Classical Music

The Listener's Companion

Edited by

Alexander J. Morin

Foreword by

Harold C. Schonberg

BOOKS

San Francisco

The Editor gratefully acknowledges the assistance of Stephen J. Haller,
who read the entire manuscript and helped in many ways to make this a better book.

Published by Backbeat Books
600 Harrison Street, San Francisco, CA 94107
Email: books@musicplayer.com
www.backbeatbooks.com
An imprint of the Music Player Network
United Entertainment Media

Distributed to the book trade in the U.S. and Canada by
Publishers Group West, 1700 Fourth Street, Berkeley, CA 94710

Distributed to the music trade in the U.S. and Canada by
Hal Leonard Publishing, P.O. Box 13819, Milwaukee, WI 53213

Cover Design by Richard Leeds
Front Cover Photo of Colin Davis by Toby Wales. © Redferns.
Text Composition by Graphic Composition, Inc., Athens, Georgia

Library of Congress Cataloging-in-Publication Data

Classical music/[edited] by Alexander Morin
    p. cm. — (Third Ear)
  Includes bibliographical references, discographies, and index
  ISBN 0-87930-638-6
   1. Sound recordings—Reviews. 2. Music—Discography. I. Morin, Alexander
(Alexander J.) II. Series

ML156.9.C58 2001
781.6'8—dc21   2001052702

Printed in the United States of America

02 03 04 05 06 5 4 3 2 1

Contents

FOREWORD

Say you are in the market for a CD of Rachmaninoff's Piano Concerto 3, so you look it up in the catalog at your dealer's shop. You find some 40 performances. Where does that leave you? Do you go by well-tested names (Ashkenazy et al.)? Take a crack at Horacio Gutierrez? Hey, what about Earl Wild? And, of course, there is Rachmaninoff himself, but in a recording some 60 years old. And there is Vladimir Horowitz. Rachmaninoff said that Horowitz played the concerto better than he himself did. Your eye drifts to the electrifying Martha Argerich. No mean virtuoso, she. But can the great, elegant Jorge Bolet be discounted? Or the superb Russian virtuoso Vladimir Feltsman? Or Yevgeny Kissin?

Help!

That is where fanatics like Alex Morin and the contributors to this book step in. They seem to have a working knowledge of every classical recording ever made and have weighed their technical and musical aspects with the rapture of a physicist discovering new particles. In this book you will find sharp critical minds that will resolve the complicated issues of A over B, X over Y. All this takes a special kind of knowledge and a kind of maniacal dedication. Plus memory. Plus taste. Go along with them. You are in good hands and better ears.

Harold C. Schonberg

ABOUT THIS BOOK AND HOW TO USE IT

Our goal in this book is to give our readers enough information about recordings for them to identify those that are most likely to satisfy their individual tastes. There rarely is a single "best" recording of a piece of music; more often, there are several that in their different ways are equally pleasing to different people. Would you rather listen to interpretations that are precise and tightly controlled or to those that are relaxed and sensuous? Do you prefer to hear them played on modern or on "period" instruments? How important is the quality of sound to you? We have tried to answer these and similar questions about every important recording of all the compositions we discuss, so you know what to expect when you consider the many choices that are available. We also discuss many recordings of music we think deserves to be called to your attention, even if it has been recorded only once.

The recommendations in the book are those of experienced and knowledgeable critics; many of them are also performers, and all of them have spent many years listening to and writing about classical music. While their opinions therefore deserve your attention, they are individuals with their own likes and dislikes; they may differ with each other, and other critics, equally experienced and knowledgeable, may reach quite different conclusions. We have tried to make our biases explicit, to provide explanations and justifications for our recommendations, and to indicate where others disagree with them. We want to give you as much help as we can, but in the end you will have to rely on your own judgement of what you hear, as well as what we say, in making your choices.

Part I of the book contains articles that discuss all the important recordings of all the major works of most of the composers, past and present, in whom you may be interested, arranged alphabetically by last name. Other composers are mentioned in some of these articles and still others are discussed in Parts II and III; you can find those you are seeking by looking at the right-hand running heads in Part I and by referring to the index at the end of the book. Part II contains articles that deal with a variety of genres, from Gregorian chant to electronic music. Part III is devoted to recordings of instruments (from the bassoon to the xylophone) that best represent the work of their greatest performers, including singers. To help you find the recordings in which you are most interested, the names of conductors or leading soloists generally appear in bold face.

We have adopted a number of space-saving devices. The recordings we recommend are indicated by the symbol ♦ in the text, rather than in lists, except for articles (especially in Parts II and III, but also in Part I) in which only recommended recordings are discussed. Record numbers are given without the prefixes and suffixes often attached to them by their producers, and they are indicated only for recommended recordings and those of particular interest or importance. Only the last names of well-known conductors and other artists are given (you can find the full names in the index if you need them), and for orchestral compositions, often only the names of conductors are cited; their orchestras may be omitted unless we have something specific to say about them. This should give you enough information to identify the recording being discussed.

New recordings appear and old ones disappear and reappear (often with different numbers) in the catalog so quickly that it's impossible to keep up with them. Information about what is new and what is available (and current record numbers) can be located in several ways: from *Schwann Opus*, a journal found in most libraries and record stores that lists most available recordings currently available in the US (though it's often incomplete or inaccurate); the twice-yearly *R.E.D. Classical Catalogue*, maintained from the database of *Gramophone* magazine in England (more complete and far more consistent than Schwann but governed by the availability of discs in the UK); or from the catalogs of producers and distributors and from their web sites on the Internet. Almost all of them are now represented there, and a good place to start is at the site called *www.Classical.Net*, which provides links to them as well as much other useful and interesting information.

Fortunately, it has become relatively easy to find out-of-print recordings; as a result of the durability of CDs, second-hand dealers have proliferated everywhere, including the Internet. To keep up to date with new releases, you may want to subscribe to *American Record Guide, Fanfare,* or similar magazines that review them. And finally, we expect to bring out a new edition of this book every few years.

As we enter the new millennium, we are in the happy position of having ready access to more of the music of the past and present than ever before. But as a result, we face an unprecedented problem in trying to sort it all out, to identify the compositions, recordings and performers that gleam like gold among the dross. We have tried to be helpful in this search, and in doing so, we hope we have conveyed the love of music that we share with our readers.

Contributors

Paul L. Althouse graduated from Harvard, where he was awarded the Leonard Bernstein Scholarship, and has a Ph.D. from Yale in Music History. He is co-chair of the Music Department at Connecticut College, and since 1976 has written regularly for *American Record Guide*, *Schwann Opus* and *Stereophile*.

Martin Anderson writes on music and economics for a wide range of publications in Europe and North America. He has been editor of *Economic Affairs* and *The OECD Observer*, has written many reviews for *Fanfare* and other journals, and publishes books on music under the imprint of Toccata Press.

Arved Ashby teaches music history at Ohio State University, where he also plays the piano in performances of new music. He has written reviews for *American Record Guide* since 1987, and his essays on Berg, Britten, Mahler, Zappa, and the relations between classical music and the mass media have appeared in scholarly journals. He recently edited and contributed to *Listening to Modernism: Re-evaluating Avant-Garde Music at the Millennium* (Garland).

John W. Barker is Professor Emeritus of History at the University of Wisconsin in Madison. His specialties are medieval and Byzantine history, but his teaching has extended to multimedia exploration of the links between music, the arts, and history in the full Western tradition. He has been a reviewer for a variety of music journals since 1957 and has written program notes for many concerts and recordings.

Peter Bates is a freelance writer, formerly a power plant tour guide, librarian, vacuum cleaner technician, social worker, teacher, and computer consultant. He has written program notes for concerts, CD liner notes, and reviews for many music journals.

Christopher Brodersen studied music history, musicology, and vocal performance at the University of Michigan and was active as a singer and instrumentalist. In 1978 he began building reproductions of historical keyboard instruments, chiefly harpsichords, and his instruments have been played in recital by such noted artists as Kenneth Gilbert and Edward Parmentier. He was Review Editor for *Continuo* until its demise in 1999.

Stephen Chakwin has studied or played just about every orchestral instrument—especially the French horn and viola—before turning to writing as his main musical outlet. He has studied musical analysis, orchestration, performance practice, and conducting with a number of distinguished musicians, and has been a reviewer for *American Record Guide* since 1980.

Ardella Crawford has taught piano, served as accompanist, and has been pianist or organist for churches. Currently she teaches English in the University of Wisconsin Colleges and reviews early music for *American Record Guide*.

Robert Aubry Davis is best known as the creator and host of "Millennium of Music", a program dedicated to music of the 1000 years before the birth of Bach and heard on about 200 public radio stations nationwide. In 1997 he helped create "The European Centuries", a national weekly one-hour program featuring live performances from European music festivals celebrating the early Baroque era through mid-19th-century Romanticism. He writes an ongoing early music column in *Schwann Opus* as well as liner notes for recordings.

Diederik de Jong is a retired Professor of Botany at the University of Cincinnati who has been a reviewer for *American Record Guide* and has hosted music programs on local radio stations for more than 30 years.

Frank K. DeWald is a music educator who has written extensively for *Pro Musica Sana*, journal of the Miklós Rózsa Society, and prepared the concert music discography for the composer's autobiography, *Double Life*. Mr. DeWald is also a composer, whose choral works are published by Boosey and Hawkes.

Gregory Dinger is a classical guitarist who also teaches guitar and composition at Bard College, SUNY/New Paltz, and elsewhere. He reviews new recordings for a number of journals and since 1985 has hosted a classical music program for radio station WDST-FM.

Sam Fagaly is Associate Professor of Saxophone and Director of Jazz Studies at Eastern Illinois University. He has recorded with the Air Force Band of the West as well as with many well-known jazz and pop artists and is recognized as a versatile performer in both classical and jazz styles.

Elaine Fine studied modern flute at Juilliard, recorder in Vienna, and baroque flute in Boston, but ultimately returned to string playing, her first love. She now plays viola in the LeVeck String Quartet, writes reviews for *American Record Guide*, teaches, coaches chamber music, and programs classical music for WEIU-FM, the radio station of Eastern Illinois University.

William J. Gatens is organist-choirmaster at the Church of the Good Shepherd in Rosemont (near Philadelphia) and is the author of *Victorian Cathedral Music in Theory and Practice* (Cambridge University Press, 1986). From 1986 to 1997 he was an announcer for WFLN-FM, Philadelphia's former classical music radio station, and has contributed reviews and articles to many journals and dictionaries of music.

Dalia Geffen is a music critic and book editor whose work has appeared on several Internet web sites. She also writes program notes for the Art of Music Chamber Players, a Boston chamber music ensemble.

Paul Geffen is an electrical engineer whose reviews of classical recordings appear on a number of Internet sites, including *Classical.net* and *Amazon.com*. In addition, he maintains a web site in honor of Sviatoslav Richter, which includes discographies for David Oistrakh, Martha Argerich, and ECM Records, and has initiated and manages E-mail lists dealing with Richter and with other great pianists.

Allen Gimbel holds degrees in composition from Eastman and Juilliard. He has won awards as a composer from ASCAP and The American Academy and Institute of Arts and Letters, has been an award-winning teacher as Associate Professor of Music at Lawrence University, and has published articles and reviews in *19th Century Music*, *Notes*, and elsewhere.

Richard S. Ginell is a reviewer for the Los Angeles *Times* and *American Record Guide* and has written program notes for several opera companies (including the Met). From 1978 to 1990, he was chief music critic of the Los Angeles *Daily News*, and has contributed hundreds of reviews and essays to the *All Music Guide To Jazz* (also published by Backbeat Books) and reviewed jazz concerts for *Daily Variety*.

William S. Goodfellow was music critic of the *Deseret News* in Salt Lake City From 1977 to 1997. Before that, he worked as an editor and music critic at the Chicago *Sun-Times*. A former educator, he holds degrees from Stanford and the University of Chicago and has written for *High Fidelity/Musical America*, *Piano Quarterly*, *Chamber Music*, and *American Record Guide*.

Philip Haldeman has been a writer and editor for *The Worldwide Adventure Travel Guide* and has published articles, reviews, and short stories in a variety of magazines, including *Digital Audio, American Record Guide, Nautical Quarterly,* and *Alfred Hitchcock's Mystery Magazine*. He has made many appearances on radio and television on the topic of science and superstition, and has consulted for *Time-Life Books, Omni, Woman's Day,* and *Bill Nye the Science Guy*.

Steven J. Haller is editor for the medical research division of a large Midwest hospital and is a longtime reviewer for *American Record Guide*. His musical tastes embrace most orchestral music from Bach through early Stravinsky, and he won't be content until every known work by Raff, Gade and Glazunov and every overture Suppé ever wrote is readily available on disc.

Roger Hecht is a reference librarian in Cambridge, MA. He once taught music in the public schools and was a freelance trombonist for thirty years. He has been collecting classical records since he was ten and is a devotee of vinyl (he builds his own tube amplifiers). He is a regular reviewer for *American Record Guide*.

Bret Johnson is an organist, choir director, and writer on contemporary music. He has written articles and reviews for *Tempo*, especially on American music, and he regularly contributes to many leading newspapers and journals.

Barry Kilpatrick is Professor of Music at SUNY/Fredonia, where he has taught trombone, euphonium, and music criticism since 1979. Principal trombonist of the Erie Philharmonic, he is a member of the Fredonia Faculty Brass and has toured with the Concord Brass. His critically acclaimed "American Music for Euphonium" (Mark Records) includes works written for him by Alec Wilder, John Davison, and Walter Hartley.

Mark Koldys is an assistant prosecutor in Michigan who has won several piano competitions in that state and performed as soloist with the Detroit Symphony. His interest in music for films led him to co-found

the Miklós Rózsa Society, and he reviews film music for *American Record Guide*.

Allen Linkowski received a B.A. in Music History from Roosevelt College in Chicago and studied conducting with René Leibowitz. He has been Fine Arts Director for radio stations in Amherst, Seattle, San Antonio, and WFMT in Chicago, is a long-time reviewer for *American Record Guide*, and was recently appointed Artistic Director of the Tacoma International Music Festival.

Stephen Long is Music Librarian at Capital University in Columbus, Ohio, and Nordic Music Archivist at Ohio State University's Music/Dance Library. He holds an M.A. in music theory and has contributed articles and reviews on contemporary music to *Tempo*, *Notes*, and *Fontes Artis Musicae*.

Timothy Lovelace teaches accompanying at the University of Texas at Austin, is a staff pianist at Ravinia Festival's Steans Institute, and has made many concert appearances. He has written articles and reviews for a variety of publications.

Ralph Lucano has degrees from Fordham and Columbia in mathematics, studied piano, but found that he preferred listening to opera. He wrote reviews for *Fanfare* for more than 10 years and has been writing for *American Record Guide* since 1976.

Joseph Magil has an M.A. in History of Art from Michigan State University. He reviews violin and viola recordings for *American Record Guide* and classical concerts for Los Cerritos *Community News,* works as a freelance editor in the Los Angeles area, and dabbles in violin repair.

Tali Makell is a conductor who studied at Peabody Conservatory and the Oberlin Conservatory of Music. He has written extensively on the subject of Nietzsche and music, was an associate producer for two recordings of Nietzsche's music (Newport Classics), and has written and co-directed a film on the life and work of the philosopher.

Donald Manildi is a pianist and curator of the International Piano Archives at the University of Maryland. His recent "Pianists as Composers" (Elan) has been critically acclaimed, and he has written hundreds of reviews, articles, and discographies for a wide array of journals, including *International Piano Quarterly*, *International Record Review*, *American Record Guide*, and *Piano & Keyboard*.

Michael Mark is a fanatic when it comes to vocal music and the light Viennese repertory, with a gargantuan collection of commercial and non-commercial recordings. He was an operatic quiz kid on national TV, works as a legal proofreader, and frequently reviews for *American Record Guide*.

Thomas McClain is a regular commentator for Nebraska Public Radio and a long-time reviewer for *American Record Guide*.

David McIntire is a composer and teacher, has studied the clarinet, and has written many instrumental, vocal and electronic works. He also writes about music and is presently teaching and learning in central Florida.

Donald Metz was trained as a church organist, and for 30 years has been Professor of Music Education at the College Conservatory of Music in Cincinnati. He is president-elect of the National Association for Humanities Education, and his articles and reviews have been published in many journals.

David Moore teaches at the Brooklyn Conservatory of Music and at William Paterson University, is principal cellist with the Queens Symphony and the Wayne Chamber Orchestra, and is program annotator for both organizations. A number of compositions have been written for him and his recordings as soloist and chamber musician may be heard on a variety of labels. He has written reviews for *American Record Guide* since 1969.

Alexander J. Morin has a Harvard Ph.D. in economics and has had several nonmusical careers, including seven years as Managing Editor of the University of Chicago Press, but all his life he has played and listened to music and read and thought about it. He has written many reviews for *American Record Guide* and *Classical DisCDigest* and for web sites on the Internet.

Kurt Moses spent most of his professional career as an aeronautical systems engineer specializing in aircraft guidance and control. His interest in classical music dates from his childhood, and after he emigrated from Germany to the US, he began to collect records as soon as he could afford them. He has been reviewing recordings for *American Record Guide* for over 20 years.

David Mulbury is an organist, recording artist, teacher, and reviewer. He is a graduate of the Eastman School of Music, has been a Fulbright scholar in Germany, and is a Fellow of the American Guild of Organists. Since 1983 he has been Professor of Organ and (in recent years) Music History at the College Conservatory of Music in Cincinnati.

Charles Parsons is Information Management Librarian at the University of Cincinnati College of Law and for 21 years has lectured at the College Conservatory of Music. As a scholar and performer, he has been involved in almost every aspect of opera research and production, is author of *The Mellon Opera Reference Index*, and has written articles and reviews for many music journals.

Tully Potter is editor of *International Classical Record Collector* (ICRC) and writes for many music journals, in particular *The Strad*. He has been collecting records for 45 years and has made a special study of performance practice as revealed in historical recordings.

Ronald E. Prather is Caruth Distinguished Professor Emeritus of Computer Science at Trinity University in San Antonio, TX. He is the co-author (with David Demsey) of *Alec Wilder: A Bio-Bibliography* (Greenwood Press, 1993), editor of the *Friends of Alec Wilder Newsletter*, and moderator of the Alec Wilder Mailing List on the Internet.

David Raymond has an M.A. in Musicology from the Eastman School of Music and has been a writer on music for the Rochester (NY) weekly *City Newspaper* since 1979. His reviews and articles have appeared in a variety of publications, and his commentaries on music and related subjects are heard weekly on Rochester's public radio station, WXXI-FM.

David Reynolds is an actor and teacher in Los Angeles, who all his life has listened passionately to classical music (especially opera). He has written many reviews of choral and vocal recordings for *American Record Guide*.

Guy Rickards is a regular contributor to *Gramophone* and *Tempo* and has written for a wide variety of other music journals. He is the author of biographies of Hindemith, Hartmann and Henze and of Jean Sibelius (Phaidon Press, 1995 and 1997), and is currently working on a monograph on the composer Harold Truscott (1914-92) for the British Music Society.

Steven E. Ritter studied woodwinds and conducting at Indiana University and the University of North Carolina at Greensboro, is an avid record collector, and has written reviews for *American Record Guide* since 1996. He is an Eastern Orthodox priest, and has contributed to several theological publications.

Harold C. Schonberg is among the best-known critics and writers on classical music in the US. He began writing reviews for *The New York Times* in 1950 and was Senior Music Critic there from 1950 until his retirement in 1980. He is the author of several standard reference books, including *The Lives of the Great Composers* and *The Great Pianists*.

Richard Traubner is the author of *Operetta: A Theatrical History*, the standard English-language work on the subject, and writes for *Opera News*, *The New York Times*, and many other publications, in addition to providing notes for operetta productions and recordings. He has translated, directed, and designed many operettas, including several Offenbach works and the first production of two zarzuelas in English, which was recorded. He is also a leading film historian, with a Ph.D. from New York University, and has programmed and lectured on film internationally.

Raymond S. Tuttle has a Ph. D. in microbiology and immunology and is Associate Director of Residence Life and Judicial Affairs at Mary Washington College in Fredericksburg, VA. He is a regular contributor to *Fanfare Film Score Monthly*, and, on the Internet, to *Classical.net*. His writing has also appeared in *Esquire* and the Miami *New Times*.

Chris Walton studied at Cambridge, Oxford and Zurich Universities and was Head of the Music Division of Zurich Central Library for ten years. He has taught music history at Oxford and Zurich Universities and in 2001 was appointed Professor and Head of the Music Department at Pretoria University, South Africa. He has written many books and articles on German Romantic music, for example Wagner, Schoeck, and Furtwängler.

Jerome F. Weber is a discographer and record reviewer who has been publishing the Discography Series monographs on composers since 1970. He contributed "Discography," "Recorded Sound", and other articles to *The New Grove Dictionary* (Revised Edition) and is past president of the Association for Recorded Sound Collections.

Robert Zierolf is Professor of Music Theory and History and Division Head of Composition, Musicology, and Theory at the College Conservatory of Music, University of Cincinnati. His scholarship is primarily devoted to 20th-century music, and he has presented papers at regional, national, and international conferences.

PART I: COMPOSERS

Carl Friedrich Abel (1723–1787)

A friend of the young Mozart, a colleague of Johann Christian Bach in London, a virtuoso on the viola da gamba (for which he wrote a good deal of music), composer of more than 200 works including 46 symphonies, 18 string quartets, and 16 concertos, Abel was in touch with the needs of his time. He did his own publishing, which may account for his conservative style, but there is a surprising lyrical gift evident in all his works and a sense of contrast that makes even his symphonic music unexpected. He's not yet appreciated at his full worth. Lovers of Mozart's early symphonies should give him a try.

Abel's symphonies come in the usual batches of six. Op. 7 has been recorded complete by Cantilena under **Adrian Shepherd** in a modern but restrained style (Chandos 8648). No. 6 was long thought to be Mozart's No. 3, K. 18, and still may be heard in that guise in **Nicholas Ward**'s nicely sprung album of early Mozart symphonies with the Northern Chamber Orchestra (Naxos 550871/2, 2CD). Opp. 10 and 17 have been recorded by La Stagione with **Michael Schneider** (CPO 999207) and the Hanover Band and **Anthony Halstead** (CPO 999214), respectively. Both are most attractive and both groups sound excellent, though the recorded sound of the Hanover Band is dry compared with La Stagione's more resonant hall.

Another fine disc of chamber music from **La Stagione** has disappeared (CPO 999209, NA). It contained two flute sonatas from Op. 6, two trios for flutes and continuo, seven pieces for viola da gamba, and a cello sonata. Another disc of flute sonatas by Bach's students contained Op. 6:5 played by **Masahiro Arita** (Denon 75025, NA). A couple of 18th century compilations of English music are available. **London Baroque** includes Op. 9:1 (Amon Ra 14), while the **Salomon Quartet** offers Op. 8:5 in an interesting program of quartets, played early music style (Hyperion 66780). There is also an odd disc by **Roy Whelden** and American Baroque that mixes Abel's music, both chamber and for solo viol, with music by Whelden, sometimes mixed into the same composition (New Albion 59). The playing is fine, but the concept is odd. You do get one complete quartet for flute, violin, viol, and continuo by Abel (if you program your player carefully) and two viol pieces. The rest is Whelden.

Abel's viol compositions come in a collection of six solo sonatas recorded by **Petr Hejný** in nicely detailed readings that show off the surprising complexity of his gamba style (Arta 46). There is also a popular suite of pieces in D minor that has been recorded several times. The most extensive version is a solidly played performance by **Laura Jeppeson** in a program including some little-known viol music by Sieur de Machy, Christoph Schaffrath, and a transcription of Mozart's Sonata for Bassoon and Cello (Titanic 183). She plays five pieces. So does **Wieland Kuijken**, but one of them is different (Denon 75659, NA). **Paolo Pandolfo** chooses three and plays them with considerable freedom (Glossa 920403). Someday someone will take this fine composer's viol music more seriously and give us a complete collection. MOORE

Joseph Achron (1886–1943)

Achron studied violin with Leopold Auer and composition with Liadov in St. Petersburg. He had a successful career as a violin soloist and wrote more than 100 pieces, about half of which were published during his lifetime. His music falls into four distinct genres that correspond to the places he lived and his musical influences (Russia, Europe, Israel, and finally the US). Much of his music is based on Jewish material, but he also wrote in other veins. His music from the '20s has indulgent chromatic harmony and bears some resemblance to Hindemith and Scriabin. He did, however, return to writing primarily Jewish-themed music after 1925 when he traveled to Palestine and then to the US.

There are many fine recordings of his short pieces. **Heifetz** recorded *Hebrew Melody* three times (RCA 61732, 61733, 61771), once with the composer's brother Isadore Achron at the piano. On RCA 61732 (Vol. 1 of "The Heifetz Collection") he also plays *Hebrew Dance, Hebrew Lullaby,* and *Stimmung.* There are other excellent recordings by **Sherry Kloss** (Protone 170), **Aaron Rosand** (Audiofon 72033), **Zina Schiff** (4-Tay 4002), and **Joseph Hassid** (Pearl 9939).

There are two extensive collections of Achron's violin music. One of mostly short pieces is by **Hagai Shaham** (♦Biddulph 021). Shaham's playing is extraordinary, and the music on this recording spans Achron's entire career. The other, by **Miriam Kramer,** includes his remarkable Violin Sonata, *Premiere Suite en Style Ancien* (which shows where Kreisler got some of his ideas), and *Children's Suite* (♦ASV 6235). FINE

Adolphe Adam (1803–1856)

Adam's work was mainly for the stage, and his only music heard much these days is the score for the ballet *Giselle* (1841). Of the two recordings of the complete ballet, **Marriner**'s (Capriccio 10568) is far superior in every way to **Fistoulari**'s (Mercury). ZIEROLF

John Adams (b. 1947)

Although Adams is usually lumped in with other minimalists, he belongs, in fact, to no school at all. Rather, he has used minimalism as a launching pad for a stream of compositions that have run the spectrum from screwball lampoons to gravely serious, even emotional, statements. Also, unlike the other principal minimalists, Adams has always wanted his music to be performed by conventional groups, so there has never been a need for a dedicated Adams equivalent of the Philip Glass Ensemble. He is a fine conductor of his works as well. His irrepressible irreverence for all that's sacred, and his penchant for raiding American pop culture (or just about anything) for inspiration will always be a problem for the stuffed shirts; but that's probably why he is, at the turn of the century, statistically the most often-played American symphonic composer. His music communicates directly, even thrillingly at times, though not always in the way the composer intended.

To my mind, the orchestra has inspired Adams's deepest, most satisfying scores, as well as his zaniest entertainments. An early work, *Christian Zeal and Activity,* is a simple devotional hymn upon which a holy roller sermon is superimposed; knowing Adams, he's probably pulling your leg. *Common Tones in Simple Time* unveils his distinctive take on minimalism, with floating orchestral textures over a pulse. Both can be conveniently heard on **de Waart**'s CD with *The Chairman Dances,* along with a grand, reverberantly recorded rendition of the zesty orchestral fanfare *Short Ride in a Fast Machine* and the gently enigmatic *Tromba lontana* (♦Nonesuch 79144). In other recordings of *Short Ride,* **Rattle** is more boisterous (♦EMI 55051); **Stephen Mosko** is smaller in scale, yet detailed and energetic (Chandos 9363).

The line on *Shaker Loops,* the piece that put Adams on the map, is that it's saturated with minimalist patterns (true enough), but it owes even more to the perpetual motion ostinatos of Sibelius, an unsung apostle of minimalism (Glass's *Floe* also blatantly borrows from Sibelius's Symphony 5). Originally written for string septet, *Loops* also exists in a string orchestra transcription, where the denser textures sometimes evoke *Pétrouchka*. **Adams**'s own recording of the orchestral version is refreshingly brisk, direct and thrusting (♦Nonesuch 79360). **Christopher Warren-Green** nearly matches him in tempo but offers somewhat softer-focused textures (Virgin 59610), and **de Waart** delivers an even hazier, weightier performance (Philips). In the septet version, **Sian Edwards** and Ensemble Modern cut a tough, abrasive profile, with more extreme dynamic fluctuations than all of the above (♦RCA 68674), superseding the roughly played recording by the **Ridge Quartet** and three ringers (New Albion).

The immediately appealing *Harmonium* expands the Adams palette of Sibelian ostinatos and floating ambiences much further to include a symphony orchestra as well as a large chorus singing poems by Donne and Dickinson. The airy, sensual performance by **de Waart** (♦ECM 21277) trumps the somewhat earthbound **Robert Shaw** (Telarc 80365); the latter disc offers a coupling, Rachmaninoff's *The Bells*, while **Adams** counters with a forceful yet luminous performance (♦Nonesuch 79549).

Grand Pianola Music nearly provoked a riot at its New York premiere in 1983 and it's easy to hear why. Part One is light and pretty at first, but before long, you become aware that Adams is now mocking minimalism, and the controversial Beethovenish Part Two is gleefully, almost intolerably vulgar (though many took it as a sincere Romantic statement and loved it). With **Adams** and the London Sinfonietta, you can't miss the point; the passages of delicacy are always countermanded in the brashest terms, though even the composer seems taken a bit aback by his deliberately awful Big Tune in Part Two (♦Nonesuch 79219). As led by **Mosko,** the Netherlands Wind Ensemble applies a patina of European polish and politeness that undercuts the jokes (Chandos), while **Ransom Wilson** captures the mockery with appropriate blunt force (Angel 47331).

Grand Pianola Music clearly forecasts the move away from minimalism in Adams's next big work, *Harmonielehre*. Now we hear many new things: gorgeously lyrical streaks of ardor and anguish, an expansion of the symphony orchestra's possibilities, reminiscences of earlier 20th century styles. **De Waart** offers a beautiful, multi-faceted performance (♦Nonesuch 79115), while **Rattle** (using Adams's revised edition) is even more full-bodied and ravishing (♦EMI 55051).

A spinoff of the opera *Nixon in China, The Chairman Dances* may be Adams's most often-played piece, where minimalist engines chug away alongside parodies of sleazy, easy-listening dance bands. **De Waart** suavely projects the nostalgia and the sleaze (♦Nonesuch 79144), **Zinman** captures more of the bounce of the rhythms (♦Argo 444454), and **Rattle**'s crisp articulation and ingrained jazz feeling really makes the piece swing (♦EMI 55051); **Mauceri** and the slightly square Hollywood Bowl Orchestra trail behind (Philips).

By now, a pattern is emerging where "serious" and "trickster" pieces (in Adams's words) alternate as if to deliberately befuddle fans and critics. On one superb **Adams**-led disc, the yin of an achingly compassionate setting of Whitman's poem, *The Wound Dresser,* is followed by the yang of *Fearful Symmetries,* a happy-go-lucky, constantly changing mosaic of syncopated jokes lashed together by minimalist motors (♦Nonesuch 79218). Again, following the beautiful *El Dorado* (♦Nonesuch 79359), we have another amusing departure, the Chamber Symphony, which conceals its homage to Schoenberg beneath pounding pulses and wild polyphony unabashedly inspired by cartoons. **Edwards** unravels all its complexities effortlessly and catch some of the antic humor of the "Roadrunner" movement (RCA), but they sound poker-faced next to

Adams himself, who brings a jaunty impudence that perfectly matches his loopy liner notes (♦Nonesuch 79219).

The Violin Concerto gets off to a fascinating start with polytonal ascending lines over a walking bass, which Adams imaginatively expands without losing the pulse, and the second movement is openly beautiful with some disturbing Ives-ish undertones. **Kremer** fiddles with enthusiastic ardor (♦Nonesuch 79360), while **McDuffie** trades some incisive detail for more elegance (♦Telarc 80494). With *Lollapalooza,* Adams indulges in pure, jumping, syncopated fun via **Tilson Thomas**'s hard-rockin' performance in "New World Jazz" (♦RCA 68798). While Adams's clarinet concerto, *Gnarly Buttons,* is both serious and mocking (Adams's recording (♦Nonesuch 79465) has more bite in that respect than **Alain Damiens** (Virgin 45351) it sounds oddly disillusioned to me.

The flagship of Adams's small output for piano, *Phrygian Gates,* was considered the first practical minimalist piece for solo piano (which leaves out Lamont Young's earlier five-hour *The Well-Tuned Piano*). **Hermann Kretzschmar** focuses on the motor energy driving the piece (RCA), but the imaginative **Gloria Cheng-Cochran** turns it into a sweeping musical time line, conjuring up waves of Liszt, Debussy and others in the piano virtuoso tradition (♦Telarc 80513). She also includes *Phrygian's* tiny, plaintive companion piece, *China Gates*.

Adams has also composed an attractive body of electronic music. *Light Over Water* combines brass instruments and synthesizer loops into a shimmering, somewhat rambling soundscape (New Albion). "The Hoodoo Zephyr" (♦Nonesuch 79311) collects seven varied pieces that offer mobile, brooding, spangled travelogues through the physical and spiritual landscapes of California and Nevada (*Bump* sounds like a close relative of "Roadrunner").

Though highly publicized, I don't think that Adams's operas contain his best music. Thus far, he has worked only with the iconoclastic, madly overpraised director Peter Sellars, who has led him into the sand trap of what one wag called "CNN Headline Opera." The question posed by *Nixon in China* is not whether or not Messrs. Adams, Sellars, and librettist Alice Goodman were kidding us, but rather, why we should care at all about the protagonists as seen through these warped lenses. Moreover, Adams's score is strewn with static imitation-Glass passages that water down his distinctive personality; only in the brief final act does he write anything halfway moving. The complete recording, led by **de Waart,** will give you the idea, though it was clearly more effective on video (Nonesuch 79177, 3CD). There is also a single disc of excerpts, but it includes nothing from the final act (Nonesuch).

The even more controversial *The Death of Klinghoffer* is undercut by its glacial pacing. Yet there are a number of choral episodes that pack emotional power in **Nagano**'s hands, some highly dramatic writing when the hijacking occurs, and a bit of Adamsian mischief when he decorates the chatter of the tourists with quotes from *Holiday for Strings* (Nonesuch 79281, 2CD). The choruses are now available on their own, so that may be the best entry into the work (♦Nonesuch 79549).

In his most daring leap yet, **Adams** wrote a pop opera about the 1994 Northridge earthquake, *I Was Looking at The Ceiling and Then I Saw the Sky,* conducting an eight- piece rock band himself (Nonesuch 79493). But this time the Trickster isn't kidding, seriously tackling rock, soul, jazz, and gospel but coming up with only two good tunes, "A Sermon on Romance" and "Three Weeks," for Sellars's dreary politically correct characters.

For those who can afford not to decide, "The John Adams Earbox" is a marvelous trip through almost every work, distilling the operas to one disc apiece, with lots of composer recordings and some scoops available nowhere else (the energetic, early-Stravinsky-influenced Slonimsky's *Earbox* and a too-controlled *Lollapalooza* from Nagano) and it's a good buy at the price (♦Nonesuch 79453, 10CD).   GINELL

Richard Addinsell (1904–1971)

Addinsell has been admired and vilified for his *Warsaw Concerto,* written for the 1941 British film *Dangerous Moonlight* (*Suicide Squadron* in the US). It has remained his most popular work and has been recorded more than 100 times, though only a few versions remain in the catalog. The film's producers thought to get permission from Rachmaninoff to use his Piano Concerto 2 for the film, decided against the idea, then asked Addinsell to write something in a similar vein. Surrounded by the scores of Rachmaninoff's Concertos 2 and 3 and *Paganini Rhapsody,* he proceeded to write the music, using as its main theme a rumba he had written as an Oxford undergraduate in the '20s.

The *Warsaw Concerto* is well played by **Martin Jones** on a disc led by Kenneth Alwyn that includes a number of other Addinsell compositions (ASV 2108). Most of the selections are film music except for *Invention,* written for BBC radio, and *March of the United Nations,* composed in 1942 for a radio "story of the men and women of the United Nations in their fight for world freedom." The longest work is the six-movement, 20-minute suite from the film *Greengage Summer* (US title *Loss of Innocence*), one of the composer's favorite scores. This is memorable, tonal, melodic, well-performed music for people who would like to explore more of his work.

The Concerto, played by **Philip Fowke,** also appears on a disc that contains much attractive music by other film composers (Naxos 554323). Also valuable is a disc by **Kenneth Alwyn** that contains a mixture of music written for films and plays and music with no such connections (Marco Polo 223732). As usual for film music, most of Addinsell's film scores were orchestrated by other musicians. This well-performed release includes themes from *Goodbye Mr. Chips, Invitation Waltz, The Isle of Apples, The Prince and the Showgirl, Tom Brown's Schooldays, Festival, Journey to Romance, Tale of Two Cities,* the *Fire over England Suite,* the *Smokey Mountains Concerto,* and the *Tune in G.* Addinsell's music is by turns joyous, introspective, tender, and vigorous; the disc is a delight from beginning to end.

No longer in circulation, but perhaps available from mail order firms, is a disc containing songs Addinsell wrote for British comedienne Joyce Grenfell, performed by **Maureen Lippman** and pianist Dennis King (Legacy 129). Also very worthwhile is a suite of Addinsell's music for *A Christmas Carol,* coupled with Dimitri Tiomkin's music for *It's a Wonderful Life,* and Cyril Mockridge's music for *Miracle on 34th Street* (Telarc 88801).   DE JONG

Thomas Adès (b. 1971)

Adès is a young composer of extraordinary facility. Almost every bar of his music, especially in later and longer works like *Asyla* and *Powder Her Face,* grips the listener's attention immediately with its intense and trenchant originality, its built-from-the-ground-up sound. Even when he moves into a Kafkaesque rendering of big-band jazz or a tango, the voice is his own. His riot of ever-shifting tone colors delights the ear, and his structures give the impression of walking a fine line between improvisation and collapse. Each piece seems in a constant, bar-by-bar flux of timbral and structural renewal; you never quite know what to expect, yet the perpetual renewal is not cruel or self-conscious.

Asyla, scored for large orchestra, is an ideal point of entry into Adès's unique and captivating world and his genius for sidestepping the obvi-

ous (♦EMI 56818). It's one of the richest and most interesting orchestral pieces I've heard in recent years—the chaconne-like slow movement is especially memorable. Also on this disc is the *Concerto Conciso* for piano and chamber group, a piece that doesn't always live down the double-edged accusations of cleverness that have hounded Adès, just as they did the young Britten. *These Premises Are Alarmed,* a toccata for large orchestra, is, however, a feast for the brain as well as the ears. . . . *but all shall be well,* scored for similar forces, dissolves after a climax of Mahlerian grandeur. Even with his largest groups, Adès' scoring stays just as transparent as it is in the Chamber Symphony for 15 players—listen there for the wry and slightly jazzy basset clarinet, the prepared piano, and the ghostly sound of the trumpeter blowing across a wine bottle.

Adès reached an earlier peak with his kaleidoscopic, over-the-top 1995 chamber opera *Powder Her Face* (♦EMI 56649, 2CD). His libretto for this deliciously depraved two-acter is a confusing welter of biography and burlesque, but his razor-sharp musical characterization is a natural for the theater. Hardly a single measure sounds like anything you've heard before. The performance could have been more beneficially blatant, but **Jill Gomez** fills out the lead role of a whorish socialite who marries into British nobility, and the composer gets a performance of verve and virtuosity from his singers and the odd, 15-player ensemble (including flexatone, accordion, double-bass clarinet, and pop-gun).

Less memorable are the earlier and generally shorter works on two discs (*Life Story* on EMI 69699 and *Living Toys* on EMI 72271). Of the two, *Living Toys* is the more interesting by virtue of its ensemble works, including the string quartet *Arcadiana* and *The Origin of the Harp* for ten players, pieces where, yet again, Adès's variety of sounds excites the ear and makes the jaw drop.   ASHBY

Jehan Alain (1911–1940)

Alain's life was tragically short, but in his 29 years he revealed a musical gift of remarkable brilliance. His father was an organ builder and he was surrounded by music from his birth. He is known primarily as a composer of organ music and his finest works are written for that instrument; we can gain through them a sense of his potential in that medium. However, his compositional interests were much broader, and it's clear he was intent on establishing himself as an orchestral composer at the time of his death. Alain's music is notable for its colorful, often exotic harmonies, and it can evince a deeply meditative atmosphere, as in *Le Jardin Suspendu,* or jubilant elation as in *Litanies,* one of his finest works for organ. His was an interesting and unique synthesis of French styles—you can hear a mingling of Debussy, Satie, Messiaen, and Dukas, along with Alain's own voice. His keyboard style is built somewhat on his formidable skills as an improviser.

The place to begin is his organ works. His sister, the renowned organist Marie-Claire Alain, has recorded his entire output for the instrument admirably; this set is unaccountably NA, but worth seeking out (Erato). Of the two complete surveys presently available, I lean toward **Kevin Bowyer**'s; his registrations are clear, his technique is brilliant, and his rhythms are clean and accurate (Nimbus 5551/2, 2CD). **Eric Lebrun** also has recorded an estimable account that has been well received, but Bowyer is superior in most respects. Lebrun's voicings are muddy at times, and his rhythms are a shade less exact (Naxos 553632/33, 2CD). This set has many virtues, though; his overall musicianship is very strong, and at budget price this is perhaps the best introduction to Alain. **Stephen Farr** has recorded a single-disc collection of his music, but it doesn't fare well next to either of the others; his registrations are not as well realized and the instrument is recorded in a rather dry acoustic space (Meridian 84282).

Alain also wrote many chamber and vocal works, as well as a substantial number of liturgical pieces. These have been collected in a 3CD anthology that further underscores his great potential (Arion 68148, 68321, and 68447). Some of the pieces are rather inconsequential, but others have great merit, such *Trois Movements* for flute and piano (in Vol. 1) or the lovely *Messe Gregorienne de Mariage* for tenor and string quartet (in Vol. 3). Even the slightest of these works displays a lively musical intellect and a warm humanity.   McINTIRE

Isaac Albéniz *(1860–1909)*

A prodigy, Albéniz made his debut as a pianist at age four. He was also a prodigious troublemaker, repeatedly running away from his parents and traveling throughout Spain, then branching out as a stowaway to Latin America and the US, all before he was 13. He settled long enough to study piano and composition in London and Leipzig, where he also took a few lessons with Liszt to perfect his keyboard technique (which was considerable, to judge from his music). However, he gave up a concert career in 1890, devoting himself to composing.

While Albéniz is remembered as one of the most sophisticated and Spanish-sounding of Spanish composers, he wrote a lot of accomplished, conventional, completely un-Spanish music, including seven piano sonatas, a concerto, and (most intriguingly) several operas, notably unsuccessful productions bankrolled by their librettist, a wealthy London banker who supported him for a time. However, it's the "Spanish" Albéniz that lives on. His magnum opus is the virtuoso piano suite *Ibéria,* whose four books (written between 1906 and 1909) combine Lisztian keyboard pyrotechnics, a very sophisticated harmonic sense (not lost on his contemporary Debussy), and a profoundly Spanish character. No folk tunes are quoted in *Ibéria,* but they didn't need to be. There are also two *Suites españolas*—also genre pieces, but shorter and more relaxed than those in *Ibéria*—and a vast number of smaller piano works.

As the Beethoven symphonies were to Karajan, so is *Ibéria* to **de Larrocha.** The Spanish pianist has made four complete recordings since the '50s, one per decade. Three are currently available, from 1962 (EMI 64504), 1972 (London 448191, with Granados' *Goyescas,* or 433926, with music of Falla), and 1989 (♦London 417887). You won't go wrong with any of them, but the most recent one has the edge in that her approach to this seductive music has grown riper, more expansive, and more satisfying with age. *Ibéria* is also in her volume in the "Great Pianists of the Century" series (Philips 456883), with music by Granados, Mompou, and Soler. Her 1959 recording of *Cantos de España* and other short pieces is also worth hearing, despite rough piano sound (EMI 64523); there's a later version, much more smoothly recorded (London 433923, with Granados's *Danzas españolas*).

Associated though she may be with *Ibéria,* de Larrocha's magisterial way isn't the only way to play it. **Jean-François Heisser** is bright and punchy (Erato 94807); another French pianist, **Roger Muraro,** does a creditable job (Accord 204522); and the Spanish pianist **Guillermo Gonzalez** is pleasingly clear and detailed (Naxos 554311, with *Suites españolas* in a bargain-priced set, 2CD). If you want to get all your Spanish piano landmarks at once, you might consider **Martin Jones**'s set, which contains *Ibéria,* the other pillar of Spanish piano literature, *Granados's Goyescas,* and lots of smaller pieces, familiar and unfamiliar, by both composers (Nimbus 5595, 4CD). The standard of playing is very high and the interpretations mostly convincing, making this a genuine bargain.

Ibéria naturally lends itself to orchestration, and Enrique Arbos and Carlos Surinach eventually orchestrated all the movements. The

arrangements sound a bit glitzy next to the piano originals, but they're very enjoyable. **López-Cobos** and the Cincinnati Symphony offer *Ibéria Suite* in a sumptuously recorded performance (♦Telarc 80470); the 1957 Minneapolis Symphony recording with **Dorati,** harsh and dry in sound, just doesn't compare (Mercury 434388). The Albéniz collection by **Bátiz** and the Mexico Symphony is zestful and colorful (♦ASV 888), and, if enough, is as good as a feast for you in this music. The celebrated **Reiner**/Chicago Symphony recording of *Navarra, Triana,* and *El Corpus en Sevilla* still sounds great, with stylish performances of music by Granados and Falla (♦RCA 62586).

As generations of guitarists have discovered, Albéniz works beautifully (and sounds even more Spanish) on the guitar. The shorter pieces of *Suites españolas* lend themselves especially well to this, and you can hear top-notch performances on Spanish/Latin-American programs by **Julian Bream** (RCA 61608, with music by Granados), **Norbert Kraft** (Chandos 8857, with Villa-Lobos, Turina, and more), and **John Williams** (Sony 36679, 46358, and 45648—the last is budget priced, coupled with Rodrigo's popular *Concierto de Aranjuez).*

If you're curious about Albéniz's music in non-nationalistic mode, you can sample his Lisztian Piano Concerto performed by **Ciccolini** and Bátiz (IMG 1607, with excerpts from the orchestrated *Ibéria Suite,* mentioned above). Three of Albéniz's well-crafted, utterly conventional piano sonatas are played by **Albert Guinovart**—prime "Guess the Composer" material (Harmonia Mundi 987007).   RAYMOND

Eugene d'Albert *(1864–1932)*

Born in England of German parents, d'Albert became a celebrated concert pianist. As an opera composer, he was not nearly as successful; his music is rarely heard these days and recordings have been few. The best known of his operas is *Tiefland* (1903), which was in the repertory of German opera houses for a while and is occasionally revived. D'Albert considered himself German and all his operas are composed to German texts.

OPERAS

Die Abreise (The Departure). This is a charming and witty comedy of manners set as a through-composed musical conversation piece. Written in 1898, it's only 46 minutes long and has but three characters, who are involved in a marital triangle. It's similar in style to Strauss's *Intermezzo,* composed 26 years later. The music is diatonic, and unlike other d'Albert operas, there's not a trace of Wagner or verismo in this high-spirited, appealing work. There are two recordings; the better one is a recent re-release of a 1978 performance from Munich first issued by EMI (♦CPO 999558). Its excellent cast of **Moser,** Prey, and Schreier sings stylishly and beautifully; they do as much for this work as can be done. The alternate version, from a 1964 Munich broadcast, is reasonably good but its singers (**Lotte Schädle,** Willi Ferenz, and Erwin Wohlfart) don't have as beautiful voices nor are they as accomplished (Calig 50964). However, Calig provides a German libretto; CPO provides only a summary of the action.

Tiefland. D'Albert's most successful opera, this is based on a Catalonian play and set to verismo music spiced up with short Wagnerian leitmotifs. There's a lot of Wagnerian recitative and many brief ariosos, and a large orchestra that's used with restraint. The score is quite tuneful and includes ballads and choral ensembles, but no crowd-rousers. The libretto is undramatic and poorly written; it seems naive and diffuse, and that may have prevented acceptance of the opera. The heavily symbolic story contrasts the lowlands, as the home of evil and corruption, with the pure air of the mountains, in which the innocent and pure of heart will prevail.

The best recorded performance, first issued by RCA in 1983 on LP, was re-released in 1989 (♦Acanta 43481). The principal singers are **Marton**, Kollo, Weikl, and Moll. Kollo suffers from some vocal strain and uncertain intonation, and Marton's voice is rather cold and full of metal, but both rise to the dramatic occasion. Weikl and Moll are excellent, and the cast is well supported by Janowski and the Bavarian Radio Orchestra. That set lacks a libretto. A 1963 German TV soundtrack has been issued at mid-price, with Rudolf Schock and **Isabel Strauss** in the leading roles and is quite effective theatrically (Eurodisc). Philips has re-issued a long-out-of print 1957 release with **Gré Brouwenstijn**, Hans Hopf, and Paul Schöffler; its dated sound detracts from some attractive singing by Brouwenstijn and Schöffler.

Die Toten Augen. Like most of d'Albert's operas, this faded from view soon after its Dresden premiere in 1916. It's the most Wagnerian of his stage works, reflecting, in particular, the musical style of *Parsifal*, yet it's also heavily indebted to Strauss's *Salome* and *Elektra*, notably in its ensembles. The story has to do with Jesus's cure of the blind wife of a Roman envoy in Jerusalem. This enables her to see her husband as the ugly cripple he is instead of the tall and handsome man she imagined him to be, but she can only love the husband of her illusions so she destroys her sight by gazing into the sun.

There are two available recordings. The older is from a 1951 Stuttgart radio broadcast, with a strong cast that includes the young **Windgassen**, Marianne Schech, and Engelbert Czubok in the leading roles (♦Myto 982185). It's a solid performance, in decent sound, that should appeal to adventurous opera lovers. It comes with a German libretto, English summary, and some excerpts from Wagner's *Siegfried* sung by Schech and Windgassen. A more recent recording has much better orchestral sound; indeed, it's a revelation compared to Myto's (♦CPO 999692). While the cast is not as good (in particular, **Dagmar Schellenberger**'s voice is not as beautiful, pure, and focused as Schech's), it's more than competent, and on balance, this is the preferred version. CPO also includes a German and English libretto.

Instrumental music. D'Albert composed two piano concertos, one cello concerto, and a symphony; all are late-romantic works reflecting the influence of Brahms and, in the piano concertos, Liszt. Both piano concertos are rather routinely played by **Piers Lane** accompanied by the BBC Scottish Symphony (Hyperion 66747). The one-movement second concerto is also available in an older but better-played disc by **Ponti** (♦Vox 5067, with several other neglected concertos by Mihály Mosonyi, Bernhard Stavenhagen, and Raff). There are several recordings of the Cello Concerto, including an old one by the great **Feuermann** (Arlecchino). A more recent issue did not please reviewers (Pan 510066), and another recent disc couples the Cello Concerto with Piano Concerto 2 (Berlin 9179).   MOSES

Stephen Albert *(1941–1992)*

Albert was beginning to enjoy a major career when he was killed in an automobile accident. Collaboration with major performers, commissions from prominent soloists and ensembles, a Pulitzer Prize, and a position on the Juilliard faculty are solid evidence of accomplishment and promise. Squarely in late 20th-century New York neo-romantic style, he was known largely in the metropolitan area with a growing interest elsewhere. His music may not have enough voice to surface from the already dated neo-romantic repertoire, and it will be interesting to see whether

it continues to be performed and recorded, but even if it isn't, several good performances exist on major labels.

Albert's self-nominated favorite composition was his 1990 Concerto for Cello and Orchestra, one of his few large-scale works not based on James Joyce's prose, commissioned by the Baltimore Symphony. **Ma**'s performance with Zinman conducting seems sure, as would be expected from this master cellist, especially because he collaborated with the composer on its composition (Sony 5796). It's colorful and masterfully orchestrated, even if we might wish for a bit more of the virtuosic given Ma's extraordinary skills. On the whole, the piece does little to rise above many other works in this style, solo or otherwise. However, this recording might stay around a while since it's on the same disc as Bloch's popular *Schelomo* (played in this case more perfunctorily by Ma and ensemble than you can hear on numerous other recordings), and more interesting, Ma's performance of Bartók's Concerto for Viola and Orchestra (in the Serly completion) on an alto violin.

Concordia (1986/88) is another concerto, though not formally so, for violin and orchestra. Albert hadn't quite adopted hard-core New Romanticism in this work, but he was on the way, as is evident in the major-chord conclusion. This bright finale doesn't quite seem to follow the previous 17 minutes of the piece. **Ilkka Talvi** is soloist with Schwarz and the Seattle Symphony in a perfectly acceptable disc (Delos 3059). On the same CD is a more successful work, equally well performed and recorded — *TreeStone I* for soprano Lucy Shelton, and tenor David Gordon. *TreeStone* exhibits Albert's fascination with *Finnegans Wake* by setting texts from Joyce's monumental novel. I prefer Cage's takes on the enigmatic Irishman's prose because I understand and value his depth and connection between artists in breaking molds of expression more than Albert's mere use of the text. The text is set nicely though, just right for the singers' quasi-melodic lines.

Albert's most acclaimed work, *RiverRun* (1984), is a symphony that won the Pulitzer Prize in 1985. Also based on Joyce's prose, it had more reviews in highly regarded publications than any other of his works. **Rostropovich** conducting the National Symphony Orchestra is adequate in all respects (Delos 1016). This work, which launched Albert's career by the visibility the award brings, has not had another recorded performance. Perhaps Rostropovich provides all there is to the music, which is topically interesting but not likely to engender contemplation of Joyce's mysteries, or Albert's.   ZIEROLF

Tomaso Albinoni *(1671–1751)*

Albinoni's life is difficult to trace. He began as a self-styled dilettante, since he was independently wealthy, at least at first, and we can find no patron who employed him. He was a violinist who helped develop the oboe concerto: we don't even know who he studied composition with, perhaps Legrenzi. His opus numbers were published between 1694 and 1722, after which he appears to have written nothing but operas; the recording industry has been singularly silent about these, though when one of them does appear momentarily, the reaction is favorable. Albinoni married an opera singer, which may have something to do with the lyrical character of his instrumental pieces.

The concerti grossi make up Opp. 2, 5, 7, 9, and 10. Right from the start they show an expressive advance over Corelli. A curious introductory disc contains Opp. 2:2, 3, 6, 5:5, 7:3, and 9:9; a miscellaneous concerto (*San Marco*); and, of course, the infamous *Adagio*—though only a few bars appear to be by Albinoni—all played by a variety of French artists (EMI 65337). The general attitude of this recording may be judged, for better or worse, by the fact that it's ordered in reverse chronology, luring the unsuspecting listener in by way of the soupy *Adagio,* then gradually back from late to early Albinoni. What this accomplishes, only St. Cecilia and the god of marketing know!

Collectors of the real Albinoni should snap up the 12 lovely Op. 5 concertos while they last. **Béla Bánfalvi,** violin, Károly Botvay, and the Budapest Strings play them pleasantly on modern instruments (Capriccio 10709). Op. 7 shows more breadth of expression and is made up of concertos for oboe(s) as well as violin. It's not completely available at present, though **Holliger** and Maurice Bourgue with I Musici were around in lively readings until recently, including Op. 2:5 and 6 as makeweights (Philips 432115, 2CD, NA). A more "early music" approach was offered by **Anthony Robson** and Catherine Latham with Collegium Musicum 90 under Standage, who mix Opp. 7 and 9 on three discs (Chandos 579, 602, 610, NA). **Evgeni Nepalo** plays Op. 7:3 and 6 with Barshai and the Moscow Chamber Orchestra in stylish readings (Russian Disc 10062).

Op. 9 shows further lyricism and maturity. It fares better at present, with a complete reading by **Felix Ayo,** violin, Holliger, and I Musici, in light, dry sound (Philips 456333, 2CD). **Scimone** with I Solisti Veneti offers lively recordings from 1969 (Erato 25593, 2CD). An "early music" approach is provided by violinist **Manze** and oboists Frank de Bruine and Alfredo Bernardini with Hogwood and the Academy of Ancient Music (♦Decca 458129, 2CD). I tend to doze off to modern instruments playing baroque music; there's no excitement to it. Manze and company, however, make it sound fresh and unexpected. Collegium Musicum 90 is brighter sounding (Chandos), with continuo of guitar, archlute, and theorbo where the Academy sticks to the customary harpsichord. It all depends what flavoring you like with your concertos. Another partial option is by oboists **Anthony Camden** and Julia Girdwood with the London Virtuosi under John Georgiadis, who play 2, 3, 5, 8, 9, and 11 on modern instruments, tastefully, brightly, and in a nicely resonant ambience (Naxos 550739). This was taken from a complete traversal of Opp. 7 & 9 (Naxos 553002 and 553035, NA).

For lovers of slow music, **Camden** & Co. provide slow movements only from no less than 18 of the Opp. 7 and 9 concertos; the disc is called "Adagio" and naturally contains a leisurely version of that work played by Capella Istropolitana (Naxos 552244). And if you'd rather not hear any real Albinoni at all, that performance also appears on "Night Music 3," as well as other slow movements from the repertoire from Corelli to Tchaikovsky (Naxos 551123). Dreamy! I might also mention that the "Heifetz of the oboe," **Malcolm Messiter,** plays Op. 9:2 in his baroque disc in fine modern style (RCA 60224).

Op. 10 returns to strings only. Considering the imagination of both scoring and melody in this set, it's amazing that there is only one version available, by **Scimone** and I Solisti Veneti, recorded back in 1981 but still fresh and enthusiastic, as Scimone usually is (Erato 18943, 2CD).

Though there are several collections of chamber music in Albinoni's output, they are not well represented in the catalogue. Opp. 4 and 6, however, adding up to 18 *Sonate da chiesa* for violin and continuo, are played with polish by **Elisabeth Wallfisch** with cellist Richard Tunnicliffe and harpsichordist-organist Paul Nicholson (Hyperion 66831, 2CD).

Opus numbers tend to be supplied by publishers rather than composers, and Albinoni is no exception, Op. 2 being both an instrumental collection and a set of 12 cantatas for voice and continuo. The cantatas have been recorded by soprano **Schlick** and countertenor **Ragin** (Etcetera 2027, 2CD, or separately on 1181 and 1204, with two cantatas by Caldara). These are early works using some of the expressive harmonies of the early baroque monodies. Schlick's voice is beautiful while Ragin is more expressive.

A *Magnificat* has been recorded in a program of same by Vivaldi, Sammartini, and Caldara, sung by the Budapest Madrigal Choir and Strings led by **Ferenc Szekeres** (Hungaroton 31259). The two by Vivaldi are familiar on records, but the rest of the disc is less well known. Albinoni's is the sparest in scoring, using only two violins and bass.　MOORE

William Albright *(1944–1998)*

Albright was composer and organist at the University of Michigan and wrote distinctive music for the organ, an instrument largely neglected by 20th-century composers outside France. His distinctively American music frequently captures an Ivesian sense of humor and originality.

Flights of Fancy, a 1992 commission by the American Guild of Organists, is representative of these ingredients. This fanciful work is pure post-Ives (listen to the New Englander's *Variations on America* before listening to Albright's piece) as it paraphrases vernacular dance music genres and a march while demanding a fully developed mastery of the instrument. Recorded only by **Pamela Decker,** her disc includes a second work by Albright, *Chasms,* a less extroverted piece than *Flights* with an obbligato timpani part (Albany 140). Two other organ works complete this disc: Herbert Bielawa's *Undertones* and Decker's own *Nightsong and Ostinato Dance.*

A more thorough sample of Albright's eclecticism is available in "Music for Organ and Harpsichord" (ARKAY 6112). Composed between 1966 and 1986, the pieces for organ (*Pneuma, Sweet Sixteenths—A Concert Rag, That Sinking Feeling—morceau de concours, In Memoriam,* and *Symphony for Organ*) rely on a variety of vernacular music ranging from boogie-woogie to tarantella. Well played by **Douglas Reed** and moderately well recorded (the organ must be the most difficult instrument to capture realistically on CD), all these works are mildly interesting, especially the symphony with added percussion parts, one of them played by Albright. The harpsichord piece, *Four Fancies,* also played well by Reed, relies again on the composer's widely ranging eclecticism, juxtaposing neo-Baroque styles with boogie-woogie. It's not as successful as the organ works, but an example of renewed interest in new and old music for harpsichord.

David Craighead is the preeminent American organist these days, and his performance of Albright's *Organbooks I* (1967) and *III* (1977) exemplify his prodigious virtuosity and interpretive ability (Gothic 58672). He presents the full spectrum of these substantial works on organs and in spaces chosen wisely for the instruments and acoustical features of the churches: I on the Aeolian-Skinner in Trinity Church, Boston, III on the Holtkamp in Park Avenue Christian Church, New York City. In these formally concise and more thoroughly composed works the composer largely eschewed his usual reliance on ragtime and other borrowings in favor of a more imaginative realm. This is the best playing of Albright's organ music in its best recording.

Albright's piano pieces are less well known, which is unfortunate for those who enjoy his vernacular-based compositions. You might think such naturally colorful music would work best on the organ, but sometimes the myriad colors achieved through registration detract from the other interesting aspects of music that borrows copiously from ragtime (Albright's favorite vernacular genre; he played the original stuff often and well) and piano-lounge music. **Thomas Warburton** is the primary proponent of Albright's piano music on recordings. He offers four works in "The Piano Music of William Albright" (CRI 674)—*Five Chromatic Dances for Piano* (1976), *Grand Sonata in Rag* (1968), *Pianoagogo* (1966), and *Sphaera for Piano and Computer-Generated Sound* (1985). I recommend his disc and Craighead's for an introduction to Albright's music; fans of this quirky stuff will likely own them already because they are the only recordings of these pieces available. ZIEROLF

Alfonso el Sabio (1221–1284)

Alfonso X was king of Castile and Leon from 1252 to 1284. At the royal court he cultivated learning and the arts, and the collection of 400 *Cantigas de Santa Maria* was drawn up under his auspices; he certainly wrote a few of the songs, but he is credited with the entire collection. Several manuscripts survive, and an additional 22 *cantigas* can be found in two supplements. These songs in honor of the Blessed Virgin take two forms: every tenth song is a *loor,* or song of praise in strophic form, and the rest are miracle stories in the form of verse and refrain, ranging from just a few verses to 25 or 30. The miracles invariably tell of deliverance from misfortune following a prayer to the Virgin for help. *Santa Maria strela do dia* and *Nenbre ssete Madre de Deus* are two of the most popular.

Unlike earlier recordings, limited to one or two verses, most recent recordings preserve the narrative line by presenting all of them. **Eduardo Paniagua** has begun to record all the *cantigas;* they are sung complete, but several selections on each disc are rendered only instrumentally. The series began on Paniagua's own label, Pneuma, and continued on Sony until that label suspended its Hispanic program. The nine Sony discs issued so far are uniformly excellent: "The Life of Mary" (♦Sony 66284, 2CD), "France" (♦60842), "Italy" (♦60843), "Castille and Leon" (♦62265), "Jerez" (♦60080), "Toledo" (♦62264), "Seville" (♦62859, 2CD), "Healing Remedies" (♦62263), and "Caballeros" (♦63018). Each of them organizes a group of *cantigas* on a common theme, and many have not previously been recorded.

I also enjoy **Savall**'s Capella Reial de Catalunya in "Strela do dia" (♦Astrée 9940), **Sequentia** in "Vox Iberica III" (♦Harmonia Mundi 77173), and **Joel Cohen**'s ensemble in "Cantigas" (♦Erato 25498), all of which include *Santa Maria strela do dia.* Other fine collections are **Micrologus** in "Madre de Deus" (♦Opus 111 30225), soloist **Esther Lamandier** in "Cantigas" (♦Astrée 7707), and **Thomas Binkley**'s ensemble (♦Harmonia Mundi 77242). Micrologus also has an earlier collection (Quadrivium). Two other collections form part of larger packages by the **Clemencic Consort** (Harmonia Mundi 2901524/27, 4CD) and **Philip Pickett**'s New London Consort (Oiseau-Lyre 433148, 2CD). WEBER

Hugo Alfvén (1872–1960)

The grand old man of Swedish music, Alfvén is known for his romanticism and the near-visual quality of his music. He was an excellent artist— almost choosing painting over music for a career—a good violinist, and a lively, engaging writer. Though he breathes the same air as other Scandinavian composers like Svendsen and Nielsen, he retains an individual voice; of his Symphony 1, he remarked late in life that it was the first symphony written in the Swedish language. Alfvén was deeply influenced by the legends and culture of the North and the sea, and remained a romantic to the end, never digressing into modern styles of composition.

SYMPHONIES

Alfvén once said his most important works were his first four symphonies (he wrote five) and a lengthy choral work, *The Lord's Prayer.* The most important recordings of the complete set are **Neeme Järvi**'s with the Stockholm Philharmonic, made between 1987 and 1992 (♦BIS, various numbers). The collector wanting all of them, with many of Alfvén's shorter orchestral works as fillers, can do no better. The performances range from good to excellent, the sound is top quality, and the notes in the program booklets are interesting and informative.

1. **Niklas Willén** provides a superlative recording (♦Naxos 553962, with 3). The work is lovely in this and **Järvi**'s versions; if anything, the latter is a little smoother and more romantic, with a lighter touch and some broadening of tempos, yet with a good deal of fire and spirit. The sound has no hint of the harshness that sometimes besets Naxos recordings.

2. It is widely regarded as Alfvén's most important symphony. It is available in a 1988 recording by **Svetlanov** (Musica Sveciae 627). The sound is very good, but the performance seems labored and at times lackluster in comparison to **Järvi**'s version. For interpretation, my first choice is **Segerstam** (♦Swedish Society 1005). This 1972 recording has been transferred very well to CD in terms of sound, and it's lively and purposeful, with attention-getting shape and meaning. The first choice, considering both sound and performance, has to be Järvi.

3. It is arguably the most accessible of Alfvén's symphonies, with its bright, joyous tone, and if you want to become acquainted with his work, **Willén**'s reading is a good place to start (♦Naxos 553729). This 1996 rendition is lively, romantic, and well-articulated—an impressive recording that provides good competition for Järvi. Unless you're attached to old recordings for sentiment's sake, you won't want another transfer from a Discofil LP (Swedish Society 1008). The sound of this 1964 rendition suffers badly in comparison with Naxos and BIS, though the performance is fine.

4. It is a stormy, erotic work in one movement that includes wordless voices. **Christina Högman** and Claes-Håkan Ahnsjö do a fine job here (BIS), though some listeners may marginally prefer the 1972 version with **Söderström**, Winbergh, and Westerberg conducting the Stockholm Philharmonic (♦Bluebell's 001). BIS has slightly better sound, though, and the inclusion of *En skärgårdssägen,* a preliminary sketch for 4, makes it a better value.

5. It stands apart from the others; the first movement was long performed as a successful concert piece on its own, and the composer worked on the remainder until his death. **Järvi** made the first (and so far only) recording of the complete symphony (BIS). Some critics think Alfvén was right in the doubts he had about the last two movements; it doesn't seem to hang together as a whole. Certainly this music conveys a sense of trouble and unease that is largely absent from his other work; in that sense, it may be his only composition at all touched by modernism.

OTHER ORCHESTRAL MUSIC

It is, perhaps, for his short orchestral works that Alfvén is best known. Many of them are delightful pieces with firm roots in Swedish folk song and legend, conveying a sense of joy and national pride. For a great introduction to the composer, **Järvi**'s rhapsodies and tone poems have been collected from the symphony discs and published separately (♦BIS 725). Here are the three Swedish rhapsodies, *Midsommarvaka* (Midsummer Vigil), *Uppsala-rapsodi* (Uppsala Rhapsody), and *Dalarapsodi* (Dalecarlian Rhapsody), along with *En skärgårdssägen* (A Legend of the Skerries) and the Suite from *Bergakungen* (The Mountain King). There are two very good recordings of *Midsommarvaka,* one led by **Edlinger** (♦Naxos 550090) and another by **Kamu** (♦Naxos 553115). The latter also has Alfvén's well-known "Elegy" from the incidental music for *Gustavus Adolphus II* and a short polka from *Roslagen.* In addition, the discs include *Uppsala-rapsodi* and the Suite from *Bergakungen,* with Symphony 1, *En skärgårdssägen,* and *Dalarapsodi* with Symphony 3, all excellently done.

If you are a firm Alfvén devotee, you may want a 1982 recording of two of his suites drawn from film scores (Sterling 1012). This is mostly forgettable music, not Alfvén at his best, but the performance and sound are good.

CHORAL MUSIC

Because of Alfvén's long involvement with choirs, some of his most important contributions to Swedish music were choral, including original compositions based on folk music and arrangements of folk songs. A marvelous performance of a number of these is by the Orphei Dranger led by **Robert Sund** (♦BIS 633). Six of these songs are for tenor and piano, and here **Folke Alin** and Ahnsjö do a fine job. The sound is excellent, as are the notes, with texts and translations. *The Lord's Prayer,* with the Norrkoping Symphony led by **Gustaf Sjokvist,** is a good digital remaster from a 1982 recording (♦Bluebell 025). It's recommended both for the moving music and for the importance the composer attached to it. Two cantatas written for the 1917 Reformation festivities in Uppsala and another called *At the Turn of the Century* are effectively led by Stefan Parkman (Sterling 1036).   CRAWFORD

Charles-Valentin Alkan *(1813–1888)*

Alkan, a child prodigy, entered the Paris Conservatoire at the age of six, where he studied both piano and organ. By the age of 24, he had built a reputation as one of the great virtuoso pianists of his day, rivaling Liszt and Thalberg. At the height of his success, Alkan, for obscure reasons, withdrew into private study for the remainder of his life, with only occasional forays into the limelight. During this period he immersed himself in the study of the Bible and Talmud, gave lessons, and composed, writing almost exclusively for the piano. His most important works are the *Grande Sonate* "Les Quatre Ages" (Op. 33) and the two sets of Etudes in all the major and minor keys (Opp. 35 and 39). These last match even Liszt's *Transcendental Etudes* in scale and difficulty. Three movements of the Op. 39 Etudes together form the Concerto for Solo Piano, which takes nearly an hour to play.

Alkan's music is very complex, exciting, and challenging to both performer and listener. Difficulty sometimes seems to be present for its own sake, and although the scores often have Liszt's energy and density, they are somewhat less agreeable. For many years after his death, Alkan's work was almost completely forgotten. Over time, however, there has been a steady revival of interest in his compositions.

The earliest available recordings of Alkan's music were by **Lewenthal** in 1965. He played the *Symphonie for Solo Piano* (Op. 39:4–7), *Barcarolle, Quasi Faust,* and *Festin d'Esope* in brilliant and aggressive readings (Elan 82276; ♦BMG 63310). In 1972, Lewenthal enlisted a number of players from the New York community to help with his second Alkan disc (Elan 82284). This contains the *Sonatine* and a number of short pieces for solo piano. It also has a wonderful bit of grotesquerie, *Marcia funèbre sulla morte d'un pappagallo,* in which Lewenthal (as conductor) is joined by singers from the Metropolitan Opera Studio, three oboes, and a bassoon.

Ogdon's only Alkan recording, the Concerto for Solo Piano, was made in 1969 (♦Philips 456913, in the "Great Pianists of the 20th Century" series). Ogdon is fearless and hard-edged and he rushes headlong into the difficult passages. His playing is neither romantic nor completely error-free, but it's full of electricity, and he manages to make this formidable music sound spontaneous, even improvised. There's nothing else like it.

Bernard Ringeissen's first Alkan disc was recorded in 1971 and contains the *Sonatine* and seven short pieces (Harmonia Mundi 190927). His choices here are restrained, and he avoids the more difficult studies from Opp. 33 and 39, giving us instead smaller and lighter works. In 1989, Ringeissen recorded seven of the Op. 39 Etudes, including the *Sym-*

phonie for Solo Piano (Marco Polo 223285). The playing here is competent but dull. The *Etudes in Major Keys* Op. 35 and the remainder of Op. 39 are on Marco Polo 223351. In "Romantic Etudes for Piano," **Ponti** tackles eight of the Etudes from Op. 39, including the *Symphonie for Solo Piano* (Vox 5151). Although he is a very capable technician, his playing tends to be glib and effortful. These earnest, driven performances are impressive but hard to like.

Another early advocate of Alkan, **Ronald Smith,** wrote two volumes on the composer and has recorded both sets of Etudes and the *Grande Sonate* (Appian 7031). The latter is Alkan's most profound work, eloquent and sweeping. In places it bears a striking resemblance to Liszt's Sonata, and anyone who admires that work will find much to enjoy here. Although Smith is to be praised for his passionate advocacy of this composer, he is only an adequate performer. His technical skills are sufficient to give us all the notes, but for depth of interpretation we must look elsewhere.

Pierre Réach recorded a fine, sensitive performance in 1991 in a very resonant acoustic. The disc includes the *Grande Sonata* and the *Sonatine* and provides an excellent introduction to Alkan (Discover 920362). **Mustonen's** lively and complete 1991 recording of the 25 Preludes Op. 31, is now sadly out of print (London 433055). **Laurent Martin** recorded the *Esquisses* (Sketches Op. 63) in 1990 (Marco Polo 223352); this is a delightful collection of short pieces (there are 48, many under a minute long). Some excerpts from this set appear on Naxos 553434, along with a few Preludes from Op. 31 and Etudes from Op. 35, the last played by Ringeissen. The Naxos disc is an inexpensive way to sample Alkan's short piano compositions.

Hamelin's recordings are all superior to the competition in both technique and interpretation, though Lewenthal comes very close. In 1991, Hamelin recorded the Concerto for Solo Piano (Music & Arts 724), and in 1993 he made the first recording of the two *Concerti da Camera,* the first of Alkan's orchestral works to be available on disc (Hyperion 66717, with Adolph von Henselt's concerto). This was followed in 1994 by the *Grande Sonate* and *Sonatine* (♦Hyperion 66794). "The Composer-Pianists," recorded in 1998, includes Alkan's transcription of the Andante from Haydn's Symphony 94 and two of the *Esquisses* (Hyperion 67050). Hamelin's "Live at Wigmore Hall," recorded in 1994, includes Alkan's transcription of the first movement of Beethoven's Piano Concerto 3 and the *Trois Grandes Etudes* Op. 76, for the hands separately and reunited (Hyperion 66765). This last work is a brilliant tour de force, half an hour in duration and in three sections. The first part is for the left hand alone, the second for the right, and the third for both hands. The writing in the first two sections is so complex that it is difficult to believe only five fingers are used. Extremely precise pedaling is the key to this sleight-of-ear.

Hamelin is the best interpreter of Alkan because of the great pleasure he finds in the music. He has a lot of fun with its twists and turns, and he's very effective at conveying his enjoyment. This makes his recordings and recitals very entertaining. The fact that he has superb technique only adds to this effect. He plays these complex and demanding pieces with great ease.

Mark Salman's "The Transcendental Piano" contains works by Beethoven and Liszt as well as the *Symphonie* (Titanic 220). Salman's approach to Alkan is too careful and too serious; he takes no risks, and the music never takes off. The only way to compete with the excellent Hamelin recording of the *Concerti da Camera* was to add more concertos. This is what **Dmitry Feofanov** did in 1995; he supplemented the first two with a third, in a speculative reconstruction, and a full-scale Concerto for Piano and Orchestra based on the Concerto for Piano Solo

(Naxos 553702). This orchestration is pleasant to listen to and interesting to compare with the solo version, but it adds nothing new. The soloist and orchestra are competent but not especially exciting.

In the third volume of an Alkan series, **Hüseyin Sermet** gives us the *Allegro Barbaro* Op. 35:5), three Fantasies Op. 41, three Preludes from Op. 31, and three Marches for piano four hands Op. 40 (Valois 4808). Most of these pieces are not available elsewhere; this is the lighter side of Alkan. **Stephanie McCallum** made a celebrated recording of the 12 *Studies in the Major Keys* Op. 35, in 1992. This is a fine performance of these lesser-known works and is in excellent sound (Tall Poppies 055). In 1995, McCallum recorded a follow-up disc that contains the *Symphonie* in a colorful and passionate reading (Tall Poppies 081).

An "Alkan Symposium" includes a few pieces for solo piano, notably *Les Regrets de la Nonnette* performed by **Ronald Smith,** but it's mainly a sampler of works for other instruments and ensembles (Symposium 1062). It's an uneven program, to say the least, and of interest only to the specialist. The **Trio Alkan** performs the *Grand Duo Concertante* for violin and piano, *Sonate de concert* for cello and piano, and the Op. 30 Trio (Marco Polo 223383). These three works comprise all of Alkan's major chamber music. They have only a little of the complexity of his more ambitious piano works but are consistently well crafted and at least as enjoyable as the chamber music of Chopin and Tchaikovsky.   P. GEFFEN

William Alwyn *(1905–1985)*

Alwyn is one of the most appealing of the romantic 20th-century British composers who entered the scene after Elgar's departure. Though composition was his destiny, he was also an accomplished professional flutist. After an unsure beginning, he produced five symphonies, several concertos, many orchestral and chamber works, two operas, film music (e.g., *Odd Man Out* and *The Fallen Idol*), and more. For a while he used a 12-tone system, more influenced by Indian music than Schoenberg, but I wouldn't associate the audible results with either; the music still sounds like the work of a romantic, expressive, and emotional composer. Rugged though some of his music may be, it's always powerful, tasteful, and beautiful. It's also broadly scaled and deeply felt. He orchestrated well, more for sonority than color, with sweeping strings and resonant brass. Even his chamber music is large-scaled in concept, and his string orchestra works have broad, sonorous textures.

SYMPHONIES AND OTHER ORCHESTRAL MUSIC

Though Alwyn wrote five symphonies (the 5th came twenty years after 4), his plan was to write a cycle of four that would carry out his personal approach to symphony writing, that is, moving away from sonata form, devising different scales, all the time using "normal" symphonic resources and Western notation. His symphonies sound bold, romantic, personal, and eminently approachable.

There are two complete cycles: **Hickox** (Chandos) and **Alwyn** (Lyrita LPs). Alwyn's recordings are very good and have great sound. If you have them, keep them, but Hickox does take these works to a somewhat higher level—enough to be noticed—and he has some great couplings. A word about sound quality: Many critics, impressed by Chandos's fine sound but apparently lacking good LP playback equipment, dismiss Lyrita vinyl. In fact, Lyrita LPs were and are classics in sound quality, and if you own decent equipment, they have more texture, presence, palpability, and range than many CDs, including Chandos's.

1. Along with 3, it is one of Alwyn's heroic symphonies. Though it starts quietly and has a beautiful, introspective Adagio, much is bold and bracing, with a mercurial, sometimes thumping II and an impressive,

brassy ending that keeps going and lifts the listener. The gap between **Hickox** (♦Chandos 9155 with Piano Concerto 1) and **Alwyn** (Lyrita 86) is greatest in this symphony, not because there are problems with Alwyn, but because this is the best recording in Hickox's series.

2. It was Alwyn's personal favorite. Its one movement in two parts grows in Sibelian fashion out of an opening bassoon motive. It's a moody, introspective work that opens up in the second part, expanding to an expressive climax in the brass. **Alwyn** (♦Lyrita 85, with *Sinfonietta for Strings*) is bold, colorful, and dramatic in the strongest performance of his series. **Hickox** is a bit slower and more molded, romantic, concentrated, and insightful, if not quite as large-scale and powerful (♦Chandos 9093, with *Overture to a Masque, The Magic Island, Derby Day Overture, Fanfare for a Joyful Occasion*). Hickox's couplings are lighter works, though *Magic Island* is a fine tone poem and *Derby Day* explores Alwyn's tonal approach to serialism. Close call.

3. It is a bold, dramatic piece with sweeping melodies, wonderful brass sonorities, and exciting militaristic passages. The stirring horn calls and serene string passages create some powerful seascapes throughout one of the greatest English symphonies since Elgar's. **Hickox** (♦Chandos 9187, with Violin Concerto) has a slightly more cohesive hold and is a little more dramatic, forceful, expansive, and dynamic than **Alwyn** (♦Lyrita 63, with *Magic Island*). The difference between the two is greater in this work and the Violin Concerto is a strong asset for Hickox.

4. It is big on the scale of 3, quite rhapsodic, brassy, almost cinematic, with an arching I that builds to a powerful climax before ending quietly. II is based on a pounding ostinato; III changes the mood, beginning softly, developing into a complex passacaglia, before ending with a powerful finality not only of the symphony but of the cycle. **Hickox** (♦Chandos 8902, with *Elizabethan Dances, Festival March*) is slightly more expansive and gripping than **Alwyn** (Lyrita 76, with 5), though I prefer the composer's sharper, more powerful rhythm in II. *Elizabethan Dances* is a sleek, light set of dances written in the style of both Elizabethan eras. Alwyn has a nice *Elizabethan Dances* (Lyrita 57 LP, with some interesting couplings by Maconchy, Bush, and Berkeley). *Festival March* is lightweight and processional in nature, smacking of Walton, but not as noble or as memorable as his marches or Elgar's.

5. ("Hydriotaphia"). This one-movement symphony is not part of Alwyn's original four-symphony plan; it's terser, shorter, and more chromatic than the others. The faster sections are rhythmic and brassy, with elements similar to 3; the slower parts are eloquent and moving, particularly the funereal final section. Comparisons between **Hickox** (♦Chandos 9196, with Piano Concerto 2 and *Sinfonietta for Strings*) and **Alwyn** (Lyrita 76, with 4) parallel those noted above: two fine performances, with Hickox a bit weightier and more cogent. Alwyn may be a little less logy in the slow movement, and his leanness results in a bit more impressionism in some lighter passages.

Sinfonietta for Strings. It is neoclassical, with solid textures and pounding rhythms (especially in I) alternating with dark, lyrical sections. II centers around a quote from Berg's *Lulu* (after a canonic passage for string trio); III is a slow, Bartókian figure. **Hickox** molds his phrases romantically and is gripping and yearning in the slow music (♦Chandos 9196). **Alwyn** is more angular and rhythmic, but less introspective and insightful, especially in the slow music (♦Lyrita 85, with 2).

Concerti grossi. are outgoing, energetic works, lighter and more classical than the symphonies, and quite inventive. All three are dedicated to musicians. 1 is for "orchestral players themselves," with solos by section leaders; 2 stands string quartet against string orchestra and is dedicated to Muir Mathieson; 3 is a spirited tribute to Henry Wood with the movements dominated in turn by brass, woodwinds, and strings. **Hickox** leads the London Sinfonia in an outstanding disc (♦Chandos 8866). **Alwyn** recorded 2 on what was not one of the best sounding Lyrita LPs (with Harp Concerto). He is slower and heavier and plods slightly more than the freer flowing Hickox.

CONCERTOS

Harp Concerto ("Lyra Angelica"). It was inspired by English metaphysical poets of the 17th century. In the notes to his own recording, Alwyn eschewed analysis so as not to distract from the "rapt mood [created by] interweaving the solo harp and strings into a continuous web of luminous sound." Half an hour long, *Lyra Angelica* is a major work. Hickox (Chandos 9065, with *Autumn Legend, Pastorale Fantasy, Tragic Overture*) and harpist **Rachel Masters** are rich, dark, and flowing, and the couplings are fascinating. Alwyn's recording with **Ossian Ellis** (Lyrita 230, with *Autumn Legend,* Concerto Grosso 2) is heavier and more plodding. It doesn't inspire and carry the listener along the way Hickox's does, and for once, Lyrita's sound lets down the side.

Oboe Concerto. The pastoral lyricism of the Oboe Concerto approaches Vaughan Williams, though it is more ruddy and full-blooded. The songful first movement is especially attractive; II is faster and more mercurial. **Nicholas Daniel** is an expressive soloist, ably led by Hickox (♦Chandos 8866, with *Concerti grossi*).

Piano Concerto 1. It is a short but evocative and inventive work that resembles Ravel's Left-Hand Concerto in many ways. It's less concerto-like than 2 and more tightly constructed. Marvelous performances by **Howard Shelley** and Hickox (♦Chandos 9196).

Piano Concerto 2. It is a bright, energetic piece, symphonic in style, with plenty of virtuosic work. It was written for the technically accomplished Cor de Groot, who was injured before the premiere and never performed it. Alwyn deleted the slow movement, here restored by his wife Mary (the composer Doreen Carwithen). Written in 1960, the work sounds more like a product of the '40s, with its touches of Gershwin, warlike brass fanfares, quartal harmonies, and rhapsodic piano writing; the main motive is a jazzy, skipping figure. **Shelley** makes a strong case for the piece (♦Chandos 9196).

Violin Concerto. It is comparable in quality to the Britten and Walton concertos. I is full of flowing melody based on gently shifting, sometimes restless rhythms. The violin floats above the orchestra with heavenly sweetness; the Adagio is sublime, with the violin hanging serenely over a green meadow of an orchestra; III is more virtuosic and fanciful, with the emphasis still on melody. A work of eloquence with the orchestra partnering the soloist. **Mordkovitch** gives a fine, lyrical performance in excellent sound (♦Chandos 9187).

CHAMBER MUSIC

Quartets. All three are full of drama and spirit. Rhythms are vigorous, melodies clear, dynamic, and often angular. No. 1 is the most bright and appealing, 2 is thorny, 3 serious and reflective, though hardly quiet. The charged sound of the **Quartet of London** and their thrusting attacks and intense, nervous vibrato overbalance the lyrical and dynamic (♦Chandos 9219, 1 and 2; 8440, 3, with Rhapsody for Piano and Strings and String Trio). Chandos's sound adds to this impression. Good performances, but they don't tell the whole story and are not as satisfying as

1 played by the **Gabrieli Quartet,** a nicely blended reading that combines angularity and lyricism well (♦Unicorn 241, LP).

Two discs with performances by Nicholas Daniel and the **Haffner Wind Ensemble** include a variety of other chamber music. Flutist Alwyn played with many British musicians; the music here includes pieces he wrote for his colleagues. It's well written with an unerring ear for melody; a French spirit, particularly reminiscent of Ravel and Poulenc, hangs over some of it. The moods vary from light-spirited (Concerto for Flute and Eight Wind instruments) to melancholy and haunting (*Music for Three Players*). The Oboe Sonata is a fine lyrical piece and the Flute Sonata is uncommonly rich. *Sonata Impromptu* uses Baroque forms and a couple of fugues, often sounding like a larger ensemble than a duet. This is rich, inventive stuff, and is wonderfully played (♦Chandos 9152, 9157)

OPERA

Miss Julie. It is based on Strindberg's play, and Alwyn's libretto is generally, but not always, faithful to the original (he adds a character, for instance). It lies well vocally, though his vocal writing lacks the astringency and twists of Britten. The opera is full of psychological subtleties, hidden meanings in the dialogue, shifting moods, and a mildly decadent Ravelian waltz. **Vilem Tausky,** with soprano Jill Gomez and baritone Benjamin Luxon**,** is excellent (♦Lyrita 121/2, LP). Gomez handles her role with ease, Luxon is solid and rugged, and Tausky paces well. Great sound.

PIANO MUSIC

Fantasy Waltzes; 12 Preludes. The Waltzes have a nostalgic Ravelian cast to them, making frequent use of skipping rhythms as opposed to the smoother Straussian variety. Though they express different moods, there is a sameness to them when heard straight through. The Preludes are more interesting, varied, dramatic, and darker. They are serial in approach, each "composed of varying note groups ranging from three to six notes" (Alwyn). **Ogden** makes a case for both works with his light touch and etched rhythm in the Waltzes, and his power and expression in the Preludes (♦Chandos 8399).   HECHT

David Amram (b. 1930)

Amram was the New York Philharmonic's first composer-in-residence in 1966-67. His predilection for cross-cultural music was ahead of its time. When writing without deliberate cross-cultural references, his style is *echt*-American, with open fifths and tonal references in a smoothly colorful orchestral texture. His frequent changes of gear into pop and ethnic styles make him sound self-conscious and point up his rather casual attitude toward continuity and concision. However, Amram's music is unfailingly pleasant to listen to, as the discs discussed below demonstrate.

RCA issued two LPs in the early '70s, one called "No More Walls" and the other containing the Triple Concerto for jazz quintet and orchestra and an *Elegy* for violin and orchestra. Neither is presently available, despite the fact that cross-cultural music is definitely "in" as we enter the new century. In the '90s **Richard Auldon Clark** provided two CDs containing primarily concertante works with orchestra (Newport Classics 85546, 85601). The latter, with concertos for violin, cello, and bassoon, is full of pleasant music played well, but suffers from a balance problem in which the soloists, particularly the bassoon, are overwhelmed by the orchestra. The other disc, also containing primarily concertante pieces for flute, trumpet, and voice, fares better. A disc of 20th-century American music by the **Atlanta Chamber Players** offers as its title piece *Conversations,* another jazz-inspired work (CM 20038).   MOORE

George Antheil (1900–1959)

Self-styled "Bad Boy of Music," Antheil was born in New Jersey of German ancestry. He spent the years following WWI in Paris, first as a pianist, then working on his image as *enfant terrible* by writing iconoclastic pieces like *Ballet mécanique* and *Jazz Symphony*. After he returned to the US in 1933, his music began to show the more romantic, patriotic mood prevalent during WWII, though it never lost the quality of unexpectedness and rapid mood contrasts evident from the beginning.

Several discs document Antheil's early scores. The most inclusive is "Fighting the Waves," played by the Ensemble Modern under **H. K. Gruber** (RCA 68066, NA). It contains the major works for small orchestra, the two works mentioned above, the title piece, for tenor, chamber group, and chorus, the 1932 Concerto for Chamber Orchestra, the 1919 *Lithuanian Night* for string quartet, Violin Sonata 1, a tiny piece for solo violin, *Printemps,* and an arrangement for orchestra of the equally diminutive but eventful *Jazz Sonata*. These are all works that should be available.

Another important disc offers earlier, longer versions of *Ballet Mécanique* and *Jazz Symphony,* as well as Violin Sonata 2 and String Quartet 1 (MusicMasters 67094). "New World Jazz" also includes the longer *Jazz Symphony,* led by **Tilson Thomas** in a particularly lively reading, coupled with jazzy works by John Adams, Bernstein, Gershwin, Hindemith, Stravinsky, and David Raksin (RCA 68798, NA). Then there is the **Mondriaan Quartet**'s disc of the three string quartets, again wildly contrasting pieces, played beautifully—well, perhaps that's not the word for Quartet 1, but the other two are more conventional (Etcetera 1093, NA).

Two piano discs give us a good idea of the young composer-pianist's style. The seemingly more inclusive program is by **Benedikt Koehlen** and contains Sonatas 2–5, *Jazz Sonata, Fireworks & the Profane Waltzes, The Golden Bird, Mechanisms, Sonata Sauvage, Sonata for Radio,* and *Sonatina* (Col Legno 31880). Koehlen emphasizes the brutal, hard-nosed side of Antheil, though even at his noisiest, he's full of contrasts. Despite all the separate titles, this disc lasts only 52 minutes, while **Marthanne Verbit** gives us 68 minutes, 17 of which are from Antheil's 45 preludes *La Femme 100 Têtes* and another 17 from his 1949 *Valentine Waltzes*. Both pianists show the volatility required for this music, but Verbit has a warmth of tone that humanizes even the most deliberately mechanical without losing their shock value. **Daniele Lombardi** gives us Sonata 3 ("The Death of Machines") and a somewhat different selection from *La Femme,* but Verbit outclasses her in verve and humor (Nuova Era 7240).

When Antheil returned to the US, his music became broader in scope and more outwardly conventional, with symphonies and other orchestral works taking pride of place. Symphony 4 (1942) was composed while he was working for the Los Angeles *Daily News,* where he was in charge of war analysis. This is a war symphony, with a nervous and troubled motive holding all four movements together; it sounds a bit like a film score, another genre espoused by the composer. There is something very authentic about **Goossens**'s 1959 recording with the London Symphony (Everest 9039) that **Kuchar** and the Ukraine National Symphony can't match, though they also play it with enthusiasm (Naxos 559033). Kuchar includes two otherwise unavailable pieces, Symphony 6 and *McKonkey's Ferry Overture*. All these works are fascinating, kaleidoscopic looks at American moods, primarily patriotic in inspiration.

Another disc of the same kind contains Symphony 5 ("Joyous"), the Spanish ballet *Capital of the World,* and a catchy rhumba movement called *Archipelago* from his Symphony 2, all played by **Barry Kolman** and the Slovak State Philharmonic (Centaur 2293). *Capital of the World*

is also available in a 1954 mono recording by **Joseph Levine** and the Ballet Theater Orchestra in brightly lit if somewhat shallow sound (EMI 66548). This is an even more vital performance by the forces that played the premiere, including the sound of Roy Fitzell's flamenco dancing, much more prominently miked and exciting than in Kolman's version, where you hardly hear the dancing. The EMI is abridged, but the immediacy of the performance and the discmates (William Schuman's *Undertow* and Raffaello de Banfield's *The Combat*) may invite you to pick up both versions.   MOORE

Anton Arensky (1861–1906)

Should you happen to think of Arensky at all these days, it's almost invariably as the composer of an often-recorded set of variations on Tchaikovsky's song "Christ in His Garden," a lovely if rather diffuse piece that sums up the essential distinction between these two composers: for all Arensky's mastery of orchestration and fluent melodic skills, there is little of the personality or invention that permeates Tchaikovsky's output. But his handful of chamber music compositions keeps his name alive, and there's much to enjoy in his admittedly limited orchestral works, while the few brief excerpts from his operas that have circulated on disc suggest it might be well worth someone's time to exhume them as well.

ORCHESTRAL MUSIC

Variations on a Theme of Tchaikovsky. It has been recorded many times, but the only recording that actually couples Arensky's arrangement with Tchaikovsky's song is **Valery Polyansky**'s, an intimate, even magical reading; it's coupled with an equally fervent Tchaikovsky *Serenade for Strings* (♦RCD 22106). **Saulius Sondeckis,** again coupled with the Tchaikovsky *Serenade,* has tempo problems and may be set aside (Sony). **Somary**'s sympathetic account at least offers a modicum of variety by adding Prokofiev's *Classical Symphony* to the Tchaikovsky you-know-what (Vanguard). There's also a **Svetlanov** recording, part of a more comprehensive survey that includes Suite 2 (Melodiya); while he indulges in a few quixotic tempo changes, he manages to make it work better than Sondeckis.

That leaves the two recordings most people are likely to remember fondly from LP, **Barbirolli** (EMI) and **Dorati** (Mercury). Here the situation is reversed; both were coupled with the Tchaikovsky *Serenade* on LP, but not on CD—fortunately in Dorati's case, as his *Serenade* is a tedious affair. His warm, genial *Variations* makes an attractive filler for Tchaikovsky's Symphonies 1 through 3 (Mercury 434391). Barbirolli's even though more affectionate reading is presently available only as makeweight for Svetlanov's sluggish Glazunov *Seasons* and over-the-top *Scheherazade* (EMI).

Symphonies. Arensky wrote his Symphony 1 at the age of 22, only a year after completing his studies in orchestration with Rimsky-Korsakov. Not surprisingly, it breaks no new ground, yet is filled with the heartfelt melody that came to him so easily. It's effectively if unimaginatively scored, with much use of folk melodies taken from Balakirev's collection. Symphony 2, written six years later, is cyclical in design, with the first movement essentially brought back as the finale (though in shortened form); its centerpiece is the soulful viola solo heard midway through the 'Romanza.' You can find several different recordings, but they're all the same coarse and raw-sounding performances by **Svetlanov** reissued many times (Mobile Fidelity, Melodiya, and in a Melodiya "two-fer," 53462). If you're fortunate enough to find **Edward Serov**'s LP of 1, hang onto it, as he turns in a much better performance than Svetlanov, more expansive in the first movement and more alert in the Scherzo and Finale (Melodiya 33 C10-09169-70 or EMI 3642).

Suites and similar works. Arensky wrote four suites for two pianos, and three are available in orchestral form. As with Tchaikovsky's suites, Arensky's are never really far from the ballet, though more generic in character. Suite 2 ("Silhouettes") is offered in a sumptuous account by **Neeme Järvi;** the problem is that to get it you have to buy his rather underplayed Scriabin *Divine Poem* (Chandos). Since the Melodiya LPs of Suite 1 with **Nikolai Anosov** (03735-6, with the Violin Concerto) and **Konstantin Ivanov** (33 C10 09085-6, with Suite 2 conducted by **Maxim Shostakovich;** also on Serov's EMI LP of Symphony 1) haven't made it to CD, **Svetlanov** pretty much has the field to himself (Suites 1 and 3 are on Melodiya as well as the above "two-fer").

Egyptian Nights is Arensky's one true ballet, commissioned for a visit to St. Petersburg by the Shah of Persia; however, that performance never came off and the ballet wasn't staged until after Arensky's death. Despite his stated recourse to "authentic" melodic sources, there's little that might be thought of as "Eastern" or even particularly exotic; still, it's lyrical and pungently colored and is set forth with sympathy and panache by **Dmitry Yablonsky** (Naxos 225028). In addition, it was recorded by **Svetlanov** (with Suite 2) and **Boris Demchenko** (Olympia), though the 'Dance of Arsinoë and the Slaves,' included on Demchenko's LP, was inexplicably omitted from the CD.

Other short works are scattered here and there. Chief among these is the Overture to *A Dream on the Volga,* based on the same Ostrovsky story as Tchaikovsky's opera *The Voyevode.* It's included with the symphonies under **Svetlanov** (though not on Mobile Fidelity). There's also a more refined LP with **Gennady Provatorov** (Melodiya C10-09967/68). By turns fanciful, lyrical, even a bit pompous, it seems close cousin to Tchaikovsky's likewise Ostrovsky-derived *The Storm.* The Prelude to *Raphael,* based on the life of the Italian Renaissance artist, may be found conducted by Svetlanov, along with the Dumas-inspired and lushly cinematic fantasia *Marguerite Gautier* and the spirited *March in Memory of Suvorov* (Melodiya 00164). Another version of the March with **Rozhdestvensky**—far breezier than Svetlanov's more measured account—is included as filler with Rimsky-Korsakov's Symphony 3 (Revelation).

CONCERTOS

Arensky wrote two concertos; the Violin Concerto shows up more often in concert, while the Piano Concerto is recorded more frequently. The rhapsodic, even impulsive Violin Concerto, structured as one movement though clearly falling into three, has until now been available primarily with the Russian violinist **Sergei Stadler** at the top of his form (Olympia 106). However, Svetlanov's Tchaikovsky Suite 3 coupled with it can readily be had elsewhere, while Shostakovich's Concerto 1 on a more recent CD (Icone 3416) is hardly a compatible soul mate. This puts the equally accomplished **Alexander Trostiansky** ahead on points for the far more stimulating pairing of Glazunov's Piano Concerto 1 and even rarer *Concerto-Ballata* for cello (Chandos 9528). **Rosand**'s soulful reading has been reissued, but the coupled Tchaikovsky and Mendelssohn concertos are expendable (Vox).

There are several recordings of the Piano Concerto to choose from. The earliest of these, by **Alexei Cherkassov** (Olympia), is still one of the better ones around, though enthusiasm is dimmed by the missing dance in the accompanying Demchenko *Egyptian Nights* suite (see above) and Vladimir Fedoseyev's rather workaday *Caucasian Sketches.* **Richard Alston** offers a warmly lyrical if less idiomatic reading, filled out with several of Arensky's solo etudes (Centaur). But couplings again tell the story,

as only **Stephen Coombs** gives you both the Concerto and the equally diverting *Fantasia on Themes of Ivan Ryabinin,* a Russian ethnomusicologist who amassed a vast collection of folk songs (♦Hyperion 66624). Since Coombs also offers the only available recording of Bortkiewicz's Piano Concerto 1, the Hyperion pretty much recommends itself.

Still, completeness requires that I also note the Melodiya CD of the *Fantasia* with **Lubov Timofeyeva** (same as Suite 2, above) as well as the Melodiya LP with **Arnold Kaplan** (same as the Piano Concerto). Unfortunately, **Maria Littauer**'s fondly remembered LP of the Concerto (Candide 31029) remains out of reach on CD, though **Felicja Blumental** (mislabeled as the *Ryabinin Fantasia* on Turnabout 34345) has surfaced, if admittedly hard to find (Ars Classicum 115939).   HALLER

CHAMBER MUSIC

Arensky's Piano Trio 1 and Quartet 2 were both written in 1894 in memory of friends and represent a purple patch in the career of this likeable but hardly original musician. A good case can also be made for Piano Trio 2, which is laid out on a larger scale than the first with particularly good inner movements, a Romanza and a Scherzo; but many ensembles who record 1 don't bother to label it as such, as if they are not even aware of a companion piece.

If you want to own both trios, it's worth tracking down the disc—still available in Europe—by the **Beaux Arts Trio,** with Ida Kavafian as violinist and Peter Wiley as cellist. Not only is their version of 1 as good as any other in the catalogue, but they top the competition in 2 by a long way. They are also very well recorded (Philips 442127). The **Borodin Trio** are insensitive in 1 and unbearably unctuous in 2, and the violinist's tuning is suspect (Chandos 7048). The **New Arts Trio** (Fleur de Son 57930), the **New Munich Trio** (Calig 50913), and the **Dussek Trio** (Meridian 84398) will all give reasonable satisfaction if the Beaux Arts version can't be found.

Trio 1, a cohesive piece with quite memorable themes, was written in memory of the cellist Karl Davydov. On its own it's often coupled with another elegiac work, Tchaikovsky's Piano Trio, and the best such coupling is by **Yefim Bronfman,** Cho-Liang Lin and Gary Hoffman, sympathetically played and well recorded (Sony 53269). A reasonable bargain alternative is by **Vovka Ashkenazy,** Richard Stamper, and Christine Jackson (Naxos 550467), although it will be superseded by the **Solomon Trio**'s performance, should that return to the catalogue.

Another favored coupling is Shostakovich's Piano Trio 2 and here the clear choice is the **Yuval Trio**'s 1986 recording, ideal in every way with glowing string tone, virtuosic piano playing and clear recording (Centaur 2443). The **Bekova Sisters** sound immature by comparison (Claudio 4013). An interesting outsider is the **Arthur Grumiaux Trio,** which does not include the great man himself but features a superb violinist in Philippe Koch; the interpretation is excellent, as is the Smetana coupling (Ricercar 131117). The dryly recorded performance by **Heifetz,** Piatigorsky, and Pennario can safely be left to fans of those players (RCA Victor 61758), but the more lyrical approach on an even older historic version by **Eileen Joyce,** Henri Temianka, and Antoni (here called Antonio) Sala retains its magic (Biddulph 059/60).

Quartet 2 is written for an ensemble with two cellos rather than two violins and its slow movement is Arensky's best-known single achievement, a set of variations in memory of Tchaikovsky; the theme is taken from one of Tchaikovsky's choruses and the composer later reworked the variations for string orchestra (see above). It's logical to couple the quartet with the older composer's *Souvenir de Florence* for string sextet, but the two British competitors both fall short of the ideal: the strangely spelt

Arienski Ensemble's performance is scrawny in both execution and recording (Meridian 84211) and the **Raphael Ensemble** is only marginally better (Hyperion 66648). This leaves the **Lake Winnipesaukee Chamber Players,** magnificently led by the distinguished Ukrainian violinist Oleh Krysa. The CD is not brilliantly engineered but you soon tune in to the sound and both interpretations are worth hearing (Russian Disc 10055). The performances by the augmented **Lajtha Quartet** of both Quartets and the Piano Quintet, with Ilona Prunyi at the piano, are adequate, and will be more attractive if they reappear on the cheaper Naxos label (Marco Polo 223811). POTTER

PIANO MUSIC

Arensky had a relatively brief but stellar career in pre-revolutionary Russia as a pianist as well as a composer. He was taught by Rimsky-Korsakov, and Rachmaninoff and Scriabin were his pupils. Recordings of his piano music are scant, but the few now available are, for the most part, well worth having. **Stephen Coombs,** who demonstrates a wonderful affinity for this music, plays a number of short pieces, including excerpts (Nos. 4 and 5) from *Près de la mer: Six Esquisses* (Hyperion 67066). Coombs has the requisite light touch for these whimsical pieces. Another excerpt from *Près de la mer* (No. 4), played by **Ossip Gabrilowitsch,** is irresistibly limpid. Although it was recorded in 1925, its sound quality is remarkable (Dante 051/52, 2CD).

Coombs and **Ian Munro** offer Suites for Two Pianos 1–4 (Hyperion 66755). They are essentially salon pieces aimed at a highly cultivated audience, and though they never quite reach the seriousness of Chopin's short works, they're highly entertaining and full of unexpected twists and turns. The two pianists harmonize seamlessly and exhibit an exquisite sense of timing, the sound is crystal clear, and these pieces are brilliantly executed. Unfortunately the same can't be said of **Daniel Blumenthal** and **Robert Groslot,** who play the same Suites and No.5 as though they were ragtime, with little delicacy (Marco Polo). A recording by **James Anagnoson** and **Leslie Kinton** of 1–4 is stodgy, with second-rate sound quality (CBC).

Gabrilowitsch and **Harold Bauer** recorded the Waltz from Suite 1 in 1929 (Dante, see above). The playing is delightful, demonstrating a high level of artistry and accomplishment, and the sound is excellent for its age. D. GEFFEN

Dominick Argento (b. 1927)

Argento is one of the most successful living exponents of American lyrical music theater; his operas, choral and vocal works are distinctive and evocative of their texts, which are always aptly selected and skillfully adapted. A prolific composer, he favors a direct and often highly illustrative musical language, preferring smaller instrumental groups in the vocal works, but he has also produced a handsome canon of larger orchestral pieces.

A very interesting recording of his 1974 opera *A Water Bird Talk,* based on Chekhov's *On the Harmful Effects of Tobacco* and Audubon's *The Birds of America,* is a wry and sour parody on unhappy marriages (Koch 7388). Also on this disc is the one-act monodrama *Miss Havisham's Wedding Night* (1981) from the famous story of the jilted bride in Dickens's *Great Expectations.* Shirley-Quirk and Linda Mabbs are joined by the Sinfonia of St. Cecilia led by **Sara Watkins.** This drama is conveyed with remarkable economy of means, yet the mood is again wry and sour rather than melodramatic.

In 1975 Argento won the Pulitzer Prize for his song cycle *From the Diary of Virginia Woolf* for voice and piano, and three performances are

currently available. Wonderfully atmospheric, the music expresses something of Woolf's serendipitous literary style by setting excerpts from the diary published by her husband after her suicide in 1941. The finest performance is by **Linn Maxwell** with pianist William Huckaby (Centaur 2092). The disc also contains the later song cycle *The Andrée Expedition,* an account of the ill-fated Swedish attempt to reach the North Pole by balloon in 1897 that ended in the deaths of Andrée and his two companions. This again is dark and memorably gripping, no mean feat over a 40-minute time span of subtle tone painting leading to the somber denouement.

The surrealistic fantasy *Postcard from Morocco* (1971) is available with the Minnesota Opera (which Argento co-founded in the '60s) led by **Philip Brunelle** (CRI 614, 2CD). It's well worth listening to this idiosyncratic music, which became his most popular work for a time. The song cycle *Songs of Spring* is also interesting, sung by **Jean Danton** with Stumpf (Albany 264, with *Elizabethan Songs* for soprano and chamber ensemble and works by Arnold Cooke and William Moylan). Worth trying too is *To be Sung Upon the Water,* a short cycle for tenor clarinet and piano (Phoenix 129, with pieces by Britten). One of his best works, the *Te Deum* of 1987, is sadly NA (Virgin). Argento has a natural flair for vocal writing, and his art songs are, along with those of Barber and Rorem, among the finest American examples. JOHNSON

Thomas Arne (1710–1778)

By all accounts, Arne was a difficult man: ill-tempered, unsympathetic, a philanderer, and erratic as a teacher, but probably the best voice trainer in London. As a Roman Catholic he was more or less disqualified from any official appointments or commissions to write for public ceremonies, so his principal spheres of musical activity were the theaters and pleasure gardens of London, where he made a precarious living. Arne's compositional technique is essentially Baroque, but his music inclines to the genial English version of the *galant* style, probably best known to present-day listeners from the symphonies of his contemporary, William Boyce. For many listeners, Arne's most impressive quality is his seemingly inexhaustible freshness of melodic invention.

INSTRUMENTAL MUSIC

There are two very different recordings of Arne's six keyboard concertos. In a 1991 recording, **Paul Nicholson** is soloist with the Parley of Instruments (♦Hyperion 66509). He uses different solo instruments according to the character of the individual pieces: 1 and 5 are played on a Kirckman harpsichord of 1778, 2 and 4 on a chamber organ built by Noel Mander, 3 and 6 on a fortepiano copied from a 1772 English model. The period-instrument orchestra has a tone that is substantial but also clear and light, while the unidentified recording venue imparts a reverberant warmth that never obscures the textures. The performances are buoyant and propulsive without sounding rushed.

Roger Bevan Williams plays them on an organ with the Glasgow-based chamber orchestra Cantilena directed by Adrian Shepherd (Chandos 8604, 2CD; also MHS). The modern-instrument orchestra has a heavier, thicker tone, less subtlety of nuance, and not quite as good ensemble as the Parley. Nearly all the tempos are slower than Nicholson's, whose readings are effervescent and seem almost effortless, no matter how intricate the figuration and ornamentation. Bevan Williams's are far less so, and by playing all the concertos on the organ, he imposes a certain uniformity of character on them; Nicholson, with his variety of solo instruments, underscores their differences in style and personality. With its slower tempos, the Chandos recording contains nearly 86 minutes of music, too long for one CD but rather skimpy for two. The Hyperion recoding, at just under 78 minutes, makes for a generous single CD.

Arne's four symphonies were published in 1767 and show the influence of JC Bach, who arrived in London in 1762, and possibly of the Mannheim symphonists, some of whose work was published in London in 1763. **Adrian Shepherd** and Cantilena recorded all four in 1985 (Chandos 8403; also MHS). These performances are more stylish and animated than their recording of the concertos. There is an earlier (1975) recording of three of the symphonies plus seven of the eight Boyce symphonies by **Kenneth Montgomery** and the Bournemouth Sinfonietta reissued as part of the EMI Baroque Series, but why settle for incomplete sets?

It appears there are no current recordings of Arne's delightful eight overtures, not even a reissue of Christopher Hogwood's 1973 LP with the Academy of Ancient Music (Oiseau Lyre). More's the pity.

A sparkling program of Arne's chamber music is presented on period instruments by **Le Nouveau Quatuor** (Amon Ra 42). The greater part of the program consists of four of the seven trio sonatas. While published in 1757 for the standard two violins and continuo, these particular four (2, 5, 6, and 7) may have been intended for flute and violin, judging from the instrumental range and choice of keys, and that's how they are performed here. The program is completed by the first of Arne's eight sonatas for harpsichord and an adaptation for solo harpsichord of an early version of Concerto 1 in C. Both are played by Paul Nicholson on a 1756 Kirckman harpsichord from the Richard Burnett collection at Finchcocks, Goudhurst, Kent.

Two works by Arne are included in a mixed program of English chamber music of the 18th century played by the period instrument ensemble **London Baroque** (Amon Ra 14; also MHS). Harpsichordist John Toll plays Sonata 2 in E Minor on the same instrument played by Nicholson on the disc described above. The ensemble also plays Trio Sonata 2, here with two violins. The rest of the program consists of music by Karl Friedrich Abel, Charles Avison, John Stanley, and Handel. Both discs are excellent.

OPERAS AND OTHER VOCAL MUSIC

Alfred was among the most highly regarded of Arne's works during his lifetime. It began as a masque—a spoken play with songs—first performed in 1740 for the Prince of Wales at his country residence, Clivenden. The score for that version included only the overture, eight vocal numbers, and a march. Arne added more music for the 1745 London premiere and revised the work again for a 1752 performance "in the manner of an oratorio" with recitatives and choruses. A score was published in 1753, but it doesn't contain the recitatives or choruses, which are now lost. **McGegan,** with an impressive quartet of vocal soloists and his Philharmonia Baroque Orchestra and Chorale, has recorded as much of *Alfred* as survives (Deutsche Harmonia Mundi/BMG 51314). Another critic has described McGegan's interpretation as "brusque." I would describe it as energetic, with some of the numbers a trifle rushed. The recorded sound is aggressive, especially the numbers for the soprano soloists, but on the whole, it's a convincing performance that really brings the work to life, even in its fragmentary condition. The final number is Arne's best-known song, "Rule, Britannia."

Artaxerxes was another of Arne's great successes, an Italian-style opera seria in English. The libretto is probably by Arne himself, adapted from Metastasio. The one recording of the work is by **Goodman** directing the Parley of Instruments (Hyperion 67051, 2CD). Like *Alfred, Artaxerxes* survives in a fragmentary state; as with so much of his music

for the stage, the original performing materials were destroyed in a theater fire. A score was published in 1762, but without recitatives and the final chorus. In 1813, Henry Bishop prepared a shortened version of the opera, and this was later published. For this recording, Peter Holman has attempted to reconstruct the 1762 version by taking as much recitative as possible from Bishop, composing the rest himself, and adapting music from Arne's *Comus* for the final chorus. The result is entirely convincing. The performance is very impressive, though there are some rough edges, only to be expected in vocal writing of such daunting virtuosity. The recorded sound, while generally good, is on the dry side, so the orchestra sometimes sounds a bit raucous, as in the opening movement of the overture.

Two of the original roles were intended for castratos. The title role is sung by countertenor Christopher Robson, whose tone is lovely but rather heady and delicate, sounding more pastoral than heroic. The other castrato role is Arbaces, friend of the hero, son of the villain, and lover of the hero's sister (business as usual for opera seria). This part is too high for a countertenor, so it's given here to mezzo Patricia Spence, whose performance is nothing short of astounding. She is so much in character that at times you can hardly believe a woman is singing. Her tone is far more masculine-sounding than Christopher Robson's. Soprano Catherine Bott as the hero's sister Mandane is clear and delicate, but sometimes overbalanced by the accompaniment. The elder statesman of the cast is tenor Ian Partridge, who gives a rock-solid performance as the villain Artabanes.

"Dr. Arne at Vauxhall Gardens" is a 1987 recording of cantatas and songs of the sort that would have entertained the patrons of London's pleasure gardens in the middle of the 18th century (Hyperion 66237). Soprano Emma Kirkby and tenor Richard Morton perform with the Parley of Instruments under **Goodman**'s direction. As Peter Holman puts it, "While no one would claim profundity for [Arne's] songs and cantatas for the pleasure gardens, they are an admirable expression of the Georgian virtues of wit, elegance, and ordered passion." Arne's inimitable lyricism, of course, is everywhere in evidence. The performances are highly accomplished, but they don't quite capture the genial elegance Holman describes. Kirkby is impressive in *The Lover's Recantation,* a virtuoso cantata written for Arne's celebrated pupil and mistress Charlotte Brent. At the same time, you couldn't describe her tone as warm and ingratiating. Morton, meanwhile, never sounds really comfortable, as if all the lines lie awkwardly for his voice, making it sound rather tight, labored, and uneven. I'm not convinced the balances are right; the instruments seem unduly prominent, at times almost covering the voices.

Kirkby, accompanied by Hogwood and the Academy of Ancient Music, includes selections from *Comus, Rosamond,* and *The Tempest* in a program that also contains songs and arias by Handel, John Frederick Lampe, and Mozart (London 458084, 2CD). GATENS

Malcolm Arnold (b. 1921)

Arnold was a prolific composer of mainly instrumental music. Much of it is light in nature, and some touches on popular and jazzy veins (including more than 80 film scores). It can be brilliant, flashy, and easy to assimilate, but he was a very serious composer, and there are undercurrents of the troubled, angry, or even violent in many of his works. The former London Philharmonic trumpeter was a brilliant orchestrator, whose "sound" derives a great deal from the instruments he uses, often in striking combinations. He's given to all kinds of melodic writing, from long tunes to ditties to short motifs; many are catchy, even breezy. Mainly a tonal composer, he has used 12-tone technique, but he's no

Schoenberg. Arnold's unique sound can be imperfectly described as jaunty, with a touch of Irish melody, some of Bartók's harmony, with Shostakovich's bite in some of the angry music, and more than a little of the haunting quality of Bernard Herrmann in some serious works.

SYMPHONIES

Arnold's symphonies are mainly the property of Vernon Handley (the only complete set), Richard Hickox, Andrew Penny, and the composer. Nearly all recordings are very good, and the conductors are unusually consistent. **Hickox** with the London Symphony goes for a big, weighty approach, with broad phrasing and tempos, abetted by Chandos's plummy sound. **Handley** and the Royal Philharmonic are direct, glossy, intense and bracing, with Conifer matching his sound. **Penny** is less potent and intense; his intimate and often ethereal style brings out an interesting side of Arnold. Fine sound. **Arnold**'s own readings are slower and more dramatic, and he got great sound from Lyrita and EMI. You can assume these traits run true in the ratings below, but do note the additional comments.

1. It sounds carefree at times but is generally pointed and at times punchy, severe, and even violent. **Hickox** (♦Chandos 9335, with 2); **Penny** (♦Naxos 553406, also with 2); **Handley** (♦Conifer, with 5); **Arnold** is more romantic and slower (♦EMI 64044, with Concerto for Two Pianos–Three Hands; *Tam O'Shanter; Solitaire* excerpts; etc.).

2. It is along the same lines as 1 but more advanced and easier to take in. It's less strident and more melodic, with a deep, funereal slow movement. **Groves** (the dedicatee) has great analog sound and a straightforward, exciting approach. The predictably broad and expansive **Hickox**'s slow Adagio is devastating and the transition to the Allegro is shocking. His 1 and 2 present a generally dark view of these works. **Handley**'s 2 comes with *A Grand Grand Overture* with organ, three vacuum cleaners, a floor polisher, gun shots, and a send-up of the *Leonore Overtures*. **Arnold**'s breezy manner works wonders in describing the woolly sheep and sleek cows in the coupled *Carnival of Animals*.

3. It is deep, with less of the deceptively breezy style of early Arnold and more brooding and yearning—it's lyrical but with stark moments. **Hickox** (♦Chandos 9290); **Handley** (Conifer: 52158); **Penny** (♦Naxos 553739), all with 4. Hickox is typically expansive, but lighter and more floating than usual. **Arnold** is the most probing (♦Everest 9001, with Vaughan Williams's Symphony 9 with Boult; ♦Phoenix 102, with *Scottish Dances*).

4. It was written during and reflects Arnold's sympathy with the Notting Hill race riots. It swings between whimsical, sad, skittish, and angry, and features a lot of percussion and Carribbean sounds. The intense **Handley** catches the range of drama and emotions well and never loses contact with the anger and mystery. He's very good with the Carribbean rhythms and his percussion in general. **Hickox** is less intense, best with the whimsical and sad but also good with the anger and exotic rhythms; this disc is his weakest. **Penny** isn't as angry either, but his light, suspended style brings out the incorporeal and mysterious in this piece very well and there is still enough drive and power to carry the finale. **Arnold** is very serious and probing as well as very, very slow (♦Lyrita 200). Try one of the others first.

5. It is often viewed as Arnold's best. It has plenty of tunes and passion, is brilliantly orchestrated, and may have his best balance between humor and sentiment. **Hickox** is good (♦Chandos 9386, with 6), but **Handley** is better because the symphony benefits from his greater control

(Conifer, with 1). The very romantic **Arnold** may be the best of all (♦EMI LP), and the coupled *Peterloo Overture*, with its clashing armies, is a knockout. **Bostock** contributes the lightest, most genial version; it's very nice (♦Classico 294, with Divertimento; Symphonic Study "Machines"; *Solitaire* excerpts; *Belles of St. Trinians*). "Machines" is a film score and sounds like its title. The less impressive *Belles* film score sounds like music hall music.

6. It is dark and full of contradictions in the way it's filled with anticipation and light textures before a quasi-triumphant finale of marches—elusive but satisfying. **Hickox** gives one of his strongest Arnold performances; it catches and holds the anticipation beautifully until his charged finale (Chandos 9386, with 5). **Handley** is slack in his weakest Arnold symphony recording; he just doesn't catch the sense of wonder (♦Conifer 16847, with *Fantasy on a Theme of John Field; Sweeney Todd; Tam O'Shanter*). The couplings are what justify my recommendation, particularly the *Fantasy*, which pits soloist against orchestra, "light and stability" vs. "satire and irony," in one of Arnold's more violent, conflicted works. *Sweeney Todd* takes a high-spirited view of the Fleet Street barber.

7 and *8.* They are difficult symphonies. No. 7 uses a 12-tone technique, though with Arnold's special voice. A tour de force of orchestration, replete with harsh staccato passages and plenty of percussion, it often burns with anger and has some of Arnold's bleakest passages as well as some of his most terrifying music. 8 is less intense and more wistful but still manages to be dark and troubled. Neither is easy to fathom. **Handley** and the Royal Philharmonic offer terrific performances (♦Lyrita). Don't start with Arnold here, but do get to hear these works.

9. It goes 7 one better. The composer had suffered terribly before its writing. It's lightly scored and enigmatic even in its one sprightly movement. The finale, a long and devastatingly soft slow movement, takes up more than half the work. This plays to the intensity that is **Handley**'s strength; his version has energy and is searing in the Lento, in great sound (♦Conifer 51273, with Concertino for Oboe; Fantasy for Oboe). The Concertino is very lyrical, with an upbeat finale, and the Fantasy is one of Arnold's difficult "contest" works. Both are very well played by Nicholas Daniel. **Penny** does a fine job, but here his lighter view of Arnold betrays him (Naxos 553540, with an interview with Arnold). This piece needs tight concentration, and that means Handley.

OTHER ORCHESTRAL MUSIC

Commonwealth Christmas Overture; Sussex Overture; Smoke; Fair Field; Beckus the Dandipratt. A knockout disc, with the inventive development of *Sussex,* the dark, mysterious, sometimes bluesy, big-city *Smoke,* and the all-out waltz fantasia *Fair Field. Christmas* invokes a bell-like holiday spirit, with a Caribbean interlude. Terrific performances from **Arnold** and the London Philharmonic in great sound (♦Reference 48).

Concerto for 28 Players. It is a complex, 12-tone work. Most of the writing is soloistic. **Mark Stephenson** and London Musici are sharp and dry, but a bit reticent and pedestrian (♦Conifer 51211, with Viola Concerto, Serenade for Small Orchestra, *Larch Trees*). The early *Larch Trees* is one of Arnold's few nature works, with a touch of Delius and an early fall chill. The Viola Concerto contrasts the dark viola tone and hints of mystery with a plethora of tunes and a light finale; it's nicely played by Rivka Golani. **Hickox,** the richer City of London Sinfonia, and an opulent recording make a more forthcoming, energetic, and convincing case for this concerto (♦Chandos 9509, with Little Suites 1-3, *Variations on a Theme by Ruth Gipps*). Doing an excellent job of catching Gipps's quirky style, Variations swings between the wistful theme and punchy marches, a waltz, and a serial variation for fun (Gipps hated 12-tone). The Suites have big, colorful sonorities with lots of brass and percussion and tuneful vigor over a number of styles.

English, Scottish, Cornish, and *Irish Dances.* They are brilliantly scored with a lot of brass. They reflect the character of their geographical titles and offer a clever blend of energy and a cloudy *gris* common to the Isles. Great stereo demo works. **Arnold** (♦Lyrita 201) and **Thomson** (♦Chandos 8867) recorded them plus dances from *Solitaire*. **Penny** and the Queensland Symphony substitute the rarer *Welsh Dances* for *Solitaire* (♦Naxos 553526). All are first-rate. Penny, my first choice, is delightful, just slightly on the light side, but with elastic, beautifully sprung rhythms and clear orchestral playing. The exuberant Thomson, the most brilliant in tone, plays up the dance element, but not as naturally or irresistibly as Penny. Arnold is generally slower, with more of the grey skies and rocky coastlines that are in this score. The others miss this aspect of the music, and for this reason he's my second choice. All get excellent sound.

Film Music. Arnold at his most versatile, from the ominous opening to *Bridge on the River Kwai* and the marches that follow, the lighter *Whistle Down the Wind* and *Hobson's Choice,* to the space-age sound of *Sound Barrier* and the sweeping, Hollywoodesque but glorious *Inn of the Sixth Happiness*. All are exhilarating and are played with all stops out by **Hickox** and the London Symphony (♦Chandos 9100).

Serenade. It is in a lighter vein but for full orchestra, and delightful with its cascading fresh opening and energetic finale contrasting with a darker II. **Ronald Thomas** (♦EMI LP, with Flute Concertos, Sinfonietta 3) has more presence and atmosphere than **Mark Stephenson,** though Stephenson's couplings are more interesting (♦Conifer 51211, with Concerto for 28 Players, Viola Concerto, *Larch Trees*). **Donald Barra**'s full, mysterious, and dark version is in many ways my favorite (♦Koch 7134, with Sinfoniettas 1 and 2, Concerto for Two Violins).

Sinfoniettas. The most convenient collection of all three is by **Pople** and his London Festival Orchestra (♦Hyperion 66332, with Concertos for Oboe and Flute 1). The performances are fast, brilliant in tone, and dominated by the woodwinds. **Barra** and the San Diego Chamber Orchestra provide an excellent and different view that's slower, with nice flow and a wonderful dark air of mystery missing from Pople and Dilkes (♦Koch 7134, with Serenade; Concerto for Two Violins). Larger in scale, but less brilliant, less flowing, and less compelling are 1 and 2 by **Dilkes** with the Philharmonia (EMI LP, with flute concertos).

Tam O'Shanter. It may be Arnold's most popular overture. Based on a Robert Burns poem about Tam's wild night and brilliantly orchestrated, it's *Till Eulenspiegel* on speed with whips. **Gibson**'s electric RCA account from the '50s is classic, with tremendous sound (♦Classic Compact Discs 2225, with works by Mussorgsky and others). Gibson's later account is much weightier but works very well and shows a darker side of the piece (♦Chandos). **Handley** is broader and dramatic but less electric (♦Conifer 16847, with Symphony 6, etc.). **Arnold**'s account is surprisingly tame (EMI 64044, with Symphony 1, Concerto for Two Pianos–Three Hands, etc.).

CONCERTOS

Arnold's short concertos often include energetic, sometimes jazzy outer movements surrounding a lyrical, often moody slow one. Most were dedicated to particular musicians and written with their approaches to their instruments in mind. The dedicatees are given in parentheses.

Clarinet. 1 (Frederick Thurston); 2 (Benny Goodman). No.1 is more lyrical and moody; 2 combines toughness with jazz elements before letting loose with a finale that some will find a lot of fun, though it can be tedious. In **Emma Johnson**'s wonderful disc of Arnold's clarinet works and woodwind ensembles, her sound is bright but full of tension and control (♦ASV 922, with Sonatina for Clarinet, Fantasy, Divertimento for flute, oboe, and clarinet; *Three Shanties for Wind Quintet*). **Thea King** is warmer, slower, and darker with Barry Wordsworth (♦Hyperion 66634, with clarinet works by Britten and Elizabeth Maconchy). She and Johnson, in their contrasting ways, take the full measure of these concertos. **Michael Collins** and London Musici are bold, bright, and nicely aggressive in both works; he's good, but I prefer Johnson for this style (1, ♦Conifer 51228; 2, ♦15004; both with other works).

Flute. 1 and 2 (Richard Adeney). No. 1 is full of flute runs and spiky writing for soloist and orchestra; it's brasher and more sardonic than 2, which is more angry and despairing, though still with energy—not all optimism is lost.

Among those who have recorded both, **Karen Jones** has a small, bright sound; her approach is less mellifluous and slightly more brittle than most and fits the optimistic 1 better than 2. Mark Stephenson and London Musici are bold and somewhat weighty (1, ♦Conifer 15004; 2, ♦51228, both with other works). **Galway**'s star vehicle has a bigger, fatter sound, more orchestral mass, and closer recording; it's decent but misses some delicacy and sharpness (♦BMG 68860, with other works for flute). **James Solum** with Neville Dilkes takes the most lyrical and melodic view, making these works more liquid and beautiful (♦EMI LP, with Sinfoniettas 1+2). **Richard Adeney** is blunter, less fluid, and more pedestrian, mainly due to the conducting of Ronald Thomas (♦EMI LP, with Sinfonietta 3, Serenade). Not bad, but it's the couplings that carry my recommendation.

Edward Beckett plays a sparkling, luminous 1 with Pople (♦Hyperion 66332, with Sinfoniettas and Oboe Concerto). **Alexa Still** uses her limpid, full sound to present 2 beautifully with great lyricism; Nicholas Braithwaite and the New Zealand Chamber Orchestra are in full sympathy (♦Koch 7140, with Gordon Jacob's Flute Concert and Thea Musgrave's Orfeo II).

Guitar (Julian Bream). The Guitar Concerto is one of Arnold's most delicate works, probably because of the quiet nature of the solo (acoustical) instrument; it's very intimate, with modal themes and a touch of light jazz. **Bream** is first-rate (♦RCA 61598, with guitar concertos by Rodrigo and Richard Rodney Bennett). His second recording for EMI was unavailable for review but well received elsewhere.

Horn. 1 (Charles Gregory), 2 (Dennis Brain). No. 1 is Arnold's most complex concerto, marked by a long, almost Mahlerian Andante of probing beauty. 2's movements are, respectively, heroic, mournful, and brilliantly bluesy. Both concertos are wonderfully played, with clean, bold sound and great control by **Richard Watkins** (1, ♦Conifer 51228; 2, ♦15004; both with other Arnold concertos).

Piano Concerto for Two Players-Three Hands. It is striking, with a complex urban-sounding I and a beautiful slow movement. Jazz dance hangs over the work, breaking out in full (and a bit uncomfortably) in III. **Phyllis Sellick** and **Cyril Smith** are outstanding, as is Arnold on the podium (♦EMI 64044, with Symphony 1, etc.). **David Nettle, Richard Markham,** and Handley are more relaxed. They accent the jazz, but miss the intensity and color of I, and are less intense than the preferable account by Arnold (♦Conifer 51240, with Symphony 2, etc.).

Piano Duet Concerto. It (Helen Pike, Paul Hamburger) is blockier, heavier, and less interesting harmonically, if more classically bravura than the other piano concerto. **David Nettle** and **Richard Markham** are solid, as are the London Virtuosi and Mark Stephenson (♦Conifer 51228, with other concertos).

Two-Violin Concerto (Yehudi Menuhin). It is more serious, modeled on the Bach Double Concerto, with touches of Bartók and Herrmann. Arnold's pyramiding of intervalic elements creates a lucid and often lyrical piece. **Kenneth Sillito** and **Lyn Fletcher** play with real energy and precision, ably accompanied by Mark Stephenson and London Musici (♦Conifer 15005, with other Arnold concertos). **Igor** and **Vesna Gruppman** are slower, darker, and more melancholy, with Barra (♦Koch, with Sinfoniettas 1, 2 and Serenade). Different views; both are excellent.

CHAMBER MUSIC
Flute Sonata, Flute Sonatina, Flute Fantasy, Shanties. These are all virtuosic, sometimes jazzy works that should appeal to flute devotees. **Galway** tosses them off with panache. The performance of *Shanties*—a delightful woodwind quintet based on sea tunes—is fine, though I prefer other performances of the concertos (♦RCA, with other works for flute).

Piano Trio; Violin Sonatas 1 and 2; 5 Violin Pieces; Cello Fantasy. They are serious, full of intensity and drive. The **English Piano Trio** plays with enthusiasm and a robust, infectious sound (♦Naxos 554237). The **Nash Ensemble** adds the Viola Sonata and substitutes Duo for Two Cellos for the Cello Fantasy in performances lighter in weight, more removed, and less robust and convincing (Hyperion 66171).

String Quartets 1 and *2.* They are Arnold at his most dark, serious, and introspective. There's a good tune here and there and a glorious chorale in 2, but if you didn't know who the composer was, you'd never guess. They sound like Bartók with an English accent. Fascinating, engrossing, and well played by the **McCapra Quartet** (♦Chandos 9112).

The **Nash Ensemble** made two other Arnold chamber music discs, both for various woodwind ensembles; they were unavailable for review (Hyperion 66171, 66172).

PIANO MUSIC
Frith gives us the mainly unknown complete piano music in fine performances (♦Koch 7162). It's arranged chronologically, and it's interesting to hear how Arnold progressed from works in a Baroque style to a more modern and mysterious Serenade with its jazz influence and on to alternately pleasant and serious works. Most of this music is entertaining and in a less complex mode than the composer's other works.

BAND MUSIC
Dances, Little Suites 1-3, Fantasy, Padstow Lifeboat. The Scottish, Cornish, and English dances are brass band arrangements of the orchestral works. The Grimethorpe Colliery Band led by **Edgar Howarth** plays with sophistication and smoothness. The English brass band sound is beautiful, but I'd like more bite, particularly in the dances, and closer, more impacting sound. Still, it's a must for brass band fans (♦Conifer 16848).

Scottish and English Dances, Tam O'Shanter, 2 Suites, Water Music, Padstow Lifeboat, marches, etc. This collection by **Jerry Junkin** and the Dallas Wind Ensemble is a must for full band lovers. The interpretations are on the romantic, weighty side, with some slow tempos–sometimes too slow (particularly in *Tam*)—but the enthusiasm of the playing and the music itself are infectious (♦Reference 66).   HECHT

Juan Crisostomo Arriaga *(1806–1826)*
Born during the upheaval between the Classical and Romantic periods, dead before he was 20, Arriaga is a hard composer to place and to interpret. Though his style matured rapidly and the symphony and string quartets are polished creations, interpretations tend to fall between classical brio and romantic indulgence, as did his life.

His first opus number is a *Nonet,* also called Overture in F Minor, a sunny piece written when the composer was 11 and had clearly been listening to early Beethoven and Rossini. Its only recording at present is by **Savall** in a disc of the early-music persuasion also containing Arriaga's only other purely orchestral works, the overture to his opera *The Happy Slaves* (age 13) and the Symphony in D (age 15). This disc presents a rather streamlined picture, with no-nonsense slow movements and lively playing (Astrée 8532). It's very short (45 minutes), expensive to boot, and deserves a prize for the most illiterate English notes of 1995.

It was upstaged later that year by **Mackerras,** who omitted the *Nonet* but added a symphony by Jan Václav Vo_í_ek, written the same year by a composer who also died young, at 34 (♦Hyperion 66800).This recording offers a more sympathetic reading. **López-Cobos** couples the two Arriaga works with an early Mozart symphony, and here arises the lack of a performance tradition (Ensayo 9728). Are we to see Arriaga as a lyric romantic or as a lively classic? Lopez-Cobos stretches the music out perhaps more than it can support without falling over. After all, the composer was only 15!

At 18, the composer wrote three string quartets that have received several recordings. The **Rasumovsky Quartet** ripped through them in 65 minutes (Philips LP, NA), the **Chilingirian Quartet** slept through them in 89 (CRD 33123, 2CD, NA), while the **Guarnieris** struck a happy, if somewhat heavy, medium, at 75 (Philips). The **Voces Quartet** seems to have the most effective balance of verve and lyricism, at 74 (♦MD+G 6030236).   MOORE

Daniel Asia *(b. 1953)*
Asia studied at Yale with Druckman and Penderecki and teaches at the University of Arizona. The recipient of many commissions, he has followed a fairly common trajectory for late 20th-century American composers, from complex, detailed serial writing to a more accessible style, redolent of the colorful, uncluttered orchestration and jazzy rhythms of Copland, Bernstein, and Adams. The New York *Times* once singled him out in an article about "The New Musical Hedonism" (or something like that), but he is more accurately described as a very serious contemporary musician who isn't afraid of the "a-word"—accessibility.

Symphony 2 (1992) is a memorial to Leonard Bernstein and a straightforward expression of Asia's own Jewishness. That comes across in the music, which is often spirited but has a constant undercurrent of melancholy. The dedication is appropriate: This symphony has some of the appeal of such Bernstein works as *Chichester Psalms* and the *"Jeremiah"* Symphony. Performed by **Sedares** with the Phoenix Symphony, it's coupled with Asia's longer but less interesting Symphony 3 (New World 804473). This 40-minute piece is put together with the utmost professionalism, but the melodic material is less impressive and the glossy orchestration and propulsive rhythms sound rather anonymous. Sedares is an Asia advocate; he also conducts Symphonies 1 and 4 (Summit 256), the virtuosic Piano Concerto (with André-Michel Schub), and the darkly colored orchestral piece *Black Light* (Koch 7372).

Asia's musical style in the '80s was more texturally complex, but attractive and challenging; some of his earlier chamber and vocal music can be sampled in Albany 106. His creative response to poetry can be heard in *Songs from the Page of Swords,* with **Asia** conducting Musical Elements, a group he co-founded (♦Summit 257). Besides the title work, this disc includes two irresistible Hebrew psalm settings for voice and guitar, in the mode of Steve Reich's *Tehillim.* As proof that Asia knows his way around a keyboard, there's a collection with pianist **Jonathan Shames** and the Bridge Ensemble that includes the seven-movement *Scherzo Sonata* and the 1989 Piano Quartet, a work whose open textures and rhythmic energy have a very "American" sound without being at all clichéd (♦Koch 7313).   RAYMOND

Kurt Atterberg (1887–1974)

Composer, conductor, cellist, music critic, civil engineer, patent office official, Atterberg did all this during his lifetime and still managed to write nine large-scale symphonies, concertos, suites, and chamber music. Together with Alfvén, Atterberg was the Swedish composer whose works were most widely played abroad during his lifetime. His music is national-romantic, with roots in Nielsen and Sibelius, suffused with the essence of (or actual borrowings from) Swedish folk music. Brilliance of coloring, intensity of expression, and broad brush strokes are his hallmarks, and in slow movements, Atterberg's superb melodic gift reigns supreme.

SYMPHONIES

1. A work of his early 20s, 1 is Atterberg's longest symphony at just over 40 minutes and shows his command of his musical craft. **Westerberg,** who has done more for Swedish music than any other conductor, leads a sensitive and committed performance by the Swedish Radio SO (Sterling 1010, with Symphony 4). It has also been recorded in an excellent performance with fine sonics by **Ari Rasilainen.**

2. A work of soaring, memorable melodies, it is sensitively interpreted by **Westerberg,** coupled with the gorgeous Suite 3 for violin, viola, and strings, an adaptation of music for Maeterlinck's miracle play *Sister Beatrice.* This may well be Atterberg's most beautiful suite (Swedish Society Discophil 1006).

3. Here the composer turned to Swedish west coast seascapes for inspiration, using lavish textures and impressionist nature-painting. In **Ehrling**'s recording it's coupled with Atterberg's fine Horn Concerto, in which hornist **Albert Linder** does the honors (Caprice 21364).

4. On the same disc as Westerberg's 1, **Sten Frykberg** offers the aptly named "Sinfonia piccola," Atterberg's shortest symphony at around 20 minutes. This is the first symphony in which he quotes actual Swedish folk tunes, rather than imitating them, showing a masterly use of them in symphonic garb. This recording was transferred from an LP with somewhat dry sonics and some surface noise. **Rasilainen** offers a better performance and excellent sonics (CPO 999639, with 1).

5. ("Sinfonia Funèbre"). Atterberg's musical language here is dark-hued and dramatic, but the music is not as funereal as the title suggests. The composer himself was not fond of this work; indeed, it seems to be an anomaly in his largely optimistic, joyous music. **Westerberg** provides a good performance (Musica Sveciae 620, with two attractive symphonic poems by Edwin Kallstenius and Oscar Lindberg).

6. It won the $10,000 First Prize in the 1928 Schubert Competition, arranged by Columbia. The work became known as the "Dollar Symphony" and was recorded by Atterberg himself, Beecham, and Toscanini. A wonderful all-Atterberg disc also contains *A Värmland Rhapsody* and *Ballad Without Words,* the latter the strongest and the most interesting; **Jun'ichi Hirokamu**'s performance and sonics are fine (BIS 553).

7 and *8.* For the very worthwhile 7, Atterberg deliberately chose the title *Sinfonia Romantica* "out of irritation with the Anti-Romantics." 8 is based on lilting Swedish folk tunes, and their melodic freshness and sweetness make it a wonderful listening experience. The two are ideally coupled under the capable baton of **Michail Jurowski** (Sterling 1026).

OTHER MUSIC

Atterberg sketched parts of his Piano Concerto in 1927 but didn't complete the work until 1934. Brahmsian in conception, it has a more symphonic than concertante character with its integrated piano part. It's coupled with the exuberant and songful Violin Concerto in fine performances by **Dan Franklin Smith** and **Christian Bergqvist,** led by B. Tommy Andersson (Sterling 1034).

The delightful ballet-pantomime *The Wise and Foolish Virgins* is a rhapsody on old Swedish folk songs and is performed by **Grevillius** (Phono Sveciae 58-1). A treatise on Swedish music says that in this ballet, Swedish folk music acquired "one of its most beautiful and genuine artistic expressions." This lovely CD is rounded out with short pieces in various instrumental combinations by other Swedish composers.

Stig Rybrant conducts the *Aladdin Overture,* a dashing, exuberant work from the fairy-tale opera of the same name (Swedish Society Discophil 1021). Nordic wistfulness and melancholy color the lovely *Suite Barocco* for woodwinds and strings and the equally fine *Suite Pastorale in Modo Antico* for strings. The two suites benefit from **Atterberg**'s expertise. The Saulesco Quartet rounds out this disc with a fine performance of the splendid String Quartet Op. 11, a lyrical work with some astringency.

Readers interested in Atterberg's chamber music would do well to consult Marco Polo 223404, a recording of miscellaneous works. His very worthwhile Piano Quintet, adapted from Symphony 6, and the impressive Sonata for Cello and Piano are on Marco Polo 223405.   DE JONG

Daniel-François Auber (1782–1871)

Destined to be forever relegated to collections of overtures along with Boieldieu, Hérold and Adam, Auber shares with them the piquant charm and fragrant bouquet of the French *opéra-comique,* which elevated to its highest level in such melodious entertainments as *Fra Diavolo, Le Cheval de Bronze,* and *Les Diamants de la Couronne.* Yet in his masterpiece *La Muette de Portici*—generally called *Masaniello* outside France—he indulged in the most passionate outbursts, telling of a firebrand revolutionary who led the people of Naples against their Spanish oppressors, and so well did he succeed that when the opera was performed in Belgium it sparked riots against Dutch rule that resulted in a declaration of independence. Thus did the Frenchman Auber plant the seeds that were to flower some 15 years later in Verdi's *Nabucco.*

ORCHESTRAL MUSIC

Overtures. Tuneful and spirited, the overtures of Auber have long been a staple at "pops" concerts and on disc. That's the *good* news. The bad news is that few of these recordings have been released on CD. Fortunately the lone collection on CD is also the best: **Paray**'s unbeatable *Fra Diavolo, Bronze Horse,* and *Masaniello,* coupled with his likewise superlative Suppé overtures (♦Mercury 434309), plus *The Crown Diamonds* in "French Opera Highlights" (♦Mercury 432014). You may find better sounding accounts of these pieces but not better performances, and that includes conductors highly skilled in "pops" fare like **Kunzel** (*Fra Diavolo,* Telarc) and **John Williams** (*Bronze Horse,* Philips)—though both collections are attractive as a whole.

Ansermet's *Fra Diavolo* and *Domino Noir* can be found, but I haven't seen them issued in the US (Decca). A rather under-energized *Masaniello* may also be heard under its alternate title of *La Muette di Portici* with **Redel** (Pierre Verany); a better one is **Markevitch**'s, as filler with the *Symphonie Fantastique* (DG). You may also find **Vonk**'s "Overtures to Comic Operas" collection, including a rather tepid *Fra Diavolo* (Ars Vivendi). Much better is the *Crown Diamonds* included in **René Leibowitz**'s "Evening of Opera" collection (Chesky 61). If you happen to purchase **Bonynge**'s complete *Domino Noir* (London), you will get the Overture and Ballet Music from *Gustave III, ou Le Bal Masqué*—yes, the same story later set to music by Verdi—as a sizable and most welcome bonus. His superlative recordings of *Marco Spada, Lestocq,* and *La Neige* have finally come out on CD as well (London).

Marco Spada is a ballet reportedly commissioned by Napoleon III as a vehicle for the two most celebrated ballerinas of the day, Carolina Rosati and Amalia Ferraris; it has no melodic connection whatever with the opera of the same name, being in fact a motley collection of airs and snatches compiled from several of Auber's most popular productions. There used to be an LP by **Bonynge,** comprising roughly two-thirds of the score, not released on CD to my knowledge (London). In its place you will find a version conducted by **Michel Quéval,** which at 90 minutes may well be the entire ballet; unfortunately, the beauties of Auber's score may be glimpsed only fitfully, thanks to Quéval's often sluggish tempos and the less than ravishing string tone of the Paris Opera Orchestra (Cybelia). A set titled simply "Ballet Gala" includes, among other things, a substantial suite called *Les Rendez-vous* arranged by Constant Lambert primarily from *L'Enfant prodigue,* as well as a shorter piece, *Pas Classique,* whose origins are less clear, both conducted by **Bonynge** (Decca, 2CD).

CONCERTOS

Auber wrote four concertos for his friend, the cellist Hurel de Lamare. One of these, in A minor, was recorded some years back by **Jascha Silberstein** and Bonynge (London), and then nearly 20 years later it surfaced again, this time on CD, with **Martin Ostertag** and Roberto Paternostro (Koch-Schwann). However, the two performances could scarcely be more different. On Koch the Auber "concerto" is downgraded to a mere "Rondo"; even more curious, what Ostertag offers is only the third movement of that concerto (if somewhat extended) to which a slow introduction has mysteriously been appended, perhaps reflecting a different edition. Performances are widely disparate as well; Ostertag is much slower than Silberstein, but more attentive to nuance and color, while his tone is less darkly hued than his colleague's but also more nasal (a minor point). Since the accompanying Popper concerto also varies widely between the two recordings—primarily reflecting the sizable array of wholesale and wanton cuts made by Silberstein—the scrupulous collector will want to have both.   HALLER

OPERAS

Auber's operas once enjoyed great popularity, but the current catalogues and a glance at the repertories of the world's opera houses indicate this is no longer the case. Even the most avid opera fan is more likely to encounter a concert performance of these works than a staged revival.

Fra Diavolo (1820). It is considered the best of Auber's stage works. It tells of an Italian bandit who only robs rich people and is finally captured when the officer on his case is tipped off by her lover, whom the bandit is planning to kill. The plot has elements of "rescue opera" but the story is neither dramatic nor tragic, and neither is the music; it keeps its distance and is, if anything, ironic. The best recording comes from

Monte Carlo and has a fine cast headed by **Gedda,** Mesplé, and Jean Barbie (♦EMI 54810).

Le Domino Noir. It was Auber's most successful opéra comique in Paris, with more than 1,200 performances from 1837 to 1909. It's set in Spain in the 18th century and is essentially a love story with a happy ending. On the way, there are complications involving the heroine, who lives in a convent and has no money; she assumes many disguises (including a black domino) but her noble lover catches up with her, and the Queen blesses their union after (because?) she inherits a fortune. It has been well recorded under **Bonynge** with Sumi Jo and Bruce Ford in the leading roles (♦London 440646). An older French radio recording has the esteemed **Jeanne Micheau** as the heroine, but its sound is much poorer (Melodram).   MOSES

Georges Auric *(1899–1983)*

Auric made his debut as a composer at age 15 and moved in the most fashionable Parisian artistic circles immediately afterwards, compiling an impressive avant-garde resumé. He was a member of *Les Six,* Cocteau dedicated his manifesto *Le coq et l'arlequin* to him, he wrote several ballet scores for Diaghilev's Ballets Russes, and he was one of the pianists in the first performance of Stravinsky's *Les Noces.* He was later a music critic and director (simultaneously) of the Paris Opéra and Opéra-Comique, and continued his association with Cocteau as composer for his great films *La Belle et la Bête* and *Orphée.* He also wrote the score for René Clair's *A nous la liberté,* and his best-known piece, by far, was for a Hollywood movie: the waltz theme from *Moulin Rouge* (1952, with José Ferrer as Toulouse-Lautrec and Zsa Zsa Gabor as Zsa Zsa Gabor). Fitted with words, "Where Is Your Heart?" made Auric the first member of *Les Six* to have a song on the Hit Parade. His earlier music, like *Les Facheux,* is definitely *Six*-ish in style, witty and colorful. He later became more experimental; his gnarly Piano Sonata in F (1931) was a notorious flop, but *Imaginées* for chamber ensemble (1968-1974) delves more successfully into atonality and improvisation.

There isn't much Auric in the current catalog. The jolly *Ouverture* for orchestra is in a 1965 **Dorati**/London Symphony recording, where it sits well with music by Milhaud, Satie, and Françaix (Mercury 34335). The Trio for Oboe, Clarinet, and Bassoon is performed by members of the Chicago Chamber Players; the all-French couplings include obscure woodwind pieces by Canteloube and Pierné (Cedille 40). His contribution to the pastiche ballet *L'Éventail de Jeanne*—a collaborative effort with Poulenc, Roussel, and others—can be heard with the Philharmonia conducted by **Geoffrey Simon** (Chandos 8356).

Auric wrote a lot of film music, and the best of it is worth preserving. His most sensitive work in this genre is *La Belle et la Bête,* which perfectly complements Cocteau's beautiful film; the complete score is available (Marco Polo 223765). If it whets your appetite, try Marco Polo 225066, which includes music for Cocteau's *Orphée* and *Les parents terribles.*   RAYMOND

Milton Babbitt *(b. 1916)*

"I want a piece of music to be literally as much as possible," Babbitt has said, underscoring his preoccupation with compositional rigor and his penchant for dense, highly concentrated musical events. He has been the major intellectual force in American serialism for 50 years, and his formidable intellect and background in both music and mathematics have insured him a lofty position in the academy. Outside academia, things are different, where his reputation as a theorist has probably overshadowed the merits of his music and enhanced his reputation as a "difficult" composer. This is a shame, because he offers great rewards to the listener who isn't put off by the prospect of twelve-tone music. Indeed, his best music has wit, charm and a sense of play that make it much more approachable than most people expect.

While many may not be able to hear the elaborate structures and pitch schema from which his music is constructed, his mastery of the idiom and sure craftsmanship are never in doubt. Repeated hearings are essential, because even the short works convey an enormous amount of information that even experienced listeners have difficulty absorbing in one pass. Babbitt's music has become progressively more overtly emotional, expressive, and witty over the years, making his more recent works an ideal starting point. There are few all-Babbitt discs; most of his works are coupled with compositions by other American composers.

Babbitt's music is extremely difficult to perform and calls for a virtuosity that most orchestras and many conductors have found difficult to deliver. Consequently, there are few recordings of his orchestral works. Try beginning with *Correspondences* for string orchestra and tape. Here Babbitt juxtaposes delicate orchestral textures with an intricate electronic filigree. **Levine** leads the Chicago Symphony on a fine disc (DG 431698, with works by Carter, Cage, and Schuller). *Relata I* is thornier, and the listener is more aware of the elaborate compositional processes being worked out. **Zukofsky** and the Juilliard Orchestra play with an ease that belies the work's difficulty (New World 80396).

Babbitt's Piano Concerto was his first orchestral work to be recorded (in 1986!) and is one of his most expansive to date. The piano plays almost continuously throughout its 25-minute length; Babbitt helps by keeping the orchestral textures transparent. **Alan Feinberg,** a longtime advocate of this composer's music, is ably supported by Charles Wuorinen and the American Composers Orchestra (New World 80346, with *The Head of the Bed*, a chamber setting of a long text by John Hollander). Soprano Judith Bettina and Parnassus give a sterling performance of the latter, but the piece loses impact because the writing is so concentrated and the text so expansive that your ears become fatigued long before it ends.

I think Babbitt is most effective in chamber and solo settings, and there are many recordings to support this. One of his most ingratiating pieces is *All Set* for jazz ensemble—not actual jazz, but the jazz idiom is refracted in Babbitt's serial language (Nonesuch 79222). "Soli e Duettini" is an outstanding all-Babbitt collection performed by the **Group for Contemporary Music,** presenting a rich and varied group of recent works for solo instruments or duos (Koch 7335 2CD). This is an ideal introduction to Babbitt's music, as these pieces are less dense and his dry sense of humor is much more evident. Works like *Whirled Series* for alto saxophone and piano, *None but the Lonely Flute* for flute solo, or *Beaten Paths* for marimba show a composer with a gentle playfulness even at his most rigorous. In *None but the Lonely Flute* (stunningly played by Rachel Rudich), Babbitt reveals the shadowy outline of the famous Tchaikovsky melody without ever actually quoting it. This piece is also wonderfully performed by **Dorothy Stone** (New World 80456). Stone takes a more languid, lyrical approach, whereas Rudich brings out the gestural brilliance of the piece. Both interpretations work well and show the expressive potential inherent in the music.

Piano works have long been among Babbitt's interests, and he has written copiously and enthusiastically for the instrument. Two collections present his most important piano pieces and both are highly recommended. **Taub** offers a broad survey of those written from the late '50s to the mid-80s (Harmonia Mundi 905160). **Martin Goldray** offers

Babbitt's "Piano Music Since 1983," which presents later works than those on Taub's disc. **Feinberg** plays five mostly brief pieces in another chamber collection (CRI 521). The latter has a nice variety to it, with *An Elizabethan Sextette* for six singers, *Groupwise* for strings, flute, and piano, and *Vision and Prayer* for soprano and synthesized tape, brilliantly sung by Bethany Beardslee.

Babbitt has composed five string quartets; only 3 and 4 are currently available. The **Fine Arts Quartet**'s excellent 1971 recording of 3 has surfaced on a beautifully remastered reissue (♦Music and Arts 707, with Wourinen's Quartet 1). The sonics are warm, and this is one of my favorite Babbitt works; it's downright lyrical and suffused with a genuine pathos. The **Juilliard String Quartet,** undaunted by its intricate complexities, gives a persuasive and highly expressive performance of 4, which is a bit more dramatic in profile (CRI 587, with quartets by Wolpe and Sessions). Both of these performances argue strongly for the music and also for the need of a complete survey of these pieces.

Two major compositions for violin and piano are presented by **Rolf Schulte** and Feinberg. *Sextets* and *The Joy of More Sextets* are substantial essays in this genre; the titles are a bit confusing because they suggest an ensemble of six rather than a duo, but they actually refer to the "sixes" that run throughout both works and inform their structures with consistent unity (New World 364). The music is typically intense, with Schulte and Feinberg handling its abrupt registral shifts and continuous flux nicely.

Babbitt was also an early pioneer in electronic music. Rather than exploring *musique concrète,* his work was done exclusively on the two RCA synthesizers built in the 1950s. These instruments were suited to his temperament and compositional interests, and he wrote a substantial number of pieces for tape and performer. An excellent survey includes the monumental *Philomel,* one of his finest compositions (New World 80466). This haunting work for soprano and tape is a brilliant setting of a John Hollander poem based on the narrative in Ovid's *Metamorphoses;* Babbitt creates a poignant and dramatic setting of the raped woman who was changed into a nightingale. It's sung by **Beardslee,** and she is its best advocate. **Judith Bettina** (Neuma 450-74, with Babbitt's *Phonemena*) gives an alternative performance, but Beardslee has better diction and a more energized, dramatic approach. But I prefer Bettina's performance of *Phonemena* to Lynn Webber on the New World disc; her singing is warmer and better integrated with the tape part.   McINTIRE

Carl Philipp Emanuel Bach *(1714–1788)*
Carl Philipp Emanuel (CPE) was the fifth son of Johann Sebastian and Maria Barbara Bach, and like his older brother, Wilhelm Friedemann (WF), he began composing at an early age. But unlike WF, CPE did not depend on his father's fame and influence to find employment; on the contrary, he spent his energies promoting his father's work after his death, preparing editions of *Art of Fugue, Well-Tempered Klavier,* and 371 of the Chorales. He secured a position as keyboard player in the court of Frederick the Great of Prussia, and though he remained in the King's service for 28 years, he was not one of Frederick's favorites (he refused to place the King's musical authority above his father's).

CPE wrote a good deal of flute music at Frederick's court. Baroque flutist **Barthold Kuijken** and harpsichordist Bob van Asperen recorded his sonatas and chamber works (Sony 53964), and **Konrad Hünteler** recorded all of the flute sonatas with cellist Anner Bylsma and keyboard player Jacques Ogg (MD+G 3484/85). Both recordings are excellent.

Perhaps the best chamber works from CPE's years in Prussia are his quartets for flute, viola, cello, and harpsichord. They are distinctive because the cello is independent of the left-hand keyboard part (in most 18th-century music the cello's main function is to reinforce the harpsichord's bass). These quartets have been recorded on period instruments by **Wilbert Hazelzet,** Wiel Peeters, Richte van der Meer, and harpsichordist Ton Koopman (Philips 416 615). Hazelzet also made a fine recording of the trio sonatas (Globe 5110).

CPE wrote three cello concertos while working for Frederick (to keep in his good graces he had to arrange them for flute, and they are extremely difficult to play). **Tim Hugh** made a fine modern-instrument recording (Naxos 553298) and **Bylsma** played them on a baroque cello (Virgin 790800). Even though the instrument was going out of fashion in CPE's time, he wrote some interesting sonatas for viola da gamba, recorded by **Siegfried Pank** and Christine Jaccottet (Berlin 9264) and by **William Hunt** with Richard Egarr (Harmonia Mundi 1910410). CPE also transcribed some of his keyboard concertos for the oboe, and **Josef Kiss** made a fine recording (Naxos 55056), as did **Holliger** (Philips 42592).

After the Seven Years War, CPE became director of music in Hamburg, a position vacated by his godfather Telemann. This was the start of a new creative period; liberated from the musical restrictions imposed on him in Prussia, he explored a style associated with Lessing's theories of sentiment ("Empfindsamkeit"). He blossomed in Hamburg, where he wrote many pieces for orchestra, including some sinfonias (the "Hamburg Symphonies") recorded beautifully on modern instruments by the **Capella Istropolitana** (Naxos 553285) and on baroque instruments by **Hogwood** and the Academy of Ancient Music (Oiseau-Lyre 417124). There is a fine recording of his earlier symphonies by **Les Amis de Philippe** (CPO 999418). The **Fiati con Tasto Köln** recorded some of CPE's very interesting wind music, including an unusual set of sonatas for fortepiano, clarinet, and bassoon (CPO 999508).

CPE wrote a small but excellent body of choral music. A fine recording of his *Magnificat,* the best known of these works, is by the **Academy of St. Martin in the Fields** (London 421148). Another rewarding composition is *Die Auferstehung und Himmelfahrt Jesu,* recorded by **Herreweghe** and the Orchestra of The Age of Enlightenment (Virgin 91498).

CPE wrote around 100 pieces for the keyboard, and there are many good recordings of his works on both harpsichord and clavichord. Harpsichordist **Gabor Antalffy** recorded 18 of his sonatas, 13 of his Rondos, and some of his Fantasies (CPO 999100), and harpsichordist **Shirley Mathews** recorded six of his sonatas from his years at Frederick's court (Gasparo 319). **Miklós Spányi** made an interesting recording of the Prussian sonatas on the clavichord (BIS 879). Though the recorded sound is odd, **Hogwood**'s clavichord recording of the sonatas and sonatinas from *Versuch über die wahre Art das Clavier zu spielen* (1753) is worth reissuing or searching out on LP (Oiseau-Lyre 589).

There are many recordings of CPE's harpsichord concertos. **Spányi** recorded all of them in six volumes (BIS, various numbers). **Ludger Rémy** and Les Amis de Philippe have a lively recording of the "Hamburg" concertos (CPO 999350), but the one I like best is the LP by **van Asperen** and the Melante '81 Orchestra (EMI/Angel 33929). CPE also wrote some multiple keyboard music. **Andreas Staier** and Robert Hill made a fine recording of his concerto for two harpsichords with Musica Antique Koln (Archiv 419256), and **Hogwood** recorded some duets with Christopher Rousset (Oiseau Lyre 40649). Both recordings include works by the other Bach brothers.

CPE wrote a small but excellent body of choral music. A fine recording of his *Magnificat,* the best known, is by the **Academy of St. Martin in the Fields** (London 421148). Other fine choral works are *Die Aufer-*

stehung und Himmelfahrt Jesu, recorded by **Herreweghe** (Virgin 91498), and *Die Israeliten in der Wüste,* led by **Christie** (Harmonia Mundi 1901321). There is also a wonderful collection of sacred songs sung by baritone **Klaus Mertens** with Ludger Rémy accompanying him at the fortepiano (CPO 999708).   FINE

Johann Christoph Friedrich Bach *(1732–1775)*

The third youngest son of Johann Sebastian and Anna Magdalena Bach became known as the "Bückeburg Bach" because he had a long and successful career at the court of Schaumburg-Lippe in Bückeburg. Like his brothers, Johann Christoph Friedrich (JCF) studied music with his father-in-law in Leipzig. Italian music was very much in fashion at Bückeburg, and JCF's patron Count Wilhelm had an extensive library of music by contemporary Italian composers and Italians as concertmaster for his orchestra as well as his court composer. After Wilhelm died, JCF remained in Bückeburg and reinforced its library with music by composers like Mozart, Haydn, and Stamitz.

JCF wrote quite a bit of music, including 14 symphonies, but comparatively little has been recorded. **Les Violins du Roy** include one of his *Sinfonias* on "Music of Bach's Sons" (Dorian 90239), and some of his orchestral music is included in the **Ensemble for 18th-Century Music's** "The Bach Boys" (Klavier 1054). **Bylsma** recorded his Cello Sonata in A with some of his father's sonatas (Sony 45945), and the **Bell Arte String Trio** recorded his trio sonatas and sonatas (Premier 1051). **Wilbert Hazelzet** offers some of his quartets for flute and strings in "Chamber Music by the Bach Sons" (Globe 5116), as well as six sonatas with harpsichordist Jacques Ogg. Oboist **Allan Vogel** includes the Trio in C major in his "Bach's Circle" disc (Delos 3214). The performers in this recording consider the last eight bars of the C-major sonata the "unofficial beginning of music's classical period."   FINE

Johann Sebastian Bach *(1685–1750)*

Johann Sebastian Bach and his music have been many different things to many different people at many different times. He seems to have thought of himself as a hard-working craftsman rather than as some sort of creative genius, but he took his professionalism seriously enough to prepare major summings up of his art, as if for some kind of posterity, almost in anticipation of the later Romantic ideal of writing for the ages. By his contemporaries he was esteemed more as performer than as composer, though some of his compositions continued to be held in high regard by musicians through the end of the 18th century. The famous "revival" of his music in the 19th century turned him into a demigod, fixing his work as the beginning of great Western art music, an attitude that survived well into the 20th. Latter-day commentators have seen him variously as a religious visionary, a dabbler in numerical symbolism and mystical imagery, or an abstract theoretician of musical science. His music continues to fascinate generation after generation of performers and listeners, who continue to discover new mysteries and meanings in his work.

The latest frenzy of attention is in progress as this book goes to press, the 250th anniversary of his death prompting accelerated productivity by the recording industry. In addition to individual projects, a major program of reissues by Teldec ("Bach 2000") and a mixture of reissued and new recordings by Hänssler ("Bachakademie") are bringing forth cycles of the "complete" works. Smaller assemblages (some ephemeral) will further confuse the availability (and identifiability) of recordings. Thus Harmonia Mundi has reissued groups of Bach recordings from its catalog as a specially packaged 20CD series called the "Essential Bach

Edition." On a smaller scale is Capriccio's 11CD "Leipzig Bach Edition," a skimpy gleaning of its resources. Still emerging is a "Bach Edition" of multi-disc boxed sets from the German Brilliant Classics label, containing a mix of older and newer recordings from various sources.

All that is on top of a long-established Bach discography that has developed with its own complexities. Much of the history of that discography has reflected the problem of how far we impose our concepts on his music. Indeed, his scores have become a laboratory for working out our understanding of performance practices through a half-century of accumulating musicological knowledge and speculation. Within the broader context of the movement to recover "authenticity" in performing Baroque music, advancing scholarly insights have prompted phases of Bach performance representing changing stages of practice. Consequently, some performances may become dated in those terms, even if their musical values transcend musicological dictates.

ORCHESTRAL MUSIC

The label for this category is arbitrary. Our idea of "orchestra" hardly corresponds to the practices of Bach's day. Certainly we are past the time when conductors ranging from Weingartner, Mengelberg, Stokowski, and Koussevitzky through Klemperer, Casals, Munch, Jochum, and Karajan would bring to bear on Bach all the resources of the 19th-century symphony orchestra. To be sure, reissues of many such "historic" recordings show that there remains an audience undeterred by anachronisms and still willing to find enduring musical values in older esthetics. Meanwhile, there are many performers who, if absorbing selectively the lessons of "authenticity" from musicologists and period instrumentalists, assimilate such lessons into compromise approaches designed to accommodate latter-day tastes.

Obviously, then, there is a spectrum of Bach-collecting tastes, and any guidance has to respect that range. As the most basic of starting points, the designation "PI" will be used for "period instruments" and "MI" for (the somewhat meaningless) "modern instruments," and variables beyond that will be pointed up along the way. For convenience, only complete sets or groupings will be considered in most cases; to call attention to the innumerable and scattered individual recordings of individual works would be of limited value.

Brandenburg Concertos

Simply to count the number of recordings over the years of this perpetually fascinating and challenging set would be daunting; there are about 45 complete sets currently in print. Many are not to be taken seriously, but a surprising number fall into the category I call "merely excellent," while a substantial minority can be recognized as truly outstanding, whether in PI or MI terms. All sets are assumed to be 2CD and without bonus selections unless indicated otherwise.

Modern instruments (MI)

The "MI" labeling here is arbitrary; for the last 45 years or so, recordings have adopted some form of compromise "historical" approach, using relatively small chamber ensembles, usually replacing the piano in 5 with harpsichord and using recorders in 2, 4, and even 5, but otherwise retaining "modern" styles of string playing. The truly old-fashioned kind of conductor-driven "orchestral" performances are hard to find nowadays, surviving almost uniquely from **Karajan** (DG), of interest mainly to nostalgia buffs between meetings of the Flat Earth Society.

Nevertheless, there is interest beyond the archeological in two examples of bygone practice recently revived. The 1932 set led by **Cortot** in a Cortot-as-Conductor album is difficult to listen to today, with its mannered, inconsistent, and totally anachronistic style, but it's a window into a Romantic spirit that prevailed in the long-lost days of yore (Koch 7705, with a Couperin suite and Brahms's Double Concerto). More enduring in both historical and musical value are **Adolf Busch's** Chamber Players 1935–36 recording of both the *Brandenburgs* and the Suites (EMI 764047; Pearl 9263; both 3CD). Notwithstanding stately tempos, young Rudolf Serkin on the piano, and other anachronisms, Busch's venture reclaimed these works for chamber-sized ensembles and served them up with affection and taste.

There is more idiosyncracy than stylishness in the performances led by **Casals** at Prades in the early 1950s (when, for instance, he replaced 2's trumpet with a saxophone!) and at the Marlboro Festival in 1964–65; those old Columbia recordings are not available (NA), but you never know when they might turn up again, likewise for nostalgia types or Casals buffs. But for old-fashioned big-band Bach that retains considerable artistic integrity for all its dated perspectives, there is the full set combined with the Suites recorded by **Koussevitzky** in 1945–49 with members of the Boston Symphony (♦Pearl 0103, 3CD). That may be supplemented by of performances from 1945–46 of 3 and 4 of both the *Brandenburgs* and the Suites (AS Disc 5721).

The full launching of historically sensitive MI recordings can be traced in landmarks by **Horenstein** (1954) and **Scherchen** (1960), but Horenstein's version is stiffly conducted and poorly recorded in soupy sound (Vox), while Scherchen's is ponderous and mannered (Theorema; Millennium). Neither is for anything but discographic reference by present standards.

Once admired as a leading exponent of "progressive compromise" sensitivity, **Karl Richter** made two recordings, but his approach now seems too rigid and unbending to be competitive (1958, Telarc; 1968, DG). Not notably distinguished but still quite agreeable are honest and dependable old sets by **Ristenpart** (Elektra; Accord 200382 and 200392) and **Günther Kehr,** though the latter can be a bit *Kapellmeisterish* (Allegretto; Vox). The eminent violinist **Josef Suk** led a disappointingly bland account by comparison (Vanguard). Canada's underrated **Bernardi's** showing is more respectable (SMS 5028). The sets led by violinists **Carl Pini** (Virgin 61403, with Violin Concertos BWV 1041-43) and **Jonathan Rees** (Omega 1008/9) offer intelligent and unmannered musicianship.

The MI category has quite a share of "merely excellent" versions. Leading that list is the long-lived **I Musici** performance, undeniably elegant and very listenable, but also rather bland (1965: Philips). **Maksymiuk's** Polish Chamber Orchestra bargain set is rather brisk in tempos and a little foursquare in pacing, but excellently played and recorded (EMI 69749, with Christmas Concertos by Corelli and others). **Menuhin** features quality soloists and undeniable musicianship in not terribly exciting but very intelligent and well-played performances (1959: Seraphim 568516). A more recent example in this line is **Rilling,** the self-appointed successor to Richter as the "compromise" assimilator of musicology into traditionally anchored interpretation; but, to my taste, his treatment is a little too polite (Hänssler, separately or in the "Bachakademie" series as Vol. 162, 92.126, 2CD). For bargain hunters, there is the polished and energetic set by **Warchal** (♦Naxos, Vols. 6 and 7 in the 8CD boxed set or separately as 554607/08, with Triple Concerto and the BWV 1057 variant on 4). Likewise lively but with less personality is **Robert Haydon Clark's** set, with the alternate horn version in 2 (Brilliant Classics, in the first two discs of their 9CD set of orchestral works and concertos, 99360).

Several conductors have made durable recordings of classic status, long praised by critics. **Baumgartner** made a distinguished MI cycle with such excellent soloists as Ralph Kirkpatrick (1959–60: DG). That version is currently NA, but his 1978 remake, again with excellent soloists, has reappeared; these are performances with enduring values of genuine taste and "traditional" style, though hampered by boomy sonics (♦RCA 61719 or 61559, with Galway leading Suite 2 and a BWV 1059 adaptation). Also satisfying in "traditional" terms is **Leppard,** always a vital and robust MI performer of Baroque music, his reissue adding desirable bonuses (♦Philips 442386 or 442387, with the Triple Concerto and Grumiaux in Violin Concertos BWV 1041-42). **Münchinger** can always be counted on for solid and lasting musicality. Of the two full sets he made in 1959 and 1974, the earlier version is still available (♦London 421027/28, with Suite 2).

Marriner holds the record for remakes. His first recording followed Thurston Dart's pioneering reconstructions of the earliest versions of each work (1971: ♦Philips 426088 or 426089); this lively Marriner I serves as the MI counterpart to Hogwood's PI cycle of "originals." Nine years later, Marriner took his St. Martin Academy through the "standard" texts, with a cast of star soloists (Szeryng, Petri, Rampal, Holliger, André Bernard, George Malcolm) for a less scholarly and more frankly box-office MI version of chamber scale (♦Philips 400076 or 422077). Then, after ten more years, Marriner made yet a third recording, first issued in a 3CD package with the Suites, now out on singles (1–4 on EMI 69877, 5–6 and Suite 1 on 69878). The overall result is a progression typical of this conductor, advancing suavity at the expense of feeling and depth—so it's Marriner III for slickness, II for glitter, I for imagination.

Several sets have individual qualities that impart special distinction. **Britten**'s carefully thought-out recording offers the insights of one great composer into the music of another (1968: ♦London 443847, with BWV 1060 and 1056 in a flute arrangement, under Marriner). At another extreme are two conductorless ensembles of crack New York City musicians who apply the minimalist principle of one player per part to MI performance. **Bargemusic** is satisfying if not very adventurous in interpretation. The **Chamber Music Society of Lincoln Center** is more impressive for verve and loving artistry, and the sound is superb (1995: ♦Delos 3185).

Finally, back on the chamber orchestra level, I think **Güttler**'s cycle is one of the best MI recordings: sensitivity to textual variants (corno da caccia for trumpet in 2) is balanced by apt vitality and polish (1991–92: ♦Berlin Classics 1145 or 1033, 3CD, with Orchestral Suites). **Pommer**'s interpretation is slightly more traditional but almost PI in scoring and wind instrumentation (1984: ♦Capriccio 10041/42, issued separately). His single disc offering four of Bach's variant versions was a noteworthy supplement (♦Capriccio 10025). Now we have the standard cycle of six together with those alternate versions in a unique "variorum" edition, enhancing the already admirable value of his performances; unfortunately, this expanded reissue is available, at least for now, only as the first pair of discs in the 10CD "Leipzig Bach Edition" (♦Capriccio 49254).

Period instruments (PI)

There are few truly low-quality recordings here, but we may distinguish between the "merely excellent" and the outstanding. All will give satisfaction, and for repeated listening you may prefer the stable to the exceptional. In the first category, I would place **Martin Pearlman,** whose version is handsomely played but bland and characterless (1993–94: Telarc). Likewise the set from **Giovanni Antonini,** which is bright, full of energy, but again without any particular profile (1996–97: Teldec). **Kuijken** is also unexceptional, save for his use of a corno da caccia in place of a trumpet in 2 (1993–94: Harmonia Mundi). Though it's much favored by critics, I would place **Pinnock**'s 1982 cycle in the unexceptional category: it's reliable and stable but rather lifeless and unimaginative (DG)

Much more enjoyable is **Lamon**'s vivacity (1993–94: Sony 66289). **Savall** is also notably energetic; PI lovers will particularly enjoy the fruitiness of the playing, and there are imagination and intelligence in evidence, but the interpretations still lack notable distinction (1991: Astrée). If it's PI energy you want, there's **Siegbert Rampe**'s La Stravaganza Hamburg group, but the extra-small ensemble takes on a rather heavy sound in hard, driven performances at generally high speed, a totality I can't recommend (Virgin). **Goodman**'s Brandenburg Consort set is less off-putting but still rather driven, featuring much energy and intelligence but ultimately rather ungracious listening (1991: Hyperion). Goodman's older ensemble, The Hanover Band, was taken over by **Anthony Halstead** in a 1991–92 recording that is attractive for judicious pacing and a sense that high-quality PI players are really enjoying the music (EMI 64571 or 64572).

Two reliable, enjoyable versions worth serious consideration are by **Koopman** (♦Erato 16163 or 16164, with Triple Concerto and a completion of unfinished BWV 1059 as an Organ Concerto) and **Parrott** (EMI: 1988, NA). Koopman leads from the harpsichord in relaxed tempos, interpolating a harpsichord Adagio in 3. **Harnoncourt**'s two pioneering cycles are somewhat more controversial (1964: Teldec 77611; 1981: 75858 or 75859, or together in 95980. 2CD, each with Suites 2 and 3). His abrasive and aggressive rethinkings are illuminating and provocative and retain lasting interest, though I'd make them backup choices rather than priorities. **Leonhardt** was somewhat less astringent, if still pungent in the use of period sounds by a very small ensemble, still a viable choice in this category (1977: Sony 62946).

Among the "puristic" or "minimalist" PI approaches, several are truly outstanding. The earliest is a special case. **Hogwood** offered not only strongly colorful PI playing but a unique textual approach (1984: ♦Oiseau-Lyre 14187 or 455700, with Two-Harpsichord Concerto 3, Violin/Oboe Concerto, and a 3-violin version of 1064). Following the earlier examples of Goberman, Dart, and Marriner, Hogwood returned to Bach's earliest versions and scorings in a documentary treatment that puts his version in a class by itself.

For those who want musicologically informed, vividly PI versions that bring special degrees of musicality to bear, four sets can be recommended. For an admirably balanced combination of scholarship with sane and reliable artistry and elegant playing, **Linde**'s 1982 cycle, with a notably generous bonus (the *Musical Offering*), is a best buy (♦Virgin 61154). On the other hand, those who like unabashedly "in-your-face" PI sound and respond to risktaking excitement may share my partiality to **Goebel** as a bracing blast of fresh air—but only, it must be stressed, if you don't mind breakneck, daredevil tempos that put off some listeners (1986: ♦DG 447287 or 447288, with Suites 1 and 4, or 423116, with Triple Concerto). **Pickett**'s bizarre theories of musical symbolism fortunately do not detract from his virtuosic and exciting readings, if you can accept his minimalist one-player-per-part doctrine (1993: ♦Oiseau-Lyre 440675).

A 1997 venture with the same scoring approach is by the Cambridge Baroque Camerata led by harpsichordist **Jonathan Hellyer Jones**—highly energetic but with no noteworthy interpretive contributions (Intim Musik 055, with an insipid reconstruction of Gamba Sonata 3, BWV 1029, as "Concerto 7," for the same scoring as 6). As the best middle ground in this group, there is the energetic and joyously musical set by the conductorless and vividly collegial **Berlin Akademie für Alte Musik,** with lots of virtuosic chance-taking but also freedom from eccentricities. It represents an outstanding choice in the PI category, compromised only by an ungenerous lack of bonuses (1997: ♦Harmonia Mundi 901634).

If not on quite the same level of boldness, Appolo's Fire Cleveland Baroque Orchestra led by **Jeannette Sorrel** offers lively and attractive performances (♦Etcetera 2047, 2CD, with a return to multiple string scorings in all but 3 and 6). The sound is vivid and the venture confirms the group's major standing on the early music scene.

Harpsichord concertos (BWV 1052-65)

Because the *ripieno* or "orchestra" in these works is a string ensemble with continuo, the distinction of PI and MI is somewhat strained here, reflecting more a matter of playing style—mainly, degree of vibrato—than choice of instruments. The only real distinction is whether Bach's designation of solo "clavier" is construed (as he probably meant) as harpsichord or as piano. Given strong partisanship over that distinction, choices for many are likely to begin (and end) on that basis.

Harpsichord(s)

A total of 13 concertos, seven for one harpsichord (BWV 1052-58), three for two harpsichords (1060-62), two for three harpsichords (1063-64) and one (actually a transcription from Vivaldi) for four (1065) survive in established form. (Solo Concerto "No. 8," BWV 1059, survives incomplete, but has sometimes been reconstructed on the basis of cantata material.) There are many individual recordings, especially of the multi-harpsichord concertos, too spread about for quick review, but there are treatments *en bloc* that can conveniently be surveyed.

There have been at least 11 variously "complete" recordings of the solo and multi-harpsichord concertos, all of LP vintage. Early cycles by **Ruggero Gerlin** (Critère/Nonesuch), **Veyron-Lacroix** (Erato/Westminster), and Ru_icková (Supraphon) are now defunct and seemingly unrecoverable. But four more of these LP ventures survive through CD reissues. There are also two "complete" projects in progress, as well as some other extended collections of significance.

Of the four reissued cycles, **Jacottet**'s with Jörg Faerber is in the "merely excellent" category—serviceable, but a respectable bargain choice rather than a prime recommendation (1978: Vox 3018, 3CD). Jacottet is never less than expert, but her playing is rather rigid, with strong but inflexible MI conducting, in rather thin sound, though its stereo directionality is unusually good in differentiating the multiple keyboards. That set's predecessor by **Leonhardt** was a pioneering venture in performing these works chamber-style, with a *ripieno* of one player per part, long a novelty; these are vital performances, but the rather harsh PI playing and dull sound somewhat handicap them now (1962–63: Atlantic/Teldec 42726, 3CD; also in Vol. 12 of Teldec's "Bach 2000" collection, 25717, 10CD).

Two other LP-derived sets are also of contrasting character. In **Pinnock**'s cumulative assemblage, the PI performances are consistently intelligent and imaginative, though they can turn tame when heard in quantity (1979, 1981–84: originally ♦DG 534325, 3CD; now MHS). Against such stable reliability stands another PI project (1985–91) by **Koopman** (♦Erato, discontinued in two 2CD sets and briefly reassembled as part of a 6CD set with the *Brandenburgs* and violin concertos; the future of the cycle is uncertain, but it deserves recovery). This is music that gives Koopman's personality full play, in renditions that are energetic and restless sometimes to the point of recklessness, but full of excitement—a cycle to relish.

The brilliant **Igor Kipnis** is responsible for two cycles, one limited and the other complete. He was in his prime (1967–70) when he made the first with Marriner and (in all but name) the St. Martin Academy. This offered the standard 1–7, plus (like Leonhardt) a reconstruction of the lost No. 8 (BWV 1059), as well as *Brandenburg* 5 and the Triple Con-

certo, the latter two items being dropped in the reissues (♦CBS 53243 or Odyssey 45616, 2CD). Kipnis's playing is stylistically sure and full of fire and energy, with suave chamber orchestra backing. Then in 1977 he joined with three other players and the Stuttgart Chamber Orchestra under Münchinger to record all 13 standard concertos. The original 5LP set (♦Intercord) was never fully reissued, though much of its content was released piecemeal as individual CDs. Those are now discontinued, but this cycle should be revived in full, for it is glorious, a perfect foil to Koopman's set and preferable to Pinnock's. Kipnis's playing had mellowed a bit, and Münchinger gave him warmer, broader backing. The CBS set remains important, recommendable in its own right, but the later cycle is a legacy that should not be lost.

Perhaps the proper successor to the Kipnis/Münchinger cycle is in the "Bach-Akademie" series (♦Hänssler 92.127/30, Vols. 127–130, 4 CD singles) in which Helmuth Rilling leads a team of soloists headed by **Robert Levin.** The pacings are unusually brisk, perhaps attributable to Levin's infectious energy and vivacity. For those who want MI string orchestra accompaniments, these are outstanding performances, vividly recorded, with unusually distinct separation of soloists in the multi-harpsichord works.

There are two more "complete" cycles, one still in the making, and both are committed to the minimalist one-per-part PI orchestra. One is by **Alessandrini** with his Concerto Italiano, of which only the first volume has been released (Opus 111). The playing is sturdy but rather hard and unbending, not encouraging so far. On the other hand, there is a series launched by the **Purcell Quartet** with Robert Woolley as lead soloist, offering wonderfully lucid, supple, vivacious, and strongly nuanced PI performances, conveying well the intimate side of these works, though with a clarity that's also rather stark (♦Chandos 0595, 0611, 0636, 0641, with Triple Concerto and *Brandenburg* 5). Especially fine, too, is the crisp spatial clarity in the multi-harpsichord works—I've never heard the interaction of the four in BWV 1065 so clearly defined. This could easily stand as the preferred entry in the minimalist category. If you one want only a smattering of this approach, **Pierre Hantal** plays and leads minimalist performances of 1 and 3 and the Triple Concerto with great vigor and flair (♦Astrée 8523, with two Preludes and Fugues).

Six other ventures, compiled from spans of recording sessions, offer partial surveys that are less than complete but still significant. **Rousset**, with Hogwood and a PI chamber orchestra of The Academy of Ancient Music, presents most of the solo concertos (1–5, 7) as well as two for two harpsichords, the two for three harpsichords, and the one for four, juxtaposed where appropriate with their solo violin counterparts (played by Jaap Schröder), or the three-violin and violin/oboe reconstructions, or the Vivaldi original; the performances are a bit on the aggressive side, but always alert and stimulating (1981–95: ♦Oiseau-Lyre 421500, 433053, 448178, 443326). The comparative element in these groupings is most valuable, and these scattered releases are now to be gathered into a coherent package. Rousset and Hogwood (as well as the corresponding Hänssler volume) also give us a chance to hear Double Concerto 2 in what may be its original form for two unaccompanied keyboards (BWV 1061a), without string orchestra, as part of a program of two-keyboard works of Bach family members (Oiseau-Lyre 440649).

An older span of recordings (1973–74, 1980–82) assembles all seven solo concertos and the three for double harpsichords in sturdy performances led from the keyboard by the reliable and intelligent **Leppard** in a bargain set (♦Philips 454268, 2CD). A still more backward-reaching collation comes in another bargain set from **George Malcolm** and Simon Preston, accompanied by Menuhin's Festival Orchestra in solo concertos 1–5 and the first two double concertos, supplemented by older mono recordings with the likes of Malcolm, Eileen Joyce, Dart, and Denis Vaughan in the first of the three-harpsichord concertos and the one for four (1965–73: EMI 572010, 2CD). The performances are strong, but the sound is harsh and wooden; this is best taken as a curiosity backup. Finally, we have **Anton Heiller**'s 1958 recording of solo concertos 1, 4, and 5, followed in 1964 by the complete multi-harpsichord concertos, in a bargain-priced reissue (Vanguard/Bach Guild 2523/24, 2CD). The orchestral work is on the heavy side, but the performances are invariably intelligent and satisfying.

Finally, there are cycles in the two "complete" packages of recent vintage. For **Warchal,** the solo concertos are distributed among four players and the performances are spirited and quite satisfying, if sometimes a tad aggressive (♦Naxos, as Vols. 3 and 5 in the boxed set of "Complete Orchestral Works" or individually as 554604/06, with the Three-Violin Concerto and a Vivaldi Four-Violin Concerto; the multi-instrument concertos were previously issued as 553505 and 554217). These recordings are excellent value at bargain prices. A less coherent cycle is offered in reliable but sometimes over-weighty performances by Christine Schornsheim and colleagues under **Burkhard Glaetzner;** the remaining four items are taken over from the 1964 **Heiller/Janigro** recordings for Bach Guild (discs 6 and 8 of Brilliant Classics 99360, 9CD). All the solo concertos (including 7), the first two-harpsichord concerto, and the four-harpsichord concerto are given

To these may be added a 1993–94 set by **van Asperen** and Leonhardt offering the multi-harpsichord works only, one disc with the three two-harpsichord concertos, the other giving the concertos for three and four harpsichords, with accompaniments provided by Melante Amsterdam, a minimalist one-per-part PI group (Virgin 545054, 545204 with *Italian Concerto* and a Prelude and Fugue, or boxed, 545336, 2CD). The well-recorded performances are meticulous and note-perfect, but a bit bloodless individually or in bulk.

There are, of course, lots of individual performances, but for comprehensive collections I would still urge Kipnis II (where are you, Intercord?) for full-blooded style, and the emerging Purcell Quartet series (Chandos) as the minimalist choice, with other backup possibilities as tastes dictate.

Piano(s)

To my knowledge, there has never been a "complete" recording of all 13 concertos on piano. For the multi-clavier works, there have been selected versions, but the prospect of all those pianists thudding away together is pretty daunting. For the solo clavier works, however, there have been no less than five more-or-less complete sets, all MI, of course. Three are of CD vintage, and all are currently available in 2CD sets or series.

The oldest is a fascinating curiosity: an assemblage of recordings made over the years by **Gould** (CBS 42270, with *Italian Concerto,* and, on organ, *Contrapuncti* 1–9 of *Art of Fugue;* reissued by Sony as 52591, concertos only). In the earlier release, 1 is with a Leningrad ensemble (1957, mono), and in the re-release, with Bernstein (1957, mono); the rest are with Golschmann (1958–69), omitting 6. Unless you're a dedicated Gould fan, his idiosyncratic style makes this a supplemental rather than a primary choice, if one still full of quirkishly inspired music-making. On a far different level is Korean pianist **Hae-won Chung**'s cycle; despite his obvious talent, the performances are cold and perfunctory, with limited imagination and insight, and no bargain (Naxos).

Somewhere between those poles are three more solo concerto cycles and two selective releases, all treating Bach's solo writing in distinctly pianistic terms. Most successful is **Schiff,** who directs the Chamber Orchestra of Europe from the keyboard in his traversal of 1–7; expressive and insightful, uneccentric and consistently musical in every way, Schiff offers the most reliable approach for those who prefer a piano in these works (1989: ♦London 425676). The same contents are offered by **Gavrilov** with Marriner (1993: EMI 65173/74, with French Suite 5, or 73641, 2CD). Aided by the smooth and carefully calculated warmth of Marriner's partnership, Gavrilov aims for more coloristic effects, some delicate and thoughtful, others less apt for the music; in all, a less consistent pianistic approach than Schiff's. Still less competitive is **Feltsman,** who leads a small group from the Orchestra of St. Luke's, and drops the Brandenburgerized 6 in favor of a heavy-handed *Italian Concerto* (1993: MusicMasters). His are high-energy performances, distinguished by obvious virtuosity, but devoid of poetry in the slow movements and too ready to mistake pounding for power in the finales.

Finally, **Kocsis** is captured in Solo Concertos 3–7, and is joined by colleagues (including Schiff) for a sprinkling of the multi-clavier works, a spirited demonstration of fitting the piano(s) into diverse textures (1973–75: Hungaroton 31695, 2CD).

Other concertos

Bach's concertos were generally written for performance by the Leipzig Collegium Musicum over which he presided, and involved a great deal of recycling through transcriptions. Thus of the 13 standard harpsichord concertos, one is a known adaptation of another composer's music (BWV 1065, from Vivaldi), while four survive in alternate versions from Bach's own hand (the two violin concertos, the two-violin concerto, and the earlier version of *Brandenburg* 4 as Solo Concerto 6). It is known that many more of the harpsichord concertos once existed in alternate versions for other instruments. Consequently, except for a few reconstructions that draw upon instrumental movements from cantatas, all of the other concertos represent pendants to the corpus of harpsichord concertos as we have it.

The starting point must be the violin concertos (BWV 1041-43). Two surviving concertos for solo violin also exist in versions for solo harpsichord: Violin No. 1 in A Minor (1041) as Harpsichord No. 7 in G minor (1058); Violin No. 2 in E (1042) as Harpsichord No. 3 in D; and Two-Violin in D minor as Two-Harpsichord No. 3 in C minor. Their long popularity with violinists has helped make them better (or at least longer) known than their harpsichord counterparts. Indeed, many old-timers like me got to know them first through the classic 1942–45 recordings by **Adolf Busch**—all three now conveniently revived (Pearl 9298).

For many, shopping for the violin concertos (all three at once, just the two solo ones, or any individual choices) will focus on a preferred soloist, especially in "traditional" MI recordings (i.e., with "standard" vibrato and variously sized string orchestras). Several "name" violinists have recorded some or all of these works more than once, further complicating choices about what is combined or mixed with what.

Those who want old-time Romantic playing can still find **Elman,** in only the solo concertos (Vanguard 8033, with Nardini and Vivaldi concertos), or, in the Double Concerto, with Kreisler (Pearl 9996, 2CD, with Beethoven, Brahms, and Mendelssohn concertos). **Heifetz,** who once played both parts in the Double Concerto by overdubbing, is still represented in his remake with Erick Friedman (RCA 6778 or 63531, with Brahms and Mozart). Perhaps the best extension of rich-toned, Romantic playing in these works is by **Stern,** probably most effectively with Perlman and Gomberg as fellow soloists and with rather weighty accompaniments led by Alexander Schneider, Mehta, and Bernstein (♦Sony 42258, with the Violin/Oboe Concerto).

Another admired set of sweet-toned and broadly paced performances is **Menuhin**'s, in a still vivid-sounding 1960 recording (Seraphim 568517, 2CD, with Violin/Oboe Concerto and Suites 1–3; alone in Royal Collection 6481). Two fine fiddlers of the traditional school are Szeryng and Grumiaux. **Szeryng,** in his final version of the three concertos, is not up to his own best standards, while accompanist Marriner is in his stage of lower-quality remakes (Philips). **Grumiaux,** on the other hand, was in fine form for the three concertos and the violin/oboe work, joining Hermann Krebbers and Heinz Holliger in high-quality performances of enduring musicality, grace, and vitality, in still-excellent sound (♦Philips 429700). Nor should **David Oistrakh** be forgotten, captured in his prime in strong, sweet, but by no means sentimentalized performances, with particularly eloquent slow movements. In the two solo concertos (1962) he also conducts, while in the Double Concerto (1961) he's joined by his son, Igor; all three are now part of a reissued collection (♦DG 447427, 2CD, with works by Beethoven, Brahms, and Tchaikovsky).

Two latter-day "Romantics" are **Perlman** and **Zukerman.** Just as Perlman joined Stern in his Double Concerto, so Zukerman joined Perlman in his set (EMI). Perlman achieves some true eloquence in the slow movements, but the whole production is hampered by heavy-handed conducting from Barenboim and dull, dated sound. On the other hand, Zukerman, leading the same orchestra (English Chamber) and joined by José-Luis Garcia, delivers clear, intelligent, and brightly recorded versions (♦RCA 60718). Both fill out their programs with the same recreation of a solo Violin Concerto in G minor derived from Harpsichord Concerto 5 in F minor (BWV 1056). Perlman subsequently recorded that transcription again, plus Harpsichord No. 1, conducting Israel Philharmonic members and joined by Ray Still in the Violin/Oboe Concerto, but the performances are edgy and dry, in rather hard and unattractive sound (EMI).

The standard three violin concertos are given suave but vigorous and sometimes eloquent performances by **Mutter,** with Accardo gracefully deferential both as conductor and solo partner; a fine specimen of her young maturity (1983: ♦EMI 47005). **Spivakov** is an even more frankly neo-Romantic interpreter, but only in the two solo concertos (RCA 61582, with violin transcriptions of harpsichord concertos and cantata material). The unjustly undervalued **Ricci** plays and leads relaxed and sweet-toned performances of the two solo concertos plus the reconstruction from BWV 1052 (♦Unicorn-Kanchana 2067). The reliable **Shumsky** is another of this tribe, but his performances of the standard three violin concertos with John Tunnell as violin 2 and conductor (plus Robin Miller in the Violin/Oboe Concerto) are disappointingly businesslike (Nimbus). If it's unapologetic and unenlightened Romanticism you want, you'll be happy with the standard three concertos as played back in 1979 by **Karl Suske** with Giorgio Krohner under Masur in old Leipzig broadcast recordings (Berlin 9310).

Takako Nishizaki is agile and serious, but burdened by overly static support from Oliver Dohnányi. Their budget release is distinguished by a curiosity among fillers: a weird Respighi arrangement of Violin Sonata BWV 1023 (1989: Naxos 550194). At a lower level of workaday performance is **Suzanne Lautenbacher** in strictly bargain-rate versions (just the three concertos on Allegretto 8057, or with the *Brandenburgs* in Vox 3008, 3CD). But an honest bargain is to be had in the recording by **Kolja Blacher** and two other fiddlers, led by Warchal: perky and attractive performances of the standard three plus a transcription of Harpsichord Concerto 1 (♦Naxos, in the 8CD boxed set or individually as 554603). The representation of the violin concertos in the Brilliant Classics set of orchestral works and concertos, on the other hand, is a muddle of performances from various sources and is best ignored.

Turning to PI performances, a rather special starting point can be found in either of two 2CD sets that attempt to combine the standard three violin concertos with all the other concertos, variously reconstructed, that constitute a "complete" edition—all but one of which, you'll remember, survive to us as harpsichord concertos (Denon, Virgin). These sets offer BWV 1041-43 with the Triple Concerto (BWV 1044), transcriptions of Harpsichord Concertos 1 (1052) and 5 (1056) as solo violin concertos, Two-Harpsichord Concerto 1 (1060), for Virgin as the usual violin/oboe derivation, for Denon as a two-violin concerto, and the Three-Harpsichord Concerto 2 (1064) as a Three-Violin Concerto. While the latter four transcriptions are not unknown in other recordings, their assemblage in this format is useful for reference. The relentlessly PI performances by **Carlo Chiarappa** and members of his Accademia Bizantina are less than top-drawer in smoothness, artistic consistency, or recording quality. On the other hand, his set is full of wonderful performances (partly to be discussed below), and very much a bargain (♦Virgin 61558).

The rest of the PI category is represented by a group of seven single-CD releases, most of quite high quality. They are perhaps best divided between those that offer only the standard three concertos and those that include supplemental works. In the first group we have the two solo concertos by **Jaap Schröder** culled from the Rousset/Hogwood series discussed above (1982: Oiseau-Lyre). His lean, almost astringent tone, together with Hogwood's quite brisk pacing, make for less-than-enjoyable repeated listening. **Kuijken** is smoother and more satisfying as soloist and conductor with La Petite Bande (Harmonia Mundi 77006).

Of the remaining five, three offer as filler a transcription of Three-Harpsichord Concerto 2 in C (BWV 1064) as a Three-Violin Concerto in D, an interesting if less-than-totally-certified addition to the Bach violin repertoire. **Standage** first recorded the standard threesome with Pinnock (DG Archive, NA). His second try, with his Collegium Musicum 90, has more personality but is still flawed by inconsistencies in the use of vibrato, while his tone is wiry and the overall sound is unpleasantly edgy (Chandos). **Lamon** with her Tafelmusik colleagues is more stable and reliable, if just a bit bland (Sony 66265). Rather more spirit, as well as outstanding attention to stylish detail and considerable expressiveness, is shown by **Wallfisch**'s assemblage with Catherine Mackintosh (♦Virgin 59319, or recombined in ♦Virgin 61558, an excellent 2CD set that I particularly recommend).

The Wallfisch/Mackintosh partnership is a reversal of roles played in **Mackintosh**'s earlier release, filled out by the Violin/Oboe Concerto with Paul Goodwin as solo partner—an outstanding disc that seems to be NA but is worth seeking out (♦Hyperion 66380). My other strong recommendation (besides Wallfisch) is **Manze**'s recording, in which flexible phrasing, discreet ornamentation, and, above all, infectious spirit make for irresistible listening (♦Harmonia Mundi 907155). The filler here is an unusual adaptation of Two-Harpsichord Concerto 1 (1060) as a Two-Violin Concerto, giving the lonely BWV 1043 a sibling at last, but one already familiar as a near-"standard" concerto in its own right.

The Concerto in C minor for Violin and Oboe, in one or another of its familiar transcriptions, will frequently turn up in a collection or as filler with the violin concertos. While there are a few other versions scattered here and there, the best ones have already been acknowledged. Generally, the MI recordings most worth attention are **Grumiaux**/Holliger/de Waart (♦Philips 420700) and the older **Stern**/Harold Gomberg /Bernstein (Sony 42258); for PI renditions, **Mackintosh**/ Goodwin/ King (♦Hyperion 66380) or **Wallfisch**/ Robson/ Nicholson (♦Virgin 61558).

Of the remaining concerto reconstructions based on harpsichord concertos (sometimes with bits from cantatas) beyond those already discussed as fillers, many came and went throughout the LP era. Noteworthy were two LPs in which **Müller-Brühl** led soloists and his Cologne Chamber Orchestra through sturdy performances of six single and multiple solo concertos, a set that would surely be worth reviving (originally Claves, briefly reissued by HNH). **Warchal** has revisited this territory on a smaller scale with updated performances of concerto reconstructions for oboe and oboe d'amore (two each) plus the oboe/violin reconstruction (♦Naxos, the first disc in the 8CD boxed set of Orchestral Works or alone as 554602). Another comprehensive approach to these transcriptions or "regained" concertos is in two discs in the Hänssler "Bach-Akademie" series, one (Vol. 131) with four for oboe or oboe d'amore, the other (Vol. 138) with four works for violin(s).

The oboe and oboe d'amore have figured prominently as beneficiaries of such reconstructions, and **Milan Munclinger** led performances of his own versions for oboe (from BWV 1059 and Cantata 35) and oboe d'amore (from 1055), as well as another for viola da gamba from 1059 and Cantata 156 (Supraphon 73150). Above all, oboist **Holliger** has been among their particular champions: three of his results (from BWV 1053, 1055, 1059) are still available (♦Philips 412851). Two of these (from 1053 and 1055) are also given fine PI performances by **Paul Goodwin** (♦Hyperion 66267, with two Telemann concertos). The same two may also be heard among handsome MI performances culled from early **Marriner** recordings with additional transcriptions for three violins (from 1064) and for violin/oboe/flute (from 1063) (♦London 440037; ♦Boston Skyline 127).

One of the most important of the transcription concertos is the "Triple" Concerto in A minor (BWV 1044) for flute, violin, and harpsichord—though, in this case, it comes not from the harpsichord concertos but survives in someone's (Bach's?) adaptation of some of his organ music. It has turned up as filler in some sets discussed above. A quite satisfying MI version may be found under **Leppard** (♦Philips 442387, with *Brandenburgs* 4–6). Another is by **Müller-Brühl** in his multiharpsichord concerto series (Naxos 553505), still another is by **Ristenpart** (Accord 205712, 2CD, with Three-Violin Concerto reconstruction and all four Orchestral Suites). A competent but somewhat perfunctory performance is part of a program—including solo Violin Concerto 2, the Two-Violin Concerto, and the reconstruction of BWV 1055 as an oboe d'amore concerto—designed to showcase members of the **Orchestra of St. Luke**'s (MusicMasters). And you may still be able to find the reissue of the mellow 1976 recording, a PI trailblazer, by **Collegium Aureum** (Deutsche Harmonia Mundi 77412, with Violin/Oboe Concerto and Harpsichord 1).

In the PI category, the leader is an imaginative Triple Concerto by **Pierre Hantaï**, who adds two particularly vivid solo harpsichord concertos (1 and 3) in an outstanding release (♦Astrée 8523). **Wallfisch** offers a generally very satisfying Triple Concerto with the two oboe concerto reconstructions (1053 and 1059), played in somewhat mannered style (♦Virgin 45190; the same BWV 1044 performance is now in ♦Virgin 61558). The original release effectively replaced an earlier recording with **Pinnock** leading a sturdy performance that shared flutist Lisa Beznosiuk with Wallfisch, with the violin/oboe standby plus the oboe d'amore reconstruction from 1044 (DG Archiv 413731). Other variable PI versions of the Triple Concerto include **Alessandrini** (Opus 111, with harpsichord concertos) and **Goebel** (DG Archiv, 2CD, with *Brandenburgs*).

Orchestral suites

Like the *Brandenburgs* and the harpsichord concertos, individual suites have had active individual lives on discs, especially the ubiquitous

No. 2—for example, Galway has recorded it at least twice, and Rampal two or three times. But most collectors will probably want the four suites as a package, especially because there is less variety among them than the *Brandenburgs*, so this section mostly considers sets. All releases are 2CD and without fillers unless otherwise indicated.

Modern instruments

The **Busch Players**'s landmark set is a historical document (like their *Brandenburgs*) that transcends the currents of changing performance; both cycles have been reissued together (♦EMI 64047; Pearl 9263; both 3CD), as have the Koussevitzky recoveries (Pearl 10103, 3CD). Intervening sets by conductors like Reiner, van Beinum, and Klemperer (not to mention individual suite recordings by Karajan, Schuricht, Knappertsbusch, Furtwängler) are now mostly discontinued relics to be hunted down by discographers or cherished by old-timers with nostalgia for "big orchestra" performances. The rule today in MI performances is fairly consistent "Baroque compromise," with smallish chamber orchestras, including harpsichord continuo.

Several worthy complete sets of the LP era were carried over onto CDs no longer available. **Richter**'s now seems rigid, however robust (DG Archiv); **Paillard**'s was more reliable if without much profile (Erato; MHS; RCA). But two sets not in print just now deserve reissue. **Münchinger**'s second full cycle (1985) was available for a while (London 414505), and an omnibus set of the conductor's Bach orchestral music is in prospect. Münchinger's approach to this music is "Dresdenchina" Bach that is either "Romantic" or "simplistic," as you prefer, but is certainly the best case for elegantly sentimental quaintness and of honest appeal to traditionalists. **Leppard**'s performances have gusto and imagination, making them one of the most enduringly satisfying MI versions; it should not be allowed to die (♦Philips).

Menuhin is much less successful in this category—tubby 1961 performances that remind one of fine old shoes, no longer in style but still comfortable if you're used to them (EMI 767350, with a very intelligent *Musical Offering*). Something of the same traditionalist style is artfully represented by **Baumgartner,** flawed only by somewhat dated sound (1978: ♦Eurodisc 69219, 3CD, with *Brandenburgs*). A parallel package of the same material in attractive performances by **Munclinger** may yet return (Supraphon). **Spivakov** took a more frankly Romantic approach, but this seems to have come and gone quickly (RCA 60360). Also shortlived was a somewhat more bland set by **Schreier,** noteworthy mainly as one of the few to include the spurious "Suite No. 5" once attributed to Bach (1990–91: Philips 432969).

Still hanging around is **Ristenpart**'s old but respectable 1960 set (Accord 205712, with Triple Concerto and three-violin reconstruction). **Kehr**'s set is also old but relatively pedestrian, and strictly for the budget-conscious (Vox 5040, with the three- and four-harpsichord concertos). Newer but likewise backward-looking in style, however well played, is **Jaroslav Dvořák**'s budget project, which is still incomplete (1989: Naxos 550244, Nos. 1 and 2).

The master of "compromise Baroque" is, of course, that rapid repeater **Marriner,** whose slick third recording (1984) has been reissued (EMI 69878, No. 1 with *Brandenburgs* 5–6, and 69879, Nos. 2–4). His second set (1978), super-refined in playing but still cool and somewhat superficial, has been reissued in a bargain set (Philips 446533, with Szeryng's three Violin Concertos). But the true "best buy" is Marriner's very first recording (1970), much fresher and more vital in character and given special zest by Thurston Dart's harpsichord continuo—in all, a striking bargain in its remastering onto a single CD in a budget series (♦London

430378). That release effaced **Rolla**'s one advantage, whose version is smooth, alert, and impeccably played, one of his best recorded ventures, but cursed by his characteristic absence of insight or individuality (Hungaroton). A much better bet is **Warchal**'s considerably more brisk and vivacious set, played with such reduced string vibrato as to be almost PI in approach, and packed onto a single CD, the closest to Marriner I on that count (♦Naxos, the final disc in his boxed set or alone as 554609).

Three other sets show even more personality. Long one of my favorites is **Pommer.**l The performance with crisp and incisive inflection, with an expert East German ensemble that played with lithe vigor in performances full of daring and clever details, is one of the most stimulating MI versions since Leppard (♦Capriccio 10011 or the second pair of discs in the Leipzig Bach Edition, augmented by two of Bach's solo harpsichord works, 49254, 11CD). One of Pommer's participants was **Güttler,** who produced a cycle of his own that is a reasonable successor, a vivacious and stylish romp, a great bargain challenging Marriner I (1990–92: ♦Berlin 9002). We also have **Rilling**—robust, flowing, and a fine statement of the "compromise" approach for the 1990s (♦Hänssler 98984 and 98978, or Vol. 126 of the "Bachakademie" series, 92.127, 2CD).

The most recent release in this category, however, represents a kind of wonderful throwback: the concert performances of 1983–85 by Camerata Academica Salzburg under **Végh** (♦Orfeo 537002). Using a chamber orchestra (with harpsichord), Végh avoids ponderousness but redeems the stereotype of "Romanticized" Bach in beautifully flowing and genuinely affectionate performances of enduring value.

Period instruments

Beginning with the first PI recording, by **Harnoncourt** (1966), and on down to the moment, the suites have been a laboratory for musicological experimentation. To be sure, that Harnoncourt trailblazer was a curiously halfway-house affair, quite venturesome on some counts (repeats, minimalist scoring for No. 2); it was also backward-looking on others (cautious tempos, incorrect double-dotting), and in somewhat overripe sound. He chose to remake his cycle in 1985, without much interpretive change but at least in improved sound. Teldec brought both versions to CD, but the second set (43051/52) has apparently been discontinued, though they are in Vol. 12 of their "Bach 2000" collection (25717, 10CD). Otherwise, the revival of the first set (Teldec 92174) seems to be his only representation for the moment.

Following Harnoncourt I, many challengers arose through the final LP years. The **Collegium Aureum** made a very cautious cycle in 1969, revived in a composite package (Harmonia Mundi). **Pinnock**'s first cycle, made in 1979 and initially issued piecemeal on LP, was much more frankly PI in ensemble sound but recorded in deadish sonics, with sometimes inventive but mostly labored, rigid, and fussy performances (DG Archiv). His second version strikes a more relaxed and vivacious note and includes four sections from cantatas; for three of them, music (from Suite 4 and two of the *Brandenburgs*) was recycled (DG Archiv 439780).

Kuijken recorded a less abrasive, more "moderate" PI version with sparkle and high spirit (1981: Harmonia Mundi 77008; MHS 523889). **Linde**'s 1982 set is suave and refined (EMI). **Gardiner**'s 1983 cycle is still more graceful; it features some astringent violin playing but otherwise mellow PI sound in thoughtful, infectious, and elegant interpretations (♦Erato 88048 and 88049 as singles, 91800 as a set). It has shamefully been allowed to go out of circulation; were it to reappear, it would be a foremost recommendation in the "moderate PI" category.

Hogwood's cycle is light, lucid, and deft, but rather cool and perfunctory (1985–88: Oiseau-Lyre 417834 and low-priced 458069, with

Two-Harpsichord Concertos 1 and 3). There was far more personality in **Koopman**'s spunky set: sturdy and emphatic readings, rhythmically vital and alert, sometimes a bit choppy and mannered, but quite bouncy. Currently NA, this set too should be revived (1988: Harmonia Mundi 7864). But the prize for assertiveness and personality has to go to **Goebel** (1982, 1985: ♦DG Archiv 415671). It won't appeal to those who dislike scrapey violin swellings, chirpy, squeaky winds, and brisk tempos, but those who respond to musical artistry and imagination will appreciate his vital agogics, his sensitive response to rhythmic effects and dance qualities, his clever embellishments and textual touches, and his innovative use of two harpsichords in the continuo; the sound is particularly close and clear. His recording is the only PI version to include the spurious "Suite No. 5," and even makes a good case for it in a minimalist performance. Not a set for conservatives, but still one of the most stimulating, adventurous, and exciting to be had.

Meanwhile, a still more experimental direction was developing in the minimalist spirit. Several recordings (Goebel, Harnoncourt I and II, Koopman, Linde, Pinnock) established the precedent of performing only No. 2 with one player per part (plus contrabass doubling), but along came four recordings that applied that practice to all four suites. Least appealing is **Gunar Letzbor**'s Ars Antiqua Austria, who offer able playing but rigid, fussy, and altogether artificial renditions best bypassed, even though they are crowded economically onto a single disc (1995: Chesky). A very distinctive case is the earliest of these experiments, a 1989 version by **William Malloch** (Koch 7037). Using the title "Suites for Dancing," Malloch takes terpsichorean cues to stress propulsive tempi that can be breakneck and unsettling, respecting all repeats while still keeping to one disc. It's certainly idiosyncratic, but it's also quite musical and well thought out, an approach not to be taken as your only choice in this music, but an exceptional treatment worth appreciative study.

The other two ultra-minimalist versions offer less stark contrasts. **Parrott** produced well-balanced and refined performances, full of lucid details (1992: EMI 754653, with Triple Concerto). **Pickett**'s cycle is more provocative, but stylistically illuminating and elegantly realized (♦Oiseau-Lyre 452000, with five concertante movements from cantatas). Whether or not you always want to hear the suites in this reduced scoring, serious collectors would do well to consider at least one representation of this approach, with Picket's perhaps easiest to live with.

The 1990s resumed the generation of recordings by PI chamber orchestras. **Robert Haydon Clark**'s recording is intelligent and alert but without much character; its principal competitive point is that it fits neatly onto a single disc (1990: Collins 30092). Usually a refreshing, even provocative interpreter, **Savall,** surprisingly, is also rather routine (Astrée). There is a lot of energy but rather aggressive PI playing in **Goodman**'s set, but the performances are rigid, harsh, and relentless (Hyperion). **Manze,** in his earlier work (mid-1990s) with La Stravaganza Köln, led an imaginative and thoroughly satisfying cycle (Denon 78965). Finally, the conductorless **Akademie für Alte Musik Berlin** made an outstanding set, a remarkable achievement of collegiality in combination with stylish artistry, perhaps the best recommendation for up-to-date realization by a PI chamber orchestra (1995: ♦Harmonia Mundi 901578/79). BARKER

CHAMBER MUSIC

Most of Bach's instrumental music dates from his stay at the Calvinist court in Cöthen, where he lived from 1717 to 1723. There he produced works of a revolutionary nature that were so advanced they would not be fully appreciated for at least a century after his death. The thought of composing unaccompanied contrapuntal works for essentially melodic instruments like the violin and the cello was new, and his example would not be followed until the 20th century. He also created the sonata for solo instrument and keyboard as we know it, for the first time giving the keyboard equal importance with the featured instrument by fully realizing its part rather than merely indicating the figured bass.

Lute suites (BWV 995-97, 1006a)

The form of the suite as used by Bach was a set of dance movements all in the same key prefaced by a prelude. The four lute suites are cut from the same cloth as the works for solo violin and cello. Highly contrapuntal and rife with quotes from Bach's religious music, they may carry a coded message. The lute has presently fallen out of favor with performers and audiences, perhaps because of its weak tone, but guitarists have adopted these orphaned works.

Paul Galbraith plays the suites on a custom-designed guitar made for him by British luthier David Rubio (Delos 3258). It has a large body, eight strings, and a tailpiece like a cello's that connects the instrument to a resonator box that rests on the floor. It has a lower range and deeper, more powerful tone than the average guitar, and is captured in mouthwatering 24-bit sound. Galbraith revels in the sonority he produces, but despite the obviously considerable research he has done on Bach's music, his performances sound glib. **Bream** has recorded BWV 996, 997, and 1006a (RCA 61603; EMI 55123). He has a broader tonal palette than Galbraith and a little greater sense of drama and ability to clarify counterpoint but sorely lacks breadth of tone. As a guitarist friend of mine once remarked, Bream sounds like a lutenist trying to play the guitar. Segovia student **Williams** has Bream's positive qualities without the dry tone and with an even greater flair for the dramatic (CBS 42204; Sony 62972, 62973).

Sonatas and partitas for solo violin (BWV 1001-6)

These are the most intricate works written for violin in the 18th century. They run such an emotional gamut that attempts have been made to discover a supposed program in them. Some hear references to the life of Christ, while others think they are autobiographical and were Bach's way of dealing with his grief for his first wife, Maria Barbara, who died in 1720. The three sonatas are in the traditional slow-fast-slow-fast *sonata da chiesa* (church sonata) form, while the partitas are dance suites.

My discussion here and elsewhere in this article is divided into two groups: recordings on modern and period instruments. These categories can't be kept rigorously separate, as there is some cross-pollination between performing styles. The popularity of these works has meant that a good number of fine performances have been recorded. Despite their highly contrapuntal nature, most violinists succeed in varying degrees at clarifying the voices Bach so cleverly suggests. I write "suggests" because the limitations of the violin made it impossible for Bach to do much more than that.

Modern instruments

In 1903 **Joachim** recorded the Adagio from Sonata 1 and the "Tempo di Borea" from Partita 1; he plays with vigor and abandon (Opal 9851). **Sarasate** recorded the Preludio from Partita 3 the following year and makes it sound like a perpetual motion study, playing much faster than people had become accustomed to (Opal 9851). In 1929, **Adolf Busch** recorded Partita 2 (EMI). He conveys little feeling in the early movements, but the Sarabande is heartfelt and the weight of the various sections of the Chaconne is astutely judged without creating an ecstatic climax at any one point as is the convention.

Szigeti recorded Sonatas 1 and 2 in the early 1930s with his trademark severity (Music & Arts) and some of his concert performances from the 1940s have been released (Music & Arts 4774). There is infinite tenderness in the Siciliano from Sonata 1, the Loure from Partita 3, and the Andante of Sonata 2, but much of the rest is overbearing. In a later set, he approaches the sonatas with great seriousness (Vanguard). He won't let you forget that you're listening to the greatest music written for solo violin. He relaxes in the partitas, however, and again plays the slower dances with uncommon tenderness. **Menuhin** recorded the first complete set of the sonatas and partitas in the mid-1930s (EMI). These are energetic performances, but there are no special insights. Menuhin's teacher **Enescu** recorded a complete set around 1940; his performances have a powerful spirituality (♦IDIS 328/29, 2CD).

Heifetz plays these works with surprising humility (RCA). This is a far more intelligent, tasteful set than many would expect from the ultimate virtuoso showman. **Szeryng**'s set from the late 1960s has a touching nobility—no one can match his ardor in the slow movements—and great purity and fullness of tone (♦DG 453004, 2 CD). **Perlman**'s account is similar in its emphasis on nobility of expression and beauty of tone, without paying much attention to period performance practice (EMI 49483, 2 CD). **Rosand**'s performances have a wise, warm, lived-in quality; this is your favorite uncle playing for you in the privacy of your living room (Vox 7901, 2 CD). **Milstein** recorded these works in the mid-1950s (♦EMI 64793, 2CD) and again in the early 1970s (DG 457701, 2CD). His technique in both sets inspires awe, but his earlier one is a bit livelier, and his enjoyment of the partitas is infectious. The partitas have been released separately (♦EMI 66870).

An interesting LP set of these works was recorded for Decca in the early 1950s by **Emil Telmanyi** and reissued in 1984 (Danacord). Telmanyi was influenced by the idea, promulgated at the turn of the century by musicologist Arnold Schering and popularized by Albert Schweitzer, that Bach's violin music was intended to be played exactly as it was notated, meaning that each voice of a three- or four-note chord was to be sustained for its written duration. In this way, it was believed, the counterpoint would come across with greater clarity. Telmanyi had a special bow made of bamboo with a mechanical frog so he could sustain three- and four-voice chords. The results are hardly inspiring. The violin sounds like a very dull organ, and, because chords are no longer rolled or broken, the music loses its rhythmic spring, which is an important part of its expression. This approach took early musical notation far too literally. In fact, Eduard Melkus found that it's impossible to play the music this way with any bow that has survived from the 17th or 18th centuries. **Rolph Schroeder** recorded these works at about the same time using a bow of similar design (Columbia).

Among recent recordings, **Mela Tenenbaum** plays with very little feeling for period style and instead sounds like an eccentric, turn-of-the-century Russian virtuoso, more intent on dazzling us with her tone, technique, and temperament than doing service to the composer (ESS.A.Y). This is a shame, as she demonstrates a deep understanding of the counterpoint. **Karl Suske** gives an intelligent, workmanlike traversal of the set, but he displays too little emotional involvement and personality (Berlin). **Stefan Milenkovich** is very straightforward in approach; his playing is crystal clear, both tonally and formally, but a bit faceless, and he attacks the notes in an unvaryingly aggressive manner that wears on the nerves (Dynamic). **Sitkovetsky** is also very intelligent and clarifies the voice leading very well, but his reading is also not emotional enough to satisfy (Hänssler).

Among recordings of selected sonatas and partitas, **Arnold Stein-**

hardt's 1966 Sonata 1 and Partita 2 suffer from inflexible tempos and a lack of feel for 18th-century style (Town Hall). **Mullova** is heavily influenced by period performance practice (Philips 434075). Her disc of the partitas is like a textbook in this respect; it's perfect, but there's no warmth or humanity in her playing. **Hahn** shows she has a mature head on her young shoulders in her intelligent recording of Sonata 3 and Partitas 2 and 3 (Sony 62793). She's a bit too serious and restrained, though, and needs to learn to loosen up.

Lara St. John, who has recorded Partita 2 and Sonata 3, is in a class by herself (♦Well-Tempered 5180). Blessed with a superb technique and flawless intonation, she gives a strong character to each movement, and, as another musician noted, when she plays Bach's counterpoint it sounds as if each voice were sung rather than bowed. She clarifies the structure of the enormous Fugue from Sonata 3 so well that it seems shorter than it really is. These are amazingly vital and insightful readings. There was an LP by **Kyung-Wha Chung** of Partita 2 and Sonata 3, in which the Allemande and Sarabande of the partita are played with much sensitivity and insight, and the Chaconne is intelligently shaped (London 6940). The Largo and Allegro assai from the Sonata are exceptionally fine.

Period instruments

Wallfisch (Hyperion), **Huggett** (Virgin), and **Lucy van Dael** (Naxos) all miss the mark. None are quite up to Bach's lofty technical demands; they don't play badly, they just don't let the listener forget how hard this music is. Also, they are not the most insightful interpreters. **Rachel Podger** is fully up to the demands of the music, but she often sounds too cheerful, refusing to explore Bach's dark side (Channel). **Sergiu Luca**'s pioneering set from the mid-1970s has held up very well (♦Nonesuch 73030, NA). Recorded under the direction of period performance practice guru David Boyden, the Juilliard-trained Luca communicates a delightful feeling of discovery as he learns to handle a baroque instrument (which he does *very* well). **Ingrid Matthews** belongs to a generation weaned on expert period instrument performances and has raised the interpretation of these masterpieces to a new level (♦Centaur 2472/73, 2CD). She plays with rare taste and understanding; her grave, noble Chaconne is unlike any other and, I suspect, close to what Bach had in mind. This is the finest complete set of these works I have heard.

Suites for solo cello (BWV 1007-12)

The six cello suites were perhaps an even bigger surprise than the works for solo violin. The cello was finally coming into its own as a solo instrument in the early 18th century, but again Bach perceived possibilities in the instrument that were unnoticed by others.

Modern instruments

Casals single-handedly resurrected the cello suites at the turn of the century (♦EMI 66215, 2CD; Monopoly 2000, 2CD). A perfectionist, he had to be dragged into the studio by his friends in the late 1930s to record them. These performances sound strangely modern in the way he strongly articulates his bowing and often lifts the bow from the string in the manner of the period instrumentalists. He characterizes each movement powerfully, as though it accompanies a scene from a film. Casals relied on imagery to aid his interpretations; he used to say the Sarabande of Suite 5 represented Christ on the road to Calvary. He was also very conscious of the overall structure of each movement, and you can feel him move the phrases along. This is one of the greatest recordings of the suites and, aside from its sound, it shows no signs of age (neither did Casals, for that matter, who began to record them when he was almost 60).

Like the works for solo violin, the cello suites have attained great popularity, so there are several very good recordings. Some miss the mark, though. **Nathaniel Rosen** is surprisingly stiff. The music doesn't flow from his cello; it's as if he has to push each note uphill (John Marks). **Gaspar Cassado** leaves a similar, wooden impression; his interpretations are stone-faced (Vox). **Dimitry Markevitch** (Gallo) has done a great service by locating two important manuscripts and using them, together with the manuscript of Anna Magdalena Bach and a more recently discovered one, to create the most thoroughly researched edition of the suites to date (unfortunately, the holograph has yet to be discovered). However, his performances are hampered by his insecure technique. **Csaba Onczay** has a secure technique but makes no effort to plumb the emotional depths of this fascinating music and is content to merely use them as vehicles for displaying his full, even, unvaried tone and secure intonation (Naxos).

Starker made a celebrated recording in the mid-1960s (Mercury). His great technical security, especially in 6, which he plays with an almost manic joy, made a powerful impression at the time, but there is little in the way of emotional depth. He re-recorded the suites in the early 1990s; his playing is less energetic, but occasionally a touch more eloquent, though the thrill is gone from 6 (RCA). **Harrell** shows an occasional insight, but too often he draws rude noises from his instrument (London, NA). **Shafran** recorded Suites 2–5 in concert in 1971, employing a consistently fast, throbbing vibrato common in Russian string playing in the early 20th century (Revelation). This often feels out of place, especially in 5, though 5:I is really impressive; here he gives the impression of a massive, oppressive force that only Fournier and Rostropovich can match. However, he plays with an unvarying intensity that is usually overbearing.

Maurice Gendron is nearly the opposite (Philips 442293, 2CD). He has a very secure technique and produces a beautiful, even tone with an attractive vibrato. His disposition is always sunny, so he can't do justice to the dark moods of 5, though his 6 is delightful. **Ralph Kirshbaum** is much like Gendron, very good in the suites with brighter moods, with a superb 6, but weak in 2 and 5 (Virgin 61609, 2CD). He draws a gorgeous tone from his 1729 Domenico Montagnana. **Yehudi Hanini** gives a personal reading with various effects inserted, like right- and left-hand pizzicato and *sul ponticello* (Town Hall, 2CD). He's not as powerfully expressive or consistently good as some others, but he has good, elastic rhythms and is nearly always tasteful.

Colin Carr has a tremendous technique (GM 2054, 2CD). His set was recorded in concert, but you wouldn't guess it from the polish of his playing and his wonderful tone. He plays a modern cello but is strongly influenced by period performance practice; he frequently lifts his bow, restrains his use of vibrato, and employs *messa di voce* swells and *notes inégales*. Carr is a gentle soul and avoids extremes of emotion, but his version is very thoughtful and peculiarly satisfying. **Boris Pergamenschikow** is also influenced by period performance practice, and like Carr, he's strong in all the suites (Hänssler 92120, 2CD). His Prelude in 1 is taken fast and off the string, and he doesn't try to thrill. He uses sparse vibrato in the slow movements to enhance expression; his approach is ruminative and very individual.

Maisky's recording includes a CD-ROM that the listener can load into a computer and follow while the music is playing (DG 463314, 2CD and CD-ROM). The recording is excellent, truthfully capturing the sound of his 1720 Montagnana, and Maisky has many insights. He's more ruminative than extrovert, with wonderful insights into the slow movements delivered *sotto voce*. He can surprise too, as he does in the Sarabande of 5, which he boldly declaims almost like an opera aria rather than in the quiet, emotionally drained manner that has been common since Casals recorded these works.

Rostropovich finally recorded the complete set in the 1990s (EMI). This is a bit sad, as by then his technique was beginning to show considerable wear, but he felt he had finally attained an adequate understanding of the music. He's still able to draw a rich, imposing tone from his superb Stradivarius, the "Duport" of 1711. Like more and more musicians, Rostropovich attaches a program of sorts to the suites. In order, he feels they convey Lightness, Sorrow and Intensity, Brilliance, Majesty and Opacity, Darkness, and Sunlight. He does a fair job characterizing each of them, and his playing shows no sign of influence by period performance practice; sustained tone is emphasized over articulation and rhythmic energy. His technical deterioration keeps him from a consistent level of execution and interpretation.

Ma has recorded the suites twice (CBS 37867, 2CD; Sony 63203, 2CD). His approach is similar in both, showing no interest in period performance practice and playing each suite in a very extroverted manner. The Sony set is recorded more closely than the CBS, and in the former he plays a magnificent Montagnana with seemingly unlimited tonal reserves. Ma characterizes each movement as very few can. Each has a strong atmosphere, like a scene in a drama, with the action and mood progressing from one to the next. Rostropovich tried to do this; Casals and Fournier succeed. It's a matter of taste to say how closely these cellists come to hitting the mark in this respect, but Ma strikes me as more involved with his own ability to shape his marvelously elastic tone than with searching for and conveying Bach's message, whatever that may be; he seems to have his own agenda and is using the music as a means of realizing it. However you feel about his fascinating interpretations, you can't deny that his second recording is one of the greatest recorded feats of tone production.

Unlike Ma, **Peter Bruns** wholeheartedly embraces period performance practice and style (♦Opus 111 30176-7, 2CD). Blessed with a superb technique and a strong, clear tone drawn from the "Pablo Casals" Carlo Tononi cello of 1730, he's capable of a very broad spectrum of expression. His use of shorter, often lifted bow strokes has nothing didactic about it, and the style he adopts for each dance is carefully matched to the mood he wishes to evoke. This is a great set; Bruns excels in each of the suites, and he surpasses all other performers on period instruments.

No cellist evokes moods as strongly as **Fournier** (♦Accord 206372, 2CD). He draws a huge tone from his Stradivarius and often employs violent attacks and huge dynamic contrasts. His Bach is much darker and more dramatic than the rest; even his 6, though ardent and hopeful, isn't as simple and cheerful as the others. He makes the music sound bigger than life, and the feelings he expresses often seem more appropriate to a Beethoven or Mahler symphony, but somehow he makes them seem very right, and these are the most gripping, powerfully moving Bach suites on CD. His re-recording a year later has better sound (♦DG 449711, 2CD), but the earlier one, which sounds as if it were recorded in concert, has a definite edge in spontaneity and boldness of expression.

Period instruments

Hidemi Suzuki has the narrowest range of expression; he's often deficient in energy and under-articulates (Deutsche Harmonia Mundi). As is often the case with period cellos, his ca. 1570 Amati has a fuzzy tone that may be more attractive in a small concert hall than in a close recording. He employs a small, five-string violoncello piccolo made in Germany in the early 17th century for 6, which Bach originally intended to be played on an instrument with five strings. The fifth string greatly facilitates execution of the high notes, but the small-bodied cello cannot

match a full-size cello's depth of tone. **Jaap ter Linden** is stodgy, without enough contrast of mood or tempo (Harmonia Mundi). In 1965, **Harnoncourt** was probably the first to record the suites on a baroque cello (MHS). He's usually not expressive enough and sounds a bit inhibited, but he finally loosens up and displays some enthusiasm in 6, which he plays on a violoncello piccolo that sounds like a kazoo.

Bylsma has recorded the suites twice, in the late 1970s (Sony 61811 and 61812) and again in the early 1990s (♦Sony 48047, 2CD). There are no major differences of interpretation among these releases, but he's a bit freer in the latter, no doubt inspired by his use of the magnificent "Servais" Stradivarius of 1701 from the Smithsonian Institution's collection. This is one of the few extra-large cellos of its time that hasn't been reduced in size to make it easier, and, as you would expect, the C string sounds glorious. It's not actually a baroque cello, having had a larger bass bar and sound post and a longer neck installed, but Bylsma plays the instrument as it might have been played in the early 19th century, with gut strings, no end pin, and a modern-style bow. He uses a Tyrolean violoncello piccolo, ca. 1700, in 6, and its sound is a big letdown after the clear, massive sonority of the "Servais." Bylsma's personality is a bit stronger than most of his rivals in the period performance crowd, and his Bach never lets you down.

Bylsma's student **Pieter Wispelwey** has recorded the suites twice, first in the early 1990s (Channel 1090, 2CD) and again in 1998 (♦Channel 12298, 2CD). The earlier recording is more outgoing and straightforward, but the later one is the most ruminative Bach on CD. Indeed, Wispelwey has turned so far inward there is a certain perversity to his almost gloomy interpretations. This isn't meant to disparage his musicianship, but listeners should be aware of the very private character of Wispelwey's discourse before investing in this set. He uses a cello built by the English maker Barak Norman in 1710 in 1 through 5 and a violoncello piccolo in 6.

Paolo Beschi, a founding member of the Italian period instrument group Il Giardino Armonico, has recorded 1 through 5 on a tonally rather threadbare Carlo Testore of 1754 and 6 on an anonymous 18th-century instrument of normal dimensions that sounds as if it has a fifth string (♦Winter & Winter 910028, 2CD). Beschi's Bach is somewhat introspective, but not nearly as much as Wispelwey's; it has very danceable rhythms and strongly articulated bowing. It's an easy-to-live-with period instrument set.

SONATAS FOR VIOLIN AND HARPSICHORD (BWV 1014-19)

Modern instruments

Menuhin and Landowska recorded BWV 1014-17 in concert in 1944; the acetates have been found and reissued (A Classical Record). This may be the slowest Bach on record. It takes them a bit over 77 minutes to play four sonatas while Sitkovetsky and Hill dispatch all six in just over 76 minutes. This celebrated duo can't hold the listener's interest, and their style sounds terribly dated too, lacking any rhythmic spring or bite. Menuhin recorded all the sonatas again with Louis Kentner in 1951 with similarly slow tempos and dated style (EMI).

Joseph Suk and Zuzana Růžičková play like very old people who should retire, with dragging, slack tempos, lack of bow control, and slow, wobbly vibrato (Lotos). **Grumiaux** and Jaccottet offer no special insights or sense of enjoyment (Philips). Their rhythms lack spring, and Grumiaux never modulates his tone; they play as if music were a job rather than a vocation. **Mela Tenenbaum** released two different recordings simultaneously, with pianist Richard Kapp (ESS.A.Y) and harpsichordist Gerald Rank (ESS.A.Y 1064–65, 2CD). The piano version is a bit stodgy and inhibited; the harpsichord version sounds much freer and more flowing. Rank even has the imagination to employ the lute stop in repeats. Tenenbaum pays little heed to period performance practice, but she and Rank have a fine feel for Bach.

Jaime Laredo and Glenn Gould recorded the sonatas in 1975 (Sony 52615, 2CD). Gould frequently proves himself a master of evoking mood, and of course the counterpoint is crystal clear. This is a real collaboration, and it's obvious that Laredo and Gould carefully rehearsed each sonata. I would recommend this set much more strongly if it weren't for the occasional slow movement that sounds as if it could only have been written by Bach under the influence of peyote (cf. 1:I and you'll know what I mean). **Sitkovetsky** and Robert Hill's recording is the most enjoyable on modern instruments (♦Hänssler 98.154). The phrases flow naturally in their hands. They refuse to plod in the slow movements, and as a result fit all the sonatas on one disc.

Gabriela Demeterová and harpsichordist **Giedré Lukšaité-Mrázková** play modern instruments with baroque tuning and style and are like a breath of fresh air (♦Supraphon 3476, 2CD). They use sensible tempos, play incisively, and shape phrases intelligently. It's clear they're really listening to each other, and the harpsichord is clearly a full partner of the violin. Demeterová draws some lovely sounds from her violin, especially in the soft passages, making moderate use of vibrato. This is a very engaging set.

Period instruments

Ivan Zěnatý and Jaroslav Tůma, who only recorded BWV 1014-17, are the least satisfying; their tempos are glacial, their rhythms metronomic, and Zěnatý plays like a student (Bonton). **Ryo Terakado** and Siebe Henstra fare little better with their complete set (Denon). **Catherine Mackintosh** with harpsichordist Maggie Cole and cellist Jennifer Ward Clarke do nothing wrong in these sonatas; the problem is that they are so reserved and faceless that their performances completely lack character (Chandos). **Wallfisch** and Paul Nicholson have little more to offer (Hyperion). **John Holloway** and Davitt Moroney play with greater involvement and confidence (Virgin). Their tempos are reasonably elastic and the phrases flow naturally, but they are hampered by poor sound. **Manze** and Richard Egarr, assisted by Jaap ter Linden on viola da gamba in BWV 1014-15, are similar in approach (Harmonia Mundi). They have excellent sound, and Manze occasionally distinguishes himself with his characteristic gentleness, but they often run out of steam and tempos drag. **Gabriela Demeterová** and **Giedré Lukšaité-Mrázková** are like a breath of fresh air (Supraphon 3476, 2CD). They use sensible tempos, play incisively, and shape phrases intelligently. It's clear that they are really listening to each other, and the harpsichord is clearly a full partner of the violin. This is a very engaging set.

Biondi and Alessandrini are supreme in this music (♦Opus 111 30127/28, 2CD). With their strong, charismatic personalities, they grab the listener by the ears immediately and don't let go for the length of the set. For once the harpsichord is recorded as a full partner, and it's clear they are really listening to the counterpoint they're playing. Phrases never plod but are forcefully shaped. Biondi frequently applies imaginative ornaments, among them his gorgeous, distinctive vibrato.

On LP, **Reinhard Goebel** and **Robert Hill** performed the sonatas on period instruments. Their tempos don't drag like so many others and they have a good deal of energy, but they lack the star quality of Biondi and Alessandrini (DG 413326, 2LP).

Sonatas for viola da gamba and harpsichord (BWV 1027-29)

The bass viola da gamba was the major solo instrument among the bowed string instruments of Bach's time. Favored by the aristocracy, es-

pecially in France, its modest tonal resources (relative to the cello) made it ideal for performances in small rooms. Its popularity reached its zenith around 1700, and the most popular style of composition for it was the solo suite, which Bach appropriated for the cello. A fretted instrument with six or more strings, a slightly curved bridge, and a flat back, the gamba eventually fell out of favor due to the difficulty of bowing without hitting other strings and the shallowness of its small tone. The instrument was thus unsuited to the concert halls that were growing in size and number in the 18th century. Its place would be taken by the cello, to whose development as a solo instrument Bach contributed more than any other composer when he wrote his six suites.

Due to the popularity of the three gamba sonatas among cellists, it's only recently that a fair number of recordings have been made using the instrument they were composed for. Gambist **Richard Boothby** has recorded them with Shalev Ad-El in clear, straightforward readings hampered somewhat by unalluring recorded sound (Chandos). **Hille Perl** and Michael Behringer take a similar approach, but they are much better recorded and gambist Perl's silken tone is a delight (Hänssler 92124). Perl also has a more natural feel for Baroque rhythms.

Paolo Pandolfo and Rinaldo Alessandrini are also blessed with good sound, and Pandolfo is fortunate to have a fine gamba, ca. 1700, attributed to the great French maker Nicolas Bertrand (Harmonia Mundi 2955218). Pandolfo's tone is warmer and deeper than Perl's, and that also characterizes his approach to the music. He takes much slower tempos in the slow movements, which he plays with great affection. **Savall** and Koopman have recorded the sonatas twice (Virgin; Alia Vox 9812). The later Alia Vox disc has superb sound, and Savall plays on a Pellegrino di Zanetto of 1550 and a Barak Norman of 1697, instruments made by two of the greatest gamba makers. Their approach is very similar to Pandolfo/Alessandrini—warm and soulful, and the deep, rich tone of the Pellegrino in Sonata 1 is a joy to hear.

Some artists consider the sound of the gamba unsatisfactory, and the sound of the cello is too large. **Bylsma** has recorded the sonatas on a violoncello piccolo, with van Asperen on the organ (Sony 45945). This is a very successful combination, due to the wider dynamic range of the instrument, with its tonal similarity to the gamba, and the full sound and sustaining qualities of the organ. Bylsma's student **Wispelwey** has taken this approach several steps further, using the violoncello piccolo, a different keyboard instrument for each Sonata (organ, fortepiano, and harpsichord, played by Richard Egarr), and a cello added for the keyboard baseline in 1 and 3. The music comes alive on this recording as on no other, and the cello is a full-fledged third voice, allowed to play out as strongly as the violoncello piccolo (♦Channel 14198).

Many recordings use cello instead of gamba, usually with a piano. **Starker** gave workmanlike readings of 1 and 2 with Gyorgy Sebok (Mercury). **Leonard Rose** recorded them with Glenn Gould (Sony). Gould is a very assertive partner, but he and Rose don't always seem to understand Bach's idiom. **Ma** and harpsichordist Kenneth Cooper are more successful (CBS 37794). Ma is much more suave than Rose, with a more elastic tone, and Cooper doesn't share Gould's occasionally bizarre ideas of articulation. **Maisky** and Argerich take a very romantic approach to this music (Philips). Maisky tenderly caresses each phrase of the slow movements, and Argerich lowers herself to the status of accompanist rather than partner.

Flute sonatas (BWV 1030-35)

The flute sonatas were composed at different times in Bach's career, and the authorship of BWV 1031 and 1033 is in doubt. There is also a lacuna of some 40 to 50 bars in the holograph of BWV 1032 that has been filled in by various editors. They are all enjoyable works, though, and make a good set. BWV 1030–32 are for flute and harpsichord, while BWV 1033–35 are written for flute and figured bass continuo.

On modern instruments, flutist **William Bennett** and harpsichordist George Malcolm have recorded the sonatas with the assistance of cellist Michael Evans in the last three (ASV 6108). Bennett has a strong tone and he and his partners give propulsive accounts. **Jean-Claude Gérard** has recorded them with fortepianist Daniel Blumenthal (Hänssler 92121). These recordings have more acoustic ambience than Bennett's, and Gérard and Blumenthal make concessions to period taste. Gérard uses a wooden mouthpiece to achieve a slight softening of his tone, and Blumenthal plays a fortepiano to achieve dynamics impossible on the harpsichord. The results are very pleasing to the ear.

For sheer tonal voluptuousness no one can match **Galway** (RCA 62555, without BWV 1032; it appears on RCA 68182.). Partnered by harpsichordist Philip Moll and gambist Sarah Cunningham, Galway falls somewhere between a romantic and period approach. **Petri Alanko** has recorded the sonatas with harpsichordist Anssi Mattila and cellist Jukka Rautasalo (♦Naxos 553754/55). Alanko has the greatest understanding of baroque style and articulation, and the contrapuntal interplay is clearer here than in other recordings. His performances are like a fresh breeze blowing away the cobwebs.

On period instruments, recordist **Michala Petri** has recorded the sonatas with jazz pianist-cum-harpsichordist Keith Jarrett (RCA 61274). These are very pert, alert readings, but the recorder lacks the tonal body of the transverse flute. **Stephen Preston** plays a baroque flute in his recording with harpsichordist Pinnock and gambist Savall (CRD 33145). The sound of his instrument is wan and vaporous, and his playing is lackluster in the sonatas for flute and harpsichord, but he perks up in the sonatas with Savall.

Trio sonatas (BWV 1036-39)

The trio sonatas are cast in *sonata da chiesa* form for two solo instruments with basso continuo, an accompaniment that usually consists of a keyboard with another instrument (viola da gamba, cello, bassoon, etc.) to reinforce the bass line. Exercises in counterpoint in Bach's hands, they were also diversions for a gathering of musical amateurs, and this enhanced their popularity. Bach composed his trio sonatas for two flutes or flute and violin.

Galway has recorded BWV 1038 and 1039 with flutist Jeanne Galway (his wife), violinist Huggett, gambist Sarah Cunningham, and harpsichordist Phillip Moll (RCA 68182). His flute dominates the mix, but the musicians are first rate and the performances are spirited. Everyone but the Galways plays period instruments. The London Baroque, a period instrument group under the direction of cellist **Charles Medlam,** has recorded all four sonatas (Harmonia Mundi 2951173). They are polished, expert, and vigorous, and the musicians artfully employ *messa di voce* swells that weave in and out of the forefront, with no one particular musician dominating the listener's attention. As a result, the counterpoint is clearer and the music is more interesting.

Musical Offering (BWV 1079)

The *Musical Offering* is more a set of exercises than a composition. Bach was summoned to the Potsdam court in 1747 to play the organ for Frederick the Great. Frederick, an accomplished flutist and amateur composer, suggested a theme for Bach to improvise and was especially pleased with Bach's performance. When Bach returned home, he set to work on a set of pieces employing various contrapuntal devices based

on this theme and sent them to Frederick as an expression of thanks for his hospitality and gifts. Some find a hidden message in this work. Musicologist Ursula Kirkendale believes it is a musical "oration" directed at the King and modeled after the rules of rhetoric as they were laid down by the Roman orator Marcus Fabian Quintilian.

Members of the **Leonhardt Consort** recorded the *Offering* in 1974 in a very straightforward reading (Sony 63189). Flutist **Masahiro Arita** and a Japanese group recorded the score in 1993 (Denon 78915). The sound is much better, and the performance is of great polish and refinement. Violinist/violist **Gottfried von der Goltz** and colleagues play the score with more vigor than others (Hänssler 92133). The use of the fortepiano in the Trio Sonata is a plus, as the keyboard can match the unusually copious dynamic notations in the other instruments' parts. The **Krozinger Musik-Collegium** recorded the *Offering,* but the recording and playing aren't competitive with the rest (FSM).   MAGIL

KEYBOARD MUSIC

Bach's "keyboard" or "clavier" works (terms used to differentiate them from the organ music) comprise 222 separate numbers in Schmieder's *Thematic Catalog,* a total that does not include the harpsichord concertos. About half are in the collections so assiduously and ingeniously assembled by Bach throughout the mature phase of his career, like *Well-Tempered Clavier* or the French Suites. At last count they added up to around 470 entries in *Schwann.*

There are several important considerations when choosing recordings of these many works. Should the music be performed on the piano, or on the harpsichord or clavichord, the instruments for which Bach wrote? If piano, there is a wide divergence of styles, from Schiff's pristine, objective approach to the more romantic approach of Tureck or Horszowski. Among harpsichordists, marked deviations are also the rule. For example, Gilbert and Leonhardt represent a strict historical approach while Landowska and Puyana use non-authentic instruments and play Bach along more liberal lines. For *Well-Tempered Clavier* and *Goldberg Variations,* some performers have even chosen the organ, though I believe these pieces aren't particularly suited to that instrument.

Some years ago, Nathan Broder wrote perceptively about these problems: "Bach probably intended some of these works for clavichord, but no doubt he expected that even those would be played occasionally on the harpsichord. Performances of Bach on the piano pose a special problem. The harpsichord with stops and coupling mechanism is capable of color variety of a type impossible to achieve on the piano. The pianist, deprived of such possibilities, tries to avoid monotony in other ways, often relying on the color properties peculiar to the piano. Actually many pianistic effects were born of the Romantic school of piano composition and are inseparably associated with it in our minds. As a result, the ordinary pianist's innocent attempts to beguile the listener while playing music not intended for his instrument often succeed only in evoking a feeling remote from Bach's. Rare are the pianists who somehow manage to keep interest alive without doing violence to Bach's style."

Because of the immense number of recordings currently on the market, the respected opinions of other reviewers have been called upon to supplement my own in the evaluations that follow, arranged mostly in Schmieder number order.

Two-part Inventions and ***Three-part Sinfonias S 772-801*** (Cöthen, 1720–23). These wonderful pieces are much more than finger exercises; they were intended by Bach as a sophisticated introduction to systematic musical thinking and composition. The F minor Sinfonia, in triple counterpoint, is one of the miracles of Baroque art. Among harpsichordists, **André Laberge** who plays a Dowd instrument with elegance (♦Analekta 3089), **Leonhardt** who recorded in a thoughtful, intellectual performance in 1974 (♦Sony 61869), and **Suzuki,** who emphasizes the lyrical and cantabile (BIS 1009), take top honors. **Kathleen McIntosh** is good, though not great (Gasparo 304). **João Carlos Martins** offers very unorthodox playing (Erato 42025).

Among pianists, **Gould** is unrivaled (♦Sony 52596). We may not always like the way he plays every piece at first, but he always makes us think about the music and has a unique way of reintroducing us to it. **Schiff** is also excellent (♦London 411974).

Duettos S 802–805 (from Clavierübung, Part III, printed in Leipzig, 1739). These are large-scale two-part inventions, and each of the four has a different constructional design. Unfortunately, they are little known in spite of the fact that they are the ultimate in two-voice composition. I recommend **Kenneth Gilbert,** playing a 1988 Tucher one-manual harpsichord after C. Vater (1738) (Harmonia Mundi France 77330) and **Jaccottet,** on an unsigned 18th-century instrument (Intercord 820.754). On piano, **Richter** provides a very intelligent and convincing account of this music (Philips 438613).

English Suites S 806–811 (Weimar and Cöthen, before 1722). An ambitious prelude in concerto style opens all but the first of these large suites. As always with Bach, each of the six is quite different in mood and the last is something special, standing apart from the others. **Peter Wachthorn**'s harpsichord recording may be the best of those currently available; he plays a beautiful instrument by Burr after a 1760 Stehlin (♦Titanic 254, 2CD). Of **Leonhardt**'s two recordings, the 1978 (♦Sony 62949, 2CD) is preferred to his 1985 version (Virgin 61157, 2CD), which is characteristically informed, if a bit academic. For the later recording, he plays a restored Lefebvre harpsichord of 1755, on which the 4' is rather weak. **Jaccottet** is straightforward and elegant (♦Intercord 830861/2, 2CD). **Colin Tilney**'s recording, though attractive, elicits some reservations (Music & Arts). The estimable **Kenneth Gilbert** can be heard in a set that includes the six English Suites, six French Suites, and six Partitas (Harmonia Mundi 290.8078, 6CD).

Schiff's piano performance is excellent, precise, and often a bit more pianistic than it needs to be (♦London 421640, 2CD). His Suite 3 is conspicuously less effective than 2 or 4, partly because it's less idiomatic on the piano and partly because he seems less engaged. **Gould** is, as usual, superb (♦Sony 52606, 2CD). One critic is impressed by **Martins** (Concord, only 4 and 5), while another harbors some misgivings about **Perahia** (Sony, 2, 4, and 5). The interpretations in **Richter**'s 1991 recording are typically thoughtful and profound, Bach-like in effect if not in idiom (Ermitage 422; Stradivarius 33333).

French Suites S 812–817 (Cöthen, 1722). Smaller in dimensions and more intimate than the earlier *English Suites,* these works were copied into the first *Anna Magdalena Bach Notebook* of 1722. Suite 6 follows somewhat later. **Moroney** wins my vote with his exquisitely musical playing—free, engaging, minutely polished—as well as the beautiful sound of his harpsichord, built by Phillips after Ruckers (♦Virgin 561653, 2CD). **Leonhardt**'s recording ranks very close and has more charm, vivacity, and appeal than his *English Suites* (♦RCA 71963, 2CD). Here he's more inclined to exploit the timbral contrasts and color of the instrument—a 1975 Rubina after Taskin, with an unusual woody quality. **Jaccottet**'s playing is also attractive, on a harpsichord by P. Jaccottet after Taskin (Intercord 820764/5, 2CD).

Among pianists, **Gould**'s playing displays both a complete immersion in the music and an astonishing precision (♦Sony 52609, 2CD). To quote a colleague, his performance is "rich and musically confident enough to haunt the senses long after all the musicologists, dissenting critics, and Dowd harpsichords have passed on." **Schiff** is more relaxed than Gould, observing all repeats in his very fine recording (♦London 433313, 2CD). **Angela Hewitt**'s playing is on the same high level, differing primarily in her fashioning of the dance movements (♦Hyperion 67121, 2CD). The miking is not as close as for Schiff. **Gavrilov** plays the Suites musically, but his approach is frequently romanticized (EMI).

Miscellaneous harpsichord suites. The Suite in A minor (S 818a) is a mature work of considerable interest, while the Suite in E-flat (S 819a) is strangely atypical but appears to be by Bach. The F minor (fragment, S 823), A major (*Partie*, S 832), and C minor (Partita, S 997), however, are all "doubtful" to some degree. For example, the F minor Suite is incomplete and the Partita in C minor was probably intended for the lute or lute-harpsichord. **Moroney** plays the Prelude from the A minor Suite with riveting panache (♦Virgin 561653, 2CD). His supremely subtle *inégales* in the "Courante" can serve as a perfect model of how to apply this technique. In the curious Suite in E-flat, his performance is discreet and gracious. Robert Hill's recording of four suites and a partita is highly regarded (Music & Arts 874). **Richard Egarr**'s performance of the Suite in A (*Partie*) and other works is less brilliant than Hill's (Globe 5150). **Alessandrini** also plays the Suite in F minor with several other works (Opus 111).

Partitas S 825–30 (Clavierübung, Part I, published in Leipzig, 1726–31). These six magnificent works represent the apogee of the Baroque keyboard suite. In them Bach systematically juxtaposed and incorporated the Italian and French manners of the age. Appropriately for Bach's "Opus 1," the Partitas are the most expansive and artistic of all his many suites, with the possible exception of the four orchestral Overtures.

Of several outstanding recordings, I find **Kipnis** particularly appealing (♦Seraphim 73700, 1, 2, and 4 only). He is extremely musical, imaginative, fresh, and technically meticulous, with wonderful digital control, and his ornamentation is a delight and in perfect style. On occasion he brings on the 16' stop, though it's unlikely that Bach played an instrument with a 16' string more than a few times in his life, if ever. Consequently, this is no longer considered strictly historical. **Rousset** on a 1751 Hemsch harpsichord (♦Oiseau-Lyre), **Jaccottet, Staier** (Deutsche Harmonia Mundi 77306, 2CD), **Robert Woolley** (Chandos 0618, 2CD), and the aristocratic **Leonhardt** (on a Dowd instrument after Mietke) all play historic instruments or replicas, and among this distinguished group Staier, Rousset, and Woolley are favored. **Ross** plays with enthusiasm, in an informed style (Erato); **Ketil Haugsand** is also very good (Simax). Two recordings by **Kirkpatrick** have been reissued and both are most desirable acquisitions. The sound in the 1952 version on a Chickering is very dry (Music & Arts 976, 4CD), making the later recording more treasurable (♦Boston Skyline, 2CD). He uses the 16' liberally in these performances.

On the piano, **Tipo**'s playing is natural and musical, quite restrained and tasteful, but lacks the stylistic integrity of the harpsichordists (EMI). For example, the pedal is occasionally used at odd times, the accents are sometimes out of place, and tempos are occasionally off. **Fiorentino** is crisp, articulate, and graceful (Appian). **Martins** is idiosyncratic and romantic (Labor). **Gould** remains your best choice (♦Columbia 42527), though **Horszowski** can also be recommended (Arbiter 113, 2 and 5 only).

On the clavichord, **Tröger** offers an excellent alternative, though the extended dimensions of the Partitas makes the music less well suited to the restrictions of that intimate little instrument than it is to the kingly harpsichord (Lyrichord 8038, 2CD).

Italian Concerto S 971 and *French Overture* S 831 (Partita in B minor) (Clavierübung, Part II, published in Nürnberg in 1735). The *Italian Concerto* is among Bach's most ebullient keyboard compositions. It's also genial, intellectual (an unusual combination), and deservedly popular.

My choices for this work are **Gilbert,** playing a 1986 Tucher harpsichord after a 17th-century Gräbner (♦Harmonia Mundi France 901278) and **Jaccottet** on a Rucker instrument (♦Intercord 820763). **Alfonso Fedi** is exciting (Arts), **Leonhardt** contemplative (Sony). There are others, including **Staier** (Deutsche Harmonia Mundi), **Rousset** (Oiseau-Lyre), **Albert Fuller** (Reference), **Olivier Baumont** (Erato), **David Schrader** (Cedille), and **Egarr** (♦EMI 69700). Of these, only the last can be recommended with confidence. But many regard **Landowska**'s 1935 performance as the best of all (♦Pearl 9265).

On the piano, **Gould**'s astonishingly artistic version stands almost alone (♦Sony 52620, with *Chromatic Fantasy and Fugue* and other works). **Schiff** is also distinguished, however, and plays the second movement much more naturally than Gould, whose tempo is dirge-like (London 433313, 2CD, with French Overture and French Suites). **Richter** offers great structural solidity and nobility of vision (♦Philips 438613). **Michelangeli** (Teldec) and **Brendel** (Philips) are fleet, but the former is far too romantic in feeling and the latter too mechanical for comfort.

Its counterpart, the French Overture, separated in key by a tritone, is one of the least known of Bach's major works. It's well-played by **Jaccottet** (see above), **Gilbert** (see above), **Rafael Puyana** in 1963 on a Pleyel (♦Mercury 434395), by **Kirkpatrick** (♦Music & Arts 976, 4CD) on harpsichord, and, as usual, by **Gould** (♦Sony 52609, 2CD, with *French Suites*), **Schiff**, and **Richter** or piano.

Well-tempered Clavier, S 846–893 (Book I: Cöthen, 1722; Book II: Leipzig, 1744). Because of the strict, elevated fugal polyphony of each of the 48 fugues, I feel strongly that these pieces, all of Bach's keyboard works, are the least suited to the piano. For other reasons (tempo, texture), they don't sound at home on the organ. Certain ones fit the clavichord ideally, but all can be played with complete satisfaction on the harpsichord. Nevertheless, dozens of piano versions are available, and, no doubt, many more will continue to appear year after year.

Among the harpsichordists, **Gilbert**'s performance is my first choice (♦Archiv 13 439, 4CD). I haven't been able to hear **Moroney,** but because I admire his other recordings so much, I would be inclined to place it alongside Gilbert's (♦Harmonia Mundi 19 01 285, 4CD). Others in the same league are **Jaccottet,** who plays a Ruckers instrument and is unmannered, unfussy, and engaging (Intercord 820.759-62, 4CD), **Vernet,** who is charmingly eccentric and discreet playing a 1624 Rucker, with fine rubato and more character than Dreyfus, and beautifully recorded (Astrée 8510 and 8539, 2CD each), **Huguette Dreyfus,** playing a 1763 Hemsch harpsichord (Denon 75638, Book I, 2CD), and **Leonhardt** (Deutsche Harmonia Mundi 77011, Book I, 2CD).

Landowska's playing is rich in insight, interest, and character, but far removed from the way Bach would have played it, contrary to her famous assertion (Book I, RCA 6217, 2CD; Book II, 7825, 3CD). **Hans Pischner** plays a Neupert harpsichord in his reissued 1965 recording. From Landowska's elaborate, over-encumbered Pleyel, his instrument is a step in the right direction, but its sound is still quite unlike a historic harpsichord or a copy of one (Berlin). Unfortunately, none of these recordings, not even the best of them—as excellent as they are—has the intellectuality, supreme consistency, and penetration into the world of the 48 as **Walcha**'s two LP versions, the first recorded for EMI (1961) and the second (1974) recorded on two harpsichords, a Ruckers of 1640 and a Hemsch of 1755–56 (Archiv). It's well past time for one or both of these classic recordings to be reissued.

Tilney's recordings are noteworthy, as he plays Book I on a clavichord and Book II on a harpsichord, and both are historic instruments (Hyperion 66351, 4CD). An organ version of both Books has been made by **Lagacé** (Analekta, 5CD).

If you must have well-tempered Clavier on the piano, **Hewitt** (♦Hyperion 67301-4, 4CD), **Schiff** (♦London 484388 and 417236, 2CD each), and **Richter** (♦Olympia 536/37, 4CD) are premier choices. **Gould** may be a bit too idiosyncratic for most tastes through this lengthy series of pieces (♦Sony 52600 and 52603, 2CD each). The revered Swiss pianist **Edwin Fischer** recorded them in the 1930s—clear, directional playing that set a high standard (Book I, Pearl 172939, 2CD; Books I and II, EMI 567214, 3CD). **Bernard Roberts**'s recording has been perceived as perfunctory by more than one reviewer (Nimbus 5608-11, 4CD). **Samuel Feinberg**'s playing is relaxed, gentle, and natural (Russian Disc 15013, 4CD). One of my colleagues was most positive about **David Korevaar**'s Book I (Musicians Showcase 82198, 2CD) and judged **Afanassiev**'s to be enjoyable, played with a minimum of pedal and well-recorded (Denon 78834, 2CD).

Our editor liked **Jandó**'s Book II (Naxos 550970, 2CD) but not his Book I (Naxos 553796, 2CD), which is over-pedaled and over-romanticized. His opinion of **Feltsman**'s Book II was that it doesn't compare well to the alternatives (MusicMasters). Some critics have complimentary things to say about the reissue of **Tureck**'s 1953 recording (DG 463305, 4CD). However, their view of **Martins** was lukewarm; the playing is fluent but lacks a Bach feel (Labor). Nikolayeva espouses an over-romanticized, rhapsodic approach to Book I (Hungaroton).

Chromatic Fantasy & Fugue in D minor S 903 (Leipzig, 1730). This great virtuosic work has been a staple of the pianist's repertoire for generations. However, it sounds much more effective on the instrument for which Bach intended it—the Baroque harpsichord.

Landowska's playing in 1936 is something of a legend, though her Pleyel harpsichord was a very distant cousin to the harpsichord Bach knew (Biddulph 31). **Jaccottet** performs the *Fantasy* with brilliance and cohesion; in the Fugue, pristine clarity, poise, and vigor reign (♦Intercord 820.763). Best of all, she eschews the eccentricity and overdramatization frequently encountered in this piece. Only in the recitative section (the most problematic hurdle for all players) does her music-making become a little static.

Newman's playing on a Tyre harpsichord bristles with electricity and fire and brings the Fugue to an exciting peroration (Vox 7520). Other highly praised recordings include **Patrick Stephens** (Americus 1003), **Alessandrini** ("energy level high, razor-sharp;" Opus 111 30258) and **Staier** (Deutsche Harmonia Mundi 77330). Critics are less impressed, for various reasons, with **Verlet** (Astrée), **Smith** (the lengthiest version, Wildboar), **Egarr** ("abrupt, violent, with a contemplative Fugue;" Globe), and **Kraus** (CBC).

Once again, **Gould** (Sony 52620) and **Schiff** (Hungaroton 11690) are the best of the piano versions.

Toccatas S 910–916 (Arnstadt, Weimar, and Cöthen). These seven flamboyant pieces all come from relatively early in Bach's *oeuvre*. We no longer possess his autograph manuscripts of any of them, only copies made by students and colleagues. In style, there are echoes of Bach's forebears, Frescobaldi and Buxtehude, so they emanate a certain fascinating archaism, yet some sections are extraordinarily brilliant.

Edward Parmentier's recording is more expressive and inventive than Newman's, on a wonderful man harpsichord in fabulous sound (♦Wildboar 9402). Newman's set on a Tyre instrument is very brilliant and energized, sometimes too tense and high-strung and seldom relaxed (♦Vox 7520). Leonhardt is magisterial in a re-release of his 1978–80 recording (Sony 60375, 2CD). Verlet is maniacal and joyous, playing the Toccatas in D, D minor, and E minor on a 1624 Ruckers in a much-admired recording (Astrée 8565). The sets by Jory Vinikour (Mandala) and Tilney (Dorian) fall below the level of the others.

Richard Tröger's clavichord version reveals the slow movements in a new light and has been deemed indispensable (♦Lyrichord 8041). This time Gould (Sony) is joined by Martins (Concord, S 913-16 only) as the most interesting of the pianists. The latter has been praised as "some of the finest Bach playing currently before the public."

Goldberg Variations S 988 (Clavierübung Part IV, printed in Nürnberg, 1742). In this, the first of the four great variation works of Bach's last decade (the others are *Canonic Variations* for organ, *Musical Offering*, and *Art of Fugue*), 30 variations are preceded by an Aria, whose bass is then "varied" in the manner of a passacaglia. With each of these late masterworks, Bach set up severe restrictions within which he was obliged to proceed, these being the canonic and fugal art as well as the retention of one key center. By successfully transcending these restrictions, he attained the zenith of his art. One of the primary decisions for the performer is whether to observe repeats for all variations (this can cause a very long elapsed time; as much as 91 minutes in Tureck's latest recording), some repeats, or none. Because Bach specified two manuals in some of the variations, the piano is certainly not the ideal instrument.

For a long time, I've been fond of the recordings by Gilbert (♦Harmonia Mundi 295.1240) and Leonhardt (♦Vanguard 2004); the latter, from 1965, is played on an Ammer harpsichord. Both artists are intellectual and sensitive. Others prefer Hill (a live recording from 1993; ♦Music & Arts 850); Masaaki Suzuki (BIS 819); Verlet (Astrée) and Rousset (Oiseau-Lyre) (both with Gallic flavor), and Christine Schornsheim (with stylish ornamentation) (Capriccio 10577. 2CD), approximately in that order; all are fine choices.

Landowska is known for an inimitable performance, which she first recorded in 1936 after playing the Variations in public for 45 years (Biddulph 31, 1936, with *Chromatic Fantasy*; Pearl 9265, 1933, with *Italian Concerto* and Partita 1; RCA 60919, 2CD, with two Fantasias in C minor, two- and three-part inventions, and Partita 2). Rousset uses a 1751 Hemsch instrument with a silvery sound and a low pitch (a=415) (♦Oiseau-Lyre 444866). He observes all repeats for a timing of 76:44, playing in a bold style with strongly marked phrasing, sometimes clipped, which doesn't occur with Leonhardt or Gilbert. In Variation 29 the rhythm is awkward. Pinnock is excellent, with superb rhythm and historical integrity, but not much suavity (Archiv 415130). His Ruckers harpsichord is miked very closely.

Good, acceptable recordings come from Karl Richter (a bit dated; Teldec, with six Partitas), Cole (Virgin), Ogg (Globe), and Hayden (Boston Skyline). Recordings with one or more reservations attached by critics are by Luc Beausejour (Analekta), Sergio Vartolo (Tactus), John Metz (Soundset), Nicholas Parle (Tall Poppies), and Christiane Hasselmeier (Koch), though all of these have received accolades as well.

In the piano field, Gould again heads the list; the fourth of his recordings (1981) is widely regarded as the definitive piano version (♦Sony 37779). Schiff (♦London 460611) and Sergey Schepkin (♦Ongaku 24107) complete a trio of pianists who have scaled Parnassus with this work. Very good recordings come from Hewitt (Hyperion), Tipo (EMI), Gershon Silbert (Bequest), Edward Aldwell (Biddulph), Lifschitz (Denon), and Robin Sutherland (D'Note). Others of no particular distinction, given the heavy competition (those listed at the end exhibit serious flaws), include Barenboim (Erato), Cecilia Li (Amati), Myung-Whun Chung (Channel), Andrei Vieru (Harmonia Mundi), Ito Eno (Music & Arts), Peter Serkin (RCA), Yudina (Philips), Feltsman (MusicMasters), Tureck (VAIA), Michael Masek (Lotos), and Martins (Labor, on an out-of-tune piano).

"Little" Preludes S 924–943. Bach left about 20 of these miniature studies, probably intended for keyboard instruction. Some of them are from the *Wilhelm Friedemann Bach Notebook.* Countless piano students have since learned and played them (and, no doubt, long since forgotten them). The following recordings, all excellent, incorporate some of them among other, larger works: Egarr (EMI 69700) and Smith (Wildboar 9501) on harpsichord, and Hewitt (Hyperion 67121) on piano.

Other single pieces

Prelude and Fugue in A minor, S 894 (Weimar, ca. 1717). Bach later revised this music and incorporated it into the "Triple Concerto" S 1044 for flute, violin, harpsichord, and orchestra. It's well played by Stephens (Americus 1003) and Egarr (Globe 5150).

Prelude and Fughetta in D minor S 899 (of doubtful authenticity) and *Prelude and Fughetta in E minor S 900.* Both of these pieces have been recorded by Martins on piano (Concord 42051).

Fantasy and Fugue in A minor, S 904 (Leipzig, ca. 1725). This piece is sometimes played on the organ. The double fugue is superb. It's offered by Verlet (Astrée 8565) and Staier (Deutsche Harmonia Mundi 77330), both on harpsichord, and by Richter on piano (Melodiya 25178).

Fantasia in C minor, S. 906 (Leipzig, ca. 1718). A well-known work, but of doubtful authenticity. It's in binary form and in a style that suggests Bach's sons. An incomplete Fugue is attached. Leonhardt recorded this on harpsichord in 1978–80 (Sony 60375, 2CD) and Richter on piano in 1991 (Live Classics 421).

Fantasy (Präludium) in A minor S 922 (Weimar, ca. 1710). A display piece of doubtful authenticity, played by Verlet on harpsichord (Astrée 8565) and Martins on piano (Concord 42052).

Fugue in A minor, S 944 (Cöthen, ca. 1720). This is Bach's lengthiest keyboard fugue and is closely related to the Organ Fugue in A minor S 543. Both are works of rushing, kinetic energy. Leonhardt plays it on harpsichord (Sony 60375, 2CD) and Richter on piano (Melodiya 25178).

Sonata in D minor, S 964. A transcription, perhaps not by Bach, of the Solo Violin Sonata in A minor, S 1003, played by Fedi on harpsichord (Arts 47253) and Richter on piano (Stradivarius 33323).

Aria variata alla maniera italiana S 989 (Weimar, ca. 1709, perhaps earlier). This little-known piece consists of an aria and 10 variations, and has been recorded several times: by Hill (Hänssler 92.102), Alessandrini on a Sidey harpsichord after an anonymous ca. 1740 German instrument (Opus 111 30258), and by Puyana on a Pleyel (Mercury 434395).

Capriccio on the Departure of his Beloved Brother, S 992 (Arnstadt, 1704). Composed when Bach was only 19 for his brother, Johann Jakob, who had joined the Kapelle of the King of Sweden, it's played on harpsichord by **Hill** (Hänssler 92.102), **Smith** (Wildboar 9501), and **Alessandrini** (Opus 111 30258), and on piano by **Martins** (Concord 42051) and **Richter** (Live Classics 461).

Prelude, Fugue, & Allegro in E, S 998. This is an unusually beautiful but atypical work, whose origin is clouded; it may have been for lute. It's played by **André Laberge** on a Dowd harpsichord after Mietke (Analekta 3089).   MULBURY/MORIN

ORGAN MUSIC

Over the past 25 years or so, a radical polarization has taken place in the organ world about how Bach should be played. Other musical fields—opera, chamber music, choral music—certainly evince differences of opinion about performance style, but that's nothing compared to the wide divergence of view among organists. This is a curious phenomenon, not generally known to the public or even to other musicians, so it's important to clarify it for the prospective record buyer. The proponents of one performance style or another can be roughly divided into three groups. Those who have recorded complete sets are indicated below by an asterisk following their names.

1. The conservative or "right wing" group is more allied to an older tradition than the others, be it French or German. Organ registration, that is, instrumental color, is viewed as an integral interpretive or architectural element. A registration is chosen that best seems to complement or project the *affect* of each individual piece. Phrasing and articulation may be either quite legato (French), conceived in terms of intervals, gestures, and melodic cells that make up the polyphonic web of the music, based upon instrumental phrasings in the cantatas, and so forth. (German). Almost any fingering or pedaling that produces musical results is used. Changes of manual, often in Baroque concerto style, are seen as important in the large works. In trio sonatas, a contrast in timbre between voices is considered artistically desirable.

Organists whose Bach interpretations fall into this category are E. Power Biggs, Helmut Walcha*, Lionel Rogg*, Michael Murray, Robert Noehren, Edgar Krapp, Walter Kraft*, and the organists featured on the Silbermann Series (Berlin)—Christoph Albrecht, Hannes Kästner, Hans Otto, Robert Köbler, and others.

2. At the other extreme—the progressive or "left wing"—is a large group of organists (including some who are very talented) who espouse an etiquette of performance first promoted by Anton Heiller, Marie-Claire Alain, and Gustav Leonhardt, further popularized by the organ faculty at Oberlin College, and now notably advocated by Harold Vogel, whose master classes have had a pervasive influence. A reaction against the ideals of the first group has been, at least in part, an impetus for these musicians' quest for an artistic and logically formulated credo, to which much thought and research have been devoted.

They view registration in Bach in a much less coloristic fashion, preferring to play most of the preludes, toccatas, fantasias, and fugues with pretty much one registration throughout. Manual changes are generally forbidden. Phrasing and articulation are primarily carried out in non-legato touches, and no cognizance is given to motives, cells, and so forth. Pedals can be played only with the toes; historical fingerings are cultivated and used whenever possible. They typically insist on recording only on organs tuned in a mean-tone temperament. Organists in this group can be quick to decry others' approaches as "unauthentic" or "uninformed," yet there is a glaring paucity of solid historical evidence to support their insistence that theirs is the only true historical style. Their recordings of the "free" organ works (those not based on chorales)

are usually monochromatic and pedantic, in keeping with the prescribed model. Because their primary emphasis is historicism rather than musicality, this is not entirely unexpected.

Organists who belong in this category are Heiller, Alain*, Leonhardt, Vogel, Rübsam*, Koopman*, Weinberger*, Lagacé, Lippincott, Fagius*, Foccroulle*, Ritchie, Kee, and Schrader.

3. In the middle is a group, the "moderates," that draws elements of its convictions from both sides. Its members are usually not doctrinaire. While there are many excellent recorded performances by these organists, much of their Bach may lack the strong imprint and distinctive character of the other, more contrasted groups. This category embraces André Isoir*, Michel Chapuis*, Christopher Herrick*, Kevin Bowyer*, Peter Hurford*, Anthony Newman, Kei Koito, Helmuth Rilling, Jean Guillou*, and Olivier Vernet*.

What, then, are the most rewarding recordings (for the listener, if not the historian) of the complete Bach organ works—about 180 works on 12 to 17 CDs?

Complete sets

Walcha's set is in a class by itself, standing at the top of the list (◆Archiv 419904, 12CD). Unfortunately, these discs are difficult to obtain. This is one of the few sets that includes *Art of Fugue,* though it doesn't contain Bach's arrangements of concertos by other composers for organ solo. The instruments heard in these recordings, made between 1954 and 1971, are in the Laurenskerk, Alkmaar, Holland (built by Frans Caspar Schnitger in the 1720s but based upon an older organ that dated back many years) and in St. Pierre-le-Jeune, Strasbourg, France (built, in part, by Johann Andreas Silbermann in 1780). The Alkmaar organ is known for its magnificent plenum and silvery sheen; the Strasbourg instrument is remarkable for its plasticity and the beauty of its flute and aliquot stops.

Walcha, who was blinded in childhood by a smallpox immunization, grew up in Bach's chosen city, Leipzig, and as a youth heard or participated in hundreds of Bach cantatas. At 20 he was assistant organist at St. Thomas and served as a Lutheran church organist until late in life. Like Bach, he was an extraordinary improvisor. Quite a few organists have performed all of Bach's organ works from memory and some have recorded all of them, but Walcha has been the only blind organist, as far as I know, to memorize and record not only the organ works but also most of the harpsichord music, the six sonatas for violin and harpsichord, and several harpsichord concertos with orchestra. Learning these masterworks "from the inside out" led him to a unique insight into the tonal world of Bach's polyphony.

Drawn from Walcha's 12CD set, two Archiv releases are easily obtainable: a program with a broad selection of larger works, the Canonic Variations, and the six Schübler Chorales 453064, 2CD), and a single disc with the Toccata and Fugue in D minor, Prelude and Fugue in E-flat, Sonata 1, and the Chorale Partita, "Sei gegrüsset" (457704).

I don't believe any other organist's playing penetrates the essence of Bach's music to the degree that Walcha's does. However, the Swiss organist **Lionel Rogg** has an excellent complete edition, with superb, elegant playing full of vitality, intensity, and bravura (◆Harmonia Mundi 290772/83, 12CD). The historic Silbermann organ in Arlesheim, Switzerland, is used for all pieces. It's not an ideal Bach organ, but it's one of tonal beauty and has been recorded in resonant, clear sound.

Like Walcha's, **Isoir**'s complete Bach is no longer listed in *Schwann.* This admirable French artist, who used both historic and modern instruments for his recordings, may well exceed all others in sheer brilliance. Most of his series was well-recorded, but the program notes were substandard (Calliope). Another of the very fine earlier sets, now reissued at budget price, is by **Michel Chapuis,** formerly professor of organ in Strasbourg (Valois 4864, 14CD). The playing is mercurial and brilliant but lacks Walcha's logic and consistency.

I would place the complete Bach editions of three British organists somewhat behind these four sets. **Christopher Herrick**'s playing is appealing and virtuosic (Hyperion). The edition uses modern organs, is well-recorded, and provides extensive program notes. Fine playing is also found in the sets by **Bowyer** (Nimbus) and **Hurford** (London and MHS), though I have a slight preference for Herrick among the three. **Vernet**'s Bach is vital and imaginative, and, if not always consistent, a better choice than many. His recordings have the advantage of top quality sound (Ligia 0104081, 18CD). A wide selection of historic organs can be heard in the complete Bach of the young French organist, **Bernard Foccroulle** (Ricercare). **Guillou**'s recordings are frequently eccentric, flashy, and not played on historic organs (Dorian).

With the exception of **Gerhard Weinberger**'s new series (CPO), which shows great promise, I'm unable to recommend any Bach played by organists of the second group. **Koopman** (Novalis; Archiv), **Fagius** (BIS), **Alain** (Erato), and **Rübsam** (Naxos) have made or are currently making complete sets. I beg the reader's forbearance as I quote from myself in an earlier review of one of these recordings: "All my copies of CDs by these organists have been sent up to the attic, where my insane grandmother occasionally, I think, plays them."

Die Kunst der Fuge (The Art of Fugue) S 1080 (Leipzig, ca. 1744–50)

For many years this was considered Bach's last work, a magnificent, if incomplete, swan song. Now some musicologists speculate that it might more correctly be placed within Bach's last decade, rather than at the very end of it. A more insightful and intriguing theory has been proposed by the brilliant Bach scholar, Randolph Currie: that Bach left it unfinished intentionally, with the tacit intimation that those select few who truly understood his art would be capable of completing it for themselves.

Bach never specified the instrument he intended for the realization of this masterwork. Consequently, today's listener has the choice of hearing it in arrangements for full orchestra, brass ensemble, reed quintet, saxophone quartet, recorder consort, piano, one harpsichord, two harpsichords, or organ. All, it should be stressed, are arrangements, and none are ideal (though some are less ideal than others). A small string or chamber ensemble, harpsichord, or organ seems the logical choice. Though each has its disadvantages, the organ — instrument of ineffable mystique, with its manifold color possibilities, its aptness for Bach's rarefied polyphony, and its ability to sustain long tones — may be the most rewarding among imperfect solutions. Another way this unworldly music can be conceptualized is by silently reading the score and hearing it within your mind.

The premier organ performances are by **Walcha** (Archiv 419904, 12CD) and **Kei Koito** (Temperaments 316016 , 2CD). Walcha's supreme intellectuality and stylistic intuition set his version (recorded on the great baroque organ in Alkmaar in 1956) apart. He performed all 18 pieces himself, including the three-voice mirror fugue, which is usually negotiated by two performers. His completion of the unfinished final "Contrapunctus 18" is the most satisfying I have heard. The recorded sound shows its age, however. Koito's recording on the 1748 Dom Bedos organ in Bordeaux is a dashing interpretation with French emphasis, in which she has chosen to reorder the movements according to her own scheme. Kenneth Weiss assists her in the two mirror fugues.

The admirable **André Isoir** has also recorded the work on the organ (Calliope 9719). I haven't heard this yet but mention it because of my high regard for his Bach playing. Other recordings are less felicitous, for various reasons: **Marie-Claire Alain** (Erato), **Johannes-Ernst Köhler** (Berlin), **Lynn Zeigler** (Calcante), **Josef Popelka** (Bonton), and **Glenn Gould** (excepts only, Sony).

The harpsichord can't offer the color possibilities of the organ, and its sameness of tone over the duration of this complex work, one and a half hours, is wearing on the listener, at least in a complete performance. Nevertheless, some unusually fine recordings are available. **Leonhardt**'s was for many years the authoritative gold standard (Vanguard Bach Guild OVC 2004, 2CD). **Robert Hill**'s is marked by energy and excitement (Music & Arts 279), **Gilbert**'s is poised and serene (Archiv 427673), and **Moroney**'s is characterized by his usual elegance and astuteness (Harmonia Mundi 295.1169, 2CD, or, with *Well-Tempered Clavier* I and II and *Musical Offering,* 290.8084, 7CD). **Koopman** and his wife, Tini Mathot, have recorded the entire work on two harpsichords (Erato 96387), certainly an unorthodox approach.

Recordings of this work by small instrumental ensembles include excellent ones by the viol consort **Phantasm** (excerpts only, Simax 1135), **Juilliard Quartet** (Sony 45937), and a period instrument group directed by **Malgoire,** in which there is an intermixture of instruments (coming in, dropping out, returning) — a practice I believe is contrary to the essence of these strict fugues (K167 040, 2CD).

While I don't recommend piano performances on esthetic grounds, distinguished recordings are available by **Aldwell** (excerpts only, Biddulph FLW 002) and by duo-pianists **Millette Alexander** and **Frank Draykin** (Connoisseur Society 4203, 2CD).

Individual recordings

In discussing discs of selected Bach organ works, we're faced with a bewildering number and variety. Here are some of the most noteworthy.

E. Power Biggs, most of whose recordings were on the Flentrop organ in the Busch-Reisinger Museum at Harvard, is always vital and engaging, infused with the spirit and musicianship of a truly great organist (Columbia/Sony).

These remarks also apply to **Robert Noehren**'s CD (Delos 3028), on the Riegger organ at Pacific Union College. He's another great artist whose technique is superior to Biggs's and has achieved even more elegant Bach performances.

Edgar Krapp has recorded the *Clavierübung,* Part III, on two Baroque organs built by Wagner in the Berlin area. This release is outstanding in all respects, with visceral, flawless playing (Berlin 1060/61).

Kei Koito's recording of the six sonatas, five concerto transcriptions, and the *Canonic Variations,* on the Schnitger organ in the Martinikerk, Groningen, Netherlands, is one of the most exceptional organ recordings of the past 25 years (Harmonic 8828/29). Her incandescent performances of extreme polish, the beautiful recorded sound, and the luxurious program booklet are all stunning. Look for her *Art of Fugue* as well (♦Temperaments 316016).

Heinrich Gurtner offers quite a different view of the six sonatas, those priceless gems, recording them on the early Baroque organ in Muri, Switzerland. Gurtner is a performer of the older school, but his playing is superb and often spiritual.

Richard Marlow, Fellow at Trinity College, Cambridge, has made a distinguished recording of the *Orgelbüchlein* (46 chorale preludes ordered according to the church year), the finest available except for Walcha's. His playing on the historic organ in the Chapel at Trinity College is both wonderfully finished and poetic. For a CD of these same chorale preludes, each preceded by a four-voice sung harmonization of the chorale, **Helmut Rilling**'s fine version is the choice (Cantate 57607/9, 3CD).

James Johnson's program at the Busch-Reisinger Museum is another outstanding disc. The CD features Preludes and Fugues in D and B minor, Concerto in D minor, Sonata 1, and five chorale preludes (Titanic 162).

Michael Murray's Bach CDs on various organs around the world offer performances by a splendid musician and meticulous technician. However, his style is firmly grounded in the legato approach advocated by Dupré and others of the Romantic French school. It's a style that arose from the great 19th century organs of the French builder Cavaillé-Coll and is not always ideal for the Baroque plasticity and transparency of Bach's art (Telarc).

Walter Kraft was among the first to record a complete set of Bach's organ works. His playing is solid and musicianly, though his tempos tend to be slow. A nice selection is available, although, unfortunately, the sound is rather dim (Vox 5059, 2CD).

Anthony Newman could be compared to those two other iconoclasts, Jean Guillou and Glenn Gould. All three are decidedly unorthodox in their treatment of Bach, and like Gould, Newman often favors extremely fast tempos. A 4CD collection called "24 Preludes and Fugues" also includes a number of the shorter chorale preludes (Vox Vol. 1, 5013; Vol. 2, 5100). In both sets the selection of works is attractive but the sound quality is mediocre.

Finally, Berlin Classics has brought out a 10CD series recorded on the organs of Gottfried Silbermann, the younger brother of the Alsatian builder, Andreas Silbermann, who worked in Saxony and knew Bach. Twelve organs, all beautiful instruments comparable to the violins of Stradivarius, are played by some of the superb organists of the former East Germany, including Christoph Albrecht, Hannes Kästner, Hans Otto, and Robert Köbler. There is some inspired, exciting playing on these incomparable instruments and the recorded sound is of premier quality, even though some of the recordings date back to the LP era. I'm not prepared to recommend any individual Bach organ discs by organists of group two—Heiller (Vanguard), Leonhardt (Sony), Vogel (Capriccio), Lagacé (Analekta), Lippincott (Gothic), Ritchie (Titanic; Raven), Kee (Chandos), Schrader (Cedille)—because I doubt they will prove rewarding to most listeners over many years. More important, I don't believe they reveal the beauty of Bach's organ music very effectively. For best satisfaction, stay with the organists of groups one and three.

MULBURY

VOCAL MUSIC

The involvement of voices, both solo and choral, adds a considerable complication to the basic distinction between MI and PI recordings in other areas of Bach's output. Questions arise about the types of vocal production of either modern conventions or as influenced by musicological reconstruction of earlier practices. The particular question of the size and character of choruses has become a serious issue of debate and distinctions in recent recordings. The following section makes some basic distinctions between "period-style" and "nonperiod-style" performances.

Cantatas (BWV 1-215)

It is impossible to cover this vast category—itself but a partial survival of the largest area of Bach's output—in any minutely systematic fashion, and it would require a discographic volume all its own. Not the least of the problems is the fact that most of the cantatas are short and are mixed with others in ever-shifting combinations. In addition, many listeners' choices will be affected by their admiration of particular singers, beyond any other critical judgments. I suspect that many record hunters will be at either of two extremes: the frenzied specialist who must have everything, or the more casual investigator who would like to pick and choose a few representative cantata recordings. There is perhaps a middle ground for some, in programs of excerpts that pop up from time to time. The **Bach Aria Group** used to present sampler programs, both in concerts and sporadically on records. However, there isn't much to commend them, though I might mention one interesting package, entitled "Gelobet seist du Jesus Christ," which demonstrates how Bach used some 15 of Luther's chorales in his own treatments (mostly in his cantatas), and is quite well performed under **Rilling** (◆Hänssler 98.101, 2CD).

It's assumed here, however, that only complete cantatas matter for our purposes. Expediency dictates two ways of providing some guidelines to collectors confronting this daunting literature, which offers many recordings by conductors whose approach has recognizable characteristics. Further, there are several ventures into "complete" recordings of the cantatas, which may be surveyed as a single category. For the rest, there are some specific cantatas so recurrently popular as to justify scrutinizing their recordings closely. The selection process is arbitrary and painful, because it omits attention to many "lesser" cantatas, but collectors may enjoy discovering them for themselves, while a sense of performer characteristics in general may be gathered from the following section.

Series and collections

As with any large corpus of music, general and "complete" approaches will involve some inconsistencies, so that even the "best" general survey will offer individual performances that have superior rivals, and collectors seeking specific cantatas will want to pick and choose. But general surveys do offer consistencies of performance style that can be relied upon as givens, once their qualities are understood. Of the comprehensive or "complete" cycles undertaken to date, one is MI and the other three are PI, each presenting a distinct musical character.

The MI version very much reflects **Rilling**'s middle-ground "compromise" approach, well established in the Richter tradition of combining historical sensitivity with warm musicianship in a distillation tailored to modern listening tastes. His ensembles—in most cases, the Gächinger Kantorei and the Bach Collegium of Stuttgart—are of appropriately moderate size and very well drilled. His soloists include, among others, sopranos Augér, Donath, Laki, and Ingebourg Reichelt; altos Hamari, Murray, Watkinson, and Watts; tenors Equiluz, Adalbert Kraus, and Schreier; baritone Fischer-Dieskau (in 56 and 82); and basses Huttenlocher, Nimsgern, Schmidt, and Schöne. The recordings, made from the early 1970s into the early 1980s, are very bright and full-bodied.

Though he has recorded them separately, Rilling omitted in this "sacred" series the final group of "secular" cantatas, stopping at BWV 200, and of those, omitting nine (15, 53, 58, 118–19, 141–42, 160, 189) that are problematical (incomplete or not authentic), for a total of 191. Hänssler has issued these variously, mainly as a series of 66 single discs, with the cantatas in random order, but allowing individual picking and choosing (◆98.801-30, 835; 98.855-87, 890-91). He has also issued selected cantatas for Christmas and Easter, grouped respectively in two 4CD boxed sets (98.836, 98.837), and most recently, all 66 of the cantata discs, plus three more containing the *Christmas Oratorio* cycle, for a total of 69 CDs in a massive three-container boxed set, and the full cantata series, with the order recast to follow the BWV sequencing, in their vast "Bachakademie" series (Vols. 1–70, 92.001-070). But Rilling has been catching up with the "secular" cantatas (BWV 201-15), now being consolidated in the "Bachakademie" sequence (Vols. 61–68, 92.061-68). As a kind of footnote, Hänssler has also issued a 2CD set gleaning the instrumental/orchestral sinfonias, sonatas, sonatinas, and whatnot from 26 cantatas, all taken from Rilling's cumulative recordings of the complete works. There have been samplings of such cantata "overtures" over the years, but this is by far the most comprehensive, for those who want such a survey.

Of more or less contemporaneous date is the first (and still the only complete) PI cycle, with conducting honors divided between **Harnoncourt** (with his Concentus Musicus Wien) and **Leonhardt** (with his Leonhardt Consort), using several different choirs all involving boy trebles. Soloists include sopranos Bonney and Kweksilber; countertenors Esswood and Jacobs; tenors Elwes, Adalbert Kraus, Equiluz; and basses Egmond, Hampson, Holl, Huttenlocher, and van der Kamp. The recordings were a revelation of new possibilities in texture, clarity, scale, and inflection, though the performances were sometimes underrehearsed and often very rough and strident, the minimalist instrumentations sometimes abrasive, and the use (most of the time) of boy trebles in place of mature soprano soloists often hard to digest. Though by no means the only performances of these works you would want to live with exclusively, they do reward continuing study. The cycle embraced BWV 1–199, less 10 problematicals (15, 53, 118, 141–42, 160, 189–91, 193) plus one alternate version (69a), for a total of 190, presented strictly in BWV number sequence, which is certainly convenient for reference.

These recordings were originally issued by Telefunken in a series of 45 2LP boxed sets, each containing a booklet of complete miniature scores. Teldec has reissued these sets in 45 directly corresponding 2CD albums (unfortunately, *not* containing the scores) and some of these are still in circulation. Teldec has also consolidated the cycle, compressing it from 90 to 60 discs, available as a single grand package (♦91765) or as a series of ten 6CD boxes (♦91755-64); and most recently they have reorganized these recordings again into four boxes of 15 CDs each (♦Vols. 1–4, 25706-9) in their "Bach 2000" series, plus a further volume (♦Vol. 5, 125710) for the "secular" cantatas. It's interesting that Leonhardt himself has returned to the cantatas in at least in one 1995 recording, using the same spare, minimalist approach, complete with boy soprano and alto soloists as well as choristers (Sony 68265).

Two new PI cycles are now in progress, though each is far from completion. **Koopman,** another major player in the PI movement, having recorded the major sacred works of Bach as well as a lot of his instrumental music, launched his challenge to the Teldec series in the fall of 1994. He uses a modest-sized PI orchestra and a chamber choir of mixed voices. His soloists include early-music veterans Schlick and Ziesak, sopranos; von Magnus, alto; Scholl and Wessel, countertenors; Agnew, de Mey, Prégardien, Türk, tenors; and Mertens, bass. His PI instrumental sound is suave but still fruity, and he consistently avoids boy trebles, using adult females in both solo and choral capacities, with often outstanding vocal work from all hands. Though his pacings are often spirited, they are far from extreme. There is more of the concert hall than the church in Koopman's approach, which honors but does not exaggerate musicological considerations. He takes the historically plausible step of setting his pitch a semitone higher than modern tuning, which may annoy some score readers, but he's unique among "completers" in adding variant movements or material, where germane, in appendices.

Erato is issuing this cycle (projected to >20 volumes) in a series of

boxes, usually 3CD or 4CD each, of which 10 have appeared at this writing. The first three (98536, 12598, 14336) collect all the cantatas that survive from Bach's pre-Leipzig years (34 of them, including "secular" BWV 208); the next two (15562, 17578) complete coverage of the "secular" cantatas (BWV 198, 201–2, 204–6, 207a, 209–15); the latest five (21629, 23141, 25488, 27315, 80220) begin the long haul through the Leipzig cantatas by covering Bach's initial cycle composed for the Thomaskirche. Thus, what may seem at first a scattershot approach, confusingly at odds with the "standard" BWV numbering (which itself is arbitrary and unhelpful), is in fact generally and intelligently chronological.

If those who find the Harnoncourt/Leonhardt approach too austere and abrasive are prepared to follow with patience, they will find Koopman's series a welcome alternative, combining musicological care with a certain "compromise" musicality. But Koopman is himself facing a new competitor, ironically one of his former students. This is **Suzuki,** who has managed in recent years to create a world-class program of Baroque performance in Tokyo with his Bach Collegium Japan. That involves a small but excellent PI orchestra and mixed-voice chamber choir (which sings very beautifully), plus a pool of very fine local soloists, including the ringing, clear-voiced soprano Midori Suzuki and the splendidly secure countertenor Yoshikazu Mera (not to slight others among this group) and to these Suzuki has selectively added Western guests like Frimmer, Türk, and Kooy.

Suzuki's pacings are sometimes a little more strait-laced than Koopman's but have dignity and flow, striking a balance between church and concert tone. The Swedish label ♦BIS has undertaken this project, at least initially releasing the recordings in individual CDs. At this writing, 12 volumes have appeared, their content sometimes thematic, sometimes arbitrary. It remains to be seen how Suzuki will finally stack up against Koopman, but this series is very much one to watch, and is easier to selectively dip into.

Not that the PI sweepstakes will end there. **Gardiner** has announced a "Bach 2000" or "Bach Cantata Pilgrimage" project with DG Archiv in which he will record Bach's cantatas, each, he proposes, "on the liturgical days for which they were composed" and in a different recording venue. Such a cycle will add much spice to the competition, and hints of its character may be gleaned in retrospect from cantatas he recorded in the 1980s (Erato: BWV 4 and 131, 99614; 50 and 118, 45979, 2CD, with Motets) and the early 1990s (DG Archiv: BWV 106, 118b, and 198, 429782; 140 and 147, 431809; 61, 36, and 62, 437327; BWV 51, Philips 411458). Some of these have an uncertain future in view of the new project, though Archiv has reissued its three earlier discs as components of the first dozen items in its new series, 463580/591).

Those who want a more conservative, less historically self-conscious approach should keep in mind **Richter,** who might have continued the musical tradition at Bach's own church but instead moved to Munich, where, with his Munich Bach Choir and Bach Orchestra, he established himself as a kind of high priest of compromise (MI) interpretation. Over two decades (1959–79), Richter recorded many cantatas as well as the larger works, and these (75 in all) have been reissued in a boxed set of 26 CDs (♦DG Archiv 439368), subdivided into five boxed albums (439 69/374/380/387/394), each focused on a church feast or liturgical occasion. A lot of splendid soloists are involved: Armstrong, Buckel, Mathis, and Stader, sopranos; Hamari, Reynolds, and Hertha Töpper, altos; Haefliger, van Kesteren, and Schreier, tenors; Adam, Engen, Fischer-Dieskau, and Moll, baritones and basses. The choral and orchestral forces are substantial but very able. Richter was greatly concerned with textual expressiveness, using heavy ritards and strong inflections, with results that for many now seem "Romantic" and old-fashioned but honor an important performance tradition. The recorded sound is widely variable, and some of it shows its age in shrillness. But conservative listeners will find these performances a treasure trove of satisfaction.

You can trace Richter's background in the broadcast recordings of his teacher, the valiant **Günther Ramin** who, occupying Bach's old post of Cantor at the Thomaskirche in Leipzig, devotedly and resourcefully maintained the traditions of Karl Straube's Bach revival there through the terrible years of WW II and the early Communist regime. From the performances he was able to organize and broadcast during 1947 through 1956, 27 cantatas have been culled. Though dated in many ways, with the edgy voices of boy choristers (and occasional solo boys) perhaps irritating to some, these remain eloquent and passionately devout performances, as few others are today (♦Berlin Classics 9091/99, 9CD). Something of the Ramin tradition is further documented by Ramin's student and successor at St. Thomas for a few years, **Kurt Thomas,** who is represented by broadcast recordings made in 1960–63 of 11 cantatas (plus the *Magnificat*); among his soloists are Grümmer, Giebel, Höffgen, Adam, and Prey.

One of Thomas's students, and a tenor soloist in these recordings, was **Hans-Joachim Rotzsch,** who succeeded Thomas as director, and from his broadcast recordings (made from the early 1970s into the next decade) we have ten CDs containing 22 cantatas plus the *Magnificat* (Berlin). The performances are variable, in a conservative and sometimes heavy-handed style, but with some fine solo work from Schreier, Adam, and Lorenz, among others. **Schreier** in turn has extended the tradition; expanding his operations from singer to conductor, he has led a few cantata recordings in addition to all of Bach's other major sacred works. His particular achievement here is a unique survey of all the "secular" cantatas (BWV 36c, 201–15) in Berlin broadcast recordings made in 1977–85: good, solidly musical MI performances with fine solo work by such singers as Augér, Mathis, Popp, Hamari, Watkinson, Adam, and Lorenz, as well as Schreier himself (♦Berlin 9220-27, 8CD).

The conservative tradition has another fleeting retrospective. **Fritz Werner** was no great conductor, but he made a series of Bach recordings for Erato in the 1960s and into the 1970s, many of which were distributed on LP by Westminster, Columbia-Epic, and MHS. A few years ago, Erato reissued a total of 13 cantatas divided between two 2CD sets (98525, 97407) that contain some genuinely warm, fluent, humane performances that will still please conservative tastes. You should also watch for a revival of the monophonic recordings of some dozen cantatas made in Vienna in the 1950s for the old Westminster label by **Scherchen,** with some fine singers of the day (such as Magda László, Rössl-Majdan, Kmentt, Poell). There were rough qualities and occasional eccentricities, but the performances were often deeply felt (with unusually expressive attention to the chorales) and retain lasting musical interest.

In the PI category, **Joshua Rifkin** has been extraordinarily influential. He has championed the idea that Bach performed his works with only one choral singer (as well as mostly one instrumentalist) per part, an idea he first launched tentatively in a recording of BWV 210 and then dramatized more aggressively in his 1981–82 recording of the B minor Mass (both Nonesuch). Between 1985 and 1989 Rifkin recorded 13 cantatas; six have been reissued, unfortunately without his probing annotations (♦Oiseau-Lyre 455706, 2CD). The loss of choral sonorities can be disturbing to some, but his singers (including Baird, Minter, Jeffrey Thomas, and Opalach) are generally excellent, with fine PI playing. Rifkin's performances are serious and artistic, hardly definitive but genuinely thought-provoking.

Directly in Rifkin's wake, and taking his work as a point of departure, his sometime tenor, **Jeffrey Thomas,** organized his own series during 1990–95; the result was a series of six single-CD volumes containing 16 cantatas (Koch). While generally following Rifkin's textual lead, Thomas conceded a small chamber choir (about 14 mixed voices) and more doubling of string parts. There was even a little overlapping with Rifkin in his varying roster of soloists, which included Baird, Nelson, Christine Brandes, Bott, Malafronte, Minter, Thomas himself, Sharp, and Weaver. The performances are tidy and attractive, sometimes outstanding, and worth seeking out.

A more strict convert to the Rifkin doctrine is **Parrott,** who has spread his application of Rifkin's ideas in a number of directions. His two discs containing cantatas mix them with items from other categories, but each is an important demonstration of the one-singer-per-part chorus combination with small PI chamber orchestra, in two major items: the "Ascension Oratorio" BWV 11 (♦EMI 749959, with BWV 50 and *Magnificat*), and the "Trauer-Ode" BWV 198 (♦Sony 60155, with two Motets). **Coin'**s series is a more moderate demonstration of quasi-minimalist style (small chamber choir and small PI orchestra) with up-to-date stylistic perspectives, begun in 1994 and so far consisting of two discs offering seven cantatas (Astrée 8544, 12853). The performances are a trifle cool, but lucid and satisfying, with fine singing from such period experts as soprano Schlick, countertenor Scholl, and tenor Prégardien.

Certainly the most prolific conductor in this category—and perhaps the most successful in assimilating PI techniques into a widely appealing performance style—is **Herreweghe.** Through the 1990s, he recorded some 30 cantatas on single discs, the first two for Virgin, the remainder for ♦Harmonia Mundi. He employs his finely honed chamber choir of mixed voices, the small but suave Collegium Vocale Ghent, with a modest but smooth-sounding PI chamber ensemble, consistently stressing handsome musicality in preference to any abrasive antiquarianism. He works with a regular circle of soloists, whose vocal qualities stress clarity and reliable artistry over any kind of flamboyance: Schlick, Mellon, Deborah York, Lesne, Scholl, Crook, Mark Padmore, Prégardien, Kooy. Herreweghe's performances are invariably serious contenders and can be relied upon for genuine satisfaction.

A curious miniseries in the PI category is led by **Pieter Jan Leusink** in very sensible and enjoyable performances by a choir of boys and men with the competent Netherlands Bach Collegium. Countertenor Sytse Buwalda is sometimes weak, but Holton and van der Meel are familiar and reliable singers, and the solo work is generally of a high order (Brilliant Classics "Bach Edition" 99363 and 99364, 5CD each). There is no system to the repertoire, and the emphasis is mainly on the less frequently recorded works. Between these two sets, a total of 31 cantatas are offered; whether there is to be more is not clear. Perhaps hard to find, this series offers good value for offbeat selections.

A specialized but quite fascinating survey is devoted to treatments of Martin Luther's many chorales for "Gelobet seist du Jesus Christ," enthusiastically performed under **Rilling;** the first disc is devoted to 18 examples from eight of Bach's cantatas (♦Hänssler 98.101, 2CD).

Sacred cantatas

4 ("Christ lag in Todesbanden"). Composed apparently in Mülhausen and then revised in 1724 in Leipzig, this Easter work is a true chorale cantata, using the full seven stanzas of Luther's chorale as text and basing its eight movements to one extent or another on the chorale melody or its components. Most recordings have followed the Leipzig version (in which double bass and extra brass doublings were added simply to strengthen texture), but the problem has been understanding the score's distinction between the three four-part "choral" sections and the four "solo" sections (two duets, two arias).

Recordings of LP days tended to treat the entire work as choral, employing choral blocks for the "solo" movements. This was done by **Shaw** (RCA) and **Roger Wagner** (Capitol), followed twice by **Prohaska** (Bach Guild), by **Werner** (Erato/MHS), and by **Riddell** (CBC). A slight fudging of that approach was followed by **Fritz Lehmann,** who used both tenor and baritone soloists, and then **Richter,** who used only a baritone. In each case, the baritone was Fischer-Dieskau, and the latter recording, generally very heavy and overly dark, has been reissued not only in the Richter omnibus series (Vol. 2, DG Archiv 439374) but also in a singer-focused single (DG 449756, with BWV 56, 82).

Two other recordings parallel Richter's large-scaled nonperiod approach. **Rilling** offers excellent choral work, but his soloists are a little tubby-voiced and overblown (Hänssler Vol. 13, 98.864, with BWV 172 and 85; "Bachakademie" Vol. 2, 92.002, with BWV 5, 6). On the other hand, **Thomas**'s 1959 Leipzig broadcast performance combines a strongly dramatic power with aptly scaled solo singing (Giebel, Höffgen, Rotzsch, Adam, plus choral boys), and can be recommended to those with traditionalist preferences (♦Berlin 9201, with BWV 11, 68).

All the PI recordings use solo against choral voices. **Harnoncourt** was the pioneer, and his small-scale approach is compelling, but his choppy pacing and his use of a boy treble soloist as well as a boys' choir is not always appealing. Equiluz is a fine tenor, but van Egmond, though a very sensitive singer, has too weak a voice to be convincing (Teldec Vol. 1, 35027, or "Bach 2000" Vol. 1, 25706). More traditional was **Gardiner,** who used a soloist only in the bass aria, with a small choir and PI orchestra (Erato, NA). **Suzuki**'s rendition is musically more satisfying, with small-scaled PI orchestra, excellent chamber chorus, and generally good solo work (♦BIS Vol. 1, 751, with BWV 150, 196).

Koopman is still better (♦Erato Vol. 1, 98536). Like Suzuki and Thomas, he uses a male alto soloist, which some may find weak, but the others (Schlick, de Mey, and the Fischer-Dieskau-ish Mertens) have just the right vocal style to match the elegant choral and instrumental work. Koopman is scrupulous in using only a single string player per part, and his mixed-voice choir is small and precise. For overall value, this is probably the most enjoyable PI version, made more interesting in that he presents the complete cantata in the original Mülhausen scoring and then, as an appendix, repeats four movements with the slightly heavier scoring of the Leipzig revision, adding musicological fascination to artistic value.

Finally, standing by themselves are three performances that cut the Gordian knot of the solo-vs-chorus problem. **Parrott** applies the Rifkin Doctrine of one performer per part with fascinating rigor, in a reduced Mülhausen scoring (without double bass or any of the cornetto and trombone extras). Thus, from his total of six singers, he has both soloists and a minimalist "choral" ensemble. Fortunately, the period-style singing and playing are outstanding, making for a musicological experience with its own artistic merit (♦Virgin 45011, with *Easter Oratorio*). **Thomas,** while using the post-Mülhausen scoring (double bass, cornetto, two trombones), is ultra-minimalism—not only one player per part, but only four singers, so that the solo/chorus distinction disappears completely. With particularly brisk tempos, he carries this work far from traditional monumentality to refreshing intimacy in one of the best of his series (♦Koch Vol. 4: 3-7233, with BWV 131, 182).

Konrad Junghänel returned to the Mülhausen scoring, with one singer or player per part (♦Harmonia Mundi 901694, with BWV 12, 106,

196). If not quite a match for Parrott in vocal quality, Junghänel's singers are quite good, and their frequent employment by this leader in madrigal singing is reflected in a tone of honest intimacy. Both Rifkin and Thomas use countertenors for the alto part, while Parrott and Junghänel stay with female contraltos, if that makes a difference.

21 ("Ich hatte viel Bekümmernis"). This expressive and expansive work, one of Bach's longest cantatas, exists in four different versions: a short original form (Weimar 1713), an expansion (Weimar 1714), and two modifications of that expansion (Cöthen/Hamburg 1720, with a change of key; Leipzig 1723). The Leipzig version has been used for most recordings, and there have been quite a few fine ones over the years.

Werner is no longer quite competitive for its now-murky sound and rather heavy approach (Erato). **Rotzsch**'s 1980–81 Leipzig recording has much better sound and good solo work (Augér, Schreier, Adam), but a plodding quality sets in early and is never quite overcome (Berlin). **Richter**'s 1970 version is more successful, and among the best recordings, if you don't mind a pious deliberateness of spirit; its advantages are fine solo oboe work and luxury casting in the solo voices: Mathis, Haefliger, Fischer-Dieskau (DG Archiv Vol. 3, 439380).

Rilling offers a more compelling kind of devoutness, with particularly fine solo singing from Augér again, Adalbert Kraus, and Schöne (Hänssler). This 1976 recording was the first nonperiod one to respect an important feature of the Leipzig version: Bach's stipulation of a group of solo singers set in juxtaposition to the full choir in three of the four choral movements. Rilling here uses the Indiana University Chamber Singers, who do very well, but the four singers he chose from their ranks for solo duties don't have pleasant voices. Moreover, at times he slips into unworkably slow tempos that undermine his overall conception and prevent an unqualified recommendation.

Bach's stipulation of soli/coro contrasts are respected in all the PI recordings, with one appropriate exception. **Harnoncourt**'s pioneering interpretation is still strong and probing, with fine solo tenor work by Equiluz, but the unnamed boy soprano is not equal to the vocal demands, especially when duetting with an adult bass (Teldec Vol. 6, 35032, or "Bach 2000" Vol. 1, 25706). Though it's only a provincial performance, there is genuine artistic insight in a Swiss Radio recording led incisively by the promising Swiss conductor, **Diego Fasolis** (♦Arts 47374, with *Magnificat* and a Motet). The soprano is mediocre, but tenor Frieder Lang and baritone Fulvio Bettini are quite good; the choral work is excellent, with a small (one player per part) and modestly PI ensemble, excellently recorded. It's worth investigating, even if it must inevitably yield to the still finer version under **Herreweghe** (♦Harmonia Mundi 290827, with BWV 42). The solo work (Schlick, Howard Crook, Peter Harvey) is relatively restrained, but is welded by Herreweghe into a deeply moving and subtly inflected interpretation of great beauty, carried out with style by his expert chamber choir and PI orchestra.

Two recordings attend to the problem of alternate versions. **Koopman,** without being fully clear about it, mixes the 1720 and 1723 versions (♦Erato Vol. 1, 98536). In the 1723 version, there are an aria for soprano, a recitative and two arias for tenor, and a recitative and duet for soprano and bass. The 1720 scoring, however, gave all the solo work to a soprano (with the bass in the duetting), and the 1714 Weimar version reversed that, giving all the solos to tenor (with duetting bass). Koopman follows the 1720 assignments of solo roles, thus eliminating the tenor, but he paradoxically honors the 1723 soli/coro concertizing in the choral movements. He adds the alternative heavier instrumentation that Bach devised in Leipzig for the third of the four choral movements, but only as an appendix.

By contrast, **Suzuki** opts consistently, and with full explanation, for the 1720 version, with no tenor and no observation of the soli/coro contrasts that belong only in the 1723 version (♦BIS Vol. 6, 851, with BWV 31). As his appendix, Suzuki gives one tenor aria and the tenor-bass recitative and duet from the 1714 version. (To help sort this out, he sensibly provides a little chart of what each version contains.) His choral and PI instrumental work is beautifully lucid, but it must be said that the solo work by Türk and Kooy, and especially the lackluster Frimmer, must yield to Koopman's team. A more assertive Schlick is joined by the splendid Mertens in particularly attractive solo work, while Koopman leads his chamber choir and orchestra with unfailing sensitivity and flair. Each of these recordings will be of value to the more specialized Bach collector.

Meanwhile, to provide exact comparison, Suzuki has also recorded the 1723 version (BIS Vol. 12, 1031, with BWV 147). Türk and Kooy are back, this time better partnered by the deft soprano Yukari Nonoshita, while the period brass contributions of the Concerto Paladino add further strength to the excellent choral and instrumental work, in a recording that by itself is a viable alternative to the Herreweghe version.

51 ("Jauchzet Gott in allen Landen"). This exuberant work is perhaps the best-known of Bach's cantatas for solo voice, and one of his most recorded compositions. Sopranos love it, and I'm tempted to wonder if—to the extent that sopranos are allowed in heaven at all—no soprano is allowed to pass the Pearly Gates without having recorded the piece! More sopranos than you can quiver a tonsil at have come and gone through this work over the years, from LP days on. They include the likes of Danco (London), Raskin (Decca), Gruberová (RCA), Popp (Accord), Ameling (Philips), Mathis (EMI), and Hendricks (EMI), any one of whom might come back in a reissue; I particularly hope for the delightful Ameling.

Among the sopranos whose recordings have survived from early years is **Stich-Randall**—that forerunner of the bleached-white sound represented today by Kirkby and Baird—who made two recordings that have floated in and out of reissue. That with Anton Heiller is included in a 4CD set (Vanguard/Bach Guild 2540), while the other, with Ristenpart, is now in a single CD (Accord 200042). In each, Stich-Randall delivers fine virtuoso singing but is just a bit cool, with a somewhat heavy and blurred orchestral sound in the Ristenpart edition, but with far better defined (if thick) orchestral work in the earlier Vanguard monophonic sound. **Bogard** is far less assertive than Stich-Randall, though no slouch in agility; her 1969 recording has been reissued (Parnassus 96-020, with BWV 202, plus A. Scarlatti and Handel items). An admired Bach and Mozart singer in her day, the late **Maria Stader** recorded the work with Richter, but there is little joy in his sober pacing while Stader sounds as if she's just working through an exercise in controlling her spread-out vocal sound (DG Archiv).

Better focused vocally is another Bach specialist of past decades, **Giebel,** who made one of the first historically informed recordings in her second go at the work in 1966 with André and the one-player-per-part Concerto Amsterdam (♦Teldec 21711, with BWV 202, 209). Her earlier effort (1961), a broadcast version, is handsomely sung, but the curiously ponderous, big-orchestra accompaniment provided by Thomas is an undeniable handicap (Berlin). In the later recording, she's confident and a shade thoughtful; this short-lived CD reissue is worth searching for, doing her much greater justice. Going back even further in the Leipzig tradition brings us to Ramin's 1948 version in the series devoted to his work (Berlin 9098, with BWV 95, 79). His soprano, **Gertrud Birmele,** though of no great repute, had an ample, well-focused, and attractive voice; despite rather heavy orchestral work and staid tempos, she conveys, if not great joy, at least genuine confidence.

Perhaps the most famous LP release is the second oldest, and something of a classic: **Schwarzkopf**'s 1950 recording, which pops up repeatedly in reissues (♦EMI 567206 or 749843, with BWV 199, 202, and arias). The mono sound is pretty antediluvian now, and the uninformed listener would be hard-pressed to discover what language is being sung. Nevertheless, Schwarzkopf's gusto in tackling this music is striking, and not only her fans will want to take this performance into account. This work became a Schwarzkopf specialty, and she made two other recordings, one in a premature and almost reckless style in 1948 (Testament 2172, 2CD), the other a concert recording from 1951 (Bella Voce 7201).

For a combination of beautifully focused singing with stylistic sensibility, you can hardly do better than **Augér:** a lovely voice, with reliably on-target pitch, and a thorough sensitivity to musical and textual values (♦Hänssler Vol. 4, 98.855, with BWV 56, 82; "Bachakademie" Vol. 17, 92.017, with BWV 49, 50, 52). She's given vibrant accompaniment by Rilling, claiming the premier recommendation for this work in any category. Nowhere near it, even in bargain-price format, is a recording in which admirably strong singing by **Ingrid Kertesi** is done in by hard and lackluster orchestral support under Mátyás Antá (Nonesuch). The reverse is true of a 1984 recording where Pommer gives sterling support, and Güttler crisply partners **Frimmer,** who has a fine voice but sounds less than comfortable stylistically or confident technically (Capriccio 49254, 11CD, with BWV 56). And if you want a zippy performance as part of an assemblage of Baroque soprano-and-trumpet pieces, there is **Ruth Ziesak** with Reinhold Friedrich and the Budapest Strings (Capriccio 10583).

As for PI versions, **Kweksilber** is not very appealing; she sounds more prissy than joyous, and Leonhardt's pacing has a fussy, huffy-puffy quality (Teldec). Two early-music prima donnas have made their bids, one of them twice. **Kirkby** struggles with some success to crank her small voice into virtuoso exertion to match Gardiner's rather ample-sounding accompaniment, and above all she shows an admirable feeling for the flow of vocal lines (1983: ♦Philips 411548, with *Magnificat*). Her American counterpart **Baird** has had two cracks at the work. Her 1986 recording with Rifkin is intimately scaled (his one-player-per-part approach) but rather sober in pacing, and Baird's thin voice seems badly strained (Oiseau-Lyre). Four years later with Thomas she was in a little firmer control of her voice, while Thomas, using a slightly more ample ensemble, paces things a bit more judiciously and supportively (♦Koch Vol. 1, 7138, with BWV 54, 55, 82).

My strongest recommendation for a period-style recording, however, is **Argenta,** with the Ensemble Sonnerie led by Monica Huggett (and using the same fine trumpeter, Crispian Steele-Perkins, heard in the Kirkby/Gardiner recording) (♦Virgin 45038, with BWV 82a, 199, currently NA but worth revival). Argenta's singing is firm and beautifully pointed, while Huggett leads elegantly crisp playing from the first fiddle desk; if you can find this one, or if it comes back, it's the PI version to have.

Finally, the most recent PI version is a special case, since it uses an expanded scoring (second trumpet, with timpani) arranged by Wilhelm Friedemann Bach. Goebel's Musica Antiqua Köln tears into it with gusto, while **Schäfer**—a soprano in the tradition of Augér (with whom she studied)—sings with brilliant security and fearless spirit (♦DG 459621, with BWV 202, 210).

54 ("Widerstehe doch der Sünde"). Dating from Bach's Weimar years, this short work (only two arias framing a single recitative, without chorus) is one of several cantatas that is exclusively for alto voice, and has accordingly become a favorite vehicle (often along with others of its scoring) both for female contraltos and for male falsettists; there is historical justification for either.

There are no really poor recordings, and their differences are partly determined by their approach to the opening aria, with its throbbing string accompaniment. Perhaps my favorite is the most extreme on that count, with Thurston Dart leading the London Philomusica in a tempo so slow that it doubles the running time others usually give it, but with eloquent and warm singing by **Watts,** in an LP I wish would be revived (Oiseau-Lyre). Thomas's 1959 Radio Leipzig recording is a broadly paced version with **Höffgen,** who pushes her matronly contralto in an undeniably earnest rendition (Berlin 9202, with BWV 82, 56). Sounding not much younger but much more animated is **Forrester**'s rich and distinctive contralto, with well-pointed support from Janigro (1964: Vanguard 64/65, 2CD, with BWV 53, 169, Bach and Handel arias).

In Rilling's 1975 recording, **Hamari** has a lighter but elegant contralto, and he gives this work some of the fastest tempos I have encountered, for a kind of 54-lite; but it's still altogether musical and enjoyable, if at the opposite pole from Watts/Dart (♦Hänssler Vol. 43, 98.805, with BWV 186, 107; "Bachakademie" Vol. 18, 92.018, with BWV 55-57). **Stutzmann** is the only female contralto to record the work with PI ensemble (under Goodman), in an appealing disc of alto cantatas; her voice has a genuine contralto richness, if with its own quirks, and she is careful with verbal values (♦RCA 62655).

Whatever one's reservations about countertenors in Bach, this cantata works well in that voice; all such singers appear with PI ensembles. **Esswood** was the first to essay the work, his light voice somewhat hampered by Leonhardt's overly punchy treatment of the opening aria (Teldec Vol. 14, 42422; "Bach 2000" Vol. 2, 25707). Another English countertenor, **Bowman,** could marshal a slightly fuller and more expressive vocal tone, backed by more cunning PI orchestral support from Robert King in an excellent disc of alto cantatas (♦Hyperion 66326, with BWV 169, 170).

Perhaps the lightest and most deft countertenor, though, is **Minter,** who is another singer careful with the words; he sings with Thomas, who gets off to a choppy start in the first aria but maintains tempos even faster than Rilling's (Koch Vol. 1, with BWV 51, 55, 82). Still faster—in, fact, the fastest of all, I think—is Suzuki; his countertenor, **Mera,** has a smallish voice but responds to Suzuki's speed with considerable lyric feeling (BIS Vol. 3, 791, with BWV 12, 162, 182). By far the strongest countertenor showing is by **Scholl,** who recorded the work twice: in 1995 with Koopman (Erato Vol. 3, 14336) and two years later in a disc of alto cantatas with Herreweghe (♦Harmonia Mundi 901644, with BWV 170, 35). With an unusually full voice, Scholl takes a notably forthright approach, in almost identical performances; but Herreweghe is able to get more meaning and inflection out of the string orchestra writing, so Scholl's second recording is preferred, if not also the winner among all male-alto competitors.

56 ("Ich will den Kreuzstab gerne tragen") and *82* ("Ich habe genug"). The two famous cantatas for solo baritone or bass (with final choral chorale in 56 and beautiful oboe obbligati in each) are regularly paired in the same package, and in quite a few fine recordings.

The picture has been dominated by that indefatigable repeater, **Fischer-Dieskau,** who has recorded 56 four times and 82 thrice. His earliest pairing was with Ristenpart, 56 in 1952 and 82 in 1953, when the young singer was first spreading his vocal wings, his voice rich and firm and already used to convey careful verbal inflection (♦DG Archiv

449756, mono, with BWV 8). A few years later, he recorded 56 again; Baumgartner paced the work more flexibly than Ristenpart and drew a more mellow vocal style from the singer, with still more attention to the words (DG, LP). In 1958, the singer redid both with Richter (♦DG: 56 in Vol. 5, 43994; 82 in Vol. 1, 439369). These recordings find him in his prime—strong and convincing, if with some hints of the fussiness he would gradually slip into. His 56 with Richter was not notably different in pacing from its predecessors, but Richter gives his 82 a much broader quality and draws deeply moving eloquence from the singer.

Fischer-Dieskau made a final stab at these two cantatas in 1983 for Rilling's series (Vol. 4, 98.855, with BWV 51 with Augér, or just the two in 98.903; in the "Bachakademie" series, 56 is in Vol. 18, 92.018, with BWV 54, 55, 57, and 82 is in Vol. 26, 92.026, with BWV 80, 81). Rilling leads with brio and intelligence, in outstanding sound, but the singer's voice shows its advancing wear and tear, prompting him to compensate with exaggerated inflections and vocal mannerisms. In all of these recordings, we're still dealing with one of the great singers of the century, and those who want to trace his vocal history will find them a fascinating sequence. But those with Richter are to be preferred for musical results, though sadly they are only available in the big reissue set rather than in a single release.

I suspect Fischer-Dieskau was in the mind of the young bass **Lorenz** when the latter recorded these two cantatas in 1984, for he seems to use his light voice to match the mellower and baritonal side of the elder singer (Capriccio). But unlike his presumed model, Lorenz seems quite uninvolved with the words and sentiments of these works, delivering rather detached performances, despite sympathetic accompaniments led by the estimable Pommer. There is also that other German baritone, **Prey,** who had an early essay (in 1960) at these two cantatas thanks to Kurt Thomas (Berlin 9202, with Höffgen's BWV 54). His young voice is smooth and satisfying, a joy to his fans; though lucid in diction, he too is somewhat detached in spirit, and Thomas's unusually broad and stately pacing, obviously sincerely conceived, is more devotional than fervent.

Absolute involvement, by contrast, is the essence of **Shirley-Quirk,** who recorded the two works in the mid-1960s with Marriner, at a time when the latter was still more interested in substance than glitz (Oiseau-Lyre LP). Like Thomas, their tempos are slow, leading to a deeply introspective mood to which Shirley-Quirk responds with profoundly moving performances, graced further by especially fine oboe partnering from Roger Lord. Unfortunately, the parent label has chosen to reissue only 82, though in a highly desirable culling of Marriner's cantata recordings of that era with Baker and Tear—a particularly recommendable CD (♦London 430260, with BWV 170, 159).

Of similar spirit is the big-hearted baritone **Mack Harrell,** but he never quite seems to get into the texts fully, while Shaw's stately accompaniments are flat and uninvolved; mono sound seems to have foreclosed CD reissue, but you never know (RCA). More suave and understated are **Souzay**'s deeply moving 1958 performances; only his BWV 58 has appeared on CD (EMI 68544, 2CD, with BWV 51, 80, 106, 140, 147). **Hotter**'s eloquent 1950 recording of 82 is still older and something of a classic (♦EMI 763198, with Brahms lieder). If spare in vocal tone, his performance is unique in the degree of noble resignation, dignity, and faith it conveys. For 56 there is a 1989 recording derived from the Bach Festival in Bethlehem, Pennsylvania; Greg Funfgeld leads a large-sounding orchestra in a conventionally solemn reading, with bass **Daniel Licht** offering smooth and sensitive singing—not a commanding version, but satisfying in traditional terms (Dorian 90127, with BWV 140 and Motet).

The remaining baritone recordings of this pair are more recent and have PI accompaniment. The first were done in the 1970s: 56 under Leonhardt, with the undistinguished **Michael Schopper** happy to get through the vocal requirements but with no commitment to the spirit of the music; 82 under Harnoncourt, with **Huttenlocher** stronger and more stylish, if just a tad tentative (Teldec Vol. 14, 42422; Vol. 21, 42577; in "Bach 2000" Vol. 2, 25707). One of the singers who participated in this series was **van Egmond,** who has only a light voice but always uses it with intelligence and gives handsomely thoughtful performances of both cantatas (Sony 60373). Brüggen's small ensemble is somewhat scrappy, if devoted.

Of the more recent PI pairings, Rifkin made an important one in 1989 (♦Oiseau-Lyre 425822, with BWV 158). Though the minimalist orchestral playing is rather astringent, **Opalach** gives the performances of his career in deeply committed and powerfully musical singing—performances that, however different on some counts, are in the same category as Shirley-Quirk's. Rifkin's epigone Thomas offers 82 in his series, though in a particularly appetizing program; the instrumental work is smoother, and bass **William Sharp** is strong of voice, elegant and stylish in expressing the messages (♦Koch Vol. 1, 7138, with BWV 54, 55, 51). **William Parker**'s 1991 recording has undeniable poignancy, since the singer was under death sentence by AIDS and the recording was a fund-raising venture. Though a fine singer, his voice is here not fully controlled or stylistically focused, while the ultra-minimalist ensemble led by McGegan sounds thin and perfunctory (Harmonia Mundi).

Another 1991 recording offers the much lighter-voiced **Kooy,** whose sometimes thin singing is nevertheless directed to verbal as well as musical clarity; indeed, his singing at times has the character of speech, not only in the recitatives but carried over into the arias (♦Harmonia Mundi 901365, with BWV 158). Herreweghe's excellent ensemble is very much an equal partner in the performance, with unusually fine effect made of the instrumental writing. All in all, this is perhaps the most enduringly satisfying of the recordings by bass-baritones with PI groups.

Kooy/Herreweghe would have had a serious challenge, though, if **Mertens** had been given a chance to record both cantatas instead of just 82. His light but smooth and mellow voice at times recalls Fischer-Dieskau, and while there is some restraint in his approach, his singing is both elegant and convincing, and he's given excellent ensemble support by Le Petite Bande led by Kuijken in a freshly diverse program (♦Accent 9394, with BWV 49, 58). On the other hand, another recording of 82 alone is simply below par, with the nondescript **Nicholas Gedge** no better than competent, matched by indifferent nonperiod orchestra work under Nicholas Ward (Nonesuch). For both 56 and 82. **Bas Ramselaar,** a Dutch bass who does some of the best singing in the Brilliant Classics series, delivers honest, unfussy, and altogether pleasing performances, with respectable PI support led by Pieter Jan Leusink.

There are again echoes of Fischer-Dieskau in the most recent recording of the pair, made in Salzburg in 1999 by **Matthias Goerne,** with excellent PI support under Norrington (Decca 466570). Goerne's singing is about as suave and elegant as you can get, though he seems at times more interested in polished surface effect than in conveying the devout texts. But augmented by an added short cantata (BWV 158) and a cantata sinfonia, this is a package of great musical attractiveness.

BWV 82 has a special supplemental history of its own, thanks to the fact that Bach seems to have vacillated in his choice of vocal range, shifting through several versions and stages (and even keys) before he settled on the ultimate low-male choice. That has allowed altos and even sopranos to stake out their claims on the piece. An early standard was set by **Baker** in the mid-1960s, one of a number of irresistible cantata recordings she made over the years, too few of which are still in print. In this 82, her luscious voice and fully engaged artistry make a performance whose reissue should be watched for carefully.

In her wake, we have **Stutzmann,** in her excellent cantata program with Goodman (1994: ♦RCA 62655, with BWV 170, 54); still, however rich and strongly conceived, their performance does not envelop the listener with the warmth and spirituality Baker achieved. It's not surprising there should be a countertenor contribution to the alto 82, and we have that from **Kowalski** (♦Capriccio 105423, with BWV 170, 53, 200). His falsetto has a considerably feminine sound—indeed, it sounds very much like Stutzmann's—and he gives a confident and musically quite convincing performance, rendered just a shade superficial, however, by the diffident nonperiod orchestral work from the St. Martin Academy under Sillito.

And, finally, for something entirely different, we have the soprano version. In a revision of the work ("82a"), Bach moved the key up a third to E minor, not only giving the vocal solo to a soprano but also reassigning the oboe obbligato to a flute. The result was demonstrated first in 1986 by **Zylis-Gara,** unfortunately hollow-voiced and tonally insecure, with a small MI group (Rodolphe 32479), and then by **Hendricks** with Schreier in a deleted EMI release. But it was a subsequent (1993) revelation, shining in **Argenta**'s superb singing with splendid PI ensemble playing led by Huggett, that provided a silvery new illumination of this lovely music, in a superlative release whose absence from the catalogue ought not be long (♦Virgin 45038, with BWV 199, 51).

80 ("Ein feste Burg ist unser Gott"). Another of Bach's chorale-commentary cantatas, this treatment of Luther's most famous hymn, words and music, became popular in recordings early on, though involving a slow process of rectifying textual problems. Composed in its initial form in Weimar in 1716 for Oculi Sunday (BWV 80a), it was recast in Leipzig in the 1730s for Reformation Sunday, with added supplemental texts. But it was still further revised after the composer's death by his son, Wilhelm Friedemann, who replaced some text passages with Latin substitutes and, above all, added his own parts for trumpets and timpani in the opening and middle choruses. Though the Latin texts have been overlooked, those added parts were taken up in some editions to create a "corrupt" version that long prevailed in recorded performances, thanks undoubtedly to its brilliant and flashy enhancement of the spirit of Lutheran celebration.

The first recording of the work to achieve popularity (using the "corrupt" edition) was made in Vienna in 1951 by **Prohaska.** It was a sturdy but rather unsubtle performance, with quite good soloists (Weis-Osborn, Rössl-Majdan, Equiluz, Berry) but somewhat woolly choral and orchestral work, in thick sound. Its reissue in the 4CD Prohaska omnibus set restores it as a kind of historical relic, but it can't match subsequent competition (Vanguard). The "corrupt" edition continued to be used by most recordings through the LP era, including **Werner** (Erato/MHS), and notably **Gönnenwein** in 1967, who not only used Wilhelm Friedemann's trumpets and drums but even added reenforcing trombones in the opening chorus. His soloists (Ameling, Baker, Altmeyer, Sotin) were superlative, with lucid choral work, but the pacing was so flabby that it's only a bargain choice even in generous reissue (EMI 68670, 2CD, with BWV 140, 147, and Motet).

For **Richter,** the title might have been paraphrased as "A Meaty Feast is Our Old Bach." His 1978 recording takes full advantage of the added instruments to create a sturdy picture of festive Lutheran affirmation, with outstanding soloists (Mathis, Trudeliese Schmidt, Schreier, Fischer-Dieskau), in particularly good sound (♦DG Archiv Vol. 5, 439 394). This is an ideal version for those who relish a "traditional" approach. Richter was anticipated by **Somary,** whose soloists (Palmer, Watts, Tear, Michael Rippon) constitute another dream team; its attractive reissue is a viable substitute for the Richter version (♦Vanguard 105, with BWV 11). There would also be validity to **Leppard**'s recording of about 1980, if Philips would ever revive it: a lively and typically intelligent rendition, with a stellar (if not always vocally well-balanced) solo group (Ameling, Baldin, Ramey).

When **Herreweghe** made his recording in 1990, he chose to follow the "corrupt" edition (♦Harmonia Mundi 901326, with *Magnificat*). But his approach—brisk, lithe, deft—is at the opposite pole from those of Gönnenwein and Richter, downplaying the grandeur and even handling the trumpets and drums with supple delicacy. His soloists (Schlick, Lesne, Crook, Kooy) are all lean-voiced early music veterans. In all, it is a novel PI projection of lightweight Lutheran cheer.

The publication of the *Neue Bach-Ausgabe* finally allowed performers to bypass the "corrupt" edition and return to Bach's Leipzig original. The first recording to venture in that direction was made in Leipzig's Thomaskirche in 1966 under **Erhard Mauersberger** (DG Archiv, NA). That was followed a decade later by the only "repeater" recording, demonstrating a case of Sinner Redeemed. Back in 1961 and early in his career, **Rilling** made a first attempt, not only using the "corrupt" edition but leading also generally undistinguished soloists (save for soprano Antonia Fahberg) and an under-rehearsed chorus and orchestra in a sloppy and ill-thought-out performance, with sluggish tempos. The reissue of this recording, as part of a set otherwise devoted to secular cantatas under Ewerhart, represents a curiosity perhaps intended to embarrass the older Rilling (Vox).

But in 1976 he was able to try again, very much to everyone's benefit. This version has more vitality and control, with more sensible tempos, a much better solo group (including Augér and Huttenlocher), and better prepared chorus and orchestra, a production more worthy of his cantata series (♦Hänssler Vol. 98.819, with BWV 115, 55, or "Bachakademie" Vol. 26, 92.026, with BWV 81, 82). Also lively and attractive as a realization of the purified edition is **Rotzsch**'s 1982 Leipzig recording, with generally fine soloists (Augér again, Wenkel, Schreier, Adam), and the Thomanerchor with boys (Berlin 2176, with BWV 79, 192, 50).

Meanwhile, the PI recordings (all, of course, with purified text) got off to a bad start with **Harnoncourt** (Teldec). The badly under-rehearsed choir (including boys) and period ensemble is terribly woolly and unfocused; despite earnest adult solo work (Esswood, Equiluz, van der Meer), the boy-soprano soloist is simply unbearable, and Harnoncourt's pacing is so consistently choppy, jerky, and nervous that one comes out wondering how Bach could have written such ugly music.

Rifkin's was a truly fresh approach; his 1985 recording has been included in the selective reissue of his cantata series (♦Oiseau-Lyre 455706, 2CD). Following his strict revisionist ideas about Bach's performing forces, he uses an ensemble of one player per part (save for doubled violins), and an excellent solo quartet (Bryden, Minter, Jeffrey Thomas, Opalach). Of course, in accordance with the Rifkin Doctrine, they as a group are also the chorus. One must therefore discard conventional expectations and accept a miniaturized performance that avoids all posturing grandeur and instead, at judiciously chosen tempos, discovers the thoughtful side of this music—an undeniably fascinating experience. Its interesting follow-up came 10 years later with tenor **Thomas**'s own recording (Koch Vol. 6, 3-7234, with BWV 140, 78). With

an excellent solo group (Bott, countertenor Daniel Taylor, Thomas himself, Sharp), Thomas pulls back from the Rifkin Doctrine, allowing a 12-voice choir and a somewhat more ample orchestra. His tempos are consistently faster, and he's not quite as lean and thoughtful as Rifkin, nor as suave and ("corruptly") sonorous as Herreweghe, but he falls neatly midway in the range of PI choices.

A 1999 modified return to tradition offers an alternative to Rifkinian strictness, in the first of the two Dutch-made 5CD cantata sets (♦Brilliant Classics 99363). **Leusink** uses the corrected edition, but with a full chorus a bit on the woolly side (boy trebles, countertenors) and PI orchestra. Ruth Holton is a bit too boyish and hooty, but the solo work is generally very good, and the robust performance stands up well as a PI compromise approach.

106 ("Gottes Zeit ist die allerbeste Zeit"; "Actus tragicus"). One of the earliest of Bach's cantatas, and an amazingly innovative work from a 22-year-old, this work dates from 1707, during the composer's time at Mühlhausen. It's certainly unusual, with its novel instrumentation of two recorders, two violas da gamba, and continuo (which all but obliterates the MI/PI distinction in performances), and with its integrated design, leading from a long sonatina through solos woven into choral textures, culminating in a quasi duet. Despite its unconventionality, it has attracted a number of recordings over the years, going back to one made in earliest LP days by **Roger Wagner** (Lyrichord).

Three more-or-less traditionalist recordings give a conspectus of changing sensitivities in performance practice. **Ramin**'s 1953 Leipzig broadcast clearly contains deep feeling and understanding, but the two recorders sound unassimilated in the instrumental ensemble, the chorus (with its biting boys' voices) is big; and the substitution of a pair of boys for an alto soloist is wrenching, even though the other soloists (Rotzsch among them) are fine (Berlin). Thirteen years later, **Richter** had a more mellow and integrated instrumental ensemble and a sizable chorus, with able soloists (Töpper, Haefliger, Adam), in a particularly solemn and weighty rendition that risks overinflating the entire tone (DG Archiv Vol. 5, 439394).

But **Rilling** got it right in 1975; the chamber instrumentation is now clear and intelligible, while the chorus is not too big, and the soloists (Hanna Schwarz, Adalbert Kraus, Schöne) catch the proper spiritual tone; the entire interpretation is highly satisfying (♦Hänssler Vol. 68, with BWV 198; "Bachakademie" Vol. 34, 92.034, with BWV 107, 108). Hardly less beautiful is a dignified and glowing performance by Stockholm ensembles, including **Hagegård** (♦Swedish Discofil 1065, with BWV 140 and *Magnificat*). Most recently, there is a well-directed but somewhat amateurishly sung performance by **Gloria Dei Cantores** in diversified Bach (Gloria Dei Cantores 028, 2CD, with BWV 78, two motets, and three organ works).

A more self-consciously "historically informed" approach was initiated by **Jürgen Jürgens** (Telefunken, NA) and by the **Collegium Aureum.** The latter (from 1968) involves the Aachen Cathedral Choir, with a superlative solo team (Ameling, Maureen Lehane, Equiluz, McDaniel), and remains a version of mellow beauty in a welcome CD revival (♦Harmonia Mundi 77461). Less endearing is another such pioneer venture by **Leonhardt;** while the spirit is good, the choral work (boys included) is scrappy, and the two boy soloists are below par, leaving only van Egmond as a vocal asset (Teldec).

In due course, the ultra-minimalist approach to "authenticity" was applied by **Rifkin** (1985: Oiseau-Lyre). His leadership was sensitive and probing, but he used only four singers, of whom only Opalach was of high quality, the others making scrawny sounds both as soloists and as the austere "chorus," the potentially bewitching alto chorale overlay on the second bass solo falling terribly flat when sung by a diffident countertenor, who also strained in the alto aria. The same strict approach, with only four singers, was followed by **Thomas;** his interpretation was likewise highly musical, aided this time by a somewhat more consistent group of soloists, with Minter making a better, if not irresistible, case for a countertenor in the alto roles (Koch Vol. 3, 3-7164, with BWV 152, 161). A third application of the Rifkin approach was **Junghänel**'s, with four able singers who provide well-balanced solo and ensemble work. He resolves the countertenor problem by using a female contralto, and his is, perhaps, the most musicallly pleasing of the PI-minimalist versions (♦Harmonia Mundi 901694, with BWV 4, 12, 196)

Other directors have been establishing a more moderate case for stylistic "authenticity": first **Gardiner** (Archiv 429782 or 463581, with BWV 118b, 198), then **Koopman** (♦Erato Vol. 1, 98536), and still more recently **Suzuki** (♦BIS 781, with BWV 71, 131). All use PI groups and crack chamber choirs, as well as fine soloists, who work in a more conventional balance. Chance and Wessel make successively better cases for a countertenor in the alto solo, though I think Mera gives the most pleasing demonstration. Suzuki's somewhat broader pacing recalls Richter's and makes his version come closer to traditionalist tastes; otherwise, Koopman gives the piece about as lively and pleasing a rendition as one might ask.

140 ("Wachet auf, ruft uns die Stimme"). Helped in no small measure by various arrangements of one particular chorale movement (familiarized as "Sleepers Awake!"), but certainly justified by its genuine musical quality, this is one of the most recorded of all Bach's cantatas. Almost from the start of the LP era, it was nearly always in the catalogue in multiple versions, under such diverse conductors as Shaw, Scherchen, and Ristenpart. Few discographic histories better display the contrasts between and within the so-called "traditional" and "authentic" categories. "Traditional" here generally means not only "modern" instrumental style but also good-sized choirs and broad pacing. Of some eight recordings in that category, all but the last are survivors from LP vintage and suggest something of the adaptability of "traditional" esthetics.

The oldest recording still available was made in 1951 in Vienna under **Prohaska** (Vanguard/Bach Guild). While the monophonic sound is quite acceptable, the performance is less so: a blowzy choir, in an uninspired reading, with solo work not even Anny Felbermayer can raise above perfunctory. Prohaska tried again in 1959; Laurence Dutoit and Hans Braun are somewhat better-matched partners in the duets, and if the interpretation is still on the heavy and reverent side, it has better choral and orchestral work and is in decent stereo (Vanguard/Bach Guild 2001, with BWV 4; or 72000, with BWV 80, 29, 50). Still more enduring is **Thomas**'s 1960 Leipzig broadcast, with the pointed tone of the Thomanerchor boys and some fine solo work led by Grümmer, caught in spacious yet nicely detailed sound (♦Berlin 9203). Thomas's tenor was **Rotzsch,** who made his own Leipzig recording; it has the same choral qualities, but the pacing is plodding at times, while Augér and Lorenz are not vocally well matched in the duets (Berlin).

Gönnenwein's 1967 recording looks promising on paper, and it has its moments, especially in Ameling's soprano work, but she's in a weak duetting match with Sotin, and the whole approach is rather overblown (EMI). You would expect some relief from **Leppard** (1981), and if his is a more intelligently detailed reading, it's still broad; Ameling returns to better effect, matched with a young Ramey trying to rein in his big

sound, but Baldin sounds like a Wagnerian heldentenor out of the water in his recitative (Philips).

Tradition is brought close to travesty by **Richter** (1977: DG Archiv). In the longest-running performance on record, some of the tempos are distended almost to breaking points (notably the opening chorus and first duet). Schreier, who sang the recitative for Rotzsch, returns here, but also to sings the tenor chorale line solo in the middle chorus in place of the usual tenor section; Mathis and Fischer-Dieskau are effective, if a little cold in the duets. You couldn't imagine a greater contrast in shifting to **Rilling**'s 1984 recording; one of the fastest performances on record, it polishes off in 6:07 the opening chorus that takes Richter 9:38. (♦Hänssler Vol. 6, 98.857, with BWV 50, 29; "Bachakademie" Vol. 44, 92.044, with BWV 143-45)! Augér returns to duet well with Huttenlocher, though they are seriously strained in the second duet by Rilling's breakneck tempo, while Baldin is again a beefy Wagnerian in his recitative. If you want a skipping, sparkling neotraditionalist romp in this work, Rilling is certainly good for the ride.

Also in 1984, **Wayne Riddell** led Canadian forces in a conventional but smooth and lucid performance; the soprano and bass soloists are undistinguished, and the whole thing might be overlooked completely save for the tiny recitative contribution of a green young tenor named Ben Heppner (CBC 5163, with Geminiani and Handel). **Funfgeld**'s 1989 recording assures us that traditionalism is alive and healthy at the Bethlehem Bach Festival (♦Dorian 90127, with BWV 56 and attributed motet). It's neither snide nor sarcastic to call his a "high-quality provincial" version; with a seemingly enormous choir and nonstellar but quite able soloists, Funfgeld produces a thoroughly intelligent, noncontroversial, and artistically satisfying performance that is worth considering.

Sharing soprano Henriette Schellenberg with Funfgeld is **Blanche Honegger Moyse,** who leads another traditionalist performance (MHS 512691; MusicMasters 7059; both with *Magnificat*). Schellenberg joins Sanford Sylvan for particularly lovely duetting, and the solo tenor sings the chorale melody; the pacing is heavily deliberate, but the singing and playing are handsomely shaped, with refined details. Something of a sleeper is a very generous release in which Stockholm performers (including **Hagegård**) deliver a glowingly musical and satisfying rendition (♦Swedish Discofil 1065, with BWV 140 and *Magnificat*).

The "authenticity" showing is a bit scantier but not lacking in either quality or variety. **Harnoncourt** kicked off with a rather conventionally paced reading with unsurprising PI instrumental work (Teldec Vol. 35, 42630; "Bach 2000" Vol. 3, 25708). He follows Richter in having his tenor, the estimable Equiluz, sing the chorale melody as a solo in the middle movement. His choir includes boys, but he also uses a boy soprano in the two duets; this may have musicological justification, but it's a musical strain, and Hampson sounds as if he's a Big Brother gingerly taking a crippled child for a perilous walk on the ice. A far less problematical use of boys is in the Knabenchor Hanover's performance, but with three adult soloists (solo tenor also taking the central chorale), led by **Heinz Hennig** (♦Thorophon 2263). It's relaxed and understated, perhaps, but musical, and it's paired with Johann Sebastian's son Johann Christoph Friedrich's setting of his father's choral texts and a motet— an interesting notion that puts papa's more imaginative methods and richer creativity in very nice perspective.

The remaining three PI recordings share brisk pacing—almost as fast as Rilling's, if better integrated—as well as what we might call "the soprano problem." **Gardiner** presides over a crisp and lean performance with lots of bounce; his chamber choir delivers energetic work, and Rolfe Johnson is unusually intelligent in the recitative—though, despite the booklet, he does *not* sing the middle chorale as a solo (♦DG Archiv (431809 or 463587, with BWV 147). But soprano Ruth Holton sounds so distractingly like a boy that Gardiner might as well have used one, since the child/adult mispairing with Varcoe still plagues the duets.

Of course, **Rifkin** means the minimalist approach of mostly one singer and player per part (Oiseau-Lyre 455706, 2CD, with BWV 8, 51, 78, 80, 147). He leads with vigor, and there is a fresh intimacy to his well-shaped conception of the work. But the problem of accepting just four solo singers (Baird, Minter, Thomas, Opalach) in place of any kind of chorus is made difficult by their badly blended vocal balances, while Baird's hooty and vibratoless soprano is uncomfortable whether in the choral or duet movements. Pulling back from strict minimalism, **Thomas** uses smallish but very well balanced choral and instrumental forces; he sings the recitative himself, while Bott offers a nice compromise between boyish and adult soprano singing, creating what sounds like a genuine dialogue between equals in the duets (♦Koch Vol. 6, 3-7234, with BWV 78, 80). In all, his recording is the best choice in the PI category for now, but there is surely more to be said about this work.

147 ("Herz und Mund und Tat und Leben"). Again we have a cantata whose popularity has been helped by various arrangements of a pair of parallel chorale choruses ("Jesu, Joy of Man's Desiring"), though by comparison with BWV 140 the work is longer and more uneven. Divided into two parts, it was first written during Bach's Weimar days, but survives as recast for later use in Leipzig.

Recordings of LP vintage now lost include one by **Kurt Thomas** (Oiseau-Lyre) and two by **Fritz Werner** (Erato, MHS). Particularly notable was a high-powered British recording under **Willcocks** with a stellar cast (Ameling, Baker, Partridge, Shirley-Quirk; King's College Choir; St. Martin Academy) that EMI would do well to revive.

At present, the MI approach is represented by four recordings, each with its virtues. The earliest (1957) is a curious piece of English provincial Bach, led affectionately by **Geraint Jones.** Helen Watts, one of my favorite singers, is outstanding; the very young Sutherland is in remote territory here, vocally quite handsome but already mushy in diction (try to guess what language she's singing!); Wilfred Brown and Thomas Hemsley labor bravely, if without great distinction. Not ideal stylistically, this is still an adequate offering in a bargain reissue (EMI 68670, 2CD, with BWV 80, 140, and Motet). A more pretentious approach was **Richter's** in 1961 (DG Archiv). Unfortunately, his solo team is uneven: Buckel and Engen on the strong side, an adequate van Kesteren, and a substandard Töpper. Tempos are contrastingly exaggerated, with a jog-trot opening chorus against sentimentalized chorale choruses, and the organ overwhelms the continuo.

Rilling weighed in (1976–77) with a more coherent version, marked by sensible tempos (no more romanticizing of the chorales) and a consistent solo team: Augér, Watts again, Equiluz, Schöne; the last disappoints only in his excessive aspiration of vowels on coloratura runs (♦Hänssler Vol. 12, 98.863, with BWV 71, 192; "Bachakademie" Vol. 45, 92045, with BWV 146). For budget-minded traditionalists, there is also a throwback to Hungarian-provincial Bach under **Matyás Antál,** sensibly if unexceptionally conducted, a little too distantly recorded, with an able lineup of local singers led by the quite fine soprano Ingrid Kertesi (Naxos 550642, with BWV 80, or 554042, with BWV 82, 202).

The PI procession for this work got off to a shaky start under **Harnoncourt** (Teldec). While quite springy in the chorales, his tempos are otherwise surprisingly stodgy. There are the recurrent boys, not only in the choir but taking the soprano and alto solos, which can be a trial;

the usually admirable Equiluz is badly hampered by the pacing, though the young Hampson is outstanding in the bass numbers. **Rifkin** offered a more successful extreme in 1985, with his one-per-part approach, reissued in a bargain package (♦Oiseau-Lyre 455706, 2CD, with BWV 8, 51, 78, 80, 140). He was the first to use a countertenor (Minter) in the alto parts, and he's joined by three excellent partners (Jane Bryden, Thomas, Opalach) who sing handsomely as soloists and are a nicely blended quartet in the choruses. The pacing is fast and deft (notably in the familiar chorales), creating an intimacy that might seem at odds with the relatively expansive character of the music but refreshing and fascinating as a challenging rethinking of the work, a unique conception certainly worth knowing.

Two 1990 recordings by British forces are particularly parallel: **Christophers** (Collins 13172, with BWV 34, 50) and **Gardiner** (♦DG Archiv 431809 or 463587, with BWV 140). Christophers has a virtuoso choir and excellent soloists (Fisher, David James, Partridge, George) who deliver consistently handsome singing. The only possible weakness in Gardiner's solo roster is Holton, whose overly boyish soprano is at least used with care; Chance makes another fine case for a falsettist in the alto parts, while Rolfe Johnson and Varcoe are unusually eloquent in their assignments, and the crack choir is highly engaged as well. Above all, whereas Christophers creates a suave and cool elegance, Gardiner infuses his performers with striking vitality and commitment to the texts, generating irresistible vitality.

Gardiner's achievement is thrown into interesting relief by the somewhat more flowing and relaxed character of **Koopman's** 1997 recording. His return to a female alto is not convincingly justified by Bogna Bartosz's lackluster singing, but Lisa Larsson is a crystal-voiced soprano, Türk a stylish tenor, and Mertens outstanding in the bass parts. If less compelling than Gardiner's version, this is still a worthy component of Koopman's unfolding series (♦Erato Vol. 7, 23141). We now have **Suzuki's** entry in his continuing traversal (BIS Vol. 12, 1031, with BWV 21). Robin Balze is an acceptable example of the male alto option, while the clear-voiced and intelligent Yukari Nonoshita is joined by the busy Türk and Kooy, in a performance that marginally outstrips Koopman's in style and grace.

198 ("Lass, Fürstin, lass noch einer Strahl"; "Trauer-Ode"). Not a part of the subsequently numbered "secular" cantatas but not a liturgical "sacred" cantata either, this "Mourning Ode" is the longest of Bach's funerary works. It was composed for Leipzig ceremonies in 1727 marking the death of Christiane Eberhardine, the estranged and staunchly Lutheran consort of the Catholic convert Augustus the Strong, Elector of Saxony and King of Poland. Its beautifully projected mood of genuine grief, its wonderful tonal effects (e.g., imitating chiming bells), and its rich instrumental scoring have made it a work of challenging but recurrent appeal to performers and audiences alike, to a degree exceeded only by its counterpart, the earlier "Actus tragicus" (BWV 106).

Among its relatively few LP recordings, you might watch for **Scherchen's** somewhat idiosyncratic but powerful CD reissue (Westminster). Perhaps you should also look for a version under **Corboz** from the mid-1970s and once in a two-LP set (Erato). Otherwise, three MI recordings are still around, representing good, better, and best. A 1960 venture drew **Robert Craft** into this unfamiliar terrain in a fascinating bit of American provincial Bach. Craft, his soloists (Marni Nixon, Elaine Bonazzi, Nico Castel, Peter Binder), and Margaret Hillis's fine American Concert Choir were all out of their normal element, and his insistence on underscoring every emotional turn made for a performance over-inflected and not quite stylish, captured in dry, very up-close sound. It's an odd item, but still interesting (Sony 62656, 2CD, with BWV 131 and Monteverdi's *Vespers*).

Rotzsch's Leipzig recording came 15 years later (1975). His is a large and spacious projection of the work, with the Thomanerchor (boys and all) and a quartet of nonstellar but very able soloists, in one of the most successful and satisfying of his Bach recordings, a welcome reissue (◆Berlin 9197). In 1983 **Rilling** assembled the elements of what should have been a distinguished recording. His ensembles and soloists (Augér, Gabriele Schreckenbach, Baldin, Huttenlocher) are stylistic veterans in fine form, and Rilling is good at capturing instrumental fine points. My only reservation is his propensity to punch out pulses with undue emphasis. Otherwise, this is a high-quality rendition, ideally paired in its single-disc release (◆Hänssler Vol. 68, 98.830, with BWV 106; "Bach-akademie" Vol. 60, 92.060, with BWV 199, 200).

The first PI recording of this great score came from Jürgen Jürgens's Monteverdi Choir with the Concerto Amsterdam led by Schröder and **Leonhardt,** joined by experienced soloists (Hansmann, Watts, Equiluz, van Egmond) in some of their finest Bach singing on discs; a lovely and beautifully satisfying performance (1966: ◆Teldec 93687, with BWV 27, 158). Leonhardt returned to this work in 1988, with more puristic intentions. The interpretation is well thought out, but only Elwes makes much of the solo numbers; a timid boy treble in the soprano solos, Jacobs as a countertenor alto, and bass van der Kamp are all below par, though with fine choral work prepared by Herreweghe (Teldec).

The chain of connections had already been extended, since **Herreweghe** made his own recording the previous year (Harmonia Mundi 901270, with BWV 78). With nicely balanced soloists (Schmithüsen, Brett, Crook, Kooy) and admirably prepared chamber choir and ensemble, this has all the beauty and smoothness that Leonhardt's recording lacks; without commanding elements but with not a single flaw, it's something more than "merely excellent" and could readily have been the leading PI recommendation but for two subsequent recordings of still more striking character.

These were **Gardiner** in 1989 (◆DG Archiv 429782 or 463581, with BWV 106, 118b) and **Koopman** in 1996 (◆Erato Vol. 4, 15562). Gardiner's solo team (Argenta, Chance, Rolfe Johnson, Varcoe) is comparable to Koopman's (Larsson, von Magnus, Paul Agnew, Mertens), and each conductor has superlative choral and instrumental forces at hand. But the interpretations differ notably. Gardiner is once again all intense urgency, especially in the choral sections, but with restless grief spilling into the work of the soloists, who sound as if they really mean the words they sing. His brisk performance runs almost eight minutes shorter than Koopman's, which has somewhat broader and more traditional tempos. But Koopman emphasizes a profound and controlled introspection that mounts to heart-piercing sadness. Each is wonderfully valid, and any Bach lover will want to experience both.

Another pair of recordings illuminate the minimalist approach pioneered by Rifkin. He has not recorded the work himself, but **Thomas,** his sometime epigone, has. His soloists (Nelson, Malafronte, Thomas himself, Sharp) are excellent, but there is a small chorus (numbers unspecified) and a modest chamber group, both sometimes rough in ensemble. The interpretation is brisk and assertive, and has an intimacy that even goes beyond what Craft attempted. But this is not a truly minimalist version, as is **Parrott**'s (◆Sony 60155, with two Motets). Parrott is a fervent convert to the Rifkin Doctrine, and he uses four singers as both soloists and "chorus" together with a mini-orchestra of 16 (including the numerous obbligatists). His stately tempos, generally much slower than Thomas's, are rather traditional, though well chosen. For some listeners the ultra-lean textures may deprive the music of its full weight and nobility, but they are worth hearing as an effort to recapture what some think was the composer's own scale of performance.

Secular cantatas

202 ("Weichet nur, betrübte Schatten"; "Wedding Cantata"). The term "secular cantata" is a catchall whose application is sometimes elusive. It includes some nonliturgical devotional works, a large number of occasional or celebratory pieces, and five quasi-dramatic compositions. At least two of the secular cantatas were composed for weddings, this one and BWV 210, "O holder Tag, erwünschte Zeit." Each is scored for solo soprano with instrumental ensemble, and they have understandably become appealing vehicles for Bach singers, especially BWV 202, the shorter of the two. Since they are such display pieces, listeners' choices will depend heavily on their preferences for particular singers.

A number of worthy recordings have fallen by the wayside, by **Danco** (London), **Seefried** (DG), and **Stader** (DG Archiv), all from LP years, and by **Hendricks** (1989) in a discontinued CD (EMI 49843, with BWV 51, 82a). Three of the very earliest survive as historical relics. **Elisabeth Schumann** made a recording in 1939, surprisingly responsible for Bach singing of that day (Pearl 9900, 2CD, with B-minor Mass, etc.) The other two feature **Schwarzkopf,** both from 1957. One derives from a concert performance in Amsterdam with Klemperer that she considers it her "best ever singing of Bach." This wonderful interpretation of knowing feminine ardor is in Schwarzkopf collections from EMI (567206, with BWV 51, 199, and arias) and Bella Voce (7201, 2CD, with BWV 51, 92, Verdi *Requiem*, etc.). A shade more careful, but likewise full of spirit, was a never-released studio recording led by Thurston Dart, who guarantees stylistic niceties and contributes a few elegant harpsichord flourishes. This shelved item has now been combined with other Bach recordings Schwartzkopf and Dart made in a series of sessions in 1957–58 (the complete BWV 199 and two cantata arias, plus Mozart's greatest concert aria) in an irresistible package no admirer of the singer or the composer should miss.

The oldest surviving LP recording is a 1954 memento of the warmhearted Viennese soprano, **Anny Felbermayer,** but Prohaska's stiff conducting and Anton Heiller's overbearing harpsichord are no assets (Vanguard). Two other recordings by German sopranos are more appealing. The refined and handsomely focused voice of **Ursula Buckel** is given gracious support by Ewerhart in an attractive set mostly devoted to secular cantatas (1965: ◆Vox 3039, 3CD). **Mathis** is somewhat more studied in vocal inflection, with more self-indulgent conducting by Schreier in his secular cantata series (Berlin 9222, with BWV 210). **Zylis-Gara**'s 1986 recording displays limited stylistic confidence, with a hooty, blowzy tone and some difficulties controlling intonation (Rodolphe).

Besides Hendricks (EMI, also with Schreier), three American sopranos have given their thoughts on the work. **Bogard** offered a somewhat small-scaled and understated version with John Moriarty that is artistic but rather unexciting (1971: Parnassus). At the opposite pole is **Battle**'s 1977 recording, dazzling but predictably operatic (RCA). A surprisingly minimalist eight-member ensemble brings lean clarity to the instrumental writing, but it's over-conducted, with Verdian exaggeration and hyper-emphasis by Levine, in high-powered sound: an overblown curiosity that sounds like Bach-meets-Zerbinetta-at-the-Go-Go-Club. Fortunately, a happy middle ground was established in 1996 by **Heidi Grant Murphy**'s crystalline soprano, radiant with a touch of girlish joy; she's given support rather than competition by the conductorless St. Luke's

Chamber Ensemble, only four players larger than the RCA group. As released in a dandy nuptial package, this is a particularly treasurable version, pretty clearly the top MI choice (♦Arabesque 6690, with BWV 210).

Murphy's virtues are thrown more into relief by two other recordings of European origins. From the depths of Slovakia comes a 1991 recording in which **Friederike Wagner,** with competent technique but an undistinctive voice, gives a rather depersonalized performance, routinely supported by Christian Brembeck, available in a bargain-level release (Naxos). More style and character are offered by Rilling in one of several recordings supplemental to his cantata series (1997); his soprano, **Sybilla Rubens,** has a healthy voice and technique but sounds edgy at times, perhaps as a result of being pushed by Rilling's sometimes rushed tempos, producing an unsettling rendition that evokes a shotgun wedding more than a joyous event (Hänssler 98.169, with BWV 206; "Bachakademie" Vol. 62, 92.062, with BWV 203, 204).

The PI category got off to an early start, if suffering numerous casualties along the way, such as **Kirkby**'s 1981 version that apparently never made it onto CD (Hyperion). The earliest PI version is still one of the best, made by the reliable **Giebel** in 1966. Long before Rifkin, she was given pioneering minimalist accompaniment by a six-member group led by Schröder and Leonhardt, in a thoroughly satisfying performance (♦Teldec 21711, with BWV 51, 209). From about the same time comes an even more endearing version by the ever-beguiling **Ameling,** with the Collegium Aureum led by Reinhard Peters, whose nonthreatening and warm playing shouldn't bother those who hate PI sound; this recording has been around in several forms, most recently in a highly attractive Bach cantata package that remains a leading choice in this category (♦Harmonia Mundi 77151, 2CD, with BWV 209, 211, 212).

Leanness of sound marks the recordings that have followed. There is much intelligence in Rifkin's 1987 version, but the minimalist PI playing is very spare, and **Baird**'s small, little-girlish voice may be too chalky and piping for some tastes (Oiseau-Lyre 421424, with BWV 209). (Rifkin had better luck with **Judith Nelson** in a fine version of BWV 210, a Oiseau-Lyre recording that never made it to CD.) **Zádori** is a very fine soprano, but her singing is also rather thin and reedy in a brusque and perfunctory rendition under Pál Németh (1990: Harmonia Mundi 9030110, with BWV 209, 210).

Good news comes from Koopman, for whom **Lisa Larsson,** though also light of voice, does some of her best Bach singing (♦Erato Vol. 5, 17578). After a particularly languorous opening movement, the performance settles into an infectious spirit of vivacity, with excellent attention to verbal inflection and some particularly rich continuo work—a very good alternative if you can't find Ameling. Also to be commended is the promising **Christine Schäfer,** whose full voice and spirited stylistic sense produce a splendid realization; she comes with frankly PI playing (one instrument per part) of great pungency, color, and intimacy from Goebel's Musica Antiqua Köln (♦DG 459621, with BWV 51, 210).

208 ("Was mir behagt"; "Hunting Cantata"). This *Jagd-Kantate* is the earliest of Bach's surviving secular odes, composed in 1716 during his Weimar years in connection with a hunting party that marked the birthday of his patron's friend and neighbor, Duke Christian of Saxe-Weissenfels. It was the first of what became a recurrent production of occasional pieces during the Leipzig years to mark festive occasions (in five cases, in honor of Augustus III of Saxony and Poland). The "libretto's" premise in BWV 208 is that despite the protests of her shepherd lover, Endymion, the goddess Diana has to take him and join Pan and the nymph Palli in praising the Birthday Boy and his wonderful hunting resourcefulness.

The score has two distinctive features. For one thing, since the work celebrates the pleasures of the hunt and the beauties of the Duke's well-regulated countryside, the music includes some of Bach's rare evocations of nature and the pastoral scene. Second, it's another of the three Bach cantatas that have achieved fame (or infamy) partly through the diverse adaptation of one of its movements (a soprano aria) into a piece with persistent independent popularity ("Sheep May Safely Graze").

The first complete recording (1961) is still with us, in a package of reissues focused on **Fischer-Dieskau** (EMI 572634, 2CD, with BWV 211, 212 and items by A. Scarlatti, Telemann, Couperin). The Berlin chorus is grandiose, while the orchestra is blurry under Forster's direction, and the two female singers—Annelies Kupper, a Diana of frayed maturity, and Erika Köth, a Palli from munchkinland—are all too distinguishable. But it's the men who give this recording some lasting value: Fischer-Dieskau is pleasantly hammy as Pan, and Wunderlich's ringing tenor reminds us how much we lost with his early death. The 1976 recording that is part of **Schreier**'s secular cantata series is a better-balanced affair. He has two thoroughly reliable sopranos in Mathis and Augér, who safely grazes her sheep with memorable radiance; Schreier himself is the sturdy tenor, and only Adam is less than commendable as a pale Pan (♦Berlin 223, with BWV 204). But the Berlin chorus and orchestra are excellent, and Schreier infuses everything with great vigor and energy, captured in strong, forward sound.

Antál's Budapest recording is less stellar but consistently reliable, if somewhat too distantly miked (Naxos 550643, with BWV 51). Among his well-matched soloists, his Diana, Ingrid Kertesi, is a standout, while István Gáti is a genuine bass rare in Pan casting—not dazzling, but an honest bargain-rate choice. There is much more style and flair in **Rilling**'s 1996 recording (replacing an earlier one of 1965, once available from Musicaphon) in the secular supplements to his cantata series (♦Hänssler 98.161, with BWV 211; "Bachakademie" Vol. 65, 92065, with BWV 209). The solo group (Sibylla Rubens, Eva Kirchner, James Taylor, Görne) is one of the most balanced, and there is a festive vivacity about this performance that is altogether apt. Rilling even adds a bonus in the opening movement of Sinfonia BWV 1046a (an earlier version of *Brandenburg* 1) to fill the lack of any stipulated curtain-raiser.

In the PI category, **Harnoncourt**'s direction in the early 1970s is sometimes brusque or heavy-handed, but he has a fine cast (Kenny, Angela Maria Blasi, Equiluz, Holl) who create quite vivid characterizations (Teldec 97501, with BWV 212; "Bach 2000" Vol. 5, 25710). **Goodman** is somewhat lighter and more deft (1985: ♦Hyperion 66169). The four singers (Jennifer Smith, Kirkby, Simon Davies, George) clearly have fun with their roles, and as a group constitute the "chorus" in its two movements, while the strict one-player-per-part instrumentation in the two "orchestral" movements increases the feeling of intimacy. Goodman goes Rilling one better by using *two* movements of Sinfonia BWV 1046a as opening and closing frames.

But for sheer spirit, you must go to **Koopman;** though he does use multiple string players in his orchestra, he also makes his four singers his only "chorus." They (Schlick, von Magnus, Agnew, Mertens) are all excellent, and the two men particularly bring a fine sense of personality to their roles (♦1995: Erato Vol. 3, 14336). If you don't mind a little over-exuberant harpsichord continuo from Koopman himself (and can do without the BWV 1046a additions), this is probably the best PI choice.

211 ("Schweig stille, plaudert nicht"; "Coffee Cantata") and **212** ("Mer hahn en neue Oberkeet"; "Peasant Cantata"). At least five of the 15-odd secular cantatas are dramatic pieces of one kind or another, with characters and plot, if sometimes symbolic or allegorical. Some of them even bear the label *dramma per musica,* and are as close as Bach ever came to the world of opera and the secular theater. Three of them have mythological bases: BWV 201, "Der Streit zwischen Phoebus und Pan" (The Conflict of Apollo and Pan); 205, "Der zufriedengestellte Aeolus" (Aeolus Appeased); and 213, "Hercules auf dem Scheidewege" (Hercules at the Crossroads). All three are available in somewhat uneven performances by soloists including Kiehr, Scholl, and Prégardien with the RIAS Chamber Choir and the PI Akademie für Alte Musik Berlin under **Jacobs** (Harmonia Mundi 901544/45, 2CD). And, as with all of the secular cantatas, they may be found in the complete series by Koopman (Erato), Rilling (Hänssler), and Schreier (Berlin).

Two more of these works present rare glimpses of Bach the comedian, writing little less than comic minioperas, comparable to the intermezzi of the contemporaneous lyric stage. One is a spoof of the craze for coffee-drinking, presenting a rebelliously addicted daughter pitted against her indignant father, composed for performance in a popular coffeehouse in Leipzig. The other is a vignette of country bumpkins acclaiming the arrival of a new village overseer, dancing and singing it up in broad Upper Saxon regional dialect. These cantatas started out separately in earliest LP days (e.g., 211 led by **Rolf Reinhardt** for Vox, 212 under **Daniel Pinkham** in a paleolithic Allegro trailblazer). More often than not, however, they've been recorded as a pair and have to be reviewed as such.

The earliest LP pairing was **Thomas**'s 1960 Leipzig recording, with Adele Stolte, Rotzsch, and Adam, issued by DG Archiv but so far not revived among the Berlin reissues. From the same year came the earliest surviving recording of the pair, reissued in a **Fischer-Dieskau** package (EMI 572634, 2CD, with BWV 208, and items by A. Scarlatti, Telemann, and Couperin). In 211, the young Fischer-Dieskau chews the scenery as the father of all curmudgeons, while Lisa Otto, if unsteady of voice, is a girlish and spunky daughter, and Josef Traxel sounds like a tongue-in-cheek Evangelist; in 212, Otto and Fischer-Dieskau clown it up like the Berlin Hilton hillbillies. Unfortunately, the farcical tone is undone by Karl Forster's ponderous accompaniments. Two decades later, Fischer-Dieskau gave the pair another try, this time with his wife, Julia Varady. In 211 he sounds more the world-weary grouch, while she's a womanly conniver, and the beefy Baldin is quite miscast as narrator; in 212, Fischer-Dieskau has sobered up, and he and Varady sing the piece fairly straight, with cool and neutral support from Marriner and his St. Martin Academy—all in an LP issue that Philips has so far chosen not to reissue (but you never know).

A pair of recordings (1965, 1966) by **Ewerhart** do honorable service in the Vox Box collection of mainly secular cantatas (3039, 3CD, with BWV 80, 202–204, 209). Claus Ocker works up a little spleen with a prickly Speiser and a supportive Jochims in 211, but Ocker and Ursula Buckel are rather well-behaved peasants in 212; Ewerhart's orchestral support is a little overblown but quite satisfactory. There is more vivid characterization in **Schreier**'s 1975 contribution to his secular cantata series. In 211 Schreier himself is an activist narrator and Mathis a strong-willed daughter who is quite a match for the somewhat spineless Adam (vocally as well as dramatically); their 212 is a fairly polite affair, and Schreier conducts well-pointed but amiable accompaniments (Berlin 9226).

Antál offers respectable value, with Ingrid Kertesi as an assertive daughter or peasant girl, while Gáti—an experienced operatic singer—suggests forceful buffo personalities in his roles and József Mukk tenors along quite supportively (1992: Naxos 550641). But brisk and superficial leadership and cavernously distant sound remove this recording from

serious competitive status. **Rilling** somewhat strains the pairing principle by placing his 1996 recordings on two separate discs in his supplemental cantata series, but they use the same singers and clearly are an integral unit (♦Hänssler: 211 in 98.161, with BWV 208 and "Bachakademie" Vol. 66, 92.066, with BWV 210; 212 in 98.163, with BWV 207a and "Bachakademie" Vol. 67, 92.067, with BWV 213). While James Taylor sounds like a somewhat surprised observer, the other two singers sound as if they are really interacting with each other. Actual dramatic characters are suggested by the beguiling Schäfer and the blustering Quasthoff—the latter delivering superbly theatrical inflection. For its combination of carefully contrived comedy with wonderful musicality, this pair of performances has to be the leading choice in the MI category.

A wide array of PI versions has been accumulating. At least three fine recordings of LP vintage are currently discontinued but would be welcome back at any time: by **Hogwood,** with Kirkby, Covey-Crump, and David Thomas (Oiseau-Lyre, 1986); **Linde,** with Rosemarie Hofmann, de Mey, and Gregory Reinhart (EMI, 1982); and **Harnoncourt,** with Hansmann, Equiluz, and van Egmond (Teldec, 1971). Harnoncourt gave 212 a second and even better try in which Blasi and Holl give boisterously humorous performances, though the accompaniments carry the rustic roughness a little too far (Teldec 97501, with BWV 208; "Bach 2000" Vol. 5, 25710). Another single of 211 only (1984) has been in and out of the catalogue, sporting thoroughly musical performances and quite effective dramatic characterizations by Monoyios, Stephen Oosting, and Ostendorf, with at least competent leadership by **Somary** (Lyrichord 8039 or Vox 9039, with BWV 53, 158, and two Motets).

The earliest surviving pairing of LP years is still unsurpassed: **Collegium Aureum** gives minimalist support that will not trouble PI-haters. Gerald English is a narrator with nicely ironic solemnity, while Nimsgern is an appropriately huffy father and robust peasant. Above all, Ameling is the daughter of your dreams, if almost too lovely and genteel as a peasant girl (♦Harmonia Mundi 77151, 2CD, with BWV 202, 209). If you can have only one recording, this would be an ideal choice.

Quite stylish and charming performances are available in a 1985 recording by the minimalist **Friends of Apollo** ensemble, the light-voiced but handsome-sounding Dawson joined by the lighter-voiced Nicolas Robertson and Stephen Alder (♦Meridian 84110). The extra-generous pairing by Dorothea Röschmann, Hugues Saint-Gelais, and Kevin McMillan is well sung but somewhat aggressive, with **Bernard Labadie** leading his Violons du Roy with considerable energy (Dorian 90199, with BWV 173a). But the most saucy of recent recordings is **Koopman**'s (♦Erato). As with Rilling, the two are given separately, but each is played with great flair and imagination, Koopman leading quite imaginative continuo work. In BWV 211 (Vol. 4, 15562), the approach is highly dramatic, with Agnew unusually caught up as narrator; Anne Grimm is a coy daughter and Mertens a highly flustered father. In BWV 212 (Vol. 5, 17578), Mertens is an earthy peasant, while Larsson has the makings of a village shrew. Koopman indulges in the novelty of adding a little chorus here and there and conjures up rustic dancing as well. These are performances to enjoy as nice foils to the more elegant renditions with Ameling.

To leave this area of Bach's output with so many cantatas still undiscussed is frustrating. Among my favorites is BWV 131, which I commend strongly to those still exploring. Many fine individual releases have slipped through the cracks, such as the fine recording of BWV 35, 169, and 170 by the wonderful young Finnish mezzo, **Monica Groop** (♦Finlandia 25325). For a thematic angle, there are parallel and only slightly overlapping discs devoted to Bach's cantatas for Christmas and

Epiphany. Four of them (BWV 40, 133, 151, 65) are given honest and satisfying renditions by nonstellar soloists with the Chorus and Orchestras of Emmanuel Music under **Craig Smith** (♦Koch 3-7462). Two of them (BWV 63, 65) receive robust performances from the Bach Choir and Festival Orchestra of Bethlehem under **Funfgeld,** with particularly fine solo work from McNair and Janice Taylor (♦Dorian 90113). And so on—so much more for you to discover for yourself.

Motets (BWV 225-30)

Written for single or double choirs, with continuo stipulated or implied but no other specified instrumentation, these are short works for occasional use, six of them authenticated and "standard." Six more, by other composers known or unknown, were placed in the Schmieder supplement (BWV Anh. 159–165). Recently, **Wolfgang Helbich,** who has dedicated himself to recording a series of the "apocryphal" Bach, has offered those extra six as a group (CPO 999235). Helbich has also recorded "The Apocryphal Bach Cantatas," six items that Schmieder reckoned as his BWV 217–222 but are now acknowledged as not by Johann Sebastian (CPO 999139, 2CD).

Though merely a category of music rather than any kind of entity, the six "standard" motets have regularly been treated as a group in recordings, and deserve our consideration thus. There have been many recordings of individual motets, some quite fine. The wonderful chorale elaboration, "Jesu, meine Freude" (BWV 227), has been a particular favorite—I still cherish my old monophonic recording by **Shaw** (RCA)—but complete cycles have been common for years. There isn't much distinction between MI and PI versions; we know Bach used instrumental ensembles in his performances, but only to double the voices, without an independent role beyond the continuo.

Of a number of sets from LP years, five deserve mention against possible reappearance. **Ramin**'s noble testament with his Leipzig Thomanerchor (1951–55) provided sensitive and earnest performances in the Leipzig neo-Baroque tradition of boys and men (DG Archiv LPs, mono). A parallel cycle offered gentler singing by a chamber choir under **Helmut Kahlhöfer** and PI doublings by the Collegium Aureum (1969: Harmonia Mundi, briefly issued here by RCA). **Schmidt-Gaden**'s Tölzer Knabenchor of boys and men provided small-scaled treatments (with solo voices in selected passages) that evoked the churchly sounds of Bach's day (1981).

A more distinctly Anglican approach—totally a cappella save for continuo in BWV 230—was offered by **Willcox** with King's College Choir, Cambridge, made in 1967 and 1970 and briefly available in reissue (♦EMI 763327). His performances are carefully, sometimes even cautiously crafted, but sung with sturdy precision in excellent sound, requiring only no objection to the all-male colors (boys and men) of a British church choir. Finally, in 1984 **Paul Hillier** led his Hilliard Ensemble, a boys-and-men Hanover choir, as well as to continuo members of the London Baroque in a small-scale realization reproducing Bach's own forces (12 to 16 singers). Not necessarily always the way to hear these works, this distinguished venture was fascinating for its lightness, clarity, and intimacy, rather than grandeur (EMI; a brief CD reissue hasn't survived but should be restored).

The tradition of full-choir performance has been durably represented in surviving recordings. **Thomas** made a cycle in the classic postwar Leipzig style (chorus with modest orchestral doubling) with warmth and sensitivity, in broad tempos and with slightly woolly boys-and-men choral sound (1958–59: Berlin 9103). The choral approach has also been demonstrated by **Marlow** and the Choir of Trinity College, Cambridge: A choir of 24 mixed voices, singing suavely with only organ continuo, with vibratoless "white" sound from the sopranos, imparts an Anglican aspect of pure and churchly ethereality (1988: ♦Conifer 15350).

With only three or four singers per part, as was Bach's practice, the Deutsche Bach-Vocalisten under **Gerhard Weinberger,** using only harpsichord continuo, deliver brisk, clinical, and rather bloodless performances (Calig). A likewise suave, polished, but rather cool cycle is given by the Vancouver Chamber Choir under **Jon Washburn:** choral forces with appropriate continuo participation (Grouse 103). Five of the motets (omitting BWV 228) are given pleasingly robust and enthusiastic performances by the Riga Radio Chorus, with MI doublings by the Riga Musicians led by **Sigvard Klava** (Audiophile Classics 101.047)

The final extreme of only one singer per part has been given two lively and vivid demonstrations, each with mixed success. The conductorless **Scholars Baroque Ensemble** uses only organ continuo and is an exercise in intimacy that totally denies any scale (Naxos 553823). **Junghänel** joins to the single-singer scoring an 11-member PI miniorchestra in varied application (♦Harmonia Mundi 77368). The singing is particularly fine, with clear diction and intense expressiveness, but many will find that this approach is minimalism carried to an extreme that does far from full justice to this magnificent music.

Two more moderate approaches benefit from the elegance of small but super-refined choral singing: **Koopman** (1987: Philips 434165) and **Christophers** (1989: ♦Hyperion 66369). Each uses continuo players, and each introduces selectively solo *Concertisten* voices in juxtaposition to the full choir. Both are sober and probing: Koopman's warm-voiced Netherlands Chamber Choir establishes wonderfully controlled detail and is vividly recorded, while Christophers' Sixteen is used to more spacious effect. With forces essentially of Bach's own size, Christophers is sparing in his use of soloists, making his version almost purely choral. The white-voiced soprano tone sounds rather Anglican, and a certain icy restraint is evident, but impeccable discipline achieves remarkably beautiful performances.

Two more examples of this type are less successful. **Kuijken** employs a 24-member mixed-voice chamber choir, with limited solo voices and careful PI doublings, admirably marshaled with refined clarity but in rather fussy renditions (Accent). **Bernius**'s version with Stuttgart forces is further down the scale: a tidy mixed-voice choir with very limited solo voices and modest PI orchestra, all polish and precision, but in rather bland understatement. Moreover, Bernius gives only the first five of the Motets (eliminating 230), a competitive handicap (1989: Sony).

Three other recordings represent intermediate approaches. The grand, weighty scale achieved in 1978 by Westminster Choir School forces under **Ehmann** is altogether traditional, but he introduces selective instrumental doublings, as well as occasional solo voices against full choir (Gothic 49052). His pacings are so spacious that the single CD format requires omission of the final chorales to BWV 226 and 229. The Stockholm Bach Choir led by **Harnoncourt** with his Vienna PI players is also sizable and mixed-voiced, but his brisk and incisively detailed performances are stimulating and enjoyable in close and vividly clear sound (♦Dorian 90113; Teldec 17430). An all-too-conventional treatment by a mixed-voice group, the Rostock Motet Choir led by **Hartwig Eschenburg,** with continuo and *colla parte* doublings from members of the Capella Fidicinia Leipzig, offers energetic but somewhat rugged and ragged singing that eventually becomes monotonous (Capriccio).

Two of the more recent recordings reflect evolving scholarly ideas of "authentic" performing possibilities, though each has highly idiosyncratic touches. In his 1986 cycle **Herreweghe** used members of his excellent mixed-voice chamber choir, three or four singers per part, without soloists, and with intimate and sensible but very PI doublings in all but one piece (♦Harmonia Mundi 901231). The exception is the great "Jesu, meine Freude" (BWV 227), which is sung by a chamber group of five solo singers with continuo only—fascinating in its clarity and intensified inflection, but erasing Bach's contrasts between larger and smaller textures. It's surprising to hear so sensitive a musician as Herreweghe sometimes slipping into tempos of jog-trotting oversimplicity; still, there's no denying the careful, responsible artistry involved.

In contrast, **Jacobs**'s 1995 recording draws upon a large, 35-member, mixed-voice choir, five solo singers, and a 15-member PI ensemble, plus three continuo players (♦Harmonia Mundi 901589). He mixes these forces almost like a painter who works freely with his palette of colors—sorting, blending, and weaving them in and out in rich, if sometimes bewildering, freedom. The combination of such imagination with dazzling precision, control, and vivacity makes this perhaps the most exciting experiment with the latest ideas of period "authenticity."

Three recordings are in a special class in that they go beyond the standard six motets and add related material. In 1973 **Schneidt** added to the six regulars the rarely heard BWV 231 and Anh. 159 (the wonderful "Ich lasse dich nicht," apparently by Bach's uncle, Johann Christoph, but sometimes attributed to Johann Sebastian), all performed robustly by the Regensburg Cathedral Choir—among the best-controlled large choirs of boys and men—with prominent PI orchestral forces led by Eduard Melkus; the set is worth tracking down (♦DG Archiv 427117 or 427142).

In Schneidt's wake came **Gardiner** (1980:♦Erato 99613, 2CD). He added the rarely heard BWV 231, the motet-like Cantata 118, the cantata torso BWV 50, and one of the "spurious" motets (an arrangement by Bach after Kuhnau). With sparing use of solo *Concertisten* and PI orchestra, Gardiner led a superbly trained mixed-voice choir, numbering in the twenties, in springy, incisive, yet expressively shaped performances, recorded with the utmost clarity.

Capping these augmented cycles is **Rilling**'s, which has its own generous array of supplements: Cantata 118, two "spurious" motets (Anh. 159 and 160), plus the Kuhnau arrangement (1990: ♦Hänssler 98.965, 2CD). Rilling returns to a chorus-only approach, with a sizable choir and a small MI chamber orchestra discreetly used for nice coloristic doublings. The performances are propulsive, flowing, and energetic, yet lyrically inflected, all with great musical appeal. The miking is a bit distant, but the sonics are among the most successful in distinguishing the two groups in the double-chorus items. All three of these sets require extra investment for a second disc, but each combines superlative performances of their kind with genuinely rewarding (if varied) supplements that put the "standard" six motets in illuminating perspective.

Obviously, the motets present a very complex picture on discs, and there can be no one-size-fits-all choice. You must sort out your preferences among several factors: large or small choir? boys or women? solo voices? instrumental doublings? PI or MI? Any Bach lover will want more than one approach to these wonderful works, and the best start might be among the narrow range offered by Rilling or Gardiner, Christophers or Marlow, and Jacobs.

Mass in B Minor (BWV 232)

Recognized for nearly two centuries as one of the supreme musical monuments of Western civilization, this enigmatic masterpiece was assembled by Bach, with extensive recyclings of his own earlier music, during his last years. It belongs with *Art of Fugue* as valedictory music

that the composer seems to have written for himself, as a kind of ultimate testament of his art, transcending practicalities of performance. Never performed in full in his lifetime, it is almost a kind of abstract music, and therefore seemingly less subject to present-day compulsions to achieve "authentic" performances—though, in fact, it has actually attracted a good deal of such attention. Whatever the approach, this work is as elusive as it is magnificent, defying any possibility of a "definitive" or "best" recording. (Note: All recordings considered are 2CD.)

Nonperiod style

The B minor Mass was the first of Bach's large-scale sacred works to achieve a complete recording, astonishingly as early as 1929 in the 78 rpm era. A labor of love under the tireless **Albert Coates,** it's wildly old-fashioned by anyone's tastes today (even with the then-novel inclusion of a harpsichord). But its solo cast included such memorable singers as Elisabeth Schumann and Friedrich Schorr, who joined in some genuinely committed vintage singing. This noble document has achieved two CD revivals, one by itself (Claremont 78-50-39/40) and the other in a package that combines it with all of Schumann's other Bach recordings (Pearl 9900, 2CD).

Though it involves a jump of some years, it's not a great stylistic leap to another historic document, a near-legendary broadcast performance recorded by the BBC in 1951 under that remarkable and versatile musical giant, **Enescu** (BBC 4008). Seekers after every scrap of Kathleen Ferrier's singing will find her at her best here, and her distinguished colleagues included Danco and Pears. The interpretation is broad and monumental; some of the ensemble work is rough; and the restored mono sound is less than ideal. But this is a performance of power and majesty, conceived by a conductor who loved and understood Bach's music with a depth that, however romantic its perspectives, still communicates.

It's only seven years more to another historical document, taking us to post-WWII German centers for a rethinking of Bach's performance style. The original powerhouse was Leipzig, where, almost in defiance of the East German regime, a new fusion of the traditions of Mendelssohn with the progress of musicology was developed under a sequence of latter-day successors to Bach at the Thomaskirche: Karl Straube, Günther Ramin, and Kurt Thomas. Their traditions were extended by Ramin's disciple, Karl Richter, relocated in Munich, and, with modifications, transferred to Rudolf Mauersberger and Martin Flämig in Dresden, plus some revivals in Leipzig again under Hans-Joachim Rotzsch and Peter Schreier.

For this work, little of the original Leipzig tradition is preserved, but it's represented by extension in **Mauersberger**'s 1958 Dresden recording (Berlin). It's a sturdy, well-sung performance, with soloists Stader, Sieglinde Wagner, Haefliger, and Adam; still, the boys as choral sopranos and altos can sometimes grate, while the generally cold and clinical interpretation eventually becomes plodding. A further extension of the modern Leipzig Bach tradition is represented in **Richter**'s two recordings: 1961 with Stader, Töpper, Haefliger, Fischer-Dieskau, and Engen, and 1969 with Buckel, Höffgen, Haefliger again, and Ernst Gerold Schramm (both DG Archiv). There are weak elements in each solo lineup, and while the interpretations are coherent and the choral work very strong, this kind of compromise between romantic traditionalism and musicological streamlining has been taken up with more compelling results in the intervening years, making Richter sound dated now.

Most nonperiod recordings since then have come in either of two categories: those by big-name conductors who bend this monumental work to their will, working mostly with large-scale forces, and those by more earnest maestros carrying on the best of the Leipzig *Kapellmeister* patterns.

One to be dismissed at the outset is **Scherchen**'s version from the 1950s, powerful in its way if you respond to his unhistorical, even ahistorical, conception of transcendent worship, but by many standards little more than a wildly eccentric ego trip (MCA). Also highly willful is **Celibidache**'s 1990 Munich concert performance; his approach is monumental and heavily romantic, with at least some of the distended tempos and idiosyncratic spirituality typical of this conductor (Exclusive). But there is also some good work, including some fine soloists (Bonney, Schreier, Scharinger among them), though the live recording has sonic shortcomings.

More serious is the case of **Karajan,** who made an early commitment to the monumental, grandly spiritual Bach style, if in his own personal way. A concert performance in Vienna is preserved in coarse-sounding mono (1950: Verona 27073/74). Here the conductor is at his most extroverted. The stellar soloists (Schwarzkopf, Ludwig, Poell, Schoeffler) include the most memorable participant, Ferrier, capturing her in her solo numbers one year earlier than in Enescu's recording. Karajan's first commercial recording of the work, made in Vienna in 1952, offers a cooler, more tightly controlled interpretation, with skillful but less individualistic solo work from Schwarzkopf again, Höffgen, Gedda, and Rehfuss (EMI 567207, mono, with Schwarzkopf and Ferrier solos and duets from Karajan's 1950 performance). Though handicapped by rather opaque choral sound, it's still a solid and refined example of "objective" modern performance style. Karajan's second commercial recording (1974) is a beautifully realized studio version in its way, with excellent soloists (Janowitz, Ludwig again, Schreier, Ridderbusch), but it's an interpretation of now introverted spirituality and overstated rhetorical gestures, within a context of almost oppressive control (DG 439696, at budget price).

Klemperer's durable 1967 recording is far less narcissistic and more consistently committed to a concept of Bachian nobility (♦EMI 763364). Klemperer's idea of Bach is almost literally timeless, in the sense that time seems to disappear: This is a *slow* performance, probably the longest ever made, but magnificently crafted, broad yet never languid thanks to the conductor's knowing flexibility. The solo team (Giebel, Baker, Gedda, Prey, Franz Crass) is well-nigh perfect, and the massive choral and orchestral forces are captured in clean and lucid stereo. One critic has described it as "a reading of true grandeur and majesty, of Michelangelesque monumentality." If that's the Bach for you, read no further.

Jochum is also committed to nobility, if in less massive terms. His two recordings have been revived in low-priced CD reissues. The 1958 version with soloists Lois Marshall, Töpper, Pears, Kim Borg, and Hans Braun is good, given additional value by a generous bonus filler, Lutheran Mass 1 under Redel (Philips 438739). But the 1980 recording, with Donath, Fassbaender, Ahnsjö, Hermann, Holl, and the same Bavarian Radio forces, is an even more fully focused performance, somewhat more clearly recorded. Jochum's nice balance of grand power with energy and refined detail makes his second version one of the most consistently satisfying "compromise-modern" recordings to be found and go back to, a top-value bargain in EMI's "double fforte" series (♦EMI 58640).

Two more high-powered podium giants have contributed recordings, both of them disappointments. A Chicago Symphony concert performance led by **Solti** in 1990 reflects an almost Karajanian ruthlessness of control, with a generally fine group of soloists—Lott, von Otter,

Blochwitz, Shimell, Howell—all but depersonalized and made to sound miniature against the calculated high points of the choral sections (London). It certainly contains exciting moments, and the chorus, if a little woolly in the upper voices, displays a marvelous range of nuance—creditable, I would guess, to its director, Margaret Hillis, one of America's great podium should-have-beens. But Solti sets this fine chorus to ruthlessly exaggerated agogic effects with really irritating staccato, detaché poundings in eighth-note runs. This may have been a striking concert experience, but it's not a recording for repeated listening.

Even weirder is **Giulini**'s 1994 concert recording at Bavarian Radio (Sony). His soloists (Ziesak, Alexander, van Nes, Keith Lewis, Wilson-Johnson) try hard, and his chorus and orchestra have been honed with Giulini's usual painstaking polish. But time after time he sacrifices rhythmic vitality to flowing line and eviscerating pulse, leaving the music as only a smooth skin without any skeleton underneath.

Recordings by other "big-name" conductors (e.g., Ormandy, Maazel) are no longer available. But one last maestro plausibly of this fraternity is not only the most persistently durable (and fecund) but also something of a bridge figure between our two main MI categories. Early in his career, in 1947, **Shaw** made not only the first American recording of the Mass but also the first anywhere to apply neo-Baroque principles, using nonstar soloists, a small, beautifully disciplined choir, and a small orchestra of crack pick-up players (RCA). His 1960 stereo remake was likewise a marvel of refinement, combining an essentially romanticized interpretive style with a new experiment in "authenticity"—the still-debated use of solo singers as *Concertisten* in juxtaposition with full *ripieno* in the choral movements (♦RCA 63529). With more individualized soloists (Saramae Endich, Adele Addison, Florence Kopleff, Mallory Walker, Ara Berberian), this Shaw II is still a very stimulating and rewarding version. His third recording, made in Atlanta in 1990, effectively repeats the combination, but with still greater choral suavity, if with a slightly less even solo team (McNair, Ziegler, Marietta Simpson, Aler, William Stone, Thomas Paul): anachronistically super-spiritualized Bach, but beautiful to hear (♦Telarc 80233).

Which brings us to what we might call the "modest maestros" currently represented. **Corboz** is one of only two conductors to make three recordings for commercial release. His first (1982) is a very well-shaped rendition, balancing vitality and reverence (Erato 45442); a subsequent recording for the same label offered still better solo and singing, but is now NA. Most recently, Corboz made a further statement in a brisk but very well-shaped and intelligent recording from concert and studio takes with his Lausanne forces and a generally able solo group: Piau, Markus Schäfer, Marcus Fink (Aria 970901). **Münchinger** is a standout in this category. His 1970 recording stresses humanity rather than monumentality in a smooth and relatively relaxed performance, graced by a heaven-sent solo roster: Ameling, Minton, Watts, Krenn, Krause (previously ♦London 440609 at bargain price, now only in the 10CD Münchinger package of Bach's "Sacred Masterworks," 455783).

Somary's 1973 recording is more in the Richter mode, offering another wonderful solo team (Palmer, Watts, Tear, Rippon) and a fine orchestra but somewhat indifferent chorus: generally convincing, but in the "merely excellent" category (Vanguard 58). From the later 1970s came a kind of vade mecum to the Richter tradition in **Marriner**'s recording (Philips). On paper the solo roster looks like a dream cast, but most of them (Margaret Marshall, Baker, Tear, Ramey) are not singing at their best, while the choral work is diffident, the tempos often quite fast, resulting in a lively but rather superficial reading.

The true continuer and renewer of the Richter tradition is, of course,

Rilling, the other conductor besides Corboz to make three recordings. Unfortunately, repetition has not meant improvement. His first version (1977) still stands as an intelligent, well-balanced, and handsomely realized "compromise" approach, with a fine group of soloists: Augér, Hamari, Adalbert Kraus, Schöne, Nimsgern (♦Sony 45615). When he undertook his second attempt (1988), he had moved toward a certain coolness and reserve in his approach (Intercord, NA). Shifting gears in 1999, his third version finds the conductor veering into high-energy exaggeration, with a tendency for his chorus and soloists to slip into unpleasant amounts of aspiration on rapid vowel-runs (Hänssler). The male soloists (James Taylor, Andreas Schmidt, Quasthoff) are fine, but the ladies are not particularly distinguished. In all, this is a letdown; Rilling's best thoughts on this work—and they are fine—are in his first recording.

One more example of the Leipzig/Dresden tradition is offered by **Schreier** in a 1991 Dresden recording (in "The Great Choral Masterpieces," ♦Philips 454108, 12CD). The soloists (Augér, Murray, Lipovsek, Schreier himself, Scharinger) are generally fine, but the tempos are often (if not always) rushed and brutally choppy, with occasionally exaggerated dynamic inflections. Despite some rewarding moments, this is not at all a comfortable presentation of this great work. The Munich tradition of Richter was also paid homage in a 1992 Bavarian Radio performance led by **Schneidt;** the discipline of Richter's large choir remains strong, and the performance is intelligent, if unexceptional, though hampered by the incidentals of concert presentation (Calig 50929).

Speaking of traditions, the United States has its own in the Bethlehem Bach Festival, where the very first complete performance of the Mass in this country was given in 1900. The current revitalizer of the Festival, **Funfgeld,** has weighed in with intelligence, stylistic sensitivity, and podium control (♦Dorian 90253). The soloists, if not of high profile, are very able, and despite some ponderous elements, this is a thoroughly satisfying rendition for those who relish a more traditional and grand-scale approach.

No music lover who wants to know and absorb this work can ever be content with only one recording. In the MI category alone, you can find a rich variety of realizations, among which should be considered the grandeur of Klemperer; the traditionalism of Jochum, Rilling I, or Funfgeld, and the polished experimentalism of Shaw II or III.

Period style

The term here refers to more than just the use of period instruments and involves a spectrum of musicologically derived insights into performance practices that might bring us back to the sounds Bach himself conceived and heard. The post-WWII trends of "compromise" style (smaller choirs and more modest MI orchestras, with either or both harpsichord and organ) resulted in what might be called 1960s Baroque. As that tradition has continued, further PI experiments have led to a distinct line of approach, parallel to the ongoing "compromise" pattern, that has also yielded important recordings of this great work.

Harnoncourt took the first full step in that new direction in 1968, using a small choir of boys and men, with experienced soloists (Rotraud Hansmann, Watts, Equiluz, van Egmond); the interpretation was marred by examples of this conductor's quirks of tempo and agogics, but was a refreshing revelation (♦Teldec 95517). He returned to the work in 1986 with a somewhat less even solo group (Blasi, Ziegler, Jadwiga Rappe, Equiluz again, Holl) and a mixed-voice choir, for a somewhat smoother remake (♦Teldec 35716).

A more dramatic shakeup came from **Rifkin** in 1982—quite possibly the single most influential recording of Baroque music ever made

(♦Elektra/Nonesuch 79036). His examination of the set of parts surviving from a hoped-for 1733 performance of the "Kyrie" and "Gloria" convinced him that Bach expected his soloists also to be his only "chorus," one singer per part. This thesis set musicology on its head, and it continues to be debated, though by no means refuted. (Rifkin's ideas further challenged the traditional concept of Bach's "choral" scoring not only in this work but in much of his sacred music in general, as we have observed.) He backed his theory by recording the Mass in 1981–1982 with a working quintet (Nelson, Baird, Jeffrey Dooley, Frank Hoffmeister, Opalach) plus three assisting singers, with a small group of period instrumentalists (including only seven string players), in a powerfully musical realization that still stands as a landmark of the "minimalist" approach.

No one since has tried to duplicate Rifkin's Spartan approach exactly, but many recordings have been influenced by his example. His closest epigone, **Parrott,** is almost as minimal as Rifkin in his 1984 recording (♦EMI 47293). His lead soloists (including such early music specialists as Kirkby, Van Evera, Covey-Crump, and David Thomas) are excellent, and are joined by five other singers as the *ripieno* in the "choruses." Tempos are springy but speedy to a degree that may put off some listeners, but Parrott joins Rifkin in bringing us as close as possible to what may have been Bach's own sound world. Just a little further removed from Rifkin is his early collaborator and subsequent apostle, **Jeffrey Thomas.** His 1992 recording uses nine solo singers (including Baird and Nelson), who join a variously-sized vocal ensemble totaling 23 at fullest strength for the choruses, with an orchestra of 28 PI players (Koch 7194). The pacing is not exaggerated and there is much to enjoy, though there are some inconsistencies of quality, and the totality is not exceptional against the competition in its class.

One more stab at recreating the composer's performing style was ventured by **King,** who leads his PI chamber group with the Tölzer Boys' Choir and adult males of the King's Consort (Hyperion). The boys (23 strong) not only sing the choral soprano and alto parts but also supply the solo singers in those ranges, leaving the adult solo roles to Rolfe Johnson and George. This supposedly reproduces Bach's own use of boys in place of females in his sacred performances, and carries the logic of Harnoncourt I to an extreme. But the weakness (in both tone and technique) of the youthful voices, and their disparity in the alto/tenor duet, as well as the very wiry string playing, will limit the appeal of this recording for many listeners, even though King leads a performance of occasional vividness and telling inflection, but mostly of sober but hyper-cautious, even fragile, dignity.

Most PI recordings since Rifkin have forged a kind of "neocompromise" style, generally employing adult soloists, small mixed-voice choirs, and modest PI ensembles. This direction has been followed to date in some 13 recordings, at least two of which can be dismissed quickly. Using minimalist forces in the Parrott tradition, **Radu** gives a fast but indifferently conceived and limp, inconsistently rendered performance, despite the presence of Baird once more (Vox). **Brembeck**'s Bratislava production offers rigidly, relentlessly punched-out rhythms, mostly fast tempos, generally diffident soloists (save for a good contralto), and a scrappy chorus, though good (and effectively, if not officially, PI) chamber orchestra playing (1992: Naxos). Neither of them can be justified by their bargain price.

Anders Elby's 1990 Swedish recording is of marginal interest; using a good-sized (42) mixed chorus, inconsistent soloists (Groop and Howard Crook as stand-outs), and a PI orchestra, Elby swims against the current in some unusually slow pacings amid his more characteristic fast ones (Proprius). On a higher level of polish are two neocompromise recordings from England and one from the United States. **Christophers** expands his chamber group, the Sixteen, to 26 singers, with a PI orchestra of 28, plus veteran early-music soloists (Dubosc, Denley, Bowman, Ainsley, George), in a performance that displays this conductor's typical polish and refinement but is also cool and unsatisfying in its objectivity (1994: Collins).

Hickox's 1992 recording is likewise depersonalized; it skillfully balances chamber-sized forces and fast tempos with a certain expansiveness of sonority, and is blessed with another good early-music solo group including Argenta, Denley, and Varcoe (Chandos 0533/34). In many ways this is a well-rounded and reliable projection of the work, even powerful at times; but the conductor's expertise can also seem like objectivity devoid of personality or any memorable qualities (and the particularly piercing PI strings may put some off). Somewhat similar is **Pearlman**'s 1999 contribution, with Boston soloists, a choir of 28, and a PI orchestra of 31 (♦Telarc 80517). This is an unmannered performance of great polish and intelligence. It, too, has a certain detached quality, without striking interpretational qualities, but with a reliability that just barely slips it into the zone of serious consideration.

Individuality is not lacking elsewhere. It marred, to some degree, a 1985 recording with **Leonhardt** leading a Dutch choir, La Petite Bande, and a lineup of experienced soloists (Poulenard, Guilamette Laurens, Jacobs, Elwes, van Egmond, van der Kamp) in a restrained but rather flaccid performance, with refined but often fussy details (Harmonia Mundi). From Germany came two recordings of the mid-'90s that justify notice. **Jacobs** made a recording of his own in Berlin, with the RIAS Chamber Choir and the Akademie für Alte Musik, plus fine soloists including Fink, Prégardien, and Görne (♦Berlin 1063). The beautifully spun-out performance reflects his stylistic authority and noble artistry, despite a few flawed details. Another musician of great ability and stylistic flair is **Hermann Max,** whose Cologne recording is rich in insights (♦Capriccio 60033).

From a little farther south, in Lugano, Switzerland, comes a sleeper from Swiss Radio forces under **Fasolis** (♦Arts 47525). A very small chamber choir and PI orchestra are joined by a group of familiar soloists (Invernizzi, Dawson, Banditelli, Prégardien, Mertens). Despite a few rough choral spots, the performance is brisk and deft; Fasolis conceives the work rather in the Münchinger tradition, de-emphasizing grandeur, which may dissatisfy those who want that quality, but there are wonderfully fresh and imaginative touches throughout.

Back to Germany, though, for a still more enterprising version, curiously intended as the aural dimension of a mimed staging of the Mass. The audio dimension stands nicely on its own as led by **Thomas Hengelbrock** (♦Harmonia Mundi 77380). The theatrical connection is not irrelevant, because Hengelbrock infuses the music, especially the choral sections, with unusual dramatic intensity; the solo sections are de-emphasized, using competent if undistinctive voices drawn from the small Balthasar Neumann Choir, which is handsomely drilled, along with the fine Freiburg Baroque Orchestra. Not at all a mainstream or reliable standby recording, but a fascinating spin on the para-minimalist approach.

Two veteran early-music conductors have contributed responsible and thoroughly praiseworthy neo-Baroque PI recordings. One, a tidily paced 1989 concert performance under **Brüggen,** was released in Europe by Philips but apparently not circulated in the United States. The other was **Koopman**'s, with his Amsterdam Baroque forces and a splendidly skilled solo quartet (Schlick, Wessel, de Mey, Mertens), in a knowing, well rounded, and spirited but judiciously paced performance

(1994: ♦Erato 98478). It's a pity that neither of these two fine recordings seems to be currently available, for they deserve serious consideration.

Which leaves us, finally, with two more conductors who are specialists in this area. **Herreweghe** has recorded the Mass twice. His first (1988) had a crack solo roster (including Schlick, Brett, Crook, and Kooy), and the conductor's Ghent chamber choir and PI orchestra (Virgin 59517). He displayed superlative control over all the differing moods and scales of the work in an approach that subordinated the monumental to the introspective and gentle, even in the lively sections. His second venture (1996) used a larger and mostly new solo team (Johannette Zorner, Gens, Scholl, Prégardien, Kooy again, Hanno Müller Brachmann) and the same ensembles, as well as essentially the same interpretive approach, though if anything refined still further (♦Harmonia Mundi 901614/15). For those who want a thoughtful neo-Baroque projection, this is a beautiful example, but it's also cool and perhaps too objective for those who expect a certain grandeur in this music.

That deficiency is amply made up by the most durable of the neo-Baroque recordings, made in 1985 by **Gardiner** (♦DG Archiv 415514). This performance represents the quintessential neo-Baroque balancing act: Gardiner has traditionalist sympathies as a choral director, while his impulses simultaneously tend toward the energetic and incisive. Benefiting from (but also bypassing) Rifkin's example and following more that of Shaw II, he elected to adopt selectively the theory of contrasted concertino and *ripieno* in the choral movements, using a substantial mixed choir with a pool of 15 soloists (including Argenta, Dawson, Chance, and Varcoe), choosing among the singers for the solo movements. The singing and playing are outstanding, and the combination of big-scale sonority with an authentic spirit of detail preserves this recording as one of the strongest recommendations in the "period" category.

Gardiner's approach is perhaps the model, consciously or otherwise, for a performance by a Swedish chamber choir of 32 mixed voices with the Drottningholm Baroque Ensemble under **Ohrwall** (Swedish Society Discofil 1092/93). Aside from the familiar Esswood, the soloists are all local, and they and the ensemble are well drilled from long experience with the work. The trouble is that the spirit of crisp efficiency makes for rather fast and glib pacings, especially in choruses, and a sense of expertise shorn of any deep expressive or spiritual commitment.

From the foregoing it should be clear that there are "period" recordings of great diversity and richness to choose from. Certainly Rifkin, Parrott, Gardiner, and Herreweghe II are among the top contenders, but others should be kept in mind by the adventurous collector.

Lutheran Masses (BWV 233–36)

If the great B minor Mass represents Bach's transcendent vision of Christian worship, the so-called "Little" or "Lutheran" Masses reflect his contributions to more routine liturgical functions. They earn the designation of "Lutheran" because they consist solely of a "Kyrie" and "Gloria," which, together with a simplified "Sanctus," were the only segments of the Latin Mass Ordinary that were carried over into Lutheran liturgy as the *Missa.* There are four of these two-movement mini-Masses (in F, A, G minor, and G) and two accepted "Sanctus" settings (C and D, BWV 237–38), plus three others incorrectly attributed. Like the great B minor Mass, these "little" Masses are "parody" works, filled with Bach's recycling of music from other compositions (mostly cantatas), reminding us of the relentless pressures under which he had to turn out a steady flow of sacred music. It's easy to shrug off these shorter Latin liturgical works, but they are full of quite lovely music and represent an important dimension of Bach's sacred output.

A few individual appearances aside, these short Masses have generally been recorded as a set. Six cycles were issued in microgroove days, the earliest of them, under **Hans Grischkat,** combining the four Masses with four of the "Sanctus" settings (Renaissance). That is no longer current, nor are two other cycles (though either might resurface any time): an early venture by the young **Hickox** on two Argo LPs, and a 2LP set with small period-style forces under **Linde** (EMI). A 1972 Dresden cycle under **Martin Flämig** (with soloists Renate Krahmer, Burmeister, Schreier, Adam) has reappeared (Berlin 9130, 2CD). A 1974 cycle under **Corboz** was valuable for including the "Sanctus" settings, but everything was presented in a heavy and old-fashioned oratorio style (Erato 97236, 2CD).

Rilling made his first recording of the four masses in 1967 (Intercord 820.510/11). Where Flämig is large-scaled, outgoing, and sometimes almost blowzy, Rilling was more introspective and smoother, if with sometimes rough choral work. He has, however, rethought and rerecorded the four, now as part of his "Edition Bachakademie," in which they are augmented with a variant item, four "Sanctus" settings, and two other Latin liturgical oddments (Hänssler Vols. 71–72, 92.071/72). In these 1992–99 recordings, Rilling is more animated than the first time around, and his soloists are among the best (Ruth Holton; Ingeborg Danz; Prégardien; and Quasthoff, Michel Brodard, or Schöne); but his big-choir approach and expansive interpretation, with modern instruments, will either endear this set to the traditionalist as warmhearted or blight it as dated for the purist. Less troubled on that count is **Schreier**'s 1993 recording; he has some fine soloists (Bonney and Bär among them), and delivers brisk, lean, vigorous performances, sometimes rather cool and businesslike, but in a highly intelligent "compromise" style (♦Philips 438873, with Magnificat, 2CD; in the Schreier Bach sacred collection, 454108, 12CD).

The first PI recording since Linde's was **Herreweghe**'s in 1989–90 (♦Virgin 91118, with "Sanctus" in D, and 91213). Despite the period instrumentation and the use of a small, tightly controlled chamber choir of 18 mixed voices, his interpretation is full of highly expressive, even romanticized inflection that may compromise the spirit of authenticity for some. A countertenor (Lesne) is used in the alto solos, and the other vocalists (Mellon, Prégardien, Kooy) are reliable veterans. In all, for elegant and pungent performances of their type, there is a lot of lovely and thoughtful listening in these two CDs. The need for a more rigorous period-style performance of the cycle has, however, been met in spades by the Purcell Quartet, in a strict application of the Rifkin approach of only one performer per part (Chandos 0642 and 0653). There are only four singers (Argenta, Chance, Padmore, Harvey), with the four players of the quartet, plus pairs of oboes and horns. Everything is spirited and vivacious, in expert renditions, but the intimate scale underplays any liturgical feeling.

Just what these Lutheran Masses really mean in functional terms has been demonstrated by **Paul McCreesh** in his remarkable recreation of an "Epiphany Mass" as it might have been celebrated in Leipzig's Thomaskirche around 1740 (♦DG Archiv 457631, 2CD). With some shortcuts (notably the truncation of the long sermons the Lutheran congregations loved), he assembles on Bach's own guidelines a long festive Mass in Lutheran style, with congregational participation in the chorales but with Bach's music as the core—not only *Missa brevis* 1 in F, but also the "Sanctus" in D, interwoven with two cantatas fit for the occasion (BWV 65, 180)—all wonderfully performed in period style with soloists Ann Monoyios, Angus Davidson, Charles Daniels, and Peter Harvey. It's one of the few recordings ever made that gives some sense of the full liturgical context in which Bach intended his sacred music to be placed. A strongly recommended demonstration.

Magnificat (BWV 243)

Most music lovers are probably unaware that this popular work is really two pieces, with essentially the same music in two distinct versions. It was originally composed for a Leipzig Christmas celebration in 1723, set in the key of E-flat, and included four short interpolated texts (two in German, two in Latin) that were interspersed among the *Magnificat*'s own Latin verses. About a decade later, for a different liturgical use (perhaps the Feast of the Visitation), Bach recast the work in D, altering some instrumental details, and above all eliminating the Christmas interpolations. Early editorial policies established the later, D major version as "definitive" (BWV 243), and it has become the standard for most performances and recordings over the years.

Original version

Marginalized as if a mere preliminary experiment (BWV 243a), the E-flat version has nevertheless teased sensibilities over the years and has achieved a recording history of its own, if a twisted one. As early as 1966, two conductors hit on the idea of using the D major version but reintegrating the four interpolations, transposed down. Unfortunately, despite an apparently able solo team (including Donath, Finnilä, Schreier, and McDaniel), **Gönnenwein** produced a performance too ponderous, sluggish, and turgid to serve any purpose; this recording has little to justify it (Bayer). On the other hand, the young **Rilling** displayed far more vigor in the same D-major-plus-interpolations approach in a Stuttgart recording (with soloists including Equiluz and Erich Wenk) that reappeared as part of a *Magnificat* collection (Vox 5095, 2CD).

Continuing his championship of this approach, **Rilling** re-recorded it in 1979 (Sony 48280, with Malgoire's Vivaldi *Beatus vir* and *Gloria*). The pacing is intelligently middle of the road, with a tidy warmth everywhere, and (save for some rough tenor work from Adalbert Kraus) outstanding soloists (Augér, Murray, Watts, Huttenlocher, Schöne). While going on to do the standard D major version (discussed later), Rilling has also made yet a third recording of the original, but this time in its full E-flat form, in a vigorous and somewhat grandly scaled performance, unfortunately relegated to an ungenerous 2CD set (Hänssler "Bachakademie" series Vol. 140, 92.140, with variant sections from the Mass and four 1998 cantatas). At least one other stab at the D-major-plus-interpolations conflation was made in 1976 by **Paul Steinmetz** (Unicorn).

The first recording of the original E-flat version fully on its own terms was **Preston**'s (1978: Oiseau-Lyre). Using a team of early-music specialists (Nelson, Kirkby, Watkinson, Elliott, David Thomas), an Oxford cathedral choir of boys and men, and a PI orchestra, recorded in an aptly churchly ambience, Preston offered a generously paced but lucid and highly convincing case for the neglected score, definitely worth seeking out (♦Oiseau-Lyre 443199, with Kuhnau and Vivaldi Motets).

Preston was followed in 1991 by **Hermann Max,** who led a substellar cast of local soloists but a crack chamber choir and PI ensemble in a more robust and bubbly performance. This was released in a fascinating package that joined not only with other Bach pieces (the two authentic "Sanctus" settings, BWV 2137–38) but also with three *Magnificat* settings by other composers (Caldara, Kuhnau-Schelle, and Anonymous [Kuhnau again?]) to provide context for Bach's achievement—a set hard to find but worth searching out (♦EMI 754426, 2CD). (It should be noted that Suzuki has brought together the Kuhnau setting and one by Zelenka with the D major version, to parallel effect, considered below.)

The original E-flat version won its latest champion in **Pickett,** who recorded a partial reconstitution of music Bach performed on Christmas Day 1724, adding Cantata 63 and "Sanctus" in D, BWV 238 (1995:

◆Oiseau-Lyre 452920). With a PI group, he used five experienced early-music singers joined by 10 others to form a five-part minichoir, three singers per part, of about Bach's own scale, and superbly blended. The pacing is early-music-brisk, full of infectious energy and insight in interpretive details. If not the only recording to own, those who love this work will find it given here a musicological and artistic recreation too important to be missed.

Standard version, nonperiod style

Entering the LP catalogue by 1950, the D major *Magnificat* has never lacked for recordings. **Prohaska**'s 1957 recording is the earliest survivor, old-fashioned in performance style but still an honest document of past practices in big-hearted Viennese fashion (Vanguard 2010, with BWV 50, 70).

The work has not attracted many of the big-name conductors who have been drawn to the larger sacred works. Notable among the rare exemplars was **Karajan**: Despite a respectable solo line-up (Tomowa-Sintow, Baltsa, Schreier, Luxon), his approach is slick, steely, coldly controlled, and orchestra-heavy, the sort of performance that is taken for penance rather than pleasure (DG). You can sadly ignore **Scherchen** too; memories of his often-stimulating Bach are done no good service by a scrappy 1963 Italian radio broadcast performance (Memories).

The "star" conductor still in the ring is **Bernstein,** from his adventurous early days with the New York Philharmonic. His 1959 recording should have everything going against it. He treats the choral movements like grandiose Elgar or Brahms, with unfortunately sloppy singing from his choir. But, if sometimes willful, the solo movements are etched with often imaginative touches. His team looks like a strange mixture on paper (Lee Venora, Tourel, Oberlin, Bressler, Norman Farrow), but they do their individual tasks admirably, and the whole thing comes off as a surprisingly interesting performance—not particularly Bachian and not really Baroque, but vintage Lenny (Sony).

Also admissible to "star" podium status is **Barenboim,** whose 1968 recording has returned in a generous but odd reissue package (EMI 764634, with Fauré's *Requiem* and *Pavane*). Even more than Bernstein, Barenboim gives us a "sock-it-to-'em" *Magnificat,* with muscular big-choir choruses (but set far back) and dramatically charged solo verses. Baker's singing alone is worth the price of admission, and she is well matched by her colleagues (Popp, Anne Pashley, Tear, Hemsley). If you like a high-power, concert-hall approach instead of churchly Bach, this is a good mid-priced choice, though the recorded sound has not worn well.

For alternatives, there are two other maestros to consider. **Marriner**'s 1990 recording offers a distressingly mixed bag: his headlong approach to some of the choral sections, intended to convey exuberance, merely results in rushed desperation (EMI 754283, with Vivaldi's *Gloria*). There is some fine singing from Murray, Heilmann, and Hynninen, but Hendricks's prissy coolness is off-putting. **Shaw**'s recording is far more balanced (◆1988: Telarc 80194, with Vivaldi's *Gloria*). Though among the shorter-running performances on disc, he never displays any sense of haste; tempos are always judicious, and there's a thoroughly musical flow from one movement to the next. His moderate-sized choir is both accurate and warm-toned, and while only the young Upshaw is a familiar name among the soloists, they all perform with skill and style. Beautifully recorded, this is a civilized and elegant realization that's bound to give lasting satisfaction.

Hovering between the "name" maestros and the *Kapellmeisters* are several conductors who have much to offer in this literature. **Corboz**'s sensible recording may yet return as a serious contender (Erato).

Münchinger is certainly to be reckoned with; his classic 1968 recording is a leisurely and comfortably paced performance, with Ameling and Watts outstanding in the handsome solo work (◆London 433175, with BWV 67, 130 or in the 10CD set of Münchinger's Bach "Sacred Masterpieces," 455783). **Richter** made his claim on the work in 1961. His big-choir, oratorio-style treatment had its following in its day, and of his highly respected soloists (Stader, Haefliger, Fischer-Dieskau) only Töpper is below par vocally. But there is a stiff and smug quality about the total effect that doesn't make for lasting satisfaction, and despite some cleaning up in the CD reissue, the sound is dull and dated.

Richter's career was an offshoot from the Leipzig/Dresden axis that is represented sequentially in this work by three contrasting recordings in a kind of tenor-to-conductor chain. We lack Ramin's thoughts, but we do have those of his successor, **Kurt Thomas.** His 1959 Leipzig recording is an earnest venture: he has the benefit of some sturdy solo work (Giebel, Höffgen, Adam), but the choirboys who sing the soprano and alto parts sound raucous and out of control, while the sonics are harsh (Berlin). Thomas's fine tenor was **Rotzsch,** who, as St. Thomas Cantor in his turn, led his own Leipzig recording in 1978 (Berlin 9164, with BWV 10, setting a German translation of the *Magnificat* for a nice pairing). Rotzsch had the boys-and-men choir in far better control, and though his pacing is stately, it's sensible and steadily moving, in a performance that stands up quite credibly. His female soloists (Shirai, Soffel) are highly able.

His tenor, **Schreier,** was to go on to record this work himself. In his case, it was a Berlin venture (1993), with the crack RIAS Chamber Choir and Bonney a wonderful standout among the soloists. In a break with his background, Schreier led a brisk and light interpretation (one of the fastest on disc), sometimes a little clipped but always deft; this is a moderately scaled MI performance (in his set of the "Little" Masses, ◆Philips 438823, 2CD, and in his 12CD set of Bach "Great Choral Masterpieces").

Ledger also used boy choristers; he recorded the work with the King's College Choir of Cambridge and the St. Martin Academy in 1976 (London 421148, with CPE Bach's *Magnificat*). The solo verses are delivered by a particularly well-balanced solo team (Palmer, Watts again, Tear, Stephen Roberts); the choruses are festive without being forced, bearing the special vocal color of the boy trebles, of course. It's back to standard forces, though, in **Rilling**'s 1995 recording: a robust, vigorous performance, with splendid solo work (◆Hänssler 98.921, with BWV 10; "Bachakademie" Edition, Vol. 73, 92.073, with short sacred pieces). There is perhaps just a bit too much rhythm-punching in the mixed-voice choral work, but those who want a full-blooded but traditional rendition will find it very satisfying.

Three other releases fit the "quality-provincial" and "near-sleeper" category. **Ohrwall**'s 1974 Stockholm recording offers a good chamber choir and orchestra, a little too distantly miked, in a somewhat restrained but careful and generally enjoyable rendition, reissued in a generous package; only the young Hagegård will be recognized among the soloists (Discofil 1065, with BWV 106, 140). **Moyse**'s 1990 release is a tad less generous, if a notch up in quality, led with vigor and intelligence (◆MHS 512691, with BWV 140). The 33-mixed-voice choir makes up in exuberance what it may lack in polish, while the soloists (Schellenberg, Mary Westbrook-Geha, John Humphrey, Sylvan), if light-voiced, sing with earnest skill; the sound is close and unusually clear, if bone-dry to an almost unpleasantly dead degree. Finally, there is the low-priced entry in which **Nicholas Ward** leads a chamber choir and orchestra in a spirited and sensible performance, with soprano Anna Crookes and tenor Timothy Robinson standing out among otherwise rather lackluster soloists;

good enough as a bargain choice, but hardly a serious competitor (Naxos 550763, with BWV 82, or 554056, with Vivaldi's *Gloria*).

Standard version, period style

The first attempt at recreating "authentic" performance style for this work was timid, made around 1966 and involving the Tölz Boys' Choir and the **Collegium Aureum** (Harmonia Mundi 054727 7411, with CPE Bach's *Magnificat*). No conductor was identified, and it's difficult to tell who (if anyone) was really in charge; the period winds sound rough and not fully assimilated, and the strings are not very different. Bach's own practice of using not only boy choristers but also soloists (two sopranos and alto) is observed; while the two male soloists (Altmeyer, Nimsgern) are just fine, the three youngsters inevitably sound overmatched, and their juvenile dimensions may disqualify it for many modern listeners.

The true launching of the PI *Magnificat* came with **Gardiner**'s 1983 recording, still triumphantly available (♦Philips 411458, with BWV 51). This is a characteristically brisk reading, one of the fastest, and you may find the crisp and propulsive choral sections either driven or ebullient, depending upon your aesthetics. And even if you have reservations about a countertenor (Charles Brett) in the alto solos, the others (Argenta, Kwella, Rolfe-Johnson, David Thomas) are alert and enthusiastically caught up in Gardiner's sweeping approach. A benchmark in its category, this recording set—and still maintains—the standard for PI versions.

The same year that brought Gardiner's powerful salvo also gave us a distinctly contrasting bombshell. Having already made his case for minimal performing forces in the B minor Mass, **Rifkin** turned to the *Magnificat* with what he has argued would have been Bach's own working resources: five singers (who take the solo verses and constitute the five-voice "chorus"), with a small PI chamber ensemble of 17 players, one per part save for two each of violins I and II (♦Pro Arte 3185, with Melchior Hoffmann's *Deutsches Magnificat* as scant filler). The pacing is generally moderate and only rarely unusual, with devoted if somewhat light-voiced singing by the five vocalists (Jane Bryden, Baird, Gall, Hoffmeister, Opalach), in a thoughtful and intimate performance.

Rifkin's recording was followed in 1989 by **Parrott**, his disciple in this approach (♦EMI 749959, with BWV 11 and 50, or 754926, with Handel's *Dixit Dominus*). Parrott relented somewhat by using a slightly larger orchestra of 22 PI players, but again only five singers. They are a cast of early-music specialists (Van Evera, Tubb, Caroline Trevor, Crook, Simon Grant) who have more robust character as individuals and as a group than Rifkin's quintet, while Parrott leads with more propulsive and even aggressive energy, in the process apparently winning the prize for the shortest-running *Magnificat* on records.

Neither of these is likely to be your only choice for this tantalizing work, but you should know either or both as remarkable experiments in rethinking performance practice, whether or not you agree with the idea. The Rifkin Doctrine denies the whole quality of contrast between soloists and choir that has become ingrained in modern expectations, and it's not an approach that has been emulated any further since Parrott, subsequent recordings tending to follow Gardiner's lead.

This was the case with two more British conductors. **Hickox** used a mixed choir of 18, a PI orchestra of 25, and a very well balanced solo group: Kirkby, Tessa Bonner, Chance, Ainsley, and Varcoe (1990: ♦Chandos 0518, with Vivaldi's *Introduzione* and *Gloria*). The solo singing is light and deft, the choral work is precise but muscular; and the lively spirit makes for a less frenetic alternative to Gardiner. **Christophers** was likewise deft and propulsive but even more elegant and precise using parallel numbers, his Sixteen (actually 18) voices and PI orchestra of

27, including a delicate theorbo in the continuo (1991: Collins 13202, with Vivaldi's *Gloria* and Caldara's *Stabat Mater*). Of the soloists, the lower voices (Alison Browner, Partridge, George) are stronger than the upper (Lynda Russell, Gillian Fisher). There is a smooth flow to the performance, but the end product seems just a bit cold and bloodless.

Three contrasting successors came from the Low Countries. **Kuijken**'s version in the late 1980s used a Dutch choir of 20 and the comparably sized PI group, La Petite Bande, with veteran soloists (Greta de Reyghere, Jacobs, Prégardien, Lika), establishing a middle ground between the extremes of Gardiner or Rifkin/Parrott with judicious pacing and a smoothly artistic rendition (Virgin 90779, with BWV 21). **Herreweghe** led his crack choir of 21 voices and PI orchestra of 25 in what is, even beyond Kuijken, the PI version that even PI-haters could love (1990: ♦Harmonia Mundi 901326, with BWV 80). His soloists (Schlick, Mellon, Lesne, Crook, Kooy) are expert, fluent, and highly sensitive; the orchestral colors are carefully under control, and the choir sings with utmost suavity. Herreweghe has become the "romantic" among PI conductors, and this is a beautifully conceived and handsomely presented performance of very broad appeal.

Koopman's 1998 recording is much more in the Gardiner tradition, with mixed chorus and PI orchestra of 24 each (Erato 23416, with *Easter Oratorio*). He displays his delight in bubbly and boisterous energy throughout, especially in the choruses, which approach Gardiner's in their zippy drive, though they are recorded a little distantly. Again the lower-voice soloists (Bartosz, Türk, the particularly mellow Mertens) outclass the upper ones (Larsson, von Magnus). An enjoyable performance in many ways, it still falls behind Gardiner's in its similarity of approach.

Much the same might be said of **Suzuki** and his Japanese forces, with Türk again as visiting tenor (♦BIS 1011). Everything is neat and tidy, in a lively and thoroughly musical conception, with fresh-voiced solo work. But if it might be overshadowed by its more stellar competition, this release has special value for its rare fillers, parallel *Magnificat* settings of the time: a long and elaborate one by Kuhnau and two shorter but livelier ones by Zelenka—a package that puts Bach's dazzling achievement into an illuminating period context.

Two more recordings fit into the "quality provincial" category. Working with local soloists, the good-sized Swiss Radio Chorus, and a quite decent PI orchestra, **Fasolis** produces another of his interesting productions in a 1994 concert recording (Arts 47374, with BWV 21 and Motet). There are some odd touches: not only does he treat the "Suscepit Israel" terzetto as a piece for choral voices (a point that continues to divide conductors), but he also uses choir sections instead of soloists for the "Et misericordia" duet. But there are imaginative touches, too, while his soloists sing consistently well and his choir is quite lucid. They respond well to his often brisk, sometimes rushed tempos. Gardiner and Hickox are better at this kind of thing, but Fasolis's release is not to be shrugged off. **J. Reilly Lewis** gives a "merely excellent" performance, with soloists, a chorus of 26, and a like-numbered PI orchestra, spaciously recorded in concert performance (1998: Newport 60155, with C.P.E. Bach's *Magnificat*). Everything is very intelligently done in what must have been a very enjoyable concert but must yield to more accomplished competition.

In all three recording categories for this work, you will want to keep in mind that the *Magnificat* nowadays will come paired with other music, and the diverse options will be a factor in your choice.

St. Matthew Passion (BWV 244)

More diffuse and multifaceted than the B minor Mass, the *Passion According to St. Matthew* is plausibly the Mt. Everest of Bach's works. It has been a challenge to a spectrum of conductors from podium egoists to "modest maestros" and from serious Bach specialists to nonentities. Despite the effort, expense, and resources called for, it has achieved well over 50 recordings over the years, ranging from the monumental to the ephemeral. (Note: All recordings considered are 3CD unless otherwise indicated.)

Nonperiod style

Many of the earliest recordings were big-name ventures and offer documentation of performing mentalities that would be unacceptable today. The most infamous example of willful, hyper-romantic bloat is **Mengelberg**'s notorious 1939 version: heavily cut and endlessly idiosyncratic, though with undeniably beautiful singing by Jo Vincent (Philips; Gramophono). How much Mengelberg's influence (e.g., broad tempos, highlighted details) persisted in Holland may be observed in **Anthon van der Horst**'s 1957 performance; at least he reined in the excesses and benefitted from new musicological knowledge. This, too, has been revived, another landmark in the evolution of performing concepts (Fidelio 1883/85).

Postwar reverberations are a particular feature of the first uncut recording (in German) to appear, which remains one of the classic renditions. Taped in concert in 1949 in a Berlin still barely rising from the wreckage of WWII, its conductor, **Fritz Lehmann,** was a noble survivor, and in Helmut Krebs he had one of the great Evangelists. Also in his cast, as a radiant Jesus, was a young unknown named Dietrich Fischer-Dieskau, in his very first recording, the one in which some of us hoary collectors first heard this remarkable singer. Briefly issued on LP by Vox, this remarkable document is sure to be revived sooner or later.

We return to eccentricity, if of a kind less easily dismissed, with **Scherchen**'s 1953 recording, now revived as part of a series devoted to the conductor (Universal/Millennium 80470; mono). His pacing is mostly brisk (save for the chorales, which are exceptionally slow) and details are sometimes exaggerated. Both choral and solo singing are variable, but the singers include the distinctive Cuenod as Evangelist and Rehfuss as a warmly human Jesus. In all, if a highly personal conception, it's powerful and dramatic. Perhaps the height (or depth) of idiosyncratic performance, however, is **Furtwängler**'s cruelly abridged yet impossibly distended 1954 concert recording, conceived in utter sincerity just months before his death. At least it had the benefit of some lovely soprano work by Grümmer and an expressive Evangelist in Dermota, with Fischer-Dieskau in his second recorded Jesus (EMI 65509, 2CD; Frequenz 051005). It's essentially a trophy for Furtwängler fans.

Furtwängler's awesomely willful excesses appear all the more bizarre when set against **Klemperer**'s magnificent 1961 recording, still kept gloriously alive (♦EMI 763058). In his case, willful podium personality meshed with artistic instincts to produce something transcendent. The pacing is leisurely, but it works logically to generate an intense and genuinely religious experience. It's brought off with superbly disciplined forces, and by great singers at their peak, led by the eloquent Evangelist of Pears and the glowing Jesus of Fischer-Dieskau in his third recording, backed by Schwarzkopf, Ludwig, Gedda, and Berry as aria soloists, plus luxurious cameos from Harper, Watts, and Geraint Evans. Klemperer distilled the essence of the "romantic" approach at its best into a performance that neutralizes any musicological reservations and invites the listener to share in its eternal vision. No Bach collector, from archreactionary to unforgiving purist, should overlook it.

Klemperer's monumentality contrasts with the more mercurial personality of **Karajan.** In a Vienna concert recording early in his postwar career, uneven sound hampers a coherently broad and grandly conceived interpretation, with fine soloists (Evangelist Walter Ludwig, Schoeffler as Jesus, Seefried, and Edelmann) led by Ferrier, whose presence alone gives the recording enduring value (1950: Verona 27070; Arkadia 211). Characteristically, Karajan's youthful artistic balance had been transformed into his mature egomania when he made his 1973 commercial recording in Berlin (DG 419789). He has outstanding work from Schreier as Evangelist and Fischer-Dieskau in his fourth Jesus, with sometimes uneven work from Janowitz, Ludwig, Laubenthal, and Berry. The performance is powerful in its way, but heavily controlled and self-indulgent.

Two other big-name conductors have weighed in with variable "big-Bach" results. **Jochum**'s old-fashioned but always honest and musically confident version is sturdy and vivacious, much less mannered than Karajan's, with some impressive solo work (Haefliger as Evangelist, Berry as Jesus, with Giebel, Höffgen, and Franz Crass among others)—a recording that may yet join his other major Bach ventures in reissue (Philips). Another frankly 19th-century conception was triumphantly achieved by **Solti**—in striking contrast to his disappointing B minor Mass—with his crackerjack Chicago forces and a splendid crew of soloists (Blochwitz, Evangelist; Bär, Jesus; Te Kanawa, von Otter, Rolfe Johnson, Krause), the only recording in its class that comes close to competing with Klemperer's (1987: ♦London 421177).

Turning to less glamorized maestros, we have some glimpses from the Leipzig-Dresden-Munich axis. From the Leipzig champion of Baroque-revival interpretation, **Ramin,** we have only a harshly abridged recording (with Lemnitz and Hüsch among the soloists, and with the same Evangelist Mengelberg had used, Karl Erb). This recording was made as an act of faith during the war years (1941), and it has been revived as a poignant document (Calig 50859, 2CD). From Dresden came a recording by **Mauersberger** made the year before he died and conducted jointly with his brother, Erhard, then director at Bach's Thomaskirche in Leipzig (1970: ♦Berlin 2144). The Mauersbergers used a choir of boys and men, with an excellent cast of local soloists, including the young Schreier in his first recorded Evangelist. Judiciously paced, carefully performed and recorded (with results far superior to Mauersberger's version of the Mass), this performance captures handsomely the best of the postwar Leipzig tradition and is important for anyone studying the evolution of performance practice for the work.

The conductor who most embodied the fusion of the Leipzig Baroque-revival style with romantic sentiment was **Richter;** he recorded the work three times. His middle version was from a concert performance in Japan in 1969, with many of his stalwart colleagues, but it's a less than memorable version that never circulated widely. The third (1979), made not long before his early death, suggests a weary overextension of energy (DG Archiv 427704). Still, it offers Schreier's best Evangelist, with the fifth and last of Fischer-Dieskau's deliveries of Jesus, plus some lovely solo work from Baker, with Mathis and Salminen among the others. It's Richter's first recording (1958), however, that survives as his most authoritative word, and it's still one to be reckoned with (♦DG Archiv 439338). What once seemed a noble "authenticity" now sounds a little dated in his very weighty and serious approach, but there is also a thoughtful nobility. Richter has the advantage of Haefliger in his first and best Evangelist; Fischer-Dieskau here takes the arias, and Seefried is outstanding among other soloists (though Töpper is a drawback).

Schreier's recording, made in Dresden in 1984, is a disappointing epilogue to this line of tradition (Philips, in his omnibus set). Though he fields an attractive team of soloists for the arias (Popp, Lipovsek, Büchner, Holl), he insists on taking the Evangelist's part himself, showing strain, while his Jesus, Adam, is over the hill. Above all, Schreier's capacities as a conductor seem unequal to this work's scale, resulting mostly in a lot of fussy miscalculations.

Gönnenwein's 1968 recording is even farther down the dead end of Kapellmeister Lane. The aria soloists are a talented bunch, with Hamari pulling forward Zylis-Gara, Gedda, and Prey; but while Franz Crass is a dignified Jesus, Altmeyer is a stiff and prissy Evangelist, and the choral work is sonorous but characterless (MHS). The elements never fuse into a meaningful entity. **Somary** is a notch up (1977: Vanguard). The solo work is highly satisfying: Haefliger is still an eloquent Evangelist and McDaniel an earnest Jesus, while Ameling, Finnilä, Seth McCoy, and Luxon each bring distinctive vocal personalities to the arias. But the choral work is a little ragged, and Somary's conception, if balanced and reverent, is rather unimaginative and even plodding at times.

A more worthy reissue is a Vienna recording by the Danish conductor **Wöldike,** one of the great specialists in Baroque choral music (1959: ◆Vanguard 85). With somewhat uneven and diverse personnel (the aria soloists are Stich-Randall, Rössl-Majdan, Waldemar Kmentt, and Berry), the performance has great warmth, feeling, and all the stylistic intelligence of its time—hardly a first choice, but a nice old friend.

Three highly successful specialists in the Bach literature have had their say. Never to be overlooked is **Münchinger's** gorgeously sung if broadly paced and somewhat stiffly led 1965 recording (◆London 455783, in his "Sacred Masterworks" set, 10CD). Pears repeats his distinctive Evangelist, and Prey is a heart-melting Jesus; Ameling and the still-lamented Wunderlich are standouts among the other excellent soloists (Höffgen, Krause); the all-male chorus, with boys in the upper parts, has a distinctive bite. As with other Münchinger recordings in this big box, this one should be restored to individual availability.

In 1982 **Corboz** presented a propulsive and direct conception of the work, aided by some distinguished soloists: Equiluz is one of the great Evangelists, and the aria singers (including Marshall, Watkinson, Rolfe Johnson) are outstanding, with Huttenlocher wonderful as well in some small dramatic parts (◆Erato 45375). In contrast to "traditional" performances, this is lively and briskly forward-moving, without affectations, representing a strong alternative to slower, more stately renditions.

Somewhere between Corboz and the Richter tradition is **Rilling,** who recorded the work twice. In his first, Rilling keeps things moving steadily, with a strong dramatic feeling (1978: Sony 79403). Adalbert Kraus is a reliable Evangelist; Nimsgern is a manly Jesus; the aria soloists (Augér, Hamari, Baldin, Huttenlocher again) are of highest quality; and even some of the short dramatic roles are taken by singers of later repute (Murray, David Thomas). Rilling re-recorded the work in 1994 with an even greater commitment to drama (◆Hänssler 98.925; "Bachakademie" series Vol. 74, 92.074). His Evangelist and aria tenor, the very promising Michael Schade, is deliberate but intense, while Görne is a Jesus somewhere between Fischer-Dieskau and Wotan. The aria soloists (Oelze, Ingeborg Danz, Quasthoff) are vocally refined, but Rilling turns more to his choir for intensity, whipping them up to frenzy in the crowd passages and driving them to emphatic inflections in the framing choruses. For those who want emotional, even theatrical expression within a "modern" compromise approach, instead of romantic grandeur in the Klemperer/Solti style, Rilling II is undoubtedly a powerful prospect. Still, Rilling I seems to me somewhat more successful as a recording to live with.

Two maestros of some repute have committed badly miscalculated recordings that deserve cautionary notice. Usually an intelligent exponent of 18th-century music, **Leppard's** broadcast for North German Radio is full of inappropriate stylistic excesses and miscalculations; achieving only limited LP circulation, this version never made it to CD (EMI). **Ozawa's** concert performance in Tokyo, despite excellent soloists (Ainsley as Evangelist, Quasthoff as Jesus, Oelze and Stutzmann among others), reveals a conductor with no sense of the work's style (Philips).

This leaves us with two "sleeper" versions from little-known sources. Taped at a 1997 concert in Utrecht is a lithe and well-planned performance under **Jos van Veldhoven,** with small-scale Dutch choral and orchestral forces (Channel 11397). Among the soloists, the best-known are Türk as a sturdy Evangelist, Scholl as a countertenor exponent of the alto arias, and Kooy in bass functions. This is a fresh and unmannered presentation that was worth release. For the budget-conscious, there is **Géza Oberfrank's** 1993 recording with Hungarian forces, for the price an indisputable bargain (Naxos 550832). József Mukk is a very able and straightforward Evangelist, and the rest of the solo team is composed of consistently capable young singers. Oberfrank's leadership is sometimes a bit stolid, but this is, in general, a reliable and honest performance, perhaps just making the "merely excellent" category by absolute standards and without stellar associations.

So rich and intricate a work can never have a "best" recording. Given the wide range of MI recordings alone, you should consider the spectrum running from the romanticism of Klemperer or Solti through the more dramatic Rilling II, the durable richness of Richter I, the special Leipzig/Dresden spirit of Mauersberger, to the deftness of Corboz.

Finally, we must note the marginal subcategory of English-language recordings, clearly directed at the Anglo-American audience. The precedent was set in 1937, in the first uncut recording of the work ever made, under **Koussevitzky**—a Good Friday concert performance captured in a 27-disc 78 rpm set by RCA Victor: stylistically chaotic and heavily tinkered with, but reflecting the conductor's very individual musicality and very sincere dedication to Bach's music, this relic has been revived as both an artistic and a historical curiosity (Rockport 5012/14, 3CD). His example was followed in another concert performance, a wartime event in 1943 under **Bruno Walter** (AS 406; Minerva A20; Phonographie 5031/32, 2CD). Only Part I survives, somewhat cut, in a heavily late-romantic style, if delivered with genuine musicality (soloists include Nadine Connor, Mack Harrell, and Herbert Janssen) and in still quite listenable sound.

Three other essentially complete English-language versions have their own curiosity value. The first full-length (if slightly cut) recording to achieve LP circulation was made in 1947–48 in London under **Reginald Jacques.** To today's ears it has a stiff, timid, and dry quality, in a diffident and outdated style, but it included some respected concert singers of its time (Elsie Suddaby, Eric Greene) and it documents the earnest British oratorio-style approach to Bach a half century ago. Its preservation is thanks to the participation of the young Ferrier (Dutton 2005, with Pergolesi's *Stabat Mater*).

A heavily abridged recording made by **Ernest MacMillan** in Toronto in the early 1950s for RCA's Canadian Beaver label is more consistent but even more bland; the big-Bach chorus and orchestra are totally old-fashioned, and among the soloists only Lois Marshall achieves much distinction. A even stranger curiosity is a festival recording conducted by no less than **Vaughan Williams,** made in 1958 during the last months of his life. Slightly cut and laced with numerous textual revisions (plus piano continuo!), carried out by routine ensembles and mostly undistinguished soloists (including Greene again), the heavily romanticized and wildly idiosyncratic performance has interest simply for conveying Vaughan Williams's impassioned commitment to the work. Of limited LP circulation, this recording has not yet achieved the CD revival that the conductor's reputation might justify.

Two more recent and more viable English-language approaches are available. Perhaps spurred by recollection of his participation while a Harvard student in Koussevitzky's 1932 performance, **Bernstein** tried his hand at his own version in 1962. Using a drastically abridged score, he chose an ill-assorted cast of singers: David Lloyd and William Wilderman are quite out of their element as Evangelist and Jesus, while only Betty Allen and Charles Bressler rise to any distinction among the others, and the choral work is diffident. The interpretation is hyperdramatic and supercharged, with a lot of highly personal spirit; yet for all its misdirections, it's actually a coherently conceived interpretation of its kind, very meticulously directed. It is, in sum, not particularly idiomatic Bach, but certainly vintage Lenny, and understandably directed toward Bernstein fans (Sony 60727, 2CD, with Bernstein analysis).

The only other upholder of the English-language approach is **Willcocks,** in a latter-day British traditionalist approach, with choral boys as well as Tear and Shirley-Quirk as experienced Evangelist and Jesus, and fine aria soloists including Lott and Alfreda Hodgson (ASV 324).

Period style

This category is led by a recording that might seem to turn "authenticity" on its head: a recreation of Mendelssohn's "revision" of the work—if not that heard in the historic performance of 1829 credited with launching the 19th-century Bach Revival, at least that used in a revival performed on Palm Sunday 1841 in Bach's own Thomaskirche in Leipzig. The score and parts that survive from that event have been used with meticulous care by PI specialist **Spering** to recreate the same text with parallel forces (♦Opus 11130-72/73, 2CD). Mendelssohn cut the work heavily (including two thirds of the arias), reducing it by about a third while also retouching the instrumentation. Spering also recreated Mendelssohn's relatively brisk tempos—surprisingly "unromantic" but apparently accurate. Jochens is an excellent Evangelist, with a capable cast of soloists (however nonstellar), a chorus of nearly 60, and an orchestra of instruments of that day. This recording is a unique document, allowing an appreciation of the early aesthetics of the Bach Revival before it was overlain by a century of weightier religiosity that became the "romantic" ideal of this great work.

The efforts to liberate it from the romantic overlay have gone through several phases (including the Leipzig-Dresden-Munich movements), culminating generally in the application of PI approaches, but involving much restudy of Bach's own documented performances—a "primitive" original in 1727, a "definitive" version in 1736, and a revival in 1740–41. The 1736 performance materials survive, and (paralleling his sensational revisionist thinking about the B minor Mass) **Rifkin**'s study led him to the conclusion that Bach used very limited forces, including no more than 12 singers, eight of whom—one per part—constituted the two "choruses." Rifkin tested his thesis in a remarkable concert performance at the University of North Carolina in 1985, but, unlike his version of the Mass, this conception of the work never made it to commercial release, nor has anyone else attempted to duplicate his undertaking, so this "extreme" approach to minimalist "authenticity" has not yet been offered on disc.

Musicological progress has influenced conductors who, while not seeking period-style "authenticity," have not lacked for historical sensitivity. The full application of musicological perspectives to "period" style has been represented in at least nine recordings, most of them still available.

The landmark venture was **Harnoncourt**'s 1970 recording, a climactic successor to his rethinkings of the *St. John Passion* (1965) and the B minor Mass (1968) (♦Teldec 42509; Bach 2000 Vol. 6, 25711, 14CD). The first PI recording, this was also the first to follow strictly and consistently Bach's stipulated division of his forces into two distinct and opposed bodies. Equiluz, sadly undervalued in reputation, is one of the most eloquent Evangelists on discs, and Ridderbusch is a dark-hued Jesus; Esswood and Bowman share the alto arias, while Nigel Rogers and van Egmond contribute handsome solo work. But boy sopranos are used, not only in the choirs but also in solo parts—more or less as Bach would have done—and Harnoncourt leads a fast and powerful performance, if sometimes a little mannered. This is aggressive "authenticity" and not to everyone's all-the-time taste, but it's a PI classic.

Harnoncourt turned to the work a second time, in a 1985 concert recording in Amsterdam, but by then he was using mixed adult voices, soloists uneven and not always idiomatic, and MI rather than PI forces (for all his historical techniques), in a less consistent and much more mannered interpretation. Properly, Harnoncourt II should be considered in our MI category, but its deletion and nonrevival—at small loss—make the issue moot.

Leonhardt's 1989 recording is somewhat in the line of Harnoncourt I; it generally honors Bach's vocal divisions and uses boy sopranos as soloists and choristers (Harmonia Mundi 7848). Prégardien's Evangelist and van Egmond's Jesus are noteworthy; countertenor Jacobs is successful as one of two substitutes for the aria contraltos, and the other male soloists (Markus Schäfer, Elwes, Mertens, Lika) are fine, even if the boy soloists are unconvincing. Leonhardt's pacing strikes a sensible balance between expressiveness and smoothness.

Gardiner's 1988 recording is relatively observant of Bach's divisions, if less strictly or consistently (♦DG Archiv 427648). The choirs are somewhat large (36 mixed voices plus 17 children) but well controlled. Rolfe Johnson's Evangelist is very individual, either mannered or assertive as your taste decides, but Andreas Schmidt is an honest and unaffected Jesus, while the other soloists (Bonney, Monoyios, von Otter, Chance, Crook, Bär, Hauptmann) are of the highest quality. Gardiner continues here his brisk approach to Bach's major works, showing great sensitivity to springy, dance-like rhythms and relishing PI colorations without neglecting at all either the dramatic or spiritual elements—in sum, an outstanding synthesis of conservative choral scale with the propulsive intensity of period style, in a release that has become the most admired and popular of all PI recordings of the work so far.

A different approach to balancing elements was developed by **Herreweghe,** the only PI two-timer in recordings, and the path-setter in not worrying about Bach's vocal divisions. His 1984 version immediately emerged as an introverted alternative to the extroverted Harnoncourt and Gardiner (♦Harmonia Mundi 901155/57). Crook sets the tone as an understated Evangelist, and Cold is a commanding Jesus; the aria soloists (Schlick, a younger Jacobs, Blochwitz, Kooy) are thoroughly accomplished, and the moderate-sized choral forces are highly polished. The whole tone is one of reverence, thoughtfulness, and contemplation, rather than drama.

Fourteen years later, Herreweghe made a second attempt (Harmonia Mundi 951676/78, 3CD, plus interactive CD-ROM). That he has become the neoromantic, if not also the New Karajan, among PI conductors is certainly suggested by this meticulously calculated performance. His soloists are mostly nonstellar. An exception is the rising tenor Bostridge, whose Evangelist is fluent but, if not entirely uninvolved, rather hard and objective; as Jesus, Franz-Josef Selig sounds magisterial but over-aged. Scholl is another standout in his creamily sung alto solos, but the others (Sibylla Rubens, Güra, Dietrich Henschel), though vocally expert and sensitive, sound depersonalized. Using even smaller choral forces this time, Herreweghe achieves even more polish and suavity of ensemble singing, with the two choirs nicely distinguished by the engineers. Much of the pacing is brisker and more flowing, and while an introspective spirit is preserved in the earlier version, here it is entombed in a cool efficiency that makes the work more a ritual obligation than a spiritual experience. Either recording may be welcomed by those who prefer this kind of reverence to PI alternatives, but I think Herreweghe I makes that case more convincingly.

Suzuki's 1999 recording is perhaps the finest Bach he has yet given us (◆BIS 1000/02). It is certainly aided by the knowing Evangelist of Türk and the gruff Jesus of Kooy, with the silvery-voiced Argenta and the quasi-contralto Robin Blaze joining fine local soloists and well-drilled, mixed-voice choral forces. But the performance is first and foremost a deft entity shaped consistently and coherently by Suzuki. This performance grabs your attention at the outset and draws you through a powerful music drama. Moreover, he has managed the most successful sonic projection yet of the spatial division Bach specified for his two bodies of performers; you hear at all times just where they are in their ever-shifting interrelationships with each other. That is a factor of great textural importance, but one much underappreciated and often overlooked. On that count alone, this is one of the outstanding realizations of the composer's intentions.

A lighter touch is represented in four other recordings, two of them dating from 1992. Koopman is close to Herreweghe I in offering an understated treatment but, in his case, sacrificing power in a rather lightweight and even diffident spirit (Erato). While certainly fully competent, the two protagonists (de Mey's Evangelist, Kooy's Jesus) and the other soloists (Schlick again, Wessel, Prégardien, Mertens) do not always measure up to the standards set by Gardiner's team. Somewhat more substantial and a bit of a sleeper is a Cologne recording by the enterprising Max (Capriccio 60046). His tempos include some that are notably high-speed, making it possible to fit the complete work onto two CDs instead of three, as a bargain issue. But there is much to respect here, not only in his interpretation but also in the latest of Prégardien's Evangelists and the warm Jesus of Mertens. Jochens contributes excellent tenor work, while only Frimmer will likely be familiar among the other capable soloists.

In a concert performance taped in Utrecht in 1996, Brüggen leads a light, brisk, intimately scaled performance, with a fine Evangelist in van der Meel and forthright solo work by a cast mostly of young local singers, though including Kiehr, Bostridge, and Kooy (Philips 454434). Another performance, made in conjunction with a video production, was led by Cleobury in 1994 in Kings College, with its famous choir and Goodman's Brandenburg Consort (Vanguard 99070). Covey-Crump is a clear-voiced Evangelist, while Michael George is a rather avuncular Jesus; the other soloists (Kirkby, Chance, Hill, David Thomas) are also familiar early music stalwarts. The choral singing immediately sets a trim and tidy tone, and everything is musically impeccable. What seems lacking, however, is a sense of spiritual meaning: The style is there, but the spirit of sacred drama is not.

These four constitute the "merely excellent" block. To them can be added a curiosity: the audio portion of a dramatized production for BBC Television cobbled up in 1995 under the always provocative direction of Jonathan Miller. Most of the singers are young and spare-voiced, though Argenta and Varcoe will be recognized as veterans among them. Paul

Goodwin, an experienced PI musician, leads them plus small choral and orchestral ensembles in a performance that is so rushed and light-weight as to suggest that everyone wanted to get it over with as soon as possible. They succeeded to the extent of matching Max in getting the full score onto two CDs (Cala United 89301, or 99137 in the otherwise useful package of all four Bach Passions, Brilliant Classics 99048).

It almost goes without saying that there is no English-language PI version. As with the much larger MI category, there is no ideal PI choice, though Gardiner is perhaps the best-rounded, with Harnoncourt I for strenuous "authenticity" and Herreweghe I for stylistic contrast.

St. John Passion (BWV 245)

Much more than the *St. Matthew Passion,* the *Passion According to St. John* has a complicated textual history involving four different versions: the original of 1724, a revision of 1725 (including music Bach soon transferred to his revised *Matthew Passion*), further changes in the 1730s, and a final version of 1749. Most recordings follow the 1724 version as filtered through that of 1749, and a few include some of the variant sections in appendices. But Rilling rightly suggested that Bach himself considered it "a work in progress" all his life, so there is no truly "definitive" score.

Nonperiod style

By virtue of its Gospel text, this Passion setting is shorter, more compact, and more tautly structured than its St. Matthew counterpart. It has thus attracted conductors less interested in monumental statements and more responsive to dramatic values. Further, unlike the Mass and *St. Matthew Passion,* the *Passion According to St. John* has not attracted the biggest of the big-gun crowd: no Klemperer or Karajan or Furtwängler or Bernstein here.

To be sure, a few "name" conductors made their bid. Ormandy recorded it for Columbia in 1968, but that's long gone. Scherchen's 1961–62 recording was coherently conceived but stylistically dated and unevenly sung (Westminster, NA). The one surviving representation of a big-name recording was made in Amsterdam in 1967 by Jochum. His is "big Bach" in the frankly romantic manner, but in its best and most big-hearted sense. Its Evangelist is among those most admired, Haefliger, with Berry as Jesus; the other soloists are seasoned veterans (Giebel, Höffgen, Alexander Young, Franz Crass). For the committed traditionalist, this is an undeniable bargain in a generous CD reissue (◆Philips 462173, with Cantata 140).

Generally this work has been left to substellar and more specialized maestros in a large number of recordings that come and go. Of those surviving or restored, primacy of chronology, if not also place, belongs to the Leipzig neo-Baroque pioneer, Ramin, whose 1954 recording has been reissued (Berlin 2015, mono). Young Haefliger's Evangelist is already impressive, and most of the other soloists (Franz Kelch, Giebel, Höffgen) are of considerable quality. On the other hand, the 80-member all-male choir is too massive, and the edgy sound of its boys' voices can become irritating after a while. Interpretational perspectives have changed over a half-century, leaving Ramin's approach rather dated. On the other hand, he appreciated the work's drama, and his utter sincerity and dedication produced a performance that still has genuine power and special qualities not to be ignored.

Those tempted by the Ramin approach will find an even more powerful and digestible alternative in Richter's 1964 recording (◆DG Archiv 453007, a bargain reissue). Haefliger is Evangelizing once more, with Prey's mellow Jesus heading a generally strong solo crew (Evelyn Lear, Töpper, Engen), and Richter delivers one of his finest recorded performances with an even bigger (90 voices!) but far more disciplined mixed choir and orchestra. The interpretation is weighty but dramatic and compelling, blending neo-Baroque consciousness with a powerfully romantic temperament. The recording remains a landmark for those who want an amply scaled but cogently shaped conception of the work.

The Leipzig tradition was continued by **Thomas** in exile, who in the late 1950s made a short-lived recording (Oiseau-Lyre LP). More notable was a fine 1975 recording under **Rotzsch,** which featured Augér as well as the first recorded Evangelist by Schreier (RCA 49181, bargain-priced). **Schreier** was to have his own say in 1988 in Dresden, conducting as well as singing the Evangelist and the tenor arias (Philips 454108, in his "Choral Masterpieces" Bach omnibus, 12CD). Holl makes a very imposing Jesus, and the other soloists (Alexander, Lipovsek, Bär) are generally capable. Schreier leads briskly and with a clarity often flawed by choppy agogics and other irritating mannerisms. He added interest to his set, however, by becoming the second conductor (and the first MI one) to include in an appendix three of the five transient numbers from the 1725 version.

Among other recordings to come and go was a thoughtful and involving one made in 1960 under **Fritz Werner,** graced by that splendid and unjustly forgotten Evangelist, Helmut Krebs (♦Erato 45443). Another transient was **Karl Forster**'s very uneven 1961 version, memorable only for the unusually impassioned Evangelist of *wunderbar* Wunderlich, if not also for Fischer-Dieskau's refined Jesus and excellent solos from Grümmer and Ludwig (EMI/HMV/Seraphim). **Münchinger**'s 1965 recording is also uneven (London). He used an all-male choir whose boys were keen-voiced but not insufferable. His Evangelist (Dieter Ellenbeck) is rather hard-toned, but Berry delivers his strongest Jesus; the radiant Ameling leads a fine solo group (Hamari, Hollweg, Prey). Many strong elements are there, but somehow it doesn't hang together as a consistent entity.

Also back with us is another mixed bag: a comfortably *Kapellmeister*-ish recording by **Gönnenwein** (1970: MHS 524463). He foolishly casts the underweight Altmeyer as the Evangelist and the wonderful Equiluz as aria tenor, instead of the other way around; to be sure, Crass as Jesus and the other soloists (Ameling again, Fassbaender, Nimsgern, Moll) sing splendidly, making for a reasonable bargain choice, if not a best buy. Less stellar and too easily overlooked among reissues is a 1971 Hungarian recording in which **György Lehel** leads a performance that beautifully balances dignity with feeling. József Réti is a dark-voiced but poignant Evangelist; the glowing Hamari is at her best, with the lilting Kalmár, among some of Budapest's world-class singers (♦Hungaroton 4024).

Corboz is one of the most important of this vintage (1977: ♦Erato 45406). His solo team is of consistently high quality: Equiluz again a superlative Evangelist, van der Meer a staunch Jesus, as well as Palmer, Finnilä, Krenn, and Huttenlocher. The steady, no-nonsense interpretation traces the Passion story's drama and suffering with nobility and dignity. Its only drawback is somewhat dull sound. Corboz is also represented in a 1994 concert performance that has some good features but is uneven and unsatisfying overall (Cascavelle 1036).

Six more recordings of the work have appeared, with varying degrees of merit. A 1987 performance under the French Baroque specialist **Paul Kuentz** quite vividly captures concert performance(s); it offers an uneven, nonstellar vocal team (only Schlick is likely to be recognized) and somewhat large ensemble forces, with relentless harpsichord-only continuo (Pierre Verany). His interpretation is sometimes thoughtful but sometimes slack, hardly up to the competition. At the opposite extreme

is **Guttenberg**'s 1991 concert performance in Munich (RCA). It involves a large choir (in occasionally blurry singing), a chamber orchestra, and an able group of soloists (Ahnsjö, Evangelist; Scharinger, Jesus; Inga Nielsen, Stutzmann, Robert Swensen, Quasthoff). The arias have a nice variety to them; the overall narrative tone is supercharged, with every dramatic point delivered in italicized capitals; and the story is more enacted than related or contemplated. This is impressive of its kind, but its vehement tone may not bear much repeated hearing.

In a better-balanced 1997 concert performance (Bayer 500007), the choral and orchestral forces are large-scaled, but the flowing pace is maintained by **Karl-Friedrich Beringer,** who makes a far better showing here than he did in a 1979 Bellaphon recording. Markus Schäfer is an able Evangelist and tenorist, but Michael Volle is better in the small roles and bass solos than Hans Griepentrog, over-strained as Jesus; Oelze and Groop are outstanding in their solos. If uneven vocally, this is an earnest and convincing performance, worthy to be placed beside Lehel's older counterpart.

Another is the most ambitious venture yet by trumpet-virtuoso-turned-conductor, the ebullient **Güttler** (1998: Berlin 1186). He combines something of Schreier's mannered briskness with Guttenberg's dramatic stress, but the tone above all is one of youth and energy. Except for the veteran Oelze, none of the soloists' names are likely to be familiar, but all are highly capable, with Christoph Genz a fresh and clear-voiced Evangelist and Egbert Junghanns a straightforward Jesus. While this recording belongs in the "merely excellent" category and might not attract much attention, it's an honest and thoroughly listenable version.

Likewise "merely excellent," if more modestly so, is a 1990 recording in which a Rilling disciple, **Eckhard Weyand,** leads his Stuttgart Choir Boys and a small chamber orchestra (Hänssler). The senior member of his cast is Adalbert Kraus, sounding just a bit tired and fussy. The only other singer who has established some repute is soprano Christine Schäfer, while the rest are young, local, and unfamiliar but entirely competent. Everything is very clean and knowing but rather bland, in a good example of quality German-*Kapellmeister*-provincial style—well recorded and a perfectly acceptable release, but unnecessary in the face of the competition.

The Weyand recording represents a curious digression for Hänssler, normally devoted to the work of its focal conductor, **Rilling.** Not to worry: Hänssler has, in fact, allowed Rilling to become the only other MI repeater in this work. Already the leading exponent of the post-Richter "compromise" approach to Bach, Rilling made his first recording in 1984 for CBS, which circulated briefly on LP and might yet be revived. This was a powerful performance. Rilling's Stuttgart chorus was particularly well disciplined, and a star-studded cast was used: Schreier is again a keen Evangelist and tenorist, and Huttenlocher is a strong Jesus, with the young Andreas Schmidt distinctive in the small part of Pilate. The ever-winning Augér, the warm Hamari, and the inimitable Fischer-Dieskau are the other soloists.

Rilling returned to the work in 1996 (♦Hänssler 98.170, 3CD; "Bachakademie" Vol. 75, 92.075, 2CD). This time the cast involved mainly young and little-known singers. Tenor Michael Schade, with a clear voice and eloquent inflection, is one of the outstanding Evangelists of recent years, and Görne is a Jesus in the Fischer-Dieskau tradition. Schmidt (with his own Fischer-Dieskau echoes) is the most recognizable of the aria soloists, but the others (Banse, Ingeborg Danz, James Taylor) are quite reliable.

Rilling uses his own composite edition that draws upon various versions with musicological savvy. Corresponding to his preference for MI over PI, however, his performance is anything but antiquarian: Charged with considerable dramatic power, strong emotional commitment, and richly musical expressiveness, it is Richter revitalized and updated. Adding further interest to an already impressive recording is an added disc (but only in the independent release, not the series volume) containing a one-hour lecture by Rilling (in English). In this he presents the five variant numbers of the 1725 version (with programming cues for recreating that version on your CD player), but unlike other recordings that do something similar, Rilling presents them in context and discusses many other details of the composer's successive revisions. It's a little tricky to follow at times, but it's the most thorough aural exposition of the matter ever attempted.

The choices here are rich: setting aside Jochum for the old-fashioned, Richter and either Rilling recording will offer dramatic satisfaction, with Lehel as a backup, and Corboz for a leaner touch.

As with the *St. Matthew Passion,* there is a subcategory of English-language recordings, in a smaller but more distinguished picture. Indeed, the very first complete recording of the work, and the first American one, was made in English translation by **Shaw** in 1950 for RCA Victor. The soloists (including Mack Harrell as Jesus, with Adele Addison, Blanche Thebom, Leslie Chabay, and Paul Matthen) are alert and effective, with refined choral and orchestral work, in a set still impressive in its mono sound; it's a pity Shaw never returned to this score.

A second English-language version was led by **Willcocks** in 1960, using the boys and men of King's College Choir (Cambridge), with a cast of distinguished British singers led by Pears as Evangelist; it has not been revived on CD (Argo). Pears himself, however, became an important part of a 1971 recording that well deserves its prolonged life (♦London 443859). The guiding force that lifted this venture from the linguistically functional to the extraordinary was **Benjamin Britten.** Leading with wonderful taste, sensitivity, and insight, he turns the piece into something of a "sacred opera," using an idiosyncratic performing edition of his own. The large chorus of boys and men is not always clear in detail or diction. Pears is a gripping and eloquent Evangelist, Gwynne Howell is a compelling Jesus, and there is variously strong work from the other soloists (Harper, Alfreda Hodgson, Tear, Shirley-Quirk). This is a very special version, not everyone's prime choice, but for its unique character and striking power not to be missed.

Period style

It was with the *St. John Passion* that **Harnoncourt** first caused a sensation in his eventual traversal of major Bach sacred works as "authentically" rethought. In his 1965 recording with his Vienna PI ensemble—actually conducted by the choirmaster, Hans Gillesberger—boy sopranos were used in both solo and choral functions, but not unsuccessfully (♦Teldec 42492). Equiluz as a matchless Evangelist and van Egmond as a bold and manly Jesus were joined by adult male soloists in a strongly organized and still compelling version.

Harnoncourt redid the work on his own in 1993, again in Vienna, in a short-lived release (Teldec 74862). While again using PI players, this time he employed an adult mixed-voice choir. The tempos are much faster, though by no means insensitive, and there are the usual quirky details typical of the conductor. In Rolfe Johnson he has a full-throated and deeply involved Evangelist and tenorist, but Holl is a somewhat ponderous Jesus this time around. Bass Anton Scharinger is strong in his solos, and Blasi and Lipovsek are outstanding in theirs. All in all, however, this recording is one in a crowd, without the force of revelation of the earlier one.

Two subsequent PI recordings clearly put Harnoncourt II into the shade (if not also Gillesberger/Harnoncourt I). The first was **Schneidt's** in 1978 (DG Archiv LP). As in the 1965 Teldec, he used boy choristers and soloists to authentic if not always artistic effect; the adult soloists, all local, were on the understated side, and the total performance had less force and profile than the 1965 trailblazer. Still, it offered a toned-down, more intimate PI alternative, and it included as an appendix the first PI recording of all five of the 1725 variants.

This set was apparently never reissued on CD, presumably retired in favor of **Gardiner's** 1986 recording (♦DG Archiv 419324). Rolfe Johnson delivered his first Evangelist, with the seasoned Varcoe as Jesus; the small "roles" were distributed widely, while the arias were apportioned to an unusually large team of two sopranos (the lovely Argenta, the pale Ruth Holton), countertenor (Chance), two tenors (Neil Archer, Rufus Müller), and a bass (Hauptmann), all of whom (as Bach's forces would have done) joined a small body of other singers to make a chorus, here totaling 23, with a PI ensemble of 33 players. There are some uneven patches, but the general quality is very high, and Gardiner fuses everything together in a vigorous, intense reading—stressing the dramatic over the devout—that has stood up very well as a prime choice ever since.

The same year (1986) witnessed another experiment with Bach's scoring. **Anthony Newman** directed a small group of PI players with a total of 19 singers constituting the chorus, among them the soloists (Newport). These are excellent American singers: Baird, Jeffrey Dooley, and Ostendorf, with Jeffrey Thomas as a splendid Evangelist, and William Sharp as Jesus. But the iconoclastic Newman's conception of the work is sometimes eccentric and quite frankly theatrical, corresponding somewhat to Guttenberg in the MI category.

But Newman started something, and a more definite exploration of the scoring came in 1989 with a recording by the Smithsonian Chamber Chorus and Players under **Kenneth Slowik** (Smithsonian 0381). With some carryovers from Newman's personnel, Slowik attempted even more specifically to use forces numerically approximating Bach's own: a PI orchestra of 27 with a vocal ensemble of only 12 including a well-integrated group of soloists (Baird, Lane, Steven Rickards, Thomas, David Ripley, Paul Rowe). Thomas is again a very effective Evangelist, and James Weaver is an honest Jesus. Not only is the performance a highly sensitive and stylish rendition of the 1749 version, but it adds all the 1725 variants in appendices as well, keyed so you can program your own choice of alternative versions.

The reduced scale of singers touches on Joshua Rifkin's arguments drawn from the composer's performing materials. Rifkin himself has never applied them to this work, but Slowik applied them effectively in his version, and so did a recurrent Rifkin disciple, **Parrott** (1990: EMI 754083, re-released as ♦Virgin 45096). Parrott used an instrumental group of 19, with only 11 singers (among them such early-music specialists as Van Evera and Tessa Bonner), including Covey-Crump (Evangelist, tenor arias) and David Thomas (Jesus, bass arias). The performance is skilled, sensitive, and polished; for some it's sure to seem spare and antiseptic even more than Slowik's version, but it offers a compelling intimacy of its own, and will interest those who want to trace performance practice back to Bach's perspectives.

It stands thus even with the subsequent appearance of **David van Asch's** 1993 ultra-minimalist recording (Naxos 550664). There, only eight adult singers (including two countertenors) are heard, with 16 players. It's all very precise and crisp, but it's only a bargain-rate alternative to Parrott. A modified pullback from minimalist extremes was offered by **Christophers,** who used a small chorus of 18 and a PI band of

21 (1989: Chandos 0507/8). The singing is superb: Partridge is a very sensitive Evangelist, with Wilson-Johnson as Jesus leading an outstanding vocal team (Kwella, David James, William Kendall, George). The tone is one of refined intimacy, resulting in a recording certainly of quality if, ultimately, only a high "merely excellent" rating.

Meanwhile, a kind of "compromise" PI tradition settled in with a series of recordings from the late 1980s onward. Within that emerging tradition, one direction was staked out by **Herreweghe** (1987: ♦Harmonia Mundi 901264/65). From his familiar circle of accomplished soloists, he mounted an evenly matched team (Crook and Peter as Evangelist and Jesus; Schlick, Catherine Patriasz, William Kendall, Kooy), plus his refined choral and instrumental forces. Exhibiting his usual sensitivity, Herreweghe avoids the dramatic and stresses a kind of nonliturgical spirituality, thus steering PI performances away from strenuous ventures into "authenticity" and back to a traditionalist spirit.

That kind of middle-of-the-road spirit was soon embodied in other recordings. For instance, **Kuijken**'s version reduces introspection to commonplace routine in a bland interpretation executed by a slightly uneven cast with a dry and lackluster Jesus (van der Kamp) at odds with a reliable Evangelist (Prégardien) and otherwise highly skilled soloists: Schlick, Jacobs, van der Meel, and van Egmond (1987: Harmonia Mundi). **Koopman**'s 1993 recording was a step up (Erato 94675). With his moderate ensembles (chorus of 27, PI orchestra of 23), his solo team offered some particularly lovely moments from Evangelist de Mey and veteran Schlick, weaker ones from countertenor Wessel, and otherwise excellent work from the rest (Kooy as Jesus; Türk, Mertens). The tone is reverent, but also rather cool and restrained, offering a conception with a rather limited profile.

Several recent recordings have seemingly tried to restore zip and a kind of secularized theatricality in approach. Such was the tone of the ever-lively **Max** (1990: Capriccio 60023). Stressing his strict adherence to the 1749 version, he returned to quasi-minimalist standards with a chorus of 17, five also serving as soloists. Prégardien is again a firm anchor as Evangelist, and Hans-Georg Wimmer is a manly Jesus; Ralf Popken's name will be the only one familiar among the other singers, who are, however, quite able. While not in any way forced or exaggerated, this is a brisk and dramatically oriented interpretation.

Andreas Kröper brought far greater intensity to a recording made in Brno in 1991 (Allegro). Judging from the unusually probing album notes, Kröper has thought a lot about textual questions, but his interpretation is unbelievably eccentric—tempos either at almost breakneck speeds or in veritable slow motion, including mannered or desensitized arias and clomping chorales. How his Moravian choir of 21 kept up with him is miraculous, though his tiny PI band of 16 is painfully rough. Virtual minimalism is furthered by the use of only four soloists: British guest James Griffett isn't bad and might be a fine Evangelist and tenorist with another conductor; bass Jirzi Klecker is also a decent Jesus; but the local soprano is too piping, the countertenor wobbly. Just to hear the living daylights beaten out of this work in such a distended, manic-depressive performance is fascinating, but this must be reckoned as one of the weirdest versions ever mounted.

Brüggen evidenced far more restraint and reverence, though with personality aplenty. His forces are more conventional: choir of 42, PI ensemble of 25. His soloists include a lot of the usual suspects, but somewhat shuffled amid a mixed bunch. Van der Meel is a deft but committed Evangelist, but the Jesus (Kristinn Sigmundsson) is heavy and gruff; among the others, Bowman and Prégardien are not up to their best, though Annegeer Stumphius and Kooy are quite good. Brüggen leads

with good stylistic sense, but this is another of the versions more dramatic than spiritual, and in this category (dominated by Gardiner), a "merely excellent" entry.

Less restrained, but safely between Kröper and Brüggen, is another venture by the energetic newcomer, **Fasolis,** in a Swiss Radio performance (♦Arts 47539). His forces are, once again, near-minimalist (choir of 18, PI band of 19). Fasolis presents a frankly dramatic case for the work, with strong touches of inflection and agogics that can sometimes seem exaggerated, falling in character somewhere between those of Schreier and Guttenberg in the MI category. But the performance is brought off by the excellent quality of the solo work. Van der Meel renews his fine Evangelist, and Mertens is ever-dependable as Jesus and bass soloist; it's back to a contralto with Claudia Schubert, who with Roberta Invernizzi and Jeremy Ovenden completes a very solid and consistent cast.

Most recent in this line is **Suzuki** (♦BIS 921/22). There is some unevenness in his cast: Türk is again a handsome Evangelist, but Chiyuki Urano is a dry and aloof Jesus; it might have been better to give that assignment to Kooy, who is, to be sure, outstanding in the other bass roles and arias. (That switch was actually made in Suzuki's subsequent recording of St. Matthew Passion.) Mera, an appealing countertenor elsewhere in Suzuki's projects, is rather pallid here, though certainly sensitive in his response to moods. Ingrid Schmithüsen and Makoto Sakurada complete the team competently. The choir of 20 and PI ensemble of 21 respond crisply to Suzuki's moderately brisk tempos. He seems to have a commitment to dramatic expressiveness, but that spirit is unevenly displayed, though at least the choral sections convey some urgency and even power. While not a top contender in its class, it makes a strong showing, given an additional boost by including the three variant arias from the 1725 version, with a useful chart plotting the changes among the versions.

A neo-traditionalist bent has also reasserted itself in two 1996 recordings. Modestly so in a concert performance taped in Portland, Oregon, where **Eric Milnes** has pursued an ambitious choral program (PCM 111). His small choir and PI ensemble are not on a par with international standards in the quasi-minimalist category, and his interpretation is no more than straightforward conventionalism, but he has a fine team of soloists: a hefty Evangelist (Mark Bleeke) and an aptly youthful Jesus (Nathaniel Watson), with the elegant alto Jennifer Lane gracing a group of otherwise local vocalists. The release remains a creditable but essentially provincial affair.

Cleobury's performance from King's College Chapel, Cambridge, is more serious. His choir of boys and men is joined by Roy Goodman's pungent Brandenburg Consort of 29 players (Columns 290241; Brilliant Classics 99050, or in its set of all four Passions, 99137, 8CD). At least vocally, the spirit here is one of British restraint, understating the drama for a more liturgical feeling. The choir is recorded spaciously, and Ainsley is a thoughtful Evangelist, while Stephen Richardson is an avuncular Jesus. Among the other soloists, Bott, Chance, and Varcoe share the conductor's restraint, and only tenor Agnew brings some intensity to his work. As a bonus, however, Cleobury includes all five of the 1725 variant numbers, thus matching Slowik and Schneidt and outstripping Suzuki (not to mention MI Schreier).

The latest approach to the question of editions and variants has been made most emphatically by **Peter Neumann** in his Cologne recording (♦MD+G 332). He simply presents Bach's 1725 version—with its new opening chorus, later transferred by the composer to end Part II of the St. Matthew Passion, plus changes and added solo numbers—as a self-contained entity on its own. The soloists (including Ruth Holton and Bogna Bartosz) are variable, if always competent, but the interpretation is carefully thought out and expertly led, constituting a persuasive case for this version. It's not likely to be your first choice, but it's an illuminating document for the serious student of Bach and this work.

There is too full and competitive an array of PI versions to make firm recommendations, but anyone interested in this work should consider Gillesberger/Harnoncourt I, Gardiner, and Slowik, with Herreweghe or Koopman among the more restrained backup interpreters, and Brüggen or Fasolis for variety.

There is an English-language appendage in this category, made in 1999 in Cleveland by the Apollo's Fire ensemble under **Jeannette Sorell** (Electra 2044). The five mostly local soloists join, with one exception, as section leaders with 17 other singers to form the mixed-voice choir, joined by a PI orchestra of 20 players. The recording venue is not quite congenial and there are rough spots in this venture, but the solo work is consistently strong and the choral and instrumental work quite decent. If there's nothing like the power of Britten's famous MI recording, there is much enthusiasm evident here and this plucky early music group certainly does itself credit. Essentially the 1724 version is used and the English translation comes through well in the solo work, but is largely lost in the choral passages.

The "lost" Passions

We know that Bach composed five Passion settings: one for each Gospel plus an alternative *St. Matthew*. Of these, only two unimpeachably authentic ones survive, the familiar *St. Matthew* and *St. John*.

A *St. Luke Passion* has also come down to us, and since the manuscript is in Bach's hand, it was for some time considered to be his and therefore listed by Schmieder as BWV 246. It is now clear that this is a work by another, unknown, composer, simply copied by Bach. Indeed, it seems strange to me that such comparatively inferior music could ever have been attributed to Bach. Inferior, but by no means without some interest and appeal of its own, even if only as a point of comparison for Bach's greater scores.

There have been three recordings. The first was made in Vienna in the early 1960s by **George Barati,** its local cast graced by a distinguished Evangelist and tenorist in Equiluz; it has apparently never had a CD reissue (Lyrichord). It was succeeded by a recording made in Tübingen under **Gerhard Rehm** and circulated on several LP labels. The respected Georg Jelden was a solemn Evangelist and eloquent tenorist, and the rest of the cast was up to high-quality provincial standards, though the sound was somewhat cavernous (Brilliant Classics 99051, 2CD, and in 99137, their package of all four Passions, 8CD). **Wolfgang Helbich,** the Master of "Apocryphal Bach," addressed the work in a 1996 recording (CPO 999293, 2CD). His Evangelist is the full-throated Rufus Müller, and the other five soloists are quite able locals, with a smallish choir and Bremen PI ensemble. Though the string playing is rough and unpleasant, the singing is generally stronger than in Rehm's version, and the sound is also superior.

To these "straight" recordings may be added a weird "re-creation" of the work by Jan Jirásek, on the basis of an idiosyncratic scheme of Carl Orff's. In this, all the arias and half the chorales are dropped, boiling the work down mostly to slightly abridged recitatives, tricked out with hokey orchestrations. Some respectable singers (Furio Zanasi, Ulrik Cold) lend themselves to this travesty, recorded in Munich under **Douglas Bostock,** for which the Leipzig master need take no blame (Classico 278).

As for Bach's known setting of the *Passion According to St. Mark,* the original work has disappeared, but it's understood that (like the Mass and *Christmas Oratorio*) it was a "parody" composition, recycling music from some of his earlier works. It has further been argued convincingly that some of the concerted numbers in the *Markus-Passion* could be identified in and recovered from known Bach compositions (Cantatas 198, 54, 7, and some chorale settings). Those recoveries (the two framing choruses, five arias, five chorales) were assembled and recorded under **Gönnenwein** (Erato LP).

But several scholars and conductors have wanted to re-create the Passion setting in full, which means, chiefly, filling in the lost Evangelist recitatives and crowd choruses (*turbae*). One attempt was made by two Polish scholars, who cobbled up the missing material themselves on the basis of corresponding segments of the *St. Matthew Passion* and the spurious *Lukas-Passion*. A performance by Polish singers and orchestra under **Joszef Bok** was taped in 1984 in Rimini, but it's quite pedestrian on all counts (Bongiovanni 2024/25, 2CD).

Two other "completion" ventures were pursued at two-year intervals thereafter. Both were built around the idea of filling in the missing Gospel narratives from a contemporaneous counterpart by Reinhard Keiser (1674–1739), a St. Mark setting that Bach knew, copied, and performed himself in Leipzig. A problem remained in that Keiser began his setting further into Mark's text than did Bach's librettist, Picander. To fill the gap, Dr. Simon Heighes of Oxford University prepared a performing edition in which he himself composed recitatives for the passages Keiser did not set, thus producing a pastiche of Bach-Heighes-Keiser. This edition was recorded in 1996 under **Goodman** (♦Musica Oscura 070970, 2CD; Brilliant Classics 99049, 2CD, and in set 99137, 8CD).

A rival performing edition was prepared and published in 1997 by Prof. Andor Gomme of Cambridge University and recorded the following year by Cambridge forces under **Geoffrey Webber** (ASV 237, 2CD). Gomme made different decisions on what recovered music to use and how, but he resolved the problem of Keiser's gap by simply starting where Keiser began and making no effort to fill in the lost Bach music for the narrative that came before. The result is also a pastiche, but a simpler one: just Bach-Keiser. Either edition is, of course, no more than a makeshift confection, and a speculative, better-than-nothing substitute for recovering a genuine "lost" work by Bach.

With a slightly shorter running time, Gomme's version under Webber (ASV) is augmented by a Psalm setting by Keiser, a generous bonus (though not very well performed).

For both musical and musicological reasons, however, Goodman's set is to be preferred. Both performances use small mixed-voice choirs, Webber's leaner in tone, Goodman's Finnish choir more full-bodied. If PI values are not very different between them, solo values are. Webber's singers are adequate; his countertenor (William Towers) is a bit hooty, but Timothy Mirfin is a very satisfying Jesus. Nevertheless, Goodman has a more experienced roster, with Covey-Crump a much stronger Evangelist than Webber's Jeremy Ovenden, however earnest he may be. To be sure, you may not like the boy treble in the two soprano arias, but Goodman's other soloists (including tenor Agnew) are fine. Above all, whereas Webber leads a staid and straightforward rendition of his edition, Goodman really digs in with a more aggressive and dramatic feeling, though here again one might simply distinguish between the choice of liturgical and theatrical dispositions thus illustrated.

Christmas Oratorio (BWV 248)

Unlike the other three major choral works, the so-called *Weihnachts-Oratorium* is not, and was never intended by the composer to be, a single, discrete entity to be heard all at once. It is a cycle of cantatas, prepared in 1734 for performance on the six successive liturgical occasions in the Christmas season and its aftermath (Dec. 25, 26, 27; Jan. 1 [Circumcision], first Sunday after New Year, Jan. 6 [Epiphany]). Each component cantata thus reflects upon a separate episode of the Nativity story, each with its own distinctive scoring; furthermore, like the Mass, it includes extensive borrowings from some previous cantatas. Nevertheless, each cantata in the set is built around tenor recitatives setting texts from the Gospels of Luke and Matthew, thereby providing a kind of serialized continuum approximating the Evangelist's role in the Passions. This unifying element perhaps prompted Bach himself in the end to inscribe the term "oratorio" at the head of this cycle's score. (Note: All recordings considered are 3CD unless otherwise indicated.)

Nonperiod style

With the mysteries of Christ's mission and the agonies of his death still far ahead in narrative perspective, this Christmas cycle lacks the dark depths of the Passions, instead sustaining a superficial if infectious tone of joy and celebration all along the way, with great diversity of textures and colors. There have been fewer recordings of the cycle than of the other three sacred monuments, mostly the work of choral and Bach specialists, though the number has been mounting in recent years. Generally, though, big-name conductors have not been drawn to it—with one exception, that big-hearted romanticist, **Jochum.** Made in 1973 for Philips, his recording is just the ticket for traditionalists (♦MHS 35185). Its soloists are as good a team as you can find (Ameling, Fassbaender, Laubenthal, Prey), and there is even a boys' choir added to the ample numbers of the Bavarian Radio Chorus and Symphony Orchestra. This is plummy, hearty, yet never ponderous Bach—a little dated in sound, but still valid in its category of stylistic approach.

Hans Grischkat's LPs, dating from the 1950s and briefly on the Renaissance and Remington labels, are long gone, but another, a rather rough Viennese job in early stereo under **Ferdinand Grossmann,** is still with us (Vox 5096, 2CD). Apart from documenting young Walter Berry as bass soloist, there is little to recommend it beyond its tenacity. Gone, too, is a noble if somewhat dated recording made in Berlin in 1955–56, begun by that grand old man **Fritz Lehmann** and completed after his death midstream by Günther Arndt (DG Archiv mono LP).

The Bach-revival traditions of Leipzig and Dresden have been represented by a number of recordings. The earliest was under Thomanerkirche Cantor **Ramin,** but it was never released in the United States. Ramin's successor, **Thomas,** made two recordings: the first for Oiseau-Lyre, now long gone, the second in 1958 just before his flight to the West (EMI 69805; ♦Berlin Classics 2191). The soloists, paladins of this kind of music in their day (Giebel, Marga Höffgen, Josef Traxel, Fischer-Dieskau), and the choir of boys and men, with a substantial Leipzig orchestra, are all quite handsomely recorded in an embodiment of the postwar Leipzig blend of neo-Baroque and early-Romantic traditions at their best.

As a kind of Leipzig offshoot, **Richter** also recorded the work twice with his own forces in Munich. The earlier venture (1958) involves a relatively nonstellar team of soloists with whom he was comfortable (Chloe Owen, Töpper, Horst Günther, Gert Lutze, Engen); the interpretation is earnest but heavy, even turgid and bloated (Teldec 97902, mono). A far more just memento of his love for this work was his second (1965: ♦DG Archiv 427236). The scale was still rather grandiose and tightly controlled, but graced by a powerhouse cast of soloists — Janowitz, Ludwig, Wunderlich (alone worth the price of admission), Crass — and it's preferable to the earlier recording.

The continuity of the Leipzig/Dresden tradition was affirmed by **Flämig** in Dresden in 1974–75 (Berlin 2065). The choir includes boys again, a very MI orchestra, and a spectrum of soloists (the velvety Augér, the rather overblown Burmeister, the slightly acidulous Schreier, a somewhat frayed Adam) in a performance of color and energy—a worthy recording of its kind, but now quite outclassed. A final contender in this line is **Schreier** himself, recorded in Leipzig in 1987 as both conductor and soloist (part of the Schreier Bach "Choral masterpieces" package, Philips 454108, 12CD). There is some good solo singing (Donath, Holl), with able choral and orchestral work (including Leopold Güttler leading the brilliant trumpet team); the pacing is brisk and lively, but there are idiosyncratic touches that restrict its overall interest.

Three recordings have disappointed despite promising solo teams. **Münchinger**'s is the earliest (1967: London). The soloists (Ameling, Watts, Pears, Krause) are of sterling quality and sing handsomely, in still-excellent sound, but the overall pacing is rather stiff and foursquare. **Ledger** led a 1976 English venture with the St. Martin Academy in a brisk but rather diffident and superficial performance. The King's College Choir (boys and men) sounds impressive but blurry and stylistically out of place, while the acoustics are quirky. It is surely the well-nigh irresistible solo roster (Ameling again, Baker, Tear, Fischer-Dieskau) that accounts for the revival of this set as a low-priced reissue (♦EMI 69503, 2CD)—an honest bargain even if it falls short of the highest interpretational standards. The third of these recordings has apparently not been kept in print, despite another fine solo complement (Schlick, Watkinson, Equiluz, Nimsgern), along with smoothly operating mixed-choral and orchestral contributions; **Corboz**'s leadership, however, is inconsistent and not up to his own best standards (Erato).

In a thoroughly competent but essentially provincial 1983 performance, the point was to show off the all-male choir, the Stuttgarter Hymnus Chorknaben, under its then conductor, **Gerhard Wilhelm;** soprano Kriztina Láki aside, the soloists were all locals (Hänssler 98.910). But Hänssler has inevitably focused on its housemaster, **Rilling.** His 1984 recording was first issued in the United States in a CBS LP set; it passed through CD reissues by Intercord, and by Hänssler themselves as a separate set (♦98.884), in several different collective packages, and finally in the comprehensive "Bachakademie" series (Vol. 76, 92.076). With veteran soloists (Augér, Hamari, Schreier, Schöne) plus his crack Stuttgart chamber choir and orchestra, Rilling offers the most stable and satisfying "compromise" MI recording around—a little old-fashioned, but stylistically alert and musically rewarding all the way.

There remain two further items in the bargain category. One is the 1992 recording by **Géza Oberfrank** and his Hungarian forces (♦Naxos 550428/30). Again offering the impressive Evangelist of József Mukk, and with consistently reliable contributions from all other hands, it's a lively, spacious, and hearty rendition, well into the "merely excellent" category, and, as such, a genuine bargain-rate contender.

But by retaining the standard 3CD format, Naxos has eroded its bargain advantage, not only against EMI's Ledger reissue but also against the latest traditionalist recording, by the Bethlehem Bach festival forces under their vigorous new leader, **Funfgeld** (♦Dorian 93183, 2CD). The mixed-voice chorus is listed at 105 singers—hard to believe in view of its excellent discipline—and the MI instrumentalists (totaling a reasonable 35) are of high quality. The soloists are young and not widely known: Bass Christòpheren Nomura is a bit gurgly, but he and the others (Tamara Matthews, Marietta Simpson, Benjamin Butterfield) are thoroughly listenable. Above all, Funfgeld maintains a spirit of rousing festivity and sacred joy, in a recording that has substance beyond a mere festival souvenir. In its 2CD format, it has real bargain status and is worth considering for those who want an honest traditionalist approach, a bit less romantic than Jochum's.

With Jochum as an unabashed extreme, the strongest choice otherwise is probably Rilling I, with Richter II (if you can find it) in the conservative middle, and the three bargain options (Ledger, Oberfrank, Funfgeld) good value for the budget-conscious.

Period style

The "authenticity" approach came to this work with a bang, via the groundbreaking 1971–72 recording by **Harnoncourt** in collaboration with Hans Gillesberger (♦Teldec 9031; "Bach 2000" edition, Vol. 6, 25711, 14CD). The PI playing is predictably aggressive, and Bach's practices were further addressed by the use of boy choristers and a boy treble soloist, as well as a countertenor (Esswood), with excellent adult work from Equiluz and Nimsgern. Pungent and convincing, this remains a classic recording, even if it initiated the zippy tempos that have come to irritate traditionalists. Gillesberger and Harnoncourt also initiated a trend in period style that, as it played out, presumed not only PI instruments but the use of boy choristers and soloists (treble *and* alto), with adult male tenor and bass.

An immediate riposte came in 1973 with all-male vocal forces and the Collegium Aureum under **Schmidt-Gaden** (Harmonia Mundi). The PI playing is still warmly cautious and unprovocative, but the choral singing is woolly, the two boy soloists are weak, the two adults (Altmeyer, McDaniel) are not of top quality, and the overall approach is timidly traditional. If that neither-fish-nor-fowl approach was little challenge to Gillesberger/Harnoncourt, a more serious one came in a 1977 recording from **Schneidt** (DG Archiv). The soloists were local and nonstellar but decent, and the performance was deft and keenly "progressive," but it has not survived.

There the PI picture stood for a decade, until a procession of still-current recordings was launched by **Gardiner**'s 1987 venture (♦DG Archiv 423232). While sporting the swift tempos typical of the established PI approach, together with its instrumental colorations, Gardiner brings warmth and humanity to a propulsive, refreshing, consistently satisfying performance, graced by his expert mixed-voice chamber choir and a wonderful batch of soloists (Rolfe Johnson as Evangelist; Argenta, von Otter, Blochwitz, Bär).

Gardiner set a standard that has yet to be beaten, though it was approached by **Herreweghe** in 1989 (♦Virgin 59530; MHS 522936). More restrained than Gardiner, Herreweghe is characteristically sensitive, intelligent, and artistic, with uniformly excellent soloists (Schlick, Chance, Crook, Kooy). More playful—energetic, crisply incisive, yet still maintaining an easy-going feeling—is a Frankfurt recording by familiar performers: a tidy mixed-voice chamber choir, the crack Concerto Köln PI group, and four soloists of the highest quality (Ziesak, Groop, Prégardien, Mertens) (1991: ♦Capriccio 60025). They are led by **Ralf Otto** in what might be called an "intimate" or "streamlined churchly" approach. Perhaps the smallest-scaled version, it's not for those of Romantic temperament, perhaps, but is a genuinely attractive application of pungent understatement, worth hearing more than once.

On the other hand, good as he is, **Christophers** seems doomed once again to the "merely excellent" bin. His recording offers crisp direction, with his sleek little mixed-voice choir (called The Sixteen, but here 18), fine PI orchestra (of 29), and an accomplished solo team (Lynda Russell, Catherine Wyn Rogers, Padmore, George). Christophers works on a scaled-down level somewhat parallel to Otto's but lacking the latter's

flexibility, in what ends up as a rather tight and clinical reading with little genuine spirit or pleasure to it (Collins).

The two of the four most recent recordings at least complement Gardiner. **Jacobs**'s is fleet but carefully thought-out (1997: ♦Harmonia Mundi 901630/31). His choir of 28 joins the outstanding Akademie für Alte Musik PI ensemble (here 34 strong), and he has a particularly fine Evangelist in Werner Güra; countertenor Scholl gives Gardiner's alto von Otter some serious competition, and the other two soloists (Dorothea Röschmann, Klaus Häger) are fine, all in all a somewhat less individualized alternative to Gardiner. In 1998 came an entry from Tokyo's **Suzuki** (♦BIS 941/42). Things are still done briskly, but with genuine dash and style, on an intelligently moderate scale, with a choir of 20 and an orchestra of 25. Their full-bodied playing shows how far PI techniques have advanced since the abrasiveness of their earlier days (e.g., Harnoncourt). The alto is the restrained but sensitive countertenor Mera, while the other fine soloists (Frimmer, Türk, Kooy) are among Suzuki's experienced German guests. This is not a spectacular version, but it's bright and thoroughly enjoyable, and a well-balanced alternative to Gardiner.

A small-scaled Otto-style version by the Boston Baroque Ensemble under **Julian J. Wachner** at a 1998 public performance is still more modestly priced (Titanic 258). Van Egmond is an interesting guest, his voice a little worn but still surprisingly agile and well used. Of the other soloists, soprano Anne Marley is quite good and the two tenors are satisfactory, but the contralto is subpar. Wachner leads with vigor and good sense, but his choir of 16 and orchestra of 27 sound a little thin or ragged. This is the kind of performance that must have pleased its audience, but it can't meet the competition. In a very unaggressive PI style, **Enoch zu Guttenberg** is more traditionalist in some ways, though his generally rushed pacing sometimes compromises what is obviously a very loving performance, with young, fresh-voiced, and very pleasing soloists (Farao 108015, 2CD, plus a third in which the conductor gives a 55-minute lecture on some of the musical highlights, of little use unless you understand German).

While Gillesberger/Harnoncourt remains a landmark classic, Gardiner is probably still the leading choice in the PI category, but Herreweghe, Otto, Jacobs, and Suzuki definitely deserve consideration for their particular merits. Moreover, as we go to press, a new recording is being issued by Oiseau-Lyre with **Pickett** leading a distinguished solo team in a version that's certain to claim serious attention.

Easter Oratorio (BWV 249)

Though no longer than some of the other major cantatas, this Easter Sunday festivity, beginning "Kommt, eilet und laufet," has come down to us as the *Osteroratorium*, placed among Bach's "major" sacred works. It has no Evangelist delivering Gospel texts but is a quasi-dramatic representation of the discovery of the empty tomb by four of Jesus's followers (a convenient vocal quartet). As with the Mass and other major works, it's a reworking of earlier music, specifically from an occasional piece of 1725 known as the "Shepherd Cantata" (BWV 249a). Indeed, a reconstruction of that cantata format has been made, and was recorded for Bärenreiter years ago by Rilling, also released for a while on a Nonesuch LP now extinct.

The *Easter Oratorio* has had a modest but respectable recording history. Of its two earliest LP manifestations, one under **Ferdinand Grossmann** for Vox is long gone, but the other, recorded in 1951 (mono) under **Prohaska**, is very much alive (Vanguard 2542; in set 2539, 4CD). A lot of the orchestral work is coarse, but the chorus is exuberant, and well-known singers (Maja Weis-Osborn, Rössl-Majdan, Equiluz, Berry) throw themselves into the piece. Among subsequent recordings of LP vintage were **Gönnenwein** for EMI/Electrola (with Zylis-Gara, Altmeyer, and Fischer-Dieskau among the soloists) and **Maazel** for Philips, made in Berlin with an equally impressive solo roster (Donath, Anna Reynolds, Haefliger, Talvela)—both of which have disappeared.

But two more recordings of that era are back with us. One is **Münchinger**'s 1968 production, a conscientiously organized performance with a Viennese choir and his Stuttgart orchestra. The latter contributes some lovely instrumental playing to complement the superlative solo work from Ameling, Watts, Krenn, and Krause. This has been variously restored as a single CD in a particularly attractive pairing (the *Magnificat*) to constitute one of the conductor's most enjoyable Bach releases (♦London 466420), or with BWV 10 (♦MHS 514905); or (backed again by the *Magnificat*) in his package of Bach's "Sacred Masterworks" (London♦55783, 10CD).

The other is **Ormandy**'s even earlier recording (1963: Sony 60261, with Bernstein's *Magnificat*). Against the churchly spirit of Münchinger, Ormandy offers a concert-hall sound with relaxed tone and traditionalist values, but on a legitimately musical level. This is Big-Band Bach, with the Philadelphia Orchestra and the Temple University Concert Choir, but the soloists (Raskin, Forrester, Richard Lewis, Herbert Beattie) include singers one can never tire of hearing. For the old-fashioned taste, this is still a comfortable choice.

The MI picture ended, appropriately, with **Rilling**'s 1980–81 Stuttgart recording (♦Hänssler 98.862, with BWV 6; "Bachakademie" series Vol. 77, 92.077, with BWV 11, the so-called "Ascension Oratorio"). Rilling's approach is, like Münchinger's, moderate in scale and churchly in feeling, but more vigorous (if sometimes a little pounding), and with comparably endearing solo work from Augér, Hamari, Adalbert Kraus, and Huttenlocher. A choice between this and the Münchinger alternative will depend on solo preferences and pairings.

It was over a decade before PI treatment came to this work, represented by three contrasting recordings. **Parrott**'s is another of that conductor's applications of the Rifkin Doctrine of minimalist forces (1993: Virgin 545011, with BWV 4). Thus he uses four experienced early-music soloists (Van Evera, Caroline Trevor, Charles Daniels, Kooy), who join with five other singers to constitute the tiny chorus, added to a small PI ensemble of 22. The performance is bright and spirited, and by no means without musical insight; but its ultra-lean textures may not appeal even to PI fans.

A direct contrast came the following year (1994) with an elegantly polished rendition by **Herreweghe** (Harmonia Mundi 901513, with BWV 66). With a mixed-voice choir of 17 and a PI ensemble of 23, the scale is modest and the textures are clean, but the timbres are full. A countertenor (Wessel) is a pallid alto, but the other soloists (Schlick, James Taylor, Kooy again) are familiar early-music experts. The tone is more reverent than boisterous, but the musicality is noteworthy. **Koopman**'s 1998 version is lively and intelligent, with a choir and PI orchestra of 24 each (Erato 23416, with *Magnificat*). But if the men (Türk, Mertens) are reliable singers, the women (Larsson, Bartosz) have modest voices, and the total is rather less satisfying than what Herreweghe offers.

Parrott's experiment should not be overlooked, but in the PI category Herreweghe is pretty much the obvious choice for now.

Miscellaneous

The chorale and the sacred song, though seeming to represent the miniature and ephemeral in the grand sweep of Bach's output, were im-

portant to him, for traditional Lutheran sacred melody was at the core of his musical soul. His sacred songs (for solo voice with basso continuo) are to be found mainly in two important collections. One is the famous (Second) *Notebook for Anna Magdalena Bach*, compiled for and by his second wife, which mostly contains keyboard pieces but includes 11 songs (though not all are on sacred texts, and a few apparently are not by Bach), reckoned as BWV 508–18. The much larger collection derives from a massive *Musikalisches Gesangbuch* published in 1736 by Georg Christian Schemelli and therefore known as "Schemelli's Songbook." It contained the words for 954 spiritual songs and arias, only 69 of them printed with music (melody and bass). The music for those 69 was prepared for the edition by Bach, and much discussion continues about how many of the melodies were his own, or how much he contributed to the bass parts.

The most comprehensive recording of this material was a series of four LPs on the old Westminster label, in which, dividing the assignments, **Rössl-Majdan** and **Cuenod** presented all 69 of the Schemelli airs, with six of the 11 from the Anna Magdalena set. Long gone, that series still deserves reissue, despite its old mono sound, as a valuable point of reference. The full Schemelli 69 appeared again, if somewhat truncated, in a 2LP recording for Christophorus (issued here by MHS), sung by tenor **Georg Jelden.**

All other recorded attention to the Schemelli songs has been selective. The most extended was a gleaning of 31 songs, sung by **Augér** and **Schreier** (each with continuo groups), interlarded with 10 four-part vocal chorale harmonizations (from the Kirnberger collection) and four chorale-based organ pieces, all supervised and directed by Rilling (1983: CBS, 2LP). **Schreier** had earlier shown his interest in the Schemelli songs. In 1974, with organist Hedwig Bilgram, he recorded 14, while soprano Elisabeth Speiser added 10 more plus two Anna Magdalena items (DG Archiv LP). Then in 1978, he recorded 20 of the Schemelli songs (duplicating four of those he sang earlier, as well as five sung by Speiser), accompanied by Karl Richter on the Silbermann organ of Freiburg Cathedral (DG Archiv 427131).

Otherwise, apart from scant samplings by a few individual singers (e.g., Giebel, Altmeyer), no serious attention was paid to the Schemelli songs until 1995, when a comprehensive traversal appeared (CPO 999407, 2CD). Of the full 69, 12 are omitted, leaving a working total of 57. **Schlick** and **Mertens** give thoughtful and moving performances, supported by van Asperen on harpsichord or organ, with cellist Wouter Möller. At least until someone else records all 69 anew, or reissues the old Westminster catchall, this recording will do nicely in introducing today's listeners to an obscure but important dimension of Bach's sacred works.

The *Anna Magdalena Notebook* has long attracted recorded samplings, and a number of single-disc programs have appeared over the years, heavily focused on the keyboard pieces but often including some of the songs. A memorable release that involved **Ameling** with Leonhardt and others included four songs (Harmonia Mundi, distributed here by RCA Victrola). Another such, a program called "Music in the Bach Household," featured the ubiquitous **Schreier** and included eight of these songs (Capriccio 10031; 49261 in the 11CD "Leipzig Bach Edition," 49254).

Of more recent vintage is a program organized by McGegan that includes three of the songs and two other vocal items sung by **Lorraine Hunt** (Harmonia Mundi 907042). Less helpful is another program presented by **Stephen Stubbs**'s Tragicomedia, in which several singers offer seven songs and two other vocal items, with two more in instrumental arrangements (Teldec 91183). The commanding anthology of this kind remains the one organized by Igor Kipnis in 1980, with nine songs sung by **Blegen** and **Luxon,** plus one more in keyboard transcription (Elektra-Nonesuch 79020, 2CD).

Bach's four-part chorale harmonizations have usually been treated as sprinklings in general Bach programs. **Schneidt** did record a fine program entirely devoted to these chorales, a release sorely missed (1979: DG Archiv). **Rilling** has recorded a number of them (most notably, matching them with Bach's Chorale Preludes for organ, in such collections as the *Orgelbüchlein*). In Hänssler's "Bachakademie" collection, the chorale treatments themselves as well as the Schemelli songs and other sacred airs, juxtaposed with appropriate organ pieces, are assembled in a vast, comprehensive, and liturgically systematic corpus in a series of eight volumes (92.078/85, all singles save the last, 2CD).

Distinctly not sacred is the curious fragment of a *Quodlibet* or medley-piece for four voices and continuo (BWV 524), a work from Bach's early years jumbling together references to popular songs of his day in boisterous hilarity. There once was a recording led from the keyboard by **Leonhardt** in a program of Bach oddments that also included two of the Anna Magdalena songs (Telefunken). Just now, however, this curiosity may be had in two lively performances as fillers in cantata collections: one in **Koopman**'s series (♦Erato Vol. 2, 12598, 3CD), the other in a set led by **Reinhard Goebel** (♦DG 457348, 2CD, with BWV 201, 206, 207, 36c).

BARKER

PDQ Bach *(1807–1742?)*

The recorded history of PDQ Bach began with a 1965 concert by Peter Schickele in New York's Town Hall, recorded by Vanguard. By the time CDs came along, 10 LPs had been made. The first five have been reissued with some additions in the form of a preliminary conversation, "In the Vanguard Vault", and another at the end of the set to introduce the previously unreleased *Sanka Cantata* (Vanguard 159-162, 4CD). The discs are presented as they were originally: The 1965 concert is still edited down, the *Quodlibet* is still cut to ribbons because of quotations from pieces under copyright (complete versions may be found in various pirates' lairs), the "Trumpet Involuntary" from *Iphigenia in Brooklyn* is still omitted (not a musical loss), and the Gross Concerto for fipple, globular, and transverse flutes is still absent, though recorded by Vanguard at the concert. I hope the tape still exists and that it and other known but unreleased works, such as Concerto for Piano vs. Orchestra and its companion, Concerto for Bassoon vs. Orchestra, both performed by Professor Schickele, will be foisted on a suspicious world.

Actually, one reason (probably not the only one) that these particular works haven't been released has to do with the many sight gags involved in their performance. Professor Schickele is being urged to make videos of PDQ Bach performances before the traditions connected with them disappear, but he's reluctant to use his pension from the University of Southern North Dakota at Hoople to pay for such a project. The Piano Concerto, no doubt, gains in poignancy when you observe the soloist milking the instrument like a cow and smoke rising from its strings at the end of the performance. In the Bassoon Concerto, it's instructive to watch the interplay between soloist and orchestra as the latter insists on playing its own cadenza. *Iphigenia in Brooklyn* has a memorable visual element, with the double-reed players isolated from the rest of the orchestra by their outfits and the fact that they make every move in unison, while the Professor's performance on a wine bottle is worth seeing, as he becomes visibly more inebriated as the piece progresses and his notes go lower, requiring him to drink down to the next pitch. Finally, he attempts an enthusiastic scale line and falls to the floor. Many other PDQ Bach works are staged in comparable detail.

There is one PDQ Bach video of the full-length opera *The Abduction of Figaro,* 144 minutes of high jinks (VAI 69027). We see the Professor conducting and participating, we see his favorite bargain-counter tenor, **John Ferrante,** in the part of the wily Turk, Opec, and we enjoy the most extended and otherwise unrecorded work by PDQ.

Some highlights of the previously mentioned Vanguard album are the oratorio *The Seasonings,* the half-act opera *The Stoned Guest,* and *Hansel and Gretel and Ted and Alice,* an opera in one unnatural act. The later LPs not yet reissued include *Missa Hilarious, Blaues Grass Cantata, "Howdy" Symphony,* and *Liebeslieder Polkas,* just to mention some of my favorites. Then Telarc took over. Their six CDs include more fine works, including *1712 Overture, Prelude to Einstein on the Fritz,* and *The Preachers of Crimetheus* (80210), *Oedipus Tex* and *Classical Rap* (80239); *Folk Song Upsettings* and *"Safe" Sextet* (80295); *Grand Serenade* and *Six Contrary Dances* (80307); *The Short-Tempered Clavier* and *Little Pickle Book* (80390); and Concerto for Two Pianos vs. Orchestra and *The Musical Sacrifice* (80376). Over the years, PDQ's style has altered, his orchestrations and harmonies have become subtler, and the humor relies less on slapstick than it used to, but the enthusiasm and joie de vivre have never been abandoned.

I should also mention *The Definitive Biography of PDQ Bach* (Random House), which tells us much more than we could ever imagine or want to know about this composer. Considering the plethora of recent knowledge that has come to light, a new edition is in order.

MOORE

Wilhelm Friedemann Bach *(1710–1784)*

The "Halle Bach" was the first son of Johann Sebastian and Maria Barbara Bach. His father was his first and most important teacher, and it was by teaching Wilhelm Friedemann that John Sebastian developed his teaching methods and materials; he wrote his *Klavierbüchlein vor Wilhelm Friedemann Bach* between 1720 and 1724, and may have written his six organ trio sonatas for Wilhelm Friedemann's study as well. Wilhelm Friedemann became an organ virtuoso, a superb improviser, and an excellent teacher. Gifted as he was, he lacked the skills to survive as a musician in the 18th century. In 1746 he secured a position at the Liebfrauenkirche in Halle that he abandoned in 1764; he was never officially employed again, and lived his last 20 years in poverty. His music sounds like a mixture of the very conservative and the very progressive. He seems comfortable with the conservative elements—he loved sequences and imitation—but most of his music is stamped with strange-sounding and oddly placed dissonances that find themselves seeking resolution in odd ways.

Two fine recordings of Wilhelm Friedemann's viola sonata come from **Nobuko Imai** and pianist Roland Pöntinen (Philips 454449) and from **Michael Zaretsky** with harpsichordist Marina Minkin (Artona, PO Box 1376, Amherst, MA 01004). Both include transcriptions of the viola da gamba sonatas by John Sebastian, as well as a sonata by Wilhelm Friedemann's brother, Carl Philip Emanuel.

Harmut Haenchen and the CPE Bach Chamber Orchestra made a fine recording of Wilhelm Friedemann's orchestral music in "Das Orchesterwerk" (Berlin 1098). One of the most interesting pieces in this recording is his *Pfingstkantate* ("Ertonent, Ihr Seligen Volker"), which seems to travel into the 20th century with its escapes from 18th-century harmony. Another recording, by the Salzburg Chamber Philharmonic Orchestra directed by **Yoon K. Lee,** includes only the Sinfonia in F (Naxos 553298). The Sinfonia in D minor under **Ormandy** is in "The Philadelphia Orchestra Plays Bach" (Sony 62345).

Wilhelm Friedemann wrote some of his best music for the keyboard and for small instrumental combinations. **Charlotte Mattax** made a beautiful recording of six of his harpsichord sonatas (Centaur 2351). Here his unusual harmonies are more graceful, perhaps because he was a fine keyboard improviser. Still, some of the harmonic resolutions in these pieces sound like puzzle boxes that have strange and unique solutions. Often his harmonic and rhythmic movement sounds disjointed, but he handles dissonance skillfully in some of the slower, more melancholy movements.

His 12 *Polonaises,* written in 1765 during the first year of his "unemployment," are captivating. They have been recorded on the clavichord by **Steve Barrell** (Globe 5035). **Konrad Hünteler** and Michael Schmidt-Casdorff's excellent recording of the six extremely difficult sonatas for two flutes (MD+G 3110844) is equally interesting. Wilhelm Friedemann's challenge here was to write duets that didn't necessitate or even imply the addition of a basso continuo, while still keeping full harmony.

Wilhelm Friedemann's and Telemann's duets are perhaps the best examples of baroque writing in this genre. His three viola duets were recorded by **Trampler** and Karen Phillips (MHS OR 398, LP) and in France by **Serge Collot** and Michael Martin (Centre Culturel de Valprivas 1001, LP), but neither has been reissued. Another reading of his viola duets comes from **Ryo Terakado** and François Fernandez, with flute duets played by **Patrick Beuckels** and Danièle Etienne and the duo for two harpsichords (Ricercar 89125).

Wilhelm Friedemann wrote 24 cantatas (he was required to write them every few weeks when he worked in Halle), but they sound like weak imitations of his father's and are not his most representative works. They are recorded very nicely in two volumes by **Hermann Max** leading Das Kleine Konzert and the Rheinische Kantorei (Capriccio 10425/26).

FINE

Mily Balakirev *(1837–1910)*

The legacy of Balakirev is twofold, first as mentor to Tchaikovsky and "The Five" and then as composer in his own right. He not only expanded upon the Slavic passion and Oriental coloring inherited from the seminal works of Glinka—traits he willingly passed on to his students Borodin and Rimsky-Korsakov—but in his compositions like *Islamey* and *Tamara* he even influenced Ravel and Debussy.

ORCHESTRAL MUSIC

Symphonies. Balakirev's Symphony 1 is a feast for the ear, a flavorful cornucopia of quasi-Oriental melodies and sumptuous colors that by rights should have taken its place alongside Rimsky-Korsakov's *Scheherazade* as a concert staple long ago. On first hearing, 2 seems almost somber by comparison, yet it has an inner vitality and rhythmic flow that carry the listener along from the staccato opening chords to the final *Tempo di polacca.*

Beecham believed deeply in 1, and his landmark recording has never sounded better than in the "Beecham Edition," with an equally fine—though mono— *Tamara* (♦EMI 63375). **Karajan**'s direct and purposeful mono recording has also been reissued (EMI 66595), but few could summon the requisite atmosphere, nuance, and color as effortlessly as Beecham. **Neeme Järvi** may be seen not as competing with but complementing Beecham's account; where Beecham offers a more comfortable, warmer reading, with faded sonics to match, Järvi's more flexible, often highly charged performance tends to indulge in greater contrasts (EMI 47505). While things may occasionally get blurred at his tempo in the opening movement, in the final romp his brisker pace seems more appropriate.

Svetlanov recorded both symphonies twice—first with the USSR Symphony (Melodiya 00151 and 00152) and again 15 years later with the Philharmonia (Hyperion 66493 or 66586). The Melodiyas have been reissued as a "two-fer" (49608), as have the Hyperions (22030), while 1 is also coupled with Rozhdestvensky's 2 (Revelation, discussed below). On Melodiya, Svetlanov offers a colorful and animated 1, perhaps closer to Järvi than the ruddy good humor of Beecham, if somewhat lacking in subtlety (likewise the sound). Perhaps the most noteworthy thing about the Hyperion remakes is his remarkable ability to make the Philharmonia sound like a Russian orchestra, even down to the strident trumpets. In terms of performance, there's little to choose, save for a broadening of tempo—evident chiefly in the Scherzo of 1—yet the Philharmonia is clearly the better orchestra. While Svetlanov has likewise expanded noticeably on his previous timings in 2, it can tolerate such treatment a lot better, and he brings out its somber colors and comfortable melodies very well.

Igor Golovchin served as assistant to Svetlanov, which might be deduced from the fact that his tempos are often only a few seconds different (Naxos). Unfortunately, it's the Svetlanov of the Hyperion remakes, not the more mercurial Melodiyas. Under Golovchin, color is spread pretty thin for all the earnest effort of the Naxos engineers, with tempos often stretched to the limit as well. Actually 1 (550792), save for the rather detached Scherzo, is a safe investment at the price; in 2 Golovchin offers a broadly conceived, expansive conception with much emphasis on low strings and brass, but the Scherzo lacks the proper swagger and the festive polonaise rhythms in the finale aren't crisp enough.

Vassily Sinaisky offers a rugged and purposeful account of the opening movement of 1—not unlike Beecham—and the buoyant finale is a strong point in his favor, but the resonant sonics, while highly colored, tend to muddy detail in the Scherzo at his fleet tempo (Chandos). Symphony 2 isn't quite so successful; as with Golovchin the music can take a more comfortable treatment and Sinaisky lavishes great warmth and care on it, but the more propulsive quality of **Rozhdestvensky**'s recording (♦Revelation 10038) makes it very special. Conducting with his heart on his sleeve, he gives a warm, robust, and richly satisfying performance that shows his obvious affection for the music, and the engineers have provided sound as hearty as the playing. This is definitely worth seeking out even if you already have the earlier Melodiya Svetlanov. Avoid **Valentin Koshin**'s sodden trudge—it's not worth buying even at budget price (Leningrad Masters, with equally dispirited accounts of *Russia* and *Islamey*).

Tamara. This evocative and highly colored tone poem, based on a poem by Lermontov, tells of a seductive but evil temptress who lures travelers into her tower bedchamber; following a night ripe with passion and reveling, her lovers invariably meet a sad fate, borne away by the flowing river as Tamara, standing by her window, blows one last kiss. **Beecham**'s sensitive reading (in mono) is included with his 1 (above); **Ansermet**'s likewise evocative recording, which dates from about the same time, was brought out in stereo on LP, but I haven't seen it on CD (London). Once again **Svetlanov** recorded the piece twice, for Melodiya and Hyperion, both times coupled with 2. The Melodiya is much better; on Hyperion his rather moderate pacing of Tamara's sensuous melodies suggests a more mature voluptuary, perhaps weary of her hedonistic exploits. **Golovchin** is even more tedious, especially in the lush middle section (Naxos, with 1). **Sinaisky** seems more interested in superficial excitement than the seductive character of the music (Chandos, with 2).

Russia and *In Czechia.* Originally titled *1000 Years, Russia* is based on three folk songs from Balakirev's seemingly endless collection and is intended to symbolize three periods of Russian history: paganism, the period of princes and popular government that gave birth to the Cossack institutions, and the Muscovite Empire. Its companion, *In Czechia* (also called *In Bohemia*), derives from Balakirev's journey to Prague and is likewise based on folk melodies of the region. Since the splendid *Russia* of **Anshel Brusilow** is not likely to show up here (◆EMI 63093), both pieces will most likely be encountered via **Svetlanov**'s Melodiya CDs. His Hyperion remake of *Russia* (with Symphony 1) is sluggish in the extreme, and **Golovchin** (with 2) is even worse, those perky folk dances falling with a dull thud on the ear. **Von Matačič**'s classic *Russia* (mono) is included in "Musiques Russes" (EMI 68550, 2CD). **Choo Hoey** offers a respectable *In Czechia* (Marco Polo 220324), if not as impetuous as Svetlanov, which has also been issued as filler for Kitaienko's Rachmaninoff Symphony 2 (Melodiya 00237). Top choice is **Sinaisky**, animated and colorful with the best sound of the lot.

Overture on Russian Themes. This is a more concise exercise combining two well-known folk tunes, one used by Tchaikovsky in the final movement of his Symphony 4 and the other by Stravinsky in *Pétrouchka*. Unfortunately, my favorite recording, with an alert Kansas City Philharmonic under **Hans Schwieger**, can be had only as makeweight for Hans Swarowsky's sluggish Tchaikovsky *Winter Dreams* (Urania 5140), and in any event is long out of print. Fortunately, **Svetlanov** carries off this plucky little piece with aplomb, both on Melodiya (with Symphony 1) and Hyperion (with 2).

Overture on a Spanish March Theme. This piece is far more elaborate, intended to depict the tragic fate of the Moors who were first persecuted and then driven out of Spain by the Inquisition. **Choo Hoey** makes a creditable effort (Marco Polo, with *In Czechia*), but the power of **Svetlanov**'s Russian brasses and the pounding tympani makes him the clear winner (◆Melodiya 00153). It's coupled with even more rarified fare: the stark and powerful music for *King Lear*—which tells far more of the story than the lone Overture included by **Sinaisky** and Hoey—and a Suite in B Minor comprising a cortege, waltz and tarantella, not available elsewhere. On another CD Svetlanov includes Balakirev's *Suite after Chopin*, a pleasant trifle bearing no relation to either Glazunov's *Chopiniana* or the more familiar *Les Sylphides* (Melodiya 00138). Hoey is quite satisfactory if you can't find the Svetlanov.

Islamey. Balakirev's best known work began life as a piano score but has been recorded in orchestral dress several times. The most familiar arrangement, skillfully fleshed out by Alfredo Casella, receives a superb performance from **Ormandy** in Sony's "Essential Classics" series (◆62647). The rather less virtuosic version by Liapunov may be found as filler with **Svetlanov**'s CD of Liapunov's Symphony 1 (Melodiya); it gets hectic at times but is still better than **Golovchin**'s tired account.

CONCERTOS

Balakirev wrote two piano concertos. The first of these ("Youth"), in one movement, is an early effort modeled on the composer's beloved Chopin. Though undeniably attractive, it's dwarfed by Concerto 2, of which only the first two movements were set down in their entirety by the composer, with the finale—remarkably like the "Dance of Terror" from Falla's *El Amor Brujo* written six years later—completed by his friend Liapunov. **Igor Zhukov**, in an ingenious coupling with two other single-movement concertos by Rimsky-Korsakov and Medtner, brings out the poetry of "Youth" but seems a bit hard toned (MK), while **Binns** sounds like he's sleepwalking through much of it (Hyperion). Thus, the clear first choice is **Shelley** (◆Chandos 9727, with Symphony 2 and *Tamara*). Unfortu-

nately only Hyperion couples both concertos; however, you could supplement Shelley with **Ponti**'s mercurial account of 2 in Volume 5 of the "Romantic Piano Concerto" series (Vox 5068).   HALLER

PIANO MUSIC

Russian composers of piano music can be divided between those who were major concert artists (Prokofiev, Rachmaninoff, the young Scriabin) and those who were not (all of the "Mighty Five"). Music for piano by the latter group is not as voluminous as from the former, and I think much of the best from the non-pianists is better when orchestrated. One could, arguably to be sure, make the case that even Mussorgsky's *Pictures at an Exhibition* is more satisfying in orchestral form, especially in Ravel's version. Balakirev's best-known work for piano, *Islamey*, is a case in point; the orchestral versions are discussed above.

That said, there are at least a dozen recordings of the piano score available, attesting to the continuing popularity of the piece in its original form. Essentially a showpiece of pianistic virtuosity in the turn-of-the-century nationalist Russian tradition, it's recorded most effectively by **Piers Lane** (EMI 2213). He takes quick tempos and doesn't try to make more of the piece than Balakirev intended. **Boris Berezovsky**'s performance serves appropriately as an encore to Tchaikovsky's Sonata in G and Schumann's *Symphonic Etudes* (EW 96516). The sound isn't as big or rich as Lane's, but clear enough to enjoy the orientalisms that Balakirev so passionately derived from the Caucasus region of Georgia. **David Lively**'s rendition is less satisfying on all counts (Discover 920118). In fact, it was this recording that introduced me to *Islamey* and led me to regard Liapunov's orchestration as musically superior even to better performances than Lively's.

Among older recordings, you have to overlook sound quality for readings by masters like **Arrau** (Philips 456706, in his "Great Pianists" set) and **Brendel** (Vox 97203). Their style may not be for modern tastes, but they have faithful followings and their musicianship cannot legitimately be assailed.

Balakirev's piano sonata suffers from comparison to the more adventuresome works by his contemporaries Scriabin and Rachmaninoff, but it has a voice different from theirs and is worthwhile. **Ronald Smith** fails by interpreting it as though it were more Scriabinesque than it actually is (Nimbus 5187, with Scriabin's Sonata 9 and *Pictures*). **Donna Amato** offers a curiously reserved reading with little to recommend it (Olympic 354, with Dutilleux's sonata). Something of a compromise is reached by **Gordon Fergus-Thompson** (Kingdom 2001, with Rachmaninoff's sonatas and Scriabin's 3rd). He's more "Russian" than Amato and less overwrought than Smith. Both Smith and Fergus-Thompson are preferable to Amato and also better recorded.

For the entire corpus of Balakirev's piano music we have **Alexander Paley**'s set (ESS.A.Y 1028, 1030, 1032, 6CD). *Islamey* and the sonata aren't performed as well as by the pianists listed above, though perhaps they have more personality, and Paley's discs include Balakirev's character pieces and transcriptions of other Russian music. **Nicholas Walker** has apparently begun a similar series, and what there is to date is considerably better than Paley's performances (ASV 940). An interesting sampler that contains the best of this music comes from **Mikhail Kollontai** (Russian Disc 288110).   ZIEROLF

Samuel Barber (1910–1981)

There has been no more craft-conscious American composer in this century than Samuel Barber. Doomed to spend most of his life in a time that was philosophically opposed to the kind of music he wrote, Barber has only of late begun to achieve the fame and respect he so richly deserves. His art—not "romantic" as he is sometimes labeled, but thoroughly modern, with an infusion of wondrous melody—now finds itself secure in the minds and hearts of performers and listeners alike. His output was not great, but every note was studied and placed in a tightly wound compositional vortex that disallowed any sort of excess. The music is serene, beautiful, brash, and quintessentially 20th century. He is one of America's best.

SYMPHONIES

1. Barber made what he called a "synthetic treatment" of the four traditional movements of a symphony into this 21-minute tone poem, one of his most cohesive scores. **Neeme Järvi**'s explosive reading has us in the first row mezzanine, but the detail shines though like a shooting star on a clear night. The Detroit Symphony is marvelous, strings fat and full, brass incisive and strong, winds warm and tangy. This one is tough to beat (♦Chandos 8958). **JoAnn Falletta** confounds those who demand big name orchestras with her idiomatic and beautifully proportioned performance with the Virginia Symphony (♦Virginia 3). **Marin Alsop** gives a crisp, highly individual reading. The Royal Scottish Orchestra makes up for its miserable *School for Scandal* with a sensational reading; it almost sounds like a different orchestra (♦Naxos 559024). Colorless winds and brass so mercilessly harsh as to be distracting mar **Zinman**'s otherwise good presentation (Argo).

Carter Nice is bothered by lack of tonal luster, and though the Ljubljana SO gives it that old college try, it fails in the competition (Vox), as does the otherwise acceptable version by **Measham** (Unicorn/Kanchana). **Walter** premiered the final version of the work, and its first recording is a fine one, but not the best available, and the old sound will prove a barrier for many (Sony). **Slatkin** leads a passionate performance, with excellent sound that is not quite as good as Järvi's. Nevertheless, the interpretation is wonderful, and it firmly places this work in the pantheon of great American symphonies (♦RCA 60732).

2. In 1964, Barber withdrew this, his last symphony, from circulation and destroyed all the parts. It had early critical success but was subsequently ignored, and this led to a crisis of confidence. Only the second movement, refashioned as *Night Flight,* was allowed performance (all three movements were devoted to evocation of the dangers and loneliness of flying). But in 1984, copies turned up in a London warehouse, and **Andrew Schenck** put together its first recording. It's a fine reading, doing justice to the score, though the New Zealand Symphony does have technical problems. At bargain price it is certainly more than acceptable (♦Vox 5091). **Järvi**'s Detroit version is in all respects superior to Schenck's; he hasn't been successful in all aspects of his American Music series, but he knows how to give definitive performances of Barber. Great sound, and a model for others to emulate (♦Chandos 9169). **Alsop** navigates this difficult score with as much skill and precision as the flying the work seeks to portray in sound. She holds nothing back, never trying to soften the dissonances or smooth out the rough edges, in what may be the best recording in an admittedly small field (♦Naxos 559024).

OTHER ORCHESTRAL MUSIC

Adagio for Strings. Taken from his early string quartet, this work, so full of pathos and cathartic passion, rarely leaves a dry eye. **Toscanini**'s championship did much to establish Barber in the public eye, giving orchestras a reason to examine his other works more carefully. Even diehard Toscanini foes should take the time to examine his early reading despite its lousy sound (RCA). There have been many fine recordings over the years, but none as emotionally compelling as **Bernstein**'s, espe-

cially his LA Philharmonic reading from the early '80s, a combination no one guessed would produce such riveting results (♦DG 427806 or 431048). But you should not overlook his earlier New York version, perhaps not so pathetically inclined, yet stirring all the same (♦Sony 63088).

Slatkin, with his fine St. Louis band, lessens the breast-beating while still moistening the eyes (♦EMI 49463). One of the earlier modern recordings by **Janigro** (Vanguard) garnered praise from some quarters but can hardly be taken seriously at a clock time of only six minutes (Bernstein took ten), and neither **Marriner** (Argo) nor **Hickox** (Virgin) really understands this work. **Levi** and the Atlanta Symphony sound great and supply us with a wonderful all-Barber disc, but his version blows by too quickly (Telarc). **Saraste**, though well recorded, is let down by his Scottish Chamber Orchestra (Virgin), and **Zinman** fails to generate enough sadness (Argo). **Järvi** has terrific sound, and the Detroit strings pull every possible wrenching aural fiber out of their instruments (♦Chandos 9169).

Tilson Thomas has sleek, slippery string tone on a Copland/Barber disc recorded by the London Symphony, and no contemporary conductor understands this music any better (♦EMI 55358). **Boughton** (Nimbus) and **Andrew Schenck** (Vox and ASV)—whose versions have been praised to the skies in other places—can be safely passed over. But don't ignore the searing, world-weary performance of **Schippers** in New York on a disc that is a desert island necessity for all Barber fans; his *Adagio* is second only to Bernstein's (♦Sony 62837).

Essays for Orchestra. Throughout his life, Barber spent much time in the world of literature. It's no wonder that the idea of musical essays was appealing to him, as their conciseness and regulated thematic structure served as the perfect model for a man so craft-conscious. All three are splendid tone poems, all are under-recorded, the third almost criminally so. **Slatkin** treats 1 as the model of serious journalism it is, stating the theme and allowing it to breathe and develop. The shattering climax is perhaps underdone, but the soft and comfy playing coupled with the satisfying overall shape make this a winner (♦EMI 49463). **Levi**'s reading, in better sound, has an ending that is lackluster, as if he decided enough had been said and laid down his baton (Telarc). **Keith Clark** and the Pacific Symphony Orchestra, in a vibrant recording, are a little fast, but intensity and drama are there, and the climaxes have punch and power (♦Albany 64).

Measham offers a solid reading that fails only because the competition is that much better (Unicorn/Kanchana), while the sound of **Schenck**'s recording, though clean and warm, fails to convey orchestral depth and detail (Vox). **Zinman** puts it all together; his Baltimore Symphony is stirring and expansive, with a winning scherzo and an effective fade-out at the end that gives a real sense of closure (♦Argo 436288). **Järvi**, likewise, turns in a superb account, with vivid sonics and high drama, passionate, and soaring. He never lets the tension wane, and the Detroit Symphony has no flaws (♦Chandos 9053). **Alsop**, in a rather quick version, is still able to paint a broad and expansive picture that is full of searing beauty and fatalistic tension; the sound is very good, and the price is very, very good (♦Naxos 559024).

No. 2, more popular than 1, is rhapsodic and dreamy, a surreal experience not unlike Schoenberg's *Transfigured Night*. **Slatkin** latches on to this idea and underlines the exotic, mysterious opening, while making the transition to the main section beautifully in a provocative reading (♦EMI 49463). On the other hand, **Levi** wastes no time moving through the opening section, robbing it of mystery, though later the orchestra makes a big, suitably raucous sound (Telarc). **Zinman** lacks the atmosphere of Slatkin, but is still nuanced and balanced, with a chord at the beginning of the scherzo that will have you jumping out of your seat. This account is completely over the top, with shadings and subtleties that make you hear it anew each time (♦Argo 436288). **Measham** is plagued by the same problems that affected his 1—a solid reading but not good enough (Unicorn/Kanchana).

Schippers has it all—Slatkin's atmosphere, Levi's sound, Zinman's fervor, and the splendid playing of the NY Philharmonic Orchestra. Though most modern orchestras handle some of the technical difficulties better, its fire and drive more than make up for the few flaws (♦Sony 62837). For some reason, **Järvi** refuses to take enough time to savor the poetry—sonically splendid while spiritually subdued (Chandos). **Golschmann** has a pioneering earnestness in one of the earlier recordings (1960), with spirit, excitement, and spacious, warm sound, though balances are skewed at times; his impassioned performance is authoritative and magnificent (♦Vanguard 4016).

No. 3 suffers from comparative neglect. This is indeed a loss, for it may be the finest of the three. At least that's what **Slatkin** would make you think. His soaring, Hollywood-style string sound and minute attention to detail add to the overt sensuality of the work (♦EMI 49463). **Schenck** doesn't have an orchestra that can compete with St. Louis, but his interpretive powers are every bit as good. His emphasis on the percussive qualities of the score makes for a volatile experience—lyrical, but a little distressing and unsettling, perhaps more of what Barber had in mind (♦Koch 7010). **Järvi** also turns in a rugged and powerful reading, highlighting elements of the piece that result in real continuity and drama; the punctuated, fleshy sound is superb (♦Chandos 9053). **Mehta** lets us down, primarily for skimpy playing time that is no bargain to the consumer, especially with other treasures available (New World).

Medea and *Cave of the Heart*. It's nice to hear Barber's ballet *Medea* in its suite format, but I can see why he decided to reduce it to the more effective concert version. Parts of the suite make little or no sense without associating them with action or movement. **Marriner,** as usual, has superb execution, but while this works well in many pieces, Barber demands *violence* (Capriccio). **Howard Hanson** provides it, but many won't like the rather rustic sound (Mercury). **Schenck** tones the piece down, eliminating some of the excitement in the 'Dance' (♦Koch 7010). Not much can be said about the 15-instrument *Cave of the Heart*—this music cries out for the wild, boisterous playing of a large orchestra, and the small ensemble doesn't do the music justice. But if you want it, it's available in Schenck's fine performance (♦Koch 7019).

Medea's Meditation and Dance of Vengeance. This is made up of what Barber considered the best parts of his *Cave of the Heart* ballet, later reduced to the *Medea* suite, and finally to this form—which is most often performed, and rightly so. **Munch** (RCA) and **Schenck** (Koch) both lead fine performances, with better sound in the former and more interpretive zest in the latter. **Schippers** supplies both in spades, turning in a reading that is intoxicating. This is a composer-approved recording by a man who conducted more Barber than anyone else (♦Sony 62837). If Schippers's Medea is a woman with jealousy and anger in her soul, **Levi** presents her as a civilized housewife; no matter, the frenzy escalates to pandemonium crazier than rush hour on Peachtree Street, the Atlanta players indulging themselves in an orgy of orchestral panic (♦Telarc 80250).

Slatkin gives us a diffuse opening that never gets going, and relief comes only in the last few bars. The energy is artificial, the pulse superficial, as if he were trying to make it exciting from outside instead of energizing it from within (EMI). But the splendiferous sound of **Järvi**

packs quite a wallop (♦Chandos 9253). He is as crazed as Schippers, but the orchestra sounds almost *too* beautiful. Schippers puts the violent passages across more forcefully, but this one is darn close.

Music for a Scene from Shelley. The verbal command "List!" from Shelley's *Prometheus Unbound* inspired Barber to create this dramatic score that seeks to fulfill the music instruction in the poem. Shelley might not have understood Barber's post-romantic blitzkrieg, but we are the richer for it. **Schenck** gives it a searing performance, and the New Zealanders play their hearts out, especially in the devastating climax (♦Vox 5019). The rich, hot sound of **Zinman** actually takes a bit of the edge away, because you can lose yourself in the prism of color and radiant melody. But too muffled is too muffled (Argo). **Golschmann** is faster than most, but doesn't feel rushed in any way. The strings sing with a passion and vitality missing in other versions, and this confident reading is simply stunning (♦Vanguard 4016). Likewise **Järvi,** whose lush sensibilities flood the air with an expectant, palpably emotional mist. This fervent interpretation, sonically splendid, is a clear first choice among modern recordings (♦Chandos 9253).

Overture to the School for Scandal. This overture, loosely suggested by Sheridan's 1777 comedy, is bouncy and brilliant, just the thing for a young composer vying for the musical world's attention. **Levi** lets the pace unfold moderately, highlighting every colorful detail, with strings that are rich and full and sound that is warm and inviting. A *refined* scandal, to be sure, but very evocative (♦Telarc 80250). **Slatkin** is less so, refusing to pause and breathe when needed, and plagued by brass that drown the strings (EMI). **Schippers** produces a high-energy reading, with bright sound, great detail, and an enthusiastic orchestra. This is Barber the tonal modernist as only the NY Philharmonic Orchestra can present him. Hang on to this disc for life (♦Sony 62837).

You can ignore **Järvi.** His slow tempos, despite great sound, make for a rather flaccid journey that offers little excitement (Chandos). **Schenck's** generally fine interpretation is undermined by his orchestra's insecure string tone (Vox). **Schwarz** leads an attractive reading that is very much middle-of-the-road, but his premiere of the orchestral version of Bernstein's *Arias and Barcarolles* and the original orchestration of Gershwin's *American in Paris* may entice you (Delos). **Zinman** gives us a very European rendition, treating the work more as a tone poem than an overture. The Baltimore strings lack some weight, but the brass are superb, and the conducting carries the day (♦Argo 436288). **Alsop** fails to convince us that this stuttering, uncertain reading is anything close to what Barber had in mind (Naxos).

Souvenirs. Originally scored for piano four-hands, this delightful work found itself transformed into a ballet when Barber was presented with the idea of working with the choreographer George Balanchine. One recording, that of **Levi** and the Atlanta Symphony, does its dance-like poetry justice. (♦Telarc 80441).

CONCERTOS

Capricorn Concerto. This delightful piece for flute, oboe, trumpet, and strings (named after Barber's home in New York) is not full of his patented big melodies, but is an amalgam of motivic ideas expertly traded off among soloists and strings. The ghost of Stravinsky hovers throughout, perhaps Barber's most obvious homage to the Master. None of the recordings is bad, and two are outstanding. **Donald Barra** gives a fine reading that suffers only when compared with others (Koch). If you like the Eastman-Rochester sound that **Howard Hanson** so consistently brought to the studio, his interpretation is fine (Mercury). **Keith Clark** puts together a truly outstanding collection of Americana (with Copland's *Saga of the Prairies* and Harris's Symphony 6) in a reading that gives us a brittle battle between combatants and chills the air instead of warming it (♦Albany 64). If Clark presents a desolate tone poem, **Slatkin** chooses to embrace tradition within the cozier confines of a modern baroque style (♦RCA 68283). Fast movements are faster and the slow one moderate. Both points of view are valid, though Clark may be more musically affecting.

Cello Concerto. This is a splendid, lyrical, 20th-century work that has received far too few performances. Barber thought highly of it, and sought to combine the songlike poetry of his Violin Concerto with the spiciness of *Capricorn.* **Ralph Kirshbaum**'s recording was well received in many quarters, not least because of his affecting traversal of the Cello Sonata (Virgin). Though you wouldn't be committing a grave sin to make this your first choice, it can't honestly be said that it's the best on the market. **Ma** comes closer to that claim, turning in a performance of great thought and subtlety, with tearful, tuneful support by Zinman, ideally coupled with Britten's wonderful Cello Concerto (♦Sony 44900). **Raphael Wallfisch** also has an excellent coupling in Shostakovich's Cello Concerto 1, but the warm sonics and generally fine playing don't top the finest (Chandos)—that is, the delectable performance by **Isserlis** with Slatkin on what has become a nearly indispensable recording. Isserlis's sound is sweet and romantic, practically perfect (♦RCA 668283).

Piano Concerto. Despite winning a Pulitzer Prize and a Music Critics Circle Award, and the overwhelmingly positive public reaction, Barber's Piano Concerto—though it may indeed be one of the most important of the century—doesn't seem to have won over an undiscerning public. There isn't a lot in it for the casual listener to grasp, aside from the beautiful second movement. But for the *discerning* listener, the riches abound, especially the crypto-atonal melodic leaps that splatter the pages of this remarkable score. The phenomenal **John Browning** gave its premiere after close collaboration with the composer, and his reading with Slatkin edges out the competition (♦RCA 60732). His second movement is sensitive and haunting, in wonderful sound that allows the instruments to breathe. Unfortunately, his even more electric collaboration with Szell is available only as an import (Sony Theta 60004, with Stern in the Violin Concerto).

Jon Kimura Parker comes in a close second, with a very urbane, metallic recording, not at all out of place. Levi's accompaniment is muscular and controlled (♦Telarc 80441). **Ted Joselson** is fine but lacking the last bit of emotional polish that Parker and Browning provide (ASV). **Abbott Ruskin** is dead in the water because of substandard sound (Vox).

Violin Concerto. Often cited as the most romantic of Barber's works—and second in popularity only to the *Adagio*—this concerto would have survived if only the first movement existed, with a melodic allure and dramatic fire that infallibly win over first-time hearers. The third movement, a pyrotechnic tour de force, was declared unplayable by Iso Briselli, its dedicatee, though later he was proven wrong by a student violinist. It's a striking contrast to the first two movements, but years of hearing the whole package have dulled our awareness of any flawed compositional schema.

Slatkin has recorded it twice, the first time with **Elmar Oliveira,** a recording loved by many, but he doesn't possess the refinement needed to jump from ultra-lyricism to ultra-virtuosity (EMI). The second Slatkin recording, with **Kyoko Takezawa,** is everything this work should be: lingering, sultry, sweet, and rapturous. The more acerbic

moments are toned down to let loose the soaring beauty of violin and orchestra (♦RCA 68283). **Perlman** does what he does best, giving us a high cholesterol performance that wears the acoustics of Boston's Symphony Hall like a warm comforter—a very European reading ably assisted by the resonant Boston strings (♦EMI 55360). **Joshua Bell** is delicate and refined, with 20-carat clarity, but doesn't have the boldness of tone of some others. Zinman makes pointed highlights of Barber the dissonant traditionalist (London).

Hu Kun provides a fresh reading—warm, sensuous, lithe, and completely at ease, the instrumental equivalent of *Knoxville* (♦Nimbus 5329). **Ricci** is not as successful. He plays tenderly, with lots of nuance in a very natural perspective, but there are technical problems and a general thinness of sound. Much ado was made of **Shaham**'s recording—bold and full of the bright lights of Hollywood—but it comes nowhere near the underlying strand of pessimism that runs through all of Barber's works, no matter how beautiful (DG). **Salerno-Sonnenberg** also fails to grasp the elusive combination of loveliness, elegance, and stoicism so necessary in this work (EMI). **Robert McDuffie,** brilliantly accompanied by Levi and his Atlantans, gives a powerhouse reading. The thick, carpeted sonic background is a perfect launching pad for his juicy, full-blooded tone, taking time where time needs to be taken (♦Telarc 80441).

But the blue ribbon goes to the recording that just about every American critic agrees on: **Isaac Stern** with Bernstein. This classic performance will probably never be surpassed, towering above all others in a collaboration that radiates sun-drenched energy and makes us feel the pulse of Stern's soaring playing and Bernstein's charged conducting in every bar. Don't miss it (♦Sony 63088). **Hahn**'s subtle maturity continues to amaze us, and she gives a loving, milk chocolate reading with Wolff and the St. Paul Chamber Orchestra; even though the strings are reduced, the intimacy and superb sound more than make up for it. An interesting new concerto by Krzystof Meyer serves as the appropriate discmate (♦Sony 89029).

CHAMBER MUSIC

Canzone for Flute & Piano. This lovely extract from the second movement of Barber's Piano Concerto is welcome regardless of format. There are many recordings in collections, but none finer than **Jeanne Baxtresser** and Israela Margalit in a wonderful disc of Barber chamber music (♦EMI 55400).

Canzonetta for Oboe & Small Orchestra. This, Barber's swan song, was originally intended for NY Philharmonic oboist Harold Gomberg. Barber, in declining health, knew he would not be able to finish it, so he wrote an Andante he thought could stand alone. The orchestration was unfinished at his death, though his intentions were fairly clear. A few recordings exist, but none is as smooth and silky, while also resigned and reflective, as that of **Keisuke Wakao** and Christoph Eschenbach, who use only piano, just as Barber left it (♦Denon 8723).

String Quartet. Barber realized the importance of this early foray into the quartet genre, so much so that he totally rewrote the last movement and excised the middle movement, which became the famous Adagio for more strings. The work is effective, but not the most memorable piece he wrote, and there aren't many recordings available. By far the best was by the old **Cleveland Quartet,** long ago buried (RCA). The **Tokyo Quartet,** in a recording with other modern works, offers the best stopgap for now, with all the attributes we associate with this great ensemble (♦RCA 61387).

The **Endellion Quartet,** recorded at some distance, is not as intense as others, but individual instruments are heard to greater effect (♦Virgin 45033). The Adagio is exquisitely done, not rushing, not trying to pull everything out of it—always a mistake, for quartets can only give so much, and they shouldn't try to imitate the larger version. The **Emerson Quartet** has never wanted for intensity, and their clean sonics, cool sound, and impeccable bow work steer them through Barber's rush-hour rhythms right between the white lines. But the unemotional Adagio sounds even faster than its six minutes suggest and completely lets the work down. The **Duke Quartet** is visceral and sharp (Collins), not unlike the Emerson, while the **Alexander Quartet** (Analekta) doesn't measure up, even against admittedly weak competition.

Serenade for String Quartet (or String Orchestra). This short, romantic ditty by the 18-year-old composer has always enjoyed a vogue in its string orchestra arrangement, but the quartet version is more effective in clarifying line and melody. As in their Quartet reading, the **Endellion Quartet** is a model of precision and light, floating, melodic charm (♦Virgin 45033). Among the orchestral readings, **Golschmann** takes the prize for this and a number of other Barber works in a terrific collection (♦Vanguard 4016).

Sonata for Cello. This was completed while Barber was still a student and very much under the spell of Brahms, whose autumnal darkness pervades much of this work. But the young Barber couldn't be suppressed, and surprises abound everywhere, giving us a hint of things to come. There are many recordings of this work, but four are something special, and you need look no further. Perhaps it's fitting that a young man should give a rich, fat, earth-moving rendition, and **Jian Wang** does just that, my favorite on disc (♦Delos 3097). **Alan Stepansky** is not far behind—intense, brusquely abrasive, but also warm in an unsentimental sort of way in a very street-smart performance (♦EMI 55400). So is **Andrés Diaz,** in a recording called "American Visions" that has stunning sound (♦Dorian 90241). **Ralph Kirshbaum,** on a disc with the Cello Concerto, gives a serious, wonderfully played reading that rounds out a fine release (♦Virgin 59565).

Summer Music (Woodwind Quintet). This may be the most popular woodwind quintet written in this century, and probably would compete successfully with any from the last as well. Originally intended as a septet for first chair players of the Detroit Symphony, the piece became a quintet and was written with the **NY Woodwind Quintet** in mind; they were intimately involved at all stages of composition. Their recording of this nocturnal romp is still the best, even with remastered sound that is warm but 40 years old (♦Boston Skyline 137). Members of the **NY Philharmonic** band together for a performance that is provocative in every way, corresponding to Barber's own description: "It's supposed to be evocative of summer—summer meaning languid, not killing mosquitoes" (♦EMI 55400). For an overseas view, you can't do any better than the clear, refined playing of the **Bergen Wind Quintet,** fresh, sparkling, and rhythmically in the groove (♦BIS 291). In and out of the catalog is the concert version by the **Marlboro Music Festival,** replete with audience noise to be sure, but worth every cough (♦Sony 46250).

PIANO MUSIC

Throughout his life, Barber devoted much time and effort to writing piano music, whether solo or as the accompaniment to his many songs. His Sonata, a favorite of many eminent pianists and a highly favored audience work, has had two classic recordings that you won't want to miss. **Horowitz** was its earliest champion, and by his performances assured

the work repertory status. No one has ever played it more brilliantly, and probably no one ever will (♦RCA 60377). But if you want more modern sound, the recording by **Cliburn** will suit nicely as it is equally vigorous, lacking only that last bit of authority (♦RCA 60415). **Ohlsson** brings a sharpness and acerbity which the composer would surely have approved. Coupled with equally persuasive Profofiev, Bartok, and Webern, this great sounding disc is an all around winner (♦Arabesque 6724). **Wild,** on the other hand, relies on a more lyrical approach, though this 85 year-old lacks nothing in technique. His coupling of his own Sonata plus those by Hindemith (3) and Stravinsky are most rewarding (♦Ivory Classics 71005).

Recordings of Barber's other piano music can be found sporadically in collections, but it is worth your while to grab a CD with all of it. Avoid **Browning;** despite the man's authority in this music and his fabulous recording of the Concerto, his playing is harsh and not sewn with the delicacy this music requires (MusicMasters). **Parkin** gives an excellent reading of most of the works, a no-nonsense *Excursions,* clearly delineated *Nocturne* and *Ballade,* and a rather sedate but effective Sonata (♦Chandos 9177). **Pollack**'s complete budget recording is an all-out exercise in high energy. This can be attractive in places, but the uniformity of approach is too extreme, despite an excellent Sonata (Naxos). **Leon McCawley** has better sound and more zest; his strokes are bold and invigorating, with a sexy, saucy *Souvenirs,* a whooping Sonata, and the inclusion of the posthumous *Interlude.* This is clearly the disc to have if you want only one (♦Virgin 45270).

CHORAL MUSIC

Agnus Dei. This choral arrangement of the famous *Adagio for Strings* has always been a crowd-pleaser, though it lacks the intensity and pathos of the string version. **Shaw**'s Festival Singers sing it as well as anyone, controlled, concentrated, and thrilling (♦Telarc 80406). Two English conductors give it a nice try, but only **Christophers** can be recommended as anywhere near Shaw (♦Collins 12872), while **Matthew Best** is just too refined and clinical, despite beautiful cathedral-style singing (Hyperion).

Prayers of Kierkegaard. This is probably Barber's most famous choral work, inspired by the existential utterings of the theologian/philosopher, who might not have approved of the fiercely dramatic setting Barber gave his prayers. **Mester** (Albany) is outclassed by two superb versions. **Shaw** sculpts a carefully crafted performance that avoids extremes while still conveying the power and emotion of the text (♦Telarc 80479). But it is again **Schenck** who provides the real emotional hits with a clean, close-up concert recording that may not be as immaculate as Shaw's but is every bit as thunderous (♦Koch 7125).

To Be Sung on the Water, Twelfth Night, others. An excellent contemporary miscellany by **Gilbert Seeley** (♦Koch 7279, with music by Libby Larsen and Stephen Paulus) is worthy of attention, as is the terrific Barber/Schuman compendium that has these plus many other choral works in great sound with great singing, conducted by **Peter Broadbent** and his Joyful Company of Singers (♦ASV 939).   RITTER

OPERAS

Antony and Cleopatra. Barber's Shakespearean opera was the winner in a bitter contest for the commission of a new opera to inaugurate the new Metropolitan Opera House at Lincoln Center in 1966. Composers and performers aligned themselves into two major groups—those supporting Barber and those supporting Bernstein—and engaged in long and acrimonious contention. The Met produced the opera in the grand manner: a huge production by Zeffirelli (who also compiled the libretto), and a first-rate cast (Leontyne Price, Justino Diaz, Jess Thomas), conducted by Schippers. The opera seemed poised for success, but instead was an almost complete disaster; its musical and dramatic elements were overwhelmed by the overproduction of the visual elements. The composer's heart was broken by its failure; subsequently he composed very little, although he continued to tinker with the opera.

In the revised version, Barber cut out most of the grandiose scenic elements, concentrated more upon the two lovers, added some new music—and eliminated Zeffirelli's name from the title page. This had its premiere in 1975 at Juilliard and also received a televised production in 1991 at Chicago's Lyric Opera. The new version is much tighter and more dramatic, yet one should not denigrate the passages eliminated by Barber; taken for what they are, they are quite effective. The only complete recording, from a 1984 Spoleto Festival production, is a worthy if not compelling performance (New World 322/4, 2CD). **Christian Badea** conducts the Westminster Choir and the Spoleto Festival Orchestra plainly and seems uninvolved.

A Hand of Bridge. The libretto of this brief one-act opera reveals the words and thoughts of two couples at a bridge game, and while it's not dramatically involving, it works well in its simplicity—a fine piece for music school production. The singers in the only recording work hard at their diction, getting most of it through; it's in their words that most of the interest lies (Vanguard 2083). **Golschmann** accompanies the text easily, with the Gregg Smith Singers and the Adirondack Orchestra.

Vanessa. Barber's first opera was a solid success, if not one that would ensure its production around the world. Most of its subsequent productions were associated with Gian-Carlo Menotti, who wrote the libretto. *Vanessa* was also filmed for television. Barber set a nostalgic tale of wealth and privilege with love gone astray and awry. Within the claustrophobic, isolated setting—an Edwardian-Gothic country house in "a northern country"—are a group of characters of strong individuality and personality. The story is strangely touching, yet with a wisp of ironic unreality and self-delusion. Barber has composed music finely complementary to the story, tonal, romantically conservative, emotionally charged, often hauntingly beautiful.

Metropolitan Opera impresario Rudolf Bing produced the opera with as good a cast as could be mustered at the time (♦RCA 7899, 2CD). Always a strong conductor, **Mitropoulos** obviously felt great affection for the music, guiding the orchestra and singers (Steber, Elias, Gedda, Resnik, and Tozzi) with sympathy. PARSONS

SONGS

Andromache's Farewell. You would think sopranos would be lining up to record this Straussian masterpiece of Barber's late years, but this is not the case. It's a tension-laden, highly emotional work about a captive woman who must give up her son to be killed, and Barber's concert scene for soprano and orchestra has an opera's worth of fission and fizz. **Arroyo,** in a justly famous recording with Schippers—on perhaps the greatest Barber album of all time—gives a radiantly heartfelt performance that would take a miracle to improve (♦Sony 62837).

Dover Beach. Victorian poet Matthew Arnold provided the lines that Barber set for baritone and string quartet. This is a dark work, unusual in its reflection of a side of the composer he hid in other works. **Hampson,** though he sings very well, doesn't have the necessary darkness of timbre to push this work over the bleary edge (DG). **Thomas Allen** doesn't have a particularly dark voice either, but his sheer musicality and ability to con-

sider and clearly express textual concerns make his rendition the finest of modern recordings (♦Virgin 45033). **Fischer-Dieskau** sings the piece with a haunting, somber, weighty tone that almost perfectly puts this spooky work across, and the 1967 sound is great (♦Sony 46727). For a woman's point of view, turn to the heavy, creamy, but somehow not quite dark enough version by **Horne** (RCA). But she is not a first choice here.

Hermit Songs. Set to poems by anonymous monks and hermits between the 8th and 13th centuries, this cycle quickly became one of Barber's most loved compositions and is one of the great song cycles of the 20th century. Rarely have feeling and expression been so wedded to the text, with a melodic element at once poignant and pithy. **Leontyne Price** made these songs famous, and Barber, once he had heard her voice, gave her the premiere. She recorded them twice, both times with the composer and both times in mono sound. Her first effort (♦Sony 46727) is in every way superior to her RCA set. In the former, she is still struggling to understand the work, and her vitality and wonder at its beauties come across brilliantly. This recording has always been a little tricky to find, but is worth the search. **Alexander** made a recording that, though intelligent and well considered, is strident in sound and lacking in interpretive nuance (Etcetera).

Sylvan also recorded them in much better sound, and this has been acclaimed by many critics. However, I find his voice lackluster and thin, missing any sort of bottom (Nonesuch). **Studer,** in a set that has been called "the Barber disc of the century" by some, turns in a strangled reading, rhythmically lax, interpretively neutral, with many vocal problems, especially pitch (DG). Aside from Price, only **Bonney** finds the true meaning and measure of this music, with a light, fragrantly tuned instrument that expresses these texts like no other and sends us away wishing we had known some of these poets (♦London 455511).

Knoxville: Summer of 1915. According to the composer, James Agee's poem was meant to express "a child's feeling of loneliness, wonder, and lack of identity in that marginal world between twilight and sleep." All recordings have this yardstick to measure themselves against. Many are successful without entirely meeting these requirements—such is the strength and durability of the music—and few actually achieve the optimum. One of these failures is **Upshaw** with Zinman (Nonesuch). There is no sense of tiredness or reverie in this vivid recording. Barber's poignancy comes across, and Upshaw sings beautifully—though sometimes stridently—as she always does, but ultimately it is Zinman who must take the blame, always too anxious to forge ahead. **Battle** and Previn present a more operatic style, with the Orchestra of St. Luke's sounding warmer and more colorful than in the Nonesuch recording. Battle weaves herself around the words, caressing and nurturing them, making them as important as the music. Previn supports her with flexible inflections and voice-sensitive phrasing (♦DG 437787).

Schippers's recording with **Leontyne Price** would seem to have an edge on all the others, considering their relationship with the composer, but alas, despite the beautiful singing—and it *is* beautiful—others have simply done more with this piece (RCA). **Ruth Golden** and Donald Barra also turn in a reading that isn't bad standing alone, but fails to rise to greater heights (Koch). Sultry, sexy, sweet, and cooled down only by a soft breeze through the magnolias, **McNair** is well-nigh perfect in her recording with Levi, as are the sound and interpretation. The playing is rich and wonderfully laid back in the beginning, lazy and lingering—this is Knoxville in 1915, after all—and her inflections are slow and sliding, taking time with the words and making sure we understand every one of them (♦Telarc 80250).

Likewise well performed is the first recording, by the wonderful **Eleanor Steber** and William Strickland (Sony). Though it must be taken seriously because of the authority of the performer and the approval of the composer, its mono sound—though hardly a serious detriment—excludes it from serious consideration as more than a supplement. Steber knew how to sing, and sing well, but where McNair tells a story, Steber seems to be looking back, mesmerized by past events. Of more immediate appeal is the version by **Hendricks** with Tilson Thomas. She's in resplendent voice—not always the case with this soprano—and is competitive with anyone. The conductor, as always, understands American music very well, and the London Symphony may well have had grits for breakfast that morning (♦EMI 55358).

Other Songs. The complete Barber songs still await their definitive interpreter. *Secrets of the Old,* a rather strong effort by **Hampson** and **Studer,** can be said to be only half a success—Hampson's half. Studer was vocally unprepared for this effort and doesn't have a firm grasp of the songs from either a technical or interpretive standpoint. Hampson is tremendous, bringing his uncanny knack for getting to the heart of a song's emotional content to every item on the disc. I only wish he had sung them all, but the set can be recommended for his performances (♦DG 435867). "Dover Beach" is the name of an album by **Thomas Allen,** and he sings wonderfully, if lacking the last bit of refinement that Hampson brings to this music (♦Virgin 45033). Avoid the disc by **Alexander**—it has bad, strident sound, and while some of her performances are fine, others are not (Etcetera). One other disc to consider is **Horne**'s warmly vibrant reading of seven Barber songs (♦RCA 68771).

RITTER

Béla Bartók *(1881–1945)*

Bartók was the last great nationalist composer. He might also be thought of as a regionalist, as his folk-musicological interests roamed freely around the southeastern reaches of the Austro-Hungarian Empire and even beyond, into Anatolia and North Africa, and all these researches influenced his works. He actually began composing in a late romantic style like Richard Strauss's. Then, in 1904, he made his first transcriptions of authentic Hungarian folk music, and thereafter his compositions underwent a profound stylistic change. It was also about this time that he became aware of Debussy's music, so he combined the Frenchman's new approach to harmony and instrumental color with the flavor of folk music. He then underwent two more major stages of development. In the early '20s, he introduced more counterpoint into his compositions, facilitated by more compact, motivic material than the longer melodies he had been using. Beginning with Violin Concerto 2 in 1938, he returned to the use of longer melodies while retaining his mastery of counterpoint.

ORCHESTRAL MUSIC

Concerto for Orchestra. This is Bartók's most popular orchestral work, commissioned in 1944 by Koussevitzky for the virtuoso Boston Symphony. It's a display piece that shows off the sections of the orchestra, most explicitly in II, 'Presentation of the Pairs.' (This is its name in the manuscript; in the published version it was somehow changed to 'Game of Pairs' and the metronome marking was lowered.)

Skrowaczewski (Vox), **Ferencsik** (Hungaroton), **Schwarz** (Delos), and **Salonen** (Sony) lead slack readings. **Leinsdorf** keeps taut control over the Boston Symphony in a fairly bland interpretation (RCA). **Haitink** (Philips) leads a reading that's also bland and unexciting until V. **Fricsay** maintains too light a mood in most of the work, robbing it of drama (DG). **Van Beinum** leads the Concertgebouw in a performance

that's superb in the odd-numbered movements but fails in the even-numbered ones (Dutton). Oddly, the same fault afflicts the recording of the premiere directed by **Koussevitzky** (Naxos). **Dorati** (Mercury) and **Stokowski** (Everest) do excellent jobs conducting, but the London and Houston symphonies around 1960 aren't up to the task. Dorati has better luck the second time around with the Hungarian State Orchestra in a good reading, though IV is too slow (Hungaroton). **Iván Fischer** is weak in all but II and III, though his reading is valuable because it has by far the finest II on disc (Philips 456575). The various pairs have great character, and Fischer gauges his humor perfectly for each "presentation."

Dutoit is good except in IV, which lacks humor, and V, which lacks excitement (London). **Bernstein** leads a bold, exciting reading marred only by a dull, humorless II (Sony 60730). V, however, will knock your socks off. **Danielle Gatti** leads a fine, thoughtfully nuanced performance with no weak movements, and he's blessed with a recording with a wide dynamic range (Conifer 51324). **Boulez** has recorded the Concerto with the NY Philharmonic (Sony 37259) and the Chicago Symphony (DG 437826). Both are fine performances whose only weakness is the lack of mystery in the introduction of I. **Solti**'s reading with the Chicago Symphony is excellent and very energetic (London 417754, NA). **Reiner**'s is a great performance (♦RCA 61504). II is nearly as good as Fischer's, and III conveys mystery, anxiety, and tragedy. **Levine**'s recording is superb, with a II nearly as nuanced as Fischer's and a finale that doesn't pull out all the stops at once but is beautifully paced with tremendous cumulative impact (♦DG 429747).

Dance Suite. This is a much spikier, more demanding score than *Romanian Folk Dances* or *Hungarian Sketches.* **Skrowaczewski** leads a decent performance (Vox), but **Boulez** is more energetic (DG) and does a much better job than in his earlier recording with the NY Philharmonic (Sony). **Dorati** has enormous drive and vigor and offers huge contrasts of tempo and dynamics (Mercury 432017), but **Solti** is just as good and has better sound and a much better orchestra (♦London, NA).

Divertimento. This is a light work Bartók wrote in just 15 days while vacationing in Switzerland in 1939. It's one of his most neoclassical pieces, and while the storm clouds that gather over *Music for Strings, Percussion and Celeste* appear here, they don't frighten as they did there. **Boulez** (DG), **Péter Csaba** (Ondine), **Dorati** (Mercury and Hungaroton), the **Orpheus Chamber Orchestra** (DG), and **Skrowaczewski** (Vox) all give good performances. **Gatti** is more atmospheric and dramatic and is recorded with a very wide dynamic range (Conifer 51324). **Solti** is very intense and dramatic (London 430352, NA).

Hungarian Sketches. These arrangements of short piano pieces are delightful vignettes of everyday life. **Fischer** does a workmanlike job (Philips), while **Boulez** is rather dull (DG). **Reiner** is more playful and energetic (RCA 61504). It's almost perverse that **Järvi** invests so much thought and attention in this minor work (♦Chandos 8895). By the time you've finished listening to his recording, he'll have you convinced that it's one of the masterpieces of the orchestral repertoire.

Music for Strings, Percussion, and Celeste. Many feel this is Bartók's orchestral masterpiece, and it's certainly a deeply personal statement. Scored for opposed string orchestras separated by percussion, it's one of the more original works of the 20th century. It's composed of four movements, and the two slow movements are so eerie and menacing that they were used to great effect by Stanley Kubrick in his horror film *The Shining.* **Dutoit** (London), **Solti** (London, NA), **Reiner** (RCA), **Skrowaczewski** (Vox), and **Ozawa** (DG) are quite similar, taking a rather impersonal, straightforward approach to this very subjective score. **Salonen** (Sony) is positively soporific.

Kubelik (Mercury) sets remarkably slow, controlled tempos in the slow movements, as does **Bernstein** (Sony). Fine as Kubelik is, he could have made more of the score's drama. Bernstein's fault is that he pursues beauty at the expense of expression. **Dorati**'s performance is a model of clarity of balance and articulation (Mercury 434357). He sacrifices speed in the fast movements as a result, and the London Symphony in 1960 wasn't quite good enough to express all the music's many moods in the fast movements. **Boulez** recorded the score twice, first with the BBC Symphony (Sony 64100, 2CD) and then with the Chicago Symphony (DG 447747), and the interpretations are very similar. He's very good in the slow movements and gets just the right vibratoless, expressionless sound at the start of the opening fugue. **Fricsay** captures the sardonic mood in II and the exuberant, triumphant mood in IV in his 1953 recording (DG 447443). **Levine** isn't quite as clear and controlled in I as Dorati or Boulez, but his II is very powerful and driven, his III wonderfully spooky, and his IV simply ecstatic (DG 429747).

At least two concert recordings by **Mravinsky** and the Leningrad Philharmonic have been released, one from 1965 (♦Melodiya 25197) and one from 1970 (♦Russian Disc 11167). No other conductor has thought as hard about this music or felt it as deeply as he did. The 1965 performance is the more polished, but the 1970 reading is electrifying. I is very imposing and II is correctly very sardonic and tightly controlled. Only in Mravinsky's hands is III not merely terrifying but tragic. IV is fast enough, with ferocious energy. Tragedy clearly becomes triumph when the fugal subject of I reappears with augmented intervals in the major mode. Both performances are more than thrilling; they are inspiring.

Romanian Folk Dances. Bartók arranged these from his popular piano pieces. **Fischer** leads a pleasant performance (Philips), but the **Orpheus Chamber Orchestra** is a little more attentive to details (DG 445541). **I Solisti Italiani** plays this music with great character and imagination (♦Denon 75040, NA).

CONCERTOS

Piano

1. This was composed in 1926 as a vehicle for Bartók's own engagements. Brusque and dissonant, with no singing melodies, it certainly must have been a shocker. **Schiff**'s approach is too romantic for this music, but he does well enough in III (Teldec). **Sandor** (Sony) and **Kocsis** (Philips) are much better, but their orchestras sound too recessed to effectively interact with them. **Jandó** is a very fine soloist, and the engineers have placed the orchestra up front with the piano in the mix (Naxos 550771). Better yet are **Anda** (DG 447399) and **Kovacevich** (Philips 438812, 2CD). The orchestras are forward and the performances are really ferocious. **Ashkenazy** tops these two with the best tempos and really virile playing (♦Decca 448125).

2. Written in 1933, No. 2 shows a considerable advance over 1 in contrapuntal technique. **Schiff** is good in I and III, but dull in II (Teldec). **Anda** is better, with a thrilling I and a percussive, primitivist III with high drama, but he's done in by a murky II (DG). **Jandó** (Naxos 550771) and **Sandor** (Sony 45835) are strong in all three movements, with Sandor excelling in II and Jandó in III. **Kovacevich** plays with great power in I and III and the orchestra has an equal role (Philips 438812, 2CD). Overall, **Ashkenazy** turns in the finest reading and displays the most refined pianism (♦Decca 448125). He makes time stand still in II and really brings out the drama in I and III. **Richter** and Maazel offer a blazing

performance that captures the music's wildness with great effectiveness (EMI 568637).

3. This was one of Bartók's last compositions, and he didn't live to play at its premiere in 1946; his student Tibor Serly had to orchestrate the last 17 bars. **Schiff** (Teldec) and **Jandó** (Naxos) are dull. **Kocsis** lacks drama in I and II and plays mechanically in III (Philips). **Ránki** turns in a delicate reading, with a humbly prayerful II (Hungaroton). **Sandor,** who played 3 at its premiere, is very fine—florid and light in I, quietly reverent in II, bouncy and nimble in III (Sony 45835). **Kovacevich** is very good in all three movements (Philips 438812 [2CD]). **Ashkenazy** is superb, with a wonderfully still II and a really celebratory III (♦Decca 448125).

Viola

Bartók did not live to orchestrate his viola concerto; Serly undertook that task and completed it in 1948. It was commissioned for **Primrose,** who played its premiere and was recorded in a concert performance with the Concertgebouw under Klemperer in 1951 (♦Music & Arts 752). He really plays his heart out, with a very individual, vibrant tone. It was at this point in his career that his playing attained a new depth of feeling. Klemperer is not the kind of conductor to hide behind his soloist, and he makes the orchestra's contributions stand out boldly. Those who wish to hear Primrose without the audience noise and mistakes may wish to seek out his LP with Tibor Serly conducting (♦Bartók Records 309, NA).

Kashkashian is technically flawless but soporific (ECM). **Wolfram Christ** is more straightforward and expressive but still makes a rather weak impression (DG). **Ma** plays the concerto on the alto violin, an instrument designed by violin maker Carleen Hutchins and held like a cello but with the same range as the viola (Sony). He plays with great intelligence and expression, but his instrument doesn't project well. **Hong-Mei Xiao** plays very well and with a strong tone (Naxos 554183). She has recorded both the Serly version and the 1995 version by Peter Bartók, Nelson Dellamaggiore, and Paul Neubauer.

Violin

1. Written in 1907-08, is in Bartók's early late-romantic style. He later repudiated this and all his other works of this kind. **György Pauk** establishes a beautifully meditative mood in I, but his II is underpowered (Naxos). **Midori** is beautiful and meditative in I, but the orchestra is too much in the background, and II is much too restrained (Sony). **Stern** is straightforward in I, but the Philadelphia strings are irresistible, and II is good and lively (Sony). **Vilmos Szabadi** is very good in I, with the right feeling of yearning, and also gets the sardonic mood in II (Hungaroton 31543).

2. This was written in 1938 at the behest of Bartók's friend Zoltán Székely; it's the first work in Bartók's late, more melodic style. **Shaham** (DG), **Midori** (Sony), **Christian Tetzlaff** (Virgin), **Mullova** (Philips), **Mutter, Menuhin** with Dorati and the Minneapolis Symphony (Mercury), and **György Pauk** (Naxos) are simply too dull and undramatic. **Szabadi** plays his part very well, but unfortunately András Ligeti is not a very involved conductor (Hungaroton). **Kyoko Takezawa** is in much the same situation (RCA), and the same problem afflicts **Szeryng** (Philips, 2CD). The premiere performance by **Zoltán Székely** and the Concertgebouw under Mengelberg has a good I, a lovely, expressive II, and a clever III (Lys 242). **Menuhin**'s recording with Furtwängler from 1953 is very passionate, and the conductor shapes the orchestral lines with great intelligence (EMI, NA).

Zukerman plays with plenty of character (RCA), but **Mark Kaplan** is even better in that respect, and Lawrence Foster is a sensitive partner

(Koch 7387). Both Zukerman's and Kaplan's discs include the original coda of the finale. **Ivry Gitlis** (Vox 5505) and **Stern** (Sony 64502) give very exciting readings. Gitlis has stupendous virtuosity and an excellent partner in Horenstein, and Stern has a great collaborator in Bernstein, with the orchestra right up front with the soloist. **Chung** and Rattle have obviously worked harder than any other team to create an integrated interpretation. Neither does anything without the other following; they play with excellent taste and great intelligence (♦EMI 54211). This is a much better collaboration than her earlier recording with Solti (London). There was a very fine LP by **Perlman** (EMI, available on CD in Europe). His playing is powerful and very exciting, and he explores a wide range of moods in II.

CHAMBER MUSIC

String Quartets

Bartók's string quartets have been the most popular set written in the 20th century, rivaled only by Shostakovich's. Beginning with 1, with its obvious blend of late Beethoven, French impressionism, and Southeast European folk music—influences that would serve him well for the rest of his career—Bartók developed an instantly recognizable, highly personal style in this idiom, moving through the arch form of 4 and 5, and ending with the unprecedented form of Quartet 6.

They have been blessed with a large number of good recordings. Among the complete sets of all six, the **Juilliard Quartet**'s 1981 recording lacks the drive, control, and clarity of their superb earlier cycles (Sony 63234, 2CD). The **Keller Quartet** is very good, and technically cleaner than some others, but they sometimes lack propulsion and are not as virtuosic as the best groups (Erato 98538, 2CD). The **Tokyo Quartet** is much more beautiful, especially in the two early quartets (RCA 68286, 3CD). Among older ensembles are the **Hungarian** (♦DG 457740, 2CD) and **Végh Quartets** (♦Auvidis Valois 4809, 3CD). Their approaches are very similar, with an intimate, conversational tone, reminding you that this is chamber music. These readings lack the flash and bigger-than-life sound of many later ensembles, but both groups clearly have the music in their blood, and one can smell the Hungarian earth as they play.

Perhaps the most accomplished of the newer groups to record this music are the **Emerson** (♦DG 423657, 2CD), **Takács** (♦London 455297, 2CD), and **Hagen Quartets** (♦DG 463476, 2CD). The Emerson takes its Bartók very seriously, and there is a pervasive air of anxiety in their readings. This feels very appropriate in these works written in the 20th-century age of anxiety. The Takács is a little like the Végh, only much more virtuosic and exhibitionistic. Their sound is often orchestral in size, and they have a very broad tonal palette. Unlike the Emerson, they like to bring out the humor of the music; the pleasure they take in performing these works is palpable, and their readings are thrilling. The Hagen approach is similar to the Takács. Their playing is very colorful and they have a big orchestral sound; they're not as propulsive as the Takács, but they carefully distinguish formal sections.

Among recordings of individual quartets, the **Arditti Quartet**'s 4 surprisingly lacks enthusiasm and involvement (Gramavision). The **Quatuor Athenaeum-Enesco** readings of 4 and 6 have the same fault (Pierre Verany). The **Sequoia Quartet**'s 3 is good, but it could use more drama and intensity (Delos). The **Vogler Quartet**'s 2 is energetic and powerful, lacking only beauty. The **Chilingirian Quartet**'s 1 and 2 (Chandos 8588) are beautiful and well balanced (RCA, NA). The **Amati Quartet** has recorded 3, 4, and 6 in the most enthusiastic performances on disc (Divox 29505). They don't have quite the polish of some of the other groups, but they have great drive. The **Juilliard Quartet** has re-leased selections from each of their three cycles (Sony 62705): No. 3 (1963), 4 (1949), and 6 (1981) are here in their entirety. 6 has the flaws of the 1981 set, but 3 has the virtues of the group's famous 1963 cycle—tremendous propulsion; excellent dynamic, tonal, and tempo contrasts; and superhuman precision. 4 reveals what the 1949 ensemble had that the subsequent ones have lacked to a degree—tremendous charisma, especially in cellist Arthur Winograd.

Violin

Sonatas. The two sonatas were written in 1921 and 1922 and were often performed by Bartók and his friend Jelly d'Aranyi. In both, **Denes Zsigmondy** is crude (Klavier). **Leslie Shank** isn't virtuosic enough and can't play with abandon (Centaur), **Guillermo Figueroa** lacks a soloist's technique (Eroica), and **György Pauk** is underpowered (Naxos 550749). **Eugene Drucker** is bland and expressionless (Biddulph). **Stern** is exciting in his old collaboration with Alexander Zakin, but Zakin is an inadequate partner (Sony). He has a much more colorful, imaginative partner in Yefim Bronfman, but by then Stern's technique was beginning to give out (Sony). **Oleh Krysa** plays with intelligence and wit, but Tatiana Chekina lacks personality. **Kremer** and Iury Smirnov are perhaps the best choice for both sonatas on one disc (Hungaroton 11655), though Kremer's later recordings are far superior. On LP, there was a fine 1979 set by **Végh** and Peter Pettinger (Telefunken 6.42417). As always, Végh's playing is not immaculate, but he's a master of nuance and of creating dark, mysterious moods.

1. **Isabelle Faust** is too mannered (Harmonia Mundi) and **Susanne Stanzeleit** is stiff and underpowered, though her partner Gustáv Fenyö is free and imaginative (ASV). **Leila Josefowicz** plays with great power, especially in III (Philips). **Menuhin** made a superb recording with the great Adolf Baller, an underrated pianist (Biddulph LAB 161). **Soovin Kim** and Jeremy Denk excel at presenting the music's half-lights during the quieter moments (Discover 920596). **Oistrakh** and Richter emphasize the score's grotesqueness and exoticism in their concert recording (Melodiya 40710, 5CD). **Kremer** and Argerich give a wild, highly improvisational reading of enormous power. This is clearly the definitive recording of this work (♦DG 427351, NA).

2. **Stanzeleit** gives a rather weak, undisciplined reading (ASV) and again **Faust** is too mannered (Harmonia Mundi). **Szigeti** and Bartók give the definitive reading in their legendary Library of Congress recital of 1940 (♦Vanguard 8008). In their hands, the music doesn't merely make sense, it becomes an organism that seems to grow before our ears. **Kremer** and Oleg Maisenberg are remarkably similar to Szigeti and Bartók (♦Teldec 13597).

Solo Violin. This sonata was commissioned by Menuhin in 1944 and is inspired by the great works by Bach. **Denes Zsigmondy** is coarse and raucous (Klavier). **Menuhin** recorded the work in 1947, but by then his technique was becoming unreliable and the strain shows (EMI, NA). **Guillermo Figueroa** plays intelligently, but lacks a soloist's technique (Eroica). **Roberto Cani**'s playing is often labored, and his conception of the work seems not to have fully matured (Agora). **Isabelle Faust** is mannered and can't let the music flow (Harmonia Mundi), and **Kovács** is too intense in I and II (Hungaroton). He plows through the phrases rather than trying to elucidate each movement's structure; he's not subtle enough in III, nor is he loose and playful enough in IV. **Christian Tetzlaff** makes the music's structure very clear, but he plays without feeling (Virgin). A deadly seriousness and lack of emotion mar **Eugene Drucker**'s performance (Biddulph).

Ivry Gitlis is strikingly virtuosic, and his I is thrilling, but he's too mannered and exhibitionistic to serve the music or clarify its structure (Vox). **Kyoko Takezawa** makes the work's structure clear, but her reading lacks drama (RCA). **Leila Josefowicz** is very dramatic, but her interpretation also lacks structural clarity (Philips). **Julia Krasko** does make the structure clear, but she doesn't have much fun doing it (Russian Disc). **Mark Kaplan** is apparently microphone-shy; he fails to relax in I and II, though his III is the most intimate and lovely on disc (Arabesque 6649).

Vilmos Szabadi plays with plenty of drama and does an excellent job clarifying the structures of I and II (Hungaroton 31558). Uniquely, his III is more playful than meditative, but his IV is too measured to be much fun. **György Pauk** plays with drama and lots of contrast in I and II, clarifying the structure beautifully; he struggles a bit in II and IV, but III is lovely and singing (Naxos 550868). **Andre Gertler** has all of Pauk's virtues without his technical limitations (Hungaroton 31635). **Stanzeleit** is excellent in all movements, and phrases in a very individual manner toward the end of I, but she could have used stronger accents in IV (ASV 852). **Kennedy** is as good as Stanzeleit and accents beautifully in IV (EMI 47621, NA).

There were two outstanding LPs. **Joseph Silverstein** plays the sonata with tremendous drive and a virtuoso technique (Columbia 5745, NA). His Fugue must be heard to be believed, and more than anyone else he brings out the machine-like quality of the music in this movement. **Robert Mann**'s account (♦Bartók Records 916, NA) is definitive. No one clarifies each movement's structure as well, without stinting on the music's drama, and only he plays the original quarter tones in the finale that were edited out of the printed score until the *urtext* was published in 1994.

Rhapsodies. These two works were written in 1928 for Szigeti and Zoltán Székely. They are arranged for both violin and piano and violin and orchestra. In the violin arrangement of both, **Faust** tends to be prissy and eccentric (Harmonia Mundi). **Székely** plays with taste, but he was clearly past his prime by 1974 (Hungaroton). **Stanzeleit** is good, helped by her more forceful partner Gustáv Feny (ASV). **György Pauk** (Naxos 550886) and **Mark Kaplan** (Arabesque 6649) are also good. **Szigeti**, with Bartók at the piano, is superb in 1 in both a studio recording and a recital from 1940 (♦Hungaroton 12326, 6CD; Vanguard 8008). **Lara St. John** is astonishing in 2 (♦Well-Tempered Productions 5185). This is the most spontaneous, wildly improvisational performance of any violin music I've heard; she possesses a virtuoso technique and tremendous charisma. **Leslie Shank** lacks charisma and can't play with real abandon in 1 (Centaur).

Among the orchestral versions, **Shaham**'s are dull and pedestrian (DG). **Kyoko Takezawa** (RCA) and especially **Chung** (EMI) are good in 1 but not quite as good in 2. **Stern** is exciting in both, especially 1 (Sony 64503).

Romanian Folk Dances. This popular work was transcribed for violin and piano by Bartók's friend Zoltán Székely. **Faust** is mannered and fussy in I and III, but good in the other dances (Harmonia Mundi). **Stanzeleit** is good in all of them (ASV). **Szigeti**, accompanied by Bartók, plays with great feeling and enthusiasm (Hungaroton 12326, 6CD; Biddulph LAB 153). **Mark Kaplan** is very stylish and has fun with the music (Arabesque 6649). **Menuhin**'s 1951 performance is very exciting, and it's clear that he and his superb accompanist, Adolf Baller, were really "on" for the recording session (♦Biddulph LAB 162, 2CD).

44 Duos for Two Violins. Bartók wrote this didactic work for violin, like *Mikrokosmos* for piano. **Perlman** and **Zukerman** (EMI), and **Eugene**

Drucker and **Philip Setzer** (Biddulph) are colorless and mechanical. **György Pauk** and **Kazuki Sawa** are delightful, with plenty of atmosphere, color, and expression and gorgeous tones (♦Naxos 8.550868).

OTHER CHAMBER WORKS

Sonata for Two Pianos and Percussion. Bartók's chamber music masterpiece, this sonata was composed in 1937. **Perahia** and **Solti** are underpowered in I and not joyous enough in III (CBS). **Geza Frid** and **Luctor Ponse**, under Dorati's direction, are very propulsive in I, a bit too fast in II, and exuberant in III (Mercury). **Bartók** and his wife **Ditta Bartók Pásztory** play with very flexible tempos (Hungaroton 12326, 6CD). They're very brooding and serious until III. The percussionists seem a bit under rehearsed. **Kocsis** and **Ránki** are powerful and virtuosic in I, very effective in II, and tremendously powerful in III (Hungaroton 12400). **Argerich** and **Kovacevich** are superb, with a brooding I, an eerie II, and an ecstatic III (♦Philips 446557, 2CD).

Contrasts for Clarinet, Violin, and Piano. This was commissioned by jazz clarinetist Benny Goodman and first performed and recorded by him with Szigeti and Bartók at the piano. **Richard** and **Lucy Chapman Stoltzman** and **Goode** are dull and meandering (RCA). **Chamber Music Northwest** (Delos 3043), **Berkes, Pauk**, and **Jandó** (Naxos 550749), and **Berkes, Miklos Szenthelyi**, and **Kocsis** (Hungaroton 31038) are all about equally fine. **Goodman, Szigeti**, and **Bartók** are very good—dark and brooding in I and a bit menacing in III (Hungaroton 12326). **Michael Collins, Chantal Juillet**, and **Argerich** are superb, with a cacophonous, menacing I (♦EMI 56816).

PIANO MUSIC

Allegro Barbaro. Composed in 1911, this became Bartók's signature piece. **Ránki** (Hungaroton) and **Kocsis** (Philips) fail to ignite the music. **Baláasz Szokolay** is good, though he doesn't provide a very strong contrast in the middle section (Naxos). **Bartók** is wild and very propulsive (Hungaroton 12326, 6CD). **Max Levinson** has Bartók's virtues and offers an even greater contrast in the central section (♦N2K 10028). **Peter Frankl** really thunders through the score (♦ASV 687).

Burlesques. **Richter**'s great strength and understanding are manifest in his two brilliant 1989 recordings of these three works (London 436451; Philips 442459).

For Children. These works start out like very simple folk songs and become more and more technically and harmonically advanced. **Mary Kenedi,** who has recorded the first two of the four volumes, is very straightforward but doesn't have a refined touch (Echiquier). **Lili Kraus,** who programs a few selections from volume I, is more playful and innocent (Vanguard 8087). **Kocsis,** in a selection from all four volumes, is very imaginative and plays the early numbers as a child might (Philips 446368, 4CD). **Bartók,** who also played selections, is very serious and straightforward, with a varied touch (Hungaroton 12326, 6CD). There was a fine LP by **Ránki**; he used a very delicate touch and his expression was beautifully wistful and nostalgic (Telefunken 6.35338).

Hungarian Sketches. In the original piano version of these charming pieces, **Richter** evokes the countryside scenes they portray with idiomatic skill (Melodiya/BMG 29465).

Mikrokosmos. This is Bartók's major didactic work for the piano. The 153 very brief pieces start out very simple and become progressively more complex, providing the student with a wide range of examples of technique and expression. **Szokolay** plays a small selection in a straightforward manner (Naxos). **Bartók** played selections and is very intense and straightforward, with a varied touch and elastic tempos (Hungaroton 12326, 6CD). **Sandor** has recorded the complete work; he's earthy and straightforward, but has a less subtle touch than Bartók (Sony).

Out of Doors. With this work, composed in 1926, Bartók exploited the full range of tone colors of the piano for the first time. **Claude Helffer** is generally clear and delicate, and playful in IV, ("Night Sounds") movement (Harmonia Mundi 1901094). **Max Levinson** is more of a powerhouse. He's very atmospheric and likes to thunder; his IV is very mysterious, his V wild and ferocious (♦N2K 10028).

Romanian Folk Dances. One of Bartók's most popular works, this collection is light and entertaining. Only **Ránki** fails to shine in this music (Hungaroton). **Kocsis** is intense and flexible and plays with great energy (Philips 446368, 4CD). **Bartók** is very propulsive and has very elastic rhythms and tempos (Hungaroton 12326, 6CD). **Lili Kraus** has a very pure feeling and is excellent at bringing out inner voices (Vanguard 8087). **Peter Frankl** is majestic in I, wild and ecstatic in VI (ASV 687).

Sonata. Oddly, Bartók only wrote one, brief sonata for his chosen instrument. **Claude Hellfer** balances the counterpoint with great clarity, and his II is more ruminative than others (Harmonia Mundi 1901094). **Kalichstein** is thrilling and sardonic in I, imposing in II, and thundering in III (Vanguard 121). **Max Levinson** is more grotesque and sardonic in I, and carefully paced. His II isn't as imposing nor his III as intense or thundering as Kalichstein's, but he finds more wit in the latter movement (N2K 10028).

Suite. Composed in 1916, this was Bartók's first major composition for piano in his mature style with original material. **Kocsis** is flaccid in I and lacks intensity in III (Philips). **Ránki** is dull in I (Hungaroton). **Claude Heffler** finds a touch of sardonic humor in I; his II is very good and his III builds well, culminating in a nostalgic IV (Harmonia Mundi 1901094). **Bartók** is very intense and serious, finding sardonic humor below the surface of I and developing a transcendent IV (Hungaroton 12326, 6CD). **Frankl** finds a hint of humor in I. II is intense and sardonic, III turbulent and thrilling, and IV reflective (♦ASV 687).

CHORAL MUSIC

Cantata Profana relates a legend of a woodsman's sons who were turned into stags. **Boulez**'s recording is beautifully sung and recorded but not very dramatic (DG 435863). **Ferencsik** has the advantage of soloists and a chorus who are native speakers of Hungarian (Hungaroton, NA). **Dorati** also has native singers and gets more drama out of the music (Hungaroton 31503).

BALLET-PANTOMIMES

The Miraculous Mandarin. A bizarre, symbolist story of man's need for a woman's love and the obstacles in his way, this is Bartók's most exciting score, strongly influenced by Stravinsky's *Rite of Spring*. Somehow, it seems to bring out the best in conductors and orchestras, and recordings of the complete score are about equally fine. **Dorati** has a great ending (Mercury 434362). **Järvi** is blessed with a recording of wide dynamic range that enhances the dramatic contrasts in the score (Chandos 9029). **Schwarz** has an exceptionally good clarinet soloist (Delos 3083). **Nagano** draws a very wide range of tone colors and dynamics from his players and again shows that he's one of the great masters of orchestral balance (Erato 23142). **Fischer** has the best clarinet soloist and does a great job characterizing the various scenes (Philips 454430). **Boulez** recorded the work twice, first with the NY Philharmonic (Sony) and later with the Chicago Symphony (DG 447747). The New York

recording is bland and underpowered, but the Chicago reading is superb, with a fine sense of the grotesque and awesome brass.

As for recordings of the Suite, which includes about the first half of the score, **Skrowaczewski** (Vox) gives a good but not great reading. **Martinon** is a bit restrained (RCA). **Dorati**'s recording with the Chicago Symphony from 1954 is excellent, with a searing intensity rarely found in performances of this or any other score (Mercury 434397).

The Wooden Prince. Like all Bartók's stage works, this odd story deals with the attempt of a man to win a woman's love. **Boulez** (DG) and **Järvi** (Chandos) are simply too slow. Only **Dorati** moves things along well enough to bring out the score's drama (Mercury 434357). **Skrowaczewski** gives a good performance with tempos similar to Dorati's (Vox 3015).

OPERA

Bluebeard's Castle. Bartók's only opera is a peculiar work. Only one hour long, with a speaker who recites a brief prologue (usually omitted on recordings) and only two characters in only one scene, it's a psychodrama whose action takes place only within the character's minds.

Dorati recorded it in 1962 with soprano Olga Szönyi as Judith and bass Mihály Székely as Bluebeard, Bartók's favorite for this role (Mercury 434325). Szönyi is serviceable and Székely is dignified. The real value of this recording is Dorati's tempos, which seem just right and move the drama along more effectively than any other conductor's. **Kertész** recorded the opera in 1965 with the husband-and-wife team of Ludwig and Berry (♦Decca 466377). The singers' relationship may have helped them understand the drama better, as this recording immediately became the benchmark for all others. Ludwig and Berry inhabit their roles like no other pair. While most Bluebeards are content to appear as remote, majestic figures, Berry wisely emphasizes his desperate romantic yearning and pathos. Just try to keep a dry eye as he sends his young wife off into his vault of memories of past loves at the end.

Adam Fischer recorded another excellent account in 1987 with Marton and Ramey (♦CBS 44523). It's fascinating to compare this with Kertész's version. The singers are just as involved in their roles, and they find new meanings in the words. Ramey just falls short at the end when it comes to emphasizing Bluebeard's pathos. **Boulez** has recorded the opera twice. His earlier account had Troyanos and Nimsgern; Troyanos is perhaps the most expressive Judith, but Nimsgern is too cold to engage with her (Sony). Many forget that it's he, not Judith, who is the main character. Recently, **Boulez** recorded it with Jessye Norman and László Polgár and speaker Nicholas Simon (DG). Both singers, especially Polgár, merely sing rather than act. Even the Chicago Symphony is bland and lackluster here.

On LP, **Solti** made a superb recording in 1979 with Sylvia Sass, Kolos Kovats, and Istvan Sztankay, a magnificent speaker (London 1174, NA). While sounding almost like a remake of Kertész's recording, it still has enough of its own imaginative touches to distinguish it, and the drama is deeply felt.

MAGIL

Arnold Bax (1883-1953)

Bax's musical English forebear was not so much Elgar or Stanford as Delius, though Bax's impressionism was less heady. Many of his images were derived from the bleak English and Scottish northern regions, the rugged Atlantic coast and the water itself. His music ranged from incisive, dramatic, and large-scale to melodic, dreamy, and languorous. He was as much a romantic as an impressionist. Much of his romantic influence came from Celtic and especially Irish literature and music (he was a passionate lover of Ireland and its people and lived on the island for a few years). He also was influenced, particularly in his early works, by a visit to Russia.

We can divide Bax's output into three periods. The early works were grand, with lush, chromatic harmonies. An abrupt change occurred around 1913, reflecting WWI, the breakup of his marriage, his passionate affair with pianist Harriet Cohen, and the execution of Irish friends during the 1916 Easter Uprising. His music grew more succinct and linear, with more balance between structure and romanticism and between chromaticism and diatonicism. It became more concise and polyphonic after 1921, notably in the symphonies. Bax tailed off in inspiration and output after Symphony 7 (1939), though he still composed more fine works than some give him credit for.

Years of composition are important for Bax, so I have indicated them below.

SYMPHONIES

The symphonies are where Bax finally worked out his inner turmoil, anger, and the conflict between man and nature that had always been with him. There is a complete set by **Bryden Thomson** (Chandos), a set in progress from **David Lloyd-Jones** (Naxos), and Lyrita analog LPs of 1, 2, and 5-7 led by various conductors.

Thomson favors thick textures and beauty and opulence of tone; he's more impressionistic and lyrical than dramatic and dynamic. The Lyritas have more tonal body, are more dynamic, and reveal more anger without slighting beauty. Both usually use the London Philharmonic; it sounds slightly better under Thomson, but not enough to detract from the Lyritas. So far, the Naxos set is more dramatic and incisive than the Lyritas, with a leaner, more crystallized orchestral tone. All provide good to excellent sound. Lyrita's is the best: close-up, rich, textured, and realistic. Chandos is more distant, broader, and occasionally swampy. Naxos is crisp, clean, and bracing.

The major couplings are discussed here or, when comparisons are warranted, under "Concertos and other orchestral music."

1 (1922) This symphony begins the struggle. It's a powerful, ferocious work, shot through with moments of beauty before ending inconclusively. **Myer Fredman**'s powerful approach to the outer movements propels urgent rhythms and builds sonorities vertically to good effect (♦Lyrita 232, with 7). I prefer him here to **Thomson**'s structured, long-range, but reticent view, though Thomson's slow movement creates more gripping tragedy (Chandos 8480, with *Christmas Eve* (1912), an opulent, stunning cross between Respighi and Liszt). **Lloyd-Jones** emphasizes the symphony's anger even more than Fredman—he hammers at the *sforzando* chords—but could use more air and openness. The trombones are a bit of an annoying laser out of the right speaker. Some like this performance more than I do (Naxos 553525, with *In the Faery Hills* and *Garden of Fand*).

2 (1926). This continues the struggle and is bleaker, more episodic, and more searching. The contrast between **Fredman** (♦Naxos 554093, with *November Woods*) and **Thomson** (Chandos 8493, with *Nympholept* [1912]) which Bax called "a perilous pagan enchantment haunting the sunlit midsummer forest") parallels that for 1. **Lloyd-Jones** leans toward Fredman, but his tempos are slower, textures more blended, the shape slightly rounder, with better sound balance than in 1. A safe choice—with a fine Royal Scottish Orchestra—but I would not be without Fredman.

3 (1929). This symphony closes the first chapter of Bax's struggle. It's rhapsodic, haunting, and difficult, with colors of a gloomy, occasionally stormy day on a rugged seashore. **Lloyd-Jones** makes the best case for this symphony, providing the required balance between the dramatic and the beautiful, all with insightful phrasing (♦Naxos 553608, with *Happy Forest*). **Thomson** leans too far to the romantic, losing the drama and missing the vital rubato phrasing that Lloyd-Jones captures in the important slow music (Chandos 8454, with *Dance of Wild Irravel* and *Paean*). **Barbirolli**'s mono LP is a classic, if lacking good sound and orchestral finesse (EMI). Avoid **Edward Downes**'s far too slack account (RCA LP).

4 (1931). This symphony is romantic, hedonistic, loosely constructed, and full of ideas and emotions that, if not all top drawer, are mostly interesting. This is **Thomson**'s least molded and most extroverted reading, well-balanced in mood, with a fine, light touch; the Ulster Orchestra plays for him with more spirit than the London Philharmonic (♦Chandos 8312, with *Tintagel*). **Handley** is poor, badly played with bad sound (Revolution LP).

5 (1932). This resumes the struggle. It's tersely argued, typical of the dedicatee, Sibelius, but still full of Bax's seascapes and storms and with a rather pagan conclusion. **Leppard**'s large-scaled reading is assured and incisive, emphasizing drama over lyricism, though not lacking in the latter (♦Lyrita 58 LP). **Thomson** is soft-grained, with broad attacks; he does particularly well in III, where he softens the bombast that sneaks into Leppard's reading, but he lacks grandeur and occasionally loses direction (Chandos 8669, with *Russian Suite*).

6 (1934). Symphony 6 is enigmatic, mystical, and evocative of the Scottish coast, from stormy to bleak to springlike. Compared to **Thomson**'s lush approach with his pastel coloring (Chandos 8586, with *Festival Overture*), **Norman del Mar** and the New Philharmonia (♦Lyrita 35 LP) are better with the dramatic and angrier music and don't wallow as much in the romantic, more Delian passages. Thomson will do, but Del Mar is worth seeking out. **Douglas Bostock** (Classico, with *Tintagel* and *Overture to Adventure*) is enthusiastic and mainstream, if not always understanding. The performance is marred by stressed orchestral playing, lack of atmosphere, and mediocre sound.

7 (1939). The struggle is over; this is happy, relaxed, and the best organized of the symphonies. The tight organization and absence of anger suit **Thomson,** who is excellent, with gorgeous orchestral sound and exquisite phrasing (♦Chandos 8628, with *Four Songs for Tenor and Orchestra*). **Leppard** doesn't produce the same finesse or tonal luster, but he's more exciting, dramatic, and involving (♦Lyrita 232, with 1).

CONCERTOS AND OTHER ORCHESTRAL MUSIC

Most of Bax's tone poems have been recorded by Thomson, whose readings have the strengths and weaknesses of his symphonies. The finest conductors of the tone poems are Boult, Barbirolli, and Handley, all of whom blend more drama, texture, and passion with beauty of tone. Still, we owe a debt to Thomson and Chandos—and Handley, too. Many of these compositions haven't been heard in over half a century.

Concertante for Piano Left Hand (1949) and *In Memoriam* (1916). Bax's rhapsodic treatment includes spooky hobgoblin rhythms, dreamy pastels, languorous melodies, and rolling piano lines. *In Memoriam* was Bax's tribute to his executed Irish friends. It's full of nostalgia, struggle, and regret, marked with a gorgeous melody, and becomes more agitated (the execution?) before peace returns. Handley and pianist **Margaret Fingerhut** are excellent (Chandos 9715, with *Bard of the Dimbovitza*).

Garden of Fand (1916). This is a kaleidoscopic, iridescent portrait of the sea (the "garden"). Everything I say about **Boult**'s *Tintagel* below applies to his *Fand* (♦Lyrita 231). **Barbirolli** is just as good—not as noble or magisterial but more passionate, surging, and involving (♦Mercury or Pye LP, with Vaughan Williams's Symphony 8 and Butterworth's *A Shropshire Lad*). **Thomson** is fine but needs more substance and is recommended only for its availability and couplings (Chandos 8307, with *Happy Forest* and *Summer Music*).

Into the Twilight (1908), ***In the Faery Hills*** (1909); *Roscatha* (1910), ***Tale the Pine Trees Knew*** (1931). Bax turned the first three listed (from an aborted opera about the Irish heroine Déirdre) into the cycle *Eire; Twilight* was the opera's overture. It's moody and lyrical with some of the sway of American southern spirituals. According to Bax, *Faery Hills* suggests "the 'Hidden People' in the innermost deeps and hollow hills of Ireland." I hear Mendelssohn, along with Bax's dramatic lyricism and heroism. *Roscatha* ("Battle Hymn") depicts the "gathering of heroes and nobles," and *Pine Trees* portrays "two landscapes dominated by the pine-trees—Norway and the West of Scotland." **Thomson** is his usual lyrical self, as is the London Philharmonic, in one of his best discs (♦Chandos 8367). **Lloyd-Jones** is lighter, less lyrical and more bracing, sparkling and Mendelssohnian in *In the Faery Hills* (♦Naxos 553525, with Symphony 1).

Northern Ballad 3 (1933), *Cortège* (1925), ***Mediterranean*** (1920/22), ***Overture to a Picaresque Comedy*** (1930), and ***Cello Concerto*** (1932). The warmly evocative *Ballad* is devoid of Bax's anger. *Cortège* is a pageant-like march, *Mediterranean* contains a touch of *Iberia*, and the Overture is lighter, reminiscent of *Till Eulenspiegel*. The underrated Concerto is lyrical, with the cello, mostly in its middle register, more vocalist than string soloist. **Thomson** (with Rafael Wallfisch in the Concerto) is in good form (Chandos 8494).

November Woods (1917). This composition, inspired by a beech woodland, is big, sometimes stormy, and romantic, with shifting pastels and touches of Wagner. **Boult** is magnificent, beautifully paced and sumptuous, with broad lines and singing phrasing. The big moments are powerful and dramatic, yet he catches the shifting, quieter colors. Great sound and playing by the London Philharmonic (♦Lyrita 37 LP, with Holst's *Fugal Overture* and Moeran's *Sinfonietta*). **Lloyd-Jones** is lightweight and intimate, less powerful and a bit faster—good, but routine next to Boult (♦Naxos 554093, with Symphony 2). **Thomson** is also lightweight but more impressionistic than Lloyd-Jones. Next to Boult, he seems understated (Chandos 8307, with *Happy Forest; Garden of Fand; Summer Music*). He's better in the coupled works.

Sinfonietta (1932) and ***Overture, Elegy, and Rondo*** (1927). Containing some of the impressionism of Symphony 3, these are more upbeat, direct, energetic, and clearly structured. **Barry Wordsworth** is a bit neutral, and the Slovak Philharmonic isn't the London Philharmonic, but they do a surprisingly idiomatic job, worth exploring (Marco Polo 223102).

Spring Fire (1913), ***Symphonic Scherzo*** (1917/33), and ***Northern Ballad 2*** (1934). *Spring Fire* is a five-movement tone poem about Spring in the forest; it's colorful, lushly orchestrated, and full of pagan sounds and celebrations. The sparer *Ballad* reflects Sibelius, and the Scherzo is from an uncompleted piano sonata. **Handley** and the Royal Philharmonic are excellent (Chandos 8464).

Symphonic Variations for Piano and Orchestra (1919). Written after the Great War and the execution of his Irish friends and at the height of his passion for Harriet Cohen, *Variations* is as big, sprawling, expressive,

and dramatic as the first two symphonies—maybe more so—ranging from dramatic to sensuous to intimate, with a strong dose of Rachmaninoff. **Fingerhut** and Thomson have the required symphonic style. Sound and balance are excellent (Chandos 8516, with *Morning Song*).

Tintagel (1919), ***Garden of Fand, Northern Ballad 1*** (1934), ***Mediterranean***. *Tintagel,* Bax's portrait of the site of King Arthur's mythical castle and "the long distances of the Atlantic as seen from the Cliffs of Cornwall on a sunny but not windless summer day," is his most dramatic and impressive sea portrait, full of noble cliffs and churning waves from deep in the ocean. *Northern Ballad 1* is "a general impression of the fiery romantic life of the Highlands of Scotland before the opening up of the country." It's the most rousing and dramatic of the *Northern Ballads,* presaging Symphonies 5 and 6. **Boult** is magisterial, full, sweeping, and noble, with great sound in all these works (♦Lyrita 231). **Barbirolli** is on the same level but more romantic, flowing, and passionate (♦EMI 2305, LP, with Ireland's *London Overture* and works by Delius). **Fallata** doesn't manage Boult's dark, heavy seas or his uncanny sense of ebb and flow, nor does she equal Barbirolli's warmth, but her less weighty, well structured, and nearly as dark-hued performance is almost as good. **Thomson**'s decent performance of *Tintagel* seems lightweight and not as tightly argued (♦Chandos 8312, with Symphony 4).

Truth about Russian Dancers (1920/26), ***From Dusk to Dawn*** (1917). *Truth* is Bax's take on Russian ballet music. It's colorful, with great melodies and without the conflict of the symphonies. *Dusk,* with its waltzes, is lighter, more sugary, and less dramatic and exciting. Excellent performances by **Thomson** and the London Symphony—not great, but entertaining (Chandos 8863).

Violin Concerto (1938). This work is not as deep as the Cello Concerto, but entertaining and upbeat, almost popularized. The work is lightly but colorfully scored and tuneful with a touch of the blues. **Mordkovitch** plays the Concerto well, but the coupled orchestral works are more interesting. **Thomson** is sprightly and less serious in the Concerto and appropriately dramatic in the other pieces (Chandos 9003, with *Golden Eagle, A Legend,* and *Romantic Overture*).

Winter Legends (1930) and ***Saga Fragment***. The listener "may associate [this] with . . . tales of the North." *Legends* is equal parts symphony, tone poem, and piano concertante. *Saga Fragment* is an orchestration of the Piano Quartet. **Thomson** gives us the music, but a conductor more flexible and with a lighter touch might do better in both works (Chandos 8484).

CHAMBER MUSIC

Cello Sonata, Legend-Sonata, Folk Tale, Sonatina. These attractive works, spanning 25 years of Bax's career, are typically lyrical, romantic and impressionistic, with a touch of the folk element. He wrote very warmly for the cello, making it a bardic singing voice without pyrotechnics. Cellist **Bernard Gregor-Smith** combines with Yolanda Wrisley for a very pleasant disc (ASV 896).

Nonet, Oboe Quintet (1931), ***Elegiac Trio*** (1916), ***Harp Quintet*** (1919), ***Clarinet Sonata*** (1934). These pieces are all played by the **Nash Ensemble** (Hyperion 66807). *Nonet* is a contemporary of Symphony 3, similarly evocative of northern England coastlines, though the weather is fairer. The Harp Quintet and *Elegiac Trio* are reminiscent of Debussy's chamber music. The Oboe Quintet is more "Irish," serious, and moving. The Clarinet Sonata isn't quite on the level of the others. This is an important and delightful disc.

Piano Trio (1946). This composition is one of the composer's best late works. The old symphonic blend of storm and impressionism is heard here in a new, less tempestuous voice. An excellent performance by the **Pirasti Trio** catches the Baxian idiom well (ASV 925, with piano trios by Stanford and Holst).

String Quartet 1 (1918), *Piano Quartet* (1922), *Harp Quintet* (1919). The String Quartet has a sprightly Dvořákian first movement, a powerfully elegiac Lento, and a finale anchored by an Irish tune. The haunting Piano Quartet begins angrily in the piano, then turns sweet and wistful, with enough whole-tone scale work to sound like Debussy. The original works better than the arrangement for piano and chamber orchestra (*Saga Fragment*). The Harp Quintet is more of a string quartet with harp coloring and percussive effects. The **English Quartet** is wonderful (Chandos 8391).

String Quartet 2 (1925), *Piano Quintet* (1915). The great Piano Quintet links early Bax with the symphonies. It's a large-scale work, barely contained in piano quintet format, and full of ideas impressive in invention, variety, instrumentation, and structure. The controlled String Quartet is one of his most contrapuntal works—note the double fugue in III—and is characterized by bold harmonies, a rich flow of melody, and colorful textures. The **Mistry Quartet** and David Owen Norris made a great Bax disc (Chandos 8795).

String Quartet 3. This blends the lightness of 1 with the thornier 2 to produce a modern, rhythmic work. It's less like "Bax" and a little like Bartók, though not as intricate or dense. Not a great work—there's a bit of excess rhetoric—but a strong one, well played by the **Amici Quartet** (GRS 31, LP).

String Quintet (1933), *Octet for Horn, Piano, and String Sextet* (1934), *Concerto for Flute, Oboe, Harp, & String Quartet* (1936), *Threnody & Scherzo for Bassoon, Harp String Sextet* (1936), and *In Memoriam* (1917). The Octet is haunting at the outset but turns lively with its Irish tunes. The dark String Quintet contains an amazing amount of variety and nature painting. The Concerto is brighter and more lively, with a beautiful cavatina for flute and an Irish jig. *Threnody* begins with dark textures starring the bassoon and bass before the bassoon leads us on a merry chase in the Scherzo. *In Memoriam* is a haunting work for an elegiac English horn, string quartet, and harp. The **Academy of St. Martin in the Fields Chamber Ensemble** is excellent (Chandos 9602).

Violin Sonatas 1 and *2* (1910, 1915). These compositions are fascinating. The freewheeling 1 was written in 1910 when Bax was having an affair with a Ukrainian girl. 2 appeared during wartime and is more seriously passionate, even harsh at times, and is thought to be about wartime events. Both have overtones of Debussy and are full-sounding. 2 may be the "better" work, but I find 1 more magnetic. **Erich Gruenberg** and John McCabe are passionate and extroverted, but there's room for a more delicate newcomer (Chandos 8845).

PIANO MUSIC

Bax was an excellent pianist and one of the few English composers who wrote major works for the instrument. His first three sonatas are large-scale and symphonic—No. 4 is more terse— and are technically difficult; some consider 2 to be the best. The smaller works are brighter and livelier. In four 2CD sets, **Eric Parkin** plays with great sympathy, though the heavier sonatas could use a darker touch (Chandos 8496/7, 9561).

CHORAL MUSIC

Enchanted Summer (1910), *Walsinghame* (1916), *Fatherland* (1907/34). *Fatherland* has a martial, patriotic air with brass flourishes, Elgarian orchestral interlude and choruses, and stirring tenor arias. (The country praised is Finland.) *Walsinghame* captures Sir Walter Raleigh's farewell to the Queen's Court. Bax at 42 was saying good-bye to his youth while reflecting another crisis with his mistress. The orchestral music is introspective with an ardent tenor and a sympathetic, resigned chorus. The opening of *Enchanted Summer* is warmly dark before sunlight appears; the work is romantic, exotic, and opulent, full of lyricism and conflict. Bax poured out many ideas, some remindful of Debussy's *Pelléas*. **Handley** conducts excellent performances, but the recording is a bit forward for the soloists (Chandos 8625).

Mater ora Filium (1921). Bax's a cappella choral music, particularly this complex masterpiece, is more sensuous, chromatic, and rhapsodic than usual in the English choral tradition. *Mater,* inspired by William Byrd, combines polyphony and rhapsody in an effluence of invention rare even for Bax. **Stephen Wilkinson** leads a romantic, full-sounding performance (♦Hyperion, with other Bax choral works). **Cleobury**'s is a less cushioned, more intimate reading, with boy trebles lending eeriness to the sound (♦EMI 47663, with choral works by Bax and Finzi). Wilkinson has the edge for his couplings, but both interpretations are valid.

SONGS

Bard of the Dimbovitza (1914). This work is based on Romanian folk poetry recited by girls spinning cloth. The music is sumptuous with elements of Debussy and Delius; the mood is warmly lush and languid, with mostly slow tempos. **Jean Rigby** sings beautifully, if with a bit of inconsequential strain. Handley and the BBC Philharmonic are in sympathy, and the sound casts an appropriate glow (Chandos 9515, with *Concertante for Piano Left Hand* and *In Memoriam*).

Four Songs for Tenor and Orchestra. These are more conventional, tuneful, romantic, and less impressionistic than *Dimbovitza*. Two are based on Bax poems reflecting an youthful romance in Russia. The first three are especially appealing, with an attractive Orientalism in 1. **Martyn Hill**'s pleasant tenor blends well with the rich orchestral accompaniment (Chandos 8628, with Symphony 7). HECHT

Amy Marcy Cheney Beach (Mrs. H.H.A. Beach) (1867-1944)

We may wonder what Amy Beach would have accomplished as composer and pianist if she had lived a century later. Largely self-taught as a composer because women were not admitted to music schools in those days, and required by her husband to give up performing, these dual talents were thwarted, first one then the other. She did compose prolifically throughout her marriage to a prominent Bostonian, and resumed a performing career after his death in 1910. A prodigy who played with the Boston Symphony as a teenager, after her marriage in 1885 she wrote the first symphony credited to a woman in the United States, the well-known "Gaelic Symphony," and a concerto she performed on a European tour immediately preceding WWI. The bulk of her work is for solo piano and songs with piano accompaniment, and all but one of her chamber pieces include the piano. All her large instrumental works were composed during her hiatus from public performance. ZIEROLF

ORCHESTRAL MUSIC

"Gaelic" Symphony. Beach's most imposing orchestral composition, this may be thought of as a respectful reply to Dvořák, who during his stay in this country suggested that American composers take their in-

spiration from the rich legacy of Negro and Indian melodies. Mrs. Beach wrote in the Boston *Herald,* "We of the North should be far more likely to be influenced by old English, Scotch or Irish songs, inherited with our literature from our ancestors." This is music of great strength and assurance, from the surging undercurrent of the strings and heroic principal theme of the opening *Allegro con fuoco* to the proud forward stride of the finale. For a long time we had to make do with **Karl Krueger**'s heavily cut performance, part of the Library of Congress's "Our Musical Past" series (Bridge), but it's superseded in every way by the Detroit Symphony under **Neeme Järvi** (♦Chandos 8958). In its sweep, its passion, its mastery of the grand gesture, Järvi's performance quite supplants any competition, and he's warmly receptive to the many supremely lyrical passages. Sound and performance are exemplary as well, making this a recording to treasure.

Piano concerto. This "magnificent romantic concerto, opening with a bold bravura cadenza and leading into some of the most melting melodies and technical fireworks a pianist could desire—plus a rich orchestra score. How could this work have remained unheard of for the last six decades?" Thus writes **Mary Louise Boehm** of this piece, which she discovered and reintroduced to concert audiences as recently as 1976. She clearly has the measure of this exuberant and warmly lyrical score, and the Westphalian Symphony under Siegfried Landau offers competent support. You may obtain the concerto either coupled with Beach's Piano Quintet on a single CD (♦Vox 7196) or as part of Vol. 6 in the "Romantic Piano Concerto" series (Vox 5069). **Joanne Polk** is more reflective in the opening movement and deeply felt in the Largo, but seems rather earthbound elsewhere (Arabesque). HALLER

CHAMBER MUSIC

Of Beach's half-dozen or so chamber works, the Piano Quintet is the most elaborate and most frequently performed these days. Often labeled post-Brahmsian, it nonetheless is distinctly American and markedly less derivative than contemporaneous music by the other "American School" composers with whom she is sometimes linked. Her Quintet highlights the piano, often merely accompanied by strings rather than integrated with them. This poses some balance problems, overcome well enough by the Endellion Quartet with **Martin Roscoe** (ASV 932) and the Lark Quartet with **Joanne Polk** (Arabesque 6738). Less successful balance and musicianship is heard from **Diane Ambache** and other musicians in the Piano Quintet, Piano Trio, and Quintet for Flute and Strings (Chandos 9752). The Chandos disc is best for those who want a broad sample of Beach's chamber music; either of the others offers a better rendition of the Piano Quintet alone. Polk has championed Beach's music in performance and recording, so perhaps that's why she provides a sense of familiarity.

For the Piano Trio, I recommend the **Macalester Trio,** who include it in "Chamber Works by Women Composers" (Vox 5029). For the Flute Quintet, a superb recording by **Eugenia Zuckerman** and the Shanghai Quartet is available (Delos 3173). It was recorded in a church and the sound is a bit odd on first hearing, but it's rich and full, and Zuckerman's absolutely first-rate playing is consistent for Beach's piece and the other music on the disc, by Arthur Foote, Ginastera, and Mozart (*Eine Kleine Nachtmusik*). By bowing out as pianist, so to speak, Beach apparently considered more carefully the possibilities for line and balance. The theme and variations form works well, and it's good to hear such a definitive performance. Perhaps more musicians will be encouraged to perform and record what may be her most underappreciated work.

The relatively late (1942) *Pastorale for Wind Quintet* is ably per-

formed by the **Reykjavik Wind Quintet** (Chandos 9174). This isn't Beach's best work, but for those interested in wind music the disc offers a good sample of 20th-century pieces by Barber, Fine, Harbison (the best piece on the disc), Schuller, and Villa-Lobos.

Joseph Silverstein and Gilbert Kalisch make a fine duo, so it's unfortunate their recording of Beach's Violin Sonata includes pedestrian music by Arthur Farwell, Foote again, and Preston Ware Orem. Obscurity has its reasons. All these works are performed to expectation, but other than those curious about unknown music there's nothing to recommend the disc (New World 80542). A better pairing is Beach's Sonata with Brahms's Op. 78 performed by **Arturo Delmoni** and Yuri Funahashi (John Marks 7281). The playing isn't nearly as good as Silverstein's and Kalisch's, but Beach's music heard side by side with the composer she is most often linked to stylistically is an advantage. There are other options, but I recommend the Silverstein-Kalisch disc just for Beach's sonata. ZIEROLF

PIANO MUSIC

Beach was an early Romantic composing piano music in the late Romantic era. Her works have more in common with Chopin and Schumann than with her contemporaries Debussy and Scriabin. Both the public and the critics loved her. As a pianist, she was dazzling, but as a composer for the piano in the *fin de siècle* United States, she was nonpareil.

Until recently, the availability of Beach's piano works on CD has been scant. In 1998 the complete works for solo piano were released: *By the Still Waters* (Arabesque 6693), *Under the Stars* (Arabesque 6704), and *Fire-flies* (Arabesque 6721) are performed superbly and consistently by **Joanne Polk.** In every piece, she knows exactly when to explode with passion and when to seethe with ethereal restraint. In 1994 **Virginia Eskin**'s "Mrs. H.H.A. Beach" provided intriguing interpretations of Beach's most famous pieces (Koch 7254). The styles of these two pianists differ widely; Polk generally gives subtler, more nuanced performances, while Eskin finds the quirky corners and revels in virtuosic passages. In sound quality, the Arabesque set is superior, with rich acoustics and voluptuous tone; the Koch CD (originally Bridge) seems distantly miked in a small studio.

In "Three American Romantics," **Mary Louise Boehm** includes Beach's longish but ingenious *Variations on Balkan Themes* in a performance that is merely acceptable; she doesn't possess Polk's finely honed elegance (Albany 293). BATES

Ludwig van Beethoven *(1770–1827)*

Beethoven was perhaps the only composer who could unambiguously wear the title of "Titan." Few men in the history of music have had his impact and enduring legacy, and if you had to choose the central figure of Western music, his name would, at the very least, be one of those at the top. For his symphonies, there is no doubt that he leads the way, but he was just as strong in every aspect of the musical art he touched. His piano music is the core of that repertory. Likewise his string quartets which are so far beyond what had come before and never surpassed to this day. Concertos, chamber music, opera, choral music, all bear his unmistakable mark, that of an artist struggling beyond human means to achieve perfection.

His was a transitory age, and he is a transitory composer, bridging the gap between what we call the "Classical" and "Romantic" periods. Though a seeker of patronage like Mozart and his teacher Haydn, he broke the chains of that bondage with his assertion of the artist as a unique, dignified prophet of society, one whose rightful duty included addressing current concerns. He marks a turning point in the history of music, and indeed of mankind, for his is the first real artistic summation of a humanism that was to indelibly, sometimes bloodily, engrave itself on the face of history.

Music suffers much violence in Beethoven's world—but is aggression the best or only way to approach this giant? We have endured a wide range of interpretations of his music since the dawn of recordings. Some are vastly introspective, seeking meaning and profundity in every bar. Others refuse to acknowledge such meaning, declaring that his constant revisions prove it was a very *human* being, complete with many flaws, who penned these works. We have had fast and slow, meditative, and flagrantly brutal Beethoven thrust on us for years, and it's impossible to decide on any one school of thought. He can stand many kinds of interpretation, revealing the riches of his energized invention afresh whenever a performance "hits home", whatever that may mean to you. It's hard to define, but with this composer, you know it when you hear it.

SYMPHONIES
Beethoven's symphonies sit at the absolute center of the Western symphonic canon. They are all the more amazing in the face of his complete deafness; he produced a "music of the spheres", an indescribable foray into musical imagination that presents humanity with a common ground for all people for all time. They remain the most played, most loved of all, and any conductor worth his salt must tackle them. Not all do them well, by any means. A good rule of thumb for determining a great Beethoven interpreter is this: If he can conquer six of the nine, he is on top of his game. It's nearly impossible to master the broad spectrum of moods and emotional postures, elegant classicism, and romantic pathos found here, but some conductors come very close. You can't hear all nine by the same conductor and expect a "hit" every time; assemblage by individual symphony is the only way to ensure success on the sublimity scale. Most of the complete sets are discussed below, with some singled out for individual symphonies.

Complete sets. You can't begin a discussion of complete sets without mentioning the numerous efforts of **Karajan,** who felt the need to make four passes at the noble canon. His first Philharmonia set displayed all the brashness of a first take, long before the trademark Karajan muddiness took hold. Fresh, vital, and with all the subtlety of a slap in the face, this set is interesting more for its reflection of the younger conductor than of Beethoven (EMI). Jumping to the opposite end of his time line, don't tread anywhere near the deadly, poisonous last reading by the great man, utterly self—absorbed in a vision of homogeneous textures that only his own mind could ever decipher (DG). His third try was much more of a success; many critics prefer it for its brilliant sound and sense of proportion. Not me—he was already over the edge at this point, in my opinion, and the 1977 sound—good as it is—doesn't compensate for interpretive waywardness. Karajan's jewel remains his 1963 set where the Berlin Philharmonic was playing like gods, and almost every move the conductor made invited the accolade of "definitive." Well, it's not quite that, but it's as close as anyone has come, and its budget price leaves you without excuse (♦DG 429036, 5CD).

Krips's traversal has garnered much attention over the years. He was a no-nonsense classicist, and for those who like their Beethoven pure, he may be the man for the job. His readings have been released in fairly abysmal CD pressings at bargain prices, and none of them did the original masters justice until Everest's transfers came along. Finally we could hear what all of the fuss was about, and I believe it was just that: fuss. At some point a conductor has to take an interpretive stand, and Krips steadfastly refused to do so. This is Beethoven clean-cut and soft-pedaled, but there can be no doubt that many will like it.

Furtwängler's name is often uttered in hushed tones of reverence, indicating his ability to inspire devotional, almost cultic feelings of loyalty. In truth, he had many important things to say about Beethoven, and it's worthwhile to at least sample some of his readings. Yet others have said far more than he, and his mystical approach to these works seems a bit cheapening and trite. He struggles to pull out of them every ounce of philosophical profundity (that Beethoven may never have contemplated). It's always an artist's prerogative to expand the vision of the original creator; this conductor was a master at that, and every subsequent artist must come to terms with him in some way. His EMI set will be the easiest to find, but you should search for the super cheapie released about 12 years ago (Virtuoso); the sound was as good as I've heard, and the price superb.

For all of **Toscanini**'s vaunted faithfulness to the composer's intentions, he made as many changes to the text as anyone. His set is either loved or hated—the latter by me—but I must in all honesty admit that his many fans are enough of a presence to preclude an immediate dismissal on my part. These are brisk, straight-to-the-point, get-out-of-my-way readings, and I can't deny the intensity that emanates from every bar. The mono sound in the latest three-set collection has never sounded better, though you can still get all nine together in RCA's older Toscanini edition.

Mengelberg is another conductor who inspires fierce loyalty or hatred. He cuts to the chase, pretending to be Beethoven's best interpretive friend, then admitting some astonishing fallacies into his readings. But you sense that he was indeed trying to serve Beethoven, as opposed to Toscanini's serving up Toscanini's *idea* of Beethoven. The Mengelberg set is in adequate sound—it will never be much better—if you desire to go the whole nine yards with him (Grammofono, 2000).

Szell always inspires debate. Some appreciate his rock-solid, clean-shaven readings, while others feel he was two steps away from a heart attack, so hard-driven and relentless were his recordings. The playing of the Cleveland Orchestra is never in doubt—no one has ever done better—and Beethoven is, after all, a rather intense, hard-driven composer. But when gas is thrown onto a fire, two things can happen: the fire grows hotter and warmer, giving off a brilliant light that illuminates everything, or the fire burns out of control and consumes everything in its path. Szell was both of these, so it's better to approach him symphony by symphony to avoid any emergency room visits (Sony).

Two other Clevelanders also had a try at complete sets, with varying success. **Dohnányi,** dull as nails on most days, still managed to produce one of the most beautiful sets on the market, with a few symphonies that can stand up against any (Telarc). **Maazel,** never progressing beyond a rather superficial understanding, offered a set that's still around but not in much demand; it's best to avoid anything from that effort (Sony). You might expect **Mackerras** to offer something new and original, but this is not the case; his are fairly standard, non-involved readings (EMI).

Weller's set has been circulating in various guises almost from the beginning of the CD era. Indeed, his was one of the first digital recordings and the original sound was lovely, but his interpretations were inoffensively neutral and unaffecting (Chandos or MHS). Likewise the sometimes underrated and sometimes overrated **Blomstedt.** You won't find a less emotionally involved set of readings. Everything is in its proper place, but the real spirit of Beethoven is missing (Berlin). **Wyn Morris** also falls into this category, offering a set with many admirable qualities, yet nothing that's likely to excite posterity (IMP).

Zinman has recorded a set based on the Bärenreiter edition (purporting to "clean up" much in the symphonies) that has been lauded in the English press, but to little effect. While the sound is great and the Zurich Tonhalle plays with remarkable buoyancy and resilience, Zinman's wild tempos and generally undernourished string section let us down far too often. (On the other hand, he does include the vestigial "10".) But several of his records are worth hearing, and are mentioned below (Arte Nova). Muti and the Philadelphia Orchestra were lambasted by virtually everyone when his set was first released, but I think time has proven its worth—many of the symphonies stand up when compared with the best. He does have a tendency to overdrive (as he shows in 5), but generally he's in the ballpark, and he offers a phenomenal 6. This is well worth considering, at least as a supplement (♦EMI 72923, 6CD).

Herbert Kegel and the Dresdeners turn in fine performances that present us with meaty, standard Central European Beethoven, something you'd be glad to hear in concert, but you may expect a little more from a recording (LaserLight or Capriccio). Ferencsik offers a very idiomatic set that rivals the competition, especially at its near-giveaway price. This was a very early digital set and has stood the test of time; it's worth considering if you're strapped for cash or are a first-timer wanting to get to know the great Ludwig (♦LaserLight 15900, 5CD). Giulini's latest collection of all nine—released separately—is altogether disappointing, despite fine playing by the Italian group and very good sound. The old master just doesn't seem up to the ferocious requirements of Beethoven's sound world any more (Sony).

Harnoncourt turned the musical world on its ear with his release of rethought, retooled, and revisited Beethoven. The Chamber Orchestra of Europe is no mean band, and Harnoncourt's ideas, though frustratingly serious for visceral impact, often prove stimulating, though those wanting geniality will be swimming upstream against a heady current (♦Teldec 46452, 5CD). Solti recorded the cycle twice with his Chicagoans, and they play with the stereotypical barrage of power they're so famous for. The second set, at full price, is the one to avoid—Brucknerian, thickly textured, and as imposing as a firewall. The first is much better (and cheaper), clean, lucid, powerful when needed, yet still lacking the last bit of orchestral refinement that Chicago has never really had (both Decca).

Klemperer was no stranger to Beethoven, and his set has rarely been a stranger to collectors over the years. "Monumental" is the word most often used to describe it, and there is some truth to the proposition, but "spacious" is even better. Klemperer simply takes his time, refusing to be pigeonholed into some sort of tradition-bound interpretive schema. But he fails as often as he succeeds, so this is not recommended for general consumption (EMI, or Music & Arts for a slightly different take).

Bernstein's Vienna set was justly acclaimed; he seemed to learn something about the composer after his first outing in New York, and the tonal luster of the VPO can't be beat. He gets most of these works just right, and his passion and seething commitment to the composer are made vivid in every note. The recording was a little close and sometimes oddly balanced for this venue, but no matter—this is one of the finest modern sets on the market, and deserves a place in every home where the name Beethoven is held in high regard (♦DG 423481, 6CD). His New York set, exciting at the time, has effectively faded from sight with the advent of the Vienna versions, with a few exceptions noted below (Sony).

The surprise of them all has to be the marvelously played, great sounding, and wonderfully conducted set by Cluytens and the Berlin Philharmonic (♦Royal Classics 703732, 5CD). At a budget price, this is one of the steals of the century, and the performances are hard to beat, coming from a source you wouldn't expect. They were recorded around the same time as Karajan's great DG set, so you know what the orchestra sounded like then. Leibowitz is the answer for those who crave a Toscanini in great sound, and it's amazing how remarkably they match each other in outlook. It's in superb remastered sound, but you must like your Beethoven even harder driven than the music naturally suggests. I like it occasionally, but couldn't live with it alone (Chesky). I wish Peter Maag had been given a better orchestra. He has been consistently interesting over the years, and several of his recordings have attained legendary status. But despite some excellent renditions of several of the symphonies, his recordings are prominently marred by scratchy, sloppy playing, and the rough sound his band makes (to be charitable) won't sit fondly in your memory. A real shame, for he deserves much better (Arts).

The periodists have of course entered the fray. Fortunately, Norrington's spew is no longer available in a set, and we should all hope EMI keeps it locked away. It wasn't just the crazy tempos (since adopted by other "modern" instrument conductors), but the soggy playing and spiritless conducting that wrecked it (EMI). Hogwood did have a real point of view and tried to establish himself by other means than just fast tempos and vibrato-less playing, but his Academy of Ancient Music, no tonal perfectionists, are too astringent for repeated hearing. Beethoven had to have a bigger sound in mind than this (Oiseau-Lyre).

Gardiner's set, as usual, was praised by nearly everyone. It's well played, almost to a fault, but the reason why it's so well liked is because of how little (compared to the others) it sounds like period instruments. These folks play so well (better than any period band I've ever heard) that you have to ask, "why bother?" Interpretively, he's rather neutral—fast, but neutral (Archiv). For the most honest approach—wind-driven, with quite rugged sound—turn to Goodman and Huggett with the Hanover Band. These recordings are full of life and vibrancy, rich in color, and so skewed against the way we're used to hearing these pieces that you really sit up and take notice. It can't be given a general recommendation because it's not the way you'll want to hear Beethoven all the time, but for a genuine re-creation of period practice, it can't be beat (Nimbus). Brüggen offers exceptionally clean playing—almost as good as Gardiner—a trademark of his Orchestra of the 18th century. His tempos are quick, deftly navigated by this virtuoso group, and he has many fine things to say about the symphonies (Philips).

Scherchen is a Beethoven conductor who gave "modern" performances before his time; his quick tempos and clean textures bear all the hallmarks of contemporary no-nonsense interpretations. He made many recordings over the years, and those interested in this conductor should investigate his versions (Enterprise, 3–6 and 8; MCA, 1, 3, 6, and 8). Haitink completed two cycles, neither particularly successful. His Concertgebouw recordings are the more beautiful, though the sloppier London Phiharmonic readings had more spunk. Neither is generally available, to no one's loss (Philips). Colin Davis has never been known as much of a Beethoven specialist, though some of his individual recordings have been quite good. His complete set on Philips had a very short shelf life in the United States, and for good reason; these performances, while full of interesting moments, are flat-footed and square, lacking strong definition or interpretive profile.

Barenboim is one of the newest entrants in the symphonies sweepstakes, and the effort is superb. Using the Berliner Staatskapelle, as underrated an orchestra as I can think of, he has pulled off the near impossible and come as close as anyone to giving us the definitive set. You can still find better individual versions, but this is something special. The dark, mahogany burnish of these readings is the ultimate in finely graded, magnificently rich and robust sound. Interpretatively, 1 and 2 are on a par with any—gorgeously managed and conducted with finesse and suppleness; 3 is splendid, a large-scale performance with small-scale details and no lack of grandeur or emotion; 4 and 8 are similar in concept, too lithe and nimble for my taste, with 8 especially lacking in grandness and swagger. No. 5 is fabulous, one of the best on disc, even giving Kleiber a run for the money; 6 is intense, too little lacking in repose, though played beautifully. No. 7 again is in the running for top honors in a very crowded field, the bravura of the horns and darkness of the sound combining for a thrilling effect, while 9 is one of the best around, full of nuance, a penetrating emotional ride that leaves you drained at the end. With a fully successful 7 of 9 symphonies (and the other two are in no way unacceptable), I will boldly say it: this is the best single collection of the nine symphonies on the market today (♦Teldec 27838, 6CD).

For **Abbado**'s Berlin swan song, he offers the punchy panache of a Harnoncourt with gleanings from the Del Mar version used by Zinman and turns in a decidedly mixed effort than nevertheless has many good moments (DG). Apart from reducing the Berlin Philharmonic to chamber orchestra size and relying on the skewed balances that come from this experiment, he does add a degree of musicality Zinman lacks, though the latter's Zurich Orchestra plays the socks off the very internationalized BPO. The brass sound fabulous—exciting and on top of their game. Nos. 1, 2, and 3 are very well done, alert, up-tempo and keenly managed. No. 4 isn't bad, though more breadth would have helped. In 5 problems begin, especially in the waltz tempo Scherzo, sounding a little silly. No. 6 is hopelessly driven and 7 is quite standard but exciting. Abbado is clueless about the humor and grandeur of 8, and his undernourished 9 is too mechanical. For a better-played conceptual set, Zinman is only a third of the price. Otherwise, pick from the Abbados when the singles come out.

1. The moment we first hear the unresolved dominant seventh chord—unheard of in Beethoven's day—we know he is already making a unique musical statement. He reveals his still strong allegiance to Papa Haydn, but with a twist: Haydn was content to rest on his considerable symphonic laurels without feeling the need to innovate, while Beethoven knew he had to strike a blaze to compete with his very popular mentor. This work is still firmly entrenched in the classical style, but we're given a minuet that's actually a scherzo and a finale that begins hesitantly, stutters, and then races. No one had paused so much in the middle of a symphonic movement before Beethoven.

Chicago for **Reiner** doesn't play in as spectacularly unified a manner as they later would for Solti; a few ragged spots spoil the sport, and the tonal luster is not the greatest. But Reiner isn't smiling; he never did, and his reading seems a little on the flat side. More humor is needed, or at least some high spirits (RCA). **Leinsdorf** reminds us that the seeds of Beethoven's later symphonies are present in the first. His 1 is brash, confident, full of youth and vigorous playing, enhanced by superb ensemble unity and warm, spacious sound. A wonderful recording, so look for it! (♦RCA 60128). **Böhm** is fabulously recorded (one of the best) and the Vienna Philharmonic is in fine form. He nevertheless leaves 1 in low gear all the way through; it's about more than just beauty of sound, and Böhm's Viennese mannerisms impart a degree of respectability to the composer at a time when he surely would have rejected it (DG).

Karajan is the model of Prussian stateliness, in the best sense of the phrase. He strikes a middle ground between the period antics of Norrington and the heavy luxuries of Böhm. Terrific dynamic control and shimmering contrasts of texture and balance make this recording most desirable (♦DG 429036). In lively, icy-clear sound, **Bernstein** approaches 1 with a swagger and eye-opening brilliance that completely hold our attention. Nothing goes unnoticed, and the Vienna Philharmonic plays like the world's premier orchestra—a most remarkable recording, like viewing a newly restored painting, this may be the best (♦DG 423481). **Walter** tries to bring some of his vaunted humanity to this early jewel, and nearly succeeds. Only some wayward phrasing and mannered exaggerations keep it out of the top rank. But if it was the only one, I could live happily (Sony).

Cluytens's account doesn't sound like Berlin. It's much smoother, more elegant of line, and completely uncluttered—unfussy and imbued with a prismatic spirit that's entirely delightful; for the money, it's hard to beat (♦Royal Classics 70373). **Klemperer** has often been criticized for his unyielding, rock-like massiveness in Beethoven, and it does seem that 1 is no place for Bruckneresque architectonic examination, but he's able to sell it, yielding not an inch to the right or left (♦EMI 66792). No one seems more polarizing than **Toscanini**, who inspires fierce devotion and detestation. I generally consider myself in the latter camp, but his 1 has many virtues, among them a drive and propulsion that never slacken or lose harmonic firmness (RCA).

Despite some of the best sound on record, **Dohnányi** remains, to my mind, hopelessly inept in most of what he has recorded. His 1 is no exception, part of a wildly inconsistent set (Telarc). **Monteux** finds just the right amount of brashness and control in his Vienna version; not known for going to extremes, he would seem ideal for a symphony that thrives in the middle of the road. Such is the case, but the fluttering, nasal oboe in I and the out of control timpani reverberation in IV make it a no-go (Decca). **Sawallisch**'s flatulent, heavy reading won't sit well with most Beethoven connoisseurs. Gone are the youthful spirits and ringing charms of fresh discovery, replaced by a crusty traditionalism that knew no younger years (EMI).

Béla Drahos's version is standard, straight-up Beethoven, clean and clear, with a small orchestra and without any special characteristics, but quite beautiful (Naxos). **Harnoncourt** is another conductor who inspires polar reactions among listeners. His 1 is not for sissies, taking its revolutionary aspect seriously while ignoring its classical antecedents—an excellent recording, but not the only one I'd want (♦Teldec 75708). **Kempe** excelled in this literature, but his recording finds him brightly caught and not at all suitable for daily fare (Seraphim).

Even at his most deranged, **Scherchen** was always interesting and challenging, and in 1 he brings us a fully realized performance that is only black-balled by dated sound (Tahra). Also consider his old Westminster recording, by no means a bad reading and can still be found if you look hard enough (MCA). **Schwarz** in the end fails to convey enough of the grandeur found in Beethoven's earliest symphonic opus (Delos). When looking for only one Beethoven recording, a good rule of thumb is to avoid chamber orchestras.

You're either committed to **Szell** over the long haul or you're not. No faults are to be found with the marvelous Cleveland instrument he built, but the cold, concrete-floor sound and clocklike forward motion don't allow enough air into the pores (Sony). **Zender** keeps things moving along, but his orchestra sounds lackluster and a little beyond their ability; tempos are fast without any offsetting values (CPO). With frighteningly precise playing and fanatical attention to long forgotten details,

Zinman came up with a real winner. His small band (50-some) won't be to everyone's taste, so it can't be considered an absolute necessity, but the interpretation and sound are fine, and it always beats period instruments. (Arte Nova).

Muti delivers a very good account of 1, articulate, intelligently realized, and the Philadelphia is in its best form. He absolved the orchestra of its Ormandy sound, but even in the late '80s they had a sheen that separated them from other bands. An outstanding reading, and budget-priced to boot; we're not often treated to recordings of past masters in such glorious sound (♦EMI 69782). The Hallé was a fine orchestra, not a great one, but Barbirolli was able to coax some marvelously supple playing out of them. It reminds me of Zinman but with more punch, and no one paid more attention to detail and nuance than this conductor (♦Dutton 1014).

2. Here Beethoven began to reach for the grand statement, stepping beyond the trial run of 1 and moving toward an ideal that would be embodied in 3, only then to be discarded while yet other symphonic concepts appear. This is a big-boned, confident work that needs an approach equally unbridled. Klemperer takes a path similar to his 1—big-band, grand, and intent on providing the requisite largeness of scale. There aren't enough synapses connecting the musical cells, and a certain ponderous quality—or lack of propulsion—rules the day (EMI). Don't let the mono sound (clear and revealing of detail) deter you from enjoying the amazing virtuosity Reiner was able to instill in the Pittsburgh Symphony, the equal of any in America at the time. It's explosive—I is almost implosive, so fast and intense are the strings—and not to all tastes, certainly not as a benchmark, but it's a unique reading, well worth hearing (♦Sony 62344).

Beecham brought Vienna to London, with a smile on his face and a cup of coffee in his hand; in this case, geniality doesn't mean slumberous, for his reading really moves. It's not available now, but grab it if you see it (EMI). In Böhm's reading the first movement might have been sent from heaven itself, so perfect are its proportions. II is quite slow, but also deliberate and convincing, not leisurely in any way. He knows just what he wants and achieves it with graceful elegance (♦DG 39681, 2CD).

Harnoncourt in no way gives short shrift to the significance of this transitory work. I is tense, almost ominous, while the second is lighter, yet clouds still darken the sky; the fourth movement is fiery and compelling, though not everyone will share the conductor's tendency to invoke the dark side in everything he attempts (Teldec). Toscanini sees Beethoven as a series of impending cataclysms, and 2 is no different. This is Beethoven as maniac, hardly a good example for the children (RCA). Menuhin's chamber-scaled performance is a little lightweight for my taste; his orchestra is superb, but the first movement could use more traction, and he deflates everything that follows (Carlton).

Morris tries to get back on track after his misguided 1 with a reading that is *vin ordinaire,* not allowed into the highest Beethovenian echelons. Giulini finds virtues in spades here: great sound, a remarkable consistency of thought and interpretation, devoid of wayward eccentricities. While not a primary choice, his fans won't be disappointed with one of the best readings in his set (Sony). Szell has many virtues in his supercharged recording, but the clammy sound continues (Sony). Overactive thyroid readings have their place, but the element of song must always be secure. Try Reiner instead, even with its mono sound.

Leinsdorf's version is as stirring as it gets. The orchestra sounds fabulous, with rich and glowing strings, and incisive, snappy winds; the tempos are moderate, convincing, and true to form. There is no finer

version of 2; it's worth hunting down (♦RCA 60130). Cluytens's reading is one of the best around. Every strand of Beethoven's delicious counterpoint is forcefully audible in a reading that respects tradition while forging its own path (♦Royal Classics 703752). Walter may come to the party dressed in a tuxedo, but don't be fooled, for underneath his patented geniality is a spine as steely as any. The outer movements are cautiously molded, suitably energetic, and laced with finely-hewn phrasing. II is radiant—only Walter could pull off such a lingering tempo, offset by a frolicking scherzo. It's one of the best (♦Sony 64460). In Sawallisch's Concertgebouw version, some lovely playing by one of the world's finest orchestras is strangely muddled by substandard sound. In his attempt to prove this a *grand* symphony, he refuses to let up at all, diligently avoiding repose (EMI).

Ever the classicist, Monteux plays down the sound of pregnant romanticism in Beethoven's transitional symphonic opus. While we must admire its clarity and stylistic consistency, it ultimately fails to move us emotionally, either as a romantic springboard or a classical pinnacle. It's not a prime recommendation even at a fire-sale price (Decca). Bernstein's Vienna recording is crisp and flagellant, offering many instances of pointed highlights and some questionable emphases. While it's not a great recording, that shouldn't stop you from acquiring his complete set (DG). His earlier New York recording far exceeds the Vienna remake. It's one of the best on records from first to last—sprightly, buoyant, and full of the irrepressible zest and zeal that were always his hallmark. The remastering is excellent (♦Sony 61835 or 47515).

You have only to listen to Karajan's bold, brash conception of 2 to silence any naysayers who would deny his status among the great conductors of the 20th century. The Berlin Philharmonic plays like gods, and this sweeping reading is like a breathless dash barefoot across the ice (♦DG 429036). Zinman's flawlessly smooth recording will raise hackles in many quarters, but I find it refreshing and stimulating. It's wind-dominated, or perhaps it just seems so because of the small number of strings. The new *urtext* coupled with Zinman's crisp articulations and subtle phrasing make for a most enjoyable experience (Arte Nova). Muti offers a rock-solid performance that successfully navigates the fine line between underdone and overwrought. Tempos are reasonable, with elegant phrasing and meaty temperament blissfully coexisting in a reading marked by superb Philadelphia playing (♦EMI 72923).

Drahos leads a perfectly acceptable reading that would more than satisfy me 90 percent of the time. There are a few problems with detail, especially in the winds—too recessed at times, lacking sharpness, and too much in the forefront at others (Naxos). Celibidache is not to all tastes, but he was one of the greatest conductors of the century, and everything he does must be examined with profound respect. His Beethoven is like the rest of his repertory, slow and carefully examined. If you're in the market for comparisons, by all means try it (EMI).

3 (Eroica). Everyone knows the story: Beethoven originally planned to dedicate this work to Napoleon, then changed his mind when he declared himself Emperor, writing "to the memory of a great man" on the score. But the real story is the arrival, finally, of Beethoven at his symphonic maturity, realizing a work of such immense significance and proportions that it dwarfed all that came before. The principle of melodic motives—one that would guide him for the rest of his career and influence countless other composers—was fully established with the opening movement. Colossal, imposing, even daunting, 3 has become a benchmark of symphonic thought, one that no conductor can ignore and that must be approached with caution.

The fleetness of **Zinman**'s approach is startling from the very beginning. Tempos are invariably fast, as much modern day period dogma insists, but here, in one of the most heroic of symphonies, we get instead an almost Mendelssohnian scherzo-like feeling, robbing the music of portent and passion. Phrases are cut short, note values almost always clipped, as if full note value had become heresy. This is not a good way to get to know this music, and what worked well for Zinman in 1 and 2 fails completely here (Arte Nova). Some would call **Leinsdorf**'s smooth version a "humanized" Beethoven. The warm, central European sound of the early '60s Boston Symphony and Leinsdorf's full, sweeping wash of perfectly rounded phrases present a Beethoven that's gorgeous to hear, while perhaps spiritually a little on the lax side (RCA). **Gardiner** has produced the best played of the period cycles. His I is like Zinman's, fast, sleek, and almost embarrassingly hurried, as if the material wasn't worth his time (Archiv).

Levine's recording amply demonstrates that the Metropolitan Opera Orchestra has become one of the foremost ensembles in the world. It's in the Szell tradition—after all, Levine worked with him—so you must expect the Szell trademarks of firmness of line, precision, brilliance of tone, and exceptional virtuosity. But Levine finds a blazing lifeline of humanistic passion that goes beyond the simple mechanics of execution, something Szell often lost sight of (♦DG 39862). **Harnoncourt** is out to make riveting points in every piece he conducts. In the *Eroica*, Beethoven seems to have accomplished this already, and the highlighting is unnecessary. What Harnoncourt lacks in his smallish orchestra, he tries to make up for with punched accents and furiously swelled crescendos. It has its moments; a Harnoncourt recording rarely bores, though it may drive you mad (Teldec).

Szell presides like a fierce warlord over a highly charged, efficient, calculated reading. Everyone is on their toes, as usual for Szell performances, and the playing is spectacular, but this is a mean machine executing orders, not bringing music to life (Sony). If you want a recording by this conductor, his Salzburg Festival recording is superior in concept, though perhaps not in execution. (Sony). **Wand**'s reading, different from the one in his complete set, manifests many of the same virtues and vices. It's traditional in flavor, correct in proportion, yet singularly absent any sense of urgency or spark. If you must have a Wand recording—something I don't recommend—stick with the set (RCA).

Peter Tiboris gives us a reverse authenticism, using Mahler's retouching and wind doublings, including trumpets in fours. It doesn't make the difference you'd expect, but it's refreshing that a conductor had the courage to pursue a project every bit as "authentic" as the authenticists would like. But it's only supplementary, not primary (Elysium). The highly underrated **Boult,** criminally cheated out of many standard repertory recordings, was allowed four delightful Beethoven excursions that deserve their place in the recording pantheon. An unerring sense of pacing and flawless phrasing mark his *Eroica* with a definite thumbs-up, until one takes into consideration the scrappy playing of the London Philharmonic and it drops out of consideration (Vanguard).

Vonk's reading is semi-predictable—a middle of the road, standard run-through that any competent conductor could produce on a good day. The difference is the marvelous playing of the St. Louis Symphony, here obscured by blurred, cluttered, canister-contained sound that stubbornly refuses to yield its treasures. At full price, no go (Archiv). **Giulini**'s brief but extraordinary tenure with the LA Philharmonic in the late '70s produced an enormous, rock-solid *Eroica*. Tempos are steady and secure, all the while maintaining a solid structure that never sacrifices harmony and melodic progression on the altar of propulsion. If you

like Furtwängler but wish for better sound, this is your choice (♦DG 47444). **Stokowski,** at age 93, finally was able to put his only *Eroica* on disc, and what a performance it is! The London Symphony plays beyond itself, as it often did for him, and this might be the best 3 ever to emerge from British shores (♦RCA 62514).

Walter's legendary touch greatly lightens this music's profundity, at the same time enhancing its humanity. It's heroic in the true sense of the word, not only noble and stoic but also compassionate, human, and filled with a zest for life. The only drawback is some coarse sound and a few mishaps by the Columbia Symphony. A real classic (♦Sony 64461). **Celibidache** took phenomenal chances every time he ascended the podium, even more than Bernstein. His art was to reveal the essence of the great composers, to seek what lies beneath the surface. For a reading splendiferous in form and architecture, look no further, but be forewarned—this may not be the *Eroica* you want to live with (EMI). **Steinberg**'s flat-footed approach will win few converts. I feels like walking through a strobe light—you may know you're moving, but everything is at half speed and you never seem to get anywhere. Movements III and IV are both fine, generalized readings, but this is hardly what we want in an *Eroica* (EMI).

Barbirolli brought a sure sense of style and keen intelligence to everything he conducted. His tempos are very slow, as if he wanted to make sure nothing went unnoticed, and indeed nothing does, but it may be considered eccentric and not a good sole choice (Dutton). **Muti**'s reading is thoroughly competent and professional, with his orchestra responding to every nuance and emotive flick of the baton. But I is too professional—a blistering charge that avoids the scenery and clings to the asphalt—and II is too stark; the fugue, always an exhilarating high point, leaves you flat and bored. Again, not a good choice for your only *Eroica* (EMI).

The word for **Toscanini**'s performance is *power*—surging, obliterating, unstoppable. His idea of the heroic, coming from his own life experiences, is that of the charging soldier, noble in struggle whether victorious or defeated, but never, *never* giving up. His myriad of loyal fans will love it (RCA). If you're put off by the Toscanini hype machine and feel the need for a quick fix without going to great expense, **Drahos** may fill the bill; for pure excitement, it beats Toscanini, though you pay a price in sound (Naxos). He and his splendid Esterházy Sinfonia supply an endearing *Eroica*, a very pliable reading that bends but doesn't break, scrupulously molded after the model of Weingartner. Those on a budget desiring excellent modern sound should consider it (Naxos). Clean-cut, superb playing and fastidious, athletic tempos are all hallmarks of **Solti**'s recording. He gives meticulous but not over-scrupulous attention to every aspect of rhythmic and melodic detail, resulting in a very good but workaday recording that you can listen to without offense, and also without much inspiration (Decca).

Monteux's recording is not a good example of his art. It's sissified and a little vulgar, with overemphasized accents—so much so that the sound is distorted—plus inconsistent phrasing within movements and blaring, distorted brass. There are more tasty *Eroica*s elsewhere (Decca). Considered by many to be a god in this music, **Furtwängler** had a special way with everything he conducted, seeking to probe that which others skimmed over. Often this resulted in much ado about nothing, but when he hit, he hit big, and this happened repeatedly in 3. The problem is the multitude of recordings that keep turning up, of varying sound quality. If you don't want to purchase the EMI set, or can't find the Virtuoso any more, try one of the postwar readings from Berlin (Music & Arts or Tahra). Otherwise, stick with Giulini.

Proportional perfection, with broad, sweeping phrases and incandescent, blazing melodic beauty, mark **Cluytens**'s one-for-the-ages recording. The Berlin Philharmonic has never sounded this good for anyone, including Karajan, and the price is close to stealing—I'd gladly pay four times the cost for this wonderful performance (♦Royal Classics 703742). **Dohnányi**'s splendidly recorded version—perhaps the best recorded—finds the Clevelanders in top form, but the performance, while it has plenty of snap and crisp, sharp-edged playing, falls into the middle of the road interpretively. You won't be disappointed, and it must be recommended, but it's not a spiritual experience (♦Telarc 80090).

Cavernous sound doesn't help the fabulous players of the Concertgebouw, and **Sawallisch**'s conducting, especially in II, is like taking a step and then wondering whether to take another, a retreating line of wounded, despondent soldiers instead of the funeral of a hero (EMI). **Böhm** offers a radiant, dazzling reading that oozes gorgeous Viennese tone. When he conducts, it's as if there were a direct pipeline from heaven. The sound is not DG's best—thin and tinny in the strings and not enough bass in the brass—but Böhm's repeat-less I is heartfelt and genuine, with a strong singing line pulled out of the orchestra like some great swooping eagle catching its prey. This is a great recording (♦DG 37368).

Bernstein's gritty, very American, very rugged account finds him and the New York Philharmonic in top form, and his combative band makes up in spirit what they lack in tonal opulence. But the finale is a letdown—disconnected, extrapolated, and drowning out important passages with questionable balances (Sony). In his Vienna reading, he shows us the very definition of introspection in the funeral march. After a I that's similar to his New York recording—though much better played—he proceeds to examine every beat and sub-beat in a microscopic manner that robs the movement of any pretense that it's a march. A sense of heavy perfume, a sort of odious fog, seems to interweave with the notes; though vital, its sluggish manner inhibits it (DG).

Like a master puppeteer, **Karajan** manipulates every aspect of his performance, coaxing the strings to near-subterranean pianissimos in order to hear the winds, and shaping the brass sound to make an impact like the explosion of a large bomb. Its rhythmic vitality is pungent and urgent, underlining everything he does, and the Vienna Orchestra sounds better than it does for Bernstein, though it doesn't always respond to Karajan in Beethoven as well as it does for Cluytens. A must have (♦DG 429036). **Klemperer**'s recording has been described as "granitic" or "monumenta", but what that really means is "insurmountable" (EMI). There is simply no point of view. Many people love this recording, but I'd avoid it unless you're collecting *Eroica*s. **Rudolf Kempe,** a vastly underrated conductor, does very well with a budget CD that's a good cheap entry into this music, but you also get a 1 and 5 that are far from the best and the sound is a little harsh (Seraphim).

4. It's understandable that after the *Eroica* Beethoven would scale back his ideas to something more manageable, but this work still has its surprises. It's as lyrical as anything he ever wrote, and he constantly challenges expectations. The mysterious opening of I should give rise to a feeling of great seriousness, but then, as Bernstein so memorably put it, what occurs is like horses breaking out of the gate—a "veritable funfest", a movement full of high spirits and joy. This is perhaps the most purely graceful of all Beethoven's symphonies, and it takes a special conductor to capture its intricacies.

Monteux's approach is utterly stylistic (♦Decca 43479). A strong classical grace of line prevails in this reading, and the playful contrasts and tempo changes make for compelling listening. He saves all the *brio* for last, in a rapid-fire, gloriously joyous finale. This is one of this conductor's best, so there's no need to bother with his San Francisco recording (RCA). Despite the brilliant playing of the Boston Symphony, **Leinsdorf**'s meticulous examination of this score leads to some rather dubious results. After three questionable movements, he recovers in IV, but it's too late, a finale without a prelude (RCA). **Klemperer**'s tempos, though leisurely, are anything but ponderous, and his rendition of 4 is excellent across the board, proving that a taut motivic line and firm bass are two basic ingredients for a successful Beethoven symphonic rendition (♦EMI 66795). This Philharmonia recording is one of the better efforts in the Klemperer Beethoven roundup, more so than his later Bavarian Radio effort (also EMI).

Harnoncourt, like Gardiner, takes an "exhilarating" approach to this work, and sells it completely. The pace is quite brisk, and you come away feeling that it's regarded as a poor cousin to 5 simply because of misjudged tempos. There's something electrifying about this recording, even if you can't imagine living with it all the time (Teldec). **Erich Kleiber** takes a middle road. The propulsion and proportion are perfect, yet he infuses every bar with such exquisite phrasing and careful nuance and shape that it's like putting an old-school interpretation into high speed. Recordings by this man are hard to come by, but the ones we have should be treasured (♦Orfeo 100841). Cold, steely, and faceless are only some of the adjectives that can be applied to **Karajan**'s recording. He was a very serious conductor, and this symphony, despite its deliberately misleading introduction, is full of smiles and warm feelings. The power is there—Karajan never lacks that—but this piece demands much more (DG).

In many ways it's a shame that a cult status has grown up around **Celibidache,** for that only alienates many listeners who have never heard his work, approaching him with the preconceived notion that he was a wildly extravagant and bizarre interpreter. His 4 is a marvel of highlighted details and carefully planned execution—not a prime choice, but worth hearing (EMI). **Toscanini** approaches Beethoven with a preconceived strategy about how the entire corpus should sound instead of taking each work on its own merits. His 4 has his usual excessive speeds, little repose, and highly charged outer movements. Yet many people revere this conductor and his style, and though I'm not one of them, I can safely preach this best-sounding-yet transfer to his large choir (RCA). I can't fault **Szell** for his insistence on exactitude and meticulous attention to detail; many feel this is where much of the beauty of a performance lies, yet sometimes such scrupulousness can stamp out, or at least cover up, the spirit of the music. Szell isn't bad, but not the best (Sony).

Sawallisch's very uneven set scores an almost perfect 10 with a lovingly guided, persuasively argued reading of 4. The acoustics are much improved, with the puffy bass reined in, and he takes full measure of every movement, emphasizing its festive nature in a perfect antidote to Karajan (♦EMI 73326). No. 4 was something of a specialty for **Bernstein,** who seemed to know exactly how this music should go. The NYPO plays up to its considerable best, and while there are smoother versions, few are as exciting (♦Sony 63079). But his Vienna reading, like Kleiber's, is one of the glories of the catalog. The carefree, party-like atmosphere he conjures up will have you dancing in the streets. You can't help yourself—you just have to smile (♦DG 423481).

Drahos has given us a fine modern cycle, and his 4 is, for the most part, a worthy competitor. It is somewhat bland, and some of the balances strike me as odd, with the oboe sounding as loud as the entire string section. You can add this with confidence if you're collecting the entire series, but it doesn't rank among the best (Naxos). Perhaps because of the string intensity of this work—lots of exposed, long-held notes in I—the thin sonics in the upper range bother me more than in some of **Cluyten**'s other symphonies. The excellence of his series slackens slightly, though II is lyrical and IV a real *perpetuum mobile* (Royal Classics).

While there is no rule that says Beethoven must always be played big and fat, many feel that the addition of faster tempos and rethought, sleeker textures only serves to make an aggressive composer even more aggressive. But in many cases it can also be refreshing, adding a degree of difference to a piece we thought we knew everything about. **Zinman**'s 4 is such a recording. The opening introduction, taken at a faster pace than usual, is neatly played and not too mysterious, more tongue-in-cheek, with a wink of the eye bringing us in on the joke. What follows is a cornucopia of dancing fairies flitting about in a lighthearted manner. Whether you agree with Beethoven's metronome markings or not, you should hear this (♦Arte Nova 59214).

Böhm and his Viennese orchestra give us a very warm, not-a-care-in-the-world rendition that pours out of the speakers like rich, molten chocolate—the diametric opposite to Zinman. While perhaps too relaxed for everyday use (Bernstein supplies the pep needed for that) this sunny, afternoon-on-the-promenade performance has many good points. Only a lack of tension and snap in several movements keep it out of the top choices (DG). **Muti** sees 4 as a precursor to 5, and consequently plays it in a tough-as-nails manner, with fast and furious tempos. Others have moved this quickly without so much adrenalin; it's intense, with little breathing room (EMI). Pieces like this would seem tailor-made for conductors like **Walter,** and this proves to be the case. Genial but not slack, he deftly guides his LA players in a reading of warmth and vitality. There's simply no reason not to recommend this. Perhaps it's the best (many feel so) and though I'm not willing to make that pronouncement, at the very least it deserves a place in any collection (♦Sony 64462).

Barbirolli offers a reading that's characteristic of all his recordings—well planned, incisive, with a knack for getting to the essence of the composer—but because of the sound (not bad, but not great either) and the fact that this isn't the best of his Beethoven, it's better reserved for his many fans or those looking for a supplement (Dutton). **Beecham**'s recording has been circulating for many years. Some swear by it, others brush it off. I think it's fully representative of his Beethoven, and he wasn't known as a Beethoven conductor, but for his supporters it will no doubt be heaven-sent (Beecham Society).

5. Whether it's fate knocking at the door, or the V-day motto, or "three quarter notes and a half," as Bernstein once said, those first four notes may be the most famous ever written—certainly the most recognized. But more important, they represent Beethoven's most concise, compressed attempt at motivic development, a phenomenal tour de force of extraordinary emotional power. Too much energy and a performance can become a brutal, vulgar display of anger; too little, and the complex intertwining of motives loses all its effectiveness.

Walter highlights many things other conductors miss—a short melodic fragment in the cellos, a slight pause at the end of a phrase—all very becoming effects that in the end rob this most emotionally charged of Beethoven's symphonies of its drive and power. There is much more to this work that Walter either misses or considers unim-

portant (Sony). **Ormandy** produced a very reliable recording that shows how this work should go, by the book, no questions asked. He manipulates the texts in a few places, adding some swelling crescendos that don't fit the music (Sony). In **Benjamin Zander**'s recording, using Beethoven's tempo markings, only I seems controversial to me, and other conductors have taken it at speeds this fast. My complaint is the short length of time the fermatas in the first movement are held—too short to be effective dramatically. Telarc's sound fails here; it's foggy, undefined, and slightly muffled, though the Philharmonia plays well.

Barbirolli's cleanly remastered mono recording is well worth knowing. The performance is electrifying, at tempos far slower than Zander's, but his pace has pulse, something often lacking in other recordings. Though not a first choice, it's something special. (Dutton). Willful, wayward, and a little nasty are only three of the many adjectives that come to mind when considering **Reiner**'s 1955 stereo recording. There is some generally sloppy ensemble and bizarre pauses in the scherzo. To be fair, many critics love it, but in all conscience I can't imagine what they see in it (RCA). There's little to complain about in **Drahos**'s recording. Tempos are moderate and the small orchestra is excellent. He navigates Beethoven's perilous articulations like a master mariner, with everyone coming away happy. Though it doesn't contain any revelations, with such a good price and performance it's tough to beat (♦Naxos 8554061).

Sawallisch gives us a hard body 5, the kind that works out at the gym for three hours a day. Forceful but not forced, he offers a reading of fiercely large proportions while achieving delicacy at key moments. The Concertgebouw is glorious, and some of the sound deficiencies affecting the rest of his cycle are absent here (♦EMI 73326, 2CD). It's hard to believe that 25 years have passed since **Carlos Kleiber** set his incandescent recording down on tape. He dusted off old interpretations, shined it up, and revved up the engine. Some consider it too "driven," but nowadays that hardly applies—he simply lets it unfold, the pattern of the notes dictating his every move. This recording would be part of my top ten all time greatest; as it is, consider it the Beethoven bargain of the century, and it belongs in your collection no matter how many others you have (♦DG 47400).

While it's wrong to interpret 4 in the same manner as 5, it's equally wrong to visualize 5 in terms of 4 or 6. **Böhm** generally falls into the same trap as Walter, offering a wealth of detail—though not as much as Walter—while depriving us of the necessary sense of dramatic urgency. Great sound, though (DG). **Leinsdorf**'s recording suffers from some bloated distortion in places, but the Boston Symphony sounds very good. This conductor was never one for cheap effects, and his slow tempos *mean* something, though many will miss the crispness found elsewhere (RCA). **Muti**'s Philadelphia recording is blessed with a natural, concert hall perspective, though often beset by fuzziness and sticky details. Its froward last movement takes it out of the running for prime consideration (EMI).

Those who fret over Kleiber's supposedly driven reading have no idea what **Monteux** has in store for them. He clocks in at one of the fastest tempos on record, his first movement devious and furious, pausing for an eternity on the fermatas. The rest is very mainstream, but the recording is plagued with tape dropout, coarse, grainy, sandpaper sound, and a scratchy and uneven London Symphony (Decca). As expected, **Zinman** takes a fleeting I and speedier than usual II, though his highlighting and articulation should be emulated by other, more famous ensembles. But this time the scherzo really *is* a joke, with a tempo so fast the basses are falling all over themselves in the trio. I don't know what he was thinking when he recorded this one (Arte Nova).

Klemperer's approach is gargantuan—Beethoven writ large for the world to see (EMI). The trouble is that 5 doesn't need that sort of treatment; we get a ponderous, plodding reading that saps all spirit. His Bavarian Radio recording on the same label fares no better. **Karajan**'s first DG series included a bold, red-blooded performance. The dramatic points are heightened but not lingered over (just listen to the held string note in I—what intensity!). This is Beethoven on steroids—supreme, heroic, taking no prisoners. It's wonderful (♦DG 429036, 2CD). You only have to listen to about ten seconds of the last movement of the Vienna **Bernstein** to see what a conductor like Zinman missed—scorching intensity, every note thick and packed with meaning (♦DG 31049). It's true that I is somewhat lacking—you'd think he'd find more here—but it's far superior to his pounding Sony recording. I hope DG will one day release his powerhouse '70's reading with the Bavarian Radio Symphony, something really special.

The Berlin Philharmonic with **Cluytens** is measured, adroitly paced, and singularly persistent in its structural integrity. He seeks to illuminate the varied facets of this work without losing emotional impact, but some slackness is all too apparent (DG). **Szell**'s forays in the concert halls often produced different results than in the studio. His long-time participation in the Salzburg Festival produced a recording (Orfeo) with a degree of spontaneity that humanizes the conductor and composer in a way unknown in his slashing, ice-pick Sony recording. The London Philharmonic was not in the best shape when **Boult** made his 1956 recording, and despite the near-miraculous restoration job on the original tapes, the sound is still a detriment (Vanguard).

The super-hot young European conductor **Christian Thielemann** presents us with a super self-conscious reading of 5. Conceptual problems abound after the first movement, not the least of them a lack of musical tension (DG). **Giulini** turns in a weighty performance, each note pregnant with significance, but his finale lacks the determination and resolve necessary to complement the struggles of the preceding three. It's recommended only as a supplement (DG). **Gardiner**'s recording set the musical world on fire when it first appeared, and the playing of the Orchestre Révolutionnaire et Romantique is astonishing, the best sounding of any period performance. If you like this sort of reconstructionism, try it—but I think Beethoven is better served elsewhere (Archiv).

Harnoncourt is always concerned with the wedding of classical sensibilities and romantic angst, the modern performance tradition with lost previous practice. In fact, this changing of Beethoven's well-proportioned argument into a psychological terror, full of anger and warlike emotion, is too much (Teldec). There are no surprises with **Toscanini**—terribly fast, pumped-up tempos accompanied by glistening string sound and hard-as-stone winds. Many love it, but it's like riding down an icy street and throwing on the brakes—out of control and moving fast, though the ride can be thrilling (RCA).

Dorati was always a capable Beethoven conductor, and his 1962 recording with the London Symphony is fine. The "Living Presence" sound inspires polar opinions among critics and collectors, and here it's quite close, with little reverb, but many details are excellently captured, and this recording stands with the best the catalog offers (♦Mercury 434375). **Kempe** shows us why he was a master conductor by the quality of his pacing—on the slow side, though the tension never falters—but his sound is echo-laden and the interpretation not good enough to sanctify it (EMI). **Steinberg** was another born Beethoven interpreter, and his Pittsburgh Symphony plays as well as any. But while I'd be happy to hear this in the concert hall, for a recording the competition is more formidable, and this one just misses consideration (EMI).

You listen to **Ozawa** and you wonder why it's even kept in the catalog—but not why he hasn't done more Beethoven. There's no sense of direction here, not a clue about how to play this music (Telarc). **Masur**'s New York recording fares little better than his Gewandhaus of old, except that it's played better. His Beethoven is middle-aged and fat, a story of the valor of days long past. Avoid it (Teldec). The Seattle Symphony with **Schwarz** is simply out of their league, with a limp, spineless reading that's only a caricature of what Beethoven should be (Teldec).

6. (*Pastoral*). You can't help but think that Beethoven must have had a wry smile on his face on the day in 1808 when the *Pastoral* had its premiere—along with the Fifth! The juxtaposition of two such different works must have been quite striking to the bewildered audience, and in fact critical opinion was divided—most of it bemoaning the "simplicity" of this "nature" symphony. In fact, it's one of Beethoven's most extraordinary compositions, an early tone painting of exquisite nuance and demure, ambrosial elegance that never fails to lift the spirits.

Abbado starts very slowly, almost bringing the first movement to a halt with his smothering, phrase-ending affectations. The finale turns Beethoven's singing apotheosis into a hyperactive, mechanical run-through, with some of the oddest balances I've ever heard recorded in the Musikverein (DG). **Zinman**'s countryside excursion can hardly be called "relaxed," unless relaxation means high-level aerobics (Arte Nova). **Drahos** is hard-pressed to do anything wrong and his account is very satisfying. It fails to exploit every aspect of Beethoven's genius, but will serve as an inexpensive, reliable introduction to this work, and the Esterházy Sinfonia is a crackerjack outfit (♦Naxos 553474). **Ormandy** leads a no-nonsense version that lacks subtlety, yet is refreshing for its directness and lack of pretension. Just listen to those strings! It's not one of the great ones, but still worth consideration (Sony).

Muti offers a stunningly successful 6, one of the best in his series. Contrary to what you might expect from a man who idolizes Toscanini, the work flows naturally and effortlessly from his baton, and the last movement in particular is an orgy of warm sentiment and good feelings (♦EMI 72923, 6CD). Many **Monteux** fans love his recording, so get your grain of salt ready. I find it absolutely relentless, over-driven, and totally lacking in repose; the in-your-lap strings with the winds five miles in the rear only exacerbate the problem. It's only for the single-minded fanatic (Decca). **Böhm** leads a lush, high cholesterol account that gushes with Viennese warmth and sentimentality, captured on a disc that boasts amazing transparency; you hear everything as if you were standing on the podium. A great reading (♦DG 37928, 2CD, or 47433). **Reiner** surprised everyone with his buttoned-down, Sunday school performance that would earn a "G" rating anywhere in the world. The only major disruption is what sounds like a thunder sheet in the storm movement. His finale substitutes high voltage for any lingering ecstasy—I usually don't like it this way, but he has convinced me (♦RCA 60002).

Long one of the jewels of **Walter**'s recorded legacy, his *Pastoral* is sensational, a sparkling, crackling, electric reading. Movement II is a little speedy, but under such control that it never seems too fast, and IV is a miracle of persuasive self-indulgence, like Olivier at the climax of a great Shakespearean drama. This is one of the best ever (♦Sony 64462). **Karajan**'s recording is full of a brimming vitality and orchestral glitter that is most attractive. He opts for a highly energized reading, and the effect is rather like looking at a beautiful, bare forest covered in ice—bracing and invigorating, but when all is said and done, still cold (DG). **Cluytens** presides over a rich tapestry of feeling, emotion, and beauty. He's unhurried, yet unyielding in his sense of rhythm—crucial in this work—

and his orchestra radiates a tonal glow equal to Böhm's (♦Royal Classics 703722).

When asked about tempo in the "scene by a brook" movement, **Klemperer** replied that it must be taken "slow enough so you can't beat it in four, and fast enough so you can't beat it in twelve." This remark was more than just supercilious; he understood the need to balance forward motion with a sense of shape and color. With great sound and fabulous conducting, this is one of the best (♦EMI 66792). **Bernstein** soft-pedals this piece with too much emphasis on a luxuriant line at the expense of taut rhythm; the finale is too flabby and episodic (Sony). Judging by his later Vienna recording, he never seemed to figure this one out. He loves it to death, phrase, bar, and note, like some sort of musical sticky paper that serves as a magnet for the doting conductor's attention (DG).

Sawallisch produces one of the best of his series. Free of any perplexing mannerisms, it may not scale the heights, but it comes darned close, and the Concertgebouw sounds like no other orchestra (♦EMI 73326, 2CD). **Harnoncourt** defies expectations here by providing a creamy reading that outdoes itself in the quest for no-frills phrasing, one of the smoothest on record. But there isn't enough contrast among movements, and though he has interesting things to say, the whole is not greater than the sum of the parts (Teldec).

Boult takes an honest, purely symphonic viewpoint that avoids Bernstein's mistakes, but his rugged individualism isn't what's needed here, just a willingness to indulge in a little common humanity—and this conductor is a little chilly (Vanguard). **Dorati** advocates a fairly intense approach, yet still conveys cordiality and warmth. There is some wonderful work with dynamics, and the London Symphony, even with the close sound, has never sounded better (♦Mercury 434375). **Szell's** close, hard sonics refuse to yield to his masterly control in this symphony. But control isn't exactly what this work requires; it needs above all an ability to breathe without a machine, and Szell definitely doesn't provide that (Sony).

Celibidache, always an acquired taste, gives an intense, lingering performance that will sound like Nirvana to some and unending to others. The Munich orchestra plays well, and all Celibidacheites will no doubt be thrilled (EMI). **Hickox,** in an early recording, is unable to provide the requisite punch and suavity; he's too uninvolved and lacks understanding (ASV). **Schwarz** runs through 6 like an early morning commuter who's late for work—there's no sense of laziness, of spending an unhurried afternoon in the country (Delos). **Steinberg** does many good things with his excellent Pittsburgh orchestra, but the sound is sharp, and it's not good enough to be mentioned alongside the greatest (EMI).

7. Aptly titled by Wagner "Apotheosis of the Dance," 7 is rivaled only by 5 in popularity. Filled with explosive rhythms and an unstoppable pulse in every movement, this work is beloved by audiences everywhere, and conductors who normally don't dabble in Beethoven feel free to take it on. There are a variety of interpretations, and everyone has an opinion about how it should be played. Only one thing is certain: the argument will continue for as long as it remains in the repertory, and it has shown a great capacity to survive even the most excessive readings.

Sawallisch's recording is one of the most overwrought, downtrodden versions in existence. The second movement II is especially more like a funeral march than an allegretto. Even the Concertgebouw's playing can't save it (EMI). **Monteux** gives a rough-riding, recklessly raw rendition that's very exciting; the finale will set you on fire, the final bars are like a long-stretching bungee jump (Decca). **Drahos** offers an excellent, black-tie reading that leaves little room for criticism or excessive

praise. It's acceptable, but lacks the dancing glory that all 7s should have (Naxos). **Walter's** gentlemanly but high-spirited romp has much going for it: smooth orchestral playing, with nary a hint of the darker side of Beethoven. His conception is holistic, with a marvelous connectivity among movements and a willingness to linger in this most driven of symphonies. It's highly recommended (♦Sony 64463).

Reiner propels us through this work in a whirlwind of energy and drive. You come away as if you've been through a seven-country tour of Europe in seven days; you see it all, but don't really absorb anything (RCA). **Zander's** recording is immaculately played and brazenly displays his correctness; the execution is flawless and the orchestral tone and sound are wonderful, but it lacks the needed *animus* (Telarc). **Bernstein's** two early recordings show that he had failed to arrive at a consistent conceptual model of this symphony. The 1964 version is better, but still suffers from heavy bowing, canyon-like, thunderous sound, and some rather wiry playing (Sony). He finally got it right in Vienna, in a thrilling performance that gives all of Beethoven's punctuations and accents (♦DG 423481, 6CD). His final performance as a conductor fittingly took place at the Tanglewood Festival where he got his start, and with the first major orchestra he ever conducted, the Boston Symphony. It's an emotionally wringing reading, as he tries to squeeze every ounce of meaning out of every note. Buy it for what it is, not as a representation of what this symphony should be; look to Vienna for that (DG).

If you're in the market for a slower, more intimate 7, **Böhm** may be your man. He uses a powerful magnifying glass to reveal every detail and sacrifices monumentality for clarity. It may be the best-recorded version of all (♦DG 37928, 2CD). **Muti's** rather cloudy recording is a little artificial in its up-tempo pacing; the effect is not unlike that of a long distance runner in a marathon. Pulling back slightly would have given the notes more room to expand and breathe (EMI). **Ormandy** is completely at sea here, in a reading that's reckless, directionally adrift, and disconnected. The orchestra, as always, is superb, but a lackluster spirit and confused podium leadership are all too obvious in a reading that is at best competent (Sony).

Once again **Carlos Kleiber** works his magic in his path-breaking mid-70s recording in which he can do no wrong. His astute fluctuations and modifications of rhythm lead to a very exciting reading (♦DG 47400). Many connoisseurs consider the NY Philharmonic Orchestra recording by **Toscanini** to be the best ever, a model of the way 7 should sound. This grossly overstates the case, and while it's certainly a great performance—maybe his best—other recordings top it. But give him his due: The New Yorkers play like madmen, and few recordings are more exciting even with the old (1936) mono sound (RCA; Grammofono 2000; Magic Talent).

If you want an exciting early recording by a great conductor, try **Stokowski** and the Philadelphia (1927) as a perfect antidote to Toscanini. The fervent beauty of orchestral sound and technical finesse are phenomenal, and it sounds as good as Toscanini's recording though it's ten years earlier (Biddulph). Avoid his internationally acclaimed BBC recording—a complete blowout from beginning to end and far too fast (BBC). **Klemperer's** 7 is mountainous—imposing, in scope the size of the universe—and way out of line. It transforms a celebration of dance into an orgy of vast, wrong-headed ideas (EMI).

The new edition **Zinman** uses is a delight—bubbly, joyous, quick but not torrid, played with spontaneity and verve. It's a real jewel in his uneven series and can stand proudly alone (uArte Nova 56351). **Cluytens's** reading is spacious in conception and noble in execution. While not blessed with any particular illumination, it ranks generally with the better ones (Royal Classics). A wild and crazy guy **Karajan** was not, but he delivers the goods in a 7 that's full of nervous energy and tightly woven rhythms, like a snake ready to strike. The finale is facile and ferocious, very exciting (♦DG 429036, 5CD). **Colin Davis** appeared on the scene in the late '50s, and one of his first triumphs was a cogently shaped and skillfully executed 7. The Royal Philharmonic was at a peak, and this young man's performance still thrills us today (♦EMI 69364, 2CD).

Though **Boult**'s London Philharmonic had seen—and would see—better days, his rock-solid reading has an indefatigable sense of proportion, honesty, and reluctance to "interpret." This is impossible, of course, but if you like your Beethoven straight up, it's for you (♦Vanguard 11, 3CD). There's a lot of pleasure in the crispness and muscle in **Steinberg**'s performance. Nothing is slack, dystrophic, or insufficient; it's a fine performance by a great orchestra (♦EMI 66888). The 41-year-old wunderkind **Thieleman** has been raising a storm in Europe and his 7 does nothing to detract from his reputation. His reading is much more colorful and weighty than the fleet-footed Kleiber, and it's worth hearing (DG).

Harnoncourt arrives fully armed and ready for battle. His IV is especially rich in detail—just hear the pungency of the winds! But he takes his dancing very seriously, and everything sounds choreographed and too well drilled (Teldec). **Abbado** makes a moderate showing in this work, but not up to the best. Balances are slightly askew, and the sound is off (DG). **Dorati**'s 7 dances with joy and abandon, and the horns sound especially marvelous in the always-controversial Mercury sonics. He displays an uncanny knack for revealing passages we don't usually hear, and his recording is certainly illuminating (♦Mercury 462958).

In one of the most spacious 7s on record, **Kubelik** leads the Vienna Philharmonic in a smooth, whipped-butter performance that sounds beautiful but lacks pulse, deadly in life and deadly in this piece (DG). **Ashkenazy** is far too precious in his recording, as if to make obscure points others had overlooked or forgotten. His fast-as-hell tempo in IV is comical, racing to the finish line but forgetting the music (Penguin Classics). **Casals** offers a version with his Marlboro Festival Orchestra that has some nice moments but can in no way stand with the best (Sony). **Celibidache** again offers a feast of food for thought, and his fans (count me among them) will love it, but his interpretations are generally not part of the common cause (EMI).

8. Beethoven called this a "Grand Symphony," and conductors have been confused about how to interpret it for many years. It seems so small in comparison to the previous one. Was Beethoven joking? This work contains many musical "jokes"—false entrances, interrupted phrases, and a reversion to older forms (hence the real minuet in III). I believe Beethoven was quite serious in his "grand" appellation, and any attempt to play down this work is a mistake. It has a sweep and feeling all its own, and its short length shouldn't discourage you from seeing it as a fully mature composition by a spiritual son of Haydn.

Walter especially sees the Haydn relationship as integral to this piece, with beautiful, classical proportions and a longing for a more genteel manner. This is a fully convincing, all-around excellent version (♦Sony 64461). You might expect a massacre from **Szell,** but though his approach is very different from Walter's, he shows a delicious sense of humor throughout the work in a wonderful disc (♦Sony 46328). **Leinsdorf** misses the point entirely; he's not exciting or humorous, compact or spacious, wittily classical or thrillingly romantic. You wonder why he even bothered (RCA). More bad balances and misbegotten phrasing

spoil **Sawallisch**'s recording. He continually misses the tongue-in-cheek nuances, and the Concertgebouw doesn't sound like themselves (EMI). You're not likely to hear the dexterous, clean, and measured playing **Zinman** offers, but it just isn't Beethoven—tempos are at hurricane speed throughout—and the total time of 23 minutes (with repeats) tells the story (Arte Nova).

In his magical 8, **Ormandy** captures every scrumptious moment with purpose and élan. The strings are rich and full, and not one iota of geniality is sacrificed. It's a great reading (♦Sony 63266). **Drahos** treats this work as the weak sister of Beethoven's symphonies. His I is anemic and unconvincing, and the players seem unusually uninterested in any of the proceedings. Decidedly *not* recommended (Naxos). **Abbado** doesn't help his cause much with a flat, condescending reading that tries to smooth out the composer's rough edges with too much Viennese *schmaltz*. No bite, no zest, no nothing, just plain flaccid; avoid it (DG).

Monteux begins aggressively, lean, spirited, and with a real concept in mind, but he carries this approach through the entire work, and ultimately it fails. Substandard sound is only more evidence for the prosecution (Decca). His San Francisco recording is even worse, thanks mainly to the wretched sound of the orchestra. **Barbirolli** leads the scrappy-sounding Hallé in a deliciously rich performance full of nuance and cleverly gauged tempos. His judgment is unerring, and only the excellent—but still coarse—remastered stereo sound keeps it out of the number one spot. Still, if you love the symphony, you need to hear it (♦Dutton 1014, 2CD). **Klemperer** presides over a stodgy rendering that's strong on lyricism while soft-pedaling the all-important rhythms. Geniality is one thing, impotence another (EMI).

Karajan takes a husky, larger than life approach that is most gratifying. The Berlin strings are tight-knit and powerful, the brass explosive, and the winds cool and aggressive. Some portions are positively Mendelssohnian, so cleverly does he guide this behemoth of an orchestra (♦DG 429036). **Bernstein** is exciting in his New York recording, yet somewhat coarse and off-the-wall. The delicacy of II and humor of III seem out of reach (Sony). In Vienna he displayed more care and concern, and the Viennese atmosphere has him spellbound, with lots of high energy and fine phrasing (♦DG 423481, 6CD). **Cluytens**'s reading is the low point in his series. This is a lumbering elephant walk that never sparkles or glistens. Even the Berlin Philharmonic can't save it (Royal Classics).

After listening to the first two movements of **Böhm**'s 8, you're ready to proclaim it the best ever, but III and IV fall flat, especially the latter, slower than a State of the Union address (DG). **Muti**'s reading is high octane all the way, yet he never lets his enthusiasm overcome his innate musical judgment. It's a dauntless, ardent, and impetuous reading that sounds great in its concert hall perspective (♦EMI 72923, 6CD). EMI lets us down a bit in their Capitol transfers, but it doesn't matter because **Steinberg** just doesn't understand this work. No excitement, no sense of leisurely entertainment, nothing *grand* (EMI).

Harnoncourt elevates 8 to a major symphonic essay. He definitely sees it in the shadow of 7 and treats it accordingly—big, robust, ennobling—and beautifully played (♦Teldec 75709). The opening bars of **Kubelik**'s version show a reasoned tactic that almost works, and except for the lack of swagger in III, this performance would be high on the must-have list. As it is, it narrowly misses, but the sound and playing are still very fine (DG). **Casals** had a nice, lyrical manner about him in 8, but the recording is not the best by a long shot, and the orchestra sounds undernourished (Sony). The story remains the same for **Celibidache,** a rewarding experience for those willing to invest the time and spirit, but probably not the best thing to hear if you're coming to 8 afresh (EMI). **Schwarz** does better here than elsewhere, probably because 8 is so like Mozart, a composer he favors. But in the long run it doesn't compete with the greatest (Delos).

9. If you had to pick only one seminal work, one that has had perhaps the greatest influence of any piece of music ever written, it would surely be Beethoven's great choral symphony. From the "music of the future" represented by Wagner and his kind through Schoenberg and his school, or the line of Brahms and the other "traditionalists," all of them looked to Beethoven, and especially this symphony, as their starting point. The universal theme of the brotherhood of all peoples has resonated in a way that even Beethoven could not have imagined, particularly in the humanist-desolate 20th century. It's a work whose every performance is looked upon with great anticipation as an "event," and almost every major celebratory occasion anywhere in the world is graced by it. Consequently, every conductor wants to put his mark on it, but there are few who can get beyond their own egos and let this piece really speak, for its message is the antithesis of ego.

Bernstein always understood this symphony, and his Sony recording was for many years one of the best. A brash, idealistic reading that was put across with a zany sort of anything-goes verve that only he could pull off, though Arroyo and her comrades were not the best on record and the choir lacked the last bit of refinement. It has been supplanted by his go-for-broke Vienna recording, full of great music making, superbly arched long-lined phrases, thrilling climaxes, and a radiant spirit. It's not flawless—Bernstein's recordings rarely are—and he has a less than stellar quartet, but he more than compensates for any shortcomings (♦DG 463469, 2CD).

It's impossible to separate his 1989 recording from the political circumstances that gave it birth. Titled "Ode to Freedom" in tribute to the fall of Communism and the destruction of the Berlin Wall, the conductor is single-mindedly intent on wringing every last bit of meaning out of every note in the score. He even changes the German word "freude" (joy) to "freiheit" (freedom), and his mixed orchestra—primarily the Bavarian Radio Symphony, but representing all the countries responsible for the partitioning of Germany—gives a broad, highly charged reading that you won't want to hear every day. But it's magnificent in its own way, with a once-in-a-lifetime commitment by chorus and orchestra, and belongs in every serious collection (♦DG 29861).

Abbado leads a vigorous, sympathetic 9, recorded in vividly detailed, bright sound, that ranks with the best. It includes some of the finest singing on disc, with Eaglen, Meier, Heppner, and Terfel setting a standard that's not likely to be surpassed anytime soon (♦Sony 62634). **Ormandy** gives a thoroughly professional run-through, exactly what you'd expect from the "Fabulous Philadelphians." Unfortunately it never rises above that, a church-choir romp that ambles along in a self-satisfied way (Sony). Stay away from **Sawallisch**—a fat, overblown account that has little to recommend it; the whole reading is strait-jacketed by glaring indifference (EMI). **Leinsdorf** presides over a hell-bent, all-out frontal assault that's stunningly played, beautifully recorded, and way ahead of its time. Indeed, this could pass for a period performance if the orchestra weren't so obviously the Boston Symphony. His rock-solid choir is second to none in their meaty presentation. If you like aggressive 9s, this is a best buy (♦RCA 7880).

Reiner starts out with an absolutely thrilling I, a powerhouse II, a subtle, delicate III, and a percussive, joyous IV. The fabled Chicago brass is well under control, and Margaret Hillis's choir sounds terrific, as does

the quartet led by Phyllis Curtin and Florence Kopleff. Don't pass it up (♦RCA 61795). **Furtwängler** is thought to have a special authority in this music, and he *does* present a very interesting philosophical argument about how to approach it. He recorded it for the last time at the Lucerne Festival in 1954, and it's one of his best (Music and Arts; Tahra). Light does indeed emerge from the chaos, and all his forces are unreservedly committed to the conductor's vision in one of the "Great Recordings of the Century" (EMI). Some prefer one or another of his wartime recordings; the 1942 version is a standout, though the sound is quite variable in even the best transfers (Gramofono 2000). None of them is a first choice, but they are fervently recommended as supplements. You should hear at least one of the Furtwängler versions.

Drahos caps his successful series with a 9 that I wish were imbued with a greater degree of spirituality. It's immaculately performed, recorded in great sound, with an excellent choir and good soloists, It's very pleasant listening, so if you want a solid, plain-Jane reading, here you are (Naxos). **Böhm**'s Vienna recording, like his whole series, sounds great (DG). But for all his obvious affection, it goes nowhere, spinning in the circle of its own self-importance; there's not enough tension to maintain the slow tempos, and not even the magnificent Vienna State Opera Chorus and the completely professional quartet (Gwyneth Jones, Troyanos, Jess Thomas, Karl Ridderbusch) can enliven it. **Mehta** (Sony) and **Macal** (Koss) lead competent, nondescript performances that can be ignored; while getting great playing from their orchestras (especially Macal), they can't compete with the best.

Walter manages to carve a large, warm embrace out of Beethoven's granitic work. The rough places are made plain, and the rather on-the-edge playing of the Columbia Symphony only adds to the sense of spontaneity. Despite their enthusiasm, the choir isn't the best, but Walter manages to mold them into a cohesive unit that responds well to Beethoven's demands (♦Sony 64464). Forget **Karajan**'s last two 9s, but the first set the standard for a generation. With wide open, sweeping playing by the Berliners that takes your breath away, this explosive recording is one of the most powerful readings on disc, aided in no small measure by Janowitz and her quartet and a stellar Vienna Singverein (♦DG 47401).

Stokowski's reading belongs almost entirely to Beethoven and very little to the conductor. It's one of great warmth and passion, devoid of the great sonic statements he liked to make in other works. This is a visionary recording by one of the great conductors of the 20th century; look for it (♦Decca 452487). For **Klemperer**, what starts out as magnificent in I quickly turns into one of the slowest, most pathetically crippled accounts on record; it's not a good conclusion to his series (EMI). For a better take on his work, look to his concert version with the same orchestra prior to the studio taping; there is much more detail, though the conception remains essentially the same (Testament).

Norrington's recording established the revisionist pattern. Literal adherence to the metronome markings with little or no concern for musical results has become an axiom of the movement, especially for this conductor. The period instruments offer small consolation in tonal suavity, though the Schütz Choir—Norrington's true forte—sounds wonderful (EMI). **Herreweghe,** also with authentic instruments, embraces period dogma ad nauseam, taking I at the tempo of a Sousa march. The scratchy strings just add to an already musically offensive performance (Harmonia Mundi). A flabby, disjointed IV spoils **Harnoncourt**'s otherwise acceptable reading; despite some great singing by the Arnold Schoenberg Choir, it's simply too willful to tolerate (Teldec).

Gardiner, for some reason, decides to make a merry-go-round out of III, the emotional heart of this piece, spoiling what is otherwise a fine performance, period caveats aside (Archiv). **Hogwood** has an interesting point of view, and he's not just a period hack, but many will be put off by the Academy of Ancient Music's grating sound; stay away unless you know and like this conductor (Oiseau-Lyre). **Mackerras,** a periodist at heart, presents a recording full of antique theories, but with his light articulation and approximate adherence to Beethoven's metronome markings, this could be an alternative for those wanting "informed" historical practice without the abrasion of old instruments (Classics for Pleasure).

Kubelik presents us with a stunningly beautiful reading. The perspective is middle row, middle hall, and the interpretation nearly flawless. His steady pulse and fusion of passion and control, all captured in glorious mid-'70s sound with good definition and presence, are truly exceptional. The soloists (Donath, Berganza, Ochman, Thomas Stewart) and Bavarian Radio Chorus are dead-on and radiant (♦DG 459462, 2CD). **Muti** also gives an excellent reading, in splendid sound, with a willingness to linger and an unwillingness to indulge himself. Studer and Morris fortify the top and bottom of the soloists with some angelic singing, and the Westminster Choir is superb as always. The Philadelphia Orchestra has never sounded better, and at the budget price it's hard to think of a better modern version (♦Seraphim 73284). The sound of **Cluytens**'s 9 conspires against the performance—there's way too much echo with a consequent loss of definition—and the conductor panders to his own waywardness in a search for nonexistent dramatic points (Royal Classics).

Szell gives a sturdy performance with superb articulation and clear, unswerving choral sound. It's a little on the metallic side but overall represents a faithful representation of the composer's wishes, though many will not like the ascetic approach (Sony). **Dohnányi** shows off the beauties of his Cleveland Orchestra in a recording that's excellent on all counts. The sound is clear and refined, the pacing apt, and only the rather fast slow movement keeps it out of first place; fans of this conductor shouldn't hesitate (Telarc). **Zinman**'s joke of a recording should never have been released. Like Norrington, he strives for metronomic accuracy at the expense of any sense of natural rhythm or flow. The choral work is excellent, but part of the same misguided sludge (Arte Nova). With **Previn** it's black tie and tux all the way, in a reading that's well executed but a long way outside his realm of expertise; it's surprising that it remains in the catalog (RCA).

Many consider the **Toscanini** edition to be the last word in humanistic profundity, and it's far from an unacceptable reading. But he sees 9 the same way he sees all Beethoven, and by now you know whether you like it or not (RCA). As I've said before, any recording by **Celibidache** is bound to strike interest and fear in the hearts of many. It bears repeating. If this conductor brings out the best in your musical sensibilities, by all means go for his 9, for you won't be disappointed. But if you're new to the work, better start elsewhere (EMI).

OTHER ORCHESTRAL MUSIC

Beethoven's overtures always had a purpose; there are four for his only opera *Leonore* (later *Fidelio*) alone. Throughout his career he wrote incidental music for plays and ballets, and most of the overtures to these pieces have remained firmly in the active repertory. His two greatest are undoubtedly *Leonore 3* and *Egmont,* and they have received the largest number of performances. Few conductors have bothered to record all of them; most are content with two or three, usually as fillers to the symphonies, though a few have dedicated entire discs to them.

Among the complete or almost-complete sets, **Szell** packs a punch, though his Cleveland Orchestra doesn't sound quite as sharp here as they do in Mozart. *Leonore 1* and *2* are both fine, though they lack the respite in the slower parts needed to set the more active sections in a better light. *Egmont* isn't paced very well, but *Coriolan* is one of the best—not rushed, with a good sense of dramatic urgency. But overall, this disc is just too harried, and Beethoven turns into an ogre in Szell's readings (Sony).

Levi's collection, completed over four years, betrays its variance in time with an equal variance in sound. Much of the album is cramped and stuffy, with little or no room for the active timpani. *Egmont* sounds almost like a Mexican hat dance, the one-in-a-bar tempo is so quick. *Creatures of Prometheus* is fast too, but without the sensitivity of phrasing that makes fast tempos tolerable. *Coriolan* is powerful, heavy, measured, and flowing, the best performance in an otherwise perfunctory disc (Telarc). **Gunzenhauser** offers good value in a disc with seven overtures: smoothly blended though perhaps a little flaccid in approach, it's a fine introduction to this music for the price (♦Naxos 859972). **Marriner** offers great sound and very satisfying performances that are only somewhat lax in spirit; he includes extended excerpts from *Creatures of Prometheus* (♦Capriccio 10548/49).

If anyone could convey the storm and drive of the overtures, it would surely be **Harnoncourt,** and that proves to be the case. These rugged readings are thrilling, though they may be too much for repeated hearings; get them as a supplement (♦Teldec 90876). But his delightful *Creatures of Prometheus* deserves no such stipulation; this performance gets a bar-to-bar attention rarely lavished on incidental music (♦Teldec). **Halasz** gives a sloppy, perfunctory performance that could have been very good with a little more spirit and a cleaner ensemble (Naxos). **Mackerras** and the Scottish Chamber Orchestra bathe us in a brightly lit, exceedingly sharp-edged *Creatures* that is aglow with vibrant, highly defined playing (Hyperion 66748).

Abravanel and the Utah Symphony grace us with a wonderful set of incidental music to *Egmont* and *Creatures,* with a peppery, lilting performance of Schubert's *Rosamunde* thrown in for good measure; you can't go wrong with this disc (♦Vanguard 8084, 2CD). **Daniel Harding**'s enthusiasm carries over to his period instrument Deutsche Kammerphilharmonie, but the metallic, twanging strings prove a particularly difficult hazard to overcome (Virgin). The echo drowns out important detail, and the dryness obscures the sonic bloom. *Ruins of Athens* and *Leonore 1* and *2* fare the best, with well formed performances that are quite alluring. *Egmont* blows by like an F-5 tornado on a hot Texas day. *Fidelio* is exciting, but none of this compensates for the sloppy playing.

Skrowaczewski may have given us the best complete set ever recorded. The *Leonores* are all superb, paced according to dramatic structure and not just for bombastic effect, effectively executed, and served up with great string playing from the Minnesota Orchestra. *Egmont* is disappointing due to reverberant sound, but it's still a rollicking reading, and at Vox's two-for-one price, this disc is a real steal. You won't find better Beethoven overtures offered anywhere at any price (♦Vox 5099, 2CD). The complete *Ruins of Athens* has never been so well served as by the golden touch of **Beecham,** coupled formerly with a robust, lyrical Mass in C, but it's sadly NA at the moment. Pray for its return (EMI).

Taken in measured doses, **Toscanini** can be stirring in this music. *Egmont* responds well to his attentions, while *Coriolan* works better in a less hurried fashion. If you're a fan, this is pure Maestro, and you know what you're getting. Sound precludes it as a first choice, but the conductor's fans won't let that get in the way. It's a shame he didn't record all of them (RCA). **Masur** and the Gewandhaus turn in large, central European readings that are a little sloppy, a little lightweight in conception, and ultimately a bit soft in the middle. It's nice to hear such a large orchestra take them on, but this isn't the group to do it (Philips). **Karajan** was a master of these pieces, and his set (when it appears again) will be a priority (DG 427257). His huge Berlin band plays these works with phenomenal sweep and majestic beauty, though sometimes he tends to be cool and slightly removed emotionally (DG). Nonetheless, he can't beat Skrowaczewski.

Abbado gave a 1991 New Year's Concert that sported a brilliant, sparkling reading of the incidental music to *Egmont,* with a dynamite overture. Also on the program was an equally persuasive *Leonore 3* (♦DG 435617). This *Egmont* supplants **Szell**'s riveting but old recording (Decca). You'll find a rapid-fire, blazing account of *Coriolan* by **Stokowski** paired with his *Eroica* (♦RCA 62514). **Böhm** offers a carefully wrought series of overtures as part of his symphony set (♦DG 437368 and 437928, 2CD). Every melodramatic moment is milked for maximum effect, and the sound is a study in palpability. A vigorous *Egmont,* a Haydnesque *Creatures of Prometheus,* and a coarse and strenuous *Leonore 3* make for pleasurable listening. Only his *Fidelio* is second-string, too ambitious and rowdy. **Reiner** doesn't fare well in the overtures; his *Coriolan* is nauseatingly bombastic, blaring, and brutal (RCA).

Fidelio finds a friend in **Muti,** who gives it a weighty symphonic treatment that adds several dimensions to this one-dimensional work. *Consecration of the House* is equally good, with whirlwind virtuosity from the Philadelphians, and *Leonore 3* has some gorgeous string playing in a reading of uncluttered finesse (♦EMI 72923, 6CD). **Klemperer**'s *Egmont* is by-the-book and pedantic, though captured in great sound (♦EMI 63611). *Creatures of Prometheus* is slovenly and insecure, but his three *Leonores* are sensational—1 and 2 close to the best available. *Fidelio* is blaring and offensive, with *Coriolan* slightly more effective. *Consecration of the House* has great breadth and power, while *King Stephen* is saucy and a little flirtatious. **Drahos** offers a disappointing set, not at all up to his generally high quality (though emotionally neutral) symphonies (Naxos).

Bernstein's *Creatures of Prometheus* is wonderfully breezy, skimming along at a rapid pace. *Egmont* is one of the finest on disc, ranging from mysterious and elemental to a fleeting gasp for breath. *Coriolan* is vital—just listen to how he draws passion from the Vienna strings! *Fidelio,* alas, is a bit tame and metronomic. *Leonore 3* has always been something of a specialty for this conductor, and its rich textures and immaculate ensemble prove the case. Look for his Bavarian Radio performance if DG ever decides to re-release it; it's brilliant. *King Stephen* is flat-out the best on disc: high voltage, sonically lustrous, and overwhelming (♦DG 423481). **Dorati** offers brisk, powerful performances of *Creatures of Prometheus* and *Leonore 3,* and while some may consider them too hard-driven, the London Symphony plays as if to the manner born. *Egmont* is iridescent, full of drama and vividly potent excitement. *Consecration of the House* is glowingly radiant, full of pomp and panoply (♦Mercury 434375 and 462958).

It's not surprising that Beethoven, having once been enthralled by Napoleon's European adventures and subsequently turning against him, would set his mind to composing a piece in honor of the Great Vanquisher, Wellington. But *Wellington's Victory* ("Battle Symphony") is a rather cheap work, full of sleazy effects that no doubt had their intended response from his audience. There are few recordings available, and for-

tunately most of them are very good. Your choice comes down to sound (very important) and discmates (equally important). **Kunzel** gives one of the best modern recordings, in vivid sound that puts even the most dedicated speaker system in danger of faltering. His Cincinnati Pops plays as well as any, and Liszt's *Hungarian March* and *Battle of the Huns* make good couplings (♦Telarc 80079). We also have the peerless playing of **Ormandy** and his Philadelphians; he really unleashes a storm in this work, and the *1812 Overture* that serves as the principal attraction here is well worth the few bucks it will cost you (♦RCA 7731).

Ondrej Lenárd does what he can with his forces, but his CSR Symphony can't match Ormandy in a cost/quality comparison (Naxos). The same holds true for **Maazel** and Bavarian Radio forces (RCA); if you're going to shell out that kind of money, stick with Kunzel. But **Dorati** brings a lot to the table in his classic disc, not least some spectacular effects in one of Mercury's early hallmark releases (♦Mercury 434360, with *1812*). RITTER

CONCERTOS

Beethoven began his musical life as a pianist. That was his instrument, and it dominated his output until very nearly the end of his life. It's significant to note that the piano—or some earlier incarnation of it—is his instrument of choice in six of the nine complete concertos (including his own transcription of the violin concerto), and that he chose to begin and end the concerto-writing phase of his career with piano works. In addition, he wrote one violin concerto (a fragment of another exists in a version completed by other hands), the so-called "Triple" concerto, which combines violin, cello, and piano in solo roles, and several short concertante works featuring flute, bassoon, and violin.

Piano

The first and last piano concertos share a common key: E-flat major. The early E-flat was written in 1819 when the composer was a mere lad of 14. It was probably created for his own use, and, though its content hardly indicated the surpassing genius waiting in the wings, it's an accomplished piece requiring much technical skill to perform. This bit of early Beethovenia was almost consigned to obscurity, as all that remained of the work was a composer-corrected piano part marked for the orchestral ritornelli. The Swiss composer-musicologist Willy Hess came to its rescue and created a performing edition complete with cadenzas, and the great Swiss pianist Edwin Fischer played the premiere in Germany in 1943.

The first of the five major piano concertos is in B-flat major, published as Op. 18. Beethoven began work on the piece around 1788 and revised it several times. It achieved what is believed to be its final form in 1798 and was published in 1801 after the succeeding C major concerto, giving it its position of No. 2 in the canon of five. Its well-known first-movement cadenza wasn't written until 1809. The B-flat major rondo published as WoO 6 is almost certainly in the finale for an earlier version (perhaps 1793). The piano and orchestral parts were finished by Beethoven's student Carl Czerny and published in 1829. Listening to this music demonstrates the composer's genius in realizing that a new ending was definitely in order.

It's believed that Beethoven made his Vienna debut as a pianist with the concerto now known as No. 1, the C major Op. 15, composed in 1795 and revised five years after his performance. It's a grand work and shows its young creator beginning to explode the boundaries set by Mozart. Nos. 3, 4, and 5 (composed between 1800 and 1809), in C minor, G major, and E-flat major (the last nicknamed the "Emperor") are the finest of the batch, with No. 4 holding pride of place with the greatest concertos ever written. It breaks from the tradition by beginning with a passage played by the soloist preceding the orchestral introduction. It was also the last of his concerts Beethoven played in public; hearing loss drove him from the concert stage, and he was unable to play the premiere of the "Emperor." He wrote no further works in the genre; except for a later attempt that was left incomplete.

The Beethoven concertos stand among the most often-recorded masterpieces, and sorting through the hundreds of available offerings is mind-boggling. But hidden among the dozens of versions of each work are a few that stand out, and while no list can be considered definitive, the following recommendations should afford the listener much pleasure.

Complete sets. Ever since Schnabel recorded the first complete cycle in the '30s, almost every world-class pianist has set down his or her view of this most challenging group of works. Some, like Rubinstein, Serkin, and Brendel, have recorded them several times, with surprisingly different results as these extraordinary musical thinkers sought to cull yet more secrets from this rich musical vein.

First, two cycles that include all (in one case) or most (in the other) of the composer's concerted works. DG, in its comprehensive 87CD "Complete Beethoven Edition" issued in 1997, collected all the works for solo instrument and orchestra (including fragments completed by other hands) in Vol. 2 of this massive enterprise (♦453707). Among the versions available to them in their own catalog by such pianists as Kempff and Zimerman, they chose the first of the two cycles recorded by **Pollini** with the Vienna Philharmonic under two different conductors. Böhm was involved in the project between 1976 and 1978, recording 3 through 5, but died before 1 and 2 could be taped. That task fell to another distinguished Beethovenian, Jochum, who completed the series in 1982.

Pollini is a superb pianist and notable Beethoven interpreter, but also maddeningly uneven. The best readings in the cycle are those with Böhm. Those with Jochum, though beautifully realized, are a mite glib. But there is so much to treasure in this sumptuously packaged set that it's well worth acquiring, including a fine reading of the early E-flat WoO 4 in a reading by **Eva Ander** and the Berlin Chamber Orchestra under Peter Guelke. Pollini's second cycle with Claudio Abbado and the Berlin Philharmonic (DG 439770) is well played but with no real interpretive point of view.

The other complete cycle comes by way of two Philips "Duos". Vol. 1 (♦442577) holds 1-4 and the two violin Romances; Vol. 2 contains the "Emperor" with other works (♦442580). The performer is **Kovacevich**, one of the finest Beethoven pianists now before the public, brilliantly accompanied by Colin Davis leading the BBC (1-4) and London Symphonies (5). These performances, recorded in the late '60s in excellent sound, remain among the best currently available versions. Also in Vol. 2 is that early E-flat concerto in a fine live recording by **Lidia Grychtolowna** with the Folkwang Chamber Orchestra led by Heinz Dressel. Missing from the Philips volumes but included in the DG set is the piano version of the Violin Concerto, to be discussed later, and the short Romance for piano, flute, bassoon, and orchestra (composed around 1786). The Rondo WoO 6 (the original finale for Concerto 2) is only included in the DG set.

Apart from these two complete editions, there are many sets devoted exclusively to the five concertos. I have several personal favorites, but if I were to choose just one, it would be **Perahia** with the Concertgebouw under Haitink's perceptive leadership (♦Sony 44575, also available singly). Perahia has a thorough understanding of each concerto and

plays with the simple unaffected manner of a true master. Nothing is forced; we get the music straight from the heart, soul, and fingers of a great musician. Haitink, who has also recorded this music with Brendel and Arrau, is at his best throughout the cycle. The great Dutch orchestra is always a treat to encounter, and the sound is superb.

Brendel is another of the great pianists of our time, and he has recorded the cycle four times. The first came in the '60s during that early period of his career when his playing was endowed with freshness of spirit and more adventurous than he tended to become as he matured (Vox 3502). These early recordings employed a variety of orchestras and conductors. No. 1 (and the *Choral Fantasy* that fills out the set) were recorded with the Stuttgart Philharmonic and Wilfried Boettcher; Nos. 2, 3, and 4 were led by Heinz Wallberg with the Vienna Volksoper Orchestra (2) and Vienna Symphony (3 and 4). The young Mehta, who offers the most vital leadership of the three, conducts 5. The orchestral playing may fall short of the highest standards, but Brendel's playing is as penetrating as any. The remastered sound is good, and at a budget price this is very much worth obtaining.

Brendel went on to record the cycle with Haitink and the London Philharmonic, and all that remains of that is a masterly "Emperor," coupled with one of the finest readings of the *Choral Fantasy* ever committed to disc (Philips 434148). His next version, taped in concert with Levine and the Chicago Symphony, has never appealed to me (Philips 456045). Brendel's playing is unimpeachable, the Chicagoans play brilliantly as usual, but Levine's contribution is brash and short on subtlety. Exciting, yes, but in the long run, not satisfying.

The crown jewel of this pianist's recordings of the cycle is his most recent, involving the inspiring participation of the Vienna Philharmonic and Simon Rattle (♦Philips 462781). Rattle is one of the most imaginative Beethoven conductors, and the two have, musically speaking, hit it off. Brendel's playing has become more natural and less studied over the last few years, and this registers in every bar of these magnificent readings. Philips has provided its usual high quality engineering. This, along with Perahia's set, belongs at the top of my recommended list.

We have to go back into recorded history to find similar excellence. **Kempff** is one pianist who certainly provided it. Passing by his earlier forays into this literature in the 78 rpm era, we can turn to the two magnificent cycles he recorded for DG. In the '50s (in mono) with Paul van Kempen and the Berlin Philharmonic, Kempff's playing is bristling with imaginative touches (♦DG 435744, with the two solo Rondos Op. 51). You can savor the relish he feels for this music in every bar. Unlike most pianists who choose from a variety of Beethoven cadenzas, he plays his own. The mono originals have been beautifully transferred.

Kempff returned to the cycle with the advent of stereo in the following decade. Again the orchestra is the Berlin Philharmonic, ably led by Leitner. Though the playing isn't quite as magical, he still has much to say about these works and the cycle is well worth having. It has been reissued in two "Doubles"; Vol. I (454400) holds 1–4, Vol. 2 (459403) contains the "Emperor" along with Wolfgang Schneiderhan's superlative account of the Violin Concerto, Oistrakh's beautiful version of the two Romances, and the Triple Concerto in a reading with Anda, Schneiderhan, and Fournier, with Fricsay conducting.

Schiff is one of today's most individual pianists. He has his own strong ideas, and his cycle has provoked controversy. Some have found it boring, others revelatory; I think it's brilliantly and thoughtfully realized. The conductor is the ubiquitous Haitink, the orchestra the redoubtable Staatskapelle Dresden (Teldec 13159, with a stimulating "Appassionata" sonata). A cycle that has justifiably achieved classic status is

Fleisher's with the Cleveland Orchestra led by Szell (Sony 48397, budget-priced, with an outstanding reading of the Triple Concerto with Stern, Rose and Ormandy and the Philadelphia, or 42445, with Mozart's Concerto 25). Fleisher was well on his way to becoming one of America's greatest pianists when this set was taped in the '50s and early '60s. He was a Schnabel student and showed remarkable insight into these works even at this early stage in his career. Szell is a formidable accompanist, somewhat tight-lipped but authoritative, and the Cleveland Orchestra plays magnificently. This is offered at a budget price and is definitely worth the modest investment.

You may not think of **Rubinstein** as a Beethoven pianist, but he obviously felt a strong attraction to these works, recording three complete sets in addition to separate versions of 3 and 4. It's the complete cycles that interest us, and in the late '50s and again between 1963 and 1967 he gave us two versions of unassailable quality. The first stereo edition, with Krips and the Symphony of the Air (the former NBC Symphony), was taped quickly in a series of sessions in 1956. The results are ebullient and exciting. He follows the Busoni edition of the first-movement cadenza of 3 by excising its introductory bars (he restored them in his two later recordings) and uses Busoni's emendations (and some of his own) in the Beethoven cadenzas for 1-4. This remains one of my favorite cycles and sounds better than ever in its remastered form in the "Rubinstein Edition" (uRCA 53012, with Sonata 18 and Haydn's *Andante con Variazioni*).

Between 1963 and 1967 Rubinstein rerecorded the cycle, this time with excellent support from Leinsdorf and the Boston Symphony. He obviously rethought this music, because there is further refinement in his approach and a newly revealed classical poise. The boundless energy found in so much of his playing is still evident, but it's more focused. RCA, once again, has worked wonders in refurbishing the originals in the "Rubinstein Edition" (63057, 1+3; 63058, 4+5; 63059, 2, with a superb reading of Brahms's Concerto 1). Hearing this new remastering has reawakened me to its very special qualities.

The final Rubinstein cycle was recorded in 1975 when the pianist was in his 90th year, and the playing is remarkable for one of such advanced age; indeed, any pianist would be thrilled to play as well, though a bit of the former almost limitless virtuosity is gone and we can sense the pianist being more careful. What remains, however, is a lifetime of acquaintance with this music and a life-affirming spirit that overrides any technical deficiencies. The London Philharmonic plays beautifully for the young Barenboim, who provides accompaniments squarely in the Central European tradition, and the transfers are excellent (RCA 63077, 1+2; 63078, 3+4; 63079, 5 and a 1975 reading of Sonata 18).

Arrau was another master pianist who turned his attention to this music more than once. His first complete cycle, partnered by Galliera and the Philharmonia, was reissued with the group of sonatas he recorded in the '50s (EMI 67379). The set briefly appeared in the early '90s, and if you find a copy, grab it; it contains some superb playing. His second cycle was with Haitink and the Concertgebouw in the '60s, and it remains a remarkable achievement. Arrau's Beethoven may not appeal to all listeners; to some, he may seem to be probing too obviously. But I've always admired his pianism, his uniquely rich sound, and his stimulating probity that causes you to think seriously about whatever he's playing. Philips has remastered the set and included it in 14 CDs devoted to his complete Beethoven recordings. The sound is better than ever; it's a treasurable document.

There is a final Arrau set from his later years, with Colin Davis and Staatskapelle Dresden (Philips 422149, 3CD). The playing reveals little

wear and tear, but his tempos have slowed considerably. The two performances from this cycle that really stand out are 4 and 5; they have been released in first-rate remasterings on a single mid-priced disc (Philips 464681). These are among my favorite performances of both works.

A remarkable cycle comes from a pianist who is all but unknown to American audiences but ranks with the finest in the world: **Peter Rösel,** whose playing, via recordings, I have admired for years. He's a perceptive interpreter and has never disappointed me. His cycle is played with the unaffected artistry and unfailing insight that grace all his work on records (♦Berlin 2136, with the early Rondo WoO 6). The naturalness and simplicity of his expression bring rewards with each rehearing. Claus Peter Flor and the Berlin Symphony provide first-rate support.

Backhaus is often in disfavor among so-called connoisseurs. He offers no-frills performances, getting right to the heart of the matter, whatever he's playing. He could seem brusque at times, but his was an honest pianism devoid of artifice. His stereo set remains one of my favorites (Decca 433891, with a stunning reading of *Diabelli Variations*). Backhaus's integrity and no-nonsense approach win the day, as does the sterling contribution of Schmidt-Isserstedt and the Vienna Philharmonic.

Gilels made two cycles for EMI. Only 4 and 5 of the earlier set remain available (discussed below), but the set he made with Szell has been reissued (EMI 69506, 1-4; 69509 contains 5, several shorter pieces, and Dvořák's Symphony 8). There's no doubt of his mastery of works he played for a lifetime, and Szell provides strong, if, at times, inflexible support. These are readings I occasionally turn to because of my great admiration for the pianist and the glorious playing of the Cleveland Orchestra.

Yet a third version from Cleveland has a further claim on my affections: **Ashkenazy**'s third and finest cycle, which he directs from the keyboard (Decca 421718, with an imposing reading of the *Choral Fantasy*). He performs his dual role superbly; only in the "Emperor" do I miss the presence of a strong figure on the podium. As for his earlier traversals, I seem to have missed his outing with Mehta but not the one with Solti in Chicago (Decca 443723, 3CD, with *Bagatelles* Op. 126 and *Für Elise*). The pianist is, as always, sensitive to the demands of this music and the conductor provides his usual intense, muscular style of music-making.

Another disappointing set comes from **Gould,** a pianist I admire greatly (Sony 52632). Three remarkable conductors were involved in this venture: Golschmann, Bernstein, and Stokowski. Things start with great promise with Gould and Golschmann delivering a brilliant reading of 1, complete with the pianist's own rather Regerian cadenza. No. 2, with Bertstein at the helm, is also a crackling reading. Things start to go downhill in 3, where some disturbing mannerisms begin to creep in from both soloist and conductor. No. 4 is even worse, as self-indulgent a reading as I've ever heard; the second movement plods along to the point of impending stasis. Gould saves his most perverse playing for the opening of the "Emperor," where he drags the music out, inflecting every note of those imposing arpeggios to the point of distraction. Things achieve a degree of normalcy after that, and Stokowski, not averse to musical perversity on occasion, leads an imposing reading.

Two current pianists offer interesting thoughts on the cycle. Everything **Zimerman** plays is worth hearing; he's one of the most thought-provoking performers before the public today. He's a man of strong opinions, and his music-making reflects this. His pianism is the stuff of which legends are made; few are blessed with his technical prowess and tonal beauty. He's also a profound musical thinker, and this is clearly evident in each reading in his remarkable set (DG 435467). Nos. 3-5 were recorded with Bernstein and the Vienna Philharmonic, but as in the case of Pollini and Böhm, the conductor died before the project was completed. Rather than accept another maestro, Zimerman led 1 and 2 from the keyboard. These are brilliant, high-spirited readings perfectly attuned to the music. The performances with Bernstein, as you'd expect, are more heavily laden; this conductor was nothing if not emotional. Here he almost goes over the top (especially in 4), but the music-making is so captivating, the pianism so exquisite, that I'm willing to overlook a bit of self-indulgence.

A second thought-provoking cycle comes from **Uchida,** whose pianism and interpretive sensibilities have gone from strength to strength. Her playing through all five is simply superb. You can feel that she has really thought carefully about this music and about her response to it. She's partnered by one of the greatest conductors of our time, Kurt Sanderling, who leads the Bavarian Radio Orchestra in 1-4 and the Concertgebouw in 5 (♦Philips 434468, 1+2; 446586, 3+4; 462586, 5, with a stunning reading of the Variations in C minor).

Barenboim's two cycles give little cause for rejoicing, which is sad because he's a pianist I much admire. The first, from the late 1960s, though displaying his usual sensitive pianism, is hampered by the often stodgy leadership of the aging Klemperer (EMI 63360). There's no doubt of the solidity and profundity of this conductor's Beethoven at its best, but when solidity degenerates into stolidity, problems ensue, especially when performing this mercurial music. Not all is lost; there are some remarkable things about this set. No. 1 has some amazing moments, especially in the brilliant reading of its finale, and the *Choral Fantasy* that rounds out the release is a great performance; I will keep the set around for its many insights. Barenboim's second set, where he directs the Berlin Philharmonic from the keyboard, doesn't present him at his best (EMI). He sounds tired and bored, though of course he plays well. I've heard him in far better form in some of this music in concert in Chicago.

A new set of the five comes from **Garrick Ohlsson,** whose ongoing series of the sonatas moves from strength to strength; he's fast becoming one of the finest Beethoven pianists of his generation. With the *ad hoc* American Sinfonietta led by Michael Palmer, the playing is brilliant and classically poised, with the extra *frisson* created by the fact the cycle was recorded in concert at the 1998 Bellingham Festival. As if the outstanding performances weren't enough, Ohlsson played a special piano, one of the remaining 1876 Steinways built to commemorate the American centennial. This is by no means a period instrument but a fully modern piano masterfully refurbished, and its special sound alone makes the set a mandatory acquisition. (For information, call the Festival at (360) 676-5997 or go to <www.bellinghamfestival.org>.)

A couple of sets are stellar examples of period performance. There are strong feelings regarding the use of so-called authentic instruments. Some can't bear what they feel is their anemic timbre, and there are credible esthetic questions to be asked about the validity of an attempt to return to an earlier age. You can try to recapture the sound of Beethoven's time (or a reasonable approximation of it), but an epoch once past is lost and gone for ever.

However, two period versions stand apart from a group that includes the rather tepid and small-scaled **Steven Lubin** with Hogwood (Oiseau Lyre) and, with the exception of a truly vital "Emperor", the glib and at times metronomic **Melvyn Tan** and Norrington (Virgin). The palm definitely goes to **Robert Levin,** who, with Gardiner and Orchestre Revolutionaire et Romantique, has provided readings of scope, depth and vivid imagination. Levin improvises his own cadenzas—as, most likely, did the composer—and throughout this undertaking there is an enlivening sense of adventure (DG Archiv 453438, 1+2 and Rondo WoO 6; 47608, 3+4; 447771, 5 and the *Choral Fantasy,* with two improvised cadenzas as an appendix).

The other period set offers the sensitive artistry of **Jos Immerseel.** The Dutch fortepianist isn't as extroverted as his American colleague, but his more intimate approach is equally rewarding. He plays Beethoven's cadenzas more conservatively, and is blessed by excellent support from Bruno Weil and the Canadian period ensemble Tafelmusik (Sony 68250, 1+2; 62824, 3+4; 66365, 5 and the Violin Concerto).

Two historic sets round out this survey. The great English pianist **Solomon** recorded 2-5 in mono between 1944 and 1955. These were issued in a 2CD set (EMI 65503, with the pianist's 1945 recording, the first of two, of the "Moonlight Sonata"). No. 3 preserves an extraordinary partnership with Boult, who leads the BBC Symphony. Nos. 2 and 4 were taped with Cluytens and the Philharmonia, and it's said the two didn't click on this occasion, though Solomon's playing is as immaculate and profound as you could wish. A happier musical relationship graced the mighty "Emperor" as Solomon, joined by Herbert Menges and the Philharmonia, gave us a stellar reading, one that should remain in the catalog. Solomon and Menges also joined forces in 1956 for stereo recordings of 1 and 3 that I've always admired (EMI 67735, 2CD, with Sonata 27 and the Grieg and Schumann concertos).

Finally to the pioneering set that started it all: **Schnabel**'s recordings in London between 1932 and 1935 for EMI, with Sargent leading the London Symphony in 1 and 5 and London Philharmonic in 2-4, are now available again (♦Pearl 9063, 3CD, filled out by a couple of short pieces and a transcription of a 1947 concert performance with the Columbus Philharmonic led by Izler Solomon). Schnabel's Beethoven was a special mixture of passion and profundity, and these recordings capture his special way with this music. There are some quirky rhythmic mannerisms and the occasional technical gaffe, but they mean nothing in the face of music-making as remarkable as this. I should note that Naxos is bringing this set out in new transfers, but the fine versions presently available should satisfy most collectors.

1. My favorite recording of 1 is, without a doubt, the vital and sparkling version by the young German pianist **Lars Vogt** with Rattle (♦EMI 56266). This is the youthful composer brought to life, a reading bristling with high energy. Vogt opts for Gould's Regerian cadenzas, playing them brilliantly. Also very much in contention is the Argentinian firebrand **Argerich** with Sinopoli; her brilliance allied with a classical poise makes this an imposing reading (♦DG 445504). Sinopoli, like Rattle, was a sympathetic partner. There's an additional version of each concerto from Argerich worth mentioning. Her 1992 concert recording in Amsterdam lacks the *frisson* of her studio version; her playing remains first rate, but she's brought down by the sleepy conducting of Heinz Wallberg (EMI 56974). Far better is her reading of 2, a brilliant account she leads from the keyboard (EMI 63575).

If I've avoided **Rudolf Serkin** until now, it's because the better of his two stereo cycles (with Ormandy and Bernstein in the '60s) remains incomplete (2, with Ormandy, has never been reissued). What is available is definitely worth exploring. No. 1, with Ormandy and the Philadelphia, allows us to hear this great and much beloved Beethovenian in a grand reading, with Ormandy and his fabulous players giving marvelous support (Sony 42259, with 3). The cycle with Ozawa finds the pianist in less than inspired form, probably due to the conductor's lackluster contribution (Telarc 80061, 3CD, minus the *Choral Fantasy,* which is coupled with 3 on 80063).

The recording of 1 in **Perahia**'s complete set (Sony 42177) vies with the best for our attention, as does **Fleisher**'s (Sony 47658, with 3). **Richter** didn't have all five concertos in his active repertoire, sticking to 1 and 3. There are several editions of 1, and two of them especially are worth our attention. His second recording session with an American orchestra brought him to Boston's Symphony Hall, where he played an imposing version with Munch (RCA 6804, with sublime readings of Sonatas 12 and 22). Another notable outing finds him with a great Russian conductor, Kondrashin (Russian Disc 11041, with 3). By 1988, when he returned to this work (28 years after the Munch taping), he had slowed his pace considerably, seeming to forget that this is music by the youthful Beethoven, not a late piano sonata. As with every Richter performance, there is something to be learned. The playing, as always, is superb. However, this performance misses the mark. The conductor on this occasion was Eschenbach (RCA 61534).

Eschenbach, in his former role of pianist, is the perpetrator of an extremely eccentric reading of 1 with Karajan (Philips 456763). **Michelangeli** also takes his time with this work, but his is a more compelling reading than the Richter/Eschenbach. The playing is beautifully crafted and his mastery and intense concentration are compelling. This is a pianist you accept on his own terms or not at all. Giulini and the Vienna Symphony offer superb support (DG 449757, with 3).

I first heard 1 on an old Columbia LP with **Gieseking** and an unnamed conductor (probably Karajan). I remember it as classically pristine with every note in place and, of course, beautifully played. That reading has never made it to CD, but his 1937 recording with Hans Rosbaud has surfaced in an excellent transfer (APR 5511). Typical of this pianist, it's a classically restrained reading, very worthwhile, especially for collectors of historical recordings.

Weissenberg is an outstanding pianist whose readings of 1 and 2, partnered by a lush, overblown Berlin Philharmonic under Karajan, leave me cold (EMI 66090). There's no doubt of the magnificent execution by all concerned; these are beautiful and sumptuous performances, and Weissenberg's tone is shimmering—but it's more about the participants than the composer. Another version that has caused some doubts is of abiding interest because of Toscanini, leading a 1945 performance by **Ania Dorfmann** (RCA 60268, with 4 by Serkin). This represents one of the maestro's rare performances of the score and, as expected, it's intense and fast-moving. Dorfmann has technique to burn, but I've always felt uncomfortable with this performance because she seems a bit hard-pressed. She's as expressive as possible considering the circumstances, but it's all a bit unsettling. Happier interpretive ground is reached by **Anda,** a truly great but currently underappreciated pianist. He offers a superb performance with Kubelik, another great conductor who never received his due (Orfeo 271921, with Brahms's Concerto 2). This is a brilliant, unforced reading that lets the music shine through.

2. Three legendary pianists have left their thoughts on 2 for posterity. **Kapell** was one of the most brilliant pianistic lights to shine in the last half of the 20th century. He left us a well-nigh ideal recording, made in 1946 in Carnegie Hall under Golschmanní's lucid direction. It was my first introduction to this delightful score, and it remains a favorite (uRCA 08994, in the comprehensive "William Kapell Edition"). A recent, somewhat cleaner and quieter transfer has been withdrawn due to copyright problems (Dutton 9701, with the celebrated Kapell/Koussevitzky Khatchaturian Concerto and three Shostakovich preludes).

While **Gould**'s performance with Bernstein remains one of the best, Sony's comprehensive "Glen Gould Edition" (Sony 52688, with Bach's

Concerto 1), taped in concert in 1957 with Ladislav Slovák, is another notable version. The recording presents a rare opportunity to sample Gould's art under concert conditions, a few years before he reteated permanently to the controlled confines of the recording studio, with Gould offering his usual brilliant pianism and astute musicianship in a work he obviously adored. Avoid the release with Ernest MacMillan because of its poor sound and performance, which add nothing to our appreciation of either pianist or composer (CBC 2015). This should have stayed in the vaults.

The recently unearthed version by **Myra Hess** is a great disappointment; she's not at her best in this performance, taped by the BBC in 1960 with Sargent and the BBC Symphony (BBC Legends 4028, with 5). To make matters worse, the sound is well below the standards of both the BBC and the year 1960. On a happier historical note is **Schnabel**'s second (postwar) version of the work with Issay Dobrowen (Testament 1020, with 5). This was part of what was to have been a second complete cycle, but as it turned out, only the last four were recorded. Some may prefer the earlier version with Sargent, but this one also displays the pianist's unique way with Beethoven and is to be treasured.

In **Kissin**'s sparkling rendition with Levine the young pianist shows himself to be sensitive to the requirements of this music and the "Emperor" with which it's paired (Sony 62926). Periodists will find much to enjoy with either **Levin** and Gardiner (Archiv 453438) or **Immerseel** and Weil (Sony 68250). **Richter** never recorded 2, but he did leave an engaging version of the work's original finale, the Rondo in B-flat, with Sanderling, in Vol. 2 of DG's massive "Complete Beethoven Edition" (453707).

3. With 3 and 4, we come to the mature Beethoven of the so-called "Middle Period". Pianistically and interpretively, both are tough nuts to crack, a challenge to any pianist. Technique alone won't suffice here; I think of the very disappointing versions of the cycle by **de Larrocha** and Chailly, gratefully deleted in this country, at least, from the Decca catalog. Fortunately there are a number of superb versions of each concerto available.

One of the great readings of 3 is by **Annie Fischer,** one of those rare artists who seemed to penetrate to the soul of this composer. Late in 1957 she taped a performance of 3 under another great but underappreciated maestro, her Hungarian compatriot Fricsay. This comes in one of the most valuable volumes in DG's "Beethoven Edition", Vol. 20, devoted to historical recordings (u453804). That she is at one with this music is evident in this granitic reading that explores every nook and cranny of the score. It's one of those special performances for which recorded sound was invented. As if this weren't enough of a prize, another Fischer/Fricsay version has turned up, recorded in concert in Berlin in 1957. This, in addition to all the qualities inherent in the studio recording, has an explosive passion of the kind usually released only before an audience. Sadly, the source tape is afflicted with severe distortion in spots, but this isn't enough to keep me from recommending this astounding performance (Palexa 0515, with Mozart's Concerto 22). Maybe a pristine copy exists in the archives of German Radio and will surface one day.

There are other commanding performances of 3. I return to **Serkin** and recommend his powerful account with Bernstein (Sony 42259, with 1, and elsewhere). Then, too, there are **Fleisher**'s commanding performances with Szell (Sony 47658, with 1). The outstanding **Perahia**/Haitink recording is also offered as a single (Sony 39814, with 4). **Uchida**'s cycle should be high on anyone's list, but even out of that remarkable achievement her readings of 3 and 4 are uniquely high in quality. The conductor is Sanderling, who leads the great Concertgebouw (Philips 446082).

Another winning version of 3 comes from **Firkušny** with Susskind (Seraphim 69018, with 5). Firkušny, despite being pigeonholed into his native Czech repertoire, was an artist who brought his sensitive musicianship to bear on a wide variety of music, illuminating everything he played. Here is Beethoven by a master. He was Klemperer's choice for a recording of the complete cycle that never took place because of contractual problems; what a cycle that would have been! **Michelangeli** and Giulini give a strongly profiled reading (DG 449757, with 1). Here, as in everything he played, Michelangeli's pianism is mind-boggling. Fortunately, musical values aren't sacrificed on the altar of perfection.

Gilels's profound reading of this work is available in a version with Szell, this time in a 1969 concert from the Salzburg Festival with the Vienna Philharmonic (Orfeo 484981, with *Egmont* overture and Symphony 5). We can't leave out **Rubinstein**'s elegant and classically poised reading with Leinsdorf, beautifully remastered in the "Rubinstein Edition" (RCA 63057, with 1). His classic 1944 reading with Toscanini sounds fresher than ever in its "Rubinstein Edition" refurbishing and is important as the only recorded collaboration between these two stellar artists (RCA 63014, with intense readings of Sonatas 18 and 23). The performance is *sui generis.*

The great Swiss pianist **Edwin Fischer** was more than just another figure from the past. There are few to whom special interpretive gifts are given, who bring more than just technique, feeling, and knowledge to the performance of a piece of music. Fischer was such an artist. At his best he penetrated far beneath the notes to reveal the essence of each work he played. He can be heard playing (and conducting the Philharmonia from the keyboard) in one of the most illuminating readings of 3 ever set down (♦Testament 1169, with Concerto 4). This and its discmate are models of Beethoven interpretation and should be experienced by all who love this music.

Now on to another visionary and his final thoughts on this complex work. **Schnabel**'s 1947 version with Issay Dobrowen is another journey into a rarefied world where each note speaks volumes (Testament 1021, with 4). Once again periodists are directed to **Levin** and Gardiner (Archiv 457608, with 4) and **Immerseel** and Weil (Sony 62824, also with 4).

4. No. 4, composed between 1804 and 1807, is one of the greatest of all concertos. It's at once gentle, serene, and profound, with turbulent undertones. Nothing like it had ever appeared before. A piano concerto that begins with a brief entrance by the soloist? Unheard of. But it was Beethoven's nature to break the bonds of convention, and if he expanded the physical boundaries of the piano concerto in 3 he shattered its esthetic bounds in 4. In all its aspects this is one of the most profound and remarkable Classical works ever conceived. It stands alone.

We're fortunate to have so many outstanding recordings available. **Serkin** left several recordings of a work he loved and understood. Skipping an incomplete (first movement only) 1933 concert performance with his brother-in-law Fritz Busch on the podium (Danacord), we turn to the 1944 concert with Toscanini (RCA 60268, with 1). Unlike the hurried feeling of Dorfmann's performance of 1 with which it's coupled, Serkin is very much his own man, matching the fevered maestro note for note. This is a fascinating document of a stimulating partnership. One of the pianist's supreme achievements in this music is his 1962 collaboration with Ormandy (Sony 42260, coupled with 5). Here is a real meeting of minds, resulting in a probing and beautifully executed reading.

Another exalted reading has been unearthed, made to celebrate the 50th anniversary of the Marlboro Festival in Vermont. The summer refuge for musicians, founded in 1951, was where Serkin was Artistic Director until his death in 1991. Here is a wondrously lyrical reading led by his longtime colleague Alexander Schneider. This set also includes Serkin's powerful performance of the annual Festival closer, the *Choral Fantasy,* dramatically conducted by son Peter (♦Sony 89200, 2CD, with chamber works by Dvořák and Janáček).

Curzon was one of the pianistic treasures of the last century, but because he hated to record he had a discography far too limited for an artist of his stature. He recorded a notable version of 4 in 1954 with Knappertsbusch (Decca 427126, with 5), and we're blessed to have a relatively modern version in a 1997 reading with Kubelik (Audite 95459). I like the pianist's poetically expansive performance, and Kubelik's contribution is equally inspired.

Another superior reading comes from **Gilels,** this time with the Philharmonia under Leopold Ludwig in 1957 (Testament 1095, with 5; Philips 45679, part of the "Great Pianists" series). This is on a much more exalted level than his later version with Szell; it's one of the finest ever made of the work. Still another sublime reading comes from **Edwin Fischer,** who leads the Philharmonia from the keyboard (Testament 1169). **Clara Haskil**'s probing and intimate performance of 4 is a real treasure. Her sparse discography is cause for regret because she's another of those rare artists who understood what this music is about (Decca 425968). Carlo Zecchi and the London Philharmonic offer unimpeachable support.

Schnabel is in a special category where both the composer and this particular concerto are concerned. He made three recordings. Critical consensus votes in favor of the earliest (1933) with Sargent, in the Pearl compendium mentioned earlier, and in ♦Philips 456961, Vol. 89 of the "Great Pianists" series. Though this is a recording for the ages, I'm also fond of his 1942 version with Stock and the Chicago Symphony (RCA 61393, with 5). Stock was another of the underrated great or near-great conductors of the first half of the 20th century who was overshadowed by the likes of Toscanini, Stokowski, and Koussevitzky, who led orchestras on the East Coast while Chicago was considered a provincial backwater. His striking accompaniments for Schnabel in both concertos make us wish he had recorded a complete cycle. Schnabel is certainly in fine form on this occasion, and the sonic restoration is first rate. His final version (1946) with Dobrowen is also a valuable contribution to the catalog. A shade more intimate than the earlier readings, this pianist never stopped seeking new meaning from those works that are always "better than they can ever be played" (Testament 1021, with 3).

Though my favorite **Rubinstein** version of 4 is his graceful Boston version with Leinsdorf (RCA 63058; with 5 in Vol. 58 of the "Rubinstein Edition"), I find a special fascination in his 1947 reading with Beecham (Testament 1154, with Saint-Saëns's Concerto 2; RCA 63082, in the "Rubinstein Edition"). This is the first of four readings that he made of music he dearly loved, and it is an extroverted and exceptionally robust one, seconded in his opinion by Beecham, who on more than one occasion spoke of his general dislike of Beethoven. A real oddity is Rubinstein's choice of the cadenzas by Saint-Saëns, a practice he abandoned in his later three recordings, returning to Busonized Beethoven.

Gieseking recorded the work on three occasions, beginning in 1939 in Dresden with Böhm (APR 5512, with 5). Versions with Karajan (EMI 66604, with 5) and Galliera (EMI 62606, also with 5) followed in the '50s. Gieseking displays his classical restraint in all three, but Böhm and Galliera offer the best support. Karajan cares more about orchestral sonority than about Beethoven on this occasion, or so it seems; he's too thick and weighty for this work. **Katchen,** another pianist who died much too young, recorded a complete cycle in the '60s with Piero (then Pierino) Gamba. Only 3-5 have been reissued (♦Decca 440839, 2CD, with *Choral Fantasy*). These performances have to be included with the finest in the catalog. Katchen was a magnificent pianist and his feeling for Beethoven's music is evident in every bar.

Though **Arrau**'s magnificent versions with Galliera (EMI) and Haitink (Philips) represent perhaps his finest achievements on record, I have a strong affection for his final outing with Colin Davis (Philips 416144, with the C minor Variations). This expansive reading allows the music to breathe, and though some may regard his later recordings dull and tedious, I find some of them (this included) searching and profound. His concert taping with Bernstein and the Bavarian Radio Orchestra is marred by the conductor's over-emotionalism (DG never transferred to CD).

A more youthful approach comes from the provocative **Hélène Grimaud,** in an inspired partnership with Masur and the NY Philharmonic (Teldec 26869, with Sonatas 30 and 31). **Hungerford**'s version is derived from a concert performance with an unidentified orchestra and conductor; it has much to say about this music, as would be expected from one of the finest Beethoven pianists of his generation. The sound is a bit rough, but the set is very much worth acquiring, both for the concerto and the solo works by Beethoven, Schubert, Chopin and Brahms (Vanguard 76/79 4CD).

Reiner's probing accompaniment enhances **Cliburn**'s stylish if slightly immature reading (RCA 7943, with 5). Some of the finer versions are locked into multidisc sets—**Kempff**/van Kempen, **Arrau**/Haitink, **Brendel**/Wallberg, **Brendel**/Rattle, and **Backhaus**/Schmidt-Isserstedt—so it's a pleasure to mention other fine performances available as singles: **Perahia**/Haitink (Sony 39814, with 3, one of the highlights of his cycle); **Kempff**/Leitner (DG 447402, with 5); and **Uchida**/Sanderling (Philips 446082). I hope the superb **Pollini**/Böhm will also be made available singly soon.

A couple of historical versions are interesting. **Backhaus**'s 1929 reading with Landon Ronald (Biddulph 037, with 5) allows us to hear the pianist in an early phase of his career (though I have no complaints about his later Decca version), and the classic recording by **Novaes** with Klemperer allows us to hear a great pianist who never really received her due in the recording studio (Vox 5501, 2CD, with Chopin and Schumann concertos).

For period instrument fans, **Levin**'s riveting performance with Gardiner is one of the most stimulating ever recorded (Archiv 457608; with 3), and I also like the **Immerseel**/Weil reading (Sony 62824, with 3).

5. Beethoven's final foray into concerto form was also his grandest; no wonder it was nicknamed "the Emperor". This concerto has attracted every pianist imaginable into the recording studio, starting in the '20s with recordings by **Frederic Lamond** and **Backhaus,** the former with Goossens (Biddulph 042, with Sonatas 8, 12, and 14), the latter with Landon Ronald (Biddulph 037, with 4). Literally dozens of pianists have followed those pioneers into the recording venues of the world. Needless to say, we can't evaluate them all. I've been listening to performances of this music for at least 30 years, so the process can be simplified.

Parental perspicacity put **Horowitz**/Reiner on the turntable early in my life, and that recording has remained a favorite to this day (♦RCA 7992, with Tchaikovsky's 1). A virtuoso reading, certainly, but what playing! And what support from Reiner and the RCA Victor Symphony!

Another soon-to-be favorite came my way later: the Columbia LP with **Serkin** and Ormandy. Bless Sony for reissuing this treasure (♦47269, 3CD, with Brahms, Mozart, and Schumann concertos and Strauss's *Burleske*).

Still another was added to the list in my early teens when I discovered **Schnabel.** His first version with Sargent really knocked my socks off, restricted sonics and all (Pearl 9063). A few years later RCA restored his 1942 reading with Stock and my hometown orchestra. That became my favorite of all, and remains to this day (♦RCA 61393, with 4)—but not before **Rubinstein** almost stole my affections with his hell-bent-for-leather reading with Krips. I still love that performance, exquisitely remastered in the "Rubinstein Edition" (♦RCA 63036, 3CD). His middle version of the work with Leinsdorf, sounding better than ever in the same sumptuous edition, is also high on my list (RCA 63058, with 4). This performance retains some of the previous high spirits, but with added refinement.

Personal favorites aside, there are other magnificent performances of this endlessly fresh masterpiece that have caught my attention and enriched my experience as time has gone by and my love for this music has deepened. In 1951 **Edwin Fischer** recorded what can only be described as a sublime rendition with Furtwängler—one of the great Beethoven conductors of the past century. This reaches summits few dare to attempt and even fewer attain. It's available in at least three editions: the original CD reissue (♦EMI 6100, with Sonata 7), the most recent transfer in the "Great Pianists" series (EMI 456769, 2CD, with Sonatas 23 and 31 and Mozart), and, best-sounding of all, the Japanese import (Toshiba-Angel 11008, with no coupling). This version has especially vivid sound; if you can find it, grab it.

Apart from the early **Serkin**/Ormandy recording, there are two more Serkins that are worth discussing. He first recorded the work in 1942 with Walter, about eight years before his recording with Ormandy. This has the vibrant playing of the 39-year-old pianist with vital support from Walter. The transfer is excellent (Sony 64489, with the Schumann concerto). In 1963 he made a thrilling reading, this time with Bernstein at the helm (Sony 37223, 42260 with 4, and elsewhere). Alas, his last recording with a rather sleepy Ozawa isn't in the same league as its predecessors (Telarc).

Gieseking made at least four recordings of 5, starting in 1931 with Walter and the Vienna Philharmonic (APR 5512, with 4). This was followed in the early '50s by a Karajan-led taping (EMI 66604, with 4), and finally in 1955 came a stereo version with Galliera (EMI version 62607, with 4). Of these three I like the Walter and Galliera versions; Karajan is again too heavy-handed. Then came a surprise from German radio: a 1944 stereo recording with the Grosser Berliner Rundfunk Orchester conducted by Artur Rother (♦Music & Arts 815, with the Schumann concerto), the finest of the lot. It's large-scaled and powerful. Rother and his orchestra offer strong support, and the sound is surprisingly good. I know the provenance of this recording is upsetting to many (including me). The sound of artillery fire heard here is only one reminder of the horrors perpetrated by Germany during that time period in European history. But there's no denying that this is a great performance by one of the last century's greatest pianists.

A **Michelangeli** 1975 concert performance (in stereo) is under Celibidache's commanding leadership (Music & Arts 4296, with Haydn's D major Concerto). Here the sometimes wayward pianist is at the height of his powers in a towering reading that has to be heard to be believed. This is a far different Michelangeli than the marmoreal figure he too often presented to the public. The sound is quite good.

We're fortunate to be able to hear **Curzon** in three different versions of this concerto. The first was taped with the Vienna Philharmonic under Knappertsbusch in the late '50s (♦Decca 467126). It has all the virtues of a Curzon performance: sovereign technique put to the service of the music. Decca's latest remastering is an improvement over previous incarnations and offers the considerable bonus of a sublime performance of 4 by the same artists. In 1999 the BBC issued a 1971 concert performance with the BBC Symphony under Boulez. Here the pianist is at his finest, aided by Boulez's vibrant support, another musician who can occasionally put music into the deep freeze (BBC 4020, with Mozart's Concerto 26). Finally came the most individual version of all, with Kubelik (Audite 95459, with 4). This is the broadest and most heavily inflected performance of the three. The pace is slower, and for the first time, in the finale there is a hint of those rhythmic hiccups so loved by his teacher Schnabel. It's a grand reading.

Kovacevich's fiery version with Colin Davis is one of the best (Philips; see above), but also worth your attention is his later reading with the Australian Chamber Orchestra, which he directed from the keyboard (EMI 2184, with a dynamic performance of a chamber orchestra version of the *Grosse Fuge*). This too is an imposing performance. **Kissin**'s superb reading with Levine is also first class (Sony, with 2), and seek out **Cliburn** with Reiner for a performance that has stood the test of time (RCA 61961, with Rachmaninoff's Concerto 2).

An early stereo recording worth noting (though it shows its age) is the 1959 version by the superb **Mindru Katz** with Barbirolli (Dutton 1014, 2CD, with Symphonies 1, 5, and 8 and *Egmont* overture). The BBC has released a 1957 concert recording by the much-revered **Myra Hess** with Sargent, highlighted by a poignant rendering of the slow movement (BBC 1023, with 2). **Novaes** would have benefitted from stronger orchestral support than that given her by the Bamberg Symphony led by Perlea (Vox 5512, 2CD, with Mozart). Perhaps it's the sonic deficiencies that weaken what appears to be a strong reading. Additionally, there is an alternative version from **Gould**: the audio track of a CBC telecast with An_erl and the Toronto Symphony (Sony 52687, with Strauss's *Burleske*). The pianist's quirky approach to the start of the work remains, though he's not quite as exaggerated as with Stokowski. Otherwise this is a strong, clear reading.

Outstanding single issues from complete cycles include the usual suspects. **Kempff**/van Kempen is more colorful than his later version with Leitner, though the latter is no slouch (DG 47402, with 4). **Perahia**'s vibrant account is unique (Sony 42330). The "Emperor" is one of the highlights of **Uchida**'s cycle (Philips 4625815, with a sterling performance of the C minor Variations). Not to be forgotten is **Arrau**'s stimulating reading, one of his finest records (Philips 464681, with 4). And to close up shop on this most popular of concertos, we have the exhilarating period performances by **Levin** and Gardiner (Archiv 47771, with the *Choral Fantasy*), **Immerseel** and Weil (Sony 63365, with the Violin Concerto), and **Tan** with Norrington and the London Classical Players (EMI 49965, with the *Choral Fantasy*).

Concerto in D major. This stepchild of the violin concerto came into being in 1807, a year after the original was completed. Clementi, always on the lookout for new works to publish, requested the transcription while visiting Vienna. Beethoven, short of money at the time, complied, and a new (sort of) work was born. Beethoven stuck to the original orchestral parts, while adding a necessary left-hand piano part to what is basically the solo violin line. What's really striking about the piece is the composer's first-movement cadenza (he left none for the original), a fasci-

nating concoction that includes a solo tympani part. (**Schneiderhan** plays a violin transcription of the cadenza in his DG version of the original with Jochum). Whether this "new" concerto really works is purely a matter of taste. It's fascinating to hear, but I agree with the consensus on the superiority of the original.

The versions by **Barenboim,** serving as both pianist and conductor, with the English Chamber Orchestra (DG "Beethoven Edition" 453707), **Jenö Jandó** with the Nicolaus Esterházy Sinfonia under Béla Drahos (Naxos 544288), and **Pietro Spada** with the Philharmonia led by Alexander Gibson (ASV 911) are all first rate. I suppose it would be too much to hope for a CD issue of **Peter Serkin**'s excellent reading with Ozawa, so the RCA LP will remain on my shelf. In **Menuhin**'s last recording of the violin concerto, he appeared not as violinist but as conductor of the piano version, played by Duchable (EMI 56875, with Piano Concerto 2).

Violin

Sixteen years before Beethoven wrote his great D major Violin Concerto, he began a concerto in C major. Only 259 measures of the opening movement survive, and there is no trace of what would have been the following two movements. The work, as completed by Wilfried Fischer (published in the early '70s) is included in DG's "Beethoven Edition" in a fine performance by **Gidon Kremer** with Emil Tchakarov (DG 453707). Though of interest to those studying the development of the composer's style, it's not in the same league as the later Op. 61.

It should come as no surprise that the composer's concerto for violin and orchestra dates from 1806, the year that saw the completion of such masterworks as the three "Rasumovsky" quartets and Piano Concerto 4. Like its pianistic cousin, the violin concerto is an intensely lyrical and intimate work, at once simple yet profoundly difficult. It was written for the 26-year-old violinist Franz Clement, who played the premiere in 1806. In the age of recorded sound, every important violinist has left his own version to posterity. Given the dozens of recordings, it's surprising how few have its true measure. In discussing them, I'll start with the pre-stereo era, where you meet those versions touched by true greatness.

At the top of my list is the uniquely perceptive and powerful 1934 recording by the temperamental **Bronislaw Huberman** led by the young George Szell. He penetrates beneath the surface of the work and delivers it with a special insight missing from many performances with big-name violinists; once you've heard this reading, you'll never hear the work in the same way. There are three transfers of the original English Columbia 78s that deserve our attention. The finest, I think, is Bryan Crimp's; he is a master of the art of transferring old recordings to CD, and this one is as fine sounding as you're likely to hear (♦APR 5506, with a crackling reading of the four-movement version of Lalo's *Symphonie Espagnole*).

The next transfer of choice is Keith Hardwick's, which is almost as sonically impressive as Crimp's offering (EMI 63194, with the violinist's astounding reading of the "Kreutzer" sonata with pianist Ignaz Friedman). It appears to have been deleted, so grab it if you find it. The third transfer should have turned out better than it did and is all the more irritating because its discmate has been so beautifully done. Naxos has been releasing some gems in its ongoing historical series; the problem here is that two different producers are responsible for the final product. Mark Obert-Thorn has done a marvelous job with the Tchaikovsky violin concerto that fills out the disc, but David Lennick has imparted an unpleasant nasality to the violinist's tone as well as a couple of other flaws, such as a slightly faulty tape join at 4:08 into II. (Even Hardwick isn't perfect at that spot in the score; Crimp is flawless). Also, must so much noise reduction be employed, robbing the recording of its natural ambience? In any event, the performance is what matters, and everything by Huberman deserves a place in any serious collector's library.

Another magic traversal of this music is by the little-known German violinist **Josef Wolfsthal,** recorded in 1929 with Manfred Gurlitt. Wolfsthal, who died at 32 in the 1931 Berlin flu epidemic, was already a great violinist when this superb recording was made. It has a spiritual purity and beauty of sound that make it one of the most transcendental readings the work has ever had. It's tucked away in Vol. 20—historical recordings—in DG's "Beethoven Edition" (♦453804), which, considering its contents, is a mandatory purchase for anyone interested in the composer and great music making.

Kreisler was one of the legendary violinists of the first half of the last century, whose humanity and warmth as well as his remarkable insight infused everything he played. He recorded the concerto twice. The better-known version with Barbirolli dates from the '30s when his playing was starting to decline, and it's his 1926 reading with Leo Blech that lets us hear his glowing version when his sovereign technique was still in full flower (Naxos 110909, Vol. 1 of the complete Kreisler concerto recordings). Fortunately, this transfer by Obert-Thorn allows us to hear the glowing warmth of Kreisler's tone, though little can be done with the rather dim orchestral sound (the ear adjusts). Another Obert-Thorn mastering of this concerto and other early Kreisler electrical recordings is available (Music & Arts 290, 2CD). As fine as that is, I think the Naxos is marginally better and at a much lower price.

Heifetz with Toscanini and the NBC Symphony was always a notoriously bad-sounding recording, but, lo and behold, the Obert-Thorn magic has transferred what was sonic dross into (almost) pure gold. Most will appreciate this reading, as I do, but not all; some may regard Heifetz as cold and superficial and Toscanini as too intense. It's a spectacular performance, stunningly played with a vital contribution (not too driven for me) from the maestro (♦Naxos 110936, with another superb transfer, the Heifetz/Koussevitzky Brahms concerto in another glorious performance). Whether or not you warm to Heifetz's playing, this supreme example of the violinist's art demands to be heard.

Szigeti is another artist who had special insight into this work. He recorded it on several occasions with ever-increasing tonal acidity. The first, made in 1932 with Bruno Walter and the British Symphony, finds him in his technical prime but is compromised by the early sound; the disc also has the violinist's legendary reading with Hamilton Harty of the Brahms concerto (Pearl 9345). Pearl is noted for its aversion to any kind of noise reduction and seems to revel in hiss and scratch, but the readings are worth the effort. He recorded it again in 1947 with Walter, this time with the NY Philharmonic. The performance is superb, despite some acidity in Szigeti's tone, and provides what I think is Walter's finest recording of this score. The engineers have done a splendid job of sonic refurbishment, and this is definitely worth your attention (Sony 64459). A welcome bonus is the Milstein/Walter version of the Mendelssohn concerto.

Menuhin had a notable history with this concerto, and four of his recordings stand out. His classic reading with Furtwängler has been beautifully refurbished in the "Great Recordings of the Century" series (♦EMI 69799, with Mendelssohn's Concerto). Don't overlook two other collaborations with Furtwängler, both of them concert performances recorded in 1947: a remarkable Lucerne Festival reading (Testament 1109), and what some regard as an even more committed version with the Berlin Philharmonic (Music & Arts 708, in deficient sound). An-

other rewarding reading is the beautifully recorded 1960 account with Silvestri and the Vienna Philharmonic, just about as potent as his recordings with Furtwängler (EMI 67310, 3CD, budget-priced, with other concertos).

In the '50s Menuhin made with Steinberg what was to become one of my favorites; this poetic reading has resurfaced, coupled with an equally intensely felt performance of the Brahms concerto (EMI 68550). There is still another treasurable Menuhin performance, with David Oistrakh leading the Moscow Philharmonic in a ravishing 1963 account (BBC 4019, with Mozart's *Sinfonia Concertante*). But avoid what proved to be his last recording of the work (as soloist; his last recording of anything was as conductor of the piano version with Duchable for Virgin) in the '60s with Klemperer. Both seem completely out of sorts and the music suffers as a result.

Milstein has always been one of my favorite violinists and his 1950 account with Steinberg in Pittsburgh is high in my regard. This poetic reading has resurfaced, with an equally intense Brahms Concerto (EMI 68550). His later stereo recording with Leinsdorf and the Philharmonia is currently available only in a 6CD anthology (EMI 64830). **Georg Kulenkampff** was a young violinist who met a tragically early death, from polio in 1948. His 1936 recording with Schmidt-Isserstedt is another of those heavenly readings the phonograph was made to capture. Forget the bowdlerized coupling of the Schumann concerto and revel in one of the Beethoven's finest recordings (♦Dutton 5018).

Exalted readings didn't evaporate with the advent of stereo. **Heifetz** returned to the work in 1955 in an invigorating version with Munch, available in beautifully remastered sound (RCA 68980). In 1962 the great German violinist **Wolfgang Schneiderhan** joined Jochum to record a version that just about equals the best of the past in a superb remastering (DG 447403, with Mozart's Concerto 5). **Kremer's** vital imagination and superb musicianship have yielded one of the finer versions of the past decade, partnered by the equally stimulating Harnoncourt and the superb Chamber Orchestra of Europe (Teldec 74881).

Fans of the violinist known as **Kennedy** will find much to think about in a reading that drags on for some 50 minutes (compared to Heifetz's 38!). That he somehow manages to bring it off is due in no small part to Tennstedt (EMI 54574). **Mutter's** lyrical and warmhearted performance, with glowing support from Karajan, is available in several configurations, including Vol. 2 of the "Complete Beethoven Edition" (DG 453707). Not to be overlooked is **Aaron Rosand's** superb outing; he's one of the great violinists of our time, whose lack of proper recognition is disgraceful (Vox 7902). This can compete with the finest, with excellent support from Inouye and Monte Carlo forces.

Three other master violinists deserve mention. **Grumiaux** left some superb accounts. His venerable reading with Beinum never made it to CD (Philips; Epic in the United States), but his two later versions did, one with Galliera (Philips 426064) and another with Colin Davis (Philips 420348). Grumiaux was a major interpreter of this work, and while Galliera's version is currently NA, Davis's should be readily available. Philips also offers a superb rendition with **Herman Krebbers,** a former concertmaster of the Concertgebouw, in its complete concerto collection (442580). Both of **David Oistrakh's** two EMI versions are NA, the earlier one with Sixten Ehrling (Testament 1032) and his stereo edition with Cluytens (69261), but you can find a 1965 performance with Herbert Albert (Melodram 2834). **Szeryng** is represented by a recording conducted by the distinguished Hans Zender (CPO 999474, with Symphonies 1 and 6).

There is a marvelous account by the exceptional young **Frank Peter**

Zimmermann under Jeffrey Tate (EMI 73283). Admirers of **Pinchas Zukerman** should turn to the recording he made in the '70s with Barenboim (RCA 435099). Fans of the venerable **Isaac Stern** are better off with his imposing '60s reading with Bernstein (Sony 63153) than with his later outing with Barenboim, when his playing had started to decline (Sony 42613). **Ginette Neveu**'s version was recorded in concert in 1949 under Hans Rosbaud. Here was a very special artist whose life was cut short in a plane crash later that year. She was to have recorded the work for EMI, but this performance remains a special memorial to what might have been (Tahra 355, with interviews and other concert performances).

Francescatti's account with Walter and his LA-based Columbia Symphony is intimate and lyrical (Sony 47659). **Ida Haendel** should have had a much bigger career than she was granted: She easily ranks with any of the distinguished practitioners of her art. Her illustrious reading with Kubelik has resurfaced (Testament 1083, with a glowing account of Bruch's Concerto 1). **Vera Beths** with Bruno Weil and Tafelmusik offers an inward and intimate period version that presents this familiar score in a very special light (Sony 63365, with van Immerseel's "Emperor").

There are three special recordings, two from one of the finest violinists of our time, another from a young artist who plays with a vision well beyond her years. **Perlman**'s 1980 recording with Giulini and the Philharmonia deserves its nomination as one of the "Great Recordings of the Century" (♦EMI 66952). This was the first great reading of the digital era and remains a benchmark for its breadth, warmth, and humanity. He recorded it again in 1986 with Barenboim and the Berlin Philharmonic, an equally poignant and probing version, with all concerned creating an atmosphere in which time seems to stand still (EMI 495670).

Hilary Hahn, still in her teens, is well on her way to becoming one of the major violinists of the new century. She possesses a flawless technique complemented by an extraordinarily beautiful tone, always in the service of the music. Her taste and humanity are rare in one so young and raised in an era dominated by computer games and trash that passes for culture. A clue to her artistic vision comes from the fact that she idolizes Fritz Kreisler—that most human of the great violinists of the past—and she brings a Kreislerian warmth and depth to her amazing recording, helped by the strong support of Zinman and the superb Baltimore Symphony. The coupling of Bernstein's *Serenade,* with its shades of Shostakovich and Stravinsky, is an imaginative choice.

Pianist-conductor Mikhail Pletnev has made a transcription of the violin concerto for clarinet. Soloist **Michael Collins** makes a strong case for this version of the work, as does Pletnev's accompaniment with the Russian National Orchestra (DG 457652, with Mozart's Clarinet Concerto).

Romances. The two lovely *Romances* make a fitting postscript to our discussion of the violin concerto. They were actually composed in the reverse order of their publication, hence the discrepancy in their numbering: No. 2 was written in 1798, 1 dates from 1801-02. Though they now stand by themselves, they were probably conceived as alternate slow movements for the C major Violin Concerto Beethoven failed to complete.

As in the case of the D major, many violinists have recorded these delightful miniatures, and any of the following versions should be satisfactory: **Accardo** with Giulini (Sony 53287); **David Oistrakh** with Goossens, with the great Russian violinist in his prime (DG 47427, 2CD, with other concertos); **Grumiaux** with Haitink (Philips "Duo" 442577,

2CD, with Piano Concertos 1-4 played by Kovacevich); **Szeryng,** also with Haitink (Philips "Duo" 46521, in Vol. 1 of his complete violin sonatas with Haebler); **Menuhin** and Furtwängler, as a filler for their great Lucerne Festival performance of the D major concerto (Testament 1109); and finally the superb **Shaham** with the conductorless Orpheus Chamber Orchestra (in DG's "Beethoven Edition" Vol. 2, 453707).

Francescatti's account with Walter and the LA-based Columbia Symphony is intimate and lyrical (Sony 47659). **Ida Haendel**'s illustrious reading with Kubelik has resurfaced (Testament 1083, with a glowing account of Bruch's Concerto 1). **Vera Beths** with Bruno Weil and Tafelmusik offers an inward and intimate period version that presents this familiar score in a very special light (Sony 63365, with van Immerseel's "Emperor" Concerto). In **Menuhin**'s last recording of the D major, a work he treasured throughout his long career, he appeared not as violinist but as conductor of the piano version, played by Duchable (EMI 56875, with Piano Concerto 2).

"Triple" concerto

Beethoven's concerto for piano trio and orchestra, the so-called "Triple" concerto, was composed between 1804 and 1805. Contrary to those who denigrate the work, it's richly lyrical and melodic, superbly crafted, and filled with countless delights. There are several fine recordings, and it's logical to start with the most star-studded version: **Richter, Oistrakh,** and **Rostropovich** with Karajan and the Berlin Philharmonic (♦EMI 66954, in the "Great Recordings of the Century" series). The reading is larger than life and a wonder to behold given the talent (genius would be a better word) in this production. Richter had qualms about the performance, especially the second movement, and made no bones about it; he wanted a remake that was denied him. Despite the great pianist's concerns, this is a most imposing performance that has never sounded better than in its remastering.

Another version with this illustrious band of soloists, recorded during a concert in Moscow with Kondrashin conducting, has to be placed in the category of might-have-beens (EMI 72016, in "Rostropovich: The Russian Years", 13CD). All we have of this magnificent account is the first movement. I asked Rostropovich about the location of the missing final two movements and he said, "I don't know".

Karajan recorded the piece with his Berlin orchestra and yet another stellar trio: **Zeltser, Mutter,** and **Ma** (DG 453707). This too is an exceptional reading, if not as high-powered as the EMI version. My favorite recording is long gone: **Serkin, Laredo,** and **Parnas** with the Marlboro Festival Orchestra led by Alexander Schneider, once available in a "Masterworks Portrait" (CBS 44842). Also currently missing is the fine account from the **Beaux Arts Trio** with Haitink and the London Philharmonic (Philips 420231).

But there's a bounty of other first-rate versions. They include readings by **Zacharias, Hoelscher,** and **Schiff** with Masur (EMI 47427); **Barenboim** (as both pianist and conductor), **Perlman,** and **Ma** with the Berlin Philharmonic (EMI 55516); **Rösel, Christian Funke,** and **Jürnjacob Timm** with Herbert Kegel (Capriccio 10150); the **Istomin-Stern-Rose Trio** with Ormandy (Sony 465439); **Arrau, Szeryng,** and **Starker** with Inbal (Philips 442580, 2CD); **Browning, Zukerman,** and **Kirschbaum,** with **Eschenbach** and the London Symphony (RCA 68964); **Jandó, Dong-Suk Kang,** and **Maria Kliegel** with Béla Drahos (Naxos 554288); and finally, the **Hendl/Corigliano/Rose** version, recorded in 1949 with Walter (Sony 64479). Will some enterprising label please bring back Weingartner's historic account? I'd love to hear it again.

Quartets

Of all the cycles of Beethoven's works, it's in the 16 string quartets, composed between 1798 and 1826, that he most reveals his musical truths. In these all-encompassing compositions we can trace his development as he moved out of the shadows of Haydn and Mozart and became his own man, taking the form to realms never before imagined. It may be considered excessive to suggest that they represent Beethoven's greatest music, given the quality of his entire output, yet in the quartets we find an ineffable quality that is sometimes missing elsewhere. From the brilliant, high-spirited and adventurous works of Op. 18 to the richly expansive middle quartets and finally to the rarefied air and dense compactness of the otherworldly last works, the composer bared his soul to us as in no other form. As his life was cut short at the early age of 56, a time we currently classify as "middle age", how much further could he have gone with, say, another decade of creative life? To what new and uncharted territories would those last quartets have led?

Since the days of shellac 78s, the Beethoven quartets have drawn the finest string quartets into the recording studio. Illustrious ensembles such as the Busch, Budapest, Calvet, and a host of others have left some or all of this timeless cycle to posterity. But as insightful and revealing as those jewels from the past are, there's no shortage of modern recordings that convey the essence of this music, and there are several versions that deserve consideration.

One of my top choices is controversial: the powerful, dynamic, at times driven accounts by the **Emerson Quartet** (◆DG 447075, 7CD). I find this ensemble's intensity riveting and exciting, often keeping me on the edge of my seat. Their technical prowess is awesome, their ensemble flawless, yet they are probing and sensitive where required. This is very much a conception for our time, Beethoven for the post-industrial age, but no less valid on that account. The sound is excellent, and the set contains superb annotation by Michael Steinberg.

A set recorded between 1972 and 1974 by the great **Vegh Quartet** offers one of the most penetrating versions of the cycle (◆Valois 4400, 8CD for the price of 4). Their probity and identification with this music are things of wonder. The players had already arrived at a late stage of their careers when the set was taped, so there remains the occasional intonation discrepancy. However such blemishes are negligible in the light of their accomplishment. This is nourishing and thought-provoking music-making.

Almost at this level of achievement is the **Talich Quartet** (Calliope 9633/39, 7CD, also available singly). Here is another ensemble that places the music before technical finesse, though their playing is well-nigh impeccable. I'm especially moved by their readings of the middle and late works, but the six of Op. 18 are also top drawer. Also outstanding are the sensitive and probing versions by the **Lindsay Quartet,** which now calls itself simply "The Lindsays" (ASV, in three boxes, 8CD, or in a single box, MHS). Here is impeccable musicianship allied with a unique grasp of the material. Some intonation problems creep in occasionally during the late quartets, but given the general high quality of the performances, it's never bothersome.

If it's high energy and superb technical finish you require, look no further than the budget box from the **Alban Berg Quartet** (EMI 66408, 7CD). They recorded the cycle twice, and the later version, taped in concert and wonderfully spontaneous, was available in several EMI multi-disc boxes that, unfortunately, are NA. But their first version was a stimulating exposition of this music, and the engineering (as with The

Lindsays) is top drawer (EMI 66408, 7CD). This group has recently begun a new cycle with outstanding versions of Op. 18 (ASV 1111/13, 3CD). Another budget box, and a cycle that deserves its classic status, is by **Quartetto Italiano** (◆Philips 454062, 10CD). This ensemble was among the finest of its generation and was justly revered from the '50s to the '70s. Here too is perceptive music-making that all but defies criticism. Philips has remastered the sound for this reissue, removing the shrillness that spoiled the earlier CD release (in three mid-priced boxes).

One of the most sumptuously played and plushly recorded cycles comes from the **Tokyo String Quartet,** taped when the group was at the height of its powers (◆RCA 61621, 9CD, with the Op. 14:1 quartet arrangement and the delightful String Quintet Op. 29 with Zukerman on viola; also available in three 3CD boxes). For sheer beauty of playing this is hard to equal, and its musical values are equal to the best available. Another set that shouldn't be overlooked is the excellent edition by the Chicago-based **Vermeer Quartet** (Teldec 76457, 9CD, also available in three 3CD sets). Then there is the controversial set from the **Amadeus Quartet,** reissued in a slim-line budget box (DG 46314, 7CD). The controversy concerns the tone quality of first violinist Norbert Brainin (some find his rather wide vibrato annoying) and the feeling in some quarters that the ensemble has a tendency to skim over the surface of some of these works. I've always been drawn to this group's playing, finding their unique timbre and personal approach fascinating and stimulating.

The **Guarneri String Quartet** has been playing together for over 35 years, and in person their Beethoven is a thing of wonder, though neither of their two recorded cycles does them real justice. Of the two, I prefer the earlier set from the late '60s and early '70s. They were young and energetic, just starting out on a new and exciting journey, and the playing shows it in its vitality (RCA, three 3CD sets). The later set has never really grabbed me, beautifully and knowingly executed as it is (Philips, in two 2CD sets and four singles). Another cycle that proved disappointing came from the **Juilliard Quartet** (Sony, three 3CD boxes). It just doesn't represent this formidable ensemble at its best. Nostalgia buffs can turn to the remastered version by the venerable **Fine Arts Quartet** that graced the Chicago chamber music scene for almost three decades. Their stereo cycle, recorded in the '60s, was how many learned this music, and if not a first choice, will bring back many happy memories (Everest, one 2CD and two 3CD sets).

Also notable is the excellent set from the now disbanded **Cleveland Quartet** (Telarc 80475, 8CD). These are beautifully realized readings, perhaps not as penetrating as some, but certainly belonging among the better versions. Finally, before moving on to notable single and historical versions, I must mention the thrilling accounts from the San Francisco-based **Alexander String Quartet** (◆Arte Nova 63637, 9CD, also available singly). These brilliant and intense performances immediately grab your attention and never let go. Don't think they are one-dimensional, glossy readings; these players more often than not penetrate beneath the surface of the music, bringing it vividly to life. There are more searching readings of the late quartets, but even here the playing is so riveting that you can't help but be won over. The sound is excellent, and the best news of all is that the discs are offered at super-budget price.

Readers may be wondering where DG's "Complete Beethoven Edition" figures in the string quartet equation. The company chose to divide these works into three separate volumes, each with a different ensemble. The first set is the most fascinating of the batch (453760, 3CD).

Not only does it contain the vibrant Amadeus Quartet versions of the complete Op. 18 but it also offers some other little treasures, such as the first version of Op. 18:1 played by the brilliant Hagen Quartet and some rare shorter pieces played by another excellent ensemble, the Mendelssohn Quartet. Rounding out the set is the Amadeus reading of the quartet arrangement of Op. 14:1. The middle quartets are offered in thrilling readings, by the Emerson Quartet (453764, 2CD). The final box comes as something of a disappointment. The late quartets are offered in '70s recordings by the LaSalle Quartet, and while there is no doubt of the general excellence of their playing, there's more to this music than is revealed here. All these complete versions include the *Grosse Fuge.*

The Beethoven quartets have been cornerstones of the recorded chamber music literature for so long that the catalog is filled with treasurable versions of these inexhaustible works. The glorious 1953 cycle by the **Hungarian Quartet** has fortunately been reissued (EMI 67236, 7CD). This budget-priced offering contains some of the most perceptive readings in the catalog, and the mono sound is quite good.

The **Busch Quartet** should have recorded a complete cycle but didn't. No other ensemble had a more profound sense of what this music is all about. This is music-making on a level that no longer exists; everything sounds so right that you're sure it's what Beethoven really intended. These musicians never draw attention to themselves; their expression is completely natural and unforced. What they did record of the 16 quartets isn't easy to find, and, unfortunately, to gather it together will entail some duplication. Also, most of this material was recorded in the 78 rpm era, so the sound, though perfectly acceptable for its time, will be hard for listeners used to the silent wonder of digital recordings. But the ear adjusts and the magic of these performances is more than worth the effort.

Probably your best option is to obtain EMI's 4CD set that holds most of the late quartets—12, 14, 15 and 16, plus 9, 11, and Op. 18:1. Missing are 13 and the *Grosse Fuge,* but these can be found in a set with the rest of the last quartets and a chamber orchestra setting of the *Grosse Fuge* (Pearl 53, 3CD). EMI's transfers are quieter; Pearl seems to have a fondness for surface noise that's carried to extremes, but here I didn't find it objectionable. A further addition to the Busch Quartet discography holds 1941 recordings of 7 and 13 (with its later alternative ending), included in the Pearl set and in a "Masterworks Portrait" release (Sony 46545).

Another great ensemble that significantly increased our knowledge of this literature is the renowned **Budapest String Quartet,** a name synonymous with "quartet" for more than a third of the 20th century. Many of us got our first exposure to the Beethoven quartets from the Budapest's traversals. Unfortunately, by the time the stereo versions were taped they had reached a period of technical decline; their intonation had become faulty, sometimes to the point of distraction. Yet I still treasure the old LPs of the middle quartets, with all their frailties, and there are still a couple of remnants of that cycle to be found (Sony 46545, 7+8; 47665, 9, 10, and *Grosse Fuge,* in the "Essential Classics" series). To really hear the Budapest at their best, you have to go back to the mono era. Some of the best transfers have appeared in the now sadly defunct "Masterworks Heritage" series (♦Sony 2870, 1, 4, 6, 9, and 11, and the string quintet with violist Milton Katims; ♦62873, 12, 14, 15, and 16, and the Minuet from 5). These performances are among the very best ever recorded and the sonic restoration is little short of miraculous.

In the early '50s the group recorded a complete cycle of excellent quality, and from that set Sony has reissued Op. 18 (52531, 2CD). But thanks to Bridge Records, the recorded saga of the Budapest is not yet complete.

The Quartet was in residence at the Library of Congress from the '40s to the '60s, and Bridge is assembling a complete cycle recorded in concert as preserved on broadcast acetates and tape. Already available, in two boxed sets, are the middle and late quartets (Bridge 9099, 9072, 3CD each). The sound is variable (sometimes quite rough), but the extra vitality of these players in concert is well worth hearing through any sonic vagaries. In the earlier concerts their playing is technically superior to those taped in the '60s, where there are some moments of suspect intonation.

The late quartets are superbly presented by the **Yale Quartet** (Vanguard 72, with *Grosse Fuge*). These are some of the most perceptive renditions of late Beethoven in the catalog. Another glorious edition of the "Final Five" comes from the **Hollywood String Quartet,** that splendid group of studio musicians who just happened to get together for chamber music sessions that some brilliant A&R person at Capitol Records had the perspicacity to record. These are splendid readings and we're lucky to have them in such superb transfers (Testament 3082, 3CD, with *Grosse Fuge*).

Two French groups were pioneers in taking the quartets into the studio. The **Capet Quartet,** who made the first recording of Debussy's quartet, can be heard in 14 and 15 (Biddulph 099), while the equally renowned **Calvet Quartet** presented gripping performances, superbly transferred.

I have recently come across a fairly young group that's putting together a series of such superb quality in interpretation, technical finish, and recorded sound that it's fast becoming my favorite ensemble in this repertoire. The **Leipzig String Quartet,** founded in 1988 by members of the great Leipzig Gewandhaus Orchestra, offers playing of such sheer musicality and unforced eloquence as to almost defy criticism. So far, three discs have been issued (♦MD+G 3070707, 7+Op. 14; 3070852, 9+10; 3070820, 14+16). From the softest whisper to the boldest accent, all is presented without a hint of coarseness and in kaleidoscopic tonal variety. This could turn out to be the best of contemporary cycles.

Quintet

Mozart was definitely the inspiration for the Quintet for Piano, Oboe, Clarinet, Horn, and Bassoon; both are masterpieces, though some critics regard the Beethoven as inferior to its predecessor. Fortunately, performing artists and record companies have disagreed with this assessment, and there is a marvelous assemblage of recordings; any of the following are excellent and can be chosen without hesitation.

One of the best is by **Kuerti,** with a brilliant ensemble of Canadian wind players; this is vitally intense and perceptive music-making, and everything on the disc is superbly rendered (CBC 1137, with Mozart and Witt piano quintets). **Barenboim** is equally perceptive with members of his Chicago Symphony and Berlin Philharmonic—a delight from start to finish (Erato 96359, with Mozart piano quintet). Another superb account comes from **Perahia** with the English Chamber Orchestra Winds (Sony 42099, with Mozart Piano Quintet). The reading by **Rudolf Serkin** and the Marlboro Festival Winds is also distinguished (Sony 47296). The great pianist's participation in chamber music is all too rare on record, and this is a most valuable addition to his Beethoven discography.

You shouldn't overlook **Richter**'s winning account with members of the Moragues Quintet (Philips 438624, 2CD), or the superb historical account by **Gieseking** with members of the Philharmonia Wind Quartet and Brain's outstanding version with members of his Wind Ensemble (BBC 4048, with the Mozart Horn Quintet, Brahms's Horn Trio, and short works by Dukas and Marais). Periodists need only seek out the thrilling account from **Robert Levin** and the Academy of Ancient Music Chamber Ensemble; it's that good! (Decca 455994; with Horn Sonata and Mozart Piano Quintet).

Beethoven arranged the work for piano quartet, and the excellent version from **Ax**, Stern, Laredo, and Ma should fill the bill nicely (Sony 53339, with Schumann Piano Quintet).

Septet

The Septet Op. 20, scored for strings and winds, is one Beethoven's finest early chamber works. One of the best versions I've heard was taped in 1988 by Oleg Kagan and colleagues; it's one of the most intense accounts in the catalog (Live Classics 104). Other notable readings are by the **Nash Ensemble** (Virgin 64109, 2CD, with a fine account of the Clarinet Trio), **Melos Ensemble** (EMI 6975, 2CD, with Wind Octet), **Gaudier Ensemble** (Hyperion 66513; with an excellent reading of the rarely-heard Wind Sextet for Two Horns and String Quartet), and members of the **Berlin Philharmonic Octet** (Nimbus 5461, with Hindemith Octet).

Sonatas

Cello. These five ground-breaking sonatas derive from all three periods of Beethoven's creative life—early, middle, and late. The first two were published as Op. 5; they were composed in 1796 during a trip to Berlin and premiered at the court of Friedrich Wilhelm II of Prussia, an amateur cellist and devoted (and generous) patron of music and musicians. Beethoven had no model on which to base these works, for Bach's sonatas for viola da gamba were entirely different and neither Mozart nor Haydn had written any such pieces, so the 26-year-old genius set out to create an entirely new genre. The sonatas give almost equal time to cello and keyboard and became the model for the Classical-Romantic sonatas of Brahms and others to follow.

There are several notable editions of the complete cycle by some of the greatest cellists and pianists of the past and present. Each team has much to say about this music, so there is no "best" version; the curious music-lover will want to have more than one.

The great French cellist **Fournier** left three superb recordings of all five, each with a superior pianist. The first arrived in the '40s when he was joined by **Schnabel**, who was no shrinking violet in any musical undertaking. Fournier holds his own, and this turned out to be a most rewarding partnership. Why it hasn't been reissued by EMI, who made the recording, or at least turned over to Testament, is puzzling; until a proper transfer arrives, I'll stick with my Electrola LPs. The cellist's first stereo recording of the cycle was in 1959 with the eccentric **Friedrich Gulda.** The then young pianist was on his best behavior, and the resulting performances remain among the most rewarding and stimulating (DG 437352, 2CD). Fournier's last cycle was recorded in 1965 with another great Beethovenian, the aristocratic **Kempff.** Fournier's understanding of these works had deepened, and this remains one of the finest sets produced in the last century. It's also the only Fournier cycle to include the three sets of variations (♦DG 45301, 2CD).

Two other formidable artists produced superb cycles, but it's not what you might expect from them. One of the most eagerly awaited sets in the early '60s was taped by **Rostropovich** and **Richter,** two of the most commanding musicians of their time. That this set was beautifully played and well recorded has never been in doubt, but there remains a certain coolness to the proceedings, the much anticipated sparks never really igniting. (As the set didn't include the variations, Philips added the sparkling version by Maurice Gendron and Jean Françaix to their most recent reissue.) But the set to have with these two great artists is

the one taped in 1964 at the Edinburgh Festival. This has all the fire and intensity lacking in the studio version, and the sound is good (♦Doremi 7731, 2CD).

Another fiery and committed version from Edinburgh, taped six years later, came from the always committed husband and wife team of **du Pré** and **Barenboim** (EMI 73332, 2CD, with the variations; 63015 *sans* variations). Every note the cellist played bristled with burning energy. Her innate musicianship always served the music, and is true on this occasion, shortly before her career was cruelly cut short. Barenboim's contribution is equally stimulating, and it remains one of the finest sets available.

Some musicians transcend their instruments by their remarkable musical insights. Such an artist was the pioneering **Casals,** who recorded two cycles in the '30s along with one set of variations (the seven on Mozart's "Bei Männern" from *The Magic Flute*) with two pianists, **Horszowski** in 1, 4, and 5 and **Otto Schulhof** in 2 and 3 (Pearl 9461, 2CD). The variations were recorded in 1927 with his longtime colleague Cortot. Casals was already well into his 60s when most of these recordings were made, but his playing was still commanding, with his great humanity and understanding shining through every note. He was in his late 70s when his second cycle was taped between 1951 and 1953. He was blessed with Serkin as partner, whose superb contribution adds immeasurably to the value of this set. Casals plays remarkably well for his age, and given the superb remastering, this is well worth exploring (Sony 58985, 2CD, with both sets of *Magic Flute* variations).

A set recorded in 1954 came from two legendary artists, the superb cellist **Piatigorsky** and the nonpareil English pianist **Solomon.** Without doubting the authority of these beautifully played readings, they're too cool and restrained for my taste (Testament 2158, 2CD, with a passionate account of Brahms's Cello Sonata 1 with Rubinstein). If you're seeking intensity in this music, then **Maisky** and **Argerich** are what you want; their committed music-making brings everything into strong relief. Every note conveys life-affirming energy. I recommend buying it in DG's "Beethoven Edition", where the packaging and annotation are superior and it's offered at mid-price (Sony 453748, 2CD, with all three sets of variations). Another excellent set is by **Ma** and **Ax;** Ma is a passionate exponent of these works and few pianists play with more sensitivity than Ax (Sony 42446, 2CD, with the variations).

A recent release brings us exquisite readings by **Harrell** and **Ashkenazy** (♦Decca 466722, 2CD). The 1984 sessions found these artists at their considerable best and their performances join the distinguished company of the finest available versions. The set is filled out by a thrilling reading of the Op. 17 Horn Sonata in a 1974 account by Tuckwell and Ashkenazy. The remastered sound is first rate.

A superb set is offered by two of the finest authenticists around, **Bylsma** and **Immerseel.** The two Dutch artists prove that "original" instruments can provide full-blooded sound and committed and sensitive readings. I'm surprised that they include only one of the variation sets, that on "Ein Mädchen oder Weibchen" (Sony 60761).

Variations. Beethoven wrote his three sets of variations for cello and piano between 1796 and 1801. They reflect both his mastery of the form and his respect for the subject matter. Two of them utilize themes from Mozart's *Magic Flute*, "Bei Männern, welch Liebe fühlen" and "Ein Mädchen oder Weibchen". The third shows the composer's great admiration for Handel, using a theme from *Judas Maccabeus,* "See, the Conqu'ring Hero Comes". These delightful pieces are well served in the complete cycles and other recordings discussed above.

Horn. This piece remains a challenge to the instrumentalist, and there are four remarkable versions from which you can choose without hesitation. The 1944 recording by the irreplaceable **Dennis Brain** with pianist Denis Matthews remains a unique historical document (Testament 1022, with Clarinet Trio). Another brilliant virtuoso, David Pyatt (current Principal Horn of the London Symphony) has included the work in an outstanding recital (Erato 21632, with music of Hindemith and others). Two more British players fill out the list, both using period instruments. The reading by **Anthony Halstead** with fortepianist **Robert Levin** tingles with excitement and is my first choice among modern recordings (Decca 455994, with Horn Sextet and Mozart piano quintets). Also notable is the the budget-priced account by **Andrew Clark** and Geoffrey Govier (EMI 72822 with Horn Sextet).

Violin. These 10 works, composed between 1796 and 1812 (the revision of the last sonata was probably completed in 1815 before its publication a year later), cover nearly two decades of Beethoven's creative life; you can literally hear the form blossom and expand as the years go by. Among such treasures a favorite can't easily be selected; we must succumb to the magic of whichever one is currently being heard. Fortunately the catalog holds an embarrassment of riches; there's a version for every taste.

Of the modern readings my vote goes to the blazing dynamism of **Kremer** and **Argerich.** These committed performances bring this music vividly to life, and there's never any sense of the routine. I recommend the presentation in DG's "Beethoven Edition"; not only is it lavishly packaged but the annotation is superb (453743, with shorter works for the two instruments in notable performances by Menuhin and the young David Garret).

For most collectors, especially those who prefer their music-making at a lower emotional temperature, there is the classic edition by **Perlman** and **Ashkenazy** (Decca 421453, 3CD). These are warmly and beautifully played, by no means lacking in energy, and while they break no new interpretative ground, they serve this music well. Those who want just to sample this cycle should turn to their superb "Kreutzer"; the remastered sound is excellent (Decca 458618, with 5). **Mutter** is an imposing and stimulating violinist who spent a year touring the world with these works before recording the cycle in concert with her regular partner, the remarkable **Lambert Orkis.** One of the finest violinists of our time, she makes an impressive case for her strong ideas about these sonatas. In the very different venue of the listening room I find some of her mannerisms disturbing, while admiring her individuality. Her admirers (and I am one) need not hesitate, but others get closer to the essence of the music (DG 457619, 3CD, with short Beethoven trifles as encores).

More on track are the superb accounts by **Aaron Rosand** and his wife, the remarkable **Eileen Flissler,** recorded in 1961 (♦Vox 3503, 3CD). Their attention to detail and commitment to the music, with absolutely no sense of artifice, combined with the excellence of the playing, make this one of finest stereo versions. Admirers of **Stern** will find much pleasure in his recordings with **Istomin** (Sony 64524, 3CD). The tonal luster of this beloved artist's earlier years was a thing of the past by the time they were made in the late '70s and early '80s. Nevertheless he's still in relatively good form and there's never any doubt of this illustrious duo's command of the music.

Kempff was involved in two complete cycles. The later one with **Menuhin** was recorded in 1970, off the cuff, it's said, with few if any rehearsals (DG 439433 and 439436, 2CD each, with *Variations on a Theme* of Mozart WoO 40 and Rondo WoO 41). The spontaneous music-making by two of the towering artistic presences of the last century is never less than fascinating. Menuhin's tone by this time was no longer at its most refined, but the musical values on display far outweigh any of the superficial glitches. Kempff's earlier cycle was taped in 1952 with another great violinist, **Wolfgang Schneiderhan,** and the music-making in this reissue can't be praised highly enough (♦DG 463605, 3CD). These two artists are at one with the spirit of the music and their warmth and humanity shine forth in every bar.

The number of reissues flooding the market gives us the opportunity to reacquaint ourselves with old friends—often in improved sound—or to discover previously unencountered old recordings. We can hear the vital playing of **Ida Haendel** in a release that offers—along with recent recordings of works by Enescu, Bartok, and Szymanowski, partnered by Ashkenazy—a bonus disc that includes among its treasures a quicksilver account of 8 in a glorious partnership with the lamented **Noel Mewton-Wood** (Decca 455488, 2CD). It's quite extraordinary, a unique account as imposing in its way as the famous RCA recording by Kreisler and Rachmaninoff.

Kreisler's complete cycle has recently been reissued again. Previous transfers have obscured not only the great violinist's remarkable way with this music but also the substantial achievement of the much underrated **Franz Rupp,** remembered today as the accompanist of legendary contralto Marian Anderson. No complete cycle of anything is flawless, but given Kreisler's stature, the three singly available discs are of substantial historical interest (Biddulph 80201, 3CD).

Equally special, indeed profound, is another reissue, recorded at the Library of Congress during a series of recitals in early 1944 by **Szigeti** and **Arrau,** who were driven from Europe by the advent of Nazism and the outbreak of war. Both violinist and pianist were at the height of their considerable powers, and this is an important document of a style and depth of performance that are gone forever. The sound takes some tolerance but the ear adjusts, and it will take more than surface noise and imperfect sonics to keep me away from these remarkable re-creations (♦Vanguard 8060/63, 4CD).

One great violinist who leaves me cold in this repertoire is **Heifetz,** who recorded the cycle with **Emanuel Bay** and **Brooks Smith** (RCA 61747, 3CD). Without disparaging the talents of those two outstanding pianists, it's the violinist who dominates the proceedings in repertoire that is, after all, a dialog between two strong voices. To make matters worse, the sound is boxy and airless (with the exception of the "Kreutzer", which was recorded in stereo). There's no denying the legendary Heifetz mastery and his unique pure, silvery tone, but Beethoven somehow gets lost in the equation.

The youthful and high-spirited outings by the young **Zukerman** and **Barenboim** include a release with the two joined by du Pré in Tchaikovsky's Piano Trio, a substantial bonus to say the least (in two EMI "double fforte" 2CD sets). **Szeryng**'s edition with **Haebler** is filled out with the two *Romances* (Philips 445521 and 446524, 2CD each). Finally, one of the greatest cycles of all came from **Grumiaux** and **Haskil;** "timeless music making" says it all (♦Philips 442625, 5CD).

Several of the sonatas have received individual recordings of substantial merit. It's a great loss that the legendary duo of **Adolf Busch** and son-in-law **Rudolf Serkin** didn't leave a complete cycle. However, what is currently available of their unique partnership is definitely worth acquiring: Op. 12:3 (EMI 65308, 4 CD, with several of the string quartets), 5 and 7 (EMI 63994, with Bach Solo Partita 2), and 9 (Pearl 0019, with 3 and 5). **Milstein** is another great violinist who, alas, didn't make a complete set, but we can get an idea of how wonderful it would have been in superb readings of 8 and 9 with **Artur Balsam** and 5 with **Firkušny** (EMI 66874). A notable version of 9 comes from his last recital, taped when he was in his 80s and still playing remarkably well (Teldec 95998). The brilliant German violinist **Gerhard Tachner** is represented by an astonishing 1945 reading of the "Kreutzer" with **Gieseking** (Bayer 200053, with the Franck sonata) and excellent 1955 accounts of 3 and 5 with the brilliant **Edith Farnadi** (Tahra 352/53, 2CD, with works by others).

One of my favorite versions of 9 is by **Szeryng** and **Rubinstein,** beautifully refurbished in the "Rubinstein Edition" in a disc that also holds marvelous readings of 5 and 8 (RCA 63040). Other great readings of the ever-popular "Kreutzer" came from **Heifetz** with **Moiseiwitsch** (EMI 64929, 2CD); **Szigeti** with **Bartók,** again at the Library of Congress in 1940 (Vanguard 8008); **Huberman** and **Ignaz Friedman** (EMI 63194); **Thibaud** and **Cortot** (EMI 64057, 3CD, with piano trios); and **Kulenkampff** and **Kempff** (in DG's "Beethoven Edition" 453804, a collection of historical performances). **Kulenkampff**'s reading with the young **Solti** (who was a formidable pianist) can't be recommended in the over-filtered transfer recently released.

Trios

Clarinet. The Trio for Clarinet, Piano, and Cello Op. 11 also exists in a version with violin substituting for its wind counterpart; I prefer the clarinet version. My longtime favorite remains the brilliant reading by **Stolzman, Rudolf Serkin,** and **Alain Meunier** (Sony 217296; with the Piano Quintet and Trio Op. 121a). Stolzman is featured in another outstanding account with **Ax** and **Ma** (Sony 57499, with Mozart and Brahms). There is a fine old version recorded in 1944 by **Reginald Kell, Denis Matthews,** and **Anthony Pini** (Testament 1022).

Piano. Although the piano trio had acquired great refinement and sophistication in the hands of Haydn and Mozart, it took the genius of Beethoven to take it further, expanding the roles of its principal participants (piano, violin, and cello) to give the form new depth and breadth. Each instrument was allowed a more prominent voice in the musical conversation, so that a real "trialogue" was achieved in these groundbreaking works. This inspired those who followed, from Schubert and Schumann to Debussy and Ravel, to pick up where Beethoven left off and chart new territory. Once the door had been flung open, the seams burst.

Collectors have a rich variety available, and your choice depends on how complete a set you want. Completists have two choices. DG's "Beethoven Edition" offers the basic cycle of Opp. 1, 70, and 97 plus the early Trio in E-flat WoO 38, the two sets of variations, and the late Allegretto WoO 39, in elegant readings by **Kempff, Szeryng,** and **Fournier.** The 5CD box also includes the Allegretto in E-flat and the trio arrangement (Op. 38) of the Septet in E-flat Op. 20 with the **Beaux Arts Trio,** and the trio arrangement of Symphony 2 with **Eckart Besch, Thomas Brandis,** and **Wolfgang Boettcher** (♦453751). Omitted is the violin version of Clarinet Trio Op. 11 (the clarinet version is included in another volume in the series). The **Beaux Arts Trio** all by themselves offer all of the above plus the violin version of Op. 11 in equally strong performances (Philips 43231, 5CD).

There are many other excellent sets. Among the finest are the **Ashkenazy-Perlman-Harrell Trio,** which includes the basic cycle, the early E-flat trio, the two sets of variations, and the Allegretto (EMI 47455, 4CD); the classic **Istomin-Stern-Rose** edition, which contains the first eight trios, including the early E-flat, the two sets of variations, and the late B-

flat Allegretto (Sony 64510, two 2CD sets); the warm, romantic **Borodin Trio,** which offers most of the standard material (Chandos 8352, 4CD); and the original **Beaux Arts Trio** before Isidore Cohen replaced founding violinist Daniel Guillet (Philips 438948, 3CD), which has a quality of new discovery not quite present in the later set, excellent though that is. Here are the first eight trios, the violin version of Op. 11, and the two sets of variations.

There are two editions I find especially stimulating even in the most August company. The first is the passionate set by **Barenboim, Zukerman,** and **du Pré** (♦EMI 63124, 3CD). If the music-making sometimes seems to go over the top, it's always faithful to the spirit of the composer. These are riveting performances by three young musicians untempered by too many years of performance. The set holds Opp. 1, 70, 96, the two sets of variations, and the two Allegrettos. This is potent stuff. The other outstanding traversal is by the ever-vital **Trio Fontenay,** whose spirited energy is ideal for this music. These brilliant readings have plenty of gravitas where required and can be recommended without qualification (♦Teldec 73281, 3CD). The set includes Opp. 1, 70, 96, the variation sets, and the violin version of Op. 11.

There are also some notable single versions that demand attention. Two superb entries are in the "Casals Edition". In one, **Casals** is joined by pianist **Eugene Istomin** and violinist **Joseph Fuchs** in imposing renditions of the Op. 70 pair, conceivably Beethoven's greatest in the form (Sony 58991, with *Handel Variations*). Then Casals and Istomin are joined by **Alexander Schneider** for equally imposing readings of the "Archduke" and Op. 11 (Sony 58992). A historic version of the "Archduke" I find unjustly underrated is by **Solomon,** with violinist **Henry Holst** and cellist **Anthony Pini,** more vividly transferred in Dutton 7015—with the great Solomon/Boult reading of Concerto 3—than in APR 5503, with solo works of Brahms and Chopin. This is a quiet, intimate reading, notable for its dignity and serenity; don't overlook it.

A more extroverted performance comes from the **Rubinstein-Heifetz-Feuermann** trio, heard to best advantage in RCA's splendidly remastered "Rubinstein Edition" (63012, with the group's equally invigorating reading of Schubert's Trio 1). This is a brisk, energetic reading, brilliantly executed. However, the palm in the "Archduke" sweepstakes goes to a recording made in 1928 by the legendary **Cortot-Thibaut-Casals Trio** and recently reissued in "Great Recordings of the Century" in a remastering so vivid you'd think it was recorded in the early '50s (♦EMI 67001, with an equally striking transfer of Schubert's Trio 1). This is one of the greatest recordings ever made, as close to definitive as it's possible to achieve. Anyone who loves Beethoven has to have this disc. Also there is a superb reading by **Richter** and two members of the Bolshoi Quartet (Philips 438624, 2CD, with piano and wind quintet, Sonatas 18 and 28, and the two solo Rondos Op. 51).

Periodists have not been forgotten. A superb recent coupling of the "Ghost" and "Archduke" trios has come from the fabulous Dutch trio of **Immerseel, Beths,** and **Byslma.** They offer perceptive and incisive readings of great power and authority that stand among the best available (♦Sony 51353).

Strings. While not to be counted among his major chamber pieces, the five string trios for violin, viola, and cello, composed in the 1790s (some believe as preparation for the Op. 18 String Quartets), are delightful and fascinating. They are of substantial interest to the collector, and are available in several excellent editions. My favorite is by the young **Leopold Trio,** whose readings are refined and have the energy needed to realize fully the composer's intentions. The sound is worthy of the playing, and these performances should remain at the top of the list for the foreseeable future (Hyperion 67253, 1+5; 67254, 2-4). Another fine account comes from the **Grumiaux Trio,** outstanding in whatever repertoire it tackles and this i s no exception (Philips 456317, 2CD, budget priced). Also recommendable are two superstar versions: **Mutter, Bruno Giuranna,** and **Rostropovich** (DG "Complete Beethoven Edition" Vol. 9, 2CD), and **Perlman, Zukerrnan,** and **Harrell** (EMI 54198, 2CD). And the legendary team of **Heifetz, Primrose,** and **Piatigorsky** left two of these works: 3 (RCA 7873, with Brahms and Schumann) and 5 (RCA 7870, with works by Spohr). Period instrument devotees are directed to **L'Archibudelli** (539161, 3+5; 48190, 2-4).

Miscellaneous wind music

Beethoven wrote quite a bit of chamber music featuring wind instruments, and to discuss all of it is beyond the scope of this volume. However, the completist can turn to a fine set with the Consortium Classicum (CPO 999658, 4CD), and the "Complete Beethoven Edition" offers a survey by the likes of the Berlin Phlharmonic Wind Ensemble, the Philip Jones Brass Ensemble, and other fine wind aggregations (DG 455779, 2CD). A single-disc compilation features the excellent Wind Soloists of the Chamber Orchestra of Europe in Octet Op. 103 and Sextet Op. 7,1 among other works (ASV 807). In another addition to the growing Dennis Brain discography, the Sextet for Two Horns and String Quartet is given an extraordinary reading, with Alan Civil and the English String Quartet (BBC 4066). The same work is given an outstanding period performance by **Andrew Clark,** Roger Montgomery, and Ensemble Galant (EMI 72822). And to conclude, **Rampal**'s outstanding collection of the complete chamber music for flute is pure delight, and at budget price, too (Vox 5000, 2 CD).

PIANO MUSIC

From the beginning of Beethoven's career to the point where encroaching deafness made it impossible for him to perform, he was a virtuoso pianist, and the bulk of his earlier music was written for the keyboard, mainly for his own use. The 32 piano sonatas, composed between 1793 and 1822, encompass his major contribution to piano literature and to this day remain the most important body of work in the repertoire. Haydn and Mozart were important models at the beginning of the young Beethoven's career, especially Haydn, but it wasn't long before he expanded the boundaries set by his illustrious predecessors and went his own way, expanding the form and bringing it to a plane never imagined by his forebears.

The sonatas remain one of the ultimate challenges for pianists, and many of them, especially the so-called "name" sonatas, remain popular with the concert-going public (and record collectors), attesting to the enduring quality of the music. As the piano's capabilities expanded, Beethoven's music continued to stretch the limits of the instrument. The "Waldstein", Apppassionata", "Hammerklavier", and 28, 30, 31, and 32 remain among the most challenging works in the repertoire, though the difficulties found in any of these 32 masterpieces should never be underestimated.

In addition to the sonatas, Beethoven wrote for the piano in other genres. There are several collections of short pieces called "Bagatelles" and several imposing sets of variations, the most notable being the "Eroica" Variations, based on thematic material from the finale of his Symphony 3, and the most amazing of all—his last piano composition—the 33 *Variations on a Waltz by Diabelli,* one of the great masterpieces in the entire keyboard literature. The completist will want

every note Beethoven left us. Fortunately it's all there for the tenacious collector.

Bagatelles

There are three major sets of *Bagatelles:* Op. 33, dating from 1802, and the much later Opp. 119 (1823) and 126 (1824). These are at once quirky, imaginative, and eccentric. There are several versions worth mentioning. **Kovacevich** plays with his usual flair and offers one of the finest versions of the three sets (♦Philips 426976). **Brendel** is equally at home in this strange sound world; his earlier version is fresh and vital (Vox 5112, 2CD, with other Beethoven miscellany), but his 1996 reading is among the best available (♦Philips 456031). **Jandó** is a distinguished Beethoven player and his disc is quite good, but it lacks the imagination of the best performances (Naxos).

It's unfortunate that **Pletnev,** in his collection of smaller pieces, opted not to record all three sets, giving us only Opp. 33 and 119 (DG 457493, 2CD). He plays them brilliantly, and they are a welcome addition to the catalog. You either like **Gould** or you don't; there's no middle ground where this pianist is concerned. If you're a fan (and I am), you will find his readings of Opp. 33 and 126 fascinating (Odyssey 45822, 2CD, with Sonatas 15-18 and 23 and "Eroica" Variations). **Schnabel** only left two sets of the *Bagatelles,* and as usual, they're stunning (Op. 33: Pearl 9123, 2CD, with other Beethoven piano works; Op. 126: Pearl 9142, 2CD, similarly coupled). **Denis Matthews** made an excellent version of the three sets in 1958, well worth hearing (Vanguard 8073), and another Englishman, **Bernard Roberts,** left a marvelous account of Op. 126 (Nimbus 5017, with Polonaise in C and "Eroica" Variations). Not to be ignored is Serkin's superb reading of Op. 119 (Sony 44837, with "Diabelli" Variations).

The most familiar Beethoven trifle is *Bagatelle WoO 58, Für Elise.* Brendel includes it in his Philips collection, and there is even a version recorded in 1932 by Schnabel (Pearl 9063).

Sonatas

Complete sets

Every comprehensive collection should contain a complete set. More adventurous collectors will want more than one, since no single interpreter, no matter how perceptive, can encompass the overwhelming wealth of material in this massive body of work. Some will want to sample several versions of favorite or especially stimulating pieces. It remains fascinating, as you listen to this endlessly engaging music, to chart the development of both composer and instrument. From the first bold F minor triadic statement of 1 to the final pianissimo C minor chord of 32 come limitless musical dramas and lyrical songs, struggles and resolutions designed for a lifetime of study and reflection.

There is no shortage of complete sets; quantity doesn't always signify quality, but there are a select few versions that reside side by side at the top of Everest. One of the finest comes from the great Hungarian pianist **Annie Fischer.** Though a most reluctant recording artist, she recorded eight of the sonatas in the late '50s and early '60s (EMI 69215, 4CD, with Schubert and Schumann). Then came four taped for the BBC (IMP 5691722). All these readings reveal extraordinary artistry and a special feeling for Beethoven.

But even these notable achievements couldn't prepare us for her superlative performances recorded between 1977 and 1992 and withheld from release by the pianist until they were made available after her death (♦Hungaroton, 10CD, various numbers). It has been reported that she recorded the entire cycle in a series of very short takes, painstakingly pieced together by her producer. What resulted from this Herculean effort is one of the most probing and revealing traversals ever committed to disc. She was a fanatical perfectionist, and her extraordinary instinctive feeling for this music is tellingly revealed throughout a series of performances that pays renewed dividends on each rehearing. They seem carved out of granite and seem to get as close to the core of each sonata as is humanly possible. It's as if we're experiencing the very act of creation.

Backhaus is one of the pianistic titans of the 20th century, cast in the mold of honest, no-frills musicianship, with a phenomenal technique that served him to the end of his life. He recorded the complete cycle twice for Decca; the "Hammerklavier" is exclusive to the '50s mono set and was reissued to complete the stereo traversal (♦Decca 433882, 8CD). The set is striking for its perspicacious objectivity; here too are granitic, no-nonsense readings in which Beethoven, not the pianist, is the focus of attention. Some have found Backhaus cool and marmoreal, but for me he's direct, probing, and involving. The dramatic "Appassionata" is bold and full of fire; the early works are stimulating in their pristine Classical clarity. Few have revealed the secrets of the final three sonatas as thoroughly as this German master. And as noted by Stephen Kovacevich—a superb Beethovenian in his own right—no other pianist understood what the "Hammerklavier" is all about—and listening to Backhaus's stunning reading I'm inclined to agree with him. It's one of the landmark recordings of this challenging and troubling work.

We're also fortunate to have several examples of Backhaus's art as revealed in the concert hall. Decca recorded the pianist's 1954 Carnegie Hall recital, and the resulting 2LP set, unavailable for decades, is prized by pianophiles. It includes striking performances of four sonatas, including the finest reading of the delightful and ebullient 25 ever committed to disc. Philips deserves praise for including the complete recital in their "Great Pianists of the 20th Century" series (456716, 2CD). We must also be grateful for a release giving us two of the pianist's late appearances at the Salzburg Festival (Orfeo 53001, 23, and 32; 30091, 12, 14, 17, and 26). These valedictory performances are real treasures for admirers of this beloved artist.

While **Kempff** recorded several of the sonatas in the 78 rpm era (and marvelous readings they are; available in several Dante reissues), it's his two cycles for DG—in mono in the '50s and a stereo remake in the '60s—for which he's justly famous. Kempff has been accused of offering lightweight Beethoven, but nothing is further from the truth. This pianist had a vivid imagination, a shimmering tonal palette, and an encompassing mastery of the cycle. Most connoisseurs opt for the earlier set, finding it fresher and more involving (♦DG 447966, 8CD).

It's indeed special, but so is the later set, especially as offered in DG's "Beethoven Edition". The remastered sound is a significant improvement over previous incarnations, and the lavish presentation is a bargain at mid-price (DG 453724, 8CD). Granted, Kempff's response to the "Appassionata" is somewhat muted; others reveal more of the work's dramatic fire. But if blazing drama isn't his forte, subtle and perceptive pianism are part and parcel of his musical arsenal, and his special way with this music shouldn't be missed. Those wishing to sample Kempff's Beethoven without investing in the complete cycle can go to DG 444704, which offers the remastered versions of 8, 14, 21, and 23, and DG 453010, a "Double" that offers some of the finest playing from the later set, remastered versions of 27-32.

One of the finest Beethovenians on the scene today is the Austrian pianist **Brendel**. He was already making great recordings of the complete set in his 20s, a feat he was to repeat three times. His first set was recorded in the early days of his career for Vox. The LPs were plagued by noisy surfaces that were the bane of record collectors, but through the snap, crackle, and swish it could be determined that something remarkable was going on. Here was a pianist to watch, and he went on to fulfill everyone's expectations and is today one of the recognized masters of the piano. Thanks to excellent remastering, we can return to those old recordings and encounter some of the finest Beethoven performances currently in the catalog (♦Vox, six budget-priced 2CD sets). The playing is fresh and vital, perceptive beyond the pianist's years, and it remains one of the best sets available.

Brendel went on to record two more complete sets. Sonically they represent a significant improvement, but interpretively the situation is not so simple. He still plays Beethoven with a probity and understanding not given to many pianists, but he has become more calculating with the passing years, sometimes lacking the imagination and freshness of the first cycle. Of the later versions, the final one is generally superior, revealing Brendel's complete mastery of his subject. His "Hammerklavier", recorded in concert in 1995, is one of the finest it has ever received. He told me at the time of its release that he felt it's the closest he has come to realizing this music (Philips 446093, with 26). Whatever qualifications I may have concerning this reading, Brendel's final thoughts deserve to be heard (Philips 446909, 10CD, also singly). His middle cycle (Philips 412575, 11CD) is also notable but NA. Philips has issued a "Duo" containing six of the so-called name sonatas (438730); the performances are among the best around.

Arrau belongs among the unique and visionary. The great Chilean pianist not only probed deeply into every corner of everything he played but had great technical command and tonal beauty. The cycle he recorded in the 1960s remains glorious, especially in its latest remastering (♦Philips 462358, 14CD, budget-priced, with variations and concertos). The "Hammerklavier" takes top honors, but everything here is magnificently rendered. There are some earlier Arrau recordings that demand attention too. EMI's 5CD memorial set, issued in 1991, offers 10 sonatas in extraordinary accounts. While I don't warm to his rather ruminative approach to the "Waldstein", others are given commanding readings; 32 is especially visionary, superb by any standards (67379, with the five concertos and the C minor Variations).

Two more examples of Arrau's unique art demand notice. One is a performance of the "Appassionata" taped in concert in 1959 by Swiss Radio (Ermitage 149, with Schumann, Debussy, and Chopin). Imposing as he was in the studio, he was a freer spirit in the concert hall, as evidenced by this excellent sampling of his artistry. Not to be missed is an album that offers a younger Arrau (aged 26 to 36) in recordings derived (mainly) from German radio between 1929 and 1939 that includes thrilling readings of two large-scaled early sonatas, 3 and 7 (Music & Arts 1060, 2CD). Here is a young pianistic lion, bursting with youthful energy, placing his considerable prowess at the service of some amazing music. It's a must for pianophiles.

Goode must be counted among today's major Beethoven interpreters. At his best, his readings are among the most satisfying available; at other times, he can be downright pedestrian and just plain boring. Fortunately, he's at his considerable best in his complete set (♦Nonesuch 79328, 10CD). Here is playing of consummate power, tempered by a winning lyricism, enhanced by a feeling for the myriad coloristic opportunities of his instrument. This set has real stature and can receive an unqualified recommendation.

Taub is another gifted American pianist, and his cycle is one of the more challenging (Vox, five budget-priced 2CD sets). He's an imaginative pianist and an intellectually probing artist. By using facsimile copies of the original manuscripts, he feels he can get closer to the language and unique structure of each sonata than by following the progression of notes on the usual printed page. If he weren't such a gifted interpreter and master of his instrument, this would seem like posturing, but Taub is sincere in his quest and this is one of the more stimulating sets, made even more appealing by the pianist's detailed (and illustrated) annotation.

Controversy seems to dog **Barenboim.** That he's one of the most gifted musicians in the world today is seldom disputed; it's the disposition of those gifts that evokes criticism. He's a master pianist, often achieving greatness; as a conductor he arouses strong, often negative, opinions. Living in Chicago, in the center of this musical storm, gives me a useful observation point. That Barenboim is totally absorbed in whatever music he performs is never in doubt. The problem with his conducting, as with his approach to music making in general, has been a tendency to over-extension that leads to an occasional lack of focus. More recently his appearances—in concert and on record—have resulted in some superb achievements, notably a revelatory Mahler Symphony 7 in Chicago and a superb set of the Beethoven symphonies with the Berlin Staatskapelle (Teldec). I mention all this because it's relevant to a discussion of his two recordings of the complete sonatas that have generated their share of divided opinion.

The earlier set was recorded between 1966 and 1969 when he seemed bent on recording the entire piano repertoire (EMI 72912, 10CD, budget-priced). This cycle offers remarkable pianism and insight. The playing displays an amalgam of youthful fire and sage wisdom and is tonally alluring as well; even in the later works Barenboim displays an understanding far beyond his years (between 24 and 27). The later set was digitally recorded between 1981 and 1984 and offers more maturity (DG 463127, 9CD, budget-priced). There's less sniffing around the flowers and a more tightly focused, direct approach. The "Waldstein" remains controversially slow in both readings, but I'm impressed by this expansive account and glad to have both sets at my disposal.

Though **Ashkenazy** isn't considered a Beethoven pianist per se, his discography boasts an impressive number of recordings devoted to this music, including three complete cycles of the piano concertos. Recorded in 1971-81, his sonata cycle is an impressive achievement (Decca 443706, 10CD, budget priced, with *Andante favori,* the composer's original slow movement for the "Waldstein"). Ashkenazy is a master pianist and a sensitive musician. At his best, his performances always have something notable to say, but sadly, his devotion to conducting has caused some coarseness to creep into his playing. Fortunately, this isn't a problem here, and listening to these renderings is pleasurable for their beauty and substance. I wish Decca had included his earlier and truly remarkable '60s version of the "Hammerklavier". The later one, taped in 1980, isn't quite at that level of inspiration or intensity.

A pianist virtually unknown in the United States, **Bernard Roberts** is much admired in his native England and rightly so, for his renderings of the complete sonatas are strong, direct, impetuous, and unaffected. This is the kind of natural music-making that causes the listener to revel in the glory of these marvelous works (Nimbus 1774, 11CD, super budget price). The ubiquitous **Jandó** also has the measure of the sonatas, and his is one of the finer traversals (Naxos, 9CD, super budget-priced). Sometimes he's more stolid than imaginative, but all in all, this is sound Beethoven playing, often more revelatory than might be expected. One of the more underrated pianists of our time is the English-born **Ian Hobson,** who plays, teaches and conducts at the University of Illinois. When I first heard his cycle, I was impressed by the musicality of his playing, which refuses to draw attention to itself, allowing the composer to speak unfiltered through his thoroughly schooled fingers. My opinion hasn't changed. This is fresh, invigorating playing, faithful to the spirit of Beethoven (Zephyr 111-97, 9CD, also available singly).

Volcanic and impulsively powerful, the Russian pianist **Nikolayeva** is nothing if not intense. Her readings were recorded in concert so the occasional mishap remains, but they're white-hot and searing, larger than life; they could be discomfiting to the faint of heart. At the end of the "Hammerklavier" the music seems to be literally screaming from the keyboard, such is the intensity of her playing. These unique performances are stimulating and viscerally exciting (Olympic, 9CD, with variations).

A brief venture into the historical realm brings us to the most famous cycle of all. Recorded in London in the '30s, **Schnabel**'s famous performances have been the bible for these works for almost 70 years—yet these powerful and visionary readings aren't without controversy. For one thing, there are problems with execution: Though he possessed a virtuoso technique, the occasional wrong notes or smudged passage-work were not past him. Some attribute this sloppiness to a decline in facility (he was in his 50s when the project was undertaken, hardly an advanced age), though careful listening reveals a solid technical foundation. It must be remembered that in the days of 78s splicing wasn't possible and a whole side had to be redone to correct a mishap. In Schnabel's case some rhythmic peculiarities or mannerisms slipped into his Beethoven, those famous "hiccups" that readily identify his playing (and that of some of his illustrious students, like Fleisher and Curzon).

Despite the flaws, he left us Beethoven of awesome power and integrity. I'm hard pressed to find even a few other pianists who dug more deeply into the profound slow movements. Listen to those from 7, 21, 28, 29, and the last three, for example, and try to find equally revelatory recreations; and as I have become more familiar with the impossibly difficult "Hammerklavier", even his impossibly gabbled execution of the work's outer movements have begun to reveal an elemental power that numerous wrong notes can't obliterate.

The problem is finding the best-sounding edition of recordings that even in their day could hardly be considered state of the art. The "official" CD reissue (EMI 3765) is quite good, but in trying to eliminate surface noise, the engineers at times clipped off the beginnings of notes, which is annoying, to say the least. Listeners not prepared to accept 78 rpm noise should avoid these early recordings, though as others have proved, sophisticated noise reduction can be employed without damage to the original product. EMI itself has been doing some remarkable transfers lately; they should return to this classic set and give us the best sound now possible.

The English reissue label Pearl provides transfers in multiple boxed sets that offer greater frequency response than EMI's, with a solidity and clarity that bring us closer to the pianist. However, Pearl adheres to a philosophy opposed to what it feels is excessive filtering, and those opting for this edition must be willing to put up with a generally higher level of background noise. If you wish to sample Schnabel's Beethoven on Pearl, go to a recent release containing the "name" sonatas. This offers a balanced view of the best and the more troubling aspects of the great pianist's approach and a prime example of the company's transfer philosophy (Pearl 0004, 2CD).

Another important set is the vibrant, sometimes over-the-top edition by the French pianist **Yves Nat.** Recorded between 1953 and 1955, these performances encompass some of the most committed and viscerally exciting Beethoven ever committed to disc. Nat was an extraordinary pianist who not only threw off sparks but probed well beneath the surface of whatever he played. This is a truly remarkable, often revelatory set, and should find a place in every comprehensive Beethoven collection (◆EMI 62501, 8CD, budget-priced). An imminent release of the complete sonatas by the great and unique **Alfred Cortot** is also rumored (EMI). I hope the rumors are true, as these readings could be revealing and stimulating.

The Austrian-born Canadian pianist **Anton Kuerti** has provided one of the most stimulating cycles (◆Analekta 24010, 10CD, with an excellent account of the "Diabelli" variations). These readings reveal a profound musical mind that has studied these works and knows them as intimately as anyone on the planet. Serkin and Horszowski were among his teachers, and Kuerti's artistry seems a unique amalgam of these legendary musicians, combining the former's rugged intellectual authority with the later's sensitivity and tonal refinement. But Kuerti is his own man, as his superb annotation makes clear, and repeated listening has made me appreciate the special qualities of his cycle to an ever greater degree. I wish he'd been given a fuller, less dry recorded sound, but this set is a remarkable achievement

Russell Sherman offers one of the more controversial cycles (GMR, as a complete set or in multiple 2CD boxes). Here is another distinguished pianist who knows these works inside out, but his insightful moments are contrasted with interpretive distortions and occasional technical shortcomings. The "Hammerklavier" is a case in point, where his obvious struggle with the notes preclude a coherent presentation of the content. The pianist's annotation combines scholarly insight with some truly bizarre observations. There are those who find these readings revelatory and I can respect their judgment, but you would do well to sample them before proceeding full steam ahead.

After Sherman it's a relief to turn to the brilliant and vital playing of the young Chilean **Alfredo Perl,** who offers one of the most stimulating cycles of recent years (◆Arte Nova 40740, 10CD, with "Diabelli" variations; super-budget-priced, also available singly). Perl brings an unfettered and direct view of the sonatas that certainly isn't devoid of personality. Undoubtedly his interpretations will deepen as time goes by, but as he has already penetrated and mastered so much of this material, this cycle can easily be recommended either to those on a strict budget or to seasoned listeners eager to encounter a fresh and stimulating musician.

Several noted pianists are engaged in ongoing cycles, first and foremost **Kovacevich,** one of the few great Beethovenians now before the public. In the '70s, while still in his 30s, he recorded a notable series. Even as a relatively young man he demonstrated an innate feeling for this repertoire and offered readings of great distinction, passion, and commitment of 8, 17, 18, 28, 30, 31, and 32. These stand among the best, and we should be thankful to Philips for restoring them to the catalog in their "Great Pianists of the 20th Century" series (456877, 2CD, mid-priced). In the '90s he began a new cycle for EMI. It's natural that what started out on such a high level has grown in depth and breadth in the ensuing years, and what's being offered now may stand with the best in recorded history. In common with Annie Fischer he gives the listener the feeling of true re-creative artistry, of each work being sculpted from solid granite, of secrets rooted out and revealed.

However, there's a problem for those wishing to collect this edition as it moves toward completion. Several sonatas are being rerecorded because of substandard sound, and the pianist has rethought an interpretation or two and has redone 32, for example. For those eager to sample some of Kovacevich's cycle, I recommend ◆EMI 56586 (8-11), 54896 (21, 34, 31), 56761 (5-7, 15), and 54599 (27, 28, 32). All are profound readings that pay increasing dividends with each encounter.

Perhaps the most frustrating of the great pianists on the current scene is **Pollini.** You never know what to expect from this mercurial artist. His commanding technical prowess astounds even in an era of technical wizardry, yet his playing goes from the sensitive and often revelatory to the cold, coarse, and uninvolving, often in the course of a single recital or recording. The same pianist who gave us, at 18, a still unsurpassed version of Chopin's Concerto 1 and sublime Schubert and Schumann has also provided us with a glib and uninspired cycle of Beethoven concertos with Abbado.

His Beethoven sonata recordings are no more even in quality. In the late '70s he made a notable and profound set of 28–32 that has stood the test of time (DG 449740, 2CD, mid-priced). These are, in the main, sensitive, beautifully played accounts, but none of his further ventures into this repertoire have yielded anything close to similar results. A case in point is his recent recording of 11, 12, and 21, cool readings that are more notable for their lack of commitment than for any compensating insights (DG 435472). Whether or not Pollini ends up giving us a complete cycle, I hope he will recapture the excellence of the first issue in the future.

A surprise for me has been the unfolding cycle by **Ohlsson,** a pianist whose growth as an artist has produced some marvelous recordings in the last few years. So far he has produced three outstanding installments in what promises to be an outstanding cycle (Arabesque 6638, 1, 23, and 30; 6677, 8, 14, and 21; 6737, an unusual coupling of 16 and 29). Ohlsson offers lucid and commanding performances in a series that goes from strength to strength. His monumental performance of 29 stands among the best of the modern readings.

The Canadian pianist **Lortie** has been impressive with his superb recordings of Ravel's solo works, showing the technical command and tonal palette necessary to bring off some of the most demanding piano music ever written. However, his ongoing Beethoven cycle, while beautifully played, doesn't reveal the same level of imagination—though his admirers may find more in it than I do (Chandos).

Partial sets

There are a few pianists who, had they wished (or fate hadn't intervened) could have left treasurable cycles. At the top of this list has to be **Rudolf Serkin,** one of the towering musicians of the last century. He was a profound musical thinker who at his best illuminated his chosen repertoire with an insight granted to few, and he knew these works inside and out. However, he was a reluctant recording artist, not comfortable with the frozen finality of a performance committed to tape; hence he left us only a few sonatas, several in multiple versions.

One of the most familiar Serkin discs contains the "Pathétique", "Moonlight", and "Appassionata" sonatas (8, 14, and 23). Though he recorded these works on more than one occasion, it's the stereo version of the three that remains available (Sony 37219, in the "Great Performances" series). His 1936 recording is also interesting, but an editing error by EMI, perpetuated by Philips in its "Great Pianists of the 20th Century" series, rules this performance out of court. A more important release is in Sony's "Essential Classics" series, where Serkin's massive reading of the "Hammerklavier" is coupled with the stereo version of the "Pathétique" and the rarely recorded Fantasy Op. 77 (Sony 47666).

Shortly before Serkin's death in 1991, he and his son Peter began to review some previously rejected tapes for possible release. On rehearing these performances, he was satisfied enough to permit their release and Peter completed the project. The resulting set (♦Sony 64490, 3CD) offers sonatas he hadn't previously recorded (1, 6, 12, 13, and 16) as well as alternative versions of several he recorded on other occasions (21 and 30–32). All are superb, and I have rarely heard a more spiritually exalted reading of 31 (taped in 1960). There is a version of the last three sonatas derived from a 1987 recital for Austrian Radio, but by this time, Serkin, already 81, had passed his prime and his playing had hardened. It's certainly interesting but doesn't represent him at his considerable best (DG 427498; also released on video).

Fate, which struck him down in 1956 at age 54, prevented the completion of a complete cycle by the English pianist **Solomon;** by the time he was forced into retirement by a stroke, he had recorded only 18 of the 32. Though reissued on LPs in the '80s, all but the last six (and an earlier version of the "Moonlight") languished in EMI's vaults until they were reissued in five beautifully remastered CDs (♦Testament). All but a couple were recorded in mono in the early '50s and offer Beethoven playing of exemplary refinement, elegance, technical finish, and a rare perception. Don't be fooled by this pianist's effortless execution; there's always a profound musical mind at work. Time after time, sonata after sonata, as you listen to these remarkable recordings it's easy to feel that Solomon's way is the only way. Such later works as the "Hammerklavier" and the last three have rarely been equaled and never bettered—but wherever you find yourself in this series, there is magic to hear.

The great Russian pianist **Gilels** was well on his way to recording a complete cycle but left it incomplete at the time of his death in 1985; those missing are 1, 9, 22, 24, and 32. The remainder (including the "Eroica" variations) were released in a DG boxed set available only briefly in this country as an import. Those wishing to sample the best in this set should turn to the discs holding 21, 23, and 26 (419162); 29 (410527); and 30 and 31 (419174). An alternative version of 29 is powerful but coarsely recorded (Melodiya/BMG 40121, with music of Scriabin).

Gould was another pianist who stopped short of a complete cycle. Whether or not he would have completed the series (he recorded all but ten of them) had he lived to do so is subject to speculation. Perhaps he got bored with Beethoven or wasn't interested in those remaining. In any event, even though purists may sneer, I find myself riveted by many of the Canadian genius's interpretations. The curious can indulge their fancy rather cheaply, as most of these recordings remain available on the inexpensive Odyssey label. Vol. 1 offers 1–3, 5–10, and 13 (45821, 3CD); Vol. 2 contains 15–18 and 23, and is filled out with the "Eroica" variations and *Bagatelles.* For the last three you have to go to the full-price "Glenn Gould Edition" (37036, 3CD). There are strange moments throughout both sets, but there is much stimulating and exciting pianism. The famous Gould vocal obbligatos may annoy some listeners, but they never bothered me. With Gould you take the exasperating with the revelatory and the journey is worth the effort, and his account of the "Hammerklavier" is one of the more visionary versions of this complex work (Sony 52645, with 24).

Richter, who had a huge but highly selective repertoire, made incandescent recordings of 22 of the 32 sonatas; his view was that he had nothing to say about the others. Most of those he played are available in multiple versions, some in sound that takes some tolerance but always seems to the convey the magic that's going on. The problem in discussing these recordings is that his discography is so sprawling it would take a whole chapter to do it justice, and new additions keep coming out. Recordings are available on many labels, some more representative of

his playing than others. Three large collections of his work have been released from Melodiya, Philips, and Praga. While none of them seems still to be in print as such, they can sometimes be obtained as boxed sets or individual volumes from U.S. or overseas dealers via the Internet; they're worth pursuing for the absorbing pictures they present of the range and quality of his artistry. Both contain recordings of Beethoven sonatas of varying dates, venues, and sound quality.

"Richter—The Authorized Recordings", despite its title never approved by the pianist, is nonetheless a treasure trove of remarkable performances, in nine 2CD boxed sets. In one volume (♦Philips 438486), 19, 20, 22, 23, 30–32, recorded in 1991/92, combine profound musicianship and peerless technique, resulting in performances (especially of the last three) of a rare elemental power. The two little Op. 49 sonatas (19 and 20) are magically realized, while 22, if not as fleet and airy as his early '60s version (RCA 86804), has a toughness and an integrity that are keenly projected at a more measured pace; and if the "Appassionata" lacks the manic drive of earlier renditions (Columbia LP, never on CD in the US)—his Carnegie Hall performance from the early '60s has to be heard to be believed (♦RCA 6518). The concentration and power of this later reading are compelling on their own terms, as is the pianist's favorite recording of the work, coupled with a compelling 1948 "Pathétique" and several bagatelles (BMG/Melodiya 438624, 2CD, with other Beethoven), and another 2CD set offers 18 and 28 played with similar conviction. And we have absolutely nonpareil versions of 9 and 11 recorded in the early '60s (Philips 438617).

Four volumes of "Sviatoslav Richter in Prague" (Praga 354001-15, 15CD) include thrilling performances of 10 sonatas recorded between 1959 and 1985 (354001-4). Recorded live, the sound is variable but certainly good enough to enable the listener to realize that something special is going on. A hair-raising "Appassionata" is combined with intense performances of 17 and 18, and the pianist's unique way with the "Hammerklavier" is paired with 27 and 28. The sound of this 1975 "Hammerklavier" is certainly better than that in London a year later (Stradivarius 33313), but both have much to say about this towering work. There is yet another great performance of the "Hammerklavier", taped by the BBC at the 1975 Aldeburgh Festival; the recital also includes three Bagatelles and Sonata 3 (BBC Legends 4052).

Richter's visits to the United States in the early '60s yielded some remarkable recordings. In addition to the aforementioned "Appassionate" (with which he is said to have been dissatisfied), there are volatile readings of 12 (with its fleet, lighter-than-air execution of the finale) and 22 (♦RCA 6804, with Concerto 1). There are also three 3CD sets of rare early Richter recordings including, among other treasurable readings of works by others, a riveting "Pathétique" (Parnassus 96-005/6).

Live Classics has been releasing a treasure trove of late Richter performances, including outstanding 1991 accounts of 30 and 31. Here we find the great pianist at his most rarefied in readings of two sublime masterpieces; it doesn't get much better than this (♦Live Classics 422, with Mozart's C minor Fantasy and Sonata). The second of the three volumes devoted to Richter in Philips's "Great Pianists of the 20th Century" series (456949, mid-priced) contains Sonatas 12, 17, 23, and 30–32, recorded at various venues between 1962 and 1997. The same performances have all appeared elsewhere (17 on EMI, the others on Philips), but the remasterings bring out their power and beauty with remarkable vividness.

Gieseking literally died while working on a cycle for EMI. These deserve a proper CD release, but until it comes along there is a fascinating set of an almost complete cycle he taped in 1949–5 (Tahra 395-400,

7CD). Nos. 4, 5, 7, 2, and 22 are missing, some of the sound requires your tolerance, and the piano is sometimes badly out of tune. But this is a fascinating survey by one of the last century's great pianists and is well worth hearing.

Other notable performances

Since the Beethoven sonatas form the backbone of the piano repertory, most major pianists past and present have added a number of them to their discographies. These so-called nonspecialists have plenty to say on the subject and often bring an individualistic flair to their performances.

Horszowski was a great artist who recorded only a few of these works, but what is there is definitely worth having. The "Hammerklavier" is offered in tandem with 30 and 32. Recorded around 1950, these refined and perceptive readings are among the finest in an overcrowded arena (♦Vox 5500, 2CD). In his late 90s this remarkable artist added 2 and 6 to his recorded legacy (Nonesuch 79232, with Bach and Chopin). Even so late in life (he lived to be over 100), his command was strong enough to provide a vital and engaging reading of these spirited works.

Edwin Fischer was another great artist who left too few Beethoven recordings. Everything this magician touched turned to musical gold, and the following recordings are worth seeking out. In the "Great Pianists of the 20th Century" series, we get his exuberant recordings of 23 and 31 from the '30s. The set (with Mozart, Schubert, and his unsurpassed 1951 "Emperor" Concerto with Furtwängler) provides an ideal introduction to a legendary musician (Philips 456769, 2CD, midpriced). Also worth seeking out is a disc that offers the "Pathétique" (APR 5502). We can sample Fischer's art in concert with performances of the "Waldstein," 7, and 15, recorded in 1948 and 1953 (Dante 043).

Clara Haskil was a revered artist whose Beethoven discography is also lamentably slim. Through a life plagued by illness and increasing frailty, her keyboard prowess remained unimpaired, and though her superb Beethoven is well documented by the violin sonatas she recorded with Grumiaux, her way with the piano sonatas is limited to 17 and 18 in the "Great Pianists" series (Philips 456829, 2CD). Her playing is a worthy documentation of her unique artistry. An auto accident cut short the career of the Australian virtuoso **Hungerford** in 1977. Before his death, he left delightful readings of eight sonatas that are well worth acquiring (Vanguard 76/79, 4CD).

Firkušný is still another distinguished pianist whose Beethoven is worth sampling, with imposing readings of 8, 14, 21, and 30 (EMI 66064). Two glorious sonata readings come from **Hess**, a pianist whose discography is limited simply because she hated the recording process. She was enticed in 1951 to record 30 and 31, and these stand among the finest of all time. We should be grateful to Philips for restoring them to the catalog in their invaluable "Great Pianists" series (456183, 2CD). **Moiseiwitsch** was a great pianist who left little Beethoven but all of it significant. He offered a rare combination of almost unparalled technical mastery, refined elegance, and unimpeachable musicianship, heard in a collection recorded in the '30s and '40s that includes 8, 14, and 21 (APR 5530). Superb technique and artistry put at the service of the music are not to be missed.

You probably don't expect to see **Horowitz** in a list of Beethoven players, but listening to his readings of several of the more popular sonatas causes a drastic reappraisal. Those used to the sometimes bizarre and idiosyncratic Horowitz will be surprised by his classically poised and direct way with Beethoven; his clarity of articulation and feeling of great power held in reserve serve the composer well. His recordings of 7, 14, 21, and 23 have been reissued in various couplings: 7 and 23 (RCA 68977); 7 with music of Chopin (RCA 60986); 14, 12, and 21 (RCA 60375, 14 and 21 in mono). In "Horowitz—The Complete Masterworks Recordings" there are superbly remastered editions of 14, 21, and 23, all with a variety of couplings (Sony 3467) and 8 (Sony 53457, 2CD). As a supplement to the studio recordings, we have a composite "live" performance of 28 recorded in 1967 in two venues, and while there's a definite change of mood between them, it's the only example we have of the pianist in late Beethoven and is a valuable document, hard-toned though much of the playing is (Sony 53466).

Rubinstein was careful in choosing which sonatas to play. He concentrated on a couple from the composer's earlier years and a few middle period works, leaving multiple recordings of the "Pathétique," "Appassionata," and "Les Adieux" among the popular sonatas, No. 18, a particular favorite, and single recordings of the "Moonlight" and "Waldstein". With RCA's comprehensive "Rubinstein Collection" it's possible to trace the development of his way with music he obviously adored (all numbers given below are those of the volumes in this huge set, all with various couplings). There's also an issue offering all of Rubinstein's sonata recordings during the '40s in which the transfers are generally cleaner than in the RCA "Collection", though the latter are often brighter (Dante).

His first Beethoven sonata recording in 1940, the first of two of "Les Adieux", was the also the first record he made in the United States. Though its structure is solid, this is an essentially romantic version where the pianist isn't afraid to relax the pulse here and there for expressive purposes (63011). His tempos remained remarkably consistent in the 22 years that separated this from his second version; the performance is tighter but still played with youthful enthusiasm by the then-74-year-old (63056). He made three recordings of the "Pathétique", another work suited to his temperament; all three are powerful statements and I like them all. The 1946 version is in 63010. The 1954 version is among my favorite Rubinstein records, coupled with a marvelous "Appassionata" and "Waldstein" (63033). The final version, taped in 1962 and also superb, is joined by 14, 23, and 26 (63056). In the two later versions, the pianist observes the first movement exposition repeat omitted in 1946.

Rubinstein seemed to have had a special affection for 18 and recorded it three times, starting in 1946 (63014) and ending with his last recording sessions in 1976 at the age of 90. I first came to know and love the piece via his 1954 recording (63036, 3CD), but having recently heard the earlier version, I'm beginning to think it's the finest of the three. The basic approach is the same, but there are significant, though subtle, differences; there's a boldness and strength throughout that softened over the years, especially in I. His valedictory 1976 reading is warm and affectionate, yet offers a brilliance and technical control amazing for a man of such an advanced age. His spirit remained youthful and energetic right up to the end.

Rubinstein left four recordings of the mighty "Appassionata". If any of the sonatas suited this pianist's temperament, it's surely this one. His first recording was made in 1946 and displays a fiery incandescence. The fires still burned brightly in 1954 in his first "modern" version of the work, and this volatile reading is one of his best (63033). A perfect balance of refined elegance and passion is found in the 1963 taping (63056). A final version comes to us from the soundtrack of an amateur video made in 1975 in Pasadena. Not originally intended for commercial release, RCA brought it out in "The Last Recital for Israel" on video tape and laser disc, accompanied by a CD that included a couple of the major works and some shorter pieces. The sound was well below standard for its time, and though RCA cleaned it up quite a bit, it was still a trial to listen to; also, some of the playing didn't display the 88-year-old pianist at his best. A further remastering for the "Rubinstein Collection" has done much to rejuvenate the sound, and though it's still subfusc it's certainly no worse than some of the early recordings from the 40s. Rubinstein was still able to bring off the work with consummate power and drive, and it's a timeless reminder of his enduring spirit and unflagging energy (63080, 2CD).

Finally we come to two sonatas that Rubinstein recorded only once. His brilliant and sparkling reading of 3 is among the finest in the catalog (63055). Recorded in 1963, the performance finds the pianist in perfect accord with the ebullient high spirits encapsulated in the grandest of the Op. 2 sonatas. The great "Waldstein" also received only one Rubinstein recording (63033). Fortunately, it's marvelous, if not as profoundly searching as Schnabel, Solomon, or Kempff.

A notable addendum to **Kempff**'s cycles comes from the BBC in a recital taped in 1969 (BBC Legends 4045). The great pianist is at his most seductive in the brief and somewhat enigmatic Sonata 22. This is the equal of Richter's great RCA recording from a few years earlier, and the coupled works of Bach and Schubert are equally imposing. A great recording.

In a crowded field there are a few other pianists worth your attention. **Perahia** has committed several sonatas to disc that reflect his sensitive and insightful musicianship. Any of the following are worthy additions to your collection: 7 and 23 (Sony 39344), 17, 18, and 26 (42319), and 1–3 (64397). All are beautifully recorded. **Rosen** has recorded the last six sonatas, 27–32 (Sony 53531, 2CD). These tough, probing, decidedly unglamorous readings get right to the heart of this music. Rosen is a profound thinker and brilliant pianist, and these readings are serious and no-nonsense in approach.

The young German pianist **Vogt** proved himself to be a notable Beethovenian in his recording of Concertos 1 and 2, and the same affinity for the composer shines forth in a disc devoted to works in C minor: Variations Woo 80 and Sonatas 5 and 32 (EMI 56136). These are powerful and commanding readings and I hope he will add more Beethoven to his discography. To round out this survey I must include two recordings by one of today's great pianists, the Russian **Mikhail Pletnev,** who is a profound musical thinker equipped with astounding technical facility. We're fortunate to have thought-provoking readings of the "Moonlight," "Waldstein," and "Appassionata," not lacking in commitment or passion (Virgin 45131), and "Les Adieux" is in another disc (DG 459634). An intense account of 32 was taped at the pianist's Carnegie Hall debut in 2000 (DG 471157, a twofer with music by others).

Variations

Beethoven wrote around 20 sets of variations for piano. All, of course, are of interest to the collector who wants a comprehensive collection. Those desiring a full survey of these works are directed to the early **Brendel** collection, which offers just about all of them, plus Sonatas 4 and 20 but minus the great "Diabelli" set (Vox 3017, 3CD). The then young pianist was more unbuttoned than in his later recordings and offers the kind of enthusiastic advocacy this music requires.

Variations on an Original Theme Op. 34. These striking variations, written in 1802, are given stirring readings by **Arrau,** from his early sessions in 1941 (Naxos 110603) and from 1968 (Philips 462358); **Richter** (Olympia); **Schnabel** (Pearl 9123); **Matthews** (Vanguard); and **Gould** (Sony).

Variations & Fugue Op. 35 ("Eroica"). There are a few sets of variations that stand head and shoulders above the rest. One of them is the so-called "Eroica" Variations; written in 1802, they're based on themes from Symphony 3 and Beethoven's only ballet, "The Creatures of Prometheus". The theme and 15 variations are topped off by a brilliant fugue and constitute one of his most imposing keyboard works. **Brendel** recorded them twice and both are worth having. The earlier version is in his comprehensive early ♦Vox collection; the second, joined by other, shorter, pieces, is in Philips 412227.

Arrau contributed no less than three versions, of which two are currently in circulation. In the earliest, recorded for RCA in 1941, the great Chilean master was more open and freer than in his later, more probing accounts. Though the sound of these early recordings is limited, Arrau's power and drama emerge unscathed (Naxos 110603). His equally compelling account from the '60s is also available (Philips 462358, 14CD, budget-priced, with complete sonatas and concertos and other solo works).

Richter is represented by more than one account, but I would opt for a version in fine sound (Olympia 339). Pearl has **Schnabel**'s superb reading (♦9139, 2CD, with other short pieces). The eccentric **Maria Yudina** couples them with powerful readings of the "Diabelli" Variations, in an immensely stimulating performance that shouldn't be missed (Philips 456994, 2CD); so does that other Russian master, **Nikolayeva** (Olympia 570). **Roberts** (Nimbus 5017) and **Matthews** (Vanguard 8074) are also distinguished. **Curzon**'s version stands with Brendel and Schnabel among the finest ever recorded (♦Decca 452302, with the "Emperor"). **Gould** fans will find his reading stimulating (Sony 52645, 2CD, with the C Minor and F major variations and *Bagatelles* Opp. 3 and 126).

Variations on an Original Theme WoO 80. These brilliant and perceptive pieces have fared well in recordings, beginning with **Rachmaninoff**'s stunning 1925 reading, sounding especially fine in the "Great Recordings of the 20th Century" transfer (Philips 456943, 2CD). Though eliminating about half of the 11 minute work, this rare example of the great pianist's Beethoven makes us wish he had recorded some of the major works. **Horowitz** complemented his friend and compatriot's recording with a superb one of his own a decade later (♦APR 5517). It represents the legendary virtuoso's Beethoven at its finest and this transfer is the one to have.

Reaching into the stereo era, we find **Moravec**'s superior reading (VAIA 1021)—one of the finest ever committed to disc—along with a few others that demand our attention. **Lupu** offers an imaginative rendition (Philips "Great Pianists" 456395, 2CD); **Gilels** in 1968 gave a characteristically intense reading; and the young **Brendel** provides a fresh account (Vox 3017, 3CD, part of his complete Beethoven collection). Equally fresh is **Perahia,** as part of the 1990 "Aldeburgh Recital", (Sony 46437; also available on video). **Nikolayeva**'s powerful account, like everything this remarkable pianist plays, is very much worth hearing (Olympic 569).

The probing **Arrau** made three imposing recordings of this music, beginning in the '50s (EMI 67379, 5CD, with complete piano concertos and miscellaneous sonatas), and in 1968 he made an exceptional recording (Philips 462353, 14CD, with complete piano sonatas and concertos). The final version—from the '80s—comes in tow with an expansive reading of Concerto 4 with Colin Davis, and while the insight of this remarkable artist is still quite evident, the fires burned a bit less brightly at this late stage in his career (Philips 416144).

Variations on a Waltz by Diabelli Op. 120. The great "Diabelli" variations (composed between 1819 and 1823) represent the composer's last major piano work and stand as one of the monuments of the keyboard literature. Lasting the better part of an hour, this must be one of the most challenging works ever written, rivaling Bach's "Goldberg Variations" in depth of expression and mastery of the form. Several versions demand consideration, and three of them are in Philips's "Great Pianists" series. **Schnabel**'s 1937 recording is revered for good reason (♦456961, 2CD). Few had the insights into the composer's output that he possessed and that he conveyed with conviction and passion. This is a superb rendition, and the Philips transfer is superior to that offered on Pearl, which is too noisy to bear.

Another is the highly individual reading by the Russian eccentric **Yudina.** She was a unique interpreter of anything she played and she invests this great work with a visionary strength that is, at times, overpowering (Philips 456994, 2CD). **Brendel** chose his 1976 in-concert performance for inclusion in this series, and it's a magisterial reading, worthy of one of the finest Beethovenians of our day (♦456730, 2CD). The more I hear this pianist's early Beethoven recordings, the more I'm convinced that they stand among his finest. Not only is there a winning freshness in his approach, there is that rare combination of youthful vitality and mature understanding allied with a tonal refinement that is sometimes absent later. There are two other Brendel traversals of the work. His early '60s version grabs your attention; it's beautifully remastered and offered at a budget price, a boon to collectors (Vox 5112, 2CD, with *Bagatelles*, etc.). His latest version also stands with the best (Philips 426230).

Arrau left two imposing versions; the first, recorded for US Decca in the '50s, was never transferred to CD. It would be a valuable addition to the catalog should MCA reissue it. The second is currently available in the 14CD set containing all the piano concertos and sonatas (Philips 462358). **Richter** played the Variations only during the 1970 and 1986 seasons. A 1976 performance (Music & Arts 879) and two of those recorded in 1986 (Praga 254023 and Philips 422416) have been released. His way with this music was inimitable in its power and depth of understanding and demands to be heard. Praga's sound is quite good.

Another Russian individualist with impeccable pianistic credentials is the 1966 Tchaikovsky Competition Gold Medal winner **Grigory Sokolov.** Nothing this imaginative artist does is routine, and his reading is both fascinating and challenging (Opus 104). That the younger generation of Russian pianists has something important to say is revealed in the broadly conceived reading by **Konstantin Scherbakov** (Naxos 554372). Some may be put off by a reading that takes over 56 minutes, but I find much to admire here. It's imaginatively coupled with two of Beethoven's English variation sets, on "Rule, Brittania" and "God Save the King." Not to be forgotten is the formidable **Nikolayeva**, whose powerful exposition of the work is paired with the "Eroica" Variations (Olympia 570).

Horszowski was a truly great pianist; his version of the "Diabelli" is strangely offered with Chopin's Impromptus and Concerto 1 (Vox 5511). Another legendary reading is the early stereo version from **Backhaus**—rock-solid, no-nonsense, yet deeply perceptive (Decca 433891, 3CD, with the concertos). **Barenboim** has recorded it three times. His first outing, taped while in his teens, is hard to find (MCA 9803, 2CD, with Sonatas 8, 14, and 23). A much more mature reading is in the "Complete Beethoven Edition" (DG 453733, 8CD, with other Beethoven works played by various pianists). Barenboim takes us on quite a journey in this, and also in his latest version (Teldec, 2CD, with an equally probing

reading of Bach's "Goldberg Variations"); an almost improvisatory quality pervades his playing, though, in his hands, the music is knowingly propelled. He knows the score intimately and very poignantly shares it with us.

A truly special version comes from the pianist/scholar **William Kinderman** (Hyperion 66763). His playing reveals a pianist who has studied this score in great detail and, while offering a thorough and musical reading, carefully avoids any sense of pedantry.

But there remain outstanding versions from other pianists. Though he cast some doubt on his now classic recording in a recent interview, the redoubtable **Kovacevich** need have no fear as to tire outstanding quality of his version (Philips 422969). His Beethoven playing has always been dynamic and most perceptive, and this powerful presentation is no exception. A fresh and fascinating account that displays many personal touches is to be had from **Alfredo Perl** (Ante Nova 27761; also available as part of his superb complete sonata cycle).

Though not well known in this country, the English pianist **Benjamin Frith** has contributed many wonderful recordings to the catalog; add his insightful reading of these variations to the list (ASV 6155, with the C minor Variations). Another distinguished Englishman, **Bernard Roberts,** gives us a fresh and probing reading (Nimbus 7710, with "Eroica" variations). Anything the deeply thoughtful pianist and scholar **Charles Rosen** plays is worth hearing, and his late Beethoven belongs with the finest (IMP 6700112).

Now to my favorite version of all, one that unfolds so naturally and tells its story so unaffectedly that it's a revelation each time I hear it: the reading by **Rudolf Serkin** (♦Sony 44837, with the Op. 119 *Bagatelles*). Despite the qualities of the remarkable accounts discussed above, Serkin's remains, for me, the most satisfying. He's said to have taped a stereo version in the '70s but it has never surfaced. Until it does, this remains a monument to one of the greatest artists of the 20th century.

In a new version of the work by Pollini, as so often happens with his playing, we are offered superbly controlled pianism that despite its technical strength lacks an attendant vision or spirituality (DG 459645). It's too literal for music that cries out for revelatory illumination. Finally I must mention the extraordinarily personal account by the remarkably imaginative **Andrew Rangell** (Dorian 931760). This penetrating reading has a most unusual discmate, Ravel's *Gaspard de La Nuit*—recorded in recital eight years later—is yet another reading demonstrating this pianist's artistry.

Other piano works

Andante favori. Composed in 1803 and at first destined to be the slow movement of the "Waldstein" sonata before Beethoven came to his senses and composed the haunting slow introduction to the work's finale, is one his most lyrically expressive works. **Brendel,** first in one of the most distinctive sets of his early Beethoven series (Vox 5112, 2CD), and more recently and appropriately with the "Waldstein" and Sonatas 22 and 28, offers readings of grace and simplicity (Philips 438472). Other superb renderings come from **Richter** in 1977 (Orfeo 491891; avoid the same performance on Music & Arts 1019, in inferior sound), **Moiseiwitsch** (APR 5530, with the "Waldstein" and other sonatas), **Schnabel** (Pearl), **Arrau** (Philips 416145, with the "Waldstein" and Sonata 30), and **Ashkenazy** (in his big set).

Rondos. The two rondos Op. 51 are beautifully served by **Kempff** (DG 435744, with his magnificent earlier set of the five concertos), **Richter** (Praga 254060, with *Bagatelles* Op. 126:1,4 and 6 and Chopin), and **Lupu** (Decca 448000, in his excellent set of the piano concertos with

Mehta). **Schnabel** offers them with the concertos (Pearl 9063), and **Kissin** can be heard in a disc that includes an intense reading of *Rage Over a Lost Penny* (RCA 68911). **Pletnev**'s superb readings of both Op. 51 works can be found in his Beethoven set (DG) or in Vol. 6 of the "Complete Beethoven Edition" (DG453733, 8CD), which is also an excellent source of some of the pianistic trivia.

Brendel's six-volume Beethoven also offers a comprehensive compilation of the major and minor works for solo piano. I should mention **Serkin**'s excellent account of the Fantasy Op. 77 (Sony 47666, with Sonatas 8 and 29) and **Schnabel**'s equally impressive reading (Pearl 9139, 2CD, with miscellaneous piano works). And the great pianist's blistering reading of *Rage Over a Lost Penny* can be found on Pearl. It remains one of the finest—if not the finest—versions around; so too is his outing with the rarely-encountered Polonaise in D.   LINKOWSKI

CHORAL MUSIC

The *Missa Solemnis* and the finale of Symphony 9 used to be the choral works of Beethoven most often encountered in record catalogs. Now, recordings of even the lesser-known pieces proliferate, and there are many excellent and musicologically informed performances to draw upon. They are all included in the 20-volume DG set of the complete works of Beethoven, for those who require nothing less than everything he wrote.

On the Death of the Emperor Joseph II and *On the Elevation of Leopold II.* Beethoven's first foray into the choral arena was this double cantata, composed in 1790; the two were intended to be performed one after the other. This isn't great Beethoven, and it was never performed in his lifetime, though he extracted the soprano solo "Da stiegen die Menschen an's Licht" for the sublime apotheosis of *Fidelio*. A 1953 recording of only the first part, conducted by **Clemens Krauss,** featured soprano Ilona Steingruber and an excellent bass-baritone, Alfred Poell (Originals 825, NA). While it's good overall and the soloists—especially Poell—are fine, the sound is muddy and gets muddier throughout. Krauss's Wagnerian approach, influenced by the then fashionable "heroic" concept of Beethoven, may account for its textural heaviness. Nevertheless, it's a very effective performance.

In the '60s **Schippers** conducted a fine performance featuring Arroyo and Diaz (uSony 63240). The major stumbling block here is the strange fact that it's sung in Latin instead of the original German, and why this is done is not clarified in the program notes. The filler is a lovely rendering of the concert aria "Ah, Perfido" by the great Régine Crespin. There are also recordings by **Jean-Paul Penin** (Acco) and **Boulez** (Sony, with *Meeresstille und Glückliche Fahrt*). The latter is a brief double cantata on texts by Goethe, a later work discussed below.

Recent recordings have come from ensembles influenced by the early music movement that has widened the performance parameters of 18th-century music, including Beethoven's. Both parts of the cantata are performed by the Berlin Radio Symphony and Chorus led by **Karl Anton Rickenbacher** (uKoch/Schwann 1435). The second part is not as striking as the first. The chorus is excellent and the soloists—Bodil Arresen, Markus Schäfer, and Alan Titus—are also fine. Titus's formerly light baritone has taken on a much darker and richer sound, though his lowest notes lack the heft required for some passages. The instruments are not authentic, but Rickenbacher is obviously aware of the benefits of a lighter, more articulated approach. This is equally true of the fine performance by **Matthew Best** and his Corydon Orchestra and Chorus (♦Hyperion 66880). The DG complete set offers **Christian Thielemann** with the Berlin German Opera Orchestra.

Fantasia for Piano, Orchestra, & Chorus (*"Choral Fantasy"*). Composed in 1808, this piece has only recently begun to achieve a modicum of general acceptance. A 1939 performance by **Ania Dorfmann** and Toscanini shows why it has been so little known and appreciated (Arturo Toscanini Recordings Association and several other labels). Dorfmann seems totally at sea with the piano part, perhaps a case of nerves due to performing on short notice, and Toscanini's contribution is perfunctory and, dare one say, careless.

The recording by **Barenboim,** Klemperer, and the New Philharmonia is an example of "massive" Beethoven, but despite the occasional ensemble glitches between soloist and orchestra (the aged Klemperer wasn't always easy to read)—and the fact that the John Aldis Chorus sounds utterly disengaged—the results are generally persuasive (EMI, with the Triple Concerto). It's available both as filler for Klemperer's *Missa Solemnis* and with Barenboim's performances of the complete piano concertos.

In 1991, I watched the New Year's Eve broadcast performance by **Kissin,** Claudio Abbado, and the Berlin Philharmonic, later reproduced on disc (DG). I have no qualms about Kissin or Abbado, but perhaps this isn't an area where you can expect to find either at their most characteristic. Abbado also recorded the piece with **Pollini** (DG), but the Kissin performance is now part of the complete DG set. **Brendel** with Haitink and the London Philharmonic is another mixed bag (♦Philips 34148). Brendel inhabits this musical realm as few performers do, and his approach brings the contours of the piece into sharp relief. Haitink is less effective. Brendel's earlier performance is still available in a set of the piano concertos (Vox/Turnabout 3502).

Rösel's recording with Kegel and the Dresden Philharmonic includes a number of unfamiliar vocal and instrumental soloists, and there is no enlightening information in the program booklet (Capriccio). The performance gives the impression of hasty preparation. Rösel's opening cadenza has little of the fire and imagination required to bring it off effectively, and the orchestral playing is pro forma. The vocal soloists and chorus are not at all bad. The final section is the most interesting part of the performance, but overall, this isn't a recording I can recommend. The disc includes the Triple Concerto; the *Fantasy* was obviously the filler for the concerto and was treated accordingly.

My favorite performance featured the brilliant **Demus** (DG, NA). He made a career playing historic pianos, and while I'm almost certain this performance wasn't on a period instrument, it doesn't sound quite like a modern concert grand either. Whatever the vintage, Demus's performance is among the finest. Also available are **Ax** with Mehta (RCA), **Ashkenazy,** who plays and conducts (London), and **Previn** (RCA).

There are also historical performances by **Lili Krauss** (Fnac), **Rudolf Serkin** with Bernstein (Sony) and Ozawa (Telarc), **Katchen** from 1965 (London), and **Yudina** (Arlecchino, Volume 7 of a Yudina collection). **Kuerti** (CBC), **Klien** (Vox), and **Pressler** (Philips) have also recorded the piece. They are less well-known than they should be, but they rarely disappoint, especially in this repertoire. For those who prefer the sound of early instruments, **Robert Levin**'s recording with Gardiner is worth investigating (Archiv).

Christ on the Mount of Olives (Christus am Ölberg). Composed in 1807 and revised in 1814, this work effectively demonstrates Beethoven's approach to the Italianate operatic style of the period. Again, my initial impressions of the piece were formed by the Vienna Singverein and the Vienna Symphony conducted by **Bernard Klee** in the ♦DG collection. The soloists—James King as Christ, Elizabeth Harwood as the Seraph, and Franz Crass as Petrus—are all marvelous. King and Harwood are in particularly good form, and the overall performance is quite convincing.

While perhaps not ideal, the Lyon National Choir and Orchestra under **Baudo** are certainly more than respectable (♦Harmonia Mundi). The stentorian heldentenor James Anderson as Christ is impressive, though he lacks King's psychological complexity. Monica Pick-Hieronimi navigates the difficult writing for the Seraph with confidence and precision, and Victor von Halem's Petrus is very fine. **Henk Spruit**'s recording with the Netherlands Radio Orchestra is another to consider (Belvedere).

Mass in C. Once again, DG's bicentennial collection provided my first experience of this work. Despite its impressive personnel, including Janowitz, Hamari, Laubenthal, and Ernst Gerold Schramm, with the Munich Bach Choir and Orchestra led by **Richter,** it fails to make a compelling case for the piece. That is emphatically not the case for **Gardiner**'s performance, the best of those available (♦Archiv 429779). Composed in 1807 on a commission from Prince Nikolaus Esterházy (Haydn's last patron), the work failed to make an impression at its first outing and was withdrawn soon thereafter. How different the Prince's opinion might have been had he heard this performance! From first to last, it crackles with energy and purpose. The personnel include the fabulous Monteverdi Choir, soloists Charlotte Margiono, Catherine Robbin, William Kendall, and Alastair Miles, and the Orchestre Révolutionnaire et Romantique. If ever a case were to be made for the use of period instruments in music of this time, this recording makes it, hands down. The filler includes the concert aria "Ah, Perfido" wonderfully performed by Margiono and *Meerestille und Glückliche Fahrt.*

Shaw offers a more conventional approach, with the Atlanta Symphony and Chorus (Telarc, with *Meerestille* and *Elegiac Song*). It's impossible to deny Shaw's formidable gifts as a choral director, but for a piece like this, which requires textural clarity and transparency, his approach is far from optimal. The choral sound, though impressive, is more suitable for Brahms than early Beethoven, and the vocal quartet is undistinguished, individually and as an ensemble.

Matthew Best's performance with the Corydon Singers and Orchestra is something of a compromise between these two approaches (♦Hyperion). It has all the articulatory energy of the early music style combined with choral and orchestral lushness. The vocal quartet—Janice Watson, Rigby, Ainsley, and Howell—is fine, and the overall sound is clear and transparent. The recording also has the benefit of excellent filler material, though its "Ah, Perfido" isn't as compelling as Margiono's. Others to consider are **Chailly** (London, an economical set since it includes Solti's *Missa Solemnis*), a good performance by **Colin Davis** (Philips), and **Corboz** (Erato).

Missa Solemnis. Completed in 1823, the *Missa Solemnis* is undoubtedly Beethoven's supreme achievement in choral music, though there remain pockets of resistance to this view. Nearly every major conductor of the latter half of the 20th century weighed in on this piece at some point in their careers, some more than once. There are many to choose from.

I judge performances by how well the "Sanctus" and "Benedictus" are realized; this is usually the point where many otherwise good performances go awry. Based on this criterion, the recordings by Klemperer and Karajan (♦DG 423913) are the most successful, though **Karajan**'s video performance from 1978 with different soloists is far superior (also DG). There was yet a third Karajan recording from 1986, but it

didn't measure up to the earlier ones and was deleted soon after its release. The overall approach is similar, but the quartet is only adequate, and the frequently faulty intonation of the Wiener Singverein is particularly evident.

I was surprised that **Levine**'s performance with the Vienna Philharmonic has replaced Karajan's in the DG complete set; perhaps this is because it is more recent, but it is not more compelling. At his best, Karajan really got to the very marrow of the work. Levine's performance, for all its positives, lacks the interpretive focus needed to bring off this very difficult piece, which is by turns an oratorio and a symphonic poem with chorus. **Klemperer** with the New Philharmonia is characteristically massive, but irresistible; his quartet (Söderström, Höffgen, Kmentt, and Talvela) is occasionally beset by ensemble difficulties, but does a fine job overall (♦EMI 69538). There is another, less compelling Klemperer performance with the Vienna SO.

I was brought up on **Toscanini**'s '50s studio recording, which has lost none of its dramatic power and linear integrity (♦RCA 60272). His live performance from the '40s is also noteworthy, and the quartet here—Milanov, Castagna, Björling, and Kipnis—is excellent, though the recording itself is marred by close miking of the brass (♦Arturo Toscanini Recordings Association). There are wonderful moments in this reading, though Toscanini lacked the temperament to realize successfully the sublimity of the "Sanctus-Benedictus" section; his slower than usual tempo increases the difficulty for the quartet, who gradually bring him around to a more manageable pace. There is another Toscanini performance with an amazing quartet: Rethberg, Telva, Martinelli, and Pinza (Melodram). **Böhm**'s 1955 recording is wonderful; again there are a few ensemble and pitch glitches by the quartet (Stader, Mariana Radev, Dermota, Greindl), but overall it's certainly worth investigation (♦DG 449737). Böhm's later recording is also very fine (also DG).

Shaw's performance with the Atlanta Symphony is another disappointment from an otherwise great artist (Telarc, 2CD, with Mozart's "Great" Mass). The quartet isn't undistinguished, but it's certainly a strange mix. McNair is the top voice, with Janice Taylor, Aler, and Krause, and she's simply unsuited to this music; it's great to have a singer with a good pianissimo, but quite another matter when mezzo forte is the top of her dynamic range. I have great respect for Aler's vocal artistry—in every performance I've heard, he's been vocally and musically excellent—but his clear, bell-like tenor is no match for the density of the orchestration. Taylor and Krause have something of the heft required, but along with Aler, they all swamp McNair, through no fault of their own, and are frequently lost in the tuttis. As expected, the chorus and orchestra are quite good, but Shaw's unremitting middle-of-the-road approach renders the piece lifeless. The sound is thick and dull with few high overtones. This performance lacks a clear sense of the musico-dramatic journey the work undergoes; there is little feeling for the alternating inner struggle and transcendent joy that gave birth to this most intense declaration of religious faith.

Among the period instrument adherents, **Harnoncourt**'s live recording is the most satisfying (♦Teldec 74884), though **Herreweghe**'s performance of the first three sections of the piece, also live, is marvelous (Harmonia Mundi 901557). **Gardiner**'s reading, with the same cast as his Mass in C, has its virtues but doesn't live up to that performance (Archiv).

There are also historical performances by **Walter** (Iron Needle), **Clemens Krauss** (Grammofono), **Koussevitzsky** (Pearl), and **Ancerl** (Tahra). A great deal of material to choose from!

Shorter choral works. While most of the shorter pieces can be found as fillers for the larger works, some are included in collections. Some are self-contained, like *Meeresstille und Glückliche Fahrt* and the beautiful *Elegiac Song*. Others were composed as incidental music for stage productions.

The DG set includes a number of wonderful performances of the incidental music, along with a few curiosities, including the complete *Ruins of Athens* conducted by **Abbado** (this was also issued singly) and the cantata *Der glorreiche Augenblick,* composed in 1814 for the Congress of Vienna. Not one of Beethoven's best, this half-hour work is also available from **Robert Bass** leading the Collegiate Chorale and the Orchestra of St. Luke's (Koch). The principal attraction of this recording is the first-rate singing of Deborah Voigt; otherwise the performance is competent, though marred by muddy sound.

Tilson Thomas's recording contains a number of interesting pieces, including *Meeresstille* and music from *Ruins of Athens* (Sony). **Rickenbacher**'s recording is particularly noteworthy; every performance sparkles (♦Koch/Schwann 1485). One notable rarity on this disc is the incidental music to *Leonora Prohaska,* a piece that's also included by Abbado in the DG collection. I've mentioned the lovely **Shaw** performances of *Meeresstille* and *Elegiac Song,* which are an improvement on the staid and overripe Mass in C that heads the disc (Telarc). I've also mentioned **Gardiner**'s Mass in C, with its interesting fillers (Archiv), though in general I prefer Rickenbacher. One other worthy collection is "The Unknown Beethoven", which contains a number of rarely heard choral works (Berlin). MAKELL

In addition to the recordings discussed above, you may want to consider **Barenboim**'s most recent version of the *Choral Fantasy,* conducted from the piano and joined by Perlman and Ma in the Triple Concerto; it's fervent and beautifully played (EMI 55516). **Serkin** was still in good form when he re-recorded this work with Ozawa (Telarc), but his earlier version with Bernstein remains very special (Sony). **Katchen** with Piero Gamba, originally released as a twofer (London 440839, with Concertos 3–5) sounds better than ever in the "Katchen Edition" (London 460825). Unfortunately, those hoping to obtain **Sherchen**'s classic Westminster recording of *Mount of Olives* will have to send to Japan for it (MVCW 18027). However, it may be worth asking British dealers for the classic Beecham performance of the Mass in C (EMI 64385).

Critics are divided on **Bernstein**'s *Missa Solemnis;* some praise his Sony recording, some prefer his later DG. Certainly the Sony is a good buy, giving you Serkin's *Choral Fantasy* plus Haydn's *Theresienmesse* in one box (Sony 47522), and the refurbished sound is good enough that the DG (offering only the *Missa*) isn't much of an improvement. Both performances are propulsive and dramatic, yet always at the service of the music. **Rilling**'s small chorus may be ideal for Bach but lacks the grandeur needed for Beethoven, and 79 minutes of music spread over two discs is no bargain (Hänssler). **Tate**'s forces aren't much larger, and the soloists are unappealing (EMI). **Solti** conveys the joy of the music, but tends to be larger than life without convincing the listener of the rightness of it all; still, he does have a splendid quartet, with Varady, Vermillion, Cole, and Pape (London).

The best thing about **Barenboim**'s *Missa* is the Chicago Symphony Chorus, powerful yet supple, but it takes him a while to warm to the glories of the score; the 'Kyrie' sounds almost unctuous, though matters improve thereafter (Erato). **Masur** is noble and weighty, but with an unfortunate tendency to urge things along a bit too much (Berlin). **Dorati**'s characterless reading and distant miking don't stand up to repeated

hearings (BIS). **Colin Davis** on RCA is a lot better than on Philips, brimming with warmth and conviction, and the appended *Choral Fantasy* with **Oppitz** makes a nice bonus if cost is a factor. **Ormandy** manages to get the entire work onto a single budget-priced disc; it still sounds good, but doesn't plumb the depths of the music as ably as others (Sony).

HALLER

FIDELIO

Beethoven's only opera may be an odd blend of Singspiel (the first scenes of Act 1) and music drama (the rest of the work) but that hasn't diminished its popularity. Its noble, moving story of faithful and heroic conjugal love and defiance of tyranny, set in great, thrilling music, still strikes a chord in contemporary audiences. Many famous conductors have recorded it, and the title role has been a favorite vehicle of dramatic sopranos ever since its premiere.

In addition to the many stereo recordings, there are several older mono sets that are worth consideration even though their sound isn't up to current standards. The best being a 1950 staged performance from Salzburg conducted by **Furtwängler** (♦EMI 64901). Its marvelous cast is headed by Flagstad and includes Patzak, Schöffler, Dermota, Schwarzkopf, and Josef Greindl. This is a much better performance (and cast) than any of the conductor's several studio recordings. The best stereo recording in modern sound is a studio recording led by **Klemperer;** it features a fine cast headed by Ludwig, Vickers, and Frick (♦EMI 55170).

Both conductors perform the opera as a Beethovenian symphonic structure, but Furtwängler's more flexible reading has greater emotional impact. Flagstad's great voice is, of course, unique; by contrast, Ludwig seems stretched in Fidelio's Act I aria. Patzak, with a smaller and less powerful voice than Vickers, still manages to communicate Florestan's pain and torment almost as well. Both supporting casts are very good, but Furtwängler's in the Salzburg set are perhaps the best ever to have recorded these roles. **Karajan**'s is another commendable stereo set (EMI 69290), with Dernesh as the fiery heroine, Vickers, and a very good supporting cast.

The more recent recordings of the opera (and there have been many) all fall short in one way or another. **Colin Davis** has the excellent Heppner as Florestan and the sumptuous-voiced but theatrically inert Voigt as Leonore. He conducts a dull, unexpressive performance, with a poor supporting cast (RCA). **Dohnányi** is torpedoed by poor singing on the part of the principals (London), and so is **Solti**'s Chicago recording (London). **Haitink**'s 10-year-old version has a rich-voiced heroine in Norman but she sounds uninvolved in the drama (Philips). Her partner, Rainer Goldberg, lacks vocal heft, and Haitink's conducting, though precise, lacks feeling.

Janowitz is the affecting heroine in **Bernstein**'s recording from Vienna, but Kollo is a wobbly Florestan and Bernstein's conductorial affectations and over-interpretations will annoy many listeners (DG). An older recording by **Toscanini** has poor sound, no dialogue, and a less than optimum cast, though the performance crackles with the excitement that's missing in so many recent recordings (RCA 60273). **Maazel** has the great Nilsson as Leonore, but McCracken's strangulated tenor makes this set unappealing (London).

Michael Halász's recording has a generally fine cast headed by Inga Nielsen and Gösta Winbergh, and both give good accounts of their roles; the other members of the cast, notably Moll and Alan Titus, sing very well (Naxos 660070). Unfortunately, the conductor has a small, weak orchestra (it sounds like a chamber group) to work with, and it doesn't give Beethoven's great score its due. **Barenboim** leads the Berlin Opera in another dull reading, though Domingo and Meier give excellent performances (Teldec 25249). This recording also has no dialogue but includes the four *Leonore* overtures.

An earlier version of the opera, known as *Leonore,* has been recorded by **Gardiner** (DG Archiv 453461) and **Blomstedt** (Berlin 1140). The two versions differ since each conductor made his own decisions about what to include from the 1805 and 1806 versions. (The final *Fidelio* dates from 1814.) Gardiner replaced the spoken dialog with a narrator (a poor choice) and his orchestra uses period instruments, but Blomstedt also has a much better cast, so his is the recommended version. An earlier recording from the Bregenz Festival has poor sound and not as good a cast; it should be avoided (Melodram 27085). *Leonore* is not as great an opera as *Fidelio,* but neither is it negligible. MOSES

SONGS

Beethoven's renown owes little to his songs, which don't have the melodic bounty of Schubert, the rapturous romanticism of Schumann, or the perspicacity of Wolf. There's something ungainly about even the best of them, especially when the composer chooses to worry his codas rather than light on a simple conclusion (think of "Adelaide" and "Ich liebe dich"). The melodies are terse and thematic rather than songful and don't always lie gratefully for the voice. The ambitious cycle *An die ferne Geliebte* moves awkwardly from number to number, even though Beethoven, by linking the accompaniments, surely intended exactly the opposite. Music history's most titanic personage couldn't quite scale down his genius to fit the intimate form of the German lied. His efforts are endearing all the same, and it's no wonder that recitalists are drawn to his songs. Listeners, too, whether revisiting familiar territory or exploring the songs for the first time, should find much to savor in an all-Beethoven program.

The complete songs require only three CDs, and there is no better starting point (and, for the parsimonious, ending point) than **Prey's** reasonably priced collection (♦Capriccio 10343). He sings most of them warmly and spontaneously, without straining for interpretive effect, and he's assisted in some pieces by a lusty chorus, which really adds life to the "Song of the Flea", to cite only one example. American soprano Pamela Coburn, clean and true, takes the songs best suited to a female voice (among them a surprisingly effective setting of "Mignons Lied").

Other complete or nearly complete compilations have come from **Schreier** (Berlin) and **Fischer-Dieskau** (DG), neither of whom surpasses Prey. I would nonetheless like to have at least one of F-D's Beethoven recitals, if not the complete set. A group of early recordings, which capture his voice at its most velvety, are available (♦Testament 1057), and an all-Beethoven program from Salzburg has been preserved, with Gerald Moore at the piano (♦Orfeo 140501). Admirers of the doggedly earnest **Bär** might find his all-Beethoven disc (EMI) a stimulating alternative, but even more engaging is the young **Stephan Genz** (♦Hyperion 67055). His voice has a velvet surface and a firm core; the readings are heartfelt, unaffected, and lovingly enunciated.

The first great recording of the cycle *An die ferne Geliebte* was made in 1936 by **Gerhard Hüsch,** and his combination of handsome tone and winning directness have not been bettered (♦Preiser 89202, with Schubert's *Müllerin* and *Winterreise*), though Prey, Fischer-Dieskau, and Genz are formidable competitors. **Souzay's** urbane account is in a set that includes Schumann and Brahms songs (♦Philips 442741, 2CD). **Hampson** brings his own distinctive approach to the cycle (EMI), and so does **Holzmair** (Philips)—nothing revelatory in either case, but both are commended to their admirers.

Listeners who favor a tenor interpreter might turn to the incisive, sensitive **Haefliger** (♦Claves 8907, a very mixed program) or the clarion **Heppner** (RCA, another mixed program), who isn't over-meticulous but transfixes the listener with almost Wagnerian force. More to my taste is **Gedda,** whose very appealing 1970 recording of Beethoven's *Liebeslieder* deserves reissue. At least we have Gedda's "Adelaide" and the *Ferne Geliebte* songs in one of EMI's Introuvables packages (u65685). **Wunderlich's** recording is pleasingly sung but a bit tentative and unpolished, and not well accompanied or recorded (Philips).

Listeners who want to add more variety to their Beethoven song collections will have to pick and choose among various anthologies, and the pickings are fairly slim. **Björling** made something of a speciality of "Adelaide", and it's worth seeking out one of the RCA recordings that includes the song. **Grümmer** sings "Ich liebe dich" (also known as "Zärtliche Liebe") in a set recommended for its Schubert and Mozart (♦Gala 100554, 2CD). Klärchen's songs from *Egmont* are sung by **Seefried** in a recital of Goethe lieder, along with "Wonne der Wehmut" (♦Orfeo 297921). **Wunderlich** offers gorgeous vocalizations of four songs as fillers to his recording of Schumann's *Dichterliebe* (♦DG 429933).

Some of the Italian songs are communicatively and idiomatically rendered by **Bartoli,** though her tone quality isn't always ingratiating (London). A good compendium of historic Beethoven performances can be found, with contributions from Karl Schmitt-Walter, Peter Anders, Marta Fuchs, Walther Ludwig, and others (♦Minerva 69). It may be worth buying the lieder albums devoted to Schlusnus, Erb, and Hotter for the sake of the few Beethoven songs included (♦Preiser 89208). **Hotter** is also imposing in two of the more obscure numbers, "Des Kriegers Abschied" and "Abendlied underm gestrinten Himmel" (Acanta), but the last word in grandeur must surely go to **Flagstad,** who is unsubtle but thrillingly majestic in the Op. 48 *Gellert-Lieder* and four other songs (♦Simax 1825).

The *gran scena ed aria* "Ah, perfido!" is a real oddity in Beethoven's output. Like the concert arias of Haydn and Mozart, it seems an orphan from an opera that was never written, the emotional cry of a character we know nothing about. However, Beethoven wrote clumsily for the voice; while "Ah, perfido!" has energy and passion, it's not melodically grateful or memorable. It would probably have passed into obscurity if anyone else had written it. It nonetheless has had no difficulty finding advocates, particularly among dramatic sopranos.

One of the best recordings remains **Flagstad's** of 1937 (♦Preiser 89141). The queenly Norwegian sings with surprising flexibility and abandon as well as matchless depth of tone. The sound is excellent for its time. **Nilsson** also essayed the aria, though she's too cool and brazen (DG). **Crespin's** shortness on top is offset by pointed diction and powerful declamation, the big voice sounding particularly bright and beautiful in the aria's cavatina (♦Sony 60577 or 63240). Even warmer are **Frida Leider** (Lys; hard to find) and **Eileen Farrell** (Sony; NA), and I would particularly like to see a reissue of Farrell's reading, which combines feminine softness, heroic, well-defined tone, and good stereo sound.

"Ah, perfido!" doesn't require Wagnerian amplitude; it lies within the reach of lyric and spinto sopraNos. **Callas** might have been a great exponent, but her 1963 recording, though it often blazes with life, finds her in hollow, mouthy voice (EMI). More satisfying is **Schwarzkopf** in 1954, one of the most personal and touching of interpreters (♦EMI 63201). The recitative is vividly stated; the cavatina sung with poised, silvery tone; the cabaletta lively and exciting. I wish only for better diction. The underrated **Gré Brouwenstijn** is at least in Schwarzkopf's class

(♦Philips 462071). She has a strong spinto voice with radiant top notes; her openhearted vitality and very individual way of inflecting the musical line makes her reading unusually memorable.

Steber's glowing, forward timbre and smooth, easy emission would have been just right, but in 1970 she was well past her prime (VAI). Susan Dunn, in a 1987 recital disc, is, like Schwarzkopf, surprisingly personal (in the cavatina especially), her voice creamy and voluptuous. Even better is another American soprano, Studer, who sings with bite and substance and lacks nothing in flexibility (♦DG 435617). Her ardor is perhaps a little too generalized, but she's more secure than Callas and more sumptuous than Schwarzkopf.

Beethoven, in collaboration with the Scottish collector George Thomson, wrote arrangements for more than 170 folk songs, mostly in English. He undertook the task to earn money, but he soon warmed to it. His instrumentations (for piano trio) and harmonizations of songs as familiar as "Auld Lang Syne" or as obscure as "My Harry Was a Gallant Gay" are delightful, a real ear-opener for those who could scarcely imagine the lofty Beethoven trafficking in such trifles.

DG's 1970 Beethoven Edition included a good selection of the folk songs. Most of them were appropriated by the efficient but unidiomatic Fischer-Dieskau, while the superb Alexander Young (a far more eloquent singer of the English language) sat on his hands for most of the recording sessions waiting for something to come his way—a strange error in artistic judgment by the producers. The 1998 Beethoven Edition takes a more sensible approach and deploys an army of fine English singers like Lott, Murray, Walker, Ainsley, and Allen. The problem here is one of bulk. The expensive 7CD set probably has more songs than anyone would want, but it's a splendid achievement and extravagantly recommended all the same (♦453786).

Convenient, single-disc samplers are scarce. The most useful comes from a foursome of singers: Elaine Woods, Carolyn Watkinson, Josef Protschka (surprisingly good English), and Richard Salter (♦Sony 64301). The selection is varied and generous, the singing deft and ebullient. Holzmair, in a good collection of songs (Philips), has a lighter touch than Fischer-Dieskau, but isn't ideal—he no more has the "pulse of an Irishman" than his Teutonic predecessor. The American soprano Julie Kaufmann is fresh and incisive, though oddly, she avoids the most familiar songs (Orfeo). The singers of the New York Vocal Arts Ensemble (Arabesque) have the right sort of spirit and make more of the words, even if none of them has Holzmair's polish.

What we need are reissues of two LPs made by Denis Stevens's Accademia Monteverdiana (one on Nonesuch, the other on Vanguard), and of Robert White's irresistible collection (♦RCA). White is joined by Ani Kavafian (violin), Yo-Yo Ma (cello), and Samuel Sanders (piano), and this is the team most likely to bring smiles of delight to the listener's face.   LUCANO

Vincenzo Bellini (1801–35)

The name Bellini stands for bel canto (beautiful song), a style of composition and voice production in the traditional Italian manner, with emphasis on beautiful tone, phrasing, sustaining and ornamentation of notes, and a fine command of subtle gradations and nuance. The style was also practiced by Rossini, Donizetti, and many lesser lights, yet it's agreed that even these two distinguished composers rarely equaled Bellini's long, supple, and graceful melodies. He died at a very early age, having composed a mere 10 operas, three of them (Norma, La Sonnambula, I Puritani) unquestioned masterpieces. All of his operas have been commercially recorded.

Adelson e Salvini. It's difficult to believe that Bellini composed his first opera (1825) for the music conservatory where he was studying, such are the high-flying technical demands of the voice parts, particularly the fiendishly high tessitura of the tenor role of Salvini. His home town, Catania, is the source of a number of recordings of his operas, particularly the lesser-known ones. I haven't been able to hear the first recording, a curious affair performed in Catania in 1985 by the Stockholm Kammarkor and the Drottningholm Barockensemble conducted by Anders-Per Jonsson (Bongiovanni). Most of the singers have Scandinavian names and are unknown to me. In a 1992 performance led by Andrea Licata, the voices are distant, as if recorded from the orchestra pit, and the secco recitatives are played on a particularly watery-sounding piano. It almost seems unfair to criticize the Salvini of Bradley Williams; management was lucky to find a tenor willing to attempt this unbelievably difficult music. He has a small, tightly afflicted voice, pinched throughout, but you must give the man credit for courage. The rest of the cast is adequate (Nuova Era 7154, 2CD).

Beatrice di Tenda (1833) isn't the most dramatically compelling of Bellini's operas, but it does have some strong passages among the well-crafted melodies. After many years of neglect, it was revived in Venice (site of its premiere) in 1964. Gui makes some strange interpolations and some nips and tucks in the music, but conducts a strong, very serious interpretation. Leyla Gencer never quite made it to the big leagues of international opera, but she certainly was popular in Italy and a force in the bel canto movement. Her Beatrice is forcefully sung, with many vocal explosions along the way to create drama where little exists, almost an over-interpretation. The other singers are competent (Nuova Era).

Although she rarely performed Beatrice on stage, Sutherland is considered the leading singer of the role. When she recorded it in 1966 she had undergone a sinus operation and had lost the open, clear sound that marked her earlier singing. Still, there's no doubt that her rendition of the role could hardly be bettered. That large, luxuriant, warm sound is ever present, her technical virtuosity unimpaired. Through her deep understanding of the bel canto style, she creates a viable human being out of a stock character. Veasey (Agnese) has a voice that blends well with Sutherland's and she too understands the style. This was Pavarotti's first commercial recording, and while it's a pleasure to hear that magnificent voice in its youth, it's a voice for Puccini, not Bellini. Bonynge leads a strong performance of this gloomy work (♦London 433706, 3CD).

A supplement, possibly even a substitute for Sutherland's studio recording, is an exciting performance from a 1961 concert by the American Opera Society. This is pre-operation Sutherland and here she truly earned her nickname, "La Stupenda." This is spectacular singing, with as much grace, ease, and excitement as possible. It wasn't just the occasion of her New York debut but her first appearance with her famous vocal partner, mezzo Marilyn Horne. She too sings brilliantly. Rescigno adds to the excitement, leading a rich, full-blooded interpretation (♦Bella Voce 107226, 2CD).

A 1967 performance has Freni as Beatrice, a true contrast to Sutherland's coloratura extravagance. Freni isn't considered a bel canto specialist, though she did sing several bel canto roles. Instead of emphasizing the role's vocal fireworks, she takes a more human approach, trying to infuse what real-life drama she can into the role, and as usual her voice is one of the most beautiful ever to emerge from a human throat. The others in the cast are variable in quality, and Maurizio Arena valiantly holds the Bologna forces together. The recorded sound isn't very good, but it's listenable. This one belongs to Freni fans (Legato).

Lucia Aliberti has a voice that needs a bit of tolerance from the listener. It's not exactly ugly, but it's very strange. Every note seems to be artificially produced, with distinct breaks between vocal registers, and this makes the basically sympathetic character of Beatrice sound like a tough broad. The rest of the cast isn't very good except for the dark, chocolate-sounding baritone Paolo Gavanelli, but he's not enough to save the show. **Fabio Lusi** leads Berlin Opera forces in a lethargic performance with tempos slowed down, probably to accommodate Aliberti's labors (Berlin).

In a 1992 Austrian Radio broadcast led by **Pinchas Steinberg**, Gruberová, like Sutherland, is a dead-on-target coloratura marksman, but has sharper diction and is a more vivid vocal actress, with her voice sometimes taking on an unpleasant edgy quality. The others in the cast are unremarkable (Nightingale, 3CD). In a strange mixture of nationalities, with Italians and Eastern European singers, the Monte Carlo Orchestra and Prague Philharmonic Choir are led by **Alberto Zedda.** Mariana Nicolesco is the star here, a Beatrice of the Gencer variety. She has strong support from her colleagues, but the competition from earlier recordings is too much (Sony, 3CD). The bargain price of **June Anderson**'s Beatrice is its only recommendation (Opera d'Oro, 2CD).

Bianca e Fernando. This second Bellini opera (Naples, 1826) was heavily revised for the opening of Genoa's new Teatro Carlo Felice. That's the version led by **Andrea Licata.** There are extensive cuts in the extremely long choral parts, plus some cuts to spare the tenor—but not spare him much. Gregory Kunde doesn't have the most beautiful or distinctive voice, but he's very musical. While the vocal hurdles are not as extreme as those of *Adelson,* they're high enough to daunt many a tenor, and Kunde goes over them quite well, with even a full-throated blasted out high F. When the soprano finally arrives, she takes over most of the vocal terrors, and Young Ok Shin has a beautiful, liquid silver voice, delicate of nuance, graceful, with fleetness and ease in the coloratura. Haijing Fu is an exciting singer; his baritone is a big, dark, burly growl that chugs its way through the bel canto. Licata has the orchestra sounding remarkably good, more than just another pit band (♦Nuova Era 7076, 2CD).

I Capuleti e i Montecchi. Crucial to choosing a recording of *Capuletti* is the listener's preference for a mezzo-soprano or a tenor as Romeo. Bellini composed the role (1830) for a mezzo, but for a 1966 revival, **Claudio Abbado** used a tenor for Romeo, and Scotto and Aragall make a strong case for this version. Scotto sings a delicate, childlike Giulietta with Aragall virile and strong, though he's no match for the grandly broad Tebaldi of Pavarotti. Abbado works wonders guiding the La Scala chorus and orchestra. This recording is available in several bargain-priced issues (♦Opera d'Oro 1171; Gala 100517; Verona 28001; all 2CD)

A curiously ineffective studio version from 1976 with Sills and Janet Baker as the lovers of Verona has not yet been issued on CD. Sills sings beautifully as a touchingly human Giulietta, every coloratura point carefully in place. Baker's Romeo is just as beautifully sung, but her feminine mezzo is all wrong for the role as well as shy on drama. Gedda surprisingly forces his tenor too much. But the overriding problem is **Patanè**'s bland conducting, with little excitement or involvement. In a 1985 performance at Covent Garden, Gruberová is quite the equal of Sills as Giulietta, as detailed and emotionally human, and perhaps to be preferred for a warmer, more beautiful tone. Baltsa is a forceful but not forced Romeo, strongly sung. Dano Raffanti does little with Tebaldo, though he sings idiomatically. **Muti** keeps up the rhythmic vitality of Bellini's long lines, never allowing them to droop, maintaining a real sense of movement (♦EMI 64846, 2CD).

There is little to praise about a 1991 performance from La Fenice. Ricciarelli is in poor voice, unfocused, sparing herself (and the audience) any approach to high notes or any sense of musicality or drama. Diana Montague's Romeo is pleasantly sung, again too feminine to be convincing. **Bruno Campanella** favors a slow, drowsy pace (Nuova Era). Eva Mei's bright, clear coloratura is competent, but she reveals little drama or character. More impressive is the Romeo of Vasselina Kasarova, big-toned and involved. Munich Radio forces under **Roberto Abbado** play competently but without the necessary movement of line (RCA).

Norma (1831) is often considered the greatest of the bel canto operas and the title role to be one of the most challenging in the soprano repertoire, technically and dramatically. The list of prima donnas who have undertaken it is extensive, with a variety of voice types to chose from.

Callas commercially recorded the role twice. In 1954 her Norma was an "exterior" performance, grandly sung but one-sided, expressing more the public, political side of the character and less expressive of the personal tragedy. The mature voice of Stignani may be inappropriate for the youthful Adalgisa, but she was a secure and accomplished singer, and the woolly bass of Rossi-Lemeni is strangely effective as Oroveso. The forces of La Scala led by **Serafin** are a shining example of style, catching the long lines unhurriedly, yet dramatically taut (EMI 56271, 2CD, mono). In Callas's 1960 stereo remake, she has much better colleagues. Ludwig's Adalgisa is glamorous of tone, sleek yet full-bodied, a truly sexy rival to Norma. Corelli's golden tenor is heard to advantage, emotional but not out of control, and Nicolo Zaccaria sings a smooth, somewhat sinister Oroveso. The La Scala forces, again under Serafin, play handsomely (♦EMI 66428, 2CD). There are several "off-the-air" Callas performances, but her second commercial recording is the one preferred.

Sutherland is a much more warm-toned, feminine Norma, expressing the drama through more delicate nuance. Horne's Adalgisa is excitingly sung but too forceful a personality, not the dreamy romantic called for (Decca 425488, 3CD). Twenty years later Sutherland re-recorded the role with big-name, big-voiced colleagues. Caballé is a luxurious Adalgisa, Pavarotti a handsome, rich-voiced Pollione, and Ramey the best sung of the Orovesos (♦Decca 414476, 3CD).

Caballé has little dramatic depth, is somewhat shy on the musical details, but she sang with great tonal beauty. There's nothing subtle about Cossotto's Adalgisa, more verismo drama than bel canto display. Domingo's Pollione is well sung with noble sentiment but little romantic involvement when needed, and Raimondi creates a firm, caring Oroveso. **Cillario** indulges the vagaries of his singers (RCA). A happy complement is Caballé's performance from 1974 with Vickers, an intelligent and expressive tenor with the necessary vocal weight and dramatic insight (♦Opera d'Oro 1140).

Sills, always a one-woman coloratura spectacular, fails as Norma—too light of voice, without the necessary grandeur. Verrett is an exciting Adalgisa, but Enrico di Giuseppe is unpleasant of voice and character and Plishka a very ordinary Oroveso. **Levine** leads the New Philharmonia in a vigorous verismo performance (EMI).

Scotto makes the most of the text, with much insight into character. Although her voice is sometimes squally on top and elsewhere under too much pressure, she sings a beautiful Norma, particularly impressive in pianissimo passages. Troyanos is a delicate Adalgisa who blends well with Scotto, but the unpleasant voice of Giuseppe Giacomini is a serious drawback—strangulated, squeezed, though impressively involved in the drama. Plishka sounds less secure than in his 1973 recording with Sills. **Levine** here has softened his approach to the music, still dramatically intense, but with more attention to the lyric line (Sony).

Jane Eaglen has a voice of Wagnerian proportions and sails through the role with plenty of power and ease, rich-toned throughout with a soaring top, but there's little dramatic depth, plenty of anger but little tragedy. Mei's chirping coloratura is all wrong for Adalgisa; she gets the notes, but her voice is too great a contrast to the heft of Eaglen. **Muti** rushes the music unmercifully with many flounders as a result; the cuts are insensitive and incomprehensible (EMI).

Il Pirata. A Carnegie Hall concert performance in 1959 is **Callas**'s only recording of Imogene, and the dramatic tension is almost palpable, a lesson in dramatic and musical artistry. Unhappily, Pier Miranda Ferraro and Constantino Ego are inadequate for their roles. Their field is verismo, and they can't negotiate even the simplest coloratura, often preferring to "impress" with bellowed high notes. The opera is cruelly cut, probably to accommodate the deficiencies of the tenor and baritone, but the chorus and orchestra perform well under **Rescigno**'s considerate guidance (♦EMI 66432, 2CD).

The most noted exponent of the role was Caballé. Her performance with the forces of RAI Rome, led by **Gavazzeni**, is handsomely sung. Ease of production and sheer beauty of tone, always Caballé's hallmarks, are heard at their finest. Except for some brilliant top notes Bernabé Marti is rough and raw, musically foursquare. Piero Cappuccilli not only sings beautifully but creates a dramatically tense Ernesto as well (EMI 64169, 2CD). A 1967 performance from Florence is even better (and at a bargain price). The recorded sound isn't as good as the studio-recorded EMI, but it will do nicely. Caballé is even more spectacular, her top voice in particular ringing and clear as well as her usual pianissimo singing. Cappuccilli is again a fine Ernesto. The big improvement is Flaviano Labo, whose attractive timbre is much to be preferred to Marti's. **Franco Capuana** guides the show with a sure hand (♦Opera d'Oro 1179, 2CD).

A 1994 recording from the Berlin Opera again finds **Aliberti** in a leading Bellini role, with no improvement over her other recordings. Stuart Neill and Roberto Frontali have attractive and agile voices, but without an Imogene worth listening to, the recording is nothing (Berlin).

I Puritani. Bellini's last opera (1835) calls for four singers of great technical capability, musicianship, and dramatic understanding. Of these the tenor role is the most extraordinary, demanding a voice capable of ascending to stratospheric heights, including a high F.

Callas, as usual in bel canto roles, is a major force to be reckoned with. Her vocal colorations continue to astound, and the somewhat limited drama of the text is given full force. The coloratura fireworks aren't treated as mindless display; they're integrated into a dramatic whole, sung not with bright, tweety, mindlessness but with a darkly shaded intensity. Di Stefano is an impassioned Arturo, but too often treats the role as verismo drama, screeching out the high notes with bold abandon. Panerai cuts a dashing figure as Riccardo, distinct of vocal color, if without Callas's keen insight in textual interpretation. Rossi-Lemeni goes for the drama if not for the vocal subtleties. Although **Serafin** sanctions too many cuts in the score, he leads a serious, carefully laid out performance, respecting the piece's emotion and the needs of the singers (♦EMI 56275, 3CD). An earlier Callas stage performance from Mexico City in 1952 can also be heard. She's triumphant, but her colleagues (di Stefano, Piero Campolonghi, Roberto Silva) and conductor (**Guido**

Picco) lose badly; the recording is very much a trial to the ear and sensibilities (Melodram).

In an RAI Rome performance, Freni and Pavarotti are at the top of their form, with much ardent, beautiful singing. Sesto Bruscantini and Bonaldo Giaiotti are sturdy and respectable as Riccardo and Giorgio, and **Muti** is a strong conductor (Nuova Era 2342, 3CD). This performance is also available on Legato 512, but it should be avoided; its technical quality is unbelievably bad.

Sutherland's first recording of the opera (1963) isn't available on CD, but it was almost a total loss, with only the beauty of her voice to be commended. Her colleagues are reliable at best, and **Bonynge** smothers the show in detail even while making unnecessary cuts. A 1973 remake is far superior. Sutherland remains in as fine a voice as earlier, and Bonynge has loosened up to give the opera more drive. The big improvement is Luciano Arturo; he attempts the high F (it's reasonably good) and has no difficulty with the other high notes. It's a robust performance with lots of excitement. There is a strong and sturdy Riccardo from Piero Cappuccilli, and Ghiaurov gives a gloriously sung Giorgio (♦Decca 417588, 3CD).

Rudel leads the London Philharmonic in the most complete edition and the most tightly controlled version. Like it or not, he demands and gets his way, with the singers often walking on the edge, courting vocal disaster—but it never happens. Sills isn't in her best voice here, but she's the most dramatic Elvira since Callas. Gedda struts with vocal elegance except for a train-whistle high F. Louis Quilico's burly baritone casts Riccardo in the Verdi mode, but Plishka's Giorgio is too pedestrian to be effective (EMI 34073, 3CD).

The performance led by **Muti** is almost as textually complete. He molds his forces into a coherent whole, with special effectiveness in the sustained lyric passages. Caballé sings Elvira with exquisite artistry, gentle, poignant, gracefully at ease. Kraus has the secure technique for Arturo's demands, but his voice isn't always ingratiating. Matteo Manuguerra sings a rich, darkly colored Riccardo, the best on record (EMI 69663, 3CD).

Except for some chancy top notes, Gruberová's coloratura is right on target; she's an expressive musician, paying careful attention to the text as well. Justin Lavender is an elegant Arturo, comfortable with all of Bellini's long lines and all the way to the top of the range, although he doesn't attempt the infamous high F. There's too much gravel and grit in Ettore Kim's voice for pleasant listening, but he does belt out the theatrics when given an opportunity, a glaring contrast to Francesco Ellero D'Artegna's somnolent Giorgio. **Fabio Luisi** keeps the show lively, with enough energetic pulse to prevent the long lines from sagging (Nightingale 070562, 3CD).

La Sonnambula. The only real comedy among Bellini's operas, *La Sonnambula* offers a real challenge in its leading role—the seemingly impossible combination of a prima donna singing a simple country girl. And yet it's exactly that impossibility that Callas accomplished. She recorded the role in the studio, and there are several stage accounts as well. Of these, the best is a 1955 La Scala performance led by **Bernstein**. Here she creates a truly living human being, an adolescent in emotion and voice, with every word, every note, expressing the character. Almost as impressive is Valletti's Elvino, idiomatically, romantically sung, with intelligence, although he transposes down from the role's originally stratospheric keys. Bernstein opens many of the traditional cuts and supports his singers with exceptional clarity (♦EMI 56278, 2CD, with the best sound; Opera d'Oro 1139, 2CD, with the best price; Myto

890.06). In Callas's studio recording, **Votto** leads the La Scala musicians in a routine performance, not bad, but with little of Bernstein's insight (EMI).

Almost by default, Scotto was the great successor to Callas in the role of Amina. In a 1961 performance in Venice, she and her Elvino, Kraus, sing spectacularly, both carefully calculating their musical and dramatic effects and without real depth of humanity. Ivo Vinco is an insipid Rodolfo. **Santi** sanctions the traditional cuts, and otherwise leads a controlled performance (Golden Age of Opera)

In the first of Sutherland's two recordings, we're given for the first time a carefully reconstructed full version of the opera, with many corrections to the score and innumerable cuts restored by **Bonynge.** It's academically correct, but far less successful in its emotional qualities. Sutherland is in a soft-focus haze vocally, her characterization wilted and faint, although she brightens up for the faster passages. Monti isn't up to the technical demands of his role, short in the top range, and he uses the traditional transpositions. Corena is a bumbling opera buffa Rodolfo; funny, yes, but with little humanity. Bonynge stresses the details, and the Maggio Musicale Fiorentino orchestra plays quite well but never escapes blandness (Decca). Sutherland's second recording (1980) reveals a decline in vocal powers, but experience brought her confidence and musical superiority, though she was still in a dramatic haze. Pavarotti's beautifully toned but insensitive interpretation of Elvino strangely contrasts with Ghiaurov's aristocratic Rodolfo. Bonynge conducts a stronger, more sympathetic performance than before (Decca 417424, 2CD).

A 1992 concert performance at the Concertgebouw offers good if not outstanding principals and sells at an inexpensive price. Orgonasova sings with assurance, pleasant and round of tone, but with little attention to the text. Raul Giménez is stylish with an easy top; he sings Elvino in the traditional transpositions. The secondary characters here are a real liability. **Zedda** leads the Netherlands Radio folk in a sagging, too-restrained performance blighted by silences where (presumably) audience applause has been technically removed (Naxos).

In a 1994 performance, Patrizia Ciofi is a pleasantly lightweight Amina, lacking coloratura fire. Even with Elvino's music transposed down, Giuseppe Morino still struggles mightily, strained and often strangulated. **Giuliano Carella** makes the chorus and orchestra into the real stars of the show, conducting sensitively with attention to details and flow of line (Nuova Era).

La Straniera. Both of Bellini's operatic failures (*La Straniera* and *Zaira*) were composed in the same year (1829), with their premieres a mere three months apart. All of the recordings are from stage performances. A 1968 performance in Palermo is graced by the sprightly Alaide of **Scotto,** in fine voice, lightly sailing through the coloratura, with as much drama as she can find in the piece. Elena Zilio carefully attempts the intricacies of Isoletta's music, generally with success. Tenor Renato Cioni works hard, but with less success. Domenico Trimarchi sings strongly with a fitting menace to his voice (Melodram 27039; Verona 27097, 2CD).

Caballé was a specialist in the softly floated intricacies of bel canto, and she is at her considerable best in a 1969 American Opera Society concert presentation in New York. Amedeo Zambon is brazen, loud, and wrong, but quite exciting. Bianca Maria Casoni and Vicente Sardiniero are on the rough side, but this fits in quite well with conductor **Guadagno**'s view of the opera as fast and furious. Still, this is Caballé's show, and she's quite spectacular. The sound is dis-

tant, probably recorded from the audience (Melodram 270.11; ♦Gala 100.516, 2CD).

A 1971 performance from Catania finds **Souliotis** driving hard at Bellini's delicate embroidery, as do her colleagues, Veriano Luchetti and Ugo Savarese. Only Elena Zilio attempts anything like bel canto singing (Giuseppe Di Stefano, 2CD). A performance from Trieste is respectable, not the ultimate in coloratura display but better than many. Except for a slight hardening of tone on top, **Aliberti** acquits herself quite well (better than in her other Bellini recordings). Her voice here is flexible and graceful, and she's a first-rate musician. Sara Mingardo sings Isoletta with a mountainous contralto voice; Vincenzo Bello wends his way through the vocal intricacies with ease, but his is a swallowed tenor tone, unpleasant to hear (Fonit Cetra).

Zaira. In a 1976 performance from Catania, Scotto in the title role makes a strong case for one of Bellini's neglected operas; she understands the bel canto style and injects it with drama. Too bad her colleagues do not, though **Danilo Belardinelli** leads an exciting show (Myto 971.151, 2CD). A second (1990) recording from Catania has better sound and a generally stronger cast. The problem here is the exchange of Scotto for Ricciarelli, who makes some pretty sounds but works her way with difficulty when ascending to the top voice or putting pressure on notes. Ramon Vargas sings a handsome Corismino and Simone Alaimo is a sophisticated Orosmane. **Paolo Olmi** coaxes excellent playing from his orchestra, suitable for the drama and the bel canto style (Nuova Era 6982, 2CD).   PARSONS

Richard Rodney Bennett *(b. 1936)*

Bennett is one of the most prolific and successful British composers of music in a large variety of styles, from opera to stage and incidental music, music for films (notably *Far from the Madding Crowd*), symphonies, concertos, church music, and chamber and keyboard works. He has also enjoyed a celebrated life in New York as a jazz pianist and cabaret artist, but this is just one side of a prodigiously talented musical persona. His versatility and talent make him the true heir to the traditions of Walton and Arnold, with whom his music shares many traits.

A good place to start exploring the range of Bennett's music is **James dePreist**'s disc of his Symphony 3, Violin Concerto, and *Diversions* (Koch 37341). The *Diversions* are light and airy, almost in English pastoral style, in contrast to the urbane, nocturnal Violin Concerto (played by Vadim Guzman) and the silky symphony. The concerto retains vestiges of Bennett's flirtation with the serial avant-garde in his early days, but his commitment to tonality (or at least to tonal centers) now seems unshakeable. In similar vein is the Concerto for Solo Percussion and Orchestra (1990), played by **Evelyn Glennie** and the Scottish Chamber Orchestra under Paul Daniel (RCA 61277, with music by Milhaud, Ney Rosauro and Akira Miyoshi). Percussion concertos seem to be all the rage now, and this one contains all the excitement and energy you would expect from composer and soloist.

An interesting release of wind music played by the RNCM Wind Orchestra conducted by **Timothy Reynish** is well worth exploring for two pieces, the bluesy *Elegy for Miles Davis,* which forms part of Bennett's Trumpet Concerto and is a must for all jazz enthusiasts, and the lovely tone poem *The Four Seasons,* which again shows all the dynamic and mood contrasts that typify him at his nocturnal best (Doyen 037, with a work by Irwin Bazelon). Still on the jazz theme, Bennett has collaborated with jazz saxophonist **John Harle,** who premiered and recorded his *Concerto for Stan Getz* (RCA).

Bennett has composed less of late, but his 1995 *Partita for Orchestra* was recorded by **Nicholas Cleobury** (BBC 1, with Britten's *Sinfonia*). The disc also contains some TV music, *Enchanted April,* and four of his *Jazz Songs,* in which the composer is both pianist and vocalist. The *Partita* is finely proportioned, cool and elegant with just a hint of the American pastorale (e.g., Barber's *Knoxville,* Sowerby's *Prairie*).

Not much of Bennett's film music is in print at the moment, but his score to the British TV series based on Mervyn Peake's *Gormenghast,* while not his very best effort in the genre, still possesses dramatic force and strength (Sony). JOHNSON

Alban Berg *(1885–1935)*

Berg used to be categorized as the romanticist of the Schoenberg circle: Gerald Abraham famously called him "more artist than doctrinaire." Two elements of Berg's music have conspired to make some of his works (including *Wozzeck* and the Violin Concerto) staples of the 20th century repertory: his unquenchable taste for things dramatic (he was a stage composer at heart, and even his instrumental works are theatrical, even operatic in conception) and his obsessive interest in musical autobiography. Yet it's significant that nay-sayers like Pierre Boulez have come around to Berg over the past 30 years or so. Boulez wrote the following account of his "conversion" in 1976: "There was a lot more to Berg than his immediately accessible romanticisms. What thrilled me as I went along was the complexity of his mind: the number of internal correspondences, the intricacy of his musical construction, the esoteric character of many of his references, the density of texture, that whole universe in perpetual motion."

ORCHESTRAL MUSIC

Chamber Concerto for violin, piano, and 13 winds is Berg's most rigorous and challenging, and thus his most Schoenbergian, work. The first of **Boulez**'s two recordings, with Saschko Gawriloff and Barenboim (Sony 68331), isn't played and recorded with the almost maniacal control and textural clarity of the 1977 Ensemble InterContemporain performance with Zukerman and Barenboim (DG 447405). There's a refreshing spontaneity in the former, but you soon notice how awkward the violinist's vibrato sounds next to the very straight tone of the wind ensemble, and also how the engineer has put some of those players in your lap.

The DG account is uncompromising, intransigent, technically impeccable, and not particularly likeable—this seems a different conductor than the one who less than two years later gave us such a sensuous and moving rendition of the three-act *Lulu.* The Parisian forces are recorded with dry, precise clarity: You could easily follow a single instrument through the entire performance, which may make this the choice for those studying the work. This disc also has a rare coupling in Berg's brief four Pieces for clarinet and piano Op. 5: Antony Pay and Barenboim are fine advocates, but Barenboim's Piano Sonata Op. 1 strikes me as turgid and sometimes rhythmically unfocused.

Sinopoli offers a diametrically opposed view, with wind players from the Staatskapelle Dresden and soloists Reiko Watanabe and Andrea Lucchesini, the greater flexibility and romanticism hinging as much on the loose church acoustic as on the more obvious variety of tempos (Teldec 18155). The concerto element is to the fore: Lucchesini is the most vibrant presence in this work since Richter (see below), and the winds are more a molded group than a coming together of soloists (as per Boulez). But a tendency to rush over Berg's structural junctures

lessens the cumulative impact of the music, especially the Adagio, which takes on a busy and bloated quality.

Paul Crossley and György Pauk recorded the Chamber Concerto with the London Sinfonietta and **David Atherton,** a performance that has a better structural grasp than Sinopoli's but strikes me as fussy in its detailing and unnatural in its multi-miked aural perspectives (London/Decca). **Claudio Abbado,** Stern, and Peter Serkin strike a kind of compromise between the Boulez and Sinopoli approaches, and their recording must be first choice (♦Sony 64504). Serkin is magnificent, uncovering details all other pianists have passed over and responding with sensitivity to Berg's harmonic language. Abbado is just as adept at larger musical paragraphing, but Stern has unsteady moments, as he does in the coupling, his 1962 version of the Violin Concerto with Bernstein (see below).

The performance by **Dennis Russell Davies** and the German Wind Soloists is probably the most flexible and musical (Bayer). Their sonority is rich and pleasing, and Davies is a more thoughtful pianist than Barenboim, though at times too deferential toward his partners. The coupling, however, is not very satisfying: Hans Georg Pflüger's *Metamorphosen* (1988) makes an appropriate and unusual if not particularly memorable makeweight. **Vladimir Válek** and his players don't achieve the turn-on-a-dime crispness of the Ensemble InterContemporain or London Symphony winds (Praga). The Czechs tend to get bogged down in the more emphatic moments of the score, and Jean-François Heisser doesn't provide the same feats of rhythmic dovetailing as Barenboim. Peter Csaba is a soulful violinist, but he sounds insecure and tentative next to Zukerman and Stern.

In a 1977 live recording by Richter, Kagan, and a Moscow Conservatory wind ensemble conducted by Yuri **Nicolaievsky,** Richter's piano is prominent in the mix, as you might expect (in "Sviatoslav Richter: un Portrait," ♦EMI 64429, 4CD). I've heard other players give Berg's waltz and ländler rhythms more Viennese charm, but this rather single-minded reading offers a blistering experience that won't soon be forgotten. The disc includes some applause at the end.

Orchestral Pieces Op. 6. **Ashkenazy** elicits an ungimmicky, honest performance of the three pieces from the Deutsches Symphonie-Orchester (London/Decca). It has neither the grandiose sweep of Karajan nor Boulez's unfailing attention to balance and detail, but the sound is probably the most natural on disc in this difficult-to-balance work. **Levine** and his unsurpassed Met Orchestra deliver Op. 6 with almost supernatural warmth and finesse, even suavity—but shouldn't this music sound more effortful, more apocalyptic (Sony)? Levine's couplings (*Wozzeck* fragments and *Lulu Suite* with Renée Fleming, see below) are also very sophisticated and urbane.

In this disc Levine doesn't sound like the same musician who gave us a cooler and plainer, less mannered 1987 rendition with the Berlin Philharmonic (DG). This was recorded in a Berlin church rather than the Philharmonie, and the trenchant, exciting, and impeccably prepared performance is undermined by the sound—a bit eccentric in balance, the trumpets inscrutably distant and the first-desk violins very close, the strings even changing distance in the mix. The couplings are Webern's Op. 6 and Schoenberg's Op. 16, and my only reservations concern Levine's rather overwrought account of the Webern, especially as he chooses the bloated original (1909) orchestration.

Boulez has recorded Op. 6 twice, both times with the BBC Symphony. The second fills out Zukerman's 1987 rendition of the Violin Concerto (♦Sony 68331, see below). In this 1984 rendition the conductor goes full tilt in a massive and cataclysmic reading where anything less than Boulez's acute ear and podium technique would tempt disaster. The earlier performance sounds comparatively labored, with less assured pacing and execution (Sony, with Boulez's earlier rendition of Chamber Concerto). Some listeners might prefer the analog sound to the slightly glassy digital version, but the earlier performance is tenuous by comparison.

Colin Davis and the Bavarian Radio Symphony fill out Kremer's Violin Concerto with an ill-focused Op. 6; I've heard American college orchestras do a better job with this score, and the apocalyptic hammer-blows in the finale are almost inaudible (Philips). **Dorati**'s London Symphony gave a better account of itself in a 1962 rendition (Mercury, with *Lulu Suite,* Schoenberg's Op. 16, and Webern's Pieces Op. 10). Wilma Cozart's 35mm film recording is fine: You can hear just about every detail, and the balances are much more natural than in Levine's DG issue. Still, the interpretation isn't settled enough to allow the music its cinematic evocations.

Abbado has made two recordings. The 1970 performance with the London Symphony has its good points but also a few oddities (like the intrusive drum at the opening of I), and it was recorded in the inappropriately dry acoustic of a film studio (DG). His 1992 remake is more settled as a performance (some 70 per cent longer!), and the Vienna Philharmonic with their unequaled strings and narrow-bore winds and brass fill the score with a variety of colors no other ensemble can manage (♦DG 445846).

Karajan is unmatched in this music: He and his Berliners convey the unearthly intimacy of the quieter moments of this score and also Berg's tremendous, post-Mahlerian sweep like no others (♦DG 457760). Even in the densest, pile-driving climaxes, the orchestral textures are coherent and well balanced. This was taped in the good old Jesus-Christus Church in Berlin-Dahlem, a favorite DG venue of the '60s, and the sound strikes just the right balance between detail and atmosphere.

Violin Concerto. **Zukerman** and Boulez are among the finest. There's a fascinating give and take to this unusual partnership, the modern and romantic temperaments alternately offsetting and controlling one another. Boulez's handling of the difficult and often very spare orchestral part is a cause for wonder—impulsive yet perfectly balanced and paced, cohesive yet improvisational. The earlier release (♦CBS 39741) is preferable to the "Boulez Edition" mastering (Sony 68331), since the latter introduces a half-second drop-out at 13:23 in the last movement, and as a coupling substitutes Boulez's earlier and less desirable rendition of *Orchestral Pieces.*

Kremer and Davis identify more with the devastating emotional "message" of the concerto, and Kremer digs deeper beneath the music's surface—indeed, he makes every note speak with its own particular affect and tonal profile (♦Philips 412523). The recording still sounds good, but unfortunately Davis and the Bavarian Radio Symphony are disappointingly scattershot in the *Orchestral Pieces* that fills out the disc. **Stern** and Bernstein are coarse, at times technically insecure, and certainly not a first choice, but still offer a humanity that has eluded other advocates; it makes a fairly worthy makeweight for Abbado's magnificent Chamber Concerto.

Zehetmair gives a detailed and impassioned reading, but is hampered by Holliger's inorganic tempo choices and the amateurish, inconsistent balancing of the Philharmonia (Teldec). Sinopoli has a vibrant and dead-on soloist in **Reiko Watanabe,** but as with Holliger there are indications that the conductor hasn't stood back to bring the score's de-

tails together into a larger whole (Teldec). **Frank Peter Zimmerman** and Gianluigi Gelmetti create some very affecting dovetailing in the earlier parts of the concerto, and this taut and well-proportioned interpretation reaches some fantastically impassioned climaxes further on (EMI). Only in the transfiguration and chorale are they rather flat, without quite Kremer's or Perlman's raptness.

Kyung-Wha Chung is a catalog standby in her rendition with Solti (London/Decca). Both pungent and soulful in II (with its death struggle followed by transfiguration), the Chicago Symphony is idiomatic in this music, even if Solti's interpretation lacks charm in the folkish moments and Chung is over-miked. **Perlman** is often touchingly childlike with his sweet tone, he varies his rhythm nicely, and he's not as obviously over-miked as Chung (♦DG 447445). Ozawa brings unusual rhythmic tension to the orchestral contribution, and builds the work to a true climax in II.

There are contrasts to be drawn between **Mutter** and those two super-virtuosos (♦DG 437093). She brings a restraint to this score that proves moving, holding back almost to a whisper at the beginning, and the DG engineers balance her realistically. Levine and his players have just as sure a grip on Berg's argument and offer just as much variety of nuance as the soloist: In both solo and orchestral accounts, this is one of the very best performances. The sound is unusually transparent and realistic and gives a good account of the Medinah Temple acoustic.

If sound quality isn't particularly important, Webern's 1937 recording with **Louis Krasner** (who commissioned the work) is unforgettable (♦Continuum 1004; Testament). Webern was scheduled to conduct the premiere in Barcelona the previous year but bowed out at the last moment, probably because he was overwhelmed by the circumstances—the first performance of his friend's musical testament. He gave this great work its most unabashedly romantic reading when he returned to the piece in London in 1937. You remember the phrasing in particular: He coaxed unbelievably long and gorgeous phrases from his players, and the music gives the rare sense of seeking out its own space and its own (slow) tempos. Just watch out for the sound, which derives from Krasner's 50-year-old personal acetates.

In addition to a Cleveland recording with Rodzinski (which Sony should reissue), another invaluable Krasner performance has circulated on a GM CD with Fritz Busch conducting the Stockholm Philharmonic. Here also, the interpretive freedom calls into question the authenticity claimed by some of today's academic, dry-as-dust performances of the Second Vienna School. This listener is struck not only by Krasner's skill but also by the liberties taken: Busch's freedom with the opening pulse, Krasner's touch of Viennese schmalz at the rustic ländler passage in the first movement, the fluidity in the chorale. The orchestra is very indistinct, the upper strings particularly elusive. The No-Noise system removed what must have been plentiful surface noise, but not much treble is left, there are a few large drops in volume, and the first bar is missing. As the coupling, Krasner plays another work he introduced, the Schoenberg concerto. Here Mitropoulos is the powerful, incisive, and fiercely confident conductor, and there are no problems with the 1954 radio recording apart from a little dryness. **Szeryng** made a recording in Munich with Kubelik and his Bavarian Radio Symphony that, typically for this conductor, sounds unusually casual in its choice of tempos (DG). The soloist, though, is touchingly beautiful and aristocratic.

CHAMBER MUSIC

String Quartet Op. 3. The **Brindisi Quartet** (Metronome) offers a remarkable reading of this early work: There's a sense of emotional trajectory in each movement and some real drama without a wiry ensemble sound. This British group recognizes Berg's lyricism and gives the piece a Mahlerian intensity. I also love their way with the couplings: Schoenberg's Quartet 2 and Webern's Op. 5 and early *Langsamer Satz*.

Lyric Suite (chamber version). A very fine performance by the **Juilliard Quartet** is full of original interpretive details (♦Sony 66840). For example, I've never heard quite so much pointillistic detailing in the *misterioso* III, and V is much more than an angry, virtuoso blur. The two Janáček quartets are the coupling, and there the Juilliard is more controversial: skittish and claustrophobic, the slower melodic sections coming across as aberrations on the face of disturbing, unpredictable music. The Juilliard also recorded *Lyric Suite* in 1961, when Robert Mann's intonation was more dependable and the group had a more tight vibrato (RCA). In both accounts, the quartet plays Berg's heartsick Zemlinsky quote at the end of the fourth movement with pliable phrasing and true sensitivity.

The remarkable **Vogler Quartet** is even more consistently recommendable (♦RCA 60855). They are more technically assured than the latter-day Juilliard, and they push the music to greater extremes than the Alban Berg Quartet (see below), though without the touching wistfulness of the latter and without quite managing to make Berg's finale the work's touchstone. Also, *Orchestral Pieces* would have been a far better discmate than Verdi's quartet, which comes from an entirely different tradition. The French **Ludwig Quartet** presents a *Lyric Suite* that's efficient without either dispatching the more complex passages with perfect clarity or infusing the moments of heartsick nostalgia with real blend and tonal beauty (Timpani). They do score highly, though, for their appropriate coupling: Dutilleux's *Ainsi la nuit* (1977), a suite-like sequence of shorter movements in a chromatic language similar to Berg's and a similar nocturnal, Baudelairean landscape, a fascinating work.

A more predictable pairing comes from the **Duke Quartet,** who offer the sextet version of Schoenberg's *Verklärte Nacht* alongside a *Lyric Suite* that's so self-consciously beautiful and lyrical as to lose its rhythmic backbone (Collins). A 1936 recording by the **Galimir Quartet** is of historic interest (Continuum, with Krasner's irreplaceable account of the concerto). The group handles the complex score with assurance, and the recording offers evidence of the freedom, almost romanticism, with which musicians essayed Berg's music before WWII. But it's not a reading of particular insight or authority—the finale is particularly wanting in tension—and the 78 surfaces are swishy.

I turn now to discs that contain both Berg's quartet and *Lyric Suite.* For some years, the **LaSalle Quartet** pairing was a catalog staple (DG, in a 4CD Second Viennese School box including an impressive book culled by musicologist Ursula von Rauchhaupt from the composer's sketches, diaries, and letters). The group brings great authority and insight to the music. They're extremely scrupulous in observing details of the score, but they're not particularly interested in Berg's romanticism, and the players were miked for detail in a dry acoustic that doesn't fall easily on the ear. The **Schoenberg Quartet** offers some interpretive insights, but the disc makes for difficult listening because of the leader's undependable intonation high up, and the murky, two-dimensional sound (Koch).

The young **Artis Quartet** offers the kind of lush performances rarely heard outside of daydreams (Orfeo). They're almost faultless in intonation, their corporate sound beautiful and impeccably blended. But they withdraw too much at Berg's requests for a slower tempo, so the discourse becomes listless and the structures flaccid, and there is a strange

lack of bloom and edge to the sound, as if everyone were using gut strings with no rosin. But they are much more attuned to Berg's strangely beautiful commingling of romanticism and modernism than the **Arditti Quartet,** who neglect the romantic elements of both pieces (Montaigne). The Abbey Road studio sound is too small and dry: This is chamber writing at its most orchestral, and the music needs more space.

The **Alban Berg Quartet,** who taped their namesake's two chamber pieces twice, is more successful. The later version never made it to American shores (EMI), but their 1974 recording is remarkable for its poise, beautiful playing, sensitivity, and unfailing sense of proportion (♦Teldec 21967, with Webern's Op. 5 and Op. 9 and a quartet by Erich Urbanner). Nothing is overstated, and Berg's precise score indications don't call attention to themselves as they do in the LaSalle recording, yet nothing is lacking. They have a sweet sound and an aristocratic yet intense approach, both of which really suit the obsessive autobiographical romanticism of *Lyric Suite.* If a single recording of this pairing could be recommended, it's this one.

Lyric Suite (string-orchestra version). Among the recordings of these three movements from the chamber original, **Karajan's** stands out for its gripping hyper-expressiveness, though the rather dry sound takes some getting used to (♦DG 457760). **Ashkenazy** doesn't shy away from Berg's aural luxuries and molds the phrases with marked rubato (London/Decca). Such an approach is perfect for the seven Early Songs that also appear on his disc (see below), but he stretches the structures of the outer *Lyric Suite* pieces a bit too much. **Abbado** and the Vienna Philharmonic strings strike the perfect compromise between linear thinking and harmonic lushness, and their disc is perfectly engineered (♦DG 447749). An unforgettable rendition.

Gielen produces an impeccable performance, as always, though his Cincinnati strings don't have the varied color shadings of the Vienna or the specific gravity of the Berlin (Vox). Rather better is his ultra-cheap but very well recorded release from Baden-Baden and the SWF Symphony, though here he does tend toward a certain haste in the first piece (Arte Nova). His *Allegro misterioso,* the movement that's all but impossible to hold together when taken up to tempo and with a full body of strings, qualifies as the most lucid and best drilled on record. **Boulez** and the New York strings are more neutral in their emotional commitment (Sony).

PIANO MUSIC

As with Berg's early songs, his juvenilia for piano are now being explored. Though some (such as the C minor *Klavierstück* from 1908) have an impassioned Brahmsian romanticism, most only help to confirm his reputation as a late bloomer. **Elisabeth Klein** includes a good deal of the juvenilia, including some works that were obviously formal exercises written under Schoenberg's supervision, in her set of the "complete" piano music of Berg, Schoenberg, and Webern (Classico, 2CD). Unfortunately, this Bartok student sounds past her prime, and her performances (which include Sonata Op. 1) are lumpy, slow, and incoherent. **Jean-Jacques Dunki** recorded a far better disc of Berg's early piano works, but that has disappeared from the catalog (Jecklin).

Piano Sonata Op. 1. **Jean-Francois Heisser** does a good job but doesn't include the exposition repeat, which is necessary because of the new context it creates for the opening cadential progression (Praga). His disc is filled out with the Chamber Concerto led by Válek (see above) and Berg's own rather makeshift four-hand arrangement of the Quartet, which is certainly no replacement for the original score. **Perahia,** as always, is disarmingly sincere and marvelous in the *cantabile* elements of the Sonata: He opens up the traces of Schubertian, Viennese lyricism in Berg's writing (in a Perahia retrospective, ◆Sony 63380, 4CD). **Pollini** is more stringent, presses forward more urgently, in following Berg's structural argument (DG). This makes for a fantastic development section, but elsewhere the music wants more variety, light, and shade. The piano is also strangely lacking in bass response.

In a contrasting 1958 studio recording, **Gould** is never afraid to slow down to make a point (Sony). While he's thus able to articulate Berg's structure like few others, the piece sounds too heavy and world-weary for a work written by a 23-year-old. It's when we go back to Gould's earlier performances that we can relish his youthful spontaneity and superhuman textural finesse. He recorded the piece in 1953 for the Canadian Hallmark label, but that has disappeared. A lovingly remastered disc of a 1952 CBC broadcast performance has astonishing passion, and this—despite the limited sound—must be the central recommendation for everyone except the audiophile (◆CBC 2008, with just as astonishing performances of Schoenberg and Webern, in sound even more primitive than the Sonata). A slightly more collected performance, better recorded, came from a lecture-recital Gould gave in Moscow in 1957 (◆Chant du Monde 278799). He drops the repeat, probably because of time constraints, but the rendition still accounts for Berg's youthful fire and voice-leading subtleties like no other—someone needs to reissue this performance immediately.

Finally, don't miss Dutch composer Theo Verbey's stunning orchestration of the sonata, heard as a coupling for Chailly and the Concertgebouw's Mahler 1 (London/Decca). The arrangement is so idiomatic and engrossing that it comes across as a long-lost orchestral treasure from the young Berg.

OPERAS

Lulu. There has been only one studio recording of the complete three-act *Lulu,* by Boulez, in conjunction with the 1979 Paris Opera premiere of the Cerha edition (◆DG 463617, 3CD). Chereau's revisionist staging raised a lot of hackles—he set the last scene in a *pissoire*—but the critics had nothing but praise for Stratas's intense, smart, flesh-and-blood Lulu and Boulez's meticulous if still moving account of Berg's longest score. If the recording has a drawback, it's an overall seriousness that rather short-changes some of the more ridiculous or flippant aspects of Wedekind's characters—though the farce of Act 2 comes off very well when the performance is so tight and sure of itself. Franz Mazura as Schön, though extremely sure musically, is a monochrome and unnuanced grouch, rolling his R's and delivering each line as if he had got up on the wrong side of the bed. Riegle is Alwa, very sure and agile but rather dry of voice and annoying as a character. Tear makes a rather wimpy Painter—maybe appropriate to the character, but such a naive man's death seems too tragic even for Wedekind—and he doesn't inspire the necessary fear when he returns in Act 3 as the homicidal Negro.

But then there are definite cast assets to offset such complaints: Minton is a beautiful and noble Geschwitz, Gerd Nienstedt is the best and most buffoonish Rodrigo on records, and Toni Blankenheim a carousing, wildly asthmatic Schigolch. Boulez is peerless in bringing the score together and balancing textures—more complex and changeable here than in *Wozzeck.* This isn't a perfect rendition, but it's worth hearing especially for Stratas's incisiveness: When she answers Schön's threats in her "Lied der Lulu," you're sure this is a woman who knows herself and her own worth amid all the blind passion that surrounds her.

Live recordings of this complex opera inevitably suffer some obvious blemishes. On the other hand, they also offer a chemistry between the characters not to be heard in studio accounts, even Boulez's. **Tate's** version has an audible stage electricity: for once you understand these cipherish stage people (EMI 54622, 3CD). Patricia Wise is the most believable and human of Lulus, and also has a freer and more agile vocal presence than Stratas, especially high up. She also manages a coquettishness that's not heard elsewhere. Wolfgang Schöne is a fine and upstanding Schön, if not quite as smart and dignified as Berry was for Dohnányi (see below)—much to be preferred to Mazura, at any rate. Graham Clark, the Captain in *Wozzeck,* is an autocratic Painter, Bodo Schwanbek a squally but suitably comic Athlete. Hotter is a memorable Schigolch, though compared with his account for Dohnányi he perhaps overdoes the old character when he seems to be singing with his teeth taken out. Fassbaender is a disappointing Geschwitz: She gives an overloud, hysterical, and all-round unsympathetic account of the character Wedekind once said was his story's central presence. But Peter Straka is a nonpareil Alwa, effortlessly and genuinely *sung.*

I mentioned "live" blemishes: Tate has some shaky moments, including an Act 1 Canon that almost falls apart (despite a cautious tempo) and some big orchestral moments that aren't perfectly coordinated. More seriously, knockabout stage noise interferes, especially in Act 2 Scene 1. Nor does Tate give the score the shape and sense of direction conferred by Boulez; the big orchestral moments are often a bit tenuous, Lulu's all-important cry of "Ah, freedom!" after her liberation doesn't seem quite the climax as with Stratas and Boulez, and he rattles through the preceding Film Music interlude. But those collectors looking above all for a living, breathing theatrical experience will enjoy Tate—and also the recording job, which is eminently natural and "unassisted" even if the percussion and saxophone obbligatos and the hurdy-gurdy in the London scene are often difficult to hear.

Ulf Schirmer directs a cast and orchestra assembled in Copenhagen in 1996 (Chandos 9540, 3CD). The sound is more wide-ranging than for Tate, and Straka again makes a valiant Alwa. But there's even more stage noise than in Tate's production, including some inscrutable additions made by the stage director (on-stage applause in Act 2), and Constance Hauman's small voice barely rises to the demands of Lulu's role in a theater.

Two-act versions of *Lulu* were recorded before Berg's widow died and thereby cleared the way for Cerha's "completion" of the score from the composer's manuscripts. **Dohnányi** had the unequaled Vienna Philharmonic, a huge asset in this heavily orchestral opera, and still audibly in the same orchestral tradition Berg must have had in his inner ear (London, 3CD). The playing is gorgeous, bringing out the Mahlerian ethos as only a *bona fide* concert group can. After hearing these discs, it's hard to go back to the opera house orchestras, though Levine's Met Orchestra runs them close in his *Lulu Suite* (see below). Berry is a magisterial Schön, but Silja is a blank and utterly inert presence as Lulu. Still, given the orchestral glories on display—and the sound picture, realistic if chillier and more empty-concert-hallish than Tate's—it would be a pity if these discs were thought obsolete and allowed to drop forever from the catalogue.

We can safely retire **Böhm's** 1968 account of the two-act torso with the Berlin Opera, even if orchestral and vocal details were rehearsed and placed with a very sure hand (DG). Complaints include—besides the absence of Act 3—uniformly loud, to-the-back-of-the-house delivery from the singers (with lots of hard-pressed final T's), some half-hearted characterizations (though Fischer-Dieskau is a wonderfully Machiavellian Dr. Schön), and a general stiffness of dramaturgy and phrasing.

Evelyn Lear is a prudish, starchy Lulu: I'd rather remember her for her later Met performances as Geschwitz, well played against Stratas's title character. This first recording of *Lulu* reminds us of an era when Berg was more awkward to perform than he has recently become.

For practical reasons, Berg excerpted a five-movement *Lulu Suite* from his opera shortly before he died. We now have several three-act *Lulu* recordings, but even so the suite makes for a more satisfying work on record and in concert than the *Wozzeck* fragments. **Dorati**'s 1961 recording with the London Symphony and soprano Helga Pilarczyk has been superseded for orchestral playing and singing (Mercury). For example, the Met Orchestra and Renée Fleming are stunning in **Levine**'s account (DG, with *Orchestral Pieces*, see above). Fleming and Levine's sumptuous richness in the *Lulu* pieces, with conductor and orchestra taking great care over every appoggiatura and gesture, make this the cleanest and most assured *Lulu* music we've had on record. **Abbado** objects as a matter of principle to posthumous completions, and so has never taped a complete *Lulu* (though his recent recording of the Mozart-Sussmayr *Requiem* might prophesy a change of heart). Apparently in lieu of such a complete edition, he has recorded *Lulu Suite* twice: in London with Margaret Price (DG, with *Orchestral Pieces* and *Altenberg-Lieder*) and in Vienna with Juliane Banse (♦DG 447749, with *Altenberg-Lieder* and three pieces from *Lyric Suite*). He digs deeper into the music in Vienna, and that orchestra has that unreplaceable, *echt-Wienerisch* combination of sweetness and morbidity that allows Berg's strange score to come into focus; this is gorgeous music-making, very well recorded, and an overtaxed Banse is the only drawback.

Boulez and the NY Philharmonic recorded a *Lulu Suite* that, though rather murkily engineered, wins over the Levine by virtue of its earthier approach (♦Sony 45838). Boulez also taps Blegen for a bloodcurdling scream at the heroine's murder, so the moment proves just as dramatic as it does in the opera. Like Abbado in London, **Gielen** uses a Zerlina voice: his Lulu is Battle, who proves astonishingly precise and feverish in "Lied der Lulu" (Vox). The Cincinnati Symphony, though, can't match the luster and tonal weight of the Vienna and New York orchestras.

Wozzeck. Our age seems to hear Berg's and Buechner's *Wozzeck* not as social critique but as music-hall caricature—equal parts Gogol and Benny Hill. **Barenboim**'s uneven performance with the German State Opera Berlin strikes out in a different direction (Teldec). He seems to conceive *Wozzeck* as a Mahlerian symphonic statement with vocal obbligatos. You can hear his much-vaunted debt to Furtwängler in his improvisatory, long-lined way with the interludes and the way he often brings Berg's dynamics way down, making the music teeter on silence.

The singers generally harken back to the days when *Wozzeck* was sung rather than barked. Franz Grundheber is the title character, and is a pleasure to hear even if he's just as inert in characterization as he is in Abbado's recording (see below). Meier brings rich tone to Marie, but she swallows the fate-sealing "Lieber ein Messer" confrontation in Act 2, Scene 3. More serious vocal worries come up with Graham Clark's Captain and Gunter von Kannen's Doctor: The latter is fairly blank, and the former employs some affected tricks that aren't welcome in Berg. The sound is good, but goes for naught what with all the clammering and galumphing and floorboard-squeaking going on.

In 1987, **Abbado** made a live recording at the Vienna State Opera with Grundheber as Wozzeck and Behrens as Marie (DG). It's an undeniably powerful but also grating experience, especially with the dry and one-dimensional sound image, gratuitously wide dynamic range, and lack of any definable acoustic. For better or worse, Abbado cleanses the

music of any sweetness or Viennese veneer. Indeed, Berg's orchestration has never sounded more shrill: Flutes and high oboe passages protrude, while brass outbursts in the Act 1 field scene are simply terrifying. Behrens is tremulous and her diction unclear, but she has real dramatic ability. Grundheber is something of a cipher, Heinz Zednik is predictably agile and neurotic as the Captain, and Aage Haugland is an excellent Doctor.

Neither Abbado nor Barenboim dislodges **Dohnányi**'s account, splendiferously produced with the nonpareil orchestral presence of the Vienna Philharmonic (♦London 417348). There's also plenty of chemistry between the protagonists, Wächter golden-toned and virile (if past his prime) and Silja vocally uneven but vivid and moving. **Kegel**'s 1973 performance is one of the most impeccably sung and coached productions I've heard—an experience to grab you musically and dramatically (Berlin). Its main virtues are some very fine principals. Adam's Wozzeck is confident and superbly pitched, almost lyrical, very clear at top and bottom. Gisela Schröter brings to Marie a strong and sure voice, her diction impeccable and the character feminine and vulnerable yet properly strong-willed. Konrad Rupf's Doctor is superb. The tenors are less dependable, but Leipzig Radio's recording is clean and natural, the audience virtually silent. **Mitropoulos** offered the first recording of *Wozzeck* in a 1951 concert performance taped before a Carnegie Hall audience, and it still has a claim to be the greatest despite some inaccuracies in *Sprechgesang* (♦Sony 62759, 2CD). This is a reading of great dramatic tension but also rare naturalness and musicality, graced by golden-age singing—which makes it a tonic after the vaudevillian *Wozzeck*s we tend to get nowadays. Harrell is the noblest of Wozzecks, his pitch confident and his characterization deeply moving without stooping to agit-prop histrionics. Farrell's Marie is the only performance I've heard truly *sung,* and that counts for a lot in the Bible-reading scene. Joseph Mordino is that rarest of creatures: a Captain with voice and without caricature. All the secondary roles are well done, and the NY Philharmonic—though balanced rather behind the singers—is astonishingly agile. The recording, smooth and very listenable in its remastering, does hide some orchestral detail and won't give you the lump-in-the-throat unison string phrasing in the big D minor interlude that you'll hear in modern studio recordings. Mitropoulos offers Schoenberg's *Erwartung* as the coupling; Dorothy Dow is the admirable soprano there, her period vibrato being the only hint that this isn't a chrome-plated modern rendition.

You can turn elsewhere if you're looking for verismo madness. **Boulez** conducted a famous Paris Opera *Wozzeck* in 1963, where he created a scandal by insisting the work be done in the original German and with all of 35 rehearsals. He recorded the production in 1966, with Isabel Strauss as Marie and Berry as Wozzeck, in a version that was let down by primitive sound and indifferent dramatic work from much of the cast (Sony). At about the same time, **Böhm** made a fine recording with Evelyn Lear, Fischer-Dieskau, and forces of the Deutsche Oper Berlin (♦DG 435705, with Böhm's less successful, two-act *Lulu*). Every detail falls into its proper place, as usual with this conductor, but his exactitude doesn't become oppressive, partly because of Fischer-Dieskau, who proves more vivid and identifiably a stage character than many other recorded Wozzecks. Lear is an unusually accurate Marie and Wunderlich is the ideal Andres, but the rest of the cast doesn't quite *sing* their roles the way Mitropoulos's do (Stolze is particularly hammy as the Captain, coughing and sobbing and sliding in a virtuoso but overbearing way). Mitropoulos gave Berg's phrasing more room to breathe, but many will prefer Böhm's more detailed stereo sound.

SONGS

After a period of neglect, Berg's early songs are gaining in popularity. He wrote dozens of lieder before he began studying composition with Schoenberg; indeed, Schoenberg complained that his student was at first unable to write anything but songs. In a hyper-expressive and chromatic idiom reminiscent of Wolf, these early songs were published (in part) only recently. **Fischer-Dieskau** recorded 19 in 1984 with composer-pianist Aribert Reimann, and this admirable disc is sporadically available as an import, coupled with a similarly adventurous selection of Schoenberg songs (♦EMI 63570). The great baritone fills even such juvenilia with dignity and interest, even if his voice wasn't exactly a vehicle of *fin-de-siècle* sensuousness by the mid-'80s.

Mitsuko Shirai has produced the most comprehensive and far-reaching single-disc collection of early Berg songs yet, accompanied by her pianist husband Hartmut Holl (Capriccio). She includes 12 *Jugendlieder* as well as the better-known seven *Early Songs,* four Songs Op. 2, the two "Schliesse mir die Augen beide" settings, and some others. The sound is excellent and the musicianship impeccable, but her voice has a sameness of shape and production that can wear out its welcome in anything more than small doses. **Norman** recorded *Early Songs* and 12 of Berg's pre-Schoenberg songs as a coupling for her *Altenberg-Lieder* with Boulez (Sony, see below). She sounds disappointingly premeditated in these pieces, and her performance of the pre-Schoenberg songs are arbitrary in line and phrase when compared with Fischer-Dieskau.

In terms of naturalness and unostentatious vocal resources, the finest account of Early Songs comes from **von Otter** and pianist Bengt Forsberg (♦DG 437515, with Korngold's brief Op. 18 lieder and songs by Richard Strauss). Von Otter also recorded Early Songs in Berg's later orchestration, in a very desirable disc conducted by Abbado (♦DG 445846, with *Der Wein* and *Orchestral Pieces*).

Most notable among Berg's pre-WWI works are the Altenberg songs, which followed the Op. 3 quartet that marked the official end of his schooling under Schoenberg and show him heading down an experimental path he quickly abandoned. Abbado's 1970 recording of *Altenberg-Lieder,* with the wildly inappropriate Mozartian voice of **Margaret Price,** gave us a vague idea of how these pieces should sound (DG). More recently, **Brigitte Balleys** and Ashkenazy were the first to record *Altenberg-Lieder* as music rather than curiosities (London/Decca, with *Orchestral Pieces* and the three movements from *Lyric Suite,* see above). Balleys has a sure voice of Wagnerian proportions, a better match for the music than Price's lyric instrument. She dispatches *Early Songs* fluently if with no great individuality, but I enjoyed Ashkenazy's orchestral work in the Altenberg songs, where he (and the Decca engineers) let us savor the felicities of Berg's "striving for effect" that Schoenberg criticized.

I wanted to welcome **Norman**'s three-story mansion of a voice to Berg's music, but I can't warm to her disc of the Altenberg songs, *Early Songs,* and various unpublished early lieder (Sony). Her *Altenberg-Lieder* come off best, since Boulez conducts (all the other songs on the disc are with piano accompaniment) and these adventurous pieces undoubtedly appeal to his modernist esthetic. He does a lot to clarify the heavy, ever-shifting orchestral textures, but there's also a studied quality that makes me prefer the more open, romantic approaches of Balleys/Ashkenazy and Banse/Abbado. Boulez's London Symphony has been miked for clarity, while Ashkenazy and Decca just give us an honest, concert-hall perspective on the music.

Vlatka Orsanic brings ideal clarity and technique to this difficult cycle, and Gielen and his Baden-Baden orchestra achieve a rare degree of success in bringing Berg's myriad and mannered details together into one transparent and cogent musical-literary statement (Arte Nova). Still, they're often rushed to the point of flouting Berg's metronome markings, and they miss much of the cycle's otherworldly mystery and ecstasy. Abbado and **Juliane Banse** supply such mystery in spades and also account for the score's plethora of abstract-expressionist detail (♦DG 447749). Banse is more dependable than in the *Lulu Suite* coupling, and comes closer than most to fulfilling Berg's impossible request to bring some impossibly high notes down to a pianissimo. The Vienna Philharmonic sounds glorious, and this is the most beautiful account yet of these enigmatic settings of Peter Altenberg's "picture postcard" texts.

Berg's concert aria *Der Wein* was a preparatory exercise for *Lulu,* and is one of his most neglected pieces. (T. W. Adorno insisted the composer was embarrassed by the work.) The two recordings are both fine, though the high-frequency edge for **Jessye Norman** in Boulez's CD rather limits its appeal. **Von Otter** brings a more flexible, rather smaller instrument to these slippery settings of Baudelaire, while the sound of Abbado's Vienna Philharmonic is more natural and allows you to hear more of what's going on in the orchestra (♦DG 445846). Their performance also tends to be more impulsive, the jazz inflections sexier and more idiomatic. Still, the Boulez disc is also worth getting for its excellent *Lulu Suite* (see above).   ASHBY

William Bergsma (1921–94)

Bergsma's career included teaching at Juilliard and serving as chair of the School of Music at the University of Washington. His music shows a fastidious sensitivity to the power of sound and a lively sense of harmonic romanticism. There's a quicksilver quality to his work that makes him both fascinating and disturbing, but he's too sensitive to the little moments of life to make the big statements of a William Schuman. His works are mostly found in collections, but a surprising number of discs include them.

One of my favorite Bergsma pieces is his String Quartet 2, a mysterious and uneasy piece from the war years once recorded by the **Walden Quartet** (ARS LP 18, NA). The earliest work presently listed is the short ballet score *Gold and the Señor Commandante* (1941), included in one of **Howard Hanson**'s Eastman-Rochester Symphony discs (Mercury 434307). Described by the composer as "a cheerful and inaccurate recollection of my California homeland during my first year of study in the East," it combines ethnic elements from Spain to China with momentary stops elsewhere. Hanson conducts it with vigor and affection.

Bergsma's music for piano is both early and late. **Jill Timmons**'s disc contains *Three Fantasies, Tangents* (a half-hour collection of 12 varied pieces, written in preparation for the opera *The Wife of Martin Guerre),* and *Variations,* Bergsma's quietly powerful farewell to the instrument (Laurel 852). The sound is close and lacking in ambience, though Timmons makes the best of it, playing with both power and delicacy.

The **Westwood Wind Quintet** has recorded the Concerto for Wind Quintet in a collection of major American wind pieces (Crystal 752), while **Paul Cortese** offers *Fantastic Variations on a theme from Tristan* for viola and piano with John Klibonoff (Crystal 636). These pieces demand both split-second timing and a light, alert musicality, and they're played to the hilt by these artists.

Serenade: To Await the Moon is a curious, quietly unsettling piece for small orchestra demonstrating both Bergsma's evocative power and his restlessness. It's offered by **Anthony Spain** and his Northwest Symphony, which has a rather thin-sounding string section but nonetheless plays with involvement (Albany 184). The Violin Concerto is a larger work, offered by **Edward Statkiewicz** with the Polish Radio & TV Orchestra under Zdzislav Szostak in an intense and lyrical performance in somewhat thin but adequate sound, in a large compendium of little-known American works (Vox 5158, 2CD).

Doriot Anthony Dwyer recorded an unusual disc of flute music with the Manhattan String Quartet, including a beautiful Quintet (Koch 7001, NA). Another woodwind disc by **John Russo,** clarinet, contains *Four Songs* for medium voice, clarinet, bassoon, and piano. The program is a bit miscellaneous but the songs are well done and interesting.   MOORE

Luciano Berio *(b. 1925)*

Berio is a contemporary composer with a difference: His music has an unashamed lyricism that separates it from almost every other postwar avant-gardist. He has written extensively and naturally for the voice; even his instrumental works seem vocal in their conception, and perhaps it's this quality that makes his music more accessible than that of many of his colleagues. He is not dogmatic about technique, preferring to view serialism not as some ideal culmination of history but simply as an additional means of expression. His music sounds well on whatever instruments he writes for, and his fiercely difficult works have been enthusiastically embraced by many musicians; his *Sequenzas,* for example, are routine recital pieces for conservatory students.

Berio is fascinated with the nature of language, and this runs through much of his work—*Sinfonia, Coro,* and his classic electronic piece, *Thema (Ommagio a Joyce),* all bear witness to this. He's more pragmatic in his outlook than many modernists and is comfortable working with idioms and materials that many others would avoid. (For example, I can't imagine Boulez arranging a version of "Black is the Color of My True Love's Hair" or anything by the Beatles!)

Berio's orchestral repertoire is large and varied. His most popular orchestral work is probably his *Sinfonia;* look for a single disc (Erato 88151, NA) or an excellent compilation directed by **Boulez** (Erato 98496, 5CD, NA, with works by Schoenberg, Carter, Birtwistle and others). It's a virtuoso vehicle for eight singers and orchestra (here sung by the New Swingle Singers) that seamlessly honors Martin Luther King, Jr., interprets Beckett's *The Unnamable,* rehears Mahler's Symphony 2, and does much, much more in its five movements. In lesser hands it might have been a faddish experiment; with Berio it's a profound experience that deepens with each hearing. *Sinfonia* is accompanied by *Eindrücke,* a shorter but notable work in which he creates a multilayered, multitemporal tapestry that reminds me of Birtwistle's processionals.

Boulez leads Ensemble Intercontemporain in an excellent selection of pieces for soloists with chamber orchestra (Sony 45862). The material in all of them emanates from a single line, and the performances do them full justice. *Chemins II* and *Chemins IV* are each based on one of Berio's *Sequenzas* for solo instruments, here viola and oboe respectively. *Ritorno Degli Snovidenia* uses fragments from Russian revolutionary songs to create a poignant, elegiac work for cello and small orchestra. *Corale,* for solo violin, strings, and a pair of horns, calls forth a shifting, teeming swirl of string textures. *Points on the curve to find . . .* is a glittering chamber concerto for piano.

Continuo is a remarkable piece with an almost impressionistic atmosphere. Berio here creates a work for large orchestra that unfolds slowly in a resolute, implacable adagio—"distant and descriptive." The texture has a special clarity, even in the most complex, dense passages, because of the chamberlike scoring. **Barenboim** leads the Chicago Symphony in a finely balanced reading (Teldec 99596, with works by Carter and Takemitsu). This disc is enthusiastically recommended.

Berio has written a series of pieces called *Sequenzas* for various soloists; presently there are 14, including one for voice. This series, begun in the late '50s, has explored each instrument's possibilities; they comprise perhaps the most important cycle of solo music since WW II. Berio takes an individual approach to each instrument, and the resulting body of work is surprisingly varied. **Ensemble Intercontemporain** has recorded the entire cycle so far (DG 457038, 3CD).

Ensemble Avantgarde offers an excellent selection of chamber works, with the *Sequenzas* for piano and clarinet, *Serenata I* for flute and 14 instruments, *O King,* a tribute to Martin Luther King, Jr., and *Linea* for two pianos, vibraphone, and marimba (♦MD+G 613 0754). These pieces cover a 25-year span of Berio's development. The performances are consistently strong, the recording is warm and detailed, and this makes a superb introduction to his chamber music.

A similar collection, now deleted but worth looking for, is directed by **Berio** himself (♦Philips 426662, NA). Here are two *Sequenzas* for oboe (immaculately played by Heinz Holliger) and voice (the great Cathy Berberian), plus *Différences* for five instruments and tape, *Due Pezzi* for violin and piano, and *Chamber Music,* again sung by Berberian. All of the performances may be considered definitive. An alternative recording of *Différences* by the Italian group **Contempoensemble** matches the playing on Berio's recording, but is filled out with pieces by Sciarrino, Bussotti, and Xenakis (Arts 447135).

Berio's complete piano music is only a small portion of his compositional output, and it can be heard on an excellent disc by **David Arden** (New Albion 089). There is great variety here, from the charming neoclassical *Petite Suite* to the 12-tone *Cinque Variazione* to the thorny clusters of *Sequenza IV.* The disc is filled out with a number of brief studies or occasional pieces, and even these display the composer's acute musicality.

Duetti for two violins is another remarkable cycle, resembling Bartók's *44 Duos* in many ways. Written as teaching pieces, these short works offer a wide range of styles and techniques. Members of **Accademia Bizantina** have recorded the first 34 in one of my favorite Berio discs (Denon 75448, with *Sequenza VIII* for violin, *Due Pezzi,* and *Corale*). I prefer this performance of *Corale* to Boulez's recording; it's warmer and more expressive.

Berio has written copiously for the female voice, with several important pieces composed specifically for the remarkable voice of his wife, **Cathy Berberian.** She recorded many of them, and her performances are unsurpassed. One of the loveliest is *Folk Songs,* a collection of eleven songs of different nationalities. Though a few are not authentic folk material, Berio's settings remain true to their spirit, setting off the words and the lovely melodies with a spare simplicity. Berberian's recording set the standard, and it's still the best, more than 20 years after it was made (RCA 62540). Also on this release is the fascinating theater piece *Recital I for Cathy,* a stream-of-consciousness monologue of an increasingly agitated singer waiting for her accompanist to arrive. Berberian's skills as an actress bring it off beautifully, with the London Sinfonietta conducted by Berio himself. Three songs of Kurt Weill, wonderfully arranged by Berio, complete the disc.

Another essential presentation of Berberian's artistry presents two other works written for her: *Circles,* for soprano, harp, and two percussionists (setting texts of e.e. cummings) and *Sequenza III* for solo voice. The disc is completed by *Sequenza I* for flute (here Aurèle Nicolet) and *Sequenza V* for trombone, played by Vinko Globokar (Wergo 6021). Berberian also recorded Berio's *Visage,* a profoundly disturbing work for voice and electronic tape. It's a classic, but not one for regular hearing, and many listeners may want to avoid it altogether. The unsquea-mish can hear it from Berberian on an all-Berio disc along with *A-Ronne*, a vocal work for five actors, and *Thema (Omaggio a Joyce),* another classic tape work (RCA 68302). **Christine Schadeberg** has recorded "The Great Works for Voice," a fine recital that presents *Folk Songs, Sequenza III, Chamber Music* (with texts by James Joyce), *O King,* and *Circles* all on one disc (Mode 48). She's vocally excellent, but I prefer Berberian's stronger dramatic sense; however, for those who want a more up-to-date recording, Schadeberg would be a first choice.

Luisa Castellani has also recorded *Folk Songs,* backed by Contempoartensemble; it has some fine moments but is outclassed by Berberian and Schadeberg (Arts 47376). Castellani's Italian accent is distract-ing in the English texts, and the disc is a bit short at 40 minutes. *Laborintus II* is an interesting setting of texts by Dante, but not as com-pelling as the other vocal works. **Berio** conducts Ensemble Musique Vi-vante, an elite French ensemble. Check it out in a budget-priced set (Harmonia Mundi 290862/64, 3CD, with works by Boulez and Stock-hausen); it's also available on a mid-priced single disc (Harmonia Mundi 190764), but as it is just over 30 minutes in length, the set is a much better value.

A composer as interested in literature, theater, and the voice as Berio would seem to be a natural opera composer, and he has written several such works, though few of them have been recorded. *Un Re in Ascolto,* a large-scale "musical action in two parts" based on texts by Auden, Calvino, Shakespeare, and Gotter, can be heard in a costly set with **Maazel** conducting the Vienna Philharmonic (Col Legno 20005).

Berio is also an important pioneer of electronic music, as discussed in more detail in the article in Part II.   McINTIRE

Hector Berlioz *(1803–1869)*

The French romantic composer par excellence, Berlioz nonetheless had his roots in the classical era. Beethoven, in the "Pastoral" and Symphony 9, may have opened the doors, but Gluck was still the touchstone. Yet his *Symphonie Fantastique*—a love- and drug-induced orchestral night-mare—took that genre farther than even Beethoven had imagined, just as his *Damnation of Faust* and *Romeo and Juliet* blurred the lines be-tween opera and oratorio. (Significantly, Berlioz even called the latter a "dramatic symphony.") At the same time, his efforts to translate litera-ture into music were also classically grounded. Virgil and Shakespeare were his great loves, followed by Goethe, Byron, and Scott. Hence it should come as no surprise that many of his most successful inter-preters retain their classical moorings without forgetting the world of romantic imagination his music simultaneously ushers us into. But there are exceptions, as we shall see below.

ORCHESTRAL MUSIC

Symphonie Fantastique. As the first great "romantic" symphony, the *Fantastique* has not wanted for good recordings since the dawn of the electrical era, when **Weingartner** made his in 1925 (Grammofono 2000 78850). Of those that followed through the 78 rpm and mono LP eras, two warrant special attention, and, interestingly, both emanated from Paris. One is the 1931 **Monteux**/Paris Symphony set (♦Pearl 9012), the best of several recordings that eminent Berliozian made of this piece (though his later San Francisco Symphony performances are also worth having). The other is **Walter's** from 1939, an unexpectedly compelling performance from a conductor not usually associated with this com-poser, with terrifying bells in 'Dream of a Witches's Sabbath' (VAIA 108, a dim-sounding transfer).

Otherwise it's the stereo era that has the most to offer in this bril-liantly scored opus. Like Monteux, **Munch** also recorded the *Fantas-tique* numerous times. The most famous is his 1954 Boston Symphony version, the first of two with that orchestra, a white-hot reading in which the music's romantic thrust is very much to the fore, especially in the last two movements (♦RCA 68979). (I like the richer, more contained sec-ond BSO recording too.) Even more fevered is a live concert perfor-mance from Lisbon with the French National Radio Orchestra (Auvidis 4826, mono). But if that's what you're after, you should also check out **Paray,** similarly intense and exciting in big, close-up sound (♦Mercury 434328). **Bernstein** also goes for the gut in this piece, most resound-ingly in his 1968 NY Philharmonic recording (♦Sony 47525), though in some ways his 1976 French remake is even wilder (♦EMI 73338, 2CD). Two other *Fantastiques* with a following are **Argenta's,** overly tight with steely strings (London 452305), and **Markevitch's,** a bit eccentric at times but always stimulating, with flavorful French winds (DG 447406).

Though not **Colin Davis's** first Berlioz recording, it was his 1963 *Fan-tastique* with the London Symphony that proclaimed him an important interpreter of this composer's music. Basically a classicist like Monteux, he balances that with a romantic sensibility that gives the ball scene (here with its optional cornet part) a delightful buoyancy and the 'March to the Scaffold' a disciplined punch. That performance may be had in an inexpensive "Duo" that includes his *Harold in Italy* and *Symphonie Funébre* (♦Philips 442290, 2CD). His 1974 re-do with the Concertge-bouw is more atmospheric, again with full repeats and the cornet spic-ings in the waltz (Philips 411425). **Boulez** also takes a classical ap-proach to this piece, but his 1996 recording ultimately fails to find much flexibility or drama in the writing (DG 453432). (His earlier recording with the London Symphony was even slower, yet more arresting, in the march.)

Better, surprisingly, is **Klemperer,** a bit stolid and Germanic but not uninteresting, though I wouldn't have minded more oomph in the Witches Sabbath (EMI 67034). By contrast, **Massimo Freccia** is re-markably imaginative, with a subliminal urgency to the waltz and a nicely sprung march (♦Chesky 88). No one is more imaginative than **Stokowski,** however, and in the absence of his "Phase-4" *Fantastique* (London 448955), there is a BBC Radio broadcast, less gimmicky in sound but maybe even quirkier as a performance and more driven in spots (BBC 4018).

Among a number of deletions, I also lament the loss of **Beecham's** 1959 mono *Fantastique* (♦EMI 64032) and **Martinon's** (♦EMI 69650, 2CD, with *Lélio*). However, **Muti's** wonderfully warm and romantic performance has been reissued, at a bargain price (♦EMI 73554), as has **Ormandy's,** with its superbly spooky bells in the finale (♦Sony 46329). Of a similar though softer stripe is **Kojian,** who offers a choice of bells, either the concert variety (track 5) or antiphonal church bells (track 6), all on the same CD (♦Reference 11). **Fournet** is also a little soft, which hurts his March and Witches Sabbath (Denon). **Golschmann,** on the other hand, is maybe too straightforward, with anemic chimes and a slightly punchy finale (Vanguard). **Goossens's** bells are fine, but the in-terpretation is a bit phlegmatic (Everest). That's not a problem with the superbly recorded **Zinman;** it just doesn't have much imagination or poetry, though the big moments register strongly (Telarc).

Then there is **Tilson Thomas,** whose trancelike distancing of the qui-eter pages works well enough but who comes across as flat-edged when things aren't so quiet (RCA). Despite a well-paced I and II and a memo-rably imposing March, **Karajan** seems too smoothed over in places and a mite earthbound in V (DG). (A great bell, though.) Nor does **Kubelik** really come to life in the last two movements (Orfeo), where each **Previn** (EMI), **Bátiz** (ASV), and, most damagingly, **Pinchas Steinberg** (Naxos) also disappoint. Previn's Royal Philharmonic remake, on IMP, is considerably better in this regard, but better on every count is **Mackerras** with the same orchestra, classically impassioned yet sensitive to the music's more lyrical aspects, at an irresistible price (♦Intersound 2831). By contrast **Menuhin** is just too civilized in the wilder, more grotesque episodes (Virgin). Like Davis, Klemperer, Kojian, and Mackerras, however, he gives us the optional cornet in 'Un Bal.'

That cornet can also be heard, along with a serpent and an ophicleide, in **Gardiner's** recording, one of the two period-instrument performances (Philips 434402). A bit tightly recorded (in the hall where the symphony first shocked the world), his *Fantastique* doesn't make as much of the instrumentation as **Norrington's** (Virgin) but is otherwise more exciting interpretively.

Grande Symphonie Funébre et Triomphale. Composed in 1840 for wind band, this *pièce d'occasion* can also be performed with strings and chorus. It's the first version, without either, that **Francois Boulanger** presides over (Auvidis 4836), a capable job that never quite scales the heights of **Désire Dondeyne's** 1976 recording (Calliope, once available in the US on a Nonesuch LP). (A generation earlier he also did it for Westminster, only with the chorus.) **Davis** offers the version with chorus and (I think) strings and, like Dondeyne, stirs the blood mightily (♦Philips 442290, 2CD). Along the same lines, if you want to hear what Berlioz's arrangement of the "Marseillaise" is like, check out **Zinman's** all-out rouser (♦Telarc 80164).

Harold en Italie. Though it was commissioned by Paganini, that virtuoso subsequently rejected this piece on the grounds that it wasn't enough like a concerto. Paganini was right. *Harold* isn't a concerto but rather a "symphony with viola solo." Maybe that's why some of the best performances are those that don't treat the viola as a front-and-center instrument. Just the same, it's impossible to ignore **Primrose**, who recorded the work three times. Of these, the one with Koussevitzky is the most exciting (Dutton 5013), the one with Beecham the most poetic (Sony, NA), and the one with Munch—well, for some reason this, Primrose's only stereo *Harold*, never really comes together, though it's nice to hear that patrician viola (RCA 62582). All three pale, however, before his two broadcasts with Toscanini (only fleetingly available on LP or CD), where the latter's electrifying orchestral conception has a soloist fully worthy of it.

That leaves **William Lincer** with Bernstein as the stereo choice, a boldly impassioned account (with an especially invigorating finale) in which the viola is very much part of the whole (♦Sony 60696). (A much less prepossessing Bernstein performance with **Donald McInnes** can be heard on EMI.) Nor does the viola stick out in Davis's recording with **Imai,** her warmly lyrical playing contrasting effectively with the classically proportioned yet tautly managed accompaniment, if such it can be called (♦Philips 442290, 2CD). Maxim Shostakovich also has a lot to say about this piece, though his red-blooded 'Orgy of the Brigands' exposes **Bruno Giuranna's** comparatively scrawny tone (IMP). **Joseph de Pasquale** and Ormandy are more opulent but also a bit heavy (Sony), while **Bashmet's** soulful playing basks in Inbal's sunnier but even more expansive frame (Denon).

In the low-price category, **Rivka Golani** and Yoav Talmi are better disciplined and more appealing than many of their high-priced competitors (Naxos 553034). And though I wouldn't take **Gerard Caussé's** mostly vibrato-less viola over Primrose, Gardiner's strikingly direct

view of the piece makes their period-instrument performance more than just a curio (Philips 446676).

Overtures. Even after 40 years, no one has beaten **Munch's** collection of overtures, still unrivaled for exuberance and panache (♦RCA 61400). His zesty *Roman Carnival* is a particular delight, but there is also much to be said for his incendiary *Corsaire,* outsized *Béatrice et Bénédict,* and, to top things off, blazing 'Royal Hunt and Storm' from *Les Troyens.* (Would that Beecham's wondrously poetic EMI recording, complete with chorus, were still available.)

Davis comes close, however, especially his latest recording with the Dresden Staatskapelle (♦RCA 68790). Tempos are occasionally broader, though usually not by much (*Les Francs-Juges* is, in fact, marginally faster) and, if anything, the years have brought added depth without diminishing the music's romantic impulse (e.g., *King Lear*). His earlier collection with the London Symphony, perhaps a bit more incisive, is also available—likewise with the overtures to *Béatrice et Bénédict* and *Benvenuto Cellini*—in a box of Berlioz orchestral music (♦Philips 456143, 6CD, or in an earlier single disc, 416430). Nor does **Previn** disappoint in the five overtures appended to the "double fforte" box containing Bernstein's *Symphonie Fantastique* and *Harold in Italy* (♦EMI 73338, 2CD, or earlier as a single in 2159). Tidy but exhilarating, these are classical performances in the best sense, if without effacing Davis's supremacy in that department.

One overture that isn't included in any of the above is *Rob Roy.* It is, however, part of **Talmi's** characteristically disciplined collection (Naxos 550999)—just listen to the string runs in Waverley—and **Alexander Gibson's** somewhat short-measure CD with, appropriately, the Scottish National Orchestra (Chandos 8316). The Gibson overtures to have, though, are in his Royal Philharmonic collection, played with greater dash and exuberance and at a bargain price (♦Intersound 2884). There is, however, no *Rob Roy* there—or, surprisingly, *Roman Carnival.* **Dutoit** comes in dead last, in an ill-focused collection that's zippy enough for the most part but never really digs into the music (London 452480). (His *Corsaire* comes the closest.) If you have **Paray's** *Fantastique,* you already have an outstanding *Roman Carnival* and *Corsaire,* a bit coarse but wonderfully invigorating (♦Mercury 434328). Ditto **Bátiz,** whose romantic temperament is very much on display (♦ASV 6090).

Reverie et Caprice. **Perlman** (♦DG 445549) brings a richer tone and greater animation to this Romance for violin and orchestra than the more modestly soloistic **Igor Gruppman** (Naxos 553034). But in addition to being more modestly priced, the latter has the advantage of being coupled with a better than average *Harold in Italy* (see above). The most idiomatic-sounding performance, however, is **Grumiaux's,** to be had only as part of a much bigger all-Berlioz collection (♦Philips 456143, 6CD).

CHORAL WORKS

La Damnation de Faust. Even Berlioz doesn't appear to have been entirely sure how to classify this semi-operatic, cantatalike adaptation of Goethe. "Dramatic legend" was what he ended up with, and it's true that any would-be interpreter ignores the drama at his or her peril.

That can't be said of **Munch,** whose 1954 recording still dominates the lists in many ways. Though Singher cuts a somewhat straight figure as Mephistopheles, Poleri and Danco are among the finest Fausts and Marguerites on disc. More important, with the Boston Symphony at its most alert, Munch proves as responsive to the score's quieter, more expansive moments as its hellfire and brimstone (e.g., a thrilling 'Ride to the Abyss'), nearly every page coming vividly, unforgettably to life. Unfortunately it's currently available only as part of the "Munch Conducts Berlioz" box (♦RCA 68444, 8CD). Though it was supposedly recorded in stereo, RCA claims portions of the master tape were lost, so the CDs are mono. No matter—this is still one of the great *Fausts*.

Monteux's 1962 BBC Radio broadcast is another stereo-era mono *Faust*, a performance of remarkable power and cohesion (♦BBC 4006, 2CD). Crespin may be a bit under par as Marguerite nor is Andre Turp the most ardent of Fausts. But Michel Roux makes a superbly insinuating Mephisto, as he was earlier for **Markevitch** (DG "Double," 437931), coloring the text with wit, imagination and style. Janet Baker's Marguerite is arguably the chief selling point of **Prêtre's** *Faust*, her alluring mezzo always at the service of the character, though Bacquier has his moments as Mephisto (EMI 68583, 2CD).

In every other way, however, this set must yield to **Colin Davis** (♦Philips 416395, NA), where Gedda was more secure, and to **Solti**, easily the most dramatic of the stereo *Fausts* (♦London 414680, 2CD). Less subtle than Davis (who perhaps overdoes the classicism here), this is a strongly articulated reading, not without feeling, with Von Stade a moving Marguerite, Riegel a ringing if occasionally tight-sounding Faust and van Dam a suavely menacing Mephisto.

Chung is, if anything, even more scrupulously detailed, unlike most conductors even observing the diminuendo at the end of the 'Rakoczy March' (DG 453500, 2CD). He's also blessed with three of the most beautiful voices in any recorded *Faust*—von Otter, Keith Lewis, and Terfel. Yet for all its polish and dynamism, there's something strangely impersonal about this performance, an impression not ameliorated by Lewis's strained C sharps in the love duet or Terfel's precipitous gallop through the "Serenade." (What can he have been thinking?) It would be a mistake to dismiss **Guenter Neuhold,** who has a real sense of how this music ought to go (Bayer 500017/8, 2CD). He also has in Larmore one of the most appealing of all Marguerites, her mezzo absolutely right for the ballad of the King of Thule. She's ably partnered by Keith Olsen's Faust, less so by David Wilson-Johnson as a perhaps too urbane Mephisto, in a concert taping that appears to lack a center channel. At a lower price this entry would have been much more competitive.

Nagano was as carefully detailed as Chung but to much greater effect (Erato, NA). **Dutoit** was elegant but surprisingly bland (London 444812), something true to a lesser extent of **Ozawa** (DG "Double" 453013). Unless you have to hear an all-French cast, **Fournet's** 1943 recording should be avoided; likewise **Furtwängler's** distantly miked 1950 Lucerne Festival performance, unless you (a) are a Furtwängler buff or (b) want to hear the work in German (e.g., Schwarzkopf's "Koenig von Thule").

L'Enfance du Christ.

L'Enfance du Christ. This evocative retelling of the events immediately following the birth of Christ, freely adapted from *Matthew 2,* drew from Berlioz some of his most endearingly intimate music, something all its recordings have conveyed. Though Davis's second is no longer listed (Philips), the earlier is the one to have, with its air of innocence and spontaneity, and happily it's available in a low-priced "Double Decker" that also includes a number of other vocal works (♦London 443461, 2CD). Pears is the Narrator, with Elsie Morrison and John Cameron an affecting Mary and Joseph.

There's also a lot to be said for **Munch,** though his singers are less involving (♦RCA 68444, 8CD). He shapes the score with obvious affection, from the subliminal dread of the nocturnal march in Part 1 to the serenity of the "Shepherd's Farewell," one of Berlioz's loveliest inspirations.

The question is whether you want to invest in an 8CD box to hear it. If not, **Cluytens** also shapes this music affectionately, with an even greater sense of style, something that happily extends to his singers—Gedda, Roger Soyer, Ernest Blanc, and de los Angeles, the last in particular an unforgettable Mary (♦EMI 68586, 2CD, with *Romeo* excerpts). Warmly idiomatic and flowing, this is a wonderfully "French" recording. That can likewise be said of **Jean-Claude Casadesus,** recorded in Lille (Naxos 553650/1, 2CD). But apart from its inclusion of the printed text, the only way it beats Cluytens is in the matter of price—barely—and that without a filler.

Herreweghe's is another French-derived *L'Enfance,* at a considerably higher tariff than either of the preceding two (♦Harmonia Mundi 901632/3, 2CD). Yet there's something very special about the dedicated teamwork of this performance, its dramatic points being made subtly yet unerringly, whether in Agnew's ethereal narration, Gens's moving Mary, or the harrowed Herod of Laurent Naouri. **Matthew Best's** *L'Enfance* also features an outstanding Herod, with the requisite low notes, in bass Alastair Miles (♦Hyperion 66991/2, 2CD). Indeed, for once the men outshine the Mary (Jean Rigby), given Gerald Finley's Joseph and Gwynne Howell's Père de Famille, with Aler a better-focused Narrator than he was for **Inbal** (Denon, NA). I just wish the playing and conducting better communicated a sense of the world being born anew.

Lélio, or The Return to Life.

Lélio, or The Return to Life. Despite the onetime availability of performances by **Boulez, Martinon** and **Inbal,** choices among complete recordings of this hodgepodge of a "sequel" to *Symphonie Fantastique* currently boil down to two: a German-language version led by **Rolf Reuter** (Berlin) and **Macal's** English-language recording, available separately (Koss 1017) or with his not very inspiring *Fantastique* (Koss 1012). For those who would just as soon do without the spoken portions, **Davis** presents it that way as part of his Berlioz orchestral box (Philips 456143, 6CD), and **Tilson Thomas** offers what are probably the two best sections, 'Chorus of the Shades' and 'Fantasia on Shakespeare's Tempest' (RCA 68930). None of these is a satisfactory solution, but that's partly because there really is none to this problematic work.

Messe Solenelle.

Messe Solenelle. Unexpectedly discovered in 1991, this, Berlioz's earliest large-scale work to have survived, already has had two recommendable recordings. **Gardiner's** is crisp and vital and looks directly ahead to the pieces much of this music would eventually find its way into, particularly *Benvenuto Cellini, Symphonie Fantastique* and *Requiem* (♦Philips 442137). He really puts it over with a wallop. **J. Reilly Lewis,** on the other hand, takes a more devotional view, beset with some of the expected weaknesses of an amateur choral society (♦Koch 7204). (I also don't care much for his vibrato-ridden soloists.) Yet it's his group that really seems to love the music—witness the affectionate sweep of the 'Gloria' or their savoring of the 'Resurrexit'—as opposed to the brisk efficiency of Gardiner's period band. You pays your money and takes your choice.

Requiem (Grande Messe des Morts).

Requiem (Grande Messe des Morts). Seldom performed for more than a century after its premiere, this has gone from being something of a curio—albeit a grandiose one—to a beloved Berlioz showpiece. That came about primarily through one recording, and it wasn't even the first. Indeed, Munch's landmark Boston Symphony *Requiem* wasn't even the first in stereo, but it was the first to capture both the critics' and the record-buying public's attention. It's still an attention-grabber, though today we're more keenly aware of its limitations. Even two-channel stereo couldn't fully capture the splendor and vastness of the scoring, with its large orchestra and chorus and four brass bands. Just the same, the sense of occasion comes through, thanks to Munch's fervently exalted direction and the willingness of all concerned to put themselves in his and Berlioz's hands. At present it can be had only as part of a "Munch Conducts Berlioz" box that also contains his first BSO *Fantastique* and *Romeo and Juliet,* along with his overtures collection, *Harold, L'Enfance, Nuits d'été* and *Damnation of Faust* (♦RCA 68444, 8CD).

However inadequate, we would have given a great deal had that technology been employed in **Beecham's** 1959 broadcast from London's Royal Albert Hall (♦BBC 4011). Even in mono this is in many ways the most comprehending *Requiem* of them all, with a natural sense of climax and proportion. Thus under Beecham it's the second climax in the 'Dies irae' that becomes the most moving, followed by Richard Lewis's tenor solos and the heart-swelling "Hosannas" of the 'Sanctus.' One recording that did come close to conveying the effect this work can have live was **Abravanel's,** in quadraphonic sound. With the brass bands deployed in the balconies, it was also the first to fully come to terms with the acoustics of the Mormon Tabernacle. Unfortunately, that's not how it's been reissued on CD, as the two-channel master seems to have been used, and that doesn't sound as good as the quad LP even when both are played through two speakers (Vanguard 100/01, 2CD). The performance itself is still good, with remarkably fine choral work, but without the sonic edge it must yield to the best of the competition.

For those who value nervous excitement in this often sublime music, there is **Bernstein** (Sony 47526, 2CD). Supposedly also done in quad (though it was never issued that way), it was, like **Scherchen's** (ReDiscovery 005/06), made at Les Invalides, the site of the work's premiere, and—again like Scherchen's—it has more than its share of eccentricities. Intense and highly rhetorical, it sometimes sounds more theatrical than even Berlioz might have intended. But the result is an undeniably powerful 'Tuba mirum'—here truly overwhelming—and a 'Rex tremendae' that really lives up to its name.

Another overwhelming 'Tuba mirum' can be heard from **Shaw,** whose set is also distinguished by Aler's tenor solos in the 'Sanctus' (Telarc 80109, 2CD). Otherwise this performance now seems a trifle foursquare, though the choral singing could hardly be better, not least in the quieter sections (of which, lest we forget, there are more than the other kind). Though his tenor, the sometimes bleaty Robert Tear, isn't on Aler's level (or Simoneau's, so at home in Munch's recording), **Previn** turns in one of the finest *Requiems,* expansive yet powerful, with a real sense of purpose and concentration (♦EMI 69512, 2CD). Nor does he neglect the quieter pages. I wish **Davis** had had this kind of recorded sound in his set, where the two-dimensional miking compromised what is otherwise one of the strongest conceptions of all (Philips, NA).

Levine also plays for strength, in a consciously bigger, more portentous account, with Pavarotti his semi-operatic tenor (DG 29724, 2CD). At the opposite extreme is **Ozawa,** more light and lyrical than cataclysmic (RCA 62524). That means the 'Lacrymosa' moves right along (which I like) but also that the bigger pages are denied the requisite heft. However, the faster tempos mean that, like Beecham's, the entire work can be accommodated on a single CD. That's also true of **Ormandy,** whose budget price would make it more attractive if it weren't for the close-up miking and less-than-stellar choral work, not to mention the comparatively unsubtle performance (Sony).

Another budget offering, albeit on two discs, is **Noel Edison's,** a warmly spacious account in which the choir outshines the orchestra (Naxos 554494/5, 2CD). That may not be the best balance for the 'Dies irae' but it's effective nearly everywhere else. Still, **Dutoit** offers the same

warmth and spaciousness (though maybe not as easeful a tenor) in an even more polished performance, filled out with some lesser-known Berlioz choral pieces, including the 'Resurrexit' from which come the brass fanfares that open the 'Tuba mirum' (♦Decca 458921, 2CD). But I wouldn't have minded had the Day of Judgment cracked a bit harder.

Roméo et Juliette. With Gardiner's near-variorum edition of the different versions, we can hear how Berlioz continued to refine this increasingly nonverbal exposition of Shakespeare (♦Philips 454454, 2CD). Given the track layout, some assembly is required, but it's worth the trouble to hear what the piece might have sounded like in its earlier incarnations, period instruments and all. Interpretively, Gardiner generally eschews emotion for brilliance and incisiveness (e.g., his 'Fête at the Capulets,' though Davis I is fully his equal here). There's nothing astringent about his soloists, however, especially Catherine Robbin's hauntingly beautiful mezzo (actually more of a light alto).

But there's a reason why Berlioz ended up with the score as we know it today, and that version is still best heard in the first of the two **Davis** recordings, available as part of an economical (if textless) all-Berlioz orchestral collection (♦Philips 456143, 6CD). His soprano and tenor may not be as rich-voiced or as expressive as their counterparts in his Vienna remake (Philips 442134, 2CD), but that one doesn't begin to touch the clarity and controlled passion of the earlier set. Witness the heightened tragedy of the tomb scene, made all the more affecting by its classical reserve. Likewise the disciplined choral singing, particularly in the finale, where Shirley-Quirk makes an unusually empathetic Friar Laurence.

Munch also recorded this piece twice, but only the first, in mono, is available complete, in the "Munch Conducts Berlioz" box (♦RCA 68444, 8CD). It's certainly the more finely honed of the two, even if his singers don't match the opulence of those in the 1961 stereo set. The latter, though, is where you'll hear the Love Scene at its most intoxicating, but to do so on CD you'll have to buy yet another issue of the 1954 *Fantastique,* to which it's appended as filler (RCA 68979). **Muti** takes a lighter, often more intimate view, the restraint of his Love Scene contrasting with the drama and color of the 'Fête,' here taken a bit slowly (EMI). Yet the lightness comports oddly with the magnificence of Norman's soprano, if not Aler's idiomatic tenor (maybe the best of the 'Queen Mab' songs); again no texts. **Gardelli** is also on the light side, his Austrian chorus coming across almost like a Kammerchor (Orfeo). However, his sodden 'Fête' and somewhat tentative 'Queen Mab Scherzo' don't help matters, even with Shirley-Quirk singing more firmly, if no less compassionately, than he did for Davis.

Among recordings of the orchestral music, **Giulini** takes top honors, with nearly an hour's worth of the score transmitted in wondrously heartfelt fashion. It's available, though, only with Cluytens's *L'Enfance,* though at a bargain price (♦EMI 68586, 2CD). **Talmi's** is even less expensive, on top of which he offers even more of the music—with chorus—together with two excerpts from *Trojans* (Naxos 553198). Still, his sometimes overly careful renditions fall a good way short of Giulini's poetry. **Bernstein,** by contrast, digs in with both fists and comes close to overloading the score's more superheated pages (Sony).

Te Deum. Described by Berlioz as "a tremendous work," the 1855 *Te Deum* is only about three-fifths the length of the *Requiem,* but when performed live it can make an enormous impact. Some of that is conveyed in **Dennis Keene's** recording of a 1996 concert at New York's Cathedral of St. John the Divine (♦Delos 3200). Not even **Beecham** or **Davis** served up as much of the music's grandeur, especially in the concluding

'Judex crederis,' though **Inbal** (Denon, NA) reportedly included the orchestral Prelude and Call to the Colors Berlioz added for state occasions.

Tristia. Another hard-to-classify Berlioz opus, this is in fact a grouping of two earlier choral pieces—*Méditation Religieuse* and *La Mort d'Ophélie*—with the *Funeral March for Hamlet,* all united by the subject of death. **Boulez's** controlled and vividly detailed performance works best in the last (DG 453432), though **Davis** finds more tragic grandeur (♦Philips 416431, with *Harold*). **Gardiner's** period instruments lend an antique flavor (Philips 446676). Away from the triptych, Davis's earlier recording of the first two is even more touchingly restrained, as are their discmates, which include *Sara la Baigneuse* and *L'Enfance* (♦London 443461, 2CD).

OPERAS

Béatrice et Bénédict. This, the last of Berlioz's major works, also stands as his sole operatic adaptation of Shakespeare, the comedy *Much Ado About Nothing.* Because of the humor, the composer thought it the most difficult of his operas to perform, yet until recently it has been the most readily available, beginning with the first of two **Colin Davis** recordings (♦Decca 448113, 2CD). Fresher in some respects than the remake, it offers the regal Beatrice of Veasey and no dialog (which may be a plus for some). By contrast Davis II offers a bit more of the text, sung and spoken, superior choral work and the moving but perhaps too artful Béatrice of Baker (♦Philips 416952, 2CD, NA). A Barenboim recording substituted narration for the dialog and had an intriguing cast, though the men let things down a bit (DG, NA).

The most beautifully sung, however, is arguably **John Nelson's** (♦Erato 45773, 2CD). McNair is a ravishing Hero, Susan Graham an equally appealing Béatrice, and Jean-Luc Viala a fresh-voiced Bénédict despite a tendency to overdo his energetic Act 1 aria. With a couple of exceptions, a separate cast handles the dialog, but the youthful high spirits prevail throughout. In sum, a first choice, if you can find it.

Benvenuto Cellini. To date **Davis's** has been the only commercial recording of what may be Berlioz's most imaginative opera,, with Gedda in the title role (♦Philips, NA). Never available on CD in the US, it's worth looking for in other formats, if only for the chance to hear the full-length 'Roman Carnival' scene (from which Berlioz later adapted the concert overture of the same name) with its exhilarating choral writing.

Les Troyens. This vast operatic canvas covering nothing less than the fall of Troy and Aeneas's sojourn in Carthage had to wait the better part of a century for its full-length theatrical premiere (in 1957 at Covent Garden). Yet it's unquestionably Berlioz's operatic masterpiece, a work of epic grandeur and dramatic thrust that, like the Wagner operas it is so unlike in other ways, needs a full evening for its cumulative impact to register.

That was plain in the first complete recording, stemming from the Covent Garden revival a dozen years later (Philips 416432, 4CD, NA). Again **Davis** affirmed his standing as the foremost Berlioz conductor of his generation, with equally commanding performances from Veasey as Dido and especially Vickers as Aeneas, a portrayal still unmatched for heroic sheen. It's hard to believe Philips still hasn't reissued this, but until then there's another powerful contender from **Dutoit** (♦Decca 443693, 4CD). Gary Lakes proves a variable Aeneas, but Voigt is an unusually strong Cassandra and Françoise Pollet an affecting Dido. What's more, Dutoit offers some additional music, including a scene Berlioz himself deleted from Act 1 and the Prelude he crafted for Part 2, *The Trojans at Carthage,* when he split the opera in two to increase the chance of

performances. All this is transmitted with warmth and plasticity (e.g., the poetic 'Royal Hunt and Storm'), even if Berlioz's scoring seldom cuts through the way it does with Davis. There's also a highlights disc (Decca 458208).

In mono, we have a 1959/60 concert performance (with **Robert Lawrence** subbing for Beecham) where the focus has traditionally been on Steber's committed Cassandra and Resnik's characterful Dido; for my money, however, the vocal honors go to Richard Cassilly's mostly gleaming Aeneas (VAIA 1006, 4CD). **Kubelik** (who led the 1957 Covent Garden performances) can be heard conducting portions of the opera in Italian, with impassioned work from Nell Rankin, Simionato, a bellowing del Monaco, and occasionally the prompter (VAIA 1026). Of greater interest is a CD transfer of the pioneering 1952 recording of *The Trojans at Carthage,* brilliantly if erratically conducted by **Scherchen,** with singing of comparable intensity—e.g., the Dido of Arda Mandikian (♦Tahra 143/4, 2CD). (I know this only from the old Westminster LPs.)

SONGS AND SOLO CANTATAS

Les Nuits d'été. I regret that **Colin Davis's** recording of this gorgeous song cycle is available only in the UK, as part of a 3CD set, especially since it divided them among different voices, as Berlioz intended, and included all the other songs with orchestra (Philips 462252). But the pickings are still pretty good for *Nuits* itself, beginning with **Baker's** incomparable 1967 traversal with Barbirolli (♦EMI 72640, 2CD). Unlike her 1990 remake with Hickox (Virgin), her mezzo is here at its richest and most sublime, in sensitively nuanced renditions that may take their time (e.g., "Absence") but always to spellbinding effect. In the later recording the voice sometimes hoots where it should caress, nor is Hickox's conducting as ripely romantic as Barbirolli's. However, it sometimes reveals deeper insights and includes three more Berlioz songs, even if Baker's "Zaide" can't match the Latin temperament of the piano-accompanied **Bartoli** (♦London 452667, with a touching "Mort d'Ophélie").

Another *Nuits* that likewise includes three additional songs is **Steber's** venerable 1954 mono recording with Mitropoulos (♦Sony 62356). The usually sprightly "Villanelle" seems a bit slow, but her voice is beautifully placed and controlled throughout. Indeed, it was this recording that made the cycle something of a hit in the US. The following year, however, brought us **de los Angeles,** with Munch the characterful accompanist—no more characterful than de los Angeles, however, whose brightly pointed singing still gives pleasure (♦RCA 68444, 8CD, or coupled with *Romeo,* 6068). Given her distinctive timbre, **Crespin** also makes a fine effect in this cycle (slightly reordered), especially in the haunting "Spectre de la Rose" (♦London 460973). Ansermet's luminous orchestral support doesn't hurt either. **Susan Graham,** by comparison, seems a bit shy on character, but really luxuriates in the writing, wrapping herself and the listener in its beauty (e.g., her ecstatic "L'Ile inconnue") (♦Sony 62730). Were that not enough, she and conductor John Nelson also offer arias from the operas and *Faust.*

As might be expected, **Norman** also provides a luxurious experience, but one that is at bottom too generalized in approach (Philips). **Kasarova's** voice is even richer in some ways, with a certain Slavic flavor, but she's both interpretively alive and admirably in sync with the mood of each song (RCA 68008). **Balleys'** styling is impeccably French, which adds a lot, but she's also subject to some strain, which doesn't (Harmonia Mundi). Finally, **von Otter** brings an amazingly lovely voice to this cycle, as well as a generous selection of other songs, but, as usual with this singer, a greater degree of involvement would not have been amiss (DG).

Herminie. This solo cantata, Berlioz's second try for the Prix de Rome (he finally won it on the fourth), is best known for making use of the melody that, as the *idée fixe,* would later pervade and unify *Symphonie Fantastique.* **Mireille Delunsch** reminds us what an effective display piece for soprano it can be (♦Harmonia Mundi 901522). However, **Michele Lagrange's** recording, though less compelling vocally, has the advantage of being coupled with the other Prix de Rome cantatas, including the first, *La Mort d'Orphee,* and the surviving 197 measures of the last, *La Mort de Sardanapale,* with tenor Daniel Galvez Vallejo (♦Harmonia Mundi 901542).

La Mort de Cléopatre, Berlioz's third attempt at the Prix de Rome, is even more dramatic, something best experienced by way of **Anne Pashley's** penetrating performance, her luscious soprano absolutely on top of the score (♦London 443461, 2CD). Colin Davis conducts, as he would later for **Baker** (Philips 462252). The current Baker *Cléopatre,* however, is her recording with Gibson, which is a bit more aloof in its queenly demeanor but soon pulls us in (♦EMI 68583, 2CD). By contrast everybody tries too hard in **Tourel's** recording with Bernstein, with its overt histrionics (Sony). In its defense, though, the piece does register.

GOODFELLOW

Leonard Bernstein *(1918–90)*

To pick a "musician of the century" would be a difficult undertaking. With so much talent emerging over the last hundred years, where to begin? It would have to be someone who was active and made an impact in all the major musical fields—composer, instrumentalist, conductor, and educator. Being a pioneer in the use of media wouldn't hurt, and writing a few books would help in the balloting. There is such a man. If Leonard Bernstein can't claim this coveted title, then perhaps no one can. I will state it plainly: In one of the great ironies of our musical times, for Bernstein was constantly worrying over his place in 20th-century music, he emerged fully the equal of any American composer, and he surpassed the others whose music he championed so ardently. You will be hard pressed to find another whose works are played more often everywhere, in symphony halls, theaters, and pops concerts.

SYMPHONIES

1 ("Jeremiah"). The 24-year-old composer made quite a splash with the critics when this symphony appeared. Brash, full of vigor, and replete with a young man's impatient sorrow, it's all the more poignant because of its moving finale, the prophet's concluding lamentation over the sacked city of Jerusalem. **Bernstein's** explosive recording remains the sentimental favorite after all these years, magnetically seducing us by the power of his arresting, extroverted music (Sony 60697). His only competition is himself, with a later recording that removed the sharp edges, where the passionate prayer of youth becomes an older man's philosophizing (DG). Bernstein's early performance in St. Louis (RCA, in the "Early Years" series) is interesting as a curiosity, and is quite exciting, but it can't match the New York reading, and neither can the collection of oldies on Pearl—an excellent compendium of super-early Bernstein for those of a historical bent (604).

2 ("The Age of Anxiety") is the second of Bernstein's symphonic "faith" trilogy, an obsession that lasted his entire life. After the historical and visionary ravings of Jeremiah, his next symphony, titled after W.H. Auden's poem, comes like a charge of electricity while standing in water. Entremont makes full use of his formidable equipment in his recording with **Bernstein** (Sony 60697). He's hampered by somewhat brittle piano sound, recessed and lacking impact, but Bernstein's spirit is willing even

while the sonic flesh is weak. Yet Bernstein's third traversal (the first Sony isn't competitive) is in every way superior to the earlier ones (DG 445245). Although tempos are generally faster, the sound is so improved, and Lucas Foss's intelligent, streamlined playing so fitting, that you could conceivably dispense with the second Sony altogether, if it weren't such a heartbreaking process.

3 ("Kaddish") completes Bernstein's symphonic output while at the same time keeping one foot in the dramatic theater, with sections of music not unlike those found in the later *Mass.* Here his diatribe about faith and man's lack of it calls God himself to account. This testament of accusation was evidently far too complex to be expressed in absolute music, so Bernstein resorts not only to a choir (singing the *Kaddish* in Hebrew) but also to a speaker (in English). The piece maintains an almost unexplainable cohesiveness that is found ultimately in the music and renders it effective and moving, if just a little irritating.

Bernstein's wife, the actress Felicia Montealegre, is the narrator in his Sony recording, and though a little mousy and tentative at the beginning, she rises to stirring dramatic heights during the course of the work. The NY Philharmonic plays this music like Vienna plays Mozart, with an explosive arrogance that fully fits **Bernstein's** confrontational musical dialogue (Sony). In 1977 he did a lot of revamping, considering the first version to have "too much talk." There are no more unaccompanied spots for narrator. Michael Wager is much better as speaker, less histrionic, sometimes coy, sometimes aggressive, sometimes sarcastic, and then sincere (DG 445245). Avoid the version with the Radio France Philharmonic and Yehudi Menuhin as narrator; he's sophomoric, a terrible reader, completely negating any musical virtues (Erato).

OTHER ORCHESTRAL MUSIC

Candide Overture. Perhaps the most popular tidbit in the Bernstein corpus is this rousing, tuneful overture to the stage work that so frustrated him all his life. **Zinman** is a little rushed, not as broad and sweeping as he should be, although the Baltimore Symphony is without fault (London). The St. Louis strings really carry the day, full of sweep and broad, brash melodic lines (Classics for Pleasure 2242). **Fiedler** pops out of the pack with his characteristic verve (RCA); it would be interesting if it weren't for the still unbeatable **Bernstein** recording—there's never been a more exciting reading (Sony 63085).

Concerto for Orchestra, "Jubilee Games," will not be everyone's cup of tea, especially those who look to *West Side Story* as **Bernstein's** decisive compositional achievement. It's wildly eclectic and structurally disjointed, even using aleatoric moments in part I, with flashes of serene peacefulness and violent abandon. Look for the premiere recording if you can find it, for it contained two other terrific works by Rorem and David Del Tredici. Otherwise, you'll have to settle for an import (♦DG 429231 or 447956).

Divertimento. This lovely, late jewel has been woefully underrecorded. Of the few extant versions, we're fortunate to have **Paavo Järvi's** bubbly, sensuous reading on a disc that really packs a wallop (Virgin 45295). The source is a surprise, but this bunch of Europeans has really caught the Bernstein style (Virgin 45295).

Dybbuk. Bernstein created this one-act ballet as a collaboration—one of many—with Jerome Robbins. It's a mystical work (with voices) based on the tale in Jewish folklore of the *Dybbuk*—a spirit that comes back to possess a person in order to once again inhabit the world. The composer said that every note was determined by manipulation according to the *Cabala,* the ancient Jewish system of numeration. It's unlike anything else he ever wrote. Gone are the catchy melodies and fluent rhythms, and despite some interesting moments, it's not difficult to see why it hasn't caught on. The New York City Ballet under **Bernstein's** direction gave it the best recording it will ever get (Sony 63090), although he did re-record it later in a series of suites, available only as an import (DG).

Facsimile. This 1946 ballet, another of his creations with Robbins, has a female protagonist in search of a companion, but she finds only a facsimile. The music is pseudo-Stravinskian overlaid with Bernstein's unique New York melodic style. **Zinman's** recording is excellent, but London's misbegotten balances continue to thwart him and his orchestra. **Slatkin** leads a pointed, well-mannered, neoclassical reading in St. Louis not at all out of touch with the work's Stravinskian leanings. The sound is great, the playing agile and lean (Classics for Pleasure 2242). Not unexpectedly, **Bernstein's** is again the one to beat, even though the New Yorkers are not as polished as St. Louis (Sony 60969). Unexpectedly, **Paavo Järvi** and the City of Birmingham Symphony revel in sparkling sound (Virgin 45295). Sound is again a prohibitive factor on the RCA and Pearl early issues, the excellent performances not up to the level of the later stereos.

Fancy Free. Bernstein exploded onto the ballet scene in 1944 with this jazzy, propulsive score that did much to establish him as a force to be reckoned with. Using the theme of three sailors "on the town" that he was to exploit later to even more critical acclaim, the music is everything New York and Bernstein were at the time—vivacious, energetic, carefree, and boisterous. **Slatkin** uses the Billie Holiday opening (as does Zinman), and the St. Louis orchestra enters like a rocket with those opening rim-shot furies. He rollicks all the way through, but lingers in important passages to provide a persuasive sense of loneliness (Classic for Pleasure 2242). **Zinman** finally gets in the groove in an otherwise lackluster album, allowing the orchestra to play with zeal and zest while staying atop all of Bernstein's exposed difficulties. But London's sound remains bloodless and dead.

The 1956 recording by **Bernstein** and the Columbia Symphony is as good as any on the market, with mono sound that's clear and bright. There is an astonishing vibrancy to this recording, and the playing outclasses the later Bernstein on Sony, good as that is. I don't often recommend mono recordings as a first choice, but this is the one to have (Sony 60559). **Marriner** gives us a rather foursquare issue that takes up half of a 2CD set, the other half belonging to Gershwin (Capriccio). **Robert Russell Bennett's** recording, fine as it is, is not in the same league as Bernstein and Slatkin (RCA).

Halil (Nocturne) for Flute & Strings is another of those delicious works that have been avoided for no good reason. There is a marvelous recording that does full justice to the work by flutist **Doriot Anthony Dwyer** with Sedares and the London Symphony (Koch 7142).

On the Town: Three Dances. Bernstein wisely culled this suite from the engaging dance numbers in *On the Town.* They are very appealing and always fresh and lively. This flavorful score comes through with technicolor brilliance in **Slatkin's** recording (Classics for Pleasure 2242). **Bernstein's** 1963 reading continues to set the standard, with doses of high spirits played to the hilt in great sound (Sony 60559). The RCA and Pearl historical releases are very good but, considering the sound, can't be given general recommendations. Likewise **de Waart**—good playing, but not the best, and it's a competitive world out there (Virgin).

On the Waterfront. Bernstein decided to assemble this suite from his score to the Elia Kazan film for fear of too much ending up on the editing room floor. It's a violent film, which he explosively captures in his music. **Bernstein's** 1960 recording is superb; sound, clarity, tonal allure—it's all here, masterfully garnered by the Columbia engineers (Sony 63085). His second go-round with the Israel Philharmonic lacks the sparkle of the New York version, but DG has it out in many guises, so if you pick this up along the way, don't feel the need to run out and grab the Sony. The Dallas Symphony has a long history of doing justice to American music, and **Mata** comes through with a beautiful reading, stunningly recorded, although perhaps lacking the intensity of the composer's (Dorian 90170).

Prelude, Fugue, and Riffs. This attractive little early work, written for Benny Goodman, is a perfect example of the feisty side of Bernstein's jazz roots. It has been well served on records, perhaps none better than the premiere directed by Bernstein with **Goodman** (Sony 60559). But there is strong competition, notably from Paavo Järvi with the sensational **Sabine Meyer** on clarinet (Virgin 45295), and from the brilliant **Tilson Thomas,** who routinely makes music like this exhilarating (RCA 68798). Lawrence Leighton Smith and **Stoltzman** bring some very special magic to it in warm, comfortable sound (RCA 61360, with Copland and Stravinsky). The Netherlands Wind Ensemble under **Richard Duffalo** are just too square and limp for this music, a piece that has to be played wide-eyed and with a lot of swing (Chandos).

West Side Story: Symphonic Dances. This collection, absent any of the hit tunes, has always been popular at pops concerts. The sound of **Zinman's** recording is far too dry for my taste—a problem that either resides in Baltimore's Meyerhoff hall or with the Decca engineers (London). As so often with **Bernstein's** performances, the NY Philharmonic is marvelous, with incisive rhythms, snappy jazz inflections, and soaring melody (Sony 63085). Again, **Paavo Järvi** turns in a riveting performance that's almost fully competitive (Virgin 45295).

CONCERTOS

Serenade for Solo Violin, Strings, Harp, and Percussion. Bernstein's only violin concerto, based on Plato's *Symposium*—where Socrates and friends discuss love at a dinner party—may be his finest moment as a composer, and the work is firmly ensconced in the repertory. Its compositional method is based on the text, where ideas and motives from the conversation are picked up and elaborated on in consecutive movements. Bernstein's last recording with **Kremer** is an object lesson in color intensity, a white-hot, blazing run that maintains its manic energy even in the slower movements (DG 445245). Slatkin and **Robert McDuffie** turn in a completely different style of performance, much more introspective (as befitting a conversation), less boisterous, more reflective and caring. McDuffie's tone is not as vibrant as Kremer's, and the recording seems more sanitized (EMI).

All of the sweltering passion built into this score explodes through the speakers in the recording by the work's dedicatee, **Isaac Stern.** The sound isn't great—compressed, strident, and terribly unbalanced. But no one has recorded this like Stern and Bernstein, so even with the floor-wax sound it's worth hearing (Sony). Ozawa and **Perlman,** as might be expected, give us an ornate, richly jeweled performance imbued with intoxicating colors and sensual expression. The Boston Symphony provides a tapestry of multifaceted musical manners that support and exhort the soloistic flights of fancy (EMI 55360). The young violinist **Hillary Hahn** has mastered this music, replete with Bernstein's swinging bright-lights swagger. Her tone is sweet when needed, yet she doesn't hesitate to swing the saber in the more angular and rhythmically sharp sections. But Zinman lets her down, failing to impose strict discipline on the Baltimore strings, which leads to some irregular passage-work (Sony).

Bernstein's second recording with **Francescatti** is bouncy and very Columbia-ish at this time—close up and under your eyelids. But Francescatti brings a burnished elegance to this score. It's very different from Stern's recording, not nearly as one-dimensional and monochromatic, far more lyrical but not quite as exciting—but with better sound (Sony 60559). **Hu Kun** plays an exciting performance that has found much critical acceptance, and deservedly so. Her tone is sweet and secure, while all of the typically jagged edges are in place (Nimbus 5329, with an excellent rendition of Barber's concerto).

CHAMBER MUSIC

Clarinet Sonata. Bernstein's only significant piece of chamber music is his refreshing, delightfully uplifting sonata for clarinet, written in 1941 at age 23. We have two excellent recordings. **Paul Meyer** and Eric Le Sage are splendid in a quicksilver reading that pulsates with life, with Copland, Bax, and Arnold as discmates (♦Denon 18016). **Richard Stoltzman** and Irma Vallecillo-Gray give us a bluesy, less intense, yet equally affecting reading in clear sound (RCA 62685).

Meditations from Mass. These three pieces, drawn from some of the best music in Mass, are effectively played on cello, although perhaps only a specialist will really find them necessary in this guise. If you are one, you'll do no better than the collection by **Andrés Díaz**—a warm, splendidly recorded recital (Dorian 90241, with works by Barber and Foote).

PIANO MUSIC

Composed before 1950, with the exception of *Thirteen Anniversaries and Touches,* Bernstein's piano output was limited, strange for a man who called the instrument his "first love." They are highly introspective and personal works and require an intense dedication when playing or listening to them. **Alexander Frey** exhibits just such a singular devotion, caressing these miniatures in a crystalline reading that lacks energy but compensates with attentiveness (Koch 7426). As if taking up the challenge of Frey's great effort, **Stefan Litwin** outdoes him stretching to the finish line. The piano sound is some of the most spacious and clean I have heard. (Cala 77006).

CHORAL MUSIC

Arias & Barcarolles. This late work is one of Bernstein's finest, very personal and at the same time very accessible. The two singers are critical; the music requires much nuance and pointed phrasing to be successful. We have now three fine versions. The first has **Judy Kaye** and William Sharp in the original piano four-hands version; coming as it did under Bernstein's supervision, it can hardly be bettered (Koch 7000). Schwarz was given the honor of making the first orchestral version, and **Jane Bunnell** and Dale Duesing are right at home in this style, with some very tender and moving singing (Delos 3078). **Von Stade** and Hampson grace Tilson Thomas's recording, with supple, graceful conducting and remarkably word-attuned singing (DG 439926).

Chichester Psalms. Bernstein's 1965 compositional sabbatical produced a work grounded in his usual elements of melody, odd meter rhythm, and spirituality. The piece found instant public success and remains one of his most often-performed works, with good reason. There is room for many interpretations, and no collection would be complete without **Bernstein's** own 1965 recording, in great sound and the model for any subsequent attempt (Sony 60595). He re-recorded the work later, but to far less effect than the earlier New York version (DG).

Shaw turns in an engrossing reading that falls just short of Bernstein's first effort, although the choral diction is unsurpassed (Telarc 80181). It's best to avoid **Yuraka Sado** (Erato), especially as it's coupled with a horrible *Kaddish*. **Cleobury** (EMI) has turned out many fine recordings, but why record this in an organ version? Likewise **Matthew Best,** a wonderful conductor on his worst days, who chooses the nonorchestral version. The singing is tremendous, so perhaps a perverse few may like it (Hyperion). **Hickox** makes no such misjudgement, and gives us by far the finest version from across the Atlantic (IMP 6600092).

Mass. Bernstein's commission for the opening of the Kennedy Center in Washington is replete with dated 60s-isms and turns of lyric phrases that couldn't have tied the work into a specific American cultural period more strongly. But it also stands as a landmark of American music, an eclectic summary of a time when all things were considered and most accepted. Using the structure of the Roman Mass was a stroke of genius, both for its ability to exorcize past humanitarian failures by a renewed Vatican II church and as a continuation of Bernstein's dialogue with God about the human condition—perhaps the central theme of his entire output. Some of his most inventive music was poured into this score, and it remains exceptionally popular with audiences whenever it's performed.

It should come as no surprise that the original cast recording will always be the one to hear. Patriarchally overseen by **Bernstein,** it captures the sense of occasion, due to the freshness and energy supplied by the first performers, making it one for the recorded history books (Sony 63089).

Missa Brevis. At Robert Shaw's suggestion, Bernstein reworked some of the choruses from his 1955 work *The Lark* into this 10-minute mass. It's in the tradition of medieval masses, ethereal, calming, and practical. Its only recording is coupled with **Shaw's** *Chichester Psalms*—not a bad deal (Telarc 80181).

Songfest marked the final stylistic phase in Bernstein's writing, a time when great emphasis was given to the spoken word, resulting in work not unlike Barber's in its extreme clarity and personification of text. **Bernstein** recorded it first, and that disc is certainly worth having (DG), but it's **Slatkin's** wonderfully fresh, springtime-sounding recording that will be hard to beat in the years to come (RCA 61581).

A White House Cantata (1600 Pennsylvania Avenue). In the early 70s Bernstein again turned his attention to the theater, this time to recreate episodes from the early years of the American presidency, alongside a series of responses from a black couple playing the presidential servants, an attempt to portray the inequalities of the time. Every once in a while the musicians step out of their roles to present a third story line in which the characters are rehearsing the play; in this way Bernstein (and librettist Alan Jay Lerner) were hoping to unite the two main themes. The musical, called *1600 Pennsylvania Avenue,* was one of the biggest failures of Bernstein's career. **Nagano** tries to salvage it by presenting a concert version that omits the play rehearsal. Some of the music is pleasing, but it's nowhere near Bernstein's best, and you could safely pass it up and not miss out on much. For the completist or the curious, however, it's probably the last word on this misbegotten effort, and it's unlikely that the stellar cast of June Anderson, Thomas Hampson, Barbara Hendricks, and Kenneth Tarver will ever be surpassed (DG 463448).

OPERAS AND THEATER WORKS

A Quiet Place. Bernstein's second opera incorporated his first, *Trouble in Tahiti.* It's wholly unsuccessful, one of the more depressing operas of the 20th century. I always find myself counting the moments until the *Trouble in Tahiti* parts begin. Dinah, the female protagonist, has died in a car accident, and the family is gathered at her funeral. This sets the stage for a series of *Tahiti* flashbacks that are utterly incongruous, musically and dramatically, with the super-serious, psychologically tormented libretto Bernstein concocted. Evidently the public agrees— **Bernstein's** is the only recording (DG) aside from a suite put together by **Tilson Thomas** (also DG), and it isn't currently available.

Candide. Of all Bernstein's compositions, this is the one that gave him the most trouble over the years, truly a "magnificent failure" if ever there was one. Almost universally praised for some of his finest music, this rendition of Voltaire's story was just as unanimously condemned by critics as unfit for the stage. As a result, it has endured many incarnations over the years, from full-blown operetta to a scaled-down rococo chamber version.

A good place to start is the original cast version, so you can make the same judgement past audiences had to make. The verdict in our time may well be that the music is terrific and people in 1957 were not hip enough to grasp it. The cast is great, although the sound—clear, clean mono—might be a problem for some (Sony 48017). The new Broadway cast recording is indeed worthy, but the question of "is that enough?" must be asked (RCA). **Bernstein's** last go at this piece, a "work in progress" for some 40 years, must be taken as his final say. His handpicked cast, including June Anderson and Jerry Hadley, with Adolphe Green as the narrator, gives us the *Candide* for the ages— although further attempts at staging it will no doubt continue for ages (DG 429734).

On the Town. This 1944 musical, with a superlative book by Comden and Green, tells the simple story of three sailors on a 24-hour shore leave in New York. Each character has his own short series of adventures, and in the end they all happily board ship as another trio of sailors arrives to repeat the cycle. From the torch song "Lonely Town" to the exuberantly double-entendre-laden "I Can Cook," there isn't a dull moment to be found.

Even with its sometimes crackling sound, it's hard to beat the energy and enthusiasm of **Bernstein's** 1960 recording. Nancy Walker is superb as Hildy, and John Reardon gives us a Gaby for the ages, but this might be hard to find (Sony 47154). **Tilson Thomas** decided that an updated version was needed during his tenure as director of the London Symphony, complete with an all-star cast from opera and Broadway (DG). The singing is for the most part very good, but the LSO doesn't have the flair of Bernstein's band. The newest entry has a cast with luminaries like **Judy Kaye** and Kim Criswell, who are far better attuned to this idiom. This won't offset Bernstein, but it's close (Jay 1231).

Trouble in Tahiti. Bernstein's sardonic commentary on contemporary married life contains some of his wittiest writing and most biting social criticism. We can relate to the themes presented in the piece, whether the early morning argument over breakfast or the disagreement over who should go to Junior's play (neither does). What made marriage difficult then makes it difficult now, and this work will be fresh for many generations to come, despite its rather dated musical idiom. **Bernstein** makes full use of jazz and popular song to put far more serious subjects across, and accomplishes it marvelously (Sony 60969).

West Side Story. Musical or opera? Drama or comedy? These are just a few of the questions critics and public alike have been asking for years over the singular work that established Bernstein as a major star in the musical firmament. The piece can survive many types of shading as long

as the performance itself is executed with flair and substance, for if *West Side Story* is anything, it's a virtuoso piece for dancers, actors, singers, and orchestra.

For those who don't know, the story is centered on two rival gangs and the relationship of a man and woman from each, based on *Romeo and Juliet* but set on the west side of New York City. Tony and Maria chance upon one another and fall immediately in love. Bernstein miraculously captures the local color of both gangs, giving us a portrayal of jealousy, racism, and prejudice that is as timely now as it has ever been. The tragic ending—almost unique on the musical comedy stage—left an indelible mark.

When **Bernstein** recorded it for DG, many critics balked over the choice of Carreras and Te Kanawa in the roles of Tony and Maria. How, they asked, can a Spaniard with an un-rehabilitated Spanish accent play a New York boy, while his partner lumbers along with an English accent? Read my lips: It does not matter! The singing, with very few exceptions (all admirably covered up in the studio), is superb in every respect. The orchestra is an A-plus studio group that really wails. The sound is fabulous, with a dynamic range that must be heard to be believed, and Bernstein—after years of thinking about the piece—puts his final thoughts down in digital sound (DG 415253). But I don't want to short shrift the original sound track recording, although it must be admitted that it sounds like a movie score—boxy sound, badly balanced voices, unrealistic sound stage. This is a second, not a first, choice (Sony). The recent British revival recording nicely captured in very good sound is interpretatively a non-starter in view of the competition (Jay).

Wonderful Town. You will have a wonderful time listening to this tongue-in-cheek musical about two girls from Ohio trying to make it in the big city. Taken from the popular play *My Sister Eileen, Wonderful Town* tells the story of two sisters, Ruth and Eileen, who are determined to make it big in New York, and along the way they encounter adventures and love, not unlike On the Town. But this is no sequel, and the music is every bit as wondrous as the earlier musical. It has had quite a recorded history, including the original cast with **Rosalind Russell,** now available in very good—but still old—sound (Sony). The claim to be the first absolutely complete recording, along with some excellent singing and excellent sound, makes the release directed by **John Owen Edwards** very attractive (Jay 1281). But the presses stop with the amazing, best-ever sound in the recording by **Rattle** and his crackerjack Birmingham Contemporary Music Group. The stunning portrayals by Kim Criswell, Audra McDonald, and Thomas Hampson make this the version to beat, probably for a very long time (EMI 56753).

SONGS

If all of Mozart's music was grounded in opera, so all of Bernstein's has its roots in the American musical theater. **Judy Kaye** and William Sharp recorded "Songfest," a wonderful album of selections from various musicals, and the world premier of Arias & Barcarolles (Koch 7000). The pianism is spiffy and poignant, the singing dead on target stylistically and impregnated with verve and emotion, with the best "A Little Bit in Love" on record. An old compendium of numbers spotlighting the talents of Comden and Green is available for those wishing to mine the riches of the original recordings (Sony 44760). And finally, **Upshaw,** Patinkin, and others give us a provocative album titled "Leonard Bernstein's New York" (Nonesuch 79400).   RITTER

Franz Berwald *(1796–1868)*

Berwald has been hailed as "the most commanding composer Sweden has thus far produced," and while it must be admitted there's scant competition for the title, these words of praise would no doubt be considered entirely justified by the composer. He was a fiercely independent spirit, imbued with a strong self-confidence that spurred him on to create wondrous symphonies at a time when both symphonies and orchestras capable of playing them were thin on the ground in Sweden. He put his greatest effort into his works for the stage, in their time as wholeheartedly ignored as the symphonies; even today, the domestic catalog shows only a single disc of selections from *Estrella di Soria,* which isn't very encouraging. With five complete sets of the symphonies now available as well as scattered individual pairings, it seems likely that it's in these works that his legacy will flourish.

SYMPHONIES

Berwald himself once declared, "The course of events should sometimes be interrupted by surprises; otherwise boredom ensues." Certainly there's nothing boring about his music, at its best displaying remarkable melodic and harmonic innovation, a trenchant and unexpected use of tone color that must have confounded the conservative Swedish establishment. Note, for example, the way he folds the Scherzo into the slow movement of *Sinfonie Singulière,* or in *Sinfonie Naïve* waits until the recap of the final movement to introduce an entirely new theme. Among harmonic touches too numerous to detail, you can't help noting the cheeky comments from the horns that punctuate the grand swaying theme in *Sinfonie Capricieuse* I and the almost Ivesian tone clusters in *Sinfonie Sérieuse* I. These designations were the composer's own, and probably not since Haydn were such names for symphonies so richly deserved.

Most listeners were probably introduced to Berwald through **Markevitch's** pioneering Decca LP of *Singulière* and Symphony in Eb (sometimes called *Naïve,* though the composer later had second thoughts); happily these performances have been restored (DG 457705), while those with fond memories of the Nonesuch LP of *Sérieuse* and *Singulière* with **Schmidt-Isserstedt** will find it reissued too (Accord). **Ehrling** established his credentials early on with a splendid London recording of *Singulière* and *Naïve* as well as a Swedish Radio LP of *Sérieuse,* all since brought out with the shorter pieces he recorded for Nonesuch. These remain highly praiseworthy, especially the two he did for London, which still sound resplendent (Bluebell 037), but they've been handily supplanted by his set with the Malmö Symphony (BIS 795). Here are beautiful performances by a conductor who has lived with these pieces for many years, played by an orchestra who surely have this music in their very souls. Even those who already own Ehrling's earlier recordings will want this set for *Capricieuse,* which he offers for the first time; but throughout the set there is a wonderful freshness, a compelling sense of discovery that really makes the music come alive.

Roy Goodman very nearly matches Ehrling strength for strength and includes a fragmentary early symphony ignored by everyone else; actually it sounds more like Schubert (Hyperion 67081). Save for unnecessarily brisk tempos in *Capricieuse* IV (Ehrling nudges it along too) and *Singulière* I, he does very well with the symphonies, and the open, airy sonics are a strong plus. **Ulf Björlin** recorded the symphonies and a lot more with the Royal Philharmonic; these have been spread across three CDs along with the Violin and Piano Concertos and several smaller pieces, while the symphonies have also been issued as a "Double Forte" set (EMI). Earnest and rather blowzy, *Sérieuse* IV seems a mite overwrought, and the sound is a bit thick-textured.

Although **Neeme Järvi's** set has been lavishly praised, the tempos all too often seem rushed, while his marked slowdown at the end of *Sin-*

gulière, as if this were just another "Romantic" symphony, suggests he never really understood Berwald's quirky style (DG 415502). **Kamu** offers good value, but this one-time firebrand has apparently become too "establishment" for this music, with tepid tempos in the final movements of the first two symphonies; the second disc, which includes the Piano Concerto, is better, although both CDs are lacking in inner detail (Naxos). **David Montgomery's** set is even worse; sluggish and indifferently recorded, it's no bargain even though it costs less than the two Naxos discs (Arte Nova).

Blomstedt recorded *Sérieuse* and *Naïve* with the San Francisco Symphony (London 436597), while **Salonen** did *Singulière* and *Naïve* with the Swedish Radio Orchestra (Musica Sveciae 531), and in both cases my only regret is that they never completed the series. Unfortunately, although Blomstedt recorded both in the same hall, *Sérieuse* sounds thick and over-resonant next to *Naïve,* although not enough to rule out his propulsive and richly sympathetic readings. Salonen invests both symphonies with a healthy vigor, with a felicitous delicacy in the opening movement of *Singulière,* and the engineers have done their job well. **Roberto Tigani** and his Sardinian players are exuberant but a bit too businesslike in *Capricieuse,* sailing past all Berwald's quirky turns of phrase; the disc is far more recommendable for the Violin Concerto (Bongiovanni 5074). **Dorati's** *Capricieuse* has been reissued in a Swedish Society CD as makeweight for his Sibelius 2, but his slow tempos in No. I render it noncompetitive.

OTHER ORCHESTRAL MUSIC

For many, their first acquaintance with Berwald's shorter works came with **Ehrling's** Nonesuch LP, offering the Overture and Polonaise from *Estrella di Soria,* the Overture to *Drottningen av Golconda* (The Queen of Golconda), and the tone poems *Erinnerung an die Norwegischen Alpen* (Memories of the Norwegian Alps), *Bajadärfesten* (Festival of the Bayadères), and *Elfenspiel* (Play of the Elves); of these, all but the Polonaise (which would have fit too) have been reissued along with *Sinfonie Sérieuse* (Bluebell 047). To this number **Björlin** added *Wettlauf* (Racing) and *Ernste und Heitere Grillen* (Serious and Joyful Fancies), with the full complement spread over the EMI CDs containing the symphonies and concertos.

Both overtures are included in **Roy Goodman's** set of the symphonies (Hyperion), while **Kamu** appends *Estrella di Soria* to his *Sérieuse* and *Capricieuse* (Naxos). Most enjoyable of the lot is *Estrella di Soria* is Goodman, although Björlin's splendid Royal Philharmonic horn section is a joy to hear; Kamu is exhilarating but done in by excessive echo, while Ehrling is given even more cramped sonics. In the remaining pieces, honors are divided more evenly between Ehrling and Björlin, although the latter has the edge for both ensemble and sonic impact. Collectors won over by Berwald's very special blend of humor and color will want to have both. They will also want to seek out a collection of overtures written for the Swedish Royal Theater, including two by Berwald: *Modehandlerskan* (The Dressmaker), and *Jag går i Kloster* (I Enter a Monastery) (Sterling 1009).

CONCERTOS

The Piano Concerto actually postdates the symphonies by some 10 years, although you'd never know it; it's a wide-eyed and tuneful rhapsody bearing little relation to the more harmonically innovative symphonies, thoroughly winning and surprisingly effective, given that Berwald's own instrument of choice was the violin. While the composer indicated the work could be played "without orchestra," he surely never intended that it be played without woodwinds, making **Ponti's** strings-only account all the more curious (Vox, Volume 7 of "The Romantic Piano Concerto"). **Greta Erikson's** highly enjoyable LP version could have been a contender if only the CD hadn't been reduced from stereo to mono for some strange reason (Genesis). **Marian Migdal's** fervent account (EMI Matrix 1) is much preferable to **Niklas Sivelöv's** uneventful reading (Naxos 553052, with the last two symphonies), and the fact that it's coupled with the Violin Concerto makes it all the more attractive.

Berwald was in his element in the Violin Concerto, although the piece was haughtily dismissed at its premiere despite the earnest effort of the soloist, his brother August. To be sure, this product of the 24-year-old composer sounds nothing like the symphonies; the first movement could just as well be by Spohr, the last by Paganini. On the EMI disc mentioned above, **Arve Tellefsen's** florid approach makes the most of the music, but he simply can't match the sustained singing tone and warm phrasing of **Marco Rogliano,** ably assisted by Roberto Tigani (♦Bongiovanni 5074), and **Tobias Ringborg** (with Niklas Willén) is even more austere tonally (Naxos 554287), although his coupling of Tor Aulin's Concerto 3 may be more attractive than the *Capricieuse* appended by Tigani. There's also a spirited account by **Leon Spierer** and Gabriel Chmura (Thorofon 2018). **Leo Berlin** (with Jan Krenz) leaves the others trailing behind in the finale, but his LP hasn't made it to CD (Lyssna).

Adding to the pleasures of Ehrling's set of the symphonies is the only available recording of *Konzertstück* for bassoon, nimbly played by **Christian Davidsson** (BIS); a close cousin to the Hummel Concerto, it has a puckish ribaldry all its own, all the more curious for the unexpected appearance of the familiar "Be it ever so humble . . ." in the slow movement.

CHAMBER MUSIC

Berwald's three quartets provide a profile of the composer's musical growth, from the gawky yet compelling G minor of 1818 to the more assured exercises in Eb and A minor written 30 years later. Adventurous and stimulating, they challenge the mindset of the listener as much as the skill of the performers. They didn't do well on LP, and it wasn't until the digital era that these pieces finally came into their own. The **Frydén Quartet** offers 2 and 3; while their Discofil LP also contained 1, it's not included on the CD, even though it could easily have been added to the playing time of 39 minutes (Caprice 21334). They are unbeatable in this music, with direct and inspired playing that quite overwhelms the rather thin sound. The **Yggdrasil Quartet** offers all three, and they're a force to be reckoned with, youthful and filled with zest, if perhaps miked a bit too closely (BIS 759). There are two other versions of No. 1, with the **Chilingirian Quartet** (CRD 3361)—lacking the drive and inflection of the others—and the **Lysell Quartet** in a far better and richer-sounding performance (Musica Sveciae 520).

Moreover, Musica Sveciae's coupling provides the perfect segue into the Septet in Eb, nestled in time between Quartets 1 and 2 (1828) yet stylistically sounding rather more like Hummel; no doubt it was patterned after Beethoven's model. The **Lysell Quartet** (filled out with clarinet, bassoon and double bass) gives an excellent account, making their CD (Musica Sveciae, with Quartet 1) the perfect companion for the **Frydén** pairing of Quartets 2 and 3. The **Nash Ensemble** couples Berwald's Septet with one by Hummel (not the "Military," the other one), and neither performance nor sound leaves anything to be desired (CRD 3344). Spohr's Nonet in F also makes a good companion piece, and the **Czech Nonet's** pairing is an excellent choice (Supraphon 1270). The **Berlin Octet** pairs the septets of Berwald and the sadly neglected Konradin Kreutzer and performs both with poise and clarity (Berlin 9037). The **Consortium Classicum** groups the Septet with the Piano Quintet in C

minor and the Quintet for Piano and Winds in Eb, but there are better versions of all three (Koch Schwann 310056).

While recordings of the remaining works are thinner on the ground, fortunately their quality is high. The two Piano Quintets (in C minor and A) are nicely coupled by **Eduard Mrazek** and the Vienna Philharmonic Quintet, a short disc (51 minutes) but eminently satisfying (Big Ben 872004). However, it has been handily supplanted by polished and glowing performances by **Bengt-Ake Lundlin** with the Uppsala Chamber Soloists, in excellent sound (Naxos 553970). The Piano Quintet in C minor is coupled with Piano Trios 1 and 3, with pianist **Stefan Lindgren** joining the Berwald Quartet and Lysell Trio respectively (Musica Sveciae 521); yet for all their impassioned playing and superb recording, it should be noted that Marco Polo offers all five piano trios on two separate discs (223430 and 223170, each with a different Hungarian threesome), and there used to be a very fine set with **Wilhelm Walz,** Jörg Metzger, and Arne Torger, although copies may be hard to find (Big Ben 572005). The early *Duo Concertante* for two violins and the more mature yet fresh-sounding violin/piano and cello/piano duos are beautifully played by **Ringborg** and friends (Naxos 554286).

Save for a few pieces included on **Gretchen Erikson's** piano concerto disc (Genesis), Berwald's piano output remains poorly represented. **Katia Capua** offers a very nice sampler (Bongiovanni 5082).   HALLER

Heinrich von Biber *(1644–1704)*

Biber was one of the most important German composers and Europe's greatest violin virtuoso of the 17th century. He joined the Salzburg court as Kapellmeister in 1670 and worked there for the rest of his career. He was renowned for his remarkable compositions for violin, which often require the use of *scordatura* (special tunings that make peculiar tone colors or multiple stops possible). He raised this technique to its highest level of development in his masterpiece, the 15 *Rosary* or *Mystery* Sonatas.

ORCHESTRAL MUSIC

Battalia. Biber was an early master of program music, and *Battalia* is his most popular orchestral work. Written in 1673, it's remarkable for its ambition and honesty. It employs unusual effects like *col legno battuto* (striking the string of a violin or viol with the wooden part of the bow), off-stage instruments, placing paper against the string of the violon to get a kazoo-like sound, snap pizzicato (250 years before Bartók) to represent gunshots, and polytonality. The ending, rather than rejoicing in triumph, has a lament for the dead and wounded. **Il Giardino Armonico** has vividly recorded this work, together with the *Passacaglia* for lute, Partita 7 from *Harmonia artificiosa-ariosa,* and Biber's whimsical *Sonata Representativa* (♦Teldec 21464).

Sonatae tam aris, quam aulis servientes. These "Sonatas as much for the altar as for the table," i.e., sacred and secular sonatas, were written in 1676. They require a virtuoso ensemble, with writing for violins and violas about a fourth higher than normal at the time, and a trumpeter able to play in G minor on a natural C trumpet. The **Purcell Quartet** has recorded this music nicely (Chandos), but **Rare Fruits Council** has made a more spirited recording in excellent sound (Astrée 8630). For those who like their trumpets garnished with timpani, the **Parley of Instruments** recording has been reissued (Helios 55041).

Fidicinium sacro-profanum was probably issued in 1682 to celebrate the founding of the archdiocese of Salzburg by St. Rupert in 582. This music was, once again, good for sacred or secular occasions, and could be performed by string orchestra and church choir or string orchestra alone. Taking the second option, the **Purcell Quartet** plays very well (Chandos, with other music, including *Battalia*), but the **Clemencic Consort** is livelier with more elastic tempos (Accord 200292).

Harmonia artificiosa-ariosa. These works were published posthumously. They are perhaps Biber's most demanding pieces for string orchestra, as they employ *scordatura,* which creates strange tone colors. The **Purcell Quartet** has recorded them (Chandos), but again **Rare Fruits Council** has a later recording that is more energetic, better recorded, and fits all the music onto one disc (Astrée 8572).

CHAMBER MUSIC

Rosary or *Mystery Sonatas.* Biber's masterpiece, these 15 sonatas were probably composed in the mid-1670s. They represent the 15 Mysteries of the Rosary, divided into three sets of five each: Mysteries of the Joyful Rosary, Mysteries of the Sorrowful Rosary, and Mysteries of the Glorious Rosary, respectively, which relate to Christ's Infancy, Passion, and Ascension, and are meditated upon as the Rosary is recited. The sonatas are remarkable for their tone painting and for the fact that each employs its own tuning for the solo violin, often to facilitate otherwise difficult or impossible multiple stops or to create striking tone colors. The soloist must maintain a battery of violins to make sure they stay in tune in so large a variety of tunings.

Most recordings have been by period instrumentalists, but two used modern instruments. **Susanne Lautenbacher** made one of the pioneering recordings; she's a competent violinist, but her readings are merely workmanlike (Vox), and the same can be said for **William Tortolano** (GIA). Turning to period instruments, **Marianne Rônez** is outclassed (Winter & Winter). **John Holloway** has excellent sound, but his performance lacks propulsion (Virgin). **Reinhard Goebel** has all the energy Holloway lacks, but he doesn't have a strong feel for the music (DG).

Eduard Melkus recorded the sonatas in 1967, at the beginning of the period instrument revival (♦DG Archiv 453173; MHS 524671; both 2CD). His style hardly sounds "period" by today's standards, but there is a sweetness and sympathy in his playing that serve the music well. Only Melkus plays 11:1, the first movement of the "Resurrection" Sonata, as though an event of earth-shaking importance has just occurred. He's also blessed with one of the largest, most varied continuo ensembles. **Evan Johnson** recorded these pieces in the mid-'80s (♦Newport Classics 60035, 2CD). He's a musician of rare insight, a real pioneer in exploring their tone painting. But **Gunar Letzbor** has gone beyond Johnson's achievements (♦Arcana 901, 2CD). His set is remarkable for the vividness of its tone painting; listen to his startling evocation of the Flagellation in 7. He's fortunate to have a continuo at least as large as Melkus's.

Except for Tortolano's, all the sets of the *Mystery Sonatas* end with Biber's *Passacaglia* for solo violin. It's meant to evoke the work of the Guardian Angel, and is the greatest composition written for solo violin before Bach's sonatas and partitas. **Holloway**'s recording has an unchanging tempo, and this is important since the descending dotted quarter notes of the bass line undoubtedly represent the unwavering presence of our guardian angels as they stride beside us wherever we go (Virgin 90838, 2CD). **Andrew Manze** includes the *Passacaglia* in his set of the eight violin sonatas, and, like Holloway, he sticks to one tempo to even better effect (♦Harmonia Mundi 907134/35, 2CD).

Violin Sonatas. Published in 1681, these eight sonatas were the basis for Biber's fame as a virtuoso composer for violin until the manuscript of the *Mystery Sonatas* was discovered and published in the late 19th century.

Like the latter, two of them require *scordatura.* Imaginative and quirky like the *Mystery Sonatas,* they are very enjoyable works. **Marianne Rônez** (Cavalli) recorded them but is outclassed in virtuosity and imagination by **Manze,** who is also better recorded (♦Harmonia Mundi 907134/35, 2CD). **Carol Lieberman** has also recorded them, but she occasionally plays out of tune and can't match Manze's charisma (Centaur).

Sonata Representativa is an early example of musical pirating. These humorous works, designed to imitate various animal sounds, were mostly stolen note for note from the *Musiurgia Universalis,* published in 1650 by the Jesuit musicologist Athanasius Kircher. It's a contest between **Marianne Rônez** (Cavalli), **Manze** (♦Harmonia Mundi 907134/35), and **Enrico Onofri** (♦Teldec 21464). Manze and Onofri tie.

CHORAL WORKS

Missa Salisburgensis. Recent research has attributed this and *Missa Bruxellensis* to Biber. The former was written in 1682 to celebrate the 1100th anniversary of the foundation of the archbishopric of Salzburg by St. Rupert. It employs huge forces, and Musica Antiqua Köln and the Gabrieli Consort & Players, under the direction of **Reinhard Goebel** and **Paul McCreesh,** respectively, have joined forces to record the work (DG Archiv 457611). The sound is admirably clear, and there are some fine antiphonal effects. Biber avoided complex counterpoint, as it would only have been obscured by the resonant acoustics of Salzburg Cathedral. This is a very fine recording, with strong performances all around.

Missa Bruxellensis. Written in 1701 to celebrate the founding of the Order of the Knights of St. Rupert by the archbishop, Count Thun, it uses similar forces and is stylistically similar to *Missa Salisburgensis,* but is distinguished by the greater than usual role assigned to the trumpets (the Knights were a military order). La Capella Reial de Catalunya and Le Concert des Nations have recorded the work in Salzburg Cathedral under **Savall**'s direction (Alia Vox 9808). The group makes an impressive sound in the Cathedral's echoey interior, with some of the countertenors the only weak performers (perhaps they had to strain their falsettos to fill such a vast space).

OPERA

Arminio. Arminius (Hermann in German) was the German tribal leader who defeated three legions under Varus's command in Germany in AD 9, saving Germany from Roman domination. Six years after this victory, Germanicus Caesar fought Arminius and captured his wife, Segesta. It's the conceit of the opera that Germanicus then brought Segesta to Rome in triumph and that Arminius accompanied her there, disguised as a slave, intending to rescue her. The opera then tells how Arminius sought the release of his wife, finally granted by Tiberius. In a period instrument performance of great intimacy the voices aren't always first class, but the story is amusing and **Wolfgang Brunner** moves it along at a sensible pace (CPO 999258, 3CD).   MAGIL

Harrison Birtwistle (b. 1934)

Birtwistle is often grouped with the so-called Manchester School, his powerful style similar to that of colleagues Peter Maxwell Davies and Alexander Goehr. More than those contemporaries, his point of departure seems to be the primeval, ritualistic, and inhuman world of Stravinsky's *Oedipus Rex.* He also stands out by entirely sidestepping any suggestions of dry academicism. He is first and foremost an opera composer, though he has sometimes resisted that history-laden term; even his purely instrumental works carve out their very own brand of elemental theatricality.

ORCHESTRAL MUSIC

The brief *Refrains and Choruses* for woodwind quintet was Birtwistle's first—if belated—composition. Most striking is *Verses for Ensembles* from 1969, for winds, brass, and three percussionists. *For O, For O, the Hobby-Horse Is Forgot* is a 1976 "ceremony" for six percussionists that doesn't rise to the knife-edge memorability of the other pieces. This is Birtwistle at his most savage and intense, and the **Netherlands Wind Ensemble and Percussion Group** demonstrates the particularly idiomatic, spot-on rhythmic and timbral incisiveness that also distinguishes Howarth's orchestral disc on the same label (♦Etcetera 1130).

A forbidding processional for large orchestra, *The Triumph of Time* is a key work—though a characteristically grim one—and a newcomer to Birtwistle might be better directed to a later score like *Secret Theatre*. **Elgar Howarth** and the Philharmonia are recorded with spectacular depth and bass response (Collins 13872), but an older LP by **Boulez** had more rhythmic tension (Argo). Howarth's coupling for *Triumph* is *Gawain's Journey,* extracted from the opera. The similarly depressing *Melancolia I* is more diaphanous and easier to follow, partly because of the reduced scoring for two string orchestras, harp, and solo clarinet (♦NMC 009). The discmates are *Ritual Fragment* for 15 players, and the early and otherworldly *Meridian* for 11 players, mezzo, six sopranos, and solo horn and cello. **NMC**'s church recording makes sure the female sighs of *Meridian* are properly erotic and mystical, and the London Sinfonietta's *Ritual Fragment* is to be preferred to a fussier German performance (CPO 999360).

Two other early scores can be found on an excellent disc: *Nomos* and *An Imaginary Landscape* (♦Collins 14142). The former is Birtwistle at his most savage, while in the latter brutality melds with more ritualistic, Stravinskyesque textures. The longest score on the disc is *Antiphonies* for piano and orchestra (1993). **Joanna MacGregor** is the able pianist and the Dutch Royal Philharmonic is impeccably prepared, as is to be expected, given Michael Gielen's direction. In the two early works on the disc, **Paul Daniel** and the BBC Symphony achieve the rhythmic definition that tends to elude Howarth's *Triumph of Time.*

The recent *Panic* is an exuberant concertante work for saxophone and orchestra, though with a typically chaotic darkness. Here **John Harle** joins Andrew Davis and the BBC Symphony (♦Argo 452104), but the most important, lengthy, and attractive offering on this release is the magnificent *Earth Dances* for large orchestra. Perhaps a kind of update of Stravinsky's *Rite of Spring,* this score brings evocative, quiet writing and drum-led rhythmic emphases together into a cogent and dramatic 36-minute sweep. With its beautiful orchestration and part-writing, it makes a splendid vehicle for **Dohnányi** and the Cleveland Orchestra, who are more brilliant and taut—sonically and interpretatively—than the BBC Symphony under **Peter Eötvös** (Collins 20012).

Perhaps Birtwistle's most immediately engaging and durable nonoperatic opus is *Secret Theatre* for 14 players, and there are several performances to choose from. The **Boulez** is beautifully played, and also has the most palatable and sonorous recording, with more ambience than usual for the IRCAM studios (♦DG 439910). Some find his refined style unidiomatic for Birtwistle, but I can't agree; this would be my first choice for *Secret Theatre,* particularly as the disc is so well filled (including the poetic *Tragoedia,* Birtwistle's earliest critical success). But **Howarth** and the London Sinfonietta (♦Etcetera 1052) give this score a priceless touch of harried and farcical fun that rather eludes Boulez (which is not to imply that Boulez is immune to the humor of the music). Also, the disc has a brighter sound picture than the DG.

Johannes Kalitzke and Musikfabrik NRW are also impeccably prepared and faithfully—if a little closely—recorded (CPO). But the direc-

tion and execution are fussier than on the other two, and once past the opening Kalitzke lets the structural tension sag. So Boulez is necessary in this marvelous music, though one of Howarth's couplings—the riotous, Stan Kenton-ish *Carmen Arcadiae Mechanicae Perpetuum,* which can be described as a manic "twittering machine" à la Paul Klee or a kind of demented calliope in the Ligeti manner—makes the Etcetera disc an absolute must-hear also.

OPERAS

The chamber opera *Punch and Judy* (1967) was Birtwistle's first major work for the theater, and fairly brims over with strident and brilliant instrumental effects. The characters inhabit a world where childish, timeless fable merges with murderous tantrum, and Birtwistle—often setting words purely as phonetic material—moves into a mocking and simplistic style for his librettist's puerile meters and nonsense rhymes. The music also becomes savage, but anchoring the drama are episodes of sustained chorale-like writing that invert the usual relationship between consonance and dissonance. The performance by **David Atherton** and the London Sinfonietta is extraordinarily committed and boasts exceptional ensemble despite the composer's extreme rhythmic demands (Etcetera 2014). The recording is a bit artificial in its balance between singers and orchestra.

In *Gawain* (first staged in 1991), Birtwistle's playing with time and reversibility of death takes on the full nightmarish sense of logic-within-irrationality. The story invokes supreme tests of knightly valor: the Green Knight, decapitated by Gawain in a grisly test of bravery, returns to extract his revenge just as King Arthur's evil half-sister schemes to undermine the solidarity of the court. Marie Angel, François Le Roux, the other singers, conductor **Howarth,** and the Royal Opera company all rise to Birtwistle's heroic demands, which are more overtly operatic than *Punch* (Collins 70412). But again the live recording, though commendably transparent, is rather dry and lacks depth and dynamic range, and there are also some stage noises and loud page-turns.

An all-enveloping and unforgettable experience, *Mask of Orpheus* (completed 1983) demonstrates more than any other work how Birtwistle has permanently changed the face and course of opera. His subject is not so much the Orpheus story as the timeless history—the telling and retelling—of the myth itself. We even follow Orpheus after his physical death, when his skull becomes an oracle and inspires Apollo's jealousy. True to the greatest reform operas, it's impossible to separate music and vocal styles from the drama or the singing from the acting. Most of the singing consists of vocalises or tense, single-note recitations, and there's nothing at all to be heard of the traditional set-piece. Birtwistle's electronics, created at the fabled IRCAM facilities in Paris, are an integral part of the work; this is some of the most memorable, subtle, and evocative electronic music I've heard anywhere. The performances by **Andrew Davis** and his forces in 1996 were taped, but there are no extraneous noises and the reproduction is smooth and flawless (♦NMC 050). Packaging, notes, and libretto are commendably (luxuriously) informative.

ASHBY

Georges Bizet (1838–1875)

If Bizet's *Carmen* was not only the culmination of his own creative genius but the supreme achievement of French opéra-comique, we must nevertheless marvel at the array of highly melodic and colorful scores that jostle one another good-naturedly in his estimable oeuvre. Both on stage and off, the freshness and buoyancy of the Symphony in C and *La Jolie Fille de Perth* sit beside not only *Carmen* but the sun-drenched palette of *Roma* and *L'Arlésienne* as well. Hindsight is all we have; yet in a very real sense the font of melody that first gushed forth in the Symphony was not quenched but merely replenished in the works to come; it was a harbinger (if only the Paris critics had the foresight to realize it) of a great composer who served the muse of melody in both opera house and concert hall.

SYMPHONIES

Plural? Yes, because actually there are two, although there remains some question whether *Roma* is symphony or suite. No such controversy surrounds the Symphony in C, which strangely languished in obscurity until Weingartner conducted the first performance in Basel in 1935. So intimidated was the 17-year-old Bizet by Symphony 1 (after which it was closely modeled) of his teacher, Gounod, that he suppressed the score during his life, and indeed the most fascinating aspect of a long out-of-print Kapp LP was Howard Shanet's absorbing annotations pointing up the many similarities between the two.

In turn, *Roma* might almost be construed as homage to Mendelssohn's "Italian" Symphony, right down to the third-movement procession and the exuberant final tarantella; certainly it's just as delightful as the far better known Symphony in C and deserves to be heard a lot more often. Not surprisingly, the two have frequently been recorded in tandem; for this, pride of place unhesitatingly goes to **Plasson** (♦EMI 55057), particularly in *Roma,* where he whips up a veritable tempest in the opening scene ("Une Chasse dans la Forêt d'Ostie") and fairly takes your breath away in the concluding "Carnaval." At a tempo noticeably less precipitous than **Frémaux's,** the bouncy rhythms bubble over with joy where Frémaux's more exhilarating pace merely skims the surface (EMI 69643; Klavier 11012).

Both are better than **Gardelli** (Orfeo), whose curiously measured pace in the final tarantella robs the piece of its essential spirit; the Symphony can perhaps survive his moderate tempos in the outer movements but not in the mawkish oboe solo in the Adagio, making either Plasson or Frémaux the clear winner. Moreover, Plasson is one of the few conductors to take all the repeats in the Symphony—which would seem to be de rigueur in this essentially Mozartean score—and is also the best recorded of the three. On Vol. 3 of his survey, **Bátiz** piles into the storm scene too, but the normally reliable Royal Philharmonic horns sound like they were having an off day in the opening pages; in the Symphony he takes all the repeats, but the Royal Philharmonic is really disheveled, with a distressingly quavery oboe in the Adagio (ASV). For a real Gallic performance, you might try the Lille Orchestra conducted by **Jean-Claude Casadesus,** coupled with the even rarer *Clovis et Clotilde* cantata (Erato); certainly you'll do better than the slipshod Bordeaux Orchestra and plodding tempos of **Roberto Benzi** (Forlane).

For the C major score, surely the classic version is **Beecham's**—superb playing, impeccable sense of tempo, buoyant and sparkling, a real tour de force (♦EMI 47794). The coupling is his superb *L'Arlésienne* suites, making it a bargain at any price. Few conductors bring out the sheer unbridled joy of the music like **Bernstein,** rather curiously coupled with the Offenbach/Rosenthal *Gaîté Parisienne* (Sony). **Ansermet's** poised and elegant reading offers Beecham strong competition, though a touch more effervescence wouldn't have been amiss (London). **Munch's** earlier recording with the French National Orchestra may be hard to find (Adès; you may know it as a Nonesuch LP); the later one with the Royal Philharmonic (Chesky, with Tchaikovsky's *Francesca da Rimini*—another strange pairing) is around but seems unduly brusque next to Beecham.

Martinon (DG) tends to lean on phrases a bit in the outer movements and is better recommended for the shorter Bizet pieces and works of Lalo (including the Cello Concerto with Fournier). Likewise **Dirk Joeres's** sprightly account is worth seeking out primarily for the coupled Saint-Saëns A major symphony (Carlton). Bizet's Symphony (and the Mendelssohn "Italian") were **Stokowski's** last recordings, taped with the National Philharmonic in June 1977, and both of these wondrously invigorating performances sound more youthful and cheeky than those of many conductors half his age, while the sound is open and clear (CBS). **Johanos's** recording handily belies its low cost; not only does he take all the repeats, but his crisp, alert reading is one of the best you can find at any price (♦Naxos 553027).

Haitink's spacious tempos suggest a conscious attempt to accommodate the Concertgebouw acoustics (Philips). It's warmly played and recorded if somewhat lacking in élan. **López-Cobos's** account suffers from a drastically reduced ensemble (derived from the Cincinnati Symphony) and is also miked much too closely; it sounds scrawny, and I is nothing but a blur at his tempo (Telarc). **Hickox** is properly insouciant, but the sound lacks warmth and presence (Virgin). Despite brisk tempos, **Ozawa** lacks the buoyancy of Bernstein or the flair of Beecham (EMI). **Barenboim's** rather low-voltage reading somehow got lost in the shuffle when the remainder of his EMI LP got transferred to CD—no great loss. While the pairing of the Bizet and Franck symphonies seems apt , the performances led by **Bychkov** are bland and impersonal and so is the recording (Philips). The couplings elected by the **Orpheus Ensemble**—Prokofiev's *Classical Symphony* and Britten's *Simple Symphony*—are a bit off the beaten track, but the music is presented with flair and polish and the sound is first-rate (DG).

Marriner tacks on the *Classical Symphony* too, along with Stravinsky's *Pulcinella Suite* (Decca 417734); his remake coupled with *L'Arlésienne* suites offers a better fit as well as a fresher sounding recording (EMI). **Saraste,** while polished and eminently musical, lacks the energy of some other versions (Virgin). **Gardiner,** like Plasson and Johanos, takes all the repeats, but his performance is on the bland side (Erato). **Krivine** also takes the repeats; however, his rather thoughtful approach imparts to the Symphony a serious mien I doubt the composer ever intended (Denon). While **Ko_ler** and the Slovak Philharmonic may not be the first who come to mind in this music, despite the occasional odd Slavic coloring, their work here is above approach; still, the coupled *Carmen Preludes* make for rather short measure (Opus). **Dutoit** is a worthy choice, with a particularly soulful oboe solo in the Adagio (Decca).

OTHER ORCHESTRAL MUSIC

L'Arlésienne and *Carmen.* What we know today as the music for Alphonse Daudet's play *L'Arlésienne* bears little relation to the original, being limited to the considerably revised version put together by Bizet's friend Ernest Guiraud. To be sure, the two suites generally offered on disc are the cream of the crop, yet it's good to hear the whole thing once in a while, originally conceived by Bizet as a sequence of short pieces lasting an hour and far more intimately scored than Guiraud's lush setting. It's particularly gratifying to hear Bizet's juxtaposition of the opening "Marche des Rois" with the Act V "Farandole" which some annotators would have you believe was entirely Guiraud's idea.

Robert Haydon Clark (Collins) elects consistently brisker tempos than **Plasson** (EMI); in some cases Clark's faster pace is apropos, yet overall Plasson's weightier approach and more substantial choral forces make Clark seem superficial. Either is preferable to **Rahbari,** thanks to whoever had the bad idea of including extensive excerpts from the play—in French, with no translation—often spoken over the music (Discover). Who needs that? **Gardiner** (coupled with the Symphony) offers maybe half the score in Bizet's original orchestration (Erato), but why settle for part of it?

Plasson may also be heard in the familiar *L'Arlésienne Suite 1* in full orchestral dress, along with *Carmen Suite* and *Jeux d'enfants* (EMI); however, the main reason to buy this disc is the other, more rarified material: *Les Quatre Coins* (originally part of *Jeux d'enfants), Marche Funèbre,* and, best of all, *Première Ouverture,* a fine piece clearly modeled after Rossini's *William Tell.* If you can find the Dutoit, you'll also obtain an even more exhilarating account of the *Ouverture* (Decca).

If you buy **Beecham's** Symphony, you already have the recommended *L'Arlésienne*—and don't forget his *Carmen Suite* (EMI 63379). Still, there are others to choose from as well. Many would award **Ansermet** top marks along with Beecham, both for performance (by the Suisse Romande) and sound (London); others swear by **Claudio Abbado** (DG). Those on a budget will probably be perfectly happy with **Ormandy** (RCA). **Paray's** readings of the standard *Carmen* and *L'Arlésienne* suites have the stamp of authority, but the sonics are beginning to show their age (Mercury). It's difficult to recommend **Frühbeck de Burgos;** his readings are competent and dutiful but lacking in flair (MCA). **Krivine** (coupled with the Symphony) says nothing new about the familiar *L'Arlésienne* suites, while the tambour is so far back in the hall in the final "Farandole" you can barely hear it.

You only get one suite from *L'Arlésienne* from **López-Cobos,** along with a brief serving from *Carmen;* they come off a lot better than the Symphony, but not enough to redeem the enterprise (Telarc). **Stokowski** unfortunately omits the "Intermezzo" from the second *L'Arlésienne* suite, but offers a generous helping from *Carmen;* still, the panache of his performances—taped the year before the Symphony—more than compensates even though the CD doesn't sound as good as the LP (Sony). **Bernstein's** more extensive selection has been offered twice on CD, first in the "Royal Edition" and more recently as part of the "Bernstein Century" series; either way the airy sonics can't cover up his curiously lackadaisical *Carmen* excerpts—with solo cornet standing in for the "Toreador's Song"—and (from the sound of it) tambourine but no tambour in the final "Farandole" in *L'Arlésienne.* **Karajan** makes the same mistake (DG), as did **Smetá_ek** (Supraphon).

Chung conducts crisply enough, but the murky sound makes it a total loss (DG). **Tortelier** lacks the subtlety and pastel shading of Beecham, as does the echo-ridden recording (Chandos); moreover, the decision to present the *Carmen* selections in the same order as the opera means that the suite ends rather ineffectually with the gentle final bars of the "Aragonaise." **Dutoit** emphasizes refinement and attention to detail over the grand sweep of this highly dramatic music, and the Montreal orchestra lacks the requisite weight and tonal richness (London). **Hogwood** couples Gounod's Symphony 1 and *Petit Symphonie* with a suite of his own devising from *L'Arlésienne* arranged for small orchestra, making for a rather interesting mix.

Bátiz, like Bernstein, pads out the *Carmen* suites with arrangements of the arias; if that's your cup of tea, Bátiz does it better (ASV, Vol. 1). Vol. 2 with *L'Arlésienne* doesn't fare nearly as well, thanks to rushed tempos in "Carillon" and "Farandole." **Alexander Gibson's** bracing *Carmen Suite* and accompanying *Faust* ballet sound as vivid as ever (Classic). Also still vivid are **Munch's** *Carmen* and *L'Arlésienne* suites—actually, you only get the "Farandole" from Suite 2 (with his *Gaîté Parisienne)*— all from London's Phase 4 series. And that's not all; you get *Jeux d'enfants,* Saint-Saëns's *Danse Macabre* and *Rouet d'Omphale* with Marti-

non, Chabrier's *España* and *Marche Joyeuse* with Ansermet, and Solti's *Sorcerer's Apprentice* too.

Old-timers may remember a set with Daudet's play accompanied by the complete score under **Albert Wolff** (London). There are two versions on CD following this example, and both may be avoided. **Helmut Froschauer** directs a concert arrangement sung entirely in German, which makes little sense for American audiences, though it's stylishly performed (Capriccio). Another set is even worse, giving us the entire Daudet text (in French) with Daniel Mesguich playing all the parts himself, including the women (Auvidis, 2CD). Even a solid account of the orchestral score by **Malgloire** can't keep it from sounding perverse, and the fact that he omits the Act IV "Intermezzo" doesn't help matters.

Buy the Symphony and you're likely to get *Jeux d'enfants* and *La Jolie Fille de Perth* too; recommended versions include **Ansermet** (London), **Martinon** (DG), and **Johanos** (Naxos). Special praise goes to Johanos for carrying off the gradual accelerando in the final "Danse Bohèmienne" of *Jolie Fille* surpassingly well, not an easy task; Ansermet does well too, though with Martinon the gear-switching is rather more obvious. **Dutoit** (same Decca as the Symphony) isn't long on subtlety in *Jolie Fille,* while **Bátiz** (with *L'Arlésienne)* is better in *Jolie Fille* than *Jeux d'enfants,* though given the sloppy playing of his Mexican forces it really doesn't matter much. **Martinon's** *Jeux d'enfants* as well as the two Saint-Saëns pieces are also available in a "Classic Sound" collection along with Ibert's *Divertissement* and a couple of Berlioz overtures (London).

Patrie. Bizet was stimulated by memories of the Franco-Prussian War to create the stirring overture *Patrie;* one author writes, "one can almost see the tricolor flapping briskly in the wind." The best around is **Paray,** coupled with *Carmen* and *L'Arlésienne* (♦Mercury 434321). Under **Barenboim,** *Patrie* is given a sturdy reading but falls short of the ramrod fervor of Paray, though his *Jolie Fille* is one of the best around (EMI, with *Jeux d'enfants).* Unfortunately, the appended *Carmen* and *L'Arlésienne* suites are no bargain, as Barenboim's sluggish tempos drain the music of its life blood. My favorable recommendation of **Plasson's** Symphony and *Roma* doesn't extend to the coupled *Patrie,* which is incredibly heavy-handed; it sounds more Teutonic than Gallic, and the same may be said of **Bátiz,** coupled with the *Carmen* suites. **Dutoit** with the Symphony is sturdy enough, if perhaps a bit pompous; **Ozawa** offers more of the requisite fervor, though not enough to elevate his Symphony to first tier (EMI). HALLER

OPERAS

Carmen. This may well be the most popular opera in the standard repertory. It has an enticing story, an earthy, sexy heroine, gorgeously melodic arias for all the principal singers, and even memorable music for chorus and orchestra. Any reasonably competent performance will entrance the listener; a great performance will be memorable. As you might expect, such a popular work has often been recorded, and there are half a dozen sets that merit consideration. The best are conducted by Solti, Abbado, and Beecham; all have fine casts and good sound. Your preference will be greatly affected, however, by your acceptance of the title role's characterization. These range from the witty and coquettish de los Angeles (Beecham) to the earthier Troyanos (Solti) and Resnik (Schippers).

Berganza, with Claudio Abbado, offers the best of the recorded Carmens; her portrayal encompasses all aspects of this fascinating role in the right proportions. She's well supported by Domingo, the best of the recorded Don Josés, Milnes, and Cotrubas. Abbado may not have the light and elegant touch of Beecham, but his work here can't be faulted

(♦DG 419636). A close runner-up is the cast of **Te Kanawa,** Troyanos, Domingo, and van Dam led by Solti (♦London 414489). **De los Angeles's** recording with Beecham will strike some as overrefined, but admirers of the Baronet and the Spanish diva love it (♦EMI 49240). It includes Gedda's excellent Don José, whose elegant singing fits right in with the conceptions of Beecham and his Carmen.

Many years later, Gedda partnered **Callas,** who never sang the role on stage and recorded it in the twilight of her career (EMI). Callas fans need not apologize for her effort, but it lacks conviction. **Resnik** also came late to her recording, which is further handicapped by del Monaco's crude singing (London). **Jessye Norman's** Carmen is a botched job altogether (Philips). A recent release featuring the appealing **Jennifer Larmore** is torpedoed by the insensitive and unidiomatic conducting of Sinopoli (Teldec). RCA's recording from the '60s, with **Leontyne Price,** Corelli, Freni, and Merrill, all admired singers, should be better than it is. Its main problems are a lack of French style in Price's and Corelli's singing and in the orchestral playing, which sounds too Wagnerian and unrefined, though Karajan whips up lots of excitement. In addition, Price's singing is often coarse, especially in her lower register; this role was not for her.

As for excerpts, single discs from the Solti (♦London 421300) and Abbado (♦DG 435401) recordings are recommended. Similar discs from the RCA (68021) and EMI (63075) versions are also available. Of interest primarily to devotees of the singers are **Risë Stevens,** a notable Carmen of the '40s and '50s, who can be heard with a good supporting cast (Odyssey 32102), and **Geraldine Farrar,** Martinelli, and Amato, a classy trio from an earlier era who recorded excerpts; the disc includes Farrar singing arias from other French operas (Nimbus 7872).

Les Pêcheurs de perles (*The Pearl Fishers*). This opera has existed on the fringes of the repertory, whence it has been rescued only when a great and popular tenor took up its cause. Caruso was one of the first to spark an interest in it; recent interpreters of the fisherman Nadir have included Kraus, Gedda, and Domingo. The dramatic conflict of the opera, as in Bellini's *Norma,* is that of a priestess who is torn between love and her sacred vows. It's enhanced, perhaps, by its exotic setting in Ceylon.

The available recordings use either Bizet's original version or a posthumously revised one that made some cuts in the original and changed its ending (it's a bit of a muddle). The best-sung sets use the revised version, notably a 1970 performance from Barcelona that has a top-rated cast of **Kraus,** Bruscantini, and Adriana Maliponte (♦Bongiovanni 516). These singers, as a group, are better than those in the original versions, who include **Vanzo,** Cotrubas, and Giuseppe Sarabia (Classics for Pleasure) and **Aler,** Hendricks, and Gino Quilico (EMI). A fine alternate mid-priced recording of the original version has the excellent **Gedda** as its main attraction (♦EMI 69704).   MOSES

SONGS

Recent scholarship debates the suggestion that Bizet wrote his songs as mere financial exercises. Anyone who knows the operas won't be surprised to hear his delightful treatment of text in his songs, numbering close to 50. They're charming, creative with respect to settings, operatic when the dramatic element is present, and often virtuosic for singer and pianist. **Ann Murray** and Graham Johnson attempt to compensate for the paltry history of Bizet songs on record; they present 20, imbuing them with flair, brilliance, and imagination (♦Hyperion 66976). **Sylvia McNair's** four are noteworthy (Philips 446656), and we can only hope someone of Murray's or McNair's abilities will give us the rest.

LOVELACE

Boris Blacher (1903–1975)

Blacher's music is refreshing for its crisp, angular rhythms, bright harmonies, and lean textures. It's lyrical and energetic without a speck of sentimentality; dissonant, but always tonal. He came of age as a composer in Berlin during the Weimar Republic, and though he lived through some of the most harrowing years of the century in the midst of an oppressive regime, his music is never brooding or morose. He wrote several important operas and theater works; sadly, none were available at the time of this writing. His music is heavily influenced by jazz, especially in rhythms and instrumentation, but it's rarely jazzy in an overt way.

Variations on a Theme of Paganini is Blacher's calling card, the work for which he's best known. Written in 1947, it's a zesty set of 16 variations on Paganini's famous *Caprice 24* for solo violin. The work is full of fascinating rhythmic transformations, colorful orchestration, and a fizzy playfulness. **Solti** recorded the current top choice in Vienna (♦London 452853, with Kodály's *Peacock Variations* and Elgar's *Enigma Variations*). The Variations can also be heard in an all-Blacher disc with his Piano Concerto 2 and *Concertante Musik,* with **Herbert Kegel** conducting the Dresden Philharmonic (Berlin 9015).

Blacher's piano concertos were all written for his wife, Gerty Herzog, in the years following WWII. 1 was composed in 1947 when he was writing for small orchestral forces in an effort to keep his music viable by making it practical; it's an absolute delight, with a sparkling solo part, crystalline instrumentation, and a clear, taut design that never allows any slackness. These qualities are emblematic of Blacher's esthetic and can be heard in all three concertos. 1 and 2 are fairly standard, distinguished by their rhythmic punch and lack of melodrama; 3 is a sly, witty set of variations on a theme of Clementi, ostensibly to capitalize on the success of his *Paganini Variations*. All these works are dazzlingly performed by **Horst Göbel** with Rudolf Alberth and the Bavarian Radio Symphony (♦Thorophon 2167).

Blacher's string quartets are terse and vivid statements that serve as a perfect antidote to much of the maudlin, angst-ridden music in this genre in the 20th century. Written between 1930 and 1967, they vary in their compositional processes but not in their unpretentious demeanor. The **Petersen Quartet** gets them just right in their survey of all five (♦EDA 006). The vivace passages are sparkling clean (indeed, this is some of the finest ensemble playing I've ever heard), and the slow movements never get sentimental or soupy.   McINTIRE

Easley Blackwood (b. 1933)

Recently retired from the University of Chicago, Blackwood is known for his prodigious intellect and teaching prowess. As a composer, he's known mainly by other composers and advocates of microtonality. Experiments and compositions using unequal tunings and scales encompassing more than 12 half steps, equal tempered or not, haven't survived their apparent promise to any appreciable extent. For one thing, too few microtonal pieces were composed; for another, it's no small matter for performers to master microtonal intervals of any sort—either in an exposed setting or in audiences' ears. (It's easier and consequently more successful *en masse,* as in Penderecki's *Threnody*.) Blackwood is arguably the most successful to date among composers who actually wrote in a microtonal realm (some wrote essentially panchromatic music and then microtoned it).

"Microtonal Compositions by Easley Blackwood" is highly recommended (Cedille 18). It includes three compositions: *Fanfare in 19-note Equal Tuning for Synthesizer* (Blackwood, performer), *Suite in 15-note*

Equal Tuning for Guitar (Jeffrey Kust, guitar), and *12 Microtonal Etudes for Synthesizer* (Blackwood, performer). Recorded in the early '80s, the synthesizer sounds dated to those attuned to recent computer music, but the sound is not so much the point in this music.

Although not a concert artist, Blackwood is an extraordinary pianist, especially as an interpreter of some of the last century's most esthetically difficult music (for example, his recording of Ives's *Concord Sonata*). His piano music isn't often programmed, and only his own performances are recorded. As with the microtonal pieces, this isn't a bad thing. On "Blackwood Plays Blackwood," containing Concert Etudes, Nocturnes, and Sonata, we hear the composer's intentions without prejudice (Cedille 38). ZIEROLF

Arthur Bliss (1891–1975)

Bliss's posthumous standing shows how fickle musical fashion can be. At the beginning of his career, in the 1920s, he was regarded as the *enfant terrible* of British music, writing bold and feisty scores that startled his older contemporaries. He gradually moved to the center of the British musical establishment, eventually to be seen as the very embodiment of the stiff-upper-lip, tally-ho Englishman; for the last 22 years of his life, indeed, he was Master of the Queen's Musick, a largely ceremonial post that required him to produce music for grand state occasions. And since his death his works have been largely neglected. They deserve better: Bliss can be uneven, and his harmonic identity can be elusive, but the best of his music has a bracing honesty that can excite and invigorate.

Bliss was a capable conductor, too, and left many recordings of his own music; a good number of them could be found until recently in the BBC Classics series and might still pop up in the stores now and then. His masterpiece, the 1930 choral symphony *Morning Heroes*, a tribute to the fallen of WWI, is currently unavailable, as is his finest purely orchestral piece, the moving *Meditations on a Theme by John Blow* (1955).

ORCHESTRAL AND BAND MUSIC

Bliss's first major work, *A Colour Symphony*, inspired by the symbolic associations of colors in heraldry, was written in 1922 and did much to establish his reputation as a major new voice in British music. Of the three recordings available, **Vernon Handley's** idiomatic and assured reading with the Ulster Orchestra carries the day (Chandos 7073, midpriced); it shares a CD with the dramatic scena *The Enchantress*, written in 1951 for Kathleen Ferrier (sung here by Linda Finnie), and the Cello Concerto of 1969, dedicated to Rostropovich (the passionate soloist is Raphael Wallfisch). **David Lloyd-Jones**, with the English Northern Philharmonia, comes very close behind Handley in *A Colour Symphony* and adds a superb account of the muscular ballet score *Adam Zero* (Naxos 553460). **Barry Wordsworth's** handling of *A Colour Symphony* with the BBC Welsh Symphony Orchestra is less confident than its rivals, but it's coupled with the only current recording of *Metamorphic Variations*, a late orchestral essay that gives ample proof of Bliss's feeling for instrumental timbre and his sure contrapuntal technique (Nimbus 5294).

Bliss wrote four ballets; the first of them, *Checkmate*, is still a regular item in the repertoire, and the suite of dances he drew from it is often heard in concert. The West Australian SO under **Hans-Hubert Schönzeler** makes rather heavy going of them (Chandos, with Rubbra's Symphony 5 and Tippett's *Little Music for String Orchestra*). **David Lloyd-Jones** (Hyperion 66436, with Walton's *Façade* suites) and **Handley** (Chandos 8503, with *Colour Symphony*) offer more attractive options.

Bliss's second ballet was *Miracle in the Gorbals*, a modern morality

play set in a Glasgow slum, where a Christ figure brings a dead girl to life and is murdered by the crowd. The music manages a well-judged blend of elegiac introspection and rhythmic excitement. It's joined by the "20-minute dissertation" (as the composer put it), *Discourse for Orchestra*, and a suite constructed by Christopher Palmer from the score for *Things to Come*, Alexander Korda's film adaptation of H.G. Wells's science fiction classic (Naxos 553698). Conductor **Christopher Lyndon-Gee** keeps up the pace, but he's poorly served by the Queensland Symphony Orchestra, whose strings display all the control of a horse on ice.

The music for *Things to Come* has become a classic. The original recording from 1935-36, when the ink was barely dry on the page, has the undisputable authority of **Bliss** at the helm of the London Symphony, though he shares the honors with Muir Mathieson; the sound isn't bad at all (Symposium 1203, with music by Walton, Lambert, Warlock, and Berners, all equally classic).

The score for *Things to Come* was only one of eight film scores (and Bliss composed much music for a ninth, *Caesar and Cleopatra*, before pulling out of the undertaking after a row with the director). Excerpts from three of them (none in the same league as *Things to Come*) have emerged in the "Film Music Classics" series (Marco Polo 223315): a suite from *Christopher Columbus* (arranged by the conductor Adriano), in which Bliss's English tone is colored by an heroic-Iberian quality; three orchestral pieces that seem to be all that survives of the music to *Seven Waves Away* (released in the United States as *Abandon Ship*); and *Baraza*, an "African" concert piece for piano, chorus, and orchestra from the score to *Men of Two Worlds*, followed by four other extracts.

Bliss wrote concertos for cello, violin, and piano. The Violin Concerto is currently unavailable. The Cello Concerto fares rather better: As well as **Wallfisch's** version (Chandos 7073), it can be found sharing a disc with the incisive *Music for Strings* and the slightly anodyne *Two Studies for Orchestra;* **Tim Hugh** and conductor David Lloyd-Jones offer a viable alternative at under half the price (Naxos 553383). The rambling Piano Concerto, pointedly dedicated "to the people of the United States of America" as WWII was looming (both Bliss's father and wife were American), begins as if it were a long-lost work by Prokofiev, and its steely passagework brings the Russian school to mind. With the disappearance of **Philip Fowke's** recording (Unicorn-Kanchana 2029—you might just find it in the deletion bins), the only version currently available is a reissue of the 1962 EMI original, with the Australian pianist **Trevor Barnard** accompanied by Sargent and the Philharmonia (Divine Art 2-4106). Barnard's passion can't disguise the work's lack of structural focus; the string playing is often decidedly ropey, and at under 38 minutes in length, it's hardly a crowded CD.

Bliss's only works for brass band proper are *Belmont Variations* and *Kenilworth* (Chandos 4525 and 4506). As Master of the Queen's Musick he was required to produce a number of fanfares for various state occasions: *Antiphonal Fanfare*, for three brass choirs, written for the investiture of the Prince of Wales, and *Fanfare for the Lord Mayor of London* come from the **Philip Jones Brass Ensemble** (London 430369); a handful of other such flourishes comes from the **Locke Brass Consort** under James Stobart (Chandos 6573, with other British works for brass band).

CHAMBER AND INSTRUMENTAL MUSIC

Bliss wrote four string quartets. He withdrew the first two, dating from 1914 and 1923, and those now flagged as Nos. 1 and 2 were composed in 1940 and 1950. Alternately lyrical and vigorously contrapuntal, gentle and gruff, they all display Bliss's emotional reticence and are given rather cautious performances by the **Delmé Quartet** (Hyperion 66178).

There are two Bliss quintets for wind instrument and strings: the Oboe Quintet of 1927 and the Clarinet Quintet of five years later. Gordon Hunt and the **Tale Quartet** capture the rhapsodical, elusive nature of the Oboe Quintet beautifully (BIS 763, with Britten's *Phantasy Quartet* and Bax's *Oboe Quintet*). The deeply felt Clarinet Quintet fares equally well from the **Redcliffe Ensemble** (Redcliffe 010, with clarinet quintets by Alan Rawthorne and Francis Routh). The five-minute *Pastorale* for clarinet and piano—elegant and elegiac—forms part of an intelligently chosen and buoyantly played British music recital from clarinetist **Einar Jóhanesson** and pianist Philip Jenkins (Chandos 9079).

Bliss's Piano Sonata is an expansive, Romantic piece miles away from the Stravinskian spikiness that characterized his early style. Dark and muscular, it requires considerable dexterity; **Trevor Barnard** is technically adequate but doesn't have the virtuoso technique that would bring the piece to life. It shares a disc with the 24 Preludes written by Busoni when he was 14, and stylistically the two composers are surprisingly close (Divine Art 2-5011). Rather boxy sound.

VOCAL MUSIC

Bliss's songs and song cycles are sung by **Geraldine McGreevy** (soprano), Toby Spence (tenor), and Henry Herford (baritone), accompanied by piano, violin, and clarinet (Hyperion 67188/9, 2CD). In *Elegiac Sonnet, A Knot of Riddles,* and "The Storm" (incidental music to *The Tempest*), Martyn Brabbins conducts **The Nash Ensemble.** There's a wide range of moods here, but what is striking about most of the settings is Bliss's unwillingness to open up the vocal line; few of these songs are distinguished by their melodies, as if his British stiff upper lip prevented him from really saying what he felt. There tends to be more overt expression of feeling in the piano part than in the vocal line—hardly the point of a song—so when he finally relaxes and spins out a real tune, as in *Ballads of the Four Seasons*, Li Po settings from 1923, the effect is like the sun coming out. McGreevy and Spence acquit themselves well, but Herford, who has the lion's share of the singing, does neither Bliss nor his own reputation any favors; he's consistently out of tune.

From the **Finzi Singers** under Paul Spicer, with Andrew Lumsden (organ), comes a valuable CD of choral music, with pride of place going to the sturdy, 40-minute cantata *Shield of Faith;* the powerful choral writing comes as no surprise, but the quality of the organ part makes one regret that Bliss didn't write more solo music for the instrument (Chandos 8980). After three choral miniatures (*Mar Portugues, Birthday Song for a Royal Child,* and *River Music*), the disc closes with the brass-accompanied anthem *The World is Charged with the Grandeur of God,* perhaps Bliss's best-known choral work. ANDERSON

Ernest Bloch (1880–1959)

If there is an underappreciated, underrated, and underperformed 20th-century composer, it's certainly the Swiss-American Ernest Bloch. His work, often inspired by an intense religiosity springing from his Jewish roots—but just as often not—is replete with ravishing melodies, exotic tonal landscaping, and sparkling orchestration. Highly prolific, he ventured into many types of music; orchestral and chamber works are the most successful. Bloch's recognition—on and off during his lifetime—has not yet fully arrived, but surely the day is not far off.

SYMPHONIES

Symphony in E-flat. Bloch had not intended that a symphony should spring from this collection of movements originally planned as a concerto grosso, but in the middle of the last movement he realized that motives and themes from an as yet uncomposed first movement needed to

make an appearance. After a little backtracking he completed the first movement, not unrelated to the famous B-A-C-H theme used by so many composers. The results are breathtaking—one of the finest 20th-century symphonic efforts—yet woefully ignored. **Dalia Atlas'** all-Bloch program is fabulous, like driving an expensive car over hilly terrain; what is underneath is complex and rugged, but the ride itself is smooth and soothing (♦ASV 1019).

Symphony in C-sharp Minor. This early (1903), sprawling work is a testament to the prolific inventiveness of the composer at a young age. Though it's far too long to sustain its considerable musical materials adequately, there are enough Straussian poetics in its many lively moments to warrant at least occasional hearings. **Gunzenhauser** has a vast and deep sound stage, with a huge dynamic range that has just enough reverb to cover up the many deficiencies in the Slovak strings. The orchestra is undistinguished and not bold enough (Marco Polo). Though using a smaller orchestra, **Lev Markiz** has better sound and a far more creditable ensemble, with a final result that does the symphony proud (♦BIS 576).

Trombone Symphony. The ram's horn, or shofar, used in ancient Israel, serves as a unifying motif in one of Bloch's last works on Jewish themes. Trombonist **Grigory Khersonsky** gives a fine performance, though the sound is substandard (Consonance). A better choice has **Christian Lindberg,** with Segerstam in the pilot's seat, in a trombone miscellany that's sure to please (♦BIS 538).

Israel Symphony. Though one of Bloch's least played and recorded works, it nevertheless has a lot to offer. It's good to have **Abravanel**'s recording available again; not state of the art, while committed and impassioned (♦Vanguard 4047). **Svetlanov**'s Russian State Symphony is not the most opulent of ensembles, boasting little tonal richness and bloated, fatty brass (Chant du Monde); the obviously committed performance doesn't measure up to Abravanel's.

OTHER ORCHESTRAL MUSIC

Concerto Grosso 1. Bloch's first concerto grosso came about when his students at the Cleveland Institute of Music were carping about the inadequacies of tonality in shaping the music for the next century. Bloch decided to prove to them that the essential and life-giving qualities of tonality were as abundant now as in the past, so he composed the prelude movement of the work that was to become one of his most popular. The students loved it, and Bloch knew the point had been well made. **Donald Barra** and his San Diego Chamber Orchestra have enhanced the Koch catalog considerably, with nothing deserving greater acclaim than this recording. The orchestra is superbly pointed, conceptually unified, and radar-locked onto Bloch's new-old style (♦Koch 7196). The warmer though more compressed sound of **Schwarz** does little to enhance his timid phrasing, and I have a feeling the Seattle strings weren't comfortable in this exposed setting (Delos).

Howard Hanson's recording set the standard for many years and is still one to be reckoned with. The Eastman players dig in with zest and joy, but the sound remains harsh and metallic (Mercury). **Alan Heatherington** strives for perfection but finds only acceptability (Centaur). **Yoav Talmi** goes in for a lot of pseudo-drama but in the end remains spinelessly bogged down in over-reverberant sound (Chandos). **Janos Balkanyi** never gets off the ground with his stubbed-toe attempt; it has no sprightliness or vigor (Musique Suisse). In one of the few collections with both concertos, **Agnieszka Duczmal** must be given high marks for effort (CPO), though Barra is too hard to beat. Finally, **William Steinberg**'s glorious old recording is available, with a large set of strings, in slightly substandard sound but worth the low cost (♦EMI 66555).

Concerto Grosso 2. Bloch's second attempt at this baroque form came some 20 years after the first. Unlike the earlier effort, this one is far more reserved in its romanticism, choosing construct and clarity over emotion and excitement. I prefer its often medicinal starkness to 1, finding it a microscopic distillation of Bloch's delicate craftsmanship. **Barra** and his orchestra give the definitive performance, an engaged concentration of dark hues and resonant aural allure that should stand for years to come (♦Koch 7196). Not as searing in its pronouncements as Barra, and with perhaps more of a New York sheen than a European medieval color, **Hanson**'s recording no longer has much to recommend it (Mercury). Likewise with **Duczmal,** fine as the recording is (CPO). **Balkanyi** seems more naturally suited to this more austere work, but his band is too disjointed and dispirited to pull it off (Musique Suisse).

Concerto Symphonique. One of Bloch's last works, this was written as a response to the trials of WWII, the formidable conflict affecting Bloch greatly. The pianism is extreme in its demands, the orchestra translucent and sonorous. **Golschmann** and pianist Marjorie Mitchell set the standard in a 1961 recording, capturing the jarring waywardness and sense of gravity that wear on the emotions with a sense of unrelieved pessimism (♦Vanguard 4052).

Evocations. Possibly inspired by Bloch's reading of Chinese poetry, the three movements of this highly perfumed work bear more than a passing resemblance to Debussy's *Nocturnes.* The orchestration is subtle but forceful, and **Sedares** tucks and folds every corner while letting the fragrant beauties of the work emerge in full blossom (♦Koch 7232). **David Amos** gives a fine reading in good sound, but some portions are cluttered and chewy, not as transparent as they should be (Centaur).

Four Episodes. This was designed to convey moods and national style (Chinese in particular); while not a great work, it has much to commend it. **Duczmal** reads this much better than the coupled Concerto Grossi, with wit and style (♦CPO 999096), while **Kuhn,** with a misbegotten coupling, gives a splendid performance with his crackerjack Swiss orchestra (♦Musique Suisse 6157).

In Memoriam. Dedicated to pianist Ada Clement in 1952 and using a theme she liked when Bloch was demonstrating Renaissance polyphony, this is one of the most gorgeous five-minute memorials you're ever likely to hear. It presents a far more sober point of view than pieces like Barber's gut-wrenching *Adagio.* Again **Atlas** is flawless, with a frothy, richly brewed recording (♦ASV 1019).

In the Night. Composed in 1922, this may be the darkest love poem ever written. Bloch orchestrated this miniature—a practice he often engaged in—and **David Shallon** gives a somber, fitfully angst-ridden performance (♦Timpani 1052).

Poems of the Sea. Written as a piano suite during Bloch's Cleveland Institute days, these three delightful works have all the salty zest of Debussy's *La Mer* and take only half the time. They were orchestrated two years after completion, and the results are spectacular, making it one of his most accessible works. Why they're not recorded more often is a mystery. Perhaps the superb Malmö Symphony, led by **Sakari Oramo,** is too formidable a competitor (♦BIS 639).

Suite Symphonique. Bloch's compositional prowess emerged full strength when Allied forces invaded Germany in 1944. A darker seri-

ousness of purpose now colored his works, yet largely avoiding any prolonged pessimism. Having come to abhor most of what passed for modern music, he began once again to look back to older forms for inspiration. This neo-Baroque suite is a checkerboard pastiche of detail that is caressed and lingered over by **Oramo** in a spectacular recording (♦BIS 639).

Three Jewish Poems. Early in his career Bloch relied heavily on Jewish mystical tradition as a springboard for his inspiration. He said he felt himself most successful when at his most racial, yet the listener devoid of this knowledge may be hard-pressed to detect any but the most cursory allusion to Jewishness in these flavorful works. The young American conductor **Sedares** and his New Zealand band immerse themselves in Bloch's Middle Eastern milieu with finely honed, suitably atmospheric readings in splendid sound (♦Koch 7232). **Atlas'** performance is captured in such vivid sound as to make the Royal Philharmonic sound like the Beecham group of old. Interpretively more intense than Sedares (but not necessarily better), this wins hands down in the sonics category (♦ASV 1019).

Two Interludes from Macbeth. Bloch's early opera *Macbeth* is a late romantic grand opera, and many of its motives are found in these two interludes from Acts 1 and 3. Bloch reworked them into a symphonic suite, richly melodic and orchestrally sumptuous in its Strauss-like arrogance. It's played almost to the hilt by the Royal Philharmonic, with only a few string mishaps noticeable. **Atlas** really pulls it out of the brass, aided by fabulous sound (♦ASV 1019).

Two Last Poems . . . (Maybe . . .). In 1958, and suffering from terminal illness, Bloch wrote what is thought to be his last composition. The two movements express both sadness and closure, and hope for the afterlife. Alexa Still plays a warmly caressing, slightly detached flute, wistful and fatalistically aloof, with excellent sound and support from **Sedares** (♦Koch 7232).

Winter-Spring. This early work is saturated with late Romanticism, in a manner that may surprise even the most devoted Bloch followers. *Winter* took a while to catch on, but *Spring* was an instant success. In a stunning recording, **Shallon** guides the Luxembourg Philharmonic in spectacular sound that will put a chill in your veins and a spring in your step (♦Timpani 1052).

CONCERTOS

Schelomo. Bloch's early rhapsody *Schelomo* (*Solomon*), based on the book of Ecclesiastes, is one of his most Jewish-inspired works. It's a marvel of sensuous exoticism and romantic passion stretched to the breaking point. Its evocativeness coupled with a palpable aural hologram of mystery have made it, quite deservedly, his most popular work.

There are many recordings, and one of the best has cellist **Fournier** with Wallenstein and the Berlin Philharmonic drawing wave upon wave of thrilling sound from this lumbering, finely controlled orchestra (♦DG 429155). Bernstein and the magnificent **Rostropovich,** not surprisingly, recorded the most voluptuous, spectacularly realized conception on disc. It has never been seriously challenged, from Slava's dark, flavorful sound to Bernstein's supercharged over-the-top reading. But considering the source—EMI—you'll have to hunt it down. **Julius Berger** offers decent playing, but nothing extraordinary (EBS). **Zara Nelsova** and Abravanel give us a realistic recording, not the most impassioned but good enough to stand by itself if need be (♦Vanguard 4047).

Ma, in a recording strangely titled "The New York Album," displays his phenomenal talent, no question, but he lacks the go-for-broke temperament so necessary for this work (Sony). **Harnoy** and Mackerras haven't always been successful collaborators, but this is a different story. She was born to play this music—frenzied, soulfully lyrical, a bejeweled necklace worn in an exotic locale. A fabulous performance (♦RCA 60757). **Torleif Thedèen** plays in a sea of superb clarity with conductor Lev Markiz; chamber orchestra-like sensitivity coupled with perfect balances (and fine cello playing) make this more akin to *Nights in the Gardens of Spain* than any desert mysticism. But get this and the C-sharp minor symphony that comes with it (♦BIS 576).

Stokowski and the estimable **George Neikrug** turn in my favorite reading of all, next to Bernstein. Nobody digs into this desert well like Stoky, milking it to the hilt, and Neikrug provides a whirlwind of color and excitement (♦EMI 65427). **Mari Fujiwara** has good sound, but her performance lacks passion and energy and the orchestra is a bit flaccid (Denon). **Maria Kliegel** plays with a fat, boisterous vibrato, like a loud-mouth trying to be heard in the midst of a middle Eastern market. **Gerhard Markson** and the highly adaptable National Orchestra of Ireland provide excellent support, and at a great price (♦Naxos 550519). **Georges Miquelle** gives a riveting performance, but the recording is deafeningly close and the sound too clattering (Mercury).

Ulrich Schmid turns in a very idiomatic reading coupled with Honegger's Cello Concerto, but unless the coupling is what you're after, look elsewhere (MD+G). **Alexander Kniazev** with Svetlanov offers a subtle, chamber-like reading of great delicacy; the unfamiliarity of the orchestra with this work doesn't lessen the overall effect (Chant du Monde 288165). Finally, **Leonard Rose** made great recordings with Ormandy and the Philadelphia, and this one is no exception; the sound isn't what it would be today, but at this price, it's unbeatable (♦Sony 48278). **André Navarra** and An_erl, in one of the great recordings of the past, turn in an exceptional, highly controlled version that revels in detail others miss (♦Supraphon 3169).

Violin Concerto. Despite Bloch's assertions to the contrary, this concerto is heavily Jewish-influenced, but mixed with a pseudo-impressionistic style that rarefies the former and gives concrete structure to the latter. **Roman Totenberg** gives a wonderfully idiomatic reading, made obsolete only by the quality of the competition (Vanguard). **Michaël Guttman**, in a superb ongoing Bloch cycle, continues the excellence of the undertaking (♦ASV 785). But it's **Oleh Krysa**, on Oramo's stunning disc, who takes the prize with a syrupy, deliciously vibrant tone coupled with spacious, naturally reverberant acoustics—a delight (♦BIS 639). **Hymen Bress** gives a fiery performance that makes you wonder how this work has managed to avoid the standard repertory (♦Supraphon 3169).

CHAMBER MUSIC

Quartets. The **Pro Arte Quartet** gives a very fine, completely convincing reading of Quartet 2, hopefully with more to follow. The only problem I have is the uncomfortably close sound, a trademark of many Laurel recordings (♦Laurel 826). The **Portland Quartet** has five quartets spread over three discs, sold separately. Their wonderfully maxed-out interpretations in great sound—and with no meaningful competition—make this the series to have (♦Arabesque 6543, 6626, 6627).

Piano Quintets. Bloch's two piano quintets, very early and very late, share some characteristics: They are lush, closely scored, and almost primeval in their appeal to a romanticism gone haywire. Again the **Pro Arte** (Laurel) and **Portland Quartets** (Arabesque) give very fine, recommendable readings. But this time a sleeper from the **American Chamber Players** leaps in to take the crown. Led by violist Miles Hoffman, this group surges

forth with a reading of great ebullience and vibrant warmth. The two pianists involved, Lambert Orkis and Ann Schein, are digital masters here, set off by the fluid, lustrous string tone (♦Koch 7041).

Sonatas. Though Bloch's violin music is not recorded often, what we do have has been done very well. He was very selective when he turned to the violin, leaving us little music. What there is must be approached seriously, for some of his most intimate music can be heard soaring from the instrument. Only his great force of personality saves the **Stern** recordings of both sonatas; the old Columbia sound is an exercise in frigid instability (Sony). The **Weilerstein Duo** gives us all of the music for violin, *Baal Shem* included, in readings that are fluent and purposeful, but lack the last bit of intensity (Arabesque).

Leonard Friedman continues ASV's stunning Bloch series with a recording of the sonatas that is the best choice (♦ASV 714). Great sound, great playing. Not so **Michael Davis,** the lyrical nature of the works finding him unprepared, proving him intonationally challenged (Orion). Last but certainly not least, **Heifetz** gave us a recording that includes the two sonatas; he knew this music well, and the old sound hardly gets in the way of an ageless performance (♦RCA 61739). *Hebrew Suite* is given a lithe, delightful performance by **Hyman Bress,** coupled with Navarra's great *Schelomo* (♦Supraphon 3169).

PIANO MUSIC

Bloch's piano works are not on the exalted level his orchestral music so often attained. Only two recordings of his short sonata are available, both recommended: **Myron Silberstein** gives us a mixed-composer recital in warm, inviting sound (♦Connoisseur 4208), and **István Kassai** leads us through a not-as-warm reading with more reverberant sound (♦Marco Polo 223289).

CHORAL MUSIC

America—An Epic Rhapsody. In 1927 *Musical America* offered a cash prize and performances with five major orchestras to the winner of a composition contest having to do with America. The idea was to encourage the American symphony, still at an embryonic stage at this time. ninety-two entries were submitted, and a blue ribbon panel consisting of the world's conductorial worthies—Stokowski, Koussevitzky, Damrosch, Stock, and Alfred Hertz—unanimously selected Bloch's *Rhapsody*. History has judged it differently, and the paucity of recordings is ample testimony to its paltriness. **Stokowski** is the one conductor who could possibly sell it, and just barely at that. He always believed in it, and almost makes it work (♦Vanguard 1471). **Schwarz,** on the other hand, sus a reading that takes the piece too seriously, and the result is just plain boring (Delos).

Sacred Service. This has not received a lot of attention, and indeed is not quite the mystical, profoundly religious utterance we would have expected. What we get are sensuous, romantic melodies, swollen crescendos, and powerful sentiment that feels a bit out of place in a religious service. **Bernstein** seems to be the only one offering it, and that's just as well, for it's difficult to imagine anyone else coming close (♦Sony 47533).

SONGS

There have been very few recordings of Bloch's orchestral songs. **Shallon**'s readings of four poems by Beatrix Rodes titled *Poems of Autumn* (sung by mezzo Brigitte Balleys), Psalms 144 and 137 (by soprano Mireille Delunsch), and Psalm 22 (by baritone Vincent Le Texier) are gorgeously rendered, lush, spine-tingling, and gloriously reverberant. This recording should pave the way for more (♦Timpani 1052).

RITTER

Karl-Birger Blomdahl (1916–1968)

As a rebellious, controversial composer, teacher, debater, and music director at Swedish Radio, Blomdahl was a forceful and energetic leader who left an indelible imprint on contemporary Swedish music. Nielsen and Sibelius influenced his early work, but during the '40s and '50s he studied Hindemith, Bartók, and Stravinsky, finding his own style in linear, polyphonic, often dissonant lines and rhythmic vitality. During the '50s he embraced dodecaphonic techniques while maintaining tonal centers, and became a pioneer in electronic music. His music is basically tonal, rhythmically and melodically stringent, vital and aggressive, but he is also capable of writing long-lined, lyrical, expressive melodies.

The lyrical *Pastoral Suite,* inspired by the Swedish poet Erik Lindegren, was written in 1949. It's coupled with the folk-colored Sonata for Strings by Jan Carlstedt and Ingvar Lidholm's rhythmically vibrant *Music for Strings* in stimulating performances by **Karl-Ove Mannberg** and the New Stockholm Chamber Orchestra (Acoustica 1008). Also from the '40s come the romantic Concert Overture, the neobaroque Concerto Grosso, Concerto for Violin and Strings, Symphony 2, and the neobaroque *Praeludium and Allegro* for strings (MAP 9024). These five works were influenced by an intense study of Hindemith and of baroque music. They're played in excellent recordings by **Ola Rudner** and **Stig Westerberg** conducting the Helsingborg Symphony. Rudner is also the soloist in the predominantly lyrical Violin Concerto.

Blomdahl wrote three masterly symphonies (1943, 1947, and 1951); they are heard in riveting performances by **Segerstam** and the Swedish Radio Symphony (BIS 611). 1 and 2 are three-movement works, with bustling, syncopated outer movements flanking introspective, often elegiac, long-arched middle movements. Nielsen and Hindemith stand as godfathers to 1, Hindemith to 2, but Blomdahl's personal thumb prints are never in doubt in these works, and 3, *Facets,* is considered one of the greatest symphonies written in Sweden. It won great popular acclaim when first performed at the 1951 ISCM Festival in Frankfurt. Based on a freely used 12-tone series, with tonal centers, this deeply felt symphony is in five sections played attacca. Section II, for strings only, is a heartfelt lament for the war victims of Warsaw.

Facets is Blomdahl's most recorded symphony. It's performed by **Ehrling,** coupled with the craggy ballet suite *Sisyphus* (1954) led by Dorati and the onomatopoeic *Forma Ferritonans* (1961), a stunning study in orchestral sonorism (using long-held notes and chords set off against shifting chords, with no melodies), conducted by Comissiona, all with the Stockholm Philharmonic (Caprice 21356). For *Forma Ferritonans,* written for the opening ceremonies of a new iron foundry, Blomdahl meticulously researched the iron-making process, from smelting to pig iron, and used melodic and harmonic intervals based on the periodic table. The first part is sonorous, swelling to a monstrous, ear-splitting crescendo; the second part is a heavy dance. This fine release is rounded out by soprano Elisabeth Söderström as soloist in the introspective . . . *The Journey into this Night,* based on poetry by Erik Lindegren, with Yuri Ahronovitch conducting.

Two movements from the *Sisyphus* ballet suite come from **Varujan Kojian** (Swedish Society Discophil 1037). Also here is the angular, rollicking Chamber Concerto for Piano, Woodwinds, and Percussion, written for pianist **Hans Leygraf,** who performs the work with Ehrling and the London Symphony. Ehrling also conducts the Stockholm Philharmonic in the powerful Symphony 3, an earlier recording than Segerstam's. This excellent disc is rounded out by a fine performance of the lyrical, introverted Trio for Clarinet, Violoncello, and Piano.

The two Dance Suites (1948, 1951), No. 1 for flute, violin, cello, and percussion, No. 2 for clarinet, cello, and percussion, are on a disc that also contains the Trio, here by different performers, and the 1952 oratorio *I Speglarnas Sal* (*In the Hall of Mirrors*), based on a text by Erik Lindegren commenting pessimistically on the plight of 20th-century humankind. This fine oratorio is scored for speaker, soprano, alto, tenor, baritone, chorus, and orchestra, and combines whole-tone scales with dodecaphonic techniques and jazz. **Ehrling** conducts a recording in very good mono sound (Caprice 21424).

In 1959, Blomdahl gained international fame with his space opera *Aniara,* the first of its kind. Scored for singers, chorus, and orchestra, the opera is based on a text by Swedish poet Harry Martinson, with a libretto by Erik Lindegren. It tells the story of the spaceship *Aniara,* with 8,000 humans aboard, fleeing a polluted, devastated Earth in the year 2038. On its way to Mars, the spaceship is incapacitated, spins off course, and is forever doomed to roam the dark, cold, galactic void. *Aniara* is not an experimental opera but a traditional drama set in a series of tableaux expressed musically by rhythmic narration in choruses, ensemble singing, arias, monologues, and orchestral commentary. The music combines tonal and dodecaphonic sequences with electronic episodes and jazz.

A concert version of *Aniara* is conducted by **Westerberg** (Caprice 22016, 2CD). A 20-minute suite from the opera was recorded in the '70s by **Werner Janssen** leading the Vienna Volksoper Orchestra, with electronic and *musique concrète* effects (Columbia 7176, LP); I haven't seen it on CD.

DE JONG

John Blow (1649–1708)

Next to Purcell, Blow was probably the most accomplished and imaginative English composer of the Restoration period. As a boy, he was a Chapel Royal chorister. He both preceded and followed Purcell as organist of Westminster Abbey, was appointed Gentleman of the Chapel Royal in 1674, and in the same year succeeded Pelham Humfrey as its Master of Children. He held numerous musical posts at court, and from 1687 to 1703 was Master of Choristers at St. Paul's Cathedral. For the most part, his compositions are in the same genres cultivated by Purcell, with the notable exception of music for the professional stage. Blow's only dramatic work, the chamber opera *Venus and Adonis,* was written for the court. He's well represented in the current recording catalogs; there are several excellent recordings devoted entirely to his music and many more that include his works in programs of music by Purcell and other Restoration composers.

SECULAR VOCAL MUSIC

Ode on the Death of Mr. Henry Purcell. Of all Blow's compositions, this is probably the best known to modern listeners, judging from the number of currently available recordings. It was composed and published in 1696 to a text by Dryden ("Mark how the lark and linnet sing"), and scored for two solo voices, two recorders, and continuo. It's usually sung by countertenors, but Peter Holman maintains that it was intended for high tenors, not falsettists. As the work doesn't fill a CD by itself, your choice may be influenced by the couplings.

There are two reissued recordings by the legendary **Alfred Deller.** The earlier, dating from 1959, is exceptionally exquisite and moving, with a delicacy and grace I have never heard surpassed (♦Vanguard 8108, with Michel-Richard de Lalande's *De Profundis*). The other vocal soloist is John Whitworth, and together they sing this sometimes daunting music as if it were the most natural thing in the world. In the solo "We beg not Hell our Orpheus to restore" Deller captures the quintessential Restoration triple-meter lilt with gentle "snaps" in the rhythm, while the duet "The heavenly choir, who heard his notes from high" is given with an eloquent tenderness that could melt a heart of stone.

The other recording dates from 1970 with Deller partnered by his son Mark (Harmonia Mundi 190201). While the Deller artistry is still very much in evidence, his voice doesn't have the freshness and aplomb heard in the earlier recording. The opening duet starts quite low and includes little flourishes of rapid notes that are not at all clean, and elsewhere the vocal lines sound a little too much like hard work. However, listeners may be attracted to the pieces that fill out the later disc: a *Marriage Ode* (date and specific occasion unknown) and "Cloe found Amyntas lying" from *Amphion Anglicus,* a collection of Blow's secular vocal works.

Another historic recording pairs countertenors René Jacobs and James Bowman under **Leonhardt**'s direction (Sony 60097). On the low notes near the beginning, the voices are overbalanced by the accompaniment. This is a common problem, and may support Peter Holman's tenor theory; the imbalance disappears as the vocal lines rise. The tone and intonation of the recorders are somewhat unsteady. On the whole, this is a fine performance, but it doesn't have the magic of Deller and Whitworth. The disc is filled out with six selections from *Amphion Anglicus.* The booklet is rather skimpy and doesn't include texts.

In a 1987 recording, Bowman and Michael Chance are accompanied by members of the King's Consort directed by **Robert King** (Hyperion 66253, with a Blow song and Purcell solos and duets). This is even more elegant than Leonhardt and a close rival to Deller. The flourishes at the beginning are about the cleanest I have heard. Bowman and Chance are a near perfect match in tone and execution, and they present this music with impressive control and artistry.

A more recent recording combines countertenors **Charles Brett** and **Ricard Bordas** (Pierre Verany 730077). Here again the voices are badly overbalanced near the beginning. The singers' tone is unduly fruity and precious, and the "snaps" in "We beg not Hell" are more bumpy than elegant. The disc opens with a selection of ten solos and duets by Purcell. The production is even skimpier than the Sony reissue: not even a booklet, just a two-panel folder with minimal notes and no texts.

Tenors Rogers Covey-Crump and Charles Daniels perform with members of the Parley of Instruments under **Peter Holman**'s direction (Hyperion 66578). The result is very impressive, though the tenors have to go into falsetto for the highest notes. It's a fine performance, but the opening movement sounds rushed, taken too quickly for the rapid flourishes to be clean. The disc consists entirely of music on the death of Purcell, with odes by Jeremiah Clarke and Henry Hall in addition to Blow and instrumental pieces by Godfrey Finger and Thomas Morgan.

Venus and Adonis. Blow called this a masque, but it's a fully-sung chamber opera in three acts with a prologue. It was first performed at court in 1681 or 1683 and was most likely the model for Purcell's *Dido and Aeneas* in 1689. It's certainly one of Blow's masterpieces and can stand unashamed next to Purcell's opera, even if the anonymous libretto has a much simpler story line and less psychological complexity and tension than Nahum Tate's libretto for Purcell. The one recording currently available is directed by **Jacobs** with the choir of Clare College, Cambridge, and the Orchestra of the Age of Enlightenment (Harmonia Mundi 901684). The title roles are taken by soprano Rosemary Joshua and baritone Gerald Finley; their characterizations are thoroughly convincing, and, indeed, all the solo singers are poised and polished. Two other relatively recent recordings directed by **Rooley** (Deutsche Har-

monia Mundi/EMI) and by **Medlam** (Harmonia Mundi) garnered favorable reviews, but they have disappeared from the catalogs.

A splendid program of Blow's "domestic music" under the title "Awake My Lyre" is performed by the vocal ensemble Redbyrd and the Parley of Instruments under **Holman**'s direction (♦Hyperion 66658, Vol. 20 of the "English Orpheus" series). The selections include secular pieces for various combinations of voices and continuo, three Latin devotional works, an intense *Dialog betwixt Dives and Abraham* paraphrased by an unknown Restoration poet, and three examples of what Holman calls the "symphony song," the most substantial of which lends its name to the program. These works for voices, obbligato strings, and continuo are sometimes called cantatas, but they are closer in format to the verse anthems with strings, known as symphony anthems, that figured prominently in the repertory of Charles II's Chapel Royal.

There are two instrumental works on the disc: a trio sonata in A and a ground in G minor. The performers, some of the most accomplished early-music singers and players in England, display extraordinary insight into this music's style. They capture the expressive atmosphere of each selection, running the gamut from exuberant joy to intense devotion to heartbreaking anguish, and even wry erotic humor. Another collection of Blow's songs and keyboard music appeared as Vol. 18 (Hyperion 66646), but it appears to be no longer available, at least in the US.

Among the discs that contain mostly music by Purcell but include some short works by Blow are two devoted primarily to music in honor of Queen Mary. "Whilst he abroad does like the sun" and "The sullen years are past," the only surviving music from court odes of 1692 and 1694, are included in "Music for Queen Mary," sung by Kirkby and Bostridge with the Westminster Abbey Choir and the New London Consort led by **Martin Neary** (Sony 66243, with Purcell's first birthday ode for the queen and a new compilation of the music for her funeral). "Homage to Queen Mary," a program directed by **Roderick Shaw,** includes the three elegies by Purcell and Blow published in 1695 (Globe 5029). The text of Blow's contribution, "No, Lesbia, no, you ask in vain," is a rhymed English version of "Incassum, Lesbia" set by Purcell as "The Queen's Epicedium".

SACRED VOCAL MUSIC

Blow made it clear in the dedication of *Amphion Anglicus,* addressed to Queen Anne in 1700, that he regarded himself primarily as a composer of church music. His output of secular songs and odes was considerable, but his more than 100 anthems and some twelve service settings constitute the greater part of his work, the fruit of his lifelong association with the Chapel Royal and other ecclesiastical foundations. While no one has yet recorded his complete anthems and service music, there are some significant recordings currently available.

The outstanding recording of Blow's anthems is a set by Winchester Cathedral Choir and Parley of Instruments directed by **David Hill** (♦Hyperion 67031, 2CD). This selection of 14 anthems composed between the mid-1670s and mid-1680s includes nine symphony anthems with strings; one of them, "Lord, who shall dwell in thy tabernacle?," also includes three recorders. All but one are accompanied by one player to a part, as was probably the practice in the Chapel Royal; the exception is the festive anthem composed for the coronation of James II in 1685, "God spake sometime in visions," which would have been accompanied by the full complement of the king's "24 Violins." The other works on the discs include a full-with-verse anthem, three verse anthems with organ, and a work for three solo voices and continuo, "How doth the city sit solitary," which may have been intended as a private devotional song rather than a church anthem.

Hill is inclined to be brisk, but while his tempos occasionally seem rushed, for the most part his interpretations are stylish and elegant, displaying a keen insight into the idiom, while their technical polish leaves nothing to be desired from the soloists, choir, or players. The program is well planned, exhibiting the full range of devotional expression, from exuberant joy in lively triple meter to intense penitence set to poignant chromatic harmonies.

A major anthem by Blow, "I was glad when they said unto me," is included in "Music for St. Paul's" with the choir of St. Paul's Cathedral and the Parley of Instruments directed by **John Scott** (Hyperion 67009, with Handel's *Utrecht Te Deum* and *Jubilate* and Boyce's "Lord, thou hast been our refuge"). The anthem was written for the formal opening of the new cathedral in 1697. The recorded sound, while entirely acceptable, is a trifle thin, not as rich as one would expect from St. Paul's acoustics.

Two of Blow's verse anthems are included in "Chapel Royal Anthems" performed by the choir of Christ Church Cathedral, Oxford, under the direction of **Stephen Darlington** (Nimbus 5454). The title might lead you to expect a program of symphony anthems, but these are with organ only. One of the Blow anthems, "The Lord, even the most mighty," is not duplicated in the David Hill set. The recorded sound has great presence, though it feels as if you were seated a bit too close to the organ. The disc also contains six anthems by Purcell and one each by Locke and Pelham Humfrey.

"Coronation Music for King James II" is an excellent recording, if you can find it, with the choir and orchestra of Westminster Abbey directed by **Preston** (Archiv 419613). In addition to an extraordinarily vivid and energetic performance of "God spake sometime in visions," this disc includes two short full anthems that Blow composed for the occasion. The other anthems are by William Child, Henry Lawes, Purcell, and William Turner. The 1986 recorded sound is rich and sumptuous but clear, a notable contrast with the sound of the St. Paul's recording under Scott.

GATENS

Luigi Boccherini *(1743–1805)*

The stigma of being no more than a weaker Mozart has dogged Boccherini long enough. Like CPE Bach, he sometimes seems to have bypassed the classical era and continually surprises us with an emotional expansiveness that occasionally suggests Schubert. Being a virtuoso cellist also gave him a distinctive approach. It must be noted that the Boccherini listings in *Schwann* are even more garbled than usual, making the already complex state of his discography even harder to clarify.

SYMPHONIES

All 28 symphonies are played by the German Chamber Academy under **Johannes Goritzki** (CPO 999401, 8CD boxed or available separately, various numbers). The earliest symphonic work is a 1767 *Sinfonia Concertante Op. 7,* a warmly expansive three-movement piece with solos for two violins and cello. It marks the onset of French influences in Boccherini's work, resembling Mozart's *Concertone* in mood and the layout of the solo passages. Boccherini later revised it to include a guitar part, and Goritzki includes the two very different versions in his Vol. 1. The guitar version also appears in Vol. 2 of **Giorgio Bernasconi's** series with the Accademia Strumentale Italiana, where it's misidentified as Op. 21:3 (Arts 47109). Bernasconi's version is broader than Goritzki's.

The six symphonies of Op. 12 appeared in 1771. They too are spacious pieces, including some concertante works lasting more than 20 minutes. This opus also contains less soloistic works, including the famous Symphony in D Minor, "La Casa del Diavolo," based partly on Gluck's music for the ballet *Don Juan.* **Leppard** recorded Op. 12 with the New Philharmonia in 1971 (Philips 438314, 2CD). **Goritzki's** reading is smoother and his soloists are more polished, but he omits almost all repeats and the music tends to slip by unless they are observed, as Leppard does. Also, Leppard's more assertive approach removes a bit of the sugar icing from Boccherini's already sweet cake. Both versions are on the modern side, with contemporary instruments and no keyboard continuo.

Op. 21 (1775) is a bright and bouncy collection recalling the early Mozart symphonies. These are all three-movement works, though the minuet is not forgotten, serving as finale in three of them. **Goritzki's** joie de vivre and generally light touch make a good impression and he's not as reluctant to take repeats in these compact pieces.

Op. 35 (1782) is slightly larger in scale and more brilliant, recalling the breadth of Mozart's symphonies of the same time. **Goritzki** takes the increased breadth as a mandate to omit many repeats. Even better, the classic **Giulini** C minor and Overture in D have been reissued, unfortunately coupled with a mono Vivaldi *Four Seasons* (Testament 1156). **Bernasconi** includes 1 in his collection and takes the repeats. After Op. 35, there are only 6 symphonies, Op. 37:1, 3, and 4, Op. 41 (a well-known work in C minor), Opp. 42 and 45. Bernasconi includes several of these in his series; he's a bit damp and logy. **Lamon** includes the C minor in her miscellaneous disc with Tafelmusik and Anner Bylsma (Sony 53121, NA), a bit dry-sounding, though the disc as a whole is memorable. Goritzki's is the liveliest and will do until some early music group decides to take the orchestral Boccherini seriously.

Other recordings of the symphonies are by **Eiji Hashimoto,** with a very fine student group at the Cincinnati Conservatory, including both the D minor and C minor with minimal vibrato but in sensitively phrased performances (Klavier 11062). **Ross Pople's** lively renditions seem to be gradually disappearing; only one of originally three CDs is presently listed, containing late works played neatly and with verve (Hyperion 66904). **Adrian Shepherd's** album is warm but a little sloppy (Chandos 8414).

CONCERTOS

There are 12 concertos for cello, many of which resemble the famous B-flat romanticized by Friedrich Grützmacher in the mid-19th century and still learned by most budding cellists in that bowdlerization. Leaving that version aside, they have been recorded twice complete, by **David Geringas** (Claves 50-8814/16, 3CD, NA) and **Julius Berger** (EBS 6055/57, 3CD). Both are fine players, Geringas more colorful, Berger more reliable. The scoring differs: Berger leans toward more conservative orchestrations while Geringas at times is more elaborate.

CHAMBER MUSIC

As a cello virtuoso, Boccherini's sonatas for that instrument were specifically written for his own performance and seldom published. They all ask for continuo accompaniment, so it's curious to hear his Op. 5, six sonatas for violin, with a written-out keyboard part in which the violinist is distinctly second fiddle to the piano; **Enrico Gatti,** violin, and Franco Angeleri, fortepiano, play on early instruments, balancing the sound beautifully and playing with verve (Tactus 740201). We don't have much keyboard writing from Boccherini; here he shows an effective style relying perhaps too much on Alberti bass lines but already with an individual voice in 1768. Flute alternatives for these pieces were recorded by **Sheridan Stokes** and Bess Karp on harpsichord in musically phrased but rather misleading performances, since the harpsichord doesn't compete well with the modern flute, making all the obbligatos drown out the tune in the keyboard (Orion 7821, NA). Also, all repeats were omitted, making the composer sound short-winded.

Six trio sonatas (1781) are rather similar, also recorded by **Gatti** with Laura Alvini, fortepiano, and Roberto Gini, cello (Tactus 740202). The emphasis is again on the fortepiano, with violin obbligato and the cello sticking to a basso continuo role, as in Haydn's trios, but the music is still prime middle-period Boccherini. The **Barros Classical Concert** also plays these pieces in somewhat less polished sound (Hungaroton 31613).

The cello sonatas are still being discovered; the total is given as 42 by Christian Speck in his notes for **Julius Berger**'s disc containing five recent discoveries (EBS 6011). Berger's recording employs organ for two sonatas, harpsichord alone for one, harpsichord and double bass for one, and hammerklavier for the difficult piece Boccherini wrote for Empress Maria Theresa. Berger's series appears to have been discontinued after three discs; he plays musically, and his Vol. 3 contains two short two-movement sonatas that no one else includes, G271 and 272. **Christian Benda** includes a sonata in F minor from this series in his Vol. 1, accompanied only by fortepiano (Naxos 554324). Berger uses harpsichord and double bass in his version.

Yves Gerard's G numbers are currently used for identification, but they give incomplete results since the five sonatas recorded by Berger were not known when his catalogue appeared in the late '60s. G2 in C minor has two versions, A and B. **Bylsma** and **Richard Lester** both recorded G2A with no keyboard continuo, only a second cello. Lester, like Bylsma, is an early-music-style player; he uses even less vibrato, emphasizing the chamber music aspect of the sonatas. Lester's disc is listed in Schwann as containing the five recently discovered sonatas recorded by Berger. This is not the case: the disc includes G2A, 4, 10, 17, and 565 (Hyperion 66719). **Benda** recorded G2B with all its repeats, accompanied by his brother Sebastian on fortepiano (Naxos 554324). **Isserlis** recorded it with no repeats but with a good deal of improvisation, accompanied by Maggie Cole on harpsichord (Virgin 90805, NA).

G3 is only found on a disc by **Michal Kanka** (Praga 250127, NA). G4A is the A major sonata every cellist learns. This also has two versions. G4A is in both Benda's and Lester's discs. Cellists may be surprised that Boccherini's original begins with the Allegro, followed by the Adagio, and ending with a Minuet. G5 in G is also on Benda's disc. He is a sturdy player, not subtle but accurate and agile. Isserlis is his competition in G5: His first two movements are reversed, putting the Largo first (editions are a major issue in the cello sonatas). As usual, Benda observes all repeats, Isserlis none.

G6, another well-known sonata in C, is presently available only in **Berger**'s Vol. 3, though it was on Kanka's and Isserlis's discs as well. G8 through 10 are on Bylsma's recording, 8 and 9 were on Kanka's, 8 and 10 on one by **Hidemi Suzuki,** played with a second cello and harpsichord (Ricercar 122107, NA). Bylsma is his usual fascinating self, virtuosic, punctilious about repeats, and basically "early music" in his approach, concentrating on sonority and blend with his partners. He plays the finale of G8 very fast, despite its stratospheric requirements. Suzuki, no slouch himself, does likewise, though a little less easily and taking only exposition repeats. Kanka, though more modern in technique and more off-the-string in style, acquits himself impressively as well. My ears are most satisfied by Bylsma, but it's a close call, and those who find the early music style anathema will prefer Kanka's sound.

In G9 Bylsma uses only fortepiano for accompaniment. His variety of

continuo scoring helps make his disc particularly interesting. He also plays G15 and four of the little Fugues for two cellos. Berger plays all seven fugues in his Vol. 3, which also includes G565, a curious version of the B-flat Concerto arranged as a sonata, also found in Isserlis' and Lester's discs. Lester is the only one to play G10; in both this and G565 he uses only double bass accompaniment. Sonatas 13 and 17 are in Suzuki's disc, while 14, 16, and 17 are in Kanka's, making it a pity they are out of print.

The string trio is another genre much favored by Boccherini. Op. 14:1, 4, and 5 are played by **Trio Euterpe,** along with Op. 47:1–3 (Pierre Verany 797102). Op. 14:2 is in a **Bylsma** release (Channel 3692, NA). Opp. 7, 35, and 54 are for two violins and cello instead of the customary violin, viola, and cello. Those who are counting will note that Op. 35 is also listed as containing six symphonies. This confusion is due to Boccherini's Paris publisher; Boccherini listed the trios as Op. 34 but Schwann and others use the Paris number. Further, the Schwann listings for all three trio opuses are so screwed up as to be indecipherable.

CPO appears to be working on a complete collection of the string quartets, using several different groups. Op. 2 is played by the **Sonore Quartet** (CPO 999123). These six pieces are short three-movement works in a concise, early classic style, played with warmth. Op. 8 is played by the **Venice Quartet** (Dynamic 111). Then we jump to Op. 32 with the **Nomos Quartet,** a young and brilliant-sounding group (CPO 999202). Their competition is the **Esterházy Quartet** (Telarc 95988). **Bylsma**'s stellar group's 1977 recording is still outstanding. It's a bit of a shock to go directly to Op. 33 with the **Revolutionary Drawing Room,** since their pitch is about a quarter-tone lower than that used by Nomos. Both groups are excellent, the RDR a little more aggressively nasal in early music style.

Quintets were a Boccherini specialty, particularly those with two cellos; he wrote at least 125. Since they consistently contain his most characteristic thoughts, it's amazing that no one has made a complete set. The **Boccherini Quintet** made some warmly romantic Angel LPs, but they've never been reissued on CD. A fine album of the six Op. 29 quintets played by the **Kuijken** brothers and Bylsma also has not surfaced (Seon 67022, 2LP), nor has the **Esterházy Quartet**'s disc (Telefunken 42353, LP).

Boccherini's famous Minuet is from Op. 13:5, so several groups have recorded the entire quintet, including **Alexander Schneider** and a stellar group (Vanguard 8006, with the also-famous guitar quintet, "La Retirata de Madrid"). Schneider & Co. play both works with almost Heifetz-like aggression, which to my mind doesn't fit them at all. The **Berlin Philharmonic Ensemble** gives Op. 13 a more beautiful reading, coupled with three other quintets in effective performances (Denon 2199). There once was a fascinating disc with Bylsma and the **Boccherini Quartet** containing four miscellaneous chamber works (Channel 3692, NA).

The quintets with other instruments are less common. For flute, there are six, Op. 17, recorded by **Alexandre Magnin** and the Janáček Quartet (Naxos 553719, NA). This is a lovely and sensitive reading of some little two-movement works. Another collection is without opus and perhaps not by Boccherini, though Gerard has blessed it with numbers G437-442. All but G440 have been recorded by **Rampal** and the Pasquiers (Sony 62679) while 437, 439, and 441 are played by the **Tourte Quintet** (Dynamic 2011). Rampal has been well received and contains more music.

There are 12 quintets with keyboard and strings, Opp. 56 and 57 (G407-18). **Les Adieux** recorded G410, 412, 415, and 418 (Deutsche

Harmonia Mundi 77053), while Piero Barbareschi and **Quartetto Elisa** have done all of Op. 56 (Agora Musica 215, 2CD). Both groups use an early piano and play with sensitivity. Les Adieux has the more resonant recording space; the Agora recording was made at a very low volume in a totally non-resonant acoustic, not unpleasant but a little claustrophobic. All 12 were also transcribed by the composer into string quintets with two violas (G379-390). There are, however, 12 original two-viola quintets (Opp. 60 and 61, G391-402), some of Boccherini's last works. G391, 395, and 397 have been recorded by **Ensemble 415,** also in early style, played very beautifully (Harmonia Mundi 901402).

Returning to the keyboard quintets, nine were soon transmuted into versions for guitar and string quartet. Naxos is working on a collection of which Vol. 3 seems to be the only one released, containing *La Ritirata di Madrid* (G453) and Quintet in E Minor (G451), as well as the two-cello quintet with the famous minuet. **Zoltán Tokos** and the Danubius Quartet offer polished if rather romantic readings (Naxos 550731). I wish **Richard Savino**'s set of all nine guitar quintets was still available; he balances the strings and guitar effectively in early music style (Harmonia Mundi 907026, 907039, and 907069). A good performance, both brilliant and sensitive, comes from **Jason Carter** and the Bingham Quartet (ASV 6244: *Fandango Quintet* (G448), *La Retirata di Madrid,* and the E minor quintet).

There are six short quintets, Op. 55 for strings with either oboe or flute. **Michael Faust** has recorded them with the Auryn Quartet in excellent flute versions (CPO 999382). It should be stated, however, that they seem originally to have been for oboe, and **Sarah Francis** played them with the Allegri Quartet in more incisive performances (MHS 4979, LP). Her disc called them by their Paris designation, Op. 45. There are also six sextets, Op. 23, once available in two versions, one with cellist **Richard Lester** (Capriccio), the other with **Ensemble 415** (Harmonia Mundi). Both seem to be NA, but for the record, Lester's discs were superior in verve and accuracy. These are highly imaginative pieces, fully on a level with the two-cello quintets. They are also some of the earliest string sextets in captivity.

VOCAL MUSIC

Stabat Mater is Boccherini's best-known vocal work, presently available in a rather logy performance of the 1801 revision, with string orchestra and three singers led by **Miguel de la Fuente** (Arion 68164), and in a more incisive version by **Ensemble 415** (Harmonia Mundi 901378).

MOORE

Joseph Bodin de Boismortier (1689–1755)

Boismortier is unique among French Baroque composers in that he seems to have lived solely on the royalties from his many published works (102 opuses, though not all have survived) without ever holding a royal appointment or ecclesiastical post. Truly remarkable, considering that a position at court, or even a job as music teacher to the children of a nobleman, often meant the difference between survival and starvation. Boismortier couldn't even boast of a particular skill as a performer, yet he did possess, perhaps more than any other French musician of the time, a special affinity for the capabilities of various instruments, especially those of the favorite wind instrument of the French, the transverse flute. His many flute sonatas, concertos, duets and trios have been a mainstay of flutists to this day, while his scattered works for other instruments (oboe, bassoon, viol, musette, trumpet) are no less convincing. He had his detractors while he was alive, and even today many critics label him the French Vivaldi for being overly facile and lacking in

depth, yet few composers have demonstrated his ability to write instrumental music.

A good place to start an exploration of Boismortier's flute music is an excellent disc by baroque flutist **Stephen Schultz** and harpsichordist Byron Schenkman playing six sonatas from Op. 91, at an attractive budget price (Naxos 553414). Four duets for cello and bassoon can be heard in a splendid CD entitled "Les Delices de la solitude," ably performed by **Danny Bond,** baroque bassoon, and Richte van der Meer, cello (Accent 58331, with music by Michel Corrette). The British group **Badinage** has put together a representative program of chamber music that includes such unusual items as two sonatas for two vielles (a rustic bowed string instrument popular in France at the time) along with four seldom-performed harpsichord suites (Meridian 84335).

"Ballets de Village" provides a generous sampling of Boismortier's orchestral music, expertly played by Le Concert Spirituel under **Hervé Niquet** (Naxos 554295). The disc includes several numbers scored for an orchestra containing the rustic instruments so beloved by the French upper classes at the time: the vielle, the musette (a kind of bagpipe chanter), and the hurdy-gurdy. It's a real party disc—you can have fun stumping your friends and neighbors by asking them to "name that instrument."

All of Boismortier's extant vocal music has been brilliantly recorded by **Niquet** and Le Concert Spirituel, and it fits neatly on one CD (Accord 240 1772). The *Motet a Grand Chœur* is a rousing affair full of dazzling orchestral colors, while *Motets a voix seule meles de symphonies* are a series of quieter, contemplative works for solo voice, sung here with great feeling by four distinguished soloists. I can't think of any better introduction to the vocal music of the late French Baroque than these motets. Too bad that's all there is.

BRODERSEN

Arrigo Boito (1842–1918)

Boito was only 26 when his first opera, *Mefistofele,* had its premiere. It was a fiasco, and it took him seven years to revise it. The second version was more successful, in Bologna in 1875 and at La Scala in 1881. The composer never finished another opera. His libretto for *Nerone* was completed by 1870, when he failed to persuade Verdi to set it to music. The two did collaborate on *Otello* and *Falstaff,* and it is perhaps Boito's ignominious lot to be better remembered as a librettist than a composer. (Under the pen name Tobia Gorrio, he also furnished Ponchielli with *La Gioconda.*)

When he decided to tackle *Nerone* himself, he had many years left, but the ambitious opera remained unfinished and unperformed until **Toscanini** offered an abridged version in a 1924 memorial ceremony at La Scala. (Despite Toscanini's advocacy, Gatti-Casazza refused to bring it to the Met.) The faithful conductor addressed it again at La Scala in 1948, and excerpts of this performance, with Siepi, Nelli, Frank Guerrera, and Simionato, have been preserved in very poor sound (SRO). A couple of "live" performances led by other conductors—**Franco Capuana** in Naples, 1957; Gavazzeni in Turin, 1975 (rather good)—have come and gone on specialist labels. The sole studio recording of *Nerone* was led in 1982 by the adventurous and indefatigable **Eve Queler,** with an all-Hungarian cast (Hungaroton). If you're curious, it's your only choice.

Mefistofele is a strange, lovable opera. The Italians who first heard it in 1868 were confused by its modernisms, though they seem fairly tame to us now. Static, uneventful passages alternate with moments of stunning beauty where Boito creates a sound world all his own, by turns wistful, nostalgic, and numinously uplifting. Indeed, the opera can't be fully appreciated on records if the sound is poor, though the most famous of its arias have been memorably recorded by many of the great singers of the century. The 1954 recording with **Tagliavini** as Faust (Cetra) and the 1956 with **Christoff** as an off-the-wall devil (EMI) don't do *Mefistofele* justice.

The first good recording was led by **Serafin,** and its durability is warranted by Siepi's performance of the title role (♦London 440054). He is the most urbane of devils, and the beauty, suavity, confidence, and idiomatic flair of his singing have not been replicated since. Tebaldi's Margherita is sometimes short of breath and uneasy on top, but she sings with richness, delicacy, and palpable affection. "L'altra notte" was one of her concert staples. Lucia Danieli is an effective if slightly strident Helen of Troy, but del Monaco, unfortunately, rides roughshod over the lovely contours of Faust's arias. The recording was originally begun with di Stefano in the role but never completed. Decca has issued excerpts, and while di Stefano is preferable to del Monaco, his voice isn't beautiful or malleable enough for the part, especially for anyone who can't get Gigli's timbre out of mind. The 1958 sound is not ideally spacious but holds up well.

Another Tebaldi recording, this one of a 1966 performance in New York conducted by **Gardelli,** finds her singing Elena (her debut role) as well as Margherita, to the mellifluous Faust of Bergonzi, who should have recorded the part in the studio. Ghiaurov, fresher of voice than he would be 22 years later, is a solid devil. The mono sound is fairly honest and listenable, though rather constricted (Legato).

In sonic comparison to any of its predecessors, **Rudel**'s recording is absolutely spectacular, with a wide sound stage, full-bodied choral sonorities, and a thunderous organ (♦EMI 66502). Mefistofele was one of Norman Treigle's signature roles, and though he doesn't sing as gracefully as Siepi, he's solid and commanding, and a more ingenious actor. Caballé seems distant at times next to Tebaldi, but just listen to what she does at "Spunta l'aurora pallida"—great singing by any standards and alone worth the price of the discs. Domingo's Faust is sung handsomely enough to offset its dramatic blandness, and Josella Ligi is a capable Helen, though her voice doesn't suggest the character's legendary pulchritude.

Caballé's Helen comes closer to the mark in a recording led by **de Fabritiis** (♦London 410175). She was past her best and just beginning to wobble. Ghiaurov's voice had also lost some of its plush and ease of emission, but it's still an imposing sound, able to dominate the proceedings whenever the devil appears. He's less debonair than Siepi, less incisive than Treigle, but he has a commanding, old-fashioned theatrical presence of his own. Freni is less opulent than Tebaldi and less technically stunning than Caballé, but her voice is lovely in its own way, with ample body and focus. She's a very human Margherita, with a wide-eyed innocence that makes her downfall all the more poignant. Faust is one of Pavarotti's best roles on records. He's very much the thoughtful philosopher. De Fabritiis is a straightforward conductor, and London's sound is excellent, though it won't raise the roof quite so high as EMI's.

Treigle's most direct successor as Mefistofele was Ramey, who had a similarly lithe, athletic appearance on stage and whose espousal of the opera motivated many companies to mount it for him. His theatrical effectiveness doesn't quite come across on either of his two recordings, with **Patanè** in 1988 (Sony) and **Muti** in 1995 (RCA). He enunciates the words clearly but monotonously, seldom enlivening them with any rubato or change in tone color. The voice pours out freely and strongly, oblivious to harmonic shifts and conversational subtleties. It's almost a consolation that the supporting casts in each case, aside from Domingo on Sony, are humdrum or worse.

Toscanini recorded the Prologue with bass Nicola Moscona in 1954 (RCA). The maestro's fierce intensity can't offset the constricted sound. Further historical explorations should start with the famous basses—Chaliapin, Tancredi Pasero, and Pinza—and some of the sopranos, from Muzio and Farrar to Callas and Crespin. There's no shortage of great tenors, Italian or otherwise, who have been drawn to Faust's arias.

LUCANO

William Bolcom *(b. 1938)*

Most of Bolcom's music is late 20th-century vernacular nationalist, preponderantly ragtime based. He's a fine performer of classical ragtime and his own piano music as well. Few composers in other parts of the world have retained such overt musical nationalism, and few in the United States have done so as consistently.

Of his large concert works, **Bolcom** offers the Piano Concerto as soloist with Sydney Hodkinson conducting the Rochester Philharmonic (Vox 7509, with Samuel Adler's flute concerto and unaccompanied flute sonata). The concerto is the result of a 1976 bicentennial commission, so it appropriately includes *Yankee Doodle,* snippets of marches, and jazz flavors in an eclectic mix of straightforward blends and cacophonous sounds. Like other such commissions, this work isn't performed much, perhaps because it's too securely located musically in a particular time and place. On the same disc, Bolcom's colorful, uncomplicated, and unaccompanied *Three Dance Portraits,* all vernacular based, are performed very well by **Barry Snyder.**

For a broader sample of Bolcom's large works in traditional forms, a recording with violinist Sergio Luca suffices (Argo 433077). The Violin Concerto is a tribute to pianist Paul Jacobs and a comedic treatment of all manner of styles and genres. There's a jazz flavor at times, and the concerto as a whole is reminiscent of extended jazz solos when musicians insert easily identifiable licks from other tunes into their improvisations. This collage technique rarely works well in concerto form, and it doesn't here, whether the listener knows the tunes or not. The chuckle that may result from the clever juxtaposition of disparate musics doesn't recur after a first hearing, and there isn't much else of interest. The same is true of the symphony on this disc, Bolcom's first and composed when he was still a teenager. The satire, if that's what it is, quickly becomes tiresome.

The same criticism could fairly be leveled at Ives's symphonies but generally is not, because they contain so much more of interest than Bolcom's (especially Ives's Nos. 3 and 4). That said, Bolcom's No. 3 receives a credible performance by **Lawrence Leighton Smith** and the undersized Louisville Symphony Orchestra (First Edition 0007). Composed in 1979, more than 20 years after his No. 1, Symphony 3 has more of the scope one expects from the genre but still lacks substance. However, one reviewer said of this work, "No one else . . . can quote so many styles and get away with it so easily."

The addition of text, Theodore Roethke's poem "The Rose," to Symphony 4 offered Bolcom precompositional substance to replace to some extent his usual reliance on vernacular music. But even thought it is sung well by **Joan Morris,** there really isn't any more made of the poem than there is of ragtime in other works. It's a clumsy poem anyway, merely sentimental and pseudo-profound, and in that sense, the musical setting matches it well. However, this work from 1986 generates a tension not present in Nos. 1 and 3, although the material isn't related much to the form, so the result is less than might have been.

Bolcom's main talent as composer is in the lighter realm, not paraphrasing vernacular styles but *in* them, and his 12 *Cabaret Songs* are right on the esthetic money (Music and Arts 729). Here the sardonic wit and over-the-top fun are fully realized. Vocalist **Judy Applebaum** and pianist Marc-André Hamelin capture their earthy element satisfactorily. Even the live recording is a plus; you feel close to being there. The other selections on this disc, Schoenberg's well-known *Brettl-Lieder,* with all its Berlin *angst,* and Britten's little-known *Cabaret Songs,* are not quite so successfully sung.

Bolcom's prowess as pianist is evident on recordings of his concerto and Gershwin's *Songbook;* perhaps this is the reason for his natural and secure compositions for piano, evident in 12 *New Etudes* performed well by **Hamelin** (New World 354). Completed in 1986, this fine set of pieces is the only solo acoustic music for piano to win a Pulitzer Prize. Etudes in the traditional sense of posing one pianistic problem each, the 12 are played with the aplomb and style we expect from Hamelin. A very different work, *Recuerdos,* is a duo-piano piece based on South American music; it's charming stuff and performed with appropriate panache by **Richard** and **John Contiguglia** (Helicon 10040). Other Bolcom compositions on this disc are *The Serpent's Kiss* and *Through Eden's Gates,* and arrangements of some of Percy Granger's works fill out the recording successfully. *Recuerdos* is performed ably but less well (Audiofon 72054, with duo-piano music by Debussy, Schnittke, and Weber). Second to the Contiguglias's *Recuerdos* is the very good performance by **Irina** and **Julia Elkina** (Virgin 106, with interesting duo-piano music by Corigliano, Gould, and Rorem).

A substantial selection of Bolcom's rags is played by **John Murphy** (Alba 325). The more popular rags are represented—*Ghost Rags, Eubie's Lucky Day, Lost Lady Rag,* and so on. For aficionados of this music, Murphy has the style and flavor down pat.   ZIEROLF

Alexander Borodin *(1833–1887)*

The noted Russian research chemist Alexander Porfiryevich Borodin, author of learned treatises including "On the Action of Ethyl Iodide on Hydrobenzamide and Amarine," still found time to compose occasionally, though not nearly enough. His masterpiece, the opera *Prince Igor,* was completed after his death by his friends Rimsky-Korsakov and Glazunov, who set down the overture after hearing Borodin play it on the piano. Glazunov also readied the remaining sketches of his Symphony 3 for performance. Its two movements only make us regret all the more what might have been, a tribute to a generous and gifted man who simply ran out of time.

SYMPHONIES

The fact that Symphony 3 was left unfinished at least permits all three to fit on one CD, an option offered by both **Serebrier** (ASV 706) and **Gunzenhauser** (Naxos 550238). The wonderfully brazen sound of Serebrier's Rome brasses adds greatly to the raw energy of 2 in particular; elsewhere ensemble is a bit untidy at times (not surprising, as all three were taped in concert) and the sound is a trifle opaque. In 1 Serebrier is rugged enough but seems tepid compared with others, and 3 is on the slow side as well. The disc is still a convenient way of obtaining all three symphonies; however, Gunzenhauser, at a considerably lower price, imbues 1 with more fire, and his Bratislava forces are no less proficient in 2, making the Naxos a much better buy (though individual versions of all three may be preferred, as noted below).

The best set of the Borodin symphonies ever issued was on LPs by **Loris Tjeknavorian** and the National Philharmonic (♦RCA 25098)— filled out with *Petite Suite,* the standard suite from *Prince Igor,* and a brief excerpt from the stillborn *Mlada*—and it's a pity that only 2

(coupled with *Polovtsian Dances* and *Steppes of Central Asia*) has been reissued (♦RCA 60535). Still withheld from us is Tjeknavorian's splendid and exuberant account of 1; in 2 he proceeds at a brisk pace, yet invests the music with a welcome solidity, though he does push a bit too hard in the Scherzo of 3.

In the absence of Tjeknavorian, **Andrew Davis**'s set offers excellent value (Sony 62406). Certainly 1 is on a par with Tjeknavorian, a skillful blend of lyricism and high spirits; in 2 Davis seems a trifle lightweight next to Svetlanov's massive RCA account (see below), yet the final movement pulses with energy, and Davis does very well with 3, perhaps the best choice after Ansermet (also see below). Vigorous and highly colored readings of the Overture and Dances from *Prince Igor* fill out the set. **Neeme Järvi** merely skims the surface of 1; he does well with the final movement, but I is way too fast (though the resilient Gothenburg players have no problems) and the all-important tympani are obscured; 2 is much better, rugged and energetic, but in 3 he keeps shifting gears, resulting in a curious stop-and-go effect (DG). Järvi also includes music from *Prince Igor,* but his set is of greater interest for *Petite Suite,* as well as Alexander Tcherepnin's fascinating arrangement of the Nocturne from String Quartet 2.

Svetlanov recorded all three symphonies twice, first for Melodiya and then RCA. In 1 his brassy, blowzy traversal for Melodiya (coupled with 2) is preferable to his more muted RCA remake (coupled with 3), though the final movement is too fast for comfort; it comes off better on RCA (♦62505). In the glorious and thoroughly Russian 2 I've been spoiled by Svetlanov; his massive tread in the opening measures might summon up the image of some great *bogatyr,* and there is overall a sense of Old Mother Russia lacking in most other recordings. Unfortunately both Svetlanov accounts of 3 are sluggish. **Rozhdestvensky**'s bloated, ponderous account of 1 may be set aside; his bland, uninvolved 2 and even more tepid 3 aren't much better (Chandos).

Gergiev quite sweeps the field where 1 is concerned, urging his orchestra on imperiously and embracing the rugged rhythms and bold splashes of color in a massive Russian bear hug; the Rotterdam musicians play as if inspired, spearheaded by the awesome brasses whose heft adds immeasurably to the effect of the grand climax of the opening movement (♦Philips 422996). He's equally impressive in 2, bringing out the bardic quality of the Andante and bristling with energy in the finale. **Ashkenazy** likewise couples 1 and 2, but proves disappointing; his headlong pace in 1 merely skims the surface, while the Royal Philharmonic has displayed more ravishing string tone elsewhere (London). He does better with 2, but not enough to recommend the recording.

Jun'ichi Hirokami offers more satisfying accounts of both scores, pointed and alert in 1 and actually sounding more "Russian" than Ashkenazy in 2 (BIS 726)—probably the best pairing next to Gergiev's (Finlandia). Certainly he's preferable to **Plasson,** whose hectic account of 1 makes Ashkenazy sound tired; he's better in 2, but again it's too little too late (Berlin). **Ari Rasilainen** lopes along good-naturedly in 1, but for all his attention to color and rhythm seems rather easy-going next to Gergiev (Finlandia). In 2, **Ansermet** seems of like mind with Svetlanov, but his frequent tempo fluctuations soon become disconcerting; however, his crisp account of 3 is hard to beat, and there's also a colorful *Prince Igor* Overture (London 430219 and Classic 6126).

For those on a budget, **Samuel Friedmann**'s bracing account of 2 (Arte Nova 30457, with *Polovtsian Dances* and *Steppes*) offers good value (though you can get all three symphonies with Gunzenhauser on Naxos for only a couple of bucks more). **Fedoseyev** offers the same program plus the *Prince Igor* Overture, but at a slower pace (save for *Steppes,* which is too fast), though beautifully played and recorded (Novalis 150079). **Kubelik,** though somewhat lacking in panache, offers a good account of the score (EMI). Even better is **Martinon**'s reading (♦Decca 444389 and in a "two-fer," 455632, neither currently available in the US).

Apparently out of print even in England is **Anshel Brusilow,** coupled with even richer treasure: Balakirev's *Russia* and Rimsky-Korsakov's *Skazka* (EMI 63093). You may still be able to find **Smetá_ek**'s vivacious account of 2, coupled with a highly energetic Tchaikovsky *Winter Dreams* (Supraphon 0612). The febrile **Bátiz,** with a first-class Mexican ensemble, omits the chorus in the *Polovtsian Dances* included by Tjeknavorian (ASV). **Kondrashin**'s brawny concert performance is also available (Philips 438280, with Stravinsky's *Pétrouchka).*

OTHER ORCHESTRAL MUSIC

Originally written for piano, *Petite Suite* was later orchestrated by Glazunov but retains the rich melodic vein typical of Borodin; indeed, two sections ("Intermezzo" and "Serenade") were used in the musical comedy *Kismet.* **Geoffrey Simon** crams so much music onto his 78-minute disc that there's no room for the "Intermezzo" (Cala 1029 or 1011). However, the *Requiem* (with tenor Ian Boughton) in an arrangement by Stokowski—based on the Russian tune "Tati-Tati," similar to our "Chopsticks"—is otherwise unavailable, and Simon (like Tjeknavorian) includes a chorus in the *Polovtsi March.* Pride of place in the absence of Tjeknavorian must go to **Järvi** (included with the symphonies), though this is hardly surprising given **Svetlanov**'s ponderous tempo in the finale (Melodiya, with Symphony 3); his remake is much better in this respect (RCA, with 2). Even more sluggish is **Rozhdestvensky** (Chandos, with 2), while **Gennadi Cherkassov**'s account fills out Esipov's set of Mussorgsky's *Sorochinsky Fair* (Melodiya).

There are too many recordings of the various *Prince Igor* excerpts to list in detail. Even without chorus or "Dance of the Polovtsi Maidens" **Fiedler** is at the top of the list, not least for the splendid *Russian Easter* and *Gayne* excerpts offered along with it—"Pops Caviar" indeed! (♦RCA 68132). **Bernstein** and **Ormandy** are safe choices in this repertoire as well.

While the highly evocative tone poem *In the Steppes of Central Asia* is often included as filler, conductors tend to forget that this is supposed to be a camel caravan; too many of them simply barrel through it, including **Ashkenazy, Hirokami, Fedoseyev,** and **Simon. Bernstein**'s amiable traversal may be had with the Andrew Davis set of the symphonies, though the string tone is not as luminous as it might be. **Järvi** is not as rushed as some but could do with more grandeur, while **Friedmann** (with 2) gets it just right. But if you have the **Svetlanov** you really don't need another.

The Nocturne from String Quartet 2 frequently surfaces in this company, though the specific version may vary: **Järvi** uses an arrangement by Tcherepnin that would make even Stokowski green with envy, while **Tjeknavorian** offers the version by Malcolm Sargent, and **Saulius Sondeckis** (with the Andrew Davis symphonies) employs the more familiar Rimsky-Korsakov setting.   HALLER

CHAMBER MUSIC

As a chamber composer, Borodin is best known for his String Quartet 2, whose slow movement, the famed Nocturne (the source of *Kismet*'s "And This Is My Beloved"), frequently stands alone. But there is also another quartet as well as a string quintet, a piano quintet, a piano trio, and various shorter pieces. And though they tend to be more indebted to Germanic models—specifically Mendelssohn, Haydn, Beethoven, and,

in the case of the Piano Quintet, Brahms—than the rhapsodic Quartet 2, they, like the Tchaikovsky quartets, tap a vein of Russian melody within their basically classical frames.

Most of them can be had in warmly idiomatic performances by the **Moscow String Quartet** and Moscow Trio (♦Harmonia Mundi 288141/3, 3CD). But these are not the only options. If your sole interest is in Quartet 2, you need look no farther than the **Emerson Quartet,** a sensitively played performance whose sure technique and unerring melodic impulse likewise distinguish its discmates, Tchaikovsky's Quartet 1 and Dvořák's *"American"* (♦DG 45551). No less recommendable are the **Borodin Quartet** (♦EMI 47795) and **Lark Quartet** (♦Arabesque Z6658), who sensibly couple Quartet 2 with 1, to which the Borodin in particular brings speed, suppleness, and just the right degree of incisiveness. On the other hand, the Lark responds especially well to the feminine grace of the writing (for example, the trios of the two *Scherzos*).

For the price-conscious, the **Haydn Quartet** is only a couple of notches below this level (Naxos). Completists may prefer the **Quartetto Paolo Borciani,** who offer not only the two quartets, in somewhat recessive but wonderfully lithe and lyrical performances, but also the charming *Serenata alla spagnola* and D major Scherzo, which later found its way into the Glazunov-completed Symphony 3 (♦Stradivarius 33445). By contrast, recordings of 2 by the **Cleveland Quartet** (Telarc) and **Concord Quartet** (Vox) seem a trifle uninvolved.

When it comes to the quintets, the **Moscow Quartet** beats its competition in both, the Piano Quintet being coupled with Quartet 1 (♦Harmonia Mundi 288141) and the String Quintet with Quartet 2 and the *Serenata* (♦Harmonia Mundi 288142). The livelier and more cultivated of the two recordings of the Michael Goldstein-completed Cello Sonata, with **Otto Kertész, Jr.,** is available only with the New Budapest Quartet's recordings of the quintets (♦Marco Polo 223172). The **Arcata Quartet**'s more straightforwardly "American" view of the String Quintet offers perhaps the most bracing finale, marked, but almost never played, *Prestissimo* (♦Vox 7543, with Quartet 1).

OPERA AND SONGS

"The funny thing about these Russian operas," a commentator once observed, "is that they all seem to have been written by somebody else." Among others, he was almost certainly thinking of *Prince Igor,* which Borodin worked on fitfully for the last 18 years of his life. After his death in 1887 his manuscripts and notes, many of them indecipherable, went to his friend Rimsky-Korsakov, who, with the aid of his pupil Glazunov, completed the opera. The result was the version in which *Prince Igor* was premiered at St. Petersburg's Mariinsky Theater in 1890 and, to a greater or lesser extent, has been the basis of nearly every recording.

Not so with **Gergiev**'s 1995 set, however, featuring that same theater's Kirov Chorus and Orchestra (♦Philips 442537, 3CD). Rather, its "new" edition incorporates material from various other sources and adopts a sequence of scenes (suggested by an outline thought to date from no later than 1883) that reverses the usual order of what used to be Acts 1 and 2. At the same time we still get the Glazunov-composed Overture and the material he and Rimsky-Korsakov put together from Borodin's sketches to make up the bulk of Act 3—which is more than can be said of those earlier recordings that jettisoned the last in its entirety, including the darkly savage "Polovtsian March."

This revised sequence puts the opera's high point, the "Polovtsian Dances," at the end of Act 1, perhaps a bit too early for things to peak musically. On the other hand, the new material—including a full-blown mutiny near the end of what is now Act 2 and an extended Act 3 mono-logue for Igor — strengthens those sections both musically and dramat-ically, as does the addition of a choral epilogue, recalling the Prologue, at the very end. Nor does it hurt that these are among the strongest parts of an already strong performance, thanks principally to Gergiev's im-passioned leadership, which catches not only the barbaric splendor of the dances but the ominous darkness of the eclipse scene and the dra-matic vigor of Galitsky's rebellion, and does it despite a few slower-than-usual tempos. He has also forged his singers into an outstanding team, from the Galitsky of Vladimir Ognovienko — even more effectively drawn than Mikhail Kit's somewhat light-voiced Igor or Bulat Min-jelkiev's otherwise dependable Khan Konchak — to Galina Gor-chakova's idiomatic Yaroslavna and the Konchakovna of Olga Borodina, with her sensual, wide-ranging mezzo.

For those not inclined to second-guess Rimsky-Korsakov and Glazunov, the 1890 version can be had complete from **Tchakarov** (Sony 44878, 3CD). Though seldom a match for Gergiev at his best, Tchakarov marshals his forces impressively, aided by superb work by the Sofia Na-tional Opera Chorus and some equally characterful solo singing (e.g., the Galitsky of Nicola Ghiuselev). The same Sofia chorus can be heard on **Jerzy Semkov**'s 1967 recording, badly cut (including all of Act 3) but worth having for the imposing Konchak and Galitsky of **Christoff,** who, like Chaliapin before him, sings both parts (EMI 66814, 2CD).

An earlier *Igor* also featured **Christoff** in 16 Borodin songs, a sampling without parallel in the current catalogue (EMI, 3CD, NA). In its absence, tenor **Sergei Larin** offers two of them in somewhat bari-tonal but deeply felt renditions (♦Chandos 9547, with other "Songs by the Mighty Handful"). One of them, "From the Shores of the Distant Homeland" may also be had in Glazunov's orchestration with baritone **Tord Wallstroem** a smooth-voiced soloist, along with mezzo **Larissa Dyadkova**'s authentic-sounding "At the Homes of Other Folk" (Chan-dos 9199). But Rozhdestvensky's dispiriting Symphonies 1 and 3, to which they are appended, seems a heavy price to pay.   GOODFELLOW

Giovanni Bottesini *(1821–1889)*

Bottesini's career differs from those of other virtuoso instrumentalists of the 19th century in two ways. First, he was known as a player, con-ductor, and composer, and second, his instrument was the double bass. As composer, he wrote 10 operas, six string quartets, and a considerable number of solo pieces and concertante works featuring the bass, for which there was very little solo literature. His style is conservative but harmonically imaginative and his orchestral scoring is colorful and ef-fective. His writing for piano isn't as interesting, perhaps the reason that some pieces exist in scores orchestrated by other hands.

Bass players have mined Bottesini extensively, but he has hardly been touched by anyone else. There is a disc of orchestral pieces (Bongio-vanni 2141) and one of string quartets (Dynamic 2006), neither of which has come my way. **Thomas Martin,** bassist, has four discs for ASV in which he includes three overtures and *Andante Sostenuto* for strings, as well as several songs with piano, two with bass obbligato. These are scat-tered through his bass collection, the orchestral works in Vols. 1 (563) and 3 (907), the songs in 2 (626) and 4 (1052).

Works for bass and orchestra include two concertos. The one in B mi-nor is rather Mendelssohnian. **Wolfgang Harrer** plays it with string or-chestra in a competent, rather matter-of-fact manner (Koch Schwann 1338, with *Melodie* in E minor, also scored with string accompaniment). Also on this disc is the only recording of *Grande Concerto* for two double basses and orchestra, played by **Wolfgang Güttler** and **Klaus Stoll** (see

Passione Amorosi below). **Zbigniew Borowicz** plays the concerto with a string quartet and does the same for the D major *Elegie & Tarantella,* and this scoring suits his understated style (SNE 581). He also plays *Fantaisie on "Lucia di Lammermoor," Variations on Paisiello's "Nel cor piu non mi sento,"* and *Reverie,* these with piano. **Thomas Martin** plays the concerto with string orchestra, calling it "Concertino in C Minor." His performance mumbles its phrases. **Ovidiu Badila** plays it with full orchestra, as well as the much larger Concerto in F-sharp Minor and *Gran Duo Concertante* for violin, bass, and orchestra with **Keng-Yuen Tseng.** His performances are assertive yet lyrical, head and shoulders above the competition in all three works (♦Dynamic 210).

But read on. Badila's only competition in the F-sharp minor Concerto is the rather lumpy Martin, but Martin is better balanced (ASV 563). Badila's upper strings get a bit wiry in places. As for the *Gran Duo,* things get really complex. Badila's score uses some winds, but Martin with vio-linist José-Luis Garcia is the only one to use brass and timpani, in a rather self-conscious performance. Two recordings of the *Duo* use string orchestra. **Joel Quarrington** includes it as the only Bottesini work in a disc called "Virtuoso Reality," and his reading with **Jacques Is-railievitch** is the best played of the bunch (Musica Viva 1108). This piece is hard to interpret; it sounds like a spoof of Italian operatic styles a lot of the time. Quarrington and friends play it with enthusiasm, as do Badila and Tseng, where **Massimo Giorgi** and **Diego Conti** tend to ham it up, also with strings (Nuova Era 6810). Real ham comes with **Ezio Bosso** and **Silvio Bresso,** who play with piano accompaniment (Stradi-varius 33397).

Perhaps this is the place to discuss these two latter discs. Giorgi's is called "Virtuoso Works for Double Bass and Strings" and includes a number of pieces not otherwise recorded with strings. For instance, there is another *Gran Duo* for clarinet and bass, a fascinating work he plays with **Vincenzo Mariozzi.** This piece has also been recorded by Martin with **Emma Johnson,** accompanied by a full orchestra. Johnson is marvelous! It's also on Bosso's disc, played with **Tindaro Capuano.** Another curious piece explored by Giorgi is *Passione Amorosi,* a three-movement early work, originally for two basses and accompaniment, here in a version for violin, bass, and string orchestra. Violinist Conti can't seem to take it seriously. Martin plays the 2-bass version with full orchestra in his Vol. 3 to better effect, with **Franco Petracchi.** Bosso and bassist **Leonardo Colonna** play it with piano, enthusiastically but rather inaccurately. But we aren't through yet. Add to this stew the *Grande Concerto* for two basses, which turns out to be the old *Passione Amorosi* with a new movement tacked onto the beginning. **Güttler** and **Stoll** are the only ones to play this version for orchestra with winds but no brass, scored quite subtly (Koch Schwann 1338).

The other works on Giorgi's disc are usually played with piano: *Elegie in D & Tarantella, Allegretto Capriccio, Introduction & Gavotte,* and *Fan-tasia on "La Sonnambula."* He may also be heard on another disc, also with string orchestra, in *Allegro di Concerto alla Mendelssohn* and *Capriccio di Bravura,* along with several non-Bottesini pieces (Koch Schwann 1424). Let's discuss the *Allegro,* since that sounds particularly effective with strings. Modeled on Mendelssohn's Violin Concerto, from which Bottesini has excised all the tunes — leaving only a few gestures beside which his own tunes don't sound too bad — he has written a con-siderable concerto movement with cadenza. Everyone records it with pi-ano but **Giorgi,** including Bossi, Martin, Michael Rieber (Bayer 100216)**,** and **Quarrington** (Naxos 554002). The only one who plays it with the requisite energy is Quarrington, but it isn't one of his best per-formances, and a concerto sounds silly accompanied by piano, so I'm all for Giorgi in this instance. (You'll probably end up with Quarrington's CD anyway.)

But let's finish with Bossi's disc. Besides the works already mentioned, he plays *Elegie 3 "Romanza patetica," Reverie,* and a curious piece for cello, bass, and piano, *Fantasia on "I Puritani".* This was written for Alfredo Piatti, a famous cellist, and is quite demanding. Bossi and **Massimo Polidori** don't play it all that well (it's hard to match Bossi's intonation, his vibrato is so wide), and this work seems to need an orchestra. **William Xuclá** plays it in "The Bel Canto Double Bass" (no company or number listed) with the cello omitted and cut to nine minutes from Bossi's 13. Xuclá also plays *Elegie 3, Bolero,* and other non-Bottesini pieces. He's rather scratchy and unreliable. **Martin** plays the *Sonnambula Fantasia* in full dress, with orchestra and an introduction nobody else uses. His cellist, **Moray Welsh,** is not very accurate (neither is Martin), but it's the only orchestral rendition around (in Vol. 3).

The rest of Bottesini's bass music seems to be with piano accompaniment. Some pieces are only recorded in one version, and we should mention those. He wrote fantasias or variations on a number of operatic tunes. That on Bellini's *La Straniera* is early, actually a set of variations. Only **Stefano Sciascia** plays it, in a disc with *Sonnambula Fantasia, Variations on "Nel cor piu non mi sento," Carnival of Venice Variations, Elegie 1 & Tarantella,* and *Reverie* (Rivo Alto 9405). He's a forthright player with a warm sound, not very couth at times, but if it's fantasias and variations you want, he does more than anyone else. The *Fantasia on "Beatrice di Tenda"* is played only by **Martin** (in Vol. 2). As you may have gathered, I'm not a fan of his bumbling approach, but if you want to know Bottesini in depth, you're stuck with him, since every volume has material you won't find elsewhere.

Fantasie on "Lucia di Lammermoor" is played along with *Variations on "Nel cor piu non mi sento"* and *Reverie* on two discs. The best performances are by **Yasunori Kawahara** (Largo 5123, in "Fantasy on Double Bass," with pieces by others, mostly transcriptions). **Borowicz** does the same three works more diffidently (SNE 581). For *Sonnambula Fantasie,* the best playing is by **Giorgi** with strings (Nuova Era 6810). **Klaus Trumpf** has a big, lyrical tone, but his gestures tend to misfire. He also plays *Elegie in D* and *Reverie,* the two most popular works, with other originals and transcriptions (Berlin 93962). **Sciascia** is more effective, though still a bit clumsy (Rivo Alto 9405). **Martin** is volatile, though technically pressed (in Vol. 4).

This brings us to the original pieces for bass and piano. The three *Elegies* need explanation. 1 in D is usually performed with the *Tarantelle; 2* in E minor is also called *Romanza Drammatica; 3* is also called *Romanza Patetica.* **Harrer** plays 3 well with strings, calling it *Melodie in E Minor* (Koch Schwann 1338). **Michael Reiber** plays all three elegies with *Introduzione e Gavotta* and *Grande Allegro* in rather phlegmatic readings (Bayer 100216). The best and most inclusive collection with piano is by **Quarrington,** the most technically polished and musical of the bassists (♦Naxos 554002). Curiously, he doesn't play the *Tarantelle* with *Elegie 1* (neither does Reiber), but does include all three *Elegies* and the other original bass pieces, *Grand Allegro, Bolero, Introduction & Gavotte, Allegretto Capriccio, Capriccio di Bravura,* and *Reverie.* In all of these he blows away the competition. He also plays a *Melodia* nobody else plays, even Martin.

One other disc should be mentioned. **Badila** and **Güttler** have recorded what may be Bottesini's first compositions, three *Grandi Duetti* for two basses alone; substantial compositions, not very original perhaps, but difficult and amusing (Dynamic 236).   MOORE

Lili Boulanger *(1893–1918)*

Marie-Juliette Olga (Lili) Boulanger wrote a surprising amount of very beautiful music during her short life. She was the youngest member of a prominent Parisian musical family and in 1913 was the first woman to win the Prix de Rome (for her cantata *Faust et Hélène*) in its 110-year history.

In 1916 Ricordi published Boulanger's song cycle *Clairières dans le Ciel,* 13 poems taken from Francis Jammes's *Tristesses,* a cycle comparable in musical substance and emotional intensity to Schumann's *Dichterliebe* or Fauré's *La Bonne Chanson.* There are only a few recordings, of which the best is by tenor **Martyn Hill** (Hyperion 66726). His voice is light, transparent, and free, while still having a great emotional range. Another very good recording is by soprano **Kristine Ciesinski,** though Jammes's poems are written for a man's voice and the texts make far more sense sung by a high tenor than a high soprano (Leonarda LP). The Hyperion recording includes several earlier vocal works: *Les Sirènes* and *Renouveau,* written in 1911, *Hymne au soleil* and *Pour les funérailles d'un soldat* from 1912, and a very beautiful *Soir sur la plaine* from 1913.

Another excellent disc, "In Memoriam Lili Boulanger," was a project of Emil Naoumoff, one of Nadia Boulanger's last students (Marco Polo 223636). The recording includes music by Nadia, with a fine reading by **Olivier Charlier** of Lili's three violin pieces, some piano music, a few songs, some extracts from *Clairières dans le Ciel,* and her last work, *Pie Jesu* for voice, harp, organ, and string quartet. **Isabelle Sabrié**'s performance of *Pie Jesu,* a piece Lili dictated to her sister three weeks before she died, is one of the most moving performances I have heard.

The first recording of Lili's music (made under Nadia's supervision) has been reissued; it includes *Pie Jesu, Vieille Prière Bouddhique,* and three psalm settings, with **Markevitch** leading the Orchestre Lamoureux and some excellent singers (Everest). Though I prefer the more recent recordings, this is an important part of the Boulanger discography. Markevitch also recorded her cantata *Faust et Hélène* in 1977, not yet re-released on CD (Varèse LP). Tortelier made an excellent recording of *Faust et Hélène,* Psalms 24 and 130, *D'un soir triste,* and *D'un matin de printemps* with the BBC Philharmonic (Chandos 9745).   FINE

Pierre Boulez *(b. 1925)*

Recent publicity blurbs appropriately describe Boulez as "the *spiritus rector* of the international avant-garde," yet he describes himself as being as much a descendant of Debussy as of Webern. Part of this French heritage lies in the fact that, unlike many modernists, he's intensely interested in sound — its quality and variety, its glitter and seductiveness. His compositions are great, enduring, and immensely enjoyable because they're brilliantly thought through and define their own flavor, color, and ethos: crystalline and elegant, with allusions to French "impressionism" as well as to music of East and Southeast Asia.

Collections. Several of Boulez's unpublished works, fascinating if imperfect by his standards, are in a mid-priced Col Legno disc. *Polyphonie X* was written by a 25-year-old serialist whom Messiaen likened to "a lion being flayed alive." *Poèsie pour pouvoir* dates from 1958 and is one of Boulez's rare pre-IRCAM electronic pieces, calling for tape and a fairly large instrumental ensemble. With typical ingenuity and integrity, he aims for an intercession between acoustic and electronic sonorities. Then there is the fascinating, stridently rhetorical voice of **Michel Bouquet** on the tape, to contrast with the still, poised electronic sounds. *Polyphonie X* and *Poèsie* are in rather dim mono sound, premieres recorded live at the Donaueschingen festival. **Rosbaud's** *Polyphonie X* isn't the last word in executive gloss, but it's apparently the musical surprises that caused the audience to titter on one or two occasions.

A 4CD set presents an essential cross section of the published works (Erato 98495). The earliest are *Sonatine for Flute and Piano*, the cantatas *Le visage nuptial* and *Le Soleil des eaux*, and Piano Sonata 1. **Boulez** recorded an Argo LP of *Soleil* in its first, 1958 version—one of his paroxysmal, violent settings of the surrealist poet René Char—in a reading often more dramatic than the new one, but the latter represents his latest compositional thoughts. The Erato also enjoys better sound, although soprano **Phyllis Bryn-Julson** is too close to the microphone. Later works include *Und Cummings ist der Dichter* for chorus, *Figures, Doubles, Prismes* for orchestra, and the static, less immediately interesting *Derivé*. Pitting a solo flute against two horns and string sextet, *Memoriale* is as evanescent, lyrical, and diaphanous as a soap bubble. Just as haunting is *Dialogue de l'ombre double* for clarinet and tape, a fragment of the revised version of *Domaines*, and my ideal of how prerecorded tape should be used in concert performance if it is to be used at all: not as a means of dismantling "natural" instrumental sounds, but as a sort of ventriloquism. **Alain Damiens** is the soloist and, having played the piece for years with the composer's assistance, his reading is definitive.

The third disc in the Erato set is given over to **Barenboim's** rather sloppy Orchestre de Paris performances of *Rituel*, *Messagesquisse* for solo cello against a concerted group of six, and Boulez's orchestration of his early piano pieces *Notations*. **Boulez's** own recording of *Rituel* is, by contrast, crisp and beautifully evocative (Sony 45839). Likewise, Barenboim's *Notations* can't hold a candle to **Abbado's** lithe performance with the Vienna Philharmonic (as part of a European avant-garde recital recorded live at the Wien Modern festival, DG 429260). The Sony disc also holds the brilliant and mercurial *Eclat* for 15 instruments, joined with the orchestral *Multiples*, to fill out a desirable and delectable issue.

Erato's fourth disc contains Boulez's longest and perhaps greatest score: *Pli selon pli*, his "portrait" of the symbolist poet Mallarmé. (This originated in part with the early *Tombeau for Prince Max Egon zu Furstenberg*, which can be heard on the Col Legno disc discussed above.) Transparent and crystalline, its palette fashioned from shards of glass and its thinking fiercely brilliant, *Pli selon pli* carved out a particular sound, ethos, and way of measuring musical time that no work—by Boulez or anyone else—has since followed up, let alone equaled. **Boulez** made this recording in 1981 with Bryn-Julson and the BBC Symphony. It's consistently slower than his 1969 performance (Sony 68335, with *Livre pour cordes*), with mikes diminished in number and pulled back a bit and the conductor less intent on driving home detail. The Erato *Pli selon pli* is also available in a "two-fer" (Warner 84248, with *Visage nuptial* and *Soleil des eaux*).

Orchestral and vocal works. Le Marteau sans maître is another masterpiece with strong timbral appeal. The scoring is for alto and six instrumentalists (with attack predominating in xylophone, vibraphone, and guitar), but the singer participates in only four of nine movements. Tone colors, like pitch and rhythmic vocabularies, shift constantly, kaleidoscopically, and the vocal line is sinuous. Sony has inexplicably failed to reissue **Boulez's** 1972 version with Yvonne Minton. His 1985 recording with mezzo Elizabeth Laurence is sporadically available (CBS/Sony 42619, with *Structures II* and *Notations* for piano). This is a rather quicker and more forceful reading than the 1972, with more natural microphone placement, but Boulez's interpretation has remained consistent. I would choose the earlier version for its evocativeness, the later one for its vigor.

Domaines, written for 21 instruments including solo clarinet, is a

lesser light in the Boulez canon. Its wind-dominated timbral world and disjunct gestures are less original than some of his other works, and the form less dramatically potent than the later *Dialogue* that was derived from it. Ensemble Musique Vivante made their recording in 1970, just after doing the Paris premiere under the composer, who is replaced on disc by **Diego Masson** (Harmonia Mundi). The confidence and crispness betoken the influence of Boulez's direction, but the CD mastering is abysmal and the disc clocks in at only 30 minutes!

It's almost always refreshing to hear Boulez's ensemble works directed by others: In their performance of *Eclat*, **Joel Thome** and the Orchestra of Our Time (Vox) tend to lack the suavity and intimidating confidence of the composer's Erato version, but that's all to the good. This is well worth hearing if Thome's couplings of music by Crumb and other contemporaries appeal. Unfortunately, their rendition of Boulez's "Improvisation 2" from *Pli selon pli* is marred by heavy tape noise; it sounds as if it might even have been dubbed from an LP.

Three discs of large-scale Boulez scores in recent revisions have appeared. The 43-minute *Répons* (DG 457605) is one of his major attempts to rethink the relationship between acoustic musical sounds and computer-based technology, although I find the score more interesting for the evidence it presents of his new desire to think across larger timespans, partly in response to his experience in conducting Wagner and Mahler in recent decades. You hear the new style right away in the opening tense, rhythmic, often homophonic measures. Filling out the disc is clarinetist **Alain Damiens,** once again playing the marvelous *Dialogue de l'ombre double* for clarinet and tape. Compared with his Erato version (see above), the DG is more aggressive with its multiphonic and spatial aspects and allows us to hear every detail of the transformations. **John Bruce Yeh** seems less interested than Damiens in the larger picture, relishing instead the details (Koch). The American playing style means his tone is brighter and his delivery intentionally less creamy and sustained, but the fingerwork is immaculate. Koch gives the music a deeper sound picture than DG, but without quite the same ear-catching variety of acoustic transformations.

Éxplosante-fixé is another large-scale offering, a work Boulez has been offering in various transformations since its initial conception in 1971 (DG 445833). The electronic component here might be more dated than that in *Répons*, but it's a more integral and subtle part of the conception. The work is a sort of meta-flute concerto, with three soloists and the electronic apparitions often forming separate concertante elements in themselves. The sound is a tad too bright and one-dimensional for my taste, especially after comparing it to the Erato *Memoriale*, which was also done at IRCAM. Filling out the disc are the early *Notations* in their piano form and the second book of *Structures* for two pianos, with **Pierre-Laurent Aimard** and **Florent Boffard.** The music is pungent, selfless, and relentlessly in motion.

The most recent scores recorded, although they both evolved from earlier solo pieces, are *Sur incises* for three pianos, three harps, and three percussionists and *Anthèmes 2* for violin and electronics (DG 463475). Forty years ago (the time of *Pli selon pli*), Boulez would have exploited such a group of long-ringing instruments for their tonal decay and would have used them with almost painful selectivity. At the end of the century he tends to make them whirling dervishes of vibration and cascading activity, and also pitch repetition, showing that he has mellowed in his own way. That said, I find more to interest me in the 20-minute *Anthèmes*, where the interaction and echoes between electronics and solo violin are always fresh and interesting and often witty. *Messagesquisse* fills out the disc.

Piano music. Although Boulez has referred to the "great textural density and violence of expression" of Piano Sonata 1, the piece boasts the usual fierce internal logic even at its most fustian. Helffer, Biret, and Henck offer it on their discs of all three sonatas. **Claude Helffer** is inclined to be over-emphatical, though that can be electrifying in the "rapide" of Sonata II (Montaigne 782120). **Idil Biret** is more sensitive, though the microphones are so close that in quieter passages you can hear the dampers going on and off the strings (Naxos). **Herbert Henck** has insufficient cueing and seems to pedal through II—or is it the smudgy acoustics? (Wergo) Also to be heard is **Jean-Philippe Aimard** (in Erato 98495, discussed above), the astonishing young musician who was for some years a resident pianist with Boulez's own Ensemble InterContemporain.

The difficult Piano Sonata 2 does indeed sound like the music of "a young lion being flayed alive," yet the ineffable Boulezian sense of balance and symmetry always comes through. The best account is **Pollini's** (DG 447431, with Prokofiev's Sonata 7, Webern's Variations, and a classic rendition of Stravinsky's *Three Movements from Pétrouchka*). With his magisterial rhythmic tension and almost superhuman keyboard command, Pollini avoids all the pitfalls. By comparison, the recognizably and engagingly human **Helffer** is just a bit approximate in his rhythms and ever so slightly taxed in the outer movements ; he also tends to neglect the quieter side of Boulez's dynamic spectrum (Montaigne 782120). In I, he's the slowest on record, although still shy of the composer's suggested timing. He thus prevents the music from enacting a stereotypical kind of frantic, avant-garde busy-ness, which is just what **Biret** produces (Naxos). Perhaps her tempos are partly to blame (her timing is the fastest), but she also fails to give individual events the acute focus they have in Pollini's hands. Details don't collide and fall over each other with Pollini as they do in **Henck's** hands and acoustics (Wergo). His technique is second only to Pollini's, and at first he convinces with his winningly acute sense of characterization and response to the wide dynamics of the score, but the echoey acoustic and the noisy, Ivesian approach soon become tiring.

In Sonata 3, Boulez produced an open, quasi-improvisatory "constellation" form that shows Cage's influence. Here **Henck** has a slightly better focused sound than in the other sonatas, though the acoustics are still fairly loose and that tends to make the *sforzatos* hard and the quieter passages indistinct (Wergo). **Biret** again suffers from a too-close balance, such that you can hear the pedal and damper mechanisms and also have to hear the pianist grunt before heavier efforts (Naxos). My recommendations are **Helffer** (Montaigne 782120) and **Jeffrey Swann** (Music & Arts 763). Helffer is alive to every detail of the score, but Swann is the more adroit technician and is my prime recommendation. They both enjoy almost ideal recording balances, so the music's extremes are contained and well integrated, but if good sound is primary, Swann wins out for the smoother treble response. Another fine reading, discreetly but vividly recorded and the most ably dispatched of all, is **Pi-Hsien Chen's** (Telos 006, with the 12 *Notations* and Jean Barraqué's Piano Sonata).

Boulez's two books of *Structures* for two pianos represent his most extreme journey into pointillistic, disjunct abstraction. There is documentary interest in the early concert recording of *Structures I* by **Yvonne Loriod** and **Boulez** himself, and it's a knife-edge performance, but the sound is comparatively limited (in the Col Legno collection described above). Both books are played by the **Kontarsky Brothers** in 1965 tapings made in a dry acoustic with extreme stereo separation of the instruments and some pre-echo (Wergo). In a performance that sounds far more like a heat-of-the-moment concert experience than an under-the-microscope musical experiment, **Pi-Hsien Chen** and **Bernard Wambach** team up for a volcanic account of Book II (CBS/Sony 42619, with *Marteau sans maître* and *Notations*). This proves even more exciting than the account of Book II by Aimard and Boffard (DG 445833; see above under *éxplosante-fixé*).   ASHBY

Paul Bowles (1910–99)

In classical music there have been few polymaths. Liszt, Schumann, and Wagner were all writers, but made their living primarily as composers. The American Paul Bowles, who lived in Morocco, was both a novelist and a composer. While he was known more as a writer—Bernardo Bertulucci created a film from his novel *The Sheltering Sky*—his intriguing music is finally getting the recognition it deserves.

Not many Bowles solo discs have been released, but he consistently appears in compilations of American composers. His art songs account for most of his presence, but it's not necessary to purchase compilation CDs to get a representative collection; his best ones appear in abundance in the available solo discs. His beguiling piano and chamber works are also available: the whimsical Sonata for Flute and Piano, the Suite for Small Orchestra, and the languid Sonata for Oboe and Clarinet. Throughout most of his life, Bowles functioned best as a composer of small-scale pieces, chamber works, or small orchestral pieces. Although he wrote no symphonies and only one concerto, he did compose three operas and four ballets. His music is sly and witty and sometimes languorous, reflecting the volatile whims of a proto-Beat expatriate.

Bowles's most beguiling large-scale work is the Concerto for Two Pianos, Winds, and Percussion, a dynamic piece of choppy cross-rhythms, abrupt tempo changes, and late-night smoky ambiance. The **HCD Ensemble of Frankfurt,** in the splendidly produced "Migrations" offers an artful rendition with finely articulated tone color (Largo 5131). The lyrical *Night Waltz* for two pianos, laced with post-war ennui and rumbling desperation, is played well by **Hermann Kretzschmar** and **Olga Balakleets.** Other performances make this a worthwhile purchase: the spirited and hilarious Kurt Weill-inspired *Music for a Farce,* the enchanting orchestral miniatures (originally scored for synthesizer) for *Hippolytos and Salome,* and the mysterious song cycle *Scenes d'Anabase.* The sense of drama, irony, and pacing in Martyn Hill's voice is perfect for the last piece.

The unnamed group in "Paul Bowles, An American in Paris" give the Concerto for Two Pianos, Winds, and Percussion a raucous and hurried interpretation, acceptable but unremarkable (Koch 1574). **Haridas Greif** and **Jean-François Zygel** pick up more of the frantic spirit underlying *Night Waltz* than Kretzschmar and Balakleets. Tenor Howard Haskin mangles Bowles's art songs; his style is more suitable for a Marx Brothers opera parody than a lieder performance. Soprano Jo Ann Pickens sings competently on this disc, but her voice doesn't seem robust enough for Bowles's music. Her interpretation of the "Sugar in the Cane" blues just isn't earthy. Generally, this is a disappointing CD.

In "Paul Bowles: A Musical Portrait" (Koch 7343), **Brian Staufenbiel** attempts "Once There Was a Lady" and "Three" with a fin de siècle weariness, but sounds inhibited and colorless. Unlike Hill, he lacks wit and nuance in *Scènes d'Anabase.* Fortunately, he performs better in *Cuatro Canciones de Garcia Lorca,* a premiere recording. Both the Flute Sonata and Sonata for Oboe and Clarinet are more leisurely and more atmospheric than on the Largo CD.

"The Music of Paul Bowles" (BMG 68409) offers two unique performances: the exotically rhythmic Suite for Small Orchestra and *The*

Wind Remains, a zarzuela based on Lorca's poems. The **Eos Ensemble** performs both with spunk. Tenor Carl Halvorson imbues the surreal text of *The Wind Remains* with Latin histrionics and spiky sforzando. The ensemble's rendition of Concerto for Two Pianos, Winds, and Percussion is more energetic (and louder) than the HCD Ensemble. Their "Galop" movement truly gallops, while on the Largo disc it merely prances. The difference between the two performances is striking, like comparing a party that's chaperoned to one that cuts loose.   BATES

William Boyce (1711–1779)

Master of the King's Music from 1755 until his death in 1779, Boyce spent much of his career in the shadow of Handel, whose compositions he helped promote. One of his own successes, however, was the publication, in 1760, of his eight "Symphonys"—short works largely drawn from the overtures or introductory sinfonias to his courtly odes and theatrical pieces—and they have also been successful in our day, beginning with Constant Lambert's edition in 1928.

Indeed the symphonies still dominate the Boyce listings, most of the complete sets taking full advantage of their late-baroque vitality and native charm. Though it lacks the bounce of his earlier Argo LP traversal, **Marriner**'s digital remake displays almost as much resiliency and finesse (♦Capriccio 10421), nor is **Ronald Thomas** far behind in matters of ebullience and style (♦CRD 3356). **Janigro**'s comparatively straight recording is even jauntier in places, with an especially delightful 4:II (♦Vanguard SVC 46). On the period-instrument front, **Hogwood** (♦Oiseau-Lyre 436761) and **Pinnock** (♦Archiv 419631) are no less enjoyable, though only the latter is currently listed.

Period instruments are also what you hear in **Shepherd**'s survey of the twelve Overtures and three Concerti Grossi, stylish but somewhat small-scale renditions (♦Chandos 6531 and 6541). Likewise **Standage**'s set of the trio sonatas, which offers the standard twelve with one to a part (♦Chandos 0648, 2CD), and **Peter Holman**'s, which adds another three in tangy, generally bracing performances that alternate the standard texts with concerto-grosso-like realizations for chamber orchestra; the variety is not unwelcome (♦Hyperion 67151/2, 2CD).

Holman is also in charge of a disc that includes Boyce's music for two of David Garrick's Shakespearean outings as well as the early masque *Peleus and Thetis* (♦Hyperion 66935). The prize here, though, is arguably the pastoral interlude *Corydon and Miranda,* with its splendid succession of airs and grafted-on 1758 *Birthday Ode* Overture. (There was also an earlier Hyperion CD of the "serenata" *Solomon,* well worth seeking out.) Three more courtly overtures can be heard from **Graham Lea-Cox** and the Hanover Band, along with *The Secular Masque,* Boyce's revival of a Dryden text that must have seemed dated even then (♦ASV 176). Nonetheless, he and his singers capture what drama there is in the music. Likewise his energetic, ultra-stylish romp through the grandly inventive 1739 *Ode for St. Cecilia's Day,* here in the 1740 Dublin revision (♦ASV 200). Conversely, the **Choir of New College,** Oxford, brings a cathedral-like ambiance and a properly devotional air to a collection of anthems and organ voluntaries (♦CRD 3483).   GOODFELLOW

Johannes Brahms (1833–1897)

Every 19th-century composer in the German tradition had to face the legacy of Beethoven, whose powerful, dramatic music within traditional musical forms set the standard for later generations. No one met this challenge better than Brahms, whose music combined rich romantic sentiment with a formal control unmatched by other romantics. Like Beethoven, he excelled in larger forms and chamber music, and neither

composer had much success with opera. Always self-critical, he often put his music through many revisions before reaching a final version, and he typically destroyed his sketches and early drafts. While some of Brahms's works may seem uninspired and over-wrought, virtually nothing is poorly constructed or unworthy of the composer. He was also the first composer to have a deep, scholarly interest in earlier music.

Due to its cerebral side, Brahms' music has never had the widest appeal, but his seriousness of purpose inspired the Second Viennese School and countless musicians of the 20th century. Now that time has made his music more familiar, we can appreciate his efforts all the more. He brought to his work a sensitivity and intellectual control that have been matched by few composers of any age.

SYMPHONIES

For Brahms the symphony was a noble genre, not the place for musical trifles. His Symphony 1 was labored over for years and reached completion only when the composer was well into his 40s. In no way, though, does it betray inexperience in writing for orchestra. His Serenades, Piano Concerto 1, "Haydn" Variations, and *German Requiem* all antedate it. 2 followed only a year later, but Brahms was to write a total of only four symphonies, all works of the highest rank.

Complete sets. Many will want all four as an integral set—one conductor and orchestra, boxed, and perhaps at a lower price. These do exist, but consider that the catalog also includes several complete "sets" that are available only as single discs.

Great conductors of the past have left a rich legacy of performances, often in sound that matches or nearly matches the best available today. Brahms performers can be divided between those who see him as a classicist and those who see him as a romantic. Those in the classical camp stress lean, clean textures with quick tempos and controlled emotion, while the romantics underplay his strong grip on structure and seek an emotional truth in the music.

The classicists were best represented by **Weingartner,** a conductor who knew Brahms and performed the music with his approval in the 1890s. His recordings, though, come from around 1940, much later in his career. The performances are alert and satisfying, but the early sound makes them a version for specialists (Grammofono 78764; Centaur 2128). Nonetheless, anyone who likes a crisp, virtuosic finale to 2 should hear Weingartner's version; music-making this exciting never goes out of style. Another great conductor in this vein was **Toscanini,** who took a vibrant, no-nonsense approach to everything he conducted. He has his partisans, and rightly so, but I find little satisfaction in his Brahms, where I get the impression he's trying to show the composer who's boss. The earlier recordings from the '40s (Music & Arts) are preferable to his later set of symphonies with lots of fillers (RCA).

A more modern version in this classical spirit is **Szell**'s, where the splendid playing of the Cleveland Orchestra is joined with a tensile strength that invigorates the music without smothering its lyricism; the sound is satisfactory, though less so than today's best (♦Sony 48398). This is a version for those who find Brahms too turgid and gooey; it's athletic and sensitive, but never sentimental. It's curious, perhaps ironic that Brahms approved of the classical Weingartner, for he also endorsed the performances of **Max Fiedler,** who conducted with passionate emotion and great freedom. His recordings have great historical importance for our understanding of Brahms performance, but they have been unavailable for some time.

Fortunately, though, we do have excellent older conductors who espouse this romantic tradition. Most important is **Furtwängler,** whose many recordings (mostly from concerts) testify to his command of Brahms's music. Both integral sets are excellent, probing accounts of the symphonies (♦Music & Arts 804 and ♦EMI 65513). Although the sound is fair to poor, one of these would be my desert island choice. With Furtwängler the weight and majesty of Brahms are revealed, and the slow movements mine a rich, deep vein of emotion. When listening to these performances, it's difficult to imagine the music going any other way.

In the period of more modern sonics, we have many satisfying versions by conductors now deceased or near the ends of their careers. **Sanderling** plays the symphonies as massive, weighty affairs, while never failing to dot the i's and cross the t's; his 2 sounds a bit contrived, but the others are very fine (♦Eurodisc 69220). A bit more romanticism can be found with **Jochum,** where the playing is very natural and unmannered. He conducts with wonderful freedom and seeming impulsiveness, and the slow movements are particularly passionate, with lots of molding and shaping (♦DG 449715). These early recordings (1951-56) are mono, but the sound is surprisingly good and, squeezed on two CDs, they're a great value as well.

For devotees of **Karajan** and his rich, sleek Berlin Philharmonic sound, the earlier recordings are best. Avoid his last, digital set (DG 427602) and look instead for the late '70s analog versions (♦DG 453097). His recordings from the '60s are generally even better, but these are available only singly, not as a set. **Solti**'s set is now deleted, but it's worth looking for (London 421074). The conductor's nervous hyperactivity is held in check, and the symphonies are played with an expansiveness and richness that often eluded this conductor.

Among other fine versions from this period, **Skrowaczewski**'s with the Hallé Orchestra can certainly be recommended (♦IMP 4). He molds the music with gently varying tempos and in general seeks a romantic, intimate view rather than a massive one; the music is full of spontaneity and affection. Also reliable and enjoyable are the performances by **Abravanel** (♦Vanguard 1719). His Utah Symphony compares favorably with more illustrious ensembles, and the interpretations are rich and satisfying in the Old World manner. **Abbado**'s set is more controversial (DG 435683). His emotional range is fairly wide, the Berlin Philharmonic sounds opulent, and at times (the scherzo of 4) the music is enthusiastic almost to the point of recklessness. The recording of 2 was the first released after his appointment as conductor of the Berlin Philharmonic and is very satisfying if you like gooey Brahms. Some listeners have responded well to Abbado's undeniable beauty, while others find him too indulgent and a bit dull.

Bernstein is another conductor to be reckoned with; his complete set is his later recording with the Vienna Philharmonic (DG). The earlier performances with the NY Philharmonic, though, sound more vital and exciting and merit the stronger recommendation (in the "Royal Edition": ♦Sony 47536, 1; 47537, 2+3; 47538, 4; 2-4 are in the "Bernstein Century," 61829 and 61846, and 1 can't be far behind). For those who prefer a less weighty Brahms, **Kubelik**'s lyrical, transparent style is very attractive; his interior movements and all of 2 are particularly good (Orfeo). Two other fine versions have recently been deleted but are worth seeking out: **Wand**'s warm, rich performances (RCA) and **Steinberg**'s exciting, large-scale versions would grace any shelf, particularly Steinberg's, available at budget price (MCA).

Formerly available as a set but now listed singly, **Masur**'s versions with the NY Philharmonic are mixed (Teldec). His 3 is wonderful, but 2 is static, and 4 is too soft-edged and earthbound. Of recent sets, the only one to offer a significantly new approach is **Mackerras,** who has recorded the works in a self-conscious attempt at mimicking 19th-century style (♦Telarc 80450). His orchestra of only 47 players includes period brass instruments, though the strings and woodwinds are modern. The results are interesting and musical, not rushed as with so many period instrument performances, and the sonics are terrific. This isn't a first choice, since most listeners will want more traditional weight and majesty in Brahms, but it's a valuable alternative view. Somewhat similar are **Harnoncourt**'s well played versions with the Berlin Philharmonic (Teldec 13136). As with all of his forays into the 19th century, we expect a century's accumulation of dirt and grime to be cleansed from the canvas, but these performances, though clean and brisk, are fairly conventional. 3 and 4 are the best, while 1 lacks a powerful finale and 2 is elongated by the first movement repeat.

Two recently deleted versions are worth mentioning, just in case they return or become available in closeout bins. **Dohnányi**'s set is mixed; his 1 is much admired and 3 is strong and cohesive, but 2 and 4 seem bland and uninvolved (Teldec). **Barenboim** is broad, lyrical, and somewhat self-consciously in the mode of Furtwängler. He may have modern sound, but if you want the Furtwängler approach, go for the real thing, poor sound and all (Erato).

1. It may be seen as Brahms's conscious attempt to link himself with the great Germanic symphonic tradition exemplified by Beethoven; he even alludes to Beethoven's 9th in the final movement. The music is more monumental and public than was his earlier custom, particularly in the outer movements. Along with the slighter inner movements, which are Romantic character pieces, the symphony has great immediate appeal and makes a good entry point to his music.

Many of the performances included in complete sets are also available individually, so you could look first at **Skrowaczewski** (♦IMP 2014) or **Szell** (♦Sony 46534). Two other performances mentioned above can be recommended again: **Karajan**'s virile performance from the '60s (the third of his five versions and not part of his complete set, DG 447408); and **Bernstein**'s with the NY Philharmonic (♦Sony 47535, also not part of his Vienna complete set).

Occasionally you can get an almost complete set for a bargain. **Jochum**'s performances of 1-3 are wonderfully ardent and persuasive (♦EMI 69515, a "two-fer," again different from the complete set on DG), and this can be supplemented with 4 in another "two-fer" (EMI 63518, with Tennstedt's *German Requiem*). **Rahbari**'s reading with the Belgian Radio-TV Orchestra is also ardent and broadly paced (Naxos 550280). The performance isn't bad, but the orchestra isn't at the highest level; nonetheless, the recording is attractive for its good sonics and budget price. **Ormandy**'s performance with the Philadelphia Orchestra is reliable and beautifully played, but there are no surprises (♦Sony 63287, recommended more for his 2). Last, but hardly least, we shouldn't forget **Walter**'s rich, passionate reading (♦Sony 64470). He is intimately in touch with the inner meaning of the music; all of Walter's Brahms is very fine, except for a disappointing 4.

2. The agonies Brahms endured bringing 1 to completion had no counterpart for 2, which he wrote in about five months. The congenial, pastoral nature of the music was noted from its earliest performances, and today many listeners count it as their favorite Brahms symphony. The lyricism of the first movement suggests Schubert (and Dvořák's 6, for that matter), while the finale is perhaps the most thrilling in all of Brahms. Perhaps because it's so different from his other works, some conductors respond to 2 better than to the others, stripping the music of its heavy, Germanic baggage and giving us more light and geniality.

As with 1, let's consider the complete sets that are available singly. Versions by **Skrowaczewski** (♦IMP 857), **Szell** (♦Sony 47652), and **Walter** (♦Sony 64471) are all very desirable. **Karajan** again is represented by an older performance at budget price (♦DG 429153), but for a modern, Mercedes-down-the-Autobahn approach this one is probably best of all. Among lighter versions, **Monteux**'s with the San Francisco Symphony shows that the piece is still very attractive without heavy emotional baggage (RCA 61891). His performance with the Vienna Philharmonic is even better (NA), while another "light" version—**Beecham**'s with the Royal Philharmonic—should be sought out as well. Even if you prefer the full Brahmsian treatment of Karajan or Walter, these are valuable alternatives.

Other good versions that strike an emotional middle ground are by **Barbirolli** with the Vienna Philharmonic (♦Royal Classics 6433) and **Ormandy** (♦Sony 63287). In Ormandy's case the orchestra sounds warm and wonderful, but he seems content to let the music play itself with a minimum of intervention. For the budget-minded, **Rahbari**'s performance is fine for those wanting a gooey, romantic Brahms with a jaunty finale (Naxos 550279), though this approach is better done by **Abbado** (♦DG 427643). For some listeners, Abbado's approach misses the internal strength of the music.

3. It was composed in 1883, six years after 2. It's the shortest of the four, but also the least popular and the most difficult to pull off in performance. In an age when the symphony was still a heroic genre, Brahms wrote a piece with almost no sense of triumph. All four movements end softly, giving the entire work a contemplative feel.

This is one of the best pieces in which to see the old Toscanini-Furtwängler dichotomy at work. **Toscanini** was never satisfied with any of his recordings, and history has proven him right; they are among his least satisfactory. **Furtwängler** left few recordings of 3, and none has very good sound or execution, but the essence of his art is everywhere apparent. His headlong rush in the first movement development and the screeching ritard in the final movement are but two details of his shaped, impulsive interpretation. It's certainly not the performance for a newcomer, but veterans should hear it.

It's ironic that Toscanini should have had trouble with this piece, because his followers, that is conductors who take a direct, unsentimental approach, have done very well with it. **Cantelli** (♦Stradivarius 13591), **van Beinum** (♦Dante 471), and **Szell** (♦Sony 47652) all offer excellent versions with taut, bracing rhythms. Similarly, **Levine**'s earlier performance with the Chicago Symphony (NA) is a fiery, young man's Brahms, more distinctive than his later Vienna version (also NA). **Reiner**'s 1958 reading, which still sounds remarkably good, is also quick and to the point, though he offers a broad, ripe slow movement (♦RCA 61793). Much the same can be said about **Walter:** early stereo, but fine sonics and a performance where everything sounds right (♦Sony 32225 or 64471).

Some conductors whose Brahms is generally undistinguished have made fine recordings of 3. For both **Masur** (Teldec 90862) and **Dohnányi** (Teldec, NA) 3 is the best of their four. **Norrington**'s self-conscious attempt to copy the performing style of Brahms's day is interesting, but in the end too contrived and soft-edged (EMI). In the budget category, you should certainly consider **Karajan,** coupled with the 2 described above (♦DG 429153), as well as **Kertész,** who was one of the finest Brahmsians of his day. His 3 is coupled with an excellent 4 (London 448200). Even the super budget shopper is well covered by **Rahbari,** whose 3 is a big, brassy affair that takes the music by paragraphs rather than sentences (Naxos 550278).

4. It is the most unusual, owing mainly to the structure of the final movement, a passacaglia consisting of a theme and 30 variations. The opening movement, though, is rigorous, since the main thematic material may be reduced to a single interval, a falling third. Except for the Double Concerto, 4 was Brahms's last work for orchestra; he completed it in 1885, more than a decade before his death.

Among older performances, **Furtwängler** continues to dominate for those who want a romantic, cosmic view of the piece; he makes you believe in the greatness of the work like few others. From the next generation we have many treasurable recordings: a taut but sensitive **Szell** (♦Sony 46330), a surprisingly lyrical **Reiner** (♦Chesky 6), a legendary, granitic **Klemperer** recording (EMI, NA), and a ripely romantic and beautifully shaped **Jochum** (♦EMI 69518). All of these speak at the highest levels of music making. Among the pantheon of greats, only **Walter** is a disappointment, though I think the dullness of his performance may be the engineers' fault (Sony).

From the '60s we should remember **Karajan**'s very fine, somewhat objective account (♦DG 431593); for many he strikes an ideal balance between the claims of classicism and romanticism in this piece. **Kempe**'s 1976 recording has plenty of excitement, but suffers from poor balances and some untidiness (BBC). Among more recent recordings, **Carlos Kleiber**'s is excellent if you see 4 as a life-or-death experience; it's well played, though many will prefer a more relaxed approach (♦DG 457706). Both **Bernstein** recordings are good, NY Philharmonic for a charged, younger view (Sony 47538), Vienna for mature seasoning (♦DG 457706 or 61846). **Skrowaczewski** is terrific for a deeply felt, affectionate performance; he's deeply involved with the music without losing grasp of its structure (♦IMP 897). The Berlin Philharmonic under **Abbado** is more overtly romantic, in a performance that's less probing than the best, but he ties the piece together surprisingly well (♦DG 435349).

Others are very good without being distinctive. **Ashkenazy** conducts a lovely performance, but he doesn't bring much individuality or feeling to the piece (London). **Chailly** is similar: soft-grained, lovely, but emotionally reticent (Philips). **Rahbari**'s budget version (Naxos) is in the rich and romantic vein, but not as distinguished as someone like Skrowaczewski. As in 3, **Norrington**'s small forces make an interesting alternative, though few would want to be without the warmth and richness of rival accounts; he diminishes the spirit of Brahms (EMI).

Other orchestral music

Serenades. The two Serenades are early works, written when Brahms was in his mid-'20s. Like many of his early pieces, 1 had a troubled birth; it began as a chamber piece for winds and strings but was rescored and enlarged from four to six movements. Brahms himself considered it a hybrid of serenade and symphony. Just as with the symphonies, the difficult birth of 1 eased the composition of 2, which was written more quickly and without significant revision. While the serenades lack the emotional density of the symphonies, they are nonetheless lovely pieces, expertly crafted.

Among earlier recordings, those of **Kertész** stand out for their warmth and sensuousness; the sound is good though not as clear as in the best modern versions (♦London 421628). **Slatkin**'s are similar—richly warm, civilized and lovely—but his 1 has been deleted; 2 remains a top choice (♦RCA 7920, with other orchestral works).

Other conductors stress the youthful side of the pieces and give us performances that are chipper, alert, even a bit boisterous. In this vein the two recordings by **Tilson Thomas** are first-rate (♦Sony 45932 and

47195, with other orchestral works). If you prefer both serenades on one disc, you could send to England to buy Tilson Thomas on a single CD (Sony Theta 60134) or get B_lohlávek's performances, which capture the youthful Brahms equally well (♦Supraphon 111823). **Abbado** gives warm, affectionate versions, but they're available only as part of a 5CD set (DG 449601). **Boult** is similar, relaxed and unhurried rather than impulsive and youthful (♦EMI 68655, a "two-fer"). **Stokowski**'s wonderful reading of 1 is NA but worth looking for (MCA).

Variations on a Theme by Haydn, Academic Festival Overture, Tragic Overture. Brahms left only three shorter works for orchestra. The *Haydn Variations*, based on the *Chorale St. Antoni*, were originally written for two pianos and later orchestrated by the composer. Both versions were written in 1873, the period of Symphony 1. They are far more than a series of unrelated variations. The pacing and drama are beautifully realized by Brahms, who combines a venerable old form with the richness of his romantic musical language. The *Academic Festival Overture* was written in acknowledgment of Brahms's honorary doctorate from the University of Breslau in 1879 and is a medley of four university songs cast into sonata form. It quickly became popular and today is Brahms's most accessible work for orchestra. *Tragic Overture,* composed in the same period, was described by the composer as a serious counterpart to the lighter *Academic Festival.* The *Tragic* has all the qualities of mature Brahms, but it has never achieved the renown of its more accessible brethren.

These works are so short that they are invariably coupled with larger pieces, usually the symphonies. The closest you'll come to the orchestral works without the symphonies is **Boult**'s genial performance of all three with the Serenades and *Alto Rhapsody* (♦EMI 68655, a "two-fer"). If you also want the symphonies, note that several complete sets include these three works. **Abravanel** (♦Vanguard 1719), **Skrowaczewski** (♦IMP 4), and **Szell** (♦Sony 48398) are all excellent sets that incorporate them. Otherwise, let couplings be your guide. **Monteux** did a wonderful *Haydn Variations,* but it's coupled with Haydn symphonies rather than more Brahms (♦London 452893). **Jochum**'s *Academic Festival* and *Tragic Overture* are first-rate and coupled with Symphonies 1-3 (♦EMI 69515). And finally, **Karajan** was always a strong proponent of all three pieces.

Hungarian Dances. Since the *Hungarian Dances* don't form an integral set (and besides, most orchestrations are not by Brahms), many recordings contain only selections. We have, though, several recordings of the complete 21. Most of the better ones come from Central European orchestras or conductors, where the freedom and spirit of the Hungarian style are familiar and ingrained. The Vienna Philharmonic, one of the world's finest in *any* repertory, is a superb orchestra for the *Dances,* and under **Abbado** they show lots of vitality and sparkle; the sonics for this early digital recording, however, could be more atmospheric and less strident (DG 410615 or 431594). A warmer, perhaps more mature look at Hungarian style is heard in **Suitner**'s recording; here the sonics are fine, but the performances tend to be over-civilized, with a shortage of dynamic contrasts (Denon 7459). In a similar vein—warmly affectionate rather than wild and spirited—**Dorati**'s version captures the idiom very well; this is an older recording, but the sound is good (♦Mercury 434326). In fully modern, brassy sound, **Järvi**'s reading is very free rhythmically, with slow tempos; this is for listeners who want the delights teased out of the music (♦Chandos 7072). First choice, though, goes to **István Bogár** and the Budapest Symphony; they have the authentic Hungarian idiom, caught in excellent sound and issued at budget price (♦Naxos 550110).

CONCERTOS

In the 19th century the concerto became a vehicle for virtuoso display with orchestral accompaniment. Brahms, though, resisted this trend and endorsed the principles of Mozart and Beethoven by creating a more equal partnership between soloist and orchestra. To be sure, his concertos call for extraordinary technical virtuosity, but the soloist is rarely granted the sole spotlight. Seldom has music of such difficulty been allied with works of such integrity and substance. Brahms left only four concertos, from early to late in his career.

Piano Concerto 1. Just as with Symphony 1 and Serenade 1, Brahms's first piano concerto had a difficult birth. It began as a sonata for two pianos that was recast as a symphony before emerging as a concerto; he finished it in 1858, in his mid-20s. It has an impulsiveness and audacity that make it very much a youthful work. The huge first movement, lasting more than 20 minutes, conveys a spirit of conflict, even anger. The Adagio shows Brahms at his most serene, and the Rondo finale transforms the lyrical first movement solo theme into music both emphatic and heroic.

Many distinctive older performances continue to grace the catalog. My first beloved version by **Curzon** and Szell continues as a strong contender; passionate and poised, it gets to the heart of the music without calling attention to virtuosity (♦London 425082). **Rudolf Serkin** brought more tension and vitality to the work when he partnered with Szell; this too is Brahms of great strength and authority (♦Sony 48166). **Cliburn**'s version with Leinsdorf is soft-grained by comparison, but he reveals more of the work's lyrical beauty, particularly in the slow movement (♦RCA 60357). If you prefer a slower, probing version, **Gilels**'s glowing, rich recording is a clear choice (♦DG 447446). Before his hand injury, **Fleisher,** a student of Schnabel, was one of our finest young pianists. His version with Szell is strong and intellectual in the best sense (♦Sony 63225).

Arrau's compelling version with Haitink is more romantic and beautifully played (♦Philips 456706). Both of these are coupled with fine versions of 2, as well as orchestral pieces. The rich, broadly-paced versions of both concertos by **Barenboim** and Barbirolli, recorded in 1967 when the pianist was only 27, have been reissued; instead of aggressive energy, they bring romantic depth to the music (EMI 72647, a "two-fer"). Also competitive are the probing versions of 1 and 2 by **Katchen** with Monteux (♦London 440612, at a special price).

Three concert performances also deserve mention; all have recently been deleted, but are worth looking for. **Kapell,** one of the century's finest talents until his untimely death, recorded the piece in 1953. He had the grand manner—rich romanticism coupled with astounding technique (Arkadia 736; Music & Arts 990). **Gould** performed the work with Bernstein, who so disapproved of the pianist's interpretation that he gave a speech to the audience before the performance; this version, not as perverse as this may sound, is well worth hearing and contemplating (Sony 60675). Less divisive is **Ogdon**'s reading with Stokowski, which includes rehearsal excerpts (Music & Arts 844). Any of these would make a good second or third version.

Several recent releases can be recommended. **Hough** presents modern recordings of both concertos that are excellent in every way (♦Virgin 61412). **Jandó** proves more than equal to the piece in his alert performance (♦Naxos 553182). I'm less excited by **Pollini,** whose technically alert playing lacks atmosphere (DG). **Gutierrez**'s version with Previn has too little interpretive profile (Telarc). My favorite modern version is unaccountably absent from the catalog: **Kovacevich** with Sawallisch (EMI 54578, not his earlier one with Colin Davis for IMP).

Piano Concerto 2. In this concerto (like 1), Brahms places virtuosity at the service of a deeper musical message, but the two pieces are hardly alike. If 1 exposed Brahms's fiery youth, 2, written in his late 40s, seems more mature and balanced. Instead of the customary three movements, we have four, all roughly the same length. Everything is here: a lyric-dramatic first movement, a vigorous scherzo, a warm slow movement (which shares its theme with a Brahms song, "Immer leise wird mein Schlummer"), and a light, joyful finale. This work is certainly one of the most difficult in the entire literature, so most great pianists have felt it was a challenge that had to be met.

Recordings of 2 have long been dominated by **Richter**'s, made during the Russian pianist's first American tour in 1960. Conducted by Leinsdorf, it has an incandescence that has never been bettered, and Richter's technique was phenomenal (♦RCA 56518). Several other fine versions come from this period. **Rubinstein** regarded 2 as a signature piece and recorded it several times; his 1958 version with Krips flows beautifully, with emphasis on lovely piano sound and the long line (♦RCA 61442). **Serkin**'s athletic account is no less fine than his 1 (♦Sony 37258). **Bachauer**'s ripe version with Dorati combines tensile strength with wonderful romantic sensibility (♦Chesky 36). As in 1, the slow, ruminating side of Brahms is best captured by **Gilels** in his second recording with **Jochum** (♦DG 447446).

Also first-rate is the reissue of **Backhaus**'s last recording, with Böhm; he was one of the legends of the 20th century, and you'd never guess he was 83 when it was made (EMI 72649). On the other side of this "two-fer" is **Barenboim**'s version, mentioned above; this too is very beautiful, though some may find it indulgent. Equally interesting, but for entirely different reasons, is **Schnabel**'s version with Boult (Pearl 9399). As in many of his performances, he gets only about 75 per cent of the notes, but he gets all the music! Among older versions, consider **Fleisher** and **Arrau**, both with excellent 2s to match their 1s. After their 1s, though, the 2s of **Cliburn** (RCA) and **Kovacevich** (EMI) are disappointments. **Horowitz**'s volcanic version with Toscanini may be perverse, but it makes an interesting alternative (RCA 60319).

Among more recent recordings, those of **Hough** (♦Virgin 61412, with 1) and **Jandó** (♦Naxos 550506) both stand out as wonderfully played and beautifully recorded. A new version by Ax and the Boston Symphony is sensitive and musical, but in the end too soft-grained. **Gutierrez** with Previn is just as retiring here as in 1 (Telarc)

Violin Concerto. It is to Brahms's friend and colleague, the virtuoso violinist Joseph Joachim, that we owe the Violin Concerto. While writing it, Brahms consulted extensively with Joachim, who was subsequently granted the dedication and the premiere, with Brahms conducting. Like the piano concertos, this work is remarkable for its combination of artistic depth with virtuoso display. This concerto holds a central place in the violin repertory and has attracted every violinist able to negotiate its considerable difficulties.

The older generation left us with so many riches that modern players may be excused for conceding they have nothing new to add. **Heifetz**, perhaps the most astounding of all 20th-century violinists, recorded it with several famous conductors (Koussevitzky, Szell, Toscanini), but his version with Reiner is my central recommendation (♦RCA 61742 or 61495). He tosses it off with aplomb and rock-solid technique, fearing nothing.

While we can't fault Heifetz in any significant way, some feel that his passionate virtuosity said more about the violinist than about Brahms. For them, the lush romanticism of **Oistrakh** comes closer to the ideal.

His several recordings with different conductors (my preferred one with Klemperer is currently NA) all show his lyrical approach, gorgeous but never demonstrative. An Oistrakh sampler includes the greatest violin concertos—Tchaikovsky, Beethoven, and Bach as well as Brahms (♦DG 447427). Two other spectacular versions from the past should be mentioned: **Milstein**'s broad and lyrical reading (♦EMI 66550) and **Szeryng**'s wonderfully shaped performance (♦Tahra 175).

We have many modern accounts to complement those above. **Perlman** has recorded the work with Barenboim and (earlier) with Giulini; his singing approach is common to both, but Giulini provides better support (♦EMI 47166). Two other fine modern versions come from **Mutter** (♦Philips 457075) and **Kremer** (♦Teldec 13137). Here Mutter is the ripe romantic, while Kremer is more reticent and thoughtful, though both are very desirable. **Kennedy**'s version is beautifully played, but disfigured by the violinist's own cadenza (EMI). **Stern**'s performance is forceful and exciting, but he's miked very closely (Sony). **Francescatti** is lyrical and lovely, but some may find his voltage too low for the piece (Columbia), while **Salerno-Sonnenberg** is so recklessly passionate that some may find her voltage too high (EMI).

Concerto for Violin and Cello. Composed in 1887 when he was 54, the Double Concerto proved to be Brahms's last work for orchestra. It's less popular than the other concertos. Assembling two soloists isn't always easy, and the work itself is in Brahms's "autumnal" style, which, among other things, doesn't allow for much overt virtuosity. Nonetheless, it's a strong, enjoyable piece that has attracted a number of fine recordings.

The earlier generation again left us performances as fine or finer than anything today, though the sonics are sometimes wanting. **Heifetz** and **Piatigorsky** certainly enjoy satisfactory sound, and the playing is superb (♦RCA 6778 or 63531). Also excellent but on the more lyrical and restrained side are **Francescatti** and **Fournier** (♦Columbia 64479). Among more recent issues, that of **Stern** and **Rose** are very desirable (♦Sony 46335), but avoid Stern's later recording with **Ma,** where the violinist is past his prime (Columbia 42387). The famous **Oistrakh** and **Rostropovich** version, conducted by Szell, seems a little brusque in the slow movement and heavy-footed in the finale, but the playing is big and extroverted, full of passion and strength (♦EMI 66954). Among the very old we have several fascinating versions by cellists like **Casals** and **Feuermann,** but they are recommended only for those who can tolerate the sonics. One early monaural version (1951) that does sound fairly good is **Milstein** and **Piatigorsky** (♦RCA 61485).

Fortunately we have several excellent modern versions. The **Zukerman/Kirshbaum** performance is beautifully detailed, and all tempos seem just right (♦RCA 68964). Likewise wonderful is **Kremer/Hagen,** conducted by Harnoncourt, who purports to have "rethought" the piece (♦Teldec 13137). Also very good but less special is **Perlman/Ma** (Teldec 15870).

CHAMBER MUSIC

The general public knows Brahms mostly through his orchestral music, but on the basis of quantity, it would be a mistake to represent him mainly by his symphonies, concertos, and overtures. The sonatas for violin, clarinet/viola, and cello, as well as the trios, quartets, quintets, and sextets, far outnumber the orchestral works, with no loss of grandeur or depth of expression. None is weak or unworthy of our attention. In his voluminous chamber music Brahms shows himself to be the true follower of the Viennese past he so admired: Haydn, Mozart, Beethoven, and Schubert.

Cello Sonatas. Brahms left two cello sonatas, the first written when he was about 30, the second about 20 years later. Many cellists have also appropriated Brahms' Violin Sonata 1 in G, transposing it to D in an arrangement by Paul Klengel. This version now boasts several recordings, but critics have argued that the transferral of melodic material to an inner voice is often awkward. The transcriptions haven't stopped with the Sonata in G. Recently Yo-Yo Ma "borrowed" Violin Sonata 3 in a recording with Ax, and his cello arrangement works better than Klengel's.

Among historical recordings, those of **Casals, Feuermann,** and **Piatigorsky** are invaluable for learning how Brahms was viewed a few generations back. These cellists were trained when the memory of Brahms and 19th-century performing style was still fresh, so despite the poorer sound we can look to them for special insights. Of the three, Casals is my central recommendation. His Brahms shows up in a variety of couplings, any of which is worth knowing. His 1936 recording of 2 with Horszowski is legendary (available only in a 4CD Casals collection, ◆Pearl 9935).

But there is no shortage of excellent more recent versions. From the near past, the impulsive, romantic performances of **du Pré** with Barenboim bring passion and almost reckless abandon to the pieces. They may tell us more about du Pré than Brahms, but they stand out for their involvement and commitment (◆EMI 63298). Special mention should also be made of the recording by **Rostropovich** and Rudolf Serkin; it's hard to imagine that Serkin would want the pieces as luxuriant and opulent as Rostropovich plays them, but the partnership is excellent (◆DG 410510). Less lush, but equally impassioned and tortured, are the wonderful versions by **Ma** and Ax. Here their earlier release is preferable (◆RCA 09026), but if you want to hear Ma's transcription of Violin Sonata 3, you'll need the later one (◆Sony 48191). Two versions that use period pianos can be recommended: **Peter Wispelwey** (◆CCL 5493) and **Peter Bruns** (◆Opus 30144). Neither is at all scholarly in tone, but the older pianos ease the balance problems, particularly in 2.

Violin Sonatas. These are mature works. The first was begun when Brahms was 45 and the others followed about eight years later. 3 is more concentrated than the first two, but a spirit of lyricism pervades all three. Unlike lots of 19th-century violin music, they seldom suggest virtuosity; the music is for the players and a few listeners. The mood, by and large, is one of nostalgic sweetness and tender lyricism; only the final sonata shows some signs of stress and angst. They conveniently fill one CD, so most modern performers do them as a group. Earlier generations did them one at a time, so historical versions are more scattered. Most of the great violinists of the past—Busch, Francescatti, Heifetz, Huberman, Kreisler, Menuhin, Spalding, Szigeti—now have one or more in the catalogue. Of these, perhaps the most interesting are the tough, vital interpretations of **Adolf Busch** with Rudolf Serkin, available in a variety of couplings.

These works have brought out the best in many present-day violinists. **Perlman**'s lush, rich tone is shown to wonderful advantage in his recording with Ashkenazy; these ripely romantic performances reveal his deep affection for the music, and his accompanist is superb (◆EMI 47403). Perlman's performance with Barenboim is equally interesting, with the presence of an audience bringing out an intensity he didn't find in the studio (◆Columbia 45819). **Stern**'s 1991 concert performance with Bronfman (in St. Petersburg) is one of the most satisfying of his later recordings (◆Columbia 53107). The performances, direct and unaffected, come from the heart and point up the autumnal side of the com-

poser. By contrast, the very fine versions by **Augustin Dumay** and Maria João Pires reveal Brahms' intellectual side, but still maintain a sensuous aspect. These well thought out performances are full of interesting interpretive touches (◆DG 435800). A few versions should be bypassed: **Boris Belkin** is too strong and "public" for these chamber pieces (Denon), while **Mutter** is undermined by the insensitive pianism of Weissenberg (EMI).

Clarinet/Viola Sonatas. Toward the end of his life, at a time when he felt his career was nearly finished, Brahms met the Meiningen clarinetist Richard Mühlfeld, who so inspired the composer that in a relatively short time he wrote a trio, quintet, and two sonatas for clarinet. At the urging of violinist Joseph Joachim, he went on to arrange the clarinet sonatas for viola and piano. The two sets differ in registral detail but are virtually the same. Rapid passagework in the solo part makes them a little more natural for the clarinet, but violists have with good reason cherished these works. Recordings with clarinet outnumber those with viola by a small margin.

Among clarinet versions, that of **de Peyer** with Gwenneth Prior has held sway for many years (◆Chandos 8563), just as his version with Barenboim did years earlier. De Peyer identifies beautifully with the style of late Brahms; his warm, rich tone and poised approach leave nothing to be desired, and Prior is an excellent accompanist in a well-balanced recording. Two other fine choices are available: **Stoltzman** with Goode, who bring a relaxed, loving approach to the sonatas (◆RCA 60036), and **Franklin Cohen** in a recording with Ashkenazy that is distinguished as much by fine sonics as wonderful playing (◆London 430149).

First mention among viola versions should go to **Primrose,** who more than anyone in this century made the viola a solo instrument to be reckoned with. Among his recordings, the last, with Firkušny, dates from 1958 and is monaural, but the rich, deep Primrose sound comes through splendidly (◆EMI 66065). Among more recent recordings, **Nobuko Imai** with Roger Vignoles offers lovely, somewhat restrained accounts of both sonatas; unfortunately, the piano is too reverberant (◆Chandos 8550). **Zukerman**'s widely admired version with Marc Neikrug is more extroverted and impassioned (◆RCA 61276).

Piano Trios. The opus numbers for the piano trios (8, 87, 101) suggest early and late compositions, but in fact the first, written in 1854 when Brahms was only 21, was completely revised in 1889. No one would suggest that the revision is anything but an improvement over the somewhat episodic original. The first version, though, would qualify as a major work for many other composers, and the two give the best opportunity in all of Brahms to see how he could work over and improve a piece of music. As is typical of many early works, Trio 1 is expansive, with suggestions of Schumann and Mendelssohn (in the scherzo). The later ones are shorter and more densely packed with ideas.

The three together are too long to fit on one CD, so "complete" recordings will come on two CDs with other pieces as fillers. Common additions are the Horn or Clarinet Trio or the posthumous Trio in A, which is a questionable early work (existing only in a copyist's hand). We have several wonderful collections. The **Florestan Trio** includes the clarinet and horn trios in performances characterized by intimacy and warmth; this is an excellent way to get all three in one package (◆Hyperion 67251, 2CD). The same couplings, though with less insightful playing, are available from the **Guarneri Trio** (Ottavo 29134, 2CD).

Among older issues, the set from Stern, Rose, and **Istomin** still sounds wonderfully rich and vibrant (◆Sony 64520, with later record-

ings of the piano quartets, 3CD). Also from an earlier period are the splendid performances by the **Beaux Arts Trio** and friends. They include the posthumous trio and the clarinet and horn trios, all six works on two CDs; the only drawback is an occasional problem of recording balance (♦Philips 38365). The discs by the **Parnassus Trio** are available separately: one contains Op. 8 and Brahms's Op. 36 sextet arranged for trio (♦MD&G 3030655); the second contains Trio 2 and the trio arrangement of the Op. 18 sextet (♦MD&G 3030656); the third includes the original version of Op. 8 and Trio 1 (♦MD&G 3030657). The extra items make the Parnassus set particularly desirable.

The warmly authoritative versions of 1 and 2 by Suk, Starker, and **Katchen** have not dimmed with time, and they still sound remarkably good. Katchen was one of the most admired Brahms pianists in his day, and this recording takes you to the heart of the composer (♦London 421152). The dangers of putting three well-known soloists together for chamber music are evident in the exaggerated, overplayed versions by Perlman, Harrell, and **Ashkenazy** (EMI 54725). But you should be alert for the fine, youthful recordings by the **Fontenay Trio** (Teldec, NA).

Horn Trio. Recordings will probably always be dominated by the 1933 recording by **Aubrey Brain** (Dennis's father), Adolf Busch (Hermann's and Fritz's brother), and Rudolf Serkin (Peter's father). Despite its years this performance leaps out of the grooves and makes others sound careful and sleepy. It's available with very different couplings, which should be your guide. Among modern accounts, those boxed with piano trios by the Florestan and Beaux Arts Trios are both very fine. (In the Beaux Arts set, hornist **Francis Orval** is joined by Grumiaux and Sebok, who were not members of the trio; the performance nonetheless is splendid, particularly regarding issues of balance.) As a stand-alone you couldn't do better than the budget-priced release by **Jenó Kevehází**, Ildiká Heg, and Jenó Jandó (♦Naxos 550441). Keep a lookout for recordings by hornists **Alan Civil** and **Dennis Brain;** they're NA now, but they could (and should) reappear.

Brahms intended the Horn Trio for natural (i.e., valveless) horn. To hear it that way, listen to **Ludwig Greer**'s performance with Stephanie Chase and Steven Lubin (Harmonia Mundi 907037). Critics disagree about the big-name version by **Tuckwell**, Perlman and Ashkenazy; some find it passionate and impulsive, while others feel those qualities are imposed on the music, making it sound superficial (Decca 433695).

Clarinet Trio. Again the Beaux Arts collection heads the list, with clarinetist **George Pieterson**. Pieterson is an imaginative, musical player who melds beautifully with the others (♦Philips 38365). If your main love is the clarinet, your best choice is a coupling with the Clarinet Quintet. Here either **Thea King**'s performance (♦Hyperion 66107) or **Josef Balogh**'s (♦Naxos 550391) would serve admirably. Both are solid, well-recorded versions, and the Naxos is at budget price. Unfortunately the passionate performance by **Stoltzman,** Ax, and Ma is currently NA (RCA).

String Quartets. When Brahms first ventured into the symphony and string quartet, two genres exalted by the classical composers he so admired, he became exceptionally self-critical and self-conscious. The first two, which he wrote when he was 40, were reputedly preceded by 20 attempts, all destroyed by the composer. In some cases a composer's earlier thoughts are more spontaneous and in the end preferable to pieces that are so worked-over they have no freshness. In a sense these quartets — particularly 1 — suffer from their complexity. We can't know the early quartets he destroyed, but few would deny the earnest, worked over na-

ture of those we have. Of the three, 1 is the most serious and unrelenting, while 2 is more lyrical. 3, written only two years after publication of the first two, has many folk-like themes, so Brahms was apparently relaxing his grip on this venerable genre. Nonetheless, we should note that once Brahms finally got to the level he wanted in the first two quartets, he was content to write another one quickly and then let the matter die. After 3 was published in 1876, he wrote several chamber pieces (including the more accessible string quintets), but no more string quartets.

Many performers take their cue from the complexity of the works, playing them quickly and aggressively, with scarcely a nod toward sentimentality or surface beauty. Among leading recordings in this vein, those by the **LaSalle, Sine Nomine,** and **Bartók Quartets** are NA at present. We do have, however, several complete performances that temper Brahms' austerity with warmth and lyricism. Among them, the versions by the **Alban Berg Quartet** are hard to fault on any grounds; their remarkable precision and complete technical assurance are matched with interpretive insight (♦EMI 54829, 2CD). They are easy to undervalue because they sound so opulent.

Equally perceptive and lovely but a little more yielding in spirit are the older recordings of the **Quartetto Italiano;** they make these thorny works comprehensible, and the two CDs are available for the price of one (♦Philips 456320). The strong performances of the young **Danish Quartet** bring enthusiasm but no loss of repose where needed (♦Kontrapunkt 32033/34, 2CD). The **Juilliard Quartet**'s versions are less desirable; they have some rough spots technically and less than flattering sound (Columbia 66285, 2CD).

For listeners wanting only one CD's worth, there are several releases of 1 and 2. The **Cleveland Quartet** brings a rich, warm, romantic style to these difficult pieces, and their sound is very good (♦Telarc 80346). Nearly as impressive in 1 and 2 are the **Muir Quartet,** which favors warmth and commitment over aggression and muscle-flexing. They don't rush the music, and sonics are very good (♦ADDA 581222). The **Colorado Quartet** is also satisfying, though balances favor the inner instruments (♦Parnassus 96007). Any of these would be preferable to the **Carmina Quartet** (Denon).

1 and 3 are coupled on two very fine recordings. The **Borodin Quartet** plays with a richness and emotional depth that make many rivals sound merely efficient. Their performances are certainly among the finest (♦Teldec 90889), and their 2 is also available coupled with the piano quintet (♦Teldec 97461). The **Tokyo Quartet** is more classical in spirit; they clarify Brahms's complex textures without emotional excess (♦Allegretto 8200). Only the **Orlando Quartet** couples 2 and 3; it is, though, a fine recording with good balances and fairly slow, unrushed tempos (♦Ottavo 68819). Finally, in Sony's "Masterworks Portrait" series, we have the **Budapest Quartet** in 1 (45686, with Rudolf Serkin in the Piano Quintet) and 3 (45553, with the Clarinet Quintet).

Piano Quartets. These pieces are not heard often, undoubtedly because standing piano quartets scarcely exist and the participants must be assembled on an ad hoc basis. Even so, we have wonderful recordings of this music.

Among recordings that include all three piano quartets, first mention should go to the legendary **Hollywood Quartet** recordings from the '50s. Don't confuse your notions of cinematic Hollywood with this group, which in its day was one of the finest ensembles in the world, and their performances (here with pianist Victor Aller) hold up remarkably well. The sound, monaural and a little strident, may not be ideal, but many feel these works have never been done better (♦Testament 3063).

Most listeners, of course, will want excellent performances coupled with modern sound, and for them the energetic, intense recordings of Stern, Laredo, Ma, and **Ax** will be an obvious choice. These versions are available either on two full-priced discs (♦Columbia 45846) or more economically coupled with the piano trios in a specially priced set devoted to Stern (♦Columbia 64520, 3CD). However you get them, these performances, closely recorded, are full of electricity and extroversion without ever losing the give-and-take of distinguished chamber playing. Even more economical and hardly less distinguished are the versions by the Beaux Arts Trio with Trampler, which are packaged as a "two-fer" (♦Philips 454017). With this group the imagination of pianist **Menahem Pressler** is always evident, and Philips' sound is first-rate.

A few fine single issues deserve mention. In the twilight of his career, **Rubinstein**, then 80, recorded 1 and 3 with members of the Guarneri Quartet. These performances, more congenial than fiery, beguile us without wishing to overwhelm (♦RCA 5677). Also memorable is **Emil Gilels**'s recording with members of the Amadeus Quartet This is for fans of the pianist, who was a probing interpreter of Brahms; his recording of the Op. 10 *Ballades* completes the CD (♦DG 447407).

String Quintets. Brahms's two string quintets were composed, as were Mozart's, for quartet plus additional viola. Both are fairly late works. In fact, Brahms for a time declared that Quintet 2, composed in 1890, would be his last work, so it has a self-consciously valedictory aspect. In contrast to the thorny quartets, the quintets show Brahms in a congenial mood. Even 1's finale, a half-hearted fugal movement no doubt inspired by Beethoven's third "Razumovsky" quartet, presents few challenges to the listener.

All the ingredients for superb chamber music—ensemble, unity of conception, technical expertise, and passion—shine forth in the recording by Trampler and the **Juilliard Quartet** (♦Sony 68476). The performances have real impact; nothing sounds routine or just "played through." Their playing is so fine that you're snapped to attention even if you already feel very comfortable with the music. Another fine version comes from the **Hagen Quartet** with Gérard Caussé. They bring tensile strength to these pieces and refuse to see them as the work of an older composer. There's almost a quality of nervousness about their playing that makes Brahms seem modern and vital, though this view will not be appreciated by all (♦Harmonia Mundi 901349). The **Brandis Quartet** with Brett Dean brings a different but still compelling approach. Their version of 1 isn't heavily interpreted; rather, it's warm and rich, congenial, serene, and mature. This is the version for late night listening (♦Nimbus 5488, with Bruckner's Quintet).

The most economical way to acquire first-rate performances of the quintets is to buy a package that includes additional pieces. Here you can't do better than the complete quintets plus the piano and clarinet quintets played by members of the **Berlin Philharmonic Octet** (♦Philips 46162, a "two-fer"). The performances are slightly less distinctive than the others mentioned above—particularly the Juilliard—but no one will be seriously disappointed by playing of this stature (and the other quintets are just as good).

Piano Quintet. Written when Brahms was about 30, this is acknowledged as one of the finest works of his early career. Its birth, though, wasn't easy. The earliest version was a string quintet (with two cellos) that Joachim criticized severely. Then followed a two-piano version, which Brahms premiered with Taussig in 1864; this sonata wasn't very successful either, but it has survived as Op. 34b. As a piano quintet, though, the music has achieved enduring fame. The potent combination

of driving passion, lyrical grace, and flawless formal control has made it one of the composer's most celebrated works.

As with many other pieces, a knowledge of older readings can inform our understanding and appreciation of the work and its more recent performances. One important document is the 1938 recording by **Rudolf Serkin** and the Busch Quartet. Anyone who thinks performers from this period were indulgently romantic or sloppy needs to hear it. It's not perfect in the manner of modern edited recordings, but their tensile strength and refusal to bow to sentimentality make for a rugged, clearheaded Brahms, and the sound (for the period) isn't bad (♦Pearl 9275, with Schumann's Quintet). Another historical version that should always be with us is from **Victor Aller** and the Hollywood String Quartet. This version, coupled with Schumann's Quintet and lots of Brahms on three CDs, offers one of the greatest chamber groups of its time ('50s) in rich, passionate performances that always sound idiomatic and right (♦Testament 3063).

Among modern performers, some seem intent on grabbing the piece, controlling it and wrestling it to the ground. Principal among these is **Pollini**'s performance with the Quartetto Italiano, presently NA but sure to return (DG). A similar outlook is shared by **Ashkenazy** and the Cleveland Quartet (♦London 425839); their version is quick and commanding, with playing of high voltage and concert-hall projection, taut and never dull. The likewise highly charged **Serkin**/Budapest reading is available in Sony's "Masterworks Portrait" series (♦45686)

The romantic, contemplative side of Brahms is better served by slower, more serene performances, like **Ian Brown** and the Nash Ensemble (♦CRD 3489) or **Piers Lane** with the New Budapest Quartet (♦Hyperion 66652 or in a bargain 2CD package, 22018). Perhaps the best compromise is the bargain set that includes **Werner Haas** and members of the Berlin Philharmonic Octet in the Piano Quintet along with the string quintets and the clarinet quintet. All these performances have a wonderful "old-world" feel, and the two-for-one price makes them irresistible (♦Philips 446172).

Clarinet Quintet. This is one of Brahms's last works and stands as the paradigm of his "autumnal" style. The music is subdued in both its materials and its formal layout, which avoids extreme levels of harmonic tension. The spirit is one of resignation rather than heroism. Nonetheless, the clarinet quintet is a major work, worthy to be placed with Mozart's quintet for the same forces.

Perhaps the range of possibilities can be seen most clearly in two recordings by the great German clarinetist **Karl Leister.** One of these is with a fairly young Leipzig Quartet, who don't get caught up in the nostalgia and spirit of resignation that often accompany this work. Their playing is certainly not insensitive, but their vigor and strength serve to dust the cobwebs from the piece (♦MD+G 3070719). Another of Leister's six recordings is with the Brandis Quartet, an older group of players from the Berlin Philharmonic (♦Nimbus 5515). Here the performance is warm, slow, and loving. Both are very fine, though in different ways.

For collectors who want to couple the Brahms with the Mozart, the gentle, reflective version by **Harold Wright** and the Boston Symphony Chamber Players is an excellent choice; recorded shortly before Wright's death, it's a wonderful testament to a great American clarinetist (♦Philips 442149). For a release that couples the Clarinet Quintet with more Brahms (at bargain price), the Philips "two-fer" (♦447172) includes the piano quintet and the two string quintets.

Sextets. The sextets are among Brahms's most appealing music. Both are relatively early works, the first dating from 1860 when Brahms was in his late 20s, the second about five years later, shortly after the composer's secret engagement to Agathe von Siebold was broken off. The first is reminiscent of Schubert, particularly in the expansive first movement. The second is a more complex, restless work, due perhaps to Brahms's working through the pain of his terminated love affair.

My central recommendation goes to the **Raphael Ensemble,** a young group formed in London in the '80s; this was their first recording, made in 1989. None of the players has achieved wide fame, but the ensemble is virtually flawless both in execution and in searching out the inner meaning of the music. Some may object to the skipped repeat in 1, but both works are accommodated on one disc (♦Hyperion 66276). If the repeat is important, the **Academy of St. Martin in the Fields Chamber Ensemble** includes it and manages to fit both works on one CD (Chandos 9151). The performances are certainly very fine, but they're more direct, lacking the interpretive detail of the Raphaels.

The recordings by **Stern** and friends are also excellent (♦Columbia 45820, 2CD). These are extremely full-bodied readings, majestic and generous in sound and spirit. It's unfortunate to have them spread over two CDs (and at high price), but those wanting a symphony-in-miniature approach will find their money well spent. For anyone wanting a period-instrument view (gut strings, spare vibrato), the **Archibudelli** players will fill the bill (Columbia 68252).

PIANO MUSIC

Brahms' chosen instrument as a youngster was the piano, which he pursued actively as a performer until around 1870. After this date, when Brahms was in his mid-30s, his public performances were less frequent, and limited mainly to his own music. Throughout his career, though, the piano was central to his composition and his musical thinking. His chamber music and many songs rely on the instrument, and he left two magnificent concertos. He also wrote extensively for solo piano.

The works divide neatly by period: the earliest are Scherzo Op. 4, *Ballades* Op. 10, and three large-scale sonatas, all works in a monumental, heroic style derived from Beethoven. These were followed by a decade (1853-63) in which he pursued variation form: four sets for solo piano and two for piano four-hands. Of all this music, only Sonata 3 and *Handel* and *Paganini Variations* are considered works of the first rank.

After the series of variations, Brahms wrote the lovely, congenial Op. 39 waltzes (1865), but then abandoned solo piano music until the late 1870s, when he produced the eight short pieces of Op. 76 and the Op. 79 *Rhapsodies.* These works, Brahms' version of the 19th century character piece, became the model for his late piano collections, twenty short works spread over four publications, Opp. 116-119. Brahms called most of them "Intermezzo" or "Capriccio," and all are important. Some are easily understood, but others are among the most difficult of his entire output.

All the piano music, though, is interesting in the way it chronicles the evolution of Brahms' style. In no other genre—orchestral, chamber or vocal music—is the composer's development so clear. A good knowledge of the solo piano music, even of selected examples, is an excellent means to understand Brahms in all areas.

Complete sets

The purchase of a complete set isn't usually the best way to build a collection, because it robs the listener of the benefits of multiple points of view; also, the ideal pianist for the virtuosic *Paganini Variations* may not be so compelling in the introspective late works. Nonetheless, complete (or nearly complete) sets have their virtues: a consistent viewpoint, often at a lower price, and frequently with economy of storage space.

Biret's collection is the most complete of the "complete" sets; it in-

cludes the concertos and the usually omitted study pieces (Naxos 501201, 12CD). Her playing, romantic and sympathetic, never misses the mark, but many will prefer the greater individuality of other pianists. Her set makes an excellent benchmark: fine performances of everything to compare with selected recordings of individual pieces by other artists. **Katchen**'s intensely romantic, personal collection is more compelling (London 430053, 6CD). He threw himself into the music and achieved an identity with the composer that few have matched. Occasionally his performances sound overdone to some listeners who want more serenity and polished beauty in Brahms, but Katchen belongs on a very short list.

A more classical, etched style is represented by **Rösel** (Berlin 9028-32, 5CD, with some items available separately). His playing is dynamic and alert, most satisfying in pieces requiring great technique. Least desirable is **Oppitz**'s set (Eurodisc, NA); here the bright, clear, classical style sounds too detaché, and he misses the warmth and beauty of Brahms.

Early works

Ballades. These four pieces, written when Brahms was 21, appeared as Op. 10. They show a break from the heroic rigidity of the sonatas and Scherzo, where Brahms tried to be impressive in Beethoven's shadow. Instead they draw their inspiration from Schumann's character pieces (not from the *Chopin Ballades*). Among several fine recordings, **Gilels** gains the top recommendation (♦DG 447407, with the G minor Piano Quartet). Beautifully sensitive and probing, this CD makes the *Ballades* into a major work. **Michelangeli** is similarly probing (♦Music & Arts 817, 2CD, with Busoni, Chopin, Ravel, and Schumann); his fine *Ballades* are NA (DG, with Schubert). **Kempff** is also sensitive, but aims more at elegance and refinement (♦DG 437374, 2CD). **Osorio** is another strong contender, whose warm playing lies between a classical and romantic approach; he brings many of the same qualities as Kempff, who was his teacher (♦ASV 6161). **Rösel** is fine for those wanting a more objective, etched style (♦Berlin 2095). **Sokolov**'s slow, romantic *Ballades,* filled with rubato, make the connection to Schumann clearer than usual (Opus 30103). **Rubinstein** (RCA 61862) and **Arrau** are worth looking for (Philips, NA), as is **Gould**'s austere, concentrated version (Sony 52651).

Scherzo in E-flat. *It* is inevitably a filler in larger collections. **Kempff** can certainly be recommended (see above), as can **Rösel**'s crisp, technically assured version (♦Berlin 2095, with *Ballades* and late pieces). **Backhaus**'s 1933 recording (♦Philips 9385, with *Ballades* etc.) is a valuable historical document from one of the finest Brahmsians of his period.

Sonatas 1 and ***2.*** Written when Brahms was 19 and 20, these are seldom heard, but interested collectors will be quickly won over by **Richter**'s splendid recording of both pieces (♦Praga 254059). He combined dazzling technique with a rare ability to penetrate the inner soul of Brahms. In selected repertory Richter may have been the finest pianist of the last 50 years, and his Brahms is first-rate. The only logical alternative is **Biret**'s account, lighter pianistically and less special than Richter, but for about one-third the price (♦Naxos 550351).

Sonata 3. It has been recorded much more frequently. First choice goes to **Curzon**'s legendary version, coupled with seven short, late works and Schubert's B-flat Sonata (London 448578). He steers a middle course between the youthfully impetuous performers and the cooler, objective classicists. The Sonata is tied together logically under his fingers, and he understands the large-scale drama of the work. Several other excellent performances should be placed beside Curzon. In his first recording of the solo music, **Perahia** proves himself a fine Brahmsian, with lots of interesting detail and inner tension; this CD, coupled with middle and late period pieces, offers an overview of the composer's career (♦Sony 47181). **Kempff**'s recording is a little on the elegant, understated side, but his viewpoint is no less valid (♦DG 437374, 2CD). His couplings include early works (Scherzo, *Ballades*) and the ten works that make up Opp. 76 and 79; all are wonderful and worth having. The only disappointing item is Concerto 1, which needs more strength.

Several others deserve mention. Prizewinner **Mark Anderson** presents a strong, objective account, intellectual and deliberate (♦Nimbus 5422, with Liszt and Schumann). **Osorio**'s technically assured version is also very fine, with unusually lucid accounts of Opp. 116 and 119 (♦Artek 5). **Sokolov** brings an approach that is both tonally beautiful and dramatic, though some may find him extravagant and syrupy (♦Opus 30103). A few can be passed by. **Oppitz** plays all the notes with admirable technique, but comes off sounding cold and distant (Orfeo), while **David Lively,** though deliberate and majestic, lacks excitement; his coupled *Ballades* fare better (Discover).

Some apparently deleted versions should be watched for. **Zimerman** brings individuality and impetuous youthfulness to a work that is, after all, quite youthful (DG). Also excellent is the sweep of **Gelber**'s rich, brooding version, with a fine *Handel Variations* (Denon). Of **Rubinstein**'s multiple recordings, his robust, athletic version is particularly desirable (RCA 61862, with *Ballades* and two late pieces). For a poetic, romantic view, **Lupu** is hard to beat (London). Somewhat less successful are **Arrau**, whose deep, philosophical playing gets him lost in detail (Philips), and **Ashkenazy**, a fine pianist who in this piece seems to be on automatic pilot (London).

Variations

The earliest four sets of variations (Op. 9, 1854; Op. 21:1 and 2, 1857 and 1853), along with a set for piano duet (Op. 23, 1861) have stood in the shadow of the famous *Handel* and *Paganini Variations* (Op. 24, 1861, Op. 25, 1862-63), not to mention the two-piano version of the *Haydn Variations* (Op. 56b, 1873). Taken together, they show the thoroughness of Brahms's self-study in the art of variation. The fruits of this labor would show not only in his later variations (*Haydn Variations,* Symphony 4 finale), but in the fabric and texture of almost everything he wrote.

For those wishing to traverse the entire territory the complete set by **Ian** (and where four hands are needed, **Claude**) **Hobson** is a fine, logical choice (♦Arabesque 6654, 2CDs). He/they combine superb technical control with a musicality that makes the variations much more than a series of exercises. The lesser-known pieces, though, do seem best. Some have found the *Variations on a Theme by Paganini* a bit plain, while the *Variations on a Theme by Haydn* sometimes seem earthbound. Another good overview is by **Michael Boriskin** (♦Music & Arts 4726), which includes Opp. 21:1 and 2, 24, and the 1860 *Theme and Variations in D Minor* from the Op. 18 Sextet. These are excellent performances of the direct, no-nonsense school.

Among the less often played sets, *Variations on a Theme of Robert Schumann* (Op. 9) is a filler in excellent CDs by **Biret** (♦Naxos 550350, with *Handel* and *Paganini*) and **Osorio** (♦ASV 6161, with *Ballades* and *Handel*). The two Op. 21 sets (*Variations on an Original Theme* and *Variations on a Hungarian Song*) appear together in fine, very well controlled versions by **Anderson** (♦Nimbus 5521, with Opp. 118 and 119).

Variations on a Theme by Handel. The *Handel* and *Paganini* sets have outstripped the others in popularity. The *Handel* is represented by excellent older recordings from **Cliburn** (♦RCA 60357, with Concerto 1) and **Fleischer** (♦Sony 63225, 2CD, with waltzes and both concertos). Among more modern pianists, **Biret** (see above) and **Ax** are notable contenders, though Ax's warm playing sometimes lacks a sharp interpretive profile (♦Sony 48046, with Opp. 79 and 118). Be on the lookout for possible returns of **Katchen**'s explosive version (♦London 440612, with *Paganini* and both concertos) and, in a very different vein, **Dichter**'s elegant, charming version (♦MusicMasters 67126, with waltzes and Op. 116). Another excellent version comes from **Gelber,** with his Sonata 3 (♦Denon 75959).

Variations on a Theme by Paganini. *They* exploit virtuosity more than the others and have appealed to super-technicians like **Wild** (♦Vanguard 118, with *Ballades* and Liszt). This work seems tailor-made for his unsentimental, crystal-clear pianism. **Arrau** (♦Philips 456706, 2CD, with Concerto 1) and **Michelangeli** (♦Music & Arts 817, 2CD) are similarly impressive. A few can be skipped. **Thibaudet**'s playing is brilliant and clear, but light on poetry (London 444338), while **Simon** seems too restrained (Vox 9004). Again, keep an eye open for a possible return of **Katchen.**

Music for piano four-hands

Variations. *Variations on a Theme by Robert Schumann* Op. 23 is played with great spirit by **Duo Crommelynck** (♦Claves 8711, with *Liebeslieder Waltzes* and the very early *Souvenir de la Russie*). They're preferable to the stodgy **Matthies** and **Köhn** (Naxos 553654). *Variations on a Theme by Haydn* Op. 56b, which is much better known in the orchestral version (Op. 56a), is brilliantly played by **Argerich** and **Rabinovitch**; this recording, never dull and almost overwhelming in virtuosity, belongs on anyone's short list (♦Teldec 92257, with waltzes and Sonata Op. 34b). Also worthy of consideration are the **Paratore** brothers (♦Four Winds 3009) and **Solti** and **Perahia** (♦Sony 42625, with Bartók). Less special are **Matthies** and **Köhn** (see above) and the Belgians **Steven** and **Stijn Kolacny,** whose good playing is marred by too much staccato (Eufoda 1238).

In addition to the above variations, Brahms left his Op. 34 Sonata (better known as the F Minor Quintet) in a version for two pianos, plus the Waltzes Op. 39, which can be played with either two or four hands. The popular *Hungarian Dances* are also four-hand music, though they're heard more often in orchestral versions.

In the Sonata **Argerich/Rabinovitch** are again a first choice (♦Teldec 92257), followed by the **Paratore** brothers (♦Four Winds 3009) and **Matthies** and **Köhn** (Naxos 553654). Among others, the **Mendelssohn Duo** is exciting, if not as polished as their rivals (Russian Disc 30105).

The same recommendations—**Argerich/Rabinovitch,** followed by **Matthies/Köhn** and **Mendelssohn Duo**—hold for the Waltzes. To these can be added the extroverted and spirited reading by **Tal** and **Groethuysen** (♦Sony 53285, with *Hungarian Dances*) and the splendid version by **David Allen Wehr** and **Cynthia Raim** (Connoisseur Society 4222). For a single piano, the recordings by **Biret** (♦Naxos 550355, with *Hungarian Dances*) and **Fleisher** (♦Sony 63225, 2CD, with concertos, etc.) both capture the spirit of lighter Brahms very convincingly.

Hungarian Dances aren't well represented in the catalog, but two versions mentioned above, **Tal/Groethuysen** and **Wehr/Wehr,** are both first-rate.

Mature works

After the early sonatas—works in a heroic mold—and a period dominated by variations, Brahms settled down to his most characteristic piano music: short works, modeled somewhat on Schumann, but without literary or descriptive titles. For the performer they are moderately difficult, too hard for the parlor pianist but never requiring virtuosity in the Lisztian sense. Brahms had a tough time naming these works. He had to ask his publisher Simrock for suggestions for Op. 76 before settling on "Capriccio" for the quick pieces and "Intermezzo" for the slower ones. Later he named the Op. 116 collection "Fantasias," but again called the individual pieces "Capriccio" or "Intermezzo." If nothing else, this shows his reluctance to suggest extra-musical allusions. In all, Brahms left 30 pieces in this period: 10 split between Op. 76 and the Op. 79 *Rhapsodies,* 20 spread over four publications, Op. 116-119.

Pianists today tend to record complete sets of pieces, but in the past they tended to pick and choose. Don't let this deter you from miscellaneous collections of his music, most notably by **Backhaus,** who recorded lots of Brahms in the '30s and continued relatively unimpaired up to his death in 1969. His Brahms was strong and to the point, stressing structural rather than romantic values. His four recitals currently available—all recommended— include a lot of duplications (Pearl 9385; Enterprise 192; Grammofono 78507; Magic Talent 48042).

Op. 76. While it may be logical to perform these pieces as a complete set, there is no implied requirement (as there would be in a sonata). Consequently, many famous pianists—Rubinstein, Richter, Pogorelich, Perahia—have played only one of the Op. 76 group. To get all eight, look first to **Kempff,** whose set is available at special price (♦DG 437374, 2CD). His playing, sensitive with lots of light and shade and never heavy, is clear, civilized, and deeply satisfying; this release is coupled with the Op. 79 *Rhapsodies* and earlier works, all first rate except for an undernourished Concerto 1. **Goode**'s richly probing version of Op. 76 is also excellent (♦Nonesuch 79154, with Opp. 116 and 119). He's more self-consciously philosophical than Kempff, but just as desirable. **Naomi Zaslav**'s version of most of Op. 76 is in the ripe, introspective school, but it tends to sound slow and a bit dour (Music & Arts).

Op. 79. These two *Rhapsodies* are frequent fillers in Brahms recitals, so couplings will be a factor in choosing a recording. For reliable versions of both look to **Ax** (♦Sony 48046), **Cliburn** (♦RCA 60419), **Kempff** (♦DG 437374, 2CD) and **Rösel** (♦Berlin 2095), all mentioned above. **Lupu**'s intense, glowing account is also exceptional (♦London 417599, with Opp. 117-19), while the old, monaural accounts by **Schnabel** (APR 5526) and **Solomon** (APR 7030) provide very different historical viewpoints.

Op. 116. It's probably true that more interesting recitals result from mixing early and late Brahms, but from the collector's point of view it seems a shame that pianists have not combined all of Opp. 116-119 in one CD. The catalog shows only one, **Valery Kastelsky,** who offers all 20 works, and his version is a fine example of the Russian romantic tradition— rather slow, and more concerned with sound and emotion than structure (Russian Disc 16340). Another complete set by **Ortiz** is technically fine, but deleted (Collins 1236). More satisfying overall is **Cliburn,** who offers almost all the late pieces, but spread over two CDs with other works (♦RCA 60419, 7942); his burnished sound and lyrical gift combine to make lovely Brahms. **Kempff**'s elegant, understated pianism captures the introspective quality of late Brahms beautifully; his late works are coupled with *Ballades* and Schumann in the "Great Pianists of the 20th Century" series (♦Philips 46662, 2CD).

Other recitals that include Op. 116 are mentioned above: **Goode**'s thoughtful performances with Opp. 76 and 119 (♦Nonesuch 79154) and **Osorio**'s warm, somewhat objective account (Artek 5) head the list.

Gilels' wonderful Op. 116 is coupled with his two concertos and is heartily recommended to those wanting thoughtful, romantic Brahms (♦DG 447446, 2CD). **Rubinstein** is also compelling in this music; his generosity of spirit makes the works less austere (♦RCA 61802; 61442, with Opp. 79, and 117, Concerto 2). If you prefer a serene, classical Brahms, **Katin**'s Op. 116 would be a better choice (♦Olympia 263, with Opp. 79 and 117 and *Handel Variations*). **Richter**'s late recording is coupled with *Ballades* and Op. 119, along with Bach and Beethoven (♦Live Classics 471). **Kissin**'s Op. 116 is astonishing technically, but many feel his facility gets in the way of the music (DG 445562).

As mentioned above, the historical accounts of **Schnabel** (APR 5526) and **Solomon** (APR 7030) are invaluable for comparison with more modern pianists. To these should be added **Kapell,** a dazzling, intensely romantic pianist whose Op. 116 is coupled with Beethoven, Khachaturian, Rachmaninoff and Shostakovich (♦Pearl 9277).

Op. 117. For the three *Intermezzos* that make up this group, many of the above recommendations apply. **Kempff** (♦Philips 456862), **Rubinstein** (♦RCA 61442), and **Lupu** (♦London 17599) are particularly fine choices. **Rösel**'s heartfelt but unfussy version is also satisfying; he has lots of technique, but doesn't call attention to himself (♦Berlin 2095). In addition, worthy recordings of only one or two of the *Intermezzos* can be found by pianists like **Curzon** (London 48578), **Gould** (Sony 66531), **Horowitz** (RCA 60523), **Moravec** (VAIA 1096), and **Richter** (Music & Arts 1025).

Op. 118. Here again, **Kempff** (♦Philips 456862), **Cliburn** (♦RCA 60419), **Richter** (♦Music & Arts 1025), and **Lupu** (♦London 417599) receive first consideration. Also formidable, though, are **Ax,** whose direct, warm playing seems natural for Brahms (♦Sony 48046, with Op. 79 and *Handel Variations*) and **Anderson,** whose thoughtful Brahms is also very fine (♦Nimbus 5521, with Op. 119 and Variations).

Op. 119. We have a wide choice for Op. 119. Excellent pianists like **Perahia** (♦Sony 47181), **Lupu** (♦London 417599), **Richter** (♦Live Classics 471), **Goode** (♦Nonesuch 79154), **Kempff** (♦Philips 456862), **Anderson** (♦Nimbus 5521), **Osorio** (♦Artek 5), and **Rösel** (♦Berlin 2095) have all given us distinguished versions of Brahms' last piano pieces.

ALTHOUSE

ORGAN MUSIC

Brahms's organ music consists of several early works: Preludes and Fugues in A minor and G minor, Fugue in A-flat Minor, Prelude and Fugue on *O Traurigkeit, O Herzeleid,* and his last completed work, the 11 Chorale Preludes of 1896. The first-named preludes and fugues are exuberant showpieces; the rest are more subdued in character. The chorale preludes in particular are marked by an atmosphere of valedictory resignation and introspection. It's fortuitous that the complete organ works fit comfortably onto a single CD. Several artists have recorded them, but in many cases the character of the music has proved elusive.

So far I have encountered no single recording that I can wholeheartedly recommend. **Robert Bates** comes closest, recorded on the 1996 two-manual Bond organ at Holy Rosary Church in Portland, OR (Pro Organo 7060). The sound of the organ isn't big enough to do justice to the preludes and fugues, but its understated romantic warmth and sweetness make it almost ideal for the other works. Bates clearly understands how the music ought to move, and presents it with flowing coherence and sensitive inflections of tempo. Each of the chorale-based pieces is preceded by the unaccompanied singing of the chorale melody by soprano Ruth Escher.

Another admirable recording is by **Kåre Nordstoga** on the 1998 Ryde

& Berg organ at Oslo Cathedral (Simax 1137). This instrument has all the brilliance and power demanded by the two big preludes and fugues, and Nordstoga plays them with great impetuosity and passion. While the instrument has a dark and majestic sound, it's not a romantic sound; its speech isn't smooth enough to be really lyrical, and the louder registrations have a neoclassical fizz. In general, the tender and poignant chorale preludes are the least convincing for these reasons.

Rudolf Innig plays the dark-toned Klais organ at St. Dionysius in Rheine (MD+G 3137). Like the Oslo instrument, this isn't really a romantic sound; the lively reverberation of the room tends to obscure some textural details, and this isn't helped by Innig's tendency to over-register much of the music. He makes a promising start with a slow and brooding yet coherent and lyrical *O Traurigkeit,* but in the chorale preludes the interpretations become wayward and registrations grotesque. One of the commonest dynamic markings in the chorale preludes is *forte ma dolce,* but there is precious little sweetness here.

The recordings by **Kevin Bowyer** (Nimbus 5262) and **Robert Parkins** (Naxos 550824) are best avoided. Bowyer plays the 1965 Marcussen at Odense Cathedral. Fast pieces are played as fast as possible—he has technique to burn—but the reverberation muddles the part-writing, and it all sounds tiresome and perfunctory. Parkins, who is Duke University Organist, plays on the much-recorded 1976 Flentrop in the university chapel. The big preludes and fugues are not at all bad, but in the more subdued pieces he takes painfully slow tempos and uses such minimal registration that nearly everything sounds attenuated. Innig may fail to observe Brahms's *dolce,* but Parkins tends to ignore the *forte.*   GATENS

CHORAL MUSIC

Ein deutsches Requiem (German Requiem). Brahms's choral music is dominated by this work, which was completed when he was in his mid-30s. Written before any of his symphonies and all but one of the concertos, it was Brahms' first large-scale success. Within a year of the premiere of the final seven-movement version, the piece was performed more than 20 times, from St. Petersburg to London. It was to be his longest work in any genre, the central composition in his public career.

Recordings of the *Requiem* were a bit slow in coming. The first studio version was **Karajan**'s of 1947, though an earlier concert recording by **Mengelberg** (1940) has been available on CD. Reasons for the neglect are easy to find. We could hardly expect an English or American group to record the piece during the Nazi period, while in Germany the compassionate spirit of the work hardly matched the militarism of the Third Reich.

All the monaural versions, which at present include Karajan I (his first of four), Furtwängler, Schuricht, Walter (NY and Rome), and Kempe, are worthy; lesser performances from the mono period have probably disappeared due to cultural Darwinism. Each uses large forces (particularly choral) and adopts a more ardent tone than is common today, but the sound is, of course, inferior. **Karajan** I is the most compelling of them all (EMI). Recorded in a Vienna still recovering from the war, he brought fine soloists (Schwarzkopf and Hotter) together with only a so-so chorus. The performance, though, so exalts humanity and hope that we easily forgive the unexceptional chorus and the 78 rpm swish. In a couple of exposed sections Schwarzkopf can be clearly heard helping the chorus.

In the stereo era we have had several fine versions. The weakest are those that stress the funereal aspects of the piece, with slow tempos and exaggerated dynamics. The first movement, for example, can be gor-

geous if taken very slowly (e.g., **Furtwängler, Barenboim, Previn**), but the total piece will invariably suffer. The best are those seen as a whole, where the conductor picks his spots and doesn't indulge himself in continuous lovely detail. My decades-long favorite has been **Klemperer** from 1961 (♦EMI 47238). He has a fine (large) chorus and the best soloists in Schwarzkopf and Fischer-Dieskau. She keeps a chaste, prayerful tone throughout her solo, and he, unlike many rival baritones, sounds as if he has actually contemplated the text and its thoughts on mortality.

A good alternative to Klemperer is **Gardiner,** who set out deliberately to strip the sanctimonious, Victorian veneer from the work (♦Philips 432140). Tempos, though quick, don't sound too fast and dramatic impact isn't slighted, except perhaps in the conclusions to II and III, where his smaller chorus doesn't uplift us the way a bigger group can. Another well-thought-out version is by **Levine,** who takes the outer movements briskly and concentrates the drama on II-VI (♦RCA 61349). His baritone, Hagegård, sounds a bit nasal, but Battle has just the right, innocent sound.

Another conductor attentive to pacing is **Masur,** whose *Requiem* is some 10-15 minutes quicker than the average (♦Teldec 98413). This is a recording on which critics don't agree. Some find it superficial—Brahms on cruise control with a Mozartean soprano in McNair—while others feel he brings emphasis to its positive aspects. For wonderful choral singing (from the London Symphony Chorus), **Hickox**'s version is hard to beat (♦Chandos 8942). The high, soft choral singing is splendid, and the soloists, Lott and David Wilson-Johnson, are likewise very good.

Other choral works. In addition to the *Requiem* Brahms wrote several other works for chorus and orchestra, enough to fill about two CDs. We have several good recordings of *Nänie* and *Schicksalslied* (the best known of the group) but the best, most economical solution is to get the 2CD reissue of all the important pieces (♦MHS 52497). Chief among these are James King's *Rinaldo,* conducted by **Claudio Abbado;** the other works (including Jard van Nes's *Alto Rhapsody*) are conducted by **Blomstedt.**

No one can claim to know Brahms on the basis of the symphonies, concertos, and *Requiem* alone. Throughout his career he wrote sacred and secular works for chorus, some a cappella, some accompanied by keyboard. Some of the pieces were designated as quartets, which, strictly speaking, ask for only one singer per part. In practice these works are regularly done both chorally and as chamber works.

Best known among the choral works are the *Liebeslieder Waltzes,* which appeared in two sets. Among the versions with soloists, that with **Bonney,** von Otter, Kurt Streit, and Bär is coupled with Schumann's wonderful *Spanische Liebeslieder* to make a delightful package (EMI 55430). First choice, though, would go to the old **Mathis,** Fassbaender, Schreier, Fischer-Dieskau version with pianists Karl Engel and Wolfgang Sawallisch (♦DG 423133). Equally satisfying are the choral versions conducted by **Shaw** (♦Telarc 80326) and **Gardiner** (Op. 52 only, ♦Philips 432152).

Recordings of the remaining works are hard to compare because the couplings are often different. You can hardly do better, though, than to acquire the discs by **Marcus Creed** and his Berlin-based RIAS Choir. Their performances of the vocal quartets (♦Harmonia Mundi 901593) and secular songs (♦Harmonia Mundi 901592) are as fine as any. Their recording of the motets, which are Brahms's most distinguished choral pieces, includes the recently discovered *Missa Canonica* (♦Harmonia Mundi 901591).   ALTHOUSE

SONGS

Brahms was one of the most prolific as well as one of the best lieder composers. He wrote nearly 200 songs, not including six volumes of duets, and he made arrangements of 121 folk songs from many Central European countries. His songs have remained as popular as those of his peers in this genre: Schubert, Schumann, and Wolf. He set many texts by Goethe, some by Heine and Schiller, and the rest by minor poets of the 19th century. His earliest lieder were all strophic, but starting in 1860 he wrote through-composed songs, though he never gave up the strophic style and returned to it in his final years. Many of his melodies sound so natural in expressing the words of the poem that they seem to be folk songs even when they're not—for example, "Von ewiger Liebe" and "Mainacht." In general, Brahms avoided elaborate preludes and postludes to his songs; the spotlight is always on the sung word.

Die Schöne Magelone (Romanzen). It is Brahms's only song cycle, set in prose with interspersed lyrics. The story, based on a medieval legend, tells of love lost and regained. There are 15 songs, but to understand how they fit into the narrative, it's necessary to have the spoken texts, which results in a 2CD set though the songs by themselves need only one. The best of the complete sets are by **Holzmair** (♦Ex Libris 6072) and **Prey** (♦Orfeo 116842). Holzmair's light, smooth baritone and fine diction are just as persuasive here as Prey's vocally more plush and more expressive rendition. The best of the single discs is by **Fischer-Dieskau,** accompanied by Richter (♦AS 337). Taped in 1965, this finds the baritone still in his best vocal state; as always, he is the most expressive and searching of interpreters, and he's strongly supported by Richter's clear and sensitive pianism. Another fine rendition by **Hynninen** is not in the current listings (Ondine 755).

Ernste Gesänge (Four Serious Songs). Composed when Brahms knew he was incurably ill, these are his noblest vocal works. The texts, culled from the Bible, are non-denominational expressions of faith, humility, and acceptance of death. The musical settings are stark, even harsh, yet powerful and expressive of the words. Both male and female singers have recorded these songs, and there are many fine renditions by celebrated artists. I recommend **Kipnis** (♦Preiser 89204), **Fischer-Dieskau** (♦DG 459012), **de Gaetani** (♦Arabesque 6141), and **Baker** (♦EMI 68667). An older recording by **Emmi Leisner** is also excellent but may be hard to find (Preiser 89210, part of a 2CD set). Since this work takes less than 20 minutes (all these discs include other selections, some by Brahms (Kipnis), some by other composers) the buyer should also consider the couplings.

Lieder. The best recital discs devoted exclusively (or almost exclusively) to Brahms's songs are by **Kipnis** (♦the same Preiser disc as the *Ernste Gesänge*), **Fischer-Dieskau** (♦Bayer 100006), **Prey** (♦INTC 830835), and **Margaret Price** (♦RCA 60902). These artists all have beautiful, smooth voices and excellent, natural-sounding diction, and they all know what to do with the words. Their singing is always expressive of the lyrics, achieved by the imaginative use of tonal color, not by affectations and annoying mannerisms. Other attractive releases, just below the level of excellence of the four listed above, are by **de Gaetani** (Arabesque 6141), **von Otter** (DG 429727), and **Fassbaender** (Acanta 43507). **Ludwig** has recorded a wonderful Brahms disc, but it's only available as part of a 4CD set ("Les Introuvables de Christa Ludwig," EMI 64075). If it's ever released as a single disc, it would get the highest recommendation. The young French contralto **Nathalie Stutzmann** makes an earnest effort that doesn't reach the high level of the recom-

mended versions (RCA). Of them all, I rate Kipnis and Fischer-Dieskau the best for their musical characterizations and dramatic insight.

MOSES

Havergal Brian *(1876–1972)*

Of working class origins, the mainly self-taught Brian enjoyed success before WWI and composed for a career of 80 years. He is best known for 32 symphonies, 21 coming after age 80. Elgar and Strauss were early influences, but his mature music was more compressed and full of mood changes and structures built out of germ motifs. Brian was not modern in the same way as Schoenberg, but more emotional and seemingly random—a cross between Ives and Ruggles, though more blunt and angry. His craggy, sometimes crotchety concatenation of marches, hymns, folk tunes, and lyrical and massive orchestral passages is powerful, beautiful, imposing, and often disturbing.

SYMPHONIES

Marco Polo is producing a set of Brian symphonies and orchestral works, in most cases in pairs on a single disc. They are fine readings in good sound. All recordings cited below can be rcommended.

1. ("Gothic"). This is a gargantuan treatment of Goethe's *Faust* and religious texts. Its styles range from medieval polyphony to modernism, serenity alternating with massive passages, choruses, brass choirs, and bands. Brian's best-known and most accessible major work, as played by **Lenárd,** the Slovak Philharmonic, and others reminds me of Mahler's 8 or the Berlioz *Requiem* (Marco Polo 223280). The sound could be more open, but it's good.

2. More conservative and expansive, its "Man in his cosmic loneliness" theme relates to Goethe's *Götz von Berlichingen.* **Tony Rowe** and the Moscow Symphony could use more passion but bring across an underrated symphony well (Marco Polo 223790, with *Festival Fanfare*).

3. It is Brian's longest instrumental symphony. Its huge orchestra plays an array of marches and hymn tunes, lines of melody, with frequent solo passages, outbursts of brass and percussion, masses of instruments, a duel between pianos and tympani, etc, **Lionel Friend** and the BBC are terrific (Hyperion 66334).

4. ("Psalm of Victory"). This is a fierce, difficult setting of *Psalm 68* in German. Written while the Nazis were building up, its violence (and occasional serenity) might be a prediction of Germany's destiny. **Leaper** and the Czech Radio Symphony and Slovak Philharmonic Choir are wild enough but could use more structure and a better soprano soloist. It's paired with 12, which somberly reflects Aeschylus's *Agamemnon.* Leaper is good but a bit stiff; decent sound, but 4 could use more clarity (Marco Polo 223447).

6. ("Sinfonia Tragica"). It began as an opera prelude and is more atmospheric than symphonic. The opening is spooky and magical, the rest profound and striking. Its discmate, 16, is tougher and more contrasted. **Fredman** and the London Philharmonic are stunning (Lyrita LP).

7. The last of Brian's expansive symphonies is based on Goethe's early life. It's full of splendor and reflection, with an eerie scherzo and Strasbourg bells. On the same disc, 31 grows tightly out of an opening germ; it's sprightly with a few impressive outbursts. *A Tinker's Wedding* is a lively overture with a Hovhanessian slow section. Great performances by **Mackerras** and the Royal Liverpool Orchestra (EMI LP).

8. More concentrated, it's full of drama, brooding and foreboding, contrasting power with stark beauty. **9.** is fierce and brilliantly scored, with a feeling of tight randomness. **Groves** leads the Royal Liverpool in a great 8; 9 is less cohesive and a bit bombastic. Terrific sound (EMI LP).

10. This is gripping, kaleidoscopic, but unified and original. 21 is conventional, quirky, and upbeat. **James Loughran** and **Eric Pinkett** draw surprisingly fine playing from the Leicestershire Schools Symphony. Decent sound (Unicorn LP).

11. It is at first seamless, flowing, and elegiac, then upbeat. 15's dominant Baroque figure leads to cheer, solemnity, parody, and starkness. **Row** and **Leaper** lead the National Symphony of Ireland (Marco Polo 223588, with *For Valour* and *Doctor Merryheart*). *For Valour* is warmly inspiring, *Doctor Merryheart* picaresque.

17. It offers Baroque-style counterpoint, with tension and contrast between the aggressive and lyrical. The more classical, reflective beginning of 32 leads to a cathartic funeral march before energy culminates in optimism. *Festal Dance* is a rouser, *In Memoriam* an impressive—and majorprocessional-style piece. **Leaper** leads the National Symphony of Ireland (Marco Polo 223481).

18. This combines marches, anger, oppressiveness, and funereal atmospheres. The more traditional Violin Concerto pits fierce passages against lyricism, followed by a passacaglia and a spirited, intimate finale. **Friend** leads the BBC Symphony and violinist **Marat Bisengaliev** (Marco Polo 223447, with *Jolly Miller*).

20. This is one of Brian's best, with a gripping, mutable I, a powerful Adagio, and clever light writing before a triumphant ending. 25 is a blend of breadth, steeliness, and mysterious lyricism, plus a lonely Adagio. *Fantastic Variations* is a humorous take on "Three Blind Mice." **Andrew Penny** leads the National Symphony of Ukraine. 25 is slightly better played than 20, which has some string thinness (Marco Polo 223731).

22. ("Symphonia Brevis"). Also building from an opening germ, it's stormy at times, giving way to a brooding march. The early *Psalm 23* for tenor, chorus, and orchestra is warm, in the English and German traditions. *English Suite 5* ("Rustic Scenes") depicts Shropshire (the "Reverie" is gorgeous). **Laszlo Heltay** and **Pinkett** get acceptable performances from the Leicestershire Schools Symphony and others (CBS LP). Acceptable, not great sound.

You may run into older unauthorized transcriptions of BBC broadcasts of symphonies on Aries LPs. Most are good readings (with performers mostly using aliases), but their sound ranges from somewhat acceptable to unlistenable. They will be mainly superfluous if Marco Polo finishes its project. Some are worth mentioning (if you can find them), particularly where they are the work's only recording, indicated by an asterisk: *5, 9 (better than Groves), 12, *13, 17, *19, 20 (better than Marco Polo, but with very covered sound), 22 (better than CBS and in decent sound), *23 (terrible sound), *24, 25, *26, *28, and Violin Concerto (quite good and interesting). The sound of 1-4, 8, and 14 is poor.

OTHER MUSIC

Tigers: Symphonic Movements is from Brian's first opera, a satire on British society, particularly the military. They are more evocative and programmatic and less tough and terse than the symphonies. **Leopold Hager** underlines their descriptive aspects, and the Luxembourg Radio Symphony plays well enough (Forlane 16724, 2 CD, with Parry's Symphony 3, John Foulds's *Pasquinade Symphonique* and *St. Joan Suite*). Three Cameo LPs of tone poems are amateurish performances with shrill sound.   HECHT

Frank Bridge (1879–1941)

Despite enjoying notable success during his lifetime, Bridge never made it into the top rank of British composers. The often elegiac nature of his music and the more progressive style (including Bergian atonality) of the works written after 1920 militated against popularity for all but a few pieces. He was better known as a violist and conductor and, by the end of his life and for several decades after, was remembered as Britten's teacher and for the theme of his brilliant protégé's *Variations on a Theme of Frank Bridge*. In the '60s, Britten began a revival of interest in his mentor's music, revealing a master of the English pastoral tradition to rank alongside Butterworth andin his chamber outputVaughan Williams.

ORCHESTRAL MUSIC

Enter Spring. **Groves**'s marvelously sympathetic recording of this engaging rhapsody with the Royal Liverpool Philharmonic is available as part of a fine all-Bridge program (♦EMI 66855), not to be confused with the live version from a 1978 BBC concert (BBC). Neither **Marriner** (Philips) nor **Britten** (BBC) is his equal.

An Irish Melody (Londonderry Air). More tone poem than the arrangements for string quartet (see below) or string orchestra, it uses the melody known as "Danny Boy" as its main theme. **Boughton**'s is the only available recording of the orchestral version (♦Nimbus 5366).

Lament for strings. **Groves** provides an eloquent account in the same program as *Enter Spring* (♦EMI 66855). More recently, **Leaper** coupled it with works by Elgar and Parry (Naxos).

Old English Songs: Cherry Ripe, Sally in Our Alley. Bridge arranged these pieces for piano duet or string quartet, several conductors adapting the latter to an orchestral body. **Groves** recorded *Cherry Ripe* alone (EMI), but **Nicholas Braithwaite** has made a lively version of both (Koch 7139). Best of all is **Boughton**'s with the expertly drilled English String Orchestra (♦Nimbus).

The Sea. Bridge's orchestral masterpiece (1910-11) provided him with the greatest success of his lifetime. The mood progression of its four movements gave Britten the model for his *Sea Interludes from Peter Grimes*. The pioneering **Groves** version (EMI) has been surpassed by **Handley**, captured in breathtaking sound (♦Chandos 8473); the first movement, "Seascape," is available separately (Collect 6538). **Britten**'s live performance suffers in sound and playing (BBC).

Sir Roger de Coverley. This "Christmas Dance" may be performed by string quartet (see below) or string orchestra, and—though an arrangement—is ironically one of Bridge's most performed pieces. As with *Old English Songs*, **Boughton** (♦Nimbus) has the edge over **Braithwaite** (Koch).

Suite for string orchestra. Bridge's major contribution to the great English string orchestral tradition, by turns extrovert, graceful, energetic, and high-spirited, demands virtuosity of the highest order. **Del Mar**'s recording with the recently disbanded Bournemouth Sinfonietta is very fine (Chandos 6566) but has been surpassed by **Boughton** (Nimbus). **Braithwaite** (Koch) and **David Garforth** (Chandos) both prove equal to the score's demands.

Summer. Written a few months before the outbreak of WWI, which swept away the idyll Bridge was depicting, the languid opening and close of this symphonic poem are the epitaph of an age. **Del Mar** gets to the core of the work (Chandos), but isn't preferable to **Groves** (◆EMI).

There is a Willow Grows Aslant a Brook. This "Hamlet Impression" for small orchestra (the title quotes Shakespeare's play) is one of Bridge's subtlest creations. As good as **Boughton**'s account is (Nimbus), both **Braithwaite** (Koch) and **Del Mar** (◆Chandos) penetrate more deeply to the music's heart.

CONCERTOS

Concerto elegiaco ("Oration"). For cello and orchestra, it was written in 1930, Bridge's Cello Concerto is both an anti-war protest and a lament for friends and colleagues killed in WWI. Innovative in design, it has been memorably recorded by **Isserlis** (◆EMI 63909).

Piano Concerto ("Phantasm"). Like "Oration," "Phantasm" (1931) has its roots in the nightmare of WWI and its aftermath, though it offers a wider range of moods. The lone recording is by **Kathryn Stott** (◆Conifer 175).

CHAMBER MUSIC

Cello and piano. Two recordings exist of *Elégie:* **Julian Lloyd Webber** and John McCabe give the work in its original scoring (◆ASV 807), **Lorraine Williams** and David Owen Norris in a transcription for viola and piano (ASV 1064). Webber also provides a fine account of *Scherzetto,* which is included with *Mélodie* and the D minor Sonata by both **Steven Doane** and Barry Snyder (◆Bridge 9056, with *Spring Song* and Britten's Sonata) and **Rebecca Rust** and David Apter (Marco Polo, with music by Donald Tovey).

Sonata in D Minor is an unconventional work in two unequally sized movements. Doane and Snyder navigate the compound-form finale better than any of their rivals. The account by **Rostropovich** and Britten has obvious historic value (Decca) and is superior to Rust and Apter (Marco Polo). Stronger competition is provided by **Rafael** and Peter **Wallfisch** (Chandos 8499).

Viola and piano. In 1908 Bridge produced two pieces for a viola series edited by the legendary Lionel Tertis, *Pensiero* and *Allegro appassionato.* **Paul Coletti,** accompanied by Leslie Howard, has recorded both in a fine "English Music for Viola" series that includes Rebecca Clarke's magnificent sonata (Hyperion 66687).

Phantasie Quartet in F-sharp Minor. For piano and strings, it is the third of Bridge's entries for the Cobbett Competition, which required a self-sufficient single-movement chamber work, it won second prize in 1910. Sadly, the **Dartington Trio**'s excellent performance is now NA (Hyperion). The **Amabile Quartet** couple it enterprisingly with quartets by Brahms and Turina (Summit 199).

Piano Trios. Phantasie in C Minor was composed for the 1907 Cobbett Competition, and won by virtue of its elegant telescoping of four-movement sonata form. The **Dussek Trio** have the measure of the work, giving a beautifully balanced account, nicely recorded, coupled with Trio 2 and the only available account of the three sets of *Miniatures* (◆Meridian 84290). The **Bernard Roberts Piano Trio** is even better, with superlative sound, although featuring just four of the *Miniatures* (◆Black Box 1028).

2 is unquestionably a masterpiece, one of the greatest 20th-century trios. A work of profundity and vision, its haunting atmosphere resonates long after the radiant close. The **Dussek Trio** is excellent (Merid-

ian), as is the **Borodin Trio,** whose tempos are more measured (◆Chandos 8495, with Bax's Trio); the version by the **Dartington Trio** is now NA (Hyperion). For sheer poise and quality of sound, the newest of all—from the **Bernard Roberts Piano Trio**is the finest (◆Black Box 1028).

String quartets. Bridge, like many viola-playing composers, had a special affinity with and talent for the string quartet, and wrote a dozen works for it. No one ensemble has tackled all of them on disc, but the **Brindisi Quartet** (Continuum 1035/6) and the aptly named **Bridge Quartet** (◆Meridian 84311 and 84369) have recorded all four numbered quartets. The Bridge players are splendid exponents of their diverse moods and styles in near-definitive accounts full of understanding; tellingly they couple one late and one early work on each disc (3 and 2, 4 and 1). By contrast, the Brindisi, for all their technical fluency, sometimes miss the reticence at their heart.

Among single recordings, the **Delmé Quartet**'s 2 (1915), the most popular and "English" of the four, is the finest of all, helped by the richness of sound of their 1982 recording, though the parsimonious (45-minute) playing time disappoints (◆Chandos 8426). The **Bochmann Quartet** has recorded 3 alongside works by Alan Bush and Wesley Redcliffe.

Phantasie in F Minor predates 1 by a year and is in the single span required by the Cobbett Competition rules (it won second prize). The excellent recording by the **Maggini Quartet** forms the main item of an all-Bridge program, including his smaller sets, *Novelletten* (the finest of his quartet-triptychs of miniatures), the three *Idylls,* and the tiny three *Pieces,* which culminate with a burlesque *Allegro marcato* (◆Naxos 553718). In the *Idylls,* the Maggini are marginally preferable to the **Coull Quartet,** despite the latter's superior sound (Hyperion 66718).

An Irish Melody; Old English Songs; Sir Roger de Coverley. The string quartet versions are closer in spirit to Bridge than his string orchestra settings, and there are no piano duet recordings of *Old English Songs.* Often played as a set, the **Maggini Quartet** gives deeply poetic and vibrant renditions (◆Naxos), subtler than the sometimes labored **Delmé Quartet** (Chandos 8426), though less warmly recorded.

String Sextet in E-flat. One of the later outpourings of Bridge's earlier, harmonically warmer style, the Sextet is most sympathetically played by the **Academy of St. Martin in the Fields Chamber Ensemble** (Chandos 9472).

INSTRUMENTAL AND VOCAL MUSIC

A few organ pieces aside, Bridge's instrumental output was centered on the piano. **Peter Jacobs** recorded it all to great critical acclaim in the late '80s and early '90s (◆Continuum 1016, 1018, 1019).

Bridge was an adept song writer, and many renowned singers have performed and recorded his songs, including **Ferrier** (Decca), **Flagstad** (Nimbus, Simax), and the **King's Singers** (EMI). Pride of place must go to the 2CD issue of his complete song output by singers **Janice Watson,** Louise Winter, Jamie MacDougall, and Gerald Finley, accompanied by pianist Roger Vignoles and violist Roger Chase, beautifully recorded and sumptuously documented (◆Hyperion 67181/2).   RICKARDS

Benjamin Britten *(1913–1976)*

Britten is regarded as the most important British composer of the 20th century. He composed prolifically in all forms, but was particularly concerned with vocal and choral music. He single-handedly revived English opera, neglected since the time of Purcell. His music is firmly rooted, but with an acutely modern flavor, and above all tuneful.

Most of Britten's major compositions were recorded in the '60s and '70s by Decca/London with the composer as conductor or pianist. They set an extremely high standard for performance and preserved the composer's own interpretations, and it's to these recordings that any new releases must be compared. However, there is great doubt of the ready availability of Britten's recordings in the US; Polygram doesn't always import them. The excellence of the "Britten Edition" with Steuart Bedford as Artistic Director boded well for Britten's music. However, in 1999 Collins Classics went out of business. Since the performances by The Sixteen and by Bedford in the "Britten Edition" are of such excellence, I have retained those entries in the hope that these important and valuable recordings will soon be available again.

ORCHESTRAL MUSIC

Prince of the Pagodas. There are only two recordings of Britten's single full-length ballet. When **Britten** recorded it in 1957 (London 421855), he drastically shortened the score by making more than 40 cuts (single bars to entire numbers). When **Knussen** offered it in 1989, he reinstated the cut material for a recording 20 minutes longer (♦Virgin 91103). The London Sinfonietta plays with serious commitment and refinement for Knussen, if without the brilliance and zest Britten brought to the score. Knussen, a composer in his own right, understands the careful structure of the work and tries to bring out those ideas with clarity. It's a marvel-filled work.

A Simple Symphony . It has been recorded 40 or more times, so I will simply survey a few of the more recent ones. The **Camerata Bern** play with a string sound as soft and warm as dark velvet (♦Denon 9409). Their disc includes fine performances of the *Bridge Variations* and the Prelude & Fugue for 18-Part String Orchestra. The English Sinfonia conducted by **John Farrer** have a rich, full sound (Carlton 660054). They too play the Prelude & Fugue, plus *Lachrymae* and Tippett's Concerto for Double String Orchestra. **Boughton** is heard in a sprightly and carefree performance (Nimbus 5025). The **Orpheus Chamber Orchestra** lacks lightness (DG), a quality in abundance in the performance by **Brydon Thomas** (Chandos 8376 or 6592). **Turovsky** is on automatic pilot with little excitement or pleasure (Chandos). The hard, acidic sound of the Slovak Chamber Orchestra under **Warchal** is not recommended (Campion). **Britten**'s own recording comes with the *Bridge Variations* and a no-narration version of *Young Person's Guide* (♦London 417509). The **Britten Quartet**'s performance is a particular pleasure (♦Collins 1115).

Sinfonia da Requiem. **Britten**'s recording (London) is excellent, but it may be outdone by **Rattle** (♦EMI 54270 or 47343, 2CD). He's less mellow than Britten but very virtuosic—intense, exciting, and incisive, with extraordinary clarity. **Bedford** is a bit more restrained than Rattle but a worthy second choice (Collins 1019). A fluffy start by **Pe_ek** doesn't bode well; we hear a gentle, well-played rendition with the climaxes strangely pulled back, dying away much too quickly (Virgin 90834).

A nice sampling of Britten's music (including *Peter Grimes Sea Interludes* and *An American Overture*), well-played and at a reasonable price, makes **Myer Fredman** a good choice for the *Sinfonia* (♦Naxos 553107). A concert performance by the NY Philharmonic conducted by **Barbirolli** is a historical curiosity, from a CBS radio broadcast of the work's second performance in 1941 (the world premiere had taken place the previous evening) (NMC 30). Barbirolli takes the work much more slowly than the composer, and the recorded sound is only adequate.

Suite on English Folk Tunes. Britten never recorded this, but **Rattle** is as good as it gets—incisive, exciting, yet sympathetic (♦EMI 55394).

Bernstein's view is solidly outlined, but that's not enough—beautifully played but wrong-headed (Sony). **Boughton** is dull, with little understanding of the music (Nimbus).

Variations on a Theme of Frank Bridge. This has also been recorded a great deal and I will mention only some of the more readily available. The English Chamber Orchestra has an airy outing under the lithe baton of **Alexander Gibson** (EMI). **Ronald Thomas** leads a classy, silken-sounding, precise rendition bursting with excitement (♦Chandos 6592 and 8376). **Bernstein** gives anything but a proper British performance; he's more interested in a Stokowski-like enjoyment of sheer sound (Sony 47541). There's little dramatic sense or feeling in it, but the physicality of sound is intense. The performance is slow, even ponderous, but you can savor every note as in a sumptuous banquet.

Andrew Davis seems to employ more strings than usual, but it's not a heavy performance at all—quite fleet, in fact (Teldec 73126). **Bedford** provides an intensity of feeling often overlooked by others. **Peter Csaba** is too careful, with little humor or movement (BIS). **Turovsky** is again too bland (Chandos). Far better in the smaller body of strings department is the **Camerata Bern,** in a richly detailed performance (♦Denon 9409). **Warchal** and the Slovak Chamber Orchestra (Campion), with their teeth-gritting strings, are easily outclassed by their Swiss colleagues. Again **Boughton** gives a sturdy, no-nonsense performance (Nimbus 5025, and in a 4CD collection of English string music, 5213). **Iona Brown** leads the Norwegian Chamber Orchestra with verve and excitement (Virgin 45121). The music is brilliantly played, clearly articulated, with a forward-moving pulse and élan.

Britten's recording is still around and still among the best, with his typical clarity of line (London 417509). He wrote the piece in 1937 for the **Boyd Neel String Orchestra.** They recorded it in 1953; its interest is now mainly historical (Dutton 8007).

Peter Grimes: Four Sea Interludes and Passacaglia. There are actually six interludes (including the passacaglia), but the last one (between scenes 1 and 2 of Act 3) has never been recorded separately from the opera. **Britten**'s was taken from his recording of the complete opera (♦London 414577). **Bernstein** omits the passacaglia in his 1990 "Final Concert" from Tanglewood (DG). That performance shares the same faults as his earlier recording with the NY Philharmonic, which does have the passacaglia; it's more a night in the tropics than a cold North Sea (Sony). **Bedford** is experienced and authoritative; his reading of the passacaglia is especially persuasive, building with inexorable power (♦Collins 1019).

For a reasonable performance at an excellent price, try **Myer Fredman** (♦Naxos 553107). **Pe_ek** is again perfunctory and not propulsive enough (Virgin). **Previn**'s 1974 recording is almost too beautiful, too gentle; there isn't enough tension. Still, if you like this music lush and romantic, this is the one for you, though it doesn't include the passacaglia. As excellent as **Boughton** is with smaller forces in Britten's music, he fails here; everything is wrong, from the big-barrel acoustics to the leaden performance (Nimbus). The notes are right, but oh-so-carefully played, almost with hesitation and timidity.

Andrew Davis and the BBC Symphony give a large-scale, sumptuous performance, sweeping and imposing, with lush strings, smooth as silk, blending with golden brass and woodwinds (Teldec 73126). Recordings by **Handley** (Chandos) and **Slatkin** (RCA) are adequate but of no special interest. **Järvi** is sans passacaglia and sans interest (BIS). A 1978 recording by **Ormandy** hasn't been reissued on CD, but might be of sonic if not interpretive interest.

A Young Person's Guide to the Orchestra. You may choose between versions with or without a narrator; most of the recordings are without. With a narrator, current choices are Sean Connery with **Dorati** (IMP 9002) and Michael Flanders with **Groves** (♦EMI 63177)both urbane, but Flanders is wittier. **Britten** never recorded it with narration; his version is restrained and refined (London 417509). But for over-the-top, sensuous sound go to **Andrew Davis** and the BBC; it's large-scale and imposing, and perhaps not the "correct" interpretation, but there's a lot of pleasure here (Teldec 73126). There is no pleasure in **Boughton's** dull conception (Nimbus).

CONCERTOS

Piano Concerto. A bravura piece, it is facile, shallow, and filled with brilliant, twinkling light—a puff pastry. Britten recorded a rather romantic version with **Richter** (London 407318). **Joanna MacGregor** recorded the "original" version—the usual four movements plus the original third movement, a slow "Recitative and Aria," as a kind of encore (in 1945 Britten substituted the "Impromptu") (♦Collins 1102). Ms. MacGregor is brilliant. (Collins has since released this performance [1301] with Britten's Violin Concerto but without the original third, which was the prime musical interest of the earlier disc.) **Barry Douglas** doesn't quite catch the virtuosity in the music (RCA). **Gillian Lin** provides a modest rendering (Chandos). **Robert Leonardy** and Skrowaczewski are slow, underpowered, lacking in spirit, and finally boring, not worth even the modest price (Arte Nova).

Violin Concerto. **Lorraine McAslan** has recorded a sizzling performance (♦Collins 1123, 1301). Her technique is formidable and brilliantly assertive. **Ida Haendel** is no match for McAslan (EMI 64202). For once a Britten-conducted recording loses; **Mark Lubotsky** does little with the piece (London). **Ricci** is a sorry affair, as if taped on a home recorder from the back of an empty rehearsal hall (Opus 111).

CHAMBER MUSIC

Quartets. Britten wrote three quartets (1931-1975) plus the unnumbered Quartet in D. The **Endellion Quartet** recorded the complete music for string quartet (including some brief pieces that are not formal quartets plus the viola *Elegy*) in fine performances, if not very exciting ones (EMI 47694, 3CD, NA). Any group calling itself the **Britten Quartet** would have a lot to live up to in this music (♦Collins 1025, 1115). They perform in virtuoso style, rushing in where angels—or at least timid musicians—fear to tread. Their technique is rock solid, so they can concentrate on the subtleties of the music, though their clarity needs a little help from the listener (more bass). In addition to the four quartets they include the *Simple Symphony,* rarely recorded by quartet.

The **Auryn Quartet** are on the bland side in 2 and 3; details sometimes slip, too (Tacet). The most recorded of the quartets is 1, and the **Brindisi Quartet** give an aggressive performance of expressive excitement (Conifer 196, with quartet music by Imogen Holst and Frank Bridge). The **Tokyo Quartet** is as fine as you would expect (RCA 61387). The **Sorrel Quartet** has recorded 1 and 3, plus the three divertimentos and *Alla Marcia* (Chandos 9469). Theirs is a strong, meaningful interpretation, quite gutsy in spirit—athletic in 1 and luminous in the more restrained 3.

Cello. Britten was inspired by the virtuosity of Rostropovich, for whom he composed three cello suites. With Britten conducting, **Rostropovich** plays with his customary sophistication and élan (♦London 421859 contains Suites 1 and 2 plus Symphony for Cello and Orchestra and the Cello Sonata). **Tim Hugh** doesn't just play these suites but attacks them;

his tight, tense tone is in full accord with his aggressive style, and you can often hear him breathing in his struggle to tear the music from the instrument, adding to the excitement (♦Naxos 553663). Hugh can stand proudly beside Rostropovich, and at a lower price, too. **Kim Bak Dinitzen** plays the complete works for solo cello, and accomplishes quite a bit with solid, golden tone, but lacks the daredevil, all-stops-out attitude of Rostropovich and Hugh (Kontrapunkt, 2CD). **Alexander Baillie** has recorded the (almost) complete cello music; he too lacks fire, is too workmanlike (Etcetera). **Julian Lloyd Webber** romanticizes 3 along with *Tema Sacher* in a program of "British Cello Music" (ASV). **Isserlis** attempts the intricacies of 3 to little avail (Virgin). **Torleif Thedéen** does succeed with them (BIS 446).

Rostropovich and Britten still take the lead with their recording of the Symphony for Cello; Britten manages a clarity of orchestral texture unmatched by other conductors. **Ma** and Zinman with the Baltimore Symphony combine fine cello virtuosity with little orchestral support (CBS). **Ralph Wallfisch** can be heard in a sturdy performance faithfully conducted by Bedford (Chandos 8363). **Isserlis** has Hickox as conductor in a powerful, large-scale interpretation (EMI 49716). **Truls Mork** puts less emphasis on the dark side and the chilling aspects of the music (BIS).

Oboe. Most of Britten's music for oboe was composed early in his career: the *Phantasy Quartet* for oboe, violin, viola, and cello, *Two Insect Pieces* (with piano), *Temporal Variations* (solo oboe), and the later *Six Metamorphoses after Ovid* (solo oboe). All four may be heard in superior performances by **Sarah Francis** with Michael Dussek, piano, and members of the Delmé Quartet (♦Hyperion 66776). Dussek also performs solo piano music by Britten: *Holiday Diary, Five Waltzes,* and *Night Piece.* A more nasal, French interpretation of the four pieces is by **François Leleux** (Harmonia Mundi 911556, with two pieces by Poulenc).

An impressive Britten anthology has **Sara Watkins** performing *Insect* and *Metamorphoses* along with early songs and folk-song arrangements sung by Shirley-Quirk and the Suite for Harp performed by Osian Ellis (Meridian 84119). A showcase for soloists of the London Symphony contains a fine performance of *Metamorphoses* by **Roy Carter** (EMI 55398).

CHORAL MUSIC

War Requiem. This was composed in 1962 for the dedication of the rebuilt Coventry Cathedral. An effective juxtaposition of the Latin *Requiem* and the antiwar poems of Wilfred Owen is set to music of great emotional eloquence. The forces required are immense: three vocal soloists, chorus, boys' choir, organ, chamber orchestra, and regular orchestra. **Britten** conducted the premiere and shortly after that a recording (♦London 414383). Ten later recordings and two videos have been issued, but his is still the best by far. He wanted the vocal soloists to represent countries deeply involved in WWII and chose three he was used to working with: Vishnevskaya, Pears, and Fischer-Dieskau. You might object to some of Vishnevskaya's shrillness, but the two men are immensely dramatic and sing poetically. Later recordings fail to measure up to the weight and intensity Britten draws from the orchestra.

Rattle's 1983 recording is a strong contender, however (EMI 47033). He comes nearest to the composer's view of the piece orchestrally, but is let down by his soloists (Söderström, Tear, and Allen). For sheer beauty of sound **Shaw** is in a class by himself, but Lorna Haywood has a wobble you could walk through; Rolfe Johnson and Luxon sing beautifully but without much emotional involvement (Telarc 80157). Shaw gives us the musical equivalent of a painting by Titian, but it should be an etching by Goya. **Hickox** is another contender, in one of his earliest Britten recordings (Chandos). Heather Harper is rather hard-pressed, but Langridge and Shirley-Quirk are dramatically involving. The St. Paul's Cathedral Choir and the London Symphony perform to fine effect, if, again, not with quite the necessary weight and power.

Gardiner conducts what should have been a great recording (DG). Rolfe Johnson, Skovhus, and Orgonasova sing very well and with considerable dramatic involvement, the Monteverdi and NDR Choirs sing gloriously, and the NDR Symphony plays for all it's worth. Gardiner judges the rallentandos finely, yet drives the climaxes powerfully. So what's wrong? The recorded sound is muddy and nonspecific, except for the percussion, which comes through with startling clarity. Details are unusually weak, the chorus far too distant, too diffuse. I haven't seen the video, but perhaps the visuals would compensate for the sonic difficulties.

By contrast, **Kegel's** performance is recorded in super sound, with excellent clarity (Berlin 1012). Kegel is more solemnly slow than the composer, with his own tragic grandeur. That causes a few problems for the soloists (Anthony Roden, Theo Adam, and Lari Lövass), who generally manage to sing and enunciate well. **Martyn Brabbins** leads a quite ordinary performance (Naxos). Nothing is particularly wrong, but it's not dramatic or musically involving. Still, its low price is an advantage, especially if you just want to test the water to hear what the piece is all about.

In a 1997 performance led by **Masur**, the clear, well-organized sound delineates the musical forces (Teldec 17115). Vaness actually betters Vishnevskaya, Hampson is less mannered than Fischer-Dieskau, and Hadley has a more beautiful but less distinctive voice than Pears and croons too much of the music. Assistant conductor Samuel Wong manages the chamber orchestra passages well, letting the tempos flow freely, but Masur's handling of the huge forces is bound too tightly, overly precise and restrained, with not enough excitement or power. **Derek Jarman** directs a truly strange video version, using the composer's recording as the soundtrack; it's strictly for film mavens (Mystic Fire Video).

A Ceremony of Carols has received at least 40 recordings. Your choice can be determined on the basis of four preferences: a female choir, an English boy choir, an American boy choir, or a mixture of male and female treble voices. Britten composed it for a boy choir, but there are several all-female recordings. A 1964 recording by the women of the **Robert Shaw Chorale** is one of the best (originally RCA, now ♦MHS 524314). The women of **The Sixteen** are also fine and do very well at imitating boys (♦Collins 1370). It's the best of both worlds: the distinctive timbre of the treble voice combined with the power of the adult voice, and the recorded sound is excellent.

The floating, disembodied voices of English boys are well represented by the **Westminster Abbey Choir** (Sony 62615), though the **Westminster Cathedral Choir** makes an even stronger case for the style (♦Hyperion 66220). In the American style the boys sound like real boys, with voices on the rough side, and although English, the **Christ Church Cathedral Choir** is congenial (ASV 6030). I should mention the **Vienna Choir Boys** because of their popularity (RCA 68150), but I prefer the recordings by English or American choirs. The mixed style is well sung by the **Trinity College Choir,** where the females tend to dominate (Conifer 51287). That recording also has stronger soloists than you normally hear. A collection with the **New London Children**'s **Choir** is a good bargain (Naxos 553183).

Rejoice in the Lamb. The wide-open ambience of Westminster Abbey is well recorded with Martin Neary leading the **Westminster Abbey Choir** in a performance using boy trebles in the soprano and alto parts, resulting in sound that's too diffuse and bottom-heavy (Sony). That is also a

problem in several of the other works on the disc, including a wrong-headed performance of *Canticle II* using a countertenor. In the **Trinity College** recording, Richard Marlow uses female voices along with his boy trebles (Conifer 51287). The females tend to dominate, giving the choir a very feminine sound that some may prefer to the pure but ethereal sound of boys. The warm, glowing organ is an advantage, and in general the soloists are a stronger lot than most. You get a real sense of the choir's enjoyment of this music; Marlow has them excelling in the delicate art of crescendo and diminuendo in clear and spacious sound.

The English traditional style is best exemplified by the **Westminster Cathedral Choir** (Hyperion 66126). It's even more "precious" in tone than **St. John**'s **College** (London 430097). If you're an Oxford rather than a Cambridge fan, there is the **King's College Choir** (EMI). **The St. Thomas (Episcopal) Choir** of New York has thoroughly absorbed the English tradition (Koch 7030). The men are solid, the boys typically ethereal. The **Robert Shaw Chorale** version is delightful (formerly RCA, now ♦MHS 524314).

Spring Symphony. **Britten** recorded *Spring Symphony* with Vyvyan, Norma Procter, Pears, the Wandsworth Boys, and the Covent Garden chorus and orchestra (London 425153). Fine as this recording is, **Hickox** is even better (♦Chandos 8855). The terrific London Symphony Chorus sings with absolute clarity of texture and amazing vocal effects: sweet yet brilliant, notes gently caressed yet fleet, supple, and subtle. The Southend Boys Choir is gutsy—no cuteness here, just real English lads. Tenor Martyn Hill is a worthy successor to Pears, and Alfreda Hodgson's mezzo is rich and mellow. Soprano Elizabeth Gale sounds a bit on the ditsy side, but that's partly the fault of what she has to sing. Hickox moves the music along with light-hearted drive, stressing the happy bucolic qualities.

In **Previn**'s recording, extremes of dynamics cause some problems (EMI). II has the faintest whispers (so turn the volume up) to the loudest of outbursts (so turn the volume down). Most of the *attacca* directions are not observed, breaking the piece into isolated sections. Sheila Armstrong is prim and proper, Tear rough and inhibited, and Baker's distinctive mezzo is fine opulence. It's a too-sophisticated performance, all sleek satin and silk, not plain homespun. **Gardiner** comes close to Hickox, but as good as the Monteverdi Choir is, the London Symphony folk are better (DG). Alison Hagley is the best of the soprano lot, Ainsley less forceful, but the Salisbury Cathedral Girls and Boys Choir is far less effective. DG has recorded a gentle haze less effective than Chandos' clarity.

A few recommendations for compilations of choral music: The extraordinary Dutch vocal ensemble **Quink,** with only five voices, sings virtuoso performances of the *Hymn to St. Cecilia, Five Flower Songs, Sacred and Profane, A Wealden Trio, A Shepherd's Carol,* and *The Sycamore Tree* (Etcetera 1017). Their intimate style brings a clarity and purity of sound unheard in a larger performance; it's like hearing these works with new ears, so refreshing and beguiling is their singing. The excellent ensemble **The Sixteen** has recorded three programs of Britten's choral music (Collins 1286, 1343, 1370). Finally, there is a good collection of Britten's choral and orchestral music conducted by **Rattle** with the Birmingham Symphony (♦EMI 54270, 2CD). *Hymn to the Virgin* and *Hymn to St. Cecilia* are both found in many of the Britten choral collections discussed above.

OPERAS AND CHURCH PARABLES

Albert Herring. The comic delights and musical ingenuity of *Albert Herring* have often been proclaimed. Britten took a brittle, satirical French farce by de Maupassant and turned it into a smiling appreciation of English culture and a loving exposé of human eccentricities and foibles. Autobiographical to a certain extent, the opera recounts the difficulties of Albert (and by implication others) who need to break away and grow up to lead full and happy lives.

Britten's 1964 recording captures the gentle humanity of the story, with the singers using a myriad of details to individuate each role. Pears sounds remarkably youthful in the title role, and years of stage performances had sharpened his interpretive powers; at times he scarcely sings the words, breathing them in a natural, conversational manner, his legendary diction much in evidence. Also notable is Brannigan's broadly humane Superintendent Budd; rotund of voice, he is a gentle bear. Others are equally fine (♦London 417849 or 421849, 2CD).

Even if his entry in the "Britten Edition" lacks some of the humanity of the composer's recording, **Bedford** equals and in some ways surpasses Britten. Extraordinarily clear sound puts every detail in place. The 12 players in the orchestra, with Bedford at the piano, provide a virtuoso display, every instrument producing beautiful tones, their sharp precision a delight. Tempos are sometimes slow, with a lot of rubato in the phrase cadences, almost as if to caress the more romantic pages in the score. Christopher Gillett doesn't fill the text with a multitude of subtle details and inflections as Pears does, but he creates an honest, reasonable, young-sounding Albert, beautifully sung. Others in the cast breathe the music and text as naturally and realistically as can be, right down to the carefully differentiated tiresome school children (♦Collins 7042, 2CD).

In an unfortunate coincidence of timing, Vox released a recording at the same time as Collins. The **Manhattan School of Music Opera Theater** version was recorded in 1996 in a series of readings, and long recording takes made possible a version with the spontaneity of a performance but without the distractions of acting and stage activity. The sound is excellent too, capturing the voices particularly well right down to some unobjectionable throat clearing and page turning. The orchestra plays carefully, with some excessively prominent percussion, the whole affair in need of a lighter touch. It would be unfair to compare these talented students with their more experienced counterparts, but this is a worthy recording and costs only half as much as Bedford's (Vox 7900, 2CD).

The Beggar's Opera. When Britten prepared his 1948 version of *The Beggar's Opera,* he didn't simply arrange it like the more familiar Austin version but reworked the musical material. Of John Gay's 69 tunes Britten used 55, converting them into his own personal opera. It's a much more sophisticated work than was envisioned by Gay, or even Austin; in Britten's hands it has become more complex, with heavy reliance on academic contrapuntal techniques. It all sounds a bit effete and precious, not Gay's earthy, bawdy comedy. Britten himself said it was more fun to write than to hear. The only recording also introduces a strange cut into the final scene: Instead of having the performers ask the audience to call for a reprieve for Macheath, Filch as *deus ex machina* appears with a proclamation of royal amnesty.

Bedford leads a strong performance for what it is (Britten, not Gay). Ann Murray (Polly) and Yvonne Kenny (Lucy), rivals in love and rival prima donnas, are refreshing jewels of comedy and singing; Anne Collins is a hearty Mrs. Peachum. Langridge is a manly Macheath, closely followed by the darkly evil Peachum of Robert Lloyd. Everyone else is too timid, too gentlemanly, too ladylike. If you think of the work as a Britten opera, it's OK, but if you prefer Gay's comedy more down-to-earth, less rarified, it's all wrong (♦Argo 436850, 2CD).

Billy Budd. It exists in two performing versions. Britten originally wrote a four-act opera for its premiere at Covent Garden in 1951, which went on a brief tour and then disappeared from the repertoire. For a revival in 1960 he prepared a two-act version, and it is this we now see and hear. The changes are insubstantial in over-all time but rather damaging to our understanding of the story. The main cut is the big ensemble that ends Act 1, Scene 1 (it's only some four minutes of music), in which the *Indomitable*'s crew express their faith in Captain Vere, making more sense of Vere's betrayal of that faith by allowing Billy to be condemned to death.

Happily we can hear both versions conducted by **Britten** himself. The first recording preserves the broadcast of the opera's premiere in 1951 (Erato). The search for an interpreter of Billy was difficult, and it was only at almost the last minute that the composer decided upon the American baritone, Theodor Uppman. It was a career-making performance for Uppman, who sounds appropriately youthful (he was) with a virile baritone that captures the hero's innocence. Pears, too, sounds youthful as Vere, at least compared with his later studio recordings. In fact he's a bit overwhelmed in the excised ensemble, possibly one of the reasons Britten chose to delete it. The recorded sound is radio monaural, and brief sections are missing (VAI 1034, 3CD).

Britten hand-picked the cast for his 1967 studio recording of the two-act version. Peter Glossop is a more heroic Billy than Uppman, darker in baritone timbre but textually aware. Pears, more experienced from stage performances and more mature in sound, is the perfect Vere. Michael Langdon's black bass makes for a lugubrious Claggart, but he adds to the theatrical chemistry with the intense, deeply seated feelings of an unspoken (unsung) homo-erotic triangle. Britten also has the great advantage of a stronger Dansker in Brannigan; he also finds more orchestral detail with the London Symphony than Nagano (see below), and the set includes his *Holy Sonnets of John Donne* and *Songs and Proverbs of William Blake* with Pears and Fischer-Dieskau singing respectably with the composer at the piano (♦London 417428, 3CD).

Nagano leads a more generalized orchestral show with a lighter touch, picking up on the lighter moments but glossing over some of the more dramatic episodes. Rolfe Johnson sings more easily than Pears in the high-flying passages calling for a clarion sound, but his voice sounds worn, not altogether pleasant, and surprisingly his is a surface-only interpretation. Hampson's handsome baritone is in fine shape but he remains a cipher, more concerned about vocal production than drama (Erato, 2CD). There's a monetary advantage to the Nagano recording: It requires only two CDs to Britten's three (in both recordings). London and Erato include a libretto; VAI does not.

The Burning Fiery Furnace. It is the second of Britten's church parables (1967). The only recording uses basically the original cast led by the composer, with Pears, Shirley-Quirk, Tear, Stafford Dean, and the English Opera Group (♦London 414663).

Curlew River. It is the first of the church parables. Its form was inspired by a Japanese Noh play, and all the roles in play and parable are played by men in an artificial form dictated by the performance venue, in this case a Christian church. It's presented as if by an abbot and his flock to a congregation, with processions and recessions and costuming as a ritual part of the presentation.

In **Britten**'s recording, Pears' interpretation of The Madwoman may never be equaled, his performance is so intense and detailed. With his legendary diction much in evidence, Pears creates an extraordinary creature, neither fully feminine nor fully masculine, but fully human, fully real. Shirley-Quirk tends to be a bit more arch than necessary, but he catches the controlling attitude of The Ferryman. The orchestral parts (all seven of them) were specially crafted for the members of the English Opera Group and are virtuosic, the player-creators fully living up to the demands Britten made on their talents. The 1965 recording duplicates the effect that the audience in a church would have experienced; individual voices are heard as processions pass to and fro and then settle into a stage front ambiance (◆London 421858).

A second recording was made at a 1993 London performance led by **David Angus** with the Guildhall Chamber Ensemble (Koch Schwann 1397). It has extraordinary clarity of sound and, like the composer's own recording, duplicates the effect the listener in the church would hear. Mark Milhofer as The Madwoman sings with a strangely feminine sound—delicate, artfully employed. All the soloists sing clearly, forcefully, with little in the way of overt interpretation. This is in itself a refreshing change from the perhaps too arch interpretation of the composer's own recording.

Death in Venice. Britten's setting of Thomas Mann's novel was his last opera and the culmination of his artistic and private life; the title page is inscribed simply, "For Peter." Although the only recording is led by **Brian Bedford** (Britten was too ill), the composer worked closely with conductor and artists, preserving the original cast's interpretation, and the recording is definitive. Pears' Aschenbach is the grand culmination of his distinguished career (◆London 425669, 2CD).

A rather odd video production from the **Glyndebourne Touring Opera** has Tear as Aschenbach (Home Vision and Pioneer Artists). It's probably the finest Britten work Tear has done, but the stage production is troublesome—not quite faithful to Britten's intentions.

Gloriana. Britten was commissioned to write an opera for the coronation of Elizabeth II. Able to avail himself of the festive occasion and the production facilities of the Royal Opera, he composed an opera unlike his others, the closest to a grand opera in traditional style. Its premiere in 1953 in the presence of the newly crowned queen was a major fiasco; the invited audience was more inclined to politics than the arts and their interest in the music was minimal. Critics who should have known better were displeased with it as well. As a result, it wasn't revived for ten years, and when it reappeared (and then only in a concert performance), the occasion was overshadowed again by politics, as it took place on the day of President Kennedy's assassination. Critics reassessed the opera in later performances, now finding more merit in it than at its premiere.

Finally in 1992 (18 years after the composer's death) the entire opera was recorded, and it was worth the wait (Argo 440213, 2CD). There are no weak links in the cast, **Mackerras** is a formidable conductor, and protagonist Josephine Barstow is in fine voice, eloquently portraying the monarch in all her strengths and weaknesses, touchingly human. Langridge, today's leading exponent of Britten's tenor roles, is a superior Essex, cooly sung. Mackerras takes a broad approach to the score, with emphasis on the majesty inherent in the opera, truly a labor of love.

The Little Sweep. **Britten**'s version (1955, mono) is severely undercut by David Hemmings but is otherwise a fine performance (London 436393, 430367). **Ledger**'s recording (1978) is superior in sound, with a stronger child lead, though it lacks Pears' authoritative interpretation (◆EMI 65111). Robert Lloyd for Ledger is much superior as Black Bob and Tom to Trevor Anthony for Britten.

A Midsummer Night's Dream. Of some 14 operatic settings of Shakespeare's play, only Britten's has had any kind of lasting success; it has re-mained in the active repertoire for more than 30 years. It's also the only one to be a verbatim setting of Shakespeare's text, though the play is reduced to about half its length by the librettists (Britten and Pears). The text imposed a kind of form on the work: three distinct groups—the fairies, the rustics, and the lovers/courtiers—interact with each other, but never all three at the same time. Superimposed on this structure is a theme recurrent in Britten's works: the world of night, sleep, and dreams, which can be good or evil. An ambiguity of interpretation rests on the story: The magic of Oberon and Puck, the lovers' dilemma, and the rustics' antics are all capable of tragic endings. In addition, it takes place in a most evocative place at a most mystical time: a forest at Midsummer. The music is apt, imaginative, and of surpassing beauty.

The Oberon in the original stage production and the first recording (1966, under **Britten**) was Alfred Deller, for whom the role was written (London 425663, 2CD). His voice is bright and clear, very forward sounding but hollow. Deller had little stage experience, and although he sang the role with care, there isn't much characterization or interpretation. The rest of the cast, including Veasey as Hermia and Harper as Helena, is fine. In the premiere production Pears created the comic role of Francis Flute, and it was said that in the Pyramus and Thisbe interlude, he sang a delightfully wicked parody of Dame Joan Sutherland in her finest coloratura madness. Here, though, he's heard in the male romantic lead, Lysander, a role he probably didn't perform on stage.

Hickox's 1990 recording followed close on stage performances and that makes a big difference (Virgin 53905, 2CD). All the participants sound dramatically involved, and the text is colored and enunciated with clarity and precision. Bowman emerges in triumph. His voice is much darker than Deller's—masculine yet unearthly; his Oberon is cruelly precise, each syllable carefully chosen and colored to create effect. Lillian Watson (Tytania) also outdoes her predecessor (Elizabeth Harwood)—all brilliance and very sensuous. The fairies here also outdo their predecessors. The boy trebles, soloists and chorus, sound like real boys; they're a rough-sounding lot—nasty, even—and seem to have picked up on the cruelty of Oberon's world.

Dexter Fletcher (Puck) sounds like an older teenager—a good choice, especially if you subscribe to the interpretation that Oberon wants to replace Puck with the Indian Boy (check your Shakespeare). John Graham Hall is fine as Lysander; a quick vibrato aside, he's romantic and earthy, with a dark tenor voice, but he doesn't have Pears' aristocratic bearing and ease of production. The women end up in a close tie. I might give a slight edge to Harper and Veasey in Britten's recording, but the Hermia and Helena of Della Jones and Jill Gomez are fine. As Theseus, Shirley-Quirk in the earlier recording is more youthful if not as regal as Norman Bailey. Bedford's rustics are a notable lot, but the earlier group sweeps the field.

As Bottom, Brannigan created not just a role, but one of the most extraordinary characterizations ever, and bass Donald Maxwell lacks the voice, the humanity, and the bubbling personality of his predecessor. I don't mean to denigrate Bedford's artists; it's a terrific performance all round. It's just that the Britten recording is often better, and with him conducting, the London Symphony has full-bodied, romantic sound, full of sweep, passion, and magic. Hickox leading the City of London Sinfonietta comes off well in passion, but is undercut by lack of clarity at times (a matter of recording technique?). Still, the Virgin set is impressive, and I certainly wouldn't want to pass it up—if only to hear Bowman.

Colin Davis' 1995 recording is the best of the three available, so much so that I can find scarcely anything to complain about (◆Philips 454122, 2CD). He leads an exciting performance, judicious in tempo, sensitive to the needs of the singers, with as lush an orchestral sound as you could wish, all recorded with every intricate strand audible. The major news here is Brian Asawa in the pivotal role of Oberon; his sumptuously beautiful voice and commanding presence are beyond compare. Just as impressive is McNair's Tytania, with every coloratura note in place, brilliantly sung, imperious, seductive—a vivid characterization. The four lovers sing beautifully, fresh and involved.

If Lloyd's portrayal of Bottom doesn't quite eclipse Brannigan, it's nonetheless a comedic masterpiece in its own right. Bostridge's Flute is first rate—not just finely sung, but an endearing interpretation. The New London Children's Choir, solos and ensemble, are precise in their roles as well. If I must quibble about something, it can only be a slight feeling that Carl Ferguson sounds a little mature in the spoken role of Puck, but he carries off his Shakespearean duties with aplomb, and that's a legitimate interpretation. Diction from all is unusually clear, with keen musical and dramatic characterizations. This is truly a magical performance.

Noye's Fludde. In 1958 Britten first experimented with opera in a church setting with a setting of the 14th-century pageant-play from the Chester cycle of medieval mysteries and moralities, an innocent retelling of Noah, the Ark and the Great Flood. Except for the three protagonists, children sing all the solo roles, perform as a chorus of animals, and augment the orchestral ensemble. The audience (congregation) gets in on the act as well with three hymns. It's all delightfully imaginative.

There's little to choose among the three recordings; all offer good sound and persuasive performances. But while the **Hickox** (Virgin 91129) and **Nicholas Wilks** (Somm 212) recordings are quite good, **del Mar**'s is even better, the big difference being Brannigan's superbly sung and humane Noye, the impressive Voice of God from Trevor Anthony, and the vital, exciting conducting of a performance of childlike innocence (♦London 425161, 436397; MHS 51500). Hickox has a harder clarity of precision, but, like Wilks, strikes a note of formality.

Owen Wingrave. Britten wrote *Owen Wingrave* for television (BBC 1971), making use of scenic opportunities not available on the theater stage. It has rarely been produced since. The opera is based on a short story by Henry James with ghosts (again) and a pacifist hero struggling against his family's military tradition. The only recording has an all-star cast of some of **Britten**'s favorite singers (Pears, Luxon, Sylvia Fisher, Vyvyan, Baker, Harper, and Shirley-Quirk), led by the composer. Enough said (London 433200, 2CD).

Paul Bunyan. Britten's art is deeply rooted in words and his response to words, and it's necessary for the listener of his music to respond to the text as well. Thus it should come as no surprise that he frequently chose texts of high literary quality. A number of his early works for voice are settings of texts by W.H. Auden, and it was their shared enthusiasm for the theater that led them to prepare their first large-scale work, the operetta *Paul Bunyan*. Composed in America during the winter of 1940-41, the work was first performed at Columbia University and was an instant failure with the critics, who were all too eager to point out its flaws, some also implying that it was impertinent of two young Englishmen to attempt an all-American subject. The operetta was immediately withdrawn, all hope of a production on Broadway was forgotten, and it remained unheard for 35 years. In 1976 there was a production by the BBC, and the first stage production came during the Aldeburgh Festival in the same year, with some newly revised material. American productions have included St. Louis (1984) and Minnesota (1987).

Although called a choral operetta, *Bunyan* is a hybrid, somewhere between musical comedy and opera, play and farce. Yet here, despite some confusion and lack of subtlety, are undoubtedly the seeds of the ideas to be found in later Britten operas. Filled with tunes of a youthful freshness, it illuminates Auden's mythic tale of unspoiled nature spoiled by many, perhaps the earliest example of the "innocence is drowned" theme that underlies so many of Britten's works. This is more than just a clever piece; it's deeply serious, though lightly treated and often poetic.

The only recording is from the **Minnesota** production and is almost entirely successful, though I detect a certain touch of cynicism. The role of the narrator, while well performed for what it is (a kind of down-home ballad) would have been more integrated into the whole if a more operatic style of singing had been used. Bunyan never appears on stage; his is a spoken part, talking to the other characters in a folk-friendly way and addressing the audience more omnisciently. The actor portraying him here fails to differentiate between the two sides of his character, intoning a little too majestically, thus overburdening Auden's text. This is a pleasurable work, not just a preview of greatness to come but a delight on its own terms (♦Virgin 90710, 2CD).

Peter Grimes. The best known and most often performed of Britten's operas, *Peter Grimes* lives or dies according to the talents of the singer portraying Grimes. The role requires not just ease and flexibility but a dramatic interpretation of profound depth; it won't automatically sell itself on strictly musical grounds. Four highly individual interpretations make for a difficult choice. Pears (who created the role in 1945) portrays a maddened poet, sad and fragile (London), the very antithesis of Vickers's tortured, wounded god (Philips). Their voices are quite different as well: Pears with slender, reedy sound, and Vickers the Heldentenor, self-possessed and in command of his dramatic outbursts. It's said that Britten didn't like Vickers as Grimes, finding him "too tough" in the role. Vickers also takes some textual liberties, changing some words that he seems to find offensive—yet it was he who popularized the opera (at least in the US and Canada). Langridge's Grimes is an honest, simple man, driven by circumstances beyond his comprehension, tense and full of anguish (Chandos). His portrayal of insanity is wrenchingly realistic. The monochromatic interpretation of Rolfe Johnson is far weaker, plain, and ordinary by comparison (EMI). His lyric voice is overtaxed by the high-lying passages as well.

Three of the four recordings use the choral and orchestral forces of Covent Garden, and they perform splendidly in all of them. Although the **Britten**-led recording was made in 1959 (early stereo), it has richness of sound and, most of all, a suitable ambiance of theater stage sound. Claire Watson strikes a note of aristocracy as Ellen, yet her love of Grimes is apparent, and she sings the role to perfection. James Pease is the best of the Balstrodes, gruff yet humane, richly sung. It seems as if Brannigan can do no wrong in Britten's operas, and here he is again, proving it as the pompous lawyer Swallow. As Ned Keene, Geraint Evans easily captures his sly hypocrisy. Britten's conducting is a model of clarity and drama (♦London 414577, 3CD).

Colin Davis's 1978 performance runs a bit longer than Britten's, generally indulging Vickers, whose last act, "Mad Scene," is significantly longer than that of Pears. Harper is a little too restrained as Ellen, sounding quite matronly and not really willing to get involved. Patricia Payne's Auntie is a strong, hearty woman, at ease in her vocal and neighborhood surroundings. The artists are all experienced in their roles, suitably concerned with characterization, and particularly pleasing vocally (Philips 432578; MHS 525011, both 2CD).

Haitink's 1992 recording has quite bothersome sound, lacking clarity, concentrating on richness rather than impact (EMI, 2CD). His conducting is no help either; it's generalized, on the speedy side, lacking dramatic weight and involvement. Lott is a competent Ellen, not very sympathetic sounding, and her thin voice gets swamped in the big vocal ensembles. Allen is genial enough as Balstrode; you can hear why he's valued as a friendly neighbor, but not why he's respected as a philosopher. Patricia Payne's Auntie has degenerated here; now she is unsteady and unclear. Only Keenlyside among the secondary characters makes much of an impression, here as a robust Ned Keene. The remaining lot are adequate. In general, it's a pale imitation of the real thing.

Of the three non-Britten recordings, Hickox's 1995 version is the most consistently musical (Chandos 9447, 2CD). Extreme care has been taken to observe full musical values with no alteration or distortion for dramatic effect; everything is neat, with mathematical clarity. Langridge, however, gently skirts the pitch for dramatic purposes, often with a deliberate holding back of vibrato and sliding into a pitch. It's as if Grimes lives in a tonal world of his own. Even with all his dramatic emphasis and subtleties of expression, Langridge's diction is crystal-clear. Janice Watson sings a feisty Ellen Orford, sounding ready to take on the entire borough—and a match for them all. Alan Opie's Captain Balstrode is sympathetic, finely detailed. The supporting cast is just as strong, neatly characterized, except for the shaky, fluttering, vibrato-laden Bob Boles of Graham Hall. The huge chorus sings and is recorded with clarity, all vocal parts audible and in precise alignment. Such clarity is never heard in the theater, so the singing sounds studied and not quite alive; for all the musical detail, I find the overall effect lacking in real excitement. Hickox's take on the score is lithe and agile, lean and taut, moving from strength to strength.

For the historically minded, substantial excerpts from *Grimes* are available performed by some of the original 1945 cast: Pears and Joan Cross, with Covent Garden forces conducted by **Reginald Goodall** (EMI 64727). The disc also contains an abridged *Rape of Lucretia* and some of Britten's folk song arrangements.

The Prodigal Son. It is the third of Britten's church parables. The only recording (1969) has basically the original cast (Pears, Shirley-Quirk, Bryan Drake, and Tear), led by the composer (♦London 425713).

The Rape of Lucretia. The original cast, including Ferrier, for whom the role of Lucretia was composed, appears in a recording made in 1946 in Holland, a bit less than four months after the Glyndebourne premiere; the recording is labeled as "Representative excerpts conducted by the composer" (Music & Arts 901). It seems to be a complete performance, but a note in the booklet warns us that "the Executors of the Britten Estate were unable to agree to the release of the complete recording of the opera in an edition that was published in 1946 but then withdrawn by the composer and revised (and republished) in 1947. The revisions were extensive." It's a shame the executors wouldn't let us hear the composer's original thoughts on the opera. If the revisions were as extensive as the notes imply, comparison of the two editions might be instructive, certainly of historic interest. Most of Lucretia's music is here, but the final scene of the opera with its summation by the Choruses is omitted.

The performance is superlative. Ferrier sings with grace and dignity combined with distinguished musicianship. Pears is heard in the full youthful bloom of his distinctive voice, with eloquence and diction already in evidence. Joan Cross, though, I find a little difficult to appreciate; she sounds tired, dreary, and not particularly involved. Most unusual is the plaintive Tarquinius of Otakar Kraus. He almost begs for Lucretia's love, and the rape becomes an act of desperation rather than

one of power or vengeance. Brannigan (Collatinus) can hardly be bettered. **Britten** conducts authoritatively as only he could. Notes and the complete revised libretto are included with indications of the recorded excerpts.

Hickox's 1993 *Lucretia* almost equals the composer's (♦Chandos 9254, 2CD). Donald Maxwell is Bottom in Bedford's *Midsummer Night's Dream,* and I was less than impressed by his performance; here, as Tarquinius, he redeems himself. The role lies less *profondo,* and Maxwell's bright, light voice sounds more at ease. Luxon has the more luxurious voice, though, and offers a more elegant characterization: a prince first, a womanizer second. Lucretia is the center of everyone's attention in the story, and in this recording Jean Rigby deserves a lot of attention. Hers is a tense, tragic performance, firmly, beautifully sung. She doesn't quite plumb the depths of character that Baker does in Britten's 1970 recording, nor does she have Baker's distinctive voice, but what Ms. Rigby does she does excellently.

The Male and Female Choruses (actually solo roles) are major characters in themselves, commenting on and explaining the action. Nigel Robson's tenor is quite pointed, slightly nasal, distinctive; he tends to sound more violent than the touchingly humane Pears, and a bit more cynical too. The remaining singers all equal their predecessors as well. The biggest difference lies with the orchestra and the overall interpretation. Hickox favors a more acerbic sound than Britten, with a curious but not unwarranted emphasis on the horn part. This leads to an overall feeling of bitterness, without the consolation at the opera's end that Britten found. Both interpretations are right in their own way. I wouldn't want to be without either of them.

The Turn of the Screw. It had to happen sooner or later: a new recording of a Britten opera that almost completely surpasses the original led by the composer. The most obvious difference is sound quality. **Britten**'s 1955 recording is monaural, rough and raw, weak in detail and impact (London, 2CD). The winds sound ugly. **Bedford**'s 1993 recording is all bright clarity combined with the brilliant virtuoso playing of the Aldeburgh Ensemble (all 13 of them, including the Brindisi Quartet), showing off orchestral details unheard or severely muddied in the London set (♦Collins 7030, 2CD). The second big improvement is in the performance of the boy treble Miles. David Hemmings (London), for all his sincerity, sounds strained and uncomfortable even though he created the role and was coached by the composer. Sam Pays (Collins) is vastly superior, singing securely and clearly, perhaps not quite involved enough dramatically, but his final (spoken) line, "Peter Quint, you devil!," is heartbreaking in its portrayal of innocence betrayed.

The excellent contributions of the Flora, Mrs. Grose, and Miss Jessel in the London set are easily equaled by Bedford. Lott as the Governess—the most important role—is clearly superior both as singer and interpreter to the unpleasant-sounding Vyvyan. Langridge doesn't have the unique color quality of Pears (and I will miss that sound dearly, particularly his seductive blandishments in the coloratura calls of Miles's name), but is excellent in his own way. This is an all-round superior performance and recording.

Colin Davis's 1983 recording is an attractive alternative, superior in recorded sound and in some roles to Britten's, less so in others (Philips, 2CD). Philips's sound is better than London's, but lacks the extraordinary clarity of the Collins set (it was used as the soundtrack for a rather bizarre Czech film of the opera directed by Petr Weigl). Donath is the best of the three Governesses—beautifully sung, sincerely dramatic. Ava June doesn't exactly fill the sympathetic possibilities of Mrs. Grose and Harper is miscast in the more mezzo role of Miss Jessel. Langridge gets the show off to a good start as the Prologue, but is replaced by Tear who does his best to imitate Pears as Peter Quint but does not succeed. Langridge should have sung both roles as is traditional. Davis's approach to the music is more romantic and less virtuosic than Hickox's.

SONGS

Canticles. Britten's five *Canticles* were composed between 1947 and 1974. The **Pears/Britten** recordings were made in 1961, 1972, and 1976 (♦London 425716). Boy treble John Hahessey is added in II, Barry Tuckwell (horn) in III, countertenor Bowman and baritone Shirley-Quirk in IV, and Osian Ellis (harp) accompanies in V. This is an extraordinary set, preserving performances by (almost) all the original creators of the music; the exception is the boy treble standing in for Ferrier. Pears's voice ages progressively, but his interpretive strength keeps growing; his famed enunciation of text is always in evidence. Hahessey more than holds his own. Tuckwell's horn is eloquently on display, Bowman's refined singing and Shirley-Quirk's sturdy line make the most of their parts, and Ellis's harp is the best there is.

A second set of the *Canticles* has **Rolfe Johnson** in all five, countertenor Chance (II and IV), baritone Opie (IV), Vignoles (piano), Michael Thompson (horn), and Sioned Williams (harp) (Hyperion 66498). Rolfe Johnson has the most luxuriously beautiful voice of the lot. This is the first of two recordings by Chance. It's quite wrong to replace the boy treble with a countertenor, no matter how exquisite his artistry; it produces a brittle artificiality certainly not intended by Britten. The others make strong contributions, and this is an excellent alternative for the listener put off by Pears's tenor.

In another set, led by **Bedford,** Langridge has a kind of healthy, rude security in his singing, with his curious trademark of flattening vibrato for dramatic effect much in evidence (Collins 1482). Careful gradation of dynamics and use of vocal color delineate the text. Jean Rigby is a stately Isaac, richly sung but not quite childlike, lacking a certain innocence. The two singing in unison to represent the voice of God are delicate and refined, casting a dreamlike state but lacking a feeling of command. Countertenor Ragin and baritone Gerald Finley blend well with Langridge in III. Bedford, so knowledgeable of the Britten style, accompanies at the piano in I-IV; he's passionate and powerful. V has harpist Osian Ellis recording the piece again in splendid form. The recording has additional material: the complete music and readings of *The Heart of the Matter.*

For Edith Sitwell's 1956 appearance at the Aldeburgh Festival, Britten composed additional music and chose additional Sitwell texts to complement III. The sequence was never heard again in Britten's lifetime, but in 1983 **Pears** prepared a shortened version that he performed and recorded (EMI 49257). Its first complete recording is splendid (♦Collins 1481). **Judi Dench** is superior to Pears in the readings; he sounds elderly, exhausted, possibly ill, while her supple voice warmly colors the text with dark hues.

An earlier recording of I (1985) by **Rolfe Johnson** includes *Winter Words* and *Seven Sonnets of Michelangelo* plus a few folk song arrangements (Hyperion 66209, with music by Argento). **John Stewart,** Ellen Shade, and Martin Katz are heard in a 1970 recording of II (Phoenix). Best is the singing of Shade as Isaac; she adopts a young boy's voice, sweet and light, and sings very well—a big sound but of little character interest. As part of a 1996 mainly choral program from Westminster Abbey, **Bostridge,** Chance, and Julius Drake sing a wrong-headed performance of II, the use of a countertenor a mistake (Sony).

Holy Sonnets of John Donne. **Pears** and Britten recorded these twice, in 1945 (EMI 54605) and 1967 (♦London 417428, with Fischer-Dieskau's recording of *Songs and Proverbs of William Blake* as filler for the 3 CDs of *Billy Budd*). It's sad that so many of the Pears-Britten song cycles are available only as fillers to the operas; they need to be released as an integral set. **Bostridge** and Graham Johnson have recorded the only recent version of this cycle (Hyperion 66823). Bostridge's voice is youthful sounding—no resemblance to Pears. In a program of Britten rarities, he sings with refinement and clarity and Johnson's accompaniments are impeccable.

Les Illuminations. Since many recordings add *Nocturne* and *Serenade* to this piece, much of what is said here applies to those works as well. Britten composed *Les Illuminations* for soprano Sophie Wyss, but it's sung more often by a tenor. The choice is limited for soprano recordings. **Lott** recorded it in 1988 with Bryden Thomson (Chandos 8657), but her 1994 version is stronger, more imaginative, with better support from Bedford and the English Chamber Orchestra (Collins 7037). **Pears** recorded it three times, in 1954 with Goossens, in the same year with Britten at the piano, and in 1966 again with Britten (London 417153), and recently a 1941 off-the-air recording by Pears, Britten, and the CBS Symphony has surfaced (NMC 30). The singing of **Christina Högman** is veiled, mezzo-like, too heavy, not at all estatico as requested by the composer (BIS). She blends well (too well) with the New Stockholm Chamber Orchestra, like another instrumental line, the text of little importance. Peter Csaba is the heavy-handed conductor.

Rolfe Johnson again displays his virtuosity, singing with bright beauty of tone and sensitivity to the text, fully aware of its possibilities (♦Chandos 8657). The Scottish National Orchestra plays with brilliance and imagination for Bryden Thomson. He repeated his artistry with the London Mozart Players led by **Jane Glover** (ASV 682). **Martyn Hill** is a worthy successor to Pears; his tenor is effortless, with a ravishingly beautiful quality (Virgin 90792). He performs without that stuffy, everso-proper sound that English tenors so often favor; he is warm and generous, spirited without other-worldliness. **Hickox** leads the City of London Sinfonietta in a performance a bit slower than Britten's but still vital and strongly committed. **Langridge** is heavy and awkward by comparison with Hill and Rolfe Johnson (Collins). The upper reaches of the tessitura all too often bring forth a head voice discomforting in quality. His performance is generally decent, but the competition is too strong.

Hadley has a heroic voice of operatic proportions (Nimbus 5234). The lower part of his voice is weak, fading out around low C, and he doesn't even attempt the still lower Gs at the opening of "Parade," taking the option of singing up an octave. He has a serious point of view, making "Départ" a minidrama, and there's a total lack of humor except in "Royauté." Maybe he's right; does anybody really know what these poems mean? The English Chamber Orchestra under Boughton doesn't make a good appearance. There's a lack of clarity in the string texture; inner voices and bass lines are inaudible, forcing much of the music into a duet for tenor and first violins. **Schreier**'s hard voice going full blast much of the time is hardly an aural treat (Berlin). His heavily accented pronunciation of English, with his "valls" (walls) and "floak" (flock), is almost a travesty. Kegel and the Leipzig Radio Symphony are not enough.

Ainsley has a mellifluous tone, but his voice tends to spread in sustained forte passages (EMI). The thin, steely string tone of the Britten Ensemble is striking but not to my liking, and Cleobury's accompaniment is nothing in particular. It's sad to relate that **Söderström** just wasn't up to her part by 1989—strident of voice and suspicious of pitch, in a recording that should not have been made (Arabesque). The accompaniment by the English Chamber Orchestra under Gilbert Levine is very good.

Nocturne. **Pears,** Britten, and the London Symphony still set the standard (♦London 417153). **Hill** (Virgin), **Rolfe Johnson** (ASV), and **Langridge** (Collins) are discussed in *Les Illuminations* above. **Ainsley** is not particularly imaginative in vocal interpretation; the sound effects (bell, owl, cat) of "Midnight's Bell" are very straightforward, with little animal onomatopoeia (EMI). **Prégardien** gives an outstanding performance, discussed under *Serenade* (BIS 540). **Hadley** sings out fully with little subtlety or suitability.

Our Hunting Fathers. Composed in 1936, this cycle was one of Britten's early successes. A **Pears/Britten** broadcast of 1961 was available in a BBC Records LP but isn't yet on CD. It's a remarkable recording simply for Britten's interpretation of the fantastic piano accompaniment. **Phyllis Bryn-Julson** is a triumph—absolutely spectacular! She handles the seemingly impossible with ease, and her agility in the florid vocal line and the complex text is amazing. Bedford and the English Chamber Orchestra carry all before them in a tumultuous riot of sound (♦Collins 1192; also in the 2CD set of orchestral song cycles, 7037). **Söderström's** voice is larger and warmer than Bryn-Julson's, more of an operatic sound (EMI 68552). It also tends to spread here and there, sometimes with a bit of a waver, but she knows her way around the text, and her rolled "r's" in "Rats Away" are spectacular. Richard Armstrong and the Welsh Opera Orchestra play exceedingly well but not at the fever pitch Bedford got from his English group.

Phaedra. This solo cantata was composed for the special voice of **Janet Baker,** and it may be heard as filler for *The Rape of Lucretia* (♦London 452666, 2CD). She may also be heard as the narrator in the recently published concert version of the radio drama *The Rescue,* which contains **Lorraine Hunt's** performance of *Phaedra* (♦Erato 22713). Hunt is fine: deeply involved, singing with ease, majestically tragic, with excellent diction. **Ann Murray** doesn't have Baker's opulent, creamy sound; she's less steady too, but much of the drama is intact (Collins 7038). Bedford gives her the strongest support possible. The recording by **Jean Rigby** and the Nash Ensemble is of more interest for the rare Britten chamber music it contains (Hyperion 66845).

Serenade. **Pears** recorded *Serenade* three times, in 1944 with Dennis Brain, Britten, and the Boyd Neel String Orchestra (London 425996; Pearl 9177), in 1954 with Brain and Goossens (NA), and in 1963 with Barry Tuckwell, Britten, and the London Symphony (♦London 417157). His voice ages as the interpretive qualities and recorded sound improve. **Tear's** 1970 recording is ordinary; he sounds something like Pears on an off day. Alan Civil (horn), Marriner, and the Northern Sinfonia do well. **Tear** is back again in 1979 with Giulini, Dale Clevenger, and the Chicago Symphony; it's a richer orchestral sound but little improvement for Tear (DG). **Neil Mackie,** with Tuckwell again, gives a better account; Mackie is sweet-voiced and the ever-perceptive Bedford outdistances both Tear recordings (EMI 49480). Better still is **Hill,** with Frank Lloyd (horn) and the City of London Sinfonia, Hickox conducting (Virgin 90792). Hill's beautiful voice is in full command of the *leggiero* passages—quick, agile, with no fudging, but with tempos a bit slower than Britten's. For **Rolfe Johnson,** see *Les Illuminations.*

   Hadley often ignores the markings, especially in the opening phrases (Nimbus). His voice is little used for tone painting—the cat and the mouse are hardly differentiated. Tempos are on the fast side; the opening Andante is a fast trot. For **Ainsley,** the solo horn is big, bold, and brassy, an uncomfortable contrast to his restrained singing (EMI). **Prégardien** gives the lie to expectations that only English tenors can perform Britten, and he's accompanied by a Danish horn player (Ib Lanzky-Otto) and a Finnish orchestra (Tapiola Sinfonietta) and conductor (Osmo Vänskä) (BIS 540). Prégardien has neither English accent nor mannerisms but sings with ease and control, projecting understanding and commitment to the music. Lanzky-Otto's playing is amazing—big and confident, a perfect match with the tenor. The Tapiola Sinfonietta hold their own too. It's exhilarating. **Schreier** has twice had a go at *Serenade,* in 1967 (Campion) and in 1985 (Opus). In both he is nasal and foreign to the style, with outrageous pronunciation.

Seven Sonnets of Michelangelo. **Pears** and Britten recorded the *Sonnets* three times: In early 1941 a private recording was made before the 1942 premiere (NMC 30), in 1942 just afterwards (Pearl 9177; EMI 54605), and in 1954 (♦London 425996). The NMC recording is the earliest with Pears as a solo recitalist. His vocal and interpretive assurance is amazing. Good sound, too. The definitive recording is the 1954 London version. The 1970 **John Stewart**/Martin Katz collaboration has Stewart with a big, controlled sound of no particular color or interest (Phoenix). **Rolfe Johnson** again gives a stellar performance (Hyperion 66209).

Songs and Proverbs of William Blake. It is the least recorded of the song cycles. It was written for **Fischer-Dieskau,** and his Britten-accompanied performance is available as filler for *Billy Budd* (♦London 417428). The only competition is **Luxon;** he's an improvement over F-D's somewhat stilted artifice, and has a more beautiful voice (Chandos 8514).

Songs From the Chinese. This cycle was written with guitar accompaniment for Julian Bream, and his recording with **Pears** is all cool silk and warm velvet (♦RCA 61601). **Marta Schele's** cool soprano makes for unusual listening (BIS 31). **Partridge** is well sung, but lacks the stylish grace of Pears/Bream (Ondine 779).

Folk song arrangements. Britten published eight volumes of folk song arrangements, many of them for Pears. The accompaniments (six volumes for piano, one for guitar, another for harp) are small masterpieces of invention and imagination. Some are simple; others are remarkably complex, with independent counter-melodies. There have been many recordings of selections, but recently two integral sets have been published, both excellent: **Lorna Anderson,** Regina Nathan, Jamie Macdougall, and Martin Martineau (Hyperion 66941, 2CD), and **Lott,** Langridge, and Allen with Graham Johnson (♦Collins 7039, 2CD). The Collins set offers 10 additional unpublished selections.

   If you're looking for a complete set of the orchestral song cycles, ♦Collins 7037 (2CD) contains *Quatre Chansons Françaises* (Lott), *Our Hunting Fathers* (Bryn-Julson), *Les Illuminations* (Lott), *Serenade* (Langridge), *Nocturne* (Langridge), and *Phaedra* (Murray), with the English Chamber Orchestra under Bedford. An excellent compilation.

PARSONS

Max Bruch (1838-1920)

Bruch had the unenviable fate of far outliving his era and his popularity. During his heyday in the latter half of the 19th century, he was one of the leading musicians in Europe. His symphonies and choral works were very popular then, but now he's known for just three works, Violin Concerto 1, *Scottish Fantasy,* and *Kol Nidre.* A confirmed Mendelssohnian, for Bruch melody was music's *raison d'être*. Unfortunately, except for the violin concerto, he was incapable of inventing memorable melodies like those that flowed from his paragon's pen. This is why most of his music, no matter how beautiful, has disappeared from modern concert halls.

SYMPHONIES AND OTHER ORCHESTRAL MUSIC

1. It was a great success, written at the suggestion of conductor Herman Levi after he heard Bruch's Violin Concerto 1. It has a strong I, but a weak scherzo follows. The Adagio is pleasant, but the finale still isn't on the level of I. **Masur** and the Leipzig Gewandhaus play this music with great commitment (Philips 462164 or 420932, 2CD).

2. It was Bruch's biggest symphonic failurecommercially, not artistically. A three-movement work lacking a scherzo, audiences of his time wouldn't accept it, especially because of its pervasive seriousness. **Gernot Schmalfuss** and the Wuppertal Symphony turn that seriousness into gloom (MD+G). **Masur** effectively conveys the tragedy and grandeur of the piece, and you can hear that it's a considerable advance over 1, even though that remained the more popular of the two during Bruch's lifetime (Philips 462164, 2CD).

3. Bruch's symphonic masterpiece, this is his Rhenish Symphony, celebrating the fun-loving ways of the people of his homeland on the Rhine. With four strong movements, including a fine scherzo, it deserves greater popularity. **Hickox** with the London Symphony misses the fun and excitement of the work and substitutes dull pomposity (Chandos). **Manfred Honeck** and the Hungarian State Orchestra come close to the mark, but the Hungarians are not first-rate musicians (Marco Polo). **Masur** and the Gewandhaus play with delightful enthusiasm and all four movements are ideally characterized (♦Philips 462164, 2CD).

VIOLIN CONCERTOS AND OTHER CONCERTANTE WORKS

1. It became an instant favorite because of its powerful expressiveness and memorable melodies. The alternately smoldering and melting themes of I, the dreamy and ecstatically passionate themes of II, and the explosive joy of the main theme of III are sure ingredients for a winner. There are a delightful naivete and directness that have made it a perennial favorite. A successful performance must unabashedly convey these simple emotions with full force.

McDuffie (Telarc), **Akiko Suwanai** (Philips), **Zukerman** (RCA), and **Cho-Liang Lin** (CBS) lack character, energy, and involvement. **Heifetz** is a little uneven, showing imagination and superhuman polish in most passages and mechanical playing in others (RCA 6214 or 61745). Genuine passion is missing, as it so often is in Heifetz's playing. **Menuhin**'s first account (Naxos), which he made at the age of 15, is fine for a lad but is surpassed by his 1956 recording, which has much more fire (EMI 66958). **Francescatti**'s mono recording with Mitropoulos is short on passion (Sony), but his stereo remake with Schippers (CBS, LP, NA) has plenty, and Schippers is more involved than Mitropoulos. A concert recording by **Erica Morini** survives from the '60s (Arbiter). She was only a shadow of her former self by this time, and this recording lacks her youthful fire, élan, and technical polish.

Perlman's first recording, with Previn, is distinguished by unmatched tonal opulence, though he's not the most intense interpreter of this score (EMI 69863). His remake with **Haitink** is a mechanical run-through with inferior sound (EMI). **Chung** plays with a fair amount of feeling, but Kempe fails to match it until the finale, and then only in the tutti sections (Decca). **Salerno-Sonnenberg** gives a thoughtful, tender reading that's very individual and emotionally on target (♦EMI 549429). De Waart stays in the background and leaves the show to her; I'd love to

hear her with a conductor who's more of a collaborator than a mere accompanist. **Ughi**'s account is intense and very committed, but Prêtre doesn't match his level of involvement (RCA, NA).

Gitlis plays with Heifetz-like verve and technical polish, though he lacks Heifetz's capacity for refined nuance (Vox). Also like Heifetz, he isn't genuinely passionate. This would have been a better recording if the Vienna Symphony, under Horenstein's direction, had been given more presence and less boomy sound. Gitlis often leaves Horenstein in the dust in III. **Accardo** gives a fine, tonally attractive performance with admirable collaboration by Masur (Philips 462167 or 432282, 2CD). **Milstein**'s recording is intense and exciting, and Steinberg is very involved too, but it could have used better engineering; it was recorded shortly before the advent of stereo (♦EMI 66551). **Mutter** plays with great passion and polish and is very well supported by Karajan (DG 415565, 2CD).

Stern blazes through I and III, and his II is perhaps the most impassioned on records (♦Sony 66830). Ormandy gives above-average support, and his involvement contributes greatly to this recording's success. **Shaham**'s performance is tonally gorgeous and very nuanced and committed (♦DG 427656). Sinopoli is the most involved and analytical collaborator, brilliantly underscoring everything Shaham does. The orchestral tutti outbursts never sound arbitrary or unprepared as they do with some other conductors. Sinopoli's collaboration is greatly enhanced by outstanding engineering.

2. Brahms criticized this work for beginning with an Adagio, and that seems to be the problem in interpreting it. The opening Adagio is the longest movement, and it contains some lovely if not really memorable melodies, but to play it *non troppo* as Bruch directs is a challenge. **Heifetz**'s recording follows the rule that he apparently observed throughout his careernever bore the audience (♦RCA 60927). His tempos for all three movements are among the fastest on record. His account is very dramatic, thanks partly to Solomon's sympathetic conducting, and he almost convinces you that Bruch's melodies are the most soulful you'll ever hear. **Perlman**'s tempos are very close to Heifetz's, and while his account isn't as dramatic, it's strongly felt and his tone is very seductive (EMI 49071).

Accardo's recording is a bit slower but still lovely, if not as fine as Perlman's (Philips, 2CD). **Nai-Yuan Hu** is slower still, but very stylish and suave, though his account lacks momentum (Delos). **Jacques Israelievitch** is slower still, positively soporific (Fleur de Son). The slowest of all, **Mordkovitch,** certainly observes the *non troppo* directive in I, yet she avoids inducing torpor with her intense, heavily nuanced expression and a penetrating musicianship that holds the listener's attention for the work's duration: 29:16 compared to Heifetz's 23:24 (♦Chandos 9738). Mordkovitch is bold and assertive and throws caution to the wind, making quite a few slips of the fingers and coarse sounds with her bow as a result. There are many times, however, when you feel as if you're listening to Oistrakh, so rich and musical is her tone. Too bad she couldn't have recorded it with a more assertive partner than Hickox.

3. Opening with a bold *Allegro energico,* 3 is in some ways a return to form for Bruch after 2. The melodies still aren't quite as unforgettable as those of 1, but 3:I does have a powerful first subject and a lovely, lilting second. II is beautifully subduedalmost prayerfuland III is martial and propulsive.

Accardo is fully up to the task of playing this heroic music, and Masur is an engaged partner (Philips 462167, 2CD). **Andreas Krecher** and the Wuppertal Symphony under Gernot Schmalfuss are nearly as good, with the best sound (MD+G). This lacks the older recording's energy, though, especially in the more lyrical sections. There was an LP by **Albert Pratz** with the CBC Festival Orchestra conducted by Victor Feldbrill, issued in the late '70s (CBC, NA). Pratz is a soloist on steroids, bringing much more energy to the score than Accardo, and Feldbrill follows suit. Accardo and friends are more polished and have more tonal allure, and relax more in the more lyrical sections. Pratz, however, can't be beat for excitement.

Kol Nidre. Originally scored for cello and orchestra, *Kol Nidre* (Hebrew for "All Vows") has been appropriated by violinists and violists. Based on a synagogal chant followed by a long lyrical section, the work shows Bruch's interest in ethnic music.

Casals recorded the piece in 1936; it's a very slow account, and he seems so enchanted with his own tone that he dreads coming to the end (EMI). **Fournier** played it with nobility and deep feeling, but his technique was starting to show a good deal of wear and his vibrato was slow and wobbly (DG). **Maria Kliegel** moves the work along nicely and plays with more emotional involvement (Naxos 550519). **Matt Heimovitz** is simply glorious: His involvement is total and his tone soars, transporting the listener (♦DG 427323, NA).

Violist **Yuri Bashmet** strives for hushed *innigkeit* where emotional outpouring is more appropriate (RCA). The thin tone of his Testore can't do justice to the tonal demands of this work. Violinist **Bronislaw Huberman** made an acoustic recording of an abbreviated version (Biddulph). He's more successful than Bashmet as he plays with more extroversion, but this performance is painfully short and I miss the greater sonority of the cello.

Scottish Fantasy. This is Bruch's second great work for violin and orchestra, and along with Concerto 1 has maintained its popularity since its premiere in 1881. Its success can be attributed to two things the wonderful Scottish melodies and Bruch's inspired treatment of them. The themes derived from Scottish folk songs are unforgettable. There is "Thro' the Wood, Laddie" in I, "The Dusty Miller" in II, the enchanting "I'm a-Doun for Lack o' Johnnie" in III, and the rousing "Scots wha hae wi' Wallace bled" in IV.

Most performances of this work have been influenced by two classic recordings made early in the stereo era by **Heifetz** (♦RCA 6214, 61745) and **David Oistrakh** (♦Classic Compact Discs 6337). Their approaches are very different. Heifetz is suave and sleek, with mellifluous runs, taking center stage and making little effort to interact with the orchestra. This stereo version is superior to the earlier mono recording made some 10 years earlier with the same conductor, Malcolm Sargent. It has much better sound and a greater sense of occasion; Heifetz was in rare form when he made it. Oistrakh's golden tone is irresistible in his account, and while his tempos are more deliberate than Heifetz's, his playing is more soulful. He has an outstanding partner in Horenstein, who interweaves the orchestral part with the soloist so they sound inseparable. Decca's sound is excellent in the Classic Compact Discs transfer, and Oistrakh and the London Symphony seem very present.

Akiko Suwanai (Philips), **Anne Akiko Meyers** (RCA), and **Lin** (CBS) lack character and energy, as does **Vanessa-Mae** (EMI), who can't even play some of the runs in IV. All are clearly influenced by Heifetz. **Rabin** gives a lovely account and Boult is a sensitive partner (EMI 64123, 6CD). **Accardo** and Masur are clearly in the Oistrakh-Horenstein camp and turn in a beautiful reading (Philips 462167, 2CD). Masur's contribution is considerable, and it's rare for a conductor to study a concerto score as carefully as he obviously has. **Chung** and Kempe are about as good (Decca 460976). Clearly influenced by Heifetz, Chung is more mercurial than most and really shines in the finale. Kempe is just as involved as she is and finds fascinating details in the score that elude other conductors. **Midori**'s interpretation is mostly delicate and introspective, with some fine touches and, for her, a surprisingly boisterous finale, but Mehta is a rather too restrained partner (Sony). Very vivid sound. **Perlman**'s performance is wonderfully songful and full of feeling, and here Mehta is more assertive (EMI 49071).

Other concertante music for violin includes *Romance,* a charming, lightweight work that's quite effective; *Adagio appassionato,* an appealing, short, character piece; *In Memoriam,* a mournful and intense but not morose work Bruch was quite proud of; *Serenade,* a light piece with a charming Nordic folk tune as the basis for I and a IV with an almost neoclassical feel to it; and *Concert Piece Op. 84,* written some 10 years before Bruch's death and the last work he completed for violin and orchestra. **Accardo** and Masur do an admirable job with all of them (Philips 462164 or 432282, 2CD).

CHAMBER MUSIC

String Quartets. 1 is a remarkably assured student work from Bruch's last year with his teacher Ferdinand Hiller. All four movements are strong, and the writing is thoroughly idiomatic. The **ISOS Quartet** has problems of balance, favoring the first violin excessively, and doesn't have an attractive ensemble sound (Koch). The **Mannheim Quartet** is perfectly balanced, with full, beautiful sound (CPO 999460). Curiously, though their timings for each movement are longer than the ISOS Quartet's, they impart a far greater feeling of propulsion, while the other group usually sounds static and meandering. 2 was written in 1860, four years after 1, and shows some formal development over 1. The comments made above about the ISOS and Mannheim Quartets also apply here. The Mannheimers are again the clear choice (CPO 999460).

String Quintet; String Octet; Piano Quintet. Bruch turned to writing chamber music in the last years of his life. Composed in 1919, the Quintet is a lovely, satisfying piece. The 1920 Octet is also a beautiful work; it's not written for the usual group with two cellos, but for one cello and double bass. Though the Piano Quintet wasn't published until recently, unlike the Quintet and Octet it was composed in the 1880s for an amateur musical enthusiast Bruch met while he was Music Director in Liverpool. As it was written for amateurs, its technical demands are minimal, and while this is apparent, it doesn't detract from the quality of the music. **Ensemble Ulf Hoelscher** has done a wonderful job preparing all three scores and plays them beautifully (CPO 999451).

Pieces for Viola, Clarinet, and Piano. A work of autumnal nostalgia, these eight pieces were written in 1910, when the musical world had already passed Bruch by. They are lovely pieces of heartfelt yearning for another time, somewhat reminiscent of Brahms's late works, and only the third composition up to its time that employs this instrumentation. Violist **Nobuko Imai,** clarinetist **Janet Hilton,** and pianist **Roger Vignoles** play them to perfection (Chandos 8776).

CHORAL MUSIC

Odysseus. During Bruch's lifetime, this oratorio was one of his most popular compositions, telling the story of the *Odyssey* beginning with Odysseus's stay with Calypso. The music is flowing and melodic, but the essential element of drama is missing. **Leon Botstein** leads a clean, competent performance with vocal soloists of middling quality (Koch 366557, 2CD).

MAGIL

Anton Bruckner (1824–1896)

Bruckner's life began the same year that Beethoven finished his 9th Symphony and ended the year after the first performance of Mahler's 2nd. It seems appropriate that his life should have as its end posts two of the greatest choral symphonies ever written, because no composer's music ever combined the sound and meaning of choral writing and symphonic resources more and better than his.

SYMPHONIES

The conventional wisdom is that Bruckner turned Wagner into symphonic music, but a more careful listening shows the strong influence of Schubert. He loved his fellow Austrian's music and knew much of it by heart. Bruckner's music is rich and romantic to today's ears, but its early performances often were not very skilled and audiences used to simpler fare couldn't abide its length and complexity. His friends offered advice, and his willingness to be influenced results in a nightmarishly complex array of editions and sub-editions used in performances.

Historic Bruckner recordings are not very common. Although occasional pre-WWII performances by Böhm, Abendroth, or Klemperer surface from time to time, the only significant body of pre-stereo recordings is **Furtwängler**'s. He left memorable versions of 5, 7, 8, and 9, as well as a good 4 and a powerful but incomplete 6 (the first movement is missing). His performances were volatile, with wide tempo variations and powerful dynamics. They were also very emotional, and their searing power still sounds through the sonic limitations of the recording technology. They move and astonish, but they don't instruct. Nobody could play Bruckner the way Furtwängler did and, after his death, nobody tried.

Of the major Bruckner interpreters of the post-Furtwängler era, Karajan was the most important. He combined rhythmic power with outstanding playing and achieved the same degree of transcendence, but by very different means. **Böhm** had Karajan's rhythmic integrity, but a leaner, more urgent style. He recorded a splendid 3 and 4 (Decca) and a fine version of 8 (DG). **Van Beinum** recorded the last three symphonies in disciplined but songful performances that are well worth searching out, despite their elderly recorded sound (Philips).

Among the complete sets, the best is **Karajan**'s, despite its dry sound (DG). These Berlin performances combine drama, beauty, and coherence in a way that no other approaches. It's seldom possible to recommend a complete set of anything unreservedly—artists are almost always better in some works than in others—but this is one of the few completes that's really solid in all the works. **Jochum** had some of Furtwängler's spontaneity and ability to get a singing sound out of his players. He recorded two complete cycles, one with the Berlin Philharmonic (DG) and one in Dresden (EMI). Both have inspired moments, but neither has the overall coherence of Böhm or Karajan or the bardic eloquence of Furtwängler.

Haitink's Concertgebouw set is fresh and plain spoken; it doesn't storm the heavens, but it offers a good (and inexpensive) introduction to these works (Philips). **Inbal**'s cycle is made up of early versions of the symphonies (some with Wagner quotes and anticipations), including a memorable 8 featuring a first movement with a triumphant C major coda (Teldec). It's worth hearing if only as a reminder that not all of Bruckner's revisions were bad ideas. **Georg Tintner**'s cycle, like Inbal's, uses the earlier editions (Naxos). It offers a solid, no-nonsense approach to the music with variable playing and good sound. The price, though, is unbeatable. Both Inbal and Tintner are good supplements to Karajan and Haitink.

Barenboim recorded the cycle twice. His first version in Chicago was vigorous, sometimes crude (DG). His Berlin Philharmonic remake is beautifully played but musically shallow: a Maxfield Parrish approach to an Ansel Adams composer (Teldec). **Dohnányi** recorded most of a cycle (minus 1 and 2) with the Cleveland Orchestra (Decca; some are still on Decca, some on MHS). These are beautifully played, challenging readings—superb at their best, oddly inert at their worst. **Solti** was not a natural Bruckner conductor; his Chicago cycle has good sound but superficial performances (Decca).

Giulini recorded the last three symphonies in Vienna and got polished playing but variable results (DG). His 7 isn't special, 8 has moments of eloquence but some odd slowings, and 9 is extremely slow but mesmerizing, a performance for special times of a special piece. **Tennstedt** was a compellingly spontaneous interpreter in concert, but his recordings of 4 and 8 convey only a dim shadow of his art (EMI). **Horenstein** made several Bruckner recordings, of which 8 and 9 seem to be in print most often. His performances are judicious and often intense, but not always responsive to the music's lyricism, though they have attracted some ardent devotees.

Celibidache is in a category of his own. He hated recordings, but after his death, performance tapes of 3 through 9 and some choral works from Munich were issued. At their best, the performances astonish with their intensity, aliveness, and monumental scale. At their worst, they are strange, with glacially slow tempos, oddly distorted relationships between different parts of the same movements, and marginal coherence. They're worth hearing but are not for Bruckner newcomers.

For individual symphonies, **Inbal**'s readings of symphonies 0 and 00 (written before the official 1) are fresh and compelling. 1 and 2 are starkly powerful pieces, not much like their successors; **Karajan**'s are the best bet. For 3, pride of place goes to **Böhm**'s Vienna disc for Decca if you can find it; **Haitink**'s Vienna performance is more rotund than its Amsterdam predecessor (and better for it). There are lots of contenders for 4. Spectacular ones include **Böhm** (Decca), **Klemperer** (EMI), **Celibidache** (EMI 56690), **Dohnányi** (Decca), and **Karajan**/Berlin (EMI, not DG).

For 5 there are three great modern recordings: **Dohnányi** (Decca), grand and eloquent; **Haitink** (Philips), warm and rich; **Karajan** (DG), a magnificent edifice. **Carl Schuricht**'s Vienna Philharmonic recording is not quite modern (the 1963 sound is nothing special) but the performance is inimitably natural and spontaneous (DG). You can choose between the warmth and tenderness of **López-Cobos** (Telarc 80244) and the sturdy honesty of **Klemperer** (EMI) for 6; **Dohnányi** is also worth investigating. For 7, **Karajan**/Berlin (EMI) is matchlessly beautiful in playing and sound, Karajan/Vienna (DG) is more human and vulnerable. **Celibidache** (EMI) is another special reading, and both **Jochums** are also worth hearing; they are the best of their sets. Yet it's hard to hear this music without thinking of a Vienna Philharmonic **Furtwängler** performance from 1951 with seedy sound and some off-and-on playing but the most tragically eloquent Bruckner slow movement on records (Music & Arts).

In 8, **Karajan**/Vienna (DG) is stunningly powerful; nothing else is in the same league, though the urgent, sweeping **Kubelik** Bavarian Radio performance blazes through mediocre sound (Orfeo). Also, **Schuricht**, with Vienna, combines eloquent performances of 8 and 9 in fine sound at a super-discount price (EMI, 2CD). The greatest performances of 9 are all unusual. **Celibidache** (EMI) and **Giulini** (DG) are both very slow and immensely powerful. **Dohnányi** is flowing, with a stark, Zen-like quality to the last movement that is unmatched on records. Only in this company could Karajan's three DG recordings be called ordinary. The best of them was from Vienna and was issued as part of the VPO's commemorative album. Both Berlin recordings are fine, with the later one better played and slightly more poised.

CHAMBER MUSIC

Bruckner's three string quartets are of no great moment. They usually appear as fillers for the String Quintet, which is an estimable work. Of the many fine recordings of this piece, the now-vanished **Vienna Philharmonic Quintet** was an unsurprising paragon (Decca). The **Raphael Ensemble** offers a gracious and elegant reading (Hyperion). An orchestral transcription was recorded by **Ashkenazy** with the Berlin German Symphony Orchestra (Ondine). The lovely *Intermezzo,* originally intended to be part of the Quintet, can be found in a disc that includes **L'Archibudelli**'s recording of the Quintet (Sony) as well as in the recording of the Quintet by the **Raphael Quartet** (Globe; not to be confused with the Ensemble).

CHORAL MUSIC

Bruckner grew up in an atmosphere full of choral music. He wrote it from the beginning to the end of his career and he wrote it well. Aside from a handful of secular pieces, most of his work is liturgical: six masses, over twenty motets, five psalm settings, a *Requiem,* a *Te Deum,* and so on.

The gold standard for recordings of the sacred choral works has been and continues to be a series of recordings made by **Jochum** between 1963 and 1972. These included the three numbered masses, ten of the motets, *Te Deum,* and *Psalm 150.* DG used to offer them as a 4CD box but now seems to provide only a single disc containing the masses (DG 47409). It's worth the effort to find the box, either as a remainder or an import. The sound is a little thin, but the performances are incandescent.

Worthwhile collections of the motets include the **Prague Chamber Choir** (Orfeo 327951) and the **James St. Bride**'s **Church Choir** (Naxos 550956), neither of which is complete. The mighty *Te Deum* has received a number of fine recordings; **Barenboim**'s—last seen as the improbable discmate to Barbirolli's Verdi *Requiem* (EMI)—and **Welser-Möst**'s (EMI) are two of the more compelling. The only recording of the *Requiem* currently available is fortunately a good one by **Martin Best** with the English Chamber Orchestra (Hyperion 66245). The only recording of one of the numbered masses to rival Jochum's performances is **Celibidache**'s 3 in F Minor, a huge-scaled reading that turns the work into a kind of musical crossroads where the Mozart of the *Requiem,* the Beethoven of the *Missa Solemnis,* and Arvo Pärt meet and form a common language (EMI 56702). The result is not much like traditional Bruckner, but it's immensely powerful.

Bruckner's only significant secular choral piece is the cantata *Helgoland,* a stark scene from an older Germany. **Barenboim**'s recordings in Chicago (DG) and Berlin (Teldec 16646) are both fine, but only the latter is in print at the moment. The wayward Welsh conductor **Wyn Morris** made an even more compelling recording with British forces (IMP 1042, NA, with Wagner's choral "Liebesmahl der Apostel").

ORGAN MUSIC

By all accounts, Bruckner was one of the greatest organists of his time, but he wrote only a handful of pieces (mostly preludes) for the instrument. There was once a complete set available on a Japanese Victor LP, but all that's in the domestic catalog now is a single prelude played by **Thomas Sauer** as filler on a disc of choral music (Ars Musici).

CHAKWIN

Gavin Bryars (b. 1943)

Bryars is one of the less easily classifiable figures on the contemporary British music scene. He studied philosophy and composition and was a professional jazz bassist. In the late '60s, he met John Cage, and his work took an outrageously experimental turn. For example, *To gain the affection of Miss Dwyer, even for one short minute, would benefit me no end* required its performers to manipulate over a dozen overhead speakers with fishing tackle to negate the spatial effects on stereophonic test records. He has mellowed since then, but he remains intriguingly elusive, frequently to the point of obscurantism. His work tends to be quiet, slow, and emotionally equivocal.

A 1975 LP introduced two watershed works: *Jesus' Blood Never Failed Me Yet* and *The Sinking of the Titanic* (Obscure, NA). In the former, Bryars loops the song of a London street tramp, adding instrumental layers with each repetition. The cumulative effect is devastating. In 1993, he expanded *Jesus' Blood,* adding instrumental combinations, choirs, and pop singer Tom Waits (Point 438823). This nearly 75-minute version exhausts me, but perhaps that's the point. A year later, Bryars similarly expanded *The Sinking of the Titanic* (Point 446061). The piece is a fantasia on hymn tunes played by the ill-fated ship's musicians as it sank, the acoustic properties of water, survivors' accounts, a music-box tune, and more; it demonstrates the open-ended and almost mystical nature of Bryars's work. He commented that *Titanic* need not even be played, because the concept and the accompanying research were more important.

Earlier recordings of Bryars's music feel purer. "Three Viennese Dancers" is based on a historical oddity: On a night in 1906, three famous dancers—Mata Hari, Maud Allan, and Isadora Duncan—stayed in Viennese hotels, apparently unaware of each other's presence (♦ECM 1323). *First Viennese Dance* ("M.H.") is sensually scored for French horn (played with incredible breath control by Pascal Pongy) and tuned percussion. String Quartet 1 ("Between the National and the Bristol") is the Duncan work; it moves closer to Steve Reich's minimalism and ends with a haunting coda in which the quartet plays in harmonics on distuned strings. A brief *Prelude and Epilogue,* again for horn and percussion, evokes Allan.

"After the Requiem" contains the title work, *The Old Tower of Löbenicht, Alaric I or II,* and *Allegrasco* (♦ECM 1424). The first is an emotionally draining pendant to the *Cadman Requiem* (see below) and features the searing electric guitar of Bill Frisell. The second work (which alludes to the contemplations of Immanuel Kant) brings violinist Alexander Balanescu to the fore, and the third is a quartet for saxophones that pushes their technique to the limits. *Alaric* was one of two Visigoth kings—which one is uncertain—for whom a French mountain was named. *Allegrasco* is a sort of concerto for clarinet and chamber ensemble; essentially motionless and lovely, it's inspired, says Bryars, by Busoni.

"Vita Nova" contains two works for members of the **Hilliard Ensemble**—*Incipit Vita Nova* and *Glorious Hill*—and two used in dance—*Four Elements* and *Sub Rosa* (ECM 1533). *Incipit Vita Nova,* an aria for countertenor and string trio, celebrates a birth; the Latin text and rarefied writing suggest a work from the 14th century as much as one from the 20th. This is even more true of *Glorious Hill,* written for unaccompanied countertenor, two tenors, and baritone, and set to a humanistic Latin text by Pico della Mirandola. It's remarkable that Bryars wrote this gloriously cloistered work for a production of Tennessee Williams's *Summer and Smoke*! *Four Elements* was written to accompany the dances of Water, Earth, Air, and Fire; here Bryars gives prominence to winds. Bill Frisell was the inspiration behind *Sub Rosa;* it's an "extended paraphrase of and comment on" a track from one of Frisell's albums, and features the recorder of Jamie McCarthy.

The **Balanescu Quartet** has recorded String Quartets 1 and 2, and a piece called *The Last Days* for two violins (Argo 448175). They are more intense than the **Arditti Quartet** (ECM), but the Ardittis make more of the coda. *The Last Days,* with its grave lullabies, is like Messiaen's *Quartet for the End of Time* without its spiritual consolation. Quartet 2 is no less grim than 1, but its warmer colors and passages of John Adams-like minimalism are more inviting.

Bryars's penchant for adagio writing is evident in a 1996 release that contains three examples of the composer's most haunting music (♦Point 454126). A Cello Concerto ("Farewell to Philosophy"), played by dedicatee **Julian Lloyd Webber,** supposedly alludes to Haydn and flows like a long, mournful river toward its increasingly spare conclusion. *One Last Bar, Then Joe Can Sing*—the title is not explained—was written for the percussion quintet **Nexus.** Over the course of nearly 19 minutes, untuned percussion instruments yield to tuned ones, some given a more singing quality through the use of bows. Again, the mood is muted, and tone colors shift and coalesce with majestic slowness. *By the Vaar* features **Charlie Haden,** and though it allows the great jazz double-bassist opportunities to improvise, the dark and elegiac tone are typical Bryars.

A Man in a Room, Gambling was a series of ten five-minute radio spots that Bryars produced with artist **Juan Muñoz;** five are on CD (Point 456514). To chamber music suggesting quiet, aching tragedy, Muñoz gives spoken mini-lessons in the deceptive manipulation of playing cards. The CD also contains two other works for smaller string ensembles, *Les Fiançailles* and *The North Shore.* These and *The South Downs,* an extended duet for cello and piano, are painfully lyrical, and in spite of the busy outpouring of arpeggios and similar figures, essentially static.

The most recent Bryars CD returns to vocal music (Point Music 462511). *Cadman Requiem* was originally written in 1989 in memory of a friend killed in the 1988 Lockerbie air crash. This 1997 revision joins the **Hilliard Quartet** with Fretwork, a six-viol consort. Again, the use of specialists in early music directs the outcome of this almost motionless work, as does the choice of ancient texts. *Adnan Songbook* sets love poems by Lebanese-American poetess Etel Adnan for soprano (Valdine Anderson) and chamber ensemble; following *Cadman Requiem,* the effect is almost jarring. The disc closes with the *Epilogue for Wonderlawn,* a septet giving prominence to viola and three cellos (two played by Bryars's daughters).

Among other Bryars works on disc is *The Black River,* a tone poem for soprano (the unearthly **Sarah Leonard**) and organ, based on a passage from Jules Verne's *Twenty Thousand Leagues Under the Sea* (ECM 1495). Another beautiful work, also based on Verne, is *The Green Ray,* a long aria for saxophone (**John Harle**) and ensemble (Argo 433847).

TUTTLE

Ferruccio Busoni *(1866–1924)*

Busoni was born in Italy to musical parents, who gave him his first training; he later studied in Vienna and immersed himself in German culture. In his lifetime he was primarily identified with his many transcriptions of Bach for the modern piano. (Legend persists that his wife was once introduced at a social event as "Mme. Bach-Busoni.") His work as a teacher and pianist made him a dominant figure of the late 19th and early 20th centuries. He taught in Helsinki, later at the Moscow, New England, and Vienna Conservatories, and in Bologna and Berlin. His best-

known pupil was Egon Petri, whom he considered his son and successor. In his compositions Busoni aimed for a fusion of Italian lyricism with German form and structure. They include operas, symphonic works, concertos, much piano music, chamber music, and of course, his Bach transcriptions, in which he was notably faithful to the spirit, if not the letter, of Bach's works.

ORCHESTRAL MUSIC

Prior to the '90s Busoni's violin concerto was one of a mere handful of his large works to be recorded. A late '40s recording contains a fine performance by **Szigeti,** a friend and collaborator of both Busoni and Petri; its companion, the Violin Sonata, has Horszowski as the superb pianist (Sony 52537). The only other recording is by **Adolf Busch** with the Concertgebouw under Walter (Music & Arts 861). Recorded in 1936, the sound is weak and indistinct, but the chance to hear two artists of this caliber in a rarely played piece will appeal to many.

The situation is better for other works, though two orchestral suites and a *Symphonic Tragedy* remain unrecorded. A good introduction to Busoni's orchestral music is a disc by **Werner Andreas Albert** and the NDR Orchestra that includes a number of pieces, all played handsomely and well recorded, though the playing time (55 minutes) is none too generous (♦CPO 991161). A Vox Box offers *Divertimento for Flute and Orchestra, Rondo Arlecchinesco,* and the clarinet and piano *Konzertstücke* in acceptable performances and good sound (Vox 5133, 2CD, with works by Lutoslawski and Szymanowski).

Busoni's Piano Concerto is a mammoth work, nearly 75 minutes long, scored for piano, large orchestra, and male chorus. The most apt comparison is with Mahler's symphonies, and because of the forces involved, each recording is an event. **Hamelin** captures the work's many moods well, and the sound is superb (♦Hyperion 67143). **Ogdon** is an attractive second choice—a fine performance, yielding to Hamelin only in sound, where it's very good but not up to the latest (EMI 69850). An earlier version from the '70s offered **Donohoe** and BBC forces, but it's NA (EMI), and so is a fine version by **Ohlsson** (Telarc 80207). Donohoe has been superseded by Hamelin, but Ohlsson, if reissued, is definitely worth your attention.

PIANO MUSIC

There are a number of fine Busoni piano recitals available. German pianist **Christoph Sischka** is working on a series that colleagues have praised for excellent playing and very good sound (♦Bayer 100196, Vol. 1). **Christopher O'Riley** offers a fine program (Centaur 203), and a recital by **Jeni Slotchiver** includes *Seven Elegies* and the first book of the *Red Indian Diary* (Centaur 2438). **Geoffrey Tozer** is also very good in a varied program (Chandos 9394), as is **Ogdon** (Altarus 9063). **William Stephenson** provides a series of Busoni works (Olympia 481), and **Ronald Stephenson** offers a fine program (Altarus 90410). In **Veronica Jochum**'s recital, the pianist is not up to the technical demands of the music. These discs overlap in some works and are the only source for others, so you should check the contents when making your decision. Most pianists who aren't up to the music's demands don't record it (but there are exceptions!), so Busoni recitals are usually at least acceptable.

Quite a few recordings of Bach transcriptions are available, testifying to the enduring appeal of the originals and Busoni's arrangements, which capture their spirit very well. Most offer one or two pieces combined with works by other composers. Of the fully or mostly Bach-Busoni discs, the best are by the fine Russian pianist **Demidenko** (Hyperion 66566) and the always reliable **Tozer** (Chandos 9394). In mixed recitals, **Pratt** (EMI 55293) and **Horowitz** (Sony 53466) are of surpassing interest, and **Chiu** is also excellent (Harmonia Mundi 907054). The sadly neglected **Borowsky** offered Busoni's version of BWV 542, along with a generous program of Liszt (Pearl 9235, 2CD), while **Arrau**'s 1929 recording of Sonatina 6 is available (Pearl 9928 with Chopin, Schumann, and others).

Petri was Busoni's prize pupil, close friend, and anointed successor. He was a powerful and sensitive pianist, with a remarkable style that owed a great deal to his teacher. Pearl 9078 offers him in a mixed recital, and a varied program, incomparably played and recorded in good '50s mono sound, is definitely worth seeking out (Westminster 18910 or 9348, LP).

OPERAS

Busoni's operatic masterpiece, *Doktor Faust,* was unfinished at the composer's death and completed by his friend and pupil Philipp Jarnach. No recordings are available now, but a splendid one from the late '70s, with Bavarian Radio forces led by **Leitner** and a superb cast headed by Fischer-Dieskau, should be reappearing soon (DG).

Two of Busoni's earlier operas, *Turandot* (not the same story as Puccini's) and *Arlecchino,* are each available in two versions, coupled in each case. One offers fine casts conducted by **Nagano,** with notes and translations (♦Virgin 59313, 2CD), while slightly superior performances led by **Albrecht,** which lack libretto and notes, are NA (Berlin). Since understanding the text is essential, Nagano gets a well-deserved nod. A fourth opera, *Die Brautwahl (*The Bartered Brideagain, not the same story as Smetana's) has been released in a 1993 Berlin performance led by **Barenboim.** While the singing is less than perfect, the performance is good, not likely to be duplicated any time soon, and can be recommended. Texts and translations are furnished in this first commercial recording (Teldec 25250, 2CD).

An orchestral suite from *Turandot* is led by **Muti,** in good performances and sound (Sony 53280, with works by Casella and Giuseppe Martucci).   McCLAIN

George Butterworth *(1885–1916)*

Butterworth was a promising composer who died at age 31, a casualty of WWI. He left behind a meager body of music and is best remembered for two groups of Housman settings and three instrumental pieces.

Songs From A Shropshire Lad, scarcely 20 minutes long, is a minor masterpiece. The poetry of Housman has a musical life of its own; his simple rhymes almost sing themselves. Butterworth's great achievement was finding music that so enhances the six poems as to become almost inseparable from them. Once having heard the tune for "The Lads in Their Hundreds" (to cite just one example), it becomes impossible to read the words without hearing the music. The somewhat more sophisticated settings in *Bredon Hill & Other Songs* are less well known, and undeservedly so.

One of the first recordings of the *Shropshire Lad* cycle was made in 1944 by **Roy Henderson** (Dutton). He's a bluff, dry-eyed interpreter, but his diction is crystal clear (in an old-fashioned way) and he perhaps unwittingly replicates something of the poet's own dour personality. Twenty years later, one of Henderson's pupils, **Shirley-Quirk,** recorded a better account, richer in tone and less aloof in manner (♦Saga 3336). The voice has a few rough edges, and that helps tone down any sentimental excess. Slightly less distinctive is **Luxon,** an honest, straightforward performer whose recording is most valuable where it has the least competition, in the five *Bredon Hill* songs (♦Chandos 8831). A much earlier recording by **John Cameron** (1954) also conjoins the *Shropshire Lad* and *Bredon Hill* cycles (♦Dutton 7104). Cameron is the smoothest

of these vocalists, his tone firm and manly, the words sharply defined, his approach straightforward and absolutely sincere.

Graham Trew's *Bredon Hill* (Hyperion) is less well done, and so is his recording of *Shropshire Lad*—his instincts are fine but his voice is on the dull, gray side (Meridian). **Brian Rayner Cook** is slightly more polished but likewise limited in range and color (Unicorn). More interesting is **Varcoe,** who offers something different: the *Shropshire Lad* songs with orchestral accompaniments (Chandos). He also tosses in the only available recording of the three songs grouped under the title *Love Blows as the Wind Blows.* Varcoe is an honest, capable vocalist, but his readings are less affecting than the others.

No one surpasses **Thomas Allen** for suave, handsome vocalism; his voice gives great pleasure and brings us closer to the *Shropshire Lad* songs in doing so (♦Virgin 91105). **Terfel** has another superb voice, and he has recorded all 11 of the Housman songs (DG). His charismatic appeal may have introduced Butterworth to many new collectors, and I'm grateful for the attention he's given the composer even if I regret his penchant for hyperbole. There's too much whispering and shouting here, and a faintly distasteful suspicion that Terfel feels Housman's poetry needs a good drubbing to make it presentable. He makes me appreciate Luxon's restrained, unfussy singing all the more.

The vocalists mentioned so far are baritones (high and low). The Housman settings fall gracefully from the mouth of a tenor as well, and **Rolfe Johnson**'s first recording is a particular favorite (♦IMP 1065). He sings simply and clearly, and his youthful accents lend the songs particular poignancy. He turned to the cycle again, adding two of the *Bredon Hill* pieces, but the second recordings are part of an ambitious (and slightly peculiar) set (Hyperion, 2CD). Every poem from *Shropshire Lad* is here, but more than half of them are read by the actor Alan Bates; Butterworth is just one of six composers who set those that remain.

I would be happy with Allen, and Rolfe Johnson in my collection and—most touching of allShirley-Quirk, but note that all the discs discussed above are filled out with music by other composers. About half of Butterworth's songs remain unrecorded. The most popular mate for *Shropshire Lad* is Vaughan Williams's *Songs of Travel,* included by Rayner Cook, Allen, Terfel, and (on IMP) Rolfe Johnson. Trew adds the Vaughan Williams cycle to his *Bredon Hill* disc; *Shropshire Lad* is part of his admirable anthology of Housman settings by various composers (Meridian). Luxon appends songs by Finzi; the other singers choose assorted miscellanies.

ORCHESTRAL MUSIC

Three pieces have been widely recorded: *A Shropshire Lad* (an elaboration of the "Loveliest of Trees" tune from the song cycle), *Two English Idylls,* and *The Banks of Green Willow.* All are right out of the cow-looking-over-a-gate school; all are serenely lovely even so. There are far too many recordings to discuss. I'll recommend **Marriner,** on a set that includes orchestral music by Butterworth, Vaughan Williams, Delius, and Elgar (♦Decca 452707, 2CD). Be advised, however, that most of the prominent British conductors have found Butterworth's miniatures irresistible, so choose a recording on the basis of whatever fillers you find most appealing.   LUCANO

Dietrich Buxtehude *(c. 1637–1707)*

The story of Bach walking 200 miles to Lübeck in 1705 to meet Buxtehude alerts us to look beneath the surface of his rather quiet life. Born in Denmark, his father was organist at St. Mary's church in Helsingør; he took over that position in 1658, but moved across the Baltic to Lübeck in 1668, becoming organist and *Werkmeister* at St. Mary's church there, where he stayed the rest of his life. Like Bach, he never wrote in the public form of opera and very little of his music was published in his lifetime. It has an unusually direct character, a dewy-eyed freshness of outlook, a willingness to look to folk music for his inspiration, a consistent simplicity, and a sense of humor. His music is never dull; it has the middle-Baroque freedom of instrumental writing we know from Biber and Schmelzer, the joy of expressing things directly yet with a fine technique and great sensitivity. His is an important voice, as Bach realized.

Buxtehude's vocal music is primarily in the form of solo cantatas which, like Bach's, contain some of his most attractive inspirations. They're generally on a smaller scale than Bach's; many are made up of only one or two numbers for a solo singer, one or two instrumental obbligato instruments usually including violin, and basso continuo; if this sounds like a description of a work by Schütz, that's one of the traditions Buxtehude worked with. Some of the smaller works are included by **Kirkby** in Vol. 1 of Buxtehude's vocal music (Marco Polo 224062). Her program contains nine vocal numbers, accompanied by two violins, viola da gamba, and harpsichord or organ. Contributing to the excellence of her performance is her ability to alter the color of her voice. A couple of the cantatas are written in a lower tessitura, and I had to check the notes to make sure it was still Kirkby singing.

A fine collection of larger-scale works is performed by Cantus Cöln with six singers under **Junghänel** (Harmonia Mundi 901629). Seven cantatas are included, all requiring several singers, most with trumpets, oboes, and a full string consort. **Van Immerseel** conducts the Collegium Vocale, Royal Consort, and Anima Eterna Orchestra in six cantatas (Channel 7895), two of which are duplicated by Cantus Cöln. Both are fine readings. Bowman's disc with The King's Consort under **King** includes two Buxtehude cantatas, music by Georg Matthias Monn, Johann Wolfgang Franck, JC Bach, and Handel's *Ode for the Birthday of Queen Anne* in excellent performances (Meridian 84126). The same *Lament* by JC Bach is on **Jacobs**'s disc with the Kuijken Consort and Parnassus Ensemble; it also duplicates Buxtehude's popular *Jubilate Deo*. This disc contains another Buxtehude cantata plus two by Telemann; it doesn't include translations, and some find Jacobs's style mannered to a fault.

The Freiburg Ensemble Musica Poetica conducted by **Hans Bergmann** performs "Herzlich tut Mich Verlangen" in an interesting program of 17th-century German cantatas (Hänssler 98336). A couple of reissues are worth mention. Six cantatas from recordings made from 1959 to 1967 were offered by three different groups, all good (Musicaphon 57601). The performances are not in early music style but are good modern versions. Then there are **Deller**'s two cantatas coupled with organ music played by Rene Saorgin, a curious combination of fine artists (Harmonia Mundi 190700). For 17 cantatas including chorus, trumpets, trombones, and drums, performed in fine style, look for **Koopman**'s collection, the largest and most exciting of all (Erato 45294, NA)

Membra Jesu Nostri is a set of seven cantatas celebrating Jesus's body parts from head to toe. **Koopman** also recorded this series in an outstanding performance (Erato 75378, NA). A less intimate, hence slightly less moving version is by **Gardiner** (Archiv 447298, NA). **Jacobs** recorded a particularly intimate performance in which his soloists also sang the choral parts (Harmonia Mundi 901333, NA). A reading with great personality is by **Suzuki** and the Japanese Bach Collegium, which boasts outstanding choral work in a rather resonant acoustic (BIS 871). An Italianate performance of considerable intensity, though slightly less polished, is by **Fasolis** with Swiss and Italian forces, opening with a *Sinfonia* by Johann Rosenmüller that seems to refer to a Passion chant popular in Germany and also used by Haydn and Mozart (Naxos 553787). A

choice between these two performances hinges on your preference for Suzuki's understated but nervously sensitive style or Fasolis's more extroverted reading and darker sound. **Erik van Nevel** leads a satisfactory but not outstanding performance (Eufoda 1294).

Buxtehude's chamber music is contained in two collections of seven trio sonatas each, Opp. 1 and 2. Seven sonatas seems almost heretical in this period when everything seems to be written in multiples of six, but the number appears to have been important to Buxtehude, from the seven cantatas making up *Membra Jesu Nostri* to the organ Passacaglia, sporting a seven-note bass pattern repeated seven times. These trio sonatas are unusual in that they employ a viola da gamba instead of a second violin, combining the duties of soloist and basso continuo. They have an unexpected quality, as does much of Buxtehude's instrumental music, a way of stopping unexpectedly and going off in a new direction, amusing and irrepressible.

The complete chamber music is played by **John Holloway,** violin, Jaap ter Linden, viol, and Lars Ulrik Mortensen, harpsichord (Da Capo 224003/5, 3CD). Opp. 1 and 2 get their own discs with the third made up of six more sonatas scored for different instruments. The performances are generally excellent, if not particularly volatile. The **Boston Museum Trio** gives us an alternative for Op. 1, played with more verve and the variety of an organ continuo at times (Centaur 2391). Two of the unpublished sonatas are included in "Abendmusik," **Skip Sempe**'s disc with Capriccio Stravagante, as well as four published sonatas and two keyboard pieces, all played with a string instrument supporting the continuo as well as the separate viol part (Deutsche Harmonia Mundi 77300). These couplings plus Sempe's always lively readings make this a worthwhile investment, even if you have the others.

Buxtehude's keyboard music is a little ambiguous, since he seldom bothered to specify whether he was writing for harpsichord or organ. Harpsichordist **Lars Ulrik Mortensen** has recorded six suites and the half-hour variations on the aria "La Capricciosa," as well as a number of other works also available on organ (Dacapo 224116/8, 3CD). An earlier recital by Mortensen is in Kontrapunkt 32069. He's more virtuosic than **Rinaldo Alessandrini** (Astrée 8534), though he tends to be dry in the less technically involving music, while Alessandrini has similar problems and is recorded a bit closely. Mortensen takes many opportunities for ornamentation, particularly in the organ pieces, and the mean-tone tuning adds a lot of spice to the "La Capricciosa" Variations.

Buxtehude is perhaps most famous for his organ music. It has been recorded in toto several times. Like Bach's, it consists of a number of exciting preludes and fugues and an equal number of chorale preludes. There were at least three complete versions on LP, two of which should be discussed. **Marie-Claire Alain** is one of the most imaginative performers in organ registration and her album, recorded on Swedish and Danish instruments, is a model of lively interpretations and colorful voicings (MHS OR 309/315, 7LP). She's also represented on a Haepfer-Erman organ in Chambéry in a 1984 collection (Erato 75095, NA) and in another from 1989, played on a Schnitzer-Ahrend organ in Groningen (Erato/RCA 75370, 3CD, NA).

Another complete edition that might well be re-released is by **Michel Chapuis,** whose eight LPs came complete with the sheet music, as did his Bach series (Telefunken). His light touch and lively tempos take the curse off for those of us who have had to listen to too many church organists learn something new every Sunday and play it at half tempo. His playing is clean and clear. **Rene Saorgin** recorded the complete works on historic organs from the Netherlands, Germany, and Switzerland (Harmonia Mundi 2901484/88, 5CD). He tends to be a bit heavy-handed, both with the controls and with his fingers. It's hard to hear the actual notes under all the overtones he enlists, though his recording is clear and powerful. Another complete set is in the making, played by **Ernst-Erich Sender** on Buxtehude's own Lübeck organ by the present organist at St. Mary's, who plays with the requisite energy, color, and joviality (Ornament 11446, 11450).

Piet Kee is a fine organist who mixes Buxtehude with Bach in one disc and Nicolaus Bruhns in another (Chandos 501, 539). He plays with conviction and taste. **Olivier Vernet** has recorded a complete edition, with fast tempos but lots of imagination on a fine modern French organ that sounds very appropriate to the period (Ligia 104025, 5CD). Among smaller collections, **Koopman**'s should be mentioned, though his tendency to use his Schnitger organ at full blast tends to hide the composer's details (Novalis 150048). His expressive powers are not to be denied, though his knowledge of baroque ornamentation leads him into some thickets under which the composer hides. **Hans Helmut Tillmans** offers the D minor Toccata and E minor Prelude & Fugue in an interesting disc of "Nordic Organ Music," played with clarity and vigor on Scandinavian organs (Koch Schwann 6726, with works by Grieg and Sibelius). MOORE

William Byrd *(1535/40?–1623)*

A prolific and inspired composer in many genres, Byrd was the link between the earlier generation of Taverner, Tye, and Tallis and the later Elizabethans and Jacobeans. He provided the last flowering of the Latin liturgy before it was pushed aside by the vernacular, to both of which he contributed. Besides his religious music, his compositions for viol consort, with and without vocal participation, provide a pinnacle that later composers could only hope to climb. His music for keyboard, primarily found in *My Lady Neville's Booke* and the *Fitzwilliam Virginal Booke,* is likewise on a high level.

Byrd's music for a cappella choir contains the main body of his work. Andrew Carwood and **The Cardinall's Musick** intend to record all of Byrd's works, and ASV, which has already brought out their recordings of Ludford and Fayrfax, is supporting this much larger project with commendable commitment. This group includes women rather than boys on the upper lines, against received tradition, but they sing with a minimum of vibrato and a variety of tone and volume that, together with the satisfyingly full ambience, meet our need for emotional involvement in this otherwise too-pure-sounding idiom. The series has begun with the early Latin church music, mostly unpublished in Byrd's lifetime, interspersed with the propers from various masses during the church year. The first three volumes (ASV 170, 178, 179) cover the uncollected works plus the graduals for Lady Masses in Advent, Nativity, and Epiphany, and the fourth gives us Byrd's contribution to the *Cantiones Sacrae* of 1575, a publication he shared with Tallis (ASV 197).

The performances in this series are on a high level, though less intensely ear-catching than some. The compromise of a small choir that assigns more than one voice to a part and the somewhat prominent women's voices may account for a certain lack of aural concentration in the sound. They are, however, fine readings and the first three volumes in particular contain many rare and fascinating items. The *Cantiones Sacrae* are also preferable to the alternative, excerpts from the publications of 1575, 1589, and 1591 by the **New College Choir, Oxford** (CRD 3492, 3420, 3439). These recordings vary in quality; only 3492 is outstanding, and they're sung by a rather large choir with concomitant gains in grandeur and losses in intimacy.

Chanticleer's collection includes the Masses *In Tempore Paschali* and *In Assumptione beatae Mariae Virginis,* as well as the motets *Regina Caeli, Ave Regina Caelorum,* and *Salve Regina* (Harmonia Mundi 7905182). This release demonstrates the virtues of small group performance even more effectively than The Cardinall's Musick. Perhaps it's the use of countertenors instead of female voices, but there is a greater purity of sound and a more effective balance in these readings. In choosing recordings, it should be remembered that neither the graduals nor the masses were intended to be performed separately. During the course of a mass, the Ordinary and the Proper are both employed, creating a greater variety of texture and style than is found in a grouping of the graduals alone, as here. It's a virtue of Chanticleer that they manage to make all these tiny fragments digestible, though it would have been even better if they had been banded separately for the convenience of the listener.

Recordings of the three Masses for three, four, and five voices are relatively thick on the ground, though they tend to come and go rapidly. A case in point is the **Christ Church Cathedral Choir, Oxford,** which recorded all three mixed with the propers for All Saints Day, Corpus Christi, and the Nativity (Nimbus 5237, 5287, 5302, all NA). These were traditional performances with children on top, giving them a pure sound that appeals to many, though it results in a kind of disembodied, not very grand approach that is anathema to an equal number of listeners. It depends on the character of the God you worship, I suspect. Does he suffer little children gladly, or does he prefer to have his name glorified on the most professional level? I suspect Byrd wouldn't have cared, but he isn't the one spending the money. Christ Church was excellent in its way, and their four-voice Mass is still represented, though without any graduals, in an odd disc called "Primal Fear" that includes a work with that title by James Newton Howard and Mozart's *Requiem* (BMG Milan 35716).

A collection including all three masses, also without interpolated graduals, comes from the **Tallis Scholars,** originally recorded in 1984, cool, polished readings bringing out the individual lines beautifully with only two voices to a part (♦Gimell 54945 or Philips 454895, 4CD). In **Alfred Deller**'s even earlier version, balances are a problem, since no one is allowed to upstage him, but there is much lovely phrasing in these intimate readings (Musique d'Abord 190211).

Another performance of the five-voice Mass, this time with the *Corpus Christi Graduale,* is sung by the **Winchester Cathedral Choir** (Hyperion 66837). This is a much larger choir, but they give a more controlled impression than Christ Church, though also more impersonal. They include the sequence *Lauda Sion Salvatorem* and *Pange Lingua* in Gregorian chant, as well as other works by Byrd. Hill's recording of all three masses was perhaps the best of the bunch to date (Argo 430164, NA). The **Hilliard Ensemble**'s recording is also NA, and that includes their more recent four-voice mass plus other Byrd motets and short works by other composers (ECM 1512, NA). They used only one voice per part and cultivated period pronunciation in beautifully sculpted readings.

The **Oxford Camerata** recorded only the four- and five-voice masses in lively, emotional performances, a bit less polished than the best (Naxos 550574). A version of the five-voice mass coupled with Palestrina's famous *Pope Marcellus Mass* is offered by the **Hägerston Motet Choir** (Nosag 6). This is a large choir, well-drilled but quite different from the small-scaled performances we've become accustomed to. Another recent version is from the Sarum Concert, an intimate, mixed-gender performance (ASV 6185). This group has also recorded motets from the Cantiones Sacrae worth hearing. The four-voice Mass is also available in an odd performance from Czechoslovakia, sung by the Duodena Cantitans in a down-to-earth reading for those who are curious about national styles (Supraphon 3328 or Mondo Musica 20121).

The Tallis Scholars may be heard in Byrd's Anglican Great Service, one of the few complete discs of his English church music (Gimell 54911). Another that mixes English and Latin church pieces is by the Cambridge Singers, presenting 18 pieces from various sources in a particularly clear and listenable set of performances articulated with beauty and care (Collegium 110, NA, with detailed notes).

The vocal music with viol consort accompaniment hasn't been collected by itself, but a good deal is available mixed in with music for keyboard and viols alone. I Fagiolini performs with sensitivity in an ongoing collection with fanciful titles; "The Early Byrd" and "The Caged Byrd" reflect a more or less chronological orientation (Chandos 578, 609). Besides consort songs, we have some of the Cantiones Sacrae and a few keyboard works played by Sophie Yates. I Fagiolini does the motets with single voices and attention to period pronunciation. A similar collection comes from Redbyrd and the Rose Consort with Timothy Roberts, harpsichord (Naxos 550604). This disc includes five songs with consort, seven pieces for consort alone, and two for multiple voices with viols, the latter two genres not in the I Fagiolini collection thus far. Unfortunately, no texts are given and Tessa Bonner, though accurate and musical, has a somewhat unsophisticated sound that doesn't quite seem to suit the style.

Another collection provides seven consort songs by Byrd mixed with consort pieces by Gibbons, sung by countertenor David Cordier with the Royal Consort (Globe 5159). Cordier shows a little strain in his low register but sings beautifully and the viols are excellent, smooth yet emotional. 14 songs are provided by Bowman and the Ricercar Consort, beautifully performed (Ricercar 206442, NA). A collection of eight consort songs mixed with as many consort pieces including five In Nomines is presented by countertenor Gerard Lesne with Ensemble Orlando Gibbons in serious and intense performances (Virgin 45264). Geraldine McGreevy, soprano, and Ian Partridge, tenor, sing 11 songs with Phantasm in fine style (Simax 1191).

Phantasm offers a disc containing 11 consort pieces as well as pieces by Richard Mico (Simax 1143). Byrd's major consort pieces are here, played with control and attention to balances, though they could be more sensitive to details. Capriccio Stravagante with Skip Sempe on virginal lives up to its name, orchestrating Byrd to include recorders and continuo instruments and playing the results with an intensity that will fascinate or irritate, depending on your predisposition (Astrée 8611). The largest consort collection and the most lively overall is by Fretwork, who play all the above and then some. Their collection began with various mixed-composer programs but was then collected on one disc (Virgin 45031, NA).

The keyboard music has finally been recorded complete by Davitt Moroney on six different instruments with 200 pages of notes, in one of the most important releases of the millennium (NHyperion 66551-7, 7CD). What more need be said? Sophie Yates's collection of nine pieces is played with expression, mixed with other composers (Chandos 574). I regret the disappearance of Hogwood's complete recording of My Lady Neville's Booke (Oiseau-Lyre 430484, 3CD, NA) and the eight pieces he did in his survey of the Fitzwilliam Virginal Book (Oiseau-Lyre 261, 2LP, NA), all played with his usual sensitivity. Joseph Payne's large Fitzwilliam collection is still, with its 11 selections, most of the longer works played rather heavily (Vox 5085, 2CD). And if period performances don't turn you on, there's always Glenn Gould, who plays five works with his inimitable intensity (Sony 52589).   MOORE

John Cage (1912–1992)

My first composition teacher once told me a story about John Cage. He had come to the college to perform with his ensemble, and they presented a concert in which everything was highly amplified, to the point of pain. Cage sat at a writing desk and scribbled instructions to his musicians as a part of the performance. Even his pencil was amplified, and he frequently tossed coins to determine various musical procedures for his comrades. He would toss them onto a copper plate next to his desk, also amplified; the sound of those coins hitting the plate was earsplitting, and after a few times people automatically covered their ears. By the end of the two-hour performance, only a few listeners remained. One was a young undergraduate whose musical sensibilities had been severely offended and who had stayed only to confront Cage at the concert's conclusion. "You — you mean you call that MUSIC?" she sputtered when she finally cornered the offender. Cage smiled and replied gently, "Well, you *heard* it, didn't you?"

This was Cage's fundamental tenet: that all sound was potentially music. For many, he was a fraud and a charlatan, for others a genius. His notoriety has obscured the fact that he was a dedicated composer who worked long hours on his music. Although after 1951 all his pieces were based on chance procedures, all were meticulously realized; there's nothing slipshod or imprecise about them. A glance at his scores reveals an elegance and clarity that are astonishing. In fact, his decision to use only chance procedures to create music probably made his compositional life more demanding, not less. Those who think "anything goes" in his work have misunderstood his intentions completely. Even when players are given choices, it's within very clear parameters.

Cage's emerging reputation as a diabolical imp was sealed at the premier of his most famous piece, *4'33*. Here a pianist is required to sit at the piano for four minutes, 33 seconds, and play nothing. Whatever your feelings about this (mine are mixed), the fact is that music hasn't been the same since. This work of silence has even had several "recordings," although I have chosen not to discuss them here. Personally, I find that my own performances of this work are as good as any I could buy. Most listeners are likely to feel the same.

Cage's music remains a source of controversy, and that's not likely to change for some time. What may come as a surprise to some listeners who are more familiar with his reputation than with his repertoire is that his body of work is remarkably deep and varied. Range, complexity, humor, and real beauty are in it. A number of pieces have attained the status of classics, and the number of recordings available attests to the fact that musicians *want* to play his music. For me, this is a telling point, whatever controversies may exist. Two labels, Mode and Wergo, are recording extensive surveys of his works. Mode has already released 21 volumes, only a portion of which are discussed here, and much remains unrecorded.

Reviewing available recordings of Cage's music presents a special problem: There really can be no "definitive" version of anything. He himself didn't listen to recorded versions of his works, though he often supervised recording sessions. (This was an inconsistency he cheerfully acknowledged.) Many pieces can sound completely different depending on the performer's realization, and many can be performed simultaneously with others, creating an unduplicated experience each time they are rendered. I have chosen to comment on the recordings and performances I find most interesting and to focus on those works that have been most meaningful in my listening life.

ORCHESTRAL MUSIC AND CONCERTOS

Little of Cage's orchestral music is currently available. He had great difficulty getting orchestral players (who tend to be highly conservative) to take his pieces seriously. Early performance efforts were marked by slovenly playing and often were intentionally sabotaged by disgruntled musicians. This has begun to change, and the Chicago Symphony's recording of *Atlas Eclipticalis* under **Levine** is faithfully rendered (DG 431698, with works by Babbitt, Carter, and Schuller). This piece is rather typical of Cage's music for larger forces after 1951, which tends to be nondramatic in essence and arrhythmic in aspect, creating a liberating sense of time suspended if you can enter into its spirit, or annoyance if you can't.

Seventy-Four is a late work that can be heard in two realizations with the American Composers Orchestra under **Dennis Russell Davies** (♦ECM 465140). They demonstrate that while the surface material may vary from performance to performance, the affect of the piece is consistent. This excellent disc also includes a fine reading of the 1947 ballet *The Seasons, Concerto for Prepared Piano,* and *Suite for Toy Piano* in two versions: the original, played by Margaret Leng Tan, and an orchestration by Cage's colleague, Lou Harrison. The disc presents the broadest possible view of Cage's orchestral music.

"Orchestral Works 1" presents three interesting and varied works: *101* for large orchestra, *Apartment House 1776* for four vocalists and chamber orchestra, and *Ryoanji* for four soloists with orchestra, in performances by various ensembles from the **New England Conservatory** (Mode 41). I like *Ryoanji* best; with its microtonal glissandos and asymmetrical throbbing repetitions, it's highly evocative of the famed Japanese rock garden it's named after. *Apartment House 1776* is of great interest too and has surprising emotional resonance. Cage uses musical materials from the time of the American Revolution to create a striking tapestry.

"Orchestral Works 2" presents *Etcetera* and *Etcetera 2/4 Orchestra;* although their titles are similar, their affects are not (Mode 86). Composed when Cage lived in Stony Point, New York, *Etcetera* evokes the rural countryside. A tape made outside Cage's home plays along with the ensemble, gently mixing sounds of birds and wind with the musicians. The effect is generally restful. *Etcetera 2/4 Orchestra* is a more urban-sounding work, again using a tape, this time made in the composer's New York apartment.

"The Piano Concertos" offers three pieces for piano and orchestra, with **Stephen Drury** as soloist in *Concerto for Prepared Piano and Orchestra* and *Fourteen* and **David Tudor** playing *Concert for Piano and Orchestra,* which he premiered in 1958 (Mode 57). At that performance, the work evoked a very hostile reaction; heard here, it sounds almost tame. Tudor's musicianship is undiminished in this last recording he made just before his death, and Ensemble Modern provides exceptionally colorful backup. The other two pieces are accompanied by the Callithumpian Consort of New England Conservatory.

Concerto for Prepared Piano and Orchestra is emblematic of Cage's interest in Eastern modes of thought. The piano part begins in a romantic, expressive fashion, dramatically contrasted with the orchestral accompaniment, which is more detached in manner. By the final movement, the piano has shed its conventional expressivity and melded with the Zenlike state of the accompaniment. *Fourteen* utilizes a "bowed piano," and the eerie sustained sounds it produces seem to emerge from nowhere, blending seamlessly with the generally soft, sustained pitches of the ensemble.

CHAMBER MUSIC

Cage had happier experiences working with small groups of musicians and soloists, and he composed prolifically for all manner of chamber combinations. Early in his career he wrote extensively for percussion ensembles and created a substantial body of literature in that genre alone. Even if his career had ended prior to his chance-derived music, he would still be an important composer, due in part to his rhythmic innovations. One piece that illustrates this well is *16 Dances,* written for his partner, Merce Cunningham. The various dances and interludes illustrate the Hindu "permanent emotions" (anger, sorrow, the heroic, etc.) and are spare, delicate evocations of those affects, using piano, percussion, winds, and strings. **Ensemble Modern**'s recording captures its spirit perfectly (BMG 61574).

A substantial disc by **Quatuor Helios** presents Cage's major percussion works from the late '30s and early '40s (Wergo 6203). Most impressive are the three *Constructions* for various percussion combinations; *Amores,* for prepared piano and percussion; and the intriguing *Double Music,* cowritten with Lou Harrison. These works sound as fresh and innovative today as they did when they were first performed. This set should have great appeal, even to those who are wary of Cage's later, indeterminate work.

Cage wrote a set of virtuoso studies for solo violin in consultation with **Paul Zukofsky,** who premiered and recorded the first eight (Book 1) of the *Freeman Etudes* (CP² 103). These pieces were composed following the same star maps that were used to realize *Etudes Australes* for piano. They are intriguing, highly virtuosic studies of violinistic possibility. Zukofsky fills out this fine disc of solo music with *Chorals,* a harrowing study of microtonal intervals, and *Cheap Imitation,* an arrangement of Cage's piano work of the same name. This work is lovely, suffused with a gentle lyricism. Zukofsky plays with meticulous precision, and his violin is recorded in a closeup audio-verité acoustic. Cage completed the entire set of *Freeman Etudes* upon hearing **Irvine Arditti** play the early ones, and Books 1 to 4 are presented in two discs (Mode 32 and 37). The composer indicates that the pieces are to be played "as fast as possible," and Arditti plays some of them in half the time of Zukofsky. This doesn't diminish Zukofsky's performance in any way; his phrasing is more musical, but for sheer brilliance and completeness, Arditti is the way to go.

The four *Etudes Boréales* for solo cello are similar to the *Freeman Etudes.* These and other works for cello are scrupulously performed by **Frances-Marie Uitti** in a set that includes Cage's important *Lecture on Nothing* (♦Etcetera 2016, 2CD). The *Etudes* display Uitti's amazing virtuosity; *A Dip in the Lake* gives us Cage's whimsical side in concentrated form; and the other pieces, like *26'1.1499 for String Player,* complete a good cross section of his chance-derived activities.

Cage wrote a number of substantial works for string quartet, and the **Arditti Quartet** has recorded them all. In "The Complete String Quartets" Vol. 1 they present *Music for Four* and *Thirty Pieces for String Quartet,* both written in the '80s (Mode 17). In Vol. 2 they perform *String Quartet in Four Parts* from 1950 and *Four,* written late in Cage's career (Mode 27). All are played with the Arditti's customary seriousness of intent, and you scarcely realize these are live recordings until the applause at the end. In "The Number Pieces 2," the Arditti teams up with trombonist **Monique Buzzarté** to perform *Five³* for trombone and string quartet (Mode 75). This extended essay in soft microtonal sonorities is punctuated by extensive silences and is utterly without pulse of any kind.

Listeners who want a more varied presentation of Cage's chamber music should consider the collection by **Ensemble Avantgarde** and the **Leipzig String Quartet** (MD+G 613 0701). This well-filled disc offers *Music for Eight,* two different realizations of *Five,* the wacky *Aria* (enthusiastically rendered by Salome Kammer), and a wonderful reading of *String Quartet in Four Parts.* All are beautifully played, and the recording is exceptionally sumptuous.

Toward the end of his life, Cage began writing music with an increasingly harmonic quality, creating beautiful sonorities that occur nowhere else. The so-called "number pieces" display this, and none more than his final one, *Thirteen,* completed just before his death. **Ensemble 13,** for whom it was written, offers two separate versions of the half-hour work (CPO 999 227). It's a study in sustained soft pitches, with ever-shifting color combinations, and the effect is highly meditative.

Violinist **Christina Fong** has also taken up the challenges of the number pieces and has recorded two discs of premiere performances. Her first offers three realizations of *One[6]* and one of *One[10.]* Here the notion of austerity is stretched to its absolute limit; these works consist of long, sustained pitches that completely suspend any sense of time. This disc sets a new standard for the concept of "minimalism" and is important in the sea of recent Cage releases. In the second ("OgreOgress"), she is joined by percussionist Glenn Freeman and cellist Karen Krummel. Freeman offers percussion ensemble realizations of *Three[6]* and *Six;* Fong performs *Twenty-Six* by herself; and Fong and Krummel team up for *Twenty-Three.* All these performances use overdubbing techniques and are not played in real time. The pieces are sonically richer than those on the solo violin disc and are quite ethereal, especially the two string works, which sound like electronic music. They are quite dissonant initially, but after a few moments they generate a palpable serenity.

PIANO MUSIC

The piano is central to Cage's works. It was the instrument he played all his life, and he wrote prodigiously for it throughout his career. In 1940 he also discovered the coloristic possibilities of inserting various materials into the strings, thus inventing the "prepared piano," an instrument capable of imitating a gamelan or percussion ensemble. He wrote many pieces for this modified instrument, and the large cycle entitled *Sonatas and Interludes for Prepared Piano* is a masterpiece. It has been recorded frequently and is one of his most important compositions, with a cool, detached elegance that is unique in Western music.

There are many fine recordings, but my favorite is by **Philipp Vandré,** using a Steinway "O" piano, the model Cage used to compose and develop the piece (Mode 50). The resulting sounds are remarkably rich and reveal a harmonic component in the music that isn't apparent in other versions. The piano is beautifully recorded and Vandré's playing is superb. Other versions worth hearing include **Yuji Takahashi**'s classic recording, my benchmark for this work for many years (Denon 7673). In **Aleck Karis**'s recording, though not played on the "O," he has prepared the piano well, using hardware available at the time Cage wrote this piece. Karis's realization is beautifully recorded, with a richer set of overtones and more sustained sound than most (Bridge 9081 A/B, 2CD). This release also contains a bonus disc of Cage reading his essay *Composition in Retrospect.*

Boris Berman's performance is highly regarded, and has the strong advantage of budget price; if you wish to sample the work economically, this is an ideal choice (Naxos 559042). Another popular version is by **Joshua Pierce** (Wergo 60156). **Maro Ajemian**'s recording from the '50s was the first ever made (she premiered the work in 1949) and has held

up well over the years (CRI 700). Cage himself instructed other pianists to listen to it as a reference when preparing their pianos. Although the recording quality is not on a par with more recent versions, for me the distant mono sound actually enhances the haunting atmosphere evoked by the piece.

Three major surveys of Cage's piano music are currently under way, and each is notable in different ways. Completists will be delighted by **Steffen Schleiermacher**'s series, which has the advantage of collecting large chunks of Cage's piano music into cohesive sets. Vol. 1, "The Prepared Piano," is a comprehensive survey of all the major works for prepared piano from 1940 to 1952, including *Sonatas and Interludes* (MD+G 613 0781, 3CD). Vol. 2 includes *Music for Piano 1-85* and *Electronic Music for Piano* (MD+G 613 0784 2CD), and Vol. 3 contains the pivotal 1951 composition *Music of Changes,* the first piece Cage wrote using the I Ching oracle to determine all aspects of the music (MD+G 613 0786). Schleiermacher's performances are meticulous, and the sound quality is superb, with his pianos beautifully recorded in a lush, warm acoustic.

Joshua Pierce offers several well-received discs, including "Works for Piano and Prepared Piano" Vols. I–III (Wergo 60151, 60157, and 6158). This series is notable for its comprehensive approach; Pierce includes pieces that feature voice or percussion as well as solo works. **Herbert Henck** has also recorded a faithfully rendered account of *Music of Changes* as part of this important series (Wergo 60099).

Stephen Drury has recorded selections from all points in Cage's career, and his readings are models of clarity and elegance. He has recorded few pieces for prepared piano, so far opting to focus on works for the "unprepared" instrument. "The Piano Works I" presents three of the "number pieces" that occupied much of Cage's attention for the last few years of his life and one earlier piece (Mode 47). *One* and *One[5]* are both solo works whose main features are their extensive silences and sustained sonorities. *Music for Two* utilizes a "bowed" piano sound, produced by rosined fishing line. *Music Walk* is the earliest piece in this collection, written in 1958, "for one or more pianists, at a single piano, using also radio and/or recordings." Drury's overdubbed realization of this is quite restrained, with little overlap of events. I find *One* and *One[5]* to be the most satisfying works here.

"The Piano Works 3" shows that although Cage's means of composing changed over the years, the resulting music was surprisingly consistent (Mode 63). This disc presents three important works: *The Seasons, Cheap Imitation,* and *ASLSP.* The first two were written to accompany choreography by Merce Cunningham, Cage's long-time partner and collaborator. *ASLSP* was written as a jury piece for a piano competition. *The Seasons* (1947) displays Cage's rhythmic innovations, while *Cheap Imitation* (1969) was composed as a substitute for Satie's ballet *Socrate.* Drury has also recorded "In a Landscape," a mixed recital that presents a survey of earlier pieces — some for prepared piano, some for the conventional instrument — and includes *Suite for Toy Piano* (Catalyst 61980).

Two highly appealing recitals come from **Margaret Leng Tan,** and both are strongly recommended. *The Perilous Night* and *Four Walls* are two works from 1944 (New Albion 37). The former is played on prepared piano, the latter is written for the conventional instrument with a single vocal interlude, here sung by Joan La Barbara. In contrast to many of Cage's works that are marked by emotional detachment, these pieces are characterized by an unusual intensity of feeling. Written at a time when Cage was becoming increasingly unhappy in his marriage, the pieces convey a stark loneliness that is palpable throughout the disc. Tan plays both works beautifully.

"Daughters of the Lonesome Isle" offers six pieces written from 1940 (*Bacchanale*, Cage's first work for prepared piano) to 1953 (*Music for Piano #2*, which was chance-derived) (New Albion 70). Also included are the exquisite Satie-influenced *In a Landscape*, *Suite for Toy Piano*, *In the Name of the Holocaust* (in which the pianist plays directly on the strings), and *The Seasons*. Tan's version of *The Seasons* is more extroverted than Drury's; I prefer his approach and find his playing cleaner, but many may prefer Tan's. She is one of the most persuasive exponents of Cage's music, and this is an exceptionally fine collection.

The acclaimed piano duo **Double Edge** has released a disc with examples from early and late in Cage's career (CRI 732). *Two²* for two pianos was written specifically for this pair of musicians. Typical of the late "number pieces," it has a fluid serenity throughout its span. *Experiences* is an enigmatic vignette, striking in spite of its brevity. *Three Dances for Two Prepared Pianos* is a substantial work that shows Cage at his most rhythmically energetic.

Etudes Australes is Cage's third and largest cycle of works for piano. Composed for virtuoso **Grete Sultan,** the four books of 32 etudes are among his most substantial compositions. Realized using star maps of the Australian sky, this is a major milestone in the Cage oeuvre. Sultan herself has recorded the entire cycle (Wergo 6152, 3CD). In this piece, the notes are fixed in a time-proportionate manner, but pedaling and dynamic indications are left to the musician to determine. The result is an effervescent, often jazzy-sounding stream of piano consciousness.

Anthony de Mare offers an interesting disc combining piano and vocal works by Cage and Meredith Monk (Koch 7104). His selection of piano works leans toward earlier pieces, with a balance between those for standard and prepared piano. The two composers' works complement one another nicely, and de Mare is an excellent pianist, but in the Cage pieces especially, one wishes for a stronger vocalist. His *Nowth Upon Nacht* pales beside La Barbara's recording.

CHORAL AND VOCAL MUSIC

Cage wrote enthusiastically and often for the voice throughout his career. He even took singing lessons and performed some pieces himself. Some of his vocal works are highly theatrical, such as the often-performed *Aria*, while others are much more reflective. I myself am drawn to the latter works, but I find many interesting moments throughout his vocal output. "The Choral Works 1" offers a wide selection of styles masterfully performed by the elite Danish ensemble Vocal Group Ars Nova, under the direction of **Támas Vetö** (Mode 71). This outstanding disc has many exquisite moments; chief among them for me is the 25-minute *Hymns and Variations*, a refraction of two hymns by William Billings through Cage's chance procedures. The piece is absolutely gorgeous. Two contrasting versions of *Four²* are presented, showing how separate realizations of a piece can yield different sonorities but be consistent in affect. Both versions show the consummate control of this group in singing sustained pitches. *Four Solos* is a more theatrical work, full of intriguing effects and a circuslike atmosphere.

Paul Hillier and his Theater of Voices have recorded "Litany for the Whale," a stunning disc of vocal pieces (Harmonia Mundi 907187). This disc's title work is a beautiful duo for two equal voices (here male) who sing antiphonally in a manner reminiscent of Gregorian chant. Hillier also presents more theatrical pieces like *Aria* and *Aria No. 2*, as well as the classic *Wonderful Widow of Eighteen Springs* and the lovely *Experiences No. 2*, a setting for solo voice of verses by e.e. cummings. This is an excellent sampling of all Cage's facets as a vocal composer.

Joan La Barbara's "Singing Through" is a similar collection of works for solo voice (New Albion 035). She sings with her well-known commitment and flexibility and presents a selection of pieces written between 1942 and 1984, complemented with three cabaret songs by Satie that underscore the deep affinity Cage felt for the French composer. Not to be missed is her rendering of *Nowth Upon Nacht,* written in memory of singer Cathy Berberian. Here Cage abandons his customary detachment and gives a fleeting portrait of searing grief.

THEATER AND MULTIMEDIA MUSIC

Cage enjoyed creating and in fact was notorious for what he called a "musicircus." He composed a work of that title in 1967 that he described as "an environmental extravaganza," consisting of simultaneous performances of rock, jazz, electronic, piano, and vocal music. His most famous piece of this type is *HPSCHD,* composed with the aid of computer wizard Lejaren Hiller. This was an enormous montage of audio and visual events and features seven harpsichordists playing computer-realized excerpts of Mozart, Beethoven, and others, along with 51 tapes played through 51 amplifiers, combined with colored lights, slides, and film. Nonesuch released an LP of the piece (NA) that scarcely did it justice, according to those who experienced it live. It was great fun and helped make Cage a popular fixture on college campuses. He continued to create works of this kind throughout his career, and while these pieces can often create a sensory overload, they can also become a glorious confluence of simultaneities that thrill and delight the ear.

One such work is *Roaratorio: An Irish Circus on Finnegan's Wake for 8 Irish Musicians,* an extended exploration of *Finnegan's Wake,* with Irish musicians and a 62-track tape that collects sounds from various locations in Dublin described in Joyce's book (Mode 28/29, 2CD, or Wergo 6303). This is a highly successful piece that is poignantly evocative of Ireland throughout its length and enjoyed great popularity upon its release.

"The Europeans have been sending us their operas for years, and now I'm sending them back," said Cage in explaining his massive *Europeras* project. These works are large-scale theater pieces that refract and splinter familiar operatic repertoire from the 19th century into surreal collages, where arias or events from different operas by different composers occur simultaneously. The results are surprisingly evocative, perhaps because of all the associations the operatic literature brings to us. *Europeras 3* and *4* contrast greatly in their texture and mood (Mode 38/39, 2CD). *Europera 3* is a dense, swirling stew of operatic lunacy; the effect is overwhelming, often comical. *Europera 4* is much different in mood, leaner in texture, more subdued, suffused with a constant melancholy. *Europera 5* features the late pianist Ivar Mikhashoff, who was to have been involved in all the *Europera* recordings (Mode 36). Like any conventional opera, these pieces lose the element of spectacle when heard in recordings, but a great deal remains, especially in the lovely *Europera 3.*

SPOKEN PIECES

Cage was a prolific and engaging writer, and some of his more interesting efforts have been text pieces. "John Cage reads his Diary: How to improve the world (You will only make matters worse)" is a hefty set for the die-hard Cage fan, presenting him reading lengthy excerpts from his diary (Wergo 6231, 8CD). Listening to his lilting voice can be an enjoyable experience, but eight CDs is a bit much, even for me. My favorite recording of this type is the Cage/Tudor collaboration *Indeterminacy* (Smithsonian 40804/5, 2CD). Cage was famous for his abilities as a storyteller, and here he reads 90 stories in 90 minutes. Each story lasts one minute on average; hence the short ones are read rather slowly, while the longer ones must be read quite quickly. Tudor supplies pianistic and electronic accompaniments to Cage's reading; he did them in a separate room, out of hearing from what Cage was reading, but it's uncanny how well the two entities mesh. This is one of my favorite Cage recordings; my children used to listen to it at bedtime. The stories are charming: Zen parables, stories about gathering mushrooms, and musical anecdotes.

COMPILATIONS

One of the most important documents issued in Cage's career was "The 25-Year Retrospective Concert," originally released on LP in the late '50s by producer George Avakian in a private issue (Wergo 6247, 3CD). The set is important because it was the first substantial recorded survey that allowed listeners and critics to evaluate a substantial portion of Cage's work. It's fascinating to hear the recording of *Concert for Piano and Orchestra,* in which the audience grows increasingly hostile as the work proceeds. The original LP set is also valuable for the many beautiful score excerpts it includes; Wergo's reissue is deficient in this respect.

"A Chance Operation: The John Cage Tribute" is a loving and respectful tribute to Cage's life and work following his death in 1992 (Koch 7238, 2CD). The set presents pieces offered in tribute and some of Cage's own work, from a diverse range of classical, pop, and avant-garde artists. Many, like Earle Brown, David Tudor, and Jackson MacLow, were early acquaintances and collaborators. Others are admirers of a later generation, like Laurie Anderson, the Kronos Quartet, and Ryuichi Sakamoto. I find the contributions a bit uneven, but there is much to enjoy. The discs are divided into over 80 separate tracks so the listener can take advantage of the "random" function on their CD player and create a unique listening experience each time. I tried that, but prefer to listen to the tracks in sequence. McINTIRE

Joseph Canteloube *(1879–1957)*

Canteloube was a formidable musician: a collector and anthologist of French folk songs, a biographer of Vincent d'Indy, and a fairly prolific composer. His list of works, mostly vocal, includes two operas, but he will always be known for his *Songs of the Auvergne* (1923–30), arrangements for voice and orchestra of folk songs from the region of France where he was born. These richly scored and immensely appealing songs belong in that subset of pieces that are almost never performed in concerts but thrive on recordings; many a soprano has lent her golden tones to a disc full of them.

Two classic renditions from the '60s are by the delectably refined **de los Angeles** (♦EMI 63178) and the earthier **Natania Davrath** (♦Vanguard 38/39, 2 CD). Divas who have more recently recorded the entire set are **Te Kanawa** (London 44995) and **Upshaw** (Erato 96559, 17577). Excellent versions by **Augér** (Virgin) and **Von Stade** (Sony) are NA but worth seeking out. For sheer lusciousness, the combination of **Moffo** and Stokowski in seven of the best-known songs is hard to beat, especially when soprano and conductor offer equally high-calorie versions of Villa-Lobos's *Bachianas Brasilieras 5* and Rachmaninoff's *Vocalise* (♦RCA 7831). RAYMOND

Giacomo Carissimi *(1605–1674)*

Carissimi was a happy and congenial priest with a great sense of humor who spent most of his life at the Collegio Germanico (a Jesuit institution that stressed the teaching mission of the order) in Rome. He was also an important composer, but a thoughtful and humble man who turned down many opportunities for advancement to stay loyal to his calling. He studied at the cathedral of Tivoli, then off to Assisi and Rome, where he became *maestro di capella* at the Collegio at age 24. He organized the

music for the church, oversaw the students' education, wrote a large body of mostly sacred music, and lived quietly and well, often able to give loans to parishioners and others.

Many knew of his work and came to study: Alessandro Scarlatti and other Italians heard his oratorios and absorbed them as influences, and Germans brought the music of this High Church Jesuit back to Reformation Germany. A later German who wound up in England was directly influenced by the oratorios that found their way there: The final chorus for Carissimi's *Jephthe* is lifted entire for the chorus "Hear, Jacob's God" in Handel's *Samson.* Marc-Antoine Charpentier studied with Carissimi for nearly three years in the 1650s and brought back to France both the Italian style and the Jesuit belief that religious feeling and knowledge can be both broadened and deepened in music.

Carissimi was the last of the great composers who gave us a large body of oratorios in Latin, and they are among the finest works of that (or any other) age. Thus we have scores of cantatas (from a man whom early scholars thought created the form; he actually inherited it from fellow Roman Luigi Rossi), some 15 oratorios, some 15 publications of motets, and many, many works attributed to him as *opera dubia*. Yet, as is so often the case, the recording history has been spotty. The oratorio *Jephthe* has had the strongest presence on disc, going back to an early Archiv recording from the '50s with the Norddeutscher Singkreis and on to a beautiful disc from the '70s with **Corboz** and the Gulbenkian Foundation (Erato LP 70688, NA but worth seeking out). The three motets that filled out this recording also hinted at the majesty of Carissimi's ability in that sacred form as well.

In the '60s, *Baltassar* was attempted by the obscure **Münster Kirchenmusikschule** (Turnabout LP). In the early '70s, **Linde** led a successful series of performances with the Basel Schola Cantorum of the mysterious *Historia divitis* (EMI LP 063-30.121; also NA but a worthy acquisition). This work gives full rein to Carissimi's evolutionary practices in the oratorio form, with rhetorical flourishes and extended recitative lines. The English weighed in with a cantata program prepared by **Hogwood** in his early days (Oiseau-Lyre LP 547, NA), and an excellent disc from 1984 offers a program of cantatas and arias by Carissimi and his contemporaries with the London Early Music Group and an all-star cast that puts this music into context brilliantly (♦"17th Century Bel Canto," Hyperion 66153, in and out of print). Also in the early '80s, we had a window into the breadth of Carissimi's interests with the charming Christmas cantata "Salve puellule" matched by an operatic tribute to one of the Counter-Reformation's secular saints, "Il lamento di Maria Stuarda" (Spectrum LP 174, NA).

This latter work, at least, is currently available; it's one of the few pieces offered in reliable interpretations, as part of the "Lamenti Barocchi" series with **Vartolo** and the Capella Musicale of San Petronio (Naxos 553320, in an interesting program that includes Monteverdi, Antonio Cesti, and Barbara Strozzi). The performances of the Cantus Cölln under **Jünghanel** are more than reliable. With the disassociation between Deutsche Harmonia Mundi and BMG, we can't be sure of finding either his *Jephthe* (♦DHM/BMG 77322) or the excerpt "Plorate fili Israel" (RCA 63450). **Fasolis** has been recording with the choir of the Italian Swiss Radio in Lugano, specializing in Baroque repertoire. He's joined by the instrumental ensemble Sonatori de la Gioiosa Marca for a fine performance of *Historia divitis*, matched with a far more common Old Testament–inspired oratorio, *Jonas*, and a reading of "Beatus vir" that again makes us long for more motet recordings (♦Arts 47513).

Some hard-to-find Italian labels have given us offerings as well. Milan's **Complesso Barocco** recorded *Historia divina*, calling it by its subtitle, "Dives malus" (Rivo Alto 8910), and Verona's **Institutioni Harmoniche** gives us a window into the so-called "Roman Colossal Baroque" style with a so-so reading of the cantata "Sciolto havean dall'alte sponde" and the Mass he based on his own work (Stradivarius 33344). This brings us to **Flavio Colusso,** a composer, conductor, entrepreneur, and record producer who loves Carissimi's music. With his Ensemble Seicento-Novecento, he gives us on his own Musicaimmage label every oratorio (*Cain, Lucifer, Davidis et Jonathae,* etc.), and a generous sampling of the motets. It's the one absolute for lovers of Carissimi, especially since it would encourage Signor Colusso in his plan to record all the other motets as well. However, he currently has no American distributor, and copies on these shores are rare (♦Musicaimmage 10020, 9CD). We can hope efforts like this will help bring about a real rediscovery of our modest Roman Jesuit.   DAVIS

Elliott Carter (b. 1908)

Carter's music throughout his life has dealt with the close juxtaposition of contradictory experiences. In his early music this was usually represented by spiky rhythms and rapid changes of pace within the quartal harmony favored by most American composers in the '30s and '40s. With the 1948 Cello Sonata, however, he moved to a more rarefied style, employing less tonal harmony and relating the elements in larger works by his self-styled "metric modulation," in which a basic metronome pulse stays constant through large spans of different note values that are sometimes quite complicated for the performer to follow. Then he experimented with pulling apart instrumental groups, redefining spatial placement and relationships on a concert stage, most obviously in String Quartets 2 and 3, but also in the way orchestral groups were related. For instance, the Piano Concerto included a chamber group mediating between solo piano and the main orchestra.

With his music of the '80s, Carter began to bring the groups back together spatially, confident that his style of relating certain intervals to certain groups or players was now sufficient to reflect their individuality. His most recent works show a further freedom, in which the conflict of individuality and the mass is shown in concertos where the material is differentiated by interval and the soloist is free to be expressive. His latest works are more lyrical and beautiful, while still clearly expressing his philosophy of opposites.

ORCHESTRAL MUSIC

Carter's penchant for juxtaposing different elements shows up from the start, particularly in his orchestral music, in a kind of jockeying for position with musicians wrestling on all sides. **Paul Dunkel** and the American Composers Orchestra made an LP of early Carter pieces that has now been broken up between two CDs. The earliest was the ballet suite from *Pocahontas,* detailing a dark moment in Indian-American relations with considerable drama (CRI 610). Then came Symphony 1 (1942), a less intense but warmly imaginative example of Americana (CRI 552). Finally, the triumphant and spiky 1944 *Holiday Overture* celebrated the liberation of Paris in a blaze of cross-rhythms in organized chaos (CRI 610). Dunkel's readings tend to be small scaled; I recall Mitropoulos and the New York Philharmonic lighting a considerably hotter fire with the Overture, but these are neat, clear, and lively readings of fascinating music. A suite from the ballet score for *The Minotaur* (1946) was recorded by **Howard Hanson** in 1956 (Mercury LP). The entire ballet recorded by **Schwarz** and the New York Chamber Symphony is only 33 minutes long, a relatively mainstream score of considerable strength (Nonesuch 79248).

Variations for Orchestra (1954–55) is a colorful and sensitive piece that requires recorded clarity and conductorial sensitivity to masses and soloists. A concert recording by **Michael Gielen** with the Cincinnati Symphony shows the sensitivity and, apart from audience noise, the clarity as well (New World 347). It replaces **James Levine**'s lushly recorded Chicago version, which is hard to get far enough away from to hear the details and overwhelming to the point of annoyance (DG 431698, NA).

Bernstein's recording of *Concerto for Orchestra* (1969) with the New York Philharmonic was not an unqualified success; it's messy and muddy, and recorded dryly as well (Sony 60203). There have been two more listenable versions, by **Gielen** and the SWF Symphony (Arte Nova 27773, NA) and **Oliver Knussen** and the London Sinfonietta (Virgin 7592712, NA), both in excellent sound, although Gielen's is somewhat more impressive sonically.

Carter was an admirer of Hart Crane, whose rather disturbing vision of the Brooklyn Bridge inspired *Symphony of Three Orchestras* (1976–77). This work allows the listener more breathing and imaging space than most of his music of the '60s, and it's beautifully set before us by **Boulez** and the New York Philharmonic (Sony 68334).

Three Occasions (1986–89) is a short collection of appealing pieces written for different occasions. **Gielen** plays them spaciously, with attention to both detail and atmosphere (Arte Nova 27773, NA). **Knussen** brings them closer to the listener, using a somewhat smaller string section (Virgin 7592712, NA).

Partita (1993) was recorded by its commissioner, the Chicago Symphony under **Barenboim** (Teldec 99596, NA), only to be upstaged by the composer, who made it the first movement of a three-movement, 40-minute *Symphonia: sum fluxae pretium spei* (1993–96), which was thereupon recorded by **Knussen** and the London Sinfonietta (DG 459660). To the exciting 16-minute movement recorded in rich sound by Barenboim, Carter added a long and beautiful slow movement and a brilliant finale that stretch Knussen's group to their sonic limits. I'd like a larger orchestra for this piece, but they play it well.

CONCERTOS

Carter began composing concertos rather late. His first, a Double Concerto for harpsichord, piano, and two chamber orchestras (1961), is an example of his spatial music, combining two keyboards with very different volume potential backed up by two differently instrumented groups, both with percussionists who mediate between the groups. The recording by **Paul Jacobs** and **Gilbert Kalish** with Arthur Weisberg and the Contemporary Chamber Players is excellent, carefully balanced and played with conviction (Nonesuch 79183).

The Piano Concerto followed in 1964–65. It adds a small group of semisoloists to mediate between the soloist and orchestra. The old concert recording by **Jacob Lateiner** and the Boston Symphony sounded like a cat fight and was recorded dryly (RCA). Another concert performance by **Ursula Oppens** gives a much better idea of the piece with Gielen and the Cincinnati Symphony (New World 347). I like it better than the studio recording they both did with the SWF Symphony in 1992, which is in better sound but isn't as stirring (Arte Nova 27773, NA).

Penthode (1984–85) for five groups of four instruments would be considered chamber music if it didn't involve so many players. Written for **Boulez**'s Ensemble InterContemporain, it's played with his customary smooth clarity (Erato 45364, NA).

The Oboe Concerto (1986–87) began a considerable series of solo concertos marked by the increasing lyricism of Carter's latest music. He isn't changing styles to any degree, but the space given to the soloist has a freer, less despotically controlled feeling; he's more able to sing, to indulge in rubato, perhaps. At any rate, this concerto makes pleasant listening as played by **Heinz Holliger** (Erato 45364, NA).

The Violin Concerto (1990) is another essay in lyricism with the soloist to the fore throughout most of its 26-minute span. **Ole Böhn** plays it with polish, and his somewhat reticent tone lets us hear Carter's subtle orchestral touches (Virgin 7592712, NA).

The Clarinet Concerto (1996) is a beautifully scored and very atmospheric piece, played with excellent control and personality by **Michael Collins** (DG 459660). Carter continues his exploration of breadth of phrase and the kind of floating harmonies and cloudlike orchestration I've noticed in his later work, particularly since Symphony for Three Orchestras. This and all the later concertos are full of music of broad appeal without altering one whit the composer's basic philosophy of juxtaposing life's elements.

CHAMBER MUSIC

The first piece by Carter to make official use of his technique of "metric modulation" was the 1948 Cello Sonata. It's still a challenging work in which bravura and passion alternate with jazzy and virtuoso passages. The classic performance is by **Bernard Greenhouse** and Anthony Makas, whose well-played but somewhat matter-of-fact mono reading is available (Phoenix 141). A great contrast to that rather dry recording is one by **Joel Krosnick** and Paul Jacobs in remarkably spacious sound; this is Carter for those who generally find him too in-your-face (Nonesuch 79183). Krosnick recorded it again with Kalish in a closer ambience, giving the instrumental sound more prominence (Arabesque 6682). Both performances are outstanding, yet quite different in effect.

Some strain is felt in **Barbara Haffner** and Easley Blackwood's reading, recorded rather dryly (Cedille 48). **Rhonda Rider** and Lois Shapiro take care of that problem in their warmly recorded reading, a little more spacious in sound than even Krosnick/Kalish (Centaur 2267). **David Pereira** and Lisa Moore also play with insight and energy (Tall Poppies 32). **Fred Sherry** and Charles Wuorinen maintain tension by taking a slightly faster basic pulse than usual and emphasizing the unity of tempo between movements. Sherry's warmth of tone and virtuosity carry him through, and Wuorinen, though not the equal of Jacobs or Kalish in expressivity, shows great technical fluency (Bridge 9044, NA). **Rohan de Saram** and Oppens offer a fine, large-scaled reading in rather dry sound (Montaigne 782091).

Carter's music for woodwinds was mostly written during the '40s, beginning with *Pastoral* (1941). Originally for English horn and piano (played with warmth by **Carolyn Hove** in Crystal 328), it was published for viola and is also recorded on clarinet by **John Russo** (CRS 9255) and by **Chicago Pro Musica** (Cedille 48). It's a substantial nine-minute piece showing a number of spiky aspects of Carter's then Americana style. Russo's reading is smoother than Pro Musica's rather harshly recorded performance, but his program is unsettlingly miscellaneous. **Laura Flax** gives a livelier and smoother toned performance in the Da Capo Chamber Players disc of Carter and Perle (GM 2020, NA). The Chicago group's CD includes both the jazzy *Woodwind Quintet* (1948) and the quirky, witty *Eight Etudes and a Fantasy* for woodwind quartet (1950) in the most successful performances in their disc.

Several others have coupled the *Quintet* and the *Etudes,* among them **Quintetto Arnold,** which plays them with light virtuosity that seems to eliminate some individuality (Stradivarius 33304). The most effective version is by **Ensemble Contrasts,** which has both a light texture and a

care for balance and individual personality (CPO 999453). Recordings of the Quintet alone include the **Boehm Quintet**'s nicely balanced and lightly sprung account (Premier 1006) and the **Westwood Wind Quintet,** which is warmer (Crystal 752). The programs on both of these discs are interesting and appropriate.

The five String Quartets represent Carter's most advanced thought. The first three show different stages of his exploration of spatial music. Quartet number 1 (1950–51) is a 40-minute work of great drama, in which the musicians seem to be going in different directions yet make beautiful combinations when they meet. It's a dramatic piece to watch, equally so to hear. In 2 (1959) the players are placed apart, making their meetings of minds even more poignant when they occur. In 3 (1971) the players work as duos, and for 4 (1986) they seem to join forces once more.

The first two quartets have been recorded by **Composers Quartet** in beautifully spacious sound (Nonesuch 71249). They seem to revel in the physical demands of the music and in the still moments as well. The **Juilliard Quartet** recorded 2 and 3 in 1974 (Columbia LP 32738, NA) and the first four plus the violin-piano Duo in 1991 (Sony 47229, 2CD). These recordings are more close up than Nonesuch's, but this incarnation of the Juilliard was particularly sensitive to lyricism, and their readings are very satisfying, more leisurely than the Composers Quartet. The **Arditti Quartet** has recorded not only the first four quartets plus the little Elegy for viola and piano (1943) (Etcetera 1065/6), but also 5 (1995) with the Cello Sonata, the violin-piano Duo, *90+,* and two late miniatures, otherwise unrecorded (Montaigne 782091). The Arditti's performances are the fastest of all and rather closely miked, eliminating the spatial character and a good deal of the atmosphere.

The Sonata for Flute, Oboe, Cello, and Harpsichord (1952) is a less-tense piece, approaching the spatial question through contrasted instrumental sounds. A light, bright-sounding work, it has been beautifully played and recorded by **Sollberger,** Kuskin, Sherry, and Jacobs in excellently atmospheric sound (Nonesuch 79183). The **Ensemble Contrasts** version is equally polished, but the sounds are blended rather than contrasted, somewhat burying the harpsichord (CPO 999453).

In 1974 Carter wrote his Duo for violin and piano, one of his most abstract pieces. The recording by **Paul Zukofsky** and **Kalish** is one of their few unsuccessful efforts; it's hunt-and-peck music that brought out the most mechanical tone quality from both players. (Nonesuch LP 71314, NA). **Robert Mann** and **Christopher Oldfather** tackle it in the Juilliard's quartet album with totally different results (Sony 47229, 2CD). Where Carter's demanding leaps and high-flying notes lead Zukofsky and Kalish to inexpressive accuracy, Mann plays with a tone that accepts the climbing of Everest (the composer's simile) as an emotional necessity, never giving up his expressive vibrato or his musical integrity even while occasionally slipping on the cliff. Oldfather's tone also keeps its warmth no matter what. The end result is still questionable music, but this is a worthy attempt. **Rolf Schulte** and **Martin Goldray** try it with more virtuosity and determination, taking Carter's notes as a personal affront; their tendency to attack is as tiring as Zukofsky's (Bridge 9044, NA). **Arditti** and **Oppens** are a bit dry but impressively accurate in their climb (Montaigne 782091).

Triple Duo (1983) was composed for Peter Maxwell Davies's **The Fires of London,** which explains the scoring: flute, clarinet, violin, cello, piano, and percussion. It's a lively and light-hearted piece, recalling Davies's style, perhaps, though with fewer nasty overtones than in his own music. Their performance is lively but not as precise as it might be; however, it is important, as the piece was composed for their sound

(Wergo 6278). Another good but occasionally inaccurate performance was conducted by **Jürg Wyttenbach** in atmospheric but distractingly resonant sound (ECM 839617, NA). The most satisfying to date is by the **New York New Music Ensemble,** which seems the happiest in playing with the varied sound colors Carter created (GM 2047).

Canon for Four (1984) is a four-minute piece for flute, bass clarinet, violin, and cello, recorded by **Da Capo Chamber Players** (GM 2020, NA). It shouldn't be confused with *Canon for Three* (1971) for three trumpets, recorded (twice) by **Gerard Schwarz** (Phoenix 115).

Esprit rude, esprit doux (1985) is another tiny piece for flute and clarinet on this disc, played by Patricia Spencer and Laura Flax. It also appears, done more slowly and with less aural violence, on the **Ensemble Contrasts** recording of wind music, played by Michael Faust and David Smeyers (♦CPO 999453). Another performance by **Philippe Racine** and **Ernesto Molinari** sets off the counterpoint against the resonant ambience of the recording venue in amusing fashion (ECM 839617, NA). Finally, a performance by **Sophie Cherrier** and **Andre Trouttet** is on Boulez's disc, played neatly (Erato 45364, NA).

Enchanted Preludes (1988) is for flute and cello and sounds like birds. The Da Capo players are **Patricia Spencer** and **Andre Emilianoff,** whose recording tends to shriek a bit in the flute and to be a little unsure in the cello. **Michael** and **George Faust** on the CPO CD are smoother in texture and recording but less exciting. **Philippe Racine** and **Thomas Demenga** find an effective balance between virtuosity and sound character (ECM). **Harvey Sollberger** and **Fred Sherry** are a little muffled in sound but play very effectively (Bridge 9044).

Quintet for Piano and Winds (1991) is an example of Carter's new capacity for lyricism. It was written for and recorded by oboist **Heinz Holliger** (Philips 446095). On the same disc is a spikier new piece for oboe and harp, *Trilogy,* in which he is joined by Ursula Holliger. The performances are definitive and highly expressive.

SOLO WORKS

The 1945–46 Piano Sonata is one of Carter's most often recorded pieces, despite its granitic texture and serious mien. First came **Beveridge Webster,** whose fluently dramatic reading was recorded in the '50s—though its present incarnation makes no mention of the fact, and much less the fact that it's in mono (♦Phoenix 141). But that doesn't matter much; it's good piano sound, if somewhat limited on top and bottom, and Webster is a master of technical control. **Francesco Caramiello** isn't well known in this country, but his CD, containing Ives and Copland as well as Carter's Sonata, is full of vigor and breadth, emphasizing the lyrical side of the music (Agora 182). The vital **Veda Zuponcic** was born and studied in the United States but recorded her CD in Moscow; hers is a fast and furious Carter (Melodiya 529). **Paul Jacobs,** in a miscellaneous all-Carter disc, offers a large and resonant performance (Elektra Nonesuch 79248). His concentration on voice leading and precision is telling. Finally, the intellectual but exciting **Charles Rosen** offers a disc containing all of Carter's piano music (Bridge 9090).

Eight Pieces for Four Timpani (1949/1966) are perhaps a bit much for listening to at one stretch, but that's the beauty of recordings. **Gert Mortensen** has recorded them in resonant sound (BIS 52). If that's too much, in "Percussion XX" **Jonathan Faralli** has excerpted three of them in clear, neat readings (Arts 47558).

Night Fantasies (1980) is a major 20-minute piece for piano based on chord patterns that soothe by their repetition while they disturb with their activity. **Rosen** plays it with control and sensitive articulation (Etcetera 1008). **Aleck Karis** also plays it well, but he's not as well

attuned to the major Chopin and Schumann pieces making up the rest of his disc (Bridge 9001). The excellent playing of **Stephen Drury** is coupled with Book 2 of Cage's *Etudes Australes* (Neuma 45076). Carter's feelings about the contrasts within music seem to be rubbing off on his interpreters' ideas of programming!

Changes (1983) is for solo guitar, a seven-minute piece beginning in violence and ending in darkness. **William Anderson** plays it with more winning tone (CRI 838), but **David Starobin** makes more of the contrasts within the work (Bridge 9044).

Riconoscenza per Goffredo Petrassi (1984), for violin solo, is a slow meditation with interruptions of violence. **Rolf Schulte** emphasizes the meditation, stretching the work to over six minutes (Bridge 9044), while both **Maryvonne le Dizes-Richard** (New World 80333) and **Curtis Macomber** (CRI 706) play it in about four. Macomber is best at making the contrasts tell; his control of pitch and bow strokes is admirable. **Hansheinz Schneeberger** is fastest of all; his performance sounds as if it were recorded in a church (ECM 839617, NA).

A six-minute piano piece, *90+* (1994), is included by **Rosen** in his disc of Carter's complete piano music (Bridge 9090) and by **Oppens** in the Arditti Quartet disc containing Quartet 5 and other works (Montaigne 782091). Both performances are good, but are somewhat dryly recorded. To the Carter collector, both are important for their material and for fine performances.

VOCAL MUSIC

Choral music was the genre Carter cultivated most consistently in his early years. The most complete program and most atmospherically recorded, if not the clearest in sound, is by the **John Oliver Chorale,** which, in its latest incarnation, has added two short but attractive pieces from a 1937 score for *The Beggar's Opera* to the seven works we knew before (Koch 7415). Texts are now provided, and the sound of the group is rich and full of a sonic variety that **Gregg Smith,** with his rather dry recorded sound, can't match, though Smith's Singers are commendable for their diction and musical intensity (CRI 648). Oliver's narrator misreads the word *courageous* at one point, and you can't follow most of the words without reading the text, and Smith's also contains a program of songs.

Most of Carter's songs came early and have been recorded together. The tiny, witty *Three Poems of Robert Frost* takes less than five minutes to perform, while Hart Crane's *Voyage* and Whitman's *Warble for Lilac Time* each take about six. **Rosalind Reese** sings them with feeling (CRI 648). **Phyllis Bryn-Julson** has a clear, rich soprano (Music & Arts 4900), while **Lucy Shelton** adds a recent cycle from 1994, *Of Challenge and of Love,* with words by John Hollander (♦Koch 7425). Her outstanding diction and emotional involvement provide a rebuttal for those who find Carter cold and cerebral. That goes for recent Carter as well; in Shelton's firm grasp, we're pulled into Carter's thorny world, and she demonstrates how his vocal line expresses humanity and feeling, even amid the disturbance created by John Constable's piano. She holds us together, in the role Carter intended; it's a tour de force. **Patrick Mason** sings the Frost songs to open Speculum Musicae's CD containing all three middle-period cycles, performing them in the 1980 versions for chamber group (Bridge 9014). We also get a taste of the intimate polish of **Jan de Gaetani** with Kalish in the first two Frost songs (Elektra Nonesuch 79248).

Speculum Musicae is responsible for premiering two of Carter's three chamber song cycles and has now recorded all three (Bridge 9014). *A Mirror on Which to Dwell* sets six poems by Elizabeth Bishop, strangely ambiguous, nervously changing images that Carter's music reflects. First recorded by soprano **Susan Davenny Wyner** with Richard Fitz and Speculum (Columbia LP 35171, NA), the recording with **Christine Schadeburg** and Donald Palma cuts the timing from 20 minutes to 17, a substantial difference. Both singers are good on pitch, but neither is particularly clear in diction; if anything, the balances in the new recording tend to drown Schadeburg more than the old one did Wyner. Still, the faster tempos are helpful. **Phyllis Bryn-Julson** has a version with Boulez and the Ensemble InterContemporain that solves the balance problem most effectively (Erato 45634, NA).

Syringa is an English poetic commentary by John Ashbery on the myth of Orpheus, mingled with texts from the Greek poets sung in Greek. It requires two singers who sing their different texts simultaneously, as in a medieval motet. The effect is unsettling and frustrating, since there is no real communication and neither singer is given a real opportunity to express anything clearly. Even **de Gaetani** can't make much out of this situation (CRI 610). **Katherine Ciesinski** is blessed with a clearer sound picture, and her diction is good.

In Sleep, in Thunder sets six poems of Robert Lowell. This cycle was written for the London Sinfonietta, and the first recording was made by them with **Martyn Hill,** tenor, Knussen conducting (Wergo 6278). It's a lovely performance in excellent sound. **Jon Garrison,** with Robert Black and Speculum, is a mite clearer in diction and is recorded slightly more closely, but he's vocally less distinguished.   MOORE

Alfredo Casella (1883–1947)

With Respighi, Gian Francesco Malipiero, and others, Casella deserves to be remembered for revitalizing the Italian tradition of orchestral and chamber music. His reputation has suffered, however, from having followed Stravinsky's influence too closely and from a misguided adulation for the Italian Fascist dictator Mussolini. At its best, his music is well crafted and often exuberant, the finer neoclassical scores of his later years sounding as much fun to play as to hear, while the more advanced works of his experimental period (roughly from 1913 to 1922) are the most interesting musically.

Orchestral music. La giara (The Jar), a sparkling Pirandello-based ballet, is presented in full by **Marco Balderi,** coupled with the well-known *Serenata* (Bottega Discanta). All the essentials of the work are present in the *Symphonic Suite* from which Casella later extracted it, played with élan by Orchestra della Svizzera Italiana under **Christian Benda** (♦Naxos 553706, with *Serenata* and *Paganiniana*).

Paganiniana is Casella's most popular work, at least on disc, and was written five years before his death. **Kondrashin**'s bright account is NA (Philips); the most eminent currently available is by **Muti** (Sony 53280, with works by Busoni and Giuseppe Martucci). Fine as the La Scala orchestra of 1988 plays for him, the performance (and indeed the recording) lack **Benda**'s exuberance (♦Naxos 553706).

Serenata started life as a prize-winning chamber work. This five-movement serenade is a little too indebted to the Stravinsky of *Pulcinella,* yet it's a lively and popular score, the "Cavatina" containing Casella's finest melody. **Benda** catches it just right (♦Naxos 553706) and is recorded better than **Balderi** (Bottega Discanta). Stronger competition comes from **Alun Francis,** a sparkling if more relaxed account recorded best of all and coupled with the otherwise unavailable *Divertimento per Fulvia* and Erwin Stein's arrangement for string orchestra of Casella's Concerto for String Quartet (♦CPO 999195).

Concertos. In the Cello Concerto, **Francesco Pepicelli** is a committed and fluent soloist, equal to the challenging "hornet flight" finale (♦Dy-

namic 169). For sheer virtuosity, however, **Siegfried Palm** is commanding, if less engaged expressively (Nuovo Era). The instrumentation of the Concerto for Strings, Piano, Timpani, and Percussion recalls Martinů's intense masterpiece, and Casella's is similarly somber, though less overtly tragic in mood. **Marcello Panni** directs a firm, driving account (Dynamic 169), though **Giuseppe Garbarino** has the edge (♦Nuovo Era 7143).

The Concerto for Piano Trio and Orchestra is one of the most satisfactory works for this combination, always tricky to balance. **Trio Kreisleriana** gives a sparkling interpretation, ably supported by Max Bragado Darman (♦Koch 367252, with *Sonata a tre*). **Marco Rizzi, Angelo Pepicelli,** and **Francesco Pepicelli** also give a fine performance, although the recorded sound favors them less; however, theirs is the more generous program (Dynamic 169, with the concertos listed above).

Chamber music. For the *Serenata,* **Ex Novo Ensemble** has recorded the entire original version (Stradivarius 33312, with trios by Ildebrando Pizzetti and Rota), as well as the violin-and-piano arrangements of *Cavatina* and *Gavotte* (ASV 1085). The latter recital also includes pieces for flute and piano, some short arrangements, and the Sinfonia Op. 53 for clarinet, trumpet, cello, and piano.

Of the three versions of *Sonata a tre* for piano trio, **Trio Kreisleriana** is the most accomplished, mixing passion and understanding in equal measure (♦Koch 367252, with Trio Concerto). Next to them, the **Ex Novo Ensemble** seems less in tune with the composer's vision in either of their recordings (Stradivarius and ASV). **Ex Novo** has also recorded the delightful *Sicilienne and Burlesque* and *Barcarola and Scherzo,* both for flute and piano, as well as arrangements for violin with piano of movements from *Scarlattiana* and *La giara;* the overall program is a touch unfocused (ASV 1085). The finest account of *Sicilienne and Burlesque* comes from **Aurèle** and **Christine Nicolet** (Camerata 302, with mainly Baroque couplings). **Francesco** and **Angelo Pepicelli** have also set down Casella's complete works for cello and piano (first recordings), unreservedly to be welcomed (Dynamic 135). **Naoko Yoshino**'s recording of the substantial Harp Sonata Op. 68 in a very varied recital is also recommendable (Philips 446064).

Piano music. **Bruno Canino** has begun a survey of Casella's complete piano music; at the time of writing only Vol. 1 has been released, with Sonatina, *Pavane, Variations on a Chaconne,* and the "musical poem" *A Notte Alta,* one of his finest creations (Stradivarius 33350). Canino is to be preferred in the Sonatina and nine *Pieces* Op. 24 to **Easley Blackwood** (bizarrely coupled with Szymanowski's *Masques;* Cedille) and in the Sonatina to **Gieseking,** a 1947 performance in good restored sound (Pearl). Sadly, **Giacomo Franci**'s recital, which also included *A Notte Alta,* has been deleted (Fone). However, most of the works it covered are featured in perhaps the most sparkling of all the piano music discs currently available: **Sandro Ivo Bartoli**'s (♦ASV 1023). His account of *A Notte Alta* is wonderfully atmospheric, while in the *Toccata* he is bright and commanding. In *Ricercari on the name B-A-C-H* and *Pezzi Infantili* Bartoli is challenged by the nicely poetic playing of **Luca Ballerini** in a varied program including a fine performance of the Op. 24 *Pieces* (♦Naxos 8554009, with six Studies Op. 70).

Casella's two four-hand suites from 1915, *Pagine di guerra* and *Puppazetti,* are among his best-known instrumental works. **Bartoli** and **Marcello Guerrini** are flawless in *Pagine di guerra,* inspired by newsreels of the war (ASV 1023). However, the **Dirani-Amelotti Duo** has recorded both pieces as part of an excellent program (Fone 9030, with works by Malipiero, Giuseppe Martucci, and Respighi). The **Brusca-**

Solastra Duo places the works in an even more interesting context, alongside compositions by Busoni, Malipiero, Goffredo Petrassi, and Respighi (♦Nuovo Era 7143). Tony and Mary Ann Lenti have also recorded *Pagine di guerra* with the four-hand *Foxtrot* (ACA, with pieces by Busoni, Goetz and Respighi).

Vocal music. Although Casella's prime cause was revitalizing Italian instrumental composition, he also wrote for the voice. However, aside from *La giara,* with its solo tenor, only two works are currently available. The four "funereal lyrics" *L'adieu à la vie* set poems by Tagore translated into French by André Gide. Liliane Zürcher's interpretation forms part of Giuseppe Garbarini's all-Casella program (Nuovo Era 7143). The five *Symphonic Fragments* from *Le Couvent sur l'eau* is also from his Parisian period. Anna Chiuri sings them in a mixed program with orchestral fragments from Malipiero's *Commedie goldoniane* and lightweight pieces by Carlo Pedrotti and Vincenzo Tommasini (Aurora).

RICKARDS

Mario Castelnuovo-Tedesco (1895–1968)

Like Mendelssohn, this Florentine composer was born into a Jewish banking family. At the age of 10 he began writing and publishing music and went on to study piano. Between the wars he studied composition, became friendly with Puccini and Toscanini, and began writing music for guitarist Andrés Segovia. Though he is primarily known as a composer for the guitar (he wrote more than 350 pieces for the instrument), he also wrote piano, chamber, vocal, and orchestral works and music for films and plays.

There are several excellent recordings of his Guitar Concerto 1 (the last piece he wrote before leaving fascist Italy with his family), by Eduardo Fernandez (London 455364), Norbert Kraft (Naxos 559729), Pepe Romero (Philips 416357), and John Williams (CBS 44791). Kazuhito Yamashita's recording includes Guitar Concerto 2 and Concerto for Two Guitars, played with his sister Naoko (RCA 60355). The orchestra is a bit sloppy at times, but the guitar playing is excellent. Segovia recorded the Guitar Quintet with the Chigiano Quintet in Vol. 8 of "The Segovia Collection" (MCA 10056), a disc devoted exclusively to this composer, and plays many of his solo pieces in other volumes.

One of the best recordings of Castelnuovo's guitar music is the *24 Caprichos de Goya* performed by Lily Afshar (Summit 167). Like Granados, he was fascinated by the art of Goya and wrote these pieces as companions to 24 of Goya's paintings and prints. The notes for the Afshar recording have thumbnail duplications of the paintings that are depicted in the music. *Well-Tempered Guitars* is another 24-work set, written in homage to Bach's *Well-Tempered Clavier;* it has been recorded by Duo Tedesco (Koch Schwann 1224).

He wrote two violin concertos, but only the second (based on Hebrew themes and subtitled "The Prophets") has been recorded. Heifetz (who commissioned the work) recorded it in 1954 (RCA 7872), and Perlman more recently with Mehta (EMI 54296).

Castelnuovo-Tedesco wrote many songs to the words of Shakespeare. One of his most often performed pieces, *Sea-Murmurs,* is actually Heifetz's transcription of the song "Arise" from Shakespeare's *Cymbeline.* There are several beautiful recordings, including an encore from Heifetz's final recital (RCA 61777) and Zina Schiff in "King David's Lyre" (4-Tay 4002). Other transcriptions include a vocalise played by Raymond Mase in his "Trumpet Vocalise" (Summit 185).

The composer's musical horizons expanded greatly during the '20s when he found a notebook filled with Sephardic melodies written down by his grandfather, and his interest in Jewish music contin-

ued throughout his life. "The Divan of Moses-ibn-Ezra," sung by Roberta Alexander and accompanied by guitarist Dick Hoogoveen, is a good example (Etcetera 1150). Cellist Vito Paternoster includes a *Hebrew Chant* and a setting of the *Kol Nidrei* in a recording devoted entirely to the composer's cello music (Dynamic 2013). János Starker plays *Fantasie on Rossini's Barber of Seville* in his "Virtuoso Music for Cello" (Denon 8118), and Nancy Green plays still more cello music (Biddulph 24).

Castelnuovo-Tedesco wrote some of his most interesting music for the piano. Ciccolini recorded three volumes of these works (Phoenix 095102, 0097301, 0097308), Rodriguez made the only recording of the Piano Concerto (Elan 2222), and Blumenthal plays the Piano Sonata, *Danze de Re David,* and *Questo fu il carro della morte* (Etcetera 1134). Michael McFrederick plays several short piano works in a disc that includes rather weak readings of the Cello and Harp Sonata and Sonatina for Flute and Guitar. Better versions of the latter can be heard from Susan Hoeppner and Rachel Gauk (Marquis 147) and from William Bennett and Simon Wynberg (ASV 692).

One of Castelnuovo-Tedesco's most popular pieces is *Romancero Gitano* (Gypsy Romance), a choral piece with soloists and an elaborate guitar accompaniment set to texts by Lorca. There is a pretty good recording by the Pacific Northwest Chamber Chorus and Steven Novacek, who plays the guitar part wonderfully (Ambassador), but I prefer the soloists in the performance by the New York Concert Singers (New World 80547).

FINE

Alfredo Catalani (1854–1893)

Catalani was born in Lucca only four years before his more famous compatriot Puccini. His operas defy exact categorization, with traces of romantic, melodramatic, and verismo styles in evidence. The tunes are pleasant enough, but never quite distinctive or truly memorable.

Loreley. Elda was Catalani's first full-length opera. After its premiere in Turin in 1880, it had only minimal success and languished for ten years until Catalani revised it with a shortened libretto as *Loreley* (again Turin, 1890). It's an ambitious piece modeled after French grand opera and requires a ballet, large chorus, and extravagant scenic effects.

A 1968 broadcast from La Scala is an ill-starred performance, the ill star being Suliotis (Hunt 551, 2CD). Her voice is unpleasant in the top range, where much of the role lies, and unsupported and unreliable in the middle range. Only in the rare drops to the lowest register does she sound secure—hardly the seductive voice to lure anyone to doom. None of the others sound at all comfortable. La Scala's chorus and orchestra are the best in the show. Gavazzeni molds a grandiose but lively performance. Beware the recorded sound, though; it's just barely acceptable. The Italian-only libretto is also a mess. The filler consists of excerpts from a 1966 *Nabucco* at La Scala. Suliotis is in good voice here, and although Giangiacomo Guelfi is flat in the top range, he too does well, with lots of fire and passion in their duet.

A recording from a 1982 concert performance in Lucca makes a much stronger case for the opera (♦Bongiovanni 2015, 2CD). All the singers are much more acceptable than their better known La Scala counterparts. Martha Colalillo in particular makes much of the title role.

La Wally. This is the last and most frequently performed of Catalani's operas. Both Toscanini and Fausto Cleva admired the work so much that they each named a daughter after the heroine. This is rather odd, as in the opera Wally is a strange creature. Although she has moments of visionary rapture, she is one tough girl with a mean streak and a nasty temper, at times quite irrational. Happily, Catalani wrote some sympathetic music for her. The Act 1 aria "Ebben? . . . ne andro lontano" would melt a heart of stone.

Wally was a role favored by Tebaldi, evidenced by at least three recordings, only one of which was (London) in the studio. The 1953 La Scala is the best, with a younger Tebaldi in fine form accompanied by a less powerful del Monaco (Legato 1772, 2CD). The very young Scotto is a superb bonus, as is Giorgio Tozzi. **Giulini** makes a strong case for the opera, though the recorded sound is variable. By 1968 Tebaldi had lost some of her vocal freshness, but it's still a strong portrayal, accompanied this time by the elegant Bergonzi (Intaglio 7642, 2CD). Peter Glossop is a first-rate singer with much sympathetic understanding. **Cleva**'s orchestral forces are a bit covered by the recorded sound.

London's 1969 recording was one of the last with its popular team of Tebaldi and del Monaco (♦425417, 2CD). Some of her high notes are hard pressed, but there are still many beautiful moments. She even manages to tone down some of Wally's craziness and create a more sympathetic character. Del Monaco, stentorian in excelsis, belts out his music with a fine degree of excitement appropriate to the callow Hagenbach. The Monte Carlo forces at this time weren't outstanding, but **Cleva** gets as much from them as he can, conducting with great sympathy if no particular drive.

Olivero's performance comes from the 1972 Donizetti Festival in Bergamo. As always, she puts her personal stamp on the title role with her distinctively colored voice and committed characterization (Foyer 2055, 2CD). Amadeo Zambon is a big-voiced, unsubtle Hagenbach, a worthy adversary-lover for Olivero. Silvano Carrolli is an unusually restrained, finely sung Gellner. There is some question whether Nicola Zaccaria actually sings the role of Strominger; he's good, whoever he is. **Ferrucio Scaglia** is a competent leader of his musical forces. The sound is only fair.

Pinchas Steinberg gives a good account of the score, and his Munich forces are fine. The problem is the principal singers. Marton's Wally is too tough, both as a character and in vocal production. Unsteady, hard-driven, aggressive, and angry, she's difficult to listen to. Araiza is overparted as Hagenbach; his lyric voice isn't adequate to the role's demands, as he just barely makes the notes any way he can. Allan Titus is surprisingly good as Gellner; his voice has grown since his early successes, and he easily encompasses the role's demands, musically and dramatically. PARSONS

Pier Francesco Cavalli (1602–1676)

Cavalli was one of the first composers of opera, writing some 30 of them, and also wrote much choral music. Since almost none of his music was published during his lifetime, it must be reconstructed and interpreted by musicologists. Chief among these have been conductors Raymond Leppard and René Jacobs.

CHORAL MUSIC

Missa pro defunctis per due cori (*Requiem*) has had two recordings, one good and one bad. A 1974 performance from Italian Swiss Radio led by **Edwin Loehrer** is the bad one (Accord). A 1993 recording by **Françoise Lasserre,** which includes four Marian antiphons, is a much better choice (Pierre Verany 793052). *Messa concertata* is in a similar situation. Seicento and Parley of Instruments led by **Peter Holman** is a superior performance (Hyperion 66970, with canzonas and motets), far outdistancing Sine Nomine led by **Carlo Rebeschini** (Rivo Alto).

Vespero della Beata Vergine Maria consists of vocal and instrumental works from Cavalli's *Musiche Sacre* (1656) that would have been performed in Venetian churches at Second Vespers during a Feast of the Virgin Mary. It's included in a moderate program moderately performed by the Schola Gregoriana Ergo Cantemus and the Athestis Chorus and Consort led by **Filipppo Maria Bressan,** with Cavalli's music alternating with chants and organ toccatas by Claudio Merulo and Gabrieli (Tactus 600311). A more complete version and better performance comes from the Akademia Ensemble Vocal Regional de Champagne Ardenne and La Fenice under **Lasserre**'s direction (Pierre Verany 96042, 2CD). With still more music, the best of the performances is a stellar reading by the Concertino Palatino led by **Bruce Dickey** and Charles Toet (♦Harmonia Mundi 905219, 2CD).

OPERAS

Few of Cavalli's operas have been recorded, most of them only once, but all the recordings are quite good. None can be considered definitive on musicological grounds, but all of them provide enjoyable music in enjoyable performances.

La Calisto is based on Greek myth, but it's a surprisingly modern story of sexual intrigue and cross-gender confusion—a bracing, witty comedy. The second (and more popular) of Leppard's editions was heard at Glyndebourne in 1971 (♦Decca 435216, 2CD). It has a strong cast with Baker (delightfully alternating between Diana and Jove) and Cotrubas as the much put-upon heroine. An all-Italian cast joyously attacks the opera with I Sonatori de la Giosa Marca led by **Bruno Moretti** (Stradivarius 13607, 2CD). A different 1993 reconstruction of the opera, reflecting musical scholarship since Leppard, is led by **Jacobs** in an equally successful performance (♦Harmonia Mundi 901515, 3CD).

Ercole amante is Cavalli's only opera composed for Paris, written in 1762 after Cardinal Mazarin imported him to jump-start French opera. **Corboz** leads a performance of high grandeur with a high-powered cast; Minton, Patricia Miller, Felicity Palmer, and Ulrik Cold are among the expert singers (♦Erato 12980; MHS 834719; 2CD).

Giasone is one of Cavalli's larger operas, requiring a cast of 10 singers, including two countertenors. It's a very confusing, hyperbolic mess-up of the Greek myth of Jason and the Argonauts, yet it's a splendid concoction, musically entertaining. **Jacobs**'s edition was recorded in 1988, with a fine cast of early music veterans (♦Harmonia Mundi 901282, 3CD).

Ormindo is technically a serenata rather than an opera and was the first of Cavalli's stage pieces to be revived in modern times. That revival began in 1968 at the Glyndebourne Festival with **Leppard**'s edition (♦Decca 444529, 2CD). It's a sunny, winning affair with fine singing all around. A different view of the opera is heard in a 1971 performance in Venice by **Renato Fasano** leading his splendid period orchestra, I Virtuosi di Roma (Stradivarius/Datum 12307, 2CD). This is a more astringent performance; the vocal soloists are not quite so tame.

Serse (also known as *Xerxes*) has appeared in an edition prepared by **Jacobs,** adapting the missing prologue from another Cavalli opera, *Il Ciro* (♦Harmonia Mundi 1175, 4CD). Again it offers the Concerto Vocale and a host of period experts (lots of countertenors), with Jacobs himself singing the title role. PARSONS

Emmanuel Chabrier (1841–1894)

"Dear Chabrier, how we love you!" wrote Poulenc about one of his favorite composers (one, incidentally, to whom he owed quite a lot). Chabrier has always been extravagantly, and rightly, admired by French composers, from Franck to Satie, Ravel to d'Indy. His heady combination of harmonic adventurousness, original handling of the orchestra, and ability to go from elegance to roughhousing make him an unusually appealing composer. In French music, at least, he's also an important one—a technical and aesthetic influence on Ravel, Poulenc, and Ibert.

Chabrier was famously sketched at the piano by Toulouse-Lautrec, and was himself something of a musical Toulouse-Lautrec, writing music notable for its wit, liveliness, and color. Outside France, he's known primarily as the composer of *España* and a couple of other orchestral "lollipops" (in the phrase of Beecham, who made wonderful recordings of several of them), works so readily enjoyable that it's easy to forget how original they are. Like many other 19th-century French composers, Chabrier was a confirmed Wagnerite (his first exposure to *Tristan und Isolde* compelled him to give up a respectable civil service job to become a composer); unlike any other French composer until Debussy, he adopted Wagner's chromatic freedom in an utterly personal way, mixing dissonance with modal harmony in music that often sounds more like the 1920s than the 1880s.

Chabrier wrote two grand operas, but will probably always be best known for his shorter works. There's hardly a piece by Chabrier, short or long, that doesn't illustrate his credo: "Music must be beautiful at once and all the time."

ORCHESTRAL MUSIC
There are many Chabrier collections with *España, Bourrée Fantasque, Marche Joyeuse, Suite pastorale,* and the rest; get **Ansermet** (♦London 43023) or **Paray** (♦Mercury 34303)—or both—and you won't go wrong. **Gardiner**'s recent collection with the Vienna Philharmonic was lauded everywhere, but not by me (DG). Gardiner, usually so sensitive to the nuances of individual composers, rides roughshod over the music; the recording is hard-edged; and the orchestra's plush sound is all wrong.

As mentioned earlier, **Beecham** recorded a few of Chabrier's "lollipops." His 1939 *España* has been listed as one of the 100 greatest recordings of the century, and it belongs there; it has elegance and brio and still sounds terrific. It's paired with an exciting, rather tubby-sounding 1961 recording of the Overture to *Gwendoline* in "French Favorites"—Beecham's, that is—including such rarities as Bizet's *Patrie* Overture and Grétry's *Zemire et Azor* (♦EMI 63401). The conductor's swaggering *Marche Joyeuse* is in an irresistible program of encores by Tchaikovsky, Delius, Mozart, and others (♦EMI 63412).

Plasson's survey of unusual Chabrier pieces for orchestra is NA but worth searching for, because it gives a concise but unusually complete picture of the composer: the operatic grandeur of two excerpts from *Gwendoline,* the melodic charm of *Larghetto* for horn and orchestra, and the delicious *Ode à la musique* for women's chorus and orchestra, a limpid hymn to *musique adorable* (EMI 54004). His earlier CD contains stylish performances of more familiar fare including *España, Suite Pastorale, Marche Joyeuse,* and *Fête Polonaise* (EMI 749652). **Armin Jordan**'s CD remains enjoyable despite the high-powered competition (Erato 88018). **Hervé Niquet** is let down by reverberant, thick sound, but offers the only available recording of *Lamento* for English horn (Naxos 554248).

PIANO MUSIC
Chabrier's piano music includes the original versions of popular works like *España* and *Bourrée Fantasque,* but also some remarkable extended works. *Pièces pittoresques* were compared by Franck to Couperin and Rameau, and the young Poulenc was completely seduced by them: "a harmonic universe suddenly opened in front of me, and my music has never forgotten this first loving kiss." All ten pieces last nearly 40 min-utes, so they're seldom performed or recorded as a set (Chabrier orchestrated four of the most seductive as his *Suite Pastorale*). **Casadesus** did all ten in the 1950s (Columbia), and there are complete recordings by **Pierre Barbizet** in his 1982 survey of Chabrier's piano music (Erato 95309) and **Rena Kyriakou** in her complete set (Vox 5108). Both also contain the luscious, harmonically downright decadent *Valses romantiques* for two pianos, an obvious influence on Ravel's *Valses nobles et sentimentales.* **Georges Rabol** has also recorded all of Chabrier's piano music; the price is right but the playing is dull (Naxos).

OPERAS
Like the perfect Wagnerite he was, Chabrier wanted to write operas. He completed two that were received with some respect but dogged by bad luck. *Gwendoline,* a tragedy set in England, closed after four performances when the theater went out of business; the comic *Le Roi malgré lui* shut down when *its* theater burned. *Gwendoline*'s flamboyant overture has been much recorded (by Beecham, Ansermet, Gardiner, and Paray, all mentioned above); **Plasson**'s orchestral collection includes an aria sung by soprano Hendricks (EMI 54004, NA). The entire opera is also available, led by **Jean-Paul Penin** (L'Empreinte Digitale 13059).

Le Roi malgré lui is the source of Chabrier's popular *Fête polonaise* and was recorded complete in 1984 by **Dutoit** for French Radio, also with Hendricks (Erato 45792, NA). The composer called this extravagantly inventive score "Comic opera in fancy undies," and if the libretto weren't so awful it might well be a repertory piece. Chabrier's harmonies are amazingly dissonant and freewheeling for 1887, yet they are presented in a colorful, tuneful, and completely entertaining format. What could be more French than that? Not until Debussy did a composer combine the revolutionary and the beautiful so convincingly.

The wacky, black-humored operetta *L'Etoile* is a sort of French precursor to *The Mikado;* **Gardiner**'s excellent recording has long been out of print (EMI).

SONGS
A few of Chabrier's witty songs occasionally turn up in recitals. Complete sets are available from **Ludovic de San** (Discover 920177) and **Agnes Mellon** and others (Timpani 1038), but for the ultimate in style, try to find **Bernac** and Poulenc's 1950 recordings of "L'Ile heureuse" and "Villanelle des petits canards," which were available on Odyssey LPs and briefly on a Sony "Portrait" CD, with similarly authoritative performances of songs by Poulenc, Ravel, Debussy, and Satie.   RAYMOND

George Whitefield Chadwick *(1854–1931)*
Olin Downes hailed Chadwick as "the dean of American composers," but that suggests some degree of pedantry, and Chadwick—for all his credentials as conductor, organist, teacher and above all director of the New England Conservatory—was no pedant, as the rich vein of robust Yankee humor that pervades his music amply demonstrates. Downes also adroitly described Chadwick as "snapping his fingers at the universe," paving the way for future generations of refreshingly irreverent American composers like Ives.

For all their wealth of melody and sparkling orchestration, Chadwick's symphonies are modeled closely on Brahms and Schumann. Certainly there's little about Symphony 2 that seems particularly "American," though there's a healthy vigor that immediately wins the listener over. That might be said as well of **Neeme Järvi**'s exhilarating account (♦Chandos 9334), which leaves **Julius Hegyi** panting to the rear (New World). Either is preferable to **Karl Krueger**'s staid recording, should it come out on CD (MIA).

Five years after the success of 2, Chadwick was moved to write another symphony, and so well did he succeed that 3 was awarded first prize in a competition organized by the National Conservatory in New York, adjudicated by a distinguished visitor to this country, Dvořák. **Krueger**'s recording in the Library of Congress's "Our Musical Past" series deserves our profound gratitude and respect but has been supplanted in every way by **Järvi** and the Detroit Symphony, who play the very devil out of this music (♦Chandos 9253). Both Chadwick symphonies are available from Järvi on a single disc (Chandos 9685), which offers good value for money, but you'll lose his *Symphonic Sketches* in the process, and that's a concession I'm not willing to make.

Symphonic Sketches is the best known and certainly the most original of Chadwick's "light symphonies," bursting at the seams with brash Yankee humor and melodic invention. The lean, spare sound of **Hanson**'s recording (♦Mercury 434337) suits its imagery exactly, imparting a Chaplinesque quality that makes the estimable **Järvi** (Chandos 9334, with Symphony 2) seem almost too comfortable by comparison. With two such worthy contenders to choose from, **Serebrier**'s earnest effort must be relegated to third place, as much for the dull, congested sonics as for the shortcomings of the Brno Philharmonic (Reference).

If the *Sinfonietta* lacks the sardonic edge of the *Symphonic Sketches,* it seems energetic enough, though not straying far from the Old World mold—at least until the last movement, when echoes of the earlier score can be heard. **Krueger** seems to have the measure of this rather unassuming fare despite the thin sound of the Rochester Philharmonic strings (MIA, with Symphony 3). *Suite Symphonique* for the most part suggests a recycling of earlier material; it may be had from **Serebrier** coupled with the symphonic poem *Aphrodite*—which in its shifting imagery reminds us that she not only was the goddess of love but was worshiped by sailors as well—and the deeply felt *Elegy* for Chadwick's close friend Horatio Parker (Reference 74). The sound is a bit opaque, but it is a vast improvement over Serebrier's *Symphonic Sketches.*

Serenade for Strings, written midway between Symphonies 2 and 3, is tuneful and immediately appealing, if without the purple passion of its better-known Tchaikovsky counterpart. It's performed competently by **Hobart Earle** and the American Music Ensemble Vienna—actually a group of Viennese musicians who get together to play American music (Albany 033).

As *Aphrodite* attests, Chadwick was fascinated with Greek lore, which is also reflected in a trilogy of overtures devoted to the Muses: *Thalia* (unfortunately not recorded), *Melpomene,* and *Euterpe.* Of these, *Euterpe* (the Muse of lyric poetry and music) is effectively conveyed by **Jorge Mester** in a grab bag (Albany 030); Melpomene (the Muse of tragedy) has been honored by **Serebrier** (with *Symphonic Sketches*) and **Matthew H. Phillips** as part of "Those Fabulous Americans" (Albany), with Serebrier by far the more compelling. Both must yield to **Järvi**, whose vivid portrayal and sumptuous sonics easily sweep the board (♦Chandos 9439, with Randall Thompson's Symphony 2). More of Chadwick's unique sense of humor may be heard in the concert overtures *Rip Van Winkle* and *Tam O'Shanter,* affectionate homage to Washington Irving and Robert Burns, and again Järvi is the clear winner, edging out Serebrier in *Tam O'Shanter* and standing alone in *Rip Van Winkle.*   HALLER

Cécile Chaminade (1857–1944)

Chaminade is known for a few pieces—I assume a lot of us played *Scarf Dance* in a Sunday afternoon recital—but only recently has her music been more widely heard in recital and on recordings. There are similar-

ities in style and form to Fauré, Franck, and Ravel, and she provided no progressive additions to compositional practice, but it's better to dismiss these influences for the sake of her own fluent and graceful voice. She's known primarily for her solo piano works, mainly 200 or so character pieces, a designation I favor over "salon music." An accomplished pianist, she performed with considerable success in England and her native France, but she never achieved great international acclaim for either her compositions or her playing. Much of her music seems quaint now, but as scholars and performers extend the repertoire, it should find a secure niche.

Several orchestral works, including a symphony and ballet scores, remain largely unknown, and only a few songs are heard very often; some choral music is done occasionally, and I'm curious about her only opera. If the larger-scaled chamber pieces and the piano sonata indicate the quality of these works, Chaminade's reputation, though enhanced, will most likely continue to be based on the character pieces. Two piano trios are offered as evidence, given a robust reading by the **Tzigane Trio** (ASV 965). Trio 1 also exists on recordings by the **Macalester Trio** (Vox 5029, 2CD) and **Rembrandt Trio** (Dorian 90187). The Macalester is more restrained than Tzigane but interesting, and their disc includes music by other women composers. The Rembrandt comes in last for Trio 1, but they include her *Serenade espagnole* and *Romanza appassionata,* both for violin and piano.

The charming *Concertino for Flute and Piano* is better known. Flutist **Lauren Zuker**'s performance isn't as good as several live performances I've heard, but will serve as an introduction to the piece (Cantilena 660012). A version for orchestra is more interesting, and there are recordings by **Manuela Wiesler** with the Helsingborg Symphony led by Philippe Auguin (BIS 529) and **Galway** with Dutoit and the Royal Philharmonic (BMG 9026). Galway is superb, but for this very French music I prefer Wiesler's sound, though her accompaniment leaves a good bit to be desired. The subtle French flavor is hard to capture digitally, so those who prefer Galway's superior if casual musicianship will be more than satisfied with his performance.

Many of Chaminade's piano scores are among the 20 in **Eric Parkin**'s disc (Chandos 8888). It's an excellent introduction to the composer and also wears well for those who are already familiar with her work. He plays each of these miniatures (65 minutes of recorded music) with a sure sense of the various styles required, intuitively illuminating her graceful melodies and introspective moments. **Enid Katahn** presents some of the same works and the sonata (Gasparo 247), but I recommend Parkin. For the fullest sample to date of Chaminade's solo piano music, get **Peter Jacobs**'s performances (Hyperion 66584, 66706, 66846). There may not be enough good stuff to warrant this extensive a commitment, but Jacobs presents the sonata and a panoply of music not recorded and rarely, perhaps never, heard in recital. His playing isn't uniformly good or bad; there are some oddly insecure moments that could surely have been rectified by a bit more attention to rhythmic fidelity and contrast of style and more careful recording from the producers and performer.   ZIEROLF

Gustave Charpentier (1860–1956)

Puccini had *La Bohème;* Charpentier had *Louise,* another story of illicit young love in turn-of-the-century Paris that is this composer's sole claim to fame. Fantastically popular in France until quite recently, *Louise* has never traveled particularly well, although the ecstatic, high-flying aria "Depuis le jour" is a staple of soprano recitals. Charpentier's ambitious score is far from negligible, especially when the joys of Paris are being limned, and it earned the admiration of such astute musicians as Mahler and Virgil Thomson. This "musical novel" (as Charpentier billed it) is an admirable wallow for fans of opera, Paris, or both.

Two major-label recordings of *Louise* came out in the late '70s and have been reissued on CD. **Cotrubas** and Domingo play the lovers on one (♦Sony 46429), **Sills** and Gedda on another (EMI 65299). I prefer the Sony; the leads are in fresher voice and the sound somewhat better than EMI's, although fans of Sills need not hesitate; even in her declining vocal years, she knew her way around a French opera heroine. You can hear "Depuis le jour" performed on many recital discs: compellingly by **Callas** (EMI 66466), brightly by **Battle** (DG 47114), complacently by **Te Kanawa** (EMI 69802), and—first choice—by **Fleming** in a collection called, with justice, "The Beautiful Voice" (♦London 458858). Fleming has performed the complete opera on stage quite a few times; if she ever makes a recording of the entire opera, it would be well worth hearing.

A truly authentic, truly French performance of *Louise* can be heard with the fabled **Ninon Vallin** and Thill, with Charpentier himself conducting (Teldec 30223, 3CD). The score was abridged for a 1933 film soundtrack, but that probably won't bother most people. As can be seen from the dates above, Charpentier lived well into the age of recording, and this set is filled out with composer-led versions of some of his other pieces—not terribly interesting, except for the colorful orchestral suite *Impressions d'Italie*. Also in the set is "Depuis le jour" performed somewhere underneath all the surface noise by the legendary **Mary Garden** (recorded in 1911). RAYMOND

Marc-Antoine Charpentier *(ca. 1643–1704)*

Charpentier's career falls into several phases. After studying with Carissimi in Rome, he composed for the *Comédie Française* from 1672 to 1686. At the same time he served the Duchess of Guise as music master from about 1675 until her death in 1688, a time when he also produced sacred music for the nuns of Port-Royal and other convents. He was music master at the Jesuit church in Paris from 1688 to 1698 and then received his final appointment as music master at Sainte-Chapelle. Catherine Cessac's *Marc-Antoine Charpentier* (Amadeus Press, 1995) is the latest biography.

Of 11 masses, by far the most familiar is the simple *Messe de Minuit* H.9 for Christmas Eve, based on traditional noëls. Minkowski's Musiciens du Louvre couples it with the most familiar (H.146) of four *Te Deum*s (Archiv 453479). King's College Choir offers the same coupling in less stylish but still satisfying performances (EMI 763135). The same *Te Deum* is coupled with the late masterpiece *Missa Assumpta est Maria* H.11 for six voices in a superb disc from Christie's Les Arts Florissants (♦Harmonia Mundi 901298, with *Litanies* H.83), superior to the same coupling from the St. James Singers (Teldec 12465). Still impressive is Louis Martini's version of H.146 with Jeunesses Musicales Chorale and the Paillard Orchestra (Vanguard 8075, with *Magnificat* H.74). This was Martini's remake of two of his pioneering Charpentier recordings, which began the revival of the composer's celebrity when they were first recorded in 1953–54. Two other fine versions of H.9 come from Paul Colléaux's Nantes ensemble (Arion 68015) and Kyle Brown's Virgin Consort (Gothic 49077, with *Magnificat* H.73).

The *Requiem,* or *Messe pour les trépassés* H.2 for eight voices, is a large-scale mass. Corboz led Gulbenkian Foundation forces (♦Erato 97238). Another *Messe à 8* H.3 came from Trajan Popescu's ensembles (Schwann 36, LP, NA). A *Messe à quatre choeurs* H.4 has been neglected, but Malgoire's Grand Écurie ensemble gave it the only recording so far (Erato 45614).

The other masses are on a more modest scale. Niquet's Concert Spirituel recorded *Messe* H.1 along with the first recording of a modest little *Te Deum* H.147 (♦Naxos 553175). *Messe pour le Port-Royal* H.5 is a slight work written for the nuns at the convent in Paris. Two fine recordings are complementary in choosing two different but equally appropriate mass propers and adding the *Magnificat pour le Port-Royal* H.81, from Les Demoiselles de Saint-Cyr (♦Astrée 8598) and Capella Ricercar (Ricercar 052034). *Messe* H.6 comes from the Purcell Choir of Budapest (Hungaroton 31869, with five responsories). *Messe des morts* H.7 is offered with three psalms and two other works by Concert Spirituel (♦Naxos 553173). Heinz Hennig's Hanover Boy's Choir pairs the same mass with *Messe pour le Samedi de Pâques* H.8 (Calig 50874), while Louis Devos's Westvlaams ensemble couples it with another modest *Messe des morts,* H.10 (Erato 17894).

Of the two *Te Deum*s not yet mentioned, István Zámbó's Veszprém Chorus and the Budapest Philharmonic recorded a large work for eight voices H.145 (♦Hungaroton 12920), while Yves Atthenont's Petits Chanteurs de Versailles offered the smaller H.148 (Jade 39424). Besides the three *Magnificat*s mentioned already, five others have been recorded: Concert Spirituel, H.72 (♦Naxos 553174); Petits Chanteurs de Versailles, H.76 (Jade 39425); Louis Devos's Ghent ensembles, H.79 (Erato 13734, with *Te Deum* H.146); and Savall's Concert des Nations, the modest H.80 (♦Astrée 8713, with seven other Marian pieces). An Everest LP of H.75 needs replacement.

For the nine Lamentations of Tenebrae, Charpentier composed a total of 31 settings. Cessac identifies H.96–110 (a series that includes some duplications) as a unified set, and Concerto Vocale recorded a complete group of nine that is the first choice here (♦Harmonia Mundi 901005/07, 3CD). Gérard Lesne's excellent Il Seminario also recorded a complete group of nine with only one selection duplicating Concerto Vocale (♦Virgin 545107, 545075, 759295). Louis Devos also offered a group of nine, but three are duplicated on Seminario's disc (Erato 96376, 2CD). Ensemble Gradiva sings three more lamentations unduplicated so far (Adda 581200, with a motet). Malgoire's Grand Écurie duplicated Concerto Vocale's group exactly without equaling its perfection (CBS 79320, 3LP, NA). Le Parlement de Musique offered an attractive program of three lamentations, each followed by a responsory, concluding with *Miserere* H.157. The liturgical format is correct, and the performances are very good, but the selections are chosen at random from all three days, nullifying their liturgical propriety (Opus 111 559119).

Charpentier also composed two sets of nine responsories to follow the lamentations (H.111–119 and 126–134). Concerto Vocale recorded the first set on LP, but only the first three fit into the CD reissue of the lamentations noted above. Il Seminario recorded eight responsories in the discs cited above, mostly from the second set. The Purcell Choir, as noted under masses, recorded five responsories from the second set (Hungaroton 31869).

Of the many psalm settings, Concert Spirituel offers a complete Vespers of the Virgin, including H.221, 149, 216, 150, and 210 (♦Naxos 553174). Gulbenkian Foundation forces sang *Miserere des Jésuites* H.193 (♦Erato 45175). Another *Miserere*, H.219, is featured in a Chapelle Royale disc (Harmonia Mundi 901185, with H.372, 346 and 434). Devos's Ghent ensembles sang *De profundis* H.189 (♦Erato 24232, 2CD). Olivier Schneebeli's Contrepoint ensemble sang five psalms, H.170, 215, 220, 221, and 216 (♦Adda 581190, with H.326 and 411). Le Parlement de Musique sang three psalms, H.174, 179, and 231 (Opus 111 309005).

The dramatic motets (sometimes called oratorios) are a significant genre for this composer. Les Arts Florissants recorded a number of them for ♦Harmonia Mundi: *Filius Prodigus* H.399 and *Caecilia Virgo et martyr* H.413 (mislabeled H.397, 90066); *In nativitatem* H.414 (1905124, with antiphons H.36–43); another *In nativitatem,* H.416 (905130, with the pastorale H.482); and *Le reniement de St. Pierre* H.424 (905151, with meditations H.380–389). Concerto Vocale included *Dialogus inter Magdalenam et Jesum* H.423 among a group of a dozen motets (Harmonia Mundi 901149).

For other dramatic motets, Le Concert des Nations included *Pour la fête de l'Epiphanie* H.395 and *Canticum in honorem B. V. Mariae* H.400 in the disc of Marian pieces cited above (♦Astrée 8713). Louis Devos's Ghent ensembles recorded *Caecilia Virgo et Martyr* H.397 and *In obitum* H.409 (♦Erato 24232, 2CD, with a psalm H.189 and *Luctus* H.331). Paul Colléaux's Nantes ensemble presented *Judicium Salomonis* H.422 (Arion 68037, with canticle H.355). The Contrepoint disc cited for its psalms includes *Caedes sanctorum innocentium* H.411 (♦Adda 581190). The English Bach Festival Chorus and Orchestra recorded *Judith* H.391 (Erato 45094) and *Dialogus inter Christum et peccatores* H.425 (♦Erato 71281, LP, NA). Michel Corboz's Gulbenkian Foundation forces gave us *Extremum Dei Judicium* H.401 (♦Erato 45175, with the psalm cited). Ton Koopman led an Amsterdam ensemble in *Mors Saülis et Jonathae* H.403, *Josue* H.404, and *Praelium Michaelis archangeli* H.410 (♦Erato 45822, 2CD, with three lamentations and a psalm, H.167). Louis Frémaux recorded *Dialogus inter angelos et pastores* H.420 (Erato 50098, LP, NA). Musica Aeterna's *Pestis Mediolanensis* H.398 needs replacement.

Many motets and other short sacred works are found in discs already mentioned. Ricercar Consort with countertenor Henri Ledroit assembled a notable collection of 12 secular pieces, including the autobiographical *Epitaphium Carpentarii* H.474, the cantata *Orphée descendant aux enfers* H.471, three songs from *Le Cid,* H.457-459, and Sonata H.548 (♦Ricercar 037011). Les Arts Florissants assembled 17 secular pieces, mostly new to records (♦Erato 25485). Le Parlement de Musique recorded a less interesting work, *Quatuor anni tempestates* H.335–338, in a disc containing psalms cited above (Opus 111 309005).

Among the operas and other scenic works, Christie's Les Arts Florissants twice recorded the composer's masterpiece, *Médée* H.491, the second time complete, with a splendid Lorraine Hunt as Médée (Erato 96558, 3CD). The satisfactory older version is still available (Harmonia Mundi 2901139/41, 3CD). The same group also recorded *David et Jonathas* H.490 (Harmonia Mundi 1901289/90, 2CD), with Gérard Lesne as David, previously offered by Michel Corboz with Paul Esswood in the role (Erato 71435, 3CD). Both are more than satisfactory.

Christie then recorded *La descente d'Orphée aux enfers* H.488 with tenor Paul Agnew as Orphée, a work that, after two acts bringing the couple out of Hades, is either partly lost or unfinished (Erato 11913). He also recorded *Les plaisirs de Versailles* H.480 (Erato 14774). Minkowski's Musiciens du Louvre performed *Le malade imaginaire* H.495 (Erato 45002). Les Arts Florissants gave us their namesake work, *Les arts florissants* H.487 (Harmonia Mundi 1901083). The same group recorded *Actéon* H.481 (Harmonia Mundi 901095), a *Pastorale,* H.482 (Harmonia Mundi 905130, with a dramatic motet cited above) and another *Pastorale,* H.483 (Harmonia Mundi 901082).   WEBER

Ernest Chausson *(1855–1899)*

Chausson's music is the embodiment of elegant, cultured melancholy. To some extent, so was Chausson himself. An only child raised in a cultivated, well-to-do atmosphere, he became (in the words of his teacher, Jules Massenet) "an exceptional person and a true artist." He slaved at

his composition, the more to avoid the label of "rich, talented amateur." His industry was tempered by inspiration; he left comparatively little music (although 39 opus numbers isn't bad for a composer who died at 44), but most of it is among the best 19th-century France has to offer. He was just hitting his stride when he died in one of the more celebrated of composers' deaths: the bicycle he was riding ran out of control on a hill and crashed into a wall, and he died instantly.

ORCHESTRAL MUSIC

If you encounter Chausson in a concert program, it's probably through his *Poème,* one of the most exquisite compositions ever written for violin and orchestra. This piece, much revised by the composer between 1882 and its final version of 1893, was suggested by a Turgenev story, and the richly emotional music has suggested several stories in turn (notably to choreographer Anthony Tudor, for his ballet *Lilac Garden*).

Poème was first performed by Ysaÿe, and while it's not as popular a concert work as it used to be, there is hardly a notable violinist, young or old, who hasn't recorded it since. There are excellent performances by **Perlman** with Martinon (♦EMI 47725) and Mehta (DG 423063), **Heifetz** (RCA 7709), **Francescatti** with Ormandy (Sony 62339) and Bernstein (Sony 47548), and particularly **David Oistrakh** with Munch, in which the inflammatory conductor and patrician violinist mesh very tellingly (♦RCA 6068). A beautiful **Milstein** version is not currently available (EMI).

Much less frequently encountered in concert is Chausson's Symphony in B-flat, an ample, beautiful, three-movement work nearly as good as Franck's Symphony in D minor, on which it is transparently modeled. If this symphony isn't heard live very often, it has been recorded fairly frequently; the best currently available are probably by **Munch** (♦RCA 60683) and **Paray** (♦Mercury 434389). I have reservations about their recording quality, but they both cook at a pretty high temperature. (Munch is coupled with the excellent *Poème* with Oistrakh; Paray has enjoyable works by Lalo and Henri Barraud.) There are less highly strung performances by **Serebrier** (Chandos), **Mata** (Dorian), and **Plasson** (EMI). Plasson includes *Viviane* and *Soir de Fête,* while Serebrier includes *Soir de Fête* plus two dances from *The Tempest;* better still, **Tortelier** gives you all three along with a sumptuous rendition of the Symphony (♦Chandos 9650). *The Tempest* may be heard in its entirety under **Kantorow;** it is coupled with *La Légende de Sainte Cécile* (EMI 55323).

An excellent, inexpensive introduction to Chausson's art is available. I had never heard of violinist **Laurent Korcia,** conductor Jerome Kaltenbach, or the Orchestre Symphonique et Lyrique de Nancy, but they give performances of *Poème* and the Symphony that are notable for their breadth and sympathy, and the recording includes *Viviane,* an early, quite Wagnerian symphonic poem (♦Naxos 553652).

CHAMBER MUSIC

As befits a composer of such inwardness, some of Chausson's most passionate and personal statements are in his chamber music. Possibly his greatest work is his *Concert for Violin, Piano, and String Quartet*—not a concerto, not a sextet, but a unique work in the spirit of the 18th-century *pièces en concerts* of Rameau. This passionate, civilized piece is a favorite of musicians, and of audiences when they get a chance to hear it. The definitive recording is probably the 1931 version with **Thibaud** and Cortot (Biddulph 29). If you're impatient with antique sound, try the early-'80s version by **Perlman,** Bolet, and the Juilliard Quartet (♦Sony 37814), unfortunately without a coupling, or the recording by **Pascal Devoyon,** Philippe Graffin, and the Chilingirian Quartet, with a generous coupling, Chausson's Piano Quartet (Hyperion 66907). There are no current recordings of his other major chamber works, the Piano Trio and String Quartet (his last work, completed by d'Indy).

SONGS

Chausson's refined songs have a small but honorable place in recitals. The splendid mezzo **Natalie Stutzmann** has recorded all of them (♦RCA 68342). Good performances of some of the most popular are by **de Gaetani,** ca. 1980 (♦Arabesque 6673, with songs by Debussy and Ravel), and **Souzay,** ca. 1950 (London 425975, with some lovely Fauré and a few French airs). De Gaetani includes the long and fascinating "La Caravane," a seven-minute song that has an opus number to itself (14). **Norman** includes five short Chausson songs with her coupling of *Poème de l'amour de la mer* and *Chanson perpetuelle* (Erato 45368).

Chausson's longest vocal work is *Poème de l'amour et de la mer,* for female voice and orchestra. The poem by Maurice Bouchor is sentimental and mediocre, but Chausson set it to beautiful, languorous music, sumptuously orchestrated. (His most popular *mélodie,* "Le temps des lilas," is extracted from this work.) Seldom encountered in concert, it has had a healthy life on records. **Norman**'s performance is lusciously sung but a bit dull (Erato), and there's a version by **Baker** with predictably splendid, heartfelt singing and somewhat enervated conducting by Previn (♦EMI 68667). Lovers of this work will enjoy Chausson's intense *Chanson perpetuelle,* for voice, piano, and string quartet, included in the Norman and Stutzmann collections; it has also been recorded by **von Otter** in a delectable French recital (♦DG 47752).

RAYMOND

Carlos Chávez (1899–1978)

This eminent composer played a dominant role in the musical life of Mexico as educator and founder and conductor of the Orquestra Sinfónica de México (later Orquesta Nacional). His music is nationalistic, neoromantic, and neoclassical, made up of short- to long-lined motifs and a strong rhythmic pulse, and spiced with moderate dissonance. Aaron Copland commented on his friend's music: It "is strong and deliberate, relentless and uncompromising. It is music that knows its own mind, stark and clear, no frills, nothing extraneous, earthy in an abstract way. [It] possesses an Indian quality that is at the same time curiously contemporary in spirit."

SYMPHONIES

Chavez wrote six symphonies, No. 1 in 1933, No. 6 in 1961; a seventh remained unfinished. The complete set was recorded in 1991 in excellent performances and spacious sound by **Mata** conducting the London Symphony (Vox 5061, 2CD). Nos. 1 and 2 are short, 10- to 13-minute, one-movement works. The sober, austere, dramatic 1 (*Sinfonía de Antígona*) was drawn from incidental music written in 1933 for a Cocteau production of Sophocles's *Antigone,* using Greek Dorian and Hypodorian modal scales. A large orchestra includes a heckelphone (bass oboe) and two harps. In 2 (*Sinfonía India,* 1935), his most popular symphony, Chávez is a true indigenist, using authentic Indian melodies supported by a large array of Mexican percussion.

Nos. 3 through 6 were written in a more universal, neoromantic or neoclassical style. No. 3 (1951) is a work of relentless intensity and thrust, but still with an undercurrent of Indian melos. The memorable 4 (*Sinfonía Romántica*) is made up of soaring, long-lined melodies, living up to its title. The largely neoclassical 5 (1953), for strings, is a work of taut rhythms and colors expressed in lean sonorities. In the majestic 6, Chávez uses fugues and passacaglias.

Chávez's own 1959 interpretations of 1, 2, and 4 are still available (Everest 9041). Nos. 1 and 4 were also recorded in excellent performances by **Bátiz,** coupled with strong works by Revueltas ("Musica Mexicana" Vol. 8, ASV 942; ASV 653). The nationalistic 2 is coupled with the lovely *Encamiento y Zarabanda* and three memorable works by Carlos Jiménez Mabarak as discmates, played by **Fernando Lozano** conducting different orchestras (Spartacus 221022). **Luis Herrera de la Fuente** conducts 2 with lively works by other composers. **Tilson Thomas** plays a rather tame 2, coupled with six other Latin American works and one by Copland (Argo 737). **Mata** leads 1 and 2 coupled with other attractive works (Dorian 90179).

OTHER ORCHESTRAL WORKS

Mata plays the passionate, energetic suite from the 1926–32 ballet *Caballos de Vapor* (Horsepower) ("Latin American Ballets," Dorian 90211, with Villa-Lobos's *Uirapurú* and Ginastera's *Estancia*). **Bátiz** plays *Zarabanda* for strings (minus the "Encantiamiento"), coupled with engaging works by Revueltas and others ("Musica Mexicana" Vol. 4, ASV 893). Chavez's orchestration of Buxtehude's *Chaconne,* played by Bátiz, is coupled with such Mexican favorites as Ponce's *Estrellita* and Blas Galindo's *Sones de Mariachi,* plus seven other Latin-flavored works ("Musica Mexicana" Vol. 5, ASV 894). Bátiz is superb in the vibrantly rhythmic *Toccata for Orchestra,* the earthy *Cantos de México,* the evocative *Paisajes de México,* the Coplandesque *La Hija de Cólquide,* and the dance-like *Baile* (ASV 927).

CHAMBER MUSIC

Chávez's much heralded *Toccata* (1942) was one of the first compositions written for percussion ensemble, followed by *Tambuco* in 1964. Various musicians play these outstanding works coupled with *Energia* for a nonet of winds and strings; *Xochipili Maquilxochitl* for piccolo, flute, clarinet, trombone, and six percussionists; and *La Hija de Cólquide* for woodwind quartet and string quartet (Dorian 90215)— Fine performances throughout.

DE JONG

Luigi Cherubini (1760–1842)

Perhaps no other composer of the classical era has been so unjustly relegated to the stockpile of once-thought-greats. From the age of 26, this Florentine decided that his musical fortunes would be better served by living in Paris. He was perhaps secretly trying to avoid the intense Viennese competition, though Beethoven spoke of him as the greatest living composer, and he maintained that reputation steadfastly during his Paris years. Cherubini's music is energetic, mysterious, beautiful, and full of originality. It's a shame that posterity has seen fit to put him on the back burner, though there are minute signs of change.

ORCHESTRAL MUSIC

Symphony in D. The spirit of **Toscanini** hovers over any modern recording of this symphony, and many are the challengers who have found their sonic superiority no match for the maestro's impeccable sense of proportion and his unerring balance among the more overtly classical elements of Cherubini's creation. His classic account has been reissued, and if sound isn't important, you needn't read any farther (RCA 60278, with several overtures). Fortunately, there are two worthy stereo recordings, by **Donato Renzetti** (♦Frequenz 011-042) and **Howard Griffiths** (♦CPO 999521). Both are refreshingly buoyant, though Renzetti makes the finale sparkle while Griffiths lopes along more amiably; still, better that than the mad scramble so many conductors have resorted to, including the LPs by **Brusilow** (RCA) and **Schwarz** (Nonesuch).

In the import bin you may find **Mackerras,** rather intriguingly coupled with works of Respighi and Busoni; unfortunately those works are the main reason to buy it, as Mackerras's sluggish tempos in both minuet and finale effectively rule it out (Carlton 91372). The **Prague Chamber Orchestra** (without conductor) is adroit but small-scaled (Supraphon 3429, with *Requiem* in D Minor).

Overtures. Of some 40 operas by Cherubini, only *Medea* (or *Médée*) remains viable for contemporary audiences, so it's hardly surprising that although there have been innumerable recordings of Rossini and Verdi overtures, Cherubini collections are few. Certainly the most familiar is *Médée,* and this stark and powerful curtain-raiser is available in highly dramatic readings from **Renzetti** (♦Frequenz 011-142), **Lawrence Foster** (♦Claves 50-9513), and of course **Toscanini** (RCA 60278). **Marriner** tempers the sound and fury a bit without diminishing the impact of the music (EMI 54438).

Marriner and Foster both offer five of the remaining pieces, to which each adds two more that are not duplicated. Toscanini offers both *Ali Baba* and *Anacréon* in addition to *Médée,* while only Renzetti gives you *Ifigenia in Aulide* and *Le Crescendo.* However, comparisons are not cut-and-dried, as some of Foster's readings have a breadth and scope that quite surpass Marriner, whereas the latter is more exhilarating in others. Avoid **Silvano Frontalini**'s CD, containing sodden, joyless run-throughs (Nuovo Era). You'll find noteworthy performances of *Il Giulio Sabino* and *Lodoïska* by **Howard Griffiths** (CPO 999521, with the D Major Symphony). *Anacréon,* perhaps second only to *Médée* in number of recordings, may also be had in **Karajan**'s Berlin Philharmonic "Operatic Overtures and Intermezzi" (EMI 69020), as well as filler for **Markevitch**'s *Symphonie Fantastique* (DG 447406).

CHAMBER MUSIC

Quartets. Cherubini was no slouch when it came to quartet writing; all six come from his last mature years. These quartets are not Beethoven—what is?—but their themes are memorable and worthy of greater representation on disc and in concert than they currently enjoy. The first and last, led by the admirable Monica Huggett with the London **Hausemusik** group on period instruments, are athletic and well groomed, finely tuned to the Cherubini idiom and definitely worth acquiring (♦CPO 999463). The silken tone and resonating energy of the **Melos Quartet** combine to make their set of all six a classic; it has been in and out of the catalog, and should be grabbed the moment it appears (♦DG). The **Quartet David** attempts to fill the gap with its very romantic, perhaps overly suave reading that nonetheless gives free rein to Cherubini's magnificent melodies. The reverberant sound detracts only slightly from truly outstanding performances (♦BIS 1003/5).

Sonatas. Cherubini's two sonatas for horn and strings are enjoyable, worthwhile members of the horn repertory. They have surfaced from time to time, usually in the company of other like-minded pieces. One suggestion is to get either or both of the versions by **Tuckwell,** one containing miscellaneous horn works (EMI 69395, 2CD), or the very attractive set with the string sonatas of Rossini (♦London 443838, 2CD). Another recommended collection is by **Ifor James** (EBS 6052), and there is a CD with **Luciano Giuliani** (Nuovo Era 6910). I'd also recommend **Hermann Baumann**'s collection, but I haven't been able to find it on CD (Arabesque 8084, LP). A disc of cello concertos by C.P.E. Bach contains what appears to be the only available recording of Cherubini's 13 *Contredanses,* performed by **Rolla** and the Liszt Chamber Orchestra (White Label 117).

KEYBOARD WORKS

Laura Alvini offers us the six sonatas on harpsichord in sound that is a little too spacious, with playing a little too sluggish (Nuovo Era). You may prefer these on piano, even fortepiano, but they are not currently to be found. Wait a while.

CHORAL MUSIC

Requiem in C Minor. Cherubini's first requiem—for the memory of decapitated King Louis XVI, and written after he had composed an anthem praising the revolution that did the trimming—achieved great popularity during his lifetime. Dark and brooding, the work aptly describes the sorrow of loss, while soberly attempting to reflect the seriousness of human life and choice.

Emilio Pomarico leads a respectable performance, spiritually astute though technically subpar, with some off-sounding balances (Stradivarius). **Muti** has been an indefatigable champion of this composer's choral music, and his C minor *Requiem* is Cherubini writ large, glorious for all of you wanting to bathe in large orchestras and overpowering choral sound. For classical restraint, look elsewhere, but if you want to weep, look no farther (♦EMI 49678). **Christoph Spering** and his 40-member period band project a sound very close to what Cherubini might have heard, and it's an immaculate performance. Orchestra and chorus perform well, tempos are well-judged if a little antiseptic (♦Opus 111 116). This may appeal to some, but once you've heard Muti, you won't go back. Finally, **Toscanini** forged a powerful account, complete with a sterling Robert Shaw–led chorus. However, the sound is boxy, and the appearance of the Muti makes the others dispensable.

Requiem in D Minor. This work, possibly intended for the composer's own funeral, is remarkably original. Using lower sonorities and only a men's chorus, the drama is scintillating and forceful. The quaking sonority achieved by these powerful forces makes quite a musical—and visceral—impression. **Markevitch** was one of the first to champion the piece, and his recording from the early '60s is lit by bright, cavernous sound. This works well, allowing a rugged spatial setting for the very large forces. The only drawback is the lack of real bass boom in the lower timbres, but the ripe, rich playing of the Czech Philharmonic adds to its beauty (♦DG 457744).

Not so the older recording by **Järvi** (Melodiya). With wiry strings and sloppy choral work, this rendition is best left alone, though he no doubt got the best he could out of them. **Muti**'s version is ascetic, Romanesque, and overwhelming in its bleak starkness. The forces strike with great impact, and the sound is close to perfect. The bass spectrum lacking in the Markevitch is here in full glory, and Muti takes us to the heart of this splendid work. This is the one to have (♦EMI 49301).

Messe Solonelle in D minor. Earliest of the choral works considered here, the massive *Missa Solemnis* of 1811 rivals in scope even that of Beethoven, all the more curious in that Cherubini wrote it without commission or any likelihood of hearing it performed. **Newell Jenkins** presents us with a fresh reading that's moving and effective (Vanguard 44, or 80 9140 72, 2CD, with Abravanel's *Messa di Santa Cecilia* by Scarlatti). A fine performance is also available from Rilling and his sturdy Stuttgart forces (Hänssler 98325 separately, or 98.981, 2CD, with Haydn's *Paukenmesse*).

Solemn Coronation Mass. Louis XVIII never got the chance to enjoy the accolades of the people at a glorious enthronement ceremony, and Cherubini never got to hear the music specially composed for the occasion. No matter, for the music is a misfit. It's not all joy and lightness as one would expect, but tense, somber, and otherworldly. **Muti** plays it as a solemn religious action, not a political one.

Solemn Mass in C. Roberto Tigani attempts a festal approach with some success, but some bad intonation among the singers spoils the effect (Bongiovanni). **Diaz** presents us with a fresh though slightly nasal reading that is quite moving and effective (♦Vanguard 44).

Coronation Mass. Written for the coronation of Charles X, this is a wonderful example of Cherubini at his lyrical finest. Freed from the somber aspects of a requiem and charged by the festive splendor of the occasion, this work is filled with gorgeous melodies, dramatic pauses and changes of tempo and temperament, and delicious three-part scoring (omitting the altos). **Muti** continues his fervent exploration of choral Cherubini, and makes the most of its operatic drama and superb melodic invention (♦EMI 72786). **Ferro** and his forces also turn in a deliciously vibrant, glistening reading from the early '90s that may not outshine Muti but is still well worth your time (Capriccio).   HALLER/RITTER

OPERAS

Ali Baba. Cherubini's last completed opera was not a successful return to the theater after an extended absence. Using music from his abortive 1793 *Koukourgi,* the opera proves to be quite charming musically, with agreeable tunes and a serviceable plot that is the familiar *1,001 Nights* adventure, routinely handled, with the addition of a love affair. A 1963 performance is most attractive (Nuova Era 2361, 2CD). Kraus performs with his customary brilliance, always cultivated and suave, and Stich-Randall's white, vibrato-less tone merely emphasizes her graceful musicianship. **Sanzogno** propels the La Scala orchestra along in breezy, even slick fashion. A charmingly good show all around.

Les Deux Journées. Cherubini's most successful opera, this was frequently performed throughout the 19th century but quickly disappeared at the beginning of the 20th. The libretto is supposedly based on a historical incident during the French Revolution, but the censors of Cherubini's day required the action to be moved back to the 17th century. Even so, the opera praises the virtues and ideals of the Revolution. This is really an *opéra-comique* with lots of spoken dialogue between brief musical selections. Among the 15 musical numbers there are only two arias, an overture, and two entr'actes; the rest are vocal ensembles. The music is quite charming and tuneful. Thanks to the ever ebullient **Beecham**, a 1947 performance is lively, dashing merrily along from one selection to the next (♦Intaglio 7342, 2CD). The singers are vocally agreeable, although I'm not totally satisfied with the edgy voice of Janine Micheau. It's monaural sound, but adequate.

Lodoïska. Beethoven greatly admired Cherubini's music, and it's in *Lodoïska* that we hear some musical elements that he was to use, thoroughly reworked, in *Fidelio.* Both are "rescue operas," a genre developed during the French Revolution and often based on historical incidents. The music is hardly memorable and probably would be more effective in the theater.

A 1965 Rome RAI performance is hardly representative of what the work is all about (Nuova Era 2236, 2CD). It's in Italian, and an unidentified "editor" has composed new recitatives in place of the spoken dialogue, made many cuts and substitutions from other operas, and re-orchestrated the work. The performance is hardly memorable either. **Ilva Ligabue** has a bothersome, pure, white quality to her voice that lacks the heroic scale required. Giacinto Prandelli's aristocratic tenor is well employed, although his top notes thin out. But **Muti**'s substantially complete, "original" version in French isn't much better (Sony 47290,

2CD). Despite his belief in the opera (he welds the La Scala forces into a coherent whole), there is still room for improvement. Mariella Devia sings with dramatic intent. Neither Bernard Lombardo nor Thomas Moser has an attractive voice, each preferring an unsubtle attack on their music. William Shimell at least has the dark, menacing quality required.

Médée (Medea). Gluck's so-called "reform operas" produced an array of successors, the most successful being the elevated and serious *Médée* (Paris, 1797). The spoken dialogue of the original was set to music as recitatives by Franz Lachner in 1854, and they have been used for most modern performances and recordings, usually in Italian translation. Not only is *Médée* a classically poised drama, but it also contains a splendid title role that dominates the opera. A quick glance at the list of recordings reveals a predominance of performances by Maria Callas, and indeed it was she who led the modern revival of the work. There was little serious competition during her day and practically none since.

The Callas recordings document her career and her declining vocal state: the drama always present, the voice less and less reliable. She always performed the opera in Italian in the Lachner edition. Callas is never less than Callas in her emotional involvement, but she was able to plumb the drama to a greater depth when surrounded by like-minded colleagues, which often as not she wasn't. Two recordings are outstanding. The 1953 La Scala performance led by **Bernstein** is ablaze with drama, with Callas at the peak of her vocal security and interpretive power (♦Fonit-Cetra 1019; Hunt 516; Melodram 26022). Gino Penno's Giasone is hardly subtle, but he tries hard to react appropriately to Callas's tigress. The 1957 studio recording led by **Serafin** is disappointing (EMI 66435 or Angel 63625, 2CD). You might appreciate his interpretation as "classically restrained," but too often the feeling is one of "correctness" with little true emotion. Even Callas seems beset by a sense of deliberation rather than spontaneous drama. Except for the fine Glauce of Scotto, her colleagues here are hardly an inspiring lot.

Callas's 1958 Dallas performance occurred within hours of her receipt of a telegram from Rudolf Bing dismissing her from the Metropolitan Opera, and much of the venom in her performance may have been inspired by this (Melodram 26005; Italiana Opera 10; 2CD). Happily, her Giasone was a worthy opponent: Vickers, one of the few artistic matches she ever had. Berganza, in her American debut, is the highly persuasive Néris. **Rescigno** whips the Dallas Symphony (and the audience) into a musical frenzy. By 1961 (La Scala) Callas was in vocal trouble, the bright and secure top voice in shambles (Hunt 34028, 2CD). Curiously, Vickers is distant and uninvolved in these proceedings, although there are strong contributions from Simionato and Ghiaurov. **Thomas Schippers**'s bland, slow conducting is not at all helpful.

Only Olivero came close to matching Callas. She's well represented in a 1967 Dallas production taped at the dress rehearsal (Music & Arts 670, 2CD). Her distinctive throaty soprano is passionately involved. **Rescigno** and the rest of the cast sound positively inspired. Her 1971 performance at Mantua was her only *Medea* in Italy (Myto 911.36, 2CD). Her voice is more forced here, with lots of chest tone. It's a sure-fire dramatic effect, but vocally risky. The rest of the cast is adequate at best. Still, Rescigno whips his orchestral forces into a musical frenzy worthy of Olivero's performance, and the audience responds, with extensive stretches of ovation included in the recording.

Gencer's 1968 performance is for fans of Gencer; her harsh voice is very much an acquired taste (Claque 2005, 2CD). In the same year (1968), Gwyneth Jones was recorded with what (on paper) looks like a dream cast conducted by **Gardelli** (London 1389, 2LP), but it just doesn't work. Jones, another singer with the goods for Medea, doesn't deliver; her voice wobbles to such an extent that drama is forgotten. Bruno Prevedi is a stolid Giasone, but the remainder of the cast sings beautifully.

You would hardly associate Rysanek with a comparatively bel canto role, but in 1972 she was in full cry, smoking up the stage in total abandon (Melodram 27087, 2CD). Her colleagues are a worthy lot, particularly a refined Glauce from Popp. Prevedi's dark tenor sags from pitch on occasion, but he too gets caught up in the drama. **Horst Stein,** a conductor not usually associated with this repertoire, drives the Vienna Staatsoper forces in a glorious rendition. The sound isn't very good, but the performance is astounding. This CD contains a bonus: extended excerpts from another unexpectedly fine *Medea* from Borkh. It's from Berlin, 1958, in German, conducted by **Gui.** Sass had the makings of a fine Medea, with a strong, attractive voice, but she lacked the security to carry off the demanding role. However, she was favored with a fine cast ably supported by **Gardelli** (Hungaroton 11904, 2CD)

Only the two most recent recordings are in French and use the original spoken dialogue, and neither is particularly rewarding. In a 1995 performance, Jano Tamar is impressive in the title role (Nuova Era 7253, 2CD). She's quite confident, securely in control of her gleaming voice. She begins slowly, saving the fireworks for later in the score, and when she unleashes the savagery, she does so with fury. Of the rest of the cast, only the appealing Néris of Magali Damonte is adequate. The small orchestra is lively under **Patrick Fournillier**'s spirited conducting, and the recorded sound is excellent.

The Newport *Médée* of 1997 has nothing to recommend it (85622, 2CD). Phyllis Treigle has a large voice, vibrato-laden and spreading dangerously in high sustained passages. Carl Halvorson is far too light in weight for Jason's music. He's pleasant-sounding, more teenage lover than devastated hero. The others sleepwalk through their roles. Worst of all is the extensive spoken French dialogue. It's quite beyond their capabilities, emerging as monochromatic, uninflected public orations instead of dramatic speech. The Brewer Chamber Orchestra plays period instruments, dully led by **Bart Folse,** and is poorly recorded.

PARSONS

Frédéric Chopin *(1810–1849)*

"In a good mechanism the aim is not to play everything with an equal sound, but to acquire a beautiful quality of touch and a perfect shading. There are, then, many different qualities of sound, just as there are several fingers."—Chopin, fragment from his unpublished piano method.

"Such a poetic temperament as Chopin's never existed, nor have I ever heard such delicacy and refinement of playing. The tone, though small, was absolutely beyond criticism and . . . his execution was perfect in the extreme."—Liszt

Chopin and Liszt first met in Paris in 1832, shortly after Chopin took up residence there. At that time, western Europe was decidedly under the influence of German music—Bach, Mozart, Beethoven, Weber, Schubert—and Mendelssohn and Schumann were assuming their place in the musical life of Germany and France. Chopin and Liszt represented a fresh infusion of eastern European blood into musical art, a fact that was to have more far-reaching and profound consequences than anyone could have imagined. Chopin, ardently Polish and from the beginning identified with the music of his native land, and Liszt, even then thinking of himself as Hungarian, were among the earliest nationalists.

Chopin is often thought of as a swooning romantic, and with this false image in mind, is too often performed sentimentally. Nothing could be farther from the truth. He didn't regard himself a romanticist; Bach and Mozart were the composers he revered most highly. This can further be seen by contrasting him with Liszt, Schumann, Berlioz, and Wagner, the arch-romanticists. All these composers drew inspiration from literary sources, but not Chopin. Arthur Rubinstein said of Chopin's music, "It is not 'Romantic' in the Byronic sense. It does not tell stories or paint pictures." Understanding this provides a revealing glimpse into the essence of his music. It also distinctly affects the way it's played.

Chopin was a unique, unprecedented pianist, just as his piano works are unique and unprecedented. His music requires a special approach to the instrument and distinctive qualities of tone. The kind of tone effective in Liszt, Brahms, or Rachmaninoff is, for the most part, unsuitable. Unfortunately, many of today's pianists, predicating their performances on large concert halls, disfigure his music with a tone that is too massive, strident, percussive, or overstated. In the critiques that follow, I have refrained from listing most of these pianists because it's my conviction that a stylistically true performance of Chopin, in good taste, starts with a variegated tone of subtlety and delicacy rather than with the hammered sounds produced by an overly muscular approach.

PIANO AND ORCHESTRA

Chopin left us six pieces for piano and orchestra, all composed very early in his career—a time when he felt he needed such works to launch himself on a career as a virtuoso. They include two concertos, a set of variations, a Rondo and a Fantasy, and *Andante Spianato* and *Grand Polonaise.* Of these, the two concertos occupy the most integral place in the repertoire. Chopin was harshly criticized by some of his contemporaries (Berlioz, for one) for his orchestration, as well as for his departure from traditional form in these two works, a criticism repeated to this day. But we should remember that they should not be regarded as symphonic concertos in the manner of Mozart or Beethoven but more appropriately as works in the tradition of Hummel, Field, and Ries, in which the soloist is the dominant protagonist, supported and accompanied by the orchestra. Moreover, Chopin was only 19 when he completed the F minor Concerto in 1829 and had just turned 20 when he finished the E minor in the following year, barely beyond his apprenticeship. In the entire concerto literature for piano, except for Mozart there is no parallel where works of such beauty and importance have been composed by someone so young.

The level of recordings of the concertos is very high, among the highest to be found in any category of classical music. All the recordings listed here are recommended, and every one of them will afford abundant listening pleasure. However, they have been assigned to three levels to give the purchaser some small guidance. There are, of course, many other recordings, but none of them are preferable to those discussed below.

Complete sets. For those who would like a complete set of the six works for piano and orchestra, there are four pianists to choose from, all 2CD: **Ohlsson** (Arabesque 6702), **Arrau** (Philips 438338), **Biret** (Naxos 550368), and **Simon** (Vox 5002). Each of the four offers outstanding performances of some works along with others that are less satisfactory. On the whole, I prefer Ohlsson and Biret, though all are quite fine.

Concerto 1. The E minor, Op. 10, was obviously intended to be a "grand" concerto, as you can hear from its broad dimensions and length compared to the F minor, Op. 21 (designated No. 2, though it dates from a year earlier). Its Finale, *à la Krakowiak,* is more brilliant than the F minor (*à la Mazur*), and provides a more rousing conclusion.

Four recordings of 1 can be designated as "exceptional." If ever a pianist could be said to "own" both of them, it would be **Rubinstein,** for no one played them with quite the inflection and mood he brought to them. Yet it will be seen that each of his several versions deserves a somewhat different rating. With Walter and the New York Philharmonic in 1947, he presented an incandescent live performance that heads the list (Dante 127). At the same level is **Perahia** with Mehta, a live recording of great beauty from 1989 (Sony 44922). **Ax** plays a historic piano of Chopin's time with faultless precision, and Mackerras and the Orchestra of the Age of Enlightenment provide an accompaniment that is in itself a thing of beauty (Sony 60771). **Biret** and Stankovsky play this work with hypnotic atmosphere, set in the best recorded sound of all (Naxos 550368), and **Josef Hofmann** gave a historical performance of wonderful style and grace (VAIA 1002; see "Piano solo" section below).

Four "excellent" recordings include **Rubinstein** with Skrowaczewski, made in 1961 and second to his 1947 reading only because it lacks, to a slight degree, the brio of his earlier version (RCA, Vol. 44 of the huge "Rubinstein Collection"; individual discs are gradually becoming available separately). His early 1937 recording with Barbirolli is extremely fast and supercharged (RCA, Vol. 5). **Zimerman,** as soloist and conductor of the Polish Festival Orchestra, presents a novel and interesting conception of the work, with many changes of tempo and mood—some of them baffling—and a very expressive approach, unlike the martial, solemn one so often heard. His orchestra plays more clearly and beautifully than any other Chopin concerto recording I know (DG 459684, 2CD). **Ohlsson**'s performance with Kazimierz Kord, like his Concerto 2, is a marvel of clarity, precision, and pianistic finesse (Arabesque 6702, 2CD). However, the slow tempos in I and II are disappointing and hamper the flow and natural line of the music, though the Finale is one of the most sprightly and delightful.

Eight more recordings are "very, very good." In order, these include **Arrau** with Inbal, satisfying and elegant if a bit slow (Philips 438338, 2CD). **Wild** with Sargent is technically superb, as always, but musically a little inconsistent; at times the playing seems emotionally detached, while elsewhere it's expressive and subtle (Chesky 93). **Rubinstein** with Wallenstein and the Los Angeles Philharmonic was recorded at a time when the orchestra was not what it is today, and the sound is mediocre (RCA, Vol. 17). **Novaes,** with an unidentified conductor and orchestra, plays the work very nicely, with her usual aristocratic mien, but circumspectly and without passion, though II is especially delicate and tender (Vox 5513, 2CD).

Abbey Simon and Heribert Beissel are recorded with much better fidelity, and Simon plays elegantly, with jewel-like clarity and an excellent choice of tempos, though his tone is occasionally too hard and energized (Vox 5002, 2CD). Among historical performances, **Moriz Rosenthal** is in this category and is discussed below. **Gilels** and Ormandy provide a very strong, technically meticulous reading with the fast passages sometimes hard-edged and rattled off as if they were etudes; the best moments are the lyrical passages, played beautifully and sensitively (Sony 46336). For **Argerich** and Abbado, the quiet moments are distinguished by exquisite tone, while the fast passages are hard-driven, even frenzied at times, as is often true of Argerich's Chopin (DG 449719).

Concerto 2 in F minor was actually the first to be composed. Chopin premiered both works in Warsaw before he left Poland permanently for Paris, performing the F minor in 1830 before about 800 listeners who received it with glowing enthusiasm. Its second movement had been inspired by a secret love, Konstanza Gladkowska, a young soprano he had met in the spring of 1829. It's a unique piece in the concerto literature; the middle section, akin to an operatic scena—a Polish lament—was the first to be written.

Three recordings stand out as "exceptional" in the midst of very daunting competition. **Rubinstein**'s 1946 recording with Steinberg embodies one of the most gripping performances ever recorded of any piano concerto, a confluence of brilliance, touching expressivity, infectious rhythm, and nuances of a rarely encountered perfection (Dante 127 or RCA Vol. 17). Oddly, this amazing recording was unobtainable for at least 40 years until its recent reappearance. **Perahia**'s live 1989 performance in Tel Aviv with Mehta and the Israel Philharmonic is pretty astonishing too. The pianist's fluency, subtle shadings, and brisk tempo in III, which bubbles and sparkles with incandescence, all distinguish this reading, though the orchestra fails to match the artistic feats achieved by the pianist (Sony 44922, with 1).

Zimerman, as soloist and conductor of the Polish Festival Orchestra, imparts a kaleidoscopic effect to this work, with much freedom and many changes of tempo and dynamics. His playing is sometimes heavy, but brilliant and emotional as well (DG 459684, 2CD). The orchestra plays impeccably, and the recorded sound is first-rate. However, the 2CD format of this recording (combining the two concertos) makes it expensive compared to Rubinstein and Perahia, whose releases occupy only one disc.

"Excellent" versions of 2 include two more **Rubinstein** performances. The first, with Wallenstein in 1958, is very beautiful, though not as overwhelming as his 1946 version (RCA Vol. 44). The second, his early 1931 recording with Barbirolli, like the 1937 version of 1, is very fast—probably too fast for this concerto (RCA, Vol. 5). There is a notoriously difficult passage at the end of the development section in I where the right hand has a descending run in thirds; Rubinstein tosses this off with unbelievable speed and virtuosity. It's interesting to note that in each of his subsequent recordings, this passage is played with fractionally but progressively less momentum. Finally, an unusually beautiful and polished performance by **Cécile Licad** with Previn completes this category. The playing doesn't quite have Rubinstein's fluency and aristocracy, and the Finale is a bit leisurely. Unfortunately, this CD appears to have been deleted (CBS 39153).

"Very good" recordings include **Ohlsson** with Kord and the Warsaw Philharmonic—the most prismatic of all, but after Rubinstein or Perahia something like a slow-motion picture (Arabesque 6702, 2CD). The technical finish of **Rodriguez** with Gunzenhauser is impressive, despite occasional hardness of tone (Elan 198 2402). **Arrau** and Inbal offer the pianist's typical sumptuous tone but slowish tempos (Philips 438388, 2CD). **Rubinstein** and Ormandy—his final recording of this work, which he was so closely associated with all his life—was made in 1968. Despite many beautiful moments, it's disappointing, lacking the movement and electricity of his earlier versions (RCA Vol. 69). And finally, **Simon** with Beissel is especially attractive for its Finale (Vox 5002, 2CD). **Hofmann** (VAIA 1002; see "Piano solo" section below) rounds out this category.   MULBURY

Kissin was only 12 when he recorded both concertos with Kitaenko (RCA 68378), and his readings have been received with euphoria by many critics, praising his fully formed grasp of the musical line for one so young; others find them slapdash and superficial. **Demidenko** is fluent and polished, with gossamer tone, but lacking in fire or temperament (Hyperion). **Bachauer** is sweeping and grand but lacking in tenderness or allure, with muscular accompaniments from Dorati to match

(Mercury). **Bolet** is unruffled but also uneventful, surprisingly lacking in passion or tension (London).

In Concerto 1, the recording by the 18-year-old **Pollini** has been regarded by many critics as outstanding since its earliest LP issue; one reviewer called it "as close to definitive as it gets" (EMI/Angel 69004 or 54354). **Cliburn** stops to savor the moment more than most and enjoys satisfying support from the Philadelphia under Ormandy (RCA 7945, with Rachmaninoff's *Rhapsody on a Theme of Paganini*). **Ashkenazy** is note-perfect as always, but seems strangely detached (Decca, with Glazounov's *Chopiniana*).

In Concerto 2, **Clara Haskil**'s treasured performance has been restored to vibrant life; it's filled with sensitive phrasing and limpid tone (Philips 416443, with de Falla's *Nights in the Gardens of Spain*). **Malcuzynski** is relaxed and lyrical, yet robust and fulfilling in the mazurka-styled finale (EMI 68226, with Sonata 3 and other solo pieces). **Lortie**'s powerful and energetic approach carries over to the accompanying Schumann concerto (Chandos 9061). HALLER

Variations on Mozart's "La ci darem la mano" Op. 2 (1827). The expansive Introduction and the six variations that follow are not without interest, but this piece really has to be regarded as a combination "study work" and showpiece, if a noteworthy one. **Ax**'s performance is ideal (Sony 60771). He's followed by **Biret** and **Ohlsson**, both of whom waste too much time in it, **Simon**, and **Arrau**, the last too heavy for this rather frothy work.

Fantasia on Polish Airs 0p. 13 (1828). Chopin's style is more in evidence here, which suggests his rapidly developing skill as a composer. There are boldly imaginative modulations and artistic treatment of the three themes. **Rubinstein**'s single recorded performance, with its excitement and broad, cohesive line, overshadows all the others (RCA, Vol. 69).

Krakowiak Op. 14 (1828). This totally captivating but underappreciated gem is probably Chopin's most successfully orchestrated work. A minor masterpiece, it's difficult to understand why it's so seldom heard. **Ohlsson**'s engaging and fluent performance is superior in every way and the best in his complete set (Arabesque 6702, 2CD). **Simon** is excellent, while **Arrau** and **Biret** are considerably less interesting.

Andante Spianato (1835) and ***Grande Polonaise Op. 22 (1830).*** A later version of this work for piano alone can frequently be heard and seems to me even more characteristic. Several artists have made very winsome recordings of the *Andante spianato* (**Arrau, Simon, Fialkowska**), but of the *Polonaise,* **Rubinstein**'s is by far the most exciting and stylish (RCA Vol. 69). **Biret**'s playing is not as sweeping, but she carries it off with rhythmic elan, very cleanly, and with captivating tone (Naxos 550368). **Fialkowska** is impressive too, and similar to Rubinstein, though not quite as exciting (CBC 5140). These three are followed by **Simon,** in a brilliant performance, and **Arrau,** whose playing is stately, which gives the piece an old-fashioned air.

CHAMBER MUSIC

All five of Chopin's chamber works, with the exception of the late Cello Sonata in G minor, were composed before he left Warsaw. In the *Introduction and Polonaise Op. 3,* the cello part is often played in a version edited and modified by János Starker. The Trio Op. 8 is an appealing, four-movement work, quite unique in the repertoire, at times uneven. The valedictory Sonata in G minor, Chopin's final large-scale composition, is an enduring masterwork, albeit with daunting challenges for performers, not least its gloomy, recrudescent melancholy. The other two compositions—a Grand Duo for cello and piano on a Meyerbeer theme and a set of variations for flute and piano on a Rossini theme—both without opus numbers—are very youthful and display only glimpses of Chopin's characteristic style.

The first three opuses are performed by **Ax,** Ma, and Pamela Frank (Sony 53112). The youthful Trio and the Introduction and Polonaise are played with notable elegance and success. The Sonata, however, seems awkward for them, despite some lovely moments, and the performance fails to satisfy. This disc includes a piano version of the *Introduction and Polonaise,* its manuscript only recently discovered; it's neatly played by **Eva Osinska,** though with limited tonal variety. Is she playing a historical piano here? The boxy sound and twang of certain treble notes would suggest so.

Argerich and Rostropovich recorded the Sonata and *Introduction and Polonaise* in 1980 (DG 419860). The Sonata is played in a nervous, impassioned, maybe even neurotic fashion. It's interesting how the performers contrive to make the initial statement of the exposition in I sound very different from its repeat. Several times during the performance a curious, dull thumping sound can be heard, as if someone were moving furniture in the room above. The *Introduction and Polonaise* suits the temperament and style of this duo better, but even here there are too many impatient, volcanic outbursts that distract the listener from the beauty of the music.

All five chamber works were recorded in Warsaw's Philharmonic Hall by several different performers (Canyon 00238). The Sonata breathes more naturally and is played in a more appealing manner than by Ax/Ma and Argerich/Rostropovich. **Tomasz Strahl**'s cello tone is rich and resonant, though his intonation isn't as good as the others. The Trio is played less elegantly by the **Chopin Trio** than by Ax/Ma/Frank. The program notes are in Japanese only, which is a detriment, because listeners really need information about these works and the performers.

Du Pré and Barenboim recorded the Sonata in 1971 (EMI 63184). Here the challenging piano part is wonderfully performed, but the cellist is less impressive. Her tone is sometimes rough, frequently scratchy, and her intonation is far from perfect. Nevertheless, the balance between the two instruments is excellent and the recorded sound is fresh and pleasing. Of the five versions I've heard, cellist **Maria Kliegel** performs this work with Bernd Glemser with the purest musicality and integration, and they seem most comfortable with its elusive beauty. Both play expertly and sensitively and are supported by outstanding recorded sound (Naxos 553159). This fine disc also includes the *Introduction and Polonaise* and the *Grand Duo.*

SOLO PIANO MUSIC

Collections

Complete recorded editions of Chopin's piano works have been made by **Ashkenazy** (London), **Biret** (Naxos), and **Ohlsson** (Arabesque)—all wonderful pianists, whose sets are, in each case, splendid.

Rubinstein recorded almost everything by Chopin; the main items missing from his discography are the etudes, rondos, solo variations, and *Krakowiak.* However, he recorded his far-flung Chopin repertoire three or more times, roughly as follows: 1930–46 (78 rpm), 1946–58 (LP mono), and 1958–76 (LP, stereo). All these recordings are available as part of an 82-volume, 94CD deluxe limited edition called "The Rubinstein Collection" (RCA 63000). Another compendium of only Chopin recordings is available as "The Chopin Collection" (RCA 60822, 11CD). The meticulous Rubinstein discographies by Donald Manildi, to be found in Harvey Sachs' biography and in "The Rubinstein Collection," as well as Sachs' essay on Rubinstein recordings in his book, provide more exact and extensive details.

Both **Arrau** and **Horowitz** recorded a great deal of Chopin's music, some of it memorable, though less complete. Finally, a nine-volume collection entitled "The Complete Chopin Edition," includes the chamber music and songs as well as the solo piano works, performed by many artists (DG 463047, 17CD).

Historical recordings

This section is generally limited to pianists who recorded before 1950 and not after that time, discussed in roughly chronological order.

Vladimir de Pachmann (1848–1933) was born in Odessa before Chopin's death. Of all the great pianists of yesteryear, I believe that he and Rosenthal best preserved the intrinsic nature of what Chopin's style and ethos may have been. De Pachmann's playing can be described in one word: revelatory. It was distinguished by delicacy, fluidity, spontaneity, extreme digital control, and musical characterization of a very high degree of naturalness and vividness. He indulged in few exaggerations and was very accurate. Unfortunately, his eccentricities have unjustly tarnished his reputation as an incomparable artist. Like Rosenthal, he had studied with a Chopin pupil (Mme. Rubio) and knew and played for Liszt. He also studied counterpoint with Bruckner in Vienna.

Pearl Opal 9840 offers 16 of his Chopin performances. There is a liquid, effortless Scherzo from Sonata 3, refreshingly Chopinesque; the most perfect Prelude 24 in D minor on records; a haunting "Raindrop" Prelude, full of atmosphere and quite unlike Paderewski's tick-tock version; Etude Op. 25:3, glowing with luminosity, without a hint of Arrau's stodginess; and also some pithy spoken comments by de Pachmann connected with his playing of the "Black Key" Etude.

Dante 056 and 061 present 30 of de Pachmann's Chopin recordings, including some of the same ones on the Pearl disc, as well as several pieces in two different recorded versions. There are extraordinary performances of Nocturnes in D-flat and F-sharp, which illustrate better than I have ever heard the "Chopin rubato," in which the right hand gives the illusion of absolute freedom while the left hand maintains strict rhythm; Nocturnes in G Op. 28:3 and E minor Op. posth., in which more delicate, sensitive playing can't be imagined; a stylish, quicksilver "Minute" Waltz; a zesty, powdery "Butterfly" Etude; a wonderful "Revolutionary" Etude; and an astounding modulation, in the manner the old pianists cultivated during their recitals, from the C-sharp minor of Mazurka Op. 63:3 to the A minor of Mazurka Op. 67:4.

Ignacy Jan Paderewski (1860–1941), another Pole and a pupil of Leschetizky, is better known. Pearl 9323, an all-Chopin disc, provides us with a chronological cross-section of his recordings and a glimpse of his potent musical personality. From around 1912, when he was at his peak, there are three Etudes, the C-sharp minor Waltz, and the F major Nocturne. The balance of this CD ranges from 1922 to 1937, showing the many defects in his technical equipment, some very lamentable. Etudes Op. 25:1 and 2 are magnificently played. A fine "Revolutionary" Etude follows (1928), but with some clunkers sprinkled here and there.

Paderewski was renowned for his inimitable playing of the C-sharp minor Waltz. Here his tendency to exaggerate is apparent, upsetting the rhythmic integrity of the music. In the F major Nocturne he does less bending and gives a beautiful performance. The Polonaise in E minor (1930), touted in the booklet notes as his outstanding Chopin recording, is a hodge-podge of waywardness and distortion. The "Heroic" Polonaise in A-flat (1937) is worse—a tragic testament of the rickety state of his declining keyboard capabilities.

Moriz Rosenthal (1861–1946) studied with Mikuli (a pupil of Chopin) and with Liszt, remaining in close contact with the old master until his death. Anton Rubinstein once exclaimed, "I never knew what technique was until I heard Rosenthal." A recording of the E minor Concerto (with cuts) dates from 1930–31 (Pearl 9339). While it's generally less satisfactory than Hofmann's, there are many beautiful and evocative moments, some of a singular, old-fashioned kind. There appears to be, at age 68, only the most inconsequential falling off of Rosenthal's legendary technique. The Concerto is followed by the Chopin-Liszt *Chant Polonais* "My Joys"—one of the most miraculous piano recordings ever made; then Etude Op. 10:1, still the most exciting and near-perfect version of this piece on records; plus several mazurkas, waltzes, *Berceuse*, and the "Black Key" Etude.

On Pearl 9963 we find the Chopin-Liszt *Chant Polonais* "Maiden's Wish" (with cadenza by Rosenthal), and 13 other pieces—mazurkas, preludes, nocturnes, and waltzes. Rosenthal's characteristic playing of the mazurkas is free, plastic, yet disciplined, with a great deal of chiaroscuro. It represents a middle ground between the bracing, rustic approach of Friedman and the infinitely subtle Rubinstein. For the young pianist who wishes to absorb the true idiom and ambience of the mazurkas, there could be no better study than the playing by these three great Poles.

Appian 7002 (2CD) offers Rosenthal's complete HMV recordings from 1934 to 1937 and is an excellent compilation, much of it also in Pearl's two volumes. One work exclusive to Appian is the *Nouvelle Etude* in A-flat, a Rosenthal specialty, played unforgettably. All three of these releases present extensive material on Rosenthal's life, especially Pearl Vol. 2. A fourth Rosenthal CD is an all-Chopin disc containing all the recordings issued by Pearl and Appian except the two Chopin-Liszt transcriptions (Piano Library 316).

Eugen d'Albert (1864–1932) was another Liszt pupil and keyboard titan, this time not Polish. The disc contains four of his Chopin recordings: Nocturne in F-sharp, Waltz Op. 42, and two Etudes from Op. 25, the F-minor and the "Butterfly," the last played twice in succession, as the old pianists often did with brief pieces (Symposium 1146). Each is wonderful in its own way, showing his immense facility and taste. No specific date is given for these recordings, but they originated around 1910–16. The sound is dim, making a judgment of the tone somewhat speculative, but d'Albert's artistry shines through.

Leopold Godowsky (1870–1938), another Pole (though he was born in what is now Lithuania), was largely self-taught, and possessed one of the most prodigious techniques in the annals of piano playing. Like Chopin, he seems to have played his best within a small circle of friends; in concert and in the recording studio he was inclined to be overcautious and not always communicative. He was an artist of impossibly high standards, generally uncommonly accurate in an age that didn't regard accuracy as a *sine qua non*. Of all his recordings, his nocturnes are the most treasurable. Recorded in 1928, they emanate a certain mystique, are delicate, accurate, and discriminating, and should take their place next to the recordings by Rubinstein and Wild. It's regrettable that Godowsky never completed the set. Only 12 of the 19 mature nocturnes were committed to disc, along with the Sonata in B-flat minor, which is rather lackluster (Appian 7010, 2CD).

Sergei Rachmaninoff (1873–1943) was unquestionably one of the greatest pianists of the 20th century, but I hesitate to place him among the greatest Chopin interpreters. For the most part, his playing was not very Chopinesque. Instead, it was rather typical of the virtuoso tradition of the Russian School, predicated very much on the setting of the concert hall and often rife with eccentricities, some of which are undeniably attractive. His Chopin recordings, made between 1919 and 1935 but mostly in the '20s, provide only a partial portrait of his gigantic virtuosity, which must be complemented by his recordings of his own compositions and transcriptions (RCA 61265, 10CD).

His recording of Sonata 2 has been acclaimed as one of the premier readings of this work, but it has many flaws. Movement I, logical and sweeping, lacks a Chopin "feel," and II is taken at such a precipitous tempo that not even Rachmaninoff could handle it. The Funeral March is played in his famous interpretation, *ppp* to *fff* and back to *ppp,* and is stirring. Movement IV rumbles by with blurred, cavernous sound. The A-flat Ballade suffers from injudicious tempos and many wrong notes, but the C-sharp minor Scherzo is played with great élan and stunning octaves. Best of all are a sublime though mannered Nocturne Op. 9:2 and several waltzes. Rachmaninoff knew how to give substance and style to some of the slighter waltzes, like the B minor, which Lipatti papers over. However, Rachmaninoff's C-sharp minor Waltz is subjected to a riot of tempos — not one, two, or three, but dozens!

Josef Hofmann (1876–1935), a student of Moszkowski and Anton Rubinstein, in Harold Schonberg's words was "one of the most colossal pianists in history." More and more of his recordings are currently being reissued, among them live performances of the two concertos (VAIA 1002, conductors and orchestras not identified). His playing of the E minor Concerto is certainly one of the most exceptional on record — patrician, airy, stylistically true, and of dumbfounding technical perfection. Apparently he felt less empathy for the earlier F minor Concerto, for his playing there is rather cold and disinterested; his *fio, fioritura*s are so blasé that they become annoying as the performance goes on. The Finale, however, is very fast, spiky, and effortless. In the F minor the orchestra doesn't acquit itself very well.

A sample of his solo performances is on VAIA 1047. Here is the finest "Military" Polonaise I have heard — full of verve, flowing, and not hammered out. His C-sharp minor Waltz is one of the most beautiful of all, with a perfect balance of strictness and freedom, the latter applied with great discretion. The Nocturne in F-sharp is played with wonderfully pure, delicate, tone. Scherzo 1 is effortlessly mercurial, but there are a few slips; he was human, after all!

Josef Lhevinne (1874–1944) "had elegance, and he could move listeners to tears by the sheer beauty of his tone," said Rubinstein. He was a classmate of Rachmaninoff and Scriabin in Moscow, then taught at Juilliard from 1924 to 1944, where my own teacher, the incomparable Stanley Hummel, was his student. Only 14 of his solo recordings still exist, of which just a few are by Chopin: the "Heroic" Polonaise in A-flat, Etudes Op. 10:6 and Op. 25:6, 10, and 11, Preludes 16 and 17 (Dante 008; a few of these can also be heard on Philips 200410, 2CD, and Enterprise 190). He was noted for his inimitable performances of Etudes Op. 10:11 ("Storm") and Op. 25:6 ("Hummingbird"), of which recordings have fortunately been preserved. Like Rachmaninoff, his Chopin was Russian in flavor and distinguished by startling virtuosity.

At this point, a digression is in order to mention an excellent two-volume release by Appian. Vol. 1 (7013, 2CD) offers recordings by Rachmaninoff, Lhevinne, Hofmann, Godowsky, and Rosenthal; Vol. 2 (7014, 2CD) has Friedman, Barere, Levitzki, and Horowitz. Each of 11 pianists can be heard in several Chopin works, as well as some by other composers. The provenance of the original recordings, remastering, and biographical sketches are all first class.

Alfred Cortot (1877–1962) recorded more Chopin than any of the preceding pianists. Donald Manildi aptly describes him as a "free spirit" among 20th century pianists, no doubt because of his insistence on feeling, passion, and spontaneity. There are many who extol the merits of Cortot's Chopin, but I have never been among them. To my ears, his playing falls well below the standards of quite a number of others, both historic and modern. His tone is usually undistinguished, there are bushels of wrong notes, his vertical voicing of sonorities is usually commonplace, and in most pieces his technique predictably lurches out of control at least once. Sometimes his inattention to pedaling creates a murky blur. Yes, there are passages of originality and beauty, but these are overbalanced by the serious defects.

A recent remastering presents Etudes Opp. 10 and 25 (1933–34), Preludes Op. 28 (1942), and the four Ballades (1933) — a fine production, with notes, unfortunately, entirely in Korean (Good International 2032, 2CD). Ballade 1 and several etudes are very praiseworthy. In the "Raindrop" Prelude and Ballade 4 the pitch sags, but otherwise the transfers are excellent. Cortot wasn't inclined to shy away from fast tempos; his G-sharp minor Etude from Op. 25, probably the most difficult of all, is as fast as anyone's.

Earlier versions of the Op. 28 Preludes and the Ballades (1929), along with *Berceuse* (1926) are on Music & Arts 317. The Preludes are much superior to the later, 1942 version, and several are quite nice, including the treacherous B-flat minor. The Ballades from 1929 are no better than those from 1933. Biddulph 001 presents the Ballades (1923), Sonatas 2 (1928) and 3 (1931), and Nocturne Op. 9:2. The Sonatas and Ballades are very uneven, with many errors and clumsy playing.

Music & Arts 717 contains "digitally refurbished in 1992" versions of Sonatas 2 and 3, Ballade 1, Polonaise in A-flat, *Fantaisie* in F minor, and *Barcarolle.* The remastering isn't successful; the bass sounds as if it comes from the bottom of the Baths of Caracalla, the treble sounds like a 19th century square piano. The playing is worse, especially the haplessly amateurish Polonaise in A-flat. My advice is to forget these recordings; if you have Rubinstein, Wild, Perahia, Horowitz, or Fialkowska you'll never want to listen to Cortot again.

Ignaz Friedman (1882–1948) was an artist of quite a different stripe. He studied with Leschetizky in Vienna; near the end of his career he estimated that he had given 2,700 concerts in every corner of the world. His complete solo recordings 1923–36 have been issued in a superb set containing 28 Chopin pieces that should be in every piano collection (Pearl 2000, 4CD). Probably the most remarkable are 12 mazurkas, considered by many to be the optimum recording of these works, and a very fast Nocturne Op. 55:2. Friedman had an immense technique, a super-critical ear, a wonderful melting tone, and was always original and imaginative, introducing many unique touches into his interpretations. One distraction, however, is the periodic volcanic outbursts to which he seemed prone.

Benno Moiseiwitsch (1890–1963), another Leschetizky student whom I have revered, is presented on Pearl 9192 (2CD). He's not at his best in the Chopin pieces — five etudes, Sonata 3, and *Barcarolle* — recorded in 1961, where his technique is bumpy and a number of wrong notes occur. The Largo of the Sonata, played with wondrous nuance and many revelatory surprises, is well worth the price of the set.

Mischa Levitzki (1898–1941), a Russian pianist who died too young, was influenced by Godowsky. His playing is elegant and accurate in Nocturne in F-sharp, Polonaise in A-flat, Waltz Op. 70:1, and Scherzo in C-sharp minor (Pearl 9962). The Polonaise is rather routinely played and his treatment of the "chorale" passages of the Scherzo is odd, but otherwise the technical aspects are immaculate.

Simon Barere (1896–1951) was an extraordinary pianist from Odessa who graduated from the St. Petersburg Imperial Conservatory while the October Revolution was erupting, and developed a breathtaking, practically unlimited technique. Three of his Chopin recordings, made in the mid-'30s in London, appear in a superlative release: Scherzo in C-sharp minor, Mazurka Op. 59:3, and Waltz Op. 42 (Appian 7001, 2CD). Barere was more celebrated for his Liszt (this release was awarded the Grand Prix du Disque Liszt for the Liszt selections) than for his Chopin, so it isn't surprising to find that each of these three recordings is less than ideal. Finest is the Scherzo, despite awkward tempos; the Mazurka is interesting but unduly impatient, which spoils some of its most exquisite passages; the Waltz is distorted by aberrant extremes of tempo. Another release contains Ballade 1, *Fantaisie, Andante spianato and Grande Polonaise,* and the Scherzo in C-sharp minor (Appian 7009).

Edward Kilenyi (b. 1910), a pupil of Dohnányi in Budapest and subsequently his associate at the University of Florida at Tallahassee, recorded Etudes Op. 10 for Pathé in Paris in 1937, a set that still ranks among the most exciting and musical. He had a highly developed sense of brilliance and sonority. Each of the twelve is fascinating as he plays it; the most captivating are 2–3, 5–8, and 11–12 (Piano Library 226). Some years later Kilenyi recorded both books of etudes for Columbia, recordings that cry out for reissue.

Dinu Lipatti (1917–1950) made his classic recording of the 14 waltzes in 1950. Appropriately, these have now been reissued in the "Great Recordings of the 20th Century" series, along with *Barcarolle,* Nocturne in D-sharp, and Mazurka Op. 50:3 (EMI 66956). His approach to Chopin is straightforward but elegant, with the left hand well subdued and never plunky, discreet tone, and an utterly musical result. There are exceptions: 1 in E-flat is too fast, while the B minor and D-flat Op. 70:3 waltzes have little charm. It's revealing to compare this recording to Rubinstein's 1953 version, which is even more patrician, interesting, and tonally variegated, EMI's remastered sound is unfortunately a bit cloudy.

William Kapell (1922–1953) recorded an all-Chopin LP in 1951–52 comprised of Sonata 3 and 10 mazurkas. I have held a very high opinion of this recording since its release, and having revisited it for this article; I believe it's one of the phenomenal Chopin recordings of all time. Sonata 2, taken from a live broadcast in Australia in 1953, only one week before his death in an airplane crash, has been added to the reissued CD (RCA 5998).

In Sonata 3, I has been strategically planned so that it unfolds with maximum artistic effect; it's assured, disciplined, fluent, and has a jewel-like finish. Perhaps the finest recorded version of the Scherzo ensues (with the possible exception of de Pachmann's); it's near perfect. The Largo is flowing—this movement stagnates in the hands of most pianists—yet powerfully concentrated in emotional communication. The Finale is taken at a brisk clip, probably a little too fast, so that some details are lost—but it's exciting. Despite extensive efforts to restore the quality of the original tape of Sonata 2, the sound isn't very good, but the performance is persuasive. Movement I bears a resemblance to Horowitz's concept, with less percussiveness. The mazurkas are played with marked intensity and glowing tone. Although I have a slight preference for Rubinstein's playing of all these works, Kapell's will be the favorite of other listeners and will always maintain a very high rank in the Chopin discography.

Mr. Morin finds **Sviatoslav Richter**'s Chopin generally too cool and objective, as if the pianist is never really comfortable with the music. But he says that among the pieces the great Russian master chose to record, several are outstanding for their brilliant technique, tone control, and bracing vigor: 14 etudes (eight from Op. 10 and six from Op. 25; Philips 438620); 13 preludes (Olympia 112 or 287); and the four scherzos (Doremi 7724). He's even more impressed with the playing of **Vladimir Sofronitzky,** another Russian master who is becoming more widely recognized as more of his recordings are reissued; a useful collection—if you can find it—includes 18 pieces, among them 10 mazurkas that are played with passionate conviction and great beauty (Arlecchino 41).

Individual works (modern recordings)

Allegro de Concert Op. 46. This intriguing but obscure work was composed in 1841, originally intended as a concerto movement. Consequently, its musical language and gestures are more overt than is typical for Chopin, though you could scarcely mistake it for the work of anyone else. **Arrau**'s recording is the finest I have heard—a great performance now available again (Arlecchino 136). More recently **Biret** and **Ohlsson** have made excellent recordings. Ohlsson seems to do more with this piece than Biret, and I prefer his playing by a slight margin (Arabesque 6686). However, Biret is quite brilliant, as usual, and her sound is outstanding (Naxos 550362).

Ballades. Chopin created this genre of piano music almost single-handedly, and his prototypes led to similar works with this title by Liszt, Brahms, Fauré, and others. Chopin's Ballades are distinguished by compound meters, and have two major themes. Most important, they are closely related to the literary ballad and have a narrative quality, with (except for 3) a pervasively epic, tragic ambience.

Rubinstein recorded the four ballades only once, in 1959 (RCA, Vol. 45), and he is really peerless. The uncanny tone, subtle nuance, exquisite shading, technique, eloquent expression of the essence of Chopin's idiom—all are there. His closest competitors aren't without these attributes, or most of them, but what sets Rubinstein apart is his unique ability to draw each piece together under a single, overarching, conceptual canopy, so that it coalesces perfectly. Only in 3, which Rubinstein programmed most frequently, is there a tendency (rare for him) to be over-exuberant. In another performance of this piece, live in 1970, the playing is more songful, quieter, more distilled, but the sound, unfortunately, isn't of top quality (Ermitage 127).

Perahia's Ballades are very beautiful, especially 2 and 4, while 3 is high-strung (Sony 64399). **Wild** also offers an outstanding set, in which 1 is particularly memorable, but 2 is somewhat forced (Chesky 44). Two of the four as played by **Biret** are exceptional: 1 is especially brilliant in the fast portions, and 3 is one of the most beautiful renditions on record (Naxos 550508). **Zimerman** treats these works in a way we imagine Liszt might have done—dramatic, orchestral, sonorous, wonderfully brilliant, but not without overstatement, and his tone is often too massive. Nevertheless, the fidelity of his CD is superior and the piano sounds sumptuous (DG 423090). **Ohlsson**'s ballades show many of the same traits as Zimerman's, both good and not so good. He tends to play them more lyrically but also, at times, with too much discursiveness (Arabesque 6630). Still, both pianists are thoroughly enjoyable. **Arrau** brings a rich veneer of tone and pleasing sensitivity to these works, but also ponderousness (Philips 422038, 6CD).

Among single recordings of various ballades, **Cecile Licad** (MHS 513777H) and **Michelangeli** (Foné 90F32) have each made absolutely superb recordings of 1 that are unsurpassed in beauty and nobility, though quite different. **Horowitz**'s Ballade 1 is played with vibrant artistry, originality, and polish, though here and there the tone is abrasive (RCA 60376). **Cortot, Friedman,** and **Rachmaninoff** among the older generation each left recordings of ballades without the high artistic merits of any of the above-mentioned pianists.

Barcarolle Op. 60. With Sonata Op. 58 and *Polonaise-Fantaisie* Op. 61, the *Barcarolle* suggests, both by means of its formal artifice and its harmonic richness, a newly emerging phase in Chopin's compositional art. These three works date from 1844–46. The *Barcarolle,* really an extended Venetian boat song, is one of his masterpieces, casting its long shadow forward to Brahms, Debussy, Fauré and Ravel. It's also one of Chopin's most difficult works, which explains why there are so few completely satisfying recordings, partly due to the breadth and depth of its emotional spectrum and partly due to its keyboard complexity.

Rubinstein made five recordings, in 1928, 1946, 1957, 1962, and 1964 (RCA, Vols. 4, 16, 29, 46, and 62, respectively). The fourth of these, one of his most enthralling, is the most beautiful and subtle I have heard of this piece. The fifth, made in Moscow by Melodiya, has a little more movement, but the shadings aren't as fine and the sound (or is it the piano itself?) is mildly bothersome. **Perahia**'s recording is also very lovely (CBS 39708). **Juana Zayas**'s recording is dreamy and emotional, without quite the tonal refinement of Rubinstein and Perahia (Music & Arts 1006). **Moravec** is distinguished, rather quiet at the end, which is refreshing and unusual (VAIA 1039). Both **Ohlsson** (Arabesque 6686) and **Zimerman** (DG 4230S0) have made superb recordings. Neither, however, has the emotional voltage of Rubinstein, and Zimerman finished up the piece with a flurry of disappointing etude-like rattlings. Less remarkable recordings come from **Jane Coop** (Skylark), **Arrau** (Philips), and **Horowitz** (RCA); Arrau is too slow and Horowitz too bombastic. Historic recordings of this work come from **Lipatti** (EMI), **Moiseiwitsch** (Pearl), and **Cortot,** who murders it (Music & Arts).

Berceuse Op. 57. Another of the late works, the *Berceuse* is astonishing for the labyrinthine tracery Chopin introduced for the right hand, while the left hand is confined to a rigid but hypnotic ostinato. Harmonically, the entire piece consists of only three chords! To perform it artistically requires a tempo that is neither too fast, which causes restlessness (**Friedman, Cortot**), nor too slow, which imparts a static feeling (**Perahia, Ohlsson**).

Of **Rubinstein**'s four recordings, the third, from 1958, is the best (RCA, Vol. 29), followed by the fourth (1962, Vol. 46). A live recording he made in 1970 is quite beautiful (Ermitage 127). **Jean-Marie Darré**'s performance is very good, though she doesn't achieve Rubinstein's feathery touch (Vanguard 8092). **Ohlsson** plays the piece more slowly than almost anyone else, but with crystalline delicacy (Arabesque 6686). **Perahia** is admirable, tonally superb, if somewhat static (CBS 39708). **Biret**'s playing, conversely, establishes a nice flow but is tonally heavy in a piece of the utmost fragility (Naxos 550508). **Coop** (Skylark) and **Michelangeli** (Ermitage) are unremarkable.

Among historic performances, **Paderewski** is best in the *Berceuse,* but plays it without much nuance (Pearl 9323). **Friedman** rips through it much too hastily and impersonally (Pearl 2000, 4CD). **Cortot** restlessly changes tempo in his nervous-sounding 1928 recording (Music & Arts 317), and **Godowsky** is bumpy (Appian 7013, 2CD).

Bolero Op. 19. The Spanish *Bolero* joins the Italian *Tarantella* and *Barcarolle,* the Scottish *Ecossaises,* and the Polish polonaises and mazurkas in a group of works that exhibit Chopin's great interest in national dance forms. *Bolero* is seldom played, which is puzzling,

given its unique, beguiling qualities. Only two recordings need concern us, **Rubinstein**'s (RCA Vol. 47) and **Ohlsson**'s (Arabesque 6686). Both are excellent, though Rubinstein has a little more verve and cohesiveness.

Ecossaises Op. 72. These three brief, evanescent dances date from around 1826 but weren't published until after Chopin's death. They are youthful pieces, but with his indelible imprint. **Ohlsson** has delightful élan, is rhythmically supple, and has excellent sonority (Arabesque 6686). **Stanislav Bunin** plays them much more freely and coquettishly, with a clear, light tone (DG 423618).

Etudes Opp. 10 and 25; Nouvelles Etudes. Chopin's Etudes Op. 10 were composed from 1829 to 1832, many of them prior to his arrival in Paris but the last few after he had taken up residence there. They were published in 1833, dedicated to Liszt, and established Chopin's reputation in Paris. In 1834 he wrote, "I am writing without knowing what my pen is scribbling, because at this moment Liszt is playing my studies [in the next room] and putting honest thoughts out of my head. I should like to rob him of the way he plays [them]."

The Etudes Op. 25 followed in 1832–37 and were dedicated to Liszt's paramour, Marie d'Agoult. Because of their unprecedented harmonies, treatment of the piano, and technical demands of a completely new nature, they were often regarded as subversive. Both books of etudes exerted a profound effect upon Liszt, Brahms, Debussy, Scriabin, Rachmaninoff, and others, none of whom quite achieved Chopin's artistic height in their comparable works. The three *Nouvelles Etudes* (*NE*) were composed in 1839, primarily for the independence of hands. While they are smaller in scope, they're more subtle and permeated with the characteristics of Chopin's late style.

It's difficult to make a recommendation, since in every case, even outstanding pianists play certain ones superbly while others seem run of the mill. The etudes pose so many and diverse challenges to the pianist's technical equipment; one may address a performer's strength and the next will expose a weakness. Certain of these pieces provide an acid test because they're so rarely played satisfactorily: Op. 10:3, 6 and 11 and Op. 25:6 and 8. To take care of this problem, it's best to own several recordings. To aid the reader, I have grouped the most important recordings into three categories; each of them includes both Op. 10 and 25 unless otherwise noted.

Excellent

Ashkenazy, 1975 (London 414127). This performance has just about everything and is vastly more musical and polished than his 1959 recording. His technically superlative etudes show, in this version, a heightened appreciation of Chopin's style. Tempos are beautifully chosen, and there is an evocative projection of moods in the various pieces.

Berezovsky (Teldec 73129, with *NE*). This young Russian is technically commanding and impeccable, though musically quite conventional.

Kilenyi (Piano Library 226). See historical section above.

Licad, Op. 10 only (MHS 513777H). This recording abounds in aristocratic playing and contains more of the "best" performances of Op. 10 than any other. Such tasteful, technically assured Chopin is seldom encountered and is immensely refreshing.

Lortie (Chandos 8482, with *NE*). Natural and stylish performances, with perfect technique, tonal sensitivity, and brilliance.

Rubinstein, *NE* only (RCA, Vols. 26 and 44). These recordings are by a fairly wide margin the most beautiful, and, indeed, are so extraordinary that one or both should be in the collection of everyone who loves Chopin's music.

Wild (Chesky 77, with *NE*). Wild's approach is quite similar to Ashkenazy's in choice of tempos and insistence on clarity. He has the virtue of making the etudes seem effortless, while Ashkenazy often projects the mood more intensively. Wild's Baldwin piano sounds luxurious here.

Zayas (Music & Arts 891) is a super-virtuoso with a tremendous technique who turns in a startling performance. Her tone is marvelous and there is little pounding. Op. 10:10 is unchallenged for evenness, shading, and rubato, though Ashkenazy comes close. Superb notes by David Dubal.

Very good

Arrau (EMI 7610 162, with *NE*). Poise, precision, clarity, and slower, sometimes deliberate tempos mark Arrau's 1956 account. Op. 10:2–4 and Op. 25:6 are especially fine.

Binns (Pearl 9641, with *NE*). There is some remarkably fine playing here, though Binns's touch and tone aren't up to the level of those previously listed, and his piano is out of tune in some pieces. He offers one of the best versions of the *Nouvelles Etudes,* however.

Biret (Naxos 555364, with *NE* on 555508). Moderate tempos. Her big technique makes the more daunting pieces very impressive, especially Op. 10:5 and 7. The recorded sound is superior.

Cziffra (Philips 456760, 2CD). I had high expectations of this recording, knowing of Cziffra's brilliance and fire and his transcendental technique. However, the general effect here is over-ridingly conventional, with very few high points.

Fialkowska (Opening Day 9312). With Zayas, Fialkowska performs the etudes with more velocity than anyone else and often gives a technically overwhelming impression. There is some percussive playing, however, and the sound leaves something to be desired.

Novaes (Vox 3501, 3CD). Like Cziffra, the overall effect is conventional, but there are some outstanding performances: Op. 10:2, 3, 7, and 12; Op. 25:1, 6, 9, and 11. Good sound.

Average

Ashkenazy, 1959 (Melodiya 33215). Very big, brash, muscular playing, often not very refined, but technically authoritative.

Cortot (Good International 2032, 2CD). See historical section above.

Perlemutter (Nimbus 5095, with *NE*). A rather mechanistic approach to the music, with less tonal subtlety and expressivity than others.

Saperton (VAIA 1037, 2CD, with *NE*). The Etudes were a specialty for Saperton, yet his technique and tone aren't memorable. There are many charming pianistic gestures here and there suggestive of the "old school."

To summarize: the thoroughbreds are Zayas and Fialkowska; the powerhouse is Berezovsky; the aristocrats are Licad and Lortie; the old (all around) masters are Kilenyi, Wild, and Ashkenazy.

Individual etudes

Some exceptional performances of individual etudes within collections of various other music include:

De Pachmann: Op. 10:12; Op. 25:3 and 9
Rosenthal: Op. 10:1; *Nouvelle Etude* in A-flat
D'Albert: Op. 25:9
(For these three, see the historical section above)

Arrau: Op. 10:4; Op. 25:1 (Marston 52023, 2CD). These were recorded in 1929, along with two others, and are far superior to his 1956 version of all the etudes.
Horowitz: Op. 10:3 (RCA 60376)
Moravec: Op. 25:7 (VAIA 1039)
Olejniczak: Op. 10:12, on a Pleyel piano of 1831 (Opus 111 43-9107)
Perahia: Op. 10:3 and 4 (Sony 64399)

Fantaisie Op. 49. Chopin has repeatedly, and not entirely deservedly, been labeled a miniaturist. He composed only a handful of large-scale works, and, of course, his many brief pieces are packed with significance. However, I have always found the larger pieces more fascinating, at first because of their emotional and pianistic allure, later because of Chopin's unerring and sophisticated sense of formal musical structure. The *Fantaisie,* composed in 1841, is one of the most widely played of the major works.

As is so often the case, **Rubinstein**'s performances overshadow most others. Of his two recordings, the later one, from 1962 (RCA, Vol. 46), is the finer. A marvelously intense, atmospheric 1970 performance is in only fair sound and some of the delicate shadings of the RCA are not so apparent (Ermitage 127). **Novaes**'s recording, from her legendary Town Hall recital in 1949, is both inspired and faultless, though the sound is disappointing (Music & Arts 1029, 2CD). The *Fantaisie* is one of **Arrau**'s best Chopin recordings; his lustrous tone, opulence, passion, and the scale of his playing sometimes make the piece sound more Brahmsian than Chopinesque (Philips 422038, 6CD). **Darré** plays with understanding and cohesion, but pounds at times, as so many pianists do, carried away by the intensity and drama of the music (Vanguard 8092).

One who does not pound is **Michelangeli,** whose 1960 and 1964 live recordings, though highly musical, give the impression of a careful rationing of fire and passion. Both of them have constricted, dry sound (1960, Music & Arts 817, 2CD; 1964, Ermitage 301). **Perahia** plays immaculately, as always, but the quiet moments bog down and frustrate the flow of the piece (CBS 39708), something that also bedevils **Ohlsson** (Arabesque 6686) and **Zimerman** (DG 423090). This is true to a lesser degree of **Biret,** especially in the opening, which she invests with many interesting touches (Naxos 555508). **Cortot**'s account is blemished by stretches of chaotic playing (Music & Arts 717).

Impromptus. Chopin's four Impromptus count among his lighter works, are all in A-B-A form and have a prominent improvisatory character. They embody the essence of Chopin, each in a different way.

There are many praiseworthy exponents of these accessible pieces. **Perahia**'s version is refined and full of character. He tosses off 1 with glittering velocity, while his interpretation of 3 is unusual for its slowness and restraint, which imparts an air of deep melancholy to the piece (CBS 39708). **Ohlsson**'s performance is the most original, predictably more leisurely than most, prismatic in tonal finish and details. His interpretation of 2 is the most ideal of any pianist's. He takes the time it needs to unfold, and he never resorts to the percussiveness so often heard in this work (Arabesque 6642, 2CD).

Alexander Uninsky is hard-edged and rigid where delicacy and plasticity are needed (Philips 442574, 2CD). **Arrau** plays these pieces with considerable beauty and marvelous pedaling, but there is also a heaviness that detracts from the inherent delicacy of this music (Philips 456336, 2CD). **Stanislav Bunin** plays with copious freedom, so much so that he could be accused of distorting the rhythm (DG 423618). The Bulgarian pianist **Marta Deyanova** plays freely too, though with less stretching than Bunin. She has a big style and gives an attractive performance, though her touch tends to be heavy. The sound of her piano is sumptuous, enhanced by the fidelity of the recording (Nimbus 5297). **Fialkowska** isn't blessed with such exemplary sound, but she's more discreet about sonority and touch, is very mobile, and comes close to the Chopin ideal (Opening Day 9318). **Biret**'s deft touch and idiosyncratic way result in exquisite performances, especially of the elusive 2 and 3 (Naxos 550362).

Once again **Rubinstein** excels in his two recordings, with great understanding of mood, content, expression, and tempos, delivered in an aristocratic way (RCA, Vol. 26, 1953-57; Vol. 47, 1964). In 3, he's the only artist who observes Chopin's tempo indication of *Allegro vivace* without becoming bogged down in the difficult figurations of the first and third sections. His playing of all four pieces is free, but subtly so, and he never allows freedom to inhibit the flow of the music, as many of the younger players do, with varying degrees of frustration. Rubinstein's later recording is slightly more refined than the first, and the stereo sound has more depth.

Horowitz left exceptionally beautiful accounts of 1 (RCA 60376), very fast, like Perahia's, and of 4, contained in his last recording (Sony 45818).

Mazurkas. For Chopin, the mazurka was the vehicle he repeatedly turned to for his most personal musical thoughts and his most extreme excursions of harmonic daring. Fifty-seven in all, they are among the first and final works of his life. The mazurka is a Polish country dance in 3/4 time, with displaced accents on the second and third beats. There are three basic types, but often an admixture occurs within a single piece. Some are epigrammatic, while others are substantial and profound.

Of the complete sets, **Ohlsson**'s is beautifully and thoughtfully played, accompanied by excellent notes by Frank Cooper (Arabesque 6730, 2CD). **Biret** offers a superbly and very musically played series in top quality sound at a budget price (Naxos 550358/9). **Frederic Chiu** offers fine, subtle performances (Harmonia Mundi 907247, 2CD). **Uninsky**'s set is one to pass over, as the playing quickly becomes tiresome (Philips 442574, 2CD).

While Ohlsson and Biret are good choices and will provide years of listening pleasure, choosing the Mount Everest of mazurka recordings is easy: **Rubinstein**'s last version, recorded in 1965–66, places everyone else at an insurmountable disadvantage (RCA, Vol. 50). If I were asked to identify his most exceptional recording, I would unhesitatingly name this one. What makes Rubinstein's mazurkas so extraordinary? After much thought, I believe it's his magical rhythmic eloquence, something that really defies description. He's also subtler and more expressive in tone, shading, and nuance, always chooses exactly the right tempo, and communicates a more potent, broader emotional spectrum. Here we have unquestionably one of the greatest piano recordings of all, and no collection should be without it.

For the same reasons, Rubinstein's two earlier sets (RCA, Vol. 6, 1938–39; Vol. 27, 1952–53) are also preferable to anyone else's. The first, notable for its high-spirited charm and somewhat rustic ambience, is preferred by many critics to the subsequent ones, and the second, less well known than either of its counterparts, is imbued with certain aspects of both of the others. We read over and over that as Rubinstein became older (in the 1960s and after) his playing became slower, more cautious, more self-conscious, because of age and declining technique. Nonsense! There was no perceptible falling off in his technique and control until his last few concert seasons, around 1972–73, at the age of 85–86. What is seen as caution or slowness is the result of his lifelong quest for more subtlety, more relevance, and deeper musical truth and beauty.

Music has proverbially been considered an international language. But Liszt himself (and who could know better) declared that only a Pole could fathom completely the unique musical language of the mazurkas. **Rubinstein, Friedman,** and **Rosenthal,** all Poles, are the incomparable mazurka players. A certain rhythmic quality in their playing sets their mazurkas apart from all others, something I believe is related to inflections of the Polish language. **Paderewski**'s mazurkas had this too, though his pianism wasn't on the level of the other three. Oddly, this rhythmic verve is missing in **Perlemutter**'s 16 mazurkas, though he was Polish too (Nimbus 5393), as it is in the recordings by the non-Poles — **Horowitz** (RCA and Sony), **Argerich** (DG), **Bunin** (DG), even **Michelangeli** (Foné, Ermitage) and **Kapell** (RCA), as beautifully pianistic as their mazurkas are.

Nocturnes. Like the mazurkas, Chopin's 21 nocturnes span his entire career and give a revealing picture of his developing style. They're not his most provocative or adventurous music but are subtle mood studies, intended to seduce a small, select audience in a salon setting, and are often mysterious and strange. More than any other genre, they reflect Chopin's predilection for the 19th century operatic world of *bel canto* as practiced by Rossini, Bellini, and Donizetti. He published 18 nocturnes during his lifetime. The E minor was written at 17, and two others, one in C-sharp minor, composed for his sister Ludwika, and one in C minor, were published posthumously.

Two pianists stand apart for their wonderful complete sets: Rubinstein, who recorded 19 of them three times, and Wild. **Rubinstein**'s initial recording of 1936–37 (RCA, Vol. 5) doesn't have quite the refinement of the later two. Of these, I favor the second (RCA, Vol. 26), made in 1949–50, which has a rapt, breathless beauty not as noticeable in the third of 1965 (RCA, Vol. 49), where the playing, however, is even more subtly perfumed. **Wild**'s 21 nocturnes are presented in a random order chosen by the pianist. The playing is impeccable, quite similar in many ways to Rubinstein's, with extreme finesse of touch and fine mood projection, much more straightforward than Arrau or Ohlsson. I'm reminded of the approach and style of Wild's teacher, Egon Petri. This set offers one of the most memorable recordings of the D-flat Nocturne and one of the very few great ones of the B-flat minor. There are also outstanding program notes by Victor and Marina Ledin (Ivory 70701, 2CD).

Novaes's recording of 19 nocturnes is less consistent (Vox 3501, 3CD). Some of the pieces are especially fine (Op. 18:1, Op. 27, and Op. 32:1), but others have a static feeling, and listening to the whole series, I'm struck by their overall sameness of tone color; not so with Rubinstein or Arrau, whose tone is much more varied. **Arrau** plays 21 nocturnes with gorgeous, perfumed tone, but much more languorously than Rubinstein or Wild, and he lavishes a beauty of expression on almost every phrase. Some listeners will find this over-emphatic and tire of it (Philips 546336, 2CD).

Ohlsson's recording was judged by Mr. Morin as too slow, unrhythmic, and mannered (Arabesque 6653, 2CD). I agree, though I appreciate his exquisite shadings and the dreamy, improvisatory mood he captures (often at the expense, however, of flow); there's a lot of Arrau's influence in Ohlsson's playing. **Livia Rév** presents a very nice recording, sensitive and musical if not extraordinary (Hyperion 66341, 2CD). **Pires**'s set has been highly praised, in excellent sound (DG 447096, 2CD). **Michele Boegner** has recorded them on a Pleyel piano of 1836 in a stylish, engaging performance (Calliope 9281, 2CD). **Perlemutter**'s recording of 10 nocturnes is not recommended. His left hand is often bumpy and obtrusive, and his tone and dynamics stay within a narrow range (Nimbus).

As for recordings of single nocturnes, **Horowitz**'s performances often suffer from percussive, sometimes bombastic tone, but parts of the C-sharp minor are unforgettable (RCA 60986). See the historical section for recordings by **Godowsky, de Pachmann,** and others.

Preludes Op. 28; Prelude in C-sharp minor Op. 45; Prelude in A-flat. It's said that when Chopin was about to give a public concert, he locked himself away with his piano several days in advance and played through Bach's *Well-Tempered Clavier,* which he knew by heart. His 24 preludes are thus descendants of Bach's preludes from *WTC,* composed around 100 years later, in 1836–38. The Prelude in C-sharp minor Op. 45 belongs to his late style, with its Wagnerian harmony and ceaseless modulation, and dates from around 1841.

Of all the recordings of these pieces, **Novaes**'s — part of her Town Hall recital in 1949 — is the most unforgettable, though the sound of many of them has sadly deteriorated, which will require a certain tolerance on the part of the listener (Music & Arts 1029, 2CD). The "Raindrop" Prelude is barely audible. Another immortal performance was given by **Bolet** in Carnegie Hall in 1974, an evening of unforgettable pianism, captured in one of the most treasurable releases in the "Great Pianists" series (Philips 456724, 2CD). **Richter**'s recording of 13 preludes also ranks right at the top (Melodiya 112). **Ohlsson**'s preludes may be the finest of all the volumes in his complete Chopin series and show his originality and stupendous technique (Arabesque 6629).

Following these superior versions, we come to several that are excellent but slightly less powerful in their effect: **Rubinstein**'s sole recording, made in 1946 (RCA Vol. 16); **Zayas,** with a high gloss of technical perfection, whose disc also includes the Preludes in C-sharp minor and A-flat (Music & Arts 1006); **Moravec,** for whom the reflective preludes are the most enthralling (VAIA 1039); **Darré,** always interesting and often understated (Vanguard 8092); and **Arrau,** musical and pleasing (Philips 422038, 6CD). **Zaritzkaya** is sometimes a little heavy (Naxos 550225), **Argerich** offers white-hot intensity (DG 431584), **Shelley** plays with high energy and big technique (QSV 6095), and **Perlemutter** (Nimbus 5064) completes the list. All but Perlemutter are very good. I don't think he's quite in the same league, as his playing is often routine.

There are five versions of the C-sharp to choose from, all excellent. **Rubinstein**'s recording of the piece, which he seldom played, was never released until it became available in "The Complete Rubinstein," but is very beautiful (RCA, Vol. 82). In addition, there are recordings by **Ohlsson, Zayas** (with the other preludes), **Zaritzkaya** (likewise), and **Coop** (Skylark 9902). See the historical section for recordings by **Cortot, Paderewski, de Pachmann,** and others.

Polonaises. The polonaise is the courtly, ceremonial dance cultivated by the Polish aristocracy, just as the mazurka is the dance of the peasantry. Both are in 3/4 meter, but Chopin's polonaises evoke visions of the high drama of Poland's national history. He composed eight "great" polonaises. These are supplemented by a group of nine lesser works composed during his youth.

Biret's Vol. 1 (Naxos 550360) includes seven of the great polonaises in well-conceived and beautifully executed performances, though occasionally her touch is heavy (E-flat minor and A) or she becomes boring (F-sharp minor and the middle of the E-flat minor). She's less bombastic than most in the F-sharp minor, a piece most players (including Rubinstein) pound out with varying degrees of determination, and she's clean and brilliant in the A-flat major. Her *Polonaise-Fantaisie* is cohe-

sive but not as expressive as Rubinstein's. Biret's Vol. 2 (Naxos 550361) includes *Andante Spianato* and *Grande Polonaise* plus the nine youthful polonaises. This performance of the *Grande Polonaise* is markedly more percussive than her very fine recording of the same piece with orchestra (Naxos 550368).

Ohlsson plays the large polonaises with grandeur and persuasiveness and the early ones with considerable grace and charm (Arabesque 6642, 2CD). His set doesn't include Op. 22, though this work is included in his volume of piano and orchestral pieces (Arabesque 6702, 2CD). However, **Ashkenazy** (London 452167, 2CD) and **Rubinstein** (RCA, Vol. 4, 1934–35; Vol. 28, 1950–51; Vol. 48, 1964) have the most thoroughly idiomatic feel for these works and I recommend their recordings highly. To be sure, Rubinstein's sets don't include the early polonaises, but all three do include Op. 22. The earliest version is notable for its dash, bravura, and vehemence, and for an exceptional F-sharp minor. Personally, I favor his second recording, which may be the most ideal of the recorded performances. Much of his third recording seems just a bit too sedate.

Rondos. Four longish works belong to this group, and all are youthful: Op. 1 in C minor, *Rondo a la mazur* in F Op 5, *Introduction and Rondo* in E-flat Op. 16, and *Introduction and Rondo* Op. 73 in C. The last was initially composed for piano solo; later in 1828, Chopin made an arrangement for two pianos, and this is the version most often played.

All four are played by **Barbara Hesse-Bukovska** (Canyon 3634). She's conspicuously fleet-fingered, so much so that a few details fall under the table. However, she plays musically and with a pleasant tone, and the sound is excellent. Easily the most winsome of the four pieces is Op. 73, of which solo performances are about as common as hen's teeth. The Canyon disc offers only the two-piano version of this charming composition.

Ohlsson gives us the first two rondos in ebullient performances of brilliance and style in his Vol. 2 (Arabesque 6629), and the third and fourth in Vol. 3 (Arabesque 6630). His Op. 16 is slower than Hesse-Bukovska's, but no details are glossed over and his performance is captivating and delicious. In Op. 73, known to be uncommonly difficult in its solo version, he takes theme "A" too slowly and dreamily, which gives it a stilted effect. The balance of the Rondo is better, but some parts need more velocity and forward motion.

Horowitz committed a wonderfully fresh, elegant reading of Op. 16 to disc in 1971 (Columbia 30463).

Scherzos. Chopin's four scherzos, all in 3/4 meter (unlike the four ballades, which are in compound meter), each have a different key (like the ballades). These pieces have no underlying narrative but are out-and-out virtuoso works, all marked *presto* and full of pianistic fireworks. Nevertheless, their musical content seems intensely dramatic, partly the result of two sharply contrasting theme groups, a constructional device that generates tension and conflict.

Complete sets are available from Wild, Ohlsson, Arrau, Deyanova, and Rubinstein (three versions), among others. **Wild**'s Scherzo 1 is ideally played, but the other three have an abstract quality, quite different from his Ballades (Chesky 44). **Biret** sometimes becomes too aggressive, which depreciates otherwise top-flight achievements. Nowhere is this more manifest than in her forceful treatment of the first three scherzos. However, she plays these difficult works with temperament and some abandon, and, of course, scintillating technique. Her 4 is luminous, unexcelled except by Rubinstein. The sound of this recording is superior (Naxos 550362).

If you're tired of hearing the scherzos played in a heaven-storming manner and you want to hear every note set into its exact place, **Ohlsson**'s recording is indispensable (Arabesque 6633). He takes his time with 1, using gesture and silence, but fascinating as this is, the piece never seems to get going. 2 is played more lyrically than heroically; the middle section is too slow—in fact, interminable. 3 is not really played *Presto con fuoco*, as Chopin indicated, but it's beautifully poised and tonally gradated.

Arrau's 1 is spacious and expressive, stirring at the conclusion. 2 is played in a dramatic, blustery, slightly square fashion. 3 and 4 are dreadfully slow and laborious in his 1984 recording (Philips 422038, 6CD). Those who've heard his superior 1939 recording of 3 (Marston 52023, 2CD)—atmospheric, fluent, with pinpoint control of all the parameters of pianism—will never want to hear the stuffy 1986 version again. **Deyanova** plays these works with robust—often too robust—tone. Sometimes she uses the pedal in a way that causes blurring. The middle sections of 1 and 2 lack direction, a common failing (Nimbus 5297).

Rubinstein's second and third recordings are more exciting than any of the foregoing, and though some listeners may find his second version tonally too assertive, no other version challenges these in sheer artistry. In his first recording (1932), they seem to me too fast and the piano doesn't sound any too good, with a rumbly bass and hollow octaves up higher, often not in tune (RCA, Vol. 6). The B minor Scherzos in sets I and II (1949, Vol. 26), sound positively demonic—out of character for Rubinstein. In set III (1959, Vol. 45), this quality has disappeared in favor of more naturalness, cleaner technique, wonderful digital control, superior polish, and much better sound. The lyrical section is exquisite in this version and the close is spellbinding.

Scherzo 2 in set II suffers from the unremitting force brought to bear on chords and octaves. This is otherwise an ideally formed performance, electrically charged, very fast, and clear despite the velocity. In set III we encounter an astonishing performance of the "Governess" Scherzo—brilliant, fiery, almost overwhelming in daring and power, in the grand manner. Here is a great virtuoso at the peak of his artistry, who had performed this piece all his life all over the world, and is now holding absolutely nothing back. At times the tone is too percussive (rare for Rubinstein), but the performance is a compendium of all the instrument can do in this piece. You might ask, "Would Chopin have played it like this, or been able to?," and the probable answer is no. Question No. 2: "Would Chopin have enjoyed hearing it played like this?" The probable answer is yes.

Scherzo 3, in set II, is extremely powerful, even vociferous. A commanding, intimidating technique (something Rubinstein would never have agreed he had) is heard here in all its glory. In set III this Scherzo is played in a more technically compelling manner than can be heard from any other performer, including Rachmaninoff and Horowitz. The "chorale" theme is beautifully set apart in relief from its cascading figurations, and the other runs and filigree work are like a glittering waterfall throughout the piece.

The last scherzo in Rubinstein's set II is more poised than it was in set I, capricious and rich in nuance and tonal balance. Scherzo 4, set III, is played a little less forcibly than in set II, with more subtlety, supreme polish, luminosity of tone, sumptuously delineated, and with intriguing rhythmic elasticity. It's a performance of unheard-of beauty and perfection, so hypnotic that once begun, it would be a crime to interrupt or abridge it.

There are some exceptional individual performances of the scherzos that are well worth acquiring.

1. **Horowitz** (RCA 60376): Played with his characteristic brilliance, this sovereign performance concludes with one of the most electrifying rising scales on records. **Novaes** (Vox 5513, 2CD): The most Chopinesque playing of this work, crystal clear, with wonderful style and technique, though there are a few minor slips.

2. **Licad** (MHS 513777H): An exhilarating, brilliant, idiomatic performance that makes most others seem tame. The tone is fresh and delightful, though occasionally too percussive on chords and accented sonorities.

3. **Novaes** (Vox 5513, 2CD): Atmospheric, with pearly touch and natural flow; superbly fashioned. In an unissued Columbia recording made in 1940, Novaes is more accurate but less interesting and the sound is tubby (Music & Arts 1029, 2CD). **Arrau** (1939): See complete Scherzos. **Argerich** (DG 431584): Marvelously clean playing, carefully articulated, and very exciting, with attention to sonority and tonal shading; her tempo seems eminently right for this piece. **Horowitz** (RCA 60463): Ferocious, brittle, super-charged; for Horowitz fans it's something special, but the sound is boxy and not altogether realistic.

4. **Novaes** (Music & Arts 1029, 2CDR): From her Town Hall program of 1949—amazingly fluid and brilliant, yet light and airy.

Sonatas

One of Chopin's most rarely performed works, Sonata 1 dates from 1828. Both **Ohlsson** (Arabesque 6628) and **Biret** (Naxos 550363) have included it with 2 and 3 on a single disc. For the great Sonatas 2 and 3, six pianists have performed these very demanding masterworks with such artistry that they stand at a considerable distance from all others: Rubinstein, Horowitz, Kapell, Novaes, and the "youngsters," Fialkowska and Ohlsson.

Rubinstein's three recordings of 2 vary noticeably from each other. In the 1946 version (RCA, Vol. 16), the listener feels inexorably drawn into a cauldron of turbulence and passion. The tempos are faster than anyone else's, yet the total artistic impression is satisfying. Rubinstein was one of the few who could play the Finale in a way that makes musical sense. His 1961 recording (Vol. 46) is the most consummate of the three. In I there's less excitement than in 1946 but more musicality and finesse, and it's more naturally Chopinesque. Movement II is less heavy, while the Finale closely approximates his 1946 recording, with a little more refinement. His playing of 2 in Moscow in 1964 was neither typical of a normal Rubinstein concert (for which I can attest) nor of his recordings (Vol. 62). In louder passages there was un-Rubinsteinian banging and over-pedaling, and some tempos were also atypical (for example, the Funeral March was too slow). The piano sound is curious as well, so I prefer both of his other versions.

Rubinstein's only recording of 3 (1961) is a kind of high water mark both for him and for this composition—a transcendental performance that has not been surpassed (RCA Vol. 46). The eloquent sweep, clarity, radiant musicality, and tone of I are magnificent. No one has ever made the "B" theme soar and sing like this; the piano is coaxed into masquerading as a *bel canto* singer! The same takes place in the cantilena in the right hand of III. Rubinstein imparts a grim, relentless character to the start of the Finale; then, in a kind of sorcery, dynamic musicality and phenomenal technique combine to bring this movement to a stupendous close.

Horowitz's recording of 2 may not always be exactly Chopinesque, but his conception of this music is towering and intensely persuasive. Tempos in I and II are unexpectedly slow, but a shattering climax (at the end of the "B" theme) is achieved in I. The Finale is transparent and drier than most pianists play it (RCA Vol. 62). It's a performance not to be missed.

See the historical section above for a discussion of **Kapell**'s Sonatas 2 and 3.

Novaes's sublime interpretations of 2 and 3 can be heard in two recordings of each on Music and Arts 1029 (2CD) and Vox 3501 (3CD). She performs these works with a wonderful naturalness, pacing, fire, and emotion, and a definitely feminine touch. For 2, the Vox recording is preferable because of better sound; also, in the Music & Arts release the Finale is blurred. In both there are occasional slips, despite her impressive and disciplined technique, but these aren't at all distracting.

For 3, the Music & Arts disc is first choice. This time the sound is clear, with less distortion. In the Vox version of the Finale, she unfortunately seems to have run out of steam toward the end, losing sonority and making errors. This must have been a brutally difficult piece for her; there's also a hint of fatigue in the Music & Arts version. Otherwise, these performances are both inspired and very Chopinesque, perhaps more so than any others.

Fialkowska's and **Ohlsson**'s recordings are so comparable that they can be considered a draw, higher marks going to Fialkowska in 2 and Ohlsson in 3. Ohlsson plays both sonatas briskly, with meticulous attention to details of dynamics, phrasing, and accents, as well as to the architecture, but his tone is often rather hard and the Finale of 2 is a mush. The marvel of his 3 is the Finale—hugely brilliant and exciting, an account in which the artist seems absolutely fearless. It may not be entirely as musical as Rubinstein's, but it certainly is as sweeping (Arabesque 6628). Fialkowska plays both sonatas with a warmer tone and more give and take in the flow of phrases, but within a narrower dynamic range. Her playing is always disciplined and musical, and not without a good measure of excitement (Opening Day 9318).

Other laudable recordings of the sonatas include **Biret** (1–3; Naxos); **Fiorentino** (2; APR 7036, 2CD), **Michelangeli** (2; Foné 90F32), and **Coop** (3; Skylark 9902). Less impressive are **Cherkassky** (3; Nimbus) and **Perlemutter** (2 and 3; also Nimbus).

Tarantelle Op. 43 is one of the more rarely played works but is of undeniable charm and character, with attractive themes skillfully balanced and handled transparently. **Rubinstein** plays it with incomparable panache (it was something of a specialty for him, though he recorded it only once), with perfect tempo, lightness, and admirable sonority (RCA, Vol. 45). **Ohlsson** is fleet, virtuosic, but a bit dry (Arabesque 6686). **Arrau**'s old recording is even more unbuttoned, but engaging (Marston 52023, 2CD). **Perlemutter** performs it cleanly and charmingly, but is rather prosaic, in a recording with very good, live sound (Nimbus 5393).

Variations. Op. 12, *Introduction and Variations brilliantes on* "Je vends des scapulaines" from Hérold's opera *Ludovic* is a charming and quite original composition from around 1833 that deserves to be heard more often. *Introduction and Variations on a German National Air* Op. posth. is an old-fashioned string of variations, c. 1826, of limited interest. Variation VI from *Hexaméron* (1841) is the masterpiece of that curious multi-composer work.

Ohlsson has recorded these in immaculately polished performances, with relaxed delight and discerning attention to detail, and also stylish tonal shading (Arabesque 6633). **Cziffra**'s brilliant, genial, propulsive playing of Op. 12 poses a definite contrast to Ohlsson's, yet is most attractive. He knows how to make this piece "sound," though there is less attention to detail here than in Ohlsson's recording (EMI 62880, 2CD, with two nocturnes and five etudes). **Zaritzkaya** plays Op. 12 in a more conventional way, which doesn't do as much for the piece. Nevertheless,

she offers fine, sensitive playing, with pleasing tone and fluidity (Naxos 550225).

A number of inconsequential pieces, all published posthumously, are in Ohlsson's Vol. 8 (Arabesque 6686), and Biret also recorded several of them (Naxos 550508).

Waltzes. Not all of Chopin's 19 waltzes are equal. There are eight major pieces, extending through Op. 64:3. A group of six earlier waltzes, more slender in content, includes Opp. 69 and 70 and the E minor Op. posth. Finally, there are five small, additional pieces composed during his youth and published after his death. To perform these pieces artistically, the player must have a deft touch, must strike a balance between the insistent 3/4 of the dance rhythm and the necessity for freedom and nuance, must keep the left hand subdued but supportive, and must address and express the emotion inherent in the music, which often flickers in and out like a candle flame—no mean accomplishment!

Predictably, **Rubinstein** accomplishes all this most successfully and with aplomb. He made two recordings of 14 waltzes, the first in 1953 (RCA, Vol. 29), the second in 1963 (Vol. 47), as well as individual recordings of single waltzes. The 1953 version is distinguished by more brio than the 1963, superb control of the left hand, and, in general, is an eminently subtle, supple, and sunny performance. The 1963 version is more relaxed, more delicate, understated, with more emphasis on pastel colors. We sense even greater digital control by the 76-year-old pianist, a collaboration of ear and fingers not exceeded by anyone else in the 20th century. A notable recording of an individual waltz is the C-sharp minor, from a 1970 recital; it's the most entrancing performance of this piece I've heard (Ermitage 127).

Both Arrau and Abbey Simon recorded all 19 waltzes, and it's difficult to choose between them. **Arrau** offers glowing tone, and the sound is full and excellent, but he plays them so slowly! (Philips 422038, 6CD). **Simon** performs them with much more verve and *joie de vivre,* but his tone is less evocative and the sound is inferior to Arrau's (Vox 5167, 2CD). **Peter Katin** has recorded 16 of the waltzes in random, illogical order (London 417045, budget-priced). He plays them with considerable flexibility, which never goes over into distortion. He does have a repeated idiosyncrasy—he starts a phrase slowly, then accelerates with a crescendo—which after a time becomes tiresome, and there is occasional pounding in the bass as well as some stridency in the treble

Recordings of individual waltzes are many, and, for the most part, unremarkable. I'm thinking of those in my collection by Horowitz, Bunin, Olejniczak, Fiorentino, Michelangeli, and Cortot—an impressive galaxy of pianists! But I must mention the most beautiful A minor Waltz ("Valse brillante") on record, by Horowitz (RCA 60986). It's a sublime performance of this enigmatic, deeply melancholy piece.

SONGS

Chopin's 19 Polish songs should not be compared to the lieder of Schubert, Schumann, or Liszt; they are charming, but lighter in weight and much more slender in substance, never intended to be more than divertissements. Most of them were written early in his career. Liszt made piano transcriptions of six of these songs, of which the most familiar are "The Maiden's Wish" (No. 1), "My Joys" (12), and "The Return" (15). The following recordings are all sung in the original Polish, and are listed in approximate order of their effectiveness. **Elzbieta Szmytka,** soprano, with Malcolm Martineau, piano, have achieved the most musical of the recordings. Their sensitive treatment, with close attention to the fluctuating moods in the texts, is impressive. Martineau's accompaniment is very discriminating. Szmytka's voice has fine clarity, though less color than the other three singers, and she sings in tune with superb control and expressivity. She makes the texts sound more natural than the others, in very good sound (DG 463072). Polish texts are included.

Elisabeth Söderström, with Ashkenazy at the piano, offers a generally pleasing account of these pieces. Her soprano is rich and colorful, but she's not always in tune, frequently squeezing up to the higher notes, and her vibrato is often too fast. The piano part is handled expertly and rather sonorously by Ashkenazy, who is, expectedly, the most powerful presence among the accompanists. The sound is a bit dry; Polish texts are included (London 414204).

The recording by **Young-Hee Choi** and Christophe Grasser is distinguished by their use of a Pleyel piano of 1831 for the songs and an 1852 Erard for the six transcriptions. Both instruments sound marvelous, but the Pleyel sounds fresher. Choi has a nice vibrato and a lovely tone in both the low and high ranges, but she sings out of tune on some notes. The Polish texts are not provided, and only incipits are given in French and English for the songs. Grasser's playing of the Liszt transcriptions is sparkling and tasteful, capturing their moods well, though he doesn't project the delicious evocativeness of Rosenthal, Hofmann, and Rachmaninoff in this repertoire. The recording was made in a Parisian church, so the digital sound is enhanced by some nice resonance (Quantum 6900).

Annette Celine, soprano, accompanied by her mother, Felicja Blumenthal, also recorded these 19 songs (Olympia 629). Her voice has a pleasant, dark color, but many notes aren't in tune and her tones lacks definition on certain tones. There is a sameness of treatment from one song to another. No Polish texts are given, only English translations.

MULBURY

Francesco Cilea (1866–1950)

Although critics have long maligned poor *Adriana Lecouvreur,* the opera has been a favorite of prima donnas and is revived with some frequency at their behest, much to the pleasure of audiences. Certainly Adriana is a role in which sopranos can revel in dramatic attitudes expressed through hyper-romantic music.

Magda Olivero has become something of a legend as Adriana. The composer pronounced her the "ideal interpreter" of the role when she retired in 1941. Then in 1951, at Cilea's insistence, she returned to the stage as Adriana and continued to sing the role for several more decades. In 1973 she even recorded a piano-accompanied abridged version at the age of 73! (Bongiovanni 2513). She was still in quite remarkable voice, and her interpretation of the text was still strongly insightful. Carmelina Gandolfo plays the piano accompaniments spectacularly.

A better example of Olivero's art preserves a 1959 performance in Naples that must have been one of the most emotional ever given; the audience goes berserk with appreciation (♦Melodram 27009; Phoenix 502; 2CD). Olivero could be subtle and passionate by turns, filing her voice down to an exquisite *fil di voce,* then letting it rip in full cry, all the while phrasing with musical grace and style. Corelli is hardly a model of taste and style, but he does sing excitingly, with top notes as thrilling as ever. Simionato out-belts several times Olivero in their confrontations and is fully as dramatic and as vivid a creation. Bastianini is equally grand, bold and virile, unsubtle. Up against such vocal competition, the orchestra loses, producing some really ugly sounds with chancy intonation. Conductor **Mario Rossi** does what he can under the circumstances, dutifully following his wayward singers. The sound favors the voices as well.

On the American side of the Atlantic, *Adriana* was almost exclusively the property of Tebaldi. By 1961 she and Del Monaco, her Maurizio, were a bit past their vocal prime, and the result is a nice souvenir of their careers but little else (Decca). Simionato is less forceful in the studio, but still a strong Princess. The Accademia di Santa Cecilia, Rome, is not the most happy of ensembles under the rough, pedestrian leadership of **Franco Capuana.**

In 1977 Scotto was in particularly fine voice, and it's obvious that she truly loved—and took seriously—Adriana and her problems. Praise Olivero to the skies, but praise Scotto even more. Her voice isn't as rich as Olivero's or Tebaldi's, but her attention to detail is ample compensation, making even the most trivial line spontaneous and inspired, the creation of a fully human character. Domingo is a more subtle artist than his competition in the role of Maurizio—a more sympathetic hero than is usually heard. He's in fine voice as well. Obraztsova is an imposing Princess, big, loud, even burly, tending toward coarseness. Much pleasure may be had from Milnes's Michonnet, a major artist in a secondary role usually assigned to a lesser artist; he's in luxuriant voice, approaching the text with care and nuance. **Levine** leads the Philharmonia Orchestra in a deeply committed performance, caressing many long-lined melodies for maximum effect; he finds, and brings out finely, many subtleties in an opera not known for subtlety (♦CBS 34588, 2CD).

When Sutherland and Bergonzi recorded *Adriana,* they were nearing the end of their distinguished careers. She is at times unsteady in sustained passages, and his top notes are effortful and strained, but years of experience had given both artists insight into the human side of the opera, with many delicate nuances of interpretation, and any vocal shortcomings are easily forgiven and forgotten. The forces of the Welsh National Opera under **Bonynge's** direction are splendid. He treats *Adriana* as a bel canto work with emphasis on beautiful tone and expressive long lines, with many felicitous details (Decca 425815, 2CD).

PARSONS

Domenico Cimarosa (1749–1801)

A contemporary of Mozart, Cimarosa's operas were more popular in their time than those of the Austrian master. Rossini's biographer, Stendahl, ranked him in a class with Mozart, and major singers clamored to appear in his operas. He composed more than 70 stage works, both comedies and tragedies, plus orchestral compositions. Yet of this extensive output, only two, *Il Matrimonio Segreto* and *Il Maestro di Capella,* are still performed with any regularity.

Il Maestro di Capella. This opera is a one-man show that's almost impossible to stage, as The Conductor in this brief comedy leads an orchestra through an intricate rehearsal. Unless the singer is himself a conductor, there is already a real conductor on the podium. It works best in recordings, and the best of them was a 1958 performance by Sesto Bruscantini: so Italian, so funny, and so well sung, with I Virtuosi di Roma conducted by **Renato Fasano.** Unfortunately, no CD has been issued. A 1960 recording by Fernando Corena finds the basso-buffo in high comic style, but the years of vocal distortion for comic effect have taken their toll, and vocal beauty is in limited supply (♦Decca 433036). The Covent Garden Orchestra led by **Argeo Quadri** is Corena's able partner in comedy.

The virtues of Jozsef Gregor's 1983 recording are the reverse of Corena's. Gregor has a bountiful voice with lots of tonal allure, but he is heavy-handed in the comedy. The Corelli Chamber Orchestra led by **Tamás Pál** plays with fine sound but not much spirit (Hungaroton). Somewhere between these extremes is Marcello Gatti, a happy compromise, in performance with the Orchestra Ars Cantus led by **Riccardo Cirri** (♦Bongiovanni 2184).

Il Matrimonio Segreto. At its 1793 Vienna premiere, this opera was such a hit with Emperor Leopold II that he requested the entire work as an encore after a late-night supper for the cast and audience. Its charm is immediately apparent. It's a gentle domestic comedy about a bourgeois father determined to marry his daughter to a nobleman; the problem is that she's already secretly married. This is one of the few non-Mozart operas of the 18th century to have a continuous performance history down to the present day.

The recorded sound of the 1950 performance from the Maggio Musicale Fiorentino isn't quite the best; it's monaural and muffled, and the musical cuts are numerous (♦Cetra 32, 2CD). But look at this cast: Simionato, Alda Noni, Ornella Rovero, Valletti, Bruscantini, Antonio Cassinelli. They're all Italian, all comfortable with the language and the musical style, and they put on quite a show—light, lively, and funny. **Manno Wolf-Ferrari** stirs his musical forces to a fine froth.

A 1956 recording from Teatro Piccolo Scala offers some serious competition (EMI 66513, 2CD). The recorded sound is superior and the cast—Sciutti, Stignani, Eugenia Ratti, Alva, Carlo Badioli, Franco Calabrese—are also all Italian with virtues like those of the earlier group. Sciutti and Ratti sound similar, as befits the two sisters; both are improvements on Noni and Rovero. Stignani and Alva equal their counterparts, although Badioli and Calabrese don't quite match their achievements. **Sanzogno** also doesn't quite equal the style and spirit of his competition.

Fischer-Dieskau may seem like an unorthodox choice for a buffo role, but his innate musicality and intelligence add up to a winning performance (DG 437696, 2CD). Of the rest of the cast, only Alberto Rinaldi sings with appropriate style and characterization; the others sound stylistically confused, interpretively bland. Varady has an attractive voice and a reasonable amount of characterization, but Ryland Davies lacks variety of color and interpretation. Augér sings accurately with little character, but Julia Hamari is mostly a failure. **Barenboim** leads the English Chamber Orchestra in a competent performance, missing any sense of style or involvement.

A delightfully spirited 1992 recording from Lausanne, although with excessive cuts, is a worthy performance (Cascavelle 1022, 2CD). Elzbieta Szmytka is graceful, confident, romantic, and determined. Jeannette Fischer's darker soprano is a fine contrast and complement to Szmytka, but Anne-Marie Owens is blurry with little of an interpretation. Angelo Romero gets the best of the comedy bits and sings them, not just in fine buffo style but handsomely as well. François Le Roux is a bit over the top in the foppish vein. **López-Cobos** leads the Chamber Orchestra of Lausanne in a stylish, elegant performance.

A number of other Cimarosa operas of varying merit are available. The best of them include *Le Astuzie Femminili,* one of his better efforts at comedy, with lively ensembles and some very romantic love music. A 1959 performance from RAI Naples led by **Mario Rossi** with Sciutti and Alva is a lively affair, catching the flair and humor of the piece (♦Memories 4285, 2CD). An *opera seria* by Cimarosa may not be to all tastes, but *Gli Orazi e i Curiazi* is full of good tunes in a jolly mixture with serious and comic music interchangeable. In a 1983 performance, **de Bernart** leads a strong performance with Daniela Dessi, Callas-like in vocal color but with none of the flair of her predecessor (♦Bongiovanni 2021, 2CD). *Le Donne rivali* is well performed in a 1994 recording from Perugia

(♦Bongiovanni 2983), and so is *L'Italiana in Londra* in 1986 from Savona (♦Bongiovanni 2040, 2CD).

Toscanini's incomparable overtures to *Il matrimonio per raggio* and *Il matrimonio segreto* are on RCA 60278. Cimarosa's more reverent passions surface in his *Requiem,* with Ameling, Finnilä, van Vrooman, and Widmer joining Lausanne forces under **Vittorio Negri** (Philips 422489).   PARSONS

Muzio Clementi (1752–1832)

Since the time of the first Elizabeth, the English have been enamored of Italians for their musical delight. Whole families of musicians migrated north to open arms during her reign, and this passion was undiminished in subsequent centuries. Handel was welcomed artistically not for his Teutonic heritage but for his Italian training, and Muzio Clementi also made it to England and there made history.

Clementi's first studies were in his native Rome, where he became organist at a parish church by age 13, when he came to the attention of Peter Beckford, a peripatetic Englishman of means who brought him to the family estate in Dorset. There he spent his time studying music until the now-adept keyboard artist and burgeoning composer went off to London. After some slow years as accompanist, conductor, and occasional soloist, he felt sufficiently confident in his own work (and some good reviews) to undertake a tour of the continent in 1780. At the court of Emperor Joseph II in Vienna, he had to endure one of those contests pitting performer against performer that so amused the 18th-century nobility. His opponent was Mozart, who said in a letter to his father that "Clementi . . . has not a kreuzer's worth of taste or feeling—in short, he is a mere mechanicus." Clementi's own recollection of his competitor is haunting: "Until then, I had never heard anyone play with such spirit and grace."

His reputation grew after his return to London, and by 1790 he was recognized as an important teacher, composer, performer, publisher, and, by the end of the decade, a key figure in the advancement of the piano itself. Clementi & Co. was a notable success; his young Irish student John Field was piano salesman and had the exclusive English rights to publish Beethoven's works. Realizing his real legacy would be as pedagogue, he followed up his 1801 *Introduction to the Art of Playing on the Piano Forte* with the vast, multivolume *Gradus ad Parnassum,* appearing 55 years after his Opus 1. When he died, mourners filled Westminster Abbey, and he was interred in the cloisters there.

Curiously, recent developments in classical music radio in the United States have been very Clementi-friendly. In a world where we in radio are told "not too new, not too old, not too vocal, not too heavy" (if you listen to major stations with this format, you recognize the symptoms), Clementi fits just right.

As so often in the history of recording, one champion made all the difference. In Clementi's case, that champion was formidable indeed: **Vladimir Horowitz.** This master technician saw beyond the Sonatinas (appended to the *Art of Playing),* so often a part of elementary musical lessons for the century after Clementi's death, and instead found what Beethoven had: genuine keyboard artistry. Nothing before, since, or indeed probably ever will do more honor to the composer's name. The excellent "Horowitz Plays Clementi" has his 1950 Rondo, the 1954 sonata sessions, and the scintillating *Sonata quasi concerto,* a remarkable piano reduction of Clementi's sole surviving concerto (♦RCA 7753). Three sonatas from 1964 sessions are also available (♦Sony 53466).

These are the sun; the rest must be lesser lights. This is not to denigrate in any way the excellent efforts of **Pietro Spada.** He's a good pianist with a passionate devotion to Clementi and has recorded the complete piano works (Arts 47223-37, 15CD). He was also soloist and editor for the very good series of the complete symphonic pieces with the Philharmonia conducted by d'Avalos (♦ASV 802-04). We're not supposed to think very much of these works; while they fascinated Alfredo Casella, who completed the fragmented Library of Congress manuscripts as a kind of Clementi tribute or pastiche, Spada argues for their intrinsic wholeness and grandeur. It's hard not to feel the affection Clementi put (and his audience heard) into the Great National Symphony (No. 3), with its touching variations on "God Save the King."

Ian Hobson's "The London Piano School" offers Clementi and his predecessors (Burton, J.C. Bach) and students (Cramer, Field). These are fine performances, elegantly programmed—who can resist (♦Arabesque 6594/95, 2CD)? Much less worthy is the set of the complete small chamber pieces for three instruments with Italy's **Fauré Trio** (Dynamic 19, 32, 93, 161). These aren't really piano trios; they're very much what they were published as: "Sonatas for Piano with Violin and Cello." They are works for piano with some strings unfairly along for the ride; we can imagine Clementi no more willing to give equal time in these works to his nonpiano collaborators than he was in his set of waltzes Opp. 38 and 39, scored for piano, tambourine, and triangle!

Balázs Szokolay has essayed Clementi as part of his ongoing quest through the Romantic piano literature (Naxos 550452). **Peter Katin** offers an interesting wrinkle by playing a sonata program on an original Clementi "square piano" (Athene 4). **June Chun** gives us a reading of the didactic sonatinas—didactic in the best sense. These were his "Progressive Sonatinas," starting easy and getting harder, and make for a charming program provided you didn't have to practice them every sunny afternoon when you were nine (Centaur 2439). **Nikolai Demidenko,** perhaps inspired by Horowitz, gives us "Demidenko Plays Clementi" (Hyperion). This disc includes works not part of the Horowitz series, notably the extensive Op. 40 pieces written for the composer's 1802 tour; they're strongly performed and perhaps a harbinger of a new series on a much more accessible label (♦Hyperion 66808).

It's curious and pleasant to note that one of the theme recordings that were issued 30 or 40 years ago is still in print. The old Turnabout label brought out a series of obscurities, usually world premiere recordings, with secondary or unrecorded artists and ensembles. Clementi's Piano Concerto got this treatment with **Blumenthal** and the Prague New Chamber Orchestra directed by Zedda. Called "Early Romantic Piano Concerti," it's enhanced by other still rare concertos by Clementi students Cramer and Field as well as works by Hummel, Czerny, and Ferdinand Ries. It's still revelatory, as a collection and as a way of putting Clementi in context as a catalyst for the evolution of the art of the piano (♦Vox 5111).   DAVIS

Eric Coates (1886–1957)

"The man who writes tunes" is how English composer Ethel Smyth once addressed her compatriot Eric Coates, reportedly to the latter's delight. But in fact Coates is more than that; his music bridges the salon and the concert hall without ever straying from the light-classical niche he so successfully carved out for himself. Even his most ambitious work, *The Three Elizabeths* suite—turned out in 1944 to honor Elizabeth I, the current Queen Mother, and the young queen-to-be—retains a distinctively jaunty air. At the same time, its Elgarian majesty was enough to earn it friends on these shores when it was used as the theme music for the BBC-TV version of *The Forsyte Saga,* just as the *Knightsbridge March*

and *By the Sleepy Lagoon* had done a generation before as BBC radio themes.

Besides *The Three Elizabeths,* the best of Coates would have to include the two *London Suites, Cinderella* and *The Three Bears* "phantasies," *The Four Centuries* dance suite, and any number of marches. Happily most of this is available on an economical set that includes, among other things, **Reginald Kilbey**'s outstanding *Three Elizabeths* and **Mackerras**'s lively but fanciful *Three Bears* and "Man From the Sea" (from *The Three Men*), with its invigorating counterpoint. Similarly, *The Dam Busters March* finds **Groves** at his most persuasive, as does his and **Jack Brymer**'s suavely sophisticated account of the cleverly syncopated *Saxo-Rhapsody,* one of the finest of Coates's concert miniatures (♦EMI 4456, 2CD).

Among single discs, **Malcolm Nabarro** brings a lyrical bounce and an agreeable warmth not only to the *Three Elizabeths, Three Bears,* and *London Suite,* but also to the discographic premiere of the Grieg-like *Ballad for Strings,* written when Coates was only 18 (♦ASV 2053). Volume 2 in his survey offers the only stereo recording of *The Four Centuries,* with its delicious "Hornpipe," and *The Seven Dwarfs* ballet (later reworked as *The Enchanted Garden*), as well as the full suite from *The Jester at the Wedding* (♦ASV 2075). Again, the performances are warmly attractive even if the orchestra sounds a bit small. **John Wilson** draws a response from the BBC Concert Orchestra in a collection of 17 smaller pieces, several of them otherwise unrecorded (♦ASV 2107), that is more polished than **Boult**'s in his now-deleted Coates program (IMP). But if you can find it, check out his and bass-baritone Ian Wallace's ultra-flavorful *Stonecracker John.*

Fennell's *Three Elizabeths* sounds a bit stiff next to these, despite impressive playing and recording (Mercury). Ditto his *London Suite,* though the conductor's natural dynamism pays dividends in *Covent Garden* and the familiar *Knightsbridge March.* They certainly have more impact than **Adrian Leaper**'s two *London* suites, where the somewhat laid-back performances suffer from overly recessed sound (Marco Polo). However, his disc does include the only *Selfish Giant* at present. Better in both respects is **Andrew Penny**'s follow-up, also with the Slovak Radio Symphony, which besides a tenderly molded *Sleepy Lagoon* offers a lyrical *Springtime Suite* and *Saxo-Rhapsody* and a complete *Four Ways* (♦Marco Polo 223521). As it happens, **Wilson** also includes *Springtime* on his follow-up disc (♦ASV 2112), maybe a little rushed even by the composer's yardstick, but worth having for his *Enchanted Garden*—one of the nicest recordings it has received.

Also worth seeking out are two collections that include some of **Coates**'s own recordings from the 78 rpm era (♦Happy Days 211/12, 2CD, and 52390, 2CD). Faded sound notwithstanding, most of them still set the standard interpretively—for example, his *Cinderella,* more vital than any other. (I would also like to see his LP *Three Elizabeths, Four Centuries,* and especially the two *London* suites reissued.)

Finally, even in Coates's purely instrumental music, one frequently hears an evocation of spoken texts—witness the 'Who's been sitting in *my* chair' that opens *The Three Bears* and the *Cinderella* motif heard throughout that piece. So it's not surprising that his output includes a number of songs, two CDs of which are currently available. Between baritone **Brian Rayner Cook** (♦ASV 567) and tenor **Richard Edgar-Wilson** (♦Marco Polo 223806), I marginally prefer the latter's lighter, salon-style approach to the former's straighter, more concert-oriented renditions. But died-in-the-wool Coates lovers will undoubtedly want both, especially since there are no duplications.

GOODFELLOW

Samuel Coleridge-Taylor (1875–1912)

Abandoned in infancy by his father, a doctor from Sierra Leone, and then brought up by his English mother, Coleridge-Taylor was a man in search of his roots. He studied with Stanford, was highly encouraged by the English musical establishment, and became a successful composer and conductor. We have few of his mature pieces, but *Hiawatha* and his settings of Negro melodies, as well as his later orchestral works, are strong enough to justify our interest in this somewhat shadowy figure.

Only three of the once numerous recordings of Coleridge-Taylor's music are presently listed. The Argo discs that were eliminated when that company changed hands are particularly missed. Two fine orchestral works, *Ballade* and *Symphonic Variations on an African Air,* were played by the Royal Liverpool Philharmonic under **Grant Llewellyn** in beautifully recorded and exciting readings (English Decca). Another release contained the entire *Scenes from the Song of Hiawatha* with the Welsh National Opera under **Kenneth Alwyn,** with soloists including Bryn Terfel, another excellent performance and recording (Argo 430356, 2CD).

An interesting program of lighter selections—including a *Hiawatha Overture* that doesn't appear in the complete recording, *Petite Suite de Concert, Four Characteristic Waltzes, Gypsy Suite, Romance of the Prairie Lilies,* and a suite from *Othello*—are offered by the RTE Concert Orchestra of Dublin, conducted by **Leaper,** all played adequately if not with the last degree of polish (Marco Polo 223516). At the moment, the only orchestral work available is the lovely *Romance* for violin, played beautifully by **Rachel Barton** with Daniel Hege and the Encore Chamber Orchestra in a varied program of violin concertos by black composers (Cedille 35). All that's listed from *Hiawatha* is the aria "Onaway! Awake, Beloved" in a disc conducted by Sargent (Dutton 7032).

Most of Coleridge-Taylor's chamber music is early, meaning that, though beautifully romantic and not unoriginal, it falls back on its influences more than his later works. The one disc presently available contains *Nonet* for woodwind and string quartets and the five *Fantasy Pieces* for string quartet, both written while he was studying with Stanford at the Royal College of Music (Koch 7056, NA). As the work of a teenager, they are remarkable. On the same disc are arrangements for piano trio of five of the *24 Negro Melodies,* his volume of piano pieces based on African and American songs. The trio versions are different in many ways and are not just transcriptions. The playing is warm and musical, though not very polished. Also, **Harold Wright** and the Hawthorne Quartet mixed chamber music with piano pieces and gave us another early chamber work, a lovely Clarinet Quintet recalling the mood of Brahms's piece. Violinist **Michael Ludwig** and pianist **Virginia Eskin** played a considerable 13-minute *Ballade,* and Eskin played six of the *Negro Melodies* and *Petite Suite de Concert.* These performances were good, though Eskin was a bit sloppy in the *Negro Melodies.*

Eskin's playing was better than the alternative, a complete performance of the 24 by **Frances Walker** in a clangy recording played from an odd edition that leaves out a bar in two places and makes a considerable cut in *Deep River,* while the pianist is arhythmic and tiring to listen to (Orion 7806, NA).   MOORE

Aaron Copland (1900–1990)

Copland has been called "the dean of modern American music," and it's hard to dispute the title. For years his name has—at least in the public mind—been synonymous with "the greatest American composer." Though many disagree, and not a few point out the current comparative neglect of the greater part of his works, he has stayed consistently popular with the public while other composers see their work languishing on the printed score, rarely played.

Copland began his career as a brash creator of striking modern scores that reflected the age he lived in. With Stravinsky as a lifelong idol, and even flirting with Schoenberg's serialism, at the midpoint of his career he developed a need to communicate with his audience, feeling that this key ingredient in the musical experience could be ignored no longer. He then produced his great series of ballets, forever engraving his name into the hearts of music lovers everywhere. Even so, the musically curious owe themselves a greater familiarity with his other major works.

SYMPHONIES

1 (Organ). Completed in the year Copland finished his studies with the great pedagogue Nadia Boulanger, his Symphony 1 is full of embryonic stylistic flowers that were later to achieve full bloom. The middle scherzo is the heart of the work—offbeat, jazzy, and decidedly not for the aurally nonambulatory. At the premiere, conductor Walter Damrosch said to the audience, "Ladies and gentlemen, I'm sure you will agree that if a gifted man can write a symphony like this at 23, within five years he will be ready to commit murder!" **Slatkin** avoids the dastardly deed by giving us a realistic recording that incorporates the organ part during the recording process, instead of dubbing it in later. Because of some stage distance, the brass and organ lack visceral impact, but it's natural and thrilling (♦RCA 68292). **Litton** gives us a wonderfully propulsive, high-octane reading (♦Delos 3221). Wayne Marshall handles the organ part with a breezy breathlessness, while the Dallas Symphony plays thrillingly. **Bernstein** brings his intensity to a reading full of fragrant early modernism. Rhythms are sharp and spiky, melodies laser-bright, and E. Power Biggs's playing is feisty. The sound is still great (♦Sony 63155).

2 (Short Symphony). Perhaps more familiar in its rescoring as the Sextet for Piano, Clarinet, and String Quartet, this brief work is highly rhythmic and carefully structured, yet easily accessible. Two premieres were canceled because of its complexities (Koussevitzky said it was "impossible"), but our ears are more accustomed to what shocked audiences in 1934, and it seems quite tame now. The St. Louis band under **Slatkin** dances through all the interpretive land mines with mastery and assurance in a recording that's second to none (♦RCA 68292). Where Slatkin is master of form and refinement, **Tilson Thomas** is master of living-on-the-edge excitement. His San Francisco Symphony, while not as beguiling and polished, rips through this tightly wound score like a hot knife through butter (♦RCA 68541). The often erratic London Symphony does a good job managing the exposed rhythms in this tricky work, and the engineers give **Copland** competitive sound, but the more recent recordings outpace this one (Sony). Likewise the recording by **Dennis Russell Davies,** chamber-like and balletic, but not as full and warm—always essential in Copland—as either of the RCA recordings (Pro Arte).

3. The end of WWII brought a sense of optimism and endless possibilities to the American people. Other composers, notably Roy Harris, were creating works in this old European genre that were breathing new life into a form many "progressives" thought outdated and insignificant. It's no surprise that Copland wanted his next symphony to be a major statement. It's his largest orchestral work, and what an outburst it is! If any American work of this century can musically define the elusive yet immediately recognizable pioneer spirit of America, this is it. One of his greatest and most popular themes is the basis of the work's last movement; audiences all over the world have adored the "Fanfare" for its noble simplicity and purity of ideas and spirit.

The enveloping sound in **Slatkin**'s recording provides a flattering backdrop for the brilliant St. Louis Symphony. He takes his time, letting the work unfold naturally and without pushing, especially in the scherzo. A thrilling reading, the best of recent vintage (♦RCA 60149). Yet **Bernstein**'s remains *the* great recording of the piece; nobody did it like Lenny, and the freshly remastered sound is spectacular. All its hope, optimism, and nascent pessimism are found here, each pulled and prodded to maximum effect. The New York Philharmonic plays with the uncontrolled exhilaration of a kid opening a new toy at Christmas. It's a must (♦Sony 63155). We might have hoped that Bernstein's last recording of this seminal American gem would bring new insights; alas, Copland's vigorous tone palette of Americana doesn't respond well to old age looking back. What was gained by a slight improvement in sound was lost by a lack of youthful brashness and energy (DG).

Copland liked to conduct his own works, for he could highlight what he felt was most important. The trouble is that he could also be deadly dull, and his reputation as a stern purveyor of orchestral unanimity and discipline is not strong. Such is the case with his Sony recording. The London Symphony is sloppy and tonally insecure, and with other great readings to choose from, this one doesn't stand a chance. His Everest recording, despite the thin sound, is far better, but far from a first choice. **Järvi** should have done a better job, for he had the right orchestra (Detroit), but his reading isn't as cohesive as others, and flaccid Copland always fails (Chandos).

Levi's solid, impact-laden performance makes it competitive with the best on the market; he ably adopts the wide-open frontier style that is part and parcel of this symphony. The Atlantans play splendidly, going from strength to strength in a recording that, while not quite as spacious as Slatkin's, is in every way as powerful and exciting (♦Telarc 80201). **Oue** takes a new look at this work in a careful, calculated production quite different from others. The sober, shiny sound of the Minnesota Orchestra is impressive, though I doubt the general appeal of this disc (Reference).

Dance Symphony. Copland refashioned the best music from his early ballet *Grohg* into a three-movement symphony—warm, lively, and criminally underperformed. **Slatkin** presents a superb reading, with warm, intensely sharpened string playing, punctuated with brooding, outspoken winds (♦RCA 68292). **Dorati**'s version—up to snuff in all respects except for the tonal allure Slatkin provides—is in a set that provides a cheap way of acquiring many fine Copland readings (♦London 48261, 2CD). In **Copland**'s own recording, the Londoners and the composer are in fine fettle, with his direct, sanitized conducting. This work is a marvel of pointillistic call-and-response, and this recording, though aged, is vivid and exciting (♦Sony 47232).

OTHER ORCHESTRAL MUSIC

To begin with, I must mention the singular set of recordings made by **Copland** (and a few by **Bernstein**) for Columbia over a period of about 20 years. Many pieces—eminently worthy of more recordings—are available only in this set, as are many others discussed here. Pieces like *Inscape, Three Latin American Sketches, Dance Panels, John Henry, Letter from Home, Two Pieces for String Orchestra,* and *Statements* are only to be found here. Though not always the best versions, many of them can hold their own—even in some of the more famous works—and the set is essential for the Copland completist (♦Sony 47232 for works 1922–1935 [2CD], 46559 for works 1936–1948 [3CD], 47236 for works 1948–1971 [2CD]).

Appalachian Spring: Suite. Martha Graham's 1943 commission inspired Copland to produce what many regard as the quintessential American work, though it was started in Hollywood and completed in Mexico. But his use of the old Shaker hymn "A Simple Song" forever engraved the work into the American psyche. The Suite was created in 1945 to give the piece some orchestral breathing room and allow for performances outside the original's restrictive orchestration. **Copland** made a wonderful recording with the Boston Symphony; while a little sloppy in places and not overtly extroverted, it still allows the wind and string sonority full bloom (♦RCA 61505). His relaxed, genteel manner with the London Symphony is no less effective in one of that band's more successful Copland efforts (♦Sony 42430). In an otherwise sterling album, **Kunzel** gives us a foursquare and flaccid version, with misdirected phrasing and total lack of forward motion (Telarc). **Oue** misses the point completely, with no sense of the heartfelt serenity and punchy, plucky playfulness that must be a part of any performance (Reference). **Bernstein,** as in so much of Copland's music, claimed ownership of this piece, whether in New York or Los Angeles. The Los Angeles recording has better sound, and possibly the better orchestra—really on top of its game. Everything is right—sumptuous strings, biting brass, and mellifluous winds (♦DG 31048). The New York recording is one of the—scratch that—is *the* great Copland album, probably never to be bettered. True aficionados will need both (♦Sony 37257).

Mehta does no wrong; in all respects this is a fine version at a great price, but it lacks the last bit of refinement to push it into the front rank (London). As much as **Schwarz** has done for American music, you would hope it would translate into riveting Copland, but he reins in his Seattle orchestra, softening the blows too often and making the rough places plain (Delos). **Louis Lane** supplies a wonderful reading in spectacular sound, graceful, fleeting, and born to the dance; the Atlantans play with quicksilver finesse (♦Telarc 80078). And **Ormandy,** in a remastered recording, shows us why he was one of the foremost interpreters of American music (♦RCA 63467).

Dorati, as usual, can be counted on for excellent Copland, always fine-tuned and silvery in tone despite the rough-edged sonics (♦Mercury 34301). **Boughton,** in spite of some fine playing and a good feel for the idiom, is let down by the sound (Nimbus). The City of London Sinfonia under **Hickox** is a competent ensemble that fails to convey the necessary punch and Pennsylvanian purity (EMI). **Kitaienko** offers an interesting, Moscow-colored version that's quite attractive, but hardly a first (or even second) choice (Sheffield Labs). **Susskind** and the London Symphony prove weak in the knees, especially when compared with Copland's own LSO recording (Everest). **Gunzenhauser** doesn't measure up, with a reading that's flat and lackluster (Naxos). Finally, **Koussevitzky** offers a delicious version recorded the year the Suite was born, in smartly remastered sound—well worth the stereo sonic sacrifice for such an "authentic" record (♦Biddulph 50).

Appalachian Spring. The original version for 13 instruments is rarely heard these days; the music missing from the Suite isn't essential to get the spirit of the score, and the full orchestra has a much wider variance of color. However, the original is not without interest, and **Copland**'s skill at mimicking larger orchestral sound is quite daring. He recorded this in the early '70s with an all-star cast that's not to be missed, sounding great (♦Sony 42431). **Wolff** offers a splendid performance in great sound, the best modern version (♦Teldec 46313). **Andrew Schenck** gives a rather slovenly reading, routine and uninteresting (Koch). The **Orpheus Chamber Orchestra** is not to be slighted, with excellent playing in good sound, but this work really needs the greater unity a conductor can provide (DG). The always reliable **Keith Clark** and the Pacific Symphony challenge with a beautifully played, effervescent reading that is a delight (♦Reference 22). **Davies**'s recording, while lyrical, is lacking in energy or motion, a wet-noodle approach to Copland (Pro Arte).

Tilson Thomas gives us the chamber setting in a score that **Ormandy** requested from Copland in 1954. He leads a very stirring, suave performance that will satisfy anyone wanting the piece in full orchestral dress (♦RCA 63511).

Billy the Kid. Copland's earliest populist ballet (1938) has enjoyed 60 years of continued public approval. Capturing our wild-western romantic proclivities in a score as brash and uncontrolled as the notorious William Bonney himself, the work is a standard of classical Americana. Two versions are presently in fashion: the original complete score (about 30 minutes) and the often-played Suite (about 20). **Gunzenhauser** doesn't have the orchestra to make this shine (Naxos). An older recording by **Levine** is too jaded to be competitive (EMI). **Slatkin** gives us one of the most ineffective readings of any music he has recorded (EMI).

Complete ballet lovers can rejoice at **Zinman**'s reading. I miss a fuller string sound, but his interpretation is pointed and alive, with the somewhat muffled recording actually working in favor of the music (♦Argo 40639). **Dorati** also offers a lovely rendition, very American, very sassy (♦Mercury 34301). **Tilson Thomas** leads a beautifully recorded, fully involved reading that gives a real sense of out-west ruggedness. The San Francisco strings and brass are especially vivid in their tonal allure (♦RCA 63511).

For those wanting only the Suite—and you don't miss much with it—there are greater choices. There is fine analog sound with flawless playing from **Ormandy,** though it has less impact than more modern recordings, and even some made at the time. But Ormandy was a master, and if his were the only version, I'd be content (♦RCA 6802 or 63467). **Mata**'s *Billy* is lackluster, like using water pistols instead of real guns (Dorian). Many critics prefer **Morton Gould** to Bernstein, who is said to lack the earthy homeliness needed to render this music in its pristine purity. I can't agree, but Gould is a lot of fun; his orchestra sounds great; and this is a wonderful recording (♦RCA 61667). Everything about **Kunzel** marks it as one of the best: booming sound, expert pacing, and unmannered playing, particularly by the strings (♦Telarc 80339).

Copland is on top of his score, but the London Symphony strings lack the last degree of refinement and precision, though the low brass is full and warm (Sony). **Bernstein** gives us a *Billy* for the ages, an outlaw tall in the saddle and quick on the draw. You really can't live without this, and if you take my advice on the other great ballets of Copland, you won't have to. Get Kunzel for the sound and Bernstein for the essence of Copland (♦Sony 63082). His earlier effort is interesting but not necessary (RCA, in "The Bernstein Years"). **Wolff** offers only a small selection as filler (Teldec). **Schwarz** isn't bad, but the competition is too fierce (Delos). The same holds true for **John Farrer;** the shadows of others are simply too long (IMP). But **Johanos** is able—quite economically—to give a crackerjack performance in great sound (♦Vox 5035).

Connotations. This thorny, riveting patchwork is perhaps the most difficult work Copland ever wrote, not least because of its 22-minute length. Serialism finally made a foray even into Copland's genteel world, though without the aesthetic of its German founders. The premiere sent shock waves through the world of music, and even Bernstein expressed

his dislike for it. Yet it's significant that of all his works, *Connotations* was one he chose to re-record near the end of his life. There is more clarity in **Copland**'s last recording—focused, attentive, and completely in control of every vicious serial maneuver. But he did make a rather large cut, and even so, it's two minutes slower than his first effort; the lack of excitement makes it a failure (DG). His first effort is full of frantic energy, forward motion, and makes no attempt to manufacture subtleties where none exist. The work can be like the unrelenting pummeling of a prizefighter at times, and **Bernstein**'s consistency keeps boredom far away (♦Sony 60177).

Danzon Cubano. About 10 years after *El Salon Mexico,* Copland again turned to the idea of dance hall music as the basis for a serious, popular piece. The result, more languorous and sultry than the first, has continued to be popular. **Zinman** fires off a particularly snazzy rendition (the piece was written for the Baltimore Symphony), full of zest (♦Argo 40639). **Copland**'s version lacks the punch of Zinman, but the sound is good and the pacing excellent (♦Sony 42429, or 89323, 2CD). **Bernstein** has all the punch but not the suavity and spikiness of Zinman (Sony). **Dorati** again scores highly, though many can't stand the Mercury sound, while others adore it (♦Mercury 34301). The original version of this piece—for two pianos, like *El Salon Mexico*—is not worth hearing after the orchestral versions, but if you insist, try **Noël Lee** and **Christian Ivaldi,** where you also get *Salon* (♦Arion 68375).

Down a Country Lane. A *Life* magazine commission put this short, sweetly wistful piece into the hands of thousands of school children and music programmers. **Copland**'s London Symphony recording is unsentimental, swift, and delightful (♦Sony 47236, or 89323, 2CD). But no more flowing, melodious account has been recorded than by **Wolff** and his St. Paul band (♦Teldec 77310).

Fanfare for the Common Man. A commission from the Cincinnati Orchestra in 1943 for a number of fanfares from various composers led to the creation of this beautiful, moving, optimistic prelude for brass and percussion, perhaps Copland's most played work. **Ormandy** and his Philadelphians are absolutely spectacular in an awe-inspiring performance that leaves nothing to be desired (♦RCA 68020). His earlier effort should be avoided—genteel, straight-laced, and buttoned-up (Sony). **Kunzel**'s version is brilliantly executed—full, round, with a powerhouse impact; look no further for the best modern recording (♦Telarc 80339). **Copland**'s version is broad, stately, and distinctly unemotional, as if to commemorate a head of state instead of some great utterance about mankind. He allows some intonation problems in the trumpets, but if you're buying this in a set, it might do (Sony).

Mehta gives us a recording that is too over-the-top—his insistence on exaggerated effects portrays the common man as cartoon (London). **Lane** supplies great sound, visceral impact, and cohesive playing—a winner all around (♦Telarc 80078). **David Honeyball** and the London Brass Virtuosi play well enough, but their tameness makes it sound more like a church processional (Hyperion). **Slatkin** and St. Louis, made for this type of music, turn in a pulverizing, fervent reading in a wonderful recording that will bring a tear to the most hardened among us (♦RCA 60983). **Richard Harvey** and a gathering of three brass ensembles give a suave, exceedingly stylish rendering on a disc that contains an eclectic group of brass works from many centuries (♦ASV 870).

Boughton has been moderately successful in American music, but his Copland disc isn't as idiomatic as it should be (Nimbus). **Schwarz** misses the point entirely with a lugubrious, lackadaisical account that fails to move (Delos). **Gunzenhauser** is raw—not always a detriment, but too much in the Mehta mold (Naxos). **Mester** and the London Philharmonic give a strained performance in an otherwise intriguing album called "20 Fanfares for the Common Man" (Koch). **Dorati,** excellent Coplandian that he was, allows his Detroit Symphony to send forth glorious sounds in an all-Copland album (♦Decca 430705). **Johanos** weighs in with a fine recording that is faulted only by some compressed sound, with a smattering of Copland, Ives, and Rachmaninoff (♦Vox 5035). Then of course there is the one-and-every **Bernstein,** whose mandatory Copland ballet album is self-recommending (♦Sony 63082). **Oue** lacks the brilliance and polish of the best performances, and the bass drum is a killer on the speakers (Reference).

Lincoln Portrait. This glitzy bit of Americana has always been a favorite at big occasions, and as it poses no stringent musical problems, its success is entirely dependent on the speaker's role. Few that meet that requirement. Koussevitzky had **Melvyn Douglas,** and the Hollywood effect is writ large all over the sound stage (Dutton Labs). **Henry Fonda** gave Copland perhaps the wimpiest reading on record, completely silly-sounding (Sony). **Norman Schwarzkopf** and Slatkin are in fine fettle, but I think of Desert Storm every time I hear his voice (RCA); it's not bad though. **Adlai Stevenson** didn't quite meet the expectations of Ormandy and his orchestra (Sony). **Gregory Peck** is very close for Mehta, but you still feel as if your father is lecturing you.

It would be irresponsible not to mention the American series from the New York Philharmonic, with Bernstein and a booming **William Warfield;** you'd pay a lot of money to get one work, but the whole set is worth it (♦NY Philharmonic 9904). Abravanel and **Charlton Heston** delight us with a very warm reading (♦Vanguard 4037). But best of all, **James Earl Jones** flattens us with a superlative, highly-emotive performance that must have had Schwarz giddy. The rest of the album is very nice also (♦Delos 3140).

Music for a Great City. Culled from the 1961 film *Something Wild,* this symphonic suite was commissioned by the London Symphony for its 60th anniversary. Late Copland can be very biting, and this score is a mirror of fast-paced, jarring, jazzy life in a city more akin to New York than London. No matter, the music is brisk and rigorous, and well worth the exemplary care lavished on it by **Slatkin** and his forces in a beautifully balanced recording (♦RCA 60149). Though the sonics are rather boisterous and edgy, as is the committed reading by the LSO—unusually energized—**Copland** is in fine form with all the jazzy jigsaws in this score. Only a lack of tonal warmth holds it back (Sony).

Music for Movies. This 1943 suite is made up of three early film scores: *Of Mice and Men, The City,* and *Our Town.* **Copland**'s version is pleasant and nicely done, with somewhat restricted sound (Sony). **Howarth** uses this as filler on his disc; his performances are fine, but nothing screams "desert island" (London). **Slatkin** gives us a technicolor musical paint bomb that showers us with oily, malleable melodies and crunchy rhythms—simply irresistible (♦RCA 61699).

Music for the Theater. The '20s spawned a myriad of jazz-inspired compositions. Gershwin, Stravinsky, Milhaud, and Ravel all enjoyed great success, and Copland took advantage of this to produce his first hit. This delightful work, so full of the New York persona that inhabited all of his nonpopulist works, has been dominated by **Bernstein**'s recording for years, and it still sounds great, though the competition is closing in fast on his blazing account (♦Sony 47232). His later recording has some elements missing, the tense, nervous, anticipatory exultation being far more present during his New York tenure (DG). **Levi** and company are

up to the challenge, bringing a little bit of New York to Atlanta, filling the void for a hefty modern recording (♦Telarc 80201). **Litton** tears into this piece as if it were written yesterday, so facile and spontaneous are he and his Dallas band; the contrast between movements is excellent—tender melody with forceful rhythms. This is a primary recommendation (♦Delos 3221). The St. Paul Chamber Orchestra plays well under **Wolff**—an underrated conductor—but this small group can't muster the oomph needed at critical moments (Teldec).

Our Town. **Copland** shunned the then-current trend of thick, luscious, late-romantic style in films and produced some exquisite, fine-as-china, homespun Americana for his score to Thornton Wilder's *Our Town.* His recording has all these qualities (♦Sony 46559, or 89323, 2CD). But once again it's **Slatkin** who plays the short suite with delicacy and musical allure (♦RCA 61669).

An Outdoor Overture. Written in 1958, this woefully underperformed work has a tonal cohesion and cheery outlook that should grace the concert stages more often. The London Symphony plays well for **Copland,** more competitive in the little-known works than in the great ballets (♦Sony 46559). **Lane** persuades us of his Copland credentials with an incisive, lilting reading of this neglected score (♦Sony 62401). **Keith Clark** gives a worthy effort in wonderful sound (♦Reference 22). Winners all around, and **Schwarz** also comes through with an ebullient, warm-sounding recording (♦Delos 3140).

Quiet City. This piece was originally intended for the stage; it's about a trumpeter who imagines the thoughts of people in the city, but the city feeling is almost totally absent from this reflective "country" piece. Of all Copland's works, this is probably the best suited to **Marriner**'s English group; sweet and subtle, it's just the type of piece the Academy plays to the hilt. Pick the earlier recording over the later Argo (♦London 48261). William Long plays romantically and beautifully for **Copland,** echoing age-old sentiments in every bar; the London Symphony strings sound revitalized (♦Sony 46559). Philip Collins on trumpet and William Harrod on English horn turn in sensitive performances on a Cincinnati disc by **Kunzel** that's a desert-island requirement—why look further? (♦Telarc 80339). Though it had the composer's approval, the wind band arrangement by **Donald Hunsberger** with Wynton Marsalis lacks the degree of softness needed to make a really *quiet* city (Sony). **Boughton** (Nimbus), **Hickox** (EMI), and **Wolff** (Teldec) are all respectable, but unless you feel a desire to pick up something else of theirs along the way, my other recommendations leave you without the need to do so.

The Red Pony. **Copland**'s music for his most popular film score is every bit as folksy and charming as his more popular ballets, and all the tunes—unlike the other scores—are his own, a fact he was quite proud of. His recording with the New Philharmonia is one of his most engaging, with bold, flashy sound and sensitive, feather-light playing (♦Sony 42429). **Litton**'s Copland album has wonderful, resonating sound that spotlights each section of the orchestra; his aptitude for this music shines in every bar in a sensational release (♦Delos 3221). In one of **Previn**'s earliest outings, he finds much that is persuasive in this lovely score, but the competition is too strong (Sony). **Sedares** falls victim to the same problem (Koch). From the opening radiant glistening of the strings to the thunderous and explosive bass line, you know right away that **Slatkin** and the St. Louis Symphony have produced a recording that is sonically the finest on disc. This is one of the best of his Copland series (♦RCA 61699).

Rodeo. A western battle of the sexes was the idea for this wartime ballet, the second of Copland's three great populist works that form the basis for his popularity today. The jazzy, pseudo-western feel and snazzy authentic melodies make for an elegantly tuneful experience. Though **Zinman** is spirited and soundly played, the strings are weak—or the winds and brass are overdone (Argo). **Mata**'s orchestra is fine, but he offers too little in a competitive field, failing to convince us in this persuasive music (RCA). **Morton Gould** was a superb musician who was an effective advocate for music in a style not unlike his own; I would be happy with his recording had I never known Bernstein (♦RCA 61667). The Bournemouth Symphony under **John Farrar** has lots of verve and polish, but little in the way of reflection and nuance, though it's played well (IMP). **Kunzel**'s fabulous recording allows all sorts of details to emerge. The slow portions are most effective; the first movement is a little lethargic, but the sound is gorgeous, and the minuses don't preclude a recommendation (♦Telarc 80339).

The London Symphony responds vividly to **Copland,** in a broad, spacious reading that unfolds gently and firmly, never rushed, never slack (♦Sony 42430, or 89323, 2CD). Who else but **Bernstein** could give us the most rollicking, bronco-bustin' dance-till-you-drop version ever recorded? Everything is as perfect as it can get in this life, and the bright sound fuels the high spirits (♦Sony 63082 or 36727). **Louis Lane** had two tries at *Rodeo*. The first in Cleveland is excellent but incomplete (Sony); the second (Atlanta) is superior, vigorous, and incisive in a well-rounded, sonically impressive reading, not bashful, and flushed with energy (♦Telarc 80078). **Dorati** is often underestimated in American music; his version is spirited and saturated with native feeling, one of the best available (♦London 48261).

Schwarz, usually right in the pack where American music is concerned, can't muster the vigor needed here (Delos). **Slatkin** turns in one of his most poorly gauged performances, lifeless and lackluster (EMI). **Gunzenhauser** can't get his orchestra to think American, though I like to see European orchestras take a crack at this music (Naxos). **Boughton** lacks the understanding that would probably be drowned out in excessive reverb even if he had it (Nimbus). **Johanos** saves the day in the budget department with a fine reading played with zest and sparkle (♦Vox 5035). **Tilson Thomas** has a fine feeling for this piece, as barn dance driven and two-step saturated as any on the market. But he has his orchestra let out a most disconcerting verbal "whoopie" during the final "Hoedown," and this spoils the movement, at least for repeated listening (RCA).

El Salon Mexico. After a visit to the "Salon Mexico" dance hall in 1932, Copland decided, in what was to be the first of his "popular" style works, to try to capture the authentic spirit of Mexican music—rugged, songful, and not a little violent. It has remained one of his most played pieces. **Fiedler** gives us a spunky, rollicking performance that ranks with the best—rhythms are incisive and motile—but it's mono, so take that into consideration (♦RCA 6806). **Bernstein** does us well twice. The wild, roller-coaster rhythms were made for him, and he performs as if making it up himself, in a great recording (♦Sony 60571). While not as brash and full of excitement, his second reading is as worthy as his first standard-setting effort. The sound is much better, and he takes a more lingering, seductive view of the score without sacrificing emotional content (♦DG 31672). Skip his early mono effort—good, but without the great sound (Sony).

Though broad, spacious, and well recorded, **Copland** lacks pizzazz, and the brass are too held back (Sony). **Dorati** is fine and has thrilling moments (London), but he can't compete with Bernstein, and neither

can **Marriner**'s cleanly recorded effort (Capriccio). **Zinman** and Baltimore are flaccid in a soft reading with little punch (Argo). Bernstein owns this one.

Symphonic Ode. Written between 1927 and 1929 for the Boston Symphony's 50th anniversary, Copland intended to make some sort of "grand statement" with this not-very-well-named work. **Schwarz** and his West Coast orchestra nicely handle its thrashing chordal palpitations (♦Delos 3154), and **Tilson Thomas,** in his fine disc of "modernist" Copland, offers the best version on records (♦RCA 68541). Despite a ragged beginning, **Copland**'s Londoners settle down to an effortful yet effective reading (Sony). Tilson Thomas is really the best, but if you happen to pick this up in the first volume of Sony's Copland Collection, don't go out of your way to acquire the others.

Variations for Orchestra. This is an orchestrated version of Copland's 1937 acerbic and glass-shattering *Variations for Piano*. I have always preferred the mystery and jarring brutality of the piano version, feeling that the orchestra softens the blows and adds too much color to what should be a cold, steely, monolithic composition. The St. Louis Symphony can't help adding some color, so talented are its players, but the results are satisfying, and **Slatkin** does his part, not pulling too many punches (♦RCA 68292). **Tilson Thomas** takes a cue from Bernstein's comments about this piece and presents a startling, tightly woven reading that never flags or sags, ending with a smashing finale (♦RCA 68541). Though **Copland** does a good job delineating the variations, the London Symphony isn't comfortable in this work, especially in the exposed sections, and the composer lacks the temperament to force cohesion upon them (Sony).

CONCERTOS

Clarinet, Strings, Harp, and Piano. This work has moments of Debussyian languidness and Stravinskian rhythmical awkwardness. Composed for jazz clarinetist Benny Goodman, no collection would be complete without his recording. Though Stoltzman is mandatory if there's only room for a single serving on your plate, **Goodman** has much to offer—the personages, the sound, and the occasion (♦Sony 42227 or 46559). Available only as an import—but well worth the effort if you can find it—is **Sabine Meyer**'s wonderful collection (♦EMI 56652B).

Paul Meyer turns in a sensational reading—with some slightly undercooked conducting by Zinman—on another hard to get recording (Denon). **Stoltzman** recorded this twice. Laurence Leighton Smith leads the lesser of the two performances in an album that's still highly digestible—indeed, an only meal if necessary (♦RCA 61360). But the riveting, finest all-around recording belongs to Tilson Thomas. Stoltzman seems doubly inspired, with technical and infallible interpretive powers all in high gear (♦RCA 61790).

George MacDonald does nice work while showing signs of strain in some passages, but still managing to tap into Copland's pastoral side (ASV). In an album of concertos dedicated to Goodman, **Martin Fröst** shines forth resplendently (♦BIS 893). For a more plaintive viewpoint, try **Janet Hilton**'s cool, distant version with Bamert (♦Chandos 8618). There are few really bad recordings of this work, but **Eduard Brunner**'s pinched, slow-waltz tempo rendering is among them (Koch). Finally, **Stanley Drucker** is right at home in Copland's jazzy parade of eclectic musical styles. Bernstein is not to be outdone here, of course; Drucker may not provide the height of sensuality, but his controlled, restrained reading has some attractions (DG).

Piano Concerto. This was Copland's last experiment in symphonic jazz (1926). Suggested by Koussevitzky, the premiere was a shocker to the staid Boston audiences, and critics were no quicker to catch on. It has remained on the fringe of the repertory, often praised more than played. That's a shame, for the work is broad, bold, and extremely accessible.

There are only a handful of recordings, and among them you certainly don't want to miss **Ohlsson**'s hair-raising reading with Tilson Thomas, a big man with a big heart pouring every bit of energy he has into a fabulous performance (♦RCA 68541). Mester's recording is a lively, wide-eyed tribute to the astonishing versatility and musicianship of **Earl Wild,** an exuberant trip on skis down the musical Alps (♦Vanguard 4029). **Lorin Hollander** and Schwarz turn in a very good reading, steady and in complete control, but this version doesn't sail the way some of the others do (Delos). **Copland** gives a surprisingly adroit, seat-of-your-pants performance, enhanced all the way by Bernstein's mastery of the score's rhythmical complexities (♦Sony 60177). Finally, **Gillian Lin**'s performance from the late '70s just can't muster enough energy and drive to compete with the likes of Ohlsson (Chandos).

CHAMBER MUSIC

Copland won't be remembered as a chamber composer. His thoughts, like those of Mahler, were large in scale and broadly expansive, and it was usually the orchestra that provided the more intimate moments through his use of chamber-like scoring. But two pieces are worth mention. His Piano Quartet (1950) is performed by the **Boston Symphony Chamber Players** in a recording that's probably as good as it gets (♦Nonesuch 79168). The more popular Sextet for Clarinet, Piano, and String Quartet—a twin of the Short Symphony—is given a golden reading by the same forces, making this a disc it would be a crime not to have. For a more modern take, check out the **Atlanta Chamber Players** in fine sound on a disc devoted to 20th-century music (♦ACA 20038), or the **Berlin Philharmonic Academy** (♦Thorofon 2012).

Copland's Violin Sonata is his one significant work for that instrument. We're fortunate to have several fine renditions, all offering superb playing. **Anne Akiko Meyers** and André Schub offer an excellent recording in "The American Album," with smooth sound and great playing (♦RCA 68114). **Shaham,** with Previn, turns in an equally fine reading in "American Scenes." And don't forget the great **Stern,** weighing in with his early championship of this piece in his "A Life in Music" series (Sony 64533).

An excellent recording by clarinetist Michael Collins with pianist Martin Roscoe and the **Vanbrugh Quartet** gives us some early, pre-cowboy Copland. These readings of the Sextet, Piano Quartet, and *Vitebsk* are sonic and interpretative marvels, the best of the more modern recordings (♦ASV 1081). But in the new Copland centenary set from Sony, we're treated once again to the delicious readings of the Sextet (with Harold Wright), Piano Quartet (with the Julliard Quartet and Copland at the piano), *Vitebsk* (with the same forces), and the *Duo for Flute and Piano* (with Copland and Elaine Schaffer). These are one-of-a-kind recordings that are full of excitement and effervescent joy (♦Sony 89326). The stunning Nonet is in another album of previously released Copland-led orchestral works, a nice way to collect a lot of fine music (♦Sony 89323, 2CD).

PIANO MUSIC

Copland tinkered with piano music all his life, and like Bernstein, never really produced a significant body of work for the instrument, though some of his most intimate moments are to be found here. Three pieces form the core of his pianistic explorations, all rather difficult works.

Fantasy still has critics wondering what it's all about. **Charles Fierro** seems to have discovered the meaning in his recording (♦Delos 1013).

But if you're looking for a one-stop oasis for all of Copland's piano music—including such delights as *The Cat and the Mouse* and *Down a Country Lane*—look no further than **Leo Smit,** whose set is bound to give lots of satisfaction, though better individual readings may be found elsewhere. This is a great buy (♦Sony 66345, 2CD).

Sonata is the middle pillar of Copland's piano trilogy, a piece that seems tough-going at first but more than repays repeated hearings, with its delightful combination of American snippets of melody and bold, startling harmonies. Both **Nina Tichman** (♦Wergo 6211) and **Eric Parkin** (♦Silva 1009) sparkle in this music, but nobody can top **Easley Blackwood** for superb music making (♦Cedille 5, with Ives's *Concord Sonata*).

Variations, an early composition, is like a modernist's credo; Bernstein claimed he used to empty rooms with the piece in his youth. Some still have that reaction today, but the work is a marvel of terse, concentrated expression, required study for any composition student. There are many fine recordings, none better than that by **William Masselos** (originally coupled with the Piano Fantasy on the old Odyssey label), if Sony ever sees fit to reissue it.

Meanwhile, we can make do with some excellent alternatives. **Kalish,** on the chamber disc mentioned earlier, gives a performance that only enhances the release's already great worth (♦Nonesuch 79168). **Fierro** tries to duplicate the Masselos effort quite successfully in a recording that includes *Fantasy* (♦Delos 1013). **Hough** is his usual virtuosic self in "New York Variations," an album that has garnered praise everywhere. His Copland is excellent, though I'm unsure about the composers that make up the remainder of the disc (Hyperion). **Joanna MacGregor** also has a fine feel for this music, but the remainder of her album is neither serious in intent nor consistent in compositional integrity (Collins). **Nina Tichman** is excellent—no finer reading can be found (♦Wergo 6211)—and **Parkin** continues his mastery of Americana in an all-Copland album (♦Silva 1009).

Two-piano transcriptions. If you want a real change of pace, try the album of two-piano transcriptions by pianists **Marcelo Bratkef** and **Marcela Roggeri.** The swagger and great fun they bring to pieces like *Billy the Kid, Danzon Cubano, Rodeo,* and *El Salon Mexico* (among others) will have you dancing the hoedown yourself. Colorful, enlightening playing in terrific sound (♦Etcetera 1223).

CHORAL MUSIC

Copland wrote very few choral works, with or without orchestra. One of the most popular is *In the Beginning,* a 16-minute tour de force based on the creation story. **Bernstein**'s version, in mono and very compact sound, may have had much to recommend it at one point, but no longer (Sony). **Copland**'s version with the New England Conservatory Chorus has been reissued, along with the equally enchanting *Lark,* and you need look no further for definitive readings (♦Sony 89329, 2CD). **Matthew Best** outdoes everyone else in his gorgeous version with the Corydon Singers (♦Hyperion 66219). **Cleobury** also has the measure of the work, though he's slightly cooler than Best (EMI). **William Payne** gives a remarkable reading, with spirit and fervor, in an all-American choral collection called "An American Collage" (♦Albany 98).

OPERAS

The Tender Land. Copland wrote one full-length opera, originally for NBC Television (which rejected it), then for the New York City Opera; and perhaps the reason it hasn't become a repertory staple is that it sounds like one of his ballets set to words. It doesn't have the kind of dramatic flair, the tense moments or life-threatening situations that contemporary audiences expect. It was for these very reasons that Copland decided to write the piece, wanting something that could be sung by the youth of America without too many obstacles. It's full of pure, Copland-esque warmth of heart and a Midwestern pragmatism and stoicism borne on the wings of fatal acceptance that offers many moments of poignancy. **Philp Brunelle**'s cast is all anyone could ask for, and while one may wish for more colorful vocal characterizations, it's hard to imagine a more effective rendition (♦Virgin 59207).

The Second Hurricane. Copland's first attempt at opera came in this drama full of moralistic lessons about the brotherhood of man. The work is tuneful and entertaining, and would be far more suitable for high school performance than another rehash of an ancient Broadway musical. **Bernstein**'s is the only performance, and the only one needed. He does the narration himself, and the sound, though dated and stereophonically "split" in the inimitable '50s Columbia manner, is more than serviceable (♦Sony 60560).

SONGS

Copland stayed away from this form for most of his career, but what he did leave us are absolute gems. *Twelve Poems of Emily Dickinson* is one of the staples of the repertory. Copland manages such a perfect wedding of music and text that any prospective interpreter has to take extra care to ensure that neither suavity of tone nor impeccable declamation gets in the way of the whole. **Sylvan**'s mannered, light voice would seem appropriate for this music, and really does fit it well, but his emotional coolness seems to go beyond the neutrality these poems sometimes call for. But the sound is great, and he gets inside the music (♦Nonesuch 79259). **De Gaetani** had seen better days by the time her 81st birthday tribute to Copland was recorded, and the songs lack vocal prowess (Bridge).

Alexander has made a specialty of American songs, and her efforts aren't without profit; her Copland album is rewarding, with the singer in fine voice (♦Etcetera 1100). **Bonney** recorded these songs with Previn in a successful album; her sugary, softening voice provides a valid perspective, if not the last word in interpretation. But she certainly tops the existing field (♦London 455511). The last word must go to the as-yet-unreleased LP rendition by the ever-so-charming **Adele Addison,** with the composer at the piano. Hers may not be the most beautiful voice, but her inflections and interpretive enthusiasm are better than anything committed to disc so far. Sony should provide a CD posthaste.

Copland also scored eight of these songs for orchestra in arrangements that are, while effective, not as becoming as the originals. Nonetheless, they enjoy greater popularity than the piano version because of their attractiveness in a variety of concert settings. **Upshaw** gives a definitive rendition in a disc that includes a humorous, breezily relaxed version by Hampson of *Old American Songs* (♦Teldec 77310). Tilson Thomas uses the **Mormon Tabernacle Choir** for these songs in a disc that also gives us two rarities, *Canticle of Freedom* and *Four Motets,* a very worthwhile recording (♦Sony 42140). RITTER

Arcangelo Corelli (1653–1713)

Corelli was the greatest Italian violinist of the Baroque. It was primarily through his fiery performances and highly polished compositions that the warm, vocal, Italian style of violin playing triumphed over the more ostentatiously virtuosic, impressionistic German style exemplified by Biber. (Unless otherwise indicated, all recordings discussed are by period instrument musicians.)

ORCHESTRAL MUSIC

Concerti Grossi **Op. 6.** Corelli brought the concerto grosso, a trio sonata ensemble with orchestra, to its highest level of development. These works, published the year after his death, reflect some 30 years of experimentation in the form. As in the Trio Sonatas, church and chamber forms are used, with the church style occurring in the first eight concertos and the chamber form in the last four.

McGegan and the Philharmonia Baroque Orchestra play the concertos in an intimate, unpretentious manner (Harmonia Mundi 907014/15, 2CD). The English Concert under **Pinnock** couldn't be more different (♦DG 459451 or 423626, 2CD). Though not large in number, their sound is truly orchestral, and they evoke real grandeur. (Corelli was known to have led orchestras with as many as 80 musicians.) Their tempos and dynamic contrasts are more abrupt and sound just right, in good, vivid sound. **Biondi**'s Europa Galante falls between McGegan and Pinnock (Opus 111 30147, 30155). They're more noble and restrained, and the sound is more chamberlike and less imposing than Pinnock's; *pp* markings are especially delicate. There is a greater variety of articulation, and the soloists use a lovely, Italianate vibrato.

Cantilena is a modern instrument ensemble directed by Adrian Shepherd (Chandos 8336/8, 3CD). They create a large sonority, partly by allowing vibrato in the orchestra as well as by the soloists, and articulate well, without the overly legato style that mars so many modern instrument performances of Baroque music; it's a fine account for those allergic to period sound. **I Musici,** another modern instrument group, plays the music as if it were an exercise in tone production (Philips). Certainly no string ensemble ever produced a more refined sound, but their perfectly sustained, even tone robs the music of its vitality and rhythmic spring, especially in the slow movements, and tempos are often so slow that the phrases lose all shape. Their homogenized style represented the antithesis of Baroque performance practice and style and served as a sort of negative inspiration for those who took up period instruments in the '60s and '70s. Then again, if you hate period style, this may appeal to you.

CHAMBER MUSIC

Church Trio Sonatas **Op. 1;** *Chamber Trio Sonatas* **Op. 2.** The Church Sonatas are composed in the usual slow-fast-slow-fast order of movements, while the Chamber Sonatas are dance suites all in the same key. These are among Corelli's earliest compositions; Op. 1 was published in 1681, and Op. 2 followed in 1685. The **Purcell Quartet** plays these works with a mellifluous tone and good tempo contrasts (Chandos 0515 and 0516).

Violin Sonatas **Op. 5.** had a great impact on violin playing in Europe. With his nobly melodic style, Corelli trumped the German violinists and their tendency to the bizarre and spurred the French to realize that the violin was useful for more than just dance bands. **Chiara Banchini** has a sweetly singing style, but she fails to make enough contrasts of tempo and dynamics, so the music is short on drama (Harmonia Mundi). **Elizabeth Wallfisch** is better recorded and uses a bit more contrast in tempos, but the music still comes off as a bit dull (Hyperion). **Sigiswald Kuijken** is the most technically accomplished player, with very fluently executed ornaments, and he makes plenty of abrupt contrasts of tempo and dynamics. Sonatas 1, 3, 6, 11, and 12 really come alive in his hands (Accent 48433). There was a delightful LP set by **Eduard Melkus,** who was attuned to the sweetness and drama of the music and pioneered the playing of 18th-century ornamented versions; his enjoyment is infectious (DG 2533132/33). MAGIL

John Corigliano (b. 1938)

Corigliano's music occupies a substantial place in what might be called the "New Consonance" prevalent in the last quarter of the 20th century.

Often lyrical and engaging at first hearing, it assimilates traditional forms and an eclectic musical vocabulary with an individualistic style. About 30 of his works have been recorded, many by leading conductors, soloists, and ensembles.

I suspect that in the '90s no symphony by a contemporary American composer was performed more often than Corigliano's Symphony 1 (1989), entitled "Of Rage and Remembrance" in honor of AIDS victims in general and three musician friends in particular. Both recordings, **Barenboim**'s with the Chicago Symphony (♦Erato 45601) and **Slatkin**'s with the National Symphony (RCA), are excellent. The CSO's sound is more lustrous, displaying a burnished timbre in full orchestra as well as chamber combinations. Corigliano's masterful orchestration is evident throughout, as is Barenboim's obvious understanding of the piece. Slatkin's recording offers less sonic quality and overall depth than this introspective work requires. Its musical interest is less in its thematic or formal content, so sound becomes an unusually important component of aesthetic satisfaction.

Another traditional multimovement genre continues to interest composers of the "New Consonance." Corigliano's concertos for piano (1968), oboe (1975), and clarinet (1977) are represented in recordings by major soloists and orchestras. He was closely associated with New York Philharmonic members, and the Clarinet Concerto was composed with **Stanley Drucker**'s extraordinary musicianship in mind. His recording with the New York Philharmonic under Mehta (♦New World 309) is preferable to **Stoltzman**'s with the London Symphony led by Lawrence Leighton Smith. Although Stoltzman is primarily a soloist, the piece's particular style of virtuosity seems better suited to Drucker's interpretation because it calls most of one's attention to the music, whereas Stoltzman primarily calls attention to the performer. Available now on CD, I prefer Drucker's original LP for its warmth of tone, diminished in the digital format.

I think the Oboe Concerto is the best of the three, but it's available only in **Bert Lucarelli**'s reading with the American Symphony Orchestra (♦RCA 60395). The piece begs for another recording, but the music is strong enough for listeners to enjoy his gorgeous tone, somewhat attenuated by less than adequate accompaniment led by Kazuyoshi Akiyama. I also believe the Piano Concerto deserves another recording, but until it gets one, **Barry Douglas** with Slatkin and the St. Louis Symphony (♦RCA 68100) is superior to **Alain Léfevre** with the Pacific Symphony under Carl St. Clair. Douglas's introspective interpretation is apt, and Slatkin's accompaniment is at least serviceable.

Of the several other works for soloist and orchestra, I recommend **Galway** for *Voyage for Flute and Orchestra* (1983). His virtuosity has often been a bit careless, but he plays the instrument so well that his eccentricities can be overlooked in favor of a true musical personality. The guitar has enjoyed something of a renaissance in the era of "New Consonance," and **Sharon Isben**'s performance of *Troubadours* (a set of variations) shows the guitar's modern side well in an engaging, idiomatic piece.

A superb recording of Corigliano's String Quartet (1995) is available from the **Cleveland Quartet,** marvelously played and adequately recorded (♦Telarc 80415). For some reason, chamber ensembles often sound more natural on CD than do orchestras, and the timbre of this recording is extraordinarily good.   ZIEROLF

François Couperin *(1668–1733)*

Ask any present-day music-lover to name a famous French composer of the Baroque era, and chances are he will say Rameau, with Marais coming in a distant second. But during the opening decades of the 18th century, the name on most people's lips would have been François Couperin *Le Grand* ("The Great"). The nickname was bestowed on Couperin during his lifetime and reflects the high regard in which he was held by his colleagues and contemporaries (he seems to have been a genuinely warm, likeable human being). Bach corresponded with him over a period of many years, and respected his music to such an extent that he made manuscript copies of several works for himself and his wife Anna Magdalena as well as composing an "Aria after Couperin" (BWV 587).

Couperin's music, as with much music of the French Baroque, is an acquired taste for many listeners. It's based neither on strong themes, as in Telemann or Bach, nor coloristic or virtuosic effects, as in Vivaldi or Tartini. Rather, in each isolated movement or section, Couperin seeks to delineate a particular *affect,* a feeling or mood expressed in music. Its structure is mostly melody with accompaniment, without the kind of learned devices (fugue, imitative counterpoint) that Bach employed. Special effects are few and far between; as Couperin said, "I would rather be touched by music than surprised." The appeal of his music is immediate and direct, but the listener will gain even greater pleasure and understanding if he knows the stylistic and cultural background behind it, for example the stylized dance movements (allemande, courante, sarabande, gigue) that make up much of Couperin's work.

Any investigation must begin with Couperin's vast quantity of harpsichord music. As chief harpsichordist to Louis XIV and teacher of the royal children, he was granted a royal privilege to publish his keyboard pieces and made good use of it. His harpsichord works are preserved in 26 *Ordres* (suites), for the most part consisting of pieces bearing amusing and sometimes baffling titles, such as *Les petites crémières de Bagnolet, Le Rossignol en amour, Le Dodo, ou L'amour au berceau,* or *Les baricades mistérieuses.* Fortunately, this music has been well served in complete editions and shorter collections.

The first complete set was **Kenneth Gilbert**'s in the late '70s. As undisputed master of this repertoire and teacher to many of the world's greatest harpsichordists, his recording commands respect (Harmonia Mundi 190351, 54, 57, 59, 10CD). Unfortunately, his choice of instrument is disappointing, and the sound is nothing special; even considering the budget price, I can't work up much enthusiasm for it. I *can* get excited, however, about **Christophe Rousset**'s set (Harmonia Mundi 2901442/52, 12CD). Magnificently played and recorded on several beautifully restored antique instruments, this is a milestone in the history of recorded sound, and anyone remotely interested in the harpsichord should check it out. There is another complete set in the works, by **Lawrence Cummings.** Vol. 1 has appeared, and while the playing isn't as fiery and spirited as Rousset's, the overall first impression is good, and the budget price should encourage wider exposure for this charming music (Naxos 8550961).

Throughout his life, Couperin devoted himself to the reconciliation of French and Italian tastes, principally through his chamber music. France was heavily influenced by Italian music in the waning years of the 17th century (chiefly Corelli), and a debate raged whether French music should remain "pure" or be allowed to absorb the Italianate tendencies of ostentatious display and overt virtuosity. Couperin saw no conflict; instead he managed to forge a series of magnificent sonatas that brilliantly synthesize elements of the French dance tradition (Lully) with elements of the Italian trio sonata (Corelli). Published in 1724 together with four sonatas from 1722, Couperin called it *Nouveaux concerts, ou les goûts réunis* ("Newly invented Concert Pieces, or the Tastes

Reunited"), and it's undoubtedly his masterwork. What a pity, then, that the digital age has not yet produced a complete recording!

You can hear many of the *Nouveaux concerts* by acquiring several different CDs, but that's small compensation. For example, the **Kuijkens** have recorded 8 and 9 in an excellent disc that includes the two *Pièces de violes avec la bass chifrée* (Accent 9288), or you can sample 10 and 12 in another excellent CD from the British ensemble **Charivari Agréable** that includes the viol pieces along with some harpsichord selections and music of Caix d'Hervelois and Antoine Forqueray (ASV 159). The first four sonatas, the *Concerts Royeaux,* can be heard in a magnificent reissue from the '70s by the **Kuijkens** and their colleagues (Sony/Seon 60370). What a shame that Sony couldn't fit its *Nouveaux concerts* 10, 12 and 15 on the same disc.

In 1726 Couperin tackled the question of national "taste" in music one last time, and the result was his other famous collection, *Les Nations.* The four sonatas delineate regional "types" ("La Françoise," "L'Espagnole," "L'Impériale," and "La Piédmontaise") in Corelli's trio sonata format and are among his most noble music. No other recording has come close to the remarkable achievement of Hespèrion XX (a star-studded cast with instrumentalists from all over Europe, directed by **Jordi Savall**), and we're fortunate that it has been reissued (Astrée 7700, 2CD).

Aside from the extended collections, Couperin wrote several isolated sonatas and ensemble pieces that the serious collector will want to own. Chief among these is *L'Apothéose de Lully,* a quasi-theatrical work with recitations that recounts Lully's ascent to Parnassus, where, at the conclusion, he is heard playing duets with Corelli. This fascinating work can be enjoyed in another excellent reissue from the '70s that features the **Kuijkens** among others (Sony/Seon 62941). The disc also includes three famous sonatas (one a quartet, the other two trios): *La Sultane, La Superbe,* and *La Steinquerque.* Closer to home and our own time is an excellent chamber music collection (two sonatas from *Les Nations* plus the *Treizième Concert* from *Concerts Royeaux*) that features several prominent West Coast musicians in a luminous recording (Music & Arts 825). Another collection to consider features Jay Bernfeld and Capriccio Stravagante under **Skip Sempé** (Deutsche Harmonia Mundi 77315).

Couperin wrote no operas, but there is a small but significant amount of solo vocal music that many consider his finest expressive achievement. The three *Leçons de Ténèbres* (there were originally nine) were written in the context of a tradition that the opera be silent during Lent. Singers were thus thrown out of work, so French composers began writing highly expressive solo motets for performance during Holy Week that exploited the considerable talent at their disposal. Couperin's *Leçons* are less operatic, more intimate and tender, requiring a special singer with the utmost deftness. The CD led by **Christophe Rousset,** with Les Talens Lyriques and star sopranos Véronique Gens and Sandrine Piau, comes very close to ideal (Decca 466776). However, if you come across Ensemble Lyra under **Anne Chapelin-Dubar,** snatch it up (Koch-Schwann 1293, NA). Here the two sopranos (Isabelle Eschenbrenner and Lena Hauser) are even lighter and more idiomatic, and the recording is very spacious and atmospheric.

There is also a tiny bit of organ music, consisting of two Masses, one *pour les paroisses* (for the parishes) and the other *pour les convents* (for the convents). Again, Couperin infused an old tradition with new life by supplying organ interludes (bearing a striking resemblance to his harpsichord pieces) to the plainsong of the Mass. The only available recording that includes the necessary plainchant is *Messe pour les convents,* idiomatically performed by the young French organist **Olivier Vernet** (Ligia 104041).

BRODERSEN

Henry Cowell *(1897–1965)*

I can think of no American composer so well known whose music is so seldom performed. Usually labeled an experimentalist along with Crawford and Varèse, Cowell explored new sounds on acoustic instruments and, occasionally, primitive electronic devices, without a priori restriction. Most experimental music paves the way for subsequent composers without entering the repertoire itself, and that is to date largely the fate of Cowell's work; however, the ever-increasing interest in American music may result in a renaissance for his iconoclastic compositions. Given the recent attention to consonance, it's no surprise the "American" works for which he is most often cited have been added to the catalogs, despite their inferiority to the Barber-Copland-Hanson-Harris repertoire. Fortunately, a few discs of his experimental music are well performed and recorded.

From the mid-'20s to the mid-'30s, Cowell was active as pianist and composer in the United States and Europe, and he wrote and edited articles and books on modern music, notably *New Musical Resources* (1930). He was viewed favorably by such disparate composers as Schoenberg, Webern, and Ives. (He coauthored with his wife the first biography of Ives, published in 1955.) His music includes many of Ives's innovations—indeterminacy, improvisation, tone clusters and other unique dissonances, rudimentary prepared pianos, and extreme rhythmic complexity and oddities. Like Ives and Gershwin, he embraced the spirit and vocabulary of vernacular music, and eventually looked to a variety of exotic repertoires to further extend "found material" for compositional use.

Anthony de Mare offers 10 short pieces for piano composed before 1920; the two best known, *Aeolian Harp* and *The Banshee,* require strumming and scraping the strings (CRI 837). Short works by Ives and Harrison are included, all played and recorded well. For comparison, I recommend "The Bad Boys," with Steffen Schliermacher playing these two pieces and 12 more by Cowell, three by Ornstein, and, most notably, Antheil's three sonatas (Hat Hut 6144). Schliermacher is one of the best exponents of modern iconoclastic piano music, and this disc is highly recommended for its excellent performances and sound. Together, de Mare and Schliermacher offer a well-rounded sample of the music for which Cowell is most often cited.

The piano also figures marginally in Cowell's *Trio in Nine Short Movements.* The traditional piano trio instrumentation works nicely for his last composition, and the **Mirecourt Trio** offers it and trios by Persichetti and Paul Reale in good performances of less than the best music from these composers (Music and Arts 686). Cowell's trio receives an equally good reading by **Trio Phoenix** in an all-Cowell disc that includes music for violin, cello, and piano, plus percussion for one piece, in various combinations (Koch 7205). Composed over a 40-year span, the repertoire ranges from the "Early American" *Hymn and Fuguing Tune No. 9* to atonal counterpoint in *Four Combinations for Three Instruments* to the simply bizarre *Set of Five.* It's a very interesting collection, well played and recorded. Some of these works have been recorded by others, but this one is the best in quality and stylistic diversity, performances, and recorded sound.

The **Mirecourt Trio** has added more chamber music to Cowell's recorded repertoire in the third of a series titled "Trio America," including some of Cowell's less-eccentric music for strings and piano along with piano trios by Otto Luening, Paul Chihara, and Paul Creston (Music and Arts 934). Listeners seeking Cowell's more adventuresome efforts will pass over this disc; those who favor his more moderate side or are curious about it will appreciate the fine performances and good sound. Another relatively conservative work has been issued in the "Modern Masters" series (Harmonia Mundi 906011). **David Ames** conducts the City of London Sinfonietta in Cowell's *Hymn for Strings* and pleasant but forgettable works by Creston, Dello Joio, Paul Turok, and David Ward-Steinman. The Sinfonietta's typically English string sound is ideal for this music.

A full disc of orchestral music is performed well by the Manhattan Chamber Orchestra led by **Richard Auldon Clark** (Koch 7220). Most of it is pure Americana—*Hymn for String Orchestra, American Melting Pot,* Air, *Old American Country Set,* Adagio—with *Persian Set* attesting to Cowell's interest in Asian and Middle Eastern material. Again, for the Americana pieces I find other's music more engaging, but this selection will be attractive to those not familiar with his post-'30s works and interested in Cowell as an composer or, more generally, in the most easily accepted music from the United States in this period.

Another disc adds still more Americana to the recorded repertoire—*Hymn and Fuguing Tune No. 10, Fiddler's Jig,* Air and Scherzo, and Concerto Grosso, with MacDowell's *To a Wild Rose* and Persichetti's *The Hollow Men* (Koch 7282). **Clark** appears again with the Manhattan ensemble, all performed and recorded very well. From the mid-'40s to the mid-'60s, Cowell composed 18 pieces titled *Hymn and Fuguing Tune* for a variety of ensembles. Some are included on discs mentioned above, but for a more extensive exposure to this series, Nos. 2, 5, and 8 for string orchestra are performed well by the Northwest Chamber Orchestra led by **Alun Francis,** with other music by Cowell for strings (CPO 999222).

As conductors and performers search for new repertoire, Cowell's music might see more publication, performance, and recording. I doubt that anyone has been through all of the hundreds of works he wrote, but if you were to take on such a project, it's likely that at least a few worthwhile pieces would be discovered. I, for one, would be curious. He probably wrote too much at the expense of concentration on fewer pieces of higher quality, but that's what an experimental composer often does. He had too much talent and imagination for his work to go to waste.

ZIEROLF

Ruth Crawford (Seeger) *(1901–1953)*

Some composers have brief spurts of intense creativity that produce substantial work, with relatively little activity in other periods. For Crawford, this productive period was the few years surrounding 1930. Her most fruitful era began in 1929 when she moved to New York City to study with folk musician and ethnomusicologist Charles Seeger, whom she married in 1932. Due in large part to his unfortunate attitude toward women composers, she subsequently devoted her talents and energies to folk music projects. The Woodwind Quintet (1952) is her only substantial composition after her marriage, and it's largely drawn from her earlier works.

Around 1930 Crawford composed several pieces usually labeled experimental; thus she's commonly linked with Cowell and Varèse as exploring new sonic palettes and ways of composing neither European–derived nor originated from the then-prevailing American styles of Gershwin and Copland. Three discs provide a representative sample of her music. The two pieces most commonly performed and rightly cited as exemplary are the String Quartet and *Study in Mixed Accents* for solo piano. Unfortunately, they aren't together on any of these three discs, but an advantage is that each disc is a good one.

Continuum enjoys a reputation as one of the finest chamber ensembles performing 20th-century music, and their recording is devoted entirely to Crawford (MHS 513493M). It presents *Suite for Five Winds and Piano* (i.e., the Woodwind Quintet), Violin Sonata, the first and last of nine Preludes for Piano, three songs to Carl Sandburg poetry, *Diaphonic Suites* 1 (for unaccompanied flute in this recording) and 2, two *Ricercari,* and *Study in Mixed Accents.* The performances are uniformly excellent.

A recent release of some of the same music by the **Pellegrini Quartet** and Ensemble Aventure is equally good and has a somewhat more ingratiating sound (CPO 999670). This disc offers no piano music, but does include the String Quartet as the featured work, as well as the Woodwind Quintet, all four *Diaphonic Suites* (2 played on oboe, a better choice of instrument for this piece), the second Suite for Piano and Strings, and Suite for Winds and Piano. The performances are comparable to Continuum's in excellence, and the recording quality is superior. The avid listener should purchase both, as they allow comparisons, and each provides one of the two major works.

An older recording rounds out the trio of samples of Crawford's music (CRI 658). It's actually a re-release of sorts, a compilation of four previous recordings, so there was no common ensemble. Perhaps this is why the performances are not as uniformly good, nor is the quality of recording, though it's more than merely acceptable given the engineering challenges. In comparison to the MHS and CPO discs, I prefer this one for **Ida Kavafian**'s rendition of the Violin Sonata and Patricia Berlin's lovely mezzo for *Three Songs.* The disc includes all nine Preludes and *Study in Mixed Accents* performed by Joseph Bloch. All three discs are recommended for quality of performance and recording, and because they exhibit well some of the best experimental American music of their time.

ZIEROLF

Paul Creston *(1906–1985)*

Creston was a major figure among mid-20th-century U.S. composers. Like most gifted composers—in Creston's case, extremely gifted, since he was entirely self-taught—he had his own identifiable style. In his case, complex rhythms with shifting meters are the cornerstone, along with a rich chromaticism and long, flowery melodies. His music is very colorful, often dance-like and jazzy without being jazz, and has the feel of the "big city" with its energy and brashness. He was a fine orchestrator who used a big orchestra to the fullest, but he was equally at home in quasi-baroque forms. He's clever without being too intellectual or cute. He wrote music to be heard and enjoyed, and for all its complexity, his pieces are certainly listenable. They may lack something in profundity and may not probe as deeply as some, but Creston was an American composer well worth exploring.

SYMPHONIES

No. 2 is Creston's paean to song and dance. It's his most popular symphony, big and bold, like all his music, but more direct; it's very lyrical, lively, and appealing. **Järvi** takes a big, lyrical approach abetted by a Detroit Symphony whose splendor is heard from the opening string lines (♦Chandos 9390, with Ives's Symphony 2). **David Amos**'s Cracow orchestra is overmatched, and he provides little effective direction (Koch, with *Corinthians XIII,* NA). **Howard Mitchell**'s mono recording is well-played, tighter and more directed than Järvi's. The sound is good and warm for its age, but it can't compete with Chandos (Westminster LP, with 3).

No. 3 ("Three Mysteries") is a depiction of the life of Christ—Nativity, Crucifixion, Resurrection—but the treatment isn't religious: I is a quirky, happy march; II is darkly atmospheric with an urban feeling; III turns into a joyful, skittery allegro. **Schwarz** and the Seattle Symphony do fine work, coupled with Partita for Flute, Violin, and Strings, *Out of the Cradle,* and *Invocation and Dance;* the latter two are colorful works with the last especially impressive (♦Delos 3114). **Mitchell**'s decent mono recording is superseded.

No. 5 is an outgoing, energetic, fluent work, with long, florid string melodies played against rhythmic, incisive brass and percussion. **Schwarz** again gives an excellent performance (♦Delos 3127, with *Choreografic Suite* and *Toccata*).

OTHER ORCHESTRAL MUSIC

Chant 1942; Suite for String Orchestra. Chant is a response to the events of 1942 in Europe. The music is contemplative, dramatic, uplifting, and tragic. The Suite is another of Creston's appealing pieces, with big string sonorities and striking rhythms. **Amos** leads colorful performances with members of the Israel Philharmonic (♦Crystal 508, with works by other U.S. composers).

Fantasy for Trombone and Orchestra. This is one of the more difficult and beautiful works in the trombone repertory, full of Creston's lyricism, tricky rhythms, and uptown, urban jazzy elements. **Christian Lindberg** plays the orchestral version with James DePreist (♦BIS 628, with other trombone pieces). I have always found Lindberg's tone a bit boxy (many don't agree), but he's stylish, free, and expressive, and he brings this colorful, urbane piece to life. **John Kitzman,** principal trombonist of the Dallas Symphony, gives a good, dry performance—more the orchestral player than the soloist—of an arrangement for trombone and piano. He has a more open sound than Lindberg, but I prefer both Lindberg's greater expressivity and the orchestral version (Crystal 386, also with other trombone pieces).

Gregorian Chant. This is a lyrical but stately work for strings in the style of Vaughan Williams's *Tallis Variations* and is worthy of its forerunner. An unnamed orchestra plays it beautifully, with a nice sheen (Vanguard 107, with Harris's Symphony 4).

A Rumor. This piece cleverly takes a line in the flutes and passes it around the orchestra where it spreads and grows much like a rumor, leading to a full climax. Cute, but not overly so, and entertaining. **Marriner** plays it in a fine disc of American music (Argo 845).

Sonata for Saxophone. This sonata sounds a lot like the Trombone Fantasy, with the same lyricism and rhythmic complexity, if a little less jazziness and declamatory music. **Lynn Klock** (ably accompanied by Nadine Shank) has a controlled, warm sound that sings without wailing, yet is never wanting in ear-opening facility or lyricism and is in no way square (♦Open Loop 007, with other saxophone works).

CONCERTOS

Concerto for Two Pianos is solid, exciting Creston in his motivic and motoric style, with a driven, Hindemithian I; a perfumy, evocative Andante; and a snappy tarantella finale. It's well performed by pianists **Joshua Pierce** and **Dorothy Jonas.** David Amos and the Polish Radio and Television National Symphony could inject more energy in I; otherwise, they're convincing and committed. There's a nice performance of the more famous Poulenc, too (♦Albany 112, with two-piano works by Poulenc and Nicolai Berezowsky).

CHAMBER MUSIC

Partita for Flute, Violin, and String Quartet. In the movements are named for baroque dances, the structure is concerto grosso, and there is plenty of ostinato and free melodies—Baroque in a modern setting, filled with Creston's fresh chromaticism. The work is cheerful and breezy, and the flute and violin provide a silvery and lyrical coloring. **Amos** and the Sinfonia of London are excellent (♦Harmonia Mundi 906011, with music by other American composers). So is **Schwarz** (♦Delos 3114, with Symphony 3), so the couplings are the issue.

Piano Trio is similar to the Partita in its urbane, upbeat tone, though it's more serious, with a darker coloring. The baroque-modern style is similar; the tone is more romantic. The **Mirecourt Trio** isn't perfect, but it's good and catches Creston's idiom well (♦TR 107, with Rick Sowash's *Four Seasons in Bellville*).

A good representation of Creston's band music is provided by **Robert Levy** and the Lawrence University Wind Ensemble in acceptable performances. These works are lively and colourful and display his unique chromaticism. There is a sameness to them, but taken one at a time they're good to hear, though better sound would have helped a lot (♦Golden Crest 5075, LP). HECHT

George Crumb (b. 1929)

Crumb's most "far-out" music was written in the '60s and '70s; the esthetic attitude expressed in his later scores is intended to be suggestive and descriptive, while his most recent works are more active than before. His concentration on sound and sensation, seemingly at the expense of development, may be easy to dismiss, but one does so at the risk of missing some very evocative and intense musical experiences.

Crumb's earliest works make a good introduction to his preoccupations. *Three Early Songs* (1947) are presented in "70th Birthday Album," sung by his daughter **Ann Crumb,** accompanied by the composer (Bridge 9095). They're sensitive settings of "Night," by Robert Southey and two lyrics by Sara Teasdale. The moon, memory, and sleep—subjects that mingle in Crumb's later works—are adumbrated here, in settings that are modal rather than tonal in essence and hold the listener's attention by an imagination in the service of simplicity. Ann Crumb has a lovely and expressive voice, though she frequently breaks up the phrases by too many breaths. An alternative is **Barbara Ann Martin,** in a somewhat studied performance (CRI 803).

The 1955 Sonata for Solo Cello is a beautiful improvisatory piece that has attracted many fine cellists, frequently as a contrast to Kodály's much longer Sonata. **Colin Carr** gives it a lovely and mysterious reading (GM 2031). **Peter Wispelwey** is a little more tortured, not out of place in this dark music (Globe 5089). **Suren Bagratuni** is more up-front and friendly, though his intonation is frequently sour; he couples the work with music by a little-known Armenian composer, Adam Khudoyan (Ongaku 24104). Young **Emmanuelle Bertrand** brings out a certain folk element, particularly in the variations, in a program of contemporary works she plays with conviction (Harmonia Mundi 911699).

With *Five Pieces for Piano* (1962) Crumb enters the world of atonality and sonic exploration, asking the pianist to produce harmonics and spend a good deal of time twanging strings. The sonic results are difficult to record effectively and to perform with musical coherence. **Ingrid Lindgren** is recorded in an effective ambience, but the variations in volume between loud and almost inaudible are a bit too extreme (BIS 52). **Jeffrey Jacob** solves this problem by pulling both the music and the volume together, taking 10 minutes where Lindgren took 14, but his rather dry recording doesn't do justice to some of the quiet harmonics (Centaur 2050). The most effective balance of sound and performance is in **Margaret Leng Tan**'s reading, which has ambience enough to make her harmonics audible while her more violent passages are captured with good tone (Mode 15). **Fuat Kent** gives an effective performance (Col Legno 20023, NA).

Night Music I (1963) marks Crumb's first use of Lorca's poetry, here providing texts for two of the seven nocturnes that make up this work for soprano, piano, celeste, and two percussionists. There are two versions, the first containing some improvisation, recorded by an ensemble conducted by the composer, in an effective performance with **Louise Toth** performing the songs with a throaty, Spanish coloration (CRI cassette 6008, NA). For a recording by **Joel Thome,** Crumb's notes state that he wrote out music to replace the improvised passages, and the listing in the program notes calls the result *Night Music II* (♦Vox 5144, 2CD). This performance has **Jan de Gaetani** singing a particularly magical interpretation of the weird vocal lines that inspires the instrumentalists as well.

Speculum Musicae recorded what they call *Night Music I* (1963, revised 1976) with notes, again by the composer, claiming this as the first recording of the revised version, and it's fine. **Susan Narucki** is more prominently recorded than de Gaetani, and things have a tendency to make louder bumps in the night than before—not necessarily an advantage. The texts are included, as they are not in the other versions. These latter two recordings seem to be of identical music. Who's on first, Mr. Crumb? Then there is also an actual *Night Music II,* four nocturnes for violin and piano (1964), played by the **Zurich New Music Ensemble** (Jecklin 705. NA).

Madrigals Books I and II (1965) were followed by Books III and IV (1969). The latter were dedicated to soprano **Elizabeth Suderberg,** who has recorded all four with the Contemporary Group at the University of Washington conducted by Robert Suderberg (Vox 5145, 2CD). The ambience is resonant and the performance full of interest, but it is recorded with such brilliance that it hurts the ears when you're close enough to sense the softer moments. **Anne-Marie Mühle** makes a less aggressive sound, but 32 minutes is a long time to hold the attention with one-line fragments of song superimposed on instrumental sound pictures (BIS 261). It takes the stylistic expertise and intensity of **de Gaetani** to make all 12 songs fascinating. Her recording is a little more closely miked than the others, making more of the details audible at a lower volume, and her capacity for quiet intensity and willingness to make really odd noises is unmatched (♦New World 357).

Eleven Echoes of Autumn, 1965 (1966) is a chamber piece for violin, alto flute, clarinet, and piano, written for and recorded by the **Aeolian Chamber Players** (CRI Cassette 6008, NA). This is a colorful 16-minute work that should be recorded again in more atmospheric sound, like that of the **Zurich New Music Ensemble** (Jecklin 705, NA).

Night of the Four Moons (1969) was inspired by the flight of Apollo 11, a cycle of four moon-related Lorca songs with a chamber group, recorded by the Aeolian Players with **de Gaetani** (Columbia LP 32739, NA). Though recorded rather closely, that performance had an immediacy **Barbara Ann Martin** doesn't achieve, in spite of superior sound (CRI 760). *Ancient Voices of Children* (1970) continues the Lorca settings, and Crumb says he had **de Gaetani**'s voice "very much in mind" when he wrote it. Her recording is a classic (Nonesuch 79149). Neither the less convincing **Martin** performance (CRI 803) nor Col Legno 31876, with its odd transcriptions, replaces it.

Black Angels (1970) is for electric string quartet, but for most of its length it resembles neither a quartet nor strings, because the electric amplification is supposed to be deafening; the instrumentalists have several other instruments to play, and they have to yell out numbers as

well. It's a disturbing piece, and one that David Harrington credits for giving him the impetus to found the **Kronos Quartet.** Their performance has become a theatrical event, but the piece itself is close to being one on its own (Nonesuch 79242). Interestingly, their reading is about five minutes faster than the **Concord Quartet** (Vox 5143, 2CD) or the **New York Quartet** (CRI cassette 6008, NA).

Lux Aeterna (1971) is a curious, timeless piece for wordless soprano, bass flute and recorder, sitar, and percussion, simple in idiom but moving in its use of the idea of meditations interrupted by slow, dance-like passages. This is the first of Crumb's masked pieces, and **Orchestra 2001** plays it with delicacy (CRI 723). *Vox Baleneae* (1971) is an "underwater" piece for flute, cello, and piano, the players all masked. Although the recording by **Zizi Mueller,** Fred Sherry, and James Gemmell is recorded with more clarity than atmosphere, it's played particularly well. The recording by **Erich Graf,** Walter Ponce, and Jerry Grossman was bigger-sounding and scarier, recorded under the composer's supervision (Columbia LP 32739, NA), while **Jayn Rosenfeld,** Charles Forbes, and Meg Bachman Vas are hampered by esoteric discmates (Centaur 2152, NA). The **Zurich New Music Ensemble** played it well (Jecklin 705, NA). Another performance is available on video in a film on Crumb by **Robert Mugge** (Rhapsody Films).

Four suites for amplified piano based on the zodiac make up Crumb's largest series to date of works in any form. *Makrokosmos I* (1972) was written for **David Burge,** whose resonant recording captures the otherworldly character of these 12 pieces effectively (Nonesuch LP 71293, NA). Beside his sound and scope, the less resonant and more compact performances by **Jeffrey Jacob** sound a little prosaic, though playing the suite in five minutes less time is not to be sneezed at. His proposed collection of all Crumb's piano music continues with *Makrokosmos II* in a similarly straightforward reading (Centaur 2080). **Jo Boatright**'s resonant recording and dramatic performance are impressive, on the order of Burge's (Music & Arts 1044). She also includes *Makrokosmos II,* an even wilder collection dedicated to **Robert Miller,** whose 1976 recording is highly effective (Columbia LP 34135, NA).

Christianne Mathe has also recorded both books in somewhat less sophisticated readings, though it seems unfair to criticize her for whistling out of tune (Koch Schwann 36409). A Musiques Suisses disc of both collections has proved hard to get. It should be added that Boatright's liner notes, by Steven Bruns, are particularly informative, even identifying each of the dedicatees of the 24 pieces, usually only given their initials, Elgar style. I should also mention **Robert Nasveld,** who was the first to record all of Crumb's piano music when it would still fit on three LPs (Attacca, NA).

Makrokosmos III, "Music for a Summer Evening" (1974), was written for pianists **Gilbert Kalish** and **James Freeman** and percussionists Raymond DesRoches and Richard Fitz, who perform it with great aplomb (Nonesuch 79149). **Musico Varia** is notably less successful in creating the moods of this five-movement work (BIS 261). **Fuat Kent,** Peter Degenhardt, Carmen Erb, and Hans-Peter Achberger provide a more volatile alternative (Col Legno 20023). *Makrokosmos IV,* "Celestial Mechanics" (1979), is the latest in this series, written for piano fourhands. In only four movements, it has a further subtitle, "Cosmic Dances." The **Duo Degenhardt-Kent**'s recording is rather dry-toned, though played with enthusiasm (Mode 19). An earlier reading by **Robert Nasveld** and **Jacob Bogaart** has disappeared (Attacca 8740, NA). This work is more down to earth than the previous ones, more active, less time-stretching.

Dream Sequence for piano trio and percussion (1976) is an attractively atmospheric piece with glass harmonica, bowed vibraphone, and other standard Crumb techniques, beautifully played by members of **Orchestra 2001** (CRI 803). The **Zurich New Music Ensemble** recording is a little less intense (Jecklin 705, NA).

Star-Child (1977) is a gorgeously apocalyptic work lasting 36 minutes and employing everyone in sight, including the obligatory seven trumpeters, some of them breathing down the audience's necks (a map of everyone's location in the hall is provided). A master of sound, Crumb creates a highly effective sound picture, beautifully captured by soprano Susan Narucki and trombonist Joseph Alessi with the Warsaw Philharmonic and Choir conducted by **Thomas Conlin** (Bridge 9095). This is his largest score to date.

In contrast, 1979 saw the creation of some of his most intimate pieces. *Apparition* is his first song cycle, on words from Whitman's "When Lilacs Last in the Dooryard Bloom'd"—a marvelous 18-minute work, full of nature and resignation, almost a *Song of the Earth* in mood, sung in a virtuoso performance by **de Gaetani** (Bridge 9006). *A Little Suite for Christmas, A.D. 1979* is related to the Nativity and dedicated to **Lambert Orkis,** whose sensitive recording is particularly evocative (♦Bridge 9028). **Robert Nasveld**'s performance is also excellent (Attacca 8740, NA), and so is **Marcantonio Barone,** colorful and precise (CRI 803). The best recorded sound comes from **Fuat Kent** (Col Legno 20023, NA).

Gnomic Variations (1982) is a concise and atmospheric study including many of Crumb's characteristic sounds on the piano, more traditional than many of his pieces. It's a fine vehicle for **Jeffrey Jacobs,** whose clean, alert performance is a high point in his series (Centaur 2050). *Processional* (1983) is another piano piece recorded by Jacobs (Centaur 2080) and by Nasveld (Attacca 8740, NA).

A Haunted Landscape (1984) is the only orchestral work presently available—an 18-minute demonstration of Crumb's considerable abilities in that medium. **Arthur Weisberg**'s reading with the New York Philharmonic is impressively captured (New World 326).

An Idyll for the Misbegotten (1985) is a long title for a 10-minute piece for flute and percussion, played with the requisite imagination and tension by **Zizi Mueller** (New World 357). *Federico's Little Songs* (1986) returns us to the world of song and Lorca, a children's cycle for soprano, flute, and harp. These are odd texts, replete with Lorca's imaginative juxtapositions of mood, set in an exciting sound picture and performed with warmth by **Susan Narucki,** Susan Palma Nidel, and Stacy Shames (Bridge 9069). *Zeitgeist* (1989) was written for duo-pianists **Peter Degenhardt** and **Fuat Kent** (Mode 19). It's the first of a new series for amplified pianos that bids fair to rival the *Makrokosmos* collection, and their performance and recording are convincing and atmospheric.

Recently, Crumb has begun writing works for the guitar, commissioned by **David Starobin** of Speculum Musicae. The first fruits of this involvement are heard in *Quest* (1994), a large chamber work with saxophone, harp, bass, and percussion (Bridge 9028). More recently, Crumb wrote a suite for Starobin with percussion, *Mundus Canis* (1998), recorded in his "70th Birthday Album" (Bridge 9095). This amusing study of the several dogs in Crumb's life is imaginatively realized by the guitarist with the composer on percussion.   MOORE

Bernhard Henrik Crusell *(1775–1838)*

Crusell's life was marked by a steady ascent to the center of cultural life in Stockholm in the early 19th century. He began his career as a military musician in a regimental band, then moved into a position as a court musician in Stockholm, and spent his last 30 years there. A virtuoso

clarinetist of international reputation, his small corpus is largely centered around his compositions for that instrument, which had a limited repertoire at the time. His writing for the clarinet is reminiscent of Mozart's and also reflects contemporary French styles. Though not especially innovative even in its time, his music has great charm and is always well conceived for the instrument. He also gained renown as a linguist, writing many songs, translating several important opera librettos into Swedish, and composing an opera that achieved considerable success in Stockholm.

Crusell's three clarinet concertos comprise the core of his small but notable oeuvre; they are highly enjoyable to play and eminently satisfying to audiences, and several recordings have appeared in recent years. My first choice is **Per Billman,** who plays with great panache, has a brilliant technique and a wonderfully balanced tone throughout all registers, and is ably supported by the Uppsala Chamber Orchestra conducted by Gérard Korsten (Naxos 554144). The eminent **Karl Leister** offers a fine alternative; his musicianship is beyond reproach, his tone is much warmer and darker than Billman's, and he exemplifies an older school of playing that shouldn't be ignored (BIS 345). The Lahti Symphony, conducted by Vänskä, plays beautifully but occasionally overbalances the soloist.

Emma Johnson has been enthusiastically reviewed, but I find the other two recordings much stronger. Her tone is nearly as brilliant as Billman's, and I like her enthusiasm, but her technique isn't as assured, and she has less control over her sound in passages of rapid articulation; this is especially evident in movements like the *Rondo: Allegretto* of the Op. 1 concerto, which Leister plays a full minute faster and still sounds cleaner in the difficult passagework. **Thea King**'s recording is good in many ways, but her articulation is excessively heavy (Hyperion 66708). **Antony Pay** plays very capably but with an overall lack of interpretive nuance, rarely going beyond the musical markings (Virgin 61585, 2CD, with the better-known Weber Concertos and Concertino). He conducts the Orchestra of the Age of Enlightenment himself, and for those who prefer "original instrument" recordings, this is the only one currently available.

A collection of some of Crusell's other concertante music, which has many delightful moments, features Finnish clarinetist **Anna-Maija Korsimaa-Hursti;** it includes *Introduction and Swedish Air* for clarinet, Concertino for bassoon, and Sinfonia Concertante for clarinet, horn, and bassoon (BIS 495). Crusell was a fine craftsman who never faltered in matters of taste, and his writing is always grateful for solo instruments. All these works display charm and warmth, and the soloists' musicianship is exceptionally good. The Tapiola Sinfonietta under Vänskä performs elegantly.

Crusell also wrote three wonderful clarinet quartets for salon and drawing-room performances, and these are among his finest, most ingratiating works. I enthusiastically recommend **Vänskä,** here serving as soloist in fine readings (BIS 741). He plays with great warmth and is supported beautifully by the string players. **Thea King** has also recorded these works with members of the Allegri String Quartet, but I prefer Vänskä (Hyperion 55031).   McINTIRE

César Cui *(1835–1918)*

The least-known member of the Mighty Handful, Cui used his influential position as critic to uphold the tenets of nationalism against the more European tendencies of Rubinstein and Tchaikovsky. His own music, however, is small-scaled and notable for its own European tendencies. He comes by this Eurocentrism honestly, as his father was a

French officer in Napoleon's army who decided to forgo the trip back from Moscow, married a Lithuanian girl, and settled in Vilnius.

Only one disc of Cui's orchestral works exists, pleasantly performed by the Hong Kong Philharmonic under **Kenneth Schermerhorn,** in which violinist Takako Nishizaki plays the attractive *Suite Concertante* with something less than total technical assurance but with winning musicality. Left to its own devices, the orchestra plays the *Suite Miniature* and *Suite "In Modo Populari"* with lyrical warmth (Marco Polo 220308). Two unusually lovely pieces for cello and orchestra have been recorded by **Isserlis** with Gardiner and the Chamber Orchestra of Europe in an interesting disc of Russian cello works (Virgin 91134, NA).

Chamber music is represented by a violin-piano disc played by **Peter Sheppard** and **Aaron Shorr** (Olympia 456). A winsome Violin Sonata supports the opinion of Vladimir Stasov that "for all his talent, he is committed to absolutely nothing." An idea of overall structure is flirted with, but comes to naught. *Kaleidoscope,* on the other hand, takes this attention deficit and turns it into a beautifully varied series of 24 pieces averaging only a minute and a half in length, just long enough to make their point. Sheppard and Shorr are light and airy and don't demand too much of themselves or the listener.

Cui's piano music is represented by 25 Preludes, played by **Jeffrey Biegel** (Marco Polo 223496). These are slightly longer than the pieces in *Kaleidoscope* but are as varied and attractive. Biegel emphasizes an outgoing element not always evident in Cui's pervasively gentle music. It's refreshing.

Cui's songs have been rather extensively explored. Seventeen are sung by **Christoff** in his important collection of Russian songs (EMI 67496, 5CD, unfortunately not supplied with texts). Soprano **Valentina Sharonova** sings 16 with few duplications in a disc also containing 11 by Alexander Dargomyzhsky (Russian Disc 11021). Her voice is rich and appealing, if occasionally shrill in the highest tones, and texts and transliterations are provided.   MOORE

Carl Czerny *(1791–1857)*

Despite strong praise from the curmudgeonly Brahms and acerbic Stravinsky, pianists and pedagogues know Czerny primarily for his *exercizi,* still a mainstay of many piano teachers around the world. Few are familiar with his concert music either from live performance or recordings, but he wrote a thousand or so pieces in almost all genres. A fine pianist who studied with Beethoven (whose complete piano music he reputedly played entirely from memory) and an indefatigable pedagogue, he wrote idiomatically for his instrument. Some of these pieces remain on the fringes of the repertoire today, and there are excellent recordings for those interested in the second tier of those who lived during the earliest days of the modern piano and the virtuoso music composed for it.

Czerny wrote at least 11 published solo sonatas for piano and some multipiano works in addition to chamber music that includes the piano. The sonatas, especially the early ones, are generally considered his best music other than arrangements. A fine sample comes from **Kuerti,** including 1 and 3 plus *Funeral March on the Death of Beethoven* (Analek 3141). He gives straightforward, unmannered performances in tune with this very Viennese music. A better choice is **Blumenthal,** for two reasons:

He plays with somewhat more style than Kuerti, although overall I'd rate them equally good, and he gives you 2 and 4 in addition to 1 and 3, and the extra sonatas are more than equal to the Beethoven tribute. Extensive program notes about the music and a succinct yet informative

biography of the composer add to the value of Blumenthal's discs (Etcetera 2023, 2CD).

About half of Czerny's published compositions are arrangements of other composers' music adapted for one or more pianists. Liszt, Czerny's student, was the most notable exponent of this common practice, which existed for a good practical reason: Music was not then disseminated on recordings or by radio, so you either attended concerts or the increasingly frequent solo piano recitals or went without. An interesting and very good recording of some of Czerny's four-hand arrangements comes from the **Baynov Piano Ensemble** (ARS 368381). The performers are superb solo pianists, and their ensemble work is exemplary. I admit to being partial to multi-piano music—its sound, acoustics, timbre, dynamic range, all of it—so although the music on this disc isn't really comparable to more original works, what little there is of it is artful and enjoyable (e.g., arrangements of Paganini's "La Campanella" and arias by Auber, Bellini, and Rossini in *Quator Concertante* Op. 230).

Op. 816 with the same title is on the whole less interesting, but the listener will recognize some of Mozart's opera arias, and perhaps some of Donizetti's and Meyerbeer's as well. Some of this music was intended for performance by four of Czerny's Viennese female students—all countesses, it seems—and the four parts range from easier to harder, presumably according to the original performers' abilities. Piano teachers today might find a lot of this music appropriate for their students in ensemble settings; if nothing else, audiences for this recording will get a glimpse of a kind of musical practice common 150 years ago. The program notes are informative, if more than a bit given to exaggeration of Czerny's talent.

For musical reasons, Op. 153 for four hands isn't likely to receive much attention except as one of the very few duet-concertos in the repertory, but the performance by **Liu Xiao Ming** and **Horst Göbel** is well done (SIG X78-00). **Tal** and **Groethuysen** are a good duo-piano team, and their recording of four of Czerny's more extensive compositions not based directly on others' music shows them off well (Sony 45936). Squarely in the early 19th-century genre suggested by their titles—*Grande Sonate Brilliante* Op. 10; *Sonate* Op. 178; *Overture Characteristique et Brilliante* Op. 54; and *Fantasie* Op. 226—the 70 minutes of recorded music would seem to be a fair representation of Czerny's place in his era. We should consider his recital music more frequently and positively than we generally do; if this superb performance won't accomplish that, nothing will.   ZIEROLF

Luigi Dallapiccola *(1904–1975)*

Dallapiccola was initially a black sheep among post-war Italian composers in that he gravitated to the ethos and 12-tone methods of the Schoenberg school. But even when his music bears a forceful message—he was a fierce anti-Fascist and most of his vocal works are demands for freedom—it has a rare delicacy and lyricism that draw the listener back; there is a certain truth to the cliché that he reconciled Webernesque austerity with Italianate lyricism.

Among his instrumental compositions, the piano score *Quaderno musicale di Annalibera* is the best known. It's very beautiful in its gravity and characteristic of his mature and concise, winnowed-down style of the '50s. The marvelous **Mariaclara Monetti** has recorded the set, and she relishes Dallapiccola's contrasting veins of modernism and dark, moody lyricism (♦ASV 1034, with two earlier and rather less interesting scores).

Most often recorded among Dallapiccola's choral pieces is the 28-minute, *Dies Irae*-ridden *Canti di Prigionia* (Songs of Imprisonment), the longest setting among them a harrowing prayer written by Mary Stuart before being led to the block. **John Oliver** directs the Tanglewood Festival Chorus in a performance of these typically astringent pieces (for mixed chorus, two pianos, two harps, and percussion), marrying substantial vibrato with a rather mannered dynamic range—this last exaggerated no doubt by the early digital recording, which has woolly, insubstantial lows and chalky, effortful highs (Nonesuch, with Weill's similarly severe *Recordare*). There's similar agit-prop drama in **Salonen**'s rendition with the magnificent Swedish Radio Choir, though the recording is the only one balanced so we can hear the opening choral whispers and fully enjoy the layered glimmer of the two pianos at the start of the second piece (♦Sony 68323). **Hans Zender,** working with the New London Chamber Choir and Ensemble Intercontemporain, makes less of a meal of the work, and the Londoners' singing is streamlined, lucid, and fresh—just right for the music (♦Erato 98509). In the final analysis, Zender gets the recommendation for shaping these pieces most convincingly and letting some extra light and lyricism into this fascinating, if also sometimes suffocating, music.

More desirable still are the three cycles for solo female voice and chamber ensemble, central works in Dallapiccola's output, that help fill out Zender's disc: Sometimes described as a single cycle of 13 *Liriche Greche,* these are the *Cinque Frammenti di Saffo,* the ravishing *Due Liriche di Anacreonte,* and the more excitable *Sex carmina Alcaei.* These lovely sets with their less doctrinaire language show earlier, more romantic influences—Berg, Schoenberg, even Mahler (Erato). Completing the very collectible disc are some contrasting a cappella pieces. The soprano voice of **Julie Moffat,** graceful even in Dallapiccola's punishing leaps and registral extremes, graces two of the three concerted sets. It is a pity that Erato gives no translations of the texts.

The 13 *Liriche Greche* are an ideal place to start for the Dallapiccola newcomer, and a competing account comes from soprano **Anita Morrison** and the Dallapiccola Ensemble under Luigi Suvini (Nuova Era 7109). With its more sensitive and legato phrasing, warmer if slightly less believable sound, and very slightly better pitch, this is a bit preferable to Zender's recording. Morrison is also brought forward a little more in the sound picture, while Moffat sounds as if she's standing behind the ensemble. But in the final accounting, I'd recommend Zender's disc, because more than half of the Nuova Era issue is given over to two fairly pedestrian instrumental works, *Piccolo Concerto per Muriel Couvreux* for piano and chamber orchestra and *Tartiniana Seconda* for violin and orchestra. These are ably dispatched by pianist Bruno Canino and violinist Marco Rizzi, but the music borders on substandard Respighi.

One of Dallapiccola's major theater works is his 45-minute drama *Il Prigioniero,* set during the Spanish Inquisition. (Arnold Whittall called the piece "a 12-tone *Tosca*.") It has made it to disc twice, once in German and once in the original Italian. The 1956 live Bavarian Radio recording under the great **Scherchen** has dependable but woolly mono sound (Stradivarius 10034), while **Salonen**'s 1995 version is crystal clear if also a little steely (♦Sony 68323, with *Canti di Prigionia*). So Salonen is the choice if sound is important, but it must be said that Scherchen presents this chilling portrayal of hope and dementia as an all-out stage drama while Salonen's sounds more like an oratorio.

Scherchen's primary singers, baritone Wächter and soprano Helga Pilarczyk, were prime exponents of Berg's Wozzeck and Marie after the war, and there's something dramatic and Bergian about this performance. (The lush vibraphone flourishes in Scene 2 sound like they're straight out of *Lulu*.) You do have to put up with the German translation

(Dallapiccola was a firm believer in doing opera in the local language), Waechter's mannerisms, and a balance that emphasizes the singers at the orchestra's expense. But Salonen's Bryn-Julson is an anonymous nonpresence next to Pilarcyzk, and Hynninen can't quite match Waechter's white-heat cantabile singing. Rounding out Scherchen's disc are 1964 Venice tapes of *Preghiere* and *Cinque canti,* one of Dallapiccola's very greatest works and an experience that alone would make this worth buying. The sound takes a turn for the worse in these two shorter pieces, but Mario Basiola's baritone sounds perfect for the music, and Scherchen's sure hand is again in evidence.

Ulisse, Dallapiccola's two-act opera, premiered in 1968 in Berlin under **Maazel,** and the performance, sung in German, has been made available by rescuing what seem to be radio tapes (Stradivarius 10063, 2CD). *Ulisse* is a powerful and forbidding but often poetic work, similar to Schoenberg's *Moses und Aaron* in its general style (including some choral parts in *sprechstimme*) and grand, timeless message (Homer's *Odyssey*). Schoenbergian, perhaps, but the vocal style is more lyrical and Italianate: On occasion the harmonies sound like Berg or late Stravinsky, and the instrumentation (saxophones) brings Berg to mind. I doubt it would be terribly gripping as theater unless a good stage director worked with it, and the music is also less immediately memorable than *Il Prigioniero,* not disproving the adage that Dallapiccola was best in the miniature forms of his idolized Webern.

Maazel leads an outstanding performance, with an impeccably prepared orchestra that often plays sensitively and beautifully (as in the instrumental lead-in to Scene 4), and with pillars of strength and accuracy among the singers (including the young van Dam in the small role of Pisandro, one of Penelope's suitors). Standouts are Annabelle Bernard as Calypso and Victor von Halem as King Alkinoos, though Erik Saedén's Ulysses is also exceptional. A pity there are problems with the mono sound: Balances are good, but the women's highest notes can be terribly discolored and the louder moments tend to cloud over. Some tape processing has been done (artificial reverb?), and it's hard to tell if this has improved matters or made them worse. The prompter is too audible. Still, anyone interested in the composer needs these discs—with general interest in Dallapiccola painfully on the wane these days, we're not likely to hear another performance or recording in our lifetimes. Stradivarius supplies a libretto, but no English translation.   ASHBY

Richard Danielpour (b. 1956)

Danielpour is rapidly becoming a familiar name in the classical music mainstream. Commissions from major soloists and orchestras have resulted in music that fits squarely and unabashedly into American-style "New Romanticism," music that audiences don't vociferously avoid or object to. Danielpour's statement that "music [must have] an immediate, visceral impact" resonates with those who require some semblance of familiarity for their musical experience. He favors traditional forms and relative consonance, and incorporates flavors and music from a wide variety of vernacular and other sources. Some composers capture their times well but fail to go beyond them; Danielpour offers more, and, given his enviable opportunities, we will listen with interest for his maturation in music that depends less on ephemeral programs and too careful attention to surface.

Of the half-dozen or so recordings to date, **Schwarz** and the Seattle Symphony offer a good introduction to Danielpour's desires as a composer. Recorded about the time he was resident composer with the Seattle orchestra, the three compositions—*The Awakened Heart, First Light,* Symphony 3 ("Journey Without Distance")—illustrate his attractive orchestration and what passes for lyricism in much of late 20th-century music. As with most of his works, these evocatively titled pieces are based on experiences real or imagined, although I find they succeed in the absolute realm better than with the distraction of a personalized reference.

More interesting music (better performed) is available from **Macal** and the Philharmonia (♦Sony 60779). These compositions—*Celestial Night, Toward the Splendid City, Urban Dances*—seem more personal, more merely musical, than those on Schwarz's disc. *Urban Dances* (not to be confused with Danielpour's other piece with the same title) is the most engaging. A suite extracted from a New York City Ballet commission, it's less self-conscious, even in title, than his other titled pieces and depends less on allusion for esthetic response.

Of his few works with generic titles, the only ones recorded are a Cello Concerto and *Metamorphosis* for piano and orchestra. The latter is virtually a concerto—three virtuosic movements—ably performed by **Michael Boriskin** with Joseph Silverstein and the Utah Symphony (♦Harmonia Mundi 907024). This recording also contains Perle's Piano Concerto 2, composed about the same time as *Metamorphosis*, and will interest those who wish to compare the two generations in American music. (Perle, born 40 years before Danielpour, is one of those who passed through serialism but hasn't expunged its restrictions; Danielpour has not yet reached the limits of unlimited eclecticism. Why does Perle's concerto sound fresher than Danielpour's?)

The Cello Concerto was instigated by **Yo-Yo Ma** and commissioned by the San Francisco Symphony. Even Ma's admirable artistry on this recording with Zinman and the Philadelphia Orchestra (♦Sony 66299) can't make Danielpour's or the other cello concertos on this recording (by Kirchner and Rouse) likely to receive the attention of, say, Ligeti's. **Ma**, who has commissioned and performed more contemporary music for his instrument than any other major cellist, stated, "If only one out of every 10 . . . ends up in the repertory, a huge contribution has been made." Admirable, encouraging, even necessary, but we'll need to look to the other seven.   ZIEROLF

Franz Danzi (1763–1826)

Danzi was not only a product of the fabled Mannheim school of composition but also a native son, born to a member of Stamitz's orchestra in that musical city. He studied cello with his father (leading to a position in the same orchestra at age 15) and composition with Vogler. In 1812 he moved to Karlsruhe and stayed there as conductor of the court theater until his death. His music is classical, suave, well-constructed, sometimes brilliant, and always genial. Most of what is recorded is for winds, though contemporaries insisted that his strength lay in vocal music.

Concertos. Danzi was a delightful writer of concertante music. Always an engaging tunesmith, his writing is idiomatic and fluent, and some of his more stormy passages presage the Romantic times that were to follow. One of the finest (and few) discs to have appeared in recent years is a collaboration by **James Galway** and **Sabine Meyer** (♦Denon 78911). Danzi's Flute Concerto 2 gets a vibrant, richly colored performance by Galway, while Meyer plays the socks off the *Fantasia for Clarinet and Orchestra on the Theme "La ci darem la mano."* The two join forces for the statelier Concertante for Flute and Clarinet Op. 41. The Würtemberg Chamber Orchestra sparkles under conductor **Jörg Faerber** (♦RCA 61976). **Paul Meyer** and **Rampal** engage each other in the Concertante with just as much success as the RCA crew; the couplings are two clarinet concertos by Ignaz Pleyel, excellently played by Meyer. Those wanting an all-Danzi program should stick with Denon.

The same Concertante makes its appearance on a disc that has the three *Potpourris for Clarinet and Orchestra* along with the Concertante for Clarinet and Bassoon Op. 47. **Eduard Brunner** and **Thunemann** deliver the goods in fine fashion and nice sound (♦Tudor 799). **András Adorjan** is good enough to provide us with the four Flute Concertos all on one disc; the Munich Chamber Orchestra, led by Hans Stadlmair, turns in fine performances (♦Orfeo 3812). Nicolás Pasquet's Neubrandenburger Philharmonic with **Albrecht Holder** as soloist gives us four bassoon concertos that are among Danzi's most engaging works. The sound is some of the best to come from this company, and at the price, this is a steal (♦Naxos 554273). On an album of miscellaneous horn music (with concertos by Mozart, Haydn, Francesco Rosetti, and Michael Haydn), **Baumann** gives a good try at the Horn Concerto in E, though the piece has little effect (Teldec).

Chamber Music. Obviously inspired by Reicha's example, Danzi produced a number of works for solo and grouped wind instruments that, while not as profound or adventurous as his concertos, still afford much pleasure. The three Bassoon Quartets Op. 40 are striking pieces—introspective, darkly lyrical, perhaps Danzi's best chamber works. They're not profound, but still have an ability to move us. **Robert Thompson** and the Coull Quartet give masterly, engaging renditions, revealing a side of Danzi we don't often hear (♦CRD 3503). **Mauro Monguzzi** and company are up to the challenge with a warm, flowing account of the same pieces, plus the added attraction of Bassoon Quartet 1 from Op. 46. These are fine performances, easily listened to, and gracefully indulgent on the ears (♦Bongiovanni 5520).

The Op. 50 Flute Quintets are not particularly inspiring, but despite their nominal musical substance, the **Les Adieux** ensemble plays them in a professional, dutiful manner without trying to infuse profundity into the music—clearly a wasted task (♦Musicaphon 56825). As a bonus, the *Petite Duos for Flute and Cello* are thrown in (with some nice cello writing), a good way to collect these works without resorting to miscellaneous compilations. You could do much worse than the three discs of the **Berlin Philharmonic Wind Quintet** playing the string and piano quintets. This intrepid ensemble has the Midas touch in anything it attempts, and if these benchmark recordings can't convince you of the worth of Danzi's chamber music, no one can (♦BIS 532, 552, 592).

The rather tough sound (inflexible and wooden) shouldn't deter you from latching on to the budget discs by the **Michael Thompson Quintet** of Quintets Opp. 56 and 67. The Berliners play them better, hands down, but the price is much higher, and if you want to sample, this is an acceptable alternative (Naxos). An added attraction to the Op. 56 disc is the inclusion of the Sextet Op. 10. Because this is Danzi's only foray into *Harmoniemusik,* and it's the main work on the disc, it can safely be recommended, though you might want to seek the Op. 56 Quintets elsewhere (♦Naxos 553076). The **Albert Schweitzer Quintet** gives ravishing, tonally gorgeous renditions of Quintets 1–3 that revel in their barnstorming virtuosity. Finer versions are hard to come by, and this is perfect for a high-quality sampling of these pieces (♦CPO 999180).   RITTER

Peter Maxwell Davies (b. 1934)

Davies is a remarkable composer whose music has gradually moved from an overtly antiestablishment stance to a less hectoring tone centered on a positive love of Nature and even, one feels, his fellow man. A thread that follows him through this odyssey is a fondness for medieval chant and techniques. Most of his works through the '70s are marked by the distinguishing sonorities of his chamber group, The Fires of London, consisting of violin, cello, flute, clarinet, keyboards, and other percussion instruments. His best-known work, *Songs for a Mad King* (Unicorn-Kanchana 9052), is typical of his work for this group.

Davies' quirky imagination is always interesting, though his decidedly ambiguous attitude toward religion and politics make his works unsettling, particularly his operas. In 1970 he moved to the Orkney Islands, and his music gradually developed a less dissonant character. He seems to get mellower with age and has written a number of attractively zany orchestral works and a long series of concertos for members of the Scottish Chamber Orchestra and others.

A major event is the series of recordings from Collins covering mainly his post-1970 period (few of his pre-Orkney works are available). Currently listed volumes include concertos for piano, piccolo, and trumpet; Strathclyde Concertos 5–10; Symphonies 1–6; and a variety of other pieces expertly conducted by Davies. Several concert suites are led by Cleobury, and a disc of choral music led by Simon Joly features the BBC Singers. A good collection of the most accessible of Davies's recent works is in Collins 15242, but if you're going to do more than skim the cream, be warned that only *Mavis in Las Vegas* is new. The 10 attractive Strathclyde Concertos are gradually disappearing from the catalogue; so the Collins series may be on its way out, even as it continues to record recent works.

A number of interesting recordings have appeared outside the series as well. **Isaac Stern** has recorded the Violin Concerto (Columbia 42449), and the **Arditi Quartet** the Quartet for Strings (Mode 59). Davies's organ works are played by **Kevin Bowyer** (Nimbus 5509), and his guitar music by **Per Dybro Sørenson** (Paula 63). *Farewell to Stromness* and *Yesnaby Ground* are short piano pieces, interludes in the 1980 *Yellow Cake Revue* that was one of Davies's responses to the prospect of opening a uranium mine in the Orkneys. There are performances by **David Holzman** (Centaur 2102), and by Davies himself in "A Celebration of Scotland" (Unicorn-Kanchana 9070). Davies plays seriously, downplaying the folksiness of the material, perhaps thinking more about the social intent of the pieces, while Holzman's readings are lighter, presenting the music in a more purely attractive manner. You may want both discs, since Holzman's also contains the only recording of the Piano Sonata, as well as several interesting works by other composers.

Davies's vocal works are among his most remarkable compositions. *Le Jongleur de Notre Dame* is a short masque on the same story as Massenet's opera. There's more dumb-show and instrumental playing than singing in this amusing 50-minute piece, and the music isn't particularly well-organized because it involves much participation by children. The performance by **Opera Sacra Buffalo,** a chamber group modeled on The Fires of London, has an improvised feeling (Mode 59). *The Lighthouse* concerns the disappearance of three keepers from a lighthouse in the Hebrides in 1900, and it's much more a lyrical singer's opera than the others, with only three characters, all male. The performance in the Collins series led by Davies is presumably definitive.

Resurrection, as might be expected from the title, is not your average opera. It features a rock band and pop singer and the resurrection involves an operation on a dummy, resulting in the Antichrist. A really effective performance would require great precision to make all the four-part writing understandable. The cast in the Collins recording is a little imprecise in its ensemble, but the text is supposed to be irritating anyway. It also contains no less than 24 singing commercials! Though no date is given, the music appears to be late '70s in style. It's guaranteed to leave a bad taste in your mouth, but it's fascinating, in its ghoulish way.

The Doctor of Myddfai is set to a libretto calling on Welsh mythology and homing in on our mistrust of bureaucracy and the corruption of power. The setting allows some beautiful singing, and the music is the most lyrical of Davies's operas to date; the notes hint that he's not planning to write any more. *Job* is a powerful study of Job's words, but God sounds like the choruses in Stravinsky's *Oedipus Rex,* an odd association. But then, Davies's manner is always odd.   MOORE

Claude Debussy *(1862–1918)*

Debussy was arguably France's greatest composer. Taking a hint from Wagner and the Russians, he abandoned classical forms and rules of harmony that he felt had hampered the development of French music and created sensuous compositions of an increasingly subjective nature, usually inspired by sounds and scenes from real life or by a program or story. His mature work is full of what might be called "counterpoint," but it's not of the 18th-century style that's derived from thematic materials introduced early in a piece. It's often a matter of competing sounds, voices, or other stimuli experienced in real life, the way you might hear different sounds coming from opposite directions in a modern city—an environment full of distractions. Once, when a critic demanded to know by what rules he composed, he replied, "mon plaisir." I find it nearly impossible to listen to his music without calling vivid imagery to mind.

Debussy's emphasis on color laid the foundation for the early Expressionist developments of Bartók and the New Viennese School. Indeed, he has been called the first modern composer. The music of such colorists as Penderecki and Ligeti has its roots in his works, and American film composers often imitated him. Look closely, and you will find his fingerprints on most 20th-century scores.

ORCHESTRAL WORKS

Starting with the creation of the two great orchestras of the German-speaking world, the Vienna and Berlin Philharmonic, and perhaps even going as far back as Wagner's Bayreuth orchestra, the mellow, highly blended German orchestral sound has gradually become the world's favorite. Other national styles are falling into disfavor as orchestras from Tokyo to Chicago to St. Petersburg adopt it. Because their instrumental sections didn't blend as well, older French orchestras had a broader, brighter palette than most German groups. They were distinguished by bright, superficial-sounding French-made violins; pungent woodwinds with fast, tight vibratos and very reedy tones; watery-toned French horns played with a wide, slow vibrato; and blaring brass, often with an intense, bleating vibrato in the trumpets. Aside from these tonal peculiarities, fast rhythmic figures were often speeded up. Be forewarned: It is these very characteristics that many listeners find disagreeable. They did, however, make French orchestras better able to clarify a work's structure by the use of contrasting tone colors, and competing voices were more clearly audible. Not only was Debussy familiar with this sound (though the orchestras he knew did not yet employ much, if any, vibrato), but it's surely what he had in mind as he composed.

Danses sacrée et profane (Sacred and Profane Dances). These dances were commissioned by Pleyel as examination pieces to be used by the Brussels Conservatory for the firm's new nonpedaled chromatic harp. They have a vaguely Iberian flavor, as *Danse sacrée* is based on a short keyboard piece by the Portuguese composer Francisco de Lacerda while *Danse profane* employs a Spanish melody Debussy used in two of his piano Preludes, *La sérénade interrompue* and *La puerta del vino.*

Vera Baddings and Haitink play prettily but fail to propel the music

(Philips). **Frances Tietov** and Slatkin are delicate and lovely, but don't convey the ecstasy of the last dance (Telarc). **Ossian Ellis** and Marriner have the most resonant recording and produce ravishing sonorities (♦ASV 517). The strings are dreamlike and fevered in the first dance, voluptuous and swinging in the second. The drama of this disc is enhanced by its great dynamic contrast; it's an intoxicating performance without peer.

Lily Laskine recorded the *Danses* with Piero Coppola and a pickup orchestra (Pearl 9348; Lys 295/7). The first dance really moves, while in the second, the sections are carefully differentiated, but it's not as ecstatic as Ellis/Marriner. Stokowski and the Philadelphia recorded the work with **Edna Phillips** in 1931 (Biddulph 013). This is a very relaxed reading, heavy on atmosphere but lacking drama.

Images (I. *Gigues;* II. *Ibéria:* A. *Par les rues et par les chemins* [Through the Streets and Byways]; B. *Les parfums de la nuit* [The Fragrances of the Night]; C. *Le matin d'un jour de fête* [The Morning of a Feast Day]; III. *Rondes de printemps* [Round Dances of Spring]).

Images is a set of sonic postcards, containing folk tunes from their respective countries (I is Britain, II is Spain, and III is France). There is a convention of performing just *Ibéria,* so I and III are not as well-known and often are not as well-performed. Occasionally, the movements are rearranged, placing *Ibéria* last.

Several of the complete recordings lack excitement or are otherwise too flawed to be considered: **Boulez** (Sony and DG), **Cluytens** (Basic Classics), **Dutoit** (Decca), **Haitink** (Philips), **Rattle** (EMI), **Salonen** (Sony), and **Thomas** (DG).

Rahbari gives a very atmospheric reading in a very resonant acoustic. Movement I has striking *sul ponticello* effects; IIA is good but unremarkable; IIB is heavily perfumed; IIC is again good but not special; III builds nicely at the beginning (Naxos). **Previn** is magical at the start of I, which goes very well; IIA has good, energetic climaxes, IIB is nicely atmospheric, IIC is fine, and III is lovely (EMI). **Dario Argenta** is good too, with an exciting IIC (Decca), and so is **Martinon,** with a particularly effective IIB but a weak IIA (EMI). **Levine** and the Berlin Philharmonic are good throughout (Sony 53284). **Bernstein** and the Santa Cecilia Orchestra are very colorful and expressive, especially in II, with good dynamic contrast and an excellent IIC (DG 429728). **Manuel Rosenthal** and the Paris Opéra Orchestra are colorful, energetic, and stylish, with a wide dynamic range, and they're blessed with very assertive oboes and English horns (♦Adès 205882, 2CD).

Munch and the Boston Symphony take a little while to work up some steam in I, but once they do they give a superb performance that's very exciting, in classic, early stereo (♦RCA 61956). IIB is a real standout here, both smokily erotic and ecstatic. He and the excellent Orchestre National de l'ORTF sizzle in all three movements; this reading is at least as good as the earlier one (♦Accord 220272). **Monteux** (who conducted the premiere of *Jeux* under Debussy's supervision) and the London Symphony made the definitive recording of this score (♦Philips 420392, NA). Every movement is tremendously exciting, the orchestra plays with whiplash precision and beautiful sound, inner voices are always brought out clearly, dynamic contrasts are nicely abrupt, and rhythms are thrillingly taut. The mood of each movement is located with pinpoint accuracy, and the grotesque humor of IIC is fully brought out. The sound is the best on disc. I can't recommend it highly enough; let's hope Philips sees fit to reissue it. His 1951 performance with the San Francisco Symphony is nearly as good as the later effort, but the orchestra and recording are inferior.

Stokowski and the French National Radiodiffusion Orchestra are outstanding (♦EMI 67313). Giving a thrilling, tremendously atmospheric reading, they are at least as good as Monteux and the London Symphony, and perhaps even better. **Hans Zender** recorded I and III, the least popular movements, in excellent performances, on a par with the best (♦CPO 999476). **Paray** and the Detroit Symphony play with their customary precision and energy, with IIC being the best (♦Mercury 434343). **Reiner** in Chicago is also excellent, approaching the excitement of Monteux (♦RCA 60179).

Among recordings of *Ibéria* alone, **Celibidache**'s is, as you might expect, hypnotically slow (EMI). The Munich Philharmonic produces lovely sounds and the balances are superb, but this reading is too eccentric for most people to enjoy. LP fanciers may wish to hunt down **Dervaux**'s *Ibéria* with the Orchestre des Concerts Colonne (♦Westminster 8191). Dervaux is like Munch, tending to speed up at climaxes, but not quite so passionately. The orchestra has a very authentic French sound along with a pronounced tendency (again, peculiarly French) to rush fast passages, in a very atmospheric, idiomatic performance.

There is a 1936 concert recording of the New York Philharmonic under **Toscanini** in which the sound is a bit muddy, but it's a superb performance that crackles in the outer movements and smokes in the middle (♦Grammofono 2000 78772). *Ibéria* was recorded in 1935 by **Piero Coppola** and the Orchestre de la Société des Concerts du Conservatoire in one of the best performances from any era (♦Lys 295/7, 3CD).

Jeux (Games). This is Debussy's only real ballet score, *L'après-midi* having been appropriated years after its composition by Diaghilev's Ballets Russe. It's one of Debussy's most colorful works, but it failed to make much of an impact at its premiere because of the weak story line and because *The Rite of Spring* had its premiere just two weeks later. The action of *Jeux* revolves around a young man and two girls searching for a tennis ball in a park at twilight, and this could hardly draw attention away from a savage, pagan sacrifice set to pounding, dissonant music.

Remarkably, nearly all recordings of this work are dull or, at best, aimless, and don't merit consideration. **Bernstein** (Sony), **Boulez** (DG), **Dutoit** (Decca), **Haitink** (Philips), **Maazel** (RCA), **Rattle** (EMI), **Tilson Thomas** (Sony), and **Zender** (CPO) fail to make any sense of the score.

Baudo and the London Philharmonic are colorful and have a large dynamic range; they're a bit disjointed and not too sure of their direction, but they provide a satisfactory reading (EMI, NA). **Martinon** is quite good—very colorful, if a bit prosaic (EMI 72667). The performance by Ravel disciple **Manuel Rosenthal** is highly dramatic, soaked in gorgeous colors, with great dynamic range and extreme contrasts of tempo (♦Adès 205882, 2CD). It's both thrilling and spellbinding, and you would hardly guess that this brilliant score was created to accompany some fuss about a ball.

La Mer (The Sea). While composing this masterpiece, Debussy confided to his friend André Messager that it was only by chance he became a musician rather than a sailor. The sea held great allure for him, and this isn't the first work to express that passion (cf. *Nocturnes,* III). Indeed, the sea so excited him that he found it impossible to compose while vacationing at the seashore. A good performance of *La Mer* should create at least that degree of excitement.

The following recordings may be dismissed as ranging from uniformly dull to possessing too few virtues to merit consideration: **Ashkenazy** (Decca, NA), **Baudo** (EMI, NA), **Bernstein** (Sony and DG), **Boulez** (CBS, NA, and DG), **Jean-Claude Casadesus** (Harmonia Mundi), **Celi-**

bidache (with bafflingly glacial tempos; EMI), Dutoit (Decca), Frühbeck de Burgos (IMP), Giulini (Sony), Haitink (Philips), Karajan's 1964 recording (DG), Leinsdorf (EMI), Maazel (RCA), Masur (Teldec), Muti (EMI), Ormandy (Sony and RCA), Previn (EMI), Rahbari (Naxos), Rosenthal (Adès), Salonen (Sony), Geoffrey Simon (Cala), Sinopoli (DG, NA), Slatkin (Telarc), Solti (Decca), Tortelier (Chandos), and Zender (CPO).

Barenboim is acceptable in I (De l'aube à midi sur la mer; From Dawn Until Noon on the Sea), which finally heats up toward the end, and is much livelier in II (Jeux de vagues; Play of the Waves) and III (Dialogue du vent et de la mer; Dialogue of the Wind and the Sea) (Decca). Ansermet has a few ensemble problems in I, but is very involved; II scintillates; and III is powerful, if a bit rough and ready (London). Reiner isn't very exciting in I, but II and III are much better (RCA). Martinon is very pleasant and sunny in I and II; his III presents nature without its demonic side, but it's powerful and effective just the same (EMI). Paray gives us a pleasant I marred only by a restrained ending; II sparkles and is beautifully executed; and III is powerful with a thrilling finale (Mercury). The Detroit trumpets are superb. Szell is curiously restrained in I and II, though II has an effective ending. It turns out he was saving up for III, which has an excellent opening and is very energetic, with wonderfully elastic tempos (Sony).

In a 1962 concert performance, Mravinsky makes all the right moves in I, but somehow it doesn't quite click (Russian Disc 11159). The rest of the piece really comes alive, though, in a playful II with elastic tempos and rich in incident and a dramatic III. Munch and the Boston are very good in all three movements, and III ends excitingly (♦RCA 61500). They are blessed with classic, early stereo sound from 1956. Seven years later, Munch recorded the piece again with the Orchestre National de l'ORTF in what sounds like a broadcast performance (♦Accord 220272). He was a sort of Alsatian Furtwängler, changing from day to day, and you're advised to hang on for the ride of your life. I builds very quickly, and Munch's sea really surges; the excitement continues in II, and in III he whips the orchestra into a frenzy. The recording is a bit harsh but the orchestra is very good, and nowhere will you hear a more thrilling La Mer.

Silvestri and the Orchestre de la Société des Concerts du Conservatoire play the original 1905 version, which has a few differences you might notice from the standard, revised score, especially in the trumpets at the end of III (♦Seraphim 69728). I—beginning with the sunrise in the east, which Debussy evokes with gamelan-like sounds—has an excellent buildup to a point where we finally feel we're at sea. The trumpets blare thrillingly at the end of I (these aren't mellow, German-style brass). II is exciting with a lovely ending, and III is thrilling from the start, with a wonderful climax. The orchestra also has a very strong French "accent."

Tilson Thomas and the Philharmonia open I with a very effective sunrise and are very exciting, if not as thrilling as Munch (♦CBS 44645, NA). They end I memorably with cymbals that are literally allowed to drown out the rest of the orchestra—you can just see the waves crashing against the rocks! II is equally fine, with an enchanting ending. Their III is perhaps the best, as thrilling as Munch, with apocalyptic brass and a great ending. The Philharmonia percussionists perform miracles throughout the piece with cymbals and gongs. Pray for a reissue. The version by Stokowski and the London Symphony, recorded in 1969, is also great (♦London 455152). Their dawn in I is excellent, and though it's not as dramatic as some others, the conductor has a fine feel for the swaying of the waves and, of course, a kaleidoscopic range of colors. II

is perky, with wonderfully shaped episodes and beautiful colors. III has a splendid opening and is consistently thrilling, with a great ending.

There was a fine LP by Désiré Emile Inghelbrecht and the Orchestre du Théâtre des Champs-Élysées (♦Trianon 6175). I is a bit ordinary, but II is colorful and dramatic, and III is very dramatic with good contrasts of tone color and tempo, subtly articulated rhythms and accents, and a great ending. Again, the orchestra has a very authentic French sound and the French tendency to rush fast figures. Golschman led a good performance with the St. Louis Symphony (Columbia 5155). I is a bit prosaic, with a rushed ending, but II and III are quite lively. He doesn't vary tempos as much as the other, better conductors in this piece, but he does manage to underscore the climactic episodes through sheer orchestral power. In Dervaux's recording with the Orchestre des Concerts Colonne, I and III are good but not thrilling, while II shines brightly with playing that strongly evokes nature (Westminster 8191). Very authentic French orchestral sound, with nimble woodwinds and rushed figures.

Koussevitzky's is the most celebrated older recording (Pearl). The Boston Symphony produced a vaporous, impressionistic sound, yet it lacks the energy and drama of the great performances, especially in I. This may be due partly to the rather dim sound. Coppola recorded a much better performance in 1932; it's full of drama and atmosphere (♦Lys 295/7, 3CD). Rodzinski and the Cleveland recorded La Mer in 1941 (Lys). It's not a very dramatic reading but it's very energetic, very detailed, and, above all, fast.

Toscanini's 1936 concert recording with the New York Philharmonic is in rather poor sound. It's an excellent performance, less driven than his subsequent studio recordings but powerful and idiomatic just the same (♦Grammofono 2000 78772). He and the Philadelphia made a fine recording in 1942 (RCA 60311). At the start of III it's obvious that a real storm is brewing, and we're not disappointed, though the performance is marred by a weak ending to I. He recorded it again in 1950 with the NBC Symphony (RCA 60265). This is blessed with clearer sound, and here the ending of I is powerful, but the beginning of III isn't as energetic as in the Philadelphia recording. Monteux and the Boston Symphony in 1954 were just as high energy and precise as Toscanini (♦RCA 61890). This is one of the last recordings the orchestra made before the advent of stereo, so the sound is a bit congested at the climaxes, but miles beyond what Koussevitzky was given. This performance is very dramatic, especially in II and III.

Le Martyre de Saint Sébastien (The Martyrdom of St. Sebastian). Debussy's music is part of a larger work, with texts by the Italian poet Gabriele D'Annunzio, incorporating speech, mime, dance, and oratorio. Its premiere lasted some five hours, and it has never been performed in its entirety since.

Monteux and the London Symphony offer selections for orchestra, played with real fervor (♦Philips 420392, NA). Salonen directs some selections to lesser effect (Sony), as do Rahbari (Naxos) and Dutoit (Decca). Bernstein's disc with the New York Philharmonic contains over 75 minutes of selections from the spoken, sung, and orchestral material, presented in English (Sony 60596). Fritz Weaver is both narrator and the Emperor Diocletian, and Bernstein's wife Felicia Montealegre is the saint. The essentials of the drama are preserved in the verbal sparring between saint and emperor, but Montealegre's throaty declamations of the saint's fanatical yearning for martyrdom and Weaver's near bellowing of the emperor's homoerotic demands soon wear on the listener.

The only other extensive collection is Tilson Thomas's with the London Symphony, which presents the text in the original French (Sony

48240). His singers are better than Bernstein's, and Sylvia McNair's gorgeous *vox coelestis* could convert the most skeptical unbeliever. Leslie Caron is a far more palatable saint than Montealegre, but the omission of the conflict with the emperor robs this version of drama.

There is a 1931 recording of orchestral excerpts by **Coppola** and the Orchestre de la Société des Concerts du Conservatoire (◆Lys 295/7, 3CD). The performance is confident, atmospheric, and appropriately moody.

Nocturnes. The Nocturnes, completed in 1901, have a clear, detailed program supplied by the composer. I (*Nuages*), with its dark, almost menacing mood, was inspired by a view from the Solférino bridge of the slow movement of gray clouds reflected by the Seine on a moonless night, "dying away in a gray agony lightly tinged with white." II (*Fêtes*) evokes the excitement of a procession of the Republican Guard through the Bois du Boulogne, complete with heralding trumpets, accompanying the Czar on a state visit in 1896. III (*Sirènes*) represents the nearly irresistible attraction the sea held for Debussy as he heard, and ultimately declined, its siren call, opting for a life in the concert hall.

Debussy came to believe that every sound we hear in everyday life could be reproduced by the modern orchestra, and he certainly tried to evoke impressions of the other senses too. This is his first orchestral score that gives interpreters real trouble; the difference in interpretive approaches to this and subsequent scores is extreme compared to those to the earlier ones. Some, mostly of a generation old enough to have known Debussy personally, favor brash, splashy, pungent sonorities and crisply articulated rhythms, especially in II, and, whatever the tempo, guide each phrase and movement with a sense of purpose. Others, concerned principally with producing a soft-focused, homogenized orchestral sound, wander aimlessly in a sonic fog. Of course, such black-and-white distinctions don't always apply, and there are many shades of gray.

Salonen (Sony), **Jean-Claude Casadesus** (Harmonia Mundi), **Boulez** (CBS, NA, and DG), **Dutoit** (Decca), **Frühbeck** (EMI), and **Maazel** (RCA) all lack feeling to varying degrees and are fairly bland throughout. Maazel is, however, blessed with fine, rather closely recorded sound of great clarity and a very forward-placed women's chorus with a reedy timbre reminiscent of a boy's choir that together give an interesting feel to III. **Barenboim** is tentative and plodding in I but more effective in II, despite tenuous ensemble in the central section; III is very good, with a fine chorus (Decca). **Martinon** isn't dark enough in I, but II is really festive, with wonderful offstage trumpets at the start of the central section; III lacks nuance—the sirens aren't calling Debussy, they're chasing him (EMI).

Bernstein only recorded I and II (Sony). I is very colorful and dramatic, but doesn't quite convey the "gray agony" at the end. II is thrilling, and he doesn't bother to slow down at all in the middle. **Paray** is too fast in I; II is very good, and he does slow down abruptly in the middle; III is remarkably clear, which robs it of atmosphere and seduction (Mercury). **Geoffrey Simon** is very good in I, but falls short in II and especially III (Cala). **Ashkenazy** is acceptable in I, with a good ending, better in II, slowing down just right in the middle, but sluggish in III (Decca, NA). **Tortelier** is good in I, conveying a sense of menace and ending well; he's very effective in II despite not slowing in the middle, but is brought down in III by a vibratoless high school girls' chorus that doesn't sound at all lubricious (Chandos). **Haitink** is right on target in I, though II lacks a little excitement (Philips 438742, 2CD). In III, the voices aren't enticing enough, but the wonderfully evocative use of vibrato by the solo trumpet partly compensates.

Surprisingly, **Monteux** and the Boston Symphony play the piece with intelligent phrasing and tempo relationships but little emotion (RCA). Monteux was reported to have had a low opinion of the work, and that may be why this performance ultimately disappoints. **Mravinsky** gives a very fine reading of I and II; I is dark and brooding, II bright and festive (◆Russian Disc 11167). **Rosenthal** is excellent in all three movements, though a bit brisk in III (◆Adès 205882, 2CD). **Munch** conjures up a powerful mood in I that almost ends right, goes wild in II, and does his utmost to seduce in III, with the young Debussy clearly bidding farewell to the sea at the end (◆Accord 220272). **Silvestri** and the Orchestre de la Société des Concerts du Conservatoire are only fair in I until the ending, which is very effective (◆Seraphim 69728). II is really rousing, with great dynamic contrasts, and III is ecstatic and arousing, with an excellent ending. This orchestra has an exceptionally pungent French sound.

Two recordings are in a class by themselves. **Tilson Thomas** and the Philharmonia convey a remarkably strong feeling in I with a perfect ending (◆Sony 63244, 2CD). II is superb, with an especially effective ritard near the end, III has a thrilling beginning, and the Ambrosian Singers are outstanding as the most seductive sirens. Every bar is alive and has a strong sense of direction. The powerful feeling at the climax near the end is unmatched, Debussy's farewell to the sea is deeply felt, and the final note is memorably sustained. **Stokowski** and the London Symphony don't create quite as dark a mood in I as Tilson Thomas and the Philharmonia, but they're wonderfully atmospheric and end it memorably (◆EMI 67313). II is very lively, with a great climax and ending; III isn't as dramatic as Tilson Thomas makes it but again is very atmospheric, with a superb climax and a memorable shiver in the chorus ca. 8:50, followed by the cellos and basses ca. 9:10. The ending is remarkably beautiful.

In **Inghelbrecht**'s LP, I stands out, with just the right color and mood, and well-balanced details; II and III are a bit weak (Trianon 6175). **Furtwängler** and the Berlin Philharmonic do well in I, with the right feel at the end, but they trivialize II (Music & Arts). **Toscanini** and the NBC Symphony get I right despite a very brisk tempo (RCA). II is very effective, though they seem to speed up in the middle. **Coppola** with the Orchestre de la Société des Concerts du Conservatoire and an anonymous women's chorus recorded the complete work in 1938 with excellent results (◆Lys 295/7, 3CD). **Stokowski** recorded it in 1937 and 1939 with the Philadelphia (◆Biddulph 013). This is a wonderfully atmospheric performance, with a III more languid than ardent.

Prélude à l'après-midi d'un faune. Written in 1892–94, this was Debussy's first orchestral masterpiece. Inspired by Mallarmé's poem, it's a paean to eroticism, and any successful performance must unabashedly represent the excitation of lust in a daydreaming faun. Velvety voluptuousness and the heated thrill of arousal must be balanced in the performer's tonal palette.

A few recordings miss the mark. **Giulini** sounds anemic and lethargic (Sony), as do **Karajan** (in his 1964 DG recording) and **Masur** (Teldec). Masur's and Giulini's are concert performances hampered by dull sound. **Solti**'s 1990 concert performance is a respectable, enjoyable, middle-of-the-road interpretation with fine sound (London). Along similar lines are **Ashkenazy** (London, NA), **Barenboim** (Decca), **Baudo** (EMI), **Bernstein** and the New York Philharmonic (Sony), **Frühbeck** (IMP), **Martinon** (EMI), **Ormandy** (Sony and RCA), **Paray** (Mercury), and **Previn** (EMI). **Tilson Thomas** has excellent sound and exploits the languid, sensuous qualities of the score (Sony 63244, 2CD), and **Salonen**'s is another beautifully played and recorded *Prélude* (Sony 62599).

Slatkin's account is intelligently phrased and lovely (Telarc 80071). Two high-energy performances, with a more authentic, pungent, mid-20th century French orchestral sound, are **Silvestri**'s with the Orchestre de la Société des Concerts du Conservatoire (♦Seraphim 69728) and **Dervaux**'s with the Orchestre des Concerts Colonne (♦Basic Classics 017). **Rosenthal** (♦Adès 205882, 2CD) and **Ansermet** (♦London 433711) are nearly as energetic and French sounding.

Stokowski and the London Symphony perform the work with that combination of ecstatic, erotic abandon and ravishing sonorities that were uniquely his, captured in concert in 1972 in full-bodied Phase 4 sound (♦London 455152). It's the longest *Prélude* on CD. Stokowski had already recorded the *Prélude* with an excellent New York pickup orchestra, but that performance lacks the concentration and emotion of this one (EMI 65614). **Bernstein**'s concert recording with the Santa Cecilia Orchestra is another deeply expressive, very colorful account (♦DG 429728).

Among older recordings, **Toscanini** and the NBC Symphony give their usual X-ray insight into the score with tremendous energy and precious little erotic languor (RCA). **Mengelberg** and the Concertgebouw play with surprising restraint (by Mengelberg's standards), lovely color, and intelligence in the fastest (but by no means brisk-sounding) account on CD (Biddulph). **Coppola** and an anonymous Parisian orchestra play with energy and passion (Lys 295/7, 3CD). **Stokowski** and the Philadelphia recorded the work in 1940 (Biddulph 013) This is a very languid reading, and his interpretation would change considerably in just three years, becoming more dramatic. He and the NBC Symphony recorded the *Prélude* in concert in 1943 (♦Cala 0526). There is unparalleled concentration here, and through extreme contrasts of tempo and dynamics, the logic and structure of the work are elucidated more clearly than in any other performance. The long, swooping portamentos in the strings hark back to an older, more authentic performing tradition. It's the finest *Prélude* on CD.

Première Rapsodie for Clarinet and Orchestra. This piece was composed as a competition piece for the Paris Conservatoire in 1909–10 and orchestrated in 1911. **James Campbell** and the Philharmonia under Geoffrey Simon get failing marks for a lack of propulsion (Cala). **Franklin Cohen**, accompanied by the Cleveland Orchestra under Boulez, produces ravishing sounds, but he and Boulez wander through the score aimlessly, the ending coming as a surprise rather than a climax (DG). **Sabine Meyer** and the Berlin Philharmonic conducted by Abbado sound beautiful (♦EMI 56832), but Meyer doesn't sound as gorgeous as Cohen. The middle of the piece is more animated here, and the fast section near the end is more piquant—thus the ending makes sense—and the Concertgebouw under Haitink aren't as animated as Meyer and Abbado, but they clarify the structure of the piece and the sections flow naturally into one another (Philips 438742). **V. Krasavin** and the Leningrad Philharmonic under Mravinsky give a bold, Fauvist reading, with strong contrasts of dynamics and tone colors (♦Russian Disc 11159). This concert recording isn't quite note-perfect, but it's spontaneous and strongly felt. **Gaston Hamelin** recorded the *Rapsodie* in 1931 with an anonymous orchestra under Coppola's direction (♦Lys 295/7, 3CD). The results are like the *Saxophone Rhapsody*—splashy rather than subtle and perfumed, but not as bold as Krasavin and Mravinsky.

Rapsodie for Saxophone and Orchestra. Modern performers have done poor service to this work. **Kenneth Radnofsky** and Masur play with little momentum, but do manage to give the various sections some character (Teldec). Radnofsky's impure, soft-grained tone and wobbly

vibrato are probably not what Debussy was used to hearing. **John Harle**'s account with Marriner is positively soporific (EMI). Those sections that aren't dull are reminiscent of a 1950s Hollywood Biblical epic soundtrack. To his credit, Harle does have a pure tone and a restrained vibrato.

Maurice Viard recorded the work around 1930 with a pickup orchestra led by Coppola (♦Pearl 9348; ♦Lys 295/7, 3CD). It's as different from the modern recordings as night from day. Viard's powerful, ringing tone and very fast, pulsing vibrato of unvarying speed and amplitude should sound familiar to connoisseurs of early jazz recordings. Coppola moves the music along, and the effect is very dramatic—even turbulent at times.

MAGIL

CHAMBER MUSIC

Debussy's chamber music is comparatively slight in quantity but uniformly high in quality. In 1880, the 18-year-old composer was employed as pianist in a trio that played to entertain Tchaikovsky's erstwhile patron Nadejda Von Meck, and there he wrote his *Premier Trio en Sol* (G). The score of this early effort wasn't published and performed until 1985, more than 100 years later, and there never was a Trio 2. Like many of Debussy's early works, it borders on salon music, showing the genial influence of Massenet and Schumann. It's a tuneful gumdrop of a piece, and it's not surprising that there have been quite a few recordings, mostly balanced with more substantial French piano trios. In the best of them, the **Fontenay Trio** couples it with Fauré and Ravel (Teldec 44937), the **Golub-Kaplan-Carr Trio** with Fauré and Saint-Saëns (Arabesque 6643), and the **Joachim Trio** (the most full-blooded of the three) with Ravel and Florent Schmitt (♦Naxos 550934).

The most familiar of the chamber pieces is the String Quartet, one of the masterpieces of Debussy's early maturity (before *Pelléas*). It's not exactly a youthful work (he was 30 when he wrote it), but it's still fresh and striking, "so vigorous, so thoughtful in its passion," according to a contemporary critic. Every string quartet performs it, and just about every famous group has committed it to disc; it's invariably coupled with the Ravel Quartet, and I have yet to hear a recording that really messes them up.

Among the outstanding performances is the second **Juilliard Quartet** recording; their sure ensemble and fine-grained tone sound very legitimately French, even more convincing than in the Ravel (Sony 52554, with a stunning performance of the challenging Dutilleux quartet *Ainsi la nuit*). Others worth hearing are performances by the late-lamented **Cleveland Quartet** (Telarc 80111), **Emerson Quartet** (DG 445509)— excellent performances from the '70s, very early in the group's career— and **Carmina Quartet** (Denon 75164). If you're on a budget, the **Kodály Quartet** (♦Naxos 550249, also including Ravel's delectable *Introduction and Allegro*) is as satisfying as most of the high-priced ensembles. A vintage '70s **Tokyo Quartet** coupling of Debussy and Ravel is at a bargain price (♦Sony 62413, with Fauré's beautiful Piano Trio).

Apart from the string quartet, Debussy's most enduring contributions to chamber music are three sonatas he wrote at the very end of his life: in 1915, for cello and for flute, viola, and harp, and in 1917 for violin. He was desperately ill with cancer, and France was embroiled in WWI. He saw writing these sonatas as a patriotic act, an affirmation of French musical virtues of clarity and simplicity (his name on the title page is followed by the description "musicien français"). The Cello Sonata is a bit unusual for Debussy in its elliptical, rather sarcastic vein of humor; the lyrical effusions of most cello works are few and far between. The Flute, Viola, and Harp Sonata was originally planned with oboe rather than harp, until Debussy had the happy inspiration of substituting the stringed instrument to create a delicious, brand-new (and much-imitated) sound. This is perhaps the most "neoclassical" of the sonatas, elegant and melancholy. The Violin Sonata was torn from Debussy almost note by note in the last months of his life. The most passionate and violent of the three, it suggested to Debussy's biographer Leon Vallas "a fight for life, a struggle against death."

These are all rewarding works, and among the many recordings, I recommend getting all three at once, since they fit neatly on a single CD (with room to spare). The recordings by members of the **Athena Ensemble** (♦Chandos 8345), **La Follia Ensemble** (♦Calliope 9837), and **Nash Ensemble** (♦Virgin 61427, 2CD) are all easily recommendable. They all contain Debussy's famous flute solo *Syrinx;* the Nash Ensemble's set offers a good collection of Ravel vocal and instrumental chamber music as well, an excellent value. Of special interest is a collection of recordings from the '30s by such fabled French musicians of the generation after Debussy's as flutist Marcel Moyse, cellist Maurice Maréchal, violinist Jacques Thibaud, and pianist Robert Casadesus (Pearl 9348).

There are also plenty of individual recordings of all three sonatas by outstanding virtuosos, in the context of mixed recital programs. **Rostropovich** and **Britten**'s recording of the Cello Sonata is as controversial at it is famous, but it's also wonderfully intense and imaginative (London 452995). The early '60s recording by **Starker** and **Sebok** is a good, straightforward alternative, accompanied by an interesting assortment of pieces by Mendelssohn, Martinů, Bartók and others, all beautifully played (Mercury 434358).

The Sonata for Flute, Viola, and Harp is exquisitely presented in two English recordings with other French chamber works with harp: a vintage "Classic Sound" version by the **Melos Ensemble** (♦London 452891, with one of the best recordings of Ravel's *Introduction and Allegro* and pieces by Roussel and Guy Ropartz), and a more recent performance by **Stephen Shingles** and friends that contains Saint-Saëns's appealing and surprisingly substantial *Fantasy for Violin and Harp* as well as the Ravel and Roussel pieces (♦Chandos 8621).

Debussy's difficult but rewarding violin sonata has been by far the most popular of his three late sonatas among violinists. Most present it in a French recital, as a kind of musical sorbet to clear the palate after Franck, Ravel, or Fauré. Many virtuosos have recorded it, and if the recital format attracts you, you'll be very happy with **Zukerman** and Neikrug (RCA 62697), **Mutter** and Orkis (DG 445826), **Chung** and Lupu (London 421154), **Dong-Suk Kang** and Pascal Devoyon (Naxos 550276, a passionate performance at a bargain price), or **Chee-Yun** and Akira Eguchi (Denon 75625). One historic recording is an absolute classic: a live Library of Congress performance from 1940 by **Szigeti** and Bartók, considered by many to be unsurpassed by any modern version in its strength and intensity (♦Vanguard 8008, with works by Bartók and Beethoven).

Finally, you can go whole hog with a beautiful 3CD set of all Debussy's chamber music played by artists associated with the **Chamber Music Society of Lincoln Center** (♦Delos 3167). Not only will you get performances of the great compositions that are as good as any (the musicians here include flutist Ransom Wilson, harpist Nancy Allen, cellist Fred Sherry, and violinist Ani Kavafian), you can make the acquaintance of pleasant rarities like Debussy's pieces for clarinet, beautifully played by David Shifrin, and the works for two pianos or piano four hands played, by Lee Luvisi and Anne Marie McDermott.

PIANO MUSIC

"French music is clearness, elegance, simple and natural declamation," Debussy wrote. "[It] aims first of all to give pleasure." And there is prob-

ably no more purely pleasurable body of piano music than Debussy's, unique in its combination of revolutionary harmonic and formal ideas, technical challenges, and ear appeal. He spoke naturally through the piano, and wrote music for it throughout his career.

The early pieces from the 1880s and 1890s hardly rank with the greatest Debussy, but their charm and melodious suavity, in the French tradition of Delibes and Massenet, are hard to resist. The most famous are probably the two *Arabesques* (1888), much recorded in the original version and in arrangements for guitars, marimbas, and much more. *Suite Bergamasque* (1890) contains the famous *Clair de lune,* a beautiful bit of moonlit Impressionist painting tucked among three neoclassical dance movements. (Many of Debussy's most popular pieces are embedded in his piano suites.) You can hear *Pour le Piano* (1896–1901) as a three-movement love letter to the instrument; it contains some of his most sonorously beautiful keyboard writing. Debussy wrote much of his greatest music—two sets of *Estampes, Images, L'Isle joyeuse,* and the two sets of *Préludes*—in the first years of the 20th century. The great series ended with two of his most visionary works, the Etudes (1912) and the suite *En blanc et noir* (1915).

Among complete sets, **Gieseking** will probably never be surpassed (♦EMI 65855). These early '50s performances set the standard and are still required listening for pianists or Debussyists. Because of them, Gieseking became almost completely identified with the composer. He took Debussy's call for an "instrument without hammers" very seriously. His delicacy and spectrum of colors are phenomenal, and he's infinitely refined without ever seeming inert. The salon-like early pieces are deliciously charming and nonchalant, while extroverted pieces like *Masques* and *L'Isle joyeuse* are almost violent in their concentrated energy. He seldom lingers over anything; for example, his *Des pas sur la neige* (*Préludes* I) is two minutes shorter than Paul Jacobs's.

These performances do have their share of finger flubs (he apparently found the Etudes as demanding as every other pianist), but Gieseking realized that the essential thing in playing Debussy is mastery of the pedal and the shadings it can create. There he is unsurpassed in creating soft-edged, luminous effects. The set is especially treasurable for his loving readings of the short single pieces that few pianists play, such as *Marche Ecossaise, Berceuse Héroique,* and the tiny *Hommage à Haydn.* The one caveat is the sound. For their 1995 reissue of this essential set, EMI cleaned it up as much as humanly or digitally possible. It's still sufficient to give a sense of the remarkable range of colors Gieseking commanded. If four CDs are too much, his *Préludes* are available in a separate "Great Recordings of the Century" disc (EMI 61004).

The most recommendable complete set in stereo is a bit of a surprise: strong and colorful performances by the Scottish pianist **Gordon Fergus-Thompson** (♦ASV 432). The prolific **Martin Jones** provides a very reasonably priced set, and the swimming, reverberant "Nimbus Sound" suits Debussy better than some composers (Nimbus 1773). **Peter Frankl** is pleasant and competent, just not very inspiring, although his set provides a lot of music at a bargain price and is a good introduction (Vox 5062, 3CD).

Estampes (1903) and the two sets of *Images* (1905–07), in the tripartite form Debussy favored for piano suites, are among his most popular pieces. Most pianists record them, or selections from them, at one time or another, but possibly the most beautiful coupling is by **Moravec**, whose sound is gorgeous but disciplined (extremely well recorded too), and whose interpretations are pretty much flawless to my ear. His *Soirée dans Grenade* is irresistible and truly Spanish, sexy and slightly haughty. This is Debussy playing as fine as any available. Moravec's Debussy was available in a super-cheap Vox disc (9005), now out of print; currently it's in ♦Vox 5103 (3CD, with a single *Prélude, Des pas sur la neige,* in an exquisitely desolate reading, and an excellent Chopin selection), but it's worth it.

Another strongly recommended set of *Images* and *Estampes* is by **Paul Jacobs** (♦Nonesuch 71365). You'll find his name several times in this article, and you can't do much better than his late-'70s Debussy recordings. He includes the first recording of *Images Oubliées,* an 1894 work that was discovered and published in 1978. It's a substantial work in its own right and a foretaste of keyboard glories to come. **Richter,** who could be incomparable in Debussy, recorded both several times; the best are probably a 1962 *Estampes* (DG 457667), a 1972 *Images I* (♦Doremi 7766, with a delicious *Hommage á Haydn* and a splendid *L'Isle joyeuse*), and a 1961 *Images II* (BBCL 4021).

Children's Corner Suite is one of Debussy's best-loved piano works (1906–08), a collection of nursery vignettes for his daughter Emma, written with a witty adult sensibility (for example, the parody of keyboard exercises in the opening "Doctor Gradus ad Parnassum" or the sudden appearance of *Tristan und Isolde* in "Golliwog's Cakewalk"). **Gieseking**'s performance in his complete set is charming and poetic; **Entremont** is more muscular and straightforward, but satisfying (Sony 48174, a well-planned recital that's recommendable if you want only one Debussy piano disc). The venerable **Horszowski** recorded the suite when he was 94, a remarkable performance that gives the music the poetry and density of Schumann (Nonesuch 79160, with pieces by Mozart, Beethoven, and Chopin).

The splashy large-scale *L'Isle joyeuse*—inspired by a trip to England with his mistress—is an oddity among Debussy's piano suites and collections. Well-performed, it's irresistibly propulsive and colorful. **Gieseking**'s performance is coruscating if not well-recorded; in **Weissenberg**'s masterly but icy performance, the island is apparently Greenland (DG 445567); **Thibaudet** is much more appealing (London 52022, a commodious 2CD package including *Préludes, Estampes,* and *Pour le Piano*). Maybe the best is **Richter,** in two separate live performances from 1992 (♦Live Classics 481).

When Copland called Debussy's music "poetry of the bourgeois," he may have had the two sets of *Préludes* in mind. Taken together, these 24 pieces, written from 1910–13 at the height of Debussy's career, are musical snapshots of different aspects of his physical and intellectual world, and a leisured, sensual one it was, as these imaginative little portraits of sailboats, heather, Dickens's Mr. Pickwick, fireworks, and girls with flaxen hair demonstrate.

There are a bewildering number of complete sets of *Préludes* available. A few stand out: **Jacobs**'s recording was greeted rapturously when it first appeared in the '70s, and is still outstanding (Nonesuch 73031). He had a fine structural sense as well as a delicate touch, and his *Préludes* hang together even when he takes very deliberate tempos. *La jeune fille aux cheveux de lin* is perfectly simple and natural, and he goes to town—in a very controlled way—in *Feux d'artifice* (Fireworks) and *Ce qu'a vu le vent d'ouest* (What the West Wind Saw).

What Jacobs's *Préludes* was to the '70s, **Zimerman**'s was to the '90s (♦DG 435773). If anything, I like it better; his always-thoughtful playing is technically flawless, his sound is utterly finished, and the "interpretations" don't seem like interpretations, but are so finely judged as to seem completely natural. His precise playing (e.g., the deliciously witty grace notes in *Minstrels*) and the care with which he voices chords so that every note is heard reveal what many other pianists don't: The *Préludes* are not only beautiful music but frequently revolutionary in harmonies

and timbres. Of secondary importance, perhaps, but offering plenty of poetry and musical pleasure (at a considerably lower price than Zimerman) is the 1985 set by the sorely missed **Egorov** (Classics for Pleasure 4805).

Like Chopin, whose music Debussy had edited just before he wrote his Etudes, these "studies" far transcend their educational purposes; many of them break new musical paths other composers didn't follow for several decades. The best contemporary recording is generally held to be **Uchida**'s magisterial performance, in which technical difficulties are forgotten and the musical quality of these pieces shines through (♦Philips 22412). Her main competition comes from **Jacobs,** technically polished and perhaps even more poetic (Nonesuch 79161). **Pollini** is technically impressive but basically uninvolving (DG); **Ohlsson** (in unfamiliar territory for him) is more satisfying (Arabesque 6601). Uchida's disc has no coupling, but the other three do, if this is a factor: Ohlsson *Suite Bergamasque,* Pollini an imaginative choice in Berg's Sonata Op. 1, and Jacobs *En blanc et noir* with Kalish.

Contemporary pianists tend to play the great Debussy sets as sets, although the composer probably expected them to pick and choose. That was also the attitude of older generations, whose Debussy recordings usually consist of bits and pieces, an Etude here or a couple of the more accessible *Préludes* there. (**Cortot,** who recorded both sets of *Préludes,* was an exception; his fascinating 1929–32 recordings are available in Enterprise 269.)

Of the two most famous 20th-century pianists, **Horowitz** recorded only one *Prélude* and one Etude; their chilly brilliance makes me glad he left it at that (Sony 53471). **Rubinstein,** on the other hand, recorded several of the best-known items (mostly from *Images* and *Estampes*) in the '40s. They are very enjoyable despite their thin, tinny sound, showing him to have been a colorful performer and sensitive (but not spineless) interpreter of this composer (♦RCA 61446, with French piano music by Ravel, Poulenc, and others). His performance of the slow waltz *La plus que lente* is one of the most deliciously swoony on records.

Fans of **Cliburn** will enjoy his collection of odds and ends, mostly recorded in the early '70s, including many of the most popular pieces; the most substantial is *L'Isle joyeuse* (RCA 63567). There's power when needed and some lovely shadings and colors, but this pianist and this composer don't strike me as an ideal match. More satisfying are the '50s recordings by the magisterial **Firkušný,** reissued in the "Firkušný Edition" (♦EMI 66067, 2CD). The set contains a charming *Children's Corner Suite* and *Suite Bergamasque* and an elegant *Estampes,* with some shorter pieces including a very poetic *Cathédrale engloutie;* ♦EMI 66069 contains a few *Préludes* and an aristocratic *La plus que lente,* filler for Smetana's delightful Czech Polkas and Dances. The mono sound is much better than Gieseking's, and even if you already have some of the complete sets, these are very desirable.

Debussy's playing on the piano rolls he made in 1913 show his command of the delicate colors and fluid tempo relationships needed to make his music work; they're the very definition of Impressionism. He recorded quite a few items, including a complete *Children's Corner Suite* and several *Préludes* (his *Cathédrale engloutie* is instructive, as his tempos differ significantly in places from the printed score). These are unfortunately NA. A fascinating hint of how his music sounded to contemporary pianists is heard in early recordings by **Rubinstein, Grainger,** the noted Debussy specialist **E. Robert Schmitz,** and many more (♦Nimbus 8807). Noisy sound but engrossing listening.

Debussy also enriched the four-hand and two-piano repertoire, the first at the beginning of his career, with *Petite Suite* (1889), one of those early Debussy works that gives few signs of the original genius to come but makes tuneful, delightful listening, as its plentiful recordings attest. (There is an equally popular orchestration of *Petite Suite* by Henri Büsser.) Debussy's four-hand masterpiece is one of his last works, *En blanc et noir* (1915). Like its contemporaries, the three chamber sonatas, this suite is very original structurally and harmonically, also emotionally intense, almost anguished in tone. The **Jacobs/Kalish** performance is full of color and contrasts (Nonesuch 79161, with the Etudes); the **Labeque Sisters** are more brilliantly virtuosic and more brightly recorded, and their disc contains other two-piano music, including the chaste *Epigraphes Antiques, Petite Suite,* and the composer's transcription of his orchestral *Nocturnes* (Philips 454471). **Cyril Scott** and **Stephen Coombs** present all of Debussy's music for two pianos; besides *En blanc et noir* and *Nocturnes,* there is a transcription of *Prelude to the Afternoon of a Faun* (Hyperion 55014). An interesting pendant to Debussy's two-piano works are his arrangements of pieces by Schumann, Tchaikovsky, Wagner, and other composers whose music was important to him; played by **Blumenthal** and **Groslot**, these are interesting for Debussyists as a glimpse into his workshop (Marco Polo 223378).　　　　　　　　　　　　　　　　　　　　RAYMOND

CHORAL MUSIC

La Damoiselle élue (The Blessed Damsel). Debussy composed this ravishing, heartbreaking work in piano score in 1893 and orchestrated it in 1902. It's a setting for two women's voices, women's chorus, and orchestra of portions of a poem by Dante Gabriel Rossetti that deals with a young woman's soul, recently arrived in heaven, yearning for her earthly lover.

Ozawa and the Boston Symphony, with Suzanne Mentzer and Von Stade, give an ecstatic, tonally ravishing reading (♦Sony 63244, 2CD). **Salonen** and the Los Angeles Philharmonic are a little cooler and clearer, and Upshaw's highly nuanced singing brilliantly elucidates the text, though she lacks Von Stade's impact in the lower register (Sony 58952). **Jean-Claude Casadesus** and Mireille Delünsch are close to Salonen et al. in approach but lack their emotional commitment (Harmonia Mundi). The finest version, blessed with excellent sound, is again by **Ozawa** and the Boston, but this time the narrator is Susan Graham and the damsel is the magnificent McNair, who has the virtues of Von Stade and Upshaw in spades (♦Philips 446682). Her virtuoso vocalism and the intelligent, sensuous way she caresses each syllable make this a spellbinding performance.

Pianist **Philippe Cassard,** with mezzo-soprano Doris Lamprecht, soprano Véronique Dietschy, and the Solistes des Choeurs de Lyon, have recorded the 1902 revised version of the score for piano and voices (Adès 204652). The recording is wonderfully clear and present, Cassard is a very sensitive pianist, and the chorus and soloists are very good. Those who wish to hear the voices with extra clarity may find this version attractive.

Coppola recorded the work in 1934 with the Orchestre Pasdeloup, the Women's Chorus of the Chorale St. Gervais, Odette Ricquier, and Jeanne Guyla (Lys 295/7, 3CD). It's not one of the most moving performances, but it's instructive to hear this music sung by Francophones performing so close to Debussy's time.

Inghelbrecht recorded the work in the mid-'50s with the Orchestre du Théâtre des Champs Élysées, Madeleine Gorge as the damsel, and Jacqueline Joly as the narrator. He doesn't try to highlight every detail in the score, but he effectively supports Gorge in the more emotional moments. She isn't the prettiest-sounding damsel, but she has the peculiar

virtue of sounding the most determined. She lets the listener feel that she has the single-minded purpose of reuniting with her beloved, and if she must confront the Queen of Heaven fresh upon her arrival in the afterlife to do so, so be it!

Jean Fournet and the Orchestre de la Société des Concerts du Conservatoire, with the Chorale Elizabeth Brasseur and Janine Collard as the narrator and Janine Micheau as the damsel, recorded the work in 1952 (♦London 448151, NA). Micheau's and Collard's vibratos are a bit wider than I like, but they're very expressive, and Fournet is by far the best conductor in this work. He really caresses each phrase and uses the orchestra to underscore the meaning of the text. The orchestra has a very French sound and plays ecstatically.

There is an excellent 1940 concert recording of **Toscanini** leading the NBC Symphony with alto Hertha Glatz as the narrator and soprano Jarmila Novotna as the damsel (♦Grammofono 2000 78772). Although not quite as nuanced as Fournet's, it's still an excellent reading, and Toscanini's direction is ecstatic without being as driven as it often is. The find here is Novotna, who has a remarkably powerful, secure, yet pure voice, with a timbre reminiscent of Welitsch.　　　　　　　　MAGIL

PELLÉAS ET MÉLISANDE

Debussy's only complete opera has been recorded many times since the 1942 release of **Désormière**'s fine rendition that had Irène Joachim and Jacques Jansen as the doomed lovers (Arkadia 78018). That is now a classic and some critics claim it has never been surpassed. But this work, with its mysterious and ethereal orchestral and vocal utterances, needs better sound to reveal its many beauties. Some modern recordings emphasize the orchestra's work, notably those conducted by **Abbado** (♦DG 435344), **Karajan** (♦EMI 49350), and **Boulez** (Sony). By contrast, those led by **Dutoit** (London) and **Jordan** (Erato) pay more attention to the words, which may be what the composer had in mind when he asked that the singers' declamation be half-sung and half-spoken. Still, it's difficult to resist the sound of a world-class orchestra playing this gorgeous score, as is the case in the EMI and DG sets.

As for the casts, Abbado and Karajan share the best Golaud (van Dam), but the latter has the advantage of Von Stade and Stilwell in the title roles. In the DG set, Maria Ewing's odd vocalism is sometimes hard to take, while her partner, François LeRoux, has the high, lyric baritone that's appropriate for the part, though the basic quality of his voice is not very appealing. The Erato release has a lightweight trio of protagonists, and so does the London set; in both, the orchestra is quite subordinate to the singers. In neither of those sets does the orchestra play as well nor are its singers very appealing, so my recommendation is the EMI release with the DG version as a fine alternate. For those averse to orchestral splendor in this work, the Erato set may be the best choice.　　MOSES

SONGS

Debussy's songs were a constant in his composing career and contain some of his most adventurous music. His response to Baudelaire and Mallarmé was as imaginative and subtle as Schumann or Wolf to Goethe and Eichendorff. The later the songs, the more elusively beautiful they are, pure examples of what baritone Pierre Bernac, one of their greatest interpreters, called "the mysterious alloy of music and poetry." They yield their secrets slowly, and listeners who delve into the French texts Debussy set so carefully for prosody and mood will get the most out of them.

There are surprisingly few full discs of Debussy songs; many well-known singers record a few favorites in a recital, and that's it. There was an EMI "complete" edition, apparently NA, which like most such is actually not complete, leaving out quite a few of the early songs. Other than that, it was one of the best efforts in the EMI series devoted to French song composers; the singers include **Souzay,** Ameling, Michèle Command, and Von Stade. Souzay's performances are the cream of the crop. Recorded in 1971 with the equally authoritative Dalton Baldwin, these performances, coupled with Ravel songs, were once available on EMI 63112, but it's almost worth seeking out the 3CD set to get them. These relatively late songs—*Rondels de Charles d'Orléans* (1904), *Ballades de Villon* (1910), and the tiny cycle *Le Promenoir des deux amants* (1910)—are among Debussy's most appealing, and might have been tailor-made for Souzay's admirably controlled, quintessentially French voice.

Debussy wrote his first song, *Nuit d'étoiles,* at the age of 14 in 1876, and his most famous, *Beau Soir,* at 15 or 16. Several years later came the 12 songs (and one duet) of *Receuil Vasnier,* written for Marie-Blanche Vasnier. The young composer-accompanist was infatuated with this beautiful coloratura soprano, and it shows. The Vasnier songs are much more conventional than most mature Debussy, but also much more direct, melodious, and romantic. (They also call for some high-flying flights of coloratura, in contrast to the *parlando* style of Debussy's later songs.) In a very full Debussy collection that features the first complete recording of the Vasnier songs, **Upshaw,** accompanied by James Levine, is in spectacular voice, offering vocal splendors seldom encountered among Debussy interpreters (♦Sony 67190). Her vibrant style rescues some of the early songs from banality and gives a fresh shine to the later, more familiar ones.

In striking contrast to Upshaw's directness (but no less effective) is the highly cultivated art of the great American mezzo **de Gaetani,** whose singing of *Fêtes galantes* and *Chansons de Bilitis* with Gilbert Kalish is the high point of a CD collecting her 1980s recordings of French songs, including Ravel's *Histoires naturelles* and eight by Chausson (♦Arabesque 6673). De Gaetani's voice sounds much better than it did in the original Nonesuch LPs—sometimes forced on loud sustained notes, but otherwise exquisitely precise in tuning. And the style, calm and cool on the outside, hot underneath, works beautifully in conveying the "amorous melancholy" (Bernac) of the bewitching combination of words and music in these cycles. The most beautiful example is her reading of "*Colloque sentimental,*" the concluding song of *Chansons de Bilitis.* It couldn't be better, capturing its dry-eyed but poetic desperation to a T. ("This is the kind of song on which one can spend a lifetime," said Bernac.)

Hendricks is another vibrant soprano interpreter in a collection with Béroff (EMI 47888). An appealing disc by soprano **Valente** and Lydia Artymiw pairs favorite songs by Debussy (such as *Beau Soir, Clair de lune,* and *Ariettes oubliées*) with familiar songs by Fauré (Centaur 2220). **Stutzmann** brings a rich contralto voice and elegant style to *Ariettes oubliées,* Baudelaire songs, and *Chansons de Bilitis* (RCA 60899, with Ravel's *Histoires naturelles*).

For the *Proses Lyriques* of 1892–1893, Debussy wrote both words and music. This long, dramatic cycle is seldom recorded, but there's a very effective version by the British mezzo **Della Jones,** accompanied by Malcolm Martineau, the centerpiece of an excellent French recital (Chandos 9147). Given the close relationship of text and music in Debussy's songs, it helps to have a singer who is a native French speaker; witness the very good collections by Canadian soprano **Claudette Leblanc** with Valerie Tryon (Unicorn 9133) and French soprano **Anne Marie Rodde** with a noted Debussy keyboard stylist, Noël Lee (Etcetera 1026). And the great **Bernac** spent a good part of his life on these and

other French songs; his historically important collection is on Testament 3161 (3CD). RAYMOND

Léo Delibes *(1836–1891)*

Tchaikovsky thought well enough of Delibes's ballet *Sylvia* to compare it favorably to his own *Swan Lake.* Posterity has treated Tchaikovsky's ballet scores more kindly, however, and *Coppélia* and *Sylvia* are seldom presented as evening-length entertainments any more. Suites from the two remain popular at pops concerts and on disc, however, and they usually come hand in hand. A special place must be reserved for **Monteux,** who recorded them at the end of 1953 (♦RCA 61975). His experience as a ballet conductor gives his recording a little extra bounce. While his are uncommonly graceful renditions of this music, they never mince. Furthermore, his selections are generous (six excerpts each), and he includes the tasty "Pas de Ethiopiens" from *Sylvia,* which many other conductors omit.

Robert Irving, another experienced ballet conductor, brings similar benefits to his grander-scaled 1960 recordings (♦Royal Classics 701182). **Ormandy** presents truncated versions of the suites, and while he's infectious in the famous "Valse lente" from *Sylvia* (not too "lente" here, actually), he's a little too big for Delibes's elusive charms (Sony 46550). **Lenárd** gives us five selections from *Coppélia,* four from *Sylvia,* plus (enterprisingly) excerpts from *La Source* and other music (Naxos 550080). There's nothing terribly wrong with the performances, but they're middle-European—more *gulyás* than soufflé.

Karajan is very suave in excerpts from *Coppélia,* although perhaps too self-regarding, and his set of ballet music by various composers is not a good value for those most interested in Delibes (DG 459445, 2CD). A generous selection—about 75 minutes from each ballet—has been drawn from recordings by **Jean-Baptiste Mari,** whose view of these scores is also more grand than gracious, but still well within the French tradition (EMI 67208, 2CD). Another conductor to give us more than the usual excerpts from *Coppélia* is **Mark Ermler,** who included about two-thirds of the ballet in a single 74-minute CD (Conifer 16192). His experience as Chief Guest Conductor of the Royal Ballet of Covent Garden assists him in giving the score a danceable lift, although he's less imaginative than Monteux and more relaxed than Irving.

None of the more or less complete recordings of the two ballets persuades me that these scores are without their longueurs; *Sylvia* can seem endless. Fortunately, all recordings are reissued bargains. Mercury invited veteran ballet conductors to record them in the 1950s: *Sylvia* with **Fistoulari** and *Coppélia* with **Dorati** (434313, 3CD). Both readings are athletic and straightforward; the music pleases but seldom fascinates, and Dorati's orchestra is a little coarse. **Zinman's** recording of *Coppélia* wears its years lightly but is rather bland (Philips 438763, 2CD).

Bonynge's versions of the two—with *La Source* thrown in—have been reissued in an inexpensive box (Decca 460418, 4CD). He likes spectacle but sometimes lacks imagination; his musicians are excellent, and this is a good value. Also good value, and my first choice among all the complete recordings, is **Andrew Mogrelia** (♦Naxos 553356/7, 2CD, *Coppélia* and *La Source;* ♦553338/9, 2CD, *Sylvia*). Avoiding sumptuousness, he's graceful, sparkling, and at times even sly, and his affection for this music is obvious. Comprehensive excerpts from these recordings are also available on a single disc (♦Naxos 554062).

Lakmé deserves more attention than it receives; this opera is far more than the "Bell Song" and the pretty duet for Lakmé and her companion Mallika made popular in movies and advertisements. It's French opera at its finest, almost as good as *Carmen* and certainly on a par with

Manon. In the '50s, the stratospheric **Mado Robin,** very French and girlish, recorded the role, but alas, her superior version has not been transferred to CD (Decca/London). **Mesplé,** in many ways Robin's successor, used her lightweight voice to good effect, and her fellow cast members are at least idiomatic, which counts for a lot in this opera (EMI 49430; highlights on 63447). **Sutherland**'s more mature singing doesn't disqualify her, but her mushy French and generalized interpretation drain some of the charm from the score, in spite of a good tenor and baritone in Vanzo and Bacquier (London 425485).

Natalie Dessay rejects coloratura twittering and makes the little priestess into a flesh and blood character (♦EMI 56569). Although her voice isn't distinctive, she's an admirably intelligent singer. As Gerald, Kunde is a little taxed, but he sings with sincerity, and veteran van Dam scores points as Nilakantha. Plasson's conducting is caring and knowledgeable. Finally, a highlights disc recorded between 1928 and 1936 opens a fascinating window into performance style before World War II (Malibran 110). **Germaine Feraldy**'s Lakmé, chic but human, is a classic. The transfers are a bit noisy, but the music can be heard.

TUTTLE

Frederick Delius (1862–1934)

Delius was more cosmopolitan than his British origin and reputation might suggest. Born in Yorkshire to German parents, he lived at various times in France, Germany, Norway, even Florida, and his music shows all these influences. At its best, the result is a uniquely poetic, even pantheistic, evocation of nature and the transience of life. But it hasn't always appealed to everyone, be they audiences or musicians. In fact, at this writing the catalog is as notable for what isn't there as what is, especially when it comes to the operas, songs and concertos.

ORCHESTRAL MUSIC

Beecham championed Delius's music with a fervor unparalleled before or since, so much so that his set of the orchestral music, plus *Songs of Sunset*—presenting all his commercial stereo recordings of Delius—is still the best introduction to this composer's art (♦EMI 47509, 2CD). These are still among the most satisfying recordings of *Brigg Fair, A Song Before Sunrise, Over the Hills and Far Away, On Hearing the First Cuckoo in Spring, Summer Night on the River, Summer Evening, Florida Suite, Dance Rhapsody* 2 and the early and delightful *Winternacht* (or *Sleigh Ride*). The miniature tone poems in particular are remarkable for their buoyancy and nuanced sense of line. No wonder Eric Fenby, the composer's amanuensis in his final years, wrote of Beecham that "no other conductor has yet surpassed him in conjuring up to sheer perfection the hidden beauties of Delius's scripts."

That this ability predated the stereo era may be heard in two more Beecham CDs containing, among other things, the first and in many ways still the best *Appalachia,* from 1938 (♦Dutton 7011), and the two *Dance Rhapsodies* and a *Brigg Fair* from 1946 that is in some ways even finer than its successor (♦Dutton 7028), though not so much as to warrant giving up stereo. Ditto his 1950 *Over the Hills and Far Away,* once available on Sony, as were his LP-era *Paris, Eventyr, North Country Sketches, Sea Drift* and incidental music for *Hassan.* His 78 rpm recordings of many of these pieces have been reissued in three low-priced CDs (Naxos).

Another long-time Delius advocate was **Barbirolli,** many of whose later recordings have likewise been collected (♦EMI 65119, 2CD). Ardent and impassioned, he presides over deeply felt but sometimes overly expansive renditions of *Brigg Fair, Appalachia, In a Summer Gar-*

den, *First Cuckoo, Summer Night on the River, A Song Before Sunrise* and other shorter pieces, as well as a number of arrangements from the Fenby years (e.g., *La Calinda,* the *Fennimore and Gerda* Intermezzo, and *Late Swallows*). In the absence of Hickox's London CD, this is probably the best of the stereo *Appalachias,* with its elevated poetry and exalted climaxes. Nor would one want to be without his equally exalted *Song of Summer* and rapturous "Walk to the Paradise Garden" (from *A Village Romeo and Juliet*).

Still luxuriant but not as deliberate in tempo, "Walk to the Paradise Garden" figures in another Barbirolli collection that includes similarly less protracted accounts of *First Cuckoo,* the *Irmelin* Prelude and *Fennimore and Gerda* Intermezzo, along with the only available *Idyll* (reworked from the unsuccessful opera *Margot la Rouge*)(♦Dutton 1005). Appended to these are earlier mono recordings of *Song of Summer, Two Aquarelles* (arranged from the wordless part-songs) and *A Song Before Sunris;* here, if anything, he's a bit too fast, probably to get it all on a single 78 rpm side. There's also a CD of **Anthony Collins**'s mono LPs, including *Paris* and *Brigg Fair,* lacking only that special Beecham magic (Dutton).

One who experienced that magic first-hand was **Norman Del Mar,** at one time Beecham's assistant. Maybe that's why this magic is sometimes present in his performances in a disc of shorter pieces with an especially lovely *First Cuckoo* and some Fenby arrangements (♦Chandos 6502). If you're interested in how an ultra-lush, big-orchestra approach works in these fragile essays, there's always **Ormandy,** undeniably opulent but a bit heavy in spirit and sound (Sony).

Among the present generation, **Handley** and **Hickox** have proven themselves sympathetic Delians on any number of occasions. Witness Handley's "Delius Orchestral Works," with its warmly radiant *First Cuckoo* and gorgeous *La Calinda* (♦EMI 4304). The same is true for his fanciful yet lovingly detailed *Eventyr* (Delius's evocation of Norwegian folk tales) in a disc that also includes *Brigg Fair, In a Summer Garden* and *A Song of Summer* (♦EMI 4568). **Myer Fredman** offers an even more evocative *Brigg Fair,* with perhaps overly spacious accounts of *Eventyr* and *Paris,* for about half the price (Naxos 553001). Compare that to **Andrew Davis**'s full-tariff disc of *Brigg Fair* and *Paris* among other pieces (Teldec 90845), which manages to be more incisive in the nocturnal portrait of the latter but less compelling than the strength and sensitivity of Collins, not to mention the darkly scintillating Beecham (♦Naxos 119094).

La Calinda comes from both the American slave opera *Koanga* and the even earlier *Florida Suite,* which Handley has also recorded with one of the better *North Country Sketches* (♦Chandos 8413). It's a shrouded, remote landscape he conjures up in the latter, more so than the similarly dark but somewhat more immediate Hickox does (e.g., his more animated "Dance" (also Chandos). Handley's *Florida Suite,* however, must bow to **Boughton**'s, a wonderfully rhapsodic performance that really blossoms in the climaxes (♦Nimbus 5208), and **David Lloyd-Jones,** a mite less open-hearted but also supple and flowing (♦Naxos 553535). Both, moreover, use Delius's original, as opposed to the somewhat tightened-up Beecham edition, with Lloyd-Jones filling out his CD with *Over the Hills and Far Away,* the final scene of *Koanga* and three discographic premieres, *Idylle Printemps, La Quadroone* and the irresistibly elfin *Scherzo;* Boughton's is filled out with *Summer Evening* and music of Vaughan Williams.

Meanwhile, on what might be termed "high-priced Naxos" (Marco Polo 220452), **John Hopkins** offers the first version of *Appalachia* (here called *American Rhapsody*), without chorus or soloist and incorporating such American tunes as "Dixie" and "Yankee Doodle," at about one-third the length, along with the only available *Paa Vidderne (On the Heights)*—sort of Delius's *Alpine Symphony*—and the only complete recording of the *Norwegian Suite,* a bit like Grieg but with an edge. Otherwise more appealing is **Ashley Lawrence**'s disc that includes not only a livelier rendition of the suite (minus the "Melodrama") but also a *Brigg Fair* preceded by a performance of the Percy Grainger–arranged folk song on which it's based (♦IMP 9128).

Mackerras also recorded *Brigg Fair* as part of a series of now-deleted Delius discs for Argo, parts of which have been reissued (♦Decca 460290, 2 CD). Smoothly flavorful, it's still an enjoyable performance, as are *In a Summer Garden,* the two *Dance Rhapsodies* and *North Country Sketches,* warmer here than either Handley or Hickox are. Mackerras's *Florida Suite* lacks lift, however, and its space might have been better used to restore his recording of the Violin Concerto with **Tasmin Little** to the catalog. (We also lost his *Village Romeo and Juliet.*)

When it comes to deletions, the biggest loss, apart from the operas, is Unicorn-Kanchana's "Delius Collection" (♦2071/7, 7CD). Here we not only had modern recordings by Fenby, Del Mar and Handley, in many cases of pieces not otherwise available; we also had the finest single disc of Delius songs, with Lott, Rolfe Johnson and Walker (Vol. 5), Ralph Holmes's lyrically subdued yet comprehending performances of the Violin Concerto (Vol. 2), *Suite* (Vol. 6), *Légende* (Vol. 7), three numbered violin sonatas (Vol. 4), and Thomas Allen's beautifully sung "Arabesque" (Vol. 6), and "Cynara" (Vol. 7).

CONCERTOS

Amazingly, the current catalog lists no recordings of the Violin Concerto, even though its history goes back a long way. In the days of 78s the great solo performance was by **Albert Sammons,** who premiered the piece both on and off records; the great accompaniment, however, was Beecham's for **Jean Pougnet** (briefly available from EMI). Since then there have been even more in stereo, including the aforementioned Ralph Holmes and Tasmin Little.

Little was also featured, with cellist **Raphael Wallfisch,** in the best recording to date of the Double Concerto in another now-deleted CD (♦EMI 2185), along with the latter's Cello Concerto—a worthy rival for **Du Pré**'s—and Mackerras's brilliant *Paris,* easily the finest since Beecham's. This leaves **Piers Lane**'s persuasive Piano Concerto (EMI 65742), though an even stronger case was made for it by **Philip Fowke** and Del Mar, another prize in Unicorn's "Delius Collection" (Vol. 2).

CHAMBER MUSIC

Though not generally remembered for his chamber music, Delius produced no fewer than four violin sonatas, one for cello and a string quartet. Together with the concertos, they reveal his often subliminal structural sense—more successful at some times than others—as well as his ability to bring an almost orchestral effulgence to a solo medium.

Tasmin Little offers all four violin sonatas in performances that are at once spirited and caring (♦Conifer 51315). However, it is the tonally more variable **Galina Heifetz** who really gets beneath the surface of the three numbered sonatas, bringing out their depth, passion, and yearning lyricism (♦Connoisseur Society 4224). Against this, **Louise Jones** seems straighter, even a bit angular at times (♦Meridian 84298/9, 2CD). But she offers not only all of Delius's music for violin and piano; in some ways her conception of Sonata 3 is also the closest to May Harrison's, the violinist to whom it was dedicated.

Until recently the violin sonatas were also available with the one-movement Cello Sonata—arguably the finest of the group—on two CDs, the first with **London Symphony** soloists (EMI) and the second the previously noted Vol. 4 in Unicorn's "Delius Collection," with Ralph Holmes, cellist **Julian Lloyd Webber** and, at the keyboard, Eric Fenby. Both are outstanding. Still, Lloyd Webber's remake is perhaps even more compelling, without giving up anything in the way of subtlety (♦Philips 454458). He also offers the rest of the music for solo cello, along with Grieg's, whose influence can be heard so often in Delius's earlier output. But if the coupling is unimportant, the more extroverted **Wallfisch** makes more of the soaring beauty of the writing, if without his colleague's wider range of tone and expression (♦Chandos 8499).

The String Quartet, from 1916, can be had in two forms: the original, affectionately played by the **Brodsky Quartet** (♦ASV 526), and Fenby's arrangement as "Sonata for String Orchestra" with **Nicholas Braithwaite,** conducting the New Zealand Chamber Orchestra (♦Koch 7139). The latter is an extension of the arrangement of the slow movement, 'Late Swallows,' commissioned in 1963 by Barbirolli, whose recording remains uniquely affecting. But either way, the essence of Delius comes through.

PIANO MUSIC

David Allen Wehr offers no fewer than eight Delius piano miniatures—the Three Preludes (1923) and Five Pieces (1921)—played with color and sensitivity and superbly recorded (♦Connoisseur Society 4224). Unfortunately he doesn't include the *Zum Carnival* polka that enlivened **Eric Parkin**'s selections from the keyboard music in Vol. 1 of Unicorn's "Delius Collection." Nor does he always match the latter's gift for understatement, though you wouldn't guess that from his collaboration with Galina Heifetz in the charming *Lullaby for a Modern Baby.*

CHORAL MUSIC

We're lucky to have as fine a recording as **Hickox**'s of *The Mass of Life* (♦Chandos 9515, 2CD), though in fact there has never been a bad one. Even **Groves,** whose Delius tended to be a bit foursquare, gave of his best in this mighty opus, sorting out its textures like nobody else. Of course **Beecham** is still the paragon when it comes to communicating the music's mystery and flow. But credit Hickox with conveying its strength, spaciousness and splendor, from its dramatic opening to its glorious finish, here putting one in mind of nothing so much as the Mahler 8th—no small achievement. Nor do his soloists disappoint here or in the filler, the still-underrated *Requiem,* especially the firm-voiced Peter Coleman-Wright, the baritone in each.

Even finer are **Hickox**'s *Sea Drift, Songs of Sunset* and *Songs of Farewell* (♦Chandos 9214), though no one has ever matched the ecstasy of **Sargent**'s ravishing account of the last, once available on EMI. Hickox recorded *Sea Drift* before, for Argo, with the ultra-sensitive Shirley-Quirk as soloist, but the Chandos remake with the rich-voiced Terfel is even more moving, with cleaner choral enunciation. In the majestic *Song of the High Hills,* the radiantly molded **Beecham** (EMI) and spaciously atmospheric **Fenby** (Unicorn-Kanchana) (neither are currently listed) are superior to **Rozhdestvensky**'s somewhat impetuous concert performance (IMP).

Reissues do happen, though, which is why the **Elysian Singers of London**'s recording of the complete choral songs is now available (♦Somm 210). Their performances are a bit distanced emotionally, especially compared with the old **Louis Halsey** LP of some of them. But at least it's in the stores, and given the state of the catalog and the gorgeous music, experience says to grab it.

OPERAS AND SONGS

At present only two of Delius's operas are listed, though not so long ago all six were available on CD: *Irmelin* (BBC), *The Magic Fountain* and

Margot la Rouge (Arabesque, also from BBC originals), *Koanga* (Intaglio), *A Village Romeo and Juliet* (EMI and Argo), and *Fennimore and Gerda* (EMI, in England anyway). Of these only EMI's *Village Romeo* remains, a reissue of **Beecham**'s pioneering 78 rpm set, incomparably conducted (e.g., the impassioned ebb and flow of his "Walk to the Paradise Garden" and impressionistic wedding dream), though technically, and sometimes vocally, superseded by **Mackerras**'s Argo recording (especially Hampson's Dark Fiddler). Indeed, if you can find it (and there was also a video issue), the Argo is still the *Village Romeo* of choice, given Hampson's and Helen Field's singing and Mackerras's seasoned grasp of the drama's overall shape, including its emotional rise and fall. Clearly this tragic tale of youthful love is Delius's operatic masterpiece, and it has never sounded more so than here.

There is, however, another option, from **Klauspeter Seibel** and the Kiel Opera (CPO 999328, 2CD). Neither as well sung or recorded as Mackerras's, nor as imaginatively conducted, it is nonetheless interesting to hear the work in German, which was the language of the premiere and of the original source material. What's more, Seibel's less romantic approach occasionally throws a stronger light on the musical structures.

German was also the original language of *Fennimore and Gerda,* and that's how **Hickox** recorded it, with the Danish National Radio Symphony and Chorus (♦Chandos 9589). These ears still prefer Rolfe Johnson's "Voice Across the Water" on **Meredith Davies**'s EMI recording (in English). But they would not willingly surrender the luminously expressive singing of mezzo Randi Stene, Hickox's *Fennimore,* or his more vital and colorful handling of the orchestra, especially valuable in a work in which it is arguably the most important player. The other singers are more of a draw.

Finally, the incidental music to *Hassan* probably fits in here somewhere, and typically that too was once available with **Handley** at the helm (EMI). No longer. Ditto the various song collections, though the two Dutton Beecham anthologies each contain a handful, including two versions of "Twilight Fancies," one with Beecham at the piano.

GOODFELLOW

Norman Dello Joio *(b. 1913)*

Dello Joio was a respected, much-performed and -recorded composer in the '50s and '60s, but his music isn't played much these days. Its pedigree is good, and might be described as the American common practice of mid-century, derived from Hindemith, Stravinsky, Copland, and jazz. To the mix he adds an Italianate, operatic lyricism and an interest in Gregorian Chant. (He came by both naturally: he was the New York–born son of Italian immigrants, he and his father were church organists, and his godfather was Pietro Yon, another prominent organist and composer of *Gesù Bambino.*)

Dello Joio's Pulitzer Prize–winning *Meditations on Ecclesiastes* (1956) is conducted by **DePreist** in a program with music by the similarly conservative Ronald Lo Presti and Menotti (Koch 7156). *Variations, Chaconne, and Finale,* first performed in 1947 by Bruno Walter and the New York Philharmonic, is conducted by **Sedares**, with the *Triumph of St. Joan Symphony* from an ambitious score for a Martha Graham ballet (Koch 7243). *Air Power,* a suite from a 1957 CBS television series, is full of good tunes and colorful orchestration; the original Columbia recording by Ormandy and the Philadelphia Orchestra has been reissued (Albany 250). A score deserving revival is the 1961 Fantasy and Variations, a flashy, jazzy piano concerto recorded for RCA in the '60s by **Lorin Hollander** and Leinsdorf.

Dello Joio's non-orchestral music is even more sparsely represented

on records, but the Variations and Capriccio for Violin and Piano (1948) is well performed by **Fritz Gearhart** in an all-American violin program (Koch Schwann 7268), and there is a collection of a large number of piano pieces, from three short but brilliant sonatas of the '40s to a *Song Without Words,* written in 1997 (Albany 344).   RAYMOND

David Diamond *(b. 1915)*

Diamond consistently elevates contemporary musical language to a high plateau of elegance, nobility, and grace. His large output of symphonic, chamber, and keyboard music is of such quality that it ensures him an honored place among the generation of composers who brought American music to maturity in the '40s and '50s, and he has continued to produce eloquent works of expressive breadth and clarity into his ninth decade. Years of neglect by performers and record companies have given way to major surveys of his orchestral and chamber works, which are at last bringing his music before a much wider public.

From his earliest published pieces, Diamond's hallmark has been neoclassical transparency of form, very much a European ideal in the '30s when he studied in Paris with Nadia Boulanger in what was becoming a nursery for American musical talent. His early *Vocalises* for soprano and viola (1935) are a perfect illustration and can be heard from **Lucy Shelton** and Louise Schulman (New World 80508). This disc also contains the 1950 Quintet for clarinet, two violas, and two cellos, a piece that lies on the very cusp of one of several stylistic advances in Diamond's career, at a time when he was moving away from the diatonic, modal language of the '40s toward a more openly chromatic, expressionist style.

Also on this disc are some excerpts from his meditative Preludes and Fugues for piano (1939) played by **William Black,** who joins violinist **Robert McDuffie** for Violin Sonatas 1 and 2, which are separated by nearly 40 years. No. 1 is cool, light, and untroubled, while 2 is prey to much darker, chromatically inclined thoughts, but Diamond never allows design to be subordinated to emotional need. This is an excellent release, in many ways a good place to start an exploration of Diamond's chamber music.

A disc devoted entirely to Diamond's chamber music, and which is worth hearing, is the disc by the **Chicago Chamber Musicians** and comprises the Clarinet and Flute Quintets, Concert Piece for Horn and String Trio, and Chaconne for Violin and Piano (Cedille 23). Sadly, No. 1 of the 11 string quartets is the only one currently in the catalog (Albany 229).

For Diamond's orchestral music, the 5CD ♦Delos series by the Seattle Symphony led by **Schwarz** is a towering accomplishment. I have no hesitation in strongly recommending every disc; Schwarz's empathy with and love for this music are not in doubt for a moment. In some ways Vol. 5 (3189) crowns the series, opening with the luminous and exquisitely nostalgic *Rounds for Strings* (1944) from the heart of Diamond's "modal" period, followed immediately by the slow movement from what is obviously his mature masterpiece, Symphony 11 (1992), a powerful Brucknerian tone poem of vast gesture and lyrical compass. Hearing this music impels a desire to hear the rest of the Symphony; let's hope that's not too distant a prospect. The early, dissonant *Elegy in Memory of Maurice Ravel* accompanies two Concert Pieces, a Copland-esque one for orchestra and another for flute and harp (played by the **Glorian Duo**) from four decades later. Ravel's music affected Diamond deeply as a young man, especially the dark side found in *Gaspard de la Nuit,* and some of this influence finds its way into the *Elegy.*

Vol. 1 (3093) draws entirely from the '40s, including the monumental Symphony 2 (an exact contemporary of "Rounds") and one of the finest American "war" symphonies. Its epic quality, gestural grandiloquence, and leaping rhythms set it apart from the others. Not to be missed either is Symphony 4, premiered by Bernstein in 1948; the slow movement is perhaps the finest of many elegiac movements Diamond has written, its ever-broadening lines piling on deeper and deeper intensity of feeling. Sandwiched in between is the brief, almost Milhaudian Concerto for Small Orchestra.

Vol. 2 (3103), also mainly from the '40s, highlights some of Diamond's finest incidental music, the Suite from *Romeo and Juliet* and the highly charged Symphony 3. In the midst of this lie the austere and meditative *Psalm* (1936) and *Kaddish,* the short tone poem for cello and orchestra (1989), featuring **Janos Starker.**

Vol. 3 (3119) offers three more large works from the '40s, the exquisitely Mendelssohnian Violin Concerto 2 with **Ilkka Talvi,** a piece that lingered in obscurity for nearly half a century, and the dynamic Symphony 1 (1940), the most propulsively rhythmical of the early modal works. Yet another surprise comes with the dreamy tone poem *The Enormous Room,* inspired by e.e. cummings, who had encouraged Diamond some years earlier to write the ballet suite *Tom,* based on scenes from *Uncle Tom's Cabin.* This suite opens Vol. 4 (3141), which takes a look at two works from the '60s, including the cantata *This Sacred Ground* (1962), an opulent setting (not dissimilar in vein to Copland's *Lincoln Portrait*) of the Gettysburg Address for choir and orchestra, with very good singing by the **Seattle Chorale.** The main feature here is the exceptionally fine Symphony 8 (1960), in which, as usual, clarity of expression is never obscured by grandeur of utterance, despite the growing rhetoric of Diamond's later musical language.

Symphony 5 is one of the few orchestral works from the '50s, when Diamond was living in Florence. It, too, has a more inward, questing mood, with sudden declamatory outbursts. It's played quite well by the Juilliard Orchestra under the late **Christopher Keene** (New World 80396, with works by Babbitt and Persichetti). *The World of Paul Klee* explores the limits of Diamond's astringency; it's a pity the only available recording is in such dim archival sound (CRI 634). For an excellent example of his late synthetic style, listen to the marvelous Flute Concerto (1985) played by **Alison Young** and the Bohuslav Martinů Philharmonic under Charles Johnson (Albany 308, with works by Doráti, Bernard Rogers, and Krenek).

Diamond's prodigious talent and the total integrity of his art place him at the very pinnacle of all that is finest in American aesthetic achievement. No one exploring this superb music is likely to be disappointed. JOHNSON

Karl Ditters von Dittersdorf *(1739–1799)*

In trying to analyze the appeal of certain composers, we find that folk music leads to simplicity of structure and directness of emotion, while a sprinkle of comic opera lends spice to harmonic movement and a light touch. These elements influenced Haydn and Mozart in their later works, and Dittersdorf no less. He wrote many comic operas, and his instrumental works show the effects. He's witty and tuneful, with a sense of humor even more prevalent than Haydn's. His symphonies and quartets have been recorded only recently and discovered to be well worth hearing. Before, we had pieces for musical clowning by the viola and the double bass, frequently in tandem, plus some rather silly serenades that gave Dittersdorf the reputation of being something of a buffoon. Well, being the class clown takes as much talent and more attention to timing

than being the school hero. He turns out to be a most refreshing person to have around.

Symphonies. Dittersdorf is supposed to have written more than 100 symphonies, but the *Schwann* listings (themselves woefully incomplete) barely scratch the surface, so we're only seeing the tip of the iceberg. The A minor symphony is coupled with two others in C and D and a Serenade in F by **Romeo Rîmbu** (Olympia 425). This is Vol. 2 of a series; in Vol. 3 he offers five symphonies, including the remarkable "Five Nations," containing stylized impressions of Germany, Italy, France, England, and Turkey (426), while Vol. 1 combines symphonies in C and D led by **Miron Raiu** with concertos for flute and double bass (405).

Uwe Grodd also offers "Five Nations" plus two others with equally picturesque titles, "The Battle of the Human Passions" and "The Delirium of the Composers," this last being a commentary on the *Sturm und Drang* movement and where it might lead, with seeming references to Haydn's music (Naxos 553975). A second disc under Grodd contains two symphonies (in D minor and G minor) clearly in the *Sturm und Drang* style along with a lighter work in F (Naxos 553974). Grodd is less lively than some, but quite scrupulous regarding repeats. The conductorless **Concerto Köln** are certainly lively enough in "The Fall of the Bastille," though firmly in period instrument style (Capriccio 10280, with works by François-Joseph Gossec, Jean-Baptiste Davaux, and François Martin).

The works conducted by **Hanspeter Gmür** are the more famous six symphonies (there are actually 12, but the rest seem to exist only in an arrangement for piano four-hands) based on events in Ovid's *Metamorphoses* (Naxos 553368/9). There have been several recordings of this series, notably a lively one by **Adrian Shepherd** and Cantilena (Chandos 8564, 2CD). Though not an early music group per se, they use a harpsichord; but they aren't much for program notes, a pity in such descriptive music. The Vienna Sinfonietta offers a much more romantic but less alert performance under **Kurt Rapf** (Calig 50885, 2CD, NA); a much slower reading comes from **Bohumil Gregor** and the Prague Chamber Orchestra (Supraphon 579, 2CD, NA). Gmür is also on the slow side, although the long timings have more to do with taking the repeats. His notes are detailed and helpful.

Concertos. Recordings of Dittersdorf's concertos concentrate on those for unusual instruments. He wrote examples for viola and double bass and a Sinfonia Concertante for both, and a couple of discs have recorded them together. Back in LP days, **Ludwig Streicher** made a fine disc combining the Bass Concerto, Sinfonia Concertante, and Mozart's aria with double-bass obbligato, "Per questa bella mano" (MHS 1162). Today, thanks to the greater length of the compact disc, the 25-minute Viola Concerto can be added without strain. **Lubomir Maly** and Frantiek Posta have recorded a particularly attractive performance of these three Dittersdorf pieces (Supraphon 110951). **Peter Pribyl** and Jakub Waldmann substitute a Divertimento in D for the Bass Concerto (Campion 1342). These performances are less characterful than Maly's, both in orchestral playing and in the soloists. Divertimenti from this composer are jolly and folksy, and we should hear more of them.

The Sinfonia Concertante has also been recorded by **Josef Suk** and Jii Hude in polished performances (Discover 920274, with like works by Haydn and Stamitz). All these projects hail from Czechoslovakia and have the national bucolic atmosphere, an added attraction. Dittersdorf's Harp Concerto is his only other concertante work presently listed, played tastefully by **Claudia Antonelli** with a very small orchestra (Arts 47285, with François-Adrien Boieldieu's Concerto 1 and Handel's Op. 4:6).

Chamber music. Dittersdorf's six string quartets (perhaps as a result of playing second fiddle in a 1784 quartet that included Haydn, Mozart, and Vanhal) are beautifully crafted works in three movements. They are light pieces compared to those of Haydn and Mozart, but no less subtle in their handling of simpler, more entertainment-oriented material. There are even movements that remind me of the six quartets Schubert wrote in his early days. There are three recordings, all excellently played; two of them fill out the series with two of Dittersdorf's six string quintets with two cellos, written to show off the cellistic abilities of King Frederick of Prussia. The **Schubert Quartet**'s lovely, subtle, yet forthright performances (♦CPO 999038, 999122) compare favorably with the **Kubin Quartet**'s less volatile but attractive readings (Multisonic 310477/8) and with the **Gewandhaus Quartet**'s rather devil-may-care handling (Berlin 9261, 2CD). The latter omits repeats and generally makes the works sound even less serious than they are. Now, if either Schubert or Kubin would give us the other four quintets, we could all rest easy!

The Sonata for viola and double bass, recorded by **Franz Beyer** and **Paul Breuer,** has been around since 1975 (Adagio 91009). This strange work also exists in a version for viola and piano and is best heard in that version, played with less humorous sonority, perhaps, but more in tune (SNE 569).

Operas. Dittersdorf's operas are not well-known, yet his best music seems to stem from his work in this medium. **Newell Jenkins** and the Clarion Music Society have put us in their debt by exhuming *Arcifanfano, King of Fools,* a 1776 opera buffa in a live performance from 1965 including both Eleanor Steber and Anna Russell! In an English translation by W.H. Auden and Chester Kallman, this performance is an event on several levels, although it may not document a musical masterpiece (VAI 1010, 2CD).

Doctor and Apothecary is better known, a 1786 Singspiel that has managed to maintain a tenuous hold on the repertory. Here we see Dittersdorf at his most musically amusing, although the recording, by **James Lockhart** and the Rhenish State Philharmonic, shows its age and LP origins by needing more bass (Bayer 100238, 2CD). The singers are good, particularly bass Harold Stamm and tenor Wolfgang Schöne. Unfortunately, no English libretto is provided.   MOORE

Ernst [Ernö] von Dohnányi *(1877–1960)*

Dohnányi lived through some of the most revolutionary years in the history of Western music, but he participated in none of the revolt. Instead, he carved out his own lyrical path, writing in a style that was becoming old-fashioned even while he was still a young man. Although one of Hungary's preeminent musicians, he has been overshadowed by the innovations and floristic interests of Bartók and Kodály. He was a hugely gifted pianist, and his compositional talent early came to the attention of Brahms, who arranged for the premiere of his Piano Quintet Op. 1. His subsequent neglect as a composer is due in large part to two factors: First, he kept to an intensely busy schedule as a performer and teacher for most of his life; second, he made a politically naive decision to move to Vienna following the Anschluss, which was interpreted as a pro-Nazi gesture (in fact, he was protesting an impossible political situation in Hungary). Because of this, his stock as composer plummeted, and only in recent years has much of his music been reconsidered. After the war, he came to the United States and spent his last years as a professor at Florida State University.

Dohnányi's music is characterized by an intensely lyrical melodicism and a harmonic style that owes much to Brahms. He favored variation forms, was a fine orchestrator, and had a good formal sense. His work for solo piano and his chamber music are of a very high quality. His orchestral music and concertos deserve to be better known, particularly the concertos and Symphony 2.

Symphonies. Dohnányi's two symphonies were conservative even in their time. No. 1 was written in 1900 and owes a great deal to Brahms and Tchaikovsky, whose works were current at the time. It's hardly derivative, though; even at the age of 24 he had an original and compelling voice. If there is one overriding flaw, it's an unyieldingly grim earnestness, with no hint of the dry wit that makes *Variations on a Nursery Song* so much fun. Still, the work is remarkably assured for such a young composer, and currently there are two excellent choices. **Leon Botstein**'s recording is wonderful, setting forth the symphony's full range of color and lyricism (♦Telarc 80511). **Bamert** is equally vivid and has the advantage of including *American Rhapsody,* one of the last pieces Dohnányi wrote, which melds all kinds of American thematic material into a moving whole (♦Chandos 9647).

Bamert has also recorded a dazzling account of No. 2 (♦Chandos 9455, with *Symphonic Minutes*). This work is much more ambitious, both harmonically and in orchestration. It sounds quite Brucknerian, but with more variety of color, and Bamert pulls out all the stops.

Concertos. Dohnányi's skills as a piano virtuoso inform every bar of his two piano concertos. Neither breaks new ground, but they are fine examples of the late Romantic concerto idiom, and although they were written 50 years apart, they're remarkably consistent in style. No. 1 is larger in scope, whereas 2 is a bit more compact. **Martin Roscoe** gives them every bit their due in "The Romantic Piano Concerto" Vol. 6 (♦Hyperion 66684). Anyone who enjoys the big Romantic concertos will find much to savor here.

The same goes for the two violin concertos. No. 1 was premiered in 1920 and owes much to Brahms. It's a sumptuous, spacious work in four movements and runs nearly three-quarters of an hour. **Ulf Wallin** plays with estimable vigor and a full-blooded tone, backed by Alun Francis and the Frankfurt Radio Symphony (CPO 999308, with *American Rhapsody*). Satisfying as this performance is, **Vilmos Szabadi**'s account, performed at a much higher voltage leaves it in the dust. It has a lot more forward momentum, and the Budapest Symphony under Vásáry plays with a feisty intensity that I prefer (♦Hungaroton 31759). It's coupled with a first recording of Violin Concerto 2, a much later work. This concerto (also in four movements) is much more colorfully scored than 1, with more delicate interplay between soloist and ensemble; it's much more distinctive in its thematic material.

Other orchestral music. *Variations on a Nursery Song* is by far Dohnányi's most popular work, and with little wonder. This set of variations for piano and orchestra on the tune we know as "Twinkle, Twinkle, Little Star" is a delightful masterpiece. Dohnányi dishes up a thrilling virtuoso vehicle loaded with charm and humor. There are several fine accounts to choose from, with the couplings probably a prime consideration. My top choice is **Howard Shelley,** with Bamert conducting the BBC Orchestra (♦Chandos 9733). The recording is full of sparkling detail, and Shelley gives a nuanced and polished reading with plenty of power in the big moments. This is also the only all-Dohnányi disc that contains this work; it tends to be treated as filler, but Chandos wisely places it in context with other music by the composer. It's coupled with the elegant *Suite* Op.19 and *The Veil of Pierrette,* music from a mimed theater piece of 1910; three first recordings are included in this collection.

Another excellent choice is **Mark Anderson,** with Ivan Fischer and the Hungarian State Symphony giving colorful support that's eminently Hungarian in character (Nimbus 5349). It's coupled with a good reading of Brahms's Concerto 1 but probably wouldn't be the listener's first choice for that work. The recording is well balanced, though, without the cavernous reverberance that Nimbus favors in many of their recordings. **Earl Wild**'s recording with Christoph von Dohnányi (Ernst's grandson) conducting is excellent as well, with Wild taking obvious relish in the flashy passagework (Chesky 13, with *Capriccio* and a fine rendering of Tchaikovsky's Piano Concerto 1. Chesky's remasterings of these analog recordings are exemplary. **Arthur Ozolins**'s recording is also worthy, although it doesn't have as much "oomph" as Anderson's or Wild's (CBC 5052, with Rachmaninoff's Concerto 1 and Litolff's Scherzo). Bernardi keeps the Toronto Symphony's playing crisp and clean, with no self-indulgence.

For another sampling of Dohnányi's orchestral music, try **Vásáry**'s well-filled disc with the Budapest Symphony that includes the Suite in F-sharp minor, *Konzertstück* for cello and orchestra, and the colorful *Symphonic Minutes* (♦Hungaroton 31637). The latter is a variegated suite that was intended to be a ballet; its five movements are all fairly brief (under five minutes), but full of memorable writing. The Suite is a more melancholy work; formally it follows a symphonic outline, but it is built on a smaller scale. The *Konzertstück* is a miniature cello concerto, once played by the composer's father. Csaba Onczay plays the solo part with warm intimacy, and the recording brings out the interplay between the cello and the Budapest woodwinds beautifully.

Chamber music. Dohnányi's father was a fine amateur cellist, and his son wrote enthusiastically for the instrument. **Maria Kliegel** offers a fine survey of this music in a disc that includes *Konzertstück* (backed by the Nicolaus Esterházy Orchestra led by Michael Halász), the Cello Sonata, and an arrangement of *Ruralia Hungarica* for cello and piano (♦Naxos 554468). Kliegel plays with a robust tone and obvious affection for the music. For the Sonata and *Ruralia* she's accompanied by Jandó, whose support is superlative. It's a wonderfully satisfying disc. If you're trying to choose between Kliegel and Onczay for the *Konzertstück*, I'd go with Onczay, mainly because of the more detailed recording, but cello fans shouldn't ignore Kliegel, especially at the budget price.

Dohnányi's first major success as a composer was with his 1895 Piano Quintet Op. 1, which Brahms arranged to be performed in Vienna. He wrote a second quintet in 1914. Brahms was his point of departure for this music, and although he wasn't tempted by any of the revolutionary stylistic trends that were happening at the time, he became somewhat more flexible in his approach to form as his music matured. His early chamber works tend to be meticulously classical. For Quintet 1, I recommend **Roscoe** with the Vanbrugh Quartet (ASV 985, with Quintet 2 and *Suite im alten Stil* for two pianos). A strong alternative would be the **Schubert Ensemble**'s disc of the quintets plus Serenade Op. 10 (Hyperion 66786). A more colorful pairing of chamber works has Quintet 2 linked with the lovely Sextet for piano, horn clarinet and string trio (Hungaroton 11624). **Ernö Szegedi** and the Tatrai Quartet. Hornist Ferenc Tarjáni and clarinetist Béla Kovács combine verve and refinement in these glorious performances. I especially like the Sextet; it's one of Dohnányi's best chamber works.

Dohnányi wrote three string quartets that are wonderful examples of the Romantic tradition. Quartet 1 was written around the time of Piano Concerto 1 and shows how well he had absorbed his stylistic models. Quartet 2, written in 1906, shows a much more distinctive musical per-

sonality emerging. Listeners can hear this evolution magnificently performed by the **Kodály Quartet** (♦Hungaroton 11853). This is the only disc with 1 and 2 together, and the analog sound is remastered well. Quartet 3 is from 1926 and can be heard in a wonderful performance by the **Hollywood Quartet** (♦Testament 1081, with Schubert's Quartet 14 and Wolf's *Italian Serenade*). Although recorded in 1955, the sound is warmly detailed, and the extraordinary musicianship of this group makes up for any sonic deficiency. Listeners who wish for more up-to-date sound should consider the **Lyric Quartet**'s performance (ASV 985, with Quartet 2 and Kodály's Intermezzo).

Piano music. Listeners who want to sample Dohnányi's solo piano music will find **Markus Pawlik**'s first volume of the "Complete Piano Works" a good place to start (Naxos 553332). Pawlik's playing is clean and energetic, and the price is right for this generously filled disc, which includes *Ruralia Hungarica,* the six *Concert Etudes,* and *Variations on a Hungarian Folksong.* However, Pawlik's style is slightly bland, with not enough attention paid to accents. The Hungarian language has strong accents on most first syllables, and many non-Hungarian musicians are unaware of this fact, which must be taken into account in any interpretation of this music. To hear the difference, listen to **Ilona Prunyi**'s fine recital (Hungaroton 31910). She plays three of the *Concert Etudes,* and there's a marked difference in the placement of accents in her account, which I find more characteristic. Her disc is more of a sampler; it includes some of Dohnányi's opera transcriptions, a fugue for the left hand, a couple of waltzes, and a set of variations; several of these are first recordings.

Wolf Harden has also recorded a recital containing *Ruralia Hungarica* (Marco Polo 223128), but it doesn't fare well next to Pawlik, who executes the brilliant passagework much more cleanly. Harden's disc does contain *Four Rhapsodies* Op. 11, which aren't currently found elsewhere. His playing has many fine points, including a tendency to let the slower movements breathe more, but Pawlik is superior in general.

McINTIRE

Gaetano Donizetti (1797–1848)

With Bellini and Rossini, Donizetti was one of the triumvirate of great composers of bel canto (beautiful song) operas. With its emphasis on beautiful singing, long musical phrases, coloratura ornamentation, and virtuoso display, bel canto was a singer's delight. Donizetti was a facile composer who produced more than 70 operas in Italian and French, both serious and comic. Falling out of favor with the rise of Verdi and then of the verismo school, his operas (with the exception of *Lucia di Lammermoor* and *Don Pasquale*) were rarely heard during the first half of the 20th century. Maria Callas single-handedly reawakened interest in bel canto, and with a reassessment of the genre revived its popularity. This interest was continued by artists like Sutherland, Sills, and Caballé. It's surprising how much of Donizetti's prolific output has been recorded.

Anna Bolena. Donizetti was fascinated by the Tudor queens of England and composed three operas that have an English queen as the protagonist (*Anna Bolena, Maria Stuarda,* and *Roberto Devereux*). Frequently referred to as the "Tudor Trilogy," they were never intended to be performed as a cycle but have been produced and recorded with one soprano in all three roles. There has also been an unwritten rivalry among sopranos for the roles: Caballé, Sutherland, Sills, and Gencer all performed and recorded them.

Anna Bolena was Donizetti's first major success and did much to establish his fame, but it's a long and talky work with a good deal of uninspired music. It needs great singers.

Callas never sang Maria Stuarda or Elisabetta, but she more than made her mark as Anna Bolena. The opera was revived for her at La Scala in 1957, marking a personal triumph and the true beginning of the bel canto revival. Here she is heard at her very best (♦EMI 66471; Verona 27090; Hunt 518; Melodram 260101; 2CD). Callas had such an instinctive feeling for this music that she created a total portrayal, with depths of emotion and natural musicality, all without the use of obvious effects and without obvious ornamentation. Although the tessitura of Giovanna Seymour implies a soprano, the role has become the exclusive property of mezzos. Simionato wasn't fazed by the high-flying music, giving time for strong dramatics. Raimondi easily encompasses the notes of Percy but does little with them. Gavazzeni seems to have a natural feeling for the music too; he lets it breathe with the singers, with subtle flexibility.

Gencer made several recordings of the tragic Anna; the best is from a 1965 performance at Glyndebourne (Hunt). She's in strong voice with lots of personality. Unfortunately, her colleagues aren't; none of them are really up to their roles. The orchestra is in rough shape, but the chorus sings capably. Gavazzeni knows the score but can't communicate with his wayward charges here.

A 1970 recording by **Suliotis** is substantially complete, but by the time she recorded Anna, she had lost the grip on her glorious, naturally dramatic voice (Decca). There is much beauty still present, but you can hear her working to produce the notes. For sheer variety of effect, Horne is the best of the recorded Giovannas. Well-versed in the vocal art of the period, she presents a coloratura spectacular without forcing her voice or the music. Ghiaurov shows how much impact a first-rate singer can have as Enrico, a richly sung role with dramatic impact. Silvio Varviso reveals many hidden jewels in the music, but lacks an overall concept of the piece.

Rudel leads a more cogent, strictly controlled performance, complete in every note (EMI 34031; Millennium 80355; 2CD; in "The Three Queens," DG 465967, 7CD). **Sills** doesn't have the large, full-blown voice of Callas or Suliotis, but her coloratura agility is far superior, and she works hard to create a complete characterization. Verrett is regal, but too tough as Giovanna—an easy top, but a tendency to hoarsen in the middle and lower range.

A 1975 performance from Dallas doesn't seem to be available on CD, but it finds **Scotto** in fine voice, artful, calculating—but with little of the spontaneity or freedom needed in bel canto. Giovanna as sung by Troyanos is a nice but dull young lady, rich in voice, but with ineffectual words. Fernando Previtali conducts a strong performance, but there are too many cuts.

For completeness and an all-around fine performance, **Sutherland**'s 1987 recording is hard to beat (♦Decca 421096, 3CD). Callas is a necessity, but Sutherland gives a better overall view of what the work is about. She is in fine voice (even though she was in her 60s at the time), secure, with beautiful tone, and with much sympathy for the heroine. This is one of Hadley's better recordings: quite stylish with the bravura aspects of the role, gently sympathetic when needed. Ramey is a powerful Enrico VIII, capturing the autocratic personality, making much of an unsympathetic character while singing mellifluously. The forces of the Welsh National Opera respond well to Bonynge's practiced and knowing direction; he's supportive of his singers yet never lingers, and even manages to propel the less-than-inspired portions of the music.

Gruberová seems to be in the midst of a project to record all the bel canto heroines (Nightingale 70565, 2CD). She does a fine job in a 1994 recording, with substantial help from Delores Ziegler and Helene Schneidermann, and substandard help from José Bros and Stefano Palatchi. The Hungarian Radio & Television Chorus and Orchestra are led by Elio Boncompagni in an adequate rendering.

Belisario. This is the third of Donizetti's operas in which the baritone is the principal character (preceded by *Torquato Tasso* and *Marino Faliero*). The effect is a shift in the usual vocal arrangements. The prima donna appears only in the first act and the final scene of the opera; her music is more for display than characterization, and the tenor ends up paired with the mezzo. Although the soprano lead has been called unsympathetic, the title and mezzo roles are more engaging, their duets prefiguring Verdi's father-daughter duets.

A 1969 performance from Venice makes a strong case for the opera's revival (Melodram 27051; Mondo Musica 10301; 2CD). **Taddei** is a dramatically strong Belisario, covering all emotions from tender to martial, singing strongly with fine musicality. Mirna Pecile, appropriately sympathetic and concerned, has a tight, fast vibrato with a rapid flutter and cutting edge—a marked contrast to Taddei; their duets sound too unblended. Gencer as Antonina is hardly a good example of lyricism: her voice is in big trouble, but her dramatic instincts remained strong. Gavazzeni leads a vigorous performance.

A 1970 performance from Bergamo features the elegant and sensitive Belisario of **Bruson**—finely shaded, shattered and weak when first blinded, regaining strength as the story proceeds, again becoming the noble warrior (♦Hunt 586, 2CD). A cast almost identical to the 1969 Venice performance is heard here. Pecile's Irene, now a contrast to Bruson's warm, soft timbre, retains the felicities of her earlier performance. Gencer is all prima donna, wowing her way into the affections of the audience, in splendid, huge voice, capping the show with a massive high B-flat. Adolfo Camozzo doesn't have the authority of Gavazzeni, but his leadership will suffice. The recorded sound is a trifle elderly.

Caterina Cornaro. The last Donizetti premiere he was able to supervise, the work betrays some signs of haste. It has lain dormant for a long time, revived occasionally for a super-diva like Caballé. It's a fine opera with lots of foot-tapping, sing-along tunes.

Gencer, although dramatically intriguing, has a peculiar voice, although not exactly what you expect for bel canto (Memories 4448, 2CD). She's capable of some lovely soft singing like Caballé and has a true sense of bel canto style and musicality with charisma to spare; but frequently she resorts to chest voice, bringing it high into the vocal register with explosive glottal attacks and peculiarities, all in the service of drama. Her Caterina is on the grandest of scales and personalities. Aragall is an attractive Gerardo, and Bruson moreso as Lusignano—his beautiful, rich-bodied, unforced voice, tasteful musicality, and delicacy of interpretation make him a treasure. The musical forces of San Carlo under Cillario are acceptable accompanists, but no more.

The audience's reception of a 1973 Radio France broadcast was tumultuous; **Caballé** was justly rewarded with mighty roars of applause (♦Phoenix 505; Rodolphe; 2CD). This is Caballé in excelsis! Exquisite pianissimos, heaven-storming fortes, breath control, and excitement make it a major musical event. Aragall is a distinguished, ardently romantic Gerardo; Gwynne Howell's potent black bass gives major proportions to the minor role of Mocenigo. Gianfranco Masini keeps the show brisk, but is in full sympathy with the singers. A musical bonus is 45 minutes of a 1974 Caballé concert, with the singer again in stupendous form in extended opera excerpts by Bellini, Donizetti, Rossini, and Verdi.

Denia Mazzola's 1995 stage performance in Bergamo is good, but not much compared to Caballé's effort (Agora 0462, 2CD). Her Caterina is intensely dramatic, dark-hued, but with a tendency to flap under pressure. Pietro Ball as Gerardo is at times a caricature of a provincial Italian teno—he whines, he scoops, he cries out with overt emotion, not a treat. The chorus is underpopulated, but tries hard. Gavazzeni takes a relaxed approach, beginning tired and sluggish but becoming more involved as the show progresses.

Don Pasquale. This amiable comedy has been well served on record, one of its earliest recordings (1932) setting a benchmark for quality as reissued in splendid sound—thanks to EMI's Cedar process, which has been so successful in restoring archival recordings (♦EMI 53241, 2CD). The La Scala set led by **Sabajno** preserves the classic Italian opera buffa style that has nearly vanished. Schipa remains the quintessential exponent of Ernesto, his liquid, clear tenor gently caressing the notes. The characterizations by Afro Poli and Ernesto Badini happily complement each other in traditional style. Only the acidic Norina of Adelaide Saraceni fails to please.

The 1965 recording with Corena has long been considered a standard of interpretation (♦Decca 433036, 2CD). He long ruled at the Met in the great Italian buffo roles and his style influenced many singers and listeners. More buffa than operatic, he often emphasized the words at the expense of the music. Years of distorting his voice for comic effect took its toll, but the loss in vocal beauty was more than made up for in comic and human interpretation. Sciutti's Norina tends to be glassy, but is certainly imbued with the comic spirit of the occasion. The Vienna Staatsoper forces sound sumptuous, but not in the best Italianate style under the inflexible baton of **Kertész.**

A not entirely happy performance is led by **Caldwell** (EMI 66030, 2CD). On paper it looks promising, but it must have been a bad day (or two) at the London Symphony recording venue. Caldwell is lackluster, tending to sluggish tempos. Sills's always personable voice sounds fun-filled as she easily sails through the coloratura intricacies, but her tone often loses precision and focus. Kraus, similarly favored with a distinctive voice, sings with his customary elegance, but too often the notes turn sour and forced. Gramm sounds too youthful for Pasquale, but most of all he's dead wrong for the role: nonidiomatic and too serious, regardless of how well he sings.

Muti's 1982 recording is very much a pleasing singers' affair with the conductor emphasizing the singing quality of the orchestral lines, while fully supporting the graceful antics of his cast (♦EMI 47068, 2CD). Bruscantini strikes a happy balance between buffoonery and seriousness, but Leo Nucci's Malatesta comes down firmly on the serious side. Freni's Norina is more lyrical and less soubrette than is usually heard—a happy complement to Gösta Winberg's winning, lyrical Ernesto.

A recording from the Hungarian State Opera led by **Ivan Fischer** comes as a pleasant surprise (♦Hungaroton 12416, 2CD). József Gregor is a personable Pasquale, no old codger, vocally or in spirit. He forgoes a lot of the buffoonery and sings most of the notes with real tone and intent. István Gáti is the robust, well-acted Malatesta. Magda Kalmár finds a variety of voices for the multi-sided Norina: she can be sour when the character is bitchy, yet sweetly sing the serious parts and gaily toss off the coloratura fun. Fischer keeps the show moving in a happy balance of gay spirit and touching seriousness.

Bruson seems a strange choice for a major buffo role. All too often the role is assigned to a veteran singer with more style than voice. What a pleasure it is to hear a voice at its prime and imbued with true Italian opera buffa spirit; he's one of the best Pasquales (RCA 61924, 2CD). The other voices are a well-matched lot. Mei's Norina gets a bit strained topside, but she has no difficulties otherwise and manages a clever, self-revealing characterization. Frank Lopardo usually has a throaty quality, but he masks it here through a good deal of soft singing; it gets a bit wearying at times, but he manages the role well. Thomas Allen sings smoothly, with a surprising (for him) amount of characterization and spirit. Bavarian Radio forces are led by **Roberto Abbado** in a finely judged performance, with emphasis on the more melancholy side of the music but perking up for the moments of high comedy.

The English seem to believe firmly in English opera, so we have an English language *Don Pasquale* (Chandos 3011, 2CD). Translation changes the nature of the work, obscuring the musical line and nuances, leading the audience to expect to understand more while disappointing them with lack of clarity. The performance makes a crudity out of a refined delicacy—an Italian comedy has become an English parody of Gilbert and Sullivan. **David Parry** gives the singers plenty of time to hang themselves in the overt, forced humor of the recitatives, but keeps the show on a steady track for the arias and ensembles.

L'Elisir d'amore. Although recorded with some frequency, *L'Elisir* has not always been well recorded. Too often the singing tends to the rudely comic. A 1955 performance from Florence is less than sparkling, tied down by **Molinari-Pradelli's** deliberate tempos (Decca). Gueden sings well, but is hardly a model of Italian style. Di Stefano is self-indulgent, wasting a fabulous voice in sobs, tears, and intrusive vocal effects. Renato Capecchi lacks charisma and depth of voice for Belcore. Corena was still holding the buffo mannerisms mostly in check at this time, so he sings more tastefully. In another recording, with the Rome Opera, Molinari-Pradelli destroys the show again; he still has not learned to interpret Donizetti and it's dead on arrival (EMI). Besides that, Gedda is miscast as Nemorino, too sophisticated and cool. Freni is half-hearted, weighed down by the tempos, and Mario Sereni offers nothing in voice or character as Belcore. Only Capecchi, gaily tripping through the comedy, singing grandly, brings Dulcamara to life.

Another set is also weighed down by its conductor, this time the veteran **Serafin** leading La Scala forces; usually so stylish in this repertoire, here he's just tired and sad (EMI). Rosanna Carteri as Adina has vocal problems with faulty intonation. The charmingly personable Panerai tends to bluster as Belcore; Taddei lacks the true bass depths for Dulcamara, but turns in an otherwise splendid performance.

A somewhat happier affair is led by **Bonynge;** it's also more complete than earlier versions (Decca 414461, 2CD). At least things are happy as far as Pavarotti and Sutherland are concerned. Both are in spectacular voice, with beauty as well as agility, thoroughly conversant with the bel canto style. She's a serious Adina; he's a broadly smiling delight, effervescent to the core. The English Chamber Orchestra dutifully follows Bonynge, but with little enjoyment.

The high quality of a 1977 recording from Covent Garden comes as an almost complete surprise. Domingo is not noted for comedy, Cotrubas could be shrill, Wixell is often gruff and bland, and **Pritchard** is not exactly famous as an interpreter of Italian bel canto. But the recording puts all these contentions to rest with a splendid performance (CBS 34585, 2CD). Although not the best technician in bel canto, Domingo sings so richly and interprets the role so well that you can't complain. Cotrubas also sings extremely well, with unaffected charm. Wixell's gruffness is actually just right for Belcore; he makes it part of his characterization. Geraint Evans is just about the perfect Dulcamara, striking a fine balance between comic effects and truly gracious singing. Pritchard seems to have somehow discovered true Italian buffa style, imbuing it with humanity.

In a 1989 remake, Pavarotti is in still in fine voice, a bit frayed in some high passages, but still a charmer (♦DG 429744, 2CD). Battle's silver soprano is coy, teasing, and attractively girlish. Nucci brings a hint of overkill to Belcore's blustering quite in keeping with the character. Enzo Dara sings rather than barks his way through Dulcamara's antics; his entrance aria is a bit too staid, but then loosens up to fine comic effect. The Met Orchestra under **Levine** plays a virtuoso performance, jolly and winning all the way.

Viotti's recording, other than for the Tallis Chamber Choir and the English Chamber Orchestra, is an all-Italian production, and quite a good one (♦Erato 91701, 2CD). The cast is youthful, all with attractive voices that blend well, good diction, and an innate sense of style. Alagna is a class act as Nemorino, a role beautifully sung, neatly characterized. Devia is shrill on occasion, but generally sings quite well, with a thoughtful characterization. Belcore's blustering finds a delicate interpreter in Pietro Spagnoli; he sings the role beautifully, with a more gentlemanly character than usual. Bruno Praticò is a lighter-voiced Dulcamara than generally heard, but he negotiates the patter songs with agility, spitting out the text to great effect. Viotti supports the legato line with a fine sense of style, yet allows the music to bubble along. It's an all-around good show.

La Favorite. The basic question with this opera is: "French or Italian?" Donizetti wrote the opera for Paris in 1840 in French, but it's most frequently heard in Italian translation. It's a dignified, serious opera in four acts with, somewhat unusually, a mezzo-soprano as the heroine.

La Favorite (in French) was one of the first complete opera recordings made (1910). The cast represents a style of singing no longer heard. Henri Albers sings a distinguished Alphonse, with Robert Malvini as a solid Balthazar. The singers, chorus, and orchestra of the Paris Opéra are led in an idiomatic performance by **François Ruhlmann** (♦Marston 52010, 2CD).

A 1949 performance from Mexico City has been preserved in dim sound (Legato/SRO). It's in Italian with good performances from Simionato and Siepi, and is of interest for hearing the young di Stefano in fine form. There isn't much interest in **Renato Cellini**'s conducting. A 1955 recording in Italian from the Maggio Musicale Fiorentino is a sorry affair (Decca). Simionato is in good form vocally and has a good sense of how to make the role into an Italian heroine, frequently sounding lovely; but Gianni Poggi's Fernando is an all-around embarrassment: name a vocal fault and he has it. Bastianini, although with a magnificent voice, assaults the music with violence, with damage to style and musicality. **Alberto Erede,** master of the bland interpretation, is in his usual listless, boring form.

Barbieri is in voluptuous voice in an Italian version, Gianni Raimondi pleasantly so, but Carlo Tagliabue, far past his prime, is most unpleasant. The RAI Turin chorus and orchestra are led neatly by **Angelo Questa.** A 1967 performance from Buenos Aires offers such muddy, distorted sound that it's difficult to judge the singers, but the cast is strong: Cossotto, Kraus, Bruscantini, and Vinco, and led by **Bartoletti** (Great Opera Performances). Cossotto and Pavarotti are heard together in two Italian recordings, a 1974 stage performance from La Scala led by **Nino Verchi** (♦Opera d'Oro 1196, 2CD) and a 1977 studio version conducted by **Bonynge** (Decca, 2CD). Cossotto is too Italian with little subtlety, in better voice in 1974 than in 1977. Pavarotti makes some gorgeous sounds in both recordings, phoning in any drama from long distance. The Bologna forces are slipshod.

A recording in fine sound contains a less than fine 1989 performance in Italian, conducted by **Fabio Luisi.** The singers make some pleasant sounds, but with nothing to really commend them (Nuova Era). I haven't heard a 1999 performance that sounds promising, with Ramón Vargas, Kasarova, and Anthony Michaels Moore (RCA).

La Fille du régiment. Donizetti composed *La Fille* in French, later translating it to Italian. The first major recording of the work (1967) remains a benchmark of fine performance as well as a historical souvenir (♦Decca 414520, 2CD). This was Sutherland's first venture into comedy and was one of Pavarotti's first great successes in that it was instrumental in creating the Pavarotti phenomenon. Both are in exceptional voice: fresh, strong, with a real feeling of élan and joy. Monica Sinclair is also a comic delight as the Marquise. Everyone's French seems to be Italiantinged, but with such a comic feeling that we can't complain. The recording followed performances at Covent Garden, so chorus and orchestra are well-tuned to **Bonynge**'s ebullient direction.

A 1969 Italian version from La Scala is dutifully and dully led by **Sanzogno** (Nuova Era 2239, Opera d'Oro 1147, Verona 27046; 2CD); but it does boast a charming, exquisitely sung Maria by Freni. Pavarotti is still in fine fettle, even more comfortable in his native Italian. Another Italian version from Venice in 1975 is bogged down by Sanzogno; Freni, Anna di Stasio, and Wladimiro Ganzarolli give fine interpretations, with the elegant, distinctive, nasal tenor of Kraus as Tonio (Mondo Musica 10011, 2CD).

An exceptionally fine performance in Italian from stage performances in Bologna in 1989 is marred by the Maria of Luciana Serra (Nuova Era 6791, 2CD). Serra is an experienced artist and knowledgeable in the stage department, but her voice too often takes on a cutting edge, particularly in its top range, and is generally unattractive. Her Maria is hardly a charmer, but a rather tough girl all too willing to overplay the comic elements. No problem with William Matteuzzi's Tonio, though. He not only flies freely through the famous nine high Cs, but throws in a D-flat, a D-sharp, and even a climactic high F at the end. All this is sung with a most attractive voice, sweet, bright, and youthful—a delightful characterization. **Bruno Campanella** leads a lively performance.

Although Gruberová has made some fine recordings of the bel canto repertoire, her *Fille* is not one of them (Nightingale 70566, 2CD, in French). Her voice was past its prime in 1995, worn and used with great caution. She sings like an experienced soubrette, but without Gallic charm or wit, especially heavy-handed in the "Lesson Scene." The hard, bright clarity of Deon van der Walt's tenor is no great pleasure. He hits all the Cs, but long sustained phrases aren't fully supported. The performance is cut to fit a time slot for the Bavarian Radio Symphony, whose forces, led by **Marcello Panni,** play well, if without the necessary Gallic poise.

Linda di Chamounix. This was written for the Kärntnertor Theater in Vienna in 1842. It's somewhat unusual, neither comic nor tragic but sometimes an uncomfortable mixture, although the finale is happy. The story is wrapped in a cozy sense of *lagrimosa* (weepy feelings), and the music for the villain comes dangerously close to buffo, softening the tragic situation. *Linda* is more deftly crafted than many other Donizetti operas, and a serene gentleness pervades the work. Some of the music is a bit commonplace, but there are enough melodies as well as rhythmic vitality to make for rewarding listening.

For a long time, a 1958 Naples recording was the only one available (Philips 442093, 2CD, Palladio 4101, Andromeda 2509; 2CD). It has held up very well over the years, and against modern competition. Antonietta Stella is not the most flexible of sopranos; her coloratura is labored, but she's a fetching Linda with a delicate, almost Puccinian sadness. Barbieri intones a hearty Pierotto, and the stylish Carlo of Cesare Valletti contrasts nicely with the semi-comic machinations of Giuseppe Taddei and Capecchi. As usual, bel canto authority **Serafin** leads San Carlo forces with authority and sympathy. Another recording offers a mainly Italian cast and a conductor well versed in Italian opera; Mariella Devia sails through Linda's music with ease, often jazzing up second verses of an aria with extra coloratura pyrotechnics (♦Arts 47151, 3CD). **Gabriele Bellini** whips the Orchestra of the Eastern Netherlands into a musical storm when required, then relaxes the atmosphere into a serene calm.

Gruberová is the star of a 1993 broadcast from Stockholm (Nightingale 670561, 2CD). She manages the role with ease, but without her usual spectacular quality. Her voice also sounds too vapid for the more serious Linda. Her colleagues are little more than serviceable. **Friedrich Haider** is the dutiful conductor.

Lucia di Lammermoor. This is not only the most popular of Donizetti's operas, but the most popular in the bel canto repertoire. *Lucia* and bel canto have become synonymous with Callas, who singlehandedly revived the genre.

Actually *Lucia* was never out of the standard repertoire and had several recordings prior to Callas. The earliest of note is a 1933 version from La Scala with **Mercedes Capsir** as a mechanical tweety-bird coloratura (Myto; Arkadia). Her Edgardo, Enzo di Muro Lomanto, is vocally strong but dramatically weak. Armando Borgioli's Enrico is strong in both departments. This remains more a historic document than a viable entry in the *Lucia* race. French coloratura **Lily Pons** sang Lucia at the Metropolitan Opera with great success for more than 25 years. Alas, her recording was too late; by 1954 her coloratura had become dry, forced, and sloppy (Sony, 2CD). Other than Richard Tucker's ardent but stylish Edgardo, the rest of the cast is adequate at best.

Of the historic Lucias, **Callas** remains the best and most important. She twice recorded the role commercially. In 1953 she was in spectacular voice, light as needed, saving the dark-toned pyrotechnics for the "Mad Scene," yet all the while infinitely moving (♦EMI 66438, 2CD). Her colleagues have seldom been better. Di Stefano's Edgardo is powerfully virile; Gobbi's Enrico dangerously cunning and sophisticated. Serafin is in strong command on the podium.

By 1959 a stereo version of the opera was thought necessary, but by then Callas's voice was already in trouble and it was necessary for her to sing with extreme caution, robbing the role of much of its drama (EMI). Tagliavini and Cappuccilli aren't much competition for their predecessors, barely encompassing the notes and with none of their style or drama. Serafin seems out of sorts here too. Of the several "off-the-air" Callas Lucias, the best (the best of *all* Callas's Lucias) is a 1955 performance with La Scala forces in Berlin, led by Karajan (♦EMI 63631, 2CD). It's all at fever pitch, the drama taut and tense, the singers all in fine fettle, with di Stefano again a strong Edgardo, and Panerai a noble Enrico.

Callas's successors in the role have been many, with varying virtues. Closest to her Lucia is **Sutherland,** who also recorded the role twice. Her 1961 version is undercut by the hairy-voiced Edgardo of Renato Cioni and the slow-boiling conducting of Pritchard (Decca). Merrill and Siepi are fine, though. By 1971 Sutherland is teamed with conductor-husband Bonynge, and he certainly knows the bel canto style to perfection (Decca 410193, 3CD). He heads a dramatic show and she follows his lead, maintaining a fuller voice than earlier, yet with all her legendary flexibility

and accuracy intact. Pavarotti is a heavy-toned Edgardo, but Milnes is a super-Verdian Enrico, and Ghiaurov is the best Raimondo on record.

Sills's bright-toned, almost steely Lucia is at the opposite extreme, with razor-sharp coloratura (NA). The burnished tenor of Bergonzi makes for a glorious Edgardo and Cappuccilli sings better here than he did earlier with Callas. Schippers conducts with sensitivity.

Scotto is in a similar vocal mode. Bastianini's Enrico is boldly sung, but by 1959 di Stefano is in serious vocal trouble, and Sanzogno's lifeless conducting scuttles the project (Enterprise). From the same bright-voiced school of coloratura comes **Roberta Peters** (♦RCA 68537, 2CD). She's a radiant Lucia, casting coloratura ornaments about like so many diamonds, each perfectly pitched, each phrase intact. Jan Peerce's distinctive nasal voice rolls the words with abandon, savoring every musical and dramatic nuance. The Germanic authority of Leinsdorf and the Rome Opera's seasoned orchestra make a winning combination. Standard cuts prevail.

Moffo is somewhere between the two vocal styles, more lyric than coloratura, respectable but not particularly exciting. She too recorded the opera twice. Her 1966 version has the superb Bergonzi again as Edgardo, but he's better with Sills (RCA). Prêtre offers little help. Moffo's second attempt (1972) was made for a film soundtrack; it's incomplete and poorly sung and conducted.

Caballé's 1976 version comes at mid-price, but is a curiously unadorned performance shedding traditional (unauthentic) additions, and without interpolated high notes (Philips). It's beautifully sung, but not of great interest. Carreras is a sweet-voiced Edgardo; and Vicente Sardinero is a sturdy Enrico. López-Cobos conducts competently, but routinely and boringly.

Gruberová twice sings a worthy Lucia. Both times she falls short of Callas's drama but compensates with lovely *leggiera* ease and technical assurance. The first time around, in 1983, Kraus is her technically assured Edgardo; Bruson is an elegant, stylistically correct, yet dramatic Enrico (EMI 64622, 2CD). Rescigno shapes the opera with care, all the while considerate of his singers' needs. Gruberová's colleagues in her 1992 remake are a less agreeable lot (Teldec). Bonynge seems to have given up on *Lucia,* conducting a lackluster performance.

You rarely hear a big, dramatic voice as Lucia, but **Studer**—elsewhere a Wagner-Strauss-type singer—manages the role quite well (DG 435309, 2CD). Her voice is attractive, caressing the ear with tonal allure, steady, seamless between registers, but cautiously employed, with little individuality or characterization. Domingo's Edgardo is first-rate, a true romantic hero. Pons is solid and stolid, doing little more than singing the correct notes. Ramey is at home in the bel canto style, easily negotiating the notes, but with more than a hint of preciosity. A major plus is the glamorously sung Alisa of Jennifer Larmore, a major artist in a minor role. Ion Marin brings no new insight into the opera, preferring to conduct a standardized, crudely efficient performance.

Going further against tradition is the 1997 "original" version, with Mackerras leading the Hanover Band (Sony 63174, 2CD). He not only uses period instruments, but also slices, dices, and generally exorcizes 150 years of singers' rules, interpolations, and traditions. Tempos are rigid, rhythmically precise with scarcely a hint of rubato. The orchestra has become the star in bel canto opera! Aided by the recorded clarity, you can now appreciate the imaginative orchestration, but it's quite boring in the long run. This is a singers' opera, but these singers aren't much. **Andrea Rost** takes on the title role, but even with her music shorn of interpolated difficulties she has a hard time of it. She's far too imprecise technically, has little resembling a true trill, and only a sketch of a characterization—all weak fluff and vulnerability. Bruce Ford easily encompasses what remains of Edgardo's music, but his voice is raw.

Lucrezia Borgia. For all its fine music, this is a difficult opera to bring off. It's a grim story, and there isn't much sympathy for any of the characters; the music is quite difficult, and calls for some truly spectacular singing.

Caballé made the great leap to American stardom with her 1965 concert performance with the American Opera Society at Carnegie Hall; it was very much an occasion and that sense is well caught by the recording (♦Opera d'Oro 1200; Legato 501; 2CD). She's at her spectacular best, with luscious singing combined with variety of tonal color and temperament. Perlea conducts dutifully with little understanding of the style. In the following year, Caballé recorded the opera in the studio (♦RCA 6642, 2CD). What a change! The recorded sound is much better, and she sings as beautifully as ever, but with a kind of all-purpose tone and expression. This is more a singing lesson than an opera performance. There is another major contrast in the spectacular Gennaro of Kraus, a model of bel canto perfection: his voice is free and easy, sailing through the cruelly high tessitura with elegance. Perlea is back on the podium; he's no more inspired than in the earlier performance, but at least he has the aid of authentic Italians in his RCA Italiana chorus and orchestra.

A 1966 performance has a dramatically spectacular Lucrezia in **Gencer** (Hunt). She careens through the role like a madwoman, without fear of what sounds like voice-killing dramatic effects. It's a reckless, dangerous, exciting performance. Even more surprisingly, Gencer can still sustain a tender line in the more lyrical sections of the opera. Aragall is a youthful, free-soaring Gennaro aware of the drama, and Anna Maria Rota is a big-voiced, straightforward Orsini. The San Carlo folk led by Carlo Franci are vigorous and enthusiastic. In 1973, Gencer replaced an ill Beverly Sills in a Dallas performance (Melodram). She's in a more frayed vocal estate than in 1966, less reckless, but still dramatically committed. The young, almost unknown Troyanos is a spectacular Orsini, with a lovely voice, rich and seamless throughout its range, and with a brilliant top. She is matched by Carreras's golden-voiced Gennaro. Rescigno understands and appreciates the style, and keeps the show flowing with dramatic grace. The sound, though, is quite dim, leaving a fair amount to the listener's imagination.

Although **Sutherland** was weak in the lower register by 1978, she was in good form elsewhere (Decca). It's a pleasure to hear such an easy, unforced projection, but alas, it's not a pleasure in the drama department. She's more unintelligible than usual, with little understanding of the drama. By 1978 Aragall was having vocal difficulties, which shows to ill-effect here. Horne is the vocally splendid Orsini—a virtuoso performance. Wixell's grit-afflicted voice and dull manners do little for Alfonso. Bonynge is his usual musical scholar/conductor self.

Maria di Rohan. Donizetti's penultimate opera has been ignored by the major recording companies, but has been recorded by some of the smaller firms. Like so much of Donizetti's work, it's a prima donna's opera, with its emphasis more on vocal display than on well-acted drama.

In a 1974 performance from Venice, the veteran Gavazzeni is in the pit, running a tight show yet fully sympathetic to the singers (♦Mondo Musica 10401, 2CD). Best of all, this is prime **Scotto**, completely in control of vocal technique and characterization, with little of the top voice squall that was to overcome her in later years. Tenor Umberto Grilli tends to shout and bleat with little sense of style or command, but Bruson is the epitome of elegance and refinement, beautifully sung. Elena

Zilio is the best of the Armandos, fully and finely sung. The recording favors the orchestra, sometimes at the expense of the singers.

In a mixed-bag 1988 performance, **Mariana Nicolesco** as Maria has a distinctive timbre, not particularly happy in all the fioritura; meanwhile, Giuseppe Morino tends to bleat and too often resorts to head voice, though he belts out the top notes (Nuova Era). Bernart conducts effectively. A better account of the opera may be heard in a performance from Vienna Radio led by Elio Boncompagni (Nightingale 70567, 2CD). **Gruberová** is in lovely voice, easily produced with even some semblance of characterization. Octavio Arevalo has an attractive tenor voice, but it tends to tighten under pressure. Ettore Kim's Enrico is a commanding presence.

Maria Stuarda. Of Donizetti's three "Tudor Queens," *Maria Stuarda* is the most gentle, the most delicate, and the least dramatically interesting. It also presents major musicological questions, since it exists in several versions. Donizetti wrote the opera for Naples in 1834, but production was forbidden by the king, and the composer hastily set the music to a totally new story as *Buondelmonte*. He rewrote the work again in 1835 for production in Milan. As the autograph scores have disappeared, subsequent performances rely on the edition published in Paris around 1855, an edition supposedly similar to the 1834 Naples original. Some recordings introduce material from the 1835 Milan version.

In a 1967 performance at the Maggio Musicale Fiorentino, **Gencer** is—as she is so often—variable (Hunt). Dramatic as always (perhaps too much so), she fails to create a truly sympathetic character of the tragic heroine, and is vocally exasperating with her musical tricks. Verrett is a correctly dramatic Elisabetta, Tagliavini a romantic Leicester, and Agostino Ferrin an imposing Talbot. Molinari-Pradelli is on the podium. In a substantially complete 1971 recording, **Sills** ornaments Maria's music extravagantly, a coloratura feast of spectacular impact with little in the way of drama (EMI; in "The Three Queens," DG 465967, 7CD). **Eileen Farrell**'s Elisabetta was recorded a bit too late in her career for vocal comfort, and lacks dramatic impact. Stuart Burrows is a very proper English Leicester, as Louis Quilico is a moving Talbot. Ceccato's leadership is sluggish.

Routine is the essence of a 1971 performance from La Scala, in which **Caballé** seems to intentionally give her detractors all the ammunition they need: sloppy musicality, inert rhythm, and bland characterization (Myto; Gala; Opera d'Oro). Verrett tries her best to wake up the show with flamboyant voice and personality, yet she only confuses Caballé. Cillario is the dutiful conductor. In a 1972 performance for Paris Radio that is quite a contrast, a much livelier Caballé revels in the high, sustained piano passages, even summoning a fair amount of drama for her confrontation scene with Elisabetta (♦Memories 4417, 2CD). Michèle Vilma (mislabeled as Vilma Menendez) is a regal opponent, not quite secure in her coloratura, but her rich mezzo is a fine contrast to Caballé's ethereal soprano. A young Carreras is a great pleasure as the ardent Leicester. Santi is the dutiful follower of divas.

The most complete recording is from Bologna, and is the all-around best recording as well (♦Decca 425410, 2CD). **Sutherland** creates even less of a characterization than Caballé, but other than a graceful simplicity of femininity there really is little to work with in the part. Besides, with such superb singing, who cares? Vocal technique, musicality, and sensitivity are all heard in perfect balance—an extraordinary example of her status as a major artist. Huguette Tourangeau's Elisabetta lacks Verrett's force and opulent voice, often forcing her chest tone too high into the register, yet it's an individual portrayal with genuine dramatic insight. As Leicester, Pavarotti has no competition on record. Beauty of tone, ease of production, and clear enunciation—all hallmarks of his art—are in abundance here. Bonynge leads a lively show with no tendency to dawdle (as is sometimes heard), and never underestimates the grandeur and theatricality of the work.

A 1983 recording sung in English has been reissued (EMI, now Chandos 3017, 2CD). Enough of an oddity in itself, its language is also has a mezzo-soprano in the title role: **Janet Baker.** There is historic precedent for such a transposition. Donizetti revised the role of Maria for the lower voice of Maria Malibran, but that version has not been found, so the role has been transposed anew. Rarely associated with bel canto roles, Baker has no difficulties with the fioritura, finding a multitude of colors and nuances in music and text. Rosalind Plowright easily catches the tough side of Elisabetta—a regal presence, fluidly expressed. Mackerras is hardly noted as a conductor of bel canto, so it's a pleasant surprise to hear how effective and sympathetic his conducting is; he finds a freely flowing, song-like flowering in the music.

Gruberová is almost the equal of her predecessors (Philips 426233, 2CD). Immaculately sung, with every musical point in place as part of a grand design, only a lack of spontaneity mars her performance. Baltsa is a tough-sounding Elisabetta, dramatically viable but not the most comfortable in coloratura, working hard to produce the required notes at the expense of vocal beauty. A tender, lyrical Leicester is heard from Araiza, a sonorous Talbot from Francesco Ellero d'Artegna. Patanè leads Bavarian Radio musicians in a careful, subdued performance.

Parisina d'Este. From its foreboding prelude to its melodramatic conclusion, *Parisina* is one tuneful delight after another, the epitome of a 19th-century Italian bel canto opera, packed with arias, cabalettas, duets, and good tunes. Its plot is supposedly based on a true incident at the Renaissance court of Azzo d'Este, Duke of Ferrara, and his wife, the beautiful Parisina. It's all perhaps a little too melodramatic, but the story is presented with no digressions. Love and revenge are what it's all about.

Badly cut in the ensembles, a 1964 performance from Bologna has been preserved (Giuseppe Di Stefano Records 21020, 2CD). **Marcella Pobbe** is hard-pressed in her opening aria but settles down in a bit, forcing less, and at times singing with real beauty. Renato Cioni uses his bright, forward-placed tenor in an exciting manner, sometimes suspect in pitch, but very much involved in the proceedings. Bruno Rigacci holds his small forces tightly together, propelling the action with rapid tempos. This isn't a great performance, but good enough to be enjoyable—and to show what an excellent opera this is.

A 1974 concert performance by the Opera Orchestra of New York must have been a very special event indeed, recorded from the audience in super-good sound (♦Legato 836, 2CD). The audience's excitement is almost palpable, the singers' extraordinarily so. **Caballé** is at her consummate best: seamless legato, almost total control of effects, even a real sense of character involvement, all beautifully sung. Her colleagues also sing extremely well even—albeit in a style more appropriate to Verdi than to Donizetti—but it sure is exciting! Louis Quilico as Azzo explodes volley after volley of big sound, and James Morris brings a snarl and a growl to Ernesto, turning the minor role of confidant into one of major proportions. Queler conducts with passion, power, and élan; she drives the work home.

Parisina's first commercial recording came from performances in 1997 at the Teatro Rossini in Lugo di Romagna (Bongiovanni). The opera gets off to a rocky start, the orchestra in sorry shape, with every blooper and ragged entrance emphasized by the clear recorded sound. With more participation from the strings, things improve but it's a struggle all the way. Davide Rocca is an odd-sounding, nasal bass, rather like Giorgio Tozzi with a cold, but he's the best of the lot. Pitch problems, strained passages, and flapping vibratos afflict all others. **Paolo Carignani** is on the podium.

Poliuto. This opera has a complex history: it was originally composed in Italian (for Naples, but not produced due to censor problems); it was then revised for performance in French in Paris in 1840, thoroughly reworked as *Les Martyrs,* with a new libretto by Eugène Scribe; and finally it was translated back into Italian (1848, again in Naples, shortly after the composer's death).

A 1960 performance at La Scala—an odd combination of the French and Italian versions sung in Italian—is savagely cut and in poor sound. But even in its mutilated state, it remains an important recording and historical document (EMI 65448, 2CD). This production marked the return of **Callas** to La Scala after a two-year hiatus, and Paolina was a new role for her. She sounds tentative at first (nerves?), but soon gains confidence; and although Paolina is a role secondary to Poliuto and limited in dramatic scope, she finds drama where no other could and a few pinched top notes aside, she is in grand voice. Corelli is galvanic in the title role. He weeps, he cries out—dramatically over the top—but what excitement, and what a voice! Bastianini is a dark-hued, dignified Severo. Votto, presumably responsible for this bastardized edition, follows along dutifully.

A recording from 1986 performances in Vienna reveals nearly the same edition, cuts and all, as the La Scala version (CBS). The sound is far superior, but the performance isn't. Carreras is sincere, even convincing in the title role, but without the style and excitement of Corelli. **Ricciarelli**'s Paolina is strangely beset with audible sighing and breathing (for drama?), though she's in good shape vocally. Pons pales in comparison with the far superior Bastianini. Oleg Caetani conducts a foursquare performance, with extreme tempos (very slow, very fast).

A 1988 performance from the Rome Opera is billed as *Poliuto* in its original form, but closer inspection reveals that cuts are present, as well as some anonymous tampering with the orchestration (Nuova Era). The performance barely passes muster: competent, dull, with singing more labored than inspired. **Jan Latham-König** is the competent conductor. Nuova Era usually has fine recorded sound from its taping of stage performances, but what happened here? The ambience is quite variable, and balances erratic.

A 1975 Bergamo performance of the French *Les Martyrs* has been preserved in recorded sound that is barely endurable (Myto). It's a very sad affair; the score is savagely cut, the Italian cast has difficulty with the French text, Gencer is in poor vocal estate, Mario di Felici screams his music, and only Bruson offers any semblance of musicality. Conductor **Adolfo Camozzo** hasn't the vaguest idea of what's going on. Forget this one.

Roberto Devereux. Of the three operas of Donizetti's "Tudor Trilogy," *Roberto Devereux* has been the most frequently performed, mainly due to the popularity of Beverly Sills and her outstanding portrayal of Queen Elizabeth.

A 1964 performance gets off to a rocky start with a sloppy chorus and orchestra, and a listless performance by **Gencer;** but with the arrival of Cappuccilli as Nottingham, and an enthusiastic reception of his first aria by the Naples audience, the show picks up considerably (Hunt 545; Opera d'Oro 1159; 2CD). Gencer and Rota blend well in their duets, and Gencer steadily improves in drama and fine lyric singing for a rewarding finale. Mario Rossi, usually better at this kind of endeavor, is adequate here, but fails to pick up the stage fireworks.

Caballé never recorded Elisabetta in the studio, but several examples of her lovely interpretation (her voice so eminently suitable for the role) may be heard from stage performances. A 1965 concert performance at Carnegie Hall has a very strong, bold Sara from Lili Chookasian, but Walter Alberti and Juan Oncina are pale colleagues. Cillario leads the American Opera Society chorus and orchestra. A 1972 performance from Venice is fine Caballé, but there isn't much help from her colleagues or the crude accompaniment of Bartoletti (Mondo Musica). Best of the lot is a 1977 performance from Aix-en-Provence, benefiting from the ardent Roberto of Carreras and a strong Sara by Susan Marsee, but hampered by a weak Nottingham from Vicente Sardinero (Legato 510, 2CD). Rudel conducts with a strong sense of drama.

Elisabetta was one of **Sills**'s finest roles. You can accuse her of using coloratura for verismo drama, but it works exceedingly well as she gracefully flits from one display to another. Not usually associated with bel canto endeavors, Mackerras leads the Royal Philharmonic in a cogent, sympathetic performance (♦EMI 34033, 2CD). A strikingly good complement is a 1970 New York City Opera performance with Sills ably abetted by Susan Marsee, Domingo, and Louis Quilico, with strong support from Rudel (Melodram 270107, 2CD; in "The Three Queens," DG 465967, 7CD).

Elisabetta is not a good role for **Gruberová**. Her bright, chirpy voice gives too much the impression of an empty-headed coloratura, not a tragic queen; and by 1994 her voice, while it retains a distinctive timbre, was in rough shape. Friedrich Haider guides the Strasbourg Orchestra in a no-nonsense, follow-the-singers manner.

Rosmonda d'Inghilterra. The story of Fair Rosamond lies somewhere between history and legend. Rosamond has become the mistress of King Henry II, who is estranged from his wife, Eleanor of Aquitaine. The opera was a success at its 1834 premiere, but wasn't taken up by other opera houses. It was given in Livorno in 1845, but disappeared until Opera Rara revived it in concert form in London in 1975.

The 1975 performance wasn't recorded, but in 1996 Opera Rara did record the work, fielding a strong cast to make the best case possible for its revival (♦Opera Rara 12, 2CD). The two principal ladies are a decided contrast both in the story and in their performance. Miricioiu as Eleanor may not find a sympathetic ear in some listeners; her voice is rough, with many glottal attacks, but she's earthy and compelling as the wronged wife. Fleming is in total contrast as the gentle Rosamond: her vocal technique is safe and sound, and she knows how to make her way easily through the coloratura pyrotechnics; she also knows how to get a good amount of drama from the text. Bruce Ford, always impressive in bel canto works, continues to be so here, with voice and vocal agility to spare. **David Parry** keeps the Philharmonia in line and in style with plenty of forward urgency to the movement. PARSONS

Those wishing to supplement the operas with separate versions of the overtures are pretty much out of luck; there are three volumes led by **Silvano Frontalini,** each more dispirited and slipshod than the last (Bongiovanni). We may hope that **Scimone**'s splendid recording will be reissued (Erato); until then, the few available in collections, including **Bonynge**'s *Roberto Devereux* and **Serafin**'s *Don Pasquale* and *Linda di Chamounix,* will have to suffice. Much of the same rich lyricism may be heard in **Géza Oberfrank**'s disc of three Sinfonias—actually arrangements of Donizetti's string quartets by other hands—often recalling Mendelssohn's wonderful String Symphonies (Marco Polo 223577). The early Sinfonias offered by **Roland Bayer** (along with three by Bellini)

are thoroughly delightful pieces that sound, for all the world, like Rossini (♦Koch Schwann 6733)

László Kovács offers a lyrical bouquet of Sinfonias and Concertinos for flute, oboe, clarinet, and English horn and a duo for violin and cello (Marco Polo 223701), and there used to be a similar collection led by **Jii Stárek** (Koch LP). Donizetti's ballet music for *La Favorite, Les Martyrs, Dom Sébastien,* and *l'Assedio di Calais*—as with Verdi, forced upon him by the insufferable Jockey Club—may still be found, another triumph for **de Almeida** (Philips 422844, or as a "two-fer" combined with Rossini's ballet music, ♦442553). The *Requiem,* songful—if limited in inspiration next to its successor by Verdi—is available in two recordings, led by **Miguel Angel Gomez-Martinez** (Orfeo 172881) and **Gerhard Fackler** (London 425043); since Pavarotti is the tenor soloist in the latter, that may be the safest choice. HALLER

John Dowland *(1563–1626)*

Dowland is perhaps the most easily identifiable of Elizabethan composers. His four published books of lute songs assure him a place at, or near the top, of the tree of singing birds that distinguishes that remarkable era. He also wrote a substantial amount of music for the lute alone, and his *Lachrimae* for viol consort are justly famous. His work tends to be gloomy, at times almost recalling the manneristic madrigals of Gesualdo, yet he maintains an English balance that produces light and merry music as well. A set by **Anthony Rooley** and his Consort of Musicke contains not only all of Dowland's works, but also arrangements for keyboard and mixed consort by many other hands (♦Oiseau-Lyre 452563, 12CD). This is a good general recommendation.

Lute Songs. The heart of the composer lies here. The songs may be authentically played in many ways, as the lute accompaniment is actually written in individual lines like a Bach fugue, and therefore may be performed on everything from a single lute to a viol consort, to a group of madrigal singers, or anything in-between. **Rooley** explores all the possibilities in his complete recording, choosing different scores according to the style of the song. The result presents the composer at his best. I initially thought that Rooley was over-serious, but listening to the entire collection shows a convincing variety of mood and texture. His set also includes "A Musicall Banquet," arranged by Dowland's son Robert, which contains (alongside three of Robert's finest songs) 17 others from various sources, many continental; it's a fascinating feast.

Earlier stars of the 1950s like **Deller** (Vanguard 8112; Harmonia Mundi 790245) and **Oberlin** (Lyrichord 8011) have explored the possibilities in their own inimitable ways, while the **Saltire Singers** are still with us as well, emphasizing the madrigalian possibilities (Lyrichord 8031). These four discs vary in their appeal. Deller's Vanguard disc was made in 1966, with his Consort and lutenist Desmond Dupré and is rather intense, as his voice is a bit exaggerated and always at the fore—even in the consort songs. The Harmonia Mundi recording was made in 1978 with Robert Spencer, lute, and a viol consort. Deller sings only nine songs, Spencer plays nine pieces, and the consort plays two. Deller is more relaxed and better controlled. Oberlin's disc is with Joseph Ladone, lute, and consists of 11 songs and two lute pieces. Next to Deller, he's the best known of the early countertenors; yet some may find his vibrato and somewhat insistent tone off-putting. The Saltire Singers are a fine madrigal group; they sing 13 songs. Both Lyrichord discs are approximately 45 minutes long.

A good contrast (and a good buy) is a disc by **Steven Rickards** with Dorothy Linell, lute (♦Naxos 553381). Rickards has a pure sound with more variety than either Deller or Oberlin, and good diction. He sings 19 songs, while Linell plays seven numbers (some not by Dowland).

The consort music consists of the series of *Lachrimae pavans* and 14 other dances, frequently recorded together. **The Consort of Musicke**'s performance is sonorous and satisfactory, but the competition is fierce in this area. You can't go wrong with **Savall** (Astrée 8701) or the **Parley of Instruments** (Hyperion 66637), to mention only those who have recorded the complete *Lachrimae*.

Lute music. Here is the only area where **Rooley**'s collection may not be the optimum choice. Rooley uses a variety of performers ranging from good (Rooley) to excellent (Jakob Lindberg, Nigel North), with Anthony Bailes and Christopher Wilson in-between. All are recorded in a somewhat dry acoustic, emphasizing the woody sound of the instrument. Going from this to **Paul O'Dette**'s collection, recorded in a beautifully resonant space by a player with total command of the contrapuntal potential of the instrument, is a revelation (♦Harmonia Mundi 2907160, 5CD). **Lindberg** has also recorded the complete lute music from and judging his imaginative playing for Rooley, that would be a close contender as well (BIS 722, 4CD).

Bream's explorations of the repertoire include a good deal of Dowland's lute music, available in his mammoth retrospective collection (listed under the artist rather than the composer in *Schwann*; RCA 61583, Vol. 3, "Dances of Dowland"). Bream is a nonpareil performer, though he brings a bit of guitar ethos to his lute technique, using metal-wound bass strings, and certain phrasing habits that hint at later styles. **Ronn McFarlane**'s collection of 28 pieces is smoothly played and recorded (Dorian 90148). Finally, tenor **Stephen Potter** presents ten songs and three *Lachrimae* arranged and recomposed for an odd group of lute, soprano saxophone, baroque violin, and bass (ECM 1697). The idea is to update Dowland to the 20th century, but the result makes me long for the original—the contemporary additions only proves Dowland's superiority.   MOORE

Felix Draeseke (1835–1913)

Son of the court preacher at Coburg, Draeseke entered the Leipzig Conservatory over his father's objections, and after hearing *Lohengrin* at Weimar, he wrote his own opera *König Sigurd* before turning 18. When his early symphonic poems met with disapproval from the conservative establishment, Draeseke—along with von Bülow, Cornelius, and others—made up the "New German School," and turned to the symphony instead, expanding harmonically upon the Brahmsian model. He settled in Switzerland, but faced with continued critical rejection, returned to Germany where he finally saw his operas performed; his trilogy *Christus* attained great acclaim the year before his death. Draeseke is becoming far more popular in recent years than he ever was in life, and with several labels announcing major recording projects, it seems his time may have come at last.

Draeseke struggled to merge the progressive harmonic and melodic philosophy of Liszt and Wagner with traditional symphonic form. Certainly there is rich melodic inspiration in Symphony 1, and it often recalls Wagner's early symphony. **George Hanson** clearly believes in this music; he and provides strong support for Claudius Tanski in the E-flat Piano Concerto, a potent and highly gratifying exercise in the Lisztian manner. Tanski's clarion tone and insouciant sashay through the final rondo make this a disc to treasure (♦MD+G 3350929).

Symphony 3 (*Symphonia Tragica*) remains one of Draeseke's most imposing scores. The name stems from the second movement (Grave), a massive and cathartic funeral march even rivaling the "Eroica" in intensity. Under **Jörg-Peter Weigle** the symphony at last stands revealed as a masterpiece. The likewise affecting *Funeral March*, written in memory of German soldiers slain during the Boer wars, is a generous addition, and this CD is especially valuable for collectors of late German Romantic fare (♦CPO 999581).

The AK Coburg label, under the auspices of the International Draeseke Society, has released three discs thus far. **Franco Sciannameo** and Eric Moe offer Viola Sonatas 1 and 2 on DR 0001; DR 0002 features **Barbara Thiem** in the Cello Sonata, *Ballade,* and *Barcarole,* aided by Wolfgang Müller-Steinbach, who contributes several solo piano pieces. **Martin Nitschmann** plays the Clarinet Sonata on DR 0003, and **Nanette Schmidt** offers an alternate version for violin plus the dramatic *Scene* based on themes from the unproduced opera *Bertrand de Born*. The Cello Sonata expands upon the Brahmsian model, while inhabiting a sound-world uniquely Draeseke's own; the viola sonatas, like Schubert's *Arpeggione*, were written for the now obsolete viola alta, yet it suits the standard viola comfortably. The clarinet sonata may well be the first such work of the Romantic period, and the violin arrangement is the composer's own. This is beautiful music, played with great sympathy and affection, which anyone who loves the chamber music of Brahms and Schumann will surely find well worth investigating.

Draeseke's quintet for the unusual combination of piano, violin, viola, cello, and horn is a triumph of ingenious design and color, with the horn seamlessly and sonorously blended into the resplendent whole. A coupling with Schumann's familiar E-flat Piano Quartet is as fascinating for its exploration of divergent harmonic styles as for its masterful performance by **Gottfried Langenstein** (♦MD+G 0673, with Mozart's Piano Quartet). **Claudius Tanski** has recorded *Sonata quasi fantasia* twice, first on Altarus 9030 and a year later on MD+G 3514, coupled both times with the Liszt Sonata; other than the recording, which is a bit more close up on MD+G, his essentially muscular reading is little changed—though the piece itself remains an interesting yet diffuse exercise.

Draeseke's *Christus,* subtitled "A Mystery in an Introduction and Three Oratorios," took him nearly five years to complete and comprises nothing less than a complete, history of the life of Jesus from birth through the Crucifixion and Resurrection. It fills five CDs (Bayer 100175/79), though the total time of 4:54 suggests it could have fit quite comfortably on four. While there is much that suggests Wagner—as well as Mendelssohn's *Elijah* and *St. Paul*—there are unavoidable *longueurs* as it proceeds, gradually mounting in tension along the road to Calvary. Breslau forces under **Udo Follert** are at least competent, and baritone Phillip Langshaw as Christ, though tonally spare, proves effective in a role that might tax Fischer-Dieskau. Given the committed leadership of **Uwe Gronostay** and the superbly blended singing of the Netherlands Chamber Choir (Globe 5147, with Schumann's four Songs for Double Chorus Op. 141), the Mass in A minor, written for a cappella choir, is a compelling mix of ancient and modern harmonies that consistently holds your attention.   HALLER

Jacob Druckman (1928–96)

Druckman was a leading exponent of the American experimental avant-garde of the '60s. His fascination with musical imagery, timbral contrast, and relationships of time and space in music led to a uniquely rich and kaleidoscopic mature style. For Druckman, experimentation, whether technical or musical, opened huge possibilities, and his output embraced most musical media except grand opera. There are frequent backward glances to the Italian Baroque, with direct quotes from Cavalli, Cherubini, and other composers. His few works for large orchestra are landscapes through which he filters sounds and images. Works with titles such as *Windows, Chiaroscuro,* and *Prism* evoke opposites: open and closed, light and shade, and the spectrum of what lies in-between.

Druckman was 44 years old before his first major orchestral work, *Windows* (written for Bruno Maderna), immediately won the Pulitzer Prize; it's conducted by **Arthur Weisberg** (CRI 781). The contrasts between tonal and atonal elements are focused through an imitation of late Debussy. This disc covers a critical phase of Druckman's evolution, with very fine remastered recordings, and includes **de Gaetani** singing *Dark upon the Harp,* an instrumental song cycle, and *Animus II,* a wild electronic piece. The Juilliard Orchestra led by **Lukas Foss** gives a memorable reading of Druckman's next orchestral essay, *Chiaroscuro* (New World 381, with pieces by Schwantner and Albert). *Chiaroscuro* is loaded with atmosphere and sharply defined elements of sound amid sustained and transitory backgrounds, which evolve into foregrounds and vice versa.

Druckman's concern with all these elements evolved further in *Aureole,* where the circular halo provides its own metaphor for the treatment of opposites and their reconciliation, with allusions to Bernstein. **Slatkin** and the St. Louis Symphony do the honors here (New World 318, with two pieces by Michael Colgrass). Of the four large orchestral pieces available, *Prism* explores all these elements, recorded by **Mehta** and the New York Philharmonic when Druckman was their composer in residence (New World 335, with Rochberg's Oboe Concerto).

Two chamber music discs merit special mention: The **Group for Contemporary Music** has recorded String Quartets 2 and 3 (Koch 7049). Quartet 2 is notable for its experimental technical devices, such as exaggerated ponticello, whereas Quartet 3 is more classical and retrospective. *Reflections on the Nature of Water* for marimba is like an exquisite, shimmering Japanese woodprint. These are superb performances by a very committed ensemble and are highly recommended. The other disc, by the **New York Philomusica** (on their own record label), also contains Quartet 3, with the absorbing early *Divertimento* and the coolly oriental *Bo* for percussion, harp, bass clarinet, and women's voices (NYPM 10023/5). Toward the end of his life, Druckman's imitative instincts drew him in a more romantic, even tonal direction, as this piece shows. JOHNSON

Guillaume Dufay *(1397–1474)*

Dufay (or du Fay) was the greatest composer of his generation. Between 1420 and 1458 he spent many years in Italy, notably at the court of Savoy; but from 1439 until his death, he was a canon at Cambrai cathedral. He composed sacred and secular vocal music. His principal sacred forms are the isothythmic motet in his earlier years (1420 to the 1440s) and after that the cantus firmus mass. The complete set of 13 isothythmic motets is available in a splendid disc by Paul van Nevel's **Huelgas Ensemble** (♦Harmonia Mundi 901700). Another complete recording, by a vocal and instrumental ensemble under **Helga Weber,** is less satisfactory, but it includes seven cantilena-motets (Renaissance 108, 3CD).

Dufay's early mass compositions preceded his mass cycles; they consist of single movements, or such sets as a *Gloria-Credo* or *Sanctus-Agnus* pair. They haven't been recorded often, but **Kees van Otten** has arbitrarily assembled ten of these movements into two cycles (♦Stradivarius 33440).

The mass cycles are discussed in order of composition.

Missa sine nomine. The **Clemencic Ensemble**'s version of this early

mass for three voices is neither complete nor satisfactory (Harmonia Mundi 190939, with *Missa Ecce ancilla Domini*).

Missa Sancti Jacobi. I like Andrew Kirkman's **Binchois Consort** version of this work for its beauty of sound (♦Hyperion 66997, with motets and a pair of mass movements). **Alejandro Planchart** directed the same work with a college group (Lyrichord 8013).

Missa Sancti Anthonii. Two versions are very fine, but I slightly prefer Alexander Blachly's **Pomerium** (♦Archiv 447772) to the **Binchois Consort** for its warmer vocal sound (Hyperion 66854).

Missa Caput. The anonymous *Missa Caput* formerly attributed to Dufay is certainly not his work. The last four are cantus firmus masses, based on a song or chant melody that runs throughout, usually in the tenor part.

Missa Se la face ay pale. This wedding mass, based on the composer's own song, has always been his most popular. Edith Ho's **Advent Church Choir** offers the best of the unaccompanied choral versions (♦Arsis 118, with *Missa Ecce ancilla Domini*), and the **Hilliard Ensemble** has the best of the unaccompanied one-voice-to-a-part versions (♦Hilliard Live 4). All the older recordings used instrumental accompaniment, and the best of these is David Munrow's **Early Music Consort** (Virgin 561283).

Missa L'homme armé. This mass is based on the anonymous song that was used by almost 30 composers as a cantus firmus. The **Hilliard Ensemble**'s version is an outstanding example of the group's superb intonation and pacing (♦EMI 747628, with five motets). Jeremy Summerly's **Oxford Camerata** gives a more broadly paced performance, and is almost as good (Naxos 553087, with one motet).

Missa Ecce ancilla Domini. This mass, as sung by Dominique Vellard's **Ensemble Gilles Binchois,** is among the finest Dufay discs for its fillers (mass propers probably composed for the Burgundian court) and the exquisite singing (♦Virgin 545050).

Missa Ave Regina caelorum. I also prefer the composer's last mass (1472) by Vellard's **Ensemble Cantus Figuratus** (♦Stil 0710 SAN 85, with chant propers). Miroslav Venhoda's **Prague Madrigal Singers** coupled this with the *Missa Ecce ancilla Domini* using a battery of instruments in a style no longer well regarded (Supraphon 110637), and the **Clemencic Consort** recorded the two masses in a similarly overblown fashion (Harmonia Mundi).

Dufay's smaller sacred pieces have been neglected. **Schola Hungarica** recorded many of his hymns, three-voice arrangements of chant hymns that he composed for the papal choir (♦Hungaroton 12951). The same group also recorded the newly discovered *Recollectio Festorum Beatae Mariae Virginis,* chants composed in 1457 for a feast celebrated at Cambrai (♦Hungaroton 31292). **Pomerium** recorded a smaller part of this set of chants (♦Archiv 447773, with four motets).

Over 80 secular songs, most of them in rondeau form, date from every period of Dufay's life. The complete recording by the **Medieval Ensemble** is more than satisfactory, even if individual songs have been surpassed by other performers (♦Oiseau-Lyre 452557, 5CD). Michael Posch's **Ensemble Unicorn** offers a useful selection of 17 songs, but half of them are only performed instrumentally (Naxos 553458). WEBER

Paul Dukas *(1865–1935)*

Paul Dukas was a fastidious composer, an excellent and influential teacher at the Paris Conservatoire, and a respected music critic—and he wrote *The Sorcerer's Apprentice,* which has pretty much obliterated all his other achievements. This piece deserves its status as a light classic, but it's more brilliantly scored and impeccably constructed than many heavier classics. No wonder everybody likes it! Unfortunately, those who do like it don't have many other rooms to explore *chez* Dukas; he destroyed almost all his manuscripts before his death, leaving just a handful of works.

For a good recording of *Sorcerer's Apprentice*—well, just pick your favorite conductor. There are enjoyable versions by **Bernstein** (Sony 47596 or 60695), **Ormandy** (Sony 46329), **Ansermet** (London 448576), **Kunzel** (Telarc 80115), **Stokowski** (Pearl 9488, old mono, for *Fantasia* fans), and **Toscanini** (RCA 60322, ditto), usually in a program of other light or French music. My favorite, however, is **Dutoit,** which is witty, pointed, and sumptuously played and recorded (♦London 421527).

If you like *Firebird* and *Daphnis et Chloé,* try *La Péri,* Dukas's last major work. It's an entertaining exercise in *le style Diaghilev,* with fragrant orchestration and memorable tunes (including the brass fanfare that begins it). **Ansermet**'s famous recording from the late '50s is fondly remembered by collectors (♦London 433714). **Boulez**'s approach in his 1976 version (♦Sony 68333) is a bit severe for such an exotic score, but it is splendidly played by the New York Philharmonic (as is the generous coupling, Falla's complete *Three-Cornered Hat* ballet). **Tortelier**'s track record in French music is excellent, and it's coupled with *Sorcerer's Apprentice* and some Chabrier (Chandos 8852).

For a work rarely performed in the concert hall, Dukas's rich and sonorous Symphony in C has had a surprising number of recordings over the years. **Tortelier** offers the best performance and recording and a good coupling in Dukas's *Polyeucte* overture, one of the better examples of 19th-century French Wagneriana (♦Chandos 9225). **Lawrence Foster** rivals Tortelier in white-hot intensity, and Fauré's *Pelléas et Mélisande* makes an inspired coupling (♦Claves 9102). **Armin Jordan**'s is an older recording that remains very enjoyable, including his *La Péri* (Erato 88089), while those fortunate enough to find the splendid **Martinon** will get not only an electric and beautifully nuanced symphony, but also an all too-brief-selection from *Ariane et Barbe-Bleue* (♦EMI 63160).

But there's one recording that has it all: gorgeous sound, thrilling and atmospheric music-making, and above superb conducting, from **López-Cobos** and the Cincinnati Symphony (♦Telarc 80515). You get the Symphony in C, *La Péri* and *Sorcerer's Apprentice,* all wonderfully done. **Slatkin** tries to pull off the same trifecta but fails miserably, in overwrought readings swallowed up by cavernous acoustics (RCA). In other threesomes, **Fournet** has the sound but not the fury (Denon), while **Petitgirard** is bland, and so are the sonics (OSF).

Dukas's most famous piano work is *Variations, Interlude and Finale on a Theme of Rameau,* a brainy, concise composition as close as French piano music comes to Beethoven's *Diabelli Variations.* **Johannesen** performs it in a program of mostly rare pieces (Vox 3032), and a disc by **Fingerhut** contains all Dukas's piano works, including a mammoth sonata (Chandos 8765).

That leaves *Ariane et Barbe-Bleue,* the *other* early 20th-century French opera based on Maeterlinck and written in a "symphonic" style, or if you prefer, the other opera about Bluebeard's Castle. But Dukas's most ambitious work is quite unlike Debussy or Bartók, and unlike most French operas, was admired by such non-Frenchmen as Schoenberg, Berg, and Bruno Walter. **Jordan**'s recording with Ciesinski and Bacquier is the only choice, but a good one (Erato 45663).　　　　RAYMOND

Henri Duparc (1848–1933)

Duparc is famous for what he *didn't* write: besides a few odds and ends, and a few orchestral pieces (chiefly the symphonic poem *Lénore*), his life work consists of 14 very beautiful songs, written between 1868 and 1884. A devoted pupil of Franck (whose Symphony in D Minor is dedicated to him), Duparc contracted a neurasthenic condition that made him unduly critical of his own composing efforts. And so he gave up, spending the rest of his life in solitude and steadily worsening health, dying blind and paralyzed at 85.

Duparc's refined and sumptuously romantic response to poetry makes his songs the best in France before Fauré's. They are popular in recitals but infrequently recorded. The great French baritone **Charles Panzéra**'s recordings of 13, made in 1937 with his wife Madeleine at the piano, remain a model of how to sing them in their characteristic straightforwardness and depth of feeling (♦EMI 64254). Pickings are slim among contemporary singers. **Holzmair** has a beautiful baritone voice, but is interpretively bland (Philips 46686); British mezzo **Della Jones** sounds more sumptuous, and her inclusion of three songs in a French recital (including perhaps the two best, *La vie antérieure* and *L'Invitation au Voyage*) makes me wish she'd recorded more (Chandos 9147).

Duparc orchestrated several of his more famous songs. These are undeniably attractive, but lack the immediacy of the piano originals; the scoring renders the torpid mood of *La vie antérieure* so well that it's practically immobile. Two star singers shine in these: **Baker** sings five of them with Previn (EMI 68667), and **Te Kanawa** sings seven with Tate (EMI 69802, a budget release). Duparc's *other* work *Lénore,* a short, dramatic tone poem, can be found in a French grab-bag ("The Sorcerer's Apprentice") led by **Plasson** (EMI).　　　　RAYMOND

Marcel Dupré (1886–1971)

Dupré is best remembered by his organ solos; the most popular of which are listed below chronologically. Although he was very open to different interpretations of his works, most performers differ primarily in tempo and some occasional alterations in registration. Naturally, the choice of instrument and church size makes the biggest difference.

SOLO ORGAN MUSIC

There are two ongoing series of the complete organ works: Naxos features a different instrument and performer for almost every disc; already up to seven CDs, these are very satisfying interpretations provided by some of America's top organists. **Jeremy Filsell** continues to record the complete works at St. Boniface, Sarasota, in a series of 12 discs (Guild).

Preludes & Fugues (1912). The first and third of the three are the most familiar, and have remained staples in the literature since their 1920 publication. Within a reverberant atmosphere, **Michelle Leclerc** at the cavernous La Madeleine dishes up a big sound, which sometimes causes the details to get lost; nonetheless, it's a commanding version(Motette). A fine performance is supplied by **Robert Noehren** on an unspecified 3-manual installation (♦Facet 8001). His sense of style and phrasing is superb, and the clarity is excellent. The best recording in terms of tempo, registration, clarity, and power when needed is **Pierre Cochereau** at Notre-Dame (♦FY 020). The recording was made in 1975, before he introduced the exaggerated tempos and somewhat biting registration evident in his later discs; here, everything is just right. In fact, the disc itself is an excellent investment for Dupré-ites, for it also includes *Cortège, Noël Variations,* and *Passion Symphony.* A search in LP bins may turn up all three played by the composer (Mercury 90231, "Dupré at St. Sulpice," Vol. 5)

Les Vêpres de la Vierge (1919). These 15 pieces were originally improvisations by Dupré at Notre-Dame while substituting for Vierne, here he alternates chant with organ responses. **Jean-Pierre Lecaudey** provides straightforward, reasonably clean interpretations, though the instrument is somewhat quirky (Pavane). Both **James Biery** (Afka) and **Robert Delcamp** (Naxos) deliver solid, accurate, conservative readings, though the pedal occasionally clouds the manual work on Biery's disc.

Two excellent versions must be mentioned, both for the instrument and the use of a choir: **Suanne Chaisemartin** at the marvelously resonant St. Ouen (Rouen) presides over one of Cavaillé-Coll's masterpieces (♦Motette 50251). The echo is formidable, which demands a certain compensation in the tempo. Each organ piece is preceded by appropriate chant, here by members of the St. Nicholas Choirschool (the chant appears to have been recorded later at a different site). The sound is wonderful, though sometimes muddy owing to the acoustics. A similar recording that may be the best choice comes from the very church where Dupré first created this work—Notre-Dame. **Philippe Lefebvre** alternates with chant performed by Cambridge's Schola Gregoriana (♦Herald 170). With a bit less (but still ample) echo, he does a first-rate job with good articulation and appropriate registration. On this disc, the choir organ assists the singers.

Cortège et Litany (1921). Another program favorite was originally an organ solo, which Dupré later arranged for organ and orchestra. There aren't any "best" versions of this—it all depends on your sense of appropriate tempo, volume, and whether to pull all the stops at the end. A very respectable version comes from **Michael Murray** on a two-manual Schoenstein in SS. Peter & Paul, San Francisco (♦Afka 512). Good clarity, smooth crescendos, and a "French" sound make this quite satisfying. Equally clear but with a bigger sound is **Todd Wilson** on a 4-65 stop Holtkamp at the University of Alabama (Delos). The last page is mercifully restrained. **Cochereau** commands a much larger instrument, delivering the fastest and surely the most grandiose version from Notre-Dame (♦FY 020). The 'Litany' expands smoothly until the massive combination of the two themes; on the turn of the page, the 32' Bombardes are cut in. Whether to your taste or not, it's thrilling. If you wonder how **Dupré** played it, look for "Dupré at St. Sulpice Vol. 2" in the LP bin (Mercury 90229). (For the orchestral setting, see below.)

Variations sur un vieux Noël (1922). This is one of Dupré's most frequently programmed works, a showcase for both instrument and performer. It demands an instrument with a sufficiently broad stop list to do it justice. **Janice Beck** plays with good tempo and clarity on a modest Oberthür in St.-Etienne, Auxerre (Real Music). Two rather comparable versions on similar sized Skinner organs are quite acceptable as mainstream interpretations: **Alan Morrison** (Gothic) and **Douglas Cleveland** (RBW). Morrison has the edge in engineering clarity. **John Farris** is convincing; the finale is a bit heavy but the rest is fine (Delos). **Brian Jones** does a splendid job controlling the 4-302 behemoth at West Point (Motette). For all its size, there is remarkable clarity in this recording.

For registration that has more bite, coupled with fine performances, two stand out. **Lecaudey** chose the organ in St. Rémy for his first volume of Dupré organ works because its pungency and clarity reflect the youthful nature of this literature (♦FY 020). The choice is good, as the instrument sounds the best in this selection. **Cochereau** draws upon the vast resources at Notre-Dame for his registrations, which are piquant yet fairly mainstream (♦Pavane 7382). Superb engineering provides the clarity easily lost in that cathedral, and this is the overall performance of choice. LP fans can hear **Dupré** play this piece (Mercury 90229).

Symphonie-Passion ("*The World Awaiting the Savior,*" 1924). There are many fine recordings of this. **Biery** gives a respectable though often labored version from St. Joseph's, Hartford (Afka). An interesting recording from Stockholm has **Torvald Torén** providing a somewhat objective interpretation, without much nuance (Proprius). However, the sound is bright, with clean engineering. **David Briggs** is a solid contender; he grasps the flow of the movements and makes the organ in St. George Hall (Liverpool) very listenable (Priory).

Three Frenchmen, however, take the honors. **Mathieu** at St. Antoine (Paris) controls a nicely balanced 3-52 Cavaillé-Coll with good tempos and proper registration (♦Adda 581278). **Cochereau**'s 1975 recording has excellent engineering, but a rather hard-edged sound (♦FY 020). The finale is blistering, and the last cascade of chords is too hurried, but he captures the excitement of the opening movement better than anyone; this is a powerful recording, full of drama. The very best performance I've heard is by Cochereau in the '50s at Notre-Dame with a less harried approach and more relaxed tempos, especially the final movement (Solstice 177/78, 2CD, with Vierne's). **Yves Castagnet** at St. Ouen (Rouen) vies for top honors (♦Sony 57485). The sound is massive when necessary, and the tempos less anxious. There is an awesome reverberation in the cathedral, and the 32' Pedal Bombarde is peerless.

Le Chemin de la Croix (*Stations of the Cross, 1931*). This was premiered in Brussels as 14 improvisations alternating with Paul Claudel's spoken stanzas. Both **Harald Feller** at Basilica Waldsassen (Calig) and **Chaisemartin** at St. Etienne, Caen (Esoldum) deliver thick, rather heavy performances, dictated perhaps by the respective acoustics. Inner lines are lost, even though the sound is rich. **Stephen Hamilton** offers a clear and accurate reading, but without much drama or excitement (Arkay). A very respectable performance is by **Wolfgang Gehring** at the Abbey Marienstatt (♦Christophorus 0076). The sound is a bit hard-edged (a 4-61 stop Rieger), but it seems appropriate for many of the movements. It's well articulated. Also meriting special notice is **Jacquelin Rochette** at Notre-Dame du Cap (♦Real Music 311174): the snarling Casavant makes for dramatic alternation with the Claudel verses beautifully read by Jean Marchand.

Evocation (1941). A somber work dedicated to the composer's father, first performed in St. Ouen (Rouen), Dupré's own church, as the previously dismantled organ was rededicated. **Beck** at St. Etienne (Auxerre) provides a neat, if somewhat objective interpretation (Real Music). **Torén** is more aggressive, and the hard-edged Stockholm instrument seems a good choice for this music (Proprius). Two versions are preferable. **Cochereau**'s 1975 LP includes this piece, and here the biting sound at Notre-Dame matches the overall mood (♦FY 020, not on the CD); **Castagnet** plays on the very St. Ouen organ Dupré used for the premiere (♦Sony 57485). This is a superb performance, and well engineered in this extremely reverberant church.

ORGAN AND ORCHESTRA

Cortège et Litany. Originally an organ solo, Dupré arranged it for organ and orchestra in 1921. **Filsell** has a conservative interpretation (Guild). The balance is sometimes lost as the "Litany" theme overshadows the "Cortège" near the end. The I-V-I timpani pattern at the conclusion is just too heavy. A smoother performance, with some interesting liberties taken with the score, comes from **Daniel Jay McKinley;** this is a very musical interpretation that holds the forces in balance and doesn't get carried away with bombast (♦Naxos 553922).

Symphony in G minor. This was Dupré's first attempt to combine orchestra with organ in an extended composition. **Ulrich Meldau** plays a 3-69 installation in the Kirche Enge, Zurich (Motette). The balance is excellent, but the organ lacks punch in the big moments, and distant miking loses some of the clarity. Both **McKinley** (♦Naxos 553922) and **Filsell** (♦Guild 7136) supply excellent performances. However, Filsell provides more emotion and more sweep; the sumptuous third movement is as lovely and moving a sonic tapestry as you could want.

METZ

Maurice Duruflé (1902–86)

Duruflé became *titulaire* at St. Etienne-du-Mont (Paris) in 1930, and later taught harmony at the Conservatoire. He wrote mostly for organ and voices, and his output was limited. His works are permeated with chant themes or chant-like melodies, generally cast in a modal fabric. The fluid writing and harmonic language that speak of an earlier time have made his choral music increasingly popular.

CHORAL MUSIC

Requiem (1947, revised 1961). There are three versions: for full orchestra, reduced orchestra, and organ only. While orchestral versions can't be surpassed, recommendations of organ-only versions will be made for interested choir directors and organists.

Among the full orchestra performances, **Shaw** received rave reviews, but I find the recording a bit too gentle and too remote (Telarc). The miking seems distant, and while vocal lines are very smooth, they lack personality; perhaps is was Shaw's intention. The mezzo solo on "Pie Jesu" is performed by all the second sopranos, making the movement depersonalized. **Michel Legrand** was well-received, but suffers from some out-of-synch moments and rather disappointing enunciation from the choir (Teldec). He lets too many individual orchestral lines protrude. **Hickox** has the most luxurious version, though on LP and cassette only (Argo). Boy trebles supplement the London Chorus, and while soaring in the "Christe," they disappoint in the final "In Paradisum." Otherwise, there is great sound and fine soloists. Another oldie worthy of plaudits is the original **Duruflé** from St. Etienne, winner of the Grand Prix du Disque in 1959, which is wonderful throughout (Erato).

The reduced orchestra version is popular, and Duruflé himself preferred it for its intimacy. Again, three interpretations emerge. **Dennis Keene** (♦Delos 3169) produces a Shaw-like smoothness from his singers, while the organ part is more convincing from **Michel Piquemal** (♦Naxos 553196). Both choirs and ensembles are good, as are the **Corydon Singers** (♦Hyperion 66191).

The organ-only version requires a good-sized instrument and a performer able to accommodate the many changes in tempo, rhythm, and registration. The **Westminster Choir** suffers from a distant mike and a glaring lack of choral blend (Hyperion). A better performance from England is by **St. John's College** (London). The **Hallgrimskirkja Motet Choir** from Iceland offers some wonderful sounds, especially from the luminous sopranos, but the performance lacks the needed phrasing and style (Thorofon). The **Brabants Chamber Choir** basically needs a better and larger organ for the accompaniment, though the choir is outstanding (Erasmus). The interpretation

of choice is by the **Rouen Choir,** with high marks in every category (♦Solstice 140).

Motets on Gregorian Themes (1960). Here are four very short harmonizations of chant themes set for unaccompanied mixed choir, frequently heard in high school and college choral programs. Each is a gem, and each reflects the smooth, elastic rhythm appropriate for subtle text stresses. Unless you really prefer English choirs with boy trebles, you may wish to skip the **Westminster Choir** for its rather English-sounding version, along with some hard-edged passages (Hyperion). Lack of homogeneous sound and an absence of flow rob the **Stéphane Caillat Choir** of higher marks (Erato). Two recordings are quite good: the **Michel Piquemal Vocal Ensemble** (♦Naxos 553196) has a well-balanced, adult choral sound, in a pleasant acoustical setting; and the **Brabants Chamber Choir** (♦Erasmus 160), with more remote miking in a very resonant hall, provides clear, almost cool vocal lines with perfect blend and balance.

Notre Père (Our Father, 1976). This was Duruflé's last composition, and was dedicated to his wife. Originally a single melody with organ accompaniment, he later arranged it for unaccompanied choir. Again, the **Brabants Chamber Choir** treats it in a clean, cool manner (♦Erasmus 160), while **Piquemal**'s forces do more with volume changes (♦Naxos 553196). Both versions are excellent. **Keene** chose the original, and has the melody performed by his choir's baritones (Delos); I prefer the choral arrangement.

Mass "Cum Jubilo" (1966). As with the *Requiem*, there are three arrangements of this work, and several recordings worthy of mention. It's unusual, being scored for baritone solo, baritone choir, orchestra and organ. Keene and Piquemal use the reduced instrumental version, and both interpretations are good. **Keene** has the more homogeneous choral sound (♦Delos 3169), while **Piquemal**'s orchestra plays with a bit more presence (♦Naxos 553197). Both soloists are commendable. A rewarding interpretation is heard from the Toulouse Orchestra led by **Plasson,** with Hampson as soloist (EMI 56878). **Duruflé**'s own interpretation can't be overlooked: This is the full orchestra version, and the soloist (Roger Sayer) is outstanding (♦Erato 98526). Though recorded in 1971, this remains the most satisfying recording.

ORGAN MUSIC

Duruflé wrote few organ works, as he felt comfortable only when each piece was "perfect". In keeping with most 20-century organ composers, his performance directions in the score—registration, tempo, phrasing—are detailed and specific. Thus what differentiates one performance from another has more to do with the size of the instrument, available registration, building acoustics, locations of microphones, etc.

Complete works. At least seven recordings of the complete organ works are available. In general, the best performances of any particular piece can also be found here. In every case the instrument heard is a large-scale church installation. Timings are remarkably similar, so deciding factors are style and the actual instrument.

Sometimes the church can have too much echo. **John Scott** suffers from this problem, playing in London's St. Paul's Cathedral (Hyperion). With an eight- to ten-second reverberation, the overlap muddies the water; in addition, the miking is rather remote. The organ and surroundings in Pithiviers, France, should be better suited for recording, but the instrument used by **Herndon Spillman** has a dominant pedal, close miking, and a frequently harsh quality (Titanic). **Piet van der Steen** performs on an exceptionally reedy Dutch organ in St. Bavo's

(Marcato); here a sameness prevails in much of the registration. He takes liberties with tempos, and in *Fugue on the Carillon,* makes it far more ponderous than was intended.

There are four excellent choices. **Olivier Latry** performs at Duruflé's own church, St. Etienne (Paris), on a splendid instrument (♦BNL 112508). Occasionally it seems a bit harsh in quality, and Latry likes to hang on to a final chord too long now and then, but these are the very sounds for which Duruflé wrote. **Todd Wilson** matches Latry's technique on a fine, French-styled organ in Dallas (♦Delos 3047). The tone quality is smooth, the interpretations outstanding. A topnotch performance by **David Patrick** comes from Coventry Cathedral (♦ASV 993). English organs don't usually have the best tone quality for French literature, but this instrument is quite surprising, and Patrick does a fine job. **Bernhard Leonardy**'s recording at St. Eustache is one of the best—wonderful acoustics and the 5-147 Van den Heuvel organ (Motette 12531). All complete sets include the lesser-known short works popular with some organists for their brevity and relative ease of performance.

Prélude, Adagio et Choral varié sur le thème du **Veni Creator** (1930). A prize winning composition using a familiar chant theme, this is a fine showpiece for an instrument's range and capacity. A very well-managed performance by **Marilyn Keiser** is available in clear, intelligent playing on a Holtkamp (♦Gothic 49037). **Mary Preston** offers a good larger-scaled performance from Dallas's Meyerson Center (♦Gothic 49079).

Suite Op. 5 (1933). This is a dramatic three-movement work that is among the more challenging in the repertory, a fine test piece for both organ and performer. Some of the available performances are marred by too remote miking—**Jennifer Bate** (DKP-Unicorn)—or a somewhat muddy sound—**Jean-François Vaucher** (Gallo). **Preston** provides good momentum throughout and supplies some unusual registration near the end of the "Toccata," but the acoustics of the Dallas concert hall lack the reverberation of a large church (Gothic). In technique, sound, registration, and recording quality, **John Tuttle** has the edge (♦Gothic 48629).

Prélude et Fugue sur le nom d'Alain (1942). This was was written as a tribute to Duruflé's friend, who was killed during the war in 1940. It's a somber piece; the prelude includes a short portion of Alain's own *Litanies,* and the fugue theme is a musical translation of the letters A-L-A-I-N. Many interpretations seem sluggish, especially in the fugue—as with **Alan Morrison** (ACA), **Walsh** (Priory), and **Mark Laubach** (Pro Organo). **MacDonald** provides an excellent all-around interpretation (♦Musica Viva 1104). **Lebrun** is also worth mention, though the brilliance in tone quality seems masked just a bit (♦Naxos 553196).

Scherzo (1924). This light, wistful piece, calling mostly for a subdued registration, is an infrequently recorded work from Duruflé's youth. **Laubach** plays it with too heavy a hand (Pro Organo), while **Michael Murray** captures its impish quality quite well (♦Telarc 80255). An equally respectable performance is by **Eric Lebrun** at St. Antoine, Paris—a deliberate, suave rendition (♦Naxos 553196).

CHAMBER AND ORCHESTRAL MUSIC

Prélude, Récitatif et Variations (1928). A charming chamber piece for piano, viola, and flute, here is a combination of romantic harmony and an obvious gift for melody. Seldom heard, Duruflé shrugged it off as a mere work of his youth. A bit challenging for the viola, the keyboard part lies particularly well. The recommended recording is by the **New Jersey Chamber Music Society** (♦Premier 10332).

Dances Op. 6 (1938). These three pieces are refreshing contributions to Duruflé's otherwise entirely sacred concerns. Dedicated to his teacher Dukas, and including theme fragments from Dukas's own works as a tribute, they serve as a sampler of Duruflé's orchestral style. There are frequent shifts of tempo and volume, and many solos, including one for saxophone. Rhythmic vigor aided by a percussion arsenal is offset by lush writing that wavers between Ibert's *Escales* and a film score by Korngold. It's delightful. The recording by **Duruflé** and the Orchestre National is recommended (♦Erato 98526).   METZ

Jan Ladislav Dussek (1760–1812)

Dussek began his musical career as a boy soprano in a local church in his Bohemian birthplace, but he also showed precocious talent at the keyboard, and he first made his name as a pianist. His career was peripatetic, taking him throughout Europe and England, and finally to Paris, where, in 1808, he was appointed *maître de chapelle* to Talleyrand. His importance in the history of music has been unjustly overlooked: he was a major influence in the evolution of the sonata and concerto; without his example, Beethoven's music would have doubtlessly sounded different.

Dussek wrote 16 piano concertos (one written for two pianos). Three of them—Opp. 17, 27, and *Concert militaire* Op. 40—are given sparkling performances from **Maria Garzón** and the Neues Rheinisches Kammerorchester under Jan Corazolla; all three first movements hover at the ten-minute mark, demonstrating the structural expansiveness that Beethoven was to inherit (Koch 6431). A fine, though slightly less assertive, recording of Op. 70 comes from **Jan Novotn** and the Prague Philharmonia led by Leo Svárovsk (Panton 9015); the accompanying works are two of Dussek's best-known sonatas, Op. 61, known as the *Elégie harmonique sur la mort du Prince Louis Ferdinand de Prusse* (his patron), and Op. 64, *Le retour à Paris*—he was fond of composing music about events in his life and the world about him.

Dussek's 40 or so piano sonatas constitute one of the finest resources of the Classical keyboard repertoire, building on Clementi's achievement to extend the singing tone of the instrument, with harmonic touches that point forward to Schumann and Brahms. He often uses chromatic progressions and modulations that destabilize the sense of key, and his fondness for off-beat rhythm can obscure the main pulse. Two discs by **Frederick Marvin** offer insightful, committed and communicative interpretations, albeit slightly marred by tape hiss arising from the original '70s analogs (Dorian 80110, Vol. I: Op. 18:2, Op. 69:3, and Op. 77, l'*Invocation*). Vol. 1 of Ian Hobson's survey of "The London Piano School" includes Dussek's E-flat Sonata, *The Farewell.* A full half-hour in duration, this work overflows with expressive ideas; the soulful slow movement is especially moving. (This excellent CD also features sonatas by John Burton, JC Bach, Thomas Busby, and Clementi, and a rondo by Samuel Wesley.)

The Czech label Studio Matouš has released two first-rate CDs of chamber music (using the Czech spelling of his name, "Dusík"). One contains *Grande Sonate* Op. 48, and *Three Progressive Sonatas* Op. 67 (all for piano four hands) Sonata Op. 65 for piano with flute and cello, and *Elégie harmonique.* **Hanuš Barton,** piano, is joined by Jana Macharáková, piano, Jan Ostrý, flute, and Jitka Vlašanková, cello (0046-2 131). Barton is again active in the expansive, sturdy Piano Quintet Op. 41, where members of the Apollon Quartet are joined by double-bassist Václav Hoskovec; his forthright reading of *L'Invocation* Op. 77 precedes the lyrical Op. 56 Piano Quartet—a typical blend of classical and romantic sensibilities (0020-2 131). Another trio for flute, cello, and piano, Op. 35, simultaneously soulful and buoyant, is joined with trios by Hummel and Ferdinand Ries, and flute solos by Kuhlau—played by **Brigite Kronjäger,** flute, Johannes Degen, cello, and André Desponds, piano (Jecklin 303).

Dussek was also important in the development of the harp repertoire (his mother, mistress, and wife were harpists), a fact upon which latter-day harpists have capitalized. The Italian **Roberta Alessandrini** serves up the second of the three Harp Sonatas Op. 34 and Concerto in E-flat, accompanied by the Orchestra di Mantova under Vittorio Parisi; the bright recording admits a bit of studio noise—not of the least is some frantic page-turning (Naxos 553622, with concertos by Georg Christoph Wagenseil and Jean-Baptiste Krumpholtz). Canadian **Erica Goodman** contributes the last of the three Sonatas Op. 2, to a harp recital (BIS 319, with Fauré, Marcel Tournier, Flagello, Carlos Salzedo, and Prokofiev). There's a particularly happy blend of piano and harp in a period-instrument recital from **Joanna Leach** and Derek Bell (better known as the harpist of the Irish traditional group The Chieftains), with the first and third of the *Trois duo concertants* Op. 69; here the clarity afforded by the original instruments shows up the different timbres to perfection (Athene 10). The two duos are separated by Leach's searching account of *Elégie harmonique,* where the sound of the 1832 Clementi square piano imparts an additional poignancy to the music.

The prize for the most inventive presentation of Dussek's relationship with the harp goes to **Danielle Perrett** in "Dussek and the Harp," also using period instruments (Meridian 84244). Alongside two of the Op. 34 sonatas for solo harp we find *A Favorite Duet for a Harp and Pianoforte* Op. 11, *Favorite Sonata for the Harp with accompaniments for violin and violoncello* Op. 37, and *Duo for harp and piano, with accompaniment for horn ad libitum* Op. 38—a fascinating mix of sonorities.

Henri Dutilleux (b. 1916)

Dutilleux's list of compositions is short, but of high quality. He won the Prix de Rome in 1938, but the onset of WWII prevented him from making the trip to Italy. After the war he joined French Radio (ORTF), becoming its director of musical productions from 1945 to 1963. He joined the faculty of the Ecole Normale de Musique in 1961 and the Paris Conservatoire in 1970, soon retiring to compose full-time. Besides a few early chamber, piano, and vocal works, Dutilleux's catalogue consists of just a few undoubtedly major works, eight of them for orchestra, most of them much revised by the composer since their first performances.

The composer described the salient points of his music in 1966: "First, in the realm of form, a careful avoidance of prefabricated formal scaffolding, with an evident predilection for the spirit of variation. Further, a penchant toward . . . a delight in sound as such. An avoidance of so-called program music, or indeed of any music containing a 'message', even though I do not of course deny in our art a meaning of a spiritual order. And finally . . . the absolute necessity of selectivity, of economy of means."

If there isn't much Dutilleux, there is choice, and his music is being taken up by adventurous soloists (its original performers included Munch, Szell, Rostropovich, Stern, and Ozawa). His manuscripts are calligraphic, precise and finely formed, and so is his music—full of seductive, precise yet dreamlike sounds. His best orchestral works, like Symphony 2 and *Timbres, Éspace, Mouvement,* show a remarkably sensitive ear and a sound both hard-edged and sumptuous, a worthy heir to the traditions of Debussy, Ravel, and Roussel.

The cornerstones of Dutilleux's orchestral music are two symphonies and two concertos (for cello and for violin). The symphonies, written at the beginning and end of the '50s, are relatively early works and some-what easier to grasp at first hearing than the concertos. They're conveniently coupled and beautifully performed by **Tortelier,** clearly and richly recorded (Chandos 9194).

Symphony 2 (*Le Double*) is a fascinating study in the interplay between a large and a small orchestra. **Bychkov**'s recording with the Orchestre de Paris couples this symphony with *Métaboles* and *Timbres, Éspace, Mouvement* in brilliant, rather muscular performances that make the disc an excellent introduction to Dutilleux's orchestral music (Philips 438008). So is the more recent collection of the same three pieces, with **Saraste** and the Toronto Symphony (Finlandia 25324).

The concertos come a bit later, and both were written for great soloists: the cello concerto (*Tout un monde lointain*) for Rostropovich in 1970, and the violin concerto (*L'arbre des songes*) for Stern in 1985. They are musically rich and poetically haunting; the cello concerto is particularly fine, one of the 20th century's best. **Rostropovich**'s premiere recording is available as an import (EMI 49304), but a newer version by **Boris Pergamentshikow** (also conducted by Tortelier) is magnificently played and recorded (Chandos 9565, with two shorter orchestral pieces, *Métaboles* and *Mystère de l'instant*).

L'arbre des songes was recorded by its dedicatees, **Stern** and Maazel (Sony 64508), but the palm goes to the more recent recordings by **Isabelle van Keulen** (Koch 6491) and **Olivier Charlier** (Chandos 9504, with Tortelier again), both vivid, confident performers whose tone lacks Stern's occasional acidity.

Dutilleux's most recent work, *Shadows of Time* (title originally in English), is in part a tribute to the 50th anniversary of the death of Anne Frank. The composer summed up the music, which adds three children's voices to a typically large orchestra, as "an abundance of swarming timbres with occasional bursts of violence." The Boston Symphony premiere under **Ozawa,** is preserved; its combination of musical rigor and strong atmosphere make it a worthy successor to earlier Dutilleux works (Erato 22830).

Of Dutilleux's nonorchestral works, the most substantial are the 1947 Piano Sonata and the 1976 string quartet subtitled *Ainsi la nuit* (Thus the Night). This conglomeration of new sounds is reminiscent of Berg's *Lyric Suite* and one of the greatest recent works for string quartet. The sonata can be heard in an all-Dutilleux disc by **Brian Ganz** (Accord 202442), and oddly coupled with Balakirev's Sonata, both rousingly played by **Donna Amato** (Olympia 354). *Ainsi la nuit* has been taken up by a surprising number of quartets, with especially good recordings by the **Arditti Quartet** (Disques Montaigne 782016) and the **Juilliard Quartet** (Sony 52554, with Debussy and Ravel). Both sonata and quartet are included in a set that includes *Ainsi la nuit* played by the **Sine Nomine Quartet** and the sonata by Dutilleux's wife Gabrielle Joy (Erato 91721, 2CD). An Erato "twofer" also includes Joy's sonata, with *Timbres, Éspace, Mouvement,* and *Métaboles* conducted by Rostropovich, and the symphonies conducted by Barenboim—all creditably (Erato 14068).

Two agreeable examples of early Dutilleux, tucked into all-French programs, are the Flute Sonatina (**Emanue Pahud,** EMI 56488; **Paula Robison,** Vanguard 4058) and four songs performed by baritone **Patrick Mason** and pianist Robert Spillman (Bridge 9058).

RAYMOND

Antonín Dvořák *(1841–1904)*

Perhaps the greatest nationalist composer, Dvořák blends a tight control of formal structure with a delicious sensation that the music can go anywhere at any time. An example is the effortless way all the tunes of the "New World" Symphony reappear in the finale, or the way the finale of Cello Concerto 2 turns into a gorgeous improvisation on earlier melodies. This mastery didn't come easily; in his earliest works his tendency to develop material led him down byways so often that it made his formal structure diffuse. He was later persuaded to make cuts in several early works, but the results are unsatisfactory. Half the fun of early Dvořák is the feeling of being in a Grandma Moses painting—a landscape where the details are more important than the overall design.

Of all Eastern European countries, Czechoslovakia has the most individualized orchestral sounds. Whether it's the Czech or Slovak Philharmonic, the nutty woodwinds, the brilliant brass, and the rhythmic precision and clarity of tone in the strings is inimitable. Dvořák isn't the same without these characteristics. His music is always rhythmically active, and an orchestra or conductor that can't reliably achieve that web of effortless accuracy—or destroys it with arbitrary, imposed rubato—is like sand in the wheels of the music.

SYMPHONIES

Complete sets. The nine symphonies represent Dvořák's gradually maturing style. The first four were virtually unknown and un-numbered until **Kertész** began to make trail-blazing LPs in the '60s, now reissued (♦London 430046, 6CD). His series was complete, including exposition repeats. He maintained a tight and lively atmosphere that occasionally seemed superficial, particularly in the later works, but these recordings are still valid. Near this time, **Neumann** made LPs for Artia that also circulated here. His first versions of 1 and 2 were heavily cut, and 1 was somewhat re-orchestrated. His more recent CDs are based on the original scores, and he has retained the musical involvement and punch he showed from the start. **Rowicki**'s collection is equally complete and more powerful in sound, though not as clear or as lively (Philips 432602, 6CD, apparently NA; also once available as "Duos": 446527, 1-3; 446530, 4-6; 456327). This set was famous for its bass response, still impressive.

Today there are many complete editions from which to choose. Luckily, most are available individually, and we can mix and match. **Kubelik**'s set with the Berlin Philharmonic offers a Czech conductor with a German orchestra (DG 463158; MHS 564673; 6CD). His interpretations are noteworthy, but as a group, they should be leavened with others. **Neumann** is the most idiomatically successful, as he should be with the Czech Philharmonic, but tends to be stiff and unimaginative (Supraphon "two-fers," three symphonies each).

Suitner, with the Berlin Staatskapelle, is beset with style problems and a somewhat small-sounding orchestra (Berlin; the first three are in a "two-fer" and also on single discs). **Gunzenhauser** with the Slovak Philharmonic gets the sound right, though he occasionally forces the Czechs to do things his way—usually a mistake with an orchestra so individual in sound and spirit (Naxos). **Macal,** with the Milwaukee Symphony, is frequently successful in imbuing the Americans with the Czech ethos (Koss). **Järvi** is lively, but rather generalized in his interpretations (Chandos). Both he and Macal do the symphonies one to a disc, filling in with other Dvořák pieces;or, you can get Järvi in a boxed set (Chandos 9008/13), while the fillers have also been separated out in a box, as noted below.

1 ("The Bells of Zlonice"). This was Dvořák's first orchestral work. Written at White Heat in 1865, sent to a contest in Germany, for nearly 60 years it was lost (it turned up in a Leipzig bookstore 20 years after the composer's death). Bells resound throughout, an effect achieved by an ingenious use of dissonant overtones in the woodwinds. The scoring is ahead of its time in this respect, but is frequently muddy and needs sen-

sitive balancing by conductor and engineer. **Neumann** has been well-received for both his balances and power; his 1987 version is complete (♦Supraphon 1003). **Gunzenhauser** is clearest in delineating the woodwind bell effects in a sometimes leisurely, but still a beautifully detailed performance (♦Naxos 550266). **Kubelik** is beautifully phrased, but the lush strings tend to hide the winds (DG). **Macal** gives a dark but lively reading (Koss 1024, with an outstanding *Symphonic Variations*). **Järvi** is effective and lively, but not insightful (Chandos), while **Suitner** makes cuts, omitting the kookier passages (Berlin).

2. This symphony was written immediately after 1 but revised later. It's a dewy-fresh, pastoral work that has generally been given bad press. **Gunzenhauser** gives it a beautiful Czech-sounding read, one of his best, and takes the exposition repeat (♦Naxos 550267). (If you buy his 1 and 2, you get the ten *Legends* as well, in excellent performances). **Kubelik** lets the Berlin brass loose, making the piece sound crude and dull (DG). He makes the same cuts Neumann made. And while **Neumann** may no longer cut the work, but he does let the brass take over (Supraphon). Some may feel that **Pešek** loves the music to death, but it's beautifully played and recorded (Virgin 45127). **Macal** also plays the work beautifully, with lightness and spring, but he makes cuts in the first two movements (Koss). **Suitner** does likewise, and his orchestra isn't polished (Berlin); and **Järvi** is complete, but uninvolved (Chandos).

3. This is the most Wagnerian of Dvořák's early symphonies, with a grand and spacious I, a Siegfried-in-the-sticks funeral march, and a lively romp-with-triangle finale. There's no scherzo, though the gloriously brassy major key mid-section of II gives us a satisfactory lift. There's a quote from *Lohengrin* buried in it, as well as a moment that haunted Dvořák in one of the later *Legends*l. **Gunzenhauser** doesn't linger (♦Naxos 550268), and his Czech orchestra sounds happier with him than with the overbearing **Neumann** (Supraphon). **Suitner** isn't quite large enough for the grand sections (Berlin). **Kubelik** is grand and glorious, but sabotaged by the Berlin brass, who refuses to dance in the mid-section of the funeral march (DG).

Macal does dance, but his trombones tend to be more prominent than his trumpets (Koss 1019, with an outstanding performance of the little-known tone poem *A Hero's Song*). **Järvi** handles this symphony well, and the major disc-mates (*Symphonic Variations, Carnival Overture*) are well played and interpreted with originality (♦Chandos 8575). **Pešek** is relaxed, expressive, and beautifully played by the Royal Liverpool Philharmonic (♦Virgin 90797). **Chung** also gives a beautiful reading with the Vienna Philharmonic (DG 449207, with 7).

4. This symphony is an exciting work, full of drama and good tunes. It has an exposition repeat, which 3 does not. The slow movement is a moody theme, and variations only rise to passion late in its progress. The scherzo is a swinger, with a trio that eventually unleashes the percussion—unusual in a Dvořák symphony. The finale is white-hot, almost brutal at times. **Gunzenhauser** underplays the drama, which is just as well, but he makes an odd tempo change in I, though the Czech orchestra is a major plus, as is the exposition repeat in I (Naxos 550269, with a somewhat oddly balanced 8). **Macal** gives a controlled performance, takes the exposition repeat, and makes his Milwaukee orchestra sound impressively fiery and Czech (Koss, with a moving *Noon Witch*). Kubelik is impressive but rather weighty (DG). **Neumann** is crude by comparison (Supraphon), but **Suitner** is effective (Berlin 9292, with 5). **Järvi** gives us a well-characterized reading (Chandos 1251, with an orchestration of all ten of the *Biblical Songs,* not just the five orchestrated by the composer). **Pešek** is expansive and opulent, with playing and sound to match (♦Virgin 91194).

5. This is a pellucid, pastoral piece, becoming dramatic in the finale, as do many of Dvořák's early works. It was called No. 3 when we thought Dvořák only wrote five symphonies—because his publisher assigned it a late opus number. **Gunzenhauser** plays it beautifully, but it's coupled with a less successful 7 (Naxos 550270). **Kubelik** is fine, but the Berlin brass are less than bouncy, and the strings are syrupy (DG). Kubelik takes his one and only exposition repeat here. **Neumann** lets the music play itself, which is good, but there's a change of discs between slow movement and scherzo where there should be a direct segue (Supraphon). **Pešek** puts the Czech Philharmonic through its paces with enthusiasm, and is more clearly recorded than Neumann (♦Virgin 90769). **Macal** also takes the repeat in a convincingly Czech-flavored reading (Koss, with an impressive *Golden Spinning Wheel*). **Järvi** emphasizes the contrasts and orchestral textures, but loses control in his whipped-up finale (Chandos). **Bělohlávek** (Chandos 9475) and **Sejna** (♦Supraphon 1917, with his outstanding reading of *Slavonic Rhapsodies*) give us memorable idiomatic readings with the Czech Philharmonic—Bělohlávek grander, Sejna more rhythmically exciting.

6. Here we reach the mature Dvořák. This work is modeled fairly closely on Brahms's 2 in places, though the slow movement is derived from a little-known early string quartet. The work requires sure rhythmic handling of a powerful orchestra. **Kertész** is a bit fast in I, though his observation of the exposition repeat is a major plus (London). The Czechs have it all their own way in this marvelously buoyant work, beginning with the exciting 1966 recording of **Ančerl** with the Czech Philharmonic (Supraphon 1926). The orchestra makes you think of Strauss waltzes played by the Vienna Philharmonic with Clemens Krauss: every beat is in place, but never where anyone outside Czechoslovakia would have placed it. Ančerl was more modern than his predecessor, **Talich**, whose 1938 reading of this symphony is also a must; it's from mono 78s, though beautifully transferred (♦Koch 1760, NA).

This symphony is best played by those who have it in their blood. Therefore, **Sejna** (Supraphon 111918), **Bělohlávek** (Chandos 9170), **Pešek** (EMI 59536), and **Neumann** (Supraphon 1005) are prime choices, in that order. But for tradition in its purest form, go for Ančerl; you won't regret it! **Gunzenhauser** isn't quite as comfortable, but the orchestra is Czech (Naxos 550268). **Macal** comes close, but is a little off in the Scherzo (Koss 1001). **Järvi** takes the exposition repeat, which the Czechs do not, and gives us a bit more sensitivity than is his wont (Chandos 8530). **Kubelik** offers sensitive phrasing; the Berlin Philharmonic emphasizes the Brahmsian aspect of the work, not to its detriment (DG). **Suitner** does likewise, but his orchestra is less powerful (Berlin).

7. This is the darkest of Dvořák's symphonies. It's also the most Brahmsian and the hardest to keep moving—even the Czech Philharmonic finds the textures intractable in places. Potentially, however, it's a glorious piece and the best of the Czech readings (which are outstanding). Perhaps the best is **Bělohlávek** (♦Chandos 9391), though **Neumann's** no-nonsense reading is also satisfyingly recorded (Supraphon 559). **Ančerl** is good, but working with the Hessian Radio Orchestra in a somewhat muddy recording doesn't show him at his best (Tahra). **Pešek** also lacks the lift of a Czech orchestra, though his is an interesting, light performance (Virgin). Also on the light side is **Macal**, with rapid tempos and a strong taste of Czech flavor (Koss 1009).

Kubelik whips the Berliners into a powerful and satisfying performance, and is perhaps his best (♦DG). **Gunzenhauser** is light and right, but his string section seems too small for the clarity and sweep of this work (Naxos). Of the non-Czech productions, **Rowicki's** 7-9 have been reissued; his 7 is one of his strongest performances, recorded in dark, powerful sound (Philips 456327, 2CD, with *Legends,* or 420890, with 8). **Monteux's** affection for this music comes through in every bar (♦London 433403, with Beethoven's 7). **Colin Davis** with the Concertgebouw, also in the last three symphonies, is impressively fiery (♦Philips 438347, 2CD, or 420890, combining 7 and 8), though he adds a trumpet to the string wail just before the end of the symphony (so do the Czechs, though it takes the effect out of that last heave of sound).

Giulini makes the Concertgebouw sound older and more tired, though his sensitivity to detail is well worth attention (Sony 58946). There's also an EMI Giulini, which is mildly engaging at best. He also uses trumpet aid. **Chung's** remake with the Vienna Philharmonic does likewise (DG 449207), though otherwise this is an outstanding dramatic reading, preferable to his undernourished Gothenburg account (BIS). **Järvi** is matter of fact, partly due to the drier sound than Chandos usually provides (Chandos 1211). **Suitner** suffers from small orchestral sound and a hard-bitten attitude (Berlin). **Barbirolli** with the Hallé turns in a warmly emotional performance that causes you to ignore slight imprecisions in the orchestra (Royal Classics 70399, 3CD). His album includes not only 7-9 but also *Legends, Scherzo Capriccioso,* Wind Serenade, and Brahms's Double Concerto; a Nixa box (1004) gets the Dvořák material on two discs by omitting the Brahms.

Bernstein is from the same sonic era with a similarly emotional approach: seductive rather than fiery (Sony 60561). **Szell** and the Cleveland give a dynamic but somehow forbidding reading (Sony 63151, 2CD, with 8+9, *Carnival Overture,* and works by Smetana). Fierce, it is. **Andrew Davis** is bland (Sony 45618, 2CD, with 8+9 and *Carnival*). **Dohnányi** is anything but; he and the Cleveland collaborate in an outstanding, dancy, almost Czech-sounding reading (London 417564, with 8, or London 452182, 2CD, with 8+9). **Previn's** gorgeous reading with the Los Angeles Philharmonic is worth seeking out (Telarc).

Dorati puts Dvořák into armor; you can count the rivets, and the sound is metallic (Mercury). **Rahbari** shows that the Brussels Radio and TV Orchestra is as sloppy as ever (Discover). You can't say that about **Marriner** (Capriccio) or **Jansons** (EMI), but they show little affection for the music as well. With **Sawalllisch** you get affection, but the sound is mediocre (EMI). Finally, **Harnoncourt** takes the Concertgebouw into the realm of early music in an interesting, but only sporadically stirring reading—grim and a bit string-shy (Teldec 21278). I knew vibrato was good for something; leaving it out in this symphony clarifies the textures but deprives us of passion.

8. This symphony dances, sings, and the birds call. What more do you want than the Czech Philharmonic to play it? **Talich** whips through it with such fire that you forget it's monaural (♦Supraphon 111898). **Ančerl's** is another classic performance, in better sound (Praga 254006). **Bělohlávek** (Chandos 9048) and **Neumann** (Supraphon 111960) give you somewhat more relaxed stereo performances. Neumann is probably best, and best in its coupling with 7, while Bělohlávek includes only a much abbreviated version of *Golden Spinning Wheel.* **Gunzenhauser** has the sound but lacks strings a little, though his coupling (a good 4) is rare (Naxos 550269).

Pešek in Liverpool is light and airy (Virgin 59516, with 7). **Macal** has character and couples it with the seldom-heard *Czech Suite* (Koss 1002). **Rowicki** is a bit anonymous; letting an orchestra alone in this symphony works better if either you or the orchestra are Czech (Philips).

Barbirolli is outstanding for character, though his 1959 sound is a little harsh (Royal Classics or Nixa), if less so than Talich's. Colin Davis is also excellent, very direct, with the Concertgebouw (Philips). Andrew Davis lacks personality (Sony), and so does Handley, though his version is beautifully balanced (Chandos 7123).

Mackerras loves the Czech style; he makes the London Symphony dance, though the textures aren't always convincing, and he uses the newly discovered variant of the last movement's variation theme when it returns—a version this cellist has yet to find convincing (EMI 2216). Dorati is enthusiastic but a bit stiff (Mercury). Järvi turns in a sunny performance, possibly happy to be working with mainstream literature for a change (Chandos 8666). Giulini with the Concertgebouw leads a loving though sleepy performance (Sony); his version with the London Philharmonic is better, though the brass are too reticent (EMI), as is true of Marriner (Capriccio). Rahbari in Brussels is convincing, but nothing special (Discover). Chung in Gothenburg is small in scale (BIS 452).

The Berlin Philharmonic is heard in several recordings. Kubelik makes them dance in one of his most effective performances (DG). Karajan lets them play in their own language, and his; the result sounds like Brahms and Wagner, and why not? (EMI 64325). His performance with the Vienna Philharmonic is not as naturally recorded (DG 415971). Maazel, also with the VPO, seems unsuited to the idiom (DG). Returning to Berlin, Abbado gives a beautifully planned, perhaps over-groomed reading (Sony 64303).

Meanwhile in America, Szell and the Cleveland give a benchmark performance; both orchestra and conductor are in fine form (♦Sony 38470). Dohnányi also inspires Cleveland to impressive heights, though his first movement is rather fussy (London 430728 or 452182, 2CD). Sawallisch is once again sabotaged by his engineers (EMI). Previn has beautiful sound, but his flaccid account is a sore disappointment after his excellent 7 (Telarc). Jansons is anything but flaccid, but goes too far in the opposite direction (EMI). Masur with the New York Philharmonic is admirably thorough, if a bit logy in the finale (Telarc 90847). Walter is warmer and more uplifting (Sony). This brings us back to Harnoncourt, who seems to have a love-hate relationship with Dvořák. His jerky, antiseptic performance makes me wish he'd hire the Czech Philharmonic and try his tricks on them (Telarc). The results would surely be interesting, even revelatory!

9 ("From the New World"). This is one of the best known and best loved of all of Dvořák's works, and not just in America. An intensity and fresh flavor imbue everything he wrote while visiting the United States—which may be partly a result of being exposed to new folk music, and partly due to an increased appreciation of his native land while far from home. At any rate, this symphony shows some of the most effective use of cyclic form to be found anywhere. Tunes from one movement turn up in others, until the finale develops them all at once. It is indeed a new world, adding a sort of long-term memory to symphonic form.

Beginning in Dvořák's spiritual home, Talich and the Czech Philharmonic are again the touchstone, despite monaural but good sound from 1954 (♦Supraphon 111899). Ančerl's readings are available in two versions: a 1961 stereo studio recording (♦Supraphon 1242), and a 1963 concert version in less clear sound (Orfeo). Both are excellent: Ančerl a bit more hard-bitten than Talich, but also more intense. More recent generations of Czechs have relaxed a bit, Neumann perhaps moreso than what is ideal, though thoroughly idiomatic, of course (Supraphon 110559 is a relatively recent version; 111960 is earlier and slightly

faster). Bělohlávek uses nearly the same timing, but is more attentive to detail (Supraphon 1987).

Petr Altrichter's 1991 version with the Prague Symphony is lovely, but it demonstrates the superiority of the Czech Philharmonic (Supraphon 111810). There's a live performance by Kubelik with the latter group (Denon 79728), but his Berlin versions (DG 47412 and 39663, 2CD) are much better recorded, though brass-heavy. His mono version with the Chicago Symphony is livelier than Berlin, more Czech, and more clearly recorded (Mercury 434387). Rather to my surprise, Gunzenhauser with the Slovak Philharmonic is outstanding in interpretation as well as idiomatic playing, complete with exposition repeat, highly unusual in Czechoslovakia (♦Naxos 550271, with an equally sympathetic *Symphonic Variations*).

Macal also observes the repeat in a serious and idiomatic reading, lacking only the last degree of excitement in the Milwaukee trumpets (Koss). His 1999 New Jersey Symphony performance is equally fine, a tad more relaxed in ensemble but warmer and better balanced in the brass (Delos 3260, with *Requiem*). Serebrier stands in front of the Brno Philharmonic and lets them play it their way (Conifer). Szell in Cleveland comes with 7 and 8, and an orchestration he made of Smetana's string quartet "From My Life" in a classic reading (Sony). Kertész's lively version takes the exposition repeat (Penguin 466212), but you may find a richer tonal mix in his economical "London Classics" disc (417678). (I should perhaps mention that Dvořák is said to have been unconvinced that the repeat was a good idea; but the movement is really better balanced with it, since otherwise it's one of the shortest sonata allegros he ever wrote, much shorter than the following slow movement). Pešek is disappointingly anonymous and not fully convincing (Virgin).

Kondrashin gives a warm and beautifully recorded reading, also observing the repeat (London 30702). Sawallisch does too, and he's also warm and affectionate (Seraphim 73286). Dohnányi turns in a fleeter performance, omitting the repeat (London 452182). Rowicki observes it and is dark and mellow (Philips 456327, 2CD). Järvi is in the relaxed mood we noted in his 8, complete with repeat (Chandos 8510). Suitner is impressively organized, with the repeat (Berlin 9395). Masur, in one of his first performances with the New York Philharmonic, gives a fine performance, also with repeat (Telarc 73244).

Bernstein led the Philharmonic in a hypnotically slow reading that was convincing on its own terms (Sony 60563), and followed it up with an even slower recording with the Israel Philharmonic that nobody liked (DG 427346). Both versions observe the repeat. Another repeat taker is Maazel, in a rather aggressively recorded version; he's a bit mannered at times (DG 455510). Karajan's long career can be traced by his recordings of this piece. One such recording is with the Vienna Philharmonic; not the best recorded of the bunch, it was made in conjunction with a video, and suffers in both sound and ensemble (DG 439009). His Berlin recording with 8 is impressively, wide-ranging even if not Czech in any sense (EMI 64523).

His successor, Abbado, is effective and observes the repeat; his version is dark, like Karajan's, but more folksy (♦DG 457651). Colin Davis is another repeater; his reading is direct and beautifully recorded (Philips 438347, 2CD). Giulini with the Concertbgebouw is highly individualized and detailed to within an inch of its life or beyond (Sony 58946, 2CD). His earlier version with the Philharmonia is livelier, and fans of this conductor may prefer it (EMI 68628, 2CD).

Walter's performance is noble; he gives us a muscular, basically Viennese reading (Sony 64484). Paray is also of that time; he whips the Detroit Symphony into a froth (Mercury 434317). Still another of an older generation is **Dorati,** who paces through the score with his usual precision (London 448947). Then there's **Reiner,** whose classic reading hews generally to the Viennese tradition (RCA 62587). And, of course, **Toscanini** made a famous version in 1953, full of vigor and drama (RCA 60279 or 59481). A 1975 performance by **Adam Medveczky** has reappeared, a not unusual but competent reading, without a word of notes and surprisingly divergent timings given on the back and in the folder; the latter is correct (Hungaroton 1017).

One of **Stokowski**'s 78 rpm Philadelphia recordings has been reissued. Stokowski had a lively and intense way with this piece, with very few rescorings (Grammofono 2000 78552); most will prefer his gorgeous stereo recording with the Philharmonia (62601, or in the boxed set). A 1927 English recording by **Hamilton Harty** is a fascinating return to a more unbuttoned age of interpretation, recorded surprisingly well (Symposium 1169). Available once again is **Erich Kleiber**'s 1929 version, one more interesting and revelatory peek into the past that makes me think of the wind and the weather moreso than contemporary recordings. It has also been reissued in Naxos's excellent historical series in surprisingly good sound, along with an excellent historical series in *Carnival Overture* (1948), a cut *Scherzo Capriccioso,* a whirlwind *Slavonic Dance No. 1,* and a somewhat muddy *Moldau.* **Horenstein**'s 1962 performance, original in some tempos but not notably idiomatic (Chesky 31). **Barbirolli**'s 1962 version maintains a feeling of spontaneity well worth investigating (Royal 70399, 3CD, or Nixa 1004, 2CD). Stokowski's successor, **Ormandy,** made a 1966 recording that was warm-hearted, but fat in sound (Sony 46331).

Among more recent efforts is a surprisingly inspired concert performance by **Ozawa** in which he shows an ability to relax and allow the music to speak for itself (Philips 432996). The recording is rich and clear. **Levine** takes a more dramatic approach, bringing out some interesting points in an exciting performance, recorded a bit cavernously (DG 447754). He also recorded it in similar style for RCA (NA). **Previn** (Telarc 80238) and **Inbal** (Erato 18950, 2CD) originally appeared at the same time in the early 1990s, when competition was already fierce. Neither was particularly outstanding, though Previn's command of the structure of the work was praised, as well as Telarc's fine recording. Horn player **Barry Tuckwell** takes the repeat, but otherwise sounds a bit workaday (Pickwick 851). And don't turn down your nose at **Fiedler**'s really exciting performance (RCA).

Enrique Bátiz gives a careful performance (ASV 6037). **Benjamin Zander** is more insightful and enthusiastic with the New England Conservatory Youth Orchestra, playing in Argentina, of all places (CPI 329405). Though not note perfect, this is an inspiring performance, particularly with the Geovision documentary film, which is also available. An odd program is provided by **Frühbeck de Burgos** and the Berlin Opera Orchestra, a concert recording full of affection and interesting tempos (Querstand 9802, with an obscure contemporary concerto for four bassoons). From the early music quarter comes **Harnoncourt** and the Concertgebouw, with brass blazing, repeat intact, and interesting phrases—if only you could hear the strings playing them. Still, other than some insensitive balances, it's a very interesting, highly charged reading, coupled with a better-balanced and beautifully detailed *Water Goblin* (Teldec 25254).

A large number of recordings, including some from well-known conductors, may safely be dismissed on musical or sonic grounds. Among these are **Fricsay** (DG), **Marriner** (Capriccio), **Eschenbach** (Virgin), **Tennstedt** (EMI), **Klemperer** (EMI), **Slatkin** (Telarc; beautiful recording though), and others too numerous to mention.

OTHER ORCHESTRAL MUSIC

Serenade for string orchestra Op. 22. This is a magical piece if left to its own devices, as the Czechs are capable and most others are not. If you pull out the lyricism with too much rubato in the slow passages, it falls to pieces. Nature, as we know, just sits there to be admired. Don't pick the flowers! This tendency mars **Turovsky**'s reading, which also includes *Nocturne* and the two *Waltzes,* played in a similarly arch fashion (Chandos 9484). Also to be treated with a grain of salt is **Stokowski,** whose warm and highly individual performance with the Royal Philharmonic is none too clear in its overall balances (EMI 66760). Another odd program is by **Vladislav Czarnecki** with the Southwest German Chamber Orchestra, a small ensemble conducted with little feeling (EBS, with little-known works by Janáček and Julius Klengel).

More meaty fare is provided by **Paavo Berglund,** whose coupling with Tchaikovsky's *Serenade* works well and is generally played well (BIS 243). **Karajan**'s Berlin reading is perhaps more sophisticated in its gestures for this piece; Tchaikovsky takes his heavy treatment better (DG 400038). **Scott Yoo** with the Metamorphosen Chamber Orchestra is impressive, also finding space for Grieg's *Holberg Suite* (Archetype 60105). An even more appropriate coupling is Josef Suk's *Serenade;* **Bělohlávek** with the Prague Chamber Orchestra plays these works with a natural flair (Supraphon 3157), though **Suk** with his own smaller group of 13 players makes an excellent case for an almost chamber music approach. His 1985 recording was poorly received (Supraphon 104136), but a 1996 remake is impressive, beautifully shaped, though recorded rather closely (♦Vox 7540, with the two Op. 54 Waltzes as a bonus).

Jaroslav Krček and Capella Istropolitana offer a more traditional performance, idiomatic and warmly recorded (♦Naxos 550419). Another effective coupling is Dvořák's Sextet as performed by the **Prague Soloists** (Classico 183). This unconducted group is a bit rigid in ensemble, perhaps because of that lack, and are recorded a bit dryly as well. The most popular coupling is with the Wind Serenade Op. 44, providing contrasted sonority as well as composer unity. The Czechs have the most attractive release, with **Vlček** and the Prague Virtuosi (♦Discover 920135, with the original version of *Romantic Pieces* for violin and piano, scored, like *Terzetto,* for two violins and viola). The price is right, too. Speaking of originals, another Czech group has recorded a version of the *String Serenade* without strings, a transcription by other hands of the Wind Serenade for nonet, and three of the Op. 72 *Slavonic Dances* for wind quintet (Praga 250129). For the curious.

Others who couple the two serenades by themselves include **Marriner,** whose super-neat versions make fine listening (Philips 400020). **Christopher Warren-Green** tends to be sentimental (Chandos 1172), while **Wolff** in St. Paul tends to be heavy and the recording is a bit dry (Teldec 46315). **David Golub** has trouble keeping his Padua Chamber Orchestra together (Arabesque 6697). **Hogwood** leads winning performances and includes interesting additional material, omitted from later editions (London). **Alexander Schneider**'s young musicians give lively, fresh accounts of both serenades (ASV).

Wind Serenade. This is actually for pairs of oboes, clarinets and bassoons, contrabassoon, three horns, cello, and bass. The effect is that of a country band playing some of Dvořák's most winning and perky music, complete with a march in and out. The sound of the Czech winds is particularly important; everyone else tends to sound wrong by comparison. The German **Linos Ensemble** has a rich sonority but uptight phrasing (Capriccio 10559, with the String Quintet with double bass written about the same time). A more effective reading, lacking only the insouciance of the Czechs, is by the **Nash Ensemble** (CRD 3410, with two of Krommer's lively wind *Partitas*). You'll find **Kertész** coupled with *Symphonic Variations, Noon Witch,* and *Hussites* (Decca 425061), and **Barbirolli** with Symphonies 7-9 (Royal Classics 70399 or Nixa 1004).

Czech Suite Op. 39. This is a highly attractive five-movement work, primarily pastoral, though the final *furiant* is brilliant and stirring. **Rudolf Krečmer** and the Czech Chamber Philharmonic make a hash of it with relentless rhythms and a too small string section (Discover). **Pešek** does much better with the Czech Philharmonic (♦EMI 59522, with a good Symphony 5). **Dorati** in Detroit is full of precision and energy (London 414370 or 460293, 2CD). **Wit**'s version is less hectic, with the Polish Radio Symphony radiating charm and warmth (♦Naxos 553005). **Golub** leaves a vague impression with the Padua Chamber Orchestra (Arabesque 6697). **Macal** in Milwaukee plays it with personality in a fairly close-up recording (Koss 1002).

American Suite Op. 98. This suite originated as a piano collection. It's a warm, open-hearted work similar in scope to *Czech Suite,* but very different in mood. The finest reading is by **Sejna,** though one could ask for better sound (♦Supraphon 111924). **Dennis Burkh** does give us better sound, though his performances are only good, not great (Centaur 2121). **Petr Altrichter** is note perfect, but coupled with Shostakovich's Violin Concerto 2 is an odd choice (Supraphon).

Dorati's *American Suite* with the Royal Philharmonic plus his *Czech Suite* with the Detroit Symphony make generous fillers for his final recording of *Slavonic Dances* (Decca 460293). **Pešek** hasn't much success in making Liverpool react to him as Prague might have done (EMI 59505). **Macal** has better luck in Milwaukee (Koss). **Tilson Thomas** at least made it sound American, if not Czech, and his LP coupling, the quirky *The American Flag,* was a perfect fit. Unfortunately, Sony chose to split them up for CD, putting the *Suite* and Andrew Davis's sodden Symphony 6 on one disc (60295), and the cantata plus Davis's equally dismal Symphony 5 on another (60297). A mystery reading listed in Schwann may be by Ančerl (Supraphon 111996, 2CD).

Slavonic Dances. The *Slavonic Dances* come in two batches of eight, Opp. 46 and 72. The earlier dances sound youthful and perky, the later ones powerful and nostalgic by turn. They're wonderful pieces, and by definition, very, very Czech. The earliest recording was by **Talich** with the Czech Philharmonic in 1935 (Music & Arts 658). Full of flavor and enthusiasm, though lacking a few repeats, it's an important and joyful document. *Carnival Overture* (on the same disc) is a plus as well. Talich's 1950 recording is a must, however; though mono, it's in excellent sound and totally satisfying in performance (♦Supraphon 111897). **Sejna**'s 1959 reading is also a winner in stereo, though more bass response is called for (Supraphon 1916).

More recent Czech recordings have been less successful. **Neumann** has recorded the *Dances* several times. His 1993 version (Canyon 3615), though not as effortless as Talich's, is recorded in richer sound than his 1985 readings (Supraphon 111959). **Košler** with the Slovak Philharmonic gives us a pleasant, leisurely run-through, but in deference to his budget issue, omits all repeats (Naxos 550143). Schwann, in similar mood, omits Košler's name from their listing.

Altrichter with the Prague Symphony seems not to have the touch (Supraphon 3286). That the problem is not a loss of tradition is emphasized by **Mackerras,** whose relations with the Czech Philharmonic result in a fresh and committed set of performances (Supraphon 3422). You shouldn't neglect the other partially Czech productions. **Kubelik**

with the Bavarian Radio Symphony offers a natural, if somewhat cultured reading full of felicitous touches (DG 457712). **Dorati** whips up a lot of excitement in his various recordings, to the point of nervousness: the Bamberg Symphony is rather harshly brilliant (Vox 7202); the Minneapolis is also aggressively recorded (Mercury 434384), while the Royal Philharmonic has the best sound (London 430735 or 460293).

Järvi's recording is well played but lacks personality (Chandos). **Pletnev** gives us a freshly Mozartian view of the music (DG 447056). **Levi** takes us to the sunny South, with relaxed phrasing making me think of Stephen Foster (Telarc 80497). And why not? Excitement abounds as well, but it isn't very idiomatic in places. **Dohnányi** in Cleveland is exciting but a bit crude and occasionally sloppy (London 430171). His predecessor with the band **Szell,** has his Czech credentials in hand and many love him. I find his recording a bit constricted in sound and less convincing than the Czech orchestras in idiom, but it's still the best of the American productions (Sony 48161).

Legends. These ten pieces are little known despite their beauty. The classic Czech recording is by **Sejna** and the Czech Philharmonic (♦Supraphon 111919). **Gunzenhauser** plays them almost as well with the Slovak Philharmonic, in better sound, but breaks them in half as fillers for his fine Symphonies 1 and 2 (Naxos 550266 and 67). **Kubelik** uses them as filler for his *Stabat Mater* in beautifully warm readings (DG 453025, 2CD). **Leppard** leads the London Philharmonic in polished but not particularly idiomatic versions, filling out Rowicki's last three symphonies (Philips 456327, 2CD). **Järvi** and the Bamberg Symphony do a good job but rather miss the boat in their discmate, Janáček's powerful *Sinfonietta* (BIS 436).

Slavonic Rhapsodies Op. 45. Here are three larger, more dramatic scores. Again **Sejna** and the Czech Philharmonic provide the tightest, most satisfying musical experience (♦Supraphon 111917, with Symphony 5). **Košler** and the Slovak Philharmonic are also excellent, with the little-known *Rhapsody* Op. 14 as a bonus (♦Naxos 550610). **Burkh** and the Janáček Philharmonic are idiomatic as well (Centaur 2121). **Järvi** includes No. 3 with his Symphony 2 and plays it winningly, but his symphony isn't outstanding (Chandos).

Overtures. The three overtures that make up the so-called cycle "Nature, Life, and Love"—*In Nature's Realm, Carnival,* and *Othello*—are thematically related, though they have separate opus numbers (91-93). They're somewhat uneasy bedfellows, since they each end on a melodramatic note, but that hasn't stopped them from being recorded together. **Talich** is the earliest, though the overtures were recorded at different times, *In Nature's Realm* from 1948 78s (♦Supraphon 111898, with his Symphony 8). If you prefer stereo sound, go for **Ančerl** in any of his incarnations (♦Supraphon 110605 with *Hussite* and *My Home* overtures, or ♦111927 lacking *Carnival* but including Symphony 9, while *Carnival, Hussite,* and *My Home* also come with Symphony 6 on ♦111926). **Albrecht,** also with the Czech Philharmonic, had yet to acquire the Czech touch in his 1992 concert performances (Supraphon).

Leaving the homeland, **Handley** gives us an atmospheric reading with the Ulster Orchestra (Chandos 8453, with *Scherzo Capriccioso,* or 7123 without *Othello* but with Symphony 8 and *Notturno*). **John Farrer** with the Royal Philharmonic handles the lyrical side of these works well; there are more exciting *Carnivals* about, but he does a good *Symphonic Variations* and a scintillating *Scherzo Capriccioso* (ASV 794). **Gunzenhauser** is here relegated to his true status as a non-Czech, since his recording is with the BBC Philharmonic, so he doesn't have his usual Slovak friends to help him out when he goes astray (Naxos). He gives a feeling reading of these works, albeit somewhat under-energized, plus the overtures to *Vanda* and *My Home*.

Kertész's readings of *Carnival, Othello, In Nature's Realm, My Home,* and *Hussites* have been issued in many combinations and remain among the best (♦London/Decca). The same may be said of **Kubelik,** currently available with the tone poems (♦DG). The recent attempt to recapture Philadelphia's glory years with **Sawallisch** should be avoided on both musical and sonic grounds (Waterlily Acoustics, with Liszt's *Les Préludes*).

When it comes to separate performances of this music, if you're a serious Dvořák collector you'll want them all, preferably together. Separately, you take what you get with the major works on the disc. **Sejna** has *In Nature's Realm* with *Scherzo Capriccioso* and the three early Smetana symphonic poems; they're mono but delectable (♦Supraphon 1915). An early Talich *Carnival* is available with his 1935 *Slavonic Dances,* and **Abbado** has *Othello's* number with his fine "New World" (DG 457651).

Two Marco Polo discs deserve mention as surveys of roads less traveled: *Vanda* and *Cunning. Peasant* Overtures, *Dramatic* (or *Tragic*) Overture, plus an early and un-numbered Rhapsody with Gunzenhauser and Pešek (220420), and Stankovsky offers even rarer fare: *King and Charcoal Burner, Dimitrij, Armida, Kate and the Devil, The Jacobin,* and *Rusalka* (223272).

Symphonic poems. When Dvořák returned to Czechoslovakia after his visit to the US, he wrote no less than five symphonic poems: four on subjects of Czech folklore, the last (*Heroic Song*) on no particular story. (Is the coincidence of dates with Strauss's *Ein Heldenleben* just that?) A **Talich** disc includes the first four poems (Supraphon 111900, miscued in *Schwann*: there is no *Zigeunerlieder* on this disc, but there is a *Wild Dove*). *The Water Goblin* is from 78s, and there are major cuts in *Golden Spinning Wheel.* Yes, the piece is more concise that way, but Dvořák was trying for ritual, repeating things three times in different ways. No, it's not as dramatic, but it's great! Strangely, there are few integral Czech readings presently available in one album; and since orchestras are losing their national character at the millennium, there may never be any more outstanding Czech versions, which is one reason I emphasize them here. Anyone can play the notes! But even Czech conductors can come a cropper, as in **Gregor**'s sodden efforts, spreading the tone poems and other pieces over various boxed sets without any flash of inspiration (Supraphon). **Neumann** does better, collecting all but *Heroic Song* in one well-filled disc (Supraphon 0199).

All five symphonic poems are played by the ubiquitous **Järvi** (Chandos 8798, 2CD). There's an advantage to having all five together, plus *My Home. Golden Spinning Wheel* is complete, 27 minutes to Talich's 19, and Chandos's sound is mellow, but Järvi is his customary homogeneous self, with no real identity with the music. Another collection is shared in three Naxos CDs. Investing in all three gets you the *Hussite Overture, Czech Suite, Festival March,* and *Heroic Song* by **Wit** (553005), while the Piano Concerto, played by *Jandó,* comes with *Water Goblin* (550896). The other three tone poems are conducted by **Gunzenhauser** (550598). The concerto has more committed advocates and so do the tone poems, though *Heroic Song* is well done, with a good *Czech Suite.*

Separate performances are again fillers for larger works. *Water Goblin* may be had with **Bělohlávek**'s Symphony 7 in a somewhat underpowered version (Chandos 9391). He's happier with *Noon Witch* and *Scherzo Capriccioso* (Chandos 9475, with his Symphony 5). *Wild Dove* is with his Symphony 6 (Chandos 9170), while his *Golden Spinning Wheel* comes with 8 (Chandos 9048). Time for Chandos to put them together,

I'd say. **Macal** has also done all five as fillers for his symphonies; these are rather special readings that should be available separately—a 2CD set with his *Symphonic Variations* would be my suggestion (Koss).

Harnoncourt uses *Wild Dove* to fill out his Symphony 7 and has better success with it than the symphony (Teldec 21278)—and the same goes for his *Water Goblin* (Teldec 25254, with "New World"). **Rahbari** fails to convince with his *Golden Spinning Wheel* and *Wild Dove* as fillers for his Symphonies 8 and 9 (Discover 920112/3). Unfortunately, **Kertész** never did *Wild Dove* or *Heroic Song,* but his marvelous readings of the other pieces have surfaced frequently (♦Decca 452346, a double, and divided between 425060 and 425061, with overtures and Wind Serenade).

There are a few other orchestral works that turn up as fillers, notably *Scherzo Capriccioso, Hussite Overture,* the overture *My Home,* and *Nocturne* for strings. They're all fine pieces that should be handled by Czechs. Mix and match to suit your purposes. **Ančerl** and **Sejna** do great *Hussite Overtures.* Ančerl also does *My Home,* which features a tune that became the Czech national anthem. *Nocturne* is an odd piece over a drone that stems from one of Dvořák's earliest string quartets and exists in numerous chamber arrangements. The string orchestra version is the longest and latest.

Symphonic Variations. This may come last, but it is by no means least. This work is full of felicitous events and requires great sensitivity from both conductor and orchestra. **Sejna** and the Czech Philharmonic (♦Supraphon 111919) provide a classic performance. **Gunzenhauser** offers a sensitive lyricism in his reading with the Slovak Philharmonic (♦Naxos 550271). **Bělohlávek** with the Czech Philharmonic gives a fine performance (Chandos 111987). **Mackerras** with the London Philharmonic is also beautiful and spontaneous (EMI 2216). **Järvi** with the Scottish National gives one of his best readings (Chandos 8575). **John Farrer** with the Royal Philharmonic offers a fine, lyrical performance (ASV 794), **Macal** turns in a winner with the Milwaukee Symphony (Koss 1024), and you can't go wrong with **Kertész** (Decca/London), **Kubelik** (DG), **Sawallisch** (EMI), or **Neumann** (Supraphon)—an embarrassment of riches!

CONCERTOS

Cello. 1 is very early and wasn't scored by Dvořák, though he completed a piano version. This work is long but full of interest; in fact, it shows methods of using material that came to fruition only in the much later 2. **Milos Sádlo** with Neumann and the Czech Philharmonic has the stamp of authority (Supraphon 0631), but **Werner Thomas-Mifune**'s more rhapsodic treatment and firmer tone pay greater dividends (Koch Schwann 1146).

2 (Op. 104) is the *real* cello concerto, and probably the favorite of all time for both performers and listeners, so it's no surprise that *Schwann* lists 43 versions. Six are the same performance by **Casals** with Szell, recorded in 1937 and still going strong. The Casals recording you get depends mostly on your choice of discmate. The recording as transferred by Mark Obert-Thorn is the most satisfactory (♦Pearl 9349). Casals's playing fits the straightforward attitude of the Czech Philharmonic beautifully.

Rostropovich recorded the piece with the Czech Philharmonic and Talich in a classic 1952 performance (♦Supraphon 111901). Twenty years later he recorded it again with **Ančerl** and the Toronto Symphony in a similarly paced reading but with the added *frisson* of a live performance (Tahra 136/37, 2CD). Two other Rostropovich performances are available, with Karajan and Berlin, gorgeous though rather heavy-handed (DG 447413), and with Giulini and the London Philharmonic

(EMI 49306). Rostropovich has a way of adjusting to his surroundings, but Giulini takes advantage of him, drawing out the tempo to near immobility. **Angelica May** also plays with the Czechs under Neumann, adding the other two Dvořák pieces for cello and orchestra, *Silent Woods* and *Rondo* (Supraphon 111544). May has less subtlety and so does Neumann. **Harrell** with Ashkenazy boasts superior sonics (London), but doesn't get to the soul of the music as he does with Levine (RCA 86531).

Maria Kliegel plays beautifully, though her Elgar coupling has been done better (Naxos 550503). **Raphael Wallfisch** lacks a tad in personality (Chandos 8662). **Frans Helmerson** has power but not much individuality (BIS 245). **Robert Cohen** gives a strong performance (Classics for Pleasure 4775, 2CD, with several other cello works). The great **Starker** plays with Dorati and the London Symphony in an interestingly detailed but painfully clinical recording (Mercury 432001); his remake with Slatkin is more warmly lyrical, yet with no loss of thrust (RCA 60717). **Piatigorsky** is also fine, interestingly coupled with Walton's concerto (RCA 61498). Two recordings by **Leonard Rose** are available, one hard-bitten with Rodzinski and the New York Philharmonic from 1945 (Iron Needle 1338), and a much warmer and more satisfying one with Ormandy and the Philadelphia (Sony 46337).

Speaking of hard-bitten, there's **Edmund Kurtz** with Toscanini in an unequal battle of cellists (Grammofono 2000 78636). Going to the other extreme, there's **du Pré** swooning with Barenboim and the Chicago Symphony (EMI 47614). The shortest and snappiest award goes to **Feuermann** in his 1929 whip-through in close to half an hour (Enterprise 99328). Clumsy orchestral accompaniment makes this not one for the faint-hearted. **Fournier** is represented by two performances, a tightly-knit reading with Szell in Berlin (DG 429155) and a live 1945 performance with Celibidache and the London Philharmonic (several listings with different couplings).

Ma has made two recordings so far, a sleazy one with Maazel in Berlin that is so smooth it sounds like Dvořák played on an organ (Sony 42206), and one with Masur and the New York Philharmonic that's more recognizable as an orchestral work (Sony 67173). Ma plays marvelously in both, but more straightforwardly for Masur. **Schiff** and Previn are direct and spontaneous, with a particularly fresh account of the orchestral part (Philips 434914). **Harnoy**'s performance tells us more about herself than the music (RCA), while at some 44 minutes, **Maisky** with Bernstein is clearly the conductor's show (DG).

Piano. The Piano Concerto is an ambitious piece with lovely melodies and a flavor that almost recalls Brahms's Concerto 1. Its only problem is that it isn't pianistic and pianists tend to try to do something about it, most using the edition by Vilem Kurz. A student of Kurz, **František Maxián**, recorded this version with Talich in 1951 in a marvelously light-textured performance coupled with Rostropovich's greatest version of the Cello Concerto, also with Talich (♦Supraphon 1901). His live performance with **Ančerl** isn't as well balanced (Tahra 136/37).

Firkušny recorded the Piano Concerto with Szell (Columbia LP), Somogyi (Westminster LP), and most recently with Neumann, using Dvořák's original piano score (♦RCA 60781). Before this recording, he used Kurz. In still another reading, he's joined by Ricci and Zara Nelsova in a recording of all the concertos that gives good value (Vox). **Richter** gives a poetic and winning account (♦EMI 66947). **Igor Ardasev** makes a rather dreamy piece out of it (Supraphon 3325). **Jandó** plays well, but not as well as either Richter or Firkušny (Naxos 550896). **Frantz** and Bernstein (Columbia) also can't compete with Richter, while **Ponti** (Vox) unacceptably cuts the score.

Violin. The Violin Concerto is a more cogent and concise work. It begins with a statement that either pulls you in or turns you off, depending on the performers. The ones who turn me on are predictably the Czechs. **Josef Suk** is Dvořák's great-grandson; furthermore, he's an outstanding violinist who recorded this work in 1961 with Ančerl and the Czech Philharmonic in a performance I have yet to hear matched (♦Supraphon 111928). If you like your Dvořák less seriously Czech, try **Perlman** with Barenboim for affection (EMI 47168). Both Suk and Perlman couple it with the beautiful early *Romance* Op. 11, based on the slow movement of the Op. 9 String Quartet but much altered. Suk's program also includes his grandfather Josef Suk's marvelous *Fantasy*. **Pamela Frank** has duplicated Suk's program with the Czech Philharmonic and Mackerras in a sweeter-toned and beautifully recorded version (London 460316).

Václav Hudeček, with the same orchestra under Bělohlávek, plays a dark-hued performance that is full of drama (Supraphon 3187). Instead of Suk, he includes Dvořák's seldom-played *Mazurek*, a difficult but attractive piece. **Gabriela Demeterová** with Pešek restores the Suk, but omits *Romance* in a lively but not very witty reading (Supraphon 3385). **Midori** with Mehta offers an unusually wayward but interesting reading (Sony, with *Romance* and *Carnival Overture*). **Michael Guttman** gives us *Romance, Mazurek, Scherzo Capriccioso*, and the two *Legends,* but he's badly out of tune (Carleton). **Ilya Kaler** and the Polish National Radio Symphony under Camilla Kolchinsky keep the *Romance* and add Glazunov's Concerto in performances that seem a bit on the fast side, though beautifully played (Naxos 550758).

Tasmin Little plays a relaxed interpretation of much beauty (Classics for Pleasure 4566, with Bruch's Concerto 1). **Ricci** and Sargent are available in a "Double Decca," while the eloquent **Accardo** (Philips 420895) and the dazzling **Mintz** (DG 449091) may safely be recommended as well. But lucky the buyer who may choose between the two splendid recordings left to us by **Milstein** with Steinberg (♦EMI 67250) and with Frühbeck de Burgos (♦EMI 47421). **Kyung-Wha Chung**'s heartfelt rendering is also very special (♦EMI 69806). You may also find **Stern**—eloquent if somewhat lacking—in sonic richness (Sony 42257, with the Brahms concerto).

CHAMBER MUSIC

Violin and piano. There are only three works for violin and piano, a rather Brahmsian sonata, a sonatina written in America for his children to play, and a *Ballade* in D minor, written in 1884 and misleadingly labeled Op. 15:1. There are a number of transcriptions, notably the four *Romantic Pieces* Op. 75, written along with *Terzetto* Op. 74 for two violins and viola. There's also a transcription of the *Nocturne* for strings, and *Romance* and *Mazurek* can be played with piano instead of orchestra.

Suk has pre-empted the recommendation for this field by recording all of the above down to *Notturno*, in readings that are both idiomatic and marvelously played (♦Supraphon 111466). This disc, with pianist Josef Hala, is even better than his 1971 LP with Alfred **Holeček**. Nevertheless, fine players persist in recording this lovely music. **Anthony Marwood** with Susan Tomes plays the same pieces well, but with sweetness substituting for Czech character (Hyperion 66934). **Ivan Zenaty** with Kubalek brings a poetic touch to the program, marked by a slow and soulful rendering of the last of the *Romantic Pieces*; he substitutes *Mazurek* for *Nocturne* (Discover 920265). A less generous coupling is by **Shaham** and his sister Orli in winsome and virtuoso performances of the Sonata, Sonatina, and *Romantic Pieces* (DG 449820).

If you want more, **Suzanne Stanzeleit** with Julius Jacobsen offers two discs containing all of the above, plus numerous transcriptions by Kreisler and Jacobsen: perhaps more Dvořák than we need, but played with imagination (Meridian 84274 and 84281). **Perlman**'s is one of the less satisfactory releases, with the self-effacing Samuel Sanders, containing only the Sonatina and *Romantic Pieces* in performances that feature the violin rather than the music (EMI, with Smetana's *From the Homeland*).

If you're looking for *Romantic Pieces* in their original form for two violins and viola, they may be found in *Schwann* under the name of "Miniatures;" elsewhere they're called by their Czech title, *Drobnosti*. Mostly they're recorded with the famous and beautiful *Terzetto*. The challenge of a string work in mid to high registers inspired Dvořák to write an autumnal piece with a very special mood. A disc that emphasizes pieces with odd scoring is by the **Alberni Quartet** (CRD 3457). Entitled "Hausmusik," it also includes the folksy *Bagatelles* for string trio and harmonium and a little *Gavotte* for three violins, as well as a setting for quartet of the two Waltzes Op. 54, all beautifully played. If you want heavier fare, *Terzetto, Drobnosti*, and *Gavotte* may be had, coupled with the A major Piano Quintet played by the **Chilingirian Quartet** with Jeremy Menuhin (Chandos 9173).

A still odder coupling gives us *Terzetto, Drobnosti* and String Quartet 1 by the **Panocha Quartet** (Supraphon 111451). I can't recommend the disc unless you like early Dvořák hectic and cut to ribbons, but the CRD and Chandos discs are excellent. The trio works have been coupled with Kodály's Serenade for the same scoring played with particular warmth (♦MHS 515393).

Taking *Terzetto* on its own, it's coupled with Quartet 1 by the **Stamitz Quartet** (Bayer 100145). This version of the quartet is also massively cut, as all versions seem to be—except for the Prague Quartet's recording. Quartet 9 is coupled with the *Terzetto* by the **Vlach Quartet** in a rather vibrato-laden performance (Naxos 553373). The "American" Quartet (12) joins it played by the **Prazak Quartet** in another budget issue including *Bagatelles*, with a prominent harmonium (Praga 250). For full price you can have the "American" Quintet instead of the quartet, played by the **Lindsay Quartet** (♦ASV 806). This is a beauty, though for *Bagatelles*, a Czech sound is important. But if you want all three of the fascinating works we've been discussing, the *Terzetto, Miniatures,* and Bagatelles, you can't do better than Suk's collection, played to a T (♦Lotos 48).

Piano Trios. All four Piano Trios are beautiful and varied. The **Beaux Arts Trio** played them in 1969 in clearly recorded and lovely readings (Philips 454259, 2CD). The **Golub-Caplan-Carr** trio gives an equally straightforward and polished performance (Arabesque 6726, 2CD). The **Lanier Trio** plays with feeling and much rubato (♦Gasparo 291, 2CD). Single-disc compilations tend to concentrate on Trios 3 and 4. The **Vienna Trio** breaks this trend by playing 1 and 4 in virile performances of considerable subtlety (♦Nimbus 5472). The Munich **Dvořák Trio** (Farso 108004) and an unidentified group (Tacet 88) play this pairing as well.

Why the pellucid Trio 1 is recorded more often than the grander and more memorable 2 is a puzzle. Only two individual recordings of 1 exist at present. Both the **Rogeri Trio** (Meridian 84294) and **Trio Animae** (Cascavelle 1069) couple it with the elegiac Smetana Trio. The Rogeri strings are a tad nasally, while the Animae are recorded rather closely and play a mite heavily, though with good detail. With 3 we're in Dvořák's grand period of Symphony 7 and *The Spectre's Bride*. All ver-

sions presently available are coupled with 4, the famous "Dumky." The **Kim-Ma-Ax** trio delivers an impressive, highly emotional account of both works, but 3 is less polished and a bit more exaggerated than ideal (Sony 44527).

The **Haydn Trio** Vienna shows fine ensemble detail in 3 without the exaggerations (Arabesque 6646). The **Barcelona Trio** also plays it with great sensitivity, though the finale is a bit slow (Harmonia Mundi 1901404). The **Florestan Trio** has great balance of forces, perhaps too artificial, playing with a larger sound than the Lanier but seeming to pull its punches (Hyperion 66895). Whatever happened to the **Suk Trio**'s Supraphon recording? The only Czech version of these quintessentially Czech compositions is by the **Guarnieri Trio** Prague, who haven't a clue to the heart of either piece (Supraphon 1463).

Recordings of the "Dumky" by itself are fairly thick on the ground. The **London Mozart Players** couple it with Schubert's B-flat Trio in a rather poorly balanced recording (Pickwick 1006). The **Borodin Trio** plays it with the Smetana Trio in a very serious reading (Chandos 8445). The **Beethoven Trio** adds Suk's *Elegie,* but, though they play a good "Dumky," their Smetana leaves no room for air (Camerata 467). The **Rembrandt Trio** couples the Dvořák with Brahms's B major in fine performances, a little short on Slavic temperament, but musically satisfying (Dorian 90160).

String quartets. These are at the heart of Dvořák's chamber music, containing many of his most beautiful inspirations as well as his most experimental work.

1–5. These early quartets show Dvořák exploring the bounds of musical form. The first four are long and demonstrate the Grandma Moses landscape technique of composition. Most recordings either ignore them entirely or cut them unmercifully.

The only uncut performances I know are in the complete edition by the **Prague Quartet** (DG 429193, 9CD). There are more polished readings of individual works, but if you're interested in such esoterica as where Dvořák got the idea for, say, the slow movements of Symphonies 4 and 6, or the Nocturne for strings, or the violin Romance, they're all to be found in the first five quartets. More than half the music recorded here is rarely heard. The **Stamitz Quartet** also recorded the early works; they were well received but have already disappeared (Bayer 100147/50). These are said to be more polished than the Prague readings, and seem by their timings to be complete. The rest of the Stamitz series is still listed and is generally considered as good as the Prague, smoother and less volatile.

The **Panocha Quartet** has recorded 1 (Supraphon 111451), 2 (Supraphon 111452), and 4 and 5 (Supraphon 111453). From the short timings these are either cut performances or unbelievably fast. The rest of the Panocha series is highly regarded, though most prefer the Prague and Stamitz readings by a whisker. Both Stamitz and Panocha are available as single discs. The **Vlach Quartet** is working on a series for Naxos, and, as befits their budget status, they come in fourth in this series—but an idiomatic, honorable fourth. They seem uneasy with the early works, playing 5 complete, but taking the first movement unseemly fast (Naxos 553377). The beauty of Grandma Moses is in the details. A sense of urgency makes this particular movement sound like a series of variations on a motif in which nothing stands out sufficiently to be interesting. The Prague follows each byway with care, and it makes a difference, though their I takes 15:21 to the Vlach's 12:37. Rapidity doesn't always work in early Dvořák.

6–8. 6 appears to exist only as played in the **Prague** collection. A curious piece in four or five movements, it was originally conceived as one continuous work (4 is another example of this method); first movement material reappears in different form in III and V, while the tunes from II reappear in IV, as reconstructed in the Dvořák Edition. 7 is played by the **Vlach** with 5. Their performances in general have a fluttery vibrato and a somewhat hesitant phrasing that I find less compelling than the Prague's more gutsy approach or the Stamitz's rusticity. 8 is another example of the Vlach's vibrato complicating a straightforward piece (Naxos 553372).

9–11. 9 brings on the **Melos Ensemble** in a beautifully detailed and lively reading, lightly played but not very Czech in its phrasing (Harmonia Mundi 901510). The **Vienna Quartet** is polished and rhythmically strong (Camerata 400), the **Vlach** idiomatic but somewhat vague (Naxos 553373). 10 is prime country music, and many groups have recorded it. Both the **Prague** and the **Stamitz** (Bayer 100142) emphasize the dark side of the music, finding depths and details others miss. The **Trávníček Quartet** plays it well (Opus 93512049, with 12), and so does the **Vienna**, in a nice, natural sound (Camerata 250). 11 is a big work written for a cosmopolitan European audience. The **Sine Nomine Quartet** plays it darkly and dramatically in an effective ambience, but is not very Czech in its phrasing (Cascavelle 1055). The **Vlach** (with 8) is more so, though Stamitz, Prague, and Panocha have the balance of forces even better marshaled.

12 ("American"). This is by far Dvořák's most popular chamber work, not just in the United States for its name, but everywhere, because it's folksy, concise, and easy to follow. Of course, it's also a great piece, with room for a number of interpretations. The **Stamitz** plays it in a relaxed manner, full of detail and space; they don't take the exposition repeat, though they generally do in the other quartets (Bayer 100141). The **Vlach** is also fine, lyrically expressive and rhythmically natural (Naxos 553371). A competing version on the same label by the **Moyzes Quartet** is even better (Naxos 550251). The **Melos Ensemble** couples 12 with the String Quintet in E-flat, another American work, in a low-key, lightly pointed reading, not technically perfect (Harmonia Mundi 901509).

The **Prazak Quartet** gives a straightforward performance at a budget price (Praga 250110, with *Terzetto* and *Bagatelles*). The **Trávníček** is even cheaper and satisfyingly idiomatic (Discover 920248, with 13). The **Cleveland** is burnished but a bit over the top in seriousness (Telarc 80283, with 14). The **Emerson** is big and brash, American-style (DG 45551). The **Hollywood Quartet** is also intense, but less abrasive and beautifully phrased, a classic (♦Testament 1072). The **Skampa Quartet** plays with sparkle and brio (Supraphon 3380, with Brahms). The **Budapest Quartet** comes off as a bit hard-bitten (Biddulph 140). The **Vienna** is warm and beautifully phrased (Camerata 250).

13 and **14.** These are long and lovely works. The **Panocha Quartet** programs them together in marvelous performances (Supraphon 1459), outshone only by the **Stamitz** (Bayer 100141/2) and the **Prague**. The **Vlach Quartet** comes in next (Naxos 553371 and 74). The **Talich** is idiomatic, but a bit too sunny (Calliope 9280). The **Trávníček** (Discover 920248) plays 13 in a sombrely effective style, while the **Vienna** is lighter and dancier (Camerata 400). **Sine Nomine** has a lovely balance, but it's a bit hectic and with some self-conscious slides that Dvořák would not have appreciated (Cascavelle 1055). The **Audubon Quartet** is folksy in an attractive, somehow American way (Centaur 2416). The **Alban Berg Quartet** couples it with all three Brahms Quartets in fine performances (Teldec 95503, 2CD).

In 14, we have the **Cleveland Quartet** in a finely honed reading of almost Schoenbergian intensity (Telarc 80283). The **Carmina Quartet** gives a sophisticated performance (Denon 18075). The **Moyzes Quartet** is full of idiomatic truth, tighter than the Vlach, and the price is right (♦Naxos 550251). The **Artis Quartet** is too lovely by half (Sony 53282). The **Lindsays** are fine in mood, though not very Czech in phrasing (ASV 788).

Cypresses is an arrangement of 12 early songs for string quartet. Much more concise and lyrical than the quartets, these pieces are a lovely introduction to Dvořák's early style, since they seem to be quite literal transcriptions of the original 1865 songs. The **Stamitz Quartet** plays them with intensity (Bayer 100148, with Quartet 8), and so does the **Panocha** (Supraphon 111457, with Quartet 10). The **Audubon** emphasizes the dewy freshness of the composer's love songs (Centaur 2416, with Quartet 13). The **Chilingirian Quartet** version is still listed, though the rest of their series has disappeared; their rich tone lends weight to these pieces (Chandos 8826).

Piano Quartets. There are two piano quartets, both in E-flat, Opp. 23 and 87. They're played by violinist **Josef Suk** and friends in an unbeatable combination (♦Supraphon 111464). **Firkušny** ups their ante with the Juilliard Quartet, adding the Op. 81 Piano Quintet and *Bagatelles* to the mix (Sony 45672, 2CD). Then the Suk conglomerate reappears for only the late works, Op. 87 and the Quintet, again with **Josef Hala** on piano, but playing with less verve than in their earlier disc (Lotos 45). Or perhaps you'd like to hear Suk on the viola part of Op. 87, coupled with his own Piano Quartet (GZ Opera 321). You can't lose! A more high-powered but much less idiomatic version of Op. 87 is by **Menahem Pressler** and the Emerson Quartet (DG 39868, with the Op. 81 Quintet).

Piano Quintets. There are again two, again in one key (A), Opp. 5 and 81. It's said that it was Dvořák's lack of success in revising Op. 5 that led him to try again. It was a long and discursive piece; the composer cut the first movement up, then lost interest, perhaps feeling as I do, that cutting up a Grandma Moses painting doesn't improve its effect. So what we have is a concise, but not very convincing I and a discursive but cumulatively fascinating II and III. And we have Op. 81 as a byproduct, so everyone should be happy.

Both Quintets were recorded by the Panocha Quartet in 1993 with pianist **Jan Panenka** rather late in his career; they present them in rather leisurely though highly idiomatic performances (Supraphon 111465). **Kubalek** plays them with the Lafayette Quartet in good performances (Dorian 90221) that don't obliterate memories of either **Firkušny** with the Ridge Quartet (RCA, NA) or **Richter** with the Borodin Quartet, the latter recorded at an impressive live performance (Philips, NA).

Those who don't care about Op. 5 have a wider choice, including **Firkušny** with the Juilliard Quartet, a bit wiry in the strings (Sony 45672, 2CD); **Jeremy Menuhin** with the Chilingirian Quartet in a not very Czech-sounding reading (Chandos); the **Gaudier Ensemble,** too sweet (Hyperion); **Pressler** and the Emerson Quartet, not subtle (DG); and **Kazuko Mimura** and the Talich Quartet, good but not colorful in the piano (Calliope). The **Clementi Ensemble** (ASV 6200) plays well, but their Quartet (Lotos 45) is better than their Quintet. **Josef Hala** with Suk's group is good but not ideal (Supraphon). The **Nash Ensemble** is a bit relentless (Virgin 90736), while **Accardo** and his group are poorly balanced and a bit mannered (Dynamic). The **Melos Ensemble** is lovely and old-fashioned, with spirit and all repeats taken (♦Harmonia Mundi 901510). **Peter Serkin**'s recording is a very personal reading of strength (Vanguard 8003 by itself, or as part of a 4CD set of miscellaneous works). The warm and lyrical account by **Curzon** and the Vienna remains a classic (♦Decca 448602), as does **Rubinstein**'s infectious playing with the Guarneri Quartet (♦RCA 86263).

String Quintets. The three string quintets are even more varied than the piano quintets. The first is Dvořák's Op. 1, a fine work in his early style, now available in a **Panocha Quartet** recording with Op. 97 in E-flat, written in America (♦Supraphon 111460). Then comes the Quintet with double bass, originally Op. 18, a countrified work of great charm—one of several pieces in which Dvořák attempted to insert an early version of the *Nocturne* only to take it out later. The **Stamitz Quartet** combines Opp. 18 and 97 in a superior reading (♦Bayer 100184). Another **Panocha Quartet** coupling offers Op. 18 with the String Sextet Op. 48 (Supraphon 1461). You can also find the Sextet with Quartet 10 by the **Stamitz** (♦ Lotos 34). All of these are outstanding performances. There are several more recordings of each of these works, but none are as satisfying as the above.

Slavonic Dances. The famed *Slavonic Dances* started as pieces for piano four-hands, as did *Legends,* inspiring several pianists to record them this way. **Silke-Thora Matthies** and **Christian Kohn** offer two discs containing *Dances, Legends,* and *From the Bohemian Forest* (Naxos 553137). The latter is a six-movement suite, the only one never orchestrated. There are no musical surprises in these readings, but they're beautifully performed. A tighter reading of this music is provided by **Christian Ivaldi** and **Noel Lee,** recorded more closely and played faster but less naturally (Arion 68014). The **Schnabel Duo** caught Karl Ulrich Schnabel too late in life for a convincing reading (Town Hall 49). **Igor** and **Renata Ardašev** pull them about a bit, but in an idiomatic way that makes theirs an interesting performance (♦Supraphon 0001). **James Anagnoson** and **Leslie Kinton** also play interestingly, but their recorded sound isn't easy to listen to—rather unbalanced toward the treble (CBC 1088). **Artur Balsam** and **Gena Raps** offer a leisurely and satisfyingly musical interpretation (Arabesque 6559).   MOORE

PIANO MUSIC

Dvořák wasn't a virtuoso pianist and wrote only two dozen solo and duo keyboard works, usually at the instigation of others. Although these pieces are given a minor place in his musical canon, they're sophisticated and delightful, and several good recordings are available.

The most authentic and accomplished rendition of the solo pieces is by **Radoslav Kvapil,** a Czech pianist who in the late '60s, recorded Dvořák's solo piano music on four ♦Supraphon CDs, of which only the last three are available. His playing is outstanding, and the sound is crystal clear. A second series features **Inna Poroshina** (ESS.A.Y, five volumes), who recorded many of the same pieces in the late '90s. Unfortunately, her rendition is uneven and choppy, particularly in the earlier volumes, with unpredictable and irritating variations in tempo.

Album Leaves. **Kvapil**'s playing of these three pieces (all without opus numbers) in his Vol. 2 (3376) is unfailingly beautiful and elegant.

Dumka and ***Furiant.*** 4 and 3 minutes long respectively, Dumka and Furiant were written during Dvořák's visit to England. They're lovingly performed by **Kvapil** in Vol. 3 (3398). **William Howard,** however, plays them as though they were Chopin; although his recording has its attractions, it's overly resonant, especially in the loud sections (Chandos).

Eclogues. **Kvapil**'s performance in Vol. 2 is suave and consistently beautiful and elegant. Another recording of this diminutive piece is by **David**

Buechner, whose approach is thoroughly modern; he's technically superb but lacks Kvapil's in-depth understanding (♦Connoisseur Society 4179).

From the Bohemian Forest. This consists of six short pieces for piano 4-hands inspired by the countryside of southwest Bohemia, where Dvořák bought a house. He later reworked the fifth of these, *Silent Woods,* for cello and piano and still later for chamber orchestra. **Silke-Thora Matthies** and **Christian Köhn** give a wispy and delicate rendition, with graceful little tweaks in the rhythm (♦Naxos 553138). **Karl Ulrich Schnabel** and **Joan Rowland** are competent, but not outstanding (Town Hall).

Humoresques. These eight pieces are for the most part lyrical rather than humorous and include the famous *Humoresque No. 7.* The inimitable **Kvapil,** in his Vol. 4 (3399), gives a subtle and nuanced performance in which the complex ebb and flow of tempo are unsurpassed. Another Czech pianist, **Firkušny,** is high-minded and serious, but somewhat reserved; nevertheless, in his hands these pieces are refined and aristocratic (♦Bianco e Nero 2436). And let's not forget jazz pianist **Art Tatum**'s unforgettable rendition of No. 7, available on many labels.

Impromptu in D minor (no opus number). This was published for a fashionable Czech humor magazine in 1883. **Kvapil,** in Vol. 4, provides a highly expressive performance, with many delightful changes in tempi. Another *Impromptu,* Op. 52, is in Vol. 2 of his series, as well as **Buechner**'s CD.

Legends. For four hands, *Legends* was dedicated to the famous critic Eduard Hanslick, and Brahms greatly admired them. Perhaps Dvořák's most charming piano pieces, these ten works have a dreamy quality, like stories of an imaginary land, but in Dvořák's case they probably have roots in the Bohemian past. **Ingryd Thorson** and **Julian Thurber** perform them with great feeling and delicacy; they seem to fully understand Dvořák's intentions (♦Olympia 708, 2CD). **Matthies** and **Köhn** (Naxos) are spirited, **Schnabel** and **Rowland** somewhat bland and plodding (Town Hall).

Poetic Tone Pictures. Dvořák's 13 mood pieces were composed in 1889. The evocative titles—"Twilight Way," "Joking," "At the Old Castle," and so on—can vary from CD to CD, depending on the translation. Playing them well requires a great deal of rhythmic flexibility, and **Kvapil,** in Vol. 4, is more than up to the task, displaying a great sense of drama. American pianist **Gerald Robbins**'s performance is too forceful, but not lacking in charm (Genesis). **Firkušny** recorded 3, 6, and 9 in 1969, and as with the other pieces in his disc, his approach is cool but thoughtful. **Howard** plays 1, 9, 7, and 13; although likable, his performance is quiet, precise, and ultimately dull (Chandos). **Kubalek**'s recording of "At an Old Castle" is restrained and the sound is too resonant (Dorian). In the 4-hands version, **Matthies** and **Köhn** give a spirited but less dramatic rendition (Naxos).

Suite in A Major. This was written in 1894 and orchestrated a year later. In the hands of **Kvapil** (Vol. 3), who plays it with great delicacy, this rarely performed work acquires the stature of a substantial piece.

Theme and Variations in A-flat major. This is Dvořák's most serious piano piece; it resembles the first movement of Beethoven's Sonata Op. 26. The best available performance is by the prize-winning **Buechner,** a great colorist (♦Connoisseur Society 4179). **Firkušny**'s recording demonstrates an in-depth understanding of this piece, but as with the other works in his set, it's somewhat detached (Bianco e Nero). His 1990 performance, however, inspired **Howard** to turn to this music; his playing is monochromatic, but pleasant enough (Chandos). A performance by **Poroshina** is a mixed bag, alternating between smooth and competent in the lighter parts and strained and choppy in the denser passages (ESS.A.Y). Those who can find **Kvapil**'s Vol. 1 will have a chance to hear him play this piece. It's safe to assume that the same high level of accomplishment found in the rest of his set will be evident here.

D. GEFFEN

CHORAL MUSIC

Mass in D. In 1887, Dvořák was asked to compose a work for the consecration of a new chapel at the grand residence of Lužany outside the city of Plzeň. Though intended for orchestra, vocal quartet, and choir, this version would wait five years until the composer could find time to complete it as a condition of publication. For its first performance, and since the work was premiered in a chapel, an organ version served nicely, and the work is still given in this manner, so robust and monumental is the accompaniment. This is a meticulously crafted piece, full of Dvořák's genius.

Smetáček recorded it in 1969 in splendid, tonally pure sound. You don't hear much stereo separation, but the singing is exquisite and the whole performance well-nigh perfect. The chorus has a buttery, blissfully smooth tonal gloss that obviously benefits from its dedication and understanding of the music. The Czech Philharmonic is like a dolphin in water, so acclimated are they to the style—a sensational bargain (♦Supraphon 1821). **Poliansky** offers a much more mystical performance—Russians usually do. Dvořák's melodies may seem stretched at first, but later you become convinced they could sound no other way. The Slavic diction is not as crisp as in Smetáček's recording, but the performance as a whole glows in a luscious sonic cushion and merits serious consideration, even as first choice (♦Chandos 9505).

Josef Pančík uses the organ original with a small choir—like a normal chapel setting—and though I prefer the orchestral version's more dramatic impact, this recording is quite satisfying. The singing is comfortable and caressing, with the organ well placed in its aural environment—a most desirable release (♦ECM 21539). **Heinz Hennig** and the Hanover Choir are very liturgical in concept—again with organ—but also a bit dull, with too much smoothness and leisurely tempos. Their lack of a strong rhythmic underpinning adds to the problem (Thorofon). **Friedrich Wolf** is plagued with a whining, nasal sound that does little to ingratiate itself in Dvořák's marvelous choral textures or to our ears; the recording is congested (Preiser). **Malcolm Archer** and the Bristow Cathedral Choir also take the boys-with-organ route, with far better results than Hennig. There's plenty of emotion, peppered with spicy, full-blooded treble sound and a silken, flawlessly projected bass. This is the one to get if you prefer the sound of boys to sopranos (♦Meridian 84188).

Requiem. At the peak of his fame, and only 49 years old, Dvořák in 1890 turned his thoughts to the transitory nature of existence in what may be his greatest choral work. Avoiding theatricality and bombast, the *Requiem* nonetheless is filled with charging effects and a sense of otherworldly drama. Curiously, there are only a handful of recordings. **Ančerl** recorded it many times. Unfortunately, his Forlane recording is orchestra-light—not in size, but from the over-heavy, over-harried choral singing. Interpretively he's very consistent in his attempts, but bad balances and sliding soprano singing conspire against this unattractive issue. His 1959 recording is much better, the one to have at its bargain price (♦DG 437377, 2CD). The energy level, balance, clarity, and sleek

overall proportions are as good as any ever recorded. Ančerl approaches the piece as if it had just been written, and the result is fresh, engaging, and a delight to the ears.

Sawallisch, as usual in Dvořák, brings a strong sense of form and an impregnable, unerring sense of pace. The devotional element is high—though not overdone—and the Czech Philharmonic responds in their customary fashion (♦Supraphon 4241). **Macal** has substandard soloists and his performance doesn't top Ančerl's, he has a great orchestra (New Jersey Symphony) and nothing comes close to the fabulous sound. The coupled *New World* is only average (♦Delos 3260, 2CD).

Stabat Mater. The Latin poem of the 13th-century Franciscan Jacopone da Todi has inspired many composers. The Virgin Mary contemplating her son's crucifixion provided the well for much fresh musical water through the ages, especially of the sorrowful, highly devotional kind. There's not much in the way of dramatic action; composers have always used it as a vehicle for their most intimate thoughts, so it comes as no surprise that Dvořák would turn to it after the death of his first daughter. After taking up the project, it would be another two years—and after the deaths of two more children—before the grief-stricken composer would be motivated to complete the project. His second choral work of any significance, the *Stabat Mater,* would greatly assist him in establishing his reputation outside Bohemia. In 1883, when the work was given in oratorio-crazed London, the English took him and his work to heart, assuring its repertory status and providing his first steps to musical immortality.

The work has been very fortunate on records, with few really bad performances, and the CD age has brought a plethora of riches. **Rilling**'s approach is highly devotional, a lovingly guided, peaceful, and wonderfully sung version (♦Hänssler 216663, 2CD). The perspective is somewhat distant, but the sound is as inviting as a familiar, favorite room. There isn't a sense of overwhelming sorrow here, rather a feeling of hopeful resignation, a quiet serenity that comes from acceptance of the inevitable. The soloists are splendid, not too operatic, but dead on in intonation. **Macal** gives us an intense, white-hot performance; faster than most, he blazes through the work in an uneasy, nervous manner. This is grief disconsolate; the words of comfort are said, but are only mouthed by the grieving person, staring ahead motionless. It's a unique take on this masterwork and succeeds brilliantly. The New Jersey Symphony is very good, alive and palpably resonant, with excellent soloists (♦Delos 3161, 2CD).

There's nothing exceptional about **Rahbari**'s reading. The sound is tinny, with some congestion in the climaxes, though the soundstage is broad enough. Miriam Gauci is fine as the soprano soloist, but the vocal quartet isn't as stylistically balanced as it should be, far too operatic. Rahbari doesn't pace well, and the chorus sounds under-rehearsed in spots (Discover). **Bělohlávek**'s measured, sweetened approach works very well, the Czech Philharmonic has this music in their blood, and Chandos's sound, for once, doesn't augment the echo. The large chorus is excellent and involved, though I would prefer a much lighter tenor; this one traverses the "dry and waterless land" in VI far too loudly. The soprano also has a case of the wobbles, but this recording remains a much finer effort than his earlier one (Supraphon).

If Bělohlávek doesn't quite measure up and you still want a Czech Philharmonic version, consider **Sawallisch** (♦Supraphon 3561, 2CD). This is a magnificent recording that exhibits Germanic tautness of line and rigor of construction. It's very operatic, but the conductor makes it work, intense and fervently emotional. The singers are splendidly agile and lyrical, and the orchestra is superb. This is the Supraphon of choice. **Leoš Svarovsky** and the Brno Philharmonic offer committed but slightly substandard choral work compared to the other recordings (Supraphon). There are passages where the soloists are flagrantly unbalanced, and a sense of flow is absent. The sound in general is very close, recorded at high volume and tending to harshness in the more energetic passages. The Brno group, while an excellent band, doesn't have the tonal luster of the Czech Philharmonic.

Robert Shaw's recording, the last he ever made, is stunning. It is quite simply the most moving account of this deceptively simple work that has ever been put on disc. The chorus is remarkable, exhibiting chamber qualities at one moment and producing a huge, beautiful sound that reduces you to tears the next. Shaw's ebb and flow are nearly perfect, and the Atlanta strings produce some of the most luscious tones ever recorded by this ensemble, while the winds show a vast palette of color, with clarity and subtle smoothness. This is a not-to-be-missed release (♦Telarc 80506, 2CD).

Kubelik was one of the earliest champions of this work, and his 1977 recording is still one of the best available (♦DG 453025, 2CD). There is some shrillness, but for the most part the sound remains warm and illuminating, with no congestion and ample dynamic range that displays the forces at their full strength. The chorus is excellent, and while lacking Shaw's more precise diction, they make up for it in spirit. The Bavarian Radio Symphony is as good as any, as are the soloists, with Mathis a stand-out. *Legends* is a nice coupling, in a terrific performance. **Talich**'s older recording is a sturdy, classically oriented affair with little in the way of wayward romanticism or unseemly piety. Again the Czech Philharmonic is at the top of their game; and this version, which set a high standard for so long, remains at the very least a necessary supplement. Suk's *Asrael Symphony* provides the appropriate coupling (Supraphon).

Saint Ludmilla. In 1884, Dvořak, at the invitation of the Royal Philharmonic Society, conducted his works in London for the first time, and in 1886 the Leeds Festival commissioned a "sacred oratorio"—a form completely new to him—to occupy a whole evening. He chose a nationalistic bit of hagiography as his subject, St. Ludmilla and the Christianization of Bohemia and Moravia, and concentrates primarily on the saint's struggle to put off paganism and adopt her new faith. The result contains some rather tedious non-dramatic moments, but every once in a while you perk up to hear some truly ravishing melodies and exceptional choral work. **Albrecht** and his WDR Symphony give the work about as good a reading as I can imagine, in tremendous sound. The soloists aren't especially noteworthy, but the piece doesn't pose any inordinate solo demands, and the chorus is the real star here. It's not "necessary" Dvořak, but you may be pleasantly surprised if you invest in it (♦Orfeo 513992).

Te Deum. Dvořak, anxious to make a good impression on his new employers at the National Conservatory of Music in New York, agreed to set this *Te Deum* for his first public concert in America, in conjunction with the 400th anniversary of Columbus's discovery of America. The work maintains a festive tone, uplifting and moderately inspiring, though in truth it's not one of his greater efforts. **Poliansky** is something of a letdown here, with a sluggish, uncertain feel. The forces are the same as in his wonderful *Mass in D,* but the spirit is sorely lacking in this rather powderpuff walk-through (Chandos). **Shaw** gets it right, emphasizing the festive moments with suitable fanfare and not lingering too long in the more lethargic passages—an effort that gives the work a tighter structure and avoids glossiness (♦Telarc 80287).

Rahbari has the right mood, spontaneous and joyful, but some sloppy choral and orchestral work blights his performance, along with distorted sound in some of the louder passages. Even at a bargain price, with his stilted *Stabat Mater* as discmate, this isn't a viable choice (Discover). **Smetáček** scores highly once again, full of a celebratory ecstasy that catches us right away and has us believing the piece is worth far more than it is. The clanging cymbals and vigorous choral work are glowing (♦Supraphon 1821). **Rilling,** not unexpectedly, presents a smooth, suave reading that removes some of the bite of this celebratory work, but it's so beautiful that you don't notice what you're missing. A sense of careful finesse is present in every bar (♦Hänssler 98307).

RITTER

OPERAS

Dvořak composed ten operas, and that number does not include *The Specter's Bride,* a dramatic cantata, or the oratorio *St. Ludmilla.* While several of the operas are still performed, if only occasionally, in the composer's homeland, only *Rusalka* has enjoyed international acceptance; apart from Smetana's *The Bartered Bride,* it's the most frequently performed Czech opera. Unlike Smetana, Dvořak did not restrict himself to Czech subjects; *Rusalka,* for example, is based on a story by a French author; this work, as well as some of his other operas, is devoid of nationalistic and folkloric influences. Rather, his works in this genre reflect the musical idioms of his time and his sympathies for the operas of Wagner, Bizet, Verdi, and Meyerbeer. They are conservative compared to those of Janáček, for example, and generally include set pieces, choruses, and a ballet. They're always tuneful, charming, and contain much beautiful music that is as satisfying as Dvořak's symphonic and instrumental works. Those opera lovers not acquainted with them are advised to start with *Rusalka* and then go on to *Kate and the Devil* and *Dimitri.*

Armida. This was Dvořak's last opera; its premiere took place a month before his death. The libretto is derived from Tasso's *Gerusalemne Liberata,* not one of opera's great plots. The music includes some pseudo-oriental passages and strong echoes of Wagner's *Parsifal.* There's only one commercial CD, a concert performance in Prague led by **Albrecht** with a cast of Polish and Czech singers (Orfeo 404962). Fortunately, it's strong and commendable.

The Cunning Peasant. This is the fifth of Dvořak's ten operas. It has a standard plot reminiscent of *The Bartered Bride:* a rich farmer wants his daughter to marry the son of another rich farmer, but she's in love with a poorer man. Through princely intervention, the poor suitor is made rich and everything ends happily. There's only one CD, and while its cast is fairly good, the conducting by **František Vajnar** is pedestrian (Supraphon 0019).

Dimitri. This opera tells us what supposedly happened after the death of Boris Godunov and the accession to the Russian throne of the Pretender Dimitri. Here he marries the Polish Princess Marina, falls in love with Boris's daughter Xenia, and is exposed as a fraud by Shuisky, who then shoots him. After the opera's 1882 premiere, the composer revised it several times. The music is first-rate Dvořak, symphonic in nature but not as vocally grateful as, for instance, *Rusalka.* It includes much work for the chorus. The only available CD is well conducted by **Albrecht** with a generally acceptable cast (Supraphon 1259).

The Jacobin. This opera deals with the reconciliation of a son with his aged father, after the youth has run off to Paris where he became a Jacobin during the French Revolution. The libretto is based on traditional Czech stories; the music is vintage Dvořak. It includes nostalgic arias, ecstatic duets, and splendid choruses. In a 1977 recording led by **Jiří Pinkas**, veteran Czech singers make up the fine cast, some of them familiar from other Czech opera recordings (Supraphon 2190). The sound is a bit boxy and not as well-balanced as it should be, but the performance is still enjoyable.

Kate and the Devil. Here is a charming work based on Czech folklore, unique in Czech opera for having no love interest. Instead, it's a wonderful mix of fantasy and some baser aspects of human nature. The music is witty and delightful, full of Slavonic and other dance tunes for the dance-loving heroine Kate and simple melodic writing in a folksy manner. There's more Smetana in this score than Wagner or Verdi. It's one of Dvořák's most popular operas and has been staged in the United States by the St. Louis Opera (1990). A 1979 recording, also led by **Pinkas**, is highly recommended (♦Supraphon 1800).

King and Charcoal Burner. This is Dvořák's second opera. Originally composed in 1871, it was revised several times by the composer, and again after his death—by the Director of Prague's National Theater, who shortened it considerably. The plot involves a king who gets lost in a forest, is rescued by a charcoal burner, is struck by the beauty of the peasant's daughter (who's already in love with another charcoal burner), and finally sees to it that the young lovers are united. It's an old tale well set to music in Dvořák's familiar manner, much of it based on Czech rhythms. The only available recording was made in 1989 for Czech television; it uses the cut version and, perhaps, cuts it even more, as it's only 70 minutes long (Supraphon 3078).

Rusalka. This is, by far, Dvořák's most popular opera; in the last decade or so, it seems to have conquered the major opera houses of Western Europe and the United States. This story of a water nymph who is apparently betrayed by her mortal lover evoked some of the composer's most poetic music. Rusalka's "Song to the Moon" is as beautiful and touching an aria as you'll hear in any opera, and there are other pieces of almost equal merit—so it's not surprising that it's the only Dvořák opera with more than one recommended recording.

The most recent recording is the best one yet (♦London 460568, 3CD). Conducted by **Mackerras**, who has made Czech opera his specialty, it has a wonderful cast of mainly Western singers. The title role is sung bewitchingly by Fleming, whose gorgeous, smooth tones make her the best Rusalka on records. She's joined by Heppner's glorious tenor (Prince), who proves again that he can sing lyrical and dramatic roles equally well. He too is the best Prince I've heard, on records and in the flesh. Also, the supporting cast is the best yet recorded. Still, two of the older recordings remain recommendable, though neither is as good as the London set. They are a 1961 release conducted by **Chalabala** (♦Supraphon 0013) and a 1982 recording led by **Neumann** (♦Supraphon 103641). Both casts are from the Prague National Theater and both conductors give us stylish performances, Chalabala's a bit livelier than Neumann's. Gabriela Benačková, Neumann's Rusalka, sings almost as well as Fleming, but her supporting cast, notably Ochman's Prince, is inferior to London's. Chalabala's set is on two CDs, the others needlessly spread over three.

Vanda. This opera was a failure at its 1876 premiere and at an 1880 revival. Its score has remained unpublished, and there have been only a few performances in this century. The story is derived from a Polish legend about a female ruler (Vanda) who saves her country from hostile invaders by sacrificing her life to the gods, drowning herself in the Vistula. The only available CD is a 1951 concert version for radio broadcast, led by **Pinkas**, which was released as a "historical recording" (Supraphon

3007). The mono sound is rather coarse, but listenable; and the cast, again from the Prague National Theater, interpret their roles well.

SONGS

Dvořák composed more than 100 songs and duets. While they are not the most important of his compositions, they still provide many pleasures to the listener because of their beautiful melodies, craftsmanship, and romantic ambience. Notable among these compositions are the inspired *Gypsy Songs* (which include the popular "Songs My Mother Taught Me") and the deeply felt *Biblical Songs.* The latter can be compared to Brahms's *Four Serious Songs;* both are affirmations of religious faith set to Biblical texts, in this case the Psalms. The *Gypsy Songs* are strikingly individualistic and have a folksy appeal; they are lively and tuneful settings of folk poetry and love songs that can easily stand with those of his contemporaries, Tchaikovsky and Brahms.

Not all of Dvořák's songs are currently available on CD, but several versions of the *Biblical* and *Gypsy* songs can be recommended. Since both take up less than a complete CD, they are often coupled with other Dvořák works, sometimes with those of other composers. But an all-Dvořák disc has been recorded by **Schreier**, accompanied by the splendid pianist Marian Lapšanský (♦Berlin 1080). It includes the *Gypsy* and *Biblical* songs as well as the love songs of Op. 83. While Schreier's voice isn't lush or very beautiful, he has excellent diction and a deep understanding of the texts (he sings in German). Another fine disc was made by the superb Czech soprano **Benačková**, accompanied by Firkušný (♦RCA 60823), both incomparable artists in this repertory. This includes *Gypsy* songs, four of the love songs from Op. 73, and four from Op. 83, and the three best *Biblical* songs. They're coupled with songs by Janáček and Martinů, all sung in Czech, but English translations are provided.

Baritone **Brian Rayner Cook** can be heard in the *Biblical Songs,* with orchestral accompaniment by Järvi and the Scottish National Orchestra (♦Chandos 9002). That disc is filled out with Dvořák orchestral music, all very well played. While excellent all-Czech recordings made between 1967 and 1972 of all the songs mentioned here seem to have been deleted (Supraphon 0206), there is a splendid disc of "Love Songs and Folk Duets," all by Dvořák, sung by **Ciesinski**, Grayson Hirst, and Ostendorf (♦Erasmus 084). Most are sung in Czech, the rest in German; English translations are provided, but no texts or notes. MOSES

Werner Egk (1901–1981)

This German composer wrote primarily for the theater. His tonal but at times dissonant music incorporates impressionist shadings, incisive rhythms, and elements of the ironic and grotesque. **Egk** himself leads the soloists and Radio Berlin Symphony in fine performances of two short, tuneful pieces, *Spagnola,* from the opera *Die Zaubergeige* (The Magic Violin), and *Tango,* from the opera *Peer Gynt,* and a 20-minute suite from the opera *Circe* (Berlin 9209). The *Circe* suite, *Siebzehn Tage und Vier Minuten,* highlights love duets between Circe (soprano Rosemarie Rönisch) and Ulysses (tenor Peter Schreier) and, in its dark chromaticism, has an atonal feeling. This release is rounded out with Wolfgang Fortner's *Bloodwedding Interludes,* conducted by the composer.

A less well-defined *Tango* is also on an all-Egk disc conducted by **Nikos Athinäos**, coupled with *Kleine Symphonie, Triptychon, Französische Suite nach Rameau,* and the Overture to *The Magic Violin* (Signum 86-00). The "Little Symphony" is an exuberant work of strong contrasts and energetic rhythms with echoes of Hindemith and Weill—though perhaps Egk went overboard in scoring the dense passages.

Triptychon combines dramatic and delicate music, and in the "French Suite," Egk borrows dance-like music from Rameau recast in his own mold. The Overture is a short, mostly quick-paced, Spanish-flavored work with interesting, accessible music, good performances, somewhat over-reverberant sonics, and an instrumental balance that isn't always ideal.   DE JONG

During Egk's lifetime his ten operas generally had successful premieres and made the rounds of European theaters (particularly in Germany) with varying degrees of acceptance. Since his death they are performed far less frequently and are under-represented by recordings. The two operas available both come from Munich radio broadcasts. At least two of his other operas, *Die Zaubergeige* (1935) and *Irische Legende* (1955, based on W.B. Yeats's play *The Countess Cathleen),* are worthy efforts and deserve to be recorded as well.

Egk's dramatic, imaginative opera *Peer Gynt* comes closer to catching the spirit of Ibsen's play than Grieg's beautiful but sentimental music. Egk strikingly expresses the "crazed" world of Peer in opposition to the "sane" world around him, and the atmosphere reeks of the lurid delights he encounters. A 1981 Munich broadcast led by **Heinz Wallberg** is a powerful performance, lean and taut as a trap about to snap (♦Orfeo 005822, 2CD). The large cast is headed by the Peer of Roland Hermann, an exceptional powerful singer and actor. The Heldentenor Hans Hopf is not far behind in vocal acting as Der Alte, Egk's Troll King. The three principal ladies sing quite fetchingly. The music is rich and colorful, with good songs, not just a symphonic poem with voices attached. The program notes are helpful, but there is no libretto.

Heinrich von Kleist's story *Die Verlobung in San Domingo,* on which Egk's opera is based, is a rather sordid tale of love and misunderstanding, power and politics, tied up in a web of didactic commentary. The music isn't exactly a treat either. Although effective on stage as a dramatic piece, listening reveals the music to be less melodic and less conservative than his earlier work. The lyric elements are brief and far between, with most of the vocal music a kind of super-heightened speech. The orchestra carries the rapidly progressing story effectively, with lots of tense atmosphere and expectancy.

A recording of the 1963 world premiere was led by **Egk** (♦Orfeo 343932, 2CD). Surely he was pleased with the performance; it sounds to me absolutely top-drawer. Yet again we are reminded of what a great loss was the premature death of Wunderlich; as always he's in superb form, singing elegantly with a fine degree of dramatic interpretation. Evelyn Lear too is in fine voice, making the most of her few lyric passages and creating a most sympathetic character. A libretto would have been helpful, but again there is none. Although monaural, the recorded sound is excellent.   PARSONS

Hanns Eisler *(1898–1962)*

No 20th-century composer of any repute was as committed to leftist politics and their employment as musical substance as Eisler. He was not merely a "fellow traveler"; he was a member of the Communist Party and as such was deported from the US in 1948. Like his compatriot and long-time collaborator Bertold Brecht, he was devoted to music "for the people," trying to strip away artifice from concert music and employ other arts and media in works that had an immediacy of expression neither sentimental nor overtly expressionistic. He chose the cabaret over opera, and wrote no concertos or other large-scale symphonic works not based on his songs or film scores. After his expulsion from the US, Eisler chose to live in East Germany, where he wrote polemical music

and prose. Some of his 200 or so songs, whether lieder or numbers in staged works, have remained before the public, but his orchestral music has only recently received much attention.

Cabaret music in Germany, particularly in Berlin, was an important medium for Eisler, as it was for Schoenberg and Weill before their emigration to the US. Cabaret singing is unlike lieder or opera; it requires a biting wit, a flexible range, especially in the low register, and variously colored timbres. **Gisela May** was such a singer, and she shared Eisler's political beliefs as well. Known primarily in Europe, she recorded much of Weill's pre-Broadway music and musical settings of Brecht's literary works. She gives us 13 of Eisler's songs and 16 by the similarly minded but less talented Paul Dessau, accompanied by the usual cabaret ensemble, small with mixed instrumentation (Berlin 2165). The lack of texts, either in the original German or translation, is unfortunate, but May's diction is superb. The CD is remastered from 30-year-old LPs, but the technology is so good you won't notice.

In contrast, **Fischer-Dieskau**'s disc is all Eisler (Teldec/ASV 84409). He didn't meet the requirements for cabaret music, at least as far as you can tell from this recording. Some would claim that the songs on this disc are different in style from those on May's, but actually the difference is more in interpretation than in the scores. There's always an edge in Eisler's songs, a darkness, that May captures and Fischer-Dieskau doesn't. He tries too hard, and anyway the male voice seems unsuited for these songs. Aribert Riemann's piano accompaniment is sensitive, but a small orchestra is always preferable for this kind of music. Texts with English translation are provided, but the listener is cautioned not to take the translations too literally because Eisler's changes in the original German are not consistently reflected in the translations.

Lack of an instrumental ensemble also detracts from "Urban Cabaret," a recording by soprano **Maria Tegzes** with pianist Geoffrey Burleson (Neuma 45083). Eisler shares this disc with Schoenberg's best-known pure cabaret work, *Brettl-lieder,* and more recent music by Edward Harsh in much the same style. About half the Eisler selections are lieder and the rest are solo piano works, three *Klavierstücke* and Sonata 2. Burleson accompanies and plays these rather insignificant pieces well, but Tegzes's singing is much less idiomatic and musically enlightening than May's.

"Songs and Cantatas in Exile" is another remastered selection of vocal works, much of which Eisler copiously reworked from music previously composed (Berlin 9229, 2CD). **Roswitha Trexler**'s voice is a bit light and insecure in outer registers, but she gets some songs just right. Jutta Czapski is an able accompanist, as is the Leipzig chamber ensemble for some of the pieces.

Of more recent recordings and younger performers, I highly recommend a disc that contains an hour of the best of Eisler's vocal music I know; the performances and recorded sound are superb (CPO 999 339). Most of the 34 tracks are filled with cantatas on texts by the Italian radical Ignazio Silone. **Monika Moldenhauer** sings these brief secular cantatas and songs with uncommonly clear diction, appropriate tone, and a natural sense of style; the two clarinetists, violist, cellist, and pianist are no less musical as accompanists. Like *Pierrot lunaire,* the instrumentation varies between and within multi-movement works. The excellent program notes include the mostly German texts with good English translations and more score analysis than is common. For the uninitiated, I recommend this disc even over May's, though hers are from one who was there.

Eisler's oeuvre is a musicologist's nightmare because he borrowed from himself more than any other 20th-century composer except perhaps the sly Copland. Most of his songs were recycled for various purposes different from their original venues, so we can't easily date his work based on style or compositional premise. A little 12-tone here, a sweet (usually bittersweet) tune there, some jazz flavor once in a while, sometimes all mixed up but always directly serving the text or the story on film. Eisler believed the new film medium was an ideal way to reach and politically energize the populace with anti-fascist, pro-socialist messages, and *New Grove* credits Eisler with 42 film scores; other sources give him only 17. Whatever the number, he began to write them in the {apos}20s while still in Germany, then continued during exile in the US and his final residence in East Germany. None of his film-derived music has had the success of Korngold's similarly derived Violin Concerto, but some good recordings of Eisler's variously titled instrumental works are available and worth at least cursory attention. The purely instrumental scores are primarily derived from film, but there is other music as well, especially the 15 or so orchestral suites and Chamber Symphony.

Two remastered discs provide the best broad sample of Eisler's orchestral music. **Max Pommer** leads the Leipzig Gewandhaus in Suites 1–4, most of which are reworkings of film scores; Theme and Variations on *The Long March,* largely taken from a documentary on the Chinese civil war; and Chamber Symphony for 15 solo instruments from a documentary on the Arctic region (Vol. 1, Berlin 9228). There's a large dollop of extra-musicality in these compositions that will be unavailable to most of today's audience, but they hold up pretty well as absolute music. So do the selections in Vol. 2, which is broader in scope, including some music originally for film but also some incidental music for the stage (Berlin 9233). *Goethe-Rhapsodie* is the most interesting of the six works on this disc, with the excellent cabaret singer Elisabeth Breul as soloist with the Berlin Radio Orchestra, **Gunther Herbig** conducting. Composed as a cantata for the 200th anniversary of Goethe's birth, the texts excerpted from *Faust* are overtly political, as you would expect.

For a single disc with similar samples, try **Hans Zimmer** leading the German Symphony Orchestra in Chamber Symphony, Little Symphony, five Orchestra Pieces, three Pieces for Orchestra, and *Storm Suite* (Capriccio 10500). The playing is dispirited by comparison to the Berlin remasters, but you do get the Little Symphony, one of Eisler's few works not based on film or other scores. Composed in 1932, it provides about 10 minutes of 12-tone music, a working out of Schoenbergian material a decade after he broke with his teacher over the perceived elitism of dodecaphony. **Mathias Husmann** and the Magdeburg Philharmonic offer a better recording of much of the same music (CPO 999071). *Overture to a Comedy* (Nestor's *Hollenangst*) replaces the *Storm Suite* on the Capriccio disc; all else is the same. (The booklet cover says there are nine Orchestra Pieces, but in fact there are only five.)   ZIEROLF

Edward Elgar *(1857–1934)*

Elgar was the first great English composer after Purcell, ending a hiatus of two centuries. So dramatic was the appearance of *Enigma Variations* in 1899 that it seemed to release a flood of pent-up musical energy; the 20th century was full of fine English composers who followed him. Viewed by some as the symbol of "pomp and circumstance" and representative of a dying English culture, he remains one of our greatest and most sophisticated composers.

Elgar's music is more complex than it sounds at first and doesn't reveal all its secrets at one hearing. This isn't because it's thorny, arcane, or artificially difficult. Rather, it's an emotional kaleidoscope, changing character before our ears, revealing one thread while moving another

aside. It's heroic, grand, joyful, and rapt, yet no one truly hears Elgar who doesn't mark the aching and yearning with which it's permeated. A master orchestrator, Elgar didn't write many solos, varying colors with subtle instrumental entries and exits, often within a measure. His use of melodic sequences and stepwise patterns is obvious, yet is effective in heightening emotional tension. Elgar isn't easy to perform, but the greatness of the music has drawn enough dedicated artists to produce many great recordings.

Elgar was the first composer to leave a large catalog of composer-conducted recordings of his own works, including most of the important ones. It's a landmark set, considered a touchstone of Elgarian interpretation. The performances are widely praised for their no-nonsense approach, with quick tempos, aggressive phrasing, clear textures, and none of the convoluted lingering that mars some modern versions. All this is true, but I find them rather hurried (as if rushing to fill the four-minute 78 rpm sides), often clumsy and pushing through phrases. They lack the orchestral textures, lushness, and beauty of phrasing other conductors have revealed. Regardless of how we may feel about these readings, they are important, vital, and well worth hearing for their insight into the mind of one of our greatest composers.

SYMPHONIES

1. **Boult**'s last recording, with the London Philharmonic, is big, lush, direct, and in no way softened by the conductor's age (♦EMI 64013, with *Serenade*). His power and sonorities are very appealing in I and IV, as is his dynamism in II. Some performances are more searching and yearning, particularly in III, but Boult has a vital Elgarian voice. His earlier reading is lighter and more fleet (though not really fast), with a leaner but still dark LPO (♦Lyrita 39, LP). Boult doesn't fuss over tempos or transitions or probe deeply, but he manages them so well that they seem natural, and this is one of the most elegant, unaffected versions.

Barbirolli's 1962 reading is passionate and personal. I sense he wants more opulence than the Hallé can supply, but it's plenty opulent enough (♦EMI). Tempos are slow and balances are forward, especially the heavy brass. It's fascinating, with good sound. His 1956 reading, also with the Hallé, is more powerful, sweeping, and exciting, with a II even more explosive than Slatkin's (see below). It's not as romantic as his 1962 version, but even more passionate (♦Dutton 1017, 2 CD, with *Enigma* and other works). Both Boult and the two Barbirollis are much better than the latter's last recording, a live BBC concert, which lacks the power, concentration, playing, and sound of the earlier performances.

Judd is colorful, bold, and exuberant, with moderately fast tempos, yet he's also warm and expansive (♦IMP 2019). String and brass tone are full yet crisp, with fine playing from the Hallé and excellent open sound. **Loughran** is a little like Judd but lighter, not as warm and more classical in nature (♦ASV 6082). Lines are clean and well formed; tempos are slightly more moderate, with fine balances. There is no lack of lyricism, and plenty of nobility and elegance; the sound is fine, if a bit covered, with good playing by the Hallé. **Otaka** takes a very smooth and vocal approach, with velvet strings and an ear for the long line—sometimes too long, as in I where he tends to linger preciously here and there. Not the weightiest reading, but if beauty of tone is important to you, it's well worth having (♦BIS 727, with *Introduction and Allegro*).

Pritchard's elegance, grace, and sense of clear structure and tone produce a uniquely uplifting and almost innocent 1 (IMP 912, with *In the South*). Tempos are slightly fast but not at the cost of sentiment, and they're never hurried. The BBC Symphony plays with refinement in excellent clean sound. Caveat: My copy chopped off the first few measures of *South*, but the symphony is worth it.

Menuhin is direct, bold, and exciting. There is feeling, but no excess of sentiment, and occasionally not quite enough (♦Virgin 61430, with Symphony 2 and marches). The dark brass of the Royal Philharmonic, particularly the horns, supports him with solid, broad attacks. Though lacking the last word in inspiration and refinement, this may appeal to fans of the composer's energetic recording. **Handley** gives a solid effort, straightforward, strong, and vigorous, not overly sentimental but satisfying. The finale falters occasionally, but not seriously. The fine London Philharmonic's strong brass plays out but is never crass (♦Classics for Pleasure 9018). **Slatkin** is full-blooded with the London Philharmonic's low brass a sledgehammer. Movement I is problematic; the loud parts are effectively massive, but the rubato in the slow music and many transitions are less convincing. I've never heard II driven so fiercely. The Adagio is more brightly lit and colorful than most. It's interesting if not overwhelming (RCA 60380, with *In the South*). Barbirolli's 1956 reading does this sort of thing much better.

Mackerras is sometimes small in scale, almost intimate, with angular lines, changing tempos, and lean, spiky textures—episodic and nervous, but on a human scale. The clean warm playing and fine sound balance the angular approach; interesting but not a first choice (Argo 430835, with *Cockaigne*). **Previn** takes a civilized, middle of the road path with a graceful I and a jazzy II. The Adagio is languorous and not as passionate as it could be, but Previn's Elgar has integrity (Philips 5425, with Symphony 2, *Cockaigne*, P&C Marches). **Hurst** is a bit lightweight and superficial in I and IV, with uncomfortable urging and altering of tempo, but they're listenable; II is well done, and the Adagio is warm and eloquent. The BBC Symphony plays well, and the sound is smooth, if lacking at the extreme frequencies. This is a decent budget recommendation (♦Naxos 550634, with *Imperial March*). If you want speed, try **Solti,** who reportedly patterned his recording on Elgar's. Rhythms are sharp and urgent, and it holds together well enough, but ultimately I find it too aggressive and superficial. Others think more highly of it (London 43856, with Symphony 2, *In the South, Cockaigne*).

Among other decent but not first-rate efforts, **Zinman**'s is direct and full of itself, and the Baltimore Symphony plays with panache, but too much is brassy, and there is some rushing in II and plodding in III (Telarc, with P&C Marches). **Andrew Davis** is warm, misty, and autumnal—not unattractive, but he's too relaxed, especially in I, causing this music to sound less virile than it is. Good playing from the BBC Symphony, but the other London orchestras do better. If you want Davis, avoid the muddy, covered-sounding Ultima reissues and look for the original Teldec (73278, with P&C Marches).

Among the non-contenders, **Barenboim** is the most frustrating. His Adagio is Wagnerian in the best sense of the term—warm, probing, and dramatic. Movement II is excellent, IV is good though not entirely cohesive, and it's blaring at the end. The real problem is that I is so meandering and self-conscious, with its lurching tempo changes, that listening is uncomfortable and unpleasant. Compressed, stuffy sound doesn't help (Sony). **Thomson** gives a decent II and III, but his slow tempos and sluggishness in I (especially) and IV take him out of the running (Chandos). Despite its Germanic coloring and style, **Haitink** is lightweight and inconsistent, and I hear little of the Elgar idiom in his treatment of melody and orchestral depth (EMI, with Symphony 2). **Somary** is to be avoided, with his clueless, exaggerated conducting and poor, at times amateurish playing (Claves).

Elgar's recording is fast, aggressive, angular, and very lively. Many swear by it, but I find it hurried with some clumsy phrasing. Sometimes he plows through touching moments that other conductors reveal far more effectively (EMI).

2. Boult's last recording is magisterial, with a conception that never wavers. Tempos are slow but don't lose their motion; the playing is weighty and ethereal at the same time. Everything floats and glows with warmth and light, yet there is power everywhere, including the faster sections. It's wonderfully elegant and concentrated, with sound to match, and the London Philharmonic is glorious (♦EMI 64014, with *Cockaigne*). In his earlier reading, Boult was lighter, faster, and more elegant, and the sound is equally good. Only the slow movement is not as successful as its counterpart in 1, and this version could use a bit more expansion and probing (Lyrita 40, LP).

Barbirolli's 2 is similar in style to but even better than his EMI recording of 1. The opening sets the pace, lingeringly lyrical and vast in conception; listen to the slowing down and tenderness in the introduction of the second theme. This is very personal conducting, even slower and more heartfelt and earthy than the otherworldly Boult; orchestral balances are good, as is the sound (♦EMI 64724). **Solti** is more successful here than in 1. There is no superficiality or aggressiveness; it's sleek and polished, with smooth playing from the London Philharmonic. If not as profound as Boult, he does a good job of taking the middle ground, in excellent sound (♦London 43856, with 1, *Cockaigne, In the South*).

Downes is expressive and clear-toned, also with excellent sound. Sometimes he pushes the faster sections and holds back in the slower ones, but these are just tendencies in a middle of the road but eloquent view, with nice playing by the BBC Philharmonic (♦Naxos 550635). **Andrew Davis** is warm, lyrical, sweet-toned, and dark-colored without heaviness or melancholy. He's also reflective—not the view of an aging man, but one who is serious, thoughtful, and genial. Tempos are moderate and relaxed but hardly lazy. There are more powerful and romantic readings, but few are as pleasant and comforting without being maudlin or insubstantial (♦Teldec 74888, with *In the South*).

Tate is fascinating and full of drama and strength. The weighty Larghetto gradually adds power before a shattering climax—he may be the most imposing in this movement. IV starts slowly and deliberately; at the fugue the sober becomes stately, then passionately noble in a remarkable transition. Decent sound, and the London Symphony is excellent (♦EMI 54192, with *Sospiri*). **Loughran** has the same qualities (and orchestra) as his 1: classical structure, lightness, grace, and dark tone (♦ASV 6087, with *Serenade*). **Menuhin**'s tempos are fleet without sacrificing profundity (though he's not the ultimate in emotional depth, either). He achieves both clarity and texture by allowing the low strings and brass to darken and support the tonal balance, and the Royal Philharmonic plays magnificently (♦Virgin 61430, with 1 and marches).

Gibson is a nice third choice. Tempos are slightly fast even in the Larghetto; the style is literal, textures are light, and the tonal spectrum is tilted slightly toward the treble. Not heart-wrenching, but pleasant and enjoyable, and the sound matches the approach (RCA, LP). **Handley**'s tempos are fast, but his command of rhythm and singing style maintain a jaunty flow in the opening that contrasts nicely with the slow probing in the "ghost" section. The Larghetto is eloquent but not overwhelming, and there is a bit of stiff rhythm and superficiality in III and IV. The London Philharmonic strings are sweet, the sound distant (Classics for Pleasure). **Barenboim**'s 2 is much better than his 1. There are no bizarre tempos or transitions, and the piece flows more with some nice rich textures. However, he underlines too much, and while the pacing moves the music along, it has a labored quality. Not bad, and the frequent use of portamento is endearing, but most of its best qualities can be heard elsewhere. Murky sound doesn't help (Sony, LP).

Haitink's 2 is better integrated if no more Elgarian than his 1; he gives us interesting things to hear, but this is lightweight, superficial stuff (EMI). Slatkin is the epitome of refinement, quite the opposite of his 1. Timbres are lean, with silvery strings. Orchestral textures are clear, often intimate, with soft playing so remarkable it becomes chamber music toward the end of II (the distant sound emphasizes this). Transitions are smooth, but there is little urgency, tension, or yearning; the music almost comes to a stop in I and at the fugue in IV. It's beautiful but lifeless, though it has received much praise in other quarters (RCA, with *Serenade*). Thomson is cold and superficial; there's a lack of depth, warmth, and profundity, and more of a wall of slightly vaporous sound. It's a decent performance but not competitive with the best (Chandos).

Svetlanov and the USSR Symphony give a Russian view with expected results. There are fast tempos and a great deal of passion (II is especially searching), but also edgy, unidiomatic brass playing, as well as sections where the performers just don't know what to do. It's fascinating until IV, which is much too slow, with misconceived rhythms and phrasing (EMI). My comments on **Elgar**'s 1 apply here too, but this interpretation is more convincing (♦Grammofono 78921, with Cello Concerto). It comes together better as it brings out the work's power, but I prefer the recordings recommended above.

3. Officially titled "The Sketches for Symphony No. 3 Elaborated by Anthony Payne," this is the result of Payne's effort to complete sketches the composer gathered toward the end of his life for a BBC commission. Elgar didn't finish the symphony, and the story of Payne's accomplishment (its undertaking spurred by the coming lapse of copyright that would have opened the sketches to the machinations of composers less able and dedicated) is too long to deal with here. Elgar was paring his style down when he wrote it, and the result is obvious from the first measures. They are the only part of the symphony he completed and orchestrated, and they sound very different from his earlier works. Not so the romantic second theme, which is pure Elgar. Payne inserted excerpts from the *King Arthur* incidental music, especially in II, but also in the Waltonian, chivalric IV, to great effect. The most controversial movement is the Adagio. Here Elgar was the most incomplete and cryptic, and it's the most difficult to pull off successfully. The music is a triumph, though not all Elgarians have accepted it.

Andrew Davis introduced and promoted the work, and his BBC recording is its first. It's too bad he didn't record it after the first concerts; they were better performances. But this reading, broad and dark in typical Davis fashion, makes a strong case for a powerful, inventive work. He's least convincing in the too episodic Adagio (♦NMC 053). There is also a Payne-narrated CD of excerpts in which he talks about his reconstruction; it's not required to enjoy the piece, which stands very well on its own (♦NMC 52). **Paul Daniel** is more energetic, rhythmic, dynamic, and brighter in tone. He creates more tension and drama in I, though his bright-toned, slightly-too-energetic finale is lacking in grandeur compared to Davis, who excels here. Daniel's Adagio is essential. His lyrical approach makes this properly mysterious music work in a way that Davis's does not (♦Naxos 554719). If you prefer darkish Elgar get Davis and Daniel. You might go with just Daniel if you like more energetic Elgar.

OTHER ORCHESTRAL MUSIC

Cockaigne Overture; Crown of India; Pomp & Circumstance Marches. These tend to be issued as couplings, but a fine recording by **Gibson** with the Scottish National Orchestra makes a strong case for the lightly-regarded *Crown of India* (♦Chandos 8429).

Enigma Variations. Many critics pick **Barbirolli**'s recordings for this work but disagree on which is the best. For me, it's the one with the Philharmonia (♦Seraphim 196388). It's passionate, insightful, weighty yet never heavy, with playing to match. He's inspired, natural, and the master of Elgarian rubato; phrases are molded and natural throughout the piece. No performance solves more of this work's problems. His earlier (1956) Hallé reading (Mercury) is one of the faster, more exciting *Enigmas*, but I hear little to evoke praise beyond that. The Hallé doesn't sound as good as the Philharmonia, and there are a few lapses in the playing.

There are several **Boult** recordings, and his second stereo version with the London Symphony is at or near the top of most lists (♦EMI 64748, with Holst's *Planets*). It's a counterpart to Barbirolli, more direct, with less rubato. These are portraits of flesh-and-blood human beings; tempos are faster, more energetic and have more spontaneity than his earlier efforts. Both of Boult's earlier readings are more straightforward, especially the EMI mono, which is a middle of the road benchmark; it would be rated higher but for the mono sound, its slight lack of energy and glow, and the quality of the competition, but it's still one of the most dignified and noble *Enigmas*. His {apos}60s London Philharmonic recording is less characterized, more held back, and less straightforward than the EMI mono. It's one of the most dignified and noble, and Boult's adherence to his slightly slow tempos is remarkable; some prefer it to the LSO version (♦Concerts for Pleasure 4022, with Holst's *Planets*).

Andrew Davis's third and best *Enigma*, with the BBC Symphony, is full, dark, sweeping, and sure of itself (♦Teldec 73279, with *Cockaigne, Introduction, Serenade*). He has a clear vision of each variation, and he connects each organically to the next. His Sony recording is similar—not bad, but step down one in general and two steps down in sound. He was just finding his way in his first reading (Lyrita). **Mata** gets it just about right but for a too loud oboe in "CAE" and a too slow and controlled "EDU"; otherwise, it reminds me of the Barbirolli/EMI. He combines moderately slow tempos with a tendency to lean expressively into notes and linger by giving them their full value and texture even in slurred passages. This holds up the pace slightly without impairing the line or dragging; occasionally it's a bit stiff, but not often. The London Symphony is first rate (♦Vox 9018, with Dvořák's Symphony 7).

Previn is helped immensely by the glowing Royal Philharmonic. The opening variations are slow and flowing, almost riverlike. Everything is congenial, autumnal, with an expansive "RPA" and a beautiful slow "Nimrod;" the letdown is a wavery "EDU." Generally, it's nice and sophisticated (♦416813, with *Pomp & Circumstance*). His earlier recording is similar but scaled down and not quite as expressive. Ironically, "EDU" is very strong here (EMI, LP). **Downes** is straightforward, pure-toned, almost rarefied, but also sweet and innocent. The quiet variations are exquisite, particularly "CAE," "WN," and "Dorabella." The loud ones aren't overpowering but are in proportion and don't go slack as they do with Zinman or Sargent. It's an elegantly reserved reading, aided by the delicacy of the BBC Philharmonic; the only problem is distant sound (♦Conifer 51507, with Cello Concerto).

Mehta's is the LP audiophile's *Enigma*, with great sound and a straightforward, rich performance with no extraordinary moments or serious problems. Everything is well played; the strings in "RPA" are typical of his warm approach (♦London LP, with Ives's Symphony 1). **Jochum** is warm, honest, and musical. He finds many interesting points, and he understands Elgar's rubato. The climax of "CAE" is beautifully restrained; "Nimrod" is very slow, but he maintains flow and avoids indulgence. A fine "EDU" has unusually burnished brass, with the London Symphony sounding like a German orchestra; the let-downs are loud variations that are too restrained (♦DG LP, with Brahms's *Haydn Variations*).

Monteux is fresh, entertaining, exciting, and very French with its bright colors and well-lit textures. When tempos differ from the norm, they are faster and more urgent. There is sometimes too much energy, particularly in a bumptious "Ysobel," a too fast "Dorabella," and a crass, over the top "EDU." The sound is on the bright side and shrill in loud places; the early {apos}60s London Symphony is fine, but the orchestra was in better shape later. Many people think this is one of the best, if not the very best *Enigmas*. It's never boring, but I find it a bit superficial and wanting in Elgarian insight (London 452303, with Karajan's *Planets*).

Barenboim is very personal. Great feeling creates a luminous dream world that may not appeal to everyone. "CAE," "RPA," and "BGN" are very nice, "Nimrod" sounds like two friends conversing, and "EDU" is particularly fascinating; the singing strings and smooth brass are treasurable, though the cramped sound is a serious drawback (Sony 48265, with *Crown of India* and *Pomp & Circumstance*). **Litton** combines power and size with controlled phrasing that holds back some of the flow; it can sound ethereal and floating to some, superficial and aloof to others. It's interesting, but not a top recommendation (Virgin, with *In the South* and *Serenade for Strings*). **Sargent** gives us another straightforward version with moderate tempos; he understates dynamics and tempo and is very gentle, and the fast variations lack energy. Sonically, it's small-scaled and distant (EMI).

Solti's Chicago Symphony recording parallels Elgar's brisk reading. The opening bars feature fine control, measured tempo, nice rubato, and excellent sound. The playing is good, and the loud variations aren't overdone until the crass "EDU." Solti is not the deepest prober, but this is a decent account, brightly lit yet not bright sounding because of the strings (London LP, with Schoenberg's *Variations for Orchestra*). His Vienna Philharmonic version is larger-scaled, sweeter in tone, and less subtle. It's more consistent from variation to variation but often heavy, with opaque sound. The VPO seems less mellow and full than usual (London, with works by Kodály and Blacher).

Zinman is refined, fast, and elegant. He's outstanding in the lighter and faster variations, but overrefined in the loud ones, except for a powerful, controlled "EDU." This is one of the relatively few American recordings, with the Baltimore Symphony doing well (Telarc, with shorter works). **Del Mar** is thoughtful and careful with well-considered and rarely indulgent rubato. Tempos are fast, with clear, light textures, an approach that's more neat and well-placed than elegant; its assets are accurate rhythms, note placement, and clarifying inner lines—noteworthy given the distant, cacophonous sound. The clean playing of the Royal Philharmonic helps. It's enjoyable but hardly passionate (Telarc, with shorter works).

Mackerras's earlier EMI recording is quirky and not romantic in the usual Elgarian sense. The tempos vary a bit, and the line is angular and sometimes clipped. The variations have a flawed human quality that portrays the people rather than just musical ideas. Not a first choice, but interesting (EMI, with *Falstaff*). His second version is inferior and dull, as though he was unsure what to do for an encore (Argo, with Cello Concerto).

Rattle's large-scale performance with his Birmingham Symphony is sleek, glorious in tone, beautifully played, and very impressive. You can wallow in it, but if you know the piece you might see the wizard behind the screen. Tempos lurch at times, he overdramatizes transitions, and he tends to slur lyrical passages regardless of markings, rendering textures muddy. His concern about sound often renders chords and line static. This disc has been well reviewed, but I find it indulgent and mannered (EMI, with short works). **Steinberg**'s is a decent performance marred by distant sound, a too-consistent approach, a few variations that fail to catch fire, and an uncomprehending "EDU." The star is the burnished Pittsburgh Symphony: Everything is warm, lyrical, honest, and not indulgent (Capitol, with Vaughan Williams's *Fantasia*).

Colin Davis gives a straightforward, classically oriented performance, with little rubato. Rhythms are straight, with few liberties or indulgences granted; it's buttoned down and restrained, but not stuffily, and makes me think of "big" Mozart (Philips, with *Cockaigne*). **Gibson**'s broad, honest rendition is one of the better straightforward performances and is never dull. There are a lot of good moments, some insight, and no glaring weaknesses. The problems tend to be rhythmic lapses, and they are frequent enough to cause one to look elsewhere for its virtues. Some regard it more highly (Chandos, with *Falstaff*). **Handley** could be competition for Mehta. He too is dark, with broad phrases, tempos on the slow side, and a "big orchestra" concept that's more concerned with abstract music than portraits. The problem is poor sound (EMI).

Thomson has a controlling, leisurely, and blended style that doesn't meet the color requirements of this piece. His tempos are within the norms, and he takes a broad, sweeping approach. Sometimes this leads to pleasant music making; at other times it's austere and disengaged (Chandos, with short pieces). **Dutoit** is similar to Monteux; both have an extroverted, entertaining manner, though Dutoit is colder, more efficient, and doesn't have as much fun. One dramatic and telling comparison is in Monteux's famous soft opening to "Nimrod"; Dutoit doesn't get that soft here or anywhere else, a trait he shares with Boult, but to more deleterious effect. The louder variations come off best (London, with *Falstaff*).

Leaper is on the bright side, though this is more a matter of orchestral texture than exuberance. Much is musical, but the Czecho-Slovak Symphony isn't comfortable with the Elgar idiom. The loud variations are weak, and there are awkward moments and balances (Naxos, with *Pomp & Circumstance* 1 and 4 and other pieces). **Menuhin** gives a straightforward performance that adheres to the score. It's slightly lacking in motion, and for me is nondescript. The Royal Philharmonic plays well, but not as well as for Previn (Philips, with Cello Concerto).

Marriner's Concertgebouw sounds darker, woodier, fruitier, and more spread-out than the brighter, more focused British orchestras. A more potent Elgarian presence than Marriner's might have produced something magical. There are great moments, but too much is awkward and out of place (Philips, with *Pomp and Circumstance Marches* 1, 2, 4). **Ormandy** is more Ormandy/Philadelphia than Elgar. The playing is great—big and lush, dominated by the strings, lending a broader, warmer, and larger-scaled aura than any other. The effect is hit-and-miss, with "miss" translating to superficial and smothering. This is a great orchestra with a sound that doesn't exist any more, but it's not Elgar (Columbia, with Violin and Cello Concertos, *Cockaigne*, marches).

Skrowaczewski presents Elgar as Bruckner. He seems clueless about the music. His tempos are extremely slow, his textures thick, and there's no attempt at characterization, elegance, finesse, or variation of color.

The dark, burnished, glowing sound of his Saarbrücken orchestra makes this one to wallow in, but be prepared for the absurd (Arte Nova, with Britten's Piano Concerto). **Stokowski** is interesting for his conducting and the Czech Philharmonic. It's full of rubato and tempo changes, some inappropriate. The first few notes of the "Theme" are quick, but before you reach the end, he slams on the brakes. Balances are unusual, e.g., the brassy "WMB" begins totally saturated by Stokowskian strings. The orchestra sounds terrific (London).

Boughton is delicate, reserved, and detailed, with some exquisite moments, but he's devoid of spark, energy, or passion (Nimbus, with *Cockaigne* and *Froissart*). **Bernstein**'s performance is notorious. It's not that out of the ordinary until "WN," which is too slow and deliberate to begin with before slowing down even more to a barely-in-motion cadence. What follows is an incredibly indulgent "Nimrod" that takes twice as long to play as the average. Everything after that is anticlimactic—and slower—than the movements before. Ludicrous, but some find it full of heart and feeling (DG, with *Pomp and Circumstance* 1 and 2, *Crown of India March*).

Haitink is lifeless and dull (Philips). **Levine** is more Wagner than Elgar. Everything is big, self-indulgent, and heavy. Textures are string-drenched and monochromatic, with little clarity, intimacy, or nuance (DG, with Debussy's *Images*). I have no idea what **Sinopoli**'s recording is about. Nice playing is wasted by leaden tempos, perverse ritards, superficiality, and self indulgence. The slowdown in "EDU" has to be heard to be believed; it sounds like England itself just ran aground (DG, with *Serenade for Strings* and *In the South*). **Slatkin**'s performance is, with a few exceptions, calculated, erratic, mannered, self-indulgent, and filled with exaggerations (RCA, with *Froissart* and *Cockaigne).*

The famous **Elgar** recording is from 1928, with the Royal Albert Hall Orchestra (EMI). The older version was made acoustically and is complete except for a cut in "Nimrod" (Pearl, LP). Tempos aren't the same. However, both are generally fast, and the spirit and style are similar. Rhythms are sharp and lively, with impulsive *accelerandos* and variations in tempo (some sound amateurish), and much portamento. The 1928 recording sounds better and is played better. Elgar's *Enigmas* are interesting and revealing. I think they skim the surface, but 1928 is highly thought of in other quarters.

The best of the historical recordings, and one of the two best, period, is **Sargent**'s 1945 recording with the National Symphony. It's the recording I think Elgar was trying to make, with exciting fast variations, rich slow ones, but a fast and very intense "Nimrod." With its wonderful characterizations, this reading is different from but just as good as the second Barbirolli. The restoration is excellent (♦Dutton 1202, with *In the South* led by Boyd Neel and smaller works). **Barbirolli**'s 1947 reading is fast but more urgent than Sargent and not as exquisite. It presses forward with that Barbirolli surge, but is singing and heartfelt, in decent sound (♦Dutton 1017, 2CD, with Symphony 1 and other works).

Toscanini's 1935 BBC Symphony recording is mainstream, Elgarian, often interesting and insightful, with only a few weak variations. Hearing the stately "Theme" and the way a beautiful, unusually languid ritard melts into "CAE," few would imagine it's the same conductor as in the NBC issue. The sound is good for its age (♦Iron Needle 35). His 1951 recording with the NBC Symphony is fast, brassy, and not as well played (RCA). There are some good moments in **Beecham**'s Royal Philharmonic recording, but there are many awkward ones, too. Some like it, but I think it's below average. **Hamilton Harty**'s approach is lively and animated, with generally very fast tempos and more portamento than any other. The Hallé's playing is generally good, though there are odd balances, especially in the woodwinds. I enjoy it for its energy and passion, but wouldn't count it among my favorites because of the fast tempos (Philips).

Falstaff. Andrew Davis combines many of the virtues of Barbirolli, Boult, and Mackerras in the most symphonic performance of this work. He's not concerned with storytelling as much as creating a "third symphony," though there is plenty of characterization. This recording has beautiful, dark timbres and is richer than many others (♦Teldec 6019, with other short pieces). His earlier *Falstaff* is light-textured, nice in its way, but not substantial enough or sure enough about its structure. The couplings are well played except for *Froissart,* which is a bit clunky and unassuming (Lyrita LP). If Davis (and most of the others) are too symphonic and dark, **Lloyd-Jones** is a dashing alternative. He and the English Northern Philharmonia stress narrative with clearly delineated, enthusiastic playing, very deft and very natural. The couplings are fine, with *Fan* being as good as any, though the unavailable Boult is better (♦Naxos 553879 with *The Sanguine Fan, Elegy*).

Barbirolli gives a warm, leisurely, and congenial reading—not the most dramatic or charged version, but very understanding and knowledgeable. The textures are weighty but at no sacrifice to the flow (♦EMI, LP). **Boult** is larger-scaled, and he captures the regal nature of the King Hal scenes without ignoring the lyrical interludes. He's not as subtle as Barbirolli, but he's riper and more involving (♦Testament 1006). **Mackerras**'s aggressive tempos stress excitement. His strength is his ability to stay with the hairpin turns of plot and personality at his fast tempo without sacrificing structure (♦Argo 436545). **Solti**'s is a riot, the one recording that makes me laugh, both in the bassoon passages and in the drunken sleep scene. A rollicking joy, and the London Philharmonic has a ball (♦Decca 452853).

Handley is also symphonic. He's not as dark and romantic as Davis and is more straightforward and a little reserved (Classics for Pleasure, LP). **Gibson**'s light-weight approach misses some of the weight and drama (RCA, LP). **Dutoit** is smooth, also missing most of the drama and humor (London, with *Enigma*). **Rattle** is nicely played but mannered (EMI). **Barenboim** is sharp, lean, and dramatic, if not often lyrical (Columbia). The sound is plagued with harsh string timbres. **Elgar**'s own recording is lively, mordant, exciting, and wry, with just enough sentiment (♦EMI 754837).

In the South. **Solti**'s performance is exciting and fleet but not too fast, weighty enough but not heavy, and nothing is pushed—great playing and sound (♦London 3856, 2CD, with Symphonies 1 and 2 and *Cockaigne*). **Barbirolli** didn't conduct *In the South* until the last two months of his life, and his live performance is from his last recording. Though the Hallé is hardly flawless, this is a thrilling interpretation that seethes with passion, energy, and power; even the usually serene viola passage has that famous Barbirolli surge (♦BBC 4013, with music by Walton and Britten). **Andrew Davis** is dark, weighty, and richly textured, with thoughtful phrasing and nice rubato in the slow section. The Romans are ponderous and tired, as if we're meeting them after a battle, and it works (♦Teldec 74888, with Symphony 2).

Butt is nicely balanced between the crisp and the dramatic; he gets clean playing by the Royal Philharmonic in great sound, and the strings really sing (♦ASV 619, with *Coronation March* and other pieces). **Boult** is middle of the road but hardly dull. The string tone is textured and warm, his intensity of line helps immensely, and the London Philharmonic outdoes itself (♦EMI, LP). **Silvestri**'s classic recording is more powerful and thrilling than Solti or Slatkin. It has a fury as if it's possessed, and the bright sound of the Bournemouth Symphony adds to the incandescence (♦EMI LP).

Litton's is a nice, somewhat buttoned down version, marked by control. There is good balance between the lyrical and dramatic, with fine sustained intensity in the lyrical music, and beautiful orchestral balances—not the most exciting, but well played and satisfying (♦Virgin, with *Enigma*). **Slatkin** is brisk yet smooth, with compelling playing from the London Philharmonic strings. The Roman army quick-marches a bit, but Slatkin slows down for a beautifully intimate "Moonlight" section. The piece loses its way toward the end; we think glossy rather than smooth and yearn for some muscle to go with the panache (RCA, with Symphony 1).

Boyd Neel with his orchestra was teeming with life and energy in 1947. He's not as purely visceral as Silvestri, but more exciting than most of the others. The restored sound is good enough for this almost to be considered a mainstream recording (♦Dutton 1203, with Sargent's *Enigma Variations* plus other Elgar works). **Elgar**'s recording is exciting, very fluid, with sweet violin tone and a lot of portamento. The only flaw is that "Moonlight" could use more delicacy and magic and suffers from a sour oboe (♦EMI LP).

Introduction and Allegro for Strings. **Barbirolli**'s 1962 recording is ardent and romantic, with rich string tone and fine playing by the Sinfonia of London. This is a classic, though other orchestras sound even better (♦EMI 63955, with Cello Concerto, *Elegy*). His more thrusting and dramatic 1956 reading is exciting, romantic, and more urgent than 1962. Those who want a powerful performance without the French strings of Munch's Boston Symphony recording should look into this (♦Dutton 1017, 2CD, with Symphony 1, *Enigma,* and other works). Barbirolli's 1947 mono reading is even faster and more thrusting, slightly too much so for me, but an interesting insight into his evolution as a conductor.

Boult is slightly broader, warmer, smoother, and slower, but no less powerful or ardent. He receives fine playing by the London Philharmonic and great, up-front sound (♦EMI LP, with Cello Concerto). His earlier recording with the same orchestra is leaner, lighter, and more chamber-like. The phrasing is a bit more molded, but otherwise it's more straightforward and not as passionate (♦Classics for Pleasure 4022, with *Enigma*). **Otaka** is similar to his coupled Symphony 1: beautiful, velvety string playing, sometimes too lingering, but gorgeous (♦BIS 727).

Leaper with the Capella Istropolitana (made up of strings from the Slovak Philharmonic) brings a lyrical, silvery aspect to contrast with the darker versions described above. The playing is supple and romantic, with fine rubato and molded phrasing (♦Naxos 550331, with other short works). **Andrew Davis** is slower and not as thrusting as Boult and Barbirolli. He's a lot smoother and lays back a little, occasionally losing momentum; string tone is darker without the bright top end of the others, though he gets fine playing from the BBC Symphony (♦Teldec 73279, with *Enigma, Cockaigne, Serenade*). **Munch** is colorful, charged, and dramatic, with the Boston Symphony strings adding a rich sheen unlike any other. It may be too "French" to be your only version but is highly desirable (♦RCA 61424, with Tchaikovsky's *Serenade,* Barber's *Adagio* and *Medea's Dance*). **Menuhin** is noncompetitive; playing and sound are harsh (Arabesque).

CONCERTOS

Cello Concerto. **Tortelier** (with Sargent) is more restrained than most and is especially winning in the lyrical passages (♦Testament 2025,

2CD). His sound is vocal, open, even, and burnished like fine walnut. Tempos are slightly held back, and he has a nice slow vibrato. **Navarra** is stunning, full of glowing tone and intensity (♦EMI 63955, with *Enigma* and *Introduction and Allegro*). This performance has a cohesiveness that grabs the listener. The only flaw is sound that puts the cello too far forward.

Du Pré with Barbirolli is a classic; her passion and fervor burn from the first note (♦EMI 56219, with *Sea Pictures*). She has great concentration and a complex tone that's occasionally buzzy. The rosin flies as she digs into the strings, and the thrust with which she sends the orchestra off with the main theme is visceral and typical of the entire recording. This is a very romantic, impulsive account with a lot of rubato in the slow passages; the sound is good, but bright and slightly bass-shy. Her recording with Barenboim is more romantic and slower but also more thought out and less impulsive (Columbia, with *Cockaigne, Enigma,* Violin Concerto, *Pomp & Circumstance*). The effect is smoother and softer (though there is no lack of power), and the playing is more halting. The sound is poor.

An all-Finnish production features an intense, bold, and clear-toned reading by **Arto Noras** and Saraste conducting the Finnish Radio Symphony in tight, gleaming, yet full sound. While hardly lacking in romanticism, Noras runs opposite to Du Pré's ultra-emotional view as he compellingly challenges the notion that this is an old man's farewell. Excellent, fairly close, but balanced sound (♦Finlandia 95768, with Lalo's Cello Concerto). **Truls Mørk**'s modern view is along the same lines, but more contemplative and chamber-like. Some may find it aloof, others refreshing (♦Virgin 453356, with Britten's Cello Concerto).

Maria Kliegel is also restrained, but more openly lyrical than Mørk. Her tone sings irresistibly. She displays feeling without exaggeration, walking a line between the passionate Du Pré and the golden Tortelier (♦Naxos 550503, with Dvořák's Cello Concerto). Soloist and orchestra are well balanced with fine sound—one of the top choices if your emphasis is on lyricism. **Steven Isserlis** occupies an emotional world of resignation and weariness (♦MCA 90735, with Bloch's *Schelomo*). His sound is small, pretty, clean, and lyrical; from the opening, his hushed, gentle playing and intimate phrasing set the tone. The line moves, but reluctantly, like a long sigh; the way it dies at the end is touching. **Schiff** is fine and direct, with beautiful transitions and strict attention to rhythm (♦Philips 412880). Marriner's orchestra plays well, and the sound is good.

Pieter Wispelwey will have many admirers (Channel Classics 12998, with Lutoslawski's Cello Concerto). It's very well thought out, finely honed, with clear cello and orchestral tone and careful balance between the romantic and classical. Some may find it a bit too calculated. He doesn't sing as much as Kliegel, nor is his tone as warm as Tortelier's, but he's given excellent sound and balance. **Alexander Baillie** is in tune with its coupled *Enigma* led by Downes: lightweight, lyrical, and clear-toned, with moderate tempos. It's more songlike and less pathetic than usual, occasionally touching on the fanciful and even the mysterious (♦Conifer 51507). **Maisky** is also clear-toned, broad, more sweeping and singing than weighty, and nicely reflective. Sinopoli's accompaniment has a fullness that comfortably envelops the soloist, and there is little of the self-indulgence that elsewhere afflicts his Elgar. The problem is that the coupled *Enigma* isn't competitive; still, this is a budget issue and may be useful for that reason (♦London 460624, with *Enigma Variations, Serenade*).

Ma is intense, with a wiry sound and fast vibrato that some find irresistible, though it's unrelenting (Columbia 44562, with four other Cello

Concertos, or 39541 with Walton's Concerto). He's more intense than romantic, his intonation is impeccable, his technique astounding. Everything is thought out, deeply felt, and never dull. The sound is only adequate. A must for Ma fans, but perhaps too mannered and intense for others. **Robert Cohen**'s second recording is bigger and more forward than his first, his manner darker and more serious (♦Argo 436545, with Mackerras's *Enigma* and *Froissart*). His earlier version with Del Mar is small, reedy, and pleasant, but lacks intensity (Classics for Pleasure 9003, with *Elegy, In the South*).

Starker gives the oddest performance of all; some will find it compelling, others irritating (RCA, with Delius and Walton). His tone is small and reedy but also liquid and facile. He seems to be improvising and taking liberties, but the rubato is well calculated and he uses a lot of portamento. Slatkin's straightforward accompaniment works well. **Harrell** has a strong legato and a good big sound (London, LP). His tempos are slow and deeply felt, and his performance has intensity and control. However, it's a bit tight, and there is an occasional buzz in his sound. It's well regarded, with fine sound, but a bit anonymous and dry. **Fournier** is regal and dignified, with a nice tenor quality (DG, LP). His line is simple, elegant, and plaintive. The recording helps the cellist by placing the orchestra well back, but it hurts the orchestral balance; decent sound otherwise.

Lloyd-Webber has a rich tone and a weighty vertical line (Philips, NA). He sits on notes and doesn't move forward as well as others, making it a bit dull and lacking in lyricism. I don't hear maturity or the last ounce of insight. The sound is quite good, and Menuhin appears to be in accord with Webber's conception. **Felix Schmidt** is pedestrian (IMP, with Vaughan-Williams). The cello is back in the orchestra, sapping some of its personality. **Ralph Kirshbaum**'s sound is small, and his playing is whiney, effete, and tentative (Chandos, with *Falstaff*). The tempos are too slow for playing so lacking in intensity.

Rivka Golani plays Elgar's sanctioned viola version put together by Lionel Tertis; the performance (with Handley) is a stunner (♦NA). Everything is more lyrical and less heavy; the notes seem to move along with greater celerity because they lie closer together on the string. Golani's sound is beautiful and sweet, on the light side, but dark in color. She plays with grace and deftness, her intonation and technique are impeccable, and the sound is exceptional.

Beatrice Harrison with Elgar producing one of his best performances on the podium is a classic, lyrical, warm, and insightful; it's one of the best recordings ever made of this work (♦Grammofono 78921, with Symphony 2). **Anthony Pini** takes a broad approach, and van Beinum (with the London Philharmonic) matches with an accompaniment more symphonic than usual. Tempos are moderate, and phrasing is expansive though not drawn out. The sound is mediocre, with Pini's big tone quite far forward; with first-rate sound, this would be a major contender (Everest 3141, LP). Many people swear by **Casals.** That depends on whether your interest is in the cello or the piece. He essentially makes this the *Casals* Cello Concerto with an extremely romantic, indulgent reading. He does it brilliantly, though, and his fans will be interested.

Violin Concerto. In **Zukerman**'s first recording he plays with a small, sweet sound that is probing and assertive without being demonstrative. The opening is quick, the violin entry natural and effortless; he plays the multiple stop passages naturally and with control, though II could use more backbone. Barenboim's conducting is a little soft and stretched out, but this is one of the best versions (♦Sony LP). Another try, this time

with Slatkin, has been well received, but I find it unmoving and bland (RCA). Beautifully as he plays, Zukerman seems less involved than before. Slatkin, while fine in the orchestral interludes, misses ardor and urgency elsewhere. There is something flat and overly lyrical about the whole thing, and the violin is much too close.

Ida Haendel's gorgeous sound is dark and sweet, but always vocal and capable of many colors (♦Testament 1146). Many call Boult's conducting slow and distended, but I find it gripping. His tempos allow Haendel to probe the composer's heart without fireworks, lingering on each turn of phrase. She's mature and understanding, yet enraptured by the music. Some passages filled with downbeats can be ponderous, and there are places in III where the intensity lets up. Nevertheless, this is a wonderful reading, and the sound is gorgeous. Haendel turned in a very different (live) performance that many may prefer, with Pritchard and the BBC Symphony (♦BBC 91942, with *Polonia*). Tempos are quicker, the style more straightforward, lighter, fleeter, and, though she was seven years older for this recording, more youthful. *Polonia,* with its blend of Elgar's style, Chopin, and colorful Eastern European melody, is a nice bonus.

Hugh Bean (with Groves) is self-effacing, with a small, lyrical sound, and not much intensity (Classics for Pleasure 4632, with Violin Sonata). His style is relaxed and his pace leisurely; he finds things in the music no one else does. The Liverpool Philharmonic strings could be sweeter and things get ponderous at times, but the sound is good, with excellent balance. **Sitkovetsky**'s tone is small but dark and complex; there is something nostalgic and autumnal in his playing that is very British (♦Virgin 45065). His approach is internalized, almost chamber-like at times, though he has more intensity than Bean. The balance has the soloist almost in the orchestra to the point where he occasionally sounds like another voice of the Royal Philharmonic. This can be disconcerting, but if you get used to it, it becomes an advantage. Menuhin conducts like someone who has spent a lifetime with the work, and the sound is rich and full.

For those who want a red-blooded performance, try **Igor Oistrakh** (♦Olympia 242). The accompaniment by Valentin Zhuk and the Moscow Philharmonic is quite good, if occasionally headlong, but this is Oistrakh's show. Close violin sound reveals all his robust, complex tone. He plays with a lot of rubato, portamento, and slowish slurs, but never overindulges. He has a good sense of this music and stays within its limits, with not a lot of mystery but plenty of enthusiasm and heart. **Kwung-Wha Chung** gives a good, lightweight performance that occupies a middle ground of intensity (London). Solti lets loose in the orchestral interludes, but usually matches his soloist, with good open sound and playing by the London Philharmonic.

Accardo has a similarly light, deft touch, but is more reticent and less passionate (Collins, with Walton's Concerto). That Hickox is not of the same mind can be heard from the violinist's retiring entrance after an outgoing orchestral introduction. Accardo is small-scaled, discreet, and dignified in the Elgarian manner; his technique is dazzling, but there is no digging in, nor is his intonation perfect. I can't recommend this generally, but I like it for its silvery and ethereal quality. **Dong-Suk Kang** has a terrific technique (though with a few pitch problems) and he handles the Elgar style well, if not with the last word of expression or subtlety (Naxos 550489, with *Cockaigne,* or 553233 with Sibelius's Concerto). His sound is bright and can get steely in the loud high register. Leaper and the Polish Radio Orchestra provide good support, though too-close miking of the soloist accentuates the brightness and makes the orchestra sound as if it were in another room. Others like this more than I do, but it's a good budget choice.

Menuhin's performance with Boult is inferior to his earlier one with the composer, though Boult leads with vigor and appropriate tempos (EMI, with Delius's Concerto). Menuhin's bright, small sound can be sweet, especially in the upper registers, but it can also be thin and whiny with too fast a vibrato. He ties the music together well, but others have more technical mastery, though ironically, it's in the less technically demanding II where Menuhin falters the most. **Kennedy** with Handley features a beautiful dark tone, a pleasant slow vibrato, and impeccable technique. It's straightforward and direct but lacks personality (EMI). A plus is the way the recording integrates the violin with the orchestra. Kennedy's second recording, with Rattle, is less controlled, even improvisatory, and Rattle isn't always in sympathy (EMI). The cadenza is the high point, as if when free of Rattle's stick he can express himself. Both recordings have been better received by other critics.

Takezawa and Colin Davis can't seem to make up their minds (RCA). The opening starts off slowly, then speeds up, but when the big lyrical theme enters on the violin, the tempo is very slow. I hear more technique than insight, and Takezawa could use better accompaniment. **Perlman** is hardly idiomatic (DG). From the obstreperous opening onward, there is no Elgarian *nobilmente,* and the Chicago Symphony's playing under Barenboim is rough and edgy. Perlman's tone sobs and throbs—some violin runs could be part of a Gypsy rhapsody—and there is little rubato. The sound has no depth and is dull and edgy, with Perlman too far forward.

Menuhin's recording with Elgar is one of the most famous. The composer was so struck by the 16-year-old violinist that he gave one of his most inspired performances. It's magical, full of life and insight. Menuhin's technique is a marvel, his beautiful tone has none of the strain of his later recordings, and the sound isn't bad at all (♦EMI 65020, with *Enigma*). **Albert Sammons**'s 1928 performance was the concerto's first complete recording (♦Novello 901, with Cello Concerto). His sound is small but sweet and fluid; his high register is gorgeous and silvery and his technique astounding, with every note in place. Tempos are quick, not urgent, with Sammons poised, never forcing. It's a very natural, fluid performance, in sound good enough to be enjoyable.

Alfredo Campoli and Boult are at their most fluid with moderate, flowing, and understanding tempos that provide a solid background for his sweet and very lyrical sound. This is a light, elegant performance, and because Campoli's sound is small, the forwardness of this {apos}50s-style recording doesn't seem overbalanced (♦Decca 675 LP). **Heifetz**'s classic account is typically bright and virtuosic, yet there's no lack of feeling. Wallenstein's accompaniment is fitting and reasonably balanced (RCA).

CHAMBER MUSIC

Piano Quintet. The **New London Quintet**'s light, lyrical reading is delightful. People who think of the Quintet as Brahmsian and dark may be surprised by how it sounds with lightly inflected playing at a fairly quick tempo. The secret is a flow of melody that rolls off the instruments with full *tenuto* and legato (♦HNH, LP). The **Mistry Quartet** with David Owen Norris gives a big, dark piano sound with up-front recording. This is a romantic, probing interpretation that combines rubato and some underlined slow tempos to examine the quiet nooks and crannies, with drama in the big moments. The phrasing is often deliberate and occasionally exaggerated, but never with a loss of flow (♦Argo 433312, with String Quartet).

The **Coull Quartet** with Allan Schiller is stylishly romantic with a touch of nostalgia but no excess weight. String tone is a little less pol-

ished than in their recording of the Quartet, partly because of ASV's more acerbic sound. None of this is objectionable, and there's always flow to the line; it's recommendable, especially if you also want Frank Bridge's great Quintet (♦ASV 678). The **Maggini Quartet** with Peter Donohoe glowingly emphasizes the work's Brahmsian aspect. Phrasing is long-lined and full, with warm, blended sound, and Donohoe's tone is big and noble. The sound is warm and natural, if slightly soft-focused (♦Naxos 553737, with the Quartet). The **Medici Quartet** with John Bingham is passionate and colorful, with little blended smoothness of tone. Everything is bright and individualistic; attacks are sharp, the tone lean. The sound is clear but harsh, exaggerating the high voltage approach, making for unpleasant listening (Meridian).

String Quartet. The **Coull Quartet** may give the warmest performance, with beautiful string tone and a natural, beguiling flow (♦Hyperion 66718, with Bridge's *Three Idylls* and Walton's Quartet). The **Gabrieli Quartet** provides another warm performance, though a little more romantic and inflected, with not quite as much flow (♦Chandos 8474, with Walton's Quartet). The **Brodsky Quartet** is full bodied and lyrical, with the slow movement given more emphasis and breadth than usual. Textures are warm and full, and there is no lack of power; the sound is clear if a bit heavy (♦ASV 526, with Delius's Quartet). The **Mistry Quartet**'s reading is very similar to their Piano Quintet: deliberate phrasing, some slow, very elastic tempos, and real passion when required. Fascinating, dramatic, romantic, and a bit episodic, Mistry is not as flowing as some, but they never bog down either (♦Argo 433312, with Piano Quintet).

The **Maggini Quartet** is lyrical and introspective, with tempos that sound slow because of their weight but are actually rather fast. Pleasant listening, but they don't probe as deeply as they could (Naxos 553737, with Piano Quintet). The **Medici Quartet**'s performance is similar to their Quintet, though less driven. It still has energy, the sound remains lean, but the recording isn't as fierce as its coupling. It's well done if you like the approach, which I don't (Meridian).

Violin Sonata is the third work from Elgar's renaissance that produced the Quartet and Quintet and is in the same autumnal mode. **Midori** gives a dark-colored, big-toned, romantic performance. Always Elgarian and careful not to be overtly demonstrative, she will rank first with many. Robert McDonald's warm pianism matches and equally partners the soloist (♦Sony 63331, with Franck's Violin Sonata). **Hugh Bean** (with David Parkhouse) is more reserved with a more straightforward flow; his sweet tone is irresistible. It's very different from but on a par with Midori; some may find him more Elgarian (♦EMI LP, with String Quartet). **Lorraine McAslan**'s and John Blakeley's leaner, angular approach is in some ways more elegant and searching. Rhythms are sharper; the sound is leaner, sometimes with a subtle honk in the low register that may bother lovers of sweet or dark tone (♦ASV 548, with Walton's Violin Sonata). **Sidney Weiss** (with Jeanne Weiss) is direct like Bean, but less sweet and flowing, smaller in tone like McAslan, but brighter, less searching, and more intense, making the work more aggressive and youthful. The sound is a bit wiry (Crystal 633, with Violin Sonatas by Strauss and Walton). In a CD entitled "Elgar: Rediscovered Works for Violin," **Marat Bisengaliev** and pianist Benjamin Frith include "small" works for violin, including *Chansons de nuit et de matin* and *Etudes Characteristiques* in glorious interpretations (♦Black Box 1016).

CHORAL AND OTHER VOCAL WORKS

The Apostles is the first of a planned trilogy about the Christian Church and may be Elgar's grandest and most colorful oratorio. It represents a new direction in terms of harmony and structure from the big choral works that culminated in *Gerontius*. It's operatic in scope, uses Elgar's biggest orchestra, and takes the listener through events and places with great beauty and power. **Boult** is magnificent, moving and flowing, with great structure and drama. He's consistently noble and magisterial in a work that cries out for those qualities. The strongly grounded bass could be the earth upon which the Church is built. Boult does this with steady and inexorable dedication that never loses sight of the goal. Helen Watts reminds us of Janet Baker and Robert Tear is his usual ringing self, the other singers are nearly as good, and the John Aldis Choir and London Philharmonic are peerless, in glorious analog sound (♦EMI 64206). **Hickox** is less noble. His textures aren't as weighty (nor is the sound), and he's more floating and airy, even billowy. He doesn't move as inexorably forward as Boult, but allows the music to ebb and occasionally drift. Sometimes this produces insight, but I miss Boult's fortitude and purpose. Hickox gets fine performances from the London Symphony Orchestra and Chorus. Bryn Terfel is a decided asset, but I prefer Watts to Alfreda Hodgson, who hoots occasionally; tenor David Rendell strains and lacks Tear's ringing qualities. Boult is for the long haul; Hickox is almost as good and has some grander moments. I prefer Boult, but some critics have favored Hickox (Chandos 8875/6, 2CD).

Caractacus is one of Elgar's freshest, most optimistic works, though it tells the story of Britain's defeat at the hands of the Romans. It contains stirring choruses, a gorgeous love duet that permeates the score, and a stirring "Triumphal March." Much is inspired by nature, particularly Elgar's beloved woodlands. **Groves** has real luminescence; the playing is incisive, with wonderful drama and color, and he moves things along vigorously and naturally. Tear and Armstrong are noble and strong, and if Peter Glossop's Caractacus is not the best, it's still powerful, marred only by an occasional wobble (♦EMI, LP). **Hickox** doesn't light up the score quite as much. He's softer rhythmically, more symphonic in scale and sound, with a more formal choral style; he moves, but without the inevitability of Groves. The soloists are good, though not as good as Groves's (Chandos 9157, 2CD, with *Severn Suite*).

Choral Songs. These are less known than the other works reviewed here; they were written from the composer's very early days to his last years, long after his major works were completed. Elgar himself didn't set much store by most of them, but they are beautifully written and cover a wide range of emotion and expression. Most are short songs or motets. A complete collection led by **Donald Hunt** is beautifully performed, with moderate tempos and balance in the choirs (♦Hyperion 66271, 2CD). **Paul Spicer** leads the Finzi Singers in 22 a cappella songs. He's proper in style, slower and more deliberate in tempo, and precise in rhythm, with a more vertical structure than Hunt. The balance is airy and tilted to the sopranos (Chandos 9269).

Handley covers much of the same material, but the choral sound is darker, stressing the mid-range rather than the treble, with softer attacks and more blended lines. Tempos are faster, but the atmosphere is more ethereal (♦Hyperion 67019). **Louis Halsey** leads his singers in a beautiful collection of 10 songs. The choral tone is full, with real strength in the bass and interior voices. The sound is romantic, almost modern, with hints of Britten's choral music to come (♦Argo 607 LP, with Delius songs). **Boult**'s collection of 10 songs with the BBC Chorus was more orchestral in sound and less ethereal than many choral recordings, but neither he nor the at-times edgy chorus is in top form. Its main interest is that it contains discussions of Elgar with Boult and with the composer's daughter, Carice (Elgar Society 001, LP).

Coronation Ode was written for Edward VII's coronation, but its performance was postponed because of the king's appendicitis. The libretto may seem pompous, but it contains some stirring and lovely music. **Gibson** led the Scottish National Orchestra and Chorus (♦Chandos 6574, with *Spirit of England*), followed a year later by **Ledger** and the New Philharmonia (EMI 3345 LP, with Elgar's arrangement of "God Save the King" and Parry's *I Was Glad*). The romantic Gibson emphasizes Elgar's rubato, wallowing only occasionally. Ledger is more straightforward and unmannered, but when warmth is called for, he can bog down, something Gibson never does. Gibson has the better soloists, particularly soprano Teresa Cahill and the imposing bass, Gwynne Howell. Gibson uses women in the a cappella "Peace Gentle Peace;" Ledger uses boys. Chandos's church-like acoustic is larger and more distant than EMI's solid and revealing sound. Both have their appeal, but Gibson includes the only recording of *Spirit of England*.

Dream of Gerontius. **Boult**'s performance is dignified and regal, but not lacking in drama or passion. It features outstanding orchestral playing and choral singing plus sound that fills the room. Everything is controlled but nothing is rigid; Boult presides, he doesn't dictate, nor does he push his broad tempos—a great help to the chorus, particularly in "The Demons." Robert Lloyd is imposing and very dark; Watts is clear-toned; Gedda's tenor is on the heavy side, and his manner is operatic but very effective—a dying man in the flesh more than the spirit (♦EMI 66540, 2CD, with *Music Makers*).

Hickox is for those who like Boult but not Gedda. His performance is more molded and floating in phrase, and he lacks Boult's noble intensity; he's more loving and devoted than powerful or exciting. Davis is a lyrical Gerontius; Gwynne Howell sings well except for occasional unsteadiness; Felicity Palmer sings with understanding but is stressed in louder passages (♦Chandos 8641, with works by Parry). **Barbirolli**'s recording is a classic for Baker's deeply felt Angel and his robust, red-blooded conducting. His heartfelt, surging tempos and passionate phrasing make this like no other performance. Richard Lewis is strong and clear-toned, but Kim Borg is wooly and flat. Good sound, but not as big as Boult's (♦EMI 73579).

Baker doesn't repeat her astounding performance for **Rattle,** but you can forgive her problems in the high register, and she's wonderful at the end. Shirley-Quirk is understanding and solid, but a bit soft. The chorus is good, especially in the Angel choruses, where it sings like seraphs, and "Praise" has real power. John Mitchinson is intelligent, less intimidated, and more agonized than most; but he strains in Part II, and his dialog with the Angel isn't comfortable. Rattle conducts boldly, with drama, dynamism, and broad expression. He phrases a lot within the line, usually effectively, and the sound is spacious and wide ranging. Not a first choice—it might be for some with better singers—but Rattle's drama is very compelling and many lovers of the work will want it for that.

Britten is dramatic and operatic in a different way. His tempos are faster and more driving; sometimes this is exciting, at other times we miss something, e.g., the big choruses lack coherence. He reveals interesting aspects of this work, but those who don't like Peter Pears—the wooly tenor, the tight crooning at times, and the heaviness—had best avoid it. I find him slightly out of place, but other than some strangulation during "Take Me Away," he sings well enough. Minton is more soprano than alto, brightening a role that should be more somber, but she adds a refreshing aspect to it; Shirley-Quirk is excellent. The London Symphony plays cleanly and the sound is excellent. Not my favorite, but some find it one of the best (London).

Gibson is laid back, with the big moments restrained. There are moments of beauty, particularly in soft passages, but not enough is stirring or involving, and too much is static, flat, and erratic. Tear is solid, Alfreda Hodgson is a sensitive Angel, but Luxon lacks the dark tone for the Priest (he's better as the Angel of the Agony). Gibson may be interesting as a fourth recording, and the sound is spacious and clear (CRD). **David Hill** tries for intimacy, but without flow, coherence, or cogent orchestral balances. The result is pedestrian, even amateurish. The soloists aren't bad, but neither they nor the distant, diffuse sound present a good enough case (Naxos).

Sargent's classic first recording is famous for the young, virile tenor of Heddle Nash and the sonorous Angel of Gladys Ripley. The low male roles are divided and well taken by Dennis Noble and Norman Walker. Sargent conducts straightforwardly, with tempos on the quick side, and with great energy and style. The sound is quite good for 78s (♦Testament 2025, with Cello Concerto). He made his second mono recording in the {apos}50s with a sublime, young-sounding Richard Lewis, along with Marjorie Thomas and John Cameron (both fine, if not quite as resonant as their predecessors) with the Liverpool Philharmonic and an exemplary Huddersfield Choral Society (♦World Record Club 658/9, LP). It's generally slower, more romantic and soft-textured than the first—though the "Devils" chorus is a knockout—but the pacing is convincing, and this one has much better sound.

The Kingdom. Intended as the second part of *The Apostles, The Kingdom* became an oratorio on its own. It's more reflective, with a greater degree of pain and searching than the more operatic *Apostles,* with more emphasis on the chorus. Because most of the tempos are slow, it's equally plausible for a conductor to think of the work as an extended movement or as a series of connected episodes, and how you feel about this issue may determine your preferences. **Boult** said he thought *Kingdom* a better work than *Gerontius* and conducts as if he believes it. He brings out nobility and grandeur in a performance consistent with his *Apostles.* Seeing the work as a huge arch, he involves the listener gradually but inexorably as he builds to the resplendent midpoint. His sound is big, warm, and blended. In Mary's grand aria, "The Sun Goeth Down," Margaret Price is peerless in her power and lyricism. The other soloists (Minton, Young, and Shirley-Quirk) and the London Philharmonic and Chorus are excellent. Grand analog sound, though not as open and imposing as that for Boult's *Apostles.*

Slatkin with the same orchestra and chorus is not as grand and is more episodic. He's also quite slow. His textures are more revealing in the climaxes—you can hear individual brass parts better—but the overall weight isn't as imposing. He's of the "connected episodes" school, taking sections more individually, creating some "hotter" climaxes. I don't find him as involving or impressive as Boult, though if you're looking for something more dramatic and exciting, Slatkin is good in spite of some wobbly soloists (RCA, with Elgar orchestrations of Bach and Handel). **Hickox** also thinks in terms of "connected episodes," but his tempos are faster, and while he's idiomatic, he sometimes skates over the surface of the work. Also, the recorded sound is at times poorly balanced and opaque (Chandos). Boult's older recording is much clearer in the chorus, too. Hickox's soloists are fine (Marshall, Palmer, Davies, Wilson-Johnson), but Boult's are better.

The Light of Life is one of Elgar's last "preparatory" works before *Enigma;* the text concerns Jesus restoring the sight of a blind man. A serene work with touches of Mendelssohn, it's less heroic than some of the earlier oratorios, but signs of the upcoming *Gerontius* are every-where. *Light* is best known for the beautiful introductory "Meditation," but the music that follows is finer and more Elgarian than some critics allow, with strong arias for tenor and soprano. **Groves** is direct, even earthy as he digs into the work, and he has some great solo singing by Marshall, Watts, Robin Leggate, and Shirley-Quirk (♦EMI 64732). **Hickox** is more fully textured and more glowing, making the work sound a bit grander (♦Chandos 9208). He also secures more polished playing from the London Symphony and Chorus than Groves does from his Liverpool forces, but his solo singing isn't quite as accomplished. Davies is dramatically fine, as is Shirley-Quirk, but his voice is shaky. Hickox is probably the choice, but both are worth having.

The Music Makers. This is one of Elgar's last choral compositions. A complete setting of Arthur O'Shaughnessy's poem, it's a generally sad reflection of Elgar's life, complete with quotations from many of his works, the most beautiful and obvious being "Nimrod" from *Enigma*. It lacks the verve of his earlier more famous oratorios and isn't as popular, but it's one of his finest compositions, one that yields its dark inner secrets slowly but with great reward. **Boult** is rich in tone, direct, natural, and flowing, with fine choral singing, the great Baker, and excellent sound (♦EMI 66540, 2CD, with *Gerontius*). **Thomson** is large-scaled and powerful, with a grand sweep to its pacing. It may not be the best performance, but it's one of the more overwhelming and would serve well as an introduction to the work. Linda Finnie is moving and the London Philharmonic Orchestra and Chorus are fine. The sound is big and cavernous, with the chorus distant, but this fits Thomson's interpretation (♦Chandos 9022, with *Sea Pictures*).

Hickox is large-scaled and has great ebb and flow. Many will like it for these qualities, but I find it somewhat puffed up and removed in tone. Felicity Palmer's contribution is stern but nicely characterized, and the London Symphony Orchestra and Chorus are excellent. My interpretive doubts aside, dull, dim sound limits my recommendation to marginal (EMI LP, with *Sea Pictures*). **Andrew Davis** is darker, less heroic, more intimate and episodic. He doesn't carry the listener forth the way Thomson does, but his probing and reflectiveness are probably truer to the spirit of the work. Jean Rigby is bit reticent in the low notes, but she's fine elsewhere, dark and expressive, as are the BBC Symphony and Chorus, in typically clear Teldec sound (♦Teldec 92374, with other pieces).

Scenes from the Saga of King Olaf is based on Longfellow's poem about the Scandinavian saga. The music ranges from romantic to martial to sad to pensive, and even mystical in the opening and closing passages. Written for three soloists, chorus, and orchestra, the best parts are the choral passages, many of them stirring, but there are also some moving solos. The "Death of King Olaf" is often fare for choral societies. Not Elgar's greatest oratorio, it's still fine music that presages what was to come, particularly *Gerontius*. **Handley** leads a sympathetic performance with the London Philharmonic Orchestra and Choir. Teresa Cahill and baritone Brian Rayner Cook are excellent; Langridge strains in the high register and has some flawed intonation, but this isn't a serious impediment (♦EMI 65104, with the Organ Sonata arranged for orchestra by Gordon Jacob and other works).

Sea Pictures. Elgar's only complete song cycle (he began another) was written for alto Clara Butt. It requires a large range and strong low notes; singers with good top registers should fare best, but with the dearth of great altos, many mezzos have recorded it.

Janet Baker's (with Barbirolli) is the most famous and respected recording. She's brilliantly concentrated and focused, sustaining the line beautifully, with wonderful expression and points of phrasing. Barbirolli matches her with tempos on the slow side, dark and weighty orchestral sound, and loving and gentle phrasing. Only the last song lacks intensity (◆EMI 56219, with Cello Concerto). **Birgitta Svendén** offers rich, lyrical singing of great power for a mezzo, with colorful, knowledgeable conducting. Not the most dramatic in terms of enunciation or interpretation, but worthwhile for its magnificent sound, phrasing, and joy (◆Forlane 16642, with Zemlinsky and Mahler songs).

Della Jones (with Mackerras) emphasizes the dramatic over the romantic, turning each song into a scene. Mackerras's phrasing is angular, his tempos are slightly fast, and the orchestra has cut and thrust, especially in the dramatic and stormy moments. Jones is lighter than most. Her voice isn't gorgeous, but it's attractive, with good high notes. She uses it to the fullest extent dramatically, to the point of breaking into speech. The engineers balance the orchestra well. Not for those who put vocalism first, this may be the most dramatically convincing entry (◆Decca 452324).

Rosemarie Lang's issue is frustrating (BIS, with songs by Wagner and Gösta Nystroem). While she has the voice for the work, her heavy German badly colors the music, making the text impossible to understand. Hans Frank and the Helsingborg Symphony make the work seem German, with a full sound and some beautiful phrasing, though the end is distended. Thomson offers a broad, orchestral-style reading, characterized by long-lined, sustained phrasing. Tempos are moderate, and there is considerable weight and breadth. However, **Linda Finnie** creates undesirable tension by lending an operatic cast to her singing that's pushy and reveals a few uncomfortable quirks in her voice (Chandos, with *Music Makers*).

Handley's tempos are very slow, which swamps the third and fifth songs: They simply run aground. **Bernadette Greevey** has a big voice that sounds good and strong in the other two, but you hear a honk in V as she tries to project power through the slow tempos (Classics for Pleasure). **Felicity Palmer** sings well most of the time, pushing too hard occasionally in the louder places (EMI, NA, with *Music Makers*). Hickox is competent, but displays no special insight, and his phrasing is rather ordinary. (To be fair, it's hard to tell how much of this is the conducting and how much is EMI sound that's thick, murky, lacking detail, and bleaches orchestral color to a monochrome.)

Barbirolli's second recording is from his last recorded concert. His tempos are *very* slow, far too slow in the last song, and his pulse heavy and very romantic. **Kirsten Meyer** may have been a bit past her prime, her vibrato slow and occasionally honky on long notes and her diction not the best, but she's a true alto, strong on the bottom and on top. She has the right caramel sound for the work and sings with real conviction. It's a very serious, passionate, but often ponderous performance (Intaglio).

Starlight Express. Elgar's incidental music for Lena Ashwell's fairy-tale play about children who "unwumble" the mistakes of adults by "expressing" their spirits into Star Caves where they are lit by starlight (Sympathy) is the composer's largest stage work. He often recalled the innocence of his childhood by the Severn River and used tunes he had written then for later works. He did this in *Starlight Express* and added many new ones. The familiar poignant, yearning melodies are there, but with a far lighter touch. It's far longer and more sweeping than his other light works. **Handley** with the London Philharmonic gives us a touching account that brings Elgar's vision alive. Valerie Masterson and Derek Hammond Stroud are the fine soloists (◆EMI 711, LP).　　　HECHT

Heino Eller (1887–1970)

If Rudolf Tobias occupies roughly the same position in Estonian musical history as Elgar in England, Eller is the Vaughan Williams—the man who followed in the footsteps of the pioneer, consolidating his achievements. Like Vaughan Williams, Eller was a much-esteemed teacher; his students range from Tubin, Estonia's most important symphonist, to Pärt, the leading figure among today's modern mystics. He wrote vigorously throughout his long life, leaving a rich legacy of works—chiefly orchestral, chamber, and instrumental pieces—that have yet to be systematically explored in the studio, and what recordings there are have tended to repeat the same pieces.

The best place to start is with the exquisite early tone-poem *Dawn,* a work of Rachmaninovian richness. It features in the first of **Neeme Järvi**'s two anthologies of Estonian orchestral music, in the company of two other important Eller works, the dignified *Elegia* for harp and strings and the often Elgarian Five Pieces for String Orchestra (Chandos 8525, with Kaljo Raid's Symphony 1). *Dawn*'s sister-score *Dusk* (sometimes translated as *Twilight*) follows in Järvi's Vol. 2 (Chandos 8656, with works by Artur Lemba, Rudolf Tobias, Veljo Tormis, and Pärt).

Two all-Eller orchestral discs may be harder to find. The Finnish label Forte, only intermittently available even in Estonia, put together a CD in memory of conductor **Peeter Lilje,** leading the Estonian Radio Symphony Orchestra in *Dawn, Dusk, Elegia,* and *Five Pieces,* joined by the symphonic poem *Phantoms* and the "symphonic picture" *In the Shade and in the Sunshine* (0020/2). In another disc **Viktor Pikaizen** is soloist in the Violin Concerto, and again we have *Dawn, Dusk, Phantoms,* and *The Singing Fields,* another symphonic poem, with the ERSO conducted by Lilje except for *The Singing Fields,* which is led by **Vello Pähn** (Antes 31.9123). The ropey playing suggests that the material in common comes from the same sessions.

Eller also composed a number of pieces for piano, among them four sonatas. So far all that has made it onto CD are the early, Scriabinesque Preludes, recorded by that faithful defender of the Estonian musical heritage, **Vardo Rumessen** (ProPiano 224520).　　　ANDERSON

Georges Enescu (1881–1955)

Violinist, teacher, pianist, conductor, and composer, Enescu was the most important Romanian musician of the 20th century. He was a creature of his time. Strongly in the Symbolist camp, he wrote music of an often fevered, hothouse quality that's very chromatic and drenched in color, with long melodies that may seem to meander aimlessly at first hearing. Like Bartók, he first presented himself as a nationalist composer, with his vaguely Eastern European flavored *Romanian Poem for Orchestra* Op. 1, and later began to exploit the actual folk music of his country (not neglecting its large Gypsy population). He occasionally wrote music with strong folk influences, for example, Violin Sonata 3, but usually was content to suffuse his works with a pervasive Romanian aroma.

SYMPHONIES

1. It was the first large-scale work that revealed Enescu's mature character. In three movements, fast-slow-fast, it established the symphonic pattern he would follow from then on. **Rozhdestvensky** lacks propulsion (Chandos); **Horia Andreescu** leads an energetic, immaculately played account of the work, with well balanced orchestral details (Olympia 441); and **Cristian Mandeal** conducts an equally fine performance (Arte Nova 37314). The most intensely committed reading is led by **Remus Georgescu,** recorded in 1942 (Lys 313).

2. This is Enescu's longest symphony. **Rozhdestvensky** again produces a lethargic reading (Chandos). **Mandeal** gives a structurally coherent performance of this massive score (Arte Nova 34035), but **Andreescu**

yields nothing to him in coherence and somewhat surpasses him in enthusiasm (Olympia 442). The martial III is more rousing in his hands, though Mandeal's delicacy can be equally effective; compare how the two treat the clarinet solo at the beginning of II—under Andreescu it's agitated, under Mandeal it's languid.

3. Scored for large orchestra and, in the last movement, wordless chorus, this is Enescu's symphonic masterpiece and a work of ravishing beauty that deserves far greater popularity in the West. **Baciu** leads a very committed account with plenty of drama. His forces are not top-drawer, though, nor is he given first-rate sound, but his enthusiasm and feeling for the music are unparalleled (Marco Polo 223143). **Andreescu** has better forces and clearer sound, but his account doesn't flow quite like Baciu's (Olympia 443). **Mandeal** leads the best-recorded performance with Romania's best orchestra, the "Georges Enescu" Bucharest Philharmonic (Arte Nova). (This is the same orchestra the composer conducted in his recording of the Rhapsodies and Symphony 1; his name was added when he died in 1955.) Unfortunately, **Mandeal** can't generate nearly the same level of excitement as Baciu or even Andreescu. **Rozhdestvensky** is given excellent sound too, but his tempos drag, obscuring the work's structure (Chandos).

Chamber Symphony. For 12 solo instruments, it was Enescu's last composition, written in 1954. It's again in three movements, like the others. The scoring is even more transparent than the Octet or *Decet,* the melodies delicate and ambiguous in mood. **Baciu** does a masterly job leading his forces through this very personal, recondite music (Marco Polo 223143).

OTHER ORCHESTRAL MUSIC

Intermezzos for String Orchestra. These are two brief mood pieces—you could call them humoresques. **Andreescu** gives a performance of fine gradations of color and feeling (Olympia 444). **Mandeal** can't match Andreescu's mastery in conveying emotional tints and half tones (Arte Nova).

Orchestral Suites. Suite 1 is full of interesting touches, from an entire movement played in unison by the violins to passages scored for chamber ensemble, showing Enescu's propensity for grabbing the listener's attention with striking effects and juxtapositions. **Lawrence Foster**'s recording lacks intensity and emotional commitment (Erato). **Iosif Conta** leads a strong performance, with well-balanced sound revealing the score's dynamic range (Marco Polo 223144). **Enescu**'s own account, recorded in 1943, is just as intense and committed as Conta's, but the relatively boxy sound doesn't let the music breathe as it should (Dante 091). **Andreescu**'s account is more meditative, even tragic, than Conta's or Enescu's (♦Olympia 444). Better than anyone else, Andreescu knits this fine score into a coherent interpretive whole. **Mandeal**'s recording fails to catch fire in I; the other movements are good though, and II is quite beautiful (Arte Nova).

Suite 2 is a delightful excursion into neoclassicism from 1915, with Enescu getting the jump on Prokofiev and Stravinsky in exploring this style. This work, based mainly on 18th-century dances, doesn't have the long, sinuous melodies of the mature Enescu. **Conta** leads an enthusiastic reading (Marco Polo), while **Mandeal** (Arte Nova 37855) and especially **Andreescu** (Olympia 495) match him in feeling and surpass him in polish and recorded sound. While Andreescu is robust and heavy, **Foster** is very stylish and light and really brings the score to life (♦Erato 24247).

In Suite 3 (*Villageoise*), Enescu reprises the success of 2 while adding some of the rustic character of Violin Sonata 3 and *Impressions of Childhood,* mixed with Debussyan impressionism. **Rozhdestvensky** gives an indulgent reading on the slow side (Chandos). **Mandeal** (Arte Nova 37855) and **Andreescu** (Olympia 495) each recorded it with excellent results. **Foster** brings out the score's delicate impressionism better than anyone else and conducts with great feeling (♦Erato 24247).

Overture on Popular Romanian Themes. The first work Enescu created after WWII is led by **Mandeal** in a dramatic, committed reading (Arte Nova 37863); **Andreescu** conducts with less passion and concentration (Olympia). **Constantin Silvestri** leads a traversal of searing intensity, but his old recording can't compare with the modern sound of Mandeal (Marco Polo 223144).

Romanian Poem. The work that first showed Enescu's nationalist leanings, it has a vaguely Eastern European flavor and is quite accomplished for a first opus, not outliving its welcome at a length of nearly half an hour. **Foster**'s account is pretty (Erato), but **Andreescu** leads a very cleanly executed, structurally clear reading that's more soulful and dramatic (Olympia 443).

Romanian Rhapsodies. These two pieces are Enescu's most popular works, at least in the West. They're quite light, especially 1, and are unique in Enescu's *oeuvre* for their lack of seriousness; no doubt they were written in an attempt to gain popularity. Most non-Romanian conductors don't know how to let their hair down and go wild in these works. Even **Stokowski** doesn't quite get it, gorgeous as his account of 1 is (RCA). **Rozhdestvensky** drags the introduction and lacks flexibility in 1, but gives a lush, colorful account of 2 (Chandos 9537). **Neeme Järvi** is even stiffer than Stokowski in 1, but his 2 is more successful, due, no doubt, to its more languorous, less mercurial character (Chandos). **Dorati** is energetic but not very flexible (Mercury). **Foster** isn't red-blooded enough and doesn't swing (Erato).

The Romanian maestros tend to use much more flexible tempos and springier rhythms. Among these, **Mandeal** has the least feel for the Rhapsodies; his tempos don't bend, nor do his rhythms spring in 1, and 2 lacks the commitment of the best performances (Arte Nova). **Andreescu** obviously takes more delight in these scores, and 2 is played with special commitment (Olympia 442). Among modern versions, **Conta**'s are the best, with the most freewheeling tempos; unfortunately, they aren't as well recorded as Andreescu's crystal-clear readings (Marco Polo 223146). The finest recordings of both are by **Georgescu** and the Bucharest Philharmonic (♦Lys 313). Recorded in 1942, they sound better than their age. The woodwind and viola soloists have an uncanny feel for the ethnic idioms of this music that you'll hear nowhere else, and they are real virtuosos too, though the ensemble as a whole is not the most polished.

Symphonie Concertante. For cello and orchestra, this dignified work fits the tonal and technical characteristics of the cello beautifully. **Franco Maggio-Ormezowski** is good (Erato) but not quite up to the level of **Marin Cazacu,** who recorded it with Andreescu in a stately reading. Though, in a few of the more technically demanding passages, his intonation is only approximate (Olympia 444).

Vox maris. This is a strange, fascinating work that Enescu worked on from 1929 to about 1950. Scored for a large orchestra with offstage chorus, no basses, and a solo tenor representing a sailor, it avoids bombast and is delicate and brooding, depicting death at sea. **Andreescu** shapes the score expertly, with an unerring feel for mood and great control of his huge ensemble (♦Olympia 496). A libretto would have helped guide the listener through the tenor parts sung in Romanian.

CHAMBER MUSIC

Cello Sonatas. The two cello sonatas, like the string quartets, share the same opus number though they were written decades apart; 1 was a student work from 1897, 2 was written in 1935. 1 inhabits the same world as *Concert Piece* for viola and Violin Sonata 1, while 2 reveals a world of color that the young Enescu could not have dreamed of. It's also a very personal work. **Rebecca Rust** has recorded 1, but she's technically not up to the task (Marco Polo). **Cătălin Ilea** is a very fine cellist who has recorded both with Nicolae Licare# (Olympia 642).

Concert Piece. For viola and piano, it is the only work Enescu wrote while still a student at the Paris Conservatoire that has found popularity. A meditative piece that beautifully exploits the tone and character of the viola, it has a distinctly wistful, French character. **Yuri Bashmet** gives a rapt reading lacking propulsion (RCA). **Cynthia Phelps,** principal violist of the New York Philharmonic, offers a more flowing version; her playing is greatly enhanced by the deep tone of her magnificent Gasparo da Salo viola, which makes Bashmet's Testore sound pitifully threadbare by comparison (Cala 0510). **Imai** really makes the music move; her 1690 Andrea Guarneri viola has nearly as sweet a tone as Phelps's massive instrument (BIS 829). **Alexandru Radelescu** recorded the work with the composer at the piano in 1943; he has a good feel for it, but the performance is marred by his sometimes shaky technique (Dante).

Decet (*Dixtuor*). For winds and Enescu's next foray into writing for a large-scale chamber ensemble after the Octet, *Decet* is remarkable for its fusion of rustic folk idiom with classical forms, with a Romanian Christmas carol as the main theme of I. The prismatic colors and the skillful way he maintains each instrument's individuality are largely responsible for this work's just popularity. The pungent, Eastern European sonorities of the winds of the Iasi Moldova Philharmonic under **Ion Baciu** are a pleasure to hear (Marco Polo). **Andreescu** leads a more accomplished group of musicians in a lovely performance of crystal-clear balance, but I miss the spunk of the Iasi group (Olympia 445). The **Oslo Philharmonic Wind Soloists** play just as well as Andreescu's musicians, but they lack his concentration and careful balances (Naxos 554173).

Impressions of Childhood. This is a remarkable set of ten miniatures for violin and piano depicting scenes witnessed in childhood, with a powerful folk character similar to that of Violin Sonata 3. They are exceptional and valuable for their vivid, wholly unsentimentalized depiction of the world from a child's perspective. **Kremer** has recorded them with Oleg Maisenberg in their superb "Impressions d'Enfance" disc (♦Teldec 13597). Their playing is wonderfully strange and spontaneous and under perfect technical control.

Octet for Strings. Enescu's first chamber work for large forces, it can be analyzed as one enormous sonata movement. The air of *fin-de-siècle* France wafts from every page. The **Voces** and **Euterpe Quartets** join forces in the piece, and their performance is committed and passionate, though occasionally the technical shortcomings of some of the players are evident (Marco Polo). **Andreescu** leads a much cleaner and no less impassioned reading, with very transparent sound (Olympia 445). The **Academy of St. Martin in the Fields Chamber Ensemble** is by far the best recorded and most polished ensemble, and the music is ravishing in their hands, with wonderful ensemble effects (♦Chandos 9131).

String Quartets. Enescu's two string quartets share the same opus number, but they were composed 31 years apart: 1 in 1920 and 2 in 1951. There remains a general similarity in style between them, with their long melodies and hothouse chromaticism, but the later quartet is nearly half the length of the earlier one and a bit more terse in expression. Both are works of strange, ravishing beauty. The **Voces Quartet** is a very strong, accomplished ensemble that plays with great concentration (Olympia 413). The **Quatuor Atheneum Enescu** is just as virtuosic a group (CPO 999068), but while the Voces stresses the drama of these works, this one stresses their color, and the difference is enhanced by the close recording of the Voces and the more distant microphones of the Atheneum.

Violin Sonatas. Written in 1897, Sonata 1 harks back to Brahmsian classical romanticism. Enescu at this time was still searching for his personal compositional style, yet this is an enjoyable work. **Vilmos Szabadi** and Márta Gulyas give a polished reading (♦Hungaroton 31778). With Sonata 2, Enescu felt he had finally found his voice; the harmonies are more chromatic, the melodies longer than in earlier works. **Yair Kless** gives a committed reading (Tacet), but he's greatly outclassed by Szabadi, who plays with real charisma, drama, and dazzling technique. Gulyas is also a top-flight virtuoso and a boldly expressive musician. **Enescu** himself recorded the Sonata in 1943 with Lipatti (♦Dante 091). Their playing is achingly sensitive, even enchanting in spots, but not as bold in the climaxes as Szabadi and Gulyas, though their performance yields nothing to the Hungarians.

Sonata 3 ("in the Popular Romanian Style") is Enescu's most popular violin sonata, and there is no other like it. In few of his compositions did Enescu try so hard to evoke his country's folk idioms, especially the wonderful freedom of a Gypsy playing a violin. He creates many exotic sonorities and goes so far as to indicate the use of quarter tones. **Stern** and Zakin are equal to the score's demands and play with admirable clarity, though without the mystery and tender feeling of Enescu and Lipatti (Sony). Enescu student **Ida Haendel** and Ashkenazy are blessed with state-of-the-art digital sound (Decca). Ashkenazy is as interesting as Lipatti, but Haendel's technique occasionally shows some wear around the edges, her tone has thinned out a little, and, in I and II, her performance lacks contrasts of color and dynamics. This may be in part because she must work to be heard over Ashkenazy's assertive playing. **Szabadi** and Gulyas liven up the music with striking tempo contrasts and precisely executed rhythms (♦Hungaroton 31778). Szabadi has a very full, attractive tone and more than enough technique to handle the score's demands. This account makes up in clarity what it lacks in mystery. **Gilles Apap** and Eric Ferrand N'Kaoua play this sonata very stylishly (♦Apapaziz 99). They revel in the wealth of tone colors and Apap has a real soloist's temperament and technique.

Menuhin doesn't have quite the same range of shades and half tones as his teacher Enescu, though his technique is far more secure (Biddulph 066). Despite his shortcomings and the fact that his sister Hephzibah can't match Lipatti's pianism, this is a fine reading. Though made seven years earlier, it has much stronger, clearer sound than Enescu's 1943 recording. The Menuhin duo recorded this work again in the mid-'60s, with fine sound and excellent results (EMI, NA).

Enescu and Lipatti are models of *Innigkeit* in a score that tempts others to bang away (♦Dante 091-92). In passages where most violinists are declamatory, Enescu sounds almost importunate. No other violinist comes close to him in gradations of color and dynamics and the ability to hold listeners spellbound while playing at a low dynamic level. Lipatti's pianism is without peer, and at times he and his godfather (they knew each other since Lipatti's birth) seem to be communicating telepathically.

MAGIL

Donald Erb (b. 1927)

Though it appears to be little known outside the US, Erb was selected to write the article on orchestration for the *Encyclopedia Brittanica*. His music shows why: It's a lively and listenable compendium of effective pieces for every conceivable instrumental grouping. The earliest recorded Erb is from 1962, when he was 35. He seems to spring full-blown into atonality, but his sonic virtuosity and lively feeling for the common touch are such that we hardly notice the notes. The suggestions and eventfulness of the music make up its considerable appeal, with hints of tonality that become more pervasive in his later scores.

A good deal of Erb's music was recorded in the '60s and '70s, but most of the earlier works have disappeared along with the LP catalog. A few pieces have been re-recorded or transferred, among them *Sonneries* for brass quintet (1961), in **Summit Brass**'s "American Tribute" (Summit 127). This three-movement suite is replete with sound effects, jazzy inflections, and Erb's customary conciseness, taking less than ten minutes. From 1962 we have a Sonata for Harpsichord and String Quartet, played by **John White** with the Koch String Quartet, reissued in a fascinating all-Erb disc (CRI 593). Erb has a fondness for the harpsichord; it turns up unannounced in a number of his '60s compositions. The rest of this entertaining disc consists of larger and later chamber works, including such instruments as the harmonica. Another piece that might have been in this collection is Three Pieces for Brass Quintet and Piano (1968), played by the New York Brass Quintet with James Smolko on piano, and conducted by a young **Matthias Bamert** (CRI LP 323, NA).

Other LP collections from this period that could well be reissued include **Donald Johanos** and the Dallas Symphony playing brilliant performances of *Symphony of Overtures, The Seventh Trumpet,* and *Percussion Concerto* with Marvin Dahlgren (Vox/Turnabout LP 34433). The Louisville Orchestra made an Erb disc with **Louis Lane** including *Christmasmusic, Autumnmusic, Spatial Fanfare,* and the Trombone Concerto with Stuart Dempster. The concerto has been recorded by **Ava Ordman** with Catherine Comet and the Grand Rapids Symphony in an enthusiastic reading in which the soloist blows up a storm (Koss 3302). But the much more concise performance by the dedicatee, Dempster, who has a particular flair for such things, is more authentic, particularly in the didjeridoo imitations.

Another Dempster collaboration, *In No Strange Land* (1968), enlisted the participation of another well-known avant-garde instrumentalist, Bertram Turetzky, on double-bass. This long (for Erb), 17-minute piece for trombone, bass, and electronic tape is an amusing response to Nonesuch's series of taped projects. Overside was a chamber piece for instrumentalists with two synthesizers played live, called *Reconnaissance* (1967) (Nonesuch LP 71223, NA). For Dempster and tape, Erb wrote *...and then toward the end...* (1971), which opens "Drawing Down the Moon," a chronologically arranged collection of wind compositions (New World 80457). This disc contains works for symphonic band as well as solo pieces.

Lynn Harrell, cellist extraordinaire, was the recipient and performer of the 1977 Cello Concerto, recorded with Slatkin and the St. Louis Symphony in a dramatic performance (New World 80415). *Aura II* is a solo piece, complete with vocal effects and bells and whistles, in which Harrell shows off his humming as well (New World 80457). The contrabassoon seems an odd subject for a concerto, placing it directly up Erb's alley. This monsterpiece is played with venom by **Gregg Henegar** with Harold Farberman and the London Philharmonic, a sonic treat not for the fainthearted (Leonarda 331). Further adventures in the underworld

are provided by *Five Red Hot Duets* for two contrabassoons, lending a *je ne sais quoi* feeling to the performance by Henegar and Bradford Buckley (Albany 92). Since there's little one can do to make these instruments funnier than they are, Erb is reduced to writing counterpoint, an amusing idea in itself and one he resorts to more often in his later works. These are serious productions, lasting longer than the concerto. A sonic feast for moles, complete with bent tones, subsonic growls, and an occasional daring foray into the upper reaches of the bass clef, they are played with true artistry.

Erb's concerto penchant next turned to the clarinet, for which the services of **Stoltzmann** were requisitioned. This work, replete with drama and activity, is recorded with conductor Catherine Comet and the Grand Rapids Symphony (Koss 3302). It features an electronic tape played on a cassette recorder and a raucous cadenza with percussion accompaniment, also some bending and breaking tones, harmonic effects, etc.

Not content with altering the playing techniques of a single soloist, Erb next wrote a Concerto for Orchestra (1985). The New Zealand Symphony recording with **James Sedares** is complete with gallon water jugs and another specially prepared cassette of indescribable character. This powerful piece should infiltrate orchestras everywhere (Koch 7417).

The brass section is focused upon next. Erb insists in the notes that theirs is a serious concerto, and we must believe him, since it contains references to a Lutheran chorale and emphasizes the most serious section of the orchestra, which can kill with a single note. Erb's music of the later '80s grew in expressivity and serious intent, and this piece has considerable power, played by the brass of the St. Louis Symphony under **Slatkin** (Albany 92). Another Lutheran chorale engaged Erb's attention in *Watchman Fantasy* for violin, amplified piano with digital delay, and synthesizer (1988), all played by the same person. This also is a serious piece, in which harmony and melody tend to have at least equal billing with sound effects and banshee wails, played with great beauty by **Gregory Fulkerson** and **Audrey Andrist** (Albany 92).

Solstice (1988) is a single movement for chamber orchestra, in which the composer makes the group sound like a full orchestra by using a large percussion section and lots of doubled woodwinds. **Sedares** and the New Zealand Symphony (Koch 7417) make a more impressive sound than **Edwin London** and the Cleveland Chamber Symphony (Albany 342), partly due to a grander playing style, partly because their recording is better balanced.

Woody (1980) is for solo clarinet, written for Stoltzmann in memory of Woody Herman. It's played by **Ross Powell,** who evokes not only the shade of jazz but some multiphonics as well (New World 80457). *Symphony for Winds* (1989) is another of the grand-sounding works Erb wrote in the {apos}80s and would clearly make a high-school band (for which it was written) sound invincible. *Drawing Down the Moon* (1990), on the other hand, shows us that the piccolo, much maligned by orchestral players who have to sit near it, doesn't have to be deafening. This piece pits it against percussion for 15 minutes of mystical descriptions and only at the end does it become obstreperous. It's a very attractive, witty piece played by **Jan Gippo** and **Kirk Brundage.**

Ritual Observances (1992) carries a mystical motif into the orchestra, in which the percussion is replete with synthesizer, amplified piano, harmonicas, slide whistles, and telephone bells, while the string section, not to be outdone, taps their strings with chopsticks. This isn't a funny piece, however, but carries Erb's recent penchant for surrounding a pedal point with sound to a moody, sometimes terrifying intensity. It's played by the Saint Louis Symphony, for which it was written, under **Slatkin** (New World 80415). The latest piece on Catherine Comet's concerto disc with the Grand Rapids Symphony is the Violin Concerto (1992), a generally light-textured work of considerable beauty of sound (Koss 3302). **Miriam Fried** plays it with assurance.

Suspecting that his sound-oriented style didn't lend itself to the string quartet, Erb has tried to keep away from the genre, but he allowed himself to be talked into one by the **Cavani Quartet.** The result is a 20-minute piece incorporating more counterpoint than usual but still recognizable as Erb in its sound structures. A fugue that starts with the tune tapped on the strings with chopsticks and continues in pizzicato is only one of its interesting features (Albany 92). That was actually Erb's second quartet. A third came in 1995, a strong piece in one movement recorded by the **Audubon Quartet** (CRI 857).

Evensong (1993) was written for the Cleveland Orchestra but was recorded by the New Zealand Symphony under **Sedares** (Koch 7417). It's one of Erb's darkest scores, in a disc of dark-hued later works, but it's also one of his most thematically oriented, continually interesting in direction as well as sound.

Then comes a disc of chamber and solo music from 1994–5 (New World 80537). There's not much room for pedal-points and chopsticks in *Remembrances* for two trumpets, played by **David Spencer** and **Ryan Anthony,** which keeps us consistently entertained with different mutes and styles. In the course of both the Sonata for Solo Violin, played by **Gregory Fulkerson,** and that for harp, played by **Yolanda Kondonassis,** the chopsticks and vocal chords are called into play, while the title track, *Sunlit Peaks and Dark Valleys,* is a trio for clarinet, violin, and piano emphasizing an elegy for the victims of the Oklahoma City bombing, played by the **Verdehr Trio.** *Changes,* for clarinet and piano, is played by **Ross Powell** and **Jo Boatright;** it's full of all sorts of effects, notably thunder effects in the piano and foghorn-like multiphonics in the clarinet flutter-tonguing. The piano metamorphoses into something resembling a vibraphone at one point, presumably with the help of two musical assistants credited for the performance. As in all of Erb's work, there is an active visual concomitant.

Recent music for strings includes Quartet 3 (mentioned above), *Suddenly It's Evening* (1997), played by **Jeffrey Krieger** on his electronic cello, *Three Pieces for Double Bass Alone* (1999) with the redoubtable **Bertram Turetzky,** and the earlier *Three Poems for Violin and Piano* (1987), played by **James Stern** and **Andrist** (CRI 857).   MOORE

Ferenc Erkel *(1810–1893)*

Budapest is the place to be if you wish to hear on a regular basis the two Hungarian national operas by Erkel, *Hunyadi László* (1844) and *Bánk Bán* (1861). More than other East European operas, Erkel's are very much under the spell of Italian opera—specifically the bel canto works and early Verdi. His two best-known operas employ the cavatina-cabaletta construction quite prominently, demand virtuoso florid singing from many of the principals, and contain sweeping Italianate ensembles and patriotic plots that suggest the young Verdi. Hungarian elements coexist nicely with and complement Western elements as well. The *verbunkos* form is quite prominent in the orchestral and vocal writing, and it's hard to tell what is folk and pseudo-folk. And of course both operas contain the czardas form.

An accomplished pianist and an active conductor in the opera houses of Buda and Pest, Erkel wrote with an understanding of voices and orchestra. If the librettos he was furnished sound stilted, well, chalk that up as something he also picked up from Italian opera of the time. *Hunyadi László* (actually *László Hunyadi*—in Hungarian the family name comes first) and *Bánk Bán (Lord Bank)* are based on historical incidents

and present many real persons, but you don't have to be steeped in historic-folkloric knowledge to appreciate them. If many Russian works with complex and obscure historical or mythic plots have found success in the West with audiences largely unfamiliar with Russian history and myth, why can't Erkel's lovely scores enjoy a similar fate?

The only recording of *Hunyadi László* dates from the '80s, boasts an impressive cast, and the contributions of the Male Chorus of the Hungarian People's Army and the chorus and orchestra of the Hungarian State Opera under **János Kovács** are of a very high standard (Hungaroton 12581, 3CD). This is a tale of political shenanigans in 15th-century Hungary. The Hunyadi family is the victim of conspiracies against the oldest son László, most particularly by his nefarious father-in-law to be. László is executed, much to the dismay of his mother Erzsebét, a strong character who sings some extremely demanding arias, including one recorded by Lillian Nordica. Sylvia Sass, the best known of the soloists, is quite impressive vocally and dramatically in this Verdi-like role. Magda Kalmár as Hunyadi's significant other is also strong, as are tenor Dénes Gulyás in the title role and a strong supporting cast, baritone Sándor Sólyom in particular. Listeners should read the multilingual booklet (including an English translation of the libretto) with care; it ably disentangles the complex musical text and historical elements.

The only recording of *Bánk Bán* has its flaws, but they seem minor against the 1969 performance's strengths (Hungaroton 11376). Lord Bank, his wife Melinda, and their child are victims of medieval Hungarian political intrigue, spearheaded by the German-born Queen Gertrude. Eventually Bank kills the Queen, Melinda goes mad and drowns herself and the child, and Bank presents himself to the King for punishment.

Karola Agay is the chief glory of this 1969 recording; as Melinda her command of the role's pyrotechnics is confident and her vocal sweetness is impressive. The veteran Jósef Simády's sweet lyric tenor isn't always as rock-solid as we might wish and his upper register sounds a bit tight, but he's still a tower of strength as Bánk Bán, thanks to his utter immersion in the role; his characterization and artistry are exemplary. Erzsébet Komlóssy as the opera's main meanie Queen Gertrude shows off her rich mezzo to advantage. The others, especially baritones Sándor Sólyom-Nagy and the veteran György Malis are impressive as well. (Hungary has had a good baritone track record in recent years, beginning with Alexander Sved.) The supporting cast is good: **Ferencsik**—an underrated conductor in the West—leads con amore, and the Budapest Philharmonic and Hungarian State Opera Chorus are invigorating. Notes and an English-Hungarian libretto are a big help.

Two discs of mostly solo piano music are stirringly and imaginatively interpreted by **István Kassai** (Marco Polo 123317/8). These separately available CDs include fantasies and transcriptions by Erkel plus a potpourri by his son Sandor (1846-1900). Comparisons with the operatic pianism in works by Liszt are inevitable, and it's amazing how well Erkel's assorted operas adapt to the keyboard. Liszt was of course a greater talent than Erkel *père* and *fils,* but these pieces cleverly develop their material and make exhilarating demands on a pianist. Definitely fun listening; Erkel was more than a two-opera composer.   MARK

Manuel de Falla *(1876–1946)*

No composer of the 20th century so completely distilled his country's musical voice as Spain's Manuel de Falla. Indeed, that proved the key to his success, as he found himself able to bring the folk and popular idioms of his native land (particularly Andalusia) into a classical context and, ultimately, to an international stage. The opera *La vida breve* and the ballets *El amor brujo* and *The Three-Cornered Hat* were all conceived for the theater and, in their final form, had their premieres outside Spain. At the same time, he was often able to invest his Spanish-flavored music with international influences; witness the French impressionism of *Nights in the Gardens of Spain* or the Stravinskian neoclassicism of the Harpsichord (or Piano) Concerto.

ORCHESTRAL WORKS

"The Essential Falla" comes remarkably close to living up to that billing. Included in two well-filled discs are **Frühbeck de Burgos**'s *El amor brujo* and *Nights in the Gardens of Spain* (the latter with **de Larrocha**), **Horne**'s Popular Spanish Songs, and **Dutoit**'s *Three-Cornered Hat,* with the Harpsichord Concerto, four Spanish Pieces, *Psyché, Homenaje* to Debussy, and the *Vida breve* "Interlude" and "Dance" thrown in for good measure (♦Decca "Double-Decca" 466128, 2CD). Most of these will be discussed below, but a fair proportion are among the finest recordings these pieces have had, making this an irresistible bargain, especially for the beginner.

El amor brujo (*Love, the Magician*). Possibly Falla's greatest work, this vivid evocation of love and witchcraft among the Andalusian gypsies began as a theatrical entertainment for the dancer Pastora Imperio, completed in 1915. A decade later a pruned and reordered version, this time a full ballet with an expanded orchestra, was premiered in Paris, and that has understandably dominated the lists ever since.

Stokowski had a notable recorded history with the latter, beginning with his 78 rpm set with the Hollywood Bowl Symphony and mezzo Nan Merriman (♦Pearl 9276). Darkly sensuous, it still stirs the blood, but not as much as his 1960 remake with the Philadelphia Orchestra and Shirley Verrett; it is a 300 per cent performance if ever there was one (though the earlier mono recording can still give it a run for its money in the popular "Ritual Fire Dance"). Unfortunately this has yet to be issued on CD in the US (it was included in Sony's 1993 3CD French anthology "Musique Espagnole"). There is, however, a BBC Radio performance from 1964 that is, if anything, even more electrifying (♦BBC 4005). The problem is (1) the interpretation itself didn't need to be any more hyper, and (2) the BBC Symphony is not the Philadelphia, nor is mezzo Gloria Lane the young Verrett. Still, it's an exciting specimen of live Stokowski.

But he's far from the only option. **Frühbeck,** in the Decca set, is wonderfully flavorful, leaning into the accents and rhythms lustily, with a gypsy-sounding soloist in Nati Mistral. I wouldn't have been disappointed had they included **Dutoit**'s instead, a gutsy yet polished performance in which the music's inner fire still comes through (♦London 430703). Another winner is **Geoffrey Simon,** perhaps a bit broadly intoned but otherwise a big, Stokowski-style *Amor* in which he and mezzo Sarah Walker really dig into it (♦Chandos 8457), as do **Mata** and Marta Senn (♦Dorian 90210). This last has the added advantage of including the only available stereo recording of the *Homenajes* in their orchestral form.

Among others, **Reiner** is orchestrally first-rate, though Leontyne Price tries a little too hard to gypsify her singing (RCA). **Giulini** and de los Angeles, conversely, are maybe a bit too elegant and restrained, but nonetheless manage to deliver the goods (♦EMI 64746). So does Grace Bumbry with **Maazel,** though the opening might snap and crackle a bit more (♦DG 447414). Were that not enough, the 1915 *Amor,* with spoken dialogue, can be heard in a number of recordings, most satisfyingly from **López-Cobos** and Alicia Nafé; this one subtly yet strongly characterized musically and dramatically (though 44 minutes seems short

measure for a full-priced CD) (♦Denon 75339). Nor should you dismiss **Josep Pons,** with his somewhat laid-back "Fire Dance" and crooning, lovingly detailed "Pantomime" (♦Harmonia Mundi 945123). His guttural soloist sounds as though she's being strangled and the orchestra may fall a bit roughly on the ears, but this is the real Spanish sound, metallic and slightly pinched, with an inner energy in the playing and a no less authentic gypsy. After that come **Luis Izquierdo,** also with Senn, similarly authentic-sounding but not held together as well (Nuova Era), and **Diego Dini-Ciacci,** well enough acted and sung (and attractively priced) but a bit too careful musically (Naxos).

El sombrero de tres picos. As with *El amor brujo, The Three-Cornered Hat* comes in two versions, the first being the 1917 pantomimic farce *El Corregidor y la Molinera* (*The Corregidor and the Miller's Wife*). But even before that was finished, the Russian impresario Diaghilev suggested that it be recast as a ballet. The original can be heard in another **Pons** recording (Harmonia Mundi 901520), but despite its reduced length it's the ballet that stands as the greater achievement; in many people's minds it is the supreme musical embodiment of Spain.

Accordingly it has been very well served on records, something that's still true despite the departure of some of the best. Thus the suavely colorful **Dutoit** can be seen as a worthy successor to Ansermet (who led the 1919 premiere), lacking only the last drop of Andalusian flavor (♦Decca 466128, 2CD). Similarly **Bátiz** (♦IMP 2028) and **Pons** (♦Harmonia Mundi 901606) recall in their different ways the superbly Spanish **Jesus Arambarri** recording from the mid-'50s (NA); Bátiz catches the sultriness of the bristling dance rhythms and Pons the edgy, ultra-brilliant sound of the woodwinds (something his sometimes deliberate tempos allow us to savor in full).

For Spanish flavor, though, it's hard to beat **Jorda,** who may not have been a great conductor per se but was a great Falla conductor. Witness the way he digs into the "Dance of the Miller's Wife," "Miller's Dance" and the final *jota,* darkly dramatic and spirited despite the English orchestra and soloist (♦Everest 9000). An English orchestra doesn't hurt **Tortelier** either, the somewhat drawn-out opening song notwithstanding; elsewhere he brings real excitement to the rhythms without short-changing the music's more languorous episodes (♦Chandos 8904). Then there is the breezily exhilarating **Mata,** a bit glossed over in places but very much inside the idiom (♦Pro Arte 581).

Boulez manages to be both clear and imposing, even if he does weigh into the dances with more strength than verve (Sony). **Schwarz** likewise makes his points tellingly, if not always as idiomatically as some (Delos). And if for some reason Pons doesn't seem to put as much energy or flamboyance into the original — *The Corregidor and the Miller's Wife* — neither did the composer. Pons also offers the only recording of the unpublished incidental music to *El gran teatro del mundo,* much of it borrowed from other composers, including Gaspar Sanz and Victoria (Harmonia Mundi 901432).

CONCERTOS

Noches en los jardines de España. An example of Iberian impressionism to be ranked with those of Debussy and Ravel, *Nights in the Gardens of Spain* has the advantage of being truly Spanish, albeit with French influences. Yet it's Moorish Spain Falla is evoking here, at least at the outset, as the ghosts of his country's past mingle with the shadows of its present — again the gypsies of his beloved Andalusia — with the piano functioning almost like a guitar.

De Larrocha's digital recording with Frühbeck, available either in the Decca set or on its own (♦London 430703), is if anything even darker and more ruminative than her earlier ones. (There was also a wonderfully atmospheric video with Dutoit.) But **Rubinstein** was no slouch when it came to the Spanish idiom either, as his various recordings of *Noches* attest. Perhaps the best was with Jorda, where his limpid pianism, like the accompaniment, still has plenty of spark and steel where needed (♦RCA 68886). The later version with Ormandy is more solemn and mature, an aristocratic view of these three nocturnes (♦RCA 61863). It's not as aristocratic as **Curzon**'s, however, whose remotely reflective 1945 78s were best heard in an all-Jorda CD (Dutton, NA).

Frühbeck also offers first-class support to the more disembodied **Gonzalo Soriano,** each proving sensitive to the music's color and atmosphere (♦EMI 64746). **Fingerhut,** with Simon, takes the piece slowly, underlining its mystery and impressionism; again, though, the climaxes register (♦Chandos 8457). Even more deliberate are **Carol Rosenberger,** luminously recorded but otherwise more prosaic (Delos), and **Josep Colom** with Pons, nonetheless authentic in flavor and sound (Harmonia Mundi). Much cheaper are the fluency and freshness of **Thiollier** (Naxos).

Further down the list, the Chicago Symphony sounds good but **Barenboim** doesn't bring much subtlety to the piano part (Teldec). (Conductor Placido Domingo is better in that regard.) Conversely, it's pianist **Joaquin Soriano** who injects the spark into an otherwise choppy collaboration with Serebrier in a disc that includes a similarly dispiriting account of the Piano Concerto (ASV).

Piano Concerto. Actually, it's the Harpsichord Concerto, from 1926, which sounds better on that instrument with its clipped articulation. **Falla** himself recorded it this way in 1930, still the most antique-sounding rendition (the piece was written for Landowska); it can be had in an invaluable collection of historical performances (♦Almaviva 0121, 4CD). **Kipnis** is far more virile and colorful, but thanks to the miking and purposeful clarity of Boulez's accompaniment, never seems out of bounds. Indeed, the latter succeeds in placing the piece firmly in the 20th century (♦Sony 68333 or 53264). **John Constable** and Rattle also bring a 20th-century sensibility to their drier and more intimate rendition (♦Decca 466128, 2CD). The most intimate of all, however, is the **Schirmer Ensemble,** which, despite sounding a bit reined-in, exhibits a welcome streak of mystery and nostalgia (♦Naxos 554366). Against that, **Luis Vidal** with Pons seems banished to far right field (Harmonia Mundi) and **Rafael Puyana** with Mata sounds muffled; otherwise his is the most delicately baroque (Dorian).

PIANO MUSIC

Barring a couple of pieces of lost juvenilia and the transcriptions, all Falla's piano music can be fitted onto a single CD, which is exactly what **Miguel Baselga** (BIS 773) and **Martin Jones** (Nimbus 5621) do (though the latter's is available only as part of a 5CD box). Between the two, Baselga's playing falls a bit more easily on the ear, though he sometimes misses the manly thrust of the more virile essays, which is hardly the case with Jones's generally rougher renditions.

De Larrocha is a better choice for the really important pieces, however (♦EMI 64527 or ♦RCA 61389). In each she offers idiomatically inflected performances of both the four Spanish Pieces and *Fantasia Baetica* (turned out in 1919 for Rubinstein), though the newer RCA tends to be warmer in spirit and in sound. (Again, the harder edge is more typically Spanish.) She's nearly outdone in the *Fantasia* (the finest of all Falla's keyboard works), by **Esteban Sanchez,** who really pours it on in this without once distorting the piece (♦Ensayo 9735). Since he also includes the Pieces and six other selections, that might give him the edge,

especially since several of those not included can be heard in first-class performances by **Len Vorster** in a pair of low-priced issues (♦Naxos 554366 and 554498).

Interestingly, both Baselga and Jones do include one of the transcriptions, *Homenaje "Le tombeau de Claude Debussy,"* originally written for guitar. As might be imagined, there have been many recordings of it in that form, but I keep going back to **Segovia**'s—not the horribly recorded Almaviva live performance, however.

CHORAL MUSIC

Atlantida. Falla intended this scenic cantata about Columbus, Hercules and ancient Atlantis to be his crowning achievement, and in it he tried to attain a universal quality. The result was to distance it from nearly everything that gives his music its greatest interest. At least that's the way it seems from what survives, because *Atlantida* remained unfinished at his death and had to be completed by his former pupil Ernesto Halffter. Still, there are moments of great beauty, with a chance to hear some of Falla's extended choral writing, much of it (especially in Part 3) recalling the glory of earlier Spanish masters.

Blessed by some gorgeous singing (Estes, Berganza, etc.), **Edmon Colomer**'s is a more-than-decent representation of this problematic work (♦Auvidis Valois 4685, 2CD). However, **Frühbeck**'s pioneering recording gave it a sharper interpretive profile (♦EMI 65997, NA). There is also a mono disc of highlights with **Ansermet** that preserves parts of Halffter's earlier realization (Cascavelle 2005).

OPERA

La vida breve (*The Short Life*). Completed in 1905, this proved to be Falla's first big success in Paris and later back home in Madrid. A *Cavalleria Rusticana*-type tale of love and betrayal, the opera's chief distinctions are its incorporation of Iberian musical culture within a partly Puccinian, partly verismo frame and the principal character of Salud, the girl whose paramour abandons her with tragic results.

Despite promising ingredients, only one of the three available recordings can stand alongside the best the analog era had to offer, and that is **Mata**'s (♦Dorian 90192). With Marta Senn as a movingly vulnerable Salud and tenor Fernando de la Mora as a fine Paco, the opera's earthier aspects are strongly underlined, especially in the flamenco sequence (here largely improvised). Pons's *cantaor* likewise rings true, but there is little sense of a staged performance, nor is the rest of the singing anything to write home about (Harmonia Mundi). While **López-Cobos** has some good ideas about the music, he's let down a bit by his soloists, beginning with the offstage voice in Act 1 (Telarc). This leaves **Frühbeck** with de los Angeles (EMI); it is still worth seeking out, as is **Luis-Antonio Garcia Navarro** with Berganza (DG), though it has yet to be issued on CD in the US.

El retablo de maese Pedro. A one-act opera in which all the characters, including the non-puppets, are puppets, *Master Peter's Puppet Show* is a remarkable concoction drawn from Cervantes's account of Don Quixote coming to the rescue of yet another imaginary heroine. And just as remarkably, nearly all the available recordings have something to offer.

Mata, in one of his final outings, combines elements of Spanish antiquity and courtly life with a modern, albeit somewhat subdued, tang (♦Dorian 90214). He also has what is arguably the best of the female Trujamans (the boy narrator of the play within the play). **Maurizio Dini-Ciacci** is even spicier, at about a third the price (♦Naxos 553499), with **Pons** the most imaginatively colored and accented, occasionally recalling the quieter pages of *El amor brujo,* with which both of these are coupled (♦Harmonia Mundi 945213). And though **Robert Ziegler**'s cast is perhaps the least well endowed vocally, their characterful singing makes up for some of that, as do a number of interesting interpretive touches (ASV 758). Then there is **Halffter,** a 1966 live performance that even in mono captures not only the piece's theatrical immediacy but also its distinctively Castilian air (Almaviva 0121, 4CD).

SONGS

Siete Canciones Populares Españolas (*Seven Popular Spanish Songs*). These songs of 1914 still loom large in the Falla catalog, often in arrangements for violin, cello, and even bassoon, where they are usually billed as "Popular Spanish Suite for (insert your favorite instrument) and Piano." But no solo instrument can come close to the vocal inflections that are an intrinsic part of this cycle, given its folk origins.

Just check out **de los Angeles,** at 68 a bit less resplendent than of yore but superbly stylish, with Pons likewise in the Halffter orchestration (♦Harmonia Mundi 901432). Except for her earlier recordings—of which one, with pianist Gonzalo Soriano, is part of a "Spanish Songs" anthology (♦EMI 65061, 4CD)—you'd have to go back to **Maria Barrientos** (with Falla at the keyboard) or **Supervia** to find something comparable (Almaviva 0121, 4CD). Still, for sheer vocal prowess, no one beats **Horne** in the original piano-accompanied setting, though she can't match de los Angeles's insights (♦Decca 466128, 2CD). Between the two **Senn** recordings, the singer sounds more at ease with Mata leading the Berio orchestration (♦Dorian 90210) than with pianist Maria Rosa Bodini (Nuovo Era 6809); either way, she really throws herself into it. López-Cobos likewise opts for Berio, his mezzo (**Alicia Nafé**) proving no less sensitive to the idiom (♦Denon 75339). Best of all, perhaps, is **Suzanne Danco,** whose 1953 recording with Ansermet leaves little unsaid about this music, mono sound notwithstanding (♦Cascavelle 2010).

Soprano **Merlyn Quaife** offers admirably felt performances of not only the *Popular Spanish Songs* but also a dozen other Falla songs in a single low-priced CD (♦Naxos 554498). In an earlier installment she can also be heard in two other vocal works, *Psyché* and *Soneto a Cordoba* (♦Naxos 554366); she nearly displaces even de los Angeles in the first (♦Harmonia Mundi 901432), but not quite.   GOODFELLOW

Johann Friedrich Fasch *(1688–1758)*

Such are the vagaries of fame and fortune that Fasch, while well known in Leipzig (where Kuhnau brought him as a young man), Hamburg (he was a dear friend of Telemann), Dresden (court composer Pisendel championed his efforts), and Berlin (CPE Bach knew him through his son), he spent 36 years—over half his life—in the provincial town of Zerbst. As organist and Kapellmeister, he wrote ceremonial music for local nobility.

Sometimes, there is the happy occasion where an artist who records puts a neglected composer on the map (I think of Nadia Boulanger's groundbreaking efforts on behalf of Monteverdi in the 1930s). This is the case with **Jean-François Paillard** and his 1968 recording of Fasch's music. Anyone who ever owned the original RCA disc remembers it with fondness. Paired with a side dedicated to Pachelbel and his *Canon,* many listeners discovered both a new depth in a familiar composer and the merits of the almost unknown younger contemporary of Bach. It is, happily, still in and out of print (♦Erato 98475); seek it out, it's in cut-out bins everywhere, lost in listings like "German Baroque, misc." or tucked under "Pachelbel." Remind yourself how, before some of the excesses of the Original Instrument Police, a compromise between authenticity and pure musicianship lent grace and immediacy to unfamiliar music.

Wynton Marsalis clearly listened. Both in his Baroque program "Wynton Marsalis: The London Concert" (Sony 39061) and his even more sparkling live performance in 1993 (♦Sony 57497), he pays tribute to Paillard by performing the Concerto in D for Trumpet, 2 Oboes, Strings, and Continuo with intensity and verve. Leppard, his conductor, clearly has all of Paillard's innate musicality and sense of instrumental compromise. Much less successful is a recording of various 18th century trumpet concertos (Deutsche Schallplatten 1062).

Fasch was not a trumpet virtuoso himself, and his 61 concertos for the instrument are but a fraction of his output. Many of his 16 masses, four operas, and 12 cantata cycles are lost; what we have is treasurable. Occasionally, early music festivals feature some of this vocal material; sadly, none of his masses are on disc. Our single stand-in is the cantata "Gehet ein zu seinen Thoren" in "Baroque Christmas Music from the University of Leipzig," recorded by the Leipzig University Choir (Thorofon 2275, with other very interesting repertoire).

Fasch was an accomplished violinist and by necessity an organist, but his musical heritage will clearly be carried on by the wind and horn players who appreciate the many often doubled combinations of their instruments, using themes that musically bridge the late Baroque to early Classical style. Various artists come together to give us two oboe concertos, two for flute and oboe, one for two oboes and bassoon, and one for two violins (MD+G 3100309). Two other releases expand this range. The **Accademia Bach** give a workmanlike reading of four more works—one for oboe, two for two oboes, and one for flute and oboe—that don't duplicate the MD+G disc (Dynamic 129). In "Overtures and Concertos," we can add yet another flute and oboe concerto, a four-oboe concerto (!), and the Violin Concerto in A Minor, giving us a hint of Fasch's mastery on his own instrument (Dynamic 201).

In keeping with the theme of sensitive baroque interpreters not in the rigid thrall of period instruments, we must note **Richard Kapp,** who for a short time left his New York Philharmonia Virtuosi to work with the Kiev Pro Musica for a program of bassoon concertos (ESS.A.Y 1041). Another in that camp is **Christopher Warren-Green,** whose admirable London Chamber Orchestra featured John Wallace in the Concerto in E scored for the stunning trio of trumpet, oboe d'amore, and violin (♦Nimbus 7016).

Original instruments are represented by **Niels Sparf** and his ensemble with a concerto for trumpet, two oboes, and strings (Naxos 553531) and, more convincingly, the Capella Savaria with **Pal Németh** conducting. Following Paillard, Németh mixes some of Fasch's 19 symphonies with the Bassoon Concerto in C that Kapp also recorded (Dynamic 199). Most recently, the same ensemble brought us three of the more than 90 overtures or orchestral suites (♦Dynamic 233).

Finally, two recordings also hark back to earlier efforts. Many years ago, **Konrad Ragossnig** whetted our appetites for Fasch with a D minor guitar concerto (Turnabout 34547, NA; possibly in Vox Box 3022). The **Accademia Farnese** recorded this and a concerto by Johann Ludwig Krebs (Mondo Musica 96030), and even before Paillard, **Hans-Martin Linde** found some of the recorder and transverse flute sonatas for performance on one of the earliest Archive discs (3173, NA). The **Collegium Pro Musica** mined this territory nearly four decades later for another recording (Dynamic 186). Finally, Berlin brings together a stable of its eminent soloists in a recording of oboe sonatas (1069).
                    DAVIS

Gabriel Fauré *(1845–1924)*

Fauré began studying in Paris at age 9 at the École Niedermeyer, and stayed there 11 years. The school's job was to produce church musicians, and at first he studied mainly Renaissance and Baroque church music, but he later entered Saint-Saëns's class, where he was introduced to the forbidden contemporary sounds of Liszt, Schumann, and Wagner. This musical seesawing continued throughout his career. He was an organist and choirmaster at several Paris churches, and wrote religious choral music (including his popular *Requiem*), but he also founded the progressive Société Nationale de Musique with d'Indy, Lalo, Duparc, and Chabrier, and wrote songs and instrumental music that were as harmonically adventurous as any in France before Debussy. In 1905 he took over the Paris Conservatoire; his students there included Ravel and Nadia Boulanger. He retired in 1920, aged 75 and afflicted with deafness, but with some great works left in him, including the song cycle *L'Horizon chimérique,* the Piano Trio, and the String Quartet.

A young music critic named Claude Debussy once called Fauré "the master of charms," and while Debussy didn't mean it as a compliment, his remark does contain a bit of truth. Fauré's music has always had the reputation of being a delicate, quintessentially French wine that doesn't travel well. The "master of charms" was also a master composer, but the very nature of Fauré's output prevents many people from thinking of him as great. There are no complete Fauré symphonies or concertos; he expressed his deepest musical thoughts in chamber works, songs, and piano pieces in such Chopinesque forms as Barcarolle, Prelude, Nocturne, and Impromptu.

Fauré was born in the year of Wagner's *Tannhäuser* and died in the year of Gershwin's *Rhapsody in Blue.* Throughout all the musical upheavals that chronology suggests, his own music retained a classical calm and balance, no matter how passionate its temper or adventurous its harmony. On the composer's centennial in 1945, Aaron Copland said: "Fauré belongs with that small company of musical masters who knew how to extract an original essence from the most ordinary musical materials. To the superficial listener he probably sounds superficial. But those aware of musical refinements cannot help but admire the transparent texture, the clarity of thought, the well-shaped proportions. Together they constitute a kind of Fauré magic that is difficult to analyze but lovely to hear."

ORCHESTRAL MUSIC

As noted above, there isn't much of it (and most of it wasn't orchestrated by Fauré), but it's very enjoyable, and in the case of his orchestral masterpiece *Pélleas et Mélisande,* genuinely moving. Also, quite a bit of it can fit on a single CD. There are excellent Fauré orchestral collections, featuring the *Pélleas et Mélisande* suites, *Dolly* (originally for piano duet), and *Masques et Bergamasques,* conducted by **Tortelier** (Chandos 8952) and **John Georgiadis** (Naxos 8553360). Between them these discs have just about everything (with a little duplication).

Andrew Davis leads the Philharmonia in a lovely *Pélleas et Mélisande* in a variable but mostly enjoyable French program, the rest of which is led by Ormandy (Sony 62644). **Enrique Bátiz**'s program includes not only *Pélleas* but also such rarities as the surviving two movements of the early Violin Concerto, the late and utterly delicious *Masques et Bergamasques,* and the incidental music to *Shylock* (ASV 686).

The popular *Pavane* appears in many French recital discs. Originally for chorus and orchestra, it has been arranged for orchestra alone, flute and harp, flute and guitar, saxophone, string quartet, and Barbra Streisand. Apart from the discs listed above, there are recommendable versions by **Dutoit** (London 21440, with *Requiem* and *Pelléas et Mélisande*), **Ansermet** (ditto, London 452304), and the **Orpheus**

Chamber Orchestra in a rather short CD (DG 449186, with *Masques et Bergamasques* and some Ravel and Satie). I should also mention historical recordings by **Koussevitzky** and the Boston Symphony (Biddulph 44, with Hanson's Symphony 3) and **Barbirolli** (Dutton 1002, a varied French program).

The closest things to a concerto in Fauré's oeuvre are two works for piano accompanied by a rather reticent orchestra, the early *Ballade,* praised by Liszt, and the very late *Fantaisie,* a short work as lucid and subtle as the best of the solo piano music and songs. **Johannesen,** excellent in French music, is excellent in these in a fascinating catch-all of French piano music from Franck to Milhaud (Vox 3032, 3CD). Good individual recordings of the *Ballade* are by **Casadesus** and Bernstein (Sony 47548, with Franck's Symphony), **Lortie** and Frühbeck de Burgos (Chandos 8773, with Ravel's piano concertos), and **Wild** and Sargent, whose 1967 recording sounds excellent and whose couplings, Chopin's and Liszt's First Concertos, are very appropriate (Chesky 93). The recording by **Stephane Lemelin** with the CBC Vancouver Orchestra is attractive, also with attractive but highly contrasted couplings, concertos by Saint-Saëns and Roussel (CBC 5178). Fauré's protégé **Marguerite Long,** one of his finest interpreters, recorded the *Ballade* in the '30s (Biddulph 35; see below).

CHAMBER MUSIC

Fauré is to French chamber music what Schumann and Brahms are to German, and it doesn't suffer from the comparison. Many passages in these works give rise to the idea of Fauré as merely a gentle, reflective, rather bland composer. They're as turbulent and anguished—and as perfectly fashioned—as anything by Brahms. They divide naturally into examples of each genre: one early and "accessible," one late and "difficult" (which in Fauré's case never means difficult to listen to).

Violin Sonatas. No. 1 is one of Fauré's most popular works, and one of the loveliest late-Romantic sonatas; 2, seldom played, is in Fauré's gnomic but beautiful late style. There are several excellent recent discs containing both: by **Mayumi Fujikawa** and Osorio (♦ASV 6170); **Krysia Osostowicz** and Susan Tomes (♦Hyperion 66277); and **Dong-Suk Kang** and Pascal Devoyon (♦Naxos 550906). They are instructively different in style—Fujikawa lithe and wiry, Osostowicz lusher and more relaxed, Kang full-blooded romantic—but they're all good.

If you'd like a superstar violinist in the popular 1, you can't do better than **Zukerman** with Neikrug, who also offer elegant performances of the Debussy and Franck sonatas (♦RCA 62697). **Heifetz**'s old recording is worth hearing too (RCA 61735, with Prokofiev's Concerto 2 and Sarasate's *Zigeunerweisen* among other virtuoso pieces).

Cello Sonatas. Fauré's two cello sonatas have also fared well on recordings. **Steven Doane** and Barry Snyder are smooth, authoritative, and enjoyable (♦Bridge 9038). **Isserlis** and Devoyon are intensely dramatic (♦RCA 68046); no one would think Fauré dull here! In an earlier recording, Isserlis and Devoyon also perform 2 with other short Fauré cello pieces (Hyperion 66235). There are classic '60s performances by **Tortelier** and Jean Doyen (Erato).

Piano Quartets. The two piano quartets are more popular than the quintets. The G Minor Quartet Op. 14 is probably the most played of Fauré's chamber works after Violin Sonata 1 and has been recorded many times. They make an excellent, popular CD pairing. I especially recommend the vibrant, beautifully recorded performances by the **Ames Piano Quartet** (♦Dorian 90144); **Domus Chamber Ensemble** (♦Hyperion 66166); **Nash Ensemble** (CRD 3403); **Fauré Quartet of**

Rome (Claves 9015); and **Villa Medici Ensemble** (MD+G 3040536). A superstar conglomeration wouldn't seem to bode well for these delicately calibrated works, but Fauré brings out the best in musicians, and the foursome of **Ax**, Laredo, Stern, and Ma plays these works marvelously too (Sony 48066).

Good **Beaux Arts Trio** performances of the Piano Quartets are on separate CDs with good couplings. They're joined by violists Kim Kashkashian in 1 (Philips 422350, with Fauré's Piano Trio) and Lawrence Dutton in 2 (Philips 434071, with Saint-Saëns's Trio).

Piano Quintets. These two seldom-recorded works, which contain some of the darkest and most violent moments in Fauré's chamber music, enjoy a really fine recording by **Domus** joined by violinist Anthony Marwood (♦Hyperion 66766).

All four piano quartets and quintets are collected in acceptable readings by German musicians (♦Vox 5073). While the mid-'60s performances and recordings are not as tonally lustrous as many of the others mentioned, they're a good, inexpensive introduction to some sublime music. Some notable French musicians offer mid-priced recordings of all the sonatas and the piano trio (EMI 62545) and the quartets and quintets with the string quartet (EMI 62548).

Piano Trio, String Quartet. Fauré's last two chamber works—the last of all his works—are profoundly beautiful. The Trio is passionate and powerful, with some immediately memorable themes. Besides the **Beaux Arts Trio** recording mentioned above, there are recommendable versions by **Trio Fontenay** (♦Teldec 44937, with Debussy and Ravel trios) and by the **Golub/Kaplan/Carr Trio** (♦Arabesque 6643, with Ravel and Saint-Saëns). A coolly elegiac leave-taking and a remarkable example of contrapuntal mastery, Fauré's only string quartet is about as typical of music in the decade of *Wozzeck, Oedipus Rex,* and *le jazz hot* as a Palestrina mass. This work isn't recorded often, but the elegantly melancholy disc by the **Miami String Quartet** is an outstanding introduction; the two Saint-Saëns quartets coupled with it will be a nice surprise to most chamber music fans (♦Conifer 51291).

Two Biddulph discs offer an array of chamber music performances by musicians who knew Fauré and were admired by him. On ♦Biddulph 035, pianist **Marguerite Long**, Jacques Thibaud, Maurice Vieux, and Pierre Fournier play Fauré's dark, turbulent Piano Quartet 2 (Long, who was thanked by the elderly Fauré for her "perfect, ideal performances," also plays a few solo pieces and *Ballade* with orchestra). **Thibaud** is also on ♦Biddulph 116, playing Violin Sonata 1 with Cortot. **Casadesus** and the Calvet Quartet play Piano Quartet 1; the **Krettly Quartet** plays the String Quartet, which was brand new music at the time of the recording (1928). There is plenty of suavity and charm in these authentic readings, but they also dig beneath the surface. If you're not put off by aged sound, these are enthralling performances of some of Fauré's greatest music.

RAYMOND

PIANO MUSIC

Cortot considered Fauré the greatest French composer at the turn of the 20th century, but his solo piano music remains misunderstood today. Even more than the popular *Requiem,* the piano music inhabits a world of ultra-sensitivity girded with searing passion. Cortot identified these elements as "reason and fantasy," and his recording of Violin Sonata 1 with Thibaud (Biddulph 116) balances those qualities exquisitely. Too often, pianists choose one over the other, and the solo piano music becomes either lifeless or quirky.

Some of the stylistic difficulties are revealed in the titles of the works themselves, borrowed from Chopin; they include nocturnes, bar-

carolles, waltzes, preludes, impromptus, a ballade, a set of variations, and a mazurka. Clearly inspired by Chopin, the writing is nonetheless more subtle, and as an antidote to those who would play his music as if it were Chopin, Fauré advised pianists to avoid interpretive excess in performance. However, many pianists have followed his directive too earnestly, reducing the music to rigidity and inflexibility.

Unfortunately, Cortot recorded none of Fauré's solo works, but **Marguérite Long**'s incomparable recordings should prove instructive to all pianists (♦Biddulph 35 or Pearl 9927). Like Cortot, Long knew the composer. The handful of Fauré recordings she left us is full of color, expression, and tasteful rubato. Long's student, **Jean Doyen**, seems to have learned little from his teacher; his set of the complete works is jeopardized by playing that's careful to the point of stodginess (Erato). Naxos has divided the complete works between two French pianists, **Jean Martin** and **Pierre-Alain Volondat**; Volondat is as willful as Martin is stiff and prosaic. If Vox returns **Evelyn Crochet** to the catalogue, that budget set would be one of the best collections in any price range.

Stott's first traversal of Fauré is as rhapsodic as Volondat's, but it's salvaged by her more refined pianism; this set contains almost half the works (♦Conifer 51751, 2CD). Her interpretations became more focused when she later committed all the music to disc (♦Hyperion 66911). Occasionally she still makes us too aware of her virtuosity, but for many, her inspired performances will be a clear first choice. Those who have doubts may acquire a one-disc sampler (Hyperion 67064). **Collard** offers a suave and often satisfying view of the composer, even if his phrasing is less inflected than Stott's (♦EMI 691492 and 62687). **Crossley** is admired by many for his balanced approach, though the bright piano and sound are less than subtle (CRD). **Rogé** is not sensitive to the music's many changes of color (London), and **Albert Ferber** is earthbound (Saga). Have they not appreciated Long's varied expression, or **Rubinstein**'s magical sound in Nocturne 4 (♦RCA 61446), or **Horowitz**'s desolate Nocturne 13 (♦RCA 60377)?

Johannesen's recordings from the '60s are being released on CD, and when complete, they should be close to definitive (♦VAIA 1165, Vol. 1). A set devoted to works by many French composers includes Johannesen's later recordings of a few of the solo pieces and strong performances of Fauré's two compositions for piano and orchestra, the *Ballade* Op. 19 (orchestrated soon after it appeared in its solo version) and the *Fantaisie* Op. 111 (♦Vox 3032). The former is better known and more frequently recorded, but many consider the *Fantaisie* a more cohesive work, even if its introversion diminishes its audience appeal. **De Larrocha**'s recording was perhaps the best (London, not yet on CD), but Johannesen's version of both works is preferable to **Collard**'s solid but occasionally routine accounts (♦EMI 47939). Bernstein's passionate conducting is an inspiring counterpart to **Casadesus**'s urbane pianism in the *Ballade* (♦Sony 47548).

As for Fauré's two-piano works, **Casadesus** was joined by wife Gaby for a charming performance of the *Dolly Suite* (Sony, NA), but **Stott**'s with Martin Roscoe is more imaginative (see the Hyperion collection above). Stott and Roscoe also include *Souvenir de Bayreuth,* a whimsical quadrille Fauré devised with André Messager on themes from Wagner's *Ring.* **Collard**'s *Souvenir* and *Dolly* with Bruno Rigutto (EMI, as above) are sophisticated but hampered by boxy sound.

LOVELACE

CHORAL MUSIC

Fauré's *Requiem* originally had only five movements. In 1893, the composer added the "Offertoire" and "Libera me" but retained the small orchestra from the 1888 version. (This version was edited by modern choral conductor/composer John Rutter, among others, and is considered most authentic.) Fauré's publisher later requested a version for full orchestra, and Fauré probably farmed out the task to a pupil. Although its expanded orchestration adds nothing to the music's impact, this 1900 version was more popular until the appearance of Rutter's edition in the early '80s.

Rutter's recording remains deeply satisfying (♦Collegium 109). Although his interpretation is surpassingly gentle, the fresh, attentive singing of the Cambridge Singers avoids excessive sweetness. This is one of the few recordings that never contradicts Fauré's dictum that this *Requiem* represents a happy deliverance by death, not a day of wrath. Soloists Caroline Ashton and Varcoe are outstanding, the former for her boy-soprano-like voice and the latter for his simple yet fervent singing in "Libera me." Fauré's simple and lovely *Cantique de Jean Racine* is a fine coupling. Ross Pople moves the English Singers along a little more quickly, but his approach, save for additional brass, is essentially the same as Rutter's, and at super-budget price is highly recommendable (♦Arte Nova 30467, with *Cantique* and *Messe Basse*). Matthew Best and the Corydon Singers produce an almost disembodied sound (Hyperion 67070). Soprano Mary Seers also imitates the white tones of a boy soprano, while baritone Michael George sounds more mature.

David Hill and the Winchester Cathedral Choir also use Rutter's edition (Virgin 45318, with *Cantique*). Hill replaces the women with boys, however, and their piping sound and intonation are not ideal. Argenta is womanly and Keenlyside histrionic. Willcocks's classic (and inexpensive) version also uses boys, with the King's College Choir, Cambridge (EMI 69858). Again, the English boys aren't quite what this work needs, and the treble and baritone soloists are quavery. Cleobury's digital remake with the same choir has a better baritone in Bär, but he races through the opening 'Kyrie' and violinist José-Luis Garcia slides through "Sanctus" all too sweetly (EMI 49880). Guest and the St. John's College Choir, Cambridge, tell about the same story as Cleobury, but their rendition feels more emotionally detached (London).

Herreweghe also tries to replicate Fauré's original concept, but in an alternative edition by Jean-Michel Nectoux that allows more brass (♦Harmonia Mundi 901292). Like Hill, Herreweghe's choir includes both children and adults, but here the French children's sound is pleasantly reedy. Agnès Mellon is the movingly childlike soprano soloist, and Kooy's small but handsome baritone is also attractive. Overall, this reading is a bit more dramatic and less polished than Rutter's, but its likable modesty is winning. The coupling is the five-movement *Messe des Pêcheurs de Villerville*, which Fauré co-wrote with Messager. Marlow and Trinity College, Cambridge, also use Nectoux (Conifer 15351, with *Cantique*). It's similar to Herreweghe but without the appealing sound of the French choir.

Marriner is a good choice among more fully scored versions (Philips 446084, with *Pavane* and short works by Fauré pupils). He moves the music along without fuss, justifies the use of larger forces in the few big moments, but otherwise preserves the work's churchly intimacy. McNair is eerily beautiful and Thomas Allen is mature and eloquent. Shaw and his polished Atlantans are strong, and this is a good first choice for those who want the Rutter edition with bigger sound (Telarc 80135). Blegen sings well but not with the affecting purity she displayed at the start of her career. Another Metropolitan stalwart, bass James Morris, brings a much darker voice than customary to his solos. It was daring to replace Fauré's specified baritone with a bass, yet Morris sings poetically.

A less polished entry from Andrew Davis is compromised by solo work from Popp and Nimsgern that tends to be lachrymose, a quality shared in lesser degree by the choral singing (Sony 67182). Their uneasy compromise between piety and drama is tolerable at a budget price. Ozawa's insistence on near inaudibility, in spite of using the fuller scoring, might seem pious, but it's self-regardingly precious, smoothed out, and glib (RCA). The Tanglewood Festival Chorus is amazingly responsive to this view of the score, wrong as it is. Hagegård is flat and Bonney's lovely voice avails little when she's forced to sing a zombie-like "Pie Jesu." The balance of the CD contains songs performed by both soloists; these are much better.

Giulini's Philharmonia recording is a sensuous mistake (DG). His tempos are maddeningly slow and the recording suffocates in its own piety. The Philharmonia Chorus sings unintelligibly, and Battle uses too much vibrato; Andreas Schmidt is more appealing, and he does an uncanny Fischer-Dieskau imitation in his second solo. Michel Legrand also favors slow tempos (Teldec). Again Bonney is unfairly challenged by the conductor's wrong-headed concept, though Hampson sings his two solos beautifully. I know there are many fans of Cluytens's 1962 stereo recording (EMI). Nevertheless, I resist its gluey tempos and the very ordinary singing of the chorus. The only thing that redeems it is de los Angeles's "Pie Jesu." In the baritone solos, Fischer-Dieskau is typically unctuous.

Those looking for a good version of the Hamelle edition could choose Barenboim (EMI 64634). His tempos tend to be extreme (at either end) and his interpretation is occasionally dread-inspiring—not what Fauré had in mind. Nevertheless, it's an imposing version, with good choral work by the Edinburgh Festival Chorus and Armstrong and Fischer-Dieskau as the mature soloists. The choral version of *Pavane* is one of the couplings.

In spite of fruity singing from the small choir and soloists, Nadia Boulanger's recording from 1948 is a remarkable document (♦EMI 61025). She introduced this work to London in 1936, and as can be seen from the recordings listed above, England has not yet let go of it. The sound is dim, but this plaintive, almost morbid performance has a humility that many others lack. A 1953 recording from Roger Wagner and his Chorale has a similar sound but not a similar incandescence (EMI).

TUTTLE

SONGS

Apart from the *Requiem*, Fauré is probably best known for his remarkable series of songs, written from 1863 to 1922 (two years before his death). Except for some early songs—including a few to the same Verlaine texts Debussy used—they're not exactly crowd-pleasers. Aaron Copland said that "only repeated hearings will make clear how filled they are with deep emotion." In a more technical performance note, Pierre Bernac said tersely, "as usual—no rubato whatever." Overemoting is not welcome in a Fauré song.

Bernac also wrote that "Fauré's melodies follow a direct line along which his music becomes always more subtle in form and harmony, and likewise, purer and more restrained in expression." They fall pretty neatly into three periods: 1863–1887, including many of the most popular songs; 1887–1906, including his greatest cycle *La Bonne Chanson*; and 1906–1924, a period that included four cycles, among them *L'Horizon Chimérique* and *Chanson d'Eve*. Even at their most extroverted, they are anything but showy, but the distilled essence of poetry and music in the late works is unique in its seductive subtlety. A complete and very recommendable set with Ameling, Souzay, and Dalton Baldwin, originally released in 1977, is now available (♦EMI 764079, 4 CD). Three discs collect fine performances by **Sarah Walker** and Tom Krause (CRD 3476/78).

Most single-disc collections include some from each period. We're lucky that Fauré lived long enough to coach and encourage singers who were able to record their informed interpretations. The first such, baritone **Charles Panzéra,** remains one of the most notable and satisfying. Several of his songs are in a French collection (EMI 64254), and his famous recording of *La Bonne Chanson* is available (Pearl 9919, with an even more famous recording of Schumann's *Dichterliebe* with Cortot). Panzéra's heir was **Souzay,** who was faithful to Fauré throughout his recording career, both early, in a 1955 song recital (London 425975) and late, in the late '70s (Denon 2252).

Among sopranos, **Hendricks** brings freshness and vibrancy to Fauré (EMI 49841) and **Yakar** sings in a sure French style (Virgin 61433, with songs by Chabrier, Bizet, and Hahn). **Stutzmann,** one of the richest-voice mezzos around, performs a Fauré recital exquisitely (RCA 61439). Baritones must tread carefully on a road traveled by Bernac and Souzay, but a recent recital by **François le Roux** is very satisfactory (REM 311175).

The Verlaine cycle *La Bonne Chanson* (*The Good Song*) is an aptly named work, and one of the glories of French vocal music. It presents odd challenges to a singer, since it is (to quote Bernac once more) "entirely devoted to the expression of happiness and joy" found in a very satisfying relationship (a marriage, to read the poems, though both words and music were written by two unhappily married men— Fauré was carrying on an affair with a younger woman). Be that as it may, the result is quintessential Fauré, luminous and subtle. **Souzay** is untouchable in this piece, and recorded it several times; besides the early '70s recording in the EMI set, there is a beautiful 1960 mono effort, also with Dalton Baldwin (♦Philips 420775), and even a digital version (Denon).

American baritone **Patrick Mason** sings a beautiful *La Bonne Chanson;* he also provides his own straightforward and gracious translations of the Verlaine poems (♦Bridge 9058). Satisfying on its own, this is a fascinating counterpart to Souzay's 1960 recording; while the timings of individual songs differ hardly at all, the two singers sound markedly different. The smooth-voiced **Holzmair** is easy to listen to but not as penetrating interpretively (Philips).

Fauré also arranged *La Bonne Chanson* for piano quintet. Most listeners prefer the original, but there are beautifully sung versions of the arrangement by two of the most satisfying contemporary singers, **von Otter** (DG 47752) and **Sanford Sylvan** (♦Nonesuch 79371). Von Otter's is part of a French song collection, but Sylvan's is all Fauré, including the late cycle *L'Horizon chimérique,* and he gives accompanist David Breitman the chance to solo in two *Barcarolles.*

Fauré's cycle *La Chanson d'Eve,* completed in 1910, is an interesting female counterpart to *La Bonne Chanson.* Charles Van Lerbergh's poems tell of Eve's delight in the Garden of Eden and her gradual discovery of sin and death, in simple language and with exquisite imagery. This subtle concoction of poetry and music was perfect for the style of mezzo **Jan De Gaetani,** whose 1981 live Aspen Festival performance is available (Bridge 9023). If a live performance (or the coupling, Druckman's *Dark Upon the Harp*) doesn't appeal, **Ameling** sings it in a pure and satisfying way in the EMI complete set, and there is an excellent studio performance by mezzo **Janet Baker,** one of the last recordings by this refined singer (Hyperion, with other Fauré songs).   RAYMOND

Morton Feldman (1926–1987)

Morton Feldman never received the recognition that came to John Cage, his friend and mentor in New York in the early '50s, and remained a connoisseur's composer until his death. Ironically, there has been an explosion of interest in his work since then. Composer William Bland tellingly wrote that "aural satisfaction appears to be the sole arbiter in all Feldman compositions, the intention being to 'wash' a period of time with a general hue." That period ranged from minutes to several hours, especially in his later works. Few composers have been so sensitive to the possibilities inherent in one note played beautifully by exactly the right instrument at precisely the correct time.

Recordings of Feldman's work tend to be beyond reproach because inferior or insensitive musicians can't find gratification in this music. Unfortunately, these recordings tend to go out of print very quickly. The Hat Hut label, for example, has released more than a dozen all-Feldman discs since 1990, but limited-edition pressings make many of them difficult to find. Some of the casualties include the haunting opera *Neither* (Hat Hut 102) and *Piano, Violin, Viola, Cello* (Hat Hut 6158)—sad, because no alternative recordings are currently available.

An excellent place to start is the Piano and String Quartet, a 79-minute work that has been gorgeously recorded by the **Kronos Quartet** and Aki Takahashi (♦Nonesuch 79320). The piano plays arpeggios and the strings play sustained chords; the work flits dreamlike at the edge of inaudibility and intangibility. Once you surrender traditional expectations about what music is supposed to do, you're overwhelmed by its ethereal beauty. Another excellent choice is the String Quartet, in a recording by the **Group for Contemporary Music** (♦Koch 7251). To paraphrase Messiaen, this is a quartet for the time of ends.

"The Ecstasy of the Moment" is a grand bargain; the three CDs sell for the price of one (♦Etcetera 3003, 3CD). The performances are by the **Barton Workshop,** and the music spans 34 years, from 1947's *Only* to 1981's *Bass Clarinet and Percussion.* This is an important Feldman collection, though it omits the composer's longest works. Several premiere recordings can be found here. Attractive shorter works can also be found in a collection by the **New Millennium Ensemble** (♦Koch 7466). These include *For Frank O'Hara, De Kooning* (Feldman was heavily influenced by writers and artists of his era), *Bass Clarinet and Percussion,* and *Instruments I.* Another varied collection—*False Relationships and the Extended Ending, The Viola in My Life I-III,* and *Why Patterns?*— contains some of the composer's best works played by various musicians (♦CRI 620).

New Albion's three Feldman CDs are typically distinctive. The first contains *Three Voices,* which the composer described, not inaccurately, as "gorgeous" (New Albion 018). Largely wordless, but with a culminating text by Frank O'Hara, it was written for soprano **Joan La Barbara** to perform live with two pre-recorded voice parts. La Barbara is also featured in works for voice with or without instruments (New Albion 085). The music is even more austere and personal, and the disc contains two performances of *Only,* the earliest Feldman work to be recorded (1946). *Rothko Chapel* is a contemplative masterwork for chorus with viola, celesta, and percussion (♦New Albion 039). Here it's performed by the **UC Berkeley Chamber Chorus;** the coupling is *Why Patterns?,* which might be described as three concurrent solos for flute, glockenspiel, and piano, played by performers from the **California EAR Unit.**

Two more CDs are important additions to the Feldman discography. A 1994 release contains shorter works: *Routine Investigations* (an example of the composer's talent for ironic titles?), *The Viola in My Life I and II, For Frank O'Hara,* and *I Met Heine on the Rue Fürstenburg* (Auvidis 782018). The members of **Ensemble Recherché** look like students and play like Zen masters. A second disc consists solely of the intriguing *Words and Music,* with text by Samuel Beckett (Auvidis 782084).

Pianist **Aki Takahashi**'s interpretations received the composer's blessing. Two discs on the Japanese ALM label seem to be out of print, but in addition to the Nonesuch disc mentioned above, there is her series of piano works. Vol. 1 includes seven, from the early *Illusions* to two masterful later pieces, *Piano* and *Palais de Mari* (Mode 54). Subsequent volumes—not with Takahashi—have been devoted to vintage recordings of early works (Mode 66) and the complete works for violin and piano (Mode 82/83). Two other discs of solo piano music are recommendable, one by **Marianne Schroeder,** which also includes *Piano* and *Palais de Mari* (Hat Hut 6035), and another by **Roger Woodward** that features the 87-minute *Triadic Memories* (Etcetera 2015, 2 CD). An alternative version of *Triadic Memories,* which I haven't heard, is by **Markus Hinterhauser** (Col Legno 31873, 2CD).

The major labels have largely ignored Feldman. A beautiful exception comes from **Tilson Thomas,** who conducts a professional-quality student orchestra in the shimmering *Coptic Light* for piano and orchestra (with Alan Feinberg) and *Cello and Orchestra* (with Robert Cohen) (♦Argo 448513). A rival account of *Coptic Light* led by **Michael Morgan** seems gross in comparison, and *Durations I-V* has been done better elsewhere (CPO). Conductor **Hans Zander**'s versions of *Coptic Light* and *Cello and Orchestra* deserve higher praise; the "two-fer" adds *Flute and Orchestra* and *Oboe and Orchestra* (♦CPO 999483). All four works are very fine; *Coptic Light* is the most austere (but watch out for the "explosion" near the end!), and *Oboe and Orchestra* is the most lapidary.

For Samuel Beckett depicts an end game (the title of a Beckett play) in which the player/musicians have run out of possibilities and must make the same moves again and again. There is activity but no warmth, and the music gently persists in hitting its head against the wall. However, because the repetitions are imperfect and the layers of sound don't line up the same way each time, it isn't static. Recordings by the **Vienna Klangforum** (Kairos 1201) and **Kammerensemble Neue Musik Berlin** (CPO 999647) are excellent.

Crippled Symmetry, a strange and rarefied trio for flute, vibraphone/glockenspiel, and piano/celesta, has appeared on three 2CD releases in spite of its 90-minute length. The most recent, by members of the **California EAR Unit,** is the least expensive, probably the easiest to find, and totally satisfactory (♦Bridge 9092). Curious listeners can track down the other two (Col Legno 31874 and Hat Hut 60801/2). Feldman's most extreme music (at least in terms of length—four hours!) is *For Philip Guston.* Again, the **California EAR Unit** is exquisitely sensitive, and an enhanced CD including Feldman's remarks and a photo montage is an exciting bonus (♦Bridge 9078, 4CD). The alternative is also well regarded (Hat Hut 61041/4, 4CD).

Intimidated? Two very short works might appeal to the skittish. *Out of "Last Pieces"* was recorded by Bernstein (of all people) in the '60s in *"Music of Our Time"* (Sony 61845). It's not one of Feldman's best works, however. Shorter and better is *Madame Press Died Last Week at Ninety,* a tender elegy to the piano teacher Feldman had when he was 12, included in John Adams's "American Elegies" (Nonesuch 79249).

TUTTLE

Brian Ferneyhough *(b. 1943)*

Ferneyhough is known for his uncompromising, rigorous approach to composition; it's unashamedly intellectual and probably won't appeal to those seeking more conventional musical expression. Regarded as the father figure of the "New Complexity" movement, his music is fiercely virtuosic and uses many extended techniques in its instrumental and vocal writing. The scores are densely notated to reveal many layers of precise performance instruction, in what Ferneyhough calls an "almost neurotic emphasis of detail," requiring a kind of superhuman concentration to learn and perform. No one sight-reads a Ferneyhough piece.

His orchestral writings are slim and almost none have been recorded, probably owing to their technical demands. However, many examples of his solo and chamber works are available. The **Arditti Quartet** has recorded his major works for string quartet in "Brian Ferneyhough 1," presenting Quartets 2 and 3, *Adagissimo,* and *Sonatas for String Quartet* (Disques Montaigne 789002). They are entirely at ease with the demands of this music, and it's less taxing when heard on stringed instruments, making this a good starting point for the curious and essential listening for the converted. "Brian Ferneyhough 2" continues with more performances by Arditti, here in Quartet 4, with Irvine Arditti as soloist in *Terrain* for violin and ensemble, plus two solo pieces for guitar and double bass (♦Disque-Montaigne 782029).

Ed Spanjaard leads the fearless Nieuw Ensemble through *La Chute d'Icare* for clarinet and chamber ensemble and *Etudes Transcendentales* for flute, oboe, soprano, harpsichord, and cello (Etcetera 1070). The former is a highly concentrated chamber concerto, the latter a nine-part song cycle with changing instrumentation for each song. This is one of Ferneyhough's most affecting works, despite the hyper-activity of the instrumental writing. The two ensemble works are complemented by solo pieces for piccolo, violin, and bass flute (this last with tape).

Ferneyhough is fascinated by individual virtuosity, and this is aptly demonstrated by a disc of solo pieces played by members of the Australian ensemble **Elision** (Etcetera 1206). *Time and Motion Study I* and *II* explore the limits of the physically possible in instrumental technique for bass clarinet and cello, respectively. The cello piece uses electronics in a striking way, creating a forbidding landscape. *Bone Alphabet* is a percussion tour de force, *Kurze Schatten II* an extended study in microtones and microactivity for guitar, and *Unity Capsule* an exhaustive examination of sonic potentials for flute. All these performances are breathtaking in their execution.

Funerailles for string septet and harp is also notable and can be heard in a hefty compilation conducted by **Boulez** with Ensemble Intercontemporain (Erato 98496, 5CD, NA). This collection features many outstanding performances of works by several contemporary composers (e.g., Birtwistle, Carter, Berio, Xenakis, et al.), and is well worth seeking out. *Prometheus* is a fairly early work that is well played by the **Senor Ensemble** (CRI 652, with works by Rano Steiger, Reynolds, and Joji Yuasa). It's less concerned with extended technique than his later music and has some interest, but I was more drawn to the other works on the disc.

Carceri d'Invenzione III for winds and percussion is part of an important cycle that occupied Ferneyhough throughout the '80s, the third in a series of works for chamber groups or soloists (Accord 205772). The disc is filled out with other chamber and solo works including *Prometheus, La Chute d'Icare,* and *On Stellar Magnitudes.*

McINTIRE

Zdeněk Fibich *(1850–1900)*

Often joined with Smetana and Dvořak in musical history, Fibich was the youngest of the three and the least concerned with nationalism. His music doesn't rely on folk song but rather on its own individuality. Still, Fibich did two things that make him both an individualist and very

Czech. First, he was a diarist in music, writing his impressions in the form of countless little piano works that trace the progress of a passionate love. Anyone who knows Czech opera, particularly Janáček, knows how deeply and insightfully the Czechs express themselves concerning love and human relationships. Also, along with his operas, Fibich wrote a series of distinctive melodramas, spoken words accompanied by music, culminating in the impressive *Hippodamia* trilogy. Originality in concept coupled with the concentration of effort to carry out his ideas at length make him an important composer.

There are three symphonies; the first is early but beautiful, the latter two employ material from the diary. All are lovely, warm-hearted works. The earliest recordings were by **Sejna** and the Czech Philharmonic, made in the '50s in clear mono sound (♦Supraphon 1920/21, LP). Stereo recordings from the '70s and '80s were played by the Brno Philharmonic under **Petr Vronsky, Jirí Waldhans,** and **Belohlávek** (Supraphon). These were worthy performances, but Brno isn't Prague and the orchestra sounds wiry in the strings and a little less sophisticated.

Along came the ubiquitous **Neeme Järvi** with the Detroit Symphony (Chandos). His recorded sound is better, but he loses most of the Czech flavor, stamping through the fast movements without much interest. Then the Czech Philharmonic got themselves a non-Czech leader, **Albrecht,** who recorded Symphony 3 with them in a hurried and almost brutal manner (Orfeo). Most recently, the Razumovsky Symphony under **Andrew Mogrelia** has recorded 1 and 2 (♦Naxos 553699). This orchestra is a pickup group containing personnel from several Prague orchestras and they play with warmth and enjoyment. The recorded sound is excellent and the price is right.

There are a number of symphonic poems and overtures. Those investing in **Sejna**'s Symphony 1 get his lovely *At Twilight* and the cantata *The Romance of Spring.* Both may also be found in idiomatic performances by the Prague Radio Symphony under **Frantisek Vajnar** along with the early tone poem *Spring* and the bucolic overture, *A Night at Karlstein* (Supraphon 103405). A complementary collection with the Prague Symphony under **Vladimír Válek** brings us the overtures *Comenius* and *The Fall of Arkona* and the symphonic poems *Toman and the Wood Nymph* and *Záboj, Slavoj, and Luděk* (Supraphon 18232011). Odd man out is the tone poem *The Tempest,* only available at present with Albrecht's Symphony 3 (Orfeo 350951), though formerly found with Vronsk's Symphony 1 (Supraphon 1091).

The earliest chamber work recorded is a Piano Trio from 1872 that was never included in Fibich's work list. A fine stereo recording is in the Supraphon archives, once available on LP but presently missing (1617). The two early string quartets and Theme and Variations are played by the **Kocian Quartet** (Orfeo 439981), Quartet 2 and the Variations by the **Dolezal Quartet** (Arta 72, with Smetana's Quartet 2). The Doleal is more enthusiastic but the Kocian is excellent as well. There's also a Piano Quartet, available from **Ensemble Villa Musica,** coupled with Fibich's major chamber work, the Piano Quintet (MD+G 3040775). The latter was originally scored for clarinet, horn, violin, cello, and piano and is the version played here. If you're collecting Fibich, this is clearly the disc to have.

Two other recordings couple the Quintet with a Sextet by Dohnányi, also a fascinating piece. The **Endymion Ensemble** (ASV 943) gives both a lively reading, while the **Acht Ensemble** (Thorofon 2377) is a little more laid back. There used to be an echt-Czech version of the Quintet played by the augmented **Fibich Trio** (Supraphon LP 1617, NA, with the Piano Trio), and another with pianist **Radoslav Kvapil** and the Suk

Quartet of the Quintet's later incarnation for strings and piano (Panton 1425, NA). Both were excellent.

The complete collection of 376 autobiographical piano snippets was recorded over several years by **Marián Lapšanský** on 12 Supraphon CDs, now gradually disappearing from the catalog even before they all were released. They are beautifully performed and recorded; the only trouble is that the subjects treated by the pieces are frequently not listed in the program notes. What good is a diary without subject matter? Fibich worked well in short forms; these little gems contain the heart of his inspiration and are remarkably expressive. If you're not sure you want to trace his development so extensively, try **William Howard**'s well-played disc of excerpts (Chandos 9381).

Fibich wrote a number of operas, but the only ones ever recorded are *Sárka,* about the legendary Amazon also immortalized by Smetana in *Má Vlast,* and *The Bride of Messina,* on a Schiller story. Fibich's fondness for the leitmotif and a through-composed attitude toward opera are well in evidence. In *Sárka,* **Jan Stych** leads the Brno Opera (Supraphon 36, 2CD) in a performance as fine as the one it replaced by **Krombholc.** *The Bride of Messina* is performed by the Prague National Theater conducted by **Jílek** (Supraphon 111492, 2CD; listed as one disc by *Schwann*). Both are good, serviceable stereo recordings, a little congested in the climaxes but more than adequate.

The melodrama (with music accompanying a spoken text) fascinated Fibich, and we have several examples of his work in this genre. Two are conducted by **Sejna** (Supraphon 111922, with two of Novak's symphonic works). *Christmas Day* and *The Water Goblin* are folk tales collected and versified by Jaroslav Erben, whose works inspired Dvorak in his late symphonic poems. The recordings are mono but good, the music more folk-influenced than usual. Fibich's largest musical composition is also a melodrama, this time on *Hippodamia,* as dramatized by Sophocles and Euripides and expanded by Jaroslav Vrchlick.

There are three opera-length works, *The Courtship of Pelops, The Atonement of Tantalus,* and *Hippodamia's Death.* They are held together by a series of leitmotives and are an experience unlike any other: There is no singing, but the spoken text requires a similar control of phrasing. There is a spoken chorus as well. These works were recorded in the early '80s, the first conducted by **Krombholc,** the other two by **Jílek,** on six CDs, two for each (Supraphon 3037). The performances are impressive, the music fascinating. MOORE

John Field *(1782–1837)*

Field was one of the most successful composers of his day and much in demand as a performer. Born in Dublin, he was playing in public by the age of ten, was apprenticed to Clementi in London, and spent his teenage years demonstrating fortepianos in Clementi's showroom. In 1802 he left England, traveled in Europe for a few years, and finally settled in Russia, where he spent the rest of his life. He wrote seven concertos, four piano sonatas, and 18 nocturnes. His early sonatas and concertos are conventional, following Classical models, while the later ones are more romantic and unpredictable. The nocturnes are the most characteristic of his works. They are short, atmospheric, and dreamy, and are among the first compositions to depart from the Classical style and embody the sensual and indefinite Romantic spirit. Like Chopin, all of Field's compositions include the piano.

O'Conor recorded a fine set of nocturnes (♦Telarc 80199). He plays a Hamburg Steinway, and although this disc includes only the first 15, it makes an excellent starting point. The recording is warm and resonant, ideal for the music. O'Conor's recording of the sonatas and remaining nocturnes is also very good (Telarc 80290). The first disc in **Frith**'s series includes nine nocturnes and two sonatas (♦Naxos 550761). He combines virtuoso technique with a smooth sound that resembles what we know of the composer's own performing style. He also plays the concertos expertly, with David Haslam and the Northern Sinfonia providing fine support (Naxos 553770, 1+3; 553771, 2+4). This series is highly recommended.

O'Rourke has recorded all the nocturnes, sonatas, and concertos for Chandos. His survey of Field's music is the most extensive, running to eight discs. The concertos, with the London Mozart Players conducted by Bamert, are on 9368, 9442, 9495, and 9534, the sonatas are on 8787, the nocturnes on 8719/20. O'Rourke has also made a disc of other short piano works, many of which are otherwise unavailable (♦Chandos 9315). The fourth disc of concertos also features chamber music, including a *Quintetto* for piano and string quartet and two *Divertissements* for piano and strings, in premiere recordings.

Hobson included one Field sonata (Op. 1:1) in Vol. 2 of his "London Piano School" series (Arabesque 6595), where it's presented alongside contemporary works by George Fredrick Pinto, Johann Baptist Cramer, and Clementi. Hobson's playing is high-spirited and clear. **Staier** has recorded Concertos 2 and 3 on an 1802 Broadwood fortepiano with Concerto Köln (♦Teldec 21475). In addition to giving us the sound the composer would have heard (these works were published in 1816), Staier includes one of the nocturnes as the middle movement of a concerto. It's likely that Field did the same.

Spada has recorded the sonatas as part of a series (Arts). He tries to emphasize the dramatic elements of the music; alas, the music doesn't support this approach—it's pleasant rather than profound.

P. GEFFEN

Irving Fine (*1914–1962*)

Fine was born in Boston and spent most of his career in and around that city, teaching composition and theory at Harvard, Brandeis, and the Berkshire Music Center at Tanglewood, where he died at the age of 47 after conducting a performance of his Symphony. He was strongly influenced by Stravinsky's neoclassicism as well as by Schoenberg's serialism and wrote music that makes use of the best features of both; his serial music never sounds atonal, and his neoclassical music sounds modern, clean, and beautifully crafted. He wrote equally well for vocal and chamber music ensembles and orchestra. His open, clean lines, expertly constructed counterpoint, lyrical phrases, and sharp wit place him on an equal footing with his more-often-recorded contemporaries—Copland (who often praised him) and Bernstein (who often imitated him).

Perhaps Fine's most recorded piece is *Partita for Wind Quintet*. There are several good recordings, including those by the **Reykjavik Wind Quintet** (Chandos) and **Boehm Quintet** (Premiere), but my favorite is by the **New York Woodwind Quintet** (♦Nonesuch 79175). This recording includes *Notturno for Strings and Harp*, String Quartet, *Serious Song—A Lament for String Orchestra*, and *The Hour Glass* (a cantata on poems by Ben Jonson). There is another excellent recording of the String Quartet by the **Juilliard Quartet** that also offers *Notturno*, the hilarious *Childhood Fables for Grownups*, and the extraordinary *Fantasia for String Trio* (♦CRI 574).

Joel Spiegelman made an excellent recording of Fine's orchestral music (♦Delos 3139). It includes the Symphony (which, like his string quartet, uses serial techniques), *Diversions for Orchestra*, and the quintessentially neoclassical *Toccata Concertante*. Spiegelman arranged Fine's *Music for Piano*, which he calls "Music for Orchestra," and the title

piece is *Blue Towers*, a charming miniature. **Scott Yoo** includes a lovely reading of *Serious Song* in his recording of American music for chamber orchestra (♦Albany 194). The **Leinsdorf** LP of the Symphony, *Serious Song*, and *Toccata Concertante* has been reissued (Phoenix 106), but the **Boston Symphony Chamber Players** LP that includes a wonderful reading of *Fantasia for String Trio* has not yet reappeared (RCA).

Fine wrote some wonderful choral music. The **Gregg Smith Singers** include two sets of choruses from *Alice in Wonderland* (beautifully performed but with a primitively recorded piano), *The Hour-Glass*, and *McCord's Menagerie* (♦CRI 630). This recording includes great performances of the Violin Sonata by **Kavafian** and the song cycle *Mutability* sung by mezzo-soprano **Eunice Alberts,** both with Fine at the piano. The **New Amsterdam Singers** include two pieces from *The Choral New Yorker*—made up of four pieces set to poems that were published in *The New Yorker* during the '20s and '30s—in "American Journey" (Albany 108). The entire set came out in 1977 in "America Sings 1920–1950" in a recording by the **Gregg Smith Singers** (Vox LP 5353, not yet on CD).

FINE

Gerald Finzi (*1901–1956*)

An ardent champion of neglected composers, a voracious reader with a penetrating intelligence—these are components of that compositional wonder and remarkable human being, Gerald Finzi. With music ultimately rooted in the thoughts of Elgar and Vaughan Williams, he walked in these giant footsteps while concentrating on a less bombastic, more introverted expression. The pastoral nature so ingrained in English composers is still there, to be sure, yet he makes it far more personal, intense, and expressionistic than his mentors. We're lucky in that most recordings of his music are excellent, but fortune disfavors us in that so much more needs to be done to capture his works adequately on records.

Orchestral music. The first performance of the lovely *Eclogue* for piano and orchestra (originally to be the middle movement of a projected piano concerto) took place at a memorial concert some four months after the composer's death. It makes us long to hear what a complete concerto would have sounded like, and the reading by **Martin Jones** with Boughton and the English String Orchestra is not only the only one available but the only one you need (♦Nimbus 5366). This super compilation includes a number of fine works by Bridge and Parry, so you have many reasons to rush out and buy the disc. You can also obtain *Eclogue* in an album that includes the Vaughan Williams and Delius piano concertos (Classics for Pleasure), but the Nimbus is required listening.

Of all Finzi's works, *Love's Labours Lost* has probably had the most chaotic history. Originally a commission for a BBC Radio performance, he eventually stripped it of its singers and added more instruments to the sparse scoring. The piece follows the action of the play, but that's not required to enjoy this entertaining music. Two performances are available: **Boughton** and the English String Orchestra (♦Nimbus 5101 or 5210, 4CD—and while you're there, enjoy the Prelude in F minor for String Orchestra and the Romance in E-flat) or see below for the supersteal from **Griffiths** (♦Naxos 553566).

Concertos. The Cello Concerto is one of Finzi's most difficult and challenging works and one of his most important. It has a haunting, questioning mood that can only be likened to Elgar. Its one recording sets the standard: **Wallfisch** and the Royal Liverpool Philharmonic under Handley (♦Chandos 8471). Don't miss this if you want to get to the essence of Finzi's art.

The Clarinet Concerto is probably Finzi's most popular piece and with good reason. It attempts to be assertive but in the end relies on the tried and true pastoral feel of the British countryside, with a strong dose of melancholy thrown in. I can think of no clarinet concerto as lyrical or fluid; the instrument serves as the protagonist throughout, never intruded upon by the orchestra. **Alan Hacker** isn't assertive enough, as if the clarinet were taking the part of the sheep instead of the shepherd, and the ambient sonics do nothing to correct this problem (Nimbus). **Thea King** gives us a marvelous version, sweet and tonally secure, full of a bittersweet nostalgia that keeps the tears flowing, and the Philharmonia Orchestra under **Alun Francis** plays like a dream (♦Hyperion 66001).

Michael Collins's excellent version with Hickox and the City of London Sinfonia is more assertive and aggressive but works like a charm. You might find it somewhere, though it has been deleted for a while (Virgin). **Stoltzman** offers one of the best versions, altogether secure in his technique while luring us on like a Pied Piper, a common occurrence with this musician (♦RCA 60437). **Robert Plane**'s recording is attractive not only for the Concerto (which is fine, though no better than the best) but also for the price, which is the best. The delight is in the couplings, including an orchestral arrangement of *Bagatelles,* a Suite from *Love's Labours Lost, Introit in F* for solo violin and orchestra, *Romance in E-flat* for string orchestra, and *Severn Rhapsody.* This is a fabulous collection of some missing links in Finzi's output, admirably led by **Howard Griffiths** with the Northern Sinfonia. At the price, you can't possibly lose (♦Naxos 553566).

Andrew Marriner and father Neville give a sensitive, gentle account of this work on a very well played disc (great sound, too). Of course, the Academy of St. Martin in the Fields does the honors (♦Philips 454438). But pride of place, with the others standing in the dust, goes to the fabulous **Emma Johnson,** who manages to morph her clarinet into a minstrel of bygone days, singing like an enchantress tunes we've never heard before even though they sound so familiar. Groves is the able accompanist, and the quite rare Stanford Concerto is the deserving partner (as on King's recording—also very well done). Don't miss it (♦ASV 787).

Chamber music. The miniature delights of the five *Bagatelles for Clarinet* have shown up in many places, none better than the recording by **Emma Johnson,** the premier clarinetist in Britain today (♦ASV 787). Also worth considering, as part of an omnibus of clarinet lore, is **de Peyer**'s version; he's as consistent a player as the instrument has known over the years (♦Chandos 8549). **Stoltzman** offers a lovely rendition of the Concerto and *Bagatelles* arranged for him by Lawrence Ashmore (best known as the composer of the music for the movie *Arachnophobia*), along with *The Four Seasons* and *Greensleeves.* This is one to hunt for (♦RCA 60437).

Choral music. There is only one recording of Finzi's varied choral music, and it's excellent. **Paul Spicer** and his Finzi Singers give us almost 80 minutes of sheer exquisiteness in ten of these pieces. Sensitive and fragile, they give us the essence of Finzi's art without sacrificing any of the power and emotional strength of the ensemble. Though there are slight problems of balance in some numbers, this is a disc for the ages (♦Chandos 8936).

Finzi's cantata *Dies Natalis* was the logical outcome of his interest in literary and rhapsodic metaphysics and ideas. This work, based on Thomas Traherne's *Centuries of Meditation,* is a sweet, illuminating piece that attempts to put into music Traherne's vision of the world as seen through a child's eyes. Both versions currently available are recommendable. **Martyn Hill** sings stoutly and with great assurance with Hickox and the City of London Sinfonia, a mid-priced disc of great attraction (♦Virgin 65588, with Holst's *Choral Fantasia* as the worthy discmate). **Rebecca Evans** breaks the tenor tradition for this work, the first woman to record it in over 50 years, and gives a supple, limpid, and moving performance (♦Collins 51285). She amply conveys the child's wide-eyed wonder in a joyous yet reflective tone that wins the day, and the inclusion of several other lovely pieces in their only manifestation adds to the attraction of this sterling disc.

The wistful, light-as-a-feather voice of **Bostridge** makes his Marriner collaboration truly fine; such sensitive interpretation of the text is a rarity (♦Philips 454438). **Ainsley** and Best give a good performance, though Ainsley's light voice displays some vocal carelessness. But since its companion is the only recording of the beautiful *Intimations of Immortality,* it's recommended by default (♦Hyperion 66876).

The brevity of life is the subject of *A Farewell to Arms,* a moving two-movement piece that Finzi took a long time to write. See above for **Handley**'s already emphatically recommended reading (♦Collins 51285). Baritone **Richard Brunner** is altogether unacceptable in a piano version; the sound is hollow and his voice is blurry and undernourished (Gasparo). If you can find it, **Hill**'s recording with Hickox is wonderful, aptly matched with *Dies Natalis* and the Clarinet Concerto (Virgin 90718).

The lovely, pensive *Requiem da Camera* is another example of an unheeded call to record more of Finzi's music. Fortunately, at least some record companies are listening, and the recording by Hickox showcasing **Varcoe**'s considerable talents isn't likely to be bettered any time soon (♦Chandos 8997).

Songs. You should avoid the abortive effort of **Robert Brunner** (Gasparo), who can't hold a candle to the fluid, mellifluous sighings and longings of **Hill,** Varcoe, and Clifford Benson on piano, who give us hard-to-beat renditions of the cycles *Earth and Air and Rain, Till Earth Outwears, A Young Man's Exhortation,* and *Before and After Summer.* These are superb readings by any standard, all based on Finzi's favorite author, Thomas Hardy. Their emotional gamut ranges from introspective responses to nature to laments over mankind's propensity to war. The sound is first class, the interpretation without fault; this is one of the best albums of its kind (♦Hyperion 66161, 2CD). RITTER

Nicolas Flagello (1928–1994)

Flagello was perhaps the most effective exponent of the American lyrical post-romantic ideal in the generation that followed Barber. His profound belief in the expressive power of music is manifest in every piece. A major factor behind the effectiveness of his music is its strong, neo-classical sense of shape and structure. Flagello's sensibilities and aspirations were firmly rooted in his Italian background, and he spent a number of years in Italy in the '50s. His finest works date from the '60s, when the style he espoused was at its most unfashionable.

The wistful nostalgia of his works for violin and piano is beautifully captured by **Setsuko Nagaka** and Peter Vinograde in the mysterious Piano Sonata (1962) and the brooding Violin Sonata from the same year (Albany 234). There is often an inwardness about Flagello's music that makes it especially poignant and the pieces played here are masterful, taut mood pictures. The Suite for Harp and String Trio is particularly eloquent. His orchestral pieces are numerous, and a particularly good disc has **David Amos** and the New Russia Orchestra playing the brief but elegiac *Andante Languido* and the more extended *Serenata* (Albany

143, with interesting works by Gould and Vittorio Giannini). Amos's understated and thoughtful performances do justice to this refined and dignified music, and this recording deserves a strong recommendation.

Restraint yields to greater exuberance and more powerful drama in Flagello's major choral work, *The Passion of Martin Luther King* (1968), recorded by **James DePreist** (Koch 7293, with Schwantner's *New Morning for the World*). The piece sets liturgical texts interspersed with King's writings and speeches; its dark mood is shot through with bursts of light. It's one of the finest examples of American dramatic oratorio, superbly played and recorded.

Equally worthy is a recording of Piano Concertos 2 and 3, *Credendum* for violin and orchestra, and two overtures, again led by **Amos** (Vox 7521). **Oliveira** gives a convincing reading of *Credendum*, a mature work of great contrasts of mood and dynamics. The two piano concertos are surprisingly polarized. The ghostly *Capriccio* for cello and orchestra and the graceful *Contemplazioni di Michelangelo* are conducted by **Flagello** in clean performances (Phoenix 125). One of America's most neglected modern romantics has at last (albeit posthumously) gained real time in the record catalog and his music is worth exploring.

JOHNSON

Friedrich von Flotow *(1812–1883)*

Flotow wrote more than 20 operas, but his enduring fame rests on only one, *Martha*, and perhaps the overture and a single aria ("Jungfrau Maria") from *Alessandro Stradella*. A pirate recording of *Stradella* with **Donath** has floated around on a couple of different labels. It does justice to the opera but may be difficult to find. *Martha* itself is kept alive primarily by its two best-known numbers, Harriet's "Last Rose of Summer" (which didn't originate with Flotow) and Lionel's "Ach, so fromm," which has been recorded as "M'appari" by Italian tenors since Caruso's time. The score's best music, however, is in its ensembles, which have an immediately captivating melodic beauty.

Martha is an uncommonly tuneful, accessible opera, handicapped by a trivial plot (a bored aristocratic lady plays a cruel trick on a young rustic only to fall in love with him in the end) and by its very passé simplemindedness (no profundity, no sexual overtones, no real angst—the aggrieved Lionel is just a crybaby with a penchant for lyrical utterance). It's an easy opera to love all the same, ideal for cozy home listening.

Robert Heger was over 80 when he recorded the opera (♦EMI 69211, 2CD). Having grown up in a tradition that took *Martha* seriously, he saw no need to condescend to it. He leads the score confidently and affectionately, and his singers perform with like conviction. Rothenberger is lovely in the title role, her voice flexible enough for the coloratura of the character's other aria, her diction wonderfully clear and pointed, her demeanor apt for both Lady Harriet and her alter ego Martha. Gedda's Lionel is stylishly sung, in bright, flowing tones, and has a salutary touch of dignity. Prey's Plunkett is hearty and amiable, and his low notes have uncommon depth for a baritone; he delivers an ebullient account of his Porter song. Fassbaender partners both him and her mistress well, molding the words clearly, singing strongly, and refusing to disappear into the crowd.

A recording led by **Wallberg** is almost as good (Eurodisc and RCA). Doris Soffel is a good Nancy, though less trenchant than Fassbaender. Ridderbusch, a real bass and a very suave one, sings almost as personably as Prey. Jerusalem in his pre-Wagnerian days was a promising lyric tenor, and he often brings more grace and a more natural air to Lionel's music than Gedda. Popp's voice is a bit tarter than Rothenberger's, but

it's just as agile and has more body and color; she's a blander actress but a fine Harriet nonetheless.

The best of *Martha* fits nicely on a single highlights disc, and **Berislav Klobucar**'s recording of excerpts is indispensable (♦EMI 34050). Rothenberger is Martha, and she's joined by the delightfully dowdy Nancy of Hetty Plümacher and Frick's amiable, spirited, and suitably roughcast Plunkett. Lionel is sung by the irreplaceable Wunderlich, absolutely peerless in the duets and the graceful ensemble finales of Acts 2 and 3. His warm, melting tones make the lilting melodies sound like great music. Look for the European CD reissue (EMI 252215), grab the cassette if you see it, or find a second-hand copy of the old Angel LP—but don't miss it.

LUCANO

Carlisle Floyd *(b. 1926)*

Possibly excepting *Treemonisha* and *Porgy and Bess*, it's interesting that the three quintessentially American operas were composed in the mid-'50s—Copland's *The Tender Land*, Moore's *The Ballad of Baby Doe*, and Floyd's *Susannah*. They share a rural setting, sociopolitical elements both overt and covert, and modest musical forces and requirements.

Of the three, *Susannah* has had by far the most performances. Curtin sang the title role many times and is unfortunately heard only on the recording of the 1962 premiere by the New Orleans Opera Association led by long-time New Orleans conductor **Knud Anderssen** (VAIA 1115). The disc lacks high quality sound, balance, and presence, but with Treigle and Cassilly, Curtin portrays masterfully the troubled foil for Treigle's machinations as the preacher. Curtin and Treigle sang these roles often with the New York City Opera with more secure and professional associates.

With a couple of exceptions, a more recent set provides a better *Susannah* (Virgin 45039). The exceptions are the two principals—Studer is not nearly as convincing as Curtin, musically or dramatically, and Ramey doesn't measure up to Treigle for the same reasons. However, Hadley as Susannah's brother is superior to Cassilly, and **Nagano** conducting Lyon Opera forces provides a secure backdrop. The sound is excellent and uniform except for Studer's part, which I believe was dubbed in after everything else was recorded. Excellent program notes, an interview with the composer, and the libretto are included. Nearly 50 years after its composition, the Cold War paranoia and McCarthy-era turmoil that surely provided a subtext for *Susannah* are probably lost for today's listeners, especially in recordings. Neither of these discs captures that, but I doubt that any recorded performance faithful to the score can.

Floyd has composed several other operas, all later than *Susannah*, but only *Markheim* has been recorded. (I've heard rumors of more: *Of Mice and Men*? San Francisco production?) Based on Robert Louis Stevenson's story of the same title, Floyd composed this one-act opera with Treigle in mind for the title role. The recording features him with the New Orleans Opera, again conducted by **Anderssen** (VAIA 1107). The disc is remastered from the 1966 premiere, and you will immediately notice the extraordinary amount of audience coughing and other extraneous noises. No libretto is included, and the notes are primarily on the performers. *Markheim* lacks the arias and other attention-getting features of *Susannah*, but Treigle is in fine voice.

ZIEROLF

Arthur Foote *(1853–1937)*

Foote had a remarkable musical instinct and intellect that are reflected in works of great originality and refreshing Yankee spirit; he excelled in short orchestral works and chamber music that, combined with his enviable longevity, made him, in Karl Krueger's words, "the Nestor of the distinguished group of New England composers." Even among later generations who found much of the New England School's music not sufficiently modern or assertively American, Foote's Suite in E for strings and *Night Piece* for flute and strings remained popular, and, with increased acceptance of our musical heritage, his other music is being rediscovered as well, a strong tribute to its staying power.

ORCHESTRAL MUSIC

Four Character Pieces after "The Rubáiyát of Omar Khayyám." Rather subtly colored compared to *Scheherazade* or *Antar,* they remain highly evocative just the same. This music was very special to **Krueger,** whose recording remains unchallenged; we may hope for its swift reissue, originally coupled with Amy Beach's *Gaelic Symphony* (Our Musical Past 105, LP).

Francesca da Rimini. Based on the same tragic Dante tale of forbidden love as Tchaikovsky's far more familiar symphonic poem, while nowhere as intense as that masterpiece, it's an impassioned and deeply felt tone poem that could easily pass for Dvořák. **Krueger** in his recording for the Society for the Preservation of the American Musical Heritage (MIA 127, LP) limns the shifting images adroitly but seems more comfortable with the rapt fervor of the doomed lovers, without bringing out the surging winds of the inferno as thrillingly as **Mester** (♦Albany 030, with music of Chadwick, Arthur Bird, and Frederick Shepherd Converse).

Suite in D minor. Perhaps Foote's most extended work for orchestra— "practically a symphony," he called it—the Suite is in four movements, and there's a hearty good humor to the outer two. Recorded by **Krueger,** perhaps this too will resurface eventually (MIA 122, LP).

Suite in E. This piece for strings remains Foote's most popular work; introduced by Max Fiedler with the Boston Symphony in 1908, it was frequently scheduled by Koussevitzky as well. **Richard Kapp** has performed the original four-movement version, but unfortunately never recorded it in this form, so it continues to be offered as a suite in three movements, notably by **Kenneth Klein,** also recommended for the hard-to-find couplings by other American composers (♦EMI 49263 or Albany 235).

CHAMBER MUSIC

Piano Quintet. A free and fluid exercise, it combines elements of romantic and impressionist styles in thoroughly engaging fashion. It's offered by **Mary Louise Boehm** and colleagues in a strong performance, in the company of similar music by Juan Orrego-Salas and Diamond (Albany 176). A more practical choice at a lower price is probably **James Barbagallo** as the able pianist with the Da Vinci Quartet; they bring out the winsome and amiable qualities of the music in easy-going and spontaneous fashion (♦Marco Polo 223875 or Naxos 559009, with Quartets 2 and 3). They also present an excellent case for Quartet 1 and the Piano Quartet, coupled with the *Nocturne and Scherzo* for flute (♦Naxos 559014). The *Nocturne* is better known as *Night Piece* and is often played with string orchestra, but the original version with string quartet has an intimate quality that remains very special. If the Piano Quartet sometimes suggests the fourth piano quartet Brahms never wrote, repeated hearings reveal more of Foote's own musical personality, and the same may be said of Quartet 1, with its echoes of Schumann and Mendelssohn spun out in wonderfully lyrical fashion. This disc too deserves a strong recommendation.

Five Poems. For piano, it is the original form of *Four Character Pieces,* and can be heard from **Virginia Eskin** (Northeastern 223, with Second Suite and piano music by Beach). Eskin does as well as anyone could hope in conveying with ten fingers all the color and Eastern atmosphere of the orchestral suite. On another disc, flutist **Fenwick Smith** is joined by pianist Randall Hodgkinson for *Sarabande and Rigadoun, Nocturne and Scherzo, Three Pieces,* and *At Dusk* (Koch 7494, with music by Copland). Foote's First Suite for piano is an early piece, nicely played by **Emily Corbato** but a trifle colorless next to its discmates by Roy Harris and Ernest Bacon (Orion 85486, LP).

Violin Sonata. Sentimental and dramatic, it gives the pianist a lot to do as well; it's played with aplomb by **Silverstein** and Kalish (New World 80542, with Beach's Violin Sonata and music by Arthur Farwell). The rest of Foote's output for violin is also highly enjoyable; five works are offered along with the Sonata in full-blooded performances by **Kevin Lawrence** and Eric Larsen (♦New World 80464). *Three Character Pieces, Melody,* and *Ballade* are also played by **Sarah Johnson** and Peter Kairoff, but her tone is a bit hard-edged for this lush music (Albany).

HALLER

Lukas Foss (b. 1922)

If you're looking for an eclectic composer equally at home in styles from neoclassicism and folk Americana to modernism and neoromanticism, try sampling the works of Lukas Foss. Unfairly dubbed "the poor man's Bernstein," Foss has created compelling works in all these forms. While his compositions aren't always successful, they're consistently intriguing. A student of Hindemith, Foss sometimes adopts the idiosyncrasies of his teacher: lush orchestrations and daring experiments, like dissonant counterpoint fused with *fugato.* Some of his late vocal works incorporate broad swatches of humor. "Humor is absolutely essential to me," he claims. "Being serious without humor is not being serious enough."

This humor makes a bold entrance in *Thirteen Ways of Looking at a Blackbird* and *Chamber Selections* (Koss 1006). In the former, Foss set absurdist poet Wallace Stevens's loopy verse to music with hilariously bizarre results. Mezzo-soprano **Evelyn LaBruce** performs the Schoenbergian *sprechtstimme* with wit and grace. In the modernist works *Paradigm* and *Curriculum Vitae with Time Bomb,* Foss satirizes academic pretension. While these chattering pieces make their points early, they're worth listening to at least once. Balancing the program are *Three Early Pieces,* romantic works Foss wishes he could still write today. The performances are warm and charming.

"Orchestral Works by Lukas Foss" is another curious amalgam, mixing two neoclassical works with an atonal symphonic poem, all conducted by **Foss** himself (New World 375). He says the opening of his *Renaissance Concerto* is "part flute cadenza, part chorale, and part circus music." Carol Wincenc performs this pastiche of Rameau, Melville, and Monteverdi well, weaving together its sprightly and melancholic moods. Baroque fanfares and antiphonal dialogues are coupled with a fugal finale in *Salomon Rossi Suite,* a not-too-challenging piece that the Brooklyn Philharmonic plays competently. The otherworldly *Orpheus and Euridice,* both ominous and dissonant, puts a modernist spin on the old fable. This programmatic score, with its knocking percussion and rumbling strings, would make excellent film music. Foss's orchestra produces unsettling effects, particularly in the duet of the ecstatic lovers, and Menuhin's keening violin is worth the price of the disc.

Ode for Orchestra, Song of Songs, and *With Music Strong* contains some of Foss's most notable music (Koss 1004). *Song of Songs* is an orchestrally dense cycle based on four of the Biblical love songs. Carolann Page sings these surprisingly secular songs competently, although a little stiffly; she downplays the eroticism in "Come, My Beloved," but skillfully conveys righteous rage in "By Night on My Bed." The early *Ode for Orchestra* is a paean to those killed in WW II; its somber mood and percussive effects owe much to Bartók's (and perhaps Lutoslawski's) *Concerto for Orchestra*. **Foss** conducts the Milwaukee Symphony Orchestra in a lean, muscular rendition. *With Music Strong* is a tour de force, beginning in minimalism and ending with luxuriant choral fugues. While about a third too long, it has intriguing compositional twists.

In his early years, Foss was entranced with American folk opera, whose era was mercifully short. Inspired by composers like Moore (*The Devil and Daniel Webster*), he wrote a folk opera based on a Mark Twain short story, *The Jumping Frog of Calaveras County*. It's an entertaining piece of Americana, despite uneven singing and a superfluous eleven-minute narration (Newport 85609). Bass Kevin Deas sings the four-flusher Stranger with delightful guile. Lulu's Song, well sung by **Julianne Baird,** portrays the character's vulnerable side. The humor in *Jumping Frog* may be hokey, but the concluding chorale is entrancing.

An excellent remastering benefits *Time Cycle, Phorion,* and *Song of Songs,* originally recorded between 1958 and 1961 (Sony 63164). **Bernstein** conducts the Columbia Symphony and New York Philharmonic in the ambitiously modernist *Time Cycle,* sung valiantly by Adele Addison, and the intriguing neoclassical/atonal *Phorion.* Tourel performs *Song of Songs* with more authority than Carolann Page. When she sings "For love is stronger than death," you believe her. (Her rendition also appears in the Bernstein "Royal Edition," Sony 47533.)   BATES

Stephen Collins Foster *(1826–1864)*

Although some of Foster's purely instrumental music has been preserved and recorded, his fame rests on his songs, which, for all their simplicity, have proved irresistible to many singers. Björling made a specialty of "I Dream of Jeannie," Paul Robeson's "Old Kentucky Home" is as bittersweet and affecting as any German lied, and even the redoubtable Dame Clara Butt once recorded a hearty, stately rendition of "Old Folks at Home." The list could be extended to include dozens of the renowned opera singers of the century, but I'll resist the impulse and focus on only the most interesting all-Foster discs.

First accolades should go to **Richard Crooks,** whose 1937 RCA recordings of ten songs have been reissued by Nimbus and other labels. The tenor is a forthright, ringing interpreter who avoids operatic excess but doesn't command much nuance. **James Melton,** about a decade later, was sweeter and more pliant, but his RCA recordings may never return. The two Nonesuch LPs with **de Gaetani** and Leslie Guinn from the '60s or '70s vitalized Foster's cause and made even sophisticated ears perk up. They addressed the songs with such deep respect and affection that the old chestnuts sounded new again, and important. De Gaetani's ethereal, haunting account of the little-known "Slumber, My Darling" is altogether exquisite, alone worth the price of the CD reissue, even with some of Vol. 2 missing (◆Nonesuch 70158).

Hampson appears to love the songs just as much, and in "American Dreamer" he brings a light, silken touch to many old favorites (◆Angel 54621). His accompanists, like those on Nonesuch, play a variety of instruments but keep their contributions modest. Not so **Robert White,** who opts for full-blown orchestral arrangements contrived by conductor Charles Gerhardt (◆RCA 5853). It may seem like a risky idea, but the tenor brings it off persuasively, with gorgeous, crystal-clear diction and tonal beauty.

More topical is a release that concentrates specifically on the Civil War songs (Helicon). The singers, led by **Linda Russell,** are unpolished but communicative; Foster wouldn't have been surprised to hear amateurs in his music. Russell is joined by **Julianne Baird,** Frederick Urrey, and others in another generous collection of fairly unusual material (◆Albany 119). Baird, an early-music stalwart, is surprisingly charming. Listeners who prefer choral arrangements of the songs (with solo interjections) should seek out the **Gregg Smith Singers** (Vox) or the **Robert Shaw Chorale** (◆RCA 61253). Both recordings have attained classic status, but Shaw's will probably be easier to find.   LUCANO

Jean Françaix *(1912–1997)*

Françaix wrote his first pieces at age 6, and many more of them after that, in every available musical genre. His best-known music has a Parisian boulevard flavor: witty, ironic, melodic, and perhaps a bit cynical—or in the words of *Grove's Dictionary,* "a very individual art, highly polished and classically reserved": Examples of this are his once-popular *Piano Concertino* (a surprising success in the atonal musical world of the '30s), the delectable oboe concerto *L'Horloge de flore* (The Flower Clock), or any of his chamber pieces for winds with or without piano.

There are three excellent recordings of *L'Horloge de flore;* your choice will depend on your taste in couplings. **John De Lancie** also does Strauss's concerto and Ibert's unusually gritty *Symphonie Concertante* (RCA 7989); **Lajos Lencsés** offers the Ibert, then switches to English horn for Honegger's *Concerto da Camera,* a work as cool and delicious as a lemon sorbet (CPO 999193); **John Anderson** (Nimbus 5330) performs the Strauss and Martinů concertos.

There are more ambitious pieces in Françaix's huge oeuvre, including a Violin Concerto (in quintuple meter throughout!) and an idiosyncratic symphony (for example, the minuet movement has a tango as its trio). Both are available in very enjoyable performances led by **Françaix** (Erol 97002); he also leads a recording of his Piano Concerto (at 17 minutes almost twice as long as the *Concertino*) with his daughter Claude in an extremely variable collection of French piano concertos (Vox 5110). She plays her father's delightful *Concertino* with **Dorati** (Mercury 434333). In addition, he leads his Suite for Violin and Orchestra (Vox 5114) and Rhapsody for Viola and Small Orchestra (Koch). *Symphonie d'Archets* (for bows, i.e., string orchestra) is exceedingly well written in a tidy, neoclassical way. The **Arion Ensemble**'s performance is pretty good (Ottavo 109459), but as with its discmate, Frank Martin's *Etudes,* I hope for a recording by a top-notch, large string orchestra.

Françaix is in the category of 20th-century composers whose works musicians love to play—and if they play wind instruments, they're particularly well served. There are quite a few collections available, and most performances are equal to the music's lightness and wit. Outstanding are a collection from the **Prague Wind Quintet** (◆Praga 250126) and a selection of flute music with **Astrid Frohlich** (◆Orfeo 388961). An ideal introduction is the **Gaudier Ensemble**'s dapper performances of the Clarinet Quintet, the suite *L'Heure du Berger,* and the Octet, composed for exactly the same forces as Schubert's—imaginative chamber music society programmers, please note (◆Hyperion 67036).

Françaix also wrote operas, ballets, and an oratorio on the most unboulevardier subject of *L'Apocalypse de St. Jean,* but only the last is currently available (Wergo 6632).   RAYMOND

César Franck *(1822–1890)*

Just as French and German influences unite in the name of Belgian-born César Franck, so do 19th-century classicism and romanticism in his music. Nor is that the only uneasy dichotomy in his life. A piano prodigy as a child, he nonetheless proved to be a late bloomer as a composer; his finest pieces date from his last two decades, and though today he's probably best remembered for his orchestral music, for the greater part of his career he earned his living as an organist. Even at this late date people tend either to love his music or hate it, and even those who love it are unlikely to love all of it. But happily there is plenty of each to choose from.

SYMPHONY

"The expression of impotence pushed to dogmatic lengths" was how Gounod dismissed Franck's Symphony in D Minor at its premiere in 1889. Well, Gounod's symphonies are largely forgotten, but Franck's, despite (or maybe because of) its odd combination of Wagnerian mysticism and Bachian rigor, is alive and well in both our concert halls and the record catalog, though its popularity was perhaps even greater a generation or two ago.

Then as now, the conventional wisdom was that the 1961 **Monteux/Chicago Symphony** recording was pretty much the last word on the subject, and I certainly wouldn't want to be without it (♦RCA 63303). Here, in their sole stereo collaboration, the Reiner-trained CSO lends a Germanic heft to the French maître's idiomatic grasp of the work's classical/romantic underpinnings that's really quite striking. But that's not the only way Monteux conducted the piece, as anyone who knows his two earlier recordings with the San Francisco Symphony can attest. There the classicism was invested with a Gallic lightness and fluency only fleetingly apparent in the stereo remake. Unfortunately neither is available today, but you can get a fair approximation of their effect from, of all people, **Boult,** whose beautifully proportioned 1960 Reader's Digest account can be heard in first-class sound in a generally outstanding all-Franck CD (♦Chesky 87).

From the same generation of conductors, **Beecham** likewise brought a classical-cum-romantic sensibility to this piece, though only his 1940 78 rpm recording is available at present (♦Dutton 2003, 2CD), finely proportioned if without the clarity of his 1957 mono remake. (There was also a stereo redo from 1959: EMI 63396, with Lalo's Symphony.) **Toscanini,** not surprisingly, was the most classically controlled of all and is still worth hearing (♦RCA 60320). However, the same concept was even more successfully realized by **Cantelli**—in full stereo—in an RCA recording most recently available on EMI.

At the opposite pole is **Stokowski,** whose blatantly Wagnerian view can be heard at its most resplendent in a reissue of his 1970 "Phase-4" recording (♦Cala 0525). Here II is deliberately soft, with a sinuous center, and despite some taffy-pulling in the middle, the finale has genuine lift and drama, though not as much as in the live concert performance from a few days earlier (Music & Arts). Nor as much as in **Paray**'s various recordings, where the music blazes to life almost from the very first bar (in stereo on Mercury 434368, with Rachmaninoff's Symphony 2).

Munch likewise brought a keen sense of drama, and speed, to the symphony. At present his Boston Symphony recording can be had only as an import, coupled with his incendiary *Chasseur maudit* (♦RCA 29256). But there is an even more intense concert recording from Montreal—despite its 1967 date, in mono only—even if the shrillish Audivis CD is harder on the ear than the cleaner but no longer available Disques Montaigne issue. **Giulini** also made several recordings, two of which are currently listed. The first, from 1957, is not unlike Beecham's but with a greater sense of warmth and plasticity (♦EMI 67723, 2CD). The second, from 1993, takes the Italian maestro's tendency to slow down over the years to the point of unlistenability (Sony 58958). The

monumental **Klemperer,** by contrast, is also slow but manages to convey not only the music's nobility and strength but a fair amount of its warmth and lyricism as well (♦EMI 66824).

Though less rock-solid than **Mengelberg** at his best (look for the Biddulph CD), **Bernstein,** with the New York Philharmonic, recaptures some of the Dutch conductor's steel and fire in what is basically a romantic conception (♦Sony 47548). His remake with the French National Orchestra is even more overt in that regard, heightening the mystery and the ecstasy but also the air of over-indulgence (DG 445512). **Ormandy,** for his part, is reliably strong, if also a bit heavy and unimaginative; still, at the bargain price you could do worse, especially given the couplings, **Robert Casadesus**'s *Symphonic Variations* and **E. Power Biggs**'s *Pièce heroïque* (Sony 60287). Other veterans include **Fournet,** uncharacteristically plodding and lifeless (Denon), and **Barbirolli,** whose recording has clarity and feeling but somehow fails to come together (Supraphon). Nor am I partial to **Silvestri,** smeary and bombastic, with ultra-*misterioso* strings (Royal Classics).

Masur is also on the heavy side, though his finale is strong (Teldec 74863). Better are **Maazel,** vital and direct without being unduly rigid (♦DG 449720), **López-Cobos,** also a bit heavy but impressively played and recorded (♦Telarc 80247), and the darkly grandiose **d'Avalos,** a mite fulsome in places but wonderfully romantic and openhearted (♦ASV 708). **Comissiona** also leans toward the romantic but without the same sense of immersion (e.g., the odd tempo shifts in I and III), nor does his orchestra play as cleanly as some, despite some lovely tone-spinning in II (Vanguard).

The historically minded will not want to overlook **Furtwängler** or **Rodzinski,** the first represented by two very different performances (Arlecchino 140) and the second by a 1945 New York Philharmonic concert rendition (Iron Needle) that, though not so clearly recorded, is of a piece with his powerfully projected commercial recordings, both long out of print. The budget-minded will not want to overlook the earlier of two Naxos CDs, alertly conducted by the largely unheralded **Guenter Neuhold** (♦550155), who proves far more alive to this music's shadings and thrust than **Roberto Benzi,** here curiously underwhelming (553631).

OTHER ORCHESTRAL MUSIC

Le Chasseur maudit (*The Accursed Huntsman*). When it comes to the tone poems, anyone springing for Boult's Symphony will also acquire **Massimo Freccia**'s splendidly dramatic *Chasseur,* with some striking antiphonal effects (Chesky), even if it's not in the same league as **Munch**'s (♦RCA 68978) or **López-Cobos**'s, with its huge bell climax and impulsive chase (♦Telarc 80247). However, the grandest, most blazingly alive *Chasseur* of the digital era is **Muti**'s, until recently available in a CD that appended it to Karajan's somewhat bloated accounts of the Symphony and, with Weissenberg, Symphonic Variations (EMI). (Originally it was paired with Muti's perhaps overly youthful view of the Symphony.)

Among others, **Benzi** is as unenlivening here as he is in the Symphony (Naxos). Not **Fournet,** however, who, though a little weak initially, strikes sparks later on (Supraphon 110613)—more, in fact, than **Ansermet** (London) or **Cluytens** (EMI 65153), who are nonetheless blessed with orchestras sympathetic to their aims and an abiding sense of the Franck idiom. Especially so is Ansermet, who is equally in touch with *Les Eolides,* Franck's wistful evocation of the heavenly breezes (♦London 452890), where he marginally outclasses **Masur** (Teldec) and, not so marginally, Benzi (Naxos).

Ce qu'on entend sur la montagne (*What One Hears on the Mountain*). Another nature-inspired symphonic poem, it is available in a disc led by **Brian Priestman** and **Alfred Walter** that also includes Henri Büesser's orchestrations of eight small harmonium pieces (♦Koch Schwann 311105). Neither the disc nor the liner specifies who does what, but everyone seems to do his work with a will, particularly in the tone painting, so early that it anticipates Liszt's treatment of the same Victor Hugo poem.

Les Djinns. **Fournet** is likewise on top of this unlikely portrait of Arabian spirits for piano and orchestra also based on Hugo (♦Supraphon 110613). So is **Kamu** (♦BIS 137), who profits additionally from superior sound, if not a superior pianist—the lyrical Kerstin Aberg vs. Fournet's incisive František Maxian. As a performance, however, neither is a patch on the demonic but poorly recorded **Richter/Kondrashin** (Revelation 10048).

Psyché. Despite the prominence of the keyboard part, Franck classified *Les Djinns* as a "poème symphonique," as he did the multi-part *Psyché*, which besides the orchestra involves a chorus and, when performed complete, exceeds the Symphony in length. Happily that's how **Tadaaki Otaka** gives it to us, in an expansively shaped and recorded traversal of the entire piece (♦Chandos 9342). Others—Toscanini, for one—may have invested some of its pages with more drama and sensuality (definitely an element in this product of Franck's final years), but none have more completely enwrapped the listener in *Psyché*'s otherworldly serenity, and here that counts for a lot. It's capped, moreover, by yet another worthy *Chasseur*, softer in outline than most but with a subliminal power that, in the climaxes, registers with considerable impact.

CONCERTOS

As a touring piano virtuoso, Franck turned out two concertos in his youth, only the second of which has survived. Written when he was 13, it reflects the early German romanticism of Beethoven and Weber more than anything we associate with the mature Franck, and can be heard coupled with the even earlier *Variations brillantes* on a theme from Auber's opera *Gustave III* (♦Koch Schwann 311105). As played by pianist **Jean-Claude Vanden Eynden,** the latter's Chopinesque virtuosity is impressive but the variations themselves don't always hang together, in striking contrast to Franck's best-known work for piano and orchestra, the Symphonic Variations of 1885.

As with the Symphony, it's an older generation that has the most to say about this piece, beginning with **Cortot** and **Gieseking** in the 78 rpm era. Even among stereo recordings, it's hard to do better than **Curzon** or **Rubinstein,** the first combining strength and intelligence (♦Decca 466376) and the second animation and charm (♦RCA 61496). Among lower-priced issues, don't overlook **Casadesus/Ormandy** (in which the former's to-the-point pianism balances the latter's portentousnesses) (Sony 60287), the songful **Thiolier/de Almeida** (Naxos 550754), or the imposing **Fleisher/Szell,** mono only but still among the very best (♦CBS 37812).

CHAMBER MUSIC

Violin Sonata. Franck's Violin Sonata is still the most important and enduring work of its kind to come out of 19th-century France. Perhaps that's why it has been so well served on records. Indeed, you can almost choose your favorite fiddler in this piece, though some seem better suited to its uniquely recessive romanticism than others.

None more so than **Thibaud,** however, whose ultra-French reading with Cortot still sets the standard stylistically, its faded 1929 sound

notwithstanding (♦Strings 99353). By contrast, **Heifetz** never seemed a paragon of French style, yet his 1937 recording with Rubinstein is remarkable for its smoothly assured yet impassioned fiddling, as well as the latter's extroverted approach to the piano part (Strings 99325). Neither quite equals **Oistrakh** and Richter, though, who wring nearly every last drop of emotion from the writing in a live performance from 1966 that suffers from an ill-balanced mono pickup (♦Revelation 10048). Better recorded is the same violinist's early-'50s studio recording with Oborin, more contained technically and emotionally but also a bit more incisive in the finale (♦Vanguard 4080/2, 3CD). Also in the special class is a 1973 private recording with **Szeryng** and Katz (which, despite its date, sounds like mono), its sweet deliberation tugging powerfully at the heart (♦Cembal d'Amour 105).

Among the younger generation, **Perlman**'s 1969 recording with Ashkenazy continues to hold an honored place in the catalog, wonderfully poised and heartfelt even if the pianist seems a mite restrained (♦London 414128 or 452887). That complaint can't be leveled at Perlman's latest partner, Argerich, who ends up driving the proceedings in an edgily exciting live performance that often finds the two temperamentally at odds (EMI 56815). Conversely, **Shaham**'s warmly ardent traversal with Oppitz is almost too beautiful, its ravishing lyricism blunting some of the music's edges (♦DG 429729). Still, the sound itself is hard to resist, as with the gorgeously silken **Chung,** who profits from Lupu's sensitive yet involving pianism (♦London 421154). **Midori,** on the other hand, is surprisingly uninvolving in this piece, to the point of being downright dull (Sony).

Neither does **Mutter** (who leans into the writing with a will, if you can stand her vibrato) (DG 445826), nor **Zukerman** shrink from the task, even if the end result is more to be admired than loved (RCA 62697). **Suk** is gloriously expansive (♦Koch 920306); **Stern** is mostly clean and straightforward (Sony). **Mordkovitch**'s articulation is a bit stretched out, but she draws the listener into the writing (Chandos), as does **Arturo Delmoni**'s intimately scaled reading (♦John Marks 8), though the economy-minded will probably prefer the tonally less refined **Takako Nishizaki** (Naxos).

Nor have other instruments been loath to adopt this piece as their own. Still, for all **Du Pré**'s virtuosity, her cello sits heavily on the Sonata, weighing down its high-flown lyricism (EMI). Happily, **David Finckel** brings a lighter touch, along with a more naturally balanced recording (♦ArtistLed 19602). With the flute, however, the choice lies between the plummy-toned **Galway** (RCA) and the more tightly focused **Julius Baker** (VAIA). Somewhere in the middle comes the viola, with **Imai** weaving the finale together nicely (Chandos).

Piano Quintet. Apart from the Sonata, Franck's most successful chamber work is probably the Piano Quintet from 1879, and here the low-priced choice is competitive with the best. The half-lights and nuanced shadings of the Quator Ludwig with pianist **Michael Levinas** bring out the music's subtlety as well as its passion (♦Naxos 553645). Nor should you overlook **Rogé** and friends, sharper in outline and generally more intense (♦ASV 769). For intensity per se, no one matches the streamlined brilliance of the Hollywood Quartet with **Victor Aller,** in still-impressive mono (♦Testament 1077). However, **Cortot** and the International Quartet take the stylistic palm, if not the technical prize (Biddulph 029).

String Quartet. The more ponderous String Quartet is not on the same level as the Quintet, though the **Juilliard Quartet** makes a compelling case for it (♦Sony 63302), as opposed to the grainier **Bartholdy Quartet** (Christophorus).

Piano Trios. I wouldn't have minded more extroverted performances of the Piano Trios than the **Bekova Sisters** offer (Chandos 9680 and 9742). Nonetheless, it's remarkable how much Op. 1:1 (despite the numbering, not the earliest of these pieces) foreshadows the masterpieces of the composer's later years, and their lighter approach is welcome in Op. 1:2, with its salon-like middle movements. (Op. 1:3 sort of mixes the two.)

PIANO MUSIC

Hough's fluidity and insight make his disc the finest in the current catalog, capturing everything from the Bach-á-la-Liszt grandeur of the *Prélude, Choral et Fugue* to the wistful lyricism of the earlier *Plaintes d'une poupée* (Doll's Lament) (♦Hyperion 66918). However, if the *Prélude, Choral et Fugue* is your prime concern, there are also recordings by **Perahia** (Sony), **Cherkassky** (Nimbus), and **Moravec** (VAIA and Philips) to consider. The first is notable for its sparkle and substance (especially in the *Choral*), the second for its nobility, and the third for its volcanic splendor. After them come **Pratt** (EMI)—individual, but he certainly brings the *Fugue* to life—and **Kissin** (RCA), beautifully played but interpretively still a work in progress. (There is also an orchestral version, filling out Neuhold's Naxos CD of the Symphony.)

GOODFELLOW

ORGAN MUSIC

Franck's reputation as one of the greatest composers for the organ rests almost entirely on a mere twelve pieces: Six Pieces, published in 1868; Three Pieces, written in 1878 for the inauguration of the Cavaillé-Coll organ at the Palais du Trocadéro; and Three Chorales of 1890. However, he wrote many others. The *Andantino in G Minor* (1857) has almost become part of the canon with the Twelve; some short pieces appeared in periodicals in 1859 and 1867, and at the time of his death he was working on *L'Organiste,* a set of short liturgical pieces suitable for organ or harmonium. In 1905, 44 *Pièces Posthumes* written around 1860 were published, and others have surfaced, most recently a substantial Piece in A, published for the first time in 1990. None of these, however, can begin to displace the Twelve as the summit of Franck's organ compositions, and for many years, recordings of them have been issued as the complete works for organ. More recently artists have been including a selection from the others for recordings that might be described as Twelve-plus.

The sound of the French romantic organ is virtually synonymous with the instruments built by Aristide Cavaillé-Coll (1811–1899). We know that Franck had the Cavaillé-Coll sound in mind for his major organ works, and he left detailed registration instructions. While it's true that they can be played convincingly on instruments from other builders and times, I feel that recordings of well-preserved Cavaillé-Coll instruments have an authority in this repertory that most others can only approximate.

Jeanne Demessieux's 1959 recording of the Twelve, playing the Cavaillé-Coll at La Madeleine, Paris, is a long-time favorite (♦Festivo 155, 2CD). The recorded sound is excellent for its time, more listenable than some more recent, and her interpretations are outstanding. The dramatic works are fiery, while the quieter and more reflective ones are sensitive and lyrical, never perfunctory. At times her quick tempos are faster than they need to be, but these performances have all the conviction of an artist who is speaking her native musical language without a trace of self-consciousness.

Another attractive and sensitive recording of more recent vintage (1998) is by **Louis Robilliard** (♦Festivo 6921.702, 3CD). In addition to the Twelve, he plays the *Andantino in G Minor* and eight selections from *L'Organiste* on two Cavaillé-Coll organs: St. François de Sales, Lyon, and St. Sernin, Toulouse. The recorded sound is excellent. The St. Sernin organ comes across with richness and warmth; the St. François instrument sounds slightly less refined with more action noise, but it too has a fine sound. Tempos are well-chosen, avoiding extremes. I could wish for a more manic *Grande Pièce Symphonique*—it was, after all, dedicated to Alkan—but on the whole Robilliard gives almost no cause for complaint.

Daniel Roth has recorded the Twelve-plus on three outstanding Cavaillé-Coll organs: St. Mary's at San Sebastian in the Basque region of Spain, an instrument strikingly similar to the original St. Clotilde organ where Franck presided; the cathedral at Saint-Brieuc; and the gigantic organ at St. Sulpice in Paris, where Roth is organist (♦Motette 11381, 11391, 11401). These discs include the first recording of the Piece in A. Roth's tempos are decidedly on the slow side, and one of my colleagues has described his performances as "sluggish" and "pedestrian." However, I hear them as spacious, with a flexibility and nuance in phrasing that produce remarkable coherence even at slow tempos, unfolding depths of meaning in the music that might be glossed over at too fast a tempo. The recent discovery of the composer's hand-written metronome marks for Six Pieces, indicating tempos far faster than anyone would have thought, doesn't change my judgment in this case.

Jean Guillou produced a very controversial recording of the Twelve for release in 1990 to mark the centenary of Franck's death (Dorian 90135, 2CD). He plays the imposing Van den Heuvel organ at St. Eustache, Paris, where he is organist. Some listeners regard these performances as the greatest ever recorded. I find them unbearably quirky and self-indulgent—more Guillou than Franck. He freely alters Franck's registrations to produce colorful effects that sometimes strike me as tasteless and grotesque. Guillou's interpretations are undoubtedly bold, but I think they show more audacity than artistic sensibility.

Another centenary release of the Twelve is by **Michael Murray** on the Cavaillé-Coll at St. Sernin, Toulouse, a magnificent instrument superbly recorded (Telarc 80234, 2CD). These are solid and dependable performances, but somewhat dispassionate and unexciting, with little drama or lyricism. The 1977 LP by **Marie-Claire Alain** has been superseded by her 1995 set of the Twelve on the Cavaillé-Coll at St. Etienne, Caen (Erato 12706, 2CD). The performances are uneven in quality; best are *Grande Pièce Symphonique, Prelude, Fugue, and Variation,* and *Fantasy in C.* There are some fine moments in *Three Chorales,* but *Cantabile in B* and *Fantasy in A* misfire completely. The recorded sound is unpleasant—rather blatant with no real pianissimos and at times very unclear. Anyone who doesn't already love the Cavaillé-Coll sound is unlikely to be won over by this recording. Some other recordings of this instrument sound better, like the 1990 disc by **Kåre Nordstoga** of *Three Chorales* and *Grande Pièce Symphonique* (Simax 1072).

A recent addition to the catalog is a Twelve-plus recording by **Bram Beekman** on the Cavaillé-Coll at Perpignan Cathedral (Lindenberg 91, 3CD). Among the best works is the third of Franck's preliminary versions of *Fantasy in C,* which I almost prefer to the final version in Six Pieces. Beekman's performances are understated but with considerable subtlety. They will repay the attention of the connoisseur, but I suspect most listeners will find them rather dull. **André Isoir**'s 1975 recordings at Luçon Cathedral have been reissued (Calliope 9920 and 9921), but the recorded sound is not as massive as you expect from a Cavaillé-Coll. His tempos tend to be slow but not plodding, except perhaps in the *Cantabile,* where he's so slow that the phrases don't hang together. These two discs contain only eleven of the Twelve—the *Pastorale* is omitted.

Jean Langlais was Franck's third successor as organist of St. Clotilde, and his 1963 recording there of the Twelve has been reissued (GIA 272, 2CD). While touted as the "original Franck organ," the St. Clotilde instrument was so substantially altered that historians no longer consider it a genuine Cavaillé-Coll. Moreover, the recorded sound is poor; it's very dark and booming, at times sounding almost electronic. It seems as if the tone has been artificially manipulated during the remastering, and there are some very clumsy edits. This is an important historical document, since Langlais studied these works with Albert Mahaut, a Franck pupil. It's a pity the recording itself is not better.

David Sanger recorded the Twelve plus *Andantino in G Minor* at the Katarina Church in Stockholm (BIS 214, 2CD). This instrument, destroyed in a fire in 1990, was built in the mid-'70s, but included pipework from the 18th and 19th centuries. It had a warm and clear sound, well suited to the romantic repertoire, though its upperwork was over-bright for Franck and the reed were a bit clinical. Another defect is the lack of a *voix humaine,* a very distinctive color that Franck calls for in four of the Twelve. Sanger is best in the exuberant pieces, bringing to them a good sense of drama and excitement, but less convincing in the quieter and more reflective pieces. While this may not be the ideal recording of Franck, it's a precious document of a fine instrument that can never be heard again.

Another recording of the Twelve plus *Andantino in G Minor* was made in 1997 by **Gillian Weir** on the Frobenius organ at Arhus Cathedral in Denmark (Collins 70442, 3CD). The reeds were imported from France and the foundation stops are so dark and grave that only the sharpest-eared purist would notice any significant difference between this instrument and one of Cavaillé-Coll's masterpieces. Weir's performances have an aristocratic bearing but are not at all stiff or cold. Not all her tempos seem quite right to me, but tastes differ. She brings an impressive grace and lyricism to *Cantabile,* though I find the B minor Chorale and *Grande Pièce Symphonique* less convincing. Overall, it's a very fine set.

There are many recordings of selections from the organ works, and while space doesn't permit even a cursory consideration of them here, there is at least one whose historical significance demands mention. **Marcel Dupré** recorded *Three Chorales* and *Pièce Héroïque* in 1957 on the Aeolian-Skinner organ at St. Thomas Church, New York (Mercury/Philips 434311). While I find his Franck rather hard-edged and unromantic, this reissue is an important document of one of the great organists of the 20th century, whose influence on Franck interpretation was far-reaching.   GATENS

Benjamin Frankel *(1906–1973)*

Frankel is noted as a composer of dark-hued, exquisitely shaded orchestral and chamber works. He adopted Schoenberg's principles of twelve-tone row notation at an early stage, becoming liberalized rather than constrained by them; this gave free reign to his highly distinctive and rich orchestral palette and contrapuntal mastery. His eight symphonies form the core of his output, together with five string quartets, all now recorded, but his many-faceted creativity extended to film music, jazz, and the theater. Although he was born and spent his life in England, his musical language clearly reflects some of the more radical developments in Europe between the '30s and '50s while successfully avoiding any tendency toward arid intellectualism. His music has immediate appeal, is always profound, and its controlled inner tension and drama occasionally burst forth with monumental grandeur.

All currently available recordings are from CPO, most of them with the Queensland Symphony led by **Albert.** For the eight symphonies, all mature works from the late '50s onward, Albert's series is a triumph. No. 1 is a highly complex, layered work with multitonal elements that never forsakes poetic utterance (999240). It's coupled with *May Day Overture* and Symphony 5, whose smooth, silky surface and intense, warm lyricism give some idea of Frankel's expressive range. These are very creditable performances of exacting repertoire, and the orchestra and conductor expend the right amount of time and effort exploring mood and essence rather than overt gesture and effect. The same can also be said of 4 and 6, with the *pièce d'occasion Mephistopheles' Serenade* (999242).

No. 4 is more direct and straightforward, with a pastoral lilt, while 6 explores a range of contrasts between long, sinuous subjects and ironic scherzos. 2 is by far the longest and perhaps the most searching and thoughtful, whereas the one-movement 3 that accompanies it is not only the shortest but also the most upbeat (999241). Although temporarily out of the catalog, this will be reissued in 2001 in a boxed set of all eight, to coincide with the release of the final disc of 7 and 8 (999243).

If each of the symphonies has its own distinctive character, so do the concertante works. The wonderful Violin Concerto, written for and dedicated to Max Rostal, is one of the most evocative elegies to the victims of the Holocaust, brilliantly played by **Ulf Hoelscher.** The late Viola Concerto exploits the sultry sensuality of the instrument to the full with glinting nocturnal suggestion. The brief *Serenata Concertante* for piano trio and orchestra is all caprice. This disc is very highly recommended, as is an appealing collection of music for string orchestra with the Northwest Chamber Orchestra of Seattle under **Alun Francis** (999221). Frankel's intimate style is at its most eloquent in the marvelous cycle of string quartets played by the **Nomos Quartet** (999420, 2CD). Each reveals a different facet of character, and all are masterly.

Of Frankel's 100 or so incidental and film scores, *Battle of the Bulge* is one of the most memorable war film scores of the last 40 years. The release of the complete music (nearly 80 minutes) reveals a work of truly symphonic dimensions (999696). The discovery and exploration of Frankel's music on CD is a significant landmark in recorded contemporary music.   JOHNSON

Girolamo Frescobaldi *(1583–1643)*

Frescobaldi is probably best-known today for his remarkable keyboard works, which are numerous and highly inventive. His keyboard music was very influential and his influence was extended through his teaching. He was reputed to be a rather impetuous young man— his first child was born out of wedlock, and his second nearly so. A whiff of scandal seems to cloud the earlier part of his career, but following his marriage he rose steadily in the ranks of society. He was one of the greatest keyboard virtuosos of his time, but appears to have been rather limited in other respects, uncultured and lacking in either social skills or business acumen.

Frescobaldi published his first book of *Canzoni da sonare* for one to four instruments and continuo in 1628, at a time when this form was quite out of fashion. He brought the instrumental song based on the French chanson to its summit, and these works are full of invention and delight. They can be heard complete, performed by recorder virtuoso **Kees Boeke** and the early music ensemble Tripla Concordia: Vol. 1 contains all the canzoni written for two basses (♦Nuova Era 7131), Vol. II the remainder (♦Nuova Era 7250/51, 2CD). These discs are filled with wonderful playing and the music is continually fresh and interesting.

Frescobaldi's music for solo keyboard comprises the largest and most important part of his huge body of work, and there are a number of ways to approach this music. For those who simply wish to sample it, I recommend the recital offered by **Sophie Yates**, "Romanesca—Italian Music for the Harpsichord" (♦Chandos 0601). Here Yates presents a selection of Frescobaldi's works, framed by pieces by other Italian composers of that era. The disc is wonderfully varied and gives a superb snapshot of Italian keyboard music of this time. **Shirley Mathews** takes a different tack, presenting a recital of works from a single year of Frescobaldi's career, 1637 (♦Gasparo 241). They are fully mature, and Mathews plays them beautifully, bringing out all their abrupt shifts of mood. Her instrument has an especially nasal timbre, emphasizing the pungent quality of the music.

Gustav Leonhardt recorded two very important recitals. One is a grab-bag of toccatas, ricercars, partitas, and other forms composed in Frescobaldi's mid-career (♦Philips 432128, NA). Everything in this 1990 recital is performed on harpsichord. He takes a fairly measured approach, although tempos on this disc are somewhat faster than on the other one, recorded in 1979, which presents Frescobaldi's first book of *Capricci*, published in 1624 (♦Deutsche Harmonia Mundi 77071, NA). Leonhardt plays about a third of these pieces on organ, including one with an obbligato baritone part sung by Harry van der Kamp. His harpsichord has a more pungent timbre here than the one he used in the Philips recording. With many of Frescobaldi's works it's not absolutely clear what instrument they are intended to be played on, with most musicians deciding for themselves which are most grateful for either harpsichord or organ. The eminent Baroque scholar **John Butt** has also recorded this book of *Capricci,* but chooses to play all of them on organ (♦Harmonia Mundi 7907178).

The Canadian harpsichordist **Scott Ross** recorded an exceptionally fine recital of "Toccatas and Danses," briefly available as an import and well worth searching for (♦EMI 49844, NA). Ross was a consummate artist, and his musicianship is sorely missed. During his short career, he made many fine recordings, and this is an excellent example of his artistry. "Toccate Libro II, 1627" is a single-disc survey of toccatas by **Lorenzo Ghielmi** (♦Nuova Era 6799). His playing is excellent; he elects to play five of the twelve on organ.

Those who favor complete sets will want the comprehensive survey of Frescobaldi's keyboard music undertaken by **Sergio Vartolo** and others for Tactus. Vols. 1 and 2 (Tactus 580780, 580704, both 3CD) offer the complete *Toccate e partite d'involatura* published in 1637. Vartolo's seeks to be as complete as possible, and so in pieces that are based on a particular aria, such as *Partita sopra l'aria della Francesca,* that aria is included ahead of the piece, sung by an uncredited singer. Vartolo's musicianship is fine, but I prefer the performances of that specific piece by Ross and Yates, and Mathews for others. Tactus continues their series with "Canzoni all Francesca" exuberantly played by **Roberto Loreggian.** These keyboard canzoni are sparkling, highly inventive works related to the *canzoni di sonare,* but are intended to be played by a single musician.

Frescobaldi is not as well known for his vocal music, but a collection of his complete motets shows that there is much to be enjoyed (♦Tactus 580602). He was much more conservative in his vocal writing, and these works are more measured and reserved than his keyboard music. Most of them are settings for only one or two singers and are beautifully rendered by the early music group L'Aura Soave under the direction of **Diego Cantalupi.** McINTIRE

Johann Jacob Froberger (1616–1667)

Froberger is a prominent figure in mid-17th-century keyboard music, held in high esteem by musicians during his life—about which very little is known—and afterwards. We know that he studied in Vienna and with Frescobaldi in Rome, and that he traveled widely and worked as a court musician for various nobles. He is known primarily for his keyboard music; only two non-keyboard works are extant. He wrote in the common Italian forms of the day, such as toccatas, ricercars, canzonas, and French-influenced suites. His 30 suites are the foundation of his considerable reputation. His gift for thematic invention is said to have influenced Bach and seems to lead directly to that master's great fugue subjects. Froberger's contrapuntal technique is quite conservative, and his music is more sober and less dramatic than that of his teacher Frescobaldi, but he was instrumental in helping to establish a unique German keyboard style.

Several satisfying recitals are available. Harpsichordist **Sophie Yates** has compiled a wonderful introduction to Froberger with "Tombeau—German Harpsichord Music of the Seventeenth Century" (Chandos 0596). She presents a broad selection of the suites plus a few toccatas, interspersed with short pieces by other German composers of the time. Yates plays with obvious enthusiasm and great technical polish, and the disc is beautifully sequenced for contrast and variety. **David Cates** offers a superb all-Froberger disc with a good variety of the various genre pieces: four suites, plus a handful of toccatas and lamentations. Cates plays with an honest sensitivity and elegance in this highly enjoyable recital and his harpsichords are beautifully recorded (♦Wildboar 9701).

The great **Gustav Leonhardt** plays this music with more gravity than Yates or Cates, but with great freedom and authority. He has recorded two superb collections, both containing a good mix of toccatas, suites, *canzonas,* and other forms. The first is deleted but worth hunting for (Deutsche Harmonia Mundi 7923); the second is still available (Sony 62732). Both are excellent representations of this composer's work, and Leonhardt's artistry and temperament are ideally suited to it.

In the late '70s **Kenneth Gilbert** recorded Suites 1–6 and *Lamentation,* and *Ferdinand III* in a distinguished disc (DG Archiv 437080, NA). His interpretations are perhaps a shade more expressive than Leonhardt's but never inappropriate or excessive. **Shirley Mathews**'s recital offers six of the suites, two toccatas, and the *Lamentation.* Her musicianship is impeccable, comparing well to Gilbert and Leonhardt, and her instrument has a particularly full low register that is beautifully recorded and suits the melancholy air of the music (Gasparo 299).

McINTIRE

Wilhelm Furtwängler (1886–1954)

Furtwängler may be famous as a conductor, but he regarded himself primarily as a composer. His idiom was late Romantic, the main influences being Reger for harmony and Bruckner for symphonic form. In his teens and early 20s, he composed many songs, piano and chamber pieces, and a few choral and orchestral works, but each new performance brought devastating reviews. After the failure of his *Te Deum* in 1910, he was unable to complete any new work for more than 20 years. Only after he had fallen into disfavor with the Nazi authorities in 1934 did his muse break free again; thereafter he composed several large-scale chamber and orchestral works.

Alfred Walter conducts Furtwängler's early orchestral works (Marco Polo 223645) and the early choral music including the *Te Deum,* coupled with the early songs, sung by tenor **Guido Pikal** (Marco Polo 223546). The musical quality of all these works is at times dreadfully poor.

Furtwängler's later music displays a greater command of form and orchestration, but all too often sounds like late Bruckner reharmonized by Reger and played at the bottom of a swamp. All the late chamber works—the two violin sonatas and the Piano Quintet—have been recorded, the latter in a fine performance by **François Kerdoncuff** and **Quatuor Sine Nomine** (♦Timpani 1018). All three symphonies and the Piano Concerto have been recorded by Walter (Marco Polo), and the Concerto by Edwin Fischer (Dante 125). Not surprisingly, the best interpreter is **Furtwängler** himself, who manages to impart an air of greatness to his Symphony 2 in his 1953 recording with the Vienna Philharmonic (♦Orfeo 375-941). WALTON

Giovanni Gabrieli (ca. 1555–1612)

Gabrieli is associated with some of the grandest, most stirring sounds in the musical universe, yet he is only now beginning to be valued at his true worth. In his native Italy he has never been given his due; even in his lifetime he was never the top musician in Venice, only first organist at San Marco—in succession to his uncle Andrea—and after his death his countrymen did little to keep his name alive. Fortunately he was much better appreciated in Germany where he studied with Lassus in Bavaria in 1575–79. Gabrieli's most famous pupil was Heinrich Schütz—and so he has never been forgotten. In the past few decades a number of fine choral recordings have been made and some skillful players have revived the techniques that make Gabrieli's instrumental music so exciting. The clarity of digital recording has also helped to bring his famous antiphonal effects to a new generation.

To deal first with some of the traditional performances using modern instruments, Columbia's gamble in taking the Texas Boys' Choir, Gregg Smith Singers, Edward Tarr Brass Ensemble, and organist E. Power Biggs to San Marco in 1967 really paid off. Gabrieli in San Marco still sounds terrific (Sony 62426). The performers, helped by **Vittorio Negri**'s firm conducting, seem inspired by their surroundings and the choral singing is excellent. Amazingly, **Biggs**'s selection of the organ music from a decade earlier is still its only substantial representation and survives by reason of the player's outsized personality (Sony 62353). On the other hand, the famous conjunction of Chicago, Cleveland, and Philadelphia brass players organized by Columbia in 1968, also with Biggs, still sounds spectacular in its way but no longer seems truly Gabrielian (Sony 62353).

Even worse are two relatively recent discs by the London Symphony Brass under **Eric Crees** that sound careful and a little dull (Naxos). The best of Gabrieli on modern brass still comes from the **Philip Jones Brass Ensemble**, and some of these players' best work can be heard in "The Glory of Venice." It shows every sign of having been thrown together from two different '80s LPs, and the singing of the Choir of King's College, Cambridge, in the choral pieces is a little too polite, but the brass playing is breathtaking in its precision (Decca 448993).

Two discs on period instruments bring the sonorous side of Gabrieli's instrumental genius to thrilling fruition. His Majesty's Sagbutts and Cornetts—actually including a few strings as well—are expertly directed in the 16 Canzonas and Sonatas from the 1597 Sacrae Symphoniae by **Timothy Roberts**, who himself plays five organ pieces (Hyperion 66908).

Concerto Palatino, led by the brilliant cornettist Bruce Dickey and trombonist Charles Toet, play eight pieces from Sacrae Symphoniae and eight from the Canzoni e sonate that were published after Gabrieli's death, as well as two other pieces (Harmonia Mundi 901688). This fine group also joins the choral ensemble Currende in a splendid disc of music for double choir by Gabrieli and Adriaan Willaert; Gabrieli has the lion's share of the program, and one of the instrumental Canzone is included for variety (Accent 93101).

"Venice Preserved" is the apt title for an enjoyable mixed program of choral and instrumental music by Andrea and Giovanni Gabrieli, members of the Bassano clan, and Monteverdi, featuring the Gentlemen of the Chapell and His Majesty's Sagbutts and Cornetts under a modern representative of the famous family, **Peter Bassano** (ASV 122).

A recent development has been the compilation of programs of music that could reasonably have been performed in a particular place on a particular day. **Paul McCreesh** has become the guru of this kind of presentation, and in 1990 he recorded pieces by Andrea, Giovanni, and others such as might have been heard at the coronation in 1595 of Venetian Doge Marino Grimani. The sequence begins with the bells of San Marco and finishes with Giovanni's wonderful 16-part setting of Omnes Gentes. If you don't want to hear the whole service each time, individual pieces can easily be picked out, and the performances by the Gabrieli Consort and Players are very good, with four organs located in the recording venue, Brinkburn Priory in Northumberland (Virgin 7590062).

Five years later McCreesh returned to Gabrieli's music, this time on location at the Scuola Grande di San Rocco in Venice, where a video was made. The audio recording is superb and the program relates to an occasion in 1608, with five of the pieces from the Sacrae Symphoniae of 1615 included, among others (Archive 449180). McCreesh's attempt at a Venetian Easter service is less successful, mainly due to the washy acoustic of Ely Cathedral. It includes choral and instrumental works by Gabrieli but the centerpiece is Missa Congratulamini nihi by his teacher Lassus, minus the "Credo" as is thought to have been the custom at San Marco (Archiv 453427).

A Belgian disc seeks to reconstruct the music for the Feast of the Trinity at San Marco; choral and instrumental music by Giovanni is leavened with two organ pieces by Andrea. The performances by the Namur Chamber Choir and the instrumental group La Fenice, directed by cornettist **Jean Tubery,** are good if not quite as expert as the best of the others (Ricercar 207412). Finally, a fascinating disc entitled "Gabrieli Tedesco" explores his German connection, showing how versions of his choral works kept at Kassel and Nuremberg were sometimes modified to suit local tastes and conditions. Instrumental pieces in the authentic Venetian editions are interleaved for variety, and the performances by **Musicalische Compagney** are superb (CPO 999454). POTTER

Niels Wilhelm Gade (1817–1890)

Fresh and vernal as a gust of bracing Nordic air is the music of the Danish composer Niels Gade, until some 10 years ago all but unknown in this country until the enterprising BIS label introduced his gloriously romantic symphonies in performances by Neeme Järvi and the Stockholm Sinfonietta. That this initial sally should emanate not from Denmark but from Sweden is symptomatic of the early experiences of the Copenhagen-born Gade, who following the almost overnight success of his overture Nachklänge von Ossian (Echoes from Ossian) had to travel to Leipzig to hear his Symphony 1 performed most enthusiastically by Mendelssohn, who remained a lifelong friend. Only then did he finally achieve much deserved popularity in his native land, recognized today along with J.P.E. Hartmann (whose daughter he married) as a prime exponent of Danish romanticism. With two full series of the symphonies and many choral works now readily available, we can be grateful that Gade has at long last truly come into his own.

SYMPHONIES

Heard today, it seems incredible that the Copenhagen Musical Society showed no interest in Gade's Symphony 1 until prodded into action by Mendelssohn. Titled "On Sjølund's Fair Plains," it's inspired mostly by Danish folk songs; surely save for the *Ossian* Overture no other work is so immediately winning, so filled with unabashed romantic melody and uninhibited vigor. In 2 it's easy to see affectionate homage to Mendelssohn's "Italian" Symphony, more in spirit than thematic resemblance.

With 3 and 4 we come to the midpoint in the cycle, both highly attractive. Some writers have suggested that Gade's "nationalist" tendencies began receding with Symphony 3; as he became more closely associated with Mendelssohn, that quality began to fall off—an opinion easily belied by the remaining works. Certainly we can hear echoes of the "Italian" in the opening movement of 6, yet there's also a certain melancholy to remind us this work was written as therapy following the sudden death of his beloved wife Sophie. Perhaps he recalled how delighted she was by the audience's startled response to hearing a piano prominently displayed in 5, which he wrote for her as a wedding gift only four years earlier. Not surprisingly, the angular opening motif will remind many listeners of Schumann's Piano Concerto.

By the time Gade wrote his 7th, Denmark and Prussia were at each other's throats over the province of Schleswig-Holstein, but Gade wanted none of it, calling the new score "a fresh and happy symphony," and indeed it bubbles over from first note to last, beaming with sheer love of life and heartfelt pride. 8 was to be Gade's last, yet there is no evidence of weariness with music-making, merely the same seamless flow of melody that informed his very first entry into the field; surely he could have written more symphonies after that, but as he himself exclaimed "There is only one Ninth!"

It was **Järvi**'s BIS series that started it all, and these performances remain fresh and invigorating today; still, there are times when he seems a bit too impulsive, even breathless, when set against **Michael Schönwandt** and the Collegium Musicum of Copenhagen, whose likewise spirited series started out on the DMA label but has since been brought out by Marco Polo (Da Capo). Unfortunately the symphonies aren't coupled the same way, so you may experience some duplication. Many of Järvi's outer movement tempos now seem unduly brisk, with tympani miked too closely; thus in 1 Schönwandt pulls up on the reins just enough to clarify the strong dotted-note motif of the opening movement and in so doing rivals even the classic (but long unavailable) LP with **Johan Hye-Knudsen** and the Royal Danish Orchestra (Turnabout).

Likewise in 3:I Schönwandt brings out more of the impish humor of the music; yet in the final movement Järvi's far more exhilarating treatment makes Schönwandt seem bland, and Stockholm strings are superior to the Copenhagen forces. In Symphony 5 Da Capo's more pastel palette suits the music better and Järvi's clangy piano is distracting, but his mercurial treatment of the final movement is a joy to hear. In 8:I Järvi is more impetuous, yet in the final movement Schönwandt pulls ahead to bracing effect. Lovers of Gade's music will want both series for the endless pleasure of playing one against the other.

A few other isolated recordings are worth your attention. **Kitaienko** offers 1 (♦Chandos 9422), filled out with the *Hamlet* Overture and the same *Echoes of Ossian* included with *Elverskud* (see below). It's a splendid reading, getting the crisp rhythms just right like Schönwandt but without the spotlight on the piccolo that occasionally proves distracting on Da Capo. **Hogwood** offers a fascinating coupling of 4 with Johannes Frederik Frøhlich's Symphony in E-flat

(♦Chandos 9609). Save for the Scherzo, where Hogwood presses on a bit, this is an effusive and beautifully played performance with a warm and cozy ambience. **Bengt Nilsson**'s lyrical and effervescent LP of 4 with hasn't made it to CD (Öresound). Some of you may have an Aries LP of 3 and 5 attributed to one **Cesare Gabrielli**; however, this label was notorious for putting out studio dubs under fake names and this is no exception; 3 is actually by Per Dreier, 5 by Jens Schröder. Both are in respectable stereo sound.

OTHER ORCHESTRAL MUSIC

The stories of the Scottish warrior bard Ossian stirred many composers to flights of fancy; not until many decades later were they revealed to be fictional tales of heroism concocted by the Scot James Macpherson. They inspired Gade to write his first great success, the magnificent overture *Nachklänge von Ossian*, beautifully done by **Hye-Knudsen** (Turnabout); if you're lucky enough to find a Danish LP (EMI 2903111), it gives you both the overture and Symphony 1. **Jerzy Maksymiuk** ingeniously couples Mendelssohn's "Scottish" Symphony with the Gade overture, Berlioz's *Rob Roy* and Debussy's *Marche Ecossaise,* though his rather deliberate tempos make it more of a clever idea than a satisfying program (Koch Schwann). A somewhat more successful mix is **Dirk Joeres**'s CD combining the Gade with Schumann's *Overture, Scherzo and Finale,* Mendelssohn's *Fingal's Cave* (also inspired by Ossian), and William Sterndale Bennett's *The Naiads* (Carlton). Certainly either of these programs makes better sense musically than the juxtaposition of the Gade plus Christian Horneman's *Gurre* Suite with works of Norgård and his student Hans Abrahamsen written in the mid-'70s (Kontrapunkt).

Kitaienko's warm-hearted reading may be had coupled with either the cantata *Elverskud* or Symphony 1, in the latter case joined by the *Hamlet* Overture, an impassioned outing with a grand stoic dirge set against more volatile material (Chandos). This too is handsomely carried off by Kitaienko, and the sonics are warm and richly textured. In Danacord's survey of father-and-son Danish composers, **Iona Brown** offers exhilarating accounts of both *Ossian* and *Hamlet,* adding as novelty Niels Gade's son Axel's Violin Concerto 2—a fascinating comparison. **Ole Schmidt** offers glowing and affectionate accounts of both pieces—if not as impetuous as Kitaienko or Brown—but his disc is even more valuable for the suites *Sommerdag paa Landet* (Summer Day in the Country) and *Holbergiana* (CPO). The first, as the name suggests, is a sequence of bucolic images spanning the day from sunrise to evening festivities in a coastal fishing village. Schmidt is far superior to **Claes Eriksson**'s flaccid, uninspired rendition, though that CD unfortunately remains the only source of Gade's *Michelangelo* Overture (Point); he offers *Mariotta* too, but his tepid account pales beside Brown.

The 1884 bicentennial of the poet Ludvig Holberg inspired composers of both Denmark and Norway, notably Grieg's *Holberg Suite;* Gade offered his own suite depicting several characters from Holberg's comedies in the style of Molière, concluding with *Maskarade* (set by Carl Nielsen several years later). **Tamás Vetö** (DMA LP) is more exhilarating in the final section, whereas **Schmidt** treats it more like a grand and elegant Polonaise—perhaps what Gade had in mind. Those who love the *Holberg Suite* will also want Gade's two sets of *Novelettes* for strings, fresh and songful, beautifully played by **Johannes Goritzki** in the company of Asger Hamerik's Symphony 6 (CPO), while **Vladislav Czrnecki** ingeniously couples the *Novelettes* of Gade and Coleridge-Taylor (EBS 6094). Another very fine version is led by **Misha Rachlevsky** (Claves).

Gade and his father-in-law J.P.E. Hartmann collaborated on the ballet *Et Folkesagn* at the request of the choreographer August Bournonville, who played to the strengths of both; thus the sunlit beauty of the idyllic pastoral setting, containing some of Gade's loveliest music, contrasts effectively with the fantastic world of trolls, witches, and changelings conjured up by Hartmann. The set with **Harry Damgaard** is all anyone could ask for, alluringly played and recorded (♦CPO 999426). In **John Frandsen**'s EMI LPs, his brisker tempos heighten excitement, but coupled with the reverberant environs they frequently cause smearing.

You may obtain Gade's lovely and tuneful Violin Concerto as part of a set containing 26 different works by Danish composers, all played by **Kai Laursen** with varying support from orchestra and engineers (Danacord, 10CD). Unfortunately many of these studio dubs are in mono, including the Gade. An equally bizarre if far more compact presentation gives the concerto in a beautiful performance by **Anton Kontra** but only as filler for the *Öresund Symphony,* a collaboration by a Dane, Ole Schmidt, and a Swede, Gunnar Jansson, written in 1993, which seems totally perverse as discmate (BIS). Unless you can find Kontra's earlier EMI import LP with **Carl von Garaguly** conducting, your only hope may be to borrow the BIS and tape the concerto.

HALLER

CHAMBER MUSIC

Octet for strings. Written during Gade's Leipzig apprenticeship, the Octet is full of charm and melodic invention. The **Kontra Quartet** with guest violists and cellists gives a nicely mannered account coupled with early fragments (BIS 545). **L'Archibudelli** and the Smithsonian Chamber Players are interpretively more spontaneous (♦Sony 48307), and pair it with Mendelssohn's Octet more appropriately than the **South German Octet** (Stieglitz 10294, with Svendsen's Octet and Shostakovich's *Two Pieces*). The **Johannes Ensemble** includes an interesting extra, the contemporaneous *Allegro vivace in E-flat* for sextet (Kontrapunkt 32127).

Piano Trios. The B-flat Trio is a student work, full of promise, surviving as a single movement. **Tre Musici**'s sensitive account is part of an enjoyable program including trios by other Danish composers (♦Da Capo 9310). The **Copenhagen Trio** is more stolid (Kontrapunkt 32077). The F major is Gade's major contribution to the trio repertoire, but still an apprentice work. The Copenhagen plays both with *Novellettes* Op. 29 (Kontrapunkt 32127) and Tre Musici with Trio 1 by Gade's mentor Mendelssohn (♦Classico 132).

Quartets. Only one of Gade's three completed string quartets was published in his lifetime; consequently, they are identifiable only by key and year of composition.

The F major Quartet ("Wilkommen und Abschied," 1840) was abandoned in the third movement for the *Echoes of Ossian* overture. What remains is viable enough, especially given the persuasive advocacy of the **Kontra Quartet** in a program with the earlier *Allegro in A minor* and other chamber works for strings (♦BIS 545). The **Copenhagen Quartet**'s 1960s recording is beautifully phrased if less exciting; the sound quality is no match for BIS (Marco Polo 224015). Gade's music at its best has a winning charm and poise; in the F minor Quartet (1851) it's added to a *joie de vivre* that makes this piece most appealing. The **Kontra Quartet** plays it with infectious zest (♦BIS 516, with the two later quartets).

Gade wrote six movements for the E minor Quartet (1877) but only used five; it was left to composer Asger Lund Christiansen to make a definitive version from Gade's notes after the composer's death. The **Kontra Quartet** is deeply poetic, but the work itself lacks its predecessor's zip (BIS 516). The **Copenhagen Quartet** omits the fourth movement (Da Capo, as above). The D Major Op. 63 (1888) was Gade's only published quartet. This deeply backward-looking (but superbly constructed) piece sounds pre-Wagnerian though written five years after that composer's death. The **Kontra** seems completely convinced of its worth in their consummate reading (BIS 516); the **Copenhagen** is a touch less compelling (Marco Polo 224015).

String Quintets. The F minor Quintet (1837), with additional viola, is a charming student piece, nicely caught by the **Johannes Ensemble** (Kontrapunkt 32127). *Andante and Allegro appassionato in F minor* (1837) replaces the second viola with a cello; it's a delightful work, perhaps an off cut from an abandoned second quintet. The **Kontra Quartet,** with Hans Nygaard, plays with a beguiling lightness (BIS 545); they're preferable to the **Kremlin Chamber Orchestra** in Rachlevsky's misguided transcription (Claves).

The E minor Quintet Op. 8 (1844), is one of Gade's most engaging early pieces, fresh-faced if a touch brash, as befits the product of a 28-year-old. The Johannes Ensemble gives a good account (Kontrapunkt 32121, with the Sextet).

String Sextet in E-flat Op. 44. This is Gade's finest chamber work, with a near-ideal balance of form and content. The **Johannes Ensemble** is more than adequate, but would benefit from more panache (♦Kontrapunkt 32121).

RICKARDS

CHORAL MUSIC

Elverskud (Elf-Hill) was the most highly regarded (and remains the most often recorded) of Gade's many works variously termed "secular oratorio" or "romantic cantata," in which the chorus is really the central figure, commenting on or even taking part in the action. These were immensely popular because, unlike the operas of the time, which even then existed on a more rarefied plane, they could be understood and appreciated by a much broader audience. They were frequently performed to great acclaim at the many music festivals then becoming a major part of the concert scene. Though based on Danish folklore, *Elverskud* soon became highly regarded elsewhere, even inspiring Goethe to write his ballad "Der Erlkönig," which so captivated Schubert among others.

Though hampered somewhat by a weak cast, **Frans Rasmussen** directs an admirable account, unfortunately without filler (Kontrapunkt). **Kitaienko** presents the score in more sensual, even operatic terms, and includes the *Ossian* Overture as well as *Five Songs* spanning the four seasons in lyrical fashion (Chandos). **Schönwandt,** in a lean and propulsive reading, brooks no indulgence and in so doing leaves room for the delectable *Spring Fantasy* (Marco Polo).

Taking the remaining works in chronological order, *Comala* is based on the same Ossian sagas as the overture, in this case a tale that may have resonated as well with Mendelssohn since it concerns King Fingal—father of Ossian—whose beloved Comala suffers a fatal swoon upon hearing (falsely, as it turns out) that the King has been slain in battle. This may be heard from **Rasmussen** and soloists (Kontrapunkt 32180). *Kalanus* is based on a loose retelling of Plutarch's documentation of a meeting between the Indian sage Kalanus and Alexander the Great. If it doesn't quite jibe with Plutarch's account, it makes for a rousing story, with Rasmussen here joined by no less than Gedda as the noble Alexander (Danacord 310, reissued as Kontrapunkt 32072). *Korsfarerne* (The Crusaders) tells the same story of the knight Rinaldo and the temptress Armida used by Handel and Haydn in their operas, concluding with a triumphant chorus as the now chastened and renewed Rinaldo, renouncing all sins of the flesh, cries out with joy upon reaching the Holy City of Jerusalem. This is available from **Rasmussen** and soloists (BIS 465). A more extended work, *Psyche,* is quite unlike the more familiar version by Franck, first in presenting the Greek myth of Psyche and Eros (here called Amor) without filtering it through a Christian subtext and then by elevating the chorus to a far more prominent role. As heard from Rasmussen and his forces it's sung in English, reflecting its Birmingham premiere; of the other recordings, only *Comala* lacks an English translation (Kontrapunkt 32244/45). Three short cantatas, *Zion, Die heilige Nacht* (Holy Night), and *Gefion,* are grouped by Rasmussen and make an interesting supplement (Kontrapunkt 32149).

The charming *Spring Fantasy,* for all its resemblance to early Brahms, almost seems a throwback to Beethoven's *Choral Fantasy* in its combination of piano, vocalists (though no chorus), and orchestra. **John Frandsen**'s quite serviceable if sonically unexceptional account has surfaced (EMI, with *Hymnus Amoris* and *Sleep*). A better choice is the far more buoyant and radiant reading led by **Schönwandt** (Da Capo*),* but the EMI will more than suffice.   HALLER

ORGAN MUSIC
Gade's works for the organ are not extensive, but his *Three Pieces* Op. 22 are a noteworthy contribution to the repertory and have been recorded by several artists. As for the rest, there are several chorale preludes and short occasional pieces as well as some unfinished works that have never been published. Taken together, they add up to about an hour of music, and at present there is only one recording of them all, by **Ralph Gustafsson,** playing a modest two-manual Swedish instrument based on an 1845 original (BIS 496).

As for Op. 22, Gustafsson's performance is entirely competent but rather ponderous. Far better is the recording by **Thomas Murray** on the magnificent 1863 E. & G.G. Hook organ at Boston's Church of the Immaculate Conception (◆AFKA 507). Murray brings a real sense of drama to the outer pieces, though the Allegretto sounds rushed and a trifle perfunctory. The disc includes sonatas by Rheinberger and Elgar plus Bach's "St. Anne" Prelude and Fugue. **Paul Trepte** includes Op. 22 in a program played at Ely Cathedral (Gamut 532). Outer movements are fast and perfunctory, the Allegretto is too slow and sentimental with a string-celeste combination, and the sound is rather distant and jumbled in the Ely acoustic.   GATENS

PIANO MUSIC
Gade, like Grieg, was a miniaturist at heart where piano music was concerned, and his output contains only one extended work, the Sonata in E minor. The most popular items are the first set of *Aquarelles* and the four *Idylls,* but these are only the highlights of a considerable number of sketches, folk songs, scherzos, dances, and other album pieces. **Anker Blyme** has collected all of it in performances that, if wanting in excitement, are committed and full of lyricism (◆Da Capo 9115/17, 3CD). **Elisabeth Westenholtz** is mid-way through a cycle; some of her performances—such as the Sonata or *New Aquarelles*—catch the essence of Gade's inspiration very well, but in rather clinical sound (Kontrapunkt 32097, 32124). **Dirk Joeres**'s performances of *Aquarelles* and *Idylls* are in the broader context of music by "Schumann and his Friends" (IMP 1044).   RICKARDS

John Gay *(1685–1732)* and Johann Christian Pepusch *(1667–1752)*
In 1716 Jonathan Swift whimsically suggested to Alexander Pope the idea of a "Newgate pastoral, among the whores and thieves." Pope passed the idea on to John Gay, and the rest, as they say, is history. *The Beggar's Opera* (1728) may not have been the first ballad opera, but it was the first to attract the attention of a wide public. It may not have spelled the end of Handel's operatic career, as legend would have it, but its trenchant satire certainly didn't advance the cause of Italian *opera seria* in London.

Of the available recordings, the clear stand-out is by **Jeremy Barlow** and the Broadside Band, with a cast that includes noted early-music singers Sarah Walker, Adrian Thompson, Charles Daniels, Bronwen Mills, Richard Jackson, and Anne Dawson (◆Hyperion 66591, 2CD; also MHS). Actor Bob Hoskins makes cameo appearances as the beggar, the putative author of the opera. Barlow bases his performance on the third printed edition of the work (1729), as this was the first to include the bass lines Pepusch supplied for the songs. Barlow keeps the music simple, with the songs accompanied by unison violins and sometimes oboes on the melody plus basso continuo. The result is a fast-paced, animated reading that captures the racy spirit of the work. The excellent singers also prove to be accomplished actors. The libretto gives the original titles of the songs and, where known, the composers.

The Beggar's Opera continued to hold the stage well into the 19th century, but Victorian sensibilities found it unappealing, and it gradually disappeared. Nigel Playfair mounted a very successful West End revival in 1920 with music newly arranged by Frederic Austin. This version was recorded several times. The one currently available is a reissue of a 1955 recording by **Sargent** with vocalists Elsie Morison, John Cameron, Monica Sinclair, Ian Wallace, Owen Brannigan, Constance Shacklock, and Alexander Young, with a separate cast of actors for the spoken dialog (EMI 68926, 2CD). Austin's sophisticated orchestration completely misrepresents the character of the original, so that it becomes a period piece but not an 18th-century period piece. The discs come with a synopsis but no libretto. Following in the Hyperion libretto, I found the spoken dialog condensed and expurgated, Act III substantially rewritten, and 23 of the songs omitted, not counting Macheath's soliloquy, which is drastically abridged. The performance itself is very good, and the recorded sound, while somewhat dated, is quite satisfactory.

Denis Stevens and the Accademia Monteverdiana recorded some but not all of the songs (Koch 1621). One reviewer described the orchestration as anachronistic and the performance too subdued and pretty. A 1940 recording of selections from the Austin version, together with a 1925 recording of Charles Dibdin's *Lionel and Clarissa,* is available (Pearl 9917). The 78 rpm surface noise is a serious distraction.   GATENS

Francesco Geminiani *(1687–1762)*
Geminiani was a violinist and a student of Corelli. He has not received the interest he deserves for his importance as a composer and theoretician; in his day the English considered him the equal of Handel and Corelli. He was an original if not prolific composer who tended to treat the solo violinist as the protagonist in his concerti grossi, making technical demands far beyond those of Corelli or Handel.

Concerti grossi. Geminiani's concerti grossi have been somewhat popular in modern times. **Angerer** and the Southwest German Chamber Orchestra recorded the complete Opp. 2, 3, and 4 (Vox 5152, 2CD). They are played in modern style, with much legato bowing and vibrato, in spirited, attractive readings with real feeling. **Iona Brown** leads the Academy of St. Martin in the Fields in Op. 7; the Academy plays with its usual tonal refinement and these performances are stately and polished, but also stuffy and effete (ASV). The Capella Istropolitana under

Jaroslav Kreček has recorded all of Op. 2 and the first four concertos of Op. 3 (Naxos 553019). They have adopted period style, with strong articulation and chaste vibrato; these are lively readings. The Camerata Bern led by **Thomas Füri** uses lots of vibrato, but their articulation is close to period style and they obviously enjoy what they are playing (Novalis 150083).

Lamon and Tafelmusik produce one of the sweetest sounds of any period instrument ensemble (Sony 48043). They tend to be smoother and less incisive than other such groups, so their performances lack a little variety. **Biondi** and Europa Galante play Op. 3 with plenty of spunk (♦Opus 111 30172). They have more of a chamber ensemble sound and use much sharper articulation than Tafelmusik. Biondi is a very charismatic, witty soloist.

The Enchanted Forest was composed for a pantomime about the siege of Jerusalem during the Crusades. A Muslim magician has put the forest outside Jerusalem under a spell, and it's now inhabited by spirits that prevent the Christian army from felling lumber to build a siege machine. Don't look for tone painting à la Biber in this score; the music is rather conventional and, though pleasant, gives no hint of the action or story line. The Orchestra Barocca Italiana under **Ryo Terakado** gives a smooth, polished reading (Stradivarius 33359).   MAGIL

Roberto Gerhard *(1896–1970)*

The Catalan composer Gerhard lived his last 31 years in England as an exile from Franco's Spain. A pupil of Granados and Pedrell, he also studied with Schoenberg in Vienna. His earlier music was in a forward-looking nationalist style, as in his vividly orchestrated ballets and the comic opera *La Dueña*. In the '50s he adopted a more radical manner and had developed into one of Europe's leading musical figures at his death. This progress can be charted through his five symphonies: the early folkloric *Homenaje de Pedrell* (1940–41) and 1–4 (1952–67).

ORCHESTRAL MUSIC

Ballets. Gerhard's best known dance scores are *Alegrías* and *Don Quixote*. Mostly encountered in piano or two-piano reductions, **Victor Pablo Pérez** and **Edmon Colomer** have recorded all the original scores, including *Albada, interludi í dansa* and *Ariel* (Auvidis 782114, 2CD). *Pandora*, of which several different texts exist, has been recorded in a scintillating performance by **Bamert** (♦Chandos 9651, with Symphony 4).

Concerto for orchestra is one of the composer's greatest works. John Pritchard's pioneering recording hasn't been reissued, but **Bamert's** electrifying account alongside the original version of Symphony 2 is the finest Gerhard orchestral disc available (♦Chandos 9694).

Epithalamion. This phantasmagorically scored "nuptial song" requires a huge orchestra including eight percussionists, possibly recycling unused film music for Lindsay Anderson's *This Sporting Life*. The Spanish Youth Orchestra under **Colomer** is magnificent (Auvidis), disadvantaged only by the virtuosic precision of the BBC Symphony Orchestra under **Bamert** (♦Chandos 9556).

Symphonies. Victor Pérez's cycle with the fine Tenerife Orchestra is on two discs; it excludes the earlier unnumbered *Homenaje de Pedrell*, long known only for its popular finale, "Pedrelliana," which is all Pérez has set down of it (Auvidis 782113/4). **Bamert's** cycle is on five discs, issued separately coupled with concertos and other pieces, with *Homenaje de Pedrell* complete (♦Chandos 9693, 9599, 9694, 9556, 9651). Bamert's performances are more polished; helped by the rich sound, Gerhard's textures sound brighter than ever, as for example in 1 and 3 ("Col-

lages"), which has a large tape part. In 2, Bamert uses the original, unlike Pérez, who performs Alan Boustead's completion of the radical 1967–88 rewrite, re-titled *Metamorphoses*. There's no denying the passion of Pérez's set, and in 4 ("New York"), written for the New York Philharmonic, he gives the music an extra Catalan expressiveness.

CONCERTOS

Harpsichord. **Geoffrey Tozer's** recording is marred by the omission of an entry in the slow movement (Chandos). **Ursula Dütschler's** splendid performance benefits from leaner sound, better suiting the spare textures (♦Auvidis 782107).

Piano. This bracing work for piano and strings stands on the cusp of Gerhard's plunge into out-and-out modernism. **Tozer** catches its mood just right (Chandos 9556), as does **Albert Attenelle,** whose couplings—Harpsichord Concerto and *Nonet*—may be the deciding factor (♦Auvidis, as above).

Violin. **Olivier Charlier** is magnificent in this approachable yet challenging work (Chandos, with Symphony 1).

CHAMBER MUSIC

Gerhard's chamber pieces range throughout his career but are concentrated in his last 20 years. By far the best collection is the **Nieuw Ensemble's**, comprising the unusually scored *Concert for Eight*—flute, clarinet, mandolin, guitar, accordion, piano, percussion, and double-bass, fiendishly difficult to balance correctly—the piano *Impromptus*, and the three "astrological" masterpieces: *Gemini* (the title was altered from *Duo concertante* to avoid confusion with Stravinsky's), *Leo*, and *Libra* (♦Largo 5134). **Barcelona 216** provides strong competition in *Concert for Eight* and *Libra*, but have a different focus (Stradivarius 33404). This is due partly to the inclusion of the Piano Trio, an apprentice work unrecognizable as Gerhard. **Cantamen** gives the Trio a fluent, lyrical account (Métier 92012), whereas Barcelona 216 have more Iberian fire and the **Gerhard Trio** puts it into a wider Spanish context (La Mà de Guido). The *Nonet* has been recorded in a splendidly effervescent performance by members of the Barcelona Symphony Orchestra under **Lawrence Foster** (Auvidis 782107).

Gerhard's two numbered string quartets have affinities with Symphonies 1 and 3, respectively. The **Kreutzer Quartet** is fully within the idiom, the performances staying long in the mind (what a shame they didn't include the student quartet from the '20s). This short disc—38 minutes but mid-price—repays repeated listening (♦Métier 92032).

Sonata for Cello and Piano was originally written for viola in 1946; Gerhard recast it magisterially for cello ten years later, partly in his newly adopted serial manner. **Jo Cole** gives a remarkably lyrical performance, coupled with the Trio, *Gemini*, and Chaconne for solo violin, magnificently played by Caroline Balding (♦Métier 92012); **François Monciero's** account is also coupled with the Trio, *Gemini*, and guitar music by other hands (La Mà de Guido). **Amparo Lacruz's** fine performance sits well alongside *Concert for Eight* and *Libra* (Stradivarius 33404).

PIANO MUSIC

Jordi Masó has recorded all the solo piano music very sympathetically, though some of his tempos seem a touch cautious (Marco Polo 22386, with Joáquin Homs's Sonata 2). In the *Impromptus* **John Snijders** is peerless (♦Largo 5134), while in *Soirées de Barcelone*, Masó yields to **Andrew Ball** in phrasing and drive (♦Largo 5119). On the latter disc Ball and **Julian Jacobson** give stunningly virtuosic performances of the two-piano versions of ballet suites *Alegrías* and *Pandora* (the latter with percussionist Richard Benjafield).

VOCAL MUSIC

The cantata *L'alta naixença del rei en Jaume* (The Noble Birth of the Sovereign Lord King James) tells the ironic tale of the conception of Catalonian King Jaume I, whose mother substituted herself for one of her husband's mistresses. It's sung wonderfully by **Coral Cármina,** alive to every nuance. In complete contrast, *The Plague* (for narrator, chorus and orchestra), based on Camus's searing allegory of Nazi-occupied France set in plague-stricken Oran, is sung magnificently by the **BBC Symphony Chorus** with narrator Michael Lonsdale (◆Auvidis 782115, 2CD, with the best known solo song sets plus *Epithalamion* and *Sardanas I* and *II*).

Gerhard's exuberant score for his opera *La Dueña* is a real "feel-good" experience in the vibrant recording by **Ros Marbà,** who directs a predominantly young cast with great skill (◆Chandos 9520, 2CD).

The song cycle *L'infantament meravellos de Shahrazada* is Gerhard's Op. 1, unrecognizable from his later music. **Isabel Aragon** and Angel Soler couple it with a set by Homs (listed in Schwann as Agora 102, but elsewhere as La Mà de Guido 2022), **Benita Valente** and Tan Crone with Gerhard's finest set, *Cancionero de Pedrell* (in "Pedrell Songbook," ◆Etcetera 1060). **Anna Cors** sings the orchestral version radiantly, as she does the six charming *Popular Catalan Songs* (Auvidis, as above).

RICKARDS

George Gershwin *(1898–1937)*

Gershwin's death at the age of 38 ended a career that no doubt would have continued to be distinguished by works—both classical and popular—that would have quickly entered the basic repertoire. In addition to *Rhapsody in Blue* and *An American in Paris*, the Piano Concerto in F belongs in any collection of classical CDs, as does at least a generous representation of music from *Porgy and Bess*, which many consider the greatest American opera. Smaller works such as *Second Rhapsody, Cuban Overture,* and *Variations on "I Got Rhythm"* flesh out his life as a classical composer. No one can get a complete picture of the man, however, unless they acquaint themselves with the music he wrote for the stage and screen. Several of his Broadway shows have been given "authentic" recordings, and albums and compilations of his hit songs are almost numberless—even today's popular vocalists regularly pay their debt to this master of American song.

With the exception of his theater works, Gershwin's compositions are relatively short; the Concerto in F—one of the longest—requires little more than a half-hour to play. As a result, recordings of his music have a confusing mix-and-match quality. Almost any combination of the major works has been recorded at least once, as you will see below.

ORCHESTRAL MUSIC AND CONCERTOS

Maazel's Cleveland Orchestra LPs from the mid-'70s were very well recorded, and his *Rhapsody in Blue, An American in Paris,* and *Cuban Overture* make a similarly positive impression on CD (London 460612). These readings admirably balance the music's classical and pop elements; the phrasing is racy and insinuating, and Maazel successfully resists distorting Gershwin's intentions, at least as we understand them today. The only thing missing from these readings is a dash of wit. Ivan Davis brings Romantic virtuosity to *Rhapsody in Blue.* Instrumental medleys from *Girl Crazy, Funny Face,* and *Oh, Kay!* have less to recommend them, only because it's a shame to do without Ira's lyrics. (Fiedler conducts them with the Boston Pops on this disc.) A suite from *Porgy and Bess,* conducted by Frank Chacksfield, is an outright no-no because of its easy-listening excesses

Maazel's *Cuban Overture* reappears in "Gershwin Weekend" at budget price (London 436570). Mehta conducts *American in Paris* and Leontyne Price sings "Summertime" from *Porgy and Bess* on this disc, but what might attract a collector's attention are the *Rhapsody* and Concerto in F with Katchen. (The only other way to get Katchen's version of the concerto at the moment is in an expensive import set.) Unfortunately, the pianist's company lets him down. The Concerto in F is done in by a seedy 1955 recording with Mantovani and an orchestra that isn't up to the music's challenges. Even the scoring has been changed: the cymbal crash in the finale is no substitute for the tam-tam. *Rhapsody* is conducted by Kertész, often a fine conductor but here a relentless taskmaster who rushes Katchen along so furiously that even this formidable pianist gabbles some of his more difficult passages. There are no booklet notes. Fight the temptation. **Katchen's** *Rhapsody* is also in his "Great Pianists" set (Philips 456859, 2CD).

In 1971, it was considered a feat to squeeze *Rhapsody, American in Paris,* and the Concerto—65 minutes of music—onto a single LP. On CD **Previn** both played the piano solos and conducted the orchestra (EMI 66943). Now, as part of the "Great Recordings of the Century" series, a new generation of listeners has a chance to hear Previn's Gershwin—perhaps curious today, since he has shed much of his populist image with age. There's no apparent strain over his double roles; everything happens neatly and on time in these readings. Overall, they're more than satisfactory. Previn understands the music, never pushes it, and plays up the jazz inflections in the piano and orchestral parts. I wish he were a little more giving, though; at times he verges on the metronomic. Little elisions in the linking passages in *Rhapsody* are momentarily jarring. The engineering is good for its time. Previn repeated this recording feat more than 15 years later, this time with the Pittsburgh Symphony (Philips 412611; the Concerto and *Rhapsody* are also in Philips 456934, 2CD, with an assortment of his solo Gershwin performances). I haven't heard this CD, but from all accounts his approach seems to have changed relatively little in the interim.

An identical grouping is available at a super budget price from the CSR Symphony Orchestra of Bratislava (Naxos 550295). Unfortunately, they give no indication that they understand Gershwin's language; they play all the notes, but sound as if they had their noses buried in a somewhat outdated Czech-English phrasebook. **Richard Hayman,** a veteran of the "pops" format who worked with Arthur Fiedler and others, does what he can to save this recording, but there's no fighting the orchestra's unidiomatic sound. In *Rhapsody* and the Concerto, Australian pianist Kathryn Selby plays accurately but without great distinction. If you want this precise combination of works, you're much better off spending a few dollars more and acquiring Previn.

Surprisingly, **Bernstein** soft-pedals the jazz in *Rhapsody* and *American in Paris* (◆Sony 63086 and 47529). Conducting the Columbia Symphony from the piano in the former, he whips up a beefy orchestral outside and a gushingly tear-jerking interior. His pianism is as flashy and muscular as his conducting. If you can accept his cuts and the wrong-headedness of this approach, which emphasizes the music's emotional extremes, these 1958–59 recordings are fabulous, even if they say more about Bernstein than they do about Gershwin. Listen to the New York Philharmonic rip into the maxixe in *American in Paris* and you'll be convinced; Bernstein loves this music, and he'll do anything to make us feel the same way. His 1982 remake of *Rhapsody* with the Los Angeles Philharmonic is far less recommendable (DG 439528, 431048, 463465, 2CD). It's marred by slow tempos and extreme self-consciousness. In spite of its concert origins and its dogged attempts to be hip, this disappointing recording never comes alive. It's Gershwin in the style of Brahms's Concerto 1, and only compulsive Bernstein collectors will need it.

Tilson Thomas's first recording of *Rhapsody* features none other than Gershwin himself playing the piano, thanks to the composer's 1925 Duo-Art piano roll (Columbia 42240). The results are interesting, if not entirely convincing. First, Tilson Thomas uses the original Paul Whiteman Orchestra's jazz charts, and the resulting leanness hardens the music's punchy qualities. (Nevertheless, the central section is gentle.) The tempos in the outer sections are controversially fast, and the Columbia Jazz Band occasionally scrambles to keep up with their ghostly soloist. More troubling, the pianism lacks charisma. I suspect that these latter two problems are associated with the piano rolls—specifically their tempos—and not with Gershwin's playing *per se*. *American in Paris*, from 1974 with the New York Philharmonic, is competent but not really special. It's leisurely, and features soulful trumpeting in the blues section. The second half of the CD contains six "Broadway overtures" arranged by Don Rose. The Buffalo Philharmonic plays them beautifully, but it makes little sense to listen to these medleys when the complete scores have so much more to offer, not least Ira's lyrics.

A decade later, Tilson Thomas returned to the *Rhapsody*—this time in its full symphonic guise—and added *Second Rhapsody* for good measure (CBS 39699). Unstressed by "Gershwin's" speeds on the piano roll, he and the Los Angeles Philharmonic find a lot of character in the earlier work, although ultimately it's the orchestra's racy playing that is most memorable, not Tilson Thomas, in spite of the assertion that his interpretation is "modeled after Gershwin's own performances." Nevertheless, everyone involved makes a fine quarter-hour of *Second Rhapsody* (also known as "Rhapsody in Rivets"), and the conductor/pianist's attempt to restore its original orchestral parts is laudable. With the exception of the charming *Promenade* (*Walking the Dog*), the balance of the CD consists of solo works, all stylishly played by Tilson Thomas. Most are premiere recordings of his arrangements, reconstructions, or realizations of scraps from Gershwin's workbench, but what scraps!

Tilson Thomas's most recent Gershwin set, recorded in 1998, is a "100th Birthday Collection" (◆RCA 68931, 2CD). It's also his best. *Second Rhapsody* (with the conductor at the piano) and *American in Paris* eclipse the performances reviewed above, and the conductor adds a whiz-bang Concerto in F (with Garrick Ohlsson). Over 40 minutes are devoted to a neither fish nor fowl version of *Catfish Row* that interpolates sung versions of four of the *Porgy and Bess* songs; these are gorgeously performed by soprano Audra McDonald and baritone Brian Stokes Mitchell. Tilson Thomas found the right tempos throughout, and he balances showmanship and intimacy perfectly. Rhythms are sharp but they don't tear the music apart, and inner lines are emphasized without submerging the melodies. This is expert conducting, and there is luscious playing by the San Francisco Symphony. Perhaps this set is a little expensive, though, particularly because there would have been room for *Rhapsody*.

Erich Kunzel has been recording Gershwin's music for Telarc in Cincinnati almost since the label's birth. His 1981 recording of *Rhapsody* and *American in Paris* is still in the catalog, even though he has rerecorded the former (Telarc 80058). At just under 34 minutes, this was short for an LP; it's undeniably stingy for a CD that can easily hold twice as much music. One thing in its favor is the sound: this was when Telarc belonged to the "big bang" school, and no one will complain that the engineering here is dull. Unfortunately, the performances themselves can't defend this charge. Kunzel is solid but not very imaginative, and the

same can be said of pianist Eugene List, who was more exciting on his Mercury recording (see below). Kunzel chops the music into sections and disturbs its unstoppable flow. He's at his best in the middle of *Rhapsody in Blue*, where Gershwin's sentimental tune is given a big, melting treatment that's hard to resist.

Things improved greatly when Kunzel returned to *Rhapsody* a few years later (◆Telarc 80166). This time, his pianist was William Tritt, but more important than a change of pianist was a change in concept. Like Tilson Thomas in his Gershwin piano roll recording, Kunzel opts for the 1924 jazz band version, but he's much more relaxed, and the performance gains in freshness, even though it's several minutes longer. Part of the length comes from the reinstatement of 48 bars of material (mostly transitional) cut after the premiere. Most notable is the emphasis on cantabile playing—this *Rhapsody* really sings, true to the word's Greek origins. Although it's unconventional, it succeeds beautifully. The same is true of the Concerto in F. Other recordings are more electric (Kunzel and Tritt seem hesitant to play to the galleries in the first movement's final minutes), but I haven't heard any that are more sensitive, even moving. The balance between piano and orchestra is ideal; no spurious spotlighting here. The bonuses are the *"I Got Rhythm" Variations* (also done imaginatively—try the sighing strings in the third variation) and Kunzel's own arrangement of the piano solo *Rialto Ripples*, which is pure "pops" delight!

When it came time for Kunzel to record music from *Porgy and Bess*, he chose not Robert Russell Bennett's "symphonic picture" but the composer's own suite, which he called *Catfish Row* (Telarc 80086). Gershwin assembled it because of his fears that the opera wouldn't stand the test of time, and also to save material cut from *Porgy and Bess* after the Boston tryout. Compared to the other symphonic treatments of this score, *Catfish Row* is much less of a potpourri, although many of the famous numbers can be heard. Instead, Gershwin focuses on the opera's dramatic sweep; this is more a drastic abridgment than a medley. As such, it hasn't achieved the crowd-pleasing status of other arrangements—it's a more serious work, and much closer to the spirit of the opera. Kunzel leads it effectively, if without the white heat of inspiration needed to sell it.

In 1998, in honor of the 100th anniversary of the composer's birth, Telarc combined material from the three discs listed above, filled some gaps, and issued a "Gershwin Centennial Edition," subtitling it "The Complete Orchestral Collection" (Telarc 80445, 2CD). New to this release are *Second Rhapsody* (with Stewart Goodyear, piano, and like Tilson Thomas's recording, a return to the original score), *Cuban Overture*, and four encores: *Lullaby* in an arrangement for string orchestra, *Walking the Dog*, *Mexican Dance*, and, most enterprisingly, a work for chorus and orchestra called *O Land of Mine, America*. (The last two are billed as world premiere recordings.) *Mexican Dance*, based on a song called "Tomale [sic] (I'm Hot for You)," actually sounds more Arabian than Mexican; apparently it was orchestrated by hands other than Gershwin's.

Although the booklet notes don't say, the same is probably true of *O Land of Mine, America*. This was Gershwin's anonymous entry in an American anthem contest sponsored by the New York *American*. Gershwin won an honorable mention; we don't know who won first prize, and Congress eventually settled on "The Star-Spangled Banner" in 1931. It's predictably stirring and not very original, and it feels gussied up in this arrangement. The new recordings in this set were made between 1992 and 1997. None of them are as inspired as the Kunzel/Tritt CD, but then again none are as choppy as Kunzel's earliest Gershwin coupling.

A collection conducted by **Slatkin** duplicates the contents of the Telarc set described above, omitting only *Rialto Ripples, Walking the Dog,* and *O Land of Mine*—arguably no great loss (♦Vox 5007). At about one-third the price of the Telarc set, this is a remarkable bargain. These recordings were made in 1974, and they're not digital; on the other hand, the sound is magically warm—few digital recordings surpass it. Many listeners adore this set. Slatkin conducts this music intellectually and with classical sophistication, downplaying the popular elements. He's always tasteful and often meltingly lovely. Those who desire their Gershwin with pepper, however, will need to look elsewhere. His pianist is Jeffrey Siegel, who seems to agree absolutely with Slatkin's restrained and thoughtful interpretations. The Saint Louis Symphony plays the music like silk, and the excellent booklet notes are by Gershwin expert Edward Jablonski.

Leonard's father Felix Slatkin appears in a collection called "Great American Gershwin" (♦Angel 66086). He conducts *Rhapsody* and *American in Paris,* and another stalwart of the Hollywood film studios, Alfred Newman, conducts a medley from *Porgy and Bess, Variations on "I Got Rhythm," Cuban Overture,* and *Second Rhapsody.* The pianist is Leonard Pennario. The Slatkin-conducted selections are among the very best on disc. He and the Hollywood Bowl Symphony take some liberties with the music, but he has the full measure of its spirit. *Rhapsody* swaggers like a big American peacock and sizzles like fireworks on Independence Day. *American in Paris* is outstanding too; the blues tune is played with memorable insouciance. However, Newman conducts an unnecessary arrangement for piano and orchestra of *Cuban Overture.* The *Porgy and Bess* medley, arranged by Greig McRitchie and too clever by half, is also turned into a concertante work in the style of *Warsaw Concerto.* Who needs it? My recommendation, then, is for the Slatkin and Pennario contributions, and not for the spurious arrangements that Newman conducts.

Levine is another conductor/pianist who has tried his hand at *Rhapsody* (DG 431625). Wisely, he tackles the original jazz band version. He's successful at realizing the music's aggressive punch, yet the central section is given its romantic due. He also gives us *Catfish Row,* a *Cuban Overture* that's a little pushy, and an *American in Paris* that's notable for the sharp discipline of the Chicago Symphony's playing. Even the trumpet blues, loose as they are, sound premeditated to the last inflection. If Levine's *Rhapsody* is less interesting than everything else on the disc, "Mad About Gershwin" couples the rest of Levine's disc with Bernstein's self-indulgent *Rhapsody* from Los Angeles and with the second of the *Three Preludes,* also played by Bernstein (DG 445576). This CD is several dollars cheaper and has a wonderful Roz Chast cartoon cover.

"Gershwin Premiere" is the title of a disc conducted by Litton (Delos 3216). The premiere in question is actually an arrangement by Sid Ramin, with Litton, of seven Gershwin song sketches. It's called *Dayful of Song* (an allusion to a lyric from "I Got Rhythm"), and the melodies are definitely Gershwin's, even if the work itself is not. Litton scores points in the jazz band version of *Rhapsody,* walking the line between popular and classical music and providing competition for Levine and Kunzel. *American in Paris* is done swingingly, and *Cuban Overture* is awash in color and rhythm. Makeweights are *Promenade* and a string arrangement of *Lullaby.* Delos's recording is fodder for the stereophiles.

Young pianist **Fazil Say** is brash and impressively talented up to a point (Teldec 26202). His arrangements of three numbers from *Porgy and Bess* are remarkable for both imagination and finger power. Nevertheless, he seems to be trying too hard. His *Rhapsody* is spoiled by oversized orchestral sound (Masur conducts) and temperamental differ-

ences, as if a precocious brat were stomping through Masur's beergarden. *"I Got Rhythm" Variations* become a wrongheaded tribute to Webern. Say bangs and crashes in some solo works, including *Three Preludes* and a number of unfamiliar rhythmic and harmonic etudes. Tempos are too fast, and Gershwin's charm and stylishness fall by the wayside. The slower pieces are somewhat better, but Say's playing is too tense to provide much enjoyment.

Once Mercury Records entered the stereo era, it wasn't long before they made their own addition to the Gershwin discography. In 1957, **Hanson** conducted the Eastman-Rochester Orchestra in Concerto in F and the *Rhapsody* with soloist Eugene List (Mercury 434341). These are readings for those who want this music played with a minimum of jazziness, and they reflect the more old-fashioned attitude that music was either classical or it wasn't—"crossover" wasn't something people touted in 1957. If you accept the stylistic malapropisms, there's much to enjoy about this recording, which is sane and at times even stately. List's fingers aren't infallible, but he's not a dull player, Hanson is reliable as always in American music, and his young musicians sound exhilarated. From the opening percussion salvo in the Concerto, the engineering is remarkably good, though the Eastman Theater was a dry recording locale. Hanson's 1962 recording of *Cuban Overture* is in a more traditional style, and the conductor's disdain for easy effects makes this one of its best recordings.

Mercury also recorded **Dorati** and the Minneapolis Symphony in *American in Paris* in 1957 (Mercury 434329). Dorati moves right along, and I find it exhilarating—a breath of fresh air after hearing some more self-consciously "blue" readings. His taxi horns are among the best (I actually laughed when I reheard then), and the sound is splendid. If you want *American in Paris* only, Dorati is worth considering. Later in his career, he recorded Robert Russell Bennett's "symphonic picture" of *Porgy and Bess* with the Detroit Symphony (London 430712). I'm not keen on the idea of a symphonic suite from *Porgy and Bess,* yet I must admit that Bennett gets to all the good tunes in less than 25 minutes, which is more than can be said about some other attempts. Dorati has spectacular early-digital sound on his side (London/Decca's Detroit recordings still sound remarkably good), and he's affectionate, though not as sweeping as Ormandy (see below).

RCA was also quick to climb on the Gershwin bandwagon. **Fiedler**'s 1959 recordings of *Rhapsody in Blue* (with Earl Wild) and *American in Paris* have been a staple of the catalog since their release, and the Concerto in F and *"I Got Rhythm" Variations* (again, both with Wild) have hardly done less well (RCA 68792). I don't find these recordings very endearing, however. Fiedler was nothing if not efficient. Sometimes, as in his Offenbach recordings, the results are bracing; unfortunately, this is Gershwin without charm. Right from the start of the *Rhapsody,* he makes us feel that the session clocks are ticking, and woe to anyone who gets in the way of the juggernaut! There's too much tension here for even a taste of jazz to rise to the top. Wild had the misfortune to perform this music with two big-name conductors (the other is Toscanini—see below) who didn't seem to care very much about it. The sound is good for the era, but it's not the audiophile extravaganza you might expect

If it's Wild you want in the Concerto, you're much better off with a dark horse recording that involves conductor **Joseph Giunta** and the Des Moines Symphony (Chesky 98). It was recorded in the early '90s when the pianist was in his late 70s, but don't expect a notable diminution in his technical powers; Wild still has more in his arsenal than many a younger pianist. Although Giunta's tempos are not much different from Fiedler's, there's more involvement here. It can be argued, though, that Wild upstages his accompaniment. One detail worth mentioning is the use of trumpet muted with a felt crown in the second movement solo; a subtle softening and rounding of the sound is the result. Most trumpeters ignore Gershwin's request and use a regular metal mute instead.

Another Chesky release, containing the Concerto and *Rhapsody in Blue,* comes from their worthwhile audiophile series of *Reader's Digest* reissues (Chesky 56). These recordings, taped in 1962, are conducted by **Oskar Danon** with virtuoso pianist Lewenthal. All things considered, they are attractive performances. Lewenthal is enjoyably spontaneous, and Danon can't be accused of excessive premeditation either. There's an air of "let's get in the studio and have a good time" that compensates for the lack of polish; I suspect the recording sessions were quick and to the point. Some of the orchestral playing is sloppy, and Lewenthal stumbles a bit from time to time, but this can be forgiven considering the lively music-making. Danon makes some questionable interpretive decisions, however (mostly having to do with "expressive" ritardandos), and his understanding of Gershwin's style, while not absent, is relatively generalized. The packaging claims this is an all-digital recording, which it obviously is not, but the sound should have even demanding listeners smiling in approval.

There's nothing wrong with **Ormandy**'s big, friendly *American in Paris,* recorded in 1967 with his "symphonic picture" of *Porgy and Bess* (Sony 62402). Ormandy-bashing goes in and out of fashion, but few conductors had such a solid grasp on so much of the orchestral repertoire. Both of the performances are leisurely—splendidly lazy, in fact, in the "Summertime" section of *Porgy and Bess*—but no one will sleep through the Philadelphia's virtuosic traversal of these scores, which are done with the same kind of spectacle usually reserved for Wagner. Marginally slower than Dorati in *Porgy and Bess,* Ormandy is more cinematic. In Concerto in F, Ormandy is joined by Entremont; they connect the lines between Gershwin's concerto and the Ravel piano concertos, the other works on this CD (Sony 46338). At times this performance lacks spontaneity and is somewhat heavy, but at its best, there is an undeniable electricity in the dialogues between pianist and orchestra. The third movement is best of all. Jazzy? Not very. Intimate? Not at all, and Entremont has his clunky moments. Nevertheless, Gershwin the symphonist is spotlighted by this recording. Unfortunately, the engineering is a little coarse; there is much better sound on the other Ormandy disc.

A younger French pianist, Hélène Grimaud, with **David Zinman,** has coupled Ravel's G major Piano Concerto with Gershwin's Concerto (Erato 19571). One critic called it "the best performance of the Gershwin concerto we are ever likely to hear." Another found Grimaud "straightforwardly romantic," although he noted that she seemed less comfortable with the work's jazz elements than with its long-limbed melodies. In contrast, *a* third admired details of her playing, but commented that her reading was sabotaged by "good breeding," and called it "a depressingly eat-your-vegetables interpretation." Clearly this is not a "safe" recommendation, but may be one for listeners who want a more grandly classical recording of this work.

Tortelier recorded two Gershwin discs with pianist Howard Shelley. One is very good and the other is disappointing. The good one, with *Rhapsody, Second Rhapsody,* and Concerto in F was recorded in 1992 (Chandos 9092). Here, Tortelier is a free spirit, and even if there's little about his interpretations that's distinctive, he's excitable, and he pulls a huge, classical sound from the Philharmonia. The word "rhapsody" is taken at face value. Jazzy details are subsumed by the seriousness of Tortelier's approach. Shelley is like-minded; he plays the two rhapsodies

straight, and in the concerto, he moves close to Rachmaninoff, whose works he has recorded. There's nothing wrong with this. Essentially, Tortelier and Shelley are like Ormandy and Entremont in digital sound and with a correspondingly higher price tag.

Unfortunately, on his second CD, Tortelier's interpretations are tentative and smoothed out, and he shows little affinity with Gershwin's idiom. What happened in the two years that separated the recording sessions? Perhaps the change of orchestras is to blame; this time around, Tortelier conducts the BBC Philharmonic. This disc contains *American in Paris,* Gershwin's *Catfish Row* suite, *Variations on "I Got Rhythm,"* and Don Rose's arranged overtures to *Girl Crazy* and *Strike Up the Band* (Chandos 9325). Tortelier belies his French heritage with an *American in Paris* that's as staid as it can be. He skates right over the surface of most of the music and the orchestra sounds barely interested. The only really noteworthy things about these performances are the distortions Tortelier introduces—for example, a grotesque raspberry to initiate the maxixe in *American in Paris,* and an out of tune upright piano in *Catfish Row.* He's most successful with the overtures, but they're hardly reasons for getting this disc.

There are several "greatest hits" collections that feature a variety of performers. One that's even more than ordinarily eclectic includes several recordings mentioned above, including Bernstein's Columbia *Rhapsody in Blue* and Tilson Thomas's New York *American in Paris* and Los Angeles recording of *Promenade* (Sony 64060). Tilson Thomas and the Los Angeles Philharmonic also accompany vocalist Sarah Vaughan in a medley from *Porgy and Bess* and a scatty rendition of "Fascinating Rhythm." This isn't jazz as Gershwin understood it, but Vaughan's Gershwin is not to be missed. The first and last of the three piano preludes are included, but in arrangements for two pianists (the Labèque sisters) and cello (Ma). Previn's earliest recording of Concerto in F— third movement only—is here as well, as is an antiquated but still serviceable reading of *Cuban Overture* with Louis Lane conducting the Cleveland Pops. The disc opens with John Williams conducting the Boston Pops in an arrangement of "Strike Up the Band." The best reason to get this disc is the *Lullaby,* played with touching fragility by the members of the Juilliard String Quartet. This is the only all-Gershwin CD I've encountered that contains this work played as written.

"Classic Gershwin" is another variation on this formula (CBS 42516). Most of its contents are reviewed above. They include Tilson Thomas's frenzied *Rhapsody* with Gershwin's 1925 piano roll, his mannered version of *Three Preludes,* Bernstein's classic New York *American in Paris,* and, as above, Sarah Vaughan singing a medley from *Porgy and Bess.* Several of Gershwin's songs are here, but not in versions the composer would recognize. There's Cleo Laine singing "Embraceable You," flutist Rampal playing "Liza," and guitarist Williams playing "A Foggy Day." A medley of five songs as arranged for Woody Allen's film *Manhattan* is played by Mehta and the New York Philharmonic. This disc makes pleasant listening, but it's hardly integral to an understanding of the composer.

Turning to a few of the more prominent discs that feature arrangements of Gershwin's music, one of the more recent is with violinist **Bell** and conductor Williams, who also assists Bell at the piano (Sony 60659). The composer had repeatedly been asked by his friend Heifetz to write a work for the violin, but he died before he could do so. Bell plays Alexander Courage's 20-minute *Fantasy for Violin and Orchestra on Porgy and Bess,* Heifetz's arrangement for violin and piano of *Three Preludes,* and various arrangements for violin and orchestra of six songs. (In "Sweet and Low-Down," Bell is joined by the composer himself, by virtue of the piano roll.) I have no problem with this disc, except it ends up serving Bell—admittedly a wonderful, lyrical player—more than it serves Gershwin.

If it's Gershwin on the violin you want, you might just as well stick with **Heifetz** himself (RCA 61771). His 1965 recordings of *Three Preludes* and selections from *Porgy and Bess* succeed because of his refusal to play too sweetly. Similarly, if you want to hear the difficulties of *Rhapsody* divided among two pianists, you can turn to the **Labèque** sisters with orchestra (London 430726) or the **Paratore** brothers without (Koch-Schwann 1439), although Gershwin was quite capable of writing for two pianos if he had wanted to. (The Paratore disc also includes two-piano arrangements of Concerto in F, plus Percy Grainger's *Fantasy on Themes from Porgy and Bess,* which is more justified.)

No one in their right mind would want the historical recordings of this music as their only choices, yet if you love *Rhapsody* and (particularly) the Concerto, **Paul Whiteman**'s versions shouldn't be missed (Pearl 0022). Apart from their historical value, they make the music shine in a completely unexpected light. Whiteman's 1928 recording of the Concerto features pianist Roy Bargy, and, in the cornet solos, Bix Beiderbecke. The score was slightly abridged to fit on six 78 rpm sides, and the orchestration has been adapted, probably by Ferde Grofé, for use by Whiteman's Concert Orchestra. Bargy's jaunty playing is just as entertaining as the wonderfully odd sounds made by the orchestra, which numbered about 25 players at the time. There's also a nine-minute abridgement of *Rhapsody* from 1927, with Gershwin himself as the soloist. (This was his second recording of the work with Whiteman; there was an acoustic version from 1924.) Ross Gorman's opening clarinet solo is a splendid tease, and the entire recording roars with playfulness and fun, just like the decade that created it. (The disc also includes Whiteman's recordings of Grofé's *Grand Canyon* and *Mississippi Suites,* and these are even more startling than the Concerto.)

The definitive historical collection, "George Gershwin Plays George Gershwin," duplicates some of the material found in other collections but is the most comprehensive and best prepared (♦Pearl 9483, 2CD). It includes both of the composer's truncated recordings of *Rhapsody,* plus *American in Paris* conducted by Nathaniel Shilkret, with Gershwin playing both the (relatively minor) piano and celesta parts. As this wonderfully breezy recording was "supervised" by the composer (apparently Shilkret couldn't keep him out of the studio), it settles—perhaps!— questions about tempo and interpretation. The set also preserves Gershwin's Columbia recordings, made in London in 1926. These include four sides with Fred and Adele Astaire; one features the sound of Fred's dancing, with vocal encouragement from the composer; the other Columbia sides were piano solos, and they display Gershwin's keyboard virtuosity better than any other material. Eight sides from *Porgy and Bess* highlight the singing of Helen Jepson and Lawrence Tibbett (Gershwin favored Tibbett for the title role, but felt a white singer would lack credibility), conducted by Alexander Smallens and also supervised by the composer. Gershwin never recorded his Concerto, but Pearl has tracked down a 1933 Rudy Vallee Show broadcast of the composer playing an arrangement of the third movement. This can't fail to interest the ardent Gershwinophile.

The recordings in a "Historic Gershwin Recordings" compilation overlap with the Pearl discs (RCA 63276, 2CD). The composer's 1924 and 1927 versions of *Rhapsody* are here, as is Morton Gould's 1955 version, which is more jazzy than most orchestral recordings but not as exciting. Gould is also a fine but nontraditional pianist in the three Preludes and in a solo arrangement from *Porgy and Bess.* His

comprehensive suite from the opera—30 minutes long—was also recorded in 1955. It's skillfully done, but no replacement for the opera. Jepson's and Tibbett's sides from the opera are here too, as are two recordings of *American in Paris,* one with Shilkret and Gershwin and the other Bernstein's 1949 recording. It's as wonderful as the one he did almost a decade later (in stereo) for Columbia. There are good things in this set, but Pearl 9483 is a better value.

Toscanini programmed the concertante works with pianists Oscar Levant and Earl Wild. At present, however, only his 1945 recording of *American in Paris* is in the catalog (RCA 60307). (Keep your eyes open, though.) There are those who feel this recording is a serious contender. Commentator William Youngren called it "perhaps the finest fruit of this burst of affection for [Toscanini's] adopted country." I find it overly fast and not very idiomatic—neither particularly French nor particularly American. Youngren defends the tempo by comparing it to Shilkret's recording, but tempo is about all they have in common. What's more, the playing is uncharacteristically sloppy, with poor entrances and brass "clams." This one is for the conductor's fans only.

Another historic recording features pianist **Levant** in all the composer's concertante works (Sony 42514). Thanks to the 1951 movie *An American in Paris* and many appearances on radio, screen, and television, the American public associated Levant with Gershwin's music throughout the '40s and '50s. The two men were actually friends in the '30s. In spite of his famously messy personal life—which easily bled over into his public persona—Americans adored the self-hating and caustic Levant. (When cast opposite Joan Crawford in the 1946 weepie *Humoresque,* he quipped, "I played an unsympathetic role—myself!") The recordings on this CD were made in the '40s, when Levant was at the height of his powers and before his personal demons gained the upper hand. His *Rhapsody* (slightly cut) is played with vehemence, and he moves from one section to the next like a cat batting a hapless mouse. *Second Rhapsody* and *Variations on "I Got Rhythm"* are hammered out with the violence of urban warfare.

In the film *An American in Paris,* Levant plays the Concerto in F, with cinematic trickery casting him as conductor, soloist, and members of the orchestra. That scene describes his 1942 recording of the work as well: it's all Levant's fingers and forceful personality. You can't help but respect his Gershwin, but it's very nearly brutal. Only in *Three Preludes* does he allows some flowers to push up. His partners are Ormandy (*Rhapsody*), Gould (*Second Rhapsody* and *Variations on "I Got Rhythm"*), and Kostelanetz (Concerto in F).

In 1938 Gershwin, who had died the previous year, was honored by the "RCA Magic Key Gershwin Memorial Program" (RCA 63275). This radio presentation featured Jane Froman among the vocalists and Gershwin's friend Shilkret on the podium. In spite of the melancholy circumstances, this program, originally issued on ten 78 rpm sides, is a delight from beginning to end. Eight of these sides are medleys—a breeze through the choruses (and maybe a verse here or there) of three or four songs at a shot. (One side is Froman's complete rendition of "The Man I Love," and another is a choral arrangement (!) of the middle section of *Rhapsody in Blue.* I usually find the medley format less than satisfying, but the singing and playing are so charming and so redolent of the era that I'm completely disarmed.

Almost all of the 36 recordings in "From Gershwin's Time" were made while the composer was alive (Sony 60648, 2CD). This collection is a cornucopia for nostalgia buffs, and the selections are typical of the era, i.e., not necessarily the best. Most are music for dancing, and right or wrong, this is how many Americans heard their Gershwin in the '20s and '30s. The performers include obscure groups such as Borah Minnevitch & His Harmonica Rascals, the Ipana Troubadours, and the Cliquot Club Eskimos. Also present are the young Kate Smith, Fred Astaire, tasty Gertrude Niesen, and Ella Logan (1937: "Love is Here to Stay"). Some of Gershwin's piano records are here again, and Concerto in F with Bargy and Whiteman. We also hear an unlikely Fritz Reiner from 1945, conducting a bang-up "Symphonic Picture" from *Porgy and Bess.*

PORGY AND BESS

A decade ago there were several complete recordings of *Porgy and Bess;* now the only one that seems to be readily available is associated with the Glyndebourne Festival—an English institution—and conducted by **Rattle** (♦EMI 56220, 3CD). Most of the principals were born in North America, however, and a fine cast they are. Willard White is a strong, sympathetic Porgy, Cynthia Haymon a passionate and vulnerable Bess, and Damon Evans a remarkably charismatic Sportin' Life. Harolyn Blackwell (Clara) is radiant in "Summertime," and the others are fine. Rattle conducts with the ultimate in extroversion. In his hands, it's grand opera indeed, and yet he brings the swagger and showmanship of the Broadway stage to this reading as well. Several reviewers have complained about the unclear diction on this recording, although there's no consensus as to whether the fault lies with the resonant engineering or with the singers themselves.

Although BMG no longer lists it, their recording continues to be available through many retailers (RCA 2109, 3CD). Many American listeners express a strong preference for this production. Conductor **John DeMain** has been praised for being less extreme than Rattle, while remaining sensitive to both the operatic and the popular elements of the music. The Porgy is Donnie Ray Albert, the Bess Clamma Dale, and most of the large cast is associated with Houston Grand Opera. Thomas Z. Shepard, the producer of many Broadway musical recordings (the cast also took the show to Broadway), has received kudos for bringing his stage savvy to this recording. **Maazel**'s Cleveland recording of the complete opera is no longer available (London 414559, 3CD). It also had Willard White as Porgy. The consensus was that this version had good singing but little dramatic impact, so it places a clear third behind Rattle and DeMain.

Although not strictly "complete" (the original cover text notwithstanding), a 1951 studio recording can't be discounted (Sony 63322, 2CD). Original producer Goddard Lieberson and conductor **Lehman Engel** cut about 45 minutes from the score, and the results are taut and sweeping. Camilla Williams (Bess) and Lawrence Winters (Porgy) were singers with the New York City Center Opera, and a few of the other cast members were involved in the 1935 production. The smaller parts were taken from the studio chorus, and the presence of voices with less training adds drama while removing little from musical values. Williams and Winters are likeable in their roles, and you feel a chemistry between them that's absent in other recordings. June McMechen is heart-stoppingly beautiful in "Summertime," and when Inez Matthews sings "My Man's Gone Now," you believe her. The other vocal standout is Avon Long, whose oily Sportin' Life steals the show. Engel moves the music along (his expertise was in Broadway musicals) and Lieberson keeps the dramatic stakes high, including the sound effects department. The engineering, old as it is, shouldn't get in the way of any listener's enjoyment of these discs.

For those who don't want the entire score—and truth to tell, *Porgy and Bess* does have its dry spells—there are a few alternatives, in addi-

tion to a panoply of popular interpretations not to be discussed here, plus a highlights disc from the Rattle recording (EMI 54325). Most treasurable among them is a reissue of a studio recording from 1963 with Leontyne Price gloriously singing music associated with Bess, Clara, and Serena, and with Warfield as Porgy (♦RCA 63312). Another vintage performance is John W. Bubbles's seductive Sportin' Life; any Bess would have followed him on the boat to New York, "happy dust" or no. The RCA Victor Orchestra and Chorus are conducted by **Skitch Henderson,** who adds three parts of Broadway to two parts Metropolitan Opera—just about the right combination for me. It's too bad that 48 minutes of music is all we get.

Litton—a solid Gershwin conductor—has fashioned a concert suite from the opera (Dorian 90223). He's joined by several veterans of the Rattle recording, including Cynthia Haymon (Bess), Cynthia Clarey (Serena), and Damon Evans (Sportin' Life), who repeat their previous roles. This is worth considering if you want a generous selection of the opera's highlights. An alternative comes from **Kunzel** (Telarc 80434). Like Litton, he includes most of the famous numbers and also a few surprises, including the world premiere recording of material that Gershwin cut from the beginning of Act III to speed the flow of an already long evening. Kunzel conducts with spirit, although some of the tempos are daringly slow ("Summertime") or unnervingly fast ("My Man's Gone Now"). Harolyn Blackwell is memorable in the former, Angela Brown screechy in the latter. Marquita Lister's Bess and Gregg Baker's Porgy are hardly dramatic portrayals; Baker lacks authority, but he does warm up as the recording progresses. At least one reviewer found this recording dull. I like it a little better, but it's too uneven to recommend over those listed above. Note that this was Cab Calloway's last recording; he scats his way though "It Ain't Necessarily So" with his last vocal resources, and any claims this recording had of being "authentic" go right out the window in the process.

Listeners might want this CD anyway, because it contains the only currently viable recording of Gershwin's *Blue Monday.* Gershwin wrote this "vaudeville opera" over the course of two weeks for *George White's Scandals,* and it's hardly an inspiring work; the plot is a variation on the "Frankie and Johnny" theme, and the most memorable tune is our old friend the *Lullaby.* This is the world premiere recording of the original orchestration; earlier, now unavailable recordings on Vox and EMI compromised the opera in different ways. There is a *Blue Monday* on an Italian label; I haven't heard it, but its Alpine origins don't inspire a great deal of confidence (Aura 174).

PIANO MUSIC

Gershwin's piano rolls have been reissued in two volumes, so now we can enjoy his "actual" playing—after a fashion—in modern sound (♦Elektra/Nonesuch 979287 and 979370). He made about 130 rolls between about 1915 and 1929, some of his own music and some of other popular music of the era (the second volume highlights composers other than Gershwin). The rolls have been realized by Artis Wodehouse on a 9-foot Yamaha Disklavier grand, and the results are brilliant, comparable to Gershwin's records except, in addition to the sonic improvements, they tend not to be so rushed. The first disc contains early songs and instrumental pieces, plus a solo piano version of *Rhapsody* (probably the substrate for the first Tilson Thomas recording reviewed above) and a two-piano *American in Paris* with both parts played by piano roll wizard Frank Milne and realized on *two* Disklavier Yamaha grands!

"Fascinating Rhythm," a CD from British pianist **Angela Brownridge,** is subtitled "The Complete Music for Solo Piano," a precipitous claim at best (Helios 55006). The booklet amends it by saying "This recording . . . includes all the short piano pieces at present available." The centerpiece is all 18 numbers from Gershwin's *Songbook,* his virtuosic arrangements of his most popular songs. These are very well written for the piano, so pianistic that even a bumbling player can make them sound good. Brownridge is anything but bumbling, though; she's a bubbly musician who enlivens everything she touches. Taking the whole disc at once, however, there's a sameness in the program that could have been relieved had she inched out on her interpretive limb a bit more. Nevertheless, it's enjoyable, and she cuts a rug in the overture to *Girl Crazy.* Other works on this CD are *Three Preludes, Promenade,* and *Rialto Ripples.* Thirteen of the *Songbook* selections are offered by **Watts** in his "Great Pianists" set (Philips 456985, 2D). Watts was a fabulous technician and stylist at the time of these recordings, and I doubt that anyone will be disappointed with what he does here.

Jack Gibbons is more exciting than Brownridge in "The Authentic George Gershwin" (ASV 328, 3CD; separately available as 2074, 2077, and 2082). Especially with his songs, what Gershwin published isn't always what Gershwin played; after all, he was a fine pianist, and sheet music of popular songs needed to be playable by an average pianist. In search of "authenticity," Gibbons has gone back to Gershwin's 78 rpm recordings and piano rolls and painstakingly transcribed them for his own performances. You might ask, "Why hear Gibbons when Gershwin's own records and piano rolls are available?" That's certainly a valid question, and Gibbons's recordings have taken a hit from some critics as a result. It's a plus, however, to hear this music played so well—and most definitely in Gershwin's style—with the benefit of modern digital sound. Whether Gibbons had to slavishly imitate the limitations of records and piano rolls (for example, the occasional need for hurried tempos to fit the selection on a single side) is debatable. It also needs to be said that piano transcriptions of orchestral works such as *American in Paris* and *Catfish Row* aren't very interesting. Still, Gibbons's playing is full of personality, and readers may wish to give at least one of these discs a try; I recommend the middle one.

Richard Glazier is an American pianist involved in continuing the Gershwin legacy. When he was 12, he met George's brother Ira, and a lifelong affinity between Glazier and Gershwin was solidified. On his two discs, he plays transcriptions from Gershwin's piano rolls and recordings and technically challenging arrangements of the music by other pianist/arrangers, including Earl Wild and Stan Freeman (Centaur 2271 and 2486). Glazier treats the music as a living thing, subject to interpretation and reinterpretation and viewable from several different angles. This is not a purist's approach, but he's a fine pianist—not as respectful as Brownridge and not as willful as Gibbons—and these recordings are worth a try.

Earl Wild is in a class by himself with his Gershwin transcriptions (♦Chesky 32). Technically, because these are arrangements, perhaps I shouldn't mention them. However, Wild is a masterful arranger, and his incredible technique complements his obvious adoration for Gershwin's music. There's a *Fantasy on Porgy and Bess,* some brilliant variations on "Someone to Watch Over Me," and a set of *Seven Virtuoso Etudes* on other Gershwin songs. With Wild, the nearly dead art of the virtuoso piano transcription is alive again.   TUTTLE

Don Carlo Gesualdo (ca. 1561–1613)

Surely no composer is more notorious than Don Carlo Gesualdo, Principe di Venosa, whose life of violence and bizarre excess might be matched with that of his younger contemporary, the painter Caravaggio.

Gesualdo was a nobleman of the bluest blood, one of the grandees of the Spanish-ruled Kingdom of Naples; he was connected by marriage to other great families of Italy, and his maternal uncle was the great Counter-Reformation prelate, Cardinal Carlo Borromeo. He became instantly infamous in 1590 when, having caught his first wife and her lover *in flagrante delicto,* he had them murdered and publicly displayed their bodies; also, it is said, he killed a recently born daughter whose paternity he mistrusted. Don Carlo's notoriety continued during his retirement to his estates at Gesualdo where, in a life of neurotic melancholia and hypochondria, he devoted himself unreservedly to his passion for music.

As an amateur musician and composer, Gesualdo identified himself with the extremes of the musical counterpart to Mannerism in the art of the day. Though aware of the new monodic experiments that were to lead music in new directions, he clung to the secular and sacred genres of part-writing, creating a highly idiosyncratic style of his own. He was a great admirer of the radical experimenter, Luzzasco Luzzaschi of Ferrara, and he drew to his personal retinue a number of progressive musicians who shared his stylistic radicalism. Gesualdo certainly possessed a remarkable imagination and produced much fascinating music, but he had none of the creative depth or substantive range that allowed Monteverdi to move into innovative leadership of far-reaching influence and substance.

Gesualdo's music constitutes a highly personal and introverted legacy that was a dead end in its own day and forgotten for generations thereafter. If noted at all, it was for its strangeness. But it has won the belated respect of 20th-century musicians and listeners for its bizarre and anachronistically "modern" qualities. He reveled in calculated dissonance, and the wild chromaticism and harmonic eccentricity displayed in much of his writing have prompted some to see him as a prophet of latter-day atonalism. No less a modern master than Stravinsky reflected his fascination with Gesualdo's music by reconstructing a few of his incomplete sacred pieces, going on to compose a tribute to him, *Monumentum pro Gesualdo.* As with much of the music of his time and region, Gesualdo's works come to us almost entirely by means of published collections that he himself put into print. A few random keyboard pieces survive, but otherwise his output was entirely vocal, in the form either of the Italian madrigal or the Latin motet.

The number of recordings has been small but stable over the years, and they fit into three categories: those that give full or selective treatment to a published collection of madrigals or motets; those that give samplings of either madrigals or motets drawn from a number of the published collections; and those that mix examples of both madrigals and motets.

MADRIGALS

Gesualdo published six Books of Madrigals, all for five voices. The first two were printed in 1594, one of them under a pseudonym (given the sensitivity of a nobleman of his rank dabbling in composition). The next two (III–IV) appeared in 1595 and 1596, and the final two were published near the end of his life, in 1611. (A collection of six-voice madrigals was published only after his death, in 1626.) His experimental bent was evident at the outset, so the successive collections show him honing a style that was reasonably well defined from the beginning. As with all the Italian madrigalists, the subject matter was generally amorous, and Gesualdo was not unusual in choosing texts that dwelt upon the pains of love. But he *was* unusual in his intensive concentration on such themes and in the frequent extravagance of his settings. He regularly used texts that dwelt upon verbal and emotional contradictions, allowing him to highlight the juxtaposition of such opposites as *vita* and *morte*, or *gioia* and *dolore*, particularly linking "death" with "joy" in erotic suggestiveness or "sweetness" and "suffering" in seeming masochism. He constantly took advantage of opportunities for vivid word-painting to heighten the poetic messages. The wrenching emotionalism of his settings has been taken as evidence of his own tormented personality, and some passages have even been construed as autobiographical or confessional. Whatever the justice of such interpretations, there is no doubting the idiosyncratic genius of his art.

Surprisingly, there has only been one integral recording of his complete published madrigal collections, undertaken around 1965 (Arcophon). This ambitious project was apparently the brainchild of **Angelo Ephrikian**—no great musician by latter-day standards, but a devoted pioneer in reviving early Italian music. He directed a shifting group of eight singers who sang under the name of Quintetto Vocale Italiano, confirming the understanding, already established, that Gesualdo's madrigals are vocal chamber music (one singer per part) rather than "choral" works (Rivo Alto 8912; one Book per disc; curiously, Ephrikian's involvement is completely ignored in this reissue). The performances are competent but not inspired or distinctive, cautious and piling up with flat monotony; far more artistically satisfying versions of particular books or individual madrigals can be found. There is undeniable reference value in the series's completeness, but that is somewhat qualified by the individual album leaflets that give only the original texts without translations.

Recordings of complete individual publications have concentrated on the last three books. The greatest loss among LP ventures is the full Book V, carefully and stylishly performed by Rooley's **Consort of Musicke** (1984: Oiseau-Lyre); Decca should revive this. Also missed is an incomplete Book VI recording by **Cantus Köln** briefly issued by CBS. But earlier a complete Book VI was led by one of the outstanding Gesualdo interpreters, **Robert Craft,** of whom more will be said below (Columbia).

Newer recordings have filled the gaps. The complete Book IV can be had in rather acerbic performances by **Ensemble Arte Musica** under Francesco Cera, in strangely dry and disembodied sound (Tactus). Books V and VI are sung with lean excellence (if perhaps just a bit too much suave elegance) by Maurice Bourbon's Paris **Métamorphoses Ensemble,** whose members are nevertheless well attuned to stylistic nuances and textual meanings (♦Arion 68388/89). The sound is a little too spacious and reverberant, but otherwise fine.

Most effective of all are the knowingly inflected performances of the complete Book VI by a crack Italian group, **Il Complesso Barocco,** under the redoubtable Alan Curtis (♦Symphonia 94133). Curtis is the only director other than Craft to train his vocalists in singing fully natural pitches and intervals, untainted by latter-day tempered tuning. That rawness of sound makes possible the full effect of Gesualdo's biting dissonances and clashes of line. Curtis also uses discreet instrumental doublings, but goes so far as to have six items done completely by instruments rather than voices, which makes some sense for consistent listening pleasure (as well as acknowledging performance options of the day) but does injustice to the verbal point of the madrigals, all the more strange given his care for vocal technique.

There are two sampler CDs, each with merits and defects. Christie's **Les Arts Florissants** are musically more substantial, and their menu is carefully structured, systematically presenting four madrigals each from Books III–VI (1988; ♦Harmonia Mundi 901268). The sensitivity to texts and moods of seven fine singers creates powerful projections, coming close to Craft's intensity. But some instrumental doubling is allowed, and rather too much indulgence is granted to one of the three players, harpist Andrew Lawrence-King; he not only delivers a transcription of one of the Gesualdo keyboard rarities (*Canzon francese*), but he and a partner are allowed to play three of the 16 madrigals as instrumental pieces—again, legitimate by contemporaneous standards but a perversion of the verbal values of vocal works.

James Grossmith and his **Claritas** ensemble offer a program called "I Tormenti d'Amore" (1999; Etcetera). It's a comprehensive survey: three items from Book I, two each from Books II and III, three from Book IV, and eight from Book VII, though in scrambled order, obviating any picture of stylistic development. The choices are fairly representative and avoid the most famous (or infamous) items. The performances are, however, not strictly one per part but employ a small chamber choir: ten singers, two per part, with a blend so smooth and rich, reinforced by the spacious acoustics of a Cambridge college chapel, that they create a polished sound comparable to that of a larger group. So polished, in fact, that one piece after another is reduced to enervating suavity, drained of harmonic bite and emotional force, and turned into homogenized slickness. Definitely not the way to encounter this mannerist master on fair terms.

MOTETS

Despite the idiosyncrasies of his personal life, Gesualdo seems to have taken spiritual expression and liturgical composition very seriously, in a surviving legacy of 70 motets as against 122 madrigals. Some of his sacred pieces for four voices were published in 1620, after his death, but he himself saw into print only three official collections. In 1603 came two separate volumes of *Cantiones sacrae,* each called *Liber primus,* one containing pieces for five voices, the other for six and seven voices—the latter volume surviving incomplete. In 1611 he published a cycle of six-voice *Responsoria* for the Tenebrae services of Holy Week. Despite their officially polyphonic form, these motets go far beyond the stylistic norms and tastes of contemporary ecclesiastical writing to transfer to sacred texts the same intensity of spirit and exaggerations of technique he had developed in his madrigals. They are more personal "sacred madrigals" than formal liturgical motets, for all their outward applicability to church ritual.

The 1603 publications involve a range of texts, but those focused upon sin, guilt and mortality are recurrent. These emphases are even more inherent in the 1611 collection, devoted to the austere penitential rites of Holy Week that had been given new impetus by the Catholic Reformation, with their somber reflections upon suffering and death—just what Gesualdo doted on in his madrigals, after all. There have been many samplings of the 1603 publications, but there is only one integral recording of the 19 items that make up the five-voice volume, by the **Oxford Camerata** under Jeremy Summerly (1992; ♦Naxos 550742). Only 12 singers are involved, effectively two per part, but the voices are well blended and richly recorded, in sensitive if rather broadly paced interpretations. Unfortunately, a great bargain is reduced to a near-cheat by the complete omission of any texts or translations.

Far more systematic attention has been paid to the 1611 collection, *Responsoria et alia ad Officium Hebdomadae Sanctae spectantia* (Responsories and Other Materials Appropriate to the Office of Holy Week). The rituals of Tenebrae observed in the darkened churches of Passiontide involved three Nocturns of the three Matins Offices for Maundy Thursday, Good Friday, and Holy Saturday. Gesualdo composed settings for all 27 responsories to the chant settings for these services, plus two other pieces for use in Holy Week.

There have been three comprehensive recordings of this 1611 collection (all presenting just Gesualdo's music, without any chant context), two of LP vintage. The first, made in the early '70s by **Deller** and his Consort, was not complete, lacking the Responsories for the Third Nocturn of Good Friday and the two extra pieces (Harmonia Mundi 190220 contained just the Holy Thursday Nocturns; the rest of the LP series doesn't seem to have been reissued). Deller's group of mixed voices, one singer per part, was slack, ill-focused, and not very satisfying musically.

The 1990 recording by Hillier's **Hilliard Ensemble** is quite different (♦ECM 843867, 2CD). With seven male singers, they renew the Deller approach of one singer per part, which sacrifices the sheen and power that choral performance can bring. But as practiced here, the approach allows textures to be kept lucid and clean, so that these excellent singers take full advantage of all the harmonic clashes and tensions of Gesualdo's expressive and highly personal art. Recorded in the apt, chapel-like ambience of England's Douai Abbey, the Hilliards become so caught up in this music that the listener is drawn with them into their stunning performances. If there is a drawback to this wonderful set, it's the distracting flim-flammery of the trendily designed album booklet, though it does find room for the full textual materials.

Seven single-disc recordings have been devoted to two of the three liturgical divisions of this set. The nine Responsories for Good Friday were recorded in 1982 by the six male voices of **Ensemble a Sei Voci,** who also apply the reduced-scale approach in elegant but somewhat relaxed and restrained performances (Erato; MHS). The **Centro Musica Antica di Padova Madrigalisti** under Livio Picotti was recorded in the same set of Good Friday Responsories, plus five Marian motets from the five-voice *Cantiones sacrae* and the substantial six-voice *Psalm 50* that is one of the supplemental pieces to the *Responsoria* publication (1990; Argo 430832). The full ensemble of 18 mixed voices is used only for the Responsories and is scaled down to 12 for the other works; the singing is frankly choral, but quite smooth and stylish in attractive performances

Parrott leads his **Taverner Choir** in the complete cycle for Good Friday, and as expected, the performances by his all-male group are superlative in technique and expressive power (♦EMI 62977). What makes this release exceptional, however, is that, as he has done with other sacred literature, Parrott sets the music in its full liturgical context. He's the first to present any of the *Responsoria* cycles (in divisions or in full) surrounded by the full array of plainchant Antiphons, Psalms, and *Lectiones* that Gesualdo's pieces would complement as part of the three Nocturns of one day's *Tenebrae* rituals. As a result, the intense packets of spiritual contemplation of the *Responsoria* are spread out and fitted into the liturgical ebb and flow in which the composer would have heard them.

The 1987 recording by the **Tallis Scholars** led by Peter Phillips presents the nine Responsories for Holy Saturday and four Marian motets from the five-voice *Cantiones sacrae* (♦Gimell 015). The 12 mixed voices blend superbly, balancing the utmost in choral polish with deft sensitivity to verbal meanings and musical inflections; these are absolutely smashing performances, not to be missed. **Herreweghe's** recording again gives us the nine Holy Saturday Responsories, plus another four of the five-voice *Cantiones sacrae,* rounded out by a work commissioned from a modern Italian composer, Sandro Gorli, setting an Italian text under the title of "Requiem" (1990; ♦Harmonia Mundi 901320). The ensemble fields 16 singers for the Gesualdo perform-

ances, which are lucid, strongly animated, textually alert, and technically refined.

Richard Marlow led his mixed-voice **Trinity College Choir, Cambridge,** in a program that opens with choral music by Stravinsky (his *Mass* and three short pieces) and concludes with the nine Responsories for Holy Saturday, with the connection between the two composers confirmed by including Gesualdo's three 6/7-voice *Cantiones sacrae* for which Stravinsky (very freely) recreated the missing voice part (1994; ♦Conifer 51232). As always with Marlow's recordings, the choral singing is smooth and stylish; the direction is knowing, but also rather staid, while distant miking in a reverberant setting reduces clarity and makes for a rather cool spirit, far less compelling than what Herreweghe offers.

MIXED COLLECTIONS

Over the years there have been a number of recorded programs that provided cross-sectional samplings of both the sacred and secular compositions. All too often, in earlier days, the performing agency was a chorus, which could work well enough for the motets but was ham-handed in the madrigals. In a program shared with works by Monteverdi—three each of Gesualdo's madrigals and motets—we have genuinely elegant and distinguished choral performances (including two examples of the five-voice *Cantiones sacrae* and one of the *Responsoria*) by Gardiner leading his **Monteverdi Choir** with flair (Decca 440032). I've already mentioned the **Deller Consort's** LP that combines seven madrigals from various books with five motets from the *Cantiones sacrae* in one-per-part performances that no longer stand up well (Harmonia Mundi; RCA).

The outstanding CD contribution to this category is by the **Gesualdo Consort** under Gerald Place (1982; ♦ASV 6210). Stressing relative rarities, it contains six madrigals (drawn from the earlier Books II and III and a posthumous publication) and three sacred pieces (one from the *Cantiones sacrae,* two of the *Responsoria,* and a four-voice Psalm from a posthumous publication of 1620), as well as a keyboard *Gagliarda.* These pieces are intermingled with nine selections (six madrigals, three motets) by four other composers—a wonderful idea, allowing us to see how much of Gesualdo's supposed "eccentricities" were shared with or influenced by other musicians of his circle. But the idea is subverted in part by wasting the opportunity to make direct comparisons in settings of the same texts. Still, the program is invaluable, and, fortunately, the performances—generally by one singer per part drawn from ten vocalists (including Place himself)—are intelligent and reliable.

Robert Craft in his younger days became a champion of Gesualdo and produced no less than five LPs devoted to his music. He began with a collection of 15 madrigals and one motet, performed by a chamber vocal group (one singer per part) called The Singers of Ferrara, issued in 1956 with notes by Aldous Huxley (Sunset). This was followed by a program of 12 madrigals plus two of the *Responsoria* and the fragmentary seven-voice motet from the *Cantiones sacrae,* with the lost two lower voices freely reconstructed by Stravinsky; by then his group had been joined by a young mezzo named Marilyn Horne (Columbia). Next, between 1958 and 1960, Craft produced three more Gesualdo LPs for Columbia (by then in stereo). One was the complete Book VI of madrigals, as noted above. The other two were programs mixing madrigals with motets and some of the keyboard pieces, as well as Stravinsky's *Monumentum pro Gesualdo di Venosa ad CD annum* (Tribute to Gesualdo of Venosa at his 400th Anniversary), a 1960 orchestral "recomposition" of three madrigals. A selection from the latter two of those LPs—all of the middle one and eight items from the last—has been reissued (♦Sony 60313).

An early devotee of serialism, Craft has been among those who stressed Gesualdo's proto-modern sounds and techniques. At the heart of his effort was his emphasis on harmonic and tonal tensions by training his highly skilled singers to push the boundaries of pitch intonation (as Alan Curtis was later to do), rather than using pure and untempered pitch in his work with Gesualdo's music. Craft's interpretations come with an agenda of sorts and are by no means the only way to appreciate Gesualdo's music, but they remain unequaled in their piercing clarity and bracing expressiveness. BARKER

Orlando Gibbons (1583–1625)

Gibbons was foursquare in the musical life of England as the Jacobean era began. His heritage and career placed him in the very center of the highly politicized Royal Chamber as a court musician; were it not for an attack of apoplexy on Pentecost Sunday, 1625, he would have presided over the ceremony for Charles I and his new bride, Queen Henrietta Maria. He was respected and admired in his own lifetime, if careful to present his elaborate verse anthems to the deans of prominent parishes while keeping his most personal works, the keyboard and chamber pieces, mostly to himself (the exception being the 1613 *Parthenia* for King James's daughter Elizabeth, where he was joined by two elder composers of great stature: John Bull and the titan of the age, William Byrd).

Gibbons seemed destined for musical prominence. His father was master of the City Waits for Oxford and Cambridge. By age 13, he was singing in the choir of King's College, Cambridge, and by his 20th year had come under the discerning eye of a well-placed musical talent scout (some suggest Bull himself) and become an unpaid Gentleman Extraordinary. He took his music degree at Cambridge, married the daughter of an official at court, set up a home in Westminster, and gradually advanced through the musical ranks until the ultimate appointment for a musician of his time, organist of Westminster Abbey. The French ambassador visited the Abbey in 1624 and said he was "the best finger of that age." Yet even then he seemed to be a composer's composer, and remains curiously under-represented on disc.

Fully a third of the available material is from the first rediscoveries of Gibbons, roughly from Alfred Deller's first efforts through Glenn Gould to Deller again in the '70s. We begin with the magnificent work of the great proponent of keyboard music of the English Golden Age, **Thurston Dart** (Argo, various discs, unfortunately NA), some odd and inadequate recordings of the *Fantazia,* and Deller's earliest essay (Archive 3053, NA but worth seeking out).

Out of a time when the greatest composers were Catholic recusants—Tallis, Byrd, Bull—Gibbons seemed entirely devoted to the Anglican sacred service. Aside from two complete settings of the Service, he also wrote Evensong settings for Whitsunday and Easter, 17 hymn tunes for George Wither's 1623 book, and 40 verse anthems of stunning originality. Weaving their way from solo to chorus, a cappella or scored for organ and even viol consort accompaniment, they are the very heart of his work. There was one book of madrigals, which gave us a secular "greatest hit" ("The Silver Swan"); a couple of consort songs, including Gibbons's contribution to the genre evoking street vendors ("The Cryes of London"); some 40 fantasias for viol consort; and over 50 keyboard works.

Some of **Deller**'s work is still available: the '60s material with four madrigals (Vanguard 8103) and a more substantial early '70s recording with a mix of consort, sacred, and secular vocal pieces (Harmonia Mundi 190219). Sadly, two of the influential recordings from the "second generation" in early music from the '70s are no longer in print:

Trevor Pinnock's keyboard offerings (Vanguard 71.262) and the wonderful and influential work of **David Wulstan** with the Clerkes of Oxenford—a must-find! (♦Nonesuch 71374).

There are four recordings of Gibbons's sacred material available, and each is worthy, with some unduplicated pieces on each. We can begin with the **Choir of New College, Oxford.** The unique pieces on this recording are a complete performance of the Second Service, and it's a necessity for Gibbons's devotees (♦CRD 3451). Six years later, Jeremy Summerly brought his **Oxford Camerata** to the chapel of Hertford College to tackle some of the same material but contrasted the Evensong pieces from the Second Service with those from the "Short Service." Also using organ continuo and featuring a contrasting performance of the extensive "Fantazia of four parts," Summerly is quieter and perhaps more languid, taking his time with each setting. It's equally wonderful, and at its bargain price deserves a home in any collection where sacred music is valued (♦Naxos 553130).

A 1994 disc featuring organist John Butt with the **University of California Berkeley Chamber Chorus** and the Berkeley Festival Consort of Viols has the virtue of illustrating how the consort accompaniment illuminates the texts Gibbons so carefully chose (♦Centaur 2308). It includes "This is the Record of John," one of Gibbons's most simple and affecting pieces, and our only recording of "Blessed are they that fear the Lord." The performances are of a very high order and are highly recommended. A disc from the **Chancel Choir of the Episcopal Church of the Incarnation** in Dallas directed by Kevin M. Clarke offers good performances distinguished by a handful of anthems not available elsewhere (Pro Organo 7062).

Some collections have attempted to show the range of Gibbons's artistry in the old Deller Consort manner by mixing sacred and secular vocal with consort works. Most successful (and again a bargain) is the **Rose Consort of Viols** with Red Byrd (♦Naxos 550603). They argue convincingly for the range of competency in the composer's *oeuvre,* from keyboard dances to "Glorious and Powerful God" for voices and viols, from popular dance settings for consort to the stunning reworking of the "In Nomine" theme from Taverner's *Missa Gloria tibi trinitas.* Purchase of this single disc should be first for neophytes; from here they can decide on more vocal, keyboard, or chamber music after listening to Gibbons in his entirety at this level of advocacy.

Gibbons provided a theme for the Utrecht Festival in the late 1990s, and two projects resulted. One mixes consort and instrumental pieces of Byrd and Gibbons and features the **Royal Consort** with David Cordier (Globe 5159). It's undistinguished and misattributes "Ye Sacred Muses" (on the death of Tallis) to Gibbons, who was only two when the great master died. **Richard Egarr** (also of Cambridge) gives us a good grounding of the range of keyboard pieces (Globe 5168), and is matched by **Joseph Payne**'s 1991 essay with all five "mask" settings for keyboard (BIS 539). A little of Glenn Gould's Gibbons is appended to a William Byrd reissue (♦Sony 52589); no, it isn't a virginal, and it isn't branded with the early music movement stamp of approval, but how can we deny his sheer joy and reverence in music-making?

And happily, there is a new project afoot. **Mark Levy** with his Concordia Ensemble has begun a series of the complete consort works. Volume I features four *In Nomine* settings, the entire 1621 collection of *Fantazias,* and the marvelous music with "the Great Dooble Bass." As passionate and convincing in performance as he is in his album notes (which are in themselves an eloquent plea for rediscovery of Gibbons's work), Levy is a welcome harbinger of what we hope for the composer in the 21st century (♦Metronome 1033). DAVIS

Alberto Ginastera (1916–83)

Ginastera described his music as having "melodic motives whose expressive tension has a pronounced Argentine accent." His sense of duality, whether tonal, dissonance juxtaposed with consonance, contrasts in orchestration, or serial repetitiveness contrasted with chorale-type writing, permeated his music. He divided his career into three distinct periods: "Objective Nationalism," a period of basically tonal music that incorporates dissonance (1935–1948); "Subjective Nationalism," a period containing implicit rhythms and melodic motifs of the pampas (1948–1954); and his "Neo Expressionist" period (after 1954).

Most of Ginastera's vocal music comes from his "Objective Nationalism" period. Soprano **Olivia Blackburn** made a wonderful recording of *Dos canciones, Cinco Canciones populares Argentinas,* and *Las horas de una estancia* with pianist Alberto Portugheis (ASV 902). Tenor **Raúl Giménez** recorded the *Canciones populares* with pianist Nina Walker (Nimbus 5107, with songs by other Argentine composers).

Alberto Portugheis has recorded all of Ginastera's piano and chamber music (ASV 880, 865). The latter, in addition to *Danzas Argentinas,* 12 *American Preludes,* and Piano Sonata 1, offers his Cello Sonata, *Pampeana #2,* and a transcription of his song "Triste" played by the composer's wife, Aurora Natola-Ginastera. Other exceptional recordings of his piano music are by **Santiago Rodríguez** (Elan 2002) and **John Novacek,** who includes *Danzas Argentinas* in his recording of music with Spanish themes (Ambassador 1014).

Portugheis includes a performance of *Pampeana #1* (with violinist Sherban Lupu) and the Piano Quintet (with the Bingham String Quartet), a very interesting and forward-looking work, in the song recording mentioned above. Ginastera's String Quartet 1 comes from his "Neo Expressionist" period, while his Quartets 2 and 3 employ more serial writing. The **Quarteto Latino Americano** (Elan 2218) recorded 1 with quartets by Revueltas and Villa-Lobos, and the **Lyric Quartet** recorded all three, with Olivia Blackburn singing the vocal part in the very beautiful 3 (ASV 944).

An interesting feature of Ginastera's music is his fascination with the open strings of the guitar, which he uses as a sort of signature in his Guitar Sonata and in many of his orchestral pieces as well. My favorite recording of the Guitar Sonata is by **Alexander-Sergei Ramírez** (Denon 78931). Much of Ginastera's orchestral music has only recently been recorded, for instance by the Uruguayan conductor **Gisèle Ben-Dor,** who has given us *Panambi* and *Estancia* with the London Symphony (Conifer 51336). Ben-Dor also has recorded *Variaciones Concertantes,* a fine concerto for soloists within the orchestra, with the Israel Chamber Orchestra (Koch 7149). On the same recording she has two versions of *Glosses on Themes of Pablo Casals,* one for string orchestra and one for full orchestra with 39 percussion instruments, piano, and harmonium.

Pampeana #3—a "Pastoral for Orchestra"—also has fascinating orchestration that incorporates unlikely pairings of instruments and an extroverted and bombastic percussion section. **Mata**'s recording is remarkable (Dorian 90178). The musicians in the all-Venezuelan Simon Bolivar Symphony play superbly, and despite Ginastera's drastic textural contrasts the recorded sound remains intimate, clear, and full. One of Ginastera's most popular pieces is his Harp Concerto, which also employs unusual colors and a large percussion section. There are two good recordings by **Ann Hobson Pilot** (Koch 7261) and by **Nancy Allen** (ASV 654).

FINE

Umberto Giordano (1867–1948)

Andrea Chénier is the best known of Giordano's dozen operas, but a few others have been recorded, and *Fedora* has had sudden spurts of popularity when singers of stature took up its cause. Those curious about the less familiar works may want to consider a 1998 studio recording of *Il Re* (Stradivarius), or a 1988 *Cena delle Beffe* (Bongiovanni). More interesting is *Madame Sans-Gêne,* a comedy with dark undercurrents that follows the fortunes of a plucky laundress from the French Revolution to Napoleon's court. **Freni** sings the title role in a 1999 stage performance (Dynamic). The sound is of studio quality, and the supporting cast, in Freni's home town of Modena, is solidly professional.

Fedora. Late in her career, **Freni** became something of a Giordano advocate, and *Fedora* was the opera she chose for her farewell appearances on several opera stages. The title role offers an aging prima donna strong dramatic opportunities without taxing her range or stamina, and Freni sang it with conviction and still-beautiful tone. A 1993 live recording from La Scala partners her with Domingo (who gets the opera's one big tune, "Amor ti vieta," popularized by Caruso), and it's worth having despite poor sound (Legato). Of the available studio recordings, the best is by Gardelli, with the inimitable **Olivero** (♦London 433033). An actress of the old school, she sings through the words, infusing each one with meaning yet making it all sound natural. Her voice still has some purity and float, though it's close to threadbare. Del Monaco is a sturdy partner, and the sound is excellent. The recording led by Patanè pairs **Marton** with Carreras and is best left to their most uncritical admirers (Sony).

Andrea Chénier. I owe (or so I thought) most of my affection for *Chénier* to the 1941 recording conducted by de Fabritiis, simply because it's such an exquisite pleasure to hear **Gigli** sing the title role (♦EMI 69996; Arkadia 78012). His voice is liquid, ringing, and incomparably beautiful, and if his acting is on the lachrymose side, the tenor's sincerity is irresistible. Maria Caniglia is a fiery, somewhat strident Maddalena, Gino Bechi a robust Gérard. The sound captures the voices with adequate fidelity, though it doesn't do justice to the orchestra and vocal ensembles.

In the years since, I have seen and heard the opera many times and have come to feel it's as close as possible to being performer-proof. Even if the singers are merely competent, it's possible to be swept away by the tuneful, bustling, colorful music. The characters themselves are so artificial it's difficult to care about them; they gesture and speechify and never resemble real human beings. No one in *Chénier* is sympathetic — not the title character, not the tempestuous Maddalena, not even the often-admired Madelon, whose decision to sacrifice her grandchild to the Revolution is loathsome rather than admirable. Perhaps Giordano was shrewder than he's given credit for; he somehow managed to create an opera that vividly depicts the French Revolution indiscriminately dehumanizing everything in its path.

Not even **Callas** could do much with Maddalena, and she never recorded it in the studio, though you can hear her in a 1955 performance (Rodolphe). There's no need to look beyond the commercial recordings, however, and there are a half-dozen good ones, including the Gigli already mentioned.

Tebaldi, del Monaco, and Bastianini often sang the opera together, and their recording, led by **Gavazzeni,** was the first in stereo and still sounds good (♦London 425407). Tebaldi brings her enthralling warmth and sincerity to Maddalena, the vocal quality as weighty and beautiful as you could wish. Del Monaco's unvaried blaring can be tiresome, but his consistency lends him a kind of integrity that fits the character. Bastianini's dark, handsome baritone is in fine shape.

More pliant and charismatic than del Monaco but no less prodigal of voice is Corelli, with **Santini** (♦EMI 65287). It's a particular thrill to hear him flesh out the phrases of his Act 2 "Credo," which might have been written for him. His acting is crude, even more self-indulgent than Gigli's, but he's believable as both poet and hero. Stella's Maddalena is not unlike Tebaldi's, though it's stronger on top and weaker in the middle. She commands all the traditional *accenti,* and her words have animation and temperament. Gérard is sung by Mario Sereni, whose voice was unusually phonogenic, sounding larger and more resonant than it did in the theater.

Levine's is a more subdued affair, neatly sung by Scotto, Domingo, and Milnes in typical form, though only Scotto has much individuality (RCA). Domingo's voice tends to narrow on top, and that makes him less exciting than Corelli. **Chailly** has a weak Gérard in Nucci, an often ravishing Maddalena in Caballé; you don't mind that she treats the music as if it were a singing exercise designed to highlight her pianissimos and long-breathed phrasing. Pavarotti's splendid diction—he articulates every syllable with relish—makes him a believable poet, and he sings strongly and vibrantly, with a good dollop of heroic abandon. Chailly is a lackluster conductor, but the sound is first-class, and the performance is enhanced by cameos from Ludwig, Varnay, Krause, and Kathleen Kuhlmann. This is an account worth having (♦London 410117).

The strained, sometimes ugly singing of Marton and Carreras make **Patanè**'s recording less desirable, but it's still effective in a disheveled way, filled with raw passion and theatrical vitality (Sony). So is the 1989 **Viotti,** with Maria Guleghina, Franco Bonisolli, and Bruson (Capriccio). Neither of these is likely to become anyone's favorite *Chénier,* but they'll give you your money's worth and an adequate picture of what the opera is about.   LUCANO

Mauro Giuliani *(1781–1829)*

Although the classical guitar is closely associated with Spain, many of the greatest names in its history have been Italian. Giuliani was the greatest virtuoso of the early 19th century, and along with the Spaniard Fernando Sor, the best of the many player-composers of that period. He composed a wide range of music: etudes of varying levels of difficulty (including a famous set of studies for the right hand), character pieces, sonata-form works, variations (his favorite form), more than 100 songs, multi-movement chamber music for guitar and other instruments, and three concertos for guitar and chamber orchestra. In his concert-level pieces, and to some extent in his easier music intended for amateurs, Giuliani balances highly crafted Viennese writing with a concern for creating idiomatic musical textures derived from the guitar's unique tuning (its open strings are tuned in fourths, not the fifths of the violin and cello). An orchestral quality is often notable in his guitar writing, and even when his themes (or treatments of them) are not especially distinguished, his use of the instrument can hold one's interest.

Concertos. The fleet-fingered **Pepe Romero** is well-suited to Giuliani, and he has recorded the "Complete Guitar Concertos" (Philips). However, **Williams**'s second take on Concerto 1 is more interesting (♦Sony 63385). Based on research suggesting a more operatic style for this music, Williams dismisses his earlier recording in favor of an approach that's more "dramatic . . . [opening] the door to continual variety of tempo and mood." Two other points in this disc's favor: he performs the concerto on an 1814 Guadagnini (a make used by Giuliani), and he presents (on his usual concert instrument) a new version of Schubert's *Arpeggione* Sonata arranged for guitar and string orchestra. His playing is Apollonian perfection.

Chamber music. Giuliani wrote most of the best guitar chamber music

of this period, finding a balance between the instrument's natural role accompanying the flute or violin, the need to keep all the players' parts interesting, and strictly musical concerns. The musicians who play these pieces are apt to be the most interested in them, but they also make excellent background music. **Perlman** and Williams include a Sonata in E minor in a disc otherwise devoted to Paganini (CBS). For more variety, look for a disc by the colorful virtuoso **Kazuhito Yamashita,** including *Gran Duetto Concertante* with Galway, the E minor Violin Sonata with Swensen, and a Serenade for violin and cello with Elizabeth Anderson (♦RCA 60237). Yamashita and Galway also include the Op. 85 Sonata in their "Italian Serenade" (RCA). Although there are guitar duos with more precision, there may never be a pair with the artistry of **Bream** and **Williams,** who give a red-hot account of the *Variazioni Concertante* in "Together Again" (RCA).

Solo guitar music. Playing Giuliani's music well requires a balance of refined musicality, a sense of color, and, when necessary, great virtuosity. In the last decade or so it has also benefitted from a new level of musicology. In the '60s and '70s it was not uncommon for great players like Bream and Williams to edit out sections of pieces and recompose endings, arguably with excellent results; today, the best players are more apt to present the music as Giuliani wrote it, even using period instruments.

Although there are some all-Giuliani discs, many of the best performances of his works are on records with other music. Some of his solo pieces have become recital and recording warhorses, like the Grand Overture Op. 61, several of the *Rossiniane,* and his Variations on a Theme (Handel's "Harmonious Blacksmith"). A wonderful performance of the latter (though with a missing variation and a revised ending) is by **Williams** (♦Sony 62425, with music by Paganini, Scarlatti, and Villa-Lobos). **Bream** was perhaps the first to have the sense of color needed for the operatic Giuliani, and reissues of his *Rossiniane* (a six-piece cycle) are recommended. Op. 121 and the Grand Overture (one of his favorite recital pieces) are examples of Bream at his best (♦RCA 61593; 61591 for Op. 119). **Eliot Fisk** plays *Rossiniane* even more dazzlingly in one of his best collections, "Bell 'Italia" (♦MusicMasters 67070).

After you've heard those, you won't be interested in **Segovia**'s performance of the first movement of Sonata Op. 15, his only substantial Giuliani recording (mistakenly included in MCA's "The Romantic Guitar"). For a less Dionysian approach, **Manuel Barrueco** offers *Gran Sonata Eroica* and *Variations on Folies d'Espagne* in performances distinguished by their razor-sharp attack and elegance (♦Vox 3007).

As for all-Giuliani discs, I recommend three. **David Russell** takes on all the big pieces as part of his excellent series devoted to single composers (♦Telarc 80525). Russell plays without affectation and with a disarmingly easy virtuosity, as well as wonderful tone. Chilean **Luis Orlandini** does a superb job with all six *Rossiniane* (CPO). **David Starobin,** playing on a replica of an early 19th-century guitar, has a particularly interesting disc, including only one warhorse (*Grand Overture*) among a selection of shorter pieces and two sets of variations (♦Bridge 9029). He also includes two wonderfully chromatic pieces for the older 5-string guitar by Antoine de l'Hoyer apparently "arranged" by Giuliani. His playing is first-rate and the instrument sounds fuller than expected.
                                                                     DINGER

Philip Glass *(b. 1937)*

For a time in the '80s, Philip Glass was the most popular composer in America, drawing huge audiences from both the classical avant-garde and pop worlds with his arpeggiated, repetitive, often surprisingly romantic, relentlessly tonal music. Eventually his style would embrace almost every format, from solo piano to full-blown operas and several genres unto themselves. Alas, Glass turned out to be perhaps overly prolific, for along with some undoubtedly beautiful things, like many an overworked, write-on-demand, 18th-century composer he has also turned out a lot of warmed-over dross. So you have to be selective when sampling his recordings, which, in order to make this shoe fit, are herein divided into some unorthodox categories.

EARLY MUSIC

Glass's earliest recordings reveal the stark, hypnotic, stripped-down, uncompromising beginnings of minimalism. *Two Pages, Contrary Motion, Music in Fifths,* and *Music in Similar Motion* gradually expand the instrumental palette (Nonesuch 79326), while *Music With Changing Parts* inflates the time frame to an hour of heavy-duty repetition for organs, winds, and voices (Nonesuch 79325). For hardcore cultists only.

Music in Twelve Parts contains over three hours of slowly evolving, arpeggiated, scalar sheets of sound that will either send you into an ecstatic trance or drive you mad. But it also has rare (for Glass) tinges of jazz feeling (Part VII), his sole tone row (Part XII), and signposts that point toward *Einstein On The Beach.* While the first **Philip Glass Ensemble** recording (♦Virgin 91311, 3CD, NA) has a blaring intensity that eludes the gentler remake (♦Nonesuch 79324, 3CD), the latter still definitely gives you the message. The last big early work is the often exhilarating *Dance* for either the Glass Ensemble or solo organ, where elements of his later romanticism start to seep into the patterns (♦CBS 44765, 2CD). Thicker, less airborne performances of Dances 2 and 4 on a pipe organ can be found in **Donald Joyce**'s all-Glass program (Catalyst 61825). Be careful with the early works; it's easy to overdose.

OPERAS

The opera *Einstein On The Beach* was the breakthrough for the entire minimalist movement, instantly dividing the musical community along strict love-it-or-hate-it lines, and it also marked the culmination of Glass's early style. Much like *The Rite of Spring, Einstein* still retains its kicky freshness and shock value today—a sure sign of greatness—and the original **Glass Ensemble** recording, though trimmed, will give you a buzz every time (♦CBS 38875, 4CD). The remake restores about 35 minutes of music but mutes the original's exuberance (Nonesuch 79323, 3CD).

Glass's second opera, *Satyagraha,* came as a total surprise to those who were turned on by *Einstein,* with arpeggios and scales repeated in groups instead of evolving brief patterns, and with passages of contemplative beauty and grandeur replacing the old electronic fury. Written for traditional opera companies like the **New York City Opera** to perform (♦CBS 39672, 3CD), it marked the beginning of Glass's mainstream style that he continues to rework today.

The third opera in the "portrait" trilogy, *Akhnaten,* recorded by the **Stuttgart Opera** (♦CBS 42457, 2CD), continues along much the same lines as *Satyagraha,* but now with a tragic monumentality and an ingenious distancing effect at the close (contemporary tourists wandering through Egyptian ruins). A single disc, "Songs From the Trilogy" (CBS 45580), contains excerpts from all three operas, but I don't think it includes their best music (especially *Einstein*); "Glassmasters" offers a much better selection (♦Sony 62960, 3CD).

With his score to Act V of that massive beached whale, *the CIVIL warS,* Glass's writing became even more conventionally operatic, with ecstatic passages affirming the triumph of tonality, some spoken weirdness, and hints that his innovations were beginning to ossify into for-

mulas. **Dennis Russell Davies** and the American Composers Orchestra make a vigorous, openly Verdian case for the work, with Laurie Anderson doing an arch spoken turn as the young Mrs. Lincoln (♦Nonesuch 79487). And Glass's homage to Debussy, *La Belle et la Bête,* an "opera" written to be played along with the Cocteau film, is worth a spin with the **Glass Ensemble** (Nonesuch 79347, 2CD).

THEATER MUSIC

A thin membrane separates Glass's operas and his theater pieces; the differences, perhaps, are in scale and portability. *The Photographer* doesn't hold up well today; played by violinist **Paul Zukofsky** and the Glass Ensemble (CBS), it sounds like a prophetic cross-section of Glassian clichés that would eventually overrun much of his writing (the voices will curl your spine). The highly electrified score for the multimedia *1000 Airplanes On the Roof* (Virgin) starts promisingly in a high-tech crescendo of synthesizers which, alas, quickly gives way to the same old Glass patterns (**Linda Ronstadt**'s vocalises sound like out-takes from *Star Trek*). *Hydrogen Jukebox* is a far more substantial piece, with a seditiously stimulating text by Allen Ginsberg that seems to fire up Glass's imagination and indignation (♦Nonesuch 79286). He reaches back to his early style as well as finding new textures to play with, touching upon jazz, India, Spain, which suited Ginsberg's interests to a T (he occasionally lends his exuberant voice to his poems).

CONCERT MUSIC

Glass's contributions to mainstream concert life are mostly to be avoided. While only five of the nine dances from *In the Upper Room* appear on a disc from an ensemble led by **Michael Riesman,** the used arpeggios on display won't make you want to hear more (CBS). The Violin Concerto—recorded by **Kremer** (DG 437091) and the more lyrical **McDuffie** (Telarc 60494)—confirmed Glass's arrival into the big time, but the piece is no big deal, a mere vertical inflation of standard Glass arpeggios and duplets with a nice slow movement (DG). Likewise, *Itaipu* and *The Canyon,* two parts of a "portraits of nature" symphonic trilogy (Sony 46352), and *The Light* (Nonesuch 79581) are overstuffed permutations of the same old thing. Symphony 2 is mostly a bore, though the Finale tries to find a way out with some mildly stimulating polytonal patterns, and I like the jazzy second movement of its discmate, Concerto for Saxophone Quartet (Nonesuch).

Symphony 3 really lifts off the ground in II with a brilliant, invigorating, neoclassical workout for 19 string players, but the clichés are back in the very next movement, the pall lifting partially in the dashing unison finale (♦Nonesuch 79581). I'd like to love Symphony 5—a 97-minute, 12-movement choral work that combines texts from several religions and philosophies—for its overwhelming ambition and compassion. Yet Glass again has to fall back on his old habits for sustenance; only from the eighth movement onward does he bring forth some interesting ideas, and after leading us to the brink of a grand, beautiful apotheosis near the end, he suddenly darkens into a subdued minor key, thoughtful yet frustrating (Nonesuch 79618, 2CD).

There's even a disc of solo piano music, where **Glass** plays soporific renditions of his usual patterns (CBS). Yet within his string quartets, you can often find some inspired writing, especially the gorgeous romantic melody in 4's slow movement. Symphony 2 ("Company") sums up the Glass esthetic in four succinct little movements totaling only 7½ minutes, a perfectly proportioned miniature. The **Kronos Quartet** recorded it twice; the first is in a grab-bag album of this and that (Nonesuch 79111), the second, somewhat less intense recording is part of their disc of Quartets 2–5 (♦Nonesuch 79356). A broader-paced, softer-focused treatment for string orchestra by **Christopher Warren-Green** and the London Chamber Orchestra also works quite well (Virgin 59610).

POP MUSIC

While invading all aspects of high culture, Glass has also bent over backwards to cultivate links with popular culture. In *Glassworks,* a loosely linked suite of short pieces that got his CBS contract off to a lucrative start (CBS 37265), he doesn't compromise his idiom, only the quality of his ideas; brevity here is a definite virtue. One *Glasswork,* the serene *Façades,* became one of his most popular numbers; a rival version with **Warren-Green** and the London Chamber Orchestra is even more relaxed and expressive (Virgin 59610). Don't blame singers **Ronstadt,** Bernard Fowler and the Roches, or lyricists Paul Simon, David Byrne, etc., for the fatiguing *Songs From Liquid Days,* a pop song cycle riddled with third-rate Glass formulas (CBS).

The "Low" Symphony takes selections from rock singer David Bowie's austerely moving experimental album *Low* and transforms them into Glass rhapsodies. This audacious idea works gorgeously when Glass hews close to the Bowie/Brian Eno material, but collapses when he retreats to his treadmill in the second and third movements. **Davies** and the Brooklyn Philharmonic officiate (♦Point 438150).

FILM MUSIC

Film has elicited a lot of Glass music that usually serves its background function quite well, though its value apart from the cinema is mixed. The score for *North Star* is a good example of his early style, easy to assimilate since the ten excerpts are only a few minutes each (♦Virgin 91013). Another film score that sounds great without the pictures is *Koyaanisqatsi,* in which Glass's trademark arpeggios generate a swirling, exhilarating undercurrent to the speeded-up images of the American rat race. While the original soundtrack contains only 46 minutes of the score (Antilles 422-814042), the **Glass Ensemble** and Western Wind recorded an expanded, uninterrupted 73-minute version in 1998 that makes much more organic sense, though the performance itself is gentler (♦Nonesuch 79506). The sequel *Powaqqatsi* has some passages of rhythmic ecstasy when its Third World influences are raging and is, on the whole, a very underrated score (♦Nonesuch 79192).

Mishima gets bogged down in recycled formulas that are better sampled in Glass's peaceful distillation in Quartet 3 (Nonesuch 79113); the **Kronos** performance of the latter is more refined and subtle than their earlier recordings on the soundtrack (♦Nonesuch 79356). The lyrical, somber *Dracula* score was written for Kronos to accompany the famous Bela Lugosi film; it sounds better without the visuals (Nonesuch 79542). Skip *The Thin Blue Line* unless you like droning film dialogue over the usual droning duplets (Nonesuch), and *The Secret Agent* is pretty static, though Glass makes darkly rich use of the solo English horn and cello (Nonesuch). Like *Powaqqatsi, Kundun* sounds best when it assimilates exotic cultures and leaves Glass's clichés behind (Nonesuch), and *The Screens,* a lovely collaboration with the Gambian kora virtuoso **Foday Musa Suso,** is definitely worth a listen even though much of the genre-hopping score falls well outside the scope of this book (Point 432966).   GINELL

Alexander Glazunov *(1865–1936)*

Glazunov in some sense may be seen as bridging the gap between Tsarist Russia and the 20th century; yet though he managed to survive the ravages of the Bolshevik Revolution, much of his music did not, held by the "intellectuals" of the time to be typical of the "bourgeois art" that must

be left behind. Yet these "bourgeois" qualities—richly colored textures, flowing melody, and a hearty embrace of all that was Mother Russia—still find favor with Russian audiences and in the West as well.

SYMPHONIES

Glazunov completed eight symphonies, and fragments of two others have surfaced on disc. Save for the survey by Neeme Järvi and his German forces, nearly all the recordings you're likely to find are by Russian orchestras and conductors. The best of the lot for both sound and performance are those led by Svetlanov, though they may be hard to find (Melodiya). In some cases older recordings by Rozhdestvensky or Fedoseyev may be preferable, and new series are ongoing from Naxos and Chandos as well. Thus buyers are encouraged to pick and choose.

Symphony 1 bubbles over with high spirits, and not surprisingly has been recorded several times. I've been spoiled by **Yevgeny Akulov**'s splendid recording, unfortunately imported only as a mono LP (Melodiya). **Neeme Järvi** is at his best here (♦Orfeo 093101, with 5). All four Russian conductors are sluggish to varying degrees, with **Fedoseyev** (Vox) more spirited in the first movement and both **Poliansky** (Chandos, with the Violin Concerto) and **Svetlanov** (Melodiya, with *The Kremlin*) pulling ahead in IV. Fedoseyev and **Rozhdestvensky** (Olympia) have mushy strings; Svetlanov is beset by horrendous echo. Sadly, slipshod ensemble and slow tempos render the budget issue by **Anissimov** not worth the money—a shame, as his coupling of 2 and 7 is the best around (Naxos).

Symphony 2 immediately compels attention with a stentorian brass fanfare, soon transformed into a rugged and purposeful Allegro; there's a festive finale and much of interest in between. Two recordings sweep the field: **Anissimov** (♦Naxos 553769, with 7) and **Poliansky** (♦Chandos 9709, with *Coronation Cantata*). Both offer a hearty account of the outer movements, though Anissimov lingers a bit more over the Scherzo; more to the point, given the low cost of the Naxos and the rarity of the Chandos filler, it would be better to have both than quibble over details. **Järvi** just skims the surface, and only offers *Concert Waltz 1* as filler (Orfeo). **Fedoseyev** is let down by congested sonics (same Vox Box as 1) and **Rozhdestvensky** by raw-sounding brasses (Olympia), though both do well with the music. **Svetlanov** is preferable sonically but saddled with the tedious *Song of Destiny* as filler (Melodiya), while **Boris Khaikin**'s stylish account hasn't been brought out on CD (Melodiya).

Symphony 3. Not the most inventive of the lot, 3 is filled with heartfelt melodies and sonorous writing for the brass. Järvi would be an obvious choice (Orfeo, with *Concert Waltz 2*) along with the Russians, here including **Rozhdestvensky** (Olympia 120, with *Lyric Poem*), **Svetlanov** (Melodiya 00024, no coupling) and **Anissimov** (Naxos 554287; see below), but not **Fedoseyev** (at least not on CD). But **Yondani Butt** pulls ahead of all of them, with a fresh, joyous account suggesting that he and the London Symphony were really enjoying themselves (♦ASV 903). You may find an earlier pressing by Butt with the symphony all by itself (ASV 581); the newer one contains excellent performances of *Stenka Razin* and the two Serenades as well, making it a much better buy. Unfortunately, as with 2, **Khaikin**'s 3 is missing in action (Melodiya). Also, only Anissimov includes the vestigial Symphony 9, a single movement arranged from the composer's posthumous sketches by **Gavriil Yudin;** however, his sluggish reading can't compete with Yudin's own (Olympia 147, with Kabalevsky's *Romeo and Juliet* led by Kitaienko).

Symphony 4 is as close to a true "Pastoral" Symphony as Glazunov ever came. The English horn sets the pace with a lovely melody, later taken up by the strings. A nasal and mawkish solo can drag down all that follows, and sadly such is the case with Anissimov, Butt (ASV), Weller (Ars Musici), Poliansky (Chandos), **Polyansky,** and worst of all, Järvi. Rozhdestvensky's horn is the most mellifluous of all (Olympia); Svetlanov's soloist laboriously inches his way along from one note to the next (Melodiya), while both Anissimov and Fedoseyev (Vox) suffer from nasal string tone.

Unfortunately **Rozhdestvensky's** disjointed account of the final movement makes it difficult to recommend his performance, and the others have their problems too, chiefly undue haste; that includes **Järvi** (though his orchestra can take it), **Weller, Polyansky,** and **Anissimov** (theirs can't). Conversely, **Butt** is strangely listless, while **Svetlanov** is vigorous but not enough so to offset his laborious account of 1. Thus **Fedoseyev,** acrid strings or no, is probably the best of a sorry lot. If you find a remaindered copy of **Hans Schwieger's** recording, grab it; his Kansas City ensemble may not be a world-class orchestra, but sounds like one in this crisp, alert reading (♦Urania 5142).

Symphony 5. For me, 5 is the finest of Glazunov's symphonies, culminating in a finale every bit as exciting as Tchaikovsky's 4th. **Rozhdestvensky** is sluggish and dispirited, as are **Järvi** and **Polyansky,** while **Butt** is even worse, and **Fedoseyev's** ponderous account hasn't made it to CD. **Anissimov's** tensile strength and strong brass presence are both in his favor (Naxos 553660, with 8). Nevertheless, despite his hectic tempo in 4:IV, **Weller** is the best choice, an exciting performance taped in concert (♦Ars Musici 1153)—though **Svetlanov** is very good too, and it's unfortunate that it comes with such a tedious 4. If mono sound isn't a concern, there's also a very good concert recording conducted by **Mravinsky,** coupled with an equally fine Prokofiev 5 (Russian Disc 11165). Still waiting in the wings is the splendid LP with **Konstantin Ivanov** (Melodiya).

Symphony 6. Of the Russians, **Svetlanov** comes off best, but the massive echo covers up detail (Melodiya). **Anissimov's** is one of his better efforts, not a subtle account but rugged and very well recorded (Naxos 554293). **Rozhdestvensky** sounds tired throughout (Olympia), while **Fedoseyev** (not on CD) tends toward hysteria in the opening movement. There's also a CD of 6 and 7 derived from old mono LPs with **Golovanov,** badly played with weird and wayward tempo changes (Arlecchino). Thus the buyer may safely choose between **Järvi** (♦Orfeo 157201) and **Butt** (♦ASV 904). Butt has a better orchestra (the London Symphony) but Järvi conducts with a bit more gusto, though the noble strains of the finale resonate more with Butt. Here again there was an earlier pressing, coupled differently (ASV 669), but 904 is the one to buy.

Symphony 7. A paltry few bucks for **Anissimov's** 2 also gets you the best 7 around (♦Naxos 553769), since **Rozhdestvensky** is too slow, save for the Scherzo, which is rushed to the point of absurdity (Melodiya). **Svetlanov** is slowest of all, except for the Scherzo, which is way too fast. **Järvi** hurtles through the symphony at a breakneck pace, while **Golovanov's** inept mono reading should have remained in the archives.

Symphony 8. **Svetlanov's** earlier LP with the Moscow Radio Symphony is more animated than his CD with the USSR Symphony (Melodiya), but either is preferable to **Rozhdestvensky's** sluggish account (Olympia). **Fedoseyev** is a lot better but unavailable on CD. **Anissimov** is overly genial in I but bluffs his way through the last movement adroitly (Naxos, with 5). Overall, **Järvi** leads the pack, with a far more urgent reading of the final movement and a much more immediate recording (♦Orfeo 093201).

OTHER ORCHESTRAL MUSIC

Ballets

All three of Glazunov's ballets are from the turn of the century, when the composer was at the height of his powers and the St. Petersburg Ballet was at its peak.

The Seasons is the best of the three (and also the shortest), an effortless font of melody culminating in an exhilarating "Autumn Bacchanale." While **Svetlanov** is one of the few to include the "Satyre" variation as part of the "Bacchanale," he takes "balletic" tempos to an extreme (Melodiya, also in an EMI "two-fer"). But he sounds positively ebullient next to **Anissimov's** impossibly bloated account (Naxos). **Ansermet** saunters along at a comfortable pace until "Autumn," when he speeds off in a shower of fallen leaves (London). **Järvi** has this music in his blood and coaxes some ravishing sounds from his orchestra, but he seems strangely reserved in the "Bacchanale" and the resonant sonics mute detail (Chandos).

Lenard seems to model his performance on Ansermet, taking the "Bacchanale" at a bracing clip but otherwise a pretty stodgy affair (Marco Polo). Even slower is **Albert Wolff's** disc, of greater interest for its inclusion of Massenet's *Scènes Alsaciennes* and *Pittoresques* (London 433088). **Ashkenazy** is solidly in the Ansermet tradition, emphasizing comfortable tempos until the rather hectic "Bacchanale;" since the appended *Nutcracker* is even worse, this set may be disregarded (London). Sonically **de Waart** may be warmly recommended, though I find his rather measured pace in the "Bacchanale" more tolerable than his hectic treatment of the closing pages (Telarc).

But the best *Seasons* in the catalogue at any price is by **Robert Irving,** coupled with his equally marvelous Scarlatti/Tommasini *Good-Humored Ladies* and Bach/Walton *Wise Virgins* (♦EMI 65911). Irving gets the "Bacchanale" just right—an exhilarating experience—and his lovingly shaped and pastel-hued reading makes the music sound fresh and new. If mono sound is no barrier, much the same satisfying experience may be had from **Roger Désormière** on an excellent transfer of a much-loved LP (EMI 66829).

Raymonda. Set in France in the Middle Ages, Glazunov's grand ballet—much longer than *The Seasons*—only really comes alive when the Saracens stride on stage in Act II, and the colorful wedding festivities in the final act rival even *Swan Lake*. Despite claims to the contrary, the only truly complete recordings are by Svetlanov (Melodiya) and Anissimov (♦Naxos 553503/4). Others boasting varying degrees of completeness are Algis Zhuraitis and Viktor Fedotov (both IMP). **Zhuraitis** was taped "live in concert" at the Bolshoi and sounds like it, a slapdash, devil-may-care romp with the audience whooping and hollering even when one section after another is cast aside; the sound is typical Russian engineering, edgy and brittle at times, yet the listener can't help but be caught up in the excitement. **Fedotov** offers more of the music than Zhuraitis, but performance and sound leave a lot to be desired, and both sets still take 2 CDs.

Most of us grew up with **Svetlanov's** set; it's extroverted and passionate, though marred by some raw sounds from the Bolshoi brasses, and his penchant for whipping up the final bars adds an extra *frisson* of excitement, but the sound shows its age. Fortunately, the best recording is also the least expensive, the splendid set by **Anissimov.** He revels in this music, embracing these languorous melodies in a most seductive fashion and supported by the engineers with a warm glow that really makes the music come alive (Naxos).

There are several suites from *Raymonda* on CD, and you'll have to accept some duplication because no two offer the same selection. **Järvi** includes not one note from Act III, which contains the most colorful music in the ballet, but what he does give us is top drawer, affectionate, and lushly played, making us wish all the more that the producers had him do the whole thing (Chandos). **Butt** offers an extended selection coupled with Symphony 6 (ASV). For those willing to settle for less than 20 minutes, **Fedoseyev** makes it an attractive filler for *Scheherazade (*Canyon).

Ruses d'Amour, also called *Lady Soubrette,* despite its Russian coloring seems like a painting by Watteau, a pastiche making use of early French melodies including "Jai du bon tabac" familiar from Saint-Saëns's *Carnival of the Animals* and ending with an Offenbach-styled *fricassée.* First heard via the pioneering LP with **Yuri Fayer,** the piece has since surfaced on CD, first with **Zhuraitis** (Olympia) and more recently with **Svetlanov** (Melodiya). All may be confidently set aside in favor of the splendid performance by the Romanian State Orchestra led by **Andreescu,** who conducts this pastel-shaded repast in thoroughly winning fashion, alternately vigorous and tender, coquettish and sentimental (♦Marco Polo 220485).

Tone poems

Many people were introduced to Glazunov through his evocative tone poem *Stenka Razin,* telling of the exploits of the infamous Cossack brigand and built upon a masterly working-out of the familiar "Song of the Volga Boatmen." Early recordings of *From the Middle Ages,* a splendid set of medieval images culminating in the grand departure of the Crusaders, and *Scènes de Ballet,* the fanciful "Marionettes" set beside heady dance rhythms, showed that for all Glazunov's adherence to strict design there is a wealth of lush color and ebullient Russian melody suffusing much of this music. Those wishing to explore this richly rewarding fare will find a number of avenues open to them.

With the entry of Melodiya onto American shores came a flood of releases by **Svetlanov** and the USSR Symphony, many now apparently endangered species; these included new versions of *The Sea, The Forest,* and *Oriental Rhapsody* (00156); *Scènes de Ballet* and *Suite Caractéristique* (00160); *From the Middle Ages* (00157); music for Oscar Wilde's *Salomé* (00158); and the two *Preludes to the Memory of Stassov and Rimsky-Korsakov* (00163), along with older recordings including *Finnish Fantasy* and *Stenka Razin* (00161). These older performances unfortunately suffer from the raw playing all too familiar to collectors of Russian LPs, but the sessions taped in 1990 offer sumptuous sonics and invigorating performances, even on occasion a lyricism not always associated with Svetlanov, as in *Ballade, Spring* (00156), and *Lyric Poem* (00161). Admittedly, tempos sometimes seem rushed and annotations are almost nonexistent, but these performances speak with authority and are all worth searching for.

Igor Golovchin studied with Svetlanov, but you'd never know it from his bland, ponderous recordings, which all too often render their budget price irrelevant (Naxos). At his best, as in the two musical tributes *To the Memory of Gogol* and *To the Memory of a Hero,* his massive tempos make for a grand display—though Svetlanov isn't quite as ponderous—while he appears more world-weary than decadent in the music for *Salomé.* He does well enough with the stirring *Ouverture Solennelle* and *Finnish Sketches,* but *Finnish Fantasy* is dreadful and *Karelian Legend* not much better. Yet another attempt is of value only for *Two Preludes "In Memoriam"* (though Svetlanov is better), as his *Suite Caractéristique* is colorless and flaccid and *Song of Destiny* is tedious music to begin with. **Konstantin Krimets** does better; *From Darkness to Light* is a turgid affair (much like the music itself) and *Stenka Razin* is sadly

dispirited, but his disc is worth having for *Fête Slave* and other short pieces (Naxos). *From the Middle Ages* is broadly drawn if not as stimulating as Järvi's, while *The Kremlin* is better than the import LP with **Aldo Ceccato** (RCA). Odd man out is **Anissimov,** whose *Scènes de Ballet* isn't much better than the *Seasons* coupled with it (see above).

A number of separate versions of these pieces are also readily available. Four marvelous performances by **Järvi** have been recycled by Chandos together (♦7049) and separately: *From the Middle Ages* (8804), *Stenka Razin* (8479), and *The Sea* and *Spring* (8611). They're all top of the line; moreover, Järvi's *Scènes de Ballet* is still the best around, since **de Waart** merely skims the surface (Telarc) and **Rozhdestvensky**'s excellent version is dragged down by his dispirited Symphony 6 (Olympia); likewise **Lenard** by his *Seasons.* An otherwise dreary release is notable for **Fedoseyev**'s impassioned reading of *To the Memory of a Hero,* though **Veronika Dudarova**'s brusque account of the tone poem *The Forest* (Icone) has been superseded by **Anissimov**'s splendid version (Naxos 554293, with Symphony 6).

Earlier releases by Marco Polo have proved far more rewarding than the later Naxos series; of these, Vol. 1 led by **Kenneth Schermerhorn** is of special interest for *Epic Poem* and *Spring* (220309) and Vol. 2, **de Almeida** conducting, has *Song of Destiny* and *Salomé* (220445). The two *Overtures on Greek Themes* are split between them. Volume 3 (also de Almeida) brings together *Oriental Rhapsody, Karelian Legend,* and *From Darkness to Light* in highly stimulating performances (220444), while Vol. 4, the weak link in the chain, offers barely adequate accounts of *Carnaval* Overture and other short pieces conducted by **Andreescu** (220487). The best *Carnaval* remains **Fiedler**'s, fortunately reissued in a splendid sounding "high-performance" CD (♦RCA 63308). You'll also find a gorgeous account of *Oriental Rhapsody* in **Dutoit**'s splendid collection of such pieces (Decca, reissued on ♦MHS 514975).

CONCERTOS

Cello. Concerto-Ballata was written for Casals and is perfectly attuned to his rhapsodic style. There is a very fine performance by **Yegor Dyachkov** on the same disc as Piano Concerto 1 (below). You may also be able to find **Boris Pergamenschikov**'s passionate reading, but the rather dissonant 1966 Cello Concerto by Boris Tishchenko coupled with it is hardly a fitting disc-mate (Musica Mundi). **Alexander Rudin**'s deep, sonorous tone suits this music beautifully, and he seems to have awakened Golovchin from his usual stupor (♦Naxos 553932).

Piano. Although the first of Glazunov's two piano concertos was written only two years after Rachmaninoff's 3rd, both structurally and melodically it seems closer to Liszt, being essentially in theme and variations form, while Concerto 2 even hews to the single-movement format of the Liszt E-flat major. The recording by the composer's daughter **Elena Glazunov** remains something of a collector's item, more for sentimental than musical reasons (Telefunken LP). **Richter**'s classic rendition of 1 boasts unsurpassed pianism but faded sonics (Melodiya), while **Ogdon** merely skims the surface of 1:I and his EMI LP hasn't come out on CD. **Alexei Nasedkin**'s performance of 1 shows its age sonically but is at least relatively easy to come by, either accompanied by 2 (played by **Dmitri Alexeiev**) and the Violin Concerto (Chant du Monde) or Liapunov's Concerto 2 (Russian Disc)

The best choice lies between **Stephen Coombs** (♦Hyperion 66877) and **Karl-Andreas Kolly** (♦Pan 510084). These performances complement each other very well, with Coombs's pearly tone and broadly lyrical treatment nicely balanced by Kolly's sparkling fingerwork and generally more impetuous approach. Either is preferable to **Oxana Yablon-skaya,** who fairly trudges through 1—no bargain (Naxos 553928). Those who don't mind buying two discs will find Concerto 1 played by **Maneli Pirzadeh** (Chandos 9528, with the *Concerto-Ballata* for cello and Arensky's Violin Concerto) and 2 played by **Matthew Herskowitz** (Chandos 9622, with Yuli Konyus's Violin Concerto and Karl Davidov's Cello Concerto 2). Both soloists offer a fresh and stimulating view of this highly romantic fare.

Violin. The Violin Concerto remains the most popular of all Glazunov's works. Personally I find this curious; it's certainly melodious, but relatively uneventful until the blazing "Red Square" finale. However, it has been recorded by some formidable talents, including **Heifetz,** whose elegant and luxurious traversal, ably seconded by Walter Hendl, is gratifyingly combined with his likewise unsurpassed Sibelius Concerto and Prokofiev's Concerto 2 (♦RCA 7019). Others may prefer a more flamboyant, heart-on-sleeve rendition like that of **Fodor;** however, the CD (if there was one) must have been short-lived (RCA). **Boris Belkin** seems prosaic next to Fodor, and the appended Shostakovich concerto may not be to everyone's taste—not mine, for one (Denon). It's also the discmate on **Perlman**'s recording, a beautiful performance that shows off his velvet tone to advantage (EMI 49814).

If you prefer Prokofiev's Concerto 1 as discmate, you'll want **Mutter**'s reading, rich-toned and romantic (Erato 75506). An even better coupling for my money is the Tchaikovsky Concerto, but **Vengerov** isn't the answer, as he seems to be standing to one side observing both pieces from a distance (Teldec). **Shumsky** paints this essentially rhapsodic piece in broad strokes, reserving his fire for the exuberant finale; more interesting is the fact that it is coupled with Järvi's *Seasons,* thus offering Glazunov's two most popular works on one CD (Chandos 8596). **Julia Krasko** sounds like she's off on a cloud somewhere, all luscious tone and precious little forward motion until the finale (Chandos, with Symphony 1).

Semyon Snitkovsky's solid if unexceptional reading is included in the same set as Symphonies 1, 2, and 4 (the Vox Box mentioned above; you may also see it on Chant du Monde, coupled with the two Piano Concertos). **Andrea Marcovici**'s reading may be of greater interest for the conductor, Stokowski; it was taped in concert and used to be a London set (Intaglio). The classic recording by **Oistrakh** is available (Omega 1025). **Milstein**'s also classic recording with Steinberg has been reissued (♦EMI 67250), but his remake with Frühbeck de Burgos (EMI) remains in limbo. The hopelessly indulgent reading by **Leila Josefowitz** may be set aside (Philips).

I should note for the sake of completeness that Glazunov also wrote a concerto for saxophone, which has been recorded with some frequency. I have never heard a bad performance, so you can choose freely among those available.

CHORAL MUSIC

Little of Glazunov's choral music has been brought out on CD. However, you will find two versions of *The King of the Jews,* intended to accompany a stage production in which Christ himself never actually appears; the music is luminous and transcendent with only occasional splashes of color and is presented in splendid fashion by **Rozhdestvensky** (♦Chandos 9467) and also **Poliansky,** who appends the music for *Salomé.* **Golovchin** takes eight minutes longer and the music suffers for it (Naxos). Avoid the Turnabout LP with **Siegfried Köhler,** should you happen to find it in some resale bin; he simply dispenses with the vocal portions altogether.   HALLER

CHAMBER MUSIC

One of the most important people in Glazunov's life was Mitrofan Belyayev, who made his fortune in the wood business and spent it supporting and publishing music. Belyayev, a violist, held chamber music sessions at his home every Friday. Glazunov attended these sessions regularly, along with many of the leading Russian composers of his day, and it was for these soirees that he wrote much of his chamber music.

Glazunov wrote seven string quartets, a set of five novelettes, an elegy, a suite for string quartet, a string quintet, a saxophone quartet, and a few collaborative pieces with his colleagues. The **Shostakovich Quartet** recorded many of his chamber works for Moscow Radio. Particularly interesting is their 1974 recording of Suite Op. 35 (a piece that became popular in a later orchestral arrangement) and Quintet Op. 39 with two cellos, like Schubert's C major quintet (Olympia 542). Another Shostakovich Quartet recording called "A Russian Birthday" contains works with movements written by Glazunov and other Russian composers to celebrate the name-day of their friend and patron Belyayev (Olympia 575).

The **Hollywood String Quartet** made a fantastic recording in 1956 of Glazunov's colorful early *Novelettes* (Testament 1061), and the **Lyric String Quartet** also recorded them (Meridian). These pieces, like much of Glazunov's chamber music, are well worth hearing.

After Belyayev died in 1903, Glazunov virtually stopped writing chamber music, but he returned to it in 1920 and 1930 to write his Quartets 6 and 7 (Olympia 526), and again in 1928 to write an *Elegy in Memory of Belyayev* (Olympia 542). Like the quartets in the birthday recording, Glazunov created a theme based on the pitches found in Belyayev's name: B-flat, A, and F (B-La-F). The **Dante Quartet**'s "Les Vendredis" includes several pieces written for Belyayev's soirees and is another fine tribute to him (ASV 6229).

PIANO MUSIC

Though some would place Glazunov's creative prime between 1899 and 1906, he wrote some of his best piano music after he became director of the St. Petersburg Conservatory in 1905 (after which he had little time to write). These late works include a stunning set of four Preludes and Fugues, a beautiful *Idylle,* and a Fantasy for two pianos (Marco Polo 223154). There are two exceptional sets of Glazunov's complete piano music (each in four volumes) by **Tatjana Franová** (Marco Polo 223151/54) and **Stephen Coombs** (Hyperion 66833, 44, 55, and 66).

FINE

Reinhold Glière *(1875–1956)*

Glière survived the October Revolution more comfortably than Glazunov and straddled the shifting political tides more adroitly than Prokofiev or Shostakovich, adapting his own conservative musical language and skillful use of ethnic color and rhythm to the needs of the moment while preserving the epic grandeur and rich narrative quality of Mother Russia and serving as mentor to Prokofiev, Miaskovsky, and Khachaturian. To Western audiences his fame rests primarily on his ballet *The Red Poppy,* with its popular "Russian Sailors' Dance," and the monumental symphony *Ilya Murometz,* images of Russia present and past that effectively frame his continued appeal.

SYMPHONIES

Symphony 1. Glière wrote three symphonies, culminating in *Ilya Murometz.* He completed 1 even before graduating from the Moscow Conservatory in 1900 and believed it sustained the popular character and mood of the Russian people; certainly its youthful vitality and tuneful good humor remain unquestioned. **Gunzenhauser** directs a spirited performance, very well played (Marco Polo 220349 or ◆Naxos 550898, with *Sirens*); **Downes** benefits from richer sound but nudges a bit in IV (Chandos 9160, with *Red Poppy*). We may hope for a reissue of **Boris Khaikin,** released in stereo by Dutch Melodiya but mono here. **Glière's** own recording is purely for archivists; it's turgid and bloated (Consonance 81-3001, mono, with *Harp Concerto*).

Symphony 2. Commencing with a glorious epic theme in the horns, there's a pungent Russian flavor and a warmly expressive quality to 2; in the whirlwind finale, ruddy-cheeked dancers in colorful garb swirl to the strains of furiously strumming balalaikas before a fervent hymn ushers in the sonorous close. **Keith Clark** is estimable (Marco Polo 223106 or Naxos 550899, with *Zaporozhye Cossacks*), but must yield to **Downes's** sumptuous account, with the horns standing proud (◆Chandos 9071, with *Cossacks*). Delos's highly touted "VR²" process produces a panoramic spread, dark, rich and sonorous yet with no sense of depth or inner detail, a pity given **Macal's** hearty and outgoing approach (3178, with *Red Poppy*). **Glière's** own recording is inadequate on both ensemble and sonic grounds (Consonance 81-3002, mono, with Soprano Concerto).

Symphony 3. (*Ilya Murometz*). Sprawling, brawling, massive, sumptuously appointed, lasting well over an hour if played uncut (which it seldom is), Glière's final symphony celebrates the legendary hero, last of the bogatyrs, and his wondrous exploits at the dawning of Holy Mother Russia. Glière deploys his immense forces with consummate skill in music of great richness and strength; it's mystical, evocative, filled with color, very Russian, and very wonderful.

Given its length, it's not surprising that recordings are often cut. If the cuts are judicious, they may not be noticeable and may even improve the flow. In his 78 rpm set with the Philadelphia Orchestra, **Stokowski** reduced the score to roughly 45 minutes (Biddulph 005); when he rerecorded it with the Houston Symphony, he brought it down to 38 mesmerizing minutes (◆EMI 65074, with Charles Loeffler's *Pagan Poem*). **Rachmilovich's** heavily cut reading is even more dimly recorded than on 78s and is for archivists only (EMI 66886, with Kabalevsky's Symphony 2). **Ormandy** recorded it in mono for Columbia and stereo for RCA, both cut and both NA.

The first complete recording was **Scherchen's** mono Westminster set, a stunning achievement that still sounds remarkable, unfortunately unavailable on CD. It took 80 minutes; **Harold Farberman** takes 93 but recorded it straight through without editing, making undue haste impractical. This may be the most expansive, sonically stupendous *Ilya Murometz* ever set to disc, and if tempo is no problem, it may be the only one you'll ever need (◆Unicorn 2014, 2CD). **Downes** is note-complete and enjoys superlative support from the BBC players and his engineers, warmly romantic and sumptuously recorded (◆Chandos 9041). **Johanos** is also complete but more impetuous, and the recording, while perfectly respectable, can't compete with Downes (Marco Polo 223358 or Naxos 550858).

With the dark, rich sound of a Russian orchestra, **Rakhlin's** set has some cuts but it's an estimable reading, deeply atmospheric and poetic; moreover, the cuts at least come at logical points in the narrative (Russian Disc 15025). That cannot be said of **Talmi,** who seems to be making cuts only to permit slower tempos and still get it on one disc; unfortunately the cuts (which bring it down to 66 minutes) seem awkward, though the performance and recording are first rate (Pro Arte 589). **Golovchin's** reading is also cut at all the wrong moments (Russian

Disc), yet longer than Rakhlin's due to somewhat slower tempos, and nowhere approaching Downes's sonic richness (Russian Disc 11358).

OTHER ORCHESTRAL MUSIC

Ballet music. The Red Poppy is Socialist Realism at its most poetic. The Chinese tea-house dancer Tao-Hoa intervenes in a coolie uprising to spare the gallant Russian captain she loves. Shot by her jealous manager, who's in league with the capitalists, with her last breath she passes on to another the red poppy that serves as a symbol of her love and also Communism itself, an association made even more blatant by the *Internationale*. (This association was not lost on the Party bosses, who changed the name to *The Red Flower* to avoid any cynical comments about "the opiate of the masses.") In addition to the "Russian Sailors' Dance," there are many other colorful scenes, while the quaint "American" touches may draw an unintended smile. Yet strangely the "American Dance" is missing from **Anichanov's** "complete" version, as is the dance just before the Act II finale (◆Naxos 553496, 2CD). Since this still leaves roughly an hour of music heretofore unavailable, the set can be recommended, particularly given his highly colored and strongly rhythmic treatment, while the darkly sonorous recording enhances the vaporous milieu of the opium den in Act II.

Macal's *Red Poppy* Suite has the same ambience problems as his Symphony 2, at times sounding positively gelatinous, while he starts out so briskly in the "Russian Sailors' Dance" he has nowhere else to go (Delos). **Downes** is better if all you want is a suite (Chandos 9160, with Symphony 1). There were two suites recorded by **Yuri Fayer,** a stereo LP on Angel/Melodiya and a shorter mono Vanguard, the only one with the "American Dance." Both remain NA, along with **Scherchen,** which filled out his *Ilya Murometz.*

The Bronze Horseman, based on Pushkin, is rarely staged nowadays, perhaps because it calls for a huge flood at one point. The lovers Evgeni and Parasha meet under the statue of Peter the Great on the senate square in St. Petersburg, but Parasha is drowned in the flood and the distraught Evgeni believes the statue has come to life, chasing him through the streets of the city until he falls dead of exhaustion. "Hymn to the Great City" is thrilling in its grandeur and sonority. There used to be an Angel/Melodiya LP suite with **Zhuraitis** and the Bolshoi, and there's a version with **Dmitri Liss** and the Ural Philharmonic (◆Russian Disc 10037, with *Zaporozhye Cossacks*), neither approaching the refined playing and smooth sound of the BBC Philharmonic under **Downes** (◆Chandos 9379, with *Horn Concerto*). But this refinement comes at a price, as the more rough-hewn yet passionate and visceral playing of the Russians is thrilling to hear. Forget **Anichanov;** he includes only four excerpts and leaves out "Hymn to the Great City" (Marco Polo 223675, with overtures).

Glière drew upon his earlier tone poem *The Zaporozhye Cossacks* for his ballet *Taras Bulba,* homage to the great Cossack hero also celebrated by Janáček's and on screen by Franz Waxman. Glière's treatment of Taras and his ill-fated sons is neither as cinematic as Waxman's nor as richly poignant as Janáček's, touching on moments of sorrow and humor in equal measure. While the Cossack dances don't resurface in the suite, there are many Polish and Ukrainian folk tunes, including one you'll recognize from Tchaikovsky's "Little Russian" Symphony. It's wonderfully played by the Odessa Philharmonic under **Hobart Earle,** but the coupled *Rasputin* suite by Evgeny Stankovich is grating and discordant (ASV 988).

Ballet Suite 1 first saw life as *Sheep's Spring,* based on a play by Lope de Vega; for all the flashing castanets and tambourines it's pretty pallid stuff. *Ballet Suite 2* is set in Greece, telling of the encounters of Chrysis with Sappho, Dionysus, and Aphrodite; there's a fair amount of oriental coloring but again it's rather shapeless. **Glière** led both in performances of historical interest only (Consonance 81-3000, mono). **Zhuraitis** offers a much better performance of Suite 2 (Icone), but instead of his Suite 1 (also Melodiya, LP), you get the Duets for violin and cello; granted, his Suite 1 was mono (unlike Suite 2), but then so is the composer's version. Not fair.

Short Pieces. As musical caretaker of all the Russias, Glière knew no equal, tirelessly working on behalf of the folk traditions of Azerbaijan and Uzbekistan as well as his native Ukraine. A marvelous disc brings it all together in superb performances by the BBC Philharmonic led by **Sinaisky** (♦Chandos 9518). Glière's first opera, *Shakh-Senem*, reflected his fascination with Persia; the Overture evokes the call of the muezzin as much as the inevitable *Scheherazade* and *Caucasian Sketches*. *Holiday at Ferghana* and *Gyul'sara* derive from Uzbek sources, with rich colors and rhythms evoking the Arabian Nights, though *Ferghana* celebrates a canal building in Uzbekistan. No doubt the raucous brass fanfares startled Chicago audiences when Glière re-dedicated it to the Orchestra's Golden Jubilee. *Overture on Slavonic Themes* combines the familiar "Slava!" with the Polish national anthem. *Heroic March for the Buryiat-Mongolian ASSR* is an admittedly political exercise, sinister references to *God Save the Tsar* callously thrust aside by the *Internationale*.

Anichanov is much less stimulating than Sinaisky and cuts a couple of minutes from *Gyul'sara* (Marco Polo 223675, with a skimpy *Bronze Horseman* suite). Import stores may have LPs of *Gyul'sara* by **Mukhtar Ashrafi** (Melodiya D 2440/1) and *Shakh-Senem* by **Grigori Stolyarov** (Melodiya D 04154/55, with operatic excerpts led by the composer), mono but filled with raw-edged excitement. *Triumphal Overture*, written for the 20th anniversary of the October Revolution, was included by **Svetlanov** in his "Overtures by Soviet Composers" (Melodiya C10 21717 004) and by **Gauk** in a mono LP (Heritage 1205), both hard to find.

The heroism and carefree nature of the Zaporozhye Cossacks, who rallied the Ukraine peasants against Polish rule under their leader Taras Bulba, strongly appealed to Glière; however, the immediate inspiration for his tone poem is the marvelous Repin painting of the Cossacks laughing heartily as they compose a scathing letter to the Turkish Sultan, a laughter heard clearly in the music before dancing and drinking ensue. **Clark** is very good (Marco Polo or Naxos); **Downes** (Chandos) is richly recorded but gets hectic near the end (both with Symphony 2). **Dmitri Liss** offers characterful playing and crisp dance rhythms that really make the music come alive (♦Russian Disc 10037, with *Bronze Horseman*).

The Sirens is a voluptuous and seductive portrayal of the sea nymphs who tempted Ulysses and his men. **Gunzenhauser** does very nicely and the sound is first-rate (Marco Polo 220349 or ♦Naxos 550898, with Symphony 1). On a mono LP *The Sirens* is conducted by **Gauk**, *Zaporozhye Cossacks* by **Rakhlin**, and *Holiday at Ferghana* by **Kondrashin**, authoritative but outclassed in both ensemble and sound (Melodiya 33 M10-39547/48).

CONCERTOS

Glière wrote five concertos, for horn, harp, cello, violin, and coloratura soprano. The Horn Concerto is thoroughly appealing and gratifying for the soloist. **Hermann Baumann** plays it expertly, but the brief fillers (by Saint-Saëns, Chabrier, and Dukas) make for a rather skimpy repast (Philips 416380). **Marie Luise Neunecker**'s massive, gutsy tone contrasts with Baumann's more mellow sound (Koch Schwann 1357, with

Glière, Glazunov, and Vissarion Shebalin). If an all-horn collection isn't a priority, **Richard Watkins** does a beautiful job (Chandos 9379, with *Bronze Horseman*). You should still be able to find the pioneering mono recording by **Valerie Polekh** with the composer conducting (Classic Editions CE 6, with works by Fikret Amirov, Prokofiev, and Glinka).

The Harp Concerto may seem like a throwback to 19th-century romanticism, filled with arpeggios and other busywork for the soloist, yet it never descends into the bland, willowy "harp music" dreaded by recitalgoers; it's a fresh and assertive work and can give the harpist quite a challenge. **Rachel Masters** plays it very well (Chandos 9094), but **Osian Ellis**'s more forceful treatment blows away the cobwebs (♦London 430006). The Chandos disc has **Eileen Hulse** as an agile and winning soprano in the Coloratura Concerto; however, this piece with its wordless melisma is well suited to **Sutherland** (Decca 430006, with Harp Concerto). Avoid **Evgenia Miroshnichenko**; her vocalism is adequate to the task but isn't enough to salvage Glière's recording of Symphony 2 (Consonance 81-3002, in mediocre stereo). Likewise **Olga Erdeli**, whose Harp Concerto (appended to Symphony 1 in Consonance 81-3001) is at least of historical value, since it was written for her aunt Ksenia Erdeli.

Only Glière completists will want the Cello Concerto, a laborious exercise lasting three quarters of an hour, and the strained, laborious account by **Sergei Sudzilovsky** doesn't help matters any (Olympia 592 or MHS 515614, with Alexander Mosolov's Cello Concerto). The Violin Concerto, completed after Glière's death by his student Liatoshinsky, was offered by **Boris Goldstein** in a mono LP, now hard to find (Melodiya).

CHAMBER MUSIC

Glière's eight duets for violin and cello combine the lyricism of Tchaikovsky and Rachmaninoff with the distant and refined world of Debussy. They're beautifully played by **Eleonora** and **Yuli Turovsky** (Chandos 8652, with Stravinsky, Nikolai Tcherepnin, and Prokofiev) and **Ernö Sebestyen** and **Martin Ostertag** (Koch Schwann 1727, with Kodály and Ravel). Either is preferable to **Sergei Kravchenko** and **Yuri Semionov**, who take up precious space with the Ballet Suite (Icone); Semionov is expressive but relegated to the background by Kravchenko's quavery, strident violin. Glière devotees will want the CD combining the duets with music for two violins and two cellos played with warmth and polish by the **South African Chamber Music Society** (Koch 920526). HALLER

Mikhail Glinka (1804–1857)

Glinka is given credit for originating the forms and styles that dominated Russian music for most of the 19th century. For a self-styled dilettante, that's doing pretty well. Up until the 1830s, this rather bland, Italianate composer gave no indication that he would become the first Russian nationalist, but from 1832 on he turned out increasingly original works using folk styles as his guide. He had an original ear for scoring, a lively sense of drama and, despite his personal tendency toward hypochondria, a positive musical attitude that makes his mature works a joy to listen to.

Orchestral music. Most of Glinka's works for orchestra are late and concise, and almost all can be contained on one well-filled CD. The most important are two Spanish overtures (*Jota Aragonesa* and *Summer Night in Madrid*), *Kamarinskaya*, and *Valse-Fantasie*. **Svetlanov** made an LP of these plus excerpts from *Ruslan and Ludmilla* in 1968 with the then-USSR Symphony in clear if somewhat brash sound. For some reason, the lovely *Valse-Fantasie* was left off the CD reissue, but the little

Symphony on Russian Themes and incidental music from *Prince Kholmsky* were added (Chant du Monde 278819). The performances are exciting. In 1992, a further Svetlanov survey appeared, mainly covering the music from Glinka's two great operas, *Krakowiak, Mazurka,* and *Waltz* from *A Life for the Tsar* and both ballet sequences from *Russlan & Ludmilla,* as well as *Chernomor's March,* the overtures to both operas and an early *Andante cantabile and Rondo* (Melodiya 166). Again the sound is serviceable, the performances scintillating.

Volume 31 of Svetlanov's huge "Anthology of Russian Symphony Music" fills in some gaps with two early overtures, Glinka's transcription of a Hummel Nocturne, and two choral numbers, notably *Prayer* (Melodiya 167). This unusual program also contains four rare orchestral works by Alexander Dargomyzhsky. More recently, **Fedoseyev** has recorded a mix of the major orchestral works with some of the operatic pieces with the Moscow Symphony, including *Valse-Fantasy,* but along with more sophisticated recorded sound and smoother interpretations have come slow tempos and a general loss of character (Saison Russe 388114). **Tjeknavorian**'s recording gave us more of Khachaturian's *Gayne* than we ever thought we'd hear, but he turned out to be lethargic and sloppy even there, and his Glinka disc with the Armenian Philharmonic is dispiriting (ASV 1075). It includes the four major orchestral works and excerpts from *A Life for the Tsar.*

Back when the world was made of vinyl and occasionally 10 inches in diameter, several other orchestral works appeared in mysterious Russian issues, notably a Polonaise based on a Spanish bolero theme (1854) and an attractive Polka, originally for piano 4-hands. Another disc contained a *Pas de Deux* and *Pas de Trois,* presumably intended for *A Life for the Tsar.* So the supply of Glinka orchestral works on CD is not yet exhausted.

Chamber music. All of Glinka's chamber music is early, so don't expect too much. Before he left Russia to tour Germany and Italy as a young man, the late Beethoven string quartets hit him like a ton of bricks and he wrote one in response. A second came after he had absorbed the material more. Both have been recorded with enthusiasm, if not with great polish, by the **Anton Quartet** (Sonora 53003). Another worthwhile collection contains the little-known Septet, the better-known Sextet, and two potpourris on Italian operas, *Serenade on themes from Donizetti's Anna Bolena* and *Divertimento on themes from Bellini's La Sonnambula,* all played by the Russian National Symphony Soloists Ensemble featuring pianists **Mikhail Pletnev** and **Leonid Ogrinchuk** in fine performances and good recordings (♦MHS 515120 or Olympia 529). The same program minus the Septet is played by **Kun-Woo Paik** and **Yves Henry** and another fine group (Sonora 53002). A good performance of the Sextet alone is by **Capricorn,** along with the rare Sextet by Rimsky-Korsakov (Hyperion 66163).

The Viola Sonata in D minor is another early work, a piece in two movements not quite finished by Glinka. It has a Schubertian lyricism. **Imai** and **Pöntinen** offer a mellow reading in their interesting "Russian Viola" disc (BIS 358, with Shostakovich's Sonata and short works by Rubinstein, Glazunov, and Stravinsky). **Bashmet** and Mikhail Muntian play it in a polished, rather intense reading (RCA 61273, with sonatas by Shostakovich and Nikolai Roslavets). A finale was added by Dmitriev; this version was recorded by **Svetlana Stepchenko** and Zoya Abolitz in a rather heavy performance (Russian Disc 10035, with Anton Rubinstein's Sonata). **Norbert Blume** and Olga Tverskaya play an early music performance of considerable warmth on an almost all-Glinka program: *Trio Pathétique, Valse Fantasie, Variations on The Nightingale,* and

Alexander Alyabiev's Piano Trio (♦Opus 111 30230, part of a "Music in St. Petersburg" series).

Trio Pathétique is a curious little piece of considerable charm. Originally written for clarinet, bassoon, and piano, it was rearranged for violin, cello, and piano, which has had more recordings than the original version. A fine performance of the original is in the disc containing the Viola Sonata mentioned above, with **Colin Lawson,** clarinet, and Albert Grazzi, bassoon. Another interesting disc is by **Charles West,** Bruce Hammel, and Landon Bilyou in a wind program including Mozart's Quintet K 452 and Bartók's *Contrasts* (Klavier 11072). The Glinka is played with spirit. The string arrangement is played beautifully by the **Borodin Trio,** with a soulful performance of Arensky's Trio 1 (Chandos 8477). The **Romantic Trio** plays the Glinka more smoothly (RCD 10401, with Rachmaninoff's *Elegaic Trio 1* and Shostakovich's Trio 2). A curious version substituting viola for cello is played by **Trio Apollon,** along with a similar rearrangement of Beethoven's Clarinet Trio and Mozart's "Kegelstatt" Trio (Koch 920500).

Piano music. While Glinka's piano music is fairly extensive, little of it is particularly deep; it was written for the salon and shows little of the involvement with Russian folk material that we get from the operas and some of the orchestral music and songs. **Victor Ryabchikov** is recording all of it by genre. His Vol. 2 contains the variations and Vol. 3 the dances, in delicately phrased if somewhat under-energized readings, suitable to the salon (BIS 980/1). **Francesco Bertoldi** plays a varied program on a less flattering piano, but with sensitivity (Nuova Era 7232).

Choral music. There is only one recorded choral work, a 15-minute setting of a *Prayer* with words by Lermontov. **Svetlanov** recorded it with other rare material by Glinka and Dargomizhsky (Melodiya 167). More vocal works were once heard on the 10-inch Melodiya LPs mentioned above, including a choral-orchestral *Tarantella* (1841) and "Moldavian Gypsy," a lovely aria sung by Zara Dolukhanova with choir and orchestra.

Operas. A Life for the Tsar, or *Ivan Susanin,* was Glinka's first major operatic effort. It's full of Russian and Polish music, both vocal and in two major ballet sequences. It's long but not dull. Christoff sang the title role in a 1957 recording under **Markevitch,** with Stich-Randall and Gedda; 155 minutes, no libretto, but a memorable performance by all concerned (EMI 69698, 2CD). A complete performance (200 minutes) was recorded by the Sofia National Opera under **Ivan Marinov,** with a fine Ivan in Ghiuselev but little else to inspire you and no English libretto (Balkanton 10032, 3CD). Another complete recording appeared soon after from Sofia, conducted by **Emil Tchakarov,** with Boris Martinovich singing Ivan (Sony 46487, 3CD, 209 minutes). This version boasted a libretto, but the singing is controversial in places. One major advantage of all three recordings is that they use Glinka's original libretto, while at the time everyone in Russia was recording the Soviet version omitting all references to the Tsar.

The Bolshoi recording under **Mark Ermler** with Nestorenko singing Ivan uses the Soviet text, which also involves considerable cutting (HMV 1651123, 3LP, NA). So does the older 1947 recording conducted by **Alexsander Melik-Pashayev** (Preiser 90365, 2CD). Both of these Russian recordings are sung in a national style that no one else duplicates. With the onset of *glasnost,* the Bolshoi reverted to the original version and recorded a video of a 1989 staging at the Bolshoi under **Alexander Lazarev,** also featuring Nesterenko (Teldec 4509-92051, 175 minutes).

Ruslan and Ludmilla is a fairy tale opera that balances the patriotic realism of *A Life for the Tsar.* It's Glinka's masterpiece and never fails to enthrall me, even though no version contained a libretto until recently. I discovered the work through **Kondrashin**'s exciting mono recording with legendary vocalists from the Russian pantheon (Voce della luna 2000, 3CD). This Bolshoi recording was complete, but whether it now comes with a libretto is a question; my Westminster LPs did not. Then nothing happened for 25 years or so, until the Bolshoi recorded the opera again in 1979 with **Yuri Simonov** conducting and Nesterenko singing the title role (Melodiya 29348, 3CD). Maybe it was the tradition of my youth, but this version struck me as less involving; though it was in big, broad stereo and had some good singing, it also cut an entr'acte and part of the grand finale, for no apparent reason.

The most recent version, by the Kirov Opera under **Gergiev** in a 1995 live recording, is complete and beautifully sung, with no really weak points. What's more, there's a libretto, and if you buy the "Deluxe Limited Edition," you get a video of the somewhat stilted staged performance (Philips 446746, 3CD, 202 minutes). It should be said that all the recent Russian videos from this source are worth seeing for the costumes, the faces, and the fact that these traditions won't last forever. I treasure them all, as I do my old Kondrashin recording. Gergiev is very fine, and I'm happy to have it.

Songs. Glinka wrote many songs. The Russians made LP collections of all of them in Melodiya LPs, sharing them among several singers, as they also did for Tchaikovsky and other composers. These have not been transferred to CD, more's the pity. **Christoff** recorded 13 of them in remarkable performances reissued in an album containing songs by many Russian composers (♦EMI 67496, 5CD). There are no texts, but it's an important collection nevertheless. Soprano **Natalia Gerasimova**'s contrasting collection contains 25 songs without texts or even English titles but sung in fine style (♦RCD 16017). Alto **Lina Mkrtchyan** sings 16 songs in an attractive, dusky voice, perhaps too often hushed in quality and not very clear in diction (Opus 111 30227).

Nineteen songs, including the long cycle *A Farewell to St. Petersburg,* are sung by baritone **Leiferkus** in a particularly expressive manner (♦Conifer 51264). An odd program combines orchestrations of 11 songs sung by tenor **Vladimir Bogachev** and bass **Nikita Storojev** with three songs by Rimsky-Korsakov and his one-act opera *Mozart and Salieri,* all conducted by Turovsky with I Musici di Montreal (Chandos 9149). The opera has had better readings, but the orchestrations may interest you. Soprano **Galina Gorchakova** sings five songs in a Russian collection entitled "Memories of Love"; her operatic style works variably on the lighter material (Philips 446720). MOORE

Christoph Willibald Gluck (1714–1787)

As a composer Gluck is important in the developmental history of opera, but his operas are more admired than loved. He attempted to reform what he regarded as contemporary abuses of opera, shearing it of ornamental excess and virtuoso display and reintroducing a seriousness of purpose, with emphasis on the text and dramatic values.

Alceste. There are two versions of *Alceste:* the 1767 original, in Italian, composed for Vienna, and a major revision of 1776, in French, for Paris.

Callas sang the French version of the opera, but in Italian. Her 1954 performance at La Scala is a formidable interpretation, vocally strong and solid throughout, with grand Italian passion in lieu of French classicism (♦Melodram 2.009, 2CD). Renato Gavarini is a shaky Admeto and Paolo Silveri an elderly High Priest, but Panerai brings a distinctive timbre and youthful enthusiasm to Apollo. Giulini guides the opera with a steady, sympathetic hand.

In 1956 **Flagstad** recorded the Vienna edition in Italian (Decca). By this stage of her career her voice had taken on an opaqueness that frequently fails to project or register. Odd Italian pronunciation and bland characterization don't help. Raoul Jobin, also a veteran singer, uses odd Italian, with strained, dry, and monotonous singing. The young Thomas Hemsley in three roles is coolly dignified and detached. Geraint Jones has a sure grip on the musical style, albeit with a lack of dramatic energy.

A 1983 recording of the French revision with **Jessye Norman** is more impressive (♦Orfeo 027823, 2CD). She's in fine form, warm and vibrant, with all her vocal virtues and vices. Gedda is cool and elegant, with exquisite diction; Tom Krause and Bernd Weikl are equally impressive. Baudo has his Bavarian Radio forces playing with reasonable lightness and delicacy, the more solemn aspects of Gluck's music coming naturally to them.

Iphigénie en Aulide. This is the first of Gluck's operas composed for Paris (1774). Unlike his other French operas, it's not dependent for its impact on a single artist, but the musical felicities and the drama are divided equally between the titular heroine, Clytemnestre, and Agamemnon.

A big name, big voice performance led by **Böhm** from the 1962 Salzburg Festival is not exactly *echt* Gluck, sounding too much like mid-19th-century German melodrama, but it's impressively sung (Orfeo 428962, 2CD). Borkh is a tougher than usual Iphigénie, almost the equal of Ludwig's harridan Clytemnestre. James King is the clarion Achilles, Berry a sonorous Agamemnon.

Richard Wagner's edition is an oddity, with a darker, thicker texture than the more classical original (RCA 32236, 2CD). Moffo is a moving Iphigénie; Trudeliese Schmidt a less than forceful Clytemnestre. Ludovic Spiess sings a burly, wrong-voiced Achilles, Fischer-Dieskau an arch, ineffective Agamemnon. Bavarian Radio forces play dutifully for **Kurt Eichhorn.**

As usual **Gardiner** sets a brisk pace, and here it truly works, the action revealing itself more vigorously than in the other Gluck operas (♦Erato 45003, 2CD). Lynne Dawson isn't much as Iphigénie, her glassy voice and cheerful demeanor at odds with the tragedy. Von Otter serves up an imposing, vengeful Clytemnestre, a dramatic contrast to van Dam's deeply moving, tragic Agamemnon. Aler is a brilliantly confident Achilles.

Iphigénie en Tauride. This setting of the latter portion of the tragic Greek legend came late in Gluck's Parisian career (1779), the next to last of all his operas. Although often regarded as his most perfect opera, it has had a difficult time on records.

Callas sang only four performances, in Italian, at La Scala in 1957, and on the opening night she was in excellent form, her voice darkly dramatic, firm and steady, but she must struggle against her vocally miscast colleagues and the stolid, heavy-handed conducting of Sanzogno (EMI 65451; Melodram 26012, 2CD). Gluck's music for Oreste and Toante is simply too high for Dino Dondi and Anselmo Colzani, but Francesco Albanese is a pretty-voiced Pilade. Transpositions, musical rewrites, and cuts are of little help, and the sound is murky. This is strictly for Callas fans.

Sonic difficulties also plague a 1964 performance in French from the Teatro Colón (Chante du Monde 278769, 2CD). Of great interest, though, is **Crespin**'s Iphigénie, a grand performance of vocal power and emotion, majestic, tragic, yet a model of classic reserve. Robert Massard is a robust Oreste, Guy Chauvet a bullish Pylade, and Victor de Narke a sturdy Thoas. Georges Sébastian's conducting is weak, flaccid, and lethargic. Gardelli leads a 1982 Bavarian Radio performance that has little to recommend it; Gluck's musical style is treated as if it were Italian melodrama. **Lorengar** is an attractive heroine, but there is only musical ugliness from Walton Groenroos and Franco Bonisolli. Fischer-Dieskau is miscast as Thoas.

For his 1985 recording Gardiner chose a group of musically sound, vocally attractive, but dramatically weak singers (Philips 416148, 2CD). The performances by **Diana Montague,** Aler, Thomas Allen, and René Massis are competent but uninvolving, and Gardiner himself comes across as overly serious, but ineffective. In his La Scala performances, **Muti** ignores period stylistic niceties in an attempt to create some musical excitement (Sony 52492, 2CD). Using slower tempos and broader phrasing than Gardiner, he infuses dramatic life into the opera, a large-scale canvas in contrast to Gardiner's delicate watercolor. **Vaness**'s Iphigénie rings out boldly in an impassioned performance, approaching Callas in intensity. Allen again is musically sound and adjusts to the new scale, adding some drama as well. Gösta Winbergh sings a sound, full-blooded Pylade. As Thoas, Giorgio Surian is forceful but not forced.

Best of the lot is the impressive performance by the Boston Baroque led by **Pearlman** (♦Telarc 80546, 3CD). Goerke is powerfully dramatic and vocal strong in the title role, ably supported by the plangent Oreste of Gilfry and a mellifluous Pylade by Vinson Cole.

Orfeo ed Euridice. The musicological complexities of Gluck's best known opera are extreme. There are five versions: (1) the original 1762 version for an alto castrato Orfeo in Italian; (2) a 1769 adaptation by Gluck raising the title role to soprano castrato, not produced in modern times and not recorded; (3) Gluck's 1774 revision in French with much new music and a tenor hero; (4) Berlioz's 1859 version in French using a female alto as Orphée; and (5) an 1889 publication by Ricordi of a conflation of the Italian and French versions using a female alto. No two recordings are exactly alike in the music used.

In 1947 Ferrier recorded an abridged version of the Italian original. She's at her consummate best, her voice rich and distinctive, ably assisted by Ann Ayers and Zoe Vlachopoulos with Glyndebourne Festival forces led by **Fritz Stiedry** (♦Decca 433468). Ferrier died before she could record the entire role in the studio, but a 1951 broadcast from Amsterdam finds her in excellent voice, with a deep contralto that sounds unlike any other, a combination of classic dignity and opulent singing (♦Verona 27016, 2CD). The Netherlands Opera Orchestra responds well to **Charles Bruck**'s leadership, carefully supporting the singers' involvement.

One of the best recordings (1956) is of the French tenor version with a meltingly beautiful, classically poised hero sung by Simoneau (♦Philips 434741, 2CD). Danco is coolly elegant, while Pierrette Alarie dances her way through the coloratura delights of Amour. **Rosbaud** has found a happy compromise between classically poised solemnity and tragedy and romantic passion. An equally stylish French version from the 1955 Aix-en-Provence Festival by Gedda and **de Froment**—possibly the best of all the *Orfeos*—has yet to be issued on CD (EMI). But the tenor can be heard in a performance from the 1967 Edinburgh Festival with Sutherland as Euridice, conducted by **Bonynge** (Verona 28018, 2CD).

Renato Fasano leads I Virtuosi di Roma in a stylish performance of the Italian conflation, but with a lack of drama (RCA 78962, 2CD). Verrett has a few difficulties with the lower reaches, but her top voice peals out brilliantly along with a sympathetic touch of drama. Moffo's Euridice is beautifully intoned, but vague as to any dramatic ideas. Judith Raskin is a sprightly Amore. **Karl Richter** leads a disheartening perfor-

mance of the 1762 Italian version with the Munich Bach Choir and Orchestra (DG 453145, 2CD). It's nervous and fidgety alternating with calm, oratorio-style coolness. A baritone Orfeo is an awkward rarity, but Fischer-Dieskau gives an intelligent interpretation. Janowitz is a pale Euridice and Moser is a blank as Amore.

Solti's 1969 recording from Covent Garden is a peculiar amalgamation, mainly the 1762 original plus various odds and ends (♦Decca 417410, 2CD). It's a dramatic show, perhaps a bit hard-driven, but capturing the deep-seated emotions inherent in the music. Horne is assured and commanding, a virtuoso performance. Lorengar's Euridice is weak, but Donath's Cupid is a delightful characterization, adroitly sung. **Muti** infuses Italian color into his very English forces (the Philharmonia) in an Italian version (EMI 63637, 2CD). Baltsa sings a tough-guy Orfeo with Margaret Marshall a contrasting feminine Euridice. Gruberová's Amore sparkles with coloratura fire.

The 1982 recording of a Glyndebourne production uses the conflation (sung in Italian) for mezzo-soprano (Erato 45864; Denon 295; 2CD). Janet Baker is a refined hero, but sounds cloudy and dull. Speiser is a strong Euridice, but Elizabeth Gale barely fills the requirements of Amore. **Leppard** leads a stylish performance enhanced by the complete ballet music.

In Berlioz's French edition, von Otter lacks a solid lower register and is limited in emotional depth (EMI 49834, 2CD). Hendricks is a delicate Euridice; Brigitte Fournier a perky French soubrette for Amour. **Gardiner** keeps the show light and lively, with faster tempos failing to catch the nobility of the opera. For his second recording, Gardiner chose the 1762 version in Italian, with Ragin as a countertenor hero. While setting a brisk tempo for the English Baroque Soloists, Gardiner still gets a fuller, weightier sound. Ragin's voice is delicate, more comfortable in the quieter moments, with less color and emotional range. McNair is also delicate as Euridice. Cyndia Sieden's Amore is a bright but simple characterization.

A plain, original Italian version also has a countertenor, Michael Chance, as Orfeo; he catches the drama and sings with exquisite refinement and tonal beauty (♦Sony 48040, 2CD). Argenta is a sparkling Euridice, but the use of a boy treble just doesn't work. **Bernius** sets some brisk tempos for the period instrument group Tafelmusik, but they generally work well.

Podles is the only artist to have recorded *Orfeo* in both French and Italian versions. In a 1992 conflation version sung in French, Marie-Noëlle Callatays and Raphelle Farman with the Capella Brugensis led by **Patrick Olivero** are her cohorts (Forlane 16720, 2CD). In 1998 she sang the same version in Spain, but in Italian (Arts & Music 47536, 2CD). **Peter Maag** leads the Galacia Symphony with Aria Rodrigo and Elena de la Merced as Euridice and Amore, respectively. In both recordings the sole interest is Podles. Her Orfeo/Orphée is distinguished, firmly intoned with a lovely voice, but a bit shallow in interpretation.

Larmore is the opulent-voiced, emotionally rich hero in a performance of the Berlioz French version from the San Francisco Opera (♦Teldec 98418, 2CD). Upshaw is a delightfully human Euridice, emotionally involved; Alison Hagley a sprightly Amour. **Runnicles,** using modern instruments, strikes a happy compromise between period and modern practices of timbre and tempos.   PARSONS

Leopold Godowsky *(1870–1938)*

After too many years of neglect, Godowsky's piano music is finally being given the serious and thorough attention it deserves from both pianists and scholars. As with Liszt, his output is divided between original works and transcriptions, all couched in a late-romantic idiom that reveals the most intimate knowledge of the capabilities of both instrument and performer. Indeed, Godowsky's polyphonic resourcefulness produced a type of piano writing nearly unparalleled for its richness and imagination. While some works are only within reach of the most lavishly equipped virtuosos, many others don't require superhuman abilities. In any case, all of them are eminently worth investigation.

Most of the significant Godowsky works can now be had in superb recorded performances. Yet a warning must be given: the CDs by **Madge** are to be avoided; his inept pianism is a total misrepresentation of the music (Dante). On a much higher level are two pianists now in the midst of complete surveys of Godowsky's output: **Carlo Grante** and **Konstantin Scherbakov.** Especially recommended are the latter's account of 16 piquant and charming Godowsky transcriptions of baroque pieces (Marco Polo 223795) and three Bach-Godowsky solo violin works, impressively transformed into sonorous piano writing (Marco Polo 223794). Grante offers strong competition in the latter (Music & Arts 1039); he can also be heard in the three Bach-Godowsky cello suites (Music & Arts 1046) and in twelve Schubert lieder in Godowsky's beautifully crafted elaborations (Music & Arts 984).

Turning to original works, the 12-part *Java Suite,* written in the mid-'20s, is a masterly evocation of oriental idioms and sonorities; it's extremely well played by **Esther Budiardjo** (ProPiano 224529). In a completely different style, Godowsky's 24 *Walzermasken* imaginatively reflect the nostalgic spirit of old Vienna; they are superbly performed by **Ilona Prunyi** (Marco Polo 223312).

Today's leading Godowsky interpreter, however, is **Hamelin,** and his two recordings are essential for all lovers of great pianism. His miscellaneous program offers the monumental *Passacaglia* and a varied assortment of shorter pieces, both original and transcribed (CBC 1026). Of even greater significance is a set containing all 54 of Godowsky's *Studies on the Chopin Etudes,* delivered with a pianistic nonchalance and sense of color and style that beggar description (Hyperion 67411/2, 2CD).

MANILDI

Hermann Goetz *(1840–1876)*

Goetz studied with von Bülow in Berlin before moving to Zürich, where he hoped to cure his chronic tuberculosis which, unfortunately, claimed him at the early age of 36. The small number of pieces he left reflects both his short life and his extremely self-critical nature, yet they span a fairly wide range, including a symphony, three concertos, and two operas, the last (*Francesca von Rimini*) left incomplete at his death. Shaw proclaimed Goetz a finer composer than Schubert, Mendelssohn, or Schumann; while that may seem extreme, the warm melodies and highly effective scoring common to his lamentably brief output compel investigation by all who worship the Romantic muse.

Goetz's F major Symphony remains his most substantial orchestral work. In this earnest if rather conventional score, he seems most inspired in the outer movements, particularly the high-spirited finale. **Werner Andreas Albert** and his Hanover players have the measure of this highly attractive work, and the warm ambience suits this music (CPO 999076). Still, even with the less polished Monte Carlo Opera Orchestra, **Edouard Van Remoortel** seems more characterful (♦Genesis 105) where Albert smooths out the contours somewhat. Only Albert offers the Violin Concerto—more of a *Konzertstück,* actually—warmly reminiscent of Bruch though underlying the predominantly lyrical mood is an affectionate playfulness that suffuses the closing pages. Gottfried Schneider is the excellent soloist.

Goetz's Piano Concerto 1, a graduation exercise set aside and only rediscovered after his death, is modeled after Liszt, less concerned with display for its own sake than a sequence of absorbing yet essentially unrelated episodes lacking only the maturity that would mold them into a seamless whole. The more ambitious B-flat Concerto seems closer to Sinding or Grieg, relaxed and bucolic save for the final Rondo with its stark rhythms spelled by lyrical chorale-like episodes. **Volker Banfield**'s enthusiastic embrace (♦CPO 999 098) contrasts with **Ponti,** who in the B-flat Concerto (in Vol. 5 of Vox's "Romantic Piano Concerto" survey) merely breezes along in his patented virtuoso mode, while **Paul Baumgartner** plods awkwardly, all but tripping over his own shoelaces and getting no support from the scrappy Beromünster ensemble (Genesis LP). Unfortunately Baumgartner's sonorous piano is more compelling than Ponti's colorless instrument or Banfield's clangorous model.

Der Widerspanstigen Zähmung (The Taming of the Shrew) largely eschews Wagner's *leitmotif* principle in favor of more large-scale forms, yet exhibits strong resemblances to *Die Meistersinger,* premiered six years earlier. Absent the faded Urania set or the better recorded Melodram, the curious must make do with the Overture. In *Francesca da Rimini,* Goetz treats the familiar story more lyrically than Tchaikovsky, and the Overture sets the scene in somber fashion. The *Frühlings-Ouvertüre* (Springtime) breathes the same fresh Mendelssohnian air as Goldmark's sunny counterpart. **Albert** seems strangely tepid here, while CPO has unwisely spread all three overtures across two CDs with the Symphony (999076) and choral works (999316), making **Van Remoortel**'s disc a more attractive package (♦Genesis 105).

Goetz's chamber music may be seen as expanding upon Mendelssohn and Schumann, in the Piano Quintet perhaps even unto Wagner. **Gerald Robbins** and colleagues offer music for piano and strings, including the Quintet in C minor (with double bass instead of second violin), the expansive Quartet in E major, and the almost Brahmsian Trio in G minor, the latter his Op. 1 yet remarkably polished nonetheless (Genesis 113, 2CD). They're passionately rendered, and save for the congested Quartet, the sonics belie their age. A similar collection with the **Göbel Trio** suffers from colorless playing and poor balances, with the piano far overshadowing the other players (CPO). The Trio is given first-class treatment by the **Abegg Trio** (Intercord 860.867, with Friederich Kiel's Trio in G major).

Adrian Ruiz plays Goetz's piano music with sweep and sensitivity, bringing out its bittersweet, Schumannesque quality (Genesis 107). This may be supplemented by **Timothy** and **Nancy LeRoi Nickel** (Arsis 114, with Schumann and Mendelssohn) or **Tony** and **Marianne Lenti** (ACA 20009; "Forgotten Piano Duets" Vol. 1) in the G minor Sonata for piano 4-hands.

Nenie (Elegy) is based upon the same Schiller poem as Brahms's *Nänie* and is a lamentation over the demise of earthly beauty, represented for Schiller by the untimely slain Orpheus, Achilles, and Adonis. While Brahms seeks consolation in eternity, Goetz takes the gods to task for such a grievous loss, gradually finding balm in transfiguration. *Psalm 137* ("By the Waters of Babylon") makes effective use of the dramatic possibilities inherent in the Biblical text, yet ends quietly, perhaps hesitant to expose audiences to the violent imagery central to the story. Both are strikingly set forth by **Albert,** aided by silvery voiced soprano Stephanie Stiller in the psalm (CPO 999316).

HALLER

Karl Goldmark *(1830–1915)*

There was a time around the turn of the century when Karl Goldmark was a force to be reckoned with both in the concert hall and the opera house. It wasn't easy to be an active partisan of both Brahms and Wagner in those days, but he managed to pull it off, and, what's more, combined in his own music the best of both worlds, the warm Viennese romanticism of the *Rustic Wedding Symphony* and the gentle lyricism of the A minor Violin Concerto set beside the lush orientalism of *Sakuntala* and *The Queen of Sheba*. Hungarian by birth, Goldmark spent most of his life in Vienna, frequently hiking over hill and dale with his good friend Brahms, yet he wrote "just as a sheep is branded by its owner, so Hungary put its brand on me and I have never lost it." This heady mix of Hungarian color and Viennese song informs everything Goldmark wrote, much to his benefit; more to the point, we might thank him for laying the groundwork for this book, as it was his great-nephew Peter Goldmark, a pioneer in television, who is generally credited with the development of the long-playing record.

ORCHESTRAL MUSIC

Rustic Wedding Symphony. What makes it particularly frustrating to try to recommend a *Rustic Wedding Symphony* is the fact that the top contender has not yet been reissued on CD. **Previn**'s LP was one of the finest things he has given us (♦Angel 37662); he clearly understood that there is nothing unpolished or unrefined about this "rustic" piece, and the warm yet translucent sonics bring out even more of the music than in the equally fine version by **Bernstein** (♦Sony 61836). Even this spirited account can't match the feeling of spontaneity, of intimate music-making, that Previn and his splendid Pittsburgh players evoke from the very first notes, while the Sony, though cleaned up a bit, still sounds bass-heavy next to the Angel LP.

Abravanel's hearty reading has been brought out several times (most recently Vanguard 10). There's a jovial, high-spirited quality to the playing that disarms all criticism, and that may be said as well of the two Enescu *Rhapsodies* coupled with it. Harder to find may be the more subtly shaped and refined recording by **López-Cobos** (Decca 448991; MHS 512160). The Los Angeles Philharmonic plays beautifully for him, but he merely skims the surface of the opening movement and goes way too fast in the final "Wedding Dance." At first blush **Butt**'s combination of the symphony's naive imagery with the more colorful and sensuous *Sakuntala Overture* may seem inspired, but for all the splendor of sound and performance he fails to sustain inner flow or bring out the rich vein of humor in this music (ASV).

Michael Bartos is better in a beautifully played and warmly recorded account filled out with the lovely *Springtime Overture*—perhaps the best overall choice after Previn or Bernstein (Newport 85503). **Gunzenhauser**, like Bartos and Abravanel, takes the opening theme and variations too quickly; surely this richly textured processional deserves to be savored at greater length, and the final "Wedding Dance" needs more splashes of color, more uninhibited abandon than he summons up (Naxos). **Hubert Reichert**'s version is a pretty tepid affair until the final movement, and the congested sonics don't help any (Vox).

Symphony 2. Perhaps if this piece had a catchy title like *Rustic Wedding* it might be played more often. Every bit as songful and well crafted as its predecessor, there's nothing even vaguely programmatic about it, though echoes of the *Springtime Overture* suffuse the first movement. The best choice is **Michael Halász,** who makes an excellent case for the music (♦Marco Polo 220417). **Butt** is more relaxed in the Scherzo—to good effect—but he's hectic and breathless in the final movement, and seems to have been miked too closely as well (ASV).

Violin Concerto. It was **Milstein**'s beautiful recording of this concerto—seconded marvelously by Harry Blech and the Philharmonia—

that first introduced most listeners (myself included) to this wonderful score (EMI, now on ♦Testament 1047, with Lalo's *Symphonie Espagnole* in mono and lacking the 'Intermezzo'). For every ointment there is a fly, and it must be noted that Milstein makes a small cut in the piece; thus both for completeness as well as on solid musical grounds you will also want **Perlman**'s reading, which sings from first note to last (♦EMI 47846, with Korngold's Concerto). **Vera Tsu**'s performance is nicely turned and a bargain (Naxos 553579, also with Korngold). **Sarah Chung** is fervent and lyrical, but the resonant soundstage pretty much reduces everything to her shrill, strained top, with the orchestra little more than a vague murmur behind her (EMI).

Coupled with the tepid Reichert *Rustic Wedding* is **Ricci**'s early take on the Violin Concerto, with his formidable virtuosity quite overwhelming this gentle fare. Two other performances by Ricci are available, one a dimly recorded, rough-hewn broadcast, the other a more recent and better sounding account notable primarily as one of the few extant recordings of Saint-Saëns's Concertos 1 and 2 (both on 111). Certainly the latter is the Ricci to go with, both for sound and performance.

Overtures. Of the seven concert overtures written by Goldmark, only *Sappho* and *Aus Jugendtagen* remain to be recorded. It would be nice if Polydor would reissue the splendid *Im Frühling* by **Fiedler.** No one else can match his heady romp, though **Bartos** will more than suffice (Newport, with *Rustic Wedding*). **Gunzenhauser** shapes Goldmark's vernal melodies affectionately if a trifle blandly (Naxos, also with *Rustic Wedding*), while **András Kórodi** suggests a lazy summer day more than the bracing gusts of spring (Hungaroton).

In Italien is vaguely Italianate in its principal theme, and the central episode with its violin trills and bird calls recalls *Im Frühling*. My favorite recording remains **John Lanchbery**'s Australian LP, which lopes along affectionately (♦EMI 7596). **Gunzenhauser** and **Butt** aren't too far behind, with the limp and shapeless **Kórodi** again bringing up the rear. The Royal Philharmonic horns really shine in the richly colored (if over-long) *Sakuntala Overture,* a product of Goldmark's love for all things exotic that culminates in a grand peroration, perhaps a better reason to buy the ASV than Butt's *Rustic Wedding.* Here Kórodi does much better, but if you can find Lanchbery's LP, you'll get a marvelous *Sakuntala* as well as the even rarer Scherzo in A and the ballet music from *The Queen of Sheba.* (Incidentally, Lanchbery's *Rustic Wedding* is no slouch either; it's on EMI 7595 if you can find it.)

The more extended *Prometheus Bound* derives from Aeschylus, rather than the account by Herder that inspired Liszt, but tells the same basic story of Prometheus punished by the gods for daring to give fire to mankind. Here **Butt** (with Symphony 2) is truly in his element, working up this turbulent music to a fare-thee-well compared to **Kórodi,** whose collection has little but convenience to recommend it (Hungaroton); Conlon tempers the fury with moderation (EMI, with Violin Converto). That leaves only *Penthesilea*—based on the story of Achilles's tragic demise—which may be heard from **Michael Halász** (Marco Polo, with Symphony 2). HALLER

OPERAS

Of Goldmark's six operas, the most famous is *Die Königin von Saba* (The Queen of Sheba). It was fairly popular in the late 19th century but hasn't been heard much since, and as far as I know, it's the only one to have been recorded. Strongly influenced by Wagner's early works, with lots of tone color and melody, it tells the story of the illicit love of the Queen of Sheba for one of Solomon's courtiers, who rejects her but ultimately dies in her arms. A fine recording from 1981 was re-released in 1986 (♦Hungaroton 12179). It's a pity it has disappeared from the listings; nothing has taken its place. MOSES

Henryk-Mikolaj Górecki (b. 1933)

I doubt that any other symphony composed in the last quarter of the 20th century has been recorded more often than Górecki's Third (nine of them, by my count), and the disc by Upshaw, **Zinman,** and the London Sinfonietta is reputed to be the best-selling classical recording of all time (Nonesuch 79282). Composed in 1976, this "Symphony of Sorrowful Songs" was noticed almost immediately via radio broadcasts in Europe beginning with the premiere over German NPR in 1977, but the 1991 Nonesuch recording was ultimately responsible for its widespread popularity, especially in England, where it was high on the pop charts, and the United States. Corigliano's Symphony 1 has probably had more live performances, but Górecki's 3 remains a top seller a decade after the Nonesuch release.

Response to this symphony, and to an extent to this recording, is sociologically and musically dichotomous. Some critics and musicians appear to be skeptical of its great popularity, assuming that the piece must lack substantial esthetic value if it reaches the egalitarian public, that there isn't really much difference between Górecki's 3 and myriad Windham Hill discs. Others suspect that Nonesuch's promotion, combined with Upshaw's ubiquitous presence, sold the disc regardless of its musical merit or lack of it; still others, more charitably, simply find it the epitome of the "New Consonance," which generally sells better than Old Dissonance across the board. There is some truth to all these more or less cynical perspectives: it *is* gloriously consonant; Nonesuch *was* aggressive, and Upshaw is everywhere these days; and like a recording of Gregorian chant a few years ago, the symphony does provide the New Age folks with austere, mellow sounds.

So does the symphony have merit approaching its popularity? Will it last or be relegated to the '90s as a period piece? I know only this: it's extraordinarily well crafted, it engages beyond the first few hearings, and it's multivalent—it has a beautiful surface but also reaches a deeper structural and historical node of consciousness. As for the Zinman/Upshaw recording, it quite simply fulfills the music's requirements to a near-perfect degree. I find some of the negative comments on the piece and recording churlish or wrong-headed, although I'm glad we have widespread, even heated, discourse about a recent piece of art.

The soprano sings relatively little in this piece, but the text and her music are critical to its full understanding. The words speak of sorrow, of loss, and of faith. Some recordings, including Nonesuch, provide the brief texts with English translations ("sorrowful songs" is not quite what the title implies in Polish), but the listener need not follow every word. The text-painting is holistic, not word for word. If you don't know this symphony, borrow it from a library or a friend and follow the immense palindromic canon that comprises the first movement, note with care the challenge to humanity provided by the texts, and simply give yourself over to the sound. You might then add to the sales of this phenomenally popular work; if not, at least you'll know what everyone else is listening to.

Of the nine recordings, I've heard five. The London Sinfonietta disc sounds better than the others, and they play this deceptively difficult music extremely well. Zinman got the tempos just right (one reviewer wrote that it doesn't matter much; on the contrary, it matters a great deal), and Upshaw's voice has a sheen, an ideal timbral connection to the (mostly) string orchestra. Several of the other recordings have merit, and for those who own Zinman/Upshaw and enjoy the symphony, a second purchase will be worthwhile. Some of them include other good music by Górecki; Nonesuch makes do with just the symphony.

Two Polish sopranos have recorded 3 twice each—**Zofia Kilanowicz** with the Polish State Philharmonic, Jerzy Swoboda conducting (Vox 7511), and the Polish Radio Symphony led by Antoni Wit (Naxos 550822). Kilanowicz is excellent on both, and some will prefer her native tongue for the text over Upshaw's vicarious Polish; of the two, I prefer Naxos. **Stephania Woytowicz** has recorded it with the Polish National Radio Orchestra, Jerzy Katlowicz conducting (Olympia 313), and the Berlin Radio Symphony led by Wlodimierz Kamirski (Koch-Schwann 36130). I recommend the Wit/Kilanowicz discs over either of Woytowicz's offerings; there is much to commend from both sopranos, but the overall recording quality and orchestral playing are slightly superior in the Vox and Naxos offerings. Of these four, only Wit approaches Zinman's all-important mastery of tempo. I've read that a relatively recent recording by the Royal Philharmonic (on their own label) with **Susan Griffin** and Yuri Simonov is very good, but I can't comment on it from personal experience (Intersound 282G). I've also heard good reports, again unconfirmed by my ears, of one by the Gran Canaria Orchestra with **Doreen de Feis** and Adrian Leaper (RCA 68387).

When a piece becomes so popular, it's natural to see what else the composer has written in the same form. In Górecki's case, the preceding symphonies share little with 3. By the mid-'70s, several composers known for serialism, sound mass, dissonant counterpoint, or electronic music, all turned to "New Consonance" at about the same time—Pärt, Penderecki, and Rochberg, for example. Composed in 1959 and 1973, respectively, Górecki's 1 has virtually no similarities with 3, but 2 is on the way to it. I don't find much in these symphonies, but if you're interested, get the recording of 1 by the Cracow Philharmonic Orchestra with **Roland Bader** (Koch-Schwann 31041); 2 comes from the Fricsay Symphony Orchestra with **Tamás Pál** (Stradivarius 33324). Both include other Górecki pieces, but *Three Pieces in Olden Style* and *Beatus vir* are better done elsewhere.

Górecki preceded his counterparts in embracing "New Consonance," as is evident in *Three Pieces in Olden Style* (1963). These short works are modal, consonant, haunting, and reflective. Wonderful in their own right, they also predict the effect of his music in the '70s. The best recording of these aptly titled works is by a fine ensemble, I Fiamminghi (Belgian despite the name), conducted by **Rudolph Werthen** (Telarc 80417 and 89111; unless there's a misprint in *Schwann,* the second is about a third as expensive as the first. I suspect, but don't know for sure, that the same performance is recorded on both).

Telarc 80417 also contains Górecki's *Little Requiem for a Polka* (1993) and *Good Night* (1990). *Little Requiem* is a four-movement work, much of which is an obvious extension of "New Consonance" techniques. *Good Night* is a requiem, marvelously scored for soprano, alto flute, three tam-tams, and piano. **Elzbieta Szmytka** sings this music very idiomatically, and the instrumentalists are equally right on. Several works by other composers are offered on Telarc 89111. Best known are Corigliano's *Elegy* and the string quartet version of Pärt's *Fratres,* plus Hovhaness's *Prayer of St. Gregory.* Those who know these works will enjoy the recording's ambience—only natural reverb from the Belgian church where the disc was made. I like I Fiamminghi and look forward to hearing more from them.

Zinman and the London Sinfonietta provide a comparably good if somewhat different reading of *Little Requiem* and *Good Night,* again with Upshaw (Nonesuch 79362). This is as reliable as the performers would lead you to expect, though I prefer I Fiamminghi's recording for its more natural sound. The third piece on this disc is Górecki's Concerto for Harpsichord and Strings (1980), performed well by soloist **Elizabeth Chojnacka** with Markus Stenz conducting the same always reliable orchestra. The Concerto has its champions, perhaps because there isn't much for the instrument in that genre. **Cecile Perrin** and Yuli Turovsky conducting Musici de Montreal include two other wonderful pieces, Pärt's *Tabula rasa* and Schnittke's Concerto Grosso 1 (Chandos 9590). I prefer the Chandos disc only because the variety of music is welcome.

Although the keyboard figures are active in the manner of harpsichord music in the Concerto, I much prefer the piano for this short, very intense piece. **Anna Górecka,** the composer's daughter, plays up a storm with able accompaniment by the Amadeus Chamber Orchestra conducted by Agnieszka Duczmal (Conifer 51246). The pounding, repetitive figures at the outset of the first movement and the flourishes that follow provide instant and constant motion for its four-minute duration. The piano again is the preferred instrument for the Ravelian ostinatos and the character that pervades the lively second and last movement, also just four minutes long. I recommend this recording for the concerto alone, but *Three Pieces in Olden Style* are given a sensitive performance and other music, especially Grazyna Bacewicz's Concerto for String Orchestra and Rudolf Barshai's arrangement of Shostakovich's String Quartet 8, make the disc a sure thing.

Choral music has been a staple of composers east of the Iron Curtain in the last quarter of the 20th century. The choral traditions in that region are ancient, and the Slavic and other languages differ much more in speech and song than Western European tongues. Three of Górecki's contributions to this repertoire are on a fine disc from **John Nelson** and the Czech Philharmonic Orchestra and Choir that includes *Beatus vir* (1979), a potent work for full forces (Argo 436835). Chant, luminous chords, and a rich solo for bass Nikita Storojev will be just right for Górecki fans but too unrelentingly dark for others. *Totus tuus* (1987), an a cappella work dedicated to Pope John Paul II, is likewise rich and dark, but may be merely dreary for others. This is a fine choir, so I would have preferred another of Górecki's choral works to his orchestral *Old Polish Music* (1969) to complete the disc.

The differences in choral singing noted above are most evident when comparing three discs by musicians of different nationalities. The Krakow Philharmonic Orchestra and Chorus conducted by **Roland Bader** perform Górecki's works in his native tongue (Koch-Schwann 31201). It's enlightening for *Miserere* and *Totus tuus,* the latter every bit as good as the Czech singers in the Argo recording. The all-strings *Choros I* fills out the time well enough. Native diction notwithstanding, I prefer *Miserere* by the Danish National Radio Choir led by **Jesper Grove Jørgensen** because it's paired with Gubaidulina's stunning *Alleluia* (Chandos 9523). For an all-Górecki choral disc that features *Miserere* I recommend **John Nelson** conducting the Chicago Symphony Orchestra Chorus (Nonesuch 79348). It's a bit heavy for my taste, too ponderous, but some will prefer the weight of the sound with the choristers' generally heavier voices for this slow-moving, pervasively consonant music.

English choral sound is equally distinctive and immediately recognizable. **King's College Choir, Cambridge,** offers a clearly recorded, very straightforward rendition of *Totus tuus* and two works each by other "New Consonance" composers—*Magnificats* by Pärt and Tavener, along with Pärt's *Beatitudes* and Tavener's *Funeral Ikos* (EMI 55096). The choir, conducted by Cleobury, produces the finely honed sound we expect from them. For full-bodied American sound, you might prefer **Robert Shaw**'s recording of *Totus tuus* (Telarc 80406). His Robert Shaw Festival singers provide good weight for Górecki's piece as well as for Pärt's *Magnificat-Antiphonies,* Barber's *Agnus Dei* (the choral version of *Adagio for Strings*), Frank Martin's Mass for Double Chorus, and Schoenberg's underappreciated *Friede auf Erden.*

Kronos usually doesn't exhibit the polish and refinement of longer-established groups, but they give a good performance of Górecki's quartets (Nonesuch 79319). Both pieces include a strong flavor of folk dance, more obvious in the first than the second. Symphony 1 ("Already It Is Dusk") is less interesting than 2 ("Quasi una Fantasia"). The latter can easily be read as a text for the darkly colored events Górecki experienced in modern Poland. Hope and faith are apparent as well, as clearly so as in Symphony 3 in this strangely beautiful work. The Kronos disc is highly recommended as the only recording to date of both quartets on a single disc, even over the **Silesian Quartet**'s excellent recording of the more impressive 2 (Olympia 375).

Devotees of Górecki's Symphony 3 will want to explore his other works, perhaps with multiple recordings of the same music. The all-Górecki discs provide that in abundance, and those not all-Górecki offer better music by others than is usually the case—generally excellent performances and recordings of Pärt, Gubaidulina, Schoenberg, and Tavener, frequently better than on discs that feature those composers.

ZIEROLF

François-Joseph Gossec *(1734–1829)*

Gossec learned much in Paris from Rameau and Stamitz, composing his first symphonies under the influence of the Mannheim School. But his most immediate and lasting fame came with his *Requiem* (*Grande Messe des Morts*) which greatly impressed Mozart and in its antiphonal effects surely influenced Berlioz. When the Revolution broke out, Gossec became one of the custodians of *Musique pour les citoyens,* turning out a great number of hymns, anthems, and other patriotic pieces including the popular *Marche lugubre* and what became the definitive arrangement of Rouget de Lisle's *Air des Marseillais.* With the defeat of Napoleon and restoration of the monarchy, Gossec retired from public life, content in his legacy as (in Adam's words) "the torch-bearer for men of greater genius whose achievements eclipsed his own."

Of Gossec's 50-some symphonies, few are available on disc. A pioneering LP by **Jacques Houtmann** and the Liège Symphony Orchestra (Musique en Wallonie 4) offered three in top-flight performances, listed in the (unfortunately French-only) booklet as Op. 5:1 in F and Op. 6:5 in G minor, plus the grandiose *Symphonie à dix-sept parties* (that is, the orchestra divided into 17 groups of players!). There's also a mono recording by **Georges Tzipine** (EMI 69830, with Méhul's Symphony 2 under Fernand Oubradous and other short pieces from the Revolution). Fortunately there's no duplication between Houtmann's LP (should you be lucky enough to find it) and the splendid disc by **Bamert** and his London Mozart Players, another exceptional entry in his "Contemporaries of Mozart" series that draws on both Opp. 5 and 12 (♦Chandos 9661).

Though generally intended for wind ensemble rather than symphony orchestra, Gossec's music for the Revolution should be noted, and is included in collections by **Roger Boutry** (EMI 49473), **Malgoire** (CBS 45607), **Lucien Mora** (Cybelia 825), **Claude Pichaureau** (Erato 45006), and **Plasson** (EMI 49470). Most of these include the *Marche lugubre,* while Pichaureau offers Gossec's arrangement of what was to become *La Marseillaise* along with several other important works.

Of the 12 quartets credited to Gossec, at least six (his Op. 14) offer the option of substituting flute for first violin, and in that form served as models for Mozart. They're played with admirable energy and flair by **Aurèle Nicolet** and the Nouveau Trio Pasquier (Dom 50) and with great élan by **Patrice Bocquillon** with the Millière String Trio (Koch-Schwann 310 081).

Gossec's major contribution to the choral literature is the *Requiem*, but the choice of recording is complicated by the fact that no two versions are even remotely alike. The original setting that so fascinated Mozart, lasting close to 99 minutes, is offered by **Jacques Houtmann** and his Liège forces in a boxed set that remains essential for anyone who wishes to have some idea of the massive scope of the piece (Koch Schwann 313041, 2CD). We have two other recordings each purporting to represent the composer's long-lost revision, both far more concise yet bearing little relation to each other. **Louis Devos** omits both the alto part and the penultimate "Lux aeterna," and the remainder of the score is extensively changed as well, now lasting 74 minutes (Erato 75359); **Herbert Schernus** includes "Lux aeterna" but omits other sections (including several choruses) heard on Erato—along with the tenor part—and comes in at just over an hour (Capriccio 10616). The more recent Erato and Capriccio recordings are much clearer than the Koch Schwann, and yet the "Tuba mirum" comes off with far better effect under Houtmann; still, given the remarkable disparity between the performing editions, it's almost impossible to recommend one over the others, and listeners looking ahead to the *Requiems* of Cherubini and Berlioz will surely want all three.

The circumstances surrounding the composition of *Dernière Messe des Vivants* remain something of a mystery as well, not the least for the curious title ("Last Mass for the Living"); yet this was Gossec's last major work, perhaps intended to complement his "first mass for the dead," the often-performed *Requiem*. Though divided into the standard sections, the "Agnus Dei" is preceded by a motet, "O salutaris hostia," and the work ends with a prayer for those in power—in this case Napoleon. The only recording, directed by **Dominique Rouits,** seems unduly lethargic, or perhaps the work itself simply lacks the power and imagination of the *Requiem,* and the distant miking of the chorus doesn't help (Koch-Schwann 13 078).

The *Te Deum* calls for two choirs and a fairly large orchestra, much of it proceeding in a majestic, even triumphant manner. Save for the rather pinched tone of soprano Jill Feldman, the Sorbonne forces under **Jacques Grimbert** give a taut and compelling account, and the sonics are entirely satisfactory (Adda 581123).   HALLER

Louis Moreau Gottschalk *(1829–1869)*

Listen to *Bamboula* or *Banjo* by this New Orleans-born Jewish/Creole composer and prepare to be astonished when you check his birth and death dates. Gottschalk was the first Third Stream composer, meaning that he combined European, black, and Latin influences into his own jaunty, ebullient idiom a century before it became fashionable. You can hear the Cuban danzon, the Brazilian samba, American ragtime and jazz, pre-echoes of Granados, Milhaud, Joplin, Copland, and dozens of other future composers in Gottschalk's music, along with Stephen Foster, patriotic anthems, Chopin, and Berlioz. More than just a history lesson, it's also lots of fun—for the performer as well as the listener—because his brilliantly crafted piano works are a comfortable physical pleasure for the hands.

So why isn't this music heard or recorded more often? Snobbery mostly, for Gottschalk never aspired to follow the serious Germanic path to profundity, preferring to go his own merry pan-global way. Even after the Gottschalk centenary in 1969, when he was feted in a fit of looming

American Bicentennial madness, his presence faded quickly, and nearly all big-name pianists and conductors continue to steer clear of him. We await some eager, energetic classical cat with a jazz bent to rediscover this stuff.

ORCHESTRAL MUSIC

Eugene List was the foremost Gottschalk champion of the 20th century, and his biggest recorded monument is an indispensable bargain-priced box that contains all the surviving orchestral works and a couple of latter-day orchestrations of piano pieces (♦Vox 5009, 2CD). Recording in Vienna with Igor Buketoff and Berlin with Samuel Adler, List could assemble the financially draining orchestras and bands called for by the composer, and while their performances are occasionally somewhat creaky, you can't hear this naively grandiose side of Gottschalk anywhere else. Among the recorded premieres are Symphony 2 ("A Montevideo")—actually a rhapsody that begins solemnly and reaches a lively apotheosis on "Yankee Doodle"—two endearingly reverent marches for orchestra and band, and even a perky, 13-minute, Latin-rhythm-spiced "opera," *Escenas Campestres.* Alas, the CD edition omits List's endearing spoken lecture on Gottschalk that opened the LP version.

Symphony 1 (*La Nuit de tropiques*). After the ultra-Romantic, Berliozian, untropical opening movement, this piece explodes into a boisterous, native-percussion-laden Brazilian samba, a startling window into the 20th century. **Buketoff** was the first conductor to use Gottschalk's massive original orchestration with band reinforcements; after an urgent opening movement, Buketoff barely achieves swinging liftoff with his elephantine Viennese forces (♦Vox 5009, 2 CD). **Abravanel** uses a reduced instrumentation without the band, yet this eloquent, exuberant performance catches the spirit more convincingly (♦Vanguard 9). **Richard Rosenberg** uses his own smallish edition based on Gottschalk's autograph, and though he rushes through I and his Hot Springs Festival strings are of variable quality, this performance can be recommended for its extensive, courageously steaming rhumba/samba grooves in II (♦Naxos 559036).

Grande Tarantelle. Using a dashing orchestration by Hershy Kay, both List (♦Vox 5009, 2CD) and **William Tritt** (♦Telarc 80112) swagger along with irresistible verve; Tritt is treated to especially sumptuous sound. **Reid Nibley**'s performance is more elegantly turned but still propulsive (♦Vanguard 9). **Rosenberg** opts for a small, quaint-sounding wind/string orchestra arrangement from 1874, and his pianist lacks joie de vivre (Naxos 559036).

PIANO MUSIC

The sheer pleasure **List** got from performing Gottschalk's music shows in his pioneering 1956 album of 12 piano pieces (♦Vanguard 4050). His playing is simplicity itself, unpretentious, unaffected, yet at the same time no one could mine the nuances and express the character of this music as winningly. He pulls many subtleties out of *Bamboula*, gives *Banjo* a folksy personality, avoids the treacly temptations of salon pieces like *The Last Hope* and *The Dying Poet,* and closes with a propulsive *Tournament Galop*. The sound is mono but well-balanced.

Alan Mandel presents the most comprehensive single package of piano music—40 pieces—which he plays with plenty of panache but not always the greatest technical control (to cite one example, the final bars of *The Union* are loaded with missed notes). But the spirit is right, and his selection of standards and rarities, acceptably transferred, comes at a tempting low price (♦Vox 3033, 3CD). **Klaus Kaufmann** made a strong impression with a 12-selection album that presents a more flamboyant portrait of Gottschalk than most of his colleagues (♦Koch Schwann 310035, NA). Often he grabs holds of the rhythms, sometimes stabbing at them, adding some imaginative phrasing of his own; his dancing *Souvenir de Porto Rico* is the most convincing performance I've heard.

Philip Martin is a prolific Gottschalk man of our time, with three volumes of piano music, yet with his refined European sensibility he's not one for all seasons (Hyperion 66459, 66697, 66915). His tempos tend to be leisurely, relaxed, more at home laying on the sentiment of the salon pieces with a shovel than reacting to the Latin rhythms, though he does find more poetry than most in the Chopinesque pieces. **Georges Rabol** is also very polished and elegant, but owing perhaps to his Creole ancestry, he finds more life in Gottschalk's rhythms and even includes a rare performance of the inventive sequel to *Banjo, Second Banjo* (Opus 111 50-9114).

Amiram Rigai is another Gottschalk specialist from way back; though sometimes restrained in impulse, on occasion he's capable of much rhythmic vitality and variety in rubato, unafraid to take off a bit from the markings. There are a number of Rigai albums from different decades (Decca DL710143, NA; MHS 3135, NA; Smithsonian/Folkways 40803), and the performances of the same pieces can differ (the Deccas often have more character). A compilation from **Leonard Pennario's** two LP albums actually contains one of the best selections of first-rate Gottschalk material among the single-disc entries (Angel 64667). But Pennario's performances are mostly bland, dynamically compressed, even tame, and that simply won't do.

As part of a program entitled "The American Romantic," **Alan Feinberg** chooses to emphasize Gottschalk's schmaltzy side with *La Chute des feuilles* (played more slowly than Martin but with less heart-on-sleeve emotion) and *Illusions perdues,* concluding with a touch of fancy bombast in *God Save the Queen* (Argo 430 330). **Richard Burnett's** program is another species altogether, played on historic pianos from Gottschalk's time (Amon Ra 32). Yet hearing these poorly maintained Erard, Graf, and somewhat improved Broadwood instruments makes you realize how much better Gottschalk's music fits on modern pianos (besides, he preferred Chickerings).

Ever the entrepreneur responding to public demand, Gottschalk arranged several of his works for piano duet and also wrote originals for that format that subsequently became better known as piano solos. **Alan Marks** and **Nerine Barrett** offer 13 numbers, but they can't really swing the rhythms and the pianos sound tinny, watery, and distant; it's like listening in the wrong end of an airplane hangar (Nimbus 5324). **List,** Cary Lewis, and Brady Millican receive thinner reproduction in five pieces (♦Vox 5009, 2CD); the instruments sometimes sound like player pianos. Yet they offer more convincing performances than Marks and Barrett; the delicately turned *Ses Yeux* has much more life, *Radieuse* and *Ojos Criollos* are crisper and livelier, *La Gallina* is sharper in rhythm.   GINELL

Morton Gould (*1913–1996*)

Of all 20th-century American composers, Gould may have had the best ear for sound. Like Mahler, he heard the symphony orchestra as an entity, not as a medium for amplifying preconceived music. This attitude makes his light, popular pieces fun to play and his more complex creations clear and attractive. His love for popular and jazz styles makes his music some of the most effective and appealing to audiences written in this century.

Gould's earliest recorded work appears to be *American Symphonette*

2 (1935), which, by the usual perversity of fate, contains one of his most popular pieces, "Pavane," as its slow movement. **Mester** is good, partly because of the idiomatic playing of the Louisville Orchestra (Albany 13, 2CD), but **Kenneth Klein** is even better in the rowdy parts with the London Philharmonic (Albany 202; EMI 9462). Klein couples it mostly with pieces with the word "American" in their titles, including the only recording of *American Ballads* and six *Spirituals for Strings* from a possible 11 once recorded by the composer (RCA 2686, NA). Mester's album gets more esoteric, including two major pieces, *Symphony of Spirituals* and the Viola Concerto (the latter played just adequately) plus several shorter works. Gould himself conducts *Columbia* and an unfortunately abridged version of *Soundings,* while Lawrence Leighton Smith does *Housewarming, Flourishes & Galop,* and the symphony and concerto. Between the two you have an interesting collection of Gould's orchestral music, most of it unduplicated elsewhere.

The only piece in Klein's disc available elsewhere is the well-known *American Salute,* based on "When Johnny Comes Marching Home," which no frequenter of outdoor summer concerts can avoid. Surprisingly, there is only one other version presently listed, in a miscellaneous program of American tub-thumpers conducted by **Fiedler** (RCA 6806), who was a classic piece of period Americana in his own right. Either performance will do; this piece plays itself. Another collection gives us examples from throughout Gould's career, beginning with the 1938 Piano Concerto, a considerable and fascinating piece played by Randall Hodgkinson. The others are *Showpiece* for orchestra, a 20-minute work of great energy and color, and a lovely suite called *String Music,* played by the Albany Symphony under **David Alan Miller** (Albany 300).

Gerard Schwarz's CD with the Seattle Symphony contains both complete works and excerpts, including the band suite *Formations* and *Concerto Grosso for 4 Violins* from the unfinished Balanchine ballet *Audubon,* as well as excerpts from TV documentaries and "Pavane" rearranged by Gould to feature trumpeter Jeffrey Silberschlag (Delos 3166). The orchestra sounds ill at ease with these scraps, but *Formations* is an exciting and amusing suite of marching band impressions and *Concerto Grosso* is a major work not recorded elsewhere. If you really want to hear Gould's TV music, **David Amos** recorded a substantial selection from *Holocaust* with the Cracow Philharmonic (Koch 7020, NA).

The suite from the ballet *Fall River Legend* (1946) is perhaps Gould's most-recorded work. It forms part of another all-Gould disc played by **Sedares** and the New Zealand Symphony in a lush and resonantly recorded reading (Koch 7380). **Schenk's** performance with the same orchestra is less broadly paced (Koch 7181). The old **Hanson** version with the Eastman-Rochester Orchestra is brightly recorded and contains a hi-fi *Spirituals for Orchestra* as well (Mercury 432016). If you prefer your *Spirituals* smoother in recorded texture, there's **Susskind** and the London Symphony (Everest 9003). Both of these recordings were demonstration quality in the '60s and still hold up well.

Returning to *Fall River Legend,* **Levine** conducts a less sonically impressive but livelier 1955 version with the Ballet Theatre Orchestra in bright mono sound (EMI 66549 or 61651). But if you want to know how the piece really ought to be played, go for **Gould** himself, who was a fine conductor and recorded the suite twice, in 1960 (RCA 61505) and 1978 (♦Citadel 88130). The latter contains a number of other Gould pieces, some otherwise unrecorded. Finally, if you want to know the whole ballet, plus a personal history, there's **Milton Rosenstock's** recording, the complete 47-minute score plus a 27-minute conversation between Gould and Agnes de Mille (Albany 35). Rosenstock is a bit stiff; his dances are not as subtly sprung as some.

Sedares's disc (Koch) also contains two works not otherwise available, *Foster Gallery*, a suite conducted by JoAnn Falletta, and an a cappella work, *Of Time and the River,* sung by the Gregg Smith Singers under John Daly Goodwin. *Foster Gallery* was once available in a 1978 version with the composer and the London Philharmonic, along with *Spirituals* (Crystal Clear LP 7005, NA). Until that reappears, this one will do just fine. *Of Time and River* first appeared in an all-choral Gould disc from 1991 (Koch 7026), containing two more recent works, the curiously balanced *Quotations* and the two-part *A Cappella.* That disc was not well received at the time. *Of Time and the River* is a 34-minute setting of passages from Thomas Wolfe, lovely but rather meandering for its length. This disc as a whole is interesting but perhaps not essential.

Latin-American Symphonette is one of Gould's most memorable pieces, consistently inspired and catchy. **Hanson**'s Eastman-Rochester LP was a little overpowering in places but stirring nevertheless. **Abravanel**'s with the Utah Symphony has been reissued; it's fine, more sophisticated though not as exciting (Vanguard 9). **Gould**'s version includes the two middle movements (RCA 61505 or 61651), reason enough for getting ◆Citadel 88130 instead, which includes the entire piece. A reissue of **Felix Slatkin**'s dynamic reading with the Hollywood Bowl Orchestra would be welcome (EMI 63738, NA).

Symphony 4 ("West Point") is an effective piece in two movements, I representing men without women at West Point (an antiquated concept), with a quiet reference to thoughts of death in the form of a *Dies Irae* quotation and a marching machine to complete the picture; movement II is a jollier martial movement. Its first recording, by **Fennell** and the Eastman Wind Ensemble, was brightly done, using real feet for the marching section (Mercury 434320, with strong band symphonies by Hovhaness and Gould's teacher Vittorio Giannini). A newer version by the **University of Georgia Wind Symphony** is smoother-sounding but less ear-catching and programmed with less interesting material (Summit 247). Also, the marching machine is not really audible.

Few discs containing single works by Gould should be mentioned. **Alan Mandel** includes the short *Prelude & Toccata* for piano in his "American Piano I" in a performance that needs lots of oil; the machine slows down and jerks along in a way I'm sure Gould didn't intend (Premier 1013). A lovely piece for strings, harp, and vibraphone called *Harvest* is recorded by **David Amos** and the New Russia Orchestra in a program that includes music by Vittorio Giannini and Flagello; it shows an affectionate resemblance to Roy Harris (Albany 143). The catchy 15-minute 1938 *Folk Suite,* written for the High School of Music & Art at the same time as Copland's *Outdoor Overture,* is on another Amos disc in a program of Rózsa, Menotti, and Marc Lavry (Kleos 5103).

The 1984 Flute Concerto is a major work, played by **Keith Bryan** with Zuohuang Chen and the Slovak Radio Symphony of Bratislava (Premier 1045, with John la Montaine's concerto). *Derivations* for clarinet and band is a short but interesting piece, found in a historical issue by **Benny Goodman,** for whom it was written (Sony 42227), and in a better-recorded and idiomatic performance by **John Bruce Yeh** (Reference 55). Both programs are jazz-oriented. **Mirian Conti** plays *Pieces of China,* a piano suite combining the pentatonic scale with jazz licks in a program primarily of works by Persichetti (Albany 299). Prize-winners of the Murray Dranoff International two-piano competition play an enjoyable suite called *Two Pianos* energetically in an interesting American program (Vanguard 106).

There are a lot of fascinating Gould works not recorded or presently missing. I've always been fascinated by his 12-tone *Jekyll & Hyde Variations,* which Mitropoulos did with the New York Philharmonic. Gould's

disc of *Spirituals for Orchestra* and *Foster Gallery* has been mentioned, but there's also one with *Burchfield Gallery* and *Apple Waltzes* with the American Symphony (RCA 5019, NA), and another with *Vivaldi Gallery* and *Venice,* two more major pieces we need. Then there's a chamber disc containing *Concerto Concertante* for violin, piano, and wind quintet, and *Cellos* for two cello quartets, played by **Masako Yanagita** and others (MusicMasters LP 20140). This last may be available from MHS. Finally there are the *Dance Variations,* once recorded with panache by **Stokowski** and later by **Amos** in an infinitely inferior performance (Koch 370022, NA). The songs from Gould's dramatic productions, *Billion Dollar Baby, Enter Juliet,* and *Something to Do* were in a worthy release that shouldn't have disappeared (Premier 1016, NA, with songs by Jerome Moross). MOORE

Charles Gounod (1818–1893)

Emile Zola's description of *Faust* as "the music of a voluptuous priest" may be extended for better or worse to much of Gounod's output, in the end turning from the stage of the Paris Opéra to the most inward and deeply religious creations, including *Mors et Vita* and the *Requiem.* If it's the more sensual side of Gounod that emerges in *Faust*—not least for the lush "Walpurgisnacht" ballet, unfortunately all too often omitted in performance or on disc—we may appreciate all the more Marguerite's angelic apotheosis. While the two symphonies by the 37-year-old Gounod may seem like willful discursions, they're no less winning for all that, and in presaging the third ("garden") act of *Faust* they may be seen as welcome harbingers of the fertile flow of melody to come. Thus, with the great success of *Faust,* Gounod had finally come full circle.

SYMPHONIES

Tuneful and ebullient, Gounod's two symphonies unabashedly portray the lyrical gifts of the composer already well known to us from his works for the stage. Written at a time when proper French composers were expected to write operas, not symphonies, neither will reveal any great strides forward in Gounod's musical development—we must remember that *Faust* was still three years away—yet both are so thoroughly delightful that this will surely be of no concern to most listeners. Gounod's Symphony 1 served his pupil Bizet so well as a model that the younger composer suppressed his own C major Symphony out of deference to his teacher; ironically, it's the Bizet we hear most often today. Symphony 2 perhaps remains farther down in Gounod's résumé, yet is no less attractive.

Plasson received a warm recommendation when his performance first came out on LP; however, enthusiasm even then was guarded, given his sober approach to the "Rhenish" theme of 2:I (it sounds more like Brahms than Schumann)—or for that matter its counterpart in Symphony 1—as well as the engineers' failure to bring out either the clarion trumpet calls in 1:IV or the tympani that exuberantly punctuate the final measures (EMI 63949). Since then we have had a fresh-sounding and winning account from **John Lubbock,** which expands upon the felicities of Plasson in many ways; still, he too adopts a rather too comfortable tempo in 2:I (though the music flows better than with Plasson) and also seems rather breathless in the Scherzo (ASV 981).

You will also find separate accounts of 1 with **Hogwood** (London)—an animated reading with wonderfully plangent wind playing, unfortunately with too few strings for full effect—and of 2 with **Jean-Louis Petit** (Arion), who fields the "Rhenish" theme with great panache but trudges through the Scherzo as if half asleep. It's coupled with Gounod choral music that may not be to all tastes. However, any shortcomings these versions might have are as nothing next to **Franz Lamprecht**'s turgid and dreary readings with echo-ridden sonics to boot (Electrecord).

Fortunately, **Marriner,** the most recent addition to the catalog, is also the best. (♦Philips 462125). For all the welcome momentum imparted to the opening sally of 1, there is a lyrical cast that is immediately winning; Marriner never pushes this essentially guileless music beyond comfortable bounds, for all the hearty good spirits of the final movement. In 2 he makes the "Rhenish" theme soar in gloriously buoyant fashion; it's a pity he omits the repeat. Marriner is the one to buy, and he benefits from a beautiful recording as well.

Gounod's *Petite Symphonie* for winds is a delightful piece, especially the crisp and captivating Scherzo. Unfortunately, two of the best versions, by **Barbirolli** (Pye 14082) and **de Waart** (Philips 6500-163), seem to have fallen through the cracks. However, **Hogwood** (coupled with 1) will more than suffice. **Michael Goodwin** treats the music with tenderness and affection, if without that last ounce of vigor that would set this performance alongside the others (CBC). In "A Serenade for You from France," **Jii Stárek** seems a bit nonchalant in the Scherzo, but his CD offers music by Godard (Suite) and Offenbach (Serenade) that you're not likely to find elsewhere (Koch-Schwann). **Alexander Brezina** has been taken to task for sluggish tempos (Orfeo); **Barry Faldner** has the Chicago Symphony soloists at his disposal, but I'm not sure Milhaud's chamber symphonies make an appropriate coupling (Koch).

OTHER ORCHESTRAL MUSIC

The ballet music from *Faust* is frequently encountered apart from the opera, usually combined with other such pieces. A number of performances have entered and left the catalog so often that it's difficult to be sure whether an LP ever made it to CD, including Ormandy (Columbia) and Fricsay (DG). Others have at least shown up sporadically, including **Mackerras** (EMI) and **Karajan**'s Philharmonia recording (EMI), while his Berlin Philharmonic version—like the EMI coupled with a heavily cut Offenbach *Gaité Parisienne*—is available in a DG "Double" (437404). The *Faust* ballet is coupled with a more complete *Gaité Parisienne* by **Dutoit** (London) as well as by **Solti** and the Covent Garden Orchestra in a British Decca "Ballet Gala" (448942); of these Dutoit may be more appealing, thanks to Solti's blistering treatment of the concluding "Dance of Phryné."

Covent Garden forces may be heard to better effect in **Gibson**'s rousing performance (♦Classic 2449); this label specializes in high-tech reissues of classic RCA and London recordings (you probably won't find them in the store, but they have an 800 number: 457-2577). Another "Ballet Gala," this one from **Bonynge**, is taken from the opera, and thus the introduction to the opening dance is missing while the "Dance of Phryné" segues directly into the ensuing duet—a most disconcerting experience (Decca). Apparently EMI chose to present the ballet separately in their release with **Plasson** so it could be recycled without such intrusions in a 2CD set of "Ballets d'Opéras." **Zinman**'s performance has been issued a couple of times, most recently as part of a Philips "Duo" as makeweight with his *Coppélia*.

My favorite is still **Paray** in "French Opera Highlights," as much for the plangent sound of the woodwinds as for his spirited performance (♦Mercury 432014). While **Marriner** (coupled with the symphonies) actually pulls ahead of Paray in a couple of places—particularly his more expressive "Les Troyennes"—elsewhere he occasionally seems to lose interest. In "Ballet Music from Famous Operas," **Bernstein** gives the music his usual ultra-romantic treatment, drawing out some pas-

sages but building to an exhilarating climax, but he cuts the appended "Dance of the Hours" (Sony 47600). Several recordings, including Paray, Karajan (DG), and Zinman, also include the buoyant Waltz from Act II as a bonus.

The *Funeral March for a Marionette* is known to most people as the theme music of Alfred Hitchcock's TV show. You may safely pick it up as part of **Paray**'s "Marches and Overtures à la Française" (♦Mercury 434332) or **Fiedler**'s "Classics for Children" (RCA), or, for that matter, coupled with Gibson's *Faust* ballet, though Paray omits the repeat.

HALLER

CHORAL MUSIC

The most familiar of Gounod's large-scale religious works is the indestructible *St. Cecilia Mass*. I'm fond of **Markevitch**'s recording, which cuts through much of the treacle (♦DG 427409), but **Prêtre**'s more relaxed account from the '80s has good soloists and better sound (♦EMI 47094; HMV 568337, with interesting fillers). The three-part Latin oratorio *Mors et Vita* is a lengthy, slow-moving, peaceful meditation on Death, Judgment, and Resurrection, and it incorporates (in its first part) as placid a setting of the *Dies irae* as you'll ever hear. **Plasson,** with excellent soloists, should suffice to satisfy anyone's curiosity (♦EMI 54459).

OPERAS

Faust. For quite some time, and through no inherent flaw, *Faust* has been a problem. Ideally we want beautiful voices, idiomatic diction, and a sympathetic conductor, recorded in excellent sound. Unfortunately, we can't find it all at the same time on records. It's a delight to hear the words perfectly enunciated and slotted into place on the musical line, but the pleasure is rare. The great French singers are long gone, and to turn to the *Faust* snippets recorded by Vallin, Plançon, Thill, and others is to realize what we've lost. Thill's recordings are especially indispensable, and the 30 minutes of *Faust* excerpts he left us in the late '20s unveil a ringing, heroic voice deployed with both fervor and finesse (♦Bongiovanni 1145).

Gratification of a different kind comes from the famous recordings by Caruso, Farrar, Amato, and Journet *circa* 1910 (RCA). Journet aside, there's nothing particularly French about these artists, but their vibrant personalities and full-throated vocalism also bring the opera to life. Nothing enhances *Faust* quite so much as great voices, and they're as precious as impeccable elocutionists. It's worth remembering that *Faust* was once the most popular opera in the world, and it was customarily sung, and relished, not only in French but also in German, Italian, and English.

Collectors who want a complete recording and place linguistic considerations above everything else must turn to the 1930 **Henri Büsser** (Malibran) or the better-sounding, oddly abridged (no aria for Valentin) 1948 **Beecham** (Preiser). There is only one great singer among both casts, Journet in 1930, the last of the great French Mephistos. The other voices have little allure; worse, they're fairly inexpressive, as if the performers feel that uttering the words is enough to put the opera across. Roger Rico, Beecham's Mephistopheles, is at least lively and personable, though his tone is light and shallow. More typical is Beecham's Marguerite, Geori Boué, who has some sweet, tender moments but is more often blank. "Je ris," she says, and you don't believe it for a second.

When **Cluytens** recorded *Faust,* he looked beyond the borders of France for his three principals (EMI). His other Pathé recordings of about the same time, *Carmen, Pearl Fishers,* and *Mireille,* drew heavily on native talent, but his *Faust* was more cosmopolitan, relying on the chorus and supporting players to provide some idiomatic flavor. De los Angeles's French is less precise than Geori-Boué's, but she is far more adept at conveying emotion through the voice. Gedda, always a reliable French stylist, also muffs a vowel or two, but listen to how sensuously their timbres melt into the phrases of the Act 3 duet. Beecham's pair, pinched and poker-faced, don't have the same magic. Cluytens's Mephisto is Christoff, famous in the role and widely admired. He has presence and theatrical vitality, but he's also coarse in tone, vulgar and overbearing, and comes close to spoiling the entire performance.

Cluytens remade *Faust* in stereo in 1958 with almost the same cast (EMI). The graceful Valentin of Jean Borthayre was replaced by the more extroverted Ernest Blanc; Rita Gorr rather than Danielle Michel is Marthe; and the sparkling (though very feminine) Liliane Berton improves on the somewhat sluggish Siebel of Martha Angelici. More significant is the vast sonic advancement. The voices in 1953 had a layer of fuzzy distortion around them; in 1958, they're much more cleanly recorded. Christoff files a bit of the roughness away from his tone, but he's still repellent. Gedda now manages the phrase "ou se dèvine la présence" in one breath up to the top C, and de los Angeles comes a little closer to suggesting (if not actually executing) the trills in the "Jewel Song." They were slightly fresher five years earlier, the tenor's voice especially having lost some of its buoyancy. Both recordings (Christoff aside) are enjoyable; the better sound of the second gives it a strong edge (♦EMI 69983).

I wish Christoff's devil had been exorcized from Cluytens's performances and replaced by Siepi, the best Mephistopheles of the '50s and '60s. He's the brightest spot in **Cleva**'s Metropolitan Opera recording (originally Columbia—hope for a reissue). Siepi is an affable fiend, masterful when need be but unfailingly charming. His voice rolls out smoothly and sonorously, and he easily dominates every scene in which he appears. (His Mephisto would grow more polished and vivid with time, so it's worth seeking out one of the later, unauthorized Met recordings that team him with Björling's Faust.) His colleagues in 1950 sound less involved in their parts. Steber is a bright, fluent, vacuous Marguerite. Conley's voice also flows lyrically, but the polished surface is undermined by pinched, nasal tone. Neither of them offers a focused characterization; after energetic spurts, they tend to slip into neutral and coast (like so many of the singers, American and otherwise, who took up the same roles in the years to come).

Pretty much the last gasp of a distinctively French style came in **Gianfranco Rivoli**'s studio recording, even if it was made in Vienna (♦VAI 1143). The Vienna Opera Chorus is heavy-footed next to its French counterpart on the Cluytens recordings, and the orchestral playing isn't impeccable. Paul Bicos's pedestrian Valentin hasn't the tonal fullness of his predecessors on EMI, but Berton is once again a delightful Siebel, and Rehfuss's Mephistopheles is not unlike Rico's: idiomatic, light but dashing, and articulate. Marguerite and Faust are also native French speakers, but they hail from Quebec. Alarie is a flexible, proficient soprano. Her basically pretty voice has a touch of astringency, but it's clear and forward. Her real-life husband, Simoneau, is an extraordinary Faust despite a few liabilities. His highest notes tend to be weak and wooden. He could use some of Gedda's (not to say Björling's) ring and penetration, though he delivers the top C of the aria in a finely gauged *voix mixte* (Thill managed it even better). His middle range is sweeter and warmer than Gedda's, and he has a masterly control of dynamics and legato. The *messa di voce* comes easily (and repeatedly) to him, and his words are lovingly shaped. His opening lines have plenty of variety and declamatory force, and he's the most dulcet of lovers in the Act 3 duet.

Bonynge couldn't be more different (♦London 421240). The cast pretty much ignores niceties of style and diction and just sings the hell out of the music. This *Faust* is my refuge when I start to lament the (apparently permanent) extirpation of the French vocal school. If we'll never have Vallin, Thill, and Journet back, Sutherland, Corelli, and Ghiaurov afford ample comfort, at least to voice lovers. All three sing with arresting tonal beauty and plenitude, never sounding tentative or stretched, and the music not only withstands the onslaught but thrives on it. Sutherland has the biggest, easiest high notes of any Marguerite on records and the best trills for the "Jewel Song." Corelli and Ghiaurov are larger than life, ignoring the fine points of characterization in favor of vocal splendor. Yet they and Sutherland always connect with the music, singing it with passion and commitment. Bonynge opens the standard cuts to include Marguerite's spinning song and Siebel's "Si le bonheur" in Act 4. It's an exhausting, overwhelming performance, for better or worse a far cry from Beecham and Rivoli.

After Bonynge, it became customary to record *Faust* complete. It also became the norm to cast singers from just about anywhere, without regard for stylistic or conceptual coherence. *Faust*'s Frenchness would quickly grow vestigial, honored only in the singing of some of the choruses or an occasional native in a minor role. Paradoxically, the diversity would result in performances that became more and more generalized, more ecumenically noncommital. Where Sutherland and her colleagues left a distinctive mark, their successors would walk into the studio, put in a few days' work, and, like perfunctory cooks, whip up an uneven, largely savorless meal.

Alain Lombard leads a slow, ponderous *Faust,* partly redeemed by the honest, vigorous, but unblandishing Mephisto of Plishka (Erato). Caballé has some lovely moments, and Aragall is an intermittently ardent Faust, but both of them have distracting vocal problems (her gulpy attacks, his intonation) and seem to lose interest in the proceedings.

Prêtre is more appealing with the Paris Opéra orchestra and chorus (♦EMI 63090). Domingo has some of Corelli's vocal largesse, without the slurps and sobs, and his French is better. He maintains a cleaner line but never duplicates the explosive thrills, and he's a vague actor. Ghiaurov's Mephisto, second time around, is more varied and subtle, less solid of voice. Freni's Marguerite is often lovely and affecting. She sang the role many times on stage, and if her French is imperfect, she certainly knows what the words mean. Her voice, for the most part, has its characteristic warmth and sheen; only some lack of ease and freedom diminish the performance. Allen is a suave, full-tongued Valentin, the best on records since Blanc 20 years earlier.

Davis evinces no particular affection for the opera (Philips). He has, in Nesterenko, a Mephisto almost as bizarre as Christoff. Te Kanawa is an aloof, droopy Marguerite (Sutherland's singing has far more rhythmic and harmonic life); Araiza is a strained Faust. **Plasson,** like Prêtre and Davis, puts Faust's usually omitted drinking song in place of the "Walpurgisnacht" ballet, which is consigned to an appendix (EMI). The old French style is fitfully ascendant in his performance: chorus and orchestra are from Toulouse, and Mephistopheles is sung by van Dam, though too dryly and timidly to put him in a class with Siepi, let alone Journet. Studer is a diligent Marguerite with occasional stirrings of life; she's at her most absorbing in the spinning song and the confrontation with Mephistopheles that follows. Richard Leech brings good schoolboy French and a basically agreeable timbre to Faust, but he's monotonous, singing too often in full voice without any timbral shading or dynamic play. Hampson is an earnest, lightweight Valentin. The stodgy Plasson administers the *coup de grâce,* conducting without any particular sense of direction and banning any high interpolations from his singers. Of minor interest is an appendix of numbers originally in *Faust* but removed by Gounod.

Carlo Rizzi gives us different variants, but his performance of the opera proper is lethargic, as though his own wallowing in the music were more important than the singers' contributions (Teldec). Gasdia is a diffident Marguerite, agile and sometimes pretty. Hadley addresses his more expansive music with Italianate strength, but his soft singing has too much wispy falsetto. Ramey's Mephistopheles could use more *savoir faire,* but he's firmer than Plishka, more sonorous than van Dam, and far less unkempt than Christoff or Nesterenko.

Lombard, Plasson, Davis, and Rizzi all miss much of the essence of *Faust,* through poor casting or stolid leadership or outright uneventfulness. Prêtre gets a bit closer to the heart of the matter; Cluytens, Christoff notwithstanding, closer still. Bonynge is in a category of his own. The Busser and Beecham performances are relics of a vanished era, and so, less authentically, is Rivoli. The perfect *Faust* recording has yet to be made, and probably never will be.

Roméo et Juliette. This opera has always lagged behind *Faust* in popularity, and though it's easier to cast—baritone and bass have relatively small roles—it hasn't been recorded as often. The first time was, astonishingly, in 1912 under **François Ruhlmann** (Malibran). Journet's mellow Friar Laurence is the most impressive performance. Yvonne Gall's wan Juliet and Agustarello Affre's robust Romeo are less striking, and the murky sound will discourage most listeners from making their acquaintance. The next studio recording didn't come until 1953 (Decca). **Erede** is the conductor, and his Francophone cast is neither incompetent nor unpleasant—the meioses suggesting that they're not all that memorable either. Jean Micheau is a lucid, slightly acidulous and mature Juliet, the Canadian tenor Raoul Jobin an intense, macho Romeo. The drama and language are fairly well served, the beauty of the music somewhat slighted.

With one exception, the other recordings have come from EMI, and the first was only a set of excerpts conducted by **Lombard,** good enough to make us wish the whole opera had been done (♦EMI 65290). Gedda sings Romeo with fervor and finesse, his high notes clean and ringing, his diction excellent. Carteri's Juliet has something of a sharp edge, but her voice is firm and incisive, her acting thoughtful and intelligent. Michel Dens delivers a quicksilver account of his "Queen Mab" ballad.

When the same conductor led a complete recording in 1968, the supporting cast was still French, but the two leads were from a different world. There is, nonetheless, something quite likable about Freni and Corelli. They mangle the language but sing with uninhibited passion and fullness, their duets are saturated with Italianate warmth and a kind of controlled lustiness. She has the lightness and wide-eyed ingenuousness for her "Waltz Song," and he disembogues a huge top B-flat at the end of his aria and then fines it down to a gentle *piano* (electronically assisted, perhaps, but he did manage much the same effect in the opera house). Advocates of proper French style have sniffed at this *Roméo,* but it's enjoyable in its own idiosyncratic way.

Plasson is more refined and more complete (EMI). Malfitano is a careful, tasteful Juliet with an efficient, generic-soprano voice. Bacquier's Capulet, Gino Quilico's Mercutio, van Dam's Laurence, and Charles Burles's Tybalt are, to a man, expert and individual. Kraus's Romeo is also distinctive, his lean, penetrating voice unmistakable for

anyone else. His demeanor is unfailingly elegant and chivalrous (if never impetuously youthful), his timbre pleasing (if never particularly beautiful).

Domingo, **Felix Slatkin**'s Romeo, is rather like a well-behaved Corelli (RCA). There's much of the same tonal succulence and amplitude, governed with more restraint and finesse. He's an undemonstrative performer, except in the most generalized way, and he never sounds young and impulsive. Swenson, his Juliet, is blander still, a pretty cipher. She has all the coloratura skills she needs and some tonal sweetness, but her singing is almost devoid of expression. Ollmann is a bumptious Mercutio, Susan Graham an unusually fine Stephano. The other cast members are phlegmatic and unnoticeable.

That leaves *faute de mieux,* the second **Plasson** recording as the most recommendable *Roméo* (♦EMI 56123). The smaller roles are in fairly good hands, with van Dam repeating his Laurence and the others (presumably from the Toulouse Opera) idiomatic in diction and comfortable with the style. Keenlyside was a perverse choice for Mercutio, however: why a stiff British baritone when there must have been a French alternative? Gheorghiu is a womanly rather than a girlish Juliet, but she sings gorgeously, in warm, creamy, freely produced tones. Plasson once again opens the standard cuts, and in the Act 4 "Potion Aria" ("Amour ranime mon courage") Gheorghiu is heart-stoppingly beautiful. She's no more Juliet than Sutherland is Marguerite, but this is remarkable singing. Alagna, a far less polished vocalist, isn't on the same level; they're an odd couple, operatically. His diction is superior to Corelli's, Domingo's, and Kraus's, and at times (the duet "Ange adorable," for example), he strikes just the right note of youthful wonder. Too often, unfortunately, he emits strange little bleating sounds, and they remind us that for all his scruffy, photogenic appeal, he doesn't have much of a voice—or else his technique still has a long way to go. EMI's sound is superb.

Whichever studio recording you choose, it should be supplemented with an indispensable unauthorized issue: the 1947 Met performance led by **Emil Cooper,** starring Sayão and Björling (Myto). She's the most limpid and lyrical of Juliets, and his Romeo is not only the most consistently handsome in tone but also the most technically accomplished. They loft the musical lines into poetic flights with peerless ease and freedom.

Other operas. Philémon et Baucis and *Le Médicin malgré lui* have had one French recording apiece, *Sapho* two. The Gounod devotee may have some trouble finding them. The composer's third most popular opera, *Mireille,* has three available studio recordings, of which the most interesting are the EMIs. **Cluytens** had the engaging Janette Vivalda in the title role, the articulate Dens as Ourrias, and the young Gedda as Vincent. **Plasson** assembled another mostly French team, among them the reliable van Dam and Bacquier (♦EMI 49653). His Vincent was one of the most admired and cultivated French tenors of the past half century, Alain Vanzo, past his prime but still eloquent. Taking the part of her operatic namesake is Freni, doing very well indeed. I might criticize her linguistic expertise and her homey effusiveness, but the beauty of her timbre remains irresistible. Her willingness to record three Gounod roles makes her, at the very least, a creditable champion of a composer whose star has fallen in the past century and who needs loving attention from singers of Freni's stature.

SONGS

Gounod published about 200 songs, intended more for the salon or parlor than the concert stage. They're tasty confections but not all that nutritious, short on musical development and harmonic interest. They've had considerably less attention on records than those of Duparc and Hahn, not to mention Fauré and Ravel, and all-Gounod recital discs are rare. The classic one was **Souzay**'s from the '70s, and while his voice may have lost some of its spin, it could still waft the gentle fioritura of "Serenade" with gossamer lightness (EMI Pathé, NA). Canadian baritone **Bruno Laplante** is not quite in Souzay's class, but he's been a diligent proponent of French song and his Gounod disc is serviceable and pleasant (Analekta).

Listeners who want a female voice can turn to the tremulous **Isabelle Vernet**, worthwhile because she duplicates few of the items Laplante sings (Ligia). **Van Dam** has a more imposing voice than any of these others, but he performs, rather charmlessly, only a handful of Gounod songs in a mixed disc (EMI). The pickings are slim indeed, and Gounod's *mélodies* would almost be a lost cause were it not for Hyperion and the tireless **Graham Johnson**. A 2CD set divides the labors among three fine artists (Lott, Murray, Rolfe Johnson) who sing reasonably good French and also address the rarely heard Italian and English songs (♦Hyperion 66801).

Soprano **Annick Massis** and mezzo Brigitte Desnoues take us past the art songs to offer a collection of sacred music for voice, violin, piano, and organ entitled "Harmonies Célestes" (♦Ligia 0202011). Much of it is on the sugary side but lovely enough to invite repeated listening. Two of Gounod's most familiar pieces are here: the "Ave Maria" adapted from Bach, and "Repentir," known in English as "O Divine Redeemer." No trouble at all finding other recordings—everyone, it seems, has tackled "Ave Maria," and "O Divine Redeemer" has somehow gotten itself pegged as a Christmas song. You can find grandiose statements of the latter from Sutherland, Te Kanawa, Tebaldi, Norman, Studer, and Dame Clara Butt. I prolong discussing it only to recommend the stunningly beautiful rendition by Stuart Burrows in a disc of Christmas songs that includes Freni's "Ave Maria" (♦Belart 461240).   LUCANO

Percy Grainger (1882–1961)

Composer, pianist, linguist, inventor, musical ethnologist and antiquarian—even at this late date it's hard to pigeonhole Australian-born Percy Grainger. Yet for the better part of a century much of the world was content to classify him as an arranger of folk songs like *Country Gardens* and *Shepherd's Hey* and the composer of similar trifles. That, however, is beginning to change, especially on records, where his unique voice is at long last coming to the fore—at once cheerful and sad, exuberant and reflective, with an occasional touch of violence, something true of the man himself.

ORCHESTRAL MUSIC

The Warriors is Grainger's most ambitious orchestral piece, an 18-minute "imaginary ballet" premiered in 1917. It's indicative of the renewed interest in his work that, where for something like 50 years there were no recordings, at this writing there are three, two others having come and gone. All are recommendable. **Geoffrey Simon** exploits the sometimes orgiastic music's livelier and more colorful aspects (e.g., the *Pétrouchka*-like opening) without muting its wilder harmonies or near-Ivesian complexities (♦Koch 7003). Neither does **Gardiner**, despite his more classical approach, building to a climax of almost Waltonian firmness (♦DG 445860). His version, however, is available only as a discmate to Holst's *The Planets*, whereas Simon's leads off a similarly outstanding all-Grainger collection that includes *Hill Songs 1* and *2,* the well-loved *Irish Tune from County Derry* (better known in this country as "Danny

Boy"), and *Suite on Danish Folk Songs.* Similarly, **Hickox**'s more open-air rendition is preceded by the charming *Youthful Suite* and seven arrangements of the more popular pieces Grainger wrote around 1950 for a recording with Stokowski (♦Chandos 9584).

Hickox's recording is Vol. 6 in Chandos's "Grainger Edition," currently up to 15 volumes, nearly all of which can be recommended. Because of its systematic organization, however, no single disc provides an overview of the essential Grainger. Better for that purpose is Simon's CD (Koch), Gardiner's Philips collection (see "Vocal music" below), and a now-deleted **Rattle** disc, aptly titled "In a Nutshell" (♦EMI 56412, NA). Rattle gives us not only *The Warriors* but also the title suite, the Stokowski version of *Country Gardens,* a pair of Debussy and Ravel arrangements, and one of the best recordings ever of the band suite *Lincolnshire Posy.*

Vol. 1 in the "Grainger Edition" is also a Hickox-led orchestral disc, with a more restrained *In a Nutshell,* along with such delicacies as *Blithe Bells* (a celestial "ramble" on Bach's "Sheep May Safely Graze"), a far-off-sounding *Colonial Song,* a rarefied *Walking Tune* (in its wind-band scoring), and the sprightly passacaglia *Green Bushes* (♦9493). It also contains the energetic *English Dance,* something of a *Warriors* in miniature.

Despite primitive sound, it's **Stokowski** who serves up the most sinuously exotic and rhythmically exciting *In a Nutshell,* in a 1945 Hollywood Bowl performance with Grainger himself at the keyboard (♦Archive Documents 2003). Ditto their *Danish Folk Song Suite,* though here the acetates are in pretty bad shape. Still, I prefer this disc, with Grainger's incomparable Grieg Concerto, to his later attempt at it and the *Danish Folk Song Suite* with Per Dreier (Vanguard 8205). The best of the *Danish Folk Song Suites,* however, may be Hickox's in Vol. 11 of the Chandos series, a Scandinavian-themed disc that features, besides a variety of choral settings, an equally flavorful account of *To a Nordic Princess,* Grainger's wedding gift to his bride, Ella (also presented at the Hollywood Bowl) (♦9721).

Danish Folk Song Suite and *To a Nordic Princess* also figure in **Keith Brion**'s "The Power of Love," albeit in somewhat coarser, more nasal performances. Grainger often liked that, however, and there is much to be said for Brion's tangy *Colonial Song* and agreeably bouncy *Green Bushes* and *Country Gardens,* not to mention the bargain price (Naxos 554263). **Fennell,** by contrast, sometimes downplays the more adventurous harmonies (e.g., in *Children's March*) in his too closely miked but still beguiling collection of shorter pieces (Mercury 434330). **Kenneth Montgomery**'s "Famous Folk-Settings" is more laid back, a mid-priced anthology that goes beyond its title in its enjoyable mix of the familiar and the unfamiliar (Chandos 6542).

Children's March can also be heard in Brion's disc of Grainger's band music in its first and lengthiest version (Delos 3101). Again the performances are flavorful if not always as clean as they might be, but there are some interesting arrangements of Franck, Fauré, and Bach, as well as Sousa's of *Country Gardens* (not bad at all). However, an even more imaginative setting of *Children's March,* with voices, is in Chandos's Vol. 8, which includes such substantial wind pieces as *Hill Songs 1* and *2*—among Grainger's most evocative scorings—and *The Power of Rome and the Christian Heart,* with conducting honors divided between **Timothy Reynish** and **Clark Rundell** (♦9630).

Still, most people would agree with Grainger that his masterpiece for winds is *Lincolnshire Posy,* from 1937, which can be heard in Chandos's Vol. 4, another Reynish/Rundell assembly of band pieces (♦9549). Even finer, though, are **Fennell**'s two recordings. The first, from 1958, is still virile and has impact without shorting the innate charm of the English folk songs that provide the suite's basic material (♦Mercury 432754). While the second, from 20 years later, doesn't pack quite the same punch, it makes up for it in added refinement and more subtly woven textures (♦Telarc 80099). Nor should you overlook **James Westbrook,** who not only savors textures and sonorities a bit more but also includes seven additional Grainger wind settings (♦Phoenix 119)—or, if you can find it, Rattle's disc containing the military-band scoring, where everything registers.

In a less imposing vein, there are also a number of chamber collections—what Grainger called "room music"—all featuring the **Academy of St. Martin in the Fields Chamber Ensemble.** The earliest contrasts the quivering intensity of the song "Shallow Brown"—one of Grainger's most moving settings—with airier and more intimate renditions of *Molly on the Shore, Shepherd's Hey, The Immovable Do,* and *Handel in the Strand,* among others (♦Chandos 9346). Some of the same pieces can be heard in Chandos's Vols. 13 and 14, but in tangier and more vital performances and with a greater number of novelties, including the early *Theme and Variations* (♦9746) and, at an opposite pole, the forward-looking *Free Music* (♦9819). Vol. 13 also contains the more appealing of the two recordings of *Scandinavian Suite* for cello and piano.

PIANO MUSIC

In a way, Nimbus found themselves in the same spot as Chandos when it came to their survey of Grainger's piano music featuring **Martin Jones** (♦Nimbus 1767, 5CD). No single disc covers every aspect of Grainger's art, so they issued one that did, "Country Gardens and Other Piano Favorites," incorporating selections from all five, including some of the transcriptions and music for more than one player (e.g., the two-piano version of *Children's March*) (♦7703). It's a more than decent compromise, if you don't mind the ultra-spacious recorded sound. Still, I wouldn't want to be without some of the original compositions in Vol. 1, such as the good-humored *English Waltz* and precocious *Saxon Twi-play* (♦5220), or the multiple-piano settings of things like *The Warriors* and Delius's *Dance Rhapsody 1* in Vol. 5 (♦5286).

Jones can be an uneven player, sometimes a bit clumpy (e.g., *The Immovable Do*) but elsewhere smooth as silk. Tempos likewise go from too slow (*Rosenkavalier Ramble* and several of the arrangements in Vol. 2) to as fast as humanly possible. But the overall impression is more than favorable and, more important, at times no one comes closer to Grainger's own style (e.g., the rollicking *Molly on the Shore* and *In Dahomey,* which seem to burst from the keyboard).

That style can be heard on some otherwise dim-sounding 78 rpm transfers on Pearl and a number of other labels, revealing **Grainger** to have been in many ways the wildest of all interpreters of his music. Yet even at his most slapdash, you sense an innate understanding and control, most of which, remarkably enough, also comes through on his Duo-Art piano rolls, lovingly restored on yet another Nimbus CD. His Duo-Art *Rosenkavalier Ramble* may be less intoxicating than his "live" recording (see below), but there's no mistaking the pianist, and nobody plays *Jutish Medley* like Grainger himself (♦Nimbus 8809).

Among other solo CDs, none is more impressive from a technical standpoint than **Hamelin**'s (Hyperion 66884). Generally fleet, clean and virtuosic, he brings an astonishing elegance and imagination to some of these pieces. At the same time, though, he often misses their rustic, semi-improvisatory air. Thus his *Shepherd's Hey* is never really unbuttoned, nor does his *Scotch Strathspey and Reel* (on the chanty "What Shall We Do With a Drunken Sailor") compare with the looser, more

spontaneous-sounding Jones. The loosest, most freely imaginative *Scotch Strathspey* of all, however, is **Ronald Stevenson**'s, where it closes his "Salute to Scotland," a unique collection that includes Grainger's *Songs of the North*—minus voices—and Stevenson's own richly expansive solo transcription of *Hill Song 1* (♦Altarus 9040).

Like Hamelin, **Eugene List** seldom seems to unbend in this music, his performances ranging from the ultra-clarity of *Jutish Medley* to a cooler and interpretively more tentative *Country Gardens.* This CD, however, lets you hear Grainger himself romp through the latter, as well as *Rosenkavalier Ramble,* recorded live in 1957 (Vanguard SVC-99; her performances can also be heard in 8205). **Janine Snowden** falls somewhere in between, in a disc mostly made up of transcriptions that never quite match Grainger's fire but also avoid the dullness of the over-careful List (ASV 2117).

As with the orchestral and band music, much of Grainger's keyboard output consists of arrangements of his own and other people's compositions, often for more than one piano. Hence, *The Warriors* and pieces like *Lincolnshire Posy* and *Hill Song 1* are also available in versions for multiple pianists. Unfortunately the most invigorating of the *Lincolnshire Posy,* featuring **Jones** and **Richard McMahon,** is NA (♦AVM 3029). Worse, the same disc offered one of the two best *"Porgy and Bess" Fantasies,* the other being **Penelope Thwaites** and **John Lavender**'s (♦Pearl 9631), also NA. Short of these, Thwaites and Lavender serve up *Posy* crisply and cleanly, if without Jones and McMahon's verve, in another four-hand Grainger CD (Pearl 9611), followed by **Richard** and **John Contiguglia,** whose performance is strangely held back in places—something also true of their appended *Hill Song 1* and *Children's March* (Helicon 1004).

Thwaites and Lavender have likewise recorded the two-piano versions of *Hill Song 1* and *Children's March,* along with *The Warriors II,* which has little connection with the 1917 score (♦Pearl 9623). Their *Children's March* is more compactly recorded than Jones and McMahon's and even more exuberant. *Hill Song,* however, really needs the wind scoring or the version Simon offers for winds, harmonium, piano and strings.

Another Thwaites and Lavender disc, Vol. 10 in the "Grainger Edition," features them along with a number of other pianists in more multi-keyboard pieces, such as a sprightly but purposeful *Green Bushes* and disciplined *Zanzibar Boat Song* (♦Chandos 9702). I prefer Jones and McMahon's virile energy in the first, however, as well as their increased languor in the second. Likewise their joyous energy in *The Warriors*—which gains a bit of clarity in its two-piano version—though a case can be made for Thwaites & Co.'s more detailed climax. (And despite Chandos's misprinted timings, their recording is complete.)

VOCAL MUSIC

As with the orchestral music, Chandos claims primacy in the Grainger vocal catalog, having issued four CDs of the choral music (liberally sprinkled with orchestral pieces) and three of the songs. The essential single-disc Grainger choral anthology, however, comes from **Gardiner,** whose great-uncle Balfour Gardiner was the composer's fellow student at Frankfurt and lifelong friend (♦Philips 446657). This may be the most stimulating Grainger collection of any kind since **Britten**'s, once available on London.

Part of its success lies in Gardiner's refusal to sentimentalize even the familiar pieces, such as *Irish Tune From County Derry,* "I'm Seventeen Come Sunday," or "Brigg Fair." Witness the heart-rending instrumental tremolos in "Shallow Brown" or the undiluted spice of the *Merry Wed-*

ding, with its pungent wind writing, and *The Bride's Tragedy*, opulently scored but still rhythmically a bit off-center. I still prefer Britten's looser view of some of these pieces; at times Gardiner and his forces seem almost too precise and unyielding. Nevertheless this is the way to go at present, if only a single CD of the choral music is wanted.

If you want more, however, there are some attractive options. Vol. 3 in Chandos's "Grainger Edition," for example, offers a comparably flavorful "Seventeen Come Sunday" and "Brigg Fair" along with "Early One Morning," an extended and harmonically unsettled *County Derry Air,* and—a favorite of the composer's—*The Lonely Desert-Man Sees the Tents of the Happy Tribes* (♦9499). Vol. 5 adds to that more rarities (e.g., *The Widow's Party, The Sea Wife* and *Dreamery*) as well as maybe the most unconventional of all *Country Gardens* and Grainger's haunting wordless vocal duet recasting of *Colonial Song* (♦9554).

Vol. 9 is generally more somber and introspective, including a number of first recordings (an early student *Scherzo* and *Random Round* for voices and guitars, sporting some uniquely Graingerian harmonies) and a *Danny Deever* that manages to be even more harrowing than Gardiner's. Finally, Vol. 11 is the above-mentioned Scandinavian collection, recorded in Denmark and, like the others, comprehensibly directed by Hickox (♦Chandos 9721).

By contrast Polyphony, under **Stephen Layton,** presents a more rarefied view of some of these pieces than Hickox (e.g., their "Dollar and a Half a Day," intimate to the point of withdrawal). In their "At Twilight" they include some rarities of their own, such as Grainger's translations of Grieg's *Four Psalms* (Hyperion 66793), and their follow-up disc has the advantage of grouping Grainger's settings of Kipling's *Jungle Book* together for the first time, including the Holstian *Hunting-Song of the Seonee Pack* (♦Hyperion 66863).

Some of the same material, but with piano accompaniment, can be heard in Chandos's three song collections, beginning with baritone **Varcoe,** whose "Lost Lady Found" proves almost as effective as the choral version. In "Shallow Brown," unfortunately, the advantage works the other way, but throughout I'm impressed by his sensitivity and style, whether in four *Songs of the North* or in settings of Kipling, Longfellow, even Arthur Conan Doyle (♦Chandos 9503).

That same sensitivity to the Grainger idiom is present in mezzo **Della Jones**'s volume, and not just because Varcoe partners her in several selections. Witness her "Sprig of Thyme," "Proud Vesselil," and "Variations on Handel's 'The Harmonious Blacksmith,'" a reflective vocalization on what would become the lively *Handel in the Strand* (♦Chandos 9730). To a lesser extent the same may be said of tenor **Martyn Hill,** though the voice itself becomes wearing after a while (Chandos 9610). Which, despite Grainger's multiple scorings of the same material, is seldom the case with the music. GOODFELLOW

Enrique Granados (1867–1916)

Granados, best known for his piano music and songs, wrote his most famous music in the 20th century. Like Brahms, he looked resolutely backwards, drawing inspiration from 18th century Spanish song and the paintings of Goya. His music is at once colorful and conservative, filled with wistful melody and bracing rhythms. His output is small, but he is the among the most approachable of Spanish composers, his untimely death all the more tragic because he was so slow to bloom.

PIANO MUSIC

After the ubiquitous *Spanish Dance No. 5,* Granados' best-known piano work is the suite *Goyescas,* his homage to painter Francisco Goya.

Recordings of *Goyescas* are legion, but vanish from the catalogue as they yield to **Alica de Larrocha**'s many accounts, particularly her 1977 performance (♦London). In color, imagination, pacing, and technical mastery, she has not been matched. Her countryman, **Eduardo del Pueyo,** is less overt (Philips 442751), and **Eric Parkin** is better for a streamlined alternative (♦Chandos 9412). The exciting **Ciccolini** lacks subtlety (EMI), and **Martin Jones** is surprisingly stiff (Nimbus). In concert **Michel Block** is expressive and spontaneous and a fine supplement to de Larrocha (♦ProPiano 224518), and **Nicholas Zumbro** plays with clarity and searing intensity (♦Fidelio 9004). Some will prefer Zumbro's organization to de Larrocha's intoxicating playing. **Douglas Riva**'s performance fails to take off (Naxos). **Jean-Marc Luisada** is well-suited to the quixotic *Goyescas* in a deleted disc (DG). **Hisako Hiseki**'s account is the closest contemporary challenge to de Larrocha; indeed, his colorful pianism has been praised by de Larrocha herself (♦LMG 2031).

Marylene Dosse is elegant and vivacious in the complete piano music (♦Vox 5075/76, 2CD). The fourth movement from *Goyescas,* "Laments, or The Maiden and the Nightingale," is a favorite excerpt among pianists. Equally special recordings come from **Hess** (once on EMI), **Rubinstein** (♦RCA 61261), and **Wild** (♦Ivory Classics 70805). Despite a constricted recorded venue, **Thomas Rajna**'s pianism was notable for its tonal beauty, even if a greater interpretive profile was needed (CRD).

In the smaller works, **de Larrocha** is again desirable. The sound of the early Hispavox recordings (frequently found on EMI) is disappointing, so look for *Spanish Dances* on ♦RCA 68184. **Emilio Brugalla** is a scintillating rival to de Larrocha in *Dances* (♦LAMA 2023), and **del Pueyo** plays idiomatically (♦Philips 442751). **Rosa Torres-Pardo** has a certain flair, if little subtlety (Naxos). **Block** is positively sultry in seven of the *Dances* and three of the *Escenas Poéticas* (IMP 6700042).

LOVELACE

OPERA

Granados wrote seven works for the stage: four zarzuelas, 2 "poems," and the opera *Goyescas.* The opera is brief, and its music is in large part an elaboration of previously composed piano pieces. When it was first performed at the Metropolitan in New York, the producers asked for an additional, purely orchestral number. The composer obliged with the *Intermezzo* that has taken on a life of its own in the concert hall. *Goyescas* is Spanish verismo, and at its premiere, it was appropriately paired with *Pagliacci.* Granados came to New York for the occasion, and he met his tragic death on his return to Spain, when his ship was torpedoed by a German submarine in the English Channel.

The ancient Decca recording with **Consuelo Rubio** as Rosario is long gone, but there's no need to lament its demise. **Ros-Marbá** leads a scintillating modern performance; the leads are Maria Bayo, whose fresh voice floats and soars, and the elegant tenor Ramón Vargas (♦Auvidis 4791). I suspect the original Met performance (with Martinelli and de Luca in the cast) was a more high-powered affair, but these Spanish artists have a flair of their own and sing with spirit and involvement. The recording is more than satisfactory; there's no need to regret that it's the only one around.

SONGS

Granados published only 32 songs, and of these, the twelve *Tonadillas* and seven *Canciones Amatorias* are the best known and most often performed. The *Tonadillas escritas en estilo antiguo* (their full title) are nostalgic evocations of the world Goya captured in his paintings—*"ensueños de un tiempo pasado,"* perhaps, to borrow the haunting refrain of the third of the "Maja Dolorosa" songs. They're readily approachable, and once heard, they stay in the mind forever.

Soprano **Maria Lluisa Muntada** recorded all 32 songs for the Spanish LMG label in 1998, and because no one else has essayed a complete set, her enterprise is praiseworthy. Her singing, unfortunately, is not all that alluring, tending toward the shrill and unpolished. You'll do well to seek better recordings of fewer songs, starting with those of the perfect Granados interpreter, **de los Angeles.** She could put a smile in her voice or fill it with languorous warmth. The bottom register is always solid, the top steady and shining, the words lovingly shaped. For years, her Granados recordings were scattered about in various EMI LPs, but the company finally brought them together in one place as part of a four-disc set entitled "Songs of Spain" (♦EMI 66937). They deserve issue on their own, but at least they're available, and among them are some previously unpublished accounts of *Canciones Amatorias* recorded in concert. Also included is one of the soprano's favorite encore pieces, "Adios, Granada," where she accompanies herself on guitar.

The handful of songs recorded by **Berganza** are in a 2CD DG anthology, but some later recordings are on Claves. Berganza is softer than de los Angeles and more artless, less inclined to turn each song into a finely cut jewel and less striking because of it. **Caballé**'s all-Granados disc includes *Canciones Amatorias* and ten *Tonadillas,* sung to (unattributed) orchestral accompaniments, plus four additional songs with piano (♦RCA 62539). The orchestra takes some of the spice out of the music, and Caballé's singing is a bit bumpy. Her low notes are weaker than de los Angeles's or Berganza's, and her hallmark glottal attacks disrupt the smooth line, but her voice at its best is stunningly beautiful.

Even so, I prefer the Granados of **Lorengar,** who recorded all the *Tonadillas* and six of the *Canciones Amatorias* with de Larrocha at the piano (♦London 433917). Her top notes are the most ravishing of all, and I'm not disturbed by the prominent vibrato, which lends flavor and individuality to her singing. Like Caballé, she's weak at the bottom, but as the voice rises, the notes shine like ripples in a sunlit stream. **Supervia**'s vibrato is even more pronounced, and so rapid it seems to give the voice a serrated edge. Her 1932 recordings of seven *Tonadillas* are nonetheless irresistible (♦VAIA 1001). She's earthy, heartfelt, and deeply communicative, and no one except de los Angeles makes the words so zesty.

For whatever reason, British singers dominate the list of non-Spanish performers who have left us substantial Granados samplings in mixed recitals. **Jill Gomez** (Saga) and **Della Jones** (Chandos) are enjoyable and deeply immersed in the music. A spirited disc from the Songmakers' Almanac entitled "¡España!" offers eight *Tonadillas;* **Ann Murray** appropriates the most familiar but leaves "El majo olvidado" to a baritone (Richard Jackson), as Granados intended (Hyperion). **Margaret Price** sings seven *Tonadillas* (including the "Maja Dolorosa" trio) gorgeously (♦Orfeo 38831). That's about all there is, and it's really enough. You primarily need the de los Angeles recordings, then a couple of others to add scope and variety.　　　　　　　　　　　　　　LUCANO

Edvard Grieg *(1843–1907)*

Grieg is, without question, the greatest Norwegian composer. Many of his works, for instance the Piano Concerto and *Holberg Suite,* have established themselves in the core repertoire of orchestras and soloists around the world. Others, like *Peer Gynt Suite 1,* are imprinted indelibly on the popular consciousness. He was happiest working in smaller forms, and it's no accident that, the Piano Concerto aside, his most enduringly popular works are miniatures or groups of miniatures where

his gift for lyricism can be heard to best advantage. His orchestral works consist mainly of suites and short tone poems, though there is an early symphony; in his chamber output there are three sonatas for violin and one for cello, all with piano, as well as two string quartets (though the second was never completed).

Grieg was a tireless advocate of a Norwegian and more generally, Scandinavian identity in music, rather than the predominantly German esthetic prevailing in Nordic music in his time. However, he resorted to quotations of folk melodies only rarely. He was adept enough as a pianist to premiere his Concerto, and often accompanied his singer wife, Nina. For most of his life he lived in Bergen on the west coast, rather than in the capital, and when he died all of Norway grieved.

ORCHESTRAL MUSIC

Neeme Järvi's highly regarded complete recording of all of Grieg's orchestral music, issued in 1993 as a 6CD set (DG), is no longer available outside Germany, although some individual compilations have appeared from time to time. The recording quality was high and the performances also, in the main. For almost all the works there are versions of equal if not greater merit more readily available

Elegiac Melodies. Comprising *The Wounded Heart* and *The Last Spring,* these two works for string orchestra are among Grieg's most popular orchestral miniatures. **Abravanel** is very sympathetic, though in cramped sound, but as part of a bargain package of Grieg's orchestral music, this is an unbeatable value (Vox 5048, 2CD). There are fine accounts with various couplings of other Grieg works from the conductorless **Orpheus Chamber Orchestra** (♦DG 23060), **Mata** (ASV), and **Tadeusz Wojciechowski** (Conifer, 2CD). The best of the budget versions comes from **Leaper** (Naxos 550330) and the best recorded from **Handley** (Chandos 8524). Of mixed-composer programs, **Barbirolli**'s 1957 performance has been beautifully restored (Dutton 1013), while **Wojciech Rajski** combines delicacy of feeling and a virtuosic quietude (♦BIS 461).

Holberg Suite (properly "In Holberg's Times," sometimes translated as "Of Holberg's Days"). Holberg was an early 18th-century Danish playwright known as the "Molière of the North." Originally composed for piano, the string orchestra incarnation of the Suite has become a staple of the concert and recorded repertoire with over two dozen versions available, generally coupled with other Grieg works. Both of **Karajan**'s are excellent, though the earlier one (♦DG 19474) sounds more fresh and alive than that made in 1981 (DG 39010). The **Orpheus Chamber Orchestra** plays with compelling attack (DG), as do the Seattle strings for **Gerard Schwarz** (Delos) and the Norwegian Chamber Orchestra for **Terje Tennesen,** though the latter are perhaps too few in number (BIS). **Abravanel**'s is one of the best performances in his bargain set (Vox 5048, 2CD), and there are exceptionally alive readings from **Boughton** (Nimbus), **Duczmal** (ASV) and, rather more quirky with the same Swiss Chamber Orchestra as Duczmal, **Mata** (ASV). **Marriner** is less impressive and (as one critic said) even histrionic in places (Philips).

Lyric Suite. Orchestrations of four numbers of the fifth set of *Lyric Pieces,* these usually make a delicate coupling for *Holberg Suite.* **Järvi**'s is beautifully played and recorded (DG 27807), though more idiomatic though no more affecting than **Handley** (Chandos 7040). **Schwarz** conducts with evident sympathy (Delos), though **Barbirolli** has the edge on all of these (♦Dutton 1012). **Abravanel** also has the measure of the music (Vox), as does **Thomas Dausgaard** (Rondo Grammophon).

Norwegian Dances. Originally written for piano, these dances—more popular than but not the equal of the later *Symphonic Dances*—are best known in their orchestral guise. Most recordings couple the two sets, as for instance **Abravanel,** who clearly relished their gaiety; sound is less of a problem here than in other items in his set (Vox). His account, slightly saccharine, is generally to be preferred for its sense of color to **Petri Sakari**'s, though the Iceland Symphony plays very well for the latter (Chandos). Neither can really compete with **Barbirolli,** recorded at the height of his powers (♦Dutton 1012), or **Ormandy** (♦Sony 53257); **Järvi** is typically sparkling (DG). Next to them, **Suitner** (Berlin) and **Edlinger** (Naxos) sound ordinary. Contrary to *Schwann,* **Bernstein** is represented by the second set only (Sony).

Norwegian Melodies. There is little to separate **Leaper** (Naxos) and **Dausgaard** (Rondo Grammophon) in these two sparkling arrangements of earlier piano pieces. *Schwann* is incorrect in listing a version by **Barbirolli;** it's actually the *Norwegian Dances* mentioned above).

Old Norwegian Romance. An alternative version of this set of variations exists for two pianos. Two fine orchestral recordings exist: **Beecham**'s, though older and also cut, is the more enjoyable (♦EMI 66966), though **Sakari**'s is well shaped (Chandos 9071).

Peer Gynt (incidental music). There are only two recordings of the complete incidental music Grieg wrote in 1874 to Ibsen's play. The 1978 set conducted by **Per Dreier** has much to commend it (Unicorn 2003/4, 2CD), but **Järvi**'s, with an outstanding cast including Barbara Bonney, is better played and an outstanding value (♦DG 23079, 2CD; a one-disc selection is also available, 27325).

Of the discs containing selections, three exist providing 12 of the 23 numbers. The finest is by **Marriner,** with the incomparable Popp, using a German translation (♦EMI 47003), closely followed by **de Waart** with Ameling (Philips 11038). **Beecham,** also using a German text, presents only 10 numbers but includes the Piano Concerto (EMI), as does **Fjeldstad** (London 448599). **Salonen,** by contrast, presents 17 numbers with Hendricks (Sony 44528). A most bizarre effort comes from the **Netherlands Guitar Trio,** with eight numbers (and the *Holberg Suite* and *Elegiac Melodies*) in guitar arrangements (Etcetera 1039).

Peer Gynt Suites 1 and 2. 1 in particular is very popular and there are around 30 recordings available. Most are accompanied by 2, which never duplicated 1's success. For many, **Karajan**'s '80s recording is the classic account, and it remains unsurpassed (♦DG 39010). **Bernstein**'s is another classic, though he seems less engaged in some of the more restrained numbers (Sony 63156). **Fiedler** was a master of this kind of repertoire, though his 1957 recording sounds its age, as does **Ormandy**'s on the same label (RCA). Although not as well played as Karajan's, **Handley**'s versions are sensitive and exciting by turns, in first-rate sound (♦Chandos 7040; 1 reissued on 8524). **Felix Slatkin** is also vibrant (Telarc 80048, with Bizet's *Carmen* Suites). In the budget section, **Maksymiuk** turns in nicely phrased though not very exciting performances (Naxos 550864). **Abravanel**'s are more than adequate, if not the best (Vox).

Sigurd Jorsalfar (incidental music). **Järvi**'s account of the complete 1872 score (♦DG 23079, 2CD, with *Peer Gynt*) is superior in sound to **Per Dreier**'s pioneering account (Unicorn). **Barbirolli** (Dutton) and **Suitner** (Berlin) present only excerpts.

Sigurd Jorsalfar (symphonic suite). Extracted from the incidental music in 1892, this has become one of Grieg's more popular orchestral works, especially the concluding "Homage March," often performed separately, for instance by **Fennell** (Mercury) and **Ormandy** (Sony). **Karajan** had an affinity for Grieg, and his account has been brilliantly

remastered (♦DG 19474). Next to this, **Abravanel**'s well-played 1975 recording suffers for its dated sound (Vox). Of the modern recordings, **Järvi** is typically exciting (DG 27807), but **Rozhdestvensky** catches the variations in mood more acutely (♦Chandos 9113). The accounts from **Handley** (Chandos) and **Maksymiuk** (Naxos) are less virtuosic but still worthy, part of more popular programs.

Symphonic Dances. Grieg's orchestral masterpiece, there are many excellent recordings of these sparkling (though not very symphonic) dances. **Abravanel**'s nicely paced and phrased 1975 performance is not in the same sonic league as its competitors (Vox). However, he's more convincing than **Edlinger** (Naxos) or **Wojciechowski** (Conifer). Sound quality is not a great problem for **Beecham**'s 1959 outing (EMI 66966) or **Barbirolli**'s (Dutton 1012), both brilliantly restored. However, few releases can rival the warmth of sound provided for **Handley** in a wonderfully sympathetic reading with the Ulster Orchestra (♦Chandos 8524) or the electric **Rozhdestvensky** with the more virtuosic Royal Stockholm Philharmonic (♦Chandos 9113). Both of these are to be preferred, albeit marginally, to **Marriner** (Hänssler 98128). **Sakari** has also recorded this, though it's unaccountably confused in *Schwann* with Glière's Symphony 2 (Chandos 9071).

Symphony in C. Grieg's only completed symphony has been recorded by **Järvi** (DG) and **Kitaienko** (Virgin), both now NA. However, **Kamu**'s performance is splendid (BIS 200; reissued with the original version of the Piano Concerto, ♦BIS 200619).

CONCERTOS

Piano Concerto. There is no room to cover adequately the legion of recordings this most popular of concertos has received. At any one time there are probably 60 or 70 different versions in circulation, not counting multiple issues of the same performance with different couplings, like those of **Dubravka Tomsic** (Unison-Navarre) or the fine **Jandó** (Naxos). They range in date from the late 1920s (**Ignaz Friedman,** Enterprise Piano Library 271) and early 1930s (**Gieseking,** APR 5513) to the present day. Many pianists have tackled it more than once. Champion in this respect is **Rubinstein,** with no fewer than six highly regarded accounts in circulation, available in various issues: five are for RCA (1942 with Ormandy; 1949 with Brahms 2 under Doráti; 1956 with Tchaikovsky 1, 63037; 1958 under Krips and two with Wallenstein; and 1961 either with Tchaikovsky 1, 62162, or Rachmaninoff 2, 63060)—plus a video under Previn (Decca).

Lipatti's account was hailed by one critic as "a collector's piece for the sense of wonder complementing transcendental virtuosity," it's available on three different labels (APR, Dante, and Philips). There are also many fine accounts no longer in circulation, like those from **Fleisher** and **Freire** (both Sony), **Katchen** (Decca), and **Ogdon** (EMI). Both currently available recordings by **Michelangeli,** not the most natural interpreter of this work, date from about the same time during WW II (Enterprise 53003; Magic Talent 48058).

One of the most celebrated recordings was made by **Kovacevich** in 1971; its most recent reissue was acclaimed by a reviewer for its "wholly natural, intimately poetic phrasing" and "delicately glistening fingerwork." Coupled classically with the Schumann Concerto, which Grieg used as a partial model, this release also includes Grieg's Sonata and offers exceptional value (♦Philips 446192). Fine as that subtle recording still sounds, more recent ones are more incisive, for instance **Perahia** (who shares Kovacevich's conductor, Colin Davis); he brings a Mozartian poise not usually heard in this work, however much he relishes the Romantic idiom (Sony 44899). **Lars Vogt** (with Rattle) is more brittle and less in tune with accepted notions of the work's poetry, making his reading slightly eccentric but fascinating (EMI 54746). Of the other versions coupled with the Schumann concerto, those by **Zimerman** (DG 39015), **Entremont** (Sony 46543), and—at budget price—**Jandó** (Naxos 550118) possess the vital blend of poetry and vigor the work demands.

There are many recordings with different couplings, though few are more satisfying than **Lupu**'s wonderful account with the London Symphony under Previn in Philips's "Great Pianists" series (456895). One novel coupling, with Kuhlau's Concerto, is by **Amalie Malling,** in very sensitive performances captured in rich sound and highly recommendable (◆Chandos 9699). **Pöntinen** pairs his reading with Tchaikovsky's 1 (BIS). **Fingerhut** doesn't show quite the same affinity for the work in a beautifully prepared performance (Chandos). **Richter** is valuable in an exciting if unsubtle 1977 live performance under Kondrashin that's no match in terms of sound with the best rivals (Praga, with Dvořák). **Cliburn**'s reading was dismissed by one critic as "rhythmically clumsy" and "a very superficial response" (RCA); **Wild**'s, coupling Liszt and Saint-Saëns, was regarded by the same reviewer as "notably workaday."

Of the all-Grieg issues one of the most polished is **Curzon**'s justly acclaimed 1959 version (London 448599). **Lowe Derwinger**'s original version is of special interest (Grieg, unable to write a second concerto, made seven versions of the A minor); it has many differences in scoring from the familiar one (BIS 619, reissued as ◆200619).

CHAMBER MUSIC

Grieg tended to write his non-vocal music either for orchestras of varying size or solo piano (though there are several piano duet works or arrangements). Formal chamber music as such, with its standard genres like the sonata or string quartet, was of less appeal. Nevertheless, he felt the need to rise to the challenge at various stages of his career, producing some of his most satisfying larger-scale designs in the process.

Andante con moto **for piano trio.** The sole recording is by members of the **Raphael Quartet** and pianist Jet Röling, in a disc with Grieg's complete output for string quartet (Olympia 432).

Fugue in F minor **for string quartet.** The **Kontra Quartet** benefits from superior sound (BIS 543), but the **Raphael Quartet** seems more engaged by the music (◆Olympia 432; not a piano trio arrangement as listed in *Schwann*). The Kontra couples this with Grieg's unfinished two-movement Quartet 2, whereas the Raphael uses Julius Röntgen's completion, plus *Andante con moto*.

Intermezzo in A minor **for cello and piano. Julian Lloyd Webber** and **Bengt Forsberg** give a very fine account of this marvelous little piece (◆Philips 454458, with the Cello Sonata and Delius works for cello). **Øivin Birkeland** and **Havard Gimse** are almost as entrancing (Naxos 550878).

Sonata for cello and piano. Over a dozen versions of this wonderfully lyrical and romantic work exist. **Lloyd Webber** and **Forsberg** are very persuasive, as in the *Intermezzo* (Philips), but are surpassed by **Isserlis** and **Hough** who take a lighter, less grand manner with the music, to its benefit (◆RCA 68290). Their couplings (Liszt and Rubinstein) may not appeal to all; indeed, couplings for this lone sonata may be a prime consideration, whether Rachmaninoff (**Mikael Ericsson** and **František Malý,** Bonton), Chopin (**Claude Starck** and **Riccardo Requejo,** Claves 703) or, more oddly, Franck's Violin Sonata (**Robert Cohen** and **Roger Vignoles,** CRD) or Martinů (**Hayashi Duo,** Fone). The most satisfying couplings of all are the *Intermezzo* with Grieg's solitary Piano Sonata

from **Birkeland** and **Gimse,** who turn in a performance of precision and intensity (Naxos).

Sonatas for violin and piano. The three sonatas as a group, of which there are well over a dozen available versions, often bring out the best in their performers. The most eloquent of all—mixing youthful elegance and passion in 1 and 2, while matching Grieg's conceptual breadth in 3—comes from **Augustin Dumay** and **Pires,** magnificently recorded (◆DG 37525). **Dong-Suk Kang** and **Pöntinen** take a slightly more fiery line but lose some of the charm of Grieg's lyricism (BIS 647), also a feature of the otherwise sensitive accounts by **Sitkovetsky** and **Davidovich** (Orfeo) and **Lydia** and **Elena Mordkovitch** (Chandos). At budget price, the most exciting account is by the young Norwegian duo **Henning Kraggerud** and **Helge Kjekshus,** whose performance of 3 outshines all its rivals even though the recorded sound does not (Naxos 553904).

There is a fine rendition from **Shumsky** with **Seymour Lipkin** (Biddulph 008). **David Oistrakh**'s 1957 recording of 1 with **Oborin** is hampered by less than satisfactory sound (Russian Revelation), unlike that of 2 in 1972 (Praga 250048). **Heifetz**'s 1936 and 1955 recordings of 2 are available separately in two 2CD sets (both RCA). The most fascinating historical account of 3 is by **Kreisler** and **Rachmaninoff** (1928), though it's only available in 10- or 11CD anthologies (RCA).

String Quartets. 1 is a curious mix of expressive moods that requires no mean effort to mold into a coherent whole. In the finest performances it has a winning charm, as with the **Shanghai Quartet,** hailed as "arguably the most compelling performance of this endearing score since the original Budapest Quartet's trailblazing HMV 78s from 1937" (Delos 3153). The **Petersen Quartet** combines it with the two movements that are all Grieg completed of 2 in wonderfully controlled and recorded accounts (◆Capriccio 10476, 1 reissued on 14862). Neither the **Kontra Quartet** (BIS) nor the **Wilanow Quartet** (Accord) suggest the same degree of understanding of Grieg's often disparate structures.

Various completions have been made of 2. The most satisfying is by Grieg's Dutch friend, Julius Röntgen, used by the **Raphael Quartet,** although half of the finale is entirely Röntgen's invention (◆Olympia 432, not in a piano trio arrangement as *Schwann* lists it). Levon Chilingirian's completion is played by the **Chilingirian Quartet** (Hyperion 67117).

RICKARDS

PIANO MUSIC

Eva Knardahl, Einar Steen-Nøkleberg, Gerhard Oppitz, and Geir Henning Braaten have surveyed all of Grieg's piano music for BIS, Naxos, RCA, and Victoria, respectively. The Knardahl and Steen-Nøkleberg series also include arrangements of music not originally written for the keyboard, as well as folk songs arranged for the piano.

It's a particular pleasure to listen to **Steen-Nøkleberg,** who is a master pianist and in just about every bar gives you the sense of an interpretive human being behind the fingers. His 14CD edition is the most inclusive and a delight from beginning to end; I can't think of a single track where he doesn't sound as if he's completely at one with the music and enjoying his assignment. If there's any fault, it's his occasional tendency to make melodies stand out too strongly from their backgrounds, so that some notes poke out of the texture (as in the well-known *Nocturne* Op. 54:4). More rarely, he indulges in rhythmic mannerisms and tends to err on the side of over-pedaling. But I emphasize that the Naxos cycle contains some of the most spontaneous and idiomatic Grieg performances in the catalog, at less than half the price of Knardahl's, and with excellent sonics. The Naxos and BIS sets stand out for the ringing transparency of the piano's overtones, with the former having greater transparency and the latter more body.

No one knowing the *Lyric Pieces* and wanting to take on some new territory should miss Steen-Nøkleberg's Vol. 4, where the pianist is so joyful and sensitive in the *Holberg Suite* that he makes you forget the orchestral version (♦Naxos 550884). Vol. 3 is also a must for the lovely *Poetic Tone Pictures* (♦Naxos 550883). Not everyone will warm to the 152 *Norwegian Melodies* settings, but the super-budget price makes it easy to explore these lesser corners of Grieg's piano output (♦Naxos 553391/93). And Steen-Nøkleberg is always interesting, even in these small and simple nationalist settings, none of them much longer than a minute, and it helps that he alternates between piano, clavichord, organ, and harmonium in *Norwegian Melodies*.

In the name of utter completeness, Steen-Nøkleberg includes several sets of incidental music, some with chorus and actors (speaking in rhymed English translations for their minimal interjections, though with colorful Norwegian accents). Music from *Peer Gynt* appears in different forms and sequences on three of his discs; the familiar two suites are complete with chorus and some dramatic acting-out (Naxos 553397), but with Järvi's complete incidental music available with orchestra (DG), it's hard to see why anyone would take to the piano versions.

Grieg's negligible musical contribution to the 19-minute *Bergliot* setting (not to be confused with his song cycle on the same subject) consists for the most part of recitative-like punctuations and chord tremolos in silent-movie style. But it's hard to imagine more beautiful performances, and the dramatic interjections—though not of Stratford-on-Avon skill or subtlety—will leave you with an enhanced sense of the dramatic import of each of these famous pieces. More scrapings from the bottom of the barrel are in Vol. 14, which includes a set of children's pieces, some song transcriptions, an organ fugue, and early versions of two movements from the Op. 7 Sonata (Naxos 553400).

Knardahl doesn't cover quite as much material in her 10CD series, and she uses no actors in the incidental music. (Her sixth disc, BIS 109, conveniently pairs the two *Peer Gynt* suites with *Sigurd Jorsalfar*.) Most of Grieg's Norwegian arrangements are found in Vol. 8 (BIS 111), while Vol. 10 includes the Piano Concerto alongside the Op. 35 *Norwegian Dances* and *Romances* Op. 53. Knardahl's cycle is in each instance almost as recommendable as Steen-Nøkleberg's, though the sonics are less consistent and Steen-Nøkleberg has more poise. Those wanting to sample Knardahl might try her 78-minute "Grieg Collection" sampler (BIS 51). The series continued with two discs from pianist **Love Derwinger**, Vol. 11 offering 23 shorter works plus the original 1868 version of the Piano Concerto, and Vol. 12 various unpublished pieces without opus number. Comparing this last disc with Steen-Nøkleberg, I find Derwinger rather overblown and uninteresting in interpretation and his acoustic too resonant.

Oppitz's cycle is more pared down, the *Lyric Pieces* housed in a 3CD box and the remaining works in a separate 4CD package. RCA's recording is probably the finest of any of the sets and individual discs listed here—only Naxos runs it close—but Oppitz's Bösendorfer has a brittle sound that doesn't allow for much tonal shading, and his dances and other fast pieces tend to sound graceless. He's a fine musician, but on this and other evidence, not always imaginative and sensitive.

Without a doubt, the central piano works in Grieg's portfolio are the 66 *Lyric Pieces*, written between 1864 and 1901, and organized into ten books. **Steen-Nøkleberg** excels here as elsewhere (Opp. 12, 38, 43, 47, ♦Naxos 553394; Opp. 54, 57, 62, ♦Naxos 5533945; Opp. 65, 68, 71,

♦5533946). These are among the finest performances, regardless of price. I haven't been able to track down all of **Henning Braaten**'s discs, but on the evidence of his Vol. 6, he's a pianist of real musicality and technical accomplishment, if without Steen-Nøkleberg's glimmer of showmanship (Victoria 19030, with the Op. 54 *Lyric Pieces,* the second *Peer Gynt* suite, presented here with neither chorus nor narration, and the three *Sigurd Jorsalfar* pieces).

Gieseking recorded one of the first *Lyric Pieces* surveys shortly before his death in 1956 (31 pieces: ♦EMI 66775, 2CD, with some humming audible from the pianist). With compact, fairly close, and warm mono sound that needs no excuses, this is a necessary accompaniment to any other account you might have. It could well be a first choice for those who resist the virtuosic, concert-hall renditions of steel-fingered, modern pianists like Gavrilov. Sounding like a supremely gifted peasant of the piano (those who don't listen closely might find him a bit square), Gieseking never strains for effect, never plays to the gallery, displays no conservatory gloss. This is domestic rather than concert-hall musicmaking, always shaped subtly and beautifully. There is a noble simplicity here, abetted by the Arrau-like depth of Gieseking's sound—he lets you forget that the piano does its work with hammers. So often, as in the famous "March of the Dwarfs" (taken quite slowly), he makes me feel that more outwardly exciting interpretations miss the point. His couplings are just as wonderful: 17 equally personable and distinguished Mendelssohn *Songs without Words*, recorded during the same period. Six 1948-vintage recordings of Grieg duplicating those on the first disc of the set fill out a distinguished package, one of the very best testimonies to this great pianist's art.

Knardahl's tone is robust and her conceptions honest and straightforward (♦BIS 104/6, 3CD). Her folklike approach is similar to Gieseking's, but she's not always as careful to avoid unsupported tone in climaxes (e.g., the Norwegian "Stumping Dance" from Op. 17), and you won't quite hear Gieseking's engrossing, multi-layered musicality—the kind of artistry that hides artistry. There are moments where Knardahl is more immediately felicitous and smile-inducing than anyone, as in her completely idiomatic account of the momentary pauses in "Homesickness" from the Op. 57 *Pieces*. But if forced to make a decision, I would generally prefer Steen-Nøkleberg and Gieseking.

Peter Katin lands somewhere between Knardahl's simplicity and Gieseking's introverted dignity, but he doesn't offer quite the musical detail of either, and his louder dynamics are ill-contained by a clattery and uncontrolled acoustic (Unicorn, 3CD). Also, beware the gradual CD corrosion that has made my copy of his Vol. 3 all but unplayable. By contrast, **Daniel Adni** offers the suavest of the surveys (nine works, most of them from Books I and II, were dropped to fit his 1973 edition of all the rest onto a "twofer," ♦EMI 68634). Adni makes some of the music sound as poetic and evocative as Satie and other numbers as nostalgic as Rachmaninoff, and EMI gave him a particularly rounded piano tone. He sparkles wonderfully in "Butterfly" (Book III), where he opens up all the giddy tensions of the piece. Steen-Nøkleberg tries for even more detail here, perhaps *too* much, with minute changes in tempo that I haven't heard elsewhere, but it's this same attention to detail and sense of fun that make him a real delight in the middle section of "Shepherd Boy" (Op. 54:1). And Adni stiffens up when he comes to the beautiful "At the Cradle."

Moving to single-disc recitals, **Gilels**'s account of 20 *Pieces* has won glowing praise over the years (DG). Listening to DG's new 20-bit "Originals" mastering, I find him detached and often depressing for all his great interpretive skills and pianistic address. His dynamic shadings are unique in "Lonely Wanderer," but his tone wants for variety, and many of the slower pieces take on a catatonic, *Parsifal*-like solemnity. (Surely the melancholy, almost abstract introversion heard in the outer sections of his "Homesickness" is more appropriate to Abbé Liszt than to Grieg.) He tries for poised musicality rather than charm in the Op. 47 "Album-blatt," and the Op. 65 "Ballade" is drawn out to a treacly four minutes.

Gavrilov takes on 24 of the *Pieces* and does something very different with them (DG). His judgment is more fallible in terms of tempo (especially slow tempos: "Shepherd Boy" reaches an incredible 5 1/2 minutes). He also treats some of the faster works like etudes, creating effortless clarity with brilliant if extremely well-supported tone. Not everything works, but I hear more personality and variety in Gavrilov's playing than in Gilels's. It's clear that he loves this music, and I prefer his single-disc selection to just about any other available (though I'm compelled to note that you can pick up two of the Steen-Nøkleberg discs for just about the cost of any one of these others).

Rubinstein's 1953 recordings of the Op. 24 *Ballade* and 10 *Lyric Pieces* have been remastered, coupled with the 1942 concerto he recorded with Ormandy (RCA). Rubinstein fans shouldn't hesitate. The concerto is predictably beautiful, impeccable, intense, and aristocratic, and the 20-bit remastering has come up with an astonishingly clear image of the musicians. But there's some regrettable surface wear on the 78s and some listeners may be unhappy with the distant balance of the soloist. The 20-minute *Ballade,* Grieg's stringent and substantial answer to Schumann's *Symphonic Etudes,* provides the mainstay of Rubinstein's closely-observed solo segment. Also included are 11 of the *Lyric Pieces,* which he essays with typical clarity and artlessness.

Andsnes's recital need not fear competition from either Gilels or Gavrilov—his technique is stunning, and this isn't an album to be dismissed lightly (Virgin). But his sound is almost as grim and anonymous as Gilels's, and there's no particular personality or charm in evidence. I prefer Steen-Nøkleberg and Knardahl in almost every case. The former instills more interest in the blustery Op. 7 Sonata with his greater variety of tone and chord-weighting (♦Naxos 550881), not to mention his more obvious Lisztian virtuosity (appropriate to this score), and his piano is less closely miked than Andsnes's. And Steen-Nøkleberg unfolds the melody of the slow movement much more beautifully. Andsnes adds six smaller pieces as well as the complete Op. 43 and Op. 54 sets, Grieg's most widely played. He presents the Op. 54 "Scherzo" and "Procession of the Trolls" as big-boned concert pieces, with a huge tone, and I don't think the music takes to his heavy and sophisticated approach. The Op. 43 "Erotik" is deeply poetic, but his posture seems pretentiously misty next to Gieseking, Knardahl, and Adni.　　　　　ASHBY

SONGS

Grieg composed 140 songs, many of them dedicated to his wife Nina, a noted singer who became his favorite interpreter. The inspired melodic appeal of these songs, especially the early ones, is one of their most endearing characteristics. Most of them are strophic, many are modeled on Norwegian folk poetry and use Norwegian texts; some are set to German poems. The piano parts are often highly developed, with short preludes, interludes, and motivic imitations of the vocal lines. The subjects are much the same as those of the other lieder composers of the 19th century: love gained and lost, nature's wonders, broken promises, and personal grief. While he was obviously influenced by preceding generations, Grieg wrote in his own, easily recognizable style.

Several of his songs have achieved wide popularity, for example, "Solveig's Song," "Ein Traum," and, above all, "Jeg Elsker Dig" (I Love

Thee); the last has been recorded by every Scandinavian singer from Flagstad to von Otter. **Flagstad,** with her unrivaled popularity, was a very effective advocate of her countryman's songs. She was the first to record *Haugtussa*, one of his finest vocal works, a setting of part of a Norwegian epic poem. Many of Flagstad's recordings have been deleted from the listings, but there is one disc that is made up of mostly Grieg songs (♦Nimbus 7871). With her huge voice and somewhat glacial approach to lieder, she wasn't always convincing in these songs that obviously were close to her.

The best of the modern, single-disc collections are those by **von Otter** (♦DG 437521) and **Per Vollestad** (♦Simax 1089). Von Otter is among the most intelligent of present-day singers, and her interpretations are always meaningful, beautifully shaped, and utterly convincing. Her somewhat cool voice, fine diction, and nuanced phrasing are just right. Vollestad has a smooth, secure baritone; his diction and emotional probing are also quite effective. He sings 34 songs (almost a quarter of Grieg's output), and includes some rarely heard items like "The Minstrel" and "To a Waterlily."

Listeners wishing to buy all or most of Grieg's songs should consider either of two sets. Seven discs of songs have been issued in a 24CD set that includes all the piano and chamber music as well (Victoria 19038/43, 19072). The Norwegian soprano **Marianne Hirsti** does most of the work, assisted by several others including Vollestad and baritone Knut Skram. Hirsti has a cool, pure soprano voice, not as rich and colorful as von Otter or Flagstad, but it will appeal to listeners who value her folksy style and unpretentious manner. As with most complete sets, not all discs are equally good; the best of the seven are discs 1 (♦19038) and 3 (♦19040, which includes *Haugtussa*).

Monica Groop, a Finnish mezzo, can be heard in the three volumes that have so far been issued in another set (♦BIS 637,787, 957). Groop is a more expressive singer than Hirsti but lacks von Otter's more probing delivery of the words. Another notable recital is by **Hagegård,** which includes many of the less familiar songs (RCA, 2CD). His smooth but undramatic delivery makes his work seem a bit bland compared to von Otter and Groop.　　　　　MOSES

Charles Tomlinson Griffes (1884–1920)

Despite his mature career's brevity—some ten years in all, though his earliest efforts date back to 1898—it would be hard to overestimate Griffes's importance to American music. His early music was Germanic in inspiration, but the success of works such as *Tone Pictures, The White Peacock,* and *The Pleasure Dome of Kubla Khan* have tended to pigeonhole him as an American impressionist. However, later works like the Piano Sonata and Preludes show him moving toward a more vigorously individual style. A capable pianist (he earned a living as a piano teacher at a boy's school), the bulk of his output is for the keyboard while several other works feature the instrument.

ORCHESTRAL MUSIC

The Pleasure Dome of Kubla Khan. **Charles Gerhardt**'s atmospheric 1968 recording of this sumptuously orchestrated tone poem attracted much critical acclaim on LP; its CD reissue is still recommendable (Chesky 112). Front-runner for sheer beauty of playing is **Ozawa** with the Boston Symphony in a 1976 all-Griffes program (♦New World 273), although the sound is no match for **Gerard Schwarz,** a fine reading in Seattle that includes the otherwise unavailable *Bacchanale* (Delos 3099). **Leo Botstein,** with an enthusiastic youth orchestra, is not in the same league (Town Hall).

The White Peacock. The 1919 orchestration of the 1915 piano original is Griffes's most popular score. **Gerhardt** set the pace in the '60s with a refined version (Chesky 112) that has been matched by **Schwarz** (Delos 3099). These are preferable to **Litton** in a varied American program (Dorian) and **Kitaienko** in a curious mix of Russian and American trifles (Sheffield Lab).

CONCERTOS

Poem for Flute and Orchestra. Griffes's one concertante work is delightful, if not a major piece. **Joseph Mariano**'s nicely phrased account, conducted by Howard Hanson, still sounds good for its age (Mercury 34307), against which **Angela Jones** in "Mostly French" seems slightly pallid (Discover International). **Scott Goff** combines the best elements of both (♦Delos 3099). George Barrère's reduction for flute and piano has also been recorded, most persuasively by **Jennifer Stinton** (Collins Classics), but the orchestral version is preferable.

CHAMBER MUSIC

The Kairn of Koridwen. Running to over fifty minutes, Griffes's largest work is a dance drama on a Celtic subject. Scored for wind septet and piano, it's occasionally evocative of his English contemporary Arnold Bax. **Ensemble M** under Emil de Cou present the whole score reverentially in rich sound (Koch 372162). By contrast, **Perspectives Ensemble** gives a more vivid, involving account of a condensed "concert" version, roughly two-thirds of the original, that loses little of its essence. Coupled with Piano Sonata and the first recordings of *Japanese Melodies* and the complete *Indian Sketches*, theirs is a better value (♦Newport 85634).

Sketches based on Indian themes for String Quartet. The 1998 CD reissue of the **Budapest Quartet**'s 1943 recording of Nos. 2 and 3 (the only ones then published) was acclaimed for its "rapt beauty that is quite unforgettable" in the powerful *Lento e mesto.* The **Kohon Quartet** in 1970 were more earthbound but still sympathetic (Vox). **Perspectives Ensemble** is the only group to record all three, a fine performance in very good sound in an all-Griffes context (♦Newport 85634).

Tone Pictures. Despite *Schwann*'s insistence to the contrary, the current recordings of these three pieces are all of the 1919 version for piano, wind and string quintets (the earlier 1915–16 winds-and-harp arrangement is unavailable). The **New World Chamber Ensemble** is let down by two-dimensional sound (New World). The **New York Chamber Ensemble**'s excellent performance is livelier and more brightly recorded (♦Albany 175, with Piston, Rorem, and Copland), as is that by members of the **Seattle Symphony** (Delos 3099).

PIANO MUSIC

The only complete recorded cycle of Griffes's piano music, at least of his finished works, is by **Michael Lewin**'s excellent interpretations in sometimes clinical sound (♦Marco Polo 223850 and 225163). He is to be preferred—for example in *De profundis*—to **Denver Oldham**, whose "Collected Works for Piano" doesn't even include all the published works (e.g., the *Fantasy Pieces* included in the LP original). Well played and excellently documented, it boasts very good sound in transfers from 1981 (New World 80310). **Tocco** has recorded all the published and several unpublished works, available variously on the Gaspara and Kingdom labels, but his well-conceived accounts are marred by harsh sound. **Noël Lee**'s collection of the "essential" Griffes piano music — *Tone Pictures, Fantasy Pieces, Roman Sketches,* and Sonata — has long been NA (Nonesuch).

Fantasy Pieces. Comprising a *Barcarolle, Notturno* and Scherzo written piecemeal during 1912–15, this set shows Griffes fully assimilating impressionism. The most evocative current recordings are by **Lewin** (Marco Polo 223850) and **Garah Landes** (a pupil of Earl Wild), both fully alive to all the poetry and warmly recorded (♦Koch 370452). The rival versions by **Tocco** (Gasparo) and **Poul Rosenbaum** (Kontrapunkt) are less convincing but have much to commend them as interpretations; however, sound quality is a drawback in both cases. The middle movement, *Notturno,* erroneously listed as an independent piece in *Schwann* (not to be confused with the incomplete *Notturno* of ca. 1906) has been recorded separately and atmospherically by **Carole Rosenberger** in a nocturnal recital, "Night Moods" (Delos).

The Pleasure Dome of Kubla Khan. **Tocco** first tackled the piano original of Griffes's great orchestral score (Gasparo 234 or 1007), but **Lewin**'s playing has greater depth and atmosphere (♦Marco Polo 225163).

Preludes. The best version currently available of these three elusive, concentrated pieces is by **Rosenbaum,** fully grasping their transitional manner moving beyond that of the Sonata (♦Kontrapunkt 32215). **Lewin** (Marco Polo 225163) and **Oldham** (New World) are also fine, if a little less compelling, with cleaner sound than either Rosenbaum or **Tocco** (Gasparo).

Roman Sketches. The third of Griffes's larger piano sets and by far the best known, if only for the popularity of *The White Peacock* (the other movements are *Nightfall, The Fountain of the Acqua Paola,* and *Clouds*). **Oldham** is swifter than most but loses little of the poetry—witness his beautiful playing of *Clouds;* however, the pieces are played in order of composition and interspersed irritatingly between other works (New World). **Lewin** is more expansive in a strong reading (♦Marco Polo 223850). **Tocco** couples the set with Preludes and MacDowell's Sonata 4 (Gasparo) and is more consistent in treatment than **Rosenbaum,** who one critic found "at his best in . . . the haunted, almost hallucinatory *Clouds*" but "steely, unyielding" in *The White Peacock* (Kontrapunkt). Contrary to *Schwann,* **Rosenberger** has not recorded the set, only *The Fountain of the Acqua Paola* alongside pieces by Debussy, Liszt, and Ravel (Delos).

The White Peacock is much recorded separately. **Joseph Fennimore** provides a remarkable account—with the Sonata—from a live 1974 concert, but in rather constricted sound (Albany 102). **Roger Shields** benefits from a clearer recording in a strong reading, coupled with *The Fountain of the Acqua Paola* as part of a fascinating survey, "Piano Music in America, 1900–45" (Vox 3027, 3CD).

Sonata in F. Griffes's fifth and last essay in the genre (1917–18) is in three linked movements (yet usually printed as only one or two tracks). **Fennimore** takes the introduction's "Feroce" marking as the watchword for a mercurially exciting live account, well over a minute faster than his nearest rival, but in comparatively poor sound (Albany). **Oldham** is over two minutes slower, achieving greater clarity at the expense of passion (New World 80310). **Rosenbaum** has greater drive and power (Kontrapunkt), but the happiest choice is **Landes,** closer in time to Oldham than Fennimore, but compelling in his emotional thrust as well as the best recorded (♦Koch 370452). **Lewin** is only marginally less involving, his tempos between Fennimore and Oldham (Marco Polo 223850). **Diane Walsh**'s account is less intense, but recommendable with its couplings (including *The Kairn of Koridwen,* Newport 85634), a more appropriate setting than **Constance Keene**'s of Beethoven, Dussek, Haydn, and Hummel (Protone).

Symphonic Phantasy for 2 pianos. Griffes's only two-piano works are arrangements, this one of his early orchestral work and another of Humperdinck's *Hansel and Gretel* Overture. **Lewin** and **Janice Weber** play with complete command in a thrilling account (Marco Polo 225163).

Tone Pictures. **Oldham** plays these three pieces in compositional, not published sequence. His performance is highly sympathetic (New World 80310), but **Landes** is more attuned to their delicate expressive heart (♦Koch 370452) as is **Lewin** (Marco Polo 223850). **Rosenbaum**'s accounts are rather mixed (Kontrapunkt).

VOCAL MUSIC

Griffes was a fine song writer, though his vocal music has been comparatively neglected on disc. **William Parker** sings six songs with great gusto alongside others by Arthur Farwell, Charles Cadman, and Ives in an album named for Griffes's *An Old Song Re-sung* (New World 80463). **Sherill Milnes** proves even more persuasive in four early German settings plus *Song of the Dagger,* coupled with **Phyllis Bryn-Julson** in *Four Impressions for Voice and Piano* and *Three Poems of Fiona MacLeod* (♦New World 273). In the *MacLeod* songs **Louise Toppin** can't match Bryn-Julson's radiance, though hers is a nicely phrased recording (Troy 322).   RICKARDS

Ferde Grofé *(1892–1972)*

Like Gershwin and Copland, Grofé was an American original. Though classically trained, the lure of "pop" music brought him to Paul Whiteman's orchestra, where he was acclaimed for his orchestration of Gershwin's *Rhapsody in Blue.* Now audiences took notice of Grofé's own music, beginning with *Broadway at Night* and *Metropolis* and expanding to encompass all America with images of the Mississippi River, Death Valley, Niagara Falls, and most of all the Grand Canyon. While other American icons followed, among them the *Hollywood* and *Tabloid Suites, Knute Rockne,* and *Henry Ford,* Grofé will always be remembered for the *Grand Canyon Suite,* for, as he wrote, "This is our music you hear, surging forth, singing up to every one of us."

At one time, every child could whistle "On the Trail," which, as "Callllll forrr Philip Morrrrisss!" might be the first great advertising jingle. Yet if the shifting colors of Grofé's Grand Canyon landscape have faded, you'd never know it from *Schwann,* which lists 15 different versions. Of course Americans grew up with this music and American conductors love to play it.

Fiedler revels in this music, sauntering along the trail and close-miking the wind machine in "Cloudburst" (♦RCA 6806). **Bernstein**'s version has been issued three times, first with **Kostelanetz**'s *Mississippi Suite* (CBS 37759), then in the "Royal Edition" (Sony 47544), and finally in the "Bernstein Century" (♦Sony 63086). Exuberant and unabashed, it still sounds great whatever the version. Don't think **Ormandy** might be too refined; he plays it to the hilt and so does his great band, rhapsodic and colorful (♦Sony 62402). **Morton Gould**'s recording is a true "stereo spectacular;" the horns are shunted all across Manhattan Center, an echo chamber is mixed in, and it offers edge-of-your-seat excitement (♦RCA 61667).

Kunzel even repeats "Cloudburst" with real thunder, but it seems studied next to Gould or Fiedler (Telarc). **Gerard Schwarz** draws out "Sunrise" but really piles into "Cloudburst" and is afforded full, rich sound (Delos 3104), closely matched by **Maazel,** the massive 'Cloudburst' fielded handily by the Sony engineers (52491). Shattering climaxes distract from **Hanson**'s earnest effort (Mercury). **Felix Slatkin**

gives it the full technicolor treatment and offers *Death Valley Suite* as a bonus (♦Angel 66387). **Abravanel**'s Broadway background proves an asset, and despite some thin string tone from the Utah Symphony still sounds first-rate (Angel 64307). **Dorati** is spectacularly recorded but terminally boring (London).

Grofé's own reading is even more tepid but still better than the vapid, monotonous Piano Concerto (with Sanromá) coupled with it (Everest). **Stanley Black** receives lavish "Phase 4" treatment, and he's far more animated than Dorati, but the coupling (Ives's *Second Orchestral Set*) may not be to all tastes (London 448956). If the Royal Philharmonic under **Bátiz** doesn't swing like the local boys, they give it the old Eton try, and the sonics are quite in keeping (IMP 1613). **William Stromberg** is a disappointment; he has made many superb recordings of film music and should be right at home here, but the Bournemouth strings lack the opulence this music needs, and his lackluster reading (with sound to match) is barely worth the budget price (Naxos 559007).

Hanson, Slatkin, Bátiz, and Stromberg as well as the early Bernstein all add the *Mississippi Suite,* flavorful images of the "Father of Waters" set beside a puckish "Huckleberry Finn" and jubilant "Mardi Gras." All share the same virtues as their more famous discmate; but best of all is a disc by the wonderful **Beau Hunks** offering the original Paul Whiteman arrangement, pungent with the colors of banjo, saxophone, "wha-wha" trumpet and piano in full Gershwin mode—a real treat (♦Basta 9083). This disc offers still more treasure: *Broadway at Night, Metropolis,* and *Three Shades of Blue,* like *Rhapsody in Blue* "making an honest woman out of jazz." Stromberg alone offers the *Niagara Suite;* we hear the thunder of the falls in the tympani, the finale rich with the sights and sounds of a bustling hydroelectric plant. Coupled with Slatkin's *Grand Canyon* is **Grofé**'s own reading (in mono) of *Death Valley Suite,* trenchant images of desert water holes and swirling sandstorms that cry out for a modern recording.   HALLER

Sofia Gubaidulina *(b. 1931)*

The leading living Russian composer, Gubaidulina has achieved international status in the last decade or so for ingeniously crafted and personally expressive music that is engaging upon first hearing. Unlike so much music of the late 20th century, her work holds up well to repetition and may well provide an ongoing basis for post-Soviet art. The unfortunate aspects of contemporary Russian life are deeply if not always obviously embedded in her ultra-personal music, and a nascent spirituality pervades almost all her work. The unique surface of her compositions is more than a chimera; in much the same enigmatic way as Shostakovich's music, it draws a view of life as having meaning despite, or perhaps in addition to, the angst and ennui that pervade post-WW II music in the US and much of Europe.

About 100 recordings of Gubaidulina's 50 or so compositions are available on major labels by prominent artists and ensembles. As with all great music, multiple recordings allow comparison and varying interpretations of her compositions, which range from masterful large-scale works to intimate chamber pieces.

Offertorium is the best known of the large pieces, a violin concerto dedicated to Gidon Kremer. The title refers to two things, possibly three: (1) the primary theme, Frederick the Great's theme used by Bach for his *Musical Offering;* (2) truncation of the theme one note at a time successively from the beginning and end, so that it appears to sacrifice itself before being redeemed palindromically as it's rebuilt note by note; and (3) perhaps as a reflection of Gubaidulina's spirituality. Of the two recordings, **Kremer**'s with Dutoit and the Boston Symphony (DG

27336) is in all ways superior to **Oleh Krysa**'s with James DePreist and the Stockholm Philharmonic (BIS 113). Kremer's playing is secure, appropriately introspective even in virtuosic passages, and the highly integrated accompaniment matches the soloist's apparent understanding of the piece's multiple meanings. A bonus on Kremer's disc is the composer's *Hommage á T. S. Eliot*, a seven-movement work including three settings of Eliot's *Four Quartets*. Gubaidulina's settings are first rate, and the ensemble led by Kremer is unfailingly true to the spirit of this provocative music.

Rejoice is an effective duet based on Ukrainian philosopher Grigory Skovoroda's "spiritual lessons." The counterpoint between two great performers, **Kremer** and **Ma,** is also superb in the coupled Shostakovich Quartet 15 (CBS 44924). One reviewer finds the duet too long at 30 minutes, but for me this contemplative music is just the right length. The extreme demands on the performers are handled better by Kremer and Ma than by **Kagan** and **Gutman** (Live Classics 121).

The three pieces on Berlin 1113 are the best introduction to Gubaidulina's music: *Concordanza, The Seven Last Words,* and *Meditation on the Bach Chorale "Vor deinen thron tret ich hiermit."* You could then proceed to *Offertorium* and *Alleluia* among the larger works and to *Rejoice* and *Hommage* next. The three pieces are from each of the last three decades. All are without text; all offer an intense, personal, enigmatic spirituality. The titles suggest a particular religious reference, but I hear no overt program. Even Messiaen's similarly titled but not texted pieces reveal more of him than Gubaidulina does of herself. Unlike too many composers who name their works merely for titillation or ease of discussion, Gubaidulina reveals a genuine spirituality and unadorned directness.

Concordanza is the earliest of the three compositions, written when she was emerging from the "mistaken path" that Shostakovich urged her to continue. Despite several reviewers' misgivings, I hear a mature composer who did indeed progress further but presents music easily comparable to Schnittke's, with whom she is sometimes unfavorably compared, and to her own subsequent compositions. Her craft kept pace with her ideas, as is evident in *The Seven Last Words*. Although textless, the orchestra and solosts—cello and bayan (a type of accordion)—take on the dramatic character usually presented vocally in compositions with this title. This music, like most of Gubaidulina's, is more profound than most that has come from Eastern and Central Europe in the last quarter of the century, and the occasional uncommon sounds from some of the instruments are less for effect than for the expression of musical ideas.

Meditation on the Bach Chorale "Vor deinen thron tret ich hiermit" is from the '90s, when Gubaidulina became known internationally, and illustrates in rich timbres and meanings her religious devotion and regard for Bach's music. She may regard Bach's solid faith and rigorous attention to compositional integrity as akin to her own, and she finds in this chorale more to compose, as Bach did himself in his chorale-based works and as Stravinsky and Berg did in their borrowings from Bach's borrowings.

A counterpoint to these spiritually redolent works is the Concerto for Bassoon and Low Strings. Decidedly post-modern, the soloist is required to scream and play multiphonics. Many pieces since mid-century require such addenda, but Gubaidulina's makes more of an impression than most. Anyway, most bassoonists like to do that sort of thing. Soloist **Harri Ahmas** does it as well as anyone, I suppose, if indeed it's him screaming in a studio recording that also contains *Concordanza* and *Duetto II* for cello and chamber ensemble (BIS 636). Ilkka

Palli is soloist in the latter with the Lahti Chamber Orchestra, Osmo Vänskä, conductor.   ZIEROLF

Alexandre Guilmant *(1837–1911)*

Guilmant was one of France's premier organists and teachers (Nadia Boulanger and Marcel Dupré were among his pupils). A prolific composer (more than 400 works), his music is characterized by clarity of form and the use of older forms like fugues. He and Andre Pirro edited many collections of early organ music, and in 1894 he and d'Indy founded the Schola Cantorum.

Many critics identify his eight sonatas for organ as his finest efforts. Only one complete set is available (**Ben van Oosten** at St. Ouen, Rouen [♦MD+G 4340/42, 3CD], and it's a beauty: Some of the timings are on the slow side, but the sound, from what many consider Cavaillé-Coll's finest installation, is wonderful.

There are also some excellent performances of individual sonatas. 1 may be his best, and two excellent interpretations are by **Jane Watts** at Westminster Abbey (♦Priory 237) and **Odile Pierre** at St. Sernin (RCA 37395); you may want to try **Ursula Hauser** as well (Pan 510049). 4 is available from **Martin Rost** at St. Jacob's in Ilmenau, Thuringen, on a bright 3-manual Walcker (♦Thorofon 2247), and you can hear it on a 1891 Mustel harmonium played by **Joris Verdin** (Ricercare 206252). For 6, we also have Pierre and Hauser. **Susan Armstrong-Ouellette** provides the brightest, cleanest performance of 7 at the Basilica of Perpetual Help, Boston, on a 3-78 Hutchings (♦Afka 538). Good performances also come from **David Briggs** at Truro Cathedral (Motette 11541) and **Henk van Putten** at the 3-66 Schyven in Notre-Dame de Laeken, Brussels (Lindenberg 60). 8 is played by **Briggs** (♦Motette 11541).

Guilmant arranged two symphonies for organ and orchestra; 1 is based on Sonata 1 and Symphony 2 on Sonata 8, though some contend it was written as a symphony first. There are two quite respectable versions. **Simon Preston** with the Adelaide Symphony has the edge in 1, with a slightly larger organ presence (♦ANC 770008); **David di Fiore** is just fine and the Auburn Symphony is one to watch (Ambassador 1019). Again, there are several choices for 2: **Franz Hauk** with the Ingolstadt Philharmonic provides a clear, clean interpretation (♦Guild 7187), while **Ian Tracey** and the BBC Philharmonic have the benefit of the organ and acoustics of Liverpool Cathedral (♦Chandos 9785). Both are excellent, but I prefer the orchestral smoothness and organ power on the Chandos recording.

Some of Guilmant's pieces in organ albums ("Pieces in Different Styles" and "The Practical Organist") were arranged for orchestral accompaniment. *Marche elegiaque* and *Funeral March 2* are played with understanding by **Hauk** and the Ingolstadt Philharmonic (♦Guild 7187); a lovely piece—*Adoration*—also with Hauk may be the most rewarding (♦Guild 7185).

Some incidental pieces have been heard enough to merit mention. One of the most popular is *March Upon Handel's "Lift up your heads,"* and is heard to good advantage from **Watts** (♦Priory 237). **Frederick Swann** at St. Andrew's, Honolulu, is also fine (♦Gothic 49092); **John Scott** from St. Paul's is ponderous but rewarding (Guild 7128), **van Putten** (Lindenberg 60) and **Carlo Curley** (RCA 3556) are adequate. *Grand Triumphal Chorus* is repetitious, but the acoustics and high-pressure reeds at Westminster Abbey help **Christopher Herrick** turn in a good performance (MHS 3855). *Prelude, Theme, Variations and Finale* is a well-crafted work, nicely done by **Marie Ducrot** at Notre-Dame, St. Omer (♦Carthagene 730519). *Marche funèbre et chant séraphique* was written in memory of the composer's mother and premiered at the inauguration of the organ at Notre-Dame, Paris in 1868. **Pierre** has two recordings differentiated primarily by the presence or absence of synchronization of the arpeggios with the Pedal theme; ♦RCA 37395 is better than Motette 11251. A decidedly slower but very effective performance comes from **Jan Mulder,** also at St. Sernin (♦Festivo 6921652).   METZ

Reynaldo Hahn *(1875–1947)*

The useful French phrase *petit maître* might have been invented to describe Reynaldo Hahn, one of the most fragrantly Parisian of composers. Nowadays he's probably best known as an intimate friend of Proust and the model for Jean Santeuil in *A la Recherche du temps perdu.* But he was a respected composer, pianist, and conductor, and the epitome of French musical virtues: elegance, urbanity, melodiousness. "With each passing day I grow fonder of balance, moderation, elegance," he once wrote. "The Himalayas, Michelangelo and Beethoven are beyond my ken."

Like Offenbach, another composer who became a symbol of *musique à la française,* Hahn was born far away from the City of Light, in Caracas, Venezuela. He came to Paris at the age of three and stayed there, becoming a permanent part of the city's cultural life as pianist, composer, salon fixture, music critic for *Le Figaro,* and friend of the great (including Sarah Bernhardt). Near the end of his life he was appointed director of the Opéra (he was noted for his conducting of Mozart's operas), and he also had a thriving career as an operetta composer, crowned by the very successful and occasionally revived *Ciboulette* (1923).

Hahn is best known as a song composer. He wrote his first songs as a teenager, and at least one of them ("Si mes vers avaient des ailes," to a text by Victor Hugo) is still performed frequently. His elegant craftsmanship and impeccable taste are amply displayed in his songs, which please most when presented in a small group. *En masse* they can lack variety and vitality, as the full-disc recitals by **Graham** (Sony) and Hill (Hyperion), well-sung as they are, demonstrate. A survey by **Lott** and Graham Johnson, among others, is a livelier affair, but two discs of Hahn is a lot (Hyperion 67141, 2CD). For most listeners, a small bouquet of his best-known *mélodies* will suffice: **Yakar**'s set, with songs by Bizet, Chabrier, and Fauré, is pleasing and idiomatic (♦Virgin 61433).

One of Hahn's most delightful works is *Le Bal de Béatrice d'Este,* a suite in the spruce neoclassical style of Ravel's *Tombeau de Couperin* or Poulenc's *Suite Française.* It's full of good tunes, given added charm by Hahn's scoring for winds, percussion, piano, and harp. An excellent performance is led by **Stephen Richman** in a charming French program with Ibert, Milhaud, and Poulenc (♦Music & Arts 649). Another, led by **Jean-Pierre Jacquillat,** is a highlight of a disc called "La Marseillaise" (EMI 747647). A more ambitious, but still charming work, is his 1931 Piano Concerto, performed by **Coombs** and Jean-Yves Ossonce, most appropriately paired with the Piano Concerto by his composition teacher (and admirer), Massenet (Hyperion 66897).

Hahn's operettas never caught on outside France, but *Ciboulette* was recorded in 1982 with the chirpy French coloratura **Mesplé** as the farm girl heroine (whose name means "chives"). This recording is currently NA, but fans of operetta may want to look for it (EMI 498732). Hahn's score is a particularly graceful example of the delicate charms of "opera's wayward daughter," to borrow the excellent phrase of Saint-Saëns.

RAYMOND

(Jacques) Fromental Halévy *(1799–1862)*

Halévy composed more than two dozen operas, but his fame, such as it is, now rests on a single work, *La Juive.* Often hailed as the very model of a 19th century grand opera, it was a spectacular success at its 1835 premiere in Paris, where it became a repertory staple for the next 100 years. Its success seemed as much due to its melodramatic story and spectacular stage settings as its melodic content. Its great aria, "Rachel, quand du Seigneur," has been a favorite of tenors since Caruso.

The plot is one of the most improbable of any opera: Rachel, the heroine, is supposedly the daughter of a Jew, Eleazar, but turns out to be the daughter of a Cardinal. Unfortunately for her, the Cardinal finds this out only after he has her tossed into a boiling cauldron for presuming to fall in love with a Christian prince, nephew of the Holy Roman Emperor, who fooled her into believing he was just a Jewish artisan. Nothing happens to him. Eleazar is also put to death, presumably for having adopted the Cardinal's castoff daughter. Wagner, and especially Mahler, admired this work; its first scene clearly anticipates the opening tableau of *Die Meistersinger.*

The only commercial recording dates from 1986 (Philips 420190). The cast ranges from very good (Varady and Furlanetto) to adequate (Carreras). Conductor **de Almeida** cut the score from four to three hours, but all the big moments are there. *La Juive* represents an operatic style that's fallen into disrepute, so it's unlikely it will be seen on any stage soon. However, it's one of the best examples of 19th century grand opera as it was practiced in Paris before Wagner and Verdi changed the rules, and this recording is the only way opera lovers can hear it these days.   MOSES

Johan Halvorsen *(1864–1935)*

Halvorsen combined in his music the best of both worlds, grand and richly textured symphonies to rival Svendsen's set beside fanciful images of trolls and sprites in the manner of *Peer Gynt.* Yet of all his impressive output, the only piece most people know is the stirring *Entry of the Boyars,* which keeps his name alive at pops concerts the world over. As composer and conductor for the National Theater of Christiania (now Oslo), Halvorsen contributed music for more than 30 plays in as many years, and in his trips abroad was influential in introducing the music of Norway to a wider audience. The relatively few recordings of his music suggest that the esteem in which he was held by his countrymen was richly deserved and readily transcends cultural bounds.

Symphonies. All three of Halvorsen's symphonies date from the '20s, but they breathe the same bracing Nordic air as Svendsen's written 50 years earlier. In 1, crisp dotted rhythms propel the dance-like opening motif, spelled by a nostalgic oboe melody; echoes of Grieg may be heard in the yearning Andante, with the scherzo—more wistful than rugged—calling to mind *Lyric Suite;* the final rondo suggests a great slumbering giant gradually awakening, leading to what might be a troll dance. **Ole Kristian Ruud** offers the only recording (♦Simax 1061).

2 opens with a great striding motif representing "Fate," yet it's not a somber exercise. The pioneering recording by **Karsten Andersen** (♦NKF 50014) could hardly be more dissimilar to **Ruud**'s (Simax 1062), whose purposeful treatment can be set against Andersen's more massive approach. The Simax disc is more resonant, though the low brass registers more compellingly with the older NKF.

Andersen better conveys the impact of the music, but only Ruud offers 3. A more concise work, it opens once again with Halvorsen's beloved oboe over muted strings, then builds to a more aggressive, even vaguely cinematic outpouring, a rapt Andante like the eye of the hurricane giving way to the driving and energetic finale. Ruud's strong support makes it all the more imperative to have both recordings of 2, as much for comparison as for the additional material.

Other orchestral music. While little by the Norwegian composer Rikard Nordraak survives today, his name lives on in Halvorsen's affectionate homage *Nordraakiana,* derived from his music for Bjørnson's drama *Mary Stuart in Scotland.* **Ruud**'s splendid reading merely enhances the attractions of the disc with his symphonies (Simax 1061). **Andersen**'s Symphony 2 also offers *Scenes from Norwegian Tales.* Both *Mascarade* and *Suite Ancienne* are performed by **Ari Rasilainen** (NKF 50033). Though Holberg's *Mascarade* is far better known from Nielsen's trenchant setting, the buffoonery of the play was tailor-made for Halvorsen's gentle satire.

Suite Ancienne, also written for a Holberg play, begins with a blaze of Handelian glory ('Intrada') and ends with a spirited 'Bourrée'. **Rasilainen** is more ebullient than **Andersen,** the recording more colorful than the NKF LP. Rasilainen also offers Halvorsen's heartfelt eulogy to Bjørnson. Still crying out for reissue are **Øivind Bergh**'s LP of music for the stage (NKF 30 039) and *Fossegrimen* coupled with *Mascarade* (NKF 30029). A *fossegrim* is a sprite who lives beneath a waterfall and plays the violin; Halvorsen not only mastered the Norwegian hardanger fiddle but used it throughout the Suite, including the spectacular 'Devil's Dance.'

Both of Halvorsen's *Norwegian Rhapsodies,* like Svendsen's, are based on folk melodies and filled with buoyant *springdans* and *halling* rhythms. They're coupled with Svendsen's by **Ruud** (Simax 1085), who splashes the colors about with greater abandon than **Andersen** (NKF 50013); however, Andersen offers a wealth of additional material, including the dashing and rhapsodic *Norwegian Festival Overture* and the graceful rococo-styled *Bergensiana.* Since it also includes *Passacaglia after Handel* and a rather breathless *Entry of the Boyars,* it makes a useful Halvorsen sampler.

Stage music. Simax is bringing out all of Halvorsen's stage music, and the first two volumes promise much. **Terje Mikkelsen** offers *Gurre, Askeladden,* and *The Merchant of Venice* on one (♦1198) and *The King, Vasantasena,* and *Tordenskjold* on the second (♦1199). The performances are committed and affectionate, in first-rate sound.

HALLER

Asger Hamerik (1843–1923)

Son of a noted theologian, Hamerik received private lessons from Gade and JPE Hartmann (both related to his mother) while still in his teens. He studied with von Bülow and Berlioz, whose grandiose proclivities Hamerik mirrored in his own *Hymne à la Paix* calling for two organs and 12 harps, unfortunately now lost. Following the production of his opera *La Vendetta* in Milan, he moved to Baltimore, where from 1871 to 1898 he was Director of the Peabody Institute. There, he formed an excellent orchestra and introduced many new works by Scandinavian composers before spending his remaining years in Copenhagen. His legacy was continued by his son Ebbe Hamerik, who became a noted composer in his own right.

All of Hamerik's symphonies date from his stay in the United States—as well as his *Nordic Suites* on folk melodies. As the ongoing Naxos/Marco Polo survey progresses, we may find further evidence of a talent that might profitably be set beside Gade and Nielsen, combining rich lyricism with a genuine harmonic ingenuity and sense of humor worth greater investigation. Most people were introduced to Hamerik

through a set that offered *Symphonie Spirituelle* (No. 6) conducted by **Ole Schmidt,** *Requiem,* Piano Quintet, and a brief piece for cello, *Concert-Romance* (Kontrapunkt (32074/75, 2CD). This still seems to be the only source of the *Requiem* and Quintet, and is a good starter set for those who can find it. *Requiem,* which only takes 47 minutes, is notable for the brass fanfare that opens the 'Dies Irae,' clearly modeled after the 'Tuba Mirum' of his mentor Berlioz. It's also unusual in giving the solo line to a mezzo, here sung by Minna Nyhus in suitably dramatic manner.

For future releases that may expand upon this nucleus, we must look to Da Capo, who have issued the first four of Hamerik's seven symphonies, and there is an account of *Spirituelle* on CPO. Since the entries are egregiously garbled in *Schwann,* it should be noted that 1 and 2 are on ♦224076, 3 and 4 on ♦224088, with the Helsingborg Symphony led admirably by **Thomas Dausgaard;** a third installment with 5 and 6 has been announced. **Johannes Goritzki** with the Deutsche Kammerakademie Neuss is even more bright-eyed and bushy-tailed than Schmidt in the pioneering Kontrapunkt set, and Gade's *Novelettes* make an attractive bonus (♦CPO 999516). In their estimable "father and son" series, Danacord combines Asger Hamerik's rapturous *Jewish Trilogy* and Romance for cello with music by his son Ebbe (♦526).

HALLER

George Frideric Handel (1685–1759)

Handel was a commercial composer of his time, making a very profitable living out of his music by courting public tastes, especially in the theater. It's therefore ironic that for generations his reputation with the public was based largely on two works—*Water Music* and *Messiah*—whose inordinate popularity virtually swamped awareness of, or interest in, the rest of his enormous output. While Chrysander's old, comprehensive *Händelgesellschaft* edition of Handel's works has long been available, the 1955 launching of the more critical *Hallische Händel-Ausgabe* has provided a firmer foundation and inspiration for performers. But recordings have played a vital role in the recent public discovery of Handel's output, especially for the operas and oratorios; in that sense, his status today is a success story of phonographic history.

ORCHESTRAL MUSIC

Water Music (WM)

Though the plushly re-orchestrated "Suite" made by Hamilton Harty (or successors) still has devoted admirers, and though there are occasional reversions to the old sequence of the full 20 movements in the Chrysander edition, the recordings considered here follow the new critical edition dividing the music into three suites by key (F, D, G). The real distinction is between recordings that use period instrument sound and techniques and those that don't. An additional consideration is that some releases give added music—even the full *Royal Fireworks Music (RFM)*—while most do not. On the other hand, there are a number of recordings that give only one or two of the three suites, or arbitrary excerpts, and are accordingly not considered.

Modern instruments (MI)

Of the non-period recordings, there are close to 30 officially current—some not seriously competitive but none really bad, and many quite worthy. Among LP-to-CD survivals, **Dieter Kober**'s Chicago recording is below par (Allegretto, with *RFM*). **Paillard**'s old recording has genuine amiability and Gallic clarity, but the playing and sonics seem rather soupy now, and there is more insight elsewhere (Erato, with *RFM*). At least he was more responsible than **Scherchen,** whose wildly eccentric version is a somewhat dubious revival (Millenium). By contrast, Handel-veteran **Helmut Koch**'s Berlin Radio recording offered intelligent, if somewhat stolid and Germanically correct playing; it would be a valid contender but is disqualified as incomplete, since it gives only the first two of the three suites (1974: Berlin, with *RFM*).

Another conductor who specializes in music of this era, **Ross Pople,** gives a quite unexceptionable rendition, some occasional embellishments aside (Arte Nova). **Warchal**'s version is also unexceptional, but reliable at low price (Naxos, with *RFM*). Likewise paired, and a truly superior bargain, is **Leppard.** This one of the oldest recordings still current, and it is still one of the best, generously scaled but warmly inflected recordings combining style with vibrant artistic personality (♦Philips 442388, with *RFM,* or in a 9CD set, 454363). "Generously scaled" is an understatement for the four trumpets and eight horns of the Concertgebouw under **van Beinum**—still sumptuous and rousing in 1958 mono sound (♦Philips 420857, with Bach's Suite 2).

Kubelik contributes much less noteworthy insight in a heavy-handed run-through (DG, with *RFM*). By contrast, **Muti** produces a big-orchestra version that stands up very well for warmth and musicality (♦Seraphim 73288). Less tied to the past, **Schwarz** offers a vigorous and assertive recording, full of stimulating ideas and clever touches (Delos, with added lecture disc, or MHS). His particular distinction is an unparalleled exploration of embellishing repeated sections, to a degree either adventurous or excessive (as you prefer), but it's all more calculated than graceful, with a bit too much harpsichord at times, in hard and dry sound.

Münchinger achieved a better balance of qualities in a neat and tasteful, but somewhat understated performance, stronger on delicacy than pomp (1983: London, with *RFM*). Something of the same character can be found in **Menuhin**'s older recording, which is unspectacular but full of elegant details and is rendered attractive by its reissue in bargain format (1963: ♦EMI 573347, 2CD, with Op. 6:11-12 and violin sonatas). Among other recordings in the Leppard tradition, **Gibson** is zestful, frankly reveling in modern, large-orchestra sound (Chandos). **George Malcolm** is more modest in scale, with a crisp rightness of spirit, reliable and satisfying (ASV). **Preston**'s knowing, but slightly cool and antiseptic rendition is somewhat parallel (London, with *RFM*). All are superior to **Hickox**'s very uneven run-through (IMP). **Robert Haydon Clark**'s relatively diffident reading has little distinction (Collins).

Some conductors have made their mark through repetition. **Boulez** is seemingly out of his element, but is actually quite intelligent here. His earlier version, with the Hague Philharmonic, suffers from dated and scrappy sound (Elektra/Nonesuch). His subsequent recording with the New York Philharmonic is more forthright and better sounding; unfortunately, the CD reissue is abridged by about half (CBS, with *RFM*). But the champion repeater is **Marriner,** who has made no less than four recordings, all currently on CD. The first is elegantly played, buoyant and hearty in spirit—one of the few peers of Leppard's larger-scaled classic (1971: ♦Argo 414596, with *RFM*). Marriner II is still elegant and bouncy, with slightly cleaner playing and some interpretational refinements, but with a sometimes over-prominent harpsichord (1979: Philips). Marriner III is again elegant but more restrained, less spontaneous, and in somewhat muted sound (1988: EMI). Marriner IV is also highly polished and it recaptures some earlier vitality in excellent, robust sound (1993: ♦Hänssler 98.939, with *RFM*). Of this series—an object-lesson in the perils of remakes—the third seems absolutely pointless. I recommend I and then IV.

With only two notches against Marriner's four, **Mackerras** has shown better reason for a renewed attempt. In his first, the winds of the Prague Chamber Orchestra contribute nice color, but his approach is broad, of almost Victorian amplitude—a little heavy and stiff, in somewhat boomy sound (1976: EMI/Seraphim, 2CD, with Menuhin's *RFM*, etc.). Mackerras II, with the Orchestra of St. Luke's, sounds like a different conductor: tempos are faster, but with repeats and variants added, with fascinating embellishments, and other fine points (1991: Telarc). Speed hasn't relaxed his rigid pulse, and the sound is dry and brittle.

Two chamber groups more or less eliminate conductors. **János Rolla** is first-desk leader with the Franz Liszt Chamber Orchestra in a lively and carefully thought-out version, with some fine wind playing (Hungaroton). The much-admired **Orpheus Chamber Orchestra** is lighter, more deft, but rather superficial, with too much domination by the strings (DG, with *RFM*). Both capture the sensitive interaction of the musicians, but they lack the interpretive profile a conductor can bring.

Three other chamber groups offer what might be called a minimalist approach, though with modern instruments. **Camerata Bern,** a small string band augmented by wind players, delivers a crisp and incisive performance, with the winds and harpsichord overbalancing the strings for a change (Denon). **Dirk Vermeulen** leads his 24-player Prima La Musica, apparently using modern instruments but with minimal string vibrato and a theorbo added to the continuo (René Gailly). **Edward Carroll**'s version is even more extreme: strings are only one player per part, opposed directionally as a separate choir against the winds, in surgically detailed sound (♦Newport 60012; Infinity 62384). These three might come close to the balances Handel would have had on the Thames barges. For those accustomed to latter-day orchestral sonorities, they will probably sound scrawny and undernourished, but they're beautifully played and worth considering as backup versions.

Period instruments (PI)

Of some thirteen PI recordings of *Water Music*, 10 are currently available. Most involve chamber groups of well under 30 players, sometimes adding timpani to the D Major Suite and often incorporating the variant F major movements.

An early version by **Collegium Aureum** was so cautious you were hardly aware of period sound at all (DHM). The next two, by contrast, adopted the in-your-face attitude cultivated by some early PI groups. **Malgoire** is full of unusual touches, sometimes imaginative, but often weird, with crazy switches in instrumentation—catchy the first time, but not likely to wear well (1973: Sony, with *RFM*). **Harnoncourt** is, as always, provocative and willful, but just too rough, harsh, and eccentric to bear much repetition (1978: Teldec). In the same year, **Hogwood** delivered a lucid, direct, nicely pointed rendition—a bit cautious and even cold in character and dry in sound, but thoroughly stylish and reliable (Oiseau-Lyre or London, 2CD, both with *RFM*).

Soon **Gardiner** weighed-in with his first recording, lively and unfailingly musical, piquant in its use of instrumental colors, with particularly raspy and not fully tamed (but bracing) horns (1980: Erato). Gardiner II was not unjustified as a second try, with the period sound more in control, but the sometimes personalized interpretation largely repeated from I (1992: ♦Philips 434122). Meanwhile, along came **Pinnock,** using the two-suite order of Samuel Arnold's 1788 edition: a balanced, stable reading, somewhat bluff and sedate rather than penetrating, the instrumental colors rich rather than blatant (no timpani here), his small group sounding quite full-throated in ample sound (1985: ♦DG Archiv 410525 or in the "Orchestral Works" set, 463094, 6CD). His is almost the ideal PI version for those who hate period instruments.

Linde is small-scaled but tangy (with bracing timpani introduced), sometimes rather relaxed, but generally with real artistic imagination, in clear but spacious sound (1984: ♦Virgin 61240 or in 561656, 2CD, with *RFM* and Op. 3). It's certainly more satisfying than **McGegan** (1987: Harmonia Mundi). His pacings are brisk, there are many textual insights, the playing is crisp and bright, and the sonics are excellent, but the whole conception seems dry and picky, not one to enjoy endlessly.

The '90s have continued to yield important recordings. **Koopman** is aggressive and fussy, but with polished playing that avoids earlier PI abrasiveness (Erato). Much sensitivity and imagination is displayed, but not enough to wear well; leading from the keyboard, Koopman bangs away, embellishes amply, often overshadowing the ensemble as if he wanted to turn this music into one long harpsichord concerto. In the end it's just too irritating. On the other hand, **Savall** seems a bit of a throwback (Astrée, with *RFM*). One of the most free in re-ordering the movements, he blatantly exploits PI sounds and is lavish with his own personal agogics and inflections—a kind of Harnoncourt with class. It's an exhilarating ride, but you need a rest when it's over, and you may hesitate to remount.

Interpretational stability returns in the two latest versions, if with editorial twists. **Lamon** and Tafelmusik revert essentially to the old Chrysander sequence, but in an intelligent, uneccentric, highly musical, and handsomely played performance (Sony). **Norrington** chooses to follow the movement order of Arnold's 1788 edition, which effectively mixes together the pieces in D and G into a single entity for a two-suite format (♦Virgin 45265, with *RFM*). He and his London Classical Players enjoy their instrumental sounds in an energetic but thoughtfully paced rendition, emphasizing warmer colors—and a robust recording.

The two latest versions set an illuminating pattern of matching the score not with other music by Handel (such as *RFM*), but with the contrasting "Water Music" (*Hamburg Ebb' und Fluth*) by Telemann. For this pairing, **Paul Dombrecht**'s Il Fondamento fields 22 players in a brisk and alert rendition that nevertheless lacks much individuality (Passacaille). But we have a far more compelling realization of the pair by **Robert King** and his ensemble (♦Hyperion 66967). King reverses the usual minimalist tendencies of PI performances and uses nearly 40 players for an unusually sonorous barge-full. (After all, a contemporaneous account of the original events speaks of "50 instruments.") Most important, this is a highly vital rendition, with delicacy, energy, inflection, and embellishment—all pursued to perfection in handsome sound. King is a strong first in this field, but many well-matched choices remain after that.

Royal Fireworks Music (*RFM*)

Original version. Here we not only have the issue of period and non-period instrumentation, but also the existence of this music in two forms: the original version for some 50 martial (wind and percussion) instruments apparently used for the first outdoor performance, and the orchestral version Handel preferred for concert purposes, with strings included. The PI movement in orchestral music began with an experimental 1961 recording of the original scoring on old instruments, under the eccentric **Richard Schulze**. It was an ill-conceived disaster, and its long-gone LP release is so awful that it's a priceless treasure (Vox). One year later, **Mackerras** assembled 73 London players (on modern instruments) in a better-organized re-creation of the outdoor scoring. Mob control required somewhat rigid interpretation, but the sound was certainly exhilarating in its LP release (Vanguard). Mackerras tried again 16 years later, with about 70 London

players, a little better controlled and more cleanly recorded, but stiff and lumpish (EMI).

Stokowski worked up his own special take on the original scoring (1962: ♦RCA 7818). Using even more winds than Handel, he added "an enlarged body of strings" for a total of 125 players. This wasn't Handel's full-orchestra version blown-up, but the wind scoring with strings doubling for extra gloss. The old wizard's control over this horde was remarkable, imposing some very emphatic dynamic and agogic effects, and producing a sumptuous sound rather like a gigantic orchestral organ, topped-off by a repeat track of the last movement with added fireworks. The same year also saw **Paillard** assemble 41 French players to produce a far less spectacular version (Erato, with *WM*). It's lean, clean, incisively conducted, and benefits from modern French wind sound (piquant reeds, edgy brass), as well as from a nice open-air quality in the recording. **Somary** initiated another round in 1972, leading about 50 London players in perhaps the best combination yet of big sonority and stylish shaping, with an unusual clarity of line (♦Vanguard 4017 or 71176, with *WM* excerpts).

The first PI attempt since Schulze was by **Michel Piguet** and David Tarr, using 39 players plus seven added flutes, somewhat raucous, but decently shaped (1976: Erato). In contrast came **Fennell**'s sonic spectacular with about 40 players from the Cleveland Orchestra, treating the original text freely—adding piccolo, trombones, bass drum, even cymbals—and quite unstylishly (1978: Telarc). Brilliant playing and dazzling sound, but Handel as John Philip Sousa.

Robert King's venture was dubiously billed as the "first ever recording on period instruments of the original 1749 scoring," but his results excuse anything (1989: ♦Hyperion 66350, with *Coronation Anthems*). His 62 players deliver a pungent but smoothly controlled sound-feast, the most musical version since Somary's, and musicologically sound to boot. Most recent is a recording by **Manze** that's coarse and raw, but gives exciting hints of authenticity (1992: Denon, with *WM* excerpts.). There has also been a silly version by **Anthony Newman,** using a reduction for brasses and organ (Vox).

Orchestral version, modern instruments. Handel's alternate and preferred version, with string parts, has tempted many non-specialist name conductors to apply a big-orchestra treatment. Some, like the amiable but bland **Previn** (Philips), are no longer current, while still with us are the tidy but impersonal **Kubelik** (DG, with *WM*), the expansive and almost blowsy **Boulez** (Sony, with *WM* excerpts), and the brisk and ebullient **Gibson** (ASV). Using the old Harty adaptation are the taut, unbending **Szell** (London, with *WM* excerpts) and the harsh **Dorati** (Mercury, with Harty's *WM* Suite).

Some of the most satisfying recordings are those on a smaller scale, by modern chamber orchestras. **Menuhin** made an elegant—if rather stiff—version in 1968 (EMI, with organ concertos, etc.). **Helmut Koch**'s 1975 recording is reliable, but a bit rigidly Germanic (Berlin, with partial *WM*). My preferred choice is again one of the most durable, by **Leppard**: robust, meaty, full-blooded, with a satisfying, sturdy bass line—grand but not fulsome (♦Philips 442388, with *WM,* or in 454363, 9CD). Not far behind, if a bit leaner, is **Marriner** I; a few textual liberties are taken, but this is a springy, brisk, alert, color-sensitive rendition, brightly recorded, good fun at each hearing (1972: ♦Argo 414596, with *WM*). Marriner again did himself no good with a remake that is broader, more self-conscious, even pompous, and in rather muffled sound (1980: Philips). **Mackerras** warrants checking out (Novalis).

Preston leads a beautifully played rendition, well-shaped but a little fussy and, overall, rather taut and cold (London, with *WM*). **Münchinger** is more ingratiating: tidy but unfussy (though note his replacement of the opening note with a drum-roll!), reliable, comfortable, and easy-going, almost "easy listening" Handel (♦London 417743, with *WM*). The **Orpheus Chamber Orchestra** is still more relaxed and cheerful, almost to the point of casualness (in spirit only; the playing is alert), in wonderfully vivid sound (DG, with *WM*). A real sleeper in this class, however, and not to be overlooked for its age, is **Munclinger's** jaunty but well-balanced performance (1973: Supraphon). **Warchal** offers a sturdy, unexceptional—but reliable—rendition at bargain price (Naxos, with *WM*). **Kober** made a specialty of this work in Chicago performances, but his CD reissue is a respectable souvenir rather than a competitive choice (Allegretto).

Orchestral version, period instruments. In 1973 came the first two PI performances of the full-orchestra version, and they couldn't have been more different. Though it had some tangy wind playing, the instrumental style was hardly provocative in **Collegium Aureum's** recording, led in gentlemanly fashion by Franzjosef Maier (Harmonia Mundi). By contrast, **Malgoire** offered his usual choppy, rough playing and aggressive tempos—a brash and attractive rendition (Sony, with *WM*).

After a decade, the period big-guns moved in. First was **Hogwood**: colorful but tightly controlled and unsmiling, if vividly recorded (1981: Oiseau-Lyre or London, 2CD, with *WM*). Next came **Gardiner**, more assertive and extroverted, strong on period color and emphatic in rhythmic pulse, in full sound (1983: Philips). **Pinnock** accepted the challenge in one of his most spirited recordings: ebullient and highly colored, with bold brass playing, and a sassy snare-drum taking the opening note (1984: ♦DG Archiv 447279 or 415129, or in "Orchestral Works," 463094, 6CD). **Linde's** version was short-lived: fruity in color, relaxed and playful in style (1984: EMI/Virgin).

The '90s have given us more widely contrasting versions. **Savall** is powerful, full of clever textual fine points, pungent and gutsy in playing, clearly and closely recorded (♦Astrée 8512 or 9920, with *WM*). **Valentin Radu** offers guts only with plodding direction and scrawny playing (Helicon, with *WM* excerpts). Relief came from **Norrington**, a beautifully recorded performance full of energy and color (♦Virgin 4565, with *WM*). Finally, we have **Lamon**: crisp, tidy, sonorous, ungimmicky, thoroughly satisfying (♦Sony 63073, with double-wind concertos).

Concertos

Opus 3. Of Handel's two collections called *Concerti grossi*, the first set of six (plus a substitute), called Op. 3, joins winds to the strings for rousing and delectable music long attractive to recording artists. My heart still belongs to the pioneering recording of the standard six, made in early LP days by the **Boyd Neel Orchestra,** with the irrepressible Thurston Dart-ing all over the keyboards—a classic I wish would be revived (London). Other fine MI recordings of the basic six were made on LP by **Mackerras** (EMI) and **Paillard** (Erato and MHS). The extended set (the regular six plus "4b") was done by a number of groups, of which the best is **Leppard** (♦Philips 454363, in a 9CD boxed set of Handel's "Complete Orchestral Works," a desirable treasury in itself).

Variously satisfying recordings of LP vintage have made it onto CDs, but **Malcolm** (ASV) and **Rolla** (Hungaroton) are discontinued, and only stolid **Günter Kehr** (Allegretto) is still with us. An excellent recent recording including "4b" is by **Pommer** (♦LaserLight). **Marriner** has recorded the standard set twice. His remake for Philips is out of the catalogue at present, but his 1964 recording is superior in every way—

spontaneity, sound quality, playing, spirit, plus the participation of Thurston Dart (♦London 430261). Giving him good competition is his St. Martin Academy under his successor, **Iona Brown,** in an exuberant, richly flavorful, and vividly recorded release (♦Hänssler 98918). A definitive choice among the four non-period leaders is hard to make.

The PI picture for Op. 3 has likewise been rich. Like Paillard, **Malgoire** combined the basic six with a complete Op. 6 (Odyssey), while **Harnoncourt's** extended Op. 3 is also now combined with his Op. 6 (Teldec). This means that, for now, their presentations can only be had in a large package. Both offer interesting details and effects worth hearing; but for repeated listening, Malgoire's brusque coarseness and Harnoncourt's willful eccentricities can become irritating.

The basic six have been recorded by PI stars: **Gardiner** (1980: ♦Erato 45981), **Pinnock** (1984: DG Archiv), and **Hogwood** (1989: Oiseau-Lyre), to which may be added **Linde's** set with "4b" (1984: ♦Virgin 61162, or in 561656, 2CD, with *WM* and *RFM*). Pinnock and Gardiner are similar in color, but the former is a little lighter and more graceful in touch, while Gardiner is much more imaginative in the fine points of detail and scoring. Hogwood shares with him some care for details (also using an archlute in his continuo), tossing in an extra movement discovered for 6. But Hogwood seems tense and even curt much of the time, against Gardiner's more spontaneous flow and sense of fun. Linde is in a class by himself, the most mellow of the lot, vivacious but relaxed and unforced, reveling in piquant colors.

Further variety has been added by the most recent PI recordings, by **Lamon, Goodman,** and **Minkowski.** For the last, balances are unduly skewed to favor the winds, while there is little interpretive insight. Lamon, on the other hand, leads spirited, imaginative performances in spicy PI color. Goodman's readings are a little leaner in sound and broader in pacing, but likewise full of stylish insights. And Goodman, alone of all current versions, includes the neglected "4b" plus the extra movement for 6, thus constituting the completest "complete" Op. 3 recording yet.

Opus 6. More than 25 complete recordings of the Op. 6 *Concerti grossi* have been made over the past six decades. A pioneering but incomplete undertaking was undertaken in 1929, with **Ansermet** leading a pickup orchestra (led by Primrose, with Leslie Heward on harpsichord) in only six of the full 12; though the sound is dated, the efforts made to deal with stylistic details were quite progressive for the time, justifying its revival as a discographic document (Koch 7708). If Ansermet's venture was the great-granddaddy among recordings, the true granddaddy of them all was the first complete set, a landmark in the revival of Baroque music, made between 1936 and 1938 by **Boyd Neel**—a document revived on CD (Pearl 9164, 2CD). Neel, joined by Thurston Dart, made a second cycle in early LP days for Decca/London.

I cut my teeth on the classic 1946 set by **Adolf Busch** (with Horszowski on harpsichord!), another document now reissued (LYS 143/45, 3CD); the sound is dated of course, but the music-making is noble still. Other sets of the LP era, mostly fine but now deleted, include Fritz Lehmann (DG Archiv), Marriner (London), Menuhin (Angel), I Musici (Philips), Paillard (Erato/MHS, with Op. 3), Kurt Redel (Vox), Scherchen (Westminster, reissued in England by Millenium, 3CD), Alexander Schneider (RCA), August Wenzinger (DG Archiv), and—Lord help us!—Karajan (DG).

The I Musici set briefly made its way onto CD, as did two more carry-overs from LP, by **Paul Angerer** (Vox) and **Rolla** (Hungaroton), all giving performances that are reliable—if lacking much interpretive character. In 1961, **Menuhin** produced a respectable and often enjoyable LP cycle (utilizing the extra wind doublings), whose CD revival has been incorporated in an attractive cut-rate series of two 2CD sets (♦EMI 573344, 1-10; 573347, 1-12, with Violin Sonatas and *WM*). But the most valuable transfer is **Leppard**'s, though to date it's only in his omnibus album (♦Philips 454363, 9CD). It's important to keep this durable set alive; animated by his imaginative harpsichord continuo, these are handsomely robust and flowing performances to be enjoyed endlessly.

The Op. 6 graveyard is crowded further with sets of CD vintage that haven't lasted long. The St. Martin Academy led by **Brown** made a fine set that was distinguished by its suavity of sound in satisfying renditions not untouched by remnants of 19th-century romanticism, but with a spacious and sensual perception of Handel's writing (Philips). Fortunately, she made a new set with the latter-day Academy (♦Hänssler 98900/02). She's interesting in her rather free use of the surviving oboe parts, and she embellishes cadenzas nicely, while John Constable contributes unusually delightful continuo realizations on harpsichord and organ. Anyone who has ever seen Brown lead this group knows the tremendous energy she brings to their playing; these are, accordingly, performances of great vitality, as well as finesse and interpretive resourcefulness, all superlatively recorded. I'm tempted to rate this a first choice in the nonperiod category.

Less striking but still worthy was a short-lived set by **I Solisti Italiani** (Denon). Apparently discontinued, too, is the **Guildhall String Ensemble**'s recording (three RCA single CDs, boxed set from MHS). The style is a kind of Leppard Lite, with handsome playing, if a bit romanticized and with weak harpsichord presence. A Hamburg recording under **Emil Klein** is a cut further down in personality, but it's respectable in the bargain-priced category (three single Arte Nova CDs).

Two current sets offer solid musical values. **George Malcolm** is one of the masters of conveying Baroque music in valid 20th-century terms, and his set is characterized by innate intelligence and good taste—not notably exciting, but altogether musical (♦ASV 303, 3CD, or singles 6163-65). The **Orpheus Chamber Orchestra** is remarkable for the unity and elegance of ensemble it maintains without a conductor, but that absence also deprives its performances of some degree of personality (♦DG 447733, 3CD). These recordings are a joy to hear for their beautiful, imaginative playing, though I think an ultimate superficiality deprives them of enduring satisfaction.

Finally, two sets offer historically-informed style without period instruments. **Pommer** is always spirited and full of imaginative touches (♦Capriccio 10021-23, three separate CDs). Even more striking is **Turovsky**'s Montreal set; the players arbitrarily alternate using or avoiding vibrato, often employing a crisp, *détaché* technique that sounds to me prissy and affected; this kind of crossover approach has won admiration in some quarters, but I can't see it as likely to satisfy either side in the period/nonperiod controversy (Chandos, 3CD).

The first PI recording of the full Op. 6, by **Collegium Aureum,** was very restrained and unprovocative in its string playing, though adding gentle tang by employing some of the supplemental oboe and bassoon parts; its CD reissue is available in England (1975: Harmonia Mundi). All six subsequent full recordings are still in circulation. **Malgoire** offers vigorous but choppy playing, in close and vivid (if dark) sound. He employs double continuos and also the added oboe parts, but so discreetly that they're barely evident, while his strings use some vibrato, minimizing the period character (1976–78: Sony/Odyssey, with Op. 3). **Pinnock** likewise uses the added wind parts unobtrusively. His string sound has the wiry, sawing quality typical of PI playing, and while there is some

flow and grace to his direction, his tempos are slow and sometimes stately in the extreme, so tedium sets in after a while (1982: DG Archiv).

Harnoncourt is typically provocative. Throwing caution to the winds, he introduces woodwind doublings into all 12 works to create thicker, more orchestral timbres than were probably Handel's intentions (1983: Teldec, with Op. 3). Continuo keyboards (organ, harpsichord) are under-emphasized until they pop out for unexpected solos or cadenzas, and the tempos exhibit Harnoncourt's propensity for push-pull pacing. More recently, we have **Hogwood** in Boston again (1993: ♦Oiseau-Lyre 436845, 3CD); his is the only PI set to eschew the added wind parts altogether, while experimenting imaginatively with continuo textures (including archlute). The string playing is a little richer and less abrasive than Pinnock's, and the tempos are consistently faster and more energetic. Indeed, Hogwood digs in with much more inflection than Pinnock, though the unbending absence of real warmth can generate a certain blandness after a while. (Of course, Handel never expected any of his published cycles to be heard completely in one sitting.)

Of the more recent recordings, **Standage**'s is issued on three separate CDs (Chandos). The wind additions are honored; the performances are lively, incisive, carefully crafted, in lean period style, clearly recorded. But they soon take on a kind of relentless quality, the rhythms punched out with limited inflection or flexibility, falling short of consistent satisfaction, perhaps the least enjoyable of the current versions. By contrast, **Manze,** the new helmsman of Hogwood's Academy of Ancient Music, leads the group in a superb set (♦Harmonia Mundi 907228/29). A bargain to begin with in its tight 2CD format, it features performances of eloquence and infectious vitality, brisk but never forced. A certified Baroque virtuoso violinist, Manze contributes wonderful cadenzas and ornaments that add a feeling of zestful chance-taking. This isn't the old plush Handel, but dramatic and swaggering.

For now, Manze's recording is the clear winner in the PI category. Two recent single discs, however, prompt relaxation of our rule of completeness. They are starkly contrasted. **Christie** offers highly idiosyncratic rethinkings of five of these pieces (Harmonia Mundi). The continuo is richly diverse; woodwinds are introduced, not just in the works for which they are specified and in their *ripieno* doublings, but also in the concertino as string substitutes and soloists. Imaginative ornamentation and other touches make these performances a fascinating experience and a stimulating supplement to whichever full set you might choose. By contrast, **Martin Pearlman** offers the first six concertos, completely avoiding any winds, in resourceful, imaginatively shaped, and refreshing interpretations, which are lucidly recorded (♦Telarc 80253). I have long hoped that Telarc and Pearlman will someday give us the other six to complete an outstanding cycle in the latest (and still quite emphatic) period style.

Organ concertos. Handel supervised publication of six organ concertos, Op. 4 (1738), but not the posthumous Op. 7 set of six more—nor the four supplemental ones (13-16) that were prepared or arranged by other hands and leave gaps (marked "*organo ad lib.*") in places where Handel would have improvised as soloist. Whether to include all 16, or stop with the first dozen, and how to respond to the *ad lib.* interpolation demands, adds further complexity to the dichotomy of period or nonperiod playing.

In the latter category, the earliest set giving the full 16 survives on CD: **E. Power Biggs**'s 1958 recording on the Great Packington organ built after Handel's own design for the Earl of Aylesford, joined by members of the Royal Philharmonic under Boult (Sony/Odyssey). It still has its admirers, and Biggs is his usual cheerful self. But his playing is superficial, there are few interpolations and little embellishment, and the big-orchestra accompaniments (without harpsichord) contribute a stable but stodgy character, in somewhat hollow sound. **Marie-Claire Alain** was less flashy in 1964, in a level-headed, unpretentious, musically satisfying set. The interpolations were conservative, and the performances might seem a little dated stylistically, but they certainly make good listening. Boston Skyline has projected a 3CD reissue of which only the first two have appeared, carrying the cycle through Op. 7:5.

Regrettably departed is **Eduard Müller**'s thorough, conscientious, and quite satisfying 1966 set, which not only presented two versions of Op. 4:3, but recorded Op. 4:4 as first used by Handel—with a choral segue into the "Hallelujah" chorus of *Athalia* (DG Archiv). During 1967–70, **Simon Preston**, with Menuhin and his Bath Festival Orchestra, made a series of recordings of all but 16, using editions by Neville Boyling (♦EMI 72676, 1-10; 72637, 11-15 with *RFM*, etc., in two 2CD bargain-priced sets). Made in four different locations on as many different organs (including the Great Packington Church), there is a certain inconsistency of timbres and sonics, and the orchestral placement shifts about disconcertingly, often at distances in sometimes cavernous settings. Preston is never less than accomplished and sympathetic, with intelligent interpolations (sources not given) where appropriate (and unusually so in Op. 4), though with very limited improvisation or embellishment. Menuhin seems to take a consistently stately and neutral view of this music. Though never dull, the performances sometimes have a dutiful quality about them and lack the playful or extroverted spirit Handel surely wanted. Still, *faute de mieux,* this is one of the best sets to be had in this category, and certainly a good buy.

Among other recordings now lost is **Lionel Rogg**'s 1975 cycle; despite some flaws, it was noteworthy for its treatment of interpolations and movement extensions (EMI). The greatest loss has been **Malcolm**'s 1976 recording, which augmented the full 16 with the short sonata from the early oratorio, *Il trionfo del Tempo* (♦Argo D3D-4, 4LP). Hogwood prepared the edition (and played imaginative harpsichord continuo), and in two concertos the solo part is played on harpsichord, not organ. The tempos were generally brisk and propulsive, with lively embellishments and carefully planned interpolations from chamber and keyboard pieces by Handel; three different organs were used, with some variations in ambience, but generally in broad and full-blooded sound. This much-admired set cries out for CD restoration, in which case it would lead the non-period crowd.

Following it not only in chronology but also in regrettability as yet another deletion is **Peter Hurford**'s set issued only briefly in both LP and CD formats (1985: London). Not only the full 16 and the oratorio sonata, but supplemental music to 6 round out a generous, if rather sober cycle—with good embellishments and improvisations by Hurford, and sensible interpolations based on pieces by Handel or other contemporaries. A modern Dutch organ is used, with a sizable orchestra (including harpsichord), in straightforward, often crisp, but somewhat depersonalized performances.

It has been common for recordings to present just Opp. 4 and 7 without 13–16. Such was the set by **Jaroslav Tuma** playing a flavorful Czech church instrument with the warm-toned Prague Virtuosi under Vlček, without harpsichord continuo, involving little elaboration, and only basic interpolations in Op. 7; it's pleasant but hardly distinguished (Supraphon, 3CD). The old Telefunken recording by **Karl Richter** as soloist and conductor has been reissued (1959: Teldec, 3CD): handsomely played, if on a grandiose Munich church organ, with admirable

improvisations and embellishments, the staid and stately performances and the tubby sonics are all a bit dated now, making this more a document of evolving performance practice than a fully viable realization for latter-day listening.

Opus 4:6 has its own history in Handel's alternative (indeed, original) version for harp and has enjoyed many recordings in that form over the years. But Argo someday simply must restore to us **Thurston Dart**'s bewitching version as a double concerto with his reconstruction of a lost part for solo lute. (**Bream**'s adaptation for RCA of the Dart reconstruction as a two-lute concerto simply won't do as a substitute.) Another reconstruction used in a performance led by **Andrew Lawrence-King** is closer to the mark, but is still short of Dart's in imagination (DHM). In all, a decidedly skimpy harvest in nonperiod terms just now.

The news is a little better on the PI front. The earliest 16-concerto cycle again came from Collegium Aureum, in which **Rudolf Ewerhart** used four different organs of highly distinctive but generally large dimensions, while the ensemble's quasi-period instruments are so blandly recorded that they sound more mellow than pungent. There is no harpsichord, the interpolations and embellishments are minimal, the pacing is relaxed, and the ambience is spacious (1967: Harmonia Mundi). In the mid-'70s, Harnoncourt's long-time collaborator, **Herbert Tachezi,** was given a chance to shine in a set of Opp. 4 and 7 only (♦Teldec 91188, 2CD). Aside from a church organ used in one concerto, the recording was made on a small chest organ of intriguing pungency, which Tachezi plays with ebullient imagination, spontaneously improvising embellishments and interpolations. Harnoncourt's accompaniments (with harpsichord continuo) are rather brusque and hard, darkly recorded, but they don't overly encumber this durable and justly admired set.

Around the same time, the 16 concertos were recorded by **Daniel Chorzempa;** there was for a while a CD reissue by MHS, but for now this cycle can be had only in a 9CD set (Philips 454363). Chorzempa plays an organ dating from about 1780 in a small church in Haarlem, a dandy old instrument with lovely tone and deliciously audible mechanism, while Jaap Schröder contributes well-modulated accompaniments in fruity period colors (with harpsichord continuo). Chorzempa introduces resourceful, virtuosic embellishments and interpolations, and even some warm-up introductions to begin a few of the concertos just as Handel himself is reported to have done. The only problem is that his pacing tends to be broad, sober, and overly drawn-out, especially in slow movements.

Preston's second round, this time with Pinnock, has been assembled (1982-83: ♦DG Archiv 435037, 3CD) and there is also a one-CD sampler (DG 447300). Preston used a single-manual chamber organ of 1766 for the first round (Op. 4), and a unique church organ of 1789–91 for the second (Op. 7, 13-15). The two locales yield differing ambiences: the museum setting for Op. 4 contrasts with the larger, more colorful organ and airier setting for the rest. Op. 16 is once again omitted, and for Op. 4:6, Preston yields to Ursula Holliger in the alternate harp version. Interpolations, mostly based on other Handel pieces, are embellished nicely; his playing is more cheerful and relaxed this time. Pinnock provides correspondingly gracious support (with some theorbo variety in the continuo), his PI players displaying a warmth of tone that wouldn't offend anyone in these amiable and mostly understated renditions.

Koopman made his cycle both as soloist (doubling on continuo) and leader of his Amsterdam Baroque Orchestra (1984: ♦Erato 75223, 4LP). His vehicle is an 1831 Dutch organ, quite similar to Handel's theater instrument despite the date, and he plays up a storm of embellishments and improvisations. He turns the opening movement of Op. 7:4 into a concerto for two organs and plainly relishes the interaction with his ensemble. The orchestral work is pungent PI playing at its best, and this whole set is one of the finest Koopman has done, as well as perhaps the closest we can get to what Handel's audiences heard. Erato has made up a set (91932) fitting Opp. 4 and 7 onto only two discs—a wonderful bargain, if denying us 13–16; a one-disc sampler (45613) is apparently discontinued.

Two other cycles are quite in contrast. All 16 have been recorded by **van Asperen** in two installments, Op. 4 as a single disc and Op. 7 plus 13–16 in a 2CD set (Virgin 45174, 45236). For the former, he uses a 1958 Goetz & Gwynne organ built after 17th-century models, in the latter a four-stop continuo organ by Noel Mander. We're told nothing more about them, but each sounds rather small and chamber-scaled, lacking a little of the flair Handel might have required. He offers relaxed, nononsense performances, with intelligently chosen interpolations and elegant embellishments in Op. 7, and leads agreeable chamber ensembles of the Orchestra of the Age of Enlightenment, with harpsichord and theorbo continuo. The results, if lacking any bold new insights, and devoid of Koopman's excitement, are reliable and thoroughly enjoyable, in superlative sound.

Paul Nicholson with Goodman is somewhat disappointing (Hyperion). Like Koopman, he tidily fits Opp. 4 and 7 onto two discs, but bypasses the last four works. Goodman, who has tinkered with the instrumentation, leads from the continuo harpsichord and also does solo violin work—and is the presiding spirit. Nicholson plays admirably at a recreation of an organ Handel designed and played while serving the Duke of Chandos at his Cannons residence. He adds imaginative embellishments and elaborations, but is somewhat lacking in true Handelian panache, while Goodman's shaping of these works makes them sound powerful and richly colored, but also rather brusque and fussy—energetic and aggressive rather than genial or showy. He uses the harp alternative in Op. 4:6, and provides the first revival of Op. 4:4 with the *Athalia* "Hallelujah" chorus since Wenzinger. The recording venue is hard on orchestral sound. It's certainly an important recording, but not satisfying enough to displace Koopman. And so we have the sad irony that in both the non PI and PI categories, the preferable recordings—Malcolm/Marriner and Koopman—are not conveniently available at this writing.

Miscellaneous concertos. There remains a miscellany of smaller or minor concertos: the three for oboe (plus a further *Sonata à 5*); the isolated C major *Concerto Grosso* nicknamed after Handel's original inclusion in performances of his ode, *Alexander's Feast;* several short orchestral concertos or overtures, some of which include material used in *WM* and *RFM*; and three *Concerti à due cori* for double wind choir with strings and continuo, which are mostly the composer's own arrangements of successful tunes into "Handel's Greatest Hits" pastiches used as fillers in his oratorio performances.

All of these are given delightful performances by **Leppard** in the Philips boxed set (454363). The three oboe concertos, elegantly played (with ambitious embellishment) by Holliger, plus the *Sonata à 5,* the "Alexander's Feast" concerto (*AF*), and other oddments, may be had separately (Philips 426082). There are two cycles in bargain-priced releases: rather superficial performances by **Anthony Camden** (Naxos) and somewhat stiff ones by **Victor Hussu** with a Russian ensemble (Infinity). Much more pleasing are attractive performances played and conducted by **Sarah Francis** (♦Unicorn-Kanchana 9153, with five oboe

sonatas). Otherwise, the only serious competition in nonperiod instrumentation would be the suave old program recorded by **Marriner** and his Academy in its early prime—another recording crying out for reissue (Argo). Marriner's smooth recording of *AF* (1980) is currently out of print (Philips).

In the PI column, the oboe concertos plus *Sonata à 5* and *AF* have been given blatant and highly colored period sounds by **David Reichenberg** and Pinnock's English Concert in a 1985 release out of print just now, though *AF* alone has reappeared in new couplings (DG Archiv 447279, with Pinnock's orchestral *RFM,* or in his orchestral set, 463094, 6CD). A much milder PI version of that concerto was a bonus in **Collegium Aureum**'s set of Op. 6 (DHM); a more astringent one is included with **Manze**'s recording of *RFM* (Denon).

The *Concerti à due cori* have sometimes been represented by two out of the three, paired with other Handel music: thus **Karl Richter** (DG Archiv LP), or, on period instruments, **Gardiner** (Philips) and **Pinnock** (DG Archiv). There is also a version in **Menuhin**'s Handel miscellany (EMI 72637, 2CD, with organ concertos, etc.). **Leppard**'s commanding 1967 MI recording of all three has been reissued (MHS 512929). A less energetic—but intelligently presented and superbly lucid—1981 recording under **Pommer** is a valid alternative, albeit without any added material (♦Berlin 2169).

The first PI recording of all three is the fruity 1983 realization by **Hogwood,** now to be had in a splendid omnibus, bargain-priced set (♦Oiseau-Lyre 455709, with *WM, RFM,* etc.). Equally tempting is **Tafelmusik**'s recording, paired with an outstanding *RFM:* colorful and spirited performances in admirably clear stereo (1997: ♦Sony 63073). Among a number of programs of miscellaneous orchestral works, **Mackerras**'s is particularly attractive, containing two concertos prefiguring *RFM,* an Op. 3 concerto, and various overtures or orchestral pieces from six operas and four oratorios (♦Novalis 150108). Sadly, his bracing account of the Concerto in F remains NA (Vanguard LP, with *RFM*).

CHAMBER MUSIC

Handel's chamber compositions, even more than his orchestral works, involve a lot of self-borrowed and recycled music. His chamber output was initially represented in three printed collections published by John Walsh during the 1730s: the sonatas for single solo instruments and basso continuo, whose anchor publication, Walsh's Op. 1, has a complicated history of changes and supplements, plus additional pieces identified by latter-day scholarship; the trio sonatas, in the two publications dubbed Op. 2 and Op. 5 by Walsh, also has additional pieces more recently added.

Long-time collectors have had the benefit of two LP projects that attempted comprehensive coverage of Handel's chamber music. One was undertaken between 1978 and 1983 by members of the **Academy of St. Martin in the Fields Chamber Ensemble** and issued in two cherishable sets, one containing 24 solo sonatas (Philips 412444, 5LP), the other with 20 trio sonatas (412439, 4LP). These sets were briefly available subdivided into a series of CD releases, discontinued for now, it seems, though gradual re-re-issue in Philips's "Duo" series may be in prospect.

The other project was undertaken at about the same time by a pool of players calling themselves **L'Ecole d'Orphée**. Containing a total of 48 items, organized by classification, their work was first issued by CRD as a series of five 2LP sets that were also brought out by MHS. In 1991, CRD reorganized the material into a series of six CD volumes in more coherent groupings (3373-78), unfortunately dropping four items—significant losses because of their rarity on records—and crudely limiting the track cues to complete works only, instead of individual movements. The Philips recordings involved more or less modern instrumental style, whereas the CRD performers used period instruments and playing style. The work by the latter is invariably expert and accomplished, but the Philips performances are distinguished by greater suavity and sheen. Reference will be made to these two projects in the categorized surveys below.

Two ventures cutting across the two major divisions of the sonatas offered a nice introductory sampling from both. One was a 2LP set in which the **Smithsonian Chamber Players,** using instruments from the Institution's collection, presented three solo sonatas from Op. 1 and five trio sonatas from various sources, attractive and worthwhile (1981: Smithsonian). In the other, a group of four players (including the formidable Manze) calling themselves the **Cambridge Musik,** gave thoughtful and highly colored PI performances of 14 items: ten solo sonatas (nine of them from Op. 1), two individual solo movements, plus two trio sonatas from Op. 2 (1995: Globe).

Solo sonatas. Sorting through close to 50 possible works (some spurious or dubious) to establish the working base of authentic solo sonatas is complex and vexing, as is the establishment of ambiguous instrumentation—not to mention the maze of their overlapping and diversified treatment in recordings. The various Walsh editions of Op. 1 eventually involved a total of 14 solo sonatas, of which four are now recognized as not by Handel. Chrysander published all 14 in his addition, adding a 15th from a manuscript source, some bearing stipulated assignments (violin, flute, recorder, oboe), but all conceivably playable on violin. Musicologists and editors have been adding other sonatas and sonata fragments to the pile, also with varied scoring.

While the Philips omnibus identified some 24 solo sonata works, the CRD series recognizes 25. A recent effort at replicating the Philips approach presents 20 sonatas as a kind of extended "Opus 1" (♦Hyperion 66921/23, 3CD). The PI performances by **Elizabeth Wallfisch** and others are vibrant and colorful, in superb stereo sound. For those who want the working repertoire in state-of-the-art realizations, this can be strongly recommended.

The presently expanded list of Handel's solo sonatas provides a shifting pool of works that recordings have drawn upon with great variety. Individual sonata recordings are too numerous to be considered, but there have been many that focus coherently on subcategories or groupings and accordingly require attention. Chrysander's collated "Opus 1" has long attracted violinists. Indeed, two of them have claimed all 15 of its items for their instrument in comprehensive LP recordings: **Julian Olevsky** (Westminster) and **Henri Temianka** (Everest). And in the early years of the PI movement, **Eduard Melkus** made a 2LP collection of ten sonatas, eight of them from the old Op. 1, including two usually given to flute and to oboe (DG Archive).

All through the LP era, a group of six or seven of the Op. 1 sonatas came to be a standard focus of violinists—thus, **Alexander Schneider** (Columbia), **Grumiaux** (Philips), and **Suk** (Supraphon). The only survivor of that crop is the 1967 recording by **Menuhin** with Malcolm: slightly sugary, but a bargain reissue (♦EMI 573347, 2CD, with Op. 6:11-12 and *WM*). More recently, **Iona Brown** offered seven of the old Op. 1 sonatas, plus two additional ones, and a short *Fantasia* in beautifully warm and vibrant performances (Philips 412603, 2CD).

Three CD singles embody the fruits of latter-day understandings about the authentic violin sonatas. In Vol. II of the CRD series (3374),

John Holloway gives somewhat tense and wiry renditions of five of the Op. 1 sonatas plus two sonata movements. More recently, a program of six basic sonatas, only three from the old Op. 1, is played by **Ryo Terakado** (♦Denon 75858). And we have a more generous program augmenting the same six with two more, plus two isolated sonata movements, played by **Rachel Barton** (♦Cedille 032). Both of these use period playing style and inventive embellishment. Terakado is leaner, more deftly colored and inflected, while Barton uses more vibrato and has a more romantic spirit, though she's full of flair and stylistic sensitivity. Both are valuable contributions, as much complementary as competitive.

The remainder of the solo sonatas, as variously assigned to wind soloists, have prompted at least three recorded surveys, all of LP vintage but reissued on CD. A 2CD Philips set in its bargain-priced "Duo" series (♦446563) collects from the older LPs all but the violin sonatas—that is, six recorder sonatas, three oboe sonatas, and five flute sonatas—plus three trio sonatas from the other Philips set, all in highly intelligent and beautiful MI performances—a wonderful bargain. Meanwhile, "The Complete Wind Sonatas" were recorded in 1973–74 by **Frans Brüggen** on recorder and flute (Sony), all in clear, deft, yet sensitive PI performances of 17 items (six recorder sonatas and two individual movements; four flute sonatas and two oboe sonatas and an individual movement).

In 1985, members of **Camerata Köln** recorded thoughtful, probing performances of 16 works (seven recorder sonatas plus a trio, four flute sonatas, and four oboe sonatas), with all the recorder items in Vol. II, the rest in Vol. I (Harmonia Mundi 77152). To those should be added a lovely set in which the **Ricercar Consort** presents serious and reliable realizations of seven recorder sonatas and seven flute sonatas (Ricercar). It should be noted that each of these surveys presents items the others do not, or variant versions.

Flute sonatas. Of the wind sonatas, those for flute have long enjoyed recorded attention. A basic repertoire of ten sonatas (seven from the old Op. 1 plus the three so-called "Halle" sonatas) was recorded in LP days by such flutists as **John Wummer** (Westminster) and of course **Rampal** (Erato/CBS Epic). **Robison**'s excellent cycle has happily been revived and may be considered the leading comprehensive MI choice (♦Vanguard 102/3, 2CD). **William Bennett**'s elegant performances of a scant five existed for a while in a CD single (Philips), but have now been subsumed into the Philips "Duo" set of wind sonatas described above. **Peter-Lukas Graf**'s rather coolly efficient recording of the three "Halle" sonatas plus four items from Op. 1 appears to have slipped into limbo (Claves). A recent release presents seven sonatas from Op. 1 in gracious and very enjoyable performances by **Robert Stallman** (VAIA).

Otherwise, comprehensive recordings of the flute sonatas are currently dominated by period versions using wooden instruments. **Stephen Preston**'s gentle and reflective performances of eight items (the three "Halle" sonatas, four from Op. 1, and one from manuscript sources) constitute Vol. I in the CRD series. On another CD, the three "Halles," three from Op. 1, and two others are given accomplished and stylish treatments by **Barthold Kuijken** (♦Accent 9180). Both are more than competitive with Brüggen and even the Hyperion mega-"Opus 1" set. In all, I recommend the Kuijkens to those who just want a fine single-disc recording.

Recorder sonatas. As the PI movement has proceeded in the last three decades, the recorder sonatas have come to outstrip the flute sonatas in interest. **Brüggen**'s early recording of the standard six (four from Op. 1

and two manuscript items) caught him in the first flush of virtuosic youth in the early '60s and merits cherishing by LP collectors (Telefunken/Teldec). Also distinguished among long-gone LP versions were two elegant recordings by **Linde** of four sonatas from Op. 1, first with Leonhardt and August Wenzinger (DHM), then with Hogwood and a gambist (EMI).

A survivor from LP origins is **Clas Pehrsson,** whose thoughtful and attractive recordings of the standard six is still to be had (1982: BIS). Among the recordings in larger cycles, **Philip Pickett** in Vol. VI of the CRD series (five Op. 1 sonatas, two of miscellaneous origin, and a rare trio sonata) is still impressive for his nervous energy, while **Michael Schneider** makes a stylish and sensitive statement in roughly the same material in the Camerata Köln series (DHM). I have also warmed to **Frédéric de Roos**'s thoughtful performances in the Ricercar set cited above.

Michala Petri is close to ideal, for a while in a CD single (♦412602) now deleted and subsumed in the Philips "Duo" set discussed above (♦446563). Her well-focused tone and imaginative embellishments are fitted into some very attractive continuo collaborations (mostly with bassoon). Her remake doesn't display any interpretational progress, but rather a lightening of her approach to accommodate a new experiment in partnership (1990: RCA); whatever the interest in the RCA venture, my preference remains with her earlier work. Previously a jazz pianist, Keith Jarrett draws upon his improvisational experience to work out his keyboard role on the harpsichord with imagination, if not always with stylistic aptness. There are elements of both serious musicianship and of a crossover celebrity stunt.

There is a sense of restraint and a muted expressiveness in **Marion Verbruggen**'s recording, but hers are certainly thoughtful and satisfying performances (Harmonia Mundi). Her release competes with an earlier and quite stylish disc featuring **Hugo Reyne** (Harmonia Mundi). Sensible and well-inflected performances of seven sonatas are offered by **Peter van Heyghen** (Accent), but I much prefer the more-or-less-standard six as done with vitality and with unusually rich and imaginative embellishments by **Dan Laurin** with the brothers Suzuki as partners (♦BIS 955). Finally, there is **László Czidra** in perky and enjoyable renditions of the four Op. 1 sonatas with some other pieces, including items for two recorders (Naxos). In all, choosing between these options can get to be hair-splitting, but the Philips "Duo" set of the comprehensive wind sonatas (♦446563, with Petri I) is the best bargain in all its components, and just behind is the 3CD Hyperion set of the solo sonatas.

Trio sonatas. In this corner of the chamber output there is somewhat less confusion about disputed works or sorting out controversies of scoring. To the six trios of Op. 2 and the seven of Op. 7 (some of which involve self-borrowings by Handel or his editors), there have been added the three so-called "Dresden" sonatas, and upwards of four sonatas found in various sources. There is also a set of six trio sonatas for two oboes (or oboe and violin) with basso continuo, which one story dates to 1696, when Handel was only ten or eleven, but these are increasingly dismissed as doubtful in authorship—if not entirely spurious. The chief variable in recording these works is the choice of the two top instruments. In the published collections two violins are assumed, but flexibility is often exercised, as in the additional trios, even when scorings appear to be stipulated.

Early LP recordings treated this literature very back-handedly; aside from a Danish recording of Op. 5 on the Haydn Society label, there were only partial sets or samplings. All was made right by the 4LP set by the **Academy of St. Martin in the Fields Chamber Ensemble,** whose contents were briefly available in CD transfers—deletions surely deserving reissue (Philips, 2CD). The ASMF players presented the 13 sonatas of Opp. 2 and 7, the three Dresden sonatas, and the four supplemental works. The performers didn't feel bound by the strict two-violin formula (where it was normally assumed), and varied the scorings freely for variety, while playing with color and zest.

L'Ecole d'Orphée, while honoring the varied scorings of the additional trios, strictly followed the two-violin formula for Opp. 2 and 7 (CRD: Vol. III for Op. 2; Vol. IV for Op. 7; Vol. V for the Dresden and three other trios; Vol. VI for a single trio). The wiry, sometimes harsh sound of the period fiddles and the frequent recourse to dynamic swellings (now rather out of fashion) can become a little tiresome, but otherwise the period instruments are used intelligently in playing full of spirit and with stylistic insight.

The only serious challenge to the Philips and CRD cycles has been a pair of singles offering Op. 2 and Op. 7 alone (♦Harmonia Mundi 901379, 901389). **Charles Medlam**'s expert London Baroque PI ensemble shows how it can be done by also remaining strictly with the two-violin scoring, but in leaner, more silvery tone, and in brisker, more mercurial pacing that makes the competition sound staid. Beyond that, there was a sampler program of five trio sonatas and one solo sonata from Op. 1 played by members of Pinnock's PI **English Concert** (DG Archiv).

The six 1696 trio sonatas attributed to Handel's tender youth attracted a certain amount of attention in the LP era, with complete sets recorded in the '60s and '70s by Michel Piguet et al. (DG Archiv), by Holliger and friends (Philips), and by Rold Roseman and the Brewers (Nonesuch). These are all gone now; the fact that this set wasn't included in the Philips and CRD collections—though a token one was among the items dropped from the latter in the transfer from LPs to CDs—perhaps speaks to the consensus as to their non-Handelian origins. The only new recording of the CD era is by the **Convivium** ensemble, led by Elizabeth Wallfisch. The annotations treat these works as unestablishable attribution, and argues that their scoring is for oboe and violin, not two oboes. But all six (plus one of the Dresden Trios) are given lovely and lively performances, leaving listeners to decide their authenticity (♦Hyperion 67083).

KEYBOARD MUSIC

One of the supreme keyboard players of his day, especially as organist, and famous as an improviser, Handel nevertheless devoted a comparatively small part of his legacy to formal writing for organ and harpsichord—and most of that only in his earlier years. Much of his creative imagination for the organ thereafter would go into his improvisations, and his fullest treatment of the instrument is preserved in his organ concertos. Otherwise, his organ output is represented by short and relatively trifling pieces that are often regarded as equally written for harpsichord. For that instrument specifically there are the great series of eight suites or "Lessons" published in 1720 (reprinted 1733), supplemented by a large number of other modest pieces transmitted in publications or manuscripts.

Little snippets and samplings aside, Handel's keyboard music is not very extensively represented on CD these days. In 1978–80 **Edgar Krapp** made a series of LPs covering the composer's entire keyboard output. He used distinguished instruments—harpsichord, virginal, organ—mostly of period vintage (including the Reichel organ in Halle's

Marktkirche on which Handel played as a youth), in somewhat dry but solid and reliable playing (Eurodisc). To my knowledge, this series has never been transferred to CD, but it is a collector's treasure. There have been small samplings and anthologies played on the organ. An arbitrary collection of "Organ Works" recorded by **Leo van Doeselaar** in 1984 is virtually all there is just now if you want Handel on the solo organ (Etcetera).

Of course, the distinction between Handel's organ and harpsichord music is artificial, with much overlapping in recorded selections. There have been a few recordings focusing on the shorter pieces (e.g., by **Janos Sebestyen** in an old Turnabout LP). But there were two important two LP ventures that, with considerable overlapping, sampled the "extra" suites of the 1733 collection plus a number of other odds and ends, mostly brief: one by **Luciano Sgrizzi** (1973: Erato/MHS) and the other by **Zuzana Růžičková** (1978: Supraphon). Sadly, both have gone the way of Krapp's marathon traversal. There have also been single-disc samplers of that kind: **Pinnock**'s rather unbending performances of four of the 1733 extra suites, plus the G major *Chaconne* was briefly reissued (1982: DG Archiv, with the "Harmonious Blacksmith" variations from Suite 5 added). Still with us, however, is **Kipnis**'s masterful and stylish program: the fifth of the 1720 suites ("Harmonious Blacksmith" and all), two of the 1733 suites, and a number of short pieces—ideal as an introduction or cross-sectional representation of Handel's harpsichord music (1981: Elektra/Nonesuch 79037).

A more recent survey takes the variations form as its focus: five suites with variation movements and two other variation pieces are played with spirit and flair by **Byron Schenkmann** (♦Centaur 2436). Another survey by **van Asperen** offers four complete suites (three from 1720) and two variation pieces, performed assertively but recorded just a bit clangorously (Sony 68260).

Otherwise, most recordings have been devoted either in full or mainly to the eight "Great" suites (plus the *Chaconne* sometimes called No. 9) of the 1720 publication. **Landowska**'s recordings of five of the suites in the '30s and some others thereafter was a pioneering venture. Though somewhat antiquated now, they're still interesting documents of a great performer and her contribution to the restudy of this music for its proper instrument. There have been various LP issues and CD samplings, but the most complete has been assembled by Pearl (9490). The great scholar-harpsichordist **Thurston Dart,** while never able to record all the suites, at least gave us the first four in performances of typically special insight—played in a free and improvisational style that surely captures Handel's own spirit—in a Oiseau-Lyre LP that cries out for CD reissue despite its dated sound.

Idiosyncratic playing of a different order is represented by the same four suites tackled by **Glenn Gould** in 1972—not on his usual instrument but on a harpsichord (SMK). Whereas Gould was famous for playing the piano to make it sound like a harpsichord, here he plays a harpsichord to sound like a piano (or to sound like a piano trying to sound like a harpsichord); some genuinely fascinating moments come amid sections of incoherence or virtual travesty, capped by Gould's private humming descants. It's more like a home tape than a serious commercial release, and definitely not the way to start your Handel experience.

Complete recorded cycles of the suites have not been rare. The most commanding of the vinyl-era projects was a 5LP set made with flair and devotion by **Paul Wolfe** that combined the standard eight with the other, unnumbered suites for a total of 16 (Expériences Anonymes); a gleaning of six suites from that project has been reissued, still much worth having (♦Lyrichord 8034, 2CD). A more modest venture was **Colin**

Tilney's traversal of only the standard eight (DG Archiv). His stylish, sensitive, altogether satisfying performances were made on two interesting period instruments, and the set's disappearance is regrettable.

Fortunately, the CD era has brought a number of new cycles. **Blandine Verlet**'s version of the standard eight suites from LP days (1973) has been reissued, with spacious and leisurely—but often superficial—performances in unpleasantly thin and metallic sound (Astrée 8655, 2CD). **Kenneth Gilbert**'s recording of the same eight has been reissued in a bargain-priced set that is somewhat dry but intelligent and thoughtful (♦Harmonia Mundi 190447/48). In 1984, at the peak of his tragically brief career, Gilbert's protégé **Scott Ross** recorded them on a wonderfully fruity-sounding copy of a 1733 Blanchet harpsichord (♦Erato 45452, 2CD). The springy performances reflected Ross's meticulous scholarship, stylistic confidence, and artistic imagination. By contrast, **Anthony Newman** plowed his aggressive way through the 1720 suites in sometimes illuminating but too often harsh performances; his frequent avoidance of repeats allowed all eight to be crammed onto one tightly packed CD (Newport).

Apparently discontinued are the conventional eight performed with some imagination but some exaggerations by **Laura Alvini** (Nuova Era). **Alan Cuckston** recorded them in 1990, plus a 1733 suite and some shorter pieces. The performances are earnest, but rather superficial and somewhat clangorously recorded, not much of a bargain even at their low price (Naxos). By contrast, the cycle by **Paul Nicholson** represents a recording plateau (1994: ♦Hyperion 66931/32, 2CD). The "Eight Great" are joined with the interesting *Six Fugues or Voluntaries for Organ or Harpsichord* and two other fugues in performances of stylistic rightness and artistic merit. These renditions flow naturally, with some particularly clever embellishment of repeats; the instrument is unidentified but admirably recorded. For this fundamental literature, this is the recording to live with.

Two newly projected series have made contrasting starts. **Eberhard Kraus** has launched a "Complete Works for Harpsichord" series with two CDs containing the first seven of the eight 1720 Suites, played with rather stiff and emphatic rigidity, but varied among three old instruments and recorded robustly (EBS 6101/02). For her "Harpsichord Works, Vol. 1," **Sophie Yates** has chosen to begin not with the 1720 collection but rather with the first six suites of the 1733 publication. Her flowing, colorful, and stylistically refined performances bode well for her series (♦Chandos 0644).

Finally, there are the pianists. A century ago or less, Handel's solo keyboard works were considered "piano music," but now we have far less Handel on the piano than the Bach on the piano we still encounter. The most recent of such rarities is the venture by erstwhile jazz pianist **Keith Jarrett**, who has recorded a program of four of the 1720 suites, one from 1733, and two additional ones (ECM). He's plainly serious in his shift of musical worlds, but his approach is quite pianistic and personal. His experience with jazz rubato is evident, but so too are influences from Chopin—and the spirit is as much Romantic sentimentalism as Baroque clarity.

Even more frankly pianistic are renditions of the standard suites by two Russian performers in bargain-priced releases (EMI). In the first, **Richter** plays Nos. 2, 3, 5, and 8, while **Gavrilov** does Nos. 1, 4, 6, and 7; in the second, continuing into the 1733 supplements, Richter plays the so-called Nos. 9, 12, 14, and 16, while Gavrilov takes Nos. 10, 11, 13, and 15. Richter plays with great fluency and sensitivity, Gavrilov rather more strictly and objectively. If anything, these piano ventures demonstrate the great difficulty of transferring Handel to that instrument. Whereas Bach's keyboard writing can achieve a kind of transcendent abstraction with which the piano can connect, Handel's harpsichord writing is too idiomatically conceived for that instrument to adjust easily to a shift of medium.

CHORAL MUSIC

Sacred and ceremonial works

Latin works

Roman Vespers. Though born and bred a German Lutheran and dying an Anglican, the staunchly Protestant Handel did compose Roman Catholic liturgical music during his youthful visit to Italy (1709), constituting his rare (though not unique) attention to Latin texts. Specifically, there are eight Latin settings dating from that Italian visit, seven of them composed in Rome. Six have been claimed as components of a Vespers service celebrated in Rome in 1707. The actual occurrence of such an event is speculative—without any hard evidence—and there are liturgical incongruities involved. But the grouping of the "Roman (or Carmelite) Vespers" has been taken up with little question in many quarters, and two recordings have appeared.

The first offered a grouping of six of the liturgical settings. That much-touted world premiere featured accomplished but distinctly operatic soloists, with a chorus and MI orchestra from Philadelphia, conducted with pedestrian ponderosity by **Michael Korn** (1985: RCA). Two years later, **Parrott** added a seventh item, while incorporating the entire cycle in plainchant material to re-create a full Vespers liturgy for Our Lady of Mount Carmel (♦EMI 49749 or Virgin 561579, 2 CD). His forces include experienced early-music soloists, with the Taverner Choir, a chant schola, and the PI Taverner Players in stylish and idiomatic performances. Whether or not you accept the premise of "Carmelite/ Roman Vespers," Parrott's recording is certainly important.

Individual items from those seven have appeared individually and in various combinations over the years. The most popular has been the stunning *Dixit Dominus,* which—with its dazzling use of choral forces and its anticipations of such later masterpieces as *Israel in Egypt*—can truly be called Handel's first work of genius. Of some 18 recordings over the years, my favorite has long been the exciting **Willcocks,** with a fine array of soloists (1965: ♦Angel LP 36331). In its absence, there are ten current recordings. In the lead is the newest, under **Minkowski,** a rousing performance with dash and energy that comes closest to Willcocks, with three more of the Carmelite-associated pieces (*Saeviate tellus, Laudate pueri, Salve Regina*) and with quite compelling singing from soloists Annick Massis and Magdalena Kožená (♦DG Archiv 459627).

Otherwise outstanding are the recordings led by the very brisk **Christophers** (♦Chandos 0517, with *Nisi Dominus*), the more balanced **Preston** (♦DG Archiv 423594, with *Nisi Dominus* and *Salve Regina*), the incisive **Gardiner** (♦Erato 45136, with *Coronation Anthem I*), and the gutsy **Diego Fasolis** (♦Arts 47560, with *Dettingen Te Deum*), all with PI forces. Also variously satisfactory are **Cleobury,** spoiled by blurry sound (London 455041, 2CD), **James Litton** (MHS or MusicMasters, with Vivaldi's *Dixit*), and **Anders Ohrwall** (BIS, with Op. 6:6). In a class of its own is a ruthlessly minimalist performance by the **Scholars Baroque Ensemble,** one singer per part—a plausible and interesting approach, done with spirit and commitment, but ultimately too spartan a realization of this wonderful music (Naxos 553208, with *Salve Regina, Nisi Dominus*).

Other Latin works. In addition to the "Vespers" items, there are individual offerings. *Laudate pueri* is handsomely presented in a **McNair** program (♦Philips 434920, with *Silete venti* and Mozart) and by **Zádori**

(Hungaroton). Much less satisfactory is an old recording under **Deller** (Harmonia Mundi 1901054, with *Nisi Dominus* and *Salve Regina*). The solo motet *Haec est Regi virginum* can be heard in a valuable program of "Marian Cantatas and Arias" by the rich-voiced **von Otter** (♦DG Archiv 439866). *Saeviat tellus* from the "Vespers" was recently available, together with the two remaining Roman (but non-Vespers) motets, *O qualis de coelo sonus* (for Pentecost) and *Coelestis dum spirat aura* (in honor of St. Anthony of Padua) in another program by the admirable **Zádori** (Hungaroton, with *Silete*). A parallel collection has **Christiane Baumann** singing *Coelestis* with the Vespers *Salve Regina* (Christophorus, with *Silete*).

One further Latin work—a curiosity possibly dating from a later visit by Handel to Venice in 1729—is the solo motet for soprano (or castrato), *Silete venti,* whose Latin text (of unknown authorship) is an extra-liturgical expression of Christian joy over the love of Jesus. In LP days, it served as a brilliant vehicle for the likes of Ameling (Philips), Bogard (Cambridge), and Jennifer Smith (DG Archiv). But there are two beautiful current versions in releases already mentioned, by the elegant **Dawson** (♦Chandos 0517, with the two *Psalms*) and by the silver-toned **McNair** (♦Phillips 434920, with *Laudate pueri* and Mozart's *Exsultate*). To these should be added the agile **Zádori** in a previously mentioned release (Hungaroton, with motets), a leaner, keener rendition by **Kirkby** (Capriccio, with two concerti grossi), and the reissue featuring **Christiane Baumann**—a kind of Sutherland-Lite soprano (Christophorus). You might keep your eye out for a version by the perceptive **Ann Mackay** (ASV, with *Agrippina* cantata). The first five are with period instruments, and any of the six can be recommended, with Baumann's ranked lowest.

German works

Despite his German and Lutheran origins, Handel contributed little to German musical literature, sacred or secular. The earliest of the few compositions is a *St. John Passion* that was first performed in 1704 in Hamburg and survived in a manuscript without composer identification. It could have been a work of the then 19 year old Handel, and for some time it was considered his. More recent scholarship has discredited its status, thus leaving it as a curious but anonymous contribution to the discography of German Passion music. However you regard it, it has enjoyed no less than four recordings, two of which (involving cosmopolitan casts and PI ensembles) are currently available: a concert performance under **Florian Heyerick** (René Gailly), and a somewhat more stylish studio version under **Németh** (Hungaroton).

Brockes Passion. Handel's major German work is a setting of the Passion poem by his friend, the Hamburg poetaster Barthold Heinrich Brockes. It was composed in 1716–17 after Handel had already settled pretty definitely in England. He responded to the quirky text with a quirky score, but one full of interesting and lively ideas. An early recording under **August Wenzinger** featured a generally stellar cast (DG Archiv, 3LP). Fortunately, we have an accomplished PI version under **McGegan,** with a fine international cast making an altogether satisfying case for this curiosity (♦Hungaroton 12734/36, 3CD).

Deutsche Arien. Providing an interesting appendix to the *Brockes Passion,* this is a group of songs to nine pious and uplifting poems that Handel set in the mid-1720s (apparently his last-ever use of German texts) for soprano, obbligato instrument, and continuo. They have attracted many sopranos over the LP years (Mathis, Speiser, Kirkby). A CD remake by **Speiser** is still current (Jecklin), but a 1988 recording by **Christian Högman** may be discontinued (BIS 403, with a cantata, arias, and sonata). Czech soprano **Irena Troupová** is earnest, if without much personality (Matouš, with two Italian cantatas). Most recently, the deft and light-voiced **Monoyios** recorded the set attractively (♦Capriccio 10.767, with two trio sonatas). But my own preference is for a 1980 recording by the more mature-voiced and beautifully artistic **Augér,** issued as a memorial to the singer, treasurable even without any added repertoire (♦Berlin 9050).

English works

Handel's recurrent contributions to dynastic and state occasions throughout his long career in England began even before his former Hanoverian patron came to the throne as George I. The first two commissions came during the reign of Queen Anne.

Ode for the Birthday of Queen Anne. During his second visit to promote Italian opera in London, Handel received a double commission in late 1712, his first to set English texts. The first part of the assignment was the *Ode for the Birthday of Queen Anne* ("Eternal source of light divine"), in which he succeeded in fusing his new mastery of Italian vocal style with the traditions of Purcell. He also set at the outset a high standard of invention, which he was to sustain through all his court commissions. Bypassing an old and mediocre **Deller** recording (Vanguard), the commanding version was long an elegant and stylish PI performance led by **Preston** (♦Oiseau-Lyre 421654, with *Foundling Anthem*). It has been followed more recently by a slightly more lively PI version under **Robert King** in "Handel: Music for Royal Occasions" (♦Hyperion 66315).

Utrecht Te Deum and Jubilate. This was the second part of the double commission, also for performance in early 1713; it was Handel's first great non operatic success in England. This fine assimilation of post-Purcellian Anglican form and style (again with Italianate infusions) was recorded a number of times on LP (e.g., by Wöldike, Geraint Jones)— one of this vintage being rough (*Te Deum* only) under Harnoncourt (Teldec). Another is a superlative PI presentation under **Preston** (originally Oiseau-Lyre, with Vivaldi's *Gloria,* now in an irresistible bargain package of choral Handel (♦London 455041, 2CD). Since then, a newer PI version led by **John Scott** has appeared in an interesting program (Hyperion, with anthems by Blow and Boyce), but the performance is disappointingly pallid, partly due to the omission of timpani parts used to fine effect by Preston and Harnoncourt. Accordingly, Preston's recording is much to be preferred.

Queen Caroline Te Deum. Handel's next court appearance followed quickly, as did Queen Anne's death. In 1714 he presented the work in D major known as the *Queen Caroline Te Deum.* It was first performed at the Chapel Royal for the new King, George I, though it was named after a subsequent Queen. Of its two recordings, **King**'s in his "Royal Occasions" program (♦Hyperion 66315) is just a bit more stylish and idiomatic than the nevertheless fine (but less British) **Wolfgang Helbich** (CPO, with *Funeral Anthem*).

Chandos Anthems. Handel was never ordained official composer to the court, though he did give keyboard instruction to royal princesses. Limited court opportunities and a lapse in operatic activities prompted him to accept a short-term position as a household musician at the lavish country estate of Cannons—being built by James Brydges, a filthy-rich bureaucratic profiteer, soon to be the newly-minted Duke of Chandos. During his residence there in 1717–18, the composer's chief product was a series of 11 psalm settings for small vocal and instrumental forces for use in his patron's pretentious chapel. These so-called "Chandos Anthems" are delightful works, showing Handel refining his skills in treating English texts and including material he borrowed for later use. Individual recordings have drawn upon them from time to time, but the best versions have been part of three extended LP series.

An early venture under **Alfred Mann** that got as far as Nos. 1-6, with excellent American soloists, has been reissued and again deserves attention (Vanguard). Thereafter, at intervals, **Willcocks** recorded six of them (two each to three LPs) with fine soloists, the King's College Choir, and the ASMF. Of those recordings, only 10 ("The Lord is my light") has resurfaced on CD (London, with *Israel in Egypt*).

However, the commanding recordings remain. One is the 1987–89 series with superlative soloists and The Sixteen choir and PI orchestra under **Christophers** (♦Chandos 0554/57, 4CD, or singles 0503-5, 0509; also MHS). A new series, entitled "Music for Chandos," has been initiated, containing 4, 6, and 11, and uses minimal forces that perhaps approximate Handel's smallness of scale more justly (L'Empreinte Digitale). As performed by a partly French ensemble under **Graham O'Reilly,** these are scrawny in sound, unidiomatic and mediocre in artistry, and of little promise for the future, leaving the Christophers recordings unchallenged.

Coronation Anthems. Handel's next opportunity for state music was the coronation of George II in 1727. The four glorious *Coronation Anthems* begin with the stunning one-movement "Zadok the Priest" (long a separate favorite in recordings) and continue with three multi-movement pieces in standard Anglican anthem-style. Complete recordings of the set were recurrent over the LP years, attracting the likes of Menuhin (EMI), Pritchard (ASV), Bernardi (CBC), and Ledger (EMI), all using modern instruments, and all out of print.

Three versions survive, one PI, two MI. In the latter category is **Marriner**'s 1984 recording, which offers balanced mixed-voice choral and MI forces in refined but just a little cool renditions (Philips). The other non-period version is the first complete version and still my favorite: **Willcocks**'s 1963 recording, in a super-best-buy choral set (♦London 455041, 2CD). The 1981 recording by **Preston** and Pinnock (with two *Due cori* concertos) strikes a judicious and forceful balance between choral substance and period sound in gratifying clarity (♦DG Archiv 447280).

Among subsequent PI versions, **King** is equally lucid, but he's on the lighter side and lacks a degree of rhetorical power (1989: Hyperion). **Willcocks** is disastrous (1996: Columns). He leads a Dutch choir with blurred diction and a local, not very able, PI orchestra in stiff, provincial, and utterly uncompetitive renditions—one more reminder of the risk conductors take in returning to a scene of former triumphs.

Wedding Anthem. After nine more years came Handel's Wedding Anthem ("Sing unto God"), composed for the 1735 nuptials of the Prince of Wales (his erstwhile enemy) and a German princess. Its words were taken from various Psalm texts, which Handel set with flair and color. Not a major work, but a very enjoyable one, it's effectively delivered in its only recording, under **King** in his "Royal Occasions" program (♦Hyperion 66315).

Funeral Anthem for Queen Caroline. The next assignment, was an unhappy one: the creation of a long *Funeral Anthem for Queen Caroline* ("The ways of Zion do mourn"). Handel was, in fact, devoted to the long-suffering consort of George II and grieved over her death in 1737. He responded with a work for performance at her burial a month later, using selected scriptural texts woven into a hymn of praise. Out of these he created a work for chorus (with optional solos) and orchestra more than

40 minutes long, stretching the idiom of the Anglican anthem to the scale of a cantata or near-oratorio and breaking new ground in extended choral writing.

Its first LP recordings were in German, but the breakthrough was the 1978 MI version by **Gardiner.** Since Handel himself reused the entire Anthem as the original Part I of *Israel in Egypt* (changing the textual "she's" for Caroline to "he's" for Joseph), Gardiner's incisive reading has been reissued as an appendix to his version of the oratorio (♦Erato 45399, 2CD). Three subsequent PI recordings explicitly followed Handel's recycling intentions, with the Anthem as Part I of their complete versions of *Israel.* **Harry Saltzman**'s rousing concert performance was for a while available in a pair of audiotapes (1985: Newport 30005), but never, alas, on CD. **Parrott** is lucid and finely detailed (1989: ♦Virgin 561350). Most recent is the lean 1993 recording under **Christophers** (♦Collins 70352, 2CD). Any of these will give great musical satisfaction, but must, of course, be considered in conjunction with the oratorio. As it happens, the only recording of the Anthem on its own just now is **Helbich**'s version, a powerful PI performance handicapped only slightly by mixtures of accents and dictions, in somewhat over-reverberant sound (1993: ♦CPO 999244, with *Caroline Te Deum*).

Dettingen Te Deum and ***Dettingen Anthem.*** George II's quixotically unexpected participation in a British victory in 1743 prompted a celebration for which Handel composed two formal works now known by the battle's name: the *Dettingen Te Deum,* Handel's last Anglican work, and the accompanying *Dettingen Anthem* ("The king shall rejoice"). The history of the *Te Deum* has been spotty to say the least, and largely of the LP era. Of ten commercial recordings (five of them sung in German translation, two of those under the same conductor, **Wolfgang Gönnenwein**), the most fully satisfactory was the first PI version, a brilliantly stylish and sonorous performance by **Preston** (1984: ♦DG Archiv 410647). This production also added the only recording to date of the Anthem and appears to be unavailable. One more German-language version of the *Te Deum* alone is a 1968 broadcast performance under **Helmut Koch** (Berlin). Language aside, Koch distorts the work by awarding all but the bass solos to choral sections—an antiquated perversion to be avoided. Fortunately, we now have a spirited English-language PI recording by **Fasolis,** one of two concert performances in a very successful pairing (♦Arts 47560, with *Dixit Dominus*). Accent problems are minimal and despite somewhat cavernous sonics, this is a credible replacement for Preston.

Foundling Anthem. Handel's ceremonial music ended not with a work for a court occasion, but as a contribution to the charity to which he became so bountifully devoted in his last years: the Foundling Hospital. For its opening, in addition to the first of what became regular fund-raising performances of *Messiah,* Handel presented what has become known as the *Foundling Anthem* ("Blessed are they that considereth the poor and needy"). It's something of a pastiche; texts mostly from the Old Testament were fitted to adaptations mostly of earlier music (from *Funeral Anthem* and *Susanna*), concluding with a variant of *Messiah*'s "Hallelujah" chorus. In fact, it works very well in its own right, and was superbly recorded by **Preston** (Oiseau-Lyre)—a CD reissue now apparently discontinued, but much in need of restoration. A reasonable substitute is another fine PI performance led by **David Hill,** currently available only in a fine bargain package (♦London 455041, 2CD). Otherwise, the only separate version is an older recording made in 1989 in Handel's native city, Halle, and released in an anthology of Halle composers—musically adequate, but with badly blurred diction, and thin sound (Berlin).

Secular cantatas

With a few exceptions, these are all in Italian, and almost all date from the composer's stay in Italy in 1706–11. Most are brief quasi-dramatic solo vignettes in operatic style for salon audiences of the day (especially in Rome, where fully staged opera was forbidden). There are lots of them: about 70 for solo voice with basso continuo, close to 30 for voice with obbligato instrument(s) or ensemble and continuo, plus some 20 duets and a few trios with continuo, and finally a half-dozen extended dramatic cantatas for two or more singers with ensemble or quasi-orchestral instruments and continuo.

Over the years, recordings have dipped into this repertoire with erratic selectivity, in varying combinations of one genre or mixes of two or more, sometimes also interspersing bits of Handel's instrumental music as spacers—not to mention selections dropped into anthologies of broader scope. The carnage has been great among the products of LP vintage, and even among CD ventures, so keeping track of worthy recordings is difficult. Furthermore, the number and diversity of these tidbits, plus their overlapping appearances on different discs, make it impossible to give detailed comparisons for each individual item. Nevertheless, some current programs of this material can be noted as worth attention while they last.

Some of the best samplings are now apparently discontinued. Two releases featured the fleet-voiced **Zádori** in one continuo-only cantata, one ensemble, and ten duets (♦Hungaroton 12565/65, 2CD). Two programs were built around the expert **Kirkby,** one containing four ensemble cantatas (♦Oiseau-Lyre 430282), the other presenting two continuo cantatas, three duets, and a trio (♦Oiseau-Lyre 414473). All of these offer performances of outstanding style and artistry; they surely deserve reissue and merit hunting by collectors.

Just how superior those releases were is pointed up by a parallel program of four continuo cantatas and three duets, given vocally unattractive and stylistically uncomfortable performances by soprano **Isabelle Poulenard**—a current release only for the collection that must have everything (Astrée). There are at least two old LP programs of ensemble cantatas I wish would come back: one by **Marjanne Kweksilber** with three items (Telefunken), and even more, one by a favorite singer of mine, contralto **Helen Watts,** fabulous in three items (♦Oiseau-Lyre 60046).

One format that has become quite popular is a mixture of diverse vocal and instrumental pieces. A fine sampler mixes one continuo and two ensemble cantatas (one of them Handel's only setting of Spanish), fragments of a dramatic cantata, and three duets in later English adaptations, with the movements of Harpsichord Suite 5 ("Blacksmith") by excellent singers **Faye Robinson** and Ostendorf (♦Helicon 1007). A more curious approach is taken by soprano **Yvonne Kenny** and bass Shirley-Quirk, who offer an Italian cantata each, separated by an oboe sonata but intermingled with three of the *Deutsche Arien* and an Italian duet (♦Meridian 84157). Three additional mixed-bag programs focus on **Baird**'s accomplished but bleached voice. One contains four continuo cantatas with a gamba sonata and a harpsichord suite (♦Meridian 84189). Another, "Handel in Italy," combines two continuo and one ensemble cantata with the Op. 2:8 trio sonata (Newport); and a third, "Handel: the Italian Years," offers three ensemble cantatas with an instrumental trio by Telemann and a Vivaldi cantata (Dorian). Two sopranos offer warmer and more emotionally committed singing: the forceful **Bott** delivers two ensemble cantatas alternating with three trio sonatas (Chandos), while the sweeter-voiced **Ellen Hargis** gives one continuo and two ensemble cantatas and an opera aria, mingled with four instrumental pieces (Wildboar). All three sopranos, by the way, include one of Handel's more frequently recorded cantatas, *Tra le fiamme*. Yet another soprano, **Roberta Invernizzi,** combines three continuo cantatas with flute, violin, and trio sonatas (Stradivarius). Finally in this category, we have two countertenors: **Ragin,** who mixes three continuo and one ensemble cantata with the two oboe sonatas (Channel), and **Lesne,** who gives vocally and (period) instrumentally zesty performances of one continuo and three ensemble cantatas, spaced by trio sonata Op. 5:4 (Virgin, 2CD, with Scarlatti cantatas).

Of programs devoted exclusively to cantatas, two volumes have appeared in a series entitled "Cantates Romaines," with the lean-voiced but earnest and able **Kiehr,** first in one continuo and four ensemble cantatas (including the Spanish piece), then, joined by countertenor Scholl, in three continuo cantatas, a dramatic cantata, and one duet (Accord). Much more forceful, zesty performances are by soprano **Lina Maria Akerlund** of three substantial ensemble cantatas, including the Spanish (♦Accord 201102). Two programs by fine countertenors are worth seeking out: the bright and agile **Kowalski** in four continuo and one ensemble cantata (Capriccio), and the richer, more mellow-voiced **Ledroit** in six continuo cantatas (♦FY/RCA 112). A third, by "sopranista" **Angelo Manzotti,** offers a very generous program that overstrains the singer's small, undistinguished, and not always fully controlled voice (Bongiovanni). Six of the unusual cantatas for bass voice (three continuo-only, two ensemble) are sung by **Jean-Luis Bindina** (Stradivarius).

Several cantatas of unusually dramatic character have found particular favor as display pieces for singers. One is the continuo cantata *La Lucrezia* ("O Nume eterni!"), the lament of the noble Roman lady ravished by the Tarquin prince. It received memorable LP recordings by Baker (Philips), Bogard (Cambridge), Murray (EMI), and Davrath (Vanguard). At present, it's represented in programs by **Invernizzi** (Stradivarius) and by Mei and Gens (discussed below), as well as in the somewhat incongruous male-alto version by **Lesne** in his aforementioned disc (Virgin). Another powerful monologue is the ensemble cantata *Armida abbandonata* ("Dietro l'orme fuggaci"), the plaint of Tasso's lovelorn sorceress. Put to words by Prince Francesco Ruspol, it was written for the soprano Durastanti with whom Handel was to enjoy a long association. Early LP recordings by Giebel (Oceanic), Woytowicz (Philips), Davrath (Vanguard), Kweksilber (Telefunken), and above all, Baker (Angel/EMI), set a high standard. It's met on a small scale by **Kiehr** (Accord), done appealingly by **Hargis** (Wildboar), but is most powerful by **Murray** in a program of three especially fine cantatas (♦Collins 15032). A third remarkable dramatic vignette is the ensemble cantata *Agrippina condotta a morire* ("Dunque sarà pur vero"), a monologue of Nero's mother facing her death. Fine LP versions by **Giebel** (Oceanic) and especially **Bogard** (Cambridge) have not been abundantly replaced. You may still find the one in which **Mackay** gives a musically brilliant but emotionally somewhat bland performance (ASV). Much more force and temperament is shown by **Zádori** in a superb three-cantata release now NA (♦Hungaroton)—a particular tragedy, for it includes a fine performance of the grandly extended *Delirio amoroso*—which is performed with even greater power by **Murray** in her already recommended release (♦Collins 15032). All three of these cantatas have sensibly been combined in a single release by **Gens** (♦Virgin 545283) and **Mei** (♦Teldec 24571). Gens has a somewhat astringent voice and strong theatrical flair. Mei's voice is fuller and riper, but while no slouch at dramatic expression—she comes particularly alive as Lucrezia—she probes a shade less into these characters's shifting moods. Both have excellent support from small PI groups, and both recordings

are valuable, though in a crunch Mei's might give just a tad more musical satisfaction.

One of the few cantatas Handel wrote in England (rather than in Italy), the extended *Cecilia, vogli un sguardo* (for soprano, tenor, and ensemble) was once in a fine LP by **Jennifer Smith** and John Elwes (DG Archiv). The almost unique example of an English cantata, *Look down, harmonious Saint*—a Cecilian ode Handel used in connection with *Alexander's Feast*—once sung rather ponderously by Theo Altmeyer (DHM), may now be found in a beautifully stylish performance by **Ainsley** as filler in Robert King's recording of *Acis and Galatea* (♦Hyperion 66361/62, 2CD). There are a number of short English songs credited to Handel, most of which are spurious and few of which have ever been recorded.

Six more extended dramatic cantatas—some of them almost mini-operas—survive complete, and five of them have been recorded. The earliest, *Clori, Tirsi e Fileno* ("Cor fedele") was long thought to survive only in fragments, and these were recorded in the above-mentioned Helicon release (1007). The discovery of its full manuscript score has made possible two complete recordings so far, one done with style and spirit by **Lorraine Hunt,** Jill Feldman, and Minter (♦Harmonia Mundi 907045), another somewhat less classy but spirited version by **Suzie le Blanc,** sopranist Jörg Waschinski, and David Cordier (♦NCA 97 05828). A shorter mini-drama, *Il Duello amoroso* ("Amarilli vezzosa"), is included by **Kiehr** and Scholl in "Roman Cantatas" Vol. II (Accord); yet **Kwella** and Denley did it with even more flair and style (1984: ♦Hyperion 66155, with two other fine ensemble cantatas). The longer pastorale *Aminta e Fillide* ("Arresta il passo") is given its only recording, fresh and bright, by **Kwella** and Gillian Fisher (♦Hyperion 66118). By far the most popular of these dramatic cantatas is *Apollo e Dafne* ("La terra è liberata"), which dramatizes Ovid's tale of the nymph Daphne's escape from Apollo's sexual harassment—a story that has attracted full operatic treatment over the centuries. Handel's cantata has had no less than seven recordings, four of LP vintage. The one by **Giebel** and Fischer-Dieskau was outstanding, something DG ought to revive.

PI treatment began with a 1985 version by the clear-voiced **Judith Nelson** and the gruff David Thomas, in rather harsh sound (Harmonia Mundi 1905157). Less than pleasant PI playing under **Harnoncourt** somewhat handicaps an otherwise powerful and highly dramatic performance by the more operatic but masterful voices of Alexander and Hampson (♦Teldec 44633, with Telemann's *Ino*). The period instrumental work is much smoother, if less intense, in **Standage**'s 1994 recording, but the silvery-voiced Argenta is too cool and girlish, while Michael George is a bit woolly, if energetic (♦Chandos 0583). Their couplings may help sway the choice between them: Chandos offers a fine version of the ensemble cantata *Crudel tiranno Amor,* another of the rare later works, written in 1721 as a London vehicle for Durastanti. A spirited and highly dramatic PI performance by Karina Gauvin and Russell Braun with **Labadie**'s Les Violins du Roy has a particularly effective pairing with the Latin motet *Silete venti* (♦Dorian 90288). By far the most extended and developed of the dramatic cantatas is *Aci, Galatea e Polifemo*, a *serenata á tre* composed for performance in Naples in 1708. A one-act chamber opera, it might well be put with the Italian operas save that it wasn't meant for the stage. It treats the same Ovid story of a tragic love triangle that Handel returned to in his English masque, *Acis and Galatea*. Beyond one tiny borrowing transferred to the later work, the earlier is a completely independent score and full of fine things. Its only recording is also fine, dashingly sung by **Kirkby,** Watkinson, and David Thomas (♦Harmonia Mundi 901253/54, 2CD, with three flute sonatas). Finally, on a smaller scale, we have the Italian duets, short multi-movement pieces, many (but not all) dated to 1710–11. They're trifles, if very pretty ones, and often interesting for Handel's first use of tunes or ideas he was to recycle into his later works in England. Indeed, some are thought to be preliminary studies of material for larger use, tried out experimentally. Extended groups of these duets have been melded into cantata recordings, as by **Poulenard/Comoretto** (Astrée) and **Zádori/Esswood** (♦Hungaroton 12564/65). Another is a fine but lamentably deleted recording of three duets with two continuo cantatas by **Nelson/Jacobs,** deserving reissue (♦Harmonia Mundi 431004). There have also been several releases entirely devoted to these duets. Nine of the ten given by Zádori and Esswood were offered in stylish and attractive performances by **Fisher/Bowman** (♦Hyperion 66440). A program of nine duets by a quartet of singers and players calling themselves **Favella Lyrica** is pleasing if less accomplished (Koch 3-7298). Roughly the same repertoire (though stressing what is pegged as Handel's post-Italy "Hamburg Duets") is offered in thinner singing by a pair of sisters, **Dörte** and **Heidrun Blase,** with more pallid continuo work (Thorophon). Two singers of **La Venexiana** present all ten of the soprano/alto duets; they're stylistically skillful but vocally unappealing (Cantus). All in all, the Hyperion discs remain the best starting-point for this repertoire.

OPERAS

Theatrical conventions of Handel's day dictated the subject matter as derived almost invariably from ancient mythology, history (Hellenistic, Roman, Medieval), or from specified areas of literature (epic, romance). Adding to this artificiality were strict conventions of form—limiting the complex plot action to recitative while using set pieces (arias, duets, ensembles) to express vignettes of emotional situations or character dimensions at a given moment. Handel's operas were shaped within these conventions, though by no means slavishly tied to them, for he was capable of breaking out or stretching them with his very individualistic experimentation. And though the idiom can seem stiff and formulaic as judged by 19th-century standards, there isn't one of Handel's opera scores that doesn't contain wonderful jewels of vocal writing, and many can prove surprisingly moving dramatically.

This was the idiom to which Handel dedicated his creativity through almost four decades, representing some four-fifths of his long career. Having tested the waters in Hamburg (in German), he achieved his first mastery and successes in Italy; he then committed himself to giving Italian operas to the London public. With declining public interest in the idiom, Handel began (at first reluctantly) to move into the eventual replacement idiom of English oratorio. His successes in that field blotted out his operas by his last years, and left them neglected and largely ignored until revivals in our century began drawing attention to them.

The postwar years saw a mounting momentum of stagings (from brilliant to horrendous) paralleling a growing tide of recordings. Indeed, the two processes have cross-fertilized. Many recordings, not only of operas but also oratorios, have been the byproducts of such prestigious events as the annual Handel Festivals in Halle and Göttingen. In addition, the operas have been a particular stimulus to, and beneficiary of, the PI movement of the past few decades. Indeed, of all the Handel operas recorded to date, not one—major or minor—has lacked at least one PI recording, and often it has been the only treatment. At the same time, the operas have become a treasure-house of jewels to be sampled by singers in aria anthologies. In the LP years, such samplings were assembled as display vehicles for individual singers, most of whom (with

such exceptions as Horne and Souzay) tended to be primarily specialists in early music. In more recent years, CD programs have developed thematically focused approaches.

A striking case in point is the series of programs worked up by Roy Goodman in collaboration with **Kirkby.** The first was called "Opera Arias and Overtures from the first half of Handel's Operatic Career (1704–1726)," drawing systematically and chronologically nine operas of that period (♦Hyperion 66860). The second, called "The Rival Queens: Opera Arias and Duets," draws on five operas from 1726–28, when Handel balanced his assignments between his two competing divas, Cuzzoni and Bordoni. Kirkby takes the roles written for the latter, while **Bott** sings those of the former (Hyperion). By sampling each opera mainly in groups of scenes or numbers, you get a better sense of the progression of Handel's operatic writing. Newcomers to that idiom might find these helpful introductory tools, as well as galleries of superbly apt and lovely singing and playing. It will be interesting to see if these performers extend this series further.

Another thematic departure was launched in 1986 by McGegan, in a program of "Arias for Senesino" with countertenor **Minter** (♦Harmonia Mundi 905183), followed by "Arias for Montagnana" with bass **David Thomas** (♦907016), "Arias for Cuzzoni" with soprano **Lisa Saffer** (♦907036), and "Arias for Durastanti" with soprano **Lorraine Hunt** (♦907056); the four single discs were sensibly reissued in a boxed set (29071/74, 4CD). No one claims that these singers match the voices of the greatest castrato of Handel's day, Francesco Bernardi (called Il Senesino, "the Sienese"), the leading bass, or two of the finest soprano singers, for all of whom the composer tailored so many of his roles. But the idea of examining in such a focused and systematic way the repertoires (and, hence, the vocal characteristics) of each of those past singers allowed valuable insights into the sources and agents of Handel's creative inspiration, in reliable and impressive modern realizations by fine singers fully comfortable in this literature.

Of course, singers continue to appear in CD programs of miscellaneous Handel arias designed as showcases for their individual talents. Among sopranos we have **Te Kanawa** in a nicely diversified program of vocal and orchestral excerpts from ten different operas fused into a silly pastiche called "The Sorceress" (Philips); Hogwood's Academy of Ancient Music contributes nice PI things, but Te Kanawa's singing, however lovely, isn't very idiomatic. **Swenson** is another star using this literature for display, showing off in six arias (three each from *Giulio Cesare* and *Semele*) as well as seven by Mozart (EMI). **Baird** is a more fully certified Handel veteran. She shows her artistic skills (overcoming her very thin vocal sound) in 13 arias: six from Italian operas or cantatas, seven from English oratorios. Seven of these items are taken from already-released recordings of complete works in which she has appeared, the rest are new to discs and will delight her fans (Newport).

Bayo is a less striking but very promising soprano who, with Skip Sempe leading PI accompaniments, artfully sings an Italian cantata, the Spanish cantata, and eight arias from three different Italian operas (♦Astrée 8674). Jumping back and forth between soprano and castrato roles in selections from four operas, the wonderful mezzo **Murray** is given sturdy PI support by Mackerras (♦Forlane 16738). The castrato literature is given female treatment by the rich-voiced French contralto **Stutzmann** in a fine release that draws upon six operas plus the *Aci* cantata in vividly dramatic and colorful realizations (♦RCA 61205).

In a veritable classic, the unique **Marilyn Horne** digs into four castrato arias from *Rinaldo,* plus female airs from that and another opera, plus castrato arias from three other operas, ten in all (♦Erato 45186).

Teams of female singers have also drawn upon the cross-gender realms. In a program called "Arie e Duetti d'Amore," soprano **Piau** and contralto **Banditelli** offer ten selections for soprano and/or castrato from eight operas, appealingly sung, with a trio sonata and a *Concerto á 4* (Opus 111).

The most common solution to the problem of casting Handel's (and other composers') castrato roles in recent years has been the countertenor, a singing voice that can only be a pale counterpart to the trumpeting of male-soprano eunuchs. To be sure, there have appeared lately a few male singers who reject the label of countertenor and advertize themselves as "sopranistas," singers who have trained their falsetto singing naturally (apparently without anatomical sacrifice) in the castratos' soprano range. Such is **Angelo Manzotti,** whose plummy voice is closer to what we would call mezzo-soprano in color, but whose gender will puzzle your party guests in listening tests. Backed by a PI group, he sings ten selections from five operas plus *Aci* (Bongiovanni). **Jean-Loup Charvet** is rather less attractive and not always secure; he sings one aria each from five operas, while the PI group adds some orchestral excerpts, a harpsichord transcription, and an irrelevant chamber quartet, all under the silly title "The Passions of the Soul" (Mandala).

A more familiar style of countertenor singing is offered by the reliable, firmly focused voice of veteran **Bowman** in 12 "Heroic Arias" from eight operas (♦Hyperion 66483). He faces challenges from some of the newer countertenors. One is **Scholl,** whose voice is firm and slightly feminine, and whose singing style is quite expressive. In 1988 he made a program called "Heroes" with Norrington (PI). Arias from three Italian operas and two English oratorios, plus arias by Hasse, Gluck, and Mozart (♦Decca 466196) was followed by a totally Handelian anthology of scenes and excerpts from six operas. The PI Akademie für Alte Musik Berlin is a full partner in orchestral sections, and the disc includes the complete *Alexander's Feast Concerto* (♦Harmonia Mundi 901685). Another emerging star is **David Daniels,** who shows that countertenor singing really can be lovely. His program of 12 arias from six different operas is exceptionally well-chosen and excellently sung, with admirable PI support from Norrington (♦Virgin 5 45326).

As already seen, some programs mix arias from operas and oratorios. One such is "Greatest Arias," produced by **Ostendorf,** with seven items from his complete Handel recordings of three works, and six from as many he has not recorded—involving seven singers and representing a nice survey program for its own sake as well as a sampler for the label (Vox). As for Italian and English mixes by just one star soloist, there is the calculated brilliance of **Battle,** singing nine zingers from three operas and five English works (EMI; MHS). By far the best of such mixtures is by the formidable **Terfel,** who is simply smashing in 14 arias or recitative/aria pairings from five operas and six oratorios, plus *Dettingen Te Deum*—not all of which, however, were originally for bass (♦DG 453480). Terfel is simply astonishing in his shifts of vocal color and expression to recreate the mood of each dramatic item—this is great Handel singing!

Two programs go rather beyond just assembling individual arias or scenes for the featured vocalist. Countertenor **Graham Pushee,** clear and agile of voice and knowing in style, joins Paul Dyer's PI Australian Brandenburg Orchestra in a program of representative selections, orchestral and vocal, from just three operas (*Alcina, Giulio Cesare, Rinaldo*), all quite handsomely done (ABC 8.770014). The other presents soprano **qwqa`qq`a** with Lamon's Tafelmusik in over 76 minutes drawn from only two operas, *Alcina* and *Agrippina* (♦Analekta 23137). Five arias from the one and four from the other are interlarded with

overtures and ballet numbers to convey, if not a coherent digest of the two operas, at least very substantial samplings, and solid introductions to the character of Handelian opera.

Finally, for the instrumentally inclined, programs of overtures have turned up from time to time. One from the early '70s in which **Karl Richter** led rather pompous readings of the *Sinfonie* to five operas and four oratorios has been revived (DG 457903). There is an especially fine set of curtain-raisers to eight operas conducted by the sympathetic **Leppard** (Philips 422486), and a 2LP series mixing 12 opera and seven oratorio overtures and sinfonies assembled by **Bonynge** (Decca 466434, so far reissued only in Australia, with other 18th-century overtures). Seven items from various dramatic scores were recorded by **Pinnock** (PI); only those for the English works have reappeared (DG 419219, with *RFM* and *AF*).

A more recent PI venture is a generous grouping of overtures from four operas and three oratorios by the Baroque Orchestra of Montreal under Joël Thiffault (Atma 2157). The music is wonderful and some of the solo work is splendid, but the ensemble is marred by brusqueness and the kind of mannerisms that the PI approach is supposed to have outgrown by now. Still in the PI department, **Sillito** led the ASMF in an elegant collection of overtures to five operas and one oratorio (Capriccio). (A program of overtures and other pieces by Mackerras is also noted above under "Orchestral Music.")

For a while, also, there was a very attractive program of ballet music (from *Alcina* and *Il pastor fido/Terpsichore*) by **Gardiner** that's worth seeking out (Erato). That, in fact, replaced an also lovely early **Marriner** program of ballet music (*Alcina, Il pastor fido, Ariodante*), an LP whose contents seem to have been denied full CD reissue and is greatly missed (Argo). Two more recent recordings have added some new slants. One is a serious effort by **Peter Holman** and his Parley of Instruments to recover orchestral and ballet music from five operas that the composer wrote in his earliest period, in Hamburg, both certain of survival (*Almira, Rodrigo*) and uncertain (*Nero, Florindo, Daphne*), with an early oboe concerto tossed in for good measure (♦Hyperion 67053).

The other, "Handel at the Opera," might more fittingly be labeled "Handel's Greatest Opera Hits Without Voice or Vibrato," or "Handel Without Hooting and Scraping." **Standage** leads his PI Collegium Musicum 90 in a program of excerpts from seven operas—not only the predictable overtures and dance movements, but five particularly familiar arias in which the vocal line is taken (even with apt embellishments) by a solo violin or oboe. It's elegantly played, to be sure, and if you just want a bath in authentic Handelian Muzak, this is for you. At least it's still a far cry from **Beecham**'s deliciously irresponsible old pastiche-arrangements, such as his Elgarian "Love in Bath" pseudo-ballet (EMI).

As for recordings of complete operas, out of Handel's total of 39 surviving, no less than 34 have made it in more or less full versions, some a number of times over. Still awaiting treatment at this writing are *Arianna in Creta, Arminio, Deidamia, Lotario*), and *Silla*. This is not considering pasticcio confections Handel hastily assembled from bits and pieces of his other music: *Alessandro Severo, Giove in Argo,* and *Oreste*. For those available on discs, the following discussion will consider them in alphabetical order, with first production date in parentheses. My discussion will be brief in cases where only one recording has been made, since your choice is either that or nothing.

Admeto, Rè di Tessaglia (1727). This is the story of the wifely devotion of the Thessalian queen Alcestis, going back to Euripides via intermediary adaptations. Its one recording, by early-music expert **Alan Curtis,**

has happily been reissued (1979: ♦Virgin 61369, 3CD). This was a pioneering venture in recording Handel opera with period instruments and with countertenors taking castrato roles. The cast is excellent, and it's a landmark in Handel opera recording.

Agrippina (1709). This opera takes a flippant look at court shenanigans under Roman emperor Claudius, reintroducing us to some of the characters from the next and nastier reign of Nero, which we have already met in Monteverdi's *L'incoronazione di Poppea*. Reckoned as the sixth opera Handel composed, it's his third to survive his first stage masterpiece, with skillfully etched characters and amusingly exploited situations. Two quite good recordings have been made by two leading PI conductors, **McGegan** (♦Harmonia Mundi 907063/65, 3CD) and **Gardiner** (♦Philips 438009, 3CD).

Both conductors have made not-always-wise decisions on reassigning castrato roles. Thus, countertenor Ragin's punkish Nero for Gardiner opposes McGegan's rather girlish soprano, Wendy Hill; Gardiner's Chance makes a slightly stronger countertenor presence as Ottone than does McGegan's Minter. Gardiner takes the prize for luxury casting by tossing in no less than von Otter for the three minutes worth of Juno. On vocal and purely musical grounds, Gardiner seems to be the logical choice. But McGegan's version resulted from a staged production—his first at the Göttingen Festival, and his first use there of the Freiburg Baroque Orchestra—and that charges the recitatives with crackling vividness and allows a genuine sense of theater, against Gardiner's concert-reading spirit. Neither recording can be disregarded.

Alcina (1735). This is the third opera with a libretto based on material in Ariosto's great Renaissance epic, *Orlando furioso* that together have become known as the "Ariosto Trilogy," though they were never meant to be an organic entity. As with the preceding *Ariodante,* Handel exploited the availability of Mlle. Sallé's French dance troupe to include extensive and highly evocative ballet sections in *Alcina,* which also makes good use of the chorus and contains solo numbers of exceptional pathos and beauty.

Much of this opera's recording history has been identified with the career of Sutherland, with whose rise to stardom it was intimately involved. Her earliest experiment with the title role of the amorous sorceress, in a 1959 Cologne Radio production with an early PI group under **Leitner,** has been circulated variously, presently in sets from Melodram and Verona. Another historic release documents the Zeffirelli production at Venice's La Fenice in 1960 with **Rescigno** conducting—the triumph that, together with her Covent Garden *Lucia* the previous year, established her as a true superstar (Bella Voce).

With her husband **Bonynge** signing on as conductor, Sutherland moved quickly to capitalize on her success with a commercial recording (1961: Decca 433723, 3CD, with *Giulio Cesare* excerpts). By then, she had entered a phase of mannered, sonically lovely but blurry singing, with her special lower Slobovian diction, that made her as much the problem as the prize of this recording. However, she was given an unusually strong team of colleagues: Berganza in Carestini's castrato role of Ruggiero; Monica Sinclair as the latter's true love, Bradamonte; Sciutti as the sorceress's sister, Morgana; Alva as her beloved Oronte; Flagello as the resident wise man Melisso; plus the luxury casting of Freni in the minor role of Oberto (originally for boy soprano). Bonynge's conducting is crisp and dramatic, in an edition that restores some of the music so brutally hacked out in the Zeffirelli production, but it's still heavily cut and trimmed to accommodate the star focus on Sutherland and takes many textual liberties.

That London recording has become so much of a classic that it unfortunately overshadowed a subsequent and far more responsible version. Made in 1985 in conjunction with a staged production, it appeared first as a 4LP set, then in one of EMI's transitory CD reissues (♦49771, 3CD). Using the complete score (with two appended numbers Handel himself had cut), **Hickox** leads a beautifully molded and well-integrated performance, with quite mellow PI playing and an extraordinarily refined and consistent cast. In the title role, the superb and much-lamented Augér is less flamboyantly narcissistic than Sutherland, and more beautifully expressive; he is backed by an equally outstanding Della Jones in the castrato part of Ruggiero and splendidly stylistic and artistic singing from the rest of the crew.

A bold new challenge has appeared in **Christie**'s recording (♦Erato 80233, 3CD), taped in June 1999 at performances during Robert Carsen's sensational—but dramatically perverted—production in Paris (which traveled to Chicago thereafter, minus Christie and a few cast changes). While Carsen's distortions still poison his notes and synopsis and are represented in booklet photos, the recording allows us to detach from them a truly remarkable performance. Fleming out-divas Sutherland in the title role, her singing rich and full-blooded, and her dramatic instincts sometimes generating almost unbearably powerful emotion—a portrayal of riveting power. For all that, Dessay as Morgana almost steals the show with her vocal agility and theatrical flair. The remaining leads (Susan Graham, Kathleen Kuhlmann, Timothy Robinson) are also vocally splendid and dramatically effective, while Christie gives snappy leadership. This recording eliminates almost all the ballet music, but its vivid feeling of theatrical presence will guarantee its attractions. Bonynge/London will always have its appeal to Sutherland fans; but in the end, the Hickox/EMI set does the most balanced justice to this great opera.

Alessandro (1726). This is one of two operas in which Alexander the Great is the central protagonist in complicated romantic entanglements—not a very flattering portrait here. The opera's two recordings represent the performing-approach paradigm in reverse. **Kuijken**'s 1979 recording is a model of PI treatment (♦Harmonia Mundi 77110, 3CD): Jacobs, at his artistic peak as a virtuoso countertenor, is brilliant in the title role; the spare-voiced Poulenard is sometimes grating as one of the two ladies after him; the rest of the cast are of high quality. It only lacks a little more sense of theatrical drama. On the other hand, a concert performance recorded in Warsaw in 1988 under **Mieczyslaw Nowakowski** seems a throwback to discredited esthetics: a turgid modern orchestra, a conductor and cast (seemingly mostly American) who display little stylistic sense, and even less artistry. It may have been a valiant effort in its time and place, but it's hardly competitive, and I wonder why the Berlin producers bothered with its issue (Studios Classique).

Almira (1705). This was Handel's earliest opera, dating from his youthful days in Hamburg, and it's clearly an apprentice work. The story is set in medieval Castile, and the libretto follows the curious local custom of having many of the arias in Italian with the rest of the libretto in German. The tangled text resulted in an uneven score, but a surprisingly competent one that already sounds like the Handel to come. In the only recording, the cast is lively and able, but ultimate credit belongs to Baroque harp virtuoso **Andrew Lawrence-King,** who took leadership of the Fiorina Musicali ensemble for this venture, and marshals their wonderful PI colors with particular skill (1994: ♦CPO 999275, 3CD). Not the recording for a Handel-opera novice perhaps, but one a devotee shouldn't miss.

Amadigi di Gaula (*1715*). This was one of the last theatrical gasps of chivalric doings that go back to a late-Medieval romance. It's the usual story of amorous tangles, studded with recurrently attractive music. Its only recording was **Minkowski**'s first Handel-opera venture, using his sometimes gruff PI ensemble, Les Musiciens du Louvre, with a very able cast dominated by the powerfully dramatic Stutzmann (1989: ♦Erato 45490, 2CD).

Ariodante (*1735*). This is the second of the Ariosto Trilogy operas, its plot based on material in the poet's *Orlando furioso* transferred to an imaginary Scotland. The score is strikingly rich, not only in dramatic solos, but in its unusual use of chorus and the addition of ballet episodes at the end of each act.

Its first recording was made in Vienna in 1971 under **Stephen Simon,** a valiant and enterprising Handel champion, but a less than distinguished conductor (RCA). It was heavily cut, but included some excellent singing. Since then, the opera has had three superb and fully complete recordings: two of PI type, under **McGegan** as a byproduct of his 1995 Göttingen Festival production (♦Harmonia Mundi 907146/48, 3CD), and under **Minkowski,** recorded in concert in 1997 (♦DG Archiv 457271, 3CD). As an intermediary step between them and Simon, **Leppard** recorded it in 1979 with an MI orchestra and a stellar cast of singers in a set that happily has been reissued (♦Philips 442096; MHS 534426, 3CD).

The three casts are, in fact, tightly competitive. For castrato Carestini's title role, all three use a mezzo-soprano. Leppard has Baker, magnificent in her dramatic expressiveness. McGegan's Hunt is surprisingly close to Baker in vocal sound, and her projection of the music is a joy to hear. Minkowski has the intense von Otter, whose virtuosic range of moods is stunning, in the trousers role (originally for contralto) of the villainous Polinesso. Leppard strangely miscalculates with countertenor Bowman, a fine singer, but simply too weak in this part. McGegan's Jennifer Lane offers a richer voice and a weightier characterization, while Minkowski's Podles uses her dark contralto in a compelling portrayal of melodramatic evil. The two soprano roles—one a mature, deeply feeling woman (Ginevra) against a younger, more impulsive, and cruelly victimized one (Dalinda)—require both vocal and dramatic distinction. Leppard's Mathis and Burrowes sing gorgeously, but are not clearly differentiated vocally or dramatically. McGegan's Gondek and Saffer make the distinction aptly and tellingly, as do Minkowski's Lynne Dawson and Verónica Cangemi, who also sing with greater vocal sheen. Of the lesser characters, neither McGegan's wooden Rè di Scozia nor Minkowski's routine Denis Sedov can come near the young Ramey, whose rich voice gives the character real presence in Leppard's cast.

These comparisons reveal competitive values that balance out pretty well for the singers. Leppard's recording is marked by his flowing, spacious, but probing leadership and will appeal to those who dislike period instruments for its compromise approach and frankly modern operatic singing. Between the other two, McGegan is more crisp and springy in his pacing, finding space to add a group of five variant numbers to Act II—a unique asset. Minkowski is sometimes rough and aggressive, but propulsive and lively in his way too. The former's Freiburg Baroque Orchestra and the latter's Les Musiciens du Louvre are quite rich in period color, especially in the ballet episodes. McGegan's cast, refined by the experience of staged production, is just a tad more of a dramatic ensemble, if that's a key factor. But, obviously, we're faced with a joyously vexing embarrassment of riches in these three recordings, and I'd go to the gallows mute before I would make a definitive choice among them.

Atalanta (*1736*). This is a light and totally artificial pastorale of romantic tests and loyalty triumphs, meant to cultivate the favor of the newly married Prince of Wales. Not a profound or great work, it's nevertheless filled with delightful music. Its one recording (complete, and with an added scene variant), was made in 1985 as part of **McGegan**'s early work in Budapest (♦Hungaroton 12612/14, 3CD). He has the crack Cappella Savaria PI ensemble and a fine cast of experienced local singers. A minor jewel in Handel's crown, but a bright one.

Berenice (*1737*). This opera draws freely upon a terribly tangled piece of the Hellenistic history of Ptolomaic Egypt and makes a typically tangled Baroque plot out of it. Handel was on the last great plateau of his operatic output and, as always, he achieved some wonderfully lovely music in this late score—even though he was struggling with a rival company, his London audience was slipping away from him, and a stroke prostrated him just after he finished the opera. Though its overture has long been a concert favorite, the full opera has been ignored and was recorded only in 1994 as part of singer-turned-producer Ostendorf's dedicated program of bringing Handel's neglected operas to discs (♦Newport 85620, 3CD). **Palmer** gives brisk leadership, with a tidy PI band and a generally fine cast of singers, which by that time had become a working recording team. A highly commendable recording that the serious Handel collector can't afford to overlook.

Ezio (*1732*). This was the last time Handel used a libretto by Metastasio. The latter is thus responsible for making this Baroque mush out of the historical career of the Roman general Aëtius at the 5th-century court of Emperor Valentinian III, a commander most famous for defeating Attila the Hun in 451, familiar to Verdi-lovers from the latter's *Attila*. Of the opera's two recordings, the first (1993) was from a staged performance in Berlin conducted by **Brynmor Llewelyn Jones** (Deutsche Schallplatten 1051, 2CD). Only countertenor Christopher Robson's name might be recognized, but the local singers in the rest of the cast are consistently able. The problem is that the performance is in German translation, seriously damaging its general value. The other recording followed the next year in Ostendorf's series (Vox, 2CD). Unlike Jones, he played fast and loose with Handel's vocal casting. The PI playing under **Richard Aulden Clark** is pungent. Following Handel's own practice, intermissions are filled by two of the composer's organ concertos (Op. 4:2 and 4), with Somary—usually a conductor, but here as soloist—in a recording ambience noticeably different from that of the opera itself.

Faramondo (*1738*). This opera adapts a Venetian libretto placed in a semi-imaginary world of Frankish and Cimbrian Germans adrift in the second century BC. It was set by Handel under the most trying circumstances, following a terrible stroke and convalescence, and then the loss of his beloved patroness queen Caroline, while the public's desire for his Italian operas was fading. Though his resources forced scoring economies, he had a good team of mostly new singers who evoked a musically handsome score. Ostendorf and his working ensemble brought us a first recording that still stands alone (♦Vox 7536, 3CD). Made in 1996, it follows familiar patterns, with a particularly jumbled response to Handel's original casting. Whatever the details, the singing is very fine, and the weak element is the rather scrawny, lackluster, and apparently under-rehearsed PI orchestra with which conductor **Palmer** can only do so much. But he risks even more by scattering the movements of *Concerto Grosso* Op. 6:4 through the intermissions as Handel might have done—music now too familiar in high-quality recordings to be acceptable when done this weakly.

Flavio, Rè di Longobardi (*1723*). This opera belongs to Handel's first phase of really great operatic writing. Its plot is an even more than usually silly piece of pseudo-Medieval nonsense, and Winton Dean has suggested that Handel may have used it, and its situations, to make some fun of *opera seria* conventions even as he followed them (mixing serious with satirical in ways that may have confused the audience of his day). The fact that the score is actually full of consistently lovely and imaginative music has been demonstrated by its only recording, from a staged production in Innsbruck in 1989 (♦Harmonia Mundi 901312/13, 2CD). With great energy and style, **Jacobs** leads Ensemble 415, which makes its own flavorful contributions in the purely orchestral sections. An excellent international cast is superlative in artistry and conviction, and notable for the dramatic fervor with which it tears into the recitatives. If not the Handel opera to start with, it's splendidly realized.

Floridante (*1721*). This opera has another of those ridiculous plots set in pseudo-antiquity, but the situations and characters are the point, as always, and Handel makes skillful and appealing musical use of them. The virtually complete first recording resulted from a concert performance at the 1990 Göttingen Festival under **McGegan** (Hungaroton). Using countertenor Minter in Senesino's castrato title role, and fine, mostly Hungarian singers, McGegan offered a reasonable account (slightly cut). There subsequently appeared a single disc of excerpts, which, in fact, constitute almost half the full version, giving a fair sense of what's in the score (♦CBC 5110). With the disappearance of McGegan's full set, this CBC release is a valid stopgap, and even a worthwhile supplement, especially since its singers are slightly more satisfying vocally. The PI Tafelmusik Baroque Orchestra plays more smoothly than its Hungaroton counterpart, the Capella Savaria, and Baroque expert **Alan Curtis** draws much more rousing and pointed playing from his players than McGegan does from his.

Giulio Cesare in Egitto (*1724*). One of the first Handel operas revived in this century, this opera has become by far the most recorded. Indeed, its recording history meshes revealingly with landmarks in its modern staging history. And along the way, it illustrates the transition from casual attitudes about casting and carving up the score for present-day consumption to a more scrupulous quest for authenticity.

The first two LP recordings, both from 1952, presented heavily abbreviated scores and adjusted gender-casting: one done mostly by Swiss singers under **Goehr** (Concert Hall/Handel Society), and the other by mostly Viennese singers under **Swarowsky** (Vox). At the same time, staged productions could draw star singers, as in a series of theater performances preserved in historic recordings. A 1955 performance at La Scala was led by **Gavazzeni**, with Christoff (hopelessly miscast as Cesare), Barbieri, and Corelli among the floundering cast. A little better is a 1965 Bavarian Radio transcription under **Leitner,** with Berry, Popp, Ludwig, and Wunderlich, currently on CD from no less than three labels (Orfeo, Verona, Melodram). Finally, there is a 1971 production at Venice's La Fenice, with Christoff again, and **Rescigno** conducting (Mondo Musica). In all of these, the score was heavily cut, castrato roles arbitrarily reassigned, and any idiomatic sensibilities sacrificed to celebrity casting.

A transition was evident by the late '60s. RCA's 1967 recording documented the New York City Opera's production led by **Rudel,** designed to showcase Treigle's portrayal of Cesare as an aging roué, but serving to catapult Sills to stardom. Dramatic values were still the priority, but despite heavy cutting and gender adjusting, Baroque style was respected in scoring (if with romanticized feeling) and in selective embellish-

ments. Then DG issued its 1969 Munich recording, which may well resurface some day on CD. This set presented the uncut score in full for the first time, though still with adjusted gender casting: it's still stellar, though, with Fischer-Dieskau (at his fussiest as Cesare), Troyanos, Hamari, Schreier, and Franz Crass, but all weighed down by **Richter**'s stately, dull conducting. Elements of those two versions came together in a 1968 production at the Teatro Colón in Buenos Aires, where Sills, Treigle, and Maureen Forrester joined Schreier and Crass, again under **Richter.** Excerpts from a tape of that production have appeared recently, in unfortunately poor sound but offering an interesting juncture of styles (VAIA 1184). More style, if less quantity, was offered by **Bonynge**'s program of selected arias, featuring Sutherland, Horne, Margreta Elkins, and Monica Sinclair—material now available as part of London's *Alcina* reissue.

In 1985 **Mackerras** recorded an English National Opera production in a reasonably responsible performing edition (EMI; now ♦Chandos 3019, 3CD). Here the first efforts were made to match Handel's castrato assignments, with Tolomeo sung by countertenor Bowman and Cesare by Baker, other outstanding singers including Valerie Masterson, Sarah Walker, and Della Jones. Most striking of all, the production was given in English translation—still the only such presentation of Handel's Italian operas in commercial recordings. This old curiosity may not be pure Handel, but it's something special and treasurable.

The drive for authenticity is illustrated in four recordings. All seriously address the problem of castrato roles (Cesare, Tolomeo), and all but one use period instruments. A 1989 production under **Marcello Panni** is vigorous and intelligent, with little-known singers ranging from adequate to excellent (Nuova Era). A recording made at the 1991 Festival de Beaune is also based on a staged production, presenting the most complete score (plus appendices) in the most authentic style (♦Harmonia Mundi's 90385/87, 3CD + 1 free). Early-music specialist **Jacobs** conducts with sensitive nuances and genuine fluidity. Schlick is a somewhat cool Cleopatra, but Larmore is an admirable Cesare, and Fink and Marianne Rorholm strike powerful mother-son sparks, while Ragin is a bizarrely fierce Tolomeo and Visse makes a specialty of Nireno.

Malgoire's 1995 recording came as this erratic conductor's best Handel opera work to date. The score is slightly cut and the tone is more mellow and lyric than theatrical (Astrée). Bowman, as the first countertenor Cesare, is somewhat pallid and hooty, though Dawson is a vibrant Cleopatra. the other players provide support that is stylish but a bit less forceful in dramatic terms. While you can admire and enjoy much in this recording, priority must still go to Jacobs.

Peter Mark, director of the Virginia Opera, takes us back to the realm of Rudel's version. In 1997, he mounted a production in which he cut the score more drastically than Rudel, losing a good 100 minutes (Koch). He assigns to countertenors not only the two castrato roles, but also the contralto role of Sesto. A nice souvenir if you saw the production, and perhaps a *Cesare* Lite for the timid seeker after a shortcut introduction to the work; but if it's a viable stripped-down *Cesare* you want, you're better served by the durable Sills/Treigle/Rudel version, even after 30 years.

Giustino (*1737*). This opera makes an utterly wild fantasy out of the rather dull life story of the Byzantine Emperor Justin I (518–527), nephew and predecessor of the great Justinian. Long overlooked, the score is full of fine musical moments and dramatic situations. The only recording derives from **McGegan**'s 1994 Göttingen Festival production (Harmonia Mundi). The cast includes Chance, soprano Dawn Kotoski (who is simply splendid), and Minter, who at least makes a plausible troublemaker. The period playing of the Freiburg Baroque Orchestra is rather strident, but the production-shaped instincts of the cast give the recitative sections believable dramatic punch, even with little sense of stage action. Not a great recording of a great Handel opera, but a quite satisfying lesser one, not likely to be replaced for some time.

Imeneo (*1740*). This opera purportedly deals with love-triangles and pirates in some kind of Greek antiquity. Originally billed as an operetta for its London production, it was trimmed down as a serenata for a Dublin presentation two years later under the title of *Hymen.* This is Handel's penultimate Italian opera, eked out as the idiom was almost without a public. Such was its failure that he pillaged it for recyclings, including items you will recognize from *Messiah.*

Its early representation on records is a broadcast transcription of a 1960 performance led by **Horst-Tanu Margraf** at the Halle Handel Festival, a strangely abridged torso (cut down by about half), with voice-casting arbitrarily muddled, the action transferred to Venice at Carnival time, and the text translated into German. There is little need for this resurrected relic (Berlin). Fortunately, Ostendorf gave us a more responsible recording (Vox). With only one castrato and a trousers mezzo in his reduced company, and only five characters in all, casting is quite simple. Ostendorf himself, happily still singing then, is wonderful as the humorously blustering title character, almost an anti-hero. The expressive Fortunato takes the trousers part of the hapless Tirinto convincingly, and two light sopranos, Baird and Hoch, are sisters caught in a silly love quadrangle. Opalach is fine as the pompous windbag Argenio. The performing edition makes a conscientious collation of the 1740 original version with new material from its 1742 transformation, and a small PI group is led even-handedly by **Palmer.** A curiosity, but an interesting one for the serious Handel collector.

Muzio Scevola (*1721*). This was a multi-composer curiosity meant to capture public attention by the dueling reputations of Handel and Giovanni Bononcini, rivals on the London opera scene. A recycled libretto—a dumb conflation of stories from Livy on early Roman history—had three acts, so a local musician, Filippo Amadei (or Mattei) was hired to do a hack job on Act I, and the remaining two were given to Bononcini and Handel. (The latter's contribution won hands down in public opinion.)

The only recording is an Ostendorf production, which gives Handel's complete Act III, prefaced by the Overture and three arias from Bononcini's Act II, augmented by two arias from an earlier opera by the latter to a different libretto with the same title (Newport). I wish for more of Bononcini (and even some of Amadei/Mattei), if only for background, but there's no denying the quality of Handel's music (so good that he pillaged some of it for use in later works). **Palmer**'s squarish and flat pacing is more of a handicap than a help to the singing, and the PI playing is quite raw, in rather stifling sound. Still, the cast is excellent and enjoyable to hear, and this is our only access to a novel episode in Handel's operatic career.

Orlando (*1733*). This was the first of the so-called Ariosto Trilogy, the three operas whose librettos derive from *Orlando furioso,* and in some ways the most innovative. The combination of text and available singers called forth such original features as the magisterial character of Zoroastro, conceived for the bass Montagnana and sometimes viewed as anticipating Mozart's Sarastro; and, for castrato Senesino, Orlando's mad scene, the granddaddy of many such operatic displays to come. (Senesino, by the way, disliked it for its unconventionality and never

created another Handel role.) The score is filled with one ravishing number after another.

The first recording was a 3LP set made in 1970, one of those enterprising but hasty Vienna jobs done under the uninspiring **Simon.** His version was seriously cut, but had an impressive lineup of singers (RCA). A 1985 staged performance at Venice's La Fenice was taped with **Mackerras** conducting (Mondo Musica 10502, 3CD). Since then, the opera has received two complete recordings in the PI category: by **Hogwood,** with mostly familiar English early-music singers (◆Oiseau-Lyre 430845, 3CD), and by **Christie,** with a cast of mostly young and less well-known singers (◆Erato 14636, 3 CD). The key casting point, of course, is how to deal with the castrato leading role. Mackerras has Marilyn Horne to barrel and bluster through the title role, working up a stormy mad scene. Hogwood uses the distinguished countertenor Bowman, a refined artist who gives almost too sensitive a characterization. Christie uses a mezzo, Patricia Bardon, who offers a stronger vocal tone and a more manly characterization. In musical terms though, I wish Bardon's assignment had been given to a contralto with a more graceful and appealing vocal personality and stronger voice, but she outdoes even Hogwood's veteran Catherine Robbin as Medoro—a role written for the *travesti* contralto Francesca Bertolli, rather capriciously given by Mackerras to the vocally uneven countertenor Jeffrey Gall.

Of the two ladies, Angelica requires a soprano of mature femininity and gets it superbly in Hogwood's radiant Augér. Nevertheless, Christie's handsome-voiced Rosemary Joshua at least matches her with a cleanly-focused tone and greater ardor. Dorinda calls for a lighter but virtuosic touch, if with thoughtful qualities, and all that is beautifully done by Rosa Mannion, a standout in Christie's cast; she gives Hogwood's predictably perky Kirkby a real run for the money. Mackerras's Cuberli and Adelina Scarabelli have the least vocal merit but are dramatically lively. Christie's one weak link is bass van der Kamp, whose lightweight Zoroastro pales against the greater heft and character of Hogwood's David Thomas, while Giorgio Surjan creates a well-rounded portrayal somewhere between them in strength. Christie's singers, too, generally outshine the other two casts in their vocal embellishments.

Mackerras leads a propulsive and intense performance appropriate to its on-stage origins, but his recording will inevitably be of prime interest to Horne admirers, leaving the other two as the true contenders. Both are good recordings, each worthy of recommendation. But while Hogwood is fine, with nice instrumental colors, it has an overall evenness that becomes almost blandly consistent. Christie's leadership is not only smoother, but has more lilt and flow, more flexibility and inflection. This proves to convey more depth and power in a more fully integrated dramatic conception of the work that reflects its honing in staged performances at the Aix-en-Provence Festival. You won't go wrong with Hogwood, but you'll do a little better with Christie.

Ottone, Rè di Germania (*1723*). This fancifully treats the historical event of Byzantine princess Theophano's marriage to the future German Emperor Otto II. It lay neglected for 170 years until, almost simultaneously, two separate ventures brought it to discs: **McGegan**'s production for the 1992 Göttingen Festival (◆Harmonia Mundi 907073/75, 3CD), followed in 1993 by **Robert King**'s recording, also based on a staged production (◆Hyperion 66751/53).

Here we face a deliciously difficult choice. McGegan's recording is one of the best of his Handel series, slightly fuller in his conflations of Handel's revisions than King. On the other hand, McGegan can be fussy and occasionally rigid, with aggressive period sound from the Freiburg

Baroque Orchestra. King, though less sharply detailed, offers smoother orchestral playing, shaping lines more musically, allowing the music to breathe, and allowing his singers greater expressive play. The casts are each fine and evenly balanced. McGegan's two female leads, Saffer and Gondek, have a dramatic edge over their (still excellent) counterparts, Claron McFadden and Jennifer Smith, while his Patricia Spence is musically more compelling than King's Denley. But King has the advantage with his male singers: countertenors Bowman and Visse create more forceful characters than McGegan's Minter and Popken, though Michael George for the former and Michael Dean for the latter are roughly comparable. In sum, no definitive choice can be made between these two sets, each of which can be recommended.

Partenope (*1730*). This opera derives distantly from myths about one of Odysseus's amours along his journeys, a lady who was supposedly the foundress and queen of Neapolis, or Naples—which actually derives from a Cumaean settlement at the present site first called Parthenope. Never mind, for the names and titles in this Baroque plot of criss-crossing love tangles have little to do with any actual time, place, or people. But it is, in the abstract, a lively amorous comedy and it's perhaps that fact, rather than any distinction of the score itself, that has made it a singularly recurrent work in recent stagings. Its one recording is a prime example of the authenticity approach, the first ventured by **Kuijken**, with the virtuosic countertenor Jacobs in the difficult role of Arsace. Krisztina Laki is sparkling in the soprano title part; the other singers are excellent, backed by Kuijken's flowing and able conducting and his Petite Bande's bracing period playing (1979: Deutsche Harmonia Mundi).

Il pastor fido (*1712/34*) and *Terpsichore* (*1734*). These are really the same work, with a recording history as complicated as the score's evolution. Handel revised the work for two revivals in 1734—in which he expanded it with a fancy, French-style ballet-prologue carrying the latter title and involving a number of self-borrowings. There were two terribly mangled and abridged recordings of the opera in LP years, under **Lehman Engel** (Columbia, 1953) and **Ennio Gerelli** (Cetra, 1958), and its ballet music has been raided frequently in recorded samplings. Thus is **Lamon** (Sony), not to mention **Beecham**'s, old, totally phony, but wonderfully delicious "Pastor Fido Suite" for modern orchestra.

Eventually **McGegan** came to the rescue, in two phases. As the first of his Göttingen Festival projects, he prepared a careful, responsible, and only slightly fussy PI performance of the third (1734b) version of the opera itself, with a cast that mixed Esswood with some fine Hungarian singers (♦Hungaroton 12912/13, 2CD). He followed this with a single disc that offered the *Terpsichore* prologue as a separate work augmented by ballet music from *Alcina* and *Ariodante* (Hungaroton). Alas, both of these releases appear to be discontinued just now, but this dramatically empty-headed, yet musically charming pastorale-opera should not be unavailable.

Poro, Rè dell'Indie (*1731*). This is the second of Handel's operas using a libretto derived from Metastasio, and also his second featuring Alexander the Great as a protagonist, here as a paragon of magnanimity. Handel's score is a good one, though not one of his greatest; it's also one of three in which a leading role (Alessandro) was given to a tenor. The earlier of its two recorded performances derives from a 1958 Halle Festival performance, and predictably, it's sung in German translation (Berlin, 3CD). Aside from a rather good soprano (Philine Fischer), the cast is dramatically adequate but vocally undistinguished and strongly Germanic, while the conducting of **Horst-Tanu Margraf** is heavy-handed and the sound dull.

A more idiomatic alternative is the 1994 recording led by **Fabio Biondi.** His treatment of vocal casting complicates rather than replicates the composer's own vocal typing (Opus 111). Fortunately, the singing is excellent. By strictly following the original 1731 score, however, Biondi denies us three fine arias that Handel added in the 1732 revival for the great bass Montagnana. The recording was made at a concert performance and is seriously lacking in dramatic spirit, but the PI playing of Europa Galante is aptly colorful, the direction is lively, and the recorded sound exceptionally clear.

Radamisto (*1720*). This opera initiated the first of the two great plateaus of Handel's operatic output. Its typically tangled Baroque plot places us in ancient Armenia and the Caucasus (don't ask!) and prompts a score full of lovely moments and striking effects—the famous arias "Cara sposa" and "Ombra cara" being only two of them. A 1962 performance deriving from a Halle Festival production is belatedly available, done, of course, in German translation, and using a wildly free adaptation of Handel's original version of the score (Berlin). While there is some good singing, **Margraf**'s typically foursquare conducting is no help, in a recording essentially of documentary interest.

A more fully realized version comes from the production prepared by **McGegan** for Göttingen in 1993 (Harmonia Mundi). For this he used the heavily revised score Handel made for his first revival in 1720, eight months after its highly acclaimed premiere. Dealing with shifting rosters of his day's world-class singers, Handel kept changing his vocal casting, and McGegan's choices of counterparts are not always ideal, though the singers are excellent. The weak element is McGegan himself. His straightforward continuo harpsichord playing is good support for the drama of the recitatives, but his flat, bland, inflexible conducting does little to shape the orchestral accompaniments, and his ensemble—this time the Freiburg Baroque Orchestra—is uncompromising in PI sound. Still, until something better comes along, and at least favored by fine singing, this is a must for Handel collectors.

Riccardo Primo, Rè d'Inghilterra (*1727*). This shows us a Richard the Lion-Hearted we don't find in the movies. The starting point is the bare fact that Richard I of England was, while on his way to the Third Crusade, blown ashore on the island of Cyprus. He proceeded to seize Cyprus from the Byzantine usurper, Isaac Komnenos, and where he then married Berengeria of Navarre. Out of no more than that, opera librettists constructed a typical Baroque plot of love tangles and intrigue.

Its first recording was an obscure release of a Göttingen Festival performance under **Günther Weissenborn,** involving Rothraud Hansmann and Esswood in the cast, sung in German, and issued on a Brazilian label. Its only successor and only serious recording was not made until 1996, under **Christophe Rousset** (♦Oiseau-Lyre 452201, 3CD). Rousset and his singers create a well-shaped performance with skill and style, using the PI sounds of his Les Talens Lyriques to particularly pungent effect. The fact that this recording was made at Fontevrault Abbey in France, where the real King Richard was buried, may or may not add a seal of approval, but it's clearly a major contribution to the grand line of authenticity-motivated recordings.

Rinaldo (*1711*). Handel's first Italian opera for London, this was also his first smash hit and was revived many times thereafter. It was one of many operatic treatments of a favorite dramatic episode—involving conflicts of love and duty—drawn from Tasso's epic *Gerusalemme liberata*. **Malgoire**'s 1977 PI version was its first full-length recording, with a strong cast including Cotrubas, Watkinson, and Esswood (♦Sony 34592, 3CD).

Horne's interest in the castrato title role involved her in staged productions that made their way onto records. A 1975 version by **Lawrence Foster** circulated via an LP collector's label, and a 1989 performance at Venice's La Fenice, with **John Fisher** conducting, came out commercially (Nuova Era). (In between, in 1982, Horne made an aria program for Erato that was dominated by four items from this opera.) Heavily cut and laced with on-stage noises, the 1989 performance has a taut theatricality, catching Horne's intense, gutsy, and uniquely personal singing in dramatic context, even if the rest of the cast is hardly up to her standards. **Malgoire**'s reading, with a peppiness undaunted by studio conditions, gives us balanced and consistent access to the full score. The picture is about to be altered drastically, I expect, by the impending appearance of Hogwood's recording with Fink, Bartoli, and David Daniels heading the cast (Oiseau-Lyre).

Rodelinda, Regina de' Longobardi (1725). This opera brings us back again to the medieval Italian Lombard Kingdom. It's a story of deep conjugal devotion tested by suffering, in the same category as Gluck's *Orfeo* and *Alceste* and Beethoven's *Fidelio*. Popular with Handel's audiences, it has (like *Giulio Cesare*) another of those recording histories that exemplify the evolution of performance approaches to Handel's operas.

An abridgement (little more than highlights) constituted a 1953 LP from Stuttgart (Period). A Sadlers Wells production in 1959, in English translation conducted by **Charles Farncombe,** was briefly represented (in paleolithic sound) in a collector's LP set and has been reissued. It's of interest for its prestigious cast, which included Sutherland and Baker (Memories). **Brian Priestman** made the first full-length recording in 1964, and his cast—Stich-Randall, Forrester, Young, and Watts among them—revealed a generation of singers who could balance vocal beauty with stylistic sensitivity (Westminster). That's a recording worthy of revival.

It was Sutherland, together with husband **Bonynge,** who pursued a more free-wheeling and modernizing commitment to this opera. Their clear focus on her talents and person can be traced through two stages. Their 1973 Holland Festival production has been issued (Bella Voce). By the time they made their commercial recording in 1985, Sutherland was already seriously aging, and her mannered attempts to disguise that fact only highlight the ruin of a previously impressive portrayal (London). Ramey steals the show as the villainous Garibaldo, chewing up the scenery in his recitatives and making the most of the one aria left him.

Bonynge's approach involved star values, a good-sized orchestra, and a score heavily trimmed down for modern operatic tastes. The authenticity movement finally caught up with this opera in two recordings of the '90s, under **Michael Schneider** (Harmonia Mundi) and **Nicholas Kraemer** (♦Virgin 45277, 3CD). Both use period instruments; Schneider's playing is rather harsh and very dryly recorded, while Kraemer is a bit smoother and in more gratifying sound. Each follows essentially the original 1725 version, with some later additions (Schneider giving one item more than Kraemer). Their differences are not great, but the latter has slightly more dramatic sense, while his pace is often more flowing. With the apparent disappearance of both the Bonynge and Schneider recordings, Kraemer gives reliable value for now.

Rodrigo (1707). Aamong Handel's earliest operas, this opera dates from a production in Florence during his Italian residence. Its plot is pegged to the dissolute career of the last Visigothic king of Spain in the early 8th century, turned into a fanciful tale of intrigue and conflicting loyalties culminating in the redemption of the title character. Indeed, it was originally presented under the title of *Vincer se stesso è la maggior vittoria* (*To Conquer Oneself is the Greatest Victory*). The opera long survived incomplete, but its lost sections have gradually been recovered, and a few small remaining gaps were filled in (through transfers from other Handel music or composition of new recitative passages) by Alan Curtis, an edition used for the first full production of the opera since 1707.

Charles Farncombe took up the newly recovered material in productions he conducted in 1985 and 1987, the latter of which yielded an LP made for local distribution. A concert performance by **Curtis** himself was the basis for the opera's debut recording (♦Virgin 545897, 2CD). He leads a dandy little PI orchestra, with veteran soloists, all excellent, but with Piau particularly appealing as Rodrigo's long-suffering queen, and Banditelli in one of her best recorded performances in the title role. In all, a stylish vindication of a newly reclaimed work of precocious imagination.

Scipione (1726). This opera inflates a fanciful tale of the great Roman general Scipio, illustrating the virtues of restraint and renunciation. Uneven in both plot and score, the work still has lovely moments. It has apparently captivated somebody at FNAC, which has issued two separate recordings. One, a 3LP set now long gone, documented a Radio France performance in 1979, in English translation by forces of the Handel Opera Society under **Farncombe,** with some outstanding singers (Masterson, Watts, Esswood). In 1993 FNAC captured a production at the Beaune Festival with **Rousset** leading his PI group, Les Talens Lyriques (♦592245, 3CD). His cast is led by the light-voiced but agile Ragin in Senesino's title role, and the silvery Piau as his love-interest. The others are generally fine.

Serse (1738). This takes place in a fairy-tale ancient Persia, with only the names of Xerxes and a few other characters relating in any way to the great Achaemenid kingdom of antiquity. Characters are patched onto a Baroque plot whose setting hardly matters. In the final agonies of his operatic business, Handel found the imagination to produce a score of ravishing freshness and imaginative vitality, with sentiment, humor, and pathos in a nice mixing of *seria* and *buffa* elements in an almost Mozartian spirit. (It is, of course, the opera that opens with the famous aria "Ombra mai fu," or "Handel's Largo," a grateful address to a shade tree.)

This is a score that has understandably prompted a number of stagings in recent years. Its recording history offers another small (if lurching) digest of performing attitudes and trends over the decades. Broadcast recordings preserve two early performances, both from 1962, and both involving celebrity singers with modern orchestras in terribly mutilated editions. One, with Milanese forces led by **Piero Bellugi,** can boast Alva, Panerai, Freni, and Cossotto in an altogether 19th-century conception of the piece (Melodram). The other, a heavy-handed performance with mostly local singers for Bavarian Radio under **Kubelik,** is of interest solely for the lovely singing of Wunderlich, a tenor in the castrato title role (Verona).

A compromise approach—reasonably full score, MI forces, some sense of style, but mostly standard operatic singers—was represented in **Priestman**'s 1965 recording, circulated for a while as a 3LP set (Westminster). It merits reissue for the sake of some very handsome singing by a vocally distinguished cast including Forrester (in the castrato lead role), Popp, and Brannigan. Then came the first and only PI version, led by **Malgoire** (1979: Sony). Once again, the voice-casting is confused. The *primo uomo* title role written for castrato Caffarelli is satisfactorily taken by a mezzo, the ever-warm-toned Watkinson, but the trousers role of Arsamene, written for a contralto, is given here illogically to countertenor Esswood. The two sopranos, Hendricks and Rodde, as well as mezzo Ortrun Wenkel, are fine in the female roles. There followed two more-or-less retrograde approaches. One is a dutiful but altogether provincial version, done with mostly little-known American singers and the Polish Radio Chamber Orchestra under **Duczmal,** which serves no recognizable purpose (Studios Classique). The other is a theater performance conducted by **Ivor Bolton** in Munich, essentially a modern-opera conception, though graced by such able cast members as Kenney and Murray (Farao).

Fortunately, we now have **McGegan**'s version for the 1997 Göttingen Festival (◆Conifer 51312, 3CD). His casting unnecessarily creates the same kind of vocal confusion that Malgoire perpetrated. But while McGegan's Malafronte and Thomas fall just slightly short of Malgoire's Watkinson and Priestman's Brannigan, they're certainly splendid in their own right, while outstanding work is contributed by Jennifer Smith and the strikingly handsome-voiced Brian Asawa, one of the new countertenors reaching star status. Above all, McGegan's cast has both a theatrical and an ensemble feeling resulting from working together in staged performances. Using the PI Hanover Band, he generates smooth and propulsive direction. In all, he has matched Priestman's achievement in updated terms, while quite eclipsing Malgoire, in a coherently stylish and satisfyingly musical realization. Other recordings may come, but McGegan's is clearly the best to date.

Siroe, Rè di Persia (*1728*). This opera is a kind of *King Lear* in ancient Persian masquerade. The libretto is one of the few by Metastasio that Handel used. The only recording was the second Handel opera venture organized by singer Ostendorf as producer, in which he was still consolidating his working team (Newport). Ostendorf is his usual superb self vocally and dramatically as the dippy old king; Baird and Andrea Matthews offer contrast between the former's bleached tone and the latter's richness. Of the two castrato roles, the lesser one is taken by the unimpressive countertenor Steven Rickards, while the title role, for Senesino, is tackled with sturdiness by the able and always enjoyable Fortunato. **Palmer** leads a somewhat scrappy PI band, but the sum total is effective and valuable.

Sosarme, Rè di Media (*1732*). This brings us again to a Persian never-never land, though its libretto derives from an earlier text about a king of Portugal—all of which reminds us that the situations and characters are what count, not the setting. Its score is less flamboyant than usual, with an emphasis on thoughtful and introspective scenes in lovely solos and moving duets, illustrating Handel's continuing experimentation on his second great plateau of Italian opera composition.

This has the distinction of being one of the first Handel operas to be given a full-length recording: **Anthony Lewis**'s classic 1955 version, which has been resurrected (Theorema). Nearly four decades passed before the second recording appeared: Ostendorf's production with **Somary** (◆Newport 85575, 2CD). The time gap dramatizes the great difference in performance approach that evolved over the years. Lewis's version is dated in more than instrumental and recorded sound, but the conductor's love of this music is evident, and the incomparable Thurston Dart's ebullient harpsichord continuo playing remains a joy to hear—his spirit particularly animates the recitatives, which are delivered with great dramatic expression. Somary uses period instruments and assembles a cast representative of the fine Handel singing that can now be fielded.

There are, as always, voice problems. Of the two original castrato roles, Lewis gave Senesino's title role to countertenor Deller, in one of his rare recordings of a complete opera. Deller's voice is *sui generis,* and his self-indulgent sound can be wearisome. Somary used the richly androgynous low-alto voice of Fortunato, which is very satisfying musically. For the other castrato role of Argone, Lewis used a high tenor, John Kentish, while Somary employed the workaday countertenor Raymond Pellerin. For the *travesti* role of Melo, written for a female contralto, Lewis has the matchless Watts, whose vocal beauty can't be fully supplanted by Somary's choice of a countertenor—even though he's the stylish Minter. But Lewis's Margaret Ritchie, ever limited vocally, is totally eclipsed by the agile and ringing sound of Baird (who is particularly compelling in her embellishments), while Jennifer Lane's warm mezzo likewise surpasses Lewis's Nancy Evans and Aler is a far more complete vocalist than Lewis's William Herbert in the role of the tormented Lydian King. Somary's conducting is more propulsive than Lewis's. Whatever the nostalgia for the latter's landmark recording, the Newport is the clear preference for our day.

Tamerlano (*1724*). This is a fanciful adaptation of fanciful stories of the captivity of the Turkish Sultan Bayazid I after his defeat (1402) by the conquering Tamerlane. It's one of the most interesting Handel operas, breaking out of normal *opera seria* conventions in casting (giving the important role of Bajazet to the usually disfavored tenor voice) and in form.

A carefully performed (if not particularly dramatic) first recording, synthesizing Handel's three very different performing versions, was made in 1970 by **John Moriarty,** with generally handsome and sensitive singing (Cambridge). Two PI recordings followed, by **Malgoire** (Sony) and **Gardiner** (◆Erato 99772, 3CD). Both cope with the problems of length and variant numbers by following the initial 1724 version, but with cuts—Gardiner's reasonable and plausible, Malgoire's more drastic and sometimes brutally disfiguring. Gardiner's conducting is far more insightful and probing than Malgoire's energetic superficiality. Some of the latter's cast compare well, especially in the countertenor handling of castrato roles. Jacobs makes a more subtle and complex Tamerlano than Gardiner's Ragin, fine as he is, while Malgoire's Ledroit bests Gardiner's Chance in vocal strength and flair. Indeed, the key to the comparison is that Gardiner's performance—recorded in concert after going through staged productions in Lyons and Göttingen—integrates his cast into an idiomatic totality with far more Handelian integrity and compelling theatricality than Malgoire. Gardiner's has been hailed as the finest Handel opera recording ever made—it certainly leaves Malgoire's version as a miscalculation of essentially supplemental value.

Teseo (*1713*). This opera dates from early in Handel's establishment of what became permanent English residence. Its Italian libretto is an adaptation of a French text that Quinault had written almost 40 years earlier for setting by Lully as his *Thésée,* and Handel responded with a mixture of French and Italian vocal and theatrical style. The score is of mixed quality but has some fine dramatic situations and a remarkable portrait of the woman scorned in the hysterical Medea, a character to be matched only later in the century by Mozart's Elettra in *Idomeneo.* This unjustly ignored work has its only recording under PI conductor **Minkowski** (1992: ◆Erato 45806, 2CD). His casting selections only expanded the confusion of Handel's vocal typings, but the singing is generally fine. Minkowski's leadership can sometimes be rough, but is generally strong.

Tolomeo, Rè di Egitto (*1728*). This sets the last libretto prepared for Handel by his valuable collaborator, Nicolas Haym. It's based freely on an episode in the history of Hellenistic Egypt, involving the rivalry between Kings Ptolemy VIII (or IX) Soter and Ptolemy IX (or X) Alexander, two sons of the ruthless Queen Cleopatra III—no, not Liz Taylor (*she* was Cleopatra VII), but her grandmother. The quite bloody historical events were turned into the usual libretto labyrinth of amorous and political intrigue, allowing the usual dramatic situations and character vignettes in some wonderful musical moments. The only recording is one of the ventures of that indefatigable Handelian producer, John Ostendorf (Vox). The singers are all thoroughly capable, and while the pickup chamber orchestra is undistinguished, **Richard Auldon Clark**'s leadership is steady if not particularly varied or probing. The fine continuo harpsichordist, Bradley Brookshire, is rung in at intermissions to contribute two of Handel's suites as fillers.

ORATORIOS

Messiah (1742ff)

Early revisions. The outlandish and obsessively outsized attention given by recordings to this work requires a section alone, in which (perhaps more here than anywhere else) the task is as much one of classification as it is of evaluation or recommendation. There are many different *Messiah*s, one for each and every taste, perverted or otherwise. Handel started it all by constantly tinkering with it, devising new or variant numbers through his repeated revivals for different casts. There is now no such thing as "the" *Messiah,* though the Ebenezer Prout edition and its byproducts made it seem there was for many generations. The recognition in recent years that some variety and diversity can be achieved by drawing selectively on the range of variant numbers introduces new factors of choice. There is also the wide range and subdivisional spectrum of performance styles and scales to choose from— from elephantine traditionalism to extreme concepts of authenticity, from modern to period, from macro to micro. It's a discographic thicket we must enter. (Note that all CD recordings cited in this section are 2CD sets unless otherwise indicated.) After Handel's own revisions, the first steps away from his initial 1742 version, the next landmark in transformation came with Mozart's rescoring in 1789 for a performance in Vienna as *Der Messias.* Published in 1803, it became a primary basis for the further re-orchestrations that were imposed regularly for some 150 years thereafter, and that have still not altogether disappeared. On this count, the interesting (if sometimes bizarre) anthology called "A Collector's Messiah" samples the kinds of things that went on in recordings made between 1899 and 1930 (Koch).

The chief exponent of the Mozart edition has been **Mackerras,** who first recorded it in 1974—appropriately, in Vienna—using the German translation Mozart employed, and with fine soloists (♦DG Archiv 427173). He later (1988) recorded the Mozart version anew, using the original English text, with splendid soloists, members of the Royal Philharmonic, and the huge Huddersfield Choral Society (ASV). Mackerras believes the Mozart scoring provides the ideal orchestral compromise for a modern performance with a large chorus—which here, unfortunately, sounds rather muddy and blurred.

Since Mackerras, five other conductors have recorded the Mozart scoring. One, who had already given us a small-scaled period *Messiah,* is **Christophers,** who recorded it for BBC with young soloists, the BBC Philharmonic and the Huddersfield chorus again, and again using the English text (*BBC Music Magazine* supplements VI:4-5, with added CD-ROM material). There is also a weak English-language Mozart version made in New York under the inept leadership of **Lyndon Woodside** (Koch Schwann). Other versions using the German words are by **Corboz** (Erato), **Rilling** (Hänssler), and **Malgoire** (Astrée). Only the last of

these uses a PI ensemble, all the others using MI forces of varying scale. You may sort out your choice of factors: Mackerras's Archive recording remains generally unsurpassed, vocally and interpretively, but in its absence Rilling's is an excellent performance that runs a very close second.

Modern instruments. The most steadfast champion of a modified (if Prout-leavened) Mozart scoring was **Sargent,** who made four recordings (three of them with the Huddersfield chorus). The third (1959) still survives (Classics for Pleasure, mono), with sturdy soloists in the British oratorio tradition, and the second (1947), with an even more traditional cast, has also been reissued (Dutton). But Sargent's Edwardian-imperial style is so dated now, and the performances are so heavyhanded, that this approach represents mainly historic rather than artistic value, save for nostalgic Anglophiles. A domestic demonstration of how degenerate the hoary Victorian tradition could become is **Ormandy**'s stylistic horror, with a total hash of number-cutting and reordering, miscast soloists, a quasi-Prout orchestration, and America's answer to Huddersfield, the Mormon Tabernacle Choir—its recent deletion should elicit few tears (Sony).

The most important podium personality in shaping perceptions of *Messiah* in our time was **Beecham,** who recorded the work three times (1927, 1947, 1959). A great conductor, Beecham is now remembered as a Handelian either with romantic nostalgia or puristic horror. Capable of the most infuriating arrogance and wilfulness, he loved Handel's music deeply, sometimes to the extent of thinking he understood it better than Handel himself. Thus, Beecham could sometimes inflict on it what we can recognize as savage wounds and mutilations, even as he brought to it a nobility of spirit and a warmth of sensual beauty. Above all, while latter-day musicology (which he detested) might view him as the last ogre of the bad old days, it must be owned that it was Beecham who rescued Handel from the monster aberrations of the festival *Messiah*s that had become standard in the 19th century, with orchestras in the hundreds and choruses literally in the thousands. Though heavily abridged, Beecham's first recording was also the first attempt at a complete recording, and its relatively stripped-down forces and revitalized tempos helped shatter the traditions of Victorian ponderosity. Interesting now as a historical document, this 1927 recording has been reissued (Pearl; Grammophono). Beecham's second recording (1947) has also been revived (♦Biddulph 059/61, 3CD, with three choruses from *Israel in Egypt* and other Handel and Bach tidbits). Textually the most complete of his versions and using celebrated oratorio stars of the day (Elsie Suddaby, Marjorie Thomas, Heddle Nash, Trevor Antony), this is musically the most satisfying of the three, and still worth hearing. Still available is his final recording, surely the most extraordinary treatment ever made of the work. With a stellar roster of wonderful soloists (Vyvyan, Sinclair, Vickers, Tozzi) and a large chorus, Beecham used an explosive expansion of Prout's orchestration devised by Eugene Goossens and Beecham himself for a full Straussian symphony orchestra, with piccolos, plentiful brass, harps, triangle, cymbals, the works. The resulting circus reminds me of Mel Brooks's imaginary boomerang musical, *Springtime for Hitler,* so awful it's delightful, and so rousingly, handsomely performed at that! I suspect that Handel the musician would have been appalled, while Handel the man of the theater would have loved it (and then sobered up the next day). Handel it is not, of course, but for those whose *Messiah* spirit is more that of New Year's Eve than Christmas Eve, there it is (RCA 09026, 3CD).

For those seeking the spirit of Beecham and the letter of Prout updated, in a rip-roaring, old-fashioned *Messiah* performed to a fare-thee-well, with updated orchestration and unpedantic style, there is **Andrew Davis**'s rousing recording, blessed with another stellar cast: Battle, Quivar, Aler, Ramey (♦EMI 49027). Anyone wanting a big-hearted and frankly modernized *Messiah*, without reduced forces, period instruments, or any audible musicological illumination, this is the *only* recording, standing quite apart for quality in its class. A 1979 recording (in still very handsome sound) by **John Alldis** is more soberly influenced by the spirit of Beecham II, relying mainly on the Prout edition (Sparrow 1560, 2CD). Alldis, a seasoned choral conductor well-versed in the work, leads beautifully lucid choral work, with lovely singing by his soloists (Lott, Hodgson, Langridge, Cold); there are some noble moments, but much of his pacing is foursquare and with little insight. For traditionalists who want a little less of Davis's pizzazz and none of Beecham III's outrageousness, this throwback performance is a sensible but not exciting choice.

Beecham's revisionist revelations were in time superseded by new ones from **Scherchen.** The first (1954) of his two LP recordings was inaccurately touted as "the original Dublin version" of 1742, but it *was* the first to return to Handel's own instrumentation (Westminster). Using British soloists, a small chorus, and a very small orchestra, it was also the first to introduce one of the variant numbers into the otherwise standard Prout sequence. Bold in its expressive freshness, if sometimes eccentric in tempos and with no recognition of opportunities for embellishment, this recording now belongs to history; both it and its subsequent (artistically inferior) stereo remake are now unavailable, though the 1954 recording was briefly reissued in England in a 3CD set (Nixa). It caused a sensation in its time and marked the beginning of a new authenticity movement in performing the work. The subsequent stage of PI performance was yet to come, but Scherchen established the model of using Handel's scoring and reduced forces that soon became standard.

The first response to Scherchen came from **Boult,** in two recordings that maintained essentially the Prout sequence (Decca/London). The second, a stereo remake with Sutherland, Bumbry, Kenneth McKeller, and Joseph Ward, using a good-sized chorus with a reduced, Handelian orchestra, demonstrated that the stately and traditional style of singing could work with scaled-down instrumentation. It remains a worthy choice (London). Boult's example soon produced imitators. An attractive one was made in 1961 by his chorus-master in the first recording, **Frederic Jackson,** with a splendid batch of soloists (Saga).

The Boult recordings consolidated the mainstream into which fall most of the recordings that have appeared over the last four decades—many no longer in print and hence not considered here. This might be called the compromise approach, definable as using modern instruments in Handel's own scoring, combined with whatever stylistic and textual variations were chosen. One of the best of that type is **Mackerras**'s first recording, using a sensibly-sized choir and orchestra, with Baker memorably leading a superb group of soloists (Harwood, Esswood, Tear, Herincx). Mackerras was the first conductor to break the Prout barrier to score content, introducing a number of refreshing variant numbers and adding extensive embellishment. Conducted with spirit and imagination, this remains one of my enduring recommendations for the liveliest fusion of musicology with tradition (♦Angel 62748).

For another successful melding of musicology with musicality, there is the late **John Tobin.** Editor of this work for the *Hallische Händel-Ausgabe,* Tobin not only wrote extensively about it, but regularly conducted and recorded his own performing edition, including some vari-

ant numbers, using modern instruments, a good-sized choir, and some fine soloists. Long prized by connoisseurs, his 1976 recording was difficult to find on LP, and at present is quixotically available only in audiotape format (Protone). But it's worth seeking out for its profound scholarship, inspired by passionate musical conviction and a lingering love for Victorian stateliness, mixed with a delight in vocal theatrics and dramatic interpretive effects.

Hardly more accessible, apparently, is the work of another celebrated Handelian, **Leppard.** He hews to the Prout sequence, but has a distinguished solo group (Palmer, Watts, Ryland Davies, Shirley-Quirk), as well as reasonably balanced and appropriate choral and orchestral forces (♦Erato 45447). His characteristic combination of stylistic feeling with robust musicality makes his recording a successful demonstration that traditional sensibilities of grandeur and expressiveness can survive nicely in the compromise approach; it's a recording to seek out and treasure.

Sometimes the compromise approach had its excesses and extremes. Sutherland's recording with Boult seems have inspired her and her husband, **Bonynge,** to make their own attempt, while employing the same choral and orchestral forces as Mackerras. They use only a few variant numbers and concentrate on adding embellishment. Sutherland does this in wild overabundance, quite unbalancing the rest of the uneven solo quartet while all kinds of instrumental cadenzas and ornaments are worked into the playing (London). It remains an intriguing curiosity, if only as a study in musicology gone haywire. At another extreme is no less a titan than **Klemperer,** with a starry quartet (Schwarzkopf, Gedda, Grace Hoffman, Jerome Hines), a good-sized choir and a stripped-down Handelian orchestra (Angel). The reading is highly idiosyncratic, mastodonic in its stateliness, using the standard Prout sequence. It's often lovely artistically, but freighted with too heavy a dose of Germanic Romanticism to sustain the compromise approach very coherently. If not Romanticism, at least a Germanic spirit infuses the 1973 attempt to fuse the continental Baroque performing style of **Karl Richter** with British soloists and ensemble forces on a Boultian scale, but the results are generally stately to an often ponderous degree and devoid of much vitality. The recent reissue of this recording, intended to honor Richter, seems rather pointless (DG). Even more pointless for the general market is a performance not only Germanic, but in German: a 1973 Berlin production under **Helmut Koch** (Berlin). The pacing is ponderous and old-fashioned (though he does draw upon a few variant numbers), and the only possible interest it might have today is for fans of Schreier or Adam, heard among the soloists.

Running to the other extreme was **Bernstein**'s idiosyncratic response to the compromise approach in the early '60s. His soloists were a musical and artistic lot, but the Westminster Chorus contributed grand-scaled renditions of the choral sections in a throwback to the "traditional" style. On the other hand, for his orchestra, drawn from NY Philharmonic players, Bernstein designed a stripped-down Handelian scoring with touches of Mozart/Prout thrown in, but using harpsichord and organ quite prominently. Most important, he not only cut the score heavily but re-arranged its order drastically, transforming it from three to two parts. That the revival of this weird affair is part of Sony's new round of tributes to the conductor makes sense, for it really tells us more about Lenny than it does about George Frideric.

Fortunately, a good antidote to such excesses is **Somary**'s very careful delivery of the same Prout sequence: excellent soloists, well-balanced choral and instrumental forces, a splendid sense of style, rather in the Leppard tradition (♦Vanguard 4018/19). Not notably exciting or venturesome, it survives as a smoothly reliable vindication of the compromise approach in a version of solid quality. **Westenburg**'s 1981 recording is in the same vein (♦RCA 63317). His elements of compromise include ventures into variant numbers and careful attention to embellishment, at the same time involving a full-blooded choral sound and soloists (Blegen, Ciesinski, Aler, Cheek) whose singing style is more operatic than antiquarian. It's a set that will give lasting satisfaction.

Several maestros have recorded *Messiah* more than once, using the compromise approach. **Colin Davis** made his first recording in 1967 with a sonorous choir and orchestra and a well-balanced solo group including Harper, Watts, and Shirley-Quirk. It's still in the Prout sequence and with minimal embellishments, but everything is done in an efficient but airy manner that has sometimes prompted complaints of blandness and superficiality. It has generally won praise and survives as a reliable model of compromise authenticity (Philips). Why Davis chose to try again, however, isn't clear. His second recording, made in Munich, though not without solo virtues, is an unidiomatic reading by the Bavarian chorus and orchestra under sadly deteriorated leadership (Philips).

Nor did **Marriner** do anybody any favors with his remakes. His first recording was a recreation of the version Handel used for the 1743 London premiere, in an edition prepared by Hogwood, who plays organ continuo (♦London 444824, bargain-priced). Ameling leads a fine quartet (Anna Reynolds, Langridge, Gwynne Howell) in a vitally paced and suavely rendered recording that remains one of the most stylish and elegant examples of the compromise approach, with musicology and artistry in total accord. While operating in Germany, Marriner subsequently made a German-language recording that was briefly (and rather needlessly) circulated, its language effectively reducing its interest to American buyers and for our purposes (EMI). Then, in 1992, Philips captured a live performance celebrating the work's 250th anniversary, with Marriner leading his Academy forces again. The female soloists (McNair, von Otter) were fine, but the males (Chance, Hadley, Robert Lloyd) were weak, and the overall direction cool and diffident. For no discernible reason, Philips has kept this version alive, but it's one more demonstration that Marriner's recurrent practice of re-recording Handel has been ill-advised.

With his two recordings, **Robert Shaw** produced sharply contrasting and distinctly individual results. His first was a very carefully thought-out and handsomely realized recreation (mostly) of Handel's 1752 performing edition (RCA, 3LP). His soloists were uniformly excellent and ventured good embellishments, the chorus and orchestra were quite close to Handel's size, and the pacing was lively and vivacious. An outstanding example of the compromise approach and one of Shaw's finest achievements on records, its unavailability for many years is a great loss. Some 20 years later Shaw produced a second recording altogether different from his first. With only a few variant numbers added, he returned to the Prout sequence, using a modest orchestra and a very large chorus, with a somewhat limp solo lineup, in a broader, more stately rendition, more traditional in character, crisply executed, but a bit calculated and cold (Telarc).

The more recent compromise *Messiah*s are a mixed lot. The problems of mixing nationalities is illustrated by two of them. In a 1982 concert performance in Stockholm **Ohrwall** used his own, somewhat cut edition and led local forces (a 35-member chorus, 21-member orchestra). His three British soloists (Kenny, Esswood, Hill) are idiomatic enough, but his bass (Magnus Lindén) and the chorus have accent problems. This was probably an illuminating performance for local audiences, but is a rather routine interpretation that has little to offer (Proprius). The

same can be said of a concert performance taped at Copenhagen Cathedral with local forces under **Morten Topp,** at least using some variant numbers (Classico). The better-known **Scimone,** normally active in Italian music, might seem out of his element here, but his 1989 combination of London's Ambrosian Singers with his Solisti Veneti works well, and most of his soloists do very fine work. While he tinkers with Handel's scoring, Scimone encourages embellishments, elicits imaginative continuo work, and in general directs with a lively and spirited hand—it will give pleasure (Arts).

Solti's Chicago recording is probably the most exciting version available. Absorbing some ideas from the PI camp (including some variants), he seeks brisk clarity with crack modern forces, including an accomplished solo quartet: Te Kanawa, Anne Gjevang, Keith Lewis, and Howell (♦London 414396). His version is far from Victorian grandeur and quite compelling in its dynamism and crisp intelligence—the *Messiah* for the fast-track generation. In drastic contrast, a British recording under **Owain Arwel Hughes** represents a kind of misguided nostalgia trip (IMP). Handel's scoring is respected, but both chorus and orchestra are large, with an uneven solo group. The Watkins Shaw edition is used, introducing some variant numbers, but stylistic insights are minimal, and the pacing is stodgy and heavy-handed, evoking the poorer side of tradition that the likes of Boult and Leppard avoided.

More honest and straight-forward is a respectable cut-rate version, made at New York's Trinity Church under **Owen Burdick** (♦Naxos 554511/12): the traditional Prout sequence is used, but embellishments are ventured and with a chorus of 20 (with soloists drawn therefrom) and MI orchestra of 20, the flavor approaches PI minimalism; spirited musicality makes it a fair bargain. Still better is a high-quality performance unexpectedly transmitted under odd evangelical sponsorship and strange packaging, offering a capable solo team, in the Watkins Shaw edition again (more variants). Led by **Timothy Dean,** the instrumental work is excellent and the choral sections are done with particular imagination, all in splendid sound (Guild). A real sleeper in its class!

Two other recordings from small or obscure labels are less commendable. In a Canadian project, **Gerald Fagan**'s big chorus is ill-disciplined, the small orchestra is rather scrawny, and his generally quite good soloists are put to work with more embellishments than you've heard since Bonynge (Opening Day). Still less worth consideration is a version from **Ross Pople.** He has given us some quite good recordings of 18th-century orchestral music, but his production here sounds ill-rehearsed, with little careful thought behind it—mostly capable soloists, but a scrappy chorus and rough orchestra, recorded in dry and deadish sound (Arte Nova). Such ventures are just not competitive at any price.

Likewise not seriously competitive but curious is a 1994 recording in which the Vienna Boys' Choir and Chorus Viennensis join a British chamber orchestra and mostly British soloists under **Peter Marschik,** a Sängerknaben alumnus and now director of the group (Capriccio). The neo-Boultian framework is conservative (Prout sequence with only two countertenor variants; minimal embellishments), and though the tang of boys' voices is certifiably Handelian, the choral accents here are no help, nor are the British soloists particularly distinguished. But the soprano is Max Emanuel Cencic, an alumnus of the choir—not a boy soprano, but one of the new breed of cultivated male sopranistas, and a fine singer with a surprisingly attractive and full soprano. A few miscalculations aside, Marschik imparts genuine vigor and unusually imaginative shaping to this performance—some of the choruses are remarkably exciting. Otherwise, the main appeal here is to those who must have everything the Vienna Boys' Choir do.

To sum, I suggest Mackerras as a first choice, with Marriner and Leppard as outstanding backups; Solti for intensity or Somary for dignity and the best of traditionalism; with Andrew Davis for those who want a rousing old-time Proutian feast.

Period Instruments. Overlapping the compromise line of *Messiah* recordings has been the parallel full authenticity approach, with period instruments as the main point, and exploration of variant numbers and differing editions is common. There have been 20 such recordings. As this approach has evolved, it has also spawned two sub-categories, which we might call "normal" and "minimal".

The very first—and still among the very best—was **Hogwood** (1979: Oiseau-Lyre 430488). He makes the most careful of any recorded recreations of the composer's own datable preforming editions, that of 1754, which is well documented. The soloists (Kirkby, Nelson, Watkinson, Elliott, David Thomas) are skilled early-music specialists who set a standard for scaled-down (rather than operatic) vocalism in this work, while the use of a British church choir (with boy trebles, which Handel normally used) further departs from traditional timbres to restore the choral sound to which the composer was accustomed. The PI sound has character without being exaggerated. Hogwood shapes the work as a carefully controlled entity, but there are certainly moments of great expressive and dramatic power within established Baroque scale. If this isn't an immediately thrilling performance, it's one of solid artistic and scholarly reliability to which we can return with satisfaction.

Two successors followed promptly. **Malgoire,** though professing to offer the original Dublin version of 1742, in fact produced a textually very confused edition that incorporated variants from later versions (CBS). Experienced soloists are joined by a precarious solo treble. The boys of a cathedral choir again color the choral sound, while the PI ensemble is smallish and strident. The interpretation is characteristically quirky, with fussy details and exaggerated rhythmic emphases, though there are redeeming moments of beauty and excitement. Those qualities were notably absent in **James Weaver**'s recording (1980: Smithsonian). He scrupulously presented a version based on Handel's 1754 and 1758 performances, with appropriate variants, boy trebles in the chorus, and careful observance of period practices. His soloists were often outstanding, but his hyper-cautious leadership resulted in a bloodless and rather neutral reading.

As the big guns moved in, **Harnoncourt** made his bid with a concert performance in Stockholm, using a local choir and a United Nations of soloists in a babel of accents (1982: Teldec). The smallish instrumental ensemble is brilliantly adept and adds much more embellishment than the soloists do, but is also happy to show off all the mannerisms and colors that period playing had developed by then. Harnoncourt follows essentially the Prout sequence with minimal variants, but his leadership constitutes a compendium of his worst eccentricities in what is surely the most disastrous and expendable of the "authentic" recordings.

Gardiner proved to be quite different. While again following Prout's basic sequence (with a few variants), he's far better in observing niceties of period performance (1983: ♦Philips 411041, 3CD). His choir is all-adult and virtuosic, but with a boy treble joining a superb roster of soloists (Marshall, Robbin, Brett, Rolfe Johnson, Robert Hale). The instrumental sound is frankly revisionist in the strings, but rich and excellently integrated, and the entire performance is highly musical, if you don't mind predominantly brisk tempos—"Authenticity without tears," as one critic described it.

Profundity is clearly the goal of **Pinnock,** who follows the variant contents of Handel's 1745 and 1759 versions (1988: ♦DG Archiv 423630). He also deals with a vexing problem previous recordings avoided by including the horns we know were used by Handel, but for which no parts survive, here doubling the trumpets an octave below. Pinnock's soloists (Augér, von Otter, Chance, Crook, Tomlinson) are generally outstanding, his all-adult choir agile, and his orchestra fruity and well regulated. He can be brisk where required, but he mostly prefers broad and spacious pacings, making his reading less streamlined than some, and perhaps a little closer to traditional sensibilities—in other words, the most middle-of-the-road of these versions.

It was certainly put into further relief by **Parrott**'s subsequent recording (1988: EMI, reissued by Virgin). Using Handel's 1753 performing version, with very few variants and modest embellishment, employing a generally fine group of early-music soloists together with a small mixed choir (of 22) and a substantial orchestra (34, including horns), Parrott closely matched Handel's own norms to produce an attractive if understated and thoughtful performance.

A certain plateau was reached—if not in artistry, at least in musicology—by **McGegan**'s California recording, constituting a unique "variorum" version that purports to assemble all the variant material Handel devised over the years as he accommodated different singers and rethought segments of the work (1990: Harmonia Mundi 907050/52, 3CD). A total of 17 variants are presented, interesting enough in themselves. But they are also grouped in careful juxtaposition to a working performance of the Prout sequence, so disposed on the three discs that, through CD player programming, you can theoretically organize any one of nine different versions known during the period 1741–61. It's a fascinating idea, somewhat compromised in the realization by a few mistakes in edition-sorting and the omission of still other valid variants. Above all, the performance itself is disappointing. The soloists are very uneven, and the one-size-fits-all mixed choir (of 42) and orchestra (32, horns included) don't always match Handel's diverse scoring balances. There are some lovely vocal moments and some interesting inflections here and there, but there are needless idiosyncracies and patches of diffidence. Allowing for some hitches, this recording has genuine archival interest but is seriously flawed in musical values.

"Back to Boult" might be **Hickox**'s motto, who seems to seek the older maestro's brand of compromise between the new musicology and the old values (1991: ♦Chandos 0522). While the adult choral and orchestral forces closely approximate Handel's norms (24 and 31; no horns), the PI playing is smoother and less provocative than that of previous years. The 1750 version is used, which means few variants; embellishments are kept to a minimum. The pacing is moderate, avoiding the breakneck treatments found elsewhere and thus bridging the gap between ultra-authentic styles and more conventional tastes. The young Terfel, in one of his first recordings, is the now-predictable standout in an otherwise somewhat bland solo lineup. Given the competition, this admittedly fine recording is the one for which I coined the expression "merely excellent".

More frankly in the revisionist camp is **Christie,** who, peerless in French Baroque music, has made some interesting lunges into Purcell and is now making abrupt stabs at Handel (1993: Harmonia Mundi). And "abrupt" is the word here; all the elements are in place, with justly balanced forces (mixed choir of 25; orchestra of 33, horns included); a selective edition incorporating a few variants but hewing mainly to the traditional sequence, with modest embellishments; a solo group of young, tidy-voiced early-music adepts who are willing to be fitted into a controlled and conductor-oriented conception more tightly disciplined than even Hogwood's. It's all crisp, incisive, careful, and rather antiseptic, as well as international in accents—less a word on the subject than a footnote, not adding much to what we already understand of this music.

Something of the same verdict can be given for a more palpably British *Messiah* led by **Cleobury** (1992-93: Argo). The famed King's College Chapel Choir, Cambridge, with boy trebles, is joined by Roy Goodman's Brandenburg Consort and a consistently fine solo group in a version with a fairly familiar choice of variant numbers and intelligent embellishment. This is a rendition that jogs along quite well but seems not wholly coherent as an entity and is another unexceptional entry. Of the same vintage is a curiosity led by erstwhile early-music singer **Mark Brown,** an international confection in which he joins four capable singers from his Pro Cantione Antiqua vocal consort with a Czech chorus who seem unsure what language they are singing and a brave but rough Slovak PI ensemble (1992: Carlton). Brown has lots of good ideas and tries hard to pull it together, but accents, under-rehearsal, and over-strain make it all foredoomed.

As the progress of PI performances has unfolded, it has created a kind of normalist mainstream. Meanwhile, an alternative minimalist approach had been taking shape along the way, one that has gone beyond forces reduced to those Handel used and moved to forces reduced beyond the composer's accustomed norms, in quest of an even greater intimacy of texture and streamlining of spirit. The first such effort, under **Koopman,** was assembled from separate concert performances in Rimini and Utrecht (1983: Erato). Harry Christophers's mixed-voice chamber choir, The Sixteen (here actually 17) plus 17 instrumentalists—including Koopman himself on either harpsichord or organ as the only continuo player—offer a stripped-down sound that turns numerical authenticity, in Handel's terms, quite on its head. A basically standard score is used, with almost no variants. The soloists are inconsistent in their degrees of ornamentation (as well as accents). Koopman's ebullient spirit dominates and, though expertly rendered, the performance is breezy and lightweight, endlessly inflected and interpreted, but lacking the weight and spaciousness that also deserve consideration. In all, this version makes me think of an engineer removing as many components of a structure as he can before it collapses.

As if he thought he could do it better on his own, **Christophers** took his Sixteen (now 19 mixed voices), organized his own PI ensemble (20; only organ continuo), and engaged a group of outstanding young soloists (Dawson, Denley, David James, Maldwyn Davies, George) who were soon to make their mark in early music, setting them to basically the standard edition spiced with a few variants and with carefully controlled embellishment (1986: ◆Hyperion 66251/52). In contrast to Koopman's self-indulgence, Christophers stresses verbal clarity and nuance, within lithe, springy, propulsive pacing without a hint of brashness or lack of dignity. All is crystalline elegance, its closeness and intimacy serving not to diminish the work but to give it a new freshness. One of the very first minimalist *Messiah*s, this remains one of the very best.

Employing a mixed chorus of 21 with an orchestra of 24 (including himself on harpsichord), **Martin Pearlman** raised the limits of minimalist boundaries close to those Parrott had already set (1992: Telarc). Following basically the 1741 version, Pearlman interpolates some later variants. Like Christophers, he paces things briskly, but with more bracing energy. He allows or encourages his excellent young soloists to embellish rather excessively, while his PI players flaunt their revisionist

timbres rather more than many traditionalists might tolerate. It's exciting, but not at the top of its subcategory.

For minimalist quality at minimum price, there is the extraordinary recording by the enterprising Scholars Baroque Ensemble, led by **David van Asch** (1992: ◆Naxos 559667/68). The orchestra is only 15 players (two trumpets, timpani, and organ/harpsichord, with 11 strings) and the chorus is 14 singers, including the soloists. (Handel always had his soloists sing with the chorus, something rarely followed in recording. In fact, the bass section-leader and soloist is also the director, van Asch himself.) The 1742 text is augmented with a few of the now-familiar variants, the non-star soloists do little embellishing, and the whole spirit is that of ensemble chamber music, in brisk pacing with almost salon or small-chapel intimacy. This is maxi-minimalism, as far from the Crystal Palace monsters as you can get, and not a *Messiah* for the masses, but it's unexpectedly good fun, especially at its bargain price.

The bargain market was the apparent target of **Valentin Radu** with a mixed chorus of 20 and an orchestra of a mere 13 (oboes, trumpets, timpani, one organ/harpsichord player, plus seven—count 'em, seven!—strings), with outstanding female soloists and weak male ones, in the 1749 version with few variants (1994: Vox). Radu over-strains to be an interpreter in a reading full of exaggerations, extreme contrasts, and constant fussing. Too much ado with too little.

The most recent authentic *Messiah* recordings suggest that the minimalist movement may by now have crested (or bottomed out). This oratorio's latest demonstration of its international attractions features Japan's most active and exciting specialist in Baroque music, **Masaaki Suzuki** (BIS). His forces conjoin two Japanese soloists with two British veterans and his Japanese mixed chorus of 21 and PI orchestra of 19 in the 1753 version. There are inevitable accent problems, and these performers have too much competition to command the highest recommendation, but they do themselves proud on their own terms, and the conductor delivers a light and brisk reading full of insights and buoyant energy.

Of about the same proportions (chorus of 22, orchestra of 21) is a performance by the Apollo's Fire chorus and Cleveland Baroque Orchestra under **Jeannette Sorrell,** derived from two church concerts in 1994 and 1995 (Onda 1). The soloists—who also sing as part of the choir—include such outside talents of note as sopranos Baird and Brandes and countertenor Steven Rickards. The edition is fairly traditional in sequence, and there are some rough moments, but there is a splendid feeling of bounciness and adventure in a committed, highly musical performance.

Bringing together trends others had already developed, **McCreesh** represents a happy terminus (◆DG Archiv 453464). Taking the 1754 version as his text, he pulls back from minimalist extremes; his mixed choir of 24 sings with spirit and fine diction, while his period orchestra of 40 (including horns) is excellent. The soloists are all young newcomers but they sing with style and sensitivity, and they are charmingly liberal in their embellishment of lines and cadences. Tempos are fast and energy is high, all in the service of a coherent conception of the total work. The new shapings and inflections McCreesh brings to one section after another give the word "freshness" a new meaning. It not only sums up much of what previous practice has contributed but demonstrates that a truly probing and perceptive performance can still give this old warhorse new vitality.

Decades of relentlessly repeated recording have yielded quite a few truly memorable versions, and in the PI column, a few exceptions aside, almost all have something of value. There can never, ever, be a "best" recording of this elusive work, but I'm inclined to put McCreesh at the top of my PI list, in the very select company of Hogwood, Christophers, Pinnock, Gardiner, and Hickox.

Italian oratorios

Oratorio, like opera, was an invention of 17th century Italy, as the sacred (and unstaged) counterpart to secular (staged) drama. It was from its century-old traditions that Handel borrowed, adapted, and transformed what he then made into his own invention, English oratorio, as a successor to his first-chosen idiom, Italian opera. But before he did that, as a resident and citizen of England, he learned his trade at the source during his residence in Italy (1706-11), and in the process he produced two specifically Italian oratorios, one allegorical, the other sacred. (Not considered here is the later Italian *pasticcio* of 1734, put together from other works by the composer, and never recorded.)

Il trionfo del Tempo e del Disinganno (1707). This launched Handel's Italian oratorio ventures. Ironically, it was this same work, though utterly transformed and augmented, that he made into his very last English oratorio after he had cobbled up an intermediary Italian revision in 1737. The text is an allegorical debate between the personifications of Time and Disillusion, with Beauty and Pleasure chiming in. It was written by one of Baroque Rome's leading intellectuals, the scholar and poet Cardinal Benedetto Pamphili, and Handel's setting proved that he was thoroughly comfortable with such large-scale Italian forms.

Its first recording (in the original 1707 version) was by **Minkowski** (1988: ♦Erato 45351, 2CD). He fields a fine group of experienced soloists together with a flavorful PI ensemble, providing all one might ask in a recorded realization. Nor is it displaced by a curious challenger, recorded in 1998 by Music from Aston Magna led by **Daniel Stepner** (Centaur 2431/32, 2CD). The four singers and a small PI band give a musically bright performance, but make the strange decision to perform the arias in the original Italian while the recitatives are in English. This split-personality character is justified by the fact that Handel himself seems to have done this in one of his revivals, but its awkwardness is only made worse by a translation full of jarring and anachronistic slang. Buyers may be further confused by use of the English title Handel used for his drastic recasting of this work into his last English oratorio—with which it should not be confounded. Best to stick with Minkowski.

But now there is an alternative of a very different kind. Convinced of this oratorio's distinct integrity, despite long neglect and indifference, **Joachim Carlos Martini** has undertaken to recreate it—not in its original 1707 form—but in terms of Handel's revival in 1737, keeping it in Italian (if under the revised title of *Il trionfo del Tempo e della Verità*)—but adding new music, notably a number of fine sections for a chorus, not previously involved (♦Naxos 55440/42, 3CD). There are some arbitrary decisions or questionable interpolations, and the casting of pairs of rather undifferentiated sopranos makes for some vocal monotony. But Martini brings off a lively and sonorous performance (if somewhat cavernously recorded) in a unique release that allows us to follow better the processes by which Handel went on to transform this piece into the very different version that was to be his last oratorio.

La resurrezione (1708). Officially entitled *Oratorio per la Resurrezione de Nostro Signor Gesù Cristo,* this was composed for performance in the palace of the Marchese Ruspoli, one of Handel's powerful and appreciative patrons in Rome. It's a sacred drama in which the actual crucifixion and resurrection of Christ occur offstage and are interpreted at two levels: through the perceptions and reactions of three of his followers (Mary Magdalene, Mary Cleophas, and St. John), and through the sparring between a triumphant angel and the humiliated Lucifer. A clever piece, it's full of wonderful contrasts of moods and imagery, while displaying Handel's innate flair for oratorio form as well as his youthful imagination in full flower. Though Handel later quarried the work for material to be reused in later years, its revival in our time, through no less than five recordings, has shown it to be a beautiful and substantial score that can stand on its own.

The discovery of Handel's own conducting score by **Rudolf Ewerhart** gave us our first full access to the work, and he accordingly gave it its pioneering recording in 1960 (Vox). Unfortunately, his rather uneven soloists, unnecessary choir, and overweight orchestra, diffidently conducted in dim sound, made his version merely a stopgap curiosity. It served its purpose but is now long gone.

After a long lapse, four very fine PI recordings appeared (all 2CD), under **Hogwood** (1982: ♦Oiseau-Lyre 421132), **McGegan,** who had been Hogwood's assistant in 1982 (1990: ♦Harmonia Mundi 907111/12), **Koopman** (1990: Erato), and **Minkowski** (♦DG Archiv; MHS 524495). Each cast has something to offer in the five roles. None of them is totally superior, but Hogwood's has the most character, with Minkowski and McGegan relatively equal, and Koopman trailing on points. In overall leadership, Hogwood is crisp and stylish, while McGegan can be a little pushy and brusque and Koopman somewhat fussy. Minkowski is robust and hearty, falling between Hogwood and McGegan. He also avoids Koopman's excessive tricks with instrumentation (including the unwise use of a trombone in the continuo, following only Ewerhart in that misinterpretation of the score). No one recording is absolutely preferable, and each will give satisfaction; with a gun to my head and facing a desert island, I guess I'd say McGegan.

English oratorios

As with the Italian operas, the English works have also have been drawn upon for programs of selected arias. An old example of the type is a 1957 program featuring tenor **Richard Lewis** (Dutton 4003, with British folk songs). The orchestral accompaniments led by Sargent are rather plush and dated in style, but Lewis shows why he was one of the finest British oratorio singers of the mid-century. A newer example of the genre features an outstanding Handel tenor of more recent generations, **John Elwes,** with the St. Luke's Chamber Ensemble in "Music Inspired by the Hebrew Bible": selections from five oratorios, balancing instrumental and vocal pieces for a nicely varied sampling of the idiom (♦Arabesque 6720).

An assemblage by producer John Ostendorf is particularly worth citing (Newport), paralleling an earlier one of both Italian and English material partly drawn from his complete Handel recordings (Vox). In this case there are five selections from his *Joshua* but the remaining eight items were all recorded separately, from *Acis and Galatea, Joseph and his Brethren, Messiah,* and *Semele.* Six of the producer's working stable of singers are represented, with **Palmer** conducting a PI group. It serves doubly as a sampler of some of Handel's most appealing English solos, but also as a reminder of Ostendorf's important recording service to this literature. There is also a half-disc of five countertenor solos from four Handel oratorios sung by the mellow-voiced **Kowalski** (Capriccio, with Bach arias). It may be noted that oratorio and operatic arias are often mixed, as in some programs discussed above. Finally, among many transitory choral programs, we may cite a worthwhile survey of choruses from oratorios, 13 selections from as many works, under **Stephen Simon** (Arabesque).

As for complete works, there are some 25 (including *Messiah*), plus one incidental score, all of which have been recorded at one time or another. The category of oratorio of course covers a wide range of sub-types, some sacred, some secular; some dramatic and some not; masques and grand odes as well. As with the Italian operas, our consideration is organized alphabetically by title as the most convenient means of access.

Acis and Galatea (*1718*). This belongs to the well-established English idioms of the pastorale and the masque. It was first presented by small forces at Cannons for the Duke of Chandos and then revised variously for a series of public performances in London beginning in 1732. Drawing minimally upon the earlier *Aci, Galatea, e Polifemo* cantata (see above), it was Handel's first success with an English-language dramatic work for the English public. It has become one of his more frequently performed and recorded works.

A flash of interest in later 18th-century Vienna prompted one of those Mozart rescorings for Baron van Swieten, a version that itself has received no less than four recordings, all of them sung in the German translation used by Mozart (all 2CD). Three of them are by PI conductors who seem to find this version more worthy of their attention than the original; thus we have **Schreier** (♦Orfeo 133852), **Hogwood** (♦Oiseau-Lyre 430538), **Pinnock** (DG Archiv), and **Spering** (Opus 111). Spering's cast has the most vividly sung Polyphemus in bass Peter Lika, a kind of Handelian Osmin, but his other singers aren't distinguished. Hogwood's Dawson and Pinnock's Bonney are equally eloquent and beautiful as the soprano nymph, but the former's George (such a fine English monster for King) is below par in German and yields to Pinnock's blustery John Tomlinson as Polyphemus.

Schreier's cast (Mathis, Rolfe Johnson, Robert Gambill, Robert Lloyd) are not only the most consistently matched and excellent, but also offer the most appropriate Mozartean vocal sound, making it almost into a kind of Baroque *Così fan tutte*. It's also Schreier, with his MI forces, who best captures a Mozartean orchestral sound and spirit, especially in the wind colors. Pinnock is energetic but sometimes monotonous, and uses a harpsichord continuo, whereas Hogwood introduces the more Mozartean fortepiano, gives more flowing shape to the piece, and has richer choral work. I recommend Hogwood for PI fans, and Schreier for overall success; Spering is interesting mainly for his pairing.

Handel's original English-language version has achieved five PI recordings framed by five MI versions (all but one 2CD). The first complete recording was a valiant venture of the early '50s under **Walter Goehr,** with a fine cast of familiar English oratorio singers, spread over a 3LP set (Concert Hall/Handel Society). This was soon blown out of the water by a recording led by **Boult,** with Sutherland caught in the first bloom of her stardom, backed by the unique Peter Pears, with David Galliver and a peerless Polyphemus by Brannigan—a treasurable set that deserves CD reissue (♦Oiseau-Lyre). It was closely, if by no means fully, approached by an even more stylishly sensitive and scrupulously shaped version led by **Marriner** in 1977, with a fine cast (Argo).

A Stour Festival production worked up under **Deller** for Harmonia Mundi (released here briefly by RCA) embodied an even more minimalist chamber approach, with a decent enough cast but with coarse playing under Deller's unsettled leadership. A kind of throwback approach—good-sized MI orchestra, full chorus—was ventured as recently as 1991 by **Schwarz** in Seattle: harpsichord continuo, some embellishments, two unimpressive tenors, a promising soprano (Dawn Kotoski), and a quite decent Polyphemus (Opalach)—a respectable performance, but conducted with squarish insensitivity and extreme tempos, and in utterly botched sound (Delos).

Somewhat rosier, fortunately, is the prevailing picture of PI recordings, all but one also using the soloists in the kind of mini-chorus Handel originally employed. These were initiated in 1979 by **Gardiner** (♦DG Archiv 423406). His singers' names are their own recommendations (Burrowes, Rolfe Johnson, Martyn Hill, Willard White), and though Gardiner's tempos can sometimes be exaggerated, his sense of the whole is beautifully eloquent. This was bested only by **King** in 1989, with forces closely approximating those Handel used (♦Hyperion 66361/62, with "Look down, harmonious saint"). King has an unusually strong cast: the slightly unseasoned but very fine Claron McFadden as Galatea, Ainsley as one of the best Acises, Covey-Crump as an unusually lovely Damon, and George as the most deliciously overplayed Polyphemus since Brannigan.

Somary's version is respectable, if on a distinctly lower level (Newport). Of the singers, only Ostendorf is outstanding as Polyphemus, in the Brannigan/George category; Baird's spare singing makes her sound too girlish and aloof, while the tenors are pedestrian. Somary gives relatively superficial and uninspired leadership to an unpolished (under-rehearsed?) instrumental ensemble. The recording organized by Ostendorf is still less substantial, in which he switched to producer and abandoned his wonderful role of Polyphemus to the stiff and disinterested Kevin Deas (Vox). Baird repeats her cool and elegant Galatea, but such is the blandness of her tenors that she gives the best sense of dramatic involvement. The small chamber choir and a very rough and strident PI group is given brusque and choppy direction by the self-conscious **Valentin Radu**—a recording to be ignored.

Another ultra-minimalist approach by **David van Asch** is more interesting (Naxos). In an effort to recapture the texture of the 1718 performance at Cannons, van Asch uses an orchestra of only eight players and has his four singers (as did Marriner's) join as the mini-chorus. The two title roles are quite well sung; Van Asch himself sings Polyphemus with vocal competence but without much character. Through brisk tempos and a couple of cuts, the piece can be crammed onto a single CD, which certainly makes this a bargain for the budget-conscious.

The most recent recording, under **Christie,** is quite similar to van Asch in performing scale and editorial decisions; despite some quirks, it comes close to recreating a pure and strict 1718 version (Erato 25505). There is much merit in the cast: Sophie Daneman is a warm and womanly Galatea, Paul Agnew an admirably ardent Acis, while Alan Ewing compares favorably to the best of the Polyphemuses. The fly in the ointment, however, is Christie himself, whose generally superficial direction is elegant but lifeless and altogether bland beside King's vitality. Fine possibilities here unrealized, then. In all, for this work, King is clearly king for now.

Alceste (*1750*). This not an integral work at all, but a set of incidental pieces for a grand dramatic production on the story of Alcestis (no relation to Handel's Italian opera *Admeto* on the same tale). The venture never came off, the spoken text has since been lost, and Handel reworked much of the music for other purposes. Still, there is enough of a score to constitute what some have been willing to consider a masque and others categorize as a semi-opera after the model of Purcell, and there are lovely things in it. It has had a carefully prepared recording under **Hogwood,** with lovely solo work from Kirkby, Nelson, Cable, Elliott, and Thomas (♦Oiseau-Lyre 443183). That is now NA, but not even stopgap value can be found in the variable and heavily accented singing and sloppy PI playing of a French recording under **Franck-Emmanuel Comte** (Absalon).

Alexander Balus (*1748*). This is one of those relative stepchildren among the oratorios. Its subject matter certainly hasn't helped: a particularly dreary episode in 2nd-century BC Hellenistic history involving a contemptible pretender to the Selucid Kingdom of Syria, Alexander Balus (more properly, Balas), and his shifty treatment by the ambitious King of Egypt, Ptolemy VI, whose daughter Cleopatra Thea was married to Alexander. The only favorable portrait of this shabby pretender is in the extra-scriptural *Book of Maccabees I,* because he showed favor to the Hasmonean rebel Jonathan, brother of Judas Maccabeus, thus winning high regard from the Jews. That was the only real source for the Rev. Thomas Morell's shallow libretto. If most of the characters in this flat saga are cardboard, they sometimes come alive, and Handel made the most of the promising situations.

This was the last of Handel's oratorios to be recorded properly and in English. It came in one of those delayed collisions typical of the strange workings of disc biz. Just as had happened earlier with *Joshua,* the work was suddenly discovered and recorded in the same year (1997) by the same two conductors for the same two labels (both 2CD): **Robert King** (♦Hyperion 67241/42) and **Rudolph Palmer** in another of Ostendorf's productions (Newport 85625). There are differences in performing editions: Palmer follows Handel's redistribution of some numbers in his 1754 revival, whereas King essentially sticks to the original 1748 layout, though he does include some extra music that Handel transferred in 1754 from his moribund *Alceste* score. Each conductor has the benefit of fine singers with whom he has worked regularly, but King's cast is generally (though not entirely) a bit stronger. Some may find the boy trebles in King's good-sized choral group (38) a bit more edgy than Palmer's mixed-voice choir (24); but Palmer's period group plays with much less polish than does King's, while the Newport engineers place the orchestra as if across the street from the closely miked singers. In this instance then, King is very much the preferred choice.

Alexander's Feast, or The Power of Music (*1736*). This sets an adaptation of Dryden's "Ode for St. Cecilia's Day." The original text was identified with the once-famous Cecilian celebrations of London's musicians. It in fact tells a story that developed in late antiquity of the musician Timotheos, whose playing on the emotions of Alexander the Great precipitated the burning of Persepolis. It is, thus, not a true dramatic work, but a narrated evocation without stipulated characters. It's brilliantly conceived, and it shows Handel awakening to the real possibilities of the British audience he was unexpectedly beginning to generate for English-language musical drama. The score is full of music of the most wonderful imagination and beauty, constituting Handel's first true masterpiece in English oratorio form. Popular with his audiences (and a mainstay of his revivals during his later years), it has also had a generous recording history—six efforts in all, half of them with period instruments (all either 2LP or 2CD).

I learned to love the work in its first recording, made in the '50s by forces of Cornell University under **Robert Hull** (Concert Hall/Handel Society). **Deller** was somewhat more coherent and pretentious in the early '60s, with quite good soloists familiar from his circle, but diffident choral singing and weak orchestral playing under his shallow leadership (Vanguard, with *Birthday Ode*). A rather provincial performance sung in German translation, made in Halle under **Sanderling,** never circulated much (Eterna). The culmination of MI performances on LP came with **Ledger**'s 1978 recording (♦Angel 3874). He was the first to include the often-scorned final three numbers, and his lean and stylish performance with the King's College

Choir, English Chamber Orchestra, and excellent soloists would do well today in a CD reissue.

The first PI version was a 1978 set with a Swedish Choir and **Harnoncourt**'s Concentus Musicus Wien: highly accomplished solo work, odd choral accents, and this conductor's typically abrasive instrumental work and idiosyncratic interpretation (Telefunken). But a plateau was reached with two CD versions: **Gardiner**'s concert performance at the 1987 Göttingen Festival (Philips 422053), and **Christophers**'s 1990 recording (♦Collins 70162). Both add concertos we know Handel specifically incorporated into performances of the work at various times: Gardiner gives the "Alexander's Feast" concerto, Christophers gives Op. 4:6 for harp, 4:4 for organ. Christophers includes the extra numbers on the non-Dryden texts at the end, Gardiner does not. Gardiner spreads the solos among five singers, only one of whom (Watkinson) has a strong personality; Christophers retains the standard number of three (Argenta, Partridge, George), all excellent. The Collins sound is more carefully controlled and fuller than Gardiner's. Given the seeming disappearance of the Gardiner recording, Christophers is the logical recommendation, and a deserved one, for this rousing work. (This was one of the Handel works that Mozart adapted, but so far no one has recorded that.)

L'Allegro, il Penseroso, ed il Moderato (*1740*). This was Handel's first exploitation of the poetry of Milton, adapted by the composer's sometime collaborator, Charles Jennens, who added a concluding segment of his own (the "Il Moderato" Part III). The unique result is a kind of cross between allegorical cantata (symbolic figures in a long debate of philosophical ideals) and pastorale (including wonderful evocations of the British countryside and rural life) in a succession of contrasting vignettes and mood pieces. Its novelty and unconventionality have served to discourage attention, while the problems of reconciling Handel's constant revisions for his various revivals can be daunting—as well as making each performing edition a slightly different work. Nevertheless, its sum total is a ravishing score that's irresistible once encountered.

Of six recordings (all 2LP or 2CD), the first two were marked by the arbitrary excision of Part III, on the specious grounds that Jennens was not Milton, but they were both fine efforts in their own terms. A splendid set of 1960 benefitted from Thurston Dart's last participation in a Handel vocal recording as matchless continuo performer (Oiseau-Lyre). A lineup of expert, highly individual, and beautifully artistic soloists joined accomplished choral and orchestral forces under **Willcocks** in a still cherishable achievement that appears in a bargain-priced reissue (♦Decca 460287, with *Ode for St. Cecilia's Day*). No less attractive—if not as elegantly British and more forthrightly American—was **Frederic Waldman** with his Musica Aeterna and a numerically reduced but handsomely artistic solo team, another set that gave lasting satisfaction in its time (Decca).

The British/American dichotomy was renewed as more scholarly approaches set in, above all including at last the previously scorned Part III. **Gardiner**'s 1980 recording was the first to do so, with a group of highly able soloists, his Monteverdi Choir and his PI English Baroque Soloists, producing a performance of vitality and sparkle (♦Erato 45377). A touch less elegant but in some ways more pungent was an early venture by **Martin Pearlman** and his Banchetto Musicale, who also included Part III (and used the movements of Concerto grosso Op. 6:1 as overture and intermezzo). His five soloists (among them the very fine Nancy Armstrong and the since-familiar James Maddalena) were less polished than Gardiner's Brits, but still quite effective (Arabesque 6554).

A real challenge to Gardiner has come from **King** (♦Hyperion 67283/84). He also includes Part III, and uses an abbreviation of Op. 6:0 as his substitute overture, while allowing his organist an improvisation to introduce the fugal finale to Part II just as Handel might have done. Coping with the problems of vocal assignment, King also uses five soloists, all of them outstanding (Gritton, Anderson, McFadden, Agnew, Neal Davies). Gardiner might have a slight edge for extra-refined choral work, but it's difficult not to vacillate between his and King's versions. Both bring this wondrous music to life in its full glory.

As a kind of bizarre epilogue, we have a 1989 Berlin Radio recording, whose five soloists—apparently young and obviously gifted—are mostly unknown here save for countertenor Kowalski, whose rich contralto quality never sounded more maturely feminine (Berlin). The chorus is beautifully balanced and expertly drilled, while the MI orchestra is crisply proficient, all led by **Rolf Reuter,** who is alert and stylistically intelligent down to including Part III. But there is a fundamental problem: the performance is in German (under the title of *Der Fröhliche, der Nachdenkliche, und der Mässige*). It's true that Anglocentrism can become a near-paranoid fixation when we confront Handel's English works sung in German as German performers have been wont to do (after all, they gave him to us!). In this particular case, though, such translation is simply unacceptable. Milton's own words matter; they are a prime point of the work, as is Handel's explicit response to them. A pity, for good musical value goes to waste in this recording.

Athalia (1733). This was based on Racine's adaptation of the accounts in the *Book of Kings* and *Book of Chronicles* of the tumultuous life of the Queen of Judah, daughter of King Ahab and his Phoenician Queen Jezebel, who sought to draw the Hebrews to the worship of Baal. It's Handel's third oratorio, again fielding Old Testament lore in his testing the waters of English-language drama during his troubles with continuing Italian opera. With this skillfully crafted drama, Handel was clearly finding his way more securely into the genre he was creating. In the early '70s, **Simon** made a single LP of excerpts, about a half-length abridgement, leading Viennese forces with soloists Augér, Shane, Wolff, and Michalski (RCA).

Not until 1985 did the work receive its first full recording under **Hogwood** (Oiseau-Lyre). Using an Anglican church choir and period instruments, he assembled a memorable cast that approximated Handel's own vocal team, including a boy soprano and a countertenor. Handel's Anna Strada was probably a heavier soprano than Kirkby, but the latter's silvery singing is ideally calculated to contrast with Hogwood's title diva, Sutherland, who brings an apt degree of regal vocal grandeur and operatic flamboyance to this Klytämnestra-like role. Bowman, Rolfe Johnson, and David Thomas do yeoman service to their parts. Oiseau-Lyre's long discontinuation of this important recording is inexcusable.

As some relief, however, comes a recording from a series of live performances in Germany by Frankfurt forces (1996: ♦Naxos 554364/65, 2CD). The German soloists and chorus have few accent problems but generally weak English diction, and conductor **Joachim Carlos Martini** leads with more stability than inspiration. Elizabeth Scholl is no match for Sutherland's temperament, but the most familiar singer, Schlick, is an eloquent Josabeth. Annette Reinhold's weighty contralto makes a strong Joad, with the other singers quite satisfactory. Not brilliant, it's still a solid effort, adequately covering this work for now, and a genuine bargain.

Belshazzar (1745). This uses the last of the librettos that Charles Jennens (collaborator on *Messiah* and two other oratorios) prepared for

Handel. Jennens drew on both Old Testament and Classical Greek writings to assemble, beyond pious moral preachment, a quite effective moral parable of the triumph of a virtuous prince (Cyrus) over a degenerate one (Belshazzar)—who at least, like Don Giovanni, sticks to his guns and goes to his death still true to himself. Reduced to sideline status is the commanding spiritual presence, the Prophet Daniel. Far more compelling is Belshazzar's mother, Nitocris, who is at once an archetypal parent anguishing over her son's folly and a personality of profound sensitivity and decency in her own right. Handel etched some sharply drawn character delineations and took advantage of fine situations (the handwriting on the wall is artfully spooky, the diverting of the Euphrates strikingly evocative), while his command of choral writing allowed him again to portray the contrast of peoples (the reckless Babylonians, the valiant Persians).

German performers and audiences seem to have particular partiality to this work, judging from their generation of at least four (three of them in German) out of the six recordings it has received. A heavily cut version of the early '50s with a Berlin cast and forces conducted by **Helmut Koch** was briefly circulated here (Vanguard/Bach Guild), while an even more drastically abridged Stuttgart performance under **Hans Grischkat** had a short and obscure life (Period), both of which deserve little beyond mention. But bulking a little more seriously is a 1975 recording that gave the score virtually complete, though of course in German (Berlin). The only cast member of note is the young Schreier, whose acidulous voice makes him aptly into a kind of punk king. The others are variable, while the chorus is enthusiastic but not well-blended and the orchestra is accomplished but listless. The ultimate problem is conductor **Dietrich Knothe,** who shows some occasional vitality, but generally just plods vacuously through the score.

The first English-language recording also came out of Germany, one of **Rilling**'s first productions in the early '60s. Released here for a while by Vox, it was substantially cut, and the cast of American, German, and Norwegian singers brought together quite a mix of accents. Most of the cast was rather routine, but Wilfrid Jochims invested Belshazzar with some vitality, while standout Sylvia Stahlman, if not vocally handsome, brought real feeling and verity of character to Nitocris.

The two PI recordings were the first to use substantially complete scores, carefully based on the first production of 1745, but assimilating some subsequent changes. **Harnoncourt**'s 1975 contribution was one of his first ventures into Handel's vocal works (Teldec 35326 or 10275, 3CD), and **Pinnock** made his recording in 1990 (DG Archiv 431793, 3CD). Differences of date and temperament result in quite different approaches. Fired by his new and experimental instrumental resources, Harnoncourt pushes their colors relentlessly, pursuing brash and provocative agogic effects and inflection and generally exploiting dramatic feeling. Fourteen years later, Pinnock was committed to more moderate and less abrasive instrumental sound, he has a choir with far better diction than Harnoncourt's Swedish chorus, and generally prefers lovely sound to striking effect.

Such differences are also reflected in the solo work. Harnoncourt's singers are committed to theatrics and willing to take risks. His Belshazzar, Robert Tear, portrays a character of fully rounded decadence, a kind of Handelian Herod, whereas Pinnock's Rolfe Johnson, if brash and rakish, sometime sounds almost heroic. Pinnock's Augér is a warm-spirited and motherly Nitocris, brooding in regal introspection, while Harnoncourt's Felicity Palmer is more varied and assertive in vocal color. The travesty female mezzo role of Daniel is pretty two-dimensional, and both casts use countertenors; Harnoncourt's Esswood has a more admonitory dignity, while Pinnock's Bowman is slightly heavier of voice. In the female mezzo role of Cyrus, Pinnock's Robbin makes him a precocious young man of vivacity but hardly adult caliber, whereas Harnoncourt's Maureen Lehane, if matronly in tone, suggests a stronger, more aggressive personality. And so it goes. Each performance is valid of its kind, and each will favor different tastes.

The Choice of Hercules (1751).

This is closer to a cantata than an oratorio, at well under an hour in running time. And in fact, there is a secular cantata by Bach, *Hercules auf dem Scheidewege* ("Hercules at the Cross-roads"), BWV 213, composed in 1733, on exactly the same subject. That subject is the formative moment in the young life of the hero Hercules at which he must make an irreversible choice between a life of pleasure and a life of virtue (the two alternatives personified by importunate characters). The text was apparently written by Morell, the last of Handel's scrivener-collaborators, and was based on immediate models. It was probably created so the composer could fit it to music left over from the abandoned theater project *Alceste*—a score from which he took materials used in other works of this period, too, but that provided the bulk of the music for this one in particular. The resulting work had little independent life of its own, but was performed as an appendage in his late revivals of *Alexander's Feast* to flesh out a full evening's entertainment.

Of its two recordings, the first was made in 1975 by **Ledger** with a distinguished British cast (EMI), the second in 1982 by **Pommer** with a cast of international voices and accents (♦Capriccio 10019). Handel meant the part of Hercules for either travesty mezzo or alto castrato, but both of these recordings use a countertenor. Bowman's full voice is familiar and well employed for Ledger, while Pommer's Alaine Zaepffel is lighter and more feminine in sound, but thoughtful. Pommer's Venceslava Hruba-Freiberger is not quite in a class with Ledger's more seductive Harper as Pleasure. But it's much harder to choose between the lovely, dusky sternness of Ledger's Watts or the just plain beautiful singing of Pommer's Augér. Ledger makes good use of the King's College Choir and the ASMF, but the overly spacious recording venue makes for rather murky and veiled sound, whereas Pommer's Leipzig choir and MI orchestra are recorded with far greater vividness. The advantage of availability just now speaks obviously for Pommer, which, allowing for variable diction problems, is certainly quite satisfying musically.

Deborah (1733).

This adapts from the *Book of Judges* a blood-and-thunder story from the early history of the Hebrews in their struggle with the Canaanites. Tthe title character is the Prophetess and Judge who prompts another woman to seduce and destroy an enemy general (anticipating the Apocryphal story of Judith). The score was hastily assembled, with plentiful self-borrowings, at a time of difficulty for Handel's operatic commitments and when the success of the revived *Esther* suggested that cultivating the public's new interest in English-language drama—at least with sacred justifications, during the Lenten season when secular theaters were closed—was a good idea. Despite the work's flaws and patchwork character, it was well received by the public, and Handel was able to revive it a number of times over the years.

Floating around is a single disc of wretchedly recorded excerpts from a concert performance at the 1970 Maggio Musicale Fiorentino, ham-handedly conducted by **Muti** with soloists of various nationalities (including Cotrubas). Its only interest is the featured solos of Norman—who is so far from the amateurish pickup that she's hardly audible (Memories). Happily, the work has received a more proper treatment from **King,** with his small PI orchestra and two Anglican church choirs (♦Hyperion 66841/42, 2CD). His solutions to gender-casting aren't always ideal, though Abinoam, written for the great bass Montagnana, is finely realized by George. But the sum total turns out to yield some fine listening, something lovers of Handel and Baroque music should not neglect.

Esther (1718/32).

Originally called *Haman and Mordecai,* this tells the Old Testament story of the Jewish Queen of Persia as filtered through Racine's treatment. This is Handel's (and music's) first English oratorio. It began as an experiment during Handel's residence at Cannons (1718) and then was extensively overhauled for public performances in London (in which, for the only time with his English oratorios, he had the production staged). While his opera company was fighting for its life, Handel still saw such a venture as peripheral, and even borrowed a good deal of the music from earlier works (such as the *Brockes Passion*). Though the score is uneven, it's nevertheless full of fine things, especially in its less cluttered original form. Above all, it shows his recognition of the possibilities of the chorus, not only in the old sense of Greek drama, but also as the embodiment of a people.

Its debut recording came in 1984 by **Hogwood** (Oiseau-Lyre 414423, 2CD), followed by **Christophers** in 1995 (♦Collins (70402, 2CD), both of whom use the original 1718 form of the work. (I wish one of them had used some of the later revisions to illustrate Handel's practices of transformation). Both have strong casts. I prefer the dignity of Kwella and the thoughtful sensitivity of Rolfe Johnson as Esther and Ahasuerus for Hogwood to the fuller but heavier characterizations by Lynda Russell and Thomas Randle for Christophers. Between the latter's firm-voiced Argenta and Hogwood's Kirkby as the Israelite Woman, any choice is difficult. Otherwise, Christophers's singers display slightly stronger profiles than Hogwood's. Both recordings employ refined PI groups: Hogwood uses a choir including boys, as Handel would have, and tends to pace in dignified stateliness, while Christophers is a bit faster, more dramatically urgent, with a crack chamber choir of mixed voices and slightly closer, brighter sound. (He also throws an orchestrated oboe sonata as an intermezzo.) I wish the Oiseau-Lyre recording, long deleted, could be restored, but Christophers is the welcome reality now.

Hercules (1745).

This might well be called "The Death of Hercules," or even better, "Dejanira," after the tormented wife who, out of misguided jealousy, tries to recover the love of Hercules by using magic she misunderstands, instead causing his agonizing destruction. The libretto was derived from Sophocles and Ovid and offers a wonderful dramatic plot full of poignantly human characters and motivations of a timeless nature. Usually classified as a "secular oratorio," it is, along with its predecessor of the previous year, *Semele,* an example of English opera in all but name and history. Not appreciated in its day, it has continued to be neglected in ours. Yet any fair acquaintance reveals it to be a true masterpiece.

Demonstrating that even attention can be damaging if it's misguided, we have an taping in really awful sound of a 1958 performance at La Scala conducted by **von Matačič.** The score was cut and reshaped to fit modern operatic tastes, with a celebrity cast (including Schwarzkopf, Corelli, Barbieri, Bastianini, and, in the title role, Jerome Hines). It's now on CD, for what it's worth (Golden Melodram, 2CD).

Fortunately, *Hercules* has had two substantial commercial recordings—both of them somewhat cut, however. The first, with Viennese chorus and orchestra under the capable **Priestman,** had the kind of cast he worked with for his Westminster recordings of Handel operas—Forrester, Luis Quilico, Stich-Randall, Young—all essentially of operatic type (1966: RCA). Only in 1982 did we have the first PI recording, based on a performance for the Göttingen Festival by **Gardiner,** with a cast of mostly young and fresh-voiced singers: Tomlinson as a brooding hero, and Walker as a compellingly tormented Dejanira; plus Jennifer Smith and Rolfe Johnson, among the others (♦DG Archiv 447 689, 2CD).

Into the breach has come a curious anomaly belatedly issued, a Leipzig Radio recording dating back to 1984 (Berlin). The fact that it's in German would prompt immediate dismissal were it not for some interesting points. In the first place, it follows the Chrysander edition faithfully and gives the full score complete for the first time on discs. Second, it's a remarkably good performance. The conductor is the knowing **Wolf-Dieter Hauschild,** who has a fine MI orchestra and one of Europe's best choirs (the Radio Leipzig Choir) at his disposal. He also has some interesting soloists, however unfamiliar their names are here. Hauschild prefers Handel's grandeur and dignity to his impassioned theatricality, so a spirit of serious and thoughtful but heavy detachment weighs down the production, reins in the singers, and deflates what dramatic tension could have been generated. That limited projection of true music drama, plus the inevitable objection of language renders this release a flawed stop-gap until we have a new and proper recording, if not a restored Gardiner set.

Israel in Egypt (*1739*). This is the second of the three works that Handel introduced in the year that began his decisive shift in creativity from Italian opera to English oratorio. Unlike the intensely dramatic (veritably operatic) *Saul* that preceded it, *Israel in Egypt* is not narrative but (like *Messiah* to come) contemplative; there are no characters and (unlike *Messiah*) the soloists are along for the ride, providing breathing spaces for the true protagonist, the chorus. The work is indeed a grandiose choral ode, in which the chorus creates great tonal pictures that describe or reflect upon the deliverance of the Children of Israel from Egypt and their passage of the Red Sea.

The work evolved in stages, as Handel decided in the process to recycle intact his long *Funeral Anthem for Queen Caroline,* which is all but totally choral. Its opening words, "The ways of Zion do mourn," became "The sons of Zion do mourn," with the feminine pronouns made masculine to turn it into "The Lamentation of the Israelites for Joseph" as Part I. The new music became Parts II and III. This totally unconventional work puzzled the public, which never took to it. In publication, the opening Anthem was re-detached and the remaining two parts were published separately (as Parts I and II), leaving it something of a Michelangelesque torso. (And with an abrupt beginning without any orchestral introduction, a deficiency remedied in many recordings by using either the introduction to the *Funeral Anthem* or an overture from another oratorio.) Even in such confusion, however, it stands as one of the very greatest extended works ever written for massed human voices.

It has been treated well, if not always wisely, by recordings; there have been some 16 over the years, most of them giving only the latter two parts (all 2LP or 2CD). The earliest was a staid and reliable performance by established English soloists (Elsie Morison and Richard Lewis among them) under **Goehr** (Concert Hall/Handel Society). Its needless flaw was the strange omission of the potent trombones (which Handel had also used in *Saul,* but rarely elsewhere), reducing a lot of Handel's effects to anemia. More vigorous and integral was a Berlin Radio performance under the rock-solid **Helmut Koch,** sung in German (Vanguard/Bach Guild).

Sargent made no improvement, giving the work the old-fashioned grandiose treatment (EMI/Angel). Though he had fine soloists, he introduced the pernicious practice of economizing on the two bass soloists by replacing them in their duet (their only appearance) with braying men's choral sections (EMI/Angel). Further, knowing better than Handel again, he also eliminated the trombones (saving more fees!) and otherwise touched up the scoring, topping it all off with a number of arbitrary cuts.

The advent of stereo at last allowed recordings to do justice to Handel's recurrent use of powerful double-choral writing. **Abravanel** was the first to exploit this, using forces in Utah (where there is a strong choral tradition), with fine local soloists (augmented by the young Bumbry) in a rousing performance (Westminster). Alas, there are flies in the ointment: more of those arbitrary cuts, and the discreet replacement of those troublesome trombones with French horns. A massive and sometimes powerful 1959 concert performance by the huge Dessoff Choir and the Symphony of the Air under **Paul Boepple** used the complete score (trombones and all), with fine local soloists but that silly choral duet again instead of two basses (Vox). Flaws continued to plague even as fine a version as **Frederic Waldman**'s: a really thorough and stylish delivery of the full score, with outstanding soloists, but still that stupid choral duet instead of bass soloists (Decca).

The first plateau of solid achievement was reached by **Mackerras** (1970: ♦DG Archiv 429530); everything is correctly in place, with a splendid team of soloists and a massive choir in a performance of majesty and weight. This is the ideal choice for those who like traditional feeling without period instruments. For contrast there is a much lighter and more deft version: well-balanced forces of Oxford's Christ Church Cathedral (with boy trebles), the English Chamber Orchestra, and a generally good solo group, led by **Preston,** who adds the "Cuckoo and Nightingale" organ concerto, as Handel himself once did, as a makeshift overture (1975: London 443470, with Chandos Anthem 10). It's a bargain for those who like stylish clarity as against weight and power.

Something of the same qualities can be heard in **Gardiner**'s first recording (1978). Still using modern instruments and a modest choir, with soloists mostly drawn from it, Gardiner's trademarks of brisk, springy rhythms, incisive articulation, and illuminating details make this one of the strongest arguments for clarity over power, though there is certainly strength in the large double-choral segments (♦Erato 45399). This release includes Gardiner's recording from the same year of the *Funeral Anthem* with its original wording, thus recovering all the material, if not the sequence, of Handel's full original version.

Something of Gardiner's spirit can be found in a 1981 Radio Leipzig performance; the local soloists are little better than adequate (though the two basses are fine), but **Wolf-Dieter Hauschild** draws some magnificent work out of his choir and orchestra. The handicap is the singing in German translation, and I wish this conductor might be given a chance with English-competent performers (Berlin). Ten years later we still find a German performance relentlessly sung in German and clinging to the outmoded old two-part format. **Heinz Hennig,** an experienced performer of Baroque music, leads his Hanover Boy's Choir and a PI group in a musically competent but undistinguished performance, with good soloists, among them the celebrated Jacobs, obviously in the last phase of his singing career. This has only local German appeal (Thorophon).

Attention to the *Funeral Anthem*'s important links to what we think of as *Israel in Egypt* prompted most newer recordings to restore it in Handel's original scheme of a coherent three-part work. The first to do this was **Harry Saltzman** in 1985 concert performances (♦Newport). Unfortunately, Newport chose never to release this on CD but only in a pair of cassettes, which sadly doomed it to obscurity and short life. While his soloists, drawn from the choral ranks, were undistinguished, they were fully adequate, and the performance as a whole is one of powerful energy, artistic excitement, and stylistic insight, marred only by obtrusively American-accented diction. Despite the lack of studio polish, the closely miked clarity is unique for realism and detail. This version deserves survival somehow.

Parrott picked up the torch with a superb recording (1990: ♦EMI 54018, reissued as Virgin 561350). For the full three-part score, he used a superb solo group of early-music specialists (Argenta, Emily van Evera, Timothy Wilson, Rolfe Johnson, David Thomas, Jeremy White), his Taverner Choir (32 mixed voices, but with male altos and a "white" tone) and a 40-member PI orchestra, getting sonorities and balances just right. The only drawback is that his pace is sometimes a bit relaxed and sedate, rendering some of the choruses more understated than they ought to be. **Gardiner** gave it another try by documenting his performances at the 1990 Göttingen Festival (Philips). Once more he deals only with the latter two parts; again, he uses (very fine) soloists from his choristers, but this time he has his PI group. The interpretation is again lucid and energetic, even more finely recorded than last time, and yet, to my taste, lacking something of the vitality and meaning of his first recording.

Christophers is also disappointing (Collins). Interpretively, he presents an outstanding performance, with generally ideal tempos and well-judged phrasing and shaping. His choir, The Sixteen, sings with wonderful clarity and precision, and the period orchestral playing is fine. Unfortunately, the soloists, taken from the choir personnel, are indifferent to weak and (if splendid in Renaissance music) out of place here. The choir of only 26 singers is spread too thin to give sufficient thrust, especially in the double choruses. The choir placement is so distant in so much reverberation that their clarity is blurred and there's little spatial distinction between their two-choir divisions. Nor is much contributed by a more recent recording, made in Copenhagen in 1998 under **Morten Topp** (Classico). He makes a gesture towards revised perceptions by including at least a reduction (about half) of the Funeral Anthem Part I, and he leads an intelligent performance, with strong choral singing and good solo work. But there are occasional accent problems, and the overall quality isn't enough to place this version high on the list.

On the other hand, the latest recording suggests that enlightened perspective on this work has finally settled in securely. **Cleobury** offers the integral three-part version. An able solo quartet (Gritton, Chance, Bostridge, Varcoe), supplemented as needed, sing admirably, and the trebles of the King's College Choir avoid the edginess that boys' voices often have, while the Brandenburg Consort provides lucid support. While it all seems to work at first, Cleobury's blandly brisk pacing leads to an inescapable sense of perfunctory neutrality that sacrifices spacious dignity without any gain in energy. If the double-choral effects are reasonably realized by the engineers, the King's College acoustics blur a good deal of the part-writing, and the all-important trombones seem to have been exiled to the vestry, diluting the pomp and solid foundation they should contribute. In all, this version lacks the spirit-raising vitality with which this music should overflow, and that both Gardiner I and Parrott achieved.

Israel in Egypt is a work as elusive as it is magnificent, and there may never be a truly perfect recording; there certainly is none just now, so the best recommendations are Mackerras (if you can find it) for non-period instruments and power, and either Parrott or Gardiner for period style and clarity (and I prefer Gardiner I, which also offers much more music for less money).

Jephtha (*1752*). This is Handel's last great oratorio masterpiece and his last original work. The composer was 66; his health was declining, and he was losing his sight—though not his inspiration, despite his mounting difficulties at putting pen to paper. He was becoming, if not bitter, at least more deeply introspective, and brooding, like the religious man he was, on God's reasons for inflicting suffering on his children. Such a frame of mind naturally drew him to the libretto Morell prepared for him.

The grim story of Jephte (or Jephtha) has been, over the centuries, perhaps second only to that of Job in attracting artistic treatments of the theme of a man trapped and tormented by his faith in God. As sketched in the *Book of Judges,* it tells of the early Hebrew leader who vows, in return for victory over his people's enemies, to sacrifice the first thing he meets upon returning home; that proves, with horrific irony, to be his beloved daughter. Morell cobbled up a quasi-happy ending that saves the daughter (for a life as a kind of Hebrew nun), giving a Christian softening to this vestigial echo of Biblical human sacrifice. But that must have seemed anticlimactic to Handel, who devotes the bulk of the work to probing the dark mysteries of the human condition, which can bring the shift from the heights of glory to the depths of misery he was learning to know all too well. (One show-stopping chorus begins, "How dark, O Lord, are thy decrees/All hid from human sight," and ends, "Whatever is, is right.") The result is one of the composer's most humane and moving works, not to be missed either to appreciate Handel or to discover what art can contribute to deepening our understanding of human life.

The considerable German interest in Handel's oratorios produced a German-language recording in 1970 led with dignity and solemnity by **Helmut Koch,** circulated briefly and to be recalled now only for the appearance of the young Schreier in the title role (Eterna). By that time, however, the actual debut recording of the work had already appeared, in 1969 under **Somary** (reissued in England as ♦Vanguard 08.509173, 3CD). With his fairly traditional but excellent choral and orchestral forces, Somary had a virtual dream cast: Alexander Young as a heroic Jephtha; the wonderful Watts compellingly human as his outraged wife Storgè; Reri Grist as their perky daughter Iphis; Forrester formidable as Jephtha's would-be-son-in-law Hamor (an alto role actually written by Handel for countertenor, and so assigned in all other recordings); and a boy treble as the *deus ex machina* Angel. With only one item cut, this beautifully molded performance still gives rich non-period performing value.

It was challenged by an equally handsome recording by **Marriner** in 1979, with a chorus of boy trebles and men plus the ASMF and another outstanding cast—Rolfe-Johnson a more bluff and straightforward Jephtha and Esswood notably fine as Hamor, with splendid work also from Margaret Marshall, Alfreda Hodgson, Christopher Keyte, and Kirkby as an ethereal Angel (Argo). Where Somary offered some degree of vigor, Marriner emphasized suavity, with operatic stylizing in solo movements but a stateliness in the choral movements; Argo's recorded sound is a bit veiled, Somary's more open.

Three PI recordings appeared all but simultaneously in 1979. The first was, predictably, by **Harnoncourt** (Telefunken/Teldec). He brought to this venture his usual combination of insight and eccentricity, his emphasis upon intensified drama, and a multinational cast of variable quality. The second PI version should have been a guaranteed winner but is less than perfect: **Gardiner,** represented in a live performance at the 1988 Göttingen Festival (Philips). There are some cuts—unnecessary in the abstract, though understandable in the concert hall for so long a work—and at the head of the cast Nigel Robson is a rather lackluster Jephtha, earnest but diffident both dramatically and vocally. The rest of the cast is good news, however; von Otter is a powerful Storgè, while soprano Dawson and countertenor Chance make a noteworthy pair of lovers and Varcoe is an aptly brotherly Zebul. Gardiner has particularly lucid choral and PI forces, and he sustains a brisk precision throughout. His conception of the score is tragic, the concentration of public performance serving to tighten a sense of contemplation and profundity.

If Gardiner views the work as tragedy, there is a return to Harnoncourt's sense of the dramatic in a 1992 recording (Berlin). **Marcus Creed** presides over forces mixing mostly English with German singers, at a time when a Handel vocal performance in Germany no longer automatically mandated German language. The cast is dominated by Ainsley, whose ringing and emotionally diversified portrayal is the best Jephtha since Young. Oelze is a lovely Iphis and countertenor Köhler is a satisfactory Hamor, while Denley creates another powerful Storgè and Julia Gooding pops in as the Angel. Creed seems to have worked out his own edition of the score, and he loses no opportunity to impart intense urgency, even at the expense of profundity, in tempos regularly faster than Gardiner's. His choir is nicely disciplined, and his orchestra represents an early recorded appearance of the Akademie für Alte Musik Berlin, rapidly becoming one of the best PI bands in Europe, here quite matching the pungency of Gardiner's effects.

There is, thus, no ideal recording for now, but Gardiner is perhaps the best general choice, with Creed quite impressive and not to be scorned at a more moderate price, while those with more traditional tastes should look or lobby for Somary to be restored.

Joseph and his Brethren (1744). This is one of the lowliest stepchildren among the oratorios, almost never heard today, though it had good success with Handel's own public. Its retelling of the Biblical story is filtered through subsequent treatments and emerges as a confused muddle. Uncharacteristically, Handel wrote a totally fresh score, altogether free of his usual self-borrowings. The verdict of past commentators—that there are some fine moments amid indifferent surroundings—is essentially just, but from Handel even the routine is worth hearing. The work had to wait until 1996 for its first and only recording by **King,** with a fine cast that exactly matches Handel's vocal scorings, a choir of boys and men and his PI group (♦Hyperion 67171/73, 3CD). Not a high priority for Handel novices, but a necessity for Handel specialists.

Joshua (1748). This is the last of Handel's blood-and-thunder Old Testament epics celebrating Jehovah's triumph through his Chosen People. From one perspective, it's just a grim story of fanatic Good Guys conquering other people on God's mandate (modern-day parallels are optional). The libretto is full of pious doggerel, and the characters are simplistic and flat. Joshua himself is a remote and one-dimensional zealot; most of the talking is left to a noble but stuffy elder, Caleb, whose daughter and a drippy young officer she loves are the closest things in the piece to human beings. But it's the music that counts, and fortunately this is a score full of some truly wonderful things, notwithstanding all its borrowings and swappings from other works (not to mention other composers). Of course, Handel always responded well to the Good Things of Life—battles, human disasters, natural upheavals—and so there are several of his delightful pictorial sections (Jericho's walls collapse, the sun and moon are halted).

Commercial attention to this work came in 1990 when (in the record industry's normally strange way of working) two recordings were made at the same time, by **King** (♦Hyperion 66461/62) and **Palmer** (♦Newport 85515), both with period instruments (and both 2CD). Each makes carefully considered editorial choices for different details, but the real contrast is in approach. King uses a numerically closer approximation of Handel's working forces than Palmer, whose own period players are rougher and more strident than King's suave group. In fact, Palmer aims at intensity and analytical clarity, directing forcefully, rather rigidly, with little nuance, whereas King is constantly shaping lines and imparting flow while illuminating details along the way, in richer tonal sonority.

The respective casts respond accordingly. Take the title character, who is little more than a sanctimonious Terminator: King's Ainsley is splendidly lyrical and lovely, which is almost making too much of the role; less handsome vocally, Palmer's Aler is aptly straightforward. The usually excellent George is slightly mushy as Caleb for King, while the manly and ringing Ostendorf is more alive and interesting for Palmer. Of the lovers, for Caleb's daughter we have the sweet but smallish and bland voice of Baird (Palmer) against the light but idiosyncratic and more assertive brightness of Kirkby (King), so you must decide if you like your virginal purity to be fluttery or piping. Handel wanted a mezzo-soprano for young Othniel and we get that from Palmer in Fortunato, whose strong singing projects the character's youthful ardor well. King gives us a countertenor instead: the distinguished Bowman delivers elegant musicality and lovely singing but suggests little personality. Each recording has its points, and if a choice must be made, it ultimately depends on whether you prefer Palmer's dramatic bent or King's greater musicality.

Judas Maccabaeus (1747). This was Handel's blatant trading on the Duke of Cumberland's victory over the Scots and the Stuart cause in April 1746, using a treatment of the Jewish hero as a hardly veiled salute to the "Bloody Butcher of Colloden." If its sublimated jingoism makes it a kind of Handelian counterpart to Shakespeare's *Henry V,* it's still a score full of rousing and beautiful music. A popular standby in the composer's day and repertoire, it has long been second in popularity only to *Messiah* among Handel's oratorios, as reflected in its ample recording history.

Of some 14 recordings, we can dispose quickly of the German-language ones. There were some celebrity versions (with various degrees of reduction), honestly meant for the German market. A 1954 Berlin concert performance under the distinguished **Fricsay,** with the likes of Häfliger, Stader, and the young Fischer-Dieskau, was documented in a "historic" release (Melodram). A drastically cut 1963 performance by **Kubelik** is still honestly musical in its old-fashioned way, and of lasting interest for Wunderlich as Judas (Orfeo 475992). Two others featured Schreier, the first in a minor role in a 1966 performance under the stolid **Koch,** which featured Häfliger again as Judas, with other notables (Janowitz, Töpper, Adam) in the cast (Berlin). Schreier was then promoted to the title role in a 1983 studio recording under **Gönnenwein,** with Donath and Lipovšek along as well (Deutsche Harmonia Mundi).

Meanwhile, the first English-language recording was among the first of **Abravanel**'s mid-50s recordings in Utah (Concert Hall/Handel Society). There were lots of cuts, and the soloists were mostly locals, but they sang intelligently and the choral work was fine. He made a second try in stereo around 1959, this time giving the full Chrysander score and mixing in with local soloists such rising notables as John McCollum in the lead, Arroyo, and the young Bumbry, then a contralto (MCA). Conceived on the grand scale of traditional oratorio performance, it's still a musically rousing and satisfying version.

Two subsequent rush jobs in Vienna had short LP lives. **Thomas Scherman**'s from the mid-'60s is heavily cut, capitalizing on the tired

Jan Peerce as Judas, and with Arroyo again, but otherwise coarse and undistinguished (Vox). Conscientiously complete, on the other hand, was a recording by the dogged if uninspiring **Simon**, his soloists including a frayed Barry Morell in the title role, with a crystalline Blegen and sturdy Simon (RCA). (Both of these, by the way, had alarmingly hideous jacket covers.)

From further in the 1970s came two particularly fine examples of stylish compromise versions, alert to progress in historical and stylistic perspectives but still with ties to the best traditions of richly vocal and polished MI performance. **Somary** offers fine choral work and consistently wonderful solo singing from Harper, Watts, Young, and Shirley-Quirk, its only drawback being that it's heavily cut (♦Vanguard 4071/72, 2CD). But **Mackerras** was Chrysander-complete (1976: ♦DG Archiv 447692, 3CD). His chorus offered the bite and pungency of boy trebles with men, plus another high-powered lineup of soloists: Baker, Palmer, Ryland Davies, Shirley-Quirk again. Despite the fullness of length, Mackerras drew it all into an effective entity, nicely balancing lovely singing with an ebb and flow of dramatic tension.

The PI approach of historical accuracy was brought to bear on this score all of a sudden, in three recordings made in a bunch in 1992. The first was by **King** (♦Hyperion 66641/42, 2CD). Using a performing edition that carefully sorts out Handel's own insertions, transfers, and changes ("O had I Jubal's lyre" is out, but "See the conqu'ring hero comes" stays in), King leads with gusto and energy, and with full-blooded playing that will allay the fears of those who dislike period sounds. Whether martial or contemplative, the music continues to flow and bounce, and the trumpets-and-drums militarism never sounded so thrilling. Jamie MacDougall is a rather lightweight Judas, if earnest, while the other soloists (Kirkby, Denley, Bowman, George) are familiar early-music experts.

Second in the PI line was a surprising demonstration of German cosmopolitanism by **Thomas Fey,** with a chorus of 37 and a PI orchestra of 27, both based in Heidelberg (Christophorus). The edition is pragmatic, drawing on a diversity of variant numbers, and it's sung, quite well, in English, by young local soloists hardly familiar here. Although this set is somewhat outclassed by the competition, it's by no means to be shrugged off, especially at a bargain price.

Finally, the end of 1992 brought **McGegan,** a recording made in California with his Berkeley chorus (rather too obtrusively American in accents) and Philharmonia Baroque Orchestra (Harmonia Mundi). His Judas, de Mey, is a sensitive lyric tenor of great taste, but he sounds out of his element here, and David Thomas, whose smallish bass voice can be used with such style and agility, sounds a bit tired and uncommanding as Simon. Still, mezzo Patricia Spence is quite competitive, while soprano Saffer is outstanding and particularly stylish in her embellishments. McGegan's leadership is steady and vigorous, though nowhere near as insightful as King's. What gives McGegan's recording unique interest is an editorial innovation: deciding to follow mostly the strict 1747 version, he then provides eight variant numbers in an appendix (recalling his variorum treatment of *Messiah*), all crammed into two very well-packed CDs.

There is obvious value in all three PI versions, though for musical satisfaction I suggest King. For non-period approaches, the truncated versions of Somary and even Abravanel will provide immediate pleasure, at least until the restoration of the transcendent Mackerras recording.

The Occasional Oratorio (1746).
This is an occasional oratorio indeed: a confection cobbled up to boost public morale in London in the weeks before the Duke of Cumberland finally defeated Bonnie Prince Charlie and ended the Stuart threat to the Hanoverian government. It has no plot or narrative, so it's really a contemplative oratorio (like *Israel in Egypt* or even *Messiah*) rather than a dramatic one; more properly, its text is simply a piece of propaganda, denouncing treason and rebellion and anticipating divinely guaranteed victory and peace. To convey all this, Handel hastily assembled a score with far more than his usual quantity of self-borrowings: bits of *Athalia* and *Deborah,* great slabs of *Israel,* the anthem *Zadok the Priest* and bits of the Op. 6 concerti, as well as nuggets of Telemann, Arne, and even Martin Luther. But it's rather fun watching these recyclings whiz by, and there's also a lot of new music, which isn't as bad as the commentators so long told us. In fact, the whole silly thing really works rather well as a piece of musical puffery, at least as it's finally served up in its long-delayed debut recording by the indefatigable Handel excavator, **King** (♦Hyperion 66961/62, 2CD). A fine group of soloists give it their very fine all, and the choral work is quite exciting at times. A fascinating novelty, if you don't take it seriously.

Ode for St. Cecilia's Day (1739).
This sets Dryden's poem beginning "From Harmony, from heav'nly Harmony." The text was written for the London Cecilian celebration of 1687 and was set then by Giovanni Battista Draghi (c1640–1708), whose score has been recorded (Hyperion). Handel decided to set it anew himself and give its debut performance on the saint's traditional feast day (November 22) as the third of his new and boldly English works in the (for him) pivotal year of 1739. Given its subject matter, it might well be considered with the other celebratory odes discussed above, but it wasn't meant for court or dynastic occasions, as were virtually all of the others; it was intended for public concert use, paralleling the previous Dryden-texted work, *Alexander's Feast.* And, if not as long as that, it's still extended and ambitious in scope. Dryden's reflections on the different kinds of music and musical effects gave Handel perfect cues for imaginative display, and his score is one of his happiest and most flamboyant.

Of eight recordings, two are very special and will appeal to those less interested in matters of stylistic propriety. From about 1960 comes a slightly overblown treatment by **Bernstein,** with Adele Addison and John McCollum as the quite handsome soloists; its ebullient and romanticized approach works largely through the conductor's sheer will-power (Sony). Another rather romanticized treatment is also shaped by a remarkable personality: **Benjamin Britten,** conducting an Aldeburgh Festival performance in 1967 (BBC 8009, with Britten pieces). Harper and Pears are strong soloists, with instrumentalists including Julian Bream, Philip Jones, and Philip Ledger. It's a rousing affair, somewhat more in the British tradition than Bernstein.

The earliest recording of all, a tasteful if slightly dated version under **Anthony Bernard,** with Stich-Randall and Young, has resurfaced (Accord). Two recordings feature the King's College Choir with MI orchestras: **Willcocks,** with April Cantelo and Partridge, made a fine 1967 recording with lovely moments (London 460287, with *L'Allegro*), but there is still more eloquence and style in the other King's recording under **Ledger** with the particularly beguiling Jill Gomez and the ringing Robert Tear (1982: ♦ASV 512). For idiomatic MI performance, Ledger's is the one to have.

Of course, the PI movement made its bid, first with **Harnoncourt;** his soloists (Palmer, Rolfe Johnson) are outstanding, but the Swedish choir's English is badly muddled and Concentus Musicus is rough and unpolished (Teldec). A far more coherent, accomplished, and satisfying version is **Pinnock**'s 1985 recording with Lott and again Rolfe Johnson as superlative soloists; the range of moods and colors is particularly well captured, and this is the preferred PI approach as of now (♦DG Archiv 419220). The same year also brought a rather retrograde version by forces of Handel's home town, Halle, but **Kluttig**'s direction is no more than serviceable (Berlin); Monika Frimmer is a soprano I have admired elsewhere, but neither she nor tenor Büchner can come near their British counterparts, and both they and the choir offer blurred English diction. Not competitive at any price.

Note, however, that this score was another that was Mozartized. There is a quite commendable PI recording of that—in German translation, of course—under **Spering**, with a much inferior *Acis and Galatea* (Opus 111). Mozart's adjustments are interesting and quite effective, including the transfer of the last aria from soprano to a bass. Mertens renders it with diffidence, but Schlick and Prégardien are very strong soloists.

Samson (1743). This was first presented between the Dublin premiere of *Messiah* in 1742 and its first London performance in 1743. Though this work was slow to win its eventual popularity, it confirmed Handel's irreversible commitment to English oratorio, now that his career in Italian opera lay in ruins. For his decisive plunge into the new idiom of English drama he turned again to the poetry of Milton, specifically the blind poet's highly personalized verse-drama about the blinded Hebrew hero, *Samson Agonistes*, as adapted by Newburgh Hamilton. Drawing on his operatic experimentation, he established his now recurrent practice of casting his protagonist with the previously unfashionable tenor voice. Above all, he could draw on his choral skills to blend the traditions of ancient Greek drama that Milton evoked with his own Old Testament vision of the Hebrews in conflict with their enemies.

For all of this great music-drama's lofty stature, it has had only five complete recordings. A heavily cut performance, sung in German by a local cast led by **Günther Weissenborn** at a Göttingen Festival, was quite musical, but its circulation was brief in a 3LP set on the Everest label in its shady days. The first really serious recording came in 1962 from Utah under **Abravanel** (♦Vanguard 131/32, 2CD). Despite a number of cuts, it catches the grandeur of the score, with Peerce as an operatically individualistic Samson and the clear-toned Curtin as Dalila (and some lesser parts as well)—one of the few documentations of a full role by this wonderful American artist and, overall, still a quite satisfying rendition.

The first stab at a complete recording—using a composite text mixing the 1743 versions with changes in later revivals—came in 1968 with **Richter**'s set (DG Archiv, reissued by MHS, 4LP). His impressive cast was headed by the stylish Alexander Young, who creates a Samson of dignity and nobility; his Dalila, Arroyo, was a duly sensual tease; Norma Procter was a little overripe in tone but still a sensitive Micah, while the remaining cast sang with polished artistry. The problem was Richter's static, bland, undramatic view of the work, with ponderous tempos that often let one's attention drift.

The MI approach was given its fullest realization ten years later by **Leppard,** in a version essentially based on the 1743 original score as collated in the Chrysander edition and presented in full for the most complete recording then made. This was originally issued here by RCA (1978: 4LP—with probably the ugliest jacket cover in history) but then reissued (♦Erato 45994, 3CD), only to be dropped since then. A slightly weak link is Robert Tear in the title role, whose gurgly singing isn't always pleasant, but who still projects a genuinely tragic figure, a weary giant who is led through suffering to renewed purpose. The rest of the cast is a ticket to heaven. Baker is a mature, perhaps a bit matronly but

worldly-wise Dalila, and Watts is a melting Micah anyone would treasure as a friend; Shirley-Quirk is a paragon of paternal anguish as Manoa, while Luxon is an aptly sneering braggart as Harapha; Burrowes, Lott, and Langridge are luxury casting in smaller roles. Above all, if somewhat traditional in spirit, Leppard captures quite consistently the powerful dramatic spirit of the work, in a landmark performance whose absence from circulation is disgraceful.

Two PI recordings followed. **Harnoncourt**'s was from a 1992 concert performance, with a cast of mixed backgrounds and quality (♦Teldec 74871, 2CD). Rolfe Johnson portrays a younger, lighter hero—a deceived youth, cut off in his prime and kinda mad about it—lucid and fresh-voiced but a little short on tragic depth. Alexander delivers a lovely soprano Dalila as young and sensual, in contrast with the more womanly mezzo Baker. Harnoncourt follows one of Handel's revival decisions and transfers Micah from a contralto to a countertenor—in this case Kowalski, who has a warmly feminine if not particularly beautiful voice that's intelligently used here but no match for Watts's gorgeous singing. As Harapha, Alastair Miles is a superbly thundering bully—the role's best realization anywhere—but Scharinger is a mush-mouthed Manoa to be forgotten.

The minor female-role singers are particularly fine: Angela Maria Blasi and Maria Venuti, the latter's breathtakingly daring "Let the bright Seraphim" seriously challenging Leppard's Lott and nearly stealing the show. The Arnold Schoenberg Choir is admirably crisp in its singing, but with blurry diction that only adds to the mixture of accents. Most serious is Harnoncourt's drastic cutting, omitting some 18 numbers (though, admittedly, not all the losses are grave). The residue is a stripped-down, streamlined, more concentrated drama, which Harnoncourt projects in a performance that is unconventional, brash, and musicologically provocative but refreshing.

There couldn't be a more contrasting rival than **Christophers** (1996: Collins 70382, 3CD). His performing edition again uses essentially the 1743 original but with some leavening; thus he follows Handel's later practice of replacing the original funeral march with the famous Dead March from *Saul*, and he gives the first realization of a choral conclusion to the famous "Let the bright Seraphim" aria at the end. His cast, though mostly of non-stellar rank, all sing very handsomely, and his chamber choir The Sixteen (here 20 strong) sings with beautiful clarity, with accomplished period playing. It's all neat and elegant, but, ultimately, also thin and superficial, with little sense of dramatic meaning or thrust. There is still ample room for a more balanced but fully complete version in the PI category, while Abravanel will do in the MI corner; but the nonperiod Leppard recording is still the one to hunt (or hunger) for.

Saul (1739), with a fine libretto drawn by Jennens from the *Books of Samuel I and II*, was the first of the three great compositions premiered in 1739, marking Handel's serious commitment to English-language works as the last embers of his career in Italian opera were flickering out. From his operatic background, however, in his new appreciation of what might be made of the oratorio form, he produced one of the great musical tragedies of the Baroque or any other era. The leading characters are brilliantly etched and the instrumental scoring is among the richest Handel ever produced. (So extensive, too, are the exclusively orchestral sections that the Bärenreiter label was once able to make up an entire LP devoted to them).

This work has earned 10 recordings over the years, only three of them with period instruments and only two of them substantially complete. An important landmark was by **Wöldike**, recorded in Vienna in 1962

(Vanguard 112/13, 2CD). This involved a Danish choir of men and boys, a slack Viennese orchestra, and an international cast of soloists with strange accent mixes. Thomas Hemsley was weak of voice but strong in character as Saul, but Watts was unforgettable in the castrato role of David, with strong singing also from Vyvyan as Saul's daughter Michal and Herbert Handt as his son Jonathan. Serious cuts were inflicted, but this was the first recording to demonstrate the work's power and grandeur. A curious, and of course cut, 1971 performance recorded in concert was circulated for a little while by the Swiss VDE label (3LP). It was done bravely in English, and surprisingly well much of the time, under a Shanghai-born Chinese conductor, **Chen Liang-Sheng,** its cast including no less than Andrew Foldi (Saul) and Cuenod (David), plus Della Jones in two minor roles.

It was only a year later that the first truly complete recording appeared, by **Mackerras** (♦DG Archiv 447696; MHS 534832, 3CD). Its Saul, Donald McIntyre, is rather staid and static, but Bowman is a strong countertenor David, Ryland Davies a sturdy Jonathan, Sheila Armstrong and Margaret Price each lovely (if just a bit oversized vocally) as Saul's two daughters, and John Winfield an interesting *travesti*-tenor Witch of Endor. Mackerras retains something of traditional festival grandeur and paces things in rather stately fashion, but brings compelling power to the choral and orchestral sections.

The final word on the semi-traditional approach came in 1981 from **Ledger** (EMI). The cast was fine, beginning with deeply felt portrayals of Saul and Jonathan by Allen and Tear; Esswood was another strong countertenor David, with Margaret Marshall and Sally Burgess lovely as the two daughters and Martyn Hill as another *travesti* Witch. Ledger's leadership was vigorous, but again there were some musically disappointing cuts; above all, the great reverberance of King's College Chapel made for a harmfully blurry recording.

The PI approach began in 1985 with a concert performance under **Harnoncourt** (Teldec). His cast is headed by Fischer-Dieskau, who pulls out all the dramatic stops in his melodramatic portrayal of the neurotic Saul, while his wife, Julia Varady, plays a haughty Merab. Thoroughly in their element are Rolfe Johnson as a staunch Jonathan, Esswood back as David, and Elizabeth Gale as a sweet Michal, plus the all-purpose tenor Helmut Wildhaber playing five small roles (including the Witch). But the mix of accents becomes distracting, and the Vienna choir is almost unintelligible. As always, Harnoncourt has interesting ideas, but they are projected brusquely, in a heavily cut edition. This is a powerful but flawed realization that would have only qualified endorsement even it were not soon followed by one of the great Handel oratorio recordings.

For such is the version under **Gardiner,** again from a concert performance, at the 1989 Göttingen Festival (♦Philips 426265, 3CD). The cast is remarkably well balanced and of consistent quality: Miles as a genuinely tragic personality, Ragin a countertenor David of vitality, Ainsley a ringing Jonathan, Dawson a warm-voiced Michal, Don Brown a brooding Merab, plus another tenor Witch. The choral singing and the period orchestral timbres are magnificent, and handsomely captured by the engineers.

Gardiner set an awesome standard for any who follow, and it's bravely challenged, if not wholly met, by two PI recordings from Germany, both made at concert performances in 1997. The first was led by **Peter Neumann** following staged presentations in Cologne (♦MD+G 3320801, 3CD). The cast is again international, but accent problems with the English text are this time minimal. Predictably, the veteran Elwes is a standout as a dramatically compelling Jonathan. The sturdy-voiced American bass Gregory Reinhart is more gloomy than paranoid as Saul, but undeniably powerful. Matthias Koch is a very lightweight countertenor David, but the other singers are satisfactory and comfortable in their roles. Most important is Neumann's very forceful leadership; he conjures up majestic choral sound, gets a lot out of Handel's rich instrumentation, and generates a great deal of excitement at the right times, especially the end—all recorded quite lucidly.

The other German recording, made in Frankfurt under **Joachim Carlos Martini,** likewise has an international cast, with English diction ranging from barely adequate to excellent (Naxos 554361, 3CD). Swiss-born Stephan MacLeod is vocally strong but makes Saul into more of an irritated grandfather than a raging and paranoid king. Countertenor David Cordier is likewise weak as David. The familiar Schlick (Michal) and tenor Knut Schoch (Jonathan) are excellent vocally but have diction problems. American soprano Claron McFadden, however, is outstanding; she invests the role of the scornful Merab with real personality, and also reclaims the Witch of Endor from conventional "travesty" assignment to a tenor. The orchestra is excellent but miking balances aren't ideal, and Martini's direction, if serious and committed, yields on points to Neumann's greater alertness. A good performance at the price, but not fully competitive beyond that.

While Neumann's energy is a nice foil to Mackerras's stateliness, any claims by either to clear recommendation have to be nullified by Gardiner's incontestable priority

Semele (1744). This is, perhaps with *Hercules,* the closest Handel came to writing a genuine English opera, though he himself never staged it but presented it entirely as a concert work, while his unappreciative audience was shocked by what some called "a bawdy opera". It tells Ovid's story of the young princess who, as one of Jupiter's paramours, is goaded by the jealous Juno and by her own vanity to make Jupiter appear to her in all his blazing glory, which inevitably consumes her, though not before the child she carries is rescued to become the great Dionysus. The libretto was derived from a prototype by Congreve prepared for and used by an earlier composer, John Eccles. Handel's interest may have been prompted by some analogies that could be drawn with a court scandal of the moment, involving a mistress of George II. The libretto nevertheless provided solid inspiration for him to produce one of his most rapturously beautiful scores—and for Handel that is truly something!

The work has been treated generally quite well on records. The debut recording was in the mid-1950s under the musicologist and conductor **Anthony Lewis,** whose approach is somewhat dated now but was loving and sensitive, abetted by the stylish continuo realizations of the great scholar-musician, Thurston Dart (Oiseau-Lyre). The rich-voiced Vyvyan long set a standard for vocal beauty in this role; William Herbert as her Jupiter was strained almost beyond his vocal capacity, but he was honestly musical and suggested real character; Watts had little to do as Iris after all the many cuts were made, but Anna Pollack was a wonderfully nasty Juno, and the lesser roles were handled with style. This recording made me an instant slave to the work, and I cherish it still; it would be nice to have this classic restored on CD.

Some two decades passed before it was superseded by **Somary** (1973: Vanguard). Again heavily (if differently) cut, it offered a better-balanced cast. Armstrong is a little more girlish as Semele, while Tear is a vocally more supple if somewhat blustery Jupiter. Following Handel's own (and dramatically sensible) practice, the roles of Ino and Juno are given to the same singer, in this case the wonderful Watts, who plays artfully with the double identity. Diaz is sonorous in his likewise-precedented double assignment as Cadmus and Somnus. Mark Deller is a travesty of his father Alfred as the cipher character of Athemas—which actually was first sung for Handel by a countertenor (though in the only revival by a castrato). Felicity Palmer is fetching as Iris. The sound is spoiled by mismanaged miking and shifting balances, no more than adequate in the remastering. But if you can accept the flaws and the truncation for a streamlined version, musically rendered at bargain price, this reissue is one to consider.

How good Somary's recording is can be appreciated by comparing it with a recording made the following year (1974) and recently resurrected (Berlin). **Koch** was a staunch proponent of Handel and championed his oratorios in a number of recorded performances—all, of course, sung in German for his local audiences. His conception of Handel in heavy stateliness and stiff grandeur is somewhat dated now, and his deliberate, weighty pacing is particularly out of place in this work, which drags badly in his hands, in an almost uncut version. Drained of its Baroque zest, this witty parable of sensuality and ambition becomes almost a dark tragedy, with surely unintended suggestions of Wagnerian anachronism—Juno as a vindictive Fricka, helped by a Somnus-turned-Fafner as she grimly pursues her husband, a youthfully tenorized Wotan who is reduced to swooning over a kind of sopranified Erda, while Athemas stands by as a befuddled (countertenor turned baritone) Gunther. The only reason to have a recording such as this is to appreciate how much better all the others are.

Happily, new heights were scaled by **Gardiner** in the only PI recording to date (1981: ♦Erato 45982, 2CD). A number of cuts are still made, but the performance is wonderfully lithe and stylish, revealing new subtleties and delicacies of orchestral color. There are standout portrayals: Rolfe Johnson is an elegant and godlike Jupiter, Burrowes glows as Semele, Della Jones is a forceful Juno, Lloyd is a movingly paternal Cadmus, and Thomas is a superbly sleepy Somnus; the others are also admirable. Reissued at an irresistible bargain price, this set is an enduring treasure.

It now has either complementary pairing with or serious competition from **John Nelson,** who, in the wake of a concert performance in New York in 1985, eventually transferred at least some of his cast to London in 1990 for a studio recording (♦DG 435782, 2CD). Nelson opted for a fully complete score (omitting an oddball number that Handel himself dropped, though, curiously, Gardiner includes it in his version). Going far beyond Gardiner's energy, Nelson displays a highly charged approach, with tempos sometimes forced or driven and often hard on his singers, and creates a propulsive excitement and dramatic force, eventually appearing just right after all.

His approach is particularly congenial to his title-role soprano, Battle; beautifully agile in her virtuosic singing, she rejects the oratorian coolness of preceding Semeles to create a strikingly theatrical character, a spoiled young centerfold sexpot, narcissistic and compulsively ambitious. Aler, smooth-toned and vocally dexterous, makes a more ardent and more achingly mortal-sounding Jupiter than most of his rivals. With his tidy, dry yet penetrating bass, double-assigned Ramey is dignified as Cadmus and funny as Somnus; McNair brings Iris to life ably as a foil to Juno's fussing. With his part given complete for the first time on records, Chance is a bit hooty as Athemas but manages to make the character a little less freakish than usual.

But the show is virtually stolen by Horne, who avoids her usual practice of singing the all-purpose character named Marilyn Horne. Matching what Watts achieved for Somary in differentiating her two charac-

ters, Horne convincingly suggests the love-struck young Ino as quite distinct from the jealous goddess, with Juno-disguised-as-Ino an artful fusion of the two. To top it all off, Nelson's MI orchestra plays robustly, and he further uses his chorus, beautifully clear and disciplined, to achieve stunningly powerful effects, all in close, sharp, precise sound. For now, accordingly, we're left with the choice between Gardiner's musicologically stylish and musically elegant (and somewhat cut) version, and Nelson's highly dramatic and supercharged (and complete) version that departs so refreshingly and convincingly from the traditional oratorio style.

Solomon (1749). This is little short of a miracle. In some ways it's a smug paean of self-congratulation to the English Enlightenment, with the wise King George II being honored in the character of Solomon. But this work also allowed Handel to combine the great choral power he had developed in *Israel in Egypt* with the delicate intimacy exhibited in the contrasting *Susanna* composed at the same time. There is no plot in a conventional sense, but each of the three acts is focused around small-scale interactions of sublime beauty (Solomon with his beloved Queen; Solomon judging the two Harlots; Solomon receiving the Queen of Sheba) set within blockbuster frames of staggering grandeur and pageantry.

Its history on records is an odd saga with a happy ending. The first chapter was writ wrong by **Beecham** who, in 1956, recorded his version of the score (Angel/Seraphim). That involved not only a complete reorchestration but an unbelievably savage deconstruction of Handel's music, chopping, reshuffling, throwing out almost half of it and smashing the rest down to a two-act travesty (literally throwing out the baby in the process). Having committed these horrors (which would never have been accepted from any other conductor), Beecham in his supremely self-confident arrogance then had the nerve to give the surviving farrago a beguilingly beautiful performance, aided by a distinguished cast (baritone John Cameron as Solomon; Young as the High Priest Zadok; Elsie Morison as Pharaoh's Daughter, the Queen; and Marshall as the Queen of Sheba). For better or worse, this curiosity has long been unavailable, but you never know when it might come out at us again.

Stages of progress were exhibited, however, in two subsequent recordings. In 1968 RCA issued a version under **Simon,** whose admirable Handelian enterprise was too little matched by forceful leadership. This was closer to Handel than Beecham, but the score was still heavily cut, especially in Act III. **Somary** followed in 1974 (Vanguard, reissued in England as 08 5086.72). Stylistically far superior to Simon, Somary offered incisive tempos, a crack orchestra (English Chamber) and an alert, sonorous choir, representing the best of progressive performance esthetics (historically sensitive but still pre-period, and still connected to the grand oratorio traditions), lucidly recorded. Armstrong, singing both Queens and the First Harlot (and sounding everywhere delectable) left Palmer with only the bitchy Second Harlot. The men were more uneven: Diaz noble but rather too heavy as Solomon, Tear fussy and mannered as Zadok, and the woolly Michael Rippon merely adequate as the Levite. Somary also made a number of cuts, different from Simon's.

Somary set the standard for years, until there appeared what is certainly among the greatest of Handel oratorio recordings, plausibly *the* greatest. This was made in 1984 by **Gardiner** in connection with that year's Göttingen Festival (♦Philips 412612, 2CD). It has one drawback: the same cuts that Somary made, plus one more, leaving us still longing for absolutely everything Handel wrote for this work. Otherwise, Gardiner brings a musicality, a technical superiority, and an exuberant energy that far outclass every previous recording, capturing both the grandeur and the gentle human warmth with equal success.

The cast is excellent, musically and dramatically. The role of Solomon was composed for a travesty mezzo, and Gardiner reclaims it from the bad old tradition of giving it to a baritone: Watkinson's rich, creamy, yet steady mezzo is neither clearly feminine nor androgynously pseudo-masculine, producing an apt neutrality of sound in a delivery that has a sincere nobility about it. Argenta is a bewitching Queen; Joan Rodgers and Della Jones are the most moving Harlots on records. Only Hendricks, with a precise but somewhat keen edge to her voice, reveals some distracting mannerisms (a throatiness in both diction and vocal color), which, if hardly disastrous, leave me somewhat dissatisfied. Reduced to the minority, the men are fine: Rolfe Johnson doesn't efface memories of Young, but is straightforward without being bland; Varcoe, with a light voice but solid musicianship, gives the only acceptable rendition the rather vacuous role of the Levite has yet had on discs. Gardiner's choir is only some 30 in number but sings with full-blooded clarity. This is also the first version with period instruments, which contribute some particularly delectable wind sounds. To the obvious verdict I add only one more suggestion: anyone who is not bowled over by this magnificent music in this magnificent recording has to be brain-dead.

Susanna (1749). This contrasts with the mature oratorios of this period, so freighted with grandeur and festivity. Perhaps as a refreshing novelty amid all that, Handel was happy to turn to small-scale drama celebrating the triumph of private virtue and honor over deceit and corruption, set in a small and essentially rural context. The chorus, which serves to comment as well as participate in crowd scenes, is still restrained in function, while the instrumentation is on a small and limited scale. The vivid evocation of rural life looks back to *L'Allegro* and even *Acis* in its naturalistic imagery, prompting Winton Dean to call it "an opera of English village life." At the same time, the moralizing is not hammered at but demonstrated in the drama, with tired old clichés about honor and chastity coming movingly alive in the genuine warmth of the 63-year-old composer's humane realization.

The plot is, of course, moralizing and quasi-Biblical, derived from the Apocryphal sections of the *Book of Daniel*. It tells how Susanna, wife of a wealthy Jewish merchant, spurns the advances of a pair of lustful village elders, who then vindictively charge her with adultery, her vindication secured by the Prophet Daniel in one of the most laughable exposures of inconsistent testimonies in the history of judicial reporting. Handel responds to this theme with a subtlety of understatement that contrasts strikingly with the blazing overstatement of the sibling *Solomon* of the same year.

Such understatement may explain in part this work's all but total neglect until 1990, when **McGegan** led a concert performance in Berkeley (♦Harmonia Mundi 907030/32, 3CD). His PI group is rather lean but effective, while the chorus has superlative balance and weight, in dry but lucid concert-hall sound; above all, his leadership shapes the performance with obvious love and understanding. Though the choral passages are beautiful, the soloists are the prime concern, in one lovely segment after another. For a change, too, it doesn't seem as if the Bad Guys are having all the fun: the two Elders sound like manic-compulsives, characterized with delicious panting hypocrisy by the insinuating tenor of Jeffrey Thomas and the sinister bass of David Thomas—matched brothers in name and carnality. The role of the husband, Joachim, written for a *travesti* mezzo, is here taken by countertenor Minter, somewhat

lacking in relative weight but expert in vocal execution and characterization, as always. William Parker is perfect as both Susanna's father and the Judge. The precocious Prophet Daniel (aka Counsel for the Defense) was originally sung for Handel by a boy treble but is taken here by Jill Feldman, whose thin, reedy, pointed voice is used to fine characterizational effect. The heaviest burden falls on the Susanna, Lorraine Hunt; though there are occasional touches of veiled and hooty sound, she brings off her part with great warmth and expressiveness. No lover of Handel's music should miss this wonderful work, at last given its due by McGegan.

Theodora (1750). This has nothing to do with Justinian's notorious Empress (notwithstanding the misguided cover art of one recorded release). Unique among Handel's religious oratorios, it deals not with Old Testament subjects, nor even with New Testament material, but with a story of the early Christian faith. Derived by the pious Rev. Morell from a tale of Christian martyrdom, it tells of a noble Roman lady who is a Christian amid the final great persecution under the Emperor Diocletian, and of the Roman officer, Didymus, who loves her and stands by his woman to the cruel end, while other characters lurk about and variously wring their hands. The superficial theme is the impregnability of true Christian faith, and this allows Handel to use his chorus tellingly in pious reflections. But Handel also recognized this as really a study in the purity of love, loyalty, and self-sacrifice, sustained by the hope of the individual for rest after suffering. Its score is full of music of indescribable beauty, and Handel was frustrated that his audiences were indifferent to it. He himself thought his greatest single masterpiece was not the Hallelujah chorus from You-Know-What, but this work's little choral triptych, "He saw the lovely youth". Not to know *Theodora* is not to know Handel at his most noble and humane.

Appreciation has begun to come to this great work only in recent decades, and has led to three recordings, each of merit. The first was long its only exposition, and a glowing one: **Somary**'s debut recording in 1968 (Vanguard). He made a number of cuts, most of them ones that Handel himself made in his performances, plus some *da capo* repeats. With a reliable British chorus and orchestra, he leads in what could be called a progressive traditional style of intelligent pre-period esthetics, linked to but not bound by the grand line of oratorio sensibilities. His cast is vocally handsome. Harper as Theodora and Maureen Lehane as her confidante Irene render their parts with feeling, and Young is an asset, as always, as Septimius, Didymus's friend. That role was written for an alto castrato, Antonio Guadagni (who was later to create the role of Orfeo in Gluck's opera); the fine contralto Forrester takes over the part with particularly strong and memorable singing. The other soloists are reliable.

The first of the two PI recordings was **Harnoncourt**'s, a 1990 concert performance (Teldec). He made the same cuts as Somary plus a few more, making for a significantly reduced but more taut and compact score. And it is propulsiveness and vigor that he constantly seeks, in contrast to Somary's concentration on introspection and nobility. The cast is international in its accents but fairly uniform in quality. Alexander makes a light and more girlish but pure and poignant title character. Her Didymus is here a countertenor, Kowalski, who has an unusually rich contralto voice for his tribe, if sometimes gurgly or not totally in control. The other soloists are thoroughly satisfying musically. The Arnold Schoenberg Choir sings with great sonority, if slightly muddy diction, and Concentus Musicus Wien plays lustily, with some nice variations in continuo instruments.

Finally came **McGegan** with his Berkeley recording (♦Harmonia Mundi 907060/62, 3CD). Not only did he give the score complete for the first time but also included a variant number—at the price, of course, of an additional disc. In general, his cast compares favorably with those of his predecessors. Against the lightweight Alexander, Lorraine Hunt is more womanly with her stronger voice; Minter, another countertenor Didymus, is lighter and more agile than Kowalski (much less Forrester). Jennifer Lane is pretty well matched with her rivals as Irene, while David Thomas brings more character to the minor role of Valens than does the barking Scharinger. Only in the case of Septimius, a minor part, does McGegan's man, the choppy Jeffrey Thomas, yield to his competitor, the more stylish Blochwitz. McGegan's chorus lacks the sonority of Harnoncourt's, but sings with clarity and idiomatic diction. His period players are far less abrasive and more colorful than Harnoncourt's, and the continuo work is even more varied. On the other hand, comparisons repeatedly reveal that Harnoncourt is less rigid and more probing in his conducting, achieving some powerful effects especially in choral sections that McGegan never approaches. The sound is dry, but detailed and analytic.

The curse or blessing of these choices is that no one can be exclusively recommended: McGegan for completeness and a fine idiomatic cast; Harnoncourt for greater dramatic punch if less idiomatic style; Somary for a more traditional musicality, expressiveness, and beauty of vocal work. With the torturer at my toenails I might opt for McGegan as the best compromise priority, with the other two tied for second place according to taste.

The Triumph of Time and Truth (1757). This is the end of the line. But it's a line that fittingly brings us back to the beginning, in that it's a re-working of Handel's very first oratorio—not an English oratorio, but the first of his two for Italy, *Il trionfo del Tempo e del Disinganno* of 1707, an extended musical debate for four allegorical characters. Three decades later, in 1737, Handel plugged a space in his repertoire by overhauling this work, recasting some sections for chorus, and offering it, still in Italian, under the more direct title of *Il trionfo del Tempo e della Verità*. Then, 20 years later still, in 1757, with his eyesight all but totally gone and no longer able to pursue fully original composition, Handel turned back to this Italian work again. This time he had Morell adapt the Italian text into English and he revised and expanded the original music, adding new material (itself mostly borrowings from others of his works) to create his new-old and last oratorio.

No one would pretend it's great music, but it's attractive listening, and it has been made handsomely accessible in a 1982 recording in which **Darlow** leads a fine chamber choir with what was effectively Roy Goodman's PI Hanover Band in nascent form (♦Hyperion 66071/72, 2CD). Sopranos Gillian Fisher and Kirkby, countertenor Brett, tenor Partridge, and bass Varcoe constituted the deft solo team, in admirable recorded sound.   BARKER

Howard Hanson *(1896–1981)*

One of the most conservative and approachable of 20th-century American composers, Hanson wrote tonal and romantic music when romanticism was not in vogue. He exulted in melody, and his rich harmony was both mainstream and distinctive enough for there to be "Hanson chords." The musical hints of his Scandinavian background led some to call him the American Sibelius, but he was more melodic and colorful than the Finnish master.

Hanson was the first American winner of the Prix de Rome, an award that took him to Italy to study with Respighi. He was also dean of the Eastman School of Music for 40 years, where he taught or influenced many American composers while creating an "Eastman sound" that was less biting and urban than New York's Juilliard School. He was a strong conductor of his own and other music, mostly in a famous series of Mercury LPs issued during the '50s and '60s. They are collector's items prized for their dramatic, visceral sound, with great staging. The brightness in the violins was aptly softened in CD reissues that otherwise caught most, but not all, of the originals' special qualities.

Symphonies. Hanson's seven symphonies are consistently romantic. The cyclical 1 ("Nordic") was written in Italy and is the most powerful, with rugged, often march-like themes that appear in each movement. No. 2 ("Romantic") is Hanson's most famous work (particularly its signature theme). It's less rugged, more brooding, and more lyrical than 1 and less derivative of Sibelius and Nielsen. No. 3 returns to the world of 1, paying tribute to the efforts of Hanson's Scandinavian forebears in settling the American West by evoking their "rugged and turbulent character [and] religious mysticism." Anchored by a fervent chorale theme, it ranges from the industrious to the triumphant, with a modernistic finale. No. 4 ("Requiem") honors the death of Hanson's father and was the composer's favorite among his works. It's less romantic, more concise, and thematically spare than its predecessors, but no less expressive, and perhaps owing to its nature as a requiem, it's also more polyphonic.

Hanson described the fifteen-minute 5 ("Sinfonia Sacra") as "an attempt to invoke some of the atmosphere of tragedy and triumph, mysticism and affirmation" of Easter. It's a tightly structured, dramatic, and conflicted work; with its short phrases, passages of eerie beauty, and a spirited march, it doesn't sound all that "religious." No. 6 seems to stem from the relative terseness of 5 and is Hanson's most dissonant and rugged symphony, with a militarism and darkness not heard in the earlier works. It's based on a three-note motif explored in six movements of contrasting mood. No. 7 ("Sea Symphony") is Hanson's only choral symphony. Set to texts by Whitman, it represents a summation of and farewell to his career, combining his early style with the more concise writing that followed.

Schwarz's complete set with the Seattle Symphony on Delos includes 1 and 2 (♦3073, with *Elegy in Memory of Serge Koussevitzky*), 3 and 6 (♦3092, with *Fantasy Variations on a Theme of Youth*), 4 (♦3105, with *Lament for Beowulf, Merry Mount Suite, Pastorale;* and *Serenade*), and 5 and 7 (♦3130, with *Piano Concerto* and *Mosaics*). Delos also issued 2, 4, 6, and 7 with several of the above couplings (♦3705, 2CD). You can buy this set and rest content, not only with the symphonies but with a solid collection of other Hanson works. Schwarz's style is laid back and lyrical, flowing, and plush. Sit back and let the music fill the room. His orchestra is polished and rich; Delos's sound is dark, blended, and a bit covered.

Strong competition is provided by **Hanson**'s Eastman-Rochester Symphony recordings of the first three symphonies on Mercury: 1 and 2 (♦32008, with *Song of Democracy*) and 3 (♦34302, with *Elegy in Memory of Serge Koussevitzky* and *Lament for Beowulf*). They are more riveting, muscular, charged, dramatic, and passionate, as well as less flowing than Schwarz's versions; tempos tend to be a bit faster. Mercury's punchier sound helps bring out themes and instrumental colors more than the Delos acoustic, but it isn't as lush. You don't wallow as much as sit up in your chair. The Rochester orchestra is enthusiastic if not as polished as Seattle. Hanson isn't better than Schwarz; he's different and equally valid.

Kenneth Schermerhorn has begun a new set with the Nashville Symphony. In 1 he brings out the Sibelian qualities, particularly the Finn's tendency to break up long lines into shorter motifs. Tempos are slower, the mood reflective and inward. Some may find this penetrating, others lacking in excitement and power. It's certainly interesting, and the couplings are more than worth the price of the disc (◆Naxos 559072, with *Merry Mount Suite, Pan and the Priest,* and *Rhythmic Variations on Two Ancient Hymns*).

There are several other good recordings of 2. **Slatkin**'s sumptuousness goes beyond Schwarz's and takes Hanson's most romantic symphony almost to Rachmaninoff with the slowest and most expansive tempos. His St. Louis Symphony is even better than Seattle, and the sound is surprisingly warm and glowing for early digital (◆EMI 47850, with Barber's Violin Concerto). **Charles Gerhardt** blends Hanson's strength with Schwarz's lyricism and adds tension and sinew to the line to create the most gripping performance, as opposed to Hanson's powerful reading. The National Philharmonic is as good as the Rochester orchestra, and the sound is natural and expansive (◆Chesky 112, with Copland's *Billy the Kid* plus works of Gould and Griffes).

Hanson made a second recording of 2 with the Mormon Youth Symphony (◆Citadel 88110, with *Song of Democracy* and *Merry Mount Suite*). It's broader than his Mercury and more rugged. The orchestral playing won't make you forget St. Louis or even Rochester, but it's good and there is commitment from players struck with the occasion of a Hanson festival. **David Montgomery** fails to capture the work's romanticism; his rough-sounding Jena Philharmonic is a more serious flaw, and this budget disc is not a good value (Arte Nova, with Symphony 4, *Elegy*).

Schwarz is pretty much uncontested in 4 through 6, except for **Siegfried Landau**'s underrated 6 with the Westphalian Symphony. Still, Schwarz's 6 is tighter and more coherent, powerful, and convincing. What makes Landau tempting is the excellent coupling (Excelsior 5257, with Piano Concerto and Schuman's Symphony 7 by Abravanel). **Montgomery**'s 4 is not recommendable (Arte Nova, with 2). **Hanson**'s monos of 4 and 5 (Mercury) compare in style with his stereos, but Schwarz is very good in both, and stereo is an obvious advantage. Avoid the "electronic" stereo version of 4 on Mercury Golden Imports LP; it was transferred out of phase and sounds like it.

In 7, **Schwarz**'s blended, near-impressionistic account is interpretively fine and very well played. The hitch is sound that makes it hard to tell what the chorus is singing. **Hanson**'s version with the World Youth Chorus (Interlochen) and the National Music Camp High School Choir has the commitment, fervor, and occasion of all the Hanson-Citadel reissues and takes the same broad, powerful view. It also has big sound and bass. Still, No. 7 is sensuous and delicate enough to require more polish and finesse than these players can supply, particularly the slightly rough chorus (◆Citadel 88116 with *Lament for Beowulf, Pan and the Priest, Extended Theme,* and *Rhythmic Variations on Two Ancient Hymns*). Even so, this powerful performance is attractive, and Hanson lovers are going to want this disc for the recorded premiere of *Pan* and the Variations. *Pan* is dramatic, with more than the usual touch of Sibelius, while the Variations are American "hymn tune" string works. (Schwarz's companion works are also important.)

Other orchestral music. Many of Hanson's orchestral, choral, and chamber works are coupled with **Schwarz**'s symphony series. There is also a compilation of these fine performances on Delos (◆3150, 4CD). **Hanson** also recorded many of his other orchestral works for Mercury,

mono and stereo, some as couplings to the symphonies as noted. The performances follow the pattern of the Hanson Mercuries, and even those monos had fine, powerful sound. Any of these discs and their works are worth acquiring if you're still buying LPs. The couplings with **Schermerhorn**'s Symphony 1 are all excellent.

Mosaics is a masterly set of variations inspired by the mosaics at Palermo Cathedral. The variations are of interval relationships rather than melodies. The work sounds very much like its name: think of a lushly colorful tapestry viewed from different angles and vantage points of light. **Schwarz**'s beautiful performance is full and colorful (Delos 3130, with Symphonies 5 and 7 and Piano Concerto). **Hanson**'s sharply etched and punchier account is more dramatic and exciting but less beautiful—not an ideal combination in this work (Mercury LP, with Piano Concerto and John La Montaine's *Birds of Paradise*).

David Fetler leads the Rochester Chamber Orchestra in a splendid disc. (Other performers include the Meliora Quartet; Brian Preston, piano; David Craighead, organ; and Eileen Malone, harp.) The well-known Hanson trademarks are present, but I hear additional elements as well. *Nymphs* is a ballet set in the Scandinavian forested hills and fjords, evoking pastoralism, majesty, and rich pictures of the sea. The Organ Concerto is a luxuriant and complex fantasia-like work, evoking the sonorities of similar French pieces and rich in modal lyricism. *Concerto da Camera* is an early, vigorous work, another fantasia, full of piano arpeggios, sounding like an American Brahms. *Yuletide Pieces* are short piano works. Fine performances and sound (◆Albany 129, with *Four Pieces for Chorus*).

Concertos. The Piano Concerto is more lively, upbeat, and jazzy than most Hanson and is more driven by rhythm than by instrumental coloring and melody. **Rosenberger,** with Schwarz and the Seattle Symphony, is decent and well played but too laid back and smooth (◆Delos 3130, with Symphonies 5 and 7 and *Mosaics*). To get the energy and impact of this piece in good sound, try **List** (◆Excelsior 5257, with Symphony 6 led by Siegfried Landau and William Schuman's Symphony 7 with Abravanel). The MIT Symphony is no Seattle, but it plays well enough. David Epstein conducts with more spirit and rhythm than Schwarz, but it's List's powerful, idiomatic playing that carries the show. **Alfred Mouledous**'s account with the composer and the Eastman-Rochester Symphony may be more spirited than List—the rhythms are more sharply etched—but this wasn't one of the great sounding Mercuries, and List plays with more authority than the good but comparatively lightweight Mouledous (◆Mercury LP, with *Mosaics* and La Montaine's *Birds of Paradise*).

Chamber music. Hanson wrote his exuberant String Quartet while in Rome. His interest in lines and counterpoint derived from his admiration for Palestrina is obvious, as are the Stravinskian rhythms. The work is thorny, cerebral, and more neoclassical than we expect from this ultra-romantic composer, though still tonal and approachable. The **Lyric Art Quartet** is outstanding, and the sound is excellent (◆Citadel 88119, with Randall Thompson's two string quartets).

Piano music. Hanson wrote solo piano music before his studies with Respighi opened him to orchestral possibilities. The romantic Hanson is here with (in the words of Thomas Labe) "the bold outlines, the soaring melodies, the layered climaxes, the penchant for unpredictability, the subtle northern flavor," rich colors and a touch of the French rhapsodist. Labe completed the unfinished Piano Sonata; *For the First Time* is an arrangement of an orchestral work. **Labe** plays like a Rachmaninoff pianist to good effect (◆Naxos 559047).

Choral music. Hanson liked to write choral works to religious texts, including three psalms for four-part chorus (some with organ, one with baritone solo) and *A Prayer for the Middle Ages* in eight parts. All are in his broad symphonic sound with his patented harmonies and reflect his interest in Lutheran hymns, Bach, and Palestrina. The Roberts Wesleyan College Chorale led by **Robert Shewan** isn't sleek, but they sing in tune with a unique "town church choir" sound that has its appeal in these orchestral-sounding works (♦Albany 129, with many orchestral works).

The early *Lament for Beowulf* was inspired by the Anglo-Saxon epic. It powerfully—and starkly—captures the militaristic feeling of the poem along with the grief and sense of loss over the hero's death. **Hanson**'s recording with the Eastman-Rochester Orchestra and Chorus is lean, strong, and rhythmic, though it accents the orchestra too much over the set-back chorus. Otherwise, Mercury's focused and punchy sound fits the work well (♦Mercury 34302, with Symphony 3, *Elegy in Memory of Serge Koussevitzky*). **Hanson**'s second reading with the Mormon Youth Chorus and Orchestra is broadly taken and strong. The mix of youthful playing and singing with mature conducting replaces the energy and drive of the Mercury with power and breadth. The sound stage is huge and the bass immense (♦Citadel 88116, with Symphony 7, *Pan and the Priest, Extended Theme,* and *Rhythmic Variations on Two Ancient Hymns*). **Schwarz**'s reading doesn't muster the excitement of the first Hanson or the breadth of the second, and the choral sound is diffuse, but it's coupled with the only good Symphony 4 (♦3105, with Symphony 4, *Merry Mount Suite,; Pastorale,* and *Serenade*).

Dies Natalis is a rich orchestral set of variations based on a Lutheran Christmas chorale. *Lumen in Christo* for women's chorus and orchestra is written to sacred texts based on light. *Lux Aeterna* is a free orchestral rhapsody with viola obbligato inspired by Palestrina ("letting lines flow through melodies," as Hanson put it). *The Mystic Trumpeter* is less interesting, though narrator James Earl Jones is excellent. The performances by **Schwarz** and the Seattle Symphony and Chorale are fine, though the choral sound is a bit covered and thick (♦Delos 3160). All but *Dies Natalis* are first recordings.

Song of Democracy, set to Whitman poems, was written for the 50th anniversary of the National Education Association. Hanson wanted the piece to be performed by school orchestras and choirs, but this didn't prevent him from turning out a stirring, dramatic, and powerful work. **Hanson**'s first reading with the Eastman-Rochester orchestra and Eastman Chorus is fine, with good sound, sharing the powerful, thrusting quality of his other Mercury recordings (♦Mercury 32008, with Symphonies 1 and 2). His second reading with the Mormon Youth Chorus and Symphony is broader, larger in scale, and more reaching. A possible first choice, it has a sense of occasion and commitment, and the youthful voices are fitting for a work written for an educational group. It offers excellent analog sound, a bit forward with huge sound staging and bass, and clear choral enunciation (♦Citadel 88110, with Symphony 2 and *Merry Mount Suite*).

Timothy Seelig conducts a version for male voices and wind ensemble. It becomes almost a different piece with its darker timbres (not just from the absence of women but from the absence of violins as well), slower tempos, reduced drive, broader, rounder textures, and darker, deeper sound. The sense of tragedy it conveys may not fit Whitman's stirring words about democracy, but this performance is moving and touching.

Opera. *Merry Mount*'s great success at the Met in the '30s seemed to guarantee it a place in the repertory, but aside from a few successful

revivals, this never happened. The story, based on Hawthorne's "The Maypole of Merry Mount," concerns a Puritan minister's unleashing of his dormant hedonism and his resultant fall over an obsession with a woman. The music is romantic, stirring, and full of effusive, often modal melody. Much is centered around an opening hymn that's hard to forget. The orchestration is lush and substantial.

The only full recording is a broadcast transcription from the '30s led by **Serafin**, with baritone Tibbett and the Metropolitan Opera. The sound is noisy and barely passable, though it's clear that Tibbett sounded magnificent (Naxos). **Hanson** led a fine, hard-to-find stereo LP of excerpts in good sound that whets our appetite for the whole thing (♦Mercury LP). Supposedly a recording was taped in Seattle, but I know nothing of any release plans.

There are orchestral suites drawn from the opera. **Schwarz**'s is one of his better performances (♦Delos 3105, with Symphony 4, *Pastorale,* and *Serenade*). **Schermerhorn**'s reading is even better—a little more direct and less broad, which works well in this music (♦Naxos 559072, with Symphony 1, *Pan and the Priest,* and *Rhythmic Variations on Two Ancient Hymns*). I prefer both to **Hanson**'s second reading with the Mormon Youth Symphony (CIT 88110, with *Song of Democracy* and Symphony 2). That one has the same commitment as the others in this series, but it's a bit heavy and lacks the finesse and flair of Schwarz's Seattle Symphony, something this music needs. I haven't heard **Hanson**'s Mercury with the Eastman-Rochester Symphony, but I know of it as a classic (and expensive) LP.   HECHT

John Harbison (b. 1938)

Whether you view him as a radical conservative or a conservative radical, Harbison's music is memorable. At its heart is a deep and compelling lyricism welded to a formidable grasp of the composer's craft. Youthful studies in viola, tuba, and piano were completed at Princeton and Harvard, including study with Sessions and Babbitt. These early experiences, plus his work as a conductor, have given him a thorough grounding in writing for instruments and voices. Musicians enjoy performing his music because it's so gratefully written for their instruments. Harbison also has strong literary inclinations, even writing the libretto to his recent opera *The Great Gatsby,* and this sensitivity to text gives his vocal writing added point and poignancy. His ear for harmony is sure, and his distinctly American voice evokes Gershwin and jazz as easily as more classical influences like Stravinsky and Sessions, whose influence is deeply ingrained in his music.

Harbison has written three symphonies so far; Nos. 1 and 3 have been recorded. No. 1 shows his mastery of orchestration in a clear and traditional four-movement plan. His writing is sinewy and expressive without any tendency toward excess, and his use of the orchestral palette is colorful and transparent, never muddy. It's led by **Ozawa** with the Boston Symphony (♦New World 80331, with Olly Wilson's *Sinfonia*).

If 1 shows his restraint, 3 offers a more unbuttoned Harbison, but without any sacrifice of clarity. It's in five sections that play continuously, traversing a wide array of moods and textures and showing impressive artistic growth. This is a humdinger of a symphony and the Albany Symphony under **David Alan Miller** outclasses many better-known orchestras (♦Albany 390). The disc includes *The Most Often Used Chords* and Flute Concerto. The former, which made me grin when I first heard it, is a witty and knowing play on some oversimplified "fundamentals of music" found in blank music-writing books; the latter is a Stravinskian essay in flights of fancy. The scoring is crystalline, and flutist Randolph Bowman conveys a sense of ease and weightlessness in the darting lines of his part. This disc is essential listening for those interested in the composer.

The Viola Concerto is a superb piece—a wonderfully balanced four-movement work that's among the finest vehicles for this subdued instrument. **Laredo** puts it across beautifully, with Wolff directing the New Jersey Symphony (♦New World 80404). The composer's first-hand experience with the instrument is evident in the way he keeps its small voice present at all times, never overwhelmed by the orchestra. He has also written a concerto for the more brilliant voice of the violin, played by his wife, **Rose Mary Harbison,** in a disc filled out with a good selection of his choral music and *Recordare* for chamber ensemble (♦Koch 7310).

Harbison was awarded the Pulitzer Prize in 1987 for his cantata *The Flight into Egypt.* This is a "Christmas" work, though it's very introspective and challenging, examining "the dark side of Christmas," as the composer says in his notes (♦New World 80395). This disc is completed with two other strong pieces: *The Natural World,* a trio of poems set for soprano and chamber ensemble, and Concerto for Double Brass Choir and Orchestra. The former is a colorful work elegantly sung by **Janice Felty;** the latter is a harkening back to Gabrieli written for the brass players of the LA Philharmonic that offers some jangling, crunchy dissonances but is made accessible through its rhythmic brio.

Two excellent all-Harbison discs offer fine surveys of instrumental and vocal music, and both are enthusiastically recommended. "At First Light" presents four stunning works in a variety of settings, all written between 1980 and the mid-'90s (♦Archetype 60106). The first, *Due Libri dei Mottetti di Montale,* is a dazzling setting of poems by Eugenio Montale for soprano and chamber ensemble. **Lorraine Hunt** sings with the grace and loveliness she's noted for, beautifully accompanied by the Greenleaf Chamber Players. *Snow Country* for oboe and strings is a melancholy study in shadings. *Chorale Cantata* features **Upshaw** and oboist Peggy Pearson in a setting of texts by Martin Luther and poet Michael Fried that uses Luther's chorale tune "Aus tiefer Not" as thematic material.

"The Boston Collection" gives us three strong duo works and Harbison's fine Sonata 1 for piano (♦Archetype 60104). The Duo for Flute and Piano is the earliest piece here, written in 1981; the others are all from the late '80s. I like best the *Fantasy Duo* for violin and piano (dazzlingly played by **Rose Mary Harbison** and Robert Levin) and the Sonata. This single-movement sonata ("Roger Sessions In Memoriam") is a fine work that displays all his best qualities as a composer.

It has been recorded three times, and all are worthy accounts. Each pianist brings a distinctive personality to the music, but your choice will depend in some degree on what you wish to hear with it. **Judith Gordon** plays it wonderfully in the "Boston Collection" disc. **Robert Shannon**'s version is paired with a fantastic performance of Ives's "Concord Sonata," one of the best available; Harbison's piece sits well besides the colossal "Concord," sounding almost like a fifth movement to that work (♦Bridge 9036). **Ursula Oppens** includes it in her sweeping survey of "American Piano Music of Our Time" (♦Music & Arts 862, 2CD). Here it's placed in a different context, alongside 12 other post-war American composers. Of these, I favor Gordon's; she highlights the work's impressionistic qualities, has the most tonal variety, and makes the most of its dramatic shifts.

Harbison's interest in the theater has borne fruit with a number of notable works: the chamber opera *Full Moon in March* (CRI 454, NA), the ballet *Ulysses' Bow* (Nonesuch 79129, NA), and most recently his large-scale opera *The Great Gatsby.* Premiered to a generally positive reception, it has not been released at the time of writing. McINTIRE

Roy Harris (1898–1979)

Harris is readily identifiable by his continuous chordal movement, interpreted as the American wide-open spaces by most listeners. His love for full triads lends clarity to this movement, as does a use of block harmony that sounds simple, even crude, but gives the illusion of simplicity to what is actually a subtle instability. Thus he can imply an emotion, then take it back by invoking its opposite, like a landscape seen in sunlight, then under clouds, or the brighter and darker aspects of American history, to give it a more cosmic spin. Ain't music wonderful?

SYMPHONIES

1 (1933). This symphony shows us Harris with his style already in place but nowhere to go, full of ideas and atmosphere but a bit jumpy in syntax and undecided in direction. **Mester**'s Louisville performance emphasizes the music's somewhat scrappy character but is a lively reading clearly recorded (Albany 12). **Koussevitzky** in Boston gave it more convincing grandeur in a radio broadcast from 1934 (Pearl 9492).

3. Written four years later, this has remained Harris's most popular symphony. It progresses from a sort of fragmentary gloom to a visionary, almost Philip Glassian arpeggiated section (as subtly orchestrated, however, as Glass is predictable and ham-handed), building to a stirring Allegro that gradually fragments into a tragic chorale, underscored by timpani; it makes a powerful statement. **Koussevitzky** commissioned and recorded it in a 1942 reading that is still unrivaled for performance (Pearl 9492), though **Bernstein** also has a way with this piece in his two recordings with the NY Philharmonic in 1961 (♦Sony 60594) and 1985 (DG 19780). The latter is in particularly good sound, but the first is more driving, and it's coupled with some indispensable music by Diamond and Thompson.

There have been other memorable versions, notably by **Toscanini** (Dell'Arte 9020, NA)—terse and vehement—and **Hanson** (Mercury LP, NA)—dramatic and exciting in sound. **Ormandy** (RCA LP, NA) and **Hendl** (Desto LP, NA) aren't much on atmosphere, though Ormandy is notable for restoring a couple of passages during the difficult arpeggiated section that nearly everyone else cuts, including Koussevitzky and Bernstein. The only one who closes these cuts today is **Neeme Järvi,** whose Detroit interpretation has little else to recommend it, rushed and matter-of-fact as it is (Chandos 9474). **Mata** in Dallas is spacious but not very convincing or involved and makes the cuts (Dorian).

4 ("Folksong Symphony" for chorus and orchestra). This work puts Harris's concept of what constitutes a symphony to the test. These settings are curious, since the chorus sticks to the melody and words fairly strictly, rhythmic vagaries aside, and the orchestra surrounds them with typical Harris chords that threaten to derail them at every turn. This is fascinating and frequently moving, but tends to make the entire work sound experimental. There are two recordings, both good, neither great. **Abravanel** and his Utah forces were the more polished and better recorded in 1975 (Angel LP 36091, NA) but **Golschmann** is what's available, from 1960 (Vanguard 4076 or 107).

5. This symphony is a three-movement work of considerable beauty. It's a pity that the only available reading, by **Robert Whitney** and the Louisville Orchestra, though effectively played, suffers from some cuts and re-orchestrations that the composer later changed his mind about too late for the recording (Albany 12).

6 ("Gettysburg"). This is a tribute to Lincoln and the dead of the Civil War. It's deeply felt and powerful, and the Pacific Symphony gives it a stirring reading, in spite of the tempos chosen by **Keith Clark,** which tend to speed up gradually in each movement, not trusting the composer to hold his own without special pleading (Albany 64).

7. This is a one-movement Passacaglia, in which the underlying melody goes through an amazing number of changes in 19 minutes. Its first and only recording is still available, a fine mono version by **Ormandy** and the Philadelphia Orchestra (Albany 256).

8 and *9.* Both are played by **David Alan Miller** and the Albany Symphony in excellent performances recorded in fine sound (Albany 350). No. 8 is a light-textured piece setting scenes from the life of San Francisco's patron saint, St. Francis of Assisi. It's a lovely, positive work with a considerable piano part in its later stages. No. 9 is a more ambitious and emotionally ambiguous work written for Philadelphia, with quotations from the Constitution and Whitman's *Leaves of Grass.* These are strong compositions that make me wish someone would record Harris's other six symphonies.

OTHER ORCHESTRAL MUSIC

Harris's other orchestral works are less well documented on recordings than they should be. His early overture on *When Johnny Comes Marching Home* makes a surprisingly scrappy effect compared to his later work, but it provides a sample of his pre-Symphony 3 music. This and the more impressive late *Epilogue to Profiles in Courage: JFK* are played by the Louisville Orchestra conducted by **Mester** and **Robert Whitney** (Albany 27). Another short patriotic piece, *American Creed,* is included by **Schwarz** in an otherwise all-Copland disc (Delos 3140). A couple of attractive but poorly played scraps, *Chorale for Strings* and *Prelude & Fugue for Strings,* are included in an all-Harris disc conducted by **Harris** (Citadel 88114).

Elegy and Dance is led by **Jacob Avshalomov** with the Portland Youth Symphony in a rather muddily recorded disc (CRI 664). An attractive short suite, *Memories of a Child's Sunday,* is done beautifully by the Albany Symphony under **David Alan Miller** (Albany 350). A couple of works for concert band, *Cimarron* Overture and *West Point Symphony,* were played acceptably by the UCLA Wind Ensemble under **James Westbrook** and recorded on the now-defunct Bay Cities label (1002 & 1008, NA), but they have yet to find a place for reissue.

CONCERTOS

The early Piano Quintet was rearranged in 1960 into a Concerto for Piano and Strings, played by the composer's wife, **Johana Harris,** and a barely competent youth orchestra conducted by the composer (Citadel 88114). Also on this disc is a 1968 *Concerto for Amplified Piano, Brass, Percussion, & Basses,* an interesting, rare example of late Harris in a lively, sometimes jazzy idiom.

The 1949 Violin Concerto, in a form as free as a bird, which the violin tends to resemble, is given a fine performance by **Gregory Fulkerson** with the Louisville Symphony under Lawrence Leighton Smith (Albany 12).

CHAMBER MUSIC

String Quartet 2 (*Three Variations on a Theme*) is an early and lively work. The **Emerson Quartet** seems to be trying to make it sound more mainstream than it is; though they play it well, it's stylistically uncomfortable in their hands (New World 80453). The Violin Sonata, a strong work from 1942, was played beautifully by **Alexander Ross** and Richard Zimdars (Albany 105, NA). One of Harris's last works is a lovely one-movement duo for cello and piano, written for and recorded by **Terry King** and Johana Harris (Music & Arts 603).

PIANO MUSIC

Piano music made up a relatively small part of Harris's output, and it tends to be in miniature in form, though interesting. **Johana Harris** has recorded it all in versions that will be important historically, since most of the music was written for her (CRI 118). However, the recording is a bit boxy and **Richard Zimdars**'s disc of this material is just as good and includes the otherwise unavailable Violin Sonata, played by Alexander Ross (Albany 105, NA).

CHORAL MUSIC

There is only one CD of Harris's choral works; it includes major early compositions, notably *Symphony of Voices,* an a cappella setting of three of Walt Whitman's poems, and two other a cappella works, *Whitman Triptych* for women's chorus and *Three Songs of Democracy* for mixed chorus (Albany 164). There is also a 28-minute *Mass* with organ, an *Easter Motet* with brass and organ, a *Madrigal* for women's chorus and piano, and finally, an early a cappella setting of *When Johnny comes Marching Home.* All this is important material, but the **Roberts Wesleyan College Chorale** of Rochester, New York, isn't a distinguished group. Their sound is congested, and they have a distinct tendency to go flat.   MOORE

Lou Harrison *(b. 1917)*

Harrison is a prominent member of the "maverick" school, along with John Cage and Harry Partch, his slightly elder contemporaries. Some of his early percussion works are collaborations with Cage, while his involvement with just intonation and building and composing for American gamelan orchestras relates to Partch's work. To these elements must be added study with Schoenberg and a love for building elaborate melodies over a drone. Not infrequently these seemingly mutually exclusive elements proceed simultaneously; in the course of an extended work, movements in several styles will alternate in a piquant and pleasant fashion. Harrison has created an effective blend of his own inventions and predilections with Western aggregations like the classical orchestra. This survey is organized chronologically within each category; detailed discussion is limited to works with more than one available recording.

SYMPHONIES

Symphony on G (1948–61). This is technically Harrison's first, meaning the first finished. It is a dramatic, predominantly 12-tone score, though including the gently folksy sound of a tack piano and a sort of scherzo-suite consisting of a 12-tone waltz, a polka, "a song" and "a rondeau." **Gerhard Samuel**'s 1968 recording is serviceable, if a little dry in sound (CRI 715).

Elegiac Symphony. This was begun in 1942 but hung fire until 1976, making it Harrison's second. This monumental work is one of the composer's most impressive compositions, beautifully played in its many lyrical sections by **Dennis Russell Davies** and the American Composers Orchestra (MusicMasters 7021). The rhythmically complex second movement is a bit scrappy in ensemble, but the performance as a whole is successful. Meditative music contrasts with expressive, wailing, Schoenbergian chromaticism in the final movement.

3 (1982). This symphony was composed for the Cabrillo music festival, whose orchestra plays it under the indefatigable **Davies** (MusicMasters 7073). Perhaps less compelling than the first two as a whole (the finale is a bit long), it contains another multi-part scherzo and is altogether attractive.

4 (1990–95). This is a strong work, though the inclusion of narrated text (Coyote stories) as an extended finale, which Harrison ends with a tale about diarrhea, seems like gratuitous bad taste, a disease he sometimes suffers from. Otherwise, the symphony is very effective, including a fine 'Stampede.' The setting of these Indian tales is interesting: partly narrated, partly sung, and the words are audible, unlike some of his vocal works. The performance by **Barry Jekowsky** in "A Portrait" includes several other works, not all of them orchestral (Argo 455590).

OTHER ORCHESTRAL MUSIC

Generally speaking, the orchestral pieces conducted by **Davies** are well played and recorded. I also recommend a disc containing *Pacifika Rondo* (1963), a fascinating seven-movement study of musical styles around the Pacific (Phoenix 118). The unsophisticated sound of the Oakland Youth Symphony under **Robert Hughes** doesn't detract from the effect of this sometimes bizarre mixture of Eastern and Western instruments, nor does the close up, incipiently raw sound typical of Desto LPs.

Piano Concerto (1985). This is an effective four-movement work featuring what Harrison calls a "Stampede," originally a wild elaboration of an estampie. The live performance is by the unlikely combination of **Keith Jarrett** on piano with the Japan Philharmonic under Naoto Otomo (New World 366). The percussion section is not always synchronized with the soloist. Despite this, the work comes off well, with Harrison's sense of balance between consonant and dissonant music dramatically juxtaposed.

Suite for Violin and Strings. This is Harrison's arrangement of his Suite for Violin and American Gamelan (1974). It's a lovely work, quite different from the original in sound, and it's beautifully played by **Maria Bachman** with Sedares and the New Zealand Symphony (Koch 7465). The original is played by **David Abel** with gamelan (New Albion 15).

CHAMBER MUSIC

The chamber category is large, including early works for percussion and late ones for the American gamelan, as well as a few more traditional chamber works and some scores written for ballet, the two latter categories being mainly middle-period.

Concerto for Flute and Percussion (1939). One of Harrison's earliest works, this eight-minute, three-movement piece is all based on ostinatos, including such odd instruments as a turtle shell, a pod-rattle, Chinese tom-toms and the guiro. Both **Rachel Rudich** (CRI 568) and **Manuela Weiser** (BIS 272) are effective. Weiser is slightly more lively and incisive and recorded a little closer to the microphones than Rudich. However, the program as a whole is the selling point for both discs, and this piece is the only duplication.

Double Music. This is a collaboration with John Cage in which each composer was responsible for his own simultaneous instrumental lines in the way medieval organum was produced. The piece is mainly bells and gongs and makes a festive sound, and the wavering pitch on some of the instruments is amusing. This work is in both the **New Music Consort**'s disc (New World 80405), where it takes over six minutes, and in "A Portrait" (Argo 455590) at more than four minutes, making a virtuoso piece out of it. The rhythmic accents are clearer and the kooky sonorities funnier in the slow version, but the Argo is an important disc for other reasons.

Canticle 3 (1941, 1989). This piece for ocarina and percussion is a substantial and haunting 15-minute work, intended to evoke ancient Mexico. The original version is on Dynamic 221, the 1989 revision is on Mu-

sicMasters 60241, in which the ocarina part is more decorated. It seems the early version is more evocative, but that may be a function of the more leisurely performance, which takes five minutes longer.

Solstice. The composition is a half-hour ballet scored for an octet including celeste and tack piano. The complete score is conducted by **Davies** (MusicMasters 60241). **Jekowsky** includes a little over half the score, recorded more warmly and played with more panache (Argo 455590). Still, the total effect benefits from the inclusion of the darker pieces included by **Davies.**

Suite for Cello and Harp (1949) and *Suite for Cello and Piano* (1995). Both pieces are played by **Nina Flyer** with Dan Levitan and Josephine Gandolfi (Koch 7465). The earlier suite is more dissonant and technically demanding. Both are beautiful.

Harp Suite and *Suite No. 2.* These are different scorings of the same music. **Beverly Bellows,** harpist, plays *Serenade, Beverly's Piece* (with percussion), *Bill & Me,* and *Avalo* (with celeste) (Phoenix 118; New Albion 55). **John Schneider,** guitar, with Amy Shulman, harp and percussion, plays *Jahla, Waltz, Threnody, Sonata in Ishartum,* and *Beverly's Piece* in a recording that separates the harmonic elements for presentation in just intonation (Bridge 9041). Finally, New Albion includes all of the above pieces except *Threnody,* transcribed for guitar and played by **David Tanenbaum.** Choosing is difficult, though I find the just intonation idea a bit less convincing than the others, partly because that disc required more experimental rearrangement than the others.

Concerto for Violin and Percussion (1940, 1959). This is another piece combining different aspects of Harrison's work, using some of his oddest percussion scoring (suspended lengths of plumber's pipe, flower pots, coffee cans, coil chimes from a clock, etc.) combined with the 12-tone system in spots. **Janna Lower** is musical, though her violin is frequently a split-second behind the percussion (New World 80382). **Enrico Balboni** tends to sound bored when asked to play slowly, letting both his pitch and his vibrato slip, particularly in the slow movement (Dynamic 221). **Antonio Nuñez** plays slightly more slowly than the others, with an almost jazzy, relaxed attitude (Pan 510103). He comes off the best, despite one spot where the zipper gets off track in the finale, also a problem passage in both the other recordings.

Concerto in Slendro (1961). For violin, two tack pianos, and percussion, this 10-minute piece with its pentatonic, lively simplicity makes a good contrast with the Violin Concerto and appears with it on both the Dynamic and Pan discs. Again **Nuñez**'s insouciant precision is more effective than **Balboni**'s more nervous and less intonationally precise performances. **Maria Bachmann** is tight and dramatic, though the recording seems artificially balanced (Argo 451590).

String Quartet Set (1979). This piece, played by the **Kronos Quartet,** is a major work in five movements (CRI 613). It's cross-cultural, with emphasis on the European tradition—but what tradition? It opens in a two-voice style recalling medieval polyphony with its open fifths. Then comes a semi-chromatic Plaint, an estampie with percussive taps on the instruments for emphasis, a short homage to the French rondeau, and finally a long Turkish piece, totally monodic. Surprisingly, all this works as only a Harrison amalgam can.

Ariadne (1987). This is a two-movement work for flute(s) and percussion in which the musical elements may be arranged to suit the players. Luckily, there are two recordings to demonstrate this. **Rachel Rudich** and Kory Grossman (CRI 568) take 10 minutes, **Leta Miller** and William

Winant take eight. Rudich plays alto flute and piccolo while Miller sticks to the common or garden flute. If I were to choose one, it would be Rudich by a whisker for its dramatic organization, though her tone is on the thin side. Miller is recorded very closely and lacks ambience.

During the early '70s, Harrison began to assemble and build instruments for his American gamelan orchestra, for which he has composed a great deal of music. All of it is played by groups associated with, or built by, the composer and his colleague William Colvig.

KEYBOARD MUSIC

Harpsichord Sonatas (1934–43). According to the composer, these six Scarlattian miniatures were originally intended for either cembalo or piano. **Kirkpatrick** plays them on harpsichord in his fascinating program, recorded in 1961 (Music & Arts 977). They have also been arranged for guitar and harp by **John Schneider,** who plays them with Amy Shulman (Bridge 9041). In emphasizing the virtues of just intonation, Schneider plays the works much more slowly than Kirkpatrick, taking 21 minutes as opposed to nine. I'm inclined to the originals, though the Bridge disc is interesting too.

Piano music is given us by **Michael Boriskin** (Koch 7465) and by **Anthony de Mare** (CRI 837). Many works are early and dissonant, particularly Sonata 3. Both programs are fun, only overlapping in three tiny waltzes. Both are well-played, Koch in an all-Harrison disc, CRI one in with 35 minutes of mostly unfamiliar Harrison plus Ives and Cowell, some of which may be familiar. De Mare loses points by trying to sing "May Rain."

VOCAL MUSIC

Mass for St. Anthony (1939–1954). Originally written for choir and percussion, this anti-Fascist piece, begun the day Hitler entered Poland, ended up as a work accompanied by trumpet, harp, and strings. It has Harrison's customary stylistic variety and unexpected combinations of sounds, though it seems less iconoclastic than usual. The **Oregon Repertory Singers** are adequate interpreters but not outstanding (Koch 7177).

Rapunzel (1954). It's hard to categorize much of Harrison's music. This is technically an operatic setting of a version of the fairy tale by William Morris, in no less than six acts. Anyone else would have called this 54-minute piece a one-act opera in six scenes. It's mainly in an idiosyncratic version of the 12-tone system, which should scare no one, as Harrison's music is always quite user-friendly and he finds place for his almost medieval love of the drone. Although clarity is at a premium in the only recording, the omission of a libretto is inexcusable (New Albion 93). The tenor (John Duykers) fights against a rather dry tone, usually with success. Soprano **Patrice McGinnis** as Rapunzel is pleasant-voiced, though none too clear in diction, while mezzo Lynne McMurtry, whose function as the witch is mainly that of elevator girl, has a wide vibrato that doesn't clarify matters for those of us who would like to follow Morris's text. Still, it's a fascinating work.

Homage to Pacifica (1991). This composition—is a six-part, 37-minute cantata for soprano, choir, bassoon, and American gamelan—was commissioned by the Gerbode Foundation for Pacifica radio (MusicMasters 67091). Harrison lets his politics hang out here, not always to good effect. It begins with a curiously Eastern setting of "We Shall Overcome," sung winsomely by **Jody Diamond,** and goes on to list all of the public radio call letters. Then comes a virulent passage by Mark Twain on the Philippine War, followed by the testimony of Chief Seattle to the effect that whatever man does to the earth, he does to himself. There are

also a couple of poems by Harrison, intended to shock. All this is set to singularly pastoral music with choral lines so inexpressive that the emotional intent of the words is lost. Altogether, this work calls Harrison's esthetic into question. MOORE

Johan Peter Emilius Hartmann (1805–1900)

While the works that graced the Royal Theater in Copenhagen during the 19th century owe much to composers who emigrated there from other lands, one of the greatest Danish composers was native-born. Warmly romantic and outgoing, Hartmann raised the Theater to a new level, first working with Hans Christian Andersen on *Liden Kirsten*—his greatest success—and then joining with a kindred spirit, Adam Oehlenschläger, a collaboration that lasted for the rest of his life and gave birth to some of Denmark's most stirring efforts for the stage. With his son-in-law Niels Gade, Hartmann spearheaded the Danish Romantic movement, and we may see in his music the beginnings of the nationalistic trend that would soon envelop all of Scandinavia.

Hartmann's two symphonies may be more freewheeling than the more classical works of Christoph Weyse, but are not at the point where a distinctive voice clearly emerges. The influence of Schumann and Spohr (especially his Symphony 3) is everywhere evident, though with a few stylistic quirks; for example, the final movement of 2 sounds as though we tuned in midway through. Only 1 has previously surfaced on disc, a sluggish LP by **Wöldike** (DMA, coupled with an equally dispirited *Yrsa* Overture); thus, **Thomas Dausgaard**'s disc is the one to have for both of these charming and melodious scores (♦Dacapo 224042).

The Valkyries of Hartmann's *Valkyrien* bear scant resemblance to the fierce warrior maidens of Wagner's opera (which Hartmann probably didn't know). Where Wagner freely adapted the Nordic legends to his own philosophy, Hartmann was content to take them at face value, modifying the 12th-century text to create a more romantic saga, a forbidden love of Viking for Valkyrie that can be resolved only by intervention of the Norse god Odin. It's almost nonstop melody, sounding very much like *Giselle* and not far removed from the ballet music Verdi was writing for the Paris Opéra. There is a very fine set with spirited leadership by **Jurowski** (♦CPO 999620, 2CD).

In addition to *Liden Kirsten,* a number of other overtures can be heard, primarily from his collaboration with Oehlenschläger. Chief among the available recordings is **Dausgaard**'s survey, which offers *Yrsa, Axel og Valborg, Correggio* and *Hakon Jarl* in first-rate performances and rich, full-blooded sonics (♦Da Capo 224097). Most compelling of all is the saga of Hakon Jarl—also immortalized by Smetana—whose heathen forces are soundly defeated by the Norwegian warrior Olav Trygvason to bring Christianity to the Northern countries. Also on the Da Capo disc is a rather curious piece, *Guldhornene* (The Golden Horns), basically a melodrama of the kind already employed by Weber for the Wolf Gorge scene in *Der Freischütz*. This fascinating work is presented in thoroughly compelling fashion, aided by Bodil Udsen's sonorous declamation.

On one of a series of CDs spotlighting Danish father-and-son composers, **Jean-Pierre Wallez** piles into the warlike strains of *Hakon Jarl* even more than Dausgaard, and also offers the spirited hunting overture *En Efterårsjagt* as well as music by Johan's son Emil Hartmann, which makes for a stimulating comparison (Danacord 510). HALLER

Karl Amadeus Hartmann (1905–1963)

For decades just a name in musical dictionaries, Hartmann was known to the public (if at all) for his principled "internal emigration" from

Hitler's Third Reich (refusing to allow any of his music to be performed in Nazi-occupied territory) and as director of the ground-breaking *Musica Viva* concerts in post-WW II Munich. In the '80s his music began appearing on disc to considerable critical acclaim.

Symphonies. Hartmann left eight numbered symphonies (1–6 in post-WW II revisions). Two complete cycles exist, the first jointly by **Fritz Rieger** (1), **Kubelik** (2, 4–6, 8), **Leitner** (3), and **Macal** (7) with the Bavarian Radio Symphony, in raw-sounding but very idiomatic accounts (Wergo 60187, 4CD). Recently, **Ingo Metzmacher**'s series has been regrouped as a medium-priced set (♦EMI 56911, 3CD; the references below are to the original separate issues).

No. 1 ("Essay Towards a Requiem") is the only one to employ a voice (a mezzo-soprano solo). **Rieger**'s electrifying account with Doris Soffel (Wergo) has been surpassed by **Metzmacher,** with the best soloist of all, Cornelia Kallisch (EMI 55424, with Martinů's *Memorial to Lidice* and Schoenberg's *A Survivor from Warsaw*). There is also a spirited version from **Leon Botstein** with Jard van Nes (Telarc).

No. 2 ("Adagio" for large orchestra) is Hartmann's most recorded work. **Kubelik** (Wergo) and **Metzmacher** share the honors here, the latter version coupled with No. 5 and one of the best accounts of Stravinsky's Symphony in Three Movements I've heard (EMI 56184). **Rickenbacker** is less intense but coupled with the unnumbered *Sinfonia tragica* (♦Schwann 312952). **Dohnányi**'s glowing rendition is only available with Mahler's 9 (Decca), while **Zender**'s appears in a wide-ranging collection (Col Legno, 8CD).

No. 3, derived in part from *Sinfonia tragica,* is one of the deepest. **Leitner** plumbed its depths most authoritatively (♦Wergo); **Metzmacher** is better recorded although curiously coupled (EMI 55254, with Ives's *Robert Browning Overture*).

No. 4 started life in 1934 as a symphonic concerto for string orchestra with soprano solo in the finale. In the late '40s Hartmann rewrote it, replacing the finale with a purely orchestral version. One of his most immediate and intense works, it has a visceral impact in **Kubelik**'s hands (Wergo) that **Metzmacher** can't match, despite more polished playing (EMI 54916, with Messiaen's *Et exspecto resurrectionem mortuorum*). The most impressive is the most recent, by **Christian Poppen** with the Munich Chamber Orchestra, superbly recorded and matching intensity with a fine grasp of the music's structure (♦ECM 465779).

No. 5 ("Symphonie concertante" for winds and double-basses) was, in its original guise, a trumpet concerto (only the slow movement, 'Lied,' now survives, recorded by **Juoko Harjanne**, Finlandia 26837). In this more relaxed, jovial score **Metzmacher** comes into his own with superior sound and playing (♦EMI 56184). **Kubelik** is still a reasonable second choice (Wergo), preferable to **Herbig** (Berlin, with 6 and 8).

No. 6 is the greatest of the symphonies, its *Toccata variata* second movement one of the repertoire's great white-knuckle rides. It's a severe test for recording engineers, the large percussion section all too easily reduced to a clatter by the ferocious tempos. Sound quality lets **Kubelik** down (Wergo), while **Botstein**—superbly recorded and very exciting—can't quite keep the ensemble together at the end (Telarc). **Herbig** doesn't take the same risks (Berlin), which leaves **Metzmacher** the clear leader, with acutely calculated tempos and the best playing of all (♦EMI 55612, with excellent versions of the Op. 6 sets of pieces by Berg and Webern).

Numbers 7 and 8 are coupled in **Metzmacher**'s series, performances whose ultra-clear textures allow the buried lyricism to shine through (♦EMI 56427). Their orchestral and recording balance puts them ahead of **Macal** in 7 and **Kubelik** in 8 (Wergo); in 8, **Herbig** isn't in the same league (Berlin).

Other orchestral works. Concerto funèbre is one of Hartmann's most eloquent scores; this violin concerto has been recorded several times. **André Gertler** made a highly sympathetic recording with Ančerl (1968), still available in decent sound (Supraphon 111955, with two Hindemith concertos). Neither **Spivakov** (RCA) nor **Christian Edlinger** (Thorofon) generates the same intensity, and fortunately **Hans Maile**'s labored account is now NA (Schwann). **Zehetmair** (as conductor as well as violinist) stresses equally the protest against tyranny and the elegy for its victims (♦Teldec 97449), while **Isabelle Faust** provides the most moving account (ECM 465779, with the sole version of the remarkable Chamber Concerto for Clarinet, String Quartet and String Orchestra with **Paul Meyer** and the Petersen Quartet); these are the market leaders.

Gesangsszene is a symphonic cantata for low voice and orchestra and was left unfinished at Hartmann's death, though in performable condition, with the final few lines spoken rather than sung. **Fischer-Dieskau** first recorded it, a marvelously subtle rendition (Wergo, with Symphonies 1–8), which **Wolfgang Schöne** can't quite equal (EMI, as above). Finest of all is **Nimsgern,** in which (at conductor Rickenbacker's direction) the final spoken words are underpinned most effectively by a low timpani roll (♦Schwann 312952).

Miserae is a symphonic poem inscribed, as early as 1933, to the memory of the victims of Dachau; for many years Hartmann regarded it as his Symphony 1. **Metzmacher** has recorded it as an appendix to his series (EMI 56468, with *Gesangsszene*).

String Quartets. No. 1 dates from 1933 and is subtitled "Carillon" from the name of a competition it won three years later. No. 2 is a more mature work, although like 1 it shows the influence of Bartók. Both have been recorded by the **Pellegrini Quartet** in clear sound, a touch too closely miked (CPO 999219).

Solo piano and violin music. **Siegfried Mauser** recorded all the extant solo piano music on one disc, and **Ingolf Turban** made an equally impressive recording of the solo violin works, some of it from the '20s (Claves). Unfortunately, both are NA.

Opera. Simplicius Simplicissimus, Hartman's great chamber opera, is a powerful indictment of tyranny, like Hindemith's *Mathis der Maler* using the terrors of Germany's historical past as a metaphor for Hitler's Reich. Originally written in 1934–35, the 1955 revised version has been impressively recorded by **Heinze Fricke** (♦Wergo 6259).

RICKARDS

Hamilton Harty (1879–1941)

Harty took over the Hallé Orchestra from Beecham in 1920 and over the course of 13 years not only expanded upon its virtues but built it to a position of great prominence and pride in Britain. He brought about a veritable Berlioz revival at home and also toured the United States, where he was hailed as "the Irish Toscanini." Yet in spite of the enthusiastic reception given his own compositions in both orchestral and vocal fields, to a modern generation he seems destined to be known only for his colorful rescorings of Handel's *Water Music* and *Royal Fireworks Music* suites, at one time as popular as Stokowski's Bach arrangements. The reader will soon realize that without the Chandos label there would be no chapter on Harty; we must be grateful for their enthusiastic support, for he is one of the finest composers the British Isles have ever produced.

Orchestral music. Surely the most winning example of all Harty's orchestral works is the *Irish Symphony*, affectionate memories familiar to this lad from County Down, all clothed in warm and comfortable textures and filled with an abundance of lively tunes. Images of Lough Neagh and the Antrim Hills give way in the final movement to a retelling of the decisive struggle between Irish and English forces at the Battle of the Boyne, commemorated noisily each year in Ulster, and as you might expect, the Ulster musicians led by **Bryden Thomson** throw themselves into this music with deep feeling and passion in their splendid recording (♦Chandos 8314). It's filled out with the hearty *Comedy Overture,* chipper woodwind writing and emphatic punctuation by the tympani leavened by a wrenching theme in the clarinet that tugs at the heartstrings even as the livelier passages brush away the tears. Here Thomson's moderate tempos blunt the caustic wit somewhat, though playing and sonics are beyond reproach.

On another disc, Thomson offers Harty's *John Field Suite,* a tuneful and gently scored pastiche derived from piano pieces of another Irish composer; the fantasy *In Ireland,* an affectionate portrayal of two Dublin street musicians (flute and harp); and Harty's arrangement of the much loved *Londonderry Air* along with the familiar *Water Music Suite* (Chandos 6583). *In Ireland* is included in the disc with the Piano Concerto (Chandos 8321; see below), but even more welcome is the rousing and poignant *With the Wild Geese,* the name given to the Irish regiments who fought alongside the French in the Battle of Fontenoy in 1745. Thomson's sturdy reading is nicely complemented by **Alexander Gibson** in "Music of the Four Countries," the other countries being England (Ethel Smyth's overture to *The Wreckers*), Scotland (Hamish MacCunn's *The Land of the Mountain and the Flood*), and Wales (Edward German's *Welsh Rhapsody*)(♦Classics for Pleasure 4635).

Concertos. Given Harty's own proficiency at the keyboard, it's not surprising that he wrote a piano concerto; the result is far less a virtuoso display than a lush Romantic concerto in the manner of Rachmaninoff, though with enough Celtic flavor to give the game away. **Malcolm Binns** clearly has the measure of the first two movements, yet, surprisingly, fairly slogs his way through the final Irish jig (Chandos 8321). The Violin Concerto was written for Szigeti, and the composer accordingly played down the Irish flavor somewhat. Indeed, much of the first movement has a rather Brahmsian cast, though the jaunty final rondo seems to bring out the leprechaun in Harty. **Ralph Holmes** gives a marvelous performance (Chandos 8386, filled out with the rather substantial *Variations on a Dublin Air,* also for violin).

Vocal music. Harty wrote his eloquent setting of Keats's *Ode to a Nightingale* for his wife, the soprano Agnes Nicholls, who performed it at the premiere. Evocative and warmly satisfying, it's beautifully sung by **Harper** (Chandos 8387). While the companion piece, *The Children of Lir,* is described as a symphonic poem, it also contains a wordless melisma for soprano. Thomson fields the shifting imagery with aplomb, and the recording is first-rate.

Originally released on the five none-too-well-filled CDs listed above—basically reproducing the LPs—Chandos has since reissued its Harty material as a 3CD boxed set (7035), and also brought out the three discs separately (7032, Violin and Piano Concertos; 7033, *Lir, Ode, Dublin* and *Londonderry Airs;* 7034, *Symphony, Overture, In Ireland, Wild Geese*). Unfortunately, in the process they have jettisoned both the *Water Music Suite*—no great loss—and the *John Field Suite.* Thus for Harty collectors unwilling to compromise, the original CDs are preferred.   HALLER

Johann Adolph Hasse *(1699–1783)*

Hasse was one of the most prolific composers of his day, with over 50 operas to his credit plus innumerable *serenades, feste teatrale,* and *intermezzi.* A close collaborator of Metastasio, Hasse set all of that prolific librettist's texts (some in multiple versions), a major achievement in itself. His operas were quite popular throughout Europe, even in distant England, for their easy flow of singable melody. Yet they're rarely performed today, and only one of Hasse's *opera seria* has been recorded, plus a few of his comic *intermezzi.*

Cleofide. This piece is an altered version of Metastasio's *Alessandeo nell'Indie.* The only one of Hasse's serious operas recorded so far, it's a lengthy and majestic work, full of inventive melody, and given its full due by **Christie** and Capella Coloniensis (♦Capriccio 27193/196, 4CD). The cast reads like a list of expert period singers: Kirkby, Mellon, and a plethora of countertenors (Ragin, Wong, and Visse). It's quite a grand display, not to everyone's taste with its countertenors and feminine "white tone" singing, but worthy of more than a cursory hearing.

La Contadina. This is an intermezzo that started life as *Don Tabarano,* later transformed musically as well as in title to *Il Tabarano* and then to *Don Tabarano finto Turco per amore,* with other variations along the way. This confusion of titles led to the work being attributed to Pergolesi, a matter only recently corrected. An extensive array of manuscripts attests to its popularity. Its structure is similar to Pergolesi's *La Serva Padrona* of five years later; Pergolesi knew a good model when he heard it. As usual in these matters, the plot is simple and simpleminded, with emphasis on cunning and deceit.

The work puts a lot of responsibility on its two singers, and a 1991 performance finds Susanna Rigacci and Romano Franceschetto singing the leading roles with reasonable flexibility, not-too-acidic tones, and a lot of purpose. The Orchestra da Camera in Canto can be a bit scrappy but not enough to interfere, and **Fabio Maestri** drives the show along with just the right feeling for timing and merriment (♦Bongiovanni 2128). A recording from the '70s by I Solisti del Maggio Musicale Fiorentino led by **Ephrikian,** with poor singing by Jolanda Meneguzzer and Ugo Trama, is best forgotten (Rivo Alto).

Larinda e Vanesio. This intermezzo had its origins in Molière's *Bourgeois Gentilhomme.* It's another tale of feminine wiles winning a wealthy husband. A 1992 recording from Catania's Palazzo Biscari is a sonic disaster, with the reverberation of a huge Gothic cathedral (Bongiovanni). The tiny voice of Silvia Piccollo gets lost in the shuffle, although, when audible, she creates a lovely character rather than the shrew that Larinda could be. Giorgio Gatti's Vanesio is a comic delight. **Salvatore Carchiolo** is on the podium.

Piramo e Tisbe. Hasse called this work an *intermezzo tragico,* one that uses the same musical forces as a comic intermezzo but tells a tragic story, the legendary love of Pyramus and Thisbe. However, it doesn't have the brief proportions of an intermezzo; in fact, it's a major and worthy musical work. A rather bland 1984 recording has Schlick as Piramo (originally for castrato, here a "trousers" role for mezzo-soprano), Suzanne Gari as Thisbe, and Michel Lecocq as Thisbe's father. Capella Clementina is led by **Helmut Müller-Brühl** (Koch-Schwann, 2CD). Schlick is back again in 1993 as Piramo; nine years have made little change in her voice (Capriccio). Ann Moneyiff is now Thisbe, a more delicate creation, and Wilfred Joches a stronger Father. La Stagione is led by **Michael Schnada.** There's less music though, more of an abridgement (or is this the 1770 revision of the 1763 original?).

A 1997 performance at the Scuola Grande di S. Giovanni Evangelista in Venice is quite attractive (♦Mondo Musica 10100, 2CD). Marina Bolgan (Tisbe) and Svetlana Sidorova (Piramo) are almost indistinguishable from each other, both coyly glassy and wilting. The Accademia di San Rocco has an acidic period instrument sound and plays quite well for **Evenezia Mario Merigo.** The orchestra is more enjoyable than the singers.

La Serva scaltra. This is an intermezzo filled with comic satire and, typical of the genre, a female outwitting a male and snaring him into marriage solely for financial security. In a 1979 recording, strings and harpsichord from Staatskapelle Berlin under **Suitner** play attractively and Brigitte Eisenfeld, very much the operetta soubrette as Dorilla, chirps pleasantly (Berlin 9114, 2CD, with Pergolesi's *La Serva Padrona*). She and the orchestra seem to have found the correct musical idiom. Reiner Süss (Balanzone) has not. He has a pleasant enough voice, but tends to bark his music like a German officer. At least much of the recitative is omitted.

A 1989 performance has a charmingly committed Bernadette Lucarini and Giorgio Gatti singing with gusto and real involvement with the characters and their situation—and somehow managing to ignore what's going on in the orchestra pit. The sounds produced by the nine-member instrumental ensemble from the Sassari Symphony Orchestra (seven strings and two bassoons) are some of the most outrageous ever recorded. There's no agreement on which pitch to tune to and their intonation is catlike at best; they don't even agree on tempo. **Gabriele Catalucci** was on the podium, presumably busy just cuing the singers (Bongiovanni). PARSONS

(Franz) Joseph Haydn *(1732–1809)*

The first thing about Haydn's music most people notice is the amount of it. Comparisons among composers are seldom useful, but here they're inevitable. Where Beethoven and Mozart each wrote eight or nine great symphonies, there are at least 30 by Haydn that can be safely called great and considerably more for which the accolade could be seriously proposed. Mozart wrote 10 great string quartets (more or less), and all of Beethoven's 16 are great. Hans Keller, in his excellent monograph, designates "only" 45 of Haydn's quartets as great, leaving another 20 or so without that label. Haydn's 43 piano trios are probably the greatest little-known treasure of the classical era. And the man found time to write more than 60 keyboard sonatas that at their best are comparable to anyone's, two magnificent oratorios, over a dozen masses, concertos for violin, cello, trumpet, horn, keyboard, flute organ, (perhaps) clarinet, and a large body of other music—songs, operas, divertimenti, miniature symphonies, chamber pieces for the now-extinct baryton, etc. He also found time to travel, to be Mozart's friend, and to occupy the unenviable position of Beethoven's composition teacher.

Once we get past the sheer quantity of Haydn's music, we have to learn to hear it. He wrote on several levels at the same time. He wanted to make his music accessible to the unsophisticated or inattentive because then, as now, they were the majority of the audience. On the other hand, he was an intelligent, witty, and sensitive person and built subtle touches into his music to please himself and his more knowledgeable listeners. Listen, for example, to the slow movement of Symphony 51. At first, it seems to be a serene landscape, as placid as can be. Then it dawns on you (or it doesn't, Haydn doesn't care) that the melody is being carried by a solo horn on stratospherically high notes, answered by its companion sinking lower and lower into the bottom of the bass register. Or

a movement will begin—like the finale to Quartet Op. 76:5—with a cadence that normally means "the end." Or it will be like a limerick—the finale of the two-movement Piano Sonata 58—that wanders into a minor key but can't keep a straight face and winds up happily back in the silly poem.

Listening carefully to Haydn is almost always rewarding. There's an odd instrumental touch here and there or a melody that's been turned upside down and hidden in an inner voice that can hardly wait for you to notice it, like a wink from the composer or those odd details in medieval pictures or friezes that turn out to be caricatures of the local grandees or the artists' families or just an interesting bunch of people from around town. And it's always there with a straight face.

No composer's music covers a wider—or more human—range of expression than Haydn's. His music is a world that encompasses black despair, convulsive rage, mystery, romance, happy country life, simple well-being, inner monologues, and a sheer numinous transcendence that only Beethoven and Bruckner could match. In all this writing, so much of it so magnificent, Haydn more or less created the rules for the classical sonata allegro form that was to dominate our music for the next century and beyond, created forms for other symphonic and sonata movements that persist to this day, and set up ways to look at melody and harmony that were eagerly used—and rebelled against—by generations of his successors. In a way, composers are still working out the implications of some of the issues that Haydn first put on the table in the late 1700s. In the perceptive words of critic David Hurwitz, "to a remarkable degree, virtually all musical roads lead back to one of two composers: Haydn or Bach." All later composers, for better or worse, are Haydn's children.

There's more than enough musical treasure here for a lifetime's exploration. This article can reveal only some of that vastness, but if you start with the recommendations here, you will be led to a good understanding of the special humanity of this giant among composers. Yet Haydn is more poorly served on disc than any other major composer. There are important recordings in print, including multi-disc sets, that are invisible to the current catalog, while listings persist that document long-vanished discs or fail to disclose important information about existing releases. The recordings mentioned here do exist and the numbers given here are real numbers, or at least were at one time.

SYMPHONIES

The symphonies cover a tremendous territory. The currently accepted inventory is about 106, but there's always a chance of a new one turning up. They range in size and complexity from early works, not very much different from what CPE and JC Bach were writing, to the Palladian splendors of the dozen London symphonies that capped his series.

Complete and partial sets

For a while we were living in a kind of Haydn heaven, with series in progress from many sources: Adam Fischer with the Austro-Hungarian Haydn Orchestra on Nimbus (modern instruments); Goodman with the Hanover Band on Hyperion, Hogwood with the Orchestra of the Age of Enlightenment on Oiseau-Lyre, Weil with Tafelmusik on Sony (all with old instruments); Harnoncourt with various ensembles (some old, some new) on Teldec; and lesser lights on Naxos. There was also the time-honored Dorati set on Decca (modern instruments), which has appeared from time to time as a low-priced box. The tides receded too quickly. Hogwood's set disappeared from the catalog before it was more than half completed, although as this is being written, it appears that it's being reissued and continued in England. Goodman's vanished without a trace more than a year ago. Fischer marches bravely on and Harnoncourt has turned his attention to Bruckner and Dvořak. It's impossible to tell how committed Sony is to a full series with Weil. This leaves Dorati and Fischer and the various Naxos ensembles as the only likely candidates for complete series in the catalog.

Dorati's recordings (modern instruments) date from the late '60s and early '70s. They still sound fine, but the orchestral playing (the Philharmonia Hungarica with some guest principals) is variable. The strings generally sound good but a little scrappy; the winds (leaving aside such highlights as Ifor James's star turn in the high horn part in 51) are serviceable rather than inspired. Dorati's leadership is solid (sometimes stolid), although some movements—for example, the otherworldly 49:I—are superbly carried off. Minuets tend to be elephantine, in an odd 19th-century tradition. Dorati's achievement was remarkable for its time. We now understand the nervous, mercurial aspect of Haydn's music better than he did, but it's still a good survey of this music.

Fischer understands the nervous side of the music but doesn't always act on this understanding. He's livelier than Dorati, but where Dorati had a (sometimes) lean and scrappy orchestra executing a (sometimes) pedantic conception of the music, Fischer has a rich-toned ensemble (with some positively regal horn and string sonorities) playing a (sometimes) earthbound Haydn. All the performances that have appeared so far are at least decent, though the London symphonies don't really soar. Fischer seems to be a kind of updated Dorati, more of a solid reference than a collection of outstanding inspiration. The Nimbus sound can seem a little recessed and cavernous, but the playing is a constant delight.

Goodman's performances on early instruments had irresistible dash and fire. His energy was even more powerful than Fischer's and didn't have its neurotic edge. On the other hand, he was an ardent proponent of the keyboard continuo, whether harpsichord or fortepiano, and gave us recordings that sounded like keyboard concertos. This isn't necessarily a bad result, but it's hard to believe it's what Haydn had in mind, especially if you know the relative carrying power of a harpsichord and even a small orchestral ensemble.

Harnoncourt, as usual, went his own way. He recorded early- to mid-Haydn with Concentus Musicus Wien and late Haydn with the Concertgebouw. His performances go in and out of print unpredictably and get reissued with different couplings and different numbers, so treat the numbers here with care; for example, there are at least three different incarnations of his "Surprise" symphony. His performances of the late works often seem over-emphatic and driven (98 and 99 were least marred by this, 100 can take this treatment without much harm). The earlier works are less hectored, but still lacking the repose and charm that can balance their energy. The best of Harnoncourt's recordings so far is a memorably furious 45 (Teldec 25914). Nos. 98 and 99, with something approaching a smile on an otherwise grim countenance, are also fine (Teldec 46331).

Hogwood (early instruments) is Goodman's opposite. Following the thoughts of Haydn scholar James Webster, he dispensed with the keyboard continuo entirely. I'm agnostic on the subject and can enjoy the symphonies with or without it. Hogwood's performances are full of a bluff heartiness that's a little less dynamic than Goodman's but also a little more nuanced. I suspect that the better English Haydn performances in the 18th century resembled these recordings, and I think that this, despite some tiredness in the middle-period symphonies, has been an enjoyable romp through the cycle. I hope it reappears in our catalog soon.

Weil's performances have been elegant and energetic, but a little surfacy. The recorded sound is spectacularly good, but the performances don't leave much of an impression.

Other interpreters have made their mark in these works. Ansermet recorded a memorable set of the Paris symphonies (82–87), but it's out of print; watch for a reissue (London). The playing was variable, but the poise and clarity of proportion are classic in both senses. Beecham's Haydn had lots of style and some depth (EMI 64389, 93-98, and Dutton 2003, 93, 99, 104). Bernstein recorded the Paris (Sony 47550, 2CD) and London sets (Sony 47533, 3CD, and 47577, 2CD) with the New York Philharmonic. These are beefy performances without much refinement or any discernible sense of style. He also recorded 88, 92, and 94 with the Vienna Philharmonic—vigorous performances that were more refined than the New York readings but still lacked poise and balance (DG 445554).

Böhm recorded little Haydn, but his disc of 88, 91, and 92 with the Vienna Philharmonic is not only one of the great Haydn discs but also one of the great symphonic recordings. It was last seen as a budget issue (DG 429523); if you see it, snap it up, even if you found his Mozart sometimes sleepy or stuffy. His Haydn is the real thing. Britten was a superb Haydn conductor. His concert performance of the "Farewell" Symphony—a coldly furious performance complementary to Harnoncourt's fiery one—was once available on a cassette with dim sound mercifully obscuring some instrumental fluffs; it has been reissued in England by Decca and will probably cross the Atlantic sooner or later. Meanwhile, listeners can console themselves with a slightly scaled down but loving reading of 95 with excellent sound and playing and wonderful discmates—Mendelssohn, Mozart, Debussy, and Beethoven (BBC 8008).

Frans Brüggen has recorded a number of excellent performances with the Orchestra of the 18th Century (Philips). His performances are very expressive and exploit the range of color available on old instruments. Haydn's writing is often closely attuned to nuances of instrumental tone, and Brüggen's readings demonstrate the depth of the composer's awareness of color. His London symphonies aren't in the current catalog, but his Paris set (Philips 462111, 2CD) is the finest around and contains an announcement for a forthcoming set of *Sturm und Drang* symphonies. Keep an eye out for it and for reissues of the Londons. Critics rightly value Colin Davis's recordings of the London symphonies with the Concertgebouw as classics, and their low price is an extra incentive to potential buyers (Philips 432286, 4CD).

Jochum's set of the Londons with the London Philharmonic offers balanced readings, a little lacking in point and fiber, but lovingly shaped and beautifully played (DG 437201). They're also low-priced. Karajan recorded both the Paris and the London symphonies (DG 945532, NA), and also recorded some of them for EMI (NA). Although his Mozart could be powerful and flowing, his Haydn was always a little earthbound. His best performances were of 104, which he built memorably.

Klemperer made a series of recordings that were collected into a now-vanished box (EMI 63667, 3CD). Since the box sometimes shows up in remainder stores and the performances may well be reissued as part of the EMI "Klemperer Edition," it's worth addressing them here. This is big-ensemble Haydn. The best performances are 98 and 101, which are trim, bracing and laced with wit. The worst are 92 and 95, which try to be classical readings but blur into heaviness and sogginess from time to time. In between are 88 and 104, which are virtually indestructible, and 100 and 102, which don't quite have the focus of 98 and 101 but still come across as classic big-scale Haydn. The quality of the readings more or less matches their chronology—the best readings are the oldest (1961), the worst are the latest (1972). The sound is no problem and the playing is alert and polished in the early readings and still decent in the last ones.

Kuijken seemed to be recording a survey for Virgin that vanished into oblivion with that label's acquisition by EMI and the resultant extinction of most of its inventory. The performances were fresh and memorable and ought to be returned to print as soon as possible, but there's good news on this front. The jewel of the series so far, the Paris symphonies with the Orchestra of the Age of Enlightenment, has been reissued as a "two-fer" [PLACEHOLDER]. This is one of the great bargains of the Haydn catalog. Perhaps Kuijken's recordings with La Petite Bande will follow; a recording of 103 and 104 is worth looking for (Deutsche Harmonia Mundi 77362).

Marriner and **Leppard** recorded a number of symphonies in the '70s that have been collected in a budget box (Philips 454335, 10CD). The theme of the box is the "name symphonies," and, because Haydn symphonies are irresistible targets for people who like to give names to things, this means that the series goes from some of the earliest, "Morning, Noon, and Evening" (6–8), to the last, "London" (104). The set contains 29 symphonies, all sparklingly performed. The orchestral forces are a little sparse for the Londons, but the performances work anyway. This is as good a survey of Haydn symphonies as there is and would make a fine beginning for a collection.

Szell's Haydn was rightly prized, and it's a shame that only a disc containing 92, 94 and 96 (Sony 46332), and the first volume of the Londons (Sony 45673, 2CD) seems to be in print. His cool, dry approach, which freeze-dried the music of so many other composers, made his Haydn fizz like champagne, and the music's sly wit seems to have brought out whatever sense of musical humor this conductor had. The lean sound he liked to get from his violins was also fine here.

Walter left memorable recordings of 88 and 100, full of joy and song (Sony 64485). They make you want to sing along and to regret that he never recorded "The Creation." Yes, there are the usual Bruno Walter problems: rhythms are soggy, the playing is variable, and there is audible relief when the loud, scary part of the "Military" symphony is over, but they don't matter a bit. This is an essential disc. The New York Philharmonic's 1954 recording of 102 was also added to the disc but isn't in the same league. It's technically better in playing and conducting, but much less vivid as a performance.

There isn't much of a legacy of older recordings for this composer. The 19th century undervalued Haydn and didn't know much of his music, and only Walter and Toscanini are among the major conductors of the first part of this century who seem to have paid much attention to it. In **Toscanini**'s recording of 31 from the '30s, the horns are technically adept but wanting in spirit (Iron Needle 1397). He offers a characteristically tense and meticulous NBC performance of 88, with a similar reading of 94 (RCA 60281). The sound is airless, the playing is drilled out of almost all individuality, but there's tremendous rhythmic power. A Dennis Brain-led horn quartet recorded 31 under **Jack Westrup**, but only the first movement made it onto LPs; watch for a reissue (EMI). Nos. 86, 92, and 100 appear in **Walter**'s prewar readings from London, Paris and Vienna, respectively, but they're not especially memorable (Grammofono 2000 78629). They're nothing like the loving performances he recorded for Sony at the end of his career.

Symphony 88, beloved of Brahms, was a favorite, however, and there are memorable recordings by **Furtwängler** (DG 447439, with one of the greatest of all Schubert 9ths), **Clemens Krauss** (various labels, including Preiser 90112, with Johann Strauss performances of a vanished and

stylish age, and Koch 7011, with other historic performances). There's also a **Koussevitzky** recording of the finale thrown in as a makeweight in a set containing his Sibelius 7, Beethoven 3, and Mozart 40 (Biddulph 29, 2CD). He returns, this time playing the whole thing, with symphonies 94 and 102 (Pearl 9185, 2CD). The readings are propulsive and dramatic; the sound is so-so. **Herman Abendroth**'s Leipzig recording, with 96, has a good reputation (Tahra 106, 2CD). **Toscanini**'s view of the piece can be heard with 88, as mentioned above, or with Cherubini, Mozart, and Dvořák (RCA 59481).

No. 96 brings a dapper **van Beinum** reading (Dante 472, with 100 and some Mozart), **Celibidache** and the Berlin Philharmonic, before he slowed way down and fled from the recording studio (Grammofono 2000 78774, 2CD), and a chipper **Walter** New York performance, less vibrant than his later ones but with a little more fiber (Sony 64486). Symphony 97 has **Beecham** (Dutton 7019 or Biddulph 041), while 98 has fiery **Fricsay** (Enterprise 4213) and tough **Toscanini** (Dante 401). No. 99 is another that gets a Toscanini reading (RCA 60282, with 101 and the lovely *Sinfonie concertante*), as well as Beecham (Dutton 2003, in a collection including 93 and 104 plus Brahms and Franck).

Symphony 101 has an **Ansermet** reading (Dante 456), no fewer than four **Toscanini** issues—the NBC version with 99 mentioned above, plus NY Philharmonic readings with Brahms and Mozart (Magic Talent 48049), Respighi, Sibelius, Weber, and Wagner in concert (Iron Needle 1335), and with Beethoven and Mendelssohn (RCA 60316). No. 104 gets two issues of a performance attributed to **Furtwängler,** but the attribution isn't clear and, whoever conducted, the reading is nothing like his 88 (Iron Needle 1382 or Russian Compact Disc 25004, both with the Beethoven 7th).

Individual symphonies

For those who wish to assess these symphonies by work rather than by performer, here's a breakdown by period with recommended performances. Don't overlook the Marriner/Leppard survey discussed above. It's a great bargain.

Early symphonies

6–8 ("Morning, Noon, Evening"). These little pieces have the grace, wit, and felicity of utterance to make them favorites now, just as they were when first written to show off the orchestra of one of Haydn's employers. **Nicholas Ward**/Northern Chamber Orchestra (Naxos 550722); **Chmura**/National Arts Center Canada Orchestra (CBC 5085).

22 ("The Philosopher"). Haydn's philosopher paces to a walking bass and intones back and forth between pairs of English and French horns. By the finale, he seems to be in a better frame of mind as the winds chuckle to one another and the strings rush around. **Orpheus Chamber Orchestra** (DG 427337); **Ward**/Northern Chamber Orchestra (Naxos 553005); **López-Cobos**/Lausanne Chamber Orchestra (Denon 75660).

26 ("Lamentation"). Haydn wove plainchant from the lamentations of Jeremiah into the first and second movements of this stormy work, which looked forward to the dark *Sturm und Drang* period that followed. **Harmut Haenchen**/CPE Bach Orchestra (Berlin 1013); **Ward**/Northern Chamber Orchestra (Naxos 550721).

31 ("Hornsignal"). Exciting hunting calls and daring high wire acts by the horn players mark this dashing work. **Haenchen**/CPE Bach Orchestra (Berlin 1028); **Mackerras**/Orchestra of St. Luke's (Telarc 80156).

Sturm und Drang (Storm and Stress) symphonies

These works, written between 1766 and 1773, are full of strong emotions and minor keys. Here are anger and frustration (45), sorrowful contemplation and desperate energy (49), dark moods lit by sudden serenity (44, 52), and sheer display and good humor (50, 51, 48). A fine set in chamber music style by **Pinnock** and The English Concert was once available and is now a candidate for reissue (Archiv), and a set by **Frans Brüggen** is promised soon (Philips). Most of them are contained (in fine performances) in Vol. 3 of **Fischer**'s ongoing set (Nimbus 5530, 5CD), but the catalog does not now list an integral set of these works. Here are recommendations for some representative symphonies.

43 ("Mercury"). It's not clear where the name came from, since the piece is no more or less mercurial than any number of others, but it's full of energy. **Weil**/Tafelmusik (Sony 48370).

44 ("Mourning"). Haydn asked that the darkly serene slow movement be played for his funeral. In its symphonic setting, it's surrounded with forceful minor-key movements, including a stern minuet with a radiantly consoling trio. **Haenchen**/CPE Bach Chamber Orchestra (Berlin 1013).

45 ("Farewell"). Famous for its acted-out leave-taking in the finale, this symphony is full of anger, frustration, and unease. Look for a reissue of **Britten**'s classic performance. **Harnoncourt**/Concentus Musicus Wien (Teldec 25914).

49 ("La Passione"). The symphony begins with a long slow movement. Is it contemplative or is another sort of passion meant? The rest of the piece crackles with dark minor-key energy. **Haenchen**/CPE Bach Chamber Orchestra (Berlin 1013).

51. It has no nickname and is much less moody than the others. On the other hand, this symphony has spectacular writing for the horns, incongruously fitted into the ostensibly simple pastorale of the slow movement. **Weil**/Tafelmusik (Sony 48371).

59 ("Fire"). This piece has no more to do with a physical fire than 43 has to do with the god, planet, or metal Mercury. Nevertheless, the fire of genius and the fire of energy flash through this work. **Harnoncourt**/Concentus Musicus Wien (Teldec 90843).

Transitional symphonies.

These were written between the *Sturm und Drang* and Paris works and are a variable lot. A few of them are memorable, most are not.

60 ("Il distratto"). Haydn cobbled this together out of music for a comedy about an absent-minded fellow, and later in life, he referred to the piece as "that old pancake." Its humor is a little too explicit, with all sorts of sudden shifts of direction and a massive retuning by the strings, yet it's fun to hear and to play. **Ward**/Northern Chamber Orchestra (Naxos 553005); **Haenchen**/CPE Bach Chamber Orchestra (Berlin 1027).

64 ("Tempora mutantur"). "Times change and we change with them." This symphony takes its name, and perhaps its unsettled and unsettling character, from this phrase. Odd, pulsing string writing and unsettled harmonies. **Haenchen**/CPE Bach Chamber Orchestra (Berlin 1092).

Paris symphonies (82–87)

Written in 1785–86 for a Masonic concert organization with a large and superb orchestra, this set of six works is full of variety and melody. The Paris audiences were quite sophisticated, and Haydn wanted to show that his music was worthy of them—it was.

Sets. Complete sets are thick upon the ground. **Brüggen** is the finest of a fine group (Philips 462111, 2CD). Almost equally good is **Kuijken** with The Orchestra of the Age of Enlightenment (Virgin, 2CD, a "two-fer"). The Tafelmusik set led by **Weil** is a little more taut and less colorful than

Brüggen's but has energy, lovely playing, and spectacularly good recorded sound (Sony 66295/96). These are all old-instrument recordings. A fine modern instrument version comes from **Marriner** (Philips 438727, 2CD, a "two-fer"; MHS 522370Y). Neither **Bernstein**'s coarse readings (Sony 47550, 2CD) nor **Karajan**'s heavy ones (DG 445532, 2CD) are compelling. There are no individual symphony performances listed in the catalog worth a detour from any of the recommended sets.

Late transitional symphonies

These are lovely works, including the immortal 88, with its deeply beautiful slow movement and glorious finale and the equally inspired "Oxford" (92), with its sinister ticking in the slow movement and whirlwind finale. The other three are pretty special too.

88. One of the most beloved of all symphonies, with its pastoral opening movement, songful slow movement, stamping dance with rustic trio, and wonderful machine of a finale. Lots of good performances here: **Böhm**/Vienna Philharmonic (DG 429523); **Walter**/Columbia Symphony (Sony 64485); **Glover**/London Mozart Players (ASV 6167); **Weil**/Tafelmusik (Sony 66253).

89. This piece lives in the shadow of 88 but is charming in its own right. **Böhm**/Vienna Philharmonic (DG 429523); **Weil**/Tafelmusik (Sony 66253).

90. The composition is a big-scaled C major work that looks back to the brilliance of the Paris symphonies. **Weil**/Tafelmusik (Sony 66253).

91. This symphony offers pleasing variations in the slow movement and an airborne finale. **Orpheus Chamber Orchestra** (DG 437783); **Drahos**/Nicolaus Esterházy Sinfonia (Naxos 550769).

92 ("Oxford"). In the words of H. Robbins Landon, this work "artlessly combines the greatest contrapuntal mind since J. S. Bach with a rich symphonic style." He left out "joyful" and "vibrant." **Böhm**/Vienna Philharmonic (DG 429523); **Szell**/Cleveland (Sony 46332).

London Symphonies (93–104)

These twelve masterpieces are among the greatest artistic creations of the 18th century. They were written between 1791 and 1795 for a pair of concert tours of England. For beauty, power, and range, there is no comparable symphonic body created in so short a time.

Sets. The gold standard for modern-instrument sets of these works is **Colin Davis** with the Concertgebouw in a pair of mid-priced sets (Philips). The playing has classical lightness and sympathetic shaping, allowing Haydn's superbly built structures to shine forth. A more mellow (and mid-priced) set from **Jochum** with the London Philharmonic is also worth investigating (DG 37201, 4CD). **Szell**'s recording of the first six is spirited and energetic (Sony 45673, 2CD, budget-priced). **Beecham**'s set of the same six is an interesting contrast, with even more spirit, more relaxation, but some unwelcome heaviness at times (EMI 64389, 2CD). **Bernstein**'s New York performances are heavy-handed and coarse (Sony 47553, 3CD; 47557, 2CD).

Karajan's set is out of the catalog but likely to be reissued at any time (DG). There were some fine moments and movements, but overall these are heavy and strangely inert readings. **Fischer**'s set combines a rich-toned chamber orchestra sound with a fairly lean interpretive approach (Nimbus 5200, 5CD). It's less individual than the others, but wears well. **Brüggen** made fine recordings of these works on period instruments, but they seem to be out of the catalog (Philips). If they're reissued, they're worth buying for their instrumental color and the insight of the conductor. **Slatkin**'s readings with the Philharmonia are well judged and well played but don't have much individuality (RCA 68425, 92, 99, 100; 62549, 94, 98, 104).

93. A stern introduction leads to a sunny work. **Goodman**/Hanover Band (Hyperion 66532).

94 ("Surprise"). **Szell**/Cleveland (Sony 46332); **Monteux**/Vienna Philharmonic (Decca 452893).

95. Haydn's last minor-key symphony, but the storm clouds are short-lived. **Britten**/English Chamber Orchestra (BBC 8008); **Goodman**/Hanover Band (Hyperion 66532). Look for a reissue of **Reiner**'s fine recording with an ad hoc orchestra in New York.

96 ("Miracle"). **Szell**/Cleveland (Sony 46332).

97. The last and biggest of Haydn's brilliant C major symphonies. See the sets above.

98. Is the moving Adagio a tribute to Mozart, whose death upset Haydn deeply? See the sets above.

99. Another Adagio reflecting the loss of a friend, Marianne von Genziger. See the sets above.

100 ("Military"). Aggressive percussion to set a martial mood. **Walter**/Columbia Symphony (Sony 64485); **Harnoncourt**/Concertgebouw (Teldec 74859).

101 ("Clock"). It ticks in the slow movement. **Monteux**/Vienna Philharmonic (Decca 452893); **Beecham**/Royal Philharmonic (Classics for Pleasure); **Goodman**/Hanover Band (Hyperion 66528).

102. Another remarkable slow movement. See the sets above.

103 ("Drum Roll"). It rolls in various ways in various performances; Haydn's notation is open to different possibilities. **Kuijken**/La Petite Bande (Deutsche Harmonia Mundi 77362); **Beecham**/Royal Philharmonic (Classics for Pleasure 4530).

104 ("London"). A huge and powerful work, a fitting end to a remarkable series. **Hickox**/Collegium Musicum 90 (Chandos 0655); **Kuijken**/La Petite Bande (Deutsche Harmonia Mundi 77362).

Sinfonia concertante. This isn't really a symphony and isn't part of the London set. It's a hybrid work combining elements of symphony, concerto, and concerto grosso, designed to display solo violin, cello, oboe, and bassoon. Soloists/**Fischer**/Austro-Hungarian Haydn Orchestra (Nimbus 5518). There's also a stiff **Toscanini** reading (RCA 60282). **Claudio Abbado** once led a lovingly detailed reading with the Chamber Orchestra of Europe (DG 423105), but it has vanished from the catalog.

CONCERTOS

Haydn wrote concertos for a wide variety of instruments. Although his keyboard and violin concertos have been overshadowed by Mozart's and then by Beethoven's, they are fine works and those for cello, horn, and trumpet can stand up to any rivals.

Cello. There are fine recordings of 1 by **Ma** (Sony 36674), **Du Pré** (with Barbirolli, EMI 69707, 2CD, and with Barenboim, EMI 47614 and 66948), **Rostropovich** (with Britten, Decca 430633, and with Iona Brown, EMI 49305), **Starker** (Delos 3062), and **Christine Walevska** (Philips 438797, 2CD, with other Haydn works). Similarly, 2 has recommendable recordings, coupled with 1 by **Ma, Du Pré** (EMI 66948), **Rostropovich** (EMI 49305), **Shafran** (Melodiya 40724), and **Walewska.**

Clarinet. The newly discovered clarinet concertos attributed to Haydn

exist only in a recording by **Dieter Klöcker** (Orfeo 448971). They don't sound like important music, whoever wrote them.

Flute. Haydn's flute concerto is similarly minor in stature and can be found in a fine performance by **Rampal** (Sony 62649).

Horn. Haydn wrote several concertos for horn, but only two survive. Of these, the second is considered spurious by some authorities, though it has the sound of genuine Haydn. **Tuckwell**'s performances are as good as it gets in this music and have the advantage of the Rostropovich/Britten Cello Concerto 1 and a fine reading of the trumpet concerto by Alan Stringer as discmates (London 340633, mid-priced). For those who must go beyond this, **Ifor James** is a fine soloist, though with a pronounced vibrato (EBS 6052), and **Ab Koster** plays 1 with a variety of other Haydn horn music (Sony 68253).

Keyboard. Haydn is credited with 15 keyboard concertos. Of these, one (15) is lost. There are also several others attributed to him that may or may not be his. These concertos are performed on harpsichord, organ, or piano (modern or fortepiano). A set intended to be comprehensive was recorded by **Ilse von Alpenheim;** some of these performances have been reissued on CD, the rest will undoubtedly follow (Vox). I have listed the concertos for which there are performances in print.

1 (C major). The piece exists in rather stolid performances by **F. Klinda** (Point 267180) and by **Franz Lehrndorfer** on harpsichord (Tuxedo 1049).

2 (D major). **Alpenheim** is dutiful on harpsichord (Vox 5017, 2CD), **Rosenberger** on piano is more lively and nuanced (Delos 3061). There are also performances by **Franz Haselböck** on organ (Orfeo 158871) and **Gloria d'Atri** on piano (IMP 964).

3 (F major). This is listed as 6 in the Hoboken catalog and is really a concerto for violin and keyboard. There are several recordings, but the best of the performances is by **Accardo** (violin) and **Bruno Canino** (harpsichord) (Philips 438797, 2CD). The others are ordinary.

4 (F major). The finest performance is by **Gerrit Zitterbart** (piano) with the Schleierbach Chamber Orchestra led by Thomas Fey; it's a supple and expressive reading with wit and drama (Hänssler 98354). **Alpenheim**'s performance is solid and stolid (Vox 5017). **Ax** (piano) is stronger than Alpenheim but less imaginative than Zitterbart (Sony 48383). It is listed as 3 in Hoboken.

5 (G major). The concerto offers the same story as 4, except that there is also a fine piano version by **Rösel** (Berlin 9294 CD, with decent performances of 6 and the cello concertos).

6 (D major). This is *the* Haydn keyboard concerto. Not only are the reliable **Alpenheim,** the decent **Rösel,** and the eloquent **Gerrit Zitterbart** in the running (see above), but also such heavyweights as **Argerich** (DG 349864) and **Kissin** (RCA 7948). There are also piano versions from **Ax** (Sony 48383), **Helen Chang** (Naxos 550713), and **Davidovich** (Supraphon 3265), and harpsichord versions from **Landowska** (Enterprise 230 or Biddulph 032) and **Pinnock** (DG 431678). None is negligible, but of the piano versions Zitterbart wears the best while Pinnock's harpsichord sound and concept are more likely to appeal than Landowska's.

9 (C major). **Alpenheim** is the only game in town.

Lira organizzata. This was a kind of hurdy gurdy; it has not been revived, and the five concertos for two lire organizzata that Haydn wrote now exist only in the form of concertos for flute and oboe. These are performed by **Robert Dohn** and **Lajos Lencsés** with the Slovak Chamber Orchestra (CPO 999182) and by **Rampal** and **Pierlot** with Rolla and the Franz Liszt Chamber Orchestra (Sony 39772, 2CD, with the oboe and flute concertos and Tchaikovsky's *Nutcracker Suite* [!]).

Trumpet. Haydn's trumpet concerto was a late work of deceptive simplicity and is one of the great works for the instrument. **Alan Stringer**'s version is solid and quite acceptable and comes with the great advantages of mid price, good sound, and peerless performances of the horn concertos by Tuckwell and Marriner and Cello Concerto 1 by Rostropovich and Britten (Decca 430633). Other fine versions include **Ludwig Güttler** (Capriccio 10010), **Wynton Marsalis** (several different Sony issues, the cheapest of which is 437846), **Gerard Schwarz** (Delos 3001), **Rolf Smedvig** (Telarc 30232), and **John Wallace** (Nimbus 7016). On a different level are the noble (but diverse) virtues of **Crispian Steele-Perkins** (IMP 6600662) and **Helmut Wobisch** (Vanguard 2535).

Violin. There were four violin concertos, of which three (1, 2, and 4) survive. **Accardo** offers fine performances (Philips 438797, 2CD, mid-priced). **Kantorow**'s are warmer and more spontaneous (Cascavelle 1053, a single disc that costs almost as much as the Philips set). **Rainer Küchl** offers an even lovelier performance of 1 and 4 (Nimbus 5518, with *Sinfonia Concertante*). **Sitkovetsky** offers the same two concertos in more prosaic performances (Supraphon 3265, with the D major keyboard concerto and the Concerto for Violin, Keyboard and Orchestra).

MISCELLANEOUS WORKS

It's impossible to cover all the various pieces defying classification that Haydn wrote, but some of them must be discussed.

The Seven Last Words of Christ on the Cross is a series of slow movements written for a Good Friday service. It exists in versions for keyboard, string quartet, orchestra, and soloists, choir, and orchestra, and an arrangement for soloists and string quartet created for the Juilliard Quartet. The plan behind the piece was that at a religious service there would be a series of sermons based on Christ's words, each of which would be followed by a slow piece about 10 minutes long.

The keyboard version is set forth magnificently by **Akl** (Discover 920503) and **McCabe** (Philips 443785, 12CD); there's nothing to choose between them, except that Akl is quite cheap and hard to find. String quartet versions exist by the **Borodin,** dark and impassioned, a vision of the world of Symphony 49 (Teldec 92373); the lyrical **Delmé,** beautifully recorded (Hyperion 66337); the rich and earnest **Festetics** (Quintana 903043); the businesslike **Kodály** (Naxos 550346); the supple and transparent **Kuijken** (Denon 78973); **Kremer** and colleagues, who offer virtuosity on fire (Sony, NA); the magisterial **Lindsay** (ASV 853); the slinky **Mosaïques** (Astrée 8743); the dark splendor of the **Talich Quartet** (Calliope 9250); and the old gold of the **Vienna Concerthall Quartet** (Preiser 93071, mono).

An interesting and moving approach combines fine quartet readings by the **Vermeer Quartet** with a series of sermons by renowned preachers and a narration by Jason Robards (Alden 123046). The choral-orchestral version is well represented by **de Almeida** with Russian forces (odd winds, but wonderful choristers, especially the basses), Viennese forces under **Scherchen** (Vox 9816, with Mozart works) and **Harnoncourt** (Teldec 101222). The **Juilliard Quartet** offers an odd hybrid version with four distinguished soloists that tries to combine the best of the quartet and choral versions and ends up with an unsatisfactory blend, including the glowing F-sharp major slow movement from

Quartet Op. 76:5 as a kind of replacement for the stark A minor interlude in Haydn's original (Sony 44914). It's a lovely piece but out of context. Approach with caution.

Haydn, like any other self-respecting 18th-century composer, turned out many occasional works, including a constellation of divertimentos. These weren't intended for close scrutiny, and all that need be said is that the series by Viennese forces under **Manfred Huss** is more than adequate (Koch Schwann 312862). Huss has also recorded all the overtures (Koch Schann 1723 and 1484). Much more worth investigating are the "scherzandos," a series of six miniature symphonies written when Haydn was 29. They're challengingly similar to the best of his later works, with many of the same sad marches for slow movements and lively minuets. Huss and his Viennese players present these pieces superbly (Koch Schwann 1443).

CHAMBER MUSIC

What can we make of Haydn's almost superhuman productivity in this area? Even more spooky is the high quality of the works. Whether he was writing string quartets of near-orchestral sonority, an unending series of baryton trios, the elegant little London trios for flutes and cello, or even the rustic/elegant Divertimento for horn, violin, and cello that sounds as if it was put together for an afternoon impromptu, there's always music-making full of life and song.

String quartets

These are the centerpieces of Haydn's chamber output. Their quality was recognized from the beginning, although twits of various kinds bestowed silly names—"The Frog," "How Do You Do?" and so on—on many of them. They've remained alive and played since they were first published and are doing well in the current catalog.

The use of period instruments inspires the kind of fervor and disregard for facts that normally characterize sectarian disputes in religion and politics. Here it isn't much of an issue for most listeners. Modern strings are usually played at a higher pitch, with A over middle C being 440 or so cycles per second; older strings are usually played at a lower pitch, sometimes a good half step below the current norm. This, plus the different construction of the instruments—no chin rests or floor pegs, different supports inside, gut instead of steel or steel-wound strings, and so on—gives the old instruments a gentler, more transparent sound, less aggressive, more mellow. There are also different techniques available and appropriate on each type of instrument, and different ideas about vibrato and bowing. Most listeners can take an ensemble on its own terms, easier to do now than in the early days of old instrument revival, when the sound and intonation of some playing were difficult to endure.

Complete sets. Four major ensembles have recorded or appear to be recording complete cycles, two on modern and two on period instruments.

The **Lindsay** (ASV) and **Kodály Quartets** (Naxos) are modern ensembles. The Lindsays are British, the Kodálys Hungarian; ASV is a high-priced import label, Naxos is, of course, a super-budget label. Thus, all other things being equal, deciding which to buy should be easy. Unfortunately, all other things are not equal. The Lindsay cycle in progress is the group's second foray through these works and it shows (some of the recordings from the earlier survey are available as mid-priced ASV discs and are worth investigating, though they're not as good as the new ones). The power, freedom, and consistent insight these players bring to this music make the Kodály performances seem like sight-readings. The volumes of the new cycle that have appeared so far (1057, Op. 22:2,5,6; 937, Op. 33; 938, Op. 54; 582, Op. 55; 906, p. 76; 1076 and 1077) have easily dominated the listings, with a level of performance unmatched by such fine groups as the **Tokyo** and **Alban Berg Quartets.**

What the Lindsays do through sheer quality, the Kodálys do through value. By every standard except back-and-forth listening, their performances are fine. The players are technically skilled, they play well individually and as a group, and they know Haydn's idiom and convey the stature and humanity of the music. But they just don't have either the lived-in feel of some ensembles that have played the works over time or the electricity that sometimes comes when an artist or group encounters a new piece and suddenly "gets" it. If you have a limited budget or are unsure of whether Haydn quartets are for you, the Kodály performances are safe recommendations; their performances are available on 23 CDs (Naxos 502301).

The old-instrument sets don't divide in quite the same way. Both groups are highly skilled, with one having, perhaps, a slight technical edge, but the other the deeper musical insight. The **Mosaïques Quartet** is recording for the French Astrée label, the **Festetics Quartet** for Arcana and Quintana. The Mosaïques is a Western European group with French leanings, while the Festetics is Hungarian. Although both use old instruments and seem to advocate similar performance practices, they sound quite different. The Mosaïques often create a solo-plus-ripieno effect, with the sound and personality of the first violin dominating the readings. The cello is the next strongest instrumental voice, but it follows at a considerable distance, while the second violin and viola are often musically negligible and close to inaudible. The Festetics, on the other hand, have a choral sound with four instrumental voices more nearly matched in strength and personality. Their approach is more introverted and lyrical, while the Mosaïques—or, to be accurate, that group's first violin—is more extroverted. It probably says more about the vagaries of classical record distribution than about the taste of our noisy, chattering age that the Mosaïques performances seem to be securely in the catalog while the Festetics are hard to find. Both offer superb playing and close attention to the sense of the music. The Festetics will likely last longer in the mind, if not the catalog, but both repay attention.

The **Tatrai Quartet**'s performances of the quartets are quite vigorous and rough around the edges and the sound is gritty (Hungaroton 410001, 25CD). Between the wiry playing and the coarse sound, I find little to like in them. Lovers of extreme string playing may feel differently.

Op. 20 (Sun). This is Haydn's first set showing the scope of his genius in this form. The **Lindsay** recording is a strong first choice. The **Kodály** performances are on Naxos 550701 and 550702. The older Lindsay recordings are distributed among three mid-priced discs that include other Haydn quartets as well (ASV 6144, 6146, 6147). The **Mosaïques** are on Astrée 8784.

Op. 33 (Russian). These quartets again have the current **Lindsay** reading (see above), the old one (ASV 6146), and the **Kodály** (Naxos 550788/89). There's a **Mosaïques** as well (Astrée 8594, 2CD). The **Festetics** are on Quintana 903002 (with Op. 42).

Op. 50 (Prussian). These present the by-now familiar choices. The Kodálys are on Naxos 855383/84.

Opp. 54 and **55**. Haydn's next two sets have three pieces per set instead

of the usual six. The **Lindsay** numbers for both are listed above; the **Kodály** numbers are Naxos 550395 (Op. 54) and 550397 (Op. 55). There is a period instrument recording by the **Salomon String Quartet** of Op. 55 with superb sound and packaging, but the performances are bland compared to the best of the competition (Hyperion 66972).

Op. 64 (Tost). This set brings a few new faces to the party. The **Borodin Quartet** offers a big-boned reading of 2 ("The Lark") challengingly coupled with Beethoven's "serioso" and Schoenberg's 2—three masterpieces (MK 418019). A joyous and airy reading comes from the **Hagen Quartet** (DG 423622, with a serene 1 and a stark Op. 74:3, "The Rider"). The old **Lindsay** recording has an elegant "Lark," more like a pheasant (ASV 6145). The **Salomons** are bland (Hyperion 67011/12) and the **Kodálys** their usual sturdy selves (Naxos). The **Budapest** (Bridge), **Flonzaley** (ASV), and **Léner Quartets** (Repertoire 5006) offer various historical readings of parts of this set that are of limited value.

Op. 71. This is another three-quartet set. The **Kodály** performance is on Naxos 550394. There's also a mellow recording by the **Chilingarian Quartet** (Chandos 9146).

Op. 74. The three-quartet set has the **Kodály** (Naxos 550396), with some Czech complements from the **Talich** (Calliope 9241 and 6617) and **Vlach Quartets** (Praga 250098).

Op. 76 (Erdödy). This has the peerless **Lindsay** mentioned above, the **Kodály** (Naxos 550314/550315), and an elegant and low-priced **Tokyo Quartet** set (Sony 53522). There are more recordings of this than of any other set, but the Lindsays are miles ahead of all competitors in quality of performance, and the Tokyo and Kodály—in that order—are superb low-priced alternatives. There's no need to look beyond them.

Op. 77 (Lobkowitz). The set offers two quartets and the piquant incomplete *Op. 103* (slow movement and minuet), which rounds it out. Look for the **Festetics** (Quintana 1903001). A good but not outstanding alternative is the **Franz Schubert Quartet** (Nimbus 5312).

String trios

These are next in importance in the realm of Haydn's chamber music. They're probably the greatest body of classical music outside the general repertoire, and their neglect is incomprehensible. There's a fine comprehensive set by the **Beaux Arts Trio** (Philips 454089, 9CD). I've written about it from time to time, but I must admit that I've underestimated its integrity and its ability to stand the test of time and repeated listening. It's not only the only game in town, but the best that's likely to come along. It's a terrific reference set and, if you can afford it, is well worth the price, both for the superb music and the quietly elegant performances.

Rival performances are scarce, but the following are worth mentioning: **Abegg Trio**, a fine young German ensemble using modern instruments (39 and 41, Tacet 89); **Beths, Bylsma,** and **Levin,** three of the finest musicians in the old instrument community (25,26,30, Sony 53120); **Höbarth, Coin,** and **Cohen,** strong performances on old instruments, tantalizingly nuanced differently from the Beaux Arts (Harmonia Mundi 901314, 32–34; 901514, 38–40; 901277, 43–45); **Vienna Piano Trio** in coarse performances to be avoided (Nimbus 5535, 32, 38, 39, 45). **Kogan, Gilels,** and **Rostropovich** isn't in the catalog but still shows up in stores from time to time, and if you see it, don't hesitate; it has superb playing in Haydn's Op. 33 as well as Mozart's K 564 and Schumann's Op. 63 (Melodiya 10-00547).

Baryton trios

If performances of the piano trios are scarce, those of the baryton trios are almost unheard-of. The baryton was an instrument with characteristics of both cello and guitar, and Prince Nikolaus Esterházy, Haydn's patron, played it. Haydn dutifully composed 125 known trios for the instrument. Professor John Hsu of Cornell is a baryton player and his ensemble, the **Haydn Baryton Trio,** has recorded six of them (Dorian 90233). The performances seem adequate and the music is pleasant but not especially deep. A rival group, the **Esterházy Baryton Trio,** recorded seven, remarkably managing to overlap with the Hsu group on only one, No. 107 (EMI 69836). The performances seem comparable. There's also a recording of (unspecified) trios by the **Geringas Baryton Trio** (CPO 999094).

London Trios

These lovely pieces from 1794–95 were written for two flutes and cello and have been memorably recorded twice by **Rampal,** the first with Stern and Rostropovich (Sony 37786), the second with Wolfgang Schultz, flute, and Georges Audin, bassoon (Sony 48061). Presumably, if he had recorded it a third time, he would have assembled the forces that Haydn originally wrote for! Both performances are fine. Those wishing to hear Haydn's original scoring should seek out the **Kuijkens** and Hantai, where the four trios are coupled with the Op. 5 flute quartets (Accent 9283). The Divertimento for horn, violin, and cello is well performed by Ab Koster with **L'Archibudelli** (Sony 68253) as well as by **John Cerminaro,** M. Larinoff, and Toby Saks (Crystal 679).

KEYBOARD MUSIC

Haydn's piano sonatas are only a little better known than his piano trios and represent another great treasure of classical music. Yet they remain in the shadow of Mozart's sonatas (lesser music) and Beethoven, whose sonatas built upon Haydn's.

Complete sets. There are two outstanding integral sets. One is by **John McCabe,** a British composer and pianist (Philips 443785, 12CD in a budget box), the other is by **Walid Akl** (Bourg or Discover, 14CD). (It's impossible to tell from *Schwann* what the Discover disc numbers are, but the Bourg series appears in seven 2CD boxes numbered 30–43.) Both play a modern piano, and both include works beyond the standard sonatas. McCabe offers supple, keenly observed performances; Akl's are more mercurial and more Gallic in style and sound. Akl has very close sound (immediate or claustrophobic, depending on your perspective); McCabe is more recessed and rounded. Both sets are superb.

Jenö Jandó, Naxos's resident pianist, has been working his way through the cycle. His performances lack the fizz of Akl's and the deep integrity of McCabe's but are solid and rewarding, worth the Naxos budget price for those who wish to learn about these works without having to make a major investment. The mature sonatas are already in print and the rest are doubtless in the pipeline (553127, 36–41; 550844, 42–47; 553128, 48–52; 53–58, with the F minor Variations; 550845, 59–62; 550657).

Among less complete sets, those of **Brendel** (Philips 416643, 4CD), **Gould** (Sony 52623, 2CD), and **Schiff** (Teldec 17141, 2CD) are all significant. Brendel includes 11 sonatas, ranging from the stormy C minor and B minor middle-period works through the sublime last handful and the great F minor Variations. His readings are a little detached and perhaps a shade drier than necessary. On the other hand, the gentle glow that lit his legendary performance of the *Diabelli Variations* is present through much of this set and is a delight to experience.

Gould plays the last six sonatas in vastly different performances. Where Brendel may be said to define the mainstream, Gould goes off in rivulets of his own. It's necessary, although perhaps obvious, to say that what Gould plays is not always, perhaps not often, related to what Haydn wrote; dynamics are exaggerated, tempos are stretched in bizarre ways. These are less performances of the sonatas than dramatizations from the point of view of an undisciplined genius. The strait-laced are warned.

Even the strait-laced will have no difficulty with Schiff's set, a miracle of wit, lyricism, and beautiful playing. It collects a handful of the mature sonatas and presents them with ease and elegance. My only quarrel is that there are not five more discs.

Other performers. Among the various other recordings of these works, it's easier to keep track by performers than by works. There are a handful of artists whose Haydn is always worthwhile. **Gilels, Kissin,** and **Richter** have recorded various sonatas superbly. **Horowitz** made memorable recordings of 58 (Sony 53466) and 62 (Enterprise 530026), and **Andre Watts**'s 58 is perhaps the most mercurial of all (EMI 64598). **Ax**'s recordings are solid and musical without quite attaining inspiration (Sony 53635), while **Jane Coop**'s are plain-spoken but deeply eloquent (Skylark 8501).

Rubinstein's F minor Variations are glamorous but superficial (RCA). Also to be avoided is **Ohlsson,** with empty, clattering technique (Arabesque). Sonata 50 was recorded beautifully by both **Clara Haskil** (Tahra 291) and **Myra Hess** (APR 7012, 2CD) as well as (coarsely) by **Lili Kraus** (Vox). A wonderfully inflammatory recording of Sonata 33 by **Anthony Newman** on pedal harpsichord once existed; if it's ever reissued, it will be worth hunting down (CBS).   CHAKWIN

CHORAL MUSIC

Die Jahreszeiten (*The Seasons*) is less eventful, less dramatic, and more religious than *The Creation.* The "characters" don't do much besides tend their gardens in the best of all possible worlds while God looks down benignly. The text is pietistic and didactic, and Haydn himself didn't approach it with much enthusiasm. There are perfunctory touches: the formulaic coloratura, the abundance of arias that end exactly the same way (with a half-scale run up to the tonic). But the old master extended himself in furnishing ingenious orchestral touches, and his melodies, if not on the *Creation* level, are still fairly catchy. *The Seasons* benefits most from a snappy approach; sententiousness won't do.

Karajan's first *Creation* is a great recording, but his *Seasons* (with two of the same soloists) is a lesson in how not to perform Haydn. The ponderous tempos and bloated choruses make the work seem interminable. Most critics prefer **Böhm**'s genial, affectionate 1967 recording, where the Vienna Singverein and Vienna Symphony perform with an almost proprietary naturalness (♦DG 457713). Janowitz sings radiantly, and Talvela, despite some bumptiousness, brings to his arias a vocal weightiness fit for a Sarastro. Not everyone has a kind word for Schreier, however. **Gönnenwein** is less buoyant than Böhm but not all that different in outlook (♦EMI 64548). His male soloists, Gedda and Franz Crass, are superior to Schreier and Talvela, and the chipper Mathis, who made a specialty of Hanne, is effervescent and meticulous. No recording has a better solo trio.

Dorati is in the fair-to-middling class; the much livelier **Harnoncourt** is subverted by his soloists. **Marriner** has some advocates and is a good bargain; his solo team—Mathis, Jerusalem, and Fischer-Dieskau—is interesting, but only Mathis sounds entirely comfortable

(Philips). The ideal tenor soloist for *The Seasons* was Wunderlich, and an inexpensive recording of a 1959 concert performance has fortunately been preserved (Bella Voce 7204). The conductor is the rather pedestrian **Hans Müller-Kray**; the American bass Keith Engen is a mellow, winning Simon. Less enticing are the conscientious soprano (Giebel) and the limited monaural sound.

Gardiner's vigor and bite are just what *The Seasons* needs, and despite some clipped choral enunciation, his 1990 recording ranks with the best (♦Archiv 431818). He has an ear for the telling detail, and his English Baroque Soloists play with great gusto. Bonney and Rolfe Johnson are limber and youthful, but Schmidt lacks the necessary bass richness. Not unlike Gardiner in its sweeping impulsiveness but more grandly scaled is **Solti**, whose *Seasons* easily outclasses both of his *Creations* (♦London 436840). The Chicago Symphony Chorus, recorded in concert in 1992, sounds cautious at first but quickly gains confidence; the splashy conclusion to "Autumn" is truly intoxicating. Soprano Ruth Ziesak also needs a little time to warm up, but she's sprightly and flexible once she does. Uwe Heilmann and René Pape (a genuine bass) have appealing voices and personalities, and no conductor has had a more responsive orchestra than the Chicago Symphony.

Only one of the two great English-language recordings is presently available, and I'd choose it over any of its German competitors: **Colin Davis**'s wonderful performance (♦Philips 289464). Two of his *Creation* soloists, Harper and Shirley-Quirk, are here joined by the sunny-voiced Ryland Davies; the BBC Chorus and Orchestra perform buoyantly, palpably relishing the job. All the performers (choristers included) enunciate clearly, and hearing the words in English really helps bring the music to life. I'm still hoping for a reappearance of **Beecham**'s 1958 recording, which has been out of the catalog too long (EMI). Two of his soloists are particularly engaging (Elsie Morison and Alexander Young), and the conductor leads the Royal Philharmonic and his own Choral Society with his unique blend of elegance and down-to-earth vitality.

Masses. Haydn's 14 Masses span his career. He wrote the first when he was still a choirboy in Vienna, the last when he was 70. In their variety and fecundity, and in the light they cast on the composer's maturation, they can justly be compared with Beethoven's symphonies or Mozart's piano concertos; the last six are very great works of music indeed. The names and Hoboken catalog numbers (not the traditional ones, all of them preceded by H. XXII) and nicknames of the most familiar are as follows: 4 Great Organ, 5 St. Cecilia, 6 St. Nicholas, 7 Little Organ, 8 Mariazeller, 9 Time of War (Paukenmesse), 10 Heiligmesse, 11 Nelson (Missa in augustiis), 12 Theresienmesse, 13 Creation (Schöpfungsmesse), 14 Harmoniemesse.

The most convenient way to acquire all of them is to buy the midpriced collection shared by three conductors (♦London 448518, 7CD, many available separately). **Preston** leads 4–6 and two earlier Masses, **Willcocks** takes 11, and the rest go to **Guest**, whose work in this repertory is consistently laudable. His performances are both stately and incisive, marked by excellent choral singing and generally fine soloists. They're not only good introductions to the masses but also recordings to live with contentedly despite the somewhat diffuse sound of King's College Chapel.

Collectors who don't want to start with a complete set, or who want to explore different approaches, have no shortage of choices. **Preston**'s *Cäcilienmesse* is certainly adequate, but this longest of Haydn's masses makes the most extreme demands on the soloists. More imposing than Preston's soprano and bass are Popp and Moll with **Kubelik** (♦Orfeo

032822). The soprano solos are particularly florid, and though Popp dashes through them smartly, Stader, with **Jochum** (DG 437383), is more impressive still—though even she doesn't toss off "Quoniam tu solus sanctus" from the "Gloria" with the spectacular flair of the great Jennifer Vyvyan in an old Haydn and Mozart recital disc that eminently deserves reissue (London).

Willcocks once recorded the *Paukenmesse* with a superb team of soloists (EMI), but his *Nelson Mass* is on the sedate side (London). **Marriner** offers a more exciting reading, with lusty, operatic singers, in an inexpensive double that includes 7, 10, and 12—the perfect entry-level recording for the curious newcomer (♦EMI 568592). Even more exuberant is **Bernstein**, whose pairing of 9 and 11 is a nice bargain (♦Sony 47563, 2CD). The soloists are a bit too distant and the sound lacks overall crispness (more so in 9, recorded in 1973 as part of an antiwar protest at Washington Cathedral), but just listen to Blegen's dancing soprano in the opening of the *Nelson Mass* and you'll be hooked. Bernstein's *Harmoniemesse* fills out his recording of *The Creation,* and he brings wonderful verve to the rollicking, surprising "Benedictus" and "Dona nobis pacem" (Sony 47560). If your ideas of how these movements should sound have been too heavily influenced by Bach and Beethoven, try Haydn for a completely different perspective.

Nos. 9 and 11 are the most recorded. **Pinnock**'s account of 11 (Archiv 435853) is coupled with the grandiose *Te Deum* commissioned by the Empress Maria Theresa to honor a visit from Lord Nelson and Lady Hamilton. More bracing than Pinnock (who also recorded 6 and 12; some find him pedantic rather than inspired) is **Weil**, whose ongoing series for Sony includes recordings of 7 (♦53368), 9 (♦66260), 10 (♦68255), 11, and 12 (♦62823). Good soloists, lovely orchestral playing, and irresistible momentum characterize these performances, which should extend to a complete set.

Levine brings a Beethovenian grandeur to 9 (DG), and still honorable is the old recording led by **Wöldike** (Vanguard). The always stimulating **Harnoncourt** is poised somewhere between the traditionalists and the period-instrument fundamentalists for 9 and 11 (Teldec). A second **Bernstein** recording (1984) surpasses his first (Philips). Among the other meritorious recordings are offerings from **Jochum** in 6 and 7 (Philips), **Sigiswald Kuijken** in 14 (Harmonia Mundi, with the *Te Deum*), and **Jeffrey Thomas** in 7 and 11 (Koch). An unprepossessing pairing of 4 and 6 conducted by **Friedrich Wolf** suggests how the masses might sound in an actual liturgical context (Preiser). Recorded at Vienna's St. Augustin Church, these are professional performances with an appealing homespun directness. **Hickox** has launched a complete series for Chandos, and with each new installment, it bids fair to challenge the best older recordings. Guest's performances have more grandeur and more individual soloists, but Hickox's vivacious, superbly executed readings are a winning alternative.

The Seven Last Words of Christ on the Cross. Haydn wrote four versions of *Seven Last Words,* for orchestra, string quartet, piano, and chorus with soloists. Whatever the performing forces, it's not easy to bring off this sequence of adagios, but the oratorio form of the work is the least austere.

Scherchen's old recording is a bit thin sonically and vocally (MCA), but there are three fairly good modern ones along with an impudent oddity. **Harnoncourt** is assured and trenchant. He certainly knows how to draw expressive singing out of a chorus, but his soloists are merely adequate (Teldec). So are the four Russians under the direction of **de Almeida,** who leads the Moscow Symphony in a weighty and often moving reading (Somm). It's always a thrill to hear those deep Russian basses in the chorus. **Rilling,** a practiced choral conductor, is the most satisfying (♦Hänssler 98.977). He chooses sensible tempos and has four excellent soloists, all of whom deserve recognition (Pamela Coburn, Ingeborg Danz, Uwe Heilmann, Andreas Schmidt). The oddity is a performance that conjoins soloists (Valente and de Gaetani among them) and the **Juilliard String Quartet,** a combination of performers (and performing versions) Haydn never envisioned (Sony). The singers introduce each movement, then leave the rest to the strings. It doesn't really work, and few critics like it.

Die Schöpfung (*The Creation*). This is the greatest and most recorded of Haydn's vocal works. Along with Bach's *Christmas Oratorio,* it's the most glorious example of sustained jubilation in Western music. Not only must the choir be well balanced and technically proficient, it must also sing with faith and feeling. Performances can be accurately evaluated as soon as the chorus makes its second appearance. If we don't hear real joy as they marvel at the newly created world ("Und eine neue Welt entspringt auf Gottes Wort"), we know they're out of touch with something essential. No less important are the soloists, who are entrusted with most of the music.

A selective discography must dismiss quite a few recordings out of hand because the singers are either uninteresting or vocally inadequate. This deficiency disqualifies **Wand** (Accord), **Jochum** (Philips), **Kuijken** (Accent), **Koch** (Berlin), **Kubelik** (Orfeo), **Bernstein** (DG but not Sony), **Harnoncourt** (Teldec), and **Weil** (Sony). Each of these conductors has at least one loyalist among critics but fails to win general approbation.

On the other hand, some of the earliest recordings are worth preserving mainly for the sake of the soloists. In 1956, **Markevitch** presided over the first great *Creation* on records, with the Berlin Philharmonic and St. Hedwig's Choir (♦DG 437380). It's a powerful, incisive account, yet never slights the beauty of the music. Kim Borg's grim bass makes him sound like a warrior archangel, but he holds your interest. The tenor is ordinary, but Seefried is one of the loveliest of soprano soloists, exquisite in the gossamer flights of "Nun beut die Flur," limpid and warmhearted everywhere else. **Karl Forster**'s recording was graced by the equally gratifying Grümmer, whose voice was richer than Seefried's (♦EMI 62595). Once again the tenor disappoints, but the bass is the inimitable Frick, even blacker than Borg but far more amiable. Forster leads the Berlin Symphony and the same chorus as Markevitch, and both the orchestral playing and choral singing have a nice old-fashioned roundness.

Not quite on the same level but still enjoyable is **Wöldike** with the chorus and orchestra of the Vienna State Opera (Vanguard). This was the first stereo recording (1958) and still sounds pretty good. The three archangels— Stich-Randall, Dermota, and Frederick Guthrie—are unforgettably individual, but the Adam and Eve are poor; Stich-Randall and Guthrie would have been much superior. Haydn himself used only three soloists in his performances, but many modern conductors deploy more, usually to deleterious effect. Too often the second soprano or bass is inferior to the first, and we end up feeling cheated. **Münchinger,** an expert choral maestro, made the same mistake as Wöldike. He should have further exploited his Gabriel and Raphael, Ameling and Krause, but his 1967 recording droops with the arrival of their replacements as Adam and Eve (London).

Such is not the case with the recording that remains my (and most critics') choice: **Karajan** in 1966, with the Vienna Singverein and Berlin

Philharmonic (♦DG 449761). Here is the grandest, strongest performance of all. The choral singing and orchestral playing are expressive and rock solid, and the soloists are extraordinary. Janowitz is a lustrous Gabriel and Eve, Berry a pliant, sonorous, eloquent Raphael. Fischer-Dieskau is Adam, and for once, a second performer is not a letdown. Better still is Wunderlich, whose zest, flexibility, and vocal beauty are still unmatched. You'll never hear a more thrilling "Mit Würd und Hoheit"—an object lesson in how expressive a great voice can be. Wunderlich died before the recording was completed, so a few of the tenor passages were supplied by Werner Krenn. A sixth soloist makes a guest appearance in the final chorus—no less than Ludwig, who was married to Berry at the time and was dragooned into singing the alto lines when she dropped by the studio.

No recording after Karajan's (including his own remake) has reached the same high level, but many of them have been enjoyable and, more important, complete. Karajan, like Forster, makes a deplorable cut near the end of the second Adam-Eve duet, presumably to spare his singers a tricky coloratura flight. Modern conductors tend to be more conscientious, but most of the older recordings are also complete. A good (and underrated) one is led with fiery dedication by **Frühbeck de Burgos** (♦EMI 569343). Two of his soloists (Donath, van Dam) are first class; the third (Tear) dry but capable. **Dorati,** whose devotion to Haydn is unmatched by any other conductor on records, made a complete recording with a decent trio of archangels but a poor Adam and Eve (London). He's oddly lethargic, scarcely bestirring himself to point up Haydn's picturesque orchestral imagery. He also shares a problem with Frühbeck: Both lead English choruses, and they don't deliver the words with the natural, conversational flair of the best German and Austrian assemblages.

Bernstein in 1969 has the same handicap, though this time the chorus is American (Sony). He offers a multitude of felicitous details, but he also turns fussy from time to time, for example ruining the great 'Heavens are telling' chorus by draining the exuberance out of it and weighing it down with profundity. His soloists are Raskin, who sounds skittish, the gravelly John Reardon, and the elegant Alexander Young, all of whom (together with the chorus) would have been much more comfortable and effective singing in English. An opportunity was missed here. Bernstein's second recording is more eccentric than his first, the recitatives in particular drawn out too lugubriously (DG).

Both of **Solti**'s recordings, with the Chicago Symphony and Chorus, are marked by a sort of frenetic efficiency and are unredeemed by their soloists (London). The second, despite some (live-performance) blemishes, is better than the first. Even so, the heavens tell the glory of God rather breathlessly, and the first Adam-Eve duet is unusually frolicsome, as if they had other things on their minds. The much-acclaimed **Gardiner** is, if not frenetic, very much on the brusque side; characteristically, he seems embarrassed by any trace of old-fashioned grandeur (Archiv). His soloists are lightweights, unable to muster enough voice to flesh out the musical lines.

Levine has moments of splendor, but his Swedish chorus sings with frosty detachment and his soloists are too far in the background (DG). **Marriner**'s second recording is sabotaged by dial-twiddling engineers (EMI). The stereo effects are so exaggerated you wonder if the conductor needed semaphore flags to communicate with his performers. The exceptional talents of soprano Bonney and tenor Blochwitz are wasted here, and the disillusioning Adam-Eve pair again keep us on the side of the angels. Marriner's first outing, bolstered by decent soloists (Mathis, Aldo Baldin, and the redoubtable Fischer-Dieskau), is more of a piece, but it's tidy and respectable rather than majestic (Philips).

Rilling made two recordings (1982 and 1993), and the second (♦Hänssler 98.938) is the more noteworthy, with special attention paid to niceties of instrumentation and vocal ornamentation. The well-disciplined Gächinger Kantorei erupts on the word "Licht" without telegraphing it ahead of time, and all the choruses are sung with firm, full-bodied tone. The bass soloist is the light baritone Andreas Schmidt, and he doesn't have all the bottom notes or the flexibility required. Soprano Christine Schäfer embellishes her parts liberally, and tenor Michael Schade is clean, forthright, and responsive to the words. The solo parts of the great choruses, "Der Herr ist gross" in particular, are rendered with exceptional clarity.

Everyone should have a recording of *The Creation* in English. The most appealing is perhaps the 1974 **Willcocks,** despite the usual problems with the over-reverberant acoustics of King's College Chapel (♦HMV 72764, readily and cheaply available in the UK). The soloists—Harper, Tear, Shirley-Quirk—have healthy voices and are unafraid to sing out personally and flamboyantly. Genteel reserve is not an incurable British affliction, but you'd never know it if you came across **Hogwood**'s recording (Oiseau-Lyre) before hearing Willcocks's. Hogwood's soloists are timorous and anemic, unable (and certainly unwilling) to raise their voices in uninhibited song.

Rattle has a better trio: Augér, Langridge, and the verbally dexterous but vocally negligible David Thomas (♦EMI 54159). This performance has life and vigor, and the big moments are richly satisfying. Joy wells forth from the performers as they share their delight in recounting what each new-created day brings. The vivacious soloists ornament freely, somersaulting cheerfully through their embellishments. The infectious zeal of the performance is irresistible, some unrefined and over-theatrical moments notwithstanding.

The best-sounding English recording is **Shaw**'s, and the choral singing, as you would expect, is of the highest quality (Telarc). The three male soloists are passable; the two ladies (Upshaw, Heidi Grant Murphy) far more than that. Shaw uses an English translation of his own devising, and it clarifies much of the syntax at the expense of the poetry. The conductor, ever the gentleman, is prone to understatement, so for all its technical expertise, this performance is far less rousing than Rattle's. So is **Somary**'s, loud enough but weak and small-scaled (Newport).

Stabat Mater. Once all but unknown, *Stabat Mater* now has several fine recordings and is no longer dismissed as second-rate Haydn. Like Rossini's *Stabat Mater,* it's not invariably solemn, but the writing for the four soloists is so inventive you'll come away humming the tunes. There are four good recordings available. **Bernius** is a good buy; Ahnsjö, his tenor soloist, is especially fine (♦Vox 5081, 2CD, with Pergolesi and Vivaldi). Once again, **Pinnock** (Archiv) divides opinion: Is he breathing life into the music or merely illustrating a scholarly viewpoint? **Harnoncourt,** with the charming Bonney as soprano soloist, is livelier (Teldec). Perhaps the safest recommendation is **László Heltay:** clean sound, well-balanced choral singing, and two superb soloists in Augér and Rolfe Johnson (♦London 433172).

OPERAS

Haydn wrote 24 operas (not all survive), and despite their neglect, they must be considered a significant part of his output. Those that have been recorded are delightful, despite their long-windedness and formal rigidity. Haydn lacked Mozart's gift for creating memorable characters in swift, sharp strokes; we find no Susanna or Donna Elvira. Musical development generally takes precedence over dramatic eventfulness, and

the vocal writing can be rather instrumental in nature. Even the difficult passages don't always flatter the voices, and few of the melodies stick in the mind. The operas might prove tedious in the theater, but they invite exploration in the home; the compact disc offers the perfect means for patient discovery.

A guide to the recordings in this case need not compare performances of a given work so much as direct the collector to the few performances that are available; there's little competition to speak of. Pride of place goes to the eight Esterházy operas lovingly recorded by **Dorati** for Philips with an array of superb singers: *L'Infedeltà Delusa* (Mathis, Hendricks); *L'Incontro Improvviso* (Marshall, Jones, Ahnsjö); *Il Mondo Della Luna* (Augér, Von Stade, Alva; ♦432420); *La Vera Constanza* (Norman, Donath); *L'Isola Disabitata* (Zoghby, Alva); *La Fedeltà Premiata* (Cotrubas, Von Stade, Alva); *Orlando Paladino* (Augér, Ameling, Shirley; ♦432434); and *Armida* (Norman, Burrowes, Ramey; ♦432438). It's difficult to cite favorites, but the three given special recommendation are good starting points. *Il Mondo Della Luna* is an effervescent, cunningly orchestrated comedy with a dark side; *Orlando,* one of Haydn's most popular operas in his own time, has both comic and tragic elements; and *Armida,* a pure opera seria, is perhaps highest in sheer musical inspiration. *L'Incontro Improvviso,* a wacky, colorful comedy in the Turkish vein, is a good place to go next.

Hungaroton has also given us recordings of *La Fedeltà Premiata* and *L'Infedeltà Delusa,* well conducted by **Frigyes Sándor** and capably but less glamorously cast. **De Almeida**'s *L'Infedeltà* is long gone (Chant du Monde); **Kuijken**'s doesn't challenge Dorati's, though it may draw the period-instrument crowd. A recording of *L'Isola Disabitata* led by **David Golub** does present Dorati with stiff competition; it's as good overall and sometimes better (Arabesque). From Hungaroton comes the best recording of *Lo Speziale* (also known as *The Apothecary*). The conductor is **György Lehel;** four accomplished Hungarian singers are in the cast. The earliest of Haydn's surviving operas, the brief, frothy *La Canterina,* also has a recording on Hungaroton and an even more appealing one with Brenda Harris and D'Anna Fortunato (Newport).

Haydn's last opera, *L'Anima del Filosofo* (better known as *Orfeo ed Euridice*), is not from his Esterházy days and isn't among his greatest stage works, but oddly, it has been the most often recorded. Excerpts appeared as early as 1951, led by **Swarowsky** for the old Haydn Society label. Three fairly good complete recordings were issued in the '90s: **Michael Schneider**'s (Harmonia Mundi, with Prégardien, Schmiege, and McFadden); **Leopold Hager**'s (Orfeo, with Swensen, Donath, Greenberg); and **Hogwood**'s (♦Oiseau-Lyre 452668, with Bartoli and Heilmann). All are worthy, but Bartoli's theatrical zest and verbal flair are irresistible, even if her timbre isn't always pleasing. She undertakes both Euridice and the coloratura role of the Genie and in so doing walks in the footsteps of Sutherland, who made Euridice something of a specialty in the '60s and couldn't resist appropriating the florid aria of the Genie as well.

Sutherland can be heard with Gedda's Orfeo in a bootleg recording conducted by **Bonynge** (Myto; Melodram). It won't please the fundamentalists, and the great soprano is not at her crispest, but her enterprise deserves commendation—no one else was bothering much with Haydn's operas at the time.

SONGS AND CONCERT ARIAS

Haydn's 46 songs are just that, not lieder in the Schubert or Schumann fashion. Among them are not only German pieces but also English canzonettas, and they include one remarkable Shakespeare setting, "She

Never Told Her Love." Many singers have been drawn to them, and I can hear the echoes of many voices in my mind (going back to Elisabeth Schumann at least) blithely capering through the "hurly burly" of "The Sailor's Song." **Fischer-Dieskau**'s late-'50s recording is gone (EMI), along with **Pears**'s of a few years later (Decca). Tenor **James Griffett** recorded 14 English songs in 1977 (Pearl) and 12 of them again five years later, his clean diction and lithe, well-focused voice perfectly matched to the material (♦Teldec 97503). **Ameling** recorded all the songs in 1981, a laudable undertaking that deserves CD restoration (Philips).

In Ameling's absence, **Augér** will do nicely. Her fresh, glowing performances afford a perfect introduction, especially to six of the English canzonettas (Berlin 9044). **Schreier**'s recital on the same label comprises 13 German and two Italian songs, sung *very* seriously and intensely. The rarity of the material is self-recommending, but **Holzmair** is a more satisfying performer, in a mixed recital of German and English songs (♦Philips 454475). Despite a slight (and charming) accent, he's quite touching in "The Spirit's Song" and "She Never Told Her Love."

Two of Dorati's opera recordings are filled out with concert arias. Tenor and baritone do the honors after *L'Incontro Improvviso*, and soprano **Mathis** gives a recital of her own after *Il Mondo Della Luna* (though here the conductor is Armin Jordan). Some of Mathis's choices are duplicated by **Berganza,** not at her youthful best but still limber and enthusiastic (♦Erato 98498). **Augér** adds three arias to her Oiseau-Lyre recording of the two great solo cantatas, *Berenice* and *Arianna a Naxos*. It was replaced by a reissue that appended some Mozart opera arias but omitted the texts (♦Decca 440414). *Berenice* is a powerful, flamboyant piece that once enjoyed an incandescent recording by Jennifer Vyvyan (London); Augér addresses it as well as anyone since.

Arianna has proved more popular, perhaps because of its familiar subject. It was originally written with keyboard accompaniment and has been so recorded by **von Otter** (Archiv), **Bartoli** (Decca), **Carolyn Watkinson** (Virgin), and **Judith Nelson** (Koch), among many others. **Berganza** has recorded both versions: a marvelous account with pianist Felix Lavilla in 1977 (Decca), and a less flexible reading with an orchestra led by Marcello Viotti in 1990 (Claves). **Augér** also sings it with orchestra, and you won't go wrong with her. To be lamented is the disappearance of the Haydn arias recorded by the impassioned Bethany Beardslee (Monitor) and the elegant Léopold Simoneau and Pierrette Alarie (Canadian RCA).

Like Beethoven, Haydn wrote instrumental arrangements for many folk songs of the British Isles. Samples have come and gone on various anthology discs, and **Fischer-Dieskau** and **de los Angeles** famously recorded the Welsh air "All Through the Night" as a duet in German (EMI). **Janet Baker** once devoted most of an EMI LP to Haydn's Scottish songs (with Menuhin playing the violin parts). **Griffett** provides ample consolation for the demise of the Baker recording with a disc titled "Will Ye Go to Flanders?" (♦Ars Vivendi 1142). He pretty much has the field to himself, but there's also an interesting collection where two of Haydn's piano trios (17 and 21) set off **Ann Mackay**'s charming singing of 11 songs (♦Meridian 84222). **Wunderlich,** unfortunately, sings seven of the songs in German, which won't do, but at least his voice gives great pleasure in itself (Philips). LUCANO

Michael Haydn (1737–1806)

Franz Joseph's younger brother was the Archbishop of Salzburg's music director from 1762 until his death. He was thus Mozart's boss, and the two had great respect for each other, so much so that Haydn "lent" Mozart his Symphony 16, to which Mozart added a slow introduction for its concert performance (it appears as Mozart's 37 in the Köchel catalog). In return, Mozart "lent" Haydn several chamber works. Such borrowing was commonplace at the time, when composers had to supply large quantities of music, often at short notice.

In his own time Michael Haydn was best known as a composer of church music; he wrote more than 360 religious compositions, including masses, passions, oratorios, and shorter works. He also composed some 40 symphonies, as well as operas, chamber pieces and more. His older brother is said to have told friends that if they wanted to hear great religious music, they should listen to Michael's, not his. Weber was among his pupils, and Haydn's wife, Maria Magdalena Lipp, was a well-known soprano of the day.

Symphonies. Haydn wrote more than 40 symphonies. The best collection is in a set with the Slovak Chamber Orchestra led by **Warchal** (CPO 999591, 6CD, also available separately). The performances have been highly praised, and the sound is superb. Eight of them are played by **Harold Farberman** and the Bournemouth Sinfonietta in splendid performances with excellent sound at a budget price, a true bargain and a good introduction to these works (Vox 5020).

Nos. 21 and 30–32 are well played by the German Chamber Academy of Music led by **Johannes Goritzki** (CPO 999179), and the same group offers 34–39 (CPO 999379), in good performances and sound. The London Mozart Players, famous for their 1950 recordings under Harry Blech, have been reconstituted under **Bamert.** They offer 6, 9, 16, 26, and 32 in splendid performances, another excellent introduction to Haydn's instrumental music (Chandos 0352).

The Helsingborg Symphony under **Hans Peter** presents 18 and 31, plus two unnumbered symphonies in D and B flat; performances and sound are good (BIS 481). Two others led by **Adam Fischer** are also excellent (Nimbus). Another fine disc offers 18, 19, and 29, with the Warsaw Sinfonietta under **Wojciech Czepiel** (Arts 47314). Avoid a recording by Capella Savaria under **Németh** (Hungaroton 31706). All five symphonies are available elsewhere, and the sour tone of the band is a particularly bad example of period instrument practice.

Concertos. An excellent performance of the Trumpet Concerto is offered by **Armando Ghitalla,** long-time trumpeter of the Boston Symphony, with John Moriarty and the Copenhagen Chamber Orchestra (Crystal 7600). **Wynton Marsalis,** with Leppard and the English Chamber Orchestra, does a superb job with the Concerto for Trumpet and Horn. MHS once offered an LP of the concertos for trumpet, horn, and viola and organ, splendidly played by the Paillard ensemble. Watch for a reissue from them or from Erato, their original source. Several other concertos are available, mostly as fillers for recordings of music by other composers. Couplings will largely determine your choice among them.

Chamber music. Haydn also wrote much chamber music, but it's poorly represented on disc. **Concilium Musicum** offers three quintets, but their intonation is poor and it's weakly played (Koch 310084). A more attractive alternative is **L'Archibudelli** playing three quintets (Sony 310084). Two violin concertos, a *Divertissement* in D, and the "Applausus" Sinfonia are played by **Peter Sheppard** and Parnassus Ensemble, but in poor sound with shrill ensemble tone and thin string tone (Meridian 84243). A trio for viola, cello, and double bass is well played and recorded (Bayer 100296, with several works by other composers).

Choral music. Haydn's masses rival his brother's in ability and power. One of the best is the *St. Theresa Mass* of 1801, written for Maria Theresa, wife of Emperor Francis I, who sang the soprano part in the first performance. A splendid performance comes from **Zsolt Szefcsik,** the Jeunesse Musicales Choir, and the Erody Chamber Orchestra (Hungaroton 31865). The disc includes a Gradual, Offertory, and Te Deum, all beautifully performed in excellent sound.

The *St. Gotthard Mass* of 1792 gets a fine performance from the Zurich Boy Choir and Munich Chamber Orchestra under **Christoph Poppen** (Tudor 7046). The disc includes four Graduals, an Offertory, and a setting of the *Anima Mea*, all performed with style and spirit and well recorded. The *Spanish Mass in C* is offered by Capella Savaria with the Kodály Chorus, under **Németh** (Hungaroton 317655). The singing is excellent, but the tone of the period instrument ensemble is poor; the recorded sound is acceptable.

The *St. Hieronymus Mass* was written for the name day of Archbishop Coloredo, Mozart's nemesis. It's offered by Ensemble Philidor, with St. Jacob's Choir, under **Eric Baude-Delhommais** (BIS 859). BIS's high standards are observed, and the disc includes a group of motets and other short religious works. The sound is excellent. A second performance, featuring the Freiburg Boys Choir, Baroque Soloists, and Philharmonia Ensemble under **Raimund Hug,** is also excellent (Ars Musici 0972). This disc is filled out with works by Johann Georg Albrechtsberger, best known as a teacher of the young Beethoven.

The *St. Leopold Mass,* together with a German *Magnificat,* a *Notturno,* and a setting of the Vespers, is presented with soloists, organ, and the Collegium Instrumentale Brugense and Capella Concinite led by **Florian Heyerick** (René Gailly). It has been highly praised, and the sound is excellent. The same performance was previously issued on Vox 92006, where it also drew high praise. The *St. Aloysius Mass* is available in a recording by the Hanover Girls Choir, with soloists and ensemble under **Krysztof Wecrzyn** (Ars Musici 1113). It's fascinating music, well recorded and adequately played. The filler is a *Miserere* by Hasse, also attractive and adequately played. The only reservation is the short playing time of the disc, 51 minutes, but no other recordings are available.

The always reliable **Rilling** offers a *Requiem Mass* that serves as filler for his performance of Josef Haydn's *Seven Last Words* in the vocal version (Hänssler 918977). The sound and performance are good.

Stage music. Only one stage work is currently available: *Der Bassgeiger zu Worgl,* a German-language comedy. A performance by **Goritzki,** soloists, and the New German Chamber Orchestra, with a group of overtures and dances filling out the disc, is well done in excellent sound (CPO 999513). Goritzki also does an excellent job with excerpts from Haydn's incidental music to the "Turkish" play *Zaire,* which Mozart started to turn into an opera but abandoned (CPO 919513, with two Nocturnes). A performance of the *Mythological Operetta,* actually incidental music for a play of that name, was once offered on a Qualiton LP and would be a worthwhile acquisition should it reappear on CD.   McCLAIN

Hans Werner Henze *(b. 1926)*

In the '50s and '60s, Henze was often mentioned along with Boulez and Stockhausen as the most promising of the immediate postwar generation of European composers. Since then, his visibility has diminished compared to theirs, perhaps because Boulez has achieved major status as a conductor in addition to his compositions, and Stockhausen because of his varied and extensive output. Henze's music seems dated by comparison. He explored serialism and electronic music but chose not to follow either to any great extent. Invariably stylish, rarely dissonant, and usually lyrical even when using some elements of serialism, he has composed in all the traditional genres with some success but without much influence or substantial following. Some appreciate his music

more for its leftist texts than for the music. Much of his extensive output has been recorded, but rarely more than once, so a comparison of recordings is seldom possible. Fortunately, many recordings by reputable performers on major labels remain in circulation.

Symphonies 1–6 were composed between 1947 and 1969; no two are alike, and to some extent they make up for western Europe's meager contribution to the genre after Mahler's death in 1911. All six have been remastered very well, with **Henze** conducting the Berlin Philharmonic in the first five and the London Symphony in 6 (DG 429854). They show his varying sides as composer of music reflective to bold, from chamber orchestration to full, including revolutionary songs reflecting his commitment to Communism (he lived in Cuba and East Germany for a time). Excellent recordings, liner notes, and sound quality make this attractive to Henze's supporters and others curious about the mid-century symphony in Europe.

A curious pairing offers *Telemanniana* and Piano Concerto 2 (CPO 999332). Reviewers are less than uniformly enthusiastic about the music, but they agree that the performance of the concerto by **Rolf Plagge** and the Northwest German Philharmonic Orchestra, Gerhard Markson conductor, is very good. Both pieces were composed in 1967 but are quite different, illustrating Henze's penchant for avoiding a consistent style. *Telemanniana* is not so much a paraphrase of the Baroque German's music as a recomposition, much as Stravinsky did with Bach's and Mozart's music. I'm probably in the minority in finding *Telemanniana* one of Henze's best works; most prefer the symphonies or operas. But it's less self-conscious, always a problem with Henze's music, and certainly less polemical than many of his vocal pieces. An alternative recording of the 50-minute Concerto is by **Eschenbach,** with Henze conducting the London Philharmonic (DG 499866). For an alternative recording of *Telemanniana,* it's coupled with songs from his opera *The English Cat,* discussed below (MD+G 3040881).

Another disc of music varied by date, style, and medium has been remastered from earlier Decca recordings (London 430342). One of Henze's first and best compositions, *Apollo et Hyazinthus* (1948) features the harpsichord, ably played by John Constable, with orchestra. *Companes Para Preguntas Ensimis* (1970) is for viola (Hiroturni Fukai as soloist, with chamber orchestra); Brenten Langheim is the soloist in Violin Concerto 2, all accompanied by the London Sinfonietta in their usual fine form, led by **Henze.** The accompaniment to the Concerto includes a tape of Hans Magnus Engenberger's poem *Hommage to Gödel,* with musicians and speakers positioned in the audience. For obvious reasons, full experience of this spatial arrangement would be more effective live than on disc.

Henze has usually employed traditional media, including string quartet, and the indefatigable **Arditti Quartet** performs Quartets 1–5 (Wergo 60114, 2CD). Composed over 30 years, they illustrate the range of Henze's thinking in absolute music better than his symphonies composed over a similar span. These five quartets range from mildly dissonant to mildly microtonal to mildly aleatoric. Henze has tempted me and many others with his obvious talent, and these pieces don't allay my suspicion that he will never harness it to write at least a few great pieces—but there's a lot here, especially in the Arditti's laudable performance.

The guitar has had something of a renaissance in the 20th century, and some of Henze's works for this delicate instrument are exemplary. *Royal Winter Music: First and Second Sonatas on Shakespearean Characters* is a good example of Henze's compositional eclecticism. Much is serial but not obviously so; some is programmatic but not vividly so.

David Tanenbaum's performance is exceptional, as is the sound quality; unamplified guitar isn't the easiest of instruments to record (Audiophone 72029). The disc is short at 47 minutes (why not more of Henze's guitar music?), but recommended for those who like modern guitar music or Henze or both. I think **Bream** is over-praised (BMG), but **Reinbert Evers** is a nearly acceptable alternative, though his tempos are more languorous and the result is less satisfying than Tanenbaum's rendition (MD+G 3110). A third recording is by **Dietmar Krebs;** in all ways it's the least of the three. Tanenbaum is again soloist in *To an Aeolian Harp,* Henze conducting the accompaniment by Ensemble Modern (Ars Musici 859). Composed for the guitarist, this four-movement work is less interesting than the sonatas but comparably well performed.

Opera is the ideal medium for the expression of Henze's radical political views, but even the most talented composers may miss a musical point in favor of a polemic (see Bernstein's *Mass,* for example). This is true of *The English Cat,* in which Henze satirizes in a peculiar and visually interesting way much of what he sees as decadent Western politics. Unfortunately, the only recording I know is largely amateurish (Wergo 6204). Good liner notes at least let the audience in on the greedy cats' machinations. *The Young Lord* is another political morality tale set as an opera—an upper class British fellow is an ape who screams and sings as he tries to educate Germans in proper social behavior. The music is typically eclectic, as needed for such a spectacle, but the recording of a mixed bag of singers conducted by **Dohnányi** with the Deutsche Oper Orchester is very good (DG 445248).

The Bassarids was composed in the late '60s to a libretto by Chester Kallman and W. H. Auden (Stravinsky's librettists for *The Rake's Progress*). It was widely praised and had something of a run but has, like a lot of Henze's music, dropped from sight despite the remarkable revival of interest in opera in the late 20th century. A good recording features tenor Kenneth Riegel as Dionysus, baritone Andreas Schmidt as Pentheus, and Karan Armstrong as The Mother, with **Albrecht** conducting the Berlin Radio Orchestra (Koch Schwann 314006).

Boulevard Solitude (1952) is for me the best of Henze's stage works. It's based on the same *Manon Lescaut* story by Prevost also used for operas by Puccini and Massenet, but unlike those operas Henze glosses over nothing, getting right to the love affair and the attributes and flaws of the characters. Postexpressionistic and post-Weill in a way, the 80-minute single act plays out splendidly with Elena Vassilieva as Manon and Jerome Pruett as des Grieux. The live performance adds immediacy, with only slight flaws that would be absent in a studio recording. Informative notes add value, but with so much music by Henze, I wonder why there are only 80 minutes on two CDs (Cascavelle 1006).

ZIEROLF

Victor Herbert (1859–1924)

Irish-born and German-educated, Herbert was for six seasons musical director of the Pittsburgh Symphony and was well known as a cello virtuoso and a serious composer with a solid résumé of orchestral and chamber music. He was also a strong proponent of composers' rights, playing a central role in founding ASCAP. Yet for most people Herbert remains best known for his enduring creations for the American lyric theater, notably *Babes in Toyland, The Red Mill,* and *Natoma.* As one whose fondest memory of *Babes in Toyland* remains the Laurel and Hardy movie, perhaps I can't speak with authority on that subject; however, it's hardly surprising that many of the choicer morsels from these scores are included among the collections that follow.

Three discs combining brief stand-alone pieces for orchestra, suites from the operettas (often with voice), and songs have been released by **Donald Hunsberger,** each named after a different Herbert piece ("Souvenir," ♦Arabesque 6529; "l'Encore," ♦6547; "The American Girl," ♦6561), and the first three volumes in **Keith Brion**'s ongoing series are at hand (Naxos 559025/26). There's also a collection called "Thine Alone," led by **Richard Auldon Clark** (♦Newport 85572). All of them are worth considering, but while Brion is more alert in *Cannibal Dance* and *Royal Sec,* his sluggish *Badinage* can't hold a candle to Hunsberger's fleet-footed account; all three do very well with *Pan Americana.*

Those primarily interested in Herbert's songs will do best with Hunsberger or Clark; Teresa Ringholz and Andrea Matthews sing beautifully, while Virginia Croskery sounds too Wagnerian. Brion's first disc (Naxos 559025) is especially valuable for the 15-minute Prelude to *Babes in Toyland.* The opening "Selections" from *Babes* and the 10-minute suite from *The Red Mill* are also offered by Hunsberger in "l'Encore," and he keeps things moving along a lot better, but Brion gives you more music from *Babes* (including a decidedly unchildlike "March of the Toys"), so this one at least is worth the duplication.

If *Pan Americana* salutes Herbert's adopted nationality, *Irish Rhapsody* is an unashamed homage to his homeland, exuberant and filled with wonderful Irish melodies. It's included by **Clark** in his Newport CD, but Brion has more fun with the last Irish jig. The other side of the coin is *American Fantasia,* deftly combining a variety of patriotic favorites from "Hail, Columbia" to a rousing "Star-Spangled Banner." It's available as part of **Slatkin**'s "American Portraits" (RCA 60983) as well as in **Kunzel**'s "American as Apple Pie," where it's joined by Herbert's *Festival March* (VoxBox, 3CD). Many will fondly remember **Ormandy**'s Columbia LP (ML 5376) including the *Irish Rhapsody, Pan Americana, American Fantasy,* and suites from *Naughty Marietta* and *The Fortune Teller,* which even in mono would be welcome on CD. Unique to Brion's Vol. 3 is *Columbus Suite,* created for the 1893 Chicago World's Fair and evoking both the fateful voyage and the discovery of a New World in fanciful fashion (♦Naxos 559027).

The more serious side of Herbert's orchestral output surfaces in the extended musical portrait *Hero and Leander,* based on Ovid's tragic tale of ill-fated love. **Krueger**'s highly respectable performance, part of his series for the Society for the Preservation of the American Musical Heritage (MIA 121), suffered by being unnecessarily stretched out over an entire LP (it takes just under half an hour). It's handily supplanted by **Maazel**'s splendid account, filled out with a suite of operetta favorites arranged for orchestra (♦Sony 52491, also with Grofé's *Grand Canyon Suite*).

It may seem strange to think of Herbert as a film music composer, but the really gut-wrenching battle music he wrote for *The Fall of a Nation* is a revelation next to the guileless melody of the operettas. **Fennell** leads about 35 minutes of the roughly 2-hour score, a fascinating sampling that will leave you hungry for more (♦Library of Congress OMP-103, with Kern's *Gloria's Romance*).

If you think you detect echoes of Dvořák's Cello Concerto in Herbert's Concerto 2, you're right; actually they're not echoes but foreshadowings, as Dvořák, then living in this country and director of the National Conservatory—where Herbert served as head of the cello faculty—lavished effusive praise on his colleague's new score, and it can hardly be a coincidence that he was stimulated to write his own concerto the following winter. Cyclical in style, with the opening theme returning in the finale, it's a glorious rush of melody with a stunning virtuoso display for the soloist. It has quite eclipsed Herbert's Concerto 1 written nearly 10 years earlier, a fresh-sounding if perhaps more naively tuneful exercise.

Harrell has recorded both concertos along with five shorter pieces, and his warm-hearted performances remain essential (♦London 417672). **Ma** has appropriately coupled 2 with the Dvořak concerto, and he does a wonderful job with both, ably supported by Masur (♦Sony 67173). **Georges Miquelle**'s lean tone contrasts effectively with Harrell's lush vibrato, but the sound seems strained next to either London or Sony (Mercury 434355, with Grofé's *Grand Canyon* and *Mississippi Suites*). **Lloyd Webber** recorded the Herbert and Sullivan concertos (EMI); like Harrell he favors broad tempos, though unlike Harrell he merely sounds bored, and like Miquelle he seems ascetic tonally but without Miquelle's energy to compensate.

Herbert's full-length operettas appear to be going begging on CD; there seem to be no recordings of *Natoma* or *Madeleine,* and while there have been samplings from *Babes in Toyland, Naughty Marietta,* and *The Red Mill* with little or no dialogue, when you compare this with Gilbert and Sullivan it's a sorry state of affairs. Herbert's once highly successful romantic comedy *Eileen* (originally titled *Hearts of Erin*) was brought out by the Ohio Light Opera Company with the orchestral score newly resurrected by **Quade Winter** (Newport). Basically the same production may be heard from an enthusiastic cast of singers ably led by **Michael Butterman** (♦Newport 85615). Newport should follow suit with the others and perhaps *The Fortune Teller,* so that Herbert's wonderful works for the stage may finally be heard on disc as they deserve.

HALLER

Bernard Herrmann (1911–1975)

Herrmann is undoubtedly best known for his colorful, imaginative movie scores, which are discussed in detail in the "Film Music" article in Part II. Around the same time he began his involvement with Orson Welles, Herrmann was also beginning a career as a "serious" composer. His cantata *Moby Dick* was premiered by Barbirolli and the New York Philharmonic, and his Symphony 1 was successfully performed over CBS radio. Throughout his career, he alternated music for movies with scores for the concert hall, and his moody, distinctive style was well suited to both. Though not one of the concert works has caught on, they're full of beautiful music. In his talent for atmosphere and melancholy turns of phrase, Herrmann's concert music often seems closer to European composers like Sibelius, Walton, and Delius than to Americans. The brilliant orchestral colors and mordant wit that flare up so effectively in his movie music occur much less often in his concert scores.

Luckily, he was an experienced conductor: director of music for CBS Radio in the '30s and leader of the CBS Symphony from 1938 to 1959. After moving to London in the '60s, he made well-received recordings of his larger works, including his opera *Wuthering Heights,* which was never performed during his lifetime. His most revivable large work is probably his Symphony 1 (1937), melodious, broadly planned, and handsomely scored, in the vein of Sibelius; **Herrmann** recorded it in London with the National Symphony (Unicorn 2063, with works by Walton and Bax), and there is a more recent version by **Sedares**—better recorded than Herrmann's, perhaps, but lacking his authoritative touch (Koch 7135). Herrmann fans will also prefer his coupling, the lovely cantata *The Fantasticks,* to Sedares's, William Schuman's *New England Triptych.* (The cantata is no relation to the Schmidt-Jones musical, but is a setting of Elizabethan poetry by Nicolas Breton, to music whose sad sumptuousness recalls Delius.) Sedares pairs the massive *Moby Dick* with the brief, beautiful orchestral elegy *For the Fallen* (Unicorn 2061).

Sedares also performs *For the Fallen,* coupling it with Americana à la Herrmann, a colorful *Currier and Ives Suite* and music from the movie *The Devil and Daniel Webster* (Koch 7224). An even better recasting of movie music into concert form is *Welles Raises Kane,* a suite of highlights from *Citizen Kane* and *The Magnificent Ambersons.* It was originally performed by Beecham, no less; **Herrmann** later recorded it with movie music from *The Devil and Daniel Webster* and *Obsession,* a late-blooming beauty from 1975 (Unicorn 2065).

While he's famous as an imaginative orchestrator, my favorite work is his sad, sumptuous clarinet quintet *Souvenirs de Voyage,* which should be a staple of the rather slim American chamber music repertoire. There are several good recordings of this gorgeous piece, the most attractive of them by **Chamber Music Northwest,** which pairs it with an equally richly hued clarinet quintet by Diamond (Delos 3088). **Herrmann**'s recording of *Wuthering Heights* seems to be out of print (Unicorn 2050/52), but you can hear one of its attractive arias sung by Renée Fleming in her American opera CD "I Want Magic!" (London 460567).

RAYMOND

Hildegard of Bingen (1098–1179)

Hildegard, who is venerated as a saint in German dioceses and the Benedictine order of monks and nuns, spent her life as a nun on the banks of the Rhine not far from Mainz. Her current fame is based on a wide variety of talents that attracted admiration in recent years, touched off by the anniversary of her death in 1979 and peaking in her anniversary year of 1998. She supervised the preparation of a manuscript of most of her music before she died, and another manuscript of her complete music was compiled at the convent shortly after her death. Only three of the 77 pieces have not been recorded. Among the favorites on records are the hymn *Ave generosa,* the antiphon *Caritas abundat,* the sequences *O Ecclesia* and *O virga ac diadema,* and the chant *O viridissima virga.*

Hildegard's music belongs to the kind of chant that flourished in the 12th century, typically hymns, sequences, and tropes developed somewhat beyond the style of the chants of the 7th to 9th centuries. Yet today her music is subjected to arrangement and recomposition that distort its original form and texture, in sharp contrast to the insistence on authentic performance practice in almost every other category of serious music. There is no evidence that her nunnery was any different in its musical practice from any other religious house of its time. Sacred music was sung during offices and mass by unison unaccompanied voices. Solo voices probably figured in some forms, such as the verse of a responsory, but vocal drones and harmonies and instrumental interludes and accompaniments are not supported by any evidence of the period.

Two discs come from the nuns of **Rüdesheim-Eibingen,** a modern convent rebuilt on the site of Hildegard's second foundation (♦Bayer 100116; ♦Ars Musici 1203). These are a solid indication of how Hildegard's music was used in liturgical observances. **Ensemble Mediatrix** is a group of professional women that sings in the same manner (♦Calig 50982). "11,000 Virgins" by **Anonymous 4** mixes some chants and polyphony of Hildegard's time with her chants for St. Ursula in one of the most rewarding releases (♦Harmonia Mundi 907200).

"Voices of Angels," by women of **Voices of Ascension,** is one of the finer collections (♦Delos 3219). Jeremy Summerly's **Oxford Camerata** alternates men and women in fine singing (♦Naxos 550998). In "Luminous Spirit," **Rosa Lamoreaux** sings Hildegard's chants effectively as soloist with discreet instrumental accompaniments (Koch 3-7443). "A Feather on the Breath of God," the initial recording of Christopher Page's **Gothic Voices,** was a best-seller for a long time, but some of these eight pieces are done better than others, and there are flaws in the Latin pronunciation (Hyperion 66039).

Sequentia has nearly completed its traversal for Harmonia Mundi of all the music found in the two surviving manuscripts. These include "Saints" (♦77378, 2CD); "O Jerusalem" (♦77353); "Voice of the Blood" (♦77346); "Canticles of Ecstasy" (♦77320); and "Symphoniae" (♦20198). While some pieces are sung with vocal or instrumental drones, others are properly unadorned, and the spirit of all the performances is exceptional. Sequentia has done more than any other ensemble to promote Hildegard's music, giving the group an undeniable cachet of excellence.

Marcel Pérès's **Ensemble Organum** introduces some individual interpretive wrinkles into "Lauds of Saint Ursula" that derive from a later era (Harmonia Mundi 901626). **Norma Gentile** sings solo in "Unfurling Love's Creation," occasionally adding a little unnecessary decoration (Lyrichord 8027). **The Augsburg Ensemble** uses instruments in some of the songs in "Celestial Stairs" (Christophorus 77205). **Tapestry** sings Hildegard's and other music with instruments in "Celestial Light," but one of the four voices lets down the team (Telarc 80456). Other recordings verge on travesty, including "Vision" (Angel), "Diadema" (Real Music), "Illumination" (Sony) and "Tönendes Licht" (Bayer).

Finally, Hildegard composed a morality play a century before any of the surviving anonymous liturgical plays. *Ordo Virtutum* represents the struggle between the virtues (each one personified) and the Devil for the individual soul. **Sequentia** has recorded it twice, both times with instrumental interludes and other works inserted to stretch it over two discs (older, Harmonia Mundi 77051, 2CD; newer, 77394, 2CD). **Vox Animae** offers a straightforward performance of the play alone that captures its style very well and makes its structure clear (♦Etcetera 1203). **Stefan Morent**'s recording is a free arrangement based on the play and other writings (Bayer).   WEBER

Paul Hindemith *(1895–1963)*

Before WWII, Hindemith was regarded as one of the triumvirate of leading radicals in 20-century composition, alongside Stravinsky and Schoenberg. His exile from Hitler's Germany—one of very few non-Jewish musicians who left—only reinforced his stature. He rapidly assumed a leading position in the United States, especially as a teacher at Yale, but by the time of his death he was regarded as an old-fashioned pedant out of touch with the modern world. Yet it should be remembered that in the immediate post-WWI period he was very much an enfant terrible; performances of his music shocked and outraged audiences, even provoking noisy demonstrations.

Unlike Schoenberg, who consciously adopted the role of revolutionary, Hindemith was no rebel, but he did delight in flouting convention, whether by composing for mechanical or electronic instruments or by grouping sonatas or concertos together in a single opus. This was part of his essentially 18th-century view of the composer's role as a craftsman with a social purpose, which informed much of his musical activity. He toured extensively as solo violist or as a member of the Amar Quartet, and after 1945 as a conductor. Some recordings survive (e.g., Koch-Schwann 311342, Pearl 9446), but EMI's 2CD set of his '50s orchestral recordings is sadly NA.

Hindemith composed in almost every musical genre, writing at least one sonata for each member of the standard orchestral complement, seven string quartets, several concertos with either chamber or full orchestral accompaniment, and a large number of orchestral works including four ballets, six symphonies, two sinfoniettas, and the magisterial *Symphonic Dances*. Although known as a viola virtuoso as well as a composer, he could also play tolerably well all the standard orchestral instruments (and several nonstandard ones). Unsurprisingly, his instrumental writing is highly expert, whether for solo or ensemble works, which helps to explain why his music has never entirely fallen out of fashion.

ORCHESTRAL MUSIC

Concert Music Op. 41. This is the first of four such works that provide a stylistic bridge between the *Kammermusik* concertos of the mid-'20s and the grander symphonic scores from the early '30s. It's for wind band; the fine, pioneering performance from **Donald Hunsberger** (Sony 44916) has been surpassed by **Roger Epple,** both with Symphony in B-flat (♦Wergo 6641).

Concert Music Op. 50. One of Hindemith's most exhilarating scores, this fourth *Concert Music* (the second and third are concertos for viola and piano respectively) telescopes elements of four-movement symphonic structure into two concentrated spans. **Hindemith** himself made a splendid recording with the Philharmonia in the '50s (EMI, sadly NA). That by **Werner Andreas Albert** is part of his survey of Hindemith's entire orchestral output (CPO, available separately or as a 6CD set). As a rule, Albert's symphonic performances suffer from limp direction and over-manicured orchestral balance; this one is no exception. **Bernstein** was much more alive to the composer's idiom; his version is thrilling (Sony 47566), but **Bělohlávek** is even better, with fewer histrionics and superior sound (Chandos 9457).

Concerto for orchestra Op. 38. Written in 1925, this seems to be the first work in the genre later made famous by Bartók; Hindemith viewed it as a species of *Kammermusik* or concerto grosso for full orchestra. **Albert**'s account is one of his better attempts (CPO 999014), though **Neeme Järvi** (Chandos 9000) and **Serebrier** (ASV 945) have the interpretive edge. There are two interesting historic versions, though **Schmidt-Isserstedt**'s (1958) is only available as part of an 8CD set (BIS), and **Rosbaud**'s (1959) has indifferent sound (Stradivarius).

Der Dämon. Of the three accounts of Hindemith's "dance-pantomime," his first ballet, **Albrecht**'s is the crispest, though the sound quality is a little unsubtle (♦Wergo 60132, with the one-act opera, *Mörder, Hoffnung der Frauen*). **Albert** was given a much better recording; it sounds tame by comparison to Albrecht but has Hindemith's rare last ballet, *Hérodiade,* as companion (CPO 999220). **Zagrosek** also gives a fine performance, setting it in the context of other music damned as *entartete* ("degenerate") by the Nazis (Decca 44182).

Die Harmonie der Welt (Symphony). One of the greatest orchestral works of Hindemith's post-war period, this has fared much better on disc than its parent opera. Two performances set the pace, by **Furtwängler** in Vienna in 1953 (EMI 565353) and **Mravinsky** in Leningrad in 1965, an electric performance marred by a bombastic treatment of the coda (Melodiya 251950). Neither **Kegel** (Berlin) nor **Albert** (CPO) is in their league, and even **Tortelier** seems at a slight interpretive disadvantage, though his is the best of the studio recordings and has by far the best sound quality (Chandos 9217).

The Four Temperaments. After *Nobilissima Visione,* this is the most popular—in concert—of Hindemith's ballets. Scored for the restrained ensemble of piano and strings (unusual for this composer), the work's "theme" is in reality a small movement constructed from three themes with four similarly sized "variations," each describing one of the four medieval humors: melancholic, sanguine, phlegmatic, and choleric. Although it's of concerto length with a sizable solo part, it's not a piano concerto in disguise, and attempts to cast it as such, like **Stefan Asbury**'s version with Gallant (Medici Quartet), can be misguided. The finest modern account is by **Siegfried Mauser** with Albert, who is in general much better attuned to the demands of the concertos than to the symphonic scores (♦CPO 999078, with the 1945 Piano Concerto). **Shelley,** with Tortelier, is also very good; the recording is richer, but this music needs a certain leanness. Mackerras provided a decent performance with **Bruno Canino,** a very sympathetic account (Novalis). Of special interest, but suffering from inferior sound, is one by **Haskil** with Hindemith himself (Orfeo C197891A).

Hérodiade. This short ballet score (Hindemith's fifth) was written for Martha Graham and has a calm, elusive character. It has remained the most obscure of Hindemith's dance works despite several recordings. There is little difference in quality between the fine performances by **Albert** (CPO 999220) and **Schenck** (Koch 7051), though CPO's sound is clearer. Couplings will perhaps decide the choice: *Der Dämon* on CPO, music by Menotti and Schuman on Koch.

Im Kampf mit dem Berge. "Struggle with the Mountain," also known as *In Sturm und Eis,* is Hindemith's most substantial film music score, for the first part of a pair of silent films by Arnold Fanck. Hindemith divided his music into six "acts," each corresponding to a reel of film, but divorced from the visual action, the music has little overt drama and is overlong. The style is also rather different from his other works of the early '20s. **Russell Davies**'s premiere account is polished if unexciting (RCA 68147), not preferable to **Helmut Imig**'s (Koch 317722); **Albert** has set down only excerpts (CPO).

Lustige Sinfonietta. This "merry little symphony" is one of Hindemith's most curious orchestral works, written in 1916 while still a student in Frankfurt but not performed until 1980. Light-hearted and parodistic, the work intersperses readings of Christian Morgenstern's poems into the orchestral fabric. Next to **Albrecht**'s pioneering account (♦Wergo 60150), **Albert**'s lacks bite but has the benefit of cleaner sound (CPO 999005).

Mathis der Maler (Symphony). This was Hindemith's first symphonic essay, written in 1933–34 on a Furtwängler commission from his still-in-progress opera centered on the 16th-century artist Matthias Grünewald. Taking his cue from Grünewald's great altarpiece at Isenheim, Hindemith based each of the three movements on one of the panels: The opera's overture represents the "Concert of Angels," the slow central movement "The Entombment (of Christ)," and the complex finale "The Temptation of St. Antony," ending with an exhilarating set of brass *Alleluias.* It is Hindemith's most recorded score, with over a dozen versions in circulation, often as part of the quintessential Hindemith orchestral program with *Nobilissima Visione* and *Symphonic Metamorphoses.*

Sawallisch with the Philadelphia Orchestra is outstanding in playing and interpretation, though the back-of-the-hall perspective may not appeal to all tastes (♦EMI 55230). It's certainly far superior to the similarly coupled but lame **Franz-Paul Decker** (Naxos), **Levi** (Telarc), and **Claudio Abbado** (DG). Strong competition was provided by **Blomstedt** in San Francisco, who substituted *Trauermusik* for *Nobilissima* (♦Decca 433 8092, seemingly NA in North America). His account of *Mathis* is nearly ideal, more than can be said for **Ormandy** (Sony; the *Metamorphoses* on this disc is conducted by Szell) or **Bernstein,** the latter too wayward though full of interesting detail (DG, with *Concert Music Op. 50*).

Horenstein is highly individual and full of insights, but his account runs into the sand in the finale (Chandos); **Bělohlávek** secures beautiful playing but lacks drama (Chandos), unlike **Mackerras** (Novalis). **Hindemith**'s 1934 recording with the Berlin Philharmonic, made just three weeks after the premiere (Koch Schwann 311342), is superior to his somewhat revisionist interpretation of the '50s (NA), and the pick of any of the historical performances, including those by **Karajan** (EMI and Orfeo).

Neues vom Tage (Overture). Hindemith detached the overture to his smash-hit satirical opera of sexual mores for concert use. It's a rattling good opener, full of bite and sarcastic good humor. **Tortelier** has its measure and with the BBC Philharmonic provides a finely paced account (Chandos 9060), marginally preferable to **Albert** (CPO).

Nobilissima Visione. This ballet is one of Hindemith's most luminous utterances, based on the life of St. Francis of Assisi and inspired by the Giotto frescoes he saw in Florence. The concert suite is one of the trilogy of his most popular scores, alongside *Symphonic Metamorphoses* and *Mathis der Maler,* yet the full score has remained one of his least known. **Rickenbacher** made a very good recording (Koch 312992).

The suite is in three substantial movements culminating in a brilliant, overwhelming passacaglia. Again, **Hindemith**'s own version is NA, but there are plenty of fine modern accounts. The two best are by **Sawallisch,** despite its back-of-the-hall sound (♦EMI 55230), and **Tortelier** (♦Chandos 9060), both of whom are entirely inside the composer's style and secure performances to match. **Albert**'s account has insufficient impetus and is disappointing (CPO), and neither **DePreist** (Delos), **Kegel,** (Berlin) nor **Levi** (Telarc) sounds entirely at home in this work. **Decker** is rather good; his reading is nicely paced and quite close to the composer's own, and it's a shame the couplings don't match it in quality (Naxos 553078). These performances are in all-Hindemith programs; the most bizarre release places it alongside Bartók's *Miraculous Mandarin* suite and Varèse's *Arcana,* conducted by **Martinon** (RCA).

Philharmonic Concerto. Hindemith's second orchestral concerto is a set of variations and was commissioned by the Berlin Philharmonic. Only two versions are currently available, led by **Albert,** whose concerto recordings are the best part of his cycle (CPO 999004), and **Kleinert** (Berlin 9270). They are equally good.

Nusch-Nuschi Dances. The three dances extracted from the early one-act nonsense opera *Das Nusch-Nuschi* (literally "The Nuts-Nuts") are early Hindemith at his most beguiling, and **Tortelier**'s account is precisely that, relaxed and jovial (Chandos 9620). **Albert,** slightly more serious, is also good (CPO 999006).

Pittsburgh Symphony. Much misunderstood—some have held it represented a first, faltering step toward a serial style—this last of Hindemith's symphonies was written for the Pittsburgh Orchestra. He seems to be consciously aiming at the hard-edged American orchestral sound found in symphonies of the period by Harris, Copland, or Schuman. **Tortelier** is easily the first choice (♦Chandos 9530), though **Kegel**'s 1985 account has much to commend it (Berlin 9391). **Albert** is typically polished but gutless (CPO). **Rozhdestvensky**'s live 1965 performance, bizarrely coupled with Bruckner's Symphony 1, is marred by poor orchestral playing and indifferent sound (Russian Revelation).

Rag Time. This rowdy fusion of a Bach fugue subject, ragtime, and Hindemith has proved increasingly popular on disc, with five versions available. Of these, **Albrecht**'s premiere account is the punchiest (♦Wergo 60150), closely followed (with warmer sound) by **Tortelier** (Chandos

9530). Next to these, **Serebrier** (ASV), **Albert** (CPO), and **Tilson Thomas** (RCA) all lack bite.

Sinfonietta in E. Despite its title, this is one of the composer's larger orchestral scores. It's also one of his least known, perhaps due to its less overtly dramatic or illustrative bearing. Although **Albert**'s lone performance is typically well played, it needs more drive (CPO 999014).

Stücke Op. 44. This is part of a series of "educational pieces for ensemble playing," the fourth and last of which are these "Five Movements" for string orchestra. More frequently recorded in the vinyl era, there are only three performances currently on CD. **Eivind Aadland**'s, with the European Community Chamber Orchestra, is the briskest (IMP 1001 2044; Carlton 30367 0158). **Albert** also has a commendable account (CPO 999301), and there is a chamber version by the **Vienna String Quintet** (Camerata).

Suite of French Dances. Hindemith made many arrangements of music by other hands, as well as scholarly editions of works by Bach, Biber, Vivaldi, Schumann, and others. This charming suite draws on Pierre d'Attaignant's *Livres de danceries* and has the same appeal as Respighi's better-known *Ancient Airs and Dances.* Both **Serebrier** (ASV 945) and **Rickenbacher** (Koch 312992) give nicely polished accounts; **Albert**'s is one of his better outings (CPO).

Symphonia serena. This curious work, Hindemith's "third" symphony, with its central movements scored respectively for winds and strings alone, is rather like an orchestral concerto and needs virtuoso treatment. It receives just that from the BBC Philharmonic under **Tortelier** (♦Chandos 9217); **Albert**'s approach for once pays dividends in the middle movements, but the outer ones are lame (CPO). Regrettably, **Hindemith**'s own version has disappeared from view. **Kegel** is worth investigating, not least for a crammed program also featuring *Mathis, Nobilissima Visione,* and the Concerto for trumpet and bassoon (Berlin 9054).

Symphonische Tänze (Symphonic Dances). Hindemith wrote five other works bearing the title "symphony" after *Mathis,* none numbered, though this should really be considered his second. One of his least-known scores, it receives a terrific performance from the BBC Philharmonic under **Tortelier,** coupled with an equally riveting account of *Pittsburgh* (♦Chandos 9530). It's superior in playing and sound to **Albert** (CPO), or to a rather dimly reproduced historic issue by **Jochum** in the late '50s (Orfeo, NA).

Symphonic Metamorphoses on Themes of Carl Maria von Weber. A work as riotously enjoyable and orchestrally virtuosic as its title is ponderous, this is the third of Hindemith's most popular scores. **Abbado** made a terrific and critically acclaimed recording in 1968 with the London Symphony (Decca 433081); his 1994 version with the Berlin Philharmonic sounds extraordinarily dull by comparison (DG). **Bernstein** (Sony 47566), **Kubelik** (Mercury 434397), and especially **Szell** (Sony 53258) give fine, high-octane performances in the bargain league, against which **Decker** (Naxos), **Levi** (Telarc), and **Davis** (Philips) don't compare well. **Albert** has the benefit of more modern sound (CPO) but lacks the verve of the first choices, **Blomstedt** (♦Decca 421523) and **Sawallisch** (EMI 55230). Although not among the leaders, **Järvi** interestingly couples his account with the original Weber pieces (Chandos 8766).

Symphony in B-flat. This is scored for concert wind band. Aside from **Albert** (CPO 999007), **Hindemith** had the field to himself, whether with the Philharmonia (EMI, NA) or the Berlin Radio Symphony (Orfeo 197891). **Reynish,** with the highly regarded Royal Northern College of

Music Winds, is bracing in an enterprising program of German wind band classics, including Schoenberg's *Theme and Variations,* Hartmann's Symphony 5, and pieces by Toch (*Spiel*) and Blacher (Chandos 9805). The Toch is also a coupling on **Roger Epple**'s brilliantly played account, alongside Hindemith's Concert Music Op. 41 and works by Hans Gál and Krenek (♦Wergo 6641).

Symphony in E-flat. This was first set down by **Boult** in a virile, driving account, albeit with the odd rough edge; the recording shows its age (Everest 9009). **Tortelier,** with the benefit of top-notch sound, is the leader again (♦Chandos 9060), easily outclassing **Albert** (CPO), though for sheer excitement **Bernstein,** who attended Hindemith's 1940 Tanglewood master classes, is peerless (Sony 47566).

CONCERTOS

Cello Concertos. The E-flat concerto is a student work, Hindemith's first of any kind on a large scale. **Angelika May** gave a sterling account shortly after it was rediscovered among the papers of the composer's brother (Musicaphon, NA); the only one available now is a committed and well-played performance by **David Geringas** (CPO 999375, with two other two Hindemith concertos).

The 1940 Concerto is well known for its second movement's lovely main theme (used by Walton as the basis of his *Hindemith Variations*). It has received some notable performances, like that by **Paul Tortelier** (Supraphon 111955). Tortelier's son, Yan Pascal, conducts the best of all, with **Wallfisch** as soloist (♦Chandos 9124). **Geringas**'s account lacks fire by comparison (DG), unlike **Starker**'s electric rendition of the solo part (RCA).

Clarinet Concerto. This concerto was written for Benny Goodman, though there is not a hint of jazz anywhere in it. The mid-'50s version by **Louis Cahuzac** conducted by the composer is NA (EMI), but there is a splendid performance by **Ulrich Mehlhart** with Albert (♦CPO 999142, with the three other concertos for winds). **Eduard Brunner** is also very good (Koch 310352), ahead of **Martin Fröst,** who is more than adequate but less compelling (BIS); both form part of "Homage to Goodman" releases.

Concert Music, Op. 48. This is the second of Hindemith's three viola concertos, the soloist accompanied by a mainly wind orchestra (as in *Kammermusik No. 5,* although larger). **Georg Schmid** was the first to record it; his account suffered from harsh sound (Koch) and was easily outstripped by **Paul Cortese** (♦ASV 931).

Concert Music, Op. 49. This is a piano concerto in all but name, the accompaniment provided by a distinctive ensemble of brass and two harps. **Paul Crossley**'s pioneering version with the Philip Jones Brass Ensemble has long been NA (Decca), leaving **Siegfried Mauser** as the pick (♦CPO 999138, sensibly coupled with *Kammermusik No. 2*). There is also an interestingly programmed performance by **Theodor Lichtmann** set alongside *Morgenmusik* and brass sonatas (Summit).

Concerto for Flute, Oboe, Clarinet, Bassoon, Harp and Orchestra (occasionally billed as *Concerto for Woodwinds, Harp, and Orchestra*). Here Hindemith seems to look ruefully back at his *Kammermusik* concertos, without attempting to recreate their boisterous style. It's gentle and low-key and receives a sparkling performance from **Bělohlávek** (♦Chandos 9457). This just has the edge over **Albert**'s fine account, though his all-wind-concerto program is more illuminating (CPO). Against two such brilliantly recorded and balanced accounts, **Rosbaud**'s has purely historical interest (Stradivarius).

Concerto for Trumpet and Bassoon. This probably unique combination works surprisingly well. The performance by **Reinhold Friedrich** and Carsten Wilkening is spot on, the two instruments cleanly balanced (♦CPO 999142); that by **Ludwig Güttler** and Eckard Königstedt is less convincing (Berlin). **Jouko Harjanne** and Erkki Suomalainen have also set down a spirited version (Alba 108).

Horn Concerto. The classic recording was by its dedicatee, **Dennis Brain,** under the composer's baton (EMI, NA). Hornists seem to have fought shy of it since, though **Maria-Louise Neunecker** has given a fine rendition, including the gimmicky touch of narrating the composer's poem from the annotations in the score (♦CPO 999375). This disc is to be preferred to **Zbigniew Zuk**'s (Zuk) if only for the other Hindemith concertos it contains.

Kammermusik. No. 1, Op. 24:1, is not really a concerto but a highly spirited if not downright iconoclastic species of concerto grosso for twelve instruments. It was clearly intended as part of the series, since Hindemith was careful to number it so, unlike its companion piece, the *Kleine Kammermusik* for wind quintet, which only the Concertgebouw set conducted by **Chailly** includes (Decca 433816). Chailly's is a particularly good performance, relishing all its subversive elements, not least the siren. **Markus Stenz**'s otherwise good account (RCA) is marred by indifferent balance—the accordion is inaudible—but is preferable to the recently reissued **Concerto Amsterdam** performance (Teldec), as is **Albert** (CPO). **Abbado** is excellent here too, closely miked and vital (EMI 56160).

No. 2, Op. 36:1, a concerto for cello, has fared very well on disc, with several excellent versions around, particularly **Harrell** (London 433816) and **Michael Stirling,** with slightly harsher sound (RCA 61730). **George Faust** has recorded a fine version (DG 56831). These are all superior in interpretation and sound to **Anner Bylsma** (Teldec). Of the recordings not linked to integral sets, **David Geringas** has the most appropriate context and yields little in persuasiveness to the competition (DG). **Thorleif Thedéen** couples his agile if slightly expressionless account with *Trauermusik* and the two Sonatas (BIS), **Natalie Savinova** with *Kammermusik No. 2* and the Octet.

No. 3, Op. 36:2, a concerto for piano, has been one of the most often recorded of the series. **Brautigam** (Decca) and **Mauser** (CPO 999138) prove to be highly idiomatic exponents, though **Ueli Wiget** outshines them (RCA). **Lars Vogt** has given a wonderfully sympathetic performance, alive to all the nuances of this subtle score (♦EMI 56831). It's a shame that **Richter**'s live 1978 recording has rather two-dimensional sound, as he had a real feel for Hindemith's music (Russian Revelation). **Gérard Van Blerk** is pedestrian by comparison (Teldec).

No. 4, Op. 36:3, is a concerto for violin. **Oistrakh** made the best recording in the '60s (Melodiya and Forlane, NA). There is an excellent modern performance from **Kolja Blacher,** whose command of the solo part is breathtaking (EMI 56160); **Konstantý Kulka** is also very good (Decca). **Michaël Guttman** is agile, though his tone is thin and a touch shrill (ASV); **Peter Rundel** is indifferently balanced (RCA); and **Jaap Schröder** is uneven (Teldec).

No. 5, Op. 36:4—of the six modern recordings of this concerto for viola, three stand out. **Kim Kashkashian**'s is a beautifully balanced performance, accompanied by the Concertgebouw (Decca). So is **Cortese**'s with the Philharmonia, whose warmth of tone casts a different light on what has often seemed a highly abrasive work (ASV 931); his account of the viola-plus-orchestral works outstrips **Georg Schmid** (Koch). **Wolfram Christ** shares Abbado's broader view and is magnifi-

cently recorded (EMI 56160), unlike **Werner Dickel** (RCA); while **Paul Doktor** sounds rather scrappy (Teldec).

No. 6, Op. 46:1, is a concerto for viola d'amore, an 18th-century instrument Hindemith revived in the '20s. **Norbert Blume** set the pace for this work and is still marginally the best (Decca), although closely followed by **Christ** (EMI 56831).

No. 7, Op. 46:2, a concerto for organ, was the final installment in the series. Of its five currently available recordings, **Martin Haselböck** has the edge, with a genuinely chamber organ sound; he also directs from the keyboard (♦Koch 312022). Otherwise, **Martin Lücker** is the most persuasive (RCA), closely followed by **Leo Van Doeselaar** (Decca). Neither **Rosalinde Haas** (CPO) nor **Albert de Klerk** (Teldec) can match them in virtuosity or sound.

Organ Concerto. This is not the seventh *Kammermusik* but a work for organ and full orchestra (1962). **Haselböck** gives it a splendid performance (Koch 312022, with *Kammermusik 7* and a piece for mechanical organ), better recorded and more insightfully played than **Haas** (CPO).

Piano Concerto. Hindemith wrote three piano concertos; the first is *Kammermusik No. 2,* the second is *Concert Music* Op. 49. The piece Hindemith regarded as his real Piano Concerto is one of his most romantic utterances. Its unfamiliarity has always struck me as inexplicable, for it's full of light and fine tunes, with a virtuosic solo part. **Mauser** is steeped in Hindemith's music, and his knowledge shows in his excellent performance (CPO 999078).

Trauermusik. This charming little piece has proved to be one of the most popular of Hindemith's works, remarkable given the circumstances of its composition; it was written in a few hours to mark the death that day of England's King George V in 1936. **Hindemith** constructed the solo part so it could be played by violin, viola, or cello, but he opted for his own principal instrument for its first broadcast, later recording it (Biddulph 087). Versions for the viola are by far the most common; I know of none for violin and two for cello, of which **Thedéen**'s is preferable (BIS). Of the modern viola versions, **Geraldine Walther**'s is heartfelt and beautifully paced (Decca 421523). It has strong competition from **Cortese** (ASV), **Kashkashian** (ECM 20002), and **Rivka Golani** (CBC), though none match **Aronowitz** (EMI 65079, with Schoenberg's *Verklärte Nacht* and Bartók's *Divertimento*). There are also recordings of the composer's viola-and-piano reduction by **Wilfried Strehle** (Nimbus) and **E. Shumsky** (Ambassador), but neither is preferable to the orchestral version.

Viola Concerto (*Der Schwanendreher*). After the rather aggressive *Kammermusik No. 5* and *Concert Music* Op. 48, Hindemith's "concerto after folk songs" is unassuming and full of charm. There is a fascinating account by **Hindemith** himself from 1939, in remarkably good sound (Biddulph 087). Among modern recordings, **Cortese**'s is the warmest, though the finale loses impetus (ASV). Next to him, **Schmid** (Koch) and **Walther** (Decca) seem thin, while **Raphael Hillyer** is not as virtuosic (Albany). **Daniel Benyamini**'s near-perfect version with Barenboim is NA (DG).

Violin Concerto. After *Kammermusik No. 4,* Hindemith only wrote one more violin concerto, in 1939 during his slow-motion flight from Nazi Germany. It's a warm and lyrical work bearing little evidence of the vicissitudes of his life at the time. A finer piece than Bartók's *Concerto 2,* it has never enjoyed the same currency. **Joseph Fuchs** made the first recording in 1958, and a fine one it is (Everest), though it would be surpassed by **Oistrakh** four years later (Forlane 16589). Next to these,

Guttman is insufficiently characterful, and his tone is simply not big enough for the work (ASV); **André Gertler** is somewhat better and has excellent couplings (Supraphon).

CHAMBER MUSIC

Clarinet Quintet. Written in just four days—straight into the five parts, to save time—this is early Hindemith at his most provocative and compelling. Both the **Villa Musica Ensemble,** using the 1923 original (♦MD+G 3447, with the Septet and Octet) and **Peter Klaus Löffler** and the Buchberger Quartet (in its 1954 revision) capture its radicalism perfectly, although the latter's sound is rather raw (Wergo 6197). The **Moscow Contemporary Music Ensemble** doesn't show the same degree of understanding (Triton).

Duet (Scherzo) for viola and cello. This is another piece dashed off in a few hours, this time as filler for the unused side of a 78-rpm disc in 1934. That classic recording, by **Hindemith** and Feuermann, is still in circulation (♦Pearl 9446; Magic Talent 48024). The only alternative is by **Wilfried Strehle** and Wolfgang Boettcher, coupled with *Trauermusik,* the F major Sonata, and pieces by Brahms and Dvořák (Nimbus 5473).

"A Frog He Went a-Courting." These variations for cello and piano are a delightful trifle written early in Hindemith's American exile. **Martin Ostertag** and Kalle Randalu throw it off with gay abandon alongside sonatas for cello, double-bass, tuba, and trombone (♦MD+G 304 0697). **Niall Brown** and **Isabelle Trüb** (Doron 3024) and **Wendy Warner** and Eileen Buck (Bridge 9088) both present it in cello-and-piano recitals.

Kleine Kammermusik. The companion piece to *Kammermusik No. 1,* this is Hindemith's only wind quintet. Most of the recordings are unremarkable. The crispest of all is by the **Aulos Quintet,** whose ensemble and intonation are impeccable (♦Koch 311632, with Eisler and Schoenberg), although the **Concertgebouw's** principals (part of the complete *Kammermusiken*) are almost their equal and more brilliantly recorded (Decca, see above). The **Berlin Philharmonic Wind Quintet,** miked so closely you can hear the keys' action, are also excellent (BIS 752, with Hindemith's *Septet* and quintets by Henze), preferable to the **Bergen Wind Ensemble** (BIS, with Barber, Jolivet, and Saeverud).

Leichte Stücke (Easy Pieces) for cello and piano. **Brown** and Trüb couple these three pieces with the three Op. 8 *Stücke, Kleine Sonate,* and *'Frog' Variations* for a varied program (Doron 3024), which makes more musical sense than **Antony Cooke** and Armin Watkins, who place these straightforward miniatures alongside sonatas by Salonen and Ludwig Thuille (Harmonie).

Minimax (Repertoire for military orchestra) for string quartet. One of Hindemith's more extended musical jokes, these parodies of military music were written for the Amar Quartet in 1922 (who were photographed, bows aslant their shoulders, "on parade"). The **Kocian Quartet** included it in their complete quartet survey (♦Praga 250113).

Morgenmusik. Hindemith left the precise instrumental disposition of his "Morning Music" to the discretion—and availability—of performers. Part of the series written for *Plöner Musiktag* ("Day of Music in Plön") in 1932—its opening item is played after dawn at the top of a tower—it's generally given as a brass quintet. The **Malmö Brass Ensemble** perform it as such with several brass and lesser-known wind pieces, including its *Plöner Musiktag* stablemate, the Recorder Trio (BIS 159). **Summit Brass** couple it with the complete brass sonatas and *Concert Music* Op. 49 (Summit). **Albert** treats it orchestrally as part of his selection of

items from *Plöner Musiktag* (CPO). In a non-Hindemith context, the **Stockholm Brass** give it a cracking performance (♦BIS 544).

Octet. Hindemith's final chamber work (1957–58) is a disappointment. The **Berlin Philharmonic Octet**'s is the most polished recording (♦Nimbus 5461), followed by **Villa Musica Ensemble** (MD+G). There are worthwhile accounts from the **Moscow Contemporary Music Ensemble** (Triton) and members of the **Arnold Wind Quintet** and **Stauffer String Quartet** (Stradivarius).

Overture to "The Flying Dutchman" as Played at Sight by a Second-Rate Concert Orchestra at the Village Well at 7 O'clock in the Morning for String Quartet. Precisely the spoof the title suggests, this anarchic little piece is available in two fine accounts, both with hard-edged sound, by the **Buchberger Quartet** (♦Wergo 6197) and the **Kocian Quartet** (♦Praga 250113).

Quartet for Clarinet, Violin, Cello, and Piano. This is one of Hindemith's greatest and most deeply satisfying chamber works. Beautifully written for all four instruments, it seems to draw the best from those who take it up. The **Incanto Ensemble** gives a flawless performance, with perfect intonation and exquisite control. Their couplings—the Clarinet Sonata and the two duets for clarinet and violin written as part of *Plöner Musiktag*—are short measure; the Clarinet Quintet could have been fitted in with room to spare (♦CPO 999302). The **Villa Musica Ensemble** is also excellent (although its intonation isn't as sweet as Incanto's), part of a marvelous program with the Heckelphone Trio and Sonata for 4 Horns (MD+G 3040537). Gilbert Kalish and the **Boston Symphony Chamber Players** are also recommendable, with Shostakovich's *Piano Quintet* as company (Arabesque).

Septet for wind instruments. The excellent performance by the **Berlin Philharmonic Wind Quintet** and friends is the best available, not least for clarity of recording (♦BIS 752, with *Kleine Kammermusik* and two Henze quintets), although the performance by **Villa Musica Ensemble** is almost as good (M+DG 3447). They and the augmented Arnold Quintet couple it with the rather pedestrian Octet (Stradivarius).

Sonata for Four Horns (without accompaniment). This is a splendid work for a quartet of horns. The **Villa Musica Ensemble** gives the most finely balanced account, in an excellent program with the Heckelphone Trio and Quartet for Clarinet, Violin, Cello, and Piano (♦MD+G 3040537). However, there is splendid competition from the **Pavilion Quartet** (CPO 999229, with Hindemith's other horn sonatas), and **Summit Brass** includes it in their survey of the brass music (Summit).

Stücke for cello and piano Op. 8. Hindemith's first published work, these three pieces show him taking his first, hesitant steps toward expressionism. **Warner** and Buck place them in the best context with the three sonatas (Bridge 9088), but for sheer virtuosity **Peter Wispelwey** and Paolo Giacometti are unmatched (♦Channel 11097).

Sonatas with piano accompaniment

During WWI, Hindemith conceived the notion of sonatas for all the standard orchestral instruments (percussion excepted), accompanied by piano. After a false start in 1919 with his Op. 11 set, he pursued the challenge seriously from the mid-'30s on, completing it in 1955 with the Sonata for Bass Tuba. With the exception of those for violin, viola, and cello, of which there are three or four each, the sonatas are all single offerings and often appear in mixed programs with works by other composers, however incongruously. Despite their reputation for sameness, they are all remarkably individual, and generally receive the most sympathetic performances when played in all-Hindemith contexts. Three labels are systematically recording all 42—CPO, MD+G, and Arts—though none are complete at time of writing. The MD+G cycle with members of the **Villa Musica Ensemble,** imaginatively programmed and excellently performed, is the finest overall (♦304 0691/7; seven discs covering 31 sonatas).

Bass tuba. Hindemith's last and one of his least engaging. There are two fine accounts, from **Abe Torchinsky** and Glenn Gould (Sony 52671; the sound is a little dry) and **Walter Hilgers** and Piret Randalu (♦M+DG 3040697). The performances of **Gene Pokorny** and Lichtmann (Summit) and **Michael Lind** and Steven Harlos (BIS) are in collections of Hindemith's brass sonatas.

Bassoon. Most available versions of this delightful sonata place it in mixed recitals, where it often seems to be just making up the numbers. **Knut Sønstevold** and Eva Knardahl give the most beautifully played and recorded performance (♦ BIS 159). **Klaus Thunemann** and Randalu are also finely judged (MD+G 304 0694).

Cello. No. 1, Op. 11:3: As we know this sonata, in its 1921 revision, it's very different from the original, the grotesque character quite at variance with its successors but in keeping with Hindemith's music of the time. The problems of balance arising from the hefty piano writing are clearly relished by **Thedéen** and **Pöntinen** (♦BIS 816, with the 1948 Sonata, *Trauermusik,* and *Kammermusik No. 3*), less so by **Ostertag** and Randalu (MD+G, with Op. 11:1, 2, 4). Only **Warner** and Buck (♦Bridge 9088) and **Brown** and Trüb (Doron 3024) place it with other Hindemith works for cello. Releases providing a wider context include **Krosnick** and Kalish with other post-WWI sonatas, including Cowell's—a real rarity (Arabesque)—while **Christophe Henkel** and George Pludermacher combine it with Pfitzner and Strauss, a coupling that would have left the latter two aghast (Sigma).

No. 2, *Kleine SonateI* is a sonatina, as its name implies. **Ostertag** and Randalu provide a beautifully balanced account, with the 1948 Sonata (♦MD+G 3040697), with only **Warner** and Buck for competition (Bridge).

No. 3 (1948) is one of the largest of Hindemith's later sonatas, in places more like a concerto. Written for Piatigorsky, it needs a big cello sound, though there are many passages of a restrained and intimate character. Curiously, there are fewer versions of this than Op. 11:3. **Ostertag** and Randalu (MD+G) are again marginally preferable to **Thedéen** and Pöntinen (BIS), but **Warner** and Buck are the best overall (Bridge).

Clarinet. One of the finest and most popular of Hindemith's instrumental sonatas, this has attracted many recordings over the years. **Ulf Rodenhäuser** and Randalu's account is exemplary for its phrasing and silky sound, coupled enterprisingly with the sonatas for flute, oboe, and English horn (♦MD+G 3040695). **Ralph Manno** and Liese Klahn are almost as good, but with a short-measure program including the Quartet for Clarinet, Violin, Cello, and Piano (CPO). **John Russo** and Lydia Walton Ignacio are imaginatively programmed with *Kleine Kammermusik* and works by Krenek, Ernst Pepping, and Toch (CRS).

Double bass. The double bass is a difficult instrument to make sing, but in the *Molto Adagio* finale Hindemith manages to do so. **Wolfgang Güttler** and Randalu present it most sympathetically (MD+G 304 0697). **Quirijn van Regteren Altena** and Peter van Henegouwen are rather less well recorded in their "Characters" recital (Olympia); likewise **Ferenc Csontos** and Balázs Szokolay in a bizarre program with sonatas by Henry Eccles, Wilfried Jentzsch, Adolf Mišek, and Vilmos Montag (Hungaroton).

English horn. It's curious that there are more recordings of this elusive piece, one of the longest of Hindemith's wind sonatas, than of the more straightforward and slighter Oboe Sonata. **Lajos Lencsés** and Shoshana Rudiakov play it with great sensitivity alongside the Heckelphone Trio (CPO 999332). There is nothing to choose between them and the intelligent performance by **Ingo Goritzki** and Randalu (MD+G 3040695); these lead the field.

Flute. The first of the later sonatas written with the complete set in mind (1936), this is one of the most enduringly popular. The classic recording by **Rampal** and Veyron-Lacroix is still unsurpassed for beauty of tone (♦Erato 45839, available only in a 2CD set), although **Peter-Lukas Graf** and Glemser come close (Claves 509307). **Jean-Claude Gérard** and Randalu are scarcely less persuasive and are set neatly among sonatas for oboe, clarinet, and English horn (MD+G 3040695). **Barbara Gisler-Haase** and Mika Mori are available either with other Hindemith wind sonatas or those by other hands (Camarata). Only **Marc Grauwels** places it with Hindemith's other flute music (Beat).

Horn. Hindemith's sonata for the French horn is a masterpiece, coming from the rich sonata-composing year of 1939. **Mason Jones** and Glenn Gould provide a brilliant, committed account, although the sound shows its age (Sony 52671), in which respect it's outclassed by both **Hans Dullaert** and Marja Bon (♦CPO 999229), and **Radovan Vlatkovic** with Randalu (MD+G 3040696). **Gail Williams** and Lichtmann feature it with the brass sonatas and *Concert Music* Op. 49 (Summit), a more apposite context than the lone Beethoven sonata of most other rivals.

Alto horn. Hindemith's sonata for alto horn (1943) can also be played on alto saxophone or French horn. A relaxed divertissement, in its saxophone incarnation the best available version is by **Pekka Savijoki** and Jussi Siirala (♦BIS 159). In its primary alto horn version, **Jones** and Gould have the edge in sheer virtuosity (Sony 52671). The piece is often played on the French horn, as by **Dullaert** and Bon, a stirring rendition (♦CPO 99929), and **Lawrence Strieby** and Lichtmann (Summit). The recording by **Radovan Vlatkovic** and Randalu is also well played (MD+G).

Oboe. **Goritzki** and Randalu give a beautifully polished account of this relatively minor two-movement sonata (MD+G 3040695), marginally better focused than **Lajos Lencsés** and Rudiakov (CPO).

Tenor trombone. No one plays this sonata quite like **Christian Lindberg** and Pöntinen, whose stunning virtuosity is captured in breathtaking sound (♦BIS 159, all-Hindemith; 258, with Berio and Martin). No other performance comes close; next to them, even **Henry Charles Smith** and Gould are disadvantaged (Sony), likewise **Branimir Slokar** and Randalu (MD+G).

Trumpet. The two oldest versions are by **Gilbert Johnson** and Gould (Sony) and **Edward Tarr** and Elisabeth Westenholz (BIS); what one has in sheer bravura, the other makes up in sound quality. For clarity of reproduction and interpretation, **Marsalis** and Judith Lynn Stillman are in a class of their own (♦Sony 47193), though there are very fine accounts by **Antonberger** and Sawallisch (EMI) and **Hannes Läubin** and Randalu (MD+G).

Viola. There are four complete sets of these sonatas, all of which have much to offer, with no clear leader. On balance, **Cortese** and Jordi Vilaprinyó are the most recommendable, the violist's warmth of tone making this repertoire—which can sound ungrateful—more appealing to the listener (ASV 978). However, for sympathy with the style of the composer, both **Nobuko Imai** and Pöntinen, in excellent sound (BIS 651), and **Kashkashian** and Levin (ECM 833309) yield nothing. These three place the three works together, and your choice may be determined more by your preference of repertoire: BIS and ASV include the "Meditation" from *Nobilissima Visione* and *Trauermusik* (ASV), ECM the four unaccompanied viola sonatas in a 2CD set. **Enrique Santiago** and Randalu place the first with Op. 11:1–3 for violin and cello (MD+G 3040691), and 2 and 3 with others for violin and viola d'amore (MD+G 3040692).

No. 1 in F (Op. 11:4), one of the loveliest, most relaxed of Hindemith's early sonatas, is far and away the most recorded of the three with piano. The most sympathetic interpretation is by **Imai** and Pöntinen, in excellent sound (♦BIS 651). They and **Kashkashian** and Levin (ECM 833309) have an apposite leanness of sonority that suits the music, unlike **Cortese** and Vilaprinyó, who are too saccharine (ASV); midway between lie **Santiago** and Randalu (MD+G). **Bashmet** and Richter are vibrant but rather rawly recorded (Melodiya and Olympia), unlike **Paul Silverthorne** and John Constable, neatly played alongside Britten's *Lachrymae* and Shostakovich's sonata (Koch). Of special interest is **Primrose** (dedicatee of 3) with Sanromá, recorded in 1938 (Biddulph 148, with Bax and Bloch).

No. 2 (Op. 25:4). By contrast with 1, the warmth of tone of **Cortese** with Vilaprinyó in this rather more angular work is revelatory (ASV 978), casting it in a very different light than their rivals. There is no clear recommendation here, with **Imai** (BIS) and **Kashkashian** (ECM) providing equally valid and well-executed accounts. **Santiago** seems a little ordinary by comparison (MD+G).

No. 3 in C (1939) is a magisterial creation. I first heard it played by **Trampler** (RCA, long NA). **Hindemith**'s own recording with Sanromá has been restored beautifully (Biddulph 087), though for quality of sound, depth of interpretation, and beauty of tone, **Cortese** surpasses the rest (♦ASV). **Imai** (BIS) and **Kashkashian** (ECM) are still of a very high order. **Santiago** sounds prosaic, not matching the grandeur of their rivals; his tone is a touch thin in the upper registers, but this version is imaginatively coupled (MD+G).

Viola d'amore (*Kleine Sonate*, Op. 25:2). Hindemith discovered the viola d'amore in the early '20s, teaching himself to play it in two months. The *Kleine Sonate* is the fruit of that endeavor (as is the later *Kammermusik* No. 6). No Hindemith recording has survived, but **Ivo Bauer,** with Randalu, gives it a committed, musicianly performance alongside Santiago's accounts of two of the viola sonatas (MD+G).

Violin. There are three integral surveys of these four sonatas, the best being by **Ulf Wallin** and Pöntinen, characterized by Wallin's sweet tone and Pöntinen's typically exemplary support (♦BIS 761). **Ida Bieler** and Randalu are almost their equal, placing the first two with the cello and viola sonatas from Op. 11 (MD+G 3040691) and 3 and 4 (where Bieler is replaced by **Thomas Brandis**) with the later viola and viola d'amore sonatas (MD+G 3040692). Both sets are better recorded than **Kagan** and Richter, whose 1978 public performances are of more than documentary interest (Live Classics 161, Vol. 10 of their *Oleg Kagan Edition*).

No. 1 in E-flat (Op. 11:1) was written while Hindemith was on active service (well behind the lines) in Flanders in 1918. Although it was originally intended as a three-movement piece, he dropped the incomplete finale. **Wallin** and Pöntinen include that fragment, the only ones to do so, making them first choice (BIS 761); **Bieler** and Randalu are no less persuasive (MD+G 3040691). **Kremer** and Gavrilov have recorded a neat if slightly detached account as part of a 2CD set (EMI).

No. 2 in D (Op. 11:2) is Hindemith's longest violin sonata and most conservative in style, not really sounding like him at all. Wallin is again the first choice (BIS 761), ahead of Bieler (MD+G 3040691).

No. 3 in E (1935). The shortest of the sonatas, this is a slight little piece, yet has proved remarkably popular on disc, with around a dozen recordings. One of the earliest was **Szigeti**'s with Carlo Bussotti in 1953, finely played, but the sound is now two-dimensional (Sony 52569). **Bieler** (MD+G 3040691) has a slight edge on **Wallin** (BIS 761) here, especially in the first movement. These lead the field, content with just this one piece.

No. 4 in C (1939), from Hindemith's best period of sonata composition, is the finest of the four. Rather neglected by violinists, aside from the three complete surveys only **Stern** from 1946 is available, with Alexander Zakin, and then only as part of a 12CD set (Sony). **Bieler** is fine, with a keen sense of purpose and appropriately light touch (MD+G 3040691). However, he's matched by Wallin, whose one-disc set may be the deciding factor (♦BIS 761).

String Quartets. Hindemith only numbered his quartets in a private notebook, but his publisher, Schott, did so arbitrarily, omitting the first of Op. 2, its successors printed as 1–6. The Hindemith Institute and Schott have officially resequenced them with Op. 2 as No. 1 and the 1945 E-flat as No. 7. The **Kocian Quartet**'s integral recording retained the old numbering with Op. 2 as No. 0. Overall—despite rather unsubtle sound—it's the best (♦Praga 250113, with *Minimax* and *The Flying Dutchman Overture* spoof). The **Danish Quartet,** omitting the parodies, features the quartets as 1–7 (CPO). Their performances are decent enough, in fine sound, no match for the Kocian in intensity though more polished in the slow movements. The **Juilliard Quartet**'s cycle—Schwann suggests it's incomplete, confused by the numbering issue—is available on three discs (Wergo 6283, 6607, 6622). They took time to grow into their task, so if in the first installment—3 and 5—they are overshadowed by the Kocian, in the later issues they are stronger rivals.

Of individual quartet recordings, the **Sonare Quartet**'s 1 and 5—part of a never-completed integral recording—doesn't show as much sympathy with Hindemith's style as those above. Two excellent historical recordings of 4, each billed as 3, also deserve attention: Hindemith's own **Amar Quartet** (Koch, with *Mathis der Maler*), and the **Hollywood Quartet** (Testament 1052, with quartets by Walton and Prokofiev).

String Trios. Hindemith's two fine trios were composed in 1924 and 1933. **Hindemith**'s own recording, with Szymon Goldberg and Feuermann, has been beautifully restored (♦Koch 311342; also Pearl, with the Duet for viola and cello). The **Deutsches Trio** has made crisp and vibrant recordings of both (CPO 999283).

Trio for Viola, Heckelphone, and Piano. The heckelphone is a baritone oboe, one of the rarer members of the wind family (undoubtedly what attracted Hindemith to write for it). Highly unorthodox in structure, this is a fascinating, enjoyable piece, the timbres of the three instruments alternately blending and clashing in its often hectic passages. The **Villa Musica Ensemble** is splendid, perfectly balanced and recorded (♦MD+G 3040537), though **Lajos Lencsés,** Gunter Teuffel, and Shoshana Rudiakov also make a fine case for one of the composer's most individual utterances (CPO).

PIANO MUSIC

Hindemith's output for the piano is of two kinds: major works, like *Ludus Tonalis* and the sonatas, and minor trifles, like the charming *Berceuse* (1921) and *Klavierstück für Josephine Grosz* (1929). Only two pianists have attempted complete surveys, **Hans Petermandl** on four discs omitting some minor or incomplete pieces (♦Marco Polo 8223335/8) but marginally preferable nonetheless—with rather better sound—to **Siegfried Mauser,** who misses nothing but is spread across five (Wergo).

In einer Nacht. Werner Bärtschi gives highly musical and delicate accounts of these expressionist miniatures, hampered by a dull acoustic and flat sound (Jecklin). **Bernhard Billeter** fares better sonically but is not as expressive (also Jecklin). **Mauser** is poorly coupled with *Suite 1922* (Wergo). **Hans Petermandl** is the most sympathetic, best-recorded, and gives the most value for money (♦Marco Polo).

Klaviermusik. For no apparent reason, **Bärtschi** omits the first of these two books of diverse, semididactic studies, which is a shame—and, indeed, short measure (Jecklin). **Mauser** (Wergo) and **Petermandl** (Marco Polo) both avoid that mistake, and are equally recommendable.

Ludus Tonalis. The pinnacle of this composer's keyboard output, along with *Suite 1922* the "essential Hindemith piano music" according to **John McCabe,** whose magnificent performance of these studies in counterpoint and fugue is illuminated by a composer's insights (♦Hyperion 66824). **Mustonen**'s reading is a brilliant exposition of pianistic virtuosity, but the coupling—Prokofiev's *Visions fugitives*—jars (Decca 44803). After these, **Petermandl** is still good, if less refined in technique (Marco Polo), while **Mauser** is over-literal (Wergo). **Roberts** takes a monumental approach, with a little loss of clarity (Nimbus), but he's safer than the error-strewn **Hüseyin Sermet** (Auvidis). Sadly, **Richter**'s account is NA (Pyramid).

Sonatas. Hindemith composed five sonatas for solo piano, but only numbered three of them. His first essay, Op. 17, was withdrawn shortly after completion and the score destroyed during WWII. **Bernhard Billeter** has reconstructed it from the composer's sketches and recorded it (Jecklin). A strange work, **Petermandl** makes it sound more appealing (Marco Polo).

Nos. 1 through 3 have been tackled by various pianists since **Gould** put them back on the map with his committed if rather idiosyncratic interpretations (Sony 52670). **Mauser**'s are split across two discs but include the original central movement of 1, replaced by Hindemith shortly after the premiere (Wergo). So do **Petermandl** (Marco Polo) and **Randalu**—the latter flawless in perfect sound—on the same disc as 1 through 3 (♦MD+G 304 0693). **Roberts** omits it and, although strong on counterpoint, is rather lackluster in sound (Nimbus). In 1941, Hindemith contemplated another sonata, but completed just one movement. Only **Mauser** has recorded it (Wergo 6214).

Sonata for two pianos. This is one of Hindemith's brightest chamber works, particularly the opening "Glockenspiel" movement. Only **Kalle** and **Piret Randalu** achieve really brilliant sound, and they maintain the highest level of virtuosity (♦MD+G 3040694). **Roberts** and **Strong** sound lethargic by contrast, in dullish sound (Nimbus).

Sonata for piano duet. The **Randalus** are again nearly flawless in this quietly marvelous work (♦MD+G 3040694). **Roberts** and **Strong** give a better account of themselves than in the 2-Piano Sonata (Nimbus), and **Nöel Lee** and **Christian Ivaldi** are also worth seeking out (Arion). Pride of historical place goes to the 1939 recording by **Hindemith** himself with **Sanromá,** in remarkably clear sound (Biddulph 087).

Suite, "1922". This delightful suite includes a March, a Shimmy, and a Boston—very subversive for the time. **McCabe** is the most sure-handed, pointing up its underlying cheekiness (♦Hyperion, with *Ludus*). **Petermandl** also has a nice light touch, though he's less overtly virtuosic (Marco Polo) and more generously coupled than **Mauser,** who gives a fine account notwithstanding (Wergo).

Tanzstücke (Op. 19). **Mauser** couples his version with *Klaviermusik Books 1 and 2* (Wergo), **Petermandl** with *Suite 1922* and *In einer Nacht,* a well-filled disc that provides a rounded picture of the early Hindemith (♦Marco Polo 223335).

OTHER SOLO MUSIC

Sonata for cello. This is one of Hindemith's most demanding solo sonatas. There are many excellent versions around, that by **Feuermann** (1934) the oldest and historic in every sense (Pearl). **Wispelwey** is breathtaking in technique (♦Channel 7495), and **Haimovitz** is also highly commendable (DG 453417). There are distinguished versions from **Frans Helmerson** (BIS) and **Erling Blöndal Bengtsson** (Danacord). **Siegfried Palm,** doyen of the avant garde, seems oddly ill at ease (Wergo).

Sonata for harp. The harp drew from Hindemith one of his most euphonious creations, a term equally applicable to **Helga Storck**'s recording, in an aptly resonant acoustic (♦MD+G 3040694). Storck's forms part of MD+G's Hindemith sonata series, while her rivals feature it in varied programs, the most interesting musically being **Loman**'s, with Britten's Suite and works by Germaine Tailleferre and Carlos Salzedo among others (Marquis).

Sonatas for organ. Like his piano sonatas, those for organ were written in a short time frame: the first two in 1937, the third, on old folk songs, in 1940 shortly after his arrival in the United States. The finest recording—which put them very much back on the map—was by **Simon Preston** (Decca, NA); none of the other accounts rival it. **Piet Kee** is most reliable, having benefitted from the advice of Franz Bozyan, a colleague of the composer at Yale (♦Chandos 9097). Kee's tempos are broad and majestic, though the over-resonant acoustic of St. Bavokerk, Haarlem, will not be to everyone's liking. **Rosalinde Haas** gets crystal-clear reproduction in her much quicker accounts, a real boon in 2, though in shaving almost five minutes (about 40 percent) off Kee's timing in 3, she rather trivializes the work (MD+G 3040696). Kee has the edge in grandeur in 1. Finest of all the available accounts are from **Kevin Bowyer** in Odense Cathedral, Denmark, combining the best qualities of his rivals (♦Nimbus 5411, with highly appropriate couplings by Schoenberg and Ernst Pepping).

Sonatas for viola. In a sense, these unaccompanied sonatas for Hindemith's own instrument get one closer to the man than any others. At least five violists have tackled them together, but the laurels are shared among **Imai** (♦BIS 571), **Kashkashian** (ECM 833309), and **Cortese** (ASV 947).

No. 1 (Op. 11:5). **Imai** has the edge in this still stylistically uneasy work, although **Cortese**'s warmth of tone is very persuasive. No. 2 (Op. 25:1) is the one with the infamous direction "Raging tempo. Wild. Beauty of secondary importance." **Cortese** fails to adapt sufficiently to its wildness, following, perhaps, **Hindemith** himself in 1934 (EMI, NA). **Kashkashian,** by contrast, is electrifying (♦ECM), outpacing **Imai**. In 3 (Op. 31:4), **Cortese** again seems less at ease with the acerbity of style than either **Imai** or **Kashkashian**. In 4 (1937), the final sonata, written while Hindemith toured America for the first time, **Cortese** comes into his own. **Imai**'s is the best of the rival accounts, less beautiful in tone perhaps but Cortese's equal in expression.

Sonatas for violin. No. 1 in G minor (Op. 11:6) is known only in fragmentary form, but has been recorded by **Kolja Lessing** (Ars Musici 0954). Nos. 2 and 3 (Op. 31:1,2) have never had the same impact as those for viola or cello. **Ilya Kaler** is the only violinist to have braved this repertoire on CD (Ongaku 103).

CHORAL MUSIC

Hindemith wrote a good deal of choral music throughout his life, much of it with at least a semididactic purpose, as for instance the still unrecorded and controversial Brecht cantata *Lehrstück.* Recordings have been few, but in recent years **Uwe Gronostay** has offered much of the larger collections, such as *Lieder nach alten texten* and six of the 12 *Madrigals,* completed in 1958, with the Danish National Radio Chorus (Chandos 9413). He recorded the other six with the excellent Netherlands Chamber Choir, with the *Six Rilke Chansons* and selected partsongs (♦Globe 5125). Gronostay's versions of the *Madrigals* are the first choice, more sympathetic than either **Fritz ter Wey** with the enthusiastic Aachen Youth Choir (CPO) or **Stefan Parkman** with the Berlin Radio Choir (Wergo).

Mass. Hindemith's most important unaccompanied choral work, the *Mass* was completed and premiered shortly before his death in 1963. It's the centerpiece of **Gronostay**'s Chandos and Globe discs, and there's nothing to choose between either performance, equally well sung and recorded. Both are preferable to **ter Wey** (CPO).

Das Unaufhörliche (*The One Perpetual*). Hindemith's longest choral work is one of his least known. He composed it in 1931 to a text by Gottfried Benn, a political adversary of Brecht, with whom Hindemith had quarrelled over *Lehrstück.* The oratorio is one of his deepest works, containing much magnificent writing for chorus and orchestra, and is crucial to understanding how the composer of the *Kammermusik* evolved into the creator of *Mathis der Maler.* **Zagrosek**'s Berlin recording suffers from less than top-notch sound but his interpretation presents the music well (Wergo 6603, 2CD). This release also contains a recording of Benn talking about the work in German, but there is no translation.

When lilacs last in the dooryard bloom'd (*Requiem for those we love*). This moving setting of Walt Whitman's Civil War–inspired verses was Hindemith's gift to the American people, written shortly after he became a U.S. citizen. A large-scale oratorio for soloists, chorus and orchestra, it had been largely overlooked until **Robert Shaw**'s groundbreaking account (♦Telarc 80132), a marvelously sympathetic performance superior even to **Hindemith**'s own by no means inadequate recording (DG, NA). There is a fine, if rather inadequately recorded Viennese performance by **Sawallisch** (Orfeo), preferable to that by **Helmut Koch** in 1966 (Berlin Classics). RICKARDS

OPERAS

Hindemith's first operatic venture was a triple-bill of one-acters on the subjects of sexuality, obsession, and punishment: *Mörder, Hoffnung der Frauen* (1919) setting an intense, expressionist text by Kokoschka (Wergo 60132, with *Der Dämon*); *Das Nusch-Nuschi* ("The Nuts-Nuts," 1920), styled a "play for Burmese marionettes" and the longest of the three, "Hindemith's most virtuoso orchestral score" according to Giselher Schubert (Wergo 60146); and most controversial of all, *Sancta Susanna* (1921)—which Fritz Busch refused to premiere—set in a convent teeming with a repressed sexuality that erupts on stage. Public protests and actions for obscenity have followed wherever it has been staged, even as late as 1977 in Rome, yet it's undeniably one of the most powerful short operas ever written. The recording by **Tortelier,** with

Susan Bullock and Della Jones, is stunning (♦Chandos 9620). That by **Albrecht** with Donath is as impressive an interpretation, but the sound quality is raw (Wergo 60106).

Cardillac (1926). This opera concerns the relationship between the artist and society, a theme developed in more depth in Hindemith's later operas *Mathis der Maler* (1938) and *Die Harmonie der Welt* (1957). A powerful recording led by **Albrecht** features the musically and dramatically detailed Cardillac of Fischer-Dieskau (♦DG 431741, with excerpts from *Mathis*). Leonore Kirschstein sings a Wagnerian-style Daughter, leaving most of the dramatics to the more capable Söderström. **Keilberth** softens the neoclassical vein of the music to a more romantic haze. Nimsgern is a less sophisticated Cardillac than Fischer-Dieskau, but he sings with more vocal body and heft (Wergo 60148, 2CD). The two ladies sing well, minus the dramatics. Albrecht takes a more acidic view of the music than Keilberth's romantic approach.

Mathis der Maler. Hindemith believed "the artist holds a position of great responsibility toward humanity as well as for art and the defense of art." Like the opera's subject, the painter Matthias Grünewald, Hindemith found himself in the early '30s at the mercy of political situations beyond his control. The result is an artist's opera and one based with reasonable accuracy on historical events, but above all it's a spiritual opera. The sensitive artist is more subject to temptations—moral, political, artistic—than ordinary mortals. Is it possible that one's own worst enemy is within? Hindemith rose nobly to the challenge to express these philosophical concepts in a clash of antagonistic worlds. Gregorian chant, Lutheran hymn tunes, and German folk songs vie with modern dissonance in support of atmosphere and text. It's a remarkable work, intellectually and emotionally satisfying.

The superb 1979 recording from Bavarian Radio led by **Kubelik** with Fischer-Dieskau and James King as the principals has almost legendary status (♦EMI 55237, 3CD), but **Albrecht**'s recording will do nicely as well (Wergo 6255, 3CD). Roland Hermann is a more robust and earthy Mathis than the refined Fischer-Dieskau; he sings firmly, heartily, dramatically. The role of Albrecht von Brandenburg is vocally difficult, with a high tessitura, and is brilliantly sung by Josef Protschka, though it's a somewhat generalized characterization without King's insights. Albrecht leads a fine, hearty performance, Kubelik a more refined and nobler interpretation.

Neues vom Tage (News of the Day, 1929). Sex and controversy also accompanied this opera, with howls of protest—and public condemnation from future Nazi Culture minister Joseph Goebbels—over the scene where the lead soprano bathes on stage. In the fuss, the trivial plot was forgotten, and the opera became a smash hit. Listening now to **Jan Latham-Koenig**'s brilliant recording of this brittle piece, you wonder where the composer of *Cardillac* and Mathis was hiding, but it's a fascinating document of its time (Wergo). RICKARDS/PARSONS

SONGS

Hindemith was a prolific composer of songs all his creative life. Most are set to German Romantic texts, but some use English verses, including Whitman poems. The songs are not melodic in the manner of the 19th-century lieder composers, but their sparse, tight construction supports the poetry, and they sound natural. Until fairly recently, they were rarely performed and recorded, but that's no longer the case.

One of the earliest programs, and still one of the best, was recorded by **Fischer-Dieskau** about a dozen years ago (Orfeo 156861). At the time, the famous baritone's vocal powers were still adequate and his interpretive abilities unrivaled. A more recent disc by the young soprano **Juliane Banse** (Orfeo 413961) is a fine complement. Banse has a lovely, fresh voice, and her program doesn't duplicate any of the songs on Fischer-Dieskau's disc. **Ruth Ziesak**'s recent recording (CPO) duplicates many of the songs on Banse's CD. She also sings six of the *Marienleben* songs, but Hindemith collectors will want the entire cycle. Ziesak is also a very fine singer; her interpretations are very similar to Banse's.

Marienleben. This 15-song cycle about the life of the Virgin Mary is set to poems by Rilke. Hindemith wrote it in the early '20s and revised it between 1936 and 1942. The revised version is performed most often; it's vocally more appealing and its piano part is more restrained. A beautifully sung recording of the revised version was made by **Janowitz** (Jecklin 574); a 1961 recording by the Wagnerian-voiced **Gerda Lammers** (Cantata) overpowers the words (and the piano) too much. A **Tourel** LP has not been rereleased on CD. The original version of the cycle was recorded by **Roxolana Roslak** (accompanied by Glenn Gould) in a set that includes songs by Strauss and Krenek (Sony 52674, 2CD). That one is for Hindemith die-hards who want a complete collection of his works.
MOSES

Lee Hoiby (b. 1926)

Hoiby is a fluent composer of ingratiatingly melodic music that combines neoclassical structures, a postromantic ethos, and subtle harmony and color to produce works that are highly accomplished and satisfying. It's puzzling that his music isn't more familiar, since it contains all the ingredients that should spell success. As a composer chiefly of romantic opera during the avant-garde meltdown of the '50s and '60s, it's possible to see how he was eclipsed, but a most welcome revival of interest in recent years, coupled with a number of new works, have ensured that his reputation is starting to gain its proper foothold. Even so, that reputation is as yet founded on very few CDs, and it's 30 years since one of his many operas (*Beatrice*) was available.

There are only three CDs devoted entirely to Hoiby's music. The one most strongly recommended is of his church music, recorded by the **Choir of Trinity Church, New York** (Gothic 49035). This disc contains some of the finest American choral music of recent years, and the relatively small forces involved do nothing to diminish its freshness, nobility, and aptness. "Hymn to the New Age," with additional brass, and his big anthem, "Inherit the Kingdom," are especially lovely. This CD was part of a series of four; the others featured a selection of American composers, and the last contains more music by Hoiby (Gothic 78932).

The first of his two piano concertos was recorded by **John Atkins** in Poland in 1966 (Citadel 88118, with John La Montaine's Concerto). The second, recorded by **Stanley Babin,** is brilliant and rhapsodic with the hint of wistfulness that is Hoiby's hallmark (MMC 2038). Very much in the Barber rather than Bernstein mold, its rhetorical and romantic breadth places it firmly in the 19th-century tradition. Hoiby himself is a fine pianist and plays the remaining pieces on the disc; his *Schubert Variations* is a superbly judged and crafted masterwork, as is the engaging sweetness of his early Violin Sonata (1952).

A recording of Hoiby's songs is also available (CRI 685). We can only hope for much more of this inspired and greatly underestimated composer.
JOHNSON

Vagn Holmboe (1909–1996)

Holmboe is considered Denmark's greatest symphonist after Carl Nielsen, with whom he shared a love for classical forms and mastery of instrumentation. He admired the discipline, logic, and efficiency of Haydn, which he emulated in his own music. Steering clear of the innovations of the '50s and '60s, he expressed himself in a language of short and long melodic lines, often using folk-derived modal inflections, diatonicism, and neoclassical affinities. If the lines appear angular or austere at times, it's because he wasn't given to emotional excess. His music has its own profile and is intellectually and emotionally satisfying. It's life-asserting, expressed by instrumental vitality, clear textures, and vibrant, rhythmic thrust. Melodic or rhythmic figures here and there remind us that his roots lie in Nielsen and Sibelius.

Holmboe wrote 13 numbered symphonies, the first in 1935 and the last in 1994. No. 1 is for chamber orchestra, and No. 4 ("Sinfonia sacra") is for chorus and orchestra and is the only one with vocal parts. No. 5 is the first in which he makes tentative use of the metamorphosis technique, in which a melodic or rhythmic motif, chord, cadence, or interval forms the basis of an entire work; this technique comes to full fruition in the magnificent 7 and was used from then on in most if not all of his works. Symphony 8 ("Sinfonia Boreale") was the first of his symphonies to be recorded, in the '60s (Turnabout 34168, with Nørgård's *Constellations* for strings). All 13 are performed by **Owain Arwel Hughes** (BIS 843/846, 6CD). The set is rounded out by the deeply felt *Sinfonia in Memoriam,* written in 1954 for the 10th anniversary of Denmark's liberation from occupation. In a letter Holmboe wrote several months before his death, he praised Hughes's work, saying that "Owain has done a very good job." I can't think of a better recommendation.

Holmboe wrote four *Symphonic Metamorphoses,* 1 ("Epitaph") in 1954, 4 ("Tempo Variabile") in 1972. His symphonic thinking in melodies, form, and structure is again evident in these impressive works. All four are led by **Hughes** (BIS 852).

Between 1939 and 1956, Holmboe wrote 13 Chamber Concertos of neoclassical cast, dating from the same time as Symphonies 2 through 8. They're well worth exploring and should appeal to any music lover interested in the soloist/chamber orchestra idiom. All are performed by various soloists conducted by **Hannu Koivula** (Marco Polo, various numbers, 4CD). This superb series reflects the robustness of the symphonies and the intimacy of the string quartets.

Concertos 11 and 12 can also be found coupled with the fine Tuba Concerto and *Intermezzo Concertante* for tuba and strings, written for and played by **Michael Lind** (BIS 802). Holmboe's broadly conceived Cello Concerto is played by **Erling Bløndal-Bengtsson** (BIS 78, with *Benedic Domino, Triade* for trumpet and organ, and Quintet for brass). All are solid, ingratiating works. The Concerto for Recorder, Strings, Celeste, and Vibraphone is a charming piece, performed by **Michala Petri** (RCA 62543, with other recorder concertos).

Holmboe completed 20 numbered string quartets, the first in 1949, and he was working on No. 21 at the time of his death. These masterly works constitute the kernel of his large chamber output. In their closely argued textures, melodic lines, and deep expressiveness, they deserve to stand next to the quartets of Bartók and Shostakovich. The **Kontra Quartet,** Denmark's leading and most active string quartet, has recorded 1–15 and is planning to record all 20 (Da Capo 9203, 1, 3, 4; 4026, 2, 5, 6; 4072, 7–9; 224101, 10–12; 4127, 13–15).

Holmboe also made important contributions to choral music. *Benedic Domino, Speravi in Domino,* and *Laudate Dominum* are fine examples of his impressive body of work, sharing a disc with Danish composer Niels La Cour's *Missa Brevis* and *Motetti Latini,* all performed by **Jesper Grove Jørgensen** (Point 5115). His imposing *Liber Canticorum* (Book of Songs), based on texts from the Old Testament and made up of

34 motets spread over 17 opus numbers, was recorded by six Danish choirs (Danica 8209/11, 3CD). This superb series has become a credo for modal neoclassical a cappella music.

On all the CDs described above, the performances range from good to excellent, as do the sonics. DE JONG

Gustav Holst (1874–1934)

Holst was an English composer of German ancestry. He and his lifelong friend Vaughan Williams took walking trips around the English countryside for inspiration, and both made great use of English folk tunes. Holst became world-famous as the composer of *The Planets*. His early compositions are in the romantic tradition of Stanford and Parry, his later ones full of modern harmony and austere beauty.

ORCHESTRAL MUSIC

In the past, it was difficult to find many of Holst's works on records. Today, most can be found in excellent digital or remastered analog sound. Because many of his compositions are relatively short, I will discuss mainly the better-known ones in discs that contain full Holst programs.

Beni Mora ("Oriental Suite"). Scored for large orchestra, this was the result of Holst's interest in Eastern mysticism. **David Lloyd-Jones** gives a fine, detailed performance (Naxos), but **Boult**'s sense of exotic adventure virtually kidnaps the listener (♦Lyrita, NA). **Holst** himself can be heard conducting a fine *Beni Mora,* though the quaint 1924 sound won't show off anyone's stereo system (♦Pearl 9417).

The Cotswolds Symphony (Symphony in F). This is one of Holst's earliest works; its main attraction, a gorgeous "Elegy," has been performed separately. His daughter Imogen suppressed the work, but **Douglas Bostock** leads the premiere recording with the well-rehearsed Munich Symphony sounding as English as can be (♦Classico 284). A two-piano version can be heard with **Anthony Goldstone** and **Caroline Clemmow** (♦Albany 198).

Double Concerto for two violins and orchestra. This was one of Holst's later, more uncompromising pieces and gained warm public acceptance. **Andrew Watkinson** and **Nicholas Ward** give a straightforward rendering (♦Chandos 9270). The aptly stringent tones of **Emmanuel Hurwitz** and **Kenneth Sillito** are unavailable (♦Lyrita, NA).

Egdon Heath. This work was hissed by a Paris audience in 1929. Holst became convinced this bleak tone poem was his best work, and (according to Imogen) held that opinion until his death. **Previn**'s reading is relatively prosaic (EMI). **Hickox** is more dramatic, but he strains a bit for effect (Chandos). **Andrew Davis,** whom I prefer, is just the opposite—subdued and autumnal—but it's hard to recommend a 14-minute filler accompanying a dull *Planets* (Teldec). By virtue of its clarity, balance, and value, your best choice is **David Lloyd-Jones** (♦Naxos 553696).

Hammersmith. This is an impressionist rendering of the London market district near the Thames. After a somber Adagio, it has a devilish dance-like motif and delicate, bittersweet melodic lines. **Hickox** feels both the drama and irony of the music, and the London Symphony is with him all the way (♦Chandos 9420). **Lloyd-Jones** (Naxos) is as good as **Boult** (Lyrita, NA), but Hickox sets a standard of potency. The original military band version has a burnished pomp and vitality, but also irony, and **Timothy Reynish**'s reading is outstanding regardless of which arrangement you prefer (♦Chandos 9697).

Lyric Movement for viola and small orchestra. This work is full of yearning melancholy. It's too bad the fine recording with violist **Cecil**

Aronowitz is kept from us (♦Lyrita, NA). Meanwhile, **Stephen Tees** plays sensitively, though without Aronowitz's passion (Chandos 9270). **Nicholas Braithwaite** gives a lyrical reading, and Vyvyan Yendoll plays expressively, but the sound is oddly constricted (Koch).

The Perfect Fool. This is the unfortunate title for some of the most magical music in the Holst canon. **Bostock**'s recording is one of the best, in demonstration-quality sound, and his disc includes groundbreaking premieres of the *Cotswolds Symphony, Walt Whitman Overture,* and *Hampshire Suite* (♦Classico 284). **Previn** is nearly as good, though not quite as atmospheric in the central "Dance of the Spirits of Water" (EMI). **Boughton** is polished and fluent (♦Nimbus, NA). **Leaper** is well played, but could use more refinement of feeling in the central section (Arte Nova). **Mackerras** has rich, burnished brass, and plays with a seamless *attacca* that emphasizes the story-like flow (♦Virgin 61510, 2CD). A skillful two-piano version is available from **Len Vorster** and **Robert Chamberlain** (Naxos).

The Planets. This is Holst's inspired masterpiece, symphonic in proportion, unprecedented in conception. Although its symbolic motifs were borrowed from astrology, it has a cool, scientific sensibility. Each "planet" has its own rarefied atmosphere, but we can't do a complete analysis, for there are now nearly 50 recordings available.

Mehta offers cool austerity and dynamic force in both his readings. Perhaps he studied Boult (who gave the premiere in 1918), for both seem to have a deep understanding of what makes this music tick. The 1971 Los Angeles Philharmonic recording is well detailed, the melodic lines finely executed (London 417677). The 1990 New York Philharmonic sounds even better, more subtle, powerful, and confident—sophisticated enough for the most critical listener—with an indescribable chilly beauty (♦Teldec 18661).

Of all the recordings, **Dutoit** is the most widely acclaimed. The sound is stunning, revealing inner details of Holst's orchestration and massive enough to blow your woofers through the wall. Magical is a word that comes to mind, though tempos are slow in the quieter sections, which are warmer and more humane than ideal (♦London 460606). **Geoffrey Simon** and the London Symphony are the best-kept secret of *Planets* recordings (♦LaserLight 14010). At super-budget price, they deliver a recording in the Boult tradition that's one of the finest ever made. It has a cool beauty and dynamic power every bit the equal of Mehta's, perfectly judged tempos, passionately shaped melodic lines, superior orchestral playing, a chorus that sounds almost possessed, and superior digital sound—all for peanuts.

The Philharmonia deserves a section to itself. This orchestra sounds amazingly similar across a 30-year time span, from Boult in 1967 to Slatkin in 1997. **Boult** never made a better recording of *The Planets* than with this group (then called the New Philharmonia). His final recording in the late '70s with the London Philharmonic has a slight advantage in sound quality (♦EMI 64748), but his deceptively straightforward 1967 account has a subtle atmosphere and concentration that haven't been duplicated (♦EMI 66934).

Rattle was the next to arrive on the Philharmonia podium, and his potent reading sounds like a more dynamic version of Boult's. Rattle is impatient with the central melody in "Jupiter," but the reading overall has attained classic status (♦EMI 9513). **Boughton** is excellent in the quieter sections, with an especially haunting "Neptune," but is undernourished elsewhere (Nimbus). **Svetlanov** has no special flavor, contrary to what you might expect (Collins). His "Mars" is the slowest, and the wordless chorus in "Neptune" is a bit thin and literal. **Gardiner**

(DG) wowed the critics, but his interpretation sounds like a lesser version of Boult's earlier one, with "Venus" taken at a speedy 7:37 vs. Boult's 8:52 (Dutoit comes in at 9:36!). For **Slatkin**, the Philharmonia plays with a wispy, exquisite delicacy but somehow doesn't make a lasting impression (RCA). All these recordings have value, but they haven't recaptured Boult's—and to an extent Rattle's—mastery.

Karajan and the Vienna Philharmonic give a valuable account. Here was a world-class orchestra with an up-and-coming German conductor who had something to say about a British masterpiece. It's a powerful reading, more emotional than Boult's (♦London 452303). His remake is self-indulgent, with stretched phrasing and a chorus abruptly cut off by the engineers (DG). Almost the same thing happens to **Levine** in an otherwise fine rendition (DG).

In the November 1969 catalog, only five recordings of *The Planets* were listed: Boult/Vienna State, Boult/New Philharmonia, Karajan/Vienna, Sargent/BBC, and Stokowski/LA. The sleeper among these is **Sargent**, who gives an appealing, oddly romantic reading (♦IMP 9104). **Stokowski** ought to have given us a great recording (EMI). Instead, it's a clipped, eccentric rendition with a toy-soldier "Mars" and a jack-in-the-box "Saturn." Perhaps he was taking cues from **Holst**'s own 1926 account, which also has clipped phrases, conditioned by the conducting style of the time (Koch). Similar, but a bit better, is the composer's antiquated acoustic recording from 1923, also with the London Symphony. It should be acquired by every serious collector (♦Pearl 9417).

Mehta's London recording triggered a '70s boom. With its "Sonic Spectacular" sticker on the shrink wrap, it became a best-seller and was followed by about a dozen others. **Steinberg** follows the composer's style, with fast outer movements; here, it works (♦DG, NA). **Haitink** is colorful and expressive, his "Mars" disturbingly relentless (♦Philips, NA). **Bernstein**'s reading is aggressive in loud sections (best is "Uranus"), analytical in quiet ones (Sony).

Previn's performance has classic status, and rightly so. "Mars" is black with menace from the very first measures, while all the other planets are beautifully rendered by the London Symphony at the height of their commitment to the conductor (♦EMI, NA). His later recording is smooth but languid (Telarc). Telarc's good sound can best be had with **Levi** and the Atlanta Symphony (♦Telarc 80466). The climax in "Saturn" could have more bite, but elsewhere Levi is finely attuned to the mystical atmosphere. After a dull "Mars," **Ozawa** gives a satisfying reading (Philips, NA), while **Maazel**'s well-recorded account has emotional commitment but is sometimes impatiently phrased (CBS/Sony). **Marriner** (Philips, NA), **Ormandy** (RCA)**,** and **Solti** (London) have excellent sound, but are mostly routine. **Susskind** (Vox) is competent but uninspiring.

Herrmann's London Phase-4 recording has cult appeal. Many (who haven't heard it?) await its rebirth, though it's one of the most bizarre—and tiresome—*Planets* ever recorded (and this from a great Herrmann fan). "Mars" has some fine percussive effects, but there's no menace at his sluggish pace, and "Venus" is a full 10 minutes of inappropriate sentimentality. The sound undermines balances, while the big bass note in "Uranus" is weak. Even though the choir is properly eerie in "Neptune," it's too late to save it.

At the dawn of the digital era, **Gibson** came along with a good performance in the refined British mold (Chandos). **Mackerras** is a potent contender in the same tradition (Virgin). **Andrew Davis**'s first recording is interesting in his use of a children's chorus in "Neptune" (EMI, NA). It works, and it's worth hearing, but the dynamic climax in "Saturn" is among the weakest, so the reading falls short. His second tra-

versal is stillborn, unable to take flight (Teldec). **Hickox** is aggressive, but also dull at critical points (IMP). **Handley** can't coax more than a routine performance out of the Royal Philharmonic, though the anguished cries of the brass at the conclusion of "Mars" are shockingly effective (Intersound).

Fair readings from the British Isles come from **James Judd** (Denon), **Wetton** (Collins, NA), **Pople** (ASV), and to a lesser extent **James Loughran** (EMI). **Goodman** is energetic, but too stern in softer passages (IMP/Carlton). In a 1996 recording temporarily available from *BBC Music Magazine,* **Tortelier** offers one of the best readings to come along in the past decade—far better than Gardiner or Slatkin—and deserves wider release. Second-tier American performances include **Williams** (Philips, NA), **Mata** (Pro Arte, NA), and **Litton** (Delos), with the latter having the best sound. These readings have fine moments, but in such a competitive field each planet must be in aesthetic apogee.

Leaper makes a strong claim among the budget releases. Though somewhat wayward, his recording with the CSR Symphony is imaginative and atmospheric (Naxos 550193). His concert recording with the Orquesta Filarmónica de Gran Canaria is well-conceived and executed (Arte Nova 27785). Either one of these might be a good choice if it weren't for Simon (see above). **Jahni Mardjani** is the lowest priced (Infinity). He and the Georgian Festival Orchestra attempt to play *The Planets* in what sounds like an abandoned missile silo. The musicians are undoubtedly giving it their best—poor intonation, bad miking and all—and Mardjani understands the music; still, how this got into such wide release (by Sony, no less) would be interesting to know. **Mark Elder**'s Proms Concert recording has a black, methodical "Mars" and a haunting rather than ethereal "Neptune," but the remaining sections are routine (BBC).

Also available are several two-piano versions and one for organ. Of the two-piano versions I know, the most sensitive is by **Richard Rodney Bennett** and **Susan Bradshaw** (♦Delos 8002). This one reveals the beauty and genius of the work, while **Vorster** and **Chamberlain** choose speedy tempos for the slow movements and a clipped articulation (e.g., in "Saturn") that reduce the sense of wonder (Naxos). **Goldstone** and **Clemmow** have recorded this version, but I haven't been able to obtain a copy for review (♦Albany 198). Finally, **Peter Sykes**'s—dare I say "organ transplant"?—is an interesting idea, but fails in the execution (Raven).

Boult's postwar recordings may be of interest to the collector. His 1945 BBC reading awaits reissue, while the 1959 stereo with the Vienna State Opera Orchestra is disappointing (MCA, NA). Neither of these recordings matches the excellence of either the 1967 or 1978 remakes, but they set the modern performance standard.

Saint Paul's Suite. This has a variety of infectious folk melodies culminating in the joyful counterpoint of "The Dargason" and "Greensleeves"—a true delight. So delightful, in fact, that this finale was quickly reorchestrated (for strings) from the Suite in F for Band. Later, the Suite in F was fully orchestrated by Gordon Jacob and called *The Hampshire Suite.* **Handley**'s recording is the most rhythmic and joyful version I've heard, and though it comes with his garden-variety *Planets*, the price is low (♦Intersound 2807). Both **Pople** (Arte Nova), and to a lesser extent **Hickox** (Chandos), are rhythmic but hard-driven and not especially engaging. **Goodman**'s comes with an even less attractive *Planets* than Handley's (IMP). My hope is that **Boult**'s straightforward and vivacious reading will be reissued (Lyrita, NA), and the same goes for **Sargent** (EMI, NA). **Holst**'s own lively recording is available in antiquated sound (♦Pearl 9417).

A Somerset Rhapsody. This gave Holst his first critical recognition. This time, **Boult**'s performance (Lyrita, NA) is outdone by **Lloyd-Jones** in an exceptionally poetic account, and though less than 10 minutes long, it tips the scales for an overall recommendation of the disc (♦Naxos 553696). **Hickox,** with excellent sound, skillfully delineates the work's alternating melody, swagger and atmosphere (♦Chandos 9420).

Suites for Military Band. These suites are lively classics of the form. **Fennell**'s joyful and rhythmic leadership of the Cleveland Symphonic Winds is a top choice for both, in demonstration sound (♦Telarc 80038). His earlier readings with the Eastman Wind Ensemble are equally good (♦Mercury 462960, mono). **Reynish** and the Royal Northern College of Music Wind Orchestra are in a class by themselves—expressive, exuberant, virtuosic, witty, and enthralling (♦Chandos 9697). **Denis Wick** is serviceable (ASV).

CHAMBER AND PIANO MUSIC

Perhaps the most evocative piece of chamber music Holst wrote is the *Terzetto* for flute, oboe, and viola. It has a velvet melancholy with a modernist soul. **James Dunham,** John Barcellona, and Peter Christ are available at mid-price (♦Crystal 647). **Richard Adeney,** Peter Graeme, and Cecil Aronowitz delivered an especially atmospheric reading that's out of the catalog (♦Argo, NA). The Quintet in A Minor for piano, oboe, clarinet, horn, and bassoon Op. 3 is given a fine reading by the **Elysian Wind Quintet,** as is Holst's Wind Quintet in A-flat Op. 14, and on the same disc is a wonderful surprise for anyone who doesn't know Gordon Jacob's Sextet (♦Chandos 9077).

Nearly all of Holst's winsome piano music is available on one CD, with radiant performances by **Anthony Goldstone** (♦Chandos 9382).

CHORAL AND VOCAL MUSIC

Choral Hymns from the Rig Veda. This contains some of Holst's most beautiful and inspired writing. These hymns, based on Sanskrit texts, come in four groups. **David Willcocks**'s performances are first-rate, with an enchanting, ethereal delicacy (♦Unicorn-Kanchana 9046). The second group was given a strong reading by **Charles Groves** (♦EMI, NA). The third group can be found with **Wetton** in a mixed program (Hyperion 66175).

Choral Symphony. Sometimes called "First Choral Symphony" (a second was planned, but never completed), this uses a wide variety of source material, from "Folly's Song" to "Ode on a Grecian Urn." The most beautiful moments are written for soprano solo, and I can't think of a sweeter voice to convey this music than Lynne Dawson's. **Wetton** is blessed with Dawson, the Royal Philharmonic, fine instrumental soloists, and superb digital sound (♦Hyperion 66660). **Boult**'s 1974 account with Felicity Palmer has barely aged (♦EMI 49638). It has Boult's uncanny ability to elicit moments of mystery, and a fine blend of chorus and orchestra.

A Choral Fantasia. This is a dynamic 18-minute piece for soprano solo, chorus, organ, strings, and percussion. Once again, Dawson is the attraction with **Wetton** and the Royal Philharmonic—but also a melancholy organ played by John Birch (♦Hyperion 66660). **Imogen Holst** is second to none as an interpreter of her father's music, and she has Janet Baker, excellent choral forces, and good remastered sound (♦EMI 49638).

The Cloud Messenger. This is one of Holst's larger concepts, based on a first-century Sanskrit drama about a poet who uses a cloud to send a message to his wife in the Himalayas. A poor premiere in 1913 caused the work to be shunned for decades. Mezzo Della Jones, **Hickox,** and the London Symphony give us the premiere recording, and it's so good that I wonder how the piece could have been neglected for so long (♦Chandos 241/6, 2CD).

The Golden Goose. Based on a Grimm fairy tale, this is ballet music for chorus and orchestra. **Wetton** gives us an excellent, ground-breaking disc in a great out-of-the-way program that includes *Morning of the Year* and *King Estmere* (♦Hyperion 66784).

The Hymn of Jesus. This was one of Holst's immediate successes and a stunning example of his special brand of ethereal harmony. Luckily, we've got a polished, forceful, tonally attractive recording by **Hickox** (♦Chandos 241/6, 2CD). The resplendent **Groves** gives superior competition (♦EMI 65128), as will Boult when it's reissued (♦London, NA).

HALDEMAN

Arthur Honegger (1892–1955)

It was merely coincidence that the serious-minded Honegger—born in France, but the son of Swiss parents—was yoked with the merry Parisians of Les Six after WWI. He wrote a few works in the music-hall idiom of the 1920s, but his real love was Bach and Beethoven, and his real ambition was to write symphonies and chamber music. However, he also loved opera, had a weakness for what might be called "choral spectaculars" (*Joan of Arc at the Stake, La Danse des Morts*), and wrote more than 40 movie scores and even a couple of spicy Parisian operettas.

Vigorous and athletic in his youth, Honegger had a heart attack while visiting the United States in 1947, leaving him sick, depressed, and bitter. In the years that remained before his death, he seriously questioned the worth not only of his own work but of all music, describing a composer as "a man who exerts himself to produce wares for which no one has any use." During his lifetime plenty of musicians and listeners had use for Honegger; he was one of the most-played 20th century composers. But only a few of his pieces stayed in the repertory after his death: Symphony 2, the "symphonic movement" *Pacific 231,* and the still exciting and endearing oratorio *King David.* That's a very small percentage of a large and interesting output. Not until a spate of recordings was released during his centennial in 1992 did most listeners get a real sense of his considerable achievement.

SYMPHONIES

Except for 2 and 3, Honegger's five symphonies rarely turn up in American orchestral programs, but all five are worthwhile. No. 1, one of the many works Koussevitzky commissioned for the 50th anniversary of the Boston Symphony, is short, aggressive, and muscular, with an Adagio of Bachian solemnity. No. 2 is a three-movement work for strings, unremittingly dark and intense until a solo trumpet chorale pierces the gloom at the very end. Both this and the grandiose 3 (*Liturgique*) are convincing but with very different evocations of the emotions, privations, and outrages of WWII; Honegger remained in Paris throughout the Occupation, and these two symphonies ring as emotionally true as Shostakovich's wartime symphonies. No. 4 (*Deliciae basilienses*—"The Delights of Basel") is the most immediately appealing of the five, with shadows occasionally peeking through a luminously orchestrated surface. Honegger's symphonic career ended as it began, in Boston: No. 5 (*De tre re*—"Of Three Ds," referring to the timpani notes that end each of the three movements) was commissioned by Munch in 1950. Written after Honegger's initial heart attack, it's a paradoxical work, emotionally bleak but strongly energetic.

Three conductors have recorded the cycle: **Baudo** with the Czech Philharmonic in the '60s (Supraphon 111566), **Plasson** with the Toulouse Capitole Orchestra in the '70s (EMI, NA), and **Dutoit** with the Bavarian Radio Symphony in the '80s (Erato 21340). Baudo's is still excellent, particularly in 3 and 5; the bright recorded sound only occasionally shows its age. Plasson's was well received and may well turn up again (4 and 5 are available on EMI 64275). Dutoit's is the most recent, and perhaps the best overall.

As for single recordings, **Karajan** pretty much owned 2 and 3 after his Berlin Philharmonic recording was released in 1973, and revisiting it now, it's easy to see why (♦DG 447435). This is the most beautifully played of any Honegger symphony recording, and the interpretations, if a bit manicured, are powerful. This conductor wasn't very convincing in much of the 20th-century repertory, but something clicked here (as it didn't with the disc-mate, Stravinsky's Concerto in D). If you only want one Honegger symphony disc, this is the one to get.

Munch was another, very different conductor who championed Honegger during his lifetime; his mono recordings of 2 and 5 with the Boston Symphony are available (RCA), as are his French National Radio Orchestra recordings of 1 and 4 (Disques Montaigne). **Neeme Järvi**'s recordings of 3 and 5 have been well reviewed (Chandos), and **Jean Fournet**'s slow and detailed reading of 3 is convincing—worth hearing if you want a performance to compare to Karajan's (Denon). **Ansermet** had a long association with his countryman's music, but his 1950s performances of 2 and 3 are NA (London). **Markevitch**'s recording of 5 is disciplined and splendidly gloomy; the recording is excellent mono (DG, reissued in the "Originals" series).

OTHER ORCHESTRAL MUSIC

Though Honegger would have disliked the idea, this very serious symphonist's best-known orchestral works are a near-pops-concert trio of short pieces. *Pastorale d'été, Pacific 231,* and *Rugby,* are often recorded—especially the second, a wonderfully realistic musical evocation of a huge locomotive gathering speed. (Honegger later insisted that this painstakingly constructed piece was "pure" music, a compositional exercise in giving the impression of increasing speed while remaining at a steady tempo—though you may prefer to think of it as a piece about a train). *Rugby* is more of the same, a raucous musical rendition of his favorite sport. *Pastorale d'été* is a calm, lyrical gem—Honegger in an impressionist mood.

There are many modern recordings of this appealing trio of works. **Honegger** himself recorded them and a few others in the '20s and '30s, and they're now available (Pearl 9459). *Pacific 231,* in particular, recorded in 1929, still sounds pretty atmospheric. (The disc includes Honegger's performance of his Prelude to *The Tempest,* probably the only piece in his catalogue noisier than *Pacific 231.*) There's no lack of personality in **Bernstein**'s 1962 performances; *Pacific 231* is massive and exciting, and *Rugby* sounds like Lenny is playing goalie on the podium. (His *Pastorale d'été* is not included in Sony 62352, although Roussel's Symphony 3 and Milhaud's *Choéphores* are; you can hear all three Bernstein renditions on Sony 60695, a French-music potpourri in stereo and mono).

Sony's recording quality is vivid but rather rough; for better sound and imposing performances, the 1992 **Plasson** collection is recommended (♦DG 435438). Plasson also includes one of Honegger's most "modernistic" works, the "dramatic symphony" *Horace Victorieux,* and a sample of his appealing film music for *Mermoz.* For some interesting, obscure Honegger, try the collection of orchestral works conducted by

Marius Constant; they range from the flamboyant early tone poem *Chant de Nigamon,* inspired by James Fenimore Cooper, to his last orchestral work, *Monopartita* (♦Erato 45862). He disliked the twelve-tone school, but this tonal (if extremely dissonant) piece is worked out with a rigor the most committed serialist could appreciate.

Speaking of film music, Honegger wrote a lot of it, and did it well. The only film score likely to be familiar to contemporary English-speaking audiences is *Pygmalion,* after Shaw's play. But his scores for Abel Gance's *Napoleon* and *Les Misérables* include some ideal examples of film music, moving and memorable in a restricted time-frame. **Constant**'s orchestral survey includes a haunting three-minute excerpt from *Napoleon* called "Les Ombres"—as memorable a bit of music as Honegger ever wrote (Erato 45862).

CONCERTOS

Honegger wrote only three works in concerto form, all of them short and sweet. There are few recordings of the once-popular Piano Concertino (1924), one of his flings with *le jazz hot*. **Oscar Levant** recorded it many years ago, and was probably an ideal soloist. **Thibaudet**'s effort is a neat, dullish performance brightly recorded (London, with the Ravel concertos and Françaix's ten-minute Concertino). **Franz Josef Hirt**'s 1953 radio recording, pretty opaque in sound, is a much more spirited affair (Gallo).

The amiable *Concerto da Camera* for flute and English horn has had better luck, with good recordings by **Schwarz** (Nonesuch, with Strauss's Duet-Concertino, NA), **Fournet** (Denon, with *Liturgique*), and **Marriner** (♦Philips 434105). I'd give the nod to Marriner; the soloists are Heinz Holliger and Aurèle Nicolet, and the program includes goodies by Honegger, Martin, and Martinů's lovely Oboe Concerto. The concise Cello Concerto also sings the blues a bit, perhaps in deference to its American origins as a Boston Symphony commission. Rostropovich's excellent recording, with **Nagano** gently nudging the jazz rhythms, is still available, coupling this delectable work with Milhaud's Concerto 1 and a piece by the Welsh composer Alun Hoddinott (♦Erato 45489).

CHAMBER MUSIC

Musicians would do well to explore Honegger's ample supply of chamber music in a set of everything from string quartets to clarinet sonatas to solo trumpet and flute works, most of it very appealing (Timpani 1012, 4CD). Honegger played violin and viola professionally, and wrote a great deal of music for strings. The quartets and most of the string sonatas are serious and rather heavy in texture, except for the Cello Sonata and a Sonata for Two Violins that is as irresistibly tart as a lemon drop. The (mostly French) performers in this set are delightful, and all four discs are available separately. If you only want one, get the wind music disc (♦Timpani 1010). Like many French composers, Honegger lightened up when writing for wind instruments, for example in the brief, bluesy Clarinet Sonata or the pleasing *Danse de la Chèvre* (Goat's Dance) for solo flute.

CHORAL MUSIC AND SONGS

Honegger's big choral works, along with *Pacific 231,* made him famous in the United States. He's still mainly known here as the composer of the "dramatic psalm" *Le Roi David* (King David), a 20th-century work even the most reactionary choral society can love. That's selling it short; this is a dramatic musical mosaic, with lots of good tunes, bright instrumental colors, and a memorable closing chorus. It completely lacks the pretentiousness of some of his other Big Utterances.

The original version of *King David* was written in 1921 for an Alpine music festival and is brightly scored for a dozen or so instruments; not much was gained when Honegger expanded the orchestra for concert performances in Paris. **Dutoit**'s 1971 reading of the original version was one of his earliest recordings; once you get used to the churchy, reverberant acoustic it still sounds fine, with native French-speaking soloists making all the difference (♦Erato 45800). The soloists are weaker in **Abravanel**'s performance from the 1960s, but the recorded sound is bright and he gives an excellent reading, as does the doughty Madeleine (Mme. Darius) Milhaud as the Witch of Endor (♦Vanguard 4038). **Ansermet**'s 1956 recording, typically light on its feet, has perhaps the best, most natural-sounding soloists of all, along with a good, small chorus (London 425621). The most recent *King David,* a recording led by **Jean-Claude Casadesus,** has been favorably reviewed (EMI).

Honegger's other important choral pieces include *Judith,* also recorded by **Abravanel** (Vanguard), and the immense oratorio *Jeanne d'Arc au Bucher* (Joan of Arc at the Stake), with text by Paul Claudel. **Ozawa** recorded this piece twice, for CBS (NA) and for DG, a performance well received in Europe but never released in the United States. And there is a late-bloomer, the moving *Christmas Cantata.* This piece opens with several minutes of Honegger's darkest, most pessimistic music, then eventually lightens into a moving quodlibet of Christmas tunes from France, Germany, and Austria. Scored for adult and children's choirs, baritone soloist, and a large orchestra, it's a difficult piece to record; there was a good one by **Martinon** (EMI, NA).

Honegger wrote a fair number of solo songs, but they're almost never sung, even by singers known for French repertoire. The few that are recorded—including *Six Poems of Cocteau* sung by **Florence Katz** (Marco Polo 223788), *Petit Cours de Moral* sung by **Von Stade** (RCA 62711), and *Paques à New-York* and *Songs of the Little Mermaid* sung by **Fusako Kondo** (in the Timpani chamber-music set)—suggest there's more material worth exploring.   RAYMOND

Alan Hovhaness (1911–2000)

One of the most prolific contemporary composers, Hovhaness is known for his unapologetic tonality; to him, atonal music is "against nature." He's preoccupied with the transcendent and noted for his use of baroque forms, such as the fugue and chorale, and of a variety of modes. His work is also heavily influenced by his Armenian heritage.

Critic Hubert Roussel described Hovhaness's music well when he wrote after the first performance of Symphony 2, "Hovhaness produces a texture of the utmost beauty, gentleness, distinction and expressive potential. The real mystery of *Mysterious Mountain* is that it should be so simply, sweetly, innocently lovely in an age that has tried so terribly hard to avoid those impressions in music." At his best, Hovhaness transports his listeners to a realm of beauty, light, and serenity; at his worst, his music can prove annoyingly repetitive. He can combine elements of Eastern and Western music in a magical way, though at times he degenerates into fuzzy Eastern mysticism or Western banality. But it must be stressed that the best of his music doesn't wear out its welcome.

SYMPHONIES

Of Hovhaness's more than 50 symphonies, only about 20 have been recorded, and many of these only once. Those best representing his work are 1, 2, 3, 6, 22, and 50.

1 ("Exile"). This was written to commemorate the Armenians persecuted in Turkey. Its three movements are characterized by startling trumpet fanfares, conveying a sense of unease. The finale consists of a triumphant chorale whose melody is seized and swept away into a fugue. **Schwarz** and the Seattle Symphony give it an excellent treatment (♦Delos 3168).

2 ("Mysterious Mountain"). This is a favorite of many Hovhaness fans, with its sweeping chorale in the strings, organ-like texture and clear, soaring trumpet, all typical of the composer's best pieces. A double fugue comprises the second of the three movements. Several recordings exist; two of the best are **Reiner**'s 1958 rendition with the Chicago Symphony (♦RCA 5733) and **Schwarz**'s 1994 release with the Seattle Symphony (♦Delos 3157). The Schwarz version is a bit more austere and restrained than the romantic Reiner, and they take a distinctly different approach to the second half of the second movement. I slightly prefer Schwarz but the sound is excellent on both.

3. This requires the largest orchestra of any of Hovhaness's symphonies. The composer characterized it as "a tribute to Mozartian classical sonata form," and it's available in a 1996 recording by the KBS (Korean Broadcasting System) Symphony with **Vakhtang Jordania** conducting (♦Soundset 1004).

6 ("Celestial Gate"). In one movement, this is available in three recordings; of these, the best is by I Fiamminghi, **Rudolf Werthen** conducting (♦Telarc 80392, with shorter pieces). In a smooth, floating, transcendent rendition of this otherworldly music, the essential dreaminess, evocative of an underwater seascape, is beautifully conveyed. **Hovhaness** as conductor brings quite a different interpretation to it (Crystal 807). The recording is fairly old so the sound isn't as good, but the interpretation is also less rich and dreamy, more ominous and raw. If you're listening for pleasure, Werthen is the clear first choice.

22 ("City of Light") and *50* ("Mount St. Helens"). If I had to recommend only one Hovhaness disc, it would be a release pairing these two pieces (♦Delos 3137). With **Hovhaness** conducting the Seattle Symphony, every movement in 22 is a gem, but it would be worth buying just for the angelic dance in III. It's all characteristic of the composer, with the organ-like texture of the strings, the solo trumpet soaring, the graceful melodies, the chorale, and fugue at the end. **Schwarz** takes the baton for 50, a commemoration of the explosion of Mount St. Helens in 1980. This is an enjoyable and highly accessible work, portraying the grandeur of the mountain before its destruction, the beauty of Spirit Lake, and finally, a vivid evocation of the explosion itself by way of a violent attack by the timpani and a passage that sounds like the dance of some triumphant volcano god.

Crystal deserves grateful mention for its efforts through the years to promote Hovhaness's music. Because many of their CDs are reissues, the sound is often inferior, but fans should buy these recordings for a couple of reasons: **Hovhaness** himself conducts many of the works, and each CD is a good value, the time usually filled out with shorter pieces. Available are Symphonies 9 ("St. Vartan"; 802), 11 ("All Men Are Brothers"; 801), 19 ("Vishnu"; 805), 21 ("Etchmiadzin"; 804), 24 ("Majnun"; 803), 25 ("Odysseus"; 807), and 31 and 49 (♦811). The last two are worth special mention. On a 1995 disc entitled "Hovhaness Treasures," the program contains the composer's own favorites, and the two symphonies especially are delightful. Two more, 39 and 46, are available in a 1993 recording led by **Jordania;** these are both good listening, and the sound is excellent (♦Koch 7208).

OTHER ORCHESTRAL MUSIC

Hovhaness wrote a large number of miscellaneous orchestral works; several are deservedly popular, often appearing as fillers in programs of his larger pieces. One of the best known is *Prayer of St. Gregory,* in honor of the saint who brought Christianity to Armenia around 301 and meant as "a prayer in the darkness." There are two equally good versions, led by

Werthen (♦Telarc 80392, with Symphony 6) and by Schwarz (♦Delos 3157, with 2). Both are deep, serene, and meditative; Werthen has a more ethereal tone and Schwarz a more purposeful one. This piece also appears on two Crystal releases (801 and 807); the latter, recorded in 1974 and conducted by Hovhaness, is even better, with a slight urgency the others don't have. The sound, however, is inferior to both Delos and Telarc.

Prelude and Quadruple Fugue, another short Hovhaness essential, appears on both these discs in equally good renditions, and they also include *Alleluia and Fugue,* a work that appears frequently. Both performances are topnotch; oddly, Werthen, for whom most of the pieces have a dreamy quality, takes the latter a bit faster than any of the others. The sound is lovely, bringing out the organ texture that often reminds me of Vaughan Williams's music. The fugue is faster than other renditions, but I quite like this interpretation.

Another contender here is in "Celestial Fantasy," played by the Slovak Radio Orchestra, Kerry Stratton conducting; the *Alleluia and Fugue* is full and beautiful with a warm, immediate sound (♦Dorian 93166). This release is my first recommendation for those wanting a good sampling of Hovhaness's shorter works. Every piece is delicious, with first class sound and execution. Included are *The Holy City; Armenian Rhapsodies 2 and 3; In Memory of an Artist; Processional and Fugue; Celestial Fantasy,* and *Psalm and Fugue.* The disc would be well worth buying just for *Processional and Fugue,* which has not been recorded anywhere else; it's divine. *Celestial Fantasy,* a quiet, meditative work, is also on Delos 3157 and Crystal 508.

An unusual work—and a favorite of mine—is *The Rubaiyat of Omar Khayyam,* a musical setting of Fitzgerald's quatrains (♦Delos 3168). Hovhaness chose several, wove them into a piece about love and the brevity of life, and set them to music of great warmth and sensuality. This love music, which Hovhaness composed for his wife, is too easily dismissed by some critics as sentimental schlock. You can easily argue that the shifting moods of the music portray the anxiety and mortality of the lover in a way that's at worst accurate and at best profound. The instrumentation is odd—it's set for solo accordion and orchestra—but it works, and the poetry is skillfully narrated by Michael York, with Schwarz conducting.

Mystery of the Holy Martyrs is another unusual piece, this time for orchestra and solo guitar, with soloist Michael Long (♦Soundset 1004, with Symphony 3). It's a tribute to Armenian Christian martyrs who died in 451, and is of great interest for its inclusion of Armenian liturgical music. Performance and sound are both excellent.

And God Created Great Whales is not one of Hovhaness's better works but is among his best known. A commissioned piece, it centers on recorded whale songs. The whale noises, though fascinating, aren't particularly melodious, sounding remarkably cow-like, but it provides a graphic illustration of Hovhaness's ability to integrate his music with nature. Two very good renditions exist by Schwarz (Delos 3157) and David Amos (Crystal 810).

CHAMBER MUSIC

Hovhaness wrote many pieces for various small instrumental groups. Generally, these aren't his strongest works, as he seemed to need the full palette of an orchestra. However, the Shanghai Quartet has collected a number of them in "Spirit Murmur," and the program—which includes four bagatelles and four string quartets—is quite strong (♦Delos 3162). Quartet 1 is an early version of *Prelude and Quadruple Fugue* for orchestra; Quartets 3 and 4 both deal with memories of the composer's childhood.

PIANO MUSIC

Composition for the piano wasn't Hovhaness's strength, though he was a capable pianist. But for those who are interested, Wayne Johnson has recorded a good program (Crystal 813), and Hovhaness himself played some of these works (Fortuna 17062). There are also two discs of the piano music played by Marvin Rosen (Koch 7195 and 7288). I miss the fullness and warmth of strings; the pieces sound simply exotic, along with their titles, such as "Love Song Vanishing into Sounds of Crickets."

CHORAL MUSIC

One of Hovhaness's best-known choral works is a setting of the *Magnificat.* There are two recordings, one on Delos (♦3176) and the other led by Robert Whitney (♦Crystal 808). I somewhat prefer the Crystal version of this otherworldly, mystical work, though the Delos—recorded in St. John's Cathedral in Denver—is newer, so the sound is better. Either the cathedral isn't the best venue for recording or the placement of microphones was poor; the choir sounds distant compared to the orchestra. However, I recommend both as valuable additions to any collection of the composer's choral work, as the Delos includes a number of smaller sacred pieces, including a setting of *The Lord's Prayer,* and Whitney pairs the *Magnificat* with *Saturn,* a strange work whose text Hovhaness wrote himself. This piece is also strangely scored, for soprano, clarinet, and piano. Composed about 1971, it's cold, stark, and alien.

Two other notable choral works are *Lady of Light,* which Hovhaness composed in 1968 as his protest against war, and *Avak the Healer* sung by Marnie Nixon (Crystal 806). The latter is the stronger work; it has more overall cohesion and more of the composer's characteristically rich string and bright trumpet passages.   CRAWFORD

Herbert Howells (1892–1983)

Howells is best known for his harmonically iridescent church music, but his passionate orchestral works have recently been revived on disc. Those who have heard the music of Vaughan Williams, Holst, and Finzi will find themselves in recognizable territory, but will soon discover Howells to be a highly individual composer with dense, soul-stirring harmonies and moving lyricism.

ORCHESTRAL MUSIC

A fine sampling of Howells's orchestral output can be heard with Hickox and the London Symphony. Vol. 1 contains six outstanding compositions, five of which are premiere recordings. One of these is Christopher Palmer's orchestration of the middle movement of an unfinished cello concerto, *Threnody for Cello and Orchestra;* it's played with deep feeling by Mory Welsh (♦Chandos 9410). Vol. 2 contains the inspiring and melodic *The B's* (following the form of Elgar's *Enigma Variations*), three Dances for violin and orchestra, and the song cycle *In Green Ways.* The Dances are powerfully emotive in the hands of Mordkovitch (♦Chandos 9557). She has just the right touch, while the competition from Malcolm Stewart is somewhat delicate and self-effacing under Handley, partly the result of a balance that seems to favor the orchestra (Hyperion).

Another compilation with Hickox, this time conducting the City of London Sinfonia, contains Concerto for String Orchestra, Suite for String Orchestra, and Serenade for Strings, all delivered with passion and sensitivity (♦Chandos 9161). Of special importance is Elegy for Solo Viola, String Quartet, and String Orchestra, inspired by Vaughan Williams' *Tallis Fantasia,* the piece that most affected the youthful Howells. It receives a beautiful, heart-wrenching performance by Matthew Souter. Stylistically loyal to the *Tallis Fantasia,* but slightly less emotive than Souter, is an earlier LP with **Albert Cayzer,** conducted by Boult (Lyrita or HNH LP, NA). An equally fine version of the Concerto for String Orchestra can be found with **Handley** and the Royal Liverpool. This disc contains Piano Concerto 2 played by **Stott,** who is insightful, polished, and compassionate (♦Hyperion 66610).

CHORAL MUSIC

Hymnus Paradisi. This is the later of two compositions that emerged from the heartbreak the composer suffered over the death of his young son. The first was *Requiem,* upon which *Hymnus* was based. Both works show how much Howells was influenced by Vaughan Williams, yet they have a modern sensibility that bridges the gap between that British master and a modern figure like John Tavener, whose cosmic liturgical harmonies owe much to Howells.

Two recordings of *Hymnus Paradisi* stand out. **Hickox** and the BBC Symphony Orchestra and Chorus offer a demonstration-class recording that captures the dense harmonies, passionate voices, and mature poignancy of this large-scale yet vividly personal work. Joan Rodgers and Rolfe Johnson are excellent soloists (♦Chandos 9744). **Handley** and the Royal Liverpool Philharmonic are just as satisfying, resplendent sound. Where Hickox is slightly more detailed and transparent, Handley is more blended, recorded less closely, and hence more ethereal-sounding in certain choral passages. Yet there's much to recommend in Hickox's smooth transparency and realism, and your choice is a matter of taste. Handley's coupling is *An English Mass,* while Hickox has *A Kent Yeoman's Wooing Song;* both are substantial, regardless of the latter's more trivial-sounding title. For Handley, singers Kennard and Ainsley deliver a highly competitive and sympathetic performance (♦Hyperion 66488).

A concert performance by **John Alexander** and the Estonian National Orchestra struggles valiantly against balance and sound problems but is a worthy interpretation (Bay Cities, NA). A fine performance by **Donald Hunt** and the Royal Philharmonic was recorded in 1977 in the reverberant acoustic of Gloucester Cathedral with the composer in attendance (BBC 56918).

Missa Sabrinensis. This is Howells's most ambitious work, ostensibly a mass but referring to the river Severn and tinted with nature's cool splendor and stellar intensity. This 76-minute work is passionately conducted by **Rozhdestvensky,** whose interest in English music pays off in spades. This is the definitive recording, and though its length may tax the patience of some listeners, its complexities, beauty, and glorious tonalities are more rewarding with each hearing. The outstanding soloists are Janice Watson, Della Jones, Martyn Hill, and Donald Maxwell, while the London Symphony Orchestra and Chorus deliver power, atmosphere, and brilliance (♦Chandos 9348).

Requiem. This may be the most hauntingly beautiful of Howells's choral works. It demonstrates a unique combination of emotion, restraint, and harmonic nuance that sets the composer off from his contemporaries. All the recordings I've heard do it justice, but the best is by **Paul Spicer** and the Finzi Singers. The engineers create a sound field of atmosphere and immediacy (a difficult achievement) and the blended, transparent articulation of the chorus seems nearly supernatural in its tonal and dynamic control (♦Chandos 9019).

Christopher Robinson and the Choir of St. John's College, Cambridge, offer a wonderful program of Howells's church music, including *Requiem,* at a super-budget price. The sound quality is the very best, and not only do the singers convey the complexities with dedication and skill but the disc makes a great general introduction to the composer's

church music (♦Naxos 554659). Another fine disc is by **Best** and his Corydon Singers. This is the first exposure I had to Howells, and *Requiem* is beautifully communicated by the participants, with a varied program that includes Vaughan Williams's *Mass* (Hyperion).

Stabat Mater. Completed in 1965, this is about the pain of the Virgin Mary on the crucifixion of Christ. Once again, **Rozhdestvensky** and the London Symphony Orchestra and Chorus deliver a gut-wrenching performance, full of anguish and despair, yet doing full justice to the ironic beauty of the score. The acoustic isn't friendly to vocal articulation, but the brasses are overwhelmingly potent and portentous, and tenor Neill Archer's delivery of the text will make you weep. This is for the strong of heart (♦Chandos 9314).

Various compilations of Howells's shorter choral music are available, much of it accompanied by organ. Again I recommend the excellent, refined readings of **Spicer** and the Finzi Singers (♦Chandos 9458 and 9021). **Edward Higginbottom** conducts the New College Choir Oxford and alternates with fine organ solos in two outstanding compilations in a spacious, atmospheric acoustic (♦CRD 3454/55). Organist **Christopher Dearnley** is another expressive soloist, with John Scott conducting the Choir of St. Paul's Cathedral (♦Hyperion 22038, 2CD).

The *Collegium Regale Service* is sung in a definitive version by the King's College Choir directed by **Cleobury**—definitive not only for the superior performance, but because it was written by Howells specifically for the Chapel acoustic (♦Argo 430205). Other pieces on the disc are imaginatively programmed to take the listener through a liturgical day. This *Service* is also well sung by the Choir of St. John's under **Robinson** (Naxos, see above). *Take Him, Earth, for Cherishing* was written on the death of John F. Kennedy and is finely conducted in the above-mentioned compilations. A complete cycle of the morning and evening *Canticles* is underway by the Collegiate Singers directed by **Andrew Millinger,** though I have not yet heard the first disc (Priory 745).

OTHER MUSIC

Chamber music. Much of Howells's chamber, piano music, and songs are spread out over multiple-composer CDs, but some are devoted exclusively to Howells. The beautiful Violin Sonatas 1-3 are especially rewarding, with **Paul Barritt** and Catherine Edward giving the music a finely expressive touch (♦Hyperion 6665). Quartet 3 ("In Gloucestershire") is played with dedication and warmth by the **Divertimenti Quartet** (♦Hyperion 55045). Sonata for Oboe and Piano has a lively, somewhat acerbic modern quality, and it's nicely done by **Sarah Francis** and Peter Dickinson (♦Hyperion 55008). **Thea King** and Clifford Benson give a polished and expressive account of the Sonata for Clarinet and Piano (♦Hyperion 22027)

Organ music. Three essential volumes of Howells's organ music are available, played by **Stephen Cleobury, Graham Barber,** and **Adrian Partington** (♦Priory 480, 524, 547).

Piano music. Howells's piano music is usually considered of lesser importance in his overall output, but sampling these often engaging works is easily recommendable with **Fingerhut**'s beautifully played and recorded compilation, including *Gadabout, Sarum Sketches, Slow Dance,* and *Cobbler's Hornpipe* among other pieces (♦Chandos 9273). Of further interest is **McCabe**'s piano traversal of *Howells' Clavichord* (20 miniatures for clavichord or piano, with such personally stamped titles as *Boult's Brangill, Rubbra's Soliloquy, Ralph's Pavane, Finzi's Rest*), and though the score indicates either clavichord or piano, I suspect Howells himself preferred the clavichord (Hyperion).

Songs. Virtually all of Howells's songs are lovingly sung by **Dawson**, Pierard, Ainsley, and Luxon, with Julius Drake at the keyboard (♦Chandos 9185, 2CD).   HALDEMAN

Johann Nepomuk Hummel *(1778–1837)*

Hummel was one of those composers condemned to be a missing link between other greater creators, yet his music can give much pleasure, and there has never been a better time to savor it, with many superb CDs available. His portraits show a genial, rotund man perhaps too well contented with himself. A pupil of Mozart, he had an uneasy friendship with Beethoven and knew Schubert, though too late to be much influenced by him. His vast acquaintanceship among composers ranged from Haydn to Liszt and Chopin and in his last years, spent at Weimar, he was close to Goethe. He was a brilliant pianist and improviser, whose pedagogical works (such as his 1828 *Piano School*) were best sellers; and although his music was never exactly path-breaking, it often foreshadowed that of Chopin, especially in the piano concertos. When he attempted a fully fledged slow movement rather than one of his graceful themes-and-variations, it tended to be impressive rather than profound.

CONCERTOS

The Trumpet Concerto is perhaps Hummel's most popular work, written, like Haydn's, for Anton Weidinger's new keyed trumpet, a treacherous and short-lived beast. **Reinhold Friedrich** gives an amazingly secure and brilliant performance on the proper instrument; Martin Haselböck conducts the Wiener Akademie, playing period instruments (Capriccio 10598, with Haydn's Concerto). Fine performers on modern trumpets include **Maurice André** (in a useful "two-fer" that sweeps up various vintage recordings, Erato 25596), **Håkan Hardenberger** (Philips 420203) and **Wynton Marsalis** (Sony 57497).

The Bassoon Concerto is a little too garrulous for its own good but has a jolly finale and is well performed by **Claudio Gonella** and the Orchestra Internazzionale d'Italia under Diego Dini-Ciacci, who himself is the soloist in the more purposeful *Introduction, Theme and Variations* for oboe and orchestra (Naxos 554280). Another good performance of the oboe work can be heard from **Jacques Chambon** in the Erato "two-fer." Among the most enjoyable miscellaneous concerted works is the *Fantasy* for viola and orchestra, which suddenly breaks into a well-known operatic aria by Hummel's teacher Mozart; it's jauntily played by **Gérard Caussé**, who directs the Montpellier-Moscow Soloists himself (EMI 754817). For the lovely Mandolin Concerto, go to **Dorina Frati**'s spick-and-span performance (Dynamic 128); the version on Erato sounds arthritic and rattly by comparison.

Should you be allergic to the mandolin, Howard Shelley plays the piano version of this concerto (*Concertino Op. 73*), with aplomb, directing the London Mozart Players from the keyboard; only occasionally do you feel the lack of a conductor (Chandos 9558). He also plays the A-flat Piano Concerto well, but he shouldn't have claimed a first recording for the delightful *Gesellschafts-Rondo*—it was done in the 1970s by **Anne Queffélec**, whose equally fine performance is in the Erato set. You can also find the A-flat Concerto coupled with an otherwise unavailable Concerto in F, but the performances by **Nikolaús Lahusen** are frustratingly soporific (Koch Schwann).

The best Hummel piano concerto disc is, without question, by **Hough,** coupling the B minor and A minor (Chandos 8507). The pianism is Olympian, bringing out the foretastes of Chopin. Bryden Thomson conducts the English Chamber Orchestra sympathetically and the recording is first-rate. Some may prefer the more delicate shad-

ings of **Hae-won Chang** (Naxos 550837). **Dana Protopopescu** is another excellent bargain choice (Discover 920117), and **Martin Galling**'s old LPs have resurfaced (Vivace 652).

Ivan Palovi offers only the A minor, but it's coupled with the only recording of the C major Concerto, played by **Pavel Ková** (Koch Schwann 311120). **Shelley**'s other disc with the London Mozart Players takes good care of the E major Concerto, which has the subtitle "Les Adieux" and boasts one of Hummel's best slow movements (Chandos 9687); it's also included in "Romantic Piano Concertos" Vol. 1, with Hans Kahn at the keyboard (Vox 5064). Even more enjoyable on this disc is the early concerto for piano and violin, really a sinfonia concertante with a central theme-and-variations movement. Hagai Shaham partners Shelley stylishly—there's a good feeling of give-and-take between the soloists, and the orchestral support is alert.

CHAMBER MUSIC

Hummel's most played and recorded chamber piece is the Viola Sonata, an early work of classical ease and charm that crops up on many recital CDs. Two all-Hummel discs include superb performances: **Luigi Alberto Bianchi** and Aldo Orvieto use modern instruments and add three enjoyable works for violin and piano (Dynamic 192), and **Jodi Levitz** is partnered by Stefano Fiuzzi on a Graf fortepiano in a disc that includes the D major Flute Sonata, the Mandolin Sonata, and the best available performance of the Mandolin Concerto, with a small orchestra (Dynamic 128). **Ralph Holmes,** with Richard Burnett also playing a Graf fortepiano, spoils the Viola Sonata's effect by playing the violin arrangement, but makes amends by including the *Nocturne* Op. 99 and the mature D major Violin Sonata (Amon Ra 12).

Hummel's Cello Sonata, which comes from his later years, has been recorded several times, best by **Boris Pergamenschikov** on a fine all-Hummel disc that also features flutist András Adorján and pianist Pavel Gililov in music for flute, cello, and piano (Orfeo 252931). Four flute sonatas are elegantly played by **Adorján** and Noël Lee in the Erato "two-fer."

Hummel's piano trios are among his freshest inspirations, spanning much of his career and treating the cello a little more generously than those of Haydn or Mozart, though the F major ends with a *Rondo alla Turca* that sadly doesn't come up to the standard of Mozart's model. The best introduction is the sparkling program by the **Beaux Arts Trio,** which has four works including the first and the last, with its sprightly *Rondo alla Russia* (Philips 446077). Pressler's command of the piano is magical, the string playing is gorgeous without ever sounding too effusive, and the recordings are worthy of the interpretations. The **Borodin Trio**'s disc is even better recorded, which merely emphasizes the insensitive pianism and out-of-tune violin; a shame, as it includes the biggest trio, 5 in E, with its eloquent slow movement (Chandos 9529). For the whole set of seven, the **Parnassus Trio** can be confidently recommended, though the late 1980s recordings are slightly less clear; the playing is stylish, with pianist Friedemann Rieger at times almost matching Pressler (MD+G 303007, 2CD).

A disc from Italy includes an enjoyable performance of the E-flat Clarinet Quartet, which has a scherzo subtitled "The Nuisance" with each instrument playing in a different meter; **Fabrizio Meloni** is the clarinettist (Naxos 554280). This work is also included in a mixed disc by **Charles Neidich** and l'Archibudelli, but the playing, though virtuosic in its way, is dry in tone and style (Sony 57968). For Hummel's three string quartets, the only available disc is luckily a good one, the **Delmé Quartet** playing with style and purpose (Hyperion 66568). The works

Runnicles is a fine conductor for this opera, never pushing too hard, allowing the music and story to unfold naturally (♦Teldec 94549). Ziesak and Larmore are more than adequate, if not especially individual. Weikl brings his customary imagination to the father, but his voice has loosened considerably over the years and the vibrato now borders on an unsettling wobble. Behrens makes a believable mother; her voice sounds a little desperate, but she uses that to her advantage. Hanna Schwarz sings the Witch with aplomb and has fun with the part. The sound is good, but does not match EMI's achievement, let alone Philips's.

Pritchard's version was a winner in its day, but time has diminished its value (Sony). Cotrubas and Von Stade are excellent children, singing with full, healthy tone and conveying the right sort of high spirits. Nimsgern has the genial tone and delivery for the father. Söderström's Witch is memorable because her interpretation is so out of the norm. When I first heard her, I thought she was very dull—no extra cackles, no scream when she's pushed in the oven, etc. Hearing it again several years later, I find her illuminating and bewitching, and realize she doesn't need to add extra effects because she has mastered the art of "less is more." Ludwig was experiencing vocal difficulties when she made this recording, so her Mother sounds edgy and acerbic. Pritchard's conducting is of the house maestro variety: well-disciplined and efficient, but otherwise routine. The sound has been cleaned up considerably for the CD, but remains rather diffuse and murky.

Solti's version is an also-ran (London). It doesn't sound as if he likes this opera very much, at least on the basis of this recording. Tempos are slow and lifeless and there is almost no forward-moving energy. The cast is variable. Popp is good, but often sounds as if she's sight reading, and her top turns shrill under pressure. Fassbaender makes a much more memorable contribution with her chocolate-brown, occasionally unsteady instrument. Berry is a lovable, robust Father and Hamari is an apt partner. Anny Schlemm's unsteady vocalism and predictable characterization aren't out of the norm for the Witch (I've heard worse in the opera house), but they're inexcusable in a major studio production. The sound is good, with some extra atmospheric effects added, but overall this performance is a big disappointment.

Fortunately, one of the best of all performances has been remastered (♦RCA 25281). **Kurt Eichhorn** leads the opera with skill and imagination; he knows how to propel the music without slowing the pace in search of orchestral details. In the cast are four singers who set standards that others must (and rarely do) match. Ludwig was in prime voice for these sessions and not only sings the Witch with precision (the top B-flat at the end of the "Witch's Ride" is thrilling) but characterizes the role with a combination of comedy and menace that would have made Humperdinck smile with delight. She cited this as her favorite recorded performance, and it's easy to hear why. Fischer-Dieskau makes the most of the Father, and Donath captures Gretel's innocence without sounding coy, while singing with disarming ease and freshness. Popp brings such verve to her Dew Fairy song that you want to skip off with her. The others in the cast are good without being as memorable. The only criticism I have is that the voices were recorded too closely; hence the sound isn't atmospheric enough.

Suitner's performance isn't particularly distinguished, but it's pleasant and enjoyable (Berlin). It also has the only male Witch on CD, and Schreier does the role ample justice, with his accurate singing and amusing characterization. **Cluytens**'s set is still viable, but only if none of the other versions are around (EMI). Seefried is the splendid Hansel, Rothenberger a beautifully sung if under-characterized Gretel, and Cluytens sounds as if he'd rather be doing something else. The famous

Karajan performance is still with us and remains a fine account. His tempos are on the stately side, which only encourages Schwarzkopf to indulge herself with cutesy "little-girl" stuff, but I find her and Grümmer's singing beautiful. For those who are interested, there is a recorded performance with Schwarzkopf and Jurinac as the siblings under Karajan's direction made for Italian radio in 1954 and sung, naturally, in Italian (Stradivarius). They sound more spontaneous than in the studio recording.

There's a set in English that preserves an excellent evening at the Sydney Opera House circa 1992 (Legato). The Norman Kelley translation is very singable (the Met also uses it) and the cast sings and characterizes well, especially **Margaret Haggart** as the Witch. **Artur Rother**'s version from the early 1940s preserves Erna Berger's lovely Gretel and Margaret Arndt-Ober's exciting Witch. The conducting is swift and sure-footed and I recommend this performance to all who love old radio recordings (Preiser).

I'll end this survey with a plea that the old Sadlers Wells performance in English return to circulation. It had a wonderful cast, excellent conducting by **Bernardi,** and warm, atmospheric sound. The Constance Bach translation sounds a little dated now, but that only enhances the set's charm.

Königskinder. This has always been *Hansel und Gretel*'s poor stepsister. Elsa Bernstein-Porges's libretto is literate and well written, though it too often embraces the moralizing tone common to many of the Grimm folk tales. On the other hand, Humperdinck's music is very rich and moving. There have been several revivals in recent years, but I think this opera will always remain a specialty. It's difficult to stage; the plot requires a gaggle of geese who are an integral part of the action in Act I and singers with strong voices who'd probably rather be singing Wagner.

Fortunately, the opera has been lucky on record, though one of the best versions, conducted by **Heinz Wallberg,** is only available in the United States as an EMI import. Donath is convincing as the Goose Girl and Dallapozza sings the Prince with handsome tone. With singers like Schwarz, Prey, Unger, and Ridderbusch in the supporting cast, the opera is very well served. An equally fine set, under the leadership of **Fabio Luisi,** stars Dagmar Schellenberger and Thomas Moser as the lovers, both very convincing vocally and dramatically (♦Calig 50 968-70). The supporting cast is excellent, as is the conducting, and the sound is superb. The only disadvantage is that Calig hasn't bothered to provide a translation, a decided hindrance to comprehending the finer points of an often poetic and wordy text.

There's also an excellent performance from 1952 starring Peter Anders and **Fischer-Dieskau** (Gala). The sound is very good broadcast mono of the period. I wouldn't recommend it as a first choice (there is no libretto), but it makes a fine supplementary edition and preserves a touching performance, containing a few minor cuts (nothing damaging).   REYNOLDS

ORCHESTRAL MUSIC

Suites from *Hansel und Gretel* come and go. **Kempe**'s Seraphim LP, for one, seems to have disappeared and it's surprising that **Rickenbacher** only recorded the Overture (♦Virgin 91494, reissued in their budget line as 61128). But Rickenbacher offers far more rarified fare, especially the lovely suite from *Dornröschen* (Sleeping Beauty)—more pastel shaded and delicately scored than Tchaikovsky's. He also offers music from *Königskinder* and *Der blaue Vogel* (The Blue Bird). **Martin Fischer-Dieskau** (Dietrich's son) gives you *Sleeping Beauty* and the prelude to *Die Marketenderin* (The Canteen Woman), but the major offering is are attractive, with a few deeper moments in the C major, influenced by early Beethoven. There is a brilliant 1957 mono performance of the G major Quartet by the **Hollywood Quartet**, coupled with that group's only Haydn and Mozart recordings (Testament 1085).

Hummel's early E-flat Partita for wind octet isn't very interesting and hardly deserves to be as frequently recorded as it is. Two groups, the **Chamber Orchestra of Europe Soloists** (ASV 812) and **Albion Ensemble** (Hyperion 55037) do it justice. His two best large-scale chamber works, the D minor Septet and the C major 'Military' Septet, include the piano as well as strings and winds. You need look no further than the performances by the **Nash Ensemble** (CRD 3418); both pianists, Ian Brown and Clifford Benson, are excellent, their colleagues are exemplary, and the recordings are superbly transparent and airy.

Hummel's Piano Quintet, arranged from the D minor Septet, has a footnote in history because Schubert's "Trout" Quintet was based on its unusual instrumentation, with double bass instead of a second violin. Although most listeners will surely prefer the septet version, the quintet is worth hearing on its own terms. The delightful period instrument performance by **Hausmusik**, coupled with the "Trout," is NA but will probably resurface (Virgin). However, **Sestetto Classico** provides an equally enjoyable performance of the Hummel and couples it with an unusual sextet by Henri-George Jérôme (MD+G 3067). A version by the **Schubert Ensemble of London** operates at a lower voltage (Hyperion 22008) and one by mainly Italian soloists with **Michele Campanella** at the piano is nicely played but not well recorded (Dynamic 8).

A disc by the **Music Collection** offering neat performances of the Piano Quintet, Viola Sonata, and E-flat Trio Op. 12, is notable for Susan Alexander-Max's twinkling playing of two period pianos. The resonant acoustic can't hide the fact that the violinist has one or two anxious moments (ASV 210).

PIANO MUSIC

Hummel was the busiest exponent of the classical piano, his fingers continually racing up and down the keyboard and recalling Count Basie's laconic comment about Art Tatum: "He didn't like space." Hummel offered a type of pianism that was virtuosic but always elegant and within the limits of the instruments of the time—you can't imagine him breaking strings. He was able to write fluent counterpoint without ever sounding academic.

A good introduction is provided by **Shelley**, who includes the fine Sonata 2, dedicated to Haydn, and six miscellaneous works (Chandos 9807). **Danielle Laval** finds a most engaging impish quality in Sonata 5 and makes light of Hummel's magnificent set of 24 Etudes, in which he summed up a lifetime of piano playing. The studies look back to Bach (a memorable *fughetta*), Scarlatti, and Mozart (another dignified *fughetta* to end the set) but also forward to Chopin and Schumann (Auvidis 4667).

If you're interested in all six sonatas, **Hobson** proves a virtuosic, stylish guide; his first volume is as good a place to start as any, as it includes the first and last works, showing how Hummel achieved a weightier style without losing sight of his roots (Arabesque 6564/6). The final Allegro vivace of Sonata 6 is one of his most engaging pieces. An inexpensive option for Sonatas 2, 3, and 5 is by the excellent Korean pianist **Haewon Chang;** she's due to record the other three as well (Naxos 553296).

CHORAL MUSIC

Haydn chose Hummel as his successor as composer to Prince Esterházy and the finest result was the *Mass in E-flat*, probably written as his first offering to his patron. It ploughs the same furrow as Haydn's late masses and Beethoven's *Mass in C*, but not quite so deeply. A venerable EMI recording can now be set aside in favor of **Martin Haselböck**'s performance with the sonorous Czech Philharmonic Choir of Brno, the Wiener Akademie, and four good soloists (Koch Schwann 1779). The disc includes *Graduale* for choir and orchestra and the lovely *Offertorium* for soprano, clarinet and orchestra. The *Mass in B-flat* is less arresting and gets a less imposing performance from an American group led by **John Eric Floreen** (Koch 7117).

SONGS

Nine of Hummel's Scottish folksong settings, accompanied by various combinations of flute, violin, cello, and piano, are pleasantly performed by **Musicians of the Old Post Road,** a group from Boston using period instruments (including a fortepiano that may have been played by Hummel). Mezzo Pamela Dellal has limited expressive means and her words aren't always clear, but the texts (four by Burns, one by Scott) are printed in the booklet. The disc, which also includes the F major Piano Trio with the Turkish rondo and Variations for Flute, Cello, and Piano, makes for relaxing listening and is well recorded (Meridian 84404).

POTTER

Engelbert Humperdinck (1854–1921)

Humperdinck is one of those one-hit opera composers who, like Mascagni, Leoncavallo, and Cilea, received overnight fame that wasn't durable. Try as he might, he was unable to recapture the public's imagination after the success of *Hansel und Gretel*, although his *Königskinder* was a success at its premiere at the Metropolitan Opera in 1910.

Hansel und Gretel. This opera premiered in Weimar in 1893 and was soon heard around the world. It was considered the ideal introduction to opera for children, though it's too long for most children to sit through without squirming and most of them aren't ready to appreciate its gorgeous orchestration and vivid counterpoint. Its critical designation as "kiddie art" has mercifully diminished over the years and performers now approach the score with more respect. It's not the easy work many people expect. The vocal lines require full operatic voices capable of singing easily within two octaves and riding over a dense orchestration. It's an enchanting opera that rewards repeated listening.

It has been fortunate in its recordings over the years, and most of the best are still available. Three of the most recent versions are quite splendid in different ways. **Jeffrey Tate** sets up a formidable challenge (♦EMI 54022). Von Otter and Bonney are fresh-voiced children, able to suggest youth without sounding condescending or cute. Hanna Schwarz and Andreas Schmidt are appropriate parents for these scamps, and Hendricks and Eva Lind are good as the Sandman and Dew Fairy. Lipovšek was a last minute replacement for Baltsa the Witch, and this is one case where Providence dealt a good hand. She sings superbly without overdoing anything and yet manages to sound sly, funny, and frightening all at the same time. The sound is excellent and Tate's direction keeps things moving.

Colin Davis's version originally came with a jigsaw puzzle in the box, though that has been deleted now (♦Philips 438013). If that weren't enticing enough, there's the sound, which is diaphanous, with every strand and texture expressed with crystalline clarity. On the whole the cast is good. Gruberová and Murray sing with precision and musicality, but sound staid next to other pairs of children. Ludwig remains a distinguished Witch, though her voice is no longer capable of the high notes and cackle that so enhanced her earlier performance for Kurt Eichhorn. Davis leads with correctness and energy. This is a "grown-up" version that makes good supplementary listening without being a first choice.

Humperdinck's *Moorish Rhapsody,* a lush, atmospheric set of picture postcards of Tarifa and Tangiers closer to *Schéherazade* than *Escales.* Unfortunately, Fischer-Dieskau omits nearly half the last movement, so you'll have to settle for the aged mono recording by **Hermann Abendroth** (Arlecchino 128).

If you're lucky enough to find **Swarowsky**'s CD, even in mono his suites from *Hansel und Gretel, Sleeping Beauty* and *Königskinder* disarm all criticism (♦Urania 5175); avoid the horrid-sounding Tuxedo ripoff (1054). You'll also want **Rickenbacher**'s magical and evocative Shakespeare Suites, originally written for Max Reinhardt's Berlin productions, filled out with the Overture to *Die Heirat wider Willen* (Dumas *père*) and the carefree *Humoreske* (♦Koch Schwann 1197). Surely no one could ever come away from this music still thinking of Humperdinck as a "one note" composer.   HALLER

Karel Husa (b. 1921)

Czech by birth, Parisian by training, an American since 1954, Husa followed the same peregrination as Martinů before him. As a child of the '20s, however, his music has taken a more thorny path. Beginning in the middle of WWII, he followed the lead of his teacher, Honegger, writing pessimistic, darkly ominous music sometimes recalling Bartók in mood and Czech folk music in its melodic and rhythmic outlines. This period culminated in the early '50s, with the powerful String Quartet 2 and the apocalyptic Symphony 1. Both works seem to swirl around looking for a place to light, finally converging on a bare octave, which his later Cornell students dubbed the Husa-tonic. His music of the 60s became more abstract in tonality and more overtly social (*Music for Prague,* 1968, *Apotheosis of this Earth,* 1971).

A teacher at Cornell since 1954 and an outstanding conductor, Husa has not been prolific as a composer and his catalog is a bit padded with rearrangements of previously conceived materials. His relatively small output is full of character, however; from his arrangements of Czech folk tunes to the mighty *Apotheosis,* he's a composer with a strong personality and a clear and colorful style. He has been the recipient of numerous awards, including a Pulitzer prize for String Quartet 3.

Symphonies No. 1 is an early but powerful work in which Czech rhythmic twists recalling Martinů are surrounded by Honeggerian counterpoint and struggle to escape. Finally, everything is overtaken by a wave of brass chorales, ending on a powerful unison. The performance by **Husa** with the Prague Symphony is effective, though its dynamic range is a little compressed (CRI 592). No. 2 (1983) is a deliberate contrast to 1, written for a Beethoven-sized orchestra with double winds and at least partially pastoral in nature. It's relatively unthreatening and written to be played by college orchestras like the Bowling Green Philharmonia that has recorded it under **Emily Brown** (Albany 321).

Other orchestral music. *Fantasies for Orchestra* is evocative and original. It's conducted by **Husa** with a Paris orchestra that plays well but isn't very precise in the rhythms of the "Capriccio" (Phoenix 128). *Mosaïques for Orchestra* (1961) is a more abstract suite of colorful pictures, played by the Stockholm Radio Symphony, also led by the composer (CRI 592).

Music for Prague is Husa's best-known work at present, a dramatic piece written in reaction to the 1986 "Prague Spring" and evoking the famous melody Smetana used to represent the warriors of Jan Hus. You can positively hear the dead arising from under Blanik Hill in this stirring call to arms. The original band piece can be heard in two fine versions, one by **Donald Hunsberger** and the redoubtable Eastman Wind Ensemble

(Sony 44916), and a more impressively recorded performance by **Husa** and the Temple University Wind Symphony that really brings the warriors into your living room (♦Albany 271). The orchestral version is played by the Martinů Symphony under **Miloš Machek** (Vienna 3023). None of the couplings seem particularly relevant to either Husa or Prague except for a disc by the Slovak Radio Symphony under **Barry Kolman** (Marco Polo 223640, NA, with Symphony 2 and *Frescoes*).

The Trojan Women is a ballet relating the story of the fall of Troy in a way that reminds the composer of the razing of Lidice by the Nazis, also commemorated by Martinů. A half-hour suite is presented by the Brno State Orchestra conducted by **Husa** in a strongly emotional reading (Phoenix 128). *Concerto for Wind Ensemble* is a concerto in the same way as Bartók's Concerto for Orchestra: Everyone gets a lot to do but there is no official soloist, so it gets listed here rather than under concertos. It shows a lightness of texture that allows the exposure of everyone's talents. The Cincinnati Wind Symphony under **Mallory Thompson** plays it with enthusiasm and the recording is excellent (Summit 192). This CD begins with *Smetana Fanfare,* a four-minute band piece celebrating the centennial of Smetana's death and quoting from his *Wallenstein's Camp.* It's impressive, though Smetana might have been disturbed at being surrounded by the sounds of the 20th century.

Les Couleurs fauves is an attempt to reproduce Husa's impressions of the wild color effects of the French Fauvist school of painters. Played with style by the New England Conservatory Wind Ensemble, it's conducted by the man who led the Ithaca High School band in the '50s when I was at school there, **Frank Battisti** (Albany 340).

Concertos. There are several works for soloists and orchestra or wind band. The earliest recorded is the *Elegie et Rondeau* for alto sax and band, available in a fine program of American concertos in a disc dedicated to the memory of the great saxophonist, Sigurd Rascher, played by **Lawrence Gwozdz** with the Martinů Orchestra under Kirk Trevor (Albany 331). This is a short but exciting piece with a lot of energy, played with virtuosity.

The Serenade for woodwinds, strings, harp, and xylophone is a recasting of a strange three-movement chamber work, *Evocations de Slovakie,* for clarinet, viola, and cello—an improvisatory, rather wild piece. It makes a good impression in a performance by the Prague Symphony with **Husa** (CRI 592). A version with piano replacing the strings, xylophone, and harp is played rather lethargically by the Westwood Wind Quintet with pianist **Lisa Bergman** (Crystal 751).

There are several concertos, for alto saxophone, percussion, and trumpet, all with band. The sax and percussion works were played and recorded well in an American band series by the Michigan State Wind Symphony under **Stanley de Rusha** (Golden Crest LP 5066, NA, with *Al Fresco,* an arrangement of a powerful '40s orchestral work).

Chamber music. Husa's series of string quartets traces his development as a composer. No. 1 is in his private mixture of Czech rhythms and Honeggerian gloom, once available in a good reading by the **Alard Quartet** (Leonarda LP 117, NA). No. 2 is a strongly thematic piece, building in rhythmic grandeur; no. 3 is more abstract in material, building up a number of exciting climaxes over its four movements. Both are played by the old **Fine Arts Quartet** with immediacy and drama (Phoenix 113). No. 4 ("Poems") is more relaxed but still relatively eventful. The **Colorado Quartet** plays its six movements with involvement and precision (Albany 259).

Evocations de Slovakie is a curiously disturbing work, improvisatory but also tightly knit thematically. There's a bit of Klezmer in the clarinet writing and some rather drunken dancing in spots. It's nicely played by the **Long Island Chamber Ensemble** (Phoenix 113). *Divertimento* for brass and percussion is an arrangement of four movements from *Eight Czech Duets*, originally written for piano four-hands. These are pungent pieces in folk style, recalling the way Bartók set folk tunes, and are conducted with style by **Lawrence Sobol** (Phoenix 128).

Chamber works made up an increasing proportion of Husa's works in the '70s. His ambitious Violin Sonata is a 35-minute blockbuster, tonally abstract but curiously haunting, played to the hilt by **Elmar Oliveira** and David Oei (New World 80493).

Landscapes for brass quintet is an ambitious, demanding three movements building long-range climaxes and holding together fragmentary motives over an 18-minute span. The **Western Quintet** plays it with conviction (CRI 592).

Sonata a Tre is a commission from the **Verdehr Trio**, consisting of violin, clarinet, and piano. It's a virtuoso piece requiring a number of contemporary playing techniques, and the dedicatees play it well (Crystal 744). *Variations for Piano Quartet* is a 20-minute piece in which the variations are more about sound than theme; the pianist spends a good deal of time twanging on the strings, to great effect. It has been recorded by one of the three commissioning groups, the **New England Piano Quartette** (Orion LP 86498, NA).

Piano music. Husa's official Opus 1 is a Sonatina for piano, written in 1943 in Prague, before he studied with Honegger and Nadia Boulanger. It shows an early form of the Czech material that comes back to his style even now. His Sonata 1 is a large work showing the serious nature of his muse. Both of these and an *Elegy* recalling material from his orchestral *Fantasies* were once available in a disc by **Mary Ann Covert**, also including Sonata 2, in musical readings, technically a little under par (Golden Crest LP 4175, NA). The dramatic and abstract 2 (1975) is available in a fine recording and performance by **Peter Basquin** (New World 80493).

Songs. The only vocal music presently available is a setting of 12 *Moravian Songs*, sung by rich-voiced soprano **Barbara Martin**, accompanied by Elizabeth Rodgers. These works show Husa surrounding folk material with his world of harmonies and instrumental colors. It's a revealing introduction to his style (New World 80493).   MOORE

Jacques Ibert (1890–1962)

The colorful orchestral suite *Escales* (Ports of Call) made Ibert famous, but he's a more interesting figure than that travel-posterish work would indicate. Consider his second most popular orchestral piece, *Divertissement*, which out-Six'es *Les Six* in good-natured cabaret rowdiness, or his witty *Hommage à Mozart*, or the excellent craftsmanship of *Bostoniana* (the only completed movement of a symphony he was writing for the Boston Symphony at the time of his death), or the dissonant, densely contrapuntal *Symphonie Concertante* for oboe and strings.

Dutoit provides an excellent portrait of Ibert (♦London 440332): a sumptuous performance of *Escales;* a brilliant reading by Timothy Hutchins of the popular Flute Concerto, the zany *Paris* suite (including a very funny send-up of a high-society restaurant band), the galumphing *Bacchanale*, and the spruce neoclassicism of *Bostoniana* and *Louisville-concert* (Ibert had excellent relations with American orchestras). *Divertissement* is missing, but Dutoit separately gives an elegant big-band performance of that piece (London 421527).

As a conductor's showpiece, *Escales* has been recorded by some showy conductors. **Munch**'s performance with the Boston Symphony is famous (RCA 61500); **Ormandy**'s with the Philadelphia Orchestra in its prime is even better, coupled with a surprisingly pointed *Divertissement* (♦Sony 62644). **Paray** is also enjoyable, though not everyone enjoys the 1950s "Living Presence" sound (Mercury 432003). **Martinon** (one of his last recordings) is coupled with two Ibert rarities, *Ouverture de Fête* and *Tropismes pour les amours imaginaires* (EMI 64276). **Fiedler**'s is one of the most delightful *Divertissements* (♦RCA 61429, coupled most appropriately with Offenbach's *Gaité Parisienne*). **Tortelier**'s performance is also fun, and the couplings are ideal for someone who wants a cross-section of early 20th-century ballet Parisian style: Poulenc's *Les Biches* and Milhaud's *Création du monde* and *Le Boeuf sur le toit* (♦Chandos 9023). Martinon's *Divertissement* is also highly regarded, and along with Tortelier's, is one of the few recordings by a French conductor of what seems a quintessentially Parisian piece (London 448571, with French "pops" by Bizet and Saint-Saëns).

Ibert sounds more like Honegger or Bartók than Offenbach in his *Symphonie Concertante*, which is coupled by John de Lancie and **Previn** with Françaix's deliciously lightweight oboe concerto *L'horloge de flores* (♦RCA 7989, also including Strauss's oboe concerto). The acidly lyrical Concerto for Cello and Wind Instruments is persuasively done by **James Kreger** and Steven Richman (Music & Arts 649, a "Salute to France" that includes Ibert's *Paris* suite in the congenial company of works by Hahn, Milhaud, and Poulenc), and by **Nathaniel Rosen** and Richard Auldon Clark (Newport 85598). This disc contains more Ibert: a good version of the zany *Concertino da Camera* with Gary Louie and a performance of *Symphonie Concertante* with stylish playing from oboist Bert Lucarelli and unacceptably scratchy playing from the Manhattan Chamber Orchestra strings.

Many saxophonists have tried the jazzy *Concertino da Camera* (wonderfully scored for a mere 11 instruments); of the current recordings other than Louie's, the bargain-priced **John Harle** is the most interesting, coupled with all sorts of interesting saxophone pieces from Glazunov to Dave Heath (♦EMI 72109). Ibert's Flute Concerto has also been recorded often. Oddly, there are no recordings currently available by Rampal or Galway; however, **Eugenia Zukerman** sounds just fine, as does **Manuela Wiesler**, coupled with equally urbane and pleasing rarities by Chaminade, Françaix, and Mouquet (BIS 529).

Fans of such 20th-century raids on the musical past as Respighi's *Ancient Airs and Dances* should try Ibert's *Suite Elisabethaine*—incidental music for a Parisian production of *A Midsummer Night's Dream* that included arrangements of Byrd, Blow, and Purcell alongside Ibert originals. **Richard Auldon Clark** presents it in a collection of familiar Ibert works including the Flute Concerto (with Eugenia Zukerman) and *Divertissement* (Newport 85531). A conductor known simply as **Adriano** includes it in a collection of unknown Ibert, including a tone poem based on Wilde's *Ballad of Reading Gaol* (Marco Polo 223508). Adriano also offers two delicious ballet scores, *Diane de Poitiers* and *La Licorne* (Marco Polo 223854), and a selection of Ibert's film scores (Marco Polo 223287). (Ibert's score for *Don Quichotte* starred the great Russian bass Fyodor Chaliapin.)

Ibert's chamber music is voluminous and varied. Every piece seems to be for a different combination of instruments, and most of them are short and sweet—or sometimes tart (you can get the works on ♦Olympia 468 and 469). The most popular chamber work is probably the jolly *Trois Pièces Brèves*, a staple of the wind quintet repertoire; besides the Olympia disc, it can be heard on Kontrapunkt 32202 (with other Ibert chamber music involving the flute); Adés 203462 (more Ibert, including his only String Quartet); and Chandos 6543 (an **Athena Ensemble** collection with compatible couplings by Gounod and Poulenc).   RAYMOND

Andrew Imbrie (b. 1921)

Imbrie's *oeuvre* is small compared to many recent composers, but even cursory listening reveals that he is a consummate craftsman whose music is painstakingly realized. Although perhaps best known as a teacher, he's a learned composer whose studies with Sessions are evidenced by his superb grasp of form and long, arching phrases, which Sessions termed "the long line." Each gesture and line is flawlessly worked out with complete integrity to the whole. He has avoided compositional movements and fads, and is difficult to categorize. His music is usually tonal, though dissonant, and it's easily recognized as American.

It's disappointing that there are so few recordings of Imbrie's orchestral music. Of his three symphonies, only 3 is currently available. It's a striking, colorful work, high-spirited and energetic. **Harold Farberman** leads the London Symphony in a fine realization (♦CRI 632). This valuable disc includes two excellent chamber works: Serenade for Flute, Viola, and Piano and the sweeping Cello Sonata.

Concertos have been a major interest for Imbrie; he has composed several, including three for piano and one each for violin, cello, and flute. Regrettably, only Piano Concerto 3 is currently available. It receives a committed reading from **Alan Feinberg,** with able support from George Rothman and New York's Riverside Symphony (♦Bridge 9091). This is coupled with Imbrie's *Requiem,* a large work for orchestra, chorus, and soprano soloist. He combines texts from the traditional requiem mass with settings of poems by Blake, Donne, and Herbert.

Imbrie's chamber music is better represented. His string quartets are central to his corpus, but of his five, only 4 and 5 are available. They receive exceptional performances from the **Pro Arte Quartet** and are strongly recommended for anyone unfamiliar with his music (♦GM 2052). This disc includes a wonderful performance of *Impromptu* for violin and piano, another of his finest works; the recording is vivid and warm, the performances beyond reproach. The **Emerson Quartet** has also released a fine recording of Quartet 4 in a compilation with other American composers (New World 80453), but their version is somewhat dry in comparison to the Pro Arte.

Parnassus has recorded a superb disc of chamber and vocal works under the direction of **Anthony Korf.** This highly recommended collection includes *Dream Sequence* for winds, piano, and strings, *Five Roethke Songs, Three Piece Suite* for harp and piano, *Campion Songs* for vocal quartet, and *To a Traveler* for clarinet, violin, and piano (New World 80441). The vocal settings are stunning, the words always placed in sharp relief, with elegant and restrained accompaniment. The instrumental pieces are colorful and highly atmospheric and show a wide range of expression. They are fairly accessible, but with challenging qualities.

Imbrie's Piano Trio 2 is a highly expressive essay in what is generally thought of as a 19th-century medium. The **Francesco Trio** has had a long association with Imbrie and it shows in every measure of their stunning recording of this work (♦Music & Arts 756, with trios by Morgan Powell, Harbison, and Lalo Schifrin). *Pilgrimage* is another notable chamber work, a striking sextet for woodwinds, strings, piano, and percussion. It sounds as if it's played by a much larger group because the woodwinds each double on more than one instrument, and because Imbrie balances each voice exquisitely. **Gunther Schuller** leads an elegant reading of this luminous work (♦GM 2019). McINTIRE

Vincent d'Indy (1851–1931)

D'Indy's artistic journey was a common one for a 19th-century composer who lived well into the 20th. One of Franck's adoring pupils,

d'Indy was also interested in "the music of the future," visiting Liszt and becoming a perfect Wagnerite. (That influence is clearly seen in his opera *Fervaal,* often described as "the French *Parsifal.*") But after WWI he lightened his musical palette, writing "neoclassical" orchestral and chamber music, much of it very pleasing. In between, he established himself as a formidable teacher, founding the Schola Cantorum in 1894, writing a four-volume course in composition and biographies of Beethoven and Franck, and editing operas by Monteverdi, Rameau, and Gluck. A dominating figure in French music at the turn of the century, he was nearly forgotten after his death, but is a better and more enjoyable composer than that fate would suggest.

D'Indy's most popular work is his celebrated *Symphony on a French Mountain Air,* a very attractive conflation of piano concerto and symphony. The "mountain air" is a catchy tune from his native Cévennes; he rings imaginative melodic changes on it and there's a fair amount for a virtuoso pianist to do. A piece worth hearing more often, it's usually taken up by French pianists like **Nicole Henriot-Schweizer** (♦RCA), **Thiollier** (♦Naxos 550754) and **Catherine Collard** (♦Erato 45821). Henriot-Schweizer's performance is exciting; Munch's power and energy (and the brash RCA recording) are not as misplaced here as they are in more delicate French music. Collard, with Janowski, is also recommendable, and the CD contains an ambitious D'Indy rarity, the symphonic triptych *Jour d'été à la Montagne* (a French counterpart to Strauss' *Alpine Symphony,* only shorter and without the 12 horns). Thiollier's performance with de Almeida (coupled with Franck's *Symphonic Variations,* which d'Indy would have appreciated, and Fauré's *Ballade,* which he probably wouldn't) is every bit as good as the others, and a great bargain.

Symphony on a French Mountain Air is the closest d'Indy comes to the standard repertory, but anyone fond of late-Romantic orchestral music will find plenty to enjoy in this composer's output. His Symphony 2 ranks high among French late-Romantic works, and he wrote many other picturesque orchestral works. Monteux's old San Francisco Symphony recording of Symphony 2 has been reissued; the performance is persuasive, but the mono sound dull and faded (RCA 61888, with *French Mountain Air* and Prelude to *Fervaal*). Monteux also recorded d'Indy's imaginative *Istar Variations,* in which the variations come before the theme; it's available with the same caveat (RCA 61900).

A very useful coupling is Symphony 2 conducted by **Plasson** with *French Mountain Air* with Ciccolini and **Baudo** (EMI 63952). There's a very good modern performance and recording led by **DePreist** (♦Koch 7280). It's paired with *Souvenirs,* d'Indy's homage to his first wife, a rich, deeply felt suite that has also been recorded by **Guschlbauer** (Valois 4686, with Symphony 3) and **Gilles Nopre** (Marco Polo 223654, with incidental music to *Medée* and *Karadec*). The lighter touch of the post-WWI d'Indy is delectably present in the *Diptyque Méditerranéen* (♦EMI 63954) and in a triple concerto for flute, cello, and piano, once on an Erato LP with **Rampal** et al. but unfortunately NA. **Prêtre's** recording of *Diptyque* includes *Poème des Rivages,* a sort of conservative answer to *La Mer* in its evocations of water, wind, and light (EMI 63954).

D'Indy's chamber music is even more rarely recorded than his orchestral music. Both string quartets are acceptably performed by the **Kodàly Quartet** (Marco Polo 223140). Another disc gathers good performances of three of his most substantial and atmospheric chamber works by the **New Budapest Quartet** and pianist Ilona Prunyi: Piano Trio 2 , String Quartet 2, and Sextet (Auvidis 4678). RAYMOND

Mikhail Ippolitov-Ivanov (1859–1935)

We're accustomed to thinking of Ippolitov-Ivanov in terms of lush sonorities and lavish use of quasi-Oriental color and rhythm, based on the familiar *Caucasian Sketches,* yet he lived well into the 1930s and thus helped bridge the gap between the Tsarist and Bolshevik eras. We may be thankful that in recent years a number of enterprising labels have expanded beyond stereotype to offer a wider range of possibilities.

Symphony 1. Those who know only *Caucasian Sketches* will find little of such effusive display in Symphony 1 (actually, it's his only symphony). Written several years later, which, in its wealth of melody and almost stifling adherence to classical form, sounds like a much earlier effort. Given the restless dotted rhythm of the opening movement and the vigorous final Allegro, there seems to be no need for a conductor; nevertheless **Gary Brain** (♦Conifer 51317) finds in the piece an unflagging energy that quite escapes **Choo Hoey** (Marco Polo), who lopes along good-naturedly (perhaps trying to make this unassuming fare seem more important than it really is) while the unfortunate imbalance between the splendid Singapore winds and the rather less winsome strings is most clearly evident in the final movement.

Caucasian Sketches. Everyone knows the first set of *Caucasian Sketches,* or at least the "Procession of the Sardar," which is often played separately. But he actually wrote two such suites; the second, compiled two years later, reflects the composer's fascination with the ancient kingdom of Iveria, neighbor to Colchis, the land of the Golden Fleece. Rooted more in nationalism than the fanciful images that make up the first suite, *Iveria* concludes with a bracing "Caucasian War March" every bit as stirring as its far better known counterpart. As it happens, Naxos is competing with themselves, offering both suites with the Ukrainian Symphony under **Arthur Fagen** (♦553405) and also with **Christopher Lyndon Gee** (Marco Polo 220369). Both favor expansive tempos for the most part; however, Fagen manages to make it all work where Gee merely sounds tired. And though Gee's Sydney players are earnest enough, they don't have this music in their hearts and souls like Fagen's Ukrainian musicians. The one problem is the "Procession of the Sardar," which both conductors take much too slowly; however, in all other respects, including sound, Fagen is the one to buy.

Those seeking only the first set of *Sketches* will find a far more varied selection to choose from. Pick of the litter is the splendid recording by **Tjeknavorian,** with its exhilarating splashes of color and well-nigh ideally chosen tempos (ASV 773). What a pity, then, that ASV took the easy way out and filled out the disc with the standard assortment of Khachaturian (*Gayne, Spartacus, Masquerade*). Close behind—though harder to find, perhaps—is an alert, richly colored account by **Gerhardt** (Menuet 160002). Color is what's missing from the bland, uninvolved reading by **Zinman,** while the engineers must have had an off day as well (Telarc).

Fedor Glushchenko offers what may be the slowest version ever set to disc, culminating in what sounds more like the Sardar's funeral procession (Chandos); in fact he takes over a minute longer than Fagen's sluggish account. On the other hand, the fastest "Sardar" ever must surely be **Rozhdestvensky**'s (Revelation 10073), of greater interest perhaps for what may be the only Russian recording of the Stokowski arrangement of *Pictures at an Exhibition.* It's a little on the raw side, but nowhere near as unrefined as **Fedoseyev,** coupled with Arensky's Piano Concerto and *Egyptian Nights* (Olympia). The much underrated **Abravanel** does very well with the suite (Vanguard SVC 8 or the earlier midpriced 5010).

Mtzyri. This is a symphonic poem, written some 20 years after the Symphony when the then 70-year-old composer was still in full command of his coloristic skills. It's based on a long narrative poem by Lermontov about a homesick lay brother who flees the monastery but dies following an attack by a panther. Until Melodiya reissues **Fuat Mansurov**'s LP (ASD 2640), **Gary Brain** will do very nicely (Conifer 513517, with the Symphony); indeed, there's little to choose between the two, save that Mansurov omits the solo soprano part.

Armenian Rhapsody. This is also included on **Brain**'s Conifer CD, as well as in a survey conducted by **Johanos** (Marco Polo 223629), and again both performances are worth having, especially since the other pieces on the Marco Polo disc aren't readily available elsewhere. Of these, pride of place goes to the suite *From Songs of Ossian,* the legendary Celtic hero who inspired many other composers including Mendelssohn (*Fingal's Cave*). The *Spring Overture* ("Yar-khmel") celebrates the euphoria that greets the long-awaited Russian spring, while *Episode from the Life of Schubert* is based in large part on the great C Major Quintet though stylistically it seems closer to Glazunov. *Symphonic Scherzo* and the blatantly jingoistic *Jubilee March* complete a fascinating package.

Turkish Fragments and *Turkish March.* Both of these pieces reflect the composer's great interest in the folk music of this region and once again will remind you of *Caucasian Sketches.* As in Symphony 1 (with which they are coupled in Marco Polo 220217) **Hoey**'s Singapore players acquit themselves well but can't match **Fagen** and the Ukrainian Symphony (Naxos 553405, with *Sketches*). HALLER

John Ireland (1879–1962)

Ireland is a distinctive English voice in 20th-century music. He taught at the Royal College of Music for 15 years, where his pupils included Britten and Moeran. He was influenced first by German Romantic and then French Impressionist styles. His later music combines the harmonic invention of the Impressionists with characteristically English modal melodies. It's traditional without being in any way conventional, and although the influence of the French school is clear, his music is simpler and more direct. His catalog begins in 1903 with *Songs of a Wayfarer,* and he's best known for his songs and piano pieces, which for many years were a staple of English music. He wrote only about a dozen orchestral works.

The songs span a wide range of subject matter and emotions. Many express a passionate inner nature, very much in contrast with Ireland's apparently uneventful life. The critic William Mann described them as "perhaps the most important [English songs] between Purcell and Britten." The texts are by Hardy, Rossetti, Masefield, Stevenson, and Housman, to name only the most famous, and the songs are precise settings that capture the moods of the poems.

An extensive collection runs 2½ hours and includes most of the solo songs, with **Lisa Milne,** Ainsley, and Christopher Maltman, accompanied by Graham Johnson (Hyperion 67261/2, 2CD). The performances are generally good, but Maltman's sense of pitch is weak. **Shirley-Quirk** and Eric Parkin give passionate, sensitive, and convincing readings of 20 songs—five to poems by Thomas Hardy, the six *Songs Sacred and Profane,* and nine others (Saga 3338).

Ireland composed piano music throughout his career. His early popular success, *Decorations* (1912), draws heavily on Debussy's Preludes for its harmonies and chromatic runs. The 1918-1920 Sonata, by contrast, is far more original and inventive. **Parkin,** who is a specialist in Ireland's music and worked closely with the composer to develop his interpretations, has recorded a large selection of the solo piano works (Chandos 9056, 9140, 9250). His playing is fine and well recorded, and he's attentive to detail. **Desmond Wright** offers a number of short piano pieces including *London Pieces* and Preludes; his playing is unimaginative, stiff, and dry (Classics for Pleasure).

John Lenehan's series includes Ireland's last piano works: the triptych *Sarnia* and *Columbine* from 1949 (Naxos 553700 and 553889). He handles this music very well, effectively conveying its lyrical and romantic qualities as well as its drama.

Ireland himself made a few recordings, including his two violin sonatas, 1 with **Frederick Grinke** and an excellent 2 from 1930 with **Sammons** (Dutton 7103). The complete music for violin and piano has been collected by **Paul Barritt** and Catherine Edwards (Hyperion 66853). In addition to the two sonatas, this disc contains four short pieces: *Berceuse* and *Cavatina,* both early works, the later *Bagatelle,* and an unpublished arrangement of *The Holy Boy* (originally for piano solo) from 1919. These musicians are competent and the sound quality is superior, but the composer's own recording is more spirited and therefore preferable.

A set of chamber works with piano features **Mordkovitch,** violin, with Karine Georgian, cello, and Ian Brown, piano, in the two violin sonatas and three piano trios, and de Peyer, clarinet, in *Fantasy Sonata* (Chandos 9377/8, 2CD). Mordkovitch's showy, extroverted style is inappropriate here and occasionally threatens to overwhelm these pieces; de Peyer, on the other hand, displays an affinity for Ireland's music. On balance, this is a successful collection, but Ireland's own recordings of the sonatas are certainly preferable. The two string quartets are performed by the **Holywell Ensemble** as part of their series of Ireland's chamber works for strings (ASV 1017). These enthusiastic performances are sometimes marred by poor intonation.

The Piano Concerto is a neglected masterpiece. Completed in 1930, it was first recorded in 1942 by the great British pianist **Eileen Joyce** (Dutton 8001). It has also been recorded by **Parkin** (Chandos 8461) and **Stott** (Conifer 15007). Joyce's is easily the best performance of the three, and Dutton's transfers from shellac 78s are very clear.

Ireland's most famous work for orchestra is the *London Overture* of 1936. It was recorded by Hickox in a solid collection of symphonic and choral works (Chandos 7074). This disc also features the young Terfel as soloist in the motet "Greater love hath no man" and "These things shall be," written for the coronation of George VI.   GEFFEN

Jānis Ivanovs (1906–1983)

This major Latvian composer, with 20 symphonies to his credit, is little known outside his native country. Happily, Campion has undertaken the recording of his orchestral works. Stylistically close to Prokofiev and Shostakovich, Ivanovs's music is rich-textured, largely tonal, melodic, with long-lined, soaring melodies, and is deeply rooted in Latvian folk music.

SYMPHONIES

1 ("Poema-Sinfonia") is a short work showing Russian influences. The three-movement *Latgalian Landscapes* expresses the beauty of the region of the composer's birth. A 1980 performance by **Sinaisky** is coupled with Symphony 2, in fine performances with somewhat over-reverberant sound (Cameo 2008).

2 and *3* are given fine performances by **Dimitri Yablonsky** (Marco Polo 223331). For 2, Ivanovs took Franck's D minor Symphony as his model. 3 shows influences of Tchaikovsky and Scriabin—the deeply felt An-

dante is based on Latvian folk songs, while the short Allegro glances at Liadov's *Kikimora*. The sonics are somewhat dry on this recording, lacking spaciousness.

4, 52 minutes long, was inspired by writings on Atlantis, including Plato. In the second movement, a vocalizing female chorus sings the praise of Poseidon in a style reminiscent of Holst's "Neptune" in *The Planets.* 4 often sounds like movie music and its frequent brassy fortissimos border on bombast. **Sinaisky** provides a fine performance and sonics, coupled with a ravishing symphonic poem, *Rainbow,* in which Ivanovs turns impressionist for harmonies and colors (Campion 2007).

5 and *12* ("Sinfonia Energica") are also performed by **Yablonsky** (Marco Polo 223332). The dramatic, dark-hued, near-expressionist 5 looks back at the horrors of WWII. 12 celebrates energy and determination in fast and slow sections. Unlike 2 and 3, the melodies of 5 and 12 are austere and angular, with 12 spiced with polytonality and linear polyphony. Fine performances but dry sonics.

11 (coupled with the expressive Andante for cello ensemble), *17* (with the symphonic poem *The Bear Ripper*), *18, 19,* and *20* (coupled with his last opus, *Novella brevis* for brass ensemble), and the Piano Concerto (coupled with the Violin Concerto) are still on Melodiya LPs.

OTHER MUSIC

The superbly lyrical Violin Concerto (1951) draws on Latvian folk melodies and was recorded by Latvian violinist **Valdis Zariņš** (Campion 2004, with the Sallinen and Sibelius concertos). Twelve of Ivanovs's wonderfully satisfying a cappella works are on a Latvian CD (Grindex 9505), coupled with the expressive *Symphony for Choir* by another fine Latvian composer, Pēteris Plakidis, with **Imants Kokars** leading the Latvian Ave Sol Chamber Choir. This release may be obtained from importers.   DE JONG

Charles Ives (1874–1954)

Ives still ranks as the most original maverick among us. Even his student pieces are full of characteristic touches. Though he was famous for dissonant music, now, at the other end of his century, we see that the clashes increase the poignance of the consonant melodies they surround. Sadly, he burned out in the early 1920s, just when dissonance was coming into power.

SYMPHONIES

1. The four symphonies span Ives's working life. The first was his graduation piece from Yale, where he studied with Horatio Parker, an outstanding romantic composer who tried to imbue young Ives with a proper respect for the classics. Love for the classics he had; respect was another matter. The symphony begins with a movement in sonata form, complete with an exposition repeat, but by the time it comes Ives has given us so much of the B theme that we aren't sure we can stand it again. **Neeme Järvi** takes the repeat (Chandos 9053) while **Tilson Thomas** does not (♦Sony 44939). If, as they say, the devil is in the details, Thomas wins hands down despite the omission, since he and the Sony engineers manage to clarify the details better than Chandos's cavernous sound will allow. Those who have **Morton Gould**'s earlier rendition for RCA (reissued in their import "Classical Navigator" series) should be warned that they are not in possession of the entire work: he made a couple of cuts. There's that devil again!

2. This is one of the first pieces Ives wrote after completing his studies; in fact, it includes a slow movement originally intended for 1 but omitted because Parker thought it didn't work. This is an important piece, in which romanticism meets the new forces of the 20th century and ultimately succumbs, but with no loss of face. Despite that ghastly dissonant thwack at the end, what we love in this symphony are those gorgeous romantic themes, some by Ives, some by others. The classic interpretation is by **Bernstein,** presently listed in no less than three couplings (Sony 60202, with Symphony 3; Sony 47568, with *Central Park in the Dark;* DG 29220, with miscellaneous short pieces). Bernstein's outgoing approach would seem ideal for Ives, but he's not fond of details: He goes for the main romantic picture and what we hear is his choice of emphasis, not Ives's. The most egregious example is the way he turns the last chord into an extended barbaric yawp instead of the eighth-note whap that Ives wrote.

This revision has unfortunately found its way into **Tilson Thomas**'s otherwise excellently detailed and satisfyingly romantic reading (◆Sony 46440). **Järvi** has rich sound but a rather generalized interpretation (Chandos), while **Stephen Sonary** is too small-scaled for the work's outgoing character (Claves). A new edition provides an exposition repeat for the second movement and various readjustments in orchestration; a recording by the Nashville Symphony under **Schermerhorn** is imminent.

3. No. 3 was written early in the century, when Ives was also composing the violin sonatas. Like them, it's a seriously light-hearted work with hymn tunes at its heart. If you like it played with conscious unsophistication, you'll like **Bernstein** (both with 2) or **Hanson** (Mercury 432755). Both go for the winsome; Bernstein follows through his phrases more seriously, Hanson's sound is clearer. **Tilson Thomas** goes to the other extreme, with careful balances and the sophisticated sound of the Concertgebouw (◆Sony 46440, with 2; 37823, with Orchestral Set 2). His edition is more recent than the others. The other available recordings, by **Marriner** (Argo 17818), **Orpheus Ensemble** (DG 39869), and **Dennis Russell Davies** (◆Pro Arte 149), tend toward the small-scaled. Marriner is tight and polite, Orpheus livelier and more individual, Davies the most freewheeling.

4. Symphony 4 is one of Ives's last works and, in the second and fourth movements, contains his most complex structures. **Tilson Thomas**'s concern for clarity makes more of its disparate elements (◆Sony 44939) than either **Serebrier** (Harmonia Mundi) or **Ozawa** (DG). He gives us something to hold onto throughout this densely textured work, several times finding important strands of touching melody that bring tears to the eyes. He includes several of the hymns Ives quotes, an idea that points up the changes Ives made in them. For instance, "Watchman, What of the Night?" turns out to be in 4/4 time, while Ives makes it a moving lullaby in 6/8. Serebrier's is a smooth and rather underenergized account of this cosmic score, further spoiled by trumpets that can't quite cut it. Ozawa rushes through the work without smelling the flowers. **Isaac Karabtchevsky** in a Venetian live reading misses the gondola in both balances and in the understanding of the music (Mondo Musica).

The musicians who have made an in-depth study of Ives tend to make the most lasting impression. Thus Tilson Thomas, an even more dedicated Ivesian than Bernstein, gets my nod in the symphonies.

OTHER ORCHESTRAL MUSIC

There are many Ives suites that aren't quite symphonies. *Holidays* is the closest, perhaps, but the first three movements tend to traverse similar arcs, from soft and mysterious to loud and raucous and back, making a somewhat unsatisfactory picture overall. On the other hand, all four movements are prime Ives, from the unexpected square-dance episode in "Washington's Birthday," complete with Jew's harp, to the wild fireworks in "Fourth of July," culminating in the chorale prelude atmosphere of "Thanksgiving," Ives's most elaborate evocation of religious emotion.

Here again, **Tilson Thomas** (◆Sony 42381) is the first with the most, bringing out details, maintaining textural continuity, and generally giving us more to listen to than anyone else. His disc includes *The Unanswered Question* (both versions) and *Central Park in the Dark*. Both pieces have an underlying string background that proceeds oblivious to the winds above. **Wolf Dieter Hauschild** has recorded an intense version of *Holidays* that has generated enthusiasm (Berlin 9008). **Zinman** is a bit too smooth and suave (Argo), while **Bernstein** is unfortunate in his coupling (Carter's Concerto for Orchestra in one of the New York Philharmonic's messiest performances), though his enthusiasm is infectious (Sony).

Then there are the *Sets* for orchestra, the first of which is one of Ives's best-known works, *Three Places in New England*. There have been many recordings. The oldest, and by no means the least successful, is **Hanson**'s (Mercury 432755). These Olympian recordings, from a single microphone suspended over the orchestra without volume adjustments, give a solid, exciting sound that is still impressive. **Zinman**'s has been described as "balletic" (not a compliment, when describing the martial and chaotic *Putnam's Camp*). **Dohnányi** (◆London 443776) gives an effective reading, coupled with the less well-known *Set 2* and works by Ruggles and Seeger.

Litton sounds rather small-scaled and is a trifle muddy in balance (basically Ives's fault, but that's why we need specialists to clarify his intent; he never heard most of this music performed). **Orpheus** also gives us a miniature performance (DG 439869), the least successful item in an interesting all-Ives disc including *Set 1* for chamber orchestra, based on orchestrations of Ives's songs, otherwise unavailable since **Gunther Schuller**'s LP disappeared (Columbia 7318). **James Sinclair**'s version of *Three Places* is coupled with a number of short pieces, some otherwise unavailable (Koch 7025). Although **Tilson Thomas** may be the most effective of all, you may not want another version of Symphony 4 and *Central Park* (◆DG 23243).

Set 2 is also in three movements but has never become as well known as its brother. It isn't as clear-cut in its images, but it's prime Ives. **Tilson Thomas** has it with Symphony 3 (Sony 37823), **Dohnányi** couples it with a fine *Three Places* and some important works by Ruggles (◆London 443776). **Gerhard Samuels** gives it a well-detailed performance, a little sloppy around the edges (Centaur 2205). This odd disc also contains a reconstruction by Larry Austin of Ives's projected *Universe Symphony*, based on 36 pages of sketches. This sounds like nothing on earth, which is, I suppose, as it should be, but 38 minutes of inchoate sound without any of Ives's usual quotes or any good tunes is an experience you may not care to repeat. Another reconstruction in a more recognizable Ives style is a projected fourth movement to Symphony 3, realized by David Porter and included under the title of *Overture to Orchestral Set 3*, performed by **Keith Clark** and the Pacific Symphony on an otherwise Ives-less disc (Varèse 47211, NA). Neither of these projects seems an integral part of the Ives canon, but they should be mentioned as examples of the bind he was in that led him to stop composing in the 1920s.

With all their emphasis on Tilson Thomas's recordings, Sony appears to have lost sight of some important material they have in their vaults. **Schuller**'s "Calcium Light Night" (Columbia LP 7138) and **Sinclair**'s "Old Songs Deranged" (Columbia LP 32969) were important collections of miscellaneous short orchestral pieces. Sinclair's CD containing *Three Places* supplements the LP collections with some fascinating firsts not done elsewhere (Koch 7025). "Ives: A Portrait," with Henry Herford, baritone, and Ensemble Modern under **Ingo Metzmacher,** gives us a number of unusual items (EMI 54552), and "Remembrance," featuring the **Detroit Chamber Winds,** is packed with good material (Koch 7182). Still, for the Ives collector, these combined vocal and orchestral collections are frustratingly programmed. The orchestral works are best kept together, as in the LPs mentioned.

CHAMBER MUSIC

The four violin sonatas seem to go together. They're based on hymn tunes and even share some material, and feel like one long meditation on life in a New England village, evoking country fiddling, philosophy, and prayer. Sonatas 2 and 4 have attained some popularity with performers, being short and more businesslike than the others. Neither the **Upper Valley Duo** in 2 (Marquis) nor **Jaime Laredo** with Ann Schein in 4 (Phoenix) are convincing in putting across Ives's quirky personality and deep thought. Sonata 2 is too light and 4 is too heavy and unvaried in approach.

Those who have recorded the complete set have generally been more successful. If they're willing to tackle the quirky writing in 1, the meditative richness of 3, and the half-hour required for each, they seem readier to appreciate the brilliance of 2 and the directness of 4. There is only one listing in *Schwann* for the complete set, played by **Gregory Fulkerson** and Robert Shannon (Bridge 2-9024). These are fine readings, less revelatory than those by **Zukofsky** with Kalish (Nonesuch LP 73025, NA), but honest, forthright performances. Zukofsky and Kalish dig deeper, observing that Ives wants the piano markedly more prominent than the violin during a great deal of the slow movement of 1, finding a whole constellation of elbow thwacks during the closing moments of 2's barn-dance scherzo, and generally pointing up the iconoclastic side of the composer while playing the notes with consummate involvement. This set should be reissued.

If this kind of Ives is too unsettling, **Daniel Stepner**'s version with John Kirkpatrick is just as insightful in a less obtrusive way (MHS 42450). Kirkpatrick was the greatest of the Ives researchers, as well as the earliest and most effective champion of his piano works, and we're fortunate that his effortless mastery of these sonatas was committed to disc. Stepner plays with commendable style and technical fluency, emphasizing the directness and basic simplicity of Ives's violin writing. A violin sonata version of three of the movements that later became *Holidays* is included, reconstructed by Kirkpatrick. MHS recordings are seldom listed in Schwann, but I suspect this set is still available.

The Piano Trio is a solitary work sharing many of the characteristics of the violin sonatas. Its two serious and mildly dissonant outer movements surround one of Ives's zaniest scherzos. It's hard to find more Ives to couple it with, though **Zukofsky,** Kalish, and Robert Sylvester managed it in their fascinating program including *Set for String Quartet, Bass, and Piano, In Re con Moto et Al,* the two *Largo Risolutos* surrounding *Halloween,* and two versions of *Largo,* with clarinet and violin and with violin alone (Columbia LP 30230). This is another issue overdue for re-release by Sony. Kalish has since recorded the Trio with Roman Lefkowitz and Ma, but Zukofsky lent a particularly Ivesian attitude to the proceedings on the old LP. Ives doesn't mix well with other composers, so the present collection of discmates has a tendency to be uneasy in his company.

The **Pacific Arts Trio** coupling is particularly unhappy (Delos, with

Korngold's Trio Op. 1). This version is further sabotaged by harsh recorded sound. The **Monticello Trio,** coupled with more modern fare and played with greater enthusiasm, has been better received (CRI 583). **Trio Matisse,** an accomplished Italian group, couples Ives with recent works by Luis de Pablo and Alessandro Solbiati. They offer a scrupulously balanced performance containing a number of minor revisions of the text and played in a sort of faux-American style, not ineffective, but a little off-putting to this native.

The two string quartets demonstrate the range of Ives's style. 1 is early, with hymn tunes treated in various styles. The opening fugue later became the third movement of Symphony 4; then two lovely and folksy inner movements lead to a jaunty march finale. 2 is completely different, one of Ives's most dissonant and deliberately chaotic pieces. It takes a stellar group to handle it effectively, one that can throw out the idea of unanimity and balance, particularly in the second movement, "Arguments," in which the second fiddle portrays a conservative who plays *Andante emasculata* while the others counter him with an *Allegro con fistiswatto.* The **Lydian Quartet** (Centaur 2069) misses the boat here, while the **Emerson** comes closer, if still lacking something in drama (♦DG 35864). Another Sony omission occurs here: The **Juilliard Quartet** did a committed job on an LP that needs to be reissued (Columbia 6427).

PIANO MUSIC

As a pianist himself, Ives did much of his experimenting on that instrument. There is a disc containing 78 minutes of **Ives** at the piano (CRI 810). It's full of interest, particularly if you try to follow the printed score of some of the pieces he purports to be playing. He never did anything the same way twice, not because he couldn't, but because his ideas changed. Some of this freewheeling creativity found its way into the printed music, i.e., the alternates to the end of the first scherzo of Sonata 1 and the remarkable differences between the two editions of 2. Besides these published differences, there are many passages in the manuscripts that have led pianists to travel other byways, some of which have become part of the accepted canon, though they don't appear in print to my knowledge.

The two sonatas account for about half of Ives's pianistic output and are the culmination of his thoughts for keyboard. The other works are mostly contained in a projected set of 24 *Studies* (13 have been found or reconstructed) and a set of *Five Takeoffs* that John Kirkpatrick edited. These works are some of Ives's most chaotic. The most complete collection is by **Alan Mandel** (Vox 3034, 3CD). He includes a great deal of music, but he's seldom outstanding in interpreting it, tending to sound didactic next to the best of the competition. No one else plays the *Waltz-Rondo* (related to Sonata 1) or the full version of *The Celestial Railroad.* The latter is a late work with parts for percussion and a second piano, related both to the Scherzo of Symphony 4 and to Sonata 2. **Anthony de Mare** recorded *Celestial Railroad* in an Ives-Cowell-Harrison disc, along with "The Alcotts" from *Concord Sonata,* transcriptions of three short improvisations, and Study 22. He plays with virtuosity and a certain flair, though his version of the railroad omits the percussion and other extras included by Mandel.

Donald Berman's "The Unknown Ives" brings together ten of the Studies, as well as *Takeoffs* and *Three-Page Sonata,* in performances that hold the music together, shaping them more naturally than Mandel though not always with as much excitement (♦CRI 811). Mandel's *Three-Page Sonata* is the only one that uses a real set of bells in the slow movement; this passage quotes from the Westminster chimes at one point. One other performance is available, by **Nina Deutsch** (Vox 5089,

2CD). She has found more odds and ends: Besides the two sonatas, she plays *Four Emerson Transcriptions* (variants on the first movement of Sonata 2), as well as her own transcriptions of the organ variations on "America" and "The Bells of Yale." Her performances are enthusiastic but a bit sketchy; many details fall by the wayside. Her *Three-Page Sonata* is best in the ragtime section. Berman plays a different edition from the others, not necessarily better, but quite different in the first movement. Mandel is the most successful in this work (♦Vox 3034).

Berman hits more home runs in *Takeoffs* than Mandel and programs them together. In the *Studies,* Mandel plays two that Berman doesn't, Berman plays one Mandel doesn't, and Ives plays one that neither does. Ives's own recording was the origin of the *Emerson Transcriptions,* so with that (if the poor sound of the originals doesn't turn you off) you can probably dispense with Deutsch.

Sonata 1 is the Cinderella among Ives's piano works. It's as long and difficult as 2, and harder to put across. Mandel is lumpy; Deutsch doesn't even try for the notes, but improvises her way through the events to considerable effect, sounding rather like Ives himself (minus the vocal commentary he sometimes gives). That doesn't constitute a recommendation, but it's a surprisingly convincing experience. What we need is **William Masselos**'s recording, originally on LP (RCA 2941), later issued in MHS 522732, in which form it may still be available, though unfortunately as part of a 2CD set with the rest not as successful. So, what with the versions by **Herbert Henck** (Wergo, NA) and **Donna Coleman** (Etcetera 1147, NA) having bitten the dust, and **Joanna MacGregor** (Collins 1107) not available on these shores, we're in trouble with this classic and don't even have Sony to blame, for once.

Sonata 2 ("Concord") is another story. There are more recordings of this than any other Ives work, and it's long and difficult. **John Kirkpatrick** made the first recording on 78s during Ives's lifetime, and his remake on LP (Columbia 7192) is another must for Sony to reissue. His is the most matter-of-fact performance, without slighting anything of the poetry or the excitement. He plays it as if he were Ives himself. Everything is unobtrusively right, from the wrong notes he deliberately introduces into *Hawthorne* to the way he plays all the climaxes in *Thoreau* without ever losing the rapt pastorale mood Ives wanted. Though he doesn't use the viola and flute as Ives directed, he incorporates those lines into the piano, which no one else does, so we don't lose Ives's thought. **Mandel** uses the flute but not the viola, and his pedaling is muddy. **Deutsch** is not a happy camper, and her instrument is slightly out of tune (from a live performance).

Louise Bessette employs her Bösendorfer to great effect, achieving some impressive cohesion, but she never plays really softly and her tendency to try to make Ives's references to the opening of Beethoven's 5th sound like Beethoven is misguided and basically un-American (Musica Viva). **Robert Shannon** is impressively concentrated and attends to details, but plays an earlier version of the work than most, one that includes only a few of the dissonant harmonic effects in "Hawthorne" and omits both viola and flute lines (Bridge 9036). Still, this is a fine performance and Harbison's Sonata is a fitting follow-up. **Hamelin** plays an even earlier version of the music, omitting all the dissonant harmonics in "Hawthorne" (New World 378). As if to make up for that, he's the most sensitive of all in the high-register clusters (using a board) elsewhere in that movement, following Ives's dynamics to the letter, and also sensitively balances the distant dissonances in "The Alcotts."

Richard Trythall is in the Kirkpatrick camp, a bit dry in sound but enthusiastic (Centaur 2285). **Easley Blackwood** is along the same lines, giving us great clarity but not much poetry, partly due to dry recorded

sound (Cedille 005). **Kalish** achieves the best of both worlds, combining Shannon's attention to detail and mood with Kirkpatrick's ongoing syntax and overall sweep (♦Elektra/Nonesuch 71337). His technical command of balances clarifies Ives's intent, and his mastery of the technical demands is never achieved by slighting the notes or tone. He's the only one to use both viola and flute inserts, both sufficiently distant to make their magical effect without disturbing the mood. His "Thoreau" is less consistently distant than either Shannon or Kirkpatrick, but the effect is there.

CHORAL MUSIC

Hello? I'm trying to get through to Sony again! They have a number of Ives works performed by **Gregg Smith** and his Singers—including nine psalm settings, three *Harvest Home* chorales, 17 songs with orchestra, and the cantata *The Celestial Country*—sitting in their library gathering dust. Smith is an ideal conductor for Ives, as Sony must have realized, since they released so much of his work on LP (6321, 7321, and 32504). None of this material is presently available, leaving us with estimable, beautifully recorded, but teddibly English accounts of *The Celestial Country* and Psalms 54, 67, 90, and 125 with **Cleobury** and the BBC Singers (Collins 14792, NA). They do include *Easter Carol* and *Crossing the Bar,* fascinating early works I wouldn't want to be without. Still, must we look to Europe for our Ives? Where is your patriotic spirit, O Sony? Oops, I forgot: they're Japanese.

Does Sony suggest I try Vox records, who have an even larger Gregg Smith collection? Well, that's good advice but Sony has a bigger collection; while Vox could probably pull together a CD's worth of Smith's Ives, Sony has at least enough for two. Cleobury has also recorded *Psalm 90* with the Choir of King's College, Cambridge in an American program (EMI 66787). If Ives's frequently experimental choral music is not your thing, *Psalm 90* was Ives's favorite of his own works, so you might try that excellent disc. Otherwise, the pickings are slim.

SONGS

If you're looking for the key to Ives, try his songs. They give a clue to his thought and distill the essence of his emotions; most of them are short, and many contain his loveliest music. There is a collection of almost all of them by four different singers (Albany 77/80, 4CD). Two are outstanding: mezzo **Mary Ann Hart** and baritone William Sharp. Soprano Dora Ohrenstein has a lovely sound but a disturbing tendency to sing flat; tenor Paul Sperry tends to be precious in expression, though he's imaginative. This collection is well recorded and presented in something approaching chronological order. A major listening problem is the lack of space between songs; yes, these are nice long discs, but even three seconds between songs would have made a big difference. As it is, it's hard to listen to.

Two singers have done a great deal for Ives over the years. **Boatwright**'s 1954 LP of 24 songs with John Kirkpatrick has been reissued (♦CRI 675, with songs by Ernst Bacon). Boatwright has an ideal voice for Ives: pure, almost childish at times, but with an underlying control and an unerring sense of pitch. In 1974, for the 100th anniversary of Ives's birth, Columbia issued an excellent set containing a number of important recordings including 25 more songs with Boatwright and Kirkpatrick (32504 plus a bonus disc of interviews, 5LP). The piano sound on the 1954 recording was slightly muffled, but that can be helped at your console.

De Gaetani and Kalish were another ideal pair for Ives. Two collections are available, one containing 17 songs (♦Nonesuch 71325) and the other 9 (♦Bridge 9006, with a work by George Crumb). These performers emphasize the richness of Ives's textures and clarify his meaning in a different way. There is an interesting program of 28 songs by **Michael Ingham,** accompanied by composer Henry Brant, who has scrutinized the Ives manuscripts and unearthed new details in many of them (AmCam 10306). Unfortunately, Ingham's voice is so uncontrolled in sound and intonation, Brant plays so rigidly, and the recording is so close up, that the interesting musical points are hard to appreciate.

Then there are some recordings of Ives and others. **William Parker** does nine in a program of American songs of Ives's period, including several of those taken from his instrumental pieces and four in French (New World 80463). These make up an unusual program, sung with something of an edgy voice, but a good alternative if you're not ready for the Albany compendium. An interesting collection of 14 German songs came from **Hampson** (Teldec 72168, NA, with more by MacDowell and Griffes). Whether or not you like his somewhat mannered performances, it's an unusual experience. Along these lines is **Upshaw**'s group of five songs orchestrated by John Adams in "American Elegies" (Elektra/Nonesuch 79249, with *The Unanswered Question*). She sings with her customary jewel-like perfection, but the reason for the disc is Adams's programming, not Ives's songs or even Upshaw's voice.

MOORE

Leoš Janáček (1854–1928)

Janáček was one of the greatest Czech composers and among the greatest operatic composers of the 20th century. He wrote music all his life, but his fame spread only with the performance of *Jenufa* in 1915, when the composer was 61. After that, he wrote many of his finest works in a remarkable burst of inspiration. Many were erotically driven, with the focal point his unrequited obsession with Kamila Stösslová, a woman 38 years his junior. Early Janáček was Dvořákian. His real voice asserted itself around the time of *Jenufa*, blending romanticism with a stark, angular, and even rough quality. Czech and Moravian folklore was an important foundation, as was his technique of adapting its melodies and rhythms.

Janáček's music often seems awkward—a quality that fooled those who completed some of his unfinished works; often they would smooth them out. Better adjectives are rich, sweet, melodic, reflective, rustic, motoric, heavy, shrill, brilliant, nervous, agitated, and most of all, original. His harmony was a distinctive blend of impressionism with quartal elements, and his key relationships could be strange. His orchestration frequently pitted odd combinations of instruments against each other, often in extreme ranges. Trumpets were brilliant, low brass heavy. His string writing could be full but also wild, chugging, and repetitive. Woodwinds are colorful and busy, and they sometimes chatter and screech. His vocal writing was difficult and pushed hard at singers' ranges. His later works moved away from the romantic and toward the more stark and austere, but his essential style was always there. As "modern" as all this sounds, Janáček was a tonal composer whose music came from the heart and is always accessible.

ORCHESTRAL MUSIC

František Jílek's set with the Brno State Philharmonic is convenient, though there are competitive and superior performances. The readings are mellow and laid back, but also insightful, neatly drawn, and song-like; you'll have to go elsewhere for weight, drive, and electricity. The Brno group is no Czech Philharmonic, but it has an appropriate and satisfying, if smallish, tone, with sweet violins, silvery flutes, and crisp ringing brass (♦Supraphon 111834, 3CD, also available individually).

Danube; Schluck und Jau; Moravian Dances. Danube is an unfinished symphonic poem in several movements treating the river as a woman, in the style of *Jenufa* and *Katya Kabanova*. The later incidental music to Hauptmann's *Schluck und Jau* is leaner and more modern. The Dvořákian *Moravian Dances* is less interesting. **Pešek** with the Slovak Philharmonic provides spirited, full-blooded performances of *Danube* and the Dances, with good intensity in sustaining phrases (♦Marco Polo 220362, with Suite for Orchestra) He's also exciting and dramatic in *Schluck und Jau*, but here I prefer **Jílek**'s atmospheric reading, particularly his slower (and more allegretto) Allegretto and his sweet strings and silvery flutes. Unfortunately, Jílek's *Danube* is flaccid and meandering. **Neumann**'s *Schluck und Jau* is as good as Jílek's and better if you prefer a larger scaled, more dramatic reading with a better orchestra, the Czech Philharmonic (♦Supraphon 1965, with *Sinfonietta, Taras Bulba,* and Violin Concerto).

Idyll, Suite for Strings, and *Lachian Dances* are early works. The Suite is Janáček's first surviving orchestral piece; it's a beauty, in the style of Dvořák, with a strong touch of Wagner. *Lachian Dances* reminds me of Dvořák's *Legends,* and *Idyll* is in a similar vein. **Jílek** seems too relaxed at first, but he isn't; these masterful performances make the pieces, especially the Suite, sound like major works, with sweet, understanding playing by the Brno strings (♦Supraphon 111520). For **Gregory Rose**'s *Idyll* and Suite the London Jupiter Orchestra is clear-toned, straightforward, but nicely romantic (♦Chandos 9195). Their *On an Overgrown Path,* an arrangement of six movements from the piano work, is excellent.

Michael Helmrath leads the Munich Philharmonic Chamber Orchestra in *Idyll* and Suite (♦Orfeo 283921). The sound is scrumptious, the playing dark and full; his romantic interpretation is more romantic and slower than Jílek's and not as compelling, but its richness has virtues. The tone poem-like *Adagio* is a bigger orchestral work with themes associated with *Sárka*. **Richard Pope**'s *Idyll* and Suite with the London Festival Orchestra have a beautiful sheen but are too romantic, with too much heaving and hauling, but it's a fine budget value and the coupled *Mládí* is terrific (Arte Nova 30501). **Conlon**'s *Lachian Dances* and *Idyll* are large-scaled but too full-blown and stiff (Erato LP).

Opera Suites. Janáček's quirky operas don't lend themselves well to suites, but there are a few. **Serebrier**'s symphonic synthesis of *Makropulos Case* is well conceived and executed and may be the best of the lot. The Talich/Smetáček suite from *Cunning Little Vixen* is acceptable, but the performance lacks wonder and romance and is too fast. *Jealousy Overture,* intended but not used as an overture to *Jenufa,* is bold and colorful, but the Prelude to *From the House of the Dead* lacks energy and weight. The Czech State Orchestra acquits itself well; the sound is dynamic but at times harsh (♦Reference 75). **Bělohlávek** conducts the Prague Symphony in the *Vixen* suite and suites from *Excursions of Mr. Brouček* (arranged by Smolka) and *From the House of the Dead* (by Jílek, including the Prelude). *Brouček* works best, with its dramatic instrumental passages. Smolka leads suites from *Excursions of Mr. Brouček* and Jílek *From the House of the Dead,* including the Prelude. *Brouček* works best, with some dramatic instrumental passages, but the excerpts from *House* seem uncomfortable out of their vocal settings. Good sound and performances (Supraphon 3436).

Sinfonietta and *Taras Bulba. Sinfonietta* is the closest Janáček came to a symphony and is his most famous work. It began as a brassy fanfare for a gymnastic celebration but expanded into a tribute to Brno, a five-movement work of amazing color and harmonic and orchestral virtuosity. *Taras Bulba* is a Russophilic symphonic rhapsody based on the Gogol story and is more opulent and expressionist than the angular, lean, and brassy *Sinfonietta*.

Among the recordings with Czech conductors and orchestras, **Ančerl**'s fast, riveting performances are masterly, with cutting rhythms, bright strings, and brilliant brass. Both works crackle with electricity and excitement, especially when played by a Czech Philharmonic that knows the music cold (♦Supraphon 111929, with Martinu's Concerto for Three Pianos). **Košler** supplies terrific, old-fashioned renditions with the same orchestra, with wailing Czech sound in the brasses, silvery strings, and ripe woodwinds. The music sings, drama and atmosphere are palpable, and the dance sections teem with life (♦Denon 17017, 2CD, with Smetana's *Má Vlast* led by Neumann and Dvořák's *Nocturne* played by the Prague Chamber Orchestra).

Neumann's readings are slightly light-weight, but they have plenty of firepower when needed, with some great moments in *Taras*. They're energetic and full of life and understanding, with nicely detailed textures and playing by the Czech Philharmonic (♦Supraphon 1965, with Violin Concerto and *Schluck und Jau*). This issue is superior in sound to the Pro Arte edition of this recording, which has no couplings. **Jílek** is laid back, as well as light, clean, transparent, and often fast. He sometimes runs through things others bring out better, and he won't bowl you over with energy or weight; his neat approach is more pleasant than stirring, but effective (Supraphon 1522, with *Danube*, Violin Concerto, *Schluck und Jau*).

There are two fine pairings with Czech conductors and non-Czech orchestras, and one with a Czech orchestra and a non-Czech conductor. **Pešek** is fresh and vital, with unusual insights, varying balances, and interesting points of phrasing, e.g., at the end of the first movement, and the prominent bass trumpets in the fanfares. The Philharmonia sounds clean and crisp—quite British without the Czech orchestras' swagger and weight (♦Virgin 91506, with Overture to *From the House of the Dead* and Violin Concerto). **Kubelik**'s accounts are bold and audacious, and the Bavarian Radio Orchestra is more enthusiastic than polished. The divided-violin setup with cellos and basses in the center right reveals a mass of weight backed by roaring low brass. His *Taras Bulba* is one the best, if not as polished as Ančerl's. The bodacious but occasionally elegant *Sinfonietta* is not quite as good and the sound is occasionally diffuse and congested, but the broad staging is impressive (♦DG 439437). **Serebrier**, with the Czech State Philharmonic, is massive and powerful. The broad soundstage and recorded emphasis on the mid-range and bass help create very dark timbres and reveal more inner parts than usual (♦Reference 65, with *Taras Bulba* and *Lachian Dances*).

Those with no Czech representation begin with **Mackerras**'s Vienna Philharmonic recording. It's broad and burnished, with colorful brass and woodwinds. The tempos are leisurely (perhaps too much so in *Sinfonietta* IV), and we get one of the more romantic and effective recordings of *Taras* (♦London 410138). His 1959 recording with the Pro Arte Orchestra is fresh with discovery and enthusiasm; it's quirky, insightful, innovative, compelling, interesting, and broad all at once. I like the clear, sweet strings and brass (though they're not entirely polished). The sound is decent early stereo that occasionally compresses climaxes (♦EMI 63779, with opera preludes). **Szell** is brilliant, deliberate, and clear-textured, with some eccentric articulations. It's virtuosic, though hardly idiomatic, and has no Czech folk quality. Still, it's an entertaining supplement (Sony 62404, with Kodály's *Galanta* and *Marosszék Dances*).

Lenárd's *Sinfonietta* suffers from detachment and lack of concentra-

tion; his *Taras* is similar but a bit better. It's acceptable as a budget choice (Naxos, with *Lachian Dances*). **Andrew Davis**'s pace is slow and heavy with little energy or electricity. Rhythms are bland, the Stockholm Philharmonic strings are grainy, and there isn't much tension. Cramped sound and odd balances, too (Finlandia, with *Fiddler's Child, Ballad of Blanik*). Both works are well played by **Rattle**, but everything is too studied and held back; we need more energy and idiomatic thrust, particularly in the lackluster *Taras*, though there are some beautiful moments in *Sinfonietta* (EMI).

For a *Sinfonietta* not coupled with *Taras Bulba*, **Ozawa** with the Chicago Symphony is brilliant like Szell but faster, brassier, much lighter, and more distantly recorded. It's more scintillating than spectacular and more stirring than what Ozawa usually produces (♦EMI 72664, 2CD, with Bartók and Lutoslawski Concertos for Orchestra and Stravinsky's *Firebird*). **Claudio Abbado** is solid, serviceable, and extremely well played. It's straightforward, cautious (particularly the slow tempo at the beginning of V), not overly exciting, but adequate. My recommendation applies to the only recording of the Zitek/Sedláček orchestration of *The Diary of One Who Disappeared* (♦DG 427313), not the issue with Bartók's *Miraculous Mandarin* (DG).

Bělohlávek has the brilliant Czech Philharmonic and good sound, but is square and lacks passion (Chandos, with Martinů's Symphony 6 and Suk's *Fantastické Scherzo*). **Neumann**'s recording isn't as good as his Supraphon reading but is slightly superior to Lenárd as a budget choice. Still, it's a little slow and dull, though the German SWF Symphony plays well enough (Arte Nova, with Violin Concerto and Suite from *Cunning Little Vixen*). **Tilson Thomas**'s recording is fast (occasionally rushed), light, and analytical. It lacks the proper bass, weight, and drive this work requires, despite fine playing by the London Symphony (Sony, with *Glagolitic Mass*).

Inbal is dark and occasionally too much on the slow side (Denon, with *Glagolitic Mass*). The third movement is mysterious in the opening, but the big chords before the final fanfares are too slow and laid back—interesting, but there are better renditions. **Previn** and the Los Angeles Philharmonic give the sleekest, plushest, and most soft-toned reading I've heard. Tempos are slow, everything is velvety but with no excess fat, and there's nary an accented note or bite. It's appealing at first, but wearisome (Telarc, with Bartók's *Concerto for Orchestra*). **Neeme Järvi**'s tempos are too slow, and energy is lacking to the point of flaccidity and weariness; the trombone passage in the third movement is so slow it's perverse. Clear textures are its only virtue (BIS, with Dvořák's *Legends*).

As for *Taras Bulba* by itself, **Bělohlávek** is clear-toned and classical, with a terrific Czech Philharmonic that sounds more Westernized than in older recordings (♦Chandos 9080, with *Fiddler's Child, Jealousy, Cunning Little Vixen Suite*—not the same one as in his "suites" disc). An excellent collection. **Jílek** is warm and lyrical, almost singing, broad but not weighty. It has an episodic quality—some transitions aren't smooth—but his instincts are genuine and convincing. The Brno State Philharmonic provides a fresh sound in another excellent collection (♦Supraphon 111521, with *Jealousy, Ballad of Blanik, Cossack Dance, Fiddler's Child, Serbian Reel Suite, Adagio*). **Gardiner** is lively, with faster tempos than Bělohlávek and fine, clean playing by the North German Radio Orchestra (DG 445838, with Rachmaninoff's *Symphonic Dances*). What's missing is the adventure and tragedy of the story.

François Huybrechts leads a warm London Philharmonic in the most opulent *Taras* I know. It's broad, slightly slow, polished, and lyrical, but never loses momentum or gets stodgy. It's not idiomatic, but that doesn't matter, and the sound is terrific (♦London LP, with *Lachian Dances*). **Kubelik**'s earlier *Taras*, with the Royal Philharmonic playing beautifully, is on the light side, graceful and lyrically insightful (♦EMI LP). Far more controlled than his DG account, it misses the tragedy and violence but is beautiful and tasteful. The sound is a little boxy, but it's an elegant box.

Masur's heavy, slow reading, with sound accentuating the bass, is similar to the coupled *Mass*. The approach doesn't work as well in *Taras*, but it may please those who like Masur's *Mass*, particularly for the Brahmsian sound of the Leipzig Gewandhaus (Philips). **Dohnányi** wastes beautiful playing by the Cleveland Orchestra in a slow, soft-edged, and aimless interpretation that makes little sense of the music (London, with Dvořák's Symphony 6).

VIOLIN CONCERTO

"The pilgrimage of a soul" was never finished, though Janáček adapted it as a prelude to *From the House of the Dead*. Completed as a concerto by Leoš Faltus and Miloš Štědroň, it's short, intense, and highly contrasted. The images suggest a dark Czech forest on a quiet winter night.

Tetzlaff gives a great performance, led by Pešek. His tone is pure and crystal clear, but strong and firm; rhythms are sharp and brilliant. The Philharmonia is an equal partner, playing with confidence and strength. This reading reveals lines, textures, and coordination we don't always catch in recordings of this work (♦Virgin 91506, with Prelude to *From the House of the Dead* and *Sinfonietta*). **Zehetmair**'s tone is sweet and round, as is the sound of the Philharmonia led by Heinz Holliger (Teldec 97449, with Berg's Violin Concerto and Hartmann's *Concerto funèbre*). It's less impressive and cohesive than Tetzlaff's reading, and Holliger isn't as good structurally (the ending is too abrupt and fast, for instance), but it has energy and sparkle. The Hartmann piece is stunning.

Christiane Edinger plays with a brighter sound and greater intensity than the others—a good thing, since Neumann's slow tempos would otherwise cause it to flag. The microphones are close to the soloist, so orchestral textures aren't as clear as they could be. It's a good bargain reading, though the coupled *Sinfonietta* is lackluster (Arte Nova 30481, with *Vixen* Suite). **Ivan Ženatý** has a beautifully sweet and firm tone. This is the most romantic and relaxed version—quite a different view, and Jílek's conducting is the slowest— but it's clean and lyrical (♦Supraphon 1522, with *Sinfonietta*, *Danube*, and *Schluck und Jau*).

CHAMBER MUSIC

Capriccio for Piano and Seven Instruments ("Defiance") and ***Concertino for Piano and Chamber Orchestra***. *Capriccio* was written for one-handed pianist Otakar Hollman and pits the piano against a strange ensemble of brass and flute/piccolo. The *Concertino* for a small string and woodwind ensemble is lighter and Stravinskian.

The classic **Firkušný** performance, with Kubelik and musicians from the Bavarian Radio Orchestra, is a marvel, combining warmth, spontaneity, strong rhythms, lyricism, and flow that is magisterial, inspired, and natural (♦DG 449764, 2CD, with *On an Overgrown Path, In the Mists*, Piano Sonata, etc.). His remake is broader, more red-blooded and colorful, and shows no signs of the pianist's advanced age. It's in excellent sound, and your choice will depend on your stylistic preferences (♦RCA 60781, with Dvořák's Piano Concerto). **Boris Berman** and the Netherlands Wind Ensemble are full of color, depth, and poignancy. *Concertino* sparkles, while *Capriccio* is sophisticated and lyrical. If not as flowing and spontaneous as Firkušný, both have depth and pathos (♦Chandos 9399).

Viktoria Postnikova and Rozdestvensky may appeal to first-timers because of the broad brass in *Capriccio* that provides a full wall of sound behind the bright piano (she darkens in *Concertino*). Rozdestvensky's leadership is colorful and dramatic and he gets a more Slavic brass sound from his French players (Orchestre de Paris) than Mackerras gets from his (♦Erato 45599, with Piano Sonata and *In the Mist*). **Ivan Klánský**'s interpretations with the Prague Wind Quintet are as appealing as Berman's, but are more Czech and fruity, more closely miked and not as seamlessly blended (♦Praga 250134, with *Tale* for cello and *Mládí*). **Mikhail Rudy** plays up Janáček's bite, sharp rhythms, and quick tempos, helped, I'm sure, by Mackerras's leadership. The Paris Opera Orchestra's piquant winds and brass and Rudy's bright piano tone produce a Janáček with a French accent (parts sound like Poulenc). It's well done, but those looking for deeper, more brooding readings may find it light and brittle (EMI 55585, with *Tale* and *Presto* for cello; Violin Sonata).

Thomas Hlawatsch and his Hungarian ensemble are better in *Concertino*. Their tone and rhythm are almost symphonic, yet there's nothing soft or overly warm. The horn tone is big but not too plush; the clarinet is bright but without the chirping heard in some performances. It's a good budget choice, but not the best available (Naxos 553587, with *In the Mist* and other piano works). The raw style of his *Capriccio* may suit some, but it lacks subtlety and misses some of the quirks and shifting moods. The couplings are interesting (Naxos 553588, with Violin Sonata and rare violin works).

Schiff and the Musiktage Mondsee Ensemble are weighty and dark to a fault. Technically, it's top notch, but you won't find the edgy, sardonic qualities that are in this music. The players never seem comfortable with the Janáček idiom (London 440312, with *Capriccio, In the Mists, Presto, A Fairy-Tale*, Piano Sonata; London 440313, with *Concertino, On an Overgrown Path*, Violin Sonata). Fans of **Hilde Somer** may enjoy her Caramoor Festival performances. Emphasizing the piano, they fare well in a bright, extroverted *Concertino*, less so in an unintegrated *Capriccio* where the instruments are out of focus (Desto LP).

By itself, *Capriccio* played in **Radoslav Kvapil**'s warm, reserved style creates symphonic seriousness and greater tension than usual; it's nice and polished (♦Nimbus 5103, with Hindemith's Concert Music for Piano, Brass, and Harps and Dalibor Vaškář's Concerto for Trumpet, Percussion and Keyboard). **Mario Papadopoulos** leads Royal Philharmonic players in a Westernized, smooth performance with warm brass sound. Unfortunately, the recording makes the brass too heavy and forward, and the piano sounds honky (Hyperion, with Piano Sonata and Stravinsky's Piano Concerto).

Mládí ("Youth"). This is a nostalgic sextet that looks back on the composer's early years. The **Prague Wind Quintet**'s 1990s reading is vigorous and idiomatic, with ripe, fruity woodwinds and horn (♦Supraphon 1354, with string quartets played by the Talich Quartet). Their later version, with mostly different players, is warmer, smoother, and less tangy, though in the same Czech tradition (♦Praga 250134, with *Capriccio, Concertino, Tale*). Both are excellent and idiomatic; I prefer the earlier one but am not as fond of the performances of the coupled quartets. The **Netherlands Wind Ensemble** is Westernized and impressive, brightly lit and colorful with fine energy, yet very elegant—an excellent disc (♦Chandos 9399, with *Nursery Rhymes, Concertino, Capriccio*, etc.).

The English **Michael Thompson Wind Quintet** version is similar but softer edged, warmer, more laid back, and less colorful. Still, it has life and is very well done (♦Naxos 553851, with quintets by Hindemith, Barber, and Larsson). **Pople** with London Festival Orchestra players is also Western, but more idiomatic, faster and more spirited and piquant.

The couplings aren't as good interpretively, but *Mládí* is worth the budget price (♦Arte Nova 30501, with Suite for Strings, *Idyll*). The **Orpheus Chamber Orchestra** account is similarly Westernized and polished but more controlled, slower, and less alive (DG, with Bartók's *Divertimento* and *Romanian Folk Dances*). The **Melos Ensemble** is mechanical and harsh; the coupled *Concertino* is also mechanical but not as harsh. Lamar Crowson is sensitive in *In the Mist* but that's not enough to recommend the disc (Angel LP).

String Quartets 1 ("Kreutzer Sonata") and *2* ("Intimate Letters"). These are often coupled without other pieces—not a good value, since they combine for less than 45 minutes of music. No. 1 is a musical recreation of the Tolstoy novella about love and adultery, with each instrument taking a character's voice and 2 is an "operatic" account of Janáček's relationship with Stösslová, with each movement a "scene." Both are impassioned, original works.

Among the Czech groups, the **Vlach Quartet** is outstanding; its balanced readings feel right, with romantic style, passion, and bite (♦Naxos 553895, with Violin Sonata and *Prohádka* for cello*)*. The latest **Smetana Quartet** performance is big and sleek, with broad rhythms and opulent tone, paced with wonderful flow (♦Denon 7547). These ultra-romantic readings, without the bite of many others, are the work of a group that has spent years with this music and is comfortable with its nuances. Their 1977 performances are just as big and romantic in tone, but less sleek and flowing (♦Supraphon LP). They probe deeper at a slower, more careful tempo, bringing out individual sections and instruments and opening up the textures.

The **Wihan Quartet**'s sound is small but sweet, with tension, tight ensemble, fine technique, and intonation that creates interest and intensity. Fast parts are brisk, with panache; slower sections are wistful but not maudlin. They're not as balanced as the Vlach, but neoclassical Janáček can be as effective as romantic (♦Matous 32). The **Prašák Quartet** is still more intense, bright-toned and sharply rhythmic, in excellent sound tilted to the treble. It's brilliant and idiomatic, but their intensity can be overpowering if you're not in the mood (Praga 250108, with Violin Sonata). The 1961 mono recording by the **Novák Quartet** is smaller in scale and not as rhythmically or tonally sharp as others, but they are understanding and idiomatic (Berlin 6203). Their sweet tone and effortless style make the works sound more youthful than usual. The **Talich Quartet** are emotionally tightly wound, stern, controlled, and less fluid and silvery than other Czech readings. They're good but won't appeal to everyone; the adequate but steely sound could use more richness (Supraphon 1354, with *Mladí*).

The German **Kreuzberger Quartet**'s performance from the 1970s bridges the serious, older performances and the energetic and intense modern readings. It's large in scale, warm, clean-toned, and virtuosic without being shrill (♦Telefunken 42179, LP). Another fine German performance is by the **Melos Quartet**. Sturdy, occasionally pensive and well-structured, they're more refined in tone and more controlled than the Kreuzberger. The beautiful, nicely balanced sound is notable; they're disciplined though never dull, and expressive in their glowing Germanic way (♦Harmonia Mundi 7901380, mid-priced).

Among British groups, the **Medici Quartet** produces stylish, lyrical performances that stress yearning. They're elegant, broader than the Czech readings, and romantic, with tension and passion plus gorgeous string sound (♦Nimbus 5113). Their earlier accounts are severe, deliberate, controlled, and inward, with forward, aggressive sound (♦EMI LP). They're dramatic and gripping, as if telling two serious stories, but

there's nothing romantic or folk-like about them. The **Gabrieli Quartet** recording is elegantly played, broad in tone, and has a nice sound. They're introspective and occasionally slow, as opposed to intense, yearning, or passionate, and they do better in the more romantic 2 (London, with Smetana's Quartet 1). Unless you prefer reserve, the Medici is better at this style. An excellent alternative is the **Vanbrugh Quartet**'s straightforward, clear-toned elegance. They're less passionate and more intimate than Medici, more assertive and idiomatic than Gabrieli, and leaner and more glistening in tone than both (♦Collins 13812, with Dvořák's Quartet 10).

The **Tokyo Quartet** combines a big, warm sound with remarkable ensemble and intonation (♦RCA 68286, 3CD, with Bartók Quartets). They're lyrical and virtuosic—perfect anti-Czech performances. The sound may put you off, though: It sounds more like a synthesizer than acoustical instruments. The **Juilliard Quartet** is dramatic, weighty, and sharply defined, particularly in the inner parts, though I sense little spontaneity (Sony). There's nothing light about the textures; No. 2 sounds more romantic than 1. The **Alban Berg Quartet** is tight-lipped, mechanical, and controlled (EMI). They play with a smaller sound that can be impressively introspective in the slower, quiet sections, but they sound metallic in the louder ones (blame the engineers for some of this). Other than some fussiness, I don't hear much expressiveness.

The **Guarneri Quartet**'s performances are mechanical, severe, and crass, with little sense of the idiom (Philips). They sound bottom-heavy, and the recording is forward and unblended. The **Hagen Quartet** is artificially and overly dramatic, with metallic extremes that make for unpleasant listening (DG). The **Vogler Quartet**'s 1 is smooth but episodic and even ugly at times (RCA, with Debussy and Shostakovich quartets). The way they exaggerate differences between tempos creates the disconcerting impression of a group showing off.

Violin Sonata. This sonata is the composer's third but only extant violin sonata and was often revised. It's haunting, and alternatively sweet, reflective, and folk-like, reflecting pro-Russian sensibilities as Janáček awaited Russian deliverance from the Hapsburgs. Much of it sounds improvisatory or conversational, and it makes grand use of the rich tone of the violin's middle register. **Tetzlaff** uses his small, lyrical sound in a nuanced, sensitive reading that brings out the conversational aspects of the work, with the sensitive Leif Ove Andsnes as accompanist (♦Virgin 45122 with Debussy and Ravel violin sonatas). **Pierre Amoyal** has a small, complex, and beautiful sound that contrasts lyrically with Mikhail Rudy's darker piano to lend a Brahmsian cast to the piece (♦EMI 55585, with *Capriccio, Concertino, Tale,* and *Presto*).

Václav Remeš's sound is a bit bright and unfocused, particularly in the low register, but his intensity has a nice Gypsy-violinist's improvisational quality (♦Praga 250108, with Quartets). The way he emphasizes short fragments over the long line is effective, and pianist Sachiko Kayahara's conventional sound and playing tie things together. It's not beautiful, but it's compelling. If you like the Prašák's quartet performances, you'll like this (**Remeš** is their first violinist). **Jana Vlachová** and František Malý are rawer, brighter, and slightly less polished than most (Naxos 553895, with *Prohádka* and Quartets).

Among the darker players, **Ulf Wallin** and Pöntinen are Brahmsian. Wallin has a small and occasionally whiny sound, and Pöntinen's flowing piano darkens the music and carries the listener along (♦BIS 663/4, 2CD, with works for piano, cello and piano, violin and piano). **Sitkovetsky**'s beautiful tone is vocal, emotional, and almost Hebraic—Janáček as Bloch—and Pavel Gililov matches him well. In many ways it's my favorite performance, if not the most idiomatic (♦Virgin 578231, with Strauss and Debussy violin sonatas). **Beverly Somach** makes a profoundly lyrical statement—on the soft side, but rich and appealing (♦MHS 512190, with violin works by Suk, Ysaÿe, and Szymanowski). **Ildikó Line** and Thomas Hlawatsch are reserved and broad (Naxos 553588, with *Capriccio, Romance, Dumka, Allegro*). **Yuuko Shiokawa**'s sweet sound combines with Schiff's dark, rolling accompaniment to flow like a lambent river—a compellingly sweet view of the composer and the best performance on the disc (♦London 440313, with *On an Overgrown Path, Concertino*).

PIANO MUSIC

Sonata October 1, 1985 ("From the Street"), *On an Overgrown Path, In the Mist.* These are the major piano works. Recordings with all three will be treated together. *On an Overgrown Path* was issued in two sets; some recordings include both, others just the first. The Sonata commemorates a carpenter slain during a demonstration demanding a Czech university in Brno. *Path* is a set of sad pieces that look back on the composer's youth and mourn the death of his daughter. The enigmatic *In the Mist* may represent Janáček dealing with personal and musical problems.

Firkušný is classic and basic. His style is moving and flowing, and his playing sounds thought-out and spontaneous at the same time. There is a rightness to the phrasing, and his tone is warm, smooth, and pleasant (♦DG 449764, 2CD, with *Capriccio, Concertino*). His remake is darker, more reflective, flowing, and legato, though he doesn't turn Janáček into Chopin the way Schiff does (♦RCA 60147). This version is very good, with richer sound, but I prefer Firkušný's greater definition, spontaneity, and inspiration.

Avner Arad is direct, with clearly articulated *tenuto* (as opposed to *legato*) and is more vertically constructed than usual. His sound and touch are full, helped by a great recording. It's not the most idiomatic performance, but it's communicative, and those who don't know this music or think it's too mystical or oblique may like his forthright approach (♦Helicon 83341). **Pöntinen** also has a big sound, with great resonance that makes Janáček sound like Brahms. He's more flowing and less clear and vertical than Arad, but he's weightier, using more left hand. The recording is excellent, and the couplings are useful and hard to get in one collection (♦BIS 663/663, 2CD, with Violin Sonata and many other small works). **Mina Miller** is a dark colorist, though more romantic as well as less weighty and sturdy than Arad and Pöntinen. Her approach is almost dewy and some may find her soft, smooth, Schumannesque style not quite right for Janáček, but it's well played, with good sound, and recommended if the style appeals (Ambassador 1020).

Kvapil also plays with a dark tone but isn't as flowing as Pöntinen or Miller or as sturdy as Arad. He's solid, searching, and more reflective than inspiring or imaginative. My recommendation is based more on his good reputation and some reviews than my own preferences (♦Unicorn 9156). **Andsnes**'s tempos are slow but with liquid flow. His sound is a little bright and bell-like, favoring the right hand, and its iridescence is hard to resist, e.g., the sparkling treble in the (very) slow movement of the Sonata. It's well thought out with a Ravelian cast, interesting if you like slow tempos and a "French" Janáček (♦Virgin 91222). **Josef Páleníček** also has a light French touch, but his tempos are more straightforward, though there's something sad and resigned about his performances, particularly in *Overgrown Path*. He's sometimes a bit mannered and understated, but I return to him often (♦Supraphon 1481).

Alain Planès is the liveliest and most extroverted. His tone is bright, not as bell-like as Andsnes or as soft as Páleníček, and his touch is

harder and more "pianistic." I thought him a bit too heavily crisp at first, but his vitality and involvement won me over (♦Harmonia Mundi 80414). **Ivan Klánský** has a light, bright sound, sometimes a bit brittle and not as flowing and deep. It has its charm, and he's very good at revealing the intricacies of Janáček's complicated musical language. It's cerebral, in a way; listening straight through reveals a bit of sameness to the playing, but it's an idiomatic and informed sameness (Kontrapunkt 32042)

Thomas Hlawatsch provides a complete collection of Janáček's solo piano works on two discs. He has a clear, bright tone and a small sound. His playing is pleasant but not exciting or searching enough to get inside the music, particularly in the more serious works in Vol. I. Vol. 2 is more recommendable, with its unusual and more folk-like works (Naxos 553586, Vol. I: Sonata and *Along an Overgrown Path;* ♦553587, Vol. 2: *Three Moravian Dances, In the Mist, Concertino*). **Gilead Mishory** is darkish, though not as much so as Pöntinen. He can generate power, but he's not cohesive. His phrasing is erratic and halting, sounding mannered and not always convincing; sometimes it seems as if he's starting over at each new phrase (Tudor). **Schiff** is soft-textured, lyrical, and often light. He doesn't seem comfortable with these moody and wistful pieces; his rhythms don't feel natural and some phrases sound affected. He offers beautiful playing, but more like romantic Chopin than Janáček (London 440312: *Capriccio, In the Mists, Presto, A Fairy-Tale,* Piano Sonata, 440313: *Concertino, On an Overgrown Path,* Violin Sonata).

Piano Sonata. **Viktoria Postnikova** plays with an unusual blend of power (her strong left hand provides a big bass foundation) and tenderness, achieving great fortissimos and stunning pianissimos. This is dramatic and sensitive pianism (♦Erato 45599, with *In the Mists, Concertino, Capriccio*). **Papadopoulos** has a neutral, "medium Brahmsian" approach and sound, revealing his English training. There's an odd phrase here and there, but he offers a fine, straightforward performance; the main problem is in the imaginative but not very useful couplings (♦Hyperion 66167, with *Capriccio* and Stravinsky's Piano Concerto). **Marian Lapšanský** takes a warm and sweet approach (Supraphon 3378, with *Diary of One Who Vanished*).

CHORAL WORKS

Glagolitic Mass. This is one of the great masses, earthy and powerful, with massive orchestration and harmonies, chugging rhythms, wild brass, and extreme, fervent writing for soloists and chorus.

Mackerras's reading of Paul Wingfield's edition of the original version is a must. Janáček made changes because of insufficient resources and the premiering players' technical deficiencies. After his death, others made more changes. The result is the version we usually hear. With Mackerras we hear the "Intrada" at the beginning as well as at the end, a restored passage for tympani solo (rather than strings), another for three sets of tympani, and other more subtle changes. The result is longer, more complex, and adventurous. His performance is excellent, in a clear-headed, forward-looking style, more exhilarating than the earthy Czech renditions and less Germanic than Western readings of the standard version (♦Chandos 9310, with Kodály's *Psalmus Hungaricus*). The "Intradas" are a bit slow, but many sections are fast, particularly the "Agneče Božij" where he refuses to linger even in the slower passages. Chandos's sound is distant and not overly clear in the choruses, but no impediment to enjoyment.

Among the standard versions, **Ančerl** is classic for its blend of drama, lyricism, authenticity, singing, and sound (♦Supraphon 111930, with works by Miloslav Kabeláč). Not as fast as his *Sinfonietta* but just as intense, Ančerl had a great sense of Janáček's angular melodic drive and bright instrumental textures, with a brilliant Czech Philharmonic. **Mackerras** and the same orchestra combine a broad, lyrical style with brilliant strings and attractively raw yet warm brass to produce power and brilliance. It's similar to Ančerl in tempos but less intense and more expansive—not as great, but close. The recorded sound is more open if not as textured. The soloists, including Söderström, are first-rate (♦Supraphon 103575).

The quirkier, more ethnic **Košler** balances romance and drama in a thrilling reading (♦GZ 0088). The Slovak Philharmonic strings are warm and shining; the middle and low brass growl. His tempos are flexible: The lyrical spots are slowish, but "Svet" chugs along. The Slovak choir and Czech soloists sing with power and clarity, in big, open sound, tipped to the dark side. **Jílek** offers a different kind of Czech reading, more subtle, less intense, and sometimes slower (Supraphon 203916, with *Amarus* led by Mackerras). With its lyricism, reserve, and languor, it's a pastoral *Glagolitic;* some may find it too laid back, but Jílek did it well. The silvery Brno strings are an asset, and the young Benačková is wonderful. **Kubelik**'s version is one of the most exuberant (DG 437937, with Dvořák's *Stabat Mater*). The mood is light and happy, with tempos slightly fast, too much so in the organ interlude (but not in "Svet," which lags a bit). You don't feel the weight of other performances, the lyricism of Jílek, or much burning excitement, but it's elegant, lithe, and spirited. Evelyn Lear and Ernst Haefliger lead some fine soloists, and the Bavarian Radio Symphony conveys the conductor's mood.

Bernstein more or less introduced the work to the West in 1965. His tempos are slow and his textures are a bit thick and weighty, as he stresses the romantic at the expense of electricity (Sony 47569, with Poulenc's *Gloria*). The result is unique, as if the orchestra responds more to Bernstein's romanticism than Janáček's elemental passion. When it works, it's compelling, but sometimes it's logy. The strings range from sweet to thin, depending on the passage; the organ is immense. It's fascinating, though some may think it earthbound. **Masur** gives the best of the dark performances (♦Philips 110358, with *Taras Bulba*). There are bits of hurrying and plodding, but generally he keeps the music moving, with fine, idiomatic soloists (particularly John Mitchinson), and the Leipzig Gewandhaus projects grandeur and enough transparency and line to keep the work from bogging down. The organ solo is a stunner, and the low brass roar. All these recordings have thick, bass-heavy sound, but Masur's is the best.

Chailly's lines are broad and his textures full (London 460213, with Zemlinsky's *Psalm 83* and Korngold's *Passover Psalm*). This is a big, dark, and warm performance, and the broad, mellow Vienna Philharmonic adds to the effect. Janáček's jagged lines are smoothed out, but the big moments are huge, and the piece sounds more homogeneous and devotional than usual. Vladimir Bogachov is the vocal star, but Eva Urbanova's small Slavic soprano is good, too. The Slovak Philharmonic Choir adds Slavic flavor. **Inbal** is the most Teutonic, with chocolate-like textures from the Deutches Symphonie (Denon, with *Sinfonietta*). The brass is broad without edge and way back in the soundstage; there are no bright Janáček fanfares, nor is there much brightness in the woodwinds. The chorus is a velvet curtain and hard to understand. Tempos are slow and occasionally the pace flags; you can wallow in it, but it becomes oppressive. It's worth a listen, but it's not a first choice.

Shaw is so lyrical and soft-textured that the work comes off as ethereal and even remote (Telarc, with Dvořák's *Te Deum*). The chorus is good but overemphasized by the engineers, rendering the Atlanta Symphony too soft and lacking in edge. **Rattle**'s reading is beautifully played by the Birmingham Symphony, but underdone in the beginning, though it eventually recovers to good dramatic effect (EMI). **Tilson Thomas** never gets the piece to jell (Sony, with *Sinfonietta*). His tempos and phrases are often erratic and don't always fit together ("Svet" is so fast it sounds scrambled despite fine playing by the London Symphony), and his textures are too light. It's more a show than a mass.

Mass in E-flat. This mass for soloists, mixed chorus, and organ was Janáček's second mass (the first was lost). He finished only the "Kyrie," "Agnus Dei," and three-fifths of a "Credo." He returned to it for his first draft of the *Glagolitic,* but removed most of that material from the later work. The mass was preserved by Vilém Petrželka, who reconstructed the texts and completed the "Credo." The result is austere, not really typical of the composer, but it has some of his acerbic edge. **Cleobury** leads the Choir of King's College, Cambridge in Petrželka's version (♦EMI 49092, with *Lord's Prayer* and Kodály's *Missa Brevis*). **James O'Donnell** directs Wingfield's new version with the Westminster Cathedral Choir (♦Hyperion 67147, with Kodály's *Missa Brevis* and *Landes Organi*). Wingfield's "Credo" is closer to Janáček's style, a bit rougher and more experimental than Petrželka's sentimental version. He also adds a "Sanctus" that is the first draft of "Svet" from the *Glagolitic.* I prefer Cleobury's fuller, richer, and closer choral sound and his greater sense of drama, but I favor Wingfield's completion. Both use male choirs with boys sounding eerie in the treble. Both make Janáček sound British.

Nursery Rhymes. This is a collection of lighter pieces for various instruments inspired by children's cartoons. The work, expanded by Janáček in number of pieces and instrumentation, is presented by the **Academi Múzických Uměni Praha** and the Netherlands Wind Ensemble in its full edition. The singing is rustic and colorful, the orchestration sparkles, with striking parallels to *Cunning Little Vixen* (♦Chandos 9399, with *Capriccio, Concertino, Mládí*). **James Wood** conducts the New London Chamber Choir and Critical Band in the chamber version. It sounds more like Klezmer music than the more punchy, driven, and folklike Chandos recording. Accomplished as it is, the singing of the other choral works tends to be softer, more elegant, and more refined than Czech choirs deliver. Recommendable if you like the style (Hyperion 66893, with *The 70,000, The Wolf's Trail, Ave Maria,* and other choral works).   HECHT

OPERAS

The Cunning Little Vixen. In this humane comedy, animals outnumber the humans. The heroine Vixen is amoral, a seducing Fox gets the heroine, a mangy lovesick dog complains, chickens fuss, frogs leap, and insects dance. The humans seem to be little better than their animal counterparts.

A 1981 recording with the Vienna Staatsoper Chorus and Orchestra led by **Mackerras** (a Janáček authority) is just about as good as an opera recording can get (♦Decca 417129, 2CD). The warm yet radiant sound of the Viennese forces is a perfect match for Janáček's luxurious music. An all-Czech cast, with Popp a most endearing Vixen, creates not just a musical ensemble but a delightful group of characters, animal and human. A 1970 recording conducted by **Gregor** remains competitive (Supraphon 3071, 2CD). Its soloists are brilliant and easier on the ear than those in the 1979 version by **Neumann** (Supraphon 3471, 2CD).

From Covent Garden comes a distinguished English cast—Lillian Watson, Diana Montague, Thomas Allen, Robert Tear—reveling in their characterizations and textual details (♦EMI 54212, 2CD). Fine conducting by **Rattle** reveals orchestral lines and details with remarkable clarity and extraordinary recorded sound. But it's in English, and that's a problem: a choice between authenticity and intelligibility. The story is self-explanatory, so perhaps it's preferable to forego understanding of the text in favor of the sheer beauty of sound of the Czech performances.

The Excursions of Mr. Brouček.

This is a most curious comedy. The story is convoluted, satirical, yet told with music of great lyric beauty. Brouček's twisted and rather alcoholic adventures take him to the moon (Part 1) and then back in time for the Hussite Wars five centuries earlier (Part 2). At times the rapturous sonorities of the orchestra and the soaring melodic fragments of the vocal lines seem at odds with the embittered story, but such beauty is difficult to ignore. Although, as usual, Janáček took great pains to write music that would reflect Czech speech patterns, I think *Brouček* would be more accessible and enjoyable in translation.

For Janáček fans uncomfortable with Czech, the 1959 performance in German from the Bavarian Staatsoper will do nicely (Orfeo 354942, 2CD). The characters are well defined vocally and quite personable. Lorenz Fehenberger's Heldentenor isn't what it used to be, but he manages a more than creditable Brouček. For impressive singing we get Keith Engen, Kurt Böhme, and the legendary Wunderlich. Wilma Lipp has no difficulties with the stratospheric music of Malinka. **Keilberth** conducts with a sure and steady hand, and the mono sound is acceptable.

A necessity in performing Janáček operas and usually in evidence in their recordings by Supraphon is a sense of ensemble in the service of musical style. A 1962 recording by **Neumann** hasn't been issued on CD, although it captures a true ensemble performance. Other than tenor Beno Blachut, none of the singers is world-class, but they're quite worthy in their endeavors. A 1980 stereo remake beautifully captures the opera's orchestral and choral delights (♦Supraphon 2153, 2CD). The Czech Philharmonic led by **Jílek** play exquisitely, full of power and poetry. Vilém Pribyl is a vivid Brouček and again there is a fine sense of ensemble. Some of the singers are guilty of the East European vocal wobble, but these are minor matters.

From the House of the Dead.

This was Janáček's last opera and he didn't quite complete it or prepare an authorized edition. Thus its musicological complexities are fearsome and there has been much tinkering with the score by editors, experts, and conductors. Although almost relentlessly oppressive (the opera is based on Dostoevski's tales of a Siberian prison), even here Janáček's faith in humanity finally triumphs.

Many listeners' first introduction to this opera was a 1954 performance in German from the Holland Festival. A "corrupt" version, it was issued in mono LP (Philips/Epic), but hasn't been reissued on CD, nor has a 1964 recording by **Gregor** (Supraphon). Although monaural in sound, this would probably be the first choice for a recording of this powerful opera.

Mackerras's 1980 recording is the first based on the final authorized (but not autograph) edition of the score (Decca 430375, 2CD). In addition, Mackerras has tinkered with it, and the result is a heavier, more assertive version than its Supraphon predecessors. The Vienna Staatsoper forces strike a majestic note, perhaps too much so, sounding beautiful but failing to capture the anguish inherent in the music. The all-Czech cast here reverts to a style heavy on vocal acid and vital characterization.

A 1979 recording offers the Chlubna/Bakala adaptation of the opera with minor changes by **Neumann** (♦Supraphon 2941, 2CD). The large cast consists mainly of Czech opera veterans, all proficient in Janáček's textual and musical style; while never neglecting characterization, they generally sing with less acid than their Mackerras counterparts. The Czech Philharmonic plays with precision and less warmth and, in a curious reversal, supplies some of the acid lacking in the singers. The choice of recordings is difficult, but the anguish and poignancy of this performance wins.

Jenufa.

The original title of the opera was *Her Foster-Daughter,* more descriptive of the story, with its equal emphasis on *Jenufa* and the Kostelnička. The most accessible and most frequently performed of Janáček's operas, it was his first operatic success (1916, when he was already over 60). It not only propelled the composer into the national limelight but encouraged him to continue composition.

A 1952 monaural recording by **Jaroslav Vogel** is distantly recorded with chorus and orchestra making a pale impression, yet it remains a classic for its solo singing (Supraphon 3331, 2CD). Possibly the best of all the recorded *Jenufa*s, Stěpanká Jelinkova is profoundly moving, progressing from youthful innocence to radiant spirituality. Marta Krásová is a strong but not profound Kostelnička. Beno Blachut has the heroic tenor voice necessary for Laca, also progressing throughout the opera, moving in his characterization and sensitivity to the text. Steva ideally needs a stronger tenor voice than the lightweight Ivo Zidek, but he does create a charming cad of a character.

A 1969 performance again uses the forces of the Prague National Theater, this time with **Gregor** conducting an almost ideal performance (♦EMI 47629, 2CD). Zidek is back as Steva, his voice remarkably unaffected by the passage of time. Nadezda Kniplová is authoritative as Kostelnička, keeping the drama well within musical bounds. Vilem Pribyl's distinctive tenor may not suit all tastes, but he's an outstanding Laca. Unfortunately Libuše Domaninska's excessive vibrato and acid tone do little to win our sympathies for Jenufa.

Supraphon's third recording comes from 1977-78, but this time it's from the Brno Janáček Opera, conducted by **Jílek** (Supraphon 2751, 2CD). Kniplová and Pribyl are back, but time has taken its toll and neither artist is equal to their earlier recording. There is however, a tonally lovely Jenufa from Benačková, almost the equal of Jelinkova, and Vladimir Krejčik sings a strong Steva.

Mackerras's traversal of the Janáček canon finds his 1982 recording in first place (♦Decca 414483, 2CD). Sumptuous playing by the Vienna Philharmonic under committed, strong leadership adds up to a passionate drama. Söderström sings a strong yet touching Jenufa, able to stand up to Randová's majestic Kostelnička. Ochman is more sweet-toned than Dvorsky, good, but a reversal of roles would have been preferable.

A wildly dramatic 1988 performance at Carnegie Hall is a worthy supplement to the Mackerras version (BIS 449; MHS 624470T, 2CD). Benačková is again a poignant Jenufa, with Rysanek the most dramatic of Kostelničkas. Ochman and Peter Kazaras are excellent as the feuding brothers and the Opera Orchestra of New York respond well to **Eve Queler**'s passionate leadership. In a 1974 performance in Italian from La Scala led by **Jerzy Semkow,** Bumbry and Olivero are intensely dramatic yet sing with wonderful sensitivity (Myto 961142, 2CD). A filler of the same cast in the first half of Act 2 performed a week later is redundant.

Kata Kabanova.

After *Jenufa, Kata* is the closest Janáček came to a conventional operatic subject. The libretto is the composer's own adaptation of Ostrovsky's *The Storm,* a domestic drama of love gone astray within a suffocating social atmosphere. It's also difficult to fit *Kata* into Janáček's optimistic view of humanity and the continuation of life.

Krombholc's 1959 recording is a worthy effort, though superceded by later ones (Supraphon). In 1976 **Mackerras** touched up the score to introduce more of the bitterness that's in the music, yet the Vienna Philharmonic plays so beautifully that you scarcely hears that bitterness (♦Decca 421852, 2CD). Instead there is a full measure of passion, sweep, and dramatic involvement. Söderström is a perfect Kata, beautifully sung, with a depth of textual understanding, expressed through the most subtle nuances and dramatic gestures. Nadezda Kniplová's hard, acid tone is apt for the hateful Kabanicha. She too finds depths of drama in the text, and Dvorsky has found the poetry and passion lacking in Blachut's 1959 performance. Superior too are Libuše Márová and Zdenek Svěhla, with inspired contributions from the rest of the cast. Decca's recorded sound, thunderstorm included, clearly elucidates Janáček's score (originally Supraphon; ♦EMI 47629, 2CD).

Mackerras's second recording, this time with the Czech Philharmonic 20 years after his first, is almost as good (Supraphon 3291, 2CD). Benačková is a fuller voiced Kata than Söderström and equally touching, Randová is a nasty but less vocally dominating Kabanicha. In a 1998 performance from the Salzburg Festival there's a lot of extraneous stage noise and interpolated vocal effects (laughter) that can be annoying; the production was more successful visually than musically (Orfeo). **Cambreling** has the Czech Philharmonic playing well, but without much of the detail found by Mackerras.

The Makropulos Affair. Janáček constructed a tragedy from Karel Capek's comedy with a principal character who provides a complex role of widely varying emotions, emotionally dead and seeking spiritual redemption. Two recordings of this strange, bewildering opera are of almost equal value with only a narrow preference dividing them. **Gregor** leads a carefully gauged performance that fully reflects the odd combination of bitterness and tenderness, ugliness and beauty (♦Supraphon 8351, 2CD). Libuse Prylova is a soprano of Slavonic shrillness, but that's not out of place in this opera, and her grand vocal gestures capture the public, bitter side of Marty. The all-Czech cast give inspired interpretations, if falling less agreeably on the ear.

Magnificent playing by the Vienna Philharmonic tips the scale by its beauty (♦Decca 430372, 2CD). Again **Mackerras** drives his musical forces to inspired heights. His edition is also a bit closer to authentic Janáček. Here too Söderström seems to have deeply penetrated the complexities of the heart and mind of a Janáček character, beautifully sung with a wealth of textual and emotional detail. PARSONS

SONGS

Diary of One Who Disappeared is a song cycle for tenor, alto, woman's chorus, and piano. The text is a set of poems in which a rich man's son explains his decision to desert his family to marry a Gypsy. **Vilém Priybl** is a good storyteller whose light, expressive tenor and way with words draw the listener in; alto Libuse Márová is Priybl's equal, and the chorus sounds ethereal (♦Supraphon). Páleníček's piano is light and expressive. The American tenor **Grayson Hirst** has a small, clean sound and presents an intimate, fresh, and compelling account, helped by the expressive pianism of Kubalek (♦Arabesque 6513). Their close communication helps convey the drama. Dark-toned American mezzo Shirley Love is a bit heavy and domineering and a slight drawback. If British tenor **Langridge** lacks the plangency of Czech tenors, he's clear-toned, sweet, and musical. He carries off the intimate and passionate music well and is matched by Graham Johnson's sensitive pianism (♦Forlane 6746, with Dvořák's *Zigeunermelodien* and songs). Jean Rigby is expressive and seductive. Their performance is intimate and well contained if not particularly dramatic.

Peter Straka is similarly intimate as opposed to operatic, but warmer, sweeter, and darker in tone (♦Supraphon 3378, with Piano Sonata). Marián Lapšanský matches his style and takes a similar approach in the piano coupling. Dagmar Peckova sings with the right darkness. **Gedda** gives an operatic cast to the work. He's in fine voice and lends his usual ardor to it (♦Supraphon 7541). His fans will be pleased; those interested in a dramatic, fuller-toned approach should also like it. Věra Soukupová's chesty alto fits well, and Páleníček supplies sensitive accompaniment.

Haefliger's German-language account mirrors Langridge's expressive style, though his sound is sightly rounder and more lieder-like (♦DG LP). Kubelik is a wonderful accompanist; Kay Griffel is a light-voiced but fine alto. This account is slightly more absorbing than **Schreier**'s reading; he's more forward, bold, and Germanic, as well as slightly less subtle and expressive. Gertrud Lahusen-Oertel's alto is lush, and Lapšanský is a fine pianist if not as brilliant as Kubelik (♦Berlin 91692, with Dvořák's *Zigeunermelodien*).

Robert Tear's English-language version is marvelous, with pianist Philip Ledger and expressive mezzo Elizabeth Bainbridge. Tear's beautifully lyrical and ringing tenor makes this music his own, and the performance draws you in — if only his diction were a little better, particularly in loud passages where Ledger, wonderful though he is with his big tone, often overbalances the voice. English in tone and style, but very enjoyable, and in excellent sound (♦Argo 692, LP).

There is a version of *Diary* orchestrated by Zitek and Sedláček, very dramatic in this guise. **Abbado** and the Berlin Philharmonic do well with it (♦DG 427313, with *Sinfonietta*). Langridge's performance is similar to his Forlane recording, though his voice is a little lighter. Brigitte Balleys contributes a warm, light alto (lighter than Rigby for Forlane) that matches Langridge perfectly. The orchestrators were afraid to create a parody of Janáček and didn't go overboard to imitate his style; they filled in more and avoided his pitting of extreme orchestra frequencies against each other. The result isn't as edgy and brilliant as Janáček might have made it, but it sounds surprisingly authentic and is very effective.

HECHT

Joseph Joachim (1831–1907)

Though revered in his day both as a violinist and composer, Joachim seems destined to be remembered more for his close friendship with Brahms than for his own compositions. He helped Brahms with his Violin Concerto, yet his own three concertos remain at the fringe of the repertory. Through Brahms, Joachim came to appreciate the conservative style of Schumann and Mendelssohn, resisting the blandishments of Liszt and in time becoming even more openly opposed to Wagner. It was he who introduced the 20-year-old Brahms to the Schumanns, a seemingly innocent action that may have come back to haunt him many years later. It was Brahms's well-intentioned support for Joachim's wife Amalie when their marriage foundered that drove the two men apart, an estrangement that wasn't resolved until Brahms wrote his Double Concerto with its magnificent violin solo and in so doing brought about a reconciliation. Thus does friendship enrich our musical legacy.

ORCHESTRAL MUSIC

A number of overtures can be found, including an extensive survey by **Roland Bader** (Koch Schwann 1514). *Elegiac Overture in Memory of Heinrich von Kleist* is more fervent than sorrowful, depicting hero more than poet; it's carried off well enough by Bader but seems slack next to **Meir Minsky**'s recording (Marco Polo or Naxos, with Violin Concerto 3).

Later pressings include the overture to *Hamlet;* unfortunately he becomes a melancholy Dane indeed in Bader's hands. Minsky is far more impassioned, though he pales next to **Leon Botstein**'s hair-raising account (IMP, with the "Hungarian" Violin Concerto). It would be easy to imagine *Overture to a Comedy by Gozzi* as a work in which the fairy world of Mendelssohn was miraculously transported to Italy, or at least it would be if Bader didn't make it sound so dull-witted and sluggish.

Botstein also gives us the Overture to Shakespeare's *Henry IV*—inexplicably omitted by Bader—not nearly as melodramatic as you might expect, yet forceful and masterfully orchestrated. By way of amends, Bader offers the Overture in C, written as a birthday gift for Kaiser Wilhelm II—a heady romp, rich with the sound of brass and drum—as well as two marches that must have appealed to Bismarck though they seem a bit lightweight for the parade ground. Sadly, considering what might have been, it's these last few pieces—not otherwise available—that most recommend the Koch CD.

CONCERTOS

Of Joachim's three violin concertos, the first, in one movement, remains unavailable; the third, composed late in life, may have had a therapeutic value, as he intended it as a eulogy for Gisela Grimm, daughter of a close friend, Bettina von Arnim, and used a song by von Arnim in the opening movement. But it was Concerto 2, the so-called "Hungarian," that carried his name around the world. In substance it's a highly melodic and smoothly flowing work, with Joachim saving his Gypsy pyrotechnics for the czárdás-styled final rondo. **Aaron Rosand**'s performance is heavily cut (Vox), effectively shifting focus to **Elmar Oliveira,** already eminently recommendable for the *Hamlet* and *Henry IV* Overtures (♦IMP 27). There used to be an LP with **Charles Treger** with much the same impulses as Oliveira, but it hasn't been restored to the catalog (Louisville). Concerto 3 exists only in a bright, tonally secure if hardly overpowering reading by **Takako Nishizaki** (Marco Polo or Naxos). On a CD largely given over to Albert Dietrich's D minor Concerto, **Hans Maile** offers two more works by Joachim, a *Notturno* and a set of variations, the latter dedicated to Sarasate (Musica Mundi).   HALLER

André Jolivet *(1905–1974)*
In the 1930s, Jolivet was a co-founder of *La Jeune France,* the group of French composers reacting against the perceived triviality of *Les Six* and the retrogression of Stravinskian neoclassicism. Among the group only Messiaen became famous, but Jolivet did become a busy and important member of Parisian musical life. He was for many years music director of the Comédie Française and taught composition at the Paris Conservatoire from 1965 to 1970.

Jolivet was a prolific composer, particularly open to the influence of music from Africa and Asia. It adds a fascinating flavor to his Piano Concerto, a splashy, raucous work unlike any other in this genre. It was in a late-60s Columbia LP by **Entremont** with Jolivet conducting (worth seeking out) and it was usefully coupled on a CD with Cello Concerto 1 and Symphony 3, again led by Jolivet (Solstice 81, NA). The combination of exotic orchestral textures and jazzy rhythms makes Jolivet's trumpet concertos and Concertino very appealing; **Marsalis** and Salonen give brilliant performances (Sony 42096). A collection of string-orchestra music, with the Savoie Orchestra led by **Mark Foster,** is available, but the small ensemble and boxed-in sound hardly do justice to the composer's aural imagination (Timpani 1027).

Jolivet's flute music, particularly *Chant de Linos,* is quite popular. **Manuela Wiesler** has done very well by it, recording the Concerto (BIS

630, with Ibert and Roussel), *Suite en concert* for flute and percussion (BIS 272), and a collection with pianist Roland Pöntinen ; besides *Chant de Linos,* there are *Incantations,* a sonata, and *Ascèses* for alto flute (BIS 549). It's a good an introduction to the music of a composer little known in America.   RAYMOND

Scott Joplin *(1868–1917)*
Sometimes fame knocks not once, but twice. Ragtime composer Scott Joplin achieved in his lifetime what few black composers before him were able to do. He took the nascent piano rag form, languishing in dance halls and bordellos, developed it, and elevated it to a popular art form. Joplin was able to make a decent living at a time when black composers weren't taken seriously by the musical establishment. However, he longed to be treated as a respectable classical composer, as is evident from his subtitles: "Reflection Rag," "Syncopated Musings," "Chrysanthemum," and "An Afro-American Intermezzo." He composed a ballet, *Rag Time Dance,* but no current recordings exist. His Scott Joplin Opera Company produced his first opera, *A Guest of Honor,* but the music is lost. He failed to get his charming second opera, *Treemonisha,* produced, partly because his publisher was too risk-conscious and possibly because of its unorthodox structure, with its climax occurring before Act III. His popularity died shortly after he did and soon his work faded into eclipse.

What Felix Mendelssohn did for Bach more than a century earlier, pianist/scholar Joshua Rifkin, composer Gunther Schuller, and others did for Joplin in the early '70s. They rescued him from oblivion and sparked a renaissance of his work that's still going strong (although with diminished fervor). His work has appeared in three films, most notably *The Sting,* and in 1976 Joplin was awarded a posthumous Pulitzer Prize.

Joplin built his fame by writing and publishing more than sixty piano pieces. If you want to hear him play, try "Elite Syncopations" (Biograph 102) for three rags from piano rolls. His *Maple Leaf Rag* isn't as exciting as you'd expect, for it lacks expressive force; however, *Magnetic Rag* fares somewhat better. The third is his idiosyncratic performance of W.C. Handy's *Ole Miss Rag,* giving insights into playing techniques of 1916. Most of the other selections on this disc are piano rolls cut in the '60s by Hal Bouleware, respecting Joplin's repeats. These charming renditions may interest the historical collector.

In "Scott Joplin Piano Works 1899–1904," **Dick Hyman** performs a hurried *Maple Leaf Rag,* slowing down only during the reprise (BMG 57993). Hyman's work is inconsistent. His *Sunflower Slow Drag* has a music box regularity to it and *The Chrysanthemum* isn't quite bittersweet enough. However, his rendition of *The Weeping Willow* effectively treads the line between restraint and sentimentality, and *The Strenuous Life* is charming, with a well-articulated ending. Despite some compelling moments, this album is a narrow miss.

For highly idiosyncratic renditions, try **John Arpin**'s "Scott Joplin: King of Ragtime" (Pro Arte 562) and "Scott Joplin's Greatest Hits" (Pro Arte 397). While his *Sugar Cane Rag* speeds by the ears and *Scott Joplin's New Rag* is on the clangy side, his *Search Light Rag* features improvisations that impart a mid-century jazzy feel. In the old standards like *Maple Leaf Rag* and *The Entertainer* he takes chances, squeezing and stretching them with humor, verve, and daring. Listen to his sly rubato in *Solace* and *Bethena Waltz* and wonder why he calls himself a "classical ragtime player." Could a key component of ragtime be its plasticity? Arpin addresses this question in intriguing ways.

For a stunningly rendered and canonical Joplin, you can't go wrong with **Joshua Rifkin**'s "Piano Rags by Scott Joplin" (Electra 979159).

Rifkin was one of the trailblazers in the Joplin revival of the early '70s and it shows in this 1974 disc. His tempo shifts and atmospheric volume dips seem exactly right. The moods he weaves in pieces like *Bethena* and *Weeping Willow* are nostalgic and rueful. I wish he'd stomped his foot during the bridge in *The Ragtime Dance* (as Arpin does so uninhibitedly), but no matter. Rifkin gives the jaunty *Country Club* an infusion of such pure swing you might just break out into a two-step.

If you can abide a persistent tape hiss that jeers from the sidelines during *pp* moments, get the budget-priced "The Complete Works of Scott Joplin" (LaserLight 17021/25, 5CD). **Richard Zimmerman** competently plays 66 numbers, arranged chronologically and sparsely notated. While Zimmerman isn't as inspired as Rifkin or as eccentric as Arpin, his renditions are pleasing and forthright. Most notable are the obscure pieces on the final disk, half of which is occupied by piano transcriptions of *Treemonisha*. Unlike many performers, Zimmerman takes the title of *A Real Slow Drag* seriously and the results emerge with gentle conviction. He also plays the newly discovered *Silver Swan Rag* with ine syncopation and the slightest whiff of sentimentality. This set is worth the money.

William Albright performs in another boxed set, "The Complete Rags of Scott Joplin" (MHS 522771H) and "Marches, Waltzes & Rags of Scott Joplin" (MHS 513562F). He plays the 52 numbers respectfully, often preserving their innate sense of fun and wonder. To his credit, he creates intriguing spans between *pp* and *ff* passages and varies tempos in the waltzes most seductively. His improvised trills are sometimes clever (as in *The Entertainer*, which needs them), but sometimes cutesy (as in *The Easy Winners*, which doesn't). If you want a well-engineered (nearly) complete set with excellent program notes and can abide some spontaneity, try this one.

"Scott Joplin: The Red Back Book" (MHS 513737K) contains piano rag orchestrations by Joplin's contemporaries E.J. Stark, D.S. De Lisle, and several uncredited others. **Gunther Schuller** and his New England Conservatory Ragtime Ensemble produced this jaunty, likable collection in 1973 and its sound is crisp and compelling today. Although many rags are hampered by uniformity of tempo (the *Sunflower Slow Drag* is anything but), some, like *The Rag Time Dance*, shine through with humor and ingenious syncopation.

Initially, there is something disconcerting about "Scott Joplin on Guitar" (Nebula 5008). You may crave the piano's bass modulation and notice that the tonal color lacks fullness; a Joplin rag on guitar isn't the same as a Bach harpsichord piece on lute. But **Giovanni De Chiaro** spins well, creating both vivacious and poignant moods, particularly in more obscure pieces like *Eugenia* and *Solace: A Mexican Serenade*. His tempo shifts in *Bethena* are only slightly short of stunning. I wouldn't want this 49-minute CD as my only Joplin disc, but it's a compelling novelty.

Even more unorthodox are the guitar transcriptions in "The Entertainer Arranged for Fingerstyle Guitar" (Shanachie 98015/116). These 16 pieces by nine performers range in style from bluegrass to 1960's American/British folk style. Some of the pieces are so freely adapted as to be barely recognizable; others are twangy, like Tom Engels's staccato version of *Nonpareil*. Still, some are slick, subtle, and even innovative.

Only one of Joplin's two operas survives — *Treemonisha*. He worked at it for the latter part of his life. It's a strange amalgam of ragtime singing and European-style operatic arias, with some debt to Puccini and other verismo composers. The closest he came to seeing it produced was an unsuccessful audition he arranged in 1915 in Harlem to attract backers. After his death, the work slept for more than five decades and

awoke in the mid-70s. T.J. Anderson orchestrated it from the piano score and it received its first complete performance in Atlanta. The only recording is an earnest performance with excellent ensemble singing, recorded in 1976 (DG 435709). **Gunther Schuller** arranged and conducted this snappy version with the Houston Grand Opera. Sopranos Carmen Balthrop and Betty Allen play the pragmatic Treemonisha and her loving mother, singing their roles with lively lyricism. Tenor Curtis Rayam as boyfriend Remus sings the didactic aria "Wrong is Never Right" with soaring portamento. The spectacular final number, "A Real Slow Drag," ends the opera in a triumphant mood that swings, in a *fin de siècle* way.   BATES

Josquin Desprez *(ca. 1440–1521)*

Desprez is arguably the greatest composer before the birth of Bach. It's best to liken him to Beethoven: moody, dark, unpredictable, capable of flights of genius that take the breath away. Take my word for it, but also take others. From Martin Luther: "Josquin is master of the notes, which must express what he desires; those other composers must do what the notes themselves dictate." As late as 1711, Andrea Adami cites him as "the greatest luminary in the science of music." When practical musical printing was invented, Josquin figured prominently in the first publications of popular songs and dances, and was the sole subject of three mass publications, editions that sold out and necessitated reprints. The Vatican Choir kept Josquin in its active repertoire for over a century after the composer's death.

Biographical details can be summarized swiftly. He may have spent his early 20s at Sainte-Chapelle working for Louis XI's chapel; by 1484 we have him in the musical circle of the Sforzas in Milan. He became singer and then choirmaster for the Papal Choir under Popes Innocent VIII and Alexander VI, forged an association with King Louis XII's court (which seems to have loosely continued until the King's death in 1515), left for Ferrara in 1503, and returned home to Condé-sur-l'Escaut a year later. He also continued a relationship with the Hapsburgs through Marguerite of Austria (Marguerite's young nephew, the future Holy Roman Emperor Charles V, loved Josquin's compositions best of all), and died as Provost of the Abbey of Notre Dame in his birthplace.

That isn't much to go on to illuminate a genius outstanding even in an age of geniuses. Fortunately, the music survives. Many recordings are in and out of print; sadly, some of those in print celebrate the "opera dubia" (like *Missa Da Pacem*), while masterpieces like *Missa Fortuna desperata* aren't currently available. Most soon will be as Peter Phillips of the **Tallis Scholars** recently told me his first priority is to record every Josquin mass, on his own label. This is right and fitting for the artists who first made an early music recording the *Gramophone* "Record of the Year." This disc pairs the middle-period *Missa La sol fa re mi* with the most recorded and most revered *Missa Pange Lingua* from Josquin's late years (♦Gimell 009). The two masses on the *L'homme armé* theme are also now available (♦Gimell 019).

For decades, Josquin's *Missa Pange Lingua* was everywhere. From the late '50s with Safford Cape and his **Pro Musica Antiqua** (Archiv) to the long-lost **New York Pro Musica** (Decca), in the '60s with **Philippe Caillard** in France and **Martin Behrmann** in Germany, the work was in record bins everywhere. Both Joel Cohen and his **Boston Camerata** and **Ensemble Organum** recorded it in the 1980s (Harmonia Mundi); only the latter is still in print as part of a boxed set and not worth seeking out. Also still available is a performance with **Ensemble Métamorphoses de Paris** conducted by Maurice Bourbon, harkening back to the 1950s idea of instrumental doubling of the voices (Arion).

The mass paired with a motet program by O'Donnell and the **Westminster Cathedral Choir** is much more reliable (Hyperion 66614). The *L'homme armé* we're most familiar with, the "super voces musicales," was given a grand opera performance by the **Prague Madrigal Singers** (Supraphon, also with instrumental doubling), as well as a reading by **Jeremy Noble** (Bach Guild). Worth seeking (or lobbying for reissue) is the **Pro Cantione Antiqua** of London performance (Archiv LP 2533.360). This should not be confused with the fiendishly difficult "sexti toni" version of the mass performed by Summerly with his **Oxford Camerata**; the companion works include two motet masterpieces, *Ave Maria* and *Absalon fili mi*, along with Jheronimus Vinders's lament on the death of Josquin, and is a fine disc even at its bargain price (♦Naxos 553428).

Some ensembles have dedicated several recordings to Josquin. **A Sei Voci** with Bernard Fabre-Garrus has combined mass and motet settings with *de Beata Virgine* (Astrée 8560); the mass dedicated to Ercole d'Este, *Hercules dux Ferrariae*, paired with the beautiful setting of the *Miserere* (♦Astrée 8601); and *Missa Gaudeamus* in the only version currently available (♦Astrée 8612). Available in France (and soon on our shores) is their pairing of *Missa Ave Maris Stella* with Marian motets, and soon after, their version of *Pange Lingua* should be here. Perhaps we can get in line to persuade this fine ensemble to continue with their cycle, and performances of the masses *Mater patris, Malheur me bat*, the exquisite *Fortuna desperata*, and others might flow forth.

The **Boston Camerata**'s old recording of *Fortuna desperata* is all we have for this lovely work (Titanic 22, NA). Likewise, **Chanticleer**'s less than satisfying version of *Mater patruis* is still sometimes available if you contact the ensemble directly in San Francisco (Chanticleer 8808). Similarly in the "it's all we have" file, a most curious disc gives us *Missa faisant regretz* (listed as "Missa Elisabeth"), with a body of Russian sacred music featuring the **Tver Philharmony Madrigalist Choral Ensemble** directed by Igor Juravlenko (Pavane 7324).

There is a sort-of other recording of this mass, paired with a sort-of reading of *de Beata Vergine*, with **Ensemble Proscenium** directed by revisionist music historian Jacques Feuillie, who believes each note was to have been sounded sharply and then ended before the next. Thus, no legato, and a general effect of a chorus with the hiccups (Cybelia 881). But wait; it gets stranger still: how about both *Pange lingua* and *Hercules dux Ferrariae*, with motets and some of the great chansons—all arranged for guitar! Well, it exists, in a transcription and devoted performance by former rock guitarist **Jeffry Hamilton Steele** (Centaur 2384); it helps to illuminate just how intricate this music is, and may help increase Josquin listenership.

Back to a tributary group: Both the originals and heirs of the **Hilliard Ensemble** have given us much treasurable Josquin. One Hilliard offering contains the most beautiful *Ave Maria* on disc, as well as two works not by Josquin (♦EMI 61302). The boys of the Hilliards joined the Medieval Ensemble of London for the must-have but currently NA pairing of *Faisant regretz* with *Missa di dadi* from Josquin's youth; find it at all costs! (Oiseau-Lyre 411937). The next Hilliard effort was *Missa Hercules dux Ferrariae* with an exquisite performance of the *Miserere* and the linked *Ave Maria/Pater Noster* that Josquin wrote as a piece to be said in the church of Condé after his death; this floats in and out of print as well, but is also invaluable to Josquin lovers (♦EMI 49960). After Paul Hillier left the group to come to America, he recorded *Missa de Beata Virgine* with a very persuasive program of Marian motets by contemporary Jean Mouton; the **Theatre of Voices** lacks the technical perfection of the

Hilliards, but it's a lovely program nonetheless (Harmonia Mundi 907136).

One of Andrew Parrot's first efforts was in 1975 as a performer with the much-missed **Musica Reservata** ensemble in a recording of Josquin's secular music (Argo, NA). He returned to Josquin nearly 20 years later with his **Taverner Consort** and Choir in a stunning disc featuring *Missa Ave maris stella*, three Marian motets, and six chansons. Among the latter is a wondrous, nearly seven-minute perfomance of "Regretz sans fin," which is how I feel about not having this masterpiece readily available, though it may still be in cut-out bins (♦EMI 54659).

Peter Urquhart is a Josquin scholar as well as director of **Capella Alamire**. His version of *de Beata Virgine* can still be acquired (MHS), but for collectors, "The Early Josquin," with *Magnificat, Missa L'ami baudechon*, and mass fragments, is a unique starting point for learning about the composer (Dorian 80131). A few motets are also part of a program including music by Antoine Busnois and Nicolas Gombert (Titanic 202).

Sometimes single motets are enough to list recordings; most are part of other large-scale programs. A singularly dedicated Josquin proponent, Alexander Blachly with his **Pomerium** ensemble, offers a piece or two on each of his discs; the three motets in the superb "Book of Hours" are especially noteworthy (♦Archiv 457586), as are the two in his brilliant "Musica Vaticana" (♦Glissando 779001).

Danish composer and conductor **Bo Holten** brought out a 1992 recording much influenced by the chronology persuasively undertaken by the late Edward Lowinsky. It's a good mix of sacred and secular, with a reading of *Missa de Beata Virgine*, some of the chansons and instrumental pieces that can be linked to Josquin's affiliation with Louis XII, and a few late motets (Kontrapunkt 32110). Herreweghe's 1986 performance of seven motets with his **Chapelle Royale** is still good (♦Harmonia Mundi 901243). There are also seven (somewhat different) motets given less passionate but very fine readings by Higginbottom and the **New College Choir**, Oxford (Meridian 84356). The **New London Chamber Choir** under James Wood has given us *Hercules dux Ferrariae*, matched with Pierre de la Rue's beautiful *Requiem Mass* and the lament ("Nymphes des bois") Josquin wrote on the death of Ockeghem, the great master of the generation before (Amon Ra 24).

Having invoked Edward Lowinsky, we must take note of the 1971 "Josquin Symposium" in honor of the 450th anniversary of the composer's death. Many came together, much was advanced, and the music was provided by **Konrad Ruhland**, who had done so much for Josquin with his seven-motet recording in 1965, which was miraculously reissued (♦Sony 60362). *Missa La sol fa re mi* is here, and seven other motets (none duplicating his 1965 disc), but sadly, no recording of Lowinsky's own favorite work, "O Domine Jesu Christe." A minor recording of this piece exists with the **Copenhagen Schola Cantorum** (Danacord 390), but how lovely it would be if one of the great Josquin interpreters would turn to this as well as other rare masterpieces.

As for secular music: does anyone remember the passion **Alfred Deller** gave to the chansons? In fact, in the four decades or so since Deller gave us a set that included the rare chansons like "Parfons regretz," only the **Clement Janequin Ensemble** had a shot at a full chanson program, in "Josquin Des Prez: Adieu mes amours—Chansons" (Harmonia Mundi 901279, NA). Even the redoubtable **King's Singers** (who gave one CD to the secular music of Lassus, one to the sacred) mixed the two in their "Renaissance" disc (♦RCA 61814). There are 15 or so pieces there (as well as a handful of motets), and it's really all we have to match the glory days when entire concerts could be dedicated to the secular Josquin.

There's a glimmer of hope in a recent issue from **Musica Antiqua** of London directed by Philip Thorby. Called "Master of Musicians," the program presents the composer in the context of his contemporaries and pupils; it's thoughtful and sensitively done, and may be the leading edge of a new generation of discovery (Signum). I hope so, because in my opinion, no finer music has ever been created.   DAVIS

Dmitri Kabalevsky *(1904–1987)*

Kabalevsky's music is difficult to categorize, at least for Western audiences; lacking the coloristic display of Khachaturian, the ebullience of Prokofiev, or the emotional extremes of Shostakovich, there is little overt Soviet propaganda in his works. He's best known for his sparkling suite *The Comedians* and the overture to *Colas Breugnon,* though Piano Concerto 3 and Symphony 2 have had their share of recordings as well. Kabalevsky never strayed beyond the traditional boundaries of tonality and harmony; he may be considered a comfortable refuge from the stifling rigor of Soviet Realism, never forsaking his Russian heritage even in his music for the Party. Those who wish to think of him as a steppingstone from Khachaturian to Shostakovich have my blessing.

Orchestral music. For all their mastery of rhythm and color, Kabalevsky's first two symphonies inhabit an entirely different world from *The Comedians*—a world not far removed from Khachaturian, with an endless flow of melody and folk tradition. No. 1, written for the 15th anniversary of the October Revolution, is based on the same poem by Vladimir Gusev (*The Year 1917*) as Shostakovich's Symphony 12 written 30 years later. There's a brooding, anguished opening movement depicting the downtrodden Russian people followed by an Allegro celebrating the triumph of the revolutionary spirit in martial, even jaunty fashion. In 2, written two years later, Kabalevsky gives his more melodic and folkloristic inclinations free rein, the restless opening Allegro giving way to a world-weary Andante and a puckish final Prestissimo with insouciant writing for the winds.

Both 1 and 2 are available from **Erwin Acél** (Olympia), whose bland, lightweight approach pales beside **Tjeknavorian**'s devastating readings (♦ASV 1032). **David Measham** seems breathless in both outer movements of 2 (Unicorn). A better choice is **Dimiter Manolov** with a fine Bulgarian orchestra (Balkanton 30078, with Miaskovsky's Symphony 5). For 4 you'll need the Olympia set of the *Requiem* (discussed below), where **Kabalevsky**'s own recording is appended; alternately somber and resolute, with an almost dreamlike Scherzo, it's essentially a distillation of themes from his opera *The Family of Taras* and quite gripping on its own terms, and despite aged mono sonics the composer offers a compelling account of the score. We could still use a modern recording, perhaps combined with the still unavailable Symphony 3 ("Requiem for Lenin").

You can hear the beloved Russian circus in every bar of *The Comedians,* the familiar 'Galop' surrounded by other equally delightful fare. **Kondrashin** is unbeatable in this music as well as Khachaturian's *Masquerade Suite,* and his coupling of both pieces with the Tchaikovsky and Rimsky-Korsakov *Capriccios* remains essential, a treasured memory of a great conductor that still sounds wonderful (♦RCA 63302). No one else even comes close, though **Abravanel** (of about the same vintage) is enjoyable (Vanguard 5010). **Lapounov** seems to be going out of his way to distance himself from Kondrashin, with wildly variable tempos culminating in a slapdash 'Epilogue' (Consonance). **Vasily Jelvakov** is like-

wise hectic in the 'Galop' (Naxos), while **Tjeknavorian** is probably best of breed after Kondrashin—but the engineers have drowned out the tympani at the end (ASV 967). No such problem afflicts **Walter Mnatsakanov,** with Piano Concerto 1 as a splendid bonus (Olympia; see below).

A better reason to buy Jelvakov's disc is his very fine reading of the music for *Romeo and Juliet,* at times strikingly close to Prokofiev's better known setting; certainly this is true of the final dirge, which could readily stand beside Prokofiev's searing imagery. At the same time, there's a cinematic feel to much of the score, as Kabalevsky seems more absorbed in setting the scene (which he does beautifully) than in delineating the characters. Many episodes come off better under Jelvakov than in **Lapounov**'s more ponderous treatment, as **Tjeknavorian** brings great tension to the opening pages while allowing the final scene to unfold with affecting gravity. However, my favorite remains **Kitaienko,** not least for its adventurous coupling with Alexei Lvov's Violin Concerto in A minor and Glazunov's fragmentary "Ninth" Symphony (Olympia 147).

In putting together his score for Romain Rolland's uplifting play about 16th-century France, *Colas Breugnon,* Kabalevsky worked closely with the author, who praised the music highly, particularly its deft use of French folk melodies. Colas, a sort of lusty Burgundian Robin Hood, fires up the villagers to overthrow the villainous Duke, who has unleashed a terrible plague on the countryside. Most people know only the witty Overture, enshrined memorably by **Reiner** (♦RCA 61958), so we're fortunate to have the entire suite from both Jelvakov and Tjeknavorian as successors to **Golschmann**'s treasured Columbia LP (ML 5152). Here **Tjeknavorian** (ASV 967) is very much in his element, whereas **Jelvakov** (Naxos) just seems to be going through the motions (and is also more diffusely recorded), while **Lapounov** (Consonance) only plays the Overture. If the suite isn't enough, **Georgy Zhemchuzhin** offers the entire score with the Moscow Theater Orchestra and Chorus and baritone Leonid Boldin ably cast in the title role (Olympia 291, 2CD).

Concertos. Kabalevsky's Piano Concerto 3, like his Violin Concerto and Cello Concerto 1, was written for the Soviet youth movement; as such it's immediately accessible if not especially profound and remains one of his most popular works. The performance attributed to **František Maxián** on Urania 5176 is also on Sound 3437, where the soloist is identified as **Pavel Stepán,** but it's ebullient and smartly played in either event. One way around this problem is to buy **James Johnson**'s disc (Centaur 2089, with music by Robert Muczynski). **Feltsman**'s LP of 2 and 3 (Melodiya 33 C 10-08015-16) is also worth seeking out; in its absence you can confidently buy a combination of 2 played by **Nikolai Petrov,** 4 by **Yuri Popov,** and **Gilels**'s legendary performance of 3, all with the composer conducting (Olympia 269). And you can complete the series with **Anatoly Sheludiakov** in 1 on another disc, which also offers the *Rhapsody* based on Kabalevsky's popular tune "School Years," probably as well known to every Russian child as "School Days" is to us (Olympia 593).

Cello Concerto 1 brims with youthful energy; 2 goes a lot deeper, setting a more brooding opening movement against a jaunty Allegro (itself combining a saxophone solo with references to the familiar *Dies Irae* before resolving the conflict in an expansive and moving finale. **Marina Tarasova**'s pairing (Olympia 292), sodden and uninvolving, is best avoided in favor of the more spirited readings by **Alexander Rudin** (Naxos 553788). **Daniel Shafran**'s account of 1 is passionate and febrile to a fault, perhaps a bit over the top but undeniably stimulating (Omega 1026, with Schumann's Concerto, Haydn's Divertimento in D, and music by Falla). No. 1 has also been recorded by the redoubtable **Ma,** a vivid rendition with Ormandy and the Philadelphia (Sony 37840, with Shostakovich's Cello Concerto 1).

No. 2 is available with **Raphael Wallfisch,** richly satisfying and effusive (Chandos 8579, with Khachaturian's Cello Concerto and Glazunov's *Chant du Menestrel*). **Isserlis** is all warm and singing tone (Virgin 90811, with Prokofiev's *Concertino* and Cello Sonata), and **Mats Lidström** is taut and compelling (BIS 719, with the Khachaturian). It has also been recorded by **Shafran** and Kabalevsky, but this is unfortunately NA (Angel/Melodiya 40065, LP).

For many, **Oistrakh** remains definitive in the Violin Concerto, secure in tone and brimming with joy and naive enthusiasm that handily come across despite the archival sound of the Soviet recording (Omega 1025, with Glazunov's Concerto and Glière's *Romance*). You can also get Oistrakh with the Shafran, Gilels, and Popov concerto recordings mentioned above, all with the composer conducting (♦Revelation 10103). Or you can seek out Oistrakh's pupil **Mordkovitch,** who combines it with the Khachaturian concerto; unfortunately she's no match for her teacher, with forced tone and low-energy orchestral playing in both pieces (Chandos 8918). A better choice is **Shaham** (DG 457064, with Glazunov).

Chamber music. The contrast between Kabalevsky's two string quartets is striking, the earlier one reflective in mood and suggesting folk music, the other (written 17 years later) showing strong Soviet influences. Both are given eloquent and sympathetic readings by the **Glazunov Quartet,** who are totally immersed in this music (Olympia 293). The Cello Sonata is played well enough by **Antony Cooke** and Armin Watkins, but their labored treatment of the accompanying Rachmaninoff piece and poorly balanced recording make it difficult to recommend (Resort 3005). At that, it's preferable to **Marina Tarasova's** soporific account (Olympia 294, with other cello pieces). Your best bet is the ever-reliable **Parnas** (Arcadia 1992), or **Timothy Hugh's** colorful and rhythmically adept reading (IMP 49, with Shostakovich and Schnittke sonatas).

Piano music. There's an assured and straightforward if not especially subtle collection of Kabalevsky's piano music by **Murray McLachlan,** including Sonata 3, Sonatina in C, and 24 Preludes, of which only the sonata (written during WWII) ventures beyond the comfortable world of Russian folk music (Olympia 266). **Mary Ann Scialdo** gives a trenchant account of the sonata in a collection that includes Scriabin Preludes and Scarlatti sonatas, all unfortunately in rather distant and muddy sound (Camtre 1). It's worth hearing even if it lacks the steely brilliance of **Horowitz** (RCA 60377). Another fine version of the sonata is offered by **Irina Zaritskaya** with six of the 24 Preludes and music of Scriabin (Christophorus 0061). **Artur Pizarro** offers splendid readings of all three sonatas plus the *Recitative and Rondo,* which despite its supposed agenda—it was written for the 50th anniversary of the October Revolution—is highly enjoyable on its own terms (Collins 1418).

Choral music. The searing and highly dramatic *Requiem* may be Kabalevsky's masterpiece. Conceived at about the same time as Britten's *War Requiem,* much of the same turbulence and pathos attend this heartfelt tribute to "those who died in the war against fascism," but there is at the same time a militant fervor that warns against such a tragedy being allowed to happen again. It's superbly performed by Valentina Levko (mezzo) and Vladimir Valaitis (baritone) with the Moscow Symphony

and Chorus directed with white-hot fervor by **Kabalevsky,** truly a landmark of Russian choral music (♦Olympia 290, 2CD, with Symphony 4).

HALLER

Vasily Kalinnikov *(1866–1901)*

Kalinnikov has only recently come into his own among Western record collectors if not, regrettably, in the concert hall. Highly regarded by his peers, he never overcame the illness and poverty that burdened him almost from his first breath, finally succumbing to tuberculosis just two days short of his 35th birthday. He completed only a handful of works, most notably two symphonies, yet every bar of his music evidences a mastery of color and form, an opulence of scoring worthy even of Tchaikovsky. Hearing the symphonies today, suffused with the endless flow of melody and profound yearning that lie at the heart and soul of Mother Russia, there's no question that they're worthy of performance by major orchestras. These qualities, revered by generations past, are not so common in the music of our own time that we can afford to be without such wondrous creations.

Kalinnikov's Symphony 1 was once a mainstay of American concert programs, championed by Damrosch, Rodzinski, and even Toscanini, who performed relatively few works by Russian composers. Though there's a melancholy cast to much of it, there is little of the pathos you might expect from a struggling young composer. The weighty motif that opens Symphony 2 will surely call to mind Borodin's 2; it returns following the haunting Andante and swaggering Scherzo to join forces with the hearty Slavic theme of the finale.

Both symphonies have been paired on disc several times. **Svetlanov's** mid-'70s recordings have resurfaced, both coupled (Chant du Monde 278926) and individually (1: Melodiya 10-00171, with Rimsky-Korsakov's *Maid of Pskov;* 2: 10-00170, with other Kalinnikov). The additional material on the Melodiya discs (if you can find them) is worth the investment; moreover, they sound better than the Chant du Monde. **Neeme Järvi** offered them separately (1: Chandos 8611, with Glazunov's *The Sea* and *Spring;* 2: 8805, with other Kalinnikov); they have since been paired, unfortunately without the other material (♦Chandos 9546). Järvi responds to this music with warmth and soul, but the sound is a problem, far too echoey in 1 and little more than a glutinous mass (save for the piercing trumpets) in 2. A pity. **Kuchar** offers highly sympathetic readings with the superb Ukraine Symphony, easily worth the low price (♦Naxos 553417). The muted sound is a problem, but Kuchar's warm embrace is irresistible.

Veronika Dudarova tends to lean on phrases a bit, particularly in both opening movements, but her performances are otherwise welcome (Olympia 511). **Samuel Friedmann** recorded 1 (Arte Nova 65414, with Glinka's *Jota Aragonesa* and *Russlan Dances*), and we may hope 2 will follow, though it would have been better to have both on one disc. Given his rather broad tempos this might not have been possible, but the music responds well to such treatment, and the recording is more detailed than Kuchar's. Symphony 1 was once available in a beautiful performance by **Kondrashin,** unfortunately not yet on CD (Angel). There are also very fine mono versions of 1 with **Golovanov** (Music Boheme 2, with *Francesca da Rimini*) and 2 with **Mravinsky** (Russian Disc 11155, with excerpts from Glazunov's *Seasons*).

Svetlanov offers the otherwise unavailable *Suite,* a large-scale and thoroughly Russian exercise rich with folk influences, coupled with the tone poem *The Cedar and The Palm* and the overture *Bylina* (♦Melodiya 10-00169). The first contrasts the harsh, cold North (*Cedar*) with the sunny South (*Palm*), while the second, as the name suggests, is bardic in nature. Svetlanov is far more spirited than **Antal Jancsovics**, who combines them with the symphonic poem *The Nymphs* and incidental music to *Tsar Boris* by Alexei Tolstoy (Marco Polo 223153). **Järvi**'s original issue of Symphony 2 includes *Cedar and Palm* but only the overture to *Tsar Boris*, which is unfortunate since he's a lot better than Jancsovics, who makes a mockery of the Allegro marking. If you buy Järvi's Rachmaninoff 3, you'll also get *Two Intermezzos*, likewise worth having (Chandos 8614). These as well as *The Nymphs* and Serenade for String Orchestra are also included with **Svetlanov**'s Symphony 2, while *Tsar Boris* (including a couple of brief fanfares omitted by Jancsovics) is coupled with Scriabin's Piano Concerto (Melodiya 10-00191). Both Melodiya and Marco Polo are recorded well enough, but Svetlanov has the edge for ensemble. We may hope that Järvi will record the whole thing.   HALLER

Imre Kálmán *(1882–1953)*

Kálmán was one of the last great composers of Viennese operettas, dominating Vienna and the stages of Germany and Austria during the first 30 years of the 20th century. Born in Hungary, he retained a strong element of Hungarian music in his operettas, also introducing stereotypical ideas about Hungarians and gypsies. Several of his operettas are still basics of the repertoire.

Die Bajadere is rarely performed today. Its East-West plot is neatly reflected in its mixture of pseudo-Oriental music, champagne-drenched waltzes, and buffo-soubrette tunes. A 1998 performance in English by the Ohio Light Opera makes a strong case for it. **J. Lynn Thompson** conducts with affection (♦Newport 85655).

Die Csárdásfürstin (The Gypsy Princess) is a winning blending of Hungarian and Viennese musical elements and one of Kálmán's most popular works. Two good 1971 recordings come from Munich. **Bert Brund** has a good pair in Moffo and Kollo (Eurodisc 610317, 2CD), but **Willy Mattes** is even better with a radiant Rothenberger and suave Gedda (♦EMI 69672, 2CD). A 1985 recording from the Vienna Volksoper finds Milena Rudiferin and Franz Waechter in good form (Denon 7933, 2CD).

Gräfin Maritza (Countess Maritza) is an appealing work, filled with many memorable tunes wedded to a romantic Viennese plot. Rothenberger and Gedda are again charmingly excellent in Munich in 1971 under **Mattes** (♦Arabesque 8057, 2CD).

Die Herzogin von Chicago (The Duchess of Chicago) mixes jazz, American dance music, waltzes, and Viennese operetta froth into a heady brew. **Bonynge** and the Berlin Symphony join with excellent soloists in a fine musical romp (♦Decca 466057, 2CD).   PARSONS

Giya Kancheli *(b. 1935)*

Kancheli's works all describe an enigmatic and unsettling concatenation of Eastern Orthodox liturgical music, Georgian folk influences, spare timbral lushness, and grating, tantrumlike outbursts that make for unexpected intrusions. Running through it all are threads of loneliness and disillusionment as rarefied as *Das Lied von der Erde* and as paralyzing as late Shostakovich. You might call Kancheli the definitive post-Cold War composer. His anxious works are desolate if often beautiful landscapes, illuminated by rare flickers of hope and humanity; they are laments for lost innocence.

SYMPHONIES

Jurowski and the Berlin Radio Symphony give us 7, Kancheli's last symphony, and 2, one of his first (CPO 999263). The listener's memory is at a loss by the time we reach the thirty-minute 7's final cadence, the long path behind us strewn with gestural carcasses as we hear the closing, tolling Ds that end the piece. Full of textural niceties, 2 is more lyrical and sinuous and reveals the influence of Georgian folk music. Jurowski is always worthy of praise, but his 7 doesn't have quite the omniscient pacing, poise, and glowing orchestral contribution of **Jansug Kakhidze**'s with the Tbilisi Symphony (♦Sony 66590). The Berlin acoustics do a better job of containing the composer's trademark climaxes (which tend, in Kancheli's words, to leave "the paint peeling from the ceiling"), but the Tbilisi hall has a warmer sound than the Berlin.

With their 3, **Welser-Möst** gives us the overall finest account of a Kancheli symphony (♦EMI 55619, with Arvo Pärt couplings). There's a luminosity to the London Philharmonic sound that's not always heard in Davies's Vienna and Stuttgart recordings of this composer. The EMI engineers also enable the extremes of soft and loud to occupy the same acoustic space, the louds not sounding gratuitous. Perhaps even more distinctive as a performance is **Kakhidze**'s 1979 recording with the Georgian State Symphony (Melodiya/Olympia), but the sound is rather fuzzy and flat next to Welser-Möst, and Kakhidze's alto voice (Gamlet Gonashvili) is balanced a bit too closely.

With its bells and juxtaposed charm and brutality, 4 might be called the most rhythmic and Stravinskian of Kancheli's symphonies. No. 5, on the other hand, is perhaps his darkest and most savage—the opening nursery-rhyme tune, with harpsichord accompaniment, is bitterly, ironically contradicted. Both scores were taped by the musicians who gave the premieres, the Georgian State Symphony under **Kakhidze** (♦Olympia 403 and Nonesuch, from a Melodiya original). These brilliant performances are powerfully designed and impeccably played, and my only reservation is the slightly hissy 1981 sound that isn't up to 5's pile-driving climaxes; the winds are also balanced a bit too closely. The disc is recommended nonetheless.

No. 6 is a more rarefied piece, from its quiet modal start to its hesitations and poignant pauses. Kancheli's hometown band and favored conductor, **Kakhidze** and the Georgian orchestra, have recorded the work twice: Their 1981 performance (Olympia) has less forceful detail, while the 1994 version (♦Sony 66590) has crisper and more transparent sound, which enables you to hear a good deal more of what's happening in the score. Kakhidze's reading itself has remained remarkably consistent.

OTHER INSTRUMENTAL MUSIC

Abii ne viderem, for viola and strings, has particular importance for Kancheli's relationship with his country. The title means "I turned away so as not to see," and refers to the anxious guilt that attended his departure at a time when atrocities and horrors were engulfing his native Georgia. **Kim Kashkashian** and the Stuttgart Chamber Orchestra under Dennis Russell Davies (ECM) turn in a very fine performance, but they don't convince you this is one of Kancheli's more distinctive compositions. Also on the disc are *Evening Prayers* for chamber orchestra and voices, where I have similar misgivings over the music itself despite a sensitive contribution from the **Hilliard Ensemble**.

Just as vaporous, although more memorable, is *Morning Prayers* for chamber orchestra, voice, and alto flute. Like *Abii ne viderem*, *Vom Winde Beweint* ("Liturgy for Solo Viola and Large Orchestra") is a clearly sincere work that still uses some stock figures (rustling strings, droning ostinatos) that can seem a little obvious. **Kashkashian** and Davies offer a well-judged interpretation that makes an excellent filler for her rendition of Schnittke's magnificent Viola Concerto (ECM 1471).

You appreciate the discretion, simplicity, and sincerity of those players when you turn to *Winde Beweint* from cellist **France Springuel** and I Fiamminghi under Werthen (Telarc). The Telarc team milks the music for all it's worth, overloading its quieter passages with gooey sentiment and making the climaxes loud and noisy, like they're from a Hollywood biblical epic.

But I've saved the best for last: *Winde Beweint* is utterly transformed in the hands of Kakhidze and the Georgia State Symphony (♦Melodiya 49958). The phrasing takes on wonderful shape and direction, thanks also to soloist **Yuri Bashmet's** rich and free sound. This is one of the better Kancheli discs in the catalog, and it's at budget price. The generous coupling is Kakhidze's equally valuable rendition of *Light Sorrow* (see below).

The recent *Simi,* for cello and orchestra, is perhaps a more rewarding solo vehicle. **Rostropovich,** the dedicatee, gives a truly inspired reading with a luminous Royal Flanders Philharmonic under Kakhidze (♦ECM 1669). There's no posturing to be heard from these great musicians, and the coupling—*Magnum Ignotum* for wind ensemble and tape, in the tradition of Stravinsky's great *Symphonies of Wind Instruments*—is a fascinating piece. Kancheli tailors his music around the intonations of the mellifluous speaking voices on the tape, and this brings him to some outright major-key tonality.

With the opening of *Midday Prayers* and its first quiet echoes of solo clarinet, triads in the piano, and violin harmonics, the listener is inducted into a mellifluous narrative and confessional of the soul. As is so often the case with this composer, loud, sudden, and dissonant exorcisms in the full orchestra lie opposite distant recollections of nursery tunes, waltz rhythms, and lonely mezzo lines from *Das Lied von der Erde.* The disc from **Davies** (♦ECM 1568) also holds *Caris Mere* for soprano and viola, a brief but in some ways even more remarkable piece. **Kashkashian** pulls a veritable orchestra of subtleties from her instrument, and her coordination with soprano **Maacha Deubner** bespeaks real musicality.

In *Night Prayers,* Kancheli uses a soprano voice as well as the soprano saxophone of **Jan Garbarek,** a tape, and the orchestra. Nightmares always appear in Kancheli, making up part of his tender and childlike naivete. In this piece the nightmares are timbral, yet at the same time he also lays out a quiet feast of sounds; the delicate tones on the tape recreate some kind of primeval wind instrument somewhere between shofar and whale song. The **Kronos Quartet** has recorded the original quartet version of *Night Prayers* (Nonesuch); the limitation to four players gives more prominence to the tape and its otherworldly sounds, but surely the composer wrote the orchestral version because he realized a quartet is not up to the score's bigger, slashing sonorities.

Lament is typically hard to categorize as symphony, rhapsody, song cycle, or otherwise (♦ECM 1656). Kancheli set a text by Hans Sahl, the German Jew who worked after WW II searching the German soul and also searching for transcendence. **Maacha Deubner's** boyish voice is used only as an incidental detail. **Gidon Kremer's** violin is a more consistent presence, but the piece is even less a concerto than it is a vocal form. After finishing his symphonies, Kancheli seems to be integrating cinematic, incidental discourse with large forms of symphonic length. *Lament* isn't as forward-directed as his symphonies, nor are details as lovingly touched in as they are in his beautiful song cycle *Exil.* But the end of this gray tapestry is still, somehow, unmistakably its end. The ECM performance is undoubtedly definitive, hosted as it is by the composer's most faithful conducting colleague (Kakhidze), his hometown orchestra (the Tbilisi Symphony), and one of the great violinists.

Trauerfarbenes Land is a 37-minute orchestral piece, or rather (as ECM's liner notes would have it) "an austere musical procession, solemn and resigned in the face of inevitable death." This is one of Kancheli's more obviously direct scores, and the Vienna Radio Symphony under **Davies** is perhaps more appropriate for this than for some of Kancheli's more radiant and nostalgic compositions (♦ECM 1646). *A la Duduki* is a companion work, though its setup of brass quintet and orchestra tends to make it sound like Renaissance or Baroque music, and the vocabulary can sound stridently Middle-Eastern.

Like many Soviet composers, Kancheli wrote a lot of music for films. An Olympia release gathers studio recordings of music from four soundtracks recorded by **Kakhidze** and **Sergei Skripka.** But the cues tend to be short, quite a few of them are popular material that might be from the films but seem to have nothing to do with Kancheli (maybe he just scored them?), and the sound is mediocre. It's a disc to be avoided.

VOCAL MUSIC

The song cycle *Exil* is Kancheli's finest piece: a feast of chastened and otherworldly sounds, with the ensemble of five players (plus tape and **Maacha Deubner's** boyish soprano) conveying more quiet evocation than tragedy (♦ECM 1535). As conducted by Jurowski, the Eastern European players are absolutely stunning for their blend and timbral delicacy, and Manfred Eicher comes up with particularly deep and rich recorded sound—particularly gratifying when it comes to the alto and bass flutes. In such a sympathetic performance, *Exil* has a rare sense of quietude that will haunt and captivate you. Not an experience to be forgotten.

Light Sorrow (sometimes translated as "Bright Sorrow") is a cantata for orchestra, boy's choir, and two boy sopranos. Kancheli finds children's voices particularly sympathetic, thinking of them as tokens of divinity in a soiled world. The choice lies between **Werthen** (Telarc) and **Kakhidze** (♦Melodiya 49958, with Bashmet's *Winde Beweint*), and again it's Kakhidze who personalizes the music and yet somehow gives it its own voice.

ASHBY

Aaron Jay Kernis (b. 1960)

In little time, Kernis has become one of today's most interesting American composers. The diversity of his mentors—Adams, Wuorinen, Subotnick, Druckman, and others—has had a powerful impact on his music, but he has found a distinctive yet stylistically diverse voice at an early age.

Symphony 1 ("Symphony in Waves") plays with watery metaphors (Argo 436287). Early Adams comes to mind, but Kernis's transgressive humor bubbles up at the end of the second movement, when Jerry Lee Lewis's rock-n-roll piano floats to the surface. **Schwarz** conducts. On the same disc is the large, mature Quartet 1 ("Musica Celestis"), influenced by medieval music and written for and performed by the **Lark Quartet.** The subtitle alludes to angels' music. While not precisely polystylistic, the work shows Kernis's receptivity to influences as diverse as Hildegard of Bingen and contemporary funk.

A second CD is dominated by *Colored Field,* a dark, apocalyptic concerto for English horn inspired by a visit to Auschwitz and Birkenau (Argo 448174). The first movement, contradicting its pastoral beginning, climaxes with orchestral assaults on soloist Julie Ann Giacobassi's innocence. Kernis aptly describes the ensuing "Pandora Dance" as "little black things slithering out of a box." Perversion is silenced in the final "Hymns and Tablets," an extended confrontation between divine law and human destructiveness, with the soloist as anguished intercessor. **Alasdair Neale** conducts. *Still Movement with Hymn* is a massive piano quartet that maintains *Colored Field*'s dark, protesting mood but is less histrionic and more subtly shaded.

Symphony 2 is also tragic. Kernis's stimulus was the Persian Gulf War, and the spiky rhythms of the opening "Alarm" are unmistakably American (Argo 448900). "Air/Ground" proceeds mournfully, never achieving rest, and "Barricade" rekindles the hostility, emphasizing the stupidity of war. *Musica celestis* is an arrangement for string orchestra of the second movement of Quartet 1, and *Invisible Mosaic III* is a riot of brilliant fragments, inspired by church mosaics. Again, touches of Adams inform this work. **Wolff** is the conductor.

Kernis returns to gentler territory in the Double Concerto for violin and guitar (Argo 460226). Jazzy outer movements surround a passionate nocturne. Here, **Wolff** conducts Cho-Liang Lin and Sharon Isbin. The disc opens with Joshua Bell playing *Air* for violin, an arrangement of an atmospheric work for violin and piano (see below). *Lament and Prayer* was written "in commemoration of the 50th anniversary of the end of World War II and the Holocaust"; **Pamela Frank**'s violin mourns with, calms, and inspires the orchestra. **Zinman** conducts these two works.

A number of chamber works played by the **Eberli Ensemble** are appealing (Phoenix 142). *Meditation,* in memory of the recently murdered John Lennon, features Kernis himself as pianist; cellist Michael Finckel creates long, elegiac lines. *Air* is heard in its original version, with Kernis's wife, Evelyne Luest, at the piano. Luest also plays *Before Sleep and Dreams,* a suite for piano that depicts a child's preparations for bed, in which darker tones suggest an existential slant. *Four Seasons of Futurist Cuisine,* a setting of Marinetti's "cookbook" cum artistic manifesto, brings the disc to an outrageous end with narration about "raw meat torn by trumpet blasts" and a "drum roll of colonial fish".

A collection titled "100 Greatest Dance Hits" also emphasizes Kernis's playfulness (New Albion 083). The polystylistic title work for guitar and string quartet climaxes with cries of "Dance Party!" and *Superstar Etude #1,* another Jerry Lee Lewis tribute, asks pianist **Christopher O'Riley,** already busy with pounding chords and ecstatic glissandi, to repeatedly exclaim "Ohhh, baby!" *Mozart En Route* for string trio retools bits of the K 563 Divertimento, American-style. *America(n) (Day) Dreams* is a setting for mezzo-soprano and ensemble of texts by poet May Swenson. Loveliest of all is "Nocturne," with texts from the *Song of Songs,* in a setting for soprano and gently chiming pianos, glockenspiels, and trumpet. Three more song cycles — *Morningsongs, Love Scenes,* and *Brilliant Sky, Infinite Sky* — further trace Kernis's development as a writer for voice (CRI 635). The latter is a particularly sensitive setting of texts dealing with the nature of reality. The singers are **Opalach,** Carmen Pelton, and Sylvan, respectively

The **Lark Quartet**'s second recording of Quartet 1 is no less accomplished than the first; if anything, it's a little more seasoned and secure (Arabesque 6727). Quartet 2 ("Musica Instrumentalis") was written in 1997 and won the Pulitzer Prize the following year. It draws upon Renaissance and Baroque dance forms; the finale is a "Double Triple Gigue Fugue (after Beethoven)," and its concentrated language and joy in what might otherwise seem to be academic contrivance make repeated listening natural.

"Dance Mix" contains the brief but notable *New Era Dance* (Argo 444454). The composer claims it was inspired by Los Angeles's 1992 riots and by the presidential race. Another inspiration was the eclectic mixture of sounds that Kernis heard in his Washington Heights neighborhood.   TUTTLE

Albert W. Ketèlbey (1875–1959)

Ketèlbey wrote a piano sonata at age 11 and won a music scholarship to Trinity College at 13, but his career took a left turn after that: He found fame and fortune throughout Britain as the composer of indelibly tuneful orchestral and piano trifles with flossy titles like *In a Persian Market, Sanctuary of the Heart,* and *In a Monastery Garden.* (Several of the piano pieces were published under the name Anton Vodorinski.) The long-lived composer's music was ubiquitous in England from the '20s through the '50s, but except for the occasional Mantovani or Fiedler recording, he never caught on in a big way in America; *we* had the jazzier, cleverer Leroy Anderson for our pops.

Ketèlbey called his descriptive pieces "narrative music"; *Grove* sums them up fairly as "sentimental pieces characterized by broad melodies and garish orchestrations." They have a firm place in the long history of English light music, and not surprisingly the extant collections are all by British conductors: **John Lanchbery** (Classics for Pleasure 4637), **Adrian Leaper** (Marco Polo 223442), and **Eric Rogers** (London 444786). All add a chorus for the big numbers like *In the Mystic Land of Egypt,* and all are very well recorded. There is a collection of 1928–38 recordings of all the favorites led by **Ketèlbey** himself (Pearl 9968).

RAYMOND

Aram Khachaturian (1903–1978)

This Russian-Armenian composer was first known for his flamboyant piano concerto, which brought him international acclaim after its composition in 1936. His 1940 violin concerto was equally successful. These two pieces display all the elements that have made him popular with listeners: accessibility, romance, color, a flavor of folk song, noisy bravado — and perhaps more poignancy, especially in the Cello Concerto and Symphony 2, than many critics have given him credit for. The suites from his ballets and incidental music, such as *Gayane, Spartacus,* and *Masquerade,* are bright, enjoyable fillers for both concert hall and compact disc. Despite detractors, who sometimes refer to his music as kitschy, vainglorious, and empty, the excitement and color of Khachaturian's work will undoubtedly ensure an enthusiastic audience for many years to come.

SYMPHONIES

Khachaturian's three symphonies, though tuneful and accessible, are not generally as well known as his concertos and the particularly well-loved ballet suites. **Tjeknavorian** offers all three in good, exciting performances (♦ASV 858, 1 and 3; 859, 2), but veteran collectors will tell you that in some cases the best recordings haven't yet made it to CD. They call for a reissue of an older Tjeknavorian LP that provides a richer recording of 1 than is now available (RCA 25203); likewise for 2 and 3, no one has really matched **Stokowski**'s LP, which steadfastly refuses to appear on CD.

Until these reappear (if they ever do), Tjeknavorian is your sole choice for 1. For 2, don't miss **Khachaturian**'s own version as he conducts the Vienna Philharmonic in a heartfelt reading of this commemoration of the October Revolution (♦London 448252). Symphony 2 is regarded as the composer's best symphony, and certainly he shows a skill and flair in handling the large musical form that can be compared to Shostakovich. This 1962 recording is very good for both sound and performance, and no one should be without it for its historical value. For another truly superior performance that brings out the inherent grandeur of the music, try **Neeme Järvi** (♦Chandos 8945). The funeral march in III is particularly compelling here, and this version is probably the best all-round now available.

For 3, try either Tjeknavorian or **Fedor Glushchenko** (♦Chandos 9321). The organ sound is better on the Chandos, but Tjeknavorian goes a bit faster and thus is lighter overall.

OTHER ORCHESTRAL MUSIC

Khachaturian's ballets have memorable, colorful moments that are very easy to excerpt; thus snippets have been recorded many times. The "Saber Dance," a piece audiences probably recognize most readily of all his music, is from *Gayane,* a Soviet ballet that takes place on a collective farm. Four suites have been taken from the *Spartacus* ballet, and another favorite is *Masquerade,* a suite based on incidental music to a play.

You can go to **Anichanov** for *Gayane* Suites 1–3 (♦Naxos 550800) and *Spartacus* Suites 1–3 (♦Naxos 550801), and to **Dmitri Yablonsky** for *Spartacus* Suite 4, with *Masquerade, Circus,* and *Dance Suite* (♦Naxos 550802). For a shorter and well-played sampler of *Gayane, Spartacus,* and *Masquerade,* try **Alexander Lazarev** (♦Erato 94677). These recordings, while not necessarily the best, past and present, are certainly very good for both sound and performance, and they give the listener an entirely adequate introduction to this music. For a more expansive (and expensive) exploration of these pieces, you can go to **Tjeknavorian**'s recordings in various all-Khachaturian releases (ASV 773, 884, 946, with other works); they're all serviceable, with decent sound.

If these colorful pieces take your fancy, look out for Tjeknavorian's *Gayane* LP (RCA). Collectors are nostalgic about these performances, fondly wishing they would be released on CD. A complete recording of the 1957 revised version of *Gayane* by **Djansug Kakhidze** has appeared, but it's marred by sound problems and a spotty performance (Russian Disc), and *Spartacus* conducted by **Khachaturian** (London 417737; Decca 460315) and *Gayane* by **Stanley Black** (London 417062) are still available, both in good recordings. I like **Järvi**'s selections on several Chandos discs; four movements of *Gayane* appear on **Orbelian**'s recording of the piano concerto, including "Saber Dance" (Chandos 8542).

The complete *Spartacus,* a ballet depicting the revolt of a Roman slave, is available from **Zuraitis** (♦IMP 992, 2CD). Despite some sonic imperfections, this recording is solid and coherent, well worth having. If budget is a problem, excerpts from this version are in one disc (♦IMP 988). These renditions bring an assurance and warmth to the music that **Järvi**'s Suites 1–3 lack, even though their sound is excellent and the Scottish National Orchestra plays with polish (Chandos). The Naxos Suites 1–3 have a less lush sound than those on Chandos, as might be expected, but the sound for 4 with its accompanying pieces is improved.

I like **Järvi**'s *Masquerade* suite (Chandos 8542) as well as **Anichanov**'s (Naxos 550802); Järvi's is a little more flamboyant. **Stanley Black** gives a big, vibrant performance of this suite (London 448252; the conductor here is mistakenly identified in *Schwann* as Khachaturian himself, who does conduct his Symphony 2 on the same disc). Apparently RCA listened to the cries of collectors a few years ago and reissued **Kondrashin**'s excellent *Masquerade* (♦RCA 63302; MHS 515725).

CONCERTOS

Cello. Two excellent but quite different modern recordings are available. My favorite by a slight margin is by **Raphael Wallfisch** with Bryden Thomson conducting the London Philharmonic (♦Chandos 8579). The sound is immediate, with strong orchestral backing. It's a flashy performance, with lots of light and color, yet with much emotion and tension that keeps it from being superficial. Wallfisch's reading is polished and beautifully shaped, with a smooth and lovely tone. For a much darker, more introspective atmosphere, try **Mats Lidstrom**'s version with Ashkenazy (♦BIS 719). The somber reading is accentuated

by his smoky tone. Both discs contain Kabalevsky's Cello Concerto 2; the Chandos also has Glazunov's *Chant du Ménéstrel,* while BIS carries a very beautiful arrangement of Rachmaninoff's *Vocalise* for cello and piano.

Piano. Without doubt, the best available performance is by **Kapell**; for the best sound, you should purchase the "William Kapell Edition" Vol. 4, a wonderfully edited and digitally remastered release that has sent reviewers into ecstasies (♦RCA 68993, with Prokofiev's Concerto 3 and some Shostakovich preludes). This version, played with Koussevitzky and the Boston Symphony, is widely regarded as Kapell's best. Another version, made in 1945 with the NBC Symphony and Frank Black, is still available, but the orchestral sound is simply awful (VAIA 1027). Kapell's playing goes a long way toward making up for deficiencies in sound, though, and the disc includes Rachmaninoff's Concerto 3, which the large set doesn't have.

My favorite among modern recordings is **Constantine Orbelian**'s rendition with Järvi (♦Chandos 8542). The piano sound is very bright, with tremendous support from the orchestra. Some reviewers have found I a bit slow, but I think the music bears it well. This version accentuates the gloriously bangy quality of the concerto, as illustrated by the opening bars of III. If you prefer a slightly more sensitive reading, **Dickran Atamian** with Schwarz offers a vibrant performance in very good sound (♦Delos 3155). An excellent choice also comes from **Oxana Yablonskaya** and her conductor-son Dmitri (♦Naxos 550799). This performance is very good, with high-quality sound, and the disc also offers *Concert Rhapsody,* which isn't often recorded.

Dora Serviarian-Kuhn, with Tjeknavorian and the Armenian Philharmonic, gives this music the steely treatment it deserves but without quite the strong orchestral support Järvi provides (ASV). **De Larrocha**'s 1977 performance is less compelling; the sound is excellent, but the music lacks fire and energy (London). There is little forward impetus at the beginning of the slow movement, which sounds like an Adagio rather than an *Andanta con anima.* The last movement, the best of the three, redeems the performance a little. **Alberto Portugheis**'s version is even worse—labored and uninspired (ASV or MHS).

Violin. Most critics agree that **David Oistrakh**'s performance is the best—the concerto was written for him—but again the sound is a problem on the old recording (Pearl 9295). It's harder to find strong recommendations here than for the piano concerto, but my top choice, taking into account both performance and listenability, is **Elman**'s 1959 rendition with Golschmann and the Vienna State Opera (♦Vanguard 8035). Elman captures the fundamental wildness of the music, giving it the primitive, raw tinge it needs, along with a wonderful richness of tone. In addition, he's in complete command, at once dominating the music and abandoning himself to it. The drawback here is the sound; it's quite listenable, but does reflect its date. **Perlman**'s 1984 performance is wonderful, but inexplicably the sound is really disappointing—dead and dull—nor do Mehta and the Israel Philharmonic keep up with Perlman's passion (EMI). You'll do no better with **Ricci**'s 1956 recording (London); the sound is good for its age, but the violin lacks richness and often seems to get lost in the distance. The recording does, however, have some beautiful lyrical moments.

Two modern recordings, though in excellent sound, are disappointing for performance. One such is **Mordkovitch**'s reading with Järvi and the Scottish National Orchestra; the slow passages are full of pathos, but she's not in full command of the furious parts, and her tone in the higher registers is a bit thin and harsh (Chandos). The orchestra is marvelous but seems at times to overbalance the violin. I like **Hu Kun**'s version better (Nimbus 5277). His approach is correct, his technique flawless, but he doesn't seem to understand the music; the violinist needs to fling himself at this concerto with a certain flair and abandon, and it doesn't happen here. The perfect modern recording is yet to be made; I'd like to hear Perlman with a different orchestra and another sound engineer.

CRAWFORD

Leon Kirchner *(b. 1919)*

Passionately intense, quirky, innovative, and often witty, Kirchner's music rarely disappoints. At times, his three string quartets, his piano sonata, even his two piano trios, sound like syntheses of Bartók and Schoenberg, with some Roger Sessions thrown in. (He studied with both Schoenberg and Sessions.) Some of his more adventurous works take substantial risks. His Pulitzer Prize–winning String Quartet 3, for strings and electronic tape, succeeds in creating an eerie and clever atmosphere, but his opera fragment, *Lily,* for soprano and chamber orchestra, is a brilliant failure. He's extraordinarily gifted as a pianist and conductor. Unfortunately, he has had only three dedicated CD releases and rare appearances in compilations.

"Leon Kirchner: Historic Recordings" is a winner, the best introduction to his works (Music & Arts 1045, 2CD). It offers a gleeful, warts-and-all program including a hissing mono recording of the Piano Sonata and two dropouts in Piano Concerto 1, as well as a haplessly patched-together *Lily.* The recordings of the three string quartets are briskly played, and **Kirchner,** as featured pianist in *Sonata Concertante,* the piano concerto, and Piano Trio 1, infuses his own works with artistry. The program notes are excellent and provide extensive documentation for each recording.

"Leon Kirchner: The Complete String Quartets" features the **Boston Composers String Quartet** under Kirchner's watchful eye (Albany 137). While earnestly and carefully played, their performances lack the raw-edge feel of the quartets on the Music & Arts CD. For example, the individual voices are more prominent in Quartet 2's lyrical adagio (played by the Lenox Quartet), and eccentricity, not technique, prowls the edge of Quartet 3 (by the Beaux Arts Quartet). To their credit, they restored the tape of electronic sounds and used it skillfully in their rendition.

Two recent works appear on "Leon Kirchner" (Nonesuch 979188): *Music for 12* and the peripatetic, moody *Five Pieces for Piano* (**Kirchner** performing). *Music for 12,* despite its democratic title, is more of a chamber violin concerto, much like Berg's in its lyrical sweep. Other pieces include Concerto for Violin, Cello, 10 Winds, and Percussion and Piano Trio 1. Kalish, Lowe, and Eskin provide a solid and subtle interpretation of the trio, but in the Music & Arts version the bursts of fury are more intense, the *sforzandi* more prominent. Nevertheless, the sound of the Nonesuch recording is excellent. Kirchner conducts the orchestral pieces on this CD with unobtrusive but consummate skill, making it a worthy addition to any collection.

Two compilations contain the only recordings of *Music for Cello and Orchestra* and *Triptych* performed by **Ma.** His virtuoso side seems stifled in *Music for Cello and Orchestra,* which appears in "Yo-Yo Ma Premieres" (Sony 66299). Flirting with modernism but married to romanticism, the piece is less engaging than Kirchner's earlier work. The chamber piece *Triptych* is more intriguing, with its quirky rhythms and faux jazz, in "Made in America" (Sony 53126). Ma and Lynn Chang give this work the disquieting edge it deserves.

BATES

Uuno Klami *(1900–1961)*

Klami is the most popular composer after Sibelius among Finnish concert audiences. During his studies he absorbed the influences of Ravel and Stravinsky, but traces of Sibelius also remain in his music. He has been lauded for introducing new a esthetic values, forms, and content into Finnish music, and his lyrical, basically tonal language is notable for its animated rhythms and bold instrumental effects.

Klami wrote two numbered symphonies. **Tuomas Ollila** introduces the first and longer of the two (Ondine 854). At times playful and capricious, the piece expresses Klami's affirmation that "composing shouldn't be taken so damned seriously." This disc also reflects his lifelong fascination with Shakespeare by including the dramatic *King Lear Overture.*

Klami's second, the "War Symphony," often dark and somber, is again performed by **Ollila** (Ondine 858). The music brings to mind Sibelius, Shostakovich, and even Tchaikovsky, its warlike atmosphere underscored by march rhythms in each of the four movements. The coupling here is *Symphonie Enfantine,* a poignant, gentle work of lovely melodies written with children in mind. This piece has also been recorded by **Kantorow** directing the Tapiola Sinfonietta, who play with sensitivity, clarity, and depth in a disc that includes *Hommage à Handel* for piano and strings with Timo Koskinen as soloist, Suite for String Orchestra, and Suite for Small Orchestra (BIS 806). Memorable melodies and a musical language tinged with impressionism mark the music on this fine recording.

Karelian Rhapsody, one of Klami's most often-performed works, is influenced by folk songs that reflect his Karelian roots and has been recorded by **Petri Sakari** (Chandos 9268, with the masterly *Kalevala Suite* and the wonderful *Sea Pictures,* his "Sea Symphony"). The latter two works are also performed by **Segerstam** (Finlandia 356). This attractive disc is rounded out by *All'Ouverture,* a colorful work that goes back to the Karelian landscape of Klami's youth—excellent performances and sonics all round. There's also a fine performance of *Kalevala Suite* by **Vänskä,** coupled with the vigorous *Cobblers on the Heath Overture* and *Theme with Seven Variations and Coda* for cello and orchestra, Klami's last concertante work, superbly performed by Jan-Erik Gustafsson (BIS 676).

Klami planned to write a 3-act ballet, *Whirls,* but the score remained incomplete. The colorful *Whirls, Act 1* has been recorded, again by **Vänskä,** coupled with the fine Violin Concerto, ably performed by Jennifer Koh, and the festive *Suomenlinna Overture.* The same conductor is featured in two orchestral suites arranged by Klami from Act 2 of *Whirls* (BIS 656). Added to this fine program is *Lemmikäinen's Island Adventures,* a rhythmically compelling, exuberant work of impressionist bent building up to a lively climax via syncopated dance rhythms. Esa Ruutunen is the sensitive baritone in "Song of Lake Küüjärvi," sandwiching a slow movement between two march themes.

The Violin Concerto, in **Ilkka Talvi**'s interpretation, is coupled with Kokkonen's ravishing Cello Concerto and Usko Meriläinen's postserial Piano Concerto 2 (Finlandia 702). I prefer Koh's performance, mentioned above. *Adventures of Lemminkäinen on the Island of Saari, Cobblers on the Heath Overture,* and *Karelian Rhapsody* were also recorded in excellent performances by **Sakari Oramo** (Ondine 859, with the dramatic *Karelian Market Place* and *In the Belly of Vipunen* for baritone, male choir, and orchestra, based on a canto from the *Kalevala).* Petri Lindros is the fine soloist.

"Meet the Composer," a set released in 1996, contains more than 140 minutes of Klami's music (Finlandia 99968, 2CD). Disc 1 combines

All'Ouverture, Sea Pictures, and *Kalevala Suite;* disc 2 contains Klami's celebrated *Cheremissian Rhapsody* for cello and orchestra, with Arto Noras as soloist. Also here are the Violin Concerto with Ilkka Talvi and the somewhat austere Piano Concerto 2 with pianist Juhani Lagerspetz; **Juhani Lamminmäki** conducts the Tapiola Sinfonietta.

A 23-verse poem by the 17th-century Finnish poet Juhana Cajanus inspired Klami to write the monumental 50-minute *Psalmus,* an oratorio in two parts for soprano, baritone, chorus, and orchestra, This deeply moving work about the transitory nature of life and how humans console themselves in the face of death is performed by outstanding soloists (Satu Vihavainen and Juha Kotilainen) with **Ulf Söderblom** (Finlandia 369). A rare glimpse of Klami as a choral composer, *Psalmus* has been called "one of those rare works that stand on a par with those of Sibelius in the musical literature of Finland." Klami's witty side is shown in the jazz-inspired *Ragtime and Blues* for two violins, clarinet, trumpet, and piano (Ondine 792, with works by Usko Meriläinen, Nielsen, and Strauss). DE JONG

Oliver Knussen *(b. 1952)*

Knussen made international news at age 15 when he stepped in at the eleventh hour to conduct the London Symphony in his own Symphony 1 (the piece has since been withdrawn). Quite an opening act, Knussen has followed it up impressively as a composer whose extraordinary knack for orchestral color reminds us of Lutoslawski, and increasingly as a superb conductor of contemporary music. He's also one of the few composers who acknowledge late Stravinsky—which he conducts brilliantly—as an influence. Knussen's output, however, has been small; experiencing burnout after writing a pair of Maurice Sendak-designed operas in the '80s, in recent years he has tended to limit himself to miniatures.

Despite its rigor and complexity, the one-movement Symphony 3 doesn't sound at all hostile, opening in a welter of dissonant color, invoking a child-like singsong theme, and bowing out in an enigmatic, quietly quizzical coda. The premiere recording by **Tilson Thomas** is NA (Unicorn), but **Ashkenazy**'s finely shaded performance serves just fine (♦RPO 7015).

Knussen is best known for his short fantasy opera *Where The Wild Things Are,* which takes off from the same idea that propels Ravel's *L'Enfant et les Sortilèges:* A misbehaving child is sent to his room and disappears into a dream/nightmare world. But Knussen goes even further than Ravel in conjuring up a deliciously wild, madly yet playfully dissonant world of sound (complete with a parody of *Boris Godunov*) that matches designer/librettist Sendak's menagerie of lovably horrible creatures. **Knussen**'s recording is a vivid trip in itself, skillfully reproducing the stage action in sonic terms alone (♦Arabesque 6535). A new composer-led recording, coupled with his other Sendak opera, *Higglety Pigglety Pop!* is due from DG.

An austere collection of chamber music, with sopranos Lucy Shelton and Lisa Saffer, pianist Peter Serkin, and **Knussen** leading the Chamber Music Society of Lincoln Center, spans about two decades, from the mysteriously alluring song cycle *Ocean de terre* to the sparely expressionistic *Songs without Voices* and a piano version of *Whitman Settings,* with time out for his archly gentle side in *Hums and Songs of Winnie-the-Pooh* (Virgin 59308, NA). But the best all-around Knussen disc is a marvelous selection of his recent short orchestral works, with the London Sinfonietta conducted *con brio* by the composer (♦DG 449572). Here he can be heard at his most approachable: the Stravinsky tribute *Flourish with Fireworks;* a sparkling potpourri of orchestral music from his other

Sendak opera *Higglety Pigglety Pop!* entitled *The Way to Castle Yonder;* a glittering Horn Concerto for Barry Tuckwell; and some very attractive smaller pieces. And *Whitman Settings,* again sung by Shelton, is far more ingratiating in this twinkling orchestration. GINELL

Zoltán Kodály *(1882–1967)*

Kodály was arguably the most important figure in 20th-century Hungarian music. His friend Bartók was the more important composer, but Kodály's accomplishments as ethnomusicologist and teacher in his native country really had no parallel. And while he's known outside Hungary mostly for a handful of popular orchestral pieces, he was a more considerable and varied composer than he's generally given credit for.

A highly musical child, Kodály played the piano, violin, viola, and cello; more conservative as a composer but as high-minded a musician as Bartók, he completed a doctorate on Hungarian folksong and began to collaborate with his contemporary in ethnomusicological field work, collecting hundreds of songs. Not only did this invigorate Hungarian musical culture, it invigorated Kodály's own art, as did his exposure to the music of Debussy. He became an international success when the orchestral suite from his opera *Háry János* was taken up by conductors like Toscanini and Mengelberg, and he produced a string of virtuoso orchestral works that have remained his most popular: *Marosszek Dances* (1930), *Galanta Dances* (1933), and *"Peacock" Variations* (1939). With their tangy Hungarian tunes and folk inflections and their richly detailed orchestration, it's no surprise that these pieces have remained 20th-century repertoire staples.

The long-lived Kodály was a revered figure in Hungary, and a well-traveled one in his very active old age, attending international musical conferences, writing, and composing until his death in 1967. He and Bartók formed a mutual admiration society; Bartók called his music "the most perfect embodiment of the Hungarian spirit." Despite the more conservative nature of his music, Kodály's Hungarianism goes far below the attractive surface of his popular orchestral pieces and is even more readily heard in his hundreds of choral works, almost unknown outside Hungary.

ORCHESTRAL MUSIC

Kodály wrote no concertos and only a single symphony (and that not until the end of his life, in 1961). However, he's amply represented in the CD catalog and on concert programs by four orchestral works.

Háry János Suite. This is Kodály's most popular work by far. This tuneful, five-movement suite is a brilliant orchestral showpiece, but it's also fairly relaxed and humorous, so the taut approach of **Toscanini** (NBC Symphony, RCA 60279) or **Solti** (Chicago Symphony, London), while exciting, seems inappropriate.

There are plenty of other recordings to fill in the gap, and quite a few authentic Hungarians to conduct them. **Fricsay**'s version with the Berlin Radio Symphony is perhaps the most flavorful and perfectly timed of all, with a wonderfully unctuous saxophone solo depicting "Napoleon's Battle and Defeat" (♦DG 457745). The Minneapolis Symphony isn't quite in the same league, but **Dorati** certainly knew his way around this piece; he recorded it several times. The Minneapolis performance still sounds good (♦Mercury 432005); the New Philharmonia version is spectacularly recorded, but is coupled with an uninteresting Dvořák "New World" Symphony (London 448947). Even better sounding is the **Gerard Schwarz**/Seattle Symphony *Háry Janos,* highly recommended if the coupling, Bartók's violent *Miraculous Mandarin,* appeals to you (Delos 3083).

Also opulently recorded and played is the most generous collection of all, by **Dutoit**: *Háry János, Peacock Variations, Marosszek,* and *Galanta Dances* (London 444322). **Szell** and the Cleveland Orchestra play *Háry János* like Haydn: unsentimental, light-textured, and with immaculate ensemble (♦Sony 48162). This CD is a real bargain, and gets the Generous Bargain Coupling Award: Prokofiev's *Lieutenant Kijé Suite* and Mussorgsky's *Pictures at an Exhibition.* **Ivan Fischer** has the most interesting coupling in *Marosszek Dances* and several of Kodály's choral songs (Philips 462824).

Marosszek Dances and **Galanta Dances.** These are often as not paired, as they are in the excellent, extroverted versions by **Ormandy** and the Philadelphia Orchestra, a good bargain in Sony's "Essential Classics" but coupled with less successful Janáček by Szell and Andrew Davis (Sony 62404). **Fricsay**'s mono recordings are outstanding (DG 457745), and the early-stereo **Dorati**/Philharmonia Hungarica version (Mercury 432005) still sounds good, if not in the Philadelphia luxury class. (Both are with the conductors' recordings of *Háry János Suite;* the Dorati performances are earlier than those mentioned below.)

Variations on A Hungarian Folksong ("Peacock" Variations). This was originally written for Amsterdam's Concertgebouw Orchestra in 1939. Immediately, and not at all surprisingly, it became a repertoire piece: it gave the Concertgebouw (and all other orchestras) a lot to chew on. It comes off brilliantly in **Leinsdorf**'s 1966 interpretation with the Boston Symphony, which sounds quite "the Aristocrat of Orchestras," as they used to call the BSO (♦RCA 63309, with a compelling Bartók *Concerto for Orchestra*). The **Kertész**/London Symphony version is also richly played and recorded, more plush than Leinsdorf's (see "Vocal Music and Opera").

This unabashed virtuoso piece responds well to **Solti**'s approach, in one of his last recordings; in this case, the virtuosos are the Vienna Philharmonic, which doesn't hurt a bit (London 452853, with Elgar's *Enigma Variations* and Blacher's sparky *Paganini Variations*). If you would like *"Peacock"* matched up with both of Kodály's sets of orchestral dances, **Leaper** with the Bratislava Symphony Orchestra is a good bargain (Naxos 550520).

Kodály's other orchestral works are less compelling than the four mentioned above, but they make pleasant listening in sympathetic hands. The early, impressionistic *Summer Evening* was memorably recorded by **Kodály** himself in old age (DG 427408). The energetic *Concerto for Orchestra,* with its propulsive and immediately memorable opening, should be played and recorded more often. The late Symphony, on the other hand, is a worthy but rather dry piece.

All Kodály's orchestral works, popular and not, are available from **Dorati** and the Philharmonia Hungarica (♦London 443006, 2CD). It's not the greatest orchestra, but their committed performances are extremely well recorded, and well worth exploring at such a reasonable price. The **Orpheus Chamber Orchestra** recording of *Summer Evening* and *Hungarian Rondo* is nicely played but a bit undernourished; the coupling of Josef Suk's *Serenade for Strings* is apt and attractive (DG 447109). **Butt** and the Philharmonia offer a recommendable recording of three Kodály rarities: *Summer Evening, Hungarian Rondo,* and the Symphony (ASV 924).

CHAMBER MUSIC

Kodály's chamber music output is quite small but includes some uncommonly beautiful works. His String Quartet 1 is long and rhapsodic; 2 is unusually constructed in two compact movements and has the same

appealing Hungarian flavor as Bartók's *Hungarian Sketches.* The **Kodály Quartet** plays them with every folk inflection in its proper place (♦Hungaroton 12362); the **Kontra Quartet** may have a little less Hungarian flavor but is beautifully recorded and offers a charming encore, a *Gavotte* for three violins and cello (BIS 564). The **Audubon Quartet** sounds rather dry in comparison (Centaur 2372). The **Hollywood Quartet**'s classic 1958 performance of Quartet 2 is very attractive (♦Testament 1072, with favorite quartets by Dvořák and Smetana).

Kodály was an accomplished cellist, and the rest of his chamber output (most of it quite early) can be described as "cello-centric." The biggest works are a relatively brief Sonata for cello and piano, a large-scale Duo for violin and cello, and a spectacular Sonata for solo cello, a half-hour work not far behind Bach's celebrated cello suites in its compositional virtuosity and emotional impact. It's irresistible to cellists with the requisite skills, and there are quite a few recordings.

The composer called **Starker**'s rendition "the Bible performance," and his recording is a classic; the coupling is the *Duo,* with Starker joined by another string legend, violinist **Joseph Gingold** (♦Delos 1015). This satisfying coupling is also well presented by **Yuli** and **Elena Turovsky** (Chandos 8427) and **Jerry Grossman** and **Daniel Phillips** (Nonesuch 79074). More recent is an intense performance of the sonatas with and without piano by cellist **Lluis Claret** and pianist **Rose Marie Cabestany** (Harmonia Mundi 1901325). **Maria Kliegel**'s collection of all the cello music (♦Naxos 553160, 554039) gathers excellent performances of the big works (her reading of the solo sonata is winningly lyrical and melancholy) and some short rarities, such as Kodály's arrangements of Bach. Kliegel's pianist is the estimable Jenö Jandó.

CHORAL MUSIC

This is the real heart of Kodály's music, and the area where his passionate concerns with folk music and universal musical education came together. Fans of *Háry János* or *Galanta Dances* may be surprised to learn that the vast majority of his catalog consists of unaccompanied choral works, large and small, many of them dramatic and piercingly beautiful. There's a collection of short pieces sung by a variety of Hungarian choruses, from the Budapest Girls' Choir to the **Hungarian Army Male Chorus** (♦Hungaroton 31697); it's listed as "Choral Music of Kodály, Vol. 3," but Vols. 1 and 2 don't seem to be currently available. Particularly recommended is Kodály's wartime *Missa Brevis,* a restrained and very moving work. He wrote versions with organ and with orchestral accompaniment; there are excellent renditions of the former by the **Netherlands Chamber Choir** (Globe 5115, with the luminous, very late choral work *Laudes Organi*) and **St. Thomas Church Choir** (Koch 7418, with Vaughan Williams's Mass in G Minor), and of the latter with the **Hungarian Radio Choir** and Budapest Symphony led by Arpad Joó (Arts 4378, with *Psalmus Hungaricus*).

Psalmus Hungaricus. This is Kodály's largest and most successful work, a fervent piece for tenor, chorus, and orchestra, written in 1922 for the union of Buda and Pest. **Fricsay**'s performance, with an excellent tenor soloist in Haefliger, is at the top of the list (♦DG 457745, with *Háry János Suite* and *Galanta* and *Marosszek Dances*). It's sung in German instead of Hungarian, but the power of Kodály's music comes through.

There are several outstanding recordings sung in Hungarian. **Kertész** has a weakish tenor in Lajos Kozma, but the interpretation and choral singing are first class (London 443488, with the complete *Háry János* and *"Peacock"*). The all-Hungarian forces led by **Joó** offer an ideal pairing with *Missa Brevis* in a mid-priced disc (Arts 47378), and the all-Danish forces led by **Mackerras** provide an interesting (and generous) pairing with Janáček's *Glagolitic Mass* (Chandos 9310). **Solti**'s brilliant last recording was of two profoundly Hungarian pieces: *Psalmus Hungaricus* and Bartók's *Cantata Profana*.

OPERA

Háry János. Called by Kodály "a musical fairytale," this is more of an operetta or musical comedy than an opera; it contains some delightful music, not all of it included in the familiar orchestral suite. The main character is a tall-tale spinner fabled in Hungarian folklore; the plot details his imaginary adventures on the battlefield, at the Viennese court, and elsewhere, but after seeing the world, János returns to the happiness of his native village and his faithful girlfriend.

The whole thing, dialogue and all, was recorded in the '80s by a Hungarian cast led by **Ferencsik,** and you can't get any more authentic than that (♦Hungaroton 12837, 2CD). Also available is a hybrid recorded in the '60s by **Kertész** (♦London 443488). All of the music is included, with Hungarian singers, and as might be expected from this conductor, it's gorgeously performed. However, the plot and dialogue were entrusted to the many voices of Peter Ustinov, who sounds more than usually pleased with himself and can be rather slow going; if you're a bigger fan of Kodály than of Ustinov, you'll want to have your CD remote at the ready. However, this mid-priced set is definitely worth considering, as it includes Kertész's beautiful performances of *Psalmus Hungaricus* and "Peacock" (and a little bonus: "The Peacock" itself, sung in Kodály's choral arrangement). RAYMOND

Charles Koechlin *(1867–1951)*

Koechlin's life was active and full of well-deserved honors. A Parisian, he studied with Massenet and Fauré, selflessly encouraged *Les Six* and other contemporary composers, and wrote a four-volume treatise on orchestration, among many other distinguished publications. We are only now learning to appreciate him as a composer of great vision and imagination. Koechlin was a nonconformist. A fastidious worker, he tended to concentrate on a particular genre, moving on when he was sure he had said all he had to say on a subject. His first 24 opus numbers are almost all vocal, either songs or choral pieces, few of which have been recorded. His works are difficult for performers, who tend to mistrust music that remains quiet for long stretches, seeming empty of technical derring-do. They require a different kind of concentration than most music of their time, more cooperation between players than customary, but the rewards are great.

ORCHESTRAL MUSIC

Only a few orchestral pieces are presently listed, and those are not the best known. Whatever happened to *Seven Stars Symphony,* Koechlin's most elaborate homage to the silver screen? It was once available in two performances, led by **Alexandre Myrat** (EMI 64369, with *Ballade* for piano and orchestra), then more solidly played and recorded, though in a less French sound, by **James Judd** (RCA 68146, with two short ballet scores, *Four Interludes* and *L'Andalouse dans Barcelone*).

Four tone poems based on Kipling's *Jungle Book* were also recorded twice, by **Segerstam** (Marco Polo 223484), played in the order Koechlin decided upon, and by **Zinman,** recorded in order of composition, with three *Poèmes* Op. 18, also from *The Jungle Book* (RCA 61955, 2CD). Zinman's is, in general, the better-played version, though not particularly sensitive to French sound. *The Bandar-Log,* a 15-minute tone poem describing monkeys, is offered separately by **Holliger** in an oddly conceived program recorded less effectively than either version above (Ars Musici 5082).

Another apparently short-lived disc is an orchestration of one of Koechlin's large piano suites, *Les Heures Persanes,* again conducted by **Segerstam** (Marco Polo 223504). This is a primarily quiet work, very subtly orchestrated and played beautifully; get it if you can. The only presently listed CD in Segerstam's series is *Le buisson ardent,* a two-part 38-minute tone poem for an orchestra including Ondes martenot, five saxophones, piano, and organ (Marco Polo 223704). The disc also contains an orchestration (and extension) of an early piece for English horn and piano, *Au loin,* and two different, equally fascinating orchestrations of another short meditation, *Sur les flots lointaines.* There's good reason for his orchestrations of Fauré's *Pelléas et Mélisande,* Debussy's *Khamma,* and Chabrier's *Bourrée fantasque*—writing for large forces inspired him to his most advanced harmonies and most exciting concepts—but don't expect a compelling symphonic argument. He seldom takes the expected route; the byways to unexpected places are what make his work consistently memorable.

CHAMBER MUSIC

More of Koechlin's chamber music is recorded than anything else. Many recordings couple it with instrumental solo music, so let's consider both realms together by instrumental category. Very little of it is for strings. Sonatas for violin and for viola have been recorded by **Marie Vlaud** and **Michel Michelakakos** with Mireille Guillaume and Martine Gagnapain, pianists, but neither string player is up to the quiet intensity Koechlin demands, and both are intonationally challenged (Skarbo 1985). The Cello Sonata was recorded by **Mats Lidstrom** and Bengt Forsberg, along with *Chansons Bretonnes* (a suite of 12 sensitive settings of folk melodies) and Pierné's Sonata (Hyperion 66979). These are performances with detail and quiet intensity that bring the music to life.

Koechlin's music for winds has claimed the attention of a number of performers. Ninety-six pieces for solo flute, based on scenes from Anatole France's novel, *La Révolte des Anges,* are challenging both to musician and composer. Forty-seven of them were published under the title *Les Chants de Nectaire;* all but two of them were recorded by **Alexa Still** with a remarkable variety of approach (Koch 7394). **Christina Singer** recorded 47 minutes' worth (25 pieces), but the greater selectivity spoils the composer's overall concept to some extent (Bayer 100106).

During WWI, Koechlin wrote a number of sonatas for both winds and strings. The Flute Sonata has been recorded by **Philippe Racine** and Daniel Cholette with the flute quintet *Primavera* and flute works by Jolivet in cool and lively performances (Claves 9003). An all-Koechlin release by **Fenwick Smith** covers more ground, including 14 *Chants,* Sonata for two flutes, and the complete *Premier album de Lilian,* as well as the flute-piano pieces from the *Second album de Lilian.* These are curious chamber collections dedicated to the actress Lilian Harvey. Book 1 is scored for soprano (Jayne West) and piano (Martin Amlin) as well as flute; Book 2 adds harpsichord and Ondes martenot.

Both books have been recorded complete by **Racine** with soprano Kathrin Graf and Cholette, along with seven monodies for Ondes martenot entitled *Vers le soleil* and the monody for flute doubling on piccolo and alto flute, *Stèle funéraire* (Accord 20123). Racine's poised, cool sound is excellent in this music; the only fly in the ointment is the absence of texts of the songs, particularly the one in Book 1 employing the words of a Palmolive soap commercial! Some of these discs may be NA, but there's a disc by flutist **Irmela Nolte,** clarinettist **Deborah Marshall,** and pianist Sabine Liebner that gives us all of Book 2 (except for the harpsichord-Ondes martenot piece) plus one excerpt from Book 1 (Koch Schwann 6729). The addition of a clarinet gives us further options, including the miniature Clarinet Sonata 1, two Pieces Op. 173b, and works for both instruments, *Pastorale*, the lovely *Sonatine modale*, and *Deux Duos*. The flute also plays *Morceau de lecture* and *Stèle funéraire*. The two wind players blend particularly well on this disc.

The oboe and its brothers, the English horn and oboe d'amore, are well represented in Koechlin's catalog. **Jacques Vandeville** plays Sonata Op. 58, a long, lively, but pastoral work; *Au Loin,* an early meditation for English horn and piano that became twice as long when Koechlin orchestrated it (Marco Polo 223704); and a considerable movement for English horn alone, *Mélopée* (Arion 68286). **Lajos Lencsés** covers later works, two *Monodies* for oboe, one for English horn, and the lovely Septet for strings, flute, and harp (CPO 999614). The two discs overlap in 14 Pieces Op. 179 and in a piece for solo English horn, *Le Repos du Tityre.* Vandeville has a somewhat dryer sound and omits two short pieces from Op. 179; Lencsés is more relaxed and is recorded more warmly. In another disc he offers the Sonata and the English horn *Monody* as well as two Sonatinas for English horn Op. 194 (Audite 97417). That disc may be harder to find but it's worth it. Lencsés is further represented by the considerable Suite for solo English horn Op. 185, which appears in a disc of monodies by Britten, Krenek, and Maderna (Bayer 800915).

The clarinet also has its opus of 14 pieces Op. 178, as well as two sonatas, the first of which is found in Koch Schwann 6729, mentioned under flute. Seven from Op. 178 are offered by **Arturo Ciompi** in Boaz Sharon's piano disc, rather dryly played and recorded (Orion 7804). The bassoon gets its innings from **Eckart Hübner** (CPO 999434). A short but lovely Sonata and three Pieces Op. 71 are joined by a huge 36-minute suite with orchestra, *Silhouettes de Comédie*. These 12 pieces cover characters from Molière, the *commedia dell'arte,* and more contemporary sources, treated with great fantasy. Hübner is a good player, though I can imagine a more unbuttoned joie de vivre in some of the *Silhouettes.*

The horn also has its Sonata, Op. 70. Recorded by **David Pyatt**, it has a lovely sound in his disc of miscellaneous horn works (Erato 21632). In the hands of **Barry Tuckwell,** it gains both stature and mystery (ASV 716). But the main items on this disc are 15 pieces for horn(s) and piano Op. 180 and 11 *Sonneries* from various sources for multiple hunting horns, the doublings all played by Tuckwell through the marvels of modern engineering. The hunting horn has no valves, so what you're hearing is the overtone series in its raw state, an experience to stretch your ears. But the best thing about this CD is Tuckwell's attitude toward the music: He allows Koechlin to control his performance more than most musicians do, following his dynamics and balances beautifully.

PIANO MUSIC

Koechlin wrote a good deal for piano. One of the earliest pieces is the 7-movement *Ballade* Op. 20, later orchestrated. As a piano solo, it seems to take too long to build up, at least as performed by **Jean-Pierre Ferey** (Skarbo 3932), who takes longer than the orchestral version by **Bruno Rigutto** (EMI 64369). However, Ferey plays the long suite *L'Ancienne maison de campagne* with more variety and humor than does the otherwise excellent **Deborah Richards** (CPO 999054). The latter plays the equally demanding *Paysages et Marines* with more verve and insight than **Boaz Sharon,** whose recording is so harsh and piercing that any musical qualities go by the board (Orion 7804).

Backtracking, Ferey also plays 12 Preludes Op. 209, more neoclassical than most Koechlin, lively and touching by turns. Richards also plays a long and lovely *Nocturne chromatique,* originally for chromatic harp, and Sharon gives us 12 tiny *Pastorales* and one excerpt from the hour-

long suite *Les heures Persanes,* later orchestrated and recorded complete by Segerstam (Marco Polo 223504). A complete recording of the piano version is by **Herbert Henck,** a fine performance that should be reissued (Wergo LP 60137, NA).

VOCAL MUSIC

There was once a disc of Koechlin songs by **Claudette Leblanc** with pianist Boaz Sharon, including both early songs and the late Op. 151, *Seven Songs for Gladys,* one of his homages to Lilian Harvey in one of her roles, all beautifully sung (Hyperion 66243). A disc of his choral music includes his religious works, sung poorly and with no texts (Skarbo 2972). MOORE

Joonas Kokkonen (1921–1996)

Kokkonen was the next Finnish composer after Sibelius of internationally acknowledged greatness, largely thanks to his magnificent (and only) opera, *The Last Temptations.* It's no exaggeration to say that this work—astonishingly, its one recording (DG) has long been NA—and Sallinen's *The Red Line* revolutionized opera in the Nordic world, placing Finland at the forefront of modern production. His modest output includes works in most standard forms, including four remarkable symphonies. Kokkonen once claimed to have composed a fifth in his head, but never wrote it down.

ORCHESTRAL MUSIC

Durch einen spiegel: Metamorphosis for strings and harpsichord. **Ulf Söderblom** secures a matchless performance (♦BIS 528, coupled with *Il Paesaggio, Sinfonia da camera,* and Wind Quintet), more alive to Kokkonen's magical tonal landscapes than **Baumgartner** (Finlandia) or **Berglund** (Ondine 860).

Interludes from "The Last Temptations." Barely hinting at the scope of the opera, even in **Vänskä**'s dedicated account, these make a fine set nonetheless (BIS 498, with Symphony 2 and the only recording of *Inauguratio*).

Music for string orchestra. This tremendous work requires virtuosity of the highest order and receives it from **Söderblom** and the Lahti Symphony. The couplings (the contemporaneus song cycle *The Hades of the Birds* and Symphony 1) make this arguably the finest Kokkonen disc ever issued (♦BIS 485).

Sinfonia da camera for strings. **Vänskä** is beautifully clear and ideally paced (♦BIS 528), delving deeper than **Baumgartner**'s by no means inadequate interpretation (Finlandia 99965).

Symphonies. **Söderblom** (1 and 3) and **Vänskä** (2 and 4) share the honors in the only current complete cycle (♦BIS 849, 2CD, with *Requiem* and *Opus sonorum,* available separately as part of BIS's complete edition, 485, 498, 508, 468). **Berglund**'s magnificent 1968 recording of 3 still sounds wonderful (Finlandia 99965), although **Söderblom** probes deeper (BIS, as above). Berglund's more recent accounts of 1 and 4 are less compelling than his Swedish rivals (Ondine); indeed, **Vänskä**'s program of 4, Cello Concerto, and *Symphonic Sketches* is the perfect introduction to the composer (♦BIS 468).

Cello Concerto. **Arto Noras** first recorded this wonderful score, and his is still the benchmark performance (♦Finlandia 99965); **Thedéen** is also splendid, in excellent sound (BIS 468).

CHAMBER MUSIC

Cello Sonata. Like Quartet 3, this sonata reworks material from *The Last Temptations.* **Noras**'s excellent rendition is unavailable on CD, but

Petja Svensson's is more than a mere stopgap (Caprice 21590, with works by Grieg, Ingvar Lidholm, and Emil Sjögren).

Piano Quintet. One of Kokkonen's earlier scores, **Tapani Valtsa** and the Sibelius Academy Quartet give a beautifully assured performance, magnificently recorded (◆BIS 458); **Jaana Kärkkäinen** and the Avanti Ensemble are equally dexterous if a touch brittle (Ondine 601 or 865).

String Quartets. Like many symphonists, Kokkonen was a master of the quartet medium. The **Sibelius Academy Quartet** provides very fluent accounts of all three (BIS 458). The **Sibelius Quartet**'s pioneering performance of 1 is even finer (that of 3 is NA, alas), but collectors will want all three works (Finlandia, as above)

KEYBOARD MUSIC

Kokkonen's acknowledged solo piano music comprises a handful of minor sets, written between 1938 and 1969. Largely overshadowed by his weightier orchestral works, the only survey of these little gems comes from **Janne Mertanen** (Alba 127). His sole organ piece, the atmospheric *Lux aeterna,* has been set down by **Kalevi Kiviniemi** (Motette) and **Seppo Murto** (◆Ondine 787).

VOCAL MUSIC

His opera aside, Kokkonen composed little for voices. If the cantata *Erektheion* doesn't compel attention the way the symphonies do, it's nonetheless a fascinating score deserving wider currency, especially with the advocacy of Satu Vihavainen, Walter Grönroos and the **Academic Choral Society** (BIS 498). Kokkonen's other available choral work (*Missa a cappella* and the motet *Lauda Sion* being NA) is the *Requiem* in memory of his wife, his last major utterance and one of his most radiant. Soile Isokoski, Grönroos, and the **Savonlinna Opera Festival Chorus** sing it most movingly (BIS 508). Kokkonen's vocal masterwork is the marvelous early song cycle *The Hades of the Birds.* Only one account exists, but any serious rival to sweet-voiced **Monica Groop** will need to be exceptional indeed (◆BIS 485).   RICKARDS

Erich Wolfgang Korngold *(1897–1957)*

A prodigy, Korngold began writing works of remarkable sophistication at age 11. Mahler, Zemlinsky, Strauss, and Puccini all hailed him, and he enjoyed considerable popularity, peaking with the opera *Die Tote Stadt* (1920) and dimming around the time of the relative failure of *Der Wunder das Heliane* (1927). Perhaps sensing the waning of his romantic star in a period of neoclassicism and atonality, Korngold went to the United States in 1934, where he "invented" the orchestral movie score as a composer for Warner Brothers. He retired from the movies in 1945 and tried to reestablish himself as a serious composer in Europe with his Violin Concerto, String Quartet 3, and Symphony in F-sharp, but never realized this ambition. Only recently has he gained the reputation he deserves.

From the beginning, Korngold composed in the manner of the late-romantic Austro-Germans (with a touch of Puccini). His music is lush and expressive, pouring forth inexhaustible melody, color, and emotion that is more complex and difficult to conduct and interpret than it sounds. Changing meters, skipping rhythms, and treacherous leaps challenge the best players, while the large scale of his works stretches the limits of their ensembles: pianos sound like quintets, string quartets like orchestras. His harmonies often grapple with the confines of tonality—Korngold can sound very modern in some performances—but the melodist in him refused to cross the line into atonality or serialism. Many people believe he never fulfilled the promise of those heady early

years, but that depends on how you view his accomplishments in Hollywood, for there he was a pioneering genius. His film music is discussed in the article in Part II.

ORCHESTRAL MUSIC

Symphony in F-sharp. Edward Downes (◆Chandos 9171, with *Abschiedslieder*) and **Kempe** (◆Varèse 5346) let the symphony speak for itself. Downes is more clear-toned and less burnished; his controlled, molded phrasing gives the music structure and coherence with lucent orchestral balances. The sound is vivid, and the BBC Philharmonic plays with clarity and strength. *Abschiedslieder* is atmospheric and well sung by contralto Linda Finnie. Kempe looks to Korngold's Viennese roots, with dark orchestral tone, lush textures, good tempos, and the right scale for each movement. The Munich Philharmonic responds as if the work were written for them. Classic, but without a coupling.

The elegant, insightful, at times chamber-like reading by **James De-Preist** and the Oregon Symphony reveals more secrets than anyone else. Sometimes he exaggerates tempos, but never without interest and effect. Beautifully played, medium in scale, clear and light in textures (yet never lacking power), and with wonderful sound, this may be a first choice for those unconvinced by this work or who have found it overblown elsewhere. The coupled suite from *The Sea Hawk* is dashing and had has great panache (◆Delos 3234).

Welser-Most (◆EMI 56169, with *Einfache Lieder*) and **Previn** (DG 453436, with *Much Ado about Nothing*) are less balanced and larger in scale. Previn is serious and tough, especially in I. The London Symphony is fine, but balances are inconsistent, and the sound is occasionally grainy. Welser-Most is a little less sensitive and occasionally halting, but the juggernaut that is the Philadelphia Orchestra gives an impressive performance, particularly in the muscular Adagio. Downes and Kempe flow more, but this is a powerful alternative. Neither **Albert** nor his orchestra can compete (CPO 999146, with *Straussiana, Theme and Variations*).

Sinfonietta. A 45-minute symphony for a huge orchestra, this was the first sign of the large-scale composer Korngold was to become. It's a beautiful, stunning work. **Bamert** rushes some tempos in I; a few rhythms are overly emphasized; a few transitions are forced and unnatural; and there is unease with the Viennese 3/4 (◆Chandos 9317, with *Sursum Corda*). It's still decent, with good sound and playing by the BBC Philharmonic, but the suave **Litton** is better at catching the Old World style of the piece. He's sensuous and slower in I, with sweet, sleek Dallas Symphony strings sounding even better than the BBC, a bit of portamento, and a nostalgic lilt (◆Dorian 90216, with Violin Concerto). **Albrecht** is more deliberate and not as charming, but there is spirit when called for; this is darker, less lyrical, and more symphonic than the others, with nice playing by the Berlin Radio Symphony (◆Varèse 5311). **Albert** is often rushed and clunky, with his orchestra hard pressed (CPO, with *Schauspiel Ouvertüre* and music from *Der Schneemann*).

Sursum Corda. This is a Straussian tone poem, broadly dynamic, charged, and exciting, with plenty of contrasting lyricism and bold brass writing. Korngold described its mood as one of "struggle and aspiration, a joyous deliverance out of storm and stress". A stunning work, it originally failed for being too modern and complex in structure. Korngold used some of its material in *Robin Hood.* **Bamert** gives a stunning, dynamic performance full of color, presence, and drama (◆Chandos 9317, with *Sinfonietta*). **Albert** is lumpy and dull (CPO, with Piano Concerto and *Much Ado about Nothing*).

Symphonic Serenade. **Bamert** and the BBC Philharmonic make this sound like the major work it is, and, with the sheen and archness of its textures and incisive articulation, a modern one (♦Chandos 9508, with Cello Concerto, Piano Concerto for Left Hand, and *Military March*). Everything is gripping and intense, with polished orchestral playing. **Mauceri,** whose performance is based on a piano recording of excerpts by Korngold, is more expansive, romantic, and darker. The Berlin Radio strings are sweeter, with less polish than the BBC's and more weight on the bottom (♦London 444170, with *Between Two Worlds* and Theme and Variations). **Albert** isn't as persuasive, with his lack of flow and cohesion in I and II (CPO, with *Baby Serenade* and Cello Concerto). He comes together by III and IV, taking a middle road between Bamert and Mauceri, but his orchestra isn't as good.

CONCERTOS

Cello. Peter Dixon is lyrical and smooth, with cello tone to match. He focuses on the long line and yearning lyricism; tempos are slow, and he's a bit understated, with soft angles and rhythms (♦Chandos 9508, with Piano Concerto for Left Hand and *Military March*). **Gabarro** is also lyrical, but more vocal, intense, and passionate (♦RCA 0185, with film score excerpts). This is the brightest, most colorful performance, with a bit of Bax's rugged seascapes, though the excellent analog sound reveals some thin violins in the National Philharmonic. **Berger** is rustic, a bit phrase-to-phrase, but with full, reedy tone (CPO, with *Baby Serenade and Symphonic Serenade*). **Albert** conducts with more definition than in the rest of his Korngold series.

Piano Concerto for Left Hand. This was written for one-armed pianist Paul Wittgenstein and may be Korngold's most complex and forward-looking work. **Hamelin**'s bright tone is modernistic enough to make Korngold sound almost like Prokofiev (♦Hyperion 66990, with Joseph Marx's *Romantisches Klavierkonzert*). The performance and the BBC Scottish Symphony under Vånskä are scintillating, with well-blended sound. (The Marx concerto is dramatic and gushing and should appeal to anyone who likes the Hollywood Korngold). **Shelley** is darker and more romantic and inward, even wayward at times, though he's technically assured; Hamelin is better integrated and more compelling (♦Chandos 9508, with Cello Concerto and *Military March*). Chandos's sound creates a covered, old-fashioned effect. **De Groote** isn't bad, but the problems that plague the rest of the CPO Korngold discs apply here, if not as seriously (with *Sursum Corda* and *Much Ado about Nothing*). There is an unwelcome heaviness to the piano sound, and lackluster playing and conducting make the piece sound more weighty than it is.

Violin. **Shaham** is ideal, with warm, romantic tone, moderate tempos, no exaggerations, and fine balances in the London Symphony under Previn (♦DG 439886, with *Much Ado about Nothing* and Barber's Violin Concerto). **Ulf Hoelscher** has just the right full tone and singing style (♦EMI LP). Conductor Willi Mattes's tempos are less romantic than Previn's, but they feel right in the most natural performance of all. The analog sound is warm and well balanced. **Vera Tsu** is romantic and full of rubato (♦Naxos 553579, with Goldmark's Concerto 1). Some might find her too indulgent, but for many it will make perfect musical sense, and there's no denying her technique and clear, open sound. Yu Long's accompaniment and the sound are exceptional. **Perlman** is romantic and soloistic, with the Pittsburgh Symphony in the background (♦EMI 47846, with Goldmark's Concerto). His sound is beautiful and not as mannered as later in his career, while Previn is sympathetic but too soft-edged. Not my favorite, but Perlman fans won't be disappointed.

Ulrika-Anima Mathé's tone is small, tightly wound, and precious. With Litton's considerable control, it may seem cloying after a while, though some may find it charming and suitably Old World (♦Dorian, with Sinfonietta). The coupling is excellent. The slow tempos of **Chantal Juillet** and Mauceri in I take getting used to, and while her small sound and fast vibrato won't appeal to everyone, there is charm and poetry here (London 452481, with Weill and Krenek violin concertos). The recording is big and open, with good balance between the Berlin Radio Symphony and soloist. The fascinating couplings, unobtainable elsewhere, may dictate purchase, but you may want another recording of the Korngold. **Stacey** and Scott Woolley are the slowest and most romantic of these recordings. There is room for this approach, and they are good at it, but **Glenn Dictorow** (the next most romantic), plays with greater intensity, fuller sound, and more virtuosity, and holds up better in the long run (Bay Cities, with Rozsa's Duo for Violin and Piano).

Among mono historicals, **Heifetz/Kurtz** is decent (Music & Arts), but **Heifetz/Wallenstein,** with the Los Angeles Philharmonic six years later, is more polished and has more tension, and the sound and orchestra are better. Heifetz's tight, silvery tone is closely miked; he creates more drive than usual and adds a disquieting element heard nowhere else (♦RCA 7963).

CHAMBER MUSIC

Piano Quintet. One of Korngold's most flamboyant, operatic chamber works, this tests the limits of the quintet ensemble to the extreme. It's full of leaps and surges and is bold and intensely romantic. The gorgeous and intense Adagio is about as close as Korngold got to atonality. The Korngold Quartet and pianist **Scot Woolley** are extroverted, committed, and passionate; their sound is big and bright and matches the size of this work (♦Varèse 302066049, with Quartet 2 played by the Lyric Art Quartet). The Danubuis Quartet and **Ilona Prunyi** capture a different and equally valid aspect of Korngold's color and passion (♦Marco Polo 223385, with Violin Sonata). Their tempos are faster, more liquid, and they play with more control, darker tone (particulary the piano), and with a reined-in, tighter ensemble that leans toward the salon rather than the orchestra stage.

A good performance if you can find it is by a group of mostly Los Angeles players with pianist **Harold Gray** (♦Genesis 1063 LP, with Piano Sonata 3). Except for some straining in the climax of II, this is a fine, stylish, middle-of-the-road reading, even warmer than Danubuis, with some of the portamento but none of the excess of the Swedish players on DG. **Bengt Forsberg**'s recording with an unnamed string quartet of Swedish players in "Rendezvous with Korngold" has received splendid reviews (DG 459631, 2CD). It's romantic, but I find everything forced. The players dig in hard and particularly exaggerate the skipping rhythms, and there seem to be swells on every other note. The effect is to lurch about with individual players cutting uncomfortably through the texture. The string players sound accomplished, but lack cohesiveness and ensemble.

The **Schubert Ensemble** of London plays well, but these English musicians don't seem at home with the style. The music making is bland and directionless in I, and the Adagio misses impulse and shaping of the line. They catch the mood in III, but it's too late (ASV 1047, with Suite for 2 Violins, Cello, and Piano Left Hand). **Kathryn Brake**'s reading with players from the Washington, D.C., area is quite the opposite. Dramatic, intense, and sometimes angry, it commands attention, but it's harsh in tone quality (a feature exacerbated by the sound). While it brings out a different side of the work, it completely misses its loveliness and romance. Interesting, but only as a fourth-or-so supplement (Albany, with Suite for Left Hand).

Piano Trio. Korngold wrote the trio when he was 13, yet it's a mature-sounding work, with great energy in the opening movement, replete with the composer's leaps, skipping rhythms, whole-tone scale lines, a quirky Scherzo, and a beautiful slow movement. Only the finale is a problem, running on a bit too long. The best performance is by the venerable **Beaux Arts Trio**. It has a lyrical, magnetic quality, enhanced by an understanding that makes the work seem to flow in a continuing stream of melody, sidestepping the emotional excesses in the score (Philips 434072, with Zemlinsky's Trio). Violinist **Glenn Dictorow,** cellist Alan Stepansky, and pianist Israela Margalit are rhapsodic and flowing, in good warm sound (♦EMI 55401, with Violin Sonata). The **Göbel Trio** is more reflective and hesitant, less flowing, and not as elegant (♦Etcetera 1043, with String Sextet played by the Berlin Sextet). The sound is decent but has the artificial quality of early digital. It's very good; the real disqualifier is the less accomplished coupling.

String Sextet. This is arguably Korngold's best chamber work; it's lush, rich, and sweet, a beautiful piece of German postromanticism. The **Rafael Ensemble** gives a magnificent performance, full of finesse and rich, dark sound (♦Hyperion 66425, with Schoenberg's *Verklärte Nacht*). The pace is broad but not slow. The very different approach of the **Flesch Quartet** is as valid as the Rafael's and makes the Sextet sound like a different, more modern piece, as if Korngold were more influenced by Stravinsky than Strauss (♦ASV 1062, with Quartet 3). Attacks are sharper, textures are brighter and leaner, and tempos are a bit faster. The **Berlin Sextet** doesn't jell (Etcetera 1043, with Piano Trio). They sound too wound up, occasionally shrill, and generally unsettled, particularly noticeable in the first violin's nervous vibrato in I. A more serious disqualifier is the synthesizer-like sound.

Suite for Piano Left Hand and String Trio. This is the third and last work Korngold wrote for left-handed pianist Paul Wittgenstein. It's in several movements and moods, including a "Groteske," a sweet Ravelian waltz, and spirited variations on a dark, rolling, Brahmsian theme. There's a fair amount of sarcasm along with sweet melodies and leaping fourths. The writing for a second violin rather than viola (with the piano filling the middle) allows for an open, nostalgic sound. **Fleisher**/Silverstein/Laredo/Ma are gripping, atmospheric, and thoughtful, with slow tempos and introspection that catch the angular, more modern side of Korngold (♦Columbia 48253, with Schmidt's Piano Quintet). The players are individualistic, with bright violins; the brilliant Fleisher dominates. **Raoul Sosa** and the Quatuor Laval are faster, smoother, more blended and romantic, and less introspective (♦SNE 606, also with Schmidt's Piano Quintet). They may seem less vital than the Sony at first—it's less "starry"—but the warmer sound, tighter structure, and better flow make them a formidable competitor, and my preference.

The **Schubert Ensemble of London** isn't bad, but it's slightly undercharacterized and bland (ASV, with Suite for 2 Violins, Cello, and Piano Left Hand). The same is true for an ensemble with pianist **Kathryn Brake.** They seem to be trying for a sweeter performance than their fierce Piano Quintet, but the result seems a little slow and "behind the curve." The real problem for them is the striking excellence of the two recommended performances (Albany, with Piano Quintet).

String Quartets. Korngold wrote the first of his three quartets at age 23. It's an ebullient, energetic work, with I powered by leaping fourths and a luminescent, songful Adagio whose sheen and color are remarkable.

No. 2 appeared in 1934 just before Korngold came to America to stay: It's lighter in tone and melodic, with a playful Intermezzo, a hypnotic, ethereal Larghetto, and a wonderful waltz finale. The post-Hollywood 3 (1945) trades youthful passion for a more romantic, at times regretful, but heartfelt maturity. It can sound quite modern in the right hands.

The **Chilingirian Quartet**'s 1 and 3 are youthful, passionate, and occasionally dreamy, particularly in 1 (♦RCA 7889). Their textures are on the lean side (but hardly thin), colorful and brightly lit, and they put real bite into the abrupt rhythmic changes. The Adagio is resplendent. Their 3 is similar, if a little fuller and more romantic. The **Franz Schubert Quartet**'s 1 is more romantically Viennese (♦Nimbus 5506, with Rezniček's Quartet 1). Textures are heavy, with plenty of rubato and portamento; rhythms are softer. The work doesn't sound as youthful as it does with the Chilingirian, whose passion and firmer structure I prefer. The **Flesch Quartet**'s reading of 1 and 2 features a small sound, tight, controlled ensemble, and clear tone (♦ASV 1035). There is a toughness and intensity in 1, but the piece is emotionally reined in compared with the Chilingirian and Franz Schubert. The Flesch approach works better in the lighter-toned 2. The smaller sound and restraint are still there, but toughness is exchanged for a more wistful, lyrical tone that gets eerie in the high harmonics of the slow movement. The exuberance of the finale is tempered, but it works.

The **Lyric Art Quartet** makes 2 a happier and less eerie piece than the Flesch (♦Varèse 302066049). Their playing is far broader, more powerful, romantic, and nostalgic. The **New World Quartet** offers a great 2 and some of the best Korngold quartet playing, period (♦Vox Box 5109 LP, with quartets by Hindemith, Bloch, etc.). This is *echt* romantic Korngold: big, full, lush, and singing from the heart. Lyric Art and New World are probably closer to the heart of this work, but Flesch, much as they do in the String Sextet, remind us that Korngold wasn't all sweetness and light.

In 3 the **Angeles Quartet** produces a terrific rival to the Chilingirian—slightly more reserved and leaner, less romantic and urgent, with a narrower vibrato and more even melodic flow. The result is elegance, refinement, and tight, unified ensemble (♦Koch 7325, with Kreisler's Quartet). The **Flesch** approach is very effective in this work, stressing the modern qualities of Korngold's most modern quartet (♦ASV 1062, with String Sextet). They're as successful here as in the accompanying Sextet, making this the more interesting of their two Korngold chamber discs. The slow movement (based on music from *Sea Wolf*) is searing.

Violin Sonata. Korngold's youthful Sonata (he was 15) is a mature masterpiece, a big rhapsodic first movement replete with leaps and exoticism, a quirky Scherzo, and a glorious Adagio. The sophisticated **Dictorow** plays with a small, well-focused sound and controlled line, partnered by Margalit's appropriately massive piano accompaniment (♦EMI 55401, with Piano Trio). **Andras Kiss** and Prunyi give a brighter, more angular, sometimes too thrusting, sharply etched performance, with the greatest tonal contrast between the pianists (♦Marco Polo 223385). Marco Polo's forward, slightly acerbic, and brightly lit sound is less coherent and balanced than EMI's. **Stacey** and **Scott Woolley** are the slowest and most romantic of these recordings. There is room for this approach, and they're good at it, but Dictorow, especially, plays with more intensity, fuller sound, and more virtuosity. He holds up better in the long run (Bay Cities, with Rózsa's Duo for Violin and Piano).

PIANO MUSIC
Sonatas. Korngold wrote his three sonatas when he was 11, 13, and 34. They are angular, powerful works, full of quartal leaps and off-beat and

skipping triplet rhythms. They exude joy, energy, and sadness, with a Viennese cast. No. 1 uses the whole-tone scale and bares the composer's sadness over the death of a friend; 2 is almost atonal at times; and 3 is refined and restrained. **Korngold** was a prodigious pianist who could make the piano sound like an orchestra in these works, and neither interpreter here can match the sheer immensity he produced in his own recordings of excerpts. **Prunyi** recorded the first two with good, dark tone, power, and definition (♦Marco Polo 223384, with *Märschenbilder* and *Much Ado about Nothing*). **Tozer** recorded all three with a lighter touch, brighter tone, and more rubato (♦Chandos 9389). The nervousness in his playing may annoy some, and he's less powerful and involving than Prunyi. **Harold Gray** produced a fine 3 (♦Genesis 1063). Combining his difficult-to-find LP and Prunyi's disc is the best way to get all three sonatas.

VOCAL MUSIC

Passover Psalm. This is for soprano, chorus, and orchestra without woodwinds and is one of the few classical works Korngold wrote while composing film scores. It's not the typical sweet Korngold of the prodigy years or the more serious composer of the Symphony, but it's a decent transitional work. The "Alleluia" is notable. **Chailly** makes a fine case for it with the Vienna Philharmonic (♦London 460213, with Zemlinsky's *Psalm 83* and Janáček's *Glagolitic Mass*).

Songs. Korngold's songs will appeal to anyone who likes Strauss lieder. **Von Otter** has produced a dramatic collection called "Rendezvous with Korngold" (♦DG 459631, 2CD). She is understanding and expressive dramatically and musically, at home in the romantic *Abschiedslieder*, the dramatic moments in *Shakespeare Songs,* and the humorous ones in *Songs of the Clown.* Bengt Forsberg is a fine accompanist. The problem is the chamber music performances in the set, though the string players are better behaved accompanying von Otter in "Marietta's Lied." **Steven Kimbrough**'s lyrical baritone provides a fine male alternative to some of the DG performances (♦Acanta). His voice may be more mellifluous than von Otter's, but he's not as insightful and expressive, and he doesn't make the same impact. Many will want both discs because Baldwin includes material von Otter does not.   HECHT

OPERAS

Korngold composed five operas, only one of which, *Die Tote Stadt,* achieved lasting success. His operatic music is written in the late romantic style of Mahler, Strauss, and their followers, spiced up with more than a dash of Puccini. It's very melodic, always well orchestrated, and often theatrically effective, but also quite predictable. Unlike some of his contemporaries like Schreker, he wasn't influenced by French impressionism, let alone the innovations of Schoenberg and Stravinsky. There has been revived interest in Korngold's operas in the last few years, and several new recordings have been issued, but except for *Die Tote Stadt,* there have been few staged performances, probably due to the banal and often poorly written librettos.

Die Tote Stadt. In this, the best and best known of Korngold's stage works, the main character, Paul, has been keeping a "temple of memories" for his dead young wife Marie, whom he adored. By chance he meets Marietta, a dancer who bears a strong resemblance to Marie, is instantly smitten, and invites her to his house. After she leaves, Marie appears to step out of the portrait he has kept and is transformed into Marietta (both roles are taken by the same singer). As Paul's apparition continues, Marietta returns to spend the night with him, but soon they quarrel, she taunts him, and Paul strangles her with a lock of Marie's hair. Finally Paul wakes up, realizes he has been dreaming, and leaves.

Korngold's lush and heavily romantic score can still hold the listener's attention, and its best numbers ("Marietta's Song" and "Fritz's Song") were once quite popular. The opera's premiere in 1920, with Jeritza as Marie/Marietta, was a sensational success, and such great opera stars as Lotte Lehmann, Richard Tauber, and Richard Mayr have appeared in it.

The best available recording has Neblett, Kollo, and Prey in the leading roles, led by **Leinsdorf** in 1974 (♦RCA 7767). A good alternate version is based on staged performances at the Stockholm Opera in 1996 (Naxos 660060). The mostly Swedish cast led by **Segerstam** is headed by Katarina Dalayman, a fine soprano (though Neblett's voice is richer) but the other singers aren't as convincing, vocally or dramatically.

Die Kathrin. Korngold's last opera, this was scheduled for a Vienna premiere in 1937 but had to be postponed until 1938, when it was canceled by the Nazi takeover of Austria. The premiere eventually took place in Stockholm in 1939 to, at best, a lukewarm reception. Kathrin, a young Swiss servant girl, is seduced by a French soldier (François) who is soon thereafter posted to Africa. Kathrin, now pregnant, goes looking for him and finally catches up with him in Marseilles, where both end up working for a nasty, lecherous nightclub owner who tries to seduce her. When he is shot, François is unjustly accused and sentenced to five years in prison. After his release, he finds Kathrin, who, with her son, has returned to her home in Switzerland. The opera ends happily with the pair and their son finally united.

The music includes several touching arias but, like the story and like Korngold's movie scores from that period, is saccharine and sentimental. In the only available recording, led by **Martyn Brabbins** in 1997, the young German lyric soprano Melanie Diener sings the title role beautifully and with much feeling, and the veteran English tenor David Rendall is a fine François, though his voice had lost a bit of its smoothness (CPO 999602).   MOSES

Joseph Martin Kraus (1756–1792)

Often called "the Swedish Mozart," Kraus was actually German by birth, settling in Stockholm at age 22. There he hoped to write for the stage as court composer for King Gustav III, who was highly impressed by his opera *Proserpine;* yet on traveling abroad he met Haydn and became fascinated with the symphony, writing largely in the prevailing *Sturm und Drang* style. We are only now coming to appreciate the great inventiveness and drama of Kraus's symphonies, and the listener will find them well worth the discovery.

Petter Sundkvist presents three symphonies (in E-flat, C, and C minor) on one disc (♦Naxos 553734) and three more (in F, A, and C) on another (♦Naxos 554472). There are also two discs from **Concerto Köln** (Capriccio 10396 and 10430), another from **Anthony Halstead** (Musica Sveciae 419), and yet another from **Martin Sieghart,** joined by Edith Peinemann in the C major Violin Concerto (Orfeo 254921). Certainly the *Sturm und Drang* style is everywhere evident; witness the opening movement of the F major in Sundkvist's Volume 2 or the C major in Volume 1. In the one symphony common to all four conductors, the C minor, despite some wiry string tone Sundkvist is highly enjoyable, while Concerto Köln is more astringent; Halstead lopes along at a rather comfortable pace, while Sieghart is more expansive.

Symphonie Funèbre, an unremittingly somber and tragic work, was, like the *Funeral Cantata,* a heartfelt response to the assassination of Gustav III. It's far more gripping under **Sieghart** than **Concerto Köln;** each drum beat is like a blow to the heart, the final Adagio more consoling with Sieghart's warm string tone. In general, the choice is largely between the fuller sound of Sieghart's Stuttgart Chamber Orchestra and the lean textures of the other proponents, with Sundkvist far surpassing Concerto Köln tonally and Halstead offering an attractive alternative. One could easily buy any or all of them without being disappointed.

The assassination of the King at a masked ball in 1792—an event that also inspired Verdi—resulted in a massive outpouring of grief from the Swedish people and compelled Kraus to write his searing and transcendent *Funeral Cantata*. Into this powerful eulogy he infused all the pain of a stunned nation. There are two superb recordings, the grandeur of **Newell Jenkins**'s moving and committed account (♦Vanguard 61) set against the thrilling period-instrument sound of **Stefan Parkman**'s Drottningholm ensemble (♦Caprice 416), though Parkman's addition of the *Symphonie Funèbre* may offset Vanguard's lower price.

Kraus's opera *Proserpine* follows the familiar myth rather closely. Pluto abducts Proserpine (Persephone) and returns to Hades amid the wailing of her mother Ceres; though Proserpine seems happy enough with Pluto, Jupiter decrees she must spend half the year with Ceres and half with her husband, whereupon the usual jubilation ensues. **Mark Tatlow** leads Stockholm forces in a taut, gripping performance, beautifully recorded (♦Musica Sveciae 422, 2CD). In contrast, *Soliman II or The Three Sultanas* is more of a singspiel following the lead of Mozart's *Abduction,* though nowhere near as sophisticated. Under **Philip Brunelle** the music bubbles from first to last, and the brio of his rendition is highly infectious (♦Virgin 91496).   HALLER

Fritz Kreisler *(1875–1962)*

Kreisler was the last of the great violinist composers. Unlike his 18th- and 19th-century predecessors, he wrote almost exclusively small-scale works with piano accompaniment. He was noted for his genial style of playing, his warm, velvety tone, and his immaculate technique, and these are needed to perform his music. He was the first violinist to use continuous vibrato, even during fast passages, and this made his tone warmer and more alive than anything people had heard before. His music lacks depth and is always placid. Menuhin said of Kreisler that his playing lacked the element of the demonic, he was so genial and civilized, and his music is the same. It's like bonbons, existing solely to give pleasure.

Violin Concerto in the Style of Vivaldi. There is one recording, by **Shaham** and the Orpheus Ensemble (DG). It's certainly in the style of Vivaldi, but it's difficult to imagine anyone mistaking it for the real thing. The performers do a very good job.

String Quartet. This is a fine work, and it's surprising Kreisler didn't try to compose anything else on this scale. Written during WWI, it recalls Wolf, Korngold, and early Schoenberg. **Kreisler** recorded it in 1935 with colleagues including cellist Lauri Kennedy (the violinist Kennedy's grandfather) in an excellent, alert performance (Monopoly 2041), and the younger **Kennedy** and friends have also recorded it (EMI 56626). It's a darker, more intense performance than Kreisler's, and equally good. **Salerno-Sonnenberg** with colleagues offers a delightfully arch reading (EMI 56481).

Shorter works. It's difficult to recommend recordings of Kreisler's large number of short, encore-type works, as they usually appear together with similar works by other composers. The rule to follow is to choose the discs by one's favorite virtuosos. However, there are some releases devoted exclusively to Kreisler.

Julia Krasko is a real virtuoso but lacks tonal allure and soul (Delos). **Bell** lacks the necessary charisma for this music (London), as does **Sitkovetsky** (Orfeo). **Stern** plays orchestral arrangements of these scores, but he was too old to meet their technical challenges by the time he made his disc (Stony). **Accardo** does a decent, workmanlike job while demonstrating the tonal properties of various famous Italian violins (Fone). **Péter Csaba,** partnered by the superb pianist Zoltán Kocsis, plays with all the warmth and affection these works require (Hungaroton 12437).

Ulrike-Anima Mathé has an intoxicating manner, though her intonation in the upper register is occasionally a bit wobbly (♦Dorian 90231). Samuel Sanders makes a great contribution from the keyboard. **Kennedy** really gets deep into this music and gives powerful, gutsy performances (EMI 55626). **Perlman** has all the qualities needed to play these scores to perfection: a warm, rich tone (after his Carnegie Hall debut, his tone was said to greatly resemble Kreisler's), a generous spirit, and a flaming virtuoso technique (EMI 47467). Those who collect vinyl might consider seeking out his superior Kreisler LPs from the '70s (♦EMI, NA). **Zukerman** also made some wonderful LPs at around the same time (♦CBS, NA).

Those who like to hear their Kreisler straight from the horse's mouth can choose from many collections **Kreisler** made from around 1900 to 1940 (♦Biddulph LAB 019 [2CD], 040, 075; EMI 64701; Monopoly 2041 [2CD]; Pearl 9324; RCA 61649 [11CD]—his complete recordings—or 68448). He was his own best interpreter, and his recordings were carefully made, so the sound is usually very good for its time.   MAGIL

Ernst Krenek *(1900–1991)*

Krenek is a neglected figure of our century. Born Czech and raised in Vienna, he was a musical chameleon, convincingly adopting several different styles throughout his career and investigating nearly every important movement of style and technique in this century. He established himself as a force to be reckoned with while still a student of Schreker in Berlin and caused an international sensation in 1927 with his "jazz opera" *Jonny spielt auf;* it was performed in more than 100 cities and translated into 18 different languages. In the mid-'30s he was writing atonal music, choosing themes that criticized the rise of Nazism, particularly in his opera *Karl V.* By 1938 he saw his performances canceled and was labeled a "cultural Bolshevist." In 1939 he emigrated to the United States and remained there for the rest of his life.

"Prolific" scarcely begins to describe the output of a composer who wrote 20 operas, five symphonies, 12 concertos, a sprawling wealth of vocal, choral, and chamber music, even finding time to investigate electronic music—after age 60! In addition, he painted and wrote voluminously, including the texts to most of his operas, extensive essays on music theory, poetry, even novels. For the curious listener, there is the problem of which Krenek to listen to; his huge corpus of music is bewilderingly varied, but consistent with his keen and questing intellect. And though he lived more than half of his life in the United States, his music is palpably European at all times.

Krenek's five numbered symphonies were all composed in the first half of his lengthy career, the first three between 1921 and 1922, the last two between 1947 and 1949. All of them owe a considerable debt to Mahler, and all are structurally rather idiosyncratic, eschewing any classic four-movement models. In these remarkably assured works you can hear a synthesis of Mahler, Zemlinsky, free atonality, and Bergian expressionism.

Of the five, all but Symphony 4 are presently available. **Takao Uki-**

gaya leads the Hanover Radio Philharmonic in a highly respectable cycle. Symphony 1 is an astounding debut for a composer barely out of his teens, a thorny work in nine sections played without pause. It's coupled with 5, which is uncharacteristically ebullient by comparison. The two works contrast nicely, though they both finish with fugues (♦CPO 999359). Symphony 2 is the largest and most Mahlerian, a much more amorphous and baffling work, and Krenek wrote it in only eight weeks! Its formal consistency is evident, but with its vast scale and atonal counterpoint, it's quite a challenge for musicians and listeners alike. Ukigaya and his comrades are undaunted and never let its swirling textures become muddy or the linear elements lose momentum (♦CPO 999255). Symphony 2 is also available in a recording led by **Lothar Zagrosek** (London), but Ukigaya has a better grasp of its structure and makes more of its contrasts. Symphony 3 is shorter, has more formal clarity, and isn't as dense as 2, making it a better starting point for the wary. It's coupled with *Potpourri,* an odd (and somewhat atypical) tonal orchestral work of unabashed jollity (♦CPO 999236).

Krenek's eight string quartets are one of the best entry points into his music. I find them (along with his piano sonatas) to be his most consistently satisfying works. They span his entire career, though there's quite a gap between 7 and 8. The early ones are heavily influenced by Bartók, though they all evince a pronounced Viennese quality. (Later, Krenek adopted Schoenberg's 12-tone technique, but wasn't dogmatic in its use.) The **Sonare Quartet** has recorded them complete in a splendid set with superb notes by Krenek himself (♦MD+G 4280, 4CD). For a more economical sampling, the single-disc release of 5 and 8 by the **Thouvenel Quartet** is worth considering (CRI 678), though the Sonare is preferable. Other chamber music for strings can be heard on a fine disc played by **Trio Rercherche** (♦CPO 999197). This disc focuses on works of a mostly expressionistic aspect from the '40s onward, including the harrowing *String Trio in 12 Stations* from 1985 and an homage to Bach, *Parvula Corona Musicalis.* In all, three works for trio are presented along with several pieces for solo violin and solo cello.

The piano was important to Krenek; besides playing it himself, he always turned to it whenever he experimented with new styles or techniques. I first became aware of his piano music through the advocacy of **Glenn Gould,** whose recording of Sonata 3 is one of his finest efforts (♦Sony 52661). It's easy to see why Gould loved the piece, with its effervescent rhythms and lean, contrapuntal textures. **Madge** is similarly committed to Krenek's music and recorded a complete survey of the sonatas under the composer's supervision (♦Koch Schwann, 2CD, NA). Madge also made an excellent disc of miscellaneous piano works that highlights Krenek's range and variety (♦CPO 999099). From the early free atonality of the sweeping *Toccata and Chaconne* through the pure entertainment of *George Washington Variations* to the introverted simplicity of *Echoes from Austria,* these works show his polystylistic ease and superb craftsmanship.

Krenek wrote a lot of vocal music, much of it to texts of his own devising. *Reisebuch aus den Osterreichischen Alpen* is an early song cycle that owes a great debt to Schubert. (Some of the songs sound so authentically Schubertian that they could easily be slipped into a Schubert recital without anyone except Graham Johnson noticing.) **Markus Köhler** sings the cycle with eloquence and a warm directness that suits it well (♦CPO 999203).

The stunning setting of *Lamentations of Jeremiah* for a cappella mixed chorus is one of Krenek's most powerful works and one of many he composed for the Roman liturgy. Written in the bleakness of 1941, the work is 12-tone in conception but with strong tonal referents to Gre-

gorian chant. It's a contrapuntal tour de force and displays his affinity for the compositions of Ockeghem, whose music he studied intently. **Gronostay** directs the Netherlands Chamber Choir in a superb performance—they never let the technical demands of the work obstruct its expressive intent (♦ Globe 5085).

Opera was a major interest throughout Krenek's life. He wrote seemingly effortlessly for the stage, and his librettos show a strong instinct for character and plot. He was somewhat dismayed that of all his works, *Jonny spielt auf* was the best known and came to represent his music to most listeners. This opera, with its intricate plot about an American jazz fiddler, a European composer, and the collision of sensibilities they represent, was notable more for its suave stylishness than for any real musical innovation. Opinions vary as to its real merits; I admit to having been disappointed when I first listened to it, having read about it for several years before I actually heard a recording. There is precious little jazz in it, mainly some pastiches of Paul Whiteman-type swing; Krenek evokes jazz more through instrumentation than through actual use of the idiom. The opera does keep getting revived, though, and **Zagrosek**'s recording makes the best possible argument for it (♦London 436631, 2CD, NA). An earlier (greatly abridged) recording is also available (Vanguard 8048), but the London recording tops it in every respect.

Der Sprung Über den Schatten (The Leap over the Shadow) came a little before *Jonny,* written in 1923 and premiered in 1924. It's a jolly little comic opera that actually has more jazz-like material than the later work—it's clearly a product of the '20s. The plot is an elaborate contraption involving members of the aristocracy trying to overcome their own conventionality, only to be thwarted by a revolution. **David de Villiers**'s direction of the Bielefelder Opera is crisp and energetic, with a fine cast (♦CPO 999082, 2CD). The recording is vivid, well balanced between orchestra and cast, and fairly free of extraneous noise (except for applause). I enjoy *Der Sprung* more than *Jonny* in some ways, perhaps because it's more consistent in tone and doesn't strain as much to make its point.

Vertrauenssache (What Price Confidence) is a brief chamber opera, composed in 1945. Its plot resembles a P.G. Wodehouse farce—it's a tale of two couples each struggling to trust their partners. It's set in Edwardian London and is full of outlandish coincidences, although its conclusion is more ambiguous than Wodehouse would allow. Krenek sets this comic scenario somewhat improbably against a lean, spiky, Schoenbergian piano accompaniment. The whole thing actually works better than you might expect, and the disc is filled out with fine performances of four *Bagatelles* for piano duet and the pivotal Sonata 4 (♦CPO 999319).

McINTIRE

Franz Krommer *(1759–1831)*

Krommer was one of the fine Czech musicians who so enriched the musical life of central Europe in Baroque and Classical times. Born in Moravia, he trained as an organist and violinist but was destined to become best known for his work with wind instruments; no doubt he got to know them during his time as a regimental bandleader. From 1795 he was a familiar figure in Vienna, and in 1818 he became the last bearer of the titles of court composer and Kapellmeister. Some 350 works by Krommer are known, and although some music of quality has undoubtedly been lost, we have enough left to demonstrate that he was a master of counterpoint and, at his best, not far behind Haydn and Mozart in skill. Although some excellent Czech-made LPs have never resurfaced on CD, he's quite well represented in the catalog.

Of at least nine symphonies by Krommer, two are lost. The two recorded by **Bamert** and the London Mozart Players, Nos. 2 and 4, are magnificent. You could be listening to Haydn, except that the deployment of the wind instruments is much more active--and, be it said, more skillful—than in most Haydn. Both, especially 4, use quite large orchestras for the time, but you never feel that Krommer is overdoing the sonority. The performances are tremendous, the recordings lifelike, and this is one of the finest discs in the "Contemporaries of Mozart" series (Chandos 9275).

Krommer's wind concertos are of superb quality. He may lack Mozart's profundity, but he writes beautifully for his soloists and the orchestral parts have real backbone. A good place to start is with a nicely planned program by flutist **Peter-Lukas Graf,** oboist **Holliger,** and the English Chamber Orchestra; each soloist has a concerto, and in between comes a delightful work for flute and oboe that for some reason is called a "Concertino," although it's as substantial as the concertos. This is one of those precious discs that sounds as good as it looks on paper (Claves 50-8203).

The various clarinet concertos are difficult to obtain without duplication. **Dieter Klöcker** and **Waldemar Wandel** do a good job with the works for two clarinets, Opp. 35 and 91, and the *Concertino Italien,* which this time really deserves its title, taking only 12 minutes to play; Hauschild conducts the Stuttgart Radio Symphony well, and the radio-derived recordings are mellow (Koch Schwann 1077). Even better in Op. 35 is the Belgian father and daughter team of **Walter** and **Anne Boeykens,** with the splendid little New Belgian Chamber Orchestra under Jan Caeyers. Boeykens senior gives the best performance I've heard of the Op. 36 Clarinet Concerto, and although the rest of the program features not more Krommer but Hoffmeister's concerto for two clarinets, it's a most melodious piece (Harmonia Mundi 1901433). **Sabine** and **Wolfgang Meyer** play Opp. 35 and 91 skillfully (EMI 49397, with pieces by Rossini).

The Czech player **Vlastimil Mareš** delivers pleasant, rustic sounding performances of Opp. 35, 36, and 91 with **Jiří Hlaváč** as his partner and the Prague Chamber Orchestra under Pešek (Supraphon 11 1596). A good bargain issue comes from the Hungarian clarinetist **Kálmán Berkes,** who dispatches the same program very musically, joined by Kaori Tsutsui and Tomoko Takashima in the works for two clarinets. He directs the Nicolaus Esterházy Sinfonia himself, and in spite of the over-resonant Budapest church acoustic, the disc is good value at the price (Naxos 553178).

Wind music is the sphere in which Krommer most closely challenges Mozart. His *Harmoniemusik*—generally written for the classic wind octet, with a contrabassoon added—is of top quality, and if his slow movements can't match Mozart's depths, his faster movements are fully comparable. A clear winner in both performance and recording is the program of three partitas by **Ensemble Philidor,** a French group playing "*instruments anciens,*" although you'd never know it, so complete is the players' command over the tricky old artifacts. They use a string bass for added clarity and are conducted by Eric Baude-Delhommais. The F Major Partita Op. 57 is a magnificent piece ending with a favorite Krommer device, an *Alla polacca.* The other two works on the disc, Opp. 73 and 79 —for the first of which the group claims a premiere recording—are almost as good, and the recordings are clear as a bell (Calliope 9264).

The **Nash Ensemble** is worth hearing in the Opp. 67 and 79 partitas, especially if you fancy the coupling of Dvořák's Wind Serenade, as the recordings still sound very good, and the playing, if not of Philidor quality, is uncomplicated and expert (CRD 3410). **Berkes** weighs in with an excellent bargain program of three partitas including Op. 57 and three marches, directing the Budapest Wind Ensemble, where he plays first clarinet (Naxos 553498). Those who like the straightforward, direct English style of wind playing will find much to enjoy in another bargain disc, featuring the **Michael Thompson Wind Ensemble** in the two Op. 45 partitas, the second in an edition with added trumpet. Another partita in E-flat calls for virtuosic horn playing by Thompson himself and Richard Berry, though it may not be by Krommer. The recordings are excellent (Naxos 553868).

Krommer often enriched his chamber music textures by using two violas—his nine beautiful flute quintets all feature just one violin, so the flute doesn't have too much high-flying competition—and the two viola parts make for a most pleasing sound. Three of these quintets are expertly played by **Bruno Meier** with one of the top Czech ensembles, the Stamitz Quartet. The G major Op. 109, Krommer's last such work dating, has a nobility that we don't always associate with the bright-toned flute. Opp. 55 and 58 both include some of Krommer's unshowy but effective fugal writing. The 1992 recordings are good (Koch Schwann 1049). The Stamitz Quartet is joined by **Mareš** for the Clarinet Quintet, which is mastered rather more convincingly than the coupled Mozart quintet (Supraphon 0017). **Klöcker** and members of the Consortium Classicum take good care of the six clarinet quartets (CPO 999141).

Not to be missed are Krommer's two likeable bassoon quartets Op. 46 with the solo instrument joined by two violas and cello. A Supraphon recording of great character has disappeared, but there is a reasonable substitute featuring **Eckart Hübner,** who adds the Mozart Duo for bassoon and cello (CPO 999297). You should still be able to obtain a good bargain version played by **John Heard** and members of the Veronika Quartet with Mary Harris, viola (IMP 02602, with Reicha's Bassoon Quintet).   POTTER

Friedrich Kuhlau (1786–1832)

Kuhlau's father, a military bandsman from Hanover, moved the family to Hamburg along with his regiment, but young Friedrich, who despite the loss of one eye became a proficient pianist, later fled to Copenhagen to avoid being drafted into Napoleon's army. There he not only introduced the music of Beethoven to the imperial court but on visiting Vienna became friends with the master himself. As a naturalized Danish citizen, Kuhlau soon made a name for himself both in the concert hall (he was a celebrated flutist) and on the stage, primarily with his score for Johan Ludvig Heiberg's fantasy drama *Elverhøj* (Elf Hill), which remains one of the most popular examples of Danish romantic theater. While numerous influences may be seen in Kuhlau's music, he remains an original, a bridge between Classical and Romantic eras colored with Danish folk melodies as well as those of his own devising.

ORCHESTRAL MUSIC

Suites from *Elf Hill* are usually found in orchestral discs devoted to Kuhlau's music. In his version, the elves are merely supporting players in a drama centering on Denmark's King Christian IV, who lived 200 years before Kuhlau's time, and the composer paid tribute to the current sovereign Frederik VI (who commissioned the work as a wedding present for his daughter) by concluding in grand fashion with the royal anthem "King Christian Stood by the Mast," also familiar from Tchaikovsky's overture. The complete score offered under **John Frandsen**'s fervent leadership is an essential addition to the Kuhlau discography, though the Danish Radio Symphony is a trifle unpolished (Da Capo 224053, earlier on 8902). The Suite as heard from **Othmar Maga** (Unicorn 9132) differs somewhat from **Johan Hye-Knudsen**'s version (Turnabout LP), but in terms of performance they are remarkably similar, and those who already have the complete score may question the need to buy Maga; however, this CD also offers four of Kuhlau's finest overtures conducted by **Serov.**

These in turn come into competition with **Schønwandt,** who offers the same overtures plus four more, including *Elf Hill* (Chandos 9648), and to make matters even more confusing, the Overture from Maga's *Elf Hill Suite* is itself recycled from an even earlier Unicorn CD of the Piano Concerto with Ponti (discussed below). Those primarily interested in the overtures will find Schønwandt's disc invaluable, if a bit drably recorded; still, comparisons sometimes favor the other recordings. Frandsen's crisp and buoyant account of the Overture to *Elf Hill* (in the complete recording) is more pleasurable than the rather emphatic readings by Schønwandt and Maga; while in *William Shakespeare* (a fantasy about the young Shakespeare and his rivalry with a local squire) both Serov and Schønwandt must bow to **Hye-Knudsen,** whose splendid disc of "Romantic Danish Overtures" is one of the treasures of the catalog (◆Sterling 1018). In *Røverborgen* (The Robbers' Castle) Schønwandt seems breathless next to Serov—and he's even more hectic in *Elisa*— yet in *Trillingbrødrene fra Damask* (The Three Brothers from Damascus) Schønwandt is strangely reserved, while in *Lulu*—which has nothing to do with Berg's angst-ridden drama—Schønwandt far surpasses Serov's tired run-through. Both of the remaining pieces, *Hugo and Adelheid* and *Trylleharpen* (The Magic Harp) fare much better.

CONCERTOS

Given Kuhlau's friendship with Beethoven, the striking motivic similarity between the opening of the Danish composer's C major Piano Concerto and Beethoven's own example in that key—written some 15 years earlier—may be considered tribute by one composer to another; but Kuhlau's work is captivating in its own right, with spirited outer movements framing a charming and all too brief Adagio. In **Felicja Blumental**'s recording, her majestic approach to the opening movement clearly points up the debt to Beethoven, though she seems a bit tepid elsewhere (Vox, reissued as Ars Classicum 1159292). **Ponti** is a good deal more energetic, though without Blumental's rich vein of poetry (Unicorn 9110). Best of all is **Amalie Malling,** a glorious outpouring of song; it's coupled with a powerful reading of the Grieg Concerto, seemingly a match made in heaven (Chandos #9699). But those who elect Ponti will be pleased to have in its place Kuhlau's otherwise unavailable Concertino for Two Horns, though the opportunity for antiphonal effects between the horn players has unaccountably been overlooked.

CHAMBER MUSIC

Kuhlau was a flutist himself, so his compositions for that instrument, particularly the three quintets that comprise his Op. 51, are beautifully put together and grateful to both player and listener, lacking only that spark of Elysian fire that would raise them to the level of Mozart and Beethoven. Interestingly, they are scored for violin, two violas, and cello rather than the usual complement. **Rampal** with the Juilliard Quartet brings out the best in this music on a well-filled disc (◆CBS 44517); **Eyvind Rafn** suffers by comparison, his bland tone coloring made worse by imprecise articulation and rhythm (Naxos 553303). Rafn has also recorded a set of Kuhlau's flute sonatas with pianist Esther Vagning, but again he has technical difficulties and the sound is brittle and over-amplified (Marco Polo 224071, 2CD). **Toke Lund Christiansen** also has problems with breath control and insecure pitch (Kontrapunkt 32160, with a much better Beethoven Quintet, 2CD). A somewhat better collec-

tion is by **Kurt Redel** and Noël Lee, nicely turned despite some dubious intonation (Etcetera 1189).

Kuhlau's lone string quartet is his last completed work. It's a polished and fluent effort, well played by the **Copenhagen Quartet** (Marco Polo 224016). This label has provided a highly recommendable 2CD set of his three piano quartets, which are exactly contemporary with Mendelssohn's; like those better-known examples, Kuhlau's are wonderfully expressive, condensing into a brief span a wide range of emotions. The performers aren't well known, but they are clearly committed to the cause. The **eSBe Quartet** with pianist Andres Meyer-Hermann offer the G minor Piano Quartet and the A minor String Quartet, both very well played (CPO 999238). You may wish to complement this with another disc containing Kuhlau's violin sonatas in excellent performances by **Dora Bratchkova,** again joined by Meyer-Hermann (CPO 999363).

HALLER

Meyer Kupferman (b. 1926)

Kupferman combines a maverick mentality with a career of college teaching at Sarah Lawrence that has kept him from more exaggerated musical styles, thus saving his work for live performers. He experiments with many contemporary techniques, always with an improvisatory feeling. Earlier compositions take these fads one or two at a time, but since the early '70s he has tended to mix his idioms without warning. Influences on his music include his Jewish background, serial procedures (notably in the "Infinities" series of the '60s, extending to more than 30 works), jazz (frequently 12-tone), and electronic manipulation of live sound (usually a live soloist surrounded by tape tracks of the soloist's own playing). Other frequent but less determining techniques include playing inside the piano and aleatoric elements. In the mid-'80s, a South American influence shows up, and occasional Oriental influences may stem from his marriage to the dancer and artist, Pai Fen.

Kupferman's career began in the late '40s, when he wrote a good deal of orchestral music, including several symphonies. During the '60s, he turned more to chamber and solo works; with the greater relaxation of the '80s, orchestral music became more frequent again. He has also written a considerable amount of music for solo instruments, notably cello, piano, and his own instrument, the clarinet, plus several pieces for flute, oboe, and guitar.

Recordings are numerous, mainly because Kupferman has always been active in promoting them. His music won the enthusiasm of Paul Kapp, whose Serenus LP label released at least seven discs of Kupferman's music. After Kapp's death, Kupferman began his own CD company, Soundspells, with more than 25 discs to date, including several reissued from LP sources. The sound on these reissues varies a bit; both Serenus and Desto tended to attenuate the low frequencies, giving their discs a rather harsh sound, while CRI's early orchestral discs lack highs to some extent. Performances vary, even during a single piece. Kupferman's music is demanding, requiring players to change their focus and style several times during a single work, and this makes for difficulties in concentration and momentary inaccuracies of ensemble and pitch. Since there are no competing performances, and nothing really egregious happens, I've kept my remarks on performance to a minimum.

SYMPHONIES

The numbers of the symphonies may be clear to the composer, but even the category of some works is hard for the listener to figure out. The earliest recorded is Symphony 2 (according to *Schwann*), or *Chamber Symphony,* according to the notes a 12-tone work written in 1950 before that system became fashionable, conducted by **Harold Farberman** (SNDS 112). The next seems to be *Little Symphony* (1952), a neoclassic score aping the mannerisms of Beethoven and others in a curiously unsettling fashion (SNDS 121). Symphony 4 (1955) and *Lyric Symphony* (1956) are both richly emotional works; 4 is a Louisville performance, coupled with *Little Symphony,* and the *Lyric* comes from **Akeo Watanabe** and the Japan Philharmonic (SNDS 111).

Then there are no symphonies until 1974, when *Twilight Symphony* appeared. Though included in Sound Phantoms's Vol. 5 of the orchestral works, both this and its discmate *Masada* are really chamber music, *Twilight* a tribute to Kupferman's father, *Masada* a work about the Holocaust. Both are in a spacious single movement with wildly contrasting styles that characterize Kupferman's music from the '70s to the present. Next is *Sinfonia Brevis #2* (Sound Phantoms's Vol. 8), a curious miniature in five movements referring to Beethoven's "Muss es sein" motive, as did Symphony 4. Then comes *Symphony for Six* (1984), clearly a chamber work (SNDS 124, Orchestral Music Vol. 10).

Jazz Symphony appeared in 1988, a 50-minute blockbuster alternating orchestral sections with songs (SNDS 104, NA). *Wings of the Highest Tower* (1988) is a three-movement symphony on patriotic subjects (SNDS 110). *Symphonic Odyssey* (1990) is also in three movements, commemorating the death of a friend in music of great variety, from dissonant passages to a Macedonian dance (SNDS 122). In 1996, *Quasar Symphony* appeared, four light-textured but fairly austere and dissonant movements, ending with one titled "Crazy Jazz" (SNDS 122). In 1997 came *Winter Symphony,* a 45-minute epic in three parts. With this work we sense an attempt to begin summing up a lifetime's experience. Kupferman keeps our interest alive through his intimate knowledge of instrumental sound and the various emotions that can be elicited by using a remarkable arsenal of expressive devices (SNDS 125). In this disc the composer conducts. He seems to be good at it; there's more unity of effort in this performance than in some others. But it's also a fine symphony.

OTHER ORCHESTRAL MUSIC

An early *Divertimento* and *Libretto* are included in SNDS 112, as well as *Atto,* a tiny piece, and *Mask of Electra,* a 9-minute chamber work with voice, not to be confused with the 1995 *Three Faces of Electra,* a dramatic 50-minute "imaginary ballet score" (SNDS 120). *Orchestral Variations* and *Ostinato Burlesca* are exciting pieces from the early period (SNDS 111). Then comes the break of the '70s, and orchestral works resume with *Challenger,* a 1983 tone poem honoring the spaceship before its tragic fall (SNDS 104, NA). *Banners* is a lively scherzo-like piece with a Mexican flavor (SNDS 113).

CONCERTOS

Concerto for Cello and Jazz Band (1962) was an early entry in the "Infinities" series, all based on the same 12-tone row. It's not orchestral, since the jazz band consists of three saxophones doubling on everything in sight, and a bass. **David Wells**'s performance of this nearly half-hour work is exemplary (SNDS 111). There are two other cello concertos from the '70s, a Fantasy Concerto for Cello, Piano, and Tape and a Concerto for Cello, Tape, and Orchestra. Both have been recorded by **Laszlo Varga,** though only the orchestral concerto is presently on disc in a fine American collection (Vox Box 5158). It's a broad and romantic piece. Another unusual jazz concerto called *Tunnels of Love* is for clarinet, bass, and drums (SNDS 118).

A spate of concertos began to appear in the '80s. The lovely Clarinet Concerto is played with smooth and lively clarity by **Peter Alexander**

(CRI 575). The piano concertos are less well represented on CD than you might expect, considering the presence of two fine pianists in Kupferman's large circle of performing friends. *Little Ivory Concerto* is almost a chamber work, accompanied by a wind quintet and string quartet in one half-hour movement (SNDS 101, NA). *The Moor's Concerto* is in an even longer movement emphasizing the romantic; shades of Tchaikovsky, Rachmaninoff, and movie scores seem to parade before us (SNDS 110). Both works are played by the excellent and sympathetic **Kazuko Hayami.**

The *Fantasy Violin Concerto* is another major work in one 40-minute movement, full of lyricism and derring-do, one of Kupferman's most beautiful concepts (SNDS 119). *Rhapsody for Guitar and Orchestra* (1980) began a continuing fascination with that instrument (SNDS 120). Kupferman's dramatic tendency has frequently led him to amplify soloists so they can compete with a full and sometimes noisy orchestra. Both his Guitar Concerto (SNDS 113) and *Hexagon Skies* (SNDS 114) are large scores calling for guitar amplification, though the latter is really six short orchestral tone poems separated by interludes for solo guitar, blending forces only at the last interlude. Most recent in this series is a colorful Concerto for Four Guitars (SNDS 124).

CHAMBER AND SOLO MUSIC

Kupferman has written a lot of chamber music, but not much has reached CD. The Bassoon Quintet is a very early piece in a determinedly slithery tonality, while the Clarinet Quintet is relatively recent and displays a variety of techniques (SNDS 108). There is also a fine Piano Quintet (SNDS 101, NA). The 1963 Jazz String Quartet is a substantial piece, played with involvement by the **Ariel Quartet** in a jazz-oriented release (SNDS 126). A more far-ranging example of Kupferman crossover is also on this disc, *Moonfingers Demon* (1998), a 14-person Halloween piece he would like to consider orchestral but that contains no doubling I can detect. Another piece for the same 14 players is the beautifully moody *A Faust Concerto* for horn and orchestra (1997), recorded with *Among the Windy Places* for violin, viola, and bassoon (1994), an unlikely but effective combination (SNDS 127).

Another crossover composition is *Ice Cream Concerto,* a large chamber work for 13 players in two movements, the second of which is a 25-minute essay in jazz style played by its dedicatees, Mexico's **Atril Cinco.** The disc includes *Must Be Hot in Mexico!* a collection of short solo pieces written for each member of the group and named after ice cream flavors (SNDS 109). It must be hot in Mexico!

A disc of cello music, both chamber and solo, is played by **Laszlo Varga** (SNDS 105). Another is by guitarist **William Anderson** (SNDS 123). **Christopher Vassiliades** has a solo piano disc of his own, Vol. 1 of a series (SNDS 115). An exciting performance of *Sonata on Jazz Elements* played by **Kazuko Hayami** has appeared, in rather brittle sound (SNDS 126). Pieces for solo flute have been recorded by other companies, *Abstractions* by **John Solum** (CRI 712), *Arcana* by **Laurel Ann Maurer** (4Tay 4006), *Chaconne Sonata* also by Maurer (Albany 167), and *O Harlequin* by **Marcia Gates** (SNDS 108). Solo trumpet is represented by **Thomas Stevens** in *The Fires of Prometheus* (Crystal 667) and by **Louis Ranger** in "Infinities 22" (Crystal 669). And I mustn't leave out the massive *Sonata Guernica* for violin and piano, recorded along with the piano quartet *Flames of Abracadabra* and *Tunnels of Love* (SNDS 118).

OPERA

Very little vocal music is available. *The Proscenium: On The Demise of Gertrude,* is a one-character, one-act opera with chamber accompaniment. The action is entirely in Gertrude's mind, seen in the form of film clips. The language seems stilted in spots, colloquial in others, and the singer speaks as well as sings. You must suspend your disbelief at rather a high level, as is frequently the case with operas in English. **Barbara Hardgrave** does a good job, but the character isn't particularly sympathetic because of the odd libretto (SNDS 107). MOORE

György Kurtág (b. 1926)

Kurtág's music—painfully brief, obsessively focused, haunted and haunting—generally sounds like an update on Webern, but then his *Kafka Fragments* for soprano and violin sounds like a latter-day composing-out of Schoenberg's *Pierrot Lunaire*. Kurtág's punishing vocal writing covers a wide range of extended techniques, and he gets as much variety from a single violin as Schoenberg does from his eight instruments. Soprano **Anu Komsi** and violinist **Sakari Oramo** present the work as a set of virtuoso concert pieces, and one piece comes across pretty much like another (Ondine). Part of the problem may be the recorded balance, which is so close that some of Oramo's note-finding is conspicuous over the rests.

Játékok (Games) is a set of 30 very short pieces for two- and four-hand piano (ECM). These seem to be character pieces in their brief and very different postures, yet the textures progress in difficulty and the set takes on a pedantic structure like Bartók's *Mikrokosmos*. The spare and disparate textures of Kurtág's piano writing are more like Webern's than Debussy's, or even Ligeti's, yet playfulness often surfaces, and he collects overtones with pedals in a kind of impressionist homage to the instrument's sonic beneficence. **Kurtág** and his wife, both very able pianists, intersperse these pieces with four Bach arrangements that become oases of stability in the journey. ECM's sound is beautifully crisp and poetic.

No disc gives a more comprehensive and hypnotic perspective on Kurtág than the **Keller Quartet's** edition of his music for quartet (♦ECM 1598). The six works show the composer creating his own introverted and often beautiful world of sound. Even when the Op. 1 quartet sounds like Webern heard through Bartók's ears, there is nothing of imitation in the music. The other pieces are all unmistakably personal, full of interest and depths that will reward repeated listening. On this evidence, Kurtág is a great composer indeed: his musical ideas are so precisely formulated as to balance on the end of a pin. The Kellers are astonishingly focused, yet have a beautiful sound that ECM's engineering catches with clarity and depth. The leader was one of Kurtág's students in Budapest, and the group's sympathy for the music shows.

The **Arditti Quartet** has recorded Quartet Op. 1, *Hommage á Milhály András* Op. 13, and *Officium breve* Op. 28 (Montaigne). The Arditti couplings (Gubaidulina's Quartet 2 and Lutoslawski's fairly frequently recorded quartet) make a less interesting context than the Keller's all-Kurtag program. Montaigne's up-front sound accentuates the Arditti's professionalism and energy while the Keller are more open to the music's poetry.

Another disc catches Kurtág in more aphoristic style, with the spotlight on violist **Kim Kashkashian** (ECM). She plays the brief and fragmentary nine *Stücke* for solo viola and *Jelek*. With clarinetist **Eduard Brunner** and pianist **Robert Levin**, she also plays Kurtág's *Hommage à R. Schumann* (ending with the ghostly "Abschied (Master Raro Discovers Guillaume de Machaut)" before the disc moves on to Schumann's works for viola, clarinet, and piano. It's a beautiful disc in its way, and also a melancholy one, but the conceptual (rather than musical) connections between Schumann and Kurtág would make a better premise for a recital than they do for a disc.

Vocal settings occupy a central position in Kurtág's output, and here the most important scores are *Messages of the Late Miss R.V. Troussova* and *Scenes from a Novel*. In both works, the singer of choice is **Adrienne Csengery** (♦Hungaroton 31821). Her vibrant, clear voice is a joy to hear, and it comes with intelligent musicianship and a natural ease with the Russian texts; she premiered all Kurtág's major vocal cycles, and her affinity for the composer is immediately audible. An earlier version of this disc included a *Troussova* performance where Csengery was accompanied by **Boulez** and Ensemble InterContemporain; rights to that were ceded to Erato, who published it in a 4CD Boulez miscellany, and Hungaroton replaced it with a performance accompanied by the just as admirable **András Mihály**.

Next to Csengary, the more boyish sounds of **Christine Whittlesey** are less memorable in *Scenes from a Novel*, and clear, dry, more up-front sound also purges the music of some of its enigmatic mystery (Sony, with a fine reading of *... quasi una fantasia ...* for piano and groups of instruments). For *Troussova*, the Sony disc pairs **Rosemary Hardy** with Ensemble Modern under Peter Eötvös. Her delivery is more personal than Whittlesey's, but Csengery is the one who truly inhabits the music and the texts. Csengery's Budapest Chamber Ensemble also sounds consistently more acclimated to Kurtág's music, more natural in interpretation.

De Gaetani sang *Scenes from a Novel* at a New York concert in 1987 with players from Speculum Musicae (Bridge, with Shostakovich's *Songs from Jewish Folk Poetry* and *Abeja Blanca* by Dan Welcher). She brings an evocative, smoky tone to the music, and with that and her free use of a strong chest voice for lower notes, she makes the music her own. In the slower songs her performance is intensely concentrated, but her slides and shout effects can also sound mannered, and a major blemish is that "Rondo" (No. 5) ends only halfway through.

An attractive student work, *Movement* for viola and orchestra, shows Kurtág's early stylistic debt to Bartók. **Kashkashian** and Eötvös include the piece in a well-planned disc that appropriately includes Bartók's viola concerto (ECM 1711). That early piece aside, Kurtág started to conceive music in longer spans and for the orchestra only in the '90s. In 1993 he was in residence with the Berlin Philharmonic, and with that orchestra **Abbado** recorded *Memorial for Stephan* and *Stele* as supplements to their magnificent performance of Stockhausen's *Gruppen* (♦DG 447761). *Memorial* is a funeral procession that moves from soft guitar strokes to despairing rage and back again. *Stele* is less predictable and probably a greater composition, though the composer doesn't give the impression of having mastered his orchestration the way he had his writing for string quartet. But it's a great pleasure to hear these Cadillac forces in such music, and the sound is just fine.

A Hungarian miscellany samples some instrumental, vocal, and choral byways. The program doesn't add up to much, and there is some quirky and unpalatable music here—Kurtág sets Pilinszky's "Alcohol" mostly to a quizzical monotone—but there are also some discoveries, like *Eight Piano Pieces* played by a young **Zoltán Kocsis**, along with **István Antal's** rendition of the same work (Hungaroton). A more worthy (if not generously apportioned) double disc documents a "Portraitkonzert" from the 1993 Salzburg Festival (Col Legno). There are some disruptive audience noises, and the whole recital sounds a bit off-mike. A pity, since the performances are generally more evocative and sensitive than the competition. For instance, **Kocsis** and Eötvös take the outer movements of *... quasi una fantasia ...* more languidly than **Hermann Kretzschmar** and Ensemble Modern on Sony (paired with *Scenes from a Novel* and *Troussova* songs, described above).

The Col Legno set also includes the fragmented *Samuel Beckett: What Is the Word,* where Kurtág gives Beckett's last prose text to a stuttering reciter who enacts recovery from aphasia. Eötvös's focused performance is preferable to **Abbado**'s hazier Viennese rendition (DG). What really makes the Col Legno discs worth seeking out is the only available recording of the 16-minute, single-movement Double Concerto for piano, cello, and two ensembles. **Kocsis** and **Miklós Perényi** are the idiomatic soloists, and they present this score as one of Kurtág's more trenchant and interesting instrumental essays.   ASHBY

László Lajtha *(1892–1963)*

Lajtha is a superb 20th-century composer who ought to be far better known. While his Hungarian compatriots, Bartók and Kodály, were ignoring symphonic form, Lajtha was writing compelling symphonies of universal appeal. Often his music is darkly romantic, with gorgeous harmonies and lush orchestrations. Like Shostakovich, he often expresses the absurdities of war, yet even when he examines the tragedy of his wartime experiences, he never entirely succumbs to pessimism. In the many works where the sun shines, he's a lively companion, full of high spirits and infectious melody. Sometimes his music is exotic and impressionistic, the result of time spent in Paris. But what lingers in the memory are a velvet-black melancholy, austere beauty, and an unfailing sense of melody that becomes more fascinating with each hearing.

ORCHESTRAL MUSIC

Lajtha completed nine symphonies, and after hearing them you may wonder at the scanty recorded legacy afforded this excellent composer. Luckily, Marco Polo has been correcting this injustice, and most of them can now be heard in superior digital sound. **Nicolás Pasquet** has given us seven volumes so far, including Symphonies 1 through 7 and an equivalent number of other orchestral works.

My own experience began with Symphonies 3 and 4 and Suite 2 (♦Marco Polo 223671), This disc gives a wide sampling of the composer's varying moods, and since it worked well for me as an introduction, I recommend it here for the same purpose. Symphony 3 is a two-movement work that displays the composer's darker callings, as does the *Molto quieto* in Suite 2, which is by turns aggressive and buoyant in the outer movements. The effervescent 4 is subtitled "Spring," with a light and rhapsodic mood and a gorgeous melody in the Allegretto. The Pécs Symphony Orchestra achieves a high level of artistry; throughout the series these Hungarians are deeply committed to their countryman's music.

Ferencsik, who knew the composer, brings high energy to Symphonies 4 and 9, along with Sinfonietta for String Orchestra from 1946 (♦Hungaroton 31452), though his exquisite approach to quieter passages leans away from Pasquet's melancholy beauty (♦Marco Polo 223670). Symphony 1, with its quasi-militaristic first movement, an eerie Andante, and a sardonically turbulent finale, gets another compelling performance by Pasquet (♦Marco Polo 223670). This disc contains Suite for Orchestra with its "Hymn Prelude" section that reaches heavenward yet is oddly earthbound, and *In Memoriam,* a 20-minute tone poem devoted to war victims. Lajtha's dark Symphony 2 in the same series sounds like a cross between Shostakovich and Sibelius; its heavy, swirling motives are exotically orchestrated, and a piano is used as an orchestral instrument (♦Marco Polo 223669). On this disc, *Variations*—composed as a self-contained concert piece, but also as film music for T.S. Eliot's *Murder in the Cathedral*—has delicate, anguished string writing and angular tonal contrasts.

Symphony 5 was conceived in a tragic vein, but where tragedy lingers in this composer's music, so do beauty and forward momentum. Symphony 6 is full of exotic, colorful orchestrations and widely contrasting moods. The use of a harp, saxophone, and 11 different percussion instruments creates a strange, organic world of sound and movement; the glassy, wandering strings and secretive woodwinds interweave with incandescent violin solos. This is one of Lajtha's most impressionistic and impressive compositions, and as a bonus the disc has the stage work *Lysistrata* (♦Marco Polo 223672). Symphony 7 is a brutal and uncompromising expression of events in the autumn of 1956 when the Soviet Union invaded Hungary (♦Marco Polo 223667). Suite 3 is lively and pleasant, but the film music for *Hortobágy* is comparatively inconsequential. I'd also put *Capriccio, Suite de ballet,* containing 77 minutes of short movements, on my list of secondary recommendations, though it too contains some fine music (Marco Polo 223668).

OTHER MUSIC

Once upon a time, all ten of Lajtha's quartets were available on Qualiton LPs, but I can find only one now, No. 10 (part of ♦Hungaroton 31453). This disc has the lovely *Magnificat* for female choir and pipe organ, *Three Hymns for the Holy Virgin,* and four Madrigals performed by **Istvan Párkai.** May we suppose that Qualiton will open their vaults for further quartet releases? Meanwhile, we have "Chamber Music with Flute Vol. 1" (♦Hungaroton 31647). "With flute" means some wonderfully atmospheric solo pieces, a flute sonata, and two trios for harp, flute, and cello. All but the solo pieces are just over 20 minutes long, and I recommend that each be heard individually, as the composer intended, not run together as so often happens with such a generous compilation. More important still are *Marionettes,* three Nocturnes, and Quintet 2, performed by a fine chamber ensemble beautifully conducted by **Gergely Matuz.** This disc is full of the composer's varying moods, and is a must-have (♦Hungaroton 31776).

Lajtha's Cello Sonata and Concerto for Cello and Piano can be heard with **Peter Szábo** (♦Hungaroton 31552, with a Dohnányi cello sonata). The Sonata is an example of Lajtha's experiments with baroque form in a modern vein, and the Concerto is a stark expression of war. Neither is for the die-hard romantic. Nor is Hungarian pianist **Klára Körmendi**'s no-nonsense traversal of Lajtha's piano music, which might be recommended tentatively, barring future comparisons in this unfamiliar repertoire (Marco Polo 223473). A listener new to this composer can't go wrong with any of the Marco Polo releases that contain at least one of the symphonies.   HALDEMAN

Edouard Lalo *(1823–1892)*

Lalo was not a late bloomer, but he certainly wasn't spoiled by early success; in fact, he didn't even find a publisher until he was 50. Almost all his music that's currently played is from the last 20 years of his life, and even such former favorites as the Overture to *Le Roi d'Ys* and *Symphonie Espagnole* don't turn up much on concert programs any more. Too bad; if Lalo's concertos or his G Minor Symphony aren't entirely free of pretension, they are also refined and full of color, in the best French tradition.

ORCHESTRAL MUSIC

Symphonie Espagnole is a scintillating, tuneful work, Lalo's best-known piece by far. It's easy to make it sound slick and inconsequential, much harder to make it sing and dance. Lalo wrote it in 1875 for Sarasate, one of the greatest 19th-century violinists, and almost every fiddler of consequence has felt compelled to record it at least once, though it isn't played much in concerts these days. Recordings by **Huberman** and the young **Menuhin** set the standard in the early '30s and are still available (Huberman in ◆APR 5506, Preiser 90118, or Classical Collector 2003; Menuhin in Biddulph 46). So are "older generation" recordings by **Heifetz** (RCA 7709, with several cuts) and **Elman** (Vanguard 8034). Of more recent vintage are an elegant mono version by **Milstein** (EMI 66552, with Bizet's *Carmen Suite* and ballet favorites by Falla and Gounod; Testament 1047, with Goldmark's rare Viola Concerto), and a barnburner, brightly recorded performance by **Ricci** (◆London 452309).

Stern's virtuosic performance from the '60s, made even more appealing by Ormandy's accompaniment, is currently NA (Sony). **Perlman**'s second recording, with Barenboim, is very good, coupled with an equally good Saint-Saëns Violin Concerto 3 (◆DG 45549; the first, with Previn, is also available in RCA 68338 or 56520). **Zukerman**'s colorful performance is an excellent bargain, with an equally appealing work, Bruch's G Minor Concerto. This is available in Sony 44717, one of the bare-bones Odyssey releases, but if you get it in ◆Sony 48274, an "Essential Classics" disc, you also get one of Zukerman's earliest Columbia recordings, Vieuxtemps's Violin Concerto 5.

The Cello Concerto is another piece that soloists perform in the recording studio more than in the concert hall. Outstanding versions are by **Leonard Rose** (◆Sony 482778, with Bloch's *Schelomo*), **Starker** (◆Mercury 432010, with excellent Saint-Saëns and Schumann concertos), and a young **Ma** (◆Sony 35848). Also interesting is a live 1973 recording by the great **du Pré**: a bit spotty, but like everything she did, spontaneous and exciting (EMI 55528).

The pickings are slimmer among Lalo's other concerted works, which tend to be agreeable but not memorable. There are a Violin Concerto, *Concerto Russe,* and *Fantasie Norvégienne,* all available in a single disc from **Ricci** (111 95040), and a Piano Concerto, appealing and tuneful if completely unoriginal. It's in an enterprising collection of oddball French concertos by Boieldieu, Roussel, Pierné and others (Vox 5110). The sound varies from good to lousy (Roussel's concerto sounds as if it was recorded under water), but it's repertoire that any Francophile or pianophile should hear once.

Lalo's ballet *Namouna* wasn't successful at its first performance, but it made an impression on at least one audience member: the 19-year-old Claude Debussy, whose vociferous applause caused him to be led out of the theater. In his music critic days, Debussy called *Namouna* "a masterpiece of rhythm and color," and you get an idea of his meaning hearing the first of Lalo's three suites from the ballet, recorded in 1957 by **Paray** (◆Mercury 434389). It's pleasing and colorful music, and you sense that Debussy got a hint for the second movement of his String Quartet from Lalo's *Serenade.* This disc includes the Overture to *Le Roi d'Ys,* once a very popular concert item. The "Living Presence" sound is grating and shallow, but the performance is undeniably exciting. **Martinon,** much better recorded than Paray, includes top-notch performances of extended excerpts from *Namouna,* as well as the Cello Concerto with Fournier, *Rapsodie Norvégienne,* and some equally enjoyable Bizet pieces (◆DG 37371, 2CD).

Lalo's single "real" symphony is an intermittently interesting piece in G minor. **Beecham** took an interest in it, and his '50s recording is the most persuasive of the few that have been made (EMI, NA).

CHAMBER MUSIC

Lalo was one of the very few mid-19th-century French composers to write a considerable amount of chamber music. These works, which include a string quartet, sonatas for violin and for cello, and three piano trios, are seldom played, but recordings are available for the curious. They reveal a composer much influenced by Schumann and Mendelssohn, but one who also knew that a chamber work isn't just an orchestral work cut down. The excellent string quartet is passably performed by the **Daniel Quartet** (Discover 920159). His piano trios are almost popular, at least on CD, perhaps because all three fit on one disc. Sets are available from the **Henry Trio** (Pierre Verany 794031), **Barbican Trio** (ASV 899), and **Parnassus Trio** (MD+G 3482).

RAYMOND

Rued Langgaard (1893–1952)

Langgaard is not as well known as some of his contemporaries in Denmark because he was always an outsider. A prodigy who wrote his first symphony at 15 and produced six more by the age of 30, then only one during the next 19 years, then at least one every year until his death, is not your ordinary composer. He was pretty much ignored by the Danish musical establishment throughout his life, his main position that of organist of Ribe Cathedral from 1940 until his death.

Music is an art that sometimes seems to mediate between a person and the world around him; the more otherworldly the composer, the harder his music has to work to explain him. Sometimes the result satisfies no one, and the composer keeps trying, tinkering with what he has written to make it more acceptable, though this may distort his original concept. Langgaard began to write symphonies in his mid-teens—long, sprawling scores that he later shortened and rearranged. Unfortunately, few of his works were performed while he lived, so he kept on tinkering with them. Along the way, his style changed: first toward the brilliance and ferocity of Nielsen's later works, then toward a neoclassicism that almost negates both his earlier Straussian romanticism and WWI-induced violence. Underlying all this, and bridging the chasms between his stylistic changes, is a visionary religiosity that led him to his opera *Antikrist,* in which good and evil meet on the musical battleground between consonance and dissonance, meditation and anger, symbols that make all his work exciting yet unsettling. The musical result is powerful because the composer is always trying to communicate something cosmic. Frequently he succeeds.

Orchestral music. All 16 symphonies have been recorded by **Ilya Stupel** and the Artur Rubinstein Philharmonic of Lodz (Danacord 401-410). This is a demanding project involving a large orchestra with occasional extras, a soprano in 2, a piano soloist in 3, tenor and chorus in 8, chorus in 14, and baritone and male chorus in 15. Although you may imagine more tightly organized performances, the orchestra plays with involvement, and Stupel renders the music with satisfying warmth, making **Neeme Järvi**'s more tightly knit performances of 4, 5, and 6 sound curiously bloodless in places by comparison. Other moments, such as the "Rustle in the Forest" opening of 4, have a more shivery effect in Denmark, and Järvi seems more moved by the excesses of Langgaard's music than he usually is by music in general (Chandos 9064).

The Danish Radio Orchestra under **Segerstam** recorded the immense Symphony 1, along with a moving performance of *From the Deep* for orchestra with choir, in a performance that takes a great deal longer than Stupel's, emphasizing its Straussian and Brucknerian grandeur (Chandos 9249). There is also a live performance of the difficult Symphony 10 by **Ole Schmidt** and a studio performance of 14 under **Schønwandt** (Danacord LP 230, NA). Stupel's orchestra sounds better than the Danes in 10, particularly in the high-register violin passages; also, he includes a number of tone poems otherwise unrecorded. Part of this excellent collection has already disappeared; better search it out while it lasts! There may someday be a recording of the early symphonies in their original form, but I'm not holding my breath, and the revised versions recorded by Stupel may turn out to be better in the end.

A curious recording combines music by Langgaard with that of his father Siegfried in a disc containing two piano concertos, one by Siegfried and one by Rued on themes by Siegfried, played by **Marshev** with the Danish Philharmonic under Matthias Aeschbacher (Danacord 535). These are both blockbusters, played well by the energetic Marshev, less well by the orchestra.

Chamber music. The major chamber works are five string quartets, recorded by the **Kontra Quartet** (Da Capo 9302, 2CD). They're numbered 2 through 6 because the original 1 was recycled into the others. There is, however, an earlier work (not included) and a set of variations (included). These were all relatively early, but they show the composer at an interesting stage, quoting from Lutheran chorales, writing counterpoint suggesting late Beethoven and harmonies resembling Schumann, using string sonorities to clarify some very interesting thoughts. This is a pleasant and important set, played with gusto.

Keyboard music. There is a good deal of keyboard music. The only piano disc I have at hand is by **Bengt Johnsson** (Danacord 369). It's listed as Vol. 1 but appears to have been preempted by Danacord 430, played by another pianist. Perhaps it's just as well, since Johnsson is a bit clumsy and is recorded on a somewhat lumpy-sounding instrument, though his performances are full of conviction, as are his liner notes. An alternative is **Rosalind Bevan,** who recorded the amusing *Insektarium,* the dissonant *Music of the Abyss, Mad Fantasy, Flower Vignettes,* and *Little Sonata* with a suitably varied tonal palette.

Langgaard's music for organ is not presently available, but he was a master at it. There was a fine Danacord LP (65) containing the first part of his three-evening work *Messis,* a 40-minute suite as colorful, in its way, as the symphonies. **Flemming Dreisig** played it with poetry, along with three short *Advent Preludes* (Classico 240).

Vocal music. Let's work our way from small works to large. There is a disc of songs sung by **Anne Margrethe Dahl** with pianist Ulrich Staerk (Marco Polo 224011). Most are early and sound like a somewhat demented Richard Strauss; the later ones pull back to sounding more like Schumann. For the dedicated, perhaps, but certainly worthwhile.

"Rose Garden Songs" is devoted to a cappella music for choir, sung by Ars Nova conducted by **Tamas Vetö** (Marco Polo 224058). The first half hour is secular and colorfully varied in style. The rest is made up of religious chorales and short motets, also fascinating, but a collection rather than a program. Also for the dedicated, but beautifully sung.

A good deal of Langgaard's music is hard to classify in genre. For instance, there is *Sinfonia Interna,* recorded by the Aarhus Symphony under **Frans Rasmussen,** a work begun in 1915 but not finished until the 1940s, if at all. Intended as his Symphony 4, it was meant to be partially staged with specific backgrounds, somewhat akin to the light show Scriabin indicated in his *Poem of Fire.* As recorded here, it includes five movements, with soprano, mezzo-soprano, tenor, and chorus. The longest movement is a 28-minute operatic scene called "The Dream," showing the composer's considerable abilities in this area. The arrangement and content of this work changed over the years, so another recording might include different material. This one is beautifully sung and played (Da Capo 224136).

Langgaard's most famous work is probably his vocal-orchestral tone poem, *The Music of the Spheres,* a 35-minute work of amazing impact, particularly considering that it doesn't rise to any kind of climax for its first half-hour. A strange work, it recalls the effect of looking up at the stars at night. There have been three recordings. EMI LP 1087 is NA; Danacord 340 was much better, with **John Frandsen** and the Danish Radio; but the richest and most effectively spacious performance is by the Danes under **Rozhdestvensky** with Gitta-Marie Sjöberg as the soprano soloist (Chandos 9517). She also sings *Four Tone Pictures,* lovely songs with orchestra.

"The End of Time" is another curious Rozhdestvensky disc (Chandos 9786). The title work consists of the prelude and three short excerpts from Langgaard's opera *Antichrist,* arranged by the composer late in life. For those who don't want two performances of the 10-minute prelude (also in Stupel's symphony collection), this version, though it covers similar ground, is in another key and differs markedly from the other, while the rest of the work makes us wish to see the opera as well as hear it. This is followed by *From the Song of Solomon,* which starts off as a beautifully Straussian setting of texts from the Bible but rather abruptly goes sour and ends on a modern, pessimistic note. Then comes *Interdict,* in which organ confronts orchestra—organ representing Langgaard, orchestra the rest of the world. The outcome is inconclusive but disturbing. Finally, *Carl Nielsen, Our Greatest Composer* is a 32-bar exclamation for chorus and orchestra to the words of the title, which the composer sent to the Danish National Radio with the direction that it should be "repeated to eternity." This performance makes a good try, repeating it no less than eight times, until the engineers fade it out gradually. The whole disc gives us a picture of the composer as a dissatisfied man, and I suspect he himself was partly to blame.

Finally comes his magnum opus, the opera *Antikrist.* Once recorded by EMI in 1986 (NA), a new version is by **Niels Muns** with the Tiroler Landestheater Chorus and Orchestra from a 1999 performance (Danacord 517, 2CD). The text reads a little like an updated and cynical *Pilgrim's Progress.* Lucifer wants to send the Antichrist into the world; God acquiesces but finally destroys the Antichrist. The moral position is a bit murky, which, judging by Langgaard's evident misanthropy, probably represents his point of view accurately. This performance seems to do the work justice, sung to great effect and recorded with realism.

MOORE

Jean Langlais (1907–91)

Blind from the age of two, Langlais went on to flourish as successor to Tournemire at St. Clotilde, producing a staggering quantity of compositions in a wide range of media, especially organ and choral. Owing to the extent of his work and the legion of interpretations, only his best-known works will be discussed

ORGAN MUSIC

True devotees will probably want a complete package. Only one exists—by **Ann Labounsky**—and a superb effort it is, the culmination of a lifetime involvement with Langlais's music as his student and later his biographer. There are eight volumes of a twelve-volume project available so far from MHS; if you write them, they'll send you a printout of the contents of each volume, which are not chronological.

Langlais's most frequently heard pieces were mostly written in the '30s and '40s. Perhaps a growing dissonance in his harmonic vocabulary dulled the appeal of later compositions. *Paraphrases Grégoriennes* is among the most popular. For "Mors et Resurrectio," **Wilma Jensen** does a masterful job controlling the gradual buildup toward the conclusion on a good-sized Casavant (♦Arkay 6117). For both "Ave Maria" and "Te Deum," **Naji Hakim** at La Trinité delivers an outstanding interpretation, allowing the chords to linger in the air before rushing on—wonderful acoustics (♦EMI 72272). **Alan Morrison** provides an energetic performance of "Fête" with good articulation and clear engineering (♦ACA 21105), while a weightier, more powerful interpretation comes from **Labounsky** at St. Pierre, Angoulême (♦MHS 524290X). As there is less clarity in this recording, a reasonable compromise would be **Joyce Jones** at the 3-79 Ruffatti in Spivey Hall (Rosenhaus 013).

Suite Médiévale (1947) gets a clean, accurate performance from **Bruno Mathieu** on the Cavaillé-Coll in resonant St. Brieuc (♦Naxos 553190), less heavy sounding than **Colin Walsh** at Salisbury (Priory 905). *Suite Française,* all ten movements of it, is heard best from **Labounsky** on the large Casavant in St. Peter's in Erie, Pennsylvania (♦MHS 424712L). The vigor and registration are first-rate. Four of the movements are performed well but with less panache by **Michael Harris** at Canterbury Cathedral (♦York 112). *Incantation* (1949) has no lack of interpreters, but some stand out. Each of these combines a potent instrument in resonant surroundings with muscular performances: **Jacques Kauffmann** (♦Skarbo 1933); **John Obetz** (♦RBW 010); **Marie-Louise Langlais** (♦Koch 31529). For sheer audio delight, try **Hakim** playing amid the remarkable reverberation of Sacre-Coeur (♦Motette 11171). Awesome.

Listeners interested in hearing how **Langlais** played his own work are urged to investigate a collection of 12 familiar pieces he recorded at Sainte-Clotilde (Solstice 01).

CHORAL MUSIC

There are at least 35 sacred vocal compositions; Langlais's three best known come from the '40s and '50s. There are several very satisfying interpretations of *Messe Solennelle* for mixed choir and organ: **Judith Hancock** (♦Koch 37228); **Kirstin Ek** (♦BIS 289); **Westminster Choir** (♦Hyperion 66270). *Missa in Simplicitate* is scored for solo voice (or unison choir) and organ. A good rendition comes from **Danielle Michel** (♦Skarbo 1933). If possible, try to find the original with **Langlais** at the console accompanying **Jeannine Collard** (♦MHS 3745). *Missa Salve Regina,* heard on Christmas Eve at Notre-Dame in 1954, is scored for three equal voices, unison, two organs, and eight brass. The original recording is still the best, but hard to find. For this, Langlais himself played the gallery organ (♦MHS 3745). Twenty-five years later, a different ensemble of musicians performed it again as a tribute. For this, **Cochereau** was the organist (♦Solstice 14).

Among Langlais's secular vocal works, the very pleasant *Breton Songs* bring out his ability to retain the simplicity of melodies amid contemporary harmonies. An interesting comparison can be made by hearing **Langlais** play these songs at Notre-Dame (♦Solstice 165) and then hearing them played by **Kauffmann** at Saint-Croix de Saint-Servan, preceded by the unaccompanied songs sung beautifully by Andrea Ar Gouilh (♦Skarbo 1973).   METZ

Libby Larsen *(b. 1950)*

Larsen writes music notable for its strikingly imaginative and original sonorities and subtle pastel shades. Her vocal and choral settings are especially apt, and her orchestral works explore a vast dynamic, tonal, and coloristic range in a strongly individual language. She's at the forefront of America's younger generation of composers, who have done so much in recent years to reestablish the ethic of evolutionary—rather than revolutionary—growth in music within a thoroughly contemporary framework. Her midwestern background seems to have established its own identity in her music; she is a cofounder of the Minnesota Composers forum, and a "minischool" of composition seems to have developed in that area.

One of Larsen's strongest works is *Missa Gaia* (Mass for the Earth) for chorus and instruments, recorded by the **Oregon Repertory Singers** (Koch 7279, with *Echoes between the Silent Peaks,* by Larsen's contemporary Minnesotan Paulus, and pieces by Barber). The fresh, crystal-clear texture of the vocal writing and the chiming bell-like instruments evoke the wide openness, even timelessness, of the Minnesotan landscape. This disc is strongly recommended, and the Paulus work, in a similar vein, won't disappoint. The award-winning Symphony 1 ("Water Music"), also has local connections, evident from the titles of the movements, which suggest a summer day (with a ghostly, nocturnal slow movement) by one of Minnesota's myriad lakes. This showpiece can be heard to great effect played by the Minnesota Orchestra under **Marriner** (Nonesuch 79147, with Paulus's *Symphony in Three Movements*). It's also in an all-Larsen disc of orchestral works led by **Joel Revsen** (Koch 7370).

This is the most important disc of her music so far (I was present at the recording sessions). "Water Music" is well worth having, as is the *Parachute Dancing* Overture, the later Symphony 3 ("Lyric"), and the tone poem *Ring of Fire,* which mark a move away from the light, airy music of the '80s toward a more concentrated, darker-hued language. This is especially so of the Symphony, whose thick harmonies and eerie interludes at times suggest the Second Viennese School overlain with occasional American vernacular elements and jazz. A disc of chamber works by various artists is also worth exploring (Innova 512).

JOHNSON

Lars-Erik Larsson *(1908–1986)*

Larsson was a Swedish organist who studied composition under Alban Berg. His early compositions can be lyrical and melodic or neoclassical. His music comes out of the sparkling cold and astringency of the North, frequently bordering on the bleak. At times he turned to polytonal and serial composition, in his later years experimenting with his own 12- tone technique, but he never settled on one style, and some of his work composed in the '60s and '70s is again neoclassical. Unfortunately, not much of his music has been recorded, but do treat yourself to what there is.

Larsson's Symphony 1 was written when he was not yet 20; it's romantic and Nordic, reminiscent of Sibelius. Symphony 2, composed about 10 years later, shows considerable development. The last movement, an ostinato, was frequently performed separately as a popular concert piece. Symphony 3 was written near the end of WWII and was first performed in 1946. Here Larsson's unique voice emerges more clearly than in the previous two; this symphony is deep and powerful.

Extremely self-critical, the composer withdrew his three symphonies for a long time, apparently believing that he was at his best with smaller forms. In 1973 conductor Sten Frykberg got permission to record 2, and Larsson remarked, "I don't know whether I was doing the right thing when I withdrew it." After its success, Frykberg persuaded Larsson to recall 3, recorded it in 1975, and again it won public acclaim. **Frykberg** recorded 3 once more in 1978, with the Helsingborg Symphony, at a concert in honor of Larsson's 70th birthday (♦BIS 96, with *Förklädd Gud*). About ten years later, **HansPeter Frank** and the Helsingborg recorded 1 and 2; both performance and sound are much better (♦BIS 426). The

1978 recording has its faults: the Helsingborg group had gained in sophistication and quality of sound by the late '80s and so, apparently, had recording techniques. But despite its warts, the essential high quality of 3 shines through, as does the beauty of *Förklädd Gud* (see below) These are the only recordings of the symphonies available, and they're well worth having.

Larsson was a master of the small work. One of his best pieces is *Little Serenade for Strings,* available either with **Salonen** conducting the Stockholm Sinfonietta (♦BIS 285) or with **Wojciech Rajski** conducting Musica Vitae (♦BIS 460). I slightly prefer the latter, both for performance and sound. **Okko Kamu** with the Helsingborg Symphony brings us Larsson's delightful *Pastoral Suite* along with the epilogue to *A Winter's Tale;* this piece is bleak and haunting, and both are served well (♦Naxos 553115). The entire incidental music for Shakespeare's play may be obtained with **Stig Westerberg** (Swedish Society 1004).

Larsson's 12 *Concertinos,* three-movement pieces each for a solo part by one of the main instruments of the orchestra, deserve special mention. All of them have been recorded (♦BIS 473, 2CD). They are dry and sharp, for the most part lacking the warmth and lyricism of the suites or the symphonies.

A sample of Larsson's personal twelve-tone technique may be found in his *Orchestral Variations,* composed in 1962 and led by **Westerberg** (♦Swedish Society 1020). This isn't exactly what one expects from 12-tone music; it seems to still have something of a tonal center—at least in spots—and is recognizably in Larsson's style, albeit more arid than his earlier music and not nearly as pleasant.

The only available choral work of the several Larsson composed is *Förklädd Gud* (God in Disguise). Both **Frykberg**'s rendition (♦BIS 96) and **Westerberg**'s (♦Swedish Society 1020) are good, though their sound is rather old (1978 and 1956, respectively). The singers are excellent, led by Hagegård for the former and Söderström for the latter. This is a delightful piece with a reader narrating the poetry between musical interludes. Its character is Nordic, with its roots firmly in the Swedish folk tradition but with a primeval longing similar to Sibelius's most wistful works.

CRAWFORD

Orlande de Lassus (1532–1594)

When Ferrante Gonzaga, agent for the Duke of Mantua, rode into the lowland town of Mons in 1544, he was on the trail of a boy reputed to have a beautiful voice. Lassus was 12, and went on to become the last of the great Franco-Flemish composers to leave his homeland and put an indelible stamp on European music. If some are more familiar with the Italianate form of his name, Orlando di Lasso, he would earn that Italian-ness as he spent his teens in a whirlwind tour of all that 16th century Italy could offer of sin and sophistication, crassness and creativity. Eventually he found his way to the prosperous and musical town of Antwerp where he was befriended by the publisher, arranger, instrument-maker and town-band leader Tielman Susato.

Then, at age 24, everything changed. Lassus was recommended for the job as court composer in Munich for Duke Albrecht V of Bavaria, and went to the place where he would live and work for the remaining 38 years of his life. There is a curious and melancholy arc to this story. We go from a time when Albrecht tried to build his chapel and court to rival Charles V, with singers and players brought in from everywhere (particularly Italy), to a time when Albrecht's son and Lassus's friend Wilhelm succeeded to power and realized that the court's finances couldn't bear the weight. Drastic cuts in the musical and social life of the court followed, and a gradual pall descended. In the best of times, Lassus and Wilhelm wrote witty letters full of polyglot puns and musical jokes, but by the end, both men had fallen into a state of withdrawal and depression; treatment for "melancholia" proved fruitless, and it was to this cause his death was ascribed.

During it all, there was music. Lassus produced scores of publications of thousands of pieces. There were 60-odd masses, over 100 Magnificat settings, 150 chansons, hundreds of madrigals, books of lieder when he mastered German, motets of every kind, works ranging from the youthful and stunning setting of the *Lamentations of Jeremiah* to his last piece, the breathtaking *Lagrime di San Pietro* ("The Tears of St. Peter")—a madrigal cycle invoking the sadness and shame Peter suffered upon betraying Christ three times before the cock crowed.

There are maybe 30 recordings of Lassus's music currently available; there used to be many more, and only a fraction of his work has been recorded. Let's first look at what we can't get any longer: **Raphaël Passaquet** once recorded both *Lamentations* and *Tears;* it's the former that is tragically lacking now (Harmonia Mundi 761/2, NA). **Simon Preston**'s '70s recordings of various masses and *Penitential Psalms* (works that so moved Duke Albrecht he had them copied on parchment, illuminated by a miniaturist, and bound in red morocco with silver clasps—it took seven years) have a few worthy successors. It's Preston's Christ Church Cathedral Choir we hear under **Stephen Darlington** in one of the Psalms, along with a mass not recorded by Preston ("Qual donna") and some motets (Nimbus 51758).

The "Bell'Amfitrit'Altera" Mass is available in at least four good English renditions following Preston's popular 1974 Argo recording of that work: **Harry Christophers**'s The Sixteen (Collins 13602), **St. John's College Choir** (EMI Classics for Pleasure 2180), **Jeremy Summerly** with the Oxford Camerata (Naxos 550836, with Palestrina), and a good program with the Westminster Cathedral Choir directed by **James O'Donnell** (♦Hyperion 66688).

The ensemble known as **Henry's Eight** have recorded the complete *Penitential Psalms* (♦Hyperion 67217/2). In performance as well as completeness it far outstrips the other available offerings: the **Czech Philharmonic Chorus** (Supraphon 112159) and the **Josquin Des Prez Chamber Choir** (Raum Klang 9606).

While **Konrad Ruhland**'s fascinating 1973 set that gave us all the major forms Lassus worked in, plus pieces by his predecessors and successors in Munich, is out of print (BASF 21192, 2CD), his 1976 recording of music for the Passion has been brought back (Sony 60360). It's incorrectly listed as the *St. Matthew Passion,* but that work is complete on a disc featuring former Hilliard Ensemble director **Paul Hillier** with Theatre of Voices and the superb Paul Elliott as Evangelist (♦Harmonia Mundi 907076). The 1984 program with Hillier back with the Hilliard Ensemble has been in and out of print, worth the cost for the *Stabat Mater* alone (Virgin 561166). However, the current Hilliards recorded the youthful, eye- and ear-popping *Prophetiae Sibyllarum* along with the moving *Requiem Mass;* it's a must-have (♦ECM 1658).

The *Requiem* is also part of a set containing all three sets of *Lamentations of Jeremiah for Holy Week* and, in the section for Easter Day, the hymn "Aurora lucis rutilat" with the *Magnificat* set on the same hymn, in marvelous performances by **Pro Cantione Antiqua** of London (Hyperion 22012, 2CD). The *Lamentations* were well recorded by Herreweghe with one of his all-star early music ensembles in 1989 (Harmonia Mundi 901299), and we can also credit him with a spare, sensitive performance of *Tears of St. Peter* (♦Harmonia Mundi 901483). It slightly outdoes the too dry **Huelgas Ensemble** version (Sony 53373) and the **Ars Nova** rendition, with its overlarge forces and excessive speeds

(Naxos 553311). It's sad to think Herreweghe has given up on the before-Bach repertoire.

Summerly's recording of masses featuring "Entre vous filles" and "Susanne un jour" (on Lassus's own chanson) is a winner (♦Naxos 550842). **Peter Phillips** has but one Lassus recording, but it's a wonder: his motet *Osculetur me* with the mass set on that motet and a selection of Marian works. The Tallis Scholars name is a sign of complete mastery in the Renaissance repertoire (♦Gimell 54918). A very interesting production directed by **Jeffrey Skidmore** features the Ex Cathedra ensemble with His Majesty's Sagbutts and Cornetts in the motet and mass *Vinum Bonum* (a nonliturgical semisacred celebration of wine), with motets and instrumental bicinia, short two-part pieces used in teaching (♦ASV 150).

The **Munich Cathedral Choir** offers a release featuring the Mass "Entre vous filles" along with the *Te Deum* and Marian motets (Christophorus 77196). It's fine, but what we need back from this label is the 1980 program from the **Vienna Motet Choir** and the Musica Antiqua of Vienna of occasional pieces—motets (often secular) and other works written for specific court occasions—with excellent citations as to the where and why of the individual pieces (Christophorus 73923, NA). The German sacred discs that are most desirable are both recent. First, the **Singer Pur** ensemble has brought us Lassus's mass setting on the Gombert chanson "Tous les regretz," with eight motets and the original chanson—this should be mandatory in recordings of this sort (♦Ars Musici 1242). Then, **Roland Wilson** and his ensembles take us to 16th century Cologne, mixing the "Susanne un jour" mass with de Monte's *Missa sine Nomine* and music of the only recently widely-recorded Jean de Castro (Glissando 779012).

A fine program that could use better performances features the **Ricercar Academy Orchestra** and vocalists in the mass on the chanson "Je suis deshéritée," along with Christmas material and the *Stabat Mater* (Stradivarius 33345). **Eric van Nevel** has a hard-to-find but worthy program with his Currende Consort of sacred and secular motets, including the humanistic works (settings of Ovid and the like) and even some of the joke and word-play motets written for Prince Wilhelm's amusement (♦Eufoda 1239). Also a tough quest is a disc from the **Choir of Trinity College, Cambridge** in which the motets are arranged along the liturgical year, going from Advent through All Saints' Day (♦Conifer 51230).

Before moving to the strictly secular material, we must note two groups that offered discs dedicated one to sacred, one to secular music. Although they call themselves the **Orlando di Lasso Ensemble,** this German group is only so-so. Most interesting in their mixed secular disc are the German lieder we rarely hear (Thorofon 2209). Better is the sacred disc dedicated mostly to Marian music, with the very interesting *Magnificat* on the madrigal "Ecco ch'io lasso il core" opening the program (Thorofon 2130).

When the early music scholar Colin Mason was part of the **King's Singers,** they gave serious attention to music of the Renaissance. Again, their secular disc ("To All Things A Season") is mostly fun, featuring some of Lassus's bawdy and humorous works the Singers often brought to a general audience (EMI 749158, NA). However, the sacred disc ("How Excellent is thy Name") is a stunner. This time, we hear the plainchant "Praeter rerum seriem" along with Josquin des Prez's perfect motet on that theme, followed by Lassus's Magnificat on the same theme—it's priceless (EMI 749157).

Let's kick off the purely secular music recordings with the one-and-only **Rinaldo Alessandrini**'s Concerto Italiano recording of the zany carnival material. When you see this ensemble on stage acting out this saucy, bawdy repertoire, you could be an 18-year-old in Naples just getting a taste of the wild side of life—nobody does it better (♦Opus 111 30-94). Don't bother with the **Toronto Consort**'s bloodless disc of chansons and madrigals (Dorian 80149). The chansons are given better life by the **Ensemble Clément Jannequin** in their 1992 recording (Harmonia Mundi 901391). I long for the time when Astrée was recording single publications entire (the 1576 chansons with the **Ensemble Polyphonique de France** or Herreweghe's lustrous recording of the 1571 motets). At least recent recordings are trying to expand the Lassus material on disc: **Ensemble de'Medici** gives us a program including instrumental pieces and some of the so-called "didactic" motets (RCM 19502).

But there is so much material to choose from. It seems that whenever a group or a label champions Lassus, the thread of commitment drifts away. It's enough to give you terminal melancholia.   DAVIS

William Lawes (1602–1645)

William and his brother Henry (1596–1662) were members of the generation after Byrd. Religious problems of the time led both to write less church music than earlier composers. William is best known for his music for strings, both viols and violins, while Henry became known for his incorporation of French *air de cour* techniques into English song. Both have mannerist elements; William's music is full of dissonant cross-relations.

There were a number of Oiseau-Lyre LPs of William's music played by the **Consort of Music,** including "Viol Consort Music" (560), "Setts for Violins and Division Viols" (564) and "Dialogues, Psalms, and Elegies" (574), this last particularly interesting as one of the few collections of his vocal music. A further collection includes 15 vocal numbers by William, made in 1996 (70972); it seems to have fallen by the wayside, as has a Henry Lawes collection from the same source (Hyperion 66135). This is turning into a wish list.

Lawes's chamber music is primarily made up of short two- to four-movement suites for various combinations, many including violins. A disc by **London Baroque** of eight Fantasia Suites for violin, viol, and organ (Harmonia Mundi 901493) is mislabeled in *Schwann* as Fantasia Suites for two violins, bass viol and organ, a different set also recorded by London Baroque (Harmonia Mundi 901423). **Music's Re-creation** has also recorded the one-violin suites in spirited readings (Centaur 2385), and the **Purcell Quartet** offers the two-violin collection at slightly livelier tempos (Chandos 552). *Royal Consort Suites* is a larger group, ten works for two violins, two viols, and two theorbos. There are two complete recordings of these pieces, by the **Purcell Quartet** (Chandos 584/5, 2CD) and **The Greate Consort** (ASV 146/7, 2CD). There is little to choose between these fine groups; though the Purcell is slightly more assertive, the Greate Consort digs deeper into the harmonies.

There are also consort sets for five and six viols, five for each grouping. Two of each are recorded by **Fretwork** (Virgin 91187, NA), while two for five viols are played by the **Rose Consort** (Naxos 550601). Both of these discs also contain more miscellaneously scored pieces not otherwise available. No one since **Thurston Dart** seems to have discovered a large collection of consorts with harp, and he only included one with the Elizabethan Consort (Argo LP 555).   MOORE

Jean-Marie Leclair (1697–1764)

The first French violinist to rival the Italians in technical expertise, Leclair was as accomplished a composer as any of them. He has a reputation among musicians, who compare him to Bach, partly based on his contrapuntal ability. Almost all his compositions are essentially violin works, frequently very demanding, with the exception of his one opera, *Scylla et Glaucus.* The difficulty of the music and its complex combination of French and Italian styles have perhaps been responsible for its rather sketchy representation on disc.

Leclair wrote four books of violin sonatas, Opp. 1, 2, 5, and 9, each containing 12 sonatas. They become more violin-specific in the later opuses; indeed, several of the earlier ones are designated by the composer as alternatively for flute. There are no complete recordings of any of them, though some players have given us single discs devoted to works from a single opus. Op. 1 is represented by **François Fernandez,** who plays 1, 3, 8, and 9 in a lively, pointed style with graceful shaping of the slow movements (Astrée 8662). Op. 5 is the most demanding—no flute alternatives here. It has been tackled by **Ryo Terakado,** who plays 4 and 6 through 11 in somewhat tentative readings in which he's rather outshone by his partners, both technically and musically (Denon). Nos. 3, 4, 6, 10, and 11 are also recorded by **Elizabeth Wallfisch** in her somewhat slapdash but lively style (Hyperion 67033).

Op. 9 is equally demanding. **Wallfisch** has recorded 2, 3, 6, and 7 (Hyperion 67068). **Fernandez** plays 2, 6, 8, and 11, doing better justice to the delicacy of their French elements than the broad lyrical strokes of which Leclair is also capable (Astrée 8568). **Monica Huggett** plays Op. 5:6 and Op. 9:7 and 9, also more convincing in the subtleties than in the bravura passages (ASV 106). **Simon Standage** plays Op. 5:7 and Op. 9:4 with harpsichordist Lars Ulrik Mortensen without benefit of a melodic continuo instrument (Chandos 531). He balances well between lyricism and virtuosity.

The eight sonatas with flute alternatives have been recorded complete four times on LP, twice by **Rampal** and once by **Christian Larde** and Barthold Kuijken. Only the last is both aware of baroque styles and beautifully played. All are NA. **Christoph Huntgeburth** plays Op. 2:1, 3, and 11 and Op. 9:2 and 7 in a relaxed way, with lovely ornaments and a warm sound (ASV 158). In the two sonatas from Op. 9, the music is significantly altered in the flute version. These two sonatas were recorded by **Rachel Brown** in "French Baroque Flute Music" in performances even more sophisticated and appealing than Huntgeburth's (Chandos 544; Op. 9:2 is incorrectly called Book 2 No. 1 on her disc). **Paul Carroll** with Badinage plays Op. 1:6 and Op. 2:1, 3, 8, and 11 in oddly muffled sound, faster than his technique will support in places (Meridian 84381). His disc also includes one of the Op. 12 duos for two violins, here transcribed for viols.

Leclair wrote two sets of six duos for two violins, Opp. 3 and 12. They are colorful and virtuoso pieces with a lovely blend of French sensitivity and Italian bravura. They have been recorded complete by **Chiara Banchini** and **John Holloway** (Erato 45013 and 45519, NA) in warmly sympathetic performances. Op: 3:4 may be found played by **Perlman** and **Zukerman** in a rather dry and clinical manner (RCA 60735). **Standage** and **Micaela Comberti** offer a warmer and more period performance of Op. 3:6 (Chandos 582).

Opp. 4, 6, 8, 13, and 14 are all scored as trio sonatas, though the musical style varies among opuses. Op. 4 is six self-styled trio sonatas, which may be heard played with polish by either the excellent **London Baroque** (Harmonia Mundi 901617) or the **Purcell Quartet** in one of their earliest recordings, with Catherine Mackintosh replacing Wallfisch (Chandos 536). The Purcell version is marked by slower tempos and a remarkable unanimity of articulation between the two violinists, recorded in a more spacious ambience than they usually employ and with a viola da gamba on the bass line, whereas London Baroque uses a cello.

Op. 13 consists of three trio sonatas and three French overtures for the same scoring and is recorded by the same two groups, **London Baroque** (Harmonia Mundi 901646) and the **Purcell Quartet** (Chandos 542). The differences are primarily a somewhat brighter sound from the Purcell, particularly effective in the more ebullient *Ouvertures,* with somewhat more depth of harmonic involvement by the London Baroque. Either choice is more polished than **Les Talens Lyriques,** whose enthusiasm tends to compromise their intonation (FNAC 592100). Finally, there's an arrangement of Op. 13:1 by the **Palladium Ensemble** for recorder, violin, viol, and arch-lute, tasty but a mixture of apples and oranges (Linn 5050).

Opp. 6 and 8 are full-length French *Ouvertures* complete with opening dotted rhythms and pseudo-fugal Allegros, both parts repeated, followed by numerous dance movements including a considerable *Chaconne.* These works are both entitled "Musical Recreation" and are further described as easy to play. The scoring is the same as for the trio sonatas. They have both been recorded by a talented and photogenic group calling themselves **Rameau**'s **Nieces,** who describe themselves as "cultivating respectful differences and disrespectful deference towards 'uncles' of all kinds" (♦Pierre Verany 794011). Their performances show a light touch, and, more important, a willingness to observe all repeats and take lively tempos in these fine pieces.

A similarly positive attitude toward Op. 6 is shown by **Collegium Musicum 90** (♦Chandos 582), while **Musica Antiqua Köln,** in one of their earliest recordings, was less successful in balancing the proportions of the movements, both in terms of repeats and tempos (Koch Schwann 1061). Op. 8 is performed by **Music**'s **Recreation,** replacing the first violin with a flute and thus diluting Leclair's blended sonorities (Meridian 84114). **La Quatrième Chambre** goes all the way, using flutes for both melody lines, which works much better (Nuova Era 7181). Finally, we have Op. 14, consisting of another shorter but highly original French *Ouverture,* still for trio sonata scoring, played with Op. 6 by **Collegium Musicum 90** in fine style (Chandos 582).

There are two collections of six concertos for violin and strings, Opp. 7 and 10. These are quite remarkable works, beginning from a Vivaldian point of view and building a French cathedral on those foundations. Both sets are played by **Standage** with Collegium Musicum 90 in performances that balance beautiful phrasing and violinistic derring-do quite effectively (Chandos 551, 564, 589). Vol. 1 is recorded at a somewhat lower level than the others, and the opuses are mixed between discs. Op. 7:3 is played in its flute alternative by **Rachel Brown** with sensitive poise in Vol. 2. Op. 7:4 and Op. 10:1, 2, and 6 are played by violinist **Daniel Cuiller** and Ensemble Stradivaria in a more volatile, hairsbreadth kind of style (Adda 581294). Perhaps most impressive is **Huggett,** who plays Op. 7:2 and 6 and Op. 10:1, while flutist Claire Guimond does Op. 7:3 with the Canadian group Arion (ATMA 22143). Huggett is particularly subtle, yet virtuosic where necessary.

Finally, the opera *Scylla and Glaucus* is the only vocal work we have by Leclair. It's an exciting opera, on a par with those of Rameau, full of dances, stage effects, choruses, and inspired music. **Gardiner** and the Lyons Opera made a highly effective recording that should be with us always (Erato 45277, 3CD, NA).   MOORE

Benjamin Lees (b. 1924)

Lees has proved the continuing viability of classical forms and fashioned them in a strong personal idiom. He works exclusively in abstract forms; the hallmarks of his style are the persistent use of intervals, constantly changing meters over a stable basic pulse, and the development of material by way of canon, fugue, augmentation and diminution. The dramatic force of his music derives from the creative tension of these interacting elements.

The massive architecture of some of his finest music is revealed in **Hobson**'s recording of Piano Sonata 4 (originally written for Gary Graffman), with the darkly Lisztian *Fantasy Variations* and a recent work, *Mirrors* (Albany 227). The Violin Concerto is a very impressive work from Lees's early career, played by **Ricci** as part of a set including concertos by Bergsma, Starer, Piston, and others that's well worth its low price (Vox Box 2, 2CD). The recording of the three violin sonatas by **Ellen Orner** and Joel Wizansky is perhaps even better(Albany 138). These pieces span nearly 40 years, and the firm, refined Sonata 3 (1989) makes a fascinating comparison with the more eclectic 1 (1953).

No survey of Lees's recorded music would be complete without investigating his magnum opus, Symphony 4 ("Memorial Candles") for soprano and orchestra, written in commemoration of the Holocaust and setting poems by Nelly Sachs, one of its survivors. The budget-priced recording led by Kuchar with mezzo **Kimball Wheeler** is very strongly recommended; no one can fail to be moved by such powerful music and texts (Naxos 559002). Another mature composition of lofty grandeur is the 1992 Concerto for French Horn and Orchestra, brilliantly played and recorded by **William Caballero** with the Pittsburgh Symphony under Maazel (New World 80503, with works by Leonardo Balada and Zwilich). The more lyrical, reflective mood emerging in his recent work is evident and notable.   JOHNSON

Franz Lehár *(1870–1947)*

With Lehár, Viennese operetta was reborn, entering a second wave of popularity that has been called the "silver" age, to differentiate it from the "golden" 19th century of Johann Strauss Jr. and his family (discussed later) and contemporaries. After the extraordinary success of *Die lustige Witwe* (The Merry Widow) in 1905, Lehár's succeeding works were eagerly anticipated by impresarios and audiences alike. Nothing quite equaled the international success of *The Merry Widow,* though several operettas came close; *Der Graf von Luxembourg* (The Count of Luxembourg, 1908) and *Das Land des Lächelns* (The Land of Smiles, 1929) are two lucrative examples.

Lehár's style in 1905 was far different from what it became in the late '20s: The frou-frou champagne bubbles you hear in the Parisian-set *Widow,* based on a play by Offenbach's librettist Meilhac, were replaced by grander, more exotically romantic motifs by the time of *Land of Smiles.* Yet the path for the future Lehár was already set in the middle of Act II of the former, when the seductive ardor of Camille's lovemaking takes on an almost Straussian thickness—Richard, not Johann. The gaiety that so distinguishes *Widow* would reappear principally in the secondary appearances of the buffo-soubrette pair in Lehár's '20s efforts.

Lehár's career was rejuvenated when, after several comparatively lean years still in Vienna around WWI, he moved to Berlin and began creating works for his great friend, the tenor Richard Tauber. This partnership created, among other works, *Paganini, Der Zarewitsch,* and *Land of Smiles,* all of which are still performed today when a respectable tenor is available. Lehár was also the most prominent operetta composer to remain in the greater Germany of the Third Reich, making a number of what might charitably be called shrewd moves during this period. He moved his very successful publishing company to neutral Switzerland and allowed his works to be performed in Allied countries as well as in occupied Europe (there, without mention of their usually Jewish librettists). He accepted Nazi awards and Nazi-backed commissions while keeping his Jewish wife out of view.

After 1945, his works—which had the advantage of continuous revivals and recordings during the wartime years—had little difficulty remaining in the public's favor. So when, in the early '50s, Walter Legge began his now-historic recordings of Viennese operettas with his wife Elisabeth Schwarzkopf (another whose career continued in Germany in the Nazi era), the Lehár works were prominently featured. Since that time, the most popular works have often been re-recorded, with *The Merry Widow* probably the most recorded of all operettas.

Die lustige Witwe. There are several complete recordings available and dozens more excerpt versions in many languages. Two complete renditions star **Schwarzkopf** (1953 and 1962), and she's divine in both. Many admire the earlier version (Otto Ackermann conducting, in good mono sound), which has been reissued several times (EMI 69520); it has Erich Kunz as Count Danilo, a very smooth baritone who isn't very theatrical. Wächter, in the later album (EMI 47178), is showier, and truly a baritone, which contrasts him nicely with a superb Gedda—the Camille on the earlier set as well, with an even more youthful presence then. The supporting casts are excellent on both; the later one has the advantage of stereo sound, and it includes a bit more spoken dialogue.

One advantage of the '50s set is that it fits on one CD, as does the very well-regarded rival version (Decca/London 436899). This has some longueurs (Robert Stolz's conducting of an unnecessary overture is one), but these are made up for by the darling Hanna of **Gueden** (without quite the sophistication of Schwarzkopf, but still delightful), Danish tenor Per Grunden's fine Danilo, and Emmy Loose repeating her enchanting Valencienne from the 1953 EMI.

Nothing subsequently recorded need dislodge these *Widows* from their prime positions on your Lehár shelf, but you do have other options. Two are from the '60s. One is a slightly abridged performance with **Rothenberger** and Gedda as Danilo, a true tenor rendition of the role (EMI 69090). For an even starrier tenor performance, turn to Schock, who pleases his many fans by occasionally going over the top, along with **Margit Schramm** as Hanna and Stolz again conducting a vibrant, well-cast performance (Eurodisc 258372). It's great fun.

Not as much theatrical glitter, unfortunately, comes from two 1994 recordings. Technically and musically they are indubitably superior to earlier versions, but neither has a Widow to rival Schwarzkopf's (or even Gueden's). Gardiner and no less than the Vienna Philharmonic really shine, with a beautifully transparent sound, but **Studer** fails to register as credible (DG 439911). Skovhus (another Danish Danilo) needs some seasoning, but I will never forget him stopping the Volksoper cold early in his career in a revue with Robert Stolz's song "Salome." The rising Austrian conductor Welser-Möst and the London Philharmonic offer a Glyndebourne Festival performance from London's Festival Hall during the season in which Glyndebourne's theater was being rebuilt (EMI 55152). **Lott** and Hampson are the stars—both acceptable, although neither sounds entirely at home in German or quite in the operetta style. Hampson even at a young age had an undeniably stagey verve, and his is a deep baritone Danilo, which is interesting. What disfigures the recording is Dirk Bogarde's silly narration; it might profitably have been cut.

A Cologne radio performance claims that it's the "original version" but has little that hasn't been recorded earlier, and an unremarkable cast that includes **Pamela Coburn**'s unexciting Widow and Viennese actor

Michael Heltau's unsung Danilo—that is, he can't really sing at all (Capriccio).

Surprisingly few English versions of this international favorite are around; the main one is from the New Sadler's Wells Opera with a new book and lyrics by Nigel Douglas—one I don't relish with quite the same enthusiasm as the old Sadler's Wells translation by Christopher Hassall, once in a lovely LP (Angel/EMI). Unfortunately, the cast in this 1986 highlights release is forgettable (Jay). In French, there have been several CDs of broadcasts or older LPs with superior casts. One (complete) has **Stich-Randall** as Missia (as Hanna is called in the Paris version) and Henri Legay as Camille (SM); the other (excerpts) has a very suave Michel Dens as Danilo, the great Raymond Amade as Camille, and an only adequate **Janette Vivalda** as Missia (EMI). This latter *Veuve Joyeuse* also offers excerpts from *Paganini* and *Land of Smiles* in French, with **Dens** the héro of both—a great set for francophile Lehárians.

Der Graf von Luxemburg. This followed *Die lustige Witwe* in 1909, another Parisian truffle; while it lacks a truly star soprano part like the Widow, the soubrette has numbers just as good, if not better. It also lacks an arresting book, so while it's performed in Central Europe—thanks to its showy title tenor part and its comedy duets—it has disappeared elsewhere. I've never cottoned to the work in performance or on disc, but can willingly tolerate a few numbers. There has been only one complete version, with an excellent **Gedda** (EMI); what may be available now are excerpts. **Schock** was also very much at home as the Count in the '60s and '70s (Eurodisc 258358). The British soprano Marilyn Hill Smith is Angèle in an English-language production from the sadly defunct New Sadler's Wells Opera (Jay). It's a charming though not very continental performance, in Nigel Douglas's very good translation (recently produced, though not recorded, by the current D'Oyly Carte Opera Company.) **Neil Jenkins** isn't quite comfortable in the German language as the Count.

Other operettas. Zigeunerliebe (Gypsy Love, 1910) and *Eva* (1911) were substantial hits in their day, but lack modern complete recordings. Excerpts in various languages are available; *Zigeunerliebe* with Schock is well-advised (Eurodisc), and *Eva* for some reason has had abridgements in Italian and Spanish. Lehár's fortunes began to decline roughly around the time of WWI, but in 1918 he enjoyed a fleeting success in Vienna with *Wo die Lerche singt* (Where the Lark Sings), and this, oddly, is available on CD. Adapted for a radio broadcast, this 1942 transmission reveals no forgotten treasures, but does have the prewar comedian Ernst Tautenhayn (Bel Age). Early '20s works tantalize with their titles: *Die blaue Mazur, Die Tangokönigin, Frasquita* (which the French used to dote on), and the French farce–based *Cloclo.* All must contain musical treasures, but none have recordings available save for occasional tidbits that may crop up, usually in Italian reissues.

With *Paganini*, in 1925, Lehár began his remarkable late career steeped in romanticism, again writing star tenor parts just right not only for **Tauber** (and subsequent tenors) but for recordings, which by 1926 could capture Tauber's voice in all its electric majesty. Any of the myriad Tauber compendia will demonstrate his utter magic with this luscious music. These operettas were well-oiled vehicles, especially geared for a star tenor, but that doesn't mean they can cruise easily on modern stages. It was difficult enough in the '20s for sophisticated Berliners to accept the stout Tauber as the wizened violinist Paganini or the young, very thin Goethe in *Friederike;* with Lehár's music and Tauber's theatrical gusto they could get away with it.

Later tenors essaying these parts include Gedda, Schock, Kollo, Dal-

lapozza, and Hadley. **Gedda** (EMI) and **Schock** (Eurodisc) approach Tauber, though without his ineffably sweet legato or his aching, sentimental poignancy. Schock is a showier performer, and you may enjoy his gusto in the more vibrant passages. Gedda comes closest to approximating Tauber's sweet side, but can still excite with a swaggering entrance song like "Schönes Italien" in *Paganini.*

What's exciting about Gedda's German-language complete versions on EMI (and there were two of him in *Land des Lächelns*) are the morsels from scores you don't know. *Friederike* (with **Dallapozza** as Goethe, which ought to have been sung by Gedda) also has some glowingly beautiful music for the soprano as well as several affecting ensembles. *Paganini,* one of the best of these late scores, is shot through with wonderfully rousing buffo-soubrette duets and spectacular chorus work, especially in Act II (EMI 65968). (Even Tauber had to appropriate a *Paganini* comedy number when he came to record his selections in the '20s, and of course he takes this into another, heavenly sphere.) *Der Zarewitsch,* however, is alternately boring or annoying. The balalaika riff on the "Volga Boatmen's Song" is cloying, and I find the soprano's famous entrance aria "Einer wird kommen" teeth-rattling. Even **Hadley,** in English, can't save the *Zarewitsch* score, and hearing his own translations unfortunately makes the lyrics seem doubly banal.

Das Land des Lächelns, however, is a different matter; it was (before *The King and I*) the musical theater's most important East-meets-West romance. Although I don't necessarily buy the story on stage, millions of middle-Europeans still do, and recordings offer great pleasure because Lehár's score is very effective in its teahouse-cum-Ringstrasse way. Yes, some of the Chinese music in Act II is Cantonese-tinkly, and the numbers with the soubrette, Mi, may at first appear something along the harmonic lines of "Chopsticks," but they do get to you after a hearing or two. Fortunately, the rest of the score is mostly sensational—for example Prince Sou-Chong's flowery entrance song, fragrant with apple blossoms, which has a wistful, far-away feeling (and a soaring center); the "tea for two" duet, a charm lesson fraught with submerged sexual tension; and the rapturous "Dein ist mein ganzes Herz," which announces its show-stopping nature from the very first notes of Lehár's spectacular introduction. His orchestral talents are amply on display in both the Viennese and most of the Chinese portions of the score, and there are genuine feeling and excitement in the finales—you may actually care for these characters.

Sou-Chong was perhaps **Tauber**'s most famous role, his imperial robes happily covering his arthritic steps. And he's hard to rival: You hear his distinctive timbre in every one of his numbers, no matter who dares to sing them. Still, **Gedda** does beautifully with Schwarzkopf (EMI 65372) and Rothenberger (EMI 69523) in his two versions, and the ladies are superb as well—certainly a bit less matronly than Tauber's partner of the '20s, Vera Schwarz. Schwarzkopf in the '50s is truly *wunderbar,* but so is Rothenberger in the following decade, both of them displaying great shading and sensitivity as Lisa. Schwarzkopf, however, gives a more distinctively youthful, personal reading, and the younger Gedda sounds more plausibly reticent as the shy Chinese prince in Vienna than he does in his later, more full-blown rendition. I grew up with the earlier recording—mono, it's true—and adored staring at the luxurious gilded Angel album cover of a Chinese girls' orchestra while being entranced by Otto Ackermann's conducting and the outright charm of the Emmy Loose–Erich Kunz secondary couple.

Land of Smiles and *Merry Widow* are the two Lehárs you should want complete, so the **Rudolf Schock–Margit Schramm** pairing of excerpts will only offer partial pleasure (Eurodisc). Schock is his usual showy self, as is **Hadley** in his excerpts in English (Telarc). The French and Hungarians, among others, have recorded other versions, but these pale when compared to those with either Tauber or Gedda. Hearing Tauber insinuate his way through the second-act love duet or the apple-blossom aria will amply demonstrate why Berlin in the late '20s was the place to be for operetta.

Two later tenors who managed to capture Tauber's ring and some of his legato tenderness were active in the Nazi era. **Karl Friedrich,** who excelled as Wagner's Walther (and you can hear why) is first rate in a series of broadcast recordings made in wartime Vienna at least nominally under the baton of Lehár himself. Friedrich's *Paganini* (Bel Age 103351) and his Octavio in *Giuditta* (Bel Age 103352) are splendid. *Giuditta,* a fairly lethargic work composed for Tauber and Novotna and premiered at the Vienna Staatsoper in 1934, comes off well in the Bel Age version, where the dialogue and production turn the work into a brisk radio play. Unfortunately, more modern German studio recordings of operettas have been dreadful, with nearly inaudible dialogue readings that should be skipped during playing.

The **Tauber-Novotna** *Giuditta* is worth seeking out for comparison (Bel Age 103352); otherwise, there are two modern versions. One, done in 1959 and quite scarce before it was released in excerpt form (London 436900), stars **Gueden** and **Kmentt** with Loose and Berry in support, with the chorus and orchestra of the Vienna Staatsoper led by Moralt, as in the '30s. It's very pleasant, Gueden especially. The English version conducted by valiant operetta champion Bonynge again has **Hadley** in the Tauber part (Telarc 80436). But somehow *Giuditta* sounded sultrier in the '30s and '40s than it does now. The Bonynge-Hadley pairing also offers an English *Paganini,* besides the already cited *Land des Lächlens* and *Zarewitsch,* each with distinctive Hilary (Eloise) Knight disc covers (Telarc). Having such comparatively unusual works in English makes them quite attractive.

Anders made several 78s of Tauberlieder when Tauber was verboten or, later, deceased, and also participated in several one-disc potpourris that must have warmed many Third Reich living rooms. But he was an excellent Lehárian. **Wunderlich** and **Björling** are two other legendary tenors whose Lehár songs are rewarding in whichever compilation you may find.   TRAUBNER

Jón Leifs *(1899–1968)*

Leifs is without doubt Iceland's most important composer, despite the ridicule meted out to his utterly unique music for much of his life. The island's stark beauty is mirrored in the extraordinary and volcanic tonal landscapes of his scores, from his quartets and string orchestra pieces, like *Elegy* and *Consolation,* to the huge orchestral arrays of *Hekla* and the *Saga Heroes* symphony, with its canyons, granite slabs and *lurs*—the ancient Norse longhorns. If the rocks and glaciers of Iceland gave voice, this is how they would sing. The soundtrack of his film biography *Tears of Stone* has been released, mainly using excerpts from his works (Music from Iceland 605).

ORCHESTRAL MUSIC

The principal items of Leifs's output depict Iceland, its legends and natural features: *Baldr* (**Paul Zukofsky**'s revelatory youth orchestra recording of this choreographic drama is NA but can still occasionally be found [CP² 106/7]), *Icelandic Overture, Geysír, Hekla, Dettifoss, Hafís* (several of these employing choruses), and *Saga Heroes.*

Fine I and II. These contrasting works were written as provisional co-

das to his unfinished third *Edda* Oratorio. **Petri Sakari** recorded them as a pair (Chandos 9433), unlike **Anne Manson** (I, BIS 1050) and **En Shao** (II, ♦BIS 930, part of a magnificent disc with the epic Organ Concerto, *Variazione pastorale on a theme by Beethoven,* and *Dettifoss*). There is nothing to choose between the performances, though the contexts are not what Leifs intended.

Galdra-Loftur. The Overture introduced the incidental music from which the *Loftur Suite* was afterwards extracted. **Vänskä** gives a sturdy performance of the Overture (BIS 830), but **Sakari** is more atmospheric and more monumental in the "Funeral March" (♦Chandos 9180, with other Icelandic works). **En Shao,** considerably faster, directs the Suite in a thrilling performance (♦BIS 1030, also including Leifs's string orchestra masterpiece, *Réminiscence du Nord*).

Geysír. Vänskä benefits from spectacular sound and a splendidly varied program including *Trilogia piccola, Icelandic Folk Dances, Trois Peintures abstraites,* and *Consolation* (♦BIS 830). The orchestra previously gave a fine account with **Zukofsky** (Music from Iceland 604, with *Peintures abstraites*—not as precise as Vänskä's—plus the only recording of *Landfall* Overture).

Hekla. Leifs's depiction of the great volcano has to be heard to be believed. **Zukofsky** set the pace in 1989 with an excellent performance that started the Leifs re-evaluation ball rolling (Music from Iceland 604). Subsequent recordings have improved sonically but not in interpretation. In "Earquake," **Segerstam** focused overmuch on eruption (Ondine 894), while **En Shao** in Iceland struck a more appropriate balance with the composer's expressive purpose (♦BIS 1030).

Icelandic Overture. One of the few Leifs works to be issued on LP (by **William Strickland,** long NA), **En Shao** secures a taut account (BIS 1030), nearly a minute swifter than **Sakari,** who managed a shade more fervor (♦Chandos 9433). Both discs include the heartfelt *Elegy* for strings; despite over two minutes difference in duration, both are excellent.

Symphony 1 ("Saga Heroes"). Sibelius' son-in-law **Jussi Jalas** misguidedly set down a cut version on LP—thankfully NA—that did Leifs's fragile reputation little good. **Vänskä,** in a performance and recording about which no superlative is excessive, revealed a work of stunning beauty and power, with huge, percussion-cluttered climaxes and brief, magical passages for six *lurs* (♦BIS 468).

CHAMBER MUSIC

String quartets. No. 1 ("Mors et vita") is a vigorous, abstract, single-movement work, unlike the intensely emotional 2 ("Vita et mors"), written in the wake of the drowning of Leifs's daughter (hence the reversal in the title). No. 3 ("El Greco") is a late work, terse but evocative. The virtuosic young **Yggdrasil Quartet**'s pioneering performances could scarcely be bettered (♦BIS 691).

INSTRUMENTAL MUSIC

The instrumental pieces have been overshadowed by the orchestral works and quartets, though **Orn Magnússon** has set down the "Complete Piano Music," a highly engaging program of Leifs at his most idiosyncratic (♦BIS 692). **Rut Ingólfsdóttir** has also recorded beautifully the two *Studies for Solo Violin* (Music from Iceland 810).

VOCAL MUSIC

The **Icelandic Opera Chorus** recorded Leifs's grand *Iceland Cantata* in 1995, splendidly engineered (Chandos 9433). More impressive in its control of extremes of pitch and dynamics is **Schola Cantorum**'s *Hafís*

(Drift Ice), coupled with three works for solo voices and orchestra, two songs Op. 14a, *The Lay of Gudrun*, and *Nótt* (Night) (♦BIS 1050). Their *Lay of Gudrun* is swifter and more dramatic than that by Thórunn Gudmundsdóttir and two colleagues, who are, however, more assured (Music from Iceland 901). The latter disc features a more sensitive *Nótt* and premiere recordings of *The Lay of Helgi, Hunding's Bane,* and *Gróa's Spell*. Most moving of all is the unaccompanied nonliturgical motet *Requiem,* another elegy for Leifs's daughter in the form of a lullaby. The Choir of Hallgrim's Church sings beautifully but sounds rushed (BIS 1030); the matchless Hamrahlid Choir may be a touch too slow, but it catches perfectly the raw howl of anguish that Leifs never allowed to break the surface (♦Music from Iceland 601, a wonderful recital of Icelandic choral music).   RICKARDS

Guillaume Lekeu *(1870–1894)*

One of the saddest blows dealt to Belgian music was Lekeu's early death. During his brief span he poured out music, most of it of high quality. Perhaps the chief stations of his life were his trip to the Bayreuth Festival and his studies in Paris with Franck, cut short by the master's accidental death. He then studied with d'Indy, who devotedly completed some of the many projects he left unfinished. The Ricercar label has issued virtually a complete edition, lovingly edited and annotated by Jerôme Lejeune and featuring committed performances by Belgian artists.

Lekeu is best remembered for his chamber works, but his orchestral output, even if it features a preponderance of slow music, includes several small masterpieces. One is the *Adagio for Strings,* probably a memorial piece for Franck, which is beautifully played by the Liège Philharmonic under Pierre Bartholomée. It's available either with an excellent Franck D minor Symphony (Ricercar 8003) or as part of Vol. 1 of Lekeu's orchestral music, including another masterpiece, *Fantaisie sur deux airs populaires Angevins,* as well as the two Symphonic Studies and *Prélude de Barberine* (Ricercar 084067). Symphonic Study 2 portrays Hamlet and Ophelia, and she comes off better than he does, though he's given arresting musical ideas. A fine alternative comes from the Liège Symphony under Paul Strauss, along with *Fantaisie contrapuntique,* a *jeux d'esprit* in which the musicians arrive at their stands in relays (Pavane 7341, with Hubert Léonard's Violin Concerto 4).

A version of the Ophelia movement with a louder ending, again conducted by Bartholomèe, is in Vol. 2 of the orchestral works with a superb *Larghetto* for cello (Marie Hallynck) and orchestra, the melodically similar *Introduction and Adagio* for tuba (Carl Delbart) and wind band, an epithalamium written for a friend's wedding, and the choral *Chant lyrique,* one of Lekeu's few upbeat pieces (Ricercar 138128). His only other choral work, the cantata *Andromède,* which won him the second Belgian Prix de Rome in 1891, is splendidly performed by soloists, a good choir, and Bartholomée with his orchestra (Ricercar 099083).

The Violin Sonata, a half-hour work of three substantial movements in Franckian cyclic style, has often been recorded. Look for accounts by Kantorow and Jacques Rouvier (Denon 72718, with Debussy and Ravel) and Augustin Dumay and Collard (EMI, NA). Lola Bobesco is not as well recorded but plays with real awareness of the style and is well supported by Jacques Genty (Pavane 7292/3, 2CD, with Franck and Fauré). The late Philippe Hirschhorn, always an interesting fiddler, is superbly partnered by Jean-Claude Vanden Eynden (Ricercar 104091). Oliveira and Robert Koenig (Biddulph 018) and Gérard Poulet and Noël Lee (Arion) are passable, but the 1938 account by Yehudi and Hephzibah Menuhin sounds as if they had just learned the piece (Biddulph).

The disc by the terrific Spiller Trio and violist Oscar Lysy of the Piano Trio and the unfinished Piano Quartet is a real bargain (Arts 47567). The fine performances by the Arthur Grumiaux Trio (Ricercar 142132) and Domus (Ricercar 104091, with the Violin Sonata) will cost you much more. The early Cello Sonata is well played by Luc Dewez and Luc Devos, but only the third of the four movements is inspired, and the first is too long; on the same disc Devos plays the impressive 1891 Piano Sonata and three enjoyable short pieces (Ricercar 143133).

Some pleasant songs and piano pieces, with Devos as the common factor, are for those who already have the Lekeu bug (Ricercar 119129), as are early works for string quartet played by the Camerata Quartet of Warsaw (Ricercar 107099) and miscellaneous early chamber pieces performed by Philippe Koch, Devos, and others (Ricercar 144127).
                                                                    POTTER

Ruggero Leoncavallo *(1857–1919)*

Leoncavallo wrote a dozen or so operas and operettas, but his renown rests entirely upon one. Occasionally, the odd aria or song will surface on a recital disc, and collectors may have come across *Gli Zingari, Edipo Re,* and *Zazà,* but the only opera that gets any attention, besides *Pagliacci,* is the one destined to be known forever as the "other" *Bohème.* With the best will in the world, it's difficult to dispute the designation. Leoncavallo's *La Bohème* will never eclipse Puccini's, even though the libretto is different enough to show the characters in a new light. The leading soprano-tenor pair are Musetta and Marcello in Leoncavallo's treatment; Rodolfo is a baritone. The music is conversational and through-composed, easy enough to listen to but seldom thrilling. The best recording is Wallberg's, with Popp as Mimi, Alexandrina Milcheva-Nonova as Musetta, Franco Bonisolli as Marcello, and Weikl as Rodolfo (♦Orfeo 023822). It makes a good enough case for the opera to reward anyone curious enough to listen to it.

Pagliacci is too often put into the "shabby little shocker" class, but it deserves more respect. If we arbitrarily define *short operas* as those that fit entirely onto a single CD, then *Pagliacci* is, for me, the greatest of short operas, surpassing even the components of Puccini's *Trittico.* It has both passion and poetry, and its characters, even when unlikable, are thoughtful and interesting (more so than their mundane counterparts in *Cavalleria*). There's a place in it for raw verismo emotionalism, but there's also room for refinement. These hotheaded Sicilians have a surprising penchant for metaphorical discourse, and a touch of refinement does not go amiss.

Cellini's recording is short on gritty melodrama but probably the best sung of all (♦EMI 66778). De los Angeles is a sympathetic Nedda with a warm, limpid middle range; Björling is a manly, ringing Canio who doesn't indulge in clichéd Italianate blubbering, and Merrill's Silvio is, at the very least, richly and beautifully vocalized. Warren's huge voice flows forth like lava from an erupting volcano; the top notes are stupendous. Cellini wisely stays out of the way and lets the singers carry the show.

You won't find comparable vocal bounty in Karajan's account, but his singers are also strong individuals and better actors (♦DG 449727). Panerai's Silvio, his voice quivering with ardor and emotion, is the most vivid on records. Taddei doesn't have Warren's top notes, but his baritone is plump and pleasing in its own right, and his words, seductive and snarling by turns, always tell. Bergonzi, an aristocratic Canio, shapes his lines expressively and passionately. Jean Carlyle also has a fine feeling for the contours of her music, and if her voice is on the pallid—even mousy side—it's still sweet and appealing, and amply strong on top. Against all expectations, she's a fine Nedda. Even the Beppe here is unusually noticeable: Ugo Benelli, a Rossini tenor of some renown. Karajan makes the La Scala orchestra sound like a great ensemble, and he has a remarkable knack for enhancing the drama without dominating the singers. The protracted string growl that concludes "Vesti la giubba" has been imitated by many conductors since, and listen to how he supports Bergonzi in the final scene, especially at "Tu mi sfidi." The La Scala choristers lack nothing in zest and authenticity.

Like Björling and Bergonzi, Pavarotti is a well-groomed Canio on the recording led by **Patanè** (London). The crispness of his diction and his natural charisma see him through a role that requires more sheer power than he commands. Freni is a lovely Nedda but not entirely persuasive, perhaps because the role wasn't in her stage repertory. The words of the *ballatella* are keenly felt, the tone strong and full, but she doesn't seem to identify with the character. You sense her heart isn't in it as she draws (skillfully, to be sure) on her arsenal of stock *accenti,* yet no Nedda on records surpasses her, and she's ravishing in the duet with Silvio. Wixell is a gritty, unidiomatic Tonio.

More promising on paper is **Santi**'s 1971 recording, but Caballé is in poor form, her voice wobbling under pressure, and Domingo, for all his tonal resplendence, is a blank, the words limp and blurry (RCA). Milnes is a forthright Tonio, similar to but less refulgent than Warren. Domingo's subsequent *Pagliacci* recordings brought some slight improvements but aren't worth seeking out.

Gardelli is more interesting than either Santi or Patanè (London, also reissued on Belart), another performance more civilized than gutsy, with one conspicuous exception. Merrill is a rich, sonorous, somewhat bland Tonio, Krause an unusually thoughtful and sensitive Silvio. Lorengar's upper notes are stronger than Caballé's or de los Angeles's, and she sings with more passion and commitment than either, though many listeners may be put off by the marked vibrato. Gardelli (like Santi and Patanè) opens the traditional cut in the Nedda-Silvio duet, which finds Lorengar at her best. McCracken's Canio comes from another world. He's angry, vehement, overwrought, sometimes remarkably ugly in timbre, but he's ham-fistedly gripping in his own frenzied way.

Callas, di Stefano, and Gobbi, with **Serafin,** are never less than interesting, though none of them sings without some strain (EMI). Di Stefano's tone turns hard and dry as he pushes for volume, and Gobbi (who ducks the high A-flat of the Prologue) sounds gaunt next to Warren, Merrill, and MacNeil. Callas is penetrating, as always, and short on vocal allure. Her *ballatella* is unlovely, but she and Gobbi offer a display of great vocal acting in the duet that follows. Panerai is the Silvio, not quite as striking as he would be for Karajan but still eloquent. Serafin's leadership, though generally admired, strikes me as too often aimless, the orchestra meandering along aloofly until the final scene.

Those who regard *Pagliacci* as a tenor's opera may be unwilling to settle for any of the Canios mentioned so far, preferring instead a singer of greater flash and power. Gigli, in the 1934 recording led by **Ghione,** is the most effervescent and vocally supple of Canios (EMI; Arkadia). He offers, perhaps, a surfeit of emotional clichés, and the joy inherent in his voice is not entirely apt for so violent a character, but his involvement is genuine and affecting, not least at the truly heartbreaking "Sperai tanto e delirio." His colleagues are less memorable, though they're all old pros. Del Monaco, with **Molinari-Pradelli,** is dour in comparison, fulminating terrifyingly but unable to soften the character's ferocity enough for us to sympathize with him (London). The ring and steely thrust of his voice are formidable even so. Gabriella Tucci is a vibrant, capable Nedda (she skips the trills before the *ballatella,* an allowable option),

and Cornell MacNeil sings the Prologue gloriously, with succulent tone and a spectacular high A-flat.

Corelli, with **von Matačič,** crosses the humanity of Gigli with the muscle of Del Monaco (♦EMI 63967). He's not without subtlety and gentleness, but his words are forcefully projected, but what really sweeps you away is the beauty and size of his voice. It's dispiriting to think we haven't heard anything remotely like it in decades. Gobbi is still a potent Tonio, and this time he (imprudently) attempts the high ending of the Prologue. His voice is worn, but his acting skills remain as sharp as ever. Von Matačič leads more dynamically than most of his Italian rivals.

None of the other *Pagliacci* recordings gets very far off the ground, even if you might pause to admire an individual performer here and there (Francesco Merli's 1930 Canio, Scotto's 1979 Nedda). **Muti** deserves a blast of opprobrium for proscribing all interpolated high notes (EMI). Pedants may applaud, but not lovers of the voice. It's more rewarding to explore the opera's extensive phonographic history, from Caruso and Scotti to Vickers and Bastianini, though you'll have to do some searching in the jumble of reissues on various labels.

It's usually difficult to name a favorite performance of an opera without some hedging or equivocating, some regretful declaration of what you are foregoing elsewhere, but if I had to have only one *Pagliacci,* I wouldn't hesitate to choose Karajan's.   LUCANO

Anatoly Liadov *(1855–1914)*

Members of the generation following the Mighty Handful grew up in a more enlightened professional milieu, but they were still subject to the same sort of personal tensions. Liadov was born with all the advantages: a family already deeply involved with music and a recognized talent of his own. However, his mother died when he was a child, and his father was an uncontrolled type like a character out of Dostoevsky, unable to care for his children, devoted to "continuous reveling and carousing," as Rimsky-Korsakov put it. He died when Anatoly was 13, leaving his son untrained, undisciplined, and unable to apply himself. You'd never guess this on hearing the jewel-like perfection of the music he completed. His orchestral scores are marvelously poetic and evocative, his piano works little gems. Unfortunately, however, it appears that his entire orchestral output would fit on one compact disc, and his piano works on perhaps two. And there seems to be little else.

Svetlanov recorded the major orchestral works (Melodiya 140). **Gunzenhauser**'s disc with the Slovak Philharmonic is performed just as well and in even better sound, and includes two Polonaises, an amusing Intermezzo, a large-scaled Mazurka, and Liadov's last tone poem, *Nénie,* which demonstrates his enthusiasm for Scriabin in his last years (Marco Polo 220348). The only major work omitted is *Russian Folk Songs;* a pity, since it would have fit on the disc. Another all-orchestral disc comes from the Mexico City Philharmonic conducted by **Bátiz** and includes *Folk Songs,* the tone poems *Baba Yaga, The Enchanted Lake,* and *Kikimora,* plus *From Olden Times, The Musical Snuffbox,* two Polonaises, and three Fanfares, otherwise unrecorded (ASV 657). This program is well recorded but played less idiomatically than either Svetlanov or Gunzenhauser.

Russian Folk Songs is recorded by **Nikolai Malko** in an interesting Russian program with the Philharmonia from early LPs (Testament 1062). The three tone poems are heard in **Neeme Järvi**'s disc with Stravinsky's 1945 extended *Firebird Suite* and Rimsky-Korsakov's *Dubinushka,* a curious juxtaposition of material, though historically significant (Chandos 8783). Another odd but interesting CD combines the same Liadov works with two scores by Nicholas Tcherepnin and the

Suite from Rimsky's *Golden Cockerel,* from the Russian National Orchestra under **Pletnev** (DG 447084). This is equally well played and recorded, though neither it nor Malko is superior to the all-Liadov programs above. **Leonid Nikolaiev** with the Moscow Conservatory Symphony isn't as polished but provides a glimpse of some rarely heard Liadov, coupling the three tone poems with 16 choral settings of Russian folk songs (Saison Russe 288144). The settings are imaginative, the singing polished.

Liadov's piano music is due for a complete survey. **Coombs** offers a well-played program including the two major sets of variations among many other pieces (Hyperion 66986). **Inna Poroshina**'s selection is quite different, and she also plays with involvement (Essay 1045). Between the two we have most of the piano works.   MOORE

György Ligeti *(b. 1923)*

Ligeti owes much to the late film director Stanley Kubrick, who appropriated his music for at least three major films: *2001: A Space Odyssey, The Shining,* and *Eyes Wide Shut.* Listeners usually unimpressed by classical music have sought out Ligeti's work solely on the basis of these films. His style began to mature in the '50s and blossomed in the '60s with impressive works for orchestra, chorus, chamber ensembles, and other genres. "Micropolyphony," the composer's term for the weblike patterns resulting from the overlapping and interweaving of similar melodic lines, is an important feature of his style. The music stays in one place, yet it shimmers and pulses like watered silk.

Unfortunately, two of the best samplers of Ligeti's music have gone to that great cut-out bin in the sky. His two most wonderful orchestral scores, *Atmosphères* and *Lontano*—individual notes coalescing to form great milky clouds of sound—received transfiguring recordings from **Claudio Abbado** (♦DG 429260). Another casualty coupled Chamber Concerto, *Ramifications,* String Quartet 2, *Aventures,* and *Lux aeterna* in excellent performances by **Boulez,** the LaSalle Quartet, and others (♦DG 423244). *Melodien* is now unavailable with the disappearance of yet another orchestral compilation (London 425623). Fortunately, you could do worse than get the original soundtrack of *2001,* since the disc includes *Atmosphères, Lux aeterna, Aventures,* and excerpts from *Requiem* along with other soundtrack music (♦Rhino 72562).

Failing that, two recordings stand out as excellent introductions to Ligeti's unusual sound world. One collection includes Chamber Concerto, two versions of *Ramifications, Lux aeterna,* and *Atmosphères* (♦Wergo 60162). These are ground-breaking performances; none is less than 30 years old, however, and the sound is dicey. A fine, varied collection by Scandinavian players contains less familiar works: Double Concerto for Flute, Oboe, and Orchestra; *San Francisco Polyphony;* String Quartet 1; *Continuum;* and *Musica Ricercata* (♦BIS 53). These discs should get the budding Ligeti admirer off on the right foot. Apparently identical performances of Double Concerto and *San Francisco Polyphony* are on another disc where **Siegfried Palm** plays the Cello Concerto to a turn and Ernest Bour conducts what is now the only available recording of the excruciatingly beautiful *Lontano,* albeit in less than complimentary sound (♦Wergo 60163).

A narrower précis of Ligeti's career is traced by his solo concertos for cello (1966), piano (1985–88), and violin (1990–92). Conveniently, **Boulez** has recorded all three (DG 439808). The Cello Concerto evokes the frosty isolation typical of the composer at this time. The Piano Concerto finds him interested in pulse, both regular and irregular—a possible result of his introduction to Central African music a few years earlier. Of the three, the heat-shimmering Violin Concerto is the most

surprising of all. Ligeti's fascination with piling meter upon meter and interference pattern upon interference pattern is taken to an extreme. This concerto's highly original timbres include a chorus of recorders and ocarinas. An alternative recording of the Cello and Piano Concertos (with Chamber Concerto) comes from **Ensemble Modern** (Sony 58945). Boulez is far more subtle, however, preferring painterly tints and shades to the Ensemble's blocky colors.

Ligeti's two string quartets are terrific. The first ("*Métamorphoses nocturnes*") finds the composer reacting to the quartets of his countryman Bartók. By Quartet 2, Ligeti's voice had matured, and his micropolyphonic experimentation was in full bloom. Both have been recorded by the **Arditti Quartet** (Wergo 60079 and Sony 62306). Fine as the earlier Wergo recording is, the Sony disc eclipses it in terms of dark passion and muscular technique. It's also better recorded, less expensive, and more complete, including two very early chamber works and the tiny *Hommage à Hilding Rosenberg* for violin and cello.

Lux aeterna for 16 voices is Ligeti's most celebrated choral work, thanks to its use in *2001.* This is another of his micropolyphonic masterpieces, and its cool, bleeding colors are the auditory equivalent of a comet passing through a meteor shower. It has been recorded superbly by **London Sinfonietta Voices** in Sony's "Ligeti Edition," along with the composer's other unaccompanied choral works (Sony 62305). Most of these come from early in the composer's career, yet there are many hints of what was to come. Ligeti is particularly inspired by nature, as by the crowing of a rooster in *Morning,* or, in *Hungarian Etudes,* by melting icicles and croaking frogs. Fascinating.

Kubrick's *Eyes Wide Shut* boosted Ligeti's piano music, specifically the second section of *Musica ricercata,* which figured prominently in the film. The first section uses only two pitches, the second only three, and so on, culminating in a "monotonous" fugue that uses all twelve; Ligeti described it as "hovering between gravity and caricature." The "Ligeti Edition" couples this work with the two books of Etudes and a preview of a single etude from the third book; the pianist is **Pierre-Laurent Aimard,** who has received the composer's blessing (Sony 62308). The Etudes are violently colorful, inspired by African music, jazz, gamelans, fractal geometry, and a sculpture by Brancusi. These polyrhythmic, "polytempo" pieces are out of the reach of all but the most accomplished pianists. (Only Conlon Nancarrow's work is so multilayered, and he composed his piano works to be played by a machine!) Aimard's playing is an act of artistic heroism.

Vol. 4 of the "Ligeti Edition" is devoted to his vocal works, notably *Aventures* and *Nouvelles Aventures* (Sony 62311). To a nonsense phonetic text by the composer, three soloists run a gamut of emotional states; the result sounds like antics in an insane asylum for Munchkins. It's very entertaining and just a little horrifying. **Phyllis Bryn-Julson,** Rose Taylor, and Omar Ebrahim have a shrieking good time of it. This volume also contains six *Nonsense Madrigals* to texts by Lewis Carroll and others, a conflation of three outrageous coloratura arias from the opera *Le Grand Macabre,* and a selection of more traditionally styled songs from early in the composer's career. With the exception of *Aventures* and its sequel, these are premiere recordings. **Michael Gielen** offers both *Aventures* and *Nouvelles Aventures* in a 1968 recording that's even more edgy—scarier, and also funnier (Wergo 60045). These two works are preceded by the complete 27-minute *Requiem,* whose waves of choral sound wash terrifyingly over the listener even in the absence of Kubrick's images. The conductor is Bruno Maderna.

Probably the most provocative of the Sony series is devoted to socalled "Mechanical Music" (Sony 62310). Most of the selections on this

CD are adaptations (not by the composer) of keyboard works for performance on a barrel organ or player piano. Ligeti's admiration for Conlon Nancarrow is no secret, and it makes sense that he would sanction player piano realizations if only for the technical impossibilities they remove. The barrel organ realizations share this advantage, and they add elements of absurdity, wheezy obsolescence, and the circus that Ligeti must find appealing. The longest continuous work is *Poème symphonique;* scored for 100 metronomes, it created a minor scandal at its Dutch premiere in 1963. A true "happening" in the Cagean sense, the work shows what sonorities result—from almost "white noise" to a solitary ticking—when the machines are precisely wound up, started together, and left to run down on their own.

Vol. 6 brings together other keyboard pieces, including works for piano four-hands, two pianos, harpsichord, and organ (Sony 62307). Ligeti is a wonderful storyteller, and this CD is worth having just to read his account of how Göteborg Cathedral almost burned down when his organ work *Volumina* was played there. It begins with all of one manual's keys depressed and all stops pulled out and continues with violent sounds you wouldn't think an organ could produce. *Harmonies,* an etude from 1967, is even more innovative, calling for an organ whose air supply has been compromised, so that microtones are the result. Originally, this was accomplished by replacing the organ's motor with a vacuum cleaner! The organist here is **Zsigmond Szathmáry.** Three ear-tricking harpsichord works (*Continuum, Passacaglia ungherese,* and *Hungarian Rock*) are played by Elisabeth Chojnacka, and the disc includes the intriguing *Three Pieces for Two Pianos,* whose middle movement is a "self-portrait with [Steve] Reich and [Terry] Riley (with Chopin in the background)," played by Irina Kataeva and Aimard.

Another CD contains the same three harpsichord pieces in earlier performances by **Chojnacka,** and *Three Pieces for Two Pianos* played by Antonio Ballista and Bruno Canino (Wergo 60100). *Trio for Violin, Horn, and Piano* (see below) is also here. There's little reason to prefer the Sony performances except for their improved sound quality.

Szathmáry plays the two etudes, and **Karl-Erik Welin** plays *Volumina* on an earlier CD (Wergo 60161). The more primitive engineering actually enhances the music's creepiness. This disc's most important contributions to the Ligeti discography are *Artikulation* and *Glissandi,* two electronic works from the late '50s. The former, as its title suggests, can be heard as a conversation without words, and, going *Aventures* one better, without human participants. *Glissandi* is also surprisingly communicative, in spite of the technique used. The disc also contains *Continuum,* a 4-minute *perpetuum mobile* for harpsichord played by Antoinette Vischer, and *Ten Pieces for Wind Quintet.*

Young Swedish pianist **Fredrik Ullén** offers an alternative to the Sony discs (BIS 783 and 983). Ligeti has blessed Kataeva and Aimard, but I find Ullén to be even better. He's in complete sympathy with the music's Rube Goldberg structures, and he plays as if the right hand doesn't know what the left is doing, which is exactly what Ligeti's polyrhythmic challenges require. He also has the requisite stony demeanor for some of the pieces and a sense of humor for others, to say nothing of a flabbergasting technique. (He also holds a doctorate in neuroscience.) Finally, Ullén's collection is more complete than Sony's.

Ligeti's 1982 *Trio for Violin, Horn, and Piano* was written after a fallow period of soul-searching. It's a bridge from the music he wrote in the '60s and '70s to today's style, which is more polystylic than its predecessors. In his annotations, Ligeti cautions the reader that all the Trio's elements "only camouflage a musical reality of an entirely different nature, which remains indecipherable." The performers are **Saschko Gawriloff,** Marie-Luise Neunecker, and Aimard (Sony 62309). *Six Bagatelles for Wind Quintet* flirt with folk music without actually quoting it, and *Ten Pieces for Wind Quintet,* which are more characteristic of the composer's later experiments with unusual timbres and polyphonic play, are played by **London Winds.** The disc ends with the stark Sonata for Solo Viola, a work from the early '90s, played by **Tabea Zimmermann** with a fine appreciation of its out-of-this-world soundscapes.

There are two recordings of Ligeti's slapstick, sex- and apocalypse-laden *Le Grand Macabre,* probably the only opera to have a prelude for car horns. A recording conducted by **Elgar Howarth** was fine for its time but doesn't reflect the composer's numerous 1997 revisions (Wergo 6170, 2CD). Material has been cut and added, sung lines have been made into spoken lines and vice versa. Also, this recording is sung in German. A more recent recording was made during the course of several live performances in Paris, sung in English and conducted by **Salonen** (Sony 62312, 2CD). He keeps this incredibly busy opera on track, and there is excellent singing from a cast that includes the stratospheric Sibylle Ehlert as the Chief of Police and Jard van Nes as the slatternly Mescalina. Among the men, countertenor Ragin offers surreal vocal thrills as the babyish Prince Go-Go, and bass-baritone Willard White cuts a ridiculous and ultimately pathetic figure as Nekrotzar, the Death-like figure whose plans for the end of the world go awry when he gets drunk on wine. TUTTLE

Magnus Lindberg (b. 1958)

Lindberg was a coconspirator in a group of young Finnish musicians who formed a "secret" music society while in college and now command the world's attention. It included the conductors Esa-Pekka Salonen and Jukka-Pekka Saraste, but Lindberg is certainly the most frequently heard composer of the Finn Pack, and also one of the most arresting figures of his postserial, postminimalist generation worldwide.

Nationalism, it turns out, is hardly on Lindberg's agenda. Rather, he is a cosmopolitan, an internationalist who owes far more to the influences of serialism, Boulez, and Lutoslawski than to the rugged epics and inward odysseys of Sibelius. Above all, Lindberg is a master colorist who uses the orchestra and electronics in flashy, gleaming, energetic bursts. He's also prolific, and although there are some major gaps in the catalog, enough of his music is available on CDs to give you a good idea of how he has evolved from a somewhat wild experimentalism toward more coherent, more attractively dramatic structures.

The Finlandia label has gathered a number of works onto a pair of CDs that give a fairly compact survey of his early radical path of the '80s and what followed. One disc (500322) includes *De Tartuffe, Je Crois* (1981) for piano and string quartet, and *Linea D'Ombra* (1981), for the novel combination of flute, guitar, clarinet, and percussion; even in its austere, restricted sound world, Lindberg's flair for dazzling instrumental color is clear. *Zona* (1983), for cello and seven instruments, is disappointing with its experimental-for-its-own-sake cello writing, though it's handled with spiky assurance by Anssi Karttunen, **Salonen** and members of the London Sinfonietta. Salonen and Avant! also make cool, colorful, transparent work of *Redroot* (1983), a rigorous, thoroughly dissonant, lightly scored reduction of a 1979–80 chamber concerto.

A second Finlandia disc (500342) contains one of Lindberg's more bizarre chamber works, *Metal Work* (1984), for accordionist **Matti Rantanen,** an unrelentingly dissonant and exciting piece of music. *Ablauf* (1983–'88), for two clarinets and percussion, is full of multiphonic clarinet effects, the whacking of two bass drums, and some vocal scatting that resembles India's *solkattu* techniques. *Twine* (1988) emerges in pianistic jolts and fragments. Another accordion piece, *Jeux d'anches* (1990–91) shows signs of Lindberg's mellowing process, very much in contrast to the more abrasive *Metal Work*.

Also on this disc is *Kinetics* (1988–89), the work that not only confirmed Lindberg's emergence as a major figure but also marked a switch in style from the fire-eating experimentalist to a more audience-friendly tone painter. The textures are softer, not quite as harmonically forbidding, the overall structure far clearer and more dramatic, the orchestrations richer than before, with some electronics used to beef things up. **Salonen** and the Finnish Radio Symphony let the more extroverted passages wash transparently over themselves, and the opening and coda emerge more slowly, with more glistening effect, than they do in the more urgent hands of **Saraste** and the Bavarian Radio Symphony. The Saraste performance can be found either in a coupling with like-minded chamber orchestra works from the same period, *Joy* and *Marea* (with Avant! on Ondine 784), or by itself (Ondine 758). In any case, both recordings of *Kinetics* are pretty spectacular, and both make the best entryways for newcomers to this composer.

"Only the extreme is interesting," thought Lindberg in the '80s, and *Action–Situation–Signification* (1982) was his most extreme manifesto, a diffuse, tough, dissonant encyclopedia of avant-garde effects that the Finnish six-man experimental Toimii Ensemble under **Salonen** performs with relish (Finlandia 372). On the same disc is the ambitious climax of Lindberg's "extreme" period, *Kraft* (1983–85), which seemed to pack all of his youthful aggressions into one half-hour explosion.

Lodged in a collection of otherwise less-forbidding later works, the highly complex *Tendenza* (1982) is tough to absorb despite its striking glissandos in the strings and precise, scampering passages (Ondine 882). With *Corrente* (1992), Lindberg works in a fragment of Purcell near the opening, alludes powerfully to Sibelius's Symphony 4 midway through, and carves out a section of flat-out minimalism down the stretch before the starkly tragic conclusion. *Corrente* exists in two versions, the original for chamber orchestra (Ondine 882) and a greatly expanded orchestral version known as *Corrente II* (Ondine 911). The latter is more powerful; the ostinatos are fleshed out by luminous, heavier orchestral scoring, and the Sibelius references are deeper, lengthier, and now form the pivotal point of the piece. Also on this disc is *Coyote Blues* (1993), not a blues in the American sense but a piece that slithers around in the sly manner of the animal while maintaining static surfaces even when there is a lot of activity within the chamber orchestra.

The 36-minute *Aura* (1993–94) was dedicated to Lutoslawski upon the elder composer's death midway through the piece's conception, yet Lindberg's scheme was already headed in the direction of the great Pole's two-part structures. You get a nebulous, unsettling feeling from the first two movements, but the piece coalesces in III and explodes with wild color in IV, topped off by a serene string chorale whose dense harmonies recall Honegger. **Knussen** fervently leads the BBC Symphony (♦DG 463184). *Aura*'s discmate, *Engine* (1996), doesn't send me; its computer-derived, Boulez-like complexities for chamber orchestra are structurally vague and unsatisfying. Lindberg has also offered the public two versions of *Arena* (1994–95); the original was scored for full orchestra, while the 1996 revision (*Arena II*) is reduced for 16-piece chamber orchestra. In both forms the work represents a further softening of his rhetoric, bringing up remnants of the past within its busy surface, its lightly transparent dissonances eventually resolving into a sustained passage of massive Mahler/Berg strings near the close. Here again the **Saraste** recording of the orchestral version (Ondine 911) makes a bigger emotional splash than the more glistening **Oramo**/Avant! reading of the chamber *Arena II* (Ondine 882), particularly the Mahlerian coda.

The most recent Lindberg piece on records is *Feria* (1997), which continues the general rhetorical and structural ideas of *Aura, Arena,* and *Corrente* right through to the "accessible" (all things being relative) conclusion (Ondine 911). Yet this work is an even more varied emotional roller-coaster ride, with tonal implications and reminiscences of Lutoslawski toward the close. Several major works—Piano Concerto (1991–94); the 40-minute *Aura: In Memoriam Witold Lutoslawski* (1994); the weird, wild, and scary *Related Rocks* (1997); the newly unveiled orchestral *Fresco* (1997–98); (1999); Cello Concerto (1999); and *Gran Duo* (2000)—have yet to be recorded. But the Finns have been astutely and prolifically documenting their own music, so keep your eyes on the L bin in major record emporiums.   GINELL

Franz Liszt *(1811–1886)*

No composer has been pilloried by the smug critical establishment with as willing a heart as Franz Liszt, in some circles rated just below Beelzebub in the pantheon of demons and blasphemers. To some extent he may have brought this on himself, with vivid musical images of Mephistopheles and hedonistic sensuality even surpassing Wagner's, until near the end of his life he renounced his sins of the flesh and assumed the title of abbé. Certainly Liszt was no saint; his affairs with the Countess d'Agoult and later the Polish Princess Karolina von Sayn-Wittgenstein (who was unable to divorce her Russian husband and marry him) provided ample fodder for the tabloids of the day. Yet at the same time there was not a more magnanimous soul; he gave freely of his wealth and time on behalf of many young musicians, and his humility and generosity contrast effectively with his public's adoring idolatry.

Already a keyboard prodigy when he began attending Paganini's concerts, the 21-year-old Liszt there had an epiphany, turning from the drawing rooms of Paris to work in earnest on developing his chosen instrument to the same virtuoso status as Paganini's violin. He did this not merely to exploit the piano for monetary gain but also to expand its harmonic and rhythmic capabilities to new heights. He soon came to the conclusion that the restrictions of structure and tonality that had bound Mozart and Beethoven were, if not yet devoid of relevance, at least limiting factors for music that depended on literary and pictorial associations. He didn't entirely abandon tonality, but in his piano music and symphonic poems he broke new ground, expanding on works like Berlioz's *Symphonie Fantastique* (which he greatly admired) and inspiring composers like Wagner, who saw in Liszt's works the music of the future. Music would never be the same again.

SYMPHONIES

Dante Symphony. Liszt originally had the idea of setting Dante's *Divine Comedy* for the stage; on realizing the formidable scope of such a project, he instead compiled an orchestral setting (hardly a "symphony" in the usual sense) in three sections: a terrifying depiction of the winds of Hell with the fearsome words "Abandon hope, all ye who enter here" sounded forth in the low brass ("Inferno") followed by a rapt and beatific "Purgatorio" and "Magnificat," with a chorus in the closing pages. **Varujian Kojian** offers Liszt's rather bombastic alternate coda as a separate track, but that's not enough to salvage his curious reading, barreling through the opening section at a truly hell-for-leather tempo and quite uninvolved thereafter (Varèse or Citadel). **Barenboim** lavishes far more care on the music—taking some 10 minutes longer—and brings out all its seething passion and mystical beauty while benefiting from far richer sound (♦Teldec 77340, coupled appropriately with "Dante" Sonata).

Masur presses ahead with a vengeance in the opening "Inferno," pointing up the snarling brass to telling effect, yet seems superficial in "Purgatorio" and "Magnificat" (EMI or MHS) where **Conlon** is more fervent (Erato 88162). **Sinopoli**'s gripping and luminous account is all the more desirable for its inclusion of Busoni's "Sarabande and Cortege" from *Doktor Faust* (DG 457614), while **Hartmut Haenchen** is primarily of interest for the appended arrangement of the organ piece *Évocation à la Chapelle Sixtine* (Capriccio 10 736). **György Lehel**'s massive opening movement makes up in sheer power what it lacks in visceral excitement, but the recording shows its age (Hungaroton 11918).

Faust Symphony. Liszt's fascination with the tale of the troubled scholar Faust and his ill-fated pact with the Devil may be appreciated from the breadth and intensity of this symphony, which is over an hour long, and in the generally heard revised version calls for chorus, solo tenor, and organ in the closing measures. There's also a version of the finale without chorus, but it's nowhere near as effective and is rarely performed, though **Iván Fischer** enterprisingly offers both (♦Philips 454460). This music resonates with **Bernstein;** he's totally immersed in the story, devastating and emotionally draining (♦Sony 47570). His overindulgent remake omits several measures from the first movement for some reason, yet still comes out nearly six minutes longer (DG). **Beecham** gave us one of the classic recordings; still, I can't help thinking that the ever urbane Sir Thomas is gazing on the proceedings from outside, for all the splendor of the Royal Philharmonic's performance (♦EMI 49260 or 63371). In the bargain range you can't do better than **András Ligeti,** highly charged and purposeful with excellent sound (♦ Naxos 553304).

Conlon lacks the last measure of white-hot intensity, yet treats the unfortunate Gretchen with great affection (Erato 88068), unlike **Ansermet,** whose undue haste renders her sad tale quite dry-eyed (London LP). The same is true of **Masur** (EMI or MHS), and also **Thomas Dausgard,** who hardly breaks a sweat in the satanic finale (Chandos). **Muti** is alternately incisive and sardonic in the outer movements, with an impassioned portrait of Gretchen, but the sound is brittle and bass-shy (EMI); likewise, **Rattle** paints all three protagonists in highly graphic terms but is let down by the gray, damped recording (EMI). **Sinopoli** fares better sonically and is also strikingly vivid (DG 449137). Both sound and performance are highly recommendable with **Solti,** his passions here entirely at the service of the music (London 417399). **D'Avalos** is served less well by the engineers, the strings coming off as a bit edgy; however, his sensitivity to rhythm and detail pays rich dividends (IMP 1071).

The Concertgebouw plays superbly for **Dorati,** but the performance tends toward the melodramatic (Philips); **Chailly,** also with the Concertgebouw, likewise benefits from impressive performance and sonics but lacks something in characterization (London). **Inbal** treats the piece like Bruckner, proceeding apace in massive blocks of sound that sound impressive but have little to do with the tense goings-on; he makes Faust sound like a weary philosopher indeed, while Mephistopheles seems not so much sinister as sated with mankind's sins (Denon). **Barenboim** shares Inbal's turgid view of the opening movement, so that even the stark and powerful Berlin brasses in Mephistopheles's hellish imagery are not enough to salvage the performance (Teldec). **Horenstein** is one of the slowest around, not lacking in cohesion yet evincing little sense of Mephistopheles's diablerie or malevolence, though his 1972 BBC aircheck (Music and Arts 744) offers a smoother blend than the ancient Vox (5504, with a mono Bruckner 8). A better choice is **Ferencsik,** not a revelatory performance but warm and knowing (Hungaroton 12022).

OTHER ORCHESTRAL MUSIC

Hungarian Rhapsodies

These heady and highly colored exercises seem like the very essence of Gypsy soul and wild abandon, even surpassing the symphonic poems in emotional impact. Of the original group of 19 for piano, Liszt and his student Franz Doppler set six for orchestra (or seven if you count *Rákóczy March*), unfortunately confusing things by numbering them differently: thus orchestral Rhapsodies 1 through 6 are equivalent to keyboard 14, 2, 6, 12, 5, and 9, while the *Rákóczy March* is 15. You can also find 2 in two different versions: the more familiar, heavily string-oriented Matthey arrangement favored by Fiedler, Karajan, Ormandy, Dutoit, and others and the original (Doppler) version with its almost Spanish-sounding trumpet introduction first championed by Scherchen and since offered by Mehta, Fischer, and Fistoulari.

No one has set them forth with the fire and smoldering passion of **Dorati,** generously coupled with Enescu's *Romanian Rhapsody* 1 in gorgeous sound and crisp, trenchant performances; moreover, Dorati even outdoes the composer by bringing out the rich, pungent sound of the cimbalom not just in 3 (where it's specifically called for) but in all others save 2 as well (♦Mercury 432015). First choice after Dorati is **Iván Fischer,** who even includes the cimbalom in 2, with Gypsy fiddling and a grand sweep that make these pieces really soar (♦Philips 456570). **Boskovsky** uses a cimbalom too, but his Liszt lacks the lilt and ardor that make his Strauss Family recordings so special (EMI). **Fistoulari** benefits from warm playing and sonics but can't match Dorati in those stirring rhythms (Vanguard). **Mehta** proves there's no Gypsy in his soul with flaccid, dispirited readings (CBS); you might expect better from **András Kórodi,** but Hungarian or not, he sounds just as sodden and tentative as Mehta except with a smaller orchestra (Capriccio).

There's nothing tentative about **Masur**—whose earnest readings perhaps lack charm but not conviction (Philips 412724)—or **Scherchen,** whose renditions are often maddeningly off the wall, yet evince a sincerity and affection that quite escape Mehta and Kórodi (MCA). The **Hungarian Folk Ensemble Orchestra** offers only 1 and 2 of the usual six, but gives you three others normally heard only with piano (13, 15 and 19) plus the *Csárdás Macabre,* not unlike what you might hear at a sidewalk cafe in Budapest (Hungaroton 10104). Many conductors have left us highly individual readings, especially **Stokowski** and **Fiedler** in 2 (both RCA) and **Karajan** in 2, 4, and 5 (DG).

The *Rákóczy March* with **Fiedler** (quite different from Berlioz's arrangement) comes with his Rimsky *Coq d'Or* suite (RCA 61497); it's also included with the Rhapsodies by **Boskovsky** along with another tasty morsel, *Hungarian Storm March*—also called *Hungarian Battle March,* thereby justifying its inclusion with *Battle of the Huns* and *Wellington's Victory* by **Lenárd** in his disc of "Battle Music" (Naxos 550230)—as well as **Kunzel** (Telarc 80079).

Tone poems

It's generally accepted that Liszt "invented" the symphonic poem, going beyond the naive tone painting of Handel and Vivaldi (and Beethoven in his "Pastoral" Symphony) to have the music tell a story or follow a program usually based on well-known works of literature or mythology; this he expanded to fuller form in his *Faust* and *Dante* Symphonies, while Wagner found in them the genesis of his operatic *leitmotif* principle. It would be disingenuous to speak of them as great music; in the main they're bombastic, banal, and way too long for their sometimes tenuous literary connotations; yet there's no question they're tremendously exciting, extremely well orchestrated (largely by Liszt himself, though his pupil Raff is often credited), and—in the right hands—highly effective. The problem is finding someone who's willing to go over the top in this admittedly emotional, even vulgar music, and surveys of all 13 are surprisingly rare, not to mention frustratingly uneven.

Haitink provided the first complete survey (Philips 438751 and 438754), still the most sumptuous sounding of all; yet there's precious little fire and passion, and you often get the impression, he considers this music beneath him, seeming cold and austere. You can't accuse **Masur** of shying away from the drama in this music, and he's more hearty and outgoing than Haitink in *Les Préludes, Tasso,* and *Mazeppa,* though neither rises above boring pomposity in the wonderfully banal *Battle of the Huns,* and the recordings sound cramped and colorless next to Haitink (EMI 68595 and 68598; MHS 522171L and 522534M). Hungaroton has issued the tone poems plus other works on five CDS though they could easily fit on four (12677–81), but **Arpád Joó**'s Budapest players lack the crisp ensemble of Haitink's London Philharmonic or Masur's Leipzig Gewandhaus, and again there's not nearly enough chance-taking from the podium. In trying earnestly to keep things from getting out of hand, Joó only succeeds in failing to work up the music as much as it deserves. He offers one of the best *Orpheus* and *Hungaria* around, but *Tasso* is a lost cause, and so is *From the Cradle to the Grave.* Thus we're faced with a daunting array of the good, the bad and the best forgotten. I'll take them in chronological order.

Ce qu'on entend sur la montagne (What One Hears on the Mountain). Liszt's first tone poem, based on a poem by Victor Hugo, is a remarkable mood painting; it does meander somewhat, but that may be forgiven in the light of such mesmerizing sonorities. **Haitink** tends to downplay the dramatic contrasts, and his unhurried traversal nicely complements the more mercurial accounts of **Joó** and **Masur.** Despite reverberant sonics, **Plasson** does a very good job with this piece as well as *Festklänge* and *Prometheus* in his second outing (Berlin 1126), though not enough to compel purchase of Volume 1 (see *Tasso*). **Butt** offers an attractive but unduly episodic overview (ASV).

Tasso: Lamento e Trionfo. This is one of Liszt's finest works; admirably concise and with memorable thematic material, it proceeds at a logical yet inexorable pace, tracing the story of the Italian poet Torquato Tasso from suffering and humiliation to ultimate triumph. Unfortunately, all too many conductors see the final procession through the streets of Rome as merely an excuse to slow to a crawl, including **Haitink, Karajan, Joó,** and even **Solti,** whose otherwise highly charged account is combined with *Les Préludes, Prometheus,* and *Mephisto Waltz* (London 417513). **Masur** does better, but better still is **Ferencsik,** unfortunately coupled with an undistinguished *Les Préludes* and *Orpheus* (Hungaroton 12446). The searing **Silvestri** pairing of *Tasso* and *Les Préludes* on an Angel LP has frustratingly been split up for CD, with *Les Préludes* tacked onto the piano concertos (Royal Classics 7445) and *Tasso* combined with Tchaikovsky's *Manfred* (Testament 1129).

Tasso, Les Préludes, Mazeppa, and *Prometheus* comprise the first of two discs by **Michael Halász,** all quite pedestrian (Naxos 550487); Vol. 2 is far better (see *Die Ideale*). **Plasson** couples *Tasso, Les Préludes,* and *Mazeppa* with *Orpheus* (Berlin), while **Iván Fischer** combines them with *Mephisto Waltz* (Quintana 903049); however, Plasson has some strange ideas about tempo, breezing through the grand statement that opens and closes *Les Préludes* in matter-of-fact fashion and becoming hectic near the end of *Tasso,* whereas Fischer does beautifully with *Tasso,* and his brazen brasses add greatly to the closing pages of *Mazeppa.* **Rickenbacher**'s impossibly tedious *Tasso* is worth putting up with for his revelatory account of the three *Funeral Odes* (Koch Schwann 1768).

Les Préludes. This work remains the most popular of all Liszt's tone poems, only later rationalized by lines from Lamartine: "What is life but a series of preludes to that unknown song whose first solemn note is sounded by death?" We had two marvelous accounts from **Paray,** first mono (Mercury), then stereo (Concert Hall); both are NA. **Stokowski**'s reading suggests he would have been an unbeatable proponent of the complete canon (Cala 0522, mono), and we may likewise regret that **Bernstein** never went beyond *Les Préludes* (Sony 47572); what a stunning *Mazeppa* he could have given us! **Fiedler** offers a fiery and potent reading that reminds us what a splendid musician he was (RCA 63532, with *Les Sylphides* and *Love for Three Oranges*), while **Scherchen,** even with the hit-or-miss Vienna State Opera Orchestra, fairly seethes with drama (MCA 9832, with *Mazeppa, Battle of the Huns,* and *Mephisto Waltz*).

Any of these—or for that matter **Masur, Joó,** or **Järvi** (Chandos 9360, with the piano concertos)—is far more compelling than **Haitink,** sadly miscast in this music, or **Muti,** whose frequent tempo changes prove distracting (EMI). **Solti** is darkly glowering in a richly satisfying account (London 417513, with *Tasso,* etc.). **Conlon** is more refined, but still absorbing (Erato 45256), as is **Iván Fischer** (with *Tasso,* etc.); **Mehta** is neither (Sony). Adding *Les Préludes* to **Dorati**'s *Scheherazade* hardly raises either one to must-buy status (Mercury). Water Lily Acoustics makes much of the technical details of their Philadelphia taping with **Sawallisch,** but to no avail, given the dead sonics and limp readings (66, with Dvořák overtures).

Orpheus. The familiar tale of Orpheus taming the wild beasts with his lute presents the composer in an uncommonly serene and reflective light. **Masur** seems strangely rushed next to **Haitink, Joó,** or **Halász,** but none of them can match **Beecham,** who's unsurpassed in this ethereal and pastel-shaded music (♦EMI 63299, with *Psalm 13* and *Ein Heldenleben*). There is a beautiful *Orpheus* in **Mehta**'s Decca CD, but the tremulous violin solo rules out his remake (Sony). **Plasson** is passionate and songful but not enough so to recommend his recording (Berlin).

Prometheus. The story of Prometheus, who gave fire to man and was roundly punished for it by the gods, clearly appealed to Liszt, who first thought of writing incidental music for Herder's play *Prometheus Unbound* and later reworked the overture as a symphonic poem. My favorite version is **Solti** (London 47513, with *Les Préludes,* etc.), but in sober fact it's difficult to find a bad recording. You might check out **Abbado,** who couples it with like thoughts on the Prometheus legend by Beethoven, Scriabin and Nono (Sony 53978).

Mazeppa. The Cossack prince Mazeppa, caught in flagrante delicto with a count's wife, was strapped naked to the back of a horse and sent headlong across the steppes; rescued in the nick of time, he became the leader of Ukraine. We hear the great striding theme of the unfortunate Mazeppa in the stentorian trombones, followed after a brief rest and recuperation by his triumphant march to glory. Even **Fiedler** (RCA 63532, with *Les Préludes*) succumbs to the temptation to take the opening trombone theme rather broadly, but he manages to pull it off—as does **Järvi** (Chandos 9360, with *Les Préludes*)—where **Haitink** merely sounds tired (Philips);

Paray (Concert Hall), **Scherchen** (MCA), and **Mehta** (Decca) show more resolve—certainly a lot better than Mehta's tepid remake (Sony), with **Masur** and **Joó** falling somewhere in between. Masur's New York remake is far more exciting (Teldec 77547, with *Háry János*), and so too is the redoubtable **Karajan** (DG 415967, with *Tasso, Les Préludes, Hungarian Fantasy,* et al., or DG 447415, with *Les Préludes* plus Smetana's *Moldau* and *Vyšehrad*). **Haitink** does very well with the swaggering final march, though at a slower pace than **Masur** and **Joó,** who along with **Fischer, Mehta,** and **Gyula Németh** (White Label 160, with Ferencsik's *Hungaria*), are among the few conductors to observe the repeat near the close.

Festklänge. Originally conceived as a wedding march for himself and the Polish Princess Karolina von Sayn-Wittgenstein (who was already married at the time), this piece was later reworked for more prosaic purposes, though further condensation would not have been amiss. While the central polonaise betrays the work's origins, the same can't be said of another theme that sounds an awful lot like "O Canada." It's not an easy piece to hold together, though some conductors, including **Masur** and **Plasson,** have managed to make the seams less noticeable. My favorite is **Solti,** a London LP; unfortunately this isn't included in his CD. You might keep an eye out for **Mark Ermler,** now hard to find but offering very fine renditions of not only *Festklänge* but also *Hungaria* and *Hamlet* (Melodiya 00033).

Héroïde Funèbre. This unrelentingly somber work is all that remains of Liszt's plans for a "Revolutionary Symphony" in five movements intended to include the *Marseillaise* and *Ein' feste Burg.* What we have left is a massive funeral march lasting close to half an hour in **Haitink**'s hands, and closer to 18 minutes for **Masur,** which should give some idea of the range of emotions involved. Somewhere in between is **Joó,** closer to Haitink than Masur, who seems more jaunty than grieving.

Hungaria. It hardly comes as a surprise that Liszt honored his native land, even if many true Magyars took him to task for favoring the Gypsy element over other components of the rich goulash that was Hungary. Nor is it surprising that the result resembles the more familiar *Hungarian Rhapsodies,* in spirit if not in structure. All too often it has been cut on disc, for example the old **Ferencsik** recording (White Label 160). Fortunately, **Joó** gives one of the best readings in his set, alert and thoroughly captivating, while **Haitink** drags out the final pages unmercifully. This is a highlight for **Masur,** who brings a pungent Gypsy flavor to the music, and is also beautifully set forth by **Ermler** (Melodiya).

Hamlet. Originally intended as an overture to Shakespeare's tragedy, it tells us more about Hamlet than about Ophelia, let alone the inexorable chain of events that destroys them both. There's little to choose between the various available versions; it's treated in dramatic and compelling fashion by all those I've heard, even **Mehta** (it's the only redeeming feature of his Sony CD).

The Battle of the Huns. Among the most terse and graphic of the set, this piece is often ill-used for that very reason, its concluding pages drawn out to the point of mere pompous rhetoric as if hoping to uncover some Great Truth that never entered Liszt's head. It's quite simply what the composer says it is: a horrific clash between Huns and Romans, who fought with such heated savagery by day that when night fell, the spirits of the slain took up their swords and had at it in renewed frenzy, with the organ finally intoning a prayer for peace. Perhaps **Scherchen** veers over the top, but I'd rather hear him, K-Mart organ and all, than the tedious heaving about of most versions, including **Haitink** and **Masur. Joó** fares better, and **Mehta** does rather well on his Australian Decca CD, but his remake is dreary (Sony), and **Maazel** is just as bad (RCA). **Kunzel** (Telarc) and **Lenárd** (Naxos) both couple it

with *Wellington's Victory,* but Lenárd's sodden effort does neither Liszt nor Beethoven any favors.

Die Ideale. Of all the tone poems, this has to be by far the heaviest—a tedious, rambling essay with dreary philosophical pretensions lasting close to half an hour. The summation from the notes for the Joó set is probably about as coherent as any: "It is about the various stages in man's life, about youth and the ideals linked with it and about the times when youth is only a memory and new ideals appear in the form of new friendships and of work." Best by far is **Michael Halász** in his second program; he almost manages to make this piece sound interesting, unlike anyone else who has essayed the work (♦Naxos 553355). Since he also offers top-rank readings of *Hamlet, Orpheus,* and *From the Cradle to the Grave,* it's more than just a bargain; it's a necessity.

From the Cradle to the Grave. For his last tone poem, Liszt took inspiration from a sketch by Count Mihaly Zichy showing man's transfiguration from babe in arms through middle age to his final rest. Unfortunately, once again the most compelling reading, by **Solti,** was set aside when they compiled the CD. Certainly he's more satisfying than **Siegfried Landau** (Vox) or **Joó,** who seem to be resigned to the fact that the grave will triumph, whereas in the middle section ('The Struggle for Life') Solti, **Masur, Haitink,** and above all **Halász** refuse to give up without a fight. Maybe that's the key to the way the Liszt tone poems should go—not with a whimper, but with a bang.

CONCERTOS

Since Liszt's keyboard music reflects his own prodigious capabilities, it comes as little surprise that the solo writing is of almost fiendish difficulty, nor that so many pianists are content to approach these pieces merely as virtuosic vehicles while treating their very rewarding poetic content in superficial fashion. Few have balanced the lyrical and heroic components of the two concertos as consummately as **Richter,** wonderfully seconded by Kondrashin; his pairing is as close to immortality as any recording is likely to become (♦Philips 446200, with the B minor Sonata). You can also find Richter doing the concertos in concert, indispensable for the *Hungarian Fantasy* he never recorded commercially (BBC 4031).

Kondrashin went on to partner the far more volatile **Janis** in 1, who's joined by Rozhdestvensky in 2, and the brilliant recordings (made in Moscow) fit Janis's clarion fingerwork like a glove (♦Mercury 432002). This too is a classic. **Katchen**'s hearty and outgoing readings with Argenta have thankfully been reissued, the brazen London Philharmonic trombones providing a very special guilty pleasure (♦Australian Decca 460831, Vol. 4 of their complete survey). You'll also have to pore through import bins for **Pennario** and Leibowitz; these are solid, satisfying readings if without Katchen's coruscating élan (RCA 29244, part of their "Classical Navigator" series).

Many recordings of Concertos 1 and 2 (there's also a 3, discussed later) are even more valuable for the appended material. By far the most extensive survey is the pair of boxed sets with **Leslie Howard,** including just about everything Liszt ever wrote for piano and orchestra (Hyperion 67401/2 and 67403/4). Satisfying if less comprehensive collections are offered by **Béroff** (♦EMI 767214) and **Joshua Pierce** (♦Carlton 02147), and **Lortie** has just begun another, starting with the *Wanderer, Lélio* and *Ruins of Athens Fantasies* (♦Chandos 9801). Howard is imperious and grand, yet rarely impetuous; these are scholarly readings (with textbook annotations to match) that are valuable as a reference source—particularly for rare pieces like *Concerto Pathétique, Grand Solo de Concert,* and *Concerto in the Hungarian Style*—rather than as the sheer entertainment they were surely meant to be. Béroff adds the *Lélio* and *Ruins of Athens Fantasies* to concertos 1 and 2, and Pierce adds Concerto 3 and the Liszt/Busoni *Spanish Rhapsody,* all of them valuable; and since both soloists are worthy proponents of the Liszt muse, it seems better to seek out both sets than split hairs choosing between them.

Several other pairings give much pleasure. That includes **Cliburn** with Ormandy, a highly satisfying coupling (RCA 7834, with Grieg's Concerto). **Douglas's** vivid and expressive account of the concertos and *Hungarian Fantasy* is by any standard—even Richter's—a splendid accomplishment (♦RCA 7916). **Freire** proves his earlier Columbia LP of *Totentanz* was no fluke with a splendid remake plus the concertos, colorful and tightly knit (Berlin 1130); and if you can find it, the concertos and *Hungarian Fantasy* played with spellbinding artistry by **Cziffra** remain indispensable (♦EMI 47640), though it's been supplanted by the "Cziffra Edition" combining the Liszt and Tchaikovsky concertos (EMI 65252).

Watts had the happy idea of coupling them with MacDowell's gloriously romantic Concerto 2—I suspect Liszt would have approved—and all three are richly satisfying with warm, full sound to match (Telarc 80429). **Tozer** is refreshingly vibrant (Chandos 9360), **Oppitz** bracing and impeccably poised (RCA 60953, with *Hungarian Fantasy*). **Brendel's** later collaboration with Haitink (concertos and *Totentanz*) is available in the "Brendel Edition" (Philips 446924) and separately (426637). You can also find his earlier recordings of all three pieces plus the Sonata and *Malédiction* in a Vox Box (5172), more swaggering than the Philips taped decades later but hampered by dismal sonics.

In concert performances of the concertos and Sonata by **Ogdon**, 1 unfortunately reflects his advancing illness (BBC 9108). **David Lively** is more convincing in the rhapsodic *Hungarian Fantasy* than in the concertos, where he seems unwilling to let his hair down (Discover). A better choice in the bargain category is **Joseph Banowetz,** more poetic than fustian, with *Totentanz* (Naxos 550187). There is a valuable document of Liszt's pupils **von Sauer** and Weingartner, who understandably demonstrate a remarkable rapport in these stirring accounts from 1938 (Pearl 9403; the earlier LP transfers had better sound).

Duchable is a powerhouse in 1, but his rushed tempos trivialize 2, and the sedate *Hungarian Fantasy* is no bonus (Erato). The same goes for **Thibaudet** (London), who also unnecessarily rewrites *Hungarian Fantasy* (so did Earl Wild, but he was more convincing). Likewise **Kocsis** does an excellent job with 1 but is dragged down by a routine 2 and a breakneck Dohnányi *Nursery Variations* (Philips). Conversely, a CD drawing together two LPs is notable more for **Jandó's** songful 2 and *Hungarian Fantasy* than **Gyula Kiss's** rather ruminative 1 and more assertive *Totentanz* (Hungaroton). **Vásáry** is refined and thoughtful, yet with no loss of impact (DG 413850).

Ivan Davis plays both works with flair, abetted by Phase 4 sound (Decca 421629). **Berezovsky** is flashy but unremarkable, further undistinguished by a bland, perfunctory *Totentanz* (Teldec). **Ax** isn't even flashy, and the Schoenberg Concerto makes a strange coupling (Sony). **Boris Berman's** readings are rapt and poetic rather than flamboyant (DG 415839), closely matched by **Arrau** (Philips 416461), if without quite the youthful abandon of his earlier recording of 1 with Ormandy. **Zimerman** has been praised effusively, but I find his rendition unexceptional (DG 423571, with *Totentanz*), which might also describe **Dichter's** nevertheless highly musical account (Philips).

Among individual recordings, pride of place surely goes to **Ogdon** in 1—taped some 20 years before the BBC version—combining power

and delicacy in an exceptional performance (♦Melodiya 33219). **Arrau** with Ormandy is more introspective and also offers the *Hungarian Fantasy* (Sony 62338, mono), while **Ozan Marsh** uses a slightly different version but seems too restrained (Vox Turnabout). **Bolet** in his prime could fend off all comers, and his Concerto 1, *Hungarian Fantasy,* and B minor Sonata have the benefit of still highly impressive sound (♦Everest 9015). **Wild's** recording shows its age sonically, but his artistry is ageless (Chesky CR93, with Chopin Concerto 1).

Rodriguez couples 1 with the Grieg and Tchaikovsky concertos in models of smoldering power and exquisitely shaded tone (Elan 2228). **Jerome Rosen** makes a nice partner for Gilels's magisterial Chopin Concerto 1 (CBS 37804). There's a good deal of flair in **Argerich's** reading, combined with the Sonata (DG 439409) or the Tchaikovsky Concerto (DG 449719). **Annie Fischer** is lyrical and fluent, a good match for Klemperer (EMI 64144, with *Midsummer Night's Dream*), while **Ousset** is highly charged and spontaneous (EMI 47221, with Saint-Saëns's Concerto 2). **Rubinstein's** 1956 collaboration with Wallenstein, also coupled with the Saint-Saëns, now seems constricted sonically (RCA 61496), but still sounds better than his 1947 version, worth having for Szymanowski's *Symphonie Concertante* (RCA 60046). **Andsnes** is loud and fast in 2, without the nobility to balance it out (Virgin).

Concerto 3 actually predates 1 and 2, but was only recently brought to light; manuscript pages were found interleaved with Concerto 1—also in E-flat—and we may thank musicologist Jay Rosenblatt for realizing that these were not mere sketches but a previously unknown work. Though lacking the polish that Liszt might have applied had he not apparently lost interest in the piece, it remains an absorbing, if brief, exercise. **Joshua Pierce** is the only one to offer all three concertos (Carlton 02147); 3 has also been recorded by **Lowenthal** (Music & Arts 803), **Steven Mayer** (ASV 778) and **Jandó** (Hungaroton 31396). Lowenthal's fanciful account is my favorite, but I'm happy to have them all.

Concerto Pathétique. This concerto is problematical; first set down for piano as *Grosses Konzertsolo,* Liszt orchestrated it a year later, calling it *Grand Solo de Concert,* and then 6 years later reworked it for two pianos as *Concerto Pathétique.* This last version in various orchestral arrangements has been recorded by **Victor Chuchkov** (AVM), **Claudio Crismani** (RS), and **Leslie Howard,** who also offers the only extant recording of the orchestral *Grand Solo de Concert* (Hyperion). Faced with the ramshackle Bulgarian ensemble on AVM and Crismani's sluggishness, Howard pretty much wins this one by default, though Liszt specialists will want all three.

Ungarische Zigeunerweisen Even more controversial, this piece is offered by **Howard** and in **Andrej Hoteev's** set of the Tchaikovsky concertos under the title *Bohemian Melodies* (Koch Schwann 6490). This seems to have been put together by Liszt's student Sophie Menter with Liszt's assistance, using melodies she provided, but Liszt suggested that she ask her good friend Tchaikovsky to orchestrate it as her own work since the two composers were not on the best of terms. Thus Hoteev treats it as a work of Tchaikovsky's in the same sodden way as the other concertos, while Howard considers it "probably written with Liszt's collaboration," but he's rather tepid in these bright dance melodies. Best of all is **Katsaris,** whose recording with Ormandy (under the title *Concerto in the Hungarian Style*) still awaits reissue (♦Angel 37888).

Grande Fantaisie Symphonique. Based on Berlioz's *Lélio,* this work is almost as rambling and garrulous as its source, the patchwork sequel to the *Symphonie Fantastique;* the far shorter *Fantasy on Beethoven's Ruins of Athens,* blending the familiar "Turkish March" with the marvelous, swirling 'Chorus of Dervishes', is a glorious pastiche all too rarely heard in concert. **Lortie** savors every phrase of the *Lélio Fantasy*, pointing up the vocal origins of the piece (Chandos 9801), while **Béroff** revels in the virtuoso passagework (EMI); **Jandó** (LaserLight 14 011) is gratifyingly swift of foot in "Brigands' Song," while **Howard** is simply tedious throughout (Hyperion). In *Ruins of Athens* he seems positively comatose, leaving the field wide open for Lortie, Béroff, Jandó, and **Philip Thomson** (Hungaroton), all safely recommendable.

De Profundis. Even Liszt devotees may be unfamiliar with his expansive setting of Psalm 130 ("Out of the depths have I called unto thee, O Lord"), a far more reflective and introspective piece than his other concertante works. **Steven Mayer** plays the piece essentially as Liszt left it, ending quietly where the manuscript breaks off (ASV 778). **Philip Thomson** (Hungaroton 31525) adds the final pages supplied by the Canadian composer Michael Maxwell, which **Howard** sets aside as "Mephisophelean," instead turning to the version prepared from the manuscript by Jay Rosenblatt with final measures by himself (Hyperion 67403/4), making the final selection as dependent on preferred version as performance.

Totentanz. A wonderfully demonic set of variations on *Dies Irae,* the familiar plainchant for the dead, this piece is every bit as compelling as the concertos and is often included with them on disc. Busoni's edition of the score, which incorporates the same *De Profundis* chorale as the earlier work, is occasionally encountered, but the so-called "final version" is played most often. **Lewenthal** combines elements of both versions, including *De Profundis*—a heady brew indeed (♦Elan 82284, with works by Rubinstein, Adolph von Henselt, and Alkan)—while **Steven Mayer** plays the Busoni "straight" (ASV 778, with *De Profundis* and Concerto 3), and **Howard** offers both. **György Oravecz**'s powerhouse account of *Totentanz* in the standard piano-orchestra setting is far more compelling than his solo piano version (Hungaroton 31461, with a virile *Hungarian Fantasy*). **Janis** and Reiner remain hard to beat in *Totentanz,* and the remainder of the program is likewise self-recommending (♦RCA 61250, with Rachmaninoff's *Isle of the Dead,* Ravel's *Rapsodie Espagnole,* etc.).

Other concertante works. Top contenders in the *Hungarian Fantasy* include **Wild** (♦Chesky 50, with the Grieg concerto and Saint-Saëns's 2) and **Cherkassky** with Karajan (DG 415967), along with **Bolet** (Everest), **Cziffra,** and **Douglas.** On London **Bolet** offers flair without panache in *Totentanz, Hungarian Fantasy;* and *Malédiction.* **Ozan Marsh** plays the Liszt/Busoni *Spanish Rhapsody* without much enthusiasm, and his *Totentanz* is the piano-only version (Vox). **Lowenthal** plays two different editions of *Malédiction,* but the one for chamber ensemble seems redundant; fortunately in both the "real" *Malédiction* and *Totentanz* he's far more persuasive (Music & Arts 803, with Concertos 1 and 3).

Ponti offers a potent *Malédiction* in Vol. 4 of the "Romantic Piano Concerto" series (Vox 5067), but at **Claudio Crismani**'s soporific tempos it becomes more of a "Bénédiction" (RS 6367). *Hexaméron* is included in **Howard**'s survey, a curious set of variations largely based on Bellini's *I Puritani* and calling for contributions from Chopin, Czerny, Sigismond Thalberg, Johann Peter Pixis, and Henri Herz as well as Liszt; it was also recorded by **List** (Turnabout LP), but once you've heard it played in concert by **Lewenthal** and five colleagues, one lone pianist hardly seems worth bothering with.

Liszt's virtuoso rewrites of Schubert's *Wanderer Fantasy* and Weber's *Polonaise Brillante* (he also noodled around with Weber's *Konzertstück*)

may be considered either affectionate homage or outright hubris; certainly the Schubert benefits greatly from the added play of winds and strings, while the Weber is simply a joy whatever the version. **Lortie** is hearty and lovingly phrased, if hardly mercurial in Schubert's grand closing fugue (Chandos, with *Lélio* and *Ruins of Athens*); **Pierce** (Carlton) and **Béroff** (EMI) are sturdy and purposeful, **Thomson** more broadly lyrical (Hungaroton), with **Howard** bringing up the rear (Hyperion).

HALLER

PIANO MUSIC

"Chopin, the aristocrat, was a pianist *da camera;* Liszt, the eloquent tribune, was a man of the stage". This perceptive comment in J.J. Eigeldinger's *Chopin, Pianist and Teacher* explains many of the fundamental differences in the piano music of these two pianist-composers. While Liszt was criss-crossing Europe in the 1830s and 1840s on concert tours, his first major works were opera paraphrases designed to dazzle his audiences. However, Brahms later said of them, "Whoever really wants to know what Liszt did for the piano will study his opera fantasies. They represent the perfection of piano technique." In 1847 he retired from the concert platform (at age 36) to settle in Weimar for "self composure and work." During these middle years he created an imposing repertoire of more serious piano compositions, such as the great Etudes, Concertos, Sonata in B Minor, and many works with a programmatic basis.

His teaching assumed more importance, and he cast a longer shadow than any other pedagogue of the 19th century, with the possible exception of Leschetizky in Vienna. Over 400 pianists studied with him, including some of the greatest virtuosos of the 19th and 20th centuries, like Tausig, von Bülow, von Sauer, d'Albert, and Rosenthal. As a teacher, he didn't discuss technique and declared, "Technique should create itself from spirit, not mechanics."

The last phase can be dated from 1861, when he left Weimar for Rome. Increasing introspection and melancholy gave rise to pieces of deep expressivity and religiosity, generally lacking overt brilliance. Gradually, the "ashen" pieces began to emerge: music of introspection (*Valse oubliée*), despair (*Aux cyprès de la Villa d'Este*), and death (*La lugubre gondola*). Some of these works embarrassed his family and friends, who found them incomprehensible. They were more futuristic than Wagner (*Bagatelle ohne Tonart, Nuages gris*) and many would not be published or played until the 1950s.

I can name only a handful of pianists who are ideal interpreters of Chopin's piano music. With Liszt, the roll of pianists who have recorded outstanding performances of his works reads like a "Who's Who" of the piano world. For ease of reference, I have organized the discussion of these recordings into four categories: (1) historical recordings by pupils of Liszt, (2) all-Liszt CDs; (3) a few memorable recordings that are part of multicomposer CDs; and (4) a cross-referenced list of recommended recordings of the major works.

Liszt pupils

Nine pupils of the master can be heard in a recording in which seven play works by Liszt (Pearl 9972, 2CD). In several cases, we sense that the performers were past their prime when these recordings were made (Sauer was 79, Lamond 73), and the sound is antiquated for all seven. However, **Eugene d'Albert**'s playing of *Au bord d'une source* alone is well worth the price of the set. By some magic, he makes the music actually sound like a brooklet, something Liszt probably did to perfection.

Unfortunately, **Moriz Rosenthal** didn't record much Liszt. Pearl 9339 contains an exquisitely evocative *Chant Polonaise* ("My Joys";

Chopin, arr. Liszt)—among the greatest recordings by any of the old pianists (also on Appian 7013, with other selections played by Rachmaninoff, Hofmann, Godowsky, and Lhevinne). Pearl 9963 has "The Maiden's Wish" (Chopin, arr. Liszt) and *Soirée de Vienne* 6 (Schubert, arr. Liszt), which by legend was one of the last three pieces Liszt played only days before his death. The last two are also available with extensive information on Rosenthal and many other piano works, mostly by Chopin (Appian 7002, 2CD).

The art of the Scotsman **Frederic Lamond** can be heard on Pearl 9911: *Liebestraum* 3; *Feux follets* (which he played at his recital in London in 1886 in Liszt's presence), where there are a few perilous moments; *Waldesrauschen; Sonnetto 104 del Petrarca; Gnomenreigen* (pretty tame, slow-moving gnomes!); *Un sospiro; Valse-Impromptu;* and the "Tarantella" from *Venezia e Napoli,* as well as three transcriptions. There are missed notes here and there, but *Un sospiro* is memorable and the playing is generally elegant. The original recordings were made between 1927 and 1936 and the sound has been very successfully remastered.

All-Liszt CDs

The Australian-British pianist **Leslie Howard** has just completed one of the most comprehensive recording projects ever attempted with his complete Liszt piano works in 57 volumes (Hyperion). It would be unrealistic to expect every piece on these 94 CDs to reach an equal artistic level, but Howard at his best is a magnificent artist. An example of an outstanding disc is Vol. 2, which contains, among other pieces, the two *Ballades, Polonaises,* and *Légends* (♦66301). His thrilling performance of *St. Francis de Paule marchant sur les flots* (St. Francis de Paul Walking on the Waters) is in a class by itself. Also look for the admirably played Waltzes in Vol. 1 (♦66201), as well as for an especially interesting disc with *Hexaméron* coupled with Liszt's famous arrangement of Berlioz's *Symphonie Fantastique* (♦66433). The final volume, containing 19 *Hungarian Rhapsodies* (67418/19) is a disappointment, for the playing is staid and careful, though all the notes are there in perfect order. For each volume, Howard has written valuable commentaries, the results of his exhaustive and penetrating musicological research into the music.

Naxos has initiated a series that offers discs with superior sound at a bargain price. Unlike the Hyperion series, where Howard has recorded the entire corpus, Naxos spreads the works among various artists. The superb Michael Ponti offers the *Fantasy and Fugue on B-A-C-H* and the *Weinen, Klagen Variations* (550408). The Canadian pianist Valerie Tryon, whose recordings have been highly praised, presents the transcriptions of David's *Bunte Blätter* in Vol. 14 (553507) and of a series of vocal works in Vol. 11 (553508). More song transcriptions are performed by Oxana Yablonskaya in Vol. 5 and by Joseph Banowicz in Vol. 6. Jenö Jandó has been assigned some of the most taxing works: the *Transcendental Etudes* (Vol. 2), the B minor Sonata with several other well-known pieces (Vol. 8), and the 19 *Hungarian Rhapsodies* (Vols. 12 and 13). In the *Rhapsodies,* his businesslike playing left me with a neutral impression, though the sound and accompanying liner notes are excellent.

"Liszt's 19 Hungarian Rhapsodies Played by 19 Great Pianists" is a splendid release that should be owned by every Liszt fan (♦VAIA 1066, 2CD). These recordings date from 1926 (Cortot, No. 11) to 1993 (Janice Weber, No. 19) and each one is a classic. Since an attempt was made to secure the best available recording of each Rhapsody for this set, it's not easy to single out the exceptional ones. Certainly Moiseiwitsch's 2, Nyiregyházi's dark and dramatic 3, Arrau's 13, and Cziffra's 16 deserve special mention. But at least four of the greatest recordings of the Rhapsodies are absent: Horowitz's 6 and 19 and Rubinstein's 10 and 12, which have probably never been equaled.

Roberto Szidon's playing of all 19 Rhapsodies is brilliant and well conceived, but the sound is shallow and dry (DG 423925, 2CD). **Janina Fialkowska**'s disc may be the premier piano recording of the '90s (♦Musica Viva 1035). Included are *Mephisto Waltz, Venezia e Napoli,* "The Maiden's Wish," "Hark, Hark, the Lark" (Schubert, arr. Liszt), "Widmung" (Schumann, arr. Liszt), *Sonetto 123 del Petrarca,* and *Transcendental Etudes* 5, 9, and 12. The playing is breathtaking, exceptionally beautiful, and strongly infused with a palpable Lisztian spirit. The recorded sound is ideal.

Although **Rubinstein** wasn't famous for his Liszt, his one Liszt CD ranks very high even in his Parnassian discography and has three of his finest recorded performances: *Funérailles* and *Hungarian Rhapsodies* 10 and 12 (♦RCA 61860). His *Liebestraum* 3 is scarcely to be excelled for sheer beauty. Rubinstein's unique tone is salient at many points in these pieces, where most pianists, even the best, tend to bang away at their instruments. Also included are the B minor Sonata, *Mephisto Waltz* 1, *Valse oubliée,* a captivating *Valse-Impromptu, Consolation* 3, and three short pieces by his namesake, Anton Rubinstein. The sound, originally mono, is a little sub par.

Several of these standard works appear on **Horowitz**'s all-Liszt CD, also a remastered mono recording, which includes the Sonata in B minor, *Funérailles, Mephisto Waltz* 1, *Consolation* 3, and *Ballade* 2 (RCA 5935). While I prefer Rubinstein's approach, Horowitz was a supreme Liszt player with an often dazzling brilliance that couldn't be duplicated.

A recording made on Liszt's own Chickering piano, now in the Liszt Academy in Budapest, is of special interest (BIS 244). **Dag Achatz** has put together a varied program, extremely well played: *Consolation* 3, *Hungarian Rhapsody* 3, *Liebestraum* 3, *Ballade* 2, *Les jeux d'eau, Nuages gris, En rêve, La lugubre gondola* 2, and *Am Grabe R. Wagners.* The sonority of this piano may be a revelation to listeners, with its transparency throughout the compass and its glassy treble.

Dezsö Ránki has recorded a wonderful disc with many of the late, less familiar works (♦Harmonia Mundi 903024). The playing and sound are faultless, and there is an especially powerful projection of mood in these fascinating pieces with their "ashen" tone color. The program includes Sonata in B minor, *Unstern!, En rêve, Klavierstück in F-sharp, La lugubre gondola* 2, *Wiegenlied, In Festo Transfigurationis, Impromptu, Sancta Dorothea, Mephisto Waltz* 4, *Mephisto Polka, Csárdás* 1, and *Csárdás obstinée.*

Jorge Bolet, another justly celebrated Lisztian, recorded a large cross section of his works in the '80s (London, at least six CDs). Bolet's musical tone and transcendental technique made for some very beautiful performances, though his tendency toward dreaminess occasionally resulted in markedly slow tempos. Among the works he recorded were *Années de Pèlerinage* Books I and II, *Venezia e Napoli, Les jeux d'eau, Bénédiction de Dieu, Ballade* 2, and other standard pieces, including the *Rigoletto Paraphrase.* These recordings should be acquired by the serious collector. Some are on London 444851 (2CD), and two volumes of Philips's "Great Pianists of the 20th Century" series are devoted to Bolet and contain a number of his Liszt performances.

Earl Wild's "The Daemonic Liszt" has *Mephisto Waltz* 1, *Mephisto Polka,* two *Etudes de Concert, Réminiscences de Don Juan,* and others (♦Vanguard 4035). The performances of this great artist are of uncommon distinction, and this recording has already—and rightly—become a classic.

To some extent, the same can be said of **Alfred Brendel**'s several collections. One offers six *Hungarian Rhapsodies* and *Csárdás obstinée* (Vanguard 4024). A 25CD set includes a wide selection of Liszt's works, some with orchestra, as well as other composers (Philips 46920). His Vox Box (5172, 2CD) earns a mixed recommendation. The four works for piano and orchestra are all available (except for *Malédiction*) in superior performances by others, but on the second disc of this set we find some of his finest playing from early in his career: Sonata in B Minor, "Dante" Sonata, *Bagatelle ohne Tonart, Czárdás macabre* in an unrivaled performance, *La lugubre gondola* 2, and *Mephisto Waltz* 1. Brendel's characteristic hard tone in the more brilliant pieces is sometimes a bit unpleasant, unfortunately accentuated by the remastered sound.

Other exceptional all-Liszt discs, all by younger pianists, include the following:

Marc-André Hamelin. Two discs are distinguished by Hamelin's wonderful pianism: Music & Arts 723 contains six works with a marvelous *La leggierezza* and *Un sospiro,* and Hyperion 66874 contains nine, with the seldom heard *Apparition* 1, a superb *Waldesrauschen,* several late pieces, and *Hungarian Rhapsodies* 10 and 13.

Stephen Hough. Two discs have sensitive and impeccable performances by one of the elite among the younger pianists: *Mephisto Waltz* 1, *Tarantella, Rhapsodie espagnole, Bénédiction de Dieu,* and others (Virgin 790700), and "Dante" Sonata, *Les jeux d'eau, La lugubre gondola* 1 and 2, *Cypresses de la Villa d'Este* 1 and 2, and others (Virgin 59222).

Zoltán Kocsis. Années de Pèlerinage Book III offers brilliant, insightful playing by this admirable artist (Philips 420174).

Károly Mocsári. "Dante" Sonata, *Fantasia and Fugue on B-A-C-H, La leggierezza,* and others—I prefer Mocsári's "Dante" to all others (Hungaroton 31203)

Jeffrey Swann. Two discs by Swann have a special slot in my library. He has a daredevil quality and sometimes misses a note, but there's a freshness and immediacy that are quite unique and can be electrifying. The sound is excellent in both: all four *Mephisto Waltzes,* the last four *Hungarian Rhapsodies,* and two *Hungarian Historical Portraits* (Music & Arts 245); two *Apparitions,* six *Consolations,* three *Csárdás,* seven *Hungarian Historical Portraits,* and *Hungarian Rhapsodies* 5 and 12 (Arkadia 113.1).

Janice Weber. 12 *Transcendental Etudes,* 1838 version—formidable playing of the earlier, more difficult version (MCAD 25890).

Krystian Zimerman. Sonata in B Minor, *Nuages gris, La notte, La lugubre gondola* 2, *Funérailles*—superlative sound and very stylish performances (DG 431780).

Exceptional recordings in multicomposer collections

Claudio Arrau. Four *Paganini Etudes, Au bord d'une source, La leggierezza,* "Hark, Hark the Lark!," *Valse mélancholique, Les jeux d'eau, Rhapsodie espagnole* (abridged) (Marston 52023, 2CD). As a student of Martin Krause in Berlin (who studied with Liszt), Arrau had an unusually close affinity with Liszt's music throughout his life. This is audible in his miraculously artistic playing of these pieces, in which the master's spirit seems to hover, wraith-like, in the background. The set includes works by Chopin, Schumann, Debussy, and others.

Simon Barere. La Leggierezza, Sonnetto 104 del Petrarca; Gnomenreigen, Réminiscences de Don Juan, Valse oubliée 1, *Rhapsodie espagnole* (Appian 7001, 2CD). Barere's 1934 Liszt recordings form part of an ex-

tensive selection of his Romantic repertoire on this release, which was awarded the Grand Prix du Disque by the Liszt Society in Budapest—a somewhat curious choice, given that there only six works by Liszt on the two CDs. Odessa-born Barere was a pianist of immense facility, who could play almost anything faster than anyone else and took pleasure in doing so. His sudden death on the stage of Carnegie Hall in 1951 was a tragic loss for the piano world. These recordings show him at the peak of his form; they're very fast, which at times, when speed substitutes for pure musicality, is a bit of a detriment.

Josef Hofmann. Etude de Concert 1, *Waldesrauschen* (Vol. 4, VAIA 1047)—still the greatest recording of this ever made (1922-23).

Vladimir Horowitz. Hungarian Rhapsody 6, *Valse oubliée* 1 (RCA 60463). Horowitz recorded the *Rhapsody* in 1947. His playing is thrilling, has never been excelled, and shows him at the peak of his almost superhuman brilliance. *Valse oubliée* was recorded in 1930. Horowitz could do things at the piano no one else could, and some of them are heard in the *Rhapsody.* He recorded *Au bord d'une source* and *Valse oubliée* 1 again during concerts in 1967 and 1970 (Music & Arts 666, 2CD). The playing is visionary, and the sound is resonant and realistic.

Edward Kilenyi. Venezia e Napoli 1 and 3, *Hungarian Rhapsodies* 8 and 15, *Rakoczy March,* and *Mephisto Waltz* 1 (Piano Library 226). These recordings date from 1937–38 (as do the Chopin Etudes Op. 10 that fill out the disc), a few years after Kilenyi completed his studies with Dohnányi. The recorded sound shows its age, but the performances are fiery and full of temperament. The *Mephisto Waltz* nearly runs off the tracks toward the end, but it's good to remember that this sort of thing happened all the time in the old days, when technical perfection was valued much less than overall effect.

Victor Merzhanov. Grandes Etudes de Paganini (Austrian Sony RCD 16 201, with Brahms's *Paganini Variations*). Merzhanov is one of the "greats" in the Russian piano school, a contemporary of Gilels and Richter. While they were students of Neuhaus, he studied with Samuel Feinberg and later taught at the Moscow Conservatory. This recording was made in the '50s and has never been equaled for technical perfection and sheer brilliance.

Cross-references for major works, with recommended performances
Années de pèlerinage
Complete:
    Swann (Arkadia 108, 2CD)
Year I, Switzerland:
    Fiorentino (APR 5583)
    Bolet (London 410160)
Year II, Italy:
    Dalberto (Denon 75500)
    Bolet (London 410161)
Venezia e Napoli
    Fialkowska (Musica Viva 1035)
    Bolet (London 411803)
Year III
    Kocsis (Philips 420174)

Etudes de Concert S 144
2. *La leggierezza* and 3. *Un sospiro*
    Hamelin (Music & Arts 723)

Etudes de Concert S 145 (Concert Studies)

1. *Waldesrauschen*
   Hofmann (Vol. 4, VAIA 1047)
   Hamelin (Hyperion 66874)
2. *Gnomenreigen*
   Perahia (Sony, 47180)

Etudes d'exécution transcendante (Transcendental Etudes)
   Bolet (Decca 414601)
   Weber, 1838 version (MCAD 25890)

Grandes Etudes de Paganini
   Merzhanov (RCD 16209; Sony Austria; "Russian Piano School")

Harmonies poétiques et religieuses
   Ciccolini (EMI 754142, 2CD, with opera paraphrases)

Hungarian Rhapsodies
   "The 19 Hungarian Rhapsodies Played by 19 Great Pianists" (VAI 1066, 2CD)

Mephisto Waltz 1
   Rubinstein (RCA 5673)
   Fialkowska (Musica Viva 1035)
   Horowitz (RCA 5935)
   Hough (Virgin 790700)
   Kapell (RCA 60921)
   Kilenyi (Enterprise 226)

Opera Paraphrases
"Liebestod" from *Tristan und Isolde* (Wagner)
   Horowitz (Sony 45818)
Overture to Tannhäuser (Wagner)
   Bolet (Philips 456724, 2CD)
Réminiscences de *Don Juan* (Mozart)
   Hamelin (Hyperion 66874)
   Bolet (London 44851, 2CD)
Réminiscences de *Lucia di Lammermoor* (Donizetti)
   Bolet (Philips 456721, 2CD)
Réminiscences de *Norma* (Bellini)
   Hamelin (Music & Arts 723)
Réminiscences de *Robert le diable:* "Valse infernale" (Meyerbeer)
   Killian (MD+G 3432)
Rigoletto Paraphrase (Verdi)
   Bolet (London 410257)
"Spinnerlied" from *Der fliegende Holländer* (Wagner)
   Wild (Onyx 104)

Sonata in B minor
   Ránki (Harmonia Mundi 9030224)
   Zimerman (DG 431780)
   Rubinstein (RCA 5673)

Since this sonata is probably Liszt's greatest solo piano work, played by nearly all serious pianists at one time or another, a few additional comments are in order. In the midst of many contenders for top billing, **Ránki** and **Zimerman** are unchallenged. Both play the piece with elevated musicality and wonderful tone. Zimerman is dramatic and rhetorical, while Ránki is subtle and extremely polished. **Rubinstein** is the clearest and most cohesive, and also one of the fastest; he requires only 26:44 compared to Ránki's 28:49 and Zimerman's 30:37. Yet his account is slightly tepid and you sense that his empathy for this work is less pronounced than with most of his other repertoire.

Brendel's early recording is notable for its powerful projection of mood, but there are a few laborious passages (Vox). **Horowitz** is fiery and intense, but this isn't one of his great recordings (RCA 5935). Two pianists who you might assume would excel in this work are actually not among the top choices—**Richter** and **Gilels.** Richter's Philips CD is very good but less interesting than the first three choices. Another recording presents his live performance in Aldeburgh in 1966, and it's one of the worst Richter recordings I've heard, full of mistakes and a lot of chaotic playing (Nuovo Era 013.6340). For sheer excitement, Gilels is unrivaled, but he too commits his share of missed notes, and his tone is frequently almost unbearable in its stridency (Theorema 121.126).

Finally, there are a few recordings which, though I've never heard them and can't comment on them, deserve to be mentioned by virtue of the fine reputation they have among connoisseurs:

Mark Anderson (Nimbus 5484)
Alexander Brailowsky (Piano Library 251)
György Cziffra (Angel 56228; APR 7021, 2CD; Philips 456760, 2CD)
Louis Kentner (Vox 5503, 2CD; APR 5514)
Minoru Nojima (Reference 25)   MULBURY

ORGAN MUSIC

Three outstanding virtuoso pieces—*Fantasia and Fugue on Ad nos, ad salutarem undam* (1855), *Variations on Weinen, Klagen, Sorgen, Zagen* (1863), and *Prelude and Fugue on B-A-C-H* (1870)—dominate Liszt's organ works, though in performance time they account for only about one fifth of his output for the instrument. The remaining four fifths may be less technically difficult, but many of them demand just as much artistic sensibility. Quite a few are very late works in the spare and cryptic idiom that Liszt cultivated in his last years. Many are reworkings—sometimes extensive—of pieces originally composed for other media, mainly orchestra or chorus. More than half are devotional or liturgical, and in many of them Liszt exploits the sustaining power of the organ in introspective meditations that seem to evoke eternity, making coherent performance that much harder.

András Virágh has recorded the "complete" organ works on the 1889 József Angster organ at Pécs Cathedral (♦Hungaroton 31701/05, 5CD). The recording doesn't include Liszt's transcriptions of works by other composers, and *San Francesco* (1880)—a piece derived from a 1862 composition for men's chorus and orchestra—is omitted without explanation. The instrument is well suited to the music: a dark and romantic sound that's ferocious in bigger registrations and intense rather than sweet in quieter ones. A lot of detail may get lost in the rich reverberation, but the overall effect is worth it. Virágh communicates a profound understanding of this music in performances that are always thoughtful and sensitive; nothing is merely tossed off. You may not agree with every interpretive or registrational decision, but this is an achievement of the first magnitude. The more I hear of others, the better I like Virágh.

Donald Sutherland is at almost the opposite end of the scale; he plays *Weinen, Ad nos,* an abridged version of *Evocation à la Chapelle Sixtine,* and an arrangement for trombone and organ of 'Cujus animam' from Rossini's *Stabat Mater* on an instrument curiously lacking in mid-range tone (Gothic). Compared with Virágh, Sutherland seems impatient and perfunctory, especially in *Weinen* and the smaller pieces. His *Ad nos* is more effective, easily the best performance on the disc, but not enough to save the whole. **Jennifer Bate** plays the Big Three plus Schumann's Op. 58 *Sketches* at the Royal Albert Hall (ASV). This is a reissue of a 1977 recording, and the recorded sound betrays its age: thin, shallow, and dry. Tempos tend to be very fast, but speed in this case doesn't produce dramatic sweep or precipitous excitement.

Hans Fagius leaves a mixed impression in his 1980 recording of the Big Three on the mid-'70s instrument at St. Catherine's Church, Stockholm (BIS 170). There is real excitement in *B-A-C-H* and *Ad nos* with ferocious organ sound and fast tempos. *Weinen,* on the other hand, seems to misfire. There's little sense of penitential brooding in the quieter variations; it all seems rather superficial.

Martin Haselböck plays the Big Three plus *Trauerode* on the 1913 Rieger organ in the Great Hall of the Vienna Konzerthaus (Orfeo 125901). The instrument makes a magnificent sound in an acoustic that's warm but not churchly, allowing details to come through with great clarity. The performances themselves are flashy and superficial. The best, oddly enough, is *B-A-C-H;* Haselböck gives it a persuasive dramatic sweep.

Marie-Claire Alain and **Daniel Roth** have recorded the Big Three on two notable Cavaillé-Coll organs: Alain at Orleans Cathedral in 1987 (Erato 88241) and Roth at St. Sulpice (Paris) in 1993 (Motette 12021). In both cases the fiery organ tone and spacious acoustic are well suited to the repertory. Alain conveys a greater sense of dramatic propulsion in the faster and louder sections, but is less convincing in the quieter or slower passages: There is little serenity and coherence in *Ad nos* and hardly any sense of the brooding, elegiac nature of *Weinen.* Roth is better in these selections, but some of his registrations are so quiet (or recorded at such a low level) that the music seems more overheard than heard. He produces some effective orchestral effects in the slow middle section of *Ad nos.*

There are far too many recordings of individual pieces from the Big Three to mention them individually. The more I hear, the more I'm convinced that there's something very elusive in Liszt's organ works, and while any number of artists can play the notes, very few can really find the music. Opinions will differ about them, but among those that deserve notice is **Karol Golebiowski**'s *Ad nos* at St. Catherine's, Stockholm (Pavane 7318, with Julius Reubke's Psalm 94 Sonata). He takes all tempos on the fast side, making the work seem less monumental, but this may be just the thing for the listener who wants to be dazzled by virtuoso technique and headlong excitement.

John Scott gives a fine reading of *Ad nos* at St. Paul's Cathedral (Guild 7128, with works by Langlais and others). He's every bit as exciting as Golebiowski, though not nearly as profound as Virágh. The recorded sound seems to accentuate the organ's upperwork to the extent that the bigger registrations sound brash and screaming, and the essential gravity of this immense instrument in an immense room is lost. The impression is far different in Scott's recording of Mendelssohn for Hyperion.

Catharine Crozier includes *B-A-C-H* in a disc of German Romantic music played at Grace Cathedral, San Francisco (Delos 3090). I prefer a more ferocious sound, but her consummate artistry does get to the music in this piece, while most others just wallow in its chromatic thickets. **Mark Laubach** includes a sensitive and highly musical reading of *Ad nos* in a disc that includes Reubke's Sonata and Edwin Henry Lemare's transcription of the *Meistersinger* Prelude (Pro Organo 7045). The instrument is a 1938 Skinner, rebuilt and enlarged in 1993 by Reuter. It too lacks ferocity for the loud sections, but the Skinner's smoothness, refinement, and color, plus Laubach's artistry, make for as lovely a performance of the slow middle section as you can hope to hear.

GATENS

CHORAL MUSIC

Liszt took his choral compositions very seriously, especially after he enrolled in minor religious orders, and you can often detect a sense of attempted profundity in them. It often fails, as it does in so much of his music. But if we begin to accept Liszt's efforts on his own terms instead of our expectations, a lot of the fog lifts, and these pieces can be exceptionally rewarding.

Christus is by far the longest, most ambitious work he ever attempted in any genre. This sprawling, utterly magnificent oratorio is heavily criticized as over-sentimental, bombastic, and religiously obtuse, but it's also one of the finest things he ever created, a splendid testament to the creative powers he struggled with all his life. It's not a *Passion* like Bach's, nor is it a religious drama. Instead, it's a spiritualized *life* that unfolds simply and naturally, the presence of Jesus woven through the work like an unheard *leitmotif.* Modern audiences haven't been kind to it, but the work was enthusiastically received after its 1866 completion in the Vatican after a three-year gestation. It's full of charm, drama, and great melodic power, one of the loveliest pieces he ever wrote.

Dorati and the Hungarian State Orchestra gave it a noble try (and a very fine one), but that recording is NA, though you might find it in the bargain bins (♦Hungaroton 12831, 3CD). But it hardly matters, as **Rilling** leaves absolutely nothing to be desired. His Stuttgart Radio Symphony and choruses sing a wonderfully subtle, meltingly radiant performance that's high on lyricism and glittering sound. The impact of the more powerful passages is striking, and if you don't feel a chill in your spine during much of this piece, your heart is hard indeed. Don't miss one of the greatest experiences of choral listening (♦Hänssler 98121, 3CD).

Liszt wrote a number of sacred works for practical use. His *Requiem* isn't very well known; **Ferencsik** and the Hungarian Army Chorus offer an interesting take on it that probably won't be to your liking, but it's the only one currently listed (Hungaroton). *Hungarian Coronation Mass* is another work with few takers, but this time there's a fine version in excellent sound by **György Lehel** with the Budapest Symphony and Hungarian Radio Chorus (♦Hungaroton 12148). *Missa Choralis,* a stunning work that has some fabulously fine-spun, delicate melodic ideas, is available in a sumptuous recording by **Heinz Hennig** and the Hanover Boys Choir (♦Ars Musici 1129, with Widor's Mass Op. 36 and Kodály's *Pange Lingua*). **Ferencsik** also recorded *Missa Solemnis,* but it's difficult to obtain; it may serve in a pinch, but I'd wait for better days (Hungaroton).

Via Crucis is getting a lot of attention these days, and strangely so, because it's not one of the composer's best works. Nevertheless, in this time of "chant" mania and meditation, it serves as a tonic for those wishing to slow down life for a while—and slow down it does, almost to a halt. Recordings that attempt to jump-start it are by and large the most successful. **Diego Fasolis**'s version in "Sacred Choral Music" isn't one of them; Liszt's rather bold experiment in the reduction of his complex harmonic schemes to serve the liturgical meaning of the words finds little help in this performance, weak and anemic in its approach. The couplings fare much better: *Ave Maria, Pater Noster,* and *Die Seligreisungen* (The Beatitudes), with some fine choral work by the Choir of Radio Svizzera, Lugano. But even at the cheap price, *Via Crucis* takes up too much space (Naxos).

A better choice for *Via Crucis* is **Andre Lynch**'s powerful recording, with a very prominent, very concentrated and substantial organ part that makes all the difference. The singing is beyond reproach, and the coupling (*Ad nos, Ad salutarem undam*) provides another rarity that's given a wonderful reading by organist Chantal De Zeeuw (♦Pierre Verany 788122). **Ebbe Munk** and the Vox Danica Chamber Choir offer an expensive but worthwhile collection of choral Lisztiana that includes *Via Crucis* (♦Danica 8145), and a similar collection is presented by the Hungarian State Chorus under **Gabor Ugrin** (♦Hungaroton 31103). If you want to sample Liszt's choral music, you can't do better than either of these last two. RITTER

SONGS

Liszt's songs, which cling tenaciously to the fringe of the standard lieder repertory, are "interesting" rather than memorable. With a few notable exceptions, the composer doesn't write melodies that lodge permanently in the mind, and when he does, he can't develop them. ("O Lieb," which was transformed into the immortal *Liebestraum* for piano, is the classic example.) Nor does he searchingly explore and lay bare the emotional heart of his chosen poetry. The songs grow on the listener as they become more and more familiar, and an all-Liszt recital can be absorbing and enjoyable (cerebrally, at least), but not everyone will find the experience a haunting one.

The composer was an inveterate reviser, and several of the songs exist in variant editions. The two albums that aspire to "completeness" both fall short. Perhaps the best library version comes from five singers (Donna Brown, Gabriele Schreckenbach, Haefliger, de Mey, and Huttenlocher); they share 74 songs, and the readings have the great advantage of variety (Adda 581084, 4CD). The booklet lists alternate, unperformed versions of the songs and supplies texts and translations. Unfortunately, both Haefliger and Huttenlocher were caught past their prime, and de Mey barely has any voice to work with at all. The two ladies are more satisfactory. Another set more modestly claimed to comprise the complete songs for tenor only and added some items missing from Adda; it also omitted some important numbers that are perfectly suited to the tenor voice, even if not specifically written for it (Thesis, 3CD). The real problem here is the performer. Much as one admires **Bruce Brewer**'s ambition, his frail voice doesn't have the resources to bring the songs to life.

Let us leap at once from sporadic competence to assured mastery. **Fischer-Dieskau**'s set, recorded in 1979 and 1981, should be the cornerstone of any Liszt song collection (♦DG 447508, 3CD). He begins with two of the most famous—"O Lieb" and "Es muss ein Wunderbares sein"—and sculpts the melodies so lovingly and colors his voice so sensitively to the harmonic shifts that they almost sound new. The 44 songs are a mix of the familiar and the little known, and hearing them sung by this particular voice seems to confer a canonical status on them all: if they're worthy of Fischer-Dieskau's artistry, they can't be all that far away from the center of the repertory. It helps greatly that he has as his accompanist a virtuoso pianist and Liszt expert, Barenboim. The liabilities are slight: The singer is less trenchant in Italian and French than in German, and his voice at the time of the recording had lost much of its nap. It was in better estate when he recorded 12 songs with Demus in 1962, and they have been reissued as part of DG's "Fischer-Dieskau Edition," coupled with six of the later Barenboim accounts. If you don't want three CDs of Liszt, this is an excellent sampler (♦DG 463508).

Gedda was an experienced singer who recorded Liszt too late in the day; the two discs he made in 1986 demand some generous forbearance from the listener (Bluebell). He could still manage the high version of the Petrarch songs, and his idiomatic command of four languages (German, French, Italian, and English) is a great asset for a Liszt interpreter, but his voice is too often dry and sour. I wish he had made the recordings about 20 years earlier, when his lean timbre had more spin and softness,

but there's still much to savor, especially in the second volume, and Gedda's many admirers may be able to listen through the flaws.

Aler has a high tenor not unlike Gedda's, and he's in healthier voice for a recital of 17 songs (♦Newport 60028). He passes over some familiar numbers but offers the four Victor Hugo favorites and the three Petrarch sonnets, bringing some elegance to the French songs and strong, easy top notes to the Italian. **Langridge** is another winning tenor, perhaps because he doesn't strain for effect but addresses the songs in a natural, responsive manner (♦Unicorn 9162). There are 18 of them on his program, all in excellent German.

Other British interpreters have done admirable service to Liszt. **Baker**'s communicative 1980 recital of a dozen songs skirts the most familiar pieces, and the singing is almost too hushed, too inward, but it's well worth hearing (♦EMI 573836, with Mendelssohn and Schumann). **Margaret Price**'s 1986 recording, with another virtuoso accompanist (Katsaris), is altogether lovely (♦Teldec 43342). It's particularly interesting to hear a soprano voice in the Petrarch sonnets, but the bracing, radiant accounts of the familiar German numbers yield even more pleasure. **Fassbaender** has given us a disc and a half of Liszt songs, but her recital with Thibaudet at the piano isn't widely available in the United States (♦Decca 430512). The nine songs on another disc show her range: bitter and ferocious in "Vergiftet sind meine Lieder," warm and affecting in "Es muss ein Wunderbares sein" and "Oh! quand je dors" (♦DG 419238).

The promising young mezzo **Marilyn Schmiege** is less intense than Fassbaender and less polished than Price. Her program of 18 songs includes the Petrarch sonnets and some French numbers (among them the strangely compelling "Joan of Arc at the Stake," also recorded by Fassbaender) but sticks mostly to the familiar German lieder (Orfeo). She's often a rough vocalist, but sings with enough commitment and imagination to merit a place in a sparsely filled arena. More satisfying is a half-Liszt recital from **Hampson,** who is as fluent in German and French as Gedda and even more persuasive in the English of Tennyson's "Go not, happy day" (♦EMI 55047, with rarely heard Berlioz and Wagner). Like Fischer-Dieskau, he brings his own sense of wonder and discovery to the familiar pieces. Soprano **Janet Obermeyer** sings 18 songs in an inexpensive disc (♦Quicksilva 6209). Her readings aren't particularly individual, but her voice is fresh and supple, and the selection is choice.

Among the out-of-print Liszt recitals that deserve reissue are the earlier recordings of Fischer-Dieskau with Demus (DG), a set by Prey (EMI), and a disc by Hildegard Behrens that was too young to die so soon (DG). Souzay's old Ducretet-Thomson 10-inch LP commands exorbitant prices from second-hand dealers; its resurrection is long overdue. Collectors who search through various anthologies may find many other recordings of Liszt's songs, a handful at a time, but Fischer-Dieskau, Price, Fassbaender, and Aler together leave little to be desired. LUCANO

George Lloyd (1913–1998)

Lloyd's music is full of sleek, flowing melodies and tonal harmonies. He used a big orchestra generously, with warm strings and sonorous brass, and he wrote well for voice and piano. His life can be heard in his music—bright optimism and humanism contrasted with bitterness and anger (particularly in the works about his experiences during WWII), as well as his English background of landscapes and history. His style is melodic like Vaughan Williams, but less folk-like and impressionistic; noble like Elgar, but not as chromatic or colorful.

Symphonies. Symphony 1 is cheerful and moving, with dark orchestration; 2 mixes dance, wistful variations, drama, marches, and a bumptious conclusion. The inventive but serious 3 ranges from sad to ominous, with melancholy string writing, fanfares, and a lively ending. Symphony 4 ("Arctic") depicts Lloyd's military service, though it's more tuneful and less strife-ridden than this suggests. Symphony 5 is a "psychological journey" of Lloyd's recovery from a nervous breakdown. The Waltonian 6 is lyrical, with free-sounding strings and a hymn-like slow movement. Symphony 7 is the longest and most tragic, at times approaching Respighi.

The outer movements of 8 are catchy and heroic (I) and Mendelssohnian (III); II is dark and broad like Dorset in winter. Symphony 9 varies from wispy and skittery to dark, with a prominent, sad Largo; III has doses of "Yankee Doodle" and a stirring march. Symphony 10 ("November Journeys") for brass was inspired by visits to cathedrals; it's a combination of walking tune, chorale, and flourishes. Symphony 11 is more "modern" and less tuneful; it's stirring but gimmicky at times, and overlong. Symphony 12 is autumnal and eloquent—a reflective valedictory but never depressed.

Lloyd's ♦Albany set is easily recommendable: 1 and 12 (032); 2 and 9 (055); 3 with *Charade* (090); 4 (002); 5 (022); 6 and 10 with *John Socman Overture* (015); 7 (057); 8 (230); 11 (060). The orchestras are the BBC Philharmonic (5–7, 9, 10), Albany Symphony (1, 4, 11, 12), and Philharmonia (8). All have warm string tone and clear brass; the Philharmonia is the best, and Albany is the least polished, though quite good. **Edward Downes** made excellent recordings of 4, 5, and 8 with the Philharmonia (♦Lyrita LPs). They're more spacious and less intense than Lloyd's. Downes and his orchestra are superior in 4, with more power and depth. Both performances of 5 are good, but Downes's sweep is slightly preferable to Lloyd's greater probing and darkness, especially in the slow movements. In 8, the Philharmonia is superior to the BBC in translating Lloyd's dark probing into real force and eloquence, making Downes sound lightweight in comparison. Both sets have good sound, particularly the more open Lyritas. **James Stobart**'s version of 10 with the London Collegiate Brass is brighter, with more intensity and balance than Lloyd's; the coupling will appeal to brass afficionados (♦Trax 114, with Wilfred Josephs's complex Concerto for Brass).

English Heritage, Diversions on a Bass Theme, Evening Song, Royal Parks, HMS Trinidad. These brass band works don't have the burnished eloquence and depth of the symphonies. The first three especially cover a wide range of expression from romantic to craggy and cerebral. They're extremely well played by **David King** and Black Dyke Mills; the sound is bit covered, but that's not a major problem (♦Albany 051).

Concertos. The first three of Lloyd's four piano concertos deal with his experiences in WWII. No.1 ("Scapegoat") is sardonic, bitter, and rueful; it's modernistic and clever, with an odd mix of Prokofiev and Rachmaninoff. No. 2 was inspired by Hitler's jig after capturing Paris; it's the toughest and angriest of the concertos, not immediately appealing but moving. No. 3 mixes vigor, fanfares, pathos, and a "knock on the door at midnight"; piano noodling is excessive at times. No. 4 is happier, spontaneous, and flowing, with touches of Rachmaninoff. **Lloyd** recorded all four with the BBC Philharmonic (♦Albany: 1 and 2 with Martin Roscoe (037); 3 and 4 with Kathryn Stott (019 and 004, with *Lily-Leaf and the Grasshopper* and other piano works). All are fine performances in good sound.

Violin Concertos 1 (with strings) and 2 (with winds) reflect Lloyd's ebullient side, though there are some fine songful passages. The violin dominates both works; they're entertaining but not as good or as consistent as the symphonies and operas. **Cristina Anghelescu** and conductor David Parry (with the Philharmonia) are energetic and committed (♦Albany 316).

Choral music. *Litany* (texts by John Donne) should appeal to fans of Vaughan Williams's *Sea Symphony*, with its big gestures and strong tunes. **Lloyd** leads the Philharmonia in a rousing performance (♦Albany 200-2). *Symphonic Mass*, Lloyd's greatest recorded work in this genre, is as rousing and sweeping as *Litany* but more inspired (though he was a nonbeliever). His integration of a single tune throughout its movements, with a variety of choral and orchestral effects and great depth and range, is brilliant. This recording is magnificent (♦Albany 100).

The late Roman text of *Vigil of Venus* is a paean to spring and love. **Lloyd**'s treatment is lyrical and full of pantheistic joy and passion that never crosses into indulgence. It's exciting and pleasant, but can be repetitious. He and the Royal Philharmonic are quite good, though the sound could use more choral focus and bass (♦Argo 430329).

Operas. *Iernin* is from Cornish history and is romantic and heroic; the music is appealing and stirring, with scenes full of pageantry, pathos, and romance. The writing is melodic but never at the expense of orchestral power or prominence. *Iernin* has an air of the American theater; it grabs your attention like a Broadway show but is in no way popularized. **Lloyd** conducts a broadcast recording with excellent sound (♦Albany 121/3, 3 CD). The rollicking, sinuous spirit of the tuneful *John Socman,* with its "manly" passages and rousing orchestra, is along the lines of *Iernin* with a nod to Vaughan Williams's *Hugh the Drover*. Lloyd conducts highlights in a fine performance (♦Albany 131).   HECHT

Pietro Locatelli *(1695–1764)*

Locatelli was the first of the modern virtuosos, achieving astonishing feats on the violin that were impossible—and perhaps unthinkable—for others. He's best known for composing the ne plus ultra of violin technique in the 18th century, *L'Arte del Violino* (The Art of the Violin).

Locatelli's Concerti Grossi Op. 1 are innovative in that they include a viola in the concertino. They also show an occasional predilection for strange, syncopated rhythms. The Capella Istropolitana is a modern instrument group led by **Krček** that has a strong affinity for period style and plays the first six concertos with vigor, relish, and virtuosity (Naxos 553445). Europa Galante under **Biondi** has recorded Op. 1 Nos. 2, 5, and 12. They are a spirited period instrument group, not afraid to tread new stylistic paths, and their performances are truly delightful (Opus 111 30104).

The Art of the Violin Op. 3 is a set of 12 violin concertos, each with two "caprices," or extended cadenzas, that contains almost all that was known about violin technique when they were published in 1733. Of course, more than mere technique is required to pull them off; a virtuoso's flair is as necessary as a virtuoso's fettle. **Susanne Lautenbacher** plays them skillfully and cleanly, but she takes the cadenzas rather slowly, which robs them of some of their thrill (Vox). **Rodolfo Bonucci** plays the cadenzas accurately and at bracing speeds, but lacks excitement (Arts 47307/10, 4CD). **Mela Tenenbaum** has all the flair you could want and then some, and she plays the cadenzas up to speed; consequently, she commits the occasional flub, but she's more likely to hold your attention during these long technical exercises than anyone else (ESS.A.Y 1043/44, 1068/1069, 4CD). **Elizabeth Wallfisch** is the lone, brave period instrumentalist offering these works; her performances are spirited, and she has the technique to handle the music's demands (Hyperion 66721/23, 3CD).

Six of the violin sonatas, Op. 8, are for violin and basso continuo; the other four are trio sonatas. They are engaging works requiring some virtuosity, but not nakedly exhibitionistic like *The Art of the Violin*. **Wallfisch** has recorded them with her group, the Locatelli Trio, with Rachel Isserlis playing the other violin part in the trio sonatas (Hyperion 67021/22, 2CD). They are fine performances, played with the same relish Wallfisch displays in *The Art of the Violin*. It appears they adopted Locatelli's name for good reason.   MAGIL

Matthew Locke *(1621/22–1677)*

Locke is a major figure in 17th-century English music, in that he connects the earlier generation dominated by Gibbons with post-Restoration composers like Purcell. Best known are his collections of chamber music and his dramatic works, which greatly influenced Purcell. A strong partisan of English music at a time when French influence was growing, Locke is often called the "father of English opera."

The only significant example of Locke's dramatic music now available is his "semiopera" *Psyche*, first performed in 1675. In this work, the play (by Shadwell) was fleshed out with extensive recitatives, airs, and choruses. Works like this—spoken plays augmented by lots of music—were outmoded by the time Italian opera became the fashion in the 18th century; they were important, though, in preparing the way for works like Purcell's *Fairy Queen* (1692). We're fortunate that the old Oiseau-Lyre recording of *Psyche,* conducted by **Pickett,** has been reissued (♦MHS 515184). A fair bit of reconstruction has been needed to bring Locke's sketchy score to life, and Pickett has done a splendid job. Anyone interested in the roots of Purcell and English opera in general will want to hear this recording.

Locke's religious and ceremonial music is missing from the catalogue, but collectors should watch for the comprehensive collection by the **Parley of Instruments** and the Choir of New College, Oxford (Hyperion 66373). His chamber music is better represented, but not by much. Two of his finest collections, *Consort in Fower Parts* and *Flatt Consort,* are brought together by the **Orlando Gibbons Viol Ensemble** (♦Alphée 9506045, 2CD). These works show much of the ingenuity and harmonic daring associated with Purcell and testify to Locke's skill away from the stage.   ALTHOUSE

Carl Loewe *(1796–1869)*

Most listeners know Loewe as the composer of fine ballads, including an "Erlkönig" that Wagner was said to have preferred to Schubert's setting. Few have heard any of his other works: the hundreds of lyrical songs and other ballads, plus symphonies, concertos, and oratorios. These lesser-known compositions have some historical importance, but we must concede that his best work is truly in the ballads. Most of his other pieces are good exemplars of the prevailing North German style but don't rise to the first rank.

The effective presentation of a ballad—essentially a poem or song that tells a story—depends critically on the listener's comprehension of the text. For this reason German ballads have been less popular than lyric songs, which often require little more than a general notion of the content. As you might suspect, Loewe is more popular in German-speaking countries, and few singers of his works have been non-German. His songs and ballads were widely recorded in the early 20th century, so historical recordings are particularly interesting.

Many issues have come and gone over the years. Several fine older singers—Rethberg, Slezak, Völker, Scheidl, Hotter, Bockelmann, Hann, Bender, and Mayr—are represented in one interesting disc (♦Preiser 89230). The recordings, which date from 1902 to 1970, vary greatly in style as well as sound, but a sympathetic listener can find just as much value in an older singer like Paul Bender as in the more recent Hotter. As for **Hotter,** his fans should also look for his recently reissued but even more recently deleted CD of 18 songs and ballads with Michael Raucheisen, recorded 1943–45 (♦Preiser 90301).

Among modern recordings, first mention must go to the ongoing complete edition of Loewe's songs and ballads on 20 CDs, all accompanied by pianist **Cord Garben.** Like Graham Johnson in his complete Schubert edition, Garben has divided up the 30 or 40 best-known pieces so that each disc includes a majority of songs most listeners will never have heard. Any of the series can be recommended to the adventurous. Two that are particularly rewarding are Vol. 6 with Moll, which includes "Heinrich der Vogler," "Prinz Eugen," and "Archibald Douglas" (♦CPO 999306), and Vol. 9 with Prégardien, which includes "Edward" and "Erlkönig" (♦CPO 999417).

The easiest way to acquire the better-known pieces is through **Fischer-Dieskau**'s set with Jörg Demus. Recorded on LPs in 1969, 1971, and 1982, these 37 songs and ballads are now available again (♦MHS 525313T, 2CD). Fischer-Dieskau was always a master at characterizing texts, so these works play to his strength. The CDs are well documented with notes, texts, and translations, so this is an ideal introduction to the composer.

For those wanting to venture further afield, one of Loewe's 15 oratorios, *The Raising of Lazarus,* is available in a fine performance, coupled with five strong choral pieces (Capriccio 10581). Perhaps more interesting is his Symphony in D Minor, which has echoes of the Beethoven 9, Mendelssohn, and Schumann, coupled with his showy Piano Concerto in A, nicely played by **Ewa Kupiec** (Koch 31539).   ALTHOUSE

Albert Lortzing *(1801–1850)*

Lortzing composed more than a dozen operas, most of them comic. He wrote his own librettos, aided by his friends. Most of his operas are characterized by a good-natured, often sentimental humor, comic characters that appeal to everyone, and an easily understood musical score that's tuneful but unpretentious and breaks no new grounds. To its detriment, it's often formulaic, sentimental, and interchangeable from one opera to the next. It's usually folksy and enjoyable and has one or two hit tunes, but lacks the deep and pointed elements that would make the music memorable. Indeed, Lortzing's scores often include reminiscences of other composers (Mozart, Spohr, Weber, for instance); they appeal to audiences because they seem so familiar and comfortable. The operas include spoken dialogue in the singspiel tradition, which may account for their limited success outside Germany and Austria. In those countries, Lortzing's operas continue to be performed frequently, especially *Der Wildschütz* and *Zar und Zimmermann.*

Hans Sachs. The story of this opera is quite similar to Wagner's *Meistersinger,* and Wagner was probably familiar with it before he composed his own opera. Lortzing, alas, is no Wagner; his score is bland and unimaginative, and this hasn't been among his more popular operas. It's fortunate that the only available CD, a cut 1950 performance from Nuremberg, has **Karl Schmitt-Walter** in the title role (Memories). He is one of those rare singers who could make you believe in any role he took on. The fascination of this work is that it illustrates so well the difference between inspired genius and mere competence.

Die Opernprobe (The Rehearsal). This is Lortzing's last completed opera; he died the day after its premiere (which he didn't see). In the only available recording, the tenor is Gedda, and the rest of the able cast is from the Bavarian Opera; **Suitner** is the fine conductor (CPO).

Undine. This presents the story of the water sprite by Fouqué that was also used by E.T.A. Hoffmann for his opera of the same name and, more memorably, by Dvořák for *Rusalka.* Unlike those operas, Lortzing's has a happy ending, in which Undine and her mortal lover live happily ever after in the realm of Kühleborn, the Prince of Waters. This is a work in the German Romantic tradition, and the comic elements introduced by the composer are incidental. It traces its descent from Weber's *Freischütz,* including magic, good and evil spirits, imaginative scenic effects, peasant dances, and folksy-sounding sentimental arias that have attracted some critics. The only recording known to me was released around 1990; it may be hard to find, but it's a fine rendition, probably from a radio broadcast (Capriccio 60017). It has an enthusiastic cast of young, fresh-voiced singers, and includes a libretto in German and English.

Der Waffenschmied (The Armorer of Worms). This comic opera takes place in Worms in the 16th century. The conventional plot is set in Lortzing's familiar style; there are two arias with catchy tunes, but the rest lacks inventive characterization, though it's well crafted and enjoyable. The only complete recording now available is by the Bavarian Opera (Calig). Its fairly good cast is conducted by **Hager,** but the disc lacks a libretto in English. A single disc of excerpts has been issued, with a cast and conductor (**Hans Fricke**) at least as good as Calig's, and it includes all the highlights of the opera (Berlin). It should suffice for all but Lortzing fans.

Der Wildschütz (The Poacher). Considered Lortzing's masterpiece, this is the most often performed of his operas. Here the composer is not his usual *gemütlich* self; it's a farcical comedy that includes some social satire, perhaps inspired by *Marriage of Figaro.* Many of the characters are a bit loony, and the story includes stock comedy situations, such as hidden identities and disguises, some double. The score has 16 musical numbers, only four of which are solo arias; the rest are duets, trios, and other ensembles, all connected by spoken dialogue. The music has the composer's usual light touch and some catchy tunes; the orchestral score is a bit more elaborate than in Lortzing's other works. It's very charming but, unlike Mozart, offers few glimpses into the human soul. The only currently available recording was made in 1980–82 in (then East) Berlin (Berlin 1143). It's a good one, with an excellent cast; **Bernhard Klee** is the able conductor.

Zar und Zimmermann (Tsar and Carpenter, or The Two Peters). This comedy deals with Tsar Peter the Great, who, the story alleges, went incognito to Holland to learn about building ships for his navy and was confused with a Russian deserter also named Peter. It's all good, clean fun, set to folksy, unpretentious music, and very enjoyable. There's only one fairly complete recording in the current catalog, a 1976 version that omits the spoken dialogue and cuts a few minor numbers; it also lacks a libretto (Acanta 42424). The cast is good, with **Popp** as Marie, Ridderbusch as the mayor, and Prey as the Tsar. Popp and Ridderbusch are excellent, but Prey's voice is uncharacteristically husky and veiled, though he's obviously well versed in the role. A fine set of excerpts issued by Odeon in Europe in 1959, with Frick, Marcel Cordes, and Helga Hillebrand, apparently never made it to CD. MOSES

OVERTURES

Lortzing's overtures are sheer delight, rich in good humor and filled with the same wealth of heartfelt melodies as the operas. The only all-Lortzing collection is a very good one (♦Marco Polo 220310). You get the cream of the crop — *Hans Sachs, Der Pole und sein Kind, Regina, Undine, Der Waffenschmied,* and, of course, *Der Wildschütz* and *Zar und Zimmermann,* and the conductors are top-notch, too. HALLER

Jean-Baptiste Lully *(1632–1687)*

It's one of the supreme ironies of music history that French Baroque music in its grandest forms (opera, orchestral suites) owes its existence largely to one man, an obscure Italian musician who rose from the depths of poverty to become the all-powerful *Maître de Musique* at the court of Louis XIV. It's unclear where and how Lully learned to play the violin, but his exceptional talent was discovered by a plenipotentiary of the king, and he was engaged as a member of Les Petits-Violons, a kind of "junior varsity" version of the more famous Vingt-Quatre Violons du Roy (Twenty-four Violins of the King). From there, he progressed rapidly to become director first of the King's ballets and later of his operas. From the premiere of his first opera in 1672 until his death, Lully reigned supreme as the malevolent godfather of French music — all those who dared oppose him were ultimately crushed.

But what about Lully's music? Historians have criticized it as "monotonous in harmony and lacking in spontaneous feeling." That's perhaps too harsh a judgment; certainly the spectacular choral and ballet numbers have immediate appeal for modern-day audiences. The cultural and linguistic differences that separate us from 17th-century France are strong; only native speakers of French are apt to notice Lully's remarkable ability to mimic the natural speech-rhythms of the language in music. His vocal writing flows easily from *récitative* to *aire* without the abrupt breaks characteristic of Italian opera; in this regard the music is almost a pre-echo of Wagner's through-composed music dramas.

We're blessed to have three of Lully's operas available in complete performances by specialists of the period — would that Italian baroque opera were as well recorded! The first of these to appear was **Christie**'s production of *Atys;* its 1988 release (there's a videotape as well) garnered much attention (Harmonia Mundi 901257, 3CD). As with so many of his recordings, Christie's realization of this work is almost a "time window" on the past, a glimpse into the resplendent age of Louis XIV. Two further, equally successful productions of Lully operas are available: *Acis et Galatée,* with **Minkowski** and Les Musiciens du Louvre (Archiv 453497, 2CD) and *Armide,* with **Herreweghe** and La Chapelle Royale (Harmonia Mundi 901456, 2CD). Both can be recommended to Baroque opera buffs.

Go straight to "L'Orchestre du Roi Soleil" for a generous sampling of Lully's orchestral music (Vox 9807). **Savall** and his period-instrument Le Concert des Nations have outdone themselves with rousing, infectious renditions of excerpts from *Le Bougeois gentilhomme, Le Divertissement royale,* and *Alceste,* using an imaginative palette of old instruments, including some lively percussion. Another highly effective collection of orchestral excerpts features the London Oboe Band under **Paul Goodwin** (Harmonia Mundi 907122). This ensemble, popular in France during the second half of the 17th century, spotlighted the newly invented oboe and bassoon, but it's not what you might think. The massed sonorities are all smoothness and suavity, nothing like the loud squawking of Renaissance shawm bands.

Lully tried his (heavy) hand at sacred music as well; his series of *Grands motets* written for the Sun King served as models for at least two subsequent generations of French composers. The music alternates between sheer resplendency, with a full panoply of chorus, trumpets, and drums, and small-scale introversion, often scored for one or two solo voices. **Hervé Niquet** and Le Concert Spirituel recorded three volumes of the *Grands motets* under the auspices of the Centre de Musique Baroque de Versailles; these have been reissued at an attractive budget price (Naxos 554397/99) This is some of Lully's most accessible music, and it would be hard to imagine more idiomatic performances.

BRODERSEN

Witold Lutosławski (1913–1994)

Lutosławski was probably the greatest Polish composer of the last half of the 20th century, one who never stopped growing and exploring. From his earlier folk-influenced pieces to his deliriously colorful later works, here is one avant-garde composer audiences grew to love, thanks to his imaginative use of the orchestra. This slightly built, impeccably dressed figure was also a superb conductor, having worked out a graceful technique for signaling passages of controlled chance.

Most of Lutosławski's discography falls into three groups. There is a six-volume hodgepodge of 1959–88 Polish recordings on Polskie Nagrania; the sound quality is wildly variable, but there are a lot of valuable performances here, many by the composer. The second batch consists of his benchmark recordings on EMI with the Polish National Radio Symphony and with Western ensembles for DG, Decca, and Philips, from 1976 through 1990. Finally, after his death, Naxos embarked on an ambitious project that will include all of his orchestral works played by Antoni Wit and the Polish National Radio Symphony—not always the best available but superbly recorded and a stupendous bargain. The following discussion is arranged chronologically by year of composition, to provide a sense of the composer's development.

Symphonic Variations (1938). Here and there are reflections of early Bartók and *Pétrouchka*, but already the composer reveals a yen for splashy orchestral color and premonitions of later effects. **Lutosławski**'s recording is wonderfully luminous; he takes evident delight in his youthful piece (♦EMI 65076). **Wit** is somewhat broader, more attuned to the 19th-century influences (Naxos.553169).

Variations on a Theme of Paganini (1941). Written in the wake of Rachmaninoff's *Paganini Rhapsody* but far more irreverent and just as flashy, this work exists in two editions, the 1941 original for two pianos and a 1978 extended version for piano and orchestra. For the two-piano version, **Argerich** and **Freire** is the great one, full of mischief and heightened dynamics (♦Philips 464043, 2CD), trumping the mellower **Paratore** brothers (CBS, NA, or Koch Schwann). **Bernd Glemser** and Wit offer a controlled, polished orchestral version (Naxos), but **Peter Jablonski** and Ashkenazy have more zip (♦London 448258, 2CD).

Symphony 1 (1947). With elements of Hindemith and Bartók strewn throughout, this is a high-spirited piece, but not yet the work of a true original. **Jan Krenz**'s 1964 performance still has a lot of brisk life (♦Polskie Nagrania 040), coming very close to **Lutosławski**, who gives it that something extra, the pointing and thrusting of the rhythms (♦EMI 65076). **Wit** is also very good: but softer-focused (Naxos).

Concerto for Orchestra (1954). A descendant of Bartók's *Concerto for Orchestra,* this has become the composer's most recorded work for two reasons: its brilliant orchestrations for virtuoso conductors to flaunt, and its tonal language that sums up his early folk-based style. **Lutosławski** lays it out for us with a contemporary edge and lots of energy (♦EMI 65305). The same orchestra under **Wit** plays it quite differently, more relaxed in the opening movement with a very dreamy coda, a

polished featherweight touch in II, and full Romantic sweep in III— a best buy (♦Naxos 553779).

Another winner comes from the unfathomably neglected **Paul Kletzki**, a seething, biting performance in gleaming 1968 Decca sound, marred only by an eight-page cut in III (♦London 448258, 2CD). **Rowicki**, the dedicatee, sets a frisky example circa 1962 (Polskie Nagrania). **Barenboim**'s opening is muscular, his Chicago brasses in full blaze, but his approach isn't as vividly characterized as the Poles; subtle episodes like the codas of I and II lack atmosphere (Erato). I prefer **Ozawa**'s earlier, light-footed, brilliantly executed Chicago performance (♦EMI 72664, 2CD). **DePreist**'s brisk treatment receives terrific sound, but the Oregon Symphony is not in the same class as the others (Delos). **Tortelier** and the BBC Philharmonic are energetic, polished, and delicate when needed, but again, others have more character (Chandos).

Musique Funébre (1955). Here we behold a new, more profoundly serious composer exploring 12-tone technique but bending it to his own expressive purposes in his first original masterpiece. **Lutosławski** puts up a stark Bartókian front in his intense performance (♦EMI 65076), while **Wit** finds more sensual beauty in the score (♦Naxos 553202), and **Tortelier** carves out an acceptable middle ground (Chandos). **Dohnányi** gives it a lean, spot-lit, chamber-like treatment (♦London 448258, 2CD); **Rowicki**'s intensity is compromised by wiry sound (Polskie Nagrania 040).

Postludes (1958). Of these three works, only the tiny *Postlude* 1 has been recorded, yet it's an important piece, for it gives fragmentary hints of the freedom to come. **Krenz** illustrates it meticulously (Polskie Nagrania 042); **Wit** is suaver and lusciously recorded (♦Naxos 554283); and **Lutosławski** is the most rugged and startling of all (♦EMI 65865).

Venetian Games (1961). Here Lutosławski has found his direction for the rest of his life. Inspired by a chance hearing of Cage's Concert for Piano and Orchestra, he incorporated carefully controlled free-form passages in his music, opening up a new, dissonant, expressively colorful, even antic world of sound—and with this weapon in hand, he ran wild in the '60s. **Wit**'s treatment is gentle, subtle, savoring the colors (Naxos), but **Lutosławski**'s recording is spikier, more dynamic, openly celebrating the fun (♦EMI 65305).

Trois poèmes d'Henri Michaux (1963). **Lutosławski**'s EMI recording of this delightful welter of choral and orchestral chaos is a vivid experience (♦EMI 65865); avoid his Polskie Nagrania rendering, which is buried in atrociously dim sound. **Wit**'s cautious yet beautifully recorded CD may be a more easily located alternative (♦Naxos 553779).

String Quartet (1964). Loaded with weird effects, the String Quartet launched another recurring Lutosławski process, a two-part series of modules with a hesitant first part and resolution in the second. The **LaSalle Quartet** (♦Polskie Nagrania 045) and **Hagen Quartet** (DG, NA) dispatch it fiercely, though the LaSalle has a clearer sense of direction.

Paroles Tissées (1965). This eerie song cycle is almost a projection of how Britten would have used chance techniques to decorate a vocal line. **Pears** eloquently reinforces the Britten analogy with **Lutosławski** at the helm (♦London 448258, 2CD); two other good composer recordings exist (EMI 65865 and Polskie Nagrania 042), but their singers lack Pears's charisma, and the London has more vivid sound. **Wit** offers an alluring alternative, and his tenor, **Piotr Kusiewicz**, is steadier than Pears (♦Naxos 553423).

Symphony 2 (1967). This symphony brings the composer's surge of controlled freedom to a mighty head in two complex movements. The

'60s seem very much in the air; indeed, the great crescendo that opens II gives you the same rush as those in the Beatles's "A Day in the Life" (the two pieces were unveiled exactly eight days apart in June 1967). You can experience this sensation most vividly in **Lutosławski**'s later recording (♦EMI 65076); his earlier Warsaw taping isn't quite as powerful (Polskie Nagrania). Though excitable in spots, **Salonen** mostly maintains a cooler head, and the sound is a trifle boxy (Sony). Again, **Wit** emphasizes its sensual aspect, and he may be the best choice for a Lutosławski newcomer (♦Naxos 553169).

Livre pour Orchestre (1968). In the glidings and shadings of this fascinating piece, **Lutosławski** and **Wit** play opposite cards: The composer is intense, intoxicating, even scary (EMI 65305); Wit is smooth, opulent, and more listenable (♦Naxos 553625). **Krenz** falls somewhere in the middle (Polskie Nagrania).

Cello Concerto (1970). Virtually a concerto for cello *versus* orchestra, this work turns into a crazed guerrilla war near the end. **Rostropovich** is easily the most combative and vividly characterized soloist, going mano a mano with Lutosławski and L'Orchestre de Paris (♦EMI 49304). **Heinrich Schiff** plays the gentle bear viciously jeered by Lutosławski and the Bavarian Radio Symphony (♦Philips 464043, 2CD); **Roman Jablonski** is a bit friskier in another Lutosławski-led recording (♦Polskie Nagrania 042). **Andrzej Bauer** and Wit project the most warmth, a viable but not all-encompassing approach (Naxos 553625).

Preludes and Fugue (1972). The composer's two-part structure is applied to another traditional form in this discursive, astringent essay for 13 solo strings, one of his lengthiest (33–35 minutes) and most difficult pieces to crack. **Lutosławski** made two excellent recordings that run a close race, the first with the Warsaw National Chamber Orchestra in sharp, close-miked sound (♦Polskie Nagrania 043), the second a slightly mellower-sounding rendition with the Polish Chamber Orchestra (♦EMI 65865).

Les Espaces du sommeil (1975). Literally "Realms of Sleep," this symphonic poem with baritone solo has an alluring dreamlike quality that ushered in a more expressive period. **Shirley-Quirk** is in firm voice for Salonen, who produces a magnificent climax (♦Sony 66280), but also seek out Lutosławski, who has the probing dedicatee **Fischer-Dieskau** and the Berlin Philharmonic (♦Philips 464043, 2CD). Wit's **Adam Kruszewski** is not in the same class, nor does the conductor make as much of an impact (Naxos).

Mi-parti (1978). Now the composer is in even greater command of his partial chance idiom, painting gorgeous soundscapes at will. As beautiful as **Lutosławski**'s first recording is (Polskie Nagrania), his remake is even more expressive and magical (♦EMI 65305), and **Wit** comes close enough with his added opulence (♦Naxos 553779). **Tortelier** gets lustrous sound but conveys minimal magic (Chandos).

Novelette (1979). In this five-part "adventure narrative," **Lutosławski**'s BBC recording (♦DG 431664) has an element of fantasy that his brusque, dry-sounding, live Polish performance lacks (Polskie Nagrania). So does **Wit,** in his more genteel way (♦Naxos 553625).

Symphony 3 (1983). Building from a fate motif not unlike the opening of Beethoven's 5th, this symphony is another culminating moment for **Lutosławski,** rolling together his experiments of two decades into a perfectly balanced two-movement shape. The composer is dramatic, enticing, and affecting at the close in a brilliantly played and recorded Berlin performance (♦Philips 464043, 2CD). For all its cathartic energy, **Salo-**

nen is handicapped by muffled sound, and the 1985 Los Angeles Philharmonic doesn't execute as well as they would for him in the '90s (Sony). **Barenboim,** surprisingly, has a more intuitive sense of the shapes of the phrases than either of them (though the free-form passages could be more unbuttoned), and he catches a Mahlerian lilt in the coda (♦Erato 91711). But **Wit** seems to have the tightest grasp of the work as a whole; he makes the long, diffuse first movement flow with amazing coherence in his first version (♦Polskie Nagrania 044); his second is more expansive and a bit better recorded (Naxos 553423).

Chains 1-3 (1982-86). Here Lutosławski invented a new musical form, where sections of each piece merge and overlap imperceptibly. *Chain* 2 is really a frisky violin concerto, 3 the most colorful, and here the discography gets a bit tangled. You can find all three together only as led by Heinz Holliger, Kazimierz Kord (with violinist **Krzysztof Jakowicz**), and Lutosławski, respectively (Polskie Nagrania 044). **Wit** splits 2 and 3 into separate discs (♦Naxos 553202 and 553625), but the former also includes a gorgeous trance-like "Interlude" written later as a link between *Chain* 2 and the Partita for Violin and Orchestra. The most incisive, imaginative performances of 2 and the Partita are by the high-powered team of Lutosławski and **Mutter** (♦DG 423696), but there is no "Interlude," and the richer of Lutosławski's two performances of 3 is also shunted over to another disc (♦DG 431664). What to do? Let price be the guide, I guess—which means Naxos.

Piano Concerto (1987). With its absence of controlled chance except at the very beginning and end and conventional bravura writing for the soloist, this concerto signals a final lyrical flowering for Lutosławski— though in this case it doesn't result in more interesting music. Of the three pianists who recorded it, **Zimerman** produces the most expression and color (♦DG 431664), followed in descending order by **Crossley**—who brings out a Bartókian element (♦Sony 67189)—and **Piotr Paleczny** (Naxos).

Chantefleurs et Chantefables (1990). The liquid glitter of this song cycle represents Lutosławski at his most alluring. **Olga Pasiecznik** is the delectable soprano on Wit's languorously warm recording (♦Naxos 554283); **Upshaw** points up the words more vividly, while Salonen conjures somewhat chillier textures (♦Sony 67189).

Symphony 4 (1993). In retrospect, Lutosławski's last major work sounds like a farewell, with its luminously sad opening clarinet melody and Mahlerian strings—and even in the more turbulent textures further on, it's the lyrical element that grabs you. **Salonen** nails its emotional essence and gets gorgeous playing from Los Angeles (♦Sony 66280), easily out-pointing the more reserved **Wit** (Naxos).　　GINELL

Edward MacDowell *(1860–1908)*

MacDowell was born in New York City and trained in Paris (Debussy was a classmate at the Conservatoire) and Germany. In 1896 he began eight years as head of the music department of Columbia University and spent his summers in Peterborough, New Hampshire. After his death, his wife established a "composers' colony" there that still exists. MacDowell was as good a visual artist as he was a composer, and much of his piano music evokes images of nature (in both its simple beauty and its awesome terror), folklore (he loved "Uncle Remus" and Cuchullainn stories), and history (real and fanciful).

He achieved international fame for his performances of his own piano concertos; Liszt invited him to play his Concerto 1 at a music festival in 1882. There are excellent recordings of the two concertos by

Thomas Tirino (Centaur 2149) and **Donna Amato** (Olympia 353), and of 2 by **Watts** (Telarc 80429). He also wrote two orchestral suites that have been recorded by **Charles Anthony Johnson** (Albany 224). **Hanson**'s 1961 recording of the first suite has also been reissued (Mercury 34337). MacDowell's four piano sonatas have been recorded by **Tocco** (Gaspari 1007) and **Keene** (Protone 2202/3), and **James Barbagallo** recorded the last two (Marco Polo 223632/3).

MacDowell began each day "sketching" melodies, and some of these made their way into his *Woodland Sketches.* His wife found a sketch of the melody that became "To a Wild Rose," perhaps the best known of these pieces, on the floor next to the wastebasket. There are excellent recordings of all ten by **Charles Fierro** (Nonesuch/Electra 71411) and **Barbagallo** (Marco Polo 223531), and a few are included in Keene's recording of the sonatas. Barbagallo's excellent three-volume collection also includes many of his other works.

MacDowell wrote several symphonic poems based on literary works: *The Song of Roland, Hamlet, Lancelot und Elaine,* and Keats's *Lamia.* They're beautifully played by **Krueger** leading the Royal Philharmonic (Bridge 9089). He also wrote two orchestral suites that have been recorded by **Johnson** (Albany 224). **Hanson**'s 1961 recording of the first suite has also been reissued (Mercury 34337).

He wrote 42 songs, some in English, some in German, and some set to his own texts. All of them have been recorded by tenor **Steven Tharp,** who sounds a bit like Wunderlich in the Op. 11 songs set to texts of Heine (Naxos 559032). FINE

Guillaume de Machaut *(ca. 1300–1377)*

Machaut was the leading poet as well as the most prolific composer of his time. He became a canon of Reims cathedral in 1340, though he was not a priest, and held that honor for the rest of his life. He wrote a dozen lengthy amorous poems honoring such figures as John II of France, Charles of Navarre, and the duke of Burgundy, but these do not prove that he gave them personal service. He composed his best-known work in the early 1360s, *Messe de Notre Dame,* to be sung every Saturday at a side altar of Reims cathedral as a memorial for himself and his brother (who was also a canon there). His motets (except for three Latin motets written during the siege of Reims in 1359) are his earliest works, and the song forms he used are lai, virelai, rondeau, and ballade. Machaut carefully prepared definitive copies of his works, arranging them in a prescribed order. These were copied into a half-dozen surviving manuscript books (three lacking the late works, the other three complete) that preserved his complete oeuvre.

Messe de Notre Dame, the only complete mass in polyphony by a known composer of the 14th century, is by far the most frequently recorded of Machaut's works. Dominique Visse's Ensemble Gilles Binchois sings it unaccompanied with one voice to a part in the context of the complete chants of the Mass of the Assumption, breaking up the intense polyphonic texture, which was not intended to be heard continuously (Harmonic 8931 or Cantus 9624). The Taverner Consort also includes the complete chants of the mass, and it attempts to render the Latin texts as the French would have pronounced them in Machaut's time, but the downward transposition is too low (EMI 747949). The Hilliard Ensemble (Hyperion 66358) and Oxford Camerata (Naxos 553833) both sing very well if you must have a version sung straight through.

About 120 of Machaut's 150 secular pieces have been recorded, but many are done poorly, and most are scattered. The excellent Orlando Consort sings 14 of his most original songs, including "Ma fin est mon commencement" (Archiv 457618). Emmanuel Bonnardot sings a fine collection of 13 monophonic songs (Opus 111 30171). The six songs that fill out Oxford Camerata's version of the Mass are superb, including a complete lai, "Le lay de bonne esperance" (Naxos 553833). Ensemble Gilles Binchois offers 15 songs in "Le vray remède d'amour" (Cantus 9625 or Harmonic 8825). The same group recorded "The Judgement of the King of Navarre" with a dozen songs inserted into excerpts from the narrative poem, although Machaut didn't intend the connection (Cantus 9626). The Clerks' Group sang nine motets, burdened only by unusually slow tempos (Signum 011).

"Le Remède de Fortune" is a poetic work that closely integrates seven songs, each exemplifying a song form of the time. Ensemble P.A.N. sang these songs as well as one other without the poetry (New Albion 068). Gothic Voices sang 13 songs, including "Douce dame jolie," the most popular song on disc (Hyperion 66087), but another 13 scattered across four later discs are even finer (Hyperion 66463, 66588, 66619, 66739). The Little Consort sings a complete lai, "Le lay de confort," stretching it out to double its normal length but still short for the capacity of a CD (Channel 0390). WEBER

Bruno Maderna *(1920–1973)*

European progressive and avant-garde composers were loosely centered in Darmstadt immediately after WWII. Maderna, Stockhausen, and Boulez were the young Turks, alternately challenging and embracing music by the Second Viennese School, principally Webern. In the late '50s they were influenced by, but without much attribution to, John Cage, Earle Brown, and other radicals from the United States. Maderna maintained a lifelong association with Darmstadt and taught composition there, his students including some of the most talented Italian composers of his generation: Berio, Nono, and Franco Donatoni. He sometimes collaborated with these composers, as he did in 1954 with Berio to found the electronic music studio in Milan, and electronic music along with leftist politics can be observed in much of their music. His most radical works were composed by the mid-'60s, often with aleatoric features, unusual instrumentation, new sounds on acoustic instruments, and the combination of live performers with tape.

Of his several concertos, the three for oboe are especially notable. The second is the most extroverted and requires the soloist to play musette and oboe d'amore as well. The performance by **Lothar Faber** is less than satisfactory and the recording is poor; the other two works on this disc are the Violin Concerto performed by **Theo Olof,** and the most interesting "concerto" of the three is *Quadrivium for Four Percussionists and Orchestra* (Stradivarius). All are conducted by Maderna, and all are live. A much better recording of *Quadrivium* is led by **Sinopoli** (DG 423246). This fine disc includes two of Maderna's late works, *Aura* and *Biogramma.* He wrote particularly well and inventively for percussion, and with the relatively large number of good percussionists these days, I predict more recordings of *Quadrivium.* A somewhat better alternative for the oboe concerto is available from **Pietro Borgonovas,** with New Music Studium Production conducted by Antonio Plotino (Dynamic 174). This disc is attractive for the varied and excellent pieces by Berio, especially *Sequenza VIII,* and Maderna's *Serenata per un satellite.*

Oboe Concerto 3 is available in a very fine recording by excellent musicians; **Frank van Koten** plays this 1970 composition, Maderna's last, with surety, handling the aleatoric material seamlessly and naturally, as does the Radio Philharmonic Orchestra with Kent Nagano (Paladino 002). Other oboe concertos on this disc are by Bernd Alois Zimmerman and Willem Frederick Bon, accompanied by the Dutch Radio Orchestra conducted by Ernest Bour. **Holliger** is likely the best-known solo oboist of his generation. Some dislike his unique sound, but his musicianship is unchallenged. His many fans will want Concertos 1 and 3; the West German Radio Orchestra of Cologne conducted by Bertini provides sure accompaniment (Philips 442015).

Two of Maderna's best works exhibit his early and late compositional practices. Concerto for Two Pianos and Instruments exists in multiple versions; the one here is the 1955 version revised from the mid-'40s original. A dense, compact work, it shows Maderna concerned with the complex sonic properties of the piano and is accompanied mostly by percussion. His conception of the concerto form is largely soloist with accompaniment rather than the typical multimovement form; this is true of the duo-piano concerto performed here very well by **Aldo Orvieta** and **Renaldo Maioli**. The Tammittan Percussion Ensemble accompanies, conducted by Guido Facchin. The later work is *Serenata for a Satellite,* an attractive piece for a mixed ensemble of 10 instruments. The aleatoric notation allows the performers much leeway, and they respond appropriately (Dynamic 2010). Other works on this valuable disc are also interesting and engaging, though not all of them are very well known: three pieces for multiple pianos by Maderna, and additional music by Germaine Tailleferre and Franco Donatoni.

Another recommended recording of engaging music is performed and recorded superbly (ADDA 581259). Maderna's *Widmung* for solo violin sounds improvisatory but is not; it's a challenging piece that was employed whole as a cadenza in his Violin Concerto. **Maryvonne Le Dizes-Richard** is soloist for *Widmung* and for Kurtag's eight Duets for Violin and Cimbalom, and is joined by Christian Poiget for Berio's *Duetti.* This disc is recommended not only to listeners but also to violinists searching for challenging, worthwhile repertoire from the latter half of the 20th century.

The Violin Concerto is available in a live recording featuring **Theo Olof** (Arkadia 34.1). Although the work was dedicated to Olof, I don't find his performance as compelling as the music demands; the concerto is a substantial work relatively undiscovered, and I hope for a recording by Le Dizes-Richard. Two other works, *Grande Aulodia* for flute and orchestra and the percussion-dominated *Aura,* complete this 87-minute disc, played by **Severino Gazzelloni** and oboist **Lothar Faber,** respectively; Maderna conducts all, and these remastered LPs provide very good sound. I haven't heard or seen a review of a recent release of the same three pieces by **Omar Zoboli,** oboe, and **Claudio Santambrogio,** flute, for *Grande Aulodia; Myriam Dal Don* for the concerto; and *Widmung,* led by Sandro Gorli (Stradivarius 33546).

After a long and marvelous history, Italian opera was stylistically truncated for the most part after Puccini's death in 1924. Dallapiccola, Berio, and Maderna have resurrected it somewhat—though of course in a modern style. Despite their protestations, none has made a connection to their predecessors' masterpieces. Maderna's *Satyricon* is derived from an incomplete but provocative ancient Roman text on the same subject as Fellini's remarkable film of the same title. It's a strange work that would surely be interesting if well staged; on disc, it's an hour-long collage of music and everyday sounds, not all of them polite. The listener may recognize quotations from a number of composers, and all manner of vernacular styles are mixed in with the equally mixed languages. A good performance by the Divertimento Ensemble of Milan is conducted by **Sandro Gorli** (Salabert 910). This isn't something you're likely to listen to frequently, but it's also not likely to duplicate anything else in your collection.

Hyperion is a serious work, a monodrama based on Hölderlin's text,

and the music is likewise serious. Serially oriented but not as angular and severe as dodecaphonic music by the Darmstadt crowd or Second Viennese School composers, it's a strong work featuring Dorothy Darrow and flutist Severino Gazzelloni with **Maderna** conducting (Stradivarius 10008). Nono's *Il canto sospeso* and selections from Schoenberg's *Moses und Aron* complete the disc. *Hyperion* has been recorded elsewhere, as have the works by Nono and Schoenberg, but Maderna and Darrow are superior interpreters, and the sound is likewise exemplary.

Electronic music was at least a passing interest for most of the Darmstadt composers. Compared with Stockhausen's *Gesang der Jünglinge,* for example, Maderna's electronic music sounds dated and relatively unsophisticated. Despite cofounding the studio in Milan and composing some electronic works, Maderna concentrated primarily on acoustic instruments. Stradivarius 33349 offers a sample of the electronic music, some with voice, as was Berio's practice also.

Berio is the most often performed Italian composer of the Darmstadt School, but I suspect Maderna's music will remain at least at the fringe of the repertory, with several good recordings of music in diverse and engaging styles.

ZIEROLF

Albéric Magnard *(1865–1914)*

Reclusive, even misanthropic, Magnard belied his studies with Massenet with four symphonies that nowhere breathe the same fragrant air as his teacher's florid music. Harmonically, he ventured beyond Franck as well—one writer speaks of "a mood of hopeful tenderness engulfed in general truculence"—though he embraced the cyclical form of Franck and Chausson, and there is a wealth of melodic and rhythmic invention throughout his limited output. This limitation we may regrettably ascribe in part to the start of WWI, when Magnard fired upon German soldiers approaching his home outside Paris and was cut down in return, his house burned to the ground along with many irreplaceable manuscripts. We may weep for what was, or we may rejoice in the music Magnard managed to leave behind, a legacy even the hounds of war cannot take away from us.

Magnard's Symphony 1 seems at times redolent of Mahler, elsewhere Bruckner's 7; certainly Mahler is evoked in the glorious closing bars, the optimism of the opening bars at last fulfilled. In the bright and confident opening sally of 2, the sunlit melodies fairly step on each other's toes in their innocent eagerness to please; the final movement scampers along gleefully, flinging clusters of notes about with abandon before bluffing its way to the final bar in an irrepressible display. Symphony 3 could serve as a microcosm of all that is Magnard, the mystical opening chorale returning to close out the symphony in grand style. If 4 often suggests that the composer is treading familiar ground, there is much to compel attention; it's alternately vigorous and idyllic with a slow movement recalling the Mahler 5.

All four symphonies were set forth in fine fashion by **Plasson** (EMI and ♦MHS 535394W, 3CD; separately, 1 and 3 in EMI 54015; 2 in 49080, with *Overture* and *Hymne à la Justice;* 4 plus *Chant Funèbre* in 47373). They are also conveniently grouped by **Ossonce** (♦Hyperion 67030, 1 and 2; ♦67040, 3 and 4). While tempos are remarkably similar, Ossonce often adds just enough more thrust to sustain interest, with more vivid and glowing colors. Thus the buyer must balance Ossonce's more stimulating readings against the additional material offered by Plasson, the fascinating *Overture* and the two achingly beautiful choral works.

In 1 **Sanderling** isn't as decisive but lingers over the more lyrical passages with loving care, while his purposeful approach in 3 makes both Ossonce and Plasson seem breathless (♦BIS 927). While his 2 and 4 take two CDs, they're priced as one, and he makes up for a sluggish 2:1 with an irrepressible account of the final movement and delivers a hearty and outgoing 4 (♦BIS 928). Though the expressive **Ansermet** reading of 3 may have surfaced on CD in England, I haven't seen it here (London LP); a pity, as it was this recording that surely introduced most listeners to Magnard's very special world.

For all its Franckist harmonies, Magnard's Quintet for Piano and Winds is closer to Fauré than Wagner, rich with memorable tunes and a trenchant wit worthy of Prokofiev. The youthful **Aura Ensemble** plays it to the hilt, with marvelous color and technique (♦Thorofon 2375); **Trio Ozi** and friends are very good indeed, but the Thorofon has the edge in overall quality (Koch 6716). The **Société des Vents de Montréal** offers a refreshing mix of affection and ebullience (CBC 1097).

Magnard's Violin Sonata may be heavier going but is played earnestly by **Augustin Dumay** and Collard (Angel 49890). The Cello Sonata is treated incisively by **Simca Heled** and Jonathan Zak (Classico 243), more expansively by **Xavier Phillips** and Huseyin Sermet (Auvidis 4807, with Piano Trio). All of Magnard's chamber music is available from Accord: the Violin Sonata plus several piano pieces in 149080, the Cello Sonata and more solo piano in 149165 or 220562, the Quintet for Piano and Winds and String Trio in 200102, the String Quartet in 149160 or 220602, and a mix of solo piano pieces and songs in 200492. All may be safely recommended.

Distant echoes of *Tristan und Isolde* permeate Magnard's warmly lyrical opera *Guercoeur*. The restless hero, now passed beyond the pale, yearns to live again, and upon being granted his wish by the deities (Beauty, Goodness, Suffering, and Truth), is returned to earth only to find both his lover and his countrymen seduced by a despot; his pleas for liberty fall on deaf ears as the populace rush upon him, weapons in hand, and the chastened Guercoeur returns to Heaven a sadder but wiser man. At times recalling the mysticism of Symphony 3, it's offered by **Plasson** with van Dam a standout (EMI 49193, 3CD).   HALLER

Gustav Mahler (1860–1922)

SYMPHONIES

Complete sets. Each Mahler symphony offered a different answer to the question of what the genre could be at the turn of the 20th century, so there's no one interpreter who consistently reveals the secrets and intricacies of all these scores. Still, it's instructive to hear all of them from one person's perspective, and some of the outstanding individual readings listed below are only available in complete boxes (some of them priced very reasonably).

Among the first and more important complete cycles (or, in this case, almost complete) is **Mitropoulos**'s set of 1, 3, 5, 6, 8, 9, and the first movement of 10, lovingly refurbished (♦Music & Arts 1021, 6CD). These mono tapes were made at the end of Mitropoulos's life (1956–60) with the WDR Orchestra Köln and the New York and Vienna Philharmonics. This is not a set for purists or audiophiles, given the occasional coughs and sneezes and orchestral gaffes, but the ensemble sound itself is always steady and extremely listenable, with no obvious distortion and few if any volume or level changes. This is blinding, revelatory music making, a counterexample to the anodyne perfection of so many of today's preening, fetishist performances. For anyone who wants to know the full emotional and musical range of Mahler's music, it's an absolute must.

Mitropoulos's legacy as a Mahlerian (and those of Horenstein, Mengelberg, and others) has been largely usurped by **Bernstein,** who left us two complete cycles (Sony and DG). He wasn't as consistent in rhythmic focus as Mitropoulos, and his decisions sound arbitrary more often than not. It also needs saying that standards in American orchestral performance, especially in wind and brass playing, have risen exponentially since the days of Bernstein's first New York cycle, in which the playing ranges from mediocre to very good, with some discipline problems, out-of-tune playing, and an assemblage of assorted vibratos. It's a pity his second cycle wasn't taped a decade earlier; by the late '80s his interpretations vacillated between lassitude and pushiness, and they became more mannered and intent on making a point as time went on, climaxing perhaps in his Vienna 5 and Concertgebouw 9 (DG), interpretations that consistently set new records for *Adagissimo* tempos.

Ozawa's cycle with the Boston Symphony often comes across as a perfectly realized blueprint, but still only a blueprint, of the music's emotional topography and spiritual journeys (Philips). (It doesn't help that the orchestra has kept almost none of the distinctive French characteristics it had in its Munch years, especially in the reeds. The players here even sound bored at times.) Ozawa's accounts of the cataclysmic 5 and 6 have precious little of the Age of Anxiety about them. Likewise, there's almost nothing of the *mit Liebe* you hear in Bernstein's interpretations—not many hints of his end-of-phrase ritards, occasionally revelatory splashes of vibrato, or personal and pliable phrasing. Ozawa's earlier 1 was eminently recommendable (see below) and gives some idea of what comes up lacking in his cycle, which founders on its stringent correctness.

Haitink taped his first cycle in 1962–71, and it's a considerable achievement except for 1 and 8 (where the second rather than the first Amsterdam recording should have been included). He and the Philips engineers are at their very best in 3, 5, 7, and 9. If you're looking for an eminently listenable cycle, this could well be it. The sound is generally paler, more hissy, and less focused than in the LPs, which leads me to think that Philips took no great interest in the remastering. (They also neglect to include the sung texts.) Haitink's second cycle, with the Berlin Philharmonic, was aborted about halfway through—for good reason, since it tends to show the conductor at his most disengaged (Philips). The earlier one is far more imposing and interesting, particularly given the prominent and colorful vintage-'60s vibrato in the Concertgebouw brass.

Someone once said that something always "happens" in a **Solti** performance. Still, his Mahler readings with the Chicago Symphony are rarely intricate, deep, or interpretively multilayered (London/Decca). One of the best qualities of his cycle is its relative consistency: His 1, 7, 8, and 9 are outstanding, and none of the others is unacceptable. The neon-lit, brass-dominated Chicago sound tends to polarize listeners, and the orchestra does sound monochromatic in quieter dynamics. At its best, this uniquely intense and brilliant orchestra is nonpareil in Mahler; the ensemble seems to demonstrate the composer's words, "Where music is, the Demon must be," but the problematic acoustics of Orchestra Hall are a drawback in these recordings.

Kubelik's set wears its years rather lightly; the sound has generally come up bright and clean, even if bass is lacking (DG). Especially in 1, 3, and 9, he was often able to show how a light and spontaneous touch enlivened the music in new and unexpected ways. But his breezy way with tempos and sometimes arbitrary phrasing don't consistently add up to much as a musical experience. In ensemble and corporate tone, the Bavarian RSO sounds dated, having neither the finesse of Klemperer's Philharmonia, nor—to move ahead a decade or so—the intensity of Tennstedt's London Philharmonic. One thing in his favor is Kubelik's seating of first and second violins, left and right, which makes some intricacies of the string writing more immediately audible.

Maazel can be counted on to get top-notch playing from any orchestra. When that group is the Vienna Philharmonic, and the engineers record them in the Musikverein "Golden Hall" with minimal miking, expectations run high (Sony). It seems the CBS engineers had an easier time with this famed acoustic than, say, the DG technicians who've had more experience there. In fact, Maazel's 3, 4, and 10's Adagio are among the very best. Yet his rather cool and calculating podium personality brings many disappointments. The big climaxes are often rushed and then swallowed (certainly there's little of the "pulling a curtain aside" quality that Bernstein gives to Mahler's perorations), the tempo choices can sound artificial, and the various speeds don't always mesh in an entirely convincing way. Still, it's easy to be intoxicated by the sound of this great orchestra run through its paces by a brilliant technician, and recorded truthfully, smoothly, and beautifully in one of the world's best concert acoustics.

As a person, **Tennstedt** was unglamorous, uncouth, and clumsy—a tough assignment for a marketing department. There's something similarly old-world and direct about the music making in his cycle (♦EMI 72941). An anachronism in our age of nonperformances, he always offered genuine interpretive intensity. He's helped in this by the London Philharmonic, which to its credit never made Mahler's music sound glib or easy. EMI offers a consistently natural recording, with little or no spotlighting, and the sound is fresh, vivid, and ear-catching, even if the highest treble isn't always completely smooth and clean at climaxes. Symphony 6 is uncharacteristically showy and two-dimensional, while 9 has an unexpected finesse, almost as if the two scores had been interchanged. No matter; if any one complete set is to be recommended as consistently putting across its own original vision, it's Tennstedt's.

Claudio Abbado is in many ways Tennstedt's opposite, and his cycle with the orchestras of Chicago, Vienna, and Berlin is recommended as a complementary view (DG). He's fascinated by the modernity and inward glances in Mahler's music, where he often achieves a jewel-like clarity and beauty that have never been equaled, but he can also be grander and more exciting than just about anyone else (as in his Berlin 1 and Chicago 2). The only objectionable performances here are a rather distended 4 and a 7 with some tempo miscalculations, and some listeners will chafe at his chamber-like approach to 8. But here and elsewhere Abbado is consistently, intensely haunting.

Inbal is always attractive but rarely inspiring (Denon). His Frankfurt Radio Symphony plays efficiently and well, but in terms of tone and tonal weight isn't quite up to the standards of Vienna, London, and Chicago. His sonics are excellent, though they could be more full and confrontational. The set is spread extravagantly over 15 discs, some of them less than 45 minutes long. The box includes *Das Lied von der Erde* but not Inbal's later performance of 10.

A very special cycle is offered by the **New York Philharmonic**—the symphonies as captured for radio between 1948 and 1982. Mahler himself was music director in New York at the very end of his life, and this fascinating set documents an orchestra so steeped in Mahler performance styles throughout much of the century that it was able to connect with the music and its sound world under a variety of conductors. The compilers of this set have chosen well and worked around some big obstacles, including CBS's wholesale destruction of all its 1948–62 radio masters. Bernstein isn't included, but his Mahler is heavily documented elsewhere. We get Barbirolli's 1959 1, a performance of typically beautiful string tone and bowing and a rendition characteristically independent of Austro-German musical fashion. Mehta's 1982 2 was the one most

heavily nominated for inclusion by the orchestra members themselves; they might have preferred it to his Vienna performance (Decca) for its crisper rhythms and firmer sense of direction.

But the New Yorkers played like an entirely different orchestra in Boulez's 1976 3: A marvelous reading of crystal-clear rhythm, firm tempos, and almost perfect tonal transparency and balance, this will be hard for him to match when he gets around to 3 in his DG cycle. Audience coughing finally begins to disappear when you arrive at Solti's 1962 4—his finest on record, though Seefried's mannered detaché articulation is something of a drawback in the finale. The conductor only pushes things ahead at the playful climax 15 minutes into the slow movement; otherwise he seems to take his time relishing the fine sound of the orchestra. **Tennstedt**'s 1980 5 is very similar to his first (studio) recording for EMI, perhaps a touch more restrained. The New Yorkers' playing, however, is if anything finer than the London Philharmonic. Mitropoulos's 6 is a superlative, predictably intense reading; Mahler's claustrophobic rhythms are sprung with incredible energy, and his horn and string lines soar above the texture.

Kubelik recorded 7 in 1981. It's a wonderfully patient but spontaneous and unaffected reading, as rich and ripe as his undervalued Mozart recordings of the same period—in all, a 7 to make you wish he had done a second cycle in the studio. Stokowski isn't quite the showman you might expect in his 1950 8. The music seems to take a lot of effort, and the choruses are stiff in their scene settings at the beginning of Part 2. The orchestra sounds much better, but Stokowski generally tends to round off the music's thrusting edges. Barbirolli gets a typically grave and beautiful sound in his 1962 9. Other readings are more obviously harrowing, but this interpretation is deeply felt, and the playing itself is stunning. Walter's *Das Lied von der Erde* dates from 1948, a few years before the renowned Decca recording he made in Vienna and his New York account (see below). Ferrier is his contralto again, and she's much more personal and vibrant than on the Decca-Vienna disc; the remastering is also vastly better.

Finally, a word or two about the presentation. By way of documentation, there are some 500 pages of fascinating text, including commissioned essays, profusely illustrated, by some of the world's eminent Mahler experts. The asking price for the box is fairly high, but there is some glorious music making here, the sound has been refurbished with loving care; and the essays comprise a book unto themselves.

1. **Walter**'s first recording is a refreshingly fresh, joyful, and unencumbered performance, and the New York Philharmonic was playing at its peak in 1954 (♦Sony 63328, mono). He's quite speedy but still evocative in the introduction, and in a similar spirit also drops the exposition repeat. The mono sound—though the strings are more vivid than luxuriant, and the fairly narrow dynamic range leaves the slow movement sounding clamorous—is lively and present enough to make you think this is stereo. His later stereo recording is slower and more sensitive, with finer-grained playing than before, but it sounds tired by comparison, especially at the final peroration (Sony).

I've heard the 1940 **Mitropoulos** only on an inferior transfer with intermittently worn surfaces, variable 78 rpm sides, and slight pitch-flutter (Theorema); the Sony mastering must be better. Mitropoulos is as electrifying in the finale as you'd expect, though the Minneapolis Symphony wasn't the most virtuoso group in the land at the time. It's a fine rendition with plenty of Mahlerian vision to it, but in the last analysis this is really a desideratum for Mitropoulos fans; the earlier Walter disc will have broader appeal.

Solti's 1964 recording is good but has neither the freshness of Kubelik nor the vision of Horenstein (London/Decca). Set beside his later disc, this London version is so soft-grained and relaxed as to seem like the work of another conductor. His Chicago rendition is simply electrifying, even if it's not a particularly revealing or deep interpretation (♦London/Decca 411731). The bright sound needs a bit of taming, but you hear more of a real acoustic space here than in other installments in his Mahler series.

Horenstein and the London Symphony are intensely Mahlerian in sound, full of color and temperament (Unicorn). However, the interpretation is seriously compromised by some ill-timed ponderous moments, most strangely at the final victory-stretches of the first and last movements. There are also some balance oddities in the recording. But there are things to learn from: Turn to the funeral march in this uneven performance, and you'll hear a master Mahlerian pulling tremendous variety and character from the music and its kaleidoscopic sequence of episodes.

Boult creates one of the grandest, most exciting conclusions on record, thanks partly to some imposing work by the London Philharmonic percussion as well as the remarkably colorful and vivid sound (Everest). En route, though, his tempos never seem to settle down, and the central section of the Scherzo is so fast that the players have some trouble keeping up with him. **Leinsdorf** gets beautiful playing from the Boston Symphony, but his direction tends to be stiff and pedantic (RCA). The tempo of I, for instance, barely picks up as it moves toward the close. In all, his Royal Philharmonic recording was much better (London). **Ormandy** is more flexible and obviously loving. He was the first to record Mahler's long-lost "Blumine" movement, in a rich and nostalgic reading (RCA). The sound is echoey but more than acceptable.

Neither of **Haitink**'s recordings is rewarding. His first, with the Concertgebouw in 1962, has a surprising rawness, and this is emphasized by an unusually high transfer level (in his Philips set). The recording, too, is grainy. The playing and sound are much better in his Berlin remake, yet there the phrasing and articulation have become lazier (Philips). I've never heard the big and lyrical D-flat episode in the finale done so strictly in time and so tediously. The bass solo in the slow movement is well-mannered and eminently in tune, which isn't a good thing.

Abbado's 1981 recording with the Chicago Symphony, typically for this conductor, is deeply thought through (DG). He's uncommonly sensitive to the quieter, more withdrawn moments in the score, and Mahler's structures take on a feeling of inevitability that almost precludes the element of surprise or exclamation; the opening "awakening of spring" verges on the catatonic. The playing is more fine-grained than under Solti. Abbado's 1989 version with the Berlin Philharmonic has similar virtues of flawless pacing and phrasing, with the added benefits of a more transparent recording and brilliant flashes of personality and individuality (♦DG 431769). This is a live recording, but the audience only makes itself heard between movements and at the end.

Chailly is uniformly dull; it sounds like an octogenarian's music-making (London/Decca). But his disc is worth hearing for the audibly distinctive culture of the Concertgebouw and the 12-minute coupling: Dutch composer Theo Verbey's stunning orchestration of Berg's Piano Sonata supplies nothing less than a new masterpiece of the fin-de-siècle orchestral repertory. **Kubelik** offers sheer, verdant freshness from first to last (♦DG 449735). This is a youthful and springlike approach, a portrait of the composer as a young man; the piece overflows with hope and spills out as if it were being written before our ears. It's important that the slow movement is played simply, not in an angst-ridden or overtly cultured way. Though the Bavarian RPO can sound a shade provincial compared to other ensembles, if anything this adds to the excitement and character of the performance. The only oddity is Kubelik's omission of the first repeat in the Scherzo. (The disc includes Fischer-Dieskau's *Songs of a Wayfarer* as the substantial filler.)

Sinopoli is mannered and unconvincing when he isn't ordinary-sounding—intensely disappointing (DG). DG's recording is dispiritingly bright and harsh, the bass response hollow. **Tennstedt** was unhappy with his 1978 London Philharmonic recording, the first he did in his cycle, so EMI released a second, live recording with the Chicago Symphony. The first disc comes up very well in its remastering, though the sound is just a little echoey. This performance is wonderfully right in every respect, natural without being in any way dull, and personal without being at all eccentric. It might not have quite the personality or splashes of unpredictable, undoctrinaire brilliance that make his later Mahler recordings invaluable, but by its side, the 1990 Chicago remake sounds labored, each movement less a vector from first bar to last than some kind of musical detour. The performance seems tired at times, and the tension sags dangerously in the finale.

Litton sports evocatively distanced trumpets toward the start of I, which has rarely enjoyed such beautiful resonance (Virgin). True to that promise, the performance is consistently lovely, well characterized, and potently played by the Royal Philharmonic. But it's also too consistently methodical, and—as usual with Litton's Mahler—the orchestra's tone production is too uniform to be idiomatic. Ann Murray is disappointing, arbitrary in line and phrase, in the coupled *Wayfarer Songs*.

Maazel searches for detail but ends up sounding more slow and mannered than revealing (Sony). His inner two movements are particularly overinterpreted, and this performance won't bear much repetition. A swift and exciting finale could have improved it, but here too there's a distinct sense of the conductor holding the music at arm's length. He also recorded this work with the Orchestre de Paris in 1980, a rendition less splendiferously played but more satisfying and spontaneous (CBS, yet to make it to CD). **Kletzki** isn't as affecting as he is in 4 or *Das Lied von der Erde,* and the Vienna Philharmonic doesn't distinguish itself as much as you might expect (EMI). The performance is predictably and refreshingly unaffected, but it also lacks quiet playing.

Kegel starts off with promising concentration and well-proportioned sound, and the Dresden Philharmonic makes you wish they made more Mahler recordings (Berlin). But this reading fails to emphasize the focal points of each movement, and Mahler's symphonic argument tends to meander. The most pleasurable aspect here is the disc's warm and ample vintage-1979 sound. A colorful but unremarkable reading comes from **Mehta** and the Israel Philharmonic (London/ Decca, with his more desirable 3). This score would seem to be designed for Mehta the orchestral showman, but the Israelis aren't uniformly dependable, and the acoustic sounds boxy.

Eschenbach and the Houston Symphony were recorded in concert deep in Mahler territory—the Vienna Musikverein—and this might account for the stunning level of playing (♦Koch 7405). This is a very rewarding reading, one of the best on record. The players' responses to his direction are always fresh, taut, and alert, and it convinces at every turn. Koch's recording, too, is clean and open, catching the famed Musikverein ambience beautifully. The only drawback is the audience noise, which does tend to settle down after the opening.

Dohnányi and the Cleveland are virtuosic and utterly transparent in sound, titanium-sleek (London/Decca). They deliver a fine performance, one with rather more life than some of their other Mahler readings. Still, I takes some time to get moving; Dohnányi is uncharacteristically mannered in the way he holds us back from the final climactic payoff of this movement, and he doesn't display any real affection for the lyrical oases of III and IV. **Inbal** turns in one of the more refreshing performances of his cycle; although the tension isn't always ideally maintained, this is a fine mixture of affectionate detailing, excellent playing, and crystalline sound (Denon). This might not be as vivid and memorable as the earlier Ozawa version, but it's still a considerable achievement.

Ozawa has recorded 1 twice, both times in Boston, and his earlier 1976 rendition is fine: artless, candid, warm-hearted, with a splendid bright-eyed sheen to the sound (♦DG 439583). Some might want thicker slatherings of neurosis, parody, and nostalgia; Ozawa reminds me of Kubelik here, partly because he entirely avoids any impressions of preciousness or sentimentality (though the Boston bass solo can get a bit mawkish). The orchestral playing is well above that of Kubelik's group, especially in the finale. Ozawa includes the "Blumine" movement that Mahler excised and places it second per the composer's original intentions. In his later recording, he omits "Blumine" and doesn't reach anything like the same level of intensity and rhythmic lift (Philips).

Mahler's symphonies together form a kind of autobiographical "meta-symphony," so can an interpreter do any single score justice while neglecting the others? **Muti**'s 1 is a beautiful model of its kind, emblematic of his deeply proficient performances of recent years, yet the reading doesn't really penetrate the music's surface. He offers more intricate layers of meaning than Solti but less in the way of idiomatic timbres and freedom of phrasing. He's not one for nostalgia or luxuriating, and his Scherzo is so fast that it loses much of its dance-like metric "catch." The lower range of the Philadelphia Orchestra sounds rather muddy in this Memorial Hall recording.

The real star of **James Judd**'s version is the Florida Philharmonic, which sounds like an internationally known ensemble (Harmonia Mundi). In interpretation he provides more musical detail than Muti, yet his interpretation has no particular charm, enthusiasm, or affection; comparing it with Walter's first rendition leaves no question of who is more memorable or has more temperament. **Segerstam** has his pedantic moments; you're made to wait patiently for I to deliver its payoff, and the tempo gets even slower as the moment draws closer (Chandos). Similarly, his considerable rhythmic-agogic touches ring hollow in the trio section of the Scherzo and the funeral march, and his tempo inflections make the finale seem endless. The orchestral playing itself is on the cool side. He includes the "Blumine" movement.

Boulez shows surprising empathy for the young Mahler, not yet the predecessor to the Second Viennese School (like Mahler's wife and a number of other luminaries, Schoenberg went on record as hating 1) but the young man still gripped by unhappy love and the morbid naïveté of German folk poetry (DG). There's an inevitability to this performance I've heard in no other, and the Chicago Symphony is in superb form. But many will want more affectionate detailing in the trio section of the Scherzo (where the clarinets have mysteriously dropped half a bar) and greater grandiosity when Mahler's seven horns come pealing in the finale. The DG sound lacks something in bloom, and the bass drum is overly prominent.

Bernstein and the Concertgebouw have many overweighted moments, particularly the Scherzo, which tends to plod (DG). ("The morning after" is how a musician friend characterizes Bernstein's take on this dance movement.) This is a heavy-weather performance that knows no grace or lightness, and it often threatens to collapse under its own weight. He adds the gratuitous (but lamentably familiar) bass drum thwack on the final note of the finale, and hits it with a vengeance. The Concertgebouw winds are resolutely New World in sound, bright-hued in neon pinks and reds. (If vivid music making is what you want, Solti in Chicago makes the music sound less like a parody of itself.)

Bernstein made less heavy weather of 1 in his earlier New York recording—a fine performance that would be easy to recommend if it had a bit more poise (Sony). He dispenses a lot of affection on the middle section of the Scherzo, but here—as opposed to the Concertgebouw rendition—he doesn't weigh the music down doing so. Much of the first part of the finale is fast—I find myself wanting him to dig into and grapple with the music more—but the conclusion is very exciting. The sound comes up very well.

Masur has transformed the New York Philharmonic, and the orchestra's newly acquired old-world sound restores this music to its central European roots (Teldec). The recording has splendid dynamic range and frequency response, but Masur's reading doesn't have the individuality and vision that distinguish the versions recommended above. What is special about the disc, though, is Hagegård's *Lieder eines Fahrenden Gesellen,* some of the most lovely, well-sustained Mahler singing ever heard on records.

2. This symphony was the first of Mahler's works to make it to recordings: **Oskar Fried** recorded the entire piece in 1923/24 with the forces of the Berlin Opera. The acoustic 78s (as remastered by Pearl) are swishy and present primitive orchestral sounds that could well have been set down 15 or 20 years earlier. Fried was coached by Mahler himself, so this is a fascinating opportunity to hear a rendition that the composer knew first hand and approved of. That said, it isn't particularly interesting or revealing, apart from the liberal portamentos; interpretation and making music seem to take a backseat to getting the orchestra to play together.

The classic recording of 2 is **Abbado**'s first version, taped in 1976 in Chicago (♦DG 453037, in a "two-fer" with his rather less desirable 4). This is one of those rare recordings where everything went right: Medinah Temple provided plenty of depth of field for the spatial-theatrical effects of the great last movement; the Chicago Symphony and CSO Chorus were at an absolute peak; Horne was then one of the great Mahler voices; and Abbado produced a performance that sparked with electricity. What's more, he drew a unique picture and mood from each movement, with "Urlicht" a hushed eye in the storm. He re-recorded the score before an audience in Vienna in 1992, and that performance has similar virtues: great clarity and rhythmic tension, faultless pacing, centered tone, with just enough kept in reserve so that the last choral cry of "being carried up to God" is the climax it must be (also DG, full price without coupling). He takes just a bit more time; this means more shaping in "Urlicht," but elsewhere (the finale, for example) the music has less fire in its belly. With her heavily rolled Rs, mezzo Waltraud Meier is more affected and heavier of voice than is Horne in Chicago. A fine performance, nonetheless, and the live recording has very fine sound.

Mehta also did 2 in Vienna, but in the Sofiensaal (Decca). He achieves more dynamic variety than Abbado, but not quite the same degree of rhythmic focus (compare the opening figures in lower strings). As a result, his performance kicks up a lot of dust from moment to moment but has less cumulative impact than Abbado's in Chicago. Neither musicians nor engineers are particularly sensitive to quieter dynamics; the sounds produced are uniformly fruity, and some of the tempo changes and climax-building methods are trivial and obvious. All that said, Mehta's mezzo is the ever-dependable Ludwig, and the Vienna Philharmonic offers its very own, irreplaceable sonic joys.

Klemperer has his admirers, and this is one of his finer Mahler recordings (EMI). As is so often the case, producer Walter Legge's natural and sweet-sounding Kingsway Hall production is the real selling point. But again, this is an account I find inferior to Abbado when it comes to pushing home the tension of structural nodes, like the ferocious, hammered-out discord before the recap of I. Klemperer disappoints in the finale, where his tempos drag—after the graves open, the dead arise (at the passage marked "Allegro energico") but don't seem to have shaken off much of their moribund lethargy.

Gilbert Kaplan's remarkable story bears retelling: wealthy publisher of a financial magazine, he consummated a lifelong love for 2 by taking conducting lessons, hiring an orchestra, and leading a series of acclaimed New York performances and then this recording (MCA). He has also re-scrutinized the score and come up with some interesting and affectionately presented interpretive details. It's a good performance all told, efficiently realized, with a particularly alert and piquant III and sound of spectacular (almost artificially wide) dynamic range. But turn to, say, Walter, and you'll immediately hear a sense of vision and telling suppleness of phrase that elude Kaplan. (This recording has been re-released by Conifer with recordings of Mahler's Welte-Mignon piano rolls and a CD-ROM version of Kaplan's *Mahler Album*, containing every photo and graphic rendering he could find of the man.)

In true **Walter** fashion, the conductor's New York reading is sensitive to Mahler's deepest veins of lyricism (Sony). The Philharmonic has rarely sounded more radiant. Walter is a bit heavy in II, but his finale (recorded a good deal later than the rest and in a different location) spills out with an overwhelming yet cogent drama that puts to shame the likes of Mehta and Kaplan. The only thing preventing a prime recommendation is a strange boxiness to the high and low registers of the orchestra. Even so, the effect is atmospheric in its own way, and for once the organ is audible toward the close, the pedals thrillingly so.

Bernstein's first recording, made in New York in 1963, is the finest of his three: a white-hot interpretation, with the Philharmonic at the top of their form and the conductor more consistent in rhythmic focus than usual (♦Sony 63159). He always took I on the slow side; here the stately basic tempo serves as a natural foundation for tremendous jumps into rhythmic intensity and also loving, leisurely incursions into Mahler's lyrical paragraphs. Tourel gives us an "Urlicht" that is one of the most heartfelt and spontaneous ever heard, and the finale is shattering. His London recording, made in 1973, operates at a markedly lower level of tension (Sony). The recording is also over-miked (no doubt necessitated by the cavernous acoustics of Ely Cathedral) and the sound a bit dry and grainy, less natural overall. The conductor also pulls the tempos around more extremely and self-consciously than he did in 1963, underlining this detail here and doting on that one there. The playing of the London Symphony is less brilliant, more soft-grained, than that of the Philharmonic.

Bernstein returned to New York in 1987 for his third try (DG). The performance overflows with affection for the music, so much so that he's constantly slowing down to the point of coming to a complete halt, and yet he somehow maintains the requisite tension from first bar to last. Ludwig and the conductor almost smother "Urlicht" with love, but the finale is hurled out with startling energy. The New Yorkers are a bit less dependable than in 1963, but DG's live recording is remarkably transparent and realistic. Compared to the earlier recordings, Bernstein's final call to resurrection inspires more gooseflesh per square inch than any other performance, though as before he tends to weigh down the close by taking a very broad approach. Although there's a lot that's

interesting here, in all, many listeners will prefer the greater tautness of his more conventional 1963 rendition.

Haitink's 1968 Concertgebouw performance is tougher-sounding than you might expect, and anyone buying his complete Amsterdam cycle will be happy with it (Philips). He's especially good at the delicate detail of the inner movements, which never falls into routine, though his finale might lack the *n*th degree of Mahlerian rhetoric. But it's surely a sign of this conductor's musical skill that he arrives at the end of the finale with such joy and naturalness, while Bernstein simply spends the last six minutes being very slow and very, very loud. In Haitink's hands, the music actually ends before you know it.

Maazel creates little sense of occasion in this most earth-shaking of symphonies; he tends to prepare grandly for climaxes, but then slides over them rather than pressing the moment home, and the performance has surprisingly little cumulative impact (Sony). In "Urlicht," Norman seems to be following the conductor rather than the other way around, and intimacy, warmth, and humanity go out the window when Mahler's little *subito piano* markings and passionate points of emphasis (the repeated "Ach, nein") are ignored.

Litton with the Dallas Symphony is similarly lacking in overall vision and impact, though not nearly as prim as Maazel (Delos). As in their 3, Delos's sonics are deep-set, realistic, and secure, and audiophiles who want to hear Mahler's brass and organ sounding out without distortion in the final climax will be happy with this. Though he doesn't put a foot wrong anywhere, Litton can't match Walter in Mahler's lyrical subtleties; nor does he have the cumulative impact of Abbado or Bernstein.

Moving from Litton to **Tennstedt,** you immediately hear the gain in interpretive character, an increased do-or-die conviction on the part of the players, and a sense that the conductor has rethought this structure on his own terms (♦EMI). Always impressive, it's nevertheless a slightly uneven reading. His "Urlicht" is the longest on records, spinning out to more than seven minutes. He unfolds the finale majestically and unerringly, with the sun-coming-out-from-the-clouds appearance of C major at Fig. 11 a moment of eye-opening beauty. But his chorus disappoints: they're lacking in sonority and lung power, and this tends to undermine the close.

After hearing Tennstedt, **Rattle**'s pedantry becomes all the more obvious (EMI). Here as elsewhere he has oriented his reading around making minutiae audible. The juggernaut element of the funeral march gets lost in the shuffle, as do any lyrical effusions. The well-drilled chorus barely rises above the instruments, but the Birmingham forces play superbly, even if without quite the tonal weight of the great orchestras. The recording also has ideal depth, but others supply greater musical and spiritual nourishment. **Neumann**'s 1980 recording with the Czech Philharmonic is taut and exciting in every bar (Supraphon). The highlight here is III, where you get to hear Mahler's barrage of percussion sounds with unprecedented clarity (in "Rute," Mahler's instruction that the rim of the bass drum be hit with a bound-together bunch of twigs is delightfully audible). The disc's main drawback is the thick, Slavic, operatic style of mezzo Eva Randova. The Supraphon engineers have been more successful than usual at managing the reverberance of the Prague Rudolfinum.

Stokowski made his recording at the age of 90, and his advanced years are probably responsible for some small variability in ensemble and balance (RCA). The tension can be impressive at moments, but it isn't consistently maintained. The finale in particular doesn't hold together as a single mise-en-scène, as it does in the finest readings. The recording has plenty of body, but is distorted a bit at the loudest moments.

Inbal is, as usual, idiomatic and dependable to a fault (Denon). There's little in his interpretation to provoke or surprise the listener, and that's surely much of what this score is about. Unlike someone like Tennstedt, Inbal creates "relative" rather than "absolute" climaxes that make the reader think "yes, this is it, this is the moment!" The Stuttgart orchestra doesn't have the sonic and timbral massiveness, the centeredness of tone, of some others. The low mastering level doesn't help, though the clarity of the climaxes is impressive. The conductor's vocalizations are often profoundly distracting. Inbal's soloists in the finale are stage front, rather than in front of the chorus.

In the straightforward category, **Ozawa** also has a claim to attention (Philips). His 2 is one of the finer installments in his cycle, though its qualities lie more in cogency and beauty than Judgment Day drama. While the Boston Symphony might be too consistently comfortable and relaxed—nowhere is heard the naked, granitic tone that the score seems to require—the playing is lovely, more assured in tone than Inbal's, and Ozawa's phrasing is always well thought out even when it's surprisingly smoothed over. Horne's voice is drier than in the Abbado discs, but still an asset. The recording is warm yet dynamic and detailed.

Solti's 1966 recording, made in London, is one of the poorest on offer; his interpretation often borders on grandstanding, even lack of musicality, and drooping levels and variability of sound suggest that the tapes have suffered with the passing years (London/Decca). The London Symphony isn't up to the level of the Chicago in his second recording (London/Decca), but I'm of two minds about the Chicago reading as well. Nowhere in the piece do you have the sense of a real, definite acoustic space. But when the organ pedals and chorus come in at the final cry of "Auferstehen!" it's a truly spellbinding moment, when in so many other performances it tends to be a bit of a letdown. More than any other, this Mahler symphony is continually aiming toward its close, and Solti realizes that like few others

Slatkin offers a reading of freshness, strength, integrity, and sincerity (Telarc). The St. Louis orchestra has a trenchant, centered sound. This is a performance in the Walter mold: There are no particular eccentricities or spectacles or surprises, and yet—as with Walter—nothing comes up missing from the musical experience. Telarc offers one of its finest recording jobs: deep-set, powerful, with spectacular bass response (the organ!), yet very believable. Perhaps Slatkin is a touch phlegmatic at the grand close, though Telarc's better account of high frequencies helps remedy that.

Rather like Rattle, **Blomstedt** in San Francisco sounds overly literal, missing some of the forest for the trees (London/Decca). Once he sets a tempo he doesn't often bend or change it and can sound calculated when he does. He consistently rushes into the climaxes in the finale, thereby understating their importance. He's best in the grace of II and the lyric-folkish moments in I, which he doesn't overstate. The sound is excellent, with an especially fresh account of the orchestral winds.

Kubelik, by contrast, is fully open to Mahler's rhetoric (DG). Also in contrast to Blomstedt, who almost specializes in poise, he tends to shy too much away from maintaining firm tempos. It's an enjoyable account, at times a thrilling one (his II is delightfully pristine without being affected). The Munich orchestral playing can sound a bit under par, though (again in contrast to Blomstedt's San Franciscans) the group always offers plenty of weight.

3. Two of the best recordings are instructively different. **Abbado** takes a naive, almost childlike view of the piece, phrasing with restraint, affection, and jewel-like beauty (♦DG 410715), while **Levine** presents it more as an orchestral showpiece, with the Chicago Symphony at the absolute peak of its powers (♦RCA 1757). Maybe there's more of Mahler's "terrifying" nature visions with Levine, but given Abbado's astonishing ability to structure the long first movement, the "storm" sequence in the development section is a true climax, and the coda really brings on an adrenalin rush. The final Adagio is the center of Abbado's conception: drawn-out and slow but also very intimate. Even their mezzo soloists are contrasting and equally magnificent: Horne is at her peak for Levine and brings a lieder singer's attention to the words, while Abbado's Norman is beautiful in a distant way, a bit like Wagner's Erda. Abbado has the irreplaceable Vienna Boys' Choir, while Levine coaches his group to overcutesy bell-ringing imitations in V. Abbado's discs were mastered at a low level, and the orchestra thereby has a rather miniaturized sound.

Recording with the same orchestra (the magnificent, irreplaceable Vienna Philharmonic), **Maazel** produced a performance of some originality (♦Sony 42403). He's more episodic than Abbado and also a bit more inscrutable, but the orchestra plays even more magnificently for him—and with more character: There's more of a subterranean growl to the lower strings and trombones (which, paradoxically, also sound more nuanced), more force to the drum strokes, and more surprise to the climaxes. Detail in the main orchestra (especially an over-insistent clarinet) tends to obscure the solo in the posthorn movement, and I'm not sure Baltsa has a Mahlerian voice.

Horenstein is more variable in tempo, perhaps to the detriment of bringing together all of I's 30 minutes (Unicorn). The London Symphony isn't as incisive or colorful as some other orchestras of this period. Horenstein has some of Abbado's gentleness and careful detailing, but not much of the structural or narrative foresight that allows that conductor's conception to work so splendidly. The middle movements are the best, with Norma Proctor admirably nuanced in the Nietzsche setting, but the finale is a bit spoiled by some out-of-tune brass playing. Listeners wanting a straightforward reading of real integrity are referred instead to Tennstedt or Salonen, who are also better recorded.

It's a bit of a surprise that it's in the quieter and more modest inner movements that **Bernstein** excels (♦Sony 61831). His I is unexpectedly mild-mannered, for instance, but there's memorable raptness in the posthorn movement and unexpected rhythmic focus in the Nietzsche setting in IV (where Bernstein doesn't over-force the accents). The 1961 sound is generally fine, an over-prominent glockenspiel notwithstanding, though some of the final chords are prematurely clipped by the engineers. Best to skip the couplings, Tourel's quivery and insecure *Rückert-Lieder* and *Kindertotenlieder,* all the more so given an all-too-obvious ventilation system.

Bernstein's 1985 New York recording was one of the first in his second Mahler cycle (DG). The interpretation tends toward heaviness, though not the willfulness that afflicts some of his later recordings. Even when he does elicit some delicacy, however, the DG team failed to reconcile it with the Avery Fisher Hall acoustic; this was one of their first attempts in this hall, and the rather limited, flattened, bloom-less sonic picture prevents any real beauty or refinement of orchestral sound. Ludwig, who worked such Mahler miracles in the '70s, is disappointingly unsteady here.

Kubelik has power and piquancy, and for once his tempos don't sound rushed or arbitrary (♦DG). The Bavarian Radio orchestra doesn't entirely measure up to current standards; if anything, the slightly rustic character of the winds adds to the performance. In the big first-movement trombone solos, it's nice to hear some juicy vibrato as an antidote to the frequently bland ("pure"?) production of later players. DG's recording offers plenty of instrumental detail in a fairly small acoustic; only when the percussionists are in full cry does it sound restricted.

Haitink's 1966 Concertgebouw 3 is possibly his finest and most fiery Mahler recording, though the orchestra didn't play as consistently well in those days as it has more recently (♦Philips, in his cycle). I is distinguished by one of the most colorful solo trombones heard outside the Eastern Bloc, a player with the kind of wonderfully wide, personal vibrato that has become rare in recent years. Haitink's contralto is Forrester, singing at her best. Philips's sound comes up quite clean and vivid if you boost the bass.

Tennstedt's is the most dramatic version since Levine and Mehta (♦EMI). He starts off smashingly, with terrifying lower brass and great thwacks on the drum. He finds more detail and interest in II than most other conductors, and the climactic passages in the posthorn movement are uncommonly exciting. Tennstedt's mezzo and posthorn player have more vibrato than usual, which is all to the good, though Ortrun Wenkel isn't nearly as controlled and finessed as Norman for Abbado or especially Horne for Levine. EMI's recording was one of their earliest digital jobs: It's clear but rich with no edginess, but you hear some mixing-desk wizardry going on and some of the resonance is cut off from final chords.

In his generally slack Israel Philharmonic recording, **Mehta** seems too intent on observing every one of Mahler's many tempo indications and fails to stitch together the massive first-movement tapestry in a convincing way (Sony). He was far better at sustaining I's broad-spanning tension in his earlier Los Angeles Philharmonic rendition, where the tempo changes are far more subtle and he manages to lead logically to the coda (♦London/Decca 443030, a "two-fer," with 1). He's also eminently optimistic and straightforward, not glancing into the darker corners of Mahler's pantheistic ode like Abbado. The Decca sound is a joy, though there isn't quite the depth of field that gives the streak of mystery to Maazel and Abbado. His Los Angeles account is one of the most consistently exciting recordings.

Barbirolli's 1969 recording has some small mistakes to suggest that the music was new to this orchestra, but I find his reading glorious, maybe for this very reason, and the playing is taut and exciting (BBC Legends). The performance is well turned and has the kind of character, subtle detail, and panoply of tone colors that are sorely missed nowadays (though his "posthorn" is improbably close). The BBC radio tapes have a touch of hiss and a good deal of conductorial grunting, but the sound is natural and transparent. Not a first choice, maybe, but not to be overlooked.

Litton's reading is not as original as Mehta's, Maazel's, or Abbado's; his performance is stricken for the most part by a fatal inability to surprise the listener (Delos). As so often in current Mahler performances, the orchestral sound is too blended and homogenized; the first trumpet and trombone are balanced too discreetly against the rest of the orchestra in I, the timpani restrained in the coda to the finale. **Inbal** is also competent and very well recorded, though not as deeply or impressively as Litton and Salonen (Denon). He's also more thoroughly steeped in the Mahler idiom than Litton, but he shows no particular interpretive insight. Rarely does the Stuttgart tone glow like some other orchestras, notably the Vienna Philharmonic.

You could say similar things of **Salonen** and the Los Angeles Philharmonic; the sound is smooth and too uniform, the interpretive view rather cool and unidiomatic (Sony). But Salonen turns up more discoveries and moments of astonishment than Litton or Inbal. He puts great store in the timbral and rhythmic refinement of the orchestra, and for

the most part they repay the honor with dividends. Sony's recording is the most transparent on offer, though it doesn't have quite the startling tonal body of, say, Levine's recording. It's not to be overlooked if sound and orchestral refinement are important criteria.

Tilson Thomas and the London Symphony are more varied and splendid (and thus idiomatic) in sound, though Abbey Road Studio 1 isn't large enough for the spatial effects Mahler calls for (Sony). He takes a consistently measured view, and his performance is exciting, though in an incidental rather than symphonic way: The movements lead to no particular culmination, and tempos tend to sound prosaically jaunty. It's wonderful, though, to hear Baker return to Mahler in IV and V and the *Rückert-Lieder*. **Wit** is more idiomatic than many of the big-name performers discussed above (Naxos). That said, he doesn't quite give the sense of digging into the music that he does in his outstanding 5; IV and V are touched by routine, and the sonics lack weight. Podles over-sings the contralto line in IV.

To be hypercritical, **Solti** doesn't find quite the nuance and sense of purpose in the score that others have uncovered; for example, the long coda to I doesn't have much joy or direction to it; II is devoid of affection and charm; and the posthorn solos are fairly prosaic (London/Decca). I heard the performance in Chicago's Orchestra Hall days before the recording, and I'd say Decca's sonics aren't all they could be in dynamic range and depth, so Solti's trademarked intensity of sound comes across as more clattery and garish than exciting.

Some sense of what the Solti could have been comes across in **Svetlanov**'s recording (Harmonia Mundi). This unusual and refreshing performance—by turns brash and sentimental—demands to be heard as an antidote to the blandness of many recent others. The brass of the Russian State Symphony (the horns especially) still show a trace of that lovable old Eastern wobble; the winds and percussion also have a hard and buzzy edge; and the bright colors are appropriate to this score. The Russian colors might not be as suitable for the middle movements; his tempo for II is too consistently slow; and Olga Alexandrova's mezzo isn't quite right in the Nietzsche setting. But Svetlanov also has an enviably sure take on the structure of the big first movement; each successive climax builds upon the previous one, and the strings really put out at the heart-stopping moment at Fig. 29. It's another performance not to be overlooked.

4. In the beginning, there was **Mengelberg**. His 4, made for Dutch radio with the Concertgebouw in 1939, is a precious document of a performance style as carried on by a friend and associate who helped keep the flame burning between Mahler's death and WWII (Philips and other labels). The idiomatic portamentos are here, and they are especially valuable in the slow movement. But we can't attribute any authenticity to Mengelberg's often artificial-sounding liberties with tempo; rather, his performance is best understood as a corrective to our latter-day reluctance to personalize or "romanticize" Mahler. The Philips production scrubbed up the sound and most of the 78 rpm surfaces but left timbres a little lifeless.

Some 30 years later, **Haitink** recorded 4 with the same orchestra and the beloved Ameling (Philips). The changes over the three decades resulted in a far straighter reading, and this is the best of Haitink's three recordings. There is the typical Concertgebouw refinement, with luminous strings, but there's also just the right amount of character, excitement, and point making. Ameling graces the finale with the perfect commingling of simplicity, boyishness, and femininity. The 1968 sound still comes up fresh.

But Haitink's 1983 remake with the Concertgebouw is a disappointment (Philips). Having perhaps more color and rhythmic energy, the lower orchestral hues are a bit darker and more varied than before, but the slow movement is surprisingly mannered, disfigured by two forced climaxes that sound rather ugly and emerge unnaturally from the structure. Alexander doesn't do much with the words; by comparison, Ameling allows you to make out every syllable. Haitink's 1992 version with the Berlin Philharmonic suffers from the bland uniformity that afflicts most of that aborted cycle (Philips). As usual, the playing, tempos, and phrasing are flawless, but there's nothing demonic about the Scherzo; the polyphonic lines come together too effortlessly in the slow movement; and in the finale McNair weighs and enunciates each word pretty much identically when so many other singers do something to convey a particular color or evocation at "Tod," "lacht," "sanftester Ruh," and so on.

Maazel is just as straitlaced and—if anything—even more serious in demeanor, but he has the indefinable interpretative subtleties of the Vienna Philharmonic to help him (♦Sony 44908). This isn't a reading to involve you so much as make you pause in quiet wonder, as you might before the chiaroscuro shadings of a Rembrandt. The strings are almost indecently radiant and the antiquated timpani have their distinctive voice. The fluid Viennese string tone is incomparable in the second theme of I, where Mahler has the Brahmsian tendency to have the cellos sing above the violas. In the finale, Battle manages the most luscious yet controlled slide imaginable at the word "lacht" (laughs). Apart from a hint of digital edge to high strings in the slow movement, the recording is fine.

Abbado does rather less to encourage the same orchestra's timbral fingerprints (DG, with 2). Still, the strings are incurably gorgeous even in his slightly soporific approach to I, and the nursery-rhyme flutes (and other wind solos) register strongly enough. He's more muscular than Maazel in the development section, and there's an appropriately off-the-cuff feel to the climaxes. Von Stade's doleful mezzo was the perfect vehicle for Mahler in the mid-'70s, but the performance is let down by a slack approach to the slow movement—the tempo is simply too slow given its lack of characterization.

Reiner offers another eminently straightforward view and fine performance (RCA). But his Chicago Symphony, playing at its peak at this time (1958), doesn't have the timbral glint in the eye of the Viennese or of Walter's New York performances. There's also something lacking when it comes to the malicious and ironic delight to be had in all the bustling detail of I and II. Reiner is at his most humane in the slow movement, but the tempo suddenly picks up at 3:10, where a bad edit leads me to think that another take was inserted. RCA's sound, at least in the latest mastering, tends toward glare at climaxes, and there is some distortion at the "opening of Heaven's gate" culmination to the slow movement.

Kubelik views 4 more as a quick and breezy jeu d'esprit than an ascent into things heavenly; he reminds us that "even St. Ursula" comes up laughing in the text to the finale. The Bavarian Radio Orchestra's relative lack of tonal blend is appropriate; the reedy winds really stand out as individual voices at the start of the Scherzo, where the music is rustic yet slightly disconcerting—never just sweet. The fast section of the slow movement has a Till Eulenspiegel brand of mischief. Only the finale disappoints: Soprano Elsie Morrison's delivery and Kubelik's fast tempo (he dispatches it more quickly than any other conductor on records) conspire to give it a rather hectored feel.

Reactions to **Klemperer** will hinge on how the listener takes to Schwarzkopf's rather mannered vocalizations in the finale (EMI). I find her boyish, rather bumpy style revealing and appropriate. Likewise, there's a particularly piquant account of Mahler's paired high woodwinds in I—a color that so often eludes later engineers and conductors. Klemperer is predictably unrushed in the first two movements and unexpectedly fast in the third. The only thing to take exception to is a certain stiffness, with the conductor refusing to push ahead in the closing page of I. Fast as it is, Klemperer's slow movement is the high point of his reading, with the luminous Philharmonia strings beautifully recorded, the first and second violins divided left and right, as usual with this conductor.

Still, I would prefer another '60s Philharmonia production to Klemperer: **Paul Kletzki**'s enchanting and sprightly reading (♦EMI 67726 and Royal Classics 6468), sporting the same reedy, unblended woodwind colors and natural sonic values but without Klemperer's rigidness. There are one or two passing fluffed notes, but nothing to limit your enjoyment of the performance. Kletzki combines something like the rightness of Haitink's first recording with the vigor and spontaneity of Tennstedt's. There's also an overall sense of relaxation without undue pokiness.

Walter made his recording with the New York Philharmonic (playing with commendable vibrato) in 1945 (Sony). Carnegie Hall sounds a bit dry, no doubt because of close microphone placement, but the performance is fine in its nonharanguing way, equal to anything recorded recently. Tempos are middle of the road, but much of Walter's virtue lies in the variety he's able to instill in the music without mauling the rhythms. Only the finale disappoints: Desi Halban offers one of the least intimate and more nervous readings I've heard. We also get eight early songs from Halban with Walter at the piano, but there it sounds as though the microphone had been taped to the singer's tonsils.

A 1953 live performance with Walter and the Philharmonic is a richer experience (Music & Arts): The cellos' bows sound longer in the second theme of I; the violinists linger in the central section of the Scherzo; and the slow movement is a touch more leisurely than before. There's more bloom and sweetness to the sound (it could almost be stereo), if also occasional peaking on the tape, the inevitable stage noise, and some virtuoso coughing. It's a special document nonetheless.

Whatever the merits of **Solti**'s second (Chicago) recording, there's an uncomfortable sense that both conducting and sound tighten up at climaxes (London/Decca). Be that as it may—I find it a difficult, unignorable flaw—this is one of the better sounding installments in Solti's Chicago cycle, and Te Kanawa's vocal luxuriance finds a more intriguing context here than it does in Ozawa's blander approach. Those wanting Solti in 4 are better directed to the New York Philharmonic set (see above). **Levine** recorded 4 with the same orchestra in 1974, and came up with a reading that's typically larger than life yet also kept on a tight leash in expression (RCA). The band sounds splendid and fresh, rhythms are well sprung, and the slow movement is beautifully shaped. But Levine, for better or worse, can never do anything untoward; conductorial skill and calculation are more in evidence than spontaneity. Similarly, the close balance of the recording flattens out the charm and variety of the music and gives the brass and winds a boxy sound.

The kind of normative reading Levine represents—tempo variation, textures, tone, and balance vigilantly watched over, just about anything overtly "inspirational" eschewed—is more attractively purveyed by **Inbal,** and his recording is also eminently transparent and realistically balanced (♦Denon 7952). He also has a lighter touch than Levine, which reaps particular rewards in the Scherzo, and he's more liberal with portamentos (almost too much so in the central pastorale section of II). His orchestra may not display the virtuoso confidence of the Chicagoans, but if anything this adds character to their performance. I do miss the tone of a great orchestra, but Denon more than compensates with excellent sound.

The Cleveland Orchestra has a recording history of its own when it comes to 4, the first of them **Szell**'s famous reading (Sony). Even at the nursery rhyme tune in trumpet and winds right before the first climax, Szell is a bit too relentlessly comfortable (Mahler instructs "Bedächtig") with his tempos in I. The balancing is also extremely careful, though there's enough character in the playing to hold the listener's interest. Rhythmic subtlety isn't Szell's strong suit: When tempo changes are made, they tend to be pretty heavily underlined. The Clevelanders are more luminous than with Boulez or Dohnányi, Szell's strings having more blend and presence. This is undoubtedly a beautiful experience, but in the final analysis I find it too controlled; there isn't an obviously human face behind the music making.

Boulez's is the most recent Cleveland account (DG). The playing is just as magnificent as expected: the orchestra's tone transparent as glass even in the largest climaxes, the intonation perfect. If I is a trifle over-refined, there's still the conductor's impeccable, dead-on pacing to reckon with. Something is definitely missing from the devilish Scherzo, though, which is too smooth in texture, easy in execution, and dovetailed in dynamic change. Juliane Banse, secure neither in breath nor pitch, was an unfortunate choice for the finale. Be all that as it may, the reading as a whole is to some extent held together by one of the most breathtaking, magically sustained slow movements on record; there's a kind of ease that transcends dullness, an intimacy born of complete mastery. Mahler describes heavenly perfection in his finale; if such is possible on our imperfect earth, it's already to be heard in Boulez's "Ruhevoll."

Dohnányi took the Clevelanders into the studio in 1993 and came up with one of the finest discs in his series (♦London/Decca 440315). His I is among the most unbuttoned on records, with strong accenting and characterization. The soloist is sardonic in the Scherzo, where the deep perspectives of the recording help us enjoy Mahler's wry horn writing. The slow movement is a bit disappointing; the tempos don't always mesh well, and Boulez does a better job of sustaining the tension. Still, he prepares the divine reappearance of G major in the strings beautifully right after the first climax. Upshaw is a very appropriate, boyish choice for the finale; the only flaw is that the microphones catch at her highest notes.

In contrast with Szell, **Tennstedt** takes the widest variety of tempos, but never to mannered effect (♦EMI 73706, budget price). This is without doubt the most interesting recording of 4 and also the most humane; every note, every phrase seems to speak. Try the return to G major in the strings after the first climax of the slow movement, where Tennstedt's phrasing is beautifully and uniquely inflected. There's just a touch of human brashness in his version of heaven, and the slightly bright sonics are perfectly appropriate — as is Popp's voice, always personable and vibrant but always in control.

Ozawa, however, is consistently routine (Philips). His tempos are resolutely middle of the road, the phrasing and climaxes prosaic, and the Boston Symphony doesn't show the poise and luminosity that one has every reason to expect. **Chailly** and the Concertgebouw have some of the same tradition-bound, middle of the road qualities, but also more variety of color, more rhythmic tension when necessary, greater lilt and charm when called for, and a soprano (the marvelous Barbara Bonney)

who digs into and conveys her text (London/Decca). This isn't the most original, interesting, or memorable performance, but it's beautifully conceived and played, and stunningly recorded. Chailly and Bonney also offer a substantial bonus: the orchestral version of Berg's *Seven Early Songs*.

Bernstein's 1960 New York recording is a bit undependable orchestrally in I and III — the winds and brass more so than the strings (Sony). Occasional braying and wayward intonation aside, this is an eloquent and enjoyable rendition, much preferable to his later reading. It's one of the finer installments in his CBS cycle, though the conductor's touch wasn't exactly light even in 1960. Reri Grist aids and abets Bernstein's quickness in the finale with her insouciant delivery and youthful, boyish voice. For his later recording, he chose a member of the Tölzer Boys' Choir, Helmut Wittek (DG). The decision to use a boy treble is entirely appropriate to the *Wunderhorn* text, which deals with a Catholic lad's wonder at the goings-on in heaven. But Mahler's line is quite wide-ranging and doesn't lie very well for a prepubescent voice. In any event, Bernstein tends to be horribly mannered. The Concertgebouw has been closely miked, more so than in its other performances in Bernstein's cycle, and this further underlies the interpretive peculiarities.

Salonen is a much happier choice — indeed, an extremely enjoyable one, a performance to renew the spirit (♦Sony 48380). Unlike Bernstein in Amsterdam, Salonen never weighs down the music. The performance made headlines when it was booed at the Salzburg Festival, and here and there in the first two movements you might still see a few snooks cocked at romantic Viennese traditions. The Scherzo is quick and full of nervous and fleeting detail, but anchoring such momentary interests is one of the most beautiful and luxuriant slow movements to be heard anywhere, the tempo daringly slow by movement's end. The Los Angeles Philharmonic is well-nigh flawless and (like the Cleveland) utterly transparent in sound, with spectacular horn work and a rare ability to float the string lines effortlessly at the beginning of the slow movement. Hendricks is the perfect partner, with her vibrant androgyny, tight vibrato, and utter security in all parts of her range.

There is an instructive comparison to be made between Salonen's smiling, intriguing quirkiness and **Colin Davis**'s pedantic detail (RCA). Davis's reading eschews lightness and charm and airiness and often fails to lift off in the climaxes. The Bavarian Radio brass can't compare with Los Angeles and Cleveland, or even Birmingham, nor are the horns always comfortable. Symptomatically, in the finale Angela Maria Blasi practically belts out the stanza beginning with "Wir führen ein englisches Leben" even though her line is marked pianissimo.

Whereas Salonen exudes a mischievous and boyish charm, **Rattle** tends to be tougher (EMI). He has clearly reconsulted the score and offers a quixotic reading. There's a disruption already in the fourth bar: He interprets the tempo for the first three bars as markedly slower than the main tempo for the first theme, a conclusion that may or may not be supported by the score. Nor does he show much evidence of heartfelt emotional investment in the piece. The verdict is still out on this innovative but rather off-putting performance.

Predictably, **Karajan** gets a leviathan string sound, wall-to-wall, all-subsuming — a womb-like sonority that evokes a bygone era (♦DG 415323). Some will also reject his usual strictness of tempo, even throughout the labyrinthine I and the tolling timpani strokes that follow the slow movement's big climax. It was part of his style to create an unerring musical shape despite the absence of large-scale tempo changes. The sounds are so beautiful and the atmosphere so consistently maintained that it's impossible to resist, and it's somehow the temporal strictness that makes such sounds possible. The slow movement is the heart of Karajan's reading; one reviewer spoke of "jaw-dropping beauty" here, and the Berliners' living, breathing, and yet unnuanced sonority is in every respect hypnotic. But the Karajan-Berlin string sound was never about mathematically exact intonation, and you'll want to look elsewhere for absolutely spot-on tuning.

5. This symphony marks a major turning point in Mahler's career and presents his interpreters with new problems. There is a new polyphonic approach, especially in III and the finale. The Scherzo almost becomes a concerto with its horn obbligato, presenting problems of balance and seating (Mahler supposedly sat his first horn up front, near the concertmaster). Even more challenging is the structure: it's in five movements, neither operatic-cinematic in juxtaposition like 2, 3, or 7, nor quasi-classical like 1, 4, and 6. The question of how to render its structure became still more complicated after Gilbert Kaplan argued in the '90s for taking the Adagietto at a faster tempo.

Part of Kaplan's argument lies in the fact that conductors who heard Mahler's own performances tended to dispatch the Adagietto in about eight minutes. Certainly **Walter,** who was first to record 5 in the days of wax shellacs (he made his only recording in New York in 1949), did not dally: his Adagietto clocks in at only 7:35. In the new transfer of this New York Philharmonic performance, surface noise is almost nonexistent and the sound is very vivid and alive, rather like an over-miked recording from the early '60s, partly because Carnegie Hall sounds quite dry (Sony, in the "Bruno Walter Edition"). The difficult II always has a firm idea of where it's going. Though drily recorded, this disc shows Walter's usual ability to bring out every ounce of character and color in the score without histrionics or haranguing.

Abbado's 1994 recording in Berlin apparently fell under Kaplan's influence in the Adagietto (DG). But the interesting thing is how the swiftness of his slow movement tends to make his reading sound as if it lacks a center, whereas Walter avoided such an impression. The performance gathers steam as it goes along. If not the most exciting or characterful reading, it's one of the more idiomatic—and beautifully played. The producer includes some applause at the end.

A number of recordings have bucked Kaplanesque trends and treated the *Adagietto* as a slow, oasis-like anchor around which the other movements gather. One such is **Ozawa,** who takes a daringly slow tempo and comes up with a heavenly reading that truly seems lost to the world, as the text to Mahler's Rückert setting goes (Philips). It's worth hearing for the 12 minutes of the Adagietto alone. But Ozawa shortchanges the more fearsome side of the symphony and doesn't instill enough rhythmic tension. He tends to stake his claims strongly enough at structural nodes in the outer movements, but the dialectic tension within sags dangerously; there's very little tension to the antiphonal exchanges between trumpet and strings in I.

With a perfectly judged tempo, a bit faster than Ozawa's, **Dohnányi** brings astute balancing and the most delicate phrasing imaginable to the Adagietto (London/Decca). But in just about all the other movements, his stunningly refined account seems a kind of interpretation in miniature. The texture is also too uniform and the sound of the orchestra diminished, except for absurdly over-miked timpani and bass drum. His phrasing is uniformly nonchalant, and even the finale never quite digs in its heels.

Other recordings are afflicted with different tempo-structural problems. **Leinsdorf** and the Boston Symphony offer some of the finest playing heard in any Mahler recording of the '60s (RCA). There are also mo-

ments on this record that are heaven-sent and unforgettable in their incisiveness and thrust. But Leinsdorf tends to undermine his own tension by not relaxing enough when asked to, and I is sabotaged by unprecedented speeds in the "Wild" episode—where he's twice as fast as the basic tempo—and an emphasis on the bass line gives it a kind of galumphing inevitability. He's also rather blank in overall interpretive detail and comes up with one of the most tepid Adagiettos on record.

Järvi is similar in that he offers a strikingly idiomatic sound without much of a structural argument to back it up: I and II sound much alike; the pianissimo cellos-and-timpani passage in II doesn't linger in the memory; the huge variety of sound colors in the Scherzo somehow fail to add up; and the Adagietto doesn't have the kind of individual touches that impress (Chandos). The sound, with transparent, natural perspectives and barely any spotlighting at all, is among the very finest this symphony has received.

Solti is a bit like Leinsdorf in that he concocts sonorities to move heaven and earth but doesn't back them up with much structural forethought (London/Decca). I also find fault with his fairly blank and unvaried approach to II and the contrapuntal finale, which he just winds up and sets loose. He's right at home in the third-movement Scherzo, which has a magnificent horn obbligato (though a bit too "assisted" in the mix), very firm bass lines, and rhythmic momentum that doesn't let up. The recording is too brightly lit, though this is less a problem in the "Solti Edition" mastering. It's a revealing reading of its kind. His live recording with the Chicago Symphony has better integrated sound, but the level of tension has dropped since the earlier rendition; furthermore, the conception isn't as well focused, and the players don't dig into the music as excitingly as before. The extraneous knocks and noises pile up, including an inscrutable squeaking at 4:56 in the first movement.

Kubelik's recording tends to falter with some different tempo miscalculations: the opening tempo of the "Funeral March" is so fast that the necessary critical tension doesn't arise between it and the faster "Wild" episodes (DG). Likewise, II and the Scherzo never quite seem to get their bearings, though there's plenty of fine playing from the Bavarian Radio Orchestra. Even Kubelik's Adagietto, though clocking in at a nonspeedy ten minutes, somehow—maybe due to the lack of truly hushed playing?—manages to sound rushed.

Karajan is splendiferous, chilling—the most beautiful recording ever made, and also the most cogently structured (DG). But this was his first recording of a composer he came to late in his career, and there's something superficial to the reading; it adds up to less than the sum of its parts. His Mahler interpretations would later take on a new, more idiomatic toughness. In 5, his luxurious attention to texture is everywhere in evidence, with woodwinds given a particularly good balance; tempos are impeccable. But his finale is typical: It becomes an orchestral showpiece, the grand conclusion to a kind of concerto for orchestra.

Inbal offers one of the better versions, the best entry in his complete cycle (♦Denon 1088). The first-movement funeral march isn't as bitter and hard-pressed as, say, Tennstedt's, but it's still a strong statement, and evocatively patient. His tempo for the Adagietto is perfect, and he sustains a remarkable level of tension here. Denon's wide dynamic range really comes into its own in the finale, which unfolds with real excitement. **Tennstedt**'s studio recording is in some ways the opposite of Karajan's: The brass snarl and bite, and the tempos are never merely comfortable (♦EMI, in his complete set). His articulation is a bit too uniform and the dynamic range narrow, though that impression might also result from the slightly recessed sonics. His Adagietto, deliciously chaste and perfectly judged, sounds like one long sigh and yet encompasses the widest span of emotions. With his perfect tempo choices and ability to maintain them, Tennstedt is generally able to create immense structural momentum and shape. His I is particularly—magnificently—trenchant, maybe the best heard anywhere. Some might think the finale a bit lightweight, but hear how very naturally and blithely it swings into action, holding something back for the very end. This is music making of very rare integrity, musicality, and vision.

Tennstedt's live recording from 1988, also with the London Philharmonic, is likewise superlative (♦EMI 49888). This performance does take some time to warm up, and there are occasional intonation smudges to deal with as well as a touch of audience noise. But by the timpani's stirring call to arms at 4:08 in III, the edge-of-your-seat impulsiveness is back, and the conclusion to this movement is a thrill. The Adagietto is perfectly judged and luscious, with stunningly fluid string sound and a touch more spontaneity to the rubato this time around. His finale has tremendous, triumphant energy, even more than before.

Gatti gives us a kind of agglomeration of the finest qualities of earlier Mahler conductors: There's something of Karajan's magical conjunction of impeccable structural foresight and sonic flair, but also a bit of Bernstein's devil-may-care attitude and Solti's cataclysmic, orchestral-sections-at-war sound (♦RCA 51318). Details are precisely placed, the climaxes are often electrifying without preempting one another, and this is a performance of rare intensity even if the orchestra isn't the last word in strength and beauty and the sonics could use a firmer bass response. If Gatti takes this music back to the studio in, say, 20 years, he could well come up with something definitive.

Sinopoli, with the Philharmonia, could have used a dose of Tennstedt's rugged artlessness (DG). His faithfulness to the score tends to call attention to itself, and his dynamic shadings sound particularly prissy in II. A similar degree of care and character in the phrasing or a greater amount of interpretive ardor and consistency might have helped offset such imbalances. The sound is among the most natural and believable this symphony has been given, with the mikes pulled a bit back in the hall. The strings, however, lack presence.

Another remarkable and intense reading comes from **Levine** with the Philadelphia Orchestra (♦RCA 5453). He manages to encompass both the lambent beauties and the bitter outbursts of the score with equal empathy, a rare achievement. The orchestra plays with beautiful tone but also with the right rhythmic tension. This was still the Ormandy era in Philadelphia, and the brilliant, weighty, and unusually wide-spanning sonics—the timpani very incisive, the violins just a bit thin—help to sharpen this group's usually opaque sound.

Bernstein's 1987 recording inspires mixed feelings, marked as it is by his usual volatility but also slowish tempos and a lack of rhythmic focus when the music isn't climaxing (DG). He tries to compensate for lack of structural forethought with eruptive climaxes, and starts off the first two movements with rather spongy articulation and insufficient rhythmic tension. The lack of tautness and crispness is a drawback in II, and he's best in the Adagietto, where his point making is effective. The finale is also alert enough—a very fine rendition, in fact—to make up for previous deficiencies.

He was more crisp and attentive to Mahler's rhythms in his 1964 New York rendition—less lumbering, even though the tempos were pretty much the same (Sony). There's more schmalz in this rendition of the trio section of the Scherzo, with its upward slides. But it has some of the drier sonics of the Sony cycle, with the result that there isn't much depth, sweetness, or mystery to the orchestra's sound, and climaxes aren't

comfortably contained. Starting right off with a solo trumpet who goes sharp on his accented (half) notes, the playing gets pretty sloppy.

Mehta's recording with the Israel Philharmonic has some of Bernstein's panache, with climaxes tellingly pushed home (Teldec). Like Bernstein, he tends to lose rhythmic focus in nonclimactic and transitional passages. The sonics really give the winds and lower brass full head, but the climaxes can be a touch blatty, and the strings are short-changed. One unsettling detail: Mehta's finale begins half a second before the Adagietto's F major chord has had a chance to die away.

Maazel has the Vienna Philharmonic more attentive than elsewhere in his cycle, and there are few of the tempo perversities that mar his 8 (Sony). But the performance only warms up in III, which comes up bright and brilliant after fairly routine tours of the "*Trauermarsch*" and II. In the long Rondo-Finale, which tends to sprawl in his hands, Maazel doesn't always escape the impression that he's treading water in the more repetitious passages. If he can't be called dramatic, he doesn't explore the score's introversions either. The sound is poetic but could use more clarity and depth.

Barenboim recorded 5 with the Chicago Symphony (Teldec). The sound is a bit less spectacular than Mehta's, without much bloom at climaxes, but it's generally fine. He shapes the Adagietto with a sure hand, and the balanced, well blended, and often suave playing is quite a change from the Solti years. Still, the finale doesn't really swing into action, and there are some rhythmic imprecisions that add up.

No such accusations of rhythmically unfocused playing can be aimed at **Haitink's** 1989 recording with the Berlin Philharmonic (Philips). Indeed, he's so infallibly right—his delineation of structure impeccable, his climaxes outwardly exciting—that it comes up missing when it comes to temperament. It's powerful, but not a hair is out of place. The tempos and general approach are similar to Tennstedt's, but there's more audible striving by the orchestra, and that means a great deal. Better to turn to Haitink's outstanding 1970 Concertgebouw reading, one of the more brazen essays in his original cycle (♦Philips, in the complete set). His finale, humorous and rising to real exuberance, is the perfect capstone to an artless but all-encompassing performance. The recording is strikingly brilliant (more vivid than the Berlin), even if there's some hiss, the bass is rather hollow, and sonic edges in full-cry tuttis aren't completely clean.

There's more character to **Neumann's** eminently respectable recording with the Czech Philharmonic; surrounded as we are nowadays by blandly internationalized sounds, it's a pleasure to hear a hint of that old Slavic bray in the brass and winds (Supraphon). This is very much a version to live with, though the very reverberant Rudolfinum tends to give the higher winds a breathy sound and the articulation a gluey, echoey quality, and also might have necessitated some of Neumann's unusually slow tempos. It's also a pity that the remastering gives the orchestra an edge I don't remember hearing on LP.

Boulez has been criticized for his emotional disengagement, yet I'd say there's a touching and refreshing purity to his approach, the excitement of a great orchestra playing magnificently, and so many interpretive decisions being impeccably, excitingly right without being merely "correct" (♦DG 453416). As always, Boulez can be counted on to unearth important details that everyone else has passed over: He brings a uniquely hesitant quality to the main theme of the funeral march, the tempo perfectly chosen, and II has the kind of rhythmic tension that's sorely missed in many other recordings. I can't remember the temperamental Vienna Philharmonic ever sounding more glorious, and the sonics are superb, with splendidly incisive strings and timpani.

While Boulez might not be a top choice, I prefer him to a good many others.

Barbirolli's often-praised account with the Philharmonia is marred by some rhythmic unsteadiness, lumpy phrasing, and plenty of moaning from the conductor (EMI). There is also a general level of orchestral ensemble that's best forgotten, though the strings are always full and vibrant. The second half of II wants a firmer sense of direction, and it's symptomatic of Barbirolli's crippling indifference toward quieter dynamics that he's more forte than pianissimo at the melancholy unison cello line, accompanied only by a timpani roll; he thereby loses what surely is the expressive heart of that movement. In this mastering, a brief but important section of the first-horn obbligato turns up missing in the Scherzo (at about 12:15); the passage sounds strangely naked without it.

Litton and the Dallas Symphony are disappointingly relaxed in the fast movements; all the devastating climaxes are beautifully but inappropriately contained (Dorian). The orchestra's sound is too homogeneous and monochromatic, and it also tends to lack tonal weight. Its consistent tepidness isn't helped by the disc's low mastering level. This is an empty musical experience.

Without having quite Tennstedt's or Boulez's temperament or sense of structure, **Chailly** does everything right without being dull or playing it safe (♦London/Decca 458860). He has the patience to let Mahler's slower tempos breathe, but doesn't cultivate a homogeneous sound in the exciting Scherzo and finale. The great Concertgebouw has great character and variety of timbre, and the generous, crushed-velvet ambience of the hall—a sound the composer knew well—is very right for Mahler. This might not be the most characterful rendition, but it makes an excellent central recommendation and is a good place to start for those approaching this music for the first time.

Finally, a magnificent performance, sonorously and spaciously if rather brashly recorded, comes from **Wit** and the Polish National Radio Symphony (♦Naxos 550528, at super-budget price). The first-movement "*Trauermarsch*" is fairly slow, just as it should be, and doesn't stoop to cinematicism. The finale is a gloriously sunny statement. Wit's rhythms have real bite in II, and in III and IV his rubato and agogic details are full of interest. The difficult horn parts are impeccably done. This would be a front-runner at any price.

6. Karajan's late conversion to Mahler struck gold with 6 (♦DG 457716). This is a performance of unspeakable magnificence—music making to haunt your deepest dreams. Given the work's relentless march rhythms, much of the difficulty in 6 lies in finding the right orchestral tone; Karajan takes painstaking care with orchestral sound and comes up with sounds that are more rugged, alive, and full of color than prettified. Especially in the "Originals" remastering, he hits on precisely the right timbres; this is tough music making, and he makes 6 seem like modern music. The fabled Berlin strings (which sound more truthful and magnificent here than on any other recording I can think of) ensure that the Andante is as gorgeous as it can be and still remain sensitive to the music's undercurrent of unspeakable pain. The finale is overwhelming, its hammer blows and final crash perfectly timed. The priceless couplings are Ludwig's nonpareil *Kindertotenlieder* and *Rückert-Lieder*.

Haitink directs Karajan's orchestra, but shows how the group tends to falter without the Karajanian toughness of approach and sonic flair (Philips). This is unremarkable, paint-by-the-numbers music making; it doesn't lack excitement but suffers from too much composure. In the absence of the Karajan push, you also get a bit tired of the dry Philhar-

monie sound, more monochromatic and less alluring than DG gave Karajan. Haitink is very good at coordinating the main climaxes of the finale, his Bruckner experience shows through. His earlier recording with the Concertgebouw is preferable in every way (Philips). The 1969 sound is on the thin side, but the playing and interpretation have a lot of character, and all the music's wide emotional vistas are encompassed, even if the finale could go to greater extremes. It's a fine example of a performance with classical leanings.

Neumann and the Czech Philharmonic are similar to Karajan in their gutsiness and rather stringently maintained tempos (♦Supraphon 111977). But Neumann tends to explore more of Mahler's brighter, less homogeneous textures: The Czech trumpets are brighter, the tuba more guttural, the brass and winds a bit more whiny and Slavic-tremulous, the percussion more jangly and less integrated into the orchestral sound. The recording is excellent if you give it a bass boost, and this magnificent reading comes on a single midpriced disc. Neumann's 1966 Leipzig account has harsh, steely sound and few of the timbral distinctions of the Czech performance (Berlin). The stereo spread of the orchestra is unnaturally wide. Neumann's interpretation, too, is more conventional. Spilling over to a second disc with only two Beethoven overtures thrown in, this is easily dispensable.

The wonder of **Horenstein**'s Mahler is that he was able to stand in front of even provincial ensembles and draw from them such idiomatic and splendid performances of a composer then played only rarely, if at all. His live 1966 recording of 6 with the Stockholm Philharmonic is a prime example (Unicorn, and a more vivid transfer from Music & Arts). The playing isn't virtuosic, sometimes even a bit tentative, but it always sounds intensely Mahlerian—alert and imbued with the right variety of colors. Unfortunately, the tempos are not sufficiently varied and inflected, especially in the finale, possibly a result of the conductor's accommodating the orchestra.

You get the feeling that march rhythms constrained **Bernstein;** whereas Karajan keeps the rhythms of the first two movements strictly in time and yet manages to instill the right degree of variety and flexibility, Bernstein is always straining against the pulse and tends to make the music sound turgid and long-winded. The earlier New York recording (Sony) is better in that regard than the 1988 Vienna performance (DG); the pulses are much better maintained, and the New York orchestra is more in tune and has a better-centered tone than the Vienna. Even so, neither Bernstein 6 blazes with quite the white-hot conviction of his 1963 2 or his Sony 7. As for the DG, it's hard to think of a recording where the Vienna Philharmonic has sounded rattier.

Kubelik is typically speedy in all but the slow movement; the effect isn't inappropriately manic (DG). While the line and tempos aren't strictly held, the Bavarians' bright, attentive, and attractive colors are appropriate to this score (a few sour or even wrong notes aside). Less distinctive are the small but accumulating imprecisions of ensemble and the raw edge of the sound in climaxes. **Solti** is dramatic and gripping in a superficial way; it's emblematic that his first movement march is on the fast side, with no irony or implicit bitterness allowed to temper the tragic heroism (London/Decca). The Chicago Symphony plays brilliantly, fearlessly, with an unexpectedly lovely contribution from the strings in the slow movement. The 1969 recording still sounds good, despite the absurdly over-miked timpani. But the finale is fatally Hollywoodish; in Solti's hands it tends to break into a kind of jaunty machismo that makes it sound like Strauss's *Heldenleben*.

Surprisingly, **Tennstedt** imbues his 6 with a similar, showbiz grandiloquence (EMI). Only the Andante moderato escapes cheap melodrama, and the too-cataclysmic-to-be-true last crash in the finale is a deafening, ultra-tragic announcement of doom. The sound is likewise bright, indulgent, and overbearing—in a word, cinematic. **Barbirolli** and the Philharmonia provide a typical Kingsway Hall recording, with a rich bloom to the sound (EMI). But the first two movements are slow and deliberate, without compensating subtlety of detail or rhythmic tension; they sound like rehearsal tempos. This conductor was famous for his grunting, and here the snorts of involvement from the podium are often extremely distracting.

Symphony 6 was astonishingly late in entering the repertory of American orchestras. **Leinsdorf** was one of the first to conduct the score in the United States, and he recorded it soon after, in 1964 (RCA). His 6 is a good deal more convincing than his 5, and the Boston Symphony's style is direct, aristocratic, gutsy, and refined. The sixth is the most classical of Mahler's symphonies, at least in structure, and something in that classicism responds well to Leinsdorf's nonindulgent but attentive advocacy. The sound is streamlined and elegant, but could use a wider dynamic range.

Hans Zender conducts the very proficient Saarbrucken Radio Orchestra in an energetic and beautiful 1973 reading that's let down only by some glare on the sound in climaxes (CPO). His tempos are open to criticism: he's too quick in the Andante moderato, especially as his finale is also one of the shorter ones on record, and he thereby also slights its pockets of repose. He drops the exposition repeat in the first movement. **Abbado** (DG) produced one of the finest 6s on records, a reading richer in bar-to-bar interpretive detail and woodwind character than Karajan's, with the Chicago Symphony more refined and sensitive than often in the past. His slow movement is as luscious as his Scherzo is trenchant, and his finale is hypnotic. But I'm not happy with DG's Galleria remastering; the sound is more opaque than I remember hearing on the LPs, and the strings are a bit dry and plasticky in fortes.

Dohnányi offers a cool, elegant, and haunting reading (♦London/Decca 466345, with 5). He makes I slightly oppressive, which is as it should be. The Andante moderato is simple and unaffected, without much give in the phrasing, yet it rises to a strong and insistent main climax. The Cleveland Orchestra is superlative, with a sound that's always seamlessly integrated and beautifully balanced without being homogeneous. Decca's sonics are wonderful, catching the glints of xylophone and discreet cowbells with alacrity and giving an imposing subterranean voice to the tuba and bass drum. This (and Levi's) will be the audiophile's choice for 6, though the performance is distinguished in its own right.

There is something almost automatic sounding to **Szell**'s performance with the same orchestra (Sony). Part of this impression comes from the live recording circumstances, with some flattening out of the dynamic range and breadth of the sound picture. There's also some audience noise. Szell's Andante is the quickest after Zender's and Järvi's and leaves uncentered his reading of the symphony as a whole. He's best in the finale, where Mahler's kaleidoscopic details are brought together into a taut and organic unity.

Maazel is unexpectedly brash in the fast music (Sony), and the Vienna Philharmonic plays a good deal more lazily than they do for Boulez (see below); the wind and brass intonation isn't always above reproach. More important is the fact that this reading is unremarkable and lacks detail by comparison with Karajan and Boulez. The slow movement, for instance, is cool but sounds more inert than evocative.

A better-played and much more alert interpretation comes from **Levi** and the Atlanta Symphony (♦Telarc 80444). The wonderful sound packs

a real punch at Mahler's cataclysms and doesn't stint on his feast of timbres; if there's a recording that gives a truer, more transparent picture of Mahler's "white noise" percussion layer (and all its complex overtones), I haven't heard it. The orchestra is a transformed group since its Robert Shaw days, their tone impeccable in climaxes and pianissimos alike; it surpasses at least two thirds of the orchestras in this listing. This is one of the very finest 6s of recent years.

Mehta and the Israel Philharmonic are efficient but atypically perfunctory, an impression not alleviated by the muddiness of the timpani and bass drum (Teldec). The sound of the group in toto is somehow both indistinct and claustrophobic. **Järvi** is uniformly fast in all movements (Chandos). (There's even room on the disc for a filler: the melodramatic, author-less *Symphonic Prelude*, which, if not written by Mahler when he was at the Vienna Conservatory, was penned by a gifted person in the same circle.) His Scherzo is so swift that it trivializes the music, his finale so speedy that it undermines its glowering and tragic edifice, and the beautiful horn solo two minutes into the slow movement starts off under the note. This comes as a disappointment after the conductor's enjoyable version of 5.

Under **Boulez**, 6 unfolds with implacable dignity and no-nonsense inevitability, but he manages to wring a lot of drama out of this music (♦DG 445835). He doesn't waste energy at the opening of the finale, for example, but paves the way for the *fff* outburst that introduces the real argument about five minutes in. I is on the slow side, and the beginning of the Andante moderato has a slightly withdrawn quality—all the better for the emotional journey to come—and this movement is graced by some of the most sensitive woodwind playing on records. Under Boulez, the Vienna Philharmonic sounds lithe, compact, pungent, and gorgeous. The sound is powerful and resonant, with an outstandingly true dynamic range.

Sinopoli takes Mahler's every cue for tempo inflection as an instigation of temporal fantasy (DG). For one, I don't think Mahler's "*a tempo, aber gemessener*" ("up to tempo, but more measured") indicates an unprecedented slow speed. He also throws in many tempo changes of his own devising. III is the slowest I've heard, but Sinopoli's phrasing sounds more warmed over than genuinely expressive. The performance as a whole strikes me as more fussily revisionist than imaginative.

Segerstam is endlessly spirited and inventive, and deserves praise for going against the "official" Mahler Society edition and reinstating the third hammer blow in the finale, which Mahler dropped for superstitious reasons (Chandos). His contribution is so rewarding in its detail, the finale so cliff-edge exciting, that I hesitate to bring up the Danish National Orchestra—not the optimal group for this music, as it turns out, the horns and strings in particular wanting for body, weight, subtleties of timbral shading, a rhapsodic bent. The wide-ranging and resonant sound do much, but the engineers didn't go out of their way to help the strings' lack of tonal heft, and there are some astonishing mishaps: The first half-second of the timpani stroke starting the Scherzo is cut off, and there's a bizarre increase in volume at fig. 98 in III. Recommended even so, and as a filler, Segerstam offers the best reading available of *Todtenfeier*, Mahler's preliminary tone-poem version of what would become the first movement of 2.

Wit has an impeccable sense of structure and pacing, and his Polish National Radio Symphony has this difficult score entirely in hand (Naxos). The sonics, too, are outstanding, though it's not a deep-set, impress-your-neighbors kind of sound. All that's missing is the last degree of interpretive personality and white-knuckle conviction, and not all the first-desk work is at a Berlin or Cleveland level of perfection: The Polish first horn has some suspect intonation in I. **Inbal** purveys his familiar trademarks of careful preparation and impeccable tempos, but again the results lack the last ounce of tonal distinction from the orchestra or the last degree of fervency or individuality from the conductor (Denon). In favor of the reading is the attention paid to the secondary lines in the part writing in the slow movement (lessening its Schubertian sweetness a bit), and, in the finale, some of the most imposing hammer blows on record.

7. This symphony is often victimized by arbitrary tempo choices. Mahler was usually profligate with his exhortations to the conductor, but in this case there may actually be too many of them; with no metronome markings to back them up, their plenitude and apparent contradictions can cause confusion. If the disparate tempos aren't coordinated, or if the conductor inserts tempo changes not called for by the score, the structure—especially in the first and last movements—tends to meander and fall apart. Maybe this has been the Cinderella among Mahler's symphonies for so long simply because it's the one conductors have most often mangled.

Though **Abbado**'s recording from Chicago (DG) has been lavishly praised, it's full of such tempo transgressions. There are other problems, like the infernal tendency of conductors (including Abbado) to slow down (with no cue from the score except a double-bar that's there only to indicate a key change) for the material that first comes up four bars after rehearsal 10. This is especially nefarious because putting on the brakes here will have to be repeated each time the material comes back, thereby pulling the movement apart. Abbado's recording also suffers from an overall lack of nuance, an unduly fast Scherzo (here Mahler specifically cautioned the conductor against speed, which tends to Disneyize the movement, making it prosaically spooky), and a rather businesslike jaunt through the second *Nachtmusik*. More's the pity that this is one of the better sounding recordings to come from Orchestra Hall, and there are many felicities of playing and conducting.

Tilson Thomas (RCA) and Ozawa are generally exemplary when it comes to tempo relations in I, but their recordings lack distinction otherwise. It really does make a difference to hear, in their hands, the first movement open as a more or less steady speeding up from the opening to the Allegro con fuoco at Rehearsal 6. My enthusiasm for Tilson Thomas and his London Symphony begins to dim, though, when I come to his rather cool approach to the nocturnal beauties of I; he doesn't really seem to enjoy the luscious passages for divided lower strings, for instance. His *Nachtmusik*s are also more efficient than charming or meaningful, and it's hard to escape the overall feeling that he doesn't have much to say about this music. But his recording does have very good sound, marked by depth, transparency, and crispness, and is worth hearing for that reason alone.

Ozawa's tempos are right, and if that were the only criterion, his recording would be a triumph (Philips). As so often in his Mahler cycle, we begin by appreciating the Boston Symphony's beautiful transparency of sound, the conductor's musicality, and the acoustics of Symphony Hall. But the performance is incapacitated by its well-heeled nature; the balance between instruments is too polite to be idiomatic, and there's a firm resolve against risk-taking when it comes to articulation and tempo. The cowbells are beautifully captured, though.

Bernstein's first recording is generally better behaved than his second, though both are better than some others in integrating Mahler's various tempos (♦Sony 60564). He doesn't pointlessly fragment I as Abbado does, and he manages to make the tempo changes mesh well despite some misjudgments. Just as important, he relishes the divided-string nocturnal passages in the development, and clearly loves the cinematic, otherworldly sounds Mahler comes up with. Moreover, the entire performance is complete on a single midpriced disc, and the 20-bit remastered sound in the "Bernstein Century" edition comes up remarkably fresh and vivid.

The New York Philharmonic plays rather better in Bernstein's remake (DG), and the live recording job is good, if harsher than the Sony. But an interpretation that was lithe, colorful, and fun in 1968 has slowed down and become more mannered and graceless by 1986. Already in the first few pages, his tempo is all over the map; in the nocturnal development material with divided lower strings, he slows down almost to a crawl to an enervating—if beautiful—effect. DG's multimiking all but purges the cowbells of their poetry, and the finale is an essay in forced and empty grandiloquence.

Tennstedt seems to spend a lot of time slowing down in I (♦EMI). The nocturnal material in the development is slow, aromatic, and beautifully played. This allows him to really make something of the big, harp-introduced "opening the curtain" passage that comes later. This symphony seems particularly suited to Tennstedt's temperament. A fair number of 7s have exciting first movements and allow the others to fade, but Tennstedt maintains tension across all five. Too bad the engineers prematurely cut off the ambience after some of the closing chords.

Haitink and the Berlin Philharmonic turn in one of their more convincing performances in character and energy, at least in I (Philips). The nocturnal material in the development is surprisingly, daringly slow, but he and the Berliners don't give it quite the radiance of Abbado, Tennstedt, or Bernstein on Sony. His Scherzo is a particular disappointment: not too fast, but with little in the way of compensating rhythmic tension.

With his Munich orchestra, decent if never plush or sonorous, **Kubelik** was more at home in the quirky "cobbler's patch" 7 than in some of the other symphonies (DG). He and the players are at their best in the middle three movements; the winds in particular have a lot of character, and the approach is everywhere fresh and genuine. But the brass, including the tenor horn in the first movement, tend to bray, and the outer movements come up rather empty, thanks to his almost-throwaway tempos and unconsidered phrasing. DG does a level-headed recording job, though—a rare instance where the mikes don't seem to home in on the percussion, especially the timpani.

There's always an unmistakable rightness to **Horenstein**'s readings of Mahler, and he's inspired in his live recording with the Philharmonia Orchestra (♦BBC Legends 4051). The concessions to be made for live conditions are some coughing, a final ovation, and occasional fluffs in the orchestra. He doesn't get the tempos entirely right in I, but with awe-inspiring crescendos from the horns, he makes the re-transition to the recap a passage of unbelievable splendor. **Levine**'s recording with the Chicago Symphony suffers from his tempo meddlings, and he does little that could be called subtle, sensitive, spontaneous, or particularly interesting (RCA). The engineers also homed in on the timpani, which can be justified at the start of the finale and maybe the first *Nachtmusik* but not anywhere else. A sonic spectacular when the recording first came out, the sound now seems rather edgy and two-dimensional.

Solti is electrifying with the same orchestra (♦London/Decca, in his complete set). He stumbles into the same skein of first-movement tempo difficulties as Abbado, and is perhaps an even worse transgressor in that respect. His exposition is riddled with unmarked tempo changes, and some exhortations in the score are misread. But his performance has great intensity and something like the cliff-edge Mahlerian sound of your dreams, and the Chicagoans make less garish sounds here than they do for Abbado. Solti comes up with an effective and fairly simple solution to the patchwork problems of the finale: simply play the hell out of the music!

I've saved the "eccentric" renditions for last. For an indication of the wild performance opposites in 7, compare **Scherchen**'s 1965 live recording with the Toronto Symphony (Music & Arts, I in 18:35) with **Klemperer**'s version with the New Philharmonia (EMI, 27:39). Scherchen was closely linked with the Schoenberg circle and might have been expected to give us some idea of their Viennese notions of Mahler performance (Webern, for one, conducted Mahler frequently). But all tempo indications are misread or ignored in I, and most of the movement goes off at such a breakneck jog that the players have some trouble keeping up. He's relatively conventional in the remaining movements, except when he sees fit to make a crescendo out of Mahler's decrescendo on the penultimate chord of the finale.

Klemperer and the Philharmonia are even more bizarre, playing the score so slowly that on its first release it had collectors running to check their turntable speeds (EMI). Only the Scherzo and second *Nachtmusik* are taken at more or less normal tempos. His speeds could have worked if the articulation had been less uniform and if he had filled the expanses with the kind of musical detail that Rattle, for one, discovers. As it is, it's marmoreal, like the real thing in slow motion. The recording still sounds good, though. It's a lesson in the perils of performance tradition and "authenticity" that Klemperer was present for each of Mahler's 20 rehearsals for the 1908 premiere of this symphony.

Rattle's live 1991 recording is different from any other version, and you should hear it no matter how many performances of 7 you've come to know (♦EMI 54344). Some might accuse him of neglecting the majesty and romanticism of the music, and I do find him obsessive at times and occasionally questionable when it comes to tempo: the Scherzo is too fast, and the rather tight-lipped finale relies too much on sheer speed and the Birmingham Symphony's virtuosity. But this is the disc I recommend as offering the best overall combination of modern sound, orchestral playing (the orchestra is world-class here), and interpretive originality and vision. There's applause at the end, but the audience is silent otherwise.

The writer, musician, and social scientist T.W. Adorno often thought of Mahler's strangenesses as an attempt to disrupt the pleasant chimera of happy "bourgeois" music making as it's heard in much of the standard repertory. If there's something Adornian "deconstruction" in Rattle's interpretation, **Boulez**'s recording positively reeks of it (DG 447756). Always one to stand a cliché on its head, he's out to defuse any symphonic presuppositions right off on the first pages. I is not only very slow, but Mahler's explosive grace notes, sforzatos, dotted rhythms, and possible tempo variations are distinctly underplayed. Boulez also explodes the traditional dichotomy of sensibilities in the middle three movements. His finale is more conventional, except that his tempos here all mesh effortlessly, and you thereby hear nothing of Mahler's "Kappelmeisterish failure" (Deryck Cooke's description of the movement). Much of this is owed to the miraculous musicianship of the Cleveland Orchestra, which dispatches everything with the crispness and quick response of chamber players. This may not be a first-choice 7, or even a good second or third choice, but it's a must for someone wanting another view.

8. This symphony was right up **Stokowski**'s alley; he gave its first American performance in 1916. His live London recording is perhaps less grand and cinematic—less indulgent—than you might expect, but every detail finds its place within a firm, masterly, beautiful conception (Music & Arts). The soloists are all good, the choruses fine in an old-fashioned, English oratorio style, and that impression is underlined by some of the stately tempos in Part 2. Too bad the mono sound isn't more inviting; it's no more than a decent if fairly murky radio broadcast for the period, with an audience that could have used a few lung transplants. Music & Arts doesn't help by giving only one access point for the hour-long Part 2.

A period piece came from **Scherchen,** whose Vienna Symphony performance dates from 1951 (Tahra). It's best described as Wagnerian; much of Part 1 has a dark foreboding (and slowness) that make it sound like the Norns foretelling doom at the beginning of *Götterdämmerung*. The solo sopranos and mezzos (a few Brunnhilde-wanna-bes among them) exemplify truck-drive-through vibratos, and some of the singers also develop a fleeting inability to count. Tahra has added artifical reverb, and the climaxes tend to break up.

Historians commonly go back to 1959 and **Horenstein**'s epochal Albert Hall performance when asked to name one event that helped launch the latter-day Mahler boom (♦BBC 4001). I know of no other recording that captures so well the vast expanse, the spatial and textural breadth, of Mahler's "symphony of a thousand." The performance gets off to a shaky start with some missed entrances and unsure rhythm, and Horenstein doesn't always maintain a taut structural line, but he's unmatched in weight of sonority and his ability to bring every detail together into a unified but vivid experience without underlining or forcing anything. The only drawbacks—and they're a fairly small price to pay for the stunning musicianship—are the absence of texts in the booklet and the profuse coughing at the beginning of Part 2. (Surely the technology exists to debronchialize such historic documents? Steer clear if noise annoys you.)

Mitropoulos holds the musical line more tautly than Horenstein; with firmer interpretive convictions and generally better-chosen tempos, he wrings more expression from the score. Unfortunately, the mono Austrian Radio tapes are hard listening: There are blurps, a pitch change or two, and shrill climaxes (Orfeo, 2CD, and on one disc in his Music & Arts set, with heavier filtering to make the sound easier on the ear but with only two tracks to Orfeo's ten). Those with some tolerance and imagination when it comes to sound will likely prefer it to Horenstein.

Bernstein's first recording, made in London in 1966, is very uneven (Sony), while his Vienna recording (♦DG 435102, from Austrian Radio tapes made at the 1975 Salzburg Festival) catches him at his most transcendent. There are some exciting moments in the London version, but the choruses are distant and woolly—which might be a good thing, considering how the soloists (especially Gwyneth Jones) scoop up to some of their notes. More worrying is the sonic peaking at the loudest climaxes. The only distinction here is the magnificent cathedral-size organ, whereas the electric instrument at the Salzburg Festspielhaus takes no prizes. You get the impression that Bernstein was particularly at home in the mysteries of Part 2, with Mahler recreating the sounds of Goethe's dramatic landscape and "holy anchorites sheltering in rocky clefts." His pliable phrasing and obvious affection for that music are very moving with the Austrians—often heavenly.

In the Salzburg version, he's far better at maintaining the tension in Part 1; there's incredible energy at the "*accende lumens sensibus*" fugue, and very little audience noise. The Vienna Boys Choir takes the prize as the strongest Mahler children's chorus on records, and the stunning solo lineup includes Margaret Price, Blegen, Baltsa, Riegel, Prey, and the wonderful van Dam (whose rare Mahler forays are all to be treasured). The final *"Alles vergängliche"* crescendo is also less mannered in Salzburg, though no less impressive. The recording is constricted at climaxes, but is fully acceptable, with the orgiastic podium thumps vividly conveyed.

Solti's version is a classic, especially satisfying in its new "Legends" remastering (♦London/Decca 460972). No account has a greater sense of occasion or blazes ever onward quite so definitively. His soloists—including Augér, Popp, and Talvela—are all very fine. The Chicago Symphony, recorded with plenty of body and resonance in Vienna, plays with great conviction as well as the necessary refinement. Solti is less sensitive to the lyricism and charm of Part 2, where I sometimes miss Bernstein's way of caressing a phrase, but these two conductors illuminate opposite sides of the work. Some of Decca's overdubbing, added ambience, and slight roll-off at climaxes are more conspicuous on CD than on LP, but the 1971 sonics are still impressive.

Haitink is lightweight, almost noncommittal in his 1971 recording (Philips). It's almost always a joy to hear the Concertgebouw, but they sound pretty perfunctory in their beginning of Part 2. Part of the problem there and elsewhere is Haitink's all too frequently casual tempos. He seems almost incapable of making rhetorical points, through tempo choices or any other means. **Kubelik** is preferable, especially with his firmer rhythms and more impulsive choice of tempos (DG). His singers, too (Fischer-Dieskau and Mathis among them), tend to bring more character to their texts and their allegorical roles in Part 2. Kubelik doesn't rush, as is his wont in Mahler, and the performance has appealing intensity and spontaneity.

Ozawa recorded 8, his first Mahler on disc, for the Boston Symphony's centennial (Philips). There's no doubt about its musicality; the well-prepared forces and the conductor's attention to detail are to be expected. But he creates the impression of an interpretation in miniature, the piece conceived as a chamber cantata that's been fleshed out with extras. His very musicality tends to rob the music of a lot of its weight and force. The soloists are able but rather faceless, and the Tanglewood Festival Chorus is less majestic in sound than tactful and round-edged.

Gielen brings great control and consummate preparation to his live 1981 Stuttgart recording, available in a single bargain-priced disc (Sony). The soloists, orchestra, and choruses are all excellent; only the woodwinds sometimes show a bit of stress. This is a richly expressive experience, with a strength of character that stems from the performers' confidence. Yet I wished he would take more time to stop and smell the roses, and charm isn't his strong suit either. The sound and balances are astonishingly good for a live recording, with just a few coughs and some concluding applause. Tensions run much less strong under **Inbal,** though the choruses have a vivid sound, and the deep and dynamic engineering (with particularly well-defined bass) adds a good deal to the performance (Denon). His "deep bells" in Part 1 sound like saucepans, and Denon fails to give internal access cues to either part.

Maazel's version is one of the stranger performances in his cycle. He's Machiavellian, a kind of anti-Bernstein: cool, impersonal, and calculated, often refusing to press on in a way that might be thought conventionally rousing. Part 1 unfolds as a disheartening series of ritards; Goethe's penitents and rocky landscape at the beginning of Part 2 seem to suit him better. **Tennstedt** can seem a bit faceless If you come to him after hearing the likes of Bernstein and Sinopoli (EMI). As if to compensate, the recording itself has great dynamic range. Still, the concentration is palpable at the beginning of Part 2; the soloists are fine; and this made a suitable conclusion to his Mahler cycle.

It's hard to recommend **Shaw** on any count (Telarc). The great choral director approaches this symphony with neither a vision nor an overview of its structure. His choruses are impressive, but in a full, rounded, unassertive way that would be more idiomatic in a Schubert partsong. His soloists are uneven, and the Atlanta Symphony is no more than dependable and a good deal less than that in their very first passage. The orchestra sounds as if it's in a different acoustic than everyone else, and there's some obvious multi-miking of the soloists.

Consider **Colin Davis**'s version a near-miss (RCA). He has wonderful choruses and some beautiful details: the delicate harp, organ, and violins passage before *"Dir, der Unberührbaren"* and the superb control of the huge final crescendo at *"Alles vergängliche."* His Bavarian Radio Symphony isn't quite at the same level as the choruses, though it's hard to tell if the lively but hard-edged sound is just being less kind to them than to the singers. Among the soloists, baritone Leiferkus is a drawback with his near-lisp and affected manner.

Abbado and his Berlin forces bring careful musicality and an almost chamber-music conception to this monumental symphony (DG). There's much musical detailing and shaping going on; nothing is forced, but nothing is understated either. In Part 2, the conductor creates the sense that a larger, grander picture is continually unfolding; we're indeed "drawn heavenward." This continually changing second half is always well integrated in sound but continually moving above and beyond, thanks partly to the conductor's crisp definition of rhythms. Terfel is the irreplaceable Pater Ecstaticus at *"Ewiger Wonnebrand,"* but every one of the soloists is outstanding. The sound is dry but naturally balanced. This release comes strongly recommended if you're looking for an intimate view of this gargantuan score.

Sinopoli is rather uneven in Part 1, where he comes up with his share of nagging Sinopolianisms (why the exaggerations in the violin solo?), and his control over the proceedings isn't as firm as that of others (♦DG 435433). But his Part 2, blazing with operatic grandeur, is a triumph; he reveals much of the drama that lies dormant in other hands. Much of the success is owed to his consistently outstanding lineup of soloists. The choruses are strong and bright, and—something far harder to achieve than might be thought—the engineers actually make all the musicians sound as though they're in the same acoustic. It's strongly recommended.

9. *Walter*'s career was intertwined with 9: He gave its posthumous premiere in Vienna in 1912, conducted it in his last concert at the Musikverein two months before Hitler marched into Austria in 1938, and finally—in a rounding-off worthy of fiction—taped it in Los Angeles as one of his very last studio recordings.

Walter's 1938 performance documents a musical Vienna that was within weeks of disappearing, never to return: The first violin was Mahler's brother-in-law, the venerable Alfred Rosé, who was concertmaster despite the fact that Austria was more or less already in Hitler's pocket by this time; this was one of the last times Mahler was heard in concert in Europe until after the war. This was pretty much the Vienna Philharmonic Mahler knew and conducted and was one of the last times Walter conducted in Europe. Except for a bit of volume difference between the 78 rpm sides, the sound is fine: The engineers had five rehearsals to set up and test their equipment, and discreet CEDAR processing has left the surfaces noise-free.

Whatever the circumstances, there's more intensity to the music making than in Walter's later stereo recording. In particular, the unison violin passages are remarkably strong. The Vienna Philharmonic's personnel and circumstances changed forever after this event, but it's still astonishing how little their sound and style has altered in the following 60 years. If there's any disappointment in the two Walter recordings, it's his consistently fast tempos, especially in the finale; he takes only about 18 minutes in 1938 when today 26 minutes has become the norm. This could well represent a more "authentic" Mahler style before the late-20th-century tendency toward elephantine tempos set in. As if to emphasize the point, he ends the finale too abruptly in both recordings; he hardly seems to follow Mahler's indication to end "*ersterbend*" ("dying away").

Whatever the pleasures of the Vienna Philharmonic in the earlier version, many will prefer the conductor's final, studio version for its fine stereo sound and the fact that Walter takes just a bit more time with the score. This 1961 reading has some of the finest and most transparent sonics the piece has enjoyed on record, at least in its 20-bit "Walter Edition" mastering (♦Sony). The Los Angeles pickup orchestra generally plays no better and no worse than a bona fide group of national class of that period, though the strings don't sound lush or plentiful. Walter's conception is modest, unforced, and effortless. It's also rather lightweight: The orchestra barely supplies the sonic heft of a modern virtuoso band. Yet nothing in the music—its nostalgia, sweetness, or dramatic extremes—comes up missing. The couplings are a lengthy interview with the conductor and a bit of the rehearsal.

Giulini and the Chicago Symphony are very special, but not to be enjoyed if you're in a hurry (♦DG 437467). Every bar is marked by his sincerity and characteristic patience and inwardness. The openings of the first and last movements are intensely beautiful, with Giulini catching perfectly the autumnal, Viennese, bittersweet quality in Mahler's writing, the sense of grace that accompanies us to the edge of the hereafter. Some will find his I and III a bit sluggish and lacking in grandiosity, and they do arguably lack something in overall shape; Giulini doesn't much respond to Mahler's common indication for climaxes to be "*bewegter*" ("more agitated"), which should entail a tempo increase. Neither is he to be rushed even in the most catastrophic transitional passages, where just about every other interpreter, even Walter, presses ahead. The finale, though, brooks no cheap melodrama and becomes one long and glorious song from start to finish. The mastering is a tad wiry and bass-shy.

Solti recorded his 9 with the same orchestra several years later, and as before in his cycle, the Chicagoans' sound is virtuosic and startlingly real (♦London/Decca). While Giulini never lets the group make an ugly or unbalanced sound, Solti is less interested in beautiful tone and more willing to court blatancy. I sounds for once truly like an apocalypse, a world and symphonic style falling apart at the seams, and the very clear digital recording lets us hear every strand of this modern symphonic fabric in decay. The approach is perhaps less appropriate to II and IV (the high violins resolutely nonsweet in the spare conclusion to the finale), and sometimes the sonic heat is turned up too high for too long. But such a sound is certainly appropriate to the wild and deathly 9 as a whole, and Solti has a vise-like grip on the listener's attention through its every moment.

Boulez took the Chicago Symphony into the more forgiving acoustics of Medinah Temple and typically tamed the Chicago tone a little (DG). There's still plenty of pungency in I's stuttering brass mottos, but now the strings have a more malleable sound and are more evenly balanced against the brass and winds. Boulez is typically expert at sifting through Mahler's passages of complex counterpoint, and no single climax preempts another. If I is superb, though, you get the impression that the emotional and textural progression traced out by the four

movements (moving from complexity to simplicity, changeability to stasis) doesn't particularly suit Boulez. The Scherzo is well played but otherwise unremarkable, and the finale is trenchant without quite erasing the impression that he's a bit bored with the music. For one thing, he doesn't demand the intensity of tone needed to put across the unison violin line leading into the recap.

Maazel and the Vienna Philharmonic are exciting, outstandingly played, and luminously recorded (CBS/Sony). But as sometimes happens in his cycle, there's the unidiomatic feeling that the long outer movements are episodic rather than cumulative, and underlining that feeling is the fact that climaxes rarely deliver the grand payoff heard in other interpretations. What the listener takes away is not the sense of a grandiose and tortuous passage into another world like Bernstein, nor the impression of a huge structure that miraculously comes together by the last bar like Karajan, but isolated moments of finely sifted sound and passages that are there to mark time. Maazel's Adagio from 10 is another matter; beautifully shaped and utterly luminous, but also more pungent and engaged than his 9, this is one of the best first-movement 10s on record.

In **Barbirolli**'s recording with the Berlin Philharmonic (♦EMI 63115), I is again a bit quick for current tastes but it has the humanity I miss in Karajan. Part of this may come from the impression that the performance wasn't over-rehearsed. It's not the kind of reading where architectural pinions are placed with great forethought and sunk deep into the bedrock like Karajan. Barbirolli doesn't seem able to find much detail in II, but the finale is the culmination it must be even if he doesn't always shake the listener to the bone and leave him breathless as Karajan does. This is an imperfect but moving, humane, and warm-hearted reading, and it's quite well recorded.

Ozawa and the Boston Symphony are alter egos to Barbirolli: impeccably prepared and paced and stunningly well played, with well-nigh perfect balance within the orchestra, but lacking emotional abandon and the necessary lift in the climactic moments (Philips). The orchestra makes some amazing sounds, but rhythm, phrasing, and articulation come across as normalized, averaged, unremarkable, and impersonal. Though lacking something in bass response, the recording job is one of the best to come from Symphony Hall.

Levine's qualities as orchestral technician and disinterest in spontaneity stand him in good stead in 9, recorded in Philadelphia (RCA). He allows himself all the time in the world at the otherworldly and serene first-movement coda, where we wait blissfully for the descending step that opened the movement to turn into a falling fifth. His patience makes a lot of wonderful things happen here and can make Karajan sound hasty. He makes II—too often a disappointment in performance—a triumph of charm and ear-catching detail without overcharging the music. At 30 minutes, his finale is the longest on record; with his penchant for rhythmic focus and ability to convey Mahlerian resignation, he sustains the half hour superbly. If there is a caveat, it might be that the movements could be better differentiated in sound and character, and that the finale wants in simplicity. The only thing preventing the strongest recommendation is the sound: There's an edge to the strings, especially in the high-lying finale passages, though this is somewhat tamable with the treble controls.

The late '70s and early '80s saw an explosion of 9s on record, and among these **Tennstedt**'s was often called exceptional (EMI). Returning to it now, especially after hearing Karajan's chamber-style transparency, his first two movements seem rather bloated, self-conscious, and ponderous. Similar things could be said about the sound, which has an unappealing edge in his cycle. The finale, though, sounds like it wandered in from a different reading; the music making is moving, perfectly paced, noble in its simplicity, and well played. The hushed and rarified ending is particularly moving—perhaps the most moving close on disc.

In 1979 **Bernstein** made his only appearance with the Berlin Philharmonic, and 9 was the forum for this collision of worlds (◆DG 435378). You can imagine the scrambling that must have taken place when he asked the players to do everything Karajan had been training them for decades to avoid: bring out isolated details in the texture, force accents, keep the tempo constantly in flux, and so on. This isn't a harmonious coming together of a conductor and orchestra, and the moments of disagreement—exhilarating tension, some would say—are many. But the climaxes are fantastic and chilling, especially in the Scherzo—Karajan had over many years taught the orchestra to build its louder sonorities from the bottom up, and that training together with Bernstein's intense, spur-of-the-moment exhortations created some otherworldly sounds. The finale is the key movement, as it must be, yet there's astonishing restraint here, and by the end you feel the conductor has in a sense liberated one of the world's great orchestras, and the orchestra has in turn handed the conductor a new sense of nobility.

This could have been something like the 9 of your dreams if a producer had been there to question some of Bernstein's stranger details and ask for a retake of some of the untidy moments where the orchestra seems less inspired than confused by the man on the podium. As it stands, the pair of discs makes a fascinating document that's to be preferred to Bernstein's other two recordings. The radio tapes are very good, and there's more noise from the podium than from the audience. As usual with Bernstein's concert recordings, no applause is included.

By 1985 Bernstein's conception had mellowed considerably and turned inward. In his Concertgebouw recording, those all-important, bittersweet upbeats in I are beautifully unhurried; the climaxes are impressive but ever so slightly blunted rather than cataclysmic (DG). The music doesn't gush. All four movements are distinguished by the dark, burnished Amsterdam horns; the watery first trumpet is less enticing. Bernstein's finale is sui generis: slow and rather shapeless, but still deeply felt, deeply moving, and never distended. After going through this beautifully played performance, you feel as though you've been transformed by hearing all three acts of *Parsifal*—and just as reluctant to talk about the experience.

Those wanting to hear Bernstein on his New York turf can turn to his 1966 recording (Sony). Certainly the mannerisms and unusual tempos are less in evidence here—but then aren't they what make Bernstein's Mahler so challenging and worth hearing? The interpretation is straightforward and the sound surprisingly good, though still on the dry side and with fairly obvious multi-miking. Less commendable is the sound of the Philharmonic itself; matching individual vibrato and intonation wasn't an obvious priority, the brass can go out of tune, and some of the climaxes tend to be pushed without the tonal support for loud dynamics that you hear in many other performances.

I had fond memories of **Kubelik**'s 9 from LP days, and hearing the performance again on CD renewed my enjoyment (DG). Once again, the Munich group isn't fully up to today's orchestral standards, but Kubelik gives a reading of such spontaneity and fluidity that many other renditions come out sounding only depressing by comparison. Like the other fine readings in his cycle, this should be released on a single disc. **Klemperer** has nobility, but of a much more low-key kind than Bernstein/Berlin; perhaps monumentality would be a better description

(EMI). The Philharmonia plays beautifully, if with no particular character and commitment, and I hangs together unusually well. The other movements are less convincing, especially the Scherzo, which is fatally slow without compensation in characterization. The dynamic range seems narrow, though the sound is very natural in the beloved late-'60s Kingsway Hall style.

All those who don't hold stereo sound as their top priority have to hear **Horenstein**'s 1966 recording with the London Symphony (◆Music & Arts 235, 2CD). Only in this listener's dreams have all Mahler's musical details, drama, grandeur, dignity, and emotional contradictions come together into such an organic, overwhelming whole. Horenstein never was one for portraying rage in music, and maybe the *Rondo-Burleske* is more heavy than menacing, but otherwise his tempos seem perfect, his characterization of each movement complete, and the tension of the drama and musical line held absolutely. For once, the finale is the summation, the transcendent culmination of the whole. The decent (mono) in-concert sound actually enhances the experience, in that we know the orchestra is really playing as beautifully as it sounds without any help from studio trickery. Horenstein here gets his most consistent orchestral response on records. Except for movement breaks, the audience is pretty much silent. This is a priceless document.

Another Horenstein live recording was taped in Carnegie Hall with the American Symphony in 1969 (Music & Arts). His integrity is again fully in evidence, but with less tension and more orchestral mishaps: For instance, the horn drops his climactic two-note phrase at the end of the exposition in I. The sound is also more vague.

Haitink elicits one of the finest performances in his Concertgebouw cycle (Philips). There's genuine tension in the *Rondo-Burleske* and a beautifully lyrical though still powerful approach to the finale, and as usual not one of his tempos can be challenged. The performance is on the cool side, partly because the dynamic range of the recording is quite narrow and the brass and percussion are placed well back. It's a moving, sometimes radiant experience nonetheless. **Neumann** produced two renditions, in Leipzig and Prague. The Czech Philharmonic version has considerable interpretive assets and some magnificent string playing (Supraphon), but the Leipzig Gewandhaus version has more substantial, up-front sound and a less casual approach to tempos (Berlin). The characterization, pacing, and recording quality are very natural and strong, and the Westernized wind sounds in Leipzig will appeal to more listeners. The pianissimos aren't entirely ethereal, and this is the only detail preventing an all-out enthusiastic recommendation.

Zender's 1977 recording is accomplished—more stylish, better played, and argued than many accounts by more famous names (CPO). His playing of the unison opening of the finale as a true, almost unmeasured recitative seems exactly the right way to do it. On the debit side, the emotions don't run quite as deep here as they do with others, and he seems to be working to avoid tempo extremes. Those spoiled by the world's great orchestras may want a more enveloping string sound or more heroic horn playing, climaxes that do more to move heaven and earth, and structural pinions that are sunk more deeply.

Zander's pacing is commendable, with a lot of well-placed detail and beautifully conceived nodal points in the structure (Telarc). He does well by dividing first and second violins, but in the final analysis he puts across little affection for the music and doesn't seem to have much to say about it. And he doesn't seem to care much about sound: The Philharmonia comes across as second-string, with unglamorous climaxes exacerbated by a distinctly unglamorous acoustic and recording that give the group little help when it comes to sweetness and body. This is an unmemorable set of discs, wanting for shape and musical nourishment.

Even though it's structurally satisfying, **Dohnányi**'s recording is emotionally disengaged (Decca). The climactic cymbal crashes in I are almost squelched, and the Cleveland Orchestra doesn't have the tonal character of the Chicago, even as heard in Boulez's recording, which is similar in overall conception. **López-Cobos**'s Cincinnati Orchestra isn't in the same league as others (Telarc). There's nothing in his unmemorable interpretation to inspire them to surpass themselves or upset the comfortable status quo. The orchestral texture is homogeneous and thereby unidiomatic; instead of a teeming, competitive polyphony, we're given a kind of pleasantly lumbering homophony, a conception that makes Mahler sound like Schubert.

Inbal has done very fine things with his Stuttgart Radio Orchestra (Denon). He's similar to Maazel, though more idiomatic, more structurally coherent, and wider-ranging in his response to the music. It's not a reading of striking originality, and his II doesn't display the elusive temporal variety within a single frame that is the mark of truly great conducting (compare Giulini). But there's enviable rhythmic control in the Scherzo, and the finale is a gem of pacing and sensitivity—the ending, one of the most genuinely rapt and hushed leave-takings in the catalog, is moving enough to make you want to observe silence well afterward. Perhaps the orchestra isn't one of the world's great ensembles, but it comes close. The sound is truthful, but maybe a bit too smooth, recessed, and nonconfrontational for this music.

The two **Karajan** recordings, the first a studio tape made in 1979 and the second live at the Berliner Festwochen three years later, are rare documents in that they have permanently changed the way people—or this writer at least—hear this music. Karajan sets up each movement with supernatural prescience and intensely organic structural thinking, with the Berliners' tone honed down to the barest essentials. No fences rushed here: There's a single climax to each movement, and it's delivered with tremendous power and clarity of vision. The microphones are close up; the Philharmonie acoustic is dry, and the orchestra takes on a kind of gray cinematicism that not everyone will like. This pair of discs has been awarded no end of plaudits, awards, and accolades, but in the last analysis I find it too emotionally tight-lipped and severe. It's certainly one way to hear the piece, and the recording makes for an overwhelming experience of its kind, especially at the finale's last climax, but I don't find Mahler's score as uniformly dour as Karajan does.

His 1979 studio recording has more timbral allure. Karajan was an unusually consistent musician, and the interpretive differences are subtle. His phrasing is more fluid and communicative at the beginning of the Andante in 1979, while the argument unfolds more naturally and a bit more quickly in 1982. If I prefer the sweeter sounds and more affectionate phrasing in the earlier discs, the less stagy 1982 rendition builds up more momentum over the four movements. The violin solos in the finale were freer and more moving in 1980, but the 1982 reading brings us to a more harrowing and less studied climax and a more hushed sense of farewell at the close.

Abbado made a live recording in Vienna in 1987, not in the Musikverein but in the more ample space of the Konzerthaus, with no audience noise whatsoever (♦DG 423564). As usual, his pacing is impeccable; the melodies are beautifully phrased without weakening the overall rhythm, every musical detail finds its place, and the orchestra is wonderfully prepared. He's the perfect interpreter of the bittersweet, nostalgic modernity of 9. He's also sensitive to the quietest dynamics, which reaps particular dividends in the first and last movements, yet the

Rondo-Burleske doesn't want for anger. The Adagio from 10 is the filler, and there the sound tends to be edgy, though the phrasing is passionate, the stratospheric violin passages totally secure. In 9, though, the sound is smooth and easy on the ear—a little distanced, even.

10. Upon his death, Mahler left behind a tenth symphony that presented a more-or-less complete horizontal structure written out in four-stave short score with instrumental cues and varying degrees of textual completion. The first movement, the 25-minute Adagio, was published in 1951. The first edition of the five-movement symphony was assembled some years later by the British musicologist Deryck Cooke, who, in his own words, limited himself to "making a performing version of the work as far as Mahler had got with it (which was really somewhere!)." In actuality, he found it necessary to fill out some textures and part writing. Over about the past 20 years, his edition has been supplemented by more recent (and often more compositionally adventurous) guesses as to how Mahler's four-stave draft should be presented. **Ormandy** recorded Cooke's first version shortly after it appeared in 1964, but that recording has disappeared after a brief CD reissue in the "Portrait" series (CBS 45882).

Cooke continued to make changes to II, IV, and V, mainly refinements of instrumentation and attempts to make the sound more "Mahlerian." **Wyn Morris** led the first recording of this second version with the Philharmonia; it was a fine job, with warm and realistic sound and some heroic work from the horns (Philips). Interpretively and in execution, though, it was handily surpassed by Levine's and Rattle's accounts, recorded in Philadelphia and Bournemouth, respectively, which arrived within a few months of each other. Rattle incorporated some additional advice from composer Berthold Goldschmidt, who had also advised Cooke.

For obvious reasons, the interpretational freedoms, decisions, and responsibilities are heavier here than in any other Mahler score. Particularly in the bare-bones texture of I, IV, and V, the conductor must decide whether to interpret the music as a sketch or as a full-scale Mahlerian experience. **Rattle,** who has more first-hand experience with this score than anyone other than Cooke himself, tends toward the second approach. Nineteen years after his 1980 Bournemouth version (♦EMI 54406), he made 10 his first recording project as director-designate of the Berlin Philharmonic (EMI). Despite the refinement of the Berlin playing, the Bournemouth is preferable; to these ears the music, often skeletal in texture, doesn't take to the increased sophistication of approach and the drier sonic picture. The opening Adagio is host to much self-conscious point making, and V has a cooler, more elegant sound that works against the music.

Inbal brings rather quick tempos to 10 and is generally low-key, possibly reluctant to bring this sketchy music from the hereafter into the bona fide Mahler canon (Denon). Though he doesn't infuse it with the deathly overtones heard elsewhere, his interpretation is haunting in its own low-profile way. **Levine** benefits from rich Philadelphia sonority and has a patient and straightforward if also sonically romantic approach (RCA). His first-movement Adagio (recorded as an independent entity some years before the rest) is glorious, but here and elsewhere his rigid tempos have a strange, desolate, almost depressing effect in this thin-textured, fragmentary music. The slightly distant ambience, though, does help fill out Cooke's textures.

Going from Levine to **Chailly** leaves no doubt that the latter hit upon the elusive, all-important balance between over- and under-interpretation of this great musical fragment (♦London/Decca 466955). His tempos are generally faster and thereby more oriented to the predominantly slow harmonic rhythm; they're also more flexible than anyone else's, which makes a world of difference. For these reasons, his conclusion seems more of a transfiguration and an arrival, and the sound has more bloom, better transparency, and a richer set of overtones than any other.

Apart from Cooke, three other editions have been heard: Joseph Wheeler approached Mahler's draft with particular caution, producing a kind of performing sketch; Clinton Carpenter had few if any editorial ambitions and tried to come up with the full Mahler experience, looking to other Mahler works for ideas on completion; and Remo Mazzelli aimed somewhere between the Cooke/Wheeler and Carpenter extremes. Mazzelli's middle-of-the-road version runs the risk of losing out with both the purists and those in search of the full Mahlerian experience. Perhaps I'm biased from having heard the Cooke for years, and I don't know the details of Mazzelli's premises, but I find a lot of his work insupportable. If Mahler's draft needs anything, it's added lines and definition and complication of the harmonies, but Mazzelli restricts himself mainly to orchestral touches (especially drum rolls) that sound like so much graffiti. **Slatkin**'s performance of the Mazzelli is good, even if it doesn't offer the cathartic experience of some others. The sound is also more streamlined—less dynamic—than EMI's sonics for Rattle-Bournemouth or Decca's for Chailly.

Das Lied von der Erde. There exists no perfect tenor for *Das Lied von der Erde;* the part demands an unrealistic combination of quiet, lyric singing and the kind of Wagnerian Heldentenor voice that can rise above a large orchestra in full cry. Since its earliest performances, it has often fallen to eminent Siegfrieds or Parsifals, and there have been few appropriate voices in recent years. There are almost commensurate demands placed on the mezzo or contralto, who (even more than the tenor) must be able to join the orchestra seamlessly as a kind of instrumental line.

Mahler specified that the even-numbered songs "can also be done by a baritone, if necessary." Over the years, relatively few performances have taken up the baritone alternative, though more such recordings have appeared recently. **Kletzki** is very special; he had a unique way of nuancing the music without getting in its way or debilitating it, and in 1959 the Philharmonia still had piquant woodwind sounds, for instance in the oboe that opens II and VI (♦EMI 62707). The male singers are perfectly matched, neither of them a dramatic or spinto voice: tenor Murray Dickie is vibrant but also unstrained and almost perfectly pitched, and Fischer-Dieskau is at his absolute peak, sweet in sonority and velvety in his phrasing. The only snag is some peak distortion, tamable to some extent by cutting the treble.

Fischer-Dieskau also did the even-numbered (mezzo/contralto) songs for **Bernstein,** with tenor James King and the Vienna Philharmonic (London/Decca). This is one of Bernstein's most visceral and extreme Mahler readings, and the entrance of the young men on horseback in the fourth song (the only point where sexual passion and the will to live erupt to the music's surface) is hectored beyond repair. The baritone's tone is drier and more worn than in Kletzki's version, and Bernstein's intensity is too over the top even for the often-angry first song. The London "Jubilee" incarnation was riddled with distortion at climaxes, though this is corrected in the newly remastered Decca "Legends" disc.

Bernstein reverted to the usual tenor-mezzo setup when he recorded it a second time in 1973 with Ludwig, Kollo, and the Israel Philharmonic

(Sony). It's a more controlled and better structured performance and one of the finer interpretations in his first Mahler cycle. Ludwig in particular sounds like a more seasoned Mahlerian than in her version with Klemperer (see below), and the sound is less intrusive, appropriately cooler and more distanced than in the EMI. Kollo is in better form in the Karajan disc, but here he appropriately combines ardency and lyricism. The sound is rather dim and inexact, but the balances are good, and I prefer it to both London/Decca's sonic strip lighting and EMI's up-front take in the Klemperer rendition. The conducting makes up for some less-than-consummate playing: don't expect consistent and utter finesse in the "Abschied" woodwind solos.

In another tenor-baritone rendition, **Rattle** recorded the work with Hampson, Peter Seiffert, and the Birmingham Symphony (EMI). The reading is marked by Rattle's usual attentiveness to detail, and Seiffert is the very rare tenor who encompasses Mahler's awkward joining of lyric and Heldentenor elements with almost perfect ease. Hampson isn't as comfortable as Fischer-Dieskau in Mahler's lower-lying passages, however, and in "Der Abschied" he and Rattle are less able than Kletzki to sustain the longer line of the music across Mahler's huge esthetic shifts and gaping silences. Hampson is closer to a Bing-Crosbyish, velvety croon than the dramatic presence of Fischer-Dieskau; thus he's distinctly better in the moments of quiet nostalgia ("Einsame in Herbst") than in the passages of heightened emotion.

The immediate distinction of **Salonen**'s recording is Domingo (Sony), who has in recent years been rescuing us from the idea that tenors of Wagnerian scale must inevitably whine and wobble. In this score, as in his Wagner forays, his earnest, Latinate, utterly secure sound comes as balm to the ears. Right away with his high, proud ascent (to be sung "with full strength," Mahler indicates), you know this is special. The great tenor is in superb voice, and I will return to this disc many times for his contribution, even though his German isn't idiomatic. I only wish he had been paired with a baritone of similar prowess and a conductor more steeped in Germanic Mahler performance traditions. Skovhus is monochromatic and not as attuned as we might wish to the intimacies of the texts, though it doesn't help that Salonen tends to turn introversion into limpness in the even-numbered songs.

The most striking of all tenor-baritone combinations, indeed a kind of once-in-a-lifetime "dream team," is the Wunderlich/Fischer-Dieskau pairing heard in a pirate edition (Myto). **Keilberth** conducts the Bamberg Symphony in this 1964 recording. The limited, murky mono sound means that not much orchestral detail comes across, but the voices and words are dependably caught. Keilberth gives Wunderlich a rather freer rein than did Klemperer, but he isn't the most imaginative of conductors. Fischer-Dieskau isn't as sweet of voice as he was for Kletzki and has a tendency to yell in the central section of "Von der Schönheit," which is also a bit unsettled rhythmically.

Whatever the merits of the famous **Klemperer** recording—the nectar-toned Wunderlich was the tenor to end all tenors, matchless in "Der Trunkene im Frühling," and Ludwig brought real emotion and awareness of the words to her songs—the results are as a whole rather undermined by the sound, which remains variable in the EMI "Great Recordings of the Century" edition: at times beefy and at times strident. The Philharmonia English horn (sounding a bit duck-like) becomes as much a stage presence as Wunderlich after the words "im Lenz" in the first movement, and the acoustic is disappointingly boxy for the tenor in "Von der Jugend." Klemperer is rather deaf to such things as the dance-like charm of "Von der Schönheit," and there's an awkward edit at 5:08 in the same song. Still, Ludwig and Klemperer are superb at sustaining

Mahler's otherworldly intensity in "Der Abschied," even if they (and the engineers) neglect a good deal of the music's glacial, Zen-like quietude.

Among Mahler's scores, *Das Lied* is the one where **Solti** seemed least at home. He taped the work twice, in Chicago and in Amsterdam. The 1992 Amsterdam version suffers from the over-miking typical of so many live recordings; the interaction of voices and orchestra smacks more of the mixing desk than a concert hall. The close mikes ruthlessly expose the fact that Lipovsek and Moser are in poor voice, the mezzo tending to hit notes below and then slide up to them, the tenor distinctly pinched and unpleasant above the stave. With the Dutch orchestra more distantly accounted for in the sound picture than the singers, I found Solti's direction over-generalized (London/Decca).

There's certainly more detail, thrust, and interpretive crispness to be heard in his 1972 Chicago recording. Kollo is in sweeter voice here than elsewhere, even if he does a bit of sliding between notes in the first song. The half-hour "Der Abschied" is something special; Minton is absolutely superb in pitch, sound, and overall control, and the first-chair Chicago winds show unbelievable breath control in their solos. Still, in comparison with some other versions, Solti sounds more heavy than impassioned in the tenor movements and more static and ritualistic than *innig* in the mezzo ones. London/Decca's sound has a particularly good take on the Chicago strings.

There are many things to like about **Levine**'s thoughtful rendition (DG). He uncovers a lot of new detail, particularly in "Trunkene im Frühling," which is often just raced through, and, as in his 9 for RCA, he isn't afraid to slow down in search of meaning. He has the redoubtable Norman and Jerusalem, the latter still powerful and believable and even sounding sweet in his high register. Norman's style has been becoming breathier in recent years, so it's a pleasure to find her controlled and well focused in sound; her voice sounds younger and more streamlined than I remembered it, though she summons the expected Normanesque sustaining power at the first "Die liebe Erde allüberall blüht auf" in "Der Abschied." Unfortunately, DG's recording is on the clinical side, and the mikes fight Jerusalem's louder passages.

Tennstedt's is a more natural conception (♦EMI 54603). His take on the tenor movements (with a secure and slightly baritonal Klaus König) is demonstrative and ungainly in the Klemperer tradition. He even out-Klempererizes Klemperer with some of his slow tempos; I and V are among the slowest I've ever heard, and they sometimes want for a stronger sense of direction. Yet even more than Klemperer, Tennstedt is able to invest the music with enough detail that the stately tempos barely register; the orchestral interludes in particular brim over with personality and event. He's rather better than Klemperer at sustaining the tension of the introverted mezzo movements (beautifully sung by Baltsa, if without much interest in the words; also, some of her German vowels don't ring entirely true), and the more realistically balanced sound helps a good deal. EMI's recording is earthy, grass-roots stuff: Some of the bigger climaxes aren't comfortably contained.

Horenstein's textures are more dark and introverted than sleek and modern, and expressive details are rather better integrated into the larger picture than they are with Klemperer and Tennstedt (♦BBC Legends 4042). He gives a more streamlined sound to Mahler's autumnal surfaces, and "Einsame im Herbst" is especially memorable for this reason. The proceedings are beautifully controlled, with the orchestral outburst at the entry of the lusty youths on horseback sounding more coherent than usual in the fourth song. There's also the benefit that the two vocalists can assume orchestral roles quite easily—thanks partly to the fact that the singers are placed a bit back—and in that sense Horenstein

conceives the piece more as a symphony with voices than something operatic or cantata-like. John Mitchinson takes a while to settle in, but Alfreda Hodgson is a superbly controlled contralto. The sound is excellent, again a bit recessed to atmospheric effect, with no audience noise. This is a prime document from one of Mahler's greatest exponents; it was recorded only a year before the conductor died, saying "my only regret in dying is that I will no longer hear *Das Lied von der Erde.*"

Walter made his famous 1952 recording in Vienna, with tenor Patzak and bona fide contralto Ferrier (London/Decca). The Vienna Philharmonic is magnificent, and Patzak's baritonal tenor is marvelous; though he was a bit past his prime and sometimes sounds it, his voice is honeyed in all registers and his diction is nuanced and miraculously clear. I can't be as enthusiastic about Ferrier. Such a true contralto sound is rare as flowers in January nowadays, but to my ears she has a strangely asexual sound, much like a male alto. Her production is consistently in the back of the throat, and her intensely fluttering, mid-century vibrato (echoed in the finale's English horn solos) also conspires to give the singer a British oratorical sound, distant from the texts and their immediate meanings. Those who better appreciate this artist should look for Decca's "Legends" remastering; the early-'80s London edition was a failure—bright and shrill.

All told, I prefer Walter's 1936 Vienna account, available in different transfers on several labels. The Dutton transfer—full-bodied and vivid, with 78 rpm surfaces less noticeable—is much to be preferred to Music & Arts. The impression on Dutton is one of more palpable excitement; the music making is consistently more inspired than in the 1952 recording. Tenor Charles Kullman covers himself in glory. I prefer him at his best even to Patzak; he and Walter vividly convey the anger of Mahler's first song, just as he hits the perfect note of devil-may-care hedonism in the drinking song (V). Contralto Thorborg, however, is rather too grand in style and wobbly in vibrato to convey the right intimacy.

Walter also made a live recording in New York in 1953, with tenor Svanholm and contralto Elena Nikolaidi (Music & Arts). The treble needs real taming here, and the acoustic is drier and boxier than in the 1936 Vienna. There's also some hum, and the Vienna has more inviting sound. There is perhaps more tension in the New York version, but there was more charm and variety in Vienna. Nikolaidi is a drawback, with her closed vowels and unsuitably huge production. The 78 rpm sides vary drastically in sound in the finale, including some disastrous changes in pitch at about 11:50.

Another early-'50s recording, in a city with as venerable a Mahler tradition as Vienna, is **van Beinum**'s with the Concertgebouw, tenor Haefliger, and mezzo Merriman (Philips). Though their now-archaic styles are similar, I find Merriman more nuanced than Ferrier and more willing to sing quietly. Haefliger, one of the top exponents of this part, is even more beautiful of voice than he was for Jochum, though his vibrato can sometimes get in the way. Van Beinum's orchestra is balanced rather far back, so some detail is lost, but the playing is predictably fine. He was a master at articulating larger structures through knowing and subtle tempo changes; the well-prepared slowing at the end of "Von der Schönheit" is symptomatic. Not least for the subtlety and detailing of the singers, this is a high priority among mono vintage recordings.

Jochum's later stereo disc with the same orchestra and singers has better (indeed, very fine) sound, but the interpretation seems a bit more provisional (DG). The larger tempo manipulations in V don't completely convince, and "Der Abschied" is marked by no particular sense of raptness. Haefliger's tone is a touch drier than with van Beinum, but the vibrato is more controlled; Merriman is better overall in the earlier recording, though still obviously one of the great Mahler voices.

Haitink's Concertgebouw rendition with Baker and James King is the finest of the Amsterdam recordings, and one of the very best available (◆Philips 462299, a "two-fer" with 9, or ◆454014, also a "two-fer" with the other orchestral song-cycles). King is no match for Haefliger; his singing is always secure and golden-toned, but there isn't much interest in the words and emotional details of the text. But Baker is miraculously intimate, and she has a unique capacity to detail her words at lower dynamics. Her intonation isn't always impeccable, but that's unimportant. No less remarkable are the cool, ashen sonorities of orchestra and hall, perfect for this music, and the conductor's supple, unobtrusive way with what Schoenberg called the "musical prose" character of Mahler's phrasing.

Reiner's classic account has some of the same virtues, including a singer of enviable intimacy in the even-numbered songs (RCA). The Chicago Symphony, too, has a lightness that isn't often heard in this music; much of the string work, for instance, is as light as eiderdown. Reiner never lets the music get heavy or coarse. Forrester connects with the texts wonderfully and also has great control; as with Merriman, you have the sense of a perfect match between music and voice, though her midcentury, wasp-in-a-bottle vibrato takes a bit of getting used to. The equation works best in "Der Abschied," a haunting rendition that shines with a beautiful, glacial perfection. But just about everywhere else I take away impressions of almost claustrophobic conductorial control, a fetishized kind of discipline.

Colin Davis's conception is similar to Horenstein's, the music thoroughly controlled in sound and profile but not deeply nuanced or inflected in dynamics and rhythm (Philips). "Einsame im Herbst" and "Von der Schönheit" are controlled to the point of inertia, but the orchestral sounds and Norman at her absolute peak (in 1981) are certainly beautiful. Philips's early digital recording is also smoother and fresher than expected. Listeners' reactions will largely depend on their reactions to Vickers, whose tone can be nagging and whose German words are almost caricaturized. But the upper part of his range has tremendous power, and he vividly conveys the drama of the tenor songs. In V, he *is* Li Po's drunkard. In the final analysis, though, Davis is more generalized in his direction than Horenstein, and the only truly memorable part of this recording is "Der Abschied," where he's not afraid to observe Mahler's rests to their full value, has the courage to take a slow tempo, and gives the music a haunting, glacial sound.

I doubt that *Das Lied* has ever been recorded more transparently or truthfully than in **Eiji Oue**'s disc with the Minnesota Orchestra (Reference). The miking is very natural, apart from a slight highlighting of the singers, and the engineering is so good you can really hear the barest brushes against the tam-tam in the finale and the quiet, staccato triplets in thirds in the flutes in I—a remarkable sound. Tenor John Villars has a hint of wobble in the first song but is otherwise trusty. Mezzo Michelle DeYoung has a remarkable ability to sing quietly yet not anonymously and with fine control; this makes for a memorable and touching "Einsame im Herbst." She manages some good dynamic effects that Oue echoes knowingly and beautifully with the orchestra. Note the subtleties of the orchestral playing, the very considerable virtues of Reference's utter transparency of sound, and the fact that Oue misses nothing in the score. This might not be a great performance, but it's certainly an enjoyable one, and audiophiles can confidently be steered toward it.

If many accounts stumble on a weak singer or noncommittal orchestral playing, the classic **Giulini** recording is marked by consistent musical commitment and consummate musicianship (◆DG 413459). The Berlin Philharmonic plays magnificently, with solos of the utmost sensitivity and tuttis of great heft and power. But this is really a singer-based rather than symphonic conception, and so it's a joy to report that his singers make an ideal pair. Araiza purveys a slightly nasalized version of Domingo's clarion tone but also a bit more technical security (he was probably half Domingo's age when he recorded this). Not every sound Fassbaender makes is beautiful, but she can be intensely dramatic and sympathetic, conveying every word and whispered sentiment with body and soul as though she wrote them. As always, Giulini never pushes, never forces, yet in his undemonstrative way he wrings every ounce of emotion and import from the music. I must include a caveat concerning the early digital sound, which is more than acceptable but still unduly opaque and sometimes a bit rough.

My runner-up for favorite *Erde* mezzos is van Nes, who is paired with Schreier under **Inbal**'s direction (Denon). She has a magnificent Mahler voice, with something of Fassbaender's soulfulness but better control. Schreier is often a trial to listen to, however—heavily Germanic-sounding, a kind of Siegfried-wanna-be with a worn upper register. As so often in his cycle, Inbal is fresh and knowingly paced but rarely inspired.

And last, something of a curiosity: apparently Mahler intended to publish a version of *Das Lied* for two voices and piano but didn't live to finish it. (Strangely, some of the words are different between piano and orchestral versions.) The recording combines tenor Moser and mezzo Fassbaender with pianist Katsaris (Teldec). The piano reduction allows the tenor to sing with new subtleties, and Katsaris is enough of a colorist to make you miss Mahler's orchestra relatively little. But Moser's voice is sadly worn and insecure, painful to hear whenever he gets loud. A boomy acoustic and bright miking don't help. Fassbaender, however, doesn't fight the microphones and is a real pleasure: she takes more opportunities for delicate shading than Moser and is in fine voice.

Das klagende Lied. This is Mahler's first surviving work, an astonishingly prescient piece he wrote as an 18- to 20-year-old. He excised the first of his three movements ("Waldmärchen") when he finally published the work in 1898, and that movement became available again when the complete autograph passed from Mahler's nephew to Yale University in 1969. The apparent suddenness of this availability explains why the 1970 Boulez recording needed a second, follow-up session with different singers: to record the necessary "Waldmärchen," well and away the longest movement of the work. (Among the two-movement recordings was a **Wyn Morris** performance that appeared briefly on Delysé and Nimbus.)

Mahler put *Das klagende Lied* through at least three rounds of revisions. In 1893 he decided to leave off I and made many revisions to II and III, revisions that show him—in addition to filling out transitions and otherwise bringing the music more in line with his current thinking—simplifying the elaborate scoring, jettisoning instruments that were no longer in general use (a passage for valveless horns), and generally making the score more practical in hope of gaining performances. Reinhold Kubik, editor of the new critical edition, has prepared a painstaking edition that presents the work as it stood in 1880. This has been recorded by **Nagano** with soloists and the Hallé Orchestra and chorus (◆Erato 21664) in a performance that is lush, nostalgic, dramatic, sensitive, and generally well sung (soprano Eva Urbanova brings up a worry or two). I've never heard the Hallé strings sound richer, darker, or more luscious. The climaxes, caught without a hint of strain, are properly grand and Wagnerian, and Erato gives a lot of depth to the orchestra and chorus.

Nagano isn't strictly comparable to the recordings of older editions of the music. The common three-movement performing version—the one most commonly heard after the "Waldmärchen" discovery—is in fact a bastardization, with neither the two-movement format Mahler chose to publish nor the instrumentation and early thoughts of the 1880 score. The point may be academic for the listener, especially when faced with a fine recording of the cobbled-together, three-movement score like **Chailly**'s (♦London/Decca 425719). Decca's sound doesn't have the depth of Chailly's later Mahler projects, and his tenor can be trying, but his offfstage wedding band kicks up enough festive dust, and Fassbaender has one of the most moving, primal Mahler voices.

Boulez, a favorite for years, unfolds this grisly tale very naturally, engrossingly, and symphonically (Sony). But rehearing this admirable account points out the conductor's sometimes generalized approach (Nagano has greater detail and more obvious eloquence), and Columbia tended to put the chorus and singers in the listener's face. **Rattle** misses out on most of the mood and atmosphere of the piece, and his singers, a bit stiff, seem reluctant to enter their characters fully (EMI). Likewise, his offstage band sounds like it's been run through a loudspeaker. **Tilson Thomas** and his San Francisco forces try to compensate for the antiseptic and boxy acoustic with garish colors and cinematic self-consciousness; the disc presents an unhappy mixture of cottony sonics and grand guignol (RCA).   ASHBY

SONGS

Mahler wrote only 48 songs, and that number includes those in his song symphony, *Das Lied von der Erde,* a small number compared to the hundreds composed by Schubert, Schumann, Brahms, Wolf and other lieder composers. But that number belies their importance to this composer's *oeuvre.* These songs are appealing, in some cases path-breaking, compositions that can surely stand on their own. But they are also the foundation on which Mahler built most of his symphonies, at the very least his first four or five, and in some respects all except his 9th and (uncompleted) 10th. He has been called by some of his critics "the song symphonist," and there's a lot of truth in that.

Mahler's songs were published in five groups. Most of them (except his early ones) are available with orchestral or piano accompaniment. In all cases, I prefer the richer and more colorful orchestral versions. He was a great orchestrator in the songs as well as in the symphonies.

Lieder und Gesänge (Songs of Youth). There are 16 songs in this group, nine to texts from *Des Knaben Wunderhorn,* a collection of old German poetry and folk song. The other texts are from various sources, some by the composer. The musical settings of several of these early works already include characteristics of the later ones, such as the use of military marches and folk songs; others were inspired by works of the older German lieder composers. Of the half dozen or so recordings in the catalog, the best are by **Baker** (♦Hyperion 66100) and **Roland Hermann** (♦Claves 50-911). Both have excellent diction, a fine command of vocal colors, and attractive voices, and they approach these songs in a direct and unaffected manner. Baker's disc includes all the songs; Hermann omits a couple of the very early ones and gives us, instead, two of the later (and greater) *Wunderhorn* settings.

Lieder eines fahrenden Gesellen (Songs of a Wayfarer). This and *Kindertotenlieder* are the only song cycles. The piano version was composed in 1883 and orchestrated a few years later. The orchestral version is symphonic in texture, which at the time was unusual for a song cycle, and it reflects the influence of Wagner and Berlioz. It's an unusually per-

sonal work; the composer, who wrote the texts, obviously identified with the Wayfarer, who is driven to despair by an unhappy love affair, as Mahler was at the time. The cycle represents a spiritual journey. The first and last songs were reworked into movements of Symphony 1, and one of the earlier ones, "Hans und Grete," also shows up in that work. Recommended recordings are headed by **Fischer-Dieskau**'s 1953 version (♦EMI 47657), **Ludwig** (♦EMI 69499), **Hampson** (♦DG 431682), and **Baker** (♦EMI 47793). They are all great Mahler interpreters, with beautiful and smooth voices and fine diction. If I had to choose only one, I'd pick Fischer-Dieskau.

Kindertotenlieder. Set to poems by Friedrich Rückert, these are among the saddest songs ever written. They are composed in Mahler's late style, contrapuntal and symphonically organized, though the orchestration is minimal. The first two songs are used in Symphony 5, which he was composing at the same time, and so is one of the Rückert songs discussed below. Another of the *Kindertotenlieder* is rhythmically similar to the introduction of the finale of Symphony 6. These songs, dealing with the death of children, are not folksy, but unusually sensitive and as complex as any Mahler wrote. Recommended recordings are, again, headed by **Fischer-Dieskau** (♦EMI 47657), **Ludwig** (♦DG 439678) and **Hampson** (♦431682). **Ferrier** with Bruno Walter is a classic recording (♦EMI 7610032). All convey the heart-wrenching despair of these songs in beautiful tones and with deep feeling.

Des Knaben Wunderhorn. These songs are set to poems from the collection of folk poetry cited above, but many of the texts were changed by Mahler to suit himself. There are 15 songs altogether; one, "Das Himmlische Leben," is usually excluded from recordings because it's the fourth movement of Symphony 4. Most of them were composed and orchestrated in 1892–96, the last two, "Revelge" and "Tambourgs' gesell," in 1899–1901. These two are judged by many to be Mahler's greatest, and they deal (as do four of the others) with military life. No less than eight are used in Mahler's symphonies 2, 3, 4, 5, 6, and 7, several more than once. Their orchestrations are elaborate and reflect their often dramatic themes.

In the recommended recordings, the two singers share some of the songs that offer a dialogue between a male and female character; that's more effective and responds better to the works than having one singer perform all of them. The best two discs are **Schwarzkopf** and **Fischer-Dieskau** with Szell (EMI 47277) and **Ludwig** and **Berry** with Bernstein (♦CBS 42202); both pairs give us expressive and sensitive interpretations, aware of the meaning of every word, and both conductors contribute luscious and detailed accompaniments. A recording by **von Otter** and **Quasthoff** is as well sung and idiomatic as the others, but the duets are only performed by one singer, which makes them less effective and interesting (DG).

Rückert Songs. These, also, don't form a cycle. The five songs are suitable for either male or female voice, except for "Liebst du um Schönheit" ("If you love for beauty's sake"), which should be sung by a female since it's obviously addressed to a male. This is the only song of the group that Mahler didn't orchestrate himself and that he dedicated to his wife Alma. Rückert's poems inspired the composer to a more subjective approach than the *Wunderhorn* texts, which are full of saints, angels, and ghost-like spirits as well as military life. By contrast, Rückert talks of love and death. Musically, the settings are more like chamber music; they're more polished and look forward to *Das Lied von der Erde* in style and spirit. Very fine, sensitively sung recordings have been made by **von**

Otter (♦DG 439928, which includes an excellent rendition of *Wayfarer*), Fischer-Dieskau (♦EMI 47657), and Hampson (♦EMI 65443, which includes a very good *Kindertotenlieder*).

Final note: the set in which the young Fischer-Dieskau performs *Wayfarer*, *Kindertotenlieder*, and the *Rückert* songs is most highly recommended; it's the single best Mahler song disc and a great bargain (♦EMI 47657).   MOSES

Marin Marais (1656–1728)

The French viola da gamba school, represented primarily by Le Sieur de Sainte-Colombe, his famous student Marais, Antoine Forqueray, and Louis de Caix d'Hervelois, is comparable in musical worth to the works of the Couperin family on the clavecin but is generally less known. However, with the upsurge in early music performance, there has been a considerable spate of recordings.

CHAMBER MUSIC

Marais published two volumes of chamber music. *Pièces en Trio* (1692) has been recorded three times, by **Musica Pacifica** (Virgin 61365, 2CD), the **Ricercar Consort** (Ricercar 206482, 2CD), and the **Hotteterre Quartet** (Telarc 77617). Like most French chamber music of the period, it's composed for two unspecified treble instruments and basso continuo. Musica Pacifica (MP) divides the two upper lines between recorder, oboe, and violin, thus clarifying each voice with a different color, while the Ricercar Consort (RC) uses two recorders or two violins, contrasting them with the basso continuo. MP sounds more like chamber music, RC more like a chamber orchestra. MP breaks up Marais's long suites into small groups; RC breaks up only the long 13-movement G minor suite, and gives us a more expansive, more serious-sounding composer. Both versions are stylistically unexceptionable. The Hotteterre's scoring resembles MP's.

The **Harnoncourts** gave an attractive reading of eight movements from the C major suite (MHS). The **Purcell Quartet**'s "La Folia" includes several suites in C and six movements from a suite from Book 3 (Hyperion 66310). Another attractive version of the E minor suite was played with flute and violin by the **Oberlin Baroque Ensemble** (Gasparo 202).

La Gamme et autres morceaux de symphonie (1723) contains only three pieces, but *La Gamme* (The Gamut) is one of the longest chamber music works in captivity. It's a little imaginary opera in which the three protagonists, who play violin, viol, and harpsichord, act like characters in an operatic *scena*, each change of mood introducing a new key of the gamut. The **Boston Museum Trio**, which has recorded the entire volume, play *La Gamme* as scored by the composer (Centaur 2129). The **Oberlin Baroque Ensemble** includes *La Gamme* in its miscellaneous collection, with a flute alternating with the violin part to add an extra character to this opera (Vox 33006, 3CD). Further, they employ a second viol to join the basso continuo instead of leaving the harpsichord to its own devices, so instead of three instruments, we have five. For some reason, they come to a complete halt midway in the piece, as if for an intermission. The Boston performance is closer to Marais's written score, but Oberlin is more colorful and perhaps more musically alert to the conventions Marais apes.

Sonata à la Marésienne is a violin sonata in a mixture of French and Italian styles, with emphasis on the Italian; it's one of Marais's most popular pieces. Again, the **Boston Museum Trio**'s performance is neat and lively, while **Spectre de la Rose** is more colorful and imaginative (Naxos 553081). These two works make up a CD by Medlam and his **London**

Baroque that employed Marais's original scoring, reissued at a low price and well received (Harmonia Mundi 2901105). The final work is a bell piece in the form of a passacaille entitled *La Sonnerie de Ste. Génevieve du Mont de Paris*. The **Boston** performance is again good chamber playing, while the **Kuijkens** give it that little extra that tells, with articulation in the viol that really sounds like bells and a slightly slower tempo that gives the ensemble room to be expressive (Harmonia Mundi 77145). If you want the volume complete, Boston is the only choice at present, but in each piece the competition is more imaginative.

VIOL MUSIC

Book 1 (1686). This was Marais's first publication and represents the state of the art of viol playing of its time. **Pierlot** and his Ricercar Consort recorded all of it in a smoothly played, resonantly recorded set; he makes the most of the serious side of Marais, represented by a tendency toward slow tempos, leading him to omit the second repeats in all the Allemandes and many of the other bipartite dances (Ricercar 205842, 3CD). Otherwise, he's a fine musician and plays this difficult and interpretively demanding music with technical polish and musical beauty. A disc by the **Smithsonian Chamber Players** contains all the two-viol pieces (Harmonia Mundi 77146). Although similar to Pierlot in sonority and performance style, they're slightly more incisive and a little clearer in balance.

A fine disc by **Savall** is accompanied by harpsichord and theorbo and is notable for the clarity of voices and musical intensity he brings to all his work (Astrée 7769). Otherwise, no major excerpts from the solo pieces of Book I are presently available. However, **John Hsu,** whose ongoing printed edition of the complete works of Marais is published by Broude, recorded excerpts from all five books on five LPs for MHS. His performances, though accomplished, are less suave than those mentioned above.

Book 2 (1702). In this much more popular volume, Marais simplified his style somewhat and wrote tuneful and relatively undemanding music. In **Markku Luolajan-Mikkola**'s selections, the playing is fine, but the balance is reticent for the soloist; you strain to hear him on occasion (BIS 909). **Laurence Dreyfus**'s disc also consists entirely of works from this volume, played without benefit of a second viol (Simax 1053). Another disc using theorbo instead of a second viol is by **Suzanne Braumann,** and includes the Suite in E minor with excerpts from Books 3 and 4 (Globe 5122). The E minor suite is also excerpted in **Juan Manuel Quintana**'s disc (Harmonia Mundi 905248). He uses harpsichord and theorbo, while **Pere Ros** employs only theorbo, but plays 12 pieces to Quintana's eight, along with a suite by Charles Dollé, *Le Mandoline* by Antoine Forqueray, while Juan Carlos Rivera plays a theorbo suite by Robert de Visée (Opus 7085).

Both the BIS and Simax issues include the largest work in Book 2, *Couplets de Folies*, variations on that famous tune lasting up to 19 minutes in some performances and including every technical move known to the Baroque era. Some play a truncated version, but **Luolajan-Mikkola** plays it all in under 17 minutes. There are also recordings by **Spectre de la Rose,** which includes a substantial piece from the D major suite, *Les Voix Humaines* (Naxos 553081), and **Cunningham,** whose reading, though less virtuosic than the others, employs the most imaginative use of the continuo group, exchanging sonority for clarity and sonic interest (ASV 112, NA).

Fantaisie in A is another popular piece on the BIS disc, played by **Hantai** (see Book 3). The *St. Colombe Tombeau* may be heard to great effect in "Musique à Versailles" by Sigiswald and Wieland **Kuijken.** Their disc is one of the most interesting and detailed studies of performance practice around (Harmonia Mundi 77145). Their version of *Tombeau* differentiates the two kinds of vibrato asked for by Marais more clearly than anyone else and gives us a really dramatic presentation of the music. Others sound tentative by comparison.

Catherine Meintz gives us 11 pieces from the B minor suite, played in a notably clear and lively manner with members of the Oberlin Baroque Ensemble (Vox 3006, 3CD). She ends with *Tombeau pour M. de Lully,* another famous work also recorded by Cunningham, giving us an opportunity to compare their styles. Both give excellent performances, but Meintz plays most of her grace notes before the beat while Cunningham makes them more dissonant by playing them on the beat. Cunningham also has an imaginative harpsichordist, Mitzi Meyerson, who plays unusually tasteful realizations of the continuo line, assisting in the dramatic presentation of this tortured music. **Dreyfus** also plays the Lully *Tombeau,* but the lack of a viol in the continuo makes this something of a specialist item.

Book 3. **Hantai** is lively and imaginative, doing well by the many cross-rhythms in the courantes and gigues. He truncates the F major Allemande, playing its double on the repeats; but just to show he's not hidebound, he plays the Courante and its double as separate pieces, following up with a very slow and lyrical Sarabande (Virgin 45266; this fine disc is hidden in *Schwann* under "Suites," and the details there reverse the Book references as well). **Savall** plays his selections with great sensitivity, using a theorbo instead of a second viol (Astrée 8761). **Cunningham** includes a fine performance of six pieces from Suite in G (ASV 112, NA), and on another disc offers suites in A minor and D (Globe 5122). Savall shows the most flair, but Hantai's program is excellent and doesn't duplicate Savall. **John Dornenburg** duplicates Savall and Hantai to some extent but uses a second viol, which Savall does not. His performances are dancier, and some slow movements are beautifully resonant, but he lacks Savall's perceptivity (Centaur 2429).

Book 4 (1717). This book is in three parts, but nearly everyone has concentrated on Part 2, the notorious *Suite d'un goût étranger* (Suite for Foreign Tastes). This 30-movement suite collects some of Marais's most exotic and difficult pieces and wends its way through a number of key centers. Keep in mind, however, that to the Parisians of the Baroque, anything outside the city was exotic. Also, tempered tuning was coming into use, making the more unusual keys more accessible.

Jean-Louis Charbonnier has recorded the entire suite, complete with countrified percussion effects in some numbers (Pierre Verany 797022, 2CD). He's not a very assertive player and tends to be drowned out by his companions, making this a rather frustrating album. **Suzanne Heinrich** and Charivari Agréable offer about half the suite mixed with excerpts from other books and four pieces played in harpsichord transcriptions (ASV 152). Heinrich is not the world's most polished player. As in his discs from Books I and III, **Savall** uses a theorbo on the lower line, thus solving the balance problem (Astrée 7727). He plays 11 pieces in a disc that's only 48 minutes long but is the most satisfying performance of this music to date.

Part III consists of more chamber pieces; though listed for three viols, they're actually in trio sonata form like those in Book I. **Music**'s **Recreation** has recorded a version played not on viols but by baroque flute and violin (Centaur 2334). This, of course, omits all double-stops and chords in the upper line, though the violin plays some of those in the second part and the arrangement doesn't leave out anything necessary to the harmony. This disc also includes a complete performance of the

A minor suite for viol and continuo from Part I, played by **Dornenburg** with considerable panache.

Book V (1725). Just as fine as the others, this book has received the least attention. Highlights include the *Tombeau* for Marais's son and an interesting piece of program music (*Tableau de l'Operation de la Taille*) describing the removal of the composer's gallbladder, with descriptive comments to be read during the performance. **Wieland Kuijken** is the only one so far to offer an entire CD from Book V (Accent 78744). He's a fine player, less distinctive than Savall but with a rich, warm sound.

Suites from Books II-V are played with a light touch by **Juan Manuel Quintana** (Harmonia Mundi 905248), with harpsichord and theorbo, and there is a very mixed program from Books II thru V by **Paolo Pandolfo,** who dramatizes his partially improvised performance with descriptions in the notes.

OPERAS

Marais wrote four operas. His greatest success was *Alcione* (1706), and there was a fine recording by **Minkowski** (Erato 45522, 3CD, NA). **Savall** has recorded instrumental excerpts, stylishly played, including the famous description of a tempest that marked the first use of the double bass in the Paris Opéra orchestra (Astrée 8525).　　MOORE

Frank Martin (1890–1974)

This Swiss composer deserves much higher status than he has yet been accorded: his music is powerful, compelling, and emotionally honest. Technically, too, it attempted—and gloriously succeeded in—something that, of all the major 20th-century composers, only Shostakovich also tackled: integration of the tonal and twelve-tone approaches to composition. The results the two men achieved are, of course, very different; though Shostakovich's music is much better known, Martin's is hardly less satisfying, and it's just as individual.

ORCHESTRAL MUSIC

The first substantial examination of Martin's orchestral music on disc was undertaken only in the '90s, with the London Philharmonic Orchestra conducted by Martin's fellow Swiss **Matthias Bamert,** who produced performances that are generally very reliable. His five Chandos CDs were cleverly planned to mix the few relatively familiar scores with those that deserve similar status. Thus the five Etudes for string orchestra and *Erasmi Monumentum* (in effect, an organ concerto) are set alongside the perky Concerto for Seven Wind Instruments, Percussion and Strings; the Etudes could do with crisper rhythmic attack (9283). They get it—only just—from the Munich Chamber Orchestra under **Hans Stadlmaier,** joined by two concertante works, the elegant *Polyptique* for violin and two small string orchestras (Martin was always concerned with contrapuntal clarity) and the understated, profound *Sonata da chiesa* for viola and strings (Koch Schwann 6732).

Two more CDs also feature the Etudes. One is an all-Martin affair from conductor-violinist **Stuart Canin** with the New Century Chamber Orchestra (NCCO), where it joins the Violin Concerto and *Maria-Triptychon,* for soprano, violin, and orchestra, the latter with the Berkeley Symphony (New Albion 086). The chamber textures of the NCCO show off the variety of instrumental color in the Etudes, though they lack that last degree of rhythmic tension and control. The Violin Concerto comes off rather better, though Canin's intrusive breathing begins to annoy, and this account of *Maria-Triptychon* (with soprano Sara Ganz) lacks polish but not drama: it's an unarguably committed performance. The Arion Ensemble under **Alexandru Lascae** couples a rather easygoing but technically secure account of the Etudes with the string orchestra version of the *Passacaglia* for organ; the other works here are by Françaix's *Symphonie d'archets* and *Variations de Concert* (Ottavo 109459).

For a man whose principal musical concern was linear, it's hardly surprising that Martin turned to the concerto: As well as the Violin Concerto, there are two for piano and one each for cello and harpsichord, as well as *Erasmi Monumentum* for organ and a handful of other concertante works, including a series of miniconcertos in the form of six *Ballades,* each around the 10 to 15-minute mark. The solo instruments are piano, trombone, cello, saxophone, viola, and flute. Martin's concern with structural strength didn't exclude a sense of humor, and there's plenty of tough twinkle in the two piano concertos, which accompany the piano *Ballade,* all ably done by **Jean-François Antonioli** with the Filarmonici di Torino under Marcello Viotti (Claves 50-8509). **Martin** himself conducts the Violin Concerto (with Wolfgang Schneiderhahn) and Piano Concerto 2 (with Badura-Skoda); the performances are obviously authoritative, but the 1971 sound shows its age (Jecklin 632).

One of Martin's best-known works, *Petite symphonie concertante,* written for Paul Sacher, can be heard from the Suisse Romande under **Martin**'s direction; he also conducts the orchestral version of the organ *Passacaglia* and *Maria-Triptychon,* with the musicians for whom it was written, Seefried and Scheiderhahn (Jecklin 645). The composer soon expanded *Petite symphonie* for full orchestra, dropping the qualifying adjective; astonishingly, it had to wait for **Bamert** in 1994 for its first recording, where the couplings are the muscular, invigorating 1937 Symphony—another first recording, long, long overdue—and, again, the orchestral *Passacaglia* (Chandos 9312).

Bamert, joined by a cohort of first-rate British instrumentalists, again does sterling work on all six *Ballades* (Chandos 9380), and on another disc **Susan Milan** (with the City of London Sinfonia under Hickox) plays the flute *Ballade* in a sparkling collection of French concertante works for flute (Chandos 8840).

CHAMBER AND INSTRUMENTAL MUSIC

Two CDs offer an ideal introduction to Martin's chamber music. One by a variety of artists including flutist Manuela Wiesler and pianist Pöntinen compiles the piano version of *Ballades* for flute and trombone with the eight *Préludes* for piano, *Etude de lecture* (Lucia Negro), and the three *Chants de Noël,* the whole rounded off with the flute-and-organ embodiment of *Sonata da Chiesa,* in passionate and communicative performances (BIS 71). The **Britten-Pears Ensemble** offers the *Ballades* for flute and for cello, Violin Sonata (a real discovery), with the early Piano Quintet and four *Sonnets à Cassandra* (ASV 1010). The *Préludes* can also be found in a glittering recital of 20th-century classics from **Diane Walsh** (Music & Arts 699, with the Barber and Bartók Sonatas and Prokofiev's Sonata 2).

In view of his outstanding gifts as a contrapuntalist, it's surprising that Martin wrote only one string quartet, in 1968—a strong, tightly argued work. The only recording currently available comes in a double album of otherwise generally forgettable 20th-century Swiss quartets from the **Sine Nomine Quartet** (Musikszene Schweiz M 57).

Martin also made an important contribution to the guitar repertoire, at the enlightened behest of Segovia: his four *Pièces brèves,* which—short though they are—establish the composer's identity within seconds. (Segovia was baffled by their innovative and utterly un-Spanish style and never played them.) **Jürgen Rost**'s recording isn't entirely technically secure (Berlin 009331, with works by other guitar composers). **Raphaëlla Smits,** whose playing is a delight, puts them at the end of an enchanting recital of "Lyrical 20th-Century Guitar Music" (Accent 8966). But the locus classicus for this work is by **Julian Bream;** he makes more extraneous noise than Smits, but also draws a far wider range of color and effects from the instrument (EMI 54901).

VOCAL MUSIC

The gem among Martin's substantial choral output is an early work he never intended for public consumption, the *Mass* for unaccompanied chorus. Composed as a private communication between himself and his God, Martin put it in a drawer and left it in silence for four decades. But once the secret was out, it soon became a choral favorite, and there are now close to a dozen recordings. Two very different ones claim our attention. **Shaw** conducts the Robert Shaw Festival Singers in a program that includes Górecki, Pärt, Barber, and Schoenberg—one of his last recordings and a well-rounded, richly textured account (Telarc 80406). In comparison with the plush, almost Romantic sound of Shaw's adults, the boy choristers of Westminster Cathedral under **O'Donnell** bring an other-worldly atmosphere, with a tone quality that's both cleaner and more sharply focused (Hyperion 67017); O'Donnell himself plays the organ *Passacaglia* and conducts Ildebrando Pizzetti's *De profundis* and *Messa da Requiem*—another a cappella masterpiece.

Martin wrote only one opera, *Der Sturm,* based on Shakespeare's *The Tempest;* it has yet to be recorded, and **Bamert**'s recording of the powerful Suite drawn from the opera—a kind of minisymphony—is as close as you can currently come to it on CD. This recording gives a good indication of what the continued neglect of the stage work is keeping from us (Chandos 9411). The Suite joins *Maria-Triptychon* (with soprano Lynda Russell and violinist Duncan Riddell—the best account on the market)—and six *Monologe aus Jedermann* (Monologues from *Everyman*), one of the past century's most darkly convincing orchestral song cycles (here with baritone David Wilson-Johnson).

But Martin was also drawn to drama in slightly less orthodox forms and wrote a considerable number of extended works that are dramatic within their less explicitly theatrical frames. The first of these was *Le Vin Herbé,* an oratorio using Joseph Bedier's modern French retelling of the Tristan legend. **Mark Shapiro** and his Cantori di New York are obviously passionate about the music, but the singing suffers from poor intonation (Newport 85670, 2CD). **Victor Desarzens**'s 1961 version offers a surer-footed interpretation, with the composer at the piano (Jecklin 581/2, 2CD). *Die Weise von Liebe und Tod des Cornets Christoph Rilke* (The Lay of the Life and Death of Cornet Christoph Rilke), to texts by Rainer Maria Rilke, is in effect an hour-long symphonic cantata for contralto and orchestra, a work of tremendous cumulative power. **Baileys** with the Lausanne Chamber Orchestra under López-Cobos (Cascavelle 1020) are outshone by the much more dramatic, more tightly focused account from **Lipovšek** and the ORF Symphony Orchestra under Zagrosek (Orfeo 164881).

The heartfelt oratorio *In terra pax* mixes religious and political intent; it was written in the last year of WWII to be performed as soon as peace was declared. The performance under **Volker Hempling** is underpowered and unfocused (Motette 40141, with *Erasmi Monumentum*); **Bamert** offers a much stronger version (Chandos 9465, with the orchestral suite *The Four Elements*). The attraction of **Corboz**'s recording is the coupling: the austerely beautiful chamber cantata *Et la vie l'emporta* (Life Won the Day), Martin's last work (Cascavelle 1014).

The next large-scale work was the stark, moving, passion-oratorio *Golgotha*. By far the strongest account of the three available comes from

Corboz, with sundry soloists and the Sinfonietta and Ensemble Vocal de Lausanne (Cascavelle 3004, 2CD). It's a live recording, with the inevitable extraneous noises that entails, and a sense of conviction that makes this powerful music instantly communicative. **Herbert Böck**'s reading doesn't have quite the same dramatic focus (Hänssler 98.327, 2CD). Both these versions are undercut in price by **Robert Faller**'s budget recording, which throws in the Mass for good measure—a false economy if you want to discover what the music is really like, but a sensibly cheap way of dipping your toe in the water (Ultima 24237, 2CD).

Ansermet's 1959 mono recording of the radiant Christmas oratorio *Le Mystère de la Nativité* (a live take of the first performance) suffers from constricted sound, although the urgency of the occasion shines through (Cascavelle 2006, 2CD). The cantata *Pilate*, based on a 1450 text by Aroul Gréban, is the coupling—a well-chosen one, since these two works effectively book-end the life of Christ. The mood, though, is very different: *Le Mystère* is dignified but optimistic; *Pilate* has all the intensity of a tragic ritual. *Pilate* is also a live recording, with all the usual offstage clicks, coughs, and shuffles, and the solo singing leaves a little to be desired, but this is the only recording on the market.

The three heart-warming *Chansons de Noël* are to be found rubbing shoulders with songs by six other French composers in an exquisite recital from **von Otter**, partnered by the ever-reliable pianist Bengt Forsberg and flutist Andreas Alin (DG (447752)—enchanting.

I leave to the end the locus classicus of Frank Martin on CD: an anthology of live recordings made by Radio Suisse Romande between 1951 and 1967 (Cascavelle 2001). **Ansermet** conducts *Petite Symphonie Concertante*, three of the four movements of the Suite from *The Tempest*, with Fischer-Dieskau in his thrilling vocal prime, and the Cello Concerto with Fournier, who commissioned it, as soloist; and as a pendant Martin himself conducts the orchestral version of the flute *Ballade* with André Pépin. Poor sound, noises off, and other distractions notwithstanding, there's a compelling passion and electricity about these performances. Cascavelle has brought this CD together with its recordings of *In Terra Pax*, *Et la vie l'emporta*, *Der Cornet*, *Le Mystère de la Nativité*, and *Golgotha* in an 8CD box (3027).   ANDERSON

Bohuslav Martinů *(1890–1959)*

Martinů wrote a great deal of music in all possible genres. His earliest works are in a romantic and impressionist idiom, but while he was studying with Roussel in Paris, his music became first jazzy, then brittle and neo-Baroque. During WWII he came to America, where his style broadened into a lushly expressive romanticism. His idiom was always based on Czech folk song; throughout all of his style changes, his melodic turns remain constant and his rhythmic ebullience keeps him moving, though he has a tendency to walk for the sake of walking, which becomes a mannerism at times.

SYMPHONIES

The first five symphonies were all written in America and mark a new breadth in Martinů's musical expression. No. 6 was written for the Boston Symphony after he moved to Switzerland in 1953.

Complete sets. There are three complete recordings of the symphonies. **Neumann** made one during 1976–77 with the Czech Philharmonic (Supraphon 110382, 3CD). (Rumor reports one from the '80s, but it seems never to have surfaced). The early recordings are good, though Neumann's besetting sin of accuracy without enthusiasm makes him irritating. He has the ideal orchestra, and just leaves it to them, though recorded balances are sometimes crude. **Neeme Järvi** with the Bamberg

Symphony is better recorded and more obviously involved, if less idiomatically natural (BIS 362, 363, 402). The same can be said of **Thomson** with the Scottish National Orchestra: exuberant, expressive, with lots of contrast, but not as effortless as the Czechs (Chandos 9103, 3CD, or separately on 8915/7).

1. **Bělohlávek** with the Czech Philharmonic brings to 1 and 6 a welcome involvement (Chandos 8950). Unfortunately, the symphonies aren't coupled (yet), and 1 isn't recorded as clearly as 6. No. 1 is with the Double Concerto, one of Martinů's strongest wartime works. Nos. 1 and 6 are also in a disc by **Arthur Fagen** with the Ukraine Symphony in lyrical performances that lack only the rhythmic snap of the Czechs, recorded in atmospheric sound (Naxos 553348). If it's the rhythm that turns you on, and if you can deal with rather thin sonics, go for **Ančerl**, whose Czech Philharmonic recordings of 1, 3, and 5 are tightest of all and played brilliantly (♦Multisonic 23, 2CD).

2. This symphony is only available outside the complete albums with **Järvi**'s 1 (BIS 362) or **Thomson**'s 6 (Chandos 8916). It's the shortest and lightest-textured of the symphonies. **Neumann** has its number.

3. This symphony is the most consistently tragic. **Neumann** does it well, but both **Ančerl** and **Sejna** (Supraphon 111924) are more intense, though less richly recorded. Both **Järvi** (BIS 363) and **Thomson** (Chandos 8917) couple 3 and 4.

4. Full of birdsong and hope, this symphony is beautifully delineated by **Martin Turnovsky** and the Czech Philharmonic (Urania 5165, NA). **Bělohlávek** made a fine 4 and 5 (Panton 811205, NA). Currently, **Bohumil Kotmel** looks interesting, coupled with the only presently available *Field Mass*, but it hasn't come my way. **Ansermet** was a champion of Martinů; his 4 is a committed performance in somewhat scrawny mono sound (Cascavelle 2007, with *Frescoes* and *Parables*).

5. This symphony expresses the tension of war, ending with a joyful, almost Beethovenian dance. **Ančerl**'s is the classic interpretation (Multisonic 23, 2CD), once available in better sound and coupled with his *Memorial to Lidice*, *Frescoes*, and *Parables* (Supraphon 1931, NA).

6. This is a dark, eerie piece full of mysterious swirls and quotations from Dvořák's *Requiem*. It was composed for the Boston Symphony, which recorded it with **Munch** in a stirring performance (RCA 3794, NA). There is another Munch live-concert recording with the Czech Philharmonic, last seen coupled with a Rozhdestvensky *Frescoes* (Panton 811122, NA). **Ančerl** also made a classic recording (Supraphon 1931, NA, with *Bouquet of Flowers*). **Bělohlávek**'s version comes with Suk's *Fantastic Scherzo* and Janáček's *Sinfonietta* in good readings (Chandos 8897). **Arthur Fagen** captures the moods effectively (Naxos 8553348, with 1). There are others, appearing only to disappear, including **Vladimir Válek** and the Prague Symphony live with a fine *Frescoes* and Martinů's only solo organ work, *Vigilia* (Praga 254050, NA).

OTHER ORCHESTRAL MUSIC

The many orchestral works are best approached in chronological order. The distinction between purely orchestral compositions and concertante works is a bit blurred, since Martinů frequently included a piano in his orchestra, then gave it an ambiguous role to play. Therefore, the sinfoniettas and *Toccata e due Canzoni* are frequently listed under concertante works, where I propose to leave them. The ballet scores will be included with the other staged works near the end of this article.

Martinů's early orchestral music is represented by a disc combining two projects, entitled "Works Inspired by Jazz and Sport" (Supraphon

3058) This is a catch-all collection containing *Half-time, La Bagarre,* and *Thunderbolt P-47* with the Brno State Philharmonic under **Petr Vronsky.** Jazz-inspired works are *Shimmy Foxtrot* from the ballet *Who Is the Most Powerful in the World?* and a short piece with chorus, *Le Jazz.* A *Jazz Suite* is listed as orchestral music, although that term is contestable for this performance, which appears to use one player to a part, even in the strings.

The Serenades are an ambiguous genre in every possible way. There are six in all, the first for chamber orchestra (1930), once available on an old Westminster LP conducted by **Henry Swoboda.** Then come four for various combinations (1932), listed as string orchestra pieces by *Schwann.* Actually, 1 is for clarinet, horn, three violins and viola; 2 is for two violins and viola; 3 is for oboe, clarinet, four violins, and cello; and 4 is for violin, viola, oboe, piano, and string orchestra (also called *Divertimento*). Finally comes a longer, later Serenade for 2 clarinets and string trio (1951). Now it gets complicated, so pay attention.

Until recently, the four numbered serenades were available played idiomatically by **Vlček** and the Prague Chamber Orchestra, with one numbered 5, actually the 1930 piece (Supraphon 2305, NA). The disc now available is by **Ensemble Villa Musica,** which plays only the chamber music works—that is, the first three 1932 Serenades, omitting the fourth, but playing the longer 1951 Serenade (calling it No. 4) and adding the Quartet for clarinet, horn, cello, and side drum (MD+G 3040774). So you need both discs if you want all six pieces, and it takes less time to play some of them than it took you to read this. Just to make matters worse, there is a *Partita* for string orchestra on the old Swoboda disc that isn't on any of the recent ones.

The later orchestral pieces are in Martinů's more lush post-WWII style. *Memorial to Lidice* is a short piece—a moving slow movement—written when Martinů heard of the Nazi blood-bath in that town in 1943. **Ančerl's** classic performance now appears in a collection of WWII pieces by Honegger and Schoenberg (Supraphon 177). More up-to-date sound is provided by **Kotmel** (Chandos 9138, with Symphony 4 and the only present recording of the wartime *Field Mass).*

The only other orchestral works presently on disc are late three-movement cycles, *Frescoes of Piero della Francesca, Parables,* and *Estampes. Frescoes* and *Parables* are in the **Ansermet** collection, played well but rather thinly recorded (Cascavelle 2007, with Symphony 4). A more satisfactory *Parables* is by **Bělohlávek,** with the only available *Estampes,* the earlier *Ricercari,* and Piano Concerto 2 with Firkušný (Supraphon 111988). *Frescoes* is on **DePreist's** disc with the Malmö Symphony, and you get a good if not great Double Concerto and **Imai's** excellent *Rhapsody-Concerto* (♦BIS 501). It's swings and roundabouts in this area, compounded by the inexplicable absence of **Ančerl's** outstanding readings of both *Frescoes* and *Parables,* once available coupled with *Lidice* and Symphony 5 (Supraphon 1931, NA), and with his Symphony 6 (Supraphon 997). And **Bělohlávek's** *Parables* and *Estampes* used to be on Supraphon 104140 (NA), with the 1953 Overture and the 1928 Rhapsody, both now unrecorded. **Kubelik's** interesting but a bit undernourished mono performances with the Vienna Philharmonic was once available (Orfeo, NA). There have been a number of good readings, but most have disappeared.

CONCERTOS

As a quasi-neo-Baroque composer, Martinů wrote a lot of works where the piano is partly soloistic but frequently reverts to a sort of basso continuo role. Sinfonia for Two Orchestras (1932) employs the piano in this way, as does the lively 1937 Concerto Grosso (only listed presently on

Supraphon 111996, 2CD, with artists unknown to *Schwann* and to me, though I hope it's the fine mono **Ančerl**). These two works plus the 1938 *Tre Ricercari* were once all together on a fine recording by **Bělohlávek** (Supraphon 381, NA); the *Ricercari* are all that's left (Supraphon 111988). They were also the filler for **Turnovsky's** classic Symphony 4 (Parliament LP 621, NA).

The best known of these works is the 1938 Double Concerto for Two String Orchestras, Piano, and Timpani, Martinů's response to the growing threat of Nazi Germany. This powerful work was first recorded by **Sejna** in a darkly violent reading with the Czech Philharmonic (♦Supraphon 111924, with Symphony 3 and Dvořák's *American Suite).* **Mackerras** has a long and active history with this work. His first recording with the Prague Radio Symphony was in 1987 (Supraphon, NA); a 1992 recording with the Brno Philharmonic was drier in sound and spirit (Conifer, NA). Presently, he's represented by a performance with the BBC Symphony in a disc containing Janáček's *Sinfonietta, Taras Bulba,* and the *Ballad of Blanik Hill,* all conducted by Rozhdestvensky (♦BBC Radio Classics 9135). Though recorded at a lower level than the Janáček, spatially it's clearer than Sejna's, and the performance is excellent (so is the Janáček).

In 1991 **DePreist** appeared with the Malmö Symphony in a lush recording that tends to blur the edges of the sound, though the performance is fine (BIS 501). **Hickox** with the Sinfonia of London appeared the same year in a polished reading lacking the vigor of the foregoing versions (Virgin). **Bělohlávek** is more idiomatic, but a little stymied by overripe microphoning and his more relaxed approach to the music (Chandos). Most recently, **Alexandros Myrat** couples the Concerto with Honegger's Symphony 2, an apt choice since the two works resemble each other in many ways and Honegger was one of the earliest proponents of the Martinů (Agora). These are concert recordings, with the perils thereof; though the performances are enthusiastic, the sound is a little wearing.

Three compositions of a similar type but in a lighter mood are *Sinfonietta giocosa* (1940), *Toccata e Due Canzoni* (1946), and *Sinfonietta "La Jolla"* (1950). These works make up an attractive program by **Vásáry** and the Bournemouth Sinfonietta, with Julian Jacobsen on piano (Chandos 8859). There have been more idiomatic recordings of all three from the Czechs—to wit, *Giocosa* by **Smetáček,** the Prague Symphony, and pianist Stanislav Knorr (Artia LP 712, NA), and the latter two by the **Prague Chamber Orchestra** with pianist Zdenek Hnat (Supraphon, NA). There was a more recent *Giocosa* by **Bohumil Gregor** with pianist Jan Panenka and the Prague Chamber Orchestra, coupled with the otherwise unavailable *Divertimento* for piano left-hand and orchestra (Supraphon, NA). That was the better of Panenka's two recordings, but it didn't equal Knorr's. However, the only alternative for any of these important pieces today is an unsubtle and dryly recorded *La Jolla* by **Jan Valta** and the Zilina State Chamber Orchestra (Opus 93501844).

Having approached the world of the Martinů concerto by the back door, let's go on to the five piano concertos. All five plus the 1938 Concertino are played with fine style and warm sound by **Emil Leichner** with Bělohlávek and the Czech Philharmonic (♦Supraphon 1313, 2CD). Individual performances of greater character have existed, but most are no longer current. **Firkušný** was closely associated with the composer, and his recordings of 2 through 4 with Pešek and the Czech Philharmonic should never have been allowed to disappear (RCA 61934, NA). At the moment, only his 2 with Bělohlávek is in print (♦Supraphon 1988). **Josef Palinicek's** 1990 3 with Neumann (Supraphon 374, NA) wasn't a patch on the one he made in the '60s with Ančerl, luckily back in print with his incandescent Janáček *Sinfonietta* and *Taras Bulba* (♦Supraphon 111929). No. 4 also received a fine performance from Palinicek and Jiří Pinkas (Supraphon LP 58591, NA). Nos. 4 and 5 are available in radio performances by **Klara Havlikova** and Czech forces, but the sound isn't good (Campion, with the Harpsichord Concerto). There was a version of 5 by its dedicatee, **Margrit Weber,** with Kubelik and Berlin, that did it justice (DG, NA).

The Concerto for Two Pianos is a fine wartime piece from 1943 only available in a rather klutzy performance by **Joshua Pierce** and **Dorothy Jonas** (Phoenix 104 or Carlton 6701732). A fine Supraphon LP was once extant, recorded in 1967 by **Vera** and **Vlastimil Lejsek** with Jiří Waldhans and the Brno Philharmonic.

The Harpsichord Concerto is a cute little number from 1935, in which that instrument is played off against a piano. Shades of C. P. E. Bach! It's played idiomatically by **Zuzana Ružičková** on her disc with Piano Concertos 4 and 5 (Campion 1321). An interesting release featuring 20th-century harpsichord concertos is by **Eva Braito,** a good alternative (Koch Schwann 31422).

Moving over to the string section, Martinů wrote two violin concertos. Both are played by **Suk** and Neumann in 1974 recordings that have yet to be superseded (Supraphon 1969, with the later *Rhapsody-Concerto* for viola). A 1946 performance of 2 by **Louis Kaufmann** is primarily for fans of this fine performer (Cambria 1063).

Martinů wrote two concertos for two violins. The first (also called *Duo Concertante,* 1937) may be had only in a 1960 reading by **Peter Rybar** and **Kurt Conzelmann** under Horenstein, along with *Concerto da Camera* for violin, piano, percussion, and strings (1941), and Quartet 6 in good mono radio performances featuring the Rybars, who were friends of the composer (Telos 23). *Concerto da Camera* may also be found with Concertino for Cello, Winds, and Percussion, and a piece by Werner Steinmetz, all played well but without much personality by **Sabine Windbacher** and the Austrian Chamber Orchestra under Ernst Theis (Musicaphon). Concerto 2 (1950) is played by **André** and **Yaga Siwy** with Barshai (Discover, with Szymanowski's Violin Concerto 2 and Prokofiev's Sonata for two violins). Their performances of the discmates have been bettered elsewhere.

For viola we have only the late *Rhapsody-Concerto* (1952), a lyrical work in two movements. There are three excellent performances. **Suk's** is classically controlled (♦Supraphon 111969), while **Imai** is darker and more subjective (♦BIS 501). A dark-horse entry is **Mikhail Tolpyga** in an intense, songful performance with a Russian orchestra (Consonance 810003).

There are two concertos for cello: one from 1930 that was heavily revised later, the second from 1944–45. They are both substantial pieces and have been recorded several times. There is also a perky Concertino with winds and percussion from 1924. At present there are two discs containing all three, by **Raphael Wallfisch** with Bělohlávek and the Czech Philharmonic (♦Chandos 9015) and by **Michaela Fukačová** with Peter Csaba and the Odense Symphony (Kontrapunkt 32256). The Chandos recording and the Czech orchestra are a distinct advantage, though Fukačová is excellent. The Concertino is also available in a less expressive reading by **Martin Rummel** with Ernst Theis and the Austrian Chamber Orchestra (Musicaphon). A concert performance of Concerto 1 by **Fournier** with Sawallisch is exciting seat-of-the-pants stuff (Cascavelle 2009). **Josef Chuchro** is a solid player, but not worth a 2CD set unless you're attracted by the discmates, Dvořák's Cello Concerto and *Stabat Mater* (Supraphon 3093, 2CD). There is also a *Sonata da Camera* for cello and chamber orchestra, presently unavailable.

The only wind concerto is for oboe (1955). Recordings are a mixed bag. **Ivan Sequardt** with Neumann is coupled with a Smetana *Festive Symphony* too heavily cut for recommendation (Supraphon). **Thomas Indermühle** is a good player, but his disc as a whole is too fast and lacks character (Camarata).

In the Baroque tradition, there are several works combining several soloists and orchestra in concerto grosso format. Most of these are presently missing from disc, but the Concerto for String Quartet and Orchestra (1930) may be found coupled with the Double Concerto and *Sinfonia Concertante* for oboe, bassoon, violin, cello, and orchestra conducted by **Hickox** in a satisfying performance (EMI 59575). In 1933 Martinů wrote a Concerto for Piano Trio and Orchestra that was temporarily mislaid. The composer promptly wrote a replacement, a Concertino. Both works were recorded by the Gobel Trio with the Pomorska Philharmonic and **Takao Ukigaya** (Thorofon 2013, NA).

That's the only outing for the Concerto, but the Concertino is in a disc by **Alexandros Myrat** with La Camarata, including the Double Concerto and Honegger's Symphony 2 in concert performances of energy if not a great deal of polish (Agora 128). There is another Concertino with the Trio Tulsa, **Paul Freeman,** and the Czech National Symphony that's better avoided (Centaur). A recording by Suk, Chuchro, and Panenka with **Neumann** and the Czech Philharmonic is languishing in the vault at Supraphon (LP 2198, NA). There you may also find performances of the Quartet Concerto and the 1936 Concerto for Flute and Violin.

CHAMBER MUSIC

Like his contemporaries Hindemith and Milhaud, Martinů wrote a lot of chamber music, much of it in odd categories. This survey runs from small to large, from the expected forms to the more individual titles.

Violin and piano works include three numbered sonatas plus an earlier unnumbered one from 1926 and a late Sonatina (1957). So says the Martinů catalog, but **Bohuslav Matoušek** and Petr Adameč have recorded two more early sonatas and an Elegy (*Evil Returns),* bringing the tally to six sonatas and the total known works for this combination to 16! All the violin-piano works are in two albums (♦Supraphon 3410 and 3412, both 2CD). Get them while they're hot! These are fine performances of rare material. **Suk** and Josef Hala played the official Sonatas 2 and 3 (Supraphon 99, NA, with *Madrigal Stanzas*). **Hanna Kotkova** and Simon Mulligan are available in idiomatic performances of Sonatas 1 through 3 plus *Czech Rhapsody* (Studio Matous 45).

The three sonatas plus the one for two violins and piano are played with sensitivity though somewhat shaky intonation by **Fredell Lack** and Timothy Hester, with Leon Spierer (Centaur 2276). Sonata 3 and *Madrigals* (written to be performed by the composer with Alfred Einstein) are in an interesting, well performed disc by **Yair Kless** and Shoshana Rudiakov (Tacet 62, with rare music by Enescu). *Arabesques, Intermezzo, Madrigal Stanzas, Rhythmic Etudes,* and *Czech Rhapsody* are played with vigor and affection by **Jan Talich** and Jaromir Klapac (GZ 305). Sonata 1, *Arabesques, Czech Rhapsody,* and Duo 1 for Violin and Cello are played with enthusiasm but some intonation problems by **Ivan Strauss** and Walter Haley, with Marek Jerie, cello (Panton 710531).

There is only one work for viola and piano, and two recordings. It's well played by **Rainer Moog** and Daniel Adni (Naxos 553916). **Robert Verebes** and Dale Bartlett also offered the Sonata in a program with sonatas by Mendelssohn and Jean Coulthard, not heard (SNE 550).

There are many cello works: three sonatas, three other collections of pieces, all from 1931, and two sets of variations. The sonatas are performed by **Jiří Hanousek** and Paul Kaspar, but so far it hasn't come my way (Centaur 2207). **Starker** and Firkušný ought to be a winner but it's not: They pull the music about unmercifully, and are poorly balanced as well (RCA). There were fine readings by **Steven Isserlis** and Bryan Evans, full of energy and imagination (Hyperion 66296, NA), and by **Roel Dieltiens** and Robert Groslot, more straightforward and perhaps even truer to the composer (Accent 8967, NA). **Christian** and Sebastian **Benda** add *Arabesques* and *Ariette,* both in their only present recording on cello (Naxos 554502). They play well together in emotionally intense readings, though their recording is a touch thin-sounding.

Individual recordings of the sonatas come from **Francois Guye** and David Lively, who play Sonata 1 along with *Slovak Variations* and music by Rachmaninoff in good but not outstanding readings (Cascavelle 10919). **Gordon Epperson** and Frances Burnett play a mannered and mumbling Sonata 2 in an otherwise American program (Centaur), while **Peter Rejto** and Eugene Rowley pull the music about and make a cut in the finale, though the rest of their disc is excellent (Summit 137).

The little 1931 cello suites (*Nocturnes, Pastorales, Miniature Suite*) are full of lovely ideas. They and the virtuoso *Rossini* and *Slovak Variations* make up the **Benda**'s Vol. 2, played with the same individuality and verve they brought to the sonatas (Naxos 554503). The same pieces minus the *Slovak Variations* but plus the tiny, jazzy *Ariette* are recorded by **Anatoly Krastev** and Krassimir Taskov in lively but somewhat unvaried readings recorded rather harshly (Gega 165). The *Nocturnes* are in the disc of piano trios by the **Bekova** sisters (Chandos 9632), while the *Pastorales* presently listed in *Schwann* are a different composition (see below). The **Hayashi Duo** has done both sets of variations in lively readings (Fone 8701, with the Grieg Sonata). **Mikael Ericsson** and František Maly played them even better (Panton 1269, NA, with *Nocturne, Pastorales,* and *Ariette*).

Separately, in *Rossini* you can get the virtuosity of **Starker** (Mercury 434358) or in a miscellaneous program of Martinů's less classifiable chamber works (Hungaroton 31674), or in **H. Zheng**'s highly varied cello program (Amati 1005). In *Slovak Variations,* there's **Bernard Gregor-Smith** in a fine Eastern program (ASV 6218) or **François Guye** (Cascavelle 1019, with Sonata 1 and Rachmaninoff).

There are a few works for wind instruments, notably a substantial flute sonata (1945). Most impressive are **Jiri Válek** and Josef Hala with Suk in a flute-oriented program containing the Sonata for Flute, Violin, and Piano, *Madrigal-Sonata* for the same combination, *Promenades* with harpsichord, and, for violin and piano, four pieces and *Intermezzo* (♦Lotos 41). The same program, substituting the Trio for Flute, Cello, and Piano for the violin pieces, is played by **Yossi Arnheim** and other Israeli and Russian immigrants in richly emotional performances (Kontrapunkt 32205). A related program of Eastern European flute sonatas is played with great polish by **Michel Bellavance** and Marc Bourdeau (Brioso 121). An unexpected coupling gives us the sonata played by **Gunilla von Bahr** and Kerstin Hindart in a program otherwise consisting of Martinů's piano music played by **Kvapil** (BIS 234). **Ezster Horgas** and Béla Simon play it in another all-Martinů program (Hungaroton 31674).

Also on this disc is Martinů's only work for clarinet and piano, the 1956 Sonatina, played by **Lajos Rozmán.** The dearth of clarinet solo music hasn't stopped **Michele Zukovsky,** who has put together two separate discs of works with prominent clarinet parts. Summit 214 contains the Sonatina and three larger works, the 1924 Quartet for Clarinet, Horn, Cello, and Side Drum; the ballet score *La Revue de Cuisine;* and perhaps Martinů's oddest piece, the *Stowe-Pastorals* for clarinet, two

violins, cello, and a quintet of recorders (not the cello *Pastorales,* as *Schwann* would have it). Written for the Trapp family in 1951, this 10-minute piece alone is worth the price of admission.

Zukovsky's other disc stretches the envelope a bit, containing transcriptions of three movements from the violin *Intermezzos* and the slow movement of the violin Sonatina and another for wind quintet of the piano piece *Merry Christmas 1941* (Summit 246). *Rossini Variations* is played in its original cello form by **Jakub Omsky** and Erik Entwhistle, and three *Sketches* for piano is performed by Gloria Cheng. This odd program also contains Serenade 3 and *Les Rondes,* a large chamber piece, sometimes called *Round Dances* (1930). These two discs are well played, but only Summit 214 is as effective as it is unusual. Finally, there is a Sonatina for Trumpet and Piano, played by **Edward Tarr** in a varied program (BIS 152).

Duos not for piano include two for violin and cello (1927 and 1958), one for violin and viola, and *Madrigals* for violin and viola (1947). The virtuosity of these works has attracted a number of players, but rather surprisingly, only one version of *Madrigals* is listed at present. Martinů wrote this effective three-movement work for **Joseph** and **Lillian Fuchs,** and their fine recording should be with us always. The only listed version is by members of the **Stamitz Quartet,** in their album of all the Martinů quartets (Bayer 100152). We're in good hands here, but there are other options, not necessarily as good. The other violin-viola duo is recorded by the **Duo Renard** in a 20th-century American disc called "The Deeper Magic" (Musicians Showcase 1035). The performance is good, if a bit heavy in places.

Oleg Krysa and **Torleif Thedéen** play brilliantly in Duo 1 for violin and cello, four-minute cadenza and all, in a program of fine works by Ravel, Honegger, and Schulhoff, in satisfactory if unnecessarily reverberant sound (♦BIS 916). The **Bekova** sisters also play this Duo well, as they do Trio 1 and *Cinq Pieces Brèves;* their Ravel Trio isn't as successful (Chandos 9452). Duo 2 is a less violent piece. There was once a Supraphon LP containing this Duo played by **Suk** and Navarra. The strings of the **Angell Trio** include it with the three piano trios (ASV 6230), while the **Tulsa Trio** leaves out Trio 3 and substitutes Concertino for Piano Trio and Strings (Centaur 2415). Tulsa has major problems with intonation in high registers, though their style is more suited to Martinů's linear writing than the Angell, who are more concerned with polish and beauty of sound. The **Bekova** sisters are also smooth to a fault in Trios 2 and 3, the cello *Nocturnes,* and *Czech Rhapsody* (Chandos 9632).

An international group has recorded the flute-violin-piano sonata and *Madrigal-Sonata,* as well as a Scherzo for flute and piano and all three piano trios in musical performances (Koch Schwann 6728). There were two Panton CDs, one containing the three trios plus *Bergerettes* played by the **Czech Trio** (811315) and another of cello pieces played by better and more idiomatically successful musicians than any of the above. I haven't been able to trace Media 7-4, in which the **Osiris Trio** plays the trios and *Bergerettes.*

Three of Martinů's more unusual trios are brought together in the **Dartington Ensemble**'s collection (Hyperion 22039, 2CD). I'm not uniformly happy with it, but it does collect many of the Madrigal compositions, including four for oboe, clarinet, and bassoon (1937) that don't seem to be recorded elsewhere. There are also *Madrigal Sonata* for flute, violin, and piano; *Madrigal Stanzas* for violin and piano; and Madrigals for violin and viola. This set also includes the Trio for Flute, Cello, and Piano and the Sonatina for Two Violins and Piano; the 1959 *Nonet* and *La Revue de Cuisine* complete the tally. The two-violin Sonatina is otherwise available only on **Fredell Lack**'s none-too-polished disc of the violin sonatas (Centaur), and it's particularly well played here by two Eastern European violinists, **Krysia Osostowicz** and **Ernst Kovacic**, with pianist Susan Tomes. The *Madrigal Sonata* is better represented by **Suk,** Válek, and Hala (Lotos 41).

The Flute Trio has received a number of recordings, but one duplicates the Dartington program to a marked degree. The **Sinfonia Lahti Chamber Ensemble** plays not only the trio but also the *Nonet* and *La Revue de Cuisine,* adding the only existing movement of a 1924 *Nonet* for good measure (BIS 653). They play with idiomatic assurance and have the benefit of a resonant recording. On the other hand, the performances by the Dartingtons that disturb me are the violin/viola Madrigals, not very well tuned, and a hokey *Revue* that tries to point up Martinů's jokes by burlesquing them at times. Good flute trios may also be had on Kontrapunkt 32205 and Hungaroton 31674, with Martinů programs to match.

The seven listed string quartets have had two complete recordings, one by the **Stamitz Quartet,** with bonuses of the violin-viola *Madrigals* and String Trio 2 (1934), otherwise unavailable (♦ Bayer 100152, 3CD), and the other by the **Panocha Quartet,** without bonuses (Supraphon 110994, 3CD). The Stamitz is more linear, the Panocha tends to smooth over things better left raw. These pieces require clarity and balance. Though both groups are excellent, the Stamitz pulls things together somewhat more tightly, and their leaner sound holds the ear better. A series by the **Martinů Quartet** includes Quartets 1 and 2; the playing is lively and polished, a fine alternative (Naxos 553782). A recording of Quartet 2 by the **New Bochmann Quartet** is raw in intonation in places (Carlton 985). A 1957 version of 6 by the **Winterthur Quartet** is part of a Peter Rybar retrospective, important for his friendship with the composer (Telos 23). Otherwise, all the old recordings once available on Supraphon have gone, the **Smetana Quartet**'s 4, the **Janáček Quartet**'s 5, **the Novak Quartet**'s 6, the **Vlach Quartet**'s 7. Sniff!

Quartets of an odder stripe include the little Quartet for Clarinet, Horn, Cello, and Side Drum available from the **Ensemble Villa Musica** (MD+G 3040774) and from the **Bohemian Ensemble Los Angeles** (Summit 214). Both are good, and both are all-Martinů discs. Then there are the 1940 Piano Quartet and the Quartet for Oboe, Violin, Cello, and Piano (1947), both available in interesting performances by a number of fine players from the 1994 **Australian Chamber Music Festival** (Naxos 553916). This disc also includes the only recordings of the 1927 String Quintet and the little-known Viola Sonata. The playing is occasionally less than perfect, but in general it's excellent.

The two Piano Quintets were once on LP, the relatively well known 2 in a couple of fine Czech readings. All there is now is 2 with **Peter Frankl** and the Lindsay Quartet, a fine performance coupled with an excellent Dvořák Op. 81 (ASV 889).

Martinů also wrote a Wind Sextet (1929) and a String Sextet (1932); the latter earned him the Elizabeth Sprague Coolidge Prize. He later added a bass part and made a string orchestra piece out of it, but the **Academy of St. Martin in the Fields Chamber Ensemble** plays the original, and does it very well too, adding Serenade 2 as a bonus and Dvořák's Sextet as well (Chandos 8771). The orchestrated version can also be heard played well by the Westphalian Chamber Philharmonic under **Frieder Obstfeld** in a program that includes music by Schreker, Hans Krása, and Pavel Haas (EDA 9). The Wind Sextet is played by the **Forras Ensemble** with more wind works by Martinů (Hungaroton 31674), and in a program of music by Poulenc and Françaix (Calig 50984).

There are also two nonets, or three, if you count the single movement from 1924 mentioned above. The 1924–25 work and the 1959 are both on **Lahti**'s disc (BIS 653), while the 1959 work is played by the **Danish Chamber Players,** along with *La Ronde, La Revue de Cuisine,* and Chamber Music No. 1, otherwise known as *Les Fêtes Nocturnes* for clarinet, harp, piano, and string trio (Kontrapunkt 32227). The latter may also be heard from the **Philadelphia Chamber Players** (Boston 1026, with Penderecki and Poulenc). But the oddest experience is provided by a 14-minute *Fantasie* (1945) for theremin, oboe, piano, and string quartet, recorded by **Lydia Kavina** with the Portland Quartet, Joshua Pierce on piano, and Kirsten Fox on oboe (Mode 76). This disc also contains original works for the theremin by Joseph Schillinger and Grainger, among others. The musical interest of the program tends to deteriorate toward the end, but it's quite fascinating sonically, and the Martinů piece is almost worth the price by itself.

PIANO MUSIC

A large number of piano works have been recorded by **Emil Leichner** (Supraphon 1010, 3CD). He has tended to get a poor press for being neither **Firkušny,** who was a friend of the composer and recorded the Sonata, *Les Ritournelles, Fantasie et Toccata,* and excerpts from *Etudes and Polkas* (RCA 87987, NA), nor **Kvapil,** an incisive pianist who plays the Sonata and *Etudes and Polkas* with rhythmic élan (BIS 234). Come to think of it, he isn't **Eleonora Bekova,** either, who has recorded the Sonata, *Fantasie et Toccata, Preludes, The Fifth Day of the Fifth Moon, Bagatelle,* and *Dumka 3,* the last three not in Leichner's collection, in agile performances (Chandos 9655).

No, what Leichner has is an unassuming good humor leavened with enough romanticism to make three hours and 20 minutes of Martinů come across with warmth and meaning. He likes the little miniatures, the three early *Puppet* Suites and *Butterflies and Birds of Paradise* that make up most of disc 1, little impressionistic pieces. Then he does the suites of *Czech Dances,* the three *Sketches in Jazz Style,* Preludes, *Les Ritournelles, Sketches of Dances, Fantaisie et Toccata,* Etudes and Polkas, *Window on the Garden,* and ends with the Sonata. He hasn't the energy of some of the other players, but he's very musical and, in the main, Martinů uses the piano as a relief from the motor he sometimes leaves running in his larger works.

Three *Czech Dances* and a Fantasy for two pianos are played rather woodenly by **Pierce** and **Jonas** on their disc with the two-piano Concerto (Phoenix or Carlton). More ebullient performances come from the **Labeque** sisters (MHS LP 1766, NA but perhaps reissued on CD).

There are a sonata and several pieces for harpsichord that have so far remained unexplored, and there is one organ work, *Vigilie,* that may be found in **Hora**'s disc (Russian Compact Disc 7, with music by Dvořák, Josef Foerster, and Janáček).

CHORAL MUSIC

There's quite a lot of choral music of different kinds. Most of the unaccompanied works are included in **Pavel Kühn**'s album, sung with unquestionable authenticity but unfortunately without printed texts (Supraphon 2232, 2CD). An alternative version of some of the madrigals and a number of unaccompanied sacred works may be found conducted by **Roman Válek** (Panton 819010). This issue contains texts and translations and is sufficiently different from Kühn's selection to be tempting.

Four late works in a folk-like style are found broken between two discs. *The Opening of the Wells, The Legend of the Smoke from Potato Fires,* and *Mikeš of the Mountains* are in Supraphon 767, while *Dandelion Romance,* which used to be in the same LP album, now serves as a pendant to the complete vocal-orchestral ballet *Spaliček* (Supraphon 752, 2CD). Also in the *Spaliček* album is *Primrose*, five duets for women's voices, piano, and violin. Another Kühn disc contains works including organ, *Mount of Three Lights* and *Hymn to Saint James*, and a late work with chamber ensemble, *The Prophecy of Isaiah* (Supraphon 751). The latter CD contains less folk-like material. There was once a better performance of *Isaiah* with **Ančerl,** in which the bass soloist was less afflicted with the vibrato disease (Supraphon LP, NA).

Bouquet of Flowers is better known, a powerful setting of folk tales for chorus, soloists and orchestra, recorded in 1955 by **Ančerl** (Supraphon 1932, NA, with his Symphony 6). Another classic Ančerl reading was of the wartime *Field Mass* for soloists, chorus, winds, and percussion, also presently NA. A modern recording of this moving work is by **Bohumil Kotmel** and the Czech Philharmonic chorus and orchestra (Chandos 9138).

Martinů's largest choral-orchestral work is the oratorio *Gilgamesh* (1955), a ritualistic retelling of an ancient Sumerian legend. Just under an hour in length, it employs a narrator, soloists, choir, and orchestra. There are two recordings, both Czech: one from 1977 by **Bělohlávek** and the Prague Symphony (Supraphon 1824), the other by **Košler** with the Slovak Philharmonic, recorded in 1989 (Marco Polo 223316). The Supraphon version has more character, but both are good.

OPERA

There are at least 16 operatic works of various sizes and shapes, and recordings exist for several. Orchestral excerpts have been recorded from *Mirandolina, Three Wishes, The Suburban Theatre,* and *Comedy on the Bridge* (Supraphon, NA).

The Miracles of Mary is a series of four stories combining song, dance, narration—you name it. It doesn't sound exactly like opera, but probably as much as *Spaliček* feels like a ballet, with its songs and operatic story line. It's touching and folksy, religious and dancy and childlike, and sounds very Czech. **Bělohlávek** and the Prague Symphony play it with warmth (Supraphon 1802, 2CD).

Julietta is a very disturbing opera in which no one has a long-term memory but everyone wants to feel that they do. It's treated with great tenderness and seriousness by everyone including the composer, who may have seen it as a metaphor for his homesickness. There have been two recordings, a much-cut one in French from 1962 conducted by **Charles Bruck** (Chant du Monde 278995, 2CD, NA), and a complete one in Czech from 1973 led by **Krombholc** (Supraphon 108176, 3CD), infinitely superior but overpriced, since at 145 minutes it would have fit on two discs.

Alexandre Bis and *Comedy on the Bridge* are little minioperas recorded together by **Jilek** (Supraphon 2140). One concerns a woman led into marital infidelity with her own husband, the other a group of noncombatants stuck on a bridge between two warring countries, neither of which will allow them to cross. Cute, but, as you see, Martinů's operas are nothing if not unexpected.

The Greek Passion is a setting of Kazantzakis's *Christ Recrucified*, about a man chosen by his village to represent Christ in a passion play trying to play the part well and killed for the attempt. The essence of the play is that Manolios is not a silver-tongued orator, and the frustrations of expressing the inexpressible are built into the opera. It's a frustrating but moving experience, just as Martinů intended. **Mackerras** and Brno forces do a beautiful job, and the opera was set in English and is here sung in that language (Supraphon 103611, 2CD).

While writing *The Greek Passion*, Martinů took some time out to write a surreal version of the legend of Theseus and the Minotaur, in French. *Ariane* is a short opera, recorded in the mid-'80s and last seen conducted by **Neumann** (Supraphon 4395, NA). It contains some of the composer's most coloratura vocal writing, particularly in the title role, apparently inspired by Callas. Celina Lindsey gives an effective portrayal.

A curious opera among curious operas is *The Marriage*, on the same Gogol story set by Mussorgsky. Written as a television opera in 1953, this fast-moving, hour-long setting is given to us in a 1958 mono recording conducted by **Václav Nosek** in Brno (Supraphon 3379). There's not much lyricism here, but it's amusing. Sung in Czech, though Martinů originally set it in English.

And finally, two early operas, *The Knife's Tears* (1927) and *The Voice of the Forest* (1935), the former a jazzy treatment of a surreal plot, the latter a touching radio opera, are conducted by **Bělohlávek** in Prague (Supraphon 3386).

BALLETS

One of Martinů's earliest works is *Istar*, a 1922 ballet on a Babylonian theme. Two suites from this gorgeously impressionistic work were recorded by **Waldhans** with the Brno State Philharmonic (Supraphon LP, NA). Another 1922 production is in direct stylistic contrast to this opulent sound. *Who Is Most Powerful in the World?* is a satirical comfort to the mouse-hearted among us, an amusingly hedonistic score of much charm, already almost recognizable as Martinů's voice, though he didn't go off to study in Paris until 1923. **Bělohlávek** recorded it with the Prague Symphony (Supraphon 3303).

Those who know the CD of jazz-inspired pieces (Supraphon 3058) will recognize the *Shimmy Foxtrot*. Paris in the '20s was a hotbed of jazz, and Martinů's next ballet, *The Revolt* (1925), continues this trend, the revolt in question being by the musical notes who rebel against bad singers, bad dance-hall music, and so on; Stravinsky is forced to retire to a desert island. This and a 1930 chess game, *Checkmating the King*, are included in Bělohlávek's disc (Supraphon 111415). He has also recorded *The Butterfly That Stamped*, a 1925 score that was never produced. Curiously, this music returns in part to the impressionist style (Supraphon 110380). These three discs are very short and could easily have been combined into two.

In a disc containing *The Amazing Flight* (translated as *The Amazing Fly)*, a 1927 ballet about flying across the Atlantic, with **Nosek** in Brno, this 25-minute score is coupled with a 16-minute suite from *The Butterfly that Stamped* and the complete *Checkmating the King* (Panton 1417, NA).

Martinů's most popular ballet is doubtless *La Revue de Cuisine*, a jazzy chamber score. We've been skirting around it in the chamber section, where it's often found in collections; for instance, the **Dartingtons** play it enthusiastically but with some exaggerated burlesques (Hyperion 22039, 2CD). **Michele Zukovsky** and the Los Angeles boys do it with a lot of sensitive phrasing, almost mysterious, reflecting perhaps the odd vision of kitchen utensils acting like people (Summit 214). The **Danish Chamber Players** are up-front in a rather dry recording (Kontrapunkt 32227). The **Lahti** group from Finland is excellent (BIS 653). But I'd go for "Music of Martinů," a catch-all disc that contains several prime items related loosely to jazz and sport, played by various Czech groups (Supraphon 3058). You get *Jazz Suite, Le Jazz*, the Wind Sextet, and three short orchestral tone poems, as well as the most insouciant *Revue* I ever hope to hear.

The climax of this early period of Martinů's compositions is the ballet *Spaliček* (1932), in which he mingles his satirical bent with a love for folk expression that stayed with him from that time on. The entire work lasts about 97 minutes and includes vocal music as well. Until it was recorded by **Jilek** in Brno, the ballet was heard only in orchestral excerpts (Supraphon 110752, 2CD). This set is filled out with two vocal works, *Dandelion Romance,* for choir with soprano solo, and *Primrose,* five duets on Moravian folk texts with violin and piano accompaniment. Martinů revised this work several times. In its original form, it ended with a setting of Erben's famous *Spectre's Bride.* Why Supraphon decided to put *Spectre* on 111090 and then delete it poses one of the record industry's typically insoluble mysteries.

SONGS

Martinů wrote few songs, but there are some interesting items. Some of his earliest works are two cycles with orchestra, *Nipponari* on Japanese texts (1908) and *Magic Nights* on Chinese poems (1918). These fascinating, impressionistic works may be heard from **Jířina Marková** and Dagmar Pecková along with *The Spectre's Bride,* all conducted by Bělohlávek (Supraphon 111090, NA).

Martinů later wrote a series of *Songs on One Page* and *Songs on Two Pages.* The one-page set is sung by **Gabriela Benačková** with Firkušny in a fascinating recital (RCA 60823, NA, with songs by Dvořák and Janáček). MOORE

Pietro Mascagni *(1863–1946)*

Mascagni had the ill fortune to have his greatest success as a composer early in his career and was never able to recapture that white-hot inspiration. His second opera, *Cavalleria rusticana* (1890), was a huge success, spawning an entire school of verismo imitations. Each of his subsequent 15 operas found less and less favor, but such was the phenomenal popularity of *Cavalleria* that opera houses continued to clamor for his works, each time hoping for another triumph but each time experiencing disappointment. A throughly trained craftsman, Mascagni wrote with a sure technique, a reasonable selection of dramatic stories often set in traditional musical forms, yet all too frequently without inspiration sustained over a long period.

Cavalleria rusticana. Mascagni's first produced opera propelled him into the front ranks of Italian opera composers. It also launched an entire genre: "verismo," in which opera portrays life at its most realistic. *Cavalleria* is usually paired with Leoncavallo's *Pagliacci,* not just in the theater but also in recordings. If it appears on only one CD it's just *Cavalleria;* if it's on two CDs, it almost invariably includes *Pagliacci.*

Mascagni was well along in years when he himself recorded *Cavalleria* (1940), and a younger man might have conducted the work at quicker tempos and more of a sense of urgency, but it holds together well, and the La Scala forces are in fine form (EMI 69987; Nuova Era 5066; Nimbus 7834; 2CD). With a little indulgence for the composer/conductor, the performance is excellent. **Lina Bruna Rasa** isn't quite musically accurate as Santuzza, but she's exciting. Gigli can tear a passion to shreds and still be as honey-voiced as ever. Gino Bechi sings a virile Alfio.

A 1953 recording has an erratic Santuzza from **Milanov,** alternately wobbly and steady, swallowed in production, yet with moments of great beauty. Björling sings beautifully but with little dramatic involvement. Alfio is excellently sung by Robert Merrill. Cellini conducts the RCA Victor Orchestra idiomatically (RCA 6510).

Callas never sang Santuzza on stage, but she easily captures the violent emotions of the role, although uneven vocally. Di Stefano's Turiddu

is from the same mold as Callas, and the two burn up the stage in their dramatic confrontation. Panerai is sympathetic as Alfio, singing with a distinctive dark burr. The La Scala forces grandly respond to Serafin's classic interpretation (♦EMI 47981, 2CD). For sheer beauty of voice it's hard to better the 1957 recording of **Tebaldi,** Björling, and Bastianini, an embarrassment of riches. Erede leads the Maggio Musicale Fiorentino chorus and orchestra in an earthy performance (♦Decca 425985).

Simionato, del Monaco, and MacNeil are the well-matched protagonists in a 1960 recording by the Accademia di Santa Cecilia led by Serafin (Decca 421807, 2CD). Big voices, grand style, with lots of Italian vigor and emotion, make up a winning performance. A 1962 recording has **de los Angeles**'s beautifully sung but dramatically unaware Santuzza. Her Turiddu, Corelli, tries to make up for her lack of dramatics by sobbing and shouting his way through the music—a coarse, brutal performance. Under the circumstances Mario Sereni's Alfio sounds noble. The Rome Opera Orchestra plays flabbily under Santini's somnolent conducting (EMI).

Karajan finds unaccustomed nuance and delicacy in the opera (DG 419257, 2CD). **Cossotto** sings a dramatic Santuzza and Bergonzi matches Björling's vocal splendors while remaining more in the true Italian style. Giangiacomo Guelfi sings a burly Alfio. By 1967 **Suliotis** was having major vocal difficulties, and they are clearly audible in her recording. She relies heavily on her chest register to bring it up high into the midrange tessitura; it's breathy and short-phrased, but undeniably dramatic. Del Monaco wasn't in good form, sounding more graceless than ever, and Gobbi sounds like he's working hard as Alfio. The Rome Opera chorus and orchestra respond lethargically to Varviso's routine conducting (formerly Decca, now Impax).

Except for Pavarotti's relentlessly forte Turiddu, Gavazzeni leads a lyrical, restrained performance. **Varady** is a lovely and loving Santuzza, dramatically convincing (Decca 414590, 2CD). A tendency toward blandness undermines Cappuccilli's Alfio. Levine leads a cogent, idiomatic performance (RCA 3091). In 1978 **Scotto** was in fine voice, and she finds hidden depths of meaning in the text. Domingo is a vibrant Turiddu, but Pablo Elvira's Alfio, while well sung, is dramatically wan.

Caballé may seem a strange choice to sing Santuzza, but she has the vocal goods, great sympathy for the character, and a favored partner in Carreras. The bloom is gone from his voice, but he still manages a creditable Turiddu. Matteo Manuguerra is possibly the best Alfio recorded, beautifully sung and dramatically aware. Muti brings Italian passion and power to the Philharmonia Orchestra (EMI 63650, 2CD).

Franco Zeffirelli used a 1983 La Scala recording as the soundtrack to a spectacular film rendering of the opera (Philips 416137, 1CD, and 454265, 2CD). Although the lip sync is awkward at times, the visual spectacle does much to distract the listener from the inadequacies of the musical performance. **Obraztsova** lurches her way through the opera in old-fashioned melodramatic form, screeching the music. Domingo sounds tired, even disinterested. As Alfio, Bruson makes some pleasant sounds, but to no avail. The La Scala chorus and orchestra sound routine, hardly inspired by Prêtre's unidiomatic conducting.

You would expect the protean soprano Norman to be an ideal Santuzza, since the music lies mainly in the middle and lower registers of the voice, precisely where she's at her strongest (Philips). But the actual timbre of her voice is wrong for the role, and she adopts a regal characterization quite out of touch with tradition and reality. Giuseppe Giacomini bellows his way through the opera, relentlessly forcing his lyric voice without a shred of nuance or musicality. The silken sounds of Hvorostovsky are an aural treat, but he's foreign to verismo tradition. Bychkov and the Orchestra de Paris raise hardly any sparks of excitement.

Anyone wanting a fresh approach to *Cavalleria* need listen no further than Sinopoli, who always strives to create something new, even if wrong and more Sinopoli than the composer (DG 429568). Mascagni's own conducting of the opera is slow, but at least it retains a sense of life; Sinopoli's performance with the Philharmonia is dead on arrival, drained of any emotion, and *Cavalleria* is all about emotion. **Baltsa** is all wrong for Santuzza; she doesn't have the vocal weight, power, or color for the role, a dead performance that fits right in with Sinopoli's concept. Domingo sings gloriously but is too restrained, and Pons sleep-sings through the role of Alfio.

An economical introduction to *Cavalleria* comes from Rahbari, who coerces his Czech-Slovak Radio forces into a coherent accompaniment (Naxos 660023). A reasonably idiomatic **Stefka Evstatieva**, a post-prime Aragall, and a solid Eduard Tumagian are the competent soloists.

L'Amico Fritz. After the lurid verismo excesses of *Cavalleria,* this is Mascagni's best-known work—and what a contrast it is! It's a lyric comedy in which the confirmed bachelor Fritz falls in love with soprano Suzel, their awkward relationship promoted and guided by Rabbi David. The music is gentle, charming, with a clear love for the protagonists. The choice of recording is an embarrassment of riches.

In 1941 **Tagliavini** was the first to record Fritz; setting a high standard, he sings with great beauty and ease and with none of the annoying Italian provincialism that so easily creeps into the role. He sets a high standard for personal charm as well. Tagliavini's real-life wife, Pia Tassinari, isn't up to his standard, but is an appealing Suzel. The ever-creative, character-filled Saturno Meletti is a delightful Rabbi David. Mascagni himself leads this RAI Turin performance (Fonit Cetra 18, 2CD).

In 1951 **Gigli** was past his prime, but still sings a cogent performance, with his daughter Rina Gigli awkwardly cast as Suzel. Afro Poli is the charming Rabbi. The San Carlo forces are led with authority by Gavazzeni (Eklipse 11, 2CD).

Valletti is just about perfect in the title role. His is a large voice, yet sweetly beautiful, expressive, with many subtle nuances of character and musicality. Rosanna Carteri is an endearing Suzel, with a most attractive voice, and Carlo Tagliabue is a most congenial Rabbi. This 1953 RAI Milan performance is led with grace and gentle sympathy by Gui (♦Bongiovanni 1098, 2CD).

If Valletti is just about perfect as Fritz, then **Pavarotti** must be absolute perfection in the role. This is one of his finest recordings (1968). Hearing it again just confirms—and renews—what all the fuss over Pavarotti was about. Here is that gorgeous voice in all its youthful, honey-toned glory, able to melt a heart of stone. Here too is the sunny Italian disposition and charming character that made him famous. And there's more: Freni too was in her prime and cast in a role and style to which she was perfectly attuned. Perhaps Vincente Sardiniero's Rabbi isn't as well characterized as his predecessors, but it will serve. Gavazzeni leads the Covent Garden forces with sympathy and understanding (♦EMI 47905, 2CD).

Livorno, Mascagni's home town, tries hard to promote the composer's music, but a 1991 recording just faces too much strong competition (Fonè). **Pietro Ballo,** Sandra Pacetti, and Armando Ariostini, with the Orchestra Accademia Strumentale Toscana led by Alessandro Pinzauti, are all pleasant, good enough for an occasional hearing but no more.

Iris. This opera deserves to be staged more frequently. The plot may tend too much toward the pathetic, but that's a fault shared by many more successful operas. Iris, an innocent Japanese maiden, is abducted by a procurer (Kyoto, the baritone) for the pleasure of a wealthy suitor (Osaka, the tenor). Although she rejects Osaka's advances, her father (the blind Il Cieco, the bass) accuses her of immorality, and she flings herself from a balcony into a sewer where she is welcomed to the Japanese Paradise. It seems to be an ideal work for staging in this age of the director, with plenty of opportunities for elaborate stage effects. The chorus and orchestra have ample occasion to show off as well, and there are plenty of big, rich, memorable tunes to go around.

In an opera so dependent on its prima donna, **Olivero** is just what's called for (♦Cetra 2023, 2CD). She's the quintessential Italian soprano, with lots of dripping emotion and characterization, all expressed through poetic musicality. The not-so-lovable tenor lead is unsettling and brashly sung by Salvatore Puma, but the equally villainous Kyoto is acutely sung by Saturno Meletti. This RAI Turin broadcast performance is urged on to sweeping emotions by Angelo Questa.

In a 1963 recording Olivero is again Iris, now past her prime, but still able to create character through subtle projection of the text to capture Iris's naivete, and she can still launch some beautiful soft tones in her upper register. A strong tenor is needed to complement Olivero; Luigi Ottolini doesn't come close. There's a lot of character in Renato Capecchi's Kyoto, but it's not a very attractive sound. Plinio Clabassi is the inadequate Il Cieco. The unidentified orchestra is actually the Concertgebouw led by Fulvio Vernizzi (Verona).

Gavazzeni conducted Rome Opera forces with authority and understanding, though the recording has some sonic problems, with occasional distortions, gaps, and interruptions, probably originating from the 1956 radio broadcast; however, in general the sound is acceptable with a real sense of presence—perhaps too much presence from the very vocal prompter (Legato 505, 2CD). **Clara Petrella** is less a fragile Japanese maiden than a hot-blooded Italian prima donna, singing broadly, grandly. Di Stefano is in fit form with lots of ripe emotion, Saturno Meletti is in impressive voice as the villainous procurer, and while Christoff's character may be blind, he rants and raves in a majestic voice, bringing nobility to a suffering soul.

From Bavarian Radio comes a satisfying 1988 performance, the first studio-made recording (CBS 45526, 2CD). Hungarian soprano **Ilona Tacit** has mastered the Italian style, and her voice is large, able to cut through the large orchestral waves, but it's not pretty. She does do a lot with the character, though. Domingo does what Domingo does best; he just sings handsomely. Pons's baritone is on the light side, pleasant enough, perhaps too pleasant for the villainous Kyoto. Il Cieco calls for a basso of impressive command; Bonaldo Giaiotti sings solidly enough, but with little characterization. Conductor **Patanè** easily matches the veteran Gavazzeni in his sweep and grandeur.

Daniela Dessi's Iris is a competent performance, but little more. José Cura manages to find some sympathy in Osaka while creating a ringing characterization. There isn't much to Roberto Servile's Kyoto; the competition shows him up. If only Ghiaurov had recorded Il Cieco earlier; 1996 was too late. The Rome Opera forces led by Gelmetti manage to get some musical honors (BMG). PARSONS

Jules Massenet (1842–1912)

"Inside every French composer is a Massenet." The young Claude Debussy, who made that remark, did not exclude himself; Jules Massenet's soft, melodious muse inspired several early Debussy works, as well as many a lesser French composer's. Among his contemporaries, Massenet was second only to Puccini in number of performances and size of bank account; unlike Puccini, he was also a respected and loved composition teacher, at the Paris Conservatoire. But this operatic master's lofty reputation fell on hard times after his death in 1912.

Massenet had a gift for ingratiating melody, a knack for clear, brilliant orchestration, and a sure theatrical sense. So why the decline? It's the price he paid for excessive popularity. *Manon* and *Werther* were two of the top three operas in the Opéra Comique's repertoire in the early 20th century, and they were frequently performed everywhere else as well. Nor did Massenet's 26 other operas go unperformed. He always aimed to please, and he hit the bull's-eye so often that more high-minded composers never forgave him for it. For many years, most of his operas were considered dead as dodos, except for *Manon* and *Werther,* and even they became much less frequently performed after the '30s and '40s. But just as Callas, Sutherland, and Sills brought obscure bel canto operas to life in the '50s and '60s, some contemporary singers have championed the forgotten Massenet, and starting in the '70s, many of his operas got their first recordings—and voilà, people actually *liked* them. With the right singers and a sympathetic conductor, even his lesser scores are diverting.

The words "pretty" and "dainty" appear frequently in descriptions of Massenet's music, and there's no getting around it: He's not a profound composer. A sensible summing-up of his status is by Martin Cooper: "If he was not much more than the *homme moyen sensuel* writing for his spiritual peers, he was a good craftsman and an excellent man of the theater. His detractors have mostly been men of higher ideals and sometimes greater potentialities, but few of them have in practice achieved anything so near perfection in any genre, however humble, as Massenet achieved in his best works."

ORCHESTRAL MUSIC

If you think of Massenet strictly as an opera composer, you'll be surprised by the amount of nonoperatic music he wrote, including no less than seven orchestral suites. All are featherweight but completely charming, and amply show off his melodic and orchestral skill. Each suite is different: 2 is titled *Scènes hongroises* and 7 *Scènes alsaciennes,* each with a fair amount of appropriate local color; 3 (*Scènes dramatiques*), is inspired by Shakespeare, and so on. **Gardiner**'s recording of 3, 4, 6, and 7 are still available (Erato 45858 and 45889), but if you like one of these suites, you'll probably like them all, and all seven can be had at a bargain price performed with requisite charm by the New Zealand Symphony and conductor **Jean-Yves Ossonce,** with the equally beguiling ballet suite from *Hérodiade* for good measure (♦Naxos 553124/5, 2CD).

Massenet's orchestral works also include an overture to Racine's *Phèdre,* available in a performance by **Paray** (Mercury), and the once-popular ballet music from *Le Cid,* available from **Marriner** with a suite from *Cendrillon* and the imperishable "Meditation" from *Thaïs* (Capriccio).

Ossonce is also the conductor on a very recommendable disc of the Piano Concerto in E-flat, a surprisingly serious and surprisingly late work (1903) by a composer who started out as a virtuoso pianist. It is of course suavely melodious, and concludes with a lively "Airs Slovaques" finale. With **Coombs** as the soloist and coupled with Hahn's equally diverting concerto, this is one of the most appealing releases in the "Romantic Piano Concerto" series (♦Hyperion 66897). You can also find it by **Marylene Dosse** in "French Piano Concertos" (Vox Box 5110) or in

an all-Massenet disc by **Ciccolini,** who also offers a good sampling of Massenet's solo pieces (EMI 84277).

Massenet also wrote two ambitious ballet scores, *La Cigale* and *Le Carillon,* as smoothly assembled and glittering in orchestration as his best operas. Both were sympathetically recorded in the '70s by **Bonynge,** and have been reissued as fillers for his complete recordings of *Swan Lake* (London 425413) and *Coppélia* (London 444836) respectively.

OPERAS

Cendrillon (Cinderella). This is the Godiva chocolate among Massenet's operas: richly flavored, exquisitely fashioned, and irresistible to anyone with a sweet tooth. The score is a perfect exercise in *le style* Massenet, abounding in 18th-century pastiche, gentle lyricism, and even some glistening fairy music quite as adept as Mendelssohn's or Verdi's. The role of Cinderella might have been written to order for Von Stade, and she's definitely the raison d'être of the 1979 recording (♦Sony 35194); her Prince, Gedda, sounds forced, effortful, and anything but young (this role, by the way, was originally written for a dramatic soprano). The supporting cast is okay, **Rudel**'s conducting sympathetic, and the reverberant recorded sound an irritating combination of brightness and cloudiness. This complaint aside, it's a most appealing opera.

Chérubin. Massenet's late operas got weaker and weaker, but *Chérubin* (1903) and especially *Don Quichotte* (1910) have quite a lot to offer contemporary audiences. *Chérubin* was written as a vehicle for Mary Garden, fresh from creating Debussy's Mélisande, and whatever its dramatic and musical shortcomings, it certainly responds well to star treatment. It may just *seem* to have a lot to offer because of the recent recording stars Von Stade, Ramey, June Anderson, and Upshaw; but this featherweight *comédie chantée* (a completely spurious sequel to Mozart's *Figaro*) is composed with surpassing skill, Massenet in his always congenial 18th-century mode, this time with a dash or two of Spanish flavoring (♦RCA 65093). Von Stade gets to do her famous Cherubino again, superbly, and Upshaw is ideally cast as Nina, the good girl to whom the lovesick Cherubino finally comes around. The conductor, **Pinchas Steinberg,** keeps everything properly effervescent.

Don Quichotte. In this opera written in 1910 for Chaliapin (he was, however, not the first to perform it; the honor went to Vanni-Marcoux), Massenet's woeful knight shares with Cervantes only a name and a penchant for tilting at windmills. Otherwise he's a dignified, idealistic figure; similarly, Massenet's Dulcinea is no village slut, but a rich, classy lady with lovers dangling after her. The opera plot centers on Quixote's rescue of Dulcinea's stolen necklace from a gang of bandits; she still refuses him, but he dies happy. The opera has hardly a memorable tune in it, but Massenet's skillful characterizations and abundant musical detail make it a pleasure to hear.

Don Quichotte is a tour de force for a leading bass and ends with one of opera's genuinely moving death scenes (though Massenet spoils it with a hectic coda). The Quixotes of choice on disc are **van Dam** (EMI 54767) and **Ghiaurov** (London 430636), both sonorous and dignified. **Chaliapin** didn't record the entire opera, but his way with the death scene can be heard in several collections of his old recordings; the easiest to find are probably Nimbus 7823 and Pearl 9812.

Hérodiade. This is a luscious retelling of the story of Salome, Herodias, and John the Baptist. It's relatively early Massenet, something of a dry run for *Thaïs,* and I have to admit that it always reminds me of the spoof opera Bernard Herrmann composed for *Citizen Kane.* However, *Hérodi-*

ade has benefitted from the increased interest in Massenet's work; besides a live version with **Caballé** and Carreras (Legato 182), there are two star-filled recordings on major labels: Sony 66847 offers a (very) live performance with Fleming, Domingo, and Dolora Zajick, conducted by **Gergiev**; with EMI 55378 you get **Plasson** with Studer, Heppner, and Hampson. The EMI has three discs and a few minutes more music than the Sony; however, Sony sensibly offers a highlights disc (♦61965), which may be the ideal solution for non–French opera addicts.

Manon. Always Massenet's main claim to immortality, and with a sufficiently charismatic soprano as the flighty teenager, *Manon* is still irresistible. The best recording is the 1956 performance with de los Angeles as Manon and **Monteux** conducting (♦EMI, NA). The *Manon*s currently in the catalog are an odd collection of hard-to-find live performances and one problematic studio recording with Sills (♦EMI 69831). The problem isn't the much-criticized soprano; her voice sometimes turns tremulous and shrill, but the performance has many beautiful and imaginative moments and is convincingly acted. Nor is there much of a problem with **Rudel**'s conducting, or the stylish Gedda and (in a rare recorded opera performance) Souzay. It's the reverberant, cavernous sound that nearly does it in, but if you can listen through it, there are sufficient rewards.

Thaïs. Nowadays, This opera is remembered mainly as one of Mary Garden's triumphs, and the source of that little sweetmeat, the "Meditation" for violin and orchestra. It hasn't been revived or recorded much, and I don't really know why; it's at least as appealing an opera as *Samson et Dalila.* There was a famously awful RCA recording in the mid-'70s with **Moffo** that quickly attained camp-classic status; I recall seeing copies in LP cutout bins.

Sills's mid-'70s recording with **Maazel** was coolly received when it first came out, but I think it's pretty good (♦EMI 65479). Again, she's often shrill and metallic, but she gets more than decent support from Gedda and Milnes, and she sure could perform this hokum convincingly. But what diva wouldn't enjoy playing this Egyptian bad girl who goes good and dies? "Sadie Thompson in the desert," somebody once called it, although one of those '50s Biblical epics with Susan Hayward and Victor Mature would be an even more appropriate parallel.

Werther. Traditionally the runner-up among Massenet's operas, *Werther* may be his best. As an adaptation of Goethe's novel, it's touch and go, but it boasts as dramatically demanding a tenor part as French opera can offer and a wonderfully sympathetic starring role for a mezzo. *Werther* is in healthier shape than *Manon* in the catalogues, with three recommendable recordings. The luxury item stars the excellent Carreras and the merely perfect Von Stade with **Colin Davis** (♦Philips 416654). In a good midpriced alternative, Gedda is a fervent Werther and de los Angeles a melancholy Charlotte, with **Prêtre** (EMI 63973), and most recently Hadley and von Otter perform with **Nagano** in a well-received release (Erato 17790; the booklet cover looks like a Calvin Klein ad, but don't let that put you off).

SONGS

"Massenet abandoned himself to his unique gift and fluency which, in his *mélodies,* led to a sugary sentimentalism. They cannot be recommended," was the tart judgement of the great baritone Pierre Bernac in his *Interpretation of French Song.* No one would put Massenet on the same lofty plane as Debussy or Poulenc, but just the same there are a surprising number of Massenet recitals available on recordings, by such estimable singers as **Didier Henry** (Marguelone 519202), **Bernard Kruysen** (Arion 68009), and **Catherine Dubosc** (201632).

RAYMOND

William Mathias (1934–1992)

Mathias was a leading Welsh composer of music of pungent vitality, often fresh, sometimes very atmospheric, and always direct in expression. He was able to evoke a nationalistic feeling in his music by using open-textured, Celtic-sounding figurations, and dance rhythms in a neoclassical, almost Hindemithian context. Indeed, although his music is far from being avant-garde, its formats and structures derive largely from European rather than "British" models. Having said that, there are parallels with Walton (in celebratory mode), with the lyrical Britten, and, in his more acerbic works, with Rawsthorne. He composed prolifically in all genres, often in a utilitarian fashion for amateurs, and left some fine church and choral works, three symphonies and some excellent chamber and keyboard music. Lamentably little is currently available on disc; this was not always so, and there is a large catalog of music from LP days ripe for reissue.

A good place to start is the disc by **Christ Church Cathedral Choir, Oxford,** of some of the best church music, including the festive anthem "I will celebrate" and another occasional work, "Let the people praise thee, O God," written for the wedding of Prince Charles and Diana Spencer in 1981 (Nimbus 5243). In between are a host of fine works, most in his mature style. The *Evening Canticles* for Jesus College, Cambridge, with their incandescent "Glorias" contrast with the shimmering remoteness of "O how amiable are thy dwellings." The *Missa Aedis Christi* written for the Christ Church choir is one of his most anguished utterances.

Anthems and settings are often given added dimension by highly independent organ accompaniment, and Mathias's facility in writing for that instrument is shown well in the disc of solo music played by **John Scott** (Nimbus 5367), including the extraordinary *Invocation,* which encapsulates his style: stunning trumpet fanfares and restless manual figurations yield to a sustained central section of sumptuous, almost exotic mysticism. The more astringent *Fantasy,* the straightforward *Processional,* the arch-like *Berceuse,* and the byzantine *Fenestra* all contribute to a disc of satisfying and varied breadth and interest, superbly played by one of Britain's leading recitalists.

Symphony 1 is upbeat, sometimes medieval in feeling, always colorful and magically atmospheric, and its intellectual discipline and integrity rank it among his strongest works. The impressionistic tone colors of the slow movement are also found in the opening of 2, a swirling maelstrom of often dramatic music. Symphony 3, one of his last works before his premature death, has a sense of fateful urgency and drive, giving way to a slow movement of deep elegy and grief, reaching vainly upward only to quail back (note the menace of Ivesian harmonies in the last movement). Two discs by the BBC Welsh Symphony Orchestra cover all three in excellent performances and recordings (Nimbus 5260, 1 and 2 with **Mathias** conducting, and 3 on 5343 with **Grant Llewellyn**). The latter also contains two contrasting tone poems, the quirky *Helios* and the glassy *Requiescat,* and the much lighter Oboe Concerto, played by David Cowley.

Also worth exploring is the Harp Concerto, one of Mathias's most delicate works (Koch 7261, with Ginastera's Harp Concerto). Of his two fine piano sonatas, the first is strongly virtuosic and slightly austere, the second more festive; they've been recorded by **Raymond Clarke** (Athene 15, with works by John Pickard). Finally, his best "pageantry" style is shown in the suite *Vivat Regina,* played by **Black Dyke Mills Band**

(Chandos 4510, a compilation of items by Edward Gregson, Gordon Langford, Vaughan Williams, et al.).   JOHNSON

(Johannes) Simon Mayr (1763–1845)

Mayr is usually remembered only as Donizetti's teacher, but to his contemporaries he was highly regarded as a rival to Rossini in opera and the leading and most prolific composer of sacred music. He wrote more than 80 operas and more than 600 pieces for liturgical use. Scarcely a note is heard today except in a handful of recordings, some of them from his adopted city, Bergamo. Much of what we hear is tuneful and listenable.

Sacred music. In the *Passion According to Saints Matthew and Mark,* Bergamo fails her adopted son in a very provincial performance led by **Pierangelo Pelucchi** (Agora 005, 2CD). It's a trial musically and is poorly recorded as well. *Requiem* is preserved in another provincial performance from Bergamo conducted by Pelucchi (Agora 131, 2 CD). The chorus and orchestra are all right, but the four soloists are a trial. *Samuele,* Mayr's 1818 oratorio, is troubled by recording dynamics in a 1996 performance in Lecco, again led by Pelucchi; the soloists are too close, the chorus too distant (Nuova Era 7273, 2CD). The performance is secure if not stellar. *Stabat Mater* 3, as led by **Pieralberto Cattaneo** in a 1998 performance in Bergamo Cathedral, has an unpleasant group of soloists, but the youthful and enthusiastic chorus and orchestra make for engaging listening (Dynamic 242).

Operas. Mayr's 1813 setting of the Medea legend in *Medea in Corinto* was once more popular than Cherubini's version; it's the best of his extensive output. In a 1969 Clarion Concerts recording, the excellent performance of **Maria Galvany** aided her rising career (Vanguard LP, NA). **Gencer** is a hair-raising, dramatic Medea in a 1977 performance at San Carlo (Myto 993.211, 3CD). Unhappily, her colleagues are hair-raising for all the wrong reasons; they are truly terrible. A strong case for the opera was made in 1993 by a most impressive cast (Opera Rara 11, 3CD). **Eaglen** sings powerfully with great agility and control, easily encompassing Medea's demanding music. Kenny's light soprano is an ideal contrast to Eaglen's, and there's also contrast between Ford and Giménez, both tenors assured and at ease in their coloratura endeavors. David Parry conducts a controlled, idiomatic performance.

Che Originali! is the only Mayr opera buffa currently recorded; it's a wickedly witty parody on amateur and professional musicians. **Franz Hauk** leads the Gregorian Chamber Orchestra in a less than vital performance, though his singers do quite well by the comedy (Guild 7167, 2CD).

La Rosa bianca e la rosa rossa is set during the English War of the Roses; it's anything but historically accurate. A 1990 Bergamo Festival performance is musically accurate and quite rewarding in its content and performance. **Susanna Anselmi** and Luca Canonici are most attractive artists (Fonit Cetra 2007, 2CD).   PARSONS

John McCabe (b. 1939)

Known mostly as a pianist of prodigious talent and wide sympathies (his recordings include all the Haydn sonatas and works by Bax, Hindemith, and many more), McCabe is also one of Britain's leading orchestral composers, whose music is increasingly making a lasting impression in concert and on disc.

Chagall Windows was inspired by the unified but contrasting colors of Chagall's stained glass windows of the tribes of Israel in Jerusalem. These are captured by McCabe's dazzling score, sounding like an orchestral concerto in **James Loughran**'s hands (EMI 67120, with *Not-*

turni ed Alba and Louis Frémaux's Symphony 2). *Edward II,* his music for David Bintley's award-winning ballet, has a visceral impact and symphonic cohesion, easily the greatest British dance score since Britten's *Prince of the Pagodas.* **Barry Wordsworth**'s complete recording is electrifying (♦Hyperion 67135/6).

Of McCabe's five symphonies, only 2 and 4 have been issued on CD. Symphony 2 is an intriguing single movement, partly inspired by Sam Peckinpah's *The Wild Bunch.* **Frémaux**'s 1972 account with the Birmingham Orchestra is beautifully paced (EMI 67120). Symphony 4 ("Of Time and the River"), not musically related to Thomas Wolfe's novel, is a study in imperceptibly metamorphosing tempos and tonality. One of the finest post-war British symphonies, it sounds like it in **Handley**'s strongly paced performance. It's coupled with the Flute Concerto written for Galway and inspired by the Atlantic Ocean as seen in Cornwall. Emily Beynon is a sensational soloist, not least in the affecting coda for alto flute (♦Hyperion 67089).

McCabe's five brass band works have been gathered in one excellently played and recorded disc by the **Britannia Building Society Band** (Doyen 030). In *Cloudcatcher Fells,* the **Black Dyke Mills Band** is peerless (♦Chandos 4509).

McCabe's first two string quartets remain unrecorded; 3, 4, and 5 illustrate his wide range of inspiration — respectively a Cumbrian mountain, Haydn, and Graham Sutherland's aquatints, *The Bees* — but stand as absolute music, especially in the **Vanbrugh Quartet**'s highly virtuosic performances (Hyperion 67078).

McCabe's recording of six of his piano pieces gives a good cross section of his output, nowhere more impressive than in the magisterial *Haydn Variations.* The couplings include Variations Op. 22 and the impressive *Gaudi,* inspired by the Catalan architect and Stockhausen's piano textures (♦British Music Society 424).

Notturni ed Alba is a combination of orchestral song-cycle and concerto for soprano; the 1973 recording by **Jill Gomez** with Loughran still sounds most impressive (EMI 67120).   RICKARDS

William Thomas McKinley (b. 1938)

McKinley is a prodigiously gifted and prolific American composer whose masterful and spontaneous assimilation of many vernacular idioms (blues, jazz, and ragtime) into a post-romantic symphonic language is unparalleled in scale and breadth. His music bursts with energy and restlessly evolving metrical and dynamic patterns and yet is extraordinarily disciplined in shape and structure; many works are cast in neoclassical variation form, extended in scope to incorporate minimalist, folk and other crossover elements while retaining a strongly symphonic character. McKinley's own career as a jazz pianist forms a strong backdrop to his music; after two decades of dodecaphonic or atonal composition, his affirmation of tonality in the '80s ushered in his mature pluralistic style.

McKinley's drive and enterprise led him to form his own record company in 1991, MMC Music, and this has greatly increased the number of his pieces on disc, together with those of many other composers. His vibrant, larger-than-life music paints a true portrait of the man himself, and the ongoing recording program should widen appreciation of a unique and diverse talent.

The only disc devoted entirely to his works (and a good place to start) includes the volatile Symphony 1, whose gentle, lilting opening yields to growing instability and riff-like episodes (MASM 2034); Piano Concerto 3, unashamedly jazz-inspired; and the highly-charged, romantic *Poems of Pablo Neruda.* These make for a good cross section of styles, and the playing by Marjorie Mitchell and the Slovak Radio Symphony under **Stankovsky** is consistently good.

For one of the best examples of McKinley's variation form, try the 1991 *Concerto Domestica,* played by the Czech Radio Symphony under **Schwarz** (MASM 2066, with music by Marga Richter). Although there are "camerata" dialogues between trumpet and bassoon (the "domestic" husband and wife), the work's dramatic and emotional growth lend it a symphonic dimension, enhanced by Steve Reich–like ostinatos, colorful and accented percussion (especially chimes, which feature strongly in McKinley's works), and tight harmonies.

McKinley has been captivated by Irish folk elements, and these abound in the dreamy and supple Piano Concerto 2 ("O Leary"), played by **Jeffrey Jacob** (MASM 2028, with music by four others). The atmospheric *Summer Dances* for violin and orchestra played by **Peter Zazofsky** is strongly recommended (MMC 2059, with violin concertos by Robert Chumbley and the gifted John Carbon). The performances on all these discs are good or very good, well recorded, and contain informative and well-considered program notes.

Clarinettist **Stoltzman** is a powerful advocate of McKinley's music and has recorded two of the clarinet concertos (2 is presently NA). No. 3 ("Alchemical") is a moody, sometimes lyrical but often chimerical (and ultimately diabolical) set of tone pictures giving full rein to Stoltzman's virtuosic powers (MASM 2031, with works by Burt Fenner and the impressive John Carbon Clarinet Concerto). Very impressive too is Concerto 3 for viola played by **Karen Dreyfus**, as full-blooded and expansive a work as any in a limited repertoire for the instrument (MASM 2047, with Walton's Viola Concerto). Symphony 3 ("Romantic"), played by the Warsaw Philharmonic under the late (and greatly talented) **Robert Black,** ranges from the brilliant to the nocturnal and is (along with the out-of-print Symphony 5) one of McKinley's finest creations (MASM 2003, with works by Carbon and John Lennon).

Fantasia Variazioni for harpsichord and orchestra is more than a neo-baroque miniature; it receives full-scale treatment with big orchestral dimensions and broad expressive range (MASM 2016, with music by four others). Similarly, *Concerto for the New World* for wind quintet and strings is another expansive set of variations (MASM 2018). McKinley at his most visceral is found in *Dallas 1963,* his tribute to John F. Kennedy (MASM 2073, with *SinfoNova* for strings and pieces by Michael Viens).

Emsdettener Totentanz is one of McKinley's most remarkable pieces for smaller ensembles, a big song cycle for voices and saxophone and string quartet, which encompasses a huge range in an almost *sprechstimme* idiom (MASM 2046). Last but not least is the dreamlike and lush Piano Quartet 1 played by the **Broyhill Chamber Ensemble** (MASM 2041, with quartets by Copland and Robert Chumbley).

JOHNSON

Nikolai Medtner *(1880–1951)*

Medtner is generally regarded as a musical conservative; he believed that the avant-garde of his time violated the immutable laws of harmony and beauty. His music has been unjustly referred to as "Rachmaninoff without the melodies," but only one who listens carelessly could make such an assessment. His music is at once lush and austere, tonally conservative, with amazingly progressive cross-rhythmic complexities, rich layering, and poignant melodies. Its devotees can be grateful for the large number of fine recordings available, with more coming along all the time. Almost everything Medtner wrote is for piano, with orchestra included only in his three concertos. He wrote one piano quintet that is

in more than one sense his crowning work, a few pieces for violin and piano, a number of songs, and all the rest for solo piano.

CONCERTOS

1. The powerful but restrained emotion of 1 is very well served by **Alexeev** (♦Hyperion 66744). Here is a completely assured and controlled yet energetic performance, with crystalline sound, lush and full strings, and crisp piano. For a more romantic interpretation, try **Madge** (♦Danacord 401). What passes for a first movement in this "through-composed" concerto is very aggressive, bright, and energetic, slightly faster than Alexeev. But the middle part, consisting of a theme and variations, is dark and brooding at the beginning, more ominous all the way through. The final movement is aggressively and brilliantly played. Altogether, Madge takes the last part considerably slower than Alexeev, but it never seems so because of the heightened energy level.

Tozer plunges into the piece with the most determination and strongest articulation of the three (♦Chandos 9039). He's also the fastest, coming in at a full three minutes less than Alexeev in the opening Allegro. The middle portion comes across as pensive, and is more sharply articulated and less dreamy than the other two versions. Tozer, playing from his gut, never leaves any doubt that he knows what he wants out of this concerto, and he gets it. But **Zhukov** gives by far the best rendition (♦MK 417087). No serious Medtner collector should be without this recording—which is, unfortunately, NA. From the opening chords, the pianist and orchestra completely possess the music; Zhukov plays with a fiery gallantry, the U.S.S.R. Radio Orchestra with a sweeping grandeur, not quite equaled in the other versions. **Scherbakov**'s recording with the Moscow Symphony Orchestra and conductor Vladimir Ziva is a fine way to try out this concerto if you're unfamiliar with it; they give a much better reading of 1 and 3 than 2 (♦Naxos 553359).

2. Written in 1926, is probably the most accessible and popular of the three—quintessentially late romantic, filled with beautiful melodies and with emotions ranging from tenderness to passion. **Demidenko** is powerful and aggressive, brilliant and assured, fully exploiting the beauties of this piece (♦Hyperion 66580). **Madge** comes in a close second (Danacord 402). His version is romantic and deliberate but powerful, with good shape and variation. Madge brings greater romance to it, especially in I where he takes risks and leaps about the piano with abandon. The mood contrasts here are wonderful.

Tozer also gives a romantic reading. His beginning is more ponderous than Demidenko's, but his playing in most of the work is lush and luminous with a good deal of depth (Chandos). His reading of II isn't as good as either Madge's or Demidenko's, as it seems to lose shape and become long and a bit plodding. **Scherbakov** is prosaic in many places and cumbersome in others, with II the best (Naxos). The orchestra seems to be trying to inject some life into the performance in III, while the piano lags. But the sound is good, with a nice balance between piano and orchestra. No collector should be without **Medtner**'s own rendition (Testament 1027). The sound is inferior, of course, though not unlistenable. Medtner himself takes the opening rather slowly, a precursor of his restrained romanticism throughout.

3. The three best performances are by **Demidenko** (♦Hyperion 66580), **Tozer** (Chandos 9038) and **Madge** (Danacord 403). Each brings a different but valid interpretation to this complex work. Demidenko has a slight edge here; he plays with power, brilliance, and energy, imparting a unique sparkle. He gives the work coherence and shape, something that isn't easy to do, especially in III; under his touch, it exudes sheer exultation. The sound is wonderful, though not quite as rich as Tozer's, whose rendition is powerful and more luminous than Demidenko's. The support from the London Philharmonic and **Neeme Järvi** is magnificent, lending a grand, sweeping openness to the work. Madge gives a leisurely, confident, almost cheerful reading to I, but III loses some of its shape and fails to cohere as well as the other two. But it's still worth having. **Ponti**'s version is idiosyncratic, interesting for purposes of comparison but not attractive for an only recording (Vox).

Medtner's own version is desirable mostly for its historic interest (Testament 1027). His reading seems pensive indeed after hearing the others. The last movement in particular is leisurely, giving a sense of triumph somewhat muted by weariness.

CHAMBER MUSIC

Piano quintet. Medtner's piano quintet is, in every sense of the word, his life work. Written over more than 40 years, this work is, more than any other, representative of both his faith and his artistic beliefs. The plainchant *Dies Irae* has a prominent place; I opens with a brooding rendition of the chant, which is transformed into a paean of joy in IV. This is an unusually straightforward composition, with easily accessible melodies and themes that reward close listening. Alexeev and the **New Budapest Quartet** give this work a marvelous reading; the string sound is full and joyous, the recorded sound excellent (♦Hyperion 66744). The second-best available version is a less forceful interpretation with the **State Prokofiev Quartet** and pianists Veniamin Korobov and Lyudmila Kuznetsova (Carlton 00582). The only other recording currently available is by **Scherbakov** (Naxos). It's much more dreamy, with less intensity than Alexeev; given the meaning and content Medtner poured into this work, Alexeev's greater intensity is more appropriate.

Sonatas for violin and piano. Collectors have two outstanding options. The first is a set with the complete works for piano and violin, played by **Manoug Parikian** and Hamish Milne (♦CRD 34934, 2CD). This is a must-have for Medtner fans, since Parikian played Sonata 2 with the composer himself before his death, thus bringing an authoritative touch to this recording. The sound is good, if just a touch strident, and the interpretations are vigorous. Also not to be missed are 1 and 2 played by **Mordkovitch** and Tozer (♦Chandos 9293). Here the sound is smoother and gentler, the reading warmer and less aggressive. Both interpretations are good. **Mateja Marinkovic** and Linn Hendry offer a sparkling version of 2, along with some nocturnes and dances (♦ASV 1044)—a clear first choice.

PIANO MUSIC

Collectors now have some excellent choices for Medtner's solo piano works, beginning with the complete piano sonatas, along with *Forgotten Melodies I* and *II,* played by **Hamelin** (♦Hyperion 67221). His treatment of these sonatas is superb. He possesses this music, shaping it beautifully and bringing to each line exactly what it calls for, whether surging power, singing wistfulness, or full richness. Here is exactly the kind of restrained romanticism Medtner's music needs, along with excellent sound. A bonus with this set is the thorough, informative notes, written by Medtner scholar Barrie Martyn, who has packed much information about both the composer and his sonatas into a small space.

Tozer is recording all of Medtner's piano works (Chandos, various numbers). His playing is warm and congenial, from the heart; his interpretations are satisfying, though in some cases less exciting than Hamelin's. **Milne**'s four CDs of various piano pieces also deserve men-

tion (CRD, various numbers). Here is a good selection of sonatas, *Fairy Tales,* and miscellaneous pieces. Milne does full justice to them, shaping them carefully and playing with romantic energy. **Adám Fellegi**'s recordings can't be recommended, especially in comparison to Hamelin and Tozer (Marco Polo). While his playing is competent, neat, and precise, he sounds as if the music is just a little out of his reach—not technically, perhaps, but interpretively.

Two notables among the several scattered recordings of various Medtner piano pieces are "Demidenko Plays Medtner" (Hyperion 66636) and "Music for Two Pianos" (♦Hyperion 66654). The former includes part of *Forgotten Melodies,* a *Fairy Tale,* a couple of sonatas, Theme and Variations, and a *Dithyramb.* All are wonderfully played, with the exception of the *Dithyramb,* which is irritatingly and self-consciously cheerful. The two-piano disc of pieces by Medtner and Rachmaninoff is a treasure, containing the best available recording of a marvelous Medtner work, *Knight Errant,* as well as his *Russian Round Dance.* **Demidenko** and **Alexeev** perform these works together in truly unforgettable performances.

Wild's recording has feeling and expertise, but the sound has a regrettable echo, making it muddy (Chesky). **Mikhail Lidsky** has recorded a lush "Night Wind" sonata Op.25:2 (Denon). Russian Disc has released some recordings of Medtner's piano works, but they generally have sound problems. There's no need to consider them when so many other fine recordings are now available.

SONGS

Medtner wrote more than 100 songs, which Geoffrey Tozer characterizes as his finest music. Strangely, not many of them have been recorded. Of the few currently available, Tozer's rendition with **Ludmilla Andrew** is undoubtedly the best; they are beautiful songs performed well (♦Chandos 9327). Another collection, by **Lydia Chernykh** and Lubov Orfenova, appeared in 1993, but it seems to be NA (Melodiya). Countertenor **Brian Asawa** has sung a few of Medtner's songs in a disc titled "Vocalise" (RCA 68903). He gives a fine reading; his voice is outstanding. Otherwise, collectors will have to depend on out-of-print LPs for further exploration of Medtner's songs.   CRAWFORD

Étienne-Nicolas Méhul (1763–1817)

Just as the declamations of Robespierre and Danton stirred the citizens during the French Revolution, so too did the composers of the time arouse passions with a vast output of patriotic fare, music that today may seem little more than *pièces d'occasion* and yet in its fervor and raw emotion, its trenchant espousal of *Liberté, Egalité, Fraternité,* still has much to say to our time. One of the most influential composers of this period was Méhul, whose works for the stage were considered advanced in their day but are now largely forgotten next to his hymns and anthems for chorus and military band. Music like this was intended to be sung by the people, on the street and in grand public spectacles; thus it's ironic that perhaps Méhul's greatest such work, *Chant National,* called for such complex forces that only experienced singers could handle it and may have heralded the beginning of the end for such amateur participation.

Symphonies. Méhul completed four symphonies, and in their day they were considered innovative. The turbulent finale of 1 grabs us by the scruff of the neck, and not surprisingly it remains the most frequently recorded of the group. Symphony 2 is strikingly reminiscent of Cherubini's D major and even more so the overture to *Anacréon,* while 3 is bright and festive, opening with a panoply of brass and in the finale swirling through the air like a Catherine wheel. Symphony 4 is in many ways the most visionary, anticipating Franck's cyclical structures by bringing back the Adagio introduction in the finale; it catches the ear in the Andante with the striking sound of solo cellos.

All four have been brought together in a splendid set by the Orchestra of the Gulbenkian Foundation led by **Michel Swierczewski**, despite some wiry string tone an important addition to the catalog (♦Nimbus 5184/5, 2CD, with *Jeune Henri* and *Trésor Supposé* Overtures). **Minkowski** with Les Musiciens de Louvre offers 1 and 2 played by period instruments, whose plangent woodwinds give much pleasure, but at the cost of a rather breathless finale in 1 (Erato). **Jorge Rotter** with the much larger Rhenish Philharmonic propels the music forward with more spirit than Swierczewski and makes an attractive supplement to the Nimbus set (Marco Polo). Harder to find may be 1 with **Rolf Kleinert** (Urania, mono, with an eccentric Schubert 6 from Scherchen)— sturdy and sympathetic with an exhilarating finale—and a stimulating account of 2 by **Fernand Oubradous** (EMI, mono, coupled with appropriate fare led by Georges Tzipine). You might also keep an eye out for **Masur**'s LP of 1 (Eterna 826090), as well as a Beecham Society issue of 2 (521, mono), though this usually reliable conductor seems strangely sluggish here.

Overtures. One of Méhul's finest works, the Overture to *Le Chasse de Jeune Henri*, remains today as loved by audiences as it is feared by horn players who must surmount the difficulty of the thrilling "hunting horn" finale. This proved no problem for the Royal Philharmonic, who played it splendidly for **Beecham** even at his bracing clip (♦Columbia ML 5029, LP). **Swierczewski** is hearty and stimulating (Nimbus, with the symphonies), while **Leppard**, in his more varied survey of "18th-Century Overtures" with the New Philharmonia, sets horns and strings on a more even footing (Philips 446659; released in the United States as "Curtain Up!" 454426). The brazen horns of the Orchestre Français d'Oratorio are heard to good effect in a set conducted by **Jean-Pierre Loré**, highlighted by Pleyel's *Requiem* (Erol 90001, 2CD), but the most glorious-sounding horns of all are in the recording by the Munich Radio Orchestra, and it's a shame that conductor **Kurt Redel** takes the exuberant closeout so slowly (Pierre Verany 786104).

The Overture for Winds in F is included in **Lucien Mora**'s "Musiques de la Revolution Française"; unfortunately it's much too staid (Cybelia 825). Far better if you can find it is **Gerhard Baumann**'s similarly titled LP (Eterna 8 26 858). Other overtures are thus far available only on LP, including Beecham's *Timoleon* and *Trésor Supposé*.

Band and choral music. With the bicentennial of the French Revolution in 1989 came a flood of recordings offering varying combinations of winds, brass, and chorus by composers of the time. For Méhul, pride of place must go to *Chant du Départ*, hailed when it was written as "a second Marseillaise"; it's offered by **Roger Boutry** (EMI 49473), **Plasson** (EMI 49470), **Claude Pichaureau** (Erato 45006), and **Malgoire** (CBS 45607), as well as in Volume 1 of **Désiré Dondeyne**'s "Anthology of French March Music" (Music Guild, 2LP). The main reason to buy Plasson is the grand *Chant National*, resplendent in its writing for three choirs and three orchestras with parts for tenor, two baritones, and bass. Since this disc gathers together some of Méhul's best work along with Berlioz's rousing arrangement of *La Marseillaise*, it may be your best bet for an overview of music of the French Revolution, but the discs by Boutry and Pichaureau are worth the duplication and Gallic completists (including this writer) will want the Mora and Malgoire as well.

HALLER

Felix Mendelssohn (1809–1847)

During Mendelssohn's short life, he exhibited amazing talents in many areas. As a musical prodigy, he has no superiors. His *Midsummer Night's Dream* overture (composed at age 17) and Octet (at 16) are far beyond what such other prodigies as Mozart, Schubert, and Bizet were writing at the same age. In addition to his musical gifts, Mendelssohn was a skilled artist (especially in watercolors), a gifted prose stylist (his letters are still worth reading), a talented linguist, and he was conversant with the cutting-edge intellectual currents of his time. He also had a talent for friendship; his friends and admirers included such diverse characters as Goethe, the English royal family, Chopin, Berlioz, Schumann, Walter Scott, Wagner (who after his death wrote shameful attacks on him), and Cherubini.

The question of whether Mendelssohn's music ever developed beyond the supreme fluency and grace of his early masterpieces has been argued for decades. Certainly his keyboard and chamber music continued to develop, and the F Minor Quartet (written after the death of his sister and soulmate, Fanny, six months before his own) inhabits a larger and darker world than the radiant one of the Octet. The degree to which his later orchestral work represents an advance from early genius remains more debatable, but the growth from the astonishing (but literal) evocations of the *Midsummer Night's Dream* overture to the psychological painting of the *Hebrides* overture and of the last three symphonies is real and obvious to any careful listener.

Mendelssohn's greatest music is probably in his chamber works, oddly neglected despite their uniformly high quality. His orchestral works remain deservedly popular. Although he is usually classified as a Romantic composer, his devotion to clarity and balance look back to the Classical era and forward to the post-Romantics. Ultimately, like all great music, Mendelssohn's transcends its time and speaks its unassuming and elegant message directly to us.

SYMPHONIES

Mendelssohn's orchestral music can be divided into three categories: symphonies, overtures, and everything else. Each category contains at least one masterpiece, and rehearsing and playing or studying it closely with score, piano, and recordings can open up a new appreciation for the inspiration and craft that went into it. Think of the garlands of flute tone woven around the strings in the slow movement of the "Italian" symphony or the many different somber colors in the "Scottish" or the sheer delight of the ophicleide (now usually tuba) part in the *Midsummer Night's Dream* overture. If the mark of a great composer is that he had things of consequence to say that nobody else said in quite the same way, Mendelssohn is securely among the greats.

Mendelssohn's symphonies fall into two subcategories: the youthful string symphonies, written when he was a teenager, and the five larger-scaled adult works. The difference between them is less important for Mendelssohn than almost any other composer. He was probably the most precocious of the major composers, and such masterpieces as the *Midsummer Night's Dream* overture and the Octet are both products of his teens. Still, the string symphonies—actually 8 has optional wind parts—are smaller, lighter, and less ambitious than the canonical five.

The string symphonies present one of those rare but happy moments in the world of recordings in which outstanding performance and sound are presented at a budget price. **Nicholas Ward**'s recordings of these pieces with the Northern Chamber Orchestra have drawn universal acclaim and should be all that most collectors need (♦Naxos 553161, 1–6; 553162, 7–9; 553163, 10–12 plus the single movement of 13). **Good-**

---

man's Hanover Band recordings are significantly more expensive but offer good performances, as well as the optional wind parts that liven up the textures in 8 (RCA 68069, 3CD). On the other hand, the recorded sound for 1 through 6 is a little unfocused.

Masur recorded these pieces with the Leipzig Gewandhaus in readings that are pleasant but somewhat generalized (Berlin 91432; also available separately as 2105 [1–6], 2106 [7, 9, 10], 2107 [both versions of 8], and 2108 [11–13]). Duczmal favors broad tempos and omits 13 (Europa, 4CD); Boughton also omits 13 but gives zestful readings of 1 through 12 (Nimbus 5141/3). Pople's performances with a British ensemble (Hyperion 66561, 3CD) and Markiz with the Amsterdam New Sinfonia (BIS 938, 4CD) are also worthy, unlike Thomas Furi and the Bern Camerata, marred by insensitivity and poor sound (Cascavelle). There's no reason to go beyond Naxos for these works unless you must have the wind parts in 8 or can't stand a bargain.

The five mature symphonies have been recorded many times. Of the complete sets, Masur offers the same virtues and caveats as his string symphonies (Teldec). Dohnányi's set with the Vienna Philharmonic is commendable for both performance and price (London/Decca 460236, 1 and 2; 460239, 3–5; you may also come across two 3CD sets, 421769 and 448514; the latter is preferable for including the *Athalie* music). Karajan's Berlin set is also midpriced and a good choice (DG 429664, 3CD). He revels in Mendelssohn's subtleties of orchestration and doesn't try to inflate the symphonies to outsized proportions. On the other hand, his recorded sound is dry and less agreeable to the ear than Decca provided in Vienna. Weller's Philharmonia set is decent without being noteworthy (Chandos 7090, 3CD). It doesn't erase memories of Sawallisch's lyrical and beautifully proportioned set with the same orchestra, now unfortunately NA (Philips 432958).

Once again, Naxos offers a fine combination of performance, sound, and price. This time the performers are Reinhard Seifried and the Irish National Symphony (♦550957, 1 and 5; 553200, 3 and 4; 2 isn't out yet, but is doubtless in the wings). Another currently incomplete cycle is by Claudio Abbado with the London Symphony. The performances are relaxed and affectionate and the sound pellucid, but DG has made a hash of the reissue process. Symphony 2 isn't available at all; 4 can be bought as a discmate to 1 (445596), 3 (427810), or 5 (415974); all that's missing is a performance of Symphony 4 backed by itself. Finally, there's a London Philharmonic set with 2 from Chailly and the rest (plus various other works) from Haitink (Philips). Like Dohnányi's, this set is spread over four midpriced discs, but it's not recommendable. Neither Chailly nor Haitink is very compelling in this music, and the orchestral playing is sometimes tired. Seifried offers the best balance of performance and value, but there's no 2. Dohnányi's is somewhat more costly, but is complete and offers better performances.

1. Matters stand pretty much as they do with the complete and almost-complete sets, with Seifried, Dohnányi, and Abbado all worth considering. Other possibilities include a rather stern Cleveland performance from Louis Lane in a budget box that includes some Ormandy reissues (Sony 63251, 2CD); Kuchar, interestingly coupled with the fully orchestrated "String Symphony 8" (Ondine 741), and a joyful version from Mas Conde and the Maastricht Symphony (Koch-Schwann 6706). Claus Peter Flor's coupling of 1 and 5 is no longer listed but is worth seeking out (RCA 60391), while d'Avalos is hectic and overwrought (IMP).

2 (*Lobgesang*; Song of Praise). Mendelssohn's choral symphony (with two sopranos and tenor thrown in) is served best by Dohnányi in a 2CD,

midpriced set with 1 and the cantata *Die erste Walpurgisnacht* (Decca 460236). Chailly, also 2CD and midpriced, has the best vocal soloists but is a less-than-compelling performance (Philips). Peter Maag, who made some fine Mendelssohn recordings, wasn't at his best in his Madrid reading, and the sound is lackluster (Arts). Performances by Schwarz (Delos) and Rilling (Hänssler) are forgettable, and so is d'Avalos (IMP). Flor's performance would be worth investigating if it were reissued (RCA 60248). Avoid 1, 2, and 3 by Dennis Russell Davies (MusicMasters or MHS), in which the entire oratorio section of 2 is omitted. For shame!

3 ("Scottish"). There are lots of good performances of this one. Recommended versions include Maag with the London Symphony, with lovely performances of the *Hebrides* overture and *Midsummer Night's Dream* excerpts (♦Decca 443578), not to be confused with the vastly inferior remake he did with Swiss forces (IMP) or his even worse Madrid version (Arts). Note, however, that Decca only offers a couple of *Midsummer Night's Dream* excerpts; the Classics Compact Discs releases are well worth the extra outlay, with the *Scottish* and *Hebrides* on ♦6191 and *Midsummer Night's Dream* on ♦6001. The bargain "Weekend Classics" issue of Maag's "Scottish" is valuable for Solti's sunny "Italian" with the Israel Symphony (433023). Also recommendable are Karajan in a single-disc excerpt from his set that includes *Hebrides* and "Italian" (♦DG 449743); Colin Davis with the Bavarian Radio Orchestra (♦Orfeo 89841); and Abbado, coupled, inescapably, with "Italian" (DG 427810).

Klemperer recorded fine versions of this work, revising the ending to meet the composer's expressed doubts about the success of the one he used. The Philharmonia recording is out of the catalog (probably temporarily), but there's a slightly more flowing version from Bavarian Radio (♦EMI 66868). Welser-Möst merely lopes along, with congested sonics (EMI); Flor's coupling of 3 and 4 is the least compelling installment of his survey (RCA), while only Mercury completists will want Dorati, and Norrington is excruciating in both 3 and 4 (EMI). Solti in Chicago seems a tad overwrought (London, with 4), while Dohnányi's remake is primarily of interest for his sumptuous *Die erste Walpurgisnacht* (Telarc).

More controversial are Harnoncourt's beautifully played, arrestingly phrased, but sometimes over-emphatic performance (Teldec 72308, with *Italian*), and Bernstein's, which is agreeably energetic but disagreeably hyped-up (Sony 47591, with 5). Levine gets beautiful playing from the Berlin Philharmonic but is bland (DG). Mitropoulos, with the same orchestra, offers an exciting (if you like it) or hectic (if you don't) performance, but the sound is indisputably poor (Orfeo 488981). Good bargain releases are by Seifried (Naxos) and Stefan Sanderling with the Royal Philharmonic (♦Intersound 2834).

4 ("Italian"). The by-now familiar suspects are recommendable: Abbado (with the coupling of your choice) and, if that's not enough, another Abbado, this time with the Berlin Philharmonic and *Midsummer Night's Dream* complete, similar except for the broader, more refined tone of the German ensemble (Sony 62826); Colin Davis; Dohnányi; and Karajan. Others worth mentioning are Gardiner, leading the Vienna Philharmonic in both the usual and Mendelssohn's revised edition (mostly squarer phrasing, plus a greatly expanded finale) in slightly over-driven performances (DG 459156), and Casals, not very refined but full of spirit (Sony 46251). Harnoncourt is lovely and fresh (listen to the urgency of the phrasing in III), the point making under control (♦Teldec 72308).

Cantelli's reading has remarkable lightness and strength (♦Enterprise 4158, mono); **Munch**'s stylish but casually played "Italian" is coupled with his sober "Reformation" (RCA 68090, mid-price), while **Levine**'s Berlin recording has the same virtues and drawbacks as his "Scottish." **Solti** in Chicago (London/Decca 414665, with 3) and Vienna (London/Decca 440476, with Shostakovich's 5!) are both very driven; his more relaxed Israel reading is more attractive (♦London 433023, with Maag's "Scottish"). **Szell** in Cleveland isn't as driven as Solti but is even more tense, and the technical finesse of the playing comes at the expense of a drilled feeling (Sony).

Toscanini, of course, was the supreme orchestral drillmaster and parts of his "Italian" reflect this, yet the lyrical feeling in I and parts of II and III show hints of sunshine behind the usual storm clouds; be prepared for desiccated sound and monochrome playing. **Ormandy**'s "Italian" is one of the boxmates of Lane's 1 mentioned above; his admirers will find it an excellent bargain, but those who find his conducting bland won't be converted by this performance (Sony 63251, 2CD). **Skrowaczewski**'s "Italian" is far more attractive than Dorati's "Scottish" (Mercury). **Klemperer** gives us a rugged "Italian" in full-blooded sound (EMI, with 3). Steinberg is expansive and warmly played (EMI 65611, with Beethoven's 7 and Wolf's *Italian Serenade*).

Bernstein offers a generously filled disc including the Violin Concerto with Zukerman, *Hebrides* overture, and the *Athalie* "War March of the Priests," but the performance is crass and not well played (Sony). **Welser-Möst** is nowhere near Presto in the final saltarello (EMI, with 3), while **Previn** is too distantly recorded (EMI, with overtures). One of the many casualties of the sale of Virgin Classics to EMI was a performance of this symphony and *Midsummer Night's Dream* excerpts by **Mackerras** and the Orchestra of the Age of Enlightenment (♦90725). These were graceful and gracious readings with playing of the highest order; if you find them in a remainder bin or as a reissue, don't hesitate. Likewise if you see **Stokowski**'s pairing of "Italian" and Bizet's Symphony in C, snap it up; these were his last recordings, and they bubble over with an infectious brio most conductors half his age couldn't summon (♦CBS Odyssey 39498).

5 ("Reformation"). This weakest of Mendelssohn's symphonies makes special demands on its interpreters. Aside from the completists recommended above (**Abbado, Dohnányi, Karajan, Seifried,** and **Masur**), there are a number of worthy versions: **Beecham** offers old sound but a wonderfully articulate performance (♦Biddulph 43); **Davis** (♦Orfeo 132851); **Flor** (RCA, with 1); **Maazel** in a midpriced 1961 recording from Berlin with surprisingly good sound, one of those startlingly fresh and intense early recordings that helped establish him on the international scene (♦DG 449720, with Franck's Symphony); **Munch**, the serious and glowingly played discmate to his "Italian" (♦RCA 68090). His 1948 "Reformation" is with the Paris Conservatory Orchestra and is redolent of a different and much more democratic era of orchestral playing (Dante 478). **Gardiner**'s is less pushed than his "Italian" (either version), yet makes less of an impression (DG). **Ančerl,** an admirable conductor, made his recording in concert with the less-than-admirable Toronto Symphony, available as part of a 3CD box; only diehard fans of the conductor will find it worthwhile (Tahra). **Paray** could sometimes do fine things in recordings, but his "Reformation" is not among them (Mercury); still, his sturdy reading is far preferable to **d'Avalos**'s tense, hectic account (IMP).

OTHER ORCHESTRAL MUSIC

Overtures. The greatest of Mendelssohn's overtures, and one of the greatest of all overtures, is *The Hebrides,* or *Fingal's Cave.* The Hebrides, of course, are islands off the coast of Scotland (the ultimate Romantic place in the early 19th century) and Fingal was the semilegendary Celtic bard whose stark verses (especially as [re]imagined by James Macpherson's alter-ego Ossian) set the early Romantic imagination alight. Mendelssohn sought to capture the wild seascape of the islands and the evocative shadows of the bardic past in this overture. Of the formidable number of formidable performances of this piece, the greatest is an urgent and inimitably fresh one by **Britten** in a disc containing equally compelling readings of Mozart, Haydn, Debussy, and Beethoven (BBC 8008). Other worthy readings include **Furtwängler** (Gramophono 78574, 2CD, or Tahra 1008, 4CD); **Beecham** (Dutton 5009); **Abbado** (DG 423104); **Maag** (Decca 443578 or 433023); **Karajan** (DG 449743, with Symphonies 3 and 4); and **van Beinum** (Dante 471).

My favorite of all Mendelssohn overtures is *Die Schöne Melusine* (The Fair Melusina), a shining, lyrical piece that prefigures Wagner's Rhine music, noteworthy since it was finished in 1833, 36 years before *Das Rheingold*. The greatest recording was **Beecham**'s (♦EMI 63407, part of the "Beecham Edition," with *Midsummer Night's Dream*). Worthy alternatives are by **Abbado** (DG 423104), **Gabriel Chmura** (♦DG 423025), and **Masur** (Berlin 2057 or 9312).

There are several worthwhile collections of overtures, by **Abbado, Marriner** (Capriccio 10708), **Masur** (Berlin 2057), and **Flor** (RCA 7905). **Chmura** is a better choice than the higher-priced Abbado (♦DG 423025). Avoid the pair of discs with **Klauspeter Seibel,** who pads things out with the preludes to *St. Paul, Elijah,* and *Die erste Walpurgisnacht* and presents the lot in dismal readings with dismal sonics to match (Colosseum 34.9007/8).

A Midsummer Night's Dream. Setting music for Shakespeare's play occupied Mendelssohn from 1826, when he was 17, through 1842, when he was 33 and had only five more years to live. His settings survive in many different forms, ranging from the overture alone through excerpts to the "complete" music for the play. Of the complete versions (not all of them equally complete), those by **Previn** (♦EMI 47163) and **Abbado** (♦Sony 62826) are outstanding, while **Brüggen** with old instruments is well worth hearing (♦Glossa 921101). **Tate**'s Rotterdam performance is finely judged without quite making it to the first rank (EMI 69864).

Of the less complete selections, **Maag** with the London Symphony is outstanding (♦Classic Compact Discs 6001), and his suite is longer than most; unfortunately, only a couple of pieces are included with his "Scottish" in Decca 443578. **Harnoncourt** offers a fresh approach (♦Teldec 74882). A lovely and uncharacteristically relaxed performance by **Szell** with the New York Philharmonic is NA, but a Cleveland disc offers a decent alternative at a budget price (Sony 48264). **Paray** does a beautiful job, coupled with his "Reformation" (♦Mercury 434396), and **Mackerras** (discussed under "Italian") is also very special. **Klemperer** is also a fine guide to this music (♦EMI 64144 or Testament 1102). **Toscanini**'s recording with the Philadelphia Orchestra in the '40s has elderly sound, but lovely playing and less of an edge than he got with his NBC orchestra and the NYPO. The readings themselves are an odd but fascinating blend of his strict approach and Stokowskian orchestral sound (RCA 60314).

The final distillation of this magical music is the overture by itself, a miraculous creation by a 17-year-old boy. Once again, **Abbado** (DG 423104, with other overtures) and **Davis** (♦Orfeo 89841, with Symphony 3), are worthy, as are **Beecham** (with *Melusine*) and **Furtwängler,** with elderly sound (Orfeo 378951).

Octet. This is a shining jewel of chamber music, but it's sometimes played by a full orchestral string section. There is a good recording by

Mas Conde with the Maastricht Symphony (Schwann 6706) and a ferocious one by the Toscanini-led NBC Symphony (RCA 60283). Thomas Furi's recording is an unhappy affair, best avoided (Camerata).

Athalie. The incidental music to *Athalie* exists in a more or less complete recording by French forces under Bernard Tétu (Koch Schwann 314282). Dohnányi's symphony set includes the Overture and "War March of the Priests" (London/Decca 460239 or 448514), while Flor included the overture in his collection (RCA 7905), and Fiedler, Ormandy, and Bernstein have all done nobly by the "War March." You'll want to supplant Tétu's *Athalie* with two discs containing the incidental music to *Antigone* (Capriccio 10 392) and *Oedipus* (10 393), both led by Stefan Soltesz. CHAKWIN

CONCERTOS

Piano concertos. Mendelssohn's two piano concertos are staples of the repertoire. Rudolf Serkin's brilliant performances are favorites for many (♦Sony 46542). Perahia is once again poetic (♦Sony 42401). Katin (London) and Shelley (♦Chandos 9215) provide a middle ground, but Schiff is more insightful (London). Edelmann plays warmly, though he's rather sluggish. Hough is, as ever, ultra-refined, but inflects too little and needs more tonal variety (Hyperion). Katsaris is headstrong to the point of lacking charm, but he includes the early A minor Concerto for Piano and Strings, which Ogdon played with more refinement (Argo). The young Joseph Kalichstein played a beautiful Concerto 1 (RCA), and he has since recorded both numbered concertos sumptuously (♦Nimbus 5112). Lympany was a strong advocate of Concerto 1, and her 1964 account with Sargent was recently reissued (♦Ivory Classics 70906), but her earlier performance with Kubelik was arguably finer (EMI). Frith is disappointing in the solo concertos, partly due to his clangorous instrument (Naxos).

Two-piano concertos. Frith and Hugh Tinney uses a similar-sounding instrument in these pieces, but the engineers have distanced the soloists somewhat, and the effect is pleasurable (♦Naxos 553416). Coombs and Munro are even more sparkling (♦Hyperion 66567) and make a nice complement to the classic Gold and Fizdale with Ormandy, once available in a Sony Masterworks Portrait. Pöntinen and Derwinger are just as scintillating and spontaneous as Coombs and Munro (♦BIS 688). Perhaps the best E major Double Concerto comes from the Pekinel sisters; their playfulness and refinement in that work and in the Mozart and Bruch Double Concertos leave us hoping they will give us the other Mendelssohn Concerto (Chandos 9711). The Paratores (Sony) and Pierce and Jonas (Vox) lack charm.

Violin and piano concerto. This would be remarkable for a composer of any age, but Mendelssohn was 14 when he wrote it. Glenn and List unearthed it in 1964, and we await a CD transfer of their exciting performance (Westminster). In the meantime, Bisengaliev and Frith (♦Naxos 553844) or Gulli and Cavallo (♦Koch 1622) are more than acceptable. Kremer and Argerich's tempos and overall characterization are almost hysterical (DG), and Csaba and Gothoni are strangely earthbound (Ondine).

The smaller works for piano and orchestra are included in some of the concerto discs mentioned above. Shelley plays *Capriccio Brillant* especially well (♦Chandos 9215), and Serkin gives a rough-hewn account (♦Sony 48166, with Brahms's Concerto 1). Lympany made a specialty of the smaller *concertante* works, and her early Decca recordings are available (♦Dutton 5506); her fresher EMI performances may be difficult to find. Kyriakou includes the A Minor Concerto with strings, but the

pleasure of the disc is diminished by primitive recorded sound (Tuxedo). LOVELACE

Violin Concerto. Mendelssohn's E Minor Violin Concerto was the first such composition of real stature after Beethoven's in 1806, 38 years earlier. Wisely, rather than trying to follow Beethoven's severely elegant classicism as his model, Mendelssohn let his fancy reign and produced the quintessential Romantic concerto. First, he dispensed with the usual orchestral introduction, having the soloist enter immediately after the orchestra established the tonality. Second, the first movement is linked directly to the second by the tenuous thread of a single note held over by the bassoon. In the beginning of the finale, the soloist seems to be pleading with the orchestra to abandon the minor mode and conclude the concerto with him in the major. It's a remarkable work filled with unforgettable melodies and striking effects, including a cadenza that's an integral part of the work, and it's no wonder it has remained the most popular of all violin concertos.

Some of the earliest recordings were of single movements in abbreviated versions. Ysaÿe recorded the finale in 1912 with piano accompaniment (♦Sony 62337, NA). A giant of a man, he had a tremendous personality to match. His playing is wonderfully reckless and full of joy. Huberman recorded II and III in 1924, also with piano accompaniment (♦Pearl 9332; Biddulph LAB 077/78). Like Ysaÿe, he possessed one of the most powerful personalities in the history of music and, again like Ysaÿe, his performance has a delightfully spontaneous, mercurial feeling, and he's just as much a virtuoso. Kreisler made his first electric recording of the concerto in 1926; it's surprisingly pedestrian—free of passion and extremes of expression (Naxos).

Szigeti's 1933 account couldn't be more different. He simply oozes personality, and the extremes of emotion are explored in this dramatic collaboration with the great Beecham and the London Philharmonic (♦Pearl 9377). A classic performance.

Milstein's first recording from 1945 is very fleet, short on feeling but long on virtuosity; the finale is especially impressive (Enterprise; Pearl; Grammofono 2000). His next recording, from 1953, is his best, preserving the virtuosity of the earlier one but presenting a greater depth of expression, though II is still blank (EMI 66551). His last, from the early '70s, has lost the virtues of the first two, but II has gained a new tenderness (DG).

Heifetz's 1949 recording with Beecham is very brisk and light, like Milstein's first, but more energetic and thoughtful, and Beecham is a fine partner (EMI 65191). His 1959 reading with Munch is almost a mechanical run-through, with tempos even faster than the earlier one though lacking much of its drive (RCA). Ivry Gitlis recorded the concerto in the mid-'50s; his account is tremendously energetic (Vox). Though I is mechanical, II is surprisingly sensitive, and III is a real roller-coaster ride. Stern's 1959 recording with Ormandy is a classic that has obviously served as the model for many musicians who came after him (CBS 36724). It avoids extremes, yet still has admirably flexible tempos. His recording with Ozawa from the early '80s shows a considerable advance in his understanding of the work over the earlier one (Sony 37204). Here, Stern is more sensitive to the structure of each phrase.

Menuhin recorded the concerto in 1952 with Furtwängler and the Berlin Philharmonic (EMI 69799). Their performance is intense, and the interpretation is straightforward and unremarkable. He did it again with Efrem Kurtz with slightly inferior results. Francescatti's recording with Mitropoulos is intense and deeply felt in I, sweet and earnest in II, and joyous in III (Sony 62339). His ringing tone is a pleasure to hear. **Michel Schwalbé** gives a good if unremarkable reading in a concert recording (Biddulph). **Szeryng** is afflicted with a wobbly vibrato in his recording with Haitink from the '70s (Philips); I is a bit sluggish, II is lovely and intimate, but III sounds as if he just isn't enjoying himself.

Chung plays with great intensity but no insight; her tone lacks body, and the finale feels rushed (Decca). **Mutter** just doesn't seem to be involved in the music (DG). Some passages in I are pretty, but II is too restrained, and she doesn't get excited enough in III. **Angèle Dubeau** gives a reading utterly without temperament or emotion (Analekta). **Robert McDuffie** offers a similar run-through (Telarc). **Shaham**'s version can't be saved by his rich tone (DG). His playing is mechanical, and he sounds uninterested in the music. His partner, Sinopoli, is more sensitive to the charms and intricacies of this score. **Perlman**'s first recording, with Previn, is very lovely; his tone is intoxicating (EMI 69863). II is distinguished by his intense lyricism. His second, with Haitink, lacks the character and tonal opulence of the first (EMI). His third, with Barenboim, is an improvement, but still doesn't equal the first (Teldec).

Zukerman sounded more spontaneous in 1969 than he does today, and he was already a master of nuance (Sony 61843). He played a fine Stradivarius back then that had a gorgeous, full-bodied tone at low dynamic levels where most other violins sound hoarse. **Cho-Liang Lin** plays the concerto with great polish and tenderness (CBS 39007). Every note is alive, and II is gorgeously vocal. He draws a lovely tone from his Stradivarius. Tilson Thomas does a fine job bringing out important orchestral detail.

As is so often the case, **Salerno-Sonnenberg** finds qualities in the music that elude others (♦EMI 49276). Her interpretation is exciting and dramatic, and she creates many moments of breathtaking beauty, all complemented by the lovely tone she draws from her instrument. She shapes her phrases with unusual intelligence and individuality, but always at the service of the music. The cadenza is remarkable in this respect. It's a shame the engineers placed the orchestra so far in the background, obscuring much of the counterpoint.

Sarah Chang gives a very standard, tasteful interpretation, but she hasn't yet made the music her own (EMI). **Leila Josefowicz** is rather like Chang; she needs to grow into this score before she can feel its emotions (Philips). **Isabelle van Keulen** has made a fine recording of the original version of the concerto with Lev Markiz (BIS 935). The differences range from the subtle to the obvious—for example, the original marking of *con fuoco* rather than *molto appassionata* for the opening Allegro, occasionally bolder orchestration, and a cadenza only a fraction of the length it is in the finished version.

There was a fine LP by **David Oistrakh** and the Philadelphia under Ormandy from the mid-'50s (♦Columbia, NA). Oistrakh played with great intelligence, making nuance and tempo adjustments to shape each phrase so it elucidates the architecture of each movement. This is one of his best recordings.

CHAMBER MUSIC

Mendelssohn worked within the forms he inherited from his classical forebears, imbuing them with delicate melody. His interest in the melodic as opposed to the thematic distinguishes him from composers of an earlier generation.

Violin sonatas. The first two are among Mendelssohn's earliest compositions. They have their charms but aren't very memorable. Sonata 3 is a mature work, but isn't as interesting as the others. **Kuniko Nagata** and Hirotoshi Kasai have recorded all three; Kasai's exceptional pianism is wasted on a partner like Nagata, whose wiry tone, nearly nonexistent vibrato, and crude execution make this disc nearly unlistenable (Talent). The recording by **Felix Ayo** and Bruno Canino is far more serviceable (Dynamic 180).

Cello sonatas. These are two of Mendelssohn's finest chamber works. Dating from his maturity, in both he treats the piano and cello as equal partners and writes very effectively for them. **Jeffrey Solow** and Doris Stevenson play them with great polish, but they're done in by the airless quality of the recording, obviously made in an acoustically dead studio (Centaur). **Starker** and Sebok recorded 2; Starker displays a greater than usual degree of emotional involvement, and Sebok is an expert, highly musical partner (Mercury 434377). **Mark Shuman** and Todd Crow play with energy and polish in a recording that captures plenty of hall ambience (ASV 6196).

Isserlis and Tan perform them on period instruments (RCA 62553). Isserlis brings out Mendelssohn's lyricism and playfulness like no one else, and Tan draws a very soft-grained tone from his 1839 Johann Streicher fortepiano. **James Kreger** and Gerald Robbins really dig into these works in a very close-up recording (♦Discover 920586). Robbins plays more aggressively than the others and also phrases more intelligently; he and Kreger are fully equal partners, but it's not for the faint of heart.

Piano trios. No. 1 is a staple of the repertoire, with its soaring melodies; 2 is less melodic but just as concentrated. **Cortot**, Casals, and Thibaud recorded 1 in 1927 (♦Monopoly 2005, 2CD; Biddulph Piano Series 2; Enterprise 99343). The performance is ardent, and Cortot is mesmerizing. **Rubinstein**, Heifetz, and Piatigorsky recorded 1 in 1950 (RCA). The result is one of Heifetz's better chamber music efforts, but the performers still fail to play with their hearts. **Hess**, Szigeti, and Casals recorded 1 in concert in 1952; Szigeti dominates, with a hypnotic degree of concentration (♦Sony 66571, NA). **Oborin**, Oistrakh, and Knushevitsky recorded both in 1948 (♦Lys 367, 371). In spite of the bad sound, you can still hear that Oistrakh is glorious, Knushevitsky is a great cellist, but Oborin is weak.

On LP, the **Beaux Arts Trio** played the trios with reserve and intimacy but no drama (Philips). Heifetz, Piatigorsky, and **Pennario** recorded 2 in 1963; the results are mechanical (RCA). The **Kalichstein-Laredo-Robinson Trio** is dominated by Laredo's violin, and the playing is a little low-key (Nimbus). The **Vienna Piano Trio** is a sensitive, well-integrated group, but they also fail to ignite this music (Vox). The **Stern-Istomin-Rose Trio** plays like equals and really digs in, but its reading isn't as poetic as some others (Sony 64519). The **Golub-Kaplan-Carr Trio** is just as accomplished; its more attuned to nuances than anyone else and give the members are the strongest sense of any ensemble thats engaged in a real dialogue, with fine recorded sound (♦Arabesque 6599). The **Trio Fontenay** is just as sensitive, but its genius is not so much in subtlety of nuance as clarity of structure and the ebb and flow of each movement's sections (♦Teldec 44947).

Quartets. The string quartet was among the earliest chamber ensembles that Mendelssohn wrote for, and he succeeded brilliantly in all six. The **Coull Quartet** has recorded the complete set, but its playing lacks fire and virtuosity (Hyperion) The **Artis Quartet** is a much better group, with a brilliant first violin (Accord 201132). Sensibly, it takes brisker tempos than the Coull, who are prone to drag.

Nos. 1 and 2, written in 1829 and 1827, are remarkable for the density and maturity of their counterpoint. The **Shanghai Quartet** gives them a good reading, but the players lack character (Delos). The **Juilliard**

Quartet lays them out with its usual authority and rich tone but could be a bit more propulsive (Sony 60579). The **Cleveland Quartet** plays 2 with fire, brilliance, and gorgeous sound (♦Telarc 80142). The **Guarneri Quartet** offers a voluptuous reading of 3 in an excellent recording (♦Arabesque 6714). The **Aurora Quartet** gives a good, workmanlike reading of 3 and 6 (Naxos).

Among period instrument recordings, the **Quatuor Mosaïques** has done 1 and 2; they are a very polished ensemble, but its playing lacks fire and can be boring (Astrée). The **Eroica Quartet** has also recorded them with far more drama; unfortunately, it lacks the Mosaïques's secure technique (Harmonia Mundi 907245).

Quintets. Mendelssohn reveled in the body of sound that a larger string ensemble could afford, and that enjoyment is evident in the two quintets. The **Berliner Streichquintet** gives them lackluster readings (MD+G). The **Raphael Ensemble** plays them with obvious relish, and the enthusiasm of the first violinist is infectious (Hyperion 66993). The **Academy Chamber Ensemble** gives a warm, moving reading of 2 (Philips 420400).

Among period instrument performances, **Hausmusik**'s version of 1 is good but unremarkable (EMI). **L'Archibudelli** is a more virtuosic ensemble, but it emphasizes brilliance over warmth (Sony 60766).

Octet. Written as a birthday present for his violin teacher, Eduard Rietz, this is probably the best-loved of Mendelssohn's chamber works. For two opposing string quartets that occasionally play as such but usually function as an octet, it's remarkable in its contrapuntal complexity; it's also a showpiece for the first violinist.

Heifetz and friends play with their customary virtuosity but little drama, and the recording gives the instruments no room to breathe, limiting their dynamic range (RCA). **Divertimenti** plays with warmth but lacks the drama and detail of the best recordings (Hyperion). The **Academy Chamber Ensemble** recorded the work twice (Philips 420400; Chandos). The Philips is preferred for its greater drama and detail, though the players are not top-notch virtuosi. The **Concertante Chamber Players** are just that, and they usually manage to infuse drama into their reading, but sometimes they run out of steam and the recording lets them down, because even though it gives a real concert hall ambience it fails to reveal detail (Helicon).

The **Cleveland and Meliora Quartets** give an exciting, polished reading and are blessed with fine sound (♦Telarc 80142). The **Guarneri and Orion Quartets** give just as exciting a performance in even better sound; details come through with great clarity (♦Arabesque 6714). The classic recording was made at the Marlboro Festival in 1965 with an all-star cast including violinists Jaime Laredo and Alexander Schneider, violist Samuel Rhodes, cellist Leslie Parnas, and the recently formed **Guarneri Quartet** (♦Sony 46251). The atmosphere was electric when it was made, and Laredo is a thrilling first violinist. The sound has held up remarkably well, with more detail audible than in many more recent recordings.
MAGIL

PIANO MUSIC

Much has been written about the supposed effect of Mendelssohn's affluence on his compositional style. To be sure, his music is often pleasant, but it's never indifferent. The solo piano works reveal a wide range of emotions in microcosm without abandoning the composer's self-avowed requirement of balance. Yet seldom do recital programs include more than a handful of Mendelssohn's output. Some performers and listeners may react to a sentimentality perceived in the music or superim-

posed by performers over the years (who can hear "Spring Song" without conjuring up images of Bugs Bunny?). Nonetheless, intimacy in Mendelssohn should never be confused with mawkishness.

Only two complete or near-complete sets of the solo music appear to be available, and both have striking attributes. **Frith** is especially attuned to the sensitivity of Mendelssohn's music, and Naxos gives him recordings to match the warmth and clarity of the performances (♦various numbers, 5CD). When Frith began his cycle, Naxos had already chosen another young artist to record the *Songs without Words,* but **Péter Nagy** can't match Frith in subtlety and refinement. Purchasers of Frith's discs may choose to acquire the *Songs* in **Martin Jones**'s traversal of the complete works at budget price (♦Nimbus 1772). Jones is imaginative and plays with ample spontaneity. He highlights the precocious youthfulness of the music, while Frith presents Mendelssohn the mature intellectual. Both if these approaches work, since a fresh intellectualism pervades Mendelssohn's entire output. The only drawback to Jones's discs is the slightly distant, over-reverberant sound; this won't disturb most collectors.

Choosing among the many accounts of *Songs without Words* is difficult. Many are available at budget price, and the intimacy of these lovely salon pieces has charmed many pianists. **Daniel Adni** (EMI), **Ilse von Alpenheim** (Philips), **Rena Kyriakou** (Vox), and **Livia Rév** (Hyperion) play them beautifully, but **Barenboim** surpasses these pianists by giving each miniature a distinct profile (♦DG 453061). **Schiff** is too quirky in his one-disc selection (London). **Gieseking**'s excerpts are required listening (♦EMI 66775, with many of Grieg's *Lyric Pieces*). With Rév, he is the most introspective, but his spellbinding finesse makes Rév seem reticent. **Ignaz Friedman** recorded nine of the *Songs* exquisitely (♦Pearl 2000), and **Ania Dorfmann**'s were magical (RCA, NA).

After the *Songs without Words, Variations Sérieuses* and *Rondo Capriccioso* are the best-known solo works. **Perahia** is poetic in both (♦Sony 37838, with the E Major Sonata, or 42401, with the concertos), and **Cherkassky** is inimitable in the latter (♦Vox 5139, with *Sonate Ecossaise* and works by other composers). **Lydia Artymiw** once had a stylish *Variations* (Chandos), and many have rightly praised **Esther Budiardjo**'s *Rondo* and other works. Often her playing needs to breathe more; it's very propulsive, but most of the time that suits this music (♦ProPiano 224524).

Many consider the sonatas empty pieces, but **Frith, Jones,** and **Perahia** (in the E major) make a good case for them (see above). **Chiu** plays them well, but isn't preferable to the aforementioned pianists; his pianism has grown since this Mendelssohn disc (Harmonia Mundi).
LOVELACE

ORGAN MUSIC

Two sets of Mendelssohn organ pieces, both with strong English connections, were published during the composer's lifetime: Three Preludes and Fugues Op. 37, dedicated to Thomas Attwood, the organist of St. Paul's Cathedral; and Six Sonatas Op. 65, commissioned by a London publishing firm. While these might be regarded as the official canon of Mendelssohn's organ works, they are by no means his only pieces for the instrument. There are several early pieces dating from 1820 to 1823, some separate preludes and fugues dating from 1834 to 1841, and a substantial number written in 1844. Most but not all of the 1844 pieces are preliminary versions of movements for the Op. 65 sonatas.

The one really complete recording of Mendelssohn's organ works, including the preliminary versions of Op. 65, is by **Rudolf Innig** (MD+G 3487, 4CD). Though currently unavailable, it's an achievement that demands attention here, and there's always the possibility of reissue or of finding second-hand copies. I suspect that only the most devoted student of these works would want a recording as complete as this. Innig chose to record on a 1910 Klais organ that I find ponderous and disagreeable. The louder registrations are heavy and turgid, striking the ear like a bludgeon, and the quieter registers lack all sweetness or delicacy. The fast movements tend to be very fast, the slow ones very slow. To his credit, his performances are never mechanical or boring, but many of them are wayward and unsteady.

Most recordings incline to either of two interpretive extremes that I call "neo-Bach" and "proto-Reger." The exponents of the first, seeing the proliferation of preludes, fugues, and chorales, conclude that the organ works are emulations of Bach and should be performed as if they were Baroque music on instruments of classic design. Many of these performances are austere and mechanical, making nonsense of the tender, song-without-words movements that are equally a part of Mendelssohn's organ style, while failing to discern the Romantic element in the movements of outwardly Baroque form. The proto-Reger interpreters view Mendelssohn as a precursor of the symphonic organ style of the late 19th and early 20th centuries. They play him on instruments of that period, often very large ones that swamp the music in thick, ponderous tone, making it sound overripe. (I would put Innig in the proto-Reger camp.) Surely the truth lies somewhere in between. The ideal instrument should combine classical clarity with romantic warmth, power for the grandiose movements with sweetness for the lyrical ones. That way the music can be clear without dryness and expressive without fin de siècle neurosis.

A notable historic recording of Opp. 37 and 65 is by **Feike Asma** on the 18th-century organ at Amsterdam's Oude Kerk (Festivo 092/3, 2CD). Asma is described in the notes as a "romantic organ virtuoso," but here he plays an early instrument with mechanical action and no registration aids, so this isn't a proto-Reger performance. It sounds like the playing of a fine musician whose technique is rather over-the-hill: tempos are slow, there are many minor slips and inaccuracies, tempos fluctuate within movements, and it's not always clear whether this is intentional. All the same, his remarkable artistry shines through the imperfections, making this well worth hearing, though perhaps it shouldn't be your only recording of these works.

Between 1973 and 1975, **Thomas Murray** produced a landmark recording of Op. 65 plus *Andante with Variations* (1844) on two mid-19th-century American organs in the Boston area: the E. & G.G. Hook (1854) at the First Congregational Society, Jamaica Plain, and the W.B.D. Simmons (1857) at the Most Holy Redeemer Church in South Boston (Raven 390). The tonal quality of these instruments almost perfectly suits these works, proving that organ tone can be romantic without being turn-of-the-century orchestral—there was life before E.M. Skinner! Murray's performances are not as impressive. While some of the larger movements have an imposing grandeur, the readings are generally mechanical and perfunctory.

James Hammann, in "The Mendelssohn Organ," has recorded all of Opp. 37 and 65 with a selection of the other works on a two-manual instrument built in 1785 by the Stumm Brothers in St. Ulrich's Church, Neckargemünd, near Heidelberg (Raven 500, 2CD). In 1845, just prior to their publication, Mendelssohn himself played the Op. 65 sonatas for friends on two other Stumm organs in Frankfurt and Kronberg. Such instruments have been characterized by organ historians as "transitional" or "early romantic." Their basic tone is warm, yet ringing and clear, with upperwork that adds brilliance when needed. There are no enclosed divisions or registration aids. It's fascinating to hear the Mendelssohn works played on an instrument of the sort the composer would have known, but Hammann's playing leaves much to be desired. He tends to be mechanical, giving little sense of the music's phrasing or trajectory, and there are too many wrong notes and minor mishaps.

Hammann's release is not the first substantial Mendelssohn recording on a Stumm organ. In 1997, **Ulrik Spang-Hanssen** recorded the "complete" organ works on the larger (three-manual) and earlier (1745) Stumm organ at the Court and City Church of St. Paul, Kirchheimbolanden, Germany (♦Classico 193-95, 3CD). The organs are similar in character; as recorded here, the larger and earlier instrument sounds a bit more brilliant, and its tuning system is better suited to the music, though it appears that some of the highest-pitched pipes cannot be tuned satisfactorily. Some listeners may find the sound a trifle raw and windy. Spang-Hanssen plays with persuasive artistry and virtuosic aplomb. His tempos tend to be brisk, and he's very free with inflections of tempo; in places this freedom verges on mannerism, but it's a vast improvement on the many mechanical interpretations we so often encounter. This set contains some of the most exciting Mendelssohn I have heard.

John Scott has combined all of Opp. 37 and 65 with the non–Op. 65 pieces of 1844 and two fugues of 1839 in a comprehensive but not exhaustive traversal at St. Paul's Cathedral in London, where he is organist (Hyperion 22029, 2CD). A very large instrument plus the cathedral's legendary reverberation make for a sound that's massive and somewhat turgid, lacking convincing presence. When Mendelssohn played at St. Paul's, the instrument was far smaller; the present organ makes these works sound rather bloated, but it hasn't completely lost its early Victorian flavor. Scott often takes a more orchestral approach to registration than Mendelssohn would have expected, while much of the playing seems emotionally detached: proto-Reger style with a sense of British reserve.

Another proto-Reger performance of the Op. 65 sonatas is by **Jozef Sluys** on the large 1884 Walcker organ at Riga Cathedral (Discover 920207). The organ tone is ponderous but basically clear, though with some distracting action noise. Sluys's playing is generally free of annoying eccentricities, but these aren't performances of great artistic insight. Those wishing to hear Op. 37 played on the same instrument will find the preludes and fugues recorded by **Vincent Genvrin,** along with Sonatas 3 and 4 and a set of Mendelssohn motets for unaccompanied choir (Hortus 008).

Among the many neo-Bach interpretations, one of the better recordings is by **Janice Beck,** who plays Op. 65 on a small but hefty-toned 1961 Beckerath at the University of Richmond (Arkay 6103). She declares the works "classic in design" and states that "this conception . . . is reflected in my performances." Her playing isn't as stiff as many, but I would welcome more inflection of the tempo. The instrument has a solid chorus with good blend and warmth but not very much tonal variety. **Peter Hurford**'s earlier recording of Op. 37 and Sonatas 2, 3, and 6 at the Rieger organ in Ratzeburg Cathedral (London 444570) might be viewed as a counterpart to Beck's Op. 65. The instrument is well recorded and makes a fine sound, though I think it's too brash for Mendelssohn. Hurford's playing is reserved and formal, clearly more baroque than romantic, but not stiff or inexpressive.

The rest of the neo-Bach landscape is pretty bleak. **Marie-Claire Alain** presents Op. 37, Sonatas 1, 3, and 6, and *Andante with Variations* on a modern Danish instrument that's more suitable for Buxtehude than Mendelssohn (Erato 96957). While the larger and louder movements have a certain grandeur, the performances are generally severe in style and sluggish in tempo. The lyrical song-without-words movements have no sense of gentle flow or lilt. In **Andreas Buschnakowski**'s 1974 recording of Op. 37 and Sonatas 2 and 6 at Zwickau Cathedral, the instrument isn't pleasant; another reviewer aptly described the mixtures as "glassy" (Berlin 0021292). The playing is clean and precise, but doesn't have much personality.

Stephen Tharp plays Op. 65 on a small 1983 Casavant in Chicago (Naxos 553583). His articulation is often choppy, and there are some peculiar registrations, at times contradicting Mendelssohn's few explicit instructions. The organ's unequally tempered tuning is rather unhappy with A-flat major in Sonata 1. **Olivier Vernet** has recorded Op. 65 on a nasty-sounding modern French organ with screaming mixtures, feeble foundations, and quiet registers that sound raw and blatant (Ligia 0104004-92). Here the Werckmeister III tuning makes a bed of nails of F minor in Sonata 1. Vernet has shown exquisite artistry in some of his other recordings, but he doesn't stand a chance trying to play Mendelssohn on this instrument.   GATENS

CHORAL MUSIC

Elijah. Pastor Schubring, an old friend of the Mendelssohn family and the second man to work on the libretto for this work, wanted the composer to emphasize the "meditative" and "spiritual" aspects of the story of the fiery Old Testament prophet Elijah. Mendelssohn, who was of course as Romantic as they made them in Protestant 1845, chose instead to paint an Elijah who was rugged and determined, much to the music world's great pleasure. The Birmingham Music Festival, already responsible for giving him other commissions (including a performance, but not a premiere, of *Paulus*), was to be the host—and what a spectacle it was, with 125 in the orchestra and a chorus of 271, all under Mendelssohn's baton. He knew few successes like it, and it has remained one of the supreme oratorios of all time.

Aside from the second most important role, that of the Israelites in the guise of the chorus, *Elijah* stands or falls on the vocal largesse and characterization of the title role. Almost all recordings have at least acceptable choral work, but that's not true for the star. Most people want the English version, certainly the one Mendelssohn would have wanted English audiences to hear (though German is the original). All recordings are 2CD.

Marriner chose to divide the roles among many singers, as do other conductors, but this is really more of a gimmick than anything else. Oratorio isn't opera, after all, and we don't visualize the vocal parts in the same way, but it looks more spectacular on an album cover to load it up with names. In this case, it has to be rejected not for the number but for the low quality of the voices. Kenny is simply horrible—flabby vocalizing that doesn't even approach the acceptable—while the Elijah of Thomas Allen has no sense of what the role is about. His Elijah has fortitude and determination, more comfortable on a psychiatrist's couch than preaching zealously to the masses (Philips).

The classic **Frühbeck de Burgos** version is still the best buy on the market, currently found in EMI's "double fforte" series. Fischer-Dieskau, despite the mannerisms (and don't we wish we had more of that today!), knows the role very well; he's suitably fierce, yet submissive to the Divine will. The rest of the cast is from Heaven as well (Gwyneth Jones, Baker, Gedda), and the wide, vibrantly deep soundstage allows every exciting word of the chorus to ring out in a gorgeous sound burst. First place, beyond a doubt (♦EMI 68601).

Another opera-sized cast graces **Paul Daniel**'s version on period instruments with the unflappable Orchestra of the Age of Enlightenment.

But a miracle! *Elijah* has been so encrusted in Victorian sentiment that the pungent winds, superbly facile strings, and above all the electrifying punctuated brass, breathe new life into this score. The Edinburgh Festival Orchestra is as good as almost any, and the sound is a wonder. Terfel is the best Elijah on records by a country mile, outdistancing even Fischer-Dieskau by several fiery chariots. Fleming is wonderfully silver-voiced, resisting the temptation to overplay her role (♦Decca 455688).

If Terfel is the most rough-edged, aggressive, but true-to-form Elijah around, surely Hampson in **Robert Shaw**'s recording is the most gentlemanly, persuading the crowds by the sheer beauty of his singing. It's almost as if a master con artist were at work, Elijah as siren instead of salty ascetic. But it works very well, and Hampson must be considered a master of the role. Bonney adds a special delight to the principal soprano role, singing with her naturally airy and light voice. There is no better choral work on disc than the Atlanta Symphony Chorus—you can hear every word in a model of vocal diction. The sound is terrific too, in one of the best *Elijah*s around (♦Telarc 80389).

You notice right away how well the London Symphony Chorus sings in **Hickox**'s recording, though the sound, wide and deep, obscures a lot of detail. Hickox has a firm grip on the score, but Willard White's Elijah is uncertain and flabby, lacking focus and tonal centering, though his dramatic instincts are good. Rosalind Plowright, Linda Finney, and Arthur Davies don't rate as highly as other casts, and their vocalizations are varied and erratic. The British press loves this recording (as do many in the States, to be honest), but it's too staid and skewed in concept—not to mention the weakness of the soloists—to compete with the others (Chandos).

Conlon's reading (in German) is like getting a blast of cold water thrown in your face: this is serious stuff, so pay attention! Even his combination of great sound, sheer dramatic power, and a fine Elijah in Andreas Schmidt, can't offset the German, the lack of an audible organ, the substandard supporting cast, and the well-playing but oddly balanced orchestra. With so many diamonds to choose from, this is quartz (EMI).

Sawallisch uses maybe the largest cast on record, but to little effect. Theo Adam has a vagrantly wobbly voice, and after about 20 measures it really grates on the nerves. Ameling is always a joy to hear, but Mendelssohn's own Leipzig Gewandhaus doesn't fare well; although the largeness of the group is a pleasure, they aren't together in ensemble, lacking the cohesion and sureness of step that mark the best performances. The aural ambiance is also rather neutral and uninteresting. The sound is very good, but it's not competitive with the best, even at the two-for-one price (Philips).

Herreweghe fires a scrappy, over the edge, get-out-of-Dodge reading directly at the unsuspecting consumer. His chorus is admirable (they always are), and the soloists, though vanilla-flavored, do all right. But his aggressiveness goes beyond the fierce (perfectly acceptable in the Daniels recording), and the constant onslaught by an aural battering ram won't wear well in the long run (Harmonia Mundi). **Masur**'s Israel Philharmonic rendition is about as well done as a German *Elijah* has been. The orchestra is especially sharp, and the chorus gives a gutsy, grand, wholly satisfying sound that suits the music well. Alistair Miles is also very good in the title role, and while he won't displace Terfel or Fischer-Dieskau, he makes the role his own, as does the wonderful Donath. If you want this oratorio in German (which you shouldn't), you can't go wrong here (♦Teldec 73131, 2CD).

Paulus. Aside from the many debates about the nature and contributions of early 19th-century Protestant church music, or even the viability of the oratorio form itself, in 1836 there was little doubt that Mendelssohn scored a resounding triumph with *Paulus*. It did much to put him on the map, and the fact that subsequent generations have chosen to ignore this chorale-heavy and dramatically impotent work in no way lessens its importance for Mendelssohn in particular and music history in general. While ignored by the major ensembles today, it's still a staple of choral and oratorio societies everywhere. This heavily pietistic work is in three parts, emphasizing Paul's conversion, travels, and a general statement about the superiority of Christianity as he practiced it. Again, all recordings are 2CD.

As in his brilliant *Elijah,* **Frühbeck de Burgos** is sensational in his reissued performance, and the work can use all the help it can get, for its dramatic impulses amount to nil. The cast is as strong as they come (Fischer-Dieskau, Donath, Hanna Schwarz, Hollweg), and the 1977 recording is in full bloom, allowing the large chorus a chance to shine. If you must have this piece—and that *is* debatable—and you want the very best, this is it (♦MHS 524869, 2CD).

After the 1836 premiere, a dissatisfied Mendelssohn cut 11 numbers from the score—a fourth of the work—before deciding to publish it. **Botstein** offers a chance to hear the missing half-hour's worth of music that the composer tried to keep from you. But despite his good sense of direction, the mediocre singing of the soloists and the slovenly choral work make this one to avoid. If you simply *must* sample the missing material, it would do in a pinch (Arabesque).

Spering scores one for the periodists. His version is enhanced by knife-sharp brass and gripping strings that give *Paulus* everything it needs. Even the more dramatic parts of the score, like the stoning of Stephen (often underplayed in Victorian performances), sound exciting here. The singing is warm and lyrical, while the soloists—an unknown lot—are well suited to their roles (♦Opus 111 30135). Another period surprise comes from **Herreweghe**. What is it about Mendelssohn that responds so well to archeological treatment? I think maybe there's been an accretion of 19th-century performance practice and an unwillingness to "let loose" that's relieved by it. Surely the composer would have responded to this immaculately sung, fabulously played rendition in diamond-bright sound. Unknown soloists grace the performance, to its credit (♦Harmonia Mundi 907584).

Hampson, a rather tuxedo-and-tails Elijah in Shaw's recording, sings like an angel for **Corboz** but doesn't have all that much to do. Yakar is fine, and the chorus has all the notable Corboz trademarks, but the orchestra has some intonation problems, and even *Paulus* has more drama than Corboz can lay his hands on (Erato). **Paul Kuentz's** recording, while offering a spacious, all-enveloping acoustic and a large-sounding chorus, also tends to diffuseness and a blurred sound. There isn't enough delineation in the choral strata, and the resulting effect is a rather muddied sound that cries out for deliverance (Pierre Verany).

Rilling offers a superbly crafted, gloriously sung recording, the best of the modern versions. Andreas Schmidt is the only name among the soloists you would recognize, but all are very solid if not always inspired performers. Yet one does struggle to find inspiration in this work, and Rilling settles for beautiful singing to make up for its inherent deficiencies. His marvelous chorus and orchestra give *Paulus* more than its due, and after playing this recording three or four times you may actually find yourself starting to love it (♦Hänssler 98926).

Die erste Walpurgisnacht. Mendelssohn was fascinated by the story of a group of Druids scaring off their armed Christian pursuers by means of subterfuge. In fact, the pagans are here considered the enlightened ones, and the Christians are mired in darkness. The composer was sincere in his Christian convictions, so we must assume that he was simply responding to the Romantic notions then passing through the air like a contagion, a symptom of his time. But this remains a woefully underperformed, great romp that should be heard more often.

The young **Masur** gives an excellent performance with his Leipzig orchestra, the chorus especially lusty and white-hot in the "First Chorus of the Druid Guards and the Heathen." The orchestra is quite good—much better than the tonally lackluster, often sloppy ensemble we hear in so many of its other recordings. Rounding out the program are wonderful performances of *Fair Melusine, Calm Sea and Prosperous Voyage,* and the Trumpet Overture (♦Berlin 2057).

The usually reserved **Dohnányi** evidently found some sympathetic vibrations in Mendelssohn's pagan cantata, for he allows the Cleveland Orchestra and Chorus to really pull out all the stops. The chorus is bold and dramatic, while the soloists (Christine Cairns, Jon Garrison, Tom Krause, Jeffrey Wells) outshine the unknown locals in Masur's recording. The pacing is temperate and even, with the drama oversized and exciting. Perhaps the reason for his success is the time he spent first recording the work with the Vienna Philharmonic, now available on a budget disc attractively coupled with the first two symphonies (♦Decca 460236), though I would stick with Cleveland if you're only looking for *Walpurgisnacht*. The superb "Scottish" Symphony coupled with it makes for a most attractive release, one of the best of the Telarc/Cleveland partnership (♦Telarc 80184). Immorally, RCA has not seen fit to reissue the spectacular **Ormandy** recording from the early '70s. It has everything: superb playing, grand singing, and sound that was okay then but would surely be phenomenal now. If it gets a reprieve, don't hesitate—it's *the* one to own (RCA).

Though long available only as an import, **Flor's** version is well worth seeking out. The singing is unswervingly excellent, and Flor's pacing betrays a real sense of Mendelssohnian fleetness and lilt. This is one to search for, though not a first choice unless you're a dedicated Mendelssohn fan (♦RCA 62513). As usual, **Corboz** finds me of two minds. There is a certain attractiveness to the way he presents his choral work: sleek, a little sluggish, and uniformly stylish. But he approaches *all* music this way, and his *Walpurgisnacht* has ozone-layer string sound and sleepy tempos that do the music no justice. Mendelssohn is a composer who is easily harmed by bad performances, and this is one of them (Cascavelle).

Other choral works. There is an excellent compilation of two of the "cantata psalms," 42 and 115, by **Herreweghe**. "Ave Maria," the middle movement of Mendelssohn's Op. 23, is also given, though there was plenty of room for the whole piece. The combined choirs of the Chapelle Royal and Collegium Vocale offer a smooth, well-blended blanket of quite alluring tone in great sound in the single most recommendable disc of Mendelssohn choral music available (♦Harmonia Mundi 901272). Herreweghe's companion volume is just as well done, making these two discs the twin towers of this repertory (♦Harmonia Mundi 901142).

Corboz has been a long-time advocate of the composer's religious works, and his album of a cappella and organ-accompanied works is very fine, if a little stilted in presentation. He has the good sense to include all three movements of Op. 23, Psalms 2, 43, and 22, and the three-part *Sacred Song*. Though his soprano soloist has difficulty negotiating pitch in several spots, the choir is outstanding (♦FNAC 592298). **Jean Sourisse** and his vocal ensemble are very good, offering clear sound and excellent singing. Only a few of the selections, such as the popular "Hear My Prayer," are well known, and as with much of this music, a little goes a long way. Though not top-drawer Mendelssohn, it could fill a gap in your collection (♦Syrius 141329).

The featured work on **Rilling**'s disc is Psalm 42, maybe Mendelssohn's finest setting. Like others of this genre, it's in cantata style, with alternating soloists and chorus. This conductor is known for the coherent excellence of his ensembles, and they don't fail him here. The sound is lusciously warm and spacious, with everything heard in complete clarity. If you know and like Rilling, you'll like this recording. The couplings are the short motet *Hora est* and a superb Dvořák *Te Deum* (♦Hänssler 90307).

Martin Flamig and the Dresden Kreuz Choir offer an all-Mendelssohn choral recital that would serve as a good introduction to this music, recorded in great sound. The Motets and Op. 39 parts 1 and 2 are offered, along with two Psalms, Op. 78, and the Op. 23 *Sacred Pieces* (Capriccio). **Christopher Robinson** and the St. John's College Choir present a very Anglicanized reading of many sacred pieces in a quite reverberant acoustic. They are rather stolid and stylized, yet there's something attractive about this recording. Perhaps it's the aura of mystery that surrounds a recording with highly blurred sound, I don't know. But it's a fine disc, in a sort of disquieting way (Nimbus).

Best and his Corydon Singers don't often let you down, and they keep that track record intact in their album of varied Mendelssohn choral pieces. The sound is slightly beset by echo, in the standard Best manner, and the choral work simply has no equal. I would rate this second to Herreweghe's effort, but those wanting a bigger sound (or the illusion of it) have found their mark (♦Hyperion 66359). **Ehmann** turns in some wondrous performances of miscellaneous Mendelssohn coupled with readings of works by Albert Becker and Heinrich von Herzogenberg in "Motets of the Romantic Era." It's useful in calling our attention to others writing at the same time (♦Cantate 57681).

Ratzinger offers an album of dispirited interpretations of various choral church pieces. Not enough is made of the floating lines and inherent emotional connotations of the works. In these days of scorned and laughed-at innocence, this kind of music must have a certain force to it, and it doesn't in these hands (Hungaroton). But **Creed** and the RIAS Chamber Choir give deeply satisfying, no-frills accounts in a collection of psalms, motets, and the *Missa Brevis*. Anything more than this can destroy the music, so this must be considered a near-perfect realization (♦Harmonia Mundi 901704).   RITTER

SONGS

Mendelssohn wrote over 100 songs. Many may strike today's listener as bland though tuneful, simple, and cheerful, ignoring the darker side of the human soul, at least compared to those of Schumann and Brahms. But we should keep in mind that these songs were mostly intended for music making in the home rather than the concert hall. Though often too relentlessly upbeat, many of them are quite beautiful, and they don't deserve to be neglected. Fortunately, there are several recorded recital programs that can be recommended.

The young German baritone **Holzmair** sings these works smoothly, with excellent diction and appealing lyrical tones (♦Preiser 93368). So does the veteran **Schreier;** he's here caught in fresh, youthful voice, though he occasionally croons a bit too much (Berlin 1107). **Margaret Price** doesn't need to croon; her more powerful, even, and (to me) more appealing voice is perfectly scaled to this music (♦Hyperion 66666). She also has the best accompanist in Graham Johnson.

Admirers of **Bonney** may want to sample her disc, which includes three pretty songs by Felix's sister Fanny (Teldec). It too is a fine recital, but Bonney's diction and phrasing aren't as good as Price's and Holzmair's. More operatic interpretations of these works were recorded by the German tenor **Josef Protschka** (Capriccio); they don't seem appropriate to me.

The ubiquitous **Fischer-Dieskau** recorded two splendid discs in 1971; they may be difficult to find, but they're worth looking for (♦EMI 64827). A set recorded later found him in poor voice (Claves 9009). A recent release pairs the young soprano **Sophie Daneman** with the more experienced baritone **Nathan Berg** in seven duets as well as 19 solo songs (Hyperion). Berg does much better than his partner, who lacks his command of vocal colors and incisive diction.   MOSES

Peter Mennin (1923–1983)

Mennin was one of the most significant of the postwar generation of American symphonists. A disciple of Howard Hanson at the Eastman School of Music, he became well known as a music administrator, heading both the Peabody Conservatory and the Juilliard School of Music. Most of his works are in large-scale symphonic forms, and his concentrated, intense style derives power from his restless, driving energy. He left nine symphonies, four concertos, a number of shorter orchestral works, and some chamber music, but no operas. Mennin may not have won the Pulitzer Prize, but he did win many other awards, and his reputation and integrity as a composer are assured.

His symphonies charted a pattern of development always keenly anticipated by his admirers. As he progressed, his music became ever more dramatic and rhetorical, perhaps reaching its apogee in the explosive 7 and the dark and brooding 8, his only overtly religious piece, where each movement is framed by a quotation from the Bible. Despite this, Mennin rarely allowed programmatic elements into his music, believing strongly in the communicative power of the abstract form. Symphony 9, his next-to-last piece, has more than an element of finality about it, a sense of tragic loss borne with courage and resignation.

Mennin's music has always been well represented on discs, but three currently available are especially worthy of mention. There is an older recording of 5 conducted by **Hanson** (Mercury 432755). However, a recording of 5 and 6 by **David Alan Miller** captures the transition from the lyrical character of his early pieces to his more restless, somber mature style (Albany 260). This disc also contains the pivotal *Concertato* "Moby Dick," whose ringing fanfares and anxious interludes vividly capture the alarums and excursions so emphatically portrayed in Melville's novel. The piece is also well recorded by **Schwarz**, with 3 and 7 (Delos 3164). Symphony 3 is a splendid introduction to Mennin's work; its pulsating drive and confident "American" feel disguise its meticulous counterpoint and continuous development of material, a form perfected in the metamorphic 7 ("Variation Symphony").

One of Mennin's strengths is the magnificent arch-like structures of his slow movements; the Adagio of 9 is a fine example, and **Christian Badea**'s recording of 8 and 9 is perhaps the most important of all (New World 371). That disc includes the early *Folk Overture*, the most Hindemithian of Mennin's shorter works. Also worth considering is **Starker**'s recording of the Cello Concerto (Louisville).

I hope that before too long there will be a recording of his symphonic testament, the 1982 Flute Concerto, which may rank as his ultimate masterpiece.   JOHNSON

Gian Carlo Menotti *(b. 1911)*

Born in Italy, Menotti studied at the Curtis Institute, where he met his musical soulmate and longtime romantic partner Samuel Barber. Before he was 30, his *Amelia Goes to the Ball* was produced at the Met. The next opera, *The Island God,* didn't do as well there, but after producing *The Medium* successfully on Broadway in 1945, Menotti was off and running, having written the first opera especially for radio (*The Old Maid and the Thief*); the first opera for television, the Christmas perennial *Amahl and the Night Visitors;* a film version of *The Medium;* and two more Broadway operas in *The Consul* and *The Saint of Bleecker Street,* both of which won rave reviews and Pulitzer Prizes.

His winning streak didn't last much longer; seemingly overnight he was almost universally scorned by "progressive" musicians and critics, who regarded his music as derivative and over-sentimentalized. But *Amahl* and *The Medium* remain among the most frequently performed 20th-century operas, and a recent wave of recordings indicates a renaissance of interest in his music. If he never bothered to follow musical trends, that's no reflection on his considerable musical and dramatic gifts.

OPERAS

Amahl and the Night Visitors. The original 1951 cast of the first (and probably still the best) opera written for television is available, led by **Schippers** (RCA 6485). This touching little work has been recorded several times since (including two additional TV tapings), but the original version in many ways remains the best. There's a fine stereo recording with **Menotti** conducting Covent Garden forces (Jay 1303).

Amelia al ballo. Recorded in the '50s at La Scala under **Nino Sanzogno,** this has long been out of print (Angel 35140). **Schippers** recorded the scintillating Overture, and it's available on a mostly Barber disc (Sony 62837).

The Consul. This much-rewarded work, in which Menotti beat the odds of producing an that opera Broadway audiences would flock to, was very effective during the Korean and Cold Wars. Its theme of ordinary lives ground down by a totalitarian bureaucracy unfortunately has never gone out of style, and the score contains some of his most laconically powerful music. The original cast led by **Lehman Engel** was recorded on LP (Decca 101). After languishing for decades, two new recordings appeared almost simultaneously in the '90s. One is a disappointment, except for another star turn by Joyce Castle (Newport 85645), but **Richard Hickox** conducting a live Spoleto Festival performance is just about perfect musically and dramatically (♦Chandos 9706). The heroine's big aria "To this we've come, that men withhold the world from men"—one of Menotti's finest moments musically and dramatically—was recorded by **Eileen Farrell** in an EMI recital (Testament 1073).

The Medium. Menotti's first try at opera for Broadway (a Grand Guignol opera, at that), *The Medium* was recorded by **Lehman Engel** soon after its premiere but hasn't been put on CD (Odyssey LPs), nor has Columbia's imaginatively produced 1970 stereo LP with **Resnik** and Blegen. However, Menotti's own 1950 movie version (which also starred the original Madame Flora, **Marie Powers**) is available (VAIA 1162, video cassette VAIA 69002). There is a fine Chicago performance, with the veteran mezzo **Joyce Castle** a smashing Madame Flora (Cedille 34). "Monica's Waltz" is sumptuously sung by **Fleming** in her American opera recital disc "I Want Magic!" (London 460567).

The Old Maid and the Thief. This was recorded in the '70s for Turnabout with a young **Blegen;** that's no longer around, but **Upshaw**'s vibrant performance of the aria "What a curse for a woman is a timid man" is in the singer's debut recital (Nonesuch 79187).

The Saint of Bleecker Street (1954). This opera won Menotti his second Pulitzer Prize. It's a story of faith versus doubt made gripping by the lurid, precisely observed Little Italy setting and his tightly written score. (If Martin Scorsese ever decides to direct opera, this is the perfect place for him to start.) The original cast recording led by **Schippers** was once available on LP (RCA 2714); I hope Hickox decides to tackle this underrated gem of American opera.

Menotti wrote several more operas after *The Saint of Bleecker Street,* none of them very successful. They are a weak lot; perhaps the best are the short operas, two of them recently recorded: the Britten-like all-male one-acter with boys' choir, *Martin's Lie,* with Hickox again (Chandos 9605), and the genuinely amusing satire *Help! Help! The Globolinks,* with John DeMain (Newport 85633). Although *Le dernier sauvage* (The Last Savage), Menotti's evening-long satire of civilization and its discontents (among them television and 12-tone music), was a flop in Paris and at the Met in 1964, I wonder if it's worth another look.

ORCHESTRAL AND INSTRUMENTAL MUSIC

Menotti's not inconsiderable instrumental output includes several large orchestral works and three concertos: for piano, for violin, and for double bass. The Piano Concerto (1945) is a tuneful, charming work, sounding like Scarlatti up to date in its glittering passagework and airy orchestration. The Romanian pianist **Sari Biro** recorded it in the late '40s, with unusual concertos by Milhaud and Leo Weiner (Pearl 9280), but the one to get is **Wild**'s effervescent, brightly recorded 1961 performance with Mester and the Symphony of the Air (Vanguard 4029, with an equally lively performance of Copland's Concerto). A similarly fleet, witty style obtains in Menotti's *Ricercare and Toccata on a Theme from The Old Maid and the Thief* for solo piano, recorded by **Michael Boriskin;** the couplings, by Ruggles and Harold Shapero, may not be to every Menotti-lover's taste (New World 80402).

Menotti's 1955 Violin Concerto, weaker than the Piano Concerto but still sweetly melodic, was originally on an LP with **Tossy Spivakovsky,** Munch, and the Boston Symphony (RCA). There are current CDs by **Ricci** (♦Reference 45) and **Walter Verdehr** (Crystal 514). Both are good, though Ricci's extroverted romantic style is better suited to the music than Verdehr's slightly vinegary tone. Ricci's conductor, Keith Clark, also leads a tauter, more colorful performance. Both violinists pair this work with Barber's luscious Violin Concerto; Verdehr adds another concerto by Alexander Arutiunian. Menotti's Double Bass Concerto, another melodious charmer, hasn't yet been recorded.

Fans of ballet music will enjoy the suite from *Sebastian,* which includes a catchy little "Barcarolle" along with more dramatic moments. **Sedares** leads an excellent digital recording (Koch 7005, with Barber's *Souvenirs*), but the old **Stokowski** 1954 stereo version with the NBC Symphony is something else again, persuasive, exquisitely colored, and remarkably well recorded (♦RCA 62517, with music from Prokofiev's *Romeo and Juliet*).

One of Menotti's finest and least classifiable works is his "sung ballet" *The Unicorn, the Gorgon, and the Manticore,* a work with a touching, profound story and a gratifyingly light musical touch. As an updating of the Renaissance "madrigal comedy," it also displays his skill at writing for a small vocal and instrumental ensemble. Unfortunately, this delightful work is currently represented on CD only by a pale, leaden performance by **Donald Teeters** and the Boston Cecilia Chorus (Newport 85621). Better to look for **Schippers**'s old LP (Angel), or wait for a new recording.   RAYMOND

Saverio Mercadante *(1795–1870)*

Mercadante was one of the most important operatic composers of the early and mid-19th century. A contemporary of Bellini, Donizetti, and Rossini, he both emulated these Italian masters and advanced the art. His use of the orchestra and his experiments in modulation and harmonic relationships surpass those of all his contemporaries, and his music was a prime influence on Verdi. He composed 60 operas, some of which get a revival from time to time, but all of which have been overlooked by the commercial recording companies. Fortunately, he hasn't been overlooked by the smaller companies. Many listeners express delight with his sweeping melodies, pulse-pumping good tunes, and fervor, along with complaints about the artificiality of his dramas and their tendency toward the fustian.

ORCHESTRAL AND OTHER MUSIC

The composer of more than 60 operas, Mercadante was still interested in instrumental and orchestral music, more so than his operatic contemporaries, and although he was busy as the director of the Naples Conservatory of Music for almost 30 years, he produced many such works.

A collection of six overtures plus a particularly attractive late chamber work makes a good introduction to the orchestral Mercadante, as well as a nice complement to the operas (Bongiovanni 2144). The overtures all have their particular pleasures: Broad cantilenas, some harmonic boldness, pert woodwinds, and idyllic scenes abound. While I'm pleased with the music, I'm less pleased with the performances by the Moldavian Orchestra led by **Frontalini.** They're adequate and firmly played, but a bit lacking in propulsive power and, worst of all, recorded at a distance in a huge, empty hall (or possibly the Grand Canyon). But for now it will suffice until the music can claim the attention of someone better.

A program of orchestral rarities is an odd mixture of the sublime and the not-so sublime, with emphasis on virtuoso display, heavily influenced by vocal music (Bongiovanni 2099.) The performances by the Warmia National Orchestra, again led by **Frontalini,** are generally not the best, lacking excitement and assuredness, but they are a passable introduction to a treasury of little-known music.

Three *Sinfonie Concertanti* are for solo flute, one or two clarinets, horn, and orchestra. Much of the music is clearly inspired by vocal music; you could, except for the range, easily substitute the human singing voice for the solo instruments. In a performance led by **Claudio Felice Sedazzari,** the sound is a bit cloudy, as are the performances by the Camerata Schubert, but there's plenty of gusto (Bongiovanni 2199).

Major opera singers and conductors have yet to take up the music of Mercadante, but major flutists have. **Rampal** (Erato 55012) and **Galway** (♦RCA 7703) have recorded the same collection of three flute concertos, both with discreet accompaniment by Scimone and I Solisti Veneti. Both soloists are strong, Rampal with a more refined, thin (French) tone, faster in tempo, and Galway with a fatter, more romantic tone, the more spectacular virtuoso.

Four flute quartets from around 1830 are models of grace and elegance, with the flute substituting for a coloratura soprano. The sweet-toned flute of **Andras Adorjan** is perfect for these rapturous solos, with the Munich String Trio providing sturdy support (♦Tudor 730).

OPERAS

Il Bravo. Mercadante based this opera on, of all unlikely sources, a novel by James Fenimore Cooper, *The Bravo: A Venetian Story.* The plot is a curious combination of *La Gioconda* and *Simon Boccanegra,* with outlaw hero and despotic Council of Ten. Carlo's father has been condemned by the Council, but the sentence won't be carried out as long as Carlo obeys the Council and acts as its official assassin (The Bravo). As with all the Mercadante operas, the only recording (1990) could be better, but it makes a strong case for the opera's revival. Strong, idiomatic conducting by **Bruno Aprea** urges the performance along admirably.

Caritea, Regina di Spagna. Musically, this is one of Mercadante's best works; the plot less so. A bracing overture promises much, and a good deal of the music is bold and brash—tough Rossini, with catchy, memorable tunes. The many ensembles (duets, trios) are splendid, the act finales large-scale affairs encouraging applause. The orchestration is imaginative, with bubbly woodwinds often prevailing. While the opera itself is a musical delight, the only recording needs a bit of forbearance (♦Nuova Era 7258, 3CD). **Giuliano Carella** leads his orchestra in a free-wheeling, exciting manner, at times encouraging them beyond their capabilities. All the singers start out tentatively but quickly improve, growing in strength throughout the performance. The voices are quite distinctive, not particularly for beauty, but for individuality of timbre. It's an exciting show, well rewarding the hearer.

Elisa e Claudio. This is Mercadante's seventh opera, a two-act *melodramma semiserio,* in which true love finds a way. It was his first opera composed for La Scala, and its popularity can be judged by the large number of manuscript copies still extant. The only recording is not ideal (it also has a fair amount of cuts), but it's better than none (Melodram 27099, 2CD). Virginia Zeani has a way with Italian opera of this period; she offers a warm, committed interpretation. I could wish for a more hefty tenor sound than Agostino Lazzari's, but he's far from pale, and it's appropriate for the much put-upon Claudio. **Ugo Rapalo** seems to identify with this music and gets everybody in the mood to like it too.

Il Giuramento. The 44th of Mercadante's 60 completed operas, This opera opened at La Scala in 1837 to great acclaim and is generally considered his masterpiece. The music prefigures early Verdi: Rossinian virtuosity was banished, and success no longer depended on the talent of one extraordinary singer. Gaetano Rossi's libretto is based on Victor Hugo's play *Angelo,* a story later adapted by Boito for Ponchielli's *La Gioconda.* It's a good piece, dramatically sound if a little confused structurally, with enough memorable tunes to satisfy artists and audience.

I have long been an admirer of **Schippers,** and I have no quibbles about his leadership (Myto 906.32, 2CD). But this is demanding music, and it's often beyond the singers, and the chorus may be the worst ever to stumble across a stage. The 1951 excerpts from an RAI performance included in the set give a better idea of the work. All the voices are Italian, and they aren't particularly attractive, but they're distinctive and seem to fit the music more comfortably (Panerai in particular). Alfredo Simonetto keeps them moving along in grand style. The libretto is included.

A 1993 performance from Nantes is in better, if not ideal, sound, and it's a far better performance than the one in Spoleto (Nuova Era 7179, 2CD). The role of Elaisa calls for a dramatic coloratura, and Giovanna de Liso is bright and chirpy, lightly fluttering, easily skirting the coloratura demands. Martine Olmeda as Bianca, Elaisa's rival in love, is the best of the cast. She has a smooth, full-bodied mezzo, which grows in strength and involvement as the complex plot progresses. The role of Viscardo is a Verdian Manrico in the making, calling for lots of heft plus an extended upper range, and Giuseppe Morino tends to be nasal with a tense, tight vibrato—not the prettiest voice, but far preferable to his earlier competition. The chorus sings decently, and they and the orchestra respond to **Giuliano Carella**'s gentle pacing. The recorded sound is constricted.

A 1984 performance (Italia 82, 2CD) has Jolanta Omilian as Elaisa, a soprano with the right weight of voice for the part, sort of a proto-Verdian soprano. She has a big voice with a soft flutter to it and is certainly the best of the three sopranos reviewed in the role. **Bruno Campanella** doesn't quite master the emotional sweep of the piece; he's adequate, but no more. The Nantes performance has more Italian passion.

Orazi e Curiazi. Roman myth, legend, and history have been the source for many opera plots, and this one combines aspects of all three. It basically revolves around Camilla, an intensely dramatic role with plenty of opportunities for vocal display. In the only recording (Opera Rara 12, 3CD), Miricioiu charges through the role with searing intensity, not the most beautiful of voices, but with a dramatic involvement that sweeps all before it—a true operatic personality. **David Parry** has the Philharmonia Orchestra playing with distinction. The score is probably uncut; Opera Rara usually does things that way.

Il Reggente. This opera treats the same subject as Auber's *Gustave III* and Verdi's *Un Ballo in Maschera,* the assassination of King Gustave III of Sweden. Like Verdi, Mercadante had difficulties with the censor: Thou shalt not show the assassination of a reigning monarch on stage. Hence the locale got shifted from Sweden to 16th-century Scotland and the King became the Regent (Il Reggente) under James VI. Otherwise, the plot is pretty much the same as Verdi's. It's one of Mercadante's finest operas, vigorously effective. The only recording is vigorous, too, rather rough and ready (Myto 905.28, 2CD). There are cuts throughout, in most cabalettas and fast ensembles. Didn't conductor **Bruno Marinotti** trust his singers, or did he know just what he was doing?

La Vestale. Here we have a hit: not just good music, but also a good performance. Mercadante seems more interested in composing music for arias that portray the emotions engendered by a dramatic event than in dramatic music for that event. Moments of recognition, of dilemma, pass quickly, understated. But the arias that follow—oh yes! They are carefully crafted, congenial to the singer's voice and the listener's ear, and apropos to the emotion portrayed. It's the old story: soprano loves tenor; tenor is believed dead; she becomes a Vestal Virgin; he isn't dead, returns in triumph, they meet in Vesta's temple; the sacred flame, untended, is extinguished; she's buried alive; tenor follows shortly. Simple, plain, but a good story well told. This isn't a great opera, but one that brings much pleasure.

In the only recording (Bongiovanni 2065, 2CD), Dunja Vejzovic is the star. She has a hefty voice but enough agility to sing these decorated strains, and she performs dramatically, as if she really believes the story. The other singers perform well except for tenor Gianfranco Cecchele, who sings heartily but with little sophistication or musicality or even the slightest idea what the role is about. The chorus sounds small, but they sing exuberantly and with real musicianship. **Vjekoslav Sutej** deserves much praise for pulling the show together and speeding it along.

PARSONS

Olivier Messiaen (*1908–1992*)

For a revolutionary figure in 20th-century music, Messiaen led an outwardly uneventful life. He was born to parents of decidedly literary leaning: his father translated Shakespeare and his mother wrote poetry for Olivier while he was still in the womb. When he came out, he was a musical prodigy, determined to become a composer at age 10 after hearing Debussy's *Pelléas et Mélisande* and entering the Paris Conservatoire at 11. He made his living as an organist (he played at La Trinité in Paris for more than 40 years) and as a harmony teacher at the Conservatoire. After WWII, his reputation as teacher and composer spread, thanks in part to his famous pupils Boulez, Xenakis, and Stockhausen, and in part to the unique appeal of his music, sweet water in the desert of postwar musical systems and -isms.

The ingredients of Messiaen's music are unusual—complex Hindu and Greek rhythmic patterns, plainchant, bird songs—and the results unique. He was "difficult" and intellectual, but he also had plenty of vital juices sloshing around inside, and so does his music, which he once described succinctly as "a theological rainbow." The theology is heavily Roman Catholic, which may cause problems for some listeners; everybody can enjoy the colors in the rainbow. Assessing Messiaen in 1945, Virgil Thomson waspishly accused him of writing music calculated "to open up the heavens and to bring down the house." But Thomson also praised "a musical technique of great complexity and considerable originality," adding, "the man is a great composer. One has only to hear his music beside that of any of the standard eclectic modernists to know that. Because his really vibrates and theirs doesn't."

ORCHESTRAL MUSIC

Mahler, who thought the symphony should contain the world, might have approved of the *Turangalîla-Symphonie.* Not only does it contain the world, it throws in heaven too, taking ten long movements to do it. "Turangalîla" is Messiaen's Sanskrit neologism combining the meanings of "a hymn to joy" and "a song of love"; the inspiration is the story of Tristan and Isolde (which also figures strongly in Messiaen's vocal works *Cinq Réchants* and *Hawari*). "*Turangalîla* means all at once love song, hymn to joy, time, movement, rhythm, life and death," said the composer—and it conveys them in a musical language that generously includes tonality, atonality, modality, and serialism. Also the colors of a huge orchestra, supplemented by a hyperactive piano part and one for *ondes martenot,* an electronic instrument whose high-pitched glissandos may recall old horror-movie soundtracks to first-time listeners.

Chung's 1990 recording with the Bastille Opera Orchestra was recorded with Messiaen's participation and full approval: "These are the correct tempos, the correct dynamics, the right feelings and the right joy!" (♦DG 39929). The composer also provided a very useful analysis and program notes. The version by the Concertgebouw led by **Chailly** is disciplined and a bit chilly, but he vividly brings out Messiaen's debt to the rhythmic Stravinsky's energy and orchestral clarity (♦London 436626). The sound is topnotch, and the orchestra plays gorgeously. **Previn**'s 1978 London Symphony recording, more relaxed and even more colorful than Chailly's, still holds up wonderfully, and is tempting at a bargain price (♦EMI 69752, with Poulenc concertos for organ and for harpsichord).

Messiaen's last orchestral work, *Eclair sur l'Au-Dela* (Illuminations from the Beyond), has been recorded by Chung and his Bastille Orchestra (DG 39929). Other than its subject, there's no sign of old age about the piece. It's music of fearsome technical complexity but also great emotional and spiritual directness: a 62-minute song of joyful expectation of the hereafter, scored for a 128-piece orchestra. It abounds in long-lined string melodies, crunchy dissonances, clanging brass and percussion, complex rhythmic schemes, and bird songs in profusion, each precisely transcribed by the composer. Birds have always been symbols of joy and jubilation for Messiaen, and one entire movement is a depiction of 48 different birds happily singing away simultaneously in the Tree of Life.

Des Canyons aux étoiles is even longer than *Turangalîla,* written after a tour of the American West in the early '70s. Ostensibly a chamber work, it's perhaps more accurately described as an immense piano concerto, displaying Messiaen's usual preoccupations with nature, bird songs, and religious import. More austere than *Turangalîla,* it's probably not for Messiaen beginners. The first recording of this work, a virtuoso effort by pianist Paul Crossley, with **Salonen** conducting the London Sinfonietta, is still the best (♦Sony 44762, 2CD, with *Couleurs de la cité celeste* and *Oiseaux éxotiques*).

Another enormous orchestral work is the rarely performed *Chronochromie* (Color of Time). **Dorati** and the BBC Symphony made a very good recording in the '60s that is worth seeking out (EMI LP). **Boulez**'s recording is technically a knockout—the Cleveland Orchestra plays this fearsomely difficult work as if it were in the basic repertory, which it surely is not (DG 45827). But his icily correct interpretation, while it presents the notes immaculately (no small achievement), seems beside the point for music of such mystic exaltation (ditto *Et expecto resurrectionem mortuorum* and *Couleurs de la cité celeste,* the perfervidly Catholic works coupled with it).

Having said that, I'll concede that the more recent Boulez/Cleveland disc of *Poémes pour Mi, Sept Haïkaï,* and *Le Réveil des oiseaux* is a splendid presentation of comparatively rare Messiaen (♦DG 453478). *Poémes* (the composer's first wife was nicknamed "Mi") is early Messiaen, requiring an orchestra and soprano of Wagnerian size and heft. (Boulez's Françoise Pollet isn't quite that, but she's very good.) The technically fascinating *Haïkaï,* a surprisingly unsensual score for this composer, offers Messiaen's impressions of Japanese scenery and music; *Le Réveil des oiseaux* is one of his most ambitious and joyous fantasias on bird songs. Boulez also does very well by *Couleurs de la cité celeste* and the clangorous, eschatological wind-and-percussion piece *Et expecto resurrectionem mortuorum,* readings full of tension and color (Sony 68332).

Messiaen old and new are brought together by Chung: his very last work, *Concert à quatre,* the haunting, late salute to Mozart, *Un sourire,* and two luminous orchestral works from the '30s, *Les offrandes oubliées* and *Le Tombeau resplendissant* (DG 445947). The early orchestral piece *L'Ascension* is fervently performed by **Stokowski** in a 20th-century collection (Music & Arts 787).

CHAMBER MUSIC

An excellent introduction to Messiaen's music is also his most popular piece, and one of his very chamber music works: *Quartet for the End of Time.* This long suite for clarinet, violin, cello, and piano was written while Messiaen was a prisoner of war and was first performed in a concentration camp in 1941. Given the circumstances, it's a remarkable statement of faith and resilience, a musical evocation of passages from the *Book of Revelation* that presents many of his musical and religious preoccupations in an easily accessible way. **Tashi**'s superbly focused performance was recorded in 1976 and is still one of the best, also a mid-priced bargain (♦RCA 7835). Perhaps the very best version—if you can find it—was recorded in 1968 by violinist **Erich Gruenberg**, de Peyer, William Bleeth, and Béroff (EMI 63947, with the short flute-and-piano

work *Le Merle Noir*). Other worthy performances (also at mid-price) are by a foursome featuring **Barenboim** (DG 23247) and by the **Walter Boeykens Ensemble** (Harmonia Mundi 7901348).

PIANO MUSIC

Messiaen's large catalogue of piano music is a treasure chest that more and more adventurous pianists are interested in exploring. Much of it is beautiful, but in some ways Messiaen in black and white is more difficult to listen to without the sauce of orchestral color. The best starting points might be some of the shorter pieces in the *Catalogue d'oiseaux,* or perhaps the fairly early *Visions de l'Amen,* a pleasing conflation of religiosity and sweetly complicated harmony.

Hakan Austbø's recordings of *Catalogue d'oiseaux* (♦Naxos 553532-34, 3CD) and *Régards sur l'Enfant Jesus* (♦Naxos 550829) are easily among the very best, and bargain-priced too. If you want to dip a toe into the river of Messiaen's piano music, try Austbø's collection of pieces that demonstrate many of the composer's musical proclivities: *Preludes,* the complex *Four Rhythmic Etudes,* and *Canteyodjaya* (Naxos 554090). **Béroff** is a sure bet in Messiaen (and just about any French music), and his *Vingt Regards* and the early, impressionistic *Preludes* remains a highlight in the Messiaen discography (EMI 7691612, 2CD). **Peter Hill**'s '80s recordings of *Catalogue d'oiseaux* were made under Messiaen's supervision and still sound very impressive (Unicorn 9062, Books 1–3; 9075, 4–6;9060, 7 and the supplement, *La fauvette des Jardins*).

The popular *Visions de l'Amen* are much recorded; Messiaenites rejoiced at the reissue of the classic 1975 recording by **Peter Serkin** and **Yuji Takahashi** (♦RCA 68907), but there are other highly recommended versions, too: from the source, with **Loriod** and **Messiaen** (Adès 203142), a softer-edged, beautifully recorded version by **Double Edge** (New Albion 45), a powerful one by **Uriarte** and **Mrongovius** (Wergo 6227), and a very satisfactory recording by **Argerich** and **Rabinovitch** (EMI 54050).   RAYMOND

ORGAN MUSIC

The organ was Messiaen's instrument. He was appointed organist at La Sainte-Trinité in 1931, where the special sonorities of the Cavaillé-Coll instrument were to become a miniature orchestral palette in his hands. Aside from each organ's unique sound and resonance, Messiaen wanted an instrument that could overwhelm the listener when necessary. The performances listed below accomplish that end.

Three collections of the complete organ works (1928-1984) deserve mention. **Jennifer Bate, Naji Hakim,** et al. set the standard (♦Jade 29491, 7CD). Performed by leading interpreters on the La Trinité organ, this set has the excitement and authenticity we seek. The sound is glorious, and listeners can enjoy the talents of six different artists. Ample liner notes aid the listener. This is my personal favorite. A close runner-up is **Gillian Weir,** who selected the large, 4-manual Frobenius organ in Arhus Cathedral, Denmark (♦Collins 70312, 7CD). Recorded in 1994, these are significant, insightful interpretations. **Hans-Ola Ericsson** is another Nordic contender, at Lulea Cathedral, Sweden (♦BIS, various numbers, 7CD). The playing is topnotch, with superb engineering and clarity.

In 1956, **Messiaen** recorded his own works at La Trinité (EMI 767400, 4CD). These historic recordings allow the listener to hear the composer at his favorite instrument. There is some fuzzy recording noise, but the interpretations should appeal to any Messiaen fan. Another older recording is by **Louis Thiry** in 1972 in St. Pierre, Geneva (Calliope 9926-28). Messiaen was effusive in his praise for Thiry, but these performances are a bit uneven.

For *Meditations,* both **Ericsson** (BIS 464) and **Christopher Bowers-**

Broadbent (♦ECM 1494) provide outstanding interpretations with excellent engineering. *Nativity* is a very popular work from 1935 and there are many good recordings, among them **Erik Bostrom**'s (Proprius 9009-15). Unfortunately you may have to buy the complete set. **Susan Landale** is wonderful in a 1986 recording from St. Vincent-de-Paul (♦ADDA 581039). *Ascension* is another early work in four movements, and **Almut Rossler** handles the challenges nicely (♦Koch 315024). *Mass of the Pentecost* gets a solid performance from **Rudolf Innig** at the 3-79 Fischer-Kramer organ in St. Bonifacius, Lingen; high marks in every category (MD+G 0622).

Probably the best one-disc sampler is from **Jean-Paul Imbert** (♦Skarbo 3925). It contains fine interpretations of *Diptyque, Celestial Banquet, Apparition of the Eternal Church, Children of God,* and *God Among Us,* all performed on the impressive instrument in St. Eustache, Paris. METZ

CHORAL MUSIC

Petites liturgies de la Présence Divine, three pieces for women's chorus and a glittering, percussion-heavy orchestra (*ondes martenot* prominent), was one of Messiaen's first compositions to get a hearing outside France; this was the piece that led Virgil Thomson to call Messiaen a great composer, and Ned Rorem to compare his music to a giant gold-plated nun. It must have sounded startling in the '40s and is still stimulating in its noisy religiosity. **Nagano** offers an excellent account (Erato), and **Bernstein**'s Columbia recording from the '60s "really vibrates," as Thomson would put it; this is the only Messiaen piece he recorded. It has been reissued in the "Bernstein Century" series with music by Feldman and Ligeti, among others, that resonates very well with Messiaen (Sony 61845).

La Transfiguration de Notre Seigneur Jesus-Christ is the closest this God-intoxicated composer came to writing an oratorio; the immense forces required for its 14 movements are marshaled very well by the Netherlands Radio Choir and Symphony under **Reinbert de Leeuw** with the indispensable Yvonne Loriod (Montaigne 782040). The digital recording encompasses the huge forces very effectively.

Messiaen's output of a cappella choral music consists of two pieces, the luminous *O Sacrum Convivium!* (the exclamation mark is *so* like the composer), and the enthrallingly complex *Rechants,* made-up language and all. They're surprisingly little recorded, so it's good to report that splendid performances of both, as well as music by Xenakis and Stockhausen, are available in "Messiaen and his Students," with the **Danish Radio Choir** (Chandos 9663).

OPERA

There are several nominees for the Messiaen *magnum opus,* but the enormous opera, *François d'Assise,* is surely a front-runner. The 1988 Paris Opera premiere with van Dam, **Ozawa** conducting, was recorded (Cybelia 833); there is also a disc of four scenes from the opera with **Fischer-Dieskau** from the 1985 Salzburg Festival (Orfeo 485982). But they have been superseded by **Nagano**'s stupendous recording of the entire opera, also recorded at the Salzburg Festival (DG 445176, 4CD). Van Dam offers his magisterial and beautifully sung performance of Francis, and the supporting cast includes a luminous Upshaw as the Angel. Is this enormous work, a series of scenes from the life of St. Francis, a "real" opera or a religious oratorio? Time and further performances will tell, but this recording reveals it as a unique and essential musical experience—like so much of Messiaen.

SONGS

All of Messiaen's music for voice and piano (there are some *mélodies,* but the term hardly describes the sprawling cycles *Hawari* and *Chants de terre et de ciel*) is collected on a set by the excellent team of **Michèle Command** and pianist Marie-Madeleine Petit (EMI 64092, 2CD). *Poèmes pour Mi,* covered in the orchestral section, is also available in a recording by **Bryn-Julson** and Mark Markham, strained and less satisfying as a performance than the Boulez-Pollet version, but interesting if you'd like to compare the composer's first and second thoughts (Music & Arts 912). RAYMOND

Giacomo Meyerbeer (1791–1864)

Meyerbeer is noted primarily as an opera composer, though he also wrote orchestral music. His early operas are in Italian in a style derived from Rossini, but his reputation rests squarely on his later six French operas (1831–64). With *Robert le diable,* he established the model for French grand opera: lengthy works with spectacular stage effects, set in exotic locales and historical periods, lots of ballet, highly charged emotions in the romantic vein, with an interest in the supernatural and the macabre. The principal roles call for heroic vocal acrobatics and are now difficult to cast. Immensely popular during his lifetime (an influence on Berlioz, Verdi, and Wagner) and for 70 years thereafter, Meyerbeer's operas fell into neglect and even disrepute as scholars and musicians disdained them as superficial and hyperinflated behemoths. They are now occasionally revived, usually with stellar casts, but have failed to reestablish their popularity or the composer's reputation. His operas have rarely been recorded in the studio and recordings are mainly derived from stage productions and radio broadcasts.

L'Africaine was Meyerbeer's last opera. The composer died while it was in rehearsal and it wasn't produced until the following year, with some uncertainties about his intentions. It's an exotic tale, with the Portuguese navigator Vasco da Gama led by an African woman to discover a sea route to India.

Muti leads a highly cut but strong 1971 performance in Italian (Memories 4213, 3CD). **Norman** is an ideal heroine, closely seconded by Veriano Luchetti. A 1972 performance from San Francisco with **Verrett** and Domingo as the compelling protagonists is attractive (♦Opera d'Oro 1185; Gala 100605, both 2CD; Legato 116, 3CD; also available on video). A 1977 Barcelona performance, sung in Italian and highly cut, is anything but authentic in style, but does offer much pleasurable singing from **Caballé** and Domingo (Legato 208, 2CD).

The last of Meyerbeer's pre-Paris Italian operas, *Il Crociato in Egitto* has few French musical effects. It was much altered to suit later casts and became known only in adulterated versions, yet it established his international reputation.

A 1990 recording presented Meyerbeer's original conception of the work as reconstructed from manuscript (♦Opera Rara 10, 4CD). Diana Montague bravely attempts the castrato role; it lies awkwardly for the soprano voice, but she presents a brave and noble sound. Kenny is much more at ease and technically secure in Palmide's flights of coloratura, and Della Jones is a sturdy Felicia. This was one of Bruce Ford's earliest recordings and he makes a remarkable debut; his voice is not only beautiful, but capable of clarion outbursts of excitement and power with great coloratura skill. The Royal Philharmonic is augmented with two stage bands capably led by **David Parry.**

In *Dinorah* Meyerbeer backed away from French grand opera style, composing more of an *opéra-comique* in a lighter dramatic and musical vein. Originally called *Le Pardon de Ploermel,* it was the last of his operas to be premiered during his lifetime. Its plot is unbelievably foolish, but there is much lovely music in it and a chance for coloratura soprano display. The only recording is a 1979 performance with a strong cast led by the light-voiced Deborah Cook as the appealing heroine (♦Opera Rara 5, 3CD). She gets strong support from Della Jones and Marilyn Hill Smith as the twin goatherds. Alexander Oliver is an attractive hero as well, joined by Christian du Plessis for some sturdy duets. **James Judd** is the sympathetic conductor.

L'Etoile du nord is the second of Meyerbeer's *opéra-comiques*. There was an excellent 1975 performance with **Janet Price** that hasn't been issued on CD (Opera Rara LP). A fine 1996 performance from the Wexford Opera Festival has been preserved, though it lacks the spectacular singing Meyerbeer would have expected (Marco Polo 223429, 3CD). **Elizabeth Futral** is a pleasure, but Vladimir Ognev as Peter the Great is not; the rest of the cast is solid.

Les Huguenots is the second (and most popular) of Meyerbeer's French operas. It is a love story set against the background of the St. Bartholomew's Day Massacre of French Protestants (the Huguenots). Containing seven major roles of heroic musical difficulties and proportions, the opera demands extraordinary singers. When produced, it was frequently billed as a "Night of Seven Stars."

A 1955 Milan Radio performance is troubled by the too-late-in-his-career Lauri-Volpi (Memories; Hunt; 3CD). However, the other three men (Taddei, Zaccaria, Tozzi) are excellent. The women are a vocally troubled lot. **Serafin** is the knowledgeable conductor, but Act V is omitted along with other cuts. If ever there was a "Night of Seven Stars" in recent times, it was the 1962 performance at La Scala (Melodram 37026; G.O.P. 701; Gala 100604; 3CD). Sung in Italian, with some major cuts and a lack of authentic style, it enlisted the musical services of Sutherland, Corelli, Ghiaurov. Simionato, Cossotto, Ganzarolli, and Tozzi. Spectacular singing all around, with **Gavazzeni** as the sympathetic conductor.

A 1971 Vienna performance by Radio Austria led by **Märzendorfer** features Gedda's estimable Raoul (♦Myto 961.141, 2CD). Of all the tenors to attempt the role in recent years, only Gedda has the necessary qualitites: a sound and florid technique combined with a wide range of interpretive nuances. His colleagues aren't up to his standards, but they make a generally good impression. Enriquetta Tarrès is shy on excitement, but sounds attractive as Valentine. The coloratura of Rita Shane is borderline astonishing with its variations on Meyerbeer's music; Jeanette Scovotti is oddly cast as Urbain, but competes with Shane in the coloratura embroidery department. Diaz sounds too youthful for Marcel but sings all the notes, and Dimiter Petkov is only a serviceable St. Bris. The performance is mutilated by heavy cuts.

Sutherland recorded the opera almost complete in the studio in 1970 (Decca 430549, 4CD). But Anastas Vrenios is inadequate as Raoul—a small voice with limited range and power and no hint of authority. Arroyo sings a lovely Valentine, but Tourangeau is troubled by the vocal intricacies of Urbain's music. Dominic Cossa and Ghiuselev are the bland Nevers and Marcel, but Bacquier is an imposing St. Bris. **Bonynge** conducts.

Almost by default, the 1989 recording from Opéra de Montpellier is the best (♦Erato 45027, 3CD). It's practically complete and in French. Richard Leech is a magnificent Raoul. Françoise Pollet does well by Valentine, but Ghylaine Raphanel (Marguerite) is shrill and Danielle Borst (Urbain) barely has the notes needed. Gilles Cachemaille is a splendid Nevers, Boris Martinovich a reliable St. Bris, and Ghiuselev is a crusty, somewhat rusty Marcel. **Cyril Diederich** leads the lively performance.

Le Prophète contains one of the most difficult tenor roles in the repertoire (Jean de Leyden, "Le Prophète"). There have been only two recordings of the opera, one from the stage, one from the studio. Gedda is the spectacular protagonist of a 1970 broadcast on RAI Turin (Laudis 2035; Foyer 2035; Myto 90318; Rodolfo 32687; 3CD). His Jean is confident, strong, with beautiful tenor tone. Horne is an athletically agile, dramatic Fidès. Margherita Rinaldi is a pleasant, acceptable Berthe, Alfredo Giacomotti and Robert El Hage less so. **Henry Lewis** conducts strongly.

In a 1976 recording that followed performances at the Met, Mc-Cracken has difficulty with the notes and must make compromises to produce them, though his Fidès is strong (♦Sony 79400, 3CD). Scotto is the preferred Berthe, soaring her way through the musical difficulties. Bastin and Hines are the powerful bass contingent. **Lewis** again conducts. There are some sonic difficulties—balances are uneven.

Robert le diable was Meyerbeer's first French opera and established the model of French grand opera, though unusually, the bass has the principal role (Bertram) rather than the tenor. A 1968 performance from the Maggio Musicale Fiorentino is in Italian and highly cut, but has some very impressive singing by Scotto, though Merighi finds the going heavy in the title role. Christoff is an inadequately prepared Bertram, and Stefania Malagù is only an adequate Alice. **Sanzogno** is the heavy-handed conductor (Melodram 37024; Hunt 549; Arkadia; 3CD).

A 1985 Paris performance in French and with most of the music gives a better impression of the opera (♦Legato 229, 3CD). Vanzo lacks some of the brilliant top notes needed for Robert, but his beautiful voice and dramatic sensibilities prevail. June Anderson is in excellent voice, singing a beautiful Isabelle, with Michèle Lagrange a pleasant Alice. Ramey has the perfect voice for Bertram, handsomely sung, suave and debonair. **Thomas Fulton** is in full control of the musical forces.

PARSONS

Nikolai Miaskovsky *(1881–1950)*

Miaskovsky affects the listener somewhat like Brahms. He doesn't try to impress you with colorful orchestration or catchy tunes, though both occur naturally in his music. He thinks in counterpoint like Bach and loves rich, ambiguous chords that roam uneasily from place to place and back again. Once you have discovered the underlying conviction and emotional depth of his thought, you may feel, as I do, that his music is second only to that of Prokofiev and Shostakovich in 20th-century Russia.

SYMPHONIES

Miaskovsky is best known for his 27 symphonies, but they haven't all appeared in the West and those that have tend to disappear rapidly. Even 21, the only one blessed with a long shelf life, is only available in a single version at present. Miaskovsky was unwilling or unable to produce music that even pretended to glorify the Soviet way of life, yet his work was too important to be ignored. Therefore, over the years, recordings were made of most of the symphonies; 4, 13, 14, 20, and 26 have never reached the West and remain a mystery to those of us without access to the scores. This article omits reference to works not presently listed as available.

1 (1908). Stylistically, Miaskovsky began composing from a strongly contrapuntal outlook. 1 begins with a fugue, though it breaks away from the structure into a more overtly emotional style in a sonata-Allegro based on the same subjects. It's not perhaps the best introduction to his music, enjoyable for the converted but a mite turgid and unvaried in texture. **Rozhdestvensky**'s recording is a little harsh in sound but welcome for filling a long-empty gap in the discography (Russian Disc 11008). Revelation 10069 contains what appears to be the same reading reproduced a little more clearly on both the high and low end; in fact, the Revelation discs seem a bit enhanced in both directions, not a bad thing in music as thick as this.

2 (1910). Miaskovsky learned fast. 2 is energetic and powerful, deeply felt and unashamedly tragic. The first of its three movements ends with a brilliantly balanced downward and upward meshing of orchestral forces, while the symphony ends with a deliberately unsettling anticlimax that presages a number of throwaway endings in subsequent works. The material is memorable and the only recording comes from the same forces and occasion as 1 (Revelation 10068). If these were public performances, as the advertising suggests, there is no audience to be heard and the playing is very fine.

5 (1918–19). Miaskovsky remarked of 5 that it was in the nature of a rest after the gloomy 4. It's full of tunes so memorable and haunting that it has become one of his most popular works and is a good introduction to the composer. There is a fine performance by the BBC Philharmonic led by **Edward Downes** (Marco Polo 223499), beautifully recorded and lacking only the fearless brass of the USSR Radio and TV Symphony with **Konstantin Ivanov** (Melodiya 3019, NA). A concert performance by **Rozhdestvensky** rushes the first movement to the point of incomprehensibility and hurries the entire symphony too much (Revelation). Wait for a reappearance of the Ivanov, which was also better recorded.

6 (1922–23). This symphony was written when Miaskovsky felt pressure from within and without to make a statement concerning the Russian revolution. The liner notes for **Kondrashin**'s 1959 performance are almost worth the investment in themselves for the story they tell, explaining why this work turned out the way it did (Russian Disc 15008). Instead of glorifying the revolution, this harrowing but very moving symphony ends with a choir lamenting those fallen in battle and makes its points with the French revolutionary tunes "Ca Ira" and "La Carmagnole" as well as the *Dies Irae*. **Stankovsky** (Marco Polo) is only adequate, **Veronika Dudarova** (Olympia) is better, but Kondrashin is incandescent. The sound is good monaural.

7 (also 1922–23). This symphony is in one movement with intervening sections separating treatments of the opening material, a strange passage in two simultaneous tonalities that sometimes blend, sometimes fight bitterly, as is Miaskovsky's wont. Of all his "modern" symphonies, this is the most impressive, concise, chilling, and moving. There is only one CD now, the Slovak Philharmonic with **Michael Halasz** (Marco Polo 223113), though the USSR Symphony led by **Leo Ginsburg** (Melodiya 163) was available until recently. As usual, the Russian version is more passionate, Halasz's reading more smoothly played and more richly recorded. The latter takes nearly three minutes longer, a telling point in a short symphony.

Symphonies 8, 9, 10, and *12* are only available presently from Marco Polo, while *11* was recorded by **Dudarova** on a Melodiya LP that should be another prime candidate for reissue. The style of these four symphonies grows increasingly spare and shows the composer approaching his unusual brand of neoclassicism. There's a feeling resembling late Sibelius in these works that would not have endeared them to the Soviets but makes them quite special. The Marco Polo readings are all beautifully recorded, though the performances tend to be somewhat lacking in fervor compared to the white-hot intensity of the Russians.

15 (1933–34). By this time, Miaskovsky had reached an effective new mode of expression. The nervous energy has become less hesitant and the dissonance content is down, but every melody in this formally conventional four-movement work is expressive and beautiful, resulting in the most consistently appealing symphony since 5. The model appears to be Tchaikovsky, whose style is suggested particularly in the lovely waltz-scherzo. **Kondrashin** gives a fine performance that has been around since the late 70s in one form or another (Audiophile 101503).

19 (1939). This work is written for concert band and, like 18, is one of Miaskovsky's most public-spirited pieces, at least in its outer movements. Its tender slow waltz of a scherzo with its bucolic interruptions and its slow movement were later transcribed by the composer for string orchestra as Op. 46a, in which form they have also been recorded, most recently by the Kremlin Chamber Orchestra led by **Rachlevsky** (Claves). I'm not convinced by the string version, but the music is attractive in either form. Two recordings exist, by **Nikolai Sergeyev** (Russian Disc 007, with 1) and by Rozhdestvensky (Chandos 9444, in a miscellaneous program of Russian band music). The former is one of their better-sounding recordings, performed with sensitivity.

21. This was, until recently, the only symphony you could count on finding on recordings. It's an attractive piece in one movement, a slow introduction of mysterious lyricism leading into a typically nervous sonata-allegro that dissipates back into the mists of the introduction in about 15 minutes. The only recording now available is played well by **David Measham** (Unicorn 2066).

22 (1941). This piece is Miaskovsky's big statement on WW II, a large three-movement work lasting 45 minutes. It concerns itself primarily with the dark side of war, but manages to rouse itself for a relatively positive finale ending with the requisite thumping of tubs. There's some fine music along the way as well. **Svetlanov**'s recording has been in and out of print since its LP appearance in the mid-'80s (Revelation 10068).

OTHER ORCHESTRAL MUSIC

Silence (1909) is a long, oppressive orchestral tone poem based on Poe's *The Raven*. It's a powerful piece in a mood rather like Rachmaninoff's *Isle of the Dead,* though without benefit of the *Dies Irae* the thematic material is a little amorphous. What is attractive about it is the unexpected way color effects take over the texture from the material. *Silence* is particularly rich in mysterious orchestral shimmers. **Stankovsky** gives a well-detailed though rather under-energetic performance (Marco Polo 223302).

Between 1928 and 1931 Miaskovsky wrote no symphonies, concentrating on smaller-scaled works and consolidating his earlier compositions. Op. 32 contains a Serenade for Chamber Orchestra, a Sinfonietta for Strings, and a *Lyric Concertino.* These compositions are attractive but odd, neoclassical and baroque in their rhythmic elements but complicated by a harmonic density suggesting more emotional depth than Miaskovsky wants to follow up on. *Lyric Concertino* is more settled, a lovely pastoral sandwich with a dark, moody slow movement for filling. These works have had a few recordings dating all the way back to 78s for the Sinfonietta, but at present the lone release is a good performance by **Samoilov** (Olympia 528).

*Greetings (*or *Salutatory) Overture* is another orchestral work from 1939, included on Olympia 528 with the Op. 32 chamber orchestra compositions. There has been some mystery about this overture since Stalin became a non-person, but the truth appears to be that it was commissioned by Soviet radio for his 60th birthday. Despite its political implications of conformity, this is a satisfying piece of relatively non-bombastic character. Sinfonietta Op. 68 (1945) is primarily a reworking of earlier material, moody and beautiful. The Kremlin Chamber Orchestra with **Rachlevsky** was favorably reviewed (Claves 9415). The Dalgat String Ensemble under **Roland Melia** is smooth and touching, well recorded (Naxos 550953).

CONCERTOS

Cello. This beautifully pastoral concerto has been championed by **Rostropovich** and is available in "The Russian Years" (EMI, 12CD). More recently it has been tackled by **Maisky**, whose romanticism, though admirable, is not quite poised enough for the job (DG). **Lloyd Webber** turns in one of his most effective performances (Philips 434106, NA). **Marina Tarasova** matches neither; her double stops are poor and she hasn't enough energy for the rapid parts of the second movement (Olympia).

Violin. In 1938 Miaskovsky wrote this lyrical piece for **Igor Oistrakh**, who recorded it with Alexander Gauk (Pearl 9295). This ancient and grainy recording is all that is presently available.

CHAMBER MUSIC

Quartets. Miaskovsky's 13 string quartets would make him an important composer even if he had written no symphonies. The **Taneyev Quartet** has recorded all of them in musical if somewhat variable performances, intonationally speaking (Russian Disc, 6CD). A strong identification with the style goes a long way, however, and there are no real competitors, present or past. The recordings are somewhat strident in the high frequencies, but that can be remedied at your console.

Cello sonatas. The only other chamber works recorded are two cello sonatas, one early, one late. Sonata 1 is a fine work in one movement alternating slow and fast material in an attractive and well-integrated way. **Truls Mørk** and Thibaudet played it with wit and warmth (Virgin 45119, NA). Sonata 2 is a warmly romantic work, bearing signs of Stalin's objection to anything dissonant but beautiful nonetheless. Both sonatas and the Cello Concerto are played by **Marina Tarasova** and Alexander Polezhaev in a lugubrious and technically undistinguished manner (Olympia). Rostropovich has recorded all the above in fine commercial recordings (NA); concert recordings of Sonata 2 and the concerto may be found in "The Russian Years" (EMI, 12CD).

PIANO MUSIC

All nine sonatas appear on 3CD sets played by **Hegedüs** (Marco Polo) and **McLachlan** (Olympia 704). Hegedüs offers well-thought-out performances, but the youthful McLachlan has the edge for drama and includes a significant number of extras, including *Reminiscences* and *Yellowed Leaves,* a considerable Sonatina, and the Prelude and Sonata-Rondo, as well as a transcription of the scherzo from Quartet 5. Other outstanding recordings of Sonatas 2–4 have existed and may resurface. **Richter**'s fine Sonata 3 may be found in two different performances, from the early '60s (Melodiya 49470) and from 1973 (Pyramid 13503).

MOORE

Darius Milhaud *(1892–1974)*

"I am a Frenchman from Provence and by religion a Jew" is the famous opening sentence of Milhaud's autobiography, *Notes Without Music.* This admirably direct statement sums up two of his musical inclinations: much of his music exhibits a sunny and relaxed Mediterranean quality, and a fair amount of it is inspired by Jewish traditions and ceremonies. But in Milhaud's 60-year career and 400-plus works, this composer's inspirations also included jazz, Brazilian pop songs and tangos,

Renaissance and Baroque melodies, folk songs, and the calculated simplicities of Erik Satie. The list, as Milhaud was only too happy to admit, includes almost nothing Germanic, unless you count a late-in-life flirtation with serial technique.

Added to this musical stew is a healthy handful of dissonant spice, ensured by Milhaud's interest in polytonality. This procedure gives his music its pungent, immediately recognizable sound. Milhaud's lesser pieces *can* be notes without music, turgid and unfocused; sometimes three keys are two too many. But his best works are more like a delightful wine with a complicated bouquet. He has as wide a stylistic and emotional range as any 20th-century composer, from winningly witty and subtle, as in much of the chamber music, to stunningly energetic and powerful, as in the polytonal clashes of *Les Choéphores* or the famous jazz fugue in *La Création du Monde.*

ORCHESTRAL MUSIC

To most music lovers, Milhaud is the composer of three extroverted, deservedly popular scores: *La Création du Monde, Le Boeuf sur le toit,* and *Suite provençale. La Création,* written for the Swedish Ballet and first performed in Paris in 1923, makes assiduous use of Milhaud's close study of jazz bands in America and Europe. It's his best-known concert work and still the most sophisticated example of "jazz at the symphony" (although Milhaud's precisely balanced chamber ensemble is no jazz band, even with saxophone and percussion added). *Le Boeuf sur le toit* (The Bull on the Roof), a toe-tapping medley of South American tunes set to a bizarre scenario by Cocteau, sounds as fresh now as it did in 1921. *Suite provençale* was long thought to be based on melodies by the 18th-century composer André Campra, but it seems Milhaud made them up, along with their sunshiny settings for orchestra. Written in the dark times of 1937, this work's uncomplicated Frenchness was almost an act of patriotism.

If the conductor can swing at all, *La Création* is irresistible. **Milhaud** recorded it in 1932, a good performance and a valuable example of French wind and brass playing between the wars (♦Pearl 9459 and ♦EMI 54604). There's also a later Milhaud performance in stereo (Charlin 2516). EMI's "Composers in Person" is the basic Milhaud disc; besides *La création* it includes his stereo recordings from the '50s of *Boeuf, Suite provençale,* and *Saudades do Brasil.* He was a rough-and-ready but persuasive conductor of his own music, and these recordings are still fun. Pearl offers rarer repertory: Milhaud conducting his Piano Concerto 1 (with Marcelle Meyer), *Printemps* (a violin concerto, though not in name), and a bit of the charming ballet score *Les Songes,* as well as a few examples of Honegger conducting Honegger.

As for the many other recordings of *La création,* **Bernstein** takes the cake, whether as a student at Tanglewood in the '40s (RCA 68101, with Stravinsky's Octet and *Histoire du soldat*), an up-and-coming contender in 1951 with the Columbia Symphony (Sony 60695, part of an entertaining collection of Lenny *à la française*), or as a graying eminence in the '70s with the French National Orchestra (♦EMI 47845, with an equally entertaining *Boeuf*). **Munch** led a robust and refined Boston Symphony performance with beefed-up strings (RCA 60585, with a rousing *Suite provençale*). **Nagano**'s version is among the best, jazzy but elegant; it's paired with a good if episodic *Boeuf* and an unexpected bonus in Milhaud's Harp Concerto, one of a seemingly infinite number of pleasing concertos this composer concocted (♦Erato 45820).

Dorati's jolly *Boeuf* is one of the better-sounding "Living Presence" CDs. It includes the original couplings: an admirably po-faced performance of Satie's *Parade* and lively short works by Auric and Françaix (♦Mercury 434335). And while the disc is very short, **Arthur Weisberg**'s

1973 pairing of *La Création* with Kurt Weill's *Threepenny Opera Suite* shows off some of the sharpest New York studio musicians of the period (Nonesuch). Milhaud also arranged this popular work for the unlikely combination of violin and orchestra, with Honegger contributing a cadenza; it was recorded in 1980 by **Kremer** (Philips LP, NA).

Milhaud wrote many other short orchestral works. The composer's friend and champion **Abravanel** in 1979 recorded *Protée*, a suite of his notably noisy incidental music for a satirical play by Claudel, and the light, tuneful ballet *Les Songes* (Angel LP, unfortunately NA). Abravanel's excellent performance of the 1917 ballet *L'Homme et son désir* (sort of a *La Création* with South American rhythms), one of Milhaud's most bizarre and original works, has been reissued, along with the 1963 choral symphony *Pacem in Terris* (1963), a setting of passages from Pope John XXIII's encyclical on world peace—proof of Milhaud's ecumenical outlook in all things (Vanguard).

He wrote 12 symphonies, or 18 if you count the six *Little Symphonies*, sparky little works from 1917–22 that average six or seven minutes apiece and are scored for some odd but flavorful chamber combinations. **Milhaud** himself recorded all six in the 1960s, and they're available in a valuable set of works familiar and strange—as good and cheap an introduction to his music as any, though it doesn't include *La création* (♦Vox 5109, 2CD).

The "real" symphonies began in 1939, the year of his arrival in the US, with a commission for the Chicago Symphony; 2, for Boston, soon followed. It takes a couple of hearings for these densely written works to click, but when they do they are revealed as melodious, bracing compositions that cover a surprisingly wide emotional range. **Milhaud** recorded both in the '50s, 1 for Columbia, 2 for Angel. Those LPs are long gone, and these works waited until 1992 for a recording by **Plasson** (♦DG 435437). Plasson also recorded Symphony 6 (which has a magical opening movement marked *"Calme et tendre",* evanescent as a dream) and Symphony 7 (DG 439939, NA in the US). Milhaud's 1968 stereo recordings of Symphony 4, a noisy commemoration of the 1848 Revolution, and 8, an appealing salute to the Rhone River inspired by Smetana's *Moldau,* are available (Erato 45841).

Almost all the symphonies have been recorded by **Alun Francis** (CPO, various numbers). The disc containing 10, 11, and 12, all products of the early '60s, is typical; you'll never mistake the Basel Radio Orchestra for the Fabulous Philadelphians, but the performances are sympathetic and well recorded, and the music, if uneven, has moments of infectious liveliness and piercing sweetness (as usual, the slow movements of all three symphonies are gems).

CONCERTOS

Milhaud's output of concertos includes some unusually pleasing works. Among available CDs, **Claude Helffer**'s collection of piano and orchestra works (Piano Concertos 1 and 4, *Ballade,* five Etudes, and the delightful *Carnaval d'Aix*) shows the composer in a wonderfully varied light; *Ballade* is a lyrical piece with more than a touch of polytonal vinegar, and the Etudes must have been considered the last word in "crazy modern music" in 1920 (♦Erato 45992). In contrast, the two concertos on this disc show a thoroughly professional composer tailoring his music to the talents of a soloist; Marcelle Meyer's light, clear touch in Concerto 1 (a relatively simple work from 1934, with characteristic touches of imagination—for example, the beginning of the 'Barcarolle' is scored for B-flat, E-flat, and bass clarinets—and the knuckle-busting virtuosity of Sadel Zkolowsky in the scintillating, almost Lisztian 4. The equally pleasing Concerto 2 is available in the Vox Box mentioned earlier, in a

performance by **Johannesen**. (Milhaud's piano concertos are models of concision; each clocks in at well under 15 minutes.)

Apart from *Le Carnaval d'Aix,* Milhaud's most familiar concertante work is probably his Cello Concerto 1. **Rostropovich**'s fine recording is coupled with Honegger's delectable Cello Concerto and a work by the Welsh composer Alun Hoddinott (♦Erato 45489). Milhaud also wrote an utterly delightful *Suite Cisalpine,* on Swiss-French folk tunes, for cello and orchestra; **Thomas Blees** performs it decently in the Vox Box, but I hope Ma will give it a go someday. The concertos for viola and for percussion (also available in the Vox Box) are less interesting; **Evelyn Glennie** recently recorded the latter (RCA). This piece, written in 1930, is not to be confused with the engaging Concerto for Vibraphone and Marimba (1947), most recently recorded by the remarkable **Peter Sadlo** (♦Koch Schwann 6145). And the previously mentioned Harp Concerto, with soloist **Fredérique Cambreling,** is a surprisingly substantial work (♦Erato 45820).

CHAMBER MUSIC

Like his competitors in the 20th-century prolificity sweepstakes, Hindemith and Villa-Lobos, Milhaud wrote reams of chamber music for every conceivable combination (and a few previously inconceivable combinations), including two quartets, 14 and 15, that can be combined as an octet. Also like them, he was faithful to the genre of the string quartet, writing 18 (one more than Beethoven, as he pointed out). A good cross-section is played extremely well by the **Parisii Quartet** (♦Auvidis 4781). 3 and 4 are comparatively dense and "modern"; 3, a memorial to a friend killed in World War I, has a memorably troubled and tragic aura, and 4 some rigorously bitonal writing. 9 and 12 are more relaxed, and parts of 12, written in memory of Fauré, are almost as luminous as Fauré's own quartet. Milhaud had the French flair for woodwind writing, and a collection by **Athena Ensemble** includes such pleasing pieces as *La Cheminée du Roi René, Suite d'Aprés Corrette,* and the brief but enchanting *Pastorale* for oboe, clarinet, and bassoon (♦Chandos 6536).

PIANO MUSIC

Milhaud wrote a lot of piano music, but is almost solely represented in recitals by *Saudades do Brazil*. These are spicily polytonal evocations of Rio de Janeiro, where he spent several years as assistant to the French Ambassador (his frequent collaborator, Paul Claudel), picking up a taste for Latin-American pop that never left him. His pupil **William Bolcom** made a deliciously languorous recording of *Saudades* (♦Nonesuch 71316, with more early Milhaud piano music, *Trois Rag-Caprices* and *Printemps*). This makes for a short CD, but Bolcom's playing and his reminiscences of Milhaud in the notes are worth it. **Alexander Tharaud**'s budget recording of *Saudades* is worth trying for two other Milhaud rarities: the passionately domestic piano suite *La Muse ménagère,* with its charming little vignettes of laundry day and reading in bed, and *Album de Madame Bovary* (Naxos 553443). Both have spoken contributions by the composer's widow, Madeleine Milhaud.

The two-piano suite *Scaramouche* has been plentifully recorded, including **Milhaud**'s 1936 recording with **Marcelle Meyer** (EMI), and the popular **Labèque** sisters include it in a recital of mostly Poulenc, performed in their high-powered style (Philips). *Scaramouche* begins a recent recital of Milhaud's two-piano music by **Pizarro** and **Stephen Coombs** (Hyperion), which includes a transcription of *Le Boeuf sur le Toit,* a bit of *Les Songes,* and such little-known but irresistible items as *Kentuckiana, Carnaval à la Nouvelle-Orléans* and *La Libertadora,* all proof that Milhaud kept his ears wide open during his travels.

CHORAL MUSIC, OPERA, AND SONGS

Milhaud's orchestral and chamber music are reasonably well represented on discs, but his huge output of vocal and choral music remains a question mark. His splendiferously noisy incidental music for *Les Choéphores* (The Libation Bearers), Claudel's bloodthirsty adaptation of Aeschylus, must have knocked its initial audience on its ears in 1916; its polytonal brass fanfares, slamming percussion, and choral chants, groans, and shouts still sound pretty wild. **Bernstein**'s 1962 recording is exciting; the chorus, orchestra, and narrator Vera Zorina are excellent, the soprano and baritone not nearly as good (♦Sony 62352). **Markevitch**'s 1957 recording may lack some of Bernstein's éclat, but not much, and the all-French cast is certainly idiomatic (♦DG 449748, mono). Both recordings are coupled with Honegger and Roussel; Bernstein has hearty, unsubtle performances of *Pacific 231, Rugby,* and Roussel's Symphony 3, Markevitch has a first-rate Honegger Symphony 5 (also mono) and an exciting *Bacchus et Ariane Suite 2* (stereo, from 1960).

Milhaud wrote plenty of operas, and a glance at some of the titles suggests he was not afraid of Big Statements: *Medée, Bolivar, Maximilien, Christophe Colombe.* But there are also his *opéras-minutes,* surprisingly effective mini-operas, and two famous one-acters: the touching *Les Malheurs d'Orphée* (The Misfortunes of Orpheus) and the shocking *Le Pauvre Matelot* (The Poor Sailor). None of Milhaud's operas, grand or minute, are currently available; a brief aria from *Medée,* performed by soprano **Natalie Dessay** in an unusual French program, is a tantalizing snippet (EMI).

This is as good a place as any to mention *Les Mariés de la Tour Eiffel* (The Newlyweds on the Eiffel Tower), a 1923 satirical entertainment by Cocteau for which five of *Les Six* (all but Louis Durey) wrote equally satirical music. Cocteau's surreal satire on French bourgeois mores of the '20s has faded, but the music stands up. Milhaud wrote three short pieces for this farrago, but the most memorable are by Poulenc and Germaine Taillefaire. **Geoffrey Simon** recorded the original orchestral versions of the music with the London Symphony (Chandos); a chamber version with the complete text, entertainingly performed, is also available (Marco Polo 223788).

A fascinating sampling of Milhaud's many songs can be heard with mezzo-soprano **Györgi Dombrádi;** the cycles range from excerpts from flower and farm-machine catalogues to the remarkable little *Soirées de Petrograd*—tiny satirical portraits of Russians of the Ancient Regime and "After the Revolution," from Pavlova to Rasputin (CPO 999408).

RAYMOND

E. J. Moeran *(1894–1950)*

Ernest John Moeran—"E.J." to the public and "Jack" to his friends— was a living casualty of WWI. A severe head wound suffered in France in 1917 led to a lifelong over-dependence on alcohol that contributed to his relatively early death. Brought up in the bleak fen country of Norfolk, he became a pupil of John Ireland after the war, but it was Ireland the country that most influenced him; there was something atavistic in this, as his father was Irish. He didn't write much—friendship with the riotous Warlock and other heavy drinkers did nothing to aid his productivity— but what we have is of good quality. Apart from the folk element, the influences of other composers are often quite palpable in Moeran's music, yet he makes the mixture peculiarly his own.

The G minor Symphony, Moeran's best-known work, is a good example of this process. The more we see the figures of Sibelius and others peering over his shoulder, the more the piece sounds like what it is: a first-rate English symphony. The pioneering 1942 recording by the

Hallé Orchestra under **Leslie Heward** has never been surpassed for lyricism, drive and sheer grandeur, and it's a superb memento of a short-lived but great conductor (Dutton 8001). The best modern version, by **Boult,** hasn't yet been transferred to CD, but the performance by the Ulster Orchestra under **Handley** will please all but the most critical, especially as the recording is excellent (Chandos 8577 or 7106).

The same artists provide the most recommendable version of the delightful Serenade in G, in its original form with two extra movements (Chandos 8808). They also do a good job with the symphonic impression *In the Mountain Country* and the three Rhapsodies; the one in F-sharp has a piano part nicely played by Margaret Fingerhut (Chandos 8639). Sinfonietta, perhaps Moeran's most accomplished orchestral work, found a worthy champion in Boult, but his studio recording hasn't made it to CD and his BBC version may be hard to find. **Del Mar** and the Bournemouth Sinfonietta come up with an excellent substitute, which has the merit of coupling the fine late Cello Concerto, written for Moeran's wife and here played by Raphael Wallfisch (Chandos 8456).

The even more beautiful Violin Concerto is well done by **Mordkovitch** with the Ulster Orchestra under Handley (Chandos 7078), but anyone prepared to risk a historic performance will find that the legendary **Albert Sammons,** captured in 1946 with the BBC Symphony under Boult, is in a class of his own. The disc also includes historic accounts of Serenade in its original form and *Fantasy Oboe Quartet* with Leon Goossens (Symposium 1201).

Moeran's chamber music, delicately flavored by folk elements, is not "important;" nevertheless it brings the listener very close to an endearing personality. A disc emanating from an Australian LP has deeply felt versions of the String Quartet in A minor by the **Melbourne Quartet** and the Violin Sonata by the group's leader, **Donald Scotts,** with John Talbot (Chandos 8465). Two recent discs contain both string quartets: the **Vanbrugh Quartet** adds *Fantasy Oboe Quartet* with Nicholas Daniel and a performance of the Piano Trio by the **Joachim Trio** (ASV 1045), while the **Maggini Quartet** adds the String Trio (Naxos 554079). These performances are all adequate, but to find what is lacking, try the historic version of *Fantasy Oboe Quartet* noted above, or the 1941 version of the String Trio by **Jean Pougnet,** Frederick Riddle, and Anthony Pini (Dutton 8014).

The piano music, most of it early and slight, has been well dealt with by **Parkin** (Stafford 2). No great claims can be made for Moeran's vocal and choral music, though it fills out one's knowledge of the man, and to obtain a fair cross-section you'd have to buy a good many CDs. The best starter is the disc by the **Finzi Singers** under Paul Spicer, which includes excellent performances of *Songs of Springtime* and the mock madrigals *Phyllida and Corydon* (Chandos 9182, with music by Warlock).

POTTER

Federico Mompou *(1893–1987)*

The Catalan Mompou was essentially a miniaturist, writing for his own instrument, the piano. As a youngster, he heard Fauré and Marguerite Long give a recital in his native Barcelona and decided to go to Paris, study with Fauré, and become a composer. Armed with a letter from Granados, he headed north but, desperately shy, turned on his heels and ran before Fauré could receive him. But he stayed in Paris for a musical education that left an indelible mark on his style; Emile Vuillermoz remarked that it was Mompou who was the true inheritor of the mantle of Debussy. To that stylistic model he added the colors and rhythms of his own country; his music may be less extroverted than that of Albéniz or Granados, but it's no less Spanish.

Almost all of Mompou's output is for the piano, his published pieces generally being collections of smaller items. One of the few exceptions is his 1963 oratorio *Los Improperios,* a setting of Christ's words on the cross (Harmonia Mundi 901482, NA).

The exquisite delicacy of Mompou's sound world has proved an irresistible draw for pianists over the years. The best-known of his collections is the set of *Cançons i danses* (Songs and Dances), composed over the course of some 50 years. Some are based on Catalan tunes; in others the "folk" melody is his own. All follow a slow-fast format. Mompou published 12 of them as a set which has proved a favorite source of recital material; **Wild,** for example, plays No. 8 with his gloriously arch sense of timing, though the '60s sound is just a tad hard-edged (Ivory 70805).

But no pianist matches the idiomatic flair and inspired rubato **de Larrocha** brings to these pieces; she knew both the composer and the milieu from which he sprang and her recordings have a buoyant authenticity all their own. On one disc she plays the 12 published together plus a later one (14) from the series, and four of his elliptical *Préludes,* one of which (11) is dedicated to her (RCA 62554). The first six *Cançons i danses,* again plus 14, feature in a sparkling anthology of Spanish music in the "Great Pianists of the 20th Century" series (Philips 456883, 2CD)—and great pianism this is.

Gustavo Romero brings some, but not all, of de Larrocha's Iberian swagger to his recording of the first 12 *Cançons i danses* (not the complete series, as the cover claims), coupled with the transparently gentle *Impressions íntims* (Koch 7185). **Hough** intersperses a program of six of the *Cançons i danses* and six *Préludes* with five other works: *Cants màgics* (Magical Songs), *Charmes, Trois Variations, Dialogues I* and *II,* and *Paisajes;* it's fine playing, but lacks the idiomatic touch that brings this coy music alive (Hyperion 66963). **Elena Riu** presents *Charmes* as the last item in a recital of explicitly "spiritual" piano music from the 20th-century (Linn 111, with works by Pärt, Sculthorpe, Tavener, and Janáček).

Between 1959 and 1976 Mompou wrote a series of 28 pieces to which he gave the title *Música Callada,* which, in the composer's words, "seeks to express the idea of a music which would be the voice of silence itself." The stylistic archetype is still Debussy, refracted through Satie's abstraction, dusted with the perfume of Spain. **Herbert Henck** movingly captures its elusive poetry (ECM 445699).

The first complete survey of Mompou's piano music is currently underway from the Catalan pianist **Jordi Masó,** with three volumes issued so far (Naxos 554332, 55448, 55457). For all that he shares the composer's origins, he fails to respond to the music's inner poetry: these are up-front, outdoor readings, with bluster replacing Mompou's shy blushes.

Only once (the 13th of the *Cançons i danses* apart) was Mompou persuaded to write for his country's national instrument, the guitar, in *Suite Compostelana,* dedicated to Segovia. You might expect it to crop up more often on CD; in one of the few versions currently available **Gordon Kreplin** features it in an attractive program with Bach's Lute Suite BWV 996 and *Mass for Solo Guitar* by American composer Robert Powell, but at under 40 minutes, it's pretty poor value for all the quality of Kreplin's playing (Ascención 104). **Antigoni Goni** brings poetry and sensitivity to her performance in a recital that includes music by Carlo Domeniconi's exquisite suite *Koyunbaba,* Rodrigo's *Invocación y Danza,* Agustín Barrios's *Un Sueño en la Floresta,* and Leo Brouwer's *El Decamerón Negro*—a first-rate disc, with the *Suite Compostelana* of choice (Naxos 553774).

Mompou also composed a number of songs, but the only recent anthology, from soprano **Carmen Bustamente** and pianist **Carlos Cebro,** has been axed, so keep your eye on the deletion bins (Discovery 920189).

ANDERSON

Stanislaw Moniuszko *(1819–1872)*

Moniuszko is the father of Polish musical nationalism, but even in these musically enlightened times his work is little known outside his homeland. In Poland his *Halka* enjoys the status of a national opera, like *The Bartered Bride* in the Czech Republic. A noted organist and conductor, he was widely traveled in Europe and, like so many other East European composers of the 19th century, incorporated western styles into his compositions. His music—he was a prolific composer of opera, chamber music, and religious works—has an irresistible tunefulness. Some detractors have dismissed it as facile, but they are overlooking the skill, sincerity, and gift for melody that characterize his work.

Halka (premiered in 1848 in two acts and then extensively revised and expanded into its definitive four-act format in 1858) has a simple plot. The peasant girl Halka, much to the despair of Jontek, who loves her, is seduced by the noble lord Janusz, to whom she bears a child. Janusz is engaged to and finally marries a wealthy landowner's daughter, and poor Halka, who is already losing her mind in Act I, spends the opera in increasing degrees of madness, leading to her suicide. In this slender plot, Moniuszko and his librettist draw sharp distinctions between the status of the nobility and the peasants. The music is heartfelt and undeniably under the influence of Italian bel canto composers, but the unmistakably Polish character of the opera's rhythms and melodies (including the inevitable mazurka and polonaise) can readily be felt.

There have been three recordings of this opera (each 2CD). **Jerzy Semkow** conducts a 1973 recording with a flair for the dramatic but isn't afraid to linger over the lyrical passages. Some listeners may find the Slavic steeliness and occasional inflexibility of Stefania Woytowicz as Halka not their cup of tea, but the intensity and musicality of her performance are undeniable. Perhaps the most ingratiating vocalism in the set belongs to Ochman as Jontek. Ochman is well known in the West and his singing has an Italianate flavor that is quite winning. All the other soloists give pleasure, and the chorus (from Cracow Radio-TV) is tops (♦Chant du Monde 27889/90, NA but worth looking for)

A 1986 performance at Warsaw's Teatr Wielki led by **Robert Satanowski** (who sanctions minor cuts) also has Ochman and Andrezej Hiolski on tap. This is faster-moving than Semkow's effort, yet somehow the lyrical, more touching elements of the work shine. Ochman is still a persuasive Jontek, but Hiolski this time was really starting to sound like a veteran. The Wielki is Poland's main opera house, so it's not surprising that the chorus and orchestra, like the soloists, have this music in their blood. Many listeners will prefer the more vocally ingratiating Halka of Barbara Zagórzanka to Woytowicz, but I find her basic sound somewhat acidic (CPO).

A 1965 recording features one of Poland's star tenors, **Bogdan Paprocki.** He's a mite too muscular, but he certainly knows the music and is involved in it. The others are also thoroughly into the work, and once again the Warsaw forces boast distinguished choral work and conducting (Polskie Nagrania). Polskie Nagrania also has several discs of *Halka* selections; however, *Halka* converts are advised to look for a recital of Slavic arias by **Zylis-Gara** that includes Halka's aria from Act II (Rodolphe). It's a shame she never recorded the role complete; her gorgeous voice is wonderful to hear in this all-too-brief excerpt.

The Haunted Manor (1864) is the only other Moniuszko opera to achieve repertory status in Poland. This four-act comedy, like *Halka,* is an appealing blend of unmistakable Polish feeling with the influence of the West—not just the influence of sunny Italy, but in some examples, such as a quartet with chorus in Act II, the feel of Berlioz. Both in its vocal writing and flattering orchestration, this is perhaps a more sophisticated score than *Halka.* In its plot, *The Haunted Manor* has types and situations taken from the comic operas of Italy, France, and Germany. Two soldier brothers vow that on their return to civilian life they will live as confirmed bachelors. That changes, however, on a visit to a family friend when they fall in love with his daughters. The man is a fierce 18th-century Polish patriot who won't have just anyone for his sons-in-law, and his daughters hatch a plan to spook our heroes when they agree to spend the night in a supposedly haunted manor. Naturally all ends well.

Of the two available recordings, the one led by **Jan Krenz** in 1986 is the best bet (♦Agora 3-509, 3CD, formerly Chant du Monde). The vocalism is for the most part of a high standard. Ochman is Stefan, Bozena Betley-Sieradzka is Hanna, while Leonard Mróz and Wiera Baniewicz are the secondary couple. Theirs are the best voices in the cast, with no major blemishes of the kind you may associate with Slavic singers. Hiolski as the girls' patriotic father and the ensemble feel of this performance are quite appealing. The recording is from Cracow, and on the evidence of this set—and the Chant du Monde *Halka*—the vocal and orchestral forces of that city rival Warsaw's.

A slightly cut 1966 effort from Warsaw offers a good ensemble feel but none of the soloists—the Siegfried-like Paprocki and **Hiolski** are in the cast—matches the beat efforts of their counterparts in the Agora set; Hiolski is better in the 1986 effort (Polskie Nagrania).

Listeners curious about the influence of Chopin on Moniuszko can best check that out in recordings of his songs, which are very simple, graceful, and affecting. There are commendable CDs by such estimable artists as Ewa Bandrowska, Hanna Rumowska-Machnikowska, and Stefania Toczyska on Polskie Nagrania and Selene, but the **Zylis-Gara** recital is the jewel here (Agora). It bears repeating: what a beautiful voice! Unfortunately many of these recordings don't stay around long and many of them lack English texts. Nonetheless, Moniuszko's vocal music is rewarding and always falls gratefully on the ear. Olympia, Selene, and Polskie Nagrania have issued recordings of his piano, religious, and orchestral music, and these discs also suggest that not all unfamiliar music deserves to remain that way.   MARK

OVERTURES

If the operas of Moniuszko speak to the Polish people in their own language, the overtures have no such ethnic limitations. Indeed, except for their Slavic rhythms there's little that points to the Polish origins of the music; they are highly melodic, passionate exercises often suggesting Auber or Donizetti. Among the three recordings, one stands out. Even though not all of the pieces largely led by **Rowicki** are in stereo, even the mono *Paria* and *Verbum Nobile* (Word of Honor) with **Grzegorz Fitelberg** and *Hrabina* (The Countess) with **Jan Krenz** have an intensity and panache that disarm all criticism, while Rowicki is just as passionate in *Halka, Flis* (The Raftsman) and *Bajka* (Winter's Tale) (♦Olympia 386).

Although **Satanowski** offers all of these plus the otherwise unavailable *Jawnuta* in excellent stereo sound, his limp, dispirited readings don't hold a candle to the Olympia team (CPO 999 113), while **Roland Bader** does very well with *Paria, Halka, Bajka* and *Verbum Nobile* but only offers brief dances from *Hrabina* and *Straszny Dwor* (Koch Schwann 1444). It's a good backup if you must have stereo; but for all of the surging pas-

sion and hair-trigger excitement that Moniuszko put into this music, the Olympia is indispensable. An excellent performance of *Bajka* is included in Grzegorz Novak's "Polish Symphonic Music of the 19th Century," a must-have if you can find it (Polish Accord 011362).   HALLER

Meredith Monk *(b. 1942)*

Monk's "performance art" is more at home in a guide to classical recordings than, say, Laurie Anderson's; her sounds are acoustic rather than electric, and her music has less of a symbiotic relationship with visual images. But over the years Monk has gone far beyond her initial classical training, devising an expanded vocabulary of purely vocal sounds that any adventurous connoisseur of singing will appreciate. Monk's way around her own vocal chords should be the envy of every singer, and she unfailingly creates a cast of nontexted vocal characters with her single voice. There's a huge and hypnotic variety of vibratos, articulation, voice ranges (Volga boatman to Shirley Temple), and timbres (pure tone to tracheotomized mosquito), and yet naivety and innocence are the first and lasting impressions.

There's plenty of wit, too. *Dolmen Music* displays the prehistoric aliens and happy-go-lucky old spinsters Monk brought to life in the '70s, and generally includes some of her most exuberant, delightfully rhythmic, and witty things (ECM 1197). *Do You Be* is one of her most gently melodic but spontaneous and evocative discs, with her variety reigned in a bit and ostinatos and counter-melodies given to varied keyboards and minimalist violin lines (ECM 1336). Even when she whoops like an air-raid siren (in the otherwise Arvo-Pärtish *Astronaut Anthem*) or brings in bagpipes (in *Wheel*), there's a sense of elegance, proportion, and quietude. This is her most immediately appealing disc, though the album "Facing North" has a similar intimacy (ECM 1482). Mostly duets with **Robert Een** backed by soft drones on organ and pitch pipes, this album is often soft-focus à la Vangelis. You'll still find the usual comic touches: *Keeping Warm* recreates sub-Arctic whoopee with the lights out, and the catchy *Arctic Bar* pictures a wordless happy hour in the Yukon.

With its variety of timbres and wordless *mise-en-scène,* "Turtle Dreams" is avant-garde Monk; the title piece evokes some of the stridency and soulful dissonance of African-American music, while *View 1* gets polytonal and also dabbles in in-your-face amplification and conflicting tunings; it's an elegantly turned piece that grows on you (ECM 1242). "Key," her disc of mannerist and minimalist "invisible theater" from the late '60s, is darker music, purged of her usual charms (Lovely Music 1051). The pretentious and far less memorable "Book of Days" has its roots in modal group improvisation, rounds, and hazy Greco-medieval exoticism (ECM 1399). Her most recent album, "Volcano Songs," is in a similarly baleful vein, though more agreeably minimalist and sparing in its wispy vocal brush strokes (ECM 1589). Included is *St. Petersburg Waltz,* a considerable piano piece lying somewhere between Tchaikovsky, Satie, and Bartók.

Finally, there is her longest work on record, the evening-length opera *Atlas* (ECM 1491, 2CD). Her orchestra here comprises 12 players and her singing cast 18, a few opera-sized voices among them, but the musicians are usually heard in groups of seven or fewer. It's certainly agreeable music, though the scenario and two-hour format stretch the musical ideas (simple ostinatos and relentlessly white-note harmonies) and transparent sonic interest to the breaking point. Larger groups have a diluting effect on Monk's work, and have diverted her—for better or worse—from her original goal of "trying for a primordial musical utterance."   ASHBY

Italo Montemezzi (1875–1952)

Montemezzi ranks among the lesser-known Italian opera composers of the early 20th century, yet his *l'Amore dei tre Re* is a most effective work with a powerfully dramatic libretto (taken from a play by Sem Benelli) well supported by lush, romantic music. The definitive recording is a 1941 Metropolitan Opera broadcast with Pinza, Moore, Kullman, and Bonelli conducted by **Montemezzi** (Eklipse 9, 2CD). Unfortunately, the CD is difficult to find.

A finely sung but dramatically wan performance with Moffo, Domingo, Pablo Elvira, and Siepi conducted by **Nello Santi** is in much better sound (♦RCA 50166, 2CD). A 1998 performance from Bregenz conducted by **Fedoseyev** is solid but stolid (Koch Schwann 6570, 2CD). Despite the presence of Dimiter Petkov, a 1973 performance at Barcelona's Liceu is a wretched affair (Arkadia 607, 2CD). A passionate performance with Petrella, Bruscantini, and Capecchi, **Basile** conducting, has long been a sentimental favorite (Fonit-Cetra 502, 2CD).

PARSONS

Claudio Monteverdi (1567–1643)

If any single composer presided over the pivotal transition from the Renaissance, with its rich but decaying language of modal polyphony, into the modern era (Baroque and beyond), with its language of homophony and tonality, it was Monteverdi. He was one of those rare figures who could simultaneously lead an artistic revolution and bring it to a peak of aesthetic achievement. The first true genius of the new form called opera (which he was crucial in defining), he left us a remarkable legacy of musical delight and dramatic power.

MADRIGALS AND OTHER SHORT SECULAR VOCAL MUSIC

Though trained, practiced, and initially employed as a string player, Monteverdi wrote little instrumental music outside his vocal works. His lifelong interest in exploring human emotions, as well as professional considerations, committed him overwhelmingly to writing for the human voice.

Central to the evolution of his vocal writing was the small form usually identified as the madrigal, though also known by other labels (*canzonetta, ciaconna, scherzo musicale,* etc.). Through his continuing experiments with this modest medium, Monteverdi paralleled and effectively bypassed the radical monodists and almost single-handedly drew vocal writing out of the idiom of small miniatures for chamber group (usually five voices) into "concerted" writing for voices and instruments. He thereby transformed the Renaissance madrigal into the Baroque cantata, making that process a central path through one of the most revolutionary periods in the history of music, in which he was the pivotal personality. We're fortunate in having a wide array of recordings that allow us to trace this fascinating process through the more than 200 pieces that survive, almost entirely in systematically compiled collections prepared by the composer.

The earliest publications show Monteverdi establishing his skills in working with vocal ensembles. *Canzonette for Three Voices* (1584, called "Book I" but never followed up) prepared him for his plunge into a series of standard five-voice madrigal collections, involving careful and discriminating choices of poetic texts. All but the first of five books of these madrigals were published during his service at the Mantuan court (I, 1587; II, 1590; III, 1592; IV, 1603; V, 1605). By Book IV, Monteverdi had established unparalleled command of this vocal form, assimilating much of the technique of the "mannerists" Marenzio and Gesualdo and bringing the madrigal to a peak of intense emotional expression.

In Book V the high level of quality was maintained but Monteverdi began his transition to what would become the "concertato" style of voices with instruments, breaking with the *prima prattica* of vocal polyphony and moving into the *seconda prattica* of "concerted" writing. For most of Book V, Monteverdi cautiously included an optional instrumental *basso seguente* that merely supported the lowest vocal line. But for the final six items the basso continuo became mandatory and integral, ultimately calling for six voices and then nine voices plus five-part strings.

In 1607 (the year of his *Orfeo*), Monteverdi's brother, Cesare, published for him a collection of *Scherzi musicali* (including three of his own) for three voices with instruments and bass. These involved metrical experimentation based on French models and dance rhythms, but the "concerted" idiom was clearly affirmed. It was only after his painful departure from the Mantua and his relocation in Venice that he returned to the madrigal in Book VI, a curiously fence-sitting combination of two divergent elements: two great five-voice madrigal cycles, *Lamento d'Arianna,* an adaptation of a long monody from a lost opera, and *Lagrime d'amante al sepolcro dell'amata* ("Tears of the Lover at the Tomb of the Beloved," or *Sestina*), and two short five-voice madrigals (all in the mannerist *prima prattica*) juxtaposed with five requiring basso continuo and a concertato madrigal for seven voices and bass, representing the *seconda prattica.*

The definitive triumph of the *seconda prattica* was clearly established in Book VII (1619), which Monteverdi called "Concerto," symbolizing the new "concerted" style. The scoring ranged from one to six solo voices with continuo, three added obbligato instruments, and the final item a *ballo*—a short theatrical piece for singing and dancing—called *Tirsi e Clori,* for two solo voices, five-voice vocal ensemble, instruments, and continuo. Only in 1632 did he return to his earlier concertato idiom, publishing a second collection under the generic title *Scherzi musicali.* Most of its pieces—described as "arias and madrigals in *stile recitativo*" ("declamatory style")—were for single voice with continuo, though two called for two singers.

In his last years, Monteverdi prepared a massive retrospective collection, assembling previously unpublished *seconda prattica* works from his mature creative life. Published in 1638 under the title *Madrigali guerrieri et amorosi,* Book VIII was divided into two parts, *Canti guerrieri* and *Canti amorosi,* ironically opposing the mirror images of War and Love in magnificent miniatures scored for one to six voices with bass and varying instrumentations. Each part also ended with theatrical pieces that Monteverdi called "works in *stile rappresentativo*" ("presentational" or "scenic" style). The "Songs of War" concluded with the dramatic madrigal or mini-opera *Il Combattimento di Tancredi e Clorinda* (1624) and the festive *ballo* in honor of Emperor Ferdinand III, *Volgendo il ciel/Movete al mio bel suon* (1636?); the "Songs of Love" ended with *Ballo delle ingrate* (1608).

As an epilogue, however, we have a posthumous "Book IX," published in 1651 by colleagues as a tribute and offering 15 concertato madrigals and canzonettas for two and three voices, five of them already printed and the rest new. Further, there are about 15 short pieces from various stages of Monteverdi's development that appeared in anthologies issued by various publishers between 1594 and 1634, only three of them included in his own publications.

Over the years, recorded attention to this large and fascinating literature has alternated between programs of selections and systematic recordings of the published collections. In earlier generations, it was common to encounter these works—certainly the five-voice madrigals—sung by a choir (small or otherwise) rather than by the more appropriate one singer per part ensemble generally accepted now.

The first of the secular publications, the *Canzonette* of 1584, received its first and only integral recording under **Sergio Vartolo** (Naxos 553316). His three female singers pretentiously take their ensemble name (Concerto delle Dame di Ferrara) from Luzzasco Luzzaschi's famous singing group of the day, and they are certainly competent vocally; but Vartolo's direction settles after a while into a bland and listless monotony, while his incorporation of some instruments and the use of an unidentified instrumental introduction aren't properly explained. There is also a projected complete recording afoot, in tandem with the *Sacrae cantiunculae* (see below); only Vol. I has appeared, containing ten of the 21 published items (Florentia Musica).

Vartolo also made the second complete recording of the *Scherzi musicali* of 1607, including the three items attributed to brother Cesare (Naxos 553317). Again, his singers and players are accomplished, but he adds some quirky percussion (a drum in Cesare's *ballo*, and castanets [!] in a few items); above all, his tempi are erratic, too fast in lively pieces, slow and flaccid in many others. This is useful as a reference, and I assume Vartolo will get around to the corresponding collection of 1632, which so far has never been recorded in full. But more vitality was offered in two LP programs that offered selections from both the 1607 and 1632 publications, under **Joel Cohen** (Vox/Turnabout) and **Albert Fuller** with Cuenod, Bressler, and others (Project 3).

There have been some comprehensive ventures addressing Monteverdi's madrigals per se, several apparently still in progress, but no truly complete traversal. Two extended LP ventures of the early '70s long stood as ambitious undertakings. One, under **Corboz,** comprised three sets totaling eight LPs and contained some 70 items, taken helter-skelter from the published collections but mostly from Books VI–VIII, including all the theatrical items as well as the two *Lament* cycles (♦Erato; MHS). While certainly hitting the high points of the repertoire, Corboz's approach was sometimes a bit sugary, with undue recourse to choral ensembles, and sometimes with what now would be taken as less than authentic instrumentation. But many fine singers were involved, the quality of musicianship was high, and the sense of commitment was genuine. Now long discontinued, this series cries out for CD reissue.

Leppard recorded the other early venture between 1969 and 1975, now restored in a generous single package — if with some identification harshly trimmed down and only Italian texts without translations (♦Philips 462243, 8CD). This traversal is more ambitious and generally more systematic. The complete contents (in printed order) are given for Books III, IV, VII, and VIII (including all their theatrical works), but then comes a mishmash of selections from the posthumous Book IX, the *Scherzi musicali* of 1632, and the supplemental anthologies. Once again, there are excesses of scale and choral expansion, while generous instrumental ensembles and Leppard's love for imaginative continuo filling don't always tally with what we now understand of period "authenticity." The roster of soloists is a veritable who's who of fine British singers of the day, though their ensemble can be very beefy and vibrato-heavy by present standards; still, some uneven moments aside, there is much fine music-making here, and some memorable moments. If you don't mind elements of anachronism and stylistic dating, you will enjoy these vigorous and colorful realizations.

Philips abandoned Leppard's project before he could finish it. The next effort was undertaken when improved stylistic standards could be established and a carefully paced approach set. The performers — **Anthony Rooley**'s Consort of Musicke — were carefully drilled in the madrigal tradition and music of the late Renaissance and early Baroque. Rooley began in 1981–83, recording Books IV and V (supplemented by

fillers from Books VII and VIII), now reissued as a bargain-priced set (♦Oiseau-Lyre 455718). In 1981 he used larger forces for a program of "Madrigali erotici" drawn from Books VII–IX, a wonderful release (♦Oiseau-Lyre 421480). Then in 1983–84 Rooley & Co. did a fascinating program for West German Radio Cologne, offering the three versions of *Lamento d'Arianna* juxtaposed with treatments of the same *Arianna* vignette by five other Italian composers of the time, an indispensable package (♦Harmonia Mundi 77115, 2CD). In 1986 Rooley shepherded two of his veterans and practiced collaborators, Kirkby and Tubb, in a delicious program of concertato "Duets and Solos," involving six madrigals and seven sacred motets plus an aria from *Ulisse* (Carlton 00442).

When delays and difficulties set in with Oiseau-Lyre, Rooley eventually shifted to Virgin, for whom, during 1989–91, he recorded Books I (♦545143, with two items from VII, including its scenic piece, *Tirsi e Clori*), II (♦759282), III (♦759283), and VI (♦791154), each on individual CDs, and, finally all of Book VIII on three separate discs (791156, without *Canti guerrieri;* 791157, without *Canti amorosi;* 791158, the three scenic works). Whether Book VII will ever be added to complete the official sequence (much less Book IX or the *Scherzi musicali*) isn't clear. Indeed, the availability of these releases in the US isn't clear: Virgin is undertaking at least partial reissues, with one new set (561570, 2CD) combining all the shorter items of Book VIII (previously in 791157/58) plus only the opening ode of the Ferdinand III *ballo* and the full *Combattimento* — a generous bargain-rate reissue that's a "best buy," save for virtually nonexistent notes and no texts or translations. Meanwhile, Rooley has become involved with Musica Oscura/Columns, for whom he has done another madrigal release considered below.

For the serious Monteverdi collector, these recordings are indispensable, and they are secure starting-points for beginners. Rooley's singers (including Kirkby, Tubb, and Agnew) are all experts in this idiom, lean and lucid in tone, and beautifully balanced and integrated as an ensemble. Likewise, the instrumental contributions in the later Books are all up to the highest standards. There is, especially in the earlier Books, a tight, cool quality that can make the music rather dry, and Rooley's substitutions of instruments for singers in two items of Book VIII trouble me. Still, these are sensitive, stylish performances that never let this great music down.

The latest comprehensive madrigal project, again a sequence of individual CDs, has been undertaken by **Alessandrini** with his vocal group, Concerto Italiano — performers who, like Rooley's, have undergone label transplants. In 1989, in what may turn out to be a prologue, Alessandrini used his six singers to create a very rewarding thematic collection of "Madrigals on Texts of Tasso," involving 15 items drawn from Books I–IV (♦Tactus 56130303). Caught up in grander ideas, he began a more systematic approach with Book VI, recorded in 1992 (♦Arcana 66). The following year, he transferred to Opus 111, resuming the series to produce Books I (♦30-117), II (♦30-111), IV (♦30-81), V (♦30-166), and a start on Book VIII (30-187, selected short *Canti* from both parts; 30-196, *Combattimento* and *Ingrate*). How the rest of Book VIII will be handled, plus Book VII and whatever else, remains to be seen.

With good if not large or distinguished voices, Alessandrini's young singers fall short of Rooley's polished team, but they also avoid his restraint and use far more expression and emotive power, while (as native Italians) paying close attention to the verbal values and inflections of the texts. The instrumental work is effectively pungent. In sum, Rooley offers more stability and elegance while Alessandrini sacrifices a degree of polish for the sake of somewhat greater emotional expression.

Besides these ambitious series, there have been recordings of individual published collections. Two early recordings of Book I on single LPs by the **Sestetto Italiano Luca Marenzio** (Angelicum/MHS) and by a California group (including Marni Nixon) led by **Roger Wagner** (Lyrichord) are long gone, as is, more regrettably, a suave (if somewhat aloof) recording of most of Book II by **Collegium Vocale Köln** (CBS). A recording of Book III led by **Maurice Bourbon** purports to represent "experimentation" with vocal groups of differing sizes. While the singing is sensitive and the recording lovely, this is just a sneaky way of trying to revive the irrelevant old ideals of choral performance for Monteverdi's vocal chamber music (Arion 68348).

Marcel Couraud's French choral performances recorded a half-century ago were admired as almost classic (released as singles by the old Haydn Society: Book IV on two LPs, with selections from Books V and VI [mostly the two *Lament* cycles] on two others). Far more valid is a pair of discs with Books IV and VI performed by I Solisti del Madrigale led by **Giovanni Acciai** (♦Nuova Era 7005, 7165). The singers are all excellent, and blended nicely into a fine ensemble. His approach falls between Rooley and Alessandrini, polished like the former but without fully matching the freer spirit of the latter. Whether or not these discs were to have been the start of a comprehensive series isn't clear, but they are worth having on their individual merits, since they offer accomplished, thoughtful performances of solid value.

Book VI also had an old-fashioned and unfortunate choral treatment by Roman forces under **Nino Antonellini** in a 2LP set briefly issued long ago by RCA. Otherwise, there is no independent representation just now. That collection's most famous components are the two madrigal cycles, the "Tears" *Sestina* and *Lamento d'Arianna*. They turn up individually in many collections, as can be observed below, but this might be the place to mention their once standard renditions by the **Deller Consort,** in variable performances in Vols. 2 and 3 of the Deller "Madrigal Masterpieces" reissues (♦Vanguard 5057, 5092).

Book VII, on the other hand, enjoys two complete recordings of quality (both 2CD). The first was made in 1987–88 by Ensemble "Concerto" (plus a small chamber choir) under **Roberto Gini,** as "Vol. III" of a Monteverdi series (♦Tactus 56031103/4, 2CD). Gini proclaimed his intention to record all the Monteverdi madrigals, but that undertaking seems to have gone no further. The second complete recording of Book VII came in 1989 from the exciting Italian vocal group La Venexiana (♦Glossa). It includes the familiar mezzo Banditelli and the splendid new bass, Daniele Carnovich and is led by countertenor **Claudio Cavina,** who sang in Gini's version as well as Alessandrini's Tactus recording.

Gini's singers generally use a heavier tone and reflect a more sensual but less imaginative approach, though there are many lovely moments (i.e., Cettina Cadelo's *Lettera amorosa*). Cavina's group is leaner in tone and often more springy and vivacious in spirit. (Cavina, by the way, scrambles the published order of the contents; Gini offers unusually thorough annotations, but gives the texts with no translations.) I recommend Cavina, but serious Monteverdi collectors will relish both sets.

Perhaps understandably in view of its fabulous contents, Book VIII has been a particular focus of recordings, both complete and selective. Other than Leppard and Rooley, no one has recorded it as an entity, but samplings abound. These either focus on one or more of the three scenic compositions (considered below) with shorter selections to round things out, or address only the shorter items.

In the second category, there were at least four programs of LP vintage, two surviving in CD transfers. Ten of the 15 shorter *Canti amorosi*

(Part II) of Book VIII were recorded by **Alfred Deller**'s Consort with assisting instrumentalists, admirable and enterprising performances for their day but somewhat dated now (1958: Vanguard). Five items each from the two Parts were recorded in rather heavy-handed performances (with lots of chorus) under **Miroslav Venhoda** (1972: Supraphon).

There are several more recent single-disc programs in our first category (short items surrounding one or another of the scenic compositions). Three, quite contrasting, include the *ballo* for Ferdinand III (*Volgendo/Movete*). For **Parrott** that work concludes a program of eight of the shorter *Canti amorosi* (1991: EMI 754333). It involves only seven singers and eight instrumentalists in characteristically light and deft but also rather cool renditions. Seven singers and nine instrumentalists are led by **Savall** in much more gutsy renditions of the *ballo* plus five items drawn from both Parts of the collection—an outstanding release (1994: ♦Astrée 8546). The ensemble Il Ruggiero (11 singers, 11 players) is ably led by **Emanuela Marcante,** offering only the *ballo* but adding *Combattimento,* with four other items from *Canti guerrieri* Part I (Tactus 561308).

The closest the posthumous Book IX has come to a complete recording is an old Italian release by four singers and two instrumentalists that provided 13 of the 15 items rather too reverently sung (Rivo Alto). **Denis Stevens** once recorded 12 selections—omitting those duplicated in Book VIII—but this is long discontinued (MHS). Otherwise, the most extensive representation is in Leppard's comprehensive set.

There were many madrigal samplings over the LP years, most of them gone. A pair of classics are two programs that drew from virtually the whole of the published output, made with a special circle of singers (including Cuenod) under the celebrated **Nadia Boulanger,** one in 1937 (Pathé/EMI), the other in the '50s (Decca). The style is terribly dated, but it represented Boulanger's pioneering advocacy of music then rarely heard or recorded and regarded as exotic "pre-Bach" antiques. The LP issues are long extinct, but sooner or later one or both will return and they should be sought out as valuable landmarks in performing history. It would also be nice if Sony would revive the pioneering **Noah Greenberg**'s program offering nine items from IV, VI, VII, and IX, including the *Sestina*—performances not always fully digested stylistically but full of verve and imagination (Columbia LP).

There are few current single-disc programs of such comprehensive scope, save for outstanding, pungent performances by the eight singers and nine players of **I Fagiolini,** with 13 items drawn from Books IV, VI–VIII, and *Scherzi musicali* (1632), including the madrigalian *Lamento d'Arianna* (Factory 316). Somewhat more skewed in repertoire is a spinoff from Alessandrini's work meant to illustrate "Le passioni dell'anima" in Monteverdi's music, such as items from Books II, VII, IX, the 1607 *Scherzi musicali,* and a supplemental anthology, combined with snippets from three operas and concluding with the *balletto* of Book VI, *Tirsi e Clori* (♦Opus 111 30-256). Older but still engaging is the bulk of a program made in 1967 under **Leppard** offering items from Books, III, IV, VI–VIII, including the madrigal *Lamento d'Arianna* and the *Ballo* for Ferdinand (EMI 73842, with abridged *Incoronazione di Poppea*).

Programs sampling just the earlier Books of the madrigals, once quite common, are now out of fashion, represented at present only by 22 items from Books II–V, given utterly unfashionable performances by the Brno Academy Choir under **Roman Válek** (Allegro), or by seven items from Books II, V, VI, and VIII, plus the Ferdinand III *ballo,* also done in doggedly choral performances by the Cologne Chamber Choir under **Peter Neumann** (MD+G).

It's rather from the concertato madrigals of the later published collections that sampler programs long have and continue to come. It's not unusual for recordings to be built around one of the scenic madrigals, filled out by shorter pieces. Two directors, McGegan and Christie, have each devised individual programs around the same two theatrical pieces, *Tirsi e Clori* from Book VII and *Il Combattimento di Tancredi e Clorinda* from Book VIII. **McGegan** recorded his *Combattimento* combination in 1987, with 11 selections from Books VII–IX and the 1632 *Scherzi musicali* (Hungaroton 12952), while his 1991 *Tirsi* combination includes 15 small pieces from the same sources (Harmonia Mundi 903014). His vocal group includes some fine singers (Zádori, de Mey, Martin Klietmann, and Mertens among them), but somehow they and the period-instrument Capella Savaria sound tentative, perhaps because of skimpy rehearsal, while McGegan's direction is stable and careful but sometimes fussy—all less than it might have been.

Christie's parallel programs are far more successful, such as the *Tirsi*-focused one with seven items from Books VII and VIII (1980: ♦Harmonia Mundi 1901068), the *Combattimento*-focused one offering nine selections from Books VII–IX and the 1632 *Scherzi* (1992: ♦Harmonia Mundi 901426). There are only a few duplications with McGegan. In his 1980 disc, Christie uses some of his most familiar singers (Mellon, Laurens, Visse, Philippe Cantor), and the selections are particularly choice, among them two that McGegan offers, the vivacious *Chiome d'oro* (Book VII) and the bewitching *Lamento della Ninfa* triptych (Book VIII), as well as the monumental *Hor ch'el ciel* (VIII).

Christie's performers put zestful and heartfelt singing into this prime repertoire that leaves McGegan's team far behind. His singers sometimes sacrifice a degree of polish for infectious vivacity (in less than ideal sound), but they offer a kind of full-blooded vocalism that many may prefer to the leaner, even bland singing style of so many early music specialists. In the 1992 program, the repertoire is less familiar but no less fine, and though his singers then were younger and less noted, Christie achieves comparable quality with much improved sound. These two programs are among the best single-disc Monteverdi releases around, ideal as an introduction to the composer's revolutionary madrigalian genius and indispensable for specialized collectors.

There are four programs of the later madrigals without any scenic centerpiece. **Leonhardt**'s respectable but slightly pallid release includes fine material from Books VI–VIII, such as the madrigalian *Lamento d'Arianna* (with a rare harpsichord "accompaniment") and the *Ninfa* triptych. Among the singers are Kweksilber and the young Jacobs, and Leonhardt's leadership (as well as all his harpsichord work) is earnest and intelligent (1979: RCA LP). **Stephen Stubbs**'s collection of "Madrigali concertati" by the Tragicomedia group is much more winning. The 14 items taken from Books VII and VIII plus the 1632 *Scherzi musicali* are excellently chosen (the *Ninfa* triptych again), and the performances are lively and handsomely sung, with a strong sense of expressive commitment and particularly colorful instrumental work (♦Teldec 91971). This release is in a class with Christie's and has a strong priority for consideration.

Important, too, if very much a special case, is a program by the vocal ensemble Chiaroscuro and members of London Baroque led by **Nigel Rogers** (1981: ♦EMI 763065). Kwella, Brett, Rogers himself, and David Thomas are among the six singers. Its angle is "Mannerist Madrigals," as represented in their concertato extension, and Monteverdi's music is revealingly juxtaposed with material by his younger contemporary Sigismondo d'India. Six choice selections from Books VI–VIII are given lean but penetrating and intense performances. If not quite on the same level of high artistry but still attractive is a program entitled "Ardo," tak-

ing its name from one of 11 of Monteverdi's later concertato pieces, chosen from Books VII–IX and the 1632 *Scherzi* (including the *Ninfa* trilogy yet again), intermixed with six instrumental pieces by four other composers of his day, all performed with spirit by singers and players of the **Quadro Asolano** in a sleeper release (♦Rivo Alto 9608).

Two important programs have also been contributed by **Jacobs** in his Concerto Vocale series. One ("Ardo Florida bella") offers 13 short selections from Books IV–IX and a supplemental anthology; the earlier pieces (save for two) are done with *basso seguente* on theorbo and all are sung with stylish verve by six singers, including Schlick, Jacobs himself, and de Mey (1981: ♦Harmonia Mundi 190184, or 2908027/29, 3CD, with madrigals by Marenzio and d'India). A follow-up features Jacobs with Helga Müller-Molinari and three players (including Christie on harpsichord and Junghänel on theorbo). The monodic *Lamento d'Arianna* is done rather heavily, but there are also five pieces for two voices from Books VII and IX juxtaposed with two contributions from a younger contemporary, Benedetto Ferrari, a solo cantata and the concluding duet that he is believed to have contributed to Monteverdi's *L'incoronazione* (1983: ♦Harmonia Mundi 7901129). These have also been issued as part of a 3CD Monteverdi set (♦Harmonia Mundi 290841/43, with motets).

That last program is a bridge to a small category of releases focused on the two-voice secular pieces. The fullest approach is represented in two discs by **Alan Curtis** with his Complesso Barocco of young Italian singers and players (♦Virgin 545293, 545302). Billed as the "Complete Chamber Duets," plus some "Selected Madrigals" (some with "dialog" effects), these programs offer 33 pieces taken from Monteverdi's concertato publications, done with flair and in good singing under Curtis's knowing direction. Some parallels are offered by the Kirkby/Tubb/Rooley program of "Duets and Solos" discussed above. Less effective is a program of 17 selections, mostly solos and duets from Books VII and IX, done unevenly by five singers and five players in a Czech release without texts or proper documentation (Studio Matous).

Two solo recitals deserve mention. One features **Montserrat Figueras,** with five instrumentalists including Koopman and Andrew Lawrence King (♦Astrée 8710). Again there is a mix of sacred and secular, with four Latin motets presented; there are six Italian selections from Books VII and IX and the 1632 *Scherzi,* among them both the monodic reconstruction of *Lamento d'Arianna* and its sacred adaptation (*Pianto della Madonna*) as well as the moving *Lettera amorosa.* Figueras sings with deep feeling in her strong and highly individual voice—a very special release of its kind. Slightly softer in tone, though hardly less spirited, is the fine mezzo **Guillemette Laurens,** who offers eight concertato pieces from Books VII–IX, the 1632 *Scherzi,* and supplemental anthologies, intermingled with seven instrumental pieces by contemporaneous composers, played with gusto by Skip Sempé's Capriccio Stravagante (Harmonia Mundi 77220).

Finally, there are adaptations of Monteverdi madrigals into Latin sacred works, a practice sanctioned (though not carried out) by the composer; rather, his close friend Aquilino Coppini published three volumes (1607–9) of motet adaptations by Monteverdi plus some from other composers. A selection of motets from madrigals in Monteverdi's Books IV and V was recorded in 1997 by chamber choir groups under **Jeffrey Skidmore,** given reverent, churchly, but quite apt performances.

A different approach was taken in 1992–93 by **Rooley** who—apparently as a counterpart to his "Madrigali erotici"—recorded seven of Coppini's motet adaptations (among them three later chosen by Skidmore) and then juxtaposed them one by one with Monteverdi's original madrigals. (Also included was the madrigal version of *Lamento d'Arianna* but adapted to the devotional *Pianto della Madonna* counterpart text.) Much of this program of "Madrigali erotici e spirituali" was recorded in the Gonzaga family's fabulous Mantuan fun-house, the Palazzo Te, as part of a film, *Banquet of the Senses* (♦Columns/Musica Oscura 070995; ♦Columns B555004, with a video-CD supplement). The one singer per part performances of the Latin adaptations predictably carry greater expressive intimacy, while the madrigals themselves seem a bit reined-in, as if to match their sacred counterparts better. Still, the singing is beautifully sensitive and this is a fascinating study in direct comparisons.

DRAMATIC WORKS

Though Monteverdi's madrigal output has been amply preserved, his theatrical works have survived only in sadly tattered fashion. Of his full length operas, or works of operatic scope, only three are preserved (one because it was published, the other two very problematically in manuscript). We know he composed and produced five more; a couple of fragments aside, the music for all of those is lost—an appalling fate for the work of opera's first great genius. There were also *balli* or short entertainment pieces Monteverdi composed in full or in part, and these also are lost. In some cases, too, we have written references to stage works without confirmation that they actually were composed or what they were like.

The three full-length operas we still have are in a category by themselves. There were, however, shorter dramatic pieces Monteverdi contributed to this or that occasion, and it's fortunate that he himself saw fit to preserve them by including them in two of his madrigal publications, Books VII (1619) and VIII (1638), at varying distances from their original times of performance.

Shorter works (*balli*, scenic madrigals)

The earliest one produced was the latest one published (Book VIII): the dramatic/choreographic spectacle *Il ballo delle ingrate* (originally *Mascherata dell'ingrate*), presented at the Mantuan court in June 1608 as part of a wedding festivity. Its dramatic premise—with the grim cooperation of Pluto (Plutone), Venus (Venere) shows Cupid (Amore) that hard-hearted women (*ingrate*) who spurn love end up going to hell and suffering eternally—is silly by our standards but was much appreciated as a thematic conceit of the late Renaissance, and appropriate to its occasion. Also for Mantua, perhaps in 1616 (after he had left the court), Monteverdi composed a short pastoral *ballo* or *balletto* entitled *Tirsi e Clori* after its two rustic characters. Written for solo and ensemble voices with instruments, it's limited dramatically but has considerable musical charm. It appeared in Book VII, only some three years after performance.

A decade after Monteverdi settled into his new position in Venice, he composed an aristocratic entertainment, apparently for the carnival of 1624–25 that involved a setting of some 15 verses from Book II of Tasso's great epic, *Gerusalemme liberata*. Under the title *Il Combattimento di Tancredi e Clorinda*, it tells how the Christian crusader, Tancred, kills a warrior in battle only to discover too late that his enemy is Clorinda, the Saracen woman he loves. Monteverdi preserves Tasso's text, sung by a Narrator (Testo), with separate singers taking only the words quoted from the two characters. Nevertheless, he intended it to be staged vividly (horses and all, it seems), and as an experiment in conveying emotion in a range of pulse possibilities and new instrumental effects (the first notated use of string tremolo and pizzicato), it's an amazing dramatic vignette.

Monteverdi published the work in 1638 as one of his "Warlike" madrigals in Book VIII, dedicated to the Hapsburg Emperor, Ferdinand III. It also included a *ballo* he wrote about two years earlier apparently for performance in Vienna in that Emperor's honor. An introductory ode followed by ensemble music for singers, instrumentalists, and dancers, *Volgendo il ciel/Movete al mio bel suon* is a piece of courtly pretension rather than dramatic substance, but the music is sonorously conceived.

The only recording that offers all four of these "lesser" theatrical works is **Leppard**'s package of the complete madrigals (Philips 462243, 8CD). His approach is quite dated now, with substantial choral groups and very full, lush string orchestra ensembles, the continuo heavily embellished. The soloists work within a conventional operatic tradition, though that isn't entirely out of place in these stage works. For *Tirsi*, the (unidentified) Clori gurgles like a dowager rather than a young shepherdess; in *Ingrate*, Harper, Watson, and Dean sing the principal roles quite nicely. Alva is too quavery as Testo, but Harper and John Wakefield are able in *Combattimento*. If there are now many recorded performances more in tune with present-day stylistic understanding, Leppard can still give pleasure and may appeal to those with old-fashioned tastes.

Perhaps the best antidote to Leppard can be found in several very fine CDs that come close to gathering all these theatrical pieces together. They all follow latter-day philosophies of "authenticity" in performing styles (single singers and players per part; period instruments, with enhanced continuo). The most recent (1992) comes from **Stubbs**'s Tragicomedia group, who combine *Ingrate* and *Combattimento* from Book VIII with *Tirsi* and the opening madrigal (*Tempro la cetra*) from Book VII (♦Telarc 90798). The singers are nonstellar but never less than able, and they respond with great feeling and power to the dramatic implications of what they sing. In musical terms, however, the focus seems to have been placed, if not less on them, then rather more on the very rich and elaborate instrumental work, with sometimes rather fussy pacing.

The results are less quirky in a 1991 program by the Red Byrd vocal group with The Parley of Instruments led by **Peter Holman,** who offer the three theater pieces from Book VIII together with the grand opening item in its *Canti amorosi* (*Altri canti d'Amor*) (♦Hyperion 66475). Here the quality of singing is a cut above Stubbs, with tenor John Potter (who sang for Stubbs but not in this role) as a fine Testo as well as an admirable soloist in Ferdinand's *ballo;* the others are also very good, responding effectively to the verbal values of their texts. Though the instrumental playing is smoother, the string sound won't please anti-PI ears, and the continuo battery is still formidable.

A somewhat better balance was struck by **Rooley** in his Book VIII (♦Virgin 791158). Its three theatrical pieces receive by far the best singing in these releases, with Agnew as soloist in *Volgendo,* Andrew King, Kirkby, and Agnew in *Combattimento,* and Tubb, Mary Nichols, and Alan Ewing (along with Kirkby as *ingrata*-in-chief) in *Ingrate*. There is again a certain restraint shown, and Rooley offers more musicality against stronger drama from Stubbs, but Rooley's renditions are by no means expressionless, and the instrumental work is not allowed to distract from the singing. Rooley is certainly a very satisfying choice for this Book VIII combination.

Comparable in musical value and even stronger in dramatic terms are *Combattimento* and *Ingrate*, combined with *Tirsi e Clori,* led by **Pickett** (♦Oiseau-Lyre 440637). Bott stars in all three, with Andrew King as her Tancredi and Tirsi; Ainsley is a forceful Testo and George is an aptly dark Plutone. The overall approach reflects Pickett's usual assertiveness, and, while this recording may be hard to find, it's outstanding for its combination of up-to-date musicology and strong dramatic values.

It's not uncommon to find *Ingrate* combined with *Combattimento*. **Malgoire**'s 1986 pairing was uneven, with Visse a countertenor who could make a convincingly feminine Venere in the former, but with András Laczó as a badly mannered Testo in the latter (CBS). Far less acceptable was **Sandro Volta**'s pairing in a 1995 set that added the monodic *Lamento d'Arianna, Lettera amorosa* and six of the Book IX or 1632 *Scherzi* miniatures—an indictable travesty of a performance (Arion).

Two more recent pairings overlap slightly in personnel. **Vartolo** recorded both works in 1995 (Naxos). Banditelli is appropriately matronly as his Venere but a rather heavy Clorinda; Patrizia Vaccari is a quite girlish Amore, while Antonio Abete sounds just a bit too chummy as Plutone; worst of all, Vartolo's leadership is slack and diffident, handicapping things badly.

Two of his male singers—meaty tenor Alessandro Carmignani and light baritone Roberto Abbondanza—reappear in a 1998 recording by **Alessandrini** in Vol. II of his exploration of Book VIII (♦Opus 111 30-196). Abbondanza is a manly Tancredi for Vartolo, but, perhaps thanks to the latter's poor direction, Carmignani is rather bland as his Testo. Swapping assignments for Alessandrini, Abbondanza is a deeply committed Testo in a brisk and exciting *Combattimento*. In *Ingrate,* the two females are not as differentiated in timbre as I would like, but Alessandrini has the advantage of Carnovich as a Plutone full of color and character. In this clear-cut confrontation of parallel material, Alessandrini's recording is definitely worth the extra price and Vartolo's no bargain, especially since Naxos prints only the text without translations and (like Arion) provides no subdivisional tracks, omissions handsomely made good by Opus 111.

Ballo delle ingrate, either by itself or with fillers, has a considerable recording history on its own. (One conductor, Denis Stevens, recorded the work three times, the third to include the long-lost second violin part he had recently discovered.) Of its many LP representations, the strangest by far was a very free adaptation into German by Carl Orff as a part of his weird Monteverdi-derived *Lamenti* trilogy, recorded in 1974–75 (Acanta and BASF LP); if ever encountered, it's not to be taken seriously.

As for more straightforward LP versions, some early accounts displayed Leppard's breadth and heaviness without his musicality. A Swiss Radio broadcast recorded under the pioneering **Edwin Loehrer** has resurfaced as a document of past tastes (Accord 2; MGB 6148, with various shorter madrigals, some done chorally). Likewise restored is another vintage recording by **Deller** (1956: Vanguard 8100, mono, with the madrigalian *Lamento d'Arianna* awkwardly sung by Deller's Consort in stereo). Deller shares leadership with Denis Stevens (in the latter's first go at the work), and with a small modern-instrument ensemble (including Denis Vaughan's busy continuo playing), he offers a kind of Leppard-Lite interpretation. While David Ward is a solemn Plutone and Cantelo a pretty Ingrata, Eileen McLoughlin makes Amore into a timid maiden aunt, and Deller himself as a countertenor Venere is just not credible. This is a performance hardly equal to subsequent competition and mainly of interest for Deller fans.

It's a leap from Deller's Leppard-Lite to Leppard-Gone-Mad with **Fausto Razzi,** whose 1993 recording came from a revisionist staged production (Nuova Era). All conductors have had to made choices about what opening *sinfonia* to use, but Razzi not only throws in interpolations (as does Alessandrini) but tinkers freely with instrumentation. While his singers are all quite good, the pacing is quirky and distended, spreading the performance a good ten minutes beyond the norm (as the

disc's only offering), and the distant miking of the singers is unhelpful. It might have worked as part of the theater experience but is hardly competitive as an audio release.

Roberto Gini's recording seemingly should be more on target, first issued in "Vol. II" of his soon-aborted Monteverdi series and then reissued independently (1988: Tactus). It's embedded in a potentially fine program of short pieces of arguably "scenic" nature, including *Lettera amorosa* and the *Ninfa* triptych. The attractive singing of soprano Cettina Cadelo is featured there, and she's also an appealing Ingrata in the large work; in the latter, however, the other singers are unexceptional, and the whole performance is rather bland. Neither of these releases offers text translation or subdivisional tracks and neither is recommended.

Christie remains the only competition for Pickett, Holman, Stubbs, or Rooley in *Ingrate* itself (1982: ♦Harmonia Mundi 7901108). Using a team of his familiar collaborators (Mellon, Laurens, Gregory Reinhart, Jill Feldman), he paces things in broad and sometimes understated terms, but fuses his elements into a beautifully sensitive performance that takes the work seriously and produces results of great sincerity and poignancy. It's paired with an absolutely gorgeous performance (by five singers and four players) of the *Sestina* from Book VI. This is one of the truly memorable and important Monteverdi releases.

Christie stands out again for the trifling but delightful pastoral *ballo* or *balletto* known as *Tirsi e Clori* from Book VII (♦Harmonia Mundi 1901068). He and his performers take a relaxed stance, bringing out its charm. **Rooley** offered a similarly leisurely perspective but with still more dance-like springiness. In a program parallel to Christie's. **McGegan** gives the work a light and much brisker treatment but with rather clipped terseness (Harmonia Mundi 903014). The two complete recordings of Book VII both play this little creampuff on a more grandiose scale: **Cavina** and his La Venexiana (Glossa) are spacious and colorful, while **Gini** (Tactus) offers more assertive singing if less stylistic substance.

Another Italian leader active in this realm, **Alessandrini,** has assembled a program culminating in *Tirsi e Clori,* given a lively performance by members of his Concerto Italiano (♦Opus 111 30-256). This thematic program (labeled "Le Passioni dell'Anima," Passions of the Soul) offers excerpts (vocal and instrumental) from two of the operas and a wide range of madrigals, including the monodic reconstruction of *Lamento d'Arianna*. The well-chosen selections offer some prime (and familiar) items, nicely done, and this is one of the few Monteverdi releases that would make a good introduction to the composer's work.

A special case of another kind is **Gardiner**'s 1982 recording as part of a program of "Balli e Balletti": our Book VII pastorale as a bookend against the Ferdinand III *ballo* (*Volgendo/Movete*), bracketing four dance segments from *Orfeo,* dance music from *Ingrate,* and the only current recording of *De la bellezza,* the *ballo* generally credited to brother Cesare that concludes the *Scherzi musicali* of 1607 (♦Erato 45984). Gardiner is backward-looking in his use of a sizeable chamber choir instead of a small vocal group in the ensemble parts, and his pacing can sometimes be fussy. Still, the admirable soloists include Kwella and Rolfe Johnson, and the program has its value as a sampler focused on Monteverdi as choreographic composer.

Finally, we have the intense dramatic miniature, *Il Combattimento di Tancredi e Clorinda,* a remarkable work recorded many times in many contexts (usually with shorter pieces). Its discography even predates LPs, and among the distinguished singers to have taken on Testo have been Max Meili (Anthologie Sonore) and Cuenod (Concert Hall Society). Some sorry Italian recordings are blessedly over and done with, but among the less anachronistic versions, three have been revived on CD with weak justification. A 1951 recording led by the pioneering **Edwin Loehrer** has been reissued in a program of madrigals he did over the years (Ermitage 138). **Corboz**'s 1978 recording is rather lethargic, despite a period-instrument group (the Baroque Ensemble of Drottningholm), and none of the singers (including the usually fine Huttenlocher) seem to feel much real commitment; its restoration seems unnecessary (Erato, with items from Books VI–VIII and Scherzi 1632). **Clemencic**'s 1977 recording has a slightly better cast and a certain lyrical quality, but it's often lethargic and no bargain (Harmonia Mundi, with *Lettera amorosa* and Ferdinand III *Ballo*).

More militantly "authentic" performances with period instruments were launched by **Leonhardt,** who recorded the work with items from Books VII–VIII; but despite Nigel Rogers as Tancredi, the performance didn't seem to crystallize very clearly, and van Egmond proved a disappointing Testo (Telefunken). By then **Harnoncourt** made a stronger bid in a 1983 program of Book VIII material; Equiluz was rather wasted as Tancredi, though Hollweg was an impassioned Testo, carrying the drama at times too far over the edge into harsh vehemence and fussy contrasts (Teldec). Recordings of this vintage were capped by a splendid program by the energetic and pungent Musica Antiqua Köln led by **Goebel,** joined by Kwella and David Thomas as stalwart combatants and with Nigel Rogers, lean of voice but deeply involved in the drama, promoted to an outstanding Testo (♦DG Archiv, with *Lamenti di Arianna and Olimpia*). Currently NA, it remains one of the best recordings ever made of the work and surely deserves reissue.

McGegan offered a generally attractive program in 1987 (Hungaroton 12952). The singing is quite good, with a nicely focused Testo from de Mey and a pert Clorinda from Zádori, but McGegan leads the fastest performance on records, sounding rushed at times. By contrast, **Gini**'s program slips into his characteristic blandness; his Testo, Carlo Gaifa, is certainly sturdy, but the overall results are routine (Tactus).

Briskness and intensity have been the hallmarks of further recordings. **Sempé**'s 1991 reading offers lively young singers and lean, fast playing, but with too much clattery harpsichord work from the leader (Harmonia Mundi, with *Lamento d'Arianna* and pieces by four other composers). **Garrido**'s 1997 recording is more successful. His singers are quite competent if not vocally distinguished, and his baritone Testo (Furio Zanassi) achieves the fastest patter passage on discs, I think. But Garrido achieves a highly dramatic rendition of great intensity and feeling. Moreover, it's presented in a fascinating programmatic context, comparing Monteverdi's treatment of sections and subjects from Tasso's *Gerusalemme liberata* (*Combattimento* and four shorter pieces) with parallel settings by 10 other composers (♦K617 617076, 2CD, or in a single CD, 617095, that retains all the Monteverdi but reduces the other composers to five). Either release is a real treasury of perspectives.

In the end, **Christie**'s 1992 recording stands out (♦Harmonia Mundi 901426). His pacing is also brisk, but it's dramatically sensitive and involving, striking a fine balance between musicality and theatricality. His light bass, Nicolas Rivenq, brings an unusual but telling darkness to Testo. It's too bad that this, one of the finest recordings of the work, like the outstanding Goebel, Pickett, and Rooley versions, may be hard to find. Nevertheless, these stand with Holman and Stubbs as the preferred recommendations.

Operas

Orfeo (1607). (All recordings are 2CD unless otherwise indicated). Of the three full-length Monteverdi operas that have come down to us, the

only one that survives with some security is *L'Orfeo, favola in musica,* created for court wedding festivities in Mantua in 1607. One of the first works of operatic form and character, it remains the earliest still performed and enjoyed regularly. In stealing the initiative from the recent Florentine inventors of opera, Monteverdi turned an experimental idiom into a viable art form, a remarkably masterful achievement for his first attempt. The new work was built upon his command of existing forms or styles — the *ballo* and familiar dance types, the madrigal, especially of the new concertato type (first emerging in the *Scherzi musicali* published later that same year), and the earlier Florentine tradition of the *intermedio* (elaborate musical-theatrical showpieces inserted into conventional dramas).

At this point, long before the formulaic elements of recitative and aria were established as structural building blocks, Monteverdi succeeded in fusing his repertoire of small forms (as well as the extensive instrumental resources at his disposal) into an entity that achieved genuine dramatic flow and enduring musical substance. Fortunately for its survival, the opera was put into print in two successive editions (1609, 1615) which, despite some small divergences, give a pretty clear idea of the music, complete with extensive indications of instrumentation.

Some have sought ways of "modernizing" this operatic antique to make it fit latter-day tastes, and two such recordings are valuable in documenting the stages by which our understanding of valid performing practice has evolved. Respighi's recreation of the score, prepared for a 1935 Milan production, is a striking example. He drew on his lifelong affection for Italian music of past eras in this labor of love, but didn't scruple to tinker with it, even interpolating some additional music, while completely recasting Monteverdi's original, highly selective, and varied instrumentation into a more consistent "orchestral" sound, very much on the pattern of his *Ancient Airs and Dances* confections. A heavily abridged recording of a 1984 concert performance under **Herbert Handt,** with rather mediocre singers, gives some idea of Respighi's intentions — earnest for their day but quite misguided by present-day stylistic expectations (Claves 50-9419).

But such modernizing efforts don't end there; witness the circulation, at least in Italy, of heavily abridged concert performances by **Jochum** (Bavarian Radio, 1954) and **Cillario** (Milan, early 1960s). By far the most bizarre, however, was **Orff**'s brutal condensation of the opera into a reduced German version as part of his tormenting of three Monteverdi scores into a confection he called *Lamenti,* which he recorded in 1974–75 with Bavarian Radio forces — now rare and of interest only as a far-out curiosity (Acanta).

The first really serious recording of the full opera goes back to a 1939 Milan performance under **Ferruccio Calusio,** apparently not yet reissued on CD (EMI). Some attempt was made to respond with modern instruments to Monteverdi's scoring, but the singers were all rooted in the verismo-oriented style of early 20th-century opera, and the heavy, solemn approach deadened any remaining dramatic spirit. **Helmut Koch**'s recording made around 1950 by Berlin Radio forces was a step forward, if still another document of badly dated performing style (Discophiles Français, distributed on LPs by Vox). The vital spirit here was the Swiss tenor Max Meili (Orfeo), long a Monteverdi champion, supported by such respected colleagues as Elfriede Trötschel (Euridice) and Helmut Krebs (Apollo); but Koch's conducting (of ample choral and orchestral forces) remained rooted in a romanticized concept of "early" music, resulting in an overall performance that was again quite reverent and stolid.

Meili/Koch remained the only recorded access to the full work until a festival performance in 1955 was organized by **August Wenzinger,** now honorably revived (♦DG Archiv 453176, 2CD). A breakthrough on many counts, this was the first to use period instruments in a conscientious approximation of the original instrumentation—a practice followed in one way or another by all recordings since. Wenzinger made a few small cuts, but the work took on new meaning with brisker pacing and a more appropriate singing style. Krebs was promoted to the role of Orfeo, and the cast included such early-music specialists as Margot Guillaume and Jeanne Deroubaix, as well as a young tenor named Fritz Wunderlich, making his recording debut as Apollo.

As "historically informed" recordings matured, two successive attempts were made in the same year (1968), in each case suggesting that return efforts are a great risk. When **Corboz** made his first venture, a Lausanne studio recording, he consolidated period-instrument usage and offered in Tappy one of the more generally admired Orfeos (♦Erato 98531). Altmeyer was a fine Apollo and the rest of the cast was reliable; as a moderate venture in "authenticity," Corboz I is still attractive. Unfortunately, he chose not to leave matters there, and in 1985 he recorded what was to be a staged production at the Aix-en-Provence Festival (Erato). In baritone Gino Quilico he offered an interesting alternative take on Orfeo, Monteverdi's vocal categories being more flexible than our own. Tappy was rung in nostalgically as Apollo, and Carolyn Watkinson illustrated a recurrent pattern in which the small role of the Messaggiera threatens to steal the show. But Corboz used a large choir of 25, and he marred his period-instrument colors with overblown continuo work, while the direction is less flowing and natural. Corboz II has understandably not survived.

Meanwhile, **Harnoncourt** pursued a far bolder course. His 1968 recording is a controversial but still exciting landmark (♦Teldec 42494). The cast is colorful: Lajos Kozma is a sometimes bland or syrupy but still lyrical Orfeo, and his Euridice, Rotraud Hansmann, is admirably pert; van Egmond brings an unusual bass-baritone flavor to Apollo, and Berberian does a double scene-stealing act as both Speranza and Messaggiera. If there are problems, they are an undue range of color, self-conscious abrasiveness in the heavy period-instrument scoring, and fussy pacing.

If Harnoncourt I was highly stimulating, Harnoncourt II appeared to be the work of a totally different mentality. Originating in a production staged by Ponnelle for the Zurich Opera, it constituted the audio dimension of a 1978 filmed version (which also circulated for a while in a video from London). The recording, issued quixotically by Teldec, reflected an effort to bring into play latter-day conventions of standard operatic style. Harnoncourt blended period instruments into the ensemble of his modern Zurich players; baritones were overworked, for both Orfeo (a still-sensitive Huttenlocher) and Apollo, while the cast was often pushed to musical overstatement and theatrical exaggeration. While lively and even attractive as part of a beautifully stylized film and not without dramatic excitement, the recording by itself represents one of Harnoncourt's less happy musical achievements.

By the time of Harnoncourt II, however, a certain level-headed standard of recorded performance had set in. In 1973 **Jürgens** assembled a propulsive if unprovocative version made in Hamburg with British singers dominating the cast (Partridge as Apollo, Stafford Dean as Plutone, Bowman as Speranza), led by Nigel Rogers strenuously tackling the elaborately ornamented vocal demands of Orfeo in his first recorded attempt at the role (DG Archiv 447703). This is acceptable but not exceptionally competitive in today's market.

A 1980 festival recording led by **Siegfried Heinrich** was even less effective musically (Jubilate LP). The instrumentation is competently handled, but the inescapably German singers (decidedly uncomfortable in Italian) of little repute or distinction (including a weak baritone Orfeo) doom this venture from the outset. The only point of interest is Heinrich's effort to deal with the anomaly of the opera's ending. Librettist Alessandro Striggio first intended the drama to end with Orfeo's brutal death at the hands of frenzied Bacchantes, as in the Greek myth. At some point in its preparation—perhaps to make it more congenial for use at a wedding celebration—the ending was altered with the intervention of Apollo and Orfeo's ascent to heaven. Whatever music Monteverdi may have written for the first ending is lost, and the second (now standard) ending is what appeared in the published editions. Adapting music from other Monteverdi works, Heinrich attempted to make a partial conflation of the two endings, in the first of two such recorded efforts of this kind.

The '80s brought two recordings that still stand as important statements. In 1983 the Chiaroscuro vocal group led by Nigel Rogers joined forces with instrumentalists led by **Medlam** to make a very special recording (♦EMI 764947). The scale is small and intimate, the pacing brisk and mercurial. Rogers himself sings his second Orfeo, by now honed into a highly personal and generally compelling assimilation of ornamental techniques with expressive style. Save for Laurens as another outstanding Messaggiera, the other singers are familiars of the British early music scene, not always Italianate but lucid and sensitive to their characters (with Varcoe suggesting a more sympathetic side of Plutone). For those who want to recapture the feeling of a tightly crafted courtly entertainment, this is an outstanding choice.

Gardiner's venture is somewhat broader and more expansive in scale, though hardly less fleet in pacing and pungent in characterizations (1985: ♦DG Archiv 419250). Baird brings pathos to Euridice, von Otter conveys the Messaggiera's agony in her task, and Willard White is another soft Plutone, while such emerging early music stars as Dawson, Argenta, and Chance have their moments. As Orfeo, Rolfe Johnson is less stylistically expert than Rogers but softens the severity of early vocal style with pleasing elements of modern operatic portrayal. Gardiner is an excellent compromise for those who want a stylish but less provocative approach.

Two more recordings scrutinized the physical scale of this opera. **Gwendoline Toth** reflects her work in a number of stage productions, honing an even more minimalist projection of the work than Rogers/Medlam (1993: Lyrichord 9002). She uses only 12 instrumentalists (including herself) and seven singers who serve as both solo characters and "chorus." Her cast is led by the singer-conductor Jeffrey Thomas (usually a Bach specialist), who is a rather cool Orfeo. The Apollo (Michael Brown) is vocally inadequate, but the others demonstrate honest involvement in the drama, and Jennifer Lane again shows how memorable the Messaggiera can be. The only American-made recording, it demonstrates the imagination and ability of groups on this side of the Atlantic, and even if it's not up to ultimate competitive standards, it shouldn't be ignored by those who love this work.

Pickett offered an even more thorough reappraisal in 1991 (♦Oiseau-Lyre 433545). Studying the possible performing situations of 1607 at Mantua's Ducal Palace while also delving into murky symbolisms of late Renaissance thought, he totally rethought how the composer's instrumental forces might have been used, in terms not only of colors but also of spatial dispositions. (His booklet essay on all this is a monograph in itself.) To be sure, his singers represent a range from satisfactory to better. Ainsley can't match either the lyric warmth of Rolfe Johnson or the period virtuosity of Rogers, but he's certainly an agile and sympathetic protagonist. Truly outstanding, though, is Bott, who enlivens all her multiple roles (La Musica, Messaggiera, Proserpina). Even if it sets few vocal standards, Pickett's recording opens up new possibilities of dramatic and spatial vividness and in its own way is every bit as revelatory as the very different Harnoncourt I. No one who wants to know this opera can afford to ignore it.

Two recordings from the later '90s have added little of significance. A 1996 recording made in Sicily as part of a Monteverdi project under **Garrido** is well-intentioned, and includes in the lesser roles some singers familiar from Italy's current early-music scene (Banditelli, Kiehr, Antonio Abete, Zanasi, Invernizzi, Türk), but the two leads (Victor Torres and Adriana Fernandez) are no better than competent (K617). The whole performance is undistinguished and is best avoided.

Only marginally better is a recording (also 1996) based on a staged production led by **Vartolo** (Naxos 554094/95). Alessandro Carmignani is not outstanding but is an able and sometimes quite affecting Orfeo, while the rest of the cast is never less than capable. But the performance is no more than that, with rather routine instrumental work. The only exceptional feature is a step beyond that first made by Heinrich in 1980 to recover the original finale: lacking Monteverdi's own music, and with no recycling from other sources, Vartolo has Orfeo and his chorus merely declaim Striggio's unset words—with an unholy amount of atmospheric ruckus—before blending (a bit redundantly, I think) into the second and surviving conclusion with Apollo. The juxtaposition is altogether jarring, though this mismanaged inclusion certainly turns an otherwise undistinguished recording into one of strong curiosity value for the specialist.

A kind of capstone was placed on the exploration of *Orfeo* by the 1995 recording that completed **Jacobs**'s cycle of the three major operas (♦Harmonia Mundi 901553/54). Based on a staged production for the 1993 Salzburg Festival, it's a superlative release. Laurence Dale makes a manly Orfeo, a shade less operatic than Johnson and less authentic in technique than Rogers, but a flexible and nicely rounded dramatic character. Rivenq is another baritone Apollo and Fink is a notably appealing Proserpina, while Larmore is another scene-stealing Messaggiera. Many of the lead singers join with others (including such notables as Visse, Scholl, and Türk) to form a 13-voice deluxe "chorus," with some 36 players as an ample but never over-used instrumental ensemble. The recording is notable for its vivid sense of presence, conveying the interplay of groupings and timbres with a spatial ambiance that rivals Pickett's efforts, and the album annotations are outstanding.

No more than any other work of importance and complexity, there can never be a "best" recording of *Orfeo*. Those with specialized period interests should consider Rogers/Medlam (EMI) and Pickett (Oiseau-Lyre), with some attention to Harnoncourt I, while those who prefer an approach more attuned to modern dramatic scales will find Gardiner worth returning to regularly (DG Archiv). For a nice balance in between, Jacobs (Harmonia Mundi) may remain the ultimate recommendation.

Arianna (1608). No, not a lost opera suddenly recovered, for this lyric tragedy of 1608 remains substantially lost. Nevertheless, the famous *Lament* by its title character has survived by itself in two adaptations by the composer himself, giving us token representation of the score.

One of these adaptations, a *Pianto della Madonna* for solo voice and continuo, with a Latin para-liturgical and quasi-dramatic text, preserves the essentially monodic character of the original music. In the

other, both the music and the words (by librettist Ottavio Rinuccini) of the original are transformed into the five-voice madrigal cycle published by the composer in his Book VI. Both versions, and especially the madrigal, have been recorded many times. These two versions allow modern editors to recreate plausible counterparts of the original opera scene.

Of several such reconstructions, **Rooley**'s unusual program is by far the most rewarding (Harmonia Mundi 77115, 2CD). With members of his Consort of Musicke and other instrumentalists, he gives us not only the reconstruction but Monteverdi's own two adaptations, juxtaposed with parallel treatments of the *Arianna's Lament* theme by five other 17th-century Italian composers. This is a set that, if not of decisive interest to opera collectors, must certainly be sought out by serious Monteverdi enthusiasts.

To be sure, this isn't the only reconstruction of the operatic *Lament*. Its monodic form (as well as the *Pianto della Madonna* adaptation) may be found in many of the collections already cited. Something of Rooley's comparative approach is represented in a series called "Lamenti Barocchi" in which both forms of the *Lament* (plus the *Ninfa* triptych of Book VIII) are mingled with lamentations by numerous other Italian (mainly 17th-century) composers, quite adequately performed by **Vartolo** (Naxos 553318-20). More concise, if wider in scope, is a program of "Lamenti" as a showcase for the highly expressive **von Otter** with Goebel (♦DG Archiv 457617), in which Monteverdi's *Arianna* monody and one other piece mingle with an interesting range of music by five other composers.

Nor have older-fashioned approaches been lacking. Respighi fitted out the refashioned vocal line with a fine post-Romantic orchestral accompaniment, a version that achieved a few recordings. And there is the eccentric recreation of the piece (in German) by Carl Orff in his bizarre confection, *Lamenti*, described above.

Il ritorno d'Ulisse in patria (1640). (All recordings are 3CD unless otherwise indicated.) Monteverdi's last two operas dating from his final Venetian years, stand today as isolated suggestions of an eleventh-hour return to the form. In fact, the composer had hardly left opera since his Mantuan days. *Il Combattimento di Tancredi e Clorinda* represented his earlier Venetian activity (1624–25). Two subsequent operas, aristocratically commissioned—one presented in Parma (1628) and another in Venice (1630)—are lost, and others are described in the composer's letters. If we had any of these, they would plug the gap until Monteverdi was prevailed upon to prepare a work for the 1640 season of the growing new world of public opera in Venice. Setting a libretto by Giacomo Badoaro based on the final books of Homer's *Odyssey*, "The Return of Ulysses to his Homeland" was the result.

There are terrible problems for the modern recovery of this work. Some aren't unique but are typical of 17th-century Venetian operas, which were devised first and foremost for singers, with instrumentation kept to a minimum and treated casually. As a result, scores like this come down to us in what seem little better than working sketches: the vocal parts over the functional bass line, sometimes adding brief four- or five-part instrumental sections to be used as introductory *sinfonie* or verse-spacing *ritornelli*. The considerable job of the modern editor is to flesh out this skeleton, while in the process deciding whether to retain the sparse Venetian theater scoring or work up a more expansive instrumentation.

Further problems for this opera are created by gross disparities between the manuscript score and the published libretto. Sections of the latter do not appear in the former, in some instances deliberately omitted, in others perhaps the result of a loss in transmission. The editor must therefore decide how many of the gaps to restore or replace. Beyond that, there has been much speculation that not all of the music we have was composed by the aged Monteverdi himself, but that he was helped by his assistants in a sort of committee project. Accordingly, there is nothing at all like an "authentic" or "original" version; each modern realization will be different.

For all that, the importance attached to any operatic survival by Monteverdi irresistibly demands attention. The result has been no less than seven commercial recordings over the years. The first was a performance by a creditable cast (soprano Maureen Lehane and tenor Gerald English as the long-suffering couple) led by **Ewerhart** in his own savagely abridged edition (Vox, 3LP). Far more responsible was the earlier of two recordings made by **Harnoncourt,** the first attempt at a full-length reconstruction (1971: ♦Teldec 42496, 3CD). His cast was led by mezzo Norma Lehrer and tenor Sven Olof Eliasson (satisfying musically but not very fully developed dramatically), with a fine international supporting group including Hansmann, Equiluz, Esswood, Nigel Rogers, van Egmond, Walker Wyatt, and Dickie. It retains interest as a valid realization.

Ten years later, Harnoncourt redid it (as well as the other two Monteverdi operas) as a trilogy for the Zurich Opera House, in Ponnelle's stylized pseudo-Baroque productions circulated in TV film versions (Teldec, 3CD). Through judicious cutting and much faster pacing, Harnoncourt reduced the opera's running time by nearly 50 minutes. His cast was somewhat more stellar, with Trudeliese Schmidt and Hollweg in the leads, while Araiza, Estes, Janet Perry, and Huttenlocher joined repeater Esswood in the lesser parts; period-instrument timbres were also more muted. It's more of a curiosity than a serious contender.

A very different recreation was attempted in 1973 by **Leppard** (CBS, 3LP), who had already pleased audiences but riled scholars with his rather free-wheeling edition of *Poppea* for Glyndebourne. In a 1979 studio recording based on his *Ulisse* production, the cast—aside from Richard Lewis (Eumete), Murray (Minerva), and Nucci Condo (a lovely Euriclea)—was mostly young rather than stellar. But the two leads were constellations unto themselves: Von Stade's plangent voice was notably apt for the long-suffering Penelope, while Stilwell's manly baritone suggested an ageless hero of passion and will power. This modern-instrument version would still please listeners of nonantiquarian and essentially theatrical tastes and should be considered for reissue. Note, however, that there is also a commercial video version made by Leppard of his initial 1973 Glyndebourne production, with Baker as Penelope and Luxon as Ulisse (VAIA).

Another video, from a 1985 Salzburg Festival production of a very freely adapted and heavily modernized version virtually recomposed by Hans Werner Henze, is splendidly conducted by **Tate** with Kathleen Kuhlman and Thomas Allen as the two leads, for an effective if anachronistic dramatic realization (Kultur). The audio dimension of that production has been released (♦Orfeo 525003, 3CD).

The first CD set was recorded in performance in Siena in 1991, using an edition and production prepared by noted Monteverdi specialist **Alan Curtis** (Nuova Era 7103/5). He tightened the action and discarded some material, notably the Olympian scene in the final act, which distorts the dramatic balance of divine/mortal interaction. He is also a minimalist in instrumentation, following Venetian norms of a small string band with lots of continuo and sparse winds. The better-known singers deliver some of the better performances: Laurens is a pre-

dictably noble Minerva, and van der Kamp's dark bass moves easily through his three "heavy" roles (Nettuno, Antinoo, Il Tempo). The two leads come off well: Banditelli's dark mezzo is rather heavy but fits the gloomy mood of much of her music, while Leroy Villanueva is a strong Ulisse; Paolo Fagotto is a vivid and scenery-chewing Iro. The rest of the cast might be called high-quality provincial, and the pit players are more than competent. While not a brilliant rendition, it at least conveys something of what a Venetian performance in Monteverdi's day might have sounded like.

There are a few parallels between Curtis's recording and **Garrido**'s, the second component of a Monteverdi opera cycle staged in Palermo in 1998 (K617 091). Three important singers from Curtis's cast reappear here. Fagotto repeats his richly hammy Iro, while Laurens is transformed into an ardent Melanto. But quasi-contralto Banditelli's repeat of Penelope now drags her part down into too much gloom. Unfortunately matching her is Furio Zanasi, whose weighty bass seems out of character, though his portrayal is undeniably impassioned.

On the other hand, whereas Curtis is draconian in editing and austere in scoring, Garrido goes to the opposite extreme. Even Harnoncourt and Leppard (in their different ways) kept strictly to what is in the musical manuscript, but Garrido takes off from what we know of operatic practices in Venice to enrich the proceedings by interpolating numerous instrumental pieces by other composers of the day. He goes still further: to supply solo or ensemble portions of the libretto for which we have no surviving music, he adapts them to several Monteverdi madrigals and even one by d'India. With all of these extras, he has created the lengthiest recorded version.

Coming between Curtis and Garrido was **Jacobs**'s recording of a staged production by the Montpellier Opera (1992: ♦Harmonia Mundi 901477/79). He makes a few very small cuts and anticipates Garrido in interpolations: a few instrumental pieces are borrowed from other Monteverdi works, plus a ballet by Lorenzo Allegri. Some missing ensemble passages are filled in with other music by Monteverdi or others, while a section of lost recitative is recreated and some liberties are taken that go beyond strictly understood Venetian instrumentation practices. But these touch-ups are more modest than Garrido's (including a small choir). Moreover, Jacobs has a more balanced and consistent cast of high quality. Fink is a handsomely realized Penelope, and Prégardien's strong tenor raises Ulisse from the usual baritone color to a more ringing heroism. De Mey creates one more vividly comic Iro, while Lorraine Hunt, Jocelyne Taillon, Visse, Hill, and David Thomas realize their characters with distinction. As a novelty, Christina Högman shifts the usual tenor character of Telemaco up to a more youthful soprano adolescence.

All these recordings have something to offer. Curtis and Garrido will interest serious Monteverdi collectors, while Harnoncourt I retains value if only as a backup. But for those who want only one recording, Jacobs is certainly the most satisfying choice.

L'incoronazione di Poppea (1642). (All recordings are 3CD unless otherwise indicated). There are unanswerable questions about how much of the music we have for this opera was actually or fully composed by Monteverdi; it's now pretty clear that the concluding duet was written by a younger associate, Benedetto Ferrari, and other parts could well have been assembled—in characteristic Venetian rush-rush fashion—as a committee work, if under Monteverdi's supervision. Whatever the uncertainties, the opera reflects the coordinating mentality of a master of lyric drama, and the result is a masterpiece that has overtaken *Orfeo* in attention and popularity through increasingly frequent recordings and staged productions.

Once again, however, grave editorial problems attend any realization of the work. It survives in two manuscripts—one from Venice, perhaps representing revisions made for a revival in 1646, after the composer's death, and one from Naples, probably relating to a production there in 1651. The latter contains more music and conforms more closely to the printed libretto by Francesco Busenello. Neither is a full score; rather, they are working sketches containing the vocal lines with continuo and written-out parts for some instrumental *sinfonie*. The editor must therefore decide which manuscript to follow and what instruments to use.

Beyond textual problems, the opera's casting shares with much of Baroque opera questions of what is acceptable or feasible. Two of the leading roles (Nero, Ottone) were written for castratos: They don't make them like they used to, so modern productions must replace them with either female sopranos or mezzos or with countertenors, or, to satisfy modern operatic stereotypes, transpose the part (e.g., Nero) down for a tenor. Further, in accordance with Venetian comedic conventions, the opera contains not just one but two "travesty" roles, silly old women sung by character-type tenors—in this instance, the two Nurses, Poppea's Arnalta and Ottavia's Nutrice—sometimes given to mezzos or cut entirely. Finally, we have two roles of the other (more familiar) "travesty" type of the adolescent boy-sung-by-female, the deity Cupid and the page Valetto (cf. Mozart's Cherubino, Strauss's Octavian), though at least the latter can be transferred to tenor.

Accordingly, a great deal of scholarship, imagination, and just plain arbitrariness have to go into every performing version, so no two are ever totally alike. But the procession of 16 recordings ("complete" or extended) that has accumulated over the years sketch the changing attitudes toward—and our understanding of—this resilient masterpiece.

The first recording was **Goehr**'s, made in Zurich in 1952 (Concert Hall Society, 3LP). He set an example by using the Venice score, but heavily cut (including the Prologue) and eliminating Nutrice entirely; likewise precedent-setting was his assignment of Nero and Valetto to tenors and Ottone and Arnalta to contraltos (the latter more matronly than comic). The Swiss singers were generally excellent, with a nice reading by the respected soprano Sylvia Gaehwiller as Poppea and Franz Kelch a dark Seneca, but the overall tone was rather staid and minimal in conveying the characters' passions. Goehr's instrumentation was free-wheeling: A string orchestra was used throughout, with characterizing choirs of recorders (for Amore) and trombones (for Seneca) at whim.

By absolute standards, Goehr's edition was a mutilated misrepresentation, but it served for a decade to suggest what might lie in this opera. Nor was it much displaced by **Ewerhart**'s first stereo recording (1962: Vox, 3LP). His edition of the Venice manuscript was even more heavily cut than Goehr's (dropping Valetto and Damigella as well as Nutrice), and using a somewhat conventional strings-with-winds-plus-continuo accompaniment. Nero was again a tenor and Arnalta (what was left of her) a contralto, but Ottone now became a countertenor. Of the mostly competent cast, Ursula Buckel was a pleasing Poppea and Eduard Wollitz a cavernously bass Seneca; the plummy-toned Eugenia Zareska was dignified but woolly as Ottavia—more like Wilde's Lady Bracknell than a wronged young wife. In all, routine and off-handed.

Modernized performing editions reached their peak with Leppard's 1962 Glyndebourne production. In its full form, his is again the Venice version with some discreet trimming, with a free and harmonically somewhat romanticized instrumentation of wind-and-string orchestra and harpsichord-heavy continuo. Unfortunately, when a recording was planned the following year, he was obliged to abridge his edition for a scaled-down release that involved wholesale discards of large passages (again the Prologue) and characters (again Nutrice). But the recording (conducted by **Pritchard**) preserved essential plot lines and the original production's character. Its "modernized" casting included a contralto Arnalta, a baritone Ottone, and tenors for Valetto and Nerone—the latter the rather too virile Richard Lewis. Magda László was a little cool as Poppea but vocally gorgeous, while Frances Bible created a believably aggrieved Ottavia and Carlo Cava a noble Seneca; also Cuenod's bit as Lucano was a welcome souvenir of that remarkable artist's work at Glyndebourne (EMI/Angel, 2LP). Cropped and distorted as it was and obviously far from authentic, it's still enjoyable in its long-delayed revival (♦EMI 73842, 2CD, with a collection of madrigals).

Leppard's edition had at least two chances for fuller exposition. A star-studded 1978 revival at Glyndebourne was led by **Rudel,** who had already brought this version to Caramoor (1986) and the New York City Opera (1973). The casting reflected a frank attempt at bringing Monteverdi's opera into "normal" operatic perspective. Thus we find a Poppea (Gwyneth Jones) who sounds like a jolly Tosca, an Amneris-like Ottavia (Ludwig), an extra-manic Manrico as Nero (Vickers), a Jack Rance of an Ottone (Stilwell), and a Seneca who sounds like Philip II (Ghiaurov), all wandering about in the same opera. Yet stars of this magnitude and temperament could make a case for "big league" Monteverdi that's passionate and exciting. Circulated unofficially in a "private" release (3LP), this is the kind of recording we can expect to resurface some day soon on CD.

Meanwhile, a video release allows access to a slightly trimmed **Leppard** version (1984), conducted by himself, at yet another Glyndebourne revival (Kultur). The cast is vocally satisfying, but most of the characterizations, under Peter Hall's direction, are rather restrained or bland, save for Ewing's passionately seductive and conniving Poppea, who alone makes a dramatic experience out of the affair.

Leppard's edition now seems quite dated, but it circulated widely in print and was used extensively. Together with his recording (however cropped) and in conjunction with his controversial adaptations of *Ulisse* and operas by Cavalli, it gave undeniable impetus to Monteverdi's acceptance by today's operatic public. The relative seriousness of this version has also been put in perspective by the recent appearance of souvenirs from other "modernized" versions of the same vintage. A 1963 **Karajan** production in Vienna is documented in thin mono sound (DG). The score was "freely adapted" (i.e., heavily abridged), with a bloated and quite anachronistic orchestration in which Karajan wallowed pretentiously. Vocal assignments were likewise updated, with tenor Stolze as a nearly hysterical Nerone and Rössl-Majdan as a ponderously matronly Arnalta. Still, there are some excellently crafted portrayals: Carlo Cava is again an impressive Seneca, while Janowitz brings unusual vitality to Drusilla; above all, Jurinac is a memorably sensual and compelling Poppea.

Still more anachronistic was a 1967 La Scala production led by **Bruno Maderna,** excerpts from which have been issued (Myto). The edition used involved the usual cuts, vocal shiftings, and overblown orchestration, the latter hardly helped by very poor mono sound. But while the singers construe their parts in an incongruously 19th-century manner, they manage to create quite compelling characters: Bumbry is a passionately sensual Poppea, di Stefano a prissy and diffident Nerone, and Gencer a fiercely vengeful Ottavia. An even more depressing relic of "normalizing" the opera is a 1966 Florence performance with both the edition and the conductor unidentified, heavily cut and compressed into a two-act format, with a tenor Nerone (Mirto Picchi), a bass Ottone

(Renato Cesari) and Senece (Christoff), and a contralto Arnalta (**Oralia Dominguez**) among the cast (Opera d'Oro). Still, however historically unstylish these mementos of the bad old days are in the Baroque Revival, they offer lessons about how this early opera might (or might not) be connected to our "standard" repertoire and sensibilities.

It was just at this time, however, that new and stricter standards of editing and performing were introduced. These were effectively initiated by **Alan Curtis** in the first of his two recordings. What eventually became a full performing edition was already in its formative stages when Curtis organized a production in 1966 at the University of California at Berkeley, recording it for the enterprising Cambridge label (4LP). His edition for the first time took some of the Naples manuscript material into account, giving the fullest presentation to date of the opera in its larger scope: the Prologue and poor Nutrice, plus other extensive scenes and segments, were finally to be heard.

Curtis's instrumentation was characteristically austere, relentlessly following Venetian practice of using mostly continuo (two opposed harpsichords for two dialoging characters) and a simple string group for ensemble passages, with very limited winds (trumpets) for a special final touch. Modern concessions were made in casting. Nero and Valetto were again tenors, Charles Bressler bouncy as the former. The two nurses were again contraltos, and mostly shorn of comic qualities, Louise Parker's Arnalta being altogether too solemn and stiff. Ottone was a countertenor (John Thomas), but not a good one. At least young Judith Nelson was a vivid Drusilla, and Bogard made an imperious Poppea. But most of the local singers weren't very strong, and the total effect was more conscientious than dramatic.

In 1974, Curtis published his edition, a scrupulous conflation of the Venice and Naples manuscripts to create the most complete digest of all the surviving music. By that time, he had organized a working production that he took on tour for some years. This resulted in his second recording, taped in performance in Venice in 1978 (Fonit Cetra 76). Curiously, Curtis II proved to be a limited counterpart to his edition, embodying far more trimming and streamlining than Curtis I, resulting in drastic omissions and the elimination of entire roles (Nutrice, Valetto, Damigella), with the recompense of a swifter and more theatrical spirit.

Recourse to a boy soprano for Amore is unsatisfactory musically. The two royal lovers are superb musically, showing what the final duet really should sound like, but this Poppea (Carmen Balthrop) is a cool kitten rather than a hot cat, while Watkinson is too womanly to be the petulant brat-emperor. Carlo Gaifa repeats from Harnoncourt I his travesty Arnalta, and Cold is a sonorous Seneca; the admirable Nelson repeats and enhances the fetching Drusilla she first created for Curtis I; Andrea Bierbaum is another splendid Ottavia. Ledroit labors manfully as a countertenor Ottone, while de Mey and van der Kamp grace small roles. Above all, and as an explicit criticism of the policies of Leppard and Harnoncourt I, Curtis II hones minimalist Venetian theater instrumentations more keenly (strings and a pair of recorders in the *ritornelli* with working continuo) and shows that it really can work in effective performance. Allowing for the cuts, Curtis II represents something of what could have been heard in the composer's own 1640 performance in Venice, just as he was soon to do in *Ulisse*.

Curtis's initial momentum was quickly taken up by **Harnoncourt** early in his career as high priest of the new "original instruments" wave of "authenticity" (♦Teldec 42547, 4CD). Textually, he outdid Curtis I by opening up still more cuts, with help from the Naples manuscript to offer the most "complete" version yet. His boldest decision, however, was to create a "reconstructed" instrumentation very much his own, using period instruments freely to interpolate lots of color and variety, all in a kind of "scholarly Leppard," if far more idiosyncratic for all the "authentic" sounds.

Nor was the casting without lapses: Nutrice was cast as a soprano, while (as Curtis II would do) Amore was given to a very shaky boy soprano. Harnoncourt's most daring choice, however, was the first female Nerone, and at that the very distinctive soprano, Söderström. Her singing is superb and her dramatic instincts are strong, but her undeniable femininity works against a convincing portrayal of a corrupt and ruthless male character. On the other hand, Donath, if just a little too cool and queenly, is a vocally lovely Poppea. Firm of voice, Esswood sings a clear and lovely Ottone, proving the viability of a countertenor in the role. Giancarlo Luccardi is a cavernous but stolid Seneca, while Gaifa, in the first of his Arnaltas, shows what the tenor-travesty concept is all about. The most compelling portrayal is Berberian's passionate and agonized Ottavia, still unmatched for gripping intensity.

That 1974 recording still stands as a landmark, striking a balance between dramatic and musical values, as in a refined concert performance. Harnoncourt's second try came five years later, in 1979, as part of his Monteverdi cycle for the Zurich Opera House in collaboration with Ponnelle (Teldec 10027, 2CD). He essentially retained the instrumentation he used previously (if more roughly played this time), but he rethought some of his casting, in line with Ponnelle's brilliant, stylized evocation of a sleazy Baroque Italian princely court (which Busenello and Monteverdi may actually have intended for their republican audience in Venice).

Nutrice was again a soprano (Maria Minetto again) and Amore a boy soprano, but Nerone and Valetto were back as tenors. In the former instance, that fitted Ponnelle's concept well, and the vocally adept Tappy plays Nero as a kind of degenerate and besotted Medici. Yakar is a bitchy and narcissistic Poppea; Esswood repeats his sensitive, beautifully sung Ottone; Trudeliese Schmidt is a tragic, intense Ottavia; and Salminen is an awesome Seneca. Janet Perry is appealing if one-dimensional as Drusilla, and Alexander Oliver pales beside Gaifa as a travesty Arnalta; Araiza is wasted in bit parts. It adds up to a lively stage presentation and can be appreciated in London's video release, but the musical standards are less consistent than Harnoncourt I, and drastic cuts are made to speed things up and accommodate to shorter space. Harnoncourt I still represents this conductor's editorial and musical values better than II.

Differing editorial approaches marked three recordings in the '80s. **Malgoire** was particularly enterprising in textual terms (1985: CBS 39728). He was the first to bypass the Venice manuscript completely and give the Naples version straight and in full. This gives us additional bits and pieces not previously recorded—above all, a scene at the end in which self-congratulating deities balance the earthly acclaim of Poppea's triumph. After hearing that, we may wonder if we've been missing all that much, but if you want what is plausibly the most "complete" recorded version of the opera, this is it.

The performance is never fully outstanding but never less than satisfactory. The cast is at least consistent in quality, with few brilliant portrayals but several fine ones. Malfitano is a cool, calculating bitch of a beauty, and Gal is another moving but comparatively understated Ottavia. Countertenor Visse is particularly fine, equally (if differently) vivid as Amore and Valetto. In fact, Malgoire's cast is only one step short of a perfect rating for "authenticity," the exception being the compromise assignment of Nero to a tenor, Elwes who is vocally more smooth than vehement, but as reasonably petulant and nasty as his handsome singing allows. Lesne is on a par with Esswood (Harnoncourt I) as a full-throated countertenor Ottone, while Arnalta and Nutrice enjoy the services of two effective travesty tenors (Ian Honeyman, de Mey), and Gregory Reinhardt is an unusually authoritative Seneca. Malgoire's edition falls somewhere between the lavish Harnoncourt I and the strict, austere Curtis in instrumentation (I or II), which does mean a lot of spare stretches with continuo only. But the chief drawback is—unusually for the sometimes unpredictable Malgoire—an overall sluggishness that makes things sometimes sound longer than they should.

It's back to Venice with **Alberto Zedda,** a specialist in critical editions of 19th-century operas, who recorded his version in a staged performance (1988: Nuova Era). The Venice manuscript is used with augmentation from Naples with a few cuts, but the instrumentation reflects a Leppard-style mentality of added harmonies and whimsically enriched scorings (extensive winds), plus extra "orchestrated" vocal passages, all of which is both anachronistic and inappropriate (the more so as rendered by modern instruments, in defiance of the by now established reliance on period instruments). The playing is sometimes rough and the pace is brisk, while casting decisions are not overly scrupulous. Nerone and Valetto are given to female sopranos, but Ottone is a female mezzo, while the two nurses are female contraltos. None of the singers carries much name recognition, and all hew to a lusty and unabashed style of 19th-century operatic singing.

Hickox's 1989 recording based on a staged production, is far more responsible and musically consequential (Virgin 790775). Textually, his performing version hews to a minimalist position (basic Venice with some substantial cuts but little textural augmentation). That means extremely spare instrumentation, sometimes reducing the continuo to almost nothing in a recreation of Venetian practice. Casting choices are sometimes inconsistent: Arnalta is taken by a travesty tenor (Adrian Thompson) but Nutrice is the matronly contralto Denley. To be sure, Valetto is given a lively soprano portrayal by the perky Juliet Booth, and Bowman's nicely rounded voice makes an earnest countertenor Ottone. But Della Jones, if musically fine as a mezzo Nerone, isn't very convincing dramatically, and a boy soprano again fails as Amore. Sarah Leonard is a more womanly Drusilla than usual, while Linda Hirst is a bleached-white and immature Ottavia. Gregory Reinhart repeats his outstanding Seneca, and as star of the show, Augér creates a Poppea of power-hungry ambition and calculated sexiness in a sensitive balance of beautiful vocal sheen and dramatic flair. In all, then, this is a strong but uneven presentation.

The early '90s brought two important new attempts. For the first component of his opera trilogy, **Jacobs** recorded a 1990 Montpellier production that is freely flexible in text but moderately stringent in texture (♦Harmonia Mundi 901330/32). He uses the Venice score with some small cuts, but augmented (in the practice of Monteverdi's day) with *sinfonie* by other composers. Jacobs also recomposes a few vocal lines, transposes others (raising Mercurio from bass to tenor), and even produces some added instrumental lines to go with vocal segments. All this is done with great taste and discretion, avoiding the Leppard/Zedda high-handedness. It is nowhere as rich as Harnoncourt I but rather less Spartan than Hickox. Above all, Jacobs views the work as a singers' opera, and gives his vocalists much freedom in shaping their vocal lines, though often at the price of leisurely pacing.

He also has an excellent cast that not only matches Monteverdi's vocal distributions as well as can be managed today but allows some interesting variations in portrayal. As a female mezzo Nerone, the admirable Laurens creates a convincingly high-strung young emperor, while the relatively light-voiced Danielle Borst is more a tenacious groupie than a calculating schemer. With a handsomely rich voice, countertenor Köhler projects a somewhat understated, almost diffident Ottone, while Michael Schopper makes Seneca a more varied character than most competitors. The two "travesty" nurses are taken by high tenor Christoph Homberger (Arnalta) and countertenor Visse (Nutrice). As a soprano Valetto, Högman is simply peerless, while de Mey is vibrant in a range of small roles (with others taken by Kiehr and Türk). And in the internationally acclaimed mezzo Larmore, we have one of the few Ottavias fully on a level with Berberian (Harnoncourt I). For those who like a balance of scholarship with musicality and theatricality, Jacobs offers an outstanding choice.

But it's seriously challenged, if in contrasting terms, by **Gardiner** (1993: ♦DG Archiv 447088). With the advice of musicologist Thomas Walker, he followed Malgoire's example in preferring Naples to Venice as a source, with only a few slight cuts. He had Peter Holman make new recreations of some *ritornelli,* but employed a far more limited instrumentation than Harnoncourt I or even Jacobs and only a bit less Spartan than Curtis or Hickox. Like Jacobs, he encourages a very free and conversational approach in the recitatives, telling in dramatic passages but also bringing unusual vitality to the Prologue.

He is a tad less "authentic" in casting than Jacobs; thus, while Nutrice is a travesty tenor (Roberto Balconi), Arnalta is the very womanly if quite sharply characterized Fink. Dana Hanchard is a boyish soprano Nerone, strong in angry moments but readily manipulated by the subtle and cunning sexuality of McNair's chilling Poppea. Von Otter is a melodramatic and overstated Ottavia, while Bott is an unusually understated Drusilla and countertenor Chance sensitively conveys the vacillation and ambivalence of Ottone. Lesser parts are all nicely done. Given the Naples variation on the text and the tighter textures, Gardiner's stands as a more scholarly alternative to Jacobs.

Almost as a kind of epilogue comes **Ivor Bolton**'s recording made during a staged performance at the 1997 Munich Opera Festival (Farao 108020). Though not explicitly indicated, the performing version (Venice with bits from Naples) seems to parallel closely (if not constitute) the Curtis edition, and the instrumentation follows Curtis and Hickox in employing only string quintet for *sinfonie* and *ritornelli,* with a generous continuo group (including two harpsichords), for a spare and preeminently vocal texture.

Casting again mixes scruples with compromise: Amore is a boy soprano, while Valetto is a tenor; of the nurses, Nutrice is a female contralto (the creaky-voiced Marita Knobel), while Arnalta is the familiar travesty-tenor characterization by Visse. Another familiar portrayal is Köhler's befuddled countertenor Ottone. The most striking innovation—surprising in that it has taken so long—is the first recorded countertenor Nerone: David Daniels has the strength and fullness of voice to bring off the music and suggests a willful, even neurotic emperor, but still without the terrifying power a castrato would have brought to the role in Monteverdi's day. The only other name of note is Moll, who is a Seneca of solemn dignity, though Ahnsjö in several small roles again shows what distinction can be found at that level. Otherwise, this cast offers very capable if not notably distinguished singing and dramatic values.

Given all the problems of recreating this opera, no single recording can offer a clearly commanding presentation. Most recordings have some insights to offer, and those seeking only one will have to make an arbitrary choice. Those who want some sense of what a 17th-century Venetian theater performance might have been like can pick from Bolton (Farao), Hickox (Virgin), and Curtis II (Fonit-Cetra). Those who want the more "complete" Naples version can find that, along with some distinctive portrayals and strict instrumental standards, from Gardiner (Archiv). Those who want freer instrumentation and distinctive portrayals should consider the classic Harnoncourt I (Teldec) and the more streamlined Jacobs (Harmonia Mundi). For those more interested in full-blooded operatic drama in more modern terms and not concerned with historical authenticity, Leppard's version surely deserves revival, if not in the old Pritchard/EMI abridgement, then in some new realization.

Finally, we need to recognize perhaps the only important program of Monteverdi operatic excerpts. It's a tribute to **Berberian** in the form of extracts from her Monteverdi recordings with Harnoncourt and contains her show-stopping solo as Messaggiera in *Orfeo* and the three solos that enshrine her unforgettable Ottavia in *Poppea,* together with three substantial concertato madrigals (including *Lettera amorosa* and the monodic reconstruction of *Lamento d'Arianna*)—in all, a wonderful introduction to Monteverdi's vocal richness as well as an encapsulation of the art of one of the great Monteverdi singers (♦Teldec 10032).

SACRED WORKS

Though Monteverdi was interested above all in the expression of human emotion, he was a professional musician required either by his job or by the general expediencies of his trade to write music for the rituals of the Roman Catholic Church. Thus sacred music is interwoven with his secular works throughout his career, its subcategories themselves interweaving as he developed from his early Mantuan days through his long service in Venice, and it involves no easy sequential division. The great pivotal masterpiece, the 1610 Vespers collection, though it comes midway in the picture, will therefore be considered last, following a survey of the other publications and their diverse content.

Shorter works

Monteverdi's very first musical publications were two collections of sacred pieces, effectively representing the completion of his studies in traditional counterpoint. The first is a set of 23 *Sacrae cantiunculae* ("Little Sacred songs") to Latin para-liturgical texts for three voices (1582), designated as "Book I" but never followed up; the second is 11 multi-part *Madrigali spirituali* for four voices to Italian texts (1583), which survives only in its bass part. The former has been sampled little, though a "complete" recording of the set is projected by Florentia Musicae, in tandem with a "complete" recording of the *Canzonette a tre voci* of 1684; only the first volume of this double cycle has appeared to date, offering 11 of the full 23 sung by eight female voices. Note, though, that seven of the *cantiunculae* have been included in the sacred program recorded by Lesne et al. considered below.

The great Mass/Vespers publication of 1610 was Monteverdi's next major venture into print with sacred music, and constituted his Janus-faced stance between the *prima* and *seconda prattica* styles. It was the latter—the "concerted" style of solo and ensemble voices with continuo and other instruments in which Monteverdi was the pioneer—that had clearly triumphed when the composer settled in Venice. His official position there was Maestro di cappella of the great Ducal Basilica of San Marco, the state church of the Venetian Republic. He undertook his work conscientiously and efficiently, overhauling and upgrading its standards. His duties included composition, an obligation he apparently accepted as a necessity rather than an artistic compulsion, but with prolific productivity.

As with his madrigals, Monteverdi used his last years to assemble systematic collections of the cream of the sacred works, resulting in the publication (dated 1640, but actually issued in 1641) called *Selva morale*

e spirituale. (The word *selva* is difficult to render precisely, for though it generally means "forest" or "grove," it can also mean "bunch" or "group.") This collection contained a full Mass setting, two Mass movements, and 29 settings of psalms, motets, and other Latin texts, plus five Italian pieces, most of them in the concertato style. This was followed in 1650 by a posthumous publication by his executors entitled *Messa a 4 voci, et Salmi,* containing another full Mass setting plus 13 psalms and a Litany, mostly in the "concerted" idiom as well. Meanwhile, a good two dozen individual Latin sacred pieces appeared in anthologies published between 1615 and 1651.

Corboz recorded virtually all of this music during the '60s (Erato/MHS, 8LP). The project omitted the two full Mass settings, but otherwise gave the 1640 and 1650 publications complete, eliminating only four items that are musical duplications and adding 18 pieces from the diverse anthologies. He used a fair-sized choir and modern instruments, and his approach is sometimes on the romantic side, but his familiar stable of soloists (including Tappy and Huttenlocher) sang intelligently. Though performance practices have moved ahead since then, this is a cycle Erato would do well to revive, if for no other reason than its excellent reference value.

Running a close second to Corboz in completeness is a project carried out in the early '80s by **Bernius** that offered the effectively complete *Selva* of 1640 plus six psalms and most of the Mass from the 1650 *Missa et Salmi* (♦Astoria 90032/34, 3CD; at least the last, if not all three of these discs, has been issued separately). A small chamber choir with period instruments and a cast of international soloists (sopranos Kirkby and Inga Nielsen, tenor Elwes) gave performances that were a step beyond Corboz's in stylistic savvy and musical satisfaction.

In his original LP series, Bernius's performances were given a liturgical ordering reflecting the fact that Monteverdi's publications were repertoires to be drawn upon for conventional ritual use. Thus his second group originally constituted a "Festive Mass in San Marco" while the third represented a "St. Mary Vespers in San Marco." The bulk of the 1640 and 1650 material represents psalms and Magnificats usable for Vespers celebrations, and it's therefore not surprising that a number of conductors have constructed plausible Vespers services focused on some feast (Marian or otherwise), usually binding together Monteverdi's contributions with the plainchant propers that would apply. (I must stress that these artificial "Vespers" conflations have nothing whatsoever to do musically with the quite distinct contents of the 1610 publication considered below.)

Denis Stevens was the first conductor to undertake such a logical conflation, in a 1978 recording of a "Christmas Vespers" that included six items from 1640 and 1650, with chant interstices, plus three motets for solo voices (two from 1640, one from a 1625 anthology). Employing soloists, chorus, and modern instrument players of his Accademia Monteverdiana, this recording is now long gone (Elektra-Nonesuch, 2LP). But the Stevens reconstruction of this festive Vespers, with the identical Monteverdi items, if without the chant contexts, has been recreated in a somewhat overblown performance by Danish forces under **Kim Glies Nandfred** (Classico). Meanwhile, a follow-up to Stevens's idea came in 1982 when **Parrott** put together a sequence of nine items from the *Selva* that would serve as Vespers for the Feast of St. Theodore, but without any chant. He applied his usual minimalist principles, using only single voices as his "chorus" in the ensemble passages, plus period instruments, all with refreshing results (♦EMI/Angel 747016, or 754886, 2CD, with *Salute* Vespers, or nine of the items in ♦Virgin 561662, 2CD, with 1610 Vespers).

In 1988 Parrott went on to another, more ambitious venture in this direction, assembling seven items from the *Selva* and mixing them with a partial "Credo" by Monteverdi's assistant, Giovanni Rovetta, plus five instrumental pieces by other contemporaries as well as selected chants, to recreate the "Solemn Mass for the Feast of Sta. Maria della Salute in Thanksgiving for the Delivery of the City of Venice from the Plague, Basilica of St. Mark, 21 November 1631." Parrott's scrupulous reconstruction of historical performance style is impressive and musically satisfying. This compilation has been reissued in wise combination with Parrott's 1982 Vespers to make an indispensable release for serious collectors (◆EMI/Angel 754886, 2CD).

Another of these liturgical reconstructions, glancingly parallel to Parrott's ventures, imagines a penitential *Vespro per la Salute* as it might have been celebrated in 1650, during the plague's aftermath, in the still incomplete votive church of Sta. Maria della Salute. It consists of five psalms and a Litany from the *Mesa e Salmi* publication of that year, with another piece from the 1640 collection and four from the anthologies, joined by a Magnificat by Monteverdi's pupil Cavalli that was actually included in the 1650 Monteverdi publication and a short responsorium by his assistant Alessandro Grandi, plus instrumental pieces by six other composers, and appropriate plainchant—all conducted by **Françoise Lasserre** (Pierre Verany 797031/32, 2CD). The eight singers and 14 period-instrument players are quite able if nonstellar, though the choir, of unspecified numbers, sounds a bit on the large side. Still, this is an enjoyable and very worthwhile counterpart to the more scrupulous Parrott set.

Four other Vespers reconstructions have been recorded, two of them directly parallel. These two attempt to recreate a Vespers liturgy in honor of St. John the Baptist, setting the same chant antiphons and the same five psalms from the *Selva*, though differing in their choice of *Magnificat* as well as in other music. One, recorded in 1987–88 under **Leonhardt**, follows the ideas of musicologist Frits Noske (◆Philips 422074): The reconstructed eight-voice *Magnificat* I is used along with a misunderstood *alternatim* hymn setting and a short anthology solo-voice motet by Monteverdi, plus five pieces by other Italian composers. In this rather lush assemblage, the chants are sung by a separate Viennese male voice choral schola, while Leonhardt leads a substantial chamber choir, a period instrument group, and nine soloists including Tubb, Laurens, Chance, Elwes, and van der Kamp. The performances are suave and stylish and recorded atmospherically.

The other reconstructed Vespers for John the Baptist was organized by **Franz Raml**, who conducts a spare group of nine singers and leads seven period instrumentalists, plus a three-man choral schola in the chant (1994: ◆MD+G 6050593). He replaces the second psalm with a 1650 counterpart while using Magnificat II from the *Selva* plus four of Monteverdi's anthology motets; sacred pieces by other composers are added. Raml follows in Parrott's footsteps by using only one singer per part in the "choral" ensembles, suggesting a more intimate ritual setting, with leaner and more lucid textures, delivered handsomely by local singers of little name recognition but considerable musicality.

Of the remaining liturgical reconstructions, in 1993 **Howard Arman** recorded a Vespers for the Feast of the Ascension (◆Capriccio 10521). Taking one psalm from the 1650 collection, Arman draws the other four, Magnificat I, and an adapted hymn, all from the *Selva*, interlarded exclusively with plainchant, without music from any other composers. He uses eight singers and 12 period instrument players, following the Parrott example of one singer per part, though still achieving weight and sonority in quite fine performances.

Another reconstruction is a Second Vespers for the Blessed Virgin Mary assembled by **Alessandrini** (◆Opus 111 30-150). Of the five psalms—using the same texts as for the 1610 Vespers but, again, with completely different music—the first is taken from an early anthology while the other four come from the 1650 publication, while the Magnificat II is from the *Selva*. Like Arman, Alessandrini adds only the appropriate plainchant, without any further insertions. To fill out the compact length of this conflation, he adds eight Monteverdi motets from diverse sources, four for solo voices, the others for five or six voices. He too follows Parrott's model of one singer per ensemble part (with instrumental doublings in the motets), but Alessandrini carries over from his madrigal recordings with the Concerto Italiano group (here six each of singers and players) a certain madrigalian spirit of heightened inflection and intimate intensity. Should you want to make a start with these liturgical reconstructions, his disc is ideal.

For those who want to avoid the subtleties (and distractions) of liturgical recreations and just hear samples of Monteverdi's own works from these major publications, we can begin with four superlative recordings. The first, led by **Roland Wilson,** addresses the psalms in the *Selva* collection (◆Sony 53363). Monteverdi presented five basic psalm texts, each in two or three alternate settings. Wilson selects one setting of each text, involving a nice diversity of scoring, and interlards them with instrumental pieces by Giovanni Picchi likely to have been used in elaborate liturgical services. The performances are colorful, sensitively inflected, and handsomely sung, in a feast of sound.

Bernard Fabre Garrus's program is admirable in musicality if less extroverted and colorful (◆Astrée 8625). It contains three psalms, a motet, and Magnificat I from the *Selva,* another 1650 psalm, and four solo motets from anthologies. The official complement of the A Sei Voci ensemble (eight singers, four players) is augmented by four more players and a small chamber choir in performances of great sensitivity and beauty.

The oldest and most durable of these outstanding programs (1981) survives in a splendid release that offers two psalms, two hymns, and a motet from the *Selva,* as well as three psalms from the *Messa e Salmi,* topped off by the novel "Prologue" Monteverdi contributed to the cooperative sacred drama, *La Maddalena* (1617). The combination nicely matches three of the composer's different settings of the same psalm text (*Confitebor tibi*). Kirkby, Partridge, and David Thomas are the wonderful singers with **Peter Holman**'s Parley of Instruments (◆Hyperion 66021).

Also splendid are two recordings from Harmonia Mundi. In 1979, **Jacobs** led his Concerto Vocale group (himself and Judith Nelson, with five players) in "Un Concert Spirituel," which included 17 sacred pieces for solo voices, including three from the 1610 Vespers, four from 1640 (including *Pianto della Madonna*), one from 1650, and others from the supplemental anthologies. This splendid assemblage was issued first as a 2LP set, but the reissue reduced it to a single CD, eliminating six items including the *Pianto* (◆Harmonia Mundi 1901032, or in 290841/43, 3CD). Even thus shorn, it's still a superb program that shouldn't be missed.

In 1986 one of the participants in that venture, **Christie,** led his Les Arts Florissants in a program identified as excerpts from the *Selva.* It contained, in fact, the great *Gloria,* two psalms and three of the five Italian spiritual madrigals from the 1640 publication, and a motet and two solo psalms from diverse sources. All are performed with lithe vivacity and authentic artistry, one singer per part, by Christie's expert group; this seems to be out of print but urgently deserves to come back (◆Harmonia Mundi 901250).

Likewise NA is a fine release involving two singers in Christie's recording, **Lesne** and Josep Benet. In 1990 they joined with two other singers and members of the Seminario Musicale and Tragicomedia ensembles in a program that is chronologically the widest-ranging sampler of Monteverdi's sacred writing (♦Virgin 791145). It begins with seven items from the 1582 *Sacrae cantiunculae,* touches on the 1610 Vespers (two instrumental arrangements), extends to the 1640 and 1650 publications (two items from each, including one of the Italian sacred madrigals from the former), with representation of the supplemental anthologies, totaling 18 selections in all. The performances are elegant and stylish, and the apparent discontinuation of this release is to be regretted (and corrected).

Two programs are compromised by ignoring the prevailing minimalist trend. A 1989 program entitled "Musiques Mariales," with **Carlo Loré** conducting (Erol), offers three items from the *Selva* (a psalm, Magnificat II, and *Pianto della Madonna*) and two from the *Messa e Salmi* (a psalm and a Litany). The solo singing is competent but the instrumental components are scrawny, and the use of a large choir inflates the ensemble writing needlessly, an effect only exaggerated by cavernous recording sound.

More pleasing is a program offering one psalm and one motet from the *Selva,* five psalms and the Litany from the *Messa e Salmi,* and four ensemble motets from Bianchi's 1620 anthology (♦Conifer 18991). These receive beautifully molded performances by the excellent mixed-voice Choir of Trinity College, Cambridge, under **Richard Marlow,** joined by four continuo players. The consistently choral approach rounds out a little too simplistically the often subtle textures of music often meant (as best we can tell) to be sung by groups of solo voices. Still, it does make lovely listening. And, on the point of lovely if overly choral performances, in 1972 **Jürgens** recorded a program of six Monteverdi sacred pieces, all but one from the *Selva,* that DG Archiv might think of reviving.

A very attractive and useful set gathers from a number of source LPs made in 1962–80, mostly MI but admirably done (Decca 458869, 2CD, bargain-priced). These include both Masses (see below) and Magnificat II from the 1619 Vespers, with five items from the *Selva* and four each from the Bianchi and Calvi anthologies.

Monteverdi's recurrent use of solo voices, sometimes exclusively, in his smaller sacred works has spawned frequent specialized programs over the years. Thus we have a collection of ten short items for one or two singers from various sources (interspersed with a few keyboard pieces by Andrea Gabrieli) by members of **Gini**'s Ensemble Concerto (Tactus 561304). Sometimes even more specialized programs serve as vehicles for featured singers. Thus we have **Kiehr** in a well-tailored program of ten solo motets (three from the *Selva,* including *Pianto della Madonna,* the rest from anthologies), interspersed with four instrumental pieces by contemporaries; Jean-Marc Aymes leads his Concerto Soave ensemble in support (♦Harmonia Mundi 901680). As noted above, the compelling program by the unique **Montserrat Figueras** offers five short solo motets (including *Pianto*) balanced against five concertato madrigals, including the monodic *Lamento d'Arianna* reconstructed from *Pianto* (♦Astrée 8710).

Such a juxtaposition of small sacred and secular solo pieces isn't unusual. A tenacious example is a 1983 program by a group led by **Kirkby** and **Tubb.** Individually expressive in solos and crisply matched in duets, they sing six concertato secular pieces plus "Penelope's Lament" from *Ulisse,* followed by seven short sacred pieces (two from the *Selva,* the rest from the anthologies). This excellent program has been leased to several labels and can be recommended in any of them, despite the inadequate

booklet material in each case (♦Carlton 00442; ♦MCA 25189; ♦IMP 881). A competitor has appeared, with soprano **Mieke van der Sluis,** countertenor **Köhler,** and instrumentalists performing a program of "Arie e Duetti" (1993: Capriccio 10470). Six of the short sacred pieces (one from *Selva,* the rest from anthologies) are followed by four short concertato secular pieces, two extracts from *Poppea,* and some instrumental tidbits. The performances are smooth but a bit understated, putting this release behind Rooley's for musical satisfaction.

Masses

Monteverdi's treatment of the Mass Ordinary seems back-handed and perfunctory, though not without importance. Comparatively disinterested in composing sacred music, he seems to have viewed the Mass as a form of outdated appeal and style at a time when shorter musical forms were allowing new expressive possibilities for liturgical composition. His seemingly sparse attention to this form may, however, reflect the vicissitudes of survival, for his letters refer to Masses now lost. What we have are only three complete Mass settings, one appearing in each of his three large publications of sacred music, and representing a category of old-fashioned polyphonic writing that he consistently designated as *da cappella.* (Each was published with a *basso seguente* for organ that is more prop than necessity.)

The earliest and most ambitious is the *Missa da cappella a 6 voci, fatta sopra il motetto "In illo tempore" dei Gomberti.* This is a six-voice polyphonic composition in the old "parody" tradition of deriving thematic material from a preexisting composition, in this case a six-voice motet by the esteemed Franco-Flemish master, Nicholas Gombert. Though this idiom was a dying art, it represented the summit of the *prima prattica,* and Monteverdi used it to demonstrate his complete command of complicated contrapuntal texture. He thus included it as the first part of his 1610 publication that otherwise contained his *Vespro della Beata Vergine,* which demonstrated his pioneering of the new *seconda prattica* of concerted writing.

The other two Masses, each entitled *Messa a 4 voci da cappella,* were in the late publications of his sacred music, the *Selva morale e spirituale* of 1640/41 and the posthumous *Messa a 4 voci e Salmi* of 1650. Reflecting the maturing style of the composer's Venetian years, these two settings are the focal works in each publication, meant to represent the *stile antico* components as against their progressive concertato content. As such, they are offered as liturgical mainstays, meant to anchor any ritual in traditionalism. They not only constitute gestures of respect toward an older style but also serve to redefine how that older style should be understood, and in the process they became powerful models for how composers for a century or more beyond should understand the *stile antico* in liturgical writing. Besides their inherent historical importance, they demonstrate Monteverdi's ability to write smooth, flowing, lucid, and even melodically appealing music within the tight constraints of austere counterpoint, as much homophonic as polyphonic.

Of these three Mass settings, the middle one (1640) has received the least attention. There have been only four full recordings. One from Russia, by the Leningrad Chamber Choir (without organ) ably led by **Valentin Nesterov,** is now hard to find (Melodiya LP). Its only full successor has been a poor version under **Ephrikian,** blurry in singing and muddy in recording (Rivo Alto, with a motet and the Litany from 1650). A smooth and appealing version by a Prague ensemble under **Petr Danek** includes a Byrd Mass and two instrumental pieces (♦Supraphon 3326-2 231). **Guest**'s suave 1965 recording is part of a valuable collection of sacred pieces, including the final (1651) Mass for a unique matching of the two late settings (♦Decca

458829, 2CD). Note that three of the 1640 Mass's movements are interspersed in Parrott's "Mass of Thanksgiving" discussed above.

The other two Masses have had a respectable if limited recording history. There have even been two instances of their sensible combination in a single release. The first was by **Christophers,** in pacings so brisk that he also found room for two six-voice motets from Bianchi's 1620 anthology (1986: Hyperion 66214). If you can't find it, automatic honor goes to **Herreweghe.** His crack 17-member choir of mixed voices (many themselves distinguished soloists) dispenses with organ and sings with flawless beauty in his somewhat more broadly paced interpretations (1990: ♦Harmonia Mundi 901355, also with one of Bianchi's six-voice motets).

If Herreweghe is a clear recommendation, there are other individual recordings past and present that should be noted. The only survivor from among several LP versions of the Gombert Mass of 1610 is very special: the recording by the Regensburger Domspätzen (with organ) under **Hanns-Martin Schneidt:** somewhat ponderous and with edgy singing from boy trebles, but of interest as a part of Schneidt's unique complete recording of the 1610 publication, discussed below (DG Archiv/MHS). Of CD vintage, we have two recordings by mixed-voice chamber choirs (without organ). The first is a quite respectable, well-shaped version under **Maurice Bourbon** (Arion 68292, with Domenico Scarlatti's *Mass*), while the second is a muddy and unstylish affair under **Gottfried Preinfalk** (Point Classics, with two Book VIII madrigals). Clearly, Herreweghe is to be preferred, though Christophers's strong feeling for polyphonic writing shouldn't be overlooked.

The 1650 Mass had a substantial LP history, with four recordings retaining the organ part. Those under **Malcolm** (Oiseau-Lyre) and **Felix de Nobel** were outstanding (Concert Hall Society); less so **Aurél Tillai** (Hungaroton). The fortunate survivor of that cohort is **Guest**'s elegant 1965 recording in the above-mentioned collection (♦Decca 458829, 2CD). **John McCarthy** was quite different; he dispensed with organ (though using occasional solo voices) but embedded the *Mass* sections in the chant propers for a post-Pentecost liturgy (MHS). Much stranger was **Deller**'s early recording (Harmonia Mundi), sung (badly) one voice per part but with doublings by trombones!

The CD era has been less prolific. An Italian venture under **Marco Longhini** is enterprising; he adds plainchant versets to the "Kyrie" and "Agnus Dei" (plus a concluding "Ite missa est") and interpolates three short motets (two from the *Selva*), which makes liturgical sense but becomes musically distracting, particularly since the singing is rather scrappy and unpolished (Nuova Era, with 1650 Litany and 1610 Magnificat II). More direct as well as more enjoyable are two performances by **Corboz** with his Lausanne Vocal Ensemble. One was recorded in 1964, reissued as filler for his set of the 1610 Vespers (♦Erato 12981, 2CD); the second was made around 1990 (Cascavelle 1025, with the 1640 *Litany* and Frank Martin's Mass). Both are smooth and without frills, but in the first the singing is warmer and the sound more glowing. Accordingly, in this 1650 Mass at least, Corboz I gives Herreweghe and Christophers an honest run for the money.

Vespers of 1610

This collection deserves a separate niche of its own, out of chronological sequence, not only for its inherent importance but also its status as Monteverdi's equivalent to Handel's *Messiah*. It is by far his most frequently recorded major work (or collection), having achieved, by present reckoning, 43 comprehensive commercial recordings. This surely makes it the most frequently recorded of any major work of the 17th century, by Monteverdi or anyone else.

Scholars have debated for some time whether Monteverdi intended his *Vespro della Beata Vergine* to be simply a quarry to be mined by musicians for their selective use according to ritual needs, or whether he meant it to be an actual Marian Vespers in its totality; or whether, beyond that, it may have been conceived for a specific ritual occasion at the Gonzaga court he served in Mantua. What we do know is that he had it published as part of his job-hunting dossier, at a time when his position in Mantua was evaporating and he needed a new post appropriate to his talents. The advertising intent is suggested by the full Latin title of the collection, which may be translated as: "Of the Most-Holy Virgin, a six-voice Mass for church choirs and Vespers for singing by several voices, with a few sacred compositions appropriate for either the chapels or chambers of princes. A work recently composed by Claudio Monteverdi . . ."

The collection's two-faced character was reflected in its division into two stylistic units, intended to demonstrate (for future employers or anyone else) Monteverdi's command of two then-alternative styles, the polyphonic *prima prattica* and the new *seconda prattica,* the "concerted" idiom of voices and instruments in diverse combinations. The six-voice Mass based on Gombert's motet *In illo tempore* represented the first style, while the remainder of the collection was described in one part book as "Vespers of the Blessed Virgin, composed in concerted style on plain chant." With employment needs urgent, Monteverdi aimed at two high-priority possibilities by having the collection printed in Venice and dedicating it to the Pope in Rome. It was Venice that presumably got the message, and knowledge of the publication must have counted in the Venetian offer of the job as Maestro di cappella at San Marco, which he took up in early 1613. The offer was one of the most important cultural decisions ever made by the Serene Republic of Saint Mark, and the rest was musical history.

The *prima prattica* Mass has already been considered above, since almost all of its recordings have treated it as an item apart. There is one exception, which is our logical starting point, for it's the only truly "complete" recording of the full 1610 publication. This was made in Regensburg in 1974/75 under **Schneidt,** and it not only gave both of the Magnificat choices (the fuller seven-voice *Primo,* but also the more spare six-voice *Secondo* alternative) and included the *prima prattica* Gombert Mass. The performances are thoughtful, and the period instrumentation is careful and fully credible; the choral work with boy trebles involves some ragged edges, but the solo work (including Esswood, Partridge, Elwes, David Thomas, and Christopher Keyte) is sensitive and highly satisfying. While not the ultimate in interpretation, this is a thoroughly successful recording, and its completeness alone makes it indispensable. Fortunately, it has been reissued (♦DG Archiv 447719; MHS 525005). (Both these sets are 2CD, as are all considered hereafter unless otherwise noted.)

Following closely but a little behind in completeness is **Corboz.** In fact, in 1966 he made the first complete recording of the Vespers only — that is, with both Magnificat settings, though without the Gombert Mass. That recording employed a substantial choir and essentially modern instruments, but had some fine soloists, including Tappy, Cuenod, and Huttenlocher (Erato/MHS, 3LP). Corboz made a second recording in 1982, also issued by these two labels (this time 2LP); it was a somewhat tighter but generally similar performance, with some different soloists and some carry-overs (Elwes, Huttenlocher), but it eliminated the second Magnificat. In preparing a CD reissue, Erato (♦12981) sensibly conflated the two versions, giving the Corboz II (1982) recording complete, then adding Magnificat II from Corboz I (1966) and completing it with Corboz's recording of a Mass—not the Gombert from the 1610 publication but the one from the 1650 collection—to make a kind of almost comprehensive counterpart to the 1610 format, and a quite worthy choice for those who wish to avoid period instruments and "authenticity."

Long before Corboz and Schneidt, however, recordings had settled into a kind of standard practice, regardless of the fine points of performing editions) (that is, the *Vespro* collection only, without Magnificat II). The '50s and '60s brought a spate of recordings, all using modern instruments, with various decisions about scoring details. **Anthony Lewis** was an early and long-enjoyed pioneer (Oiseau-Lyre), and there was much to respect in the efforts of **Hans Grischkat** to achieve a degree of instrumental integrity (Vox). Deller and his Consort made a dismal version with **Michel Le Roux** directing choral and orchestral forces, and **Denis Stevens** made two recordings (Vanguard and Koch/Schwann), the first of them an arbitrarily stripped-down version eliminating all five of the *concerto* sections.

A BBC performance of 1970 provides a mark between Lewis's recording and Gardiner's to come: **Louis Halsey** led a starry group of soloists (Cantelo, Esswood, Partridge, Elwes, David Thomas), with performers on instruments old and new (including Hogwood and David Munrow among the players), in a lively if still somewhat romanticized approach (Carlton 91877). Otherwise, the only commercial recording to survive from that era was made in California in 1967 by **Robert Craft** (Sony, with Bach Cantatas 131 and 198). Two Texas choirs and soloists partly drawn from them all sound bright-eyed and bushy-tailed, but Craft's conducting is squarish and without much sense of style, while his free instrumentation sometime sounds like hyped-up Stravinsky. However difficult it is to recommend Craft, he sounds good beside **von Matačič,** whose heavy-handed and uncomprehending concert performance in Zagreb in 1974 has been revived by two different labels for no reason I can discern (Nuova Era; Memories).

1974 did, however, produce one outstanding survivor in this category, **Gardiner**'s first recording, one of his earliest, made when he had not yet embraced period instruments or other fine points of historical authenticity. With a splendid team of soloists (Gomez, Palmer, Bowman, Tear, Langridge, Shirley-Quirk), he led a performance of energy and expressive power, one that remains exciting and genuinely enjoyable, whether or not you care about scholarly quibbles. In reviving it, Decca/London (♦43482) cleverly augmented it with a Monteverdi motet, one by Bassano, and five by Giovanni Gabrieli, taken from a still earlier LP recording (1972), but rounding out a bargain-rate release that is emphatically a "best buy" in its or any other class.

By the '70s, recordings of the 1610 Vespers had come to reflect the currents of historically informed performance, and modern instrument recordings came to an end. But more than the introduction of period instruments was involved in the landmark 1966 recording in which choral conductor Jürgens joined forces with instrumental leader **Harnoncourt** for the first "scholarly" reading. The standard contents (that is, omitting Magnificat II) were presented, but to emphasize the relationship of the chant-based movements to their sources and anchor the Vespers material to ritual use, the psalms were framed by their chant antiphons (sung by a separate choral schola under Konrad Ruhland). The results are still quite satisfying musically, as embodied in this durable recording (♦Teldec 92175). But its drawbacks—rather sedate pacing, Harnoncourt's sometimes too lavish use of period-instrument colors—can't be denied in the light of subsequent recording experience.

Indeed, both Jürgens and Harnoncourt indicated their discontent by making separate second recordings. The latter ventured his as a 1986 concert performance in Graz Cathedral (Teldec). For this, Harnoncourt retained essentially the same performing edition (with full instrumentation and separate choral schola) but tried to eclipse the earlier recording with enlarged choral forces, a more glitzy solo team (including Margaret Marshall, Palmer, Langridge, Equiluz, and Hampson), and, above all, a more intense interpretation. Unfortunately, the performance suffered from haste and insufficient rehearsal, and the sound is seriously flawed.

Meanwhile, trends in recording the 1610 Vespers had firmly bifurcated between what we may call the "concert" approach (giving only Monteverdi's compositions, without chant interpolations) and the "liturgical" approach (including chants). In the latter line, a certain "me-too-ism" was at first suggested by **Martin Flämig,** who made a recording in 1981/82 that used chant prefaces and laid on period instruments with freedom, imitating Harnoncourt to some extent. The soloists were variable, the Dresden Kreuzchor was marked by very prominent boy-treble colors, and the pacing—again, à la Jürgens/Harnoncourt—was gentle and relaxed to the point of lassitude. An honest experiment at the time, this recording isn't competitive now (Berlin).

But **Parrott**'s 1983/84 version was a major contribution to the "liturgical" line of recordings (♦EMI/Angel 61347, or ♦Virgin 561662 with nine later Vespers pieces). He was particularly concerned with Monteverdi's treatment of chant motives in his music and about liturgical contexts. He therefore not only included chant antiphons (representing the propers for a Second Vespers of the Assumption) but reshuffled the order of pieces, also interpolating one of Monteverdi's own Marian motets (from a 1624 anthology) as well as two instrumental sonatas by Giovanni Cima. In his characteristic fashion, Parrott used solo voices as much as possible in ensembles (with a solo lineup that is a roster of England's leading early music singers of the day), adding his soloists to others to make a crack chamber choir while using some of the men in a sizeable choral schola. The results are elegant, pungent, stylistically insightful, and musically refreshing. making it a still-important entry in this category.

Parrott's sense of stylistic and liturgical detail soon received a foil in **Herreweghe**'s 1986 recording (♦Harmonia Mundi 901247/48). Chant antiphons are included (though no other additions are made), and the instrumentation is sensible. The soloists (among them Mellon, Laurens, Howard Crook, Kooy, and David Thomas) are of high quality, and the vivacious, elegant singing by the modest chamber choir is particularly appealing. This is perhaps the most velvety of all the historical/liturgical recordings, and the discography could well have closed down at this point. But the inexhaustible seductions of this challenging work were to prompt no less than eight more recordings in the "liturgical" line alone.

Amid the many debates about the 1610 Vespers collection, there has been much discussion as to whether or not Monteverdi's very specific ordering of pieces was meant to represent a planned entity and to reflect a specific occasion, perhaps at the Mantua court chapel. With the advice of Graham Dixon, **Christophers** made the case for such an original venue, for a feast in honor of the Gonzaga dynasty's family saint, St. Barbara, thus "restoring" a putative first title of "Vespers for the Feast of St. Barbara" (Hyperion 22028). Movement sequence is again altered, a few textual wordings are adjusted, appropriate chant propers are put into play, and, paralleling Parrott, there are interpolations of extra music—not only two instrumental sonatas by Giovanni Amigone but Palestrina's motet *Gaude Barbara beata*—to strengthen the occasional coloring. The liturgical case is hardly convincing, and though Christophers leads a polished and sensible performance (with capable soloists drawn from his chamber choir), overall it is "merely excellent" rather than outstanding.

St. Barbara was in the air in 1988, for at the same time **Savall** accepted the premise of St. Barbara origins for the work and used appropriate chant antiphons accordingly, but without undue polemic (♦Astrée 8719). Recorded at the Festival of Ambronay Abbey, the production used an Italian choir, an international group of instrumentalists (including Alessandrini), and a solo group that joined Figueras with others mainly familiar from the Italian early music scene (including Kiehr, de Mey, Türk, Fagotto, Abbondanza, and Carnovich). The performance has more character than Christophers's, in an unusually thoughtful and introspective approach that is realized with beautiful sensitivity.

The following year (1989) brought two recordings that returned to including only Marian chant antiphons and made one shared shift of content (moving the remarkable *Sonata sopra "Sancta Maria"* to the end). **Bernius** used an international mix of soloists (including Elwes, van der Meel, and Kooy), a Stuttgart chamber choir, and Roland Wilson's distinguished Musica Fiata Köln, plus a choral schola that brought back Konrad Ruhland, all nicely shaped and satisfying, though again a recording that has to be set at the top of the "merely excellent" pile (Harmonia Mundi 7760).

Pickett's recording is more distinctive. Despite an ample instrumental force, he emulates Parrott's smaller and more intimate scale: seven solo singers (Bott, Ainsley, George among them) who join nine others to form the full choir, from whose male ranks comes the choral schola (♦Oiseau-Lyre 425823). Pickett keeps his vocal ensembles as small as he can, one singer per part, stressing, if not intimacy, then at least a kind of restless clarity. He chose to use antiphons from the Vespers for the Feast of the Virgin's Nativity, and, as in Jürgens/Harnoncourt, not just to precede but also to frame the psalms. This is scholarly in conception but more musically assertive than Parrott.

Jacobs led the contributions of the '90s with a 1995 recording that complements his series of operas (♦Harmonia Mundi 901566/67). He used the standard Marian antiphons (like Picket and Jürgens/Harnoncourt) to frame the psalms. His instrumental forces are moderate in size, and his solo team (except for Kiehr and the outstanding Scholl) are stronger in abilities than big names, but his 25-member mixed-voice choir (whose men supply the choral schola) is quite substantial. As conductor, the stylistically savvy and artistically alert Jacobs offers a myriad of refined details. He makes lucid distinctions between solo and ensemble voices; solo lines are caressing and expressive in the concertos, while the psalms pulse with rhythmic vitality, and plainchant lines are kept audible as binding features of choral textures. This is a recording of outstanding musicality.

Jacobs's comparative strengths are all the more clear compared with **Hans-Christoph Rademann**'s concert performance in the following year: Local soloists, the Dresden Chamber Choir (which does some particularly fine singing), and early-instrument groups of Dresden and Leipzig present a conventional "liturgical" approach (with standard Marian antiphons) that's colorful, enjoyable, and high-quality provincial in character, but "merely excellent" amid the competition (Raumklang 9605). A cut above this is the third recording of the Vespers made in the US, by **Martin Pearlman** in 1997 with local soloists, 23 instrumentalists, and choir of 30, all from the Boston Baroque (♦Telarc

80453). Pearlman presents a very intelligently planned performance balancing choral grandeur with soloistic sensitivity, sometimes extra slow in solo segments, but always handsomely achieved with a strong sense of ensemble. If not quite as refined as Jacobs, Pearlman is certainly competitive.

Christie's 1997 recording includes standard Marian antiphons and emulates Parrott by interpolating two instrumental sonatas by Cima (♦Erato 23139). With a choir of 27 and a period-instrument group of 19, Christie invests the larger-scaled pieces with elegance and color, but in a relaxed, gentle, and lyrical fashion in contrast to Pearlman. He has a particularly fine battery of soloists, though only Agnew is likely to be recognized by name. This is a fine performance, comparable to Jacobs if a bit less assertive.

As the "liturgical" line of recorded performances took shape, objections set in to the idea of chant interpolations. It was suggested that Monteverdi's own inclusion of the extra-liturgical *concerto* alternations were meant to replace the chant antiphons in ritual use, or that he meant the collection to be a self-sufficient musical complex that transcended or bypassed mere liturgical presentation. Whatever the justifications, expressed or implied, a clear alternate line of treatments of the 1610 Vespers emerged and has flourished in what we can call the "concert" recordings—period instrument presentations of just what Monteverdi published (less Magnificat II) as a kind of abstract if historically stylish program of sacred pieces.

The first two examples of this line involved curious overlapping, in both cases with choirs using boy trebles. In 1977 four singers of the Pro Cantione Antiqua of London and members of the cautiously period-instrument ensemble Collegium Aureum, led by Franzjosef Maier, went to Montserrat monastery near Barcelona to record the Vespers under its conductor, **Ireneu Segarra,** a basically very satisfying set (Harmonia Mundi, 2LP). As if dissatisfied, two years later three of the soloists (including George) with Maier and some of his players joined other singers (Schlick and Partridge among them) and Roland Wilson's Musica Fiata ensemble, as well as the Hanover Boys' Choir, for a recording under **Heinz Hennig** (Ars Musici 1000). The first of these two has never reached CD, while the second is an attractive if somewhat overly reverent performance, a bit dated in spirit.

In 1981 the mercurial **Malgoire** jumped onto the scene with a hastily conceived version. The international mix of soloists included some fine familiars (Esswood, Ledroit, Nigel Rogers, Elwes) as well as some clinkers (the bizarre Anfuso, whose solo recordings should always be avoided, anywhere!), but the choral and instrumental forces were under-rehearsed and this release proved short-lived (CBS, 2LP). Only a little less disappointing is the oldest of this phase of recordings, by **Ledger** in 1973 (EMI/Angel). Joining the all-male King's College Choir and David Munrow's Early Music Consort of London is a near dream team of soloists (Ameling, Burrowes, Brett, Tear, Rolfe Johnson, Hill among them). But the promise held out by such talent isn't realized; the soloists rarely sound engaged (and Tear's idiosyncratic sound may strike some as a further problem), and the choir is too big. Ledger's pacing is sometimes ponderous, often tedious in his penchant for punching out rhythms, while the acoustics of King's College Chapel hamper the sound.

In issuing Vespers recordings, most producers have been singularly mean by spreading the work needlessly over two full CDs, so something should be said for EMI's generosity in filling out its bargain-rate reissue of Ledger's recording with the full contents of another LP program of 1975 in which **Willcocks** leads the big Kings' College Choir and modern brass ensembles in blatantly modern but sumptuously thrilling performances of polychoral motets by Schütz, Scheidt, and, mostly, Giovanni Gabrieli. The sum total is an undeniable bargain, if somewhat qualified (EMI 568631).

The late '80s brought two contrasting recordings by repeater conductors. In 1987, **Jürgens** led performances in Hamburg's St. Michael's Church (Ambitus). At this point, he was ostentatiously turning his back on the "liturgical" approach he had originally pioneered and emphatically embraced the "concert" rationale. Though there are some fine singers (Schlick, Elwes, Jochens among them) and instrumentalists (13, from Roland Wilson's group and others), and though the choir sings admirably, there are conspicuous inconsistencies both in singing styles and sonic balances that rule this release out as a serious contender, for all of Jürgens's dedication.

In contrast, **Gardiner** in 1989 proved that second thoughts can have sensational results. It's likely that Monteverdi may have performed some of his 1610 Vespers music in Venice once he took up work at San Marco, but beyond printing the collection in Venice, its music has no direct connection with either the church or the city. Nevertheless, the attractions of linking them are irresistible, and Gardiner was able to conduct this collection in two sessions, recording and concert, in the great building. Its tricky acoustics were managed brilliantly to produce an astoundingly realistic sense of San Marco's physical space. (Close your eyes and you are there!) And if sound isn't enough, the performance as filmed by the BBC has been released as a video and is a splendid experience in its own right (DG).

Fortunately the performance itself is lovely, full of spirit and dramatic intensity, competitive with anybody else's. The soloists include some admirable familiars (Monoyios, Chance, Mark Tucker, Robson, and a youngster named Bryn Terfel); there is a children's choir of 13 with the mixed-voice choir of 28, plus a total of 23 period instrumentalists, all directed with incisive stylishness. And as icing on the cake, when Gardiner & Co. returned to London they made a special recording of Magnificat II, to make this wonderful release the only truly "complete" recording of the Vespers beyond Schneidt and Corboz. No one who loves this music should leave this life without experiencing Gardiner II (♦DG Archiv 429565).

Of recordings in the '90s, **Frederick Renz** with his New York Grande Bande ensemble used only ten singers plus 18 players (1993: MHS 523536). With one singer per part in much of the ensemble writing, this is a version in the Parrott-Pickett tradition of minimalism, but not as smooth or well-digested stylistically. Nevertheless, MHS has at least rounded out the proceedings with three of Monteverdi's concertato madrigals (including the *Ninfa* triptych) and rare instrumental pieces by four other composers. For all that, though, an interesting try but not a prime choice.

Another problematical minimalist recording was made by the tiny but enterprising Scholars Baroque Ensemble. Led by **David van Asch,** this group has made some plucky and plausible recordings, but this one is a miscalculation. Consisting here of nine singers and 11 players, they make the minimalist approaches of Parrott and Pickett sound like adventures with the Mormon Tabernacle Choir. Scrawny, over-strained, under-styled, this recording isn't even justifiable as a "bargain" and is altogether to be avoided (1993: Naxos).

But two recent recordings have made a better case for minimalism. One is led by **Junghänel,** with ten members of his madrigalian Cantus Cölln and 16 players of the Concerto Palatino (Harmonia Mundi 77332); the other by **Jeannette Sorrell** with nine singers of her Apollo's Fire

group (with tenor Ian Honeyman as a guest) and the Cleveland Baroque Orchestra (Eclectra 2038). Junghänel gives just the Monteverdi settings, in suave and elegant renditions as a kind of intimate liturgical concert, just a bit cool in character. Sorrell includes a few bits of chant and generates quite a lot of excitement in the spirit of a small-chapel liturgy. Both demonstrate that the minimalist approach has taken considerable hold in performing this music.

The '90s have also brought us two attempts at the perfectly feasible idea of fitting the standard 1610 Vespers collection (less Magnificat II, of course) onto a single CD. With brisk tempos, this reaches a manageable length of 78 minutes in a performance by **Ralf Otto,** with choral and instrumental forces of unspecified numbers and a group of six soloists (including Prégardien, Mertens, and George); the performance is capable and colorful, though at times the pacing is rushed or choppy (Capriccio 10516). Still, in this compact form it's a better bargain than the Naxos double.

Still more economical in its way is a recording by the ever-venturesome **Hermann Max** (EMI 754546). His performing version makes a case for an alternative or "continuo version" of the collection. His point of departure is the simplified texture of Magnificat II, which he uses as a model for reducing instrumentation throughout to only continuo instruments. The instrumental lines, he argues, are or can be subsumed in the vocal parts or otherwise eliminated: thus lost are the toccata of the opening 'Responsory', all the *ritornelli,* and the *Sonata sopra "Sancta Maria"* (which is replaced by a Frescobaldi *Ricercar*). The result boils down to a tight 77 minutes. It's little more than an experiment, of course, a kind of probing the composer's methods and alternative thoughts, but still interesting. It's also excellently performed by nine very able local soloists (including Wessel and Jochens) who join with 17 others to form a beautifully disciplined and sonorous choir, plus four continuo players. Not the prime choice, but a fascinating take as it might have been designed for the chapel of a quite poor (or skinflint) prince.

That minimalism isn't wholly triumphant is demonstrated by the most recent recordings. Two constitute something of a pair, both deriving from performances in Lugano and involving overlapping personnel. Early music veteran **Nigel Rogers** both sings and conducts one made in 1993 with the Swiss Radio chorus led by Fasoli (Azzurra 21001). **Fasoli** himself tackled the work in 1999, using different PI instrumental ensembles (Arts 47594). Both performances are thoughtful and understated, but Fasoli carries those qualities sometimes to the point of slackness, while his soloists are uneven, somewhat behind those (unidentified) for Rogers. Both conductors pay their respects to liturgical concerns by including chant antiphons.

Gabriel Garrido offers the latest version, made in 1999 in his ongoing Palermo-based series (K617 100/2). He marshals choral forces totaling 26 and 31 period-instrument players for a quite spacious and full sonority. Unfortunately, his interpretation is generally rather flaccid and unimaginative. Still, his additions are interesting. Besides a few scraps of chant, he interpolates three motets for soloists (two sung by choral sections), two of them by another composer, plus an instrumental *sinfonia* by still another. Most important, he includes both settings of the Magnificat, only the fourth to do so. To Garrido's recording may be added one more, of uncertain date and origins, and seemingly available only in a big package ("1000 Years of Sacred Music," Brilliant Classics 99452, 15CD, in a 2CD component with Purcell sacred works; no notes or texts). Pforzheim and Munich forces under **Rolf Schweizer** might suggest provincial quality, but the performance is honest and enjoyable, with full chant fleshing out good period-instrument playing, a somewhat large choir, but quite fine solo work. Not a recording to hunt down, but one to be happy with if it comes your way.

Given all the problems and divergent possibilities the 1610 collection involves, there can never be any one "definitive" recording. So much depends on the options chosen: what to include and exclude; modern or period instruments; liturgical (with chant) or concert (without them) format; large scale or small. For those satisfied with modern instruments and traditional style, Gardiner I (Decca) is the strongest choice, backed by the composite Corboz (Erato). For musical comprehensiveness, Schneidt (Archiv/MHS) is indispensable, while, in the "standard" Vespers alone, the "concert" category is clearly dominated by the satisfying and atmospheric Gardiner II (DG Archiv), with Ledger (EMI) and Otto (Capriccio) very much in the bargain-rate rear. Among the many "liturgical" approaches, Jacobs (Harmonia Mundi) and Christie (Erato) are perhaps the most satisfying realizations on musical grounds, though Herreweghe (Harmonia Mundi) should also be considered. For a more scholarly approach, Parrott (EMI) is outstanding, with Pickett (Oiseau-Lyre) following close behind. I have to say, however, with a gun to my head and the ship for the desert island about to leave, I would have to make Gardiner II my ultimate personal choice.   BARKER

Douglas Moore (1893–1969)

Moore laid the foundations of the modern American musical theater style: His many operas dealt consistently with American themes and folklore within the established 19th-century European operatic style. He also enjoyed considerable success as a composer of orchestral works, but his skill in creating dramatic set pieces that explore some of the historic issues of the American experience brought wide acclaim in his lifetime.

His first major success came in 1924 with *The Pageant of P.T. Barnum,* an orchestral suite depicting scenes from the life of the legendary showman. The Eastman Rochester Orchestra's classic recording with **Hanson** is still available after 40 years (Mercury 434319, with pieces by Carpenter, Bernard Rogers and Burrill Phillips). Stephen Vincent Benet's story of *The Devil and Daniel Webster,* with its Faustian subject matter set in a New England context, was Moore's first successful opera (1938), using Benet's libretto. The modern recording of this one-act folk tale led by **Russell Patterson** with the Kansas City Lyric Opera and Symphony (Newport 85585) is far superior to the '60s recording by the Festival Orchestra and Chorus led by **Armando Aliberti** (Phoenix 103).

Moore's best known and most popular opera, *The Ballad of Baby Doe* (1956), tells the tale of the Wisconsin beauty who remains loyal to her husband after he loses everything in the 1893 collapse of the silver market. It's offered by the Central City Opera Orchestra and Chorus led by **John Moriarty** (Newport 85593, 2CD). In the following year Moore wrote *Gallantry,* a one-act TV operatic satire on radio and television; it's quite interesting but not compelling listening, as played by the New York Chamber Ensemble led by **Stephen Rodgers Radcliffe** (Albany 173, with works by Hindemith and Menotti). It's a pity his last opera, *Carrie Nation,* is out of the catalog, as this dark fable of alcoholism is one of his most powerful works.

"American Masters" features three of Moore's best orchestral works (CRI 714, with pieces by Marion Bauer). *Farm Journal* (1948) is a suite of homespun but never banal, almost Coplandesque portraits of rural life. The more abstract Symphony in A (1945, actually his second) is informed by stylistic references to folk music, and *Cotillion* (1952) ploughs a similarly engaging furrow. The Oslo Philharmonic is led by **Alfredo Antonini** and the Japan Philharmonic by **William Strickland.**

None of this music is going to ignite the world, but there's no doubt of its craftsmanship and atmospheric appeal.

Finally, *In Memoriam* for orchestra is his most serious tone poem, dedicated "to those who die young." Its sense of loss can't be denied, and it's keenly executed in a performance by the Japan Philharmonic led by **Strickland** (Citadel 88133, with works by Diamond, Koussevitsky, and Quincy Porter). I hope his fine 1946 Clarinet Quintet, once available on a CRI LP, will reappear before too long.   JOHNSON

Ignaz Moscheles (1794–1870)

Hanslick's description of Moscheles as "the last great composer of the classical school and yet the creator of a new era" handily sums up the paradox of Ignaz Moscheles, perhaps the foremost pianist after Hummel and before Chopin. Acclaimed for his formidable keyboard prowess, he settled in London before becoming Professor of Piano at the Leipzig Conservatory at the urging of its founder Mendelssohn, where he was a devoted, even paternal mentor. One of the most respected and beloved artists of his day, his music breathes the very essence of the Romantic style, grateful to pianist and listener alike, and you will be all the better for making his acquaintance.

Moscheles's few purely orchestral works comprise a fascinating disc under **Athinäos** (♦Signum 96). The fresh and energetic Symphony in C betrays the influences of Beethoven and Mozart, yet with a melodic impulse very much Moscheles's own; the Overture to Schiller's *Maid of Orleans* deftly combines the martial and spiritual personae of Joan of Arc. Piano Concerto 6 (*Concert Fantastique*) seamlessly melds the usual three movements into one; sadly, Liu Xiao Ming's percussive tone and assertive mien prove distracting. The final rondo of Concerto 3 suggests Beethoven in an uncommonly playful mood. **Ponti,** in Vol. 2 of the "Romantic Piano Concerto" series, may be set aside; it's heavily cut and rather aggressive (Vox). Instead, you should look for a beautiful disc with **Ivan Klánský,** coupled with the Concerto for Flute and Oboe and a delightful solo work, *Bonbonnière Musicale* (♦Supraphon 1326).

Hobson is recording all eight of Moscheles's piano concertos, conducting from the keyboard as Moscheles himself may have done (♦Zephyr 116-99). Volume 1, containing 2 and 4, is splendid in every way, contrasting the Beethovenian pomp and exhilarating final *Tempo di Polacca* of 2 with the expansive and resolute 4, its robust Rondo finale joyfully working up the familiar tune "The British Grenadiers" in a manner that must have brought London audiences to their feet.

For a sampler of Moscheles's chamber music, you can hardly do better than the CD containing the *Grand Septet in D; Grand Sonata Concertante* for flute and piano; *Introduction and Scottish Rondo* for piano and horn; and two short Etudes, all wonderfully set forth by a **Hamburg** ensemble who clearly love this music very much (♦Koch Schwann 1178). Another fine recording has the Septet plus the *Grand Sextet in E-flat* and *Fantasy, Variations and Finale on a Bohemian Folk Song* played beautifully by the **Consortium Classicum** (MD+G 301 0669).

Moscheles's piano pieces are filled with virtuoso display and introspective sentiment, combining the expressive quality of Brahms with Liszt's fire and passion. **Frederick Marvin** offers an admirable account of the elegant and flowing Sonata in B-flat along with a sonata by Mendelssohn's teacher Ludwig Berger and Liszt's daunting *Grosses Konzertsolo* (Genesis 109). **Loredana Brigandi** essays all 24 of Moscheles's Op. 70 Etudes plus *Allegro di Bravura;* unfortunately, completeness comes at the cost of stiff and colorless readings and less than alluring piano sound (Nuova Era). **Ponti** only offers a representative sampling, but his lively and adept renditions present the music in a far more compelling light (Vox). **Noël Lee** effortlessly meets all of the challenges posed by the pieces in his collection (*Sonate mélancolique, Allegro di Bravura, Rondeau Brilliant* and Etudes), but fails to capture their romantic spirit (Arion). HALLER

Moritz Moszkowski *(1854–1925)*

Moszkowski is primarily known among music lovers as a composer of tidbits and salon pieces, a justified reputation, at least in part. However, his dazzling, opulent Piano Concerto in E is proof that he was well versed in handling large forms; its colorful orchestration attests to his highly developed skill at instrumentation (Beecham studied orchestration with him in Paris).

Fialkowska has recorded this scintillating but little-known concerto with the Kitchener-Waterloo Symphony (CBC 5140). Her performance casts a mesmerizing spell, shot through with her typical dash and superb polish. **Ponti**'s version with the Philharmonia Hungarica is also a thrilling tour de force (in "The Romantic Piano Concerto" Vol. 3, Vox 5066). Fialkowska plays it with a bit more fleetness, while Ponti emphasizes power. The sound is a little clearer and more immediate in the latter. This concerto is bound to please, as will either Fialkowska's or Ponti's superb playing.

The youthful German pianist **Markus Pawlik** and the Polish National Radio Symphony under Wit recorded this work in 1996 (Naxos 553989). Their pace is somewhat more deliberate, which results in less brilliance but more "heartstrings." The sound is very rich and well balanced. The orchestral suite *From Foreign Lands* fills out the disc and helps make it an excellent budget choice. Mr. Haller says that **Piers Lane** blows hot and cold, alternately flailing about and tempering passion with languor (Hyperion), while **Raekallio** is fanciful enough but the orchestra is too distant (Ondine), and **David Bar-Illan** makes a huge cut in the third movement (Audiofon).

Very stylish playing characterizes **Seta Tanyel**'s three discs of smaller pieces. She has technique to burn and plays with soul and sensitivity. In Vol. 1, alongside such decadent powder-puffs as the *Valse* Op. 34:1 and *Albumblatt* Op. 2, are the haunting *En Automne,* the surging and substantial Tarantella Op. 27:2, and the perfect encore piece, *La Jongleuse*—all of which display Moszkowski's unerring ability to write evocatively for the piano in an age that is sadly, some would say, a bygone era (Collins 1412, Vol. 1; 1473, Vol. 2; 1519, Vol. 3). The sound is full, clear, and resonant.

Swann is the ideal pianist to bring to life the 15 *Etudes de virtuosité* ("Per aspera ad astra"). He plays them with élan and delicious geniality, and is well recorded (Arkadia 112.1). Two of these Etudes, 6 and 11, pop up on **Horowitz**'s "Encores" (RCA 7755). Of course, he brings his customary startling virtuosity to bear on these pieces and turns them into incomparable performances. *Etincelles* Op. 36:6 (a favorite encore of Josef Hofmann) appears on "Horowitz in Moscow" (DG 125264); it's even more breathtaking on Music & Arts 666 (2CD). **Hough** included two of the more innocuous bon-bons in his "Piano Album 2," the well-known *Serenata* Op. 15:1 and *Valse mignonne* (Virgin 759304). Both are played with grace and suavity. Last but not least is **Bolet**'s incomparable performance of *La Jongleuse,* one of the encores in his historic 1974 Carnegie Hall recital, all of which is included in his "Great Pianists of the 20th Century" set (Philips 456724, 2CD).

The suite *From Foreign Lands* Op. 23, is nicely played by the Polish National Radio Symphony Orchestra under **Wit** (Naxos 553989, with the Piano Concerto). Moszkowski originally wrote this suite for piano duet and then arranged it for full orchestra. Six movements are each named

after a European nationality; they are short and lots of fun, a romp in assorted national costumes. *Spanish Dances* was transcribed for orchestra from the original 4-hand piano score; Mr. Haller tells me that **Ataulfo Argenta**'s performance has long been a mainstay in the London catalog, and their most recent reissue is a best buy (Decca 466376, with Debussy's *Images*). The Violin Concerto in C has at last found its way into the catalog, performed by **Thomas Christian** and the Bamberg Symphony (Koch Schwann 3672). MULBURY

Wolfgang Amadeus Mozart *(1756–1791)*

There is a saying among musicians that when the angels play for God, they play Bach, but when they play for themselves, they play Mozart. And if it's true that Otto Klemperer once said "Beethoven crashes the gates of heaven, while Mozart comes down from heaven," it was a singular insight on his part. If perfection could ever be established in any art, surely Mozart's music would serve as the model. No other composer has ever achieved such exquisite balance, heaven-sent proportions, or that elusive, innate feeling of rightness that floods the senses every time one listens to his magnificent music.

He was primarily a composer of the theater, and this is reflected in his nonoperatic music as well. From the dramatic entrance of the piano in his C minor Concerto, or the turbulent melodic constraints of the G minor String Quintet, you can hear the human voice as an inaudible but firmly realistic presence behind everything he wrote. His forte was concertos (especially piano), opera, chamber music, and choral works. His music is the definition of that old cliché, "timeless," and remains remarkably fresh and vital time and time again.

SYMPHONIES

Though the last six symphonies are rightly regarded as the summit of the classical form, Mozart was not the consistent, masterly symphonist that Haydn was. Of course, he didn't have as much time, either. He was always the pragmatist, turning out works as they were needed, and symphonies weren't always high on the list—witness the large number of serenades and divertimentos by comparison. But what he did leave in his last few years is incomparable, works that were marveled at by his and later generations, and few composers since then have even come close to the perfection found here.

Complete and partial sets. There have been a few traversals of all the Mozart symphonies. Record companies have generally avoided such undertakings because of the difficulty of selling the packages—usually around 12 or 13 CDs. Only one set can be considered an unqualified success. **Böhm** completed a series that in every way outclasses any competition. It's a wonderful, superbly recorded, utterly idiomatic and tasteful survey by one of the master Mozartians of our time. It may not be easily attainable, but it will be back, and it's worth its weight in gold (♦DG).

Philips has combined **Marriner**'s recordings of the early symphonies with **Krips**'s readings of the middle through late works. Krips's Mozart is always problematical. While providing some of the finest, cleanest, classically delineated recordings ever (with the Concertgebouw), he is too often plagued by a lack of vitality and spirit, most noticeable in the last six. His readings of 31–34 are excellent, but coupled as they are with Marriner's dubious early symphonies, this collection is a questionable purchase (Philips). In **Leinsdorf**'s set the mono sound is for the most part very good, and he's always interesting in Mozart (MCA). But it's far from the best (even at its budget price), and with so many excellent versions on the market, only those with a particular affection for this conductor should investigate it.

Mackerras brought hope to listeners when he embarked on his set with the Prague Chamber Orchestra, using a harpsichord all the way through and presenting rigorous, always-fast tempos (and lots of repeats). But his is a bland, same-color palette; this is Mozart in black and white, with little variation in texture, timbre, or textual perspective—all in all, with few exceptions, quite dull (Telarc). **Levine** has offered the entire symphonic corpus, and we might have anticipated something great, since his early Mozart was excellent and he had the nonpareil playing of the Vienna Philharmonic (DG). But the results are also curiously bland; it's as if he decided to take no point of view at all, and even the sterling craftsmanship of the Viennese can't save this nondescript set. It's a major disappointment.

Hogwood was the first to complete a period instrument roundup of all the symphonies, and the international press generally gave its full blessing. The set still sells fairly well, probably because it has been offered in multiple boxes as well as a single boxed set. I can't deny the brisk *joie de vivre* of this collection (Oiseau-Lyre 452496). Obviously much thought and care went into its production, and a couple of the individual works (like 25 and 29) are truly outstanding. Yet Hogwood's Academy of Ancient Music—while miles better than the wretched early recordings of Harnoncourt's Concentus Musicus Wien—still presents, in almost trademark fashion, an astringent, brittle style of playing that wears on the nerves after a time. It's best to choose one of the early volumes if you wish to sample this collection.

Among partial sets, **Pinnock**'s go at the so-called "Salzburg" symphonies is altogether successful, a much toned down period production that captures the special character of these young works; you won't find a better set (♦Archiv 439915). Likewise, **Kehr** supplies shapely, finely wrought performances of 26–34 that equal Pinnock's, in fine sound and at a bargain price. It's a great way to introduce yourself to these works (♦Vox 5072, 3CD).

Walter's monaural recordings of 5, 28, 29, and 35–41 are in a class by themselves, and these releases warrant careful attention by all Mozart lovers. If his last stereo recordings remain indispensable, these earlier readings show a slightly different conductor at work, often more energetic and spirited, while perhaps a little less autumnal and reflective (Sony). Stay far away from **Fricsay**; it's slow, somnambulant, late night Mozart that proves willful and disoriented, and the Vienna Symphony is hardly a band to write home about (DG). **Toscanini** is another woeful, wrong-headed Mozart interpreter. All you need to hear is his searing, perverse account of 35 to understand what his misconstrued notions of Mozart are all about. He was a wonderful Haydn conductor, but his Mozart is way out of bounds (RCA).

Marriner has several recordings, on Philips and (more recently) EMI. Avoid either, for his Mozart is sterile and lifeless; though flawlessly played by the Academy of St. Martin in the Fields and fairly well recorded, there is no sense that the composer is being treated as anyone special. Too many of the symphonies are competent, highly polished run-throughs that may be OK for department store background music, but bad for serious listening. **Kubelik** made the first digital series of the last six symphonies, and they are very good (Sony, NA). The Prague Symphony is in tip-top form, and little can be added in the way of commitment and nuance. This is a fine alternative if they are released again. **Maag** is an excellent, grossly underrated conductor who has made many fine recordings over the years. Unfortunately, his scrappy Italian band can't provide the necessary tonal luster or technical prowess to convey his many unique insights (Arts).

Early Symphonies. Arguments about the significance of Mozart's childhood symphonies abound: are they the unimpressive scribblings of a prepubescent child or the inspired utterances of a boy wonder? He *was* a wonder, of course, but that doesn't imply that we should take his childhood attempts at composition any more seriously than the youthful efforts of, say, Mendelssohn or Haydn. (In fact, perhaps we should take *them* even more seriously; Haydn's symphonic corpus is, taken as a whole, superior to Mozart's). What we do have are amazing works from a child so young; his first symphony was composed at age eight. Instead of lamenting the fact that 1 doesn't sound like 41, we should be astonished at just how much pleasure these early pieces still afford. They are by no means necessary even for the most complete collections, but if you love Mozart and explore this particular mine, you may be enchanted.

Marriner was one of the pioneers in this music, producing the first set of the early symphonies that was free of mannerisms, sharply executed, and faithfully realized. But in the process a deadly fatigue set in, and all these works take on a monochromatic hue that is most unfair to the young Mozart (Philips). **Böhm**'s Mozart is by a master, and while it's hard to say when his set will reappear, when it does, grab it—these early works haven't been done better (♦DG 453231, 10CD). **Graf**'s Salzburg Mozarteum Orchestra plays them with obvious relish and style, but with some rather strange ideas about phrasing and articulation. This is concise and tidied up Mozart; at the same time it's energetic and brisk, worth sampling at its low price (♦LaserLight 867-9, 3CD).

Nicholas Ward has produced a beautiful traversal of the early symphonies and his collection is one of the best on the market. Buttery smooth string sound and perfectly judged tempos make these discs a first choice (♦Naxos 550871-5, five separate discs). **Kehr**'s set with the Mainz Chamber Orchestra remains one of the best, a delightfully inexpensive way to invest in these works (♦Vox 5070). The sound is wonderful, the playing is thoroughly professional in all respects; the music gets all the careful attention it deserves. The early works by **Levine,** part of his complete set, aren't generally available and really won't be missed; they don't represent the conductor at his best, or even his best Mozart for that matter. Fastidious, artificially pointed, and sterile phrasing are only some of the hallmarks of these wooden performances (DG).

Mackerras also includes the early symphonies in his set, and with the exception of one disc (reviewed below), he can't be counted on as a reliable guide to these works (Telarc). The rigid tempos, strict phrasing and de-emphasis of the songful lines make them all sound similarly dull. For some reason, **Pinnock**'s set of 1–25 never seemed to garner as much attention as Hogwood's, and that's a shame, for they really raise the bar for period instrument playing. While a few of Hogwood's more adventurous readings do surpass Pinnock's, for the most part the latter's versions are vivacious and mercurial, with slow movements that linger in a most convincing way. Aside from Böhm, this may be the best set, if you can locate it (♦Archiv 437792, 4CD).

Harnoncourt gives measured, sensible readings of 10, 11, 42, and 44–46. The string tone is uncommonly good and the manner well pleasing and enjoyable, unlike his later versions (♦Teldec 25914). **Scimone** supplies enchanting, wholly considered renditions of 1–19 and 55, in excellent sound. They are treated as if greater than they are and this enhances their listening value in a fine, very intimate series (♦Arts 47100, 47101, 47277, 47278).

Middle symphonies (25–34). Often dismissed as mere entertainments, these juvenile works offer much to the discerning listener. While nowhere near the profundity and superb compositional maturity of the last six, they have a delightful, insouciant feeling that makes for eminently satisfying listening time and time again. Ignore these works only if you find charm and high spirits distasteful. (Note: 25 and 29 are discussed individually below.)

26 is lowest on the list, rarely recorded except in complete sets. **Ward** gives the best reading on the market, far outclassing the EMI Marriner (♦Naxos 550876, with 21–24). **Groves,** as expected, gives us superbly idiomatic and tasteful readings of 27, 28, and 34 (♦IMP 933). The English Sinfonia plays like Beecham's Royal Philharmonic and the spirit and sense of unbridled joy couldn't be more evident. **Beecham** himself is no slouch in 27 (Dutton), though many will prefer another coupling than the Flute and Harp concerto that's in better sound (EMI). Avoid **Wordsworth** in 27 and 28; he's not competitive at all (Naxos). **Claudio Abbado**'s Berliners play 28 like no others, but an opportunity was wasted. Why reduce this orchestra? It's smartly played and in excellent sound, but the questionable 29 and 35 should probably steer you away (Sony).

Walter may be the best choice in 28, even in mono, with 25, 29, and a glorious 35 as discmates (♦Sony 64473). 30 is another tough call, almost as ignored as 26. In this case, since the price is so low, you might opt for **Wordsworth,** though I can't say I think much of the 29 and 38 that tag along (Naxos). **Mackerras**'s 30 is one of the better versions, perhaps the lone exception (♦Telarc 80188, with 24, 26, and 27).

31 ("Paris") was an important work for Mozart, who was trying to take advantage of the Parisian love for big effects and large ensembles; any recording that shrinks it to chamber size must be ignored. This knocks out **Wordsworth** (Naxos), **Marriner** (EMI), and **Mackerras** (Telarc) right off the bat. **Ormandy** gives a deliciously vibrant, highly energetic reading with full orchestra in tow, exactly what's needed, along with an equally concentrated 30. There's no repose here—as if there were room for any—and a festive atmosphere is vividly conveyed (♦Sony 62827).

There's no sense of bloated occasion in **Beecham**'s reading; it's uptempo, feisty, and brilliantly executed, as are 29 and 34 coupled with it (♦Dutton 5008). It's evident that he thought as much of this work as 25 and 29, and it remains one of the most thrilling on record, even in mono. **Klemperer** takes a big band, monolithic approach that fits snugly into Mozart's intentions. Though not as high strung as Ormandy, the overall reading is quite effective (♦EMI 63272, 4CD). There can be no doubt that **Abbado** has kept the Berlin Philharmonic in fine fettle during his tenure; no orchestra articulates as well, and they are a perfect Mozart band. But he plays every note of 31 as if he has some kind of point to make, and the end result is like getting clobbered by a teacher who is trying to drill a lesson into you over and over (Sony).

Groves's "Paris" is completely in sympathy with its style; the strings are lush and rich and there is a relaxed, flexible manner in evidence all through it. The sound is superb; this is one for the books (♦IMP 933). **Saraste** doesn't turn in a bad performance of 32, but the pizzazz and explosiveness of the opening chords just aren't there, and the Scottish Chamber Orchestra feels featherweight (Virgin). To hear the difference, listen to **Maag** and the London Symphony: The sound is big, bold, brilliant, yet tempered in the slow section with unparalleled poetry (♦Decca 466500). This is a fabulous disc of little played and known Mozart, deserving a place in any collection. **Wordsworth** gives us a wonderful 32: It is taut, tight, and terrifically played. But his couplings (25 and 41) are lackluster, and I doubt if even the low price is worth eight minutes of playing time (Naxos).

Rifkin's 32 is hyperactive, dull, and unnecessary (Capriccio).

Levine, always iffy in Mozart, strikes a winner with 32, though there are problems with his "Posthorn" Serenade, the major work on the disc (DG). **Klemperer** gives rousing readings of 33 and 34, well played but not manic, always giving way to the lyrical element, even in the allegros (♦EMI, 63272, 4CD). **Iona Brown** leads a festive, dexterous rendition of 33 with the St. Martin Academy. Showing how fluently melodic the young composer could be, she capitalizes on every rapid tempo he provides, and the results are thrilling (♦Hänssler 98129).

Lucinda Carver and her Los Angeles Mozart Orchestra surprise us with a very efficient, never dull 17 and 34. The sound is great and the interpretation second to none (♦RCM 19603). **Barbirolli** is always worth hearing, and his 33 (along with a fine Beethoven 4) is stirring and fluid (♦Dutton 1011). **Jane Glover** (with a fine 25 and 29) turns in an outstanding performance in sound that's a little obscure, yet clear enough to let her wonderful orchestra shine through (♦ASV 717).

Graf gives us an unbeatable 34 with his splendid Salzburg Mozarteum, in stunning sound complemented by precise, spirited playing. The coupled "Haffner" is excellent, while the "Linz" is a little quick-paced to be effective, but at its low price it hardly matters (♦LaserLight 15864). **Wordsworth** gives a very nice reading with his 35 and 39, perhaps the two best late symphonies of his set (Naxos). It's worth consideration if you're on a budget, though Graf is better in all these works, and his two discs sell for a little over half the price of Wordsworth.

25. The "little" G minor marks the opening of Mozart's great series of symphonic essays. It can't be considered in the same company as the last six, but too often too little attention is paid to these middle works ("middle" being an approximate term for a composer who died at 35). Often the composer tried his hand at various styles that passed his way, only later incorporating what he learned in a more profound and serious manner. This first example of *Sturm und Drang* in his work was to find full fruition in that later, most perfect of masterpieces, the "big" G minor. This work is but a seed, a young man's experiment, and his materials are nowhere as intricate as the later pieces. But he does whip up a storm, and it remains the most popular of his teenage symphonies.

Britten uses his profound musical sensibilities to deliver a stormy, tempest-laden account that nonetheless has a slow movement as restful as the eye of a hurricane; it's an outstanding version (♦Decca 44323, 2CD). With some saucy, sprightly oboe playing in the minuet, **Abbado** comes across as tempestuous and vital, played to the hilt, but lacking any sense of stillness (♦Sony 48385). "Storm and stress" should reflect a temperament, not bolt into a manic rush for artificial devices designed to exploit "seriousness;" still, Abbado is exhilarating. **Bernstein** leads a highly lyrical account, with richness and color, but he plays down the horns, so essential to the piece. Despite excellent phrasing and dynamics, the overall effect suffers from a lack of clarity (DG).

Klemperer's reading is close to ideal. A scorching, red hot I sets the stage for the tranquil II, but even that is fraught with underlying tension, a conflict resolved tactfully by his transition-like III, culminating in a wonderful, not too fast finale (♦EMI 63272, 4CD). **Wordsworth** provides a version with an exposed underbelly. While his lyrical sensibilities can be appreciated, there isn't enough *noise* here to garner attention (Naxos). Using a miniscule orchestra (strings 5-5-3-3-1), **Pinnock** gives an acceptable, clean recording that ignores the repeats (no bad thing) and is a little calmer in his storm than, say, Hogwood, to compare peers. It's OK but not as satisfying as his early symphonies (Archiv).

Groves shows his excellent Mozartian credentials in a reading of stirring emotions and ambivalent contrasts, making Mozart's uncertain juvenilia that much more ambiguous and interesting. The English Sinfonia's excellent playing adds to the enterprise (♦IMP 6702502). **Böhm** gives a very well considered performance, as always, but is too affect-laden, imparting a gravity and heaviness that aren't really there. This may be a work of storm and stress, but only that of a teenage child imitating others and hardly feeling the burden that would bear down on him later (DG).

Glover is more than run of the mill, in outstanding sound and benefitting from obvious care in shaping and balance. The players respond with attention and devotion to the music (ASV). **Koopman** gives us a suave, toned-down production, not a bad reading but less than honest in its presentation of young Mozartian *angst* (Erato). If you insist on period instruments, **Hogwood**'s version, even with scrappier sound, provides far more satisfaction (Oiseau-Lyre). **Walter** currently has two recordings on the market, his New York (Sony) version and a very intense, volatile Vienna reading (♦Orfeo 430961). Both are worthwhile, but the Vienna's seething passion and manic mood swings make it something special. The sound is good mono.

29. It remains astonishing that an 18-year-old could have written something as refined and convivial as the A major. The last of Mozart's so-called "Salzburg" symphonies, the young composer here is beginning to strike out on his own, still intent on maintaining tight motivic control but equally intent on generating a relaxed, friendly atmosphere. The Andante in particular, with its lovely, ever-so-smooth muted strings and delightful, surprisingly biting winds, is a joy few Mozart lovers could live without. The finale is a young man's gigue, the very embodiment of youth's romping spiritual ecstasy.

The bloated, flabby rhythms and tubby sound of **Entremont**'s recording do little to enhance the already second-rate tone of the Vienna Chamber Orchestra (Sony). He really has no idea how to conduct this, and the result is a frightening example of what a bad conductor can do to Mozart. In spite of the prissiness of some of **Beecham**'s articulations and style of ornamentation in I, he recovers enough in the three remaining movements to make his recording worthwhile. II is especially poignant, quite beautiful even in mono sound (♦Dutton 5008). You will listen in amazed bewilderment when you hear how fast the Berlin Philharmonic strings can articulate the 16th notes in **Abbado**'s finale. But *allegro con spirito* doesn't mean "super fast" any more than the conductor's first movement could be called *moderato*. His II is also stretched too far—but you should hear that last movement! (Sony).

Groves and his smooth-sounding English Sinfonia give a gorgeous, entirely idiomatic rendition, full of life, sparkle, and wit. The sound is as good as it gets, and each movement is sculpted to perfection (♦IMP 922). **Klemperer** is the essence of good manners in this work, neither pulling Mozart's long-winded lines out of recognition, nor stalling the phrases, nor letting any detail slip by. It's similar to Groves, though the sound isn't quite as good (♦EMI 63272, 4CD). **Bernstein** tries to enhance this work when no enhancement is needed, even to the point of catching the Vienna Philharmonic off guard at the end of II. It's not a bad reading—Bernstein was incapable of that in Mozart—but it doesn't rank with his best (DG). **Britten** leads a vivacious, wonderfully spontaneous version, reveling in the crisp, crackling rhythms and frolicsome high spirits. The English Chamber Orchestra isn't the most tone-friendly group in the world, but their contribution shouldn't be underestimated (♦Decca 44323, 2CD).

Wordsworth makes a miserable attempt at this work with an orchestra that struggles to stay in tune. II is loved to death, pulled out of bal-ance at phrase endings, and the finale is again intonationally challenged; avoid it at all costs (Naxos). **Lucinda Carver** offers a wonderful reading, and her 17 and 34 are as delightful as any around. The excellent sound seals this release with a kiss (♦RCM 19603). **Karajan**'s 1970 version is in many ways better than his later DG, at least in terms of sound, but there is far too much "Forward, march!" and too little rose-smelling in a work full of flowers (EMI).

Walter gives an inspiring, soothing reading that seems to find the essence of Mozart—grace, charm, intense feeling, and an unalloyed spirituality. Even in mono, it's well worth your time (♦Sony 64473). **Iona Brown** and the Norwegian Chamber Orchestra conjure up some truly lovely sounds in a spirited performance of depth and substance. Its disc-mate *Eine kleine Nachtmusik* is equally affecting, a tribute to this fine conductor (♦Omega 1004). **Davies** is too brightly recorded and lacks interpretation (Discover).

De Preist, not known as a Mozartian, turns in a nominal reading, but at only 41 minutes for the entire disc, surely they're joking! (Delos, with 4 and 5). If you think you might like the "little" G minor by **Koopman,** by all means give it a try (Erato), but Hogwood's is far better, if you can find it (Oiseau-Lyre). **Glover,** always pretty much of a sure thing in Mozart, gives a fine performance in superb sound, coupled with an excellent 25 and 33, though I wouldn't want it as my only performance (ASV). **Böhm** is somewhat of an acquired taste in this work. Many love his version, seductive and as sensitive as a doting masseuse, but while not denying its virtues, I think it lacks flair and is overly caressed (DG).

35 ("Haffner"). In 1782, Mozart hurriedly assembled a serenade in honor of Sigmund Haffner, on whom the dignity of nobility was bestowed. Naturally he wanted to make a good impression, and the serenade was one of his calling cards at a time when he was also enjoying success at the Vienna Opera. Later he fashioned its four-movement form and added clarinets and flutes to the outer movements to create what we now know as the "Haffner" symphony. It foreshadows the intense motivic development of the later "Jupiter" and is certainly a supreme example of his symphonic prowess at this stage of life. Buoyant and joyous, it's as grand a work as he ever wrote.

From the opening chords of **Saraste**'s "Haffner," the ambient sound doesn't betray the fact that he uses a chamber orchestra. Like Szell, he takes the unwritten repeat in I and falters only slightly with a sluggish IV. The Scottish Chamber Orchestra is flawless (Virgin). The dry acoustics of Abbey Road Studio where **Klemperer** recorded Mozart's earlier symphonies (ending with 35) do little to flatter the Philharmonia's sound, especially the reedy, piercing oboe. Given the less than grand I and the positively lugubrious minuet, that is decidedly not one of his better efforts (EMI).

Despite a change of venue from Abbey Road to Kingsway Hall (in the middle of the first movement!), the remastered sound is wonderful in **Beecham**'s recording. In the absence of his later EMI mono recordings—no better interpretively—his hand-picked London Philharmonic and uncanny ability to present Mozart in a sympathetic manner in this early Columbia recording wins a place on any Mozart lover's want list (♦Dutton 5001). But lo and behold! The change of venue problem is solved with a new 1958 air check, though the result is still monaural (♦BBC 4027). It's well worth hearing if you can't find his next recording. The reverence many attach to his 1958 stereo version goes much deeper than the elemental and rather rude stereo sound would suggest. The conductor arrived at a more reflective manner with this work, and a more loving "Haffner" would not appear until Walter's recording. Beechamites and dedicated Haffnerites will have to have it (♦Music and Arts 631).

Kubelik's early '60s Vienna recording suffers from a sonic congestive disorder and an unattractive rawness. It's competent and professional, but singularly uninspired (EMI). His later digital recording with the Bavarian Radio Symphony is far better, offering remarkable playing and interpretation (Sony). The Berlin Philharmonic plays with power and great delicacy for **Abbado** (Sony). It's almost ideal—flowing, sturdy, and played with amazing agility. Only the overlong II, which stretches the symphony way out of proportion, precludes this as a first choice. The sound is spacious and realistic, if a little hard. **Walter** brings his incomparable sense of humanity to every bar of this piece, one of the best on record. He teases, cajoles, caresses, and consoles with an arsenal of musical insights; don't miss it for any reason (♦Sony 64473).

Böhm is rarely challenged in warmth of expression or depth of feeling. He does nothing to inhibit the wide-staged Berlin Philharmonic sound and they seem to relish digging into this classical fare. You can't go wrong with this stately, rewarding recording (♦DG 47416, 2CD). **Brown** and her Academy of St. Martin in the Fields grace us with a performance of acrobatic finesse and tonal brilliance coated in milky-warm sound. Rarely has any set of strings negotiated Mozart's dizzying displays of technical opulence with such exactitude and style. This fights for a place in the "finest ever" sweepstakes (♦Hänssler 98173).

From the opening sounds of **Reiner**'s recording, we're off to the races, and if there were any question that the Pittsburgh Symphony in 1946 was one of the best in the country, this answers it. Taking the reins in Chicago may have been a step down, judging by what we hear on his disc (Sony). The sound is superb mono, though Reiner's relentless ravings and extreme tempos may grow tiresome after repeated hearings. But what a ride! Great structural unity, perfectly gauged tempos, and resplendent, brilliant tone make **Szell** almost untouchable in this music. All movements are flawlessly judged, and the perfection of Mozart is wedded to the perfection of the Cleveland Orchestra. The experience is breathtaking, and everyone should have this, the greatest "Haffner" on records (♦Sony 46333). His Salzburg recording pales in comparison (Orfeo).

Next to Szell, I can only second **Bernstein**'s Vienna recording as worth its many accolades (♦Penguin 460615). His 35 is dark, richly hued, and always suggests tragedy beneath the surface. But what exuberance and unbridled excitement in the finale, where you can almost see the Vienna players lifted out of their seats in the final measures! **Karajan**'s recording is overwhelming in its sense of Teutonic power, producing a sound more reminiscent of Beethoven than Mozart. The Berliners show great finesse in this bloated effort, but officiousness is never a substitute for wit and grace in Mozart (DG or EMI).

Graf leads a fusion-powered, highly upbeat account that captures Mozart's vision faithfully. The Salzburg Mozarteum plays as if they own this music, and the price is great, but with so many other wonderful discs, I suggest it only as a cheap, reliable supplement (LaserLight). Compared to Graf, **Wordsworth** offers a rather slack and unexciting version that does little to ingratiate itself. The orchestra is fine, but suffers from malnutrition; it's quite underweight (Naxos).

Dohnányi rivals Szell in his approach (Decca). The sound is splendid, and he shows a degree of spontaneity and flexibility not often heard in his other recordings. **Harnoncourt** makes 35 a battle cry, not an entertainment, and his extraordinary ability to grab our attention with new and novel approaches doesn't work in a piece that was intended for pure enjoyment (Teldec). **Krips**'s Chesky account falls short of his later Philips recording, though that one also was a bit skeletal and light. **Brit-**

ten brings his usual flair and finesse to a 1972 program of miscellany that includes the "Haffner" (BBC).

36 ("Linz"). Taking advantage of the hospitality of Count Johann Joseph Anton von Thun-Hohenstein of Linz in 1783, Mozart, upon finding himself without a work on hand to honor his host, created the so-called "Linz" symphony. It reflects in its graciousness the graciousness he found in his host, who evidently showered him with kindness. The work is gloriously shorn of all darkness, bathing in a refined, agreeable light that projects gentleness and high hopes. Some conductors are at a loss in this piece, either turning it into a barnburner or embracing it in a fatal love-death. Few find the right combination of anticipatory excitement and amiable manners.

Beecham brings his customary elegance and grace to this, the most elegant and graceful of all Mozart's symphonies. I does suffer slightly from a congested start and II is a little precious for my taste, but he's always worthwhile in Mozart, and I wouldn't want to be without it (♦Dutton 5001). **Kubelik**'s Vienna recording once again fails to persuade us of Mozart's marvelous symphonic structures, due in no small part to the rather inelegant, inexpressive playing of the Vienna Philharmonic (EMI).

Böhm is very much the quintessential Mozartian, always manifesting a profound understanding of the composer's music, navigating the treacherous road between prissiness (Krips) and bombast (Karajan) with a sure and steady hand. His "Linz" is remarkable for its poise and pacing, a stunning reading (♦DG 47416, 2CD). **Saraste** is a careful Mozartian, showing some unusual turns of phrase and a nice feeling for the melodic line, but the Scottish Chamber Orchestra is understaffed and thin in a work that should be loaded with grandeur (Virgin).

After a normal introduction, **Klemperer** strides into the corral with all guns blazing, giving the Philharmonia players a chance to show just how dexterous they can be. I is very fast, but he pulls it all together, and the flying fingers of the Philharmonia strings show no signs of an emasculated Mozart. This superb reading is not for the faint of heart or those who like "Mozart for Breakfast" (♦EMI 63272, 4 CD). The over-inflated behemoth of **Karajan**'s reading does little for his Mozartian accreditation. The obnoxious timpani drown out everything they come into contact with, and the conductor's parody-like III is ponderous and paralyzing (DG or EMI).

Let me say it plainly: **Bernstein** *owns* this symphony. He recorded it three times, and each is a gem. The early Vienna version isn't available at the moment, but seek it out with a vengeance when it appears (DG). His 1966 Vienna recording is almost its equal, and better than all others; don't miss it (♦Decca 48570). **Walter** finds all manner of means to highlight the expressive delights of this work. Yet this is no dainty reading; coupled with the customary dignity of a Walter reading is a sense of muscular agility that's not afraid to allow Mozart some real punch (♦Sony 64474). **Graf** takes the Klemperer approach: Very rapid tempos in I are just borderline acceptable, but work beautifully in IV. This is the weakest of his series, but still good at the price (LaserLight).

Along with 39, this is the best of **Wordsworth**'s late Mozart series—though, while it has a lot of verve, it's not the best (Naxos). **Dohnányi**'s version is more inflexible and stoic than others in his series; aside from the great sound—though the strings are slightly thin in places—there's little here to recommend given the competition (Decca). **Abbado**'s merciless bloodletting, coupled with an insignificant 23 and a rather diffuse but well-played *Sinfonia Concertante*, offers little but swollen repeats and blurred detail; it's no threat to Bernstein (Sony). **Guttler** offers a genial, richly elegant version that is lovingly played. The only obstacle to a persuasive recommendation is the chamber orchestra, which lacks the requisite power (Berlin).

Schneider and his La Fenice Orchestra prove a real sleeper with an assertive, bold "Linz" that demands recognition. The orchestra is rich and vibrant in sound, supple and nimble in technique. It's a real surprise (♦Mondo Musica 100241). Letting **Harnoncourt** loose in this music is like releasing a bull in a china shop—you know the results even before it begins. Mozart doesn't work well in a militant environment (Teldec).

38 ("Prague"). Prague is said to be one of the darkest cities in Europe—old churches, dusky and daunting streets—yet for Mozart no place was ever to appear in a more brilliant light. The city was in a rage over *Figaro*, and *Don Giovanni* was soon to strike an equally successful chord. In 1787, the evening before Mozart was to conduct *Figaro*, he presented a concert that premiered his D major symphony, the first of the last great four. Piercing and tonally heightened because of the open-stringed key, 38 remains a mirror image of the great city Mozart so loved—dark, complex, and psychologically confused, dashing between flashes of light and moments of scarred introspection. Cut from the same cloth as *Giovanni*, it has rarely failed to please.

Despite some skewed string playing in the introduction, **Walter**'s "Prague" is a fine account, though perhaps the least desirable of his series. His infallible sense of chamber-like delicacy just doesn't carry the day in this most virile of Mozart's symphonies (Sony). **Karajan,** not usually reliable in Mozart, provides a reading with Teutonic power and magnitude fully suited to this work. The strings soar in I while III blazes with distraught glory. DG offers the better interpretation, while EMI sounds better; both are remarkably similar, as his vision of Mozart changed little over the years (♦DG 457127; EMI 66099).

The "Prague" wasn't one of **Klemperer**'s better stereo efforts (EMI). It's often weak-kneed and flabby, displaying little of the strength that characterized this conductor. But his earlier mono recording proves a spectacular effort (♦Testament 1094). The darkness of the opening is in beautiful contrast to the fitful allegro in I, the other movements equally affecting. I don't recommend a lot of mono recordings as a first choice, but this one is simply too good to pass up.

Böhm's high-powered, well-balanced version is one of the finest on record. The Berliners play as if Mozart were in the audience, so vital is their execution; it's quite marvelous (♦DG 47416, 2CD). **Beecham** can always be counted on for new insights, and his "Prague" is no exception. Masterly, fleet-footed playing mark this effort, a superb reading in good old mono (Dutton). The early Columbias are something special, but for the best sounding Beecham "Prague," try the remastered 1958 mono aircheck; it's as good as the Columbia, with better sound (♦BBC 4027). **Kubelik**'s version is pocked by glaring, flat, irritating sound (EMI). His Chicago recording is much better, but can't compete with Klemperer in the monaural sweepstakes (Mercury). Stick with his Sony digital recording if you insist on this conductor.

Britten performances are always something special, and you come away either delighted or infuriated. His "Prague" is exceptional; he uses every means at his disposal to provide an engaging, tremendously exciting reading. Just listen to the way he heightens the melodic line, or adds his own dynamic indications; Puritans, depart! Here is a real musician at work (♦Decca 44323, 2CD). **Bernstein**'s recording is a little wayward even for him, as if he didn't know how to handle Mozart's darkest symphony. The Vienna is in top form, and I'd own it as part of a collection, but it's the weakest of his last six (DG).

Blomstedt takes his time with 38, letting the drama build slowly and relying more on scale and architecture than speed and fury to make his case. The Dresden Staatskapelle plays beautifully, and the sound is excellent (♦Denon 17003). Taken at such a rapid pace with all of the repeats, you hear things twice before you realize it in **Graf**'s recording, but it's played gorgeously and with amazing dexterity (♦LaserLight 15865). Mozart's most militant symphony gets an explosive, fully martial treatment from **Harnoncourt** (Teldec). Beethoven, look out! The slashing phrases and shattering timpani will frighten almost anyone.

Wordsworth favors us with one of the wimpiest, most effete "Pragues" on record. It has no impact at all, quite the opposite of Harnoncourt (Naxos). In one of his weaker efforts, **Groves** provides a gentlemanly run-through, lacking in passion and perspective. His orchestra sounds good, but the blood runs cold (IMP). The metallic sound of the strings is an irritant in **Dohnanyi**'s reading—Cleveland's strings have always been sharp, precise, and defined (and warm), but never metallic. The performance is excellent, but not on the level of Böhm (Decca). **Košler** leads a powerful reading with a lot of potent energy, though it drags in a few spots (Opus).

39. In 1791, Mozart began a trilogy of symphonies that were produced in a very short time, only a manner of weeks. They have come to be regarded as the pinnacle of classical symphonic writing. In them, he presents an incredible span of emotions and feelings, from the rugged grace of 39 to the dark and portent-filled angst of 40 to the machine-like, rigorous perfection of the "Jupiter." 39 starts off with an introduction that takes us boldly down the wrong path, rendering us completely unprepared for the gentlemanly, charmingly deceptive melody that follows. The whole work is of a similar nature, threatening to lead into more profound waters but cracking a smile at the last minute.

Grace and charm with a fire lit under them describes **Bernstein**'s way with this music. Though the currently unavailable DG is his recording of choice, his New York version was nothing to sneeze at, and serves as a fine stopgap until DG lets the other one out of jail. But Bernstein's early way with this symphony won't be to all tastes (Sony). You hope for a stylish, easy-going, refined treatment of this work from **Giulini** in the twilight of his career, and that's exactly what he gives us. Warm, humane, and lovingly radiant, this performance is full of charm and splendor (♦Sony 48064).

Once again, **Beecham** has located the essence of a Mozart symphony and presented it to us in the most effective, communicative manner possible. He fleshes out the Mozartian shell with some explosive tempos and refuses to treat it as anything other than an eruptive, energized piece, deceptively graceful melodies to the contrary (♦Dutton 5012). For your fill of nasty Prussian cannon-fire and noisy, barroom brawling, turn to **Karajan.** Stuffy, bloated sonics and strings that cut through steel are the order of the day in both of his disastrous recordings (DG and EMI).

Both **Klemperer** recordings are highlights of his Mozartian traversal, stunningly played and marvelously agile, full of nuance and bright, singing lines. Though I'd rate his earlier concert recording higher (♦Testament 1094), the stereo studio version shouldn't be snubbed (EMI 63272, 4CD). Aside from a rather sluggish II, **Walter** is rather up-tempo in this work. You'd think he'd be more reflective and relaxed in this genial piece, but that's not the case. His polish and charm are not to be doubted, but there are better versions (Sony). **Szell** should have recorded more Mozart than he did, for this composer elicits a fire and warmth not often heard in his other outings. 39 is a good example, overflowing with ripe smoothness and silken energy that declare the reading to be near definitive. Keep your eyes open, it will be back (Sony).

Böhm leads a standard-setting effort, with the gorgeous, big-boned Berlin strings on their best behavior. From the flowing, tender opening of the Allegro to the tumbling finale, this is as close to the best as it gets (♦DG 47416, 2CD). **Saraste** is repeat-crazy, bending the work all out of proportion. The Scottish Chamber Orchestra sounds tiresome and bloodless, with far too little subtlety, grace, or poise (Virgin). **Blomstedt** takes an expansive view of this work, classically German with all that entails: weighty, well delineated, and meaty, with little time for delicacy or pleasant puffery. Repeats are taken, and this is a fine reading— *not* for vegetarians (♦Denon 17003).

Graf gives a lovely, cordial account, not too slow. His orchestra could play this in their sleep, and it's a great bargain (♦LaserLight 15865). **Harnoncourt** avoids any semblance of long-lined phrases or soaring melody, words not in his Mozartian vocabulary. He seems determined to shake our senses and make us rethink Mozart; the result is pure perversion, turning the most perfect of composers into a monster (Teldec). **Wordsworth**'s gracious, lighthearted reading suits the music well. This is a simple, fluid account that's quite lovely, though not on a par with the best the market has to offer (Naxos).

Dohnányi charges through IV, but III is nicely done. He's cold, afraid to let his emotions show in this amiable work, but it still could be termed a success were it not for the raw string sound (Decca). **Reiner**'s mono Mozart gets a new lease on life in its remastering; the lines are clean and classical, and it's a worthy performance, though not top of the list, preempted by the great stereo recordings (RCA). Stuttering articulation in the strings and equally sloppy passagework elsewhere make **Ferencsik** a nonstarter; the playing lacks suavity and finesse (Hungaroton). **Košler**'s ensemble plays very well in a traditional, warmly resonant reading that's more shaded in color than most. The sound is disarming and friendly; an excellent performance (♦Opus 2488).

40. The G minor is usually considered the greatest of Mozart's symphonic essays. While there is perhaps more sheer perfection of line, harmony, and contrapuntal writing in 41, it doesn't hold a candle to the seriousness of purpose, emotional malleability, and dramatic, concentrated cells of explosive musical ideas that are present everywhere in 40. We're at a loss to explain the sense of overt melancholy in this piece, sandwiched between two highly optimistic symphonies, all three written in a six week span of the composer's last year. But whatever his motives, Mozart shows his incredible facility in producing many flavors of music, seemingly at the drop of a hat, with little or no relation to what was happening in his life.

Walter set a standard for many years, and though his incandescent reading has many competitors, none is better. His dramatic instincts are unfailing, his sense of line and phrase unerring, and his notions of tempo and pulse utterly unequivocal (♦Sony 64477). **Britten** takes a completely wrong-headed approach, taking all the repeats in II so that it's fully half the length of the whole. Then, as if to make up for lost time, he rushes through III and takes all the repeats in IV. The sound is diffuse and cluttered (Decca). **Szell**'s account has you wondering how the symphony could ever be played differently. It's warm, big-blooded, and straight down the road, with little or no interpretive excess (♦Sony 46333).

For some reason, **Böhm**'s normally sympathetic Mozartian *zeitgeist* fails him here. The Berliners play with passion, but the conductor is curiously neutral, as if afraid to put a personal stamp on it (DG). **Giulini**'s 1965 performance is smooth, rounded, soft-sculpted marble. The sound is vibrant and creamy, nearly ideal. This is one of his finest efforts

among a not inconsiderable body of work, a great recording (♦Decca 452889). His Sony recording is also very fine, but not in the same league. Despite a splendid IV (with all repeats taken), the Vienna **Bernstein** hasn't held up as well as I expected, even though it has received great critical acclaim. The sound is strangely muffled, and this reading is more like a meditation class than a passionate, purposefully stringent exercise in Mozartian passion (DG).

Beecham, the ultimate classicist, takes a very studied, conscientious view, not suppressing fervency and emotion but keeping a tight rein on the outer bounds of expressiveness. The articulation and illumination of inner parts are most impressive, and he continues to show why he's so great in this music (♦Dutton Labs 5012). With militant, rigorous efficiency, **Karajan** bulldozes his way through this most profound of works, attempting to impose his own rather stern view on unsuspecting listeners. Brisk, imposing, and ruthlessly authoritarian, this is only for those who enjoy a particularly virulent strain of aural sadism (DG or EMI).

Klemperer yields to no one in his ability to project a solicitous, embracing warmth in this work. He invests so much charged intensity into every note that this becomes easily the most operatic of all versions. It's a splendid recording (♦EMI 63272, 4CD). **Steinberg**'s is a testament to the exquisite, towering playing of the Pittsburgh Symphony in the early 60s. This clean-cut, impeccably groomed, well-mannered reading is infused with a stirring passion that is fully convincing (♦Seraphim 69027). What worked for **Blomstedt** in 38 and 39 fails miserably here; it lacks any sort of rhythmic impetus to get it off the ground. The wonderful structural complexities are lost in a fog of cluttered counterpoint, driven by a fetid, wooden pulse (Denon).

Taking a symphony that is the height of *Sturm und Drang* and changing it into a life and death struggle of immense philosophical proportions is *sui generis* for **Harnoncourt.** The work doesn't need this kind of anal-retentive attention. His still available Concentus Musicus Wien recording isn't worth looking at (Teldec). **Wordsworth** plays Harnoncourt's nemesis in a direct and clean presentation, offering little in the way of deeper thought. He leaves a lot unsaid, but speaks plainly with no small amount of beauty (Naxos). **Graf** involves us in a relatively self-effacing, professionally competent reading that should please just about everyone, especially at the price (♦LaserLight 15829). Nothing is out of place or unexpectedly exaggerated, and Mozart speaks unhindered. The sound and playing are great.

Dohnányi's reading is fine by any reckoning. The sound is better than others in his series, and the darkness of his reading suits the music well, without Karajan's aggressive Germanic blustering (Decca). **Guttler** gives us a relaxed, unaggressive rendition that's stylish and well played, but comparatively lackluster when viewed next to a number of the others (Berlin). It's a shame RCA didn't take advantage of **Levine**'s then-peaking relationship with the Chicago Symphony at the Ravinia Festival and record all the Mozart symphonies, instead of leaving it to DG to produce his much more sterile account years later. This is a big band, extremely finessed account that will appeal even to those only remotely familiar with the composer (♦RCA 61397).

Reiner's monaural Chicago G minor never sounded this good on LP (RCA), and our great loss is the fact that he didn't record much Mozart. If you want a Reiner that's excellent in every way, go with his fabulous mono Pittsburgh reading. They played better than Chicago any day of the year back then (maybe now too), and Reiner's admirable tempos and sleek, smooth lines conspire to excellence (♦Sony 62344). You can do much worse than listen to the exceptionally smooth and warm strings that **Davies** gets from the Stuttgart Chamber Orchestra. This well-presented version wants only a certain heart's ease to push it into first rank. But if you like the coupling (Keith Jarrett playing concertos 21, 23, and 27, plus an indifferent *Masonic Funeral Music*), you may proceed with confidence (ECM). **Schwarz** gives a simple, direct account that's totally inoffensive and acceptable, but far from exceptional (Delos).

41 ("Jupiter"). In a remarkable burst of activity perhaps unparalleled in even this fecund composer's life, Mozart completed the third of a trilogy in a few weeks during the summer of 1791. The "Jupiter" was the final hurrah in his symphonic corpus, and in many ways the most magnificent in its structure. It has neither the pathos of 40 nor the sheer elegance of 39, but fits together in as perfect a manner as physical nature itself, the last movement especially being an amazing testament of canonic invention, unique in the history of music.

Saraste's recording is muffled and congested, and while the Scottish Chamber Orchestra plays with precision, the fragmented II, sleepy III, and frivolously fast finale make it a no-go (Virgin). **Walter**'s normally humanizing presence dwindles into mere officiousness in this least emotional of Mozart's late symphonies. The slow tempos allow the taut rhythmic constructions to falter and stall, and his slackening of the reins leads to a dull performance (Sony). **Beecham**'s 1934 recording is better in every way than his EMI stereo version, sounding courageously coruscating in its latest refurbishing. This work was in his blood, a fresh, diamond-sharp reading that lacks only stereo sound to be the first choice (♦Dutton 5012).

It's really too bad that the stern, militant opening of **Szell**'s recording spoils the rest of the work, though the minuet also sounds rather angry. He finds real excitement in the finale, but that's not enough to salvage it (Sony). His Salzburg recording is a much better interpretation, an interesting document of this conductor's way with Mozart outside the studio (Orfeo). It's difficult to find anything to criticize in **Böhm**'s "Jupiter." Long regarded as one of the highlights of that master's career—and therefore of Mozart recordings in general—his reading might best be described as poetry with backbone, never yielding to the temptation to over-sweeten the melody or allow the rhythms to sag. It's a beautiful recording (♦DG 47416, 2CD). His 1943 Vienna reading is also fine, but hardly competitive with the even better stereo effort (Orfeo).

Giulini again summons a sterling performance from the Philharmonia—sleek, impulsive, brimming with zest and newly minted dazzle. Though lacking Bernstein's sense of monumentality, its ardent nature makes you appreciate anew the crystal-clear, contrapuntal fireworks (♦Decca 452889). His newer Sony reading doesn't stand a chance against such a refulgent performance. You'd be right to expect a robust, electrically charged version from **Karajan,** and he doesn't disappoint, no matter which version. His "Jupiter" works in unexpected ways, the Brucknerian sound enlivening the music in a manner unknown to other conductors, and the results are intriguing and thrilling all at once. His earlier recording (♦EMI 66100) is preferable, but the DG is close.

Bernstein's gift for shedding light on the obscure and bringing hidden events to the surface is made radiantly clear in his numinous, imposing "Jupiter." The repeats put it on the grand scale, but his uncanny sense of timing and joyful, dazzling abandon make it the best on record, not to be missed (♦DG 31040 or 45548). While the spirit is willing, the sound and orchestra (Vienna) in **Kubelik**'s recording are weak (EMI). If you admire this conductor, his 1985 version serves as a stopgap (Orfeo). **Blomstedt**'s reading isn't bad at all, a solid, workaday effort that presents Mozart in an honest, pristine manner. The Dresdeners play fabulously, though I wish the conductor would rethink his repeats (♦Teldec

17003). **Reiner**'s special way with Mozart always proved the exception to the rule. Perceived as a vitriolic madman with a short baton, you'd never guess that his conductorial gestures would result in such splendid Mozart. His "Jupiter" is no exception, especially when it's put out at an acceptable price (♦RCA 6376).

Amazingly, this motivic, fragment-oriented work seems to survive **Harnoncourt**'s assaults better than any of the others, even generating real excitement in places. But mere toleration of an acceptable performance hardly merits a recommendation (Teldec). **Wordsworth**'s reading is spiritually solid but structurally soft. This piece relies on a grid-iron foundation to reveal its secrets, and his version is flaccid and featherweight, despite much lyricism (Naxos). **Graf** supplies a lot of spark, but his orchestra doesn't provide enough largeness of scale—but get his record for the G minor coupling (LaserLight). It's odd that the bookends of **Dohnányi**'s six-symphony set seem to be the best, but not when you consider how linked the "Haffner" and "Jupiter" are in their cell-like motivic puzzles. This is a good reading, deserving a higher recommendation were it standing alone. It isn't (Decca).

One of only a handful of Mozart symphony recordings in Chicago since Reiner, **Levine**'s "Jupiter" is tremendous in its flexible, life-affirming pulse and large-orchestra sense of line and sweep (♦RCA 61397 or 61708). The Hungarian State Orchestra under **Ferencsik** gives very mainstream, vanilla performances, showing ragged ensemble and rough-edged, unclear sound. Not for consideration at any price (Classical Diamonds). Though **Košler** feels a need to speed through the minuet, his reading has spunk and ambience, still infused with the darkness that pervades his other Mozart recordings but also revealing an emergence into the light by the conclusion; not a bad offering (Opus). **Schneider** gives a robust, old-fashioned reading that is as attractive as the great ones of old. Only the rather fast minuet betrays any sense of dwelling in the past; it's a fine reading, beautifully played (♦Mondo Musica 10024).

Schwarz's version with chamber orchestra is nicely recorded, but not up to the hunt; his Mozart lacks fervency (Delos). **Klemperer** pleads Mozart's last symphonic opus in a manner bespeaking greatness—a grand, benevolent version that heightens the drama while downplaying the mechanical aspects of the score. For this conductor, the "Jupiter" is an oversized intellectual challenge tempered by a lyricism and smoothness of line that only he could achieve (♦EMI 63272, 4CD).

SERENADES, DIVERTIMENTOS, ETC.

Mozart, like so many of his confreres struggling to make a living in 18th century Europe, had to resort to providing music for many workaday occasions like weddings and other celebrations. (Little seems to have changed in that regard for musicians today.) But Mozart being Mozart, even these more pedestrian forms were often invested with truly splendid music, some the equal of any he ever wrote. There's a lot of it, and many ensembles use these pieces as fillers. They're almost too numerous to be counted, and I will focus on complete discs more than on the stragglers. Many of these recordings are close to worthless, others are sublime.

Orchestral and chamber

Complete Sets. I would be remiss not to mention the complete serenades and divertimentos in three volumes from Philips. Many of these performances are truly excellent, yet others (notably those by Marriner) suffer from an intolerable stuffiness. Yet for one obsessed with collecting all these works, this is the most economical way to do so (♦Philips 422503, Vol. 3, 7CD; 422504, Vol. 4, 5CD; 422505, Vol. 5, 6CD). **Johnson** and the New York Philomusica have recorded all 17 of the numbered divertimentos in outstanding performances at budget price. If the Philips collection seems like a lot to swallow, you may find your thirst satisfied with these three 2CD sets (♦Vox 5049-51).

K 239 (*Serenata notturna*). While the American colonies were declaring independence in 1776, the 20-year-old Mozart was busy (among other things) composing his Serenade for two small orchestras, a forerunner of other great works in the genre to be produced later that year. He ingeniously used a concertante format to elicit new and varied utterances from his instruments.

Steinberg paces his classy Pittsburgh band through an object lesson in Mozartian chivalry; the sound is a little boomy, but overall it's excellent (♦Seraphim 69027). Klemperer weighs in with a reading that's one of the best around. Some can't abide the monaural sound, but it's worth the investment because of the great Symphonies 38 and 39 along for the ride (♦Testament 1094). Böhm really shows us how this music should unfold—a great, full orchestra (Berlin Philharmonic), firm bass line, and unwavering lyricism, without turning Mozart's melodies into a taffy pull (♦DG 453076, 2CD).

On a fabulous disc, Maag gives an exciting, very military-style reading that's more than satisfactory in every respect; the sound is superb (♦Decca 466500). Karajan has the right idea with his large orchestra, but his swirling homogenization of the sound renders this recording well nigh incomprehensible (DG). Boskovsky gives a rather pedantic, lumbering reading that has little charm or forward thrust. His Vienna Mozart Ensemble plays in a very lackluster, disinterested manner (Decca). Likewise Marriner and his Academy turn in a boring, unflattering performance that doesn't ring true—too much flash and too little lyrical sensibility (Philips).

At the excellent price of Tate's recording, you can hardly go wrong. The English Chamber Orchestra is well mannered and lyrical, an easy purchase decision (♦EMI 69819). López-Cobos gives a sprightly rendition (alongside the "Posthorn") that isn't good enough to stand alone, considering the stingy total timings (Cascavalle). Britten provides excellent value in a marvelous set with four symphonies that offers highly involved, startlingly refreshing playing—not to be missed (♦Decca 44323, 2CD). Végh treats us to his usual flair with a fine performance that's equal to most and eclipsed by few. As a bonus you pick up the youthful Divertimentos K 136–138 and a tasty *Nachtmusik* (♦Capriccio 49176). Rolla's version isn't bad, but he really can't compete with the others considering his full price (Hungaroton).

Claudius Traunfellner, with only *Nachtmusik* and K 136–138, also fails in the generosity department, with an offering that's quite costly (Camerata). Shuya Okatsu (Discover) and Wolfgang Sobotka (Naxos) offer little in the way of special insight or extraordinary performance, though the price can hardly be bettered. Mackerras, for some reason much more interesting in the serenades than the symphonies, fares well here; his Prague Symphony plays with intense devotion and utter attention to the conductor's wishes (♦Telarc 80161).

K 250/248b ("Haffner"). The 20-year-old Mozart set out to make an impression with this large-scale work, and the effect hasn't worn off after 200 years. Composed for a wedding of one Sigmund Haffner's sister, and actually performed the night before the big event, its grand *maestoso* opening shows that Mozart considered it an important work. Yet despite its later revisions (morphing into a symphony at one point), Mozart maintains the serenade form by the inclusion of two movements for solo violin.

Böhm gives a huge, soaring, richly textured reading that will never fail to please (♦DG 453076). Iona Brown and her marvelous Academy spirit us through a reading with quick tempos and gossamer strings, maybe the best modern version available (♦98173 or 98199, 2CD). Boskovsky has always been considered able like no other to infuse Viennese charm into his performances. I disagree with that assessment, but his "Haffner" is lovely indeed, not sentimental, and a worthy competitor (♦Decca 443458, 2CD). Marriner's reading is somewhat successful and also somewhat inconsistent (Philips). The sound is better than on many other recordings he made at this period, and some of the playing is quite stunning. But I would think twice about this one, as Brown eclipses him with his own orchestra.

Rampal, with Stern as soloist, gives a flashy, dance-till-you-drop reading that's exciting the first time through and exhausting on every subsequent hearing (Sony). Zukerman and the Los Angeles Philharmonic give a taut, experienced, exuberant rendering that sets the speakers on fire, one that would definitely have grabbed the attention of the wedding party. The sound is slightly dry, but Zukerman's politically incorrect, gorgeous solo playing offsets any possible objections (♦Sony 63254). Mackerras rounds off an excellent reading with a coupling just as outstanding in *Serenata notturna*. This is a very fine disc, with sterling playing and floating phrases shaped to perfection (♦Telarc 80161). For those experiencing period mania, you can listen with great pleasure to Weil's thinly strung band, energetic as usual, exceedingly flavorful and infused with great taste, though what's spicy to some will seem bland to others (♦Sony 47260).

K 320 ("Posthorn"). In 1779, Mozart presented an entertainment at Salzburg University, intended as an open air serenade to be played after the students had completed their examinations and were taking leave of the faculty. The posthorn (appearing in the second trio of the second minuet) was a familiar symbol to travelers, so the connotations of leaving the campus and hitting the road wouldn't be missed. It's a brilliant, highly tuneful work that hasn't ceased to win admirers since its first performance.

Végh and his Camerata Academica are anything *but* academic in their exciting, spirited romp. The orchestra isn't large, but staggeringly unified, as if it's one great instrument (♦Philips 422413). Iona Brown and her Academy lead us in a wonderfully ebullient, energized reading that grabs your feet and starts them tapping. There isn't a lot of rest time here—there never is with the Academy—but you can't help enjoying such vigorous, happy playing (♦Hänssler 98129 or 98199). Böhm's reading is a classic, full of beautiful lines, soaring melody, and a Viennese feeling that's second to none. The sound is lightly recessed but still good, without compression. If you can have only one "Posthorn," this should be it (♦DG 453076, 2CD).

Szell leads an elegant, insistent, very personal account that displays all the usual Cleveland trademarks—remarkable ensemble, gleaming string sound, and brisk tempos. But the sound is a little boxy, making this recording primarily one for his legion of fans (Sony). It's too bad Boskovsky eliminated the opening and closing marches in his version, for it's a very fine reading, uncluttered, with some truly wonderful string tone shining through the substandard recorded sound. The couplings are somewhat less worthy, making this a full-priced offering, probably not a first choice (Decca). Marriner does a fine job, including the two outside marches (as did Végh). The Academy plays like the pros time has shown them to be, and I can't complain about anything Marriner does here (♦289464, 2CD).

Abbado gives us two renderings, one with Symphonies 25, 31, and *Masonic Funeral Music* and one with the Serenade separately. Both are excellent, though they don't quite measure up to the others (Sony). Davis uses the Bavarian Radio Orchestra to create one of the best "Posthorns" around, the richly singing strings and colorful winds of that ensemble providing a melting radiance that's most alluring (♦Novalis 150013). Jiri Hynk and the Czech Philharmonic offer a spirited, warmly blended version of this seminal work, with playing that's clean and concise, bold and colorful (♦Canyon 3652). Rifkin's period-instrument effort doesn't have the spit and polish of the best modern-instrument versions (a common malady), and should be avoided on counts of sound and interpretation (Capriccio).

López-Cobos gives a very lively account, lovely and clean with little pretension, but at 52 minutes and full price, this isn't a reasonable choice (Cascavelle). Harnoncourt beats the hell out of Mozart in this and almost everything he attempts with this composer, turning an examination celebration into a field artillery day (Teldec). Mackerras is able to break away from his usual artificial Mozart and give us an alert, sensitive reading of great high spirits; the recording is very good (♦Telarc 80108). Weil offers a period-instrument performance of zany zest and rabid instrumental execution; those preferring their Mozart served up in a fanciful but exciting manner won't be disappointed (♦Sony 47260). Despite the flawless, rich sound of the Vienna Philharmonic, Levine generally gives me the shivers in Mozart. But others disagree, and if you count yourself among his fans, there's nothing especially wayward in his recording, aside from lack of warmth (DG).

K 525 (*Eine kleine Nachtmusik*). In 1787 Mozart composed what was to become his most popular work, the Serenade in G major, "A Little Night Music." We don't know what prompted this effort, but its conciseness and strength of invention place it in the rank of truly great pieces in the Mozartian—and by definition, musical—pantheon. For strings only, it has enjoyed great recordings and suffered innumerable hacks.

Szell set a rapid pace in his reading, refusing to linger over anything, yet showing his obvious devotion to the work with the care he takes in shaping phrases (♦Sony 48266). Böhm takes this piece at far too leisurely a pace. After all, it's not one of the symphonies, and its development is far more arrested. I wish the energy found in his "Posthorn" were here (DG). Steinberg's splendid Pittsburgh Symphony gives us an object lesson in masculine Mozart, with good pace, singing strings, and obvious relish of the music. The older sound has some echo, but at bargain price, who cares? (♦Seraphim 69027)

Kubelik's Vienna version is OK in bald, grainy sound, but not worth an investment (EMI). Boskovsky offers a matter-of-fact reading. This music has been played so often that it takes a very special commitment to stimulate the ears, and this doesn't have it (Decca). Harnoncourt's commitment is truly there, but so perversely as to render this gentle work unrecognizable (Teldec). Galway and the Chamber Orchestra of Europe are stylish, but so over-recorded in bright sound as to negate its other virtues (RCA). Marriner does little justice to this jewel, treating it to a pedantic run-through that in no way sparkles and sings the way it should (Philips).

But Walter is supreme in this music. He knows how to put it across, and though others have had better bands, his interpretation more than compensates for any faults. Start with his stereo recording (♦Sony 37774) and then proceed to his 1954 mono version, more energetic if not as caressing (♦Sony 64468). The Academy of St. Martin in the Fields Chamber Ensemble scores with a delightful version played by string quartet. The sound is simply gorgeous and the playing full of fire and en-

ergy (♦Philips 412269). It's preferable to the Brandeis String Quartet's recording, drowning in the Nimbus echo. Pommer is far too fast, though his orchestra plays well (Berlin). Dohnányi's earthbound, plodding sound does little service to Mozart's ebullient, feisty serenade, despite better than usual interpretation from this source (Decca). We can't talk about Mozart without mentioning Beecham, whose wartime recording should satisfy all interpretive longings—yet the sound is old, so approach it with care (♦Beecham Society 41).

For period-instrument devotees, Weil's recording could hardly be bettered, with sprightly playing and quickish tempos. This conductor usually tries to see beyond the archeological aspects of a performance (♦Sony 46695). On the same label, if you can stand Russian strings in Mozart you may want to consider Alexander Titov's version—but I would let the thought pass (Sony). Rolla has two recordings with the Franz Liszt Chamber Orchestra, and it would be foolish to buy the Hungaroton disc when you can have it for a fifth of the price—and a nice recording at that, coupled with the two shorter wind serenades (♦LaserLight 15648).

Reiner has a way with Mozart, and this piece gets the royal treatment on a disc that has Symphonies 39 and 40—no decision here! (♦RCA 62585) Turovsky and his Montreal band offer a very nice, acceptable rendering with Divertimentos K 136 and 138 in excellent sound (♦Chandos 9045). The always reliable Végh keeps his end of the bargain with an excellent recording that features Divertimentos K 136–138 ("Salzburg Symphonies") along with an excellent Divertimento K 334 and Serenade K 239 (♦Capriccio 49176). Vilmos Tatrai (of quartet fame) leads the Hungarian Chamber Orchestra in a warmly played *Night Music*. With an exceptional *Serenata Notturna* and near best-of-breed Divertimento 11, this knockout recording is even more attractive at the knockout price (♦Hungaroton 1030).

We expect pointed, well-executed and highly musical recordings from Iona Brown, and she doesn't let us down here, complete with a very good Symphony 29 and Divertimentos K 136–138 (♦Omega Classics 1004). Dorati again proves his versatility with a very well-shaped version that includes the Handel-Harty version of *Fireworks* and *Water Music* along with some rare Mozartiana, including two sets of German Dances (♦Mercury 434298). If you liked Levine's "Posthorn," you'll be enthralled with his *Nachtmusik* too, but the temperature is still too chilly for me (DG). Mackerras keeps up the good work with his Prague Chamber Orchestra, offering well turned playing with an excellent "Posthorn" as discmate (♦Telarc 80108).

I Musici supplies their typical brand of scaled-down yet flawlessly executed renderings that can't fail to please chamber lovers; an assortment of Baroque chestnuts rounds out their program (♦Philips). And for those desiring a really large-scale approach, no one gets any bigger than Karajan, who revamps this wondrous little nocturnal piece into a creature of mammoth proportions. Stick with one of the other "big name" conductors before trying this behemoth (DG). Leinsdorf offers a delicate, exquisitely nuanced reading that has a very good Symphony 40 by Levine and the Chicago Symphony (♦RCA 61552).

K 563 (*String Trio in E-flat*). The paucity of recordings of this towering masterwork is scarcely to be believed. One of the finest chamber works Mozart ever wrote, rarely has a piece for such small forces achieved this sort of majesty and inventiveness, a *tour de force* of string writing in small ensemble form. None of the current recordings can be recommended, so be sure to keep your eyes peeled for the stunningly conceived, flawlessly executed performance by Stern, Zukerman, and Rose.

You might still be able to find it, almost as an afterthought, in a set of Mozart violin concertos by Stern (♦Sony 46523, 3CD).

Others. It's impossible to list every recording of the lesser, yet in some instances highly desirable pieces. Mozart, like all composers of his time, was to some degree a slave to the fashions and trends of musical society, and as a result produced many works for varied occasions. Many of them have fallen by the wayside or exist only in single recorded versions, but others have achieved some sort of sideline status.

The D major Serenade, K 100, is given an unusually suave reading by **Boskovsky.** At the price, you can hardly go wrong (♦Decca 443458, 2CD). **Karajan** gives an amazingly relaxed, big-band reading of the "Salzburg Symphonies," K 136–138, very popular and stunningly realized here, perhaps the best on disc and a real surprise from this source (♦DG 29805). **Martin Sieghart** gives a refreshing, well-played account of these pieces with a nice-sized orchestra in good modern sound, coupled with a fine Symphony 28 (♦Discover 920288). The 18-member **Vienna Tonkünstler Chamber Orchestra** entertains with these "Symphonies" in a low-priced, immaculate recording, with playing that deserves the same description (♦Discover 920355). None of the other big names are currently represented, except for a **Marriner** disc that's best left alone (Philips).

Brown offers a superb album that contains some of the most delightfully bejeweled playing around—a must-have for dedicated divertimento fanciers (♦Omega 1004). And if you want K 136 played by a quartet, you can do no better than the **Academy of St. Martin in the Fields Chamber Ensemble.** It may be a mouthful to say, but the large-scale name of the ensemble is appropriate for their big time performance (with a wonderful *Nachtmusik* and "Musical Joke") in simply stunning sound (♦Philips 412269).

Speaking of "A Musical Joke" (*Ein musikalischer Spass,* K 522), the deadpan Harnoncourt can achieve a tepid recommendation, but not for the *Nachtmusik* that comes with it (Teldec). A better choice would be the Mozartian miscellany by **L'Archibudelli,** always a reliable period group (♦Sony 46702). **Maag** offers a wonderful *Notturno for Four Orchestras* (K 286) that makes the most of Mozart's antiphonal effects. The accompanying six German Dances are possibly the best on disc, with a marvelous *Serenata notturna* and top-of-the-line Symphony 32 added in (♦Decca 466500). **Pommer,** like Maag, gives a very fine, spacious reading of the *Notturno,* but the Decca couplings are too hard to beat (Berlin).

The excellent "Haffner" on **Zukerman**'s disc isn't well supported by his rather stuffy Serenades 4 and 5 (K 203/189b and 204/213a) (Sony). Instead, stick with **Weil**'s recording with Tafelmusik (on the only other CD that has both) for some really spirited playing (♦Sony 427260, 2CD). **Brymer** and the London Wind Soloists carry the day in jocular readings of the divertimentos for wind instruments. The major serenades aren't the best available, but they're acceptable if you want a complete set (♦Decca 455794, 2CD).

Graf offers a superb collection of marches and dances that are sharply pointed in their idiomatic style, played by his rousing Salzburg Mozarteum (♦LaserLight 15886). On another charming disc, he presents us with various dances and minuets. If you don't know these, you should really give them a try; all have Köchel numbers in the high 400's and up, and at this price, no other pair of recordings can come close to these outstanding bargains (♦LaserLight 15887). But human nature and record collectors being what they are, another fine choice for the most popular set, German Dances K 605, would be **Dorati,** already in your possession if you purchased his *Nachtmusik* (♦Mercury 434398), or **Walter** with

Haydn's spunky "Miracle" Symphony (♦Sony 64486). And mention must be made of **Leinsdorf,** but his coupling is the Szell "Posthorn"—though maybe the cheap price can persuade you (♦Sony 48266).

Harnoncourt offers a bracing, if onerous, reading of a Serenade and Divertimento K 113. He always makes you sit up and listen, but in this case, once is enough (Teldec). **Lev Markiz** is highly recommended for K 334, especially for those who prefer chamber orchestras in this music, but the coupled Symphony 33 isn't as choice (Discover). **Tate** gives us a stylish, no-exaggeration K 287 at budget price. The sound is clear and clean, with no gimmicks (♦EMI 69823).

Masonic Music is offered complete on only one integral set—**Maag** and the Vienna Volksoper Choir and Orchestra, magnificent performances in slightly substandard 1966 sound (♦Vox 5055). But you won't be missing a lot if you opt out, though the Vox price makes it difficult. The *Mauerische Trauermusik* (Masonic Funeral Music) is offered as filler on many discs, short seven-minute work that it is. Almost any of them can be recommended, for it's not hard to play. For a really good disc with a lovely, moving *Trauermusik,* try **Walter**'s Overtures album with a wonderful, best of breed *Nachtmusik* (♦Sony 37774).

Winds

The *Harmonie,* or wind band, was popular in Mozart's day because its instrumentation ensured flexibility in tonal color, ease of transportation (these bands were always on the move), a variety of instrumental combinations, and a guarantee of sound production, especially at outdoor occasions—something strings could not muster. Mozart wrote three serenades for winds and numerous divertimentos and cassations—functionally similar forms, whatever the composer wanted them to be. The serenades are each absolute masterpieces of the genre, required listening for any dedicated Mozartian.

Complete sets. The only complete set of the wind music currently available is by **Jack Brymer** and the London Wind Soloists. Its cheap price and dutiful performances may garner a slight recommendation, but the problems with the major serenades are somewhat prohibiting, as discussed below. The smaller divertimentos, written as early as 1773 in Milan and solidified stylistically in Salzburg by 1777, along with a generous sprinkling of works of "doubtful authorship," are most attractively presented. But since even the most assiduous collectors probably won't have a need for many of these, I can't honestly recommend this set (Decca).

Another collection still available but perhaps difficult to find is by the **Orpheus Chamber Ensemble.** This conductorless group should have reconsidered that choice, for most of their coddled run-throughs don't have the essence of Mozartian elegance. To be sure, their playing is beyond reproach, but their effort is far too mannered for frequent consumption (DG). The youngsters of the **Chamber Orchestra of Europe** give top-rank performances of the wind divertimentos and serenades in ravishing sound. This may be hard to find, but worth it if you're looking for an integral set (♦Teldec 46472, 5CD). Otherwise, be on the lookout for individual offerings. They have also recorded the three big serenades in very good sound on a disc (ASV) that may serve as an alternative to the scarcity of the Teldec album, but the latter is still the preferred choice.

The **Consortium Classicum** has always been a superb ensemble, but their latest offerings sound much better than their recordings of the three great serenades and four divertimentos. It's a relatively cheap acquisition, but I would advise against it as an only source (EMI). The **Italian Octet** gives proper attention to even the lowliest of notes and phrases in their excellently recorded series that spotlights the three great serenades. A whole slew of lesser but still exemplary works is added to the stew. It's a refreshing, joyous series well worth acquiring (♦Arts 47279-81, 3CD, available separately).

K 361/370a (10 in B-flat). The largest of the wind serenades in scope and instrumentation, this piece was announced as a major work and has been accepted as such ever since its first performance. The writing, using a double bass in the best performances but often substituting a contrabassoon like the one Mozart used in *Masonic Funeral Music,* is the very epitome of charm and exquisite melody, setting a standard by which all subsequent works in this form must be judged.

Brymer's London Wind Soloists evidently didn't think much of the score, they race through it so hurriedly. Their rapid tempos even give the oboes a brief scare in several places, and the sound, though clear as a bell, lacks warmth (Decca). **Colin Davis** and his Bavarian Winds are warm and genial, personifying the humanity and supreme beauty of this work. The sound is soft and pliant (♦RCA 60873). **De Waart** and the Netherlands Wind Ensemble give one of the finest performances ever recorded, unfortunately NA. The sound is clean and highly detailed, the playing extraordinary, and the scale almost operatic. Keep your eyes open for this 1968 beauty (♦Philips 420711). New York Philomusica conducted by **A. Robert Johnson** stuns us with a very smooth, blended, European sound that's as good as any on the market. The players produce ravishing tones in a subdued soundscape that's one of the highlights of the catalog (♦Vox 5014, 2CD).

Even with **Mehta** at the helm (certainly not necessary for these players), the Berlin Philharmonic Winds give a luscious, warm, and vigorous reading of this all-important work that can stand with any (♦Sony 58950). If you want a non-Mehta performance by this group, their reading on Orfeo may be to your liking, but I'd stick with the Sony. **Milan Turkovic** and the Octagon Ensemble give an unsmiling, typhoon-quick reading that takes itself too seriously and puts a frown on Mozart's face (Camerata). **Herreweghe** provides a serviceable period-instrument recording (Harmonia Mundi) that's competitive with most of its kind (like **Kuijken** on Accent), but not really up to the quality of the best non-period versions available.

Hogwood offered the best at one time, since deleted (Oiseau-Lyre). The **Champs-Elysées Wind Ensemble** provides a solid period-instrument reading that has a unified sound and fluidity of tone, but like its C minor discmate doesn't measure up to the finest modern instrument recordings (Harmonia Mundi). But **Paavo Järvi** offers a fine version at mid-price that serves as a good introduction, if not in company with the best versions (♦Chandos 6575).

Fennell has tried to record everything under the sun for winds, but the sound isn't up to the best available, despite a very good reading (Mercury). It's difficult to fault anything **Sabine Meyer** does on clarinet, and her ensemble's recording of this work assuredly falls into that category—a vigorous yet fireplace-warm performance (♦EMI 55155). The **Marlboro Festival Players** can always be counted on for deliciously subtle readings, and this one is no exception. But as in many of the discs coming from this source, the sound can be a bit tinny and raw, so better put off purchase unless you just have to have this group (Sony).

Mackerras, as part of his ongoing series, enjoys splendid sound and first-rate playing, yet much of his Mozart leaves me cold, a creeping academicism sometimes crashing the party. But if you're one of his many fans, you won't be disappointed here (Telarc). For a thrilling, one-of-a-kind experience, try the Winds of the American Symphony under **Stokowski.** He brings a razor-sharp intellect coupled with an unerring sense of what this music is all about. It's simply stunning, with concerti grossi by Corelli and Vivaldi hardly less so (♦Vanguard 8009).

K 375 (11 in E-flat). The second of the great trilogy, the E-flat was originally constructed as a sextet for two clarinets, horns, and bassoons plus optional double bass. Mozart later revised it to conform to the more normal octet with oboes, but his effort was only half-hearted, as he simply doubled the parts instead of making the additions more integral to the work, a procedure he followed scrupulously in the other serenades. He used it to attract the attention of a member of the nobility, and it had its intended effect, as it has had on all of us ever since.

The sound of the London Wind Soloists under **Brymer** is positively screeching in the last movement. Wind music always needs color, and this reading, not the most inspired, is too black and white (Decca). **De Waart**'s way with this music is intimate and involving, far more than a mere serenade—and of course, this is *not* a mere serenade. The Netherlands Wind Ensemble, so typical of players from that part of the world, can't be excelled, and the 1968 sound is as good as any from the digital era. It's hard to find, but so is gold (♦Philips 420711). This same ensemble goes it alone in their newer recording, only slightly less satisfying than their earlier effort. There are some textual differences from the first version, but these can be argued either way, and the sound is great (♦Chandos 9284).

Werner Haas and his all-star London Baroque Ensemble give us a reading in sterling mono sound that can be considered an early watershed. The interpretation is somewhat streamlined and matter-of-fact, but the playing is superb, and it's a fine supplement (Testament). The **Consortium Classicum** provides a delightful reading in great sound, but be advised that this is the original scoring, so oboes are banished. For some it may not be a priority for this reason alone, but it's still an excellent version (Novalis; an older recording is on EMI 69362, 2CD). The New York Philomusica Winds under **A. Robert Johnson** perform beautifully in a vibrant reading of the revised version. The sound is slightly underlevel but comes across as nicely fragile and sweet (♦Vox 5014, 2CD).

If you want a pleasant outing or prefer a lawn party version, then **Newell Jenkins** and the New York Woodwind Soloists are for you. Elegant, shimmering, with a finely spun lyricism unequaled by most recordings, this hall-of-fame disc held the fort for many years (♦Everest 9026). The **Sabine Meyer Wind Ensemble** brings a certain regal demeanor to this work, not at all out of place. The sound is wonderful, and the performance must be ranked with the best (♦EMI 56502). Anyone wanting a deep, dark, German coloring should seek out the disc by the **Berlin Philharmonic Winds.** Their profound understanding coupled with an innate sense of performance values makes for great listening (♦Orfeo 134851).

The **Budapest Wind Ensemble** may offer a cheap introduction to this piece (LaserLight), but for that I suggest sticking to the wonderful Vox recording. The **English Concert Winds** give a very good reading, but no better than the best, and the expense may nix any purchasing plans (Hyperion). **Charles Neidich**'s period-instrument recording is a little too prissy and stylized to be completely effective, lacking emotion and passion (Sony). A lack of vivacity and lilt should discourage you from acquiring the late '70s version by the **Danzi Ensemble** (Sony). But the **Paris-Bastille Wind Octet**'s vision of this work is quite wonderful, placing it at the front of desirable period-instrument recordings (♦Harmonia Mundi 911583). **Rolla** offers this and the C minor at a great price with few quibbles—not the best, but a good way to sample (♦LaserLight).

K 388/384a (12 in C minor). This is a powerful, penetrating piece that encompasses many of the emotional realms Mozart explored in his great operas. The spectacular, hauntingly beautiful set of variations that makes up the finale leads the listener to profound emotional and compositional depths. This is a piece as worthy as any he wrote, and though the B-flat remains his most popular composition in this form, the number of people who regard the C minor as his supreme masterwork among serenades is not small.

Davis brings us a version that's short on drama, rounding off the minor key edges and emphasizing beauty of tone and sleekness of ensemble. Tempos are highly expressive, and the music is really allowed to breathe (♦RCA 60873). **Haas** gives a no-nonsense reading that tries to bring out the hidden drama by means of artificially fast tempos. He succeeds to a point, and the fabulous London Baroque Ensemble is wonderful. Though the mono sound is excellent, it remains a supplemental choice (Testament). The London Wind Soloists under **Brymer** play better here than in the other two serenades, and for once some rich, robust sound emerges. The set is cheap, but a .333 batting average for the three serenades isn't impressive (Decca).

Consortium Classicum gives a reading very much in the Haas mode—quick tempos and lots of drama—but they're much better in phrasing and general interpretation. This is an excellent reading, though it's paired with the original scoring of the E-flat Serenade, not to all tastes (Novalis). **Johnson**'s New York Philomusica Winds perform with a seriousness and sense of gravitas that becomes this much-more-than-a-serenade serenade. As with the others in his admirable series, the sound is attractive and warm, and it's an outstanding bargain (♦Vox 5014, 2CD). The interesting but dispensable couplings are the wind versions of the *Figaro* and *Cosi* overtures.

Jenkins gives Mozart's minor mode manner a real going-over in a classic version with the New York Woodwind Soloists; don't hesitate if you come across it—it's worth every cent (♦Everest 9026). **Sabine Meyer** and her wind ensemble offer a liquid, lucid, disturbing vision of Mozart's masterpiece that is notable for its stunning breadth and consistency; it's a prime choice (♦EMI 56502). The darkness of the **Berlin Philharmonic Winds** only adds to the undercurrents of drama and tension in this dusky, caliginous work, with fine playing by a group that knows few peers (♦Orfeo 134851).

Like its E-flat reading, the **Budapest Wind Ensemble** may offer good value for the money, but there are too many other great ones to give it a thumbs-up (LaserLight). The **English Concert Winds** don't like the dark that much, adding a touch of sweetness that seeks to alleviate the minor key foreboding. It works like a charm, but the coupling and price don't push it into the checkout lane (Hyperion). **Herreweghe** loses again with a version that's too much on the acerbic side, though the darker period instruments fit right in (Harmonia Mundi). But on the same label, the intrepid players of the **Paris-Bastille Wind Octet** offer a Cimmerian, highly concentrated portrait of profound emotion (♦Harmonia Mundi 911583).

Without a doubt, the **Netherlands Wind Ensemble** remains one of the finest groups of its type in the world. Their dark-paneled reading continues in the great tradition of searing, pointed, set-the-standard wind playing from this great ensemble (♦Chandos 9284).

Others. Mozart's small wind divertimentos (published under the name "Viennese Sonatinas" for the keyboard) are enchanting works that demand little in the way of attentive listening, yet repay it with interest if offered. The **Trio Avena** offers an inexpensive way to become acquainted with these works, in close but clean sound and alert, idiomatic playing (♦Discover 920195, 2CD). The **New World Basset Horn Trio** offers rather vanilla performances, not so much for the blandness of the playing as for the blandness of the instrumentation (Harmonia Mundi). But you can count on the appetizing performances of the **Berlin Philharmonic Winds** on two separate CDs replete with other Mozartian trivia (♦Orfeo 217901, 218911).

Three divertimentos for two oboes, bassoons, and horns (K 252, 253, and 270) are given nice readings by the **Collegium dell'Arte,** the default winners in a sparse catalog (♦Sony 64557, 57230). K 287 comes across in a thrilling manner, with a savvy "Musical Joke" by the **Vienna Chamber Ensemble** using five strings and two horns, in excellent sound (♦Denon 75200). There is some happy, infectious playing of K 247 and 334 in the **L'Archibudelli** set, though the horn clams may put off some listeners (Sony). Stick instead with a proven source—**Végh**'s budget disc—for K 247 (♦LaserLight 15863). The same conductor leads four splendid discs of various concoctions of serenades, dances, and marches, showing rare understanding of the excitement and subtlety present in these pieces (♦Capriccio 10376, 10377, 10153, 10185).

OVERTURES

All of Mozart's overtures are bona fide opera overtures—the notion of an overture as a concert work wouldn't fully emerge until the Romantic era. They virtually span Mozart's career, from the youthful *Ascanio in Alba* and *Lucio Silla* to the masterworks of later life like *Figaro* and *Magic Flute.* Many of them have been recorded singly as part of miscellaneous assemblies, but no collection is complete without a disc devoted solely to the overtures.

Among the very best is **Davis,** always a very good Mozartian even in lesser moments. At one time, his early (late '60s) recording with the Royal Philharmonic set the standard. Four of the greatest overtures are available in a disc that includes Steinberg's *Serenata notturna,* Symphony 40, and *Nachtmusik* (with Pittsburgh) as icing on an already delicious cake (♦Seraphim 69027). The Staatskapelle Dresden could play this music in their sleep, and Davis's late in life manner with these works is a marvel to hear (♦RCA 56698). The same orchestra illuminates another disc with **Vonk** in almost (but not quite) as good sound, but at its super-budget price, if you're seeking only one recording, it will be tough to pass up (♦LaserLight 15885).

Though the Academy of St. Martin in the Fields plays well for **Marriner,** his overtures are too neatly packaged—slick, prefabricated, a vision of neatness but with no life (EMI). **Harnoncourt,** in a manner typical of his Mozart, incessantly destroys the line and interrupts the phrase with his loud, splattering punctuation (Teldec). **Barry Wordsworth** offers a jam-packed disc (14 overtures) at bargain price that doesn't have the most finesse yet gives a lot for the money (Naxos). A disc with **Szell**, Schippers, Walter, and Brico should be avoided because of Entremont's lousy Symphony 28 and Brico's two dreadful overture readings (Sony). **Hager,** on the other hand, gives traditional, full sounding, highly lyrical performances with the English Chamber Orchestra (♦Novalis 150041).

Weil and Tafelmusik sport a cotton-like sonority and soft, flexible string playing. He's not dogmatic about these performances, making this disc (with a wonderful *Nachtmusik*) one of the best period-instrument recordings to come along (♦Sony 46695). **Walter,** of course, was well nigh unbeatable in this music, and his Columbia Symphony recording proves this; for Mozart with a smile and nostalgic reflection, don't miss it (♦Sony 47734 or 64486). **Lubbock** offers a very fine mid-priced disc that's inoffensive and middle-of-the-road for those of a more conservative bent (♦ASV 6197). RITTER

CONCERTOS

Mozart left 40 or so concertos for a rather limited variety of instruments. These include five for violin, two for flute, four for horn, and one each for oboe and bassoon. There are also concertante works for flute and harp, and violin and viola. But by far his most important body of concerted works consists of the 27 concertos for piano, including the two multiple-keyboard works for two and three pianos.

Piano

Mozart raised the level of the keyboard concerto to a plateau not reached by any of his contemporaries or predecessors (the Baroque concerto was an entirely different form, so the works of Bach, Vivaldi, and others don't figure into this equation). His older contemporary, Haydn, may have been supreme master of the symphony, string quartet and keyboard sonata, but his concertos never met the high standard he achieved in those other genres. It was the young Mozart — himself a brilliant keyboard virtuoso — who took the form to an exalted level where it was to be expanded and intensified by Beethoven, Brahms, and the great Romantics who followed (I didn't say "improved," for Mozart's piano concertos are in an "unimprovable" category of their own). The 25 solo concertos (21 if we omit four early pieces based on works of others) are *sui generis;* from the very beginning something special is encapsulated in each and every one.

More than any other composer, it takes a special combination of qualities to play Mozart. A pianist's technique must be flawless, yet there must never be a hint of glibness. The dynamic range must not be too wide or too narrow; otherwise miniaturization creeps in, or, on the other hand, an inappropriate coarseness. This is why so many noted pianists who distinguish themselves in other repertoire are at a loss when playing Mozart. The music presents a unique paradox, though infused with an otherworldly purity and spirituality, it's also very much of this world. Mozart was both a profound student of human nature and a performer who knew the importance of virtuoso display in appealing to a fickle public, and both kinds of knowledge are part of his musical alchemy.

Complete sets

There are a special group of pianists who have solved the Mozart puzzle and we're fortunate to have their wisdom preserved for us on record. For my taste, the finest complete sets are those of Murray Perahia and András Schiff, two great pianists who were fairly young when they committed their remarkable cycles to disc. Perhaps, by a whisker, I would place **Perahia** at the top of the heap (♦Sony 46441, 12CD). Recorded between 1976 and 1984, leading the superb English Chamber Orchestra from the keyboard, Perahia produced a cycle that provides the ideal mix of purity and profundity that forms the Golden Mean of Mozart interpretation. The music flows with a deceptive simplicity; nothing is forced, nothing has to be proven. The pianist's pellucid tone is ideal, as is his understanding of the qualities required in this repertoire, and the orchestral playing is on the same high level as the pianism. Sony remastered the set in 1991 (be sure to look at the copyright date on the box before you buy), refining the sound and removing every hint of harshness or glare. Perahia offers all the concertos (with the exception of the multiple keyboard works, which he recorded elsewhere with Lupu), including the first four. This is a very special set.

Schiff is another pianist with impeccable Mozartean credentials, and his set has the added attraction of the venerable Sandor Vegh leading the Camerata Academica of the Salzburg Mozarteum (♦Decca 488140, 9CD). There is an almost otherwordly quality to Schiff's interpretations, yet he's always clearly focused and in full control of his vivid imagina-

tion. This is visionary Mozart, both of this world and beyond. Vegh's equally imaginative support and appropriately spacious sound make this set a mesmerizing experience. Schiff excludes the four early works, choosing to start his cycle with 5.

Brendel is another outstanding Mozartean who has given us a complete cycle, and thanks to the "Complete Mozart Edition" we are able to hear it in the context of the composer's complete output for keyboard(s) and orchestra (♦Philips 422507, 12CD). This pianist is clearheaded and direct, and these are brilliant and cleanly played accounts enhanced by a probing musicianship. He's accompanied by a spirited Marriner leading the Academy of St. Martin in the Fields. Marriner doesn't display the depth evinced by Vegh for Schiff, but his direction is clearheaded and lively. Brendel is joined by the superb Imogen Cooper in the two-piano versions of 7 and 10. Filling out the collection are excellent readings of the original version of 7 by the Labèque sisters with Bychkov leading the Berlin Philharmonic from the third piano; a fortepiano version of 1–4 from Haebler; the three K 107 concertos after Bach, with Ton Koopman; and Rondos K 382 and 386 (also offered by Perahia).

Philips is also home to **Uchida**'s elegantly played cycle. She offers more introverted readings than some other pianists, but this inwardness has its rewards. Her pianism is tonally opulent and is filled with many subtleties. Tate and the English Chamber Orchestra offer strong support, though a bit more sparkle and brilliance wouldn't have been out of place. **Ashkenazy** isn't a pianist we often associate with Mozart, yet his cycle, recorded between 1972 and 1987 is one of the finest. He's sensitive and stylish and his pianism is clear and direct, as is his leadership of the Philharmonia from the keyboard. The set is complete except for the first four but includes the two- and three-piano works and the two Rondos, with Barenboim and Fou Ts'ong assisting in 7 and 10 and Kertész as conductor in the Rondos (Decca 443727, 10CD).

Barenboim has now recorded two complete sets, each time conducting from the keyboard. The first offers all but the three from K 107 and 7 arid 10 for multiple keyboards (EMI 62825, 10CD). Barenboim has always been an outstanding Mozartean and this cycle, recorded between 1967 and 1974, shows the life-affirming spontaneity he demonstrated when he was still young. He's not afraid to take risks, achieving performances that, more often than not, sound as if they were created on the spot. Of course, these results took much thought and preparation, and it pays off. He may, at times, go over the top, but the results are always stimulating and scintillating. The English Chamber Orchestra is its usual responsive, unimpeachable self. Rondo K 382 is an enjoyable bonus.

Over the last several years Barenboim has produced another cycle, this time with the Berlin Philharmonic. However, with maturity came a slight loss of the earlier spontaneity, though with some gain in perception (Teldec, 9 single CDs, with Rondo K 382). If I prefer the earlier set it has nothing to do with any lack of quality in the new one. Teldec's recordings sometimes betray a harshness in orchestral sound not present in the earlier, more natural sounding EMIs.

A fine set comes from the always reliable (and often a great deal more) **Jandó,** with assisting artists and Concentus Hungaricus led by Mátyás Antál, Ildikó Hegyi, and András Ligeti. Included are all the solo and multi-piano concertos and the two Rondos (♦Naxos 506002, 6CD; 505011, 5CD; also available singly). Jandó is a marvelous pianist and his readings are generally top drawer. **Anda** was one of the finest pianists of the last century and recorded all the solo concertos (DG 429001, 10CD). Nobody who opts for Anda, who leads the Camerata Academia of the Salzburg Mozarteum from the keyboard, will disappointed. He was a remarkable artist and a knowing Mozartean. And don't overlook the outstanding cycle from **Rudolf Buchbinder,** who directs the Vienna Symphony from the keyboard (Calig, 10CD).

Those who favor period instruments are especially lucky in the case of Mozart's keyboard concertos. A set that has stood the test of time is from **Malcolm Bilson** with the English Baroque Soloists led by Gardiner. Both are vital and imaginative Mozarteans and offer brilliant and stimulating readings of the entire canon (DG Archiv 463111, with the two multiple concertos with Robert Levin and Melvyn Tan). Also to be treasured is the set featuring **Jos van Immerseel** leading Anima Eterna from the keyboard. The Dutch fortepianist is a sensitive Mozartean and these are stylish and perceptive accounts (Channel, 10CD, minus the first four, K 107, and Rondo, K 382; also available singly).

A cycle to avoid, sad to say, is the 1980 set by **Rudolf Serkin** with Abbado (DG). The great pianist was in his '80s and past his prime when this project was undertaken, and it presents him at far less than his best. He planned a complete set for Columbia a couple of decades earlier but only a few of the concertos were recorded, and they (see below) are a better testament to his remarkable Mozart. A distinguished series is now in progress from **Goode** and the Orpheus Chamber Orchestra. This is Mozart playing on the highest level—elegant, sensitive, and stylish. So far eight concertos have been recorded for Nonesuch on 5 CDs (various numbers).

Individual recordings

Among the hundreds of recorded versions of Mozart's piano concertos there are a select few that are worth the listener's attention. Any of the following represents Mozart interpretation at its best.

Among the great pianists of the last century, **Rubinstein** was perhaps the finest Mozartean of them all. His unique combination of urbane elegance and musical sensitivity are perfect for Mozart's expressive palette. Of the six concertos he played in concert he recorded five, one of them— 23, his favorite—three times. All are superb renditions of music he obviously felt and loved deeply. The three readings of 23 each delight in their own special way. The 1931 recording with Barbirolli eschews all the Romantic excesses that would be expected of Mozart performances of the period and remains potent and striking. So too the 1949 account with Golschmann. As the Grand Old Master of the piano he taped his final version in 1961 with Wallenstein as part of sessions that also produced excellent accounts of 17, 20 and 21. His love for the composer remained undimmed throughout his long career and these readings are among the finest available (◆RCA "Rubinstein Edition" 63009, 63019, and 63061). There is also a powerful and deeply-felt reading of 24 with that excellent Mozartean, Krips, one of the finest around (RCA 7968).

The elegant and perceptive Mozart of the great French pianist **Casadesus** is easily recommendable. Not all of his illustrious concerto readings have been transferred to CD (a superb rendition of 17 with Szell awaits reissue) but what we do have—21–24, 26, and 27 with Szell—is well worth acquiring (Sony 46519, 3CD). In his 1938 broadcast performance of the popular 23 with Barbirolli the artistry of these legendary musicians manages to shine through, though even a careful restoration can't improve the wretched sound or restore a couple of noticeable missing segments of music. Approach with care. Of far more significance are two Casadesus performances from the archives of the Salzburg Festival (Orfeo 536001). The first is a dynamic reading of 24 in which this elegant Mozartean is joined by the fiery Mitropoulos and the Vienna Philharmonic, taped in 1956. Joining it is a classically poised 1961 account of 27 in which the Vienna players are led by the imposing Schuricht, who, unfortunately, omits seven important measures of the opening orchestral

exposition. Both are outstanding examples of this pianist's unique way with Mozart.

Before he embarked on his complete cycle, **Brendel** taped 9 and 14 with Janigro. These two marvelous performances have been reissued as part of the "Alfred Brendel Collection" in refurbished sound and deserve a place in any comprehensive Mozart collection (◆Vanguard 4015). The Austrian master, not content to rest on his Mozartean laurels, has returned to this repertoire and is re-recording some of the later concertos with Mackerras. The first installment is devoted to the two concertos in minor keys, 20 in D minor and 24 in C minor (◆Philips 462622). These performances far surpass Brendel's earlier efforts with Marriner and are among the finest available versions of both works. At around the time he was beginning his cycle with the English Chamber Orchestra in 1967, **Barenboim** taped a magisterial reading with Klemperer that remains a classic (in Philips "Great Pianists" series, 456721, 2CD).

Curzon was a great Mozartean, but few artists were more resistant to the recording process than this distinguished English pianist. It's disheartening to know that he had agreed to tape a complete cycle for English Decca and then typically backed out of the project. Two installments are available: 20 and 24 (Philips 462622) and 221 and 27 (Philips 468367). Two other concertos with Kertész, 26 and 27, have turned up in the "Great Pianists" series some 33 years after the original sessions (◆Philips 446757, 2CD). It has been worth the wait; coupled with the pianist's superb Schubert Impromptus and "Wanderer" Fantasy from the '40s and '50s, this is a release that belongs in every pianophile's collection. In 1970, Curzon taped one of the great Mozart recordings of all time with Britten, a uniquely perceptive coupling of 20 and 27, also unapproved by the pianist and released after his death in 1982 (◆Decca 417288). The playing is on such a rarefied plane that one wonders why he failed to approve this recording.

Two more Curzon Mozart recordings have come our way from broadcast sources. In two performances from 1979, he is joined by Barenboim in 27 and this is as fine a reading of the two-piano concerto K 365 (10) as I have ever heard. The true stature of this work is revealed; the poignant Andante is moving beyond description. 27, a Curzon favorite, is also beautifully realized (◆BBC 4037, with a superb Curzon-Britten 1960 collaboration in the two-piano sonata K 448). We also have a brilliant 1974 reading of 26 with Boulez that I like even more than Curzon's studio taping with Kertész. Boulez offers a vivid and stylish accompaniment and the pianist seems more committed before an audience (BBC 4020, with Beethoven's "Emperor" Concerto).

Still another Curzon treasure comes from Bavarian Radio (◆Audite 95.4153). In collaboration with Kubelik (a notable Mozartean in his own right), we get two performances taped in 1976 of such breathtaking beauty that I was overwhelmed as I was listening to them. 21, which the pianist never recorded commercially, and 24 are two of the finest Mozart performances I have ever heard. As the audiences on both occasions were remarkably quiet and the sound is excellent, this disc can be recommended without reservation. Finally, anyone interested in early Curzon can acquire his fine recording with Boyd Neel in a well-processed reissue (Dutton 5507, with the pianist's first recording of Brahms's Concerto 1 with Bátiz conducting).

The two Mozart recordings left by the short-lived, much-lamented **Lipatti** showed him to be a profound Mozartean. His recording of Sonata 8 remains a phonographic classic, but his recording of Concerto 21 with Karajan is also of prime importance to the collector. The sound is thin but the magic of the occasion shines through (◆EMI 69792, with the Schumann Concerto). Two discs preserve the remarkable Mozart of the distinguished Czech pianist under Marriner's alert direction (Hänssler 98.142, 20 and 23; 98.955, 24 and 25). **Kempff** offered sensitive, elegant and profound readings of 8, 23, 24 and 27 with Leitner (DG 439699, 2CD), and 9, 23, and 24 appear on another disc from the same set (DG). **Gilels**'s recorded legacy didn't encompass much Mozart but one superb disc from the great Russian master belongs in every collection: a sublime coupling with Böhm of 10 (with daughter Elena) and 27 (DG 419059).

Early in what would become a special relationship, **Bernstein** taped a fresh, vital reading of 15 from the keyboard with his beloved Vienna Philharmonic (Decca 467123, with Symphony 36). The young Austrian **Till Fellner** has given us brilliant readings of 19 and 25, while the fiery **Argerich** with Alexander Rabinovitch offers a rare sample of her intense brand of Mozart in a dramatic account of 20 (Teldec 98407). Also on the disc is a dazzling reading of 10 with Rabinovitch assuming the primo role and Argerich an equally dynamic secondo. Unfortunately, Rabinovitch fills out the disc with a reading of 19 that's bloated and over-Romanticized and a blot on an otherwise excellent recording.

Christian Zacharias is a pianist who should be better known on this side of the Atlantic. A stimulating interpreter of everything he plays, in a recent release he offers a powerful account of 25 in another pianist-led performance (MD+G 3400967, with a concert aria superbly sung by mezzo Bernarda Fink and an imposing reading of the "Prague" Symphony). **Horowitz** recorded only one Mozart concerto, and it shouldn't be surprising that he chose the ever-popular 23. Partnered by Giulini, the often-eccentric virtuoso tames his wild beasts and delivers a sensitive and straightforward account (DG 423287, with Sonata 13). The refined pianism of **Pires** is the perfect vehicle for Mozart and she doesn't disappoint in the four concertos she has so far given us with Abbado (DG 437529, 14 and 26; 439941, 17 and 21). Like Brendel, **Ashkenazy** recorded several concertos before he taped his complete cycle, including a superb rendition of 20 with Schmidt-Isserstedt that hasn't yet made it to CD. But 8 and 9 with Kertész are currently available, and these sparkling readings remain among the finest available of these early but notable works (Decca 443576, with Rondo K 386).

Serkin was a great Mozartean who waited too long to record a comprehensive cycle. His discs with Abbado are most disappointing (DG; see below), but fortunately there are some earlier recordings of great distinction. Serkin's 1938 recording of 14 with father-in-law Adolf Busch is not only one of the great pianist's finest Mozart recordings but one of the greatest Mozart concerto readings ever made. It has received an excellent transfer that includes notable accounts by Busch and his ensemble of other Mozart works (♦Pearl 9286; 14 is also in Philips's "Great Pianists" series with quieter surfaces but with several concertos from the inferior Abbado cycle). This disc holds 81 minutes of sublime music-making from a bygone age (note the occasional portamentos that add charm to the proceedings). We can hear surpassing readings of 14, 17, 19, 20, 27, and 10 for two pianos with son Peter, with various orchestras led by Alexander Schneider, Szell, and Ormandy (Sony 47207, 2CD). A concerto collection offers 21 with Schneider and 25 with Szell, both outstanding (Sony 47269, 3CD), and there is a delightful Schneider-led reading of 12 and Piano Trio 3 (Sony 46255).

Horszowski was a colleague of Serkin (both taught at Philadelphia's Curtis Institute) and an equally distinguished Mozartean. He recorded nine of the concertos (9, 12–14, 17–20, and 22) with Frederic Waldman in readings that have the transparency of chamber music (Pearl 9153, 2CD). The young **Leon Fleisher** was responsible for one of the finest

readings of a Mozart concerto with his early stereo taping of 25 with Szell; it remains available in two incarnations, coupled with the pair's luminous rendering of Beethoven's Concerto 4 (Sony 37762) and as filler for the complete Fleisher/Szell Beethoven cycle (42445, 3CD).

Reaching further back into phonographic history, Vox offers three outstanding Mozarteans in notable versions of a clutch of later concertos. One gives us the superb (young at the time) **Maria Tipo** in 21 and 25, recorded in 1956 with Perlea (5515, 2CD, with 12 Scarlatti sonatas in impeccable readings). Another distinguished Mozartean, **Lili Kraus,** recorded 22 and 26 in 1950–51 with Moralt (5516, 2CD, with Sonatas 8 and 17 and more). And, finally, the inimitable **Novaes** can be heard in 9 and 20 recorded in the early '50s with Swarowski (5512, 2CD, with Sonatas 5, 11, and 15 and Beethoven's Concerto 5).

Louis Kentner is an unjustly almost forgotten pianist. A reissue finds him with the truly great—and unique—Beecham in a 1940 reading of 12, part of a treasurable collection that includes Mozart opera overtures, *Eine kleine Nachtmusik,* and Haydn's Symphony 97 (Dutton 7019). One of the great pianists of the last century, **Solomon,** left only three Mozart concertos. No one was more suited to this music, and with his luminous tone and rare sensitivity, his readings of 15, 23, and 24, taped in 1953 and 1955 with Herbert Menges, belong in every serious collection (EMI 63707).

Edwin Fischer was a remarkable interpreter of the Viennese classics and especially revelatory in Mozart. At a time when the composer's music was often performed in a demeaning, almost mincing manner, Fischer offered a masculine and profound yet elegant view that even today is striking in its uniqueness. Three superbly transferred volumes give us 20 with the pianist leading the London Philharmonic from the keyboard; what is still to my mind the finest rendition of 22 ever, led by Barbirolli (♦APR 5523); 17, with Fischer conducting his own chamber orchestra from the piano; 24 with Lawrence Collingwood (♦APR 5534, with Sonata 11 and Fantasy K 396); and 25 with Krips (♦APR 5525, with Sonata 10, Fantasy K 475, and Haydn's D major concerto). These discs hold some of the most profound Mozart playing ever recorded and are essential to every library. **Fischer**'s postwar readings of 20 and 24 with Susskind avoid the excesses of the Romantic past, bringing the music to life. Pearl is reissuing this material, and Volume 1 offers fine transfers of 10 (for two pianos), 19, 21 and 27 (0006, 2CD, with Sonata 8).

Though justly famous for his Beethoven, **Schnabel** was an equally persuasive Mozartean, and a 3CD set contains most of his Mozart recordings (EMI 63703). Included are 19–21, 25, and 27, the two-piano concerto with son Karl-Ulrich, Sonatas 12 and 16, and the A minor Rondo K 511; Sargent conducts the London Symphony in 19 and 21, Barbirolli in 27, and Boult in the two-piano work. Schnabel's Mozart is strong, avoids miniaturization, and is eminently stylish (except for a textual error in the *Larghetto* in 27 that leads to a halving of the tempo, a miscalculation only one of Schnabel's stature could bring off). Sargent and Barbirolli are a bit old-fashioned in their approach—some unstylish portamentos creep in—and it's Boult who is the finest Mozartean of the bunch, with his classically proportioned, rhythmically charged support.

Gieseking's Mozart remains controversial. While the admirable collection that held his readings of 20 and 25 (with Rosbaud) and 23 and 24 (with Karajan) has long been deleted (EMI, 2CD), there remains the pianist's 1936 recording of 9 with Rosbaud (APR 5511, with Sonata 17 and Beethoven's Concerto 1). Music & Arts has collected a series of his broadcast performances, including 9, 21, 23, and 21; the conductors include Cantelli, Markevitch, Victor Desarzens, and Volkmar Andreae (1008, with Sonatas 15 and 17).

No discussion of recorded Mozart would be complete without mention of **Clara Haskil,** the Romanian-born pianist noted for her sensitive performances. We have superb readings of 19 and 27 with Fricsay (DG 449722, with Sonata 4), and the "Great Pianists" series offers the same version of 27 with 13, 20, 23, 24, and Rondo K 386 (Philips 456826, 2CD). **Michelangeli** is a pianist surrounded by mystery and controversy. Whether or not you find his technically flawless playing amenable is a matter of taste. It's true that he often sounds cold and distant, but there's never any doubt of the purity of his pianism or his basic musical integrity. Even in a severely limited discography he found room for several concertos, starting with early recordings of 15 and 23 (EMI 63819). The digital era brought live tapings of 13 and 15 (DG 431097) and 20 and 25 with Cord Garben (DG 429353).

In addition to her remarkable Beethoven, **Annie Fischer** was a redoubtable Mozartean. Beginning in the late '50s, she started a series that included six late concerted works. In commemoration of the 200th anniversary of Mozart's death, the works were issued on three single budget-priced discs (EMI 67000, 20 and 23 with Boult; 67002, 21 and 22 with Sawallisch; and 67001, 24 and 27 with Kurtz). There is a special refinement and elegance in her playing, as well as the integrity that infuses all her performances. Unfortunately, the series has been deleted and only four of the concertos (20–23) remain available (Seraphim 68529, 2CD). A powerful reading of 22 with Klemperer from the '50s is also available but is compromised by poor sound (Palexa 0515, with Beethoven's Concerto 3). As fine as the EMI recordings are, I have grown very fond of this great pianist's home-grown Mozart: recordings of 20 and 21 (with the added attraction of Concert Rondo K 382) made in 1965 with the Budapest Symphony under Ervin Lukács (Hungaroton 31492). The Philharmonia may offer more refined playing and the recorded sound gives a very bright picture of the higher strings, but I find more fire and commitment from the pianist on this occasion.

Gould made no secret of his distaste for Mozart and left a complete set of the piano sonatas that remain an abject lesson in how not to play this music. But even the quirky Canadian contradicted himself on occasion and did leave at least one notable Mozart recording, of Concerto 24 with the CBC Vancouver Symphony under Susskind (Sony 52626).

Among the world's great pianists, **Richter** was a somewhat disappointing Mozartean. Although he placed his full technical and tonal resources at the service of the composer, something was decidedly missing—the spiritual connection that turns the superbly executed into the musically sublime. Yet he left several recordings of a few concertos and they're worth mentioning. He taped 22 with Muti (EMI 64750, with Beethoven's Concerto 3) and with Britten (BBC Legends 8010, with *Adagio and Fugue* and *Sinfonia Concertante* K 364). Both offer Britten's overblown and anachronistic cadenzas, though the latter reading is far superior to the one with Muti. The same forces also recorded an austere version of 27 (BBC Legends 8005, with "Exsultate Jubilate" and the G minor Piano Quartet, Britten at the keyboard). Mozart's more appropriate cadenzas are played this time.

Richter's fine early stereo recording of 20 has turned up in a rather strange place: Volume 20 of DG's "Complete Beethoven Edition." This is because he plays Beethoven's cadenzas in I and III and DG has sought to include every note of the master in its comprehensive offering (453304, 6CD). This is altogether a most valuable collection and Richter's account of the concerto adds to its attractiveness. Perhaps the most bizarre Richter recording comes from very late in his career: a version of 25 with

Yuri Bashmet (Teldec 94245, with Bach concertos). Not only is the playing shockingly dull and undistinguished, but, as the composer left no cadenzas, the pianist simply leaves the holes blank. Strange indeed.

In the only concerto recording **Solti** made as piano soloist, he leads the English Chamber Orchestra from the piano in a respectable reading of 20. The orchestral response is vigorous in the usual Solti manner and the pianism is suitably refined and controlled, if at times more restrained than you would expect from so volatile a personality. It's joined by high-spirited accounts of the Two-Piano Concerto with Barenboim assuming the primary role and the Three-Piano Concerto in which Solti is partnered by Schiff and Barenboim (Decca 430232). The first major Mozartean to record one of the composer's concertos from the keyboard was **Bruno Walter,** who also began his musical life as a pianist. He recorded a distinguished account of 20 with the Vienna Philharmonic in the '30s (Pearl 9940).

I don't often endorse unauthorized recordings, but Iron Needle 1336 offers a pair of performances of considerable historical significance. **Landowska,** famous as a harpsichordist and scholar who almost single-handedly aroused interest in period performance and is remembered above all for her profound Bach recordings, was also a remarkable pianist and interpreter of other composers as well. She left only one commercial Mozart concerto recording, a 1937 reading of 26 with Walter Goehr (Biddulph 013), so her insightful readings of 13 and 22 with Rodzinski are treasurable mementos of a uniquely gifted Mozartean. The 1945 sound is better than might be expected, and Rodzinski's powerful and clear leadership enhances these remarkable accounts.

Two periodists cry out for recognition. Fortepianist **Andreas Staier** is one of the most imaginative keyboard artists before the public; everything he plays represents a vivid recreation. His recordings directing Concerto Köln from the keyboard are brilliantly conceived and executed and merit the attention of every devoted Mozartean (Teldec 98412, 9 and 17; 80676, 18 and 19). Finally, there is an outstanding ongoing series from the always stimulating and invigorating **Robert Levin,** who with Hogwood is bringing these concertos to life in a unique and imaginative way. Levin improvises his cadenzas—as did the composer—and adds other effective touches as well (his ornamentation is a joy). So far eight discs have been issued, offering 1–4 (Oiseau-Lyre 466131); 9 and 17 (443328); 11 and 13 with Rondo K 386 (444371); 15 and 26, in one of this troublesome late concerto's most insightful renderings (♦455814); 17 and 20 (455607); 18 and 19 (452051); 22 and 23 (452052); and 5, 14, and 16 (Decca 458285).

No survey would be complete without mentioning **Howard Shelley**'s abbreviated series. The English pianist offers stylish and elegant Mozart playing that reveals much beneath a smooth and fluid surface. He leads the London Mozart Players from the keyboard in 9 and 17 (Chandos 9068); 12 and 19 (9256); 13 and 24 (9321); 14 and 27 (9137); 20 and 23 (8992); and 21 and 22 (9404). Special mention must be made of the minicycle of 15–19 by **Peter Serkin** and the English Chamber Orchestra led by Alexander Schneider. RCA gave their 3LP and 3CD editions a very short life, and they have been unavailable for a long time. These readings have achieved and deserve historic status, and if you find them, grab them: 14 and 15 (♦RCA 1492), 16 and 17 (1943), and 18 and 19 (2244).

Finally, Byron Janis, in a brilliant career interrupted by arthritis, never recorded a Mozart concerto in the studio, so his exquisite 1960 reading of 23 with Bernstein and the New York Philharmonic is especially valuable. He proves to be a sensitive Mozartean and the conductor provides a stylish accompaniment (in the 10CD Bernstein set available from the Philharmonic or Tower Records; the set contains many gems).

Violin(s)

It's generally thought that Mozart composed his five authenticated violin concertos (there are a couple of works that are considered spurious) in 1775, when he was only 19, though 1 may have been written earlier. What is not in doubt is the generally high quality of these works. Avoiding virtuoso display, these basically sunny, melodic, and lyrical pieces are far more difficult to bring off than meets the eye and ear. Behind their essential simplicity—as is often the case with Mozart—lies much depth and complexity. In addition, Mozart left three short concerted works for violin and orchestra: an Adagio in E major and two Rondos (in B-flat and C), composed for the Salzburg concertmaster Antonio Brunetti. Then there are the concertante works for violin and additional solo instruments: the brilliant *Concertone in A for Two Violins* and the great *Sinfonia Concertone for Violin and Viola K 364*. And finally, the might-have beens: an unfinished *Sinfonia Concertante for Violin and Piano* and another for violin, viola, and cello, both of which have been recorded in reconstructions by Philip Wilby. A lost Cello Concerto K 206a remains tantalizingly out of reach; we can hope it will be found some day.

Complete sets

The catalog is filled with glorious versions of the five concertos played by the greatest violinists of the past and present. Many are available as budget-priced "two-fers" that allow the collector to add all these marvelous works to their collections at a modest outlay. But before turning to them I should mention the set in the "Complete Mozart Edition" that holds all the concerted works that feature the violin (Philip 422508, 4CD). The concertos and other solo works are played by **Szeryng**, and the *concertante* pieces by **Iona Brown,** in superbly crafted performances.

Perhaps the finest recent version of the concertos comes from the brilliant **Pamela Frank** (♦Arte Nova 72104, 2CD, with the mini-concerto Mozart inserted into his "Haffner" Symphony). Accompanied by the Zurich Tonhalle under Zinman's sparkling direction, her performances are alive with pulsating energy while responding well to the lyricism of the music. **Grumiaux** and the London Symphony under Colin Davis also provides a superlative collection (♦Philips 428323, 2CD, with the E-flat *Sinfonia Concertante*). These sensitive and stylish readings have been versions of choice ever since their initial release in the early '60s. In **Menuhin**'s cycle leading the Bath Festival Orchestra, he offers special insights and his performances are among the best on disc (♦Seraphim 68530, 2CD, with a superb reading of *Sinfonia Concertante* led by Barshai). One of Menuhin's last recordings was also devoted to the violin concertos, in 1997 as conductor of the Vienna Chamber Orchestra, with glowing performance of 2, 3, and 5 by the young **Vadim Repin** (Erato 21660). One of the finest violinists of his generation, Repin allies a sovereign technique and tonal sweetness to true Mozartean sensibility.

Wolfgang Schneiderhan is almost forgotten today, but his tonal refinement and Classical sensibility made him an ideal interpreter. He recorded a cycle as soloist and conductor of the Berlin Philharmonic in the '60s, but only 5 survives (♦DG 447403). An earlier, equally accomplished, reading of 4, was with Hans Rosbaud, a great conductor whose scant discography makes his every record a treasure (DG 457720, with two Haydn symphonies). The mono recordings from 1956 have been beautifully transferred.

Frank Peter Zimmermann is one of the finest young violinists on the international concert circuit; he plays a wide-ranging repertoire and is a most persuasive Mozartean. He has recorded the complete cycle

with Jörg Faerber, and it's well worth your attention (EMI 69355, 2CD, with the two Rondos and *Adagio*). He also appears in a winning performance of 3 led by Sawallisch (EMI 55426, with the Brahms Concerto).

Perlman, with Levine, offers refined and intense readings that are often like the violinist himself, a bit larger than life. Here is an artist who revels in his music-making, and those who favor his approach to music won't be disappointed (DG 445535, 2CD, with Rondos and *Adagio*). **Stern**'s stereo set of the concertos evolved over several years and involved two conductors, Alexander Schneider and Szell. Whether you want to quibble about this or that, there is no doubt of this artist's love for Mozart, and his admirers won't be disappointed either (Sony 66475, 3CD, with more Mozart). Nor will those of **Szeryng,** whose cycle is part of the "Complete Mozart Edition" (Philips 422508, 4CD). With Alexander Gibson, he offers beautifully crafted accounts, using his sweet, singing tone to great effect.

Oistrakh's excellent cycle as soloist and conductor with the Berlin Philharmonic has been reissued as part of a budget series (EMI 745177, 1–3; 74578, 4+5; 74559, *Sinfonia Concertante* with son Igor and the Brahms concerto under Klemperer). These are unique readings from one of the great masters. Another excellent Oistrakh 3 is with Sargent (EMI 69331, 2CD, with Beethoven and Prokofiev).

Another violinist of great distinction is the Latvian-born, Moscow-trained **Gidon Kremer.** A profound and highly individual interpreter, he has teamed up for a cycle with another strong individualist, Harnoncourt. I find the results stimulating, but they won't please all tastes (DG 453043, 2CD, with *Sinfonia Concertante*). Fans of **Zukerman** can acquire his cycle, in which he's soloist and conductor with the St. Paul Chamber Orchestra (Sony 46539/40, 2CD, budget-priced). **Cho-Liang Lin,** with Leppard, has given us some of the finest Mozart concerto recordings ever committed to disc. All the important elements are here—style, charm, warmth, energy, tonal opulence—producing performances that have stood the test of time (♦Sony 44503, 1 and 4; 42364, 3 and 5; 47693, *Sinfonia Concertante* and *Concertone*). The series also offers an oddity: Lin includes the spurious 7, but while it's wonderful to have such a commanding performance, it's still inauthentic.

Mutter didn't conceive her set as a unified series; it's split between two labels and three conductors. It began in 1978, when, as a mere 14-year-old, she recorded 3 and 5 with Karajan. These fresh and inspired readings remain among the finest and have been beautifully remastered (DG 457746). Some years later she recorded *Sinfonia Concertante* with Marriner (EMI 54302) and 2 and 4 with Muti (EMI 69865). All fulfill the promise of her debut release.

A disappointing Naxos set features the noted Japanese violinist **Takeko Nishizaki.** 1 and 2 are led by Johannes Wildner (550414), 3 and 5 by Gunzenhauser (550063, with Rondo K 363 and *Adagio*), and 4 and *Sinfonia Concertante* again with Gunzenhauser (550332). Though generally well played, the recorded sound imparts a nasality to the violnist's tone and generally lacks refinement and a firm low end. Even at super-budget price, these recordings aren't competitive. But an excellent bargain comes from the brilliant **Christian Tetzlaff,** whose performances are stylish, spirited, and refined, with sound to match (Virgin 61841, 1, 3+5; 61842, 3, 4, and shorter pieces).

Those who favor period performance are blessed with two marvelous sets. **Simon Standage** with Hogwood offers the concertos, the two Rondos, and *Adagio* in stylish and elegant performances, enhanced by the transparency that only first-rate period execution can provide (Oiseau-Lyre 455721, 2CD). **Monica Huggett,** as soloist and conductor of the Orchestra of the Age of the Enlightenment, provides enthralling readings (♦Virgin 61576, 2CD). If I favor her a bit, it's because of her slightly sweeter sound.

Individual performances

Though many of the past century's great violinists were notable Mozarteans, they didn't leave complete cycles, choosing instead to record selected pieces. The elegance and purity of **Heifetz**'s playing made him a natural Mozartean, and his recordings are worthy additions to any library. A splendid transfer of his 1947 version of 4 with Beecham has been released; the beauty of this reading, allied to Beecham's marvelous support, make it a phonographic classic (♦Dutton 9704, with Vieuxtemps and Bruch). He went on to record a superb stereo version with Sargent (RCA, "The Heifetz Edition" Vol. ?). He also left several recordings of 5, including a 1934 version with Barbirolli (Biddulph 012) and a stunning stereo version in which he appears as soloist and conductor (RCA 61757).

Going back even further, to 1924 and the acoustic era, we have an elegant and sweetly played version of 5 from **Fritz Kreisler** in his prime, with an anonymous orchestra conducted by Landon Ronald. Though the surface noise is heavy and the orchestral sound tinny, the violinist's sumptuous tone comes through in a superb transfer (Naxos 110921, with a 1927 Brahms Concerto with Leo Blech). The ear adjusts and the results are most rewarding. Kreisler re-recorded 5 in 1939 with Sargent, now available in a fresh transfer (Naxos).

Bruno Walter left few concerto recordings, preferring to devote his discography to the symphony, but he left a jewel in his partnership with **Zino Francescatti** in 3 and 4 (Sony 64468, with *Eine kleine Nachtmusik*). Both soloist and conductor infuse these works with overflowing warmth and humanity and the remastered sound in the "Bruno Walter Edition" makes the 1958 recordings sound brand new. Another glowing Mozartean was the Polish **Szymon Goldberg**, who taped the last three concertos with Susskind in classic accounts (Testament (1028).

Concertone for Two Violins is both brilliant and tuneful—it was frankly written as a crowd-pleaser—but it doesn't represent the composer at his best. It was composed either in 1773 or 1774 and shows several influences, including some aspects of the Mannheim style and the Baroque concerto grosso. Though rarely encountered in the concert hall, it has received several excellent recordings.

At the top of the list is the excellent account by **Perlman** and **Zukerman** under Mehta (DG 415486). What makes this disc special is these artists' superb reading of the E-flat *Sinfonia Concertante*. **Cho-Liang Lin** and **Jaime Laredo** are another distinguished team, who are joined by Leppard in impeccable performances (Sony 47693, with the same *Sinfonia*). Add **Stern** and **Zukerman** to the list of excellent renditions of this subfusc bit of Mozarteana (in Stern's complete Mozart violin concertos, Sony 66475, 3CD). Also, **Szeryng** and **Poulet** offer a brilliant reading in the "Complete Mozart Edition."

Even periodists are offered a version of abiding excellence. The brilliant duo of **Monica Huggett** and **Pavlo Beznosiuk** do this music proud (Virgin 545290, with *Sinfonia Concertante*). Finally, there's what could be called a novelty version of the work, a transcription for two flutes. The **Rampal-Kudo** duo appear with the Salzburg Mozarteum Orchestra under Rampal's direction (Sony 45930, with other Baroque concertos).

Sinfonia Concertante in E-flat K 384. Mozart composed this piece for violin and viola in 1779; it isn't known who or what prompted its creation but it turned out to be one of his most sublime works. It has drawn

together some of the finest solo violinists and violists, who have provided many inspired recorded performances.

Claudio Abbado's Mozartean credentials are rarely questioned and, with two principals from the Berlin Philharmonic, **Reiner Kussmaul** and **Wolfram Christ,** offering pristine accounts of the solo parts, he has given us perhaps the finest contemporary version (Sony 66859, with Symphonies 21 and 36). Another superb rendition comes from **Christopher Warren-Green** as violin soloist and leading the London Chamber Orchestra, with **Roger Chase** (Virgin 61205, budget-priced, with an equally sterling account of *Sinfonia Concertante* for winds).

In 1982, **Perlman** and **Zukerman** were at their considerable best in a heartfelt and inspired reading, beautifully partnered by Mehta (DG 415486). The only fly in this particular ointment is the coupling: well played as it is, little can be done to save the boring *Concertone*. Another excellent reading came from **Arthur Grumiaux** and **Arrigo Pellicia** with Colin Davis (Philips 438323, 2CD, budget-priced, with Grumiaux's eloquent accounts of the violin concertos). In the '60s **Menuhin** taped an elegant reading as both violinist and conductor with the Bath Festival Orchestra, partnered by the great **Rudolph Barshai** (EMI/Seraphim, 2CD, with the violin concertos). In another notable version, taped in London in 1963, he conducted the visiting Moscow Philharmonic with the father and son team of David and Igor Oistrakh (BBC 4019, with Menuhin as soloist in the Beethoven Concerto with David Oistrakh conducting).

In 1967, **Norbert Brainin** and **Peter Schidlof,** first violinist and violist of the Amadeus Quartet, played the work with outstanding results, led by Britten (BBC 8010). This disc also holds the finer (by a wide margin) of Richter's two versions of Piano Concerto 22, with those strange Britten cadenzas in I and III, and a strong account of *Adagio and Fugue in C Minor*. Some 14 years earlier, Brainin and Schidlof recorded a notable account with Harry Blech (Testament 1157, with Schubert's C major String Quartet).

Isaac Stern has participated in several distinguished versions. A rather leisurely account pairs him with two legends, **Primrose** and Casals as conductor (Sony 58983, with Erica Morini's "Turkish" Concerto). Casals imparted a unique wisdom to everything he performed and with his two superb soloists has left us a unique version of this music. Stern can also be heard in a version taped at his 60th anniversary concert with **Zukerman** under Mehta (Sony 36692, with Bach and Vivaldi concertos).

It's not surprising that Szell dominates the proceedings in his recording with the Cleveland Orchestra; since its initial release in 1964, it has always held a prominent position in the catalog (Sony 67177, with Ormandy's *Sinfonia Concertante* for winds and Zuckerman's B-flat Rondo). Szell was an imposing Mozartean and leads a propulsive performance with two of the orchestra's noted principals, concertmaster **Rafael Druian** and violist **Abraham Skernick.** There are still many who feel that **Heifetz** was the greatest of the great violinists; listening to his sterling account with **Primrose,** conducted by the almost forgotten Izler Solomon, it's easy to see and hear why. The laser-like purity of his tone, allied to a supreme musicality, brings magic to Mozart's eloquent score. Primrose is surely an equal here, and in its latest remastering, it has never sounded better (RCA 63531, with ravishing performances of the Bach and Brahms Double Concertos).

A striking reading comes from **Gidon Kremer** and **Kim Kashkashian,** led by the always fascinating (or exasperating) Harnoncourt (DG 453043, with the violin concertos). Also worthy of attention is the brilliant team of **Mutter** and **Bruno Giuranna** with Marriner (EMI

54302, with Concerto 1), and not to be forgotten is the sparkling version by members of the **Orpheus Chamber Orchestra** (DG 429784, with *Sinfonia Concertante* for winds). As with his complete cycle of the violin concertos, **Cho-Liang Lin**'s exquisite outing with **Jaime Laredo** under Leppard brings cultured and elegant playing from everyone involved; forget the coupled *Concertone* and get this disc for the major work (Sony 47693). Those who are drawn to **Takako Nishizaki**'s concerto cycle will find much to admire in her account with **Ladislav Kyselak** directed by Gunzenhauser (Naxos 550330, with Concerto 4).

Finally, it should be noted that aficionados of period performance are very much in luck with the outstanding account by **Huggett** and **Beznosiuk,** with Huggett performing double duty as conductor of the Portland Baroque Orchestra (Virgin 545290). Those who know her playing are aware that she eschews the astringent style so offensive to many listeners and plays with a sweet and winning lyricism. Beznosiuk is an excellent partner both here and as second violinist in the coupled *Concertone*.

Winds

Bassoon. It's not known for whom Mozart wrote his brilliant Bassoon Concerto, though we do know it was composed in Salzburg in 1774. It's less well known than the other wind concertos, but it utilizes the full resources of the instrument with all the mastery of the others.

One of the finest versions is by **Gwydion Brooke,** felicitously accompanied by Beecham and his Royal Philharmonic (of which Brooke was first bassoon). Issued as part of the "Beecham Edition," it may be hard to locate but is well worth the effort (◆EMI 63408, with Clarinet Concerto and Violin Concerto 3). **Frank Morelli** with the Orpheus Chamber Orchestra also offers a vibrant account (DG 431665, 3CD). Not to be overlooked is the performance by **Dietmar Zeman** and his colleagues of the Vienna Philharmonic led by Böhm (DG 457719, with the G major Flute Concerto and Clarinet Concerto). On the same disc that holds Lothar Koch's sumptuous reading of the Oboe Concerto with Karajan is **Guenter Piesk**'s excellent account (EMI 64355). **Stepan Turnovsky** weighs in with a fine reading under Johannes Wildner (Naxos 550345, with Oboe and Clarinet Concertos), and another version in the budget category comes from **Bernard Garfield** and his colleagues in the Philadelphia Orchestra under Ormandy (Sony 62652, with Weber and Strauss).

Leonard Sharrow is a renowned bassoonist from the past, and partnered by Toscanini he gave a brilliant and intense account (RCA 60286, with other Mozart). Not to be forgotten is the fine reading by **Willard Elliot** with Abbado in that hard-to-find DG disc (415104). Finally, from **Denny Bond** and Hogwood we get a unique account on a copy of an instrument from Mozart's time (Decca 460027, 3CD).

Clarinet. Not only is Mozart's Clarinet Concerto his greatest wind concerto, it's one of his greatest works in any medium, so it's especially curious that we don't have a truly authentic source for such an imposing masterpiece. All we have is a partial autograph score for the first movement of a concerto for an earlier instrument, the bassett clarinet. The later score, finished in 1791, was written for Anton Stadler and was for an instrument closer in form to the bassett than the one generally used today. It wasn't published until ten years after Mozart's death, in an arrangement for the standard instrument by an unknown hand, with many changes made to adapt the work to a different range. Though it's not possible to arrive at a wholly accurate version of the original score, there are critical sources, including the completed 199 measures of the 1789 work that enable us to get close to one of the most sublime works from his pen.

This concerto has received many fine recordings on both the standard clarinet and its more exotic relative. If I were to choose just one, it would be the magnificent reading by **Thea King,** in which modern and historical perspectives are married in a performance of exquisite beauty. King, playing a modern reconstruction of the bassett clarinet, is joined by a superb modern instrument ensemble, the English Chamber Orchestra, stylishly led by Tate (◆Hyperion 66199, with Clarinet Quintet). Another performance that has won my affection is by the equally skilled German clarinetist **Sabine Meyer.** Here is an artist who can draw the most subtle colors from her instrument and has a special feeling for this work. She has recorded it twice on a bassett clarinet: in 1990 with the Staatskapelle Dresden under the vital direction of Hans Vonk (◆EMI 66949, in "Great Recordings of the Century," with *Sinfonia Concertante* for winds), and in 1998 with the Berlin Philharmonic under Claudio Abbado (◆EMI 556832, with unconventional couplings, Debussy's *Première rapsodie* and Takemitsu's *Fantasia/cantos*, both exquisitely played). This time she has produced a version that is at once magically transparent and kaleidoscopically tinted. She gets to the heart of Mozart's music, and I would be hard-pressed to choose between the two. EMI has reissued this performance with Pahud's Concerto 1 and the Pahud/Langlemet reading of the Flute and Harp Concertos — for those, I suppose, who would prefer an all-Mozart outing to the original 20th-century pairings (57128)

Two earlier versions are of significant interest. The first features **Jack Brymer** and the Royal Philharmonic conducted by Beecham. Beecham was a stylish if sometimes heavy-handed Mozartean, and Brymer, his principal clarinetist, was a notable master of his instrument and this concerto (EMI 63408). Together they created a memorable performance, disfigured only by the occasional nip and tuck the conductor felt necessary to "tighten up" the work. Brymer returned to this music several years later and taped a marvelous reading with Marriner (Philips 416483, with Oboe Concerto), and **Andrew Marriner** (Neville's son) has contributed a fine recording of his own, partnered by the London Mozart Players under the wonderful Jane Glover (EMI 4484, with Bassoon Concerto).

Another important reading came from **Benny Goodman,** "The King of Swing," a formidable master of the instrument. In a 1956 recording he's joined by Munch and the Boston Symphony (RCA, 68804, with Clarinet Quintet). Goodman's lustrous tone and instinctive musicality serves the music quite well, and while not a first choice, it's of definite historic significance.

One of the most notable contemporary masters, **Richard Stoltzman,** has recorded the concerto twice with the English Chamber Orchestra. The first, coupled with his transcription of the Bassoon Concerto, is conducted by Alexander Schneider (EMI 60379). In the second, he performs double duty as soloist and conductor (EMI 60723). This newer recording is filled out with the Clarinet Quintet played by the Tokyo Quartet, and those who admire this remarkable artist's sumptuous tone aren't likely to be disappointed by either.

Next come versions that are notable not only for the quality of the solo playing but also for the reputations of the conductors involved. **Alfred Prinz**'s sensitive reading with his colleagues of the Vienna Philharmonic is stylishly led by Böhm (DG 457719). **Robert Marcellus,** who served many years as principal clarinet of Szell's magnificent Cleveland Orchestra, was one of the finest instrumentalists of his generation, and we're fortunate to have his collaboration with his superb colleagues (Sony 62424, with the two flute concertos played by Eugenia Zukerman). Karajan is at his most anonymous in his two recordings. The first, recorded in 1955 in the heyday of producer Walter Legge's Philharmonia Orchestra, featured the ensemble's outstanding first clarinetist, **Bernard Walton**, who offered a cultured reading of the solo part. If only the beautifully-played orchestral accompaniment were more vital this would have been memorable (EMI 63312, in the "Karajan Edition"). The later stereo version with the Berlin Philharmonic and principal **Karl Leister**—one of the finest clarinetists around—is even more bland, thanks to the conductor's rather cold and slick approach (EMI 63472, in the "Karajan Edition" volume devoted to the Mozart wind concertos).

Much more to the point is **Charles Neidich**'s excellent account with the Orpheus Chamber Orchestra as part of that ensemble's outstanding collection of the wind concertos (DG 431665, 3CD). Also not to be forgotten is the remarkable **David Shifrin**, who gives us a notable outing with Gerard Schwarz (Delos 3020, with Clarinet Quintet). Finally, we have a superb period-instrument version by **Anthony Pay**, playing the bassett clarinet with Hogwood and the Academy of Ancient Music. This transparent, ethereally clear reading infuses this music with a serenity and nobility that add up to a special listening experience (Decca 460027, 3CD).

Flute. In 1777, through a Mannheim connection with the virtuoso flutist, Johann Baptist Wendling, Mozart received a commission to write " three short and undemanding concertos" and a pair of flute quartets for Ferdinand Dejean, a wealthy Dutch surgeon who was a gifted amateur flutist. Apparently distracted by other matters—notably a romantic infatuation with Aloysia Weber, the sister of his future wife Constanze—only two of these works emerged: one quartet and the G major Flute Concerto. Since Dejean found its original slow movement too complicated, Mozart supplied an alternative Andante. The second flute concerto was a transcription of his C major Oboe Concerto, composed about a year earlier. Mozart's often-expressed disdain of the flute is belied by the quality of both; they not only demonstrate a consummate mastery of the instrument but are musically satisfying as well. The 22-year old composer produced lyrical, richly melodic music that is easy on the ears and refreshing to the spirit.

Galway has consistently impressed me with his lyrical elegance and beauty in these concertos. He has recorded one or both of them on several occasions, but his latest, with Marriner, is not only his finest but perhaps the most rewarding now available (♦RCA 68256, with Flute and Harp Concerto). Even Marriner, who can often be anonymous on records, has provided some of the best and most affectionate Mozart I have heard from him. Add to this RCA's glowing sound and you have a record to treasure. As the performers' expansive (but never sagging) tempos add up to 77 minutes of playing time, there wasn't room for the *Andante.*

Almost at this level is the same coupling featuring **Emanuel Pahud**, the brilliant young former principal flute of the Berlin Philharmonic (♦EMI 56365). Pahud, like Galway (one of his predecessors in the Berlin post), is not only an accomplished virtuoso but, like his older colleague, has a stunning tonal palette. His readings are a trifle cooler and definitely brisker (by some six minutes) but no less heartfelt. Abbado and the Berlin Philharmonic offer refined, almost ethereal, support. Here there is room for the *Andante* and it should have been included.

Fans of the late, great **Jean-Pierre Rampal** are currently offered his readings of both concertos with Mehta (Sony 44919, with *Andante* and a Rondo). An earlier CD that holds the French master's 1966 accounts (Erato 88106) has been supplanted by one of the G major Concerto and *Andante* but replacing the D major with the Flute and Harp Concerto with the great Lily Laskine (Erato 45832). Guschlbauer leads the Vienna

Symphony in the solo works, Paillard and his ensemble accompany the duo concerto.

Of historical interest is a recording from the '30s by the legendary **Marcel Moyse** (Pearl 9118, with Flute and Harp Concerto). Moyse was to the flute as Landowska was to the harpsichord and Segovia to the guitar. This is a remarkable document. The outstanding **Irena Grafenauer** is flutist in the SCD box "Complete Mozart Edition" devoted to all the concerted wind music, partnered by Marriner (Philips 422509). The Orpheus Chamber Orchestra unfailingly offers performances of high quality, and **Susan Palma** is the excellent soloist in the G major Concerto and *Andante* in their set of most of the concerted works for winds (DG 431665, 3CD, available singly, with the C major Oboe Concerto and its transcription for flute).

Böhm was a perceptive Mozartean who left a large discography devoted to the composer's works. In addition to the complete symphonies and the major operas, he also recorded the complete wind concertos, leading the Vienna Philharmonic and principals from that orchestra. He selected only the G major work for his series and it's beautifully played (DG 457719, with Bassoon and Clarinet Concertos). Another not to be forgotten version is by the renowned **Julius Baker**, the distinguished former principal flute of the New York Philharmonic. He recorded both concertos and *Andante* with Janigro (Vanguard 54, with Vaughan Williams and Vivaldi) and the D major and *Andante* with Prohaska (Vanguard 55, with Gluck and Vivaldi).

Periodists are directed to Hogwood's outstanding set, which offers the solo wind concertos and Flute and Harp Concerto (Decca 460027, 3CD, available singly). Of the flute works, the set offers only the G major concerto and *Andante,* with **Lisa Beznosiuk** as the stylish soloist. The sound is vivid throughout the set.

Horn. Mozart was attracted early to what later became the French horn and began writing for the instrument when he only eight. His horn concertos were composed for his friend, the virtuoso Joseph Lautgeb. The works—the first three in E-flat, the final one in D—were composed between 1783 and 1791, probably in the following order: 2, 3, 4, and 1, in the standard numbering. Concerto 4 was completed by Mozart's famous (or notorious) pupil Süssmayr, who performed similar duties for the uncompleted *Requiem.*

The works have had a long and distinguished recorded history, with the palm still going to the first complete set, by **Dennis Brain** with the Philharmonia under Karajan. Brain's playing has never been equaled. There are many masters of the instrument, but this English horn player—who died tragically at age 36 in an auto crash—possessed that certain magic granted to very few. His recording was made in 1953/54 and remains a landmark in recorded history, a special blend of supreme virtuosity and insight, a oneness of music and instrument that stands unique. An excellent remastering is currently available in the "Great Recordings of the Century" series, filled out with a superb reading of the Quintet for Piano and Winds (♦EMI 66950).

In the late '40s, before recording his now-legendary cycle with Karajan, Brain set down versions of 2 and 3 with the Philharmonia and the Hallé. There are collectors who prefer the earlier versions, finding them even fresher and more vital. At this level comparisons are odious; Brain was a unique artist and anything he left demands our attention. The playing is magnificent, and this release holds other gems, such as Beethoven's Horn Sonata and Brain's first recording of Strauss's Horn Concerto 1 (Pearl 26).

For the next truly remarkable cycle of these works, we turn to a period performance by **Anthony Halstead** with Hogwood, part of the remarkable Decca set devoted to the wind concertos (♦460027, 3CD). Halstead is a complete master of a difficult instrument, the valveless horn, but like Brain, his virtuosity takes second place to a total commitment to the music. Hogwood offers strong support and Decca has supplied superb sound. Even though many listeners are averse to period performance, this is one instance where I would ignore the medium and partake of the message. Halstead uses John Humphries's recent edition and adds Süssmayr's completion of 4 as well as Humphries's reconstruction of *Concerto Rondeau* in E-flat, the final movement of a missing earlier concerto.

has the distinction of having recorded the concertos on both period and modern instruments, offering a fascinating comparison. Both are winningly brought off and each has its unique timbre. The modern instrument version offers the four concertos and Humphries's reconstructions of the finale of 4 and *Concert-Rondo* K 317. Its attractiveness is enhanced by Iona's Brown's outstanding support with the Academy of St. Martin (Hänssler 98.316). Brown's period edition includes the concertos and several short pieces in a "two-fer," along with a group of Mozart arias exquisitely sung by soprano Lena Lootens and tenor Christoph Prégardien (Virgin 61573). He also performs double duty, playing the solos and conducting the Orchestra of the Age of Enlightenment.

Periodists also have excellent choices in a recording by **Ab Koster,** accompanied by Tafelmusik led by Bruno Weil (Sony 53369, with Rondo K 371) and a version by the renowned **Hermann Baumann** with the equally distinguished Harnoncourt and Concentus Musicus Wien (Teldec 42757).

For more conventional, though no less stimulating versions, the more distinguished modern instrument accounts include the great English hornist **Barry Tuckwell**'s three complete sets. His mastery is evident in all of them. The most recent appears on the now-defunct Collins label (♦1153); it's worth searching for, as in addition to the excellence of the playing, he fills out the disc with some unusual small items. He also acts as conductor, leading the Philharmonia Orchestra. Tuckwell's 1972 version with Marriner is currently available in a mid-priced disc (EMI 69569), and there's a CD where he appears as soloist and conductor of the English Chamber Orchestra (Decca 410284). An earlier taping with the London Symphony in the '60s, when he was principal horn there, is NA. All are outstanding.

Another renowned English horn player is the late **Alan Civil,** who replaced Brain as principal in the Philharmonia, and he too recorded three complete cycles. A highly regarded outing with Kempe is NA (RCA; I don't recall a CD reissue), and his distinguished recording with Marriner is now only available in Europe (Philips 442397), which leaves us with his version with Klemperer and the Philharmonia (Testament 1102, with short pieces by Mendelssohn and Rossini). The conductor dominates the scene with rugged, measured, large-scaled orchestral contributions in his usual manner, almost relegating his soloist to an obbligato role. But Civil's playing is impeccable and the readings have a certain integrity, though it's not for all tastes. Of the Mozart concerted works, only the four concertos (in their standard editions) are offered.

A slight hint of Eastern European vibrato colors the tone of the brilliant readings by **Radovan Vlatkovic,** who is sympathetically partnered by Tate and the English Chamber Orchestra (EMI 64851, with Rondo K 371 and a substantial bonus in Strauss's Horn Concerto 1). In Karajan's second version with then principal horn **Gerd Seifert,** the orchestra is the Berlin Philharmonic, and while Seifert lacks the potent character that characterized Brain's set, he's a true virtuoso and the disc is distin-

guished for the marvelous contributions of soloist, conductor, and orchestra (DG 419057). **Günter Högner**'s fine accounts with Böhm are a worthy complement to the conductor's complete cycle of Mozart wind concertos. **Michael Thompson** scores with an outstanding set, as soloist and leading the Bournemouth Sinfonietta (Naxos 553592, with another Humphries reconstruction, a fragment in E-flat K370b). Playing a modern horn, his version is made even more tempting by its super-budget price.

In the fresh, direct, and exhilarating accounts of the Orpheus Chamber Orchestra, the honors are split between **David Jolley** (1 and 4) and **William Purvis** (2 and 3) (DG 431665, 3CD). One of the most brilliant young virtuosos to come down the pike in recent years is **David Wyatt,** whose every record has brought glowing reviews. His brilliance rings true in his 1996 readings with Marriner (Erato 17074). Though the shorter concerted pieces are omitted, we can't complain, as the disc is filled out with the substantial bonus of the Horn Quintet. Marriner and his often-recorded Academy are also present in the "Complete Mozart Edition," where the soloist is the noted **Peter Damm** (Philips 422509, with Rondo K 371).

There is never any doubt of the consummate virtuosity of **Dale Clevenger,** principal of the Chicago Symphony. He recorded his traversal of the concertos in Hungary with the superb Franz Liszt Chamber Orchestra, which he also directs. Also on this budget-priced disc is a delightful rarity, the *Sinfonia pastorella* for alphorn and string orchestra, in which the soloist is Michel Garcin-Marrou, with Malgoire and La Grande Ecurie et la Chambre du Roy (Sony 62639). Clevenger can be heard under Abbado in a brilliant account of 3, the most popular of the concertos, in the previously mentioned collection of Mozart and Haydn concertos (DG 415104). One more fine version comes from **Milos Stevove,** principal horn of the Slovak Philharmonic, with Capella Istropolitana directed by Josef Kopelman (Naxos 550118). His typically Eastern European sound adds a welcome bit of individual color.

Oboe. This lovely concerto, the progenitor of the D Major Flute Concerto, was composed in 1777 for oboist Giuseppe Ferlendis. It's a fresh and lyrical work, Mozart at his most charming, joyful and full of life and filled with soaring melodies. Several prominent oboists have recorded the work and the following versions should give pleasure.

Starting with the Philips "Complete Mozart Edition," we have an excellent contribution from the distinguished Swiss oboist **Heinz Holliger** led by Sillito. Another comes from **Randall Wolfgang** and the Orpheus Chamber Orchestra (DG 431665, 3CD). I don't normally favor Karajan's Mozart, finding it, in the main, too homogenized and string oriented, but there is one instance where I'm so enamored of the soloist that I'm willing to overlook any deficiencies in the orchestral backdrop. **Lothar Koch**'s lustrous tone is the highlight of many Karajan/Berlin recordings, and I enjoy his sound enough to recommend his version, while recognizing that its discmates have received more striking and idiomatic readings elsewhere (♦EMI 64355, with bassoon and clarinet concertos). For those who enjoy the conductor's high-calorie Mozart, all the wind concertos (minus the horn concertos) have appeared in a 3CD box (in EMI's now-defunct "Herbert von Karajan Edition").

Another choice version comes from **Douglas Boyd** as the imaginative soloist with the Chamber Orchestra of Europe (of which he is principal oboist) conducted by Paavo Berglund (ASV 808, with Strauss's Oboe Concerto). Böhm's Vienna Philharmonic reading requires a full-price duplication for those who favor his version of the G major Flute Concerto as it has been sensibly coupled it with the Oboe Concerto with soloist **Gerhard Turetschek** (DG 413737). Another treasurable recording features former Chicago Symphony principal **Ray Still** with Abbado (DG 415104, with Bassoon Concerto and Horn Concerto 3 and Haydn's Trumpet Concerto). The whole disc features present or former first chair players of the Chicago Symphony and is currently only available overseas.

The pungent tone of the period oboe is beautifully captured in **Michel Piguet**'s potent reading in Hogwood's complete set (Decca, see above; also 43392, with Clarinet Concerto).

Other concertante works

Concerto for Flute and Harp. Hoping to further his career and enhance his finances, Mozart spent six months in Paris in 1778. Though nothing spectacular or felicitous happened in those two areas, he was commissioned to write what turned out to be this magnificent piece. The work was ordered by the Comte de Guines for himself (he was an accomplished flutist) and his daughter, who played the harp. The fact that many critics have relegated this work to the category of "lesser Mozart" fails to take note that the piece is filled with glorious melodies and many imaginative orchestral felicities.

I return to the two splendid discs that offer the flute concertos, since they also offer magnificent versions of this music. **Galway,** with **Marisa Robles** and Marriner, gives us a reading that glows with warmth and affection. No one who selects this superb recording will be disappointed (♦RCA 68256). Also high on the list is **Pahud,** who is joined by **Marie-Pierre Langlemet** and their colleagues of the Berlin Philharmonic led by Claudio Abbado (EMI 56365). Pahud's playing is, as always, beyond criticism, and if this reading, in the end, lacks the resplendent warmth of Galway and others, it's still a remarkable achievement.

The legendary team of **Rampal** and **Laskine** have also given us a marvelous version (Erato 45832, with Flute Concerto 1 and *Andante*). These longtime colleagues must have performed the piece on countless occasions, and their collaboration with Paillard and his chamber orchestra represents a labor of love from two unique artists who are sorely missed. It's no surprise that flutist **Susan Palma** and harpist **Nancy Allen** turned in a brilliant account with the Orpheus Chamber Orchestra (DG 431665, 3CD). Tempos are brisk, especially in the finale, but never breathless, in one of the most refreshing and invigorating performances in the catalog.

Though I have reservations about Karajan's Mozart, a notable exception is his luxuriant reading of this concerto with flutist **Andreas Blau,** harpist **Fritz Helmis,** and the Berlin Philharmonic (EMI 69187, with Galway's Flute Concerto 1). The beauty of this performance merits a positive nod. Böhm's account is graced by the legendary Spanish harpist, **Nicanor Zabaleta,** with flutist **Wolfgang Schulz** (DG 413552, with Clarinet Concerto). **Julius Baker**'s 1962 taping with **Hubert Jelinek** under Janigro is of abiding interest (Vanguard 42), and anyone on a strict budget can safely turn to the sprightly reading from **Jiří Válek** and **Hans Müllerová,** directed by Edlinger (Naxos 550159, with Sinfonia Concertante K 297b).

Two historical versions deserve attention considering the legendary status of their participants. The redoubtable duo of **Marcel Moyse** and **Lily Laskine** (Eugène Bigot conducting) was recorded in the '30s (Pearl 9118), and Laskine appears again in a delightful reading with flutist **René Le Roy** and Beecham (Dutton 7037). And to close, there is a magical period-instrument reading from flutist **Lisa Beznosiuk** and harpist **Frances Kelly** with Hogwood (Decca 460027).

Sinfonia Concertante in E-flat for winds. This concerto for oboe, clarinet, bassoon, horn, and strings was composed during Mozart's 1778 stay in Paris and was intended for performance at the prestigious Concerts Spirituel. There is some confusion about this work since the original has disappeared, and scholars have assumed that what has come down to us is not by Mozart. If the work is indeed by an imposter, he certainly was a great imitator; so many uniquely Mozartean stylistic signatures dot the landscape of this music that whoever wrote it was a master of Mozartean inflection. In any event, it's a marvelous piece and worth including in this survey.

Of the many fine versions, pride of place must go to the vivid account by clarinetist **Sabine Meyer** who, with principals from the Staatskapelle Dresden under Hans Vonk's inspired direction, offers a reading of great distinction (♦EMI 66949, with Meyer's superb reading on bassett clarinet of the Clarinet Concerto). Another brilliant account comes from the **Orpheus Chamber Orchestra,** which always manages to bring a fresh vision to whatever music they play (DG 431665, 3CD; also available on 429764 with *Sinfonia Concertante* for violin and viola).

Karajan recorded this music twice. His classic account with the principal winds of the Philharmonia has received an excellent transfer (Testament 1091, with substantial couplings). He drew soloists from the Berlin Philharmonic for his later stereo version, and while it's beautifully played, it doesn't quite have the poignancy of the earlier one (EMI 68101, with Kremer's Brahms Concerto). Another version from the Berlin Philharmonic led by **Giulini** is predictably fine (EMI 48064, with Symphony 39). **Alexander Schneider**'s excellent reading is also worthy (ASV 803, with Bach and Vivaldi concertos). Finally, we have a snappy account from **Edlinger** and Capella Istropolitana (Naxos 550159, with Flute and Harp Concerto).

CHAMBER MUSIC

Mozart began writing chamber music as a prodigy of six and continued nearly to the end of his short life. Included are 23 string quartets; two piano quartets and one for oboe; six string quintets and others for piano and winds and for clarinet and horn with strings; six piano trios; and some violin and piano sonatas. There is also a trio for piano, clarinet, and viola, and two duets for violin and viola. Most are of the highest quality, but many, written early in his life, belong in the realm of curiosity and need detain only the completist. The current catalog offers enough notable performances to satisfy the appetite of even the most voracious Mozartean.

Duos

Mozart's string duos offer music of great beauty, depth, and technical finish. I only recently became acquainted with them from a 1979 recording by **Toshiya Eto** and **Michael Tree** (Nonesuch, unfortunately NA). But the exquisite 1968 readings by **Grumiaux** and **Arrigo Pelliccia** still grace the catalog in a budget-priced "two-fer" devoted to the complete string duos and trios (♦Philips 454023; also in the "Complete Mozart Edition," Vol. 13, at a higher price). The remastered sound is excellent. A fine alternative comes from **Perlman** and **Zukerman** (RCA 60735, with music of Leclair). Periodists can turn to the members of **L'Archibudelli,** who offer a most unusual coupling: an anonymous small-ensemble transcription of the great E-flat *Sinfonia Concertante* for violin and viola, offered under the title "Grande Sestetto Concertante" (Sony 46631). An interesting historical issue features **Szymon Goldberg** with two renowned violists: **Frederick Riddle** in the G major, recorded in 1940, and **Paul Hindemith** in the B-flat, recorded in 1934 (Music & Arts 4665, 3CD, with Mozart and Beethoven).

Quartets

Flute. The reports of Mozart's aversion for the flute are belied by the fact that his four quartets for the instrument are accomplished and beautiful. They have flourished on records and there are several distinguished versions. One of the finest young virtuosos is **Emmanuel Pahud,** former principal flute of the Berlin Philharmonic, and he's joined by three colleagues in a marvelous presentation of these works (♦EMI 56829). Another fine version is heard from **Konrad Huenteler** with colleagues; here is some of the most sensitive and tastefully realized Mozart playing I've encountered (♦MD+G 3110966).

When Columbia recorded the works in the late '60s and again in the '70s, they put together the greatest star power available: **Rampal,** Stern, Alexander Schneider, and Leonard Rose in the earlier edition (Odyssey 42601) and Rampal, Stern, Accardo, and Rostropovich in the second (Sony 42320). Both present excellent accounts. A superb rendering comes from **Paula Robison** and members of the Tokyo String Quartet (♦Vanguard 4001), and the Tokyo players are joined by **James Galway** in still another excellent performance (RCA 60442). Not to be overlooked are versions by **Carol Wincenc** and members of the Emerson Quartet (DG 431770) and by members of the **Nash Ensemble** (Virgin 61448, 2CD).

Oboe. The Oboe Quartet is one of the jewels of the repertory; it's filled with luscious melody and infectious high spirits. I've admired the playing of **Lothar Koch** since his days as principal of the Berlin Philharmonic, and he joins members of the Brandis String Quartet in an invigorating reading (♦Nimbus 5487, with Clarinet and Horn Quintets). One of his successors in Berlin, **Hansjörg Schellenberger,** with the Berlin Philharmonic Quartet, has turned his attention to this music with expectedly fine results (Denon 8003, with the same couplings). Then there are superb versions from two renowned English ensembles: the **Academy of St. Martin in the Fields Chamber Ensemble** (Philips 423833, again with Clarinet and Horn Quintets) and the **Nash Ensemble** (Virgin 61448, 2CD). Finally, there is a fine edition from **Jozsef Kiss** and the Kodály Quartet (Naxos 550437, with Horn Quintet).

Piano. Mozart's two piano quartets are among his finest chamber works and have a notable recorded history, beginning in 1934 with the still nonpareil version by **Schnabel** and members of the Pro Arte Quartet (♦EMI 63870, 2CD, with String Quintets 2, 3, and 5 and Quartet 16, or Pearl 0104, with Sonatas 13 and 16 and Schubert). This powerfully conceived, insightful reading is a phonographic classic, an object lesson in how this music should be played.

Three other historical recordings can't be overlooked. **Curzon** and members of the Amadeus Quartet in 1952 presented the epitome of Mozartean elegance and grace without sacrificing the elemental power that fills both works (♦Decca 425960, with Brain and the Griller Quartet in the Horn Quintet). In addition to his considerable conductorial skills, **George Szell** was a remarkable pianist and a redoubtable Mozartean. In 1946 he joined members of the still formidable Budapest String Quartet for excellent performances (♦Sony 47685, with fine 1967 readings of two violin sonatas with Raphael Druian). Another warm and insightful version comes from a group of sensitive Mozarteans, including **András Schiff** on fortepiano (Decca 444115). Finally, there is the outstanding reading from **Benjamin Britten** as pianist with Sillito, Abronowitz, and Heath (BBC 8005, with Concerto 27 with Richter and "Exsultate Jubilate" with Ameling).

The best contemporary versions come from **Brendel,** whose pianism is growing ever more refined, and it shows in his glowing accounts with two different ensembles. In one he joined an illustrious ad hoc group of instrumentalists (♦Philips 446001, with an equally superb reading of Schubert's "Trout" Quintet). The second brings a brilliant and radiant reading with members of the Alban Berg Quartet (♦EMI 56962, with a superb account of the quintet version of Concerto 12). Another ensemble filled with star power brought considerable commitment and insight from **Ax** with longtime collaborators Stern, Laredo, and Ma (Sony 66841). Whenever this group of superb instrumentalists gets together, it's a cause for celebration, and this offering is no exception.

A really outstanding recording comes from the **Beaux Arts Trio** joined by violist Bruno Giuranna (♦Philips 410391; also in the "Complete Mozart Edition," Vol. 14). This ensemble always offers first-rate performances and these stimulating readings are among the best available. Also very much worth considering are the elegant accounts from **Rubinstein** and members of the Guarneri Quartet (RCA "Rubinstein Edition" 63075). I'm also fond of **Peter Serkin**'s stimulating readings with Alexander Schneider, Michael Tree, and David Soyer (Vanguard 8007). Collectors on a budget should be quite satisfied with the fine versions by the **Menuhin Festival Piano Quartet** (Naxos 554274). **Kagan** offered a powerful 1982 account of Piano Quartet 1 with Richter, Bashmet, and Gutman. The disc is rounded out with a strong 1985 reading of String Quartet 15 with Victor Tretyakov (Live Classics 193).

Strings. For the collector who must have all twenty-three works, there are two marvelous choices. Pride of place goes to the "Complete Mozart Edition," in which the perceptive, refined renderings by the **Quartetto Italiano** serve this music to near perfection (♦Philips 422512, 8CD). Just about at the same level is the magnificent traversal by the **Talich Quartet,** a superb cycle by one of the world's finest ensembles (♦Calliope 9241/8, 8CD). Those seeking a fine budget version need look no further than the **Eder Quartet,** which offers not only the 23 quartets but also the *Adagio & Fugue in C minor* and the three *Divertimentos K 136–8* (Naxos, 8CD, available separately).

Perhaps the finest version of the final ten quartets (14–23) was taped in the '70s by the **Alban Berg Quartet** (♦Teldec 72480, 4CD). These readings are filled with glowing warmth and affection and, as is usually the case with this marvelous ensemble, are impeccably played. The group returned to this music in 1991, and here too we find beautiful execution, but the exquisite naturalness of the earlier edition is missing; we're led to notice the players more and the music less (EMI 63858, 5CD, also available separately). There's no doubt of the excellence of the playing, but the depth of expression so evident in the Teldec set is somewhat lacking here. The **Franz Schubert Quartet** of Vienna may not be a household name, but their Mozart playing is definitely world class. These are perceptive accounts that would grace any collection, and the set is a steal at budget price (♦Nimbus 1778, 5CD).

Next on any collector's list should be the six so-called "Haydn" quartets, certainly among the most important works in the genre. The set by the **Mosaïques Ensemble** stands head and shoulders above the rest (♦Astrée 8596, 3CD, available singly). This group plays on period instruments and that may be off-putting to some, but in this instance the playing is tonally full and opulent, avoiding the nasality and pinched sound of many such groups. The important thing here is that they are as perceptively Mozartean as we could wish; their readings are sensitive, stylish, elegant, and revelatory. The recorded sound is superb, leaving absolutely no barrier between performers and listener. Among modern versions of these works, this set is my first choice. For those who favor a more astringent style of "authentic" performance, there are the stylish and perceptive readings by the **Salomon Quartet** (Hyperion 44001/3,

3CD). Many critics greatly admire this ensemble, but I've always found their approach too dry.

The **Talich Quartet** offers exquisite readings (Calliope 241/3, 3CD, with Haydn's Quartet Op.74:3). The many admirers of the **Juilliard Quartet** will find much to enjoy in their traversal of the cycle (Sony 45826, 3CD, budget-priced, with Haydn). A couple of historic versions should be mentioned. The superb **Smetana String Quartet** gave excellent mid-'50s readings of 15, 16, and 18, while 19 is coupled with Haydn and Schubert (Testament 1117/1118). The legendary **Hollywood String Quartet** recorded a lovely 1957 version of 17 (Testament 1085, with Haydn and Hummel).

For the "Prussian" Quartets, we have a magnificent set of these remarkable works by the **Leipzig String Quartet** (♦MG+D 3070936, 2CD). These superlative readings are thoroughly idiomatic and equal to the finest in the catalog. And we turn again to the **Mosaïques** and a disc devoted to two quartets from this cycle, 21 and 23. These are very much at the level of their "Haydn" set and make an important addition to the Mozart discography (Astrée 8659).

Quintets

Clarinet. Few works reveal Mozart's genius more glowingly than the sublime Clarinet Quintet of 1789. This radiant work is as close to musical perfection as you can find anywhere, and only the very finest readings will suffice. Again we must turn to the Quatuor Mosaïques, who, with **Wolfgang Meyer** playing a basset clarinet (with its extended lower range), offer a performance of rare opulence, beauty, and refinement (♦Astrée 8736, with an equally persuasive account of the Clarinet Trio). Another sterling account comes from **David Shifrin** with the Emerson Quartet (DG 459641, with an equally fine reading of Brahms's Clarinet Quintet). A radiant performance of the work was recorded in 1966 by the renowned English clarinetist **Gervase de Peyer** with the Amadeus Quartet (BBC 4061, with a blazing account of Franck's Piano Quintet with Curzon plus the sextet from Strauss's *Capriccio*).

The late, great **Harold Wright** left two superb versions of the work. A 1968 reading was superseded by a digital version from the '90s with the Boston Symphony Chamber Players that presents an even more poignant vision (♦Philips 442149, with a rich-toned, autumnal account of Brahms's Clarinet Quintet). Also outstanding are the exquisite readings by **Thea King** and the Gabrieli Quartet (Hyperion 66199, with the Clarinet Concerto) and by **Bohuslav Zaradnik** and the Talich Quartet (Calliope 9231/3, with the complete string quintets). Don't forget **Stoltzman** with the Tokyo Quartet (RCA 60723, with the Clarinet Concert) and the readings by the **Academy of St. Martin in the Fields Chamber Ensemble** (Philips 422833, with Horn and Oboe Quintets), and the excellent account by a former Berlin Philharmonic principal, **Karl Leister,** who, joined by the Brandis String Quartet, is most persuasive in this music (Nimbus 5487, with Horn Quintet and Oboe Quartet).

Horn. Mozart composed his Horn Quintet in 1782 and gave it the unusual scoring of horn, violin, two violas, and cello. It isn't one of his greatest contributions to chamber music, though it has its moments and an inspired performance can quicken the pulse. This is why I lead off with two historical accounts. The great hornist **Dennis Brain** was an artist who could turn whatever he played into pure gold. All his recordings—including his solo turns as principal horn in the Philharmonia Orchestra—are little short of magic. He left us two recordings of the Mozart quintet, the finer of which, with the English String Quartet in 1957, vividly brings this work to life, making for a most rewarding listening experience (♦BBC 4048, with the finest account of the Brahms Horn Trio in my experience). In Brain's other recording he's joined by the Griller Quartet in another magical reading (♦Decca 425960, with the Amadeus's quartets).

There are several fine modern versions of the work. The **Nash Ensemble** offers an excellent super-budget account (Virgin 614448, 2CD, with Flute and Oboe Quartets and more), and there is an excellent reading from the **Academy of St. Martin in the Fields Chamber Ensemble** (Philips 422833, with Clarinet Quintet and Oboe Quartet). The same collection of music is offered in a superb disc by **Gerd Seifert,** former principal horn of the Berlin Philharmonic, with members of the Brandis Quartet (Nimbus 5487). An estimable version comes from **Jozsef Kiss** and the Kodály Quartet (Naxos 550437, with Oboe Quartet), and the period performance by **Andrew Clark** with Ensemble Galant is an extraordinary bargain (EMI 72822, with Mozart horn duos, Beethoven, and Brahms). Periodists also have the option of a notable reading from **L'Archibudelli** (Sony 46702, with the horn duos and other Mozart).

Piano and winds. This quintet was composed in that most fertile year, 1784, and is among Mozart's greatest works. It has been blessed with a multitude of superb recordings, and again I must list one in the "historical" category as my top choice: **Gieseking** and a magnificent ensemble from the Philharmonia Orchestra, including Dennis Brain, recorded in 1953. Here we have great musical talents combining to produce a reading of timeless quality. Its reissue is beautifully produced and filled out with an equally compelling Beethoven Piano Quintet and the Karajan E-flat *Sinfonia Concertante* (♦Testament 1091).

Among modern recordings there are none finer than the 1993 performance by Barenboim and members of his Chicago Symphony and the visiting Berlin Philharmonic (♦Erato 96359). This ad hoc ensemble plays as if they had performed together for years, and the results are most rewarding. The disc is slated for withdrawal, so if you find a copy, grab it. A dazzling recording comes from the perceptive **Stephen Hough** with the Berlin Philharmonic Wind Quintet. Finer Mozart playing is hard to find, and the disc is rounded out with wind arrangements of shorter pieces, also beguilingly played (♦BIS 1132).

Perahia's marvelous recording with the English Chamber Orchestra Wind Ensemble has stood the test of time (♦Sony 42099, with an equally superb account of Beethoven's Piano Quintet). Also high on the list of recommended versions is **Kuerti** in one of his few recorded excursions into chamber music (CBC 1137). He's joined by a superb ensemble of Canadian wind players and the playing is simply ravishing. An equally persuasive account of the Beethoven piano quintet and the rarely heard quintet by Beethoven's almost exact contemporary Anton Witt round out this fine offering.

Dennis Brain's legendary recording of the Horn Concertos has been made even better by adding to it a wonderful reading of the piano quintet by **Colin Horsley** and the Dennis Brain Wind Ensemble (EMI 66950). I haven't heard **Previn**'s performance with the Vienna Wind Soloists, but given the talent involved, the performances should be quite good (Telarc 80114). Finally, periodists have a treat in store with **Robert Levin**'s vital account with the Academy of Ancient Music Chamber Ensemble (♦Decca 444115). Few offer such stimulating music-making on or off record, and this riveting reading is an invigorating tonic.

Periodists also have a choice of other excellent versions, though two of the best, both by fortepianists, have vanished from the catalog: the superb accounts by **Malcolm Bilson** and friends (Archiv 423404) and **Andreas Staier** and others, performing as the ensemble "Les Adieux"

(Deutsche Harmonia Mundi 77221). Both offer exquisite renderings of the piano quartets, and if you come across them don't hesitate. The English group **Sonnerie,** whose members are some of the finest periodists on the scene, offers vital readings and includes the bonus of a contemporaneous transcription of the piano quintet, replacing the winds with four strings; interesting, but no substitute for the original (ASV 212).

Strings. After the string quartets, the six string quintets are the most important sequence of works. They can't be thought of as a unified group, since they represent the composer from almost the very beginning to just about the end of his creative life.

I have been enthralled by the cycle recorded between 1967 and 1975 by the **Amadeus Quartet** with guest violist Cecil Aronowitz from my first acquaintance with the original LP release (♦DG 431149, 3CD). These performances have always sounded so right to me that although there have been several other excellent versions over the years, it has remained my favorite. In addition to the standard version of 5 (which includes alterations not made by Mozart that soften the original chromatic melodic line), this set includes the music as originally written.

My next recommendation is currently available as part of the "Complete Mozart Edition," with the sterling **Grumiaux Trio** augmented by violinist Arpad Gerecz and violist Max Lesueur (♦Philips 422511, 3CD). Chamber music playing on this level is rarely encountered either on record or in the concert hall and this edition belongs in the pantheon of great Mozart recordings. This ensemble opts for the authentic version of the finale of 5. The third great performance is the superb cycle by the **Talich Quartet** and violist Karel Rehak (♦Calliope 9231/3, 3CD). This group offers great perspicacity and conviction and their account would grace any collection. The correct finale of 5 is offered, and so is a considerable bonus in a ravishing performance of the Clarinet Quintet.

The **Guarneri Quartet,** with guest violists Ida Kavafian, Kim Kashkashian, and Steven Tenenbom, recorded a marvelous cycle in the '80s. These are warm, lovingly played renditions, with the rich timbre of one of the great ensembles—a balm to ear and soul. Unfortunately these deeply felt readings are currently NA, but I'll list the numbers should you wish to find them through used record services (RCA 7770, 1+3; 7771, 4+5; 7772, 2+6). The correct finale of 5 is played.

My first exposure to these works was in performances by the long-defunct **Griller Quartet** with Primrose, who recorded five of the six in 1959, first reissued by Vanguard in its cheap "Everyman" series, perfect for the young neophyte to learn unfamiliar repertoire. Recent reacquaintance with its remastering has proved most rewarding (Vanguard 8024, 3+5; 8025, 2, 4, 6). These are marvelous performances and still rewarding to hear. Also in the historic category, the early '50s set featuring the **Budapest Quartet** has unfortunately disappeared. The great **Pro Arte Quartet** with violist Alfred Hobday can be heard in a stunning compilation of their '30s performances of 2, 3, and 5 (EMI 63870; 2CD, with Piano Quartet 1 and String Quartet 16). Not only do we have three of the greatest of the quintets but also their collaboration with Schnabel in the G minor Piano Quartet; the playing may not be absolutely perfect by today's standards but the spirit invested in these readings is unique.

None of the periodists appears to have recorded a complete cycle, but the renderings of 2, 3, 5, and 6 by **Hausmusik** is very much worth seeking out (Virgin 45169, 2CD). These are stylish and committed readings that have true Mozartean spirit. The **Salomon Quartet,** with violist Simon Whistler, has also recorded this music, but as with their quartets, I find their approach too dry to provide much pleasure (Hyperion 2005,

2CD). Much more to the point is **L'Archibudelli**'s spirited yet deeply considered readings of 2 and 3 (Sony 66259). The **Eder Quartet** and violist János Fehérvári offer a fine set, a decent choice for the collector on a budget (Naxos 553102, 1+2; 553104, 3+4; 553105, 5+6).

A collection of the quintets performed by the distinguished American period ensemble **Aston Magna** holds excellent performances of the Clarinet and Horn Quintets and String Quintet 3. My only complaints concern the sound, which is a bit too dry, and the omission of the important first-movement exposition repeat in the String Quintet; otherwise these sensitive, stylish performances are a real bargain (Harmonia Mundi 907059). And finally, Zukerman joined the **Tokyo String Quartet** in a superb performance of 2+3 (RCA 60940).

Sonatas for violin and piano. Mozart composed some 35 sonatas for violin and piano. Those we think of as *the* sonatas for the two instruments—17 to 35—were written between 1778 and 1788 and represent the composer (especially the last four) during his most accomplished period of creativity. The earlier sonatas—1 to 16—were written when he was between 6 and 13, at the time when he was a traveling child prodigy, and were in the style, fashionable at the time, where the keyboard—usually a harpsichord—dominated and the violin provided little more than a very simple obbligato, rarely a dialogue between two equal partners. The later ones are something else entirely; inspired by a set of sonatas by the now forgotten Joseph Schuster, which Mozart discovered in his travels, in these works the violin assumed a more important role. Mozart, as always, improved upon the models and produced some of his finest music, true dialogues between the instrumental partners.

Only the completist is likely to have much interest in the early sonatas (in which Mozart's father, Leopold, is likely to have had a hand). "The Complete Mozart Edition" offers all the extant works for violin and piano, including two sets of variations and several shorter pieces (Philips 422515, 7CD). For those wishing just the early sonatas, the **Gerard Poulet/Blandine Verlet** team is offered in a budget-priced set (Philips 438803, 2CD). Also available are arrangements for flute and piano of 6–10 with **Rampal** and his longtime accompanist, harpsichordist **Robert Veyron-Lacroix** (Sony 32970).

The so-called "great" sonatas have been recorded by several master violinists. Heading the list are two outstanding renderings of the final 16. The first is the 1974 edition by the great **Szymon Goldberg,** accompanied by the young **Radu Lupu** (♦Decca 448526, 4CD). Age and wisdom complement youth in these remarkable readings, which are also beautifully recorded. The well-established partnership of friends and colleagues **Perlman** and **Barenboim** also offers a remarkable recording. The two have been performing together for decades and their fresh approach brings rewarding results, in excellent sound (♦DG 463749, 4CD).

Another renowned partnership is that of **Szeryng** and **Haebler.** Their excellent accounts have appeared in two 2CD budget-priced sets (Philips 462185, 17–25; 462303, 17–35). **Zukerman**'s set with **Marc Neikrug,** mixing a substantial number of the early and late works, seems to have disappeared from the catalog (RCA, 5CD). In 1955 **Szigeti** recorded 15 of the 16 (omitting the last) with both **Horszowski** and **Szell** offering distinguished support at the keyboard. The violinist's tone may demonstrate the acidity that plagued his playing in his later years, but the musical values outweigh any technical shortcomings (Vanguard 8036/39, 4CD). **Richter** was often not at his best in Mozart, but when he joined **Oleg Kagan** in 11 of the sonatas taped in 1982, he offered some of the finest Mozart playing imaginable; the music-making has to be heard to be believed, and these performances belong in every Mozart lover's collection (♦Live Classics 102, 24, 26, 27; 122, 21–23; 123, 28, 30–32).

Stern and **Bronfman** recorded three volumes devoted to this music; both artists are in fine form and the discs are worthy additions to the catalog (Sony 53972, 17, 32, 34; 61962, 21, 25, 35; 64309, 19, 20, 22, 28). A super-budget release offers the excellent duo of **Nishizaki** and **Jandó** (Naxos 553111, 17–20; 553110, 21–23, 25; 553112, 26–28; 553590, 32–33). A well-filled disc presents the glorious partnership of **Augustin Dumay** and **Pires** in 18, 21, 26, and 27 (DG 431771), and **Yuoko Shiokawa** and her husband, **András Schiff,** provide winning period performances of 21, 27, and 32, with a bonus in the form of the six Variations K 360 (Decca 436547). **Grumiaux** and **Haskil** were one of the great musical partnerships of the last century and they recorded 18, 21, 24, 26, and 34 (reissued in a mid-priced set with the complete Beethoven violin sonatas as part of the "Clara Haskil: The Legacy" series, ♦Philips 442625, 4CD). The set originally appeared stateside as an import and may be difficult to find, but these superb performances are definitely worth a search. The original mono recordings still sound fine. Grumiaux went on to record the later sonatas with renowned Mozartean Walter Klien (in the "Complete Mozart Edition," Philips 422515, 7CD, with complete early sonatas).

My first exposure to the recording of the great Sonata 32 by **Heifetz** was an RCA LP that coupled this masterpiece with 26, both recorded in 1936. These performances have been reissued as part of the massive "Heifetz Collection" (RCA 61740, 2CD, with works by Mozart and others). As the "Edition" has been mostly deleted, this may be hard to find. Oistrakh's superb 1956 rendition with **Vladimir Yampolsky** is, however, readily available in a fine transfer (Testament 1115, with Beethoven Sonatas 3 and 9). Also worth searching out is **Mutter**'s vital realization of 21 with **Lambert Orkis** as part of "The Berlin Recital" (DG 445828, with music of Brahms, Debussy, and Franck).

TRIOS
Piano. Mozart's six piano trios, scored for piano, violin, and cello, cover a span from 1776 to 1788. The first of the set still finds the piano in command, with its colleagues more often than not in subservient roles; in the last five the composer is at his most masterful, providing a true conversation between violin, cello, and piano. The **Beaux Arts Trio** has dominated this repertoire for the past 35 years. Pianist Menahem Pressler and cellist Bernard Greenhouse participated in both of the group's two complete traversals. In the first, recorded in the '60s, the ensemble was joined by founding violinist Daniel Guilet. These remain outstanding accounts, marred for some by the violinist's rather thin tone; for me, this gives the enterprise an almost period flavor, and I've always been fond of the set for its profound musical values (♦Philips 446154, 2CD, with Clarinet Trio). It has been superseded by a second cycle recorded in 1987, which introduced violinist Isidore Cohen, formerly of the Juilliard String Quartet, whose richer tone and more powerful presence added a higher profile to an already outstanding approach to this music. These remain at the top of the list, although the inclusion of more repeats and the addition of Trio K 422 (in a completion by Stadler) require an extra disc (♦Philips 422079, 3CD; also in Vol. 14 of the "Complete Mozart Edition").

Other versions worth your attention include the brilliant **Trio Fontenay** (Teldec 12336, 2CD) and the more romantically inclined and deeply felt readings by the **Borodin Trio** (Chandos 8356/7, 2CD). The **Vienna Schubert Trio** offers a fine budget-priced edition (EMI 73350, 2CD). Periodists will find much to enjoy in classically pure renditions by **The Mozartean Players** (Harmonia Mundi 907033/34, 2CD). Also excellent are 3 and 6 in versions by the **London Fortepiano Trio** (Hyperion 662125)

A couple of single versions deserve mention, both with **Rudolf Serkin.** The first, recorded in 1968 with Jaime Laredo and Madeline Foley, finds the pianist in a relaxed reading of Trio 2 that is mellow, spirited, and affectionate (Sony 46255, with Piano Concertos 10 and 12). The other, from 1944, is played with Adolf and Hermann Busch of the Busch Quartet (Arbiter 112, 2CD, with Beethoven chamber music). Also, superb readings of 1–3 are provided by the brilliant team of **Maria João Pires,** Augustin Dumay, and Jian Wang (DG 449208).

The remarkable 1786 Trio for Piano, Viola, and Clarinet is the first such work for this combination of instruments, nicknamed the "Kegelstatt" because it was allegedly completed in a bowling alley. The featured solo instrument is the clarinet, and the viola completes the trio. It's one of the composer's finest achievements and very difficult to bring off. My longtime favorite is the 1969 recording by clarinetist **Jack Brymer** with Kovacevich and Patrick Ireland (♦Philips 446154, 2CD, with complete piano trios). These players get it right in a reading that is sheer delight. Another rendering that approaches perfection is a period performance by **Wolfgang Meyer** with colleagues from the Quatuor Mosaïques (♦Astrée 8736). This is superb music-making, and the disc is made even more desirable by the fine rendering of the Clarinet Quintet that fills it out.

Other excellent versions are by **The Nash Ensemble** (Virgin 61448, 2CD, with Horn Quintet and Flute Quartet); **Janet Hilton,** with Nobuko Imai and Roger Vignoles (Chandos 8776, with works by Bruch and Schumann); **Michel Portal,** with Gérard Caussé and Jean-Philippe Collard (EMI 55389, with Clarinet Quintet); **James Campbell,** with Rostislav Dubinsky and Luba Edlina of the Borodin Trio (Chandos 8655, with Haydn and Beethoven trios); the all-star team of **Stoltzman,** Ma (substituting cello for viola), and Ax (Sony 57499, with Beethoven and Brahms clarinet trios); and finally, the super-budget version with the Hungarian team of **Bela Kovacs,** György Konrad, and Jandó (Naxos 550439; with other Mozart works).

Strings. The delightful String Trio in B-flat—scored for two violins and cello—was started in 1777 but left incomplete. What we have—an Adagio and a Menuetto (some nine minutes of music)—is well worth hearing and is well served in the set by members of the **Academy of St. Martin in the Fields** (Philips 423833). The remaining works for string trio are scored in the familiar configuration of violin, viola, and cello. The Six Preludes and Fugues K 404a are arrangements of works of JS and WF Bach, to which Mozart supplied four of his own Adagios. These settings show his contrapuntal mastery and musical sensitivity, and they are superbly rendered by the **Grumiaux Trio** in the Philips set.

Mozart's supreme masterpiece in this idiom is the large-scaled, six-movement Divertimento in E-flat, the only string trio he ever completed. Once again, the **Grumiaux Trio** offers a superb reading (♦Philips, as above). Also worth seeking out is the fine account by **Kremer, Kashkashian,** and **Ma** (Sony 39561). The 1941 performance by **Heifetz, Primrose,** and **Feuermann** is in a class by itself (RCA 61740, 2CD; Biddulph 074). **L'Archibudelli** provides an excellent period version (Sony 46487).

PIANO MUSIC
Mozart left a healthy body of solo keyboard music. The piano, or its various ancestors, was his main instrument of expression, and he wrote

many works either for his own use or for his students. Between 1775 and 1789 he wrote some 18 sonatas and 15 sets of variation. Add to this a number of miscellaneous shorter pieces and pieces for piano duo and his output is astonishing for one who died just shy of his 37th birthday.

Though few would dare to doubt Mozart's genius, there is some argument about the quality of much of this music. Some pianists regard it as falling below his usual high standard. There are those who feel that Haydn generally achieved a higher level in his piano music, but there a number of Mozart sonatas that are unquestioned masterpieces, and so are several of the variations and fantasias and some of the shorter Rondos. At any rate, anyone who loves Mozart will want to experience as much as possible of these works.

Complete sets. For those seeking a fairly comprehensive collection, **Gieseking**'s still controversial set recorded in the 1950s is an intriguing choice (EMI 63688, 8CD). This pianist's approach to Mozart is not universally admired, most critics finding it too dry and miniaturized. He eschews the sustaining pedal, provides a rather narrow dynamic range, and ignores all exposition repeats; yet within his chosen parameters, he has much to say. His command and tonal opulence are things of wonder; this is pianism at its most subtle and intimate. In addition to the EMI set, there are a couple of other Gieseking recordings that are worth acquiring. The "Great Pianists of the 20th Century" series offers an excellent 1936 version of Sonata 14 (Philips 456790, with great recordings of Beethoven, Debussy and Ravel), and there is a performance of 18 taped in 1956 that is more dynamic than the contemporaneous studio recording (Pearl 9236, with Concertos 21+27).

Barenboim has recorded most of the solo music, and there can be no question of miniaturization in his bold and characterful approach. The complete sonatas and variations are included in a budget-priced collection (EMI 438789, 8CD) The set could have been made even more valuable had the producers included Barenboim's collection of miscellaneous works, which has always placed high on my list of Mozart recordings.

A valuable set of the complete piano music offers **Ingrid Haebler** playing the sonatas and the later sets of variations, with the earlier sets played by the Dutch harpsichordist **Ton Koopman** and the four-hand works divided between Haebler with **Ludwig Hoffmann** and the famous team of **Badura-Skoda** and **Demus** (Philips 456132, 10CD). Though no one collection can reveal all of the secrets of this music, the high standard attained here should please all who turn to this anthology as an alternative to the "Complete Mozart Edition," which offers the same performances of the variations but includes Uchida's superb renditions of several pieces, including Rondo K 511 and *Eine kleine Gigue* K 574 (Philips 452518, 5CD).

Sonatas

Complete sets. The sonatas have been lucky on record and there are superb sets that can be recommended without hesitation.

Before devoting himself virtually full time to the podium, **Christoph Eschenbach** was one of the most individual young pianists on the musical scene. In the late '60s and early '70s he made a sizable number of recordings, among them a complete set of the sonatas (DG 463137, 5CD, budget-priced). The readings are cool, clear, crisp, and stylish, but not in the least cold or miniaturized. He pairs the K 475/457 Fantasia and Sonata, as do most others, though Brendel (and Schnabel before him), are adamantly opposed to this practice. In the recent book, "Alfred Brendel on Music," he says that the fact that the two were published in one volume proves nothing. "Each of these works is an autonomous master-

piece; together they cancel each other out." On the other hand, another legendary Mozartean, Lili Kraus, was reportedly furious when CBS Records split the Fantasia from the Sonata for a single-disc reissue of some of her recordings. "Those butchers!," she is said to have exclaimed.

Schiff's remarkable collection is also most recommendable (Decca 443717, budget-priced). Schiff has always been one of the most imaginative of Mozarteans (his complete set of the concertos remains one of the jewels of the discography), and this cycle of the sonatas, recorded in 1980, only enhances his reputation; these sensitive, searching readings offer continual pleasure. Another addition to the pantheon of truly remarkable cycles is from **Uchida;** for some, she represents the ultimate in this music (Philips 422517, 5CD, with Fantasia K 475). Hers are intimate but by no means small-scaled renderings. Like Schiff, she is a searching interpreter, seeking to bring out all the deep secrets hiding in the deceptively simple writing. Those who feel that most of Mozart's solo piano music is considerably less than his best should listen to any of these three excellently conceived cycles and return enlightened. Uchida remains one of the most revealing of guides.

Also of abiding excellence is the equally stimulating cycle from **Pires** (DG 431760, 6CD, also issued singly, with the two great Fantasias). She is at once powerful, probing, and sensitive, and it's only because of the set's domestic deletion that I haven't included it with those above. Also worth noting is **Jando**'s fine set; he's a reliable and often imaginative guide through this music (Naxos 550514, 5CD, also individually). I have never liked Marta Deyanova's cycle, finding her approach a bit over-emphatic (Nimbus 1775, 6CD). The blurry, over-reverberant sound favored by this label doesn't help matters.

In the historical category, at budget price and well recorded, is one of the finest surveys of this music ever made: **Walter Klien**'s complete cycle, which is both stylish and perceptive (Vox 5026; 5046, with Rondo K 494 and Fantasia; each 2CD). As a supplement Klien also recorded several shorter pieces, including four sets of variations (Vox 5517, with four of the Concertos). Also treasurable is **Horszowski**'s glowing cycle, recorded in 1960 (Arbiter 101, 1-8, 2CD; 104, 9-18, 3CD). He was one of the great pianists and musicians of the last century, a most sensitive Mozartean, and these readings should not be missed.

No survey of Mozart's piano music would be complete without mention of the great Hungarian pianist **Lili Kraus.** Though her command diminished somewhat toward the end of her long career, her indomitable spirit remained undiminished. She made many distinguished recordings during the postwar period, including a fine sonata cycle in the '60s (Sony 47222, 4CD), but it's her 1954 traversal recorded for the Haydn Society that deserves first place in her extensive Mozart discography (Music & Arts 1001, 5CD, with other important shorter works). This is full-blooded, dramatic playing, and like Schnabel, her teacher, she realizes that this composer is fully human, that neither passion nor drive are alien to him, and that his music is a document, albeit a subtle one, of the full range of human behavior.

Though there are many triumphs among the complete cycles, there are also some disappointments. In her prime there were few more distinguished Mozarteans than **de Larrocha.** However, her series of concertos and sonatas remains basically dull and uninvolving (RCA). To hear this beloved artist at her best in Mozart turn to her set in the "Great Pianists of the 20th Century" series, where elegant and perceptive readings of 8, 10, 11, and 18 are joined by superb Bach, Handel, Haydn, and Scarlatti, all from excellent Decca originals (Philips 456886, 2CD). More than disappointing—in fact, downright disgusting—is **Glenn Gould**'s traversal (Sony 456712/13, two 2CD sets offering seventeen of the eighteen sonatas and a couple of shorter pieces). He disdained Mozart and claims to set out here to show how bad this music really is. This is distorted, poorly conceived music-making, and unless you like to indulge in self-torture, avoid it.

Arrau's set demonstrates his stunning sonority and generally probing pianism, but the gravity of his approach is at times difficult to bear in music that so often cries out for lightness of spirit. His interpretations work best in the darker works, like the minor key 8 and 14, and he can sometimes lighten his approach. But in general this is all much too serious. His admirers will want the set and will be rewarded, but the music is, for the most part, better served elsewhere (Philips 432306, 7CD).

Individual recordings. A number of single discs offer various sonatas in outstanding readings. Arrau, whose complete cycle is disappointing, supplied some fine Mozart in his 1956 Salzburg recital, giving powerful readings of Fantasia K 475 and Sonatas 12, 14 and 18 (Orfeo 459971). These are full-blooded accounts featuring the great pianist in his prime. In a disc containing some of his first recordings in the United States in 1941, the performances of 5 and 18 are worth hearing, but the recordings have been too heavily filtered for my taste (Naxos 110603).

Brendel has the proper respect for the solo works, though he has yet to give us a complete cycle. One of his finest recordings holds sterling 1966 performances of the tragic Sonata 8, coupled with other works; finer Mozart playing than this would be hard to find (Vanguard 129). A group of his solo performances recorded between 1971 and 1991 offers generally excellent readings of 8, 11, 13, and 14 (Philips 454244, with shorter works, 2CD). If I prefer the earlier version of 8, this remains a distinguished collection and a bargain, too. His recent recordings are nothing short of superb—for instance, marvelous readings of 10, 11, and 17 (Philips 462903) and 12–14 (Philips 468645).

Horowitz is not a pianist you would normally associate with Mozart, but he's an unusually sympathetic and sensitive interpreter of the composer. A fine sampling of his way with the sonatas includes 3, 10, and 13, culled from the recitals the legendary pianist gave late in his career (DG 445517). Gilels was also an excellent Mozartean, as can be heard in a collection that includes 8 and Fantasia K 397; lovers of great pianism should invest in this mid-priced set (BMG/RCA 7552, 3CD, with works by others). There are few greater Mozarteans currently on the scene than Perahia. He has given us a stunning set of the concertos, and though he doesn't believe all the solo music represents the composer at his best, there are several works he loves and respects. That shines through in glowing performances of 8, 11 and the hybrid 15—a great recording (Sony 48233). Christian Zacharias is not as well known in this country as he should be; he's one of the most imaginative and sensitive pianists around. His recording of some of the shorter pieces makes one long for more; it's superb Mozart playing (MD+G 3400961).

Among the great pianists, Richter was a most uneven Mozartean. He said he preferred Haydn and his readings of that composer were imbued with a profundity and sparkling wit that sometimes eluded him in Mozart. The "Richter Edition," all but gone from the domestic catalog but still available in Europe, offered some fine Mozart playing in 2, 5, and 13–15 (Philips 438480, 2CD). Then there is a collection recorded between 1956 and 1985 that gives classically poised readings of 2, 4, and 8; despite the occasionally rough sound, it's worth having (Praga 254025). Two more modern Russian giants have given us some notable Mozart. Pletnev offers an imposing version of 17 (BMG/Melodiya 25181) and a Gavrilov recital presents stimulating playing of 11, 12, and more (EMI).

Though Rubinstein left recordings of several Mozart concertos, his discography holds only one of the composer's solo works, an elegant reading of Rondo K 511 (RCA 63075, Rubinstein Collection, Vol. 7, with the two piano quartets).

No Mozart collection would be complete without Edwin Fischer's contributions to the catalog. He was a truly great Mozartean and we can be thankful for the reissue of some of his finest readings in excellent transfers. APR 5524 holds 11 and Fantasia K 396 (with concertos 17 and 24), while 5525 includes 10 with Fantasia K 475 (with concerto 25 and Haydn). EMI has done a poor job perpetuating Schnabel's great Mozart solo recordings, and again the independents have come forth. Pearl offers two fine reissues: 0006 is a 2CD set that includes 8 in a collection mainly devoted to the concertos; 0104 gives us 13 and 16. APR 5526 offers 12 and a Rondo, with works by others.

Annie Fischer left comparatively little Mozart so her Montreal performance of 12 is especially valuable (Palexa 0514, with Schubert and Schumann). Novaes is another great pianist who left us little Mozart, a deficiency somewhat remedied by readings of 5, 11, and 16 (Vox 5512, 2CD, with concertos 9+20 and Beethoven). Solomon's sublime reading of 13 is offered in the "Great Pianists of the 20th Century" series (Philips 456973, 2CD, with works by others). His exquisite accounts of 11 and 18 await reissue.

The hybrid Sonata 15 K 533/494 was composed over a period of two years, 1786–88. The Finale, a rondo composed in 1786, began as an exercise for one of his students, and Mozart later decided to turn the piece into another marvelous three-movement sonata. Apart from the versions offered in the complete editions of the sonatas, there are several other notable recordings. Gilels offered the work in his 1972 Salzburg recital (Orfeo 523991, along with works by Brahms, Debussy, and Stravinsky), in a superb reading. Richter also us gives us a marvelous reading in an all-Mozart disc (Praga 254026). Finally, that nonpareil Mozartean, Perahia, offers a suberb account in a truly remarkable all-Mozart recital (Sony 48233).

I close with an offering from Fazil Say, a young Turkish pianist who gives us stimulating readings of 10, 11, and 13, plus the charming *Variations on "Ah! vous dirai-je, Maman"* (Teldec 21970).

Variations and shorter works

Variations. The 15 sets of variations for solo piano are spread throughout Mozart's early career. Some are mere fluff, but others have more substance. The most well-known is the set of 12 based on "Ah, vous dirai-je, Maman," better known to us as "Twinkle, Twinkle, Little Star." The nine *Variations on a Minuet of Duport* remain one of his more substantial works, while six *Variations on Salieri's "Je suis Lindor"* are also quite diverting, as are eight *Variations on "Ein Weib ist das herrlischte Ding."*

The best course for the listener is to get a complete set and listen through them— slowly, please, to avoid overload. Gieseking's comprehensive set of the piano music (EMI 63688, 8CD) offers them all at mid price. For those who prefer a bolder approach, Barenboim's set is also part of a budget-priced release (EMI 438789, 8CD, with the sonatas). Periodists should note that fortepianist Ronald Brautigan's excellent accounts have been separated out of his complete edition of the solo piano music (BIS 1266/7, 4CD).

There are notable versions of some of the individual variations. Clara Haskil has given us stylish accounts of "Ah, vous dirai-je, Maman" and the "Duport" variations, restored to circulation in the "Great Pianists of the 20th Century" series (Philips 456829, 2CD). The same series offers Kempff's delightful reading of the delightful *Variations on "Unser dum-*

mer Pöbel" (Philips 456888, 2CD), and yet another volume offers **Uchida's** perceptive rendition of this set along with other Mozart gems (Philips 456982, 2CD). And these variations are well served by **Schiff**, as is "Ah! vous dirai-je, Maman," in a distinguished collection (Decca 421369).

Brendel has recorded the "Duport" variations twice, and if I prefer his especially fresh earlier version (Vanguard 129) to the later one (Philips 454244, 2CD), the latter is also an imposing reading. Two further performances of "Ah! vous dirai-je, Maman" are worth attention: the brilliant recording by **Fazil Say** (Teldec 21970) and the sparkling account by the often eccentric French genius **Samson François** in a musical potpourri in the "Great Pianists" series (Philips 456778. 2CD).

Fantasias. Fantasias K 396, 475, and 397 are among Mozart's finest solo piano works. Two earlier *Fantasias*, K 396 and 397, were left as fragments; the first was completed by the composer's friend Maximilian Stadler and published in 1803, and for the second, an anonymous ending was tacked on for publication, but it remains a magnificent example of Mozart's art, even in the imperfect condition in which it has been handed down to us.

A different kind of controversy surrounds the great *Fantasia* K 475. It was composed in 1785, the same year as Sonata K 457, with which it was originally published and is often paired in performances and recordings. **Brendel** strongly believes the two works should be kept separate; in *Brendel on Music*, he says that "each of these works is an autonomous masterpiece; together they cancel each other out." Philips has placed them together in its reissue of several of his recordings (456727, 2CD), though in the "Great Pianists" series it stands alone in accordance with the pianist's wishes (456727, 2CD). In any event, this 1991 reading is masterful and a valuable addition to the Mozart discography.

Other excellent versions come from **Barenboim** (EM1 63683, 8CD, with the sonatas and variations), **Edwin Fischer** (APR 5525, with Concerto 25, Sonata 10, and Haydn's D-major concerto), **Eschenbach** (DG 463137, 5CD, with sonatas), **Schiff** (Decca 433717, 5CD, with sonatas), **Uchida** (Philips 422517, 5CD, with sonatas), **Pires** (DG 431760, 6CD, with sonatas), **Egorov** (Globe 6015, with *Fantasias* by others), **Arrau** (in the "Great Pianists" series, Philips 456712, 2CD), **Klien** (Vox 5046, 2CD, with Sonatas 12–18), and **Richter** (Live Classics 422, with Sonata 14 and Beethoven Sonatas 30 and 31).

The later *Fantasias* are also well-served on disc. Excellent readings of K 396 come from **Zacharias**, who also includes a brilliant account of K 475 in his collection (MD+G 3400961), **Barenboim** (INI 47384, a now-deleted all-Mozart collection of abiding excellence; grab it if you find it), **Edwin Fischer** (APR 5524, with Concertos 17 and 24 and Sonata 11), and **Brendel** (Vanguard 129). The D-minor *Fantasia* is offered in excellent readings by Zacharias and Barenboim (see above), **Horszowski** (Nonesuch 7910, with Beethoven and Debussy; an alternative reading is also available in Arbiter 104, 3CD, with sonatas), **Pires** (DG 431760, with sonatas), and **Uchida** (Philips 412123, with sonatas 11 and 12).

Two rather unusual but distinctive recordings come from **Ernst Levy** (Marston 52021, 2CD, with Beethoven and Haydn sonatas) and from that most eccentric of Mozarteans, **Glenn Gould,** whose readings I usually despise but for which I occasionally make exceptions (Sony 45613, 2CD, with Sonatas 11–17).

Rondos and Adagio. Rondo K 511 remains one of Mozart's most eloquent and deeply felt statements for the keyboard, and its beauty has led some of the greatest pianists to plumb its depths and reveal its most intimate secrets. From the probing account by **Schnabel** (APR 5525 or Pearl 6), we move on to marvelous readings by **Rudolf Serkin** (Sony

47207, 3CD), **Rubinstein,** in one of his finest Mozart recordings (RCA "Rubinstein Edition" 63075), **Brendel** (Vanguard 129 is my favorite of his three extant recordings; the others are Philips 454244, 2CD, and Philips 462903), **Horszowski** (Arbiter 104, 3CD), **Schiff** (Decca 421369), **Uchida** (Philips 412122), **Ashkenazy** (Decca 436383, 2CD), **Barenboim** (EMI 47384), **Zacharias** (MD+G 3400961), **Konstantin Lifschitz** (Denon 78908), and **Arrau** (Philips 432306).

Rondo K 485 isn't quite as imposing as K 511, but it's certainly worth inclusion in this survey. It hasn't been as often recorded, but some remarkable artists have turned their attention to it. **Horowitz** (DG 45517, all Mozart, or differently coupled, DG 427772), **de Larrocha** (Philips "Great Pianists" 456886, 2CD), **Pires** (Denon 8072), **Barenboim** (EMI 47384), and **Zacharias** (MD+G 3400961) should satisfy the most discriminating listeners.

Adagio K 540 can be placed, along with Rondo K 511, among Mozart's greatest solo keyboard works, and it has been recorded by some great pianists. **Arrau's** version is the most expansive on record, lasting some 20 minutes; it's an extreme reading in the pianist's later, rather slow-moving style and won't appeal to all tastes (Philips 432306, 2CD). Even as an admirer of the great Chilean, I find it somewhat of an ordeal to get through. Much more to the point are **Horowitz** (DG 45517 or 456886), **Brendel** (Philips 454244, 2CD), **Barenboim** (EMI 47382), **Zacharias** (MD+G 3400961), **Lifschitz** (Palexa 507, 2CD), **Uchida** (Philips "Great Pianists" 456982, 2CD), and **Schiff** (Decca 421369).

Piano four-hands music

During Mozart's precocious childhood, he and his gifted older sister Nannerl gave four-hand recitals at home in Salzburg and in such major continental capitals as London and Paris. His first work in the genre, the so-called "Duet" Sonata K 19d, dates from his tour between 1763 and 1767 when he was seven years old. More important are four later masterpieces and the grand Sonata for Two Pianos K 448, written in 1781 and the only such work he completed. There are also other less ambitious pieces.

These works have been blessed with a number of excellent recordings. **Christoph Eschenbach** and **Justus Frantz** have given us a fine collection of the complete sonatas, adding the marvelous G Major Variations and a couple of transcriptions of works originally composed for the so-called mechanical organ (DG 435042, 2CD). **Ingrid Haebler** and **Ludwig Hoffmann** offer fine readings of the four-hand music, filled out by a completion of a fragment dating from 1782–88 by Badura-Skoda and a *Larghetto and Allegro* in E-flat played by **Badura-Skoda** and **Demus** (Philips 454026, 2CD). The same performances are also available in the Philips survey of the complete output for keyboard (456132, 10CD). Also worth mentioning is a set of the sonatas by **Ranki** and **Kocsis** (Hungaroton 11794/95, 2CD).

There are several single discs that demand attention. The two-piano sonata has been blessed with several outstanding readings. My favorite is the blazing yet sensitive performance by **Argerich** and **Rabinovitch** (Teldec 991378, with equally compelling readings of the G Major *Andante and Five Variations* and the four-hand sonatas in C and D). These artists prove that fiery commitment and Mozartean sensibility can go hand in hand. Another wonderful version of the two-piano masterpiece is the by now classic account from **Perahia** and **Lupu** (Sony 39511, with an equally exquisite reading of the great Schubert *Fantasy in F Minor*). Here are two fabulous artist lavishing their considerable talents on this glorious masterpiece. The same artists also offer marvelous readings of *Andante and Variations* and *Fantasia in F Minor*, originally composed for mechanical organ but here in a transcription for two pianos by Busoni, to fill out a disc devoted to the mulitiple-piano concertos (Sony 44915).

The third of my chosen few combined the imposing talents of **Curzon** and **Britten** (BBC 4037, with the Two-Piano Concerto with Curzon and Barenboim and Concerto 27 with Curzon). This too, is a great performance that belongs in every comprehensive Mozart collection, one of the all-time great Mozart records. A fourth superb account comes from **Schiff** and **Peter Serkin** (ECM 465062, 2CD, with the C Minor Fugue and music by Reger and Busoni in equally compelling readings).

In another reading from **Britten,** his partner is **Richter,** a pairing that needs no further comment on its quality (Music & Arts 709; with music by Britten, Debussy, and Schumann). For collectors on a budget, **Jando** and **Zsuzsa Kollar** come to the rescue with a disc that holds the two-piano sonata as well as four-hand sonatas K 119d, in D and C, and the C Major Variations (Naxos 535158). The performances are very good but lack the commitment of the finest versions. Finally, a hard-to-get import should be acquired if found: the superb duo of **Imogen Cooper** and **Anne Queffelec** is heard in magnificent readings of the Sonatas in F and C as well two works transcribed from pieces for mechanical organ (Ottavio 129242).   LINKOWSKI

CHORAL MUSIC
Mozart's years in Salzburg under the sometimes hostile patronage of the autocratic Archbishop-Prince Hieronymous von Colloredo were prolific; he wrote about 50 works for use in the Church, a feat he would never repeat. Though it's true that Mozart could compose on demand—his life is full of such instances—it remains hard to believe, as some scholars have suggested, that his neglect of this genre during the Vienna years is evidence of a lack of concern for matters religious. These early and mid-stream works are anything but trivial, showing a depth of feeling and clarity of style fully equal to anything else he produced at the time. Their neglect in the recording world isn't easy to explain, yet neglected they are, and the recordings that do make it into the catalog don't remain for long.

Complete choral music. The Philips "Complete Mozart Edition" dedicated Volumes 19 and 20 to all of Mozart's known choral works. There are some good performances in Volume 19, but the big three—Coronation Mass, C minor Mass, and *Requiem*—are not all first choices. The rest of the volume has performances by Kegel that wouldn't be recommendable as single issues, so a blanket approval is impossible for all but the most determined completeniks. Volume 20 is a different matter, replete with excellent performances (♦Philips 22520). **Harnoncourt** has attempted many, but not all, of these pieces, and his boxed set on Teldec, when available, is preferable to the Philips edition, despite the period instrument playing. But there are enough fine recordings available singly to satisfy most collectors. The music is certainly worth the investment.

Requiem. By far the greatest Mozartian mystery of all is how much of the *Requiem* is really Mozart's. The most common version, that of Franz Xaver Süssmayr, has been under fire for years, yet current thinking dispels some of his burden by denying that he had the ability to complete the work as he did. It's now widely assumed that he was working at least from sketches that Mozart left behind or outlined for him, and this story makes sense, for he's remembered only for his work on the *Requiem,* not for his own compositions. The discovery some years ago of an "Amen" fugue at the end of the "Lacrimosa" in Mozart's handwriting gives credence to the idea that there very well might have been more sketches than originally thought.

Others have tried to clean him up, notably (and most successfully) Franz Beyer; Robert Levin made an admirable attempt (more below), and C.R.F. Maunder made a radical reconstruction that makes its own persuasive argument. H.C. Robbins Landon tried to cull the resources of the original three who attempted completion, and Duncan Druce made perhaps the boldest (and most arrogant) attempt by practically recomposing the "questionable" portions. Most miss the mark, for it's obvious that Süssmayr knew what he was doing and was privy to inside information that the centuries have shrouded from sight. No matter—this is one of the most profound, humane, and ultimately ennobling works ever put to paper by any composer anywhere. It has been well served by recordings, and with the exception of nine or ten, all could serve as only choices. Of course, true lovers of this piece will have to have as many as possible.

First, a few to absolutely avoid. The international press never seemed to tire of heaping accolades on **Hickox** and the Northern Sinfonia (Virgin). It was initially offered as a budget recording, and to these ears that's exactly where it belongs, but it has been hailed as the best of *Requiems.* Dull, lifeless, emotionally adrift, underpowered, and lackluster are only a few of the descriptions that apply here. It's the great swindle among *Requiems.*

Robert Levin came up with a new version that completes some Mozart sketches while leaving the Süssmayr format essentially intact. The great shame is that its premier recording is a loser on almost all counts. This is a period-instrument chamber *Requiem* that sounds like a quartet of strings with a choir of trombones behind them. The percussion is way out of proportion to the rest of the forces, and the Boston Baroque, while not a bad band, aren't as polished as some of their European counterparts. The choir gives its all, but without an overall grandness of conception or nobility of line. **Martin Pearlman,** who must claim responsibility, takes some of the numbers at ridiculously breakneck speeds. This is a requiem, not a party, and Levin's version deserves better.

The Robbins-Landon edition used by **Weil** is in the same vein, a reckless attempt that moves at the speed of light and turns any semblance of a requiem into a pathetic parody (Sony). The normally excellent Tafelmusik bravely follows the conductor's will in this brutish butchering of Mozart's masterpiece.

Abbado uses small forces—excellently balanced—but the fast tempos and excessively reverberant sound spoil the effect (DG). The combined use of the Maunder and Levin versions is an interesting idea, but Levin's contribution sounds very un-Mozartian in many places. **Marriner**'s first recording (London) goes nowhere—bland, boring, too genteel—while the usually thoughtful **Robert Shaw,** though he has a road map, proceeds down the wrong highway time and time again by failing to convey structurally the wonderment his fabulous chorus is trying so hard to put across. **Savall, Harnoncourt,** and **Koopman** should also be avoided; all three miss the point.

Norrington provides us with a case study in one-upmanship. His Schütz Choir is fantastic, offering some spectacular singing. They, and the excellent soloists led by Argenta, have to be hyper-alert to negotiate the carnival-like tempos he takes. This rivals only the Pearlman for clownish interpretation. The version by Duncan Druce he uses isn't without interest. Druce accepts most of what Süssmayr started, but then takes off on flights of fancy that don't seem at all idiomatic. Reorchestrations abound, sounding no better than the originals, and subtle changes to the harmonies and even counterpoint are very off-putting after so long a historical time. This may be the best recorded period instrument version, with the best singing and soloists, and maybe the best orchestra, but I would have been laughing through the whole thing were I sitting in the orchestra, not a good sign in a requiem.

By far the worst modern-instrument recording is by **Giulini,** a man who always either exalts greatly or offends deeply (more of the former in his long and brilliant career). Sony should never have released it—it's flaccid, lacking sinew and muscularity, with atrophied tempos (not the slowest on record, but certainly the weakest) and blurred, fuzzy melding of the wonderful baroque counterpoint that illuminates this work. Giulini's bad phrasing extends even to the soloists, who are willful and distorted, placing emphasis on things that don't make sense. How different this is from his 1979 recording! That was one of the most dramatic ever, fairly bursting with a boldness and energy that only Böhm was to capture completely. Its budget incarnation sounds better than ever, and with the Philharmonia's extraordinary playing and a wonderful, all-star cast (Donath, Ludwig, Tear, Lloyd), this is hard to beat at the price (♦Seraphim 73702).

William Fred Scott and the Atlanta Opera Orchestra and Chorus play and sing very well, as do the soloists, but the cathedral sound is washy, with a fatal lack of clarity and detail (ACA). Scott's tempos are medium to fast, and his orchestra is reduced to a paltry sound even though they use modern instruments. He, like other misguided revisionists, uses a mishmash of corrections to the score that do nothing to improve Süssmayr. **Somary,** with some splendid choristers and soloists, is hampered by period strings that sound as if they went without food for several days—whiny, anemic, and far short of the task at hand (Vox). His 1975 recording is far too wayward and unseemly to be seriously considered. Though the sound is very detailed, this production smacks of interpretative amateurism (Vanguard).

I'm a little hesitant about placing **Barenboim**'s second recording on the "avoid" list, for it does have many virtues (EMI), Battle's angelic singing among them, but since his first recording is one of the greats, there's little reason to consider it (EMI). In his better recording (1971), he gives us a reading that is a model of clarity and proportion, as near a perfect understanding of how this work should go as we have on records. None of the tempos are in the least controversial, and spirit and reverence come across in every bar. The sound can be slightly muddy and constricted in spots, but his all-star cast (Armstrong, Baker, Gedda, Fischer-Dieskau) helps us forget any sonic deficiencies. The English Chamber Orchestra was on a roll in the early '70s, and produces a large, brilliantly warm sound that's robust and highly caffeinated. The John Alldis Choir, also on a roll during this period, pulsates with feeling and love. This recording has been subject to EMI's catalog prestidigitation, but persistent seekers won't be disappointed (♦EMI 62892).

Solti is a conductor of whom I'm always wary, for his fiercer moments are so strangulating that the essence of a piece often gets destroyed. His reading at the celebration of the 200th anniversary of Mozart's death in St. Stephen's Cathedral in Vienna has much to recommend it (London). H.C. Robbins Landon tried to come up with a new idea by forging a compendium of "authentic" Mozart revisionists—Süssmayr, Eybler, and Freystädtler. The result is a mass of changes just subtle enough to be irritating. Add to this some sloppy playing from the Vienna Philharmonic and a teaspoon of Solti's hurriedness and there's cause for concern. But the choral work of the Vienna Opera, the overall wonderful sound of the orchestra, and the terrific quartet (Augér, Bartoli, Vinton Cole, Pape) generates enough enthusiasm to make it fully convincing. The sound is that of a big, reverberant cathedral, and Solti's quick tempos begin to make sense in the context of a Roman Mass.

First prize can be awarded to **Marriner,** who gets it right. The lovely, pure singing, responsiveness to musical demands, clearly defined choral textures, and satisfying overall tonal ambiance make this a most desirable release. The Academy of St. Martin in the Fields sounds like it always does, the best chamber orchestra in the world, and the Sylvia McNair-led quartet is solid. Certain readings zero in on the essence of a work, as do certain conductors. This release scores high on both counts (♦Philips 432087).

I'm not one of those who go into ecstasy at every release by **Gardiner,** especially his period orchestra work, though I do admire him. His choir and orchestra are top notch, just as one would expect, and his ardent admirers won't be disappointed. But his *Requiem* seems to me wrongheaded and far too clinical. When this was released, Gardiner pontificated about how true authenticity lies in the Süssmayr version, yet he himself "cleans up" a lot of the writing. His heavy trombone sonority makes Mozart sound like Berlioz. This is a trombone-grounded work, not -dominated.

Welser-Möst leads a no-nonsense, sensibly paced big-band performance using the Beyer edition (as do Shaw and Bernstein). No real surprises, everything is in place, in tune, and in sync. This is very middle of the road, and a good recording with the London Philharmonic Symphony and Chorus performing very well (EMI). But as so often with this conductor, a spiritual element is missing. **Wolfgang Grohs** leads a weighty, bloated performance using a large chamber orchestra and what sounds like a very large—or at least very powerful—choir. But though the choral effects are carefully studied and meticulously managed, the reading never gets off the ground due to its lugubrious, muddied textures (Arte Nova).

Karajan's first *Requiem* (1962) is a large, exceptionally smooth, emotionally nullified reading (DG). There's no punch to the words, with each note extended to the maximum value, giving the whole an elongated, sticky texture. The Berlin Philharmonic is unusually characterless. The blurred, gooey choral textures that only Karajan at his worst could achieve, along with some strange microphone placement (cellos off in the distance) make this a nonstarter.

His second go (1976) is marked by overpowering strings (Berlin Philharmonic) and somewhat muted brass (DG 419867, 429821). The faster tempos and better articulation in the chorus coupled with better solo singing make this a great improvement over the earlier effort. But a certain coolness (problematic with this conductor) pervades the whole. Everything is in place; it's perfectly acceptable, at an acceptable price for a *requiem ordinaire,* easily tolerable and even enjoyable, without any outstanding interpretive nuance—but it doesn't enter into the mystical essence of Mozart's psyche. However, Karajan's third and final recording offers a reading of massive, granitic proportions, displaying much seriousness and gravity (DG 439023). This is a suitable interpretation, and Karajan knows how to illuminate the tragic, funeral elements of the score. The Vienna Philharmonic Orchestra and Choir are wonderful, but the soloists are too intense and operatic.

Look up the definition of "warmth" in a dictionary and you're likely to find a picture of **Bruno Walter.** His 1955 mono recording directing the New York Philharmonic, with OK sound and a marvelous cast (Seefried, Tourel, Simoneau, Warfield), reveals the humanist Mozartian commitment that he brought to everything (Sony 64480). This recording isn't so much about Mozart's feelings toward God, life, death, or anything else traditionally connected with a requiem as it is about Walter's feelings toward Mozart. It's not bombastic, subtle, or particularly profound, but it's a reflection of his view of the humanity of us all, as expressed by perhaps our greatest musical representative. Just listen to the "Agnus Dei" and dare yourself ever to be pessimistic about *anything*. Only sound precludes first-choice status here, and this is a favorite of all of us, desert island (even with the sound) for several.

Yet there's more, for there's a Salzburg performance one year later that rivals its Yankee counterpart in many ways (Orfeo 430961). The sound is much closer, and the reading underscores its devotional spirit and is imbued with great sacredness. This is a *big* reading, fully integrated, fully comprehensive, fully Bruno Walter. The Vienna Philharmonic was on its best post-war behavior, and the stellar cast (della Casa, Ira Malaniuk, Dermota, Siepi) actually out-sings the New York bunch. Walter makes a supremely personal statement in this performance, and Mozart has never known such tender caressing. Nevertheless, the Sony is the one to have if you can budget only one.

Sound isn't a problem in the first recording by **Colin Davis.** I sometimes wonder how he got these players (BBC Symphony) to scale the mountain top the way they did. The 1967 analog sound graciously surrounds his forces with a lush, full ambiance worthy of Vienna. The conductor knows Mozart very well, and the music breathes, pulsates, and flows quite naturally, totally unforced. Davis is always sensitive to the needs of the text, hushed one moment and exultant the next. The John Alldis Choir (yet again) and the cast of soloists led by Donath do everything asked for (♦Philips 438800). Davis's second recording is only a slight letdown, with giant scope and gargantuan feeling, but lacking the spirited sobriety of the Philips, though many will enjoy the beautiful sense of proportion and the rich sound of the Bavarian Radio Symphony (RCA).

Hogwood fires up the Westminster Cathedral Choir (with boys) into a blazing rendition, using Maunder's reconstruction. This version drops the "Sanctus," "Osanna," and "Benedictus" as not possibly written by Mozart, and completes the "Lacrimosa" with an "Amen" based on recent discoveries, while altering the "Agnus Dei" slightly (he accepts this as genuine). I was put off only slightly by this brazenness and was quickly won over by Hogwood's shimmering, committed reading. The soloists, led by Kirkby, are stunningly blended and colorful throughout the work, a real tribute to his interpretive power and the assured playing of the Academy of Ancient Music. Anyone demanding an exceptionally musical period performance need look no further (♦Oiseau-Lyre 411712).

Period instruments are also palatable in **Christie**'s recording (Erato). The soloists sing neatly and with the appropriate amount of gravitas. The fine orchestra lacks weight, wanting the sustaining power to keep the sound in our ears. Christie makes a good interpretive run, injecting some real feeling into the standard version, but the acoustic is too dry with the sound getting sucked out of the room, only adding to the problem of weight. Schreier strolls through the piece with a performance that's clean as a whistle, extremely understated and thoughtful (Philips). The Dresden Staatskapelle is slightly recessed, the Leipzig Radio Chorus dances on angels's wings, and the soloists are somewhat vanilla. The tempos are as well judged as any recording available, and the reflective ambivalence of the pace—not slow, but somehow "right"—allows you to take in the full measure of the music. Yet this version is anything but bland, and we're given a peaceful and quiet requiem, a softer side of Mozart that he probably would have approved.

Richter is anything but peaceful. This man lives every moment of every note. There is no subtlety—everything is portrayed in very large brush strokes that represent a consecration of faith. Richter speaks plainly; his is a fundamentalist reading, with emphasis on basics, with no deviation to the left or right. The whole performance is stamped with the plain-dress Amish-like persona of the conductor, who asks only that we hear and believe. This performance, fine as it is (in somewhat aged sound), demands other supplements.

Two of our favorites are nicely priced but somewhat constricted by old sound. **Kertész** and the Vienna Philharmonic sound as if they were recorded in a rehearsal room, with the choir so much to the fore that they often drown out the orchestra (London). But Kertész and his soloists (Ameling, Horne, Ugo Benelli, Tugomir Franc) were really "on" that day, and the performance is superb. Listen to the exquisitely proportioned "Recordare," or the faith-enhancing "Domine Jesu Christe" for a breeze of breathtaking beauty. This conductor knew how to shape a line, and for those who can get by the tolerably tubby sound, this release at budget price represents a great temptation (London).

Another version that many of us like is **Scherchen** leading the Vienna State Opera Orchestra (MCA). The sound is good, but the miking a little strange, with the trumpets and trombones seeming to be in a separate, closer room. The soloists are uniformly excellent, well rehearsed and unified in concept, with an overall arch that launches many good ideas. Some movements are slightly willful and stretched, but Scherchen strives above all for devotion and contrast. Again, great music at a bargain price.

Košler leads a surprisingly rich, exceptionally well sung version that offers much solid, crisp choral sound. His "Dies Irae" may not be as fervent as some, but his 'Domine, Jesu Christe' is every bit the equal of the best on record. The soloists, an unknown group, are up to every challenge, and the Slovak Philharmonic gives a superb reading, hampered only by slightly thin sound. This is excellent for those on a budget, but you will want to add one of the great ones eventually (Naxos). Despite some very promising moments in **Gönnenwein**'s 1961 version, the sum of the good parts doesn't add up to the equal of so many other wholes. The sound is excellent, wide, and spacious, and the performers can't be faulted. This one's problems have to be laid at the feet of the conductor, who has good initial ideas and then fails to follow them up in a consistent manner (Seraphim).

Böhm gives us the slowest realization on record, but where Giulini clogged and slogged, Böhm soars. Intense, monumental, lyrical, searching, and testamentary, only a superb Mozartian like Böhm could get away with dissecting every measure in search of profundity, and finding it. The Vienna Philharmonic plays like angels, the chorus shouts with exaltation, cowers in fear, prays in hope, and finally accepts with peace. Though the tempos test the elasticity of the work and the quartet bends to include some otherwise unnecessary breath points, it's evident that the conductor knows at every moment where he's going and how he will get there. Just listen to the "Rex Tremendae" to see how he mines riches galore from the slow pace. The sound is a model of clarity, though bathed in DG's early '70s sunshine brightness. This recording should be in every collection that takes the *Requiem* seriously (♦DG 413553).

George Guest, surprisingly, considering his typical English reserve that puts classical grace above temperament, gives us a very bouncy, lively rendition that has trumpets and trombones making quite a wallop. The boys and men of St. John's College, Cambridge, supply rounded choral lines, legato and silky, with no roughness at all. This doesn't always work well with the ample reverberation that tends to obscure them behind the excellent playing of the English Chamber Orchestra. The quartet is well blended, and David Wilson-Johnson in particular is sturdy and affecting with his full, mellifluous bass. Tempos are all middle of the road, and this could be a good choice at mid-price were it not for the muddled sound.

Probably the best alternative is **Bernstein** and the Bavarian Radio Symphony and Chorus with a wonderfully fresh group of soloists (led by Marie McLaughlin and Maria Ewing), who offer a performance of great integrity and spontaneity. Bernstein leaves no stone unturned in this massive, ardently numinous reading. The sound is perfect, and everyone is heard to full effect. Bernstein doesn't hesitate either to linger or to push forward. The opening "Kyrie" is a model of introspection, while he unleashes the fury of hell itself in the "Dies Irae." The "Domine Jesu" is insistent and persistent in its supplication. Every phrase is power-packed, and the choral textures are remarkably rich and innervating. The conductor uses the Beyer version with some modifications, and the organ really gets a chance to shine. Even with the longish timing, this stunning version gets top recommendation. You will probably want more than one *Requiem*, but this one is mandatory (♦DG 427353).

Missae brevis and other shorter works. Harmonia Mundi really puts one out of the park with an issue of eight of Mozart's "Short Masses." The 24-member choir of the Augsburger Domsingknaben (men and boys) has been drilled to perfection. The members of the choir also take the solo roles, probably a common occurrence in Mozart's time, but more probably a money-saver here. Even so, the boys are superb, and the pungent period instruments are on their best behavior. The right amount of atmosphere pervades the recording, and the organ is a welcome guest, often toned down as mere backup on other recordings. These clean-spirited readings are very precise and Mozartian without being overly delicate, which is death in this music. **Reinhard Kammler,** while not skimming over or attempting to cover up an admittedly self-indulgent age for western liturgical music, brings us into the heart of that age and persuasively moves us to consider its inherent beauties (♦Harmonia Mundi 77090, 2CD).

János Reményi's larger choir and sound are striking, though the choral work is slightly less precise than in Kammler's set. The girls' voices are softer on top, and the combined forces fill the aural spectrum very well. (The higher the "K" number, the more Mozart benefits from larger groups.) Two of the short masses, K 65 and 194, are presented here, and for those who may not want a large collection of early masses, this offers a very good single-disc alternative. The works that serve as filler (*Miserere* K 85, *Sancta Maria, Mater Dei* K 273, *Alma Dei creatoris*, *Ave verum corpus* K 618, and *Misericordias Domini* K 222) are all jewels, making up almost half the release. The concert is spirited and effervescent, a credit to all involved (♦Hungaroton 4003).

Missa longa K 262, one of Mozart's most accomplished early masses, is given a splendidly sung, acceptably played, inconsistently ornamented rendering by **Uwe Gronostay** and the RIAS Sinfonietta and Choir of Berlin. The soloists are fine, but the strings are shaky in spots, and the brass and woodwinds are too recessed, though better than in the disc-mates, Masses K 65 and 258. This isn't the cleanest reading the work has had, but it's a generally good performance, and, astoundingly, is the only realization of this magnificent piece available. It serves as a stop-gap, nothing more, and can be given only a qualified recommendation (♦Koch Schwann 313021).

Missa in C minor K 139 ("Waisenhaus"). The Choir of King's College Chapel, Cambridge, conducted by the usually reliable **Cleobury,** disappoints this time with a flaccid, nondramatic opening of Mozart's "Orphanage" mass. The smallish body of strings, undernourished bass line, and too-reverberant acoustic do little to inspire. This was Mozart's first mass, Italian "cantata" style, with sections broken up into smaller mu-

sical components given a variety of treatments, from full-blown choral to intimate operatic, and a certain largeness of scale is prerequisite. This massiveness is what is missing.

The Berlin Radio Symphony under **Marcus Creed** turns in a performance of idiomatic proficiency, warmer and less diffuse than Cleobury. The orchestra—larger and better—is also better felt, and the choir and soloists are simply wonderful. The fillers (*Misericordias Domini* K 222, *Inter natos mulierum* K 72, *Sancta Maria, Mater Dei* K 273, and *Venite populi* K 260) round out a wonderfully stylish recording with real impact, at a great price (♦LaserLight 15883).

Mass in C K 257 ("Credo"). **Harnoncourt,** part of a general recommendation (♦Teldec 72304), has to give way in this instance to **Cleobury** and the King's College Chapel Choir. Though Argo coupled this with the above-mentioned rotten *Waisenhaus-Messe* (curiously recorded at the same time), here the work is tripled with the "Coronation" Mass and *Missa Solemnis* K 337. The reading is unified, with coherent choral sound, rich bass, and a sense of real commitment. This is an upbeat, high-intensity tour of an equally upbeat work (Decca 448228).

Missa solemnis in C K 337. **Cleobury** and King's College forces again offer a gorgeous reading of this mature, highly inventive piece. From the Palestrina-like "Benedictus" to the unique and almost tongue-in-cheek humor of the "Agnus Dei," this is an astonishing work that all serious collectors should own. The King's Choir is on top of the score, the orchestra is in fine form, and Cleobury is sensitive to all of Mozart's harmonic wanderings and twists of tonality (♦Decca 448228; Philips 455032). **Neumann** tries to spice things up with the "authentically" inspired notion of adding an epistle sonata (16) to the work—as he does in his "Coronation" mass—but even this won't make you appreciate this work given his thin strings and uninspired choral work. His offering currently comes coupled with the C minor and "Coronation" Masses in a super-cheap double CD, but that's not enough (Virgin).

Once again, **Harnoncourt** gives us an energy-filled, love-it-or-hate-it wild ride with exaggerated accents, dynamics, and shading. His trombones are straight out of *Flying Dutchman,* with attacks that are incisive, swift, and slashing. The Concentus Musicus Wien isn't always the smoothest of ensembles, but here it acquits itself with dignity. The always fine Arnold Schoenberg Choir negotiates Harnoncourt's laser-like tempos with finesse. The filler pieces (*Litaniae de venerabili altaris sacramento* K 125 and *Regina coeli* K 276) are both beautifully done, with fine soloists led by Bonney. The sound is reverberant, but you'll be too enthralled to notice it (♦Teldec 90494).

Vesperae de Dominica K 321. Mozart's vespers settings are rarely recorded, let alone heard in concert, and this is a shame, for some of his most original liturgical music is to be found in these scores. More solemnity is employed and all stops pulled out in his use of orchestra, organ, brass, timpani, and bassoons. An early '90s release is a good and very cheap way to get introduced to this music, if you can find it (LaserLight 15884). Among those offering both vespers, a heavily Germanic rendition spotlights the mostly reliable Mathis with **Bernhard Klee,** and once again King's College, this time with period instruments and the fine Hilliard Ensemble separating to take on the solo parts (Berlin). The boys don't have their usual luster; part of the problem is the recording, with sound that's muddled and obscure. So the general recommendation must go to **Harnoncourt,** almost by default in this case (♦Teldec 46469). I do hope other companies and artists get on this wagon.

Vesperae solennes de confessore K 339. The choices are a little wider when it comes to Mozart's more popular "Solemn Vespers for a Confessor." No fewer than four period-instrument recordings are available, all coupled somewhat illogically with the "Coronation" Mass: **Pinnock** (Archive), **Pearlman** (Harmonia Mundi), **Koopman** (Erato), and **Hogwood** (◆Oiseau-Lyre 436585) offer robust, quickly-paced accounts that are everything their respective fans have come to expect. But Hogwood has a larger then usual period band that gives us clear, bubbly sound, with playing that is energetic and compelling. His soloists, led by the consistent Kirkby, are backed by the Winchester College Quiristers and Cathedral Choir, full of fire and fury in this fabulous fare. The version by **Cleobury** and King's College paired with the "Dominican" Mass isn't competitive. An album marketed more under Kiri Te Kanawa's name than Mozart's, with **Colin Davis** and the London Symphony (adding *Ave verum corpus* K 618, *Exultate jubilate* K 165, and the D minor *Kyrie* K 341), is not to be missed for those enjoying beautiful singing and modern instruments (◆Philips 12873).

Mass in C ("Coronation") K 317

Mass in C ("Coronation") K 317. Like a despot who forces his way to power yet truly offers his people something positive in return, so has the "Coronation" Mass claimed its spot as first among Mozart's "lesser" choral works, to the unfortunate detriment of many other equally wonderful pieces. But listen to the "Gloria;" has there ever been a more joyous piece of sacred music, one that is more marvelously wedded to the text? In the end, the work's popularity is fully deserved, yet all of the period performances charge like men on horseback driving through a crowded village.

This work has much subtlety, and only **Hogwood** comes close, but even his "Dona nobis pacem" sounds too much like a military march, though his "Credo" is quite exciting (◆London 36585). **Levine** leads the Berlin Philharmonic in a well-groomed, cheery rendition that has wonderful singing and ambiance—a very pleasing performance (◆DG 35853). **Ferencsik** gives us a reverential approach that emphasizes the Rococo spirituality Mozart infused in every bar. The singing and playing are terrific and tempos well-paced, lacking neither excitement nor repose. This might be the first choice if it weren't for the coupling, a rather lackluster run-through of the "Organsolo" Mass K 259, but at this price, who cares? (◆LaserLight 14098)

Marriner had an early go that was only partly successful (London). Its current incarnation, joined to his equally unsuccessful earlier *Requiem*, is still not much of a bargain despite its bargain price. **Cleobury**'s King's Collegers initiate us with an excellent "Kyrie," then deflate us with a rather flaccid "Gloria." The biteless strings and the unaffirming affirmation of the "Credo," along with a too-unemotional soprano in "Dona nobis pacem," drops this one into the delete bin, even though the final bars are well done, with a great, reserved dignity that is most appropriate.

The forcefully dramatic, up front, mass-as-art before mass-as-liturgy approach of **Colin Davis** probes the heights and depths, possibly some that aren't really there. The London Symphony and Chorus are virtuosic, playing and singing above themselves, and Davis's "Credo" will have you dancing in the pews. The soloists, led by Donath, are part of a great pool of Londoners recording in the late '60s and early '70s. This isn't a quiet performance—even the slower parts are just pit stops until Davis revs them up again—but a very exciting and effective one (◆Philips 438800).

Many have been attracted to **Karajan**'s earlier DG recording, made at a very special appearance of the Vienna Philharmonic on the feast of SS. Peter and Paul at the Vatican and remaining a unique document and superb musical event. This performance has been cast in several different guises, including the original that had the entire mass (with the Pope!); the extraordinary singing of Battle and the sturdy Wiener Singverein gave the congregants that day in the mid-'80s, and us forever, something very special (◆DG 429980).

Neumann has his band playing well, but fails to match the riveting excitement that Hogwood musters in the period orchestra competition. The thin strings and general lack of spirit make for a rather ho-hum experience (Virgin). **Pinnock** ignores the all-important pulse that is implicit in every Mozart work. Though Bonney sings splendidly and his chorus is red-blooded and full, lethargy reigns throughout, as if the performing forces were uncertain as to how this mass should really sound (Archiv).

Missa in C minor ("Great"), K 427

Missa in C minor ("Great"), K 427. We may never know why Mozart decided to abandon this wedding present to his new bride, Constanze, but we do know that at least some of the work was played. Perhaps Mozart knew he had embarked upon a project that was far too grand to have any practical performance value; after all, the unfinished work lasts anywhere between 50 minutes and one hour, depending on the conductor. The "Credo," already 15 minutes long and just getting underway, could conceivably hit 35 minutes if ever completed—far beyond what most church ceremonies of the day would have tolerated. But even in torso form, this work is worthy to stand on the same exalted platform that Bach's B minor Mass occupies—a testament of faith, a profoundly moving portrait of Mozart's intensely spiritual side.

Colin Davis jettisons the mysterious for the dramatic, and the brawny sound and disconcertingly brutal effect of some of the choral attacks wear thin as the work progresses (Philips). He has a point of view, and this is a good performance, but the overly reverberant sound and constant pounding of the orchestra move this one off the A list. The same is true for **Rilling**, for different reasons (Hänssler). Point of view is lacking—one cannot simply tackle a work like this without being aware of its challenges. Well sung is not always enough.

Marriner did his homework; his chamber orchestra sounds a bit smaller, the sound is soft and rounded, and the performance—though actually faster than Davis's—is not so manic and outspoken as to spoil the effect. His soloists are a who's who of singers: Te Kanawa, von Otter, Rolfe Johnson, and Lloyd. Te Kanawa has the perfect voice for this soprano-intensive work, pearly and off-white. Not the most spectacular version, but consistently excellent in all categories (◆Philips 438999).

The huge choir of the Vienna Philharmonic summons up an equally huge sound for **Levine,** and the orchestra is great. Levine has traditionally turned out acceptable, enjoyable Mozart, without any special insights to separate it from other good readings. This sensitive and stylish effort is neither stodgy or overworked, yet lacks spirituality. Battle sounds as pure and unmannered as one would expect, but her co-soprano Cuberli is a major disappointment, clearly out of her league in this company. The split violins are nice, but the sound can get confused and cluttered.

Shaw's approach on the other hand, is no-nonsense, with clarity of line and purity of tone, balanced to perfection, every note rounded and given proper length, every phrase neatly turned. The choir is stupendous, and the Atlanta Symphony plays as well as any. Yet some might be put off by this sameness of approach, a refusal to take chances to create an extraordinary event. Nonetheless, a performance this good is a rarity, and enough heights are scaled to give you a sense of dizzying performance butterflies. Very good sound, though I did lose the sopranos several times (◆Telarc 80150).

The sound wrought by **Herreweghe** is whopping, the 46-member choir aided by typically close Harmonia Mundi sonics. But the 14 period violins show some strain trying to sustain the lethargic opening "Kyrie," and though the chorus is as pure as a sine wave, it lacks grandeur in the more rambunctious passages. Soprano Oelze has a wonderful voice, and mezzo Larmore knocks the socks off Mozart's difficult runs. But the massive sound so obviously called for in the score in the passages for double chorus just don't have any steam here, and that is deadly.

Leppard knows this work very well, and everything about his recording feels right—temperament, tempo, phrasing, tone, structure, you name it. The New Philharmonia plays splendidly, the John Alldis Choir performs as we have come to expect, and the two sopranos, Cotrubas and Te Kanawa, play off one another with verve and style (♦Angel 47385). Ever since the early '60s, **Fricsay**'s recording has enjoyed a special status; he really knew this work in a way that places his reading near the top of the "must have" list. It's a huge performance, extraordinary in its depth and power, truly a sonorous wonder, and Maria Stader's singing is maybe the best around (♦DG 463612).

Not so **Gardiner**'s ponderous production (Philips). Right off in the 'Kyrie' all the primary beats are accented too heavily, giving the opening a sense of foreboding, hardly the spirit wanted at the beginning of a mass. McNair, whether ordered to do so or choosing to, sings in a vibrato-less flute tone, adding it at the end of certain notes without any rhyme or reason. Both choir and orchestra sound larger than for Herreweghe, with more bloom in the acoustic. Gardiner does a very good job delineating various strata in the choral parts, and the English Baroque Orchestra doesn't let its fans down. But the sopranos *are* a letdown, and the choir is a little top-heavy. Gardiner's rewritten string parts in "Et incarnatus est" are idiomatic and effective, but the novelty factor in this noisy period recording doesn't wear well.

The smooth, deliberate "Kyrie" in **Karajan**'s recording is intensely spiritual, not the best articulated, but does this man ever know how to build drama and forge surging climaxes! Hendricks sings radiantly, the best on disc. Karajan molds the choral presentation into a great funnel of feverish fervency, despite the fact that the Wiener Singverein is often a chorally challenged group. The Berlin Philharmonic digs into the music with real zest. The sound is soft, engulfing, and inviting, with no harshness or acerbity. Listen to the "Qui tollis" if you need a quick injection of emotional drainage. A great recording (♦DG 400067).

Great follows upon great in the monumental recording by **Bernstein** and the Bavarian Radio Symphony and Chorus. The opening is powerful, the sound crisp and clear, though not as elastic as Karajan. The acoustics in this church recording pick up all the important musical strata with remarkably focused clarity. Bernstein doesn't drag at all and invests considerable energy into every movement. His "Qui tollis" doesn't dwell in mystical contemplation upon the "sins that are taken away from the world," but exalts in the fact that they *are*. His superbly matched quartet—Augér, Von Stade, Frank Lopardo, Cornelius Hauptmann—sings this music as if it were the last thing they were ever to do. It *was* one of the last things Bernstein was to do, and is a recording for the ages (♦DG 431791).

From the opening bars of **Hogwood**'s recording, you perceive a mass of profound seriousness, not bereft of joy, but thoroughly examined and pleasingly presented. With a stellar cast (Augér, Dawson, Ainsley, Thomas) to supplement the excellent Winchester Cathedral Choir and Choristers (boys) and his period instrument Academy of Ancient Music, he gives a reverent, deliciously supple reading, ranking with the best of the nonperiod performances. The singing is just too good to pass up,

especially if you're looking for an "authentic" instrument reading (♦Oiseau-Lyre 425528).

Despite some shining playing by his period orchestra and a new edition by H.C. Robbins-Landon, **Christie** can't compete, with a less than front ranking quartet (with the same Lynne Dawson as second soprano that Hogwood used 10 years earlier). The things he does right are very exciting and his prominent use of brass is especially thrilling. But his choir, though good, isn't as formidable as on other recordings, and this piece is even more choir-dependent that the later *Requiem* (Erato). **Neumann** makes a valid attempt in his period reading, but his small body of strings and chamber choir simply can't make the joyful noise that Mozart undoubtedly envisioned at his wedding. An overall blandness seems to pervade the whole reading, and not even the faultless playing of the Collegium Cartusianum can rectify this soulless rendition (Virgin).

One of the most surprising discs I have come across is **Abbado**'s well paced, nifty version. Though you can tell that the orchestra is scaled down somewhat (as in all of Abbado's Mozart recordings), the Berlin Philharmonic still plays with such strength and gusto that you don't miss the larger group. The cast is second to none (Bonney, Augér, Blochwitz, Holl), and the choir is completely attuned to Helmut Eder's reconstructed edition. This is sensitive, lithe playing of the highest order, and one of this conductor's best recordings (♦Sony 46671). RITTER

OPERAS

By current reckoning, Mozart wrote seven operatic masterpieces. The three collaborations with Da Ponte are framed, chronologically, by the two German Singspiels, and they in turn are set off by the two great *opere serie*. As recently as the '50s, only three Mozart operas were performed with any frequency in the United States: *Figaro*, *Don Giovanni*, and *Magic Flute*. The popularity of the others, *Così fan tutte* especially, has grown, and even *Idomeneo* and *Tito* have won a secure place in the repertory. The number of available recordings is staggering. Four important conductors have recorded all seven masterpieces (Davis, Böhm, Harnoncourt, and Gardiner) and more will surely follow.

The pre-*Idomeneo* operas—*La finta semplice, Bastien und Bastienne, Mitridate, Lucio Silla, La finta giardinera, Il re pastore, Thamos*, and *Zaide*—are well served by their issues in the ♦Philips "Mozart Edition" and don't require much discussion; a blanket recommendation will suffice, with a few additional suggestions.

Harnoncourt (Teldec) offers a stimulating alternative in some cases (*Lucio Silla, La finta giardinera*). **Rousset**'s recording of *Mitridate* (Decca) is livelier than Heger's (Philips) and cast with energetic young performers, but the singers are never superior to their earlier counterparts (Augér, Gruberová, Baltsa, Cotrubas). **Goodwin** doesn't try, as Klee did in the "Mozart Edition," to reconstruct the spoken dialog, but his cast (Dawson, Blochwitz, Bär) is more winning on the whole (♦Harmonia Mundi 907205). A 1960 Stuttgart radio performance of *Zaide* conducted by **Rischner** tantalizingly stars Stader and Wunderlich, and their singing is, indeed, a joy to hear (Myto). The score is oddly abridged, the characters' names changed, the text altered, and the melodramas (the opera's most original feature) omitted. The quality of the singing makes it worth hearing, but be warned that it's far from the real thing.

As for the great operas, I don't apologize for preferring, in many cases, recordings that are 30 or more years old. They have stood the test of time, and they will continue to set standards for years to come. The engineers of the '50s and '60s could capture voices with scarcely less fidelity than their counterparts today, but if the voices are less important to you than the sound of the instruments or the space around the singers, by all means choose the most recent of the recommended recordings.

Idomeneo. In its own way, *Idomeneo* is as revolutionary as *Abduction* or *Figaro.* It's an *opera seria,* but one that finds Mozart stretching formal constraints to their limits. A record of highlights can't begin to do justice to it, but to hear it "complete," you must make choices. The opera exists in no definitive form. Mozart wrote it in 1781 for the Munich carnival and kept revising until the last minute. The role of Idamante was intended for a soprano castrato. For a 1787 Vienna concert performance, several numbers were changed or eliminated, and a new aria was given to Idamante, now a tenor part. Mozart never heard the opera again in his lifetime, and we have no way of knowing which options he preferred. Record producers and conductors have gone their own way, and no two recordings are quite alike—a situation unique to this opera and one that precludes a simple recommendation.

A good starting point, on two mid-priced discs, is **Pritchard**'s Glyndebourne performance of something resembling the 1787 Vienna revision (◆EMI 73848). The conductor is unsubtle and unobtrusive, efficient but not dynamic. Among the cast are two of the greatest Mozart singers of the century, Jurinac and Simoneau, and their contributions have not been bettered. They have seamless, uniquely beautiful voices and address the music in their own inimitable way. Richard Lewis's Idomeneo and Lucille Udovick's Elettra are less exalted but still capable.

There's considerably more music in **Schmidt-Isserstedt**'s Munich-Vienna amalgam, including both of Arbace's arias (EMI). This is the grandest, weightiest reading of all, not so fortunate in its (tenor) Idamante and Ilia as Pritchard's but distinguished by Gedda's dignified Idomeneo and Moser's fiery Elettra. A 1961 Salzburg *Idomeneo* led by **Fricsay** is the most interesting of the nonstudio recordings, worth having for Grümmer's Elettra and Lorengar's Ilia; Haefliger is the tenor Idamante (EMI).

Colin Davis gave us one of the most vivid performances, and it still holds up well (◆Philips 420130). Schmidt-Isserstedt might be carving a monument, but Davis goes all out for flesh-and-blood drama. George Shirley excels as a sturdy, flexible Idomeneo, and the others throw themselves into their roles with considerable fervor. Ryland Davies's Idamante is gallant and fluently sung, and the two ladies are well inside their roles. The version is essentially Munich and allows us to hear, for the first time in proper context, the earlier Ilia-Idamante duet and the florid version of "Fuor del mar." Arbace's arias are cut, and, oddly, Idamante is a tenor. He would remain a tenor in only one more major recording, led by **Böhm** (DG), which takes us back to Vienna, with some odd excisions (not an unusual practice for this conductor). The two leading ladies (Mathis and Varady) are fine, but the performance is otherwise unappealing.

Since 1980 or so, it has been the fashion to cast a mezzo-soprano as Idamante, regardless of which version of the opera was used. Those of us who think a tenor is a more sensible choice (from both a musical and dramatic point of view) are out of luck, but at least the high tessitura happily prevents countertenors from appropriating the role (though it may be only a matter of time before they do). **Harnoncourt** started the trend, but neither his mezzo Idamante nor her colleagues are winning performers (Teldec). **Pritchard** recorded the opera a second time in 1983, ostensibly as a vehicle for Pavarotti's Idomeneo (London). The version is mostly Munich, though the star (who earlier in his career sang Idamante) takes the simple options and Arbace's arias are disastrously assigned to an inflexible baritone. Popp and Gruberová are excellent, but Baltsa's blank Idamante fails to make a persuasive case for singing the role *en travesti.*

The first mezzo to do so was **von Otter,** in the far more consistent and sensible **Gardiner** performance (◆Archiv 431674). This version is almost pure Munich, and Gardiner, leading a band of period instruments, is the strongest conductor since Davis. His Ilia, Elettra, and Idomeneo (McNair, Hillevi Martinpelto, Rolfe Johnson) acquit themselves well without leaving a lasting impression. Arbace is, properly, a tenor, but his arias are feebly sung. **Davis**'s second recording would bring us the best Arbace yet (Uwe Heilmann) and Hendricks and Alexander outpoint their Archiv competition both vocally and dramatically (1991; ◆Philips 422537). Suzanne Mentzer's warm, powerful Idamante almost justifies a mezzo in the part. The Munich version is used, and Araiza has both the presence and the flexibility for "Fuor del mar," though his tone is often abrasive.

Levine's recording is not unlike Pritchard's second, in that it's quite obviously intended as a star vehicle (◆DG 447737). In this case, Domingo takes the title role, inserting the simplified Vienna "Fuor del mar" into the (more or less) Munich framework and singing pensively if heavily. He's not the only star: Terfel takes the small role of Neptune, Hampson is another baritone Arbace (but so fluent as to silence objections), and Bartoli is the most verbally dexterous and also the most feminine of Idamantes. Heidi Grant Murphy is a lovely Ilia, Vaness a thrilling but sometimes overwrought Elettra. The superb Met chorus affords notable pleasure in this performance, grandly led by Levine.

The great diversity of the recordings demands that you have more than one. My short list includes the first Pritchard (for the sake of Jurinac and Simoneau), Gardiner (for integrity and consistency), and Levine (for grandeur); but the 1968 Davis remains the most satisfying of all.

Die Entführung aus dem Serail (The Abduction from the Seraglio). After *Idomeneo,* the editorial problems diminish and we can concentrate instead on matters of vocal excellence. *Entführung* just may be the most difficult of the major Mozart operas to cast. The lead soprano, tenor, and bass need not only style and personality but also exceptional coloratura technique. Less agility is demanded of the secondary soprano and tenor, but they must have unusually wide vocal compasses.

Beecham's 1956 recording has consistently won plaudits from critics, even though he repositions some arias (a sensible but unscholarly liberty) and omits Belmonte's "Ich baue ganz" (◆EMI 63715). His male cast left little to improve upon: Simoneau's elegant Belmonte pours forth round, beautiful tones, yet also has thrust and strength. Frick's black bass moves with surprising alacrity through Osmin's music, while Gerhard Unger is an exemplary Pedrillo. The ladies are not on the same level. Constanze is the game but sorely taxed Lois Marshall, less secure than Stader in Fricsay's recording (DG) or Rothenberger with Krips (◆EMI 63263).

Krips is a stodgier conductor than Beecham or Fricsay, but his cast is strong enough to make his account one of the most essential. Unger and Frick repeat the roles they took under Beecham, and Gedda is a fine Belmonte, less suave than Simoneau but appealingly clean and direct. Popp is a full-tongued Blonde, not just a light, perky soubrette, and Rothenberger's Constanze is astonishing. She has all the requisite charm and agility, but she puts some real bite into her tone and keeps the words clear even in her high register. **Fricsay**'s Stader comes close in terms of vocal ease but also sounds rather mechanical (DG). She's still worth hearing, however, and so are Streich's bubbly Blonde and Haefliger's proud Belmonte.

I regret that we know the Constanzes of Sutherland and Margaret Price only from excerpts; the role thrives on big voices with virtuoso techniques. The closest we've had to a true dramatic soprano Constanze is Studer, who undertook the part for **Bruno Weil** in 1991 (♦Sony 48053). A certain blandness in her manner offsets the vocal opulence, and the performance is further handicapped by a smooth but rather too genial Osmin. Kurt Streit is a Belmonte in the Gedda mold, lean and dapper, and Weil also has a decent Blonde and Pedrillo. This recording has been pretty much ignored by the critics; it's a real sleeper.

The best Belmonte on records is Wunderlich in the first uncut recording, the 1965 **Jochum** (♦DG 459424). Here was a tenor who could sing the role with a manly, melting lyricism. Jochum is as lively and responsive a conductor as Beecham, and he transforms the performance into more than the sum of its parts. Kurt Böhme's Osmin is vivid and funny despite some vocal crudity, and Erika Köth is a sprightly but shallow-toned Constanze. The third DG recording was led by **Böhm** in 1973, and he brought us perhaps the best Osmin of all in Moll. His voice is more limber than Frick's, and his lyric instincts tend more toward bel canto than Wagnerian declamation; it's a gorgeous piece of singing. Augér's Constanze is much like Rothenberger's, less incisive but perhaps more genteel. Schreier is an intelligent and stylish Belmonte, but his desiccated voice affords little pleasure in itself. Böhm is a correct, reserved conductor, faithful to tradition but never revelatory.

The recordings by **Solti** (London), **Wallberg** (Eurodisc), **Harnoncourt** (Teldec), and (Philips) probably don't deserve to be dismissed in a sentence or two, but that's what I'm going to do. None of them offers anything that isn't bettered by the other recordings mentioned. I also regret that a 1965 Salzburg *Entführung* led by **Mehta** fails to live up to the promise of bringing Rothenberger and Wunderlich together (Orfeo). The tenor is, if anything, even more personable and imaginative than he was with Jochum, but on this occasion the soprano sounds too much the fluttery soubrette.

Gardiner (Archiv) and **Hogwood** (Oiseau-Lyre) lead period-instrument performances, and both pedantically ruin the Pasha's entrance by placing a recently unearthed, inconsequential little march just before it. Belmonte's "Wenn der Freude," already awkward in its dramatic placement, is further prolonged by extra coloratura noodling. Gardiner's Constanze (Orgonasova) and Belmonte (Stanford Olsen) are singers of some merit, but his Osmin is unqualified for the part. Hogwood's cast is worse, but both performances strike me as Mozart for marionettes. If you must have "authenticity," **Christie** is a better choice (♦Erato 25940). He leads with plenty of snap and fervor, but he also knows how to let the music breathe. His reading is dramatically strong and cleanly articulated without being punchy or antilegato. The cast, unfortunately, is more lightweight than the music dictates, and neither the unpolished Constanze (Schäfer) nor the delicate Belmonte (Bostridge) approaches the stature of the best previous interpreters.

Mackerras spurns period instruments and leads a big-boned performance of great vigor and clarity, superbly recorded (Telarc). He wisely omits the trivial march before the Pasha's entrance and consigns the long version of "Wenn der Freude" to an appendix. But his singers throw the scale off; so splendid an orchestral framework requires better voices, but this cast, however willing and competent, is sorely disappointing. (The conductor's recordings of the Da Ponte operas are similarly trammeled.) Belmonte is a pinched tenor who wrestles clumsily with the coloratura; Blondchen has no low notes and neither, more crip-

plingly, does Osmin. The Turkish soprano Yelda Kodalli is a flashy Constanze with a voice that, like Rothenberger's, gains strength as it rises but also picks up glare and stridency; her coloratura facility remains intact. She alone among the cast has the talent and flair to entice the listener back.

The recording is the sound track for a performance filmed at the Topkapi Palace, and the young, photogenic singers probably look wonderful on camera. Visual delights are beside the point when you're just hearing the CDs; the older recordings recommended above are far better sung. Mackerras's inspired conducting is the strongest selling point, but Jochum, Fricsay, and Beecham are no less accomplished.

Le nozze di Figaro (The Marriage of Figaro). Starting with *Figaro,* the plethora of recordings becomes truly daunting, and it will be impossible to do justice to all of them. I will concentrate on those that preserve individual performances so engaging that they renew themselves with each hearing.

Lest any reader accuse me of accidentally ignoring the much venerated Glyndebourne series from the '30s conducted by **Fritz Busch,** I must declare that I'm ignoring them quite intentionally. Poorly recorded and, in most cases, poorly sung, they were superseded as early as 1960 and many times thereafter. I have only one favorite among the pre-stereo accounts, and if the sound were better, I'd declare it the best *Figaro* of all. Led by **Hans Rosbaud** and recorded live at Aix-en-Provence in 1955, it has a strong, memorable singer in each of the five major roles: Stich-Randall, Streich, Lorengar, Rehfuss, and Panerai (Ca' d'Oro 1004/05; EMI 64376). The piano continuo is a drawback, and the usual cuts are taken, but it's an altogether delightful performance. No Figaro utters the words as crisply as Panerai, and no Susanna floats softer, sweeter tones than Streich.

Almost as enjoyable is **Vittorio Gui**'s Glyndebourne recording from the same year, which preserves Jurinac's luminous Countess (she would record it again for Böhm) and has a lively Figaro-Susanna pair in Bruscantini and Sciutti (EMI). On the minus side are Gui's limp conducting and the vocally pressed Count and Cherubino. The CD reissue omits Basilio's aria, though it was on the LP set, where Cuenod sang it with unctuous, reptilian delight.

The first stereo recording was also made in 1955 and remains one of the best (♦Decca 466369). **Kleiber**'s conducting is both forceful and relaxed, and he includes the two numbers most often omitted, the arias for Basilio and Marcellina in Act 4 (though the latter is sung by this recording's Susanna). Siepi's Figaro is the plushest, suavest of all, and Gueden is a tirelessly pert Susanna. Della Casa's poised Countess sings in tones pure as crystal, though, like most of the cast, she's stingy with appoggiaturas. Poell's dry Count and Danco's thin-toned Cherubino partially redeem themselves by their intelligent acting.

Most of this cast isn't particularly comfortable with the fast recitatives, a failing that was rectified when **Giulini** led a mostly Italian *Figaro;* the native speakers really make a difference (♦EMI 63266). Giulini is a marvelous conductor who unerringly chooses exactly the right tempos and perfectly balances the score's theatricality and elegance. Moffo is a warm, sexy Susanna, and Taddei's facile tongue and plump baritone make him one of the best of all Figaros. The Count and Countess are clearly from another country, but what betrays Wächter's unsuitability is not his diction but his rampageous manner. His baritone is deluxe but his bearing is all wrong. Schwarzkopf's Countess is far more aristocratic. She sings beautifully and thoughtfully and creates a believable character.

Colin Davis has a more dignified Count than Giulini, but both Wixell in this role and Wladimiro Ganzirolli as Figaro have dry, gritty voices (♦Philips 422540). Norman's Countess, on the other hand, is sumptuous, and Freni is my favorite Susanna of all. She has more voice than any of her rivals, and she utters the words with sincerity and charm, always alert to the drama. Davis works hand in hand with his singers at every point, and his conducting, if anything, got even better when he recorded the opera again in 1991 (RCA). The orchestral playing is uncannily conversational; the players add an eloquent commentary of their own to the singers' words. Varady's Countess is both spirited and melancholy, and her top notes shine. Donath's fresh timbre and vivacious manner are just right for Susanna. The other performers aren't quite in the same class.

Böhm's 1956 Figaro is graced by Jurinac's Countess, a second Susanna from Streich, and the young Ludwig's Cherubino, but is otherwise dispensable (Philips). His 1968 account is more of a piece, with a fine ensemble of mostly German singers who work smoothly together (DG). Janowitz is yet another first-class Countess who sculpts her lines flawlessly, with an enthralling tonal radiance uniquely hers. Marriner has a well-bred Count in Raimondi, a poignant Countess in Popp, and a potent Figaro in van Dam (♦Philips 416870). Hendricks's Susanna is slightly too diffident and Baltsa's Cherubino slightly too brusque and acidic, but this is a very likeable performance, further enhanced by the funny, sympathetic Marcellina of Felicity Palmer and the weighty Bartolo of Robert Lloyd.

Solti (London) and Levine (RCA) both have casts I'd love to see on stage. A quick accolade, at the very least, is due Solti's high-class (rather than high-strung) Count (Thomas Allen), beautifully sung Countess (Te Kanawa), and zesty Susanna (Popp). Ramey's Figaro is poker-faced and rhythmically square, however, and the spirited Von Stade is too inclined to drain the warmth out of her voice to suggest Cherubino's boyishness. I can't shake the admittedly subjective impression that these singers aren't all that well acquainted with each other—they came together in the studio, put in a good day's work, and went off in their own directions.

Muti might have been enjoyable, but he browbeats his cast into halfheartedness (EMI). Abbado, by contrast, sounds rather uninvolved (DG). He should have discouraged Bartoli's vulgar descents into her chest register and urged his Susanna (McNair) to stop mooning and sing. Mehta, like Giulini, has the advantage of an almost all-Italian cast, but a few buoyant moments aren't sufficient to overcome a generally prosaic traversal (Sony).

The best of the period-instrument performances is Arnold Ostman's, which includes an appendix of rarely heard variants (Oiseau-Lyre). His Countess (Augér) and Susanna (Bonney) sing prettily and sensitively, and the rest of his cast, if on the routine side, are capable. Gardiner's recording, despite the seething (and perhaps overbearing) Figaro of Terfel and the Count of the promising Rodney Gilfry, is weakly cast (Archiv).

Don Giovanni. Between its Prague premiere and its Vienna revival, Mozart fiddled slightly with Don Giovanni and never let us have his final word on the score. Posterity decided the matter for him, however, and until fairly recently, performances of the opera included Elvira's "Mi tradi" and both tenor arias and omitted the Act 2 Zerlina-Leporello duet. Our modern pedants, however, aghast at the notion of performing a version Mozart himself never heard, set us an impossible choice: simply put, do we forgo "Il mio tesoro" or "Mi tradi"? Neither, shout the traditionalists, and they are right.

The period-instrument performances are a sorry lot, but I'll only pick on the most acclaimed, by Gardiner (Archiv). In common with his conductor-sympathizers, Gardiner's tragic flaw is to settle habitually for singers of less than the highest caliber. It may be that he wants no unruly individualism compromising his dominance, or maybe he believes his own undiluted musicological vision will alchemize second-rate talents into great performers. It never happens, and despite his estimable skills as a conductor, most of his new recordings affirm (to crib Dr. Johnson's remark about second marriages) the triumph of hope over experience. Record collectors 50 years hence will unearth Gardiner's ephemeral Don Giovanni (or Ostman's or Norrington's) only if they sincerely feel that singing is a matter of ideological rather than vocal achievement. Daniel Harding is even worse: a hasty, hard-driven performance that quickly comes to seem shallow and skittish (Virgin). It's almost impossible to grasp the quality of Mozart's music here.

Giulini's remains the best studio recording (♦EMI 47260). Listen to the young Sutherland pop out the high As of "Or sai chi l'onore;" there's no hesitation, no fumbling, the notes are simply there, exactly where they ought to be, at exactly the right time. Listen in the same way to how easily Schwarzkopf sails through Elvira's divisions, how serenely she lofts her own upper notes. The difficulties don't call attention to themselves and are not an end in themselves, and her very personal, wounded Elvira makes an indelible impression, all the more so because it contrasts so strongly with Sutherland's frosty, imperious Anna. (No need to cast a mezzo as Elvira—a deplorable modern practice—when the voices are already so identifiable.)

The other cast members are also well-defined individuals. Taddei's Leporello relishes every word, Sciutti is a fetching Zerlina, Frick's black bass makes him a formidable Commendatore, and even Masetto gets a first-class interpreter, Cappuccilli, who would go on to be a much-in-demand Verdi baritone. Alva's slender, slightly nasal voice may not be great, but it's so gracefully employed you don't notice. Giulini is strong but pliant, and as in his Figaro, every tempo seems exactly right. Wächter's Giovanni is less calamitous than his Count. His free, handsome baritone is a splendid instrument, but he can't sustain the urbanity, and he blusters and hyperventilates too often. He doesn't ruin the performance entirely, but he certainly diminishes it.

Remediation is easy to find. Pinza was the best Giovanni of the first half of the 20th century, and his worthiest successor in the second half was Siepi. Unlike Wächter and most others, Siepi starts in the right place. A rake who has already seduced 1003 women in Spain alone could hardly lack confidence, and Siepi's self-assurance is impossible to miss. He doesn't try to act the part of Don Juan; he never shouts or rants, he simply becomes the character and does what comes naturally. His charisma is reinforced by his stunning vocalism. His well-upholstered bass commands attention at all dynamic levels, from dulcet mezza voce to ringing forte, and because he's singing his own language, he never feels the need to exaggerate. Corena often partnered him as Leporello, and he had a quick tongue and a substantial voice of his own.

You can hear Siepi and Corena together with Krips (London), Leinsdorf (RCA), and Mitropoulos (♦Sony 64263). With Krips, you also get Della Casa's limpid Elvira (the voice enchanting in itself), Gueden's Zerlina, and Dermota's sloppy but laudably noble Ottavio. Leinsdorf offers Nilsson's mighty Anna (thrilling when she gets all the notes out), Leontyne Price's ravishing and often impassioned Elvira, and Valletti's patrician Ottavio.

Mitropoulos's recording was made at the 1956 Salzburg Festival, and if the sound were better and the conductor less obstructionist, it would be the greatest *Don Giovanni* available. In the cast are Grümmer (a treasurable artist who, incredibly, was never asked to record a complete Mozart role), Della Casa (far more animated before an audience than in the studio), Streich, Simoneau, and Frick, an assemblage unparalleled in the LP-CD age.

No other recording has a cast on this level, but three or four of them are fairly good. **Davis**'s discerning leadership elevates his 1973 performance above the norm, and he has an excellent female trio featuring a surprisingly fluent and sophisticated Elvira from the young Te Kanawa, an even more surprisingly passionate Anna from the usually placid Arroyo, and a bewitching Zerlina from Freni (♦Philips 422541). Stuart Burrows is a supple, commanding Ottavio. **Maazel**'s account has Te Kanawa more compelling than before, an effective mezzo Zerlina in Berganza, and a tempestuous if somewhat weirdly sung Anna in Moser (Sony). Van Dam's aptly cynical Leporello is a real gentleman's gentleman, and Raimondi's Giovanni has some of Siepi's easy confidence, though he's more saturnine and sings with less variety.

Muti's *Don Giovanni* is unsettling; the conductor grabs you by the throat and doesn't let go (EMI). It's a wild, exciting ride, but we remember only three of the characters we meet along the way: Ramey's morose, carefully sung Leporello, Studer's vibrant Anna, and William Shimell's vocally bland but consistently astute Giovanni comprise the trio. Like too many modern Giovannis (but unlike Siepi), Shimell has a voice that gets lost in the ensembles, and that won't do. **Marriner** preserves Allen's suave libertine (the most unflappable since Siepi's) and Araiza's agile, uncommonly masterful Ottavio (Philips). Like Burrows and Alva, and following in the footsteps of the great John McCormack, Araiza dispatches the runs of "Il mio tesoro" fluidly, without a single unnecessary breath. Such virtuosity once seemed a matter of artistic pride, and it's disheartening that so many young, modern tenors refuse to polish their techniques to the point where they can duplicate the achievement.

The most absorbing of the digital recordings is **Harnoncourt**'s (♦Teldec 44184). He has some of Muti's ferocity but tempers it with finesse. His cast looks unpromising on paper but exceeds all expectations. Gruberová is an incisive if lightweight Anna, Bonney a lovable Zerlina, and Blochwitz a decorous Ottavio who's sometimes short of breath. Hampson's Giovanni is a little too cocky, but he knows how to use his lyric baritone gracefully and he does try to avoid overacting. Alexander's Elvira really catches fire; it's dazzlingly sung and acted for all it's worth. After Harnoncourt, the best modern recording to come along may be **Abbado**'s, a graceful, meticulous performance with an effective cast (DG). Keenlyside, like so many British Giovannis, is always a gentleman and sings with a good measure of self-assurance. Terfel proves himself more suited to playing the servant than the master, and Salminen is a Wagnerian-sized Commendatore. Patricia Pace's gentle Zerlina and Soile Isokoski's smoldering Elvira are fine, but despite some individual touches, the Anna and Ottavio are well below the top class.

Böhm's two studio recordings (DG) are spottily cast, and so are Solti's (London). **Solti**'s first recording at least has an interesting trio of ladies to commend it (Margaret Price, Sass, Popp), along with Burrows's exemplary Ottavio. His vastly inferior second has Fleming's Anna, but Terfel's histrionics in the title role make Wächter seem like a paragon of gentility. **Böhm**'s most interesting recording is a 1955 live Vienna performance sung in German (RCA). The irresistible cast is an assemblage of personable, utterly individual stylists: Della Casa (as Anna rather than her usual Elvira), Jurinac, Seefried, London, Kunz, Weber, Dermota, all more pointed, lively, and comfortable in German than they were, or would be, in Italian.

Karajan never seemed to come to terms with *Don Giovanni*. His disjointed performances are no more than intermittently impressive. I'd keep only the 1963 Vienna broadcast, though you'll need a CD player that can crank it up to pitch (Verona). Wächter's Giovanni is less frenzied than it was in the studio, and Leontyne Price's smoldering Anna (the only Mozart role she kept in her stage repertory) deserves to be remembered. Most noteworthy (because it was almost lost to history) is Wunderlich's Ottavio, which he had just begun to sing in Italian. It's an unrefined interpretation but vigorous enough to suggest what might have come had he not died so young.

One other recording deserves mention because its constellation of eight stars includes two of the highest magnitude: **Moralt**'s indifferent reading is glorified by Jurinac's melting Elvira and Simoneau's chivalrous Ottavio (Philips). You won't hear a more heartrending "Mi tradi" or a more polished "Dalla sua pace" anywhere.

Cosi fan tutte. By the '80s, this once-neglected work had become one of the most frequently performed of all operas in this country. Inevitably it had its share of trendy, make-it-relevant stagings, but I think the opera works best in productions that try to replicate the mind-set (rather than the instruments) of its period. The plot is fairly thin, and it makes no sense if we don't understand that the characters are facing an agonizingly real conflict between passion and propriety. In our own permissive society, the word "etiquette" is almost obsolete, but it was a living concept in the world drawn by Mozart and da Ponte. If the people on stage can't persuade us that they are ladies and gentlemen in the old-fashioned sense, they won't seem to be taking any risks, and their behavior will seem unaccountably artificial.

All this by way of introducing my favorite recording of the opera, **Karajan**'s aristocratic account (♦EMI 67064). Consider Simoneau's Ferrando, the best on records. He sings more beautifully than any of his rivals, with an apparently infinite range of dynamics and a round, gleaming voice that blends perfectly in the ensembles even as it maintains its distinctive glint. Just as important, he never loses his composure, even if he allows a hint of distress to creep into his tone from time to time. Bruscantini matches his courtliness; this Alfonso has a glib baritone and manipulates the others easily, without ever raising his voice. Panerai is no less articulate, and if his snappy singing is sometimes too emphatic, it suits the character. Schwarzkopf leaps Fiordiligi's hurdles with ease and creates an appealing, multifaceted character. Nan Merriman's smiling Dorabella, enlivened by the mezzo's trademark rapid vibrato, and Lisa Otto's saucy but uncaricatured Despina are on the same level. Karajan cuts some of the recitative but includes Ferrando's and Dorabella's essential second arias.

Solti's first recording is elegant and more complete than Karajan's (♦London 430101). Lorengar is a reflective Fiordiligi with incandescent top notes; Berganza a warm, delectable Dorabella. Tom Krause sings Guglielmo with uncommon grace, Ryland Davies is a lithe, mannerly Ferrando, and the two conspirators are gleefully crusty. His second is a more bumptious affair, commendable for Fleming's Fiordiligi and little else (London). **Klemperer**'s singers (especially Margaret Price and Luigi Alva) approximate the expertise of Solti's first cast, but they're sabotaged by the conductor's lethargy (EMI). **Davis** offers Caballé in her only Mozart role on commercial discs, and she has some lovely but also some indifferent moments (Philips). Baker's alert Dorabella is a little too studied, and Gedda, who should have been an interesting Ferrando, is in rather sour voice.

Jochum is more satisfying, with a cast of old pros playing marvelously off each other (DG). Seefried may have lost her flexibility and her top notes but not her charm and candor. This is an artist who never distanced herself from her audiences; she allows you to see her face so clearly you can easily tell when she's in earnest and when she's just putting you on. Merriman's Dorabella is even more vivacious than it was under Karajan, and Haefliger's Ferrando wears his stuffed shirt becomingly. Prey and Fischer-Dieskau are also strong presences, but the Italian language doesn't come easily to most of the singers. Too many of the words, and far too many of the notes, are lost in this performance.

If I wanted to jettison elegance entirely and go for the grand opera approach, I'd choose **Leinsdorf,** the first of the complete recordings and still the most extroverted (♦RCA 6677). There's nothing subtle about the players, Price, Troyanos, and Milnes among them, but they sing lustily (and remarkably accurately) and have a great time. **Levine** has one of the best of all Despinas in the ingenuous **Marie McLaughlin** but is otherwise uneven (DG). **Muti** (EMI) and **Haitink** (EMI) also have uneven casts, and **Harnoncourt** (Teldec) is too eccentric. Only a few of their hard-working singers win my sympathy. **Marriner** (Philips) is more enjoyable, and I'm occasionally lured back by Allen (a velvety Guglielmo), Araiza (a confident Ferrando), von Otter (Dorabella), and van Dam (Alfonso). I want to like **Barenboim** more than I do (Erato). It's the most interesting of his Mozart opera recordings, despite some willful tempos. Bartoli, Cuberli, Streit, and Ferruccio Furlanetto have some refreshing and individual ideas, but they don't sing well enough to compete with the best of their rivals.

Böhm recorded *Cosi* three times. The first and last (1955 London and 1974 DG) are brutally cut, but I treasure some of his cast members: the sparkling Della Casa and Ludwig in 1955, together with Dermota's fretful Ferrando and Erich Kunz's amiable Guglielmo, and Janowitz, Fassbaender, and Schreier in 1974. His 1962 recording is widely esteemed and—probably at producer Walter Legge's insistence—almost complete (EMI). The Despina and Alfonso are nothing special, but the others (Schwarzkopf, Ludwig, Kraus, Taddei) promise much. In fact, they sing remarkably well, especially Schwarzkopf, whose prime was just passing, and Taddei is the most resourceful of Guglielmos.

What bothers me about the performance is its underlying pushiness; the personalities of the singers overwhelm the personalities of the characters. I usually don't object to healthy egotism, but in this case each artist seems to be doing a star turn, greedily seeking the spotlight whenever possible. They don't blend well in the ensembles, and while they certainly have class, they overdo even the artifice that civility demands. However sporadically enjoyable, this traversal is far less satisfying than Karajan's or Solti's, or even Leinsdorf's. Indeed, pressed to choose only one of Böhm's performances, I'd opt for the first, cuts and all.

Jacobs gives the best of the historically informed performances (♦Harmonia Mundi 961663). In his determination to clarify the musical architecture, he reminds me, oddly enough, of Klemperer, though his tempos are (not surprisingly) much faster. The score is set forth with great clarity and transparency, but it's apparent even in the opening trios that every nuance, every emphasis, has been carefully fabricated and slotted smoothly into place. The period instruments whirr, buzz, and crunch delightfully all the same, and the cast is perfectly balanced. Most striking is Graciela Oddone, who sings with more verbal relish than any other Despina I've heard; she reminds me of a miniature Renata Scotto. Her exchanges with the Alfonso of Petro Spagnoli are sharp and fluent. Marcel Boone is a mellow Guglielmo, Güra a sweet-toned Ferrando, though limited in power. Gens and Fink

as the two sisters are capable but fall short of the high standards set by the others.

Die Zauberflöte (The Magic Flute). *Zauberflöte,* textually the least complicated of the Mozart operas, has endured quite a few attempts at historical reconstruction, i.e., making it sound new by making it sound old. Among others, **Gardiner** (Archiv) and **Christie** (Erato) argue their points intelligently but miss an obvious impossibility. Something can be new only once. Great works of music are timeless and have the capacity to be renewed only through the talent and imagination of the performers. It's not enough to reproduce self-effacingly the notes on the page. A Mozart singer (let's not forget that the idea of a great Mozart *conductor* is an invention of our own century) must offer us something we want to return to again and again. Gardiner's and Christie's performances are engaging enough the first time around and might serve to introduce new audiences to the music. The singers, however, give me no incentive whatsoever to hear them a second time. Will anyone miss them 50 years from now?

Beecham's 1937 *Flute* has never gone out of print, and some of his stars still shine brightly and steadily (Nimbus; Pearl; EMI). I agree with those commentators who consider the performance overrated, but Hüsch's honest, congenial Papageno and Lemnitz's warmly glowing Pamina deserve their immortality. **Karajan**'s 1950 account also justifies perpetuation for the allure of Dermota's earnest Tamino, Kunz's Papageno (as likable as Hüsch's though more drily sung), Ludwig Weber's magniloquent, deep-toned Sarastro, and above all, Seefried's exquisite, wonderfully human Pamina (EMI). Karajan's First Lady is the young Jurinac. Devotees of **Furtwängler** may prefer to hear Seefried, Dermota, and Kunz under that conductor, but I think his early-'50s Mozart opera recordings belong more in the special-interest category (EMI and other labels).

I nod affectionately toward **Fricsay** (DG), the first recording to include dialog, **Böhm** (London), and the tantalizing Salzburg **Szell** (EMI), pausing at the latter only long enough to commend the ardent Tamino of Simoneau (in liquid voice) and the tender, ladylike Pamina of Della Casa. I'm hurrying to arrive at the first great *Zauberflöte,* **Klemperer**'s in 1963, the only one of his Mozart opera recordings not crushed by his heavy conductorial hand (♦EMI 67071). It bubbles and sparkles, and it has in Popp a Queen of the Night who is more than just a deft coloratura. Her tangy voice has some dramatic-soprano bite, and she set a new standard for the role. It was the first time most of us had ever heard her, and we remembered. Just as striking was the Pamina of another newcomer, Janowitz, whose entrancing, pure-silver voice sculpts the lines with perfect aplomb. The Three Ladies—Schwarzkopf, Ludwig, Hilde Rössl-Màjdan—are the most ebullient trio ever, and they sound as magical on repeated hearings as they did at first. You remember each of them individually. The male cast, if less extraordinary, is still splendid: Gedda's forthright Tamino, Berry's unpretentious Papageno, Frick's sepulchral but rather unmalleable Sarastro.

Klemperer excises the dialog, but **Böhm** in 1964 (♦DG 449749) and all the other recordings since then include at least some of it. (Harnoncourt is an outlandish exception—he substitutes a spoken narration.) Böhm has, in Franz Crass, a Sarastro no less imposing but far more mellifluous than Frick, an amusing Papageno from Fischer-Dieskau, and one of the few performances of a Mozart role I deem perfect: Wunderlich's mesmerizingly beautiful Tamino. If Sarastro's music is sublime enough to issue from the throat of God, it's appropriate that his protégé should also sound like a young deity.

Solti's two recordings find him unusually relaxed but still alert. In 1973 he had Prey's gentlemanly Papageno, the best since Hüsch and very much in the same mold: genial but never clownish, and sung with a true lieder singer's eloquence (♦London 414568). Lorengar's Pamina is warm and guileless, and her top notes soar. Fischer-Dieskau (like London on the old Karajan set, Crass with Klemperer, and Hotter with Böhm) is one of the few Speakers you really notice. Burrows's Tamino and Talvela's Sarastro leave little cause for complaint, but Deutekom's grotesque Queen sounds like a cross between an electronic synthesizer and a Swiss yodeler. The 1990 account has a less quirky Queen in Sumi Jo, even if she takes us back to the coloratura canary-land of Berger, Streich, and Lipp. Ruth Ziesak and Uwe Heilmann are an appealing pair of young lovers, and Moll contributes the smoothest and mellowest of his Sarastros (♦London 433210). The whole is somehow more than the sum of its parts—a captivating performance.

Moll sings almost as well with **Davis,** where we find another accurate but lightweight Queen in Luciana Serra (Philips). Schreier's Tamino (for Davis—not the earlier one for Suitner) is his finest Mozart role. For once, he keeps the sputtering down to a minimum and tries to put some sugar into his voice. Margaret Price's Pamina combines fervor with an almost instrumental purity and focus. **Marriner** has a fairly strong singer in every role, though only Bär's Papageno sounds truly at ease (Philips). Studer's Queen is formidable and tremendously exciting; you're not quite sure if she's going to make it, but she does, and she's hair-raising. Te Kanawa's sedate Pamina doesn't quicken the pulse in quite the same way. Araiza is a virile, ringing, slightly stiff Tamino; Ramey a shaky Sarastro who doesn't have the right sort of deep bass for the role.

Mackerras has another dramatic soprano Queen, June Anderson, less secure than Studer and harder on the ears (Telarc). I've neglected Mackerras's recordings of the Da Ponte operas because I'm not happy with any of his casts. His *Zauberflöte* assemblage is typical. Allen is a classy Papageno, Hendricks makes some pretty sounds as Pamina (though Mackerras rushes her aria), Hadley is an outgoing Tamino, and Robert Lloyd has the depth and gravity for Sarastro. I don't have much incentive to hear them repeatedly, however.

We needn't linger long over **Karajan**'s second *Flute* (1980; DG), despite another virtuoso Queen (Karin Ott), or **Levine**'s account, which has more dialog than any other (RCA). **Harnoncourt**'s capricious tempos and gratuitous female narrator disqualify his reading (Teldec), and the EMI recordings that followed Klemperer's have little to offer. I'll praise only Moser's trenchant Queen and Moll's reliable Sarastro under **Sawallisch,** and Popp's touching Pamina for **Haitink.**

La Clemenza di Tito. This has been the luckiest of Mozart's operas on records; you won't go wrong with any of the stereo sets. The first, under **Kertész,** has Berganza's supple, warm-toned Sesto, Popp's Servilia, and Fassbaender's Annio to commend it (London). **Davis** (♦Philips 422544) has the most regal of emperors in Burrows and the most resolute of Vitellias in Baker (though she can't reach that odd, solitary high D-flat). Popp repeats her Servilia, and Minton is a capable, fluent Sesto. Berganza takes on Sesto a second time for **Böhm,** who profits further from Varady's incisive Vitellia but not from Schreier's wizened Titus (DG).

The two historically informed, period-instrument recordings are less grand, but the conductors have troubled themselves to find first-class singers. **Gardiner** has Varady, the pliant, imperturbable von Otter, and the soft-grained but stately Rolfe Johnson (♦Archiv 431806); **Hogwood**

(♦Oiseau-Lyre 444131), a less hard-driving but also less probing musician, has Bartoli, Heilmann, and Della Jones (a really vicious Vitellia). **Harnoncourt,** an apostate from the strict authenticity movement, now conducts modern-instrument orchestras, but he tries to bring to their playing some of the verve of period bands (♦Teldec 90857). His brashness is often irritating, but not in *Tito,* his best Mozart recording after *Don Giovanni.* This is a rousing account, enhanced primarily by Popp, whose ingenuous Servilia has metamorphosed into a cunning Vitellia. Langridge's voice is scratchier than either Burrows's or Rolfe Johnson's, but he's an effective Titus. Bonney is a lovely Servilia, and Ann Murray a proficient Sesto. You really won't go wrong with any of the *Tito* recordings.

A final note about the historic (pre-LP) recordings, too little and too late. Every Mozart lover should know how Pinza, Rethberg, Kipnis, et al. sounded, so I'll make three recommendations. EMI's "Introuvables du Chant Mozartien" (63750, 4CD) is a great bargain and offers the richest treasure trove of classic recordings. Two discs from Memoir (406 and 410) are less comprehensive but just as valuable. Orfeo's set concentrates on Salzburg performers 1922–83 (408955. 5CD); the 1922-2 collection is, like the others, available separately (394101) and nicely complements the EMI and Memoir offerings.

CONCERT ARIAS

Mozart wrote just over 40 concert arias, enough by modern standards to fill five CDs. There would seem to be ample material here for two or three full operas, but the concert arias are, for the most part, more formal, less dramatic, and usually lengthier than their operatic counterparts. They are self-contained *scenas,* their sentiments uttered by characters we never get to know. The most florid specimens are vehicles for vocal display rather than personal expression, and even the simpler pieces exist in an emotional void. The music is wonderful nonetheless, and the best melodies stay with you for a long time after each hearing.

Avid Mozartians will want Vol. 23 in the Philips "Mozart Edition." All the concert arias are here along with various vocal ensembles, canons, choral numbers, and alternate arias for some of the operas. The performers include such tantalizing singers as Popp, Mathis, Gruberová, Araiza, Blochwitz, and Ahnsjö. On eight CDs, it's perhaps a bit too much for the average collector, so a more sensible choice might be the inexpensive 5CD London set conducted by **György Fischer** and devoted to the pure concert arias alone (♦London 455214). The arias are grouped by singer rather than arranged chronologically, and the two sopranos entrusted with the most vertiginous coloratura flights (Krisztina Láki and Elfrieda Hobarth) are not entirely comfortable—or easy on the ear—in the stratosphere, but none of the participants is less than capable. The best impression is made by Te Kanawa, consistently lovely in timbre and free in tone, but Gruberová, Berganza, Winbergh, Fischer-Dieskau, and Corena offer much that is enjoyable.

Another good collection, though only two CDs' worth, comes from Salzburg recitals, 1956–83 (♦Orfeo 394401 and 394501). It has the great advantage of variety: 23 different singers each have an aria apiece (Mathis gets two), and all the vocal categories are covered. Outstanding, and hard to find elsewhere in this repertory, are Sciutti, Fassbaender, Simoneau, Varady, and a quartet of fine basses (Tozzi, Evans, van Dam, Moll).

Many artists, sopranos especially, have left us single discs of concert arias. A short list should include the adventurous **Donath** with various obbligato instruments (♦Acanta 43470), the lustrous and full-blooded **Margaret Price** (♦RCA 61635), and (for those who pass up the complete sets mentioned above) the industrious and reliably proficient Gruberová (♦Teldec 72302). Also notable are the youthful, delicate Oelze (Berlin), the always dependable and agile Lott (ASV), and the virtuoso (if deadpan) Dessay (EMI). Janowitz (DG) is on the sleepy, self-indulgent side but angelically lovely; Cyndia Sieden (Glossa) is an awe-inspiring technician in the difficult arias Mozart wrote for Aloysia Weber but no more expressive than Dessay, and both Mathis (Berlin) and Hendricks (EMI) fluently address not the concert arias proper but a selection of sacred pieces. Among the sopranos of the past whose Mozart recordings deserve reissue are Streich (DG) and Vyvyan (Decca).

Among tenors the paradigm is Simoneau, but most of the recordings have vanished. One aria is among the fillers to Beecham's *Entführung,* one is in Philips's "Early Years" box (a splendid "Non temer"), and another is in the Orfeo collection mentioned above. Alva, tackling all the tenor arias in a 1981 Preludio disc, is still stylish and limber, but the harsh recorded sound limits enjoyment. You may as well stick with the tenors in the London and Philips collections—and the baritones and basses, too.

Exsultate, jubilate. Far and away the most recorded of Mozart's concert pieces for soprano, *Exsultate, jubilate* is a motet rather than a proper aria, but the distinction shouldn't concern anyone. It's as exhilarating as anything he ever wrote, and few coloratura sopranos have resisted its lure. The concluding "Alleluia" has had several superb recordings on its own from sopranos (Moffo, Vyvyan, Sutherland) who treat it as a showpiece rather than an expression of religious faith. Of the many complete recordings, we can dismiss (with some twinges of regret) those that don't quite meet Mozart's florid demands, even though the artists are as estimable as Schumann, Seefried, and Gueden.

De los Angeles's tongue doesn't quite move quickly enough either, but the warmth of her manner and the distinctive texture of her voice should disarm the most churlish listener (Testament). **Berger,** caught late in the day (1956), smears some of the runs, but her voice remains astonishingly fresh, steady, and girlish (Testament). **Popp,** whom we first came to know as Queen of the Night, should have turned in an outstanding *Exsultate,* but in 1967 she was inexplicably cautious, singing prettily but too slowly and ducking the climactic high C (EMI).

I'm inclined to pass over most of the smallish, flexible voices, however exquisitely deployed (Ameling, Donath, Battle, Bonney) and the fairly neutral readings of some very accomplished lyric sopranos (Mathis, Lott, Marshall, Hendricks, Bayo). *Exsultate* is a stretch for the mezzos, so let's dispense as well with the dexterous but prickly-toned Bartoli (London) and the aging but spry Baker (London). I would not, in fact, banish any of these singers from my own collection; I'm simply reserving my endorsements for the half-dozen or so recordings I like best.

The earliest of these (1948) comes from **Schwarzkopf** in her sunniest voice, nimble in the divisions and characteristically personal in the slow middle aria (♦EMI 63201). She's secure enough to play with dynamics and vocal shadings even in the most difficult passages. The drawback is the primitive technology, which robs the Philharmonia Orchestra of presence. The usually unflappable **Stader,** in 1954, isn't quite note-perfect—an indication of how challenging the music really is. The runs aren't always articulated cleanly, and the trills are weak, but she sings an elaborate cadenza at the end of the first aria and generally keeps her tone full and round (♦DG 447334; also appended to Fricsay's *Entführung*). There's something just a bit mechanical about her singing, and in that sense she has a modern-day replica some 30 years later in **Kirkby,** punctilious but even more limited in color (Oiseau-Lyre). **Stich-Randall** in

the early 60s is more impressive than either Stader or Kirkby, despite the odd mannerism or two (disembodied tones, unwarranted staccati). She brings more variety and gravity to the text, and she flies ebulliently through the final "Alleluia" (♦Accord 20042).

Augér is less splashy, whether at Salzburg in 1973 (Orfeo) or on stage with Bernstein in 1990 (♦DG 431791). Her timbre is rather soft-grained, but the divisions are fleet and accurate, and her tone has a gentle glow. **Te Kanawa** has much of the same sweet warmth, and she brings surprising urgency to the central aria (♦Philips 412873). In 1971 her voice was not yet the creamy instrument it would become, but the trills and roulades are dispatched smoothly and easily, at a good clip. **Sutherland** recorded only the "Alleluia" in the studio, rather late in her career, but a complete 1959 Cologne radio recording has been preserved in excellent mono sound (♦Bella Voce 107.001). La Stupenda tosses off the coloratura in her own matchless way, her big voice bright and well-defined, her diction unwontedly crisp. For sheer technical mastery, she's unbeatable, but Schwarzkopf, Stich-Randall, and Augér come remarkably close.

SONGS

Mozart's entire song output can be pretty much accommodated on a single CD. I equivocate because Vol. 24 of the Philips "Mozart Edition" stretches them out to two discs by including the German church songs and the rarely heard Italian "nocturnes" for soloists and wind ensemble. The chief contributor is **Ameling,** who has the sparkle and vocal purity demanded by the songs, accompanied here by Dalton Baldwin. The soprano was slightly fresher in her earlier EMI recording with Demus, now long gone. The songs themselves don't warrant extensive collecting. They yield their secrets quickly, and new recordings generally don't have anything new to tell us. Ameling would do nicely as a single interpreter, but only an iron-willed collector could pass up other recordings of some of the songs.

We'll keep the list short. **Schwarzkopf**'s 1955 recital with Gieseking has long been regarded as a classic. She digs deeply into the songs, imprinting them with her own extroverted temperament yet never bringing too much weight to bear upon the music (♦EMI 63702). **Seefried,** more direct and spontaneous and cleaner of diction, is even better. She sings the words eloquently, and voice and music come together unforgettably. Her 1952 recordings with Moore are the more pristine (♦Testament 1026), but she's more assured and communicative in 1957 with Werba (♦DG 437348). **Stich-Randall**'s rarefied purity of line makes her seem a little distant, but the songs sound newly minted (♦Accord 201452; 1956). The less fastidious **Köth** has a winning sense of humor, and she's really engaging in the lighter songs like "Die Alte" (Berlin; 1966). **Alexander** (Etcetera), **Hendricks** (EMI), and **Bonney** (Teldec) are appealing, each in her own way, but by now we've heard it all before. (Collectors who started with any of them and worked back to Schwarzkopf, Seefried, and Ameling might justifiably feel exactly the opposite.)

A male voice in the songs makes a refreshing change, and **Schreier,** with Schiff, is forthright, sensitive, and unusually smooth (♦London 430514). **Ainsley** commands less trenchant diction, but his crisp tenor is pleasing and agile. He divides the songs with the soprano Joan Rodgers, elegantly poised and pure, in a recital that profits from the vocal contrast (♦Hyperion 66989). LUCANO

Modest Mussorgsky *(1839–1881)*

He may have been the greatest Russian composer of them all. Yet except for a generous outpouring of songs, Mussorgsky managed to complete only one opera (twice), 13 or 14 piano pieces, and a mere handful of orchestral works. Yet the opera is *Boris Godunov,* the piano pieces include *Pictures at an Exhibition,* and, thanks to his friends, even some of the things he didn't complete have found their way into the repertoire. Nearly every one of them bears witness to his bold originality and unique ability to distill his country's folk idiom into music—not to mention the darker aspects of the Russian psyche, which may have helped bring about his untimely end.

ORCHESTRAL WORKS

Pictures at an Exhibition. It isn't just Russian opera that often "seems to have been written by somebody else" (see Borodin's operas); the same can be said of some of the orchestral music. There's no better example than Mussorgsky, for when this mightiest and most revolutionary member of the "Mighty Handful" died of alcoholism at age 42, his colleagues characteristically jumped into the breach. To Rimsky-Korsakov fell the task of pulling the unfinished opera *Khovanshchina* into shape, and he went even further with two versions of *Boris Godunov* (which Mussorgsky himself had done in 1869 and 1872) and what quickly became the standard concert version of *A Night on Bald Mountain.* Similarly, Rimsky's pupil Tushmalov was the first to orchestrate parts of *Pictures at an Exhibition,* and the ensuing decades have brought us more than a dozen more efforts, along with arrangements for organ, guitar, chorus, accordions, even rock band (e.g., Emerson, Lake & Palmer).

But the most successful creator of a Mussorgsky orchestral work wasn't even Russian. He was a Frenchman, Maurice Ravel, whose orchestration of *Pictures* went on to sweep the world following its premiere by its commissioner, conductor Serge Koussevitzky, in 1922. And it's the Ravel orchestration that has dominated the catalog since its first recording, also by **Koussevitzky,** in 1930 (♦Pearl 9020). It's still a potent account, as are the early-'50s follow-ups by **Kubelik** (♦Mercury 34378) and **Toscanini** (♦RCA 60287).

Not that the stereo era need hang its head in shame. Indeed, some of the finest recordings available date from the earliest days of stereo, most prominently **Reiner**'s, long established as a classic. Thrillingly disciplined, with an eye (and ear) to characterizing each portrait individually, it not only finds the Chicago Symphony at its most impressive but also stands among the recordings with greatest impact to come out of Orchestra Hall (e.g., "The Hut on Fowl's Legs"). Unfortunately, no CD has fully captured the magnificence of the original LP or RCA's subsequent ".5" remastering. But the current "Living Stereo" issue comes closest, containing as well a number of Reiner's other successful forays into Russiana, including his tautly propulsive *Night on Bald Mountain* (♦RCA 60958).

Karajan's was another superbly disciplined recording of the early stereo era (EMI, NA). While his 1966 remake is generally broader in tone and articulation (DG), the earlier one can still raise a few goose bumps, especially in its most recent remastering (DG 447426), which packs more punch than the inexpensive "Musikfest" issue. (His 1986 digital recording was less effective than either.) Nor should **Bernstein**'s or **Markevitch**'s *Pictures* be overlooked, the first highly individual but vividly drawn (♦Sony 60693) and the second also strongly characterized, the Leipzig Gewandhaus lending the piece a dark East European flavor (♦Berlin 2139). Likewise **Szell**'s clean-cut presentation (♦Sony 48162), even if its current discmates are less compelling than its earlier Odyssey LP and cassette coupling, Richter's jaw-dropping account of the piano original.

Nor did the early digital era disappoint. **Maazel** offered an often incisive, brilliantly recorded performance, with a *Night on Bald Mountain* to match (♦Telarc 80042). No less stunning was **Solti,** solidly characterized throughout, with a steadily powerful "Bydlo" and crackling "Hut" (♦London 430446). After that came **Abbado** (♦Penguin 460633), almost as powerful but with a greater sensitivity to nuance and color (e.g., his straining "Bydlo" and delightfully shaded "Tuileries" and "Ballet of the Chicks in Their Shells"). In many ways these are still among the very best.

Despite somewhat cavernous sound, **Slatkin** is also very fine (♦Vox 7298). Moreover, what he gives us is Mussorgsky-Ravel, as opposed to the "anthology" *Pictures* he has taken to performing in recent years, made up of a variety of orchestrations. Among other recorded *Pictures,* **Dorati** seems emotionally constricted, despite a fair amount of juice (Mercury). Conversely, **Ormandy** is big and sonorous, if a bit soft around the edges (RCA). Surprisingly, **Levi** also seems a bit too cultivated in spots (e.g., his "Old Castle"), but there's no doubting his control (Telarc).

Not so **Järvi,** who, even with the Chicago Symphony, paints with a brush so broad as to admit some smeary articulation (Chandos). **Sinopoli,** by contrast, over-polishes the piece, though his accompanying *Night on Bald Mountain* is strongly delineated (DG). **Giulini** on Sony is even slower and heavier than in *his* Chicago Symphony recording (NA) but without its focus, not to mention its majesty and depth. The prize for the slowest *Pictures* in the current catalog, however, goes to **Celibidache,** whose performance, though undeniably hypnotic in places, clocks in at around 43 minutes—about eight minutes too much of a good thing; no double-time "Bydlo" here! (EMI).

Poliansky is more reasonable; his 36-minute traversal is broad but flavorful, besides being filled out with some less commonly heard Mussorgsky (Chandos), as is **Macal,** whose more direct approach includes a crisply exciting "Hut" (Delos). There are a few surprises in "Goldenberg and Schmuyle"; otherwise **Eiji Oue**'s *Pictures* just keeps rollin' along (Reference). Similarly **Sargent,** though better than you might expect (e.g., his telling underlining of details in "Bydlo" and the "Ballet of the Chicks"), who tends to skim over some of the bigger sections (Everest). Each, however, is impressively recorded.

Once past Karajan, Szell, and Slatkin, quality in the budget category drops sharply. If you can stand his tinny cymbals, there are still **Jahni Mardjani**'s ill-focused brasses to contend with, as well as his sometimes leaden tempos (Infinity). Nor is articulation the strongest point of **Daniel Nazareth**'s traversal (e.g., the shaky trumpet in "Goldenberg and Schmuyle"), but at least he and his Slovakian players put their hearts into it (Naxos). So do the otherwise ponderous **Edward Serov** and the Volgograd Philharmonic in a generously filled, all-Mussorgsky CD (Amadis). **Gilbert Levine** is more disciplined but less inspiring (LaserLight).

Over the years the only other orchestration of *Pictures* to regularly command a place in the catalog has been **Stokowski**'s, and not just with him on the podium. Darker and generally heavier on the strings than Ravel's, it eliminates some of the brighter portraits (e.g., "Tuileries" and "Limoges") and emphasizes the music's more grotesque aspects (e.g., the slithery "Hut on Fowl's Legs"), as do his various recordings. Thus on both Decca/London (NA) and Music & Arts, "Gnomus" leaps to the fore, as does the fearful majesty of "Catacombs," with a quickstep oxcart in between. Music & Art's 1963 BBC Symphony concert performance is more spirited and more imaginative than Decca/London's "Phase-4" redo, albeit less imposing. Of course there is always Stokowski's first recording of the piece, from 1939, with the Philadelphia Orchestra, to be heard with his other Mussorgsky transcriptions (Dutton 8009). But if you want to hear one of the best-ever Stokowski *Pictures*, check out EMI 65614 (NA), where he does "The Hut on Fowl's Legs" and "Great Gate of Kiev" to a turn—but in the Ravel orchestration!

Bamert's recording of the Stokowski orchestration is broader still (Chandos), highlighting its more mysterious aspects (e.g., "The Old Castle"), whereas Rozhdestvensky brings a more Slavic accent to the proceedings, along with some tonal spread (Revelation). (It's also nice to hear their slower "Bydlos.") The first time the Philadelphia recorded *Pictures* was in 1937 with Ormandy, this time in the Lucien Cailliet orchestration, in some ways even more French than Ravel's (Biddulph 046). While the rich sonorities fall easily on the ear, they reveal few new insights. Nor does Ashkenazy's arrangement depart radically from Ravel's, though he has brought some sections more in line with Mussorgsky's original piano score, with which his performance is coupled (♦London 414386). And, like Cailliet, he restores the fifth "Promenade."

That section, omitted by both Ravel and Stokowski, may also be heard in the orchestrations by Leo Funtek and Sergei Gortchakov. In recent years Masur has been the latter's foremost champion, and his 1990 recording (Teldec) did a fine job of bringing out its metallic shimmer and more aggressively Slavic edge (with a pronounced emphasis on the brass). Unhappily, that CD is no longer available, leaving Saraste, whose recording alternates Gortchakov with Funtek (Finlandia). Since his handling of the latter highlights its best sections more effectively than Segerstam's all-Funtek recording (BIS), I regret that Saraste didn't stay with the warmer, somewhat string-heavy Funtek all the way, especially since his Gortchakov segments seem a bit soft compared with Masur's.

A Night on Bald Mountain. If you have Maazel's, Markevitch's, Reiner's, or Sinopoli's *Pictures,* you already have an outstanding *Night on Bald Mountain*—the Rimsky-Korsakov version, anyway—to which company may be added the exciting Tjeknavorian recording (♦ASV 6180). At the same time, the version from the unfinished opera *Sorochinsky Fair,* with chorus and soloist(s)—which was essentially the basis for Rimsky-Korsakov's—is available as part of three different Mussorgsky collections. As "The Lad's Dream," it leads off Poliansky's *Pictures* (Chandos); as the "Dream of the Peasant Gritzko," it leads off Macal's *Pictures* (Delos); and as "St. John's Night on the Bare Mountain," it's the principal item on Abbado's non-*Pictures* Mussorgsky CD (Sony).

Of these, Macal has the clearest sound, with the singers solidly in the picture; Polyansky is the most darkly atmospheric, albeit with a tad less punch; and Abbado has the least impact, sonically or interpretively, of the lot. By contrast, his earlier Mussorgsky anthology offers an electrifying account of David Lloyd Jones's edition of Mussorgsky's original, in many ways the most daringly imaginative of all (♦RCA 61354). Were that not enough, it also includes the finest recordings to date of the early B-flat major *Scherzo* and the "Triumphal March" from the abortive collaborative opera *Mlada* ("The Capture of Kars"). Complicating things, however, is the Sony CD's inclusion of the even rarer *Intermezzo Symphonique in Modo Classico,* the last of Mussorgsky's symphonic essays.

Protestations to the contrary, Stokowski's *Night on the Bare Mountain* is pretty much an extra-eerie retooling of Rimsky-Korsakov's. If you can find it, the maestro's "Phase-4" recording is an obvious choice, though at times Bamert conjures up even more thunder and lightning

in a more natural sonic perspective (Chandos). Then, of course, there is always the "Fantasia" soundtrack. . . . GOODFELLOW

OPERAS

Boris Godunov. Mussorgsky started many opera projects in his short life, but at his death only *Boris Godunov* had been completed. It would become his most popular opera and is in the repertory of most major companies. After his death, his friend Rimsky-Korsakov decided to revise the orchestration, smoothing out Mussorgsky's stark and original harmonies, making the music more like his own. This version is now out of favor and has been replaced in most contemporary productions by orchestrations, most prominently Shostakovich's, that are based on the composer's original score. Mussorgsky revised his original work (1868) by adding the Polish scenes of Act 3 and making other changes; this 1872 version has long been preferred for performance and recordings.

The best of the available recordings are by Abbado (♦Sony 58977) and Rostropovich (♦Erato 45418). Both use Mussorgsky's original score and orchestration and conflate the 1868 and 1872 versions, sometimes unnecessarily. Both have very good sound, excellent conducting, and strong casts. Anatolij Kotcherga (Abbado) and Raimondi (Rostropovich) portray the unfortunate Tsar with warm and sympathetic singing, fine tonal coloring, and excellent diction. Abbado's supporting cast is, as a whole, a bit better than Rostropovich's (for instance, Lipovsek's Marina is better sung than Vishnevskaya's), but the Russian conductor leads a more emotionally riveting performance.

Rimsky's version of the score, with its glitzier orchestration, has been recorded in good sound under Karajan, with the excellent Bulgarian bass Ghiaurov in one of his most famous roles as the Tsar (London). Christoff's interpretation of this fascinating role is memorable (EMI mono, NA). The most famous Boris of all was Chaliapin, whose theatrically powerful recordings of highlights are again available (♦Nimbus 7823/4). Those opera lovers who want both versions in their entirety will find Gergiev's mammoth set of interest (Philips 462230, 5CD). The casts are quite good even though neither title role is sung as well as Ghiaurov and Christoff do it.

Khovanshchina (The Khovansky Affair). This opera was left incomplete at the composer's death. Two of its five acts lacked endings, and not much of the work had been orchestrated. Rimsky finished the opera, using reprises of Mussorgsky's music for the missing pages. Shostakovich published his version in 1958, based on musicologist Pavel Lamm's 1931 edition of Mussorgsky's manuscripts, and that is the edition preferred by most opera houses today. The opera deals with the political intrigues of the 1680s, when the young Tsar Peter (later known as "the Great") had to fight off several challengers to his throne, including the powerful Khovansky family, his sister Sofia, and a religious sect known as the Old Believers and their leader Dosifey (a role made famous by Chaliapin).

The best all-round presentation is, again, by Abbado, whose theatrical flair, fine cast, and excellent sound make for a gripping experience (♦DG 429758). Abbado used the Shostakovich edition except for the quiet finale; there he opted for one by Stravinsky for a 1913 Paris production. It omits the brassy fanfares that announce the arrival of Peter's troops in the other versions. Gergiev's Kirov Opera recording is a good alternative (♦Philips 432147). He also uses the Shostakovich version, without any cuts, but his cast is not as consistently excellent as Abbado's. The Rimsky version is performed by the Sofia Opera (Capriccio) and the Rome Opera (Bella Voce). The latter, a 1973 broadcast, has a superior cast (Ghiaurov, Cossotto, Siepi) but is sung in Italian and the sound is mediocre. The sound is better on Capriccio but the cast not nearly as good.

SONGS

All of Mussorgsky's songs are performed with remarkable insight and wonderful vocal control by **Christoff** (♦EMI 63025, 3CD). His are the best recorded interpretations, though they are sometimes quite theatrical. Listeners who favor a more subdued approach may turn to **Leiferkus,** but his singing is less arresting and at times too monochromatic (Conifer 51274, 51248, 51229). Many of the songs have been recorded by such fine artists as **Sergei Larin** (Chandos 9547) and **Hvorostovsky** (Philips 438872). Both present the composer's *Songs and Dances of Death,* coupled with songs by other composers or arias from Russian operas. So does the young Armenian contralto **Lina Mkrtchyan,** whose beautiful, dark voice is very attractive and who often outsings her male competitors (Opus 111, 30235). These discs will be of interest to those listeners who don't want all of Mussorgsky's songs, and they are recommended on that basis.   MOSES

PIANO MUSIC

Mussorgsky's works for piano consist primarily of the famous suite, *Pictures at an Exhibition.* Since **Richter** showed the world it was viable in its original form, a lot of pianists have recorded it. Richter's 1958 performance in Sofia is documented in the "Great Pianists of the 20th Century" series, along with his marvelous Prokofiev Sonatas 6-8 and other fine examples of the Richter legend (♦Philips 456946, 2CD). This album is a must. His 1956 Prague performance is less stirring (Praga 254034).

Horowitz is less intense, for a wonder, and his modifications of Mussorgsky's score aren't too disturbing (RCA 60526). This disc enshrines his 1947 studio performance; his later recording still lacks musical depth, though it's technically impressive (RCA 60449). One of **Kapell**'s last recordings in 1953 was of *Pictures;* it's available, but the rest of the disc does his memory less than justice (VAIA 1048). A better collection includes a 1951 performance (Arbiter 108), and, of course, there's the valuable 9CD set devoted to this pianist, including the 1951 version (RCA 68442).

Of more recent readings, **Ashkenazy** is somewhat clangorously recorded and lacks personality (London 414386). **Douglas** is more warmly recorded, but lacks energy. **Brendel** gives a monumental, well-paced reading, rather lacking in temperament (Vox 97203). **Bronfman** offers a broad and effective performance, good but not outstanding (Sony 46481). **Janis** is technically impressive and musically sensitive (♦Mercury 434346). **Pogorelich** plays a curiously individual reading, intense but too slow for most tastes (DG 437667). **Andrei Vieru** gives a low-tension, almost baroque performance (Harmonia Mundi 901616). **Noriko Ogawa** returns to the manuscript but finds nothing earthshaking there, though her performances include piano reductions of a number of other Mussorgsky pieces, mostly operatic (BIS 905). **Demidenko** is excitingly muscular (Hyperion 67018). **Pratt** is slower than most, but musical (EMI 56836). **Earl Wild** doesn't seem to find this somewhat unpianistic writing inspiring, so neither does the listener (Ivory 70903).   MOORE

Conlon Nancarrow (1912–1997)

This emigré composer (he lived in Mexico after 1940) was one of America's brilliant eccentrics. He's best known for his *51 Studies for Player Piano,* which are based on mathematical relationships of rhythm and tempo, frequently taken at tremendous speeds that usually can't be played by humans and must be realized by a machine. His hand-punched piano rolls can only be played by the composer's specially adjusted, high-powered player piano.

These pieces were originally inspired by the jazz piano of Earl "Fatha" Hines and Art Tatum, and the early ones have a strong jazz and blues feel and an outrageous sense of humor very much like Ives's. The later ones have a rarefied feel reminiscent of late Webern, while retaining Nancarrow's signature humor. Most of the Studies are available in a 5CD set (♦Wergo 6907). This is a fascinating work that rewards the casual listener and the scholar.

Pianist **Ursula Oppens** has taken up Nancarrow's cause and has recorded his demented *Tango?,* which he also made into a piano roll. The contrast between her performance on a concert grand and the recording on the composer's honky-tonk upright player piano is striking. Oppens also recorded *Two Canons for Ursula,* and her secure rhythm is remarkable (♦Music & Arts 4862, 2CD).

Nancarrow's works for ensembles are similar to the Studies in their focus on rhythm and tempo. String Quartet 1 (1945) is his major work from his early, pre-player piano period. The **Arditti Quartet** gives a taut, virtuoso reading of this already rhythmically complex work (♦Montaigne 782010).   MAGIL

Otto Nicolai (1810–1849)

The alert collector might have netted, over the years, a handful of Nicolai's songs, two recordings of the *Te Deum,* and one of the Mass in D. The composer's fame nonetheless rests almost entirely on the delightful *Merry Wives of Windsor* or, more likely, its oft-recorded overture, a compendium of the opera's best tunes. Verdi's *Falstaff* is certainly more sophisticated in its freedom from operatic cliché; Nicolai's bumptious, down-to-earth treatment of the Falstaff story relies more heavily on stock formulas but is effective nonetheless and does Shakespeare no disservice. I can understand why we seldom hear *Martha* or *Oberon* or *Königskinder,* but *Die lustigen Weiber von Windsor* (to give it its proper German title) is so accessible and so skillfully crafted that its neglect is a mystery.

There have been three stereo recordings, curiously linked in that the Annas of the first two went on to sing Frau Fluth next time around. Veteran conductor **Heger** with the Bavarian State Opera set a still-unsurpassed standard in 1963 (♦EMI 69348, 2CD). His Falstaff is the unflappable Frick, a splendid actor with an unmistakable timbre and a commanding presence. His granitic voice moves nimbly, despite its bulk, and he throws himself wholeheartedly into his portrayal. Mathis's pretty voice has enough substance to make Anna into more than a sweet young thing, and Wunderlich is a paradigm among Fentons. His account of his aria bursts with rich, incomparably juicy tone—one of the great masterpieces of tenor singing on records. The rest of the cast is less extraordinary, but Heger leads with palpable affection, and the singers deliver the dialogue with unaffected charm.

Klee boasts Moll's Falstaff, more suave than Frick but not quite so engaging an actor (♦Berlin 2046, 2CD). It's wonderful nonetheless to hear the music sung so sonorously. Having left Anna behind her, Mathis now turns out to be the best Frau Fluth on the complete recordings, her voice full and flexible, her manner properly mature. Donath's fresh, limpid Anna is captivating, but Schreier's Fenton sounds skeletal next to Wunderlich's. Klee, like Heger, is a sympathetic conductor (he leads the Berlin Staatskapelle), and he performs the opera uncut, but the dialogue is replaced by spoken narration, disruptive enough to lend the proceedings some artificiality.

Kubelik, with Bavarian Radio forces, offered yet another *Merry Wives* for our delectation (London). He found a third great Falstaff in Ridderbusch, slimmer of voice than Moll and less personable than Frick but still winning and perhaps the most aristocratic of the lot. (The character is, after all, "Sir" John Falstaff.) Ahnsjö has a sweeter voice than Schreier (though he's far below the Wunderlich class), and Wolfgang Brendel sings handsomely as Herr Fluth. Donath doesn't make the transition to Frau Fluth quite as successfully as Mathis; for all the loveliness of her singing, she sounds too girlish. This recording's Anna is a great disappointment, but the sound is excellent and the dialogue has been restored to the singers.

One notable collection of excerpts deserves mention, a set led by **Hans Löwlein** and available in Germany (DG). Three of the singers are especially noteworthy. Haefliger's Fenton approximates the Wunderlich standard more closely than either Schreier or Ahnsjö; Franz Crass's gorgeous, onyx-colored bass plumbs both the dignity and the buffoonery of Falstaff, and Evelyn Lear is an ideal Frau Fluth, playful yet womanly. Her coloratura is not only astonishingly fluent but also uncommonly telling—you can see the gleam in her eye as she schemes. It's most regrettable that these singers didn't record the opera complete.

LUCANO

ORCHESTRAL WORKS

Richly melodic, with a rhythmic elan and range of colors that elicited praise from Berlioz, Nicolai's Symphony in D has a rugged, resolute opening movement supported by a lyrical Adagio and a galumphing Scherzo, all leading up to one of the great hunting horn finales in all music. In this exhilarating feast for the horns **David Stern** stands proud, aided by rich and expansive sonics (♦MD+G 601 0832). **Rickenbacher** adopts more propulsive tempos but can't match Stern in the bracing final movement (Virgin).

Both Rickenbacher and **Jurowski** (♦Capriccio 10592) offer the same wide assortment of overtures, the well loved *Merry Wives of Windsor* set beside the strongly Verdian *Der Tempelritter* (The Knight Templar, based on Scott's *Ivanhoe*) and *Die Heimkehr des Verbannten* (The Homecoming of the Exile), while both Jurowski and Stern share the sorely neglected *Fantaisie et Variations Brillantes on 'Norma'*, Nicolai's heartfelt homage to Bellini. In this remarkable repast for piano and orchestra Friedrich Höricke's delicate touch and pearly tone with Jurowski far surpass Claudius Tanski's more matter-of-fact traversal with Stern. Only Rickenbacher offers the glorious *Weihnachtsouvertüre*, no mere string of Christmas carols but a richly satisfying work culminating in a grand choral setting of the Lutheran hymn *Vom Himmel Hoch*, an experience not to be missed. The collector seeking lush Romantic fare won't want to be without any of them.

HALLER

Carl Nielsen (1865–1931)

For many years Nielsen's music was a victim of those mindless pairings—HaydnandMozart, BrucknerandMahler, DebussyandRavel—in his case with Sibelius, where he was shrugged off as the junior partner. His music was slow to win recognition for its distinct individuality and to gain champions beyond his homeland. Robert Simpson's 1952 book on the composer and Bernstein's 1962 recording of Symphony 5 were landmarks in the slow but steady progress his music has made in the past half-century toward a secure and continuing place on the musical scene.

Nielsen grew throughout his career. With roots in the high-Romantic idiom of Brahms and the Scandinavian Romantic nationalism of Gade and Svendsen, he evolved a highly personal style marked by unsentimental craftsmanship and a deeply humanistic philosophy. He was firmly grounded in counterpoint and made regular recourse to fugal textures. He rejected emphatically the modernism of Stravinsky or

Bartók and the doctrinaire ideology of atonalism, but he wasn't afraid to experiment with new possibilities of color and harmony that could be quite astringent. At the same time, he never lost touch with his rural and peasant origins, and he returned regularly to an unforced folksiness or spontaneous lyricism.

Nielsen was recognized in his later years as Denmark's greatest living composer, and his music was performed and recorded by colleagues and disciples whose classic performances have by no means been replaced by subsequent waves of international attention. Happily, Danacord has gathered these into "The Historic Carl Nielsen Collection," in six volumes referred to below.

SYMPHONIES

Simpson's book helped crystallize the image of Nielsen as first and foremost a symphonist; save for the Wind Quintet, the six symphonies have become his most familiar and most frequently recorded music, and constitute our inevitable starting point.

The recordings by the pioneer Nielsen conductors are gathered in sequence in Vol. 1 of Danacord's series (351/53, 3CD). Recorded between 1950 and 1959, all but one of them are live performances conducted by **Thomas Jensen** (3, 4, 6), **Erik Tuxen** (1, 5), and **Launy Grøndahl** (2). Additionally, Vol. 6 (365/7, 3CD) contains two earlier recordings, one of Jensen leading 2. Combining those releases with the reissue of Jensen's Decca recordings from the early '50s (Dutton 2502), it becomes possible to assemble a complete cycle of all six done by Nielsen's most important Danish exponents. In addition, Tuxen's recordings of 3 and 5 have been reissued (Dutton 1207). All these recordings are, of course, mono, varying in quality from studio sound to coarse concert tapings, but they represent the foundation of the interpretive tradition in these works and are essential for serious study.

To date, only one other Danish-born conductor—Ole Schmidt—has completed a full recorded cycle, a measure of how much a part of the international repertoire they have become; made in London in 1973–74, it has been reissued (Unicorn-Kanchana 2000, with Simpson's outstanding written notes, or individually). Schmidt achieved earnest and certainly reliable performances, but they only rarely rise to perceptive heights. At almost the same time, **Blomstedt** made the first of two complete cycles. This was part of the most comprehensive recording of Nielsen's complete orchestral works (six symphonies, three concertos, seven shorter pieces); originally released by Seraphim in the US, only the symphonies (plus two short pieces) have been reissued (EMI 565306, 1+2; 565415, 3+4; 565867, 5+6). Blomstedt I offered good performances, but they soon proved noncompetitive. Blomstedt II, on the other hand, was made in 1988–90 during the conductor's tenure with the San Francisco Symphony; first issued as three individual CDS (♦London 425607, 1+6; 430280, 2+3; 421524, 4+5), they have now been reissued in two bargain-rate 2CD sets, with related (mostly Blomstedt) recordings added (♦Decca 460985, 1–3, with *Maskarade Overture* and *Aladdin* Suite; 460988: 4–6, with *Little Suite* and *Hymnus amoris*). Blomstedt II is a step up in interpretation, consistently of high quality—perceptive, cogently realized with splendid playing and well-balanced sound, and in some cases competitive standouts. These low-priced reissues are a clear best buy.

Two cycles were left incomplete. It's ironic that **Bernstein** never completed a full set (his sensational recording of 5 ignited the international Nielsen boom, and his controversial version of 3 helped further it); his 2 and 4 were disappointing, and though he also recorded the two wind concertos, he never got to 1 and 6. A jumping-on-the-bandwagon act by

Ormandy yielded the two missing symphonies and four shorter pieces, if in rather stiff and cold renditions; all this Bernstein/Ormandy material has been assembled in a boxed set, which is the fullest orchestral package at the moment but, it must be stressed, in rather inconsistent and uneven performances (♦Sony 45989).

There is also **Chung**'s projected cycle of Nielsen's orchestral works with the Gothenburg Symphony; between 1983 and 1992 he recorded 1–3 and 5, plus the three concertos and some short pieces, issued as four single CDs (BIS). When this project broke down, BIS borrowed 4 and 6 by **Neeme Järvi** (with the same orchestra) from DG to create a boxed set of the symphonies and concertos (♦BIS 614/16, 4CD). In turn, DG issued its set of all six with Järvi (437507). While the Järvi versions are quite satisfactory, if rarely outstanding, Chung's performances are among the best to be had and mark him, in my opinion, as the Nielsen conductor of our time, even with his series left incomplete.

Two Finnish conductors have given us cycles: **Paavo Berglund** with the Royal Danish Orchestra (RCA 7701, 1+4; 7884, 2+5; 60427, 3+6) and **Salonen,** who virtually launched his precocious career in a Nielsen cycle with the Swedish Radio Symphony (CBS/Sony 42321, 1; 44934, 2; 46500, 3+6; 42093, 44547, 5, with other Nielsen material). Whereas Berglund's recordings parallel Järvi's (substantial and consistently reliable but only occasionally top-drawer) Salonen's readings are slick and superficial, though they can't be dismissed out of hand.

Chandos has released two full cycles, each issued first as three separate CDs and then in a boxed set. **Bryden Thomson** and the Royal Scottish Orchestra began their series vigorously, but became variable in quality as they went along (8880, 1+2; 9067, 3+5; 9047, 4+6; 9163, all three). With the Royal Stockholm Philharmonic, **Rozhdestvensky** became bogged down in stolid monumentality (9260, 1+4; 9300 2+3; 9367, 5+6; 7094, all three).

Two conductors working with provincial orchestras have also recorded the symphonies on individual discs. **Edward Serov,** with the Odense Symphony, offers a series noteworthy for the shorter items used as fillers, often interesting rarities (♦Kontrapunkt 32157, 1; 32178, 2; 32203, 3; 32193, 4; 32171, 5; 32210, 6). Serov's interpretations are knowing and sound, nicely blending traditional Danish and international approaches, but let down by provincial orchestral playing and indifferent sound. **Leaper** has a really good ensemble to work with in the National Symphony Orchestra of Ireland, but his leadership is lifeless and rarely shows much insight, either stylistic or musical (Naxos). His series is less than no bargain, especially in the face of Blomstedt II.

Three new cycles appear to be in the making. Two of them have the advantage of using new critical editions of the scores, and **Douglas Bostock** makes a special point of this in his projected series (Classico, with 2, 3, and 5 now out). **Schønwandt** has achieved two discs, containing 2 and 3 and 4 and 5 (Dacapo). A third cycle by **Saraste,** so far with 3 and 6, and 4 and 5, is shaping up as unconventional, taking a sometimes divergent and provocative interpretive direction (Finlandia).

All these cycles will be referred to as necessary in considering the individual symphonies.

1. At least four recordings stand out. **Previn**'s memorable recording in his London Symphony days is a benchmark that has been reissued in England (♦RCA 21296, with 4, in the "Classical Navigator" series). A spacious, warm, full-blooded, romantic approach that caught the floodtide of Nielsen's first creative surge, it still outstrips all competition. **Chung** likewise develops a Brahmsian heft and a passionate ardor, captured handsomely in a broad, warmly shaped performance: If sought

individually, it's particularly recommended in its original issue (♦BIS 454, with an outstanding Flute Concerto and *Imaginary Journey* Overture). On the other hand, **Thomson**'s performance is a good argument for distancing the score somewhat from romantic richness, a tad less sensitive stylistically but bracingly lithe and propulsive, in one of the best items in his cycle (♦Chandos). Working in the Jensen tradition, **Blomstedt II** offers a solid balance of romantic feeling with good overall shape (♦Decca).

Kamu is slightly lower on the scale but still worth considering (Classico 115, with Sibelius's 7). He follows Thomson's path, delivering the work as a young man's score, fresh and outgoing, but without any of the romantic padding Nielsen was trying to escape. If lacking the sheen of more prestigious ensembles, his orchestra is able, and a good cut above **Serov**'s, who is in the Previn tradition but whose inadequate orchestra rules him out (Kontrapunkt). **Järvi** is meaty and rather Tchaikovskian, but a little simplistic (DG). **Berglund** is sturdy but rather too weighty (RCA), and **Rozhdestvensky** never gets off the ground (Chandos). **Ormandy**'s old Philadelphia performance is shallow and the sound is glassy (Sony). Last but by no means least is **Thomas Jensen**'s classic version, still valid in its reissue (♦Dutton 2502, with 5).

2 ("*De Fire Temperamenter*"). Nielsen's clever essay portraying "The Four Temperaments" is a wonderful interpretive opportunity, and from Jensen on, many conductors have met its challenges with imagination. **Jensen** himself, in his 1947 78 rpm recording, seen through some HMV/EMI revivals on LP, still provides a locus classicus for the work.

In this score, **Bernstein** is strangely listless and unresponsive, in what sounds more like a preliminary reading than a finished performance (Sony). **Serov**'s version is also miscalculated in some of its tempos (Kontrapunkt), while **Schønwandt** is bland, stiff, and spiritless, in mediocre sound (Marco Polo). **Salonen** is, as usual, mostly superficial, though this is probably the best (or least uninteresting) of his set, and his filler helps make him a plausible choice (CBS/Sony 44934, with *Aladdin*). More honest vitality and stylistic sense are shown by **Douglas Bostock,** brightly recorded, and using a corrected edition of the score in what is announced as Vol. 1 of a new "Carl Nielsen Edition" (♦Classico 296, with 5).

Berglund is strong, solid, and sonorous, nicely contrasting the four character types (♦RCA 7884). Their moods are more blatantly differentiated, indeed overstated, by **Järvi** (DG), and **Rozhdestvensky** is just plain ponderous and overweight, quite out of scale with this work's wit and spirit (Chandos). **Thomson** is at the other extreme; flowing and supple, in beautifully focused sound (Chandos). (His development in this work can be traced against an earlier, quite full-blooded broadcast performance on Carlton 91492, with Horenstein's 5.)

Somewhere in between come three other recordings. **Morton Gould** was grossly underestimated as a conductor (and much better, I think, than as a composer); his performance with the Chicago Symphony still stands up admirably as imaginatively shaped, spirited, heartily satisfying, and splendidly played (♦RCA 40492, with Clarinet Concerto; also in the "Classical Navigator" series, 29255). **Blomstedt II** is impeccable in his pacing, while playing and sound are admirable; he is perhaps the most direct successor to Jensen (Decca). But **Chung** digs just a bit more thoughtfully into the different humors (especially in his probing slow movement), and he leavens his choice of tempos with just the right flexibility and rubato (♦BIS 247, with *Aladdin,* or in the composite set).

In so accessible and attractive a score as this, there can be no best version, but depending on the approach you desire, the last four offer the best choices.

3. Subtitled *"Sinfonia espansiva,"* with its inspired mix of exuberance, tunefulness, waltz evocations, and pastoral reflection (including wordless solos from two singers in the slow movement), this wonderful score marks the completion of Nielsen's maturation at the outer limits of the Romantic tradition and is one of the most immediately attractive of his works.

Erik Tuxen's classic 1946 recording has been reissued, and few subsequent LPs were as effective (Dutton 1207, with 5). **Bernstein**'s extroverted 1965 recording, made in Copenhagen at the Centennial festivities, is a marvelous testament to his first enthusiasm for the composer, though flawed by one of his typical eccentricities—exaggerated slow tempos in the finale.

Two other major conductors have given us curious might-have-beens. A historical BBC recording (date unstated) by **Horenstein,** in mono sound, proves to be stiff and fussy (Intaglio). **Ehrling,** a Nielsen conductor who could knock your socks off in live performances, should have given us a full cycle of the symphonies, but this erratic, studio-hating conductor never recorded any of them commercially. A Nielsen 3 with the Danish National Orchestra, captured in concert at the Kennedy Center in 1984, is an impressive performance, but rather too calculated and curiously cool (Audiofon). **Serov** is intelligent but too rigid, though with particularly good recorded sound (Kontrapunkt). **Salonen** is even more than usually vapid and expendable (Sony). In the first disc of his series, **Schønwandt** is able to convey only a shadowy and unsettled conception of the score's rich possibilities (Dacapo).

Berglund is robust, impassioned, and meaty, in gutsy sound, if at the expense of the more delicate elements (RCA). **Järvi** follows a rather single-minded conception of the work as robustly rustic and full of earthy spirit; it's a little short on contrasts but quite infectious, with unusually good realizations of the vocalises (♦DG). **Thomson,** by comparison, is all intellect, imparting logical shape but lacking heart. At least he's not as off-base as **Rozhdestvensky,** who finds only Slavic gloom in this diverse Nordic work (Chandos). **Blomstedt II** is one of his best performances, beautifully shaped and full of penetrating rhythmic insights, and in the single-CD release it's ideally paired with his splendid 2 (♦Decca). Yet despite his small margin of superiority in the playing of his San Francisco orchestra and Decca's sharply focused sonics, my top recommendation is **Chung;** his recording best captures the work's ebullience, its dramatic tensions and releases (♦BIS 321, with Clarinet Concerto, and in the composite set).

The two latest entries are in ongoing series. **Bostock** offers a strong, propulsive, and highly effective performance (♦Classico 297). It isn't in the top echelon but acquires special interest by giving II twice, the second time with the instrumental options (clarinet, trombone) Nielsen suggested as alternatives to the vocalise singers (soprano, tenor/baritone)—a hardly adequate substitute but it's fascinating to hear the composer's original and bolder intentions. For fillers there are not only the conventional *Helios* Overture and the fullest yet realization of his hymn paraphrase in tribute to the *Titanic* tragedy but the first recordings of the composer's orchestral versions of two of his songs.

In the second disc of his series, **Saraste** presents an unconventional 3: sharply analytical, finding greater depths and more ambiguous corners in the work (Finlandia 29714, with 6). A key to this, beyond crisp delineation of inner parts and often overlooked details, is his increased emphasis on the brass parts, generating more strength and power. This isn't an idyllic 3 but a realization that draws the score closer to the harsher ground of Nielsen's subsequent major orchestral works. It may not be the "Espansiva" to live with always, but it offers a fascinating alternative perspective.

4 (*"Det Uudslkkelige"*). Nielsen called this "The Inextinguishable" in an analogy to the force of life itself. Some critics consider it the greatest of his symphonies. It's the first of two in which he responded to WWI and its aftermath, and the first to apply most fully his principles of progressive tonality in the service of a philosophical program, representing the struggle and triumph of affirmation and humane values against forces of violence and negation.

Going back to LP days and on down, the floor has been littered with recording failures, **Mehta**'s among them. **Launy Grøndahl**'s early and classic HMV/EMI presentation remains an interpretative model, but it's done in by the poor sonics of its day. **Markevitch** scored a near miss in a knowingly shaped performance spoiled by misjudged recorded sound. In this he was preceded by **Barbirolli,** whose 1963 version isn't particularly probing and was poorly recorded; it resurfaced for a while with improved sound but little competitive value otherwise (Angel). **Menuhin**'s maundering and vapid treatment is even more spineless (Virgin). **Andrew Davis** offers a lucid rendition that sacrifices momentum and emotional impact to abstract clarity (also Virgin). **Thomson** follows a somewhat similar rationale; though he makes a strong argument for this work as a spacious intellectual drama, he leaves the listener uninvolved (Chandos). Still lower in this bin is **Bernstein,** who just seems to go through the motions without any of the commitment or insight, much less the intensity, you expect of him (Sony).

Serov is intelligent if, as always, orchestrally handicapped—though he does have some compelling moments, including a lilting finale, with an unusually sharp rendering of the climactic timpani duel (Kontrapunkt). At least his work is honest next to **Salonen**'s empty slickness (Sony). **Karajan** achieved a more deceptive slickness; he seems to be generating excitement but soon proves to be creating calculated effects of shallow spectacle without conviction or feeling (DG). **Rattle**'s recording is fussy and so deliberate that it bogs down badly and becomes just plain elephantine, despite lovely orchestral playing (EMI). **Rozhdestvensky** builds to a certain ultimate power, but he's much too stolid along the way (Chandos). **Schønwandt** is hardly any better in the second volume of his cycle; he displays a degree of uncertainty and diffidence that's relieved only belatedly in a somewhat fiery finale with well-captured timpani duels, but the overall conception is muddled (Dacapo).

By contrast, **Järvi** rushes headlong in pursuit of drama, merely skimming the surface of the peaceful *Poco allegretto* interlude, and achieving powerful moments at the expense of an overall sense of shape in an interpretation not fully ripened (DG). **Berglund,** on the other hand, is able to achieve drama without sacrifice: He's in his element here, building slowly with fierce and cumulative conviction; the Royal Danish Orchestra plays its heart out for him, and the great timpani duel in the finale is perhaps the best realized on records (♦RCA). **Blomstedt II** is close behind, offering an electrifying interpretation and fervent playing, if compromised slightly by rather brittle and edgy sound (♦Decca).

Two newcomers and two old-timers need to be considered as well. **Saraste**'s recording offers a carefully thought out and powerful performance, though his tendency to linger over some passages and details sometimes dilutes the flow, while the recorded sound, like Blomstedt's, is somewhat brittle and harsh (♦Finlandia 21439, with 5; 81922, 2CD, with Violin and Clarinet Concertos, etc.). **Ulf Schirmer**'s recording is a real sleeper, offering an unforced but steadily involving and ultimately gripping account, again with a riveting timpani duel (♦Decca 452486, with *Hymnus amoris* and *Little Suite*).

Of the oldies, there is **Alexander Gibson**'s exciting, impassioned, yet remarkably well-balanced performance, a version fully justifying its revival despite the rather thin sound of his Scottish Orchestra (♦Chandos 6524, with short works by Nielsen and Sibelius). Above all, there is the most exciting version ever recorded, the white-hot performance by the underrated **Jean Martinon** in his Chicago Symphony years, a recording that countless critics have been begging ♦RCA to reissue. Awaiting Martinon, your best bets are Berglund, Blomstedt, and Schirmer.

5. The struggle between forces of darkness and light, negativism and affirmation, violence and humanity, are distilled in this symphony even more directly than in 4, in one of the great symphonic dramas. The first recording was by **Tuxen** in 1950 (Dutton 1207, with 3), but a subsequent one, under **Jensen** in 1954, still sets the standard for balanced musicality (♦Dutton 2502, with 1). **Horenstein**'s LP, monumentally eloquent if you prefer a reserved and studied approach, has also been revived (♦Unicorn-Kanchana 2023, with *Saga-Dream*). There is a later and handsomely parallel Horenstein performance in a 1971 broadcast recording (Carlton 91492, with Thomson's 2).

An Amsterdam concert recording by **Kondrashin** was a worthy memorial to a great conductor in a powerful performance more architectural than idiomatic or gripping (Philips 438283, with Sibelius's 5). Much the same can be said for **Kubelik**, whose careful but somewhat too cautious approach to the work was captured in a 1986 concert performance in Copenhagen (EMI 565182, with Dorati in Sibelius pieces). Excess caution likewise bedevils **Andrew Davis,** who only belatedly converts his massive propulsion into genuine excitement at the end (Virgin). **Rozhdestvensky** reminds me somewhat of Horenstein, but with little of the latter's sense of structural cohesion, offering merely ponderous and deliberate monumentality (Chandos).

Schønwandt again offers incoherence and uncertainty, with a Part I central section more tragic than affirmative, and fatally understated solos for side drum and clarinet; there's no stirring drama or consistency of vision. **Serov** presents some very fine details and inflections but overall is too stiff, though he has fine recorded sound (Kontrapunkt). Again, though, he has more integrity than **Salonen,** who postures his way through glitzy but empty motions (Sony). **Leaper**'s limp and lifeless idea of the work wastes some really fine playing by his Irish orchestra (Naxos).

Alexander Gibson is outstanding among the old-timers; his 1978 recording—exciting and richly satisfying—is a welcome restoration (♦Chandos 6533, with *Helios* Overture and pieces by Sibelius). The champion survivor is **Bernstein,** whose 1962 reading is one of the great Nielsen recordings (♦Sony 47598, with 3, or in the composite set). An impassioned, sweeping rendition that takes the full measure of the score's power in both its nasty and its uplifting dimensions, it's indispensable. Some may find more probing detail, if not also equal power, in **Saraste**'s version; it's certainly a fine rendition (♦Finlandia 21439, with 4). **Thomson** is altogether too calculated, with a fine realization of the relentless negativism in the first half's march episodes but with a deliberate finale lacking in joyous release (Chandos).

Berglund has a greater strength and sonority, but he also sacrifices the extrovert effects to a reserved deliberation (RCA). **Bostock**'s recording in the "Carl Nielsen Edition" has the benefit of a new critical edition of the text, which clarifies many details; it is, in addition, beautifully shaped, lucidly clear, and handsomely played (♦Classico 296, with 2). Still, the clearest challenge to Bernstein comes from **Chung** (♦BIS 370, with Violin Concerto, or in the composite set). Distinctly a chance-taker, he builds his performance entirely around propulsiveness to a nearly

reckless degree, with breathtaking results and in splendid sound. Those who prefer a better balance of structure with dramatic effects may turn to the handsomely delivered **Blomstedt II** (♦Decca). In all, Bernstein, Chung, and Blomstedt are the leading choices, with Bostock close behind.

6 ("*Sinfonia semplice*"). Long the stepchild among the Nielsen six, this problem score reflects the interruption of the composer's creative development by disillusionment over his declining health and frustration at seeing himself overshadowed by flamboyant modernists of the avant-garde. There are moments, mostly in the satirical II, where Nielsen lashes out bitterly, but there's also a great deal of reflection and just plain whimsy along the way, in a work the composer surely didn't intend to be his last symphonic statement. It easily puts off listeners and its subtle crosscurrents require careful advocacy.

Jensen made the first attempt in his 1952 recording, though he had to spare his over-stressed strings by introducing cuts (in Danacord's Vol. 1). **Ormandy** had orchestral expertise to burn but showed little understanding of the work's intricacies in a glib run-through, thinly recorded (in Sony's composite set). The most convincing projection of the score's whimsical side, with its gossamer delicacy and subtlety of instrumentation, remains that by **Ole Schmidt,** the outstanding item in his complete cycle (♦Unicorn-Kanchana). **Salonen** seems to be aiming in the same direction, but his brisk skimming underplays any satire or dark patches to produce a kind of Nielsen *Nutcracker Suite* (Sony).

Many recordings have gone in other directions, sometimes too far. **Berglund,** for example, is simply too gutsy, quite losing the dimensions of never-never-land mystery (RCA). Some conductors have even looked to other composers for stylistic reference points. It's no surprise that **Horenstein,** in a concert performance in quite decent stereo, draws on the grotesqueries of Mahler for inspiration (Intaglio 7381). On the other hand, Mussorgsky seems to be the model for **Thomson** and **Järvi;** the former creates an interpretation of ironic and finally sinister power (♦Chandos), while the latter moves even further into an idiom of obsessive grimness and almost surrealistic savagery (DG).

Rozhdestvensky always seems to have Shostakovich in the back of his mind; his analytical strictness brings a certain eloquence to III and a better-than-normal order to IV, but completely neuters the phantasmagoric I and the bizarre II (Chandos). **Serov** displays a much better grasp of Nielsen's sardonic irony, satire, and pathos, and though he's limited by his orchestra's capacities, he produces a quite respectable performance (Kontrapunkt). With a better orchestra, **Leaper** treats the work as a series of disconnected episodes (Naxos). **Saraste**'s version raises the ghost of Shostakovich-to-come in a bold performance that avoids any pussyfooting and lets the angst and whimsy fall where they may (Finlandia). It's certainly the most successful projection of the work's unsettling qualities. **Blomstedt II** offers perhaps the most balanced and objective approach, though he fails to catch all the moody delicacy of I (Decca).

Schmidt and Thomson, backed by Blomstedt and Serov, are the leading possibilities for now, but this work, so strange and flippant, has secrets still to be revealed.

OTHER ORCHESTRAL MUSIC

Concert pieces

Nielsen had little sympathy for the programmatic idiom of the 19th-century symphonic poem and only occasionally ventured into writing shorter concert pieces. Still, short works of various kinds turn up recurrently in his output and confer attractive small-scale dimensions to the image he presents in larger ones. There are four core works in this category: the wonderful concert overture *Helios,* evoking the passage of the sun over the Aegean Sea in the course of a day; *Saga-Dream (Dream of Gunnar),* the closest Nielsen came to a romantic tone-poem; the impressionistic "Nature-Scene," *Pan and Syrinx;* and the rhapsodic overture *A Fantasy Journey to the Faeroe Islands.*

There are three single-disc surveys of these works. **Järvi**'s is appealing (♦DG 447757). Its largest components are excerpts from the opera *Maskarade* and a suite from the stage music for *Aladdin* (discussed below); he renders these and the four core works with spirit, rather too fast in *Helios* but otherwise quite effective. A second program of this kind was recorded by **Rozhdestvensky** (♦Chandos 9287). To the four core works, he adds the very early *Symphonic Rhapsody* that began life as the intended first movement of a projected symphony never completed, as well as the Vaughan-Williamsy *Bohemian-Danish Folk Tune Paraphrase* for strings, plus two rarities (one a youthful venture, the other a curious response to the sinking of the *Titanic*). Rozhdestvensky is slower and heavier than most conductors in his approach to much of this material, his *Helios* Overture a slow-motion contrast to Järvi's high-speed solar journey but a poetic one for all that. If his weighty, even ponderous treatment nearly crushes *Pan and Syrinx,* it results in a *Saga-Dream* that is powerfully impressive.

A third program is again heavily weighted toward stage music (excerpts from the two operas and one play), but includes *Saga-Dream, Pan and Syrinx,* and *Fantasy Journey,* as well as Nielsen's first published work, *Little Suite* for strings, a remarkably accomplished and perennially charming youthful effort. The Odense Symphony Orchestra is undeniably a provincial group not the equal of competing ensembles, but **Vetö** draws from it thoroughly credible performances (notably of *Saga-Dream*) in a release that's worth your attention (♦Big Ben 571-011). Finally, a program of music for strings, half of it by Grieg and the other half by Nielsen—*Little Suite, Bohemian-Danish Folk Tune Paraphrase,* and *Andante lamentoso* ("At the Bier of a Young Artist")—is given quite effective performances by the **Copenhagen Young Strings** (Classico 113). (It should be noted that *Little Suite* has been a common component of anthologies of Scandinavian music over the years.)

Many of these shorter pieces are sprinkled through releases of the symphonies or concertos. The grand-daddy of that practice is the first commercial recording of *Helios,* made in 1952 (Dutton 2502, with Symphonies 1+5). Of course, many of these works are represented in Danacord's series: Vol. 2 contains concert versions of *Little Suite, Helios,* and *Saga-Dream* conducted by **Tuxen,** and of *Pan and Syrinx* and *Andante lamentoso* led by **Jensen.** The more or less standard five pieces in **Blomstedt**'s generally reserved performances are in a bargain-rate reissue of the concertos (EMI 69758, 2CD). **Gibson**'s performances are particularly fine in their reissues: a big-hearted *Helios* (♦Chandos 6533, with Symphony 5) and *Fantasy Journey* and *Pan and Syrinx* (Chandos 6524, with 4), in each case with a pair of Sibelius pieces added.

The same three works in **Ormandy**'s rather stiff and brittle renditions are included in Sony's composite package (45989). **Jan Caeyers** leads superlative performances of *Little Suite* and *Pan and Syrinx,* as well as a late theater overture, *Love and the Poet* (♦Harmonia Mundi 901489, with Clarinet Concerto). **Chung** only got around to one of these items in his aborted Nielsen cycle, a rousing *Fantasy Journey* (♦BIS 454, with Symphony 1 and Flute Concerto). But **Salonen** used a number of them as fillers: *Little Suite* with Symphony 1 (CBS/Sony 42321); *Pan and Syrinx* with 2 (44934, plus *Aladdin*); *Helios* with 4 (42093), as well as *Fantasy Journey* in his disc of wind concertos

(53276, also with *Funen Spring*), all in well played if not notably distinctive performances.

But it's **Serov,** in his too-easily-dismissed symphony series, who has been most generous and enterprising in this regard. Sometimes his performances and often the novel material transcend his below-par recordings of the symphonies themselves. Thus there is *Helios* with his 1 (Kontrapunkt 32157); two very early little pieces for strings with 3 (32203); *Pan and Syrinx, Andante lamentoso,* and *Saga-Dream* with 4 (32193); *Bohemian-Danish Folk Tune* and *Symphonic Rhapsody* with 5 (32171); *Fantasy Journey* with 6 (32210); and there are also excerpts from theater music, considered below.

Theater music

Because it's common in Scandinavia for plays and operas to share the same theaters, it also became common for dramatic productions to use the available pit and its players for plays conceived with musical components; hence the frequent occurrence of incidental scores among the works of Nordic composers like Grieg and Sibelius. Nielsen wrote such stage music throughout his career, ever more in demand as his reputation grew. Some of his contributions involved short solo songs, and most of them are assembled in Vols. 4 and 5 of a Nielsen song series (♦Rondo 8327, 8329).

There are some 15 dramatic scores, besides the two operas. While Nielsen treated most of them offhandedly, leaving them unpublished, two were substantial, and the composer took them seriously enough to publish them, at least in part. The music he wrote for a 1918 production of Adam Oehlenschläger's play *Aladdin* is the more familiar. Nielsen responded to its spirit of proto-Hollywood orientalism with a score of colorful and charming exotica, including one piece of para-Ivesian organized confusion. He immediately published three songs from his score as a set (for voice and piano), and these are in Vol. 4 of the songs series (♦Rondo 8327). But in 1926 he abstracted larger segments into a concert suite of seven orchestral movements (two with optional chorus), which has acquired some popularity.

The first recording, by **Svend Christian Felumb** in 1953, is now somewhat antiquated but still available in Vol. 2 of Danacord's series. Since then, there have been a number of recordings, by **Blomstedt** (♦Decca 425857, with *Maskarade Overture* and Grieg's *Peer Gynt Suites;* now in Vol. 1 of his symphony series, 460985), **Chung** (♦BIS 247, with Symphony 2), **Järvi** (♦DG 447757, with *Maskarade* excerpts and orchestral pieces), **Salonen** (♦Sony 44934, with Symphony 2 and *Pan and Syrinx*), and **Vetö** (Unicorn-Kanchana 9054, with *Funen Spring*). Any of these recordings will give pleasure; your choice will be affected by the couplings, though it should be noted that only Järvi and Salonen include the choral parts.

It's now possible to go beyond the Suite and the separate songs. The Danish Nielsen scholar, Torben Schousboe, has reconstructed the entire score for *Aladdin* as originally meant for use with the play, in a performing edition recorded by **Rozhdestvensky** (♦Chandos 9135). It's a delightful and fascinating romp that shouldn't be missed. It reveals just how imaginatively Nielsen responded to the play in music beyond what the Suite contains, and it also gives us a rare insight into the mechanics of a major Scandinavian theater score in full, before any filtration for concert use—*Peer Gynt,* move over!

The other major theater score Nielsen sought to salvage was composed in 1920 for a production of Helge Rode's patriotic allegory-play, *Moderen (The Mother).* The salvaging in this case proved only partial, resulting in dispersion of material into three separate categories.

Nielsen immediately published a good bit of his score, but in reduced form: eight songs (voice and piano) and five instrumental/orchestral pieces (piano), followed by alternate versions or arrangements of these and other segments. Of the eight splendid songs, several became great favorites, especially thanks to recordings by Aksel Schiøtz, while the last of them proved to be one of Nielsen's great patriotic hits (in various adaptations). The full eight as a group are in Vol. 5 of the song series (◆Rondo 8329).

Three miniatures for flute have been taken up as favorite examples of Nielsen's chamber music and may be found in a number of recordings, some discussed below. Of the original orchestral movements, all four (two scene Preludes, Menuet, and March) are available under **Serov** (Kontrapunkt 32210, with Symphony 6, etc.). **Vetö** included the Prelude to Scene 7 in his orchestral program (Big Ben 571-011). The Prelude to Scene 4 and the March, together with one of the flute miniatures and five of the songs (in their original orchestral garb), have been gathered as the major part of a valuable and highly satisfying program of (mostly) theater music conducted by **Frandsen** (◆Paula 18, with important bits from *Funen Spring* and *Grocers' Cantata*).

After the Schousboe/Rozhdestvensky *Aladdin,* the fullest Nielsen theater score available is one he composed in 1906 for Holger Drachmann's drama *Hr. Oluf han rider* (*Sir Oluf Rides Forth*), based on medieval Danish stories and songs about a knight's fatal (and wonderfully pre-Freudian) pre-nuptial encounter with the fairies. The original production was a failure, and from it Nielsen published little more than three songs in voice-piano arrangements (in Rondo's Vol. 5). But about half the original score (including the three songs and spoken passages), totaling some 37 minutes, has been re-assembled and recorded by **Vetö** in a program of Nielsen's theater music (◆BIS 641).

The indefatigable **Vetö** has been the most diligent explorer of Nielsen's extra-operatic stage music. He has recreated from manuscript sources the music for three productions presented in the outdoor theater of Dyrehavsbakken Park north of Copenhagen: for the tragedy *Hagbarth og Signe* (1910) and *Sankt Hans-Aften Spil* (St. John's Eve Play, 1913), both by Adam Oehlenschlæger, and for Harald Bergstedt's folkdrama *Ebbe Skammelsen* (1925), all for voices with small chorus and winds (the first of these calling for some early Viking horns known as *lours*). While there are no lost masterpieces here, there is a lot of really interesting and attractive music in them, and they offer valuable insights into Nielsen's stylistic development as well as his skills as a workaday musician (◆Kontrapunkt 32188).

Vetö has also dipped into five (mostly unpublished) theater scores for short selections (◆BIS 641, with *Hr. Oluf*). These extend from Nielsen's earliest such music, a flashy Prelude to a historical play, *En Aften paa Giske* (*An Evening at Giske,* 1889), to Sophus Michaëlis's play about Hans Christian Andersen's pining for Jenny Lind, *Amor og Digteren* (*Love and the Poet,* 1930), to which he contributed a brittle Overture and two songs (one of them omitted here). In between come selections from music for Ludvig Holstein's *Tove* (1908, one of four songs published), from *Willemoës,* about a Danish naval hero of the Napoleonic era (1908, two of five published songs and an orchestral Prelude), and *Cosmus* (1922, one of two unpublished songs). Once again, no spectacular finds, but a lot of lovely little gems. Vetö's offerings are duplicated by smaller gleanings from four of the scores he sampled (including the *Amor og Digteren* Overture) in **Frandsen**'s program (◆Paula 18, with *Moderen* excerpts). Note, too, that all the songs for these scores are in Rondo's Vols. 4 and 5, though only in their voice-piano forms.

One last theater score should be mentioned, a very early one (1894)

for Holger Drachmann's melodrama, *Snefrid.* Five unpublished orchestral movements are offered by **Serov** (Kontrapunkt 32178, with *Amor og Digteren* Overture and Symphony 2); he has also recorded the *Willemoes* Act 3 Prelude in another release (Kontrapunkt 32210, with Symphony 6, *Moderen,* and *Fantasy Journey*). To tie up more loose ends, the *Aften paa Giske* Overture is in **Rozhdestvensky**'s orchestral program (Chandos 9287), and that for *Amor og Digteren* has been recorded by **Jan Caeyers** (Harmonia Mundi 901489, with Clarinet Concerto, *Little Suite,* and *Pan and Syrinx*).

CONCERTOS

As with other idioms, Nielsen approached this one unconventionally, largely ignoring traditional form and exploring new structural possibilities. For his first venture into this genre, he turned to the instrument he knew best as a professional violinist (orchestral, not virtuoso). The other two resulted from his growing fascination with wind instruments, and from his intention to compose a solo work for each of his friends in the Copenhagen Wind Quintet, each with a form of its own and reflecting the personality of its dedicatee.

In LP years concerto pairings weren't unusual, especially of the two for winds, and there are two such now on CD. But the timings of all three add up neatly to the capacity of a single CD, and there are currently at least four releases that conveniently bring together the full trio. Two are Danish, one conducted by **Schønwandt** offering good but inconsistent performances (Chandos 8894), and another led by **Vänskä** where the pacing tends toward the relaxed (Kontrapunkt 32254). Most recently, we have a bargain-rate release conducted by the Dutch-born **Kees Bakels,** who demonstrates a deep knowledge of Nielsen's total style and a uncanny ability to relate each Concerto to its context in the composer's output. Above all, there is a lively cycle led by **Chung,** released first on the single CDs of his symphony series, then gathered together as a group (◆BIS 666; 614, in the Chung/Järvi composite set). Containing the nearbest Violin Concerto, one of the best Flute Concertos, and pretty much the best Clarinet Concerto, the Chung package is the one to have if you want the whole works. But an undeniable value is a reissue of **Blomstedt**'s 8LP set of Nielsen's orchestral works, revived as a bargain-rate CD (EMI 69758).

Clarinet Concerto. It enshrines its recipient, the assertive and temperamental Aage Oxenvad. Into this remarkable work—one of the most taxing and exposing ever written for the instrument—Nielsen poured some of the toughest, most astringent music of his late maturity. As fate would have it, Oxenvad was denied the opportunity to record it. The first recording was made instead in 1947 with **Louis Cahuzac** as soloist, John Frandsen conducting (Clarinet Classics 0002, with Wind Quintet and other pieces). It's an interesting memento, but Cahuzac's elegant French personality was too much at odds with the music's spirit. A more idiomatic if still somewhat restrained recording was made in 1954 by **Ib Eriksson** with Wöldike (in Vol. 2 of Danacord's series). That restrained side of the Danish temperament survives in **John Kruse**'s performance, accomplished but too much held down by the understatement and relaxed spirit that typifies Vänskä's conducting in the Kontrapunkt package.

Among other soloists who have had trouble capturing the work's strength of spirit is **Benny Goodman,** in a Chicago recording with Morton Gould; a genuinely able classical performer, Goodman is up to the work's technical demands but falls short in color and personality (RCA). **Håkan Rosengren** is a fluent and colorful player, but his approach is too relaxed and Salonen's support is bland and indifferent (Sony).

John Bruce Yeh and Dieter Kober are plucky but limited in personality and crude in accompaniment (Centaur). Philippe Cupper's performance is more polished but also rather cool and objective (Adda). Musically appealing, Janet Hilton is nevertheless much too gentle (Chandos). If you want manliness, then Kullervo Kojo will do nicely, in his strong performance with Finnish Radio forces under the probing Saraste (♦Finlandia 95873, with pieces by Sven Englund and Crusell; 81966, 2CD, with 4, 5, Violin Concerto, etc.).

I still cherish the wonderfully woody sound of John McCaw in an old Unicorn recording with Raymond Leppard that I wish would be reissued. A fascinatingly different approach is taken by Walter Boeykens, in a moving but almost too thoughtful and moody version, cast on an interestingly intimate scale (♦Harmonia Mundi, with short pieces). A parallel example of such an unconventional approach is displayed by Kevin Banks with Kees Bakels; bypassing the idea of portraying the tempestuous Oxenvad, Banks suggests the image of a thoughtful bystander reacting to all the terrible things being done to him, rather than that of a provocative antagonist joined in equal struggle—an introspective conception brought off beautifully, even if you don't agree with it (Naxos). By contrast, Stanley Drucker is a clarinetist of strong profile and his performance has long and justly been held in high esteem, but I wish Bernstein's accompaniment were not so stolid and grim (♦Sony 47599, with Flute Concerto and Hindemith's concerto, or in the composite set). Kjell-Inge Stevensson's perceptive version with Blomstedt is better balanced (♦EMI 69758, 2CD).

The last two entries are of foremost quality. Ole Schill, with Chung, brilliantly captures the work's aggressive and even abrasive qualities (♦BIS 321, with Symphony 3 and Maskarade excerpts, or in the concerto package or the composite set). Niels Thomsen, with Schønwandt, makes a well-balanced trade-off between astringency and warm-blooded strength, which probably best recaptures Oxenvad's style and character (♦Chandos 8894). Once more, there are many fine possibilities, with varying company.

Flute Concerto. This was composed for—and is a remarkably vivid portrait of—Nielsen's friend, Holger-Gilbert Jespersen. He gave what remains its best and most authoritative performance (♦Dutton 2505, with Clarinet Concerto and Maskarade excerpts). A refined yet whimsical and fully idiomatic performance in the Jespersen spirit by one of his students, the elegant Poul Birkelund, captured in a concert performance in 1958 with Jensen, is included in Vol. 2 of Danacord's series. (In Vol. 4 of that series, Birkelund can be heard alternatively in an arrangement of the Concerto for flute and piano by Emil Telmányi, recorded in 1947 with Christian Christiansen.)

Over the years, flutists have been picking up the work as a viable item for their repertoires and have recorded it among flute concertos by other composers (thus the agile and refined Aurèle Nicolet, with Masur pacing things a bit heavily in a Leipzig recording) (Philips 412728, with works by Reinecke and Busoni). Noam Buchman and Rumanian forces are enjoyable but rather too grand in scale (Olympia). Keith Bryan's recording is sprawling, diffuse, and unfocused (Premier). Petri Alanko's fine performance with Saraste is much more intense and strongly characterized (♦Ondine 802, with works by Ibert and Jolivet).

Turning to more Nielsen-focused releases, Mary Stolper is an amiable soloist with the Chicago Chamber Orchestra rather scruffy but devotedly conducted by Dieter Kober, long a Nielsen champion in the Chicago area (Centaur). Expendable for other reasons are two star figures. Rampal is, in fact, an admirably personable soloist, but he's given diffi-

dent support by conductor John Frandsen (CBS/Sony). Master-egoist Galway is memorable in a collection, not so much for his brash, vulgar, and (literally) overblown solo playing as for his far more perceptive work as conductor (RCA 6359, with Wind Quintet and short pieces). The same overblown, Galwayesque sound creeps into the work of Per Flemström (as it did somewhat into Alanko's playing), while Salonen, unexpectedly more alert than usual, offers a rather inflated accompaniment—though some may find this a strong performance (Sony 53276, with Clarinet Concerto, *Funen Spring*, and short pieces). The Galway excesses, altogether contradicting the dedicatee's portrait, are also in evidence in Gareth Davies's brash solo work with Kees Bakels, though the conductor's realization of the orchestral writing, if a bit outsized, points up just how typically Nielsenesque are its sonorities—an interesting perspective (Naxos).

Lisa Hansen is lower on the scale of sheen, with Dorrit Matson conducting: a thoroughly intelligent and tasteful performance, though the orchestral work is a bit scrawny (♦Centaur 2442, with Violin Concerto). Andràs Adorján delivers a relaxed and engaging performance, apparently following Vänskä's leisurely lead (Kontrapunkt 32254). Frantz Lemmser is even better in pointing up the work's engaging charm with Blomstedt (♦EMI 69758, 2CD). Toke Lund Christensen (a Birkelund student) is a deft and thoughtful soloist, but his work is swamped by Schønwandt's too-weighty support in too-grand sound (Chandos).

Something of the same problem afflicts Bernstein's treatment of the work, but Julius Baker's gentle playing makes for an interesting (and perhaps not inappropriate) tension of personalities in an interpretation of strong flavor (♦Sony 47599, with Clarinet Concerto and Hindemith's concerto, or in the composite set). The premier choice, however, may be a Rampal student, Patrick Gallois, who invests his playing with exactly the kind of character that recalls Jespersen's own self-portrait, in a deliberate and substantial but temperamental performance with finely pointed support from Chung (♦BIS 454, with Symphony 1 and short pieces, or in the composite set). With so many recordings to pick from, your choice will probably depend upon the coupled material.

Violin Concerto. Its stylistic ambiguities—no longer Romantic yet hardly modern—have delayed its absorption into the virtuoso repertoire, but it has slowly been attracting interest from an international range of soloists. Nielsen's son-in-law, Emil Telmányi, recorded it twice, first in 1947 in a 78 rpm version with Egisto Tango conducting and then in a 1951 concert performance with Fritz Busch on the podium. The latter was briefly available in a Danacord LP, while the former is available in Vol. 2 of Danacord's series. Kai Laursen was a fine Danish violinist and able Nielsen performer who was never able to record the work commercially, a loss suggested by a very idiomatic and skilled concert performance in 1978 with Janssons, preserved in a mediocre mono transcription as part of the violinist's massive "26 Danish Violin Concertos" set (Danacord 461/70, 10CD).

The concerto's actual LP debut was an unsatisfactory HMV venture, with Menuhin wanting the work to sound romantic while conductor (and Nielsen protégé) Wöldike disagreed. The best recording of the LP era was by the technically agile and stylistically sensitive Arve Tellefsen in Blomstedt's 8LP set, now reissued (♦EMI 69758, 2CD). But Tellefsen went on to an even better performance in his second recording, with the conductor this time Menuhin himself, a courteous but insipid supporter (Virgin). Another outstanding soloist let down by a weak conductor is Cio-Liang Lin with the diffident Salonen (Sony). Most recently, in one of their series of recordings together, **Vengerov** is full of virtuosic color, but he and Barenboim are somewhat tentative (Teldec).

The most balanced performances feature violinists who may not be absolutely the best but who do accomplished jobs with sympathetic conductors. Expressive and full-toned, **Kim Sjøgren** is backed well by Schønwandt (◆Chandos 8894). **Dong-Suk Kang** has a sweet if thinner tone but catches fire from Chung's conducting (◆BIS 370, with Symphony 5, or in the composite package). I quite like the tight, light, sharply focused tone of **Jonathan Carney,** who has a genuine feeling for the work's wit and charm, while Kees Bakels conveys better than many conductors how much this concerto belongs to the sonic world of Symphony 3 (Naxos).

There are also less stellar but quite attractive "provincial" versions. One is by **Jennifer Koh,** a warmly expressive and highly lyrical soloist with Vänskä (◆Kontrapunkt 32254). Another is by the very fluent Australian violinist **Adele Anthony,** understandingly supported by the smallish New York Scandia Symphony under Danish maestra Dorrit Matson (◆Centaur 2442, with Flute Concerto). One of the most thoughtful and songful versions is by **Henrik Hannisdal,** with warm-hearted Norwegian orchestral support under Terje Mikkelsen (◆Finlandia 81966, 2CD, with Symphonies 4+5, Clarinet Concerto, etc.). There is, then, a nice range of choices to consider in an underrated work that will be a discovery for many.

CHAMBER MUSIC

Vol. 4 of Danacord's Nielsen series contains nearly all of Nielsen's published works for chamber combinations, many of them in vintage performances by musicians closely associated with the composer, and still to be reckoned with in present-day comparisons.

Trained and initially employed as a violinist, Nielsen understandably turned to that instrument throughout most of his career, at least until his fascination was transferred to winds in his later years. Notwithstanding the fact that his first instrumental writing was a pair of simple Fantasy Pieces for oboe and piano, Nielsen took seriously to the predictable form of the sonata for violin and piano. Discarding an early attempt from his student days, he produced his official Sonata 1 in 1895; No. 2 came in 1912. They vividly represent stages of his development, 1 still drawing unashamedly upon a sunny and outgoing Brahmsian spirit, 2 on the threshold of the period that produced Symphony 4 and the two sets of piano variations, tough and probing.

No more in this form followed, but in the late '20s Nielsen returned to the violin, this time unaccompanied in the style of Bach's works (and as part of his deep study of older musical traditions), to produce two astonishingly serious and virtuosic pieces, *Prelude and Theme with Variations* and *Preludio e Presto,* meant as display pieces for his son-in-law, Hungarian violinist Emil Telmányi. Ironically, Telmányi never recorded these works. **Kai Laursen**'s stunning 1958 recordings are happily resuscitated in Danacord's Vol. 4. The same volume, however, contains the recordings **Telmányi** did make of the two Sonatas: 1 with Christian Christiansen in 1936, and 2 with Victor Schiøler in 1954. (Also in this volume is Telmányi in his arrangement for violin of the first of the Fantasy Pieces for oboe, recorded with Gerald Moore.) This violinist was never perfectly tidy in his intonation and his later playing can be a little scrappy, but there is no denying the close connection of his performances to the composer's own thinking.

Latter-day recordings have not been numerous, and for convenience, your best bet is a fine release of all Nielsen's works for violin—the two sonatas with piano, the two unaccompanied pieces—in accomplished

and thoroughly idiomatic performances by **Søren Elbæk** with Morten Mogensen (◆Kontrapunkt 32200). The sonatas themselves are given fresh but also idiomatic performances by "**The Danish Duo,**" Frank Jarlsfelt and Johannes Søe Hansen (Classico 118, with music by Peter Lange-Müller). But the most full-blooded and romanticized approach—and one that removes the music from an exclusively Danish purview—is offered by **Mordkovitch** with Clifford Benson, though unfortunately it's skimpy value without any coupled material (◆Chandos 8598).

As a practicing violinist, Nielsen was from the start drawn to the world of the string quartet. Several juvenile quartet movements and a fully complete quartet, all from the mid-1880s, are preserved in manuscript, and in 1888 he produced his only String Quintet (with viola), an ardent and attractive work just preceding *Little Suite*. Telmányi, Nielsen's second wife, and their three strapping daughters gave the Quintet its scrappy recording premiere as a family ensemble in a semicommercial Danish LP. Since then, the work has enjoyed a technically more secure performance from the augmented **Carl Nielsen Quartet** (DG 431156, with the Quartets) and an even more ripe and alert performance by members of the **Academy of St. Martin in the Fields Chamber Ensemble** (◆Chandos 9258, with Svendsen's Octet and Romance).

In 1887 Nielsen composed his Quartet in G Minor, publishing it belatedly, after revision, as his second, Op. 13. This was followed (in order of composition) by his designated 1 (1890), 3 (1897–98), and 4 (1906), actually Op. 19 but updated as Op. 44 when he revised it for publication in 1919. During the last quarter-century of his life, however, he never actively returned to the form, despite being urged to address this important idiom in his full maturity. As a result, his contributions to the quartet literature, though enjoyable and undeniably interesting as they grow along with him, are essentially reflections of his early development, when he was still acknowledging titular tonalities.

All four published quartets are found in Vol. 4 of the Danacord series: 3 recorded in 1946 by the **Erling Bloch Quartet,** the other three in the early '50s by the **Koppel Quartet.** These performances obviously reflect an established local playing tradition, but they are undistinguished artistically or sonically. There were some recordings of individual quartets over the LP years, though not in large quantity. By far the outstanding traversal was by the **Copenhagen Quartet,** released here in a series of LP singles (with various pairings) by Vox-Turnabout: warm, bighearted, sonorous performances that made a strong case for the works as genuinely enjoyable music, but, alas, never revived on CD.

Of LP-transfer or CD vintage, however, we have had four complete cycles. The oldest, a re-assemblage of '70s recordings by the **Carl Nielsen Quartet** and others, was fleshed out and reissued by the group's Quintet, plus a kindred version of the Wind Quintet (DG 431156). The performances were earnest but rather thin and superficial. Much warmer and more flowing readings of the four quartets, plus the quintet and *Andante lamentoso* (which was really for string quintet in the first place), are offered by the **Kontra Quartet,** a very attractive package (◆BIS 503/4). The **Danish Quartet** offers somewhat less polished but more intense renditions, without the Quintet but with the only recording of all five surviving quartet movements of Nielsen's student days (◆Kontrapunkt 32150/51).

Two cycles issued on pairs of separate singles, just two quartets to each disc, sacrifice any additional material. The sacrifice is justifiable if you seek a best buy, which is offered by the **Oslo Quartet** (Naxos 553908, 1+2; 553907, 3+4). Despite some slightly strained ensemble playing and sometimes weak first-violin tone, this group plays with expansive sweep, strong feeling, and confident stylistic sense in generally handsome versions. There is no such sacrificial value in the **Zapolski Quartet**'s series (Chandos 9365, 1+4; 9817, 2+3). Their fussy and idiosyncratic versions defy the composer's rejection of overblown sentimentalities and turn Nielsen's fresh and bracing ensemble writing into inchoate, pseudo-Slavic mush.

Another Slavic approach comes from the Czech players of the **Kubin Quartet** in 1 and 2 (Centaur). Their pacings are generally more brisk and certainly more vital, with lean and uncluttered tone; lyricism is stressed but not milked to death, while faster movements are full of youthful ardor. If (as I hope) the Kubins match this with a second disc to fill out the whole set, theirs would be a cycle to take seriously. The same can be said of another single CD: the **Vertavo Quartet** (two pairs of Norwegian sisters) gives fresh and exuberant performances of 1 and 2, capturing their echoes of Mendelssohn, Brahms, and Dvořák (Simax 1128). They too would do well to complete a cycle.

Nielsen's transition from strings to winds in chamber music writing is delightfully exemplified in the curious *Serenata in vano* for clarinet, bassoon, horn, cello, and double-bass. Composed in 1914 at the request of friends in a traveling ensemble who wanted a special showpiece, this short work is a charming, quasi-programmatic evocation of a (futile) serenade by a group of country musicians. Within less than a decade, Nielsen was caught up in a mounting fascination with wind instruments; his interest in Mozart's wind writing was given point as he followed the work of friends who made up the Royal Danish Orchestra's wind quintet. He wrote that great masterpiece, his own Quintet for Winds, for them in 1922.

From its success came a project that yielded as its most spectacular fruit his Flute and Clarinet Concertos, parts of his planned but uncompleted cycle of concertos for each of the five instruments (and instrumentalists) in the group. He did manage a short rain-check for the horn, *Canto serioso* for horn and piano (1928–30). But in 1921, as part of an incidental score for the patriotic play *Moderen,* he wrote three entrancing miniatures for flute (one unaccompanied, the other two with harp or viola) that further augment his wind output—which would undoubtedly have been still richer had his life not ended so very prematurely.

A number of recordings combine some or all of this music in useful groupings. The obvious starting-point is Danacord's Vol. 4, which contains pioneer recordings by musicians closely associated with the composer, recorded in 1936/7 within only a few years of Nielsen's death. The Wind Quintet was recorded by four of the five musicians for whom he wrote it: Svend Christian Felumb, Aage Oxenvad, Hans Sørensen, and Knud Lassen, with Holger Gilbert Jespersen replacing the original flutist (Paul Hagemann); the *Serenata* involves Oxenvad, Sørensen, and Lassen again, with cellist Louis Jensen and bassist Louis Hegner—the last of whom originally requested it. The playing is spare, precise, and highly personalized, and interesting particularly for clarinetist Oxenvad's only recording. (These two recordings are also on Clarinet Classics 0002, with the Cahuzac/Frandsen Clarinet Concerto.)

The combination of *Serenata* with the Wind Quintet may also be found in a recording by the **Scandinavian Chamber Players** in a program of Danish music (Classico 184), and the *Serenata* pops up here and there in chamber group programs. But Nielsen specialists will want to consider these works first of all in comprehensive collections of his full wind output. There have been three of these, two of LP vintage. The earliest, by the augmented **Lark Wind Quintet,** hasn't survived (Lyrichord and MHS), but that by the **Athena Ensemble** has been reissued (♦Chandos 8680). Since then we have the collection by the augmented **Bergen**

Wind Quintet (♦BIS 428). Both groups offer fine performances; the Athena players have a leaner sound in a very bright, close recording, while the Bergen group plays a bit more flexibly, with somewhat more feeling for sonority, if in less detailed recorded sound. The BIS program has the advantage of adding to the standard grouping two small wind trifles, one from the very beginning of Nielsen's career and the other from the very end.

There have been three trimmed-down Nielsen wind programs. In LP years, members of the **West Jutland Chamber Ensemble** offered adequate but undistinguished performances of the Wind Quintet, the three *Moderen* pieces, *Serenata in vano,* and *Andante lamentoso,* though only the last was revived for reissue (DG, in the Quartet set). But another Danish group, the **Jutland Ensemble,** is heard in the Wind Quintet, *Canto serioso, Fantasy-Pieces,* and *Moderen,* with some other Nielsen oddments (Paula 90). A third was offered by **Galway,** designed as a showcase for that celebrity flutist and dominated by the Flute Concerto (RCA 6359). For the rest, Galway blasts his way through his arrangement of *Fantasy-Pieces for Oboe* (Felumb shows how they should go in Danacord's Vol. 4) and the three miniatures from *Moderen,* joining four Danish players for the Wind Quintet. He doesn't blend well with them, but they make sure the performance still has interest and quality, if no claim to priority. It's really for Galway fans rather than Nielsen lovers.

The Wind Quintet has an extraordinary recording history on its own, as by far the single most popular, familiar, and recorded of Nielsen's compositions, with well over 30 versions traceable to date. For audiences, it contains some of his most approachable and immediately appealing music. For players, it's one of the works that re-invented the wind quintet idiom in the 20th century. As such, it has become fundamental to the repertoire of all such ensembles and has regularly been recorded in tandem with works by other composers in a discographic history that goes back over a half-century. A few such multi-composer releases stand out. Two of LP origins made it briefly to CD: the elegant version by the **Melos Ensemble** (Angel/EMI 565304, with pieces by Janáček), and one by the **Marlboro Festival Players** (Sony 46250, with Weber's Clarinet Quintet).

Among current recordings, the **Ensemble Wien-Berlin**'s fluent, precise, and perceptive reading is outstanding (Sony 44596, with Paul Taffanel's Quintet). A quite valid bargain version is by the **Oslo Wind Ensemble** (Naxos 553050, with pieces by John Fernström and Johan Kvandal). Beyond that, one risks an arid laundry-list of some dozen more recordings, among many that whiz in and out of the catalogue. While Nielsen's wind writing makes strong demands, it's comfortably within the range of any good ensemble, and the scores are so satisfying for players that it's difficult to find a really unacceptable performance nowadays. The real factor of choice will be your preference among couplings.

PIANO AND ORGAN MUSIC

Nielsen wasn't an accomplished pianist, so he never became steeped in the conventions of what piano music was supposed to be, but he turned to the instrument throughout his career as a medium of composition, creating music of great individuality and originality whether or not it sounded properly pianistic. His major statements for piano were the sturdy and post-Brahmsian *Symphonic Suite* (1894); *Chaconne* and *Theme with Variations* (both 1916–17), two cathartic works testing harsh violence against structural order, from the same rationale that produced Symphony 4; *Luciferiske Suite* (1919–20) and Three Pieces (1928), each exploring a modernistic spirit very much Nielsen's own, tough yet thoughtful. Distributed around these were a number of collections of short pieces, mostly little salon vignettes in the tradition of Grieg but with some distinctive touches, culminating in a set of 24 *Piano Pieces for Young and Old* in all keys, as much an array of miniature studies in structural and harmonic problems as didactic exercises.

Nielsen's unconventional piano output was slow to attract attention, though in the decades after his death, a number of pianists who had been associated with him or became early champions made recordings of selected items. A gleaning of these, by five different pianists, may be found occupying the bulk of Vol. 5 of Danacord's series. One is **Arne Skjold Rasmussen,** a musician of great talent who never won the international reputation he deserved. He was surely the most powerful and authoritative performer of Nielsen's piano music; his playing in his LP recordings for Fona (released for a while by Vox) didn't quite match the gripping intensity of his public performances, and the sound quality wasn't ideal, but his rugged renditions set what is still the standard in this material, and it's sad they have been out of the catalogue for so long.

However, Skjold Rasmussen set a precedent for a number of other pianists to undertake full cycles (usually adding a few trifles he omitted), which could fit conveniently onto two CDs. The tally of these cycles now totals eight. Among those lost along the way was a very intelligent set by **John McCabe** (Decca). However, two others (both of whom studied with Rasmussen) have made the transition from LP to CD. **Elisabeth Westenholz**'s performances are dutiful but not always insightful and are further flawed by some unpleasant sound quality (BIS). The American pianist and Nielsen scholar, **Mina Miller,** having made her own critical edition of the piano works, recorded them in performances that are informed, thoughtful, and introspective, but in their restraint (as with Westenholz's) they fall short of her teacher's in strength and authority (Danacord 498/99).

A cycle that draws on the longest performing experience is by **Herman D. Koppel,** a composer and pianist who received early encouragement from Nielsen and made some of the earliest 78 rpm and LP recordings of the piano works (his 1952 version of *Symphonic Suite* is in Vol. 5 of Danacord's series). A 1982–83 recording of the conventional canon found him in his 70s, and there is often a feeling of struggle—if also of abandon—in his playing. If hardly a primary choice, this documentation of interpretive connection is still worth investigating (Dacapo 224095/96). A Koppel student, the Danish pianist **Anne Oland** (who shares Funen origins with the composer) recorded the enlarged canon in 1993; her playing has a strength that recalls Rasmussen, and though it can become choppy and hard at times, offers solid insights—a kind of foil in extroversion to Miller's introversion (Paula 79/80; ♦Classico 205/6, 2CD). The most recent cycle is a genuine best buy: the British pianist **Peter Seivewright** delivers the enlarged canon in performances that are probing but thoughtful, with a strong feeling for lyric possibilities (♦Naxos 553574 and 553653).

Over the years there have been a number of single-disc samplings of Nielsen's piano music (about half of it at a time). In LP days, the most respected was an RCA release (never reissued on CD) by **John Ogdon;** the performances were more supple and fluent than forceful, but the perspective was quite valid. **Robert Hamilton**'s program was more stylistically coherent and emotionally focused (Orion). Of current samplers, the leader for effective performances and solid commitment is Norwegian **Leif Ove Andsnes** (♦Virgin 45129). Not too far behind is a very intelligent program (slightly better balanced in repertoire) by another Norwegian, **Christian Eggen** (♦Victoria 19074). There are also quite serviceable selections by **Barbara Meister** (Centaur 2254) and **Enid Katahn** (Gasparo 268; Kingdom 2019).

It's typical of Nielsen's lifelong zest in exploring new musical realms and possibilities that in his last years he discovered the organ. Invited in 1929 to produce some organ preludes, with essentially ecclesiastical purposes in mind, Nielsen pulled out one very early short piece he had filed away and incorporated it into a set of 29 Preludes for Organ or Harmonium, in which he exceeded the original intentions and created a fascinating set of miniatures (supplemented by two more Preludes published posthumously). In the following year, his fascination with the organ as an instrumental medium and his study of Renaissance polyphonic traditions resulted in *Commotio,* a monumental work over 20 minutes long. This is essentially a vast contrapuntal study, cast in an almost symphonic four-section structure of two successive preludes and fugues, conceived in monumental terms.

Nielsen's complete organ works can fit snugly onto a single CD, but only two such collections are currently available. One is by **Westenholz,** this time at the organ of Grundtvig Church in Copenhagen (♦BIS 131, with Motets). Her performances are strong and altogether worthy. **Ulrik Spang-Hansen** is still more forceful and colorful, playing a Marcussen church organ in Assens, Denmark, and recorded with vivid brilliance (♦Paula 55). Sadly unavailable on CD are either or both of the LPs of *Commotio* and selections of the Preludes by the able **Grethe Krogh.** With a background in Baroque music, **Jørgen Ernst Hansen** brought a more historical profile to his recording of *Commotio* at Holmens Church in Copenhagen (Danacord 447, with Gottfred Matthison-Hansen's Organ Concerto).

All along, *Commotio* has been a welcome challenge to organists, who have recurrently matched it in recordings with works by other composers. Cases in point are **Kevin Bowyer** (Nimbus 5468) and **Anders Riber** (Kontrapunkt 32242), in both instances joining it to organ pieces by other Danish composers. But the classic exponent of *Commotio* was **Finn Viderø,** himself a great performer of Baroque organ music and one of Krogh's teachers. Viderø made the first commercial recording for Decca/London, and a later public performance (on the Holtkamp organ in Battell Chapel, Yale University, in 1960) is in Vol. 5 of Danacord's series.

CHORAL MUSIC

Best known as an orchestral and instrumental composer, Nielsen was also a vocal master, refined in both solo and choral writing, while also producing two striking operas. One factor that has delayed recognition of this portion of his output has been language. To be sure, two of his major choral works set Latin texts, which should be no problem for musicians anywhere. But most of his vocal music involves texts in Danish, a language hardly comfortable for either singers or audiences outside Denmark. These aren't insuperable barriers, and the briefest introduction to this category of Nielsen's music will reveal the rewards it offers.

Nielsen had a strong feeling for choral writing, and he came from a land where the northern European tradition of choral societies as both cultural and social institutions created a strong market for choral productivity. It was, above all, for the world of the choral societies, and in conjunction with Nielsen's interest in Danish poetic expression, that he composed the largest body of his choral music—some 30 individual pieces or groups of pieces for unaccompanied voices: much for male choir, some for female choir, the rest for mixed voices, from very early student compositions to music written in his last year. Much of it is simple—strophic, four-square, short pieces—ranging from the sentimental to the patriotic and socially conscious to the frankly comic. Many of them are just for fun, reminding us that Nielsen, like Schubert, had his richly amiable and convivial side. The exception is the only music to non-Danish texts, a set of three Motets setting psalm verses in Latin, which Nielsen composed in 1929 for the young Mogens Wöldike, whose Palestrina Chorus was giving Nielsen experience in studying Renaissance polyphonic traditions.

All this a cappella music was given a complete and devoted recording by **Frans Rasmussen** in 1983–84 in a jam-packed CD, complete with full texts, translations, and annotations (♦Danacord 368). Little of this music is or ever has been available elsewhere, the notable exception being the Motets. **Wöldike** recorded them twice, once in 1954 with a woolly-sounding mixed choir (now in Danacord's Vol. 6), and again in 1982 with a student choir (Unicorn-Kanchana). Despite differences between them, Wöldike aimed at an austere clarity, better achieved the second time. That approach set the model for subsequent recordings, including one by the **Worcester Cathedral Choir,** with boy trebles (Abbey LP).

There was some relaxation of approach in a recording by a 27-member choir of mixed voices under **Per Enevold,** where linear clarity was sacrificed to greater warmth (BIS 131, with organ works). But Rasmussen applied a judiciously Romantic spirit, which adds expressive to liturgical character, clarifying the hybrid nature of the music and revealing its connections with the a cappella motets of Bruckner and Brahms. His approach was carried further by **Stefan Parkman** (who used Rasmussen as his choirmaster) in a program with the Danish National Radio Chamber Choir (♦Chandos 8853). Using a ripe, frankly Brahmsian richness, Parkman makes the most persuasive case yet for this carefully crafted music as more than just a threesome of antiquarian exercises.

The rest of Nielsen's choral works, long or short, all involve orchestra. There are ten occasional pieces, hymns, or cantatas commissioned for institutions or celebrations, seven of them unpublished and none given full recordings as yet. That leaves the three really important works that highlight important points in Nielsen's development. The earliest, *Hymnus amoris,* sets a Latin text that contemplates the various effects of love upon human experience and perception, an oratorio-scaled work calling for five soloists, children's choir, mixed chorus, and orchestra. Anticipating Stravinsky's *Oedipus Rex,* Nielsen had the text put into Latin to achieve a degree of objectivity, also allowing for wider accessibility in the process. Composed in 1896–97 (between Symphony 1 and Quartet 3) with an unsentimental, post-Romantic warmth, the music is a wonderfully humane and uplifting essay in life affirmation.

The second work, composed in 1903–4 (just after Symphony 2 and *Helios Overture*)is the ode *Søvnen* (*Sleep*), projecting the contrasting effects and moods of the night on a post-Brahmsian scale that recalls the shape of the older master's *Schicksalslied.* Finally, in 1921, Nielsen set a prize-winning text, *Fynsk forår* (*Springtime in Funen*), for three soloists, children's choir, mixed choir, and orchestra. Just before composing the monumental Symphony 5 and the trail-blazing Wind Quintet, Nielsen slipped into a homey, spontaneous, and lyrical character, using the evocation of the coming of spring to his home island (Fyn, or Funen) as a microcosm of nature's radiant blessings upon human life—one of his most joyously human and endearing scores.

The earliest recordings of any of these works is a thoroughly musical and well-balanced 1958 concert performance under **Jensen** and another concert performance (1953) under **Hye-Knudsen,** both in Vol. 2 of Danacord's series—good stylistic models, but in rather antiquated sound. Nielsen's protégé, **Wöldike,** in his last years recorded all three with Danish forces in more up-to-date studio versions: a vivacious *Fynsk forår* for Philips (briefly available here as a Mercury LP) and full-

blooded realizations of *Hymnus amoris* and *Søvnen* in a pairing for EMI. Unfortunately, the first of these recordings has never been reissued and is sadly missed, but the latter pairing has been revived (♦EMI 566999, with a Gade cantata). **Segerstam** conducted a choral program that combines all three; he leads muscular performances, in sumptuous sound, but his interpretations are stiff and inflexible, falling sadly short of Wöldike's, and they can't be seriously recommended (Chandos).

On the other hand, at least two of these major choral works have good individual recordings. *Hymnus amoris* is given an ardent and irresistible performance by international soloists (including Bonney and Ainsley) and Danish ensembles, handsomely recorded under **Ulf Schirmer** (♦Decca 452486, with Symphony 4 and *Little Suite;* separately in Vol. 2 of Blomstedt's symphony series, 460988, with 4–6). *Fynsk forår* can be had in two contrasting versions. **Vetö** conducts Odense forces in an earnest and enthusiastic but undeniably provincial performance, in less than brilliant sound (Unicorn 9054, with *Aladdin*). **Salonen**'s unexpectedly animated performance with Swedish forces is altogether an improvement in artistic polish and sonic color, the best of his Nielsen releases (♦Sony 53276, with Flute and Clarinet Concertos, etc.). When all is said and done, however, we still need to have Wöldike's unsurpassed recordings restored.

OPERAS

The language problem is particularly acute in this corner and has undoubtedly hindered international attention to Nielsen's two great works for the lyric stage, but there are English translations available for each, and several US productions of *Maskarade* have demonstrated its viability beyond Denmark. Recordings haven't been plentiful, but have helped alert listeners to what these operas have to offer.

Maskarade (*Masquerade*). For his second opera, Nielsen turned to the great Danish dramatist Ludwig Holberg, the "Molière of the North," and his comedy about the generational strains created by the craze in Copenhagen for masquerade balls. While the plot, full of pranks, disguises, and stock characters, is fairly standardized farce, the servant Hendrik is a sprightly counterpart to Mozart's Figaro, and Nielsen's witty and fluent music brings it all to life convincingly, with even a few Wagnerian echoes. The score was composed in 1904–6 (between Symphonies 2 and 3) and first performed in 1906. There have been criticisms of its musical unevenness and dramatic imbalances, but the first of its three acts is a superbly crafted theatrical entity, while the other two are filled with wonderfully tuneful and ebullient music, and the work as a whole is one of the most joyously delightful comic operas ever written—a work often spoken of as Denmark's national opera.

Three recordings were made with Danish forces. The first was a 1954 Danish Radio broadcast performance conducted by **Grøndahl** (in Vol. 3 of the Danacord series, without libretto). The score is slightly cut, but the stylistic sense is sure, and there are some good portrayals among singers of the mid-century generation. It remains a performance for reference, and so is one that circulated unofficially only in under-the-table LP pressings, the audio track of a 1964 televised production under **Frandsen** that captured many of the cast members of the Royal Theater's working productions of the time.

Frandsen made the first commercial recording in 1977 (♦Unicorn-Kanchana 9073/74, 2CD). The cast is largely an updating of the Royal Theater's working roster, with Ib Hansen as Jeronimus, and all the others accomplished and thoroughly satisfying (including the young Aage Haugland in a tiny role). That set's diminished availability makes **Ulf Schirmer**'s 1996 entry welcome; he uses a new critical edition of the score and is recorded in the best sound the opera has ever enjoyed (Decca 460227, 2CD). Haugland leads the cast, but his Jeronimus, sonorous and bullish, lacks some of the zest of his predecessors in the role, while a singer-by-singer comparison shows that Frandsen's cast is consistently superior in their portrayals, and his greater theatrical savvy makes for a more pointed projection of the opera's humor and warmth. There is nothing seriously wrong with Schirmer's set, save that it might be even better; another isn't likely to come along soon, so it will undeniably give pleasure, though a search for Frandsen will yield a preferable experience.

Two vocal excerpts from *Maskarade* have achieved recorded attention on their own. Jeronimus's pseudo-archaic song of nostalgia from Act I turns up sometimes among song programs, while the delightful "Dance Scene of Magdalone," in a 1939 recording with **Schiøtz** and Einar Nørby, is in Vol. 10 of Danacord's Schiøtz series (460). But many listeners made their first contact with the opera through one or more of the orchestral excerpts that have long been concert and recording favorites. The Overture itself is a recurrent filler item, as in discs by Blomstedt (Decca), Chung (BIS), Ormandy (Sony), and Salonen (Sony).

There have also been occasional assemblages of a suite from the opera, involving the Overture, the *Meistersinger*-ish Prelude to Act II, and the *Hanedan* (*Dance of the Cockerels*), one of two delightful ballet divertissements in Act III. (Why no one has taken up the other divertissement, the deliciously satirical *Ballet of Mars and Venus,* is a mystery to me.) That grouping can be found in recordings by **Serov** (Kontrapunkt 32203, with Symphony 3) and **Vetö** (Big Ben 571011, with other orchestral pieces); **Salonen** is much better (♦Sony 44547, with Symphony 5), and so is **Järvi** in his orchestral program (♦DG 447757). Old but still enjoyable is the first such suite, adding to the three common components the *Magdalone Dance Scene* (without the vocal parts) from Act I, recorded by **Jensen** (Dutton 2505, with Flute Concerto and the Erikson/Wöldike Clarinet Concerto).

Saul og David (*Saul and David*). Nielsen's first operatic venture was composed slowly in 1898–1901, between Symphonies 1 and 2, and had its premiere in 1902. Its libretto focuses the Biblical saga on a confrontation between the embattled King Saul and the noble young David, as the former's jealous descent into paranoia leads to his tragic ruin. The two main characters are drawn with intense clarity, with sub-themes of David's friendship with Saul's son Jonathan and romance with Saul's daughter Mikal. There are strong dramatic parallels with Handel's *Saul,* while Honegger surely learned from Nielsen in composing his dramatic poem *Le roi David.* Indeed, given its relatively slow action and the extensive role given to the chorus, it's easy to find Nielsen's work more oratorio than opera, a difficulty that can be accentuated in staging if the director isn't careful. Nevertheless, the drama is compelling, and the music is magnificent.

The work's recording history began in 1960 with a broadcast performance for Danish Radio conducted by Nielsen's friend and disciple, **Thomas Jensen,** using a cast seasoned by staged performances at Copenhagen's Royal Theater (♦in Vol. 3 of Danacord's series, without libretto). It has its drawbacks: The sound is dry and constricted, and Jensen imposed a number of cuts—some trivial (numerous repeats) but others substantial (e.g., in the Act IV Prelude), dispensing with some 15 to 20 minutes of music. The singers are provincial in vocal quality, but Jensen's cast has two outstanding exponents of the title roles: Otte Svendsen is a convincing David, and, despite strained vocal resources, Frans Andersson is unsurpassed in his projection of Saul's tortured personality. For all its flaws, Jensen's authoritative grasp of Nielsen's style makes this still a performance to learn from.

Its successor was another Danish broadcast performance in 1972 under **Horenstein** (Unicorn-Kanchana 9086/87, 2CD). He opted to have the work sung in a modified English translation by Geoffrey Dunn instead of the original Danish, imposing on it a distracting babel of accents and variable diction. Two stellar singers give the best renditions of their roles: Alexander Young is an ideal David of noble purity and vocal freshness, while Söderström, despite problems of accent and maturity, is a truly winning Mikal. But Willy Hartmann is a workhorse Jonathan, while Christoff is little short of a disaster as Saul: his declining vocal control and mushy-mouthed accent worked against an otherwise outstanding dramatic sensibility—a Biblical Boris gone wrong. Horenstein's powerful and probing direction can still command admiration, but the inconsistencies of this production make it primarily a relic for the specialist.

A 1990 recording is also flawed but generally more successful, again with forces of Danish Radio, but in the original Danish and with a more consistently idiomatic cast, conducted by **Järvi** (♦Chandos (8911/12, 2CD). The cast is strongest in the lesser roles: Jørgen Klint is a sturdy Abner, Christian Christiansen a gritty Samuel, and Anne Gjevang is far and away the best Witch of Endor on discs. But Tina Kiberg is too matronly a Mikal, while Peter Lindroos isn't up to David's high-soaring effusions and Kurt Westi is a weary Jonathan. Most disappointing is Haugland, from whom we might have expected a weighty and powerful Saul; his dark black bass is wasted in Nielsen's demands upon the higher range, where Haugland is thin; also, he never seems very engaged dramatically, sounding like a befuddled Hagen who has wandered into the wrong opera. What holds the performance together, however, is Järvi's urgent, propulsive conducting, which trims over ten minutes from Horenstein's running and contributes countless dramatic inflections and insights. We still lack a truly ideal recorded performance—if only we could take the best singers from each of the three versions and put them all together!—but Järvi's is the obvious choice for now.

The opera has no overture or introduction, but the subsequent acts all have wonderful orchestral preludes: The one to Act I is majestic, Act III sensuously poetic, and Act IV tumultuously stormy. These (especially the Act II) turn up here and there as fillers with larger works. All three are done quite honestly by **Serov** (Kontrapunkt 32157, with Symphony 1 and *Helios*); **Salonen** has done the Act II Prelude (Sony 53276, with Flute and Clarinet Concertos and *Funen Spring*), and so has **Vetö** in his Nielsen anthology (Big Ben 571-011).

SONGS

Part of Nielsen's reaction to late-Romantic esthetics focused on the art song, an idiom he rejected and largely avoided. He was drawn to song composition, however, by the adult education movements and patriotic cultural indoctrination in Denmark in his time, which created both a hunger and a market for a strongly national kind of poetry and song. In response, Nielsen virtually re-invented Danish vocal style, creating in his own terms a distinctly and identifiably Danish genre of song—with strong, even folksy tunes, usually setting strophic texts—that became swept up in nationalist consciousness. Readily usable by amateurs, children, and educators, many of his songs were taken up as the equivalent of traditional or folk treasures, though they never quoted actual folk music but were always completely original.

As his musical growth continued, Nielsen returned regularly to this direct and straightforward lyrical idiom without affectation, while creating within simplicity a wide range of variety. A precise reckoning is difficult because some of his songs were produced or published in alternate or repeated versions, but he has been credited with something like 250 in all. Some were written for use in stage works, while many were published in sets, and still more were contributed to large anthologies he created in collaboration with Thomas Laub. Though there are exceptions, these songs generally follow the conventional scoring of solo voice and piano.

The inevitable starting-point has long been the recordings made during 1938–43 by the beloved Danish tenor, **Aksel Schiøtz.** A collection of his song recordings has been reissued in a disc that also contains vocal pieces by other Danish composers (Pearl 9140). That group is also in Vol. 6 of Danacord's Nielsen series, with six more items from stage scores in Vol. 3, but they have also released a single disc that augments the original 15 with ten supplemental or alternate items (♦460, Vol. 10 of the Schiøtz series, including a short scene from *Maskarade* with full texts and translations). One way or another, this singer's recordings are indispensable: No one else has brought such naturalness and meaning to Nielsen's songs. Meanwhile, Danacord's Vol. 6 also includes 14 songs recorded by another distinguished singer, **Einar Nørby,** plus 20 more song recordings by 13 other singers. Some songs are duplicated in this collection, so you can compare the different but still idiomatic approaches and vocal personalities the various singers represent.

In terms of quantity, however, their most impressive treatment is in a collection called "The Lesser Known Nielsen" (♦Rondo 8319, 8323, 8325, 8327, 8329). It presents a total of 157 songs (including theater-music songs and a number of hymns), organized by sources and sung by a team whose performing standards are consistently high and reliable. The extensive booklets give full Danish texts (though, unfortunately, only curt explanations without English translations), and the final volume gives a cumulative alphabetical index to titles or incipits for the full series. In all, an invaluable reference collection, as well as a pleasure to dip into at random.

Next in order of scope is a set that offers 44 songs, organized mostly by their publication groupings, including the familiar hits that Schiøtz helped popularize (Classico 280/81, 2CD). **Ulrik Cold** employs a light, high bass voice in a somewhat dry but very clear singing style; he's a reliable interpreter, but the scanty booklet gives no Danish texts and only fragmentary English translations or summaries. Tenor **Kurt Westi**'s well-chosen program of 22 songs, including the familiar favorites, is more selective and attractive. Westi was at first touted as the successor to Schiøtz, placing on him a burden impossible to carry, but he has had a solid career in Denmark and his approach is a worthy extension of his predecessor's. Despite rather sepulchral recording sound, it's the best single-disc introduction to this material (with full texts and translations) since the Danacord Schiøtz assemblage. Far less satisfactory is a program containing 22 items (again, mostly familiar) given rather rough-and-ready performances by the rugged bass **Jørgen Klint,** with reticent accompaniments from Rosalind Bevan (Paula 56). The absence of any texts, translations, or descriptions makes this release of very limited use for those who don't already know the songs or have alternative sources of information.

There are also two single-disc programs that supplement the Rondo series in differing ways. One is a release in which baritone **Lars Thodberg Bertelsen** sings "Songs by Carl Nielsen and his Pupils": eight by Nielsen himself and 26 others by eight disciples that demonstrate Nielsen's strong yet diverse influence on this corner of his country's musical tradition (♦Danacord 472). The other program presents Bertelsen

with organist Frode Stengaard in a program that intersperses seven *Little Preludes for Organ* with 24 selections from the religious collection *Hymns and Spiritual Songs* published in 1919—including the one ("Min Jesus, lad mit Hjerte faa") that Nielsen would shortly use as the theme for the variations finale of his Wind Quintet (Rondo 8335). Full texts with English digests help give valuable access to this interesting corner of Nielsen's output. BARKER

Luigi Nono *(1924–1990)*

The most prominent Italian composers of Nono's generation were politically leftist, none more so than he. A member of the Italian Communist Party and frequent visitor to and supporter of socialist regimes, many of his works are based on texts reflecting his politics. Regardless of such messages in music, however powerful and morally defensible they may be, few last beyond their era. To the extent that they remain in the repertoire, even Bernstein's Mass (1970) and some of Verdi's operas are viewed more in abstract terms, more purely esthetic, than was the basis for understanding them when they were composed.

Nono's hour-long opera *Intolleranza* (1960) is such a work. I agree with reviewers that however valid the political points, the work suffers from overt polemics at the expense of music that engages us beyond the original social context. It might be effective if staged, but on disc one has a hard time following any sort of narrative to hold the piece together. For the curious, a live recording by the Staatsoper Stuttgart offers an acceptable performance of singing and speaking (is there a reason policemen aren't allowed to sing?), conducted by **Bernhard Kontarsky** (Teldec 97304). Among the more successful pieces with political texts, *Epitaffio* Nos. 1 and 3 are the most effective, especially given **Roswitha Trexler**'s marvelous singing and speaking, with Herbert Kegel and Horst Neumann conducting the Leipzig Radio Orchestra and Chorus (Berlin 21412).

The secular cantata *Il canto sospeso* (1956) brought Nono considerable acclaim and remains one of his more frequently performed larger scores. Rigorously serial and motivically dense, the strong political text seems out of date today, as does the difficult music that is very tied to time and place. In the latter part of the 20th century Germans have struggled with the legacy of the Nazis and, especially after the opening of the Berlin Wall, have dealt with persistent antisemitism and other issues with the hope that a more humanistic atmosphere will prevail. Music has figured in that realm, and a 1992 performance by the Berlin Philharmonic that included *Il canto sospeso* was conducted and recorded by Claudio Abbado (Sony 53360). Soloists and ensembles are superb for Nono's work and for Mahler's *Kindertotenlieder*. Strong stuff, as it was meant to be. An alternative version is conducted by Nono's teacher, Bruno Maderna; *Moses und Aron* by Schoenberg (Nono's father-in-law) is represented by its opening music, and Maderna's *Hyperion* completes the disc (Stradivarius 10008). Subject to your choice of repertoire, I prefer the Sony, which includes important printed information the Stradivarius lacks.

Most recordings of Nono's works include live performers with tape or live electronics. Composed in the '70s and '80s, these pieces reflect his concern for a less dense sonority, more subtle and colorful than the post-serial pointillism of the '50s and '60s. As one of the radical young composers at Darmstadt after WWII, Nono, like Boulez and Stockhausen, studied and admired Webern's aphoristic compositions above all else, and in a very real way extended the Second Viennese School's most modern composer's extreme attention to detail and pacing. The Darmstadt composers saw electronic music and limited aleatory music

(Boulez's term) or improvisation as necessary, but all eventually turned away from it. Nono's pieces for performers and electronics are neither as sophisticated as Stockhausen's nor as elaborate as Boulez's, and most exist in only one recording, so the listener must make do with them for now. Fortunately, all are at least acceptable for quality of sound and performance.

One piece that offers alternative recordings is *La lontananza nostalgica utopia futura,* a late work for voice and electronics that captures Nono's musical modernism and leftist politics, the latter gleaned mostly by reading the liner notes and not from the performance itself. In live performance the violinist communes with the audience by walking among its members while playing; this affects the interplay between acoustic and electronic sound that is, of course, largely lost in recording. Gidon Kremer plays it masterfully, and the spatial and timbral features are conveyed well (DG 435870). **Irvine Arditti** is violinist in an hour-long performance, a full 20 minutes longer than Kremer's rendition (Disques Montaigne 782004). In the remaining 20 minutes of Kremer's disc, he's joined by with violinist Tatiana Guidenko in Nono's all-acoustic *Hay que caminar soñando.* Of the two, the DG is preferable for Kremer's tempos, the additional duet, and superb notes than explain much about the conception and production of *La lontananza.* I also find it interesting that Russian composer Sofia Gubaidulina is credited with the electronic manipulations in Kremer's recording.

For instruments and tape, available recordings include *Das atmende Klarsein* for flute and tape, and *Sofferte onde serene* for piano and tape (Agora Musica 113). For solo or ensemble, the listener is directed to *Con Luigi Dallapiccola* for percussion, *Guai ai gelidi mostri* for mixed instruments, *Post-Pre-Ludium per Donau* for tuba, *Omaggio a György Kurtag* for trombone, and *Quando Stanno Morendo* for women's voices, flute, and cello—all with live electronics.

An interesting string quartet is performed by the **Arditti Quartet** (Montesque 789005). Titled *Fragmente-Stille,* it has also been recorded by its dedicatees, the **LaSalle Quartet** (DG 415513). The LaSalle may be unmatched for Second Viennese School and Darmstadt-style music, but the Arditti do their usual fine job. Both discs are very good, but I slightly prefer the LaSalle, perhaps because I was very impressed by a live performance I heard them give in Cincinnati. Nono mellowed musically but not politically in his later years, and this quartet from 1980 is less dense and forbidding than much of his earlier work. Fortunately, the string quartet continues to flourish as a genre, and I suspect that many will keep Nono's work on at least the edge of their repertoire.

ZIEROLF

Per Nørgård (b. 1932)

Having produced important works in almost every conceivable genre, Nørgård is the most eminent senior Danish composer and one of the finest of postwar Europe. Like many other young Nordic composers of the '50s, he initially embraced Nordic traditions, including the metamorphosis principle of organic development used by his teacher Vagn Holmboe. However, following his investigation of international trends later in the decade, he began a restless experimental period during the '60s that involved an exploration of such diverse resources as serial principles, electronics, collage, and minimalism.

One of Nørgård's most important theoretical accomplishments of this period was the invention of a principle of interval generation, the infinity series. This could be applied to a variety of scales and allowed him to create a new, dynamic polyphony with hierarchical relations involving melody, rhythm, and harmony. His application of the series to

diatonic scales in the '70s imparted a generally more consonant sound to the works from this period. He surprised his followers around 1980 with a sharp change of direction influenced by the esthetics of the eccentric Swiss poet and painter, Adolf Wölfli. The extreme contrasts of imagery and ideas reflected in Wölfli's work had an impact on Nørgård's musical language, especially in his use of dramatic, violent gestures, more stringent harmony, and abrupt changes of expressive character. In recent years, the composer has gone through a consolidation process, drawing upon resources from previous creative phases.

SYMPHONIES

Perhaps the best introduction to Nørgård's music is the Chandos series of the first five symphonies, which illuminates key junctures in his stylistic development. One of the distinguishing characteristics of his symphonic cycle is that each work has emerged as radically different in conception and expressive character from any of the others. The first CD in the series offers 1 and 2 (♦Chandos 9450). The three-movement 1 is remarkably mature for a young composer, who, while exhibiting Nordic influences, is also laying the foundation for a more individual style. **Segerstam**'s brilliant, forceful reading balances its Nielsen-like dramatic sweep with a clear delineation of its developmental processes and underlying structure.

In the concise, one-movement 2, composed after Nørgård's exploration of the European avant-garde, the infinity series is unfolded in dynamic, colorful, and varied instrumental groupings. Segerstam's account emphasizes the work's dramatic element and sensuous orchestral sonorities, while **Jorma Panula**'s somewhat slower performance clarifies frequently dense polyphonic textures (♦Point 5070).

3 is one of Nørgård's most dynamic and original achievements. Although radically different in character, the two large movements are complementary halves of an evolutionary process. The first introduces basic musical elements in a slow, monolithic unfolding that coalesces in the second in a fully realized, complex, polyphonic environment teeming with varied and unpredictable activity. This ranges from passacaglia and variation techniques to minimalism, from a Schubert quotation to Latin American musical references. Clarifying both the structure and subtle detail within dense orchestral textures, **Vetö**'s performance (♦Da Capo 224041) is slightly preferable to **Segerstam**'s (♦Chandos 9491).

If 3 can be seen as a luminous vision of a romantic utopia, 4 is a portrait of Wölfli's surreal, nightmarish world. Its subtitle, "Indian Rose Garden and Chinese Witch Lake," suggests its feverish transformation of musical images between idyllic and catastrophic extremes. More divergent conceptions of the piece can hardly be imagined than Panula's (coupled with 2) and Segerstam's (♦Chandos 9533). **Panula** presents the work as a tightly knit, concentrated statement, emphasizing its stark expressive contrasts and structure. **Segerstam**'s more expansive interpretation (50 per cent longer!) is a valid alternative and is coupled with the only available recording of the 35-minute milestone, Symphony 5 (1986–90). Divided into four contrasting sections, 5 is one of the composer's most difficult and enigmatic works, but the patient listener will find rich rewards, especially in the first and third sections. Segerstam delivers a sharply focused, richly detailed performance.

OTHER ORCHESTRAL MUSIC

An old LP (♦Caprice RIKS 54, NA) featured the first and finest recording of *Voyage Into the Golden Screen,* perhaps the composer's best known work and one of the most original monuments of the postwar avant-garde. Divided into two radically different yet complementary movements, the first presents independent, overlapping gestures and textures that interweave and collide in wave-like motions. In the second, textures coalesce and give birth to a smooth linear motion where the infinity series is presented in various instrumental groups at different tempos. **Vetö**'s more subtle exploration of the textures in the first movement is preferable to **Knussen**'s straightforward account (♦Da Capo 9001), despite the latter's greater clarity of sound. The disc is filled out with the only recording of another important orchestral work, *Iris,* which explores dense, shifting blocks of sound. **Blomstedt**'s performance is proficient, though the constricted acoustics don't always allow orchestral detail to emerge clearly.

Vetö's disc of Symphony 3 also offers two orchestral pieces: *Luna,* a masterly set of short, nocturnal mood studies, closely related in character to *Iris,* and *Twilight,* a satellite of 3 in its appropriation of gestures and the general sound world of that monumental work.

A disc devoted to works for chamber orchestra presents Nørgård at his most accessible (♦Kontrapunkt 32140). The Aarhus Sinfonietta under **Soren Hansen** presents idiomatic performances, as if the works had been in their repertoire for years. Most of them were composed during or shortly after the extended time the composer devoted to Symphony 5. Yet these works (including *Prelude to Breaking* from 1986 and *Night Symphonies-Day Break* from 1992) could hardly be more different from the frequently dense, abstract world of the symphony. Representing a lighter side of the composer, they offer an almost neoclassical clarity of texture and economy of expression.

A disc called "Fugitive Summer," devoted to Nørgård's complete works for string orchestra, is a fine introduction to his life-long artistic preoccupations, stylistic range, and use of terse, concentrated forms (♦Finlandia 25986). The pieces date from either the composer's formative years (the '50s) or the most recent period (late '80s to mid-'90s). The non-chronological sequence of the works on the disc underscores his ongoing compositional concerns, particularly the continuous transformation of materials and the interference concept of continuously shifting related gestures. The series of three *Tributes* to various composers are particularly outstanding. A highlight from the Nordic period is the rhythmically intricate *Constellations* for 12 strings (1958), standing at the crossroads between the composer's Nordic heritage and his invention of the infinity series in 1959. The **Ostrobothnian Chamber Orchestra** negotiates technical difficulties without sacrificing nuances of phrasing and dynamics.

CONCERTOS

The percussion concerto *For a Change* (1982–83), included in a set with *Siddharta* (Da Capo 224031/32), has a programmatic and technical relationship to the opera. However, the musical language of the outer movements is much harsher and more stringent than anything to be found in *Siddharta.* The extreme contrast between their Varèse-like boldness of gesture and the delicate, poetic, gamelan sounds of III brings the piece into the sphere of the Wölfli-inspired works. Soloist **Gert Mortensen** delivers an intense performance, although the orchestra seems too far in the background in relation to the always up-front percussionist.

Two of the three substantial string concertos Nørgård composed in the 1980s are in an enterprising CD (♦Da Capo 9002). *Remembering Child* is an austere viola concerto in which the soloist eloquently declaims a simple tonal melody at the beginning of the second section as the harmonic context becomes increasingly chromatic. Unlike the other string concertos, the chamber orchestra is generally used sparingly, though with occasional obtrusive outbursts. **Zukerman** gives an impassioned performance. In contrast to the formal scheme of the viola concerto, where the soloist rarely relinquishes the dominant position, the cello concerto *In Between* invigorates the genre's conceptual models by presenting a grand scheme of possible roles for soloist and orchestra. **Morten Zeuthen** is the fine cellist.

Nørgård's *Helle nacht* is one of the great violin concertos of the 20th century. This profoundly moving work exhibits an extraordinary marriage of form and content; a thorough organic development of its ideas is accomplished with inevitability and succinctness. It's divided into four movements of symmetrical pairs: The dramatic and varied outer movements are of symphonic scope with independent, layered levels of activity and virtuosic writing for the soloist; the two slower inner movements are more reflective and unified in mood. In the premiere performance, **Anton Kontra** and Kamu give an electrifying account (♦EMI 749869, NA). **Christina Astrand** and Dausgaard give a fine interpretation, although not quite equaling the urgent intensity of Kontra's reading in the outer movements (♦Chandos 9830). Astrand especially excels in the more lyrical sections, projecting a warm expressive tone and clean articulation of the solo line. Dausgaard clarifies the orchestra's inner lines and detail, which were occasionally obscured in Kontra's performance.

Nørgård's piano concerto, *Concerto in due tempi,* is coupled with Segerstam's Symphony 3. Alternately gritty and lyrical in character, with a sometimes jazz-inflected sense of rhythmic syncopation, it's one of the composer's more accessible major scores, with basic motives not so much developed as frequently repeated in new harmonic and rhythmic contexts. **Per Salo** and the Danish RSO under Segerstam's direction have an impressive command of the work's rhythmic and metrical intricacies (♦Chandos 9491).

PIANO MUSIC

Although solo piano music doesn't loom large in Nørgård's output, there is at least one major score, Sonata 2 (1957); it's among the highlights of his Nordic period. In the traditional three movements, this monumental, fiercely virtuosic work is almost bursting at the seams with attractive ideas and inventive developmental sections, but also ventures into more individual territory in its handling of complex metrical changes and polyrhythms. **Elisabeth Klein** (♦Philips 6507022, LP, NA) and **Per Salo** (♦Kontrapunkt 32147) both offer magisterial readings, with Klein perhaps having the edge due to her ability to articulate the contrapuntal lines more clearly and her greater sensitivity to phrasing and sectional contrasts. Salo has the advantage of superior sound and offers three additional piano works.

The intervening period between Sonata 2 and the next work on the disc, *Grooving* (1968), involved great stylistic development; the latter work is as spare and austere as the sonata is ornate and complex. *Turn* reflects minimalist influences, while the substantial *Achilles and the Tortoise* echoes the intricate rhythms of the sonata while anticipating the experiments of tempo found in the piano concerto.

OPERAS

Gilgamesh was Nørgård's breakthrough opera but doesn't follow operatic conventions in its lack of traditional division into acts, its unusual layout of singers, instrumentalists, conductor, and audience, and its use of words as phonetic elements. The work is successful in its evocation of a primeval world, but overall it seems only intermittently effective; in some sections there is a tiresome over-reliance on minimalist-like ostinatos in the instrumental parts and whole-tone scalar fragments in the voices. However, it achieves transcendent power in its final sections, effectively realized in **Vetö**'s performance (♦Da Capo 9001).

Norgård's third opera, *Siddharta,* is more impressive than its predecessor. It's a successful fusion of dramatic issues with large-scale architecture, offers a prodigious level of orchestral invention and gratefully written, frequently haunting vocal lines, and is anchored in a generally more sophisticated harmonic framework. Moreover, the opera's ongoing motivic development imparts large-scale organic growth. *Siddharta* is perhaps the climax to the more consonant romantic style of the '70s, but also points the way to the polarized language of the Wölfli period. **Latham-Koenig** presents a brilliantly prepared performance, and the recording creates a careful balance between soloists, chorus, and orchestra (♦Da Capo 224031).

SONGS

Nørgård's great setting of Whitman's *Seadrift* was briefly available on a rare LP (♦Sub Rosa 10, NA). Scored for soprano and an unusual combination of Renaissance and modern percussion instruments, this 22-minute work creates a sound world that is both modern and evocative of a distant time and place. Another vocal work, *Nova Genitura,* a satellite inhabiting the sound world of Symphony 3, fills out the disc. A complete list of Norgård's recorded works is available at the web site for the Danish Music Information Centre: <http://www.mic.dk>.   LONG

Vítězslav Novák *(1870–1949)*

Novák and Suk are the main representatives of the post-Dvořák generation in Czechoslovakia; both were his students. Novák had the more exploratory temperament initially, but he lacked self-confidence, leading him to contemplate suicide at one point. His music is less outgoing than Suk's, and it took him a while to balance his ideas with his expressive means. Once he did so, he fit better into the postwar generation than Suk, continuing to grow outward where Suk went inward.

ORCHESTRAL MUSIC

The earliest of Novák's recorded pieces for orchestra is Serenade Op. 9, a substantial piece, full of summertime feeling, scored in a curiously spare fashion. **Andrew Mogrelia** plays it along with the later Serenade Op. 36 in a leisurely and lyrical mood (Naxos 223649). There are curious dark patches in this work that show us sun and sand are not going to be Novák's specialty. Op. 36 is more concise and is shaped to better effect by **Bělohlávek** in a program that includes *Slovak Suite* and the song cycle, *Melancholy Songs about Love* (Supraphon 3372).

Why Supraphon didn't see fit to include the *Maryša Overture* Op. 18 while they were reissuing **Sejna**'s Novák recordings is a fair question. This dramatic, eventful tone poem was originally released along with *Slovak Suite* (sometimes called *Moravian-Slovak Suite*), and another Sejna LP contained the tone poems *In the Tatras* and *About the Eternal Longing*. All but *Maryša* were reissued in 1993 (Supraphon 682, NA), but *Slovak Suite* has since been replaced by two of Fibich's melodramas (♦Supraphon 1922). My annoyance at this messy programming has been somewhat mitigated by the release of **Talich**'s even more marvelous *Slovak Suite* in warm monaural sound (♦Supraphon 1905, with Janáček). Among its many felicities, the balance between organ and orchestra in *In Church* is so subtle you hardly notice the organ as such; it feels as if the orchestra is doing a marvelous imitation all by itself. The only competition is the aforementioned Bělohlávek release, with good stereo sound but less atmosphere (Supraphon 3372).

There have been at least two other recordings of this popular suite, one by **Pešek** with the same program as Supraphon 682 in rather slower and slightly less idiomatic performances than Sejna and Talich (Virgin 45251, NA), and one by **František Vajnar,** coupled with the late *South*

Bohemia Suite (Supraphon 1743, NA). *In the Tatras* is also available in a powerful reading by a little-known early Czech conductor, **František Stupka,** (Supraphon 1909, with fine performances of Tchaikovsky's *Pathétique* and Dvořák's *Carnival Overture*). *About the Eternal Longing* may also be heard in a somewhat more lively, less grand performance by **František Jilek** (Supraphon 3049, with the ballet-pantomime, *Signorina Gioventú*).

During the late '20s, Novák wrote two of these ballets, the other an odd satire on smoking called *Nikotina* (Supraphon 3050). Musically, these works hold together about as well as a ballet is expected to, considering the exigencies of the stories, but they contain over 50 minutes apiece of prime Novák, played well and recorded cleanly. *Nikotina* is coupled with the colorful earlier symphonic poem *Toman and the Wood Nymph,* not to be confused with the melodrama on the same tale by Fibich. This is an effective recording.

In the years just before WWI, Novak wrote a long piano tone poem called *Pan,* which he also orchestrated; this has been recorded by **Zdenek Bilek** in a pantheistic reading of warmth and atmospheric beauty (Marco Polo 223325).

South Bohemian Suite was written in 1937 in anticipation of war, beginning in pastoral peace and ending with the national anthem and an exhortation to the Taborites as they lie under Blanik Hill awaiting a call to arms. This was followed in 1941, Czechoslovakia's darkest hour, by *De Profundis* for organ and orchestra, a dissonant and powerful tone poem. Both are recorded by **Jaroslav Vogel** with the considerable overture, *Lady Godiva* (Ultraphon 1873). The sound is a little woody, from the early '60s, and there have been stronger performances, but these are adequate and idiomatic. **Pešek** offers an excellent *Lady Godiva, De Profundis,* and *Toman and the Wood Nymph* in excellent sound, probably a better bet (Chandos 9821). There was once a recording of the Suite under **Vajnar** (Supraphon 1743, with *Slovak Suite,* NA), and there is a good recording by **Douglas Bostock** (Classico 191, with the rare *Nocturnes* for voice and orchestra).

CHAMBER MUSIC

The earliest of Novák's chamber works presently available is the Piano Quintet Op. 12. There is an earlier Violin Sonata in D Minor from 1891, but it has disappeared for the nonce, and Piano Trio Op. 1 and Piano Quartet Op. 7 haven't been recorded yet. There are two recordings of the Quintet, one by the Kubin Quartet with pianist **Jírí Skovajsa** (Centaur 2191, with String Quartet Op. 35), the other with the Kocian Quartet and **Radoslav Kvapil** (ASV 998, with songs and piano music). Both are excellent, the Kocian somewhat darker in tone, the Kubin more formally compelling.

There are two string quartets. Op. 22 is a relatively outgoing three-movement piece in a folk-influenced style, cyclic in its thematic use. This was played by the **Novák Quartet** on LP (Crossroads 47). A later recording coupled it with the Piano Quintet by the **Suk Quartet** and pianist Pavel Stepan, also excellent (Supraphon 72437, NA). Op. 35 is a curious piece in only two long movements, a lyrical fugue followed by a fantasia in several interludes, adding up to a work lasting more than half an hour, oblique but fascinating.

Piano Trio Op. 27 is a short, dramatic work. Once available in a Supraphon LP, there are two recordings presently, by the **Osiris Trio** in an oddly-assorted program entitled "Folk Music" mixing Dvořak, Beethoven, Martin, Shostakovich, and Ives (Channel 13098, 2CD), and, well played and less expensive, by the **Joachim Trio** in a program including Smetana and Suk (♦Naxos 553415). Though English rather than

Czech, this group plays with virtuosity, unanimity, and enthusiasm and is recorded very well. There have been a couple of Supraphon recordings of this work over the years, notably by the **Prague Trio,** later by the **New Prague Trio** (72888, NA).

PIANO AND ORGAN MUSIC

Songs of Winter Nights is a four-movement piano suite. **Fingerhut** emphasizes the impressionistic aspects of the music; her "Storm" is particularly effective (Chandos 9489). **Lapsansky** brings out the Czech elements in a disc containing little-known works by Fibich, Josef Foerster, and Janáček (Supraphon 3016). **Kvapil** plays it straightforwardly, particularly effective in the final "Carnival Night," coupled with the Piano Quintet and some of Novák's folk song settings (ASV). **Martin Vojtisek** couples the *Songs* with the early suite *Reminiscences* and the later collection for young pianists entitled *Youth* (Panton 9007). He plays with polish and the sound is good.

Fingerhut's performance is coupled with *Pan,* a huge 55-minute tone poem in five movements. *Pan* is better known in Novák's subsequent orchestration, but Fingerhut makes a good case for it in the original, making much of its pianistic color effects and spacious moods. There have been other recordings, one by **František Maxian,** who knew Novák personally, another by **František Rauch** (both Supraphon, NA).

An earlier work, *My May,* is recorded by **Igor Ardasev,** a young Brno pianist (Supraphon 3183, with works by Smetana and Suk). There was a recording by **Rauch** that Supraphon may reissue, but this one is strong and poetic.

Novák wrote only two works for organ solo, one short early Prelude and the half-hour *St. Wenceslas Triptych* Op. 70, written under the shadow of WWII and later orchestrated. **Jaroslav Tuma** plays both works on the organ in Smetana Hall in Prague's Municipal House (Supraphon 3318, with Janáček organ music). The instrument has a sweet, fruity sound with a romantic character, while the music is characteristic of Novák's late style, effortlessly contrapuntal and rich in associations.

VOCAL MUSIC

The Storm is a hyper-cantata for vocal soloists, chorus, and orchestra. Seventy minutes long, full of drama and excitement, it makes an ideal album-mate for Dvořak's *Spectre's Bride,* a similarly dramatic piece recorded by **Krombholc** with the Czech Philharmonic and a stellar vocal quartet back in 1956. The sound is good mono. A more modern recording was released recently, conducted by **Košler,** but vocally it isn't a patch on the older version and the storm takes six minutes longer as well, easier on the musicians no doubt but not as exciting (Supraphon 3088, NA). Very little of Novák's choral music has been recorded.

He also wrote many settings for solo voice and piano of folk songs, 13 of which are sung sensitively by **Magdaléna Kožená** to Kvapil's sympathetic accompaniment (ASV 998). Otherwise, we have the eight *Nocturnes* sung by soprano **Daniela Strakova**(Classico 191). This is a lovely song cycle, full of feeling. Another is *Melancholy Songs about Love,* sung by **J. Tetourova** (Supraphon 3372). Both are well worth investigating.

MOORE

Jacob Obrecht (1457/58–1505)

Obrecht has come to be recognized as one of Josquin's greatest contemporaries. He spent his adult life in Cambrai (briefly), Bruges, and Antwerp; following so many other Netherlanders to Italy, he went to Ferrara in 1504 only to die of the plague within a year. The *New Obrecht Edition* contains 31 masses, of which nine have been recorded, and we have

recordings of half of his less than 30 motets and less than half of his fewer than 30 songs.

Jeremy Summerly's Oxford Camerata recorded a fine *Missa Caput* on the same chant cantus firmus as Ockeghem's setting (♦Naxos 553210, with two *Salve Reginas*). Peter Phillips's Tallis Scholars recorded a work of exceptional breadth for its time, *Missa Maria zart* (♦Gimell 454932). Edward Wickham's Clerks' Group give us *Missa Malheur me bat* (♦ASV 171, with four motets by Johannes Martini), and János Bali's A.N.S. Chorus also recorded the last work along with *Missa O lumen ecclesiae* (Hungaroton 31172, with two motets).

Hans Grüss's Capella Fidicinia recorded *Missa L'homme armé* (♦Querstand 9609, with Ockeghem's mass setting), and Gary Cooper's Dufay Consort offers *Missa Ave regina caelorum,* based on Frye's motet (♦Dervorguilla 102, with the motet *Salve crux*). Dietrich Knothe's Capella Lipsiensis recorded *Missa Sub tuum praesidium* (♦Berlin 3076, with an Ockeghem mass), and we have **Richard Taruskin's** *Missa Salve diva parens* (MHS 922059, 2LP, NA). The Clemencic Consort's recording of *Missa Fortuna desperata* (Harmonia Mundi, LP, NA) needs replacement. Obrecht's motets and songs, the latter mostly in Flemish, have been recorded only in scattered collections. WEBER

Johannes Ockeghem (ca. 1420–1497)

Ockeghem's date of birth is not even approximately known, and guesses range from 1410 to 1430, but the median date of 1420 seems close to the truth. Like most composers of his time, he was a singer, a basso profundo as evidenced by some of the bass lines in his works. He held high rank as a chaplain at the French royal court, residing at Tours from 1451 till his death. Of the works that survive, there are at most 15 masses (counting a separate *Credo* and a dubious work), not all of them complete cycles. Four motets are undeniably authentic, but several others are dubious. Of the recorded songs, only 22 are authentic.

Requiem is the first surviving polyphonic work of its kind, though it consists of only five movements. Coupled by the Hilliard Ensemble with the next work below, the disc makes an ideal introduction to the composer (♦Virgin 561219). Edward Wickham's Clerks' Group also offers a fine version (ASV 168, with *Missa Fors seulement*). Marcel Pérès's recording, however, fills in additional movements in a different style (Harmonia Mundi).

Missa Mi-Mi. This is a unique and remarkable work, not based on any existing melody. This and the *Requiem,* the composer's two most popular masses on records, are paired by the Hilliard Ensemble in exquisite performances (♦Virgin 561219). Wickham also has a fine version (ASV 139), and Rebecca Stewart's Capella Pratensis sings this mass with extraordinary style (Ricercar 206402).

Missa prolationum. This is another unique work, a series of double canons beginning at the unison in the first "Kyrie" and widening progressively until the first "Hosanna" is sung in canon at the octave. The Hilliard Ensemble again offers a superb performance (♦Virgin 561484, with all four authentic motets and the dubious second *Salve Regina*). Wickham's version is also excellent (♦ASV 143). Bo Holten's fine recording is coupled with the *Requiem* (Naxos 554260).

Missa cuiusvis toni. The third of these freely composed masses has no clefs, so the parts can be sung in any mode, shifting the half-step intervals in the scale. Recorded performances deal with the possibilities in several ways. Wickham performs it in the Phrygian mode, generally regarded as the most successful way to realize the music (♦ASV 189, with

Missa quinti toni). Siegfried Heinrich recorded it twice, in the Phrygian mode on one side of the disc and the Mixolydian mode on the other (♦Jubilate 15211, LP, NA). Clytus Gottwald adopted the Dorian mode, which requires too much *musica ficta* (flats inserted by the singers) (♦Bayer 100273). In a different interpretation, based on Glareanus (1547), Peter Urquhart uses a transposed Mixolydian mode (♦Dorian 80152, with *Missa sine nomine* for five voices and *Missa Fors seulement*). Wickham and Urquhart are the most compelling of the four distinctly different interpretations.

Missa Caput. All the other masses are based on existing melodies. This early work is one of Wickham's finest discs (♦ASV 186, with *Missa Ma maistresse*).

Missa L'homme armé. Written shortly after *Missa Caput,* this is another of Wickham's beautiful discs (♦ASV 204, with the dubious *Missa sine nomine* for three voices).

Missa au travail suis and *Missa de plus en plus.* Peter Phillips's Tallis Scholars couple exquisite performances of both (♦Gimell 454935). The latter is also well sung by Wickham's group (ASV 153, with the *Credo*) and by the Orlando Consort (Archiv 453419, with six songs and the lament *Mort tu as navré*).

Missa Ecce ancilla Domini. Wickham's first recording is the only available version of this work (Proud Sound 133).

The Medieval Ensemble has recorded the complete secular music, an even finer set than their similar Dufay collection (♦Oiseau-Lyre 436194, 2CD). For a collection on one disc, Romanesque offers only ten songs (Ricercar).   WEBER

Jacques Offenbach *(1819–1880)*

As a cellist, Jakob Eberst the cantor's son achieved great renown, even studying briefly with Cherubini, but it was only after adopting the name of his home town, Offenbach am Main, and joining the cello section of the Opéra-Comique that the young man became exposed to the bawdier side of the Parisian night life. Fired with enthusiasm by the examples of Auber, Hérold, and Rossini, he bought a rundown theater off the Champs-Elysées and, calling it the "Bouffes-Parisiens," embarked on a remarkable career, beginning with his own farce *Les Deux Aveugles.* When this proved highly successful, even bolder productions followed, satirizing the follies of Parisian society in the guise of Greek mythology (*Orphée aux Enfers, La Belle Hélène*) and even parodying the military in *La Grande-Duchesse de Gérolstein;* the joke wasn't lost on Bismarck, who reportedly slapped his knee and cried "But that's it exactly!" Offenbach hoped to achieve similar renown in grand opera with *Les Contes d'Hoffmann* but died before he could complete it; he would be gratified to know that this work, as much as his *opéras bouffes,* has carried his name around the world.   HALLER

LES CONTES D'HOFFMANN

Offenbach died before he could put his one great serious opera into definitive form, but until 1970 or so, audiences knew exactly what to expect: the version edited by Choudens and published in 1907. It didn't seem to bother anyone that some of the music wasn't by Offenbach at all. The baritone aria "Scintille diamant" and the septet (actually a sextet with chorus), both in the Giulietta act, are delightful pieces for all their spuriousness. Hoffmann, in his reminiscences, first meets Olympia, then Giulietta, and finally Antonia; and the listener was accustomed to hear a reprise of Giulietta's famous Barcarolle at the end of the Antonia act, even if its position there didn't make complete sense. The traditional version of the opera was fairly short and swift, and cuts (especially in the repeated verses of the arias) weren't unusual.

Of all the recordings of the Choudens edition, the most stylish and cohesive was led by **Cluytens** in 1948, with a cast of native French speakers (♦EMI 65260). No other performance matches its verbal flair and lucidity or has the same easy, natural flow. The sound distorts in loud passages, and the orchestra has no depth, but the voices generally come across cleanly (along with a multitude of "sound effects"). Doria's agile Olympia has bite and focus; Vina Bovy is a sophisticated, credibly sensuous, slightly threadbare Giulietta; and Boué's Antonia, for all its emotional vulnerability, has more vocal pallor than the character demands. The villains, like the ladies, are each assigned to a different singer, and even the poorest of them (the Dapertutto, who won't surrender to Cluytens's tempos) has ample panache. Jobin sings the title role in clean, ringing tones, but he's a grim hero.

The character could use more poetry and dreaminess, exactly the strong points of another French-Canadian Hoffmann, Simoneau, who recorded the role twice. A 1957 recording led by **Pierre-Michel Le Conte,** with a French chorus and orchestra, was short-lived and has never been reissued on CD (Epic). No one, not even Olympia, is allowed the second verse of an aria. The four villains are sung by the lively but vocally limited Rehfuss. Uta Graf is a squealing, inaccurate Olympia; Dobbs does fairly well with the other two heroines.

The source of a recording led by **Lee Schaenen** is slightly mysterious: Vienna, according to the label; Italian radio, according to Simoneau himself (Voce della Luna). This time, Pierrette Alarie, Simoneau's wife, is a nimble, sparkling Olympia; Danco, a fine singing actress, takes on both Giulietta and Antonia. London sings the villains with macho flamboyance; he's surprisingly sleek and powerful in "Scintille diamant." In both recordings, Simoneau shapes the lyrical passages exquisitely. No one else spins out the arias quite so gracefully, with an easy control of dynamics and words that have clarity and flavor. The problem is that his voice is weak on top, without enough metal for high, loud interjections. Where Jobin is thrilling, Simoneau is feeble—but I wouldn't part with either of his recordings all the same.

One tenor whose talents should have encompassed both the lyric and heroic demands of Hoffmann was Gedda, in the second **Cluytens** recording (♦EMI 763222). He comes close, but he's not at his best; I've heard the voice flow out more freely and easily in the same role in the theater. Cluytens is a more tentative conductor in 1964 than in 1948, perhaps because his cast is a conglomeration of polyglot stars rather than a smooth-working ensemble. Gianna d'Angelo is a proficient Olympia with some tonal warmth. De los Angeles, not entirely happy with the tessitura, is a vulnerable, touching Antonia. Schwarzkopf was a strange choice for Giulietta, but she throws herself into the role, which is too short for her to make much of an impression (or do much damage). London sings only Coppélius and Dr. Miracle, yielding Dapertutto to Ernest Blanc, a Belgian baritone with pealing top notes. A baritone rather than a mezzo is cast as Nicklausse, to poor effect.

The whole somehow manages to transcend the disparate parts, so if you want a stereo recording of the Choudens *Hoffmann,* this remains the best choice—better than the Sills-Treigle-Burrows performance led by **Rudel** (EMI). Sills and Treigle could be mesmerizing on stage, but neither sounds comfortable or secure on records. Burrows, a potentially fine Hoffmann, sounds too nonchalant, unwilling or unable to focus his voice around a solid core.

In 1972, **Bonynge** rocked the boat by replacing the recitative with spoken dialogue and transferring the septet (transformed into a quartet) to the Epilogue (♦Decca 417363). He kept the acts in the traditional order. Domingo comes closer than anyone to encompassing the vocal requirements of Hoffmann, and he's a pleasure to hear, his vague French notwithstanding. The resourceful Bacquier sings the villains compellingly, though his voice isn't all that juicy. Sutherland's Olympia is, predictably, marvelous, but she's also a remarkable Antonia, achieving expression through subtle vocal shadings rather than verbal nuances. Of all the recordings of *Hoffmann,* Bonynge's is the easiest to listen to, though his version is very much his own.

The floodgates opened in 1976 when de Almeida discovered more than 1,500 pages of lost music. He and musicologist Fritz Oeser (who also rescued *Carmen* from tradition) prepared a new edition of the score in 1978, and it was recorded a decade later by **Cambreling** (EMI). It's an overstuffed, disorganized performance that actually makes the opera seem weaker, though it's useful as a reference. Its strongest asset is van Dam as the four villains. **Ozawa,** two years later, rejected much of Oeser and went back to Choudens; but his performance, like Cambreling's, didn't make all that strong a case for itself (DG). We already had Domingo's Hoffmann, and Gruberová's assumption of the heroines is less stunning than Sutherland's.

Enter Michael Kaye, an American musicologist, whose first version of *Hoffmann* reverted to the spoken dialogue, expanded the role of Nicklausse, and reversed the Antonia and Giulietta acts. The Giulietta act in particular was plumped out most becomingly, though the authentic substitute for "Scintille diamant"—"Tourne, tourne miroir"—is a less-striking piece. The Venetian courtesan doesn't glide off in the traditional gondola but takes poison instead; the act ends with Dapertutto's sardonic "Ah! Maladroite." The performance led by **Tate** with the Dresden Staatskapelle and Leipzig Radio Chorus is generally enjoyable, even if Eva Lind is a wispy Olympia and Norman strains for Antonia's high notes (♦Philips 422374). On the plus side are Studer's Giulietta, sultry and flexible; von Otter's proficient Nicklausse; Araiza's Hoffmann, sometimes tight and charmless but ardent and handsome (he interpolates a few extra top notes); and Ramey's villains, solid and satisfactory if without the Gallic flair of van Dam.

Kaye's second version, conducted by **Nagano** and recorded in 1996, makes further changes (♦Erato 14330). The Septet is restored (with an altered text), and Giulietta is given the most difficult version of her aria "L'amour lui dit," so festooned with coloratura that it makes her seem a near cousin to Olympia. Nagano deploys the forces of the Lyons Opera to excellent effect; it's a particular pleasure to hear such snappy enunciation in the choruses. Many of the smaller roles are vividly assumed: Sénéchal's Spalanzani, Gilles Ragon's comic servants (all four), Bacquier's Crespel. Dubosc is a spunky Nicklausse, though she sings less well than von Otter. Van Dam again undertakes the four villains, and if some of the nap on his voice has worn down, the style is intact. Dessay is a dexterous, rapier-thin Olympia; Sumi Jo, another coloratura, dispatches her difficult aria easily but sounds brittle rather than seductive. In this version, Giulietta doesn't die but doesn't sail off either.

Leontina Vaduva's Antonia is lovely. Her tone has a slightly dull patina and the character is bland—Sutherland and de los Angeles had far more "face"—but she's never less than competent and better than Norman. As Hoffmann, Alagna sounds like a French tenor who really wants to be an Italian. He pronounces the words correctly but without much élan, and he resorts too often to Italianate sobs and explosive

emphases. His diction and no-nonsense directness are admirable; but for all his virility, he's never dapper, never a credible poet.

There simply isn't a best choice among the modern recordings of *Hoffmann.* The Philips and Erato are as good as any, though I wish I could insert Tate's Giulietta act into Nagano's performance.

LUCANO

OPERETTAS

Offenbach, the father of modern operetta, and, by extension, musical comedy, came to exemplify Second Empire Parisian gaiety (to translate the title of the famous ballet woven from his operetta themes). He had his antecedents (composer-librettist Hervé the most important), and of course his acolytes and descendants, from Delibes to Lecocq to Messager to Hahn, but all owed their operettas to some degree to père Jacques, and all remain measured, even today, against the delightful standards he set. His one-act buffooneries, written originally in the 1850s when other Paris theaters wouldn't permit full-length competition, were the models for subsequent operettas not only in France but in Britain and Austria-Hungary as well. The careers of such masters as Sullivan and Suppé were substantially influenced by Offenbach's one-acters.

The full length masterpieces that flowed from 1858, however, are the fully blooming cornerstones of the operetta/musical repertoire. They were written with the ingenious librettists Henri Meilhac and Ludovic Halévy, who were as much responsible for these marvelously satirical and silly works as Offenbach. Many of them still hold the stage internationally and have been frequently recorded. The one-act works are less recorded, as are the other Offenbach *opera bouffes,* which from time to time are revived in Europe by theaters seeking a novelty. Very seldom are the libretti left alone—in French or in English—and there's also a temptation for contemporary musical directors to have their say about the original scores or orchestrations. This is why some older recordings are particularly valuable as approximations of the original versions.

Orphée aux Enfers (Orpheus in the Underworld). Taking the principal seven *opera bouffes* in chronological order, we begin here. The original 1858 version, which made Offenbach a household name worldwide, was a two-act farrago that remains—as originally composed and written—a delightful mock-heroic musical comedy. Long after the composer had reached his creative apex, in 1874, he decided to aggrandize the original into a four-act super-spectacular for the Gaîté theater he was then running (into the red, as it turned out). The extra characters, choruses, ballets, and incidental music may have been something to see, but for the most part they weren't terribly interesting to hear, and for the most part didn't improve on the frivolous original.

By far the best *Orphée* and *Belle Hélène* were recorded in the dawn of the LP age by **René Leibowitz.** Neither (to my knowledge) has been transferred to CD. Performances of excerpts from both works recorded by Pathé during the same period have been reissued in a valuable CD (EMI 67515, with numbers from *La Vie Parisienne*). These are among the best recordings of these neo-classic delights, all conducted by **Jules Gressier** with the Concerts Lamoureux. Michel Roux is a splendid Jupiter (and Calchas in *Hélène*), Aimé Doniat an excellent Aristeus-Pluto, and the other roles are beautifully done by stalwarts of the era like Liliane Berton, Claudine Collart (also the Eurydice for Leibowitz), and Claude Devos (an appealing Orphée).

The deleted EMI rendition of the 1874 enlargement was, at the time of its release a century later, a considerable achievement for Offenbachians, and a good deal of fun despite its grandeurs. This has been supplanted by an ideal compromise of the two-act and four-act versions under **Minkowski**'s leadership for a radio production in 1998 with the Lyon Opera (EMI 56725). All ears here are on the glamorous Eurydice of Dessay and the modern sound; the supporting cast on the whole doesn't rise to a '50s level in its luxurious vivacity. Still, this is the Orphée of the moment, and, as the first modern musical comedy, a must for any comprehensive musical-theater collection.

A version in German as *Orpheus in der Unterwelt,* with fine operetta singers like Benno Kusche and Adolf Dallapoza, well-cast and nicely produced, will appeal most to those who speak that language (EMI 693600). EMI has also reissued its famous excerpts from the 1960 Sadler's Wells English version (translated by Geoffrey Dunn), a delightful production starring June Bronhill, while the Wells's successor company, the English National Opera, has much less success with its 1985 translation by Snoo Wilson (Ter/Jay). Those who saw that production, as I did, will more likely remember Gerald Scarfe's wild sets and costumes.

La Belle Hélène. This opera has possibly the best combination of antics and emotion, burlesque and beauty, and thrilling tunes plus divine orchestration of all the Offenbachs. It appeared at the Théâtre des Variétés (still standing in Paris) in 1864 and made Hortense Schneider—playing Helen of Troy—the world's first operetta diva. It's too bad we have no recordings of Schneider, but we can see and read how her beauty, charm, and sexiness made her such a huge star, easily her era's Marilyn Monroe. The role of Helen has understandably attracted sopranos wishing to emulate not only Schneider but also the legendary beauty of "the face that launched a thousand ships." It's a dream part, in a dream operetta that also defined the composition of character types and voices in subsequent works.

Strangely, we have yet to hear a legendary Helen on discs. There have been several complete versions on LP; with **Leibowitz**'s 1952 *Hélène* with Janine Linda's fine Helen is superior to any subsequent performance, but sadly is not on CD. But no one playing the title role has captured the imagination with a force to equal the legendary Schneider. **Danièle Millet** was unmemorable in the '70s (EMI 69844, excerpts only); **Jessye Norman** (oh, dear!) was fundamentally miscast in the mid-'80s; **Nicky Nancel** (Accord 290002) was for camp followers only. The role of Paris has been better done in recordings by such tenors as André Dran, Charles Burles, and John Aler. The only CD version widely available is once again in German, a mostly lugubrious performance from Munich with a worthwhile cast that includes Rothenberger, Gedda (both slightly mature-sounding) and Fassbaender in the *travesti* role of Orestes. A new Belle Hélène, *en français,* is required—and will soon appear on EMI, with Lott as the Helen under **Minkowski**'s baton.

Barbe-Bleue (Bluebeard). Offenbach wrote *Bluebeard* for the same roster of players as *Hélène,* and it followed at the Variétés in 1866. But this time the fun was mixed with ghoulish thrills and dark emotions, very much foreshadowing the composer of *Les Contes d'Hoffmann.* For this reason, and also because of the fairly tame central satire on ludicrous European royal courts, the work hasn't been as popular (or as often recorded) as it should be. The role of Bluebeard is literally—as well as figuratively—a killer, better suited to Heldentenors like Leo Slezak; such tenors today are too busy with Wagner to bother with something they must perceive (oh, so incorrectly) as "light" opera.

There is but one *Barbe-Bleue* available, a radio performance from 1967 that amply displays (but with inferior sound) the work's wonders (Memories 4591/2; Opera d'Oro 1211). There are some cuts in this long score (especially in the spectacular Act 1 finale) but the performance will send *frissons* of terror and joy down your back in dozens of places, what with the boisterous but elegant Bluebeard of Henri Legay and the supremely well-done Boulotte of Lina Dachary. If any Offenbach deserves a modern complete recording, it's *Barbe-Bleue,* and with revivals at this writing scheduled for companies in Metz and Vienna, one may surface yet.

La Vie Parisienne. This operetta was written for a theater company at the Palais-Royal that specialized in farces with songs, or vaudevilles. The 1866 result is technically the most splendid vaudeville ever written, but it's also a great operetta, with dazzling arias, ensembles, and finales. The question of how to present this piece still vexes: Is it meant to be spat out like a furious boulevard farce or sung more formally by opera types? The answer is somewhere in the middle.

Leaning entirely toward the theatrical are (generous) excerpts from the celebrated 1958 Paris revival by the **Jean-Louis Barrault/ Madeleine Renaud** acting company (Musidisc 206142). Barely sung (in some cases) and raucously played by a small orchestra, this is one of the most joyous and wonderful of all Offenbach recordings, a recreation of what so many of these vaudevilles and operettas must have seemed like in the 1860s. In its persistent gaiety and fizz, you forgive its musical limitations and wonder at the sounds produced by Pierre Bertin and Mme. Renaud as the Swedish baron and baroness and Barrault himself as the raspy Brazilian. Suzy Delair, the film star imported for the production, gives the most assured performance musically as the courtesan Métella.

Next to this, the **Plasson**-led complete performance with Crespin and Mesplé seems rather heavily overbearing (EMI 47154). I wonder, in recordings like these, why Crespin has such a great operetta reputation; I think she lacks Mesplé's sprightliness (at least early in her career). By far the worst Offenbach recording is also of *La Vie Parisienne,* a ghastly German version presented in 1998 in Vienna (where I saw it at the Burgtheater, of all august places) and Berlin (Col Legno 20100). Both Christoph Marthaler, who directed, and **Cambreling,** who conducted, should stay away from operetta. Less objectionable, if too Teutonic in a less reprehensibly old-fashioned way, is a complete Munich-based production with a starry cast that includes Rothenberger, Dallapozza, and Renate Holm (EMI 65360).

La Grande-Duchesse de Gérolstein. This must have had amazing resonance in 1867, just three years before the Franco-Prussian War. In 1870, things German weren't fashionable in Paris, including Offenbach himself, who prudently left the capital for his homeland. But in 1867, Meilhac and Halévy's loony satire on German militarism and petty grand duchies could provoke laughter not only from Parisians but also from Bismarck and other European heads of state, all gathered in Paris for the Exposition Universelle. All had to see not only the operetta but also the Grande-Duchesse herself, Hortense Schneider—preferably in private in her luxury dressing room at the Variétés.

Offenbach's score may not be as consistently winning as his other *chef-d'oeuvres,* but its high points score very well for tunefulness and dramatic effect—notably the swaggeringly sexy entrance song for the Duchess ("Ah! Que j'aime les militaires!") and the ridiculously solemn Sabre Song and parody-opera ensemble in the Act 1 finale. Things threaten to fall apart in Act 3 (they often do in three-act operettas), but several exuberant numbers redeem matters by the curtain's fall.

Earlier singers excel in individual excerpts from the 78 rpm era, but the best *Grande-Duchesse* was a stereo French-excerpts LP on Pathé that EMI briefly reissued (63415, with bits from the less felicitous, late-period *La Fille du Tambour-Major*). Eliane Lublin may not have been a truly imperial Grande-Duchesse, but Raymond Amade is a wonderful Fritz, and the orchestra (under **Félix Nuvolone**) makes us wish the whole work had been recorded then. The entire work was recorded, live, with a mostly Italian cast from a 1996 performance, with a lot of spirit, a lot of extraneous noise, a Bratislava chorus, a Graz orchestra, and no individual performances to really treasure (Dynamic 173/1-2). Also complete, but in German, is a radio performance with Enriqueta Tarrès conducted by **Pinchas Steinberg** that will appeal to those who prefer their Offenbach as performed at the Vienna Volksoper or the Munich Gärntnerplatztheater—that is, with boots rather than slippers (EMI 66373). But some will want boots in so mock-military a work.

La Périchole. In recent years this operetta has become very popular again, in France and elsewhere, and it's not difficult to fathom why. It has an exotic setting (18th-century Peru), wonderful songs, brilliant finales, and a host of comic characters and situations. Street singers performing a habañera and a seguidilla, a drunken wedding ceremony, a merry court scene involving accusations and an arrest, and a jolly jail scene all contribute to the general merriment. There's also genuine feeling and sentiment behind the humor, as exemplified by such famous numbers as La Périchole's Letter Song and her Act III song with the refrain "Je t'adore, brigand." Another boost for this operetta's reputation was administered by a Metropolitan Opera production in the '50s, recorded (LP only), revived, and published.

Pathé recorded the ideal *Périchole* on LPs in the late '50s, a mono performance starring Suzanne Lafaye and Raymond Amade as the lovers and Louis Noguera as the comic viceroy, under the superb baton of **Markevitch**. Excerpts, once again, but fairly substantial ones, were on a CD to seek out (EMI 69845). In the '70s and early '80s, Crespin, Vanzo, and Bastin under **Lombard** sought to rival this rendition (Erato 45696, NA), while Berganza, Carreras, and Bacquier under **Plasson** attempted the same (EMI, also NA). Neither really succeeded, though the sound under Plasson is richly large-scaled. Amade can't be equaled as a perfect Offenbach tenor, with Carreras utterly and unpleasantly at sea in this repertoire. Crespin and Berganza have their moments, and at times are better individually than Lafaye, but the ensemble work with Markevitch is so enthralling that his version remains definitive, worth buying an LP turntable should you find the original complete pressing.

Should there be a recording from the 1999–2000 Jérôme Savary productions at the Paris Chaillot or Opéra-Comique theaters, you'd best avoid it if you seek the original 1868 sound. It does to Offenbach and Meilhac/Halévy what Papp did to Gilbert and Sullivan with *Pirates of Penzance* in 1980, but more outrageously—and just as, if not more, hilariously.

Les Brigands. The satire behind *Les Brigands*—rather than the score— is quite possibly what's behind the current resurgence of this work in popularity. Compared to *La Périchole*, the music is distinctly B+ Offenbach: tuneful, witty, enchantingly scored, but without quite the brilliance of the former work. The story involves brigandage (read gangsterism) as a respectable trade, a conceit that Gilbert gleefully seized upon when he was called in to write a translation from Meilhac and Halévy's original. But there's also a more wearisome element of disguises and other imbroglios that doesn't play as well.

Gardiner led a well-received revival in 1988 at the Lyon Opera that's as zippy and lovely a performance as you could wish for, especially with the Fragoletto of Colette Alliot-Lugaz and the Fiorella of Ghislaine Raphanel, two young singers who shine in French operetta (EMI 49830,

NA). A pity we haven't a recording of the work with Gilbert's words— that would be something wonderful indeed: Gilbert and Offenbach!

Other works. The few recorded one-act works show how ephemeral, if intermittently delightful, these little operettas are on stage. They were originally not much more than musical skits, something along the lines of the minimusicals we saw on television comedy-variety shows years ago. Produced for a local audience in a few days or weeks, they were never meant to travel into the next two centuries, and their short formats meant that character and musical development were necessarily limited. Still, a few Offenbach trifles have survived, with some getting recordings.

A triple bill given at the Opéra-Comique in 1982 (which I saw) got a CD packaging: *Pomme d'api, Monsieur Choufleuri restera chez lui le . . . ,* and *Mesdames de la Halle* (EMI 74936, NA). The first is a romantic trifle, the second a poke at Italian grand opera pretensions, the third a drag escapade. The musical recipe for these generally consists of five or so numbers, the third or fourth of which, usually in fast tempo, is reprised as the joyous finale. One of the most delightful of the one-acters is the chinoiserie *Ba-ta-clan,* which again parodies operatic excesses with lyrics in a pidgin-Italian "Chinese." This and other Offenbach short works deserve a series of new recordings—the kind of thing Marco Polo could do well at minimal expense, providing it uses French singers.

Some small labels (like Bourg, now vanished, I fear) have over the years offered LP or CD versions of some of Offenbach's other, less successful full-length and short operettas, as well as the occasional pasticcio concocted from cuttings from his operettas—*Christopher Columbus* is the best of these (Opera Rara 2). Most of them disappear from catalogues and stores very quickly. There is also an attractive disc of the opéra-comique *Robinson Crusoe* from 1867, the best moments of which are the more *opéra-bouffe*-esque (Opera Rara 7). A better if more limited way to get to know the rarer pieces is by hearing excerpts from these— and the more familiar works—recorded on 78s by *spécialistes.* The French label Forlane has a series now on three discs, plus a fourth devoted to Hoffmann, which offers much pleasure. The third of these offers the best numbers from *Les Brigands, Le Roi Carotte, La Jolie Parfumeuse, Madame l'Archiduc* and others, ending with *La Fille du Tambour-Major,* composed one year before Offenbach's death.

Hearing Reynaldo Hahn accompanying himself in a song from *La Boulangère a des écus* is a particular joy. But the best of these ancient treasures crops up in Vol. 2 with the Russian Mme. Novikova giggling and gargling the drunken ariette from *La Périchole*—a truly intoxicating experience, and one that Offenbach no doubt would have adored.

TRAUBNER

ORCHESTRAL WORKS

Overtures. Offenbach would probably be amused to learn that many of the pieces being passed off as his overtures these days are in fact the work of other hands. The overture to *Orpheus in Hades* we all know and love was actually compiled by Karl Binder, who expanded Offenbach's brief introduction to include Orpheus's violin solo and of course the wildly popular can-can, while the familiar version of *La Belle Hélène* is generally attributed to an arranger named Haensch, in each case designed to accommodate Viennese tastes. Both *Barbe-Bleue* and *La Grande-Duchesse de Gérolstein* boast curtain-raisers fashioned by Fritz Hoffmann, with the latter including an optional insert sometimes omitted in performance; thus, one may encounter long and short versions of both pieces.

Marriner offers the original overture to *La Belle Hélène,* the familiar

Orpheus, and the short versions of *Barbe-Bleue* and *La Grande-Duchesse,* filled out with *La Fille du Tambour-Major, La Périchole, Les Deux Aveugles,* and *La Vie Parisienne* (Philips 411476*)*. **De Almeida** gives us the tableau created by Offenbach for the far more lavish 1874 restaging of *Orpheus* and five even rarer items: *Voyage dans la Lune, Die Rheinnixen, Monsieur et Madame Denis, Le Roi Carotte,* and *Maître Péronilla* (♦Philips 422057), and on his disc of arias with Von Stade makes room for the short versions of *Barbe-Bleue* and *Grande-Duchesse* plus three more (RCA 68116). *Voyage dans la Lune* and *Rheinnixen* may also be had with **Swierczewski,** along with *Orpheus* and the short form of *Grande-Duchesse* (♦Nimbus 5303).

Only a certain languor in the waltzes keeps **Frémaux** from going to the head of the list; still, he does offer the long versions of *Barbe-Bleue* and *Grande-Duchesse,* plus fine accounts of *Orpheus, Belle Hélène,* and *La Vie Parisienne* (Klavier 11040). Even with less than alluring string sound, **Karajan**'s collection still gives pleasure; he includes the long versions of *Barbe-Bleue* and *Grande-Duchesse* along with *Orpheus, Belle Hélène,* and *Vert-Vert* (DG 400044). Those with access to import labels will find joyous if eccentric accounts of six overtures with **Scherchen** (Millennium 80106, padded out with some dreary Suppé from Rudel); this is far better than **Bruno Weil**'s tedious CD, even though he offers the same pieces plus two more (Sony 53288).

You'd do better to seek out **Kunzel**'s *Vert-Vert;* he also gives you *L'Ile du Tulipatan* and both *Orpheus* and *Belle Hélène* as well as the long versions of *Barbe-Bleue* and *Grande-Duchesse,* but the novelty here is an entirely different pastiche for *La Vie Parisienne* created by Dorati (Vox 5131). Scintillating accounts of *Orpheus* and *Belle Hélène* are offered by **Paray** (Mercury 434332) and **Fiedler** (RCA 61429), the latter joined by the long version of *Grande-Duchesse;* both also include a brief suite from *Tales of Hoffmann* including the "Barcarolle." Others remain in limbo, at least on CD, including sparkling accounts of *La Vie Parisienne* from **Vilem Tausky** and *La Fille du Tambour-Major* from **Rosenthal** (both EMI).

Ballets. The only full-length ballet Offenbach wrote was *Le Papillon,* his hopes centered on a young danseuse named Emma Livry, then the toast of Paris; but after her dismaying death (her skirt caught fire when as the Butterfly she got too close to the gaslights), Offenbach salvaged a couple of pieces, including one we now know as the "Apache Dance." **Bonynge**'s recording is unfortunately available only as makeweight for his *Nutcracker* (♦London 444821).

On expanding *Orpheus* from two acts to four, Offenbach created three new divertissements for the corps de ballet. One of them, "Ballet Pastoral," is included in **de Almeida**'s disc of overtures (Philips), while **Swierczewski** offers "Ballet des Mouches," wherein Jupiter tries to attract Eurydice's attention by changing himself into a fly (Nimbus). Both conductors also present "Ballet of the Snowflakes" from *Le Voyage dans la Lune*—depicting a snowstorm on the moon—but while this scene calls for a wind machine, Swierczewski omits it and also the music written to accompany it. You may also find a set coupling **Mackerras**'s brief suite from *Gaîté Parisienne* with even more lavish fare, the ballet *La Belle Hélène* arranged by Aubert and Rosenthal (EMI 68289); but what really recommends this set is **Henry Krips**'s memorable sextet of waltzes by Emile Waldteufel, otherwise unavailable on CD.

Offenbach's best known ballet remains *Gaîté Parisienne,* but it was actually put together by Manuel Rosenthal for the Ballets Russes de Monte Carlo using selections suggested by impresario Sol Hurok and choreographer Léonide Massine. Massine had doubts about the fin-

ished product until he showed it to Stravinsky, who exclaimed, "Léonide, if you reject this score, you are an idiot; you will be rejecting what may be the greatest success of your career!" From its opening night it has never failed to prove Stravinsky right, a feast for eye and ear. Not surprisingly, **Rosenthal** himself recorded it three times, first in 1953 with the RIAS in Berlin, then again in 1977 (EMI TOCE-7153), and most recently with the 92-year-old master once again conducting his beloved Monte Carlo orchestra (Naxos). On EMI Rosenthal lingers affectionately over the magical waltz tunes, yet sails into the can-can sequence with an élan that leaves even Fiedler puffing to the rear. Unfortunately it's only available as a Japanese import, though worth looking for; the Naxos is leaden and lifeless.

Another dispirited *Gaîté* comes from **Previn;** it seems incredible that the man who gave us the frothy film score *Irma la Douce* could have missed the point so badly (Philips). **Solti** is just the opposite, piling into it with a will—exhilarating, certainly, but lacking a sense of humor (London). **Kunzel** has the advantage of lush sound, but his decision to rearrange things so that the soothing 'Barcarolle' isn't the last thing we hear pretty much rules him out (Telarc). **Munch**'s full-blown treatment is just as lavish, with some rather eccentric tempos along the way. Far better is **Dutoit,** who brings out all the joy of the music without excess or affectation (London 430718).

Next to Rosenthal, surely the conductor most affectionately remembered for *Gaîté Parisienne* is **Fiedler,** who recorded it first in 1954 and again five years later. And next to Rosenthal, surely no one knew and loved this music more; his bracing treatment has never been bettered. His first recording—a collector's item on LP—has been brought out in RCA's "Living Stereo" series (♦61847), coupled with an all-too-brief suite from *La Boutique Fantasque* and sounding as fresh as ever; you can find an even more colorful remake, coupled with his coruscating suite from *Gayne* (♦Victrola 57734). **Felix Slatkin** is a bit sentimental in the waltz scenes but has plenty of panache where it counts (EMI 67248).

If a suite will suffice, there are several to choose from, including two from **Karajan** that have been reissued numerous times (Angel and DG), as well as the **Mackerras** mentioned above and **Kunzel** (in the Vox Box with the overtures). If you buy **Bernstein**'s Bizet Symphony, as you should—either in the "Royal Edition" (Sony 47532) or the more recent "Bernstein Century" series (Sony 61830)—you will also get willy-nilly his coarse-sounding, slapdash arrangement. Far better are **Ormandy** (Sony 48279, rather curiously thrown together with Rachmaninoff's *Symphonic Dances*) and **Dorati,** whose festive treatment of both *Gaîté* and Strauss's *Graduation Ball* are coupled with Fistoulari's splendid *Giselle* (Mercury 434365).

Gaîté Parisienne is not Rosenthal's only Offenbach pastiche; several years later he wrote another, *Offenbachiana,* based on entirely different material including the familiar "Apache Dance." There's no story this time, merely a nonstop cascade of melody and color including some ribald writing for trombone and tuba that makes *Gaîté Parisienne* sound positively genteel. **Rosenthal**'s original recording still sounds respectable (Varèse LP), but it was supplanted by a stereo remake for 20th-Century Fox called *Offenbachiade,* now available in a set called "Hommage à Manuel Rosenthal" (Adés 13.283). Rosenthal fills out his latest *Gaîté Parisienne* with maybe half the score, omitting the wonderful "Apache Dance" in the process, and as in *Gaîté* he trudges through it in thoroughly dispirited fashion (Naxos). Two other delightful arrangements by Dorati, *Bluebeard* and *Helen of Troy,* have been reissued in excellent mono sound with **Joseph Levine** (EMI 67100).

CONCERTOS

Since Offenbach was an accomplished cellist long before he turned to the stage, it's not surprising that his gift for melody and color should carry over into his works for the cello, no doubt written primarily for his own use. The "Military" Concerto, written some 10 years before *Orpheus in Hades,* rather belies its title with a rich array of melody, at times suggesting bel canto; certainly if the sparkling final rondo has any fleeting "military" overtones, they are of the parade ground, not the street barricades of the time.

It's played with panache and sparkle by **Harnoy,** ably seconded by de Almeida (RCA 68420). Harnoy also offers the delightful *Concerto Rondo* with Kunzel (in the Vox Box or separately as RCD 10022; British RCA 71003). **Catalin Ilea** may be set aside, as it's heavily cut and her lush vibrato and sober-sided treatment are all wrong for this music (Olympia). The charming *Musette* for cello is included in Fiedler's splendid "Offenbach in America," with **Samuel Mayes** doing the honors (RCA 61429). **Marcel Cariven** offers a frothy assortment of fantasies and quadrilles, including many you'll recognize from *Gaîté Parisienne;* Don't let its title — "Offenbachiana" — fool you; it has nothing to do wih the Rosenthal concoction (♦Omega 1034).   HALLER

Carl Orff (1895–1982)

Orff is known for many things, including the Orff method in music education, but he's best known as the composer of *Carmina burana.* There are so many recordings of this thrilling, viscerally exciting music that a small volume could be dedicated solely to it. You'd think that with all the versions already available, the record companies would move on to something else. No fear: Old habits die hard, and by the time this book appears in print, there will probably be at least three new versions and five remastered reissues of older recordings.

Previn's earlier version for EMI has been remastered again; not having heard the newest edition, I can't adequately compare it to its former self. All the same, it has the advantages of good sound and soloists and a first-rate choir and orchestra. But it appeared nearly 30 years ago and has been superceded in all areas except for Thomas Allen, who remains one of the best exponents of the baritone solos. Gerald Finley does the treacherous tenor solo well, if without the imagination of others, and Sheila Armstrong is dull average with some wobbly tone and a wretched high D in "Dulcissime." Previn's remake has better sound and a more forthright tenor soloist (Frank Lopardo), but the rest, while good enough, isn't memorable (DG).

Ozawa has made two fine recordings. The first, with the Boston Symphony, has been considered a classic for many years, and deservedly so. This also has recently been remastered, and I'm told the new version has a slightly better bass response than previous incarnations, but the excerpt I heard didn't seem miraculously improved. The original was noteworthy for its natural, clear sound, present in the version I have (RCA 56533). The choir and orchestra are superb, and the soloists (Evelyn Mandac, Stanley Kolk, and Sherrill Milnes) not only sing well but characterize memorably. Ozawa isn't a conductor we usually remember for his sense of humor, but here he seems to be really enjoying himself. His remake is also distinguished, with even more spacious sound, but seems rather anonymous (Philips). The choir and orchestra are among the best, and the soloists (Gruberová, Aler, Hampson) are excellent — but I can't retain any special memory of this performance even after hearing it again only a short while ago.

Muti's aggressively recorded and played version will be the first choice for many; he has a fine orchestra, choir, and soloists. It has been remastered for the "Great Recordings of the Century" series, and it's pretty darn good (EMI). I think Augér has been overrated (I find her a little wily and bland), but I wouldn't seriously argue with anyone who chose it as his or her favorite.

You'd expect **Levine**'s recording to be distinguished, and up to a point it's exciting, but all his enthusiasm can't make up for a lack of passion (DG). Phillip Creech's voice was much criticized for being throaty and rough, but I think that that only adds to his characterization; he's the only one of the soloists who is at all memorable. June Anderson was, I think, a last-minute replacement for Battle (how lovely it would have been to hear her in this music). She's competent, but her voice starts to squall and wobble all over the place up high (her high D positively hurts), and she never sounds as if she's interested in what she's supposed to be singing about. Weikl was starting to get wobbly himself at about this time, and although his characterizations are apt, his intonation troubles quickly become irritating. The sound is rather hi-fi-ish and a little dull.

I sang in this work with the Atlanta Symphony under Levi and remember that we didn't have a lot of time to rehearse. Fortunately, most of the choir had sung it under Shaw's leadership and knew the piece very well. **Shaw**'s own recording sounds wonderful: clear and spacious, and the choral work, predictably, is spectacular. The soloists (Blegen, William Brown, Hagegård) are good and fit into Shaw's sedate reading very well. **Blomstedt** recorded this work with San Francisco forces and excellent soloists (Lynne Dawson, John Danhielcki, and Kevin MacMillan). The sound is superb; the recording won a Grammy and for once deserved it.

Older recordings of distinction include **Jochum**'s classic account (another remastered job), supervised by the composer himself (DG). The choir and orchestra have this music in their blood, and the soloists (Janowitz, Stolze, Fischer-Dieskau) remain among the finest to have recorded the work. **Stokowski**'s version has also survived the decades with a high reputation (EMI). He makes some cuts (eliminating extra verses of some of the choral music), and his tenor rescues the baritone a few times when the music gets too high (though other baritones have managed it); it's more interesting for its differences than for anything very musical (I do like the conductor's manic energy, however). **Tilson Thomas**'s account has its adherents (Sony). I find the sound excessively doctored and deplore the fact that some of the solo material was dubbed in later and sounds like it. The engineer made little effort to match acoustics, and the whole thing sounds like an assembly line job.

Other notable accounts include **Mata**'s version with Aler in prime voice (RCA) and **Ormandy**'s exciting rendition; he also has three good soloists (Sony). I've eliminated from serious consideration any version that uses a countertenor in the tenor solos. The singer is supposed to sound stretched and squawky; with a "male alto," it sounds just plain squawky. Others may not be bothered by this, and in that case they'll want to consider the otherwise excellent versions by **Mehta** (Teldec), **Plasson** (EMI), and **Chailly** (Decca).

Perhaps more interesting (because we haven't heard the music so many times) are the other works in Orff's *Trionfi,* of which *Carmina burana* is the third. The record companies haven't been nearly as generous with the others, and there are only a handful of recordings available, some of which aren't readily accessible in the American market. **Kegel** recorded all three, and his versions are well played and sung in excellent sound (Berlin). **Welser-Möst** also recorded all three, but his are much too polite, drearily sung, with cavernous sound. He respects the letter of the score but not the passion; if you're going to do this music, you must leave your sexual and scatological inhibitions at home.

Orff's other stage works seem to go in and out of the catalog. *Der Mond* and *Die Kluge* are delicious operas that we don't hear or see performed nearly enough. There have been fine recordings available, but these have disappeared from the catalog, at least for the time being. **Sawallisch** recorded both with Schwarzkopf and Frick in the cast, and maybe these will be reissued sometime soon (EMI). Thomas Stewart and **Popp** appeared in both operas and performed with great distinction, sadly long gone (Eurodisc). Orff's other operas based on Greek legends—*Antigonae* and *Oedipus der Tyran*—were available for a while, but have now become expensive imports. They're truly exciting, but be prepared to find your own libretto; because of copyright restrictions, DG wasn't allowed to provide any text or translations.   REYNOLDS

Leo Ornstein (b. 1892)

Ornstein's music, like that of many of his contemporaries, shows major stylistic changes over time. He began as an enfant terrible in the days before WWI, when noisy, barbaric music was less acceptable than it became in the roaring '20s. His early piano pieces used to be available on several discs, notably from Orion, but haven't remained in print. We seem determined to deny appreciation to a composer while he's still alive, an attitude Ornstein is doing his best to challenge by living to a ripe old age.

The earliest piece presently listed appears to be his 1913 Violin Sonata, played with commendable musicality by **Gregory Fulkerson** and Robert Shannon in a well-performed program of American violin works by composers like Copland, Glass, and Richard Wernick (New World 80313). Ornstein's piece is full of tone clusters not wholly disguising a strong romantic impulse. More avant-garde are *Suicide in an Airplane, Three Moods,* and *A la Chinoise,* played with serious purpose by **Daniele Lombardi** in "Futurpiano" (Nuova Era 7240, with works by Antheil and Alexina Lourie). The piano *Arabesques* are refreshingly compact as played by **Marthanne Verbit** in "Past Futurists" (Albany 70, with Sonata 4 and works by Cyril Scott). Verbit is one of the most insightful and musically convincing interpreters of early 20th-century music, handling both the brawny sonorities of *Arabesques* and the more romantic Sonata with equal expertise.

The Cello Sonata is an even more romantic piece, played by **Yehuda Hanani** and Michelle Levin in an American program (Koch 7070, NA). This positively soupy half-hour sonata might have done better for itself if coupled with another Ornstein work. We're beginning to understand that his compositions are basically emotional and more honestly so than those of most 20th-century composers. The most clear-cut example of that side of his work can be found in a disc combining the Blochian Piano Quintet and his recent String Quartet 3, played by the Lydian Quartet with pianist **Janice Weber** (New World 80509). Both of these works are powerful and gorgeous inspirations on the largest of scales, played with conviction. Ornstein is one of the few composers courageous enough to trust his own musical sense rather than subscribing to assorted isms, and it's time our new romanticism caught up to what he's been doing all along. The world will be a more beautiful place when we do.   MOORE

Johann Pachelbel (1653–1706)

Pachelbel was the teacher of Johann Christoph Bach (who was in turn the teacher of his brother Johann Sebastian Bach) and one of the most important German composers of his time. His current representation on CD is limited to many recordings of his *Canon and Gigue in D* and only a few of his other pieces.

The remarkable Canon was written in 1680 for three violins and continuo and has a two-measure bass line or "ground" that repeats 28 times during the 57-measure piece. It's written with one violin part played in canon by three violin voices that enter at two-measure intervals, when the bass begins its pattern again. The piece works very well as background music for events that require flexible amounts of time, like wedding processions and television commercials, because it can be resolved and stopped at any point. It also works as "pop" music because of its repetitions and the fact that it's instantly identifiable by its eight-note ground.

In 1968 **Paillard** recorded the Canon, along with Pachelbel's *Partita 6* and *Partie in G* (MHS; this seems to be the same performance heard on RCA 65468 and Erato 98475). He plays an arrangement that gives the three violin parts to three violin sections while a harpsichord provides a simple harmonic outline. An added viola section plays a pizzicato filler for most of the piece (near the end the violas finally play their ostinato figure with their bows—a very beautiful moment). In this orchestral arrangement the piece is expanded in length, and to maintain clarity with the added voices, the tempo is rather slow. Paillard achieves wonderful dynamic and textural contrasts.

The version of the Canon most familiar to listeners (the London LP calls itself "the record that made it famous") is a transcription by **Münchinger** (London 41193). His source was an organ version of the piece (which may have been the original), and his transcription sounds very organ-like. This recording is just a tad faster than Paillard's, but both are far slower than more recent conductors like **Slatkin**, who also offers such favorites as Borodin's *Nocturne,* Vaughan Williams's *Greensleeves,* and the Tchaikovsky Serenade (Telarc).

After **Karajan** recorded it in 1970 (DG), dozens of others followed. Recordings range from the original instrumentation to a mallet and drum version by **Harold Farberman** (Allegretto). There's a lovely recording by harpist **Yolanda Kondonassis,** who includes the Canon in "A New Baroque," with some fine Handel, Bach, Telemann, and Scarlatti (♦Telarc 80403). "Pachelbel's Greatest Hit" features **Galway** playing an embellished version of the Canon's melody against the pop beat of an electric bass, synthesizers, and strings (RCA). On the same recording he plays a version with Cleo Laine singing the words "How, Where, When?" (I would add the question "Why?")

We get to hear **Canadian Brass** play an antiphonal version in the key of E-flat (Sony and RCA); the **Hampton String Quartet** sets it as counterpoint to the song "Earth Angel"; and there is an entirely synthesized version by **Isao Tomita** and the Plasma Symphony Orchestra. This recording could be ignored if it weren't for Rochberg's fascinating *Variations on the Pachelbel Canon in D* from his String Quartet 6. There are also two rather bland orchestral performances on this disc, one conducted by Ettore Stratta and the other by Rudolf Baumgartner.

In 1984 **Karajan** recorded the Canon again in a slow, organ-like arrangement for large orchestra (DG). In the same year **Marriner** presented a lighter and happier version that includes the Gigue sandwiched between two identical readings of the Canon (Philips 416386). In 1985 **John Williams** recorded it in "Pops in Love" in a very nice arrangement that includes an organ and puts the ground normally played in the bass into some of the upper voices (Philips 16361). **Orpheus Chamber Orchestra** has a nicely flexible and lyrical reading on a recording that includes many familiar fillers: the Albinoni-Giazotto Adagio, Corelli's Christmas Concerto, Bach's "Jesu Joy of Man's Desiring," and Handel's "Largo" from *Xerxes* (♦DG 429390).

The only orchestral recording I know that includes the Canon's companion Gigue is Marriner's; however, all the period-instrument recordings include it. They are also all rather clever in their programming: If you buy the three best baroque instrument recordings, you also get an excellent library of Baroque music, with very little duplication. **Pinnock** and the English Concert play warmly and evenly, bringing out the structural aspects of the piece (♦Archiv 11518). They use a version with three violins and continuo without any added voices, aside from the harpsichord's right-hand improvisation. Orchestral arrangers try to disguise the Canon's repetition of the same material by adding voices, dynamics, and variations to relieve its monotony, and in this solid and sober reading they use a moving but reasonable tempo. The disc includes Handel's "Entry of the Queen of Sheba" from *Solomon,* Albinoni's Oboe Concerto, Charles Avison's Concerto Grosso 9, and Haydn's D major harpsichord concerto.

Goebel solves the problem of possible monotony by playing the Canon as fast as possible, and playing the cascades of thirty-second notes detached rather than legato (♦DG 427118, with two suites and an Aria with Variations by Pachelbel and three Buxtehude sonatas). **Hogwood** offers a very relaxed and light Canon that moves forward without sounding too fast (♦Oiseau-Lyre 410553). This recording includes some very nice readings of four Vivaldi violin concertos, his two-trumpet concerto, and some excellently played Gluck and Handel.

Pachelbel's choral music is sung by **Capella Sebaldina Nuremberg** (Entrée 050) and **Cantus Cologne** (Harmonia Mundi 77305). There are recordings of his organ music on LP and cassette that haven't been released on CD, but luckily **John Butt** recorded the *Hexachordum Apollinis* (Harmonia Mundi 7907029), one of Pachelbel's most important pieces, and **Piet Kee** recorded several of his *Chaconas* (Chandos 0520).

The harpsichordist/organist **Joseph Payne** has recorded several suites from 1693 attributed to Pachelbel (Bis 809) and is in the process of recording all of his organ music in a 10CD set (Centaur 2304, Vol. 1).

FINE

Ignace Jan Paderewski *(1860–1941)*

There's no question that Paderewski was one of the great pianists of our century, with sold-out recitals worldwide and command performances before the crowned heads of Europe. Yet surely none of this well-earned adulation gave the intensely patriotic Paderewski as much pride as that day in 1919 when as Prime Minister he stepped forward to sign the Treaty of Versailles on behalf of the Polish people, a peace that sadly proved all too fleeting. In his compositions virtuosity gives way to humanity; Paderewski was a proud man whose tireless effort against oppression earned him the thanks of a grateful nation quite apart from his very real influence on generations of pianists.

ORCHESTRAL MUSIC

Paderewski distilled into his "Polonia" Symphony all the intense patriotic fervor that fired his soul and fueled his art; it is a massive structure lasting well over an hour and calling for immense forces. Ostensibly intended to commemorate the failed revolt of the Poles against the Czar in 1863, the audience understood what the music was really about and easily picked up on the fleeting fragments of the Polish national anthem heard in the finale. **Jerzy Maksymiuk** gives a committed and fervent account with truly prodigious playing by the BBC Scottish Symphony and superb sound (♦Hyperion 67056). **Bohdan Wodiczko** is even more intense, but suffers from huge cuts in the outer movements (Olympia). **Roland Bader** offers Walter Rabl's colorful potpourri from the opera

Manru and uncredited arrangements of several piano pieces, including the famous Minuet in G (Koch Schwann 1735); it shares with Naxos (below) a cheerful earlier *Overture,* treated in more upbeat fashion by **Wit.**

Paderewski wrote one piano concerto, an effusive outpouring of song spurred by the polonaise and mazurka rhythms so loved by Chopin; the even more flamboyant *Fantaisie Polonaise,* a rhapsodic tribute to his homeland, is often paired with it. Current couplings include **Ewa Kupiec** (♦Koch Schwann 6550), **Karol Radziwonowicz** (Polskie Nagrania 105), **Tirino** (♦Newport 85525), **Blumental** (Ars Classicum 1159322), and **Fialkowska** (Naxos 554020). The Concerto may also be obtained separately from **Piers Lane** (Hyperion 66452, with Moszkowski's Concerto), **Wild** (Élan 82266, with Scharwenka's Concerto 1), **Barbara Hesse-Bukowska** (Olympia 302, with Paderewski's Sonata), **Piotr Paleczny** (Olympia 398, with Henryk Melcer's Concerto 1 played by Ponti), and **Regina Smendzianka** (Olympia 305, with *Polonia*). Second thoughts on the Concerto and *Fantaisie* are paired by Radziwonowicz and Smendzianka (Koch Schwann 1145).

While this seems like a formidable array, Kupiec quite sweeps the field in the Concerto, bringing together sure technique, passion and tonal beauty in a way that puts most of the others in the shade, though Tirino's virile account is a close second. Wild's fondly remembered performance now seems breathless by comparison, particularly the hectic finale (also Lane's downfall). Worst of the lot is Fialkowska, though Radziwonowicz (both times) and Paleczny seem particularly disjointed in the opening movement.

In the *Fantaisie* Kupiec is more reflective than some; here Tirino's more uninhibited account pulls ahead, and surprisingly so does Fialkowska, making this piece and the Overture the main reasons to buy the Naxos disc. Radziwonowicz simply slogs through the piece, while Smendzianka is hampered by poor orchestral support (so is Blumental in both pieces) and on Koch Schwann she's mannered and dispirited. Wild's recording of the *Fantaisie,* originally coupled with the Concerto on an RCA LP, remains unavailable on CD.

PIANO MUSIC

Save for a mannered Minuet in G, **Kupiec**'s solo recital offers fresh, dedicated playing (Koch 1176). She includes the *Tatra Album,* strangely omitted from **Radziwonowicz**'s "complete" survey (Chant du Monde 2781073, 3CD). This piece also appears in two other collections, with **Adam Wodnicki** (Altarus 9045) and **Rinko Kobayashi** (Polskie Nagrania 073). Kobayashi plays with more polish than passion; Wodnicki is preferable, though in the more substantial *Miscellanea* and the impassioned Sonata in E-flat he faces stiff competition from **Waldemar Malicki** (Adda 581186). The Sonata, played skillfully by **Andrzej Stefanski,** fills out Barbara Hesse-Bukowska's Concerto (Olympia). **Paderewski**'s own performances of five pieces may be heard, mostly taken from piano rolls and including the Minuet in G (LaserLight 14205).   HALLER

Nicolò Paganini *(1782–1840)*

Paganini was the greatest violinist who ever lived. He was scorned in his lifetime by such eminent musicians as Ludwig Spohr, who found his playing and compositions shallow and vulgar, yet even Spohr had to admit that he had raised violin technique to a new level. With Paganini began the myth of the virtuoso soloist as some sort of superman. In his day, this manifested itself as a rumor that he had sold his soul to the devil in exchange for boundless virtuosity. He made hay off the fact that only he was able to play his compositions. This was partly because he published very few works in his lifetime; it helps to make sure no one else has the opportunity to practice your scores, if exclusivity is your goal, and his heirs jealously guarded his manuscripts well into the 20th century. It's rumored that some of Paganini's music has survived only in scores created by enterprising musicians who copied what he played at his concerts.

Though he was an inspiration to the Romantics, Paganini's style is solidly classical, rooted in Italian opera. His melodies and technical tricks owe much to the coloratura tradition. His virtuosity on the guitar, tuned in fourths and a third, also seems to have inspired some of his more torturous multiple-stop configurations for the left hand on the violin, tuned in fifths.

SOLO VIOLIN MUSIC

Caprices Op. 1. The only works Paganini published in his lifetime, the 24 *Caprices* were printed in 1820. They are a summa of violin technique up to that time. Upon their publication, many considered them unplayable; since then, they have become staples of conservatory instruction, and many violinists have recorded them all.

The first complete recording was **Ossy Renardy**'s in 1940 (Biddulph). He didn't use the original, unaccompanied version, choosing instead a piano accompaniment supplied by Ferdinand David. These accompaniments were almost mandatory at one time, but they sound strange today, when the *Caprices* are usually played unaccompanied. Renardy was technically proficient but not a very charismatic or dazzling musician, and this music exists to dazzle.

The first complete recording of the original version was by **Ricci** in 1947 (IDIS). These readings are technically more than adequate, and Ricci frequently dazzles, but he's not the most expressive violinist. He recorded the *Caprices* again many years later on Paganini's own violin, the powerful "Cannon" Guarnerius del Gesù of 1742 (Biddulph). The only del Gesù to have escaped having its plates thinned out, the instrument proves to be more than Ricci can handle; many of the fast passages either don't sound at all or sound weak and hoarse at best. **Rabin** recorded eleven of the *Caprices* in 1950 at the age of 14 (Sony 60894). His playing is astonishing for one so young, not just in its technical security but in its powerful expression. He recorded the complete set in 1958; his technique here is really stunning, and this immediately became the one to beat (EMI 64560).

For a long time after this, few tried. **Perlman** recorded them in 1972; he matched Rabin for technique and surpassed him in tone and charisma (♦EMI 67257). Occasionally, as in 7 and 20, Perlman misplaces his rhythmic accents; still, there's an Italianate feel to his playing that really brings the music to life. **Accardo**'s recording is technically secure but not quite up to Rabin's or Perlman's standards technically or interpretively (DG). **Midori** isn't suited to Paganini's exhibitionism, and occasionally she shows some strain (Sony, NA). **Alexander Markov** seems to think the whole point of playing the *Caprices* is to show the strain (Erato), yet Paganini is reported to have never broken a sweat (figuratively, of course). **Ilya Kaler**'s recording is about on Accardo's level (Naxos).

Benjamin Schmid has recorded the *Caprices* with the piano accompaniment supplied by Robert Schumann. Schmid is a real virtuoso, with an effortless staccato and a flawless left hand, but he lacks the instinct to dazzle, and Schumann's Teutonic harmonies clash with Paganini's Italianate style and are definitely not what the composer seems to imply (MD+G). **Leonidas Kavakos** possesses a demonic technique and knows how to put on a show; he's a bit poker-faced, though, in the more lyrical sections (Dynamic 66). **James Ehnes** plays beautifully and has a fine technique; no one has ever played the last six more musically, and

these alone are worth the price of the disc (♦Telarc 80398). **Frank Peter Zimmerman** plays with great charm and never forgets that just because the music is difficult doesn't mean he can forget to phrase, which he does wonderfully (♦EMI, NA).

You will usually find the shorter compositions of all the major virtuoso composers of the 19th century dispersed among discs of similar music that today is usually only played as encores. In Paganini's case, the most familiar of these pieces, for solo violin or violin and guitar, include *I Palpiti, Le Streghe, Introduction and Variations on Nel cuor più non mi sento, La Campanella*, the famous *Cantabile, Il Carnevale di Venezia*, and *Moto perpetuo*. The best rule of thumb for selecting a disc is to get one by your favorite virtuoso violinist. The operative word here is "virtuoso," as Paganini's music is no pleasure to hear if the performer doesn't have a tremendous technique.

Heifetz, Milstein, Rabin, Ricci, Příhoda, Perlman, Accardo, the young Menuhin, and Fodor have recorded excellent Paganini. **Příhoda**'s Concerto 1 disc has a few short works thrown in (Biddulph 135), and so does **Gringolts**'s, in which his playing is just as effortless and lyrical as in the Concerto. **Menuhin**'s is filled out with highly expressive accounts of several *Caprices* and a stunning *Introduction and Variations*, among others (Biddulph 102). **Stefan Milenkovich** has recorded a very full recital of long-time favorites; he has an excellent technique, but other violinists have stronger character (Dynamic 165). **Massimo Quarta** has recorded a number of pieces for the first time from original versions in the surviving manuscripts; he's a superb technician who draws a beautiful tone from the "ex-Baron Knoop" del Gesù violin of 1735 (Dynamic 232).

VIOLIN CONCERTOS

1. The first concerto was recorded by **Fritz Kreisler** in 1938 (Pearl 9362). Already an old man who had been wounded in WWI and seriously injured in an automobile accident, he plays surprisingly well, and his famous warm-hearted manner is evident. The great Czech virtuoso **Příhoda** recorded the first-movement arrangement by August Wilhelmj in 1924 with piano instead of orchestra (Biddulph 135). He sounds a bit more old-fashioned than Kreisler, using more slides as he changes position. **Menuhin** recorded the complete score in 1934 with dazzling technique and tremendous charisma (Biddulph 102). **Francescatti**'s recording radiates a simple joy in music making (Sony 47661). **Rabin** (EMI), **Grumiaux** (Philips), **Vengerov** (Teldec), **Kaler** (Naxos), **Mullova** (Philips, NA) and **Viktor Tretyakov** (Melodiya) fail to convey this joy.

Midori is too introverted for this kind of music, though her technique is fully up to the challenge (Philips). **Sarah Chang** phrases intelligently but lacks charisma (EMI). **Accardo** is fleet-fingered and musically very satisfying (DG 415378; 437210, 3CD). **Shaham** (DG 29786) and **Gringolts** (BIS 999) give no hint of the fiendish difficulty of the score and play with a lovely lyricism. **Perlman** is bursting with joy and has a ravishing tone (EMI 47101). **Philippe Hirshhorn** is the most dazzling of all, in a concert recording from the Queen Elizabeth of Belgium competition of 1967 (♦Cypres 9605, 2CD). On LP, there was a wonderful recording by **Erick Friedman** where he perfectly conveyed the extremes of Paganini's style—impassioned lyricism juxtaposed with crazed exhibitionism (♦RCA, NA).

2. Published posthumously in 1851 together with 1, 2 hasn't attained the former's popularity, perhaps because of its slightly less exhibitionistic character. Often the last movement alone is played, as its recurring strokes of a little bell have endeared it to the public and earned for it the nickname "La Campanella" or "The Door Bell." **Accardo** gives a technically secure, incisive account (DG 415378; 437210, 3CD). **Uto Ughi** is just as facile but a bit more lyrical (RCA, NA). **Gitlis** is technically dazzling, lyrical, and a bit more dramatic than the others (Philips 462865, 2CD). **Ilya Kaler** is technically impeccable but relatively weak in the personality department (Naxos).

3. This concerto wasn't published until the '70s. **Szeryng** played the solo part at its 20th-century premiere, was the first to record it, and gives a satisfying account (Philips). **Accardo** has a little better grasp of Paganini's melodic style (DG 423370; 437210, 3CD).

4. Like 3, 4 wasn't published until the '70s. **Grumiaux** gives a gentle reading short on exhibitionism (Philips 462865, 2CD). **Accardo** is more attuned to Paganini's bold idiom and more involved, too (DG 423370; 437210, 3CD).

5. A product of Paganini's last years, 5 survives only in a manuscript of the solo part that includes detailed instructions for the orchestration. Federico Mompellio has realized an excellent orchestral accompaniment, with some good dialogue between the soloist and orchestra. **Accardo** does full justice to the score's technical and musical demands (DG 437210, 3CD).

6. Despite its numbering, 6 actually antedates 1 by several years. It seems to have been first performed in Milan in 1815 and survives in a manuscript with guitar accompaniment, so Mompellio has again contributed a fine realization of the orchestral score. 6 shows the influence of Viotti and isn't quite as technically demanding as the others. It also has a more serious tone. **Accardo** plays it with brilliance and sensitivity (DG 437210, 3CD).

MUSIC FOR VIOLIN AND GUITAR

Paganini played the guitar for pleasure and for composing. His music for this combination is charming and intimate. The violin usually takes the lead, and the guitar plays a chordal accompaniment. *Centone di Sonate* is the largest collection of these works. Violinist **Moshe Hammer** and guitarist **Norbert Kraft** are disciplined, well-balanced partners, though Hammer is just a bit stiff (Naxos). **Alberto Bianchi** and **Maurizio Preda** are a little more fluid and brilliant, though Preda could be a bit louder in the mix (Dynamic 34, 84, 148). The Violin and Guitar Sonatas are similar to *Centone di Sonate* in that they are also brief, two-movement works. **Scott St. John** and **Simon Wynberg** play this music as if born to the manner (◆Naxos 550759, 550690). St. John's tone is wondrously mellifluous, and he blends virtuoso brilliance and soulful cantabile like no one else.

Václav Hudeček and **Lubomír Brabec** have assembled a recital disc of four of the *Centone di Sonate,* several other works for violin and guitar, and the fiendishly difficult *Introduction and Variations* (Supraphon 3395). They are admirably balanced in a very intimate acoustic and obviously enjoy what they're playing. However, Hudeček, a flaming virtuoso, doesn't seem comfortable playing intimate cantabile lines at a moderate tempo; like a thoroughbred race horse that wasn't born for taking Sunday trots around the neighborhood, he frequently sounds as if he'd like to rip into one of the more difficult *Caprices* at any moment.

Shaham and **Göran Söllscher** are beautifully recorded and balanced in three of the sonatas and two of the *Centone di Sonate,* with a few other compositions and arrangements for violin and guitar (DG 437837). Shaham obviously enjoys the music, but he can't match St. John's lyricism. **Perlman** and **John Williams** are a winning combination in a short recital (◆CBS 34508). Perlman's tone is really gorgeous, and he and Williams have a playful manner that suits this music perfectly.

Bianchi and **Preda** have recorded the recently discovered "Lucca" Sonatas (Dynamic). The music isn't Paganini's best, and the performances have a slapdash quality.

GUITAR MUSIC

Paganini was celebrated for his proficiency on the guitar, and it should come as no surprise that he left a considerable amount of music for that instrument. **Frédéric Zigante** plays these works with taste and the right kind of sentiment (Arts 47192/95, 4CD). MAGIL

John Knowles Paine (1839–1906)

Though not the first American to write a symphony—that honor goes to George Frederick Bristow—certainly Paine may be considered the first American symphonist of any stature, as well as the first professor of music (appointed by the president of Harvard over the objections of the more hidebound faculty). His Mass in D was played to great acclaim abroad, while his two symphonies—the second becoming the first American symphony to be published in this country—were just as warmly received by Boston audiences. With the euphoria that followed WWI, the music of Paine and other composers strongly influenced by German tradition was set aside in favor of a new generation of more American-sounding composers like Copland and Ives; this we may now see as regrettable, for symphonies like Paine's still fall gratefully on the ear and still have the power to fire the emotions just as they did when the idea of being an American composer seemed little more than fantasy.

ORCHESTRAL MUSIC

Paine's Symphony 1 served notice that American composers should be taken seriously, moving the then 21-year-old George Whitefield Chadwick to marvel, "It proved we could have a great musician, and that he could get a hearing." For all its prevailing echoes of Mendelssohn and Schumann, the warmth and spaciousness of the music were qualities that appealed to Boston audiences, perhaps depending more on sheer energy than thematic diversity, yet skillfully molded into a coherent whole. Surging forward impetuously from the very first measures, **Mehta** (◆New World 374) puts **Krueger**'s estimable recording in the shade, even though this LP is one of Krueger's better efforts (MIA 103). It actually sounds better than Mehta's, with an open, airy quality that makes the warm coloring of the CD sound monochromatic by comparison. Mehta also offers the overture to *As You Like It,* energetic and captivating in the manner of Mendelssohn's *Midsummer Night's Dream,* a bright and spirited reading once again closely matched by Krueger (MIA 141).

Symphony 2, written four years later, was likewise enthusiastically received, but at just over 50 minutes in length (some 15 minutes longer than 1) didn't take quite as well to repeated hearings and was perhaps better appreciated by the critics than by the casual concertgoer. Labeled "In Springtime," it's clearly modeled after Raff's Symphony 8 written the year before, bidding winter farewell while welcoming the awakening of Nature nearly in a single breath, and in the final movement, "The Glory of Nature," rather closely resembling its counterpart in Schumann's "Spring" Symphony. Here **Krueger** doesn't fare nearly as well; the cavernous recording (MIA 120) swallows up any vestiges of sunlight, while the fact that his recording is 7 minutes shorter than **Mehta**'s (◆New World 350), despite his sluggish tempos, suggests that judicious cuts have been made en route. In the tone poem *The Tempest*—alternately stormy and fervent in the style of Tchaikovsky—**Krueger** is the only game in town (MIA 130), causing us to hope that this will be a high priority in Bridge's ongoing reissue project.

CHORAL MUSIC

Paine's first great success came with the Mass in D, the first such work by an American composer to be performed in Europe, though reports suggest that American audiences were reduced to hearing it played with organ since the orchestral parts were left behind in Germany; these were later destroyed when Berlin was bombed during WWII, and new parts were prepared under the supervision of **Gunther Schuller** for his recording (♦New World 80262). Schuller's description of the score as "a work of grandeur and haunting beauty" is reflected in the loving care lavished on every aspect of the performance, to the extent that any shortcomings seem irrelevant; soloists are first-rate, and the chorus has obviously been well rehearsed, while the St. Louis players give their very best under Schuller's committed leadership. Here is a recording that will handily repay repeated hearings for all lovers of great choral music.

The oratorio *St. Peter*, a massive and lofty work with rich writing for the chorus as well as more intimate ensembles for the 12 disciples, likewise benefits from **Schuller**'s grand vision, again boasting well-chosen soloists and a strong choral presence, ably supported by the Pro Arte Chamber Orchestra of Boston (GM 2027). Of Paine's extensive incidental music for Sophocles's *Oedipus Tyrannus,* only the Prelude survives on disc, included by **Kenneth Klein** with other music by American composers (EMI 49263; Albany 235); concert performances of the complete score suggest that Schuller might be strongly encouraged to look into this work as well.   HALLER

Giovanni Paisiello (1740–1816)

Paisiello was a prolific composer, with more than 100 operas and 40 masses plus other church music to his credit. His instrumental music includes a variety of string quartets, sonatas, piano concertos, and a harp concerto. Other than several operas, little of his music is heard today.

Concertos. To the extent that the lyricism and easy flow of melody of Paisiello's operas can be translated to the keyboard, his piano concertos will provide pleasure, though those expecting the inspiration of Haydn and Mozart will be disappointed; they contain much that is original and winsome, but little of importance. **Spada** has done yeoman service in putting the scores into playable form, and his performances have the stamp of authority (♦Arts 47120/1), but his clattery, clumsy-action instrument, scrappy ensemble, and too-careful playing must yield to **Mariaclara Monetti**'s more buoyant readings, with a modern concert grand and strong support from the English Chamber Orchestra (♦ASV 872/3). **Blumental**'s spirited accounts of 1 and 2 still give pleasure if you can find them (Ars Classicum 1159382).

Choral music. Paisiello was a favorite of Napoleon and could scarcely turn down the opportunity to direct the choir and orchestra of the Royal Chapel, for which he composed among others his *Messe en Pastorale* for Christmas 1802 as well as three motets: *Tantum ergo, Gloria Patri,* and *Tecum principium.* All four are played by soloists with the Prague Symphony under **Edoardo Brizio** (Studio), unfortunately in shrill sound with excruciating solo singing and notes all in Italian. Paisiello is better served by **Alberto Zedda**'s beautiful performance of the *Missa defunctorum,* written in 1789 for King Ferdinand of Naples following the death of his two young sons. This eloquent and deeply moving music expresses heartfelt sorrow (Fonit Cetra 92). The *Passione di Gesu Cristo is* is more meditation than Passion, but in it there is more humanity than pompous religiosity, and despite less than stellar solo work it's sensitively set forth by Warsaw forces under **Wojciech Czepicl** (Koch Europa 350-250, 2CD).   HALLER

Operas. Few of Paisiello's serious operas have been recorded, and most of the recordings of his comic operas derive from stage performances in secondary performance venues. The most important is *Il Barbiere di Siviglia,* the illustrious predecessor of Rossini's now more famous version. Paisiello's setting was so popular that at its premiere Rossini's was considered inferior and an insult to the earlier composer. The earliest recording (a 1959 studio version) remains the best: **Renato Fasano** leads I Virtuosi di Roma with an experienced set of singers (Sciutti, Monti, Capecchi, Panerai, Petri) in a charming, sparkling performance (♦Palladio 4136, 2CD). A recording from the 1982 Valle d'Istria Festival with Cuberli, Visconti, Corbelli, and Dara scores some high marks (Frequenz CAE2, 2CD). Recordings from Hungary (Hungaroton) and Marstall zu Putbus (Arte Nova) are not in the running.

Paisiello's next best known opera is *Nina, o sia La Pazza per amore.* William Matteuzzi's performance with sturdy help from Jean Marie Bima and Gloria Bandinelli, **Hans Ludwig Hirsch** conducting, is notable (♦Arts 47166, 2CD). **Bonynge** leads singers from Catania in a decent performance (Nuova Era 6872, 2CD), but **Marcello Panni**'s version from Savona doesn't offer much (Bongiovanni).

Among other Paisiello operas on CD that can be recommended are *Don Chisciotte,* a charming version from the Rome Opera (♦Nuova Era 6994, 2CD); *Fedra,* in a tough and rugged 1958 performance from RAI Milano (Memories 4502, 2CD); *Il Mondo della luna,* a rollicking 1993 performance from Bolzano (♦Bongiovanni 2173, 2CD); and a delightful 1959 RAI Naples performance with Sciutti, Gianni Raimondi, Misciano, and Bruscantini of *La Molinara* (♦Melodram 29502; Cetra 2024; 2CD). Difficult to find but worth the effort is an RAI Torino performance of *Il Re Teodoro in Venezia* with **Fasano,** Monti, and Bruscantini (♦Discoteca di Stato 993, 2CD). Paisiello's setting of *La Serva padrona* is best served by a 1991 Munich performance with **Jeanne Marie Bima** and Petteri Salomaa (Arts 47152) and a strong 1991 performance with **Anne Victoria Banks** and Gian Luca Ricci (Nuova Era 7043).   PARSONS

Giovanni Palestrina (ca. 1525–1594)

Palestrina once ranked alone as the supreme Renaissance composer. Even today, now that many composers of his own and earlier generations have been reevaluated, he's still counted among the greatest of them. His 104 masses are the core of his output and of his claim to excellence. Most of them were published during his lifetime or shortly after his death (the posthumous masses include some of his early works), and just over half have been recorded. He wrote around 250 motets — those for five voices are most numerous — as well as other sacred texts such as hymns, offertories, *Magnificats,* and *Lamentations.* He also published two books of secular madrigals (1555, 1586) and two of spiritual madrigals (1581, 1594).

Masses. The finest recent recordings of his masses have come from David Hill's Westminster Cathedral Choir of London (♦Hyperion 66266). The balance of trebles and men's voices (with both boys and men on the alto line) is ideal, and the choir is small enough to possess the flexibility of a vocal ensemble. The perfect introduction to Palestrina's music is *Missa Papae Marcelli* and *Missa brevis,* by far the two most frequently recorded of the masses. The former is a marvelous work of great clarity and beauty for six voices, published in 1567 but possibly composed on the election of Pope Marcellus in 1555. The latter has been a staple of church choirs for its lovely melodies and clear texture for four voices.

The same choir recorded six more masses in four discs. *Missa de beata Virgine* for six voices and *Missa Ave Maria* for four voices are masses of Our Lady, both based on chant melodies (♦Hyperion 66364). Both of these were first recordings, the former a majestic work of ethereal beauty, the latter a contrast in its simplicity and dignity. *Missa O Rex gloriae* for four voices and *Missa Viri Galilaei* for six voices are also first recordings, based on two motets for the Ascension that are included in the disc (♦Hyperion 66316). Both celebrate the joyful aspect of the feast, making full use of musical phrases drawn from the motets. Like the previous disc, this pairing demonstrates the contrast between four-part and six-part writing in similar masses.

Under **Hill**'s successor at Westminster Cathedral, James O'Donnell, the Westminster Cathedral Choir also sings *Missa Aeterna Christi munera* for four voices, which has been recorded a number of times; it's much shorter than those just listed and a favorite with church choirs. The disc is filled out with the chant hymn underlying the music, several motets including the great *Super flumina Babylonis,* and the great *Magnificat* in the first mode for eight voices (♦Hyperion 66490). *Missa Ecce ego Joannes* for six voices is a powerful mass for All Saints Day (♦Hyperion 67099, with a *Magnificat* in the fourth mode and five motets). Herreweghe also recorded *Missa Viri Galilaei* with added chant propers from the composer's era (Harmonia Mundi 901388).

Stephen Darlington's Christ Church Cathedral Choir of Oxford comes close to the highest standard in *Missa O Sacrum Convivium* for five voices, based on the motet for Corpus Christi by Christóbal de Morales, also here, as are a *Magnificat* in the sixth mode and two motets (♦Nimbus 5394). The same choir recorded *Missa Dum complerentur* for six voices, based on the elaborate motet for Pentecost, with four additional motets (♦Nimbus 5100).

Small vocal ensembles have recorded much Renaissance music that was once the province of choirs. Peter Phillips's Tallis Scholars has won high regard in this field. *Missa Sicut lilium* is based on the composer's motet (♦Gimell 454920, with the familiar *Missa brevis*). *Missa Nasce la gioja mia* is based on a madrigal by Giovanni Leonardo Primavera (♦Gimell 454908), *Missa Nigra sum* on a motet by Jean Lhéritier (♦Gimell 454903), and *Missa Benedicta es* on a motet by Josquin des Prez (Gimell 454901). These four masses have been recorded for the first time. They have also recorded *Missa Papae Marcelli* twice (Gimell).

Bruno Turner's Pro Cantione Antiqua has recorded a series of masses, usually filled out with chant propers, sung with greater vigor than the refined Tallis group. *Missa L'homme armé* for five voices (♦Carlton 782, with *Missa Assumpta est Maria*) and *Missa Lauda Sion* (♦Carlton 742, with the familiar *Missa brevis*) are recommended. *Missa L'homme armé* for four voices and *Missa Aeterna Christi munera* are good, but other versions are better (Carlton 772), and the same applies to their *Missa Papae Marcelli* (Carlton 702).

A useful reissue offers five fine masses. St. John's College Choir, Cambridge, offers *Missa Assumpta est Maria* and *Missa Veni sponsa Christi;* the Carmelite Priory Choir of London recorded *Missa Je suis deshéritée (sine nomine)* and *Missa Ecce ego Joannes;* and King's College Choir, Cambridge, sings *Missa Tu es Petrus* for six voices (Decca 458386, 2CD, a "two-fer"). Regensburg Cathedral Choir also recorded the last work in a set that includes their *Missa Dum complerentur,* the Westminster Abbey *Missa Papae Marcelli,* and other sacred works from Pro Cantione Antiqua (Archiv 439961, 2CD, also a "two-fer").

Schola Cantorum of Oxford sings *Missa Hodie Christus natus est,* the marvelous double-choir mass for Christmas, coupled with the *Stabat Mater* and one of the great Lassus double-choir Masses (♦Naxos 550836). The Gabrieli Consort is also very fine in this mass (Archiv 437833). Jeremy Summerly's Oxford Camerata also pairs *Missa Papae*

Marcelli and *Missa Aeterna Christi munera* (Naxos 553238). Delitiae Musicae has recorded two pairs of masses. One disc offers two masses based on motets by Jacquet of Mantua, *Missa Aspice Domine* and *Missa Salvum me fac* (♦Stradivarius 33477); the other contains two masses based on madrigals by Cypriano de Rore, *Missa Qual'è il più grande amore* and *Missa Quando lieta sperai* (Stradivarius 33423). All four are first recordings.

Ensemble Sagittarius made the first recordings of three masses, *Missa Beatus Laurentius* (♦Accord 202462), *Missa Salve Regina* (Accord 203572), and *Missa secunda* (Accord 202162) as well as the more familiar *Missa Ecce ego Joannes* (Accord 203662). Capella Palestrina recorded *Missa pro defunctis* (♦Erasmus 042), and Chanticleer also recorded this little-known mass for the dead (Teldec 94561).

An ensemble from San Petronio under Vartolo coupled *Missa L'homme armé* and *Missa sine nomine,* both for four voices; the latter is mislabeled as a different work for six voices (♦Naxos 553314). Pro Cantione Antiqua also recorded the *L'homme armé* mass (Carlton 772), and Fasolis (Arts 47521) conducted the other work. Vartolo's ensemble also recorded ten masses composed for the Duke of Mantua that were only published in 1954. Only one is set in polyphony throughout, *Missa sine nomine (Mantuana).* The other nine are alternatim masses, in which polyphony alternates with chant, showing a different side of Palestrina's approach to church music. Four of these, *Missa in festis apostolorum I* and *II* and *Missa in semiduplicibus majoribus I* and *II,* are similar in style, and all five are available in a boxed set (♦Bongiovanni 5544/45, 2CD). The other five masses are similar but slightly different in their alternatim structure. Three of these, *Missa Beatae Mariae Virginis I, II,* and *III,* are in another boxed set (♦Bongiovanni 5556/57, 2CD). The last two, *Missa in duplicibus minoribus I* and *II,* are in the final disc (♦Bongiovanni 5558).

Antonio Sanna's choir recorded two masses for the first time, *Missa Ut re mi fa sol la* for six voices and *Missa de feria* for four voices, along with a duplication of the much-recorded *Missa brevis* and a selection of motets and madrigals (Fonè 90F20, 2CD). Several masses are more than satisfactory, including Gloriae Dei Cantores in *Missa Descendit angelus* (♦Gloriae Dei 106, with *Missa Beatae Mariae Virginis II*), *Missa sine nomine* for six voices by Maarten Michielsen's Rotterdam ensemble (Erasmus 013), and *Missa Ascendo ad Patrem* by Elmer Iseler's singers (CBC 1067). Also good are *Missa de beata Virgine* for four voices by Jeunesses Musicales (Hungaroton 12921), *Missa Dies sanctificatus* by the Bristol Cathedral Choir (Priory 385) and *Missa Regina caeli* for four voices by Amor Artis Chorale (Newport 85603). Finally, *Missa Ave Maria* for six voices by King's College Choir with chant propers of the mass from the composer's own time may be reissued (HMV 3955, LP, NA).

Several masses exist in recordings that can't be recommended, including *Missa Ecce sacerdos magnus* by Lydia Davidova (Melodiya). *Missa primi toni* under Ivan Lantos is a travesty (Detour). *Missa ad fugam* under Felix de Nobel was satisfactory in its time (Philips/Epic LP), but *Missa Già fu chi m'ebbe cara* under Peter Sipple (Lyrichord) and *Missa Iste confessor* on an early Allegro LP (Lyrichord) under James B. Welch were not.

Canticum Canticorum (1584). The most familiar of Palestrina's nonliturgical works is this setting of 29 motets for five voices on Biblical texts, altogether about half of the *Song of Songs.* Pro Cantione Antiqua presents the book most effectively (♦Hyperion 66733). The Hilliard Ensemble, with the most ethereal sound, is excellent, but it's spread over two discs (Virgin 61168, 2CD). Ensemble William Byrd is also fine (Champeaux 0005). The Cambridge Singers have the largest ensemble and the fastest tempos (Collegium 122).

Lamentations. At least four sets of lamentations for Tenebrae survive. Book 3 includes settings of other texts for Tenebrae as well. Musica Contexta has so far recorded the Book 3 settings for the first two days (♦Chaconne 0617 and 0652), with another disc anticipated. Cori Spezzati has recorded the same book complete (Champeaux 0004, 2CD). A different set, the Fourth Book of Lamentations (without additional pieces), has been recorded by Pro Cantione Antiqua (♦Carlton 762).

Magnificats. Palestrina composed at least four settings of this canticle in each of the eight modes. Three of the mode 1 settings—for eight voices by James O'Donnell (♦Hyperion 66490) or Peter Phillips (Gimell 994), for five voices by Herreweghe (Harmonia Mundi 901388), and for four voices by Elmer Iseler (CBC 1067)—can be found as fillers in discs of masses. Also, a mode 4 setting is found in O'Donnell's disc (♦Hyperion 67099), and a mode 6 setting for six voices is in Darlington's (♦Nimbus 5394). Likewise, a mode 7 setting is in Timothy Brown's disc (EMI 569703), and a mode 8 setting for four voices is in Sanna's (Fonè 90F20, 2CD).

Motets. Palestrina's motets are most often encountered as fillers with the masses. The masterpiece among them is *Stabat Mater* for eight voices, a filler in two of Summerly's Oxford discs discussed earlier (♦Naxos 550836 or 553238). Camerata Nova recorded a full disc of Marian motets (Stradivarius 33375). Occasional examples of a cycle of hymns for the church year (1589) and a cycle of offertories for the church year (1593) are equally scattered on disc.

First Book of Madrigals (1555). Concerto Italiano recorded this early publication in their usual high style (♦Tactus 521601).　　　　WEBER

Hubert Parry (1848–1918)

Parry's compositions were quite influential in his time. If Elgar reestablished English music on the world stage, Parry's works—along with his scholarship and teaching—firmed up English musical standards twenty years before *Enigma Variations*. Much of his music has only recently come to our attention, thanks mainly to Chandos releases. After an early Wagnerian period, he found his own musical identity, a blend of German romanticism and clear-toned, stirring English rectitude and nobility. His music is replete with good tunes, full and solid if not particularly colorful orchestration, and real strength, sweep, and energy. Later, he would turn a bit more "modern," as the war-shaken old man tried to fit his voice into what was happening in postwar Europe, but even then the appeal is there, as it is in all his music. Parry is approachable, sensitive, and very enjoyable.

SYMPHONIES

Bamert has recorded all five symphonies (Chandos). He has control, tensile strength, and a straightforward approach to melody. His orchestral sound has sweep, but his control often makes him sound buttoned-down and neutral. The London Philharmonic is its usual warm-toned self. Chandos's sound is "tighter" and less open than usual; it's certainly good, but I prefer a more open acoustic. I recommend this set highly, but there are some alternatives.

1. The first symphony plunges into the young composer's sweeping style with a warm, tuneful slow movement and plenty of life and enthusiasm elsewhere. **Boughton** is slow and dark, with Brahmsian orchestral

sound (♦Nimbus 5296, with *From Death to Life*). His molded rubato makes the symphony sound mature, serious, substantial, but a bit logy at times. The English Symphony plays almost as well as the London Philharmonic. **Bamert** is more spirited and exuberant than usual; his tempos are faster, his rhythms more sprung (♦Chandos 9062, with *Concertstück*). He's favored by most critics.

2. ("Cambridge"). Depending on which source you read, this may or may not describe life at Cambridge University. It's full of good spirits, tunes, holiday festivals, and romance. **Andrew Penny**'s is the best performance (♦Naxos 553469, with *Overture to an Unwritten Tragedy* and *Symphonic Variations*). He and the Royal Scottish Orchestra blend a youthful, upbeat mood, fluid lyricism, and Brahmsian textures in perfect proportion—something **Bamert** doesn't quite achieve in a recording that is more serious, heavy, and generally slower (Chandos 8961, with *Symphonic Variations*). Bamert molds more than he sings, and doesn't have Penny's lift, flow, and spirit.

3. ("English"). This symphony is broadly scaled, with surging tunes, vigor, and a melancholy Adagio. It nicely incorporates features of Schumann's *Rhenish* and Mendelssohn's *Italian* symphonies. **Bamert**'s tempos are slow, and his manner is laid back, smooth, even languid; atypically, he lets things drift at times, but it's a fine reading (♦Chandos 8896, with 4). **Hager** is quick, energetic, and incisive; his enthusiasm is infectious, but sometimes he pushes a bit, and his Luxembourg Radio Symphony isn't the full-sounding, polished London Philharmonic (Forlane 16724, with works by Havergal Brian and John Foulds).

4. This is heroic, with a powerful first movement based on a stirring opening theme. This and the fourth movement are said to be seascapes, but I don't hear much of the sea. I do hear powerful, expansive music full of drama and thrust, along with a near-Elgarian Adagio. **Bamert** plays to type: energetic, clear-headed, and less broad and laid back than his 3 (♦Chandos 8896, with 3).

5. The most mature and mellow of Parry's symphonies, this sums up his career before it headed in a new direction. Its one movement is in four sections and moods. **Bamert** is forthright, moving, and well phrased, with fine energy and sumptuous texture and tone (♦Chandos 8955, with *From Death to Life* and *Elegy for Brahms*). **Boult** is a bit broader and more expansive—he probes more and uses more rubato—but there's plenty of energy (♦EMI 65107, with *Symphonic Variations, Blest Pair of Sirens,* and *Elegy for Brahms*). It's a toss-up.

OTHER ORCHESTRAL MUSIC

Concertstück. This piece reflects Parry's early admiration for Wagner. It's confused but entertaining, though little of the mature Parry is here. **Bamert** is bracing and powerful and well played (♦Chandos 9062, with Symphony 1). **Hager** is similar, but more relaxed and lyrical (♦Forlane 16724, with Symphony 3).

English Suite and *Lady Radnor's Suite.* **Leaper** and Capella Istropolitana (members of the Slovak Philharmonic) include these in a nice collection of English string music with works by Dowland, Elgar, and Bridge. It's more idiomatic than expected and a good budget choice, if not up to the Boult recording reviewed under *Symphonic Variations* (♦Naxos 550331).

From Death to Life. This is a stirring, two-part tone poem from the beginning of WWI about man's return from mourning. Parry was going in a new direction, though his style was still Germanic. **Bamert** is solid, forthright, and within Parry's concept (♦Chandos 8955, with Symphony

5). **Boughton**'s warmth and darkness yield a mysterious Elgarian quality, bogging down only briefly. Not a first recommendation, but interesting (♦Nimbus 5296, with Symphony 1).

Symphonic Variations. This flowing piece sounds like a symphony, both in its seriousness and weight of tone and in its four-group structure. **Penny** is revelatory with quick tempos, strong rhythm, structure, and drama—outstanding playing and sound (♦Naxos 553469, with Symphony 2). **Boult** made two recordings, the first as part of a wonderful Parry disc (♦Lyrita 220, with *Overture to an Unwritten Tragedy* and the *English* and *Lady Radnor's Suites*). Almost as spirited as Penny, Boult is a touch more lyrical with even better analog sound. His second performance is slower, weightier, and expansive, with a glowing brass variation (♦EMI, LP, with Symphony 5). It's very good but seems almost languid next to his Lyrita and Penny's recording.

Piano Concerto 1. Modeled after Brahms's Concerto 1, though it's more like Schumann in tone, this is a bravura work for the pianist, with startling key changes, a big cadenza, and a spacious slow movement—a decent but not great work. Pianist **Piers Lane,** Martyn Brabbins, and the BBC Scottish Symphony are solid (♦Hyperion 66820, with Stanford's Concerto 1).

CHAMBER MUSIC

Piano Quartet and *Piano Trio.* The Quartet is Parry's finest chamber work, mature and serious; the Trio is more passionate and energetic but quite assured. The performances by the **Deakin Trio** have fire and enthusiasm but lack tonal refinement, tight ensemble, and intonation, particularly in the violin; the pianist is quite good (♦Meridian 84248).

Violin Sonata (1889); *Fantasie Sonata* (1878); *Twelve Short Pieces* (1894). *Fantasie Sonata* is a substantial work, with Brahmsian skipping rhythms. *Twelve Short Pieces* are wistful and Dvořákian. The Violin Sonata is rather bland and less interesting. **Erich Gruenberg**'s small, stringy sound is enjoyable enough, though he presses at times for a bigger sound. He's least effective in the Violin Sonata. Roger Vignoles's dark piano tone helps immensely. Quite nice, but nothing special (Hyperion 66157, LP).

PIANO MUSIC

There is a flowing, Schumanesque quality to Parry's piano music that makes it ideal for calm listening. *Shulbrede Tunes* was inspired by a medieval rural house where Parry's daughter lived, and Parry reveals his heart in describing the house and its inhabitants. The Variations in D Minor are more serious and tightly constructed. *Hands across the Centuries* is modeled on Baroque forms but sounds more like Schumann and Brahms. **Peter Jacobs** plays them all with a warm touch (♦Priory 451).

CHORAL MUSIC

Invocation to Music (1895). This is a neo-baroque cantata for three soloists, chorus, and orchestra, and was one of the first works since Purcell (to whom it is dedicated) to mine the musical riches of English poetry. One of the most appealing of Parry's big choral pieces, it captivates from the onset with gentle, dignified, English lyricism and few full-blown climaxes. **Bamert** leads a lovely performance with fine singing and choral work (♦Chandos 9025).

Job. This is one of Parry's lighter choral works. There are some fine passages, but it doesn't stir the listener the way the way the others do. **Wetton**'s routine performance lacks energy, grip, and engagement, nor is there enough sweep and power in the chorus (Hyperion 67025). The soloists are good but not outstanding, and even the Royal Philharmonic

seems uninvolved. Pleasant and pretty but hardly dramatic, the distant sound goes with the interpretation.

Songs of Farewell. These are really motets in four to six parts and were written in Parry's last decade, when things weren't going well for him. The texts deal with death and concern for one's soul. This slow music is sad and somber, yet rich and varied. The performance by Richard Marlow and the **Trinity College Choir** is stunning, with a beautiful sheen and brilliant intonation—great choral work and recorded sound (♦Conifer 51155, with works by Stanford).

Soul's Ransom ("Sinfonia Sacra") and *Lotus Eaters. Ransom* is Parry's most successful oratorio. The mostly Biblical text reflected a humanistic sensibility when it wasn't in vogue. The music is a four-part vocal/symphonic poem, romantic and dramatic, with big, noble choruses, and some dramatic solo work; Elgar's influence is plain. *Lotus Eaters,* based on Tennyson's poem, was one of Parry's favorites and of a different nature than *Soul's Ransom.* Though earlier, it's more advanced harmonically, more distinctive, varied, and less foursquare. **Bamert** leads powerful, broadly paced performances, well played and sung by the London Philharmonic and Choir, with fine sound (♦Chandos 8990).

SONGS

Parry's songs have a mostly Brahmsian cast, without much Irish/British/Celtic lilt or folk quality; they're relaxing to hear. Parry was said to be overly concerned with his texts, but you can always find justification in the music. **Varcoe**'s baritone is attractive and expressive in the early *Three Songs* and 27 songs from Parry's mature and more Brahmsian *English Lyrics.* The tiny bit of strain on some high notes doesn't impair enjoyment, and Clifford Benson provides fine accompaniment (♦Hyperion 67044). HECHT

Arvo Pärt (b. 1935)

Pärt is one of the most important contemporary composers of sacred choral music. His earliest works were mostly instrumental, some in a neoclassical style reminiscent of Prokofiev and Shostakovich; later he took up serialism. In 1968 he entered a silent period, unbroken (except for his transitional Symphony 3) until 1976, when he wrote a brief piano piece, *Für Alina.* With this, which followed a thorough study of Gregorian chant and other music of the Middle Ages and Renaissance, Pärt began composing in the austere, serene style that now distinguishes his music. His works are deeply religious, many of them composed for Latin texts despite his adherence to Russian Orthodoxy. His work is often compared to—and paired with—composers like Tavener, Penderecki, and Górecki.

Listening to Pärt's symphonies in order is a good way to trace his musical journey. Symphony 1, composed in 1964, is a twelve-tone work, as is 2 from 1966. In 3 (dedicated to Neeme Järvi), the medieval influence is apparent, and on the whole the work is serene and tonal in contrast to the angst of the first two. **Järvi** gives us all three on one disc (♦BIS 434). **Paavo Järvi** (Neeme's son) made an excellent recording of 1 (Virgin 45212). The elder Järvi has also recorded 2 in a release that has a mix of earlier and later Pärt, good for comparative purposes (♦Chandos 9134). If you want to avoid the twelve-tone music, try Järvi's recording of 3 with the Gothenburg Symphony (♦DG 457647). I slightly prefer BIS, both for sound and performance, but DG has some nice pairings. You could also try Järvi and the London Philharmonic's somewhat cooler version of 3 (EMI 55619, nicely paired with Kancheli's Symphony 3).

For a sampling of the twelve-tone works, go to *Perpetuum mobile* and *Pro et Contra* for cello and orchestra, both well performed as coupled with symphonies (BIS 434). The early *Collage on B-A-C-H* is paired with 2 (Chandos), and *Nekrolog,* Estonia's first dodecaphonic work, can be found with 1 (Virgin).

As might be expected, the tonal works are recorded more frequently. One of the most popular is *Fratres,* first written in 1977 for string and wind quintets and later revised into eight pieces for various instruments. **Tamas Benedek** has recorded six versions of *Fratres* (♦Naxos 553750, with three other popular short works: *Festina lente, Summa,* and *Cantus in memory of Benjamin Britten*). Don't fear boredom with these repetitions; the music bears up well. **Rudolf Werthen** and I Fiamminghi have done an identical program (♦Telarc 80387). It's difficult to beat Telarc's sound, and I Fiamminghi's performance is reliably top-notch, but if money is a concern, go for Naxos. The only weak spot here is a short solo violin passage in the second *Fratres* that seems harsh and scratchy; the rest is beautiful.

There are a number of good recordings of the haunting *Tabula Rasa,* another work from 1977. First choice for this concerto for two violins, orchestra, and piano is the performance by the dedicatees, **Kremer** and **Tatjana Grindenko,** with Saulius Sondeckis (♦ECM 21275). But **Eleonora** and **Natalya Turovsky** are also outstanding (♦Chandos 9590), as is a 1999 version by **Shaham** and **Adele Anthony** (♦DG 457647). One last recommendation for a short orchestral work: Don't miss the luminous *Trisagion* by the Lithuanian Chamber Orchestra with **Sondeckis** (ECM 1592).

If you truly want to understand Pärt's work, I recommend going directly to his choral pieces, for they mirror the true breadth and depth of this unusual composer. These intensely religious works reflect his idea that music arises naturally out of words, especially sacred words. The music's timeless serenity, though bleak at times, always points to an unchanging, transcendent refuge for the world-weary.

From 1977, as Pärt emerged from his silence, come three works: *Missa Syllabica, Cantate Domino,* and *Sarah Was 90 Years Old.* The first is an austere setting of the Latin mass text, the second a joyful version of Psalm 95. These are impeccably performed by the **Estonian Philharmonic Chamber Choir** led by Tonu Kaljuste (♦Virgin 45276). Another fine recording of these two works is by Paul Hillier and **Theater of Voices** (♦Harmonia Mundi 907182). Despite duplications, it's worth having both discs, as some of the differing companions have not been recorded elsewhere. Hillier also gives us *Sarah,* this time with the **Hilliard Ensemble** (♦ECM 21430). This unusual work for instruments and wordless voices transmits its meaning through the simplicity of length and silence.

Several major works were composed during the '80s. Only one recording exists of the 1982 *Passio Domini nostri Jesu Christi secundum Joannem,* but it's a good one, again by the **Hilliard Ensemble,** with soloists Lynne Dawson and Roger Covey-Crump (♦ECM 21370). The same forces give us the 1985 *Stabat Mater,* with violin soloist Kremer (♦ECM 21325). Pärt completed this cycle of works devoted to the Passion in 1989 with *Miserere,* a powerful piece combining Psalm 51 with the Latin *Dies irae.* Here he departs from the familiar Gregorian chant and composes his own music in a moving and terrifying portrayal of the day of wrath, all wonderfully performed by **Hillier** et al. (ECM 21430, with *Sarah*).

There is only one recording of the 1984–86 *Te Deum,* but it's so well served by Tonu Kaljuste with the **Estonian Philharmonic Chamber Choir** and the Talinn Chamber Orchestra that it's hard to imagine a better version (♦ECM 1505). The 1989 *Magnificat* and 1990 *Berliner Messe* included here are both recorded elsewhere; *Magnificat* is available from

Cleobury and the **King's College Choir** (♦EMI 55096, with *Ikos*), and in "Out of the Night" with Andrew Parrott and the **Taverner Choir** (Sony 61753), while Stephen Layton and **Polyphony** offer both (♦Hyperion 66960). It's difficult to choose among these estimable recordings, but the Estonian choir under Kaljuste's able direction sings with a loving reverence that better conveys the rugged spirituality of Pärt's work. And the sound! The music seems to float down from the shadowy vaulted ceiling of the ancient Finnish church. Go with the Estonians. The British choirs, whose pristine sound I usually love, are a shade *too* precise and correct for this music. This is not to fault their excellent performances, especially Layton's *Berliner Messe,* a very close second to Kaljuste's version. The **Oregon Repertory Singers** and Gilbert Seeley provide another fine recording of this Mass (Koch 7177, with Lou Harrison's *Mass to St. Anthony*).

The 1988 *Magnificat-Antiphonen* is also popular; both Layton and Cleobury offer it (see above). They're good, but again I prefer the Estonians, as this piece needs their superior basses. But Cleobury is a good second choice, as is Hillier, though it's a little cold (Harmonia Mundi 907182). Two major works, the 1994 *Litany* (♦BIS 1592) and the 1998 *Kanon Pokajanen* (♦BIS 1654) have each been recorded only once; how fortunate for us that the Estonians perform them.

If you want to explore Pärt's music systematically, you should work your way through it chronologically, but if you want only one work, get *Kanon Pokajanen.* This massive piece (83 minutes) represents not a departure but a radical expansion of Pärt's style. Composed for the Old Church Slavonic Canon of Repentance, it reaches higher than any of his previous music. If this piece is a harbinger of things to come, we have only begun to hear the best of this unique counter-cultural composer.

CRAWFORD

Harry Partch (1901–1974)

Partch was an original. He began by reproducing the sounds of natural speech in vocal works blending speech patterns with self-made instruments built to parallel the pitch freedom of speech. "Historic Speech-music Recordings from the Harry Partch Archives" includes the earliest recordings from this period (Innova 401). This album also contains three major documents: a reconstruction of *Bitter Music,* an autobiographical diary of a hobo trip with musical interludes that is a practical demonstration of Partch's study of speech patterns, a 1967 recording of Partch demonstrating his preferred scale tunings and instruments, and *Harry's Wake,* a documentary by his friends that includes taped interviews with the composer. All this makes the album important to the dedicated.

Others may find a collection of later recordings more satisfying (CRI 751/54, available individually). As Partch turned to percussion instruments, he revised many of his early compositions to incorporate the new sounds. This is particularly evident in a series of works he later collected with the overall title of "The Wayward." The longest is *U.S. Highball,* much more colorful (and vocally clearer) in this version, where the complete text is printed as well. Also much altered is *Barstow,* based on hitchhiker inscriptions. Partch's scoring for adapted guitar, adapted viola, and voice is on Innova; CRI adds percussion.

An even earlier version with adapted guitar only has been reconstructed and played by **John Schneider Bridge** (Bridge 9041). Each version has its charms. Also on this disc are *Two Studies on Ancient Greek Scales,* the first two of 11 *Intrusions.* Schneider and harpist Amy Shulman play beautifully, bringing out the tuning clearly, and they are better balanced than in Partch's own Gate 5 78 rpm discs from the '50s (CRI

751). The new generation of Partch performers and inheritors of the original instruments, Dean Drummond's **Newband,** has released its own version of *Two Studies* (Mode 18). All the *Intrusions* are required listening, however, mixing song, story and instrumental sounds in an oddly fascinating way.

The Letter is another work from "The Wayward," available in two recordings, one of the original 1950 Gate 5 version (CRI 650) and a later composite from 1972 (CRI 752). Still another early work is *Lyrics by Li-Po;* ten are intoned by **Partch** (Innova 401), but the whole series of 17 has been recorded in a modern interpretation in much better sound (TZA 7012). And before we leave the CRI collection, it should be reported that in CRI 752, *Windsong* and *Rotate the Body in All Its Planes* appear in reversed order from their listings. *Windsong* is a film score turned dance piece, revised under the title Daphne of the Dunes. A new recording has been made by **Newband** (Mode 33), more virtuoso in character and more clearly recorded, including more music than in the CRI release.

The larger works are difficult to classify in genre. *The Bewitched* is called a "dance-satire," but Partch's habit of filling the stage with his sometimes immense instruments leaves little room for dancing. A 1959 recording presents this work in adequate mono sound (CRI 754). *Revelation in the Courthouse Park* is a more operatic venture alternating the basic plot of Euripides's *The Bacchae* with a modern parallel involving a rock star and his mother. This is the most "normal" sounding of Partch's recorded works, combining Western instruments with speaking actors and singers, all surrounded by his instruments. There is a good recording of this piece, which Partch never heard in his lifetime (Tomato 70390, 2CD).

Shorter works also not easily classifiable are *Plectra and Percussion Dances* ("Satyr-Play Music for Dance Theater") and *Water, Water* ("An Intermission with Prologues and Epilogues"), which mixes Partch's own instruments with ordinary ones to comic effect in his closest approach to Broadway style, and *And on the Seventh Day Petals Fell in Petaluma,* a sort of instrumental warm-up for his last major work, *Delusion of the Fury.* All but the last are included in the CRI collection, as well as several shorter works in good recordings from the '60s. *Delusion,* primarily an instrumental drama featuring Partch instruments, and perhaps his most serious piece, received an excellent performance on a Columbia LP (30576) and should be released on CD. This album included an unlisted demo disc narrated by Partch introducing all his instruments, totally different from the demo included in Innova 401. Furthermore, the notes included color photos of the instruments.　　　　MOORE

Stephen Paulus *(b. 1949)*

Paulus is becoming a major voice in contemporary music, not yet fully established but reaching for his place in the musical world. One of America's most prolific and accomplished composers, he has written music in a wide variety of genres, including opera. His music is listener-friendly, reasonably tonal, mildly inventive, with a good ear for effect and texts.

Paulus is fond of Christmas, and several recordings reflect that interest. "Carols for Christmas" is a delightful compilation of four carols composed by Paulus along with his arrangements of a dozen traditional carols (d'Note 1015). The same recording appears to be available as "Christmas Echoes" Volumes 1 and 2 (Augsburg Fortress 4–11). The **Dale Warland Singers** are the worthy artists.

The Three Hermits is the sixth and latest of Paulus's operas (1997). It's brief, based on a short story by Tolstoy, itself based on a traditional Rus-

sian tale told to the author by a wandering storyteller. It imparts a moral lesson: A traveling bishop meets three hermits and instructs them about prayer, and after his departure by ship the bishop is followed by the hermits running on the water; they have forgotten his instructions. Chastened, the Bishop assures the hermits that the way they choose to pray is acceptable to God. Paulus makes minimal demands on his performers and his listeners: a cast of eleven, a four-part choir, and a modest eleven-piece orchestra are all that is required. The music is quite tonal, tuneful, simple, gentle, direct, and intensely moving—a rare treasure of contemporary religious music. A competent recording from **The House of Hope Presbyterian Church** in St. Paul is the opera's only recording (♦d'Note 1025). A fine performance by the **Dale Warland Singers** of the opera's concluding "Pilgrim's Hymn" may be heard as part of a choral collection (♦American Choral Catalog 123).

A short choral piece, *Echoes between the Silent Peaks,* is a grouping of six songs using highly visual poetry from 8th-century China, performed with silken sound by the **Oregon Repertory Singers;** two choral pieces by Barber and Libby Larsen's *Missa Gaia* round out the recording (Koch 7279).

In Paulus's Concerto for Violin and Orchestra, **William Preucil** is the soloist accompanied by the Atlanta Symphony Orchestra led by Shaw (New World Records 363). This CD also contains Paulus's *Concertante* for orchestra and his Symphony for Strings, the Atlanta Symphony led this time by Levi. **Marriner** leads the Minnesota Orchestra in a terse performance of the Symphony in Three Movements (Elektra/Nonesuch 79147).　　　　PARSONS

Krzysztof Penderecki *(b. 1933)*

Penderecki is a prolific composer in all genres and media, and in two obviously contrasting styles. He first came to international attention with *Threnody for the Victims of Hiroshima* in the early '60s. Relatively isolated in Communist Poland, this work and subsequent "sound-mass" compositions placed him at the forefront of the European avant-garde for more than a decade. By the mid-'70s, he turned to a less dense, more consonant practice, as did so many other composers of heretofore dissonant music.

His first style was unique and, I believe, remains his most meaningful. His later music must compete for attention with the large number of diverse practitioners of New Consonance, such as Gubaidulina, Schnittke, and many others in Europe and the United States. Ligeti made the transition from sound-mass to other styles successfully, but Penderecki so far hasn't been able to recapture the talent and imagination of his earlier works. He receives many commissions—sometimes he's years late with promised pieces—and his work is performed and recorded by some of the world's greatest artists and ensembles. But I can't help wondering if composing fewer works might not rekindle the stunning originality of *Threnody.*

Originally, the piece had a generic title, and Penderecki answers enigmatically when questioned about it, but whatever its inspiration or extra-musical impetus, *Threnody for the Victims of Hiroshima* (1960) remains his most cited composition. Extreme dissonance is achieved by 52 separate string parts that require the 12 chromatic pitches plus microtones, excruciatingly slow glissandi, unusual bow placement, and other extended techniques. (The score is very interesting and recommended to those curious about posttraditional notation.) A performance time of about nine minutes requires additional works to fill discs. I recommend **Herbert Kegel** conducting the Leipzig Radio Symphony (Berlin 1012, 2CD) and **Szymen Kawalla** leading the Polish Radio Orchestra of Krakow (Conifer 168); both are very good, so your choice might be based on the other music on each. The Berlin recording includes two established masterworks, Britten's *War Requiem* and Berg's Violin Concerto. The Conifer includes Penderecki's and Nancy Van de Vate's first violin concertos with Grigori Zhislin as soloist and Van de Vate's orchestral work *Chernobyl*. Those with favorite recordings of the Berg and Britten works should probably choose the Conifer disc for the lesser-known but very worthwhile music.

Even greater dissonant sound-mass is employed in Penderecki's first opera, *The Devils of Loudun*, which may be one of the few operas as effective on disc as on stage. Dealing with religious persecution and an actual witch trial, derived from Aldous Huxley's novel and, more directly, John Whiting's play, the sounds—culminating in burning at the stake—are some of the most disturbing in all music. The score is ideal for this powerful drama, and the Sante Fe premiere in the early '70s caused much commotion, to the extent that a photograph of the set appeared on the cover of *Time*. A very good recording has been remastered from the premiere LP in good sound, with informative notes and a libretto in English, and excellent performances by soloists and the Hamburg State Opera and Chorus led by **Janowski** (Philips 44638). It's the epitome of Penderecki's '60s style, and is highly recommended.

The choral music in *The Devils* is challenging to performers and audiences alike, and more of Penderecki's choral work is available. His Roman Catholic heritage is the basis for a number of a cappella choral pieces performed by the Tapiola Chamber Choir conducted by **Juha Kuivanen** (Finlandia 450998999). The counterpoint is clean and clear, and the sound is richer than that provided by **Penderecki** conducting many of the same works sung by the Warsaw Philharmonic Choir (Wergo 6261). Composed over a 30-year span beginning with *Stabat mater* (1962), it may be that this music will achieve repertoire status for posterity. A few of these pieces are offered by Penderecki in another release, again conducting the Warsaw Philharmonic singers. Some of his lesser-known orchestral works are included, and all are well done (Sony 66284).

Penderecki's most dramatic single choral piece is *Dies irae: Oratorio for the Memory of the Victims of Auschwitz*. This powerful work from 1967 uses full vocal and orchestral forces and receives a stunning performance by the Polish Radio and TV Orchestra, **Kawalla** conducting (Conifer 185 or Vienna Modern Masters 3015). Schoenberg's late *A Survivor from Warsaw* and two of Van de Vate's tributes to the Polish people and the thousands murdered by Stalin make up a disc of remembrance and sincerely passionate music. Texts in translation add value to this highly recommended release.

Of Penderecki's recent music, I recommend Violin Concerto 2 performed by **Mutter**, for whom it was composed, accompanied by the London Symphony Orchestra with Penderecki conducting (DG 453507). In his second style, it mostly rings true and indicates his security with the more expansive means of New Consonance.

Any composer would be grateful for a multivolume set of excellent performances, and Penderecki has received that in a collection of reissues from analog recordings, masterfully transferred and packaged with sufficient information (Muza 17–21, 5CD). More than seven hours of his music features Polish ensembles for all the large works, and most of the soloists are Polish as well. Some pieces, for example *Threnody* and *Dies irae*, receive better performances elsewhere, but given the amount and variety of music, his most serious fans will have to have this release.

Penderecki has taught and maintained residences in Poland, Germany, and the United States, and he conducts his own and others' music often and well, with the world's leading soloists and ensembles. I believe his compositions will remain in the live and recorded repertoire, and that his earliest ones will leave a considerable mark on 20th-century music.   ZIEROLF

Giovanni Battista Pergolesi (1710–1736)

Pergolesi's popularity and musical influence far outweigh his musical production. Dividing his work almost equally between church and theater, his output was not large, but it was generally first-rate. His music reflects his frail constitution in its exquisite workmanship, delicacy, and tenderness of feeling. His popularity inspired a host of anonymous imitators, creating problems of attribution that recent scholarship has only begun to unravel.

CHORAL MUSIC

Pergolesi devoted the last two years of his brief life to setting liturgical texts, and of these, his *Stabat Mater*, composed during his final illness, is the most important. The work was so popular that it was the most frequently printed score during the 18th century. The soprano and alto solo parts are of great intricacy; these solos are now heard in varying combinations, using female voices, a countertenor, male sopranos and altos, and even a boy treble.

An recording by Freni and Berganza with the Scarlatti Orchestra of Naples led by **Ettore Gracis** is very operatic (Archiv 427123). **René Jacobs** sings countertenor and conducts treble Sebastian Henning and Concerto Vocale in an oddly unsatisfying performance (Harmonia Mundi). **Abbado** leads the London Symphony with Margaret Marshall and Lucia Valentini Terrani in a large-scale interpretation (DG 415103). Soprano Gillian Fischer and countertenor Chance join **Robert King** in a technically correct but uninvolving performance (Hyperion; MHS).

Harnoncourt leads a group of excellent soloists, using period instruments in a nontraditional interpretation, with tempos faster and slower than usual. Another period-instrument, lower-pitch recording has **Goodman** with two excellent, big-voiced female soloists, Elizabeth Norberg-Schulz and Stutzmann (RCA 61215). An efficient performance at a budget price has Julia Faulkner and Anna Gonda joining the Camerata Budapest led by **Michael Halasz;** Pergolesi's cantata *Orfeo* is the unusual filler (Naxos 550766). A carefully polished, cooly performed rendition with sexless-sounding soloists (Kirkby and Bowman) is led by **Hogwood** (Oiseau-Lyre 425692).

Giorgio Croci's recording is lackluster, with a troubled Ricciarelli and a genuine contralto in Manuela Custer (Tactus). Barbara Frittoli and Anna Caterina Antonacci join La Scala forces led by **Muti** for another very operatic rendition (EMI 56174). At a vocal pitch lower than other recordings, **Lesne** sings contralto and conducts Il Seminario Musicale in an intimate performance (Virgin 45292). Gens is the soprano soloist. **Dutoit** and the Montreal Sinfonietta provide sturdy support for opera stars Anderson and Bartoli (Decca 436209). Bonney and Scholl offer delicacy and excitement, accompanied by Les Talens Lyriques led by **Rousset** (♦Decca 466134).

OPERAS

Adriano in Siria. The only recording uses the recent edition by Dale Monson and was recorded in performance in 1986 (♦Bongiovanni 2078, 3CD). It's substantially complete, and what cuts there are (mainly recitatives) are indicated in the libretto. The music is complex, spectacular, ornamented, coloratura. The three trousers roles originally composed for castratos are here performed by a mezzo and two sopranos. Dessi, the best of the singers, shades her music dramatically with spinto coloring, but the others are more than adequate. The orchestra under **Marcello Panni** is minimal—mainly strings with an occasional oboe or horn obbligato. They play simply, competently, with a hint of stodginess.

Il Flaminio. This is the last of Pergolesi's operas and the second of his two full-length comedies. The somewhat cut 1983 San Carlo recording is efficient, if not particularly polished (Fonit Cetra 39, 3CD). Dessi and Fiorella Pediconi sing attractively, but Elena Zilio's voice is marred by awkward breaks between registers. The other singers make only a vague impression. Stravinsky adapted three selections from *Flaminio* for his ballet *Pulcinella;* **Panni** does similarly by using the opening of *Pulcinella* (actually a piece misattributed to Pergolesi) for an interpolated concerto by folk musicians at the conclusion of Act 2.

Lo Frate 'nnamorato. Much might be expected of a recording that comes from a 1989 La Scala performance (Angel/EMI 54240, 3CD), but the artists don't deliver, or at least they deliver very little. It's not that anyone sings badly or incorrectly, but they all sing with a mechanical, bland sameness of vocal timbre and interpretation. All the rough edges have been filed away, eyes glued on **Muti**'s baton, but a teeth-gritting kind of hilarity ensues. There's precious little distinction of voices, and few of any interest as interpreters. A 1969 RAI Naples performance isn't much of a treat either (Foyer 2026 or Memories 4132, 2CD). It's lively enough, but the singing is on the rough and ready side. **Bonisolli** in particular is bombastic and difficult to listen to.

Livietta e Tracollo. In the 18th century brief intermezzos were introduced between the acts of a grand tragic opera, from which the reforms of Zeno and Metastasio had banished any comic element. We don't hear many of them these days, but Pergolesi's examples, *Livietta e Tracollo* and *La Serva Padrona,* deserve an occasional airing. Cetra's recording is a very brief 36 minutes (Cetra 31). Couldn't something else have been included, perhaps the equally brief *La Serva Padrona?* But enough carping: This is a fine performance. The plot is as slight as can be, but both artists—Dino Mantovani and Elda Ribetti—make much of it. Not content with being very pleasant and singing with grace, they bring an ample measure of amusing comedy to the mix. The Villa Olmo Orchestra is sprightly and sparkling under the direction of **Ennio Gerelli.** The sound is '50s monaural but good.

Gerelli's recording is, more or less, the original Naples 1734 version, the one usually performed. Bongiovanni's (2111) is the first recording of the Paris 1753 version, with the title changed to *Tracollo.* The anonymous reviser has added four new episodes, two of them borrowed from another famous intermezzo, Giuseppe Sellitti's *Drusilla e Strabone* (Naples, 1735). With the added music and slower tempos, this recording takes 63 minutes compared to Cetra's mere 36. The additional music is nothing of great importance, and the plot, such as it is, isn't helped by the revisions. The Cetra singers are far more personable and inventive than their Bongiovanni counterparts, and Cetra's orchestra is more spirited, too.

A 1996 performance in Brussels offers the original intermezzo, and the period style and instruments of **La Petite Bande** give much added pleasure (Accent Live 96123). The singers are adequate but not up to the standards set by Mantovani and Ribetti.

L'Olimpiade. The last of Pergolesi's operas, the only recording is from a 1992 concert performance at the International Festival at Gerace. The opera is substantially complete except for extensive cuts in the seemingly interminable recitatives (Arkadia 129, 3CD, or Agora 093.3, 3CD). **Marco Armiliato** leads the Transylvanian Philharmonic in an aggressive, confi-

dent performance. The singers are uniformly good with two exceptions, one good, one bad. Ernesto Palacio is a stylish specialist in music of this period; his clear tenor is very much a plus. At the opposite extreme is Adelaide Negri, who alternately hurls and squawks her music; coloratura emerges as laughs, chuckles, and hiccups, sustained notes a warble. She has none of the flexibility or accuracy needed for this music. Negri aside, this is a fine recording of a lot of enjoyable music, if with little drama. An added incentive to buy it is three CDs for the price of two.

La Serva Padrona. There has been a plethora of recordings of *Serva,* most on LP, fewer on CD. Many of the RAI-derived opera recordings are again available in improved sound from Fonit Cetra. Some were the first complete performances to be issued and are fine examples of true Italian opera style of the era ('40s to '50s), with a number of treasurable individual performances. Alas, the 1949 *Serva* isn't one of them (Fonit Cetra 33). The style is there, and the sound is good, but the singing isn't. The 1954 **Carteri**/Rossi-Lemeni recording set a standard for its time (Angel 35279, LP), but was soon eclipsed by the 1960 recording by **Scotto** and Bruscantini, a delightful, sparkling performance that still sets the standard but hasn't been reissued on CD (♦Mercury 90240, LP). **Moffo** and Paolo Montarsolo (1962) are on the comedically wan side (RCA 2650, LP). Rossi-Lemeni recorded the work again in 1964 with his wife **Virginia Zeani** (Vox 50380, LP). She's fine, but he has far less voice than he did in 1954. Their German accompaniment is only vaguely Italianate.

Renato Capecchi's 1974 version is worth a search (♦Ensayo 3425). The **Capella Savaria** 1986 recording uses period instruments and is a sprightly affair; it includes some arias inserted into the early Paris performances (Hungaroton 12846). **Baird** and Ostendorf are ill at ease in the Italian buffa style—she too pallid, he too stentorian, neither projecting the text as normal speech (Omega 1016). **La Petite Bande** uses period instruments, adding an air of authenticity (Accent Live 96123).

PARSONS

George Perle (*b. 1915*)

Perle was one of the first American composers to show interest in serial technique. He studied and adapted Schoenberg's methods in an innovative way to give more coherence to the harmonic dimension of twelve-tone music and thereby created a new tonality. He also views these possibilities through the lenses of Stravinsky, Berg, Scriabin, Debussy, and Varèse. All this is explored most thoroughly in his series of string quartets (none currently available), but his very distinctive language places him at the forefront of 20th century American pioneers.

His most engaging mature work is Piano Concerto 2, brilliantly played by **Michael Boriskin** with the Utah Symphony led by Joseph Silverstein (Harmonia Mundi France 907024, 2CD, with pieces by Bach and Danielpour, originally issued with Perle's six Etudes for piano and Danielpour's *Metamorphosis,* 907124). Note especially the shimmering slow movement and the extraordinary clarity of texture of all Perle's music, which retains a chamber music feel even in the larger orchestral scores. Well worth buying and no less impressive are the six Etudes, which, if not available played by Boriskin, are at least played by **Frances Renzi** (Centaur 2301, with works by Persichetti and Rorem). Fortunately Boriskin is a most persuasive interpreter of two '80s piano works, *Sonatina* and *Lyric Intermezzo* (New World 380, with music by del Tredici and Nicholas Thorne). Each Etude is a masterly exploration of a different technical and expressive issue, executed with consummate clarity of means.

Another "must" disc contains the magnificent Serenade 3 for piano and chamber orchestra played by **Richard Goode** and the Music Today Ensemble led by Schwarz (Nonesuch 79108). This Bartókian essay in sonata form grips your attention, again by its crystal clear texture and classical shape. *Concertino* for piano, winds, and timpani is even more condensed, treating the wind parts in metamorphic style while employing an intricate and fascinating variation technique amid all the hurly-burly. *Ballade* for piano is more lush, romantic, and nocturnal. A series of wind quintets spanning 25 years played by the **Dorian Wind Quintet** is worth exploring, as are *Dickinson Songs,* sung by **Bethany Beardslee** (New World 359, with uninspiring pieces by Philip Batstone, Malcolm Peyton, and Godfrey Winham). I hope CRI soon delves further into their archives and rerelease one of Perle's pivotal works from the '60s, *Three Movements* for orchestra. JOHNSON

Vincent Persichetti *(1915–1987)*

Persichetti was one of my professors at Juilliard, where we found him to be an outstanding teacher and a friend with whom we could communicate. Even his textbook on 20th-century harmony was readable and inspiring. A true student of the '50s, I was at the time most excited by his more difficult scores, and once was emboldened to ask why he wrote so many simple-sounding band pieces when the more ambitious works seemed so much more important. I realized immediately that it was a very questionable question, but Persichetti merely got a faraway look in his eyes and replied that there were two sides to him, one as important as the other, and also that the two styles weren't really far apart.

Today, with our reaction against the musical complexities of the '50s and '60s, the lighter aspect of Persichetti, like his earlier band works and serenades, is coming into its own, and we now appreciate his friendlier side. He never shouts out what he's trying to say musically, and it's easy to overlook the subtlety and deep feeling underlying his harmonies, or the way he'll quietly point up a melody by contrasting it with a seemingly jarring accompaniment. His music lends itself to careful performances that bring out these qualities rather than concentrating on velocity and virtuosity. The still core of this composer has yet to be penetrated.

Symphonies. There are nine symphonies. The first three have never been recorded, though the composer thought highly of 3, a big American-sounding work something like Copland's 3. Symphony 4 is Haydn-like in a lucidly classical format, very American in sound. **Ormandy** and the Philadelphia offer a polished and virtuosic 1954 performance (Albany 276). Symphony 5 is for strings and is played by **Muti** and the Philadelphia (New World 370 with the Piano Concerto performed by **Robert Taub** and Dutoit). Both were taken from live performances and are recorded with a bit less clarity than in a studio, but the readings are intense and involved, just what this exciting, serious, one-movement symphony wants.

Symphony 6 is for band, a short but pithy work in four movements. It was once available in a fine reading by **Fennell** (Mercury LP, NA), more recently by **Eugene Corporon** (Klavier 11047, NA). Symphony 7 ("Liturgical") has never been commercially recorded, though it was performed at Juilliard. It's a big, one-movement work of much drama and beauty. Symphony 8 is a large four-movement piece, again in a classical format but broader and more romantic than 4. It's led by **Mester** in a neat and witty reading (Albany 24). Symphony 9 ("Janiculum") is a one-movement work celebrating the Roman god who sees the past and future simultaneously, always looking in both directions. Appropri-

ately, much play is made with a kind of distorted version of the *Dies Irae.* A fine performance by **Ormandy** was once available, coupled with William Schuman's equally moving Symphony 9 (RCA LP 3212, NA).

Other orchestral and band music. There are several works for string orchestra and several for winds. A combination is found in *The Hollow Men,* a short tone poem for trumpet and strings based on T. S. Eliot's text. This piece is a meditation, sounding something like Copland's *Quiet City.* The work also exists with organ replacing the string orchestra, and this version has been recorded by **Andrew Plog** (BIS 565) and **David Hickman** (d'Note 1002), though Hickman's front cover is ambiguous on the subject and *Schwann* obviously forgot to turn the case over, much less play the disc. Both are thoughtful performances, while **Chris Gecker** brings out its more volatile side (Koch 7282). The front cover here is also misleading, since it never mentions either Gecker or Persichetti at all, only Henry Cowell and conductor Richard Auldon Clark. *Introit* (1965) is an even shorter string piece, played with warm tone by **David Amos** in an interesting string program (Crystal 508). The only other orchestral work presently available is the atmospheric *Night Dances,* a work related to the moods of Symphony 9, played with notable sensitivity by the Juilliard Orchestra under **DePreist** (New World 80396).

When it comes to band music, the recorded tally improves markedly. The major works are contained on a well-recorded and sensitively played disc by **Amos** and the winds of the London Symphony, under the misleading title "Divertimenti for Winds" (Harmonia Mundi 907092). There is one piece by that title, played here with more polish than it had in **Fennell**'s old Mercury LP, but performance practices have smoothed out in the last 40 years, and modern recording techniques emphasize this change. Fennell's performance of *Psalm* is available, also recorded in early LP days, again less sonically smooth than Amos but radiating American sound from every pore (Mercury 462960). More modern sounds are made by the Northwestern University Symphonic Winds under **John Paynter** playing *Pageant* in a 1977 recording called "Winds of Change" (New World 80211).

Persichetti's most ambitious band works, *Masquerade* and *Parable IX,* are played by **Eugene Corporon,** the former with the Cincinnati Conservatory Wind Symphony (Klavier 11066), the latter with the North Texas Wind Symphony (Klavier 11098). Both readings are a bit faster than Amos's, but that's not necessarily an advantage in music like this, which benefits from a little breathing space. A reading of *Parable IX* faster than either was by **Robert Foster** and the University of Kansas Symphonic Band in an LP devoted to the composer's band works and including several that Amos missed: *Bagatelles;* two Chorale Preludes, *So Pure the Star* and *Turn Not Thy Face;* and Serenade for 10 Winds, Persichetti's Op. 1 (Golden Crest LP 5055). This 1978 disc might find an audience if transferred to CD.

You would expect that a composer who wrote so much music for solo instruments (25 *Parables* for every instrument imaginable) would have written many concertos, but there are only two, one for Persichetti's instrument, the piano, played by **Robert Taub** with Dutoit (New World 370), and the other for English horn and strings, played by **Thomas Stacy** and conducted by the composer (New World 80489). The Piano Concerto is a rip-snorter, full of virtuosity, while the English horn concerto is a tender, charming work. Both readings are effective.

Chamber music. The four string quartets were once available in an LP album, played and recorded rather crudely. They were welcome then, but the world needs a new reading of these strong works.

A 20-minute ballet on *King Lear* for wind quintet, piano, and timpani is an imaginative if not particularly tragic score, recorded by **John Stephens** (AmCam 10305). Note that the banding on the disc is not correct: the Persichetti is on band 7, not band 4. Another work for wind quintet is the little *Pastoral,* included in the **Boehm Quintet**'s excellent disc called "American Winds, Vol. 1" (Premier 1006). **Paul Cortese,** violist, has a disc containing both *Parable XVI* for solo viola and *Infanta Marina,* a piece for viola and piano based on a song from Persichetti's long and moving Wallace Stevens song cycle *Harmonium.* Cortese is an impressive stylist who puts these varied pieces across with poetry and virtuosity (Crystal 636).

An unexpected genre for Persichetti is his series of 15 serenades, scored for everything from full orchestra to solo piano. One of the most unusual is for flute and harp, performed by **Jennifer Stinton** and **Aline Brewer** in a lovely disc of 20th-century works called "A Contemporary Collection" (Collins 12972). Not one of the eight movements lasts more than a minute and a half, but they are little vignettes of much variety.

A good cross section of Persichetti's four-hands piano music is offered by the **Malinova** sisters (Koch 7213), who play the early Sonata, the diminutive Serenade 8, and the monster Concerto for piano four-hands that Persichetti played (and recorded) with his wife. Though the latter performance shows more energy, it's no longer available, and this is a good, if somewhat straight, reading of an important work. The **Elson-Swarthout Duo** also plays the Concerto in a larger program of 20th-century works, more poetic in the slow sections and a little more spontaneous-sounding in the virtuoso parts, though a bit less technically fluent (♦Laurel 859). There is nothing harder than to make the piano four-hands repertoire come off properly; ensemble is very hard to achieve while still sounding natural. The Persichettis' performance was unusual in its involvement with the moment.

SOLO INSTRUMENTAL MUSIC

Persichetti wrote 12 piano sonatas, not one of which is presently available. Sonata 3 was once played frequently, and 10 and 11 were in **Ellen Burmeister**'s disc with Serenade 7 (Owl LP 29). But new recordings are always surprising us, and presently we have all three sets of *Poems* for piano played with sensitivity by **Mirian Conti** (Albany 299). Balancing this collection is a disc of "20th-Century Etudes," including Persichetti's seven late *Mirror Etudes* played by **Frances Renzi** (Centaur 2301). Both of these discs are important, not only for the Persichetti works.

There are several chorale preludes and a sonata for organ. The sonata and "Drop, Drop, Slow Tears" were in a recital by **David Craighead** (Crystal LP 181). Presently, **Herndon Spillman** offers a feeling performance of the latter in a multiethnic program (Titanic 205). Persichetti spent a good deal of time in his later years writing sonatas and other pieces for harpsichord. Sonata 1 was recorded by **Carole Terry** (CRI LP 533) and 2 through 5 by **Elaine Comparone** (Laurel 838, NA). Perhaps Comparone could be persuaded to eliminate the seven Scarlatti sonatas from her program and substitute Sonatas 6 and 7. Everyone knows these mixed musical periods don't fly, and she plays good, lively Persichetti.

Many of the *Parables* are for solo instruments. They're mostly short pieces, about five minutes apiece. Crystal Records has accounted for a large number of them, all buried in large programs of other music for the instrument involved. They would do us a service by collecting all the solo *Parables* in a single disc. Until someone does that, it's difficult to talk about five-minute pieces each in a separate disc.

Vocal music. A lovely program containing three choral works is performed by the Mendelssohn Club of Philadelphia conducted by **Tamara**

Brooks (New World 80316). *Winter Cantata* is particularly touching, based on Japanese haiku and written for women's chorus, flute, and marimba. *Love* and *Mass* are for unaccompanied mixed chorus. *Mass* employs archaic-sounding quartal harmony, while the short *Love* emphasizes the tritone.

Persichetti's major song cycle *Harmonium,* based on Wallace Stevens's poems, was once available on a recording, I believe. This is an important work by a presently under-represented composer. *The Creation* should also be explored; it is an hour-long oratorio the composer thought highly of that takes its texts from many different cultures.

MOORE

Allan Pettersson (1911–1980)

Swedish composer Allan Pettersson is Scandinavia's most important since Sibelius, and internationally the strongest symphonic voice to emerge after WWII. His output includes 16 symphonies as well as string concertos, songs, and chamber music. Revered in his native land, virtually his entire output is currently available on disc, much of it in competing recordings. His most compelling works direct their forbidding forces toward a redemptive sublimity, expressed by a strikingly elevated diatonicism, which sometimes can take on a character of obsessive banality. The later works adopt a relentlessly turgid, overwritten style that rewards study but demands a most patient and devoted listener.

Pettersson often uses material taken from his *Barefoot Songs,* a remarkable set of 24 songs with texts by the composer himself. These songs are essential starting points for any investigation of his music. The one recording is superb, but no translations are provided, making serious engagement impossible for English-speaking listeners (Swedish Society 1033); six of the songs' texts are translated in Caprice 21359, but don't let the glee clublike choral arrangements on this disc be your only encounter with them. Using the songs as a starting point, a suggested path through Pettersson's major works might take the following form: (I) Symphonies 7, 8, 6, Concertos for String Orchestra, Violin Concerto 2; (II) Symphonies 3, 4, 5, 9, 2; (III) Symphonies 10, 14, 13, 15; and (III) *Vox Humana,* Symphonies 11, 12, 16.

SYMPHONIES

1 (1951). This symphony is withdrawn. Symphony 2 (1953) contains all the Petterssonian trademarks: death treads, fractured lyricism, weeping descents, a ubiquitous snare drum, diatonic fragments, violent explosions, seraphic hymn-like passages. Despite the formalist propaganda congesting most writing on the composer (including his own), this is clearly a document of a tortured childhood. The early **Westerberg** seems tentative and a bit slow (Swedish Society). The more assertive **Alun Francis** is given more modern sound, but that only serves to reveal some very wobbly winds and raunchy upper strings (CPO). Couplings don't really settle matters—perhaps there will be a BIS with Segerstam some day.

3 (1955). This is the most classically etched of the symphonies, with a clear exposition, slow movement, scherzo, and recapitulatory finale. **Segerstam** is the clear choice here, with the fine Norrköping orchestra providing truly spectacular playing (♦BIS 680). **Francis** can't compete with his inferior orchestra, but you will need his disc anyway for 4 (CPO).

4 (1959). Symphony 4 leads its concise materials through 38 minutes of intense and unpredictable development, threaded with extraordinarily beautiful, folk-like material. **Francis** is the only recording at this time (CPO 999223, with 3).

5 (1962). This is a sprawling, often mysterious work. Its long lines eventually focus on an obsessively recurrent three-note motive; the lengthy short-short-long pedal point that concludes the work is both haunting and unforgettable. **Moshe Atzmon**'s version is well played but somewhat distantly recorded, and doesn't make as overwhelming an impression as it should (BIS 480). But you'll need it anyway for Imai's Viola Concerto.

6 (1966). In my opinion, this is Pettersson's greatest symphony, though not necessarily the best introduction to his work. Two elements, a passacaglia-like bass ostinato and an intense, almost Brahmsian tune, engage in ferocious existential battle until a long, sad, folk-like tune (derived from the last of the *Barefoot Songs*) takes over for the last half of the piece to indescribable effect. Simply put, this is among Western music's greatest achievements. **Manfred Trojhan** (CPO 999124) serves as a good replacement for the brave but long-deleted **Kamu,** a sloppy and poorly recorded concert performance once circulating on a Swedish CBS LP. Trojhan gives a fine account, as does his orchestra's incredible brass section, but the same provincial English horn, flute, and string playing that mar this entire series makes us hope that BIS may come to the rescue.

7 (1967). Symphony 7 is the work that made Pettersson "famous," even (for a while) in this country. Why? Interspersed with the long, mysterious lines and violent outbursts are easily graspable minor triad ostinatos singular in their rigidity, passionately romantic gestures, and a stunningly beautiful string orchestra passage that serves as the work's climax. Most of us were first introduced to Pettersson's music when **Dorati**'s recording was issued here on a London LP; that classic performance, with Sweden's best orchestra, is now on CD (♦Swedish Society 1003, with 16). The fine **Comissiona** (a concert performance) is somewhat more deliberate, very well played and recorded, but a near miss in several important places, including the crucial string orchestra passages (Caprice). **Segerstam** is very slow, not especially well played, and rather distantly recorded, but has its rewards when the string passage is reached—it's otherworldly (BIS). **Albrecht** isn't competitive—poor orchestra, fuzzy conducting, noisy audience (CPO).

8 (1969). This is the only Pettersson work to be taken up by an American orchestra. **Comissiona** was musical director of the then up-and-coming Baltimore Symphony back in the late '70s, and he released an extraordinary performance of it in 1980 that turned many heads at the time, but is unfortunately NA (DG). **Segerstam** has a stunning opening passage (one of the most arresting expositions in the symphonic literature) and the most electrifying scherzo yet, but there is a tendency toward impatience (♦BIS 880). Nevertheless, it's well played and recorded and is the one to have with Comissiona out of the running. **Thomas Sanderling** (Kurt's son) gives a richly detailed concert performance that often misses the forest for the trees but makes an interesting supplement (CPO). **Albrecht** has the same problems as in 7 and can be safely set aside (Orfeo).

9 (1970). This symphony has the distinction of being the longest single-movement work in symphonic history, but exactly how long it's meant to be poses serious performance-practice questions. There is a 15-minute difference between its two recordings. **Francis** (CPO) tries to obey the composer's indication of a 65- to 70-minute frame, but his orchestra just can't keep up (though the lengthy unison ending is thrilling). **Comissiona** takes a safer and saner tempo, but in rather boxy sound (Swedish Philips LPs, possibly reissued in Europe). We haven't heard the last word on this daunting masterpiece.

10 (1972). Symphony 10 was written, along with 11, during a nine-month stay in the hospital where Pettersson was being treated for a kidney ailment (the medication almost killed him). This work is nothing less than an attempt to exorcize disease. As such, a good performance should be intense, resolute, strong, and focused; these qualities are achieved with flying colors by **Segerstam** in one of the most searing orchestral explosions on record (♦BIS 880, with 8). **Dorati**'s pioneering performance was in a Phono Suecia/Swedish EMI LP that might be available in Europe, but don't bother—it's ragged, out of tune, and unpolished. **Francis** is even worse: slow, tedious, even more ragged, and shrilly recorded (CPO).

11 (1973). This symphony doesn't seem to be on the same level as the other symphonies; its romantic opening, lengthy pedal points, fractured marches, and barking poundings don't seem to add up to much. **Francis** (CPO, with 10) is clearer than the fuzzy **Segerstam** (BIS, with 7), but I doubt you'll take this off the shelf that often.

12 and the cantata *Vox Humana* (1974). These two works may be considered together. Both are statements of Pettersson's revolutionary politics. Set to Latin American texts (12 is Pablo Neruda's "The Dead on the Square"), their translation into Swedish in combination with Pettersson's most turgid, overwrought late style makes a peculiar impression. I doubt there will be better performances than **Lars-Erik Larsson** for the symphony (Caprice 21369) and **Westerberg** for the cantata (BIS 55), but these pieces are better heard about than heard.

13 (1976). This is an outrageously dense, proudly inaccessible 67-minute trauma with just enough motivic repetition to keep you coming back for further confrontation. There are even some quotes from Beethoven and Rossini, a waltz episode, and what sounds like a cowboy tune all floating about in the morass. **Francis** gets credit for even being able to learn the thing, but his production is harshly recorded and out of tune (CPO). You may want to wait for further competition.

14 (1978). Along with Violin Concerto 2 of the same year, this is the strongest of Pettersson's late works. Both are built on *Barefoot Songs,* and both leave lasting and powerful impressions. **Comissiona,** with the superb Stockholm Philharmonic (♦Phono Suecia 12), is far superior to **Johann Arnell**'s glaringly recorded and sloppily played concert performance (CPO).

15 (1978). Symphony 15 is an elusive work with a long Mahlerian coda that reveals more with every hearing, and you can't go wrong with either recording. **Peter Ruzicka** (♦CPO 999223) is stunningly recorded, very well played, and considerably slower than the composer's metronome markings. It's coupled with a piece by Ruzicka making use of material from Pettersson's sketches for a 17th symphony. **Segerstam** (♦BIS 680, with 3) is six minutes faster than Ruzicka, no less well played, and decently if somewhat distantly recorded.

16 (1979). This last symphony is a saxophone concerto, somewhat similar in concept to the Viola Concerto of the same year. The astounding **Frederick Hemke** commissioned it, and you can hear him play it, with Dorati's indispensable 7 (♦Swedish Society 1003).

CONCERTOS

The three Concertos for String Orchestra are symphonies in all but name. No. 1 is one of the great works for this medium, fully comparable to Bartók's *Music for Strings, Percussion, and Celeste* and Honegger's Symphony 2. No. 3 has as its slow movement the astonishing 30-minute *Mesto,* published and often played separately. These are among Pettersson's greatest works. They are most easily obtained in **Goritzki**'s set (CPO 999225, 2CD), but you'll find a better 1 by **Westerberg** coupled with the only Symphony 12. We need a great orchestra to take these up.

Violin Concerto 1 (1949). Actually a chamber work for violin and string quartet, this is Pettersson's first substantial effort. Perhaps a bit aggressive in its avant-gardish nature, its arresting slow movement bears the mark of a master. **Ulf Hoelscher** and the Mandelring Quartet give a clear enough performance (CPO, with Pettersson juvenilia), but don't achieve the same amount of color as **Karl-Ove Mannberg** and Freskkvartetten (Caprice, probably available in Europe).

Violin Concerto 2 (1978). This is one of the most harrowing depictions of man's struggle and eventual reconciliation with pain and death in the literature. It's certainly among the most demanding concertos ever written for the instrument. **Haendel**'s performance is astounding, and it's unlikely that there will be another performance in the foreseeable future, but the CD transfer is a bit harsh (♦Caprice 21359). Try to find the LP.

Viola Concerto (1979). Pettersson's last completed work, Ruzicka discovered this in a pile of manuscripts after the composer's death. **Imai** provides its only recording (BIS 480, with Symphony 5).

OTHER MUSIC

Pettersson's most substantial chamber works are the seven Sonatas for Two Violins (1951). Many of the his stylistic imprints are presented here for the first time. These hair-raisingly difficult pieces are rendered with astonishing color, accuracy, and authority by **Josef Grünfarb** and **Karl-Ove Mannberg** (♦Caprice 21401). The more recent recording by **Matin** and **Cecelia Gelland** falls far short in technical and musical assurance (BIS 1028). Six attractive early songs are paired with the essential *Barefoot Songs* in Swedish Society 1033. Everything else is juvenilia, and truthfully of minimal musical interest; most can be found on CPO 999169 with stragglers on Koch 1651 and BIS 1028.   GIMBEL

Hans Pfitzner *(1869–1949)*

Pfitzner's works included symphonic, chamber, and choral music as well as operas and songs. His music was, to the end of his life, written in the conservative, Romantic idiom he learned in his youth. Wagner and Brahms were his musical gods; he had no use for the Second Vienna School, Impressionism, or other 20th-century compositional techniques. He was also a polemicist and a German nationalist who played a prominent part in the politicization of music during the interwar years; he was always on the conservative side. This probably hurt his reputation during the postwar period as much as his firm adherence to the musical values of his youth. Still, many of his compositions, notably his masterpiece *Palestrina* and his well-crafted songs, are still performed, and there has even been renewed interest in his chamber music.

Pfitzner's orchestral works and concertos consist of three symphonies, three concertos for cello and orchestra, single concertos for violin and piano with orchestra, and a violin and cello duo and a scherzo, both with orchestra. All these works, plus the three preludes to Ibsen's play *Das Fest von Solhaug* and two minor pieces, can be found in a set led by **Albert** (♦CPO 999249, 5CD, available individually). For listeners who only want to sample the orchestral works, I recommend CPO 999079, which includes his lovely Violin Concerto and the beautiful Duo and Scherzo.

He wrote four quartets, spanning his creative life from his student days to 1943. All are written in his conservative musical style; Brahms wouldn't have disowned any of them. All have been recorded by the

Franz Schubert Quartet (CPO 999526, 1 and 3; 999072, 2 and 4). These are skillful, revealing performances in very good sound. Other, older recordings couple one or the other of these pieces with works by other composers, and not one of them is as good.

Pfitzner also wrote several sonatas. Of major interest is the Violin and Piano Sonata, dedicated to his friend, the conductor Bruno Walter. The only available version, by the **Orfeo Duo,** is coupled with a Violin and Piano Sonata by Walter (VAIA 1155). Pfitzner's Brahmsian Sonata for Cello and Piano, played by **Christoph Henkel** and **Georges Pludermacher,** is coupled with cello sonatas by Strauss and Hindemith (Signum 6400).

The best known of Pfitzner's choral works is the choral fantasy *Das dunkle Reich,* for soloists, chorus, and orchestra. It was composed in 1929 after the sudden death of his wife. The only recent recording is by **Rolf Reutter** (CPO 999158, with two of the composer's shorter works, *Der Blumen Rache* and *Fons Salutifer*). It's a beautiful, mournful, elegy that will appeal to lovers of Brahms's *German Requiem.*

The opera *Palestrina* is Pfitzner's masterpiece. Its story deals with Palestrina's effort to write a Mass for his patron, Cardinal Borromeo, that would persuade the Council of Trent (1563) not to ban polyphonic music for church services. The music for this long work is often very beautiful (it owes a great debt to *Die Meistersinger*), but the stage action is static much of the time. A 1973 recording, stirringly conducted by **Kubelik** with a fabulous cast headed by Gedda and Fischer-Dieskau and in very good sound, is excellent (DG 427417). A more recent recording led by **Suitner** has an able but less distinguished cast (Berlin 1001). A staged Vienna Opera performance from 1964, led by **Heger,** has been released; it, too, has a fine cast but poor sound (Myto 92259).

The three preludes from *Palestrina* are available on several discs. One led by **Sawallisch** includes excerpts from the composer's other operatic success, *Die Rose vom Liebesgarten,* as well as his Overture to Kleist's play *Kätchen von Heilbronn,* for which he also wrote incidental music (Orfeo 168881). The latter and the *Palestrina* preludes are given fine performances by **Christian Thielemann** in a CD that includes excerpts from Strauss's *Guntram* and *Feuersnot* (DG 449571).

Pfitzner wrote over 100 songs. Recommended recorded recitals include those by **Fischer-Dieskau** (EMI 63659; Orfeo 036821) and **Robert Holl** (Preiser 93321), both of whom combine excellent diction with smooth, attractive singing. A historic release includes 12 songs by the renowned baritone **Hüsch,** accompanied by Pfitzner at the piano, plus performances of Symphony in C and Duo played by the Berlin Philharmonic conducted by the composer, in fairly decent sound (Preiser 90029)   MOSES

Astor Piazzolla *(1921–1992)*

Piazzolla studied piano in New York with Rachmaninoff and went to France to study with Nadia Boulanger, but his first and favorite instrument was the bandoneon, an accordion-like instrument invented in 1854 by Heinrich Band that has a series of buttons instead of piano keys. Band intended it to be used as a substitute for the organ in small churches, but around 1890 it made its way into the brothels of Buenos Aires. Piazzolla aspired to raise the bandoneon's status to that of a "classical" instrument, and believing that the tango was more than just dance music, he formed a quintet, made recordings, and toured the Americas to present the bandoneon in concert halls. Ultimately he elevated the status of the tango to that of art song.

He wrote around 50 film scores, an opera called *Maria de Buenos Aires* (Dynamic 185), and more than 300 tangos. "Piazzolla Classics" includes some of his best-known orchestral pieces performed by the **Buenos Aires Symphony** (Milan 35640), and "El Nuevo Tango de Buenos Aires" features the great tango singer **Roberto Goyeneche** (♦Milan 35797). Piazzolla also made a very intense recording of "Five Tango Sensations" with the **Kronos Quartet** (Electra/Nonesuch 979254), and "Tangos and Milongas" gives fine examples of the tango as art song (Milan 35806).

Kremer and some of his European colleagues recorded some very exciting and unusual arrangements called "Homage à Piazzolla" (♦Nonesuch 79402). **Ma**'s "Soul of the Tango" has some fine playing with a half dozen excellent tango musicians in very effective fashion, but it also has an annoying enhanced disc feature that makes it difficult to play on a computer (Sony CD-ROM 63122). He also plays an engineered duet with Piazzolla (who recorded his part in 1987, Ma in 1997). Jorg Calandrelli's arrangements with the cello playing the melody line as well as the embellishments are quite good and distinctly different from the spicy arrangements on the Kremer recording. For "classical" musicians playing tangos, I still prefer Kremer, though the Calandrelli arrangements are probably more authentic.

A remarkable recording by jazz vibraphone player **Gary Burton** includes an extraordinary performance of *Contrabajissimo* by its dedicatee Héctor Console (Concord Jazz 4887). Three great arrangements are played by the 12 cellists of the **Berlin Philharmonic** in "South American Getaway": *Fuga y Misterio, Adios Nonino* (a piece written in memory of Piazzolla's father), and *Chiquilin de Bachin,* sung by Juliane Banse (EMI 56981).

As exciting and fresh as his pure tango music is, we shouldn't forget Piazzolla's more formal music that doesn't include improvisation and isn't arranged. There are fine recordings of the flute and guitar piece *Histoire du Tango* by **Susan Hoeppner** and **Rachel Gauk** (♦Marquis 177) and **Heriberto Calvalcante Porto** and **Pierre-Paul Rudolph** (♦René Gailly 87128). Cellist **Maria Kleigel** has a terrific recording of *Le Grand Tango* (♦Naxos 550785), and marimba player **Nancy Zeltsman** has a beautiful arrangement of his *Tango Suite,* originally written for two guitars, in "Woodcuts" (♦GM 2043). One of Piazzolla's finest pieces is the 1979 Concerto for Bandoneon and Orchestra, which he recorded in Greece (Milan 35758).   FINE

Gabriel Pierné (1863–1937)

Pierné was a highly regarded conductor with the Paris Colonne Orchestra and the Ballets Russes. He wrote six operas, five ballets, and many religious choral works, but is mostly known (or used to be) for a single "lollipop": the "March of the Little Lead Soldiers" from his ballet *Cydalise et le chèvre-pied* (1923). That doesn't seem to be currently available on CD, but his agreeable *Konzertstück* for harp and orchestra, from 1903, is. **Annie Challan**'s very French-sounding recording is a small part of a tribute to conductor André Cluytens (EMI 68220, 2CD); if you'd rather have this piece with other harp works, try **Isabelle Moretti**'s collection (Koch Schwann 1142 or 1339)

Pierné's 1887 Piano Concerto isn't nearly as appealing. The outer movements are pompous; the scherzo is sparkling, if a few cuts below Saint-Saëns. You can try it in a collection of French piano concerto oddities; **Marylène Dosse**'s performance is okay, but was apparently recorded under water (Vox 5110). If you're interested, there's a more modern, more expensive recording that includes music from the ballet *Ramuntcho* (BIS 381). Pierné's chamber music is a worthwhile addition to the slim French Romantic repertory, particularly the Violin Sonata in D minor, written in 1901 for Thibaud (REM 311260, with very compat-

ible couplings by Franck and Tournemire), and the Cello Sonata (Hyperion 66979, with a very different, equally arresting sonata by Koechlin).

Pierné very successfully recast his Violin Sonata for flute; it's played by **István Matuz** and Norbert Szelecsényi, coupled with the ambitious Piano Trio, a 40-minute work that doesn't quite hang together compellingly but is full of interesting details (Marco Polo 223189). His piano music is lightweight stuff in comparison, but some agreeable salon pieces in Schumannesque style are played by **Chang Hae-Won** (Marco Polo 223115).   RAYMOND

Walter Piston (1894–1976)

Piston is at the very heart of the coming of age of American music in the middle decades of the 20th century. His substantial but not prodigious output epitomizes neoclassical elegance, a graceful wit, and fertile inventiveness. Like many of his generation and the one that followed, he studied in Paris with Nadia Boulanger, and the natural authority of his music is reinforced by impeccable academic discipline. Sometimes described as the "American Hindemith," his work possesses Hindemith's clarity of form and texture, but Piston's language is uniquely American in its atmospheric subtlety, its tendency toward an austere grandeur of utterance, and—especially in the mature works—its mellow harmonic sweetness and delicate pastel shadings.

Symphonies. Piston has always been afforded a fair wind by the record companies, and rightly so. The backbone of his output is the eight symphonies, spanning nearly 30 years, all of which are available. The most frequently played and perhaps the finest is the luminous 2, played by **Schwarz** and the Seattle Symphony as part of a survey of orchestral works (Delos 434307, 3CD, with 6 and *Sinfonietta*). Symphony 6 uses a larger orchestra and is nocturnal and seductive; *Sinfonietta* is conceived on a symphonic scale; and these three fine works represent the best of his output. Schwarz's next offering included pieces from the '50s and '60s that represent Piston at the height of his powers (Delos 3106). The ebullient 4 is a work of supreme assuredness of touch and lightness of step, and *Serenata* is a three-movement suite of sophisticated urbanity, a perfect foil for the gossamer delicacy of the *Capriccio* for harp and strings. Even more impressive are *New England Sketches,* three of Piston's few impressionistic landscape tone pictures.

Schwarz's third disc contains Piston's most famous piece, the ballet suite *The Incredible Flutist* (Delos 3128). It's easy to see why: The music is ablaze with oriental color and piquancy. This recording is the best, along with the slightly dated offering by **Hanson** (Mercury 34307, with pieces by Barber, Bergsma, and Griffes). Schwarz has the edge by presenting four more works, at least two of which were previously unrecorded: the early and very French *Suite 1* for orchestra and the remote and wistful Fantasy for English horn, harp, and strings. He also includes Piston's last work, the brief Concerto for String Quartet, Winds, and Percussion, a work imbued with poignancy and sadness, and the meditative *Psalm and Prayer of David,* Piston's only sacred piece for choir and orchestra. Schwarz consistently proves his dedication to and affinity with the music, and all three discs are well worth having.

Four other symphonies (1, 5, 7, and 8) can be found in two Louisville Orchestra recordings transferred from LP. Symphony 5, conducted by **Robert Whitney,** is an impressive sequence of sonata form, variations, and rondo, and its reconciliation of diverse materials marks the beginning of Piston's mature music (Albany 011). The recording itself is adequate but shows signs of age, and the orchestra doesn't capture the grandeur and epic nature of Piston's design. Symphonies 7 and 8 on the same disc, conducted by **Jorge Mester,** are generally better performed and in more modern sound, which is just as well, since the darkening tone of Piston's music in the '60s makes heavy demands on its interpreters. Symphony 8 especially is one of his most challenging and ultimately satisfying large-scale works.

Symphony 1, also conducted by **Mester,** is less demanding, but its stern predilection for fourths and fifths clearly establishes its Hindemithian link (Albany 044, with works by Robert Kurka and Mennin). These recordings are adequate if not spectacular, and not in Schwarz's league. The remaining symphony, 3, receives a quite good performance by the Harvard Radcliffe Orchestra led by **James Yannatos** (Albany 400, with works by the conductor). The performance available on LP for many years by **Hanson** and the Eastman Rochester Orchestra (never transferred to CD) has yet to be surpassed (Mercury).

Concertos. There are good recordings of the 1968 Flute Concerto. The better is probably by **Doriot Anthony Dwyer** (Koch 7142, with concertos by Bernstein and Zwilich; it's incorrectly listed in *Schwann* as the Piano Concertino). The other, by **Samuel Baron** with the remarkably good Billings Symphony, includes the very interesting 1967 Clarinet Concerto and several other works (Connoisseur Society 8840). There is a choice, too, for the brief Piano Concertino, but its inclusion in a reissue of a series of LPs of American concertos wins the day for both quality and budget price (Vox VB2, 2CD).

The two violin concertos, played by **James Buswell** with the National Symphony of Ukraine under Theodor Kuchar, are exceptional discoveries (Naxos 559003). Separated by over 20 years, 1 is all energy, verve, and drive, whereas 2 has the searching, questing quality born of a mature artist's growing awareness of the world's uncertainties. Its autumnal mood and downbeat temperament set it apart from the more virtuosic American violin concertos. The austere *Fantasia for Violin and Orchestra* that concludes the disc finds Piston economizing frugally with emotional material. The performances are very good, and orchestra and soloist deserve commendation for their thoroughly idiomatic contribution.

Chamber music. The Flute Quintet, in a recording of chamber works by the **1999 Australian Festival of Chamber Music,** shows Piston's affinity for the tonal qualities of the soprano instruments (Naxos 559071). He wrote surprisingly little keyboard music, which is a pity, for his grasp of the mysteries of keyboard tonality is captured in the enigmatic Piano Quartet, in which the surface tension between the lyrical string voices and the piano's quest for a more independent line creates endless musical interest. The String Sextet is one of his darkest essays; the dense suspensions of the long first movement are only partially lightened by the greater elasticity of the *energico* finale. There's an interesting Piano Quintet, too. All are beautifully played and a fantastic value.

Piston's superb legacy of quality is well represented on disc, even if some of the symphonies would benefit from more contemporary readings, and a series of the five string quartets would give an even more complete picture. His music always challenges, stimulates and handsomely rewards.   JOHNSON

Manuel Ponce *(1882–1948)*

Ponce belongs to the same revolutionary generation as Bartók, Stravinsky, Webern, and Varèse, but his music is much more in line with their contemporaries—Szymanowski, Turina, and Villa-Lobos, notable "second-string" composers of a much less forward-looking bent. Ponce is primarily known for his guitar music, most of it written for the great Spanish virtuoso Segovia. Several factors have contributed to the survival of his guitar music: (1) the advocacy of Segovia (including his recordings and concert performances) and his students and proteges; (2) the diverse forms in which Ponce composed, from brief preludes to large-scale sonatas; (3) the large quantity of his output; and (4) its overall high quality, playability, and appeal.

Ponce sought, with some resistance at first from the artistic establishment, to initiate a new era in Mexican music, drawing on European forms and techniques to express the Ibero-American sensibility. His music weaves together aspects of turn-of-the-century romanticism (the "salon" style) and neoclassicism (including Kreislerian baroque forgeries) within a generally mainstream European harmonic style (rather like Ravel), with frequent use of Spanish and Latin American harmonic, melodic, and rhythmic elements (also like Ravel). His music is completely tonal, with occasional touches of bi- or polytonality (his Four Miniatures for string quartet). He collected and harmonized Mexican and Spanish folk songs and became most famous for a huge-selling "popular" song, "Estrellita," and then had the financial misfortune of signing away the rights.

Ponce's nonguitar music is being newly explored as musicians, audiences, and record companies look for material off the beaten path, and the emergence of Latino popular culture engenders consideration of its more serious figures. The main source for this music is the six-volume "Musica Mexicana" series with **Bátiz** and the State of Mexico Symphony Orchestra, which offers many of the orchestral pieces and concertos for violin and piano, along with music by other Mexican composers (ASV).

SOLO GUITAR MUSIC

Segovia, in addition to declaring that Ponce's works "in all the literature for the guitar . . . . have the most value to me," perceptively noted that of all the non-guitar-playing composers who wrote pieces for him, Ponce had the best instinctive feel for the instrument, resulting in remarkably idiomatic writing in a variety of textures. Segovia, in fact, was closely involved in the composition of many pieces, suggesting their form or style, and "fixing" (or having Ponce revise) an occasional nonguitaristic passage. Segovia's romantic style of playing (by today's standards) was also the basis for Ponce's concept of the classical guitar. Therefore, you have to start with Segovia's recordings.

The "Segovia Collection" Vol. 6 is all Ponce and consists of three sonatas: "Mexicana," "Clásica," and "Romantica" (the latter two in the style of Sor and Schubert, respectively), plus two short pieces titled "canciones" (MCA). The playing is completely characteristic, with that unmistakable array of tone color (from meltingly lush to aridly brittle), expressive portamenti, rhythmic verve, and metric freedom. Unfortunately, "Mexicana" is a weak piece, and the other two sonatas, though enjoyable, aren't really "pure" Ponce. More satisfying repertoire, and more youthful playing (from the early '30s, on gut strings), is found in Vol. 2 of a 1927–39 reissue (♦EMI 561049): the first two movements of Sonata 3, Mazurka and *Valse,* and an abbreviated *Variations and Fugue on "Folies d'Espagne"* (only half the variations). There are a number of differences in these performances from Segovia's published editions that may be of interest to players.

Vol. 1 contains Ponce's excellent Suite in A in the style of baroque lutenist Silvius Weiss, played with great abandon, and a catchy Gigue attributed to Froberger. "Centenary Celebration" contains those two lovely canciones, three preludes (some of Ponce's most successful pieces), and my personal favorite, his *Theme, Variations, and Finale,* in classic performances from 1954 and 1962 (MCA/Decca, 4CD). While there are rough edges in Segovia's interpretations, there is real sincerity in his connection to this music.

For more up-to-date, polished interpretations, here are some recommendations. For the complete "Folies" Variations, try either **John Williams,** a student of Segovia at one time (♦Sony 47669), or **Eliot Fisk** (♦MusicMasters 67127). Unfortunately, most of Williams's all-Ponce LP hasn't been reissued (Columbia). Fisk also gives a restrained (for him), poetic account of *Theme, Variations, and Finale* and *Valse on "Für Eliot"* (♦GSP 1008), which also features Martin's *Pièces Brèves* and typically incredible Scarlatti and Paganini.

If you can find a copy, **Isbin**'s debut LP also had an exquisite version of *Theme, Variations, and Finale* (Sound Environment). I like **Barrueco**'s crisp, tasteful reading of *Sonatina Meridional* (EMI), but look for no-longer-available LPs by Segovia and Williams that contain an unpublished (but transcribable) version of the last movement. You'll find good repertoire and performances in an all-Ponce disc featuring **Jukka Savijoki** and Diego Blanco (♦BIS 255). Ponce's brief but delightful *Preludio* in baroque style is played in great Segovia manner by **Parkening,** as a solo and as a duet with harpsichord (♦EMI 11570 and 264630; Segovia's duet with Rafayel Puyana—♦Decca LP 10046—is NA); Parkening's Four Preludes, from his debut album "In the Spanish Style," are smoother and more musical than Segovia's (EMI/Angel). Williams's early Torroba/Ponce LP with all 12 Preludes is also unfortunately NA (Westminster).

CONCERTO
Ponce's Guitar Concerto ("Of the South") hasn't caught on in the way those of Rodrigo and Villa-Lobos have; in today's world it is perhaps too "Segovian." But it has appealing themes and a wonderful cadenza and succeeds in balancing the soloist with the orchestra much better than some others. **Segovia**'s rendition (with **Jorda** and the Symphony of the Air) is fine (in the "Centenary" set), though **Williams** benefits from better backup with Previn and the London Symphony (♦Columbia 44791). Their judicious cut in II also tightens the piece up a bit.

OTHER MUSIC
As mentioned above, ASV's "Musica Mexicana" series offers many of Ponce's orchestral works. Vol. 1 includes his 1940 "divertimento" *Ferial* and the 1938 *Instantaneas Mexicanas;* Vol. 2 offers only the 1943 Violin Concerto (a beautiful piece that—ruefully—quotes "Estrellita" in its slow movement) as performed by its dedicatee, **Szeryng;** and Vol. 6 has five works, including the 1929 *Chapultepec* (three symphonic sketches), *Poema elegiaco* for chamber orchestra (1935), and his 1912 Piano Concerto, with **Osorio** as soloist. That pianist has also recorded an all-Ponce recital (ASV).

For more varied repertoire (including some pieces for left hand alone and a Prelude and Fugue on a theme by Bach), I recommend a fine recording by **David Witten** (♦Marco Polo 223609). (Both this and the Osorio disc contain the original piano version of *Scherzino Mexicano,* usually found in guitar transcription.) Violin versions of "Estrellita" (arr. Heifetz) include **Perlman** (EMI: "The Art of Perlman," Vol. 4), **Shumsky** (Biddulph), and, of course, **Heifetz** himself (RCA: "Heifetz Plays Gershwin and Encores," and "Bygone Memories").

DINGER

Amilcare Ponchielli (1834–1886)
Ponchielli wrote 10 operas, but his fame rests on only one, and when we don't have the singers for it, his name disappears from sight. It doesn't help his cause that *La Gioconda* requires six large, healthy, spinto voices, one in each vocal category: a *Don Carlo* or *Trovatore* quintet plus a solid contralto. It doesn't help either that the libretto (by the same Boito who wrote *Otello* and *Falstaff* for Verdi) is too preposterous to stand on its own as drama. Only great singers can redeem *Gioconda,* but the opera has an astonishing wealth of melody and generously rewards performers who have the vocal equipment to bring it off.

When the world's opera houses could call on the services of Ponselle, Homer, Caruso, Martinelli, Gigli, Amato, and Ruffo, *Gioconda* was an audience favorite, an opera for those who prize great singers in an immensely flattering context. It could have been recorded in good sound with a first-rate cast at just about anytime in the '50s and '60s but wasn't. The best available singers never came together for the same recording, and then disappeared as the century moved toward its close. To appreciate *La Gioconda,* you'll need to dip into the archives to sample the artists mentioned above and several others, and you'll need to acquire more than one recording.

La Gioconda. Including unauthorized issues, there have been about two dozen more-or-less complete recordings. The first in stereo is still estimable: **Gavazzeni** in 1957 (London). The contralto who sings La Cieca is weak, but the other five roles are in experienced hands. Bastianini and Siepi sing as richly and beautifully as anyone since. The baritone in particular has a congenial role; one-dimensional villains fell easily within his dramatic range. Del Monaco is on his best behavior, surprisingly ardent and dignified, and credibly heroic. Simionato makes a sometimes coarse Laura, but she's always ear-catching, and the meteoric Cerquetti, who made only one other commercial recording, is an interesting Gioconda, her voice of ample weight and thrust for the role, her acting sensitive and at times fiery. Her tone doesn't expand much on top and always has a slight anxious quiver; the bottom is weakish, and yet she's still satisfying, if less compelling than Callas.

Callas recorded *Gioconda* twice with the same conductor, **Votto,** in 1952 (Cetra) and again in 1959 (EMI). She's a natural for this ugly-duckling heroine, who loses everything she has and doesn't even get a chance to sing a duet with the man she loves. She triumphs only in self-sacrifice, and the mesmerizing conviction and concentration Callas brings to "Suicidio" make it more than a show-stopper. The earlier recording has a good Laura in Barbieri and a fine Barnaba (Paolo Silveri) and Alvise (Giulio Neri). The second enjoys better sound, a solid but still green Cossotto as Laura (at least she sounds young, unlike Simionato and Barbieri), and another decent Barnaba-Alvise pair (Cappuccilli and Vinco). It's best to pass over the tenors in charitable silence.

Where Callas finds humanity in Gioconda, Milanov is more the imperious prima donna, passionate in her own way but also stagy and orotund. In 1958 with **Previtali,** she was past her best and sometimes squally, but the solidity of her low register and the molten flow of her voice remain remarkable (RCA). It's thrilling to hear the tone billow like a sail in the wind, but the soft singing is just as enchanting. I can't be the only collector who wore out some of the grooves on side 2 of the old LP set playing and replaying the magically floated "Enzo adorato . . . come t'amo." Rosalind Elias is a lightweight, incisive Laura, the voice sharply focused, and contralto Belan Amparan is the first really solid Cieca on records. Warren, a bit shaky, matches Milanov's grandiloquence, and he has some of the flair and humor that the grim Bastianini lacks. Di Stefano is romantic, affable, and in terrible shape, the upper notes strained and wooden. Previtali is a routine conductor, but this remains an enjoyable *Gioconda,* enshrining much of the grandeur of a soon-to-vanish golden age.

Like Milanov, Tebaldi waited too long to record *Gioconda;* her top in 1967 tends to be flat and juiceless. The central and lower portions of her voice are still uniquely opulent, and she approaches her role with a thorough mastery of Italian operatic tradition, every accent in place, every phrase shaped with unaffected assurance. Her colleagues are an oddly matched lot. Ghiuselev is a gritty Alvise; Oralia Dominguez a shallow Cieca. The Americans, Horne and Merrill, sing cleanly, handsomely, and aloofly. Bergonzi, who grew out of the same tradition as Tebaldi, isn't quite heroic enough as Enzo, but when he gets hold of a good melody (listen especially to "Già ti veggo . . . tu sei morta" at the end of Act 3), he knows exactly what to do with it. **Gardelli** is a lively, knowing conductor; the sound is excellent, the best of any recording to date (♦London 430042).

The Decca engineers would do even better in 1981 for **Bartoletti** (♦London 414349). His cast is another diverse assemblage, and the two singers farthest from the Italian style are, in characteristic modern fashion, too light for their roles: Baltsa and Alfreda Hodgson. Ghiaurov's tone is rusty, but his voice and temperament are appropriate. Milnes is an extroverted, zealous Barnaba with pealing top notes and plenty of dramatic presence. He's steadier than Warren, more imaginative than Bastianini or Merrill. Caballé lofts the loveliest pianissimos since Milanov and knows how to find the most becoming shape for her most rhapsodic passages, though her chest register is relatively feeble. Pavarotti carries less spinto weight than Bergonzi, but the brighter gleam of his upper range offers substantial compensation and carries him through the ensembles. His words are finely chiseled, his demeanor engagingly earnest. Bartoletti provides energetic leadership, and because this performance has no ugly moments, it would do well as an introductory recording.

Patanè is fitfully admirable (Sony). The cast, once again, is down to a single Italian: Giorgio Lamberti, an idiomatic but mundane Enzo. Marton has the volume for Gioconda but not the heart; Milnes was in better voice for Bartoletti; Ramey is a stolid Alvise. The Laura and Cieca are ciphers. To listen to the studio recordings of *Gioconda* is to witness the dissolution of a style and tradition that may never return. There are vestiges of it in Bartoletti's account, but it's pretty much gone in Patanè's. We can only hope for its resurgence in the new millennium.

As a supplement to a complete recording, the *Gioconda* enthusiast should seek out some excerpts on recital discs. Whatever we have of the Enzos of **Gigli** and **Björling** deserves hearing, not least the duet with Barnaba (De Luca or Ruffo in Gigli's case, both creepily insinuating; the resonant Merrill with Björling). **Corelli,** the best Enzo in modern times, performed the role often on stage but shied away from it in the studio, leaving us only a magnificent statement of "Cielo e mar" (EMI). He should have recorded the opera with **Crespin,** whose "Suicidio," with its titanic top B and sonorous chest register, is altogether stunning (London). Fans of Farrell, Domingo, Carreras, MacNeil, and others will find a handful of *Gioconda* snippets from their favorites. The opera's most familiar tune, which occurs in the "Dance of the Hours" ballet, isn't vocal (and hence not representative). It has been wrenched out of context and recorded innumerable times. Ponchielli, no doubt, would have come to regret writing it.   LUCANO

Francis Poulenc *(1899–1963)*

Poulenc made his name as a composer of witty songs and suave piano pieces: *mouvements perpétuels,* nocturnes, novelettes. But although he was branded as a musical lightweight in the '20s, he turned out to be a

hardworking, continually developing composer, the only one among *Les Six* to make a significant dent in the standard repertory. Certainly few who knew his work in the 20s and admired the elegant hedonism of his ballet *Les Biches* would have suspected that he would write works of such high seriousness as his song cycle *Tel jour, telle nuit* or the Mass in G major, let alone a three-act tragic opera about the martyrdom of a nunnery, *Dialogues of the Carmelites.* True, high spirits and catchy tunes are seldom far away in most of his music, but this composer demonstrated his acquaintance with the darker side of life, for example in the near-Gothic gloom of parts of the Organ Concerto or the surrealistic cantata *Le Bal masqué,* whose frantic finale is both hilarious and a bit scary.

Stravinsky once said that one of a composer's most valuable gifts was "the instant imprint of personality." I don't know who Stravinsky was thinking of, but it might well have been his friend Poulenc; a piece by this composer is recognizable from the first bar. The problem for some critics is that Poulenc was a sort of musical magpie, taking nifty bits of music he liked and weaving them into his own tapestry. Gluck's *Dance of the Blessed Spirits* is quoted obliquely in his Trio for Oboe, Bassoon, and Piano, Mozart's "Haffner" Symphony quite boldly in *Les Biches,* and Falla's *El Amor Brujo* in one of the *Improvisations* for piano. The detective work can go on and on, but no matter where the ideas come from, somehow Poulenc's music always sounds like Poulenc. And by borrowing from others so freely and lovingly, he somehow created art that was completely true to himself—one of those paradoxes that art can present but has no need to explain.

Poulenc never suffered from false modesty about his music, but he was also well aware of his place at the composers' table, as he wrote in a letter in 1942: "I know very well I am not one of those who have made harmonic innovations like Igor, Debussy, or Ravel, but I think there's room for new music that doesn't mind using other people's chords. Wasn't that the case with Mozart and Schubert?"

ORCHESTRAL MUSIC

Concertos aside, Poulenc's largest orchestral works are the *Sinfonietta* and two ballet scores, *Les Biches* (1924) and *Les Animaux modèles* (1944). The earlier work is '20s Poulenc at his most appealing, spirited and delicately hedonistic; the later score is equally appealing but ampler in scope and more warmly emotional. The most light-hearted and elegant performance of *Les Biches* was led by **Désormière** on an old London LP worth seeking in a used record shop. All other *Les Biches* seem a bit dumpy in comparison, although **Prêtre**'s performance of the whole ballet (with chorus) in a set of Poulenc's orchestral works is lively; besides *Les Animaux modèles,* the set includes the charming if overextended *Sinfonietta,* commissioned by the BBC in 1948 (♦EMI 69446, 2CD). The '60s sound is sometimes clotted, but the performances are authoritative, especially the Concerto for Two Pianos with Poulenc himself and Jacques Février—a bit slow, to accommodate Poulenc's aging technique, but still the real thing—and the delightful *Concert Champêtre* for harpsichord with Aimée van de Wiele.

The suite from *Les Biches* contains the best music, and **Dutoit**'s performance is predictably spiffy and well recorded (♦London 452937). This generous collection, an ideal introduction to Poulenc's orchestral music, includes *Les Animaux modèles, Aubade,* and several orchestrations of short pieces. You can follow it up with another desirable Poulenc/Dutoit collection featuring *Concert Champêtre* with Rogé and *Sinfonietta* (London 452665). If you would like *Les Biches* in a general French program, **Tortelier** puts it in the congenial company of Milhaud's *La Création du Monde* and Ibert's *Divertissement,* with stylish but unbuttoned playing by the Ulster Orchestra (Chandos 9023).

A nice pendant to Poulenc's orchestral music is his witty, tender setting of *L'Histoire de Babar* (Babar the Elephant) for speaker and piano, later orchestrated with pleasing Gallic clarity (auto horns and all) by Jean Françaix. **Meryl Streep,** with JoAnn Falletta conducting the New Zealand Symphony, tells a warm and endearing bedtime story (Koch 7408, appropriately coupled with Poulenc's Concerto for 2 Pianos and Ravel's *Mother Goose Suite),* but the classic *Babar* is **Peter Ustinov**'s peerless, sly performance, possibly more entertaining for parents than for children (EMI, NA).

CONCERTOS

Poulenc is most apt to be represented in a concert by one of his concertos. They cover the keyboard gamut: *Concert Champêtre* (Rustic Concerto) for harpsichord (written for Wanda Landowska), concertos for one and two pianos, and an organ concerto. All except the Piano Concerto are staples in their particular repertoires, and all (even the Piano Concerto) have been recorded many times. There is also the ballet/concerto *Aubade,* for piano and eighteen instruments, very modish in its minglings of Mozart and Stravinsky, but with its plot about Diana "condemned to chastity" surprisingly serious too (Poulenc called it "amphibious").

A handy summary of Poulenc's accomplishments as a composer of concertos is in a disc that contains Piano Concerto (with Rogé), Concerto for Two Pianos (with Rogé and Sylviane Deferne), and Organ Concerto (with Peter Hurford), all conducted by **Dutoit** (♦London 436536). Also recommended are two CDs packed with all Poulenc's concertos, stylishly performed by organist Marie-Claire Alain and pianist Duchable, among others, with **Conlon** conducting (♦Erato 21342). There are also excellent individual recordings of each concerto. Poulenc sat in on, and approved, a 1962 recording of the Organ Concerto with Duruflé and *Gloria,* both conducted by **Prêtre** (♦EMI 47723).

Organist/harpsichordist Simon Preston does the honors in a coupling of the concerto and *Concert Champêtre* with **Previn,** with one of the best recordings of Messiaen's *Turangalîla-Symphonie* (♦EMI 69752). The same pairing is provided by **Jean-Claude Casadesus:** a dryly witty *Concert Champêtre* by harpsichordist Elisabeth Chojnacka and a dark, looming, positively Gothic live recording of the Organ Concerto by Lefebvre (♦Naxos 554241). If Poulenc coupled with other French organ works appeals to you, Ian Tracey and **Tortelier** offer a beautiful, plush recording (Chandos 9271).

The Concerto for Two Pianos is also well represented on disc. In 1961, the fabled American team of **Gold** and **Fizdale** joined **Bernstein** for a predictably lively recording (♦Sony 47618; the couplings, Shostakovich's Piano Concertos, are pleasingly apt). The most celebrated of current two-piano teams, the **Labèques,** are heard in the Concerto with Ozawa, a performance that's certainly glossy but a little *too* lively; Poulenc would never have approved of their tricks with rubato (Philips 26284). The Labèques' couplings are excellent two-piano works *sans orchestre* by Poulenc and Milhaud. Another pair of sisters, the **Golabeks,** offer a more stylistically appropriate performance (Koch 7408, with *Babar).*

Pianist **Ralph Votapek** plays *Aubade* as a substantial part of an irresistible 20th-century French program (♦Music & Arts 649). **Rogé** includes it in his equally irresistible all-Poulenc disc (♦London 436536), and **Tacchino** in a disc with both piano concertos (EMI 64714). As an odd footnote, I'll mention a performance by **Gould,** of all people: a predictably bizarre, wrong-headed, fascinating performance of several

movements from *Aubade,* taken from a CBC special on music in the '20s. For Gouldians only, it's available in Sony's "Glenn Gould Edition."

CHAMBER MUSIC

A very useful chamber music collection includes the Sextet, Trio for Clarinet, Bassoon, and Piano, and Sonatas for flute, oboe, and clarinet (♦London 421581). The acoustic is a bit fuzzy while Poulenc's music is *sec,* but the selection is generous and the performances are excellent. Another good collection is a set that includes all the above plus *Rapsodie nègre* (written when Poulenc was 17), bits and pieces (some of them very bitty indeed) of incidental music for Jean Anouilh's play *L'invitation au château,* and a breezy wind quintet arrangement of *Mouvements perpétuels,* not to mention Ravel's *Introduction and Allegro* and *Pièce en forme de habañera* (♦Cala 1018, 2CD).

While his woodwind pieces are gems of dry wit, composing for strings didn't come easily to Poulenc, and his somewhat ungrateful sonatas for violin and for cello prove the point. The Violin Sonata sounds as good as it can on the recording by **Cho-Liang Lin** and Paul Crossley, with an outstanding program of Ravel and Debussy works for violin and piano (Sony 66839).

PIANO MUSIC

Poulenc pooh-poohed his solo piano music, claiming that the best of it was in the accompaniments for his songs. Perhaps so, but there are plenty of gems. Much of it is in the form of suites of short character pieces and has an attractive improvisatory quality. It's easy to imagine the composer playing away for the pleasure of a few friends at his chateau (in fact, one of the most substantial of the piano works, *Les Soirées de Nazelles,* is about just that).

Two very full discs by **Rogé** are delightful and have all the important works, if that's the right adjective (♦London 417438, 425862). Ditto **Parkin** includes some pieces Rogé misses, like *Napoli* and *Suite française* (Chandos 8637, 8847). **Olivier Cazal** sturdily performs the main works (Naxos 553929 and 553930); the second disc contains two of the most attractive suites, *Mouvements perpétuels* and *Les Soirées de Nazelles.* Poulenc's *Promenades* are dedicated to **Rubinstein,** who apparently never performed them; he did record, deliciously, *Mouvements perpétuels,* a nocturne, and an intermezzo (♦RCA 61446, with music by Debussy, Ravel, and Chabrier).

Poulenc's keyboard masterpiece is his Sonata for Two Pianos, written in the '50s for the American team of **Gold** and **Fizdale;** it's plentifully lyrical, but surprisingly desolate and violent. Gold and Fizdale recorded it in mono and in stereo (the latter in a Columbia LP with Poulenc as pianist in his Sextet), but they are disappointingly brittle for such emotionally charged music. More serious minded, if a bit cloudily recorded, is the performance by **Setya Tanyel** and **Jeremy Brown,** in a disc of all of Poulenc's music for two pianos (Chandos 8519). The rest of the music on this disc is lighter stuff, even a piece called *Elégie;* the brief "valse-musette" *L'Embarquement pour Cythère* is pure soufflé, an ideal encore piece.

CHORAL MUSIC

Gloria, first performed in Boston in 1961, is Poulenc's most popular large-scale work, and reportedly the second most frequently performed piece of French music (the first being Ravel's *Boléro).* It's not hard to see why: it expresses an uncomplicated joy that's most unusual in 20th-century music, especially 20th-century religious music. *Gloria* was recorded soon after its French premiere by **Prêtre,** in a performance witnessed and approved by the composer (♦EMI 47723, with another

Poulenc-approved recording, the Organ Concerto played by Duruflé). **Bernstein**'s 1977 performance is a bit wayward, but fresh and affectionate, and Blegen is an excellent soloist (♦Sony 47569, with Janáček's *Glagolitic Mass*).

Fans of Battle will enjoy her singing with **Ozawa**, although he picks some eccentric tempos and the recording is shallow (DG 427304). Another Ozawa *Gloria* is coupled with the more severe *Stabat Mater*, as is Janice Watson with **Tortelier** (Chandos 9341). The popular John Rutter version is nicely sung by the **Cambridge Singers** but sounds underpowered to me (Collegium 108). The most satisfying performance of this work is led by **Shaw,** coupled with an even more arresting setting, Szymanowski's *Stabat Mater* (♦Telarc 80362). **Michel Piquemal**'s *Stabat Mater* is fervent and appealing (with an excellent soprano in Danielle Borst), but the coupled *Gloria* lacks power and energy (Naxos 553176).

Shaw was one of the composer's favorite interpreters ("his tempos correspond to the rhythm of my blood," he wrote of an early Shaw recording), and the combination of purity and sensuality in Poulenc's religious choral music is beautifully served in his recording of the Mass in G, four *Petites prières,* and a selection of motets (♦Telarc 80236). The gem among Poulenc's secular choral works is the wartime piece *Figure humaine,* which ends with a luminous, downright thrilling choral paean to "*Liberté*"; it's the highlight of a joyous choral anthology by **Gardiner** (♦Philips 46116). The excellent British group **The Sixteen** recorded two discs that contained almost all of Poulenc's a cappella choral music, sacred and profane; they're out of print but seem a likely candidate for reissue (Virgin).

OPERAS

Les Mamelles de Tirésias (The Breasts of Tiresias). "Surrealist comic opera" may be an accurate label, but it hardly does this delicious work justice. It's no manifesto, but a show as tuneful as a Broadway musical, as anarchic as a Marx Brothers movie, and so tastefully bawdy that probably only a Frenchman—in fact, only Francis Poulenc—could have brought it off.

Mamelles was the first of his three operas, begun in 1939 but not finished until after the war, and first produced in 1947. Its basis is a farce by Apollinaire about a wife (named Thérèse) and husband (named Husband) who decide to change identities. They do it spectacularly: Thérèse's titular breasts turn into red and blue balloons and float away, she grows a beard, dons a smoking jacket, and reads the daily papers, just like a man. The Husband becomes a "scientific" mother, producing 40,000 babies in a day, including one who can paint just like Picasso. After many bizarre, gender-bent adventures, husband and wife go back to the way they were. Poulenc was entirely faithful to Apollinaire's play, with one exception. Apollinaire specifies the setting as Zanzibar; Poulenc kept the title but changed the scenery to Monte Carlo, a city he described as "quite tropical enough for the Parisian that I am."

The score accompanying these going-ons is, as the composer put it, "crammed with music, 200 percent pure Poulenc." It covers a range of moods, from manic to unexpectedly moving, and is flawlessly put together. After the 1953 recording of *Mamelles* was released, Poulenc wrote to his frequent recital partner, baritone Pierre Bernac: "I am insanely fond of this work. It is one of the rare things I have written where I would not change one eighth-note." And we can be grateful he never did.

Mamelles was first recorded in 1953 by a peerless cast of French performers, led by **Cluytens** with the Thérèse/Tiresias of Denise Duval, a

glamorous, leather-lunged soprano for whom Poulenc wrote his other two operas (♦EMI 65565, an import worth searching for). **Ozawa**'s 1996 recording can't compare with the old one for authenticity, but it's performed with spirit by Japan's Saito Kinen Orchestra, and it's certainly enjoyable to hear Poulenc's sparkling orchestration in modern stereo (♦Philips 456504). As Thérèse, soprano **Bonney** sounds like she's having fun, and her silvery voice is a pleasure to hear. Her husband is played very drolly by Jean-Paul Fouchecourt, whose ease with the French text makes him stand out in the international cast.

Dialogues des Carmélites. This was Poulenc's magnum opus, and probably his masterpiece, a three-act opera first produced in 1957. It's based on a successful play by Georges Bernanos, which later became a successful film and, almost untouched, the libretto for the opera. Blanche de la Force, a young woman of an aristocratic family, decides to become a nun to overcome her fear of death. As a novice in a Carmelite monastery, she experiences the painful, frightened death of the First Prioress, and fears that the same fate awaits her, but the grace necessary for a "good death" is transferred to her, and when the nuns are guillotined during the French Revolution, she can go calmly to her fate.

Poulenc's music serves the libretto completely; he took great pains to get every stress and vowel sound right while making sure that every word could be heard. He takes off musically in only two places: a gorgeous setting of the "Ave Maria" in Act 2, and a terrifying setting of the "Salve Regina" sung by the nuns as they go to the guillotine at the end of the opera. The sound of the blade cuts through the choral music at irregular intervals, and the music begins again, minus one voice at a time—a tremendous effect, on stage or on a recording.

Carmélites was a triumph at its premiere and quickly made the rounds in Europe (its U.S. premiere was on NBC TV, with a young Leontyne Price in the cast), and unlike most 20th-century operas, it has stayed in the American and European repertoire. It was also treated to an "original cast" recording of the Paris premiere, conducted by **Dervaux**, which is still available (♦EMI 49331, mono). Besides Duval as Blanche (the role was written for her), the cast includes the young Crespin and Gorr. Almost 30 years later, with **Nagano** conducting an excellent performance, modern digital stereo brings out more of the variety of Poulenc's orchestration (♦Virgin 59227). The cast is headed by the young Dubosc as Blanche, and Gorr returns from the 1957 cast, this time as the Prioress. Nagano also restores a short dialogue scene cut from the old recording. Mono or stereo, *Dialogues des Carmélites* is one of the most absorbing and moving of 20th-century operas.

La Voix humaine. Poulenc's last opera was also his only real collaboration with Jean Cocteau, the protean writer who named *Les Six:* an adaptation of Cocteau's 1932 monodrama as a mono-opera, or as Poulenc preferred to call it, a *tragédie lyrique.* In opera and play, a woman is alone on stage for 45 minutes. Her lover has dumped her, but she desperately tries to keep him on the telephone. After she confesses that she tried to kill herself with pills the night before, the conversation breaks off, and it's clear that the woman (known only as Elle) has been abandoned for good. The aging Poulenc identified with the aging Elle, and the rather soapy story is given grandeur by the breadth of his music (scored for a very large orchestra).

La Voix was first performed by Poulenc's beloved soprano **Duval,** who also recorded it with Prêtre soon after the premiere (EMI, NA). The most easily obtainable current recording is a good, midpriced version, with **Françoise Pollet** and Jean-Paul Casadesus conducting (Harmonia Mundi 7901474). **Julia Migenes**'s version, also with Prêtre, is dramatic and affecting; this reissue couples the opera with pure and finely shaded performances of some of Poulenc's choral music, especially the Mass in G and *Figure Humaine,* by the Uppsala Academic Chamber Choir (♦Erato 25598).

SONGS

If Poulenc had only left us his songs, he would still be an important composer. His 146 songs are filled with emotional depth and riotous humor, but within a surprisingly strict framework; they almost always move in calm, even rhythms and note values, seldom changing tempo, requiring perfect legato and sometimes a hazy sound he described as *"un halo de pédale,"* but no rubato. He set his native language to music meticulously, and his remarkable ability to grasp the essential emotional quality of obscure poetry is nowhere more pronounced than in the great cycle *Tel jour, telle nuit.* Eluard's poems are weird and surrealistic on the surface, romantic and passionate underneath. Poulenc's music illuminates their meaning with an art all his own.

The songs have been recorded complete on an uneven set featuring **Ameling,** Souzay, and Gedda, with pianist Dalton Baldwin (EMI 64087, 4CD). In a recent set, three of the four singers are French (almost always a plus in Poulenc)—**Dubosc,** Cachemaille, and Le Roux—and the fourth is an outstanding non-French Poulenc singer, soprano Felicity Lott, with Rogé at the piano (Decca 436991, 458859, and 460326, including the late cycles). (The complete set is also listed as Decca 460599, probably only available in larger stores or as an import.)

If you would like just a selection of the songs, there are some fine anthologies. **Lott**'s "Voyage à Paris" is an excellent introduction to Poulenc's art as a songwriter (♦Hyperion 66147). It includes *Tel jour, telle nuit,* atmospheric and witty songs to words by Apollinaire and Vilmorin, and delightful lighter fare, including the famous valse chantée, "Les Chemins de l'Amour" (words by Anouilh). Lott is heard in most of them, and sounds delicious, as does pianist Graham Johnson.

Bernac's thin, nasal, very French baritone may not be most people's idea of bel canto, but no one did Poulenc's songs more convincingly; luckily he and the composer made many recordings. *Le bestiaire, Tel jour, telle nuit,* and nine songs are included in a single disc (♦EMI 54605, mono, with Britten's *Michelangelo Sonnets* and *Holy Sonnets of John Donne* performed by Poulenc and Pears). And there are more cycles and *mélodies* from Bernac and Poulenc to investigate (♦Adés 14.114 and 14.1152; the latter includes the Flute Sonata, with the composer accompanying its first performer, Rampal).

The song cycle *Le Bal masqué,* for baritone and chamber ensemble, is one of Poulenc's most brilliant and typical works, circusy and satirical, high-spirited and bitter. Two recommendable recordings couple it, appropriately, with *Les Mamelles de Tirésias:* **Holzmair**'s performance is excellent (Philips 456504), but a 1960s recording with **Jean-Christophe Benoit** is fantastic (EMI 65565).

Poulenc is one of the few 20th-century composers who will show up in a real diva's song recitals, for example as encores in a collection by **Crespin** (London 417813), in the first recorded recital by the young **Leontyne Price** (RCA 61499), and in a delectable French recital by **Von Stade** that includes some unusual pieces by Honegger and Messiaen (♦RCA 62711). RAYMOND

Michael Praetorius *(1571–1621)*

Praetorius not only composed music, but also compiled treatises on every known musical instrument, edited *Musae Sionae,* a collection of arrangements of songs and hymns in nine volumes, and was employed as an organist. His style was less florid than Schütz's, aimed more at Protestant townsmen than at courtiers or bishops. Praetorius planned to publish eight volumes of secular dance music he had adapted from French composers but completed only one, *Terpsichore.* While his sacred works soar into the early Baroque, *Terpsichore* weaves through the late Renaissance.

Unfortunately, there is no set containing all 312 dances. Instead, there are three notable discs. "Excerpts from *Terpsichore*" is the most uninhibited. **Sally Logemann** leads the York Renaissance Band with vigor, as if she were Mistress of Misrule (Arabesque 6531). She's also adventurous with her instrumentation (Praetorius never specified which instruments to use). "Dances from *Terpsichore*" has a courtly feel, with finely measured tones and excellent dynamics (Decca 414633). I can imagine **Philip Pickett**'s New London Consort playing these infectious, saucy, and melancholy interpretations at Shakespearean festivals. Another set of "Dances from *Terpsichore*" is performed with more restraint than the other two; however, it's the only CD with vocal pieces, performed by the redoubtable soprano, Lena Hellström-Färnlöf (Naxos 553865). **Bertil Färnlöf** with the Westra Aros Pijpare ensemble reins in his crumhorns and forgoes racketts.

The devil doesn't always snare the best tunes. Praetorius must have been prescient about the recording industry's annual orgy of Christmas music, because several CDs are devoted to his sacred nativity music. The **Gabrieli Consort**'s "Mass for Christmas Morning" constructs a plausible 1620 Lutheran mass (MHS 514734L). Among its pieces are an ethereal *cantus firmus* processional, a spirited Introit with the renowned *Puer Natus in Bethlehem,* peppy organ preludes, a dramatic *Sanctus* motet, and a rousing recessional. Unfortunately, the consort gives the plainsong pieces (such as the epistle and gospel) such uninspired renditions that there'll be fidgeting in the pews.

Everything clicks in **Musica Fiata**'s "Polyhymnia Caduceatrix and Pangyrica" (Sony 62929). In exhilarating pieces like "Wie Schön leuchtet der Morgenstern," this double set paints visions of ecstatic and fervent Lutherans. The polychoral textures are ideally miked, the tempos wondrously varied, the singing transcendent. The **Huelgas Ensemble**'s "Magnificat" (Sony 480039) provides an otherworldly program of Praetorius's lesser known works. None are as lively as the Musica Fiata disc, but the singing is resplendent.

The **Hassler Consort**'s "Christmas Motets" (MD+G 6140660) features dazzling word painting in "Wachet auf" and Birgit Schönberger's scintillating "Der Morgenstern." The tempos are sprightly, the pacing acceptable. However, not only do the boy choir pieces lack boy sopranos, but "In Dulcet Jubilo" lacks jubilation as well. The inventive **David Munrow** left us "Dances from *Terpsichore* and Motets" (EMI 561289). What this 1974 recording lacks in dynamic range, it compensates for with irreverent sackbuts and shawms. In one motet, Munrow's use of an instrument-only chorus is stunning. BATES

Sergei Prokofiev *(1891–1953)*

One of the most remarkable composers of the 20th century, Prokofiev ran the gamut of styles without ever losing his own. His personal romanticism is threaded through all his work, no matter how tortured or alien the subject matter or how enthusiastically modern his style. In this, he resembles Richard Strauss, another innovator with a soft core. Like Strauss, he worked seriously and with remarkable originality in opera and has not been given his due in that area. He had great talent in describing movement and emotion in music, using meaningful phrases that have a strong impact.

SYMPHONIES

The seven symphonies are remarkably varied. There have been several complete sets, but none that handle all the styles equally well. **Rozhdestvensky** did them on Melodiya LPs, musically impressive but in rather limited sound, some of which are being reissued (Consonance). **Leinsdorf** offered nicely detailed but somewhat underpowered readings in Boston (RCA). **Weller** provided a powerful series that came closest to being recommendable for all the symphonies (London 430782, 4CD, NA). **Rostropovich** made a set that loses momentum too often (Erato, NA). **Neeme Järvi** has a good feeling for this composer, and his set has a fine 2, 3, and 4 and includes both the 1930 and 1947 versions of 4 (MHS 545111, 4CD). **Košler** brings out surprising details, though he lacks something in energy (Supraphon 91, 4CD). **Martinon** gives incisive readings that are small in scale but powerful in impact (Vox 5001 and 5054, 2CD each).

1 ("Classical"). By far the shortest, this symphony turns up coupled with longer works. It's not easy to play well, and the first movement has a curious tempo marking of quarter note equals 100, which has led a few conductors to play it slowly. Prokofiev is said to have intended the symphony to represent a tourist jauntily passing the beautiful old buildings of Paris and enjoying the view. **Koussevitzky** made perhaps the fastest recording of this piece during Prokofiev's lifetime, so the composer had a chance to complain but apparently didn't (RCA 61657). **Rozhdestvensky** also takes it fast (Consonance 815007, with 7 and two little-known early symphonic poems). Other worthy older readings are by **Ormandy** (Sony 53260), **Bernstein** (Sony 47602), **Nicolai Malko** (Classics for Pleasure 4523), and **Karajan** (DG 37253) if you prefer slower tempos. More modern versions that retain some joie de vivre are by **Järvi** (Chandos 8400), **Claudio Abbado** (DG 29396), and **Orpheus** (DG 423624). All of these last are not only excellent performances but have interesting discmates.

2. This is the ugly duckling of the symphonies, catching the composer in Paris at his most alienated moment. Stylistically, it resembles his ballet for Diaghilev, *The Steel Leap,* concerning Russia's embrace of industrialism, and both ballet and symphony glorify the machine. Still, after the deliberately brassy, mechanistic music of I comes a theme and variations full of lyricism and lightness as well as the expected mechanistic apotheosis. It's a fascinating and vital piece. Recommendations are difficult. Much depends on the recording engineers in such a densely scored yet subtly detailed piece, approaching *Rite of Spring* in complexity of texture.

Perhaps the best combination of musical phrasing and recorded clarity is **Weller**'s fast but lyrically phrased performance (London, NA). **Järvi**'s is a similar if less clearly delineated reading (Chandos 8368, with *Romeo and Juliet Suite 1*). **Martinon** is lively and powerful, though there are passages in both movements where the recording seems to lose high frequencies for a minute or so (Vox 5054). **Košler** emphasizes clarity of texture and thumb-to-nose atmosphere, sometimes at the expense of the underlying melodic impulse and onward rush of the music (Supraphon).

For that we need **Rozhdestvensky**, whose Moscow LP was a classic, though neither its performance nor recorded sound matched the polish of today's versions. **Kuchar** is tight and well recorded, though, as with Martinon, the focus of the sound seems to alter at times (Naxos, with a surprisingly lethargic 1 and a dreamy *Dreams* and *Autumn*). **Leonid Grin** gives us a fine version (Ondine 762, with *Autumn* and *Summer Night Suite).* We could use the fine hand of **Leinsdorf** in this piece, none of whose performances are presently available.

3. The third symphony is another work of considerable violence in an atmosphere of horror. It's actually the orchestral suite from the opera *Fiery Angel,* a medieval tale of obsession and exorcism, and makes great technical and emotional demands on both players and listeners. **Martinon** plays it intensely but speeds up abruptly at the climax of the first movement, tossing away the power he has built up so carefully (Vox). His brass plays the climactic phrases in one breath, but his subsequent race into darkness is disturbing. **Rozhdestvensky** only managed that in a broadcast, not in his commercial recording. **Košler** gives us more detail than anyone else, but his tempos and phrasing are a bit phlegmatic (Supraphon). **Leinsdorf**'s version had similar virtues and vices, but in a darker-sounding ambience (RCA).

Kuchar is atmospheric, but the sound has an electronic edge at times that attracts attention to itself, particularly in the scherzo's wild string glissandi, and has an unwieldy character that precludes recommendation (Naxos). **Järvi** is probably the best we've got at present, though he hasn't been uniformly praised (♦Chandos 8401). **Weller**'s was an emotionally cogent reading in a warm recording (London). **Rozhdestvensky** had a real Russian orchestra with trumpets that soared, though his recording lacked bass (Consonance). Most performances today seem too polite for this symphony.

4. This symphony also originated in music for a stage work, the neoclassical ballet *The Prodigal Son.* In 1947 Prokofiev attempted to turn it into a Soviet-style work. The two styles mix uneasily, though the changes are fascinating and add 15 minutes to the score. The original 1930 version is in the **Martinon** set, played with panache and verve in one of his best readings (Vox 5001). However, **Järvi** has staged a coup by coupling it with his excellent 3 (♦Chandos 8401) and giving us the revision with his 1 (Chandos 8400). **DePriest** plays the revision in a civilized manner (BIS 531), as do **Košler** (Supraphon), **Weller** (London, NA), and **Ormandy** (♦Sony, NA). This is in stark contrast to **Rozhdestvensky**'s heavily Russian style; he reveled in the brass and the over-the-top ending Prokofiev added, and slowed down at every possible point (Consonance).

5. With 1, 5 is Prokofiev's most popular symphony. The story about the sound of artillery going off outside Moscow just before the downbeat at its first performance is wholly appropriate to this wartime work, with its grandeur, tragedy, and nose-thumbing ending. I hope a performance by **Mravinsky** will always be available. An excellent mono concert recording demonstrates his way: a broadly paced I, an alert and mercurial II, a cumulative III, and a brisk IV full of resolution (♦Russian Disc 11165, with his powerful Glazunov 5). **Koussevitzky** recorded another powerful monaural version that should be on everyone's shelf (♦RCA 61657, with 1, the finale from *Chout* and excerpts from *Romeo and Juliet*). These are some of his greatest readings, in clear, rich sound.

Another important performance is a concert recording by **Rozhdestvensky** and the Leningrad Philharmonic in London, a wonderful resurrection of the sound of this orchestra in 1971, when it had a more distinctively Russian character than it does today (♦BBC 5691462, with shorter pieces). There's a tension that's only evident at a live concert. The sound, though not studio-clear, is good stereo, while the conductor is much more intensely involved than in his commercial recording (Consonance 815008) and is better recorded. Another interesting Russian performance is by **Mark Ermler** from 1978, who, with the U.S.S.R. State Academic Symphony, makes a beautiful mixture of the raw woodwinds and rich strings characteristic of Russian sound (Talents of Russia 16452, with *Summer Day*). There are some oddities, volume cuts, and a not very clear bass. Also, the cello scale leading into the trio is taken by a single player for some reason not evident in the score.

Kitaienko's 1986 recording with the U.S.S.R. Large Radio Symphony has great enthusiasm, though it's recorded in exaggerated sound (RCA 32042 with 1 and Audiophile 101.505 with Violin Concerto 1 appear to be the same recording, despite different names for the orchestra). The best Russian orchestral sound is from **Jansons,** who brought the Leningrad Philharmonic to Dublin in 1988 and recorded one of the fastest 5s ever at 38 minutes (Chandos 8576). The timings actually resemble Koussevitzky's, though the slow movement is faster. From the Ukraine comes **Kuchar** with an unfussy but imaginative reading somewhat spoiled by interventionist recording balances (Naxos 553056, with *The Year 1941,* a little-known three-movement suite not found anywhere else). A rival reading on the same label is by **Gunzenhauser,** recorded clearly and full of detail, though the finale is a bit stolid (Naxos 550237, with 1). The Russian way is further represented by **Ashkenazy,** who leads the Concertgebouw in an outstanding version (♦London 417314, with *Dreams*).

For the non-Russians, we return to the past for **Karajan's** 1968 Berlin recording, still considered one of the best (♦DG 423216, with 1). **Szell** drives the piece hard, and his Bartok *Concerto for Orchestra* contains a major cut (Sony). **Ormandy's** 1958 recording in Philadelphia goes as fast, but is less clipped-sounding, and the orchestra is outstanding (Sony 53260, with 1). **Dorati** in Minneapolis keeps a stiff upper lip throughout (Mercury). **Bernstein** in New York did a rather wayward reading in 1966 (Sony, with 1).

More recently, **Masur** pulled the New York Philharmonic in new directions, not successfully (Teldec). **Tilson Thomas** with the London Symphony shows imagination and attention to detail (Sony 48239, with 1), but less joie de vivre than **Slatkin,** at home in St. Louis (♦RCA 61350). **Levi** is rather charmless in Atlanta (Telarc, with 1), and **Levine** broods and blasts without emotion in Chicago (DG, with 1). Of those who have done all the symphonies, **Järvi** seems rather detached. **Martinon** is French, not Russian, but well articulated; **Košler** is sensible and full of his usual detail; while **Weller** is better balanced than the rest, and with better sound, but NA at present.

6. This is the most personal and tragic of all the symphonies. It's so very Russian that all non-Russian orchestras tend to seem a little ersatz, particularly in the opening of the slow movement, with its apparent imitation of a wailing Russian organ badly out of tune. Only the Russian winds can match that sound.

There are three different **Mravinsky** performances, all with the Leningrad Philharmonic. Best known is his studio recording, once on an Artia LP, a classic recorded with a good deal of clarity in 1959. This performance is presently NA, but two live performances are available, a 1967 radio broadcast (Praga 256004), not representative of the orchestra at its best, and a 1959 concert recording in Moscow (♦Russian Disc 10900), more driven than the studio recording, more immediate but more messy, recorded with as much impact but a bit grainy on top, as these recordings tend to be. **Martinon's** is a good, somewhat tight reading, but you miss the Russian sound (Vox). **Järvi** is weak in the strings, but makes some telling points in rich sound (♦Chandos 8359). **Dutoit** with the NHK Symphony of Japan is lean and French in aspect with thinsounding soloists (Decca). **Ormandy** and **Leinsdorf** are NA—more's the pity.

7. Symphony 7 is the Cinderella of the symphonies in several ways. It's light and balletic in style, wholly unassertive, and absolutely beautiful!

The Russians tend to make it larger than life. **Rozhdestvensky** is recorded in brash yet squishy sound that makes the piece sound loud, though the performance itself is idiomatic (Consonance 815007). **Kuchar** is heavy and graceless (Naxos); **Martinon,** though sensitive, is less relaxed than would be ideal (Vox). Even **Weller** is uncouth in his bass-heavy balances here, though his lyricism is lovely (London). A lighter and more successful performance comes from **Nikolai Malko** (Classics for Pleasure 4523). My favorite 7 was by Rozhdestvensky's father, **Nikolai Anosov,** with the Czech Philharmonic. This is their kind of piece, and the way Anosov subtly points up the details of Prokofiev's scoring without ever resorting to burlesque is a lesson to us all. **Košler** can't match it, even with the same orchestra (Supraphon).

OTHER ORCHESTRAL MUSIC

Where to begin? Perhaps with the largest orchestral works, the ballets and their suites, then the incidental scores, then the abstract works. We can save operatic suites to go along with the operas.

Ballet music

Ala et Lolly (Scythian Suite). This ballet, better known in its orchestral form as *Scythian Suite,* was Prokofiev's first commission from Diaghilev. The idea was to follow up the scandal of Stravinsky's *Rites of Spring* with another ballet from pagan Russia. In the event, Diaghilev decided not to take the chance, after Prokofiev had already composed the music. Written for an outsized orchestra, this work has always challenged sound engineers, and each recording emphasizes different aspects of the score.

One of the most satisfying was a filler in **Weller's** set of the complete symphonies, brilliant and warm in sound (London). Though **Rozhdestvensky's** version is exciting, the balances aren't good, giving us a disturbingly loud piano in the "Nocturne," among other things (BBC 9146). **Abbado** in Chicago sacrifices some violence to good grooming (DG 47419), where **Järvi** lets it all hang out (♦Chandos 8564). **Ansermet's** scrawny version is on London, *pace* Schwann (448273, 2CD). **Skrowaczewski** is metronomic and small-scaled (Vox), and **Mata** in Dallas has a great time with Prokofiev but much less fun with the coupled *Rite.*

Cinderella. This work's composition was interrupted by the political necessities of WWII and presents a less consistent atmosphere in parts of Act 3 than did *Romeo and Juliet.* Nevertheless, a complete performance is desirable. **Rozhdestvensky's** is the earliest and the best, made in 1966 and still a classic in a lively and well-played performance (♦Consonance 815002). **Previn** is sensitive, if a bit sleepy (EMI 68604, 2CD). **Pletnev** (DG 445830, 2CD) is more austere in sound and interpretation than Rozhdestvensky; I still prefer the older performance.

Prokofiev extracted three suites from *Cinderella.* As with *Romeo and Juliet,* the music is rearranged and put in a different sequence. None of the listed recordings have come this way or have been mentioned in the literature available to me.

Chout ("The Tale of the Buffoon"). This was the first Prokofiev ballet to be danced by Diaghilev's company. A satirical work, the score is sometimes brittle and off-hand, frequently dark and disturbing. There's a disembodied feeling; it's almost more about puppets and cruelty than *Pétrouchka.* The four early ballets were recorded complete by **Rozhdestvensky** in the late '80s (♦Icone 9406). *Chout* complete takes 56 minutes, and Prokofiev made two suites from it. **Martinon** (Vox) includes only 21 minutes to **Susskind's** 34 (Everest 9019). Susskind adds more lyrical moments to Martinon's predominantly lively selection and is blessed with a remarkably clear recording. **Järvi** gives us excerpts from three early ballets, playing with his usual enthusiasm and rough edges (Chandos 8729). **Abbado** gives us a fine performance, the best in his rather catchall collection (London 448273). Finally, **Koussevitzky** turns in a performance of only the "Final Dance" that blows everyone else away with its beautifully paced accelerando (RCA 61657).

On the Dneiper. Prokofiev's last ballet for the Ballets Russes, this is a 41-minute work in the **Rozhdestvensky** recording (NA) from which the composer extracted a 20-minute suite, also recorded by Rozhdestvensky (NA).

Pas d'acier ("The Steel Leap"). This ballet about Russia's entry into the industrial age glorifies machinery, though there's still a lot of lyricism in the score. **Rozhdestvensky**'s complete version lasts 30 minutes; the suite takes about 13 and is included with his complete *Cinderella* (Consonance 815002, 2CD). The complete score is NA at present and **Järvi**'s is the only other recording of the suite (Chandos 8729).

The Prodigal Son. The most famous of the early ballets, this has been recorded complete by several conductors over the years, starting with a lively version, now long gone, by **Leon Barzin**. It has the classical balance of the last two piano concertos, an aspect emphasized by **Rozhdestvensky** in his complete recording (NA). His version takes 37 minutes to **Järvi**'s 34 (Chandos) because Järvi rushes so much. The mystery version listed in *Schwann* (London 448273) is the suite, played by **Ansermet** and the Suisse Romande. The suite is quite different from Symphony 4, which elaborates on material from the ballet. I should mention the video of Balanchine's choreography danced by Baryshnikov (Nonesuch 40179).

Romeo and Juliet. This is the most famous of the three full-evening ballets Prokofiev wrote in Russia. The music raises his use of leitmotif to the Wagnerian level and the emotionalism of his art to its highest point as well. There have been many complete recordings, as well as a couple of videos. The film commemorating Lavrosky's choreography with Ulanova is a remarkable document in several respects, not least because it shows the kind of revisionism the composer had to deal with in his Soviet years. The film suffers from numerous cuts and rearrangements, including only 95 minutes of the 145-minute score. As a historical document of Soviet choreography, however, it's invaluable.

Building on the tempos favored by Lavrosky, a 1981 complete recording by **Zhuraitis** and the Bolshoi Theater Orchestra represented the state of Russian playing at the time: very ethnic, fearless and vibrato-laden brass, expressive intonation, and density rather than clarity of sound (Carleton 3). It included three numbers Lavrosky dropped even before Prokofiev orchestrated them, pieces no one else plays, orchestrated by the conductor. I happen to like the old-style Russian sound, mawkish oboes and all. Those who like a light, balletic character with the drama of Russian orchestral sound may prefer **Gergiev** with the Kirov Theater Orchestra, a sensitive performance, though perhaps too much on the delicate side (Philips 432166).

Ermler manages to turn Covent Garden into a good facsimile of a Russian orchestra, with exciting brass and a hint of vibrato in the horns. His more theatrical reading does justice to both the dramatic and the tender side of the score (Conifer 55309, NA). For instance, this is one of the few occasions where Tybalt staggers to his death with conviction. Some say there aren't enough strings, but I suspect they're devotees of the non-Russian, nonballet versions. **Kitaienko** is more dramatic still but uses the orchestrations as revised by the Bolshoi, who complained to Prokofiev that they couldn't hear the music, so he thickened it for the

occasion (Chandos 9322). Moving away from tradition to a richer symphonic sound, **Maazel** made a streamlined, sometimes glib but passionate recording (♦London 452970 or MHS 524596). **Ozawa** is a bit more generalized (DG), while **Previn** is downright dull (EMI).

Prokofiev extracted three suites from the score. The first includes mostly dances, ending with the death of Tybalt; the second includes the most dramatic and romantic moments and is the best known; and the third is predominantly lyrical numbers. He compressed and rearranged the music for the suites. Also, conductors frequently mix the numbers to suit themselves.

First consider those conductors who have made complete recordings, like **Zhuraitis** (IMP 6700842) and **Gergiev** (Philips 32819); both play excerpts directly from the ballet score. **Andrew Mogrelia** with the Czech State Philharmonic (Košice) offered a complete recording of the ballet at one time and now has excerpts from all three suites arranged in ballet order (Naxos 550380). He's one of the few who includes selections from Suite 3. He plays with insight and warmth, but his orchestra has weak strings, embarrassing at times. He also conducts two selections with the Ukrainian National Symphony (Naxos 554063).

Several conductors are represented by more than one collection. **Ančerl** did an excitingly dramatic mono LP that has now disappeared (Supraphon), though a taste may be had in a disc including three pieces not in his LP (Tahra 117, 3CD). **Skrowaczewski** is effective in two collections, an entire disc with the Cologne Radio Symphony (♦Denon 78840) and a complete Suite 2 with the Minnesota Orchestra (Vox 3016, 3CD), not to be confused with a Mercury production with an earlier, not-so-good incarnation with that orchestra.

More full-disc collections are by **Levi** in Cleveland, Suites 1 and 2 mixed and programmed well, beautifully played and emotionally satisfying (Telarc 80089); **Schwarz** in Seattle, metronomic and soulless in 1 and 2 (Delos 3710, 2CD); and **Salonen** with the Berlin Philharmonic, not the suites but larger groupings from the ballet score, played with intensity and style (♦Sony 42662). **Abbado** in concert in Berlin plays with sensitivity (DG 453439), though some recall his earlier disc with more affection. **Tilson Thomas** plays a generous selection from the ballet score, but the sound in San Francisco and his preference for transparency defeat him in the more dramatic parts (RCA). **Chung** with the Concertgebouw is sensitive and has a virtuoso orchestra, but gives us less music than others (DG 439870).

Shorter groupings coupled with other works include **Daniele Gatti**'s dramatic performances from the suites with the Royal Philharmonic (Conifer 51343) and shorter collections by **Masur** in New York (Teldec) and **Dutoit** in Tokyo (Decca), both coupled with symphonies, none of them satisfactory. Older performances include four movements from Suite 2 from **Koussevitzky,** a bit rushed in the lyrical passages (RCA 616572). Avoid **David Oistrakh** in Portsmouth: They can't get it together in any respect (Supraphon). **Saraste** is not well ordered and not well interpreted either (Finlandia). **Leinsdorf** is represented only by 36 minutes with the Los Angeles Philharmonic with odd discmates (Sheffield). He did more with Boston, but it's not available at present. His Prokofiev is generally outstanding.

The Tale of the Stone Flower. Prokofiev's last ballet is little known in the West, though **Rozhdestvensky**'s complete recording is still listed, a fine performance first issued in 1974 in clear, somewhat overmodulated sound (Russian Disc 11022, 2CD). There was a version by **Jurowski**, 13 minutes slower and spread over an extra disc, though in better sound (CPO 999385, 3CD, NA). The mystery listing in *Schwann* refers to excerpts conducted by **Varviso** with the Suisse Romande (London 448273, 2CD). The **Järvi** listings are various excerpts coupled with other Prokofiev pieces. There is a video by the Kirov Ballet of the 1957 revision by the Soviets, replete with atmosphere, with 14 numbers cut and the Scherzo of Symphony 7 inserted (Elektra-Nonesuch 40153). Still, it's authentic in its way.

Incidental music

There are a number of primarily orchestral scores written for various dramatic purposes during Prokofiev's years in Russia. Some, like the music for the Eisenstein films *Alexander Nevsky* and *Ivan the Terrible,* are better approached in the choral section below.

Peter and the Wolf. Judging recordings of this familiar work is really a matter of who is doing the narration and how. I personally grew up with **Richard Hale** and Koussevitzky, and Hale's British wit and accent seem right to me. Pearl 9487 preserves it with several early Koussevitzky Prokofiev recordings and is a valuable document in itself, though children of the digital age may find the inevitable surface noise of the 78 rpm discs troubling. **Alec Guinness,** with the Boston Pops and Fiedler seems too detached by half, recorded at a different time from the careful and antiseptic orchestra (RCA). **John Gielgud** with Jack Stamp and the Academy of London is livelier but still rather stuffy (Virgin 90786). **Previn** both narrates and conducts the Royal Philharmonic in a particularly well-integrated performance (Telarc 80126).

If you'd like to hear how it's done by a real Russian, the composer's first wife **Lina Prokofieva** narrates it with Järvi in an atmospheric, rather leisurely performance (Chandos 8511). For the moderns, **Sting** has a lively version with Abbado that should attract the attention of a child (DG 429396). **Jack Lemmon** does it diffidently and was obviously spliced in (LaserLight 15386). **Peter Schickele** goes back to his North Dakota roots with Levi, altering the story entirely (Telarc 30350). (This is better than a performance he once did in which the wolf ate Peter, ending the story in mid-bite.) The original translation from the Russian is rather basic: I was surprised to discover how many felicitous turns of phrase were seemingly invented by Hale for his Boston reading.

Lieutenant Kije. This is a suite intended for a satirical film about an imaginary soldier invented by a bureaucracy to cover up their errors. The film appears never to have been completed, but the music became one of the composer's most popular scores. There have been many good recordings, especially one by **Reiner** and the Chicago Symphony, notable for its polish and slightly manic tempos (RCA 61957 or 60176 or 68363). Another remarkable recording by **Leinsdorf** gave us the original vocal versions of two numbers (RCA 21292). In the absence of that classic, try **Slatkin** in his interesting album containing all three of the film scores (Vox 5021). Unfortunately, he doesn't include the texts. It has become common to couple *Kije* with *Alexander Nevsky,* as **Previn** does; his *Kije* is slow in spots (Telarc 80143).

Abbado with Chicago isn't always note-perfect (DG 419603). **Macal** brings out a number of subtleties in the harmonies (Koss 1016). **Sargent** has an irritatingly casual attitude toward the score (Everest 9019). **Tilson Thomas** gives a performance replete with contrasts (Sony 69249 or 63275), and **Järvi** is also colorful (Chandos 8806). There are a couple of oldies about. **Scherchen** has verve and imagination (Enterprise 4167), and **Szell,** his customary polish (Sony 48162). The mystery set listed in Schwann (London 448273) contains **Dorati** and the Netherlands Radio Symphony.

Egyptian Nights. This is an incidental piece composed in 1933 for a spectacular combining Shakespeare and Pushkin. The major part of this interesting score was recorded by the indefatigable **Rozhdestvensky** for Melodiya and in a separate issue contained a monologue not included in the suite. A performance by **Järvi** of music for *Boris Godunov* makes a single seven-minute piece out of four of the 24 numbers in the score (Chandos 8472). **Alexander Frolov** plays six pieces, fleshing out their miniature character with repeats and substituting instruments for vocalists; not a successful venture (Consonance).

Better on the same disc is **Emin Khachaturian**'s performance of *Hamlet,* a beautiful score of nine pieces and songs which Shostakovich may have been looking at when he wrote his own film score. The songs and music have a curiously Scottish flavor. This performance also contains several extra repeats to flesh out short numbers. **Rozhdestvensky** released it with his complete *On the Dneiper,* played with greater accuracy and richer sound (Melodiya 206, NA). **Vladimir Ponkin** has done it, too, though with more gloom. His disc also contains a long score for *Eugene Onegin,* intended to be played for a reading of the Pushkin poem (Russian Disc 788027). Ponkin plays the music without text in an idiomatic but rather lugubrious performance, while **Groves** stretches it out to two discs by making it part of a dramatic production of the poem in English translation. The music alone lasts an hour or so and is full of leitmotifs whose development relies a lot on the poem. Since the performance never took place, Prokofiev recycled much of the music elsewhere. Three short dance numbers are included on the same **Järvi** disc as his *Boris* excerpts.

In the spirit of recycling, I should also mention *Waltz Suite,* which consists of six numbers, the first of which forms part of *Onegin* and was reused in *War and Peace.* The others hail from *Cinderella* and incidental music to *Lermontov,* all changed just a little. This suite is conducted by **Rozhdestvensky** in a beautifully detailed but occasionally uncouth reading (Consonance 5005). **Järvi** plays it more smoothly, if with considerably less flavor (Chandos 7076, or divided between his Symphonies 5 and 6).

Summer Day is another children's piece, seven little orchestrations from a series of easy piano pieces called *Music for Children.* I can suggest **Donald Barra**'s lively performances from San Diego (Koch 7042). **Mark Ermler** is plagued by close-up microphoning (Russian Compact Disc). **Dietrich Kober** in Chicago includes a transcription for clarinet and strings by Kent Kennan of the Flute Sonata and the only non-Järvi recording of the early and attractive *Sinfonietta* (Centaur 2154). Unfortunately, the disc is plagued by weak strings.

Abstract music

Our consideration of Prokofiev's abstract orchestral works begins with *Sinfonietta,* a four-movement work that already shows his penchant for revisiting earlier music in later works. This is an appealing score. Like most of these short works, your choice depends a lot on the coupling. **Järvi** does it with the lovely Symphony 7 in an effective reading (Chandos 8442). The symphonic poems *Dreams* and *Autumn* are two other early works. These atmospheric pieces are recorded together in two releases. **Rozhdestvensky** couples them with Symphonies 1 and 7 in beautiful performances (♦Consonance 815007), while **Kuchar** does them with Symphonies 1 and 2, somewhat less convincingly though with idiomatic conviction (Supraphon). A **Rozhdestvensky** reading of *Dreams* accompanies his important Symphony 5 (BBC 9146).

Järvi's *Dreams* are less dreamy and a bit more dramatic (Chandos 8472, with his *Romeo and Juliet, Suite 2,* and excerpts from *Eugene One-*

gin and *Boris Godunov* and the two *Pushkin Waltzes*). His *Autumn* comes in another miscellaneous collection including *Lieutenant Kije,* excerpts from *Stone Flower,* and an orchestration of the last movement of String Quartet 1 (Chandos 8806). **Ashkenazy's** *Autumn* used to be with his now deleted Symphony 5; it has been recycled in London 448273, where it's buried next to a number of inferior performances.

Prokofiev wrote three very different overtures. The earliest is from the '20s, Op. 42, sometimes called the "American." It's a curious piece for winds and piano, a fascinating sonority very much of its time. **Tilson Thomas** has the only current reading, stuffed into a set with his Symphonies 1 and 5 and other works (Sony 48139, 2CD). There's a **Rozhdestvensky** version recycled with his complete *Chout* (♦Icone 9406). Then there's the famous *Overture on Hebrew Themes,* originally a work for clarinet, quartet and piano, rescored for small orchestra. The trick here is to figure out in advance which version you're getting. The orchestral version was recorded by **Martinon** (Vox 5001, 2 CD), **Abbado** (DG 29396), **Camerata Vistula** (Olympia 343), **Masur** (EMI 62542, 2CD), and **Walter Proost** (Gallo 849). Finally, there is the monster *Russian Overture,* an unbuttoned romp for large orchestra, in the **Martinon** album and also in a **Järvi** collection (Chandos 9096). Both are exciting readings, and it's a fun piece.

Divertimento is based on music from various sources, including the ballets *Trapeze* and *Prodigal Son. Symphonic Song* is an early example of Prokofiev's Russian period. There is also an orchestration of the slow movement of Piano Sonata 4. These are only available in Järvi's series. The suite *The Year 1941* is in Naxos 553056 along with **Kuchar's** Symphony 5. *Ode to the End of the War* is another quirkily orchestrated piece led by **Rozhdestvensky** (Consonance 815008), and there are four marches for military band. Unfortunately, the Russian recording of these is NA, and we must make do with the **Temple University Wind Symphony,** a good group but not drinking vodka (Albany 271).

CONCERTOS

Piano concertos

The piano concertos contain some of Prokofiev's most sparkling and unbuttoned music. No. 1 was his graduation piece from the conservatory, a show-off work to demonstrate his pianistic prowess and compositional modernity. No. 2 is a blockbuster to outdo all blockbusters and seems somehow of evil intent. No. 3 is a sunny and popular work. Nos. 4 and 5 are from his last European years (4 was written for the left-handed pianist Paul Wittgenstein); both are acerbic, neoclassical pieces that require some acquaintance to get by the deliberate dryness of the idiom. All are prime Prokofiev.

Complete sets. The earliest complete set is by **Tacchino** with Radio Luxembourg under de Froment, recorded in the early and mid-'70s, now available in an album also containing the two violin concertos and *Symphony-Concerto* for cello and orchestra (Vox 3000, 3CD). Tacchino phrases beautifully, and the sound is well balanced between piano and orchestra. The competition is stiff, however, and the orchestra is a bit scrappy in places and a little small-scaled for the rambunctious 2, though enthusiastic. In 1974 **Béroff** with Masur and the Leipzig Gewandhaus recorded commanding readings full of virtuosity and sensitive music making. The sound Masur elicits from the orchestra is rather unfocused and lacks character, however (EMI 62542, 2CD, with *Hebrew Overture* and Béroff's excellent *Visions Fugitives*).

The very next year brought us **Ashkenazy** with Previn and the London Symphony in performances adding a little more panache and rich sonority to the brew (♦Philips 452588, 2CD). Even the normally polite Previn is incited to enthusiasm. More recently, **Alexander Toradze** with Gergiev and the Kirov Orchestra shows us vivid colors and milks the music for all its worth (Philips 462048, 2CD). Two complete sets are available on individual discs. **Kun Woo Paik** is lyrical, with more room for color and detail than most (Naxos 550565/6). **Demidenko** with Lazarev shows a great variety of tone color and split-second timing between conductor and soloist, though some tempos are slow (Hyperion 66858 and 67029). Järvi's set combines the talents of two pianists: **Boris Berman** plays 1, 4, and 5, **Gutierrez** gets 2 and 3 (Chandos 8938). Both are fine, but neither outclasses Ashkenazy.

1. The first concerto was recorded by **Graffman** with Szell and the Cleveland (Sony 37806, with classic performances of 3 and Sonata 3). **Kissin** gives a polished, perhaps too controlled reading (DG 439898, with 3). **Bronfman** adds 5 to the mix, but the results are not totally engaging (Sony). His recording of 2 and 4 is also hard-bitten (Sony, with an encore of the *Hebrew Overture* with the Juilliard Quartet and klezmer-style clarinetist Giora Feidman). **Feltsman** is impressive in 1 and 2 but lacks something in bravura (Sony). The classic recording of 1 is by **Richter** and Kondrashin with a Russian youth orchestra in grainy sound (Melodiya 29468). There is another with the Prague Symphony and Ančerl worth investigating, with a whiz-bang Tchaikovsky 1 (Supraphon 110268).

2. Igor Ardasev plays this concerto with the Prague Symphony under Svarovsky in a lively and sensitive reading (Supraphon 3382, with Tchaikovsky's fascinating *Concert Fantasy*). If you like a bit more violence, try **Marian Lapsansky** with Slovak forces; this work can take it (Opus 2635). And don't forget **Bolet,** who plays 2 and 3 with the Nuremberg Symphony under Ainslee Cox (Genesis 104), though I only know his earlier 2 with Thor Johnson, which was impressive but slightly cut. And there's **Adilia Alieva** with the San Remo Symphony, about which the less said the better (Gallo).

3. When we reach 3, we find the composer himself showing us how he'd do it (♦Pearl 9470 or Magic Talent 48040). Pearl includes all the solo pieces Prokofiev recorded, not what *Schwann* indicates. This is an important document, in quite good sound for its time (1932). **Cliburn's** performance with Hendl in Chicago has surfaced again, coupled either with Schumann (RCA 62691) or Rachmaninoff's (RCA 6209). His warmth is in direct contrast to the composer's objectivity, but he had something to say.

Another voice from that era is **Janis,** whose dynamic 3 may be heard with Kondrashin in Moscow (Mercury 434333 or Philips 456850, 2CD). **Argerich** is available in no less than three couplings, on DG and Philips, all the same performance with Abbado and Berlin. You should have one of these, probably Philips 456700, 2CD. **Janis Vakarelis** with Rowicki and the Royal Philharmonic stands up surprisingly well in this august company (RPO 8003). **Dickran Atamian** is rather less dynamic and further undermined by Schwarz's picky phrasing (Delos).

4. This concerto has seldom been done on its own. **Fleisher** made a strong impression with the Boston Symphony and Ozawa (Sony 47188).

5. Concerto 5 belongs to **Richter,** whose Warsaw recording with Rowicki is beyond compare (DG 415119).

Violin concertos

The two violin concertos are wonderfully contrasted. The opening of 1 is one of the most beautiful passages in Prokofiev's music, or in music altogether, and it's amazing to realize how little the orchestra plays in a low register in this work. 2 is a complete contrast; everything is dark and earthy. These are special pieces that contrast beautifully on a program, and, are frequently recorded together.

They were recorded twice by **Stern**, in 1963 with Ormandy (Sony 38525) and in 1983 with Mehta (Sony 42439). Both are fine, straightforward readings. Balances tend to favor the fiddle, as they do in **Perlman**'s recording with Rozhdestvensky (EMI 47025) and, to some extent, in **Mordkovitch**'s with Järvi (Chandos 8709). Perlman also recorded 2 with Leinsdorf in 1966 (RCA 61454, with both violin sonatas) and with Barenboim in 1993 (Teldec 98255, with Stravinsky's concerto). He continued to mature but showed authority right from the first. Mordkovitch is full of individuality; even the opening of Concerto 1 seems impatient. **Sitkovetsky** is also recorded rather closely, but his smooth and silky sound lets the orchestra through better (♦Virgin 90734).

Kyung-Wha Chung (London 25003) and **Cho-Liang Lin** (Sony 53969) both add the Stravinsky to their discs. Chung's readings have a vulnerable quality, where Lin is more controlled, though warm. **Boris Belkin** is insightful but technically disturbing (Denon). **Gil Shaham** adds the solo Violin Sonata to his disc, giving refined and satisfying performances (♦DG 447758). **Tedi Papavrami** does the same program with a folksy personality (Naxos 553494).

Anne Akiko Meyers substitutes the five *Melodies* in outstandingly personalized readings, recorded a bit close to the violin (RCA 68353). **Vengerov** recorded both concertos but on two discs, each coupled with its Shostakovich counterpart in particularly dark, searching readings (Teldec 92256 and 13150). Vengerov's teacher, **David Oistrakh,** also recorded both, the first several times. The version with von Matačič is a good example of his forthright style with 1 (Testament 1116). **Ricci** plays a mannered, self-conscious 1; his aggressive style suits 2 better (Vox 3000, 3CD).

Turning to individual recordings, 1 is owned by **Szigeti**, whose 1935 recording with Beecham is still outstanding (♦EMI 64562). **Milstein** is beautiful but downplays the music's modern aspects (EMI 66551). **Ilya Grubert** plays with aplomb, but the rest of the disc is poorly performed (Chandos 9615). If Szigeti owns 1, **Heifetz** has dibs on 2. Of at least three versions, perhaps the one with Munch (RCA 61744) is the best. The earliest (1935), with Koussevitzky, is less mature, though sweeter in tone (RCA 61735, 2CD). **Repin** gives a light, rapid reading (Erato 10696).

Cello concertos

There are actually three works for cello and orchestra. First came a Concerto in E Minor, recorded by **Starker** on two occasions, the first with a major cut in the finale, and by **Christine Walevska**, with different cuts (Philips 434166). All are presently unavailable. The concerto was written on the cusp of Prokofiev's return to Russia and is a bit undecided in style, though a fascinating piece. Much later, the composer rewrote it for **Rostropovich,** amplifying and changing it considerably, renaming it "Symphony-Concerto." This version has been recorded several times by its dedicatee, only listed at present in his mammoth album "The Russian Years" 1950–1974 (EMI 72016, 13CD). That version is a compilation of two live performances, a rather staid I conducted by Guzman in 1972, and a fiery II and III with Rozhdestvensky from 1964. The latter performance was complete on Russian Disc 11103, NA, with the even later *Concertino*.

This attractive work deals partially with variants of material from the *Symphony-Concerto* that didn't appear in the original Concerto, so it makes an interesting juxtaposition. The first movement of Rozh-

destvensky's *Symphony-Concerto* wasn't included in "The Russian Years" because it was messily performed, though inspired, but the *Concertino* is in the set. The talented **Alexander Rudin** recorded a fine disc combining these two items (Naxos 553624, NA). Otherwise, the Concertino is presently out of the catalogue.

Symphony-Concerto is a demanding piece requiring endurance and power, as well as agile fingers in high registers and a participatory orchestra. There's an effective presentation by **Laszlo Varga** in an album containing all the concertos — agile, accurate, and virtuosic, but playful (Vox 3000, 3CD). **Maisky** does the piece justice both in technique and soul (DG 449821, with Miaskovsky's fine concerto). **Jan-Erik Gustafsson** concentrates on the lyrical side (Ondine 861, with Aarre Merikanto's Concerto 2). **Ma** gives a memorable reading with Maazel, intense but refined, almost Germanic (Sony 48382). An older but exciting version came from **Navarra** with Ančerl in 1965, precise but passionate (Supraphon 111950). A curious recording by **Truls Mørk** includes an alternative version of the finale, substituting other material for a subversive tune introduced by the composer in the original (Virgin 45310, NA). Another little slice of history! Mørk plays with a sort of introverted lyricism that's very attractive.

CHAMBER MUSIC

For a pianist, Prokofiev wrote surprisingly little music for piano with other instruments. Perhaps the times weren't conducive; Shostakovich's massive series of string quartets didn't begin until the war years, when Prokofiev's quartets and sonatas also began. Before that, there's nothing except the acerbic, almost Stravinskian Quintet for oboe, clarinet, violin, viola, and double bass. It was originally written as a ballet score called *Trapeze,* a project that fell through, and the composer recast the music in this form. The **Walter Boeykens Ensemble** plays it with other clarinet-oriented pieces including *Hebrew Overture* in accurate but not very characterful performances (Harmonia Mundi 901419). **Chamber Music Northwest** couples it with Nielsen and Loeffler in vehement but not very sensitive readings (Delos 3136). The **Southwest Chamber Music Society** does better by both Quintet and Overture (♦Cambria 1072, with Poulenc).

Cello Sonata. This sonata was written under the cloud of Soviet criticism and has occasionally received a bad press for being in a relatively pellucid C major. In the right hands, however, the grandeur and positive attitude of this lovely piece are hard to resist. It was written for **Rostropovich,** whose performances with Richter have been coming and going since the '50s (their 1950 performance was on EMI 72016, the one from 1955 on Melodiya 10-00553 or Monitor 602201). It's traditionally coupled with Shostakovich's Sonata, played by the cellist and the composer in the most authentic readings of both works. Rostropovich includes the Shostakovich in his 13CD album (EMI 72016) and substitutes the live 1950 performance of the Prokofiev, made in the presence of the composer.

The Shostakovich makes a fine discmate, and many cellists duplicate this program. **Turovsky** and Luba Edlina offer an idiomatic account of both (Chandos 8340), **Suren Bagratuni** and Adrian Oetiker hardly less so, but more episodic (Ongaku 024110). That coupling makes a short disc, so many add to it. **Isserlis** and Mustonen give lively performances, adding all of Janáček's cello music to the disc (♦RCA 68437). **Bernard Gregor-Smith** and Yolande Wrigley play only Janáček's *Fairy Tale* but add Martinů's *Slovak Variations,* all recorded somewhat cavernously and played with less personality (ASV). **Leonid Gorokhov** and Alexander Melnikov substitute Stravinsky's *Suite Italienne,* playing a fine

Prokofiev but a rather irritable Shostakovich (Supraphon). **Michaela Fukačová** and Ivan Klánský play the same program in a primarily lyrical fashion (Kontrapunkt 32216). The best in this coupling is **Truls Mørk** and Lars Vogt (Virgin 45274, NA).

Xavier Phillips and Hüseyin Sermet substitute Schnittke's Sonata 1 for Stravinsky and play an inspiring Prokofiev, but are less convincing in the more modern material and are dryly recorded (Harmonia Mundi). Substituting Schnittke's *Klingende Buchstaben* for Stravinsky, **Kim Bak Dinitzen** and Paul Coker play well in a somewhat short program (Kontrapunkt 32146). **Lev Evgrafov** and Maria Yudina add Yuri Shaporin's rare Five Pieces Op. 25 and the Adagio from *Cinderella* in a performance full of contrasts, recorded a bit dully (Russian CD 16305). Another favorite coupling is with the Rachmaninoff Sonata. **Thedéen** and Pöntinen give satisfying readings in excellent sound (BIS 386). **Ma** and Ax pull the music about, an approach that works better for Rachmaninoff than for Prokofiev (Sony). **Boris Pergamenchikov** and Pavel Gililov offer an unusual program: Nikolai Roslavets's Sonata and a *Meditation* along with Prokofiev's little-known *Ballade* Op. 15 and a waltz from *Cinderella,* all played with involvement and in good sound (♦Orfeo 249921).

Two recordings couple the Prokofiev Sonata with Elliot Carter's from the same year. **David Pereira** and Lisa Moore play this short program with expertise (Tall Poppies 32), but are somewhat upstaged by **Joel Krosnick** and Kalish, who add Poulenc's Sonata, also written in 1948 (♦Arabesque 6682). Their performances tend to emphasize the darker elements in the music. Finally, **Michael Grebanier** and Janet Guggenheim participate in a disc including the two quartets played by the Aurora Quartet in good if not outstanding readings (Naxos 553136).

Violin sonatas. The contrasts here are again great, the first a distillation of wartime feelings, the second a nostalgic and positive work originally written for flute. Recordings of both sonatas include **David Oistrakh** on two separate discs, 1 with Richter (Orfeo 489981) or with Bauer (Praga 250041), 2 with Yampolsky (Testament 1113). All are special; Oistrakh persuaded the composer to transcribe 2 for violin. For more modern interpretations, **Perlman** and Ashkenazy are in command and give us the Leinsdorf Concerto 2 as a bonus (♦RCA 61454). **Nicolai Madojan** and Elizabeth Westenholz offer lyrical performances that don't quite go over the top (Kontrapunkt 32185, with *Melodies*). The young **Yevgheny Bushkov** and Stephen Prutsman give us the Solo Sonata in performances of great promise (Harmonia Mundi 1656).

Amoyal and Chiu play with enthusiasm (Harmonia Mundi 7237), but the end result is less impressive than **Repin** and Berezovsky (Erato 10698). Both are coupled with *Melodies*. **Mullova** and Piotr Anderszewski play 1 only, in a well-organized but somewhat bloodless performance (Philips 446091, with Debussy and Janáček). **Francisca Mendoza** and Xavier Borrás do only 2 without much conviction (Albert Moraleda 1294, with Debussy). In "*Souvenir d'un Lieu Cher,*" **Dmitri Berlinsky** and Svetlana Gorakhovich play 2 in a virtuosic, rather febrile fashion (Helicon 1015, with light works by Shchedrin, Schnittke, and Tchaikovsky).

The original flute version of 2 is recorded by **Manuela Wiesler** and Pöntinen in a rather obscure Russian program that will fascinate some and irritate others (BIS 419). An all-Prokofiev program mostly of transcriptions (*Melodies* and a few of the *Visions Fugitives*) is played by **Laura Gilbert** and S. Tahmizian in lively style (♦Koch 7105). **Galway** and Argerich couple it with Reinecke and a Franck transcription that will attract mostly fans of these two composers (RCA 61615). **Michael**

Faust and Randall Hodgkinson substitute Schumann's *Romances* for Reinecke in more introverted readings (GM 2055).

There is a performance of the sonata for two violins by **Mordkovitch** and **Emma Young** (Chandos 8988, with the solo violin sonata; Schwann calls it "a solo cello sonata or for 2 violins in unison," a record for inaccurate reporting; in fact, there *is* a Solo Cello Sonata, left unfinished at Prokofiev's death). The playing is rather overblown for a neoclassical opus. The same goes for their *Melodies* for violin and piano, a transcription of *Vocalises* (Chandos 8500).

String quartets. Both are in three movements. The first is late Parisian, the second a folk-Ukrainian piece. The contrast in mood and styles makes them natural discmates, and most recordings offer them together. The **Emerson Quartet** gives a beautifully balanced, somewhat antiseptic performance, including the little-known Sonata for Two Violins in an equally careful reading (DG 431772). The **Aurora Quintet** couples them with the Cello Sonata in sensitive and well-contrasted readings (Naxos 553136). The **Claudel Quartet** is a bit overbearing but plays warmly and unanimously (SNE 587). The **Coull Quartet**'s coupling is the *Hebrew Overture,* in intelligent, lively, somewhat politely paced readings , beautifully recorded (Hyperion 55032). The **American Quartet**'s performances are particularly characterful (MHS 512302). For 2 there is the **Hollywood Quartet,** a classic reading in clear mono sound, with Hindemith's Quartet 3 and Walton's Quartet in equally committed performances from the '50s (Testament 1052).

PIANO MUSIC

Though a master of the instrument, Prokofiev never recorded any of his nine sonatas and only the third of his five concertos. He seems to have recognized his limitations, evident by the emotional dryness of his readings, technically fluent though they are. Some recordings stem from piano rolls, notoriously lacking in subtlety of touch. Magic Talent 48040 is devoted to his pianism, while the rest of his recordings are on Nimbus 8813. Whatever happened to Pearl 9470 with all the above on one disc?

Collections. Like Beethoven's, Prokofiev's piano pieces seem to represent a particularly personal side of the composer, music in which he was more willing to experiment than his more public works allowed him to do. This attitude shows up right away in his first few pieces, where he's still a student enjoying the Romantic era and yet attempting to escape it. Eighteen student works were recorded in the course of **Chiu**'s valuable 8CD survey of the complete piano music, scattered about in Volumes 5, 7 and 8 (Harmonia Mundi 907 169, 190, and 191). They are perhaps not sufficient reason for investing, but these volumes are available separately, and Chiu's somewhat dry but brilliant pianism suits the short pieces that make up the rest of the material on these volumes. They're more satisfying than **Sandor,** whose complete edition (minus juvenilia and transcriptions) was my introduction to much of this material (Vox 3500, 3CD, and 5514, 2CD, NA). Sandor is marvelously agile and enthusiastic but has a hard edge that dulls the ears after a while, whereas Chiu knows when to let up, though he's most exciting when the music is most difficult.

Marshev's "Complete Piano Music" is played in a rather romantic style that does little for the more angry side of the composer (Danacord 391/95). **Boris Berman** has recorded nine Prokofiev discs, making him almost as complete as Chiu, minus most of the juvenilia. His style is more consistently outgoing, though occasionally stiff, and he's assisted by Chandos's reverberant sound in a satisfactory collection. A new series by **Eteri Andjaparidze** has begun with some early works, Opp. 4, 11, 12, 17, and 22. The energy level seems a bit low, though the sound is excellent (Naxos 553429).

But I've been waiting to tell you about **Raekallio** (♦Ondine 947, 3CD). I would hardly have expected a pianist who hears everything Prokofiev wrote as contrapuntal to convince me of his vision, but this Finnish pianist has done just that. His care in following multiple voices through the dense thickets of Prokofiev's writing results in an emotional experience I never expected based on the more generalized performances of others. His playing is as virtuosic as you could wish, and his fascination with voice-leading isn't an exercise but an emotional conviction that imbues every line with its own personality and intent. His whole album is worth recommending; it includes the most sensitive rendition of *Visions Fugitives* I've ever heard. Another disc contains transcriptions from *Romeo and Juliet, Sarcasms, Grandmother's Tales, Etudes,* and *Toccata* (Ondine 898).

Prokofiev's transcriptions are frequently done together, as in Chiu's Volume 4 (Harmonia Mundi 907150) and 9 (907195). One way out of the morass of performances would be to invest in Chiu's Vols. 4 through 9 and Raekallio's Sonatas, though I'd keep my eyes open for more Raekallio issues. **Demidenko** does an interesting though eccentric *Romeo and Juliet,* along with a Mussorgsky *Pictures* that raises eccentricity to an art form (Hyperion 67018). **Tacchino** plays *Romeo* with personality, along with a fine Sonata 2 and 3 and the Op. 12 collection of early pieces (Pierre Verany 791022). **Todd Joselson** plays both *Romeo* and *Cinderella* with notable empathy (♦Olympia 453). **Elena Kuschnerova** does *Romeo* and Sonata 2 with agile dancing fingers but a little matter-of-factly (Ars Musici).

Finally, something should be said about "The Russian Piano School," 21 discs in two Melodiya albums (25172 and 33230) containing a large number of performances of Prokofiev's music. For instance, we have **Neuhaus** in *Visions Fugitives,* **Sofronitzky** in *Grandmother's Tales* and numerous excerpts, **Gilels** in some of the *Visions,* and **Pletnev** in Sonata 7. Volume II contains **Nikolaieva** in a marvelous Sonata 8 and her arrangement of *Peter and the Wolf,* **Mikhail Zhukov**'s *Music for Children,* and **Yekaterina Ervy-Novitskaya** in a full disc containing *Sarcasms, Visions, Romeo,* and Sonata 5.

Sonatas. Some pianists have stayed primarily with the sonatas, among them **Murray Maclachlan** (Olympia 705, 3CD). His sound is romantic, somewhat generalized, and recorded without a very wide dynamic range, not my idea of Prokofiev's sound world. **Yakov Kasman** has recorded all the sonatas on two CDs (Calliope 9606/07). He's inspired but rather disconnected.

Dealing with the sonatas in smaller groups, we first meet **Bronfman,** who has done 1, 4, and 6 (Sony 52484) and 7 and 8 (Sony 44680), with punctilious attention to Prokofiev's markings, yet not as much fantasy as these works contain. **Pletnev** lacks energy in 2, 7, and 8, sonatas in which that quality should be paramount (DG). The same three by **Glemser** aren't biting enough at times (Naxos 553021); his other disc with 1, 3, 4, and *Romeo* is more effective (Naxos 554270). **Anne-Marie McDermott** plays the late revision of 5 plus 6 and *Sarcasms* in too polished a manner (Arabesque). **Dmitri Bashkirov** plays 8 with excerpts from *Visions Fugitives* and the last of Schubert's three A minor sonatas in a pellucid manner that suits Prokofiev better than Schubert (RCD).

The "War" Sonatas 6 through 8 are still the property of **Richter,** whose recordings may be heard on a number of issues; his 2 and 9 are also available (Praga 250015). There are better-recorded readings, but none shows such musical integrity. The "Great Pianists" series gives you Sonatas 6 through 8, Mussorgsky's *Pictures at an Exhibition,* and other important Richter performances (♦Philips 456946, 2CD). Also, his "Live

in Japan" disc 2 contains a program of miscellaneous pieces mostly not recorded by him elsewhere (Memoria 991002). **Horowitz**'s 7 is important too (RCA 60377), and **Pollini**'s 7 is an experience not to be missed (DG 447431). **Ohlsson**'s 8 is perhaps too smooth for anything but comfort (♦Arabesque 6724).

Something should be said about the two versions of 5, which may seem to be not very different but include many subtle changes. I prefer the original, a neoclassical work full of touching melodies and spicy harmonies, but the softening of many harmonies and subtle changes in articulation in the revision have validity, considering the changes to the ends of each movement that Prokofiev also made. Chiu and Sandor play only the revision, Raekallio the original.

CHORAL MUSIC

Alexander Nevsky. This is a film score with a prominent choral part. Prokofiev organized the music into continuous form when Hitler's pact with Stalin made it look as if this patriotic film would not be shown. As we know, the pact was broken, and Eisenstein's film was released. The music is powerful. Prokofiev's muse worked better at one step's distance from overt patriotism; it gave his imagination more scope, and evocative images always inspired him.

Nearly all the recordings of *Nevsky* ever made are still available, attesting to the popularity of the music. **Abbado** made one of the earliest surviving versions in London, though the sound has paled against more recent issues, and the accompanying *Lieutenant Kije* and *Scythian* suites from Chicago aren't stellar (DG 47419). Other versions coupled with *Kije* come from **Reiner,** sung in English and rather laid-back (RCA 60176 or 68363), **Rossi,** enthusiastic but raw (Vanguard 8207), **Macal,** emphasizing the sadness of the score at the expense of the brutality (Koss 1016) but with an excellent alto (Janis Taylor), and **Previn,** slow but well recorded (Telarc 80143).

Järvi couples *Nevsky* with *Scythian Suite,* doing both in his colorful, straightforward fashion, also with a fine alto in Linda Finnie (Chandos 8584). Two recordings are coupled with Shostakovich symphonies, **Mata** with the oddly contrasting 9 in a particularly well-recorded performance (Dorian 90169), **Rodzinski** in particularly bad sound with a cut 10; avoid it (Stradivari 10035). **Temirkanov** conducting William Brohn's reconstruction of the original film score is interesting; it shows what Prokofiev did to turn it into the cantata version we know (RCA 61926). The trouble is, once you've heard it, you probably won't want to hear it again, since it's mostly bleeding chunks from the cantata without connecting material. The film itself has been released with this performance replacing the music on the soundtrack (RCA 62705).

Two recordings combine *Nevsky* with *Ivan the Terrible,* the other Eisenstein-Prokofiev collaboration. This was never completed (a third film was planned but never made), leaving the story in the middle, but a version with extensive dramatic narration was put together by **Abram Stasevich** after the composer's death. This was recorded by him (NA) and by **Muti** in a fine, atmospheric performance coupled with an impressively grand *Nevsky* and Rachmaninoff's "The Bells," all without texts (EMI 73353, 2CD).

The narration bothered some people and was omitted by **Järvi** in a rich soundscape (Chandos 8977) and by **Slatkin** in a sonic triumph over a less-than-impressive hall (Vox 5021, 2CD). Slatkin is very conscious of the Russian sound in these works and reproduces it with much success, also in *Nevsky* and *Kije* (performed with songs as in the film), but Vox neglects to supply texts for any of this. **Gergiev** gives an exciting reading from Rotterdam without narration (Philips 456645). And if you're interested in the original context, Image 4577 and 78 give you the two parts of Eisenstein's film in VHS or DVD formats. I understand that the DVD looks better, but the subtitles are harder to read.

The other choral works currently available are all patriotic. *Cantata for the 20th Anniversary of the October Revolution* was once available on LP in a **Kondrashin** performance, somewhat cut for political reasons. **Järvi** does it complete, with Rozhdestvensky reading the offending text (Chandos 9095). It's a rather wild piece in either version, which is probably why it wasn't popular with Stalin. After he made his preferences known, Prokofiev wrote *Zdravitsa*, a short birthday ode in as innocuous a style as he could manage (IMP 6600122). **Derek Gleeson** will do for this, since he includes Tchaikovsky's student setting of the *Ode to Joy* and the original *Romeo and Juliet Overture*, before Balakirev talked him into including a tune for Friar Lawrence. *On Guard for Peace* was the result of more brainwashing by Stalin. There have been more enthusiastic performances of both this and its discmate, Shostakovich's *Song of the Forests,* in the past—**Rozhdestvensky** did the Prokofiev works, Mravinsky the Shostakovich—but **Temirkanov**'s is the only one at present (RCA 68877).

An early choral work, *The White Swan,* a short work on a Balmont text, is included in **Rozhdestvensky**'s disc (BBC Radio Classics 9146), unfortunately without text. *Seven, They Are Seven,* a wildly modernistic setting of an ancient Chaldean text, was once recorded by **Rozhdestvensky** and is now languishing in the Melodiya files.

OPERAS

Opera was an early Prokofiev enthusiasm; one of his first compositions was *The Giant,* with music and libretto by the then nine-year-old composer. *Maddelena,* a one-act romantic melodrama, was completed in piano score by 1911, but the orchestration was never finished. Two recordings were made, but neither has survived. Mezhdurodnaya Kniga 417056 (NA) used no less than three sopranos to cover Prokofiev's difficult vocal line for the heroine (who is, indeed, schizophrenic). An interesting recording, if you can find it.

The Gambler. Prokofiev's next opera, this was based on Dostoevsky's semiautobiographical story. An expressively cogent dramatization, it suffers somewhat from its characters, who aren't really operatically colorful and therefore only occasionally evoked Prokofiev's lyrical gift. His setting follows them through their emotionally overwrought, unhappy world with enthusiasm, but there's little to inspire him to memorability, as the somewhat scrappy suite *Four Portraits and Denouement* shows, imaginative though it is. **Rozhdestvensky**'s LP set was excellent, but in terms of tight dramatic interpretation, smooth sound, and realistic sound spacing, **Gergiev** is an improvement (Philips 454559, 2CD). It's about 11 minutes shorter with no cuts evident and with a more readable translation in the libretto, though it's difficult to follow the Russian. The singers in both versions are highly competent without making a strong impression. *Four Portraits and Denouement* is only listed in a **Järvi** performance (Chandos 8803), though there was a fine recording by **Rozhdestvensky** in the not-so-distant past. Järvi's is a good reading, coupled with a suite from *Semyon Kotko,* rare and interesting fare.

Love for Three Oranges. This is such an imaginative and zany concept that it should never have been allowed to go out of print, but it has. A setting of a surrealistic play by Carlo Gozzi, it's a prime example of the Russian ensemble style of production, where everything depends on split-second timing and characterization. There was a fine Russian version

conducted by **Dzhemal Dalgat** (NA), and then there was a fine French one by **Nagano,** in neater, more spacious sound, with an equally effective cast (Virgin 91084, 2CD, NA). What will be next? Stay tuned!

The suite from the opera is hardly long enough to be a determining factor, but I should mention **Malko**'s disc containing it along with excellent readings of Symphonies 1 and 7 (Classics for Pleasure 4523). **Järvi**'s disc also contains suites from *Chout* and *Pas d'Acier* in lively performances (Chandos 8729).

The Flaming Angel. This was never performed in Prokofiev's lifetime and it's possible that it was never completed, since it leaves several questions unanswered in the plot. However, it's so full of effective scenes that companies stage it anyway. When it became clear that it wasn't going to make the boards, the composer took material from it to create his Symphony 3. The opera concerns a woman who sees visions of a fiery angel and resists the attempts of her would-be lover to distract her from her obsession, set in a medieval background including such oddly assorted figures as Faust, Mephistopheles, and the magician Agrippa. The opera reaches its climax at an exorcism in a nunnery.

The first recording was made soon after Prokofiev's death, in a French version conducted by **Charles Bruck** that's quite effective (NA). **Järvi** conducted it with a non-Russian cast singing in Russian in a colorful but not entirely convincing reading (DG 431669, 2CD, NA). Up to that point the opera had never been performed in Russia, but **Gergiev** took it on with the Kirov in 1990, and a live performance of that production was recorded, both on CD (Philips 446078, 2CD, NA) and as a video or two laser discs (070198). It has the disadvantages of pit acoustics and stage sounds, which may be why the CD disappeared, but the performance is the best yet, and the video may still be available. Those who saw the production when it came to the United States will remember it, particularly the evil little demons that represented Renata's delusions (or were they delusions?) and the amazing nude scene in the convent that ends the opera. Well, it's all there on the video. And the singing is amazing!

Semyon Kotko. Prokofiev's move to Moscow changed the character of his music markedly, and a public genre like opera more than most. *Semyon Kotko* was his first Soviet opera, a study of Russia in the middle of WWII. Though limited to more or less stock characters and situations, there's plenty of musical meat here. A complete recording was on Mezhdurodnaya Kniga LPs under **Zhukov,** but no one has seen fit to do it since, or to bring that excellent performance to CDs. An extensive suite was recorded by **Rolf Kleinert** on a Urania LP (NA), and **Järvi** has a much livelier version (Chandos 8803).

Betrothal in a Monastery. We may interpret Prokofiev's next opera as a way of avoiding political issues, but whatever his motive, this setting of a comedy by Sheridan is the most amusing opera he ever wrote, an elaborate, tender, caustic, and satirical piece that should always be with us. Unfortunately, its only really effective performance, from the point of view of characterization, is out of print. Chant du Monde 2781003 offered it with panache, with a Russian-Jewish fishmonger (Don Jerome) second to none and a solo clarinet that understood satire.

Neither of these important elements graces either of the presently available versions. **Gergiev** smooths the Russian character out of it and takes three discs for a 153-minute opera (Philips 462107, 3CD), while **Lazarev** solves the latter problem but provides even less humor than Gergiev and doesn't include a libretto (Melodiya 60318, 2CD). The orchestral suite is called *Summer Night* and, like the opera itself, isn't fortunate in its recordings. **Järvi** plays it in his usual all-purpose fashion

(Chandos 9096), while **Pletnev** is better (DG 445830, 2CD), but you have to buy his complete *Cinderella* (not, however, a fate worse than death).

War and Peace. Prokofiev's magnum opus, this is a worthy testament to his abilities and determination. It took a long time to write, and even when it was presumably finished, he added major new scenes and episodes, including a revision of the ending, replacing 18 pages in the piano score to incorporate Kutuzov's aria into the final choral peroration. This is his most Mussorgskian opera in the war scenes, his most Tchaikovskian in its individual characterizations. It rivals *Romeo and Juliet* for beautiful melodies and is a great work on stage.

There have been three serious attempts to record it. There was once a heavily cut version on three MGM LPs that I mention merely to dismiss it. Then came **Alexander Melik-Pashayev**'s stirring version from 1961, featuring Vishnevskaya as Natasha, Ivan Petrov as Ilya, Arkhipova as Helene, Alexej Krivtchenya as Kutuzov, and Alexander Vedernikov as Nikolai (BMG/Melodiya 29350, 3CD, NA). This gave us 186 minutes of the score and represents probably more of it than Prokofiev ever heard. At that time, it looked as if we would never hear an uncut version, but then **Rostropovich** defected to the United States and took up conducting, making a recording in France of the uncut opera (Erato 75480, 4CD, NA). His performance lasted 245 minutes and boasted outstanding recorded sound and a livelier performance than his usual. Vishnevskaya again sang Natasha, but not as well, nearly 30 years later. Ghiuselev did a memorable Kutuzov, and Gedda sang Anatole. The performance is enlivened with the sound effects beloved by Rostropovich—horses galore, cannon fire, and so on—and is, along with his Shostakovich *Lady Macbeth of Mtsensk,* his most valuable recording to date.

Then came **Gergiev** with not only a live performance (Philips 434097, 3CD) but a video as well (Philips 440070527). He takes 231 minutes, accounted for by faster tempos. The recording isn't bad, though congested in spots and not as well balanced or well played as Rostropovich. Nor is it better sung: Nicolai Okhotnikov as Kutuzov is the least assertive voice of the three. The great virtue of this production is the video: We see all of these people. Kutuzov becomes a character, not just a voice, and Gregoriam makes a real impression as Pierre. The stage could be more lifelike at times; the use of elevators for outdoor scenes recalls Radio City Music Hall rather than the steppes. But that's a minor quibble; the video is required watching, and the fast tempos don't hurt much. Ideally, we should have Rostropovich's CD and Gergiev's video. And the singers from Melik-Pashayev. Oh, well!

There is a suite from *War and Peace,* not by the composer, but arranged by Christopher Palmer, conducted by **Järvi** (Chandos 9096).

Story of a Real Man. Prokofiev's last opera, this was based on a Russian novel of a pilot shot down in WWII who was rehabilitated by the Soviets after losing both legs in the crash. The story is handled better than you might expect by the composer, who, you must remember, wrote all of his own librettos—and very well, too. There has been one decent recording of a 1960 Bolshoi production, well sung though rather heavily cut and rearranged, conducted by **Mark Ermler** on LP, that hasn't made it to CD. We could use a complete version of this score as the composer wrote it.

SONGS

Songs make up a small part of Prokofiev's output, but the few he wrote are choice. **Carole Farley** made two fine CDs, one with pianist Arkady Aronov (Chandos 8509, NA), the other with Roger Vignoles (ASV 669). There are no duplications, but the Chandos issue was short and had no

texts. The ASV disc includes the *Melodies* later transcribed for violin and *The Ugly Duckling,* better known as a work for soprano and orchestra though presently unavailable in that form. The Chandos needs reissue with additions and text. MOORE

Giacomo Puccini (1858–1924)

Puccini's name was not among the six carved into the proscenium arch above the old Metropolitan Opera stage—he was born too late for that—yet now we wonder how any opera company could survive without him. Often derided by critics and academics, he is beloved of audiences and performers; even an indifferently cast *Bohème* or *Tosca* is likely to sell out the house. His best operas have many studio and bootleg recordings, and they keep on coming.

Puccini's popularity and the technology of sound reproduction grew together in the 20th century. We can hear the voices of many of the artists who created their roles, and just as readily turn to modern performances in splendid stereo. Puccini enthusiasts should seek out some of the great old singers on CD reissues. Raisa and Fleta were the first Turandot and Calaf; Farrar the first Suor Angelica; de Luca the original Gianni Schicchi. Schipa was in the premiere cast of *La Rondine;* Caruso, Destinn, and Amato in the first *Fanciulla.* Toscanini led the first performance of *Butterfly,* with Storchio, Zenatello, and de Luca. Bori and Caruso sang the Metropolitan (though not the Italian) premiere of *Manon Lescaut;* and although we don't have documentation of the very earliest *Bohème* and *Tosca* singers, we have ample compensation.

The greatest singers of the century have championed Puccini. Indeed, a list of the century's most renowned Italian singers is also a list of the great Puccini interpreters. A good place to start exploring the past is a sampler entitled "The Century's Greatest Singers in Puccini" (♦Romophone 86001). Here are Gigli, Caruso, Pertile, Bori, and Muzio. They should inspire collectors to look further into the Romophone catalog and those of the other companies that specialize in historic recordings.

Modern singers have also done well by Puccini, and enjoyed the advantages of more accurate sound reproduction. The oldest recordings can't do justice to Puccini's lush orchestrations and high-flying soprano lines. Verdi was a resourceful and subtle orchestrator, but he also knew how to keep the orchestra out of the singers' way by writing noncompetitive accompaniments. Puccini, by contrast, tends to give his big tunes to everyone at once. He's especially unkind to sopranos. The whole orchestra bids "Addio" to Rodolfo, despairs with Manon Lescaut in Louisiana, and shares Butterfly's final words. It's thrilling to hear a soprano rise to the challenge and hold her own (a sympathetic conductor is absolutely essential), and if the listener isn't actually in the opera house, the achievement is best appreciated through good-sounding, modern recordings. The Puccini collector is urged to start with complete accounts that have stood the test of time, then to turn to some of the great old singers. There are also some interesting bootleg recordings, but I know of none that surpasses the best of the studio offerings—a claim diehard fans of various singers are free to dispute.

La Bohème. Just over a century old, *Bohème* has become probably the world's most popular and most performed opera. Most of the two dozen or so studio recordings are likable for one reason or another; it would take too much space to comment on each of them.

I have returned again and again to the spontaneity and Italianate flair of **Albanese** and Gigli (1938; EMI and Arkadia); the more intimate but no less authentic **Carteri** and Tagliavini (1952; Cetra); Albanese again with the fiery and authoritative **Toscanini** (1946; RCA); the perennially fresh Mimi of **Sayão** (1947; Sony); the vitality of **Callas** and di Stefano, with Moffo's classy Musetta (1956; EMI); the unaffected sincerity of **Moffo**'s own Mimi in 1961 (RCA); the full-throated vocal glamour of **Caballé** and Domingo, led by the energetic Solti (1973; RCA); the delicacy of **Ricciarelli** and the ardor of Carreras under the scrupulous Colin Davis (1979; Philips); the solid professionalism of **Scotto** and Kraus (1979; EMI); the candor and burnished smoothness of **Orgonasova** (Naxos); the bright-eyed charisma of **Gheorghiu** and Alagna, sweethearts on and off the stage (1998; Decca).

It would be difficult to forgo any of these, but there are three recordings that strike me as even more fundamental to a Puccini collection. Beecham in 1956 has the most polished pair of young lovers in **de los Angeles** and Björling, each in superb voice and utterly individual in manner (♦EMI 555236). They are, perhaps, just a little aloof at times (so is the conductor), but their singing is fresh, shapely, and disarmingly beautiful. **Tebaldi** brought a plusher timbre and more innate warmth to Mimi than de los Angeles. She recorded the opera twice, the first time under Erede in 1951 (London), more insightfully (if less vocally pristine) under Serafin in 1959 (♦London 488725). In 1951 she was teamed with the sensitive Rodolfo of Giacinto Prandelli and the flamboyant Musetta of Gueden. In 1959 she was part of an ensemble of great Italians (Bergonzi, Bastianini, Siepi, Corena) gloriously performing *Bohème* as a singers' opera. (The American soprano Gianna D'Angelo is, oddly, the most restrained member of the cast.) Yes, these poor creatures struggle and love and die, but they're Italian, so they express themselves in generous outpourings of melody. It's not entirely unsubtle — Bergonzi is the most poetic of Rodolfos, Bastianini the staunchest Marcello, and Siepi the most warmhearted Colline — but this is *Bohème* as grand opera, theatrically thrilling because of the prodigious vocal largesse. The human drama takes second place to musical grandeur.

Karajan's 1972 recording is also conceived on a fairly grand scale, but he's able to bring some intimacy to the story (♦London 421049). **Freni** and Pavarotti are an ideal Mimi-Rodolfo pair, more comfortable on top than Tebaldi and Bergonzi and more adept at bringing a realistic, human dimension to their characters. The tenor is at his youthful best; the soprano, with her combination of emotional vulnerability and vocal strength, shows why she owned the role of Mimi for a good quarter-century. She was just as lovable in her first recording, led by Schippers, but Gedda's clean-lined, ringing Rodolfo needed more pasta in the voice (EMI, 1963). The genteel Elizabeth Harwood was a strange choice for Musetta, but she was one of those imprudent singers who fluttered like a moth toward Karajan's flame. Panerai's crisp Marcello and Ghiaurov's sonorous Colline are additional assets.

La Fanciulla del West. This has always been the connoisseur's favorite Puccini opera, a departure from the blatant emotionality of its three predecessors. It has never endeared itself with the operatic public. The orchestration and musical style have grown more complex; gone are the sure-fire, easily approachable (and readily excerpted) arias and duets. The vocal writing is fairly heavy and demanding, requiring a soprano, tenor, and baritone of at least (and ideally more than) *Tosca* caliber. Performances are often cut.

The first recording wasn't made until 1950; it came from the dutiful Cetra company and no longer serves a purpose. The first stereo recordings both date from 1958. Von Matačič has **Nilsson** as Minnie, a startling choice but a delightful one, both powerful and cunning (EMI). More idiomatic is Capuana's cast, with **Tebaldi,** del Monaco, and the robust MacNeil (♦London 421595). Minnie's straightforwardness suits

Tebaldi, and she sings with her customary feeling for Puccini's music. Del Monaco is an impressive, dour hero.

Capuana's recording remains the best, but Mehta's 1977 account was the first to offer the opera complete (♦DG 419640). **Carol Neblett** is a game, mettlesome Minnie, an exciting but far from impeccable vocalist. Domingo and Milnes are their usual vigorous selves as the outlaw and the sheriff. Domingo would repeat his role in 1991 under Maazel, with the peculiar Minnie of **Mara Zampieri** (Sony). A slightly earlier recording led by Slatkin, with **Marton** and O'Neill, need not detain us (RCA).

Madama Butterfly. The premieres of *Manon Lescaut, Bohème,* and *Tosca* were greeted with acclaim, but *Butterfly* was a fiasco, its second La Scala performance immediately canceled and replaced with, of all things, *Faust.* Puccini rethought the opera, and the revision was a triumph, but anyone curious about the original version can hear it on a 1995 recording led by Rosekrans, with the conscientious **Maria Spacagna** in the title role (Vox). It will never displace the standard *Butterfly,* which has been recorded about as many times as *Bohème.*

The effectiveness of a *Butterfly* performance depends almost entirely on the heroine. The baritone has little to do, and the tenor doesn't even appear in Act 2. Casting Cio-Cio-San is almost as difficult as casting Strauss's Salome, who also needs a young voice big enough to cut through the heavy orchestration. The delicate approach sometimes works on records, where the studio engineers can contrive a just balance, and there are touching passages in the 1958 Leinsdorf recording, where both **Moffo** and Valletti sound young and innocent (RCA). They don't really fool you at the big moments, which patently demand larger voices. The conductor found them for his 1962 account with **Price** and Tucker (♦RCA 6160). Price's Butterfly is a great piece of singing, though not characterization. She's a dutiful actress, but no other soprano soars so healthily and radiantly through the high-lying effusions. Tucker is a brash and blubbery Pinkerton, but the quality of his voice discourages excessive criticism. This is the performance I turn to when I want opulent vocalism rather than dramatic verisimilitude.

Callas, by contrast, offers a meticulously detailed portrayal, Karajan conducting, yet somehow manages to conceal the care and cerebration that must have gone into it. She's always absorbing, sometimes revelatory, but seldom luscious enough in tone (♦EMI 556298). Her charming, lightweight Pinkerton is the young Gedda.

De los Angeles isn't entirely luscious either, and her lovely, distinctive voice is more womanly than girlish, but she brings an appealing open-heartedness to both her recordings. The first, led by Gavazzeni in 1954, is the more desirable (♦Testament 2168). Di Stefano is a callous, dashing Pinkerton, a role that might have been tailor-made for him, and Gobbi is just about the only Sharpless on disc you really take notice of. The 1959 stereo remake conducted by Santini has a stunningly vocalized Pinkerton in Björling, though his seriousness and innate dignity weigh against him (EMI).

The Cio-Cio-Sans of **Caballé** (EMI) and **Ying Huang** (Sony) deserve a brief appreciative nod, though Caballé's silken suavity is tepid, and the often affecting Huang isn't quite sizable enough. Butterfly was **Albanese**'s signature role, so it's a pity she never recorded it, but a 1946 Met broadcast has been preserved (and vended for an extravagant sum); admirers of the soprano might want to investigate it, or look for it on a European label that disregards American copyrights.

The 1939 Butterfly of **Toti dal Monte** has attained a legendary status in some circles (EMI). Her conductor is Fabritiis; her Pinkerton, the irresistible Gigli. Dal Monte genuinely tries to sound like a young girl, but she also utters every word with point and clarity. There's a world of nuance in her portrayal, but the voice itself, very much on the thin, shrill side, must be tagged as an acquired taste.

That leaves us with three more Italians, each of whom recorded Cio-Cio-San twice: Tebaldi, Scotto, and Freni. In both her recordings, **Tebaldi** sounds unsuitably mature, but there's no denying her emotional honesty or sympathy with the role (1951 and 1958; London). Her voice, with its solid chest register, fills out her phrases generously. The second recording, conducted by Serafin, is the more estimable of the two (♦London 452594). With Bergonzi as a gentlemanly Pinkerton, it shares the virtues of the 1959 *Bohème*: a traversal solidly grounded in an Italian performer-oriented tradition, where musical considerations take precedence over dramatic niceties.

Scotto, known affectionately to her fans as "Little Renata," doesn't have Tebaldi's vocal endowment, but she has a knack for weighting and accenting each word exactly the right way. Her voice, despite some rough patches, is particularly full and steady in her first recording, with Barbirolli in 1966 (♦EMI 63411). The conductor's deliberate approach suits her perfectly, allowing her to sculpt her phrases with care and commitment, mesmerizingly attentive to every nuance. Her fine Pinkerton is Bergonzi; her Sharpless Panerai, as vocally alert as Gobbi. The second recording, made 10 years later with Maazel, is just as painstaking, but her voice is in poorer condition, the supporting cast less appealing (Sony).

Freni strikes a balance somewhere between the two Renatas: more vocally pliant than Tebaldi, lovelier of timbre than Scotto, stronger and more luminous on top than either. She doesn't have Tebaldi's plentitude or Scotto's dramatic flair, but she's poignant and believable, without sacrificing anything in vocal glamour, and she has an inwardness of her own. The 1974 recording with Karajan would probably be my desert-island choice; it's that beautiful and touching (♦London 417577). Pavarotti is the breezy Pinkerton, Ludwig a surprisingly effective Suzuki. Freni's second *Butterfly* still has some of the magic, but conductor Sinopoli turns it into the slowest on record, an unbearable exhibition of conductorial self-glorification (DG).

Manon Lescaut. Puccini's first success, *Manon* has some dull stretches and has never been as popular as the three operas that followed it, but the world's opera houses don't ignore it, and it enters the repertory with gratifying frequency. Perhaps the best recording remains one of the earliest: Perlea in 1954, with **Albanese** and Björling (♦RCA 60573). No one has surpassed Björling's Des Grieux, sung so beautifully that you don't just wait for the most familiar moments but hang on his every word. Albanese's shining top register is her greatest strength, but she's also an engaging and committed actress, fully immersed in the drama. Her voice can be shallow and fluttery, and she sometimes sounds a little too old for the naive (if not downright nitwitted) heroine, but she's as admirable as her recorded rivals from the '50s.

Tebaldi in 1953, on a recording led by Molinari-Pradelli, is matchlessly sumptuous in the middle range, but her top notes aren't always accurately tuned (London). Her Des Grieux is the blaring Del Monaco. **Callas** in 1957, Serafin conducting, has a better tenor partner in di Stefano (even though he too pushes his voice too hard), and their exchanges are urgent, personal, and believable (EMI). Di Stefano, as always, sounds natural and unaffected; Callas is thoughtful and probing, too cerebral a heroine in the final analysis but always interesting.

The first stereo recording was Bartoletti's in 1971 (London). **Caballé** and Domingo sing handsomely as the doomed lovers, though they're less endearing than Albanese and Björling. The performance struck me as rather bland when it was first issued, but I've become increasingly grateful for the beauty of the singing. **Te Kanawa**'s Manon is also beautiful, with Chailly conducting, but she's no more persuasive an actress than Caballé, and her enthusiastic tenor, Carreras, is in poor shape (London; 1987).

Freni came to the role of Manon late in her career and recorded it twice. The first is spoiled slightly by the perverse Sinopoli, who self-indulgently favors expansive tempos and huge orchestral eruptions; it is impressively recorded (DG; 1983). Domingo's Des Grieux is slightly more assured and animated than it was 12 years earlier, but he's still on the prosaic side and sounds rather too straitlaced. Freni utters the words with the sort of idiomatic flavor only an Italian commands; her identification with the character is deep and palpable. When she recorded the role again in 1992, she had a more sympathetic conductor in Levine, and her tone was still full and lovely, even if some of the bloom was gone (♦London 440200). The top remains secure and steady, the chest register is better attached to the rest of the voice, and her words are no less deeply felt. Pavarotti is a gleaming, incisive Des Grieux. Freni and Pavarotti together match some of the Albanese-Björling or Callas–Di Stefano chemistry. This is the stereo recording of choice.

La Rondine. This was yet another departure for Puccini, a curious mixture of *Bohème* and *Traviata* without the tragedy, leavened by some Viennese froth. Two pairs of young lovers play out their romances in the salons of Paris and the Côte d'Azur. Lisette and Prunier, the Musetta-Marcello counterparts, bicker and fuss and apparently live happily ever after. The worldly Magda (the restless "sparrow" of the title) falls in love with a rustic lad, but because she's a Woman with a Past, she deems herself unworthy of him and sends him away; for all her aristocratic dignity, she turns out to be an even sillier heroine than Manon Lescaut.

Much of the music is conversational, though Magda has two well-known arias and the Act 2 ensemble "Bevo al tuo fresco sorriso" is a rapturous showstopper. It's important that the singers be comfortable with the language, and that's one of the reasons the 1966 Molinari-Pradelli recording remains a top choice (♦RCA 60459). Tenor Danielle Barioni is just a little more uncultivated than the character need be, but Sciutti and Antonio de Palma are winning and verbally adept as the secondary pair of lovers, and **Moffo** sings with warm, pretty tone and an eloquent dreaminess. Like Strauss's Marschallin, she resigns herself to her fate with high-minded composure.

Te Kanawa and Domingo, with Maazel in 1982, have bigger voices than Moffo and Barioni but smaller hearts; their singing is beautiful but dull (Sony). **Cecilia Gasdia** and Alberto Cupido, with Gelmetti in 1993, have the opposite problem: They act persuasively but don't sing beautifully enough (Italia).

The 1996 *Rondine* led by Pappano is the best alternative to the old RCA (♦EMI 556338). **Gheorghiu** and Alagna are naturals for their roles: she, glamorous and sophisticated, with a creamy voice that revels in the vaulting melodies; he, unpolished and provincial, only intermittently pleasant in timbre but always passionate. The second pair of lovers is in good hands; the sound is splendid, and excerpts from *Le Villi* make an enticing bonus.

Tosca. Serafin's 1953 *Tosca* has been extolled for more than four decades as one of the greatest opera recordings ever, and I won't put forward any heretical dissent (♦EMI 556304). Tosca, both prima donna and passionate lover, was a perfect role for **Callas;** no one has embodied the character so fully. Gobbi, though somewhat dry of voice, is her match as an actor, and the young di Stefano is an ardent romantic hero. As a totality, no other recording approaches this one, which remains essential to any operatic collection.

What's missing, perhaps, aside from good stereo sound, is some of the sensuous beauty so much a part of Puccini's music, but it's easy to find a corrective. Karajan's 1962 recording has demonstration-quality sound and the ravishingly sung Tosca of **Price** (◆Decca 466384). She can't begin to match Callas detail for detail, but her manner is persuasively hot-blooded, her voice irresistible. Taddei's Scarpia is as vivid as Gobbi's and better sung, in plumper, rounder tones. Di Stefano is again Cavaradossi, but his top notes, while strong, are now hard and unpleasant, though his fervor is undimmed. Price recorded the title role again in 1972, with Domingo and Milnes, Mehta conducting (RCA). The exterior is vocally resplendent but skin-deep.

More interesting is Colin Davis's 1976 account, where **Caballé** offers the most gorgeously vocalized Tosca of all, a miracle of shapely, long-breathed phrasing (◆Philips 412885 or 438359). Wixell is an intelligent but gravelly Scarpia; Carreras, a zealous, golden-tongued Cavaradossi.

Many other recordings, while unsatisfactory in their entirety, have tempting assets. **Gigli**, with the tempestuous but coarse Maria Caniglia in 1938, is a fluent, honeyed, and effusive Cavaradossi (EMI). **Björling** in 1957 is more dignified and pensive, though no less vocally thrilling (RCA). These are two of the greatest Cavaradossis on records, and it's a shame their Toscas are not quite on their level. Milanov with Björling (Leinsdorf conducting) at least has a good measure of prima-donna hauteur, and at her best she's quite grand, but she's too often out of control. Warren's Scarpia is imposing in a melodramatic way, and his plangent voice pours out unstintingly. Midpriced, it's worth acquiring.

So is Maazel's 1966 recording for the sake of **Corelli**'s formidable Cavaradossi, liquid and ringing, every inch the hero (London). Nilsson is a Tosca who can coolly match his volume. Her natural imperiousness is entirely apt here, and she sings with more variety and involvement than she's often given credit for. Scarpia is the rather too-calculating Fischer-Dieskau, thin of tone and ravenously devouring the scenery; Maazel is a jumpy, finicky conductor. The thrills are genuine nonetheless, even if the stars appear to be singing to an imaginary audience rather than each other.

Yet one more fine Cavaradossi comes from **Bergonzi,** though in the rather sad context of the second Callas-Gobbi Tosca, led by Prêtre in 1964 (EMI). Their contributions are best passed over in silence, along with **Carreras**'s labored second Mario in 1979, with an older and fussier Karajan (DG). Ricciarelli is his fragile Tosca.

Tebaldi and Freni each made two recordings of the opera; **Scotto,** one. These Italian sopranos address the title role with an authority born of immersion in a well-established tradition; it's a pleasure just to hear them mold the words. Freni and Scotto are really a size too small, though **Freni** at least conveyed the illusion of grandeur the second time around, with Sinopoli in 1990 (DG). Her Cavaradossi is the doughty Domingo (who is also Scotto's), her Scarpia the miscast Ramey. She had somewhat more interesting colleagues for the first recording, led by Rescigno in 1978 (London): Milnes a Scarpia in the Warren (rather than Gobbi) mold, now a bit short on top; Pavarotti a valiant Cavaradossi, the distinctive ping of his voice lending boldness and resolve to his portrayal. **Scotto** sings less beautifully than Freni but does more with the text. Her 1980 recording, conducted by Levine, found her in squally voice, and her Scarpia is the lackluster Bruson. Domingo's Cavaradossi is a redeeming feature, but not one unique to this performance (EMI).

Tosca was the role **Tebaldi** sang most often at the Met. She was no firebrand, but she seemed to identify with the character completely, even if the impression she gave was more of a great Italian soprano impersonating Tosca than of Tosca herself. It's profoundly satisfying to hear this huge, seamless voice fill out the musical lines, despite the strain at the top. She was fresher for her first recording in 1952 (London, Erede conducting), more assured and resourceful on the second, led by Molinari-Pradelli in 1959 (◆London 411871). Her tenor on the second occasion is del Monaco, unvaryingly loud and powerful; her Scarpia, the unidiomatic but compelling London.

Il Trittico. The three one-act operas that comprise *Il Trittico* seem unrelated to each other, but their librettos at least suggest the composer's original intention to score an episode from each of the three parts of Dante's *Divina Commedia.* Puccini wanted the triptych performed as a whole, even though each opera stands well on its own and calls for specific types of performers. *Il Tabarro* needs a *Tosca* trio; *Suor Angelica,* with its all-female cast, requires a lyric soprano and dramatic mezzo who are accomplished singing actors; *Gianni Schicchi,* the only story actually derived from Dante, is the composer's sole comic opera and requires a wily buffo baritone. A versatile soprano could find a starring role in each opera, but she'd have to change her partners.

Those who want *Il Trittico* in a single package have five good sets to choose from, and there's even a sixth for those on a shoestring budget in the recordings conducted by Rahbari, not top class but more than adequate (Discover). **Tebaldi,** who could switch comfortably from lyric to spinto roles, sang the three heroines under Gardelli in 1961 (◆London 411665). She's a powerful, sympathetic Giorgetta in *Il Tabarro,* abetted by the muscular Luigi of del Monaco and Merrill's faceless but handsomely sung Michele. Her Lauretta is more adult than ingenue, but she fleshes out the lines of "O mio babbino caro" magnificently. Corena is a seasoned and funny Schicchi, delivering every word with point and flavor. In *Suor Angelica,* Tebaldi and Simionato confront each other like the two old pros they are, and in the scenes that follow, the soprano is at her most overtly emotional.

Freni also recorded the three soprano roles with Bartoletti in 1993 (London). She too is at her best in *Suor Angelica,* a role she declined to sing on stage because it was too emotionally draining. On records, she's deeply affecting, and she holds her own against the frightening (and vocally disheveled) Souliotis, a real gorgon of a Principessa. Freni would have been an ideal Lauretta 20 or so years earlier, but her voice still glows. The problem with *Schicchi* is the feeble Nucci in the title role. Pons, if anything, sounds even feebler as Michele and ruins the *Tabarro* performance; it's impossible to believe he could kill a man with his bare hands. Freni has much of the passion and spinto fullness Giorgetta demands, and she has a ringing and persuasively amorous Luigi in Giuseppe Giacomini.

The other complete *Trittico*s divide the soprano roles between two or more performers. The EMI set has three different conductors: **Bellezza** for *Il Tabarro* in 1955, **Serafin** for the 1957 *Angelica,* and **Santini** for *Schicchi* a year later. The weakest of these performances is *Tabarro,* despite Gobbi's formidable Michele. The same baritone is an endearing Schicchi, and he has a radiant Lauretta in de los Angeles, who is also a heartrending Suor Angelica. Angelica's forbidding aunt is vividly impersonated by Barbieri.

Maazel conducted the three operas in a 1976 recording (◆Columbia 35912), and here again is Gobbi's Gianni Schicchi, older but no less mirthful or slick. Cotrubas is a pleasant Lauretta; Domingo a deluxe Rinuccio, the only first-class tenor to essay the part on records. He's also a potent Luigi in *Tabarro,* and his Giorgetta is the riveting Scotto, alive to every dramatic opportunity, vocally fluent and incisive. Wixell is also incisive, but his resourceful acting can't disguise the un-Italianate grittiness of his timbre. Scotto's Angelica is as pitiable as Tebaldi's or Freni's, though her voice is less attractive. Horne is a stalwart, capable Principessa, not overly imaginative.

Pappano's 1998 *Trittico* deploys the greatest variety of singers, always to sensible effect (EMI). For *Tabarro,* he has a feisty dramatic soprano in Maria Guleghina, a facile, impulsive Luigi in Neil Shicoff, and an unusually ruminative Michele in Paolo Guelfi. The Alagnas content themselves with a cameo appearance as the offstage lovers, but they take major roles in *Schicchi,* where Gheorghiu is an alluring Lauretta and her husband full of adolescent ardor as Rinuccio. He was also Freni's Rinuccio, but an uneven singer, then and now. Van Dam easily upstages both of them as a sometimes mellow, sometimes crusty Schicchi; there's plenty of plush left in the voice. The least famous singers are the principals in *Suor Angelica,* soprano Cristina Gallardo-Domas and mezzo Bernadette Manca di Nissa, and yet this is the most winning component of Pappano's set.

Each of the *Trittico* operas has at least one good recording that isn't part of a package. **Leinsdorf**'s *Il Tabarro,* with Price, Domingo, and Milnes, is the most lavishly cast if not the most searingly dramatic (RCA). It's always a pleasure to listen to these voices, which make the opera readily approachable. Panerai, another stylish veteran baritone, takes the title role in *Gianni Schicchi* in a recording conducted by **Patanè** (Eurodisc). His voice, in 1988, shows signs of age, but his tongue is as nimble as ever. Donath and Peter Seiffert make an ardent pair of lovers, and their voices, if not quite of Puccinian quality, are fresh and appealing.

One of the best recordings of *Suor Angelica* is the 1972 account led by **Bartoletti** (♦RCA, NA). Ricciarelli, with her pretty tone, slightly diffident manner, and telling diction, is an exemplary Angelica, and she interacts vividly with the articulate and imposing Principessa of Cossotto. With **Bonynge,** Sutherland would seem less of a natural Angelica than Ricciarelli, and so she is, but her huge, bright voice easily stands out in the crowd, and the fey ecstasy she brings to the final scene is transfixing. She has a sturdy, humane adversary in the dignified Ludwig, who also justifies what might seem an equally odd piece of casting (London).

Turandot. For his last opera, Puccini returned partly to the sort of blockbuster set pieces that would guarantee success. If his spectacular gestures seem too obvious at times, they're no less irresistible. There's plenty of subtle invention in *Turandot* as well, and genuine art behind the flashy orchestrations. The opera needs not only sensational sound (as anyone who's attended a performance in the opera house can attest), but also a tireless soprano with a big, carrying voice and a tenor hefty enough to stand up to her.

Callas, as always, is infinitely engrossing, but she wisely took the role of Turandot out of her stage repertory as early as 1949. She returned to it in the recording studio in 1957, Serafin conducting, and though she's taxed by it, her dramatic acumen is undiminished (EMI). Her Calaf is less suited to his part, and Schwarzkopf's Liù, while exquisitely vocalized, founders in its own artifice—she sounds as out of place as Weber's Agathe would be in the same context. The 1955 Erede recording has **Borkh,** a renowned Salome and Elektra, in the title role, more comfortable on top than Callas but less disciplined and expressive (London). Del Monaco is a relentlessly loud Calaf, Tebaldi a ravishing Liù.

Nilsson was the most commanding Turandot of her time, and she recorded the role twice, first in 1959 with Leinsdorf (RCA), again in 1965

with Molinari-Pradelli (♦EMI 5932). The earlier performance is still fairly rousing, but the primitive stereophonic sound is exaggeratedly wide and has very little depth. Less noticeable, perhaps, is the close miking of Björling to pump him up to Nilssonian size, though the unique gleam and focus of his voice aren't falsified in any way. Tebaldi, again, is a beguiling Liù, her pianissimos beautifully floated. RCA's Ping-Pang-Pong trio remains unbeaten.

There's little difference between the 1959 and 1965 Nilsson, but since the second recording is superior overall, let's turn quickly to it. The sound, while not up to the best that EMI could produce at the time, is an improvement over RCA's. Calaf was probably Corelli's finest role. The character's ardor and single-minded determination didn't stretch him dramatically, and he could pour out floods of ringing, virile, viscerally thrilling tone. Nilsson's innate frostiness is apt for the aria and Riddle Scene, but she thaws gratifyingly in the last act. Her vocal stamina and control are awesome. She tosses off "In questa reggia" without breaking a sweat; her high Cs at the end of Act 2 are sensational, and she can still surprise us by sweetly floating her final words (for which we owe thanks to Alfano's completion of Puccini's unfinished score). Scotto brings such complete conviction to Liù that you never question the character's motivation, and she sings with care and fervor. Molinari-Pradelli pretty much stays out of the way, which is fine—it's the singers' show.

Sutherland and Pavarotti, in the 1972 Mehta recording, offer a stimulating alternative: softer, more lyrical and down-to-earth (♦London 414274). Sutherland has ample vocal strength and thrust, and she takes pains to sharpen her diction and act with the voice. Pavarotti's natural eloquence and compact tone help him through a role that's really too heavy for him, and his exchanges with Sutherland have a personal involvement that eludes both Nilsson and Corelli. Caballé is a soft, exquisite Liù; Mehta revels in the score's symphonic richness, and the sound, though a bit manufactured, is stunning. Peter Pears makes a telling cameo appearance as the Emperor Altoum, Ghiaurov is the most striking of Timurs, and Krause is an excellent Ping.

None of the other recordings reach the level of Nilsson or Sutherland, and to consider them is merely to invite invective. **Marton** (Sony) and **Dimitrova** (Nuova Era) belt out Turandot's lines with sufficient volume but little vocal allure. **Caballé** (EMI) and **Ricciarelli** (DG) should have stopped at Liù, following the example of Tebaldi, who had more voice and more sense. **Mehta**'s second recording (RCA) preserves a performance—talk about authentic settings—in the Forbidden Palace of Beijing, but it's of only visual interest.

Le Villi and *Edgar.* Puccini's first two operas will never be standard repertory fare, but the curious listener may want to investigate them all the same. One soprano of stature, **Scotto,** has been ambitious enough to tackle both of them. Domingo and Gobbi partner her in *Le Villi;* Bergonzi is her *Edgar* tenor. Not even these performers suggest that the operas are neglected masterpieces, and it doesn't help (and really doesn't matter all that much) that Scotto herself is in tight, acidulous voice. *Edgar* has Puccini's first great soprano aria, "Addio, mio dolce amor," and it's worth knowing, but seek out **Price**'s performance in an RCA recital disc.

Puccini was an opera composer almost exclusively, but he left us a handful of songs, many of whose melodies will already be familiar to anyone who knows the operas. Domingo's recording is the only one you'll ever need (♦CBS 44981). Very little of the sacred music has been recorded. Conscientious British choristers offer the *Requiem, Salve Regina,* and *Vexilla Regis* (ASV). The more ambitious *Messa di Gloria* has a fine recording led by **Scimone,** with Carreras and Prey among the soloists (Erato), and another led by Inbal (Philips). *Crisantemi* (Chrysanthemums) for string quartet is nicely rendered by the **Alberni Quartet** (CRD) and the **Giovane Quartetto Italiano** (Claves); both recordings include Verdi's string quartet as well. LUCANO

Henry Purcell (1659–1695)

For many years Purcell was revered more for his reputation than from close familiarity with more than a handful of his works. In the last 30 years or so, that situation has changed dramatically, with a growth in Purcell scholarship as well as a veritable explosion of performances and recordings of his music in all genres, which has benefitted especially from developments in the use of period instruments and performance practices. While Bach and Handel can often survive the rather heavy-handed approach that was common in the 19th century and much of the 20th, I don't think Purcell can. His idiom really demands the lightness, transparency, and incisiveness best obtained by skillful playing on period instruments and the vocal techniques cultivated by early-music singers. Some readers may disagree, but in general I'm persuaded that the finest Purcell recordings have come from the late '70s onward.

Having said that, it's only fitting to pay tribute to the formidable artistry of **Alfred Deller,** who was one of the great trailblazers of the early music revival, especially in the works of Purcell. Many of his landmark recordings, particularly those made for Vanguard, are now available on CD. While in many respects they've been surpassed by the current generation of artists, it may justly be said that his example helped make their achievements possible. In his own right, Deller represents an important chapter in the history of Purcell performance and reception, and his recordings are still well worth hearing.

CHURCH MUSIC AND DEVOTIONAL SONGS

Like so many English musicians from the Middle Ages to the present day, Purcell began his career as a boy chorister, in his case as part of England's most prestigious foundation, the Chapel Royal of Charles II. Ironically, the high-water mark of Restoration church music came with the coronation of James II in 1685, but the new Roman Catholic king took little interest in his Anglican chapel, and things became even worse under the Calvinist William III. After the reign of Charles, Purcell's production of church music declined but did not cease altogether. Among his last contributions were an orchestral *Te Deum* and *Jubilate* for the St. Cecilia's Day festivities of 1694 and music for the funeral of Queen Mary in the following year.

The closest thing to a definitive recording of this repertory is the 11CD series of the complete anthems and service music by Robert King and the **King's Consort** (♦Hyperion, various numbers). The anthems fall into three main categories: full anthems (including the so-called "full-with-verse" anthems incorporating passages for solo voices in the context of works for full choir), verse anthems with organ (essentially continuo, with a theorbo included in many of these performances), and verse anthems with strings, the supreme showpieces of the Chapel Royal repertory. The performances can hardly be faulted technically. King clearly has a strong affinity for this music, and his readings have confident authority. The informative program notes explain many of the performance decisions, from the size of the instrumental ensemble to the high pitch (A = 466) used in the Chapel Royal.

As a bonus, King's series also contains Purcell's nonliturgical devotional songs for one to four voices with continuo. Apart from the Bible and Prayer Book, some of the finest poetry Purcell ever set to music is found in these pieces. Most are works of intense religious expression in the form of impassioned arioso. The soloists are outstanding, including several very accomplished boy trebles. The series is a notable achievement that will not soon be surpassed.

The choice among other recordings of the sacred music depends as much on what pieces you are seeking as on considerations of performance quality. Some very fine collections seem to have dropped from the catalogs, for example, **Trinity College, Cambridge** (Conifer), and **Christ Church, Oxford** (Archiv)—both worth getting if you can find them. A good selection of anthems, plus the *Funeral Music for Queen Mary* and a Latin psalm, has been recorded by the **Winchester Cathedral Choir** (Argo 436833). This program includes the two most popular anthems with strings: "Rejoice in the Lord alway" and "My beloved spake." A fine performance of the 1694 St. Cecilia's Day *Te Deum and Jubilate in D* is found in a disc from the **Taverner Consort** (Virgin 45061). This disc also includes "My beloved spake," two Latin psalms, "Saul and the Witch of Endor," and a set of four pavans, all in stylish performances.

While **Leonhardt** is an early-music artist of the first magnitude, I find his Purcell performances unconvincing, as if the musical language were foreign to him. Nevertheless, he has produced a good selection of anthems with strings plus three devotional songs sung by van der Kamp (Sony 53981). A good cross section of the anthems plus *Funeral Music* and *St. Cecilia Te Deum* comes from **Herreweghe** (Harmonia Mundi 901462). A recording by Summerly and the **Oxford Camerata** is less impressive as a performance but notable for a good selection of the lesser-known full anthems (Naxos 553129).

Two discs present a good selection from the devotional songs. **Jill Feldman** includes 11 of them in a disc with organist Davitt Moroney that also contains all of Purcell's solo organ works (Arcana 10). It's confined to songs for one voice, but this restriction doesn't apply to the 12 devotional songs for varying combinations of voices recorded by **Paul McCreesh** and members of the Gabrieli Consort, also including *Funeral Sentences* (Archiv 445 829). My only complaint here is that the reverberation is almost overwhelming, far too much for such intimate music.

Before leaving the anthems, it's worth mentioning two discs that combine works of Purcell with those of his distinguished contemporaries. Darlington and **Christ Church Choir, Oxford,** have compiled a disc of "Chapel Royal Anthems" including six verse anthems (without strings) by Purcell and a selection of anthems by Blow, Locke, and Pelham Humfrey (Nimbus 5454). Finally, no admirer of Restoration church music will want to be without Preston and the **Westminster Abbey Choir** in the collected music for the coronation of James II (Archiv 419613). Purcell is represented by "My heart is inditing" and "I was glad," along with works by Blow, Henry Lawes, William Child, and William Turner. This one may be hard to find, but it's worth the effort.

ODES AND WELCOME SONGS

Purcell's court duties included writing odes for such occasions as the autumn return of the king and court from Windsor to Westminster (beginning in 1680) and from 1689 to 1694 for the birthday of Queen Mary. In addition, there were odes for the annual celebrations of St. Cecilia's Day (November 22), including his most ambitious and best-known ode, "Hail, bright Cecilia" (1692). There were also odes for miscellaneous occasions such as the Duke of Gloucester's birthday and the centenary of Trinity College, Dublin. Court poetry could be insufferable, but Purcell had the talent to set the most sycophantic drivel to music of exquisite distinction. Most of the odes are not at all well known, but they're well worth exploring.

The most notable recorded monument of this repertory is the series by the **King's Consort** of the 24 odes and welcome songs (♦Hyperion, various numbers, 8CD). Here, as in his series of the anthems and service music, King displays an uncommon affinity for this material. He persuades us that this is the way it should go; it all seems right, whether it be gracefully lilting, grandiose and triumphant, sweetly languishing, or lively and dance-like. Based on research in court documents, King has concluded that most of the odes were performed with minimal scoring—mostly one player or singer to a part—and he proves his point with performances that are thoroughly convincing. His soloists are a veritable who's who of English early-music singers. Like his other set, it's unlikely that this series will be superseded any time soon.

Among recordings of "Hail, bright Cecilia," **Parrott** makes a very strong showing in an extroverted reading that captures the work's sense of festivity (EMI 47490). I find the recorded sound a trifle over-bright, and the string tone tends to be astringent, especially when combined with oboes. Generally the pacing is good, though "Wondrous machine" sounds rushed. **King**'s performance in Vol. 2 of his series is, in contrast, gentler and more delicate, even in the opening symphony with trumpets. **McCreesh** gives another lively reading with some dazzling solo singing (Archiv), though more of the tempos sound rushed than Parrott's. The most annoying feature here is the sometimes jarring change of acoustical ambience from one track to another, and there are places where the continuo seems over-realized, with jangling harpsichord and strumming theorbo. **Herreweghe**'s performance is less extroverted but still crisp and neat, though another critic has found this reading somewhat calculated: "too much efficiency at the expense of spontaneity" (Harmonia Mundi).

Of the birthday odes for Queen Mary, "Come, ye sons of art" (1694), the last of the series, is the best known. **Gardiner** directs a spirited performance that has a great sense of occasion (Erato 96553). It's coupled with a less satisfactory performance of *Queen Mary's Funeral Music*—less satisfactory because he makes it sound more like music for the theater than for a real funeral. **Pinnock** combines "Come, ye sons of art" with "Welcome to all the pleasures," the earliest of Purcell's St. Cecilia odes (1683), and "Of old, when heroes thought it base" (1690), the Yorkshire feast ode, in a good sampler (Archiv 427663).

Among other recordings of "Welcome to all the pleasures," **Gardiner** gives a curiously subdued, almost elegiac reading that's nevertheless very elegant (Philips 432114, with *Dido and Aeneas*). **Robert Glenton** offers a respectable performance that's short of the first rank (Naxos 553444). This bargain disc is worth considering, however, because it contains the first recording of "The noise of foreign wars," the unfinished 1688 welcome song for James II, left incomplete when the troubled political situation forced a cancellation of that year's festivities.

Two discs that deserve favorable mention are "Songs of Welcome and Farewell," performed by **Tragicomedia** (Teldec 95068), and a program by the **Ensemble William Byrd** that opens with the first of Purcell's welcome songs (1680), "Welcome, vicegerent of the mighty king" (Adda 581242). The Tragicomedia disc also opens with this work, concludes with the 1685 welcome song for James II, "Why, why are all the muses mute?" and in between gives two Latin elegies for Queen Mary. The Ensemble William Byrd combines the 1680 welcome song with a varied assortment of sacred and secular vocal pieces performed one-on-a-part with great energy and richness of tone.

As a pendant to the recordings of Purcell's odes, it's only fitting to mention a collection of "Odes on the Death of Henry Purcell," beautifully performed by a distinguished ensemble of vocal soloists with the **Parley**

of Instruments (Hyperion 66578). It contains works by Jeremiah Clarke, Godfrey Finger, Henry Hall, Thomas Morgan, and John Blow.

SECULAR SONGS

Of Purcell's secular songs, some 150 were written for the stage, and these are included in the **Hogwood** set of theater music discussed below. As for the rest, it should come as no surprise to those who have read this far that **King** has produced a comprehensive series of recordings (Hyperion 66710, 66720, 66730). After eliminating the theater and devotional songs and those misattributed to Purcell, there remain some 88 songs. These King recorded with a distinguished roster of soloists — Bonney, Susan Gritton, Bowman, Covey-Crump, Charles Daniels, and George — plus instrumentalists from his King's Consort. As with his other Purcell recordings, he and his colleagues bring to this project a keen affinity for the repertory, producing a reference-quality series of performances that won't soon be superseded. It's worth noting that the best-known Purcell songs come from his theater works and odes, not included in this series. Consequently, most of the songs here will be relatively unfamiliar except to Purcell specialists, but that shouldn't deter the general listener.

Even so, it's more likely that those who wish to make a first acquaintance with Purcell's songs will opt for one or more of the many fine single-disc collections. In many instances the secular songs, both theatrical and nontheatrical, are freely combined with devotional songs and works in other genres such as anthems, complete odes, and instrumental pieces. The choice among them will depend on the composition of the programs and your predilections for specific artists.

Among the programs that include the more familiar songs, a strong entry is by soprano **McNair** (Philips 446081). One reviewer described her program as "Purcell's Greatest Hits," though he had minor reservations about her unvaried tone. The program is punctuated with some instrumental pieces. Countertenor **Chance** is an outstanding Purcell exponent, and his disc consists of selections mainly from theater pieces and odes (Columns 555008, including a video CD). In an earlier release, Chance combined with countertenor **Bowman** for a disc of duets and solos including the Latin elegies for Queen Mary and Blow's "Ode on the Death of Purcell" (Hyperion 66253). Another disc of better-known songs is by countertenor **Daniel Taylor** (ATMA), whose performances are estimable but, as one critic put it, "do not efface memories of Alfred Deller."

A reissue of a late-'70s recording by countertenor **Jeffrey Dooley** and tenor Howard Crook consists mostly of airs and duets from odes and theater pieces plus some devotional songs (Lyrichord). They seem to be trying for an intimate effect, but I found the harpsichord accompaniment too busy and obtrusive. Much the same can be said for another late-'70s reissue of 18 Purcell solo songs (secular and devotional) by tenor **Partridge** with harpsichordist George Malcolm, who anachronistically colors his performance by manipulating the toe stops of his modern instrument (ASV, with Britten's song cycle *Winter Words*). Soprano **Christine Brandes** devotes most of her program to longer dramatic material, including devotional songs, rather than shorter and more popular items (Harmonia Mundi 907167). Soprano **Kirkby** and bass David Thomas present an exquisitely intimate performance of lesser-known songs and dialogues accompanied on the lute by Rooley (Hyperion 66056).

Space doesn't permit discussion of every available recording, but I should mention discs by such distinguished artists as **Argenta** (Virgin 59324), **Bott** (Chandos 0571), **Jill Feldman** (Arcana 002), **Agnes Mellon** (Astrée 8757), and **Susan Rode Morris** (Donsuemor 20601). Also worthy of note is a recording by members of the **New Chamber Opera Ensemble** of 24 songs from the "Gresham Autograph," a manuscript collection in Purcell's own hand (ASV 194). Some of the songs are unique to that source.

MUSIC FOR THE THEATER

Between 1680 and his death in 1695, Purcell furnished music for some 50 theatrical productions, most dating from the last five or six years of his life. His opera *Dido and Aeneas* (1689) will be discussed separately. His other music for the theater ranges from suites and songs for spoken plays to the so-called semioperas. A framing suite consists of a "First and Second Musick" to alert the audience to the imminent beginning of the show, an overture to introduce the show itself, and "Act Tunes" played between the acts. There might be a few songs and dances performed within the play.

Four of Purcell's authenticated works—*Dioclesian* (1690), *King Arthur* (1691), *The Fairy Queen* (1692), and *The Indian Queen* (1695)—are designated semioperas, a term probably coined by Roger North in 1728 to describe the most ambitious theatrical genre of late 17th-century England. (There is a fifth semiopera, *The Tempest* [ca. 1695] that contains one authenticated song by Purcell, but the authorship of the rest of the music is disputed.) They are still spoken plays, but with elaborate musical embellishments and staging, including fully musical scenes depicting spectacles, ceremonies, the supernatural, and pastoral allegories. Scenes like these were the only ones regarded as suitable for such treatment, and a true semiopera would have at least one in most or all of its five acts. These scenes, which owe much to the courtly masque tradition, don't advance the drama and hardly ever involve the principal characters of the play. There are also works, like *Timon of Athens* (1694), that contain perhaps one fully musical scene (in this case a masque in Act 2), but not enough to qualify it as a semiopera.

Two of the strongest exponents of Purcell's theater music are Gardiner, with his Monteverdi Choir and English Baroque Soloists, and Christie, with Les Arts Florissants. Both deliver performances of animation, coherence, and technical polish, but they differ significantly in personality, and listeners will have to decide for themselves which is more congenial.

In his recordings of *The Fairy Queen* (Harmonia Mundi 901308/09, 2CD) and *King Arthur* (Erato 98535, 2CD), **Christie** stresses the essential theatricality of the works in performances with an international flavor. His recording of *King Arthur* was made in conjunction with a 1995 staged revival of the work, and he frankly declares in his notes that it's a document of a particular production, "not a neutral interpretation," and that he doesn't "set out to offer an objective reading." In both semioperas, he doesn't hesitate to touch up the instrumentation with alternations of strings and winds as well as the addition of percussion. I think he sinks to gimmickry with the introduction of a wind machine and choral sneezes in the dance from the famous Frost Scene (Act III) of *King Arthur,* though the war-whoop that precedes "Come if you dare" (Act I) doesn't seem out of place. Where Gardiner speaks with a decidedly English accent, Christie tends to stress the French influences in Purcell's music. Whether or not you prefer his approach, his performances are splendid, richly worthy of the critical accolades they have garnered.

Gardiner has probably recorded more of Purcell's theater music than anyone else: *Dioclesian* plus the masque from *Timon of Athens* (Erato 96556, 2CD), *King Arthur* (Erato 96552, 2CD), *The Fairy Queen* (Archiv 419221, 2CD), *The Indian Queen* (Erato 96551), and *The Tempest* (Erato 96555). In general, his performances are at a slightly lower voltage than

Christie's, but I find them more subtly nuanced, intimate, and more faithful to the score. Where Christie is apt to regard the score as a kind of sketch to be turned into a finished work according to the imagination of the musical director, Gardiner approaches it more as a finished work needing only to be interpreted. The result may be a more mainstream English reading, but it's by no means dull, mechanical, or insensitive. Christie's liberties of interpretation and scoring can be very effective, but Gardiner proves that the music doesn't need them. It seems to me inappropriate to declare either Christie or Gardiner superior in this repertory. Each is excellent in his own way. My own predilection is in favor of Gardiner, largely because I like his English flavor more than Christie's Franco-international style.

There are other recordings of the semioperas that deserve honorable mention. **Hickox** and Collegium Musicum 90 have recorded the masque from *Timon* and the Act V masque from *Dioclesian* in one disc and the rest of the *Dioclesian* music in another (Chandos). Many of the same singers heard on the Christie and Gardiner discs reappear on here—first-rank early-music singing in London is evidently a small world—and the instrumental playing is also excellent. While Hickox is never less than competent, his interpretations aren't always exciting. He makes even a bacchanalian masque sound rather like a sacred oratorio.

There have been several fine recordings of *The Fairy Queen,* including **Koopman** (Erato 98507, 2CD), **Norrington** (EMI 55234, 2CD), and **Christophers** (Collins 7013, 2CD). **Leonhardt** is less satisfactory (Teldec). This recording and a disc of Purcell anthems recorded around the same time convince me that Leonhardt simply doesn't understand the personality of this music (Sony). His *Fairy Queen* is harsh, aggressive, and rather grim—not exactly the right atmosphere for an enchanted sylvan comedy.

A significant recording of *The Indian Queen* is by **Hogwood** (Oiseau-Lyre 444339, NA). Purcell left this score unfinished at his death, and the final masque for Act V was composed by his brother Daniel. Hogwood was the first to record it. The God of Dreams in Act III was sung by a boy in the first production of 1695, and here is taken by Tommy Williams, a treble whose clear tone and vocal poise belie his years. Gardiner gives this number to tenor Martyn Hill, and he omits the Act V masque. The one shortcoming of Hogwood's recording is the sound quality: hard, thin, and at times unpleasantly shrill.

The fashion for doing baroque music with as few performers as possible has infected the semioperas of Purcell. The **Scholars Baroque Ensemble,** a group that performs without a conductor, has recorded both *The Fairy Queen* and *The Indian Queen,* including Daniel Purcell's masque (Naxos). Without a firm hand on the helm, the Scholars suffer from a certain slackness of ensemble, though one reviewer has admired the "relaxed, good-natured quality" of their readings. Another minimalist recording of *The Indian Queen* is by **Catherine Mackintosh** (Linn). This chamber-music approach is simply wrong-headed for works that were intended to be dazzling spectacles, even allowing that the theaters in Restoration London were tiny by modern standards.

The most comprehensive recording of Purcell's theater music other than the semioperas and *Dido* is a set from **Hogwood** (Oiseau-Lyre 425893, 6CD). He's often a bit too aggressive and intense, calling forth a string tone so pointed as to be almost brash. It is, however, a recipe for vivid animation and the incisive delivery of the dance rhythms, and as one critic said, "it is the place to go for anyone seriously interested in this material."

Instrumental suites derived from the theater music have a long history, stretching back to Purcell's lifetime, and in 1697 there was the posthumous publication of 13 suites under the title *A Collection of Ayres, Compos'd for the Theatre, and on Other Occasions.* This was in the form of four string part books, but for modern performance it's a simple matter to expand the scoring to include the winds, timpani, and continuo ensemble of a typical Restoration theater orchestra.

There are several recordings of theater suites, and one of the most attractive is by **Lamon,** containing suites from *Dioclesian, King Arthur, The Fairy Queen,* and *The Indian Queen* (Sony 66169). Her performances are vivid and animated, but not as hard-driven as Hogwood's. Lamon shows great sensitivity to the character and flow of this music in performances of grace, warmth, and aplomb. In comparison, the very similar collection of suites (*The Fairy Queen, Dido and Aeneas, King Arthur,* and *Abdelazer*) from **Thomas Hengelbrock** seems rather cut and dried (Harmonia Mundi). There's great delicacy in some of the quieter and slower movements, but it all seems somewhat disengaged, with very little of Lamon's genial gracefulness. **Savall** has issued a critically acclaimed recording of suites from *The Fairy Queen* and *Dioclesian* (Fontalis 8583). As I recall, there were some very attractive modern-instrument recordings of the suites by **Leppard,** but they seem to have disappeared from the catalog. Look for reissues.

DIDO AND AENEAS

Purcell's best-known and most-recorded composition is also the only work in which we find him actually setting a drama to music from start to finish. There is no definitive score, and because of textual uncertainties as well as many open questions concerning performance practice, the available recordings differ considerably from one another as the various directors arrived at their own solutions. The catalog is filled with recordings by early-music specialists keen to stake their unique claim in a highly competitive territory. Some are more persuasive than others.

The recorded performance I find most satisfying overall is by **Lamon** (♦CBC 5147). It's the soundtrack for a film by the Mark Morris Dance Company, in which Dido and the Sorceress are sung by the same artist, as if they were two sides of the same person. I think that premise is a bit too Freudian for the 17th century, but the parallels between the two characters and their entourages can't have been accidental. Mezzo **Jennifer Lane** is thoroughly convincing in both. Her voice has the gravity needed for Dido, expressing a dignified, regal sadness, and as the Sorceress she uses a harder tone that evokes menace but not caricature. Baritone Russell Braun is a superb Aeneas, giving the role a strong and heroic reading while evoking tenderness where appropriate. Lamon demonstrates a keen sense of the dramatic pacing and flow of the work. The period strings are clear and crisp, yet warm and full.

Pinnock also gives a strong reading (Archiv 427624). **Von Otter** is a suitably grave Dido; her concluding "Lament" is superb. Varcoe's Aeneas may not be as macho as Braun's, but he brings a remarkable range of expressive nuance to the role, including sheer vocal power where needed. The part of the Sorceress is sung here by Nigel Rogers. In a later 18th-century source, this part is written in the bass clef; it was the custom in the Restoration theater for witches to be played by men. Rogers does well, singing the part without caricature, but I have yet to hear a really convincing male Sorceress. Pinnock shows a good sense of dramatic pacing, and his period strings have a somewhat silky sound that is effectively plaintive at the beginning of the overture.

Hogwood is more adventuresome but with mixed results (Oiseau-Lyre). In general, he seems to prefer a somewhat thin and astringent string tone in music of this period that I find less pleasant than many other period string ensembles. Bott is a grave Dido, but doesn't quite

evoke the regal sadness of Lane. Kirkby is a near-perfect Belinda, and Ainsley reads Aeneas more as a baritone lover than as a bass hero. Hogwood opts for a male Sorceress, but David Thomas makes the character sound like a pantomime wicked fairy—thanks to Roger Savage for that expression—in drag. Hogwood goes mad with sound effects in Act 2, opening the witches' scene with thunder and introducing it at every opportunity. The wind machine played through most of the false Mercury's message is just too much.

Gardiner gives a rather dark reading (Philips). There's a lot of reverberation, and the voices don't always sound forward and crisp enough. Carolyn Watkinson is a grave Dido, but with too much vibrato for my taste. Her "Lament" is heartbreaking, and here Gardiner demonstrates yet again that he knows exactly how Purcell's music is supposed to move. George Mosley as Aeneas and Teresa Shaw as the Sorceress are persuasive, though the two solo witches have vibratos too wide for the lines they have to sing.

Christie has recorded *Dido* twice, and, as in the semioperas, he favors a more French-influenced reading than most others. In his first recording, the principals are all convincing, though their diction is pretty bad in places, and Philippe Cantor is more pouty than heroic in Aeneas's grove scene soliloquy (Harmonia Mundi). As always, Christie takes very brisk tempos wherever possible, but they are sometimes at odds with his very deliberate pacing of the recitatives, so the abrupt jerking back and forth makes your head spin. The "Lament" is a complete bust: no heartbreak here, just ultra-slow and sluggish. For his second recording Christie reduced the strings to one to a part and retains the French flavor: brisk tempos, high energy levels, and technical polish (Erato).

Parrott has also made two recordings of *Dido*. In the first, from 1981, the string playing is gentle and delicate compared with the crisp ferocity of some versions (Chandos). Kirkby, Hogwood's near-perfect Belinda, is less convincing here as Dido. The role needs a voice with darker hue so that the listener can tell Dido from Belinda without having to peek at the libretto. David Thomas is an unheroic Aeneas. Parrott evidently doesn't take the witches seriously either. Jantina Noorman as the Sorceress is every inch a pantomime wicked fairy with a chorus of chipmunks. In his second recording, Parrott reduces the strings to one to a part and the chorus to two to a part with a crisper and more aggressive tone (Sony, 1994 but released in 1999). Emily van Evera as Dido and Ben Parry as Aeneas have the same shortcomings as Kirkby and Thomas in these roles. Tenor Haden Andrews plays the Sorceress like a drag queen in a snit.

Hickox brings little dramatic cohesion to his performance; he makes it sound like a song recital with oratorio choruses (Chandos). **Martin Pearlman** gives a technically polished reading that seems to me breathless and impatient, in need of a more considered dramatic pacing (Telarc). Nancy Maultsby sings Dido with a dark and dignified sound, while Braun turns in yet another stunning Aeneas.

Since the forces in *Dido* are modest compared with those in the semioperas, and since the work was never given in a public theater during Purcell's lifetime, the case for minimal ensemble is perhaps stronger here, but reduce the chorus to one to a part and the result is nonsense; witness the recordings by **Bradley Brookshire** (Vox) and by the conductorless **Scholars Baroque Ensemble** (Naxos). Brookshire's single strings are effectively supported by a large continuo ensemble, and his principal singers are well suited to their roles, especially Lane, whose Dido here is, if anything, even more impressive than for Lamon. The Scholars, in contrast, produce a thin and whiny string tone in a recording that's generally over-bright. The principals are far from first-rate, and for some reason the players use a hokey tremolando in the witches' scene.

I have yet to hear a modern instrument recording that sounds as right for the music as the best of the period instrument ones. The reissue of a 1977 recording by **Leppard** with Troyanos and Stilwell in the title roles has been praised (Erato) and is preferable to his later recording with Norman (Philips). Still in the catalog is another Leppard recording, this one of a live 1971 performance in Turin with Shirley Verrett as Dido; the sound is appallingly bad, but Verrett's portrayal is well worth hearing (Arkadia).

The recording with Baker and Raimund Herincx under **Anthony Lewis** seems to me dull and pedestrian until the "Lament," where Baker really shines (London). There is a 1959 studio recording directed by **Britten** of the edition he prepared with Imogen Holst, in which Pears is expressive as Aeneas but hardly heroic (BBC). I find Britten's detailed and over-written continuo realization (played by George Malcolm) obtrusive and annoying. The same can be said of Thurston Dart's realization with Lewis/Baker.

INSTRUMENTAL MUSIC

If we consider his output as a whole, Purcell must be viewed primarily as a composer of vocal works, whether for the church, court, theater, or domestic consumption. Even so, his brilliance as an instrumental composer is evident in the overtures, dances, and interludes that adorn his odes, symphony anthems, and theatrical scores. While independent instrumental works occupy a far less conspicuous place in his catalog, they're not negligible, and in two categories—the viol fantasia and the trio sonata—he made significant contributions.

Purcell's viol fantasias are a belated last chapter in the distinguished history of Tudor and Jacobean consort music. They're not mere antiquarian or academic exercises, but highly expressive works in a rigorous idiom where he displays the full power of his contrapuntal ingenuity. The most highly acclaimed recordings of this repertory are by **Hesperion XX** (Astrée 8536) and **Fretwork** (Virgin 45062). A strong contender at a budget price is the **Rose Consort of Viols** (Naxos 553947). Still available is **Harnoncourt**'s 1965 recording, though it's sober and just a bit stolid alongside the others (Vanguard).

In 1683, the 24-year-old Purcell published his twelve *Sonatas of Three Parts,* possibly the first trio sonatas written by an English composer. A second set of ten was published posthumously in 1697. In his preface, Purcell said that he was emulating Italian models in these works, but inevitably he left his own highly individual stamp on the music. An outstanding recording is by the **Purcell Quartet,** including the sonatas, five pavans, "Three Parts upon a Ground," and the *Chacony in G Minor* (Chandos 0572 and MHS; the CD omits the violin prelude and the two organ voluntaries that appeared in the original LPs). The performances are notable for their animation and refinement. **Hogwood** presided at the keyboard in recordings of the sonatas—the 1683 set with violinists Pavlo Beznosiuk and Rachel Podger plus Christophe Coin on the bass violin (Oiseau-Lyre 444449), and the 1697 set with Catherine Mackintosh, Monica Huggett, and Coin (Oiseau-Lyre 433190). Another noteworthy recording of both sets is by **London Baroque** (Harmonia Mundi 901438/9), though neither their discs nor the Hogwood recordings offer the additional selections that come with the Purcell Quartet versions.

Purcell's production of solo keyboard works is modest, but there are some real gems among them. It appears that **Robert Woolley**'s recording of the "complete" harpsichord works is NA, and I find no later attempts at so comprehensive a survey (Saga 9009, 2CD). **Davitt Moroney** has recorded two suites and some shorter pieces found in a recently discovered autograph manuscript (Virgin 45166). Notable recordings of the suites include those by **Kenneth Gilbert** (Harmonia Mundi 901496), **Sophie Yates** (Chandos 0587), and **John Gibbons** (Centaur 2313).

Purcell left only a handful of organ pieces, probably because most organ music of his day was improvised rather than written. Two recordings of the "complete" organ works are by **Moroney** (Arcana 10) and **Woolley** (Chandos 0553). Both are played on the same instrument, the late 17th-century organ by the expatriate English builder Thomas Dallam in the parish church of Guimiliau in Brittany. The playing is very fine in both instances, but the instrument is far more agreeably recorded for Woolley than for Moroney. The temperament is a variety of mean tone, and this makes for some excruciating sourness in nearly every piece. Woolley plays only the double organ (two-manual) version of Purcell's *Voluntary in D Minor,* and fills out his disc with works by other English composers. Moroney plays both versions of the voluntary, and adds solo devotional songs sung by soprano Jill Feldman (see above).

GATENS

Johann Joachim Quantz *(1691–1773)*

Quantz is best known among musicologists for his book *Versuch einer Anweisung die Flöte traversiere zu spielen,* a guidebook that covers just about every aspect of 18th-century musical performance practice, from the intricacies of ornamentation and articulation to the personal qualities necessary for a musician. Quantz wrote it as well as most of his 300 concertos, 350 sonatas, 47 trio sonatas, and 6 flute duets, while in the service to the flute-playing king Frederick the Great. Frederick was so impressed with Quantz that he hired him as his flute teacher at a salary of 2,000 thalers a year (C.P.E. Bach, who worked at Frederick's court as an accompanist for 30 years, earned only 300). Unfortunately, everything Quantz wrote became Frederick's property, and most of his music was never published.

Quantz's G major concerto did make it into the flute literature, and there are many fine recordings on both modern and baroque instruments. I prefer his music played on the baroque flute but enjoy **Patrick Gallois**'s modern flute recording in "Flotenkonzerte aus Sanssouci"; Sanssouci was the name of one of Frederick's castles (DG 4398962). **Galway**'s recording includes three concertos besides the G major (RCA 60247). He plays them with his usual big, bold, extroverted sound, but everything sounds pretty much the same. He doesn't have the same feel for this music as baroque flutist **Rachel Brown** with the Hanover Band (♦RCA 61903). Brown has made some other excellent recordings, including one of some unpublished flute concertos, played from manuscript and using a copy of a flute made by Quantz (♦Hyperion 66927), and another with Standage of a concerto and a trio sonata called "Music from the Court of Frederick the Great" (Chandos 0541). The **Kuijkens** (flutist Bartold and gamba player Wieland) include Quantz's B-flat Sonata in another disc called "From the Court of Frederick the Great" (♦Sony 66237), and **Camerata Köln** includes his C major trio sonata for flute and recorder (Harmonia Mundi 77172).

The only nonflute recordings of Quantz I know are one of his E-flat horn concerto played by **Uwe Komischke** and the Philharmonische Streichersolisten (Koch Schwann 3-1237), and an astounding pan flute version of his G major concerto played by **Ulrich Herkenhoff** (Koch Schwann 315032).

FINE

Henri Rabaud (1873–1949)

In Rabaud we encounter neither a musical giant nor a revolutionary, but a gifted and assured talent who was fortunate enough to be born into an influential family of musicians: His mother sang the part of Marguerite at the premiere of *Faust;* his father was professor of cello at the Paris Conservatoire; his grandfather was a renowned flute player; and his great-aunt had held leading roles in Meyerbeer and Halévy operas. By the time Rabaud entered the Conservatoire, one symphony already under his belt, his professors (including Massenet) could only wonder at a prodigious mind blessed with a keen sense of melody and orchestration. Although he completed a second symphony, neither has been heard since; rather, Rabaud has come down to us primarily as a purveyor of restrained exoticism in his once successful opera *Mârouf.*

The record collector may benefit from a wondrous example of parallel evolution in which two recordings have been issued containing nearly the same program and nicely summarizing the disparate nature of Rabaud's output: one led by **Dervaux** (EMI 63951) and the other by **Segerstam** (Marco Polo 223503). Common to both are *La Procession Nocturne,* a lushly textured tone poem based on Lenau's *Faust;* the ballet music from *Mârouf,* clearly cut from the same multicolored cloth as *Scheherazade; Eglogue,* inspired by Virgil; and *Divertissement on Russian Songs.* To these Segerstam adds *Suites Anglaises* 2 and 3.

The differences between the two aren't enough to make a clear recommendation. In *La Procession Nocturne* Dervaux avoids the ponderous tempos favored by Segerstam and brings out the low brass in an imposing manner; conversely, in the dances from *Mârouf* Dervaux seems a bit sober-sided against Segerstam's heady ebullience, while in the *Divertissement* Segerstam finds more wit and insouciance than Dervaux. Both do very well with *Eglogue,* which rounds out Dervaux's disc. The two *English Suites* appended by Segerstam, intended for a production of Shakespeare's *Merchant of Venice,* are Rabaud's arrangements of 16th-century virginal tunes by Byrd, Farnaby, and others and breathe the refinement and grace of that period; what a pity Segerstam didn't include Suite 1 as well! Perhaps these swing the balance in favor of Segerstam, though it is far better to have both. There's also a collection of "Exotic Dances from the Opera" conducted by **Eiji Oue** (RR 71), which includes the dances from *Mârouf* at tempos closer to Segerstam's than Dervaux's.

HALLER

Sergei Rachmaninoff (1873–1943)

Rachmaninoff was born in imperial Russia and died in democratic America. He was one of the greatest keyboard virtuosos of all time, and the shamefully few recordings RCA allowed him to make are stunning in their range of expression and technical facility. He was also a magnificent conductor, at least of his own work, as the single RCA disc of his Symphony 3, *Isle of the Dead,* and *Vocalise,* demonstrates. Yet much as we might wish he had given us Bach's *Goldberg Variations,* Beethoven's late sonatas and *Diabelli Variations,* and more, he remained devoted to his own works.

In retrospect, he was right to do this; his real work was as a composer. He had an individual and powerful voice, and he gave us some of the most beautiful music ever written. We think of his gorgeous *Vocalise,* arranged for every imaginable kind of musical performance, the overwhelming nostalgia of the introduction to Symphony 2, the insidiously haunting melody that opens Piano Concerto 3. Cheap and vulgar imitations of his music have appeared in movie scores and elsewhere, but its true power transcends these counterfeits. Scorned by academics for its accessibility, shunned by the avant-garde for its conservatism, his music has endured and persisted. His ability to find tunes that had never been sung before but seemed to have been known forever reached back to his beloved Tchaikovsky and to Chopin and Mozart; they guaranteed his immortality and live on today. Like all great teachers, he leads us to see and so to live more fully.

ORCHESTRAL MUSIC

Born when Wagner had ten more years to live, dead shortly after Philip Glass's ninth birthday, Rachmaninoff was no orchestral innovator. Instead, he looked to the music of Tchaikovsky, particularly the deep lyricism of *Eugene Onegin* and the darkness of *The Queen of Spades* for his inspiration. The elegance of his melodies and the vocal quality of his part writing contrast oddly with his sometimes vulgar use of percussion. In the best performances, his music is powerful, emotional, and haunting.

Rachmaninoff was a superbly gifted conductor, as his three known recordings—Symphony 3, *Isle of the Dead,* and *Vocalise*—attest. These are peerless performances, and listeners should seek them out in their reincarnations (♦RCA; Pearl). Aside from these and a couple of Stokowski recordings, there are few historical orchestral performances. There are many modern versions of Symphony 2, but the bulk of his music remains underrecorded, which is odd, considering how popular it has always been with concert audiences.

Fortunately, there are several superb collections of orchestral music. Of these, **Ashkenazy** with the Concertgebouw is preeminent (♦Decca, 3CD). It includes the three symphonies, *Isle of the Dead, The Bells,* and *Symphonic Dances;* a number of less important works are missing. Ashkenazy's flexibility and sense of color as a conductor (so different from some of his pianism) have often been noted. This set would convince any skeptics and, with a bargain price, top-notch playing, and outstanding sound, is probably all that most collectors will need to feel content. It even comes with good notes and texts.

Its closest rival is **Previn**'s set with the London Symphony (EMI). It's equally well played and almost as well recorded. Previn is a more lyrical interpreter than the urgent Ashkenazy, but his set has less music and is more expensive. **Slatkin** offers the most music and lowest price of all; he includes all that Ashkenazy offers plus almost all the pieces he omits (Vox). Unfortunately, the performances aren't very intense. **Ormandy**'s perfunctory set of the symphonies is another disappointment (Sony). He was a friend of the composer, but the attentiveness he brought to his concerto accompaniments wasn't present in his symphonic readings. **Maazel** has gorgeous Berlin Philharmonic playing, but not much to say about the music (DG). **De Waart** is ordinary (Philips), and **Svetlanov** is agreeably fervent but disagreeably crass (Melodiya).

Turning to individual pieces, Previn's recording of *The Bells* is remarkably vivid, even more than Ashkenazy's (♦EMI). *Capriccio bohémien* is not a memorable piece and has no memorable recordings; the least uninteresting is probably **Järvi**'s (Chandos). *The Isle of the Dead* has had a number of excellent readings. Of these, **Horenstein** (♦Chesky), **Mitropoulos** (Sony, in elderly mono), **Reiner** (♦RCA), and **Stokowski** (Pearl, another old one), join **Ashkenazy** at the head of the list. *Mona Vanna* has been recorded only by **Igor Buketoff** and appears with an early version of Concerto 4 (Chandos). For *Prince Rostislav,* the choice is between the dull but inexpensive readings of **Slatkin** (Vox) and **Maksymiuk** (Naxos) and **Svetlanov**'s thrashing around. *The Rock* has good performances from **Pletnev** (DG) and **Dutoit** (Decca), both paired with problematic versions of Symphony 2. *Scherzo* is an early piece and brings back the Scylla and Charybdis of Slatkin and Svetlanov. *Spring* has a quite decent recording with **Kitaienko** (Chandos), as well as the inescapable Slatkin.

Symphonic Dances, in my view, is Rachmaninoff's greatest orchestral piece. I don't know which I regret more, that RCA couldn't be bothered to record him and Horowitz in the two-piano version, or that it didn't record him conducting the orchestral version. Consolation exists in the form of two fine modern recordings: the **Ashkenazy** already mentioned and **Jansons** in an alternately suave and sinister reading with an appropriately bittersweet-sounding St. Petersburg Philharmonic, with the advantage of left-right violin placement (♦EMI, with a fine Symphony 3).

There's really no reason to look past the stellar performances and low price of Ashkenazy or Previn in the symphonies, and for 1 there are no alternatives worth bothering with except Jansons (EMI), which is fine but a lot more expensive. For 2, of course, the story is quite different, yet a close look narrows the field down rapidly: Ashkenazy, Jansons, Previn (LSO on EMI or Royal Philharmonic on Telarc, fresher and richer, respectively), and an old Stokowski (Music & Arts). The story is much the same for 3 except that there the Stokowski is a modern recording and almost as stirring as the composer's own (EMI). In the "Youth" Symphony, Slatkin is the only game in town.

The *Vocalise* has been recorded many times in many forms. The composer, Jansons, Previn, and Stokowski (with Symphony 3 on EMI or with various short pieces on RCA) are all full of elegance, longing, and nostalgia.   CHAKWIN

CONCERTOS

The four concertos are markedly different. No. 1 in F minor is an effective work originally conceived in 1890–91 but much revised in 1917, and therefore containing elements of both early and late Rachmaninoff. No. 2, the famous C minor, was written in 1901, following the composer's long bout with depression after the unsuccessful first performance of Symphony 1. It's a justly famous work, rich and powerful. No. 3, in D minor (1909), is longer and deeper. Unfortunately, this is one of several works the composer was persuaded to cut in his recording; these cuts, like those in Symphony 2, became traditional until recently. No. 4 in G minor was written in 1926 during Rachmaninoff's stay in the United States, where his style became much more elusive and pared down. It's a marvelous work that exists in two markedly different forms, the later one completed in 1941. *Rhapsody on a Theme of Paganini* is from 1934, a dramatic set of variations containing prominent references to the demonic Paganini in its use of the Gregorian *Dies Irae* chant.

Rachmaninoff's complete acoustic and electrical recordings are in a large boxed set; the quality of the originals varies, but the recordings are well reproduced (RCA 61265, 10CD). The set includes all four concertos and *Paganini Rhapsody,* with Stokowski in 2 and the *Rhapsody* and Ormandy in 1, 3, and 4, all with the Philadelphia Orchestra. There are two versions of 2, an acoustic from 1924 and an electrical from 1929. Pickwick 104 presents the 1929 version in richer sound than RCA, though the pitch is a quarter-tone higher than RCA's A = 440. Rachmaninoff as conductor is represented by *Isle of the Dead,* Symphony 3, and *Vocalise,* again with the Philadelphia. The set also includes the three sonatas Rachmaninoff recorded with Kreisler, Beethoven's Op. 30:3, Schubert's D 574, and Grieg's Op. 45:3. This album is a gem! Excerpts from the solo recordings, including most of his own pieces, are also in the "Great Recordings of the Century" series (Philips 456943, 2CD).

Complete sets. **Rachmaninoff**'s own performances of these works are hard to beat, though neither recording of 2 is in very good sound. The other concertos and *Rhapsody* are much more satisfactory. Rachmani-

noff's performances are highly individual: there are places in 2 where he does exactly the opposite of what he put in the score in terms of tempo and dynamics. His compositions have an improvisatory quality that also characterizes his performances of both his and other people's music, yet there is such warmth and integrity that everything he plays sounds better for his attentions, both technical and textual.

One performer who matches the composer's technical skills is **Wild,** who recorded all the piano-orchestral works in 1965 with Horenstein (Chandos 8521/2, 2CD; in better sound, Chesky 41, 2CD). His readings seem closely modeled on Rachmaninoff's, even to the cuts in 3. The chemistry between pianist and conductor isn't as effective as Stokowski's or Ormandy's with the composer—Horenstein doesn't have much precision as an accompanist, and ensemble is chancy at best—making these readings less satisfactory than we would hope with these two giants at work. Yet their technical address is hard to resist, the emotional power of the readings is terrific, and they are priced at a discount.

Ashkenazy recorded the complete cycle twice, with Previn (London 425576, 2CD; 444839, 2CD) and Haitink (London 421590). Both omit the *Rhapsody* but play 3 complete, making life difficult, since Ashkenazy's *Rhapsody* is only available coupled with individual concertos but never 3. He is less volatile than either the composer or Wild, and Haitink's basic stolidity sometimes carries this trend almost to somnolence. Previn is livelier, but these performances are still more characterized by warmth than excitement. The 1972 Previn readings are also available complete with the *Rhapsody* and Ashkenazy's Preludes, Sonata 2, and the two suites for two pianos, an album well worth considering, particularly at budget price (Philips 455234, 6CD). The London sound balances soloist and orchestra well in the concertos, and the performers offer perhaps the best unified and most insightful performances of all.

The readings by Ukranian pianist **Mikhail Rudy** with Mariss Jansons are also remarkably well played, unified, and insightful, though from a very different direction from that taken by Ashkenazy and Previn (EMI 737765, 3CD, with Tchaikovsky's 1, budget priced). Rudy is a master of detail and color; this is perhaps the most articulate set since Rachmaninoff's own, and Jansons gets magnificently red-blooded playing from the Leningrad/St. Petersburg Philharmonic. Rudy's performances are less heroic, more articulate, and in a more specific frame with almost chamber-music integration with the orchestra. There's nothing quite like it in the catalog, and it's a safe recommendation (along with Wild) for those who don't want to deal with the elderly sound of the composer's recordings.

Shelley with Thompson plays elegantly, though temperature and ensemble are sometimes questionable; the piano is rather forwardly balanced (Chandos 8882). **Kocsis** provides an exciting if sometimes superficial approach with de Waart (Philips 446199; 446582), while **Anievas** does a lyrical job in 1 and 4 with Frühbeck de Burgos but is held back in the rest by the sluggish conducting of Moshe Atzmon and Aldo Ceccato (EMI). **Victor Eresko** gives an *echt* Russian reading, lacking something in polish (Melodiya). **Rösel**'s performances with Sanderling are satisfying musically, but so slow there's no room for *Rhapsody* (Berlin).

1. With No. 4, 1 is the stepchild of the Rachmaninoff family. Both were heavily revised, and the results are excellent, only paling beside the more spacious inspiration of 2 and 3. **Rösel** gives us sophisticated though rather heavy readings of 1 and 2 (Berlin 9307). **Janis** made two classic recordings of 1. A 1962 version with Kondrashin is listed in two different forms: Mercury 434333 with Prokofiev 3 and some solo works, while Philips 456850 (2CD) couples it with Tchaikovsky 1, Liszt 1, and other solo works, in their "Great Pianists of the 20th Century" series. Janis has an impressive balance between virtuosity and feeling that puts him in the class of Wild and Rachmaninoff. His recording with Reiner is also worth searching out (RCA 68762).

Recordings of 1 and 4 together may be had from **Entremont** with Ormandy, in a well-filled disc including *Rhapsody* (Sony 46541). These are musical, straightforward readings that make a telling case for both the neglected sisters. **Glemser** offers the same program but at a greater emotional distance and with a less assertive orchestra (Naxos). **Thibaudet** with Ashkenazy breezes through 1 and 3 with efficiency but not much involvement (London), and **Lill** does 1 and 2 in similarly pedestrian fashion (Nimbus). **Vardan Mamikonian** plays a program of first concertos (with Liszt and Mendelssohn) with variable success, though his Rachmaninoff is good (Orfeo). **Volkov** gives another real Russian interpretation, a little short on poetry (Brioso). **Richter**'s 1955 recording with Sanderling has a rude vitality that's emphasized by the raw sound; it's one of the most exciting performances on disc (Melodiya/BMG 28467, with 2). Other recordings of considerable distinction come from **Vasary** (DG, with 2) and **Rudy** (EMI, with 4).

2. This ever-popular concerto has been recorded by most major pianists, sometimes more than once. **Rachmaninoff** himself recorded it twice with Stokowski, once acoustically and once electrically. Other early versions are still with us, notably a fine reading by **Cyril Smith,** along with an equally worthy *Rhapsody* and a lyrical Suite 2 for two pianos with his long time partner **Phyllis Sellick,** all recorded in good late-'40s mono (Dutton 4004). **Moiseiwitsch** recorded it twice, his version with Hugo Rignold making it to the "Great Pianists of the 20th Century" series (Philips 456907, 2CD), while *Rhapsody* and solo pieces may be found with the orchestral music accompanied by Walter Goehr (APR 5505). He's perhaps not the ideal pianist for Rachmaninoff; his sophistication replaces passion at times, yet his performances are fascinating.

Rubinstein is a bit slapdash in this repertory, but his recordings with Golschmann (Historical Piano Collection 132), gleaming and powerful with Reiner (RCA 4934), and particularly Stokowski (Biddulph 41), have many admirers. **Katchen**'s recording with Solti is less remarkable than his *Rhapsody* and the coupled Dohnányi *Variations on a Nursery Theme,* but is a fascinating disc for their sake (London 448604). He also recorded the same program in the early '50s with Boult and Fistoulari (Dutton 2504). **Janis**'s 2 is less impressive than his 3, but both are on a high level (Mercury 432759 or Philips 456850, 2CD). In **Richter**'s 1959 recording with Wislocki, his control and virtuosity equal the composer's, and his interpretation is full of integrity (DG 47420, with Tchaikovsky 1; Philips 456952, 2CD, with solo Rachmaninoff and Scriabin).

Kapell's outstanding 2 and *Rhapsody* are only available presently in RCA's multi-CD album devoted to this pianist. Another relatively early recording is by **Graffman** with Bernstein, a classy reading with lots of power and panache, available in several couplings. Avoid Sony 47630 with Watts's underpowered Tchaikovsky 1; either Sony 36722 with the *Rhapsody* or 63032 with 3 will do. **Entremont** with Bernstein is on the superficial side, though technically impressive (Sony). **Cliburn** is careful to a fault. His recording with Reiner may be heard with his Beethoven 5 (RCA) or with his famous Tchaikovsky 1 (RCA). **Ashkenazy**'s first readings of 2 and 3 with Kondrashin and Fistoulari from 1963 have been reissued (♦Decca 466375). They may remind you what all the fuss was about before this outstanding pianist turned to conducting.

Recordings from the CD era include **Philip Fowke** in well-balanced readings with Temirkanov (EMI 9509, with *Rhapsody*); an impressive performance by then 18-year-old **Kissin** with Gergiev (RCA 57982, with some Op. 39 *Etudes-Tableaux*); **David Golub**'s well-played but ill-at-ease collaboration with Wyn Morris (MCA); **Gutierrez**'s well-planned if not stellar readings of 2 and 3 with Maazel (Telarc); **Arthur Ozolins**'s distinctive interpretation (CBC 5108, with Healey Willan's enjoyable Concerto); **Bronfman**'s rather low-energy 2 and 3 (Sony); **Grimaud**'s diffident reading (Denon); and **Sequeira Costa**'s tasteful but not outstanding performance (INMP 6701132, with 4).

Thibaudet offers a fine performance, perhaps a little held back, with Ashkenazy (London 440653, with *Rhapsody*). **David Lively** is a bit anonymous (Discover); **Noriko Ogawa** also lacks temperament (BIS), as does **Lill** (Nimbus). **Ohlsson** goes to the other extreme, with rubato galore (Hänssler). **Glemser** gives a reading full of feeling, somewhat lacking in energy at times (Naxos).

3. The third concerto is the grandest of all. Like several of the composer's spacious works of this period, it became subject to cuts, beginning with **Rachmaninoff**'s own recording with Ormandy, and the first movement cadenza was provided with a less barnstorming alternate, which he used when he recorded the piece. These traditions were followed by almost all pianists until the late '50s, when Cliburn recorded the larger cadenza and Ashkenazy opened the last cuts in the finale. Neither may have been the first to do this, but they were the ones that impressed this listener. **Cliburn**'s 3 is otherwise good but not great, a bit lacking in forward movement but full of integrity (Philips 456748, 2CD; RCA 6209).

Ashkenazy's first and perhaps greatest reading was with Fistoulari, playing the less bombastic cadenza (Decca 466375, with his also outstanding 2). His recording with Ormandy and the Philadelphia is amazing. The normally pedestrian Ormandy, who had been conducting this concerto for some 40 years, created a superbly detailed world and made the normally skittish and shallow Ashkenazy slow down and address the music. His tone is still hard (what happened to the liquid tones of his youth heard in the Fistoulari performance?), but he expands to fill the epic framework Ormandy provides, and the result is powerfully symphonic, one of the finest readings available. It's in a low-priced collection called "Rachmaninoff in Hollywood" and is on the disc only because of the movie *Shine* (RCA 68874). Go figure.

Gilels is another who should be heard, though his 1956 recording with Cluytens makes the cuts and Cluytens isn't the world's most Russian conductor (Testament 1029). **Horowitz** made several recordings of 3. The 1932 version with Coates is coupled with Rachmaninoff playing 2 with Stokowski in 1929; it includes some alternate takes from 2 and is an important release (Biddulph 36). A live radio broadcast from 1941 with Barbirolli and the New York Philharmonic is coupled with a rip-roaring Tchaikovsky 1 (APR 5519). The excitement of this reading makes the later studio recording with Reiner seem pale (RCA 7754). Another concert performance with the New York Philharmonic and Ormandy, with less intensity than the earlier readings but better sound, is coupled with the pianist's special version of Sonata 2 (RCA 63681); still another with Koussevitzky isn't as successful (Iron Needle).

More modern recordings include **Feltsman,** remarkable for nothing but an editing error in the *Rhapsody* and the usual cuts in the finale (Sony). **Weissenberg** offers a powerfully muscular reading with Prêtre and the Chicago Symphony, a fit companion to his outstanding recordings of the Preludes (RCA 61396, midpriced). **Rösel** plays a musically satisfying if somewhat underpowered version, with 4 to back it up (Ars

Vivendi 2100166). **Lill** is musical but in stasis (Nimbus), and **Glemser** is indecisive (Naxos). **Natalia Trull** plays well, but her conductor is stiff and the orchestra small (Audiophile). **Argerich** recorded a white-hot reading live in 1982, with some rhythmic distortions that turn passion into incoherence and an uninspired accompaniment from Chailly, that may be too much for repeated listening (Philips 446673). **Thibaudet** plays a well-detailed if not very exciting performance under Ashkenazy (Decca). **Cherkassky** gives a similarly broadly paced but fascinatingly phrased performance (Decca 448401, with solo works).

The **David Helfgott** phenomenon, represented by the film *Shine*, resulted in a recording, uncut and with the more massive cadenza, best forgotten (RCA). **André Laplante** is presented in a performance that had only 15 minutes of rehearsal time, turning a potentially vital reading into a not very satisfactory recording (Analekta). **Noriko Ogawa** plays a musically detailed but rather nonpoetic account (BIS). **Bolet** is captured in a grand performance not very effectively balanced in sound (Palexa 503). **Artur Pizarro** is also hampered by a recorded balance that tends to bury his excellent reading under the orchestra (Collins 1505). **Kissin** offers an elegantly played rendition with some ravishing moments, but with plodding accompaniment by Ozawa and the Boston Symphony; it's hard to find much drama in it or to justify its release much (RCA 61548).

Levine's accompaniment for **Arcadi Volodos** approaches the Ozawa level of blandness, despite the presence of the Berlin Philharmonic. The performance is technically adroit, although in a field with so many great performances, Volodos offers nothing special. The solo pieces are far more full of life than the concerto; perhaps he would have given us a more striking reading if he had been luckier in his partner. **Lazar Berman** has a giant technique, and his recording with Abbado (Sony, NA) was impressive but musically insignificant because of its pervasive lack of drama and tension. **Berezovsky** with Duchable is exciting (Erato 18411, with 2), **Bronfman** with Salonen much less so (Sony).

4. Concerto 4 was composed in 1927 and revised in 1940, when **Rachmaninoff** recorded it. The original version has been recorded by **William Black** in a warm but somewhat careful performance with Igor Buketoff, adding 79 bars to the 1940 version (Chandos 8987). This still isn't the version as first performed, which was another 114 bars longer. I miss the revision's exciting return to the first movement climax, though there are many interesting differences here.

The revision has been recorded in complete sets by our old standbys: **Wild** is exciting but somewhat hectic (Chandos and Chesky); **Previn** is also exciting (EMI); and **Ashkenazy** is better controlled (London). **Rudy** offers both versions of the finale in his complete set, as well as jewel-like playing. **Kocsis**'s 1984 recording is neat and well balanced (Philips 456874, 2CD). **Rösel** gives a thinking man's performance (Ars Vivendi 2100166, with 3), and **Entremont**'s version with Ormandy is exciting (Sony 46541, with 1 and *Rhapsody*). **Sequeira Costa** does a pedestrian job (Royal Philharmonic), and **Lill**'s recording is also a walk-through (Nimbus). **Thibaudet** is too light and Gallic for the rich sonorities (Decca), while **Glemser** is a bit flattened out by distant sound (Naxos). **Paul Stewart** gives an effective reading (Palexa 506, with a Medtner sonata), and the old **Michelangeli** has been reissued with considerably improved sound(EMI 67258). Some swear by it, but others find it lacking in sweep.

Rhapsody on a Theme by Paganini. This is such a brilliant showpiece for both piano and orchestra that even the prominent *Dies Irae* chant seems only a guest at the feast. It's hard to get beyond the technical

derring-do and the ensemble demands to make serious music. The recording by **Rachmaninoff** and Stokowski does get beyond the notes, providing a standard few can reach. Besides the complete 10CD set of Rachmaninoff's performances and the 2CD set containing all the concertos, there is one of just the *Rhapsody*, Concerto 2, and the *Vocalise*, all conducted by Stokowski, in richer sound than the RCA sets (Pickwick 104). There is also a Naxos disc with decent sound and an unbeatable price.

Moiseiwitsch recorded both Concerto 2 and *Rhapsody* twice. His pre-war versions compare favorably with the composer's own, as Rachmaninoff himself declared (Appian 5505). By 1955, he was past his prime, and Hugo Rignold was not as well attuned to him (EMI). **Rubinstein** made two fine recordings, one with Susskind (HPC 132, with Concerto 2), and an even more impressive one with Reiner (RCA 4934, with Concerto 2, and 68886 with Chopin and de Falla). **Katchen** recorded an unusual program twice, including Concerto 2 and Dohnányi's *Variations on a Nursery Song*. The earlier version was from the early '50s with Boult and Fistoulari (Dutton 2504); his remake with Solti is in more impressive stereo sound (London 448604). Katchen had a sensitive rubato, though he's less idiomatic than some. **Ashkenazy** is excellent, both with Previn (London) and Haitink (London). **Wild** is even more impressive, but his ensemble with Horenstein isn't as tight (Chandos and Chesky). **Cliburn** made recordings with Kondrashin and Ormandy, but his tendency to wallow makes them heavy going (both RCA).

More recent versions include **Golub** in a performance marked by less than ideal rapport with conductor Wyn Morris (Pickwick), and a careful, too laid-back account by **Feltsman,** with a 13-bar editing cut in Variation 22 and the usual cuts in Concerto 3 (Sony). An exciting and well-recorded performance by **Pletnev** is somewhat spoiled by distant orchestral sound (Virgin 90724); his more recent recording with Abbado offers a better blend of forces, though the discmates aren't ideal (DG 457583). **Entremont** plays at a high technical level, but his involvement doesn't go very far (Sony). **Gutierrez** is plagued with a distant orchestra and a similar lack of involvement (Telarc).

Graffman gives an effective performance, though Bernstein hams it up a bit (Sony 63032). **Thibaudet** is too cool for the lyrical moments, though his technique is impressive (Decca). **Lill** is lacking in temperament, and the recording is poorly balanced (Nimbus). **Adilia Alieva** isn't competitive (Gallo), but **Volkov** is a fine technician, and the Moscow Philharmonic adds spice (Brioso 111). **Glemser** gives a rather vague impression (Naxos).   MOORE

CHAMBER MUSIC

Although Rachmaninoff composed mainly for the piano, his few chamber works are enchanting and well worth hearing. The most famous is the Sonata for Cello and Piano, written for his friend Anatoli Brandukov, who premiered it with the composer in 1901. Its most accessible and charming rendition is by **Ma** and **Ax** (♦Sony 46486). This highly ingratiating and melodious performance may lack the fireworks provided by Russian musicians, but the two are well attuned to each other and speak in unison. Equally good and also in excellent sound is a 1984 recording by **Schiff** and **Leonskaja,** an engaging and spirited performance that displays much depth, complexity, and artfulness (♦Philips 412732).

Less stellar performances are by **Tortelier** and **Ciccolini** (EMI), a soft and subtle presentation, as well as a midpriced reissue of a 1979 recording by **Lloyd Webber** and **Yitkin Seow,** a glib and facile affair with overly resonant acoustics (ASV). **Michael Grebanier** is lackluster and amateurish; **Janet Guggenheim**'s piano is more textured and fluid, but their recording merely skims the surface of this most accomplished piece (Naxos). **Thedéen** and **Pöntinen** are too controlled to move the listener (BIS). **Mørk** and **Thibaudet** give a modern but cold interpretation (Virgin), and **Starker** and **Shigeo Neriki** are dry and uninspired (RCA).

The two *Elegiac Trios* have been recorded on several labels. An appealing rendition of 1 comes from **Gennady Dzubenko**, Victor Abramyan, and Alexander Bourikov; this eloquent performance expertly builds to a dramatic crescendo and is full of longing (♦RCD 10401). The **Bekova** sisters convey a sense of drama but aren't entirely coherent (Chandos). The **Beaux Arts Trio**, although expert, remains somewhat earthbound (Philips). The 1947 recording by **Alexander Goldenweiser**, Dmitri Tziganoff, and Sergei Chirinsky is full of the nervous energy of a race horse (♦Dante 103).

For the best rendition of the hauntingly beautiful 2, written in memory of Tchaikovsky, look to Russian musicians. A 1976 performance by **Pavel Serebryakov, Michail Vaiman,** and **Rostropovich** is simultaneously exciting and tender; Rostropovich's playing is outstanding, and the recording quality is good (♦Russian Legacy 8408). An out-of-print 1958 mono recording with **Oborin, Oistrakh,** and **Knushevitsky** is in decent sound and worth finding; this performance is consistently beautiful and never lets the listener down (♦MK 417111). Highly expressive and driven, it makes a close second choice, particularly for Oistrakh aficionados. For a more delicate touch, there is a moving rendition by the **Golub/Kaplan/Carr Trio** (Arabesque 6739). The **Budapest Quartet** recorded this trio in 1952 at the Library of Congress (Bridge 9063). The sound quality isn't the best, but for the patient listener it offers a cornucopia of nuances. You'll find no fireworks here, just a clear and unspoiled beauty. The rendition by the **Bekova** sisters (see above) is competent but superficial, and the **Beaux Arts Trio** (also above) leaves the listener strangely unmoved.

String Quartets 1 and 2 are played by the **Budapest String Quartet** (Bridge 9063, with the D minor Trio). Although the musicianship of this seamless ensemble is never in doubt, the performance isn't truly engaging, and the sound quality leaves something to be desired. These pieces are rarely performed, and this CD seems to be the only recording.

D. GEFFEN

PIANO MUSIC

The solo piano works comprise two sonatas, two sets of variations, two of preludes, two of etudes, and three early collections of miscellaneous pieces. There are also two sets of very early works: three *Nocturnes* and four pieces originally called Op. 1, both from 1887. And there are several short pieces that never received opus numbers, from various periods.

Rachmaninoff was one of the greatest pianists of his generation. Luckily, he made many recordings, beginning in 1919 with a number of piano rolls, followed by acoustic discs during the early '20s and continuing through to the '40s with a glorious series of electrical recordings. Piano rolls, by their very nature, are a poor substitute for the real thing; there's no way that holes in a roll of paper can capture the touch of a player with the accuracy of a recording. Though they may be reproduced in up-to-date sound, gradations of volume and pedaling are crudely handled in this medium. A good representation of the possibilities and a good selection from Rachmaninoff's piano-roll recordings are available, for what they're worth (Decca 425964). "A Window in Time" consists of the same pieces presented with the aid of modern technology (Telarc 80489). The sound is even more impressive than Decca's, but the result is still one step removed from reality: a zombie with wooden gloves playing a marvelous modern keyboard.

Collections. The most comprehensive collection on LP was by **Ponti;** the playing was lively and competent, if somewhat short on poetry, and Sonata 2 was omitted (Vox 5456 and 5478, 6LP). **Ruth Laredo** recorded the major works on CD soon thereafter; less mercurial than Ponti, she gives a solid, somewhat humorless impression (Sony 48468–72, 5CD). **Shelley** made a more comprehensive survey, including both original and revised versions of Sonata 2, all the early pieces as well as those without opus numbers (Hyperion 44041-48, 8CD). His playing is the most satisfying and emotionally balanced of the complete sets. **Thiollier** showed more fire and brimstone, and his collection was nearly as inclusive as Shelley's, but his three albums have disappeared (Thesis 82004–06, each 2CD).

Here as elsewhere, **Richter** was highly selective, playing only those pieces that interested him: 11 of the *Etudes-Tableaux,* for instance, 12 of the Preludes, and a scattering of others. But what he did play is quite wonderful—richer in sonority and more passionately romantic than anyone else. Eight of his *Etudes-Tableaux* and seven of the Op. 32 Preludes are on Olympia 337, but this may be hard to find, and you may have to settle for the five Preludes in Vol. 1 of his three albums in the "Great Pianists" series (Philips 456946).

Etudes-Tableaux These pieces are divided among two collections, Opp. 33 and 39. These are brilliant late compositions, fully as important as the Preludes. **Shelley**'s are among the best of his performances, though somewhat rushed at times (Hyperion 66091). **Hobson** plays them with style, though sometimes he loses concentration (Arabesque 6609). **Nikolai Lugansky** has the advantage of the national idiom and remarkable technical fluency (Fidelio 9206). **Lill** gives one of his best performances (Nimbus 5439). Three women seem to have their number: **Idil Biret** offers a darkly powerful reading (Naxos 550347); **Constance Keene** emphasizes clarity and vitality (Protone 2207); and **Marietta Petkova** gives them an almost symphonic grandeur, recorded in concert (Doron 3026).

Op. 39 has been recorded separately by **Ashkenazy,** his second recording (Decca 417671) a bit harder in sound than his first (♦London 444845, 2CD). **Freddy Kempf** gives an outstanding reading (BIS 1042), and **Stephen Prutsman** also plays them well, with a somewhat dryer approach (Brioso 113). **Maria Pia Carola** rather misses the boat; her performances lack drama (Symposium). **Nelson Goerner** has the virtuosity and imagination needed for this music (Cascavelle 1037).

Moments Musicaux Op. 16. This collection is played by itself by several pianists. **Igor Ardasev** plays these pieces with perhaps a too uncomplicated musicality (Supraphon); **Valentina Lisitsa** is very literal and not poetic (Audiofon); **Lill** is similarly earthbound (Nimbus 5575). **Alwin Bar** is satisfyingly brooding and dramatic (Erasmus 210). **Claudette Sorel** is rather unrelenting (Emsco).

Preludes. If you combine Preludes Op. 23 with Op. 32 and Op. 3 No. 2, you get the magic number 24 (following Debussy's model). Several pianists have done this, notably **Ashkenazy** (London 443841, with his own version of Sonata 2). Another set is offered by **Agustin Anievas,** with the three early *Nocturnes* plus Liszt's Sonata and Chopin 3, played with passion and insight (EMI 69527). **Donohoe** made a less economical version, also on two discs but with no filler, in excellent readings (EMI 64787). **Marta Deyanova** managed to get them all on one well-filled CD, though her performances aren't as insightful as any of the above (Nimbus). **Peter Katin** recorded a powerful if rather monolithic version in 1972 (IMP 1081).

Lill deprives these pieces of their poetry (Nimbus), but **Constance Keene** is lyrical and colorful (Protone 1101). And one excerpt disc needs mention since it includes all of Op. 23 and the first eight of the 13 of Op. 32, along with the revised Sonata 2. Why **Wild** chose to do it this way rather than give us all the preludes together is hard to figure, but these are performances of great beauty and fascination (Chesky 114). Op. 23 by itself may be had in intense, dark performances by **Biret,** along with the Op. 3 pieces (Naxos 550348).

Op. 32 is the larger collection. **Anthony di Bonaventura** plays it by itself in musical, somewhat deliberate readings (Titanic 195). **Constantin Lifschitz** couples it with Scriabin in virtuoso but rather self-indulgent performances (Denon 80354). **Morton Estrin** joins them with late Brahms in subtle and musical readings, beautifully recorded (Connoisseur Society 4235). **Rodriguez** plays them with particular flair, along with his fine Sonata 1 (Elan 82244).

Sonatas. The sonatas are demanding in every way. Sonata 1 was written around the time of Symphony 2, during Rachmaninoff's most expansive period. It employs his favorite Gregorian chant and is in three movements taking about 40 minutes. Sonata 2 marks a crisis between his styles, being both broadly conceived and impatient. Its original 1913 version was shortened by the composer. The general impression is that the cuts were not an improvement, and many pianists now prefer the original. Horowitz recorded a compromise version of his own devising that satisfies neither faction.

Pianists who have coupled the two sonatas include **Shelley,** who uses the revised 2 (Hyperion 66047); he plays the original in an oddly titled disc called "The Early Works" with greater conviction and involvement (Hyperion 66198). **Victor Eresko** couples them in rather forbidding readings, playing the revised version of 2 (Chant du Monde). **Fergus-Thompson** gives impressive performances of both works, playing the original 2 (♦Kingdom 2007). **Rodriguez** plays both sonatas, but on different discs: Elan 82244 gives us an excitingly sustained 1 along with the Op. 32 Preludes, while Elan 82248 provides the revised 2, the Op. 3 pieces, and *Chopin Variations* with their original quiet ending.

Beret plays both sonatas (2 in the original) with larger-than-life gestures, powerful but a bit crude (Naxos 553003). **Berezovsky** couples a brilliant 1 with a marvelously played *Chopin Variations,* unfortunately omitting two variations (Teldec 90890). **Fiorentino** couples 1 with Scriabin's 1 and 4 in beautifully intense, serious readings (APR 5556). **Lill** plays 1 with the Op. 16 pieces in rather monolithic performances somewhat akin to Beret's (Nimbus 5575). And you should consider **Weissenberg**'s incandescent, demonic performance of 1, released in a collection of various composers (Philips 456988, 2CD). His version of both was once on DG 427499, in which he whipped through them in an astonishing 44 minutes!

Sonata 2 (revised) is featured by **Claudette Sorel** in a set also containing Op. 16, the early *Nocturnes,* and assorted preludes, all played with such total organization as to miss the lyrical moments (Emsco). The revised 2 is most persuasively advocated by **Wild,** along with as many preludes as he can accommodate on a single disc (♦Chesky 114). **Thibaudet** plays it with fleet-fingered glibness (Decca 458930). **Nikolai Lugansky** fails to make anything much of it (Vanguard), but **Marshev** gives a brooding performance that does make it work (Danacord 525). **Browning** offers a fine, broadly conceived 2 in the original version, with a selection of short pieces (Delos 3044).

Then there are two contrasted readings on RCA, both chosen also by Philips for their "Great Pianists" series: **Cliburn** in the original 2 (RCA 63612 or Philips 456748, 2CD) in a live performance of his own arrangement, a bit congested in sound and spirit, but fascinating nonetheless, and **Horowitz** in his inimitable compromise, recorded in 1980, coupled with his memorable live performance of Concerto 3 with Ormandy and the New York Philharmonic (RCA 63681). The Horowitz version is also played by **Nelson Goerner** in a performance rather similar to that of the arranger (Cascavelle 1037). Another arrangement of particular interest is provided by **Ashkenazy,** combining elements of both versions in a committed performance, coupled with his important reading of the Preludes (♦Decca 414417, 2CD). The original 2 is also played by **Mark Gurovsky** in a lovely but somewhat rambling manner (Sonora), and **Lill** also fails to hold it together (Nimbus). **Kocsis,** on the other hand, gives a coruscating performance (Philips 446220, with selected short pieces). **Freddy Kempf** is occasionally diffident but colorful (BIS 1042).

Variations on a Theme by Chopin and *Variations on a Theme by Corelli.* The *Chopin Variations* seemed too long to the composer at one point, and he suggested that some might be omitted. He also wrote a loud ending as an alternative to the original soft one. The late *Corelli Variations* are more concise and perhaps more subtle. **Wild** plays both sets in an outstanding 1992 recording (Chesky 58). Less overtly virtuosic than his earlier discs, these are thoughtful, lyrical performances of real depth. He takes the soft ending in *Chopin.* **Bolet** also plays the ruminative ending in his poised reading (Decca 421061). **Shelley** plays the variations with insight, using the barnstorming ending (Hyperion 66009). **Berezovsky** takes the composer at his word and omits variations 12 and 14, rather spoiling an otherwise excellent reading (Teldec 90890). **Rodriguez** plays them all, with the quiet ending, in a performance blending virtuosity with musical intensity (Elan 82248). **Biret** plays them intelligently but not very warmly (Naxos 554426). **Francesco Nicolosi** is technically assured in both, rhapsodic and tender, though the sound seems to be filtered through gauze (Nuova Era 7168).

Corelli Variations have been recorded no less than three times by **Ashkenazy.** His youthful 1958 reading is now on Testament 1046. The 1972 recording is warmer in sound, coupled with *Etudes-Tableaux* and all the two-piano works (London 444845, 2CD). Then in 1985 he recorded them again with the *Etudes* in somewhat brighter sound (Decca 417671). All his readings are outstanding. **Shelley** is also excellent, particularly for his sense of detail and artful tempo relationships. **Kathryn Stott** is also sensitive to the inner workings of this Cinderella of Rachmaninoff's works (Conifer 159).

More recently, **Vladimir Viardo** included it in an otherwise-Medtner disc, in a rather small-scaled reading (Elektra/Nonesuch). **Thibaudet** likewise misses the depths of this work (Decca). **Nikolai Lugansky** comes closer in idiom, though not approaching Ashkenazy in conviction (Vanguard 99009). **Marshev** turns in an expansive and deeply felt performance (Danacord 525), and **Pletnev** presents an involving reading on Rachmaninoff's own Steinway (DG 459634). **Mark Gurovsky** characterizes each variation with musicality, though he's not very exciting overall (Sonora).

Opp. 3, 10, and 16. These three early opuses are not usually recorded complete outside of the major collections. The five pieces of Op. 3, however, were recorded by the composer at different times. All but the *Elegie* may be heard in the complete **Rachmaninoff** album, while "A Window in Time" (Telarc 80489) contains all five pieces in earlier readings for player piano. Other recordings include **Marshev** in an effective presentation coupled with less satisfying versions of the truncated Sonata 2 and *Corelli Variations* (Danacord 525). **Rodriguez** is also excellent, substituting *Chopin Variations* for *Corelli* in more impressive versions of everything (Elan 82248).

All the early pieces were combined on one disc by **Ruth Laredo,** though her playing isn't very subtle in characterizing these varied pieces (Sony). **Hobson** omits the famous C-sharp Minor Prelude from his recording and lacks something in both temperament and lyricism (Arabesque 6685). **Shelley** plays the Opp. 10 and 16 collections with somewhat greater success, though he also lacks total commitment (Hyperion 66184). **Thiollier** plays all three opuses along with the two sets of variations in exciting, temperamental readings (Thesis 82006).

Transcriptions. Rachmaninoff as performer made a number of transcriptions of other people's music as well as his own. He recorded many of them himself, of course, but there are collections by other pianists as well. **Janice Weber** made a disc of them, played in rather pedestrian fashion (Pickwick). **Shelley**'s disc has much more character (Hyperion 66486), while **Hobson** is elegant and expressive (Arabesque 6663). **Beret** lacks the ideal light touch, but plays an interesting program (Naxos 550978). **Wild** made his own transcriptions of many Rachmaninoff songs, played with his inimitable fluency (Dell'Arte 7001).

Music for more than one pianist. This category includes the two suites for two pianos Opp. 5 and 17, a *Russian Rhapsody* from 1891, and an arrangement of the late *Symphonic Dances.* There are also six duets for piano four-hands Op. 11 and two pieces for piano six hands, plus a Romance and *Polka Italienne.* All of the above are very well played by **Edwin Bruce, Martin Jones,** and **Richard McMahon** (AVM 3026). **Ingrid Thorson** and **Julian Thurber** also play this entire collection well, though the sound is a bit lacking in atmosphere (Paula 46, 2CD). **Brigitte Engerer** and **Oleg Maisenberg** are even better in style and expressiveness, though the sound varies from piece to piece (Harmonia Mundi 901301/2, 2CD).

Less inclusive collections include one by **John Ogden** and **Brenda Lucas** of the suites, duets, and Polka coupled with work by other composers, played with clarity but aggressively recorded (Classics for Pleasure 144383, 2CD). The suites and *Symphonic Dances* are played with fine ensemble but with odd tempo choices and a side-by-side piano placement by **Shelley** and **Hilary MacNamara** (Hyperion 66375). **Argerich** and **Rabinovitch** give hell-for-leather readings of the same (Teldec 74717), less impressive than her earlier Suite 2 with **Freire** (Philips 411034). **Alexeev** and **Demidenko** play Suite 2, *Symphonic Dances,* and *Russian Rhapsody* with some Medtner in excitingly propulsive readings (Hyperion 66654). The two suites and duets are effectively played by **Cynthia Raim** and **David Allen Weir** (Connoisseur Society 4214). Most satisfying of all are **Ashkenazy** and **Previn,** whose warmly recorded suites, *Dances,* and Rhapsody are presently coupled with the Op. 33 *Etudes-Tableaux* and *Corelli Variations* (♦London 444845, 2CD).

The two suites are played by **Lyubov Bruk** and **Mark Taimonov,** a famous duo of yesteryear; their Suite 1 is special, but the recorded sound for 2 isn't as good (Philips 456736, 2CD). **Nikolay Lugansky** and **Vadim Rudenko** play both suites outstandingly in excellent recordings (Triton 18). **Wild** and **Christian Steiner** play *Symphonic Dances* and the Waltz from Suite 2 with a panache all their own (Ivory 70803). The Duets Op. 11 are played with charm by **Wolfgang Manz** and **Rolf Plagge** in the course of a Russian program (Discover 920150). **Tal** and **Andreas Groethuysen** play them even better (♦Sony 47199, with Dvořák and Rubinstein). MOORE

CHORAL MUSIC

The Bells. *The Bells* and *All-Night Vigil* were Rachmaninoff's two favorite works, and it's not hard to see why. In *The Bells* he attempts a daring musical union with Konstantin Balmont's metaphysical paraphrase of Poe's evocative poem.

Kitaienko offers the best sounding recording, luring us on a smooth, punchless journey that takes its time in making points (Chandos). **Ashkenazy**'s reading is crisp, up-tempo, and very much alive. The chorus is clean, precise, and manic, portraying a raw, earthy sense of uneasiness. He defines for us the "ebb and flow" of the tide, the "banging and clanging" of the bells in a way no other recording quite matches (♦London 455798). **Kondrashin** offers a midpriced, vintage reading of great presence that's offset by the brash primary colors of too-close sound and coarse orchestral playing (RCA).

Shaw's version has great dignity and control, though it's not a life-and-death experience. Yet his sound is superb, and the chorus is the best on record, with sparkling, diction-perfect English. Fleming is recorded in natural perspective and renders the most beautiful singing of any soprano on disc (♦Telarc 80365). In Philadelphia with **Dutoit,** detail is lost—the edges soft, neatly tucked and turned in a manner thoroughly foreign to Rachmaninoff (London). **Neeme Järvi**'s recording allows the bass line to come ringing through, and the chorus is robust, full, and vibrant. These bells don't have the visceral impact of Ashkenazy's, but they're terrifying, fierce, and warlike, adding up to a remarkable performance in full, rich sound (♦Chandos 8476). **Slatkin** gives us a beautiful opening, with well-judged tempos and nicely shaped transitions. The choir is excellent, and the sound is almost perfect, as is the St. Louis Symphony, with events rollicking along at an exciting pace (♦Vox 3002).

Spring. This marvelous, unduly neglected cantata—based on the tale of a man forced to live through the winter with his unfaithful wife—seethes with romanticism and expressionism. **Kitaienko**'s reading with the incomparable Hynninen is clearly the leader of the pack (♦Chandos 8966). The orchestra pulsates with life, painting a very realistic picture of spring descending into winter darkness. Far too much detail is lost in **Dutoit**'s recording. It's cluttered and claustrophobic, foiling the fine chorus and orchestra (London). **Slatkin** energetically gives his all in a thrilling performance, but he's also more episodic, inhibiting momentum. Yet this boxed set is too good to pass up (♦Vox 3002).

Three Russian Songs. These aren't heard often, and it's a shame, for their delightful melodies and lively poetry make for enticing listening. **Dutoit**'s recording is a nonstarter because of the failed discmates, *The Bells* and *Spring* cantata (London). **Slatkin,** on the other hand, presents us with a dramatic, colorful canvas full of instrumental *sturm* and choral *drang* (♦Vox 3002).

All-Night Vigil. This towering monument to the art of Russian Orthodox church singing stands not only as the supreme summation of that tradition, but also as one of the half-dozen or so truly great a cappella works ever composed. **Georgi Robev** offers an impassioned, high-level performance of great commitment and style, marred by the formidable acoustics of St. Alexander Nevsky Cathedral (Capriccio). **Shaw** leaves nothing to doubt or to chance. When a rumbling, overpowering sound occurs, it's because the passage is marked forte, not because of any out-of-control emotional outburst. The sound is superb, and the mellifluous, serenely calming power of this music comes through in one of the highlights of Shaw's long career (♦Telarc 80172).

Chernushenko has made many recordings, but none more thrilling and spectacularly sung than with the Glinka Choir, a life-affirming, intense reading of great emotional compass. The sound has a warm and promotive vibrancy with tremendous vigor and impact (♦Olympia 247). His later version, almost as good and in great sound, may be easier to obtain (♦Saison Russe 788050). The results of **Matthew Best** and his brilliant Corydon Singers are decidedly mixed—a model of English reserve, eloquently presented in cuffs and tails (Hyperion). **Rostropovich** elicits the most fabulous all-around performance on disc. The sound is like liquid air; the massed ensemble has a whopping impact; and the tempos are liturgical instead of meditative or reflective. This is a sleek, spectacular recording, surely one of Erato's best (♦Erato 45269).

Liturgy of St. John Chrysostom. Written five years earlier than the more popular (and far better) *All-Night Vigil*, Rachmaninoff's liturgy attempts to recreate the spirit of the Russian church. The work isn't without beauty, but hindsight knows what followed and reacts accordingly.

   Anthony Antolini spent a lot of time researching and correcting the parts for this work (Bison). His choir, not professional, sings with great dedication, though some technical hurdles ensnare them. The sound is compressed, with very little reverberation. **Abalyan** eliminates too much of the work; the entire disc amounts to less than an hour, so it's not a bargain (Sony). **Korniev** is plagued, as he is in all his Philips recordings, by muddy sound and over-the-top interpretation (Philips). **Mikhail Milkov** somehow unlocks the chorus-drowning secrets of St. Alexander Nevsky Cathedral to produce the finest version of this problematic work yet. The 1978 analog sound is just fine, with great presence, a wide spectrum, and—most important—a choir that fully understands the work and is able to compensate for its shortcomings (♦EMI 68664). The Kansas City Chorale gives us a sonically unsullied, calculated interpretation under the direction of **Charles Bruffy** (Nimbus). Though sung impeccably, with virtuosity and flair, it's too dissected for my taste.   RITTER

OPERAS

Rachmaninoff wrote only three short operas early in his career. For almost two years, he was chief conductor of Moscow's Bolshoi Opera; after his sudden resignation in 1906, he never composed another stage work, though he started several such projects.

Aleko (1892). This was the first of the three and remains the most popular (though that is a relative term). It was composed in 17 days to satisfy a graduation requirement of the Moscow Conservatory, was immediately accepted for performance and publication, and launched Rachmaninoff's career as a composer. The story is based on the Pushkin poem *The Gypsies*. The wandering Aleko joins a band of gypsies and falls in love with Zemfira. She gets tired of him and his abuse, and, like Carmen, takes up a new lover, and when Aleko catches the two in a midnight tryst, he kills them both. Under gypsy law, no retaliation or violent punishment is permitted, but Aleko is expelled from their community.

   Aleko has been recorded several times, most recently by the Bolshoi Opera led by **Andrei Tchistiakov** together with the other two operas (♦Saison Russe 288079). It's recommended for its generally fine cast, headed by Vladimir Matorin in the title role, excellent chorus, and good sound. A previous recording from 1987 can be recommended as an alternative. Evgeny Nestorenko sings Aleko, and the supporting cast is also quite good (♦Melodiya 00049). There also exists a 1973 Balkanton performance that doesn't have as good a cast or as good a chorus and orchestra as the two listed above (Capriccio).

The Miserly Knight. Rachmaninoff next set to music a somewhat shortened version of another Pushkin poem that deals with a stingy Baron

and his spendthrift son who, when his father refuses his endless requests for money, decides to poison him so he can pay off his usurious creditor. The orchestral score of this opera is more indebted to Wagner than *Aleko*, which owed more to Tchaikovsky. It has been rarely performed, even in Russia, and outside of Russia not until 1993 in a concert performance in Paris. There is only one recording, led by **Tchistiakov** with the Bolshoi Opera (Saison Russe 288079). The highlight of the work is a 23-minute monologue by the Baron as he admires the gold and treasures in his vault. The role was written for Chaliapin, and is well performed by Mikhail Krutikov.

Francesca da Rimini. This is Rachmaninoff's final stage work and is based on the well-known story in Dante's *Divine Comedy*. Rachmaninoff's setting, like his other operas, only takes an hour or so. The Saison Russe recording led by **Tchistiakov** can again be recommended. The main role, also intended for Chaliapin, is sung by Matorin, who is as effective as in *Aleko*.   MOSES

SONGS

Rachmaninoff was a great melodist, but his songs, with a few exceptions, aren't notably melodic. They are passionate, declamatory, and sometimes impressionistic; the composer was more concerned with laying bare the emotional import of the texts than with writing good tunes. The elaborate piano accompaniments demand a virtuoso player and can overwhelm the singer. Rachmaninoff's symphonies may be as approachable as Tchaikovsky's, but his songs are not. The listener needs to know what the words mean, so anyone unfamiliar with Russian must look first for recordings that include texts and translations.

   The best starting point is the generous (and slightly confusing) Chandos collection. Three discs are shared by a quartet of singers: Joan Rodgers, Maria Popescu, Alexandre Naoumenko, and Sergei Leiferkus (♦9405, 9451, 9477). The pianist is Howard Shelley. **Leiferkus** is the dominant contributor, and if he's no Chaliapin (the bass for whom Rachmaninoff wrote many of his songs), he's an interesting, vibrant interpreter, despite a somewhat dry, gritty voice. Rodgers has a sweet, fresh soprano, and she's very appealing in many of the more lyrical numbers. Rodgers and Leiferkus each have a solo disc, duplicating their contributions to the complete set (Chandos 9374 and 9644). Yet another Chandos disc was made by a fifth singer, **Sergei Larin,** who repeats some of the songs that had already been recorded (9562). If Leiferkus is no Chaliapin, Larin is no Sobinov, but he's a more interesting singer than Naoumenko and chooses a broad range of material. His voice is on the bright, penetrating side, best savored in small doses.

   Dimitri Kharitonov, a light baritone, offers a mellower alternative to Leiferkus (♦EMI 56814). Andsnes accompanies, and texts are supplied. **Hvorostovsky** has a more beautiful voice, and has included a good selection in three separate recitals, one of which—the earliest, coupled with Tchaikovsky, and the most appealing—is NA (Philips 42536, 46666). He's not a particularly imaginative singer, but it's a pleasure to listen to him. Even better is the great Armenian baritone **Pavel Lisitsian,** whose collection offers 10 Rachmaninoff songs with 14 by Tchaikovsky; the singing is gorgeous, but texts are absent (Russian Disc 15021).

   The usually reliable **Gedda** is not at his best in an EMI disc, also without texts. He's distressingly inaccurate in the famous *Vocalise* (written for the coloratura soprano Nezhdanova), despite a strong high C-sharp and a passable trill, and his forte singing is generally labored. **Robert Tear** comes fairly cheap and adds some charming Chopin fillers (Belart). His voice isn't all that beguiling, but the interpretations are earnest and intelligent. More recommendable are the haunting **de Gaetani** (Arabesque) and the colorful, richly hued contralto of **Podles** (Forlane), though each sings only a handful of Rachmaninoff songs.

A plea, finally, for a reissue of perhaps the most admired collection: **Söderström** and Ashkenazy, originally on four Decca LPs. So far Decca has given us only one parsimonious selection from the complete set, in a single CD that wasn't long on the market. You might not think one soprano could sustain interest through so many songs, but Söderström is consistently colorful, perceptive, and often breathtakingly lovely. The collector may also want to search for deleted LPs made by **Vishnevskaya** (DG), **Arkhipova** (EMI), and **Christoff** (EMI), as well for recordings of performers from the old Russian school who were alive when Rachmaninoff was composing. As for that notorious *Vocalise*, the purely orchestral recordings outnumber those with voice and piano. **Moffo** and Stokowski are rather self-indulgent in the conductor's own arrangement, but they remain irresistible (RCA).   LUCANO

Joachim Raff (1822–1882)

Swiss-born but generally considered a German composer, Raff was a major figure in the late 19th century; his symphonies filled the concert halls until Brahms began writing his own. His mastery of orchestration is reflected by the commonly held belief that he actually scored several of Liszt's tone poems. Surely Raff's finest symphony is the 5th, *Lenore*, one of the great unsung masterpieces of the Romantic era. Based on a ballad by Gottfried August Bürger, the music tells of the unfortunate maiden Lenore who despairs for her lover Wilhelm, who is slain on the battlefield. When his specter calls to her, she joins him in a wild ride, at once terrifying and thrilling, that leads even unto the gates of Hell, before she finally ascends to heaven in rapturous transfiguration.

That we may know this wonderful music at all is the legacy of Bernard Herrmann, who often championed the score in his radio broadcasts with the CBS Symphony and later recorded it with the London Philharmonic (♦Unicorn/Kanchana 2031). Herrmann sets forth this music in all its Gothic splendor, and the recording resonates with warmth and glowing vitality, bringing out details that seem muffled in **Butt**'s more dispassionate CD (ASV). **Bamert** is treated even more shabbily by his engineers; the diffuse, bland sonics render his earnest account ineffective (Koch/Schwann). **Urs Schneider** comes closer to Herrmann; his reading seems a bit too unrelenting in its visceral impact but remains a worthy contender (Marco Polo 223455). Fortunately, the most recent version is also the best since Hermann's, a rapturous account by **Nicholas Carthy** (♦Dynamic 283); if you have this plus the Herrmann, you don't need any others.

After *Lenore*, Raff's greatest achievement is his Symphony 3, *Im Walde* (In the Forest), which in its bucolic imagery and full-throated passion rivals even Beethoven's "Pastoral." For a long time, record buyers had to make do with **Richard Kapp**'s LP, which was grossly disfigured by a massive cut in the last movement (Candide). Even more frustrating, the first CD of the score by **Schneider** made the same cut, rendering the last movement unlistenable (Marco Polo). Fortunately, *Im Walde* is available complete in two different but equally stimulating readings, with **Davan Wetton** (♦Hyperion 66628, with Symphony 4), and **d'Avalos** (ASV 793, with less substantial fare). If Davan Wetton seems more impassioned in the opening movement, he permits the rapt introduction to the final tableau to unfold with surpassing breadth, and he fields the shifting images that follow with more restraint, whereas d'Avalos is inclined to simply press ahead. I'd go with Davan Wetton, not least for the substantial coupling.

While several composers have set the four seasons of the year to music, surely none has done so with quite the resolve of Raff, who parceled them out to each of his last four symphonies: 8 is Spring, 9 Summer, 10 Autumn, and 11 Winter (left unfinished at Raff's death and completed by a pupil). Symphony 8, with the Basel Radio Orchestra led by **György Lehel,** has been reissued, accompanied by *Ode au Printemps* for piano and orchestra (Tudor 784). Symphony 9, with **Jean-Marie Auberson** and the same Basel forces, is joined by the Piano Concerto (Tudor 785). Both 8 and 9 have been coupled by **Schneider,** who offers good value, but his brisk tempos, though undeniably exhilarating, often seem dictated by the need to accommodate both symphonies in one CD (Marco Polo 223362). In general, the Tudor discs are more attractive, though both conductors inexplicably omit about three minutes from the last movement of 9.

While 10 may be had with **Schneider** (Marco Polo 223321), the heavily cut *Im Walde* with it would pretty much rule it out; fortunately, **Lehel**'s recording is far better both musically and sonically (♦Tudor 786). **Francis Travis** offers a more sumptuous repast; the music fairly glows, with the lusty Basel Radio Symphony horns simply blowing the Košice forces away in the final hunt. Symphony 11 (Winter) may be enjoyed with **Mario Venzago** (Tudor 787, with the *Sinfonietta*) and **Schneider** (Marco Polo 223529, with 4). I prefer Venzago's broader stride in I, and his less precipitous tempo in IV brings out the infectious good humor of the wind writing, but his rather brisk tempo for "By the Fireside" tends to dissipate the seductive nature of the music. Sonically they're on a par, and string honors are evenly divided, but again the Basel horns are far better than their Košice counterparts.

The remaining symphonies are all worth adding to your collection, and save for 4 there's no competition for Marco Polo. The only one not conducted by **Schneider** is 1, *An der Vaterland,* offered by **Samuel Friedman;** at 70 minutes, it's also the longest (223165). For a first effort, it's well worth investigating for those willing to meet it halfway. Symphony 2 might be thought of as Raff's "Pastoral" and is effectively put across by Schneider (223630). Symphony 4 may also be had from Schneider (223529, with 11) and **Davan Wetton** (♦Hyperion 66628, with 3); Schneider has the edge for string ensemble, but the wide array of wind colors offered by Davan Wetton (not to mention his splendid *Im Walde*) makes it a more attractive proposition. Symphony 6 easily makes up in sheer energy what it lacks in melodic inspiration; it's been recorded by Schneider (Marco Polo 223638), who completed the series with 7 (*In den Alpen;* 223506).

Sinfonietta for winds is sheer delight from start to finish and makes an attractive companion for Venzago's Symphony 11 (Tudor 787), particularly since the import LP with **Leopoldo Casella** directing a Swiss ensemble was heavily cut (CTS).

Complementing Marco Polo's impressive survey of the symphonies is a disc featuring two highly evocative works, *Aus Thüringen* and *Italian Suite,* conducted by **Edlinger** (223194). Several other short pieces turn up as fillers. The overture *Ein' feste Burg ist unser Gott,* employing the Martin Luther chorale already familiar from Mendelssohn's "Reformation" Symphony, is coupled with 5 by **Schneider** and is also offered by **Pinchas Steinberg** as makeweight with 10 (Tudor 786); Schneider is more propulsive, though Steinberg's broader tempo imparts more strength of character to the closing pages. Also included with 6 by Schneider are *Dame Kobold* Overture, *Fest-Ouvertüre*—based on a German anthem we know as "My Country 'Tis of Thee"—and *Festmarsch*.

The Shakespearean overtures *Macbeth* and *Romeo and Juliet* are coupled with 2 by **Schneider,** while **d'Avalos** plays *Romeo and Juliet* and the rhapsody *Im Abend* along with 3; both versions are worth having. The *Concert Overture in F* makes an attractive bonus with Schneider's 7. If you do buy **Butt**'s *Lenore,* you'll also get a "Salon Suite" comprising what used to be called "Raff's celebrated Cavatina" as well as a *Scherzino, Canzona,* and *Tarantella,* all arranged from the Op. 85 *Morceaux*—pleasant listening, but not enough to recommend the disc.

Raff's splendid Piano Concerto is one of his most impressive achievements, striding forward much in the manner of Liszt's *Mazeppa* in the final Allegro—itself a heroic transformation of the grand theme of the opening movement. And like *Mazeppa,* the martial finale comes across more effectively when treated broadly, as **Jean-François Antonioli** does so persuasively (Claves 8806, coupled appropriately with the equally attractive *Ode au Printemps*). **Ponti** holds his own in both pieces, with the Concerto included in Vol. 4 of the "Romantic Piano Concerto" series (Vox 5067) and the *Ode* in Vol. 7 (Vox 5098); both are thrillingly put across, even though Ponti isn't inclined to stop and smell the roses in either piece and there are a few cuts in the Concerto. A more recent CD coupled both pieces in highly sympathetic readings by **Peter Aronsky** (Tudor 7035; however, I'd rather have them in the original Tudor issues coupled with 9 and 8, respectively).

While not on the same exalted level as his Piano Concerto, Raff's two violin concertos are highly melodic and offer an exhilarating workout for the soloist, in this case the estimable Michaela Paetsch Neftel (♦Tudor 7086). HALLER

Jean-Philippe Rameau *(1683–1764)*

Rameau was the reluctant hero of the French Baroque, a musician whose famous *Traité de l'harmonie* (1722), the first systematic investigation of modern harmonic practice, garnered significantly more notoriety (good and bad) than his early harpsichord compositions. He remained virtually unknown until his forties, when he had the good fortune to gain the ear of the famous La Poupelinière, the most influential music patron in Paris. Like Brahms and the symphony, Rameau came to his most successful genre (opera) late in life, at age 50. He did so brilliantly, although once again he found himself the center of controversy. Adherents to the older operatic style of Lully decried Rameau's music as "abstruse, difficult, grotesque, thick, mechanical, and unnatural." Twenty years later, during the famous "War of the Buffoons," a heated debate that raged in Paris over the relative merits of French and Italian opera, Rameau would be regarded as the champion of French music by many of the same critics who had lambasted his early operas!

Despite all the politics, and especially despite Rameau's obstinate, unyielding personality, he has come to be regarded by later generations as the epitome of French musicians, equaled in the 18th century only by Couperin. Nowadays, Rameau ranks as one of the most accessible (and recordable) of Baroque composers; only Bach, Handel, Vivaldi, and Telemann are as popular.

The logical place to start, then, is with Rameau's most characteristic music, his compositions for harpsichord. Many of these pieces will be familiar even to non-early-music audiences; titles such as *La Poule* and *Les trois mans* have been featured in countless piano recitals since the time of Liszt. Unlike many other Baroque composers, Rameau had the foresight to limit the total playing time of his harpsichord music to just over two hours, in other words, the length of two CDs. Beginning in the LP era, *Premier livre, Pièces de clavecin,* and *Nouvelles suites* have seen several excellent recordings, including those by Kenneth Gilbert, Pinnock, Christie, and Scott Ross, though only the first three have made it to CD.

However, it's the set by the young French harpsichordist **Christophe Rousset** that is by far the most stimulating (Oiseau-Lyre 425886, 2CD). With a superb original instrument and gorgeous recorded sound, this is an interpretation that underlines the dramatic, virtuosic side of Rameau, as well it should. **Christie**'s set at budget price is an acceptable alternate, aristocratic but somewhat understated (Harmonia Mundi 1901120, 2 CD). A further item to consider is Rameau's own transcription of orchestral music from his opera *Les Indes galantes* for solo harpsichord, available in a budget CD featuring **Gilbert** (Harmonia Mundi 1901028).

An adjunct to the harpsichord music is *Pièces de clavecin en concerts,* available in Rameau's own arrangements for violin, viol, and harpsichord, with optional flute part. This is, in fact, Rameau's only major set of chamber music, and offers more of the same kind of effervescent, outgoing music you find in the harpsichord suites. There have been two period instrument recordings of this material, but luckily the classic **Kuijken-Brüggen-Leonhardt** recording from 1972 has been reissued, at a budget price to boot (Teldec 77618). The sound has held up well, and the "star power" of these Belgian and Dutch period instrumentalists is undeniable.

We're fortunate to have most of Rameau's early operas available in definitive performances by specialists in French Baroque opera. His string of early operas, up to and including *Dardanus,* contains his most important theatrical works. **Christie** and Les Arts Florissants started the ball rolling in the late '80s with brilliant recordings of *Les Indes galantes* (Harmonia Mundi 901367, 3CD) and *Castor et Pollux* (Harmonia Mundi 9014435, 3CD). The latter is generally considered to be Rameau's operatic masterpiece. Then came **Minkowski** and Les Musiciens du Louvre in 1995 with their dazzling realization of Rameau's first opera, *Hippolyte et Aricie* (Archiv 445853, 3CD), followed by their equally effective production of *Dardanus* (Archiv 463476, 2CD). It's fascinating to compare the two conductors' approach to Rameau's challenging music. While Minkowski is more astute at discovering and developing the drama inherent in the score, he often chooses singers who are much too 20th-century "operatic" (with vibrato) to be believable. Christie, on the other hand, invariably selects singers with smooth, ingratiating voices and an idiomatic style, but his pacing often drags. As with so many things in life, the ideal approach would be a combination of the best elements of both, but that doesn't exist.

Many listeners, myself included, find listening to baroque opera on CD a challenging proposition, something like a long-distance romance with a beautiful woman through the mail. The missing visual element makes the difference, especially in the case of French opera, with its emphasis on spectacle and ballet. I suppose that's why the record companies have been eager to record instrumental suites from Rameau's operas; costs are greatly reduced by dispensing with all those pesky singers, and the discs inevitably sell well.

Nobody does this better than **Frans Brüggen** and the Orchestra of the 18th Century; their recordings of suites from *Les Boréades* (*Abaris*) and *Dardanus* (Philips 420240), *Les Indes galantes* (Philips 438946) and *Acante et Céphise* and *Les Fêtes d'Hébé* (Glossa 921103) fairly crackle with excitement and energy, and the recording quality ranges from good (Philips) to exceptional (Glossa). Another excellent rendition of orchestral suites comes from **McGegan** and the Philharmonia Baroque Orchestra of San Francisco, arguably America's finest period-instrument group. The disc contains suites drawn from *Platée* and *Dardanus,* and the recorded sound is of demonstration quality (Conifer 51313). An earlier recording with McGegan and the Philharmonia Baroque featured suites from *Le Temple de la gloire* and *Naïs,* both later, rather inconsequential stage works whose music is probably best enjoyed in this format (Harmonia Mundi 907121).

Finally, a disc containing Rameau's opera overtures (all 17) by **Rousset** and Les Talens Lyriques is extraordinary (Oiseau-Lyre 455293). The playing from this crack French ensemble of period instrumentalists is beyond belief: ultraprecise yet spontaneous, even a trifle capricious, as if the music were being improvised on the spot. It's a must!

Like Couperin, Rameau wrote a limited amount of sacred music; what there is fits neatly in one CD. The five Latin motets are fairly lavish productions for solo voice, chorus, orchestra, and continuo in the style of Lully, and have received well-nigh definitive performances from **Hervé Niquet** and Le Concert Spirituel (Virgin 61526).

BRODERSEN

Shulamit Ran (b. 1949)

Unlike many of her contemporaries, the Israeli-American composer Shulamit Ran shuns the neoromantic mantle and relentlessly pursues the modernist path. Her music probes and arouses, startles and amuses, calms and terrifies, often in the same piece. Winner of the Pulitzer Prize in 1991 for her Symphony 1, she has written an opera, many orchestral works, and several chamber pieces. Many of her pieces have oddly expressive titles, such as *Hyperbolae, Double Vision, Inscriptions, Hatzvi Israel Eulogie, O the Chimneys,* and *Amichai Songs.* Her music is every bit as evocative as her titles. She's exploratory, witty, and suggestive, sometimes painting the doors of development without opening them. There's no telling what she'll come up with next, except that it will be something extraordinary.

Regrettably, only a small portion of her work has been released on CD. Her best piece, *Concerto da Camera II* for chamber ensemble, plays like a mid-20th-century concerto for orchestra. It begins as a showcase for clarinet, piano, and string quartet; then the focus shifts from one instrument to the other as players compete for the stage like Japanese Kabuki performers. It has been recorded twice: by the **Contemporary Chamber Players** of the University of Chicago (CRI 609) and by the **Da Capo Chamber Players** (Bridge 9052). The former present a brisk, idiosyncratic rendition in sound that's slightly muddy at times, while the latter has a more controlled pacing, with a pronounced respect for rhythmic subtleties. Also, the Bridge release divides the three movements into discrete CD tracks, whereas CRI combines them for some odd reason.

In the other piece these two CDs share, the sensuous *Private Game* (1979), the performances are virtually equal. No surprise, since they are both excellently played by **Laura Flax** and Andre Emelianoff, Da Capo's clarinetist and cellist. Other chamber works on the Da Capo disc include Ran's evocative solo works: the Varèse-inspired *East Wind I* (1987) for flute, the exploratory and tenuous *Inscriptions I* (1991) for violin, and the playful musical essay, *For an Actor: Monologue for Clarinet* (1978). The most strikingly unique work on the Contemporary Chamber Players CD is the spooky vocal piece *Apprehensions* (1979), based on a disturbed poem by American poet Sylvia Plath. Soprano Judith Nicosia sings it with sardonic pathos.

The **English Chamber Orchestra** (Koch 7269) does a marvelous job with Ran's callow *Three Fantasy Movements* (1971/1993). Orchestrator Cliff Colnot transformed this erstwhile cello sonata into a frenetic cello concerto, but it retains much of its youthful exuberance as well as its excesses. More worthwhile on this CD is String Quartet 1 (1988-89), a robust, passionate work with motives that appear and disappear with jolt-

ing frequency. It's tautly performed by the **Mendelssohn String Quartet,** for whom it was composed.

BATES

Ture Rangström (1884–1947)

Rangström is known in his native Sweden primarily for his hundreds of songs. After studying at the Stockholm Conservatory, he made his name as a singer, a singing teacher, a music critic, and as conductor of the Göteborg Symphony Orchestra. With Atterberg, he belonged to the so-called "young generation" of Swedish composers for his progressive tendencies and interest in expressionism. In the 1910s, Swedish orchestras rebelled against his music's "modernism" (an early nickname was "Sturm-und-Drangström"). Sibelius thought him the best Swedish composer of his time.

A generally fine 3CD set of Rangström's four symphonies conducted by **Jurowski** is available for the price of two (CPO 999748, also available separately). There's little competition. **Segerstam** and **Janos Fürst,** respectively, offer Symphonies 1 and 3 (Sterling 1014). I have heard neither, but critics seem to prefer Jurowski.

Rangström's literary interests appear in his Symphony 1 (1914; "August Strindberg in memoriam"). It's thickly orchestrated and highly emotional, and it certainly suggests Strindbergian *Sturm und Drang.* Symphony 2 (1919) might be called Rangström's "Pastorale." Here he found greater subtlety than in 1, and the nature-painting in the middle movement is particularly beautiful. Symphony 3 (1929; "Song Under the Stars") is in one movement. Rangström wrote that it was "nothing more than a solo song, without words, scored for large orchestra." At 22 minutes, this is the most approachable of the four, and a good place to start for the newcomer. The last symphony, "Invocatio," is imposing. It's the Swedish answer, if you will, to Saint-Saëns's "Organ" Symphony. Jurowski's set contains three shorter pieces: *Dithyramb, Intermezzo drammatico* (music "from an [imaginary] oriental fairy play"), and *Vårhymn,* another work inspired by Strindberg.

An inexpensive collection of "Swedish Orchestral Favorites" includes Rangström's *Divertimento elegiaco* for string orchestra; **Petter Sundkvist** conducts (♦Naxos 553715). Fans of Bernard Herrmann, particularly the more elegiac moments of his score to *Psycho,* will respond to this melodic but dark and serious music. The entire disc is very desirable.

A sampling of Rangström's chamber works, unheard by me, has been released (CPO 999689). The score to his ballet *Miss Julie*—another Strindberg inspiration—has also been reissued (Swedish Society Discofil 1040).

TUTTLE

Einojuhani Rautavaara (b. 1928)

Rautavaara is probably Finland's most significant living composer and a major figure in late 20th-century music, whose broad sweep displays a fervid and devotional lyricism, glowing atmosphere, and strikingly original and compelling musical architecture. His growth as a composer reveals a fertile imagination; his diversity of taste and range of knowledge are always carefully marshaled. Each work's secrets slowly unfold as they are lit by the rays and warmth of his orchestral palette. His affirmative and opulent postmodernist idiom is often tempered by acerbic harmonies and polytonality.

His early works show a range of styles from the Waltonian Symphony 1 to the Stravinskian 2 and the postromantic 3. All three can be heard in a recording by the Leipzig Radio Symphony under **Pommer** (Ondine 740). The monumental opening of 3 and its sense of growth give a first true glimpse of mature Rautavaara. The very long phrases, expressive breadth, and strongly independent treatment of different divisions of the orchestra lend the piece an epic quality. The performances are adequate if not spectacular.

The same artists recorded the untamed Symphony 4 and exultantly cavernous 5 (Ondine 747), along with the celebrated and eerily beautiful *Cantus Arcticus,* a concerto for orchestra with taped sounds of Arctic birds. The latter can also be heard (with Symphony 3 and the idiosyncratic but lyrical Piano Concerto 1) in a budget-priced recording by **Hannu Linnu** and the Royal Scottish National Orchestra, superbly played and recorded and highly recommended (♦Naxos 554147).

Pommer's best effort by far is his reading of the deeply enigmatic Symphony 6, a work of floating textures and sudden synthesized sound bursts evoking the world of Van Gogh, whose life inspired an opera by Rautavaara; the disc includes the 1968 Cello Concerto played by **Marko Ylonen** (Ondine 819). The late '60s saw the greatest transformation in Rautavaara's music: Cantabile cello and luminous orchestra easily capture the affections.

However, the best was yet to come: three unforgettable discs by the Helsinki Philharmonic led by the flamboyant **Segerstam**. The first contains one of Rautavaara's finest works: the short tone poem *Isle of Bliss,* a vision of paradise in the dreamlike quality of the music, its gentle serenity and bird-like calls (♦Ondine 881). The delicately balanced Violin Concerto played by Oliveira glides like a bird aloft the thermals only to cascade earthward before soaring once more. The other work on the disc is *Angels and Visitations,* which shares some traits with *Isle* but has its moments of angst.

In the masterful Symphony 7 ("Angel of Light") the brightness is never dazzling, and as the passing shadows become darker the music threatens to plunge into a black hole only to be pulled out by tugging, searing strings. On a second disc it's joined by Karl Jussila playing the organ in the knotty *Annunciations,* a concerto for organ, winds, and brass (♦Ondine 869). Finally, the third disc uncovers another wonder from the late '60s, the tone poem *Anadyomene* ("Adoration of Aphrodite"), if anything more concise than *Isle* but still determinedly lost in its own world of voluptuous reverie (Ondine 921). The Flute Concerto, with Patrick Gallois, almost ballet-like, weaves golden threads, but the light only momentarily catches them. The choral work *The Last Frontier,* whose energy derives from constantly recurring ostinatos, is very intriguing.

Piano Concerto 3 (1998), commissioned and played by **Ashkenazy** and the Helsinki Philharmonic and containing all the luminous virtuosity of the earlier essays for these forces, is counterweighted by the dreamily poetic concerto *Autumn Gardens,* commissioned for the 1999 BBC Proms (Ondine 950). No doubt Symphony 8 ("The Journey"), premiered in Philadelphia in April 2000, will soon appear on disc.

Another series of major orchestral and chamber pieces includes the Double Bass Concerto "Angel of Dusk" played by **Esko Laine** and the Tapiola Sinfonietta under Kantorow (BIS 910, with Symphony 2). Unfortunately, this disc lacks depth of sound, and the solo line in the Concerto is decidedly thin. The Lahti Symphony under **Vänskä** turns in an especially luxuriant Symphony 7, played with greater urgency and transparency than Segerstam but without any loss of breadth (BIS 1038). The same can be said of the Flute Concerto and *Cantus Arcticus* (probably its best recording) that accompany it.

In a compilation of chamber pieces by different performers, sound and quality are variable (BIS 66). The disc is well filled, though, and is valuable for the dainty, almost Brittenesque *Lapsimessu,* a short mass for children's choir with small orchestra; the dark and melancholy but

richly atmospheric String Quartet 4 played by **Voces Intimae Quartet;** and the Clarinet and Flute Sonatas. *Pelimannit* (The Fiddlers) for strings is as chewy as Rautavaara's music can get.

He has proved himself adept at writing vocal and choral music. His *Vigilia,* an Orthodox cantata for unaccompanied choir recorded in Finnish, is, unlike much liturgical music, upbeat and confident as well as meditative. It's exquisitely sung by the Finnish Radio Chamber Choir under **Timo Nuoranne** (ODE 910).

A budget-priced CD of piano music played by **Laura Mikkola** reveals a Francophile side to his personality: Debussy, Ravel, and especially Messiaen stalk the pages of the Etudes Op. 42 (Naxos 554292). The much earlier *Ikonit* (Icons) and *Preludes* betray the influence of Copland and Persichetti at Tanglewood. The two sonatas from 15 years later show that Ravel has finally gained the upper hand, albeit with a keen cutting edge. These are beautifully played and recorded.   JOHNSON

Maurice Ravel *(1875–1937)*

"The only love affair I have ever had was with music," claimed Maurice Ravel. If this was his only affair, it was spectacularly consummated. Trained at the stuffy Paris Conservatoire, he came under the beneficial musical influences of Chabrier, Satie, and Fauré. Add to their gaiety and lack of pretense a dash of Spanish influence and just a bit of American jazz, and you have the compote of Ravel's musical style. While he never won the Prix de Rome, he quickly won a reputation among the avantgarde, then as a 20th-century classic, then as something even rarer: a beloved 20th-century classic.

The music often sounds like the man looked: urbane and beautifully turned out. Only a little over five feet tall, always nattily dressed, he lived in a specially decorated little country house just outside Paris, full of tiny clocks and mechanical toys. (It's still there as a Ravel museum, almost exactly as he left it.) The son of an inventor, Ravel sometimes painted the joys of mechanized sounds in exquisite detail, as in the evocation of a clock shop at the beginning of his opera *L'Heure espagnole;* and what is the unrelenting piling-on of sound in *Boléro* if not a gigantic orchestral machine?

Some complain that this music is all alluring surface and no depth, no passion. If passion were all that mattered, some pretty rotten composers would enter Parnassus—but Ravel's passionate feelings were carefully concealed beneath a lacquer of irony, wit, and consummate craft. Ravel said of critics of his "artifice," "Doesn't it ever occur to these people that I can be 'artificial' by nature?"

ORCHESTRAL MUSIC

Ravel's orchestral works are a mixed bag: a few orchestral originals (*Rapsodie espagnole, Boléro,* and *La Valse*) and many imaginative orchestrations of piano pieces (*Ma mère l'oye, Valses nobles et sentimentales, Le Tombeau de Couperin,* etc.). No symphonies here, but a remarkably varied picture gallery, and, in their attention to lapidary details of weight and color, a persuasive argument for regarding orchestration as an art, not just a craft. A conductor who can't make these perfectly calibrated pieces work doesn't belong on a podium. Rare is the conductor who hasn't at least recorded *Boléro;* most have recorded considerably more than that, and who can blame them?

Complete sets. Highly recommendable sets of Ravel's orchestral works, complete or nearly complete, are available, and none of them are full price! Some of the individual performances of larger works are highlighted below, but they all include the favorite works, and the standards of performance and recording in all of them are very high.

Boulez's stylish, precise performances from the '70s are still treasurable; the 3CD box also includes his complete 1975 *Daphnis et Chloé* with the New York Philharmonic and the Left-Hand Concerto with Entremont (Sony 45842). **Cluytens**'s Paris recordings, made in 1961 and 1962, are authoritative, and offer the distinctive vibrato of old-school French wind and brass playing, not to everyone's taste (EMI 69165). Vestiges of it remain in **Martinon**'s '70s recordings, but these are beautiful performances and a good memorial to an underrated conductor (EMI 68610). (Martinon's 1975 EMI recording of the complete *Daphnis et Chloé*, not included here and not currently available, is one of the very best.)

The elegant limning of **Dutoit** and the Montréal Symphony set the standard in French repertoire for the '80s and '90s (London 460214). **Ozawa**, regarded as an also-ran in most repertory, is first-rate in Ravel and much other French music (DG 439342). This early-'70s set (also including a complete *Daphnis et Chloé*) proved that the Boston Symphony's French tradition, begun by Koussevitzsky and further cultivated by Munch, was in excellent hands. The refined interpretations of **Claudio Abbado** (DG) and **Haitink** (Philips 438745) are enhanced by top-rank orchestras: Abbado has the London and Boston Symphonies, Haitink the Concertgebouw. Don't overlook **Skrowaczewski** and Minnesota: These recordings were hailed in the mid-'70s and still sound beautiful (Vox 5031). Vox has economically coupled them with both Piano Concertos (with Abbey Simon) and the String Quartet in acceptable performances—a good, inexpensive way to get to know a lot of Ravel.

Boléro. In terms of sheer orchestral know-how, Ravel's most popular piece is also his craftiest. ("My masterpiece," the composer called it. "Unfortunately, it contains no music.") For a piece containing no music, *Boléro* can take remarkably varied treatment. You can get it hopped-up (**Munch**, RCA 61856 or 6522), notably slinky (**Bernstein**, Sony 60565), comparatively dignified (**Boulez**, Sony 45842 or DG 38745), or very fast (**Paray**, Mercury 434306, an early stereo showpiece). The **Monteux**/London Symphony recording still sounds beautiful too, and is coupled with lots of equally beautiful Ravel, including one of the best performances ever of *Ma mère l'oye* (Philips 442542).

Another veteran conductor and French music virtuoso, **Ansermet**, offered a strongly characterized *Boléro* (Decca 448576, with *La Valse* and other French favorites like Dukas's *Sorcerer's Apprentice* and Honegger's *Pacific 231*). If you can have only one Ravel CD, **Dohnányi** and the Cleveland Orchestra offer the three "biggies" (*Boléro, La Valse,* and *Daphnis et Chloé Suite* 2) in razor-sharp performances and spectacularly detailed recordings, and midpriced too (Teldec 97439). (Dohnányi's *La Valse* is especially impressive.) For refined sorcery and hypnotic mood, the palm probably goes to the famous 1964 recording by **Karajan** and the Berlin Philharmonic. It has been reissued generously with other orchestral works given the ultra-refined but musically satisfying Karajan touch: Debussy's *La Mer* and the Mussorgsky/Ravel *Pictures at an Exhibition* (DG 447426), or *La Mer* and a magical *Daphnis et Chloé Suite* 2 (DG 427250).

Daphnis et Chloé. Ravel's orchestral masterpiece was written in 1910 for Diaghilev's Ballets Russes. The original production, with its rather thin scenario and anemic choreography, was a failure, but the complete work is now frequently recorded, and deserves to be: With the right orchestra and conductor, this amazingly sumptuous music can be overwhelming, "a vast musical fresco," as the composer described it.

The first great stereo recording of the entire ballet was probably Monteux's, in 1959. It still sounds both disciplined and ravishing (♦London

448603). (A 1955 live performance by Monteux and the Concertgebouw is in Music & Arts 812, but the sound isn't in the same class as London's.) Still ranking high is **Munch**'s incendiary account with the Boston Symphony (RCA 61846); he's a little tough and hectic, but he has undoubted authority, and the orchestral playing—mon Dieu! The most famous modern performance is probably **Dutoit**'s, an early digital recording that brought the Montréal Symphony to a willing public (London 458605). The reissue of **Previn**'s warm and artfully understated London Symphony performance is a great bargain, in fact one of the best *Daphnis et Chloé* recordings, period (♦Seraphim 73293).

Schwarz's reading is beautifully played by the Seattle Symphony, and the recording is second to none (Delos 3110); ditto **Chailly** and the peerless Concertgebouw (London 443934). Rattle's version was lavishly praised by British critics for both performance and recorded sound; you can check it out at a bargain price (EMI 69830, with *Boléro*). For a historical view, try an earlier **Munch** version with the Paris Conservatoire Orchestra, which sizzles through a still-impressive 1946 mono recording (Dutton 1201), or the early-'60s recording by **Cluytens,** with the same group (Testament 1128).

Daphnis et Chloé was for a long time mainly known by its Suite 2, the last third or so of the ballet. Most great (and not so great) conductors have had a go at it, and many of the older ones—classic recordings now at mid-price or lower—remain thoroughly recommendable: **Bernstein** (Sony 60565), **Giulini** (EMI 67723), **Karajan** (DG 27250), **Martinon** (RCA 63683), **Ormandy** (Sony 46274), and **Paray** (Mercury 34306) are easily near the top. All are coupled with congenial French repertoire (except Giulini's, a 2CD "Portrait of the Artist" effort that also includes vintage recordings of Franck, Tchaikovsky, and Britten). Bernstein's collection, divided between the New York Philharmonic and the French National Orchestra, is uneven in quality, including a sexy *Boléro* and a dullish *La Valse*. The **Stokowski**/London Symphony performance (London 455152) is only recommendable to Stoky freaks: There's no end of lush sound, but there's also a little too much messing with the score (including a brand-new sustained fortissimo chord for the chorus at the end!). **Maazel** isn't usually noted for his sensuality, but his Vienna Philharmonic disc, while it contains an overly fussy *Boléro*, also has drop-dead gorgeous versions of Suites 1 and 2 (RCA 68600).

Ma mère l'oye (Mother Goose). Originally written as a piano duet for two children of a friend of Ravel's, this work was expanded by the composer into a ballet several years later. It's the most touching evocation of childhood imaginable (except for his opera *L'Enfant et les sortileges*), innocent and adult at once, and we'd be suspicious of the humanity of a conductor who couldn't do it justice. There are some beauties in the catalog: besides the **Monteux** recording just mentioned, there are two by **Previn**, one from Pittsburgh (Philips 462938), and the other from London (DG 457589, with *L'Enfant et les sortilèges*). **Boulez, Ozawa,** and **Skrowaczewski** all give bewitching performances in their complete sets, and Boulez's newer recording of his dry-eyed but affecting interpretation is superlatively played by the Berlin Philharmonic (DG 38745). **Giulini** and the Los Angeles Philharmonic offer nicely detailed performances of this and *Rapsodie espagnole* (DG 415844), and a cherishable performance of the complete ballet by **Tilson Thomas** and the London Symphony is part of an attractive Debussy/Ravel/Satie bargain package with various conductors and orchestras (Sony 63056).

Rapsodie espagnole. This sultry, virtuoso piece is Ravel's earliest purely orchestral work, one of the few originally written for orchestra (although it does recycle an early *Habanera* for piano four-hands).

Among single-disc Ravel collections, **Reiner**'s vintage '50s Chicago Symphony performances of *Rapsodie espagnole, Valses nobles et sentimentales, Alborada del gracioso,* and *Pavane for a Dead Princess* are about as perfect as recordings get, and happily have seldom been out of print (♦RCA 60179 or 5720, with an equally laser-like performance of Debussy's *Ibéria*). From the same period, and with even more generous Ravel couplings, is **Paray**'s performance with the Detroit Symphony (Mercury 432003).

If you want a more contemporary performance and sound, there is a recommendable Ravel collection in general, and *Rapsodie espagnole* in particular, by **López-Cobos** and the Cincinnati Symphony (Telarc 80171). The Chicago version by **Martinon** is also a beaut, coupled with a sparkling *Alborada del gracioso,* a touchingly simple *Ma mère l'oye* Suite, and a superior *Daphnis et Chloé* Suite 2; it's worth acquiring no matter how many other Ravel discs you have (♦RCA 63683).

Shéhérazade (*Ouverture féerique*). This isn't a memorable piece, but it's colorful and exotic in a Ballets Russes way. The versions in the complete sets by **Boulez** (Sony) and **Martinon** (EMI) are just fine. There is a single disc containing *Shéhérazade*: **Eiji Oue**'s collection of Ravel orchestrations with the Minnesota Orchestra (Chabrier, movements from Schumann's *Carnaval,* and, of course, Mussorgsky's *Pictures;* Reference 79).

Le Tombeau de Couperin. If *Rapsodie espagnole* is hot, *Tombeau* is cool, but hardly unemotional: Ravel wrote this dance suite in part as a tribute to colleagues killed in WWI, in part as a salute to French culture itself. **Dutoit**'s performance is exquisitely played, gracious, and (very important) completely unsentimental (♦London 410254). Nearly as elegant is **Schwarz** (♦Koch Schwann 373582), who includes an interesting oddity: the fugue from Ravel's original piano suite, handsomely orchestrated by the American composer David Diamond (who met Ravel as a teenager). Schwarz includes other Ravel, Debussy, and Satie keyboard pieces, arranged with equal acumen by Diamond. Both **Boulez** recordings (in his complete Sony set and on DG) also combine precise playing with just enough warmth.

La Valse and *Valses nobles et sentimentales.* Ravel's two orchestral tributes to the waltz are strikingly contrasted. *Valses nobles,* the earlier piece, is the epitome of sophistication. The title is a take-off from Schubert, but it's also accurate. Ravel's music brings together sumptuous harmony and glittering orchestration in a combination both nostalgic and hard-edged, a Godiva chocolate in the finest gold paper. **Reiner** recorded it with notable sweep and poise (RCA 60179); **Paray**'s recording from about the same time isn't as distinguished, but it's certainly idiomatic, and is part of a very pleasing Ravel/Debussy collection, including the classic *Boléro* mentioned above (Mercury 434306). **Boulez**'s recording, a buffer between tempestuous performances of the piano concertos by Zimerman, is fascinating, with tempos on the slow side and meticulously detailed and balanced playing by the Cleveland Orchestra (♦DG 449213). Nary an eighth-note of Ravel's fabulous orchestration seems to go unheard. Another excellent *Valses nobles* is tucked into **Previn**'s collection, a slow, richly recorded version (more *sentimentale* than *noble,* maybe) coupled with more Ravel and Debussy conducted by Maazel (Seraphim 68539, 2CD).

La Valse could be subtitled "The Decline of Middle-European Civilization in Twelve Minutes of Three-Quarter Time"; nothing in 20th-century music is as elegantly scary as the maelstrom of orchestral sound Ravel works up out of some frothy scraps of waltz tunes. *La Valse* was originally written for Diaghilev's consideration as a ballet; the great impresario passed on it, but since it's one of Ravel's most kinetic pieces, the impresario may have thought that dancing would gild the lily. **Munch**'s famous Boston Symphony performance has a heady sense of irony and a downright apocalyptic ending (♦RCA 61856 or 61712). **Boulez**'s New York Philharmonic recording, not quite as ferocious, is nearly as good (Sony 45842), and his newer Berlin Philharmonic reading is even better recorded (DG 47057). **Bernstein**'s '70s recording with the French National Orchestra is disappointing, not as steamy as his fabled old New York Philharmonic performance (Sony 60565).

CONCERTOS

Ravel wrote two, both at about the same time; both are for piano, one calling for left hand only. The two-hand Concerto in G, a scintillating work written for **Marguerite Long,** has been recorded by a long list of great pianists, including Long herself, in a brilliantly nonchalant 1931 performance (Pearl 9927). It's not conducted by Ravel, as legend has it, but by Pedro de Freitas-Branco, with an instructively slow recording of *Boléro* that is definitely led by the composer. Ravel claimed that this concerto was "written very much in the spirit of Mozart and Saint-Saëns," two composers he admired for their wit, translucency of sound, and lack of pretension. The jazzy, brilliant outer movements surround a superb Adagio. He claimed to have written this spontaneous-sounding piece slowly, carefully, one bar at a time, "with the assistance of the slow movement from Mozart's Clarinet Quintet."

The Left-Hand Concerto was written for one-armed pianist Paul Wittgenstein, who created an interesting niche of 20th-century piano repertoire by commissioning music from Hindemith, Prokofiev, and Britten, among others. Wittgenstein warmed slowly to this work but eventually came to think of it as a masterpiece. One of Ravel's finest compositions, it's almost everything the G major is not: dark-hued, tragic, at times frantic (Ravel's contemporary Roland-Manuel referred to its *caractére panique*). It's also a masterpiece of the arcane technique of making a single hand at the keyboard sound like three.

Most pianists have recorded both Ravel concertos together. I recommend the dependable early digital performance of **Rogé** and Dutoit (♦London 410230). (Dutoit recorded them again for London with Thibaudet, a promising-sounding team that turned out to be surprisingly uninteresting.) I also like the still-satisfying recordings by **Entremont** with Ormandy (Concerto in G) and Boulez (Left-Hand), very appropriately coupled with Gershwin's Piano Concerto (♦Sony 46338). Slightly lower on the scale are **Béroff** and Abbado (DG 23665) and **de Larrocha** and Slatkin, the latter very sumptuously recorded (RCA 60985).

The 1960 **Samson François**/Cluytens pairing was recently reissued in the "Great Recordings of the Century" series (♦EMI 66957). François was a unique, unpredictable pianist, and his rich, wayward performances of these works are full of odd and revealing details. The award-winning coupling of the concertos by **Zimerman** and Boulez is in a class by itself for grandeur and musical detail (♦DG 449213). Also highly recommended by various reviewers are the recordings by three excellent, undersung pianists: **Thiollier** (Naxos 550753, with Falla's *Nights in the Gardens of Spain*); **Lortie** (Chandos 8773, with Fauré's *Ballade*); and **Philip Fowke** (Classics for Pleasure 4667, with Fowke's solo version of *Valses nobles*).

Argerich's famous first recording of Concerto in G coupled it with an equally brilliant 20th-century work, Prokofiev's 3, with Abbado conducting the London Symphony (♦DG 47438). DG has released this firecracker of a recording in its "Originals" series; there are no more exciting performances of either work in the catalog. It's also in Argerich's volume in the "Great Pianists of the Century" series (Philips 456700). **Michelangeli**'s fabled recording (EMI 49326, with Rachmaninoff's Concerto 4) is also available in the "Great Pianists" series (Philips 456901).

Two of the greatest performances of the Left-Hand Concerto are old: **Cortot** from the '30s, with Munch conducting, is dimly recorded but magisterial (Pearl 9491). Even better is **Casadesus**'s 1947 performance with Ormandy and the Philadelphia, which has passion, elevation, and some pretty amazing remastered sound, coupled with his self-recommending set of Ravel's piano music (♦Sony 63316). **Fleisher** and Ozawa couple the piece with other Wittgenstein commissions: Prokofiev's oddball Concerto 4 and Britten's witty *Diversions* (Sony 47188). **Michel Block**'s version is highly regarded (Zephyr 11499), and a 1937 performance by **Wittgenstein** himself, with Walter conducting the Concertgebouw, has been released (Urania 126, with another issue of Long's Concerto in G).

Ravel never wrote a violin concerto, but his short *Tzigane* contains enough difficulties to outfit several of them. It's also a flashy, appealing slice of the composer's Gypsy/Spanish side, and most celebrated violinists have had a crack at it. The currently recommendable recordings include no less than three by **Perlman**. The most desirable is a 1975 performance with Martinon (♦EMI 47725, with Chausson's *Poème* and two Saint-Saëns pieces), but you can also hear a very good digital version with Mehta (♦DG 23063, with similar French repertoire, or ♦DG 47445, with his excellent Berg and Stravinsky concertos, Ozawa conducting) and a very early recording with Previn (RCA 56520, with Sibelius and Lalo concertos).

The **Francescatti**/Bernstein reading is a classic (Sony 47548); **Bell** and Litton offer a warmer, more modern recording (London 33519); and **Chung** and Dutoit provide a pleasantly refined interpretation of this barn-burner, generously coupled with concertos by Lalo and Vieuxtemps (Decca 460007). Good versions of Ravel's original violin-and-piano version are available from **Shaham** and Oppitz (DG 29729) and **Cho-Liang Lin** and Crossley (Sony 66839). Shaham's couplings are the Franck and Saint-Saëns sonatas; Lin's are Poulenc and Debussy.

CHAMBER MUSIC

Ravel's sparse output of chamber music includes three gems of the 20th-century repertory: String Quartet in F (1902-03); *Introduction and Allegro* for flute, clarinet, and harp, sunny and fresh as a May morning (1906); and the magnificent Piano Trio, written in 1914, just before Ravel left for his harrowing period of service in WWI as an ambulance driver.

Introduction and Allegro. A recording by the **Melos Ensemble** is particularly alluring, appealingly coupled with other French chamber music with harp (♦London 452891). There are also lovely versions by harpist **Nancy Allen** (EMI 47520, with Debussy) and the **Academy of St. Martin in the Fields Chamber Ensemble** (Chandos 8621, in a French program similar to the Melos Ensemble's). An attractive **Allegri Quartet** performance is a makeweight for a fine collection of Poulenc chamber music (Cala 1018, 2CD). And the 1951 Capitol recording by the **Hollywood Quartet** has never been surpassed; it's reissued in mono, but that hardly matters with this classic performance (Testament 1053).

Introduction and Allegro is sometimes performed with an orchestral string section added to the flute, clarinet, and harp, to pleasingly lush effect. Excellent recordings are available from **Martinon** and the Chicago

Symphony (RCA 63883, a glittering Ravel program) and **Louis Lane** and the Cleveland Orchestra (Sony 63056, with pieces by Satie and Debussy).

String Quartet. There are fine current recordings by the **Juilliard** (Sony 52554), **Emerson** (DG 45509), **Tokyo** (Sony 62413, bargain priced), **Cleveland** (Telarc 80111), **Kodály** (Naxos 550249, bargain priced), and **Ysaye Quartets** (London 30434); the last-named group has particularly luscious sound. LP collectors will remember the 1966 version by the **Quartetto Italiano** at its peak; this beautiful performance has been reissued (Philips 420894, with Debussy's Quartet; 454134, with admirable performances of the Piano Trio by the Beaux Arts Trio and the Violin Sonata by Grumiaux). Neither is currently available in the United States, but they're worth seeking out.

In LP days, Ravel's quartet was invariably coupled with Debussy's. Things haven't changed in the CD age, although the greater length allows for additional works. The Tokyo Quartet adds Fauré's delectable Piano Trio, and the Juilliard adds Dutilleux's *Ainsi la nuit,* an imaginative contemporary work definitely in the French tradition.

Piano Trio. This is one of the great masterpieces of French chamber music and one of the outstanding 20th-century works for this combination. It requires real virtuosos, and certainly gets them in **Ashkenazy, Perlman,** and **Harrell,** a lineup that, unlike many superstar chamber music excursions, actually works (♦London 444318, with Debussy's violin and cello sonatas). It sounds even better in the hands of **Bell, Isserlis,** and **Thibaudet** (♦London, generously coupled with Chausson's *Concert*). Less starry, but full of emotion, are the **Borodin Trio** (Chandos 8458, with Debussy's violin and cello sonatas) and the **Joachim Trio** (Naxos 550934, a genuine bargain, with unusual couplings by Debussy and Florent Schmitt that will attract the Francophile). The **Nash Ensemble**'s performances of the Trio and the pleasantly tart Sonata for Violin and Cello are the highlights of a collection of chamber and vocal music (Virgin 61427).

Violin sonatas. Ravel wrote two, one in 1897, quite romantic in expression, the other in 1927 and definitely sounding it, particularly in the middle movement, an acerbic and witty "blues." Excellent performances of both are given by **Lin** and Crossley (Sony 66839), and by **David Oistrakh** and Suk (Praga 254016). Along with *Tzigane* and a couple of shorter Ravel violin works, Lin and Crossley also offer sonatas by Debussy and Poulenc; Suk and Oistrakh offer more Ravel, including the substantial Sonata for Violin and Cello. Oistrakh's flawless, aristocratic *Tzigane* is one of the very best. If you'd just like the sonatas, **Mordkovitch** plays both in a juicy, immediately communicative style with Clifford Benson, and a surprisingly apropos coupling in the substantial Respighi sonata (Chandos 9351).

PIANO MUSIC

Complete sets. If you don't mind mono sound (cleaned up considerably from the LPs, but still indifferent), Casadesus's 1951 traversal of Ravel's piano music is the one to have (♦Sony 63316, 2CD). The set includes everything Ravel wrote for solo piano, piano four-hands (and, in the case of *Frontispiece,* five hands), with the addition of a short violin and piano piece and an outstanding 1947 performance (in amazingly good mono) of the Left-Hand Concerto with Ormandy, mentioned earlier. **Thibaudet**'s brisk, cool renditions rank high among sets (London 433515; a one-disc selection is also available in London 48618, called "Beautiful Starry Night"). If you have a taste for the historical, check out an inexpensive set of the solo piano music (incomplete, but with the most important works included) and both concertos (conducted by Horenstein) played by the long-lived **Perlemuter,** who, like Casadesus, knew Ravel (Vox 5507). Perlemuter also recorded them in stereo (Nimbus 5005, 5011).

Two British pianists are known for their interpretations of French piano music, and offer especially good Ravel. **Crossley**'s is worth seeking out for his aristocratic style (CRD 3383/84). **Stott**'s generous selection of popular Ravel piano works (coupled with equally persuasive Debussy) is outstanding, especially in a "two-fer" (Conifer 51755). **Lortie** is also much praised, and now available in another "two-fer" (Chandos 7004), as is a rather lower-powered set from the '70s by the excellent **Rogé** (London 440836). Lortie offers an interesting appendix with Ravel's piano arrangements of *Boléro, La Valse, Rapsodie espagnole,* and *Ma mère l'oye* (Chandos 8905).

Complete sets by **Abbey Simon** (Vox 5012) and **Entremont** (Sony 53528) are bargain priced. Both have the necessary finger power; neither is overly subtle. Entremont is better recorded, and I prefer his straightforward performances to Simon's often unconvincing fussing with tempos and textures. Simon does include a rarity, Ravel's solo piano arrangement (on three staves) of *La Valse.*

Individual works. **Rubinstein**'s playing of *Valses nobles et sentimentales* is sumptuous and civilized (RCA 61446, in a French collection), and you haven't lived till you've heard **Argerich** thunder through *Gaspard de la nuit* (DG 47438, with her equally brilliant Concerto in G). This alluring nightmare of a work, Ravel's piano masterpiece, has received some remarkable recordings by remarkable pianists: **François** (EMI 56239, a perfect coupling for his Ravel piano concertos); **Michelangeli** (Music & Arts 817 or 955, or his entry in the "Great Pianists" series, Philips 456901); **Gieseking** (Pearl 9449). For pianistic and recording virtuosity, **Nojima**'s 1992 version is easily one of the best modern Ravel recordings (♦Reference 35, with *Miroirs*), and not far behind is a celebrated account by the controversial **Pogorelich,** in his element here (DG 413363).

Two great Russian pianists not immediately associated with Ravel, **Richter** and **Gilels,** give magisterial performances—both virtuosic and poetic—of individual items. Richter's *Valses nobles* and *Miroirs* are coupled with Liszt (Praga 254057); Gilels' *Jeux d'eau, Tombeau de Couperin,* and *Alborada del gracioso* are in his "Great Pianists" volume (Philips 456793). The **Labécques** play a gently compelling *Ma mère l'oye* in a collection of "childhood" music (including Bizet and Fauré) that's one of this duo's most delightful discs (Philips 420159). **Berezovsky**'s Ravel disc is a powerful experience, especially the composer's insanely difficult transcription of *La Valse,* not often recorded (Teldec 94539).

CHORAL MUSIC

An interesting corner of Ravel's small output is occupied by his single choral work, *Trois Chansons,* a mature work from 1914–15 proving that Ravel could be reliably sumptuous even when limiting himself to a cappella vocal writing. Every note tells in the finely sung performances led by **Shaw** (Telarc 80408) and **Gardiner** (Philips 38149), so the couplings may help you decide: Shaw's is an interesting 20th-century program of Britten, Debussy, Poulenc, and Argento; Gardiner's is a chaste performance of Fauré's *Requiem* and rare choral pieces by Fauré, Debussy, and Saint-Saëns. The complete Ravelian will want to check out the four cantatas the not-so-young composer wrote in competition for the Prix de Rome. He never won it, which caused a predictable Parisian musical scandal, but all of them have been recorded and offer glimpses of the splendors to come (Marco Polo 223755).

OPERAS

Ravel's largest stage work, in fact his largest musical statement, is *Daphnis et Chloé;* his two one-act operas are more modest, at least on the surface. While they are very different in subject matter, both display gorgeously and in fantastic detail Ravel's obsession with the mechanical.

L'Heure espagnole (The Spanish Hour). This is a vaudeville with a paper-thin but spicy plot. An elderly clockmaker's lively, neglected young wife entertains two suitors while he's out tending to the town clock. Hiding them both in clock cases, she relies on a muscular young muleteer to move them around—and decides to give him a try when she sees how easily he can lift up those heavy clocks. It's amusing if well performed, but Ravel's score is not for bel canto freaks. He set a short play almost word for word and seldom stops the action for anything resembling an aria or ensemble. As someone once pointed out, Ravel was more interested in the clocks than the characters, and the opening moments are a deliciously orchestrated evocation of the clockmaker's shop.

While it lends itself well to recording and fits neatly on a single LP or CD, *L'Heure espagnole* hasn't been recorded very often. The current champ is **Maazel**'s 1965 reading (♦DG 449769, 2CD, with his equally fine recording of *L'Enfant et les sortilèges*). The French cast's delivery is perfect, the sound is detailed and lucid, and Maazel's customarily antiromantic approach suits the opera perfectly. True Ravelians will want to search out **Cluytens**'s 1953 Paris Opera recording (EMI 65269). The mono sound is no match for Maazel's, but the performance couldn't be more French; it stars the legendary soprano Denise Duval, for whom Poulenc wrote his operas, in a performance both glamorous and earthy.

L'Enfant et les Sortilèges (most readily translated as "The Child and the Enchanted Things"). This is more conventionally tuneful. Ravel's model was Broadway musicals of the '20s, with lots of brief numbers, dance rhythms, and "specialties" (though I don't know of any Gershwin musical that contains singing cats, dragonflies, armchairs, and teacups). As a sophisticated evocation of childhood, and of Ravel's love of nature, it's unique and very moving.

Collaborations between great writers and great musicians don't always work, but Colette and Ravel produced a masterpiece. Because of its fantastic nature, it seldom translates well to the stage, but it lends itself beautifully to recording, and while there haven't been many, none is a dud. The '50s mono recording by **Ernest Bour** is still warm and communicative (Testament 1044). **Maazel**'s '60s version is one of his earliest and best recordings, with wonderfully idiomatic performances by a French cast, flavorful without being hammy (in the 2CD set with *L'Heure espagnole,* DG 449769). The French touch is less evident in **Previn**'s warm-hearted, well-sung recording with the London Symphony (Classics for Pleasure 2241). Previn recently made a second recording of *L'Enfant,* even more brilliantly recorded and quite as recommendable as the first (DG 457589), and his first of *L'Heure espagnole* (DG 457590). In addition to their musical satisfactions, both CDs have dandy Chuck Jones cover art.

SONGS

Like his instrumental chamber music, Ravel's output of songs is small in number but distinguished in quality, and true vocal chamber music. One of his most "modern" compositions is *Chansons madécasses* (Songs of Madagascar), written in 1925–27 for Elizabeth Sprague Coolidge and first performed at the Library of Congress. They are short but flavorful settings of supposedly authentic poems by the 18th-century poet Everiste de Parny. The first and last, evoking languid, exotic passions, are Gauguins in music; the second is a shrill diatribe against colonialism. The scoring, stripped down but sensuous, is for flute, cello, piano, and voice. A performer closely associated with *Chansons madécasses* was mezzo-soprano **de Gaetani;** her late '70s recording is exquisitely sung and declaimed (♦Nonesuch 71355). (The main coupling is Ravel's enjoyably acidic Sonata for Violin and Cello, played by Isidore Cohen and Timothy Eddy.) De Gaetani did equally well with *Histoires naturelles*—settings of brief, dryly witty sketches of animals by Jules Renard—recorded with her pianist of choice, Gilbert Kalish (Arabesque 6673, with Debussy and Chausson songs).

If you can pull off this cycle, you can sing anything in the French song repertory; among those who do are two Americans, baritone **Patrick Mason** (Bridge) and soprano **Dawn Upshaw** (Erato). Both performances are highlights of all-French programs: Mason's includes Poulenc and Dutilleux; Upshaw's is part of a fascinating program of music dedicated to soprano Jane Bathori by Milhaud, Honegger, Roussel, and many more. **Norman**'s performance of *Chansons madécasses* (directed by Boulez) isn't as coolly perfect as de Gaetani's, but it's very good and usefully coupled with other Ravel songs. **Jill Gomez**'s singing of the cryptic but fascinating *Trois poèmes de Mallarmé* is bewitching, and **van Dam** is hearty and touching in Ravel's last composition, the *Don Quichotte* songs (♦Sony 64107, with Roussel's Symphony 3).

Baritone **Gérard Souzay** was another excellent Ravelian; his Ravel and Debussy are models of French singing and style; a good collection, including a baritone take on *Chansons madécasses*, is available (EMI 631122). **Bartoli**'s characterful singing of *Chants populaires, Vocalise en forme d'Habanera, Kaddisch,* and a few other items in her French recital disc (London 52667, with pianist Myung-Whun Chung), makes me wish she would do *Shéhérazade*—and she'd be great in *L'Heure espagnole.* A very recommendable set collects all the above and some other Ravel vocal oddities (including a "Scottish Song," "Ye Banks and Braes"), performed by an all-star cast: Berganza, Norman, Mesplé, van Dam, and Bacquier (EMI 69299, 2 CDs).

Ravel's one voice-and-orchestra piece is the sumptuous *Shéhérazade,* not as famous as Rimsky-Korsakov's but almost as full of musical wonders. The recording of choice is probably **Crespin**'s, with Ansermet conducting (♦London 417813); her massive voice was in its prime in 1964, and the interpretation is sensuous and grand. But there are plenty of other good *Shéhérazades,* by such stylish singers as **Danco** with Ansermet (London 448151 is stereo, Dutton 1201 is 1948 mono but an excellent transfer), **Tourel** with a young Bernstein conducting (Sony 60695, mono), **Horne** also with Bernstein, this one from 1977 (Sony 47604—excellent, but coupled with a not-so-hot *Daphnis et Chloé*), and perhaps best of all, **Baker** and Barbirolli (♦EMI 68667, 2CD, with Chausson, Duparc, and Brahms lieder, a fine bargain). **McNair**'s recording with Ozawa has been well reviewed (Philips 446682, with Debussy's *Demoiselle élue* and Britten's *Illuminations*). RAYMOND

Alan Rawsthorne *(1905–1971)*

Rawsthorne is a difficult composer to place, which is another way of saying that he is a genuine individual whose music, if you take to it, will probably become addictive. He was an exact contemporary of Alwyn, Tippett, and his close friend Constant Lambert; his other dearest professional friend, William Walton, a fellow Lancastrian, was three years older. After brief forays into architecture and dentistry, Rawsthorne studied piano, cello, and composition at the Royal Manchester College of Music; further studies abroad included piano tuition from Egon Petri. Clarity, concision, and craftsmanship are the hallmarks of his work, which covers every genre except opera. The discs listed are all recommended, and many are on midpriced or budget labels.

Orchestral music. Of Rawsthorne's three symphonies, the most immediately appealing is 2 ("Pastoral"), with its *giocoso* country dance and, as in Vaughan Williams's "Pastoral," a soprano solo in the finale; it was digitally recorded in 1993. The seasonal text by Henry Howard, Earl of Surrey (1516–1547) is sung by the late Tracey Chadwell with the London Philharmonic under **Nicholas Braithwaite.** Symphony 1 was recorded by the same orchestra under **John Pritchard** in 1975, and 3, the composer's longest work with its moving sarabande, was performed as long ago as 1967 by the BBC Symphony under **Norman Del Mar** (Lyrita 291). All three recordings sound good, despite the disparity in dates.

Pioneering versions of *Symphonic Studies,* Rawsthorne's first major orchestral work, and the overture *Street Corner,* his most popular piece, were made by the Philharmonia in 1946 under **Lambert;** despite their sonic limitations, they breathe an inimitable authority (Pearl 0058, with music by Delius and Warlock). New recordings of *Symphonic Studies* and the Cello and Oboe Concertos are awaiting release (Naxos 554763). **Rawsthorne** conducts the Pro Arte Orchestra in *Street Corner* and the suite from his ballet *Madame Chrysanthème,* based on the Madam Butterfly story, in a collection of British music all conducted by the composers (EMI 64718).

Concerto for String Orchestra, a classic of 20th-century English string music, is the standout in a disc of music for chamber orchestra (Naxos 553567). *Concertante pastorale* for flute, horn, and strings, written to be played in the Hampton Court Orangery, is as mellow as you might expect. The brief *Light Music for Strings* is based on Catalan dances, while *Divertimento* is just as lively, ending with a jig. *Elegiac Rhapsody,* in memory of the poet Louis MacNeice, is deeply felt and passionate. The Suite for Recorder and Strings is arranged by soloist John Turner and the composer John McCabe from one for viola d'amore and piano. Conrad Marshall, flute, and Rebecca Goldberg, horn, are the other soloists, and **David Lloyd-Jones** conducts the Northern Chamber Orchestra.

Music from nine of Rawsthorne's 26 film scores, arranged by Gerard Schurmann and Phillip Lane, is all well recorded and excellently played by the BBC Philharmonic under **Rumon Gamba** (Chandos 9749). *Prisoners' March,* based on themes from *The Captive Heart,* is included along with music from two other Rawsthorne film scores in a collection recalling Ealing Studios. **Kenneth Alwyn** conducts the Royal Ballet Sinfonia (Silva Screen 177).

Concertos. Classic performances of the two piano concertos are still unsurpassed. **Lympany** plays 1 with the Philharmonia under Herbert Menges; in three movements, it ends with a tarantella making use of the revolutionary song "Bandiera rossa," reflecting Rawsthorne's Spanish Civil War sympathies. Concerto 2, in four movements—the last beginning with a popular tune that some find vulgar—has the BBC Symphony under Sargent supporting **Denis Matthews,** who also contributes four Bagatelles for piano, recorded in 1942. This historic collection is completed by the T. S. Eliot entertainment *Practical Cats,* for speaker (Robert Donat) and orchestra, the Philharmonia conducted by **Rawsthorne** (EMI 66935). **Geoffrey Tozer**'s performances of both concertos with the London Philharmonic under Bamert are only for those who must have digital recording and also want the Concerto for Two Pianos, not one of the composer's better efforts; Tamara Anna Cislowska is the other pianist (Chandos 9125).

Violin Concerto 1 is a lyrical work, 2 is more elusive, and neither has enjoyed the popularity of those for piano. Both are splendidly performed by **Rebecca Hirsh,** well backed by the BBC Scottish Symphony under Lionel Friend, who also conducts the 13-minute concert overture

Cortèges; the recordings are excellent (Naxos 554240). Concerto for Clarinet and Strings, written for Frederick Thurston, is authoritatively played by his widow **Thea King,** who prefers the virtuosic ending reconstructed from a private Thurston recording to that approved for publication by the composer; concertos by Arnold Cooke and Gordon Jacob complete the disc (Hyperion 66031).

Chamber and instrumental music. Rawsthorne wrote five string quartets but published only three, which are compact works charting his development as a composer. The **Flesch Quartet** adds the second of the unpublished works, from 1935, cutting back the overlong finale (ASV 983). **Fibonacci Sequence** gives excellent performances of Sonata for flute, oboe, and piano; Suite for flute, viola, and harp; Quintet for piano and winds, one of his finest later works; Quintet for piano, clarinet, horn, violin, and cello, a weaker piece; and Concerto for Ten Instruments, which contrasts solo instruments against groups (ASV 1061).

Another useful anthology has **Martin Outram** and Julian Rolton in the recording premiere of the Viola Sonata, an unaccountably neglected work that was lost in the war but turned up in a second-hand music shop; Peter Adams and Yoshiko Endo in the Cello Sonata; Nadia Myerscough and Endo in the Concertante for violin and piano; the Rogeri Trio in the Piano Trio; and John McCabe at the keyboard in the Piano Quintet (Naxos 554352). The Cello Sonata is also well played by **Lloyd Webber** and McCabe in a British cello anthology (ASV 592).

The Clarinet Quartet, one of Rawsthorne's best chamber works, is coupled by **Nicholas Cox** and the Redcliffe Ensemble with quintets by Bliss and Francis Routh (Redcliffe 010). Theme and Variations for two violins, which established the composer's international reputation, is presented by the **Redcliffe Ensemble** with his Oboe Quartet and works by Elizabeth Lutyens and Routh (Redcliffe 006). The Violin Sonata marked Rawsthorne's return to creativity after a three-year hiatus and was immediately appreciated. **Susanne Stanzeleit** and Julian Jacobson couple it with works by Vaughan Williams and Fricker (Cala 88036).

Piano music. Though an accomplished pianist, Rawsthorne found it difficult to write for the instrument, but the effort doesn't show in his small output—Bagatelles, Sonatina, four Romantic Pieces, Ballade, and Theme and Variations—which should make new friends in the performances by **John Clegg** (Paradisum 2). **Alan Cuckston** spreads his readings across two discs, the first including the masterly piano duet miniature, *The Creel* (Swinsty 120/21). Elegy for guitar, left unfinished on Rawsthorne's death and completed by **Bream,** has been recorded both by him (RCA 61595) and **Anders Miolin** (BIS 926).

Vocal music. Rawsthorne wrote songs throughout his career, but none of them is among his most characteristic creations. A selection ranging from *Tzu-Yeh Songs* to *Two Fish* is sung by **Sandra Dugdale** and **Martin Hindmarsh** with Cuckston at the piano in the first of his piano discs (Swinsty 120). *Canzonet,* contributed to "A Garland for the Queen" in Coronation year; *A Rose for Lidice,* written to mark the dedication of a rose garden in the Czech village destroyed by the Nazis; and *The Oxen,* composed to words by Thomas Hardy for a carol anthology, are performed by the **National Youth Chamber Choir** alongside works by Priaulx Rainier and Routh (Redcliffe 011).

POTTER, WITH THE ASSISTANCE OF TONY PICKARD

Max Reger *(1873–1916)*

Welcome to one of the most beautiful, individual of sound worlds—one that has been denied to many listeners through the blind (or deaf) prejudice of American and English critics. Reger was a towering figure in 20th-century music; had he lived longer, he would have been able to stand up for himself. His opinion of critics was typified by his celebrated rejoinder to one of them: "Sir, I am sitting in the smallest room of my house. I have your review before me. In a moment it will be behind me." After his early death, a terrible revenge was exacted by the people who live not by creating but by picking over the bones of those who do create. American critics in particular have a habit of getting on their high horses when discussing Reger—in effect doing in prose what they accuse him of doing in music.

Granted, his was a personality of contradictions. On one side was the man who engulfed vast quantities of food and alcohol; who craved honors and decorations; who related filthy stories with relish, especially if there was someone present whom he found tedious. On the other side was the deeply religious man who composed outstanding organ music and hauntingly beautiful short choral pieces; who conducted an orchestra or played the piano with infinite delicacy, often underplaying the written dynamics in his own music and achieving pianissimi quite at odds with his bullish physiognomy; the cultivated Roman Catholic who revered the Protestant Bach; the man who was capable of loyalty and tenderness in personal relationships; the joker whose sense of humor reflected his Bavarian rural background but was infinitely creative, giving rise to thousands of wisecracks and puns, such as the signature "Rex Mager" (Rex Meagre) on the receipt for a stingy concert fee. He could be bitter and then humorous, malicious and then charming. Above all, he was a devoted friend who attracted around him some of the great musicians of his time, including the Busch brothers, Fritz and Adolf.

This article, written by an avowed Regerian, seeks to provide a way in to each category of his music while also leading the converted to new delights. Anything you have read about Reger's music being difficult is likely to have been written by someone who doesn't know it well. Like all the best music, Reger's needs to be given a fair hearing, and closer acquaintance will bring admiration for all but a handful of works. Reger's music also needs careful rehearsal, which is why German discs feature so strongly in the choices below; they should be easy enough to obtain in these days of ordering by Internet.

ORCHESTRAL MUSIC

Reger always said he didn't really understand how to write for the orchestra until he became conductor of the Meiningen Court Orchestra in 1911, so let's begin near the end of his life with the Ballet Suite of 1913. It's a gorgeous little piece lasting less than 20 minutes and is given a superb performance by the Berlin Staatskapelle under **Suitner.** The charming *Concerto in the Old Style* of 1912 is equally well performed, and a fine performance of the *Beethoven Variations* has been added to the original LP for the reissue. The 1971–72 recordings have come up beautifully (Berlin 9123).

Reger's most famous orchestral work is *Variations and Fugue on a Theme by Mozart* Op. 132, and historic performances can be found from **Böhm** (DG), **van Beinum,** and **Scherchen** (CPO). But there are at least four magnificent modern ones. **Colin Davis** and the Bavarian Radio Symphony give a sharply etched performance and add a suitable Hindemith coupling, *Symphonic Metamorphoses on Themes of Weber* (Philips 422347). **Horst Stein** and the Bamberg Symphony take a slightly warmer approach and add *Variations and Fugue on a Theme by Beethoven* Op. 86 (Koch Schwann 1141). Two versions couple the atmospheric tone poem *Tondichtungen nach Arnold Böcklin* Op. 128: **Jörg-Peter Weigle** and the Dresden Philharmonic have a light touch

(Capriccio 10307), while veteran **Heinz Bongartz** takes a grander view in refurbished analog recordings with Dresden's two orchestras, the Staatskapelle in Op. 132, the Philharmonic in Op. 128 (Berlin 2177).

The hugely enjoyable *Variations and Fugue on a theme of J. A. Hiller* Op. 100 boasts one classic version. In 1963 **Franz Konwitschny** polished each variation like a jewel and took the Leipzig Gewandhaus Orchestra through the final fugue with unique brio (Berlin 0120). **Davis** (Orfeo 090841) and **Stein** (Koch Schwann 311150) provide the same contrasts as before, both offering the Ballet Suite as coupling. **Neeme Järvi** finds the Concertgebouw a plus but its famous acoustic a minus (Chandos 8794, with *Böcklin Suite*). Bargain hunters will find that sturdy old versions of the Mozart and Hiller Variations and the Ballet Suite by **Keilberth** and his Bamberg and Hamburg orchestras still come up well in a useful "two-fer" (Teldec 28175).

The *Böcklin Suite*, especially valuable for its first and third sections, "The Hermit Playing the Violin" and "The Isle of the Dead," comes in two recordings that couple it with the warm *Romantic Suite Op. 125*. **Albrecht** has the more modern recording with the Berlin Radio Symphony (Koch Schwann 311011), while **Schmidt-Isserstedt** and the North German Radio Symphony provide classic accounts from 1972 and 1967 (Acanta 43.077). *Symphonic Prologue for a Tragedy* is a powerful piece for which Reger provided a shortened version, well played by the Berlin Radio Symphony under **Heinz Rögner** (Berlin 3119, with *Romantic Suite*). Albrecht and the same orchestra play the longer version, with **Hans Maile** adding the two lovely Romances for violin with conductor Uros Lajovic (Koch Schwann 11605).

Reger's first orchestral work, *Sinfonietta* Op. 90 of 1905, used to be thought a monster—it lasts some 50 minutes! But a well-played recording works wonders, and you realize how beautiful the slow movement is with its solo violin. **Stein** does a fine job in his Bamberg series, throwing in *Concerto in the Old Style* (Koch Schwann 1354), but the converted may like to try **Bongartz**'s loving 1973 performance with the Dresden Philharmonic (Berlin 9122). Serenade Op. 95 of 1906 shows how wrong Reger was in thinking he couldn't orchestrate. It's a beautiful creation, with half the string section muted and half not, and **Jochum** used to specialize in it; a live performance with the Concertgenouw is available but only in a 4CD set (Tahra 232/5). **Stein**'s Bamberg performance is very sympathetic (Koch Schwann 1566, with *Suite in the Old Style*). The final disc in the Bamberg series is a bit of a ragbag but does include the fine *Comedy Overture* (Koch Schwann 1498).

CONCERTOS

Reger's two concertos seem to sprawl on first acquaintance but soon grow on you. The Violin Concerto, taken all around the world by Adolf Busch, has been recorded a number of times, but two discs stand out. **Edith Peinemann** gives a uniquely sympathetic performance and is well supported by Wolf-Dieter Hauschild and the Stuttgart Philharmonic; her CD is worth seeking (Amati 9005/1). **Manfred Scherzer** takes a more virtuosic view and has the superb Dresden Staatskapelle for company, conducted by Blomstedt (Berlin 9124). The classic account of the Piano Concerto by **Rudolf Serkin** is NA, but **Barry Douglas** is a suitably romantic substitute, enthusiastically accompanied by Janowski and the French Radio Symphony; they add another Serkin specialty, Strauss's *Burleske* (RCA 68028).

CHAMBER MUSIC

Reger's chamber music holds many enchantments, best exemplified by the version of *Romantic Suite* for string trio Op. 77b and D major Serenade for flute, violin and viola Op. 77a; he later composed another such pairing, the D minor String Trio Op. 141b and G major Serenade Op. 141a. A wonderful coupling of the string trios by the **German String Trio** and *gemütlich* readings of the Serenades by **Peter-Lukas Graf** and Sandor Végh are NA. Good alternative versions of the trios come from the **Vienna String Trio** (Calig 50 906) and adequate performances of the serenades from **Serenata of London** (ASV 875, with viola suites).

Of the violin sonatas, the best is the last, Op. 139, a work without any double-stopping. It's sympathetically played by **Renate Eggebrecht**, who couples it with Sonata Op. 72, and strangely has a different pianist for each (Troubadisc 01413). **Hansheinz Schneeberger** and Jean-Jacques Dünki also understand the work and pair it with Sonata Op. 122, but the violinist's vibrato won't be to all tastes (Jecklin 649). **Ulf Wallin** and Pöntinen give a straightforward performance, adding the attractive *Suite in the Old Style* and three short pieces (CPO 999643). They also offer the early Sonata Op. 1 and Op. 84, another attractive work (CPO 999452). Good but not exceptional performances of Opp. 72 and 84 come from **Robert Zimansky** and Christoph Keller (Accord 200002).

The clarinet sonatas consist of two early works, Op. 49 and a large-scale mature work, Op. 107. All are well played by **Karl Leister** and Anthony Spiri, along with two short pieces and the delicate Clarinet Quintet, Reger's last chamber work, with the Philharmonia Quartet (Camerata 371). Sonata Op. 107, the short pieces and the Quintet also come from **Eduard Brunner**, Gerhard Oppitz and the Wilanow Quartet in excellent Bavarian Radio recordings (Tudor 724). The viola versions of the sonatas have been well done by **Barbara Westphal** and Jeffrey Swann (Bridge 9075); they're preferable in Op. 107 to **Ivo van der Werff** and Simon Marlow (ASV 976, with cello suites). But admirers of the late **Ulrich Koch** will find there is a splendid size to his performance of Op. 107 with his wife Sachiko Nakamura; they're joined in the early Op. 2 Trio by Susanne Lautenbacher (Bayer 100085).

In the Cello Sonatas, the late **Ludwig Hoelscher** had no equal and in his 1974 set he was well partnered by Karl Heinz Lautner (Bayer 200 033/4). **Reimund Korupp**, on two different labels with different pianists, is variably recorded but gives excellent performances, adding three small pieces (CPO 394; Antes 31.9001). A reasonable alternative, also with extras, comes from the Danish duo Anders Grøn and Jørgen Hald Nielsen, but they're sorely tested by the difficult F minor Sonata Op. 5 (Danica 8176/7). A lovely historical radio recording of the little Sonata Op. 116 comes from **Enrico Mainardi**—who played it with Reger in his youth—and Carl Seeman (Orfeo 418971). You may still be able to find the magnificent interpretation of Op. 78 by **Leslie Parnas** and Wonmi Kim (Arcadia 1998). Of various performances of the great Piano Trio Op. 102, the best—both coupling the early Op. 2 Trio with a guest violist—are those by the **Genberg Trio** (Koch Schwann 1157) and **Trio Parnassus** (MD+G 3030751).

Reger's five canonical string quartets climax with the fourth, Op. 109, a beautiful work that ought to be in every ensemble's repertoire. Look for historic performances by the **Strub Quartet** and especially the **Busch Quartet**. All five quartets are well played by the **Mannheim Quartet**, the two of Op. 54 coupled with String Trio 1 Op. 77b (MD+G 0711); the large-scale Op. 74 with String Trio 2 Op. 141b (MD+G 0712); Op. 109 with Quartet 5 Op. 121 (MD+G 0713). Further recommendations are Op. 74 by the **Philharmonia Quartet** (Thorofon 2116) and Opp. 109 and 121 by the **Joachim Quartet** (Koch Schwann 310068). The dubious distinction of a rather weak set by the **Bern Quartet** is that it includes an early unnumbered work from 1888–89 (CPO 999069).

Of the two Piano Quartets, Op. 113 is one of Reger's few failures.

Members of the Mannheim Quartet with **Claudius Tanski** get lost in its toils, which is a shame, as the accompanying Serenade 2 Op. 141a is well done in Reger's own all-string version (MD+G 0715). These players do better with the less dense op. 133, adding the three Duos for violins Op. 131b (MD+G 0714). But first choice for the piano quartets has to be the **Fanny Mendelssohn Quartet,** whose fine musicians even manage to clarify Op. 113 (Troubadisc 01415). A team including the **Krist** brothers goes to the trouble of finding an Ibach piano, as used by Reger, but neither their playing nor the recording is up to the best standards (Telos 001, 2CD). For the Piano Quintet Op. 64 it's back to the **Fanny Mendelssohns;** three of them also do the Op. 102 Piano Trio proud (Troubadisc 01414).

In Clarinet Quintet Op. 146, a luminous work that might have heralded a fresh era of simplicity for Reger had he lived longer, **Leister** offers a recent performance as well as the one noted above. His latest partners are the Vogler Quartet, who support him well but pull the accompanying String Quartet Op. 109 around too much (Nimbus 5644). **Pierre Woudenberg** and the Schoenberg Quartet give a competent performance if you prefer the Brahms Quintet as a coupling (Koch Schwann 311502). As well as Brunner's radio performance already mentioned, there is one from West German Radio by **Franz Klein** and the Heutling Quartet that many will want for the coupling, the Mozart Quintet featuring Klein and the Amadeus Quartet (Koch Schwann 1809). The gorgeous String Sextet Op. 118 is promised from the **Vienna Sextet,** but the 1977 recording by the **Zurich Kammermusiker** is still very enjoyable (Jecklin 543).

INSTRUMENTAL MUSIC

Organ. Reger's organ music, much of it written for his friend Karl Straube, covers an immense range, from small chorale preludes to vast concert works. Although organists are Reger's main champions among musicians, they are split between those who follow Straube and give slower, more nuanced readings with traditional tempo variations and those who feel the music should be played in as virtuosic a manner as possible. It seems this dichotomy existed even in the composer's lifetime. There are advantages in using a German concert organ from the 1890–1920 period; to take just one example, as Nicholas Kynaston has pointed out, the crescendo at bar 54 of the *Fantasy and Fugue on B-A-C-H* is impossible without the Rollschwelle or Walze—a general crescendo—that was fitted to most medium to large instruments of the time. Newcomers to this rich vein of some 200 titles should perhaps start with the shorter middle-period pieces of Opp. 59, 65, 69, and 80, then proceed to the Preludes and Fugues Opp. 56 and 85; the Suite Op. 92; the nine Pieces Op. 129; and the seven Pieces Op. 145. Of the large-scale works, the Fantasy and Fugue Op. 135b and *Fantasy on Ein feste Burg* Op. 27 are perhaps the most approachable.

The enthusiast will find stray historic recordings by such great organists as Fritz Heitmann, Günther Ramin and Fernando Germani. Of the newer recordings, **Rosalinde Haas**'s complete set stands out for its thoroughness. She's of the modern school and uses a 1983 organ, which makes for a clean sound, and each of her 12 discs is arranged as a recital in itself (MD+G 3350/61). Three bargain discs are interesting. **Bernhard Haas** plays the ten Pieces of Op. 69 and three of the Preludes and Fugues from Op. 85 in Straube fashion, bringing out marvelous details (Naxos 553926). On the same organ, **Ludger Lohmann** plays the massive *Introduction, Passacaglia, and Fugue* Op. 127, nine Pieces Op. 129, and ten of the Chorale Preludes Op. 135a in more 21st-century vein (Naxos 553927).

Bernhard Buttmann breezes through the two biggest concert works, Op. 127 and *Variations and Fugue on an Original Theme,* on a modern Klais instrument (Arte Nova 67526). Contrast his versions with the far more spacious playing of the same two works by **Haas** on the 1913 Rieger of the Vienna Konzerthaus, readings full of loving lingerings and colors in a well-presented disc (Fermate 20020). An even more spacious presentation of Op. 73 comes in a splendid recital by **Christoph Bossert** on the 1909 Dalstein and Haerpfer in the Strasbourg Palais des Fêtes (EMI 544067). **Arvid Gast** is atmospherically recorded for his fine recital of five middle-period works on the famous Sauer in Berlin Cathedral; the fortissimi in the opening *Fantasy on Ein feste Burg* will sound tremendous on a good system (Motette 12041).

One of the more iconoclastic players is **Franz Hauk,** whose recital on a Klais—*Fantasy on Wachet auf,* Sonata Op. 60, *Symphonic Fantasy and Fugue,* and *Christmas* from Op. 145—is recorded in mellow fashion (Guild 7192). On a bargain disc **Donald Joyce** plays Op. 73, *Fantasy on Wachet auf,* and *Benedictus* on the organ of Norwich Cathedral (IMP 00852). *Fantasy and Fugue on B-A-C-H* and Fantasy and Fugue on the little-known chorale "Hallelujah! Gott zu loben" are well played by **Rothkopf** and **Rübsam,** respectively, on the Rieger-Sauer of Fulda Cathedral; the coupling is the two-piano version of the *Mozart Variations* noted above (Organ 7004).

Straube's pupil **Heinz Wunderlich** is worth hearing in a recital that includes two pieces for violin and organ, but the 1980 tapes are a mite fuzzy, and the organ isn't really suitable (Signum 27-00). Nor is the organ at St. Bavo, but **Piet Kee** plays sympathetically in four shorter works that share a disc with Hindemith sonatas (Chandos 9097). The same can be said for **Roger Judd,** who couples the seven *Pieces Op. 145* with selections from Opp. 59, 65 and 67 on the organ of St George's Chapel, Windsor (Herald 203). Of the many organists who program individual works, you should look especially for performances by Werner Jacob, Graham Barber, Hanns-Martin Lehning, and Franz Lehrndorfer.

Piano. Reger apparently played the piano with extraordinary finesse, which is reflected in his many short pieces. The big sets of variations demand virtuoso treatment. After many years during which Serkin was its only big-time protagonist, this major body of work is attracting the sort of player it needs. The German pianist **Markus Becker** has almost finished a complete edition that is already a landmark, as the playing is of a uniformly high standard and the instrument itself is beautifully prepared. Begin with Vols. 8 and 9, featuring the four books of *From My Diary,* short pieces of infinite variety and beauty (Thorofon 2318/19). Becker's performance of the *Telemann Variations* in Vol. 2 shows that he'll be equal to the other big sets (Thorofon 2312). This work was recorded by **Bolet,** and hopefully his version will return; **Serkin**'s rugged traversal of *Variations and Fugue on a Theme of J. S. Bach* should also make a comeback.

Meanwhile **Hamelin** has framed his whimsical versions of *Humoresques* with performances of both these "baroque" sets that raise them to new heights of virtuosity (Hyperion 66996). The more solid versions by **David Levine** are rather eclipsed (Koch Schwann 310 008). **Schiff** has also entered the fray with a live performance of the Bach set that's full of delightful touches (Teldec 99051). Levine's art is better represented by his pleasant disc of *Improvisations, Humoresques,* and Fantasy Pieces (CPO 999074). **Ulrich Urban** is worth hearing in the first book of *From My Diary* and two of the Sonatinas (Koch Schwann 1033). **John Buttrick** is a sympathetic interpreter of the six *Intermezzi* and *Träume am Kamin* (Jecklin 601).

A bargain series has so far yielded two good discs for the impecunious, though neither is as well recorded as the opposition. **Jean Martin** plays six *Pieces* Op. 24, *Silhouettes,* and *Blätter und Bluten* (Naxos 550932). **Markus Pawlik** contributes *Improvisations, Humoresques,* the early *In der Nacht,* and *Träume am Kamin* (Naxos 553331).

Reger's music for piano duet, including *Mozart Variations,* was definitively done by **Tal** and **Groethuysen,** and we must hope for a reissue (Sony). The two-piano version is not quite as good, having a different eighth variation, but it's enjoyably played by **Andreas Rothkopf** and **Wolfgang Rübsam** in a disc otherwise devoted to organ music (Organ 7004). There's also a good performance by **Evelinde Trenkner** and **Sontraud Speidel,** along with the two-piano version of *Beethoven Variations*—in this case the original, with four more variations than the orchestral version—and the *Introduction, Passacaglia, and Fugue* Op. 96 (MD+G 3300756). The heavy-handed playing of **Uriarte** and **Mrongovius** in the Mozart set is to be avoided (Calig 50893). Another version of the two-piano Beethoven set, by **Zsuzsanna Kollar** and **Gabriella Lang,** is not only very well played but offers the Schubert set by Reger's disciple Adolf Busch as one of the couplings (Koch Schwann 1230). **Schiff** and **Peter Serkin** collaborate in a buoyant account of the *Beethoven Variations* as part of a fascinating double album including music for two pianos by Mozart and Busoni (EMI 465062). Fans of **Richter** will want his live performance of the *Beethoven Variations* with **Andreas Lucewicz** (Live Classics 482).

Strings. Reger's music for solo string instruments is clearly influenced by that of Bach and is none the worse for it. As a child he wanted to play the violin but was thwarted, and he always had a feeling for the instrument. The complete Preludes and Fugues for Solo Violin are played in straightforward fashion by **Mateja Marinkovic,** but maddeningly he omits the Chaconne from Op. 117, even though the two discs take only 82 minutes (ASV 876). It looks as if **Søren Elbaek** will rectify the omission with Vol. 2 of his traversal of the solo violin music; the promising first volume includes Op. 131a and the seven sonatas for solo violin Op. 91, the seventh ending in the first of Reger's two Chaconnes (Kontrapunkt 32300/1).

The Op. 91 sonatas are also splendidly played by **Ulrike-Anima Mathé,** and she's exceptionally well recorded (Dorian 90175, 90212). However, **Renate Eggebrecht,** though a fractionally less secure player, is even further inside the music than her rivals (Troubadisc 01416). If you want just a taste of unaccompanied Reger, **Luigi Alberto Bianchi** couples a fine 1992 performance of Op. 91:7 with his famed 1977 versions of the three suites for solo viola Op. 131d (Dynamic 10).

The first of the viola suites, in G minor, is a perfect little masterpiece, and the other two go well with it. The superb Japanese violist **Hirofumi Fukai** recorded his recital of the Reger suites and Hindemith's great solo sonata Op. 25:1 back in 1981, but it still sounds superb (Signum X38-00). **Pierre Franck** plays well but offers just the three suites, very short measure (Pierre Verany 799101). **George Robertson**'s suites are all right, but his disc is more recommendable for the two flute serenades (ASV 875). **Robert Verebes** plays just Suite 1 in a general solo recital and isn't competitive (SNE 562), nor is **Zahari Tchavdarov,** who again plays only Suite 1, with sonatas by Hindemith and Shostakovich (BIS 81).

Of the three suites for solo cello Op. 131c, the best is the third, but they make a riveting sequence in the hands of a master like **Erling Blöndal Bengtsson,** who adds Ysaÿe's solo sonata (Danacord 372). **Keith Harvey** is a thoughtful player, and, as noted above, his disc also includes a fair performance of the big Sonata for Viola and Piano (ASV 976). **Wis-**

pelwey makes an appealing sound, using gut and silver-wound gut strings, and adds some lovely short pieces with piano (Channel 9596). **Rama Jucker**'s fine 1979 performances have acquired a few piano pieces as fillers on their transfer to CD (Accord 200572). **Werner Thomas-Mifune**'s 1992 readings are first-rate but expensive with no coupling (Calig 50921). The same goes for the excellent **Michaela Fukačová** (Kontrapunkt 32142). **Guido Schiefen,** on the other hand, is entitled to offer just his splendid performances of the Suites at their bargain price (Arte Nova 65428). **Feuermann**'s historic recording of Suite 1 is poorly transferred (Pearl 9443).

CHORAL MUSIC

Reger's church cantatas are simple works, not comparable with Bach's. All four are nicely performed by vocal and instrumental soloists and the **Mainz Bach Choir** under Diethard Hellmann (Christophorus 0049). But the performances of two of them by soloists and the **Stuttgart Chamber Choir** under Bernius are even better, coupled with the early three *Choruses* Op. 6 with piano and three songs for women's voices a cappella, Op. 111b (Amati 9301).

Reger's unaccompanied choral music used to be thought very difficult, but today's virtuoso choirs make light of it. Everyone should know the profound eight *Sacred Songs,* the proofs of which were found on the composer's bedside table the morning after his death. The **Netherlands Chamber Choir** under Gronostay are incomparable; their Bruckner couplings are supremely well sung and the recording is crystal-clear (Globe 5160). The **Frankfurt Vocal Ensemble** is also very good; their coupling is Frank Martin's Mass (Bayer 100084).

Of the all-Reger discs, the more recommendable is by the **Frankfurt Vocal Ensemble,** which also has the three six-part *Choruses* Op. 39 and four other sacred pieces (Thorofon 2334). The LP recital by the **Berlin Radio Choir** and Dietrich Knothe featured three *Sacred Songs* Op. 110, and only the first four of the Op. 138 songs are included in its reissue (Berlin 2001). For a coupling of Opp. 39 and 110, the **Danish National Radio Choir** under Stefan Parkman is ideal (Chandos 9298). The ten songs for a cappella male voices Op. 83, including an earlier setting of *Requiem,* are superbly sung and characterized by **Gli Scapoli** under Reza Aghamir (Vanguard 99049). POTTER

SONGS

Reger composed almost 300 lieder, but very few can be found on recital programs today. Many are good examples of turn-of-the-century Romantic songs, but they were never popular. Two reasons are usually given: Reger didn't choose suitable texts, and he was mining the same territory as his contemporary Richard Strauss, who undoubtedly was the more imaginative composer and had superior melodic gifts.

Iris Vermillion, a young, rich-toned mezzo, has recorded 21 songs (CPO 999317). It's the only such disc in the current listings but would be commendable in any event. Eight of the sacred songs, all quite brief, may be heard in a disc primarily devoted to Bruckner Motets (Globe 5100). A larger selection of sacred songs, together with similar songs by Hasse and Schoeck, is handicapped by the vocal inadequacies of the soloists (Thorofon). The best choice is a disc devoted entirely to Reger's sacred choral music, sung a cappella by the **North German Figural Choir** (Thorofon 2334). It doesn't duplicate the selections on the others and is the best introduction to this music. MOSES

Steve Reich (b. 1936)

Of all the well-known so-called "minimalist" composers, Reich made not only the most radical break with the Western music mainstream, but he has so far created the most consistently enjoyable body of work as well. There are three secrets to Reich's appeal. The first is his irrepressible use of rhythm, rooted in the syncopations of jazz, gaining further richness through his studies of drumming in Ghana. The second is that he comes up with consistently good musical ideas. A minimalist is only as good as his material—you have to present patterns that will hold the listener's interest through all that repetition—and Reich somehow manages to choose exactly the right notes. The third is that unlike many overly prolific minimalists who seem to grab every assignment thrust before them, Reich has kept his output fairly limited in quantity, and as a result there's a higher percentage of quality Reich per square foot.

And there's a fourth: he keeps reinventing himself. Like Glass, Reich first attracted notice with his most daring stuff, the early phasing pieces, and gradually worked his way toward mainstream concert life. But after getting a bit bogged down writing for orchestras, Reich turned his back on that trend in the late '80s, shrank his forces to chamber size, and bravely went back to the drawing board, experimenting with sampling and video installations, trying to invent new forms of docu-theater. So far, the track record of his later works has been spotty, yet his fans always eagerly await his next move—and how many composers in any idiom still attract that kind of anticipation?

Reich in virtually all of his phases and stages can be experienced in a giant compilation of most of his music, so if you just want to get that and be rid of the task of picking and choosing, I won't stop you (♦Nonesuch 79451, 10CD). Otherwise, read on.

EARLY WORKS

Reich discovered phasing quite by accident when two tape loops he had made of a San Francisco street preacher drifted out of phase. From that idea, he created *It's Gonna Rain*, where the voice is distorted and multiplied until it sounds exuberantly chaotic. Then he achieved truly frightening results manipulating the words of a Harlem teenager in *Come Out;* at one point, the voices develop a demonic jazzy quality. These two tapes remain to date Reich's most radical pieces; they're not for the fainthearted (♦Nonesuch 79169, with a rerecording of *Piano Phase* and the totally self-contained *Clapping Music*). In *Violin Phase,* **Zukovsky**'s abrasively hypnotic performance has been gone for decades (Columbia 7265, NA), leaving the field to **Shem Guibbory**'s faster, lighter rendition (♦ECM 1168).

Four Organs, which swaps phasing for augmentation as a maraca beats time against the increasingly sustained sounds of four electric organs, received its premiere recording at the Guggenheim Museum with a historic ensemble containing both **Reich** and Glass (they had a falling out soon thereafter) (Shandar 10.005, NA). **Bang on a Can**'s rendition is sleeker and slightly slower (♦Naxos 79481).

Reich's phasing phase, so to speak, reached its apotheosis in *Drumming,* which more than a quarter-century later sounds like a masterpiece. Anywhere from 55 to 90 minutes in length, depending upon observance of repeats, the work gradually shifts from one percussion group to another in a masterly arch; indeed, the transition from drums to marimbas and voices (Part I to Part II) is a magical moment in new music. **Steve Reich and Musicians** made two recordings; I prefer the first (♦DG 427429, 2CD), which is longer and slower and has an ecstatic, ethereal ambiance that eludes the more hectic, much shorter remake (Nonesuch 79170).

CHAMBER MUSIC

Beginning with *Six Pianos,* Reich abandoned phasing and started to develop an additive technique (introduced in *Drumming*) that would greatly increase the rhythmic element in his music, bringing it closer to the feeling of jazz syncopation. *Six Pianos* has plenty of vitality in the original version (DG 427429, 2CD), and a more percussive, brighter, noticeably different balance in the recording by **Piano Circus** (♦Argo 430380). But Reich's trimming and rescoring of the piece under the name *Six Marimbas* has an even more swinging feeling (♦Nonesuch 79138). *Music For Mallet Instruments, Voices, and Organ* channels the processes of *Four Organs* and *Six Pianos* into a mellower continuum; the **Steve Reich and Musicians** remake (♦Nonesuch 79220) is crisper and more detailed than their laid-back first recording (DG 427429, 2CD).

Music for 18 Musicians was Reich's popular breakthrough, and in some ways this hour-long journey remains his most beautiful piece. Now he introduces shifting harmonies, comes up with some great syncopated ideas for repetition, and the whole thing flows like a dream. **Reich**'s first recording has a mellow, gauzy, delicate ambiance and understated drive that gradually seduce the listener (♦ECM 1129). His remake is longer (but not slower), balanced in a completely different way, tougher in some sections, smoother in others, more uninhibitedly aware of the swinging jazzy pulse (♦Nonesuch 79448). **Ensemble Modern** was the first group other than Reich's own to perform this piece, and though at first you can sense a touch of stiffness, the precise Germans ultimately play it really well, at times indistinguishably from Reich's bands (♦RCA 68672).

The bouncy, lightweight *Eight Lines* was originally called *Octet,* but Reich altered the instrumentation slightly and renamed it; in either guise, it has become Reich's most recorded work. The disc labeled "Octet" is by the rhythmically buoyant **Steve Reich and Musicians** (♦ECM 1168), still the best choice among the three versions of *Eight Lines,* and it also includes *Music for a Large Ensemble,* a tuneful extension of the techniques used in *Music for 18 Musicians.* Flutist **Ransom Wilson** does some rearranging, expanding to 25 players, adding double bass, favoring mobile rhythms, weightier strings, and of course the flute (EMI 47331, NA). **Christopher Warren-Green** and the London Chamber Orchestra double the string contingent from four to eight players, but their performance lacks rhythmic definition (Virgin). The **Bang on a Can** version follows Reich's lean original scoring but could use springier rhythms (Naxos 79481).

Tehillim was another breakthrough; besides being Reich's first published setting of a text, it marked the beginning of his preoccupation with his Jewish heritage. It's a joyous, easily assimilated setting of four Psalms, with highly syncopated rhythms dictated by the Hebrew text and widely spaced vocal lines for female quartet. **Steve Reich and Musicians** play the chamber version with lightness of touch and thrusting rhythms, a marvelous performance but poor value at only 30 minutes (♦ECM 1215). Although a bit earthbound by comparison, **Reinbert de Leeuw** and the Schoenberg Ensemble do get the basic idea, and it's coupled with *Three Movements* (♦Nonesuch 79295). The outer portions of the Sextet for pianos and percussion flow with irresistible mechanistic and jazzy energy (♦Nonesuch 79138).

Then, once Reich got orchestral music out of his system, he took off in a totally new direction with *Different Trains* for the **Kronos Quartet,** with sampled voices and train sounds. In contrasting the trains of his childhood with those headed for concentration camps in Europe, he created a powerful work with a deeply emotional edge rare in new music (♦Nonesuch 79176). *City Life* for 18-piece chamber ensemble also uses sampled sound effects—played rhythmically on keyboards—but this time Reich keeps his emotional distance and gives us a somewhat turgidly bleak portrait of New York City (Nonesuch 79430).

ORCHESTRAL MUSIC

As minimalism became a big deal in cultural circles in the '80s, even Reich felt the pull toward writing for conventional orchestras. His first attempt, *Variations for Winds, Strings, and Keyboards*—written for and recorded by **de Waart** and the San Francisco Symphony—is a gauzy expanse of pretty busywork where Reich's rhythmic impulse is smoothed over (Philips 412214, NA). But *The Desert Music,* an orchestral/choral setting of William Carlos Williams's poetry, is a 50-minute work of imagination and vitality, evoking a fast-car journey through the deserts of the West (though Williams's poems do not). Stoked by engines of maracas and mallet instruments, and driven by **Tilson Thomas**'s energetic leadership of Reich's ensemble and the Brooklyn Philharmonia, the varying rhythmic grooves manage to lift and carry the added weight (♦Nonesuch 79101).

From here on, though, Reich seemed to lose interest in the orchestra as a vehicle to explore new directions. *Three Movements* is a warmed-over return to *Desert Music* and Sextet country with hardly a striking new idea; II is basically a superfluous orchestration of the Sextet's IV. (Nonesuch 79295). *The Four Sections* is full of ideas, beginning with a long, heavy, lyrical, un-Reichian passacaglia for strings, followed by one movement each for percussion and winds before finally starting the engines (Nonesuch 79220). The problem is that Reich's distinct sound world is mostly lost and conventionalized. **Tilson Thomas** leads the London Symphony in both recordings.

OTHER WORKS

As showcases for favored soloists, Reich started a "counterpoint" series in which the soloist makes a tape of multiple parts on different-sized instruments and then plays over that tape in live performance. *Vermont Counterpoint* for flutist **Ransom Wilson** has a deliciously light, bubbly quality (♦EMI 47331, NA). As befitting its instrument, the clarinet, *New York Counterpoint* develops a jazzy sense of swing that evokes the big band era. Here, **Richard Stoltzman** (to whom the work is dedicated) remains the swaggering champ (♦RCA 5944), out-pointing **Alain Damien**'s staccato elegance (Virgin 45351) and **Evan Ziporyn**'s somewhat square version (Naxos 79481). *Electric Counterpoint* for electric guitars and basses has attractive folk/rock rhythmic elements, as well as the best harmonic and melodic ideas in the series, all deftly handled by jazz guitarist **Pat Metheny** (♦Nonesuch 79176). All three make delightful listening.

Alas, Reich's multimedia magnum opus *The Cave* doesn't work on CD, even though the piece—essentially a video oratorio—is quite effective in the theater (Nonesuch 79327, 2CD). Meditating on the story of Abraham, Sarah, Isaac, Hager, and Ishmael, coupled with interviews where, as in *Tehillim,* speech rhythms are set to music, Reich's score is a dour, static, audio experience; you can't experience how tightly the music cues in Beryl Korot's quick-changing images on the five video screens.

Proverbs, which Reich called "a pit stop" in his career, is an anomaly, deploying the neutral, early-music **Theater of Voices** against pairs of vibraphones and organs, an austere, innocent-sounding bone thrown to the fans of the fashionable neomedieval troika of Pärt, Tavener, and Górecki (Nonesuch 79430). And what is one to make of *Reich Remixed,* where this most stringent control freak of composers allows various DJs to electronically alter and refashion his music into entirely new bite-sized pieces? Well, I thought it was great fun to hear this pop-flavored afterthought after running through Reich's entire corpus—especially the "Megamix" where *Electric Counterpoint* becomes a running subtext for a long string of Reich quotes. Don't miss it (♦Nonesuch 79552).

GINELL

Anton Reicha (1770–1836)

Reicha ran away from home at 12, became a longtime friend of the youthful Beethoven in Bonn, and ended up teaching many famous musicians at the Paris Conservatoire. He was a highly imaginative theorist and composer, best known today for his 25 woodwind quintets, which show the bright, folksy feeling for those instruments that marks most Czech composers. He wrote many other works of great interest, in a lively style that mixes Classical and Romantic elements in a frequently unexpected way.

Very little of Reicha's orchestral music has been recorded. A light, bright symphony in E-flat was once available in a lively reading by the **Prague Chamber Orchestra** (Supraphon LP 50007, NA). The Wuppertal Symphony under **Peter Gülke** is adequate in this work; the disc includes a rather confrontational *Sinfonia Concertante* for the instruments Reicha played, flute and violin, and an overture in 5/8 time in the composer's experimental mood (MD+G 3350661). Earlier Supraphon CDs of a Concerto in E-flat for two horns and another in the same key for piano—the latter coupled with one by Anton's uncle Josef—seem to have disappeared. However, four very fine symphonies are spread over two Panton discs by the Dvořák Chamber Orchestra under **Altrichter:** F minor and C minor (811026) and D and F, this last a substantial work close to three quarters of an hour long (81027).

Jan Caeyers with the Beethoven Academie offers highly characterful accounts of the F major and C minor scores for those merely wishing a sampler (Auvidis Valois 4134). Also keep an eye out for the collection by the **Cincinnati College Conservatory of Music Wind Symphony** under Eugene Corporon that includes Reicha's *Commemoration Symphony* written to honor the heroes of the French Revolution.

Most of the works on disc are chamber music, the great majority consisting of or including wind instruments. Let's begin with the all-wind works. An odd genre that Reicha cultivated to a surprising degree is chamber works for flutes and horns. A collection of the flute works is played beautifully by the **Kuhlau Quartet,** with informative liner notes (Kontrapunkt 32045). There's music for from two to four flutes here, all of it lovely and imaginative. The works for multiple horns are contained in two large collections. Op. 82 consists of 24 little pieces for three horns, and **Zdeněk** and **Bedřich Tylšar** and **Zdeněk Divoký** play them all in modern Czech style, neat and lively, with a little vibrato (Supraphon 1446). The **German Natural Horn Soloists** play them without valves or vibrato, as they would have done in Reicha's day. Musically, there's little to differentiate these fine groups, but in sound, the natural horn produces notes outside the overtone series with a hand in the bell, making for a flavor of open and stopped notes that's either disconcerting or fascinating, depending on your taste.

Op. 93 is a similar set of 12 pieces, this time for two horns and bassoon. The **Tylšars** with bassoonist **František Herman** couple them with two little-known wind works by Beethoven (Supraphon 1445, NA).

The famous wind quintet series began in 1811 with a single work that remains in manuscript. There quickly followed four sets of six each (Opp. 88, 91, 99, and 100), most written between 1817 and 1820. They have all been recorded by the lively and ebullient **Albert Schweitzer Quintet** (CPO 999022–030 and 042, 10CD, NA). This young Hamburg group recorded in a fine ambience and, although they seldom take exposition repeats and frequently take tempos almost beyond the realm of probability, their split-second ensemble and beauty of tone, not to mention their wit and rubato, are major pluses. The **Academia Wind Quintet** of Prague has an album of five works including the 1811 Quintet

Op. 88:2 and 5 and Op. 91:3 and 5 (Hyperion 22006, 2CD). The Czech national style is attractively folksy for these pieces (I could listen to Czech wind players all day!), though the playing isn't quite as polished as the Schweitzer. Notes in both sets are excellent, the Hyperion booklet full of interesting quotes from Reicha and his contemporaries, the CPO with analyses and musical examples from all the quintets, as well as Reicha's meticulous metronome markings for each movement (not necessarily followed by the players).

The **Michael Thompson Quintet** from Britain has a series so far including Opp. 88:2 and 100:5 (Naxos 550432), Opp. 88:4 and 99:6 (Naxos 553528), and Opp. 88:6 and 91:6 (Naxos 554228). These readings are decidedly phlegmatic next to either of their rivals, though it should be stated that their version of Op. 88:2 contains more music than the Hyperion version, which uses a truncated edition of the piece. The Naxos group also takes all exposition repeats; still, it lacks fire and flame. A livelier reading of Op. 88:2 coupled with other wind quintet music is provided by the **Taffanel Quintet** (Denon 8004), with a little huffing and puffing by the horn.

Most of Reicha's chamber music combines that genre with the concerto: works with one wind and strings tend to fall into that category. A fine series of quintets for a single wind instrument with string quartet was once available (MD+G 3010501/2), but all that's left is Vol. 3 (MD+G 3010515).

There is a considerable Flute Trio with violin and cello, 45 minutes long, recorded by the **Reicha Trio,** not one of the composer's most compelling works (Arta 51). Another flute work is 18 *Variations and Fantasia on a Theme of Mozart* for flute, violin, and cello. This may be heard in a rather miscellaneous program played by **Rampal,** Stern, and Rostropovich with considerable enthusiasm (Sony 44568). Six Flute Quartets Op. 98 are relatively early, ca. 1813, and somewhat recall Mozart's works in the genre, though richer in emotional content and even quirkier in subject matter. **Nicolet** recorded the first three with the Mozart String Trio, playing with vigor and musicality (Denon 9203, NA). **Konrad Hunteler**'s recording is a worthy replacement (MD+G 3110630). Let's have the other three quartets, please.

Reicha wrote an Oboe Quintet (Op. 107), but at the moment it's only available in the composer's transcription for clarinet. The real clarinet quintet is Op. 89 in B-flat. There are three recordings presently, only one of which mentions the opus number. The most unusual is **Charles Neidich** with L'Archibudelli, an early-music version with a surprisingly woody but expressive clarinet sound and involved playing on everyone's part (Sony 57968, with Weber and Hummel). **Jean-Louis Sajot** with Ensemble Karl Stamitz gives a more straightforward reading with a more polite-sounding soloist (Pierre Verany 789101, with the Octet). **Vlastimil Mareš** gives us the Oboe Quintet played on clarinet in a smooth and nicely phrased performance, joined by the Stamitz Quartet (not to be confused with the Ensemble above) (Supraphon 51). He and Neidich take exposition repeats; Sajot doesn't.

Reicha gave the bassoon three works, a quintet, a set of variations with strings, and a sonata, all recorded by **Eckart Hübner** with the Nomos Quartet and pianist Inge-Susann Römhild (CPO 999061). The two pieces with strings are strong; the sonata is the only one recorded. The playing is lively and enjoyable. The quintet was also recorded by **Daniel Smith** and the Coull Quartet (ASV, NA).

Quintet for Horn and Strings is a bright and agile piece boasting a considerable slow movement. **Klaus Wallendorf** and Consortium Classicum play it with great polish and warmth, along with *Grand Quatuor Concertant* for flute, bassoon, cello, and piano (MD+G 3010515). This is

an imaginative 35-minute work with a lot of lovely scoring ideas along its merry way.

The largest chamber work is Octet in E-flat for wind and string quartets. There are two recordings of this decorative work, one by **Ensemble Carl Stamitz** on the disc with the Clarinet Quintet, played rather politely (Pierre Verany 789101). **Consortium Classicum** seems somewhat more involved (♦Orfeo 282921, with an obscure but attractive septet by Adolphe Blanc).

A more unexpected genre is found in three string quintets of 1805–1807 with two cellos, one of which is given a soloistic role, frequently playing duets with the first violinist. **Bylsma** recorded these with L'Archibudelli in lively, virtuosic readings (Sony 53118, NA). In his usual iconoclastic way, Bylsma omits the minuet movements (perhaps added later by the composer) and records the pieces in reverse order. They are fine works that should be reissued.

Two flute sonatas have been recorded by **Yoshimi Oshima** and Jaroslav Tuma; they are attractive music, beautifully played (Arta 96). This generous disc is filled out with four fugues for piano, also worthy of note. Finally, there are six piano trios, highly expressive pieces from 1824. The first three are recorded by the **Guarneri Trio** in highly responsive readings (Supraphon 3024).

One of the earliest Reicha pieces we have is one of his relatively rare piano collections, showing both his didactic bent and his iconoclastic side as well as a certain humorous attitude toward the world in general. This is 36 Fugues Op. 36 recorded by **Tiny Wirtz** (CPO 999065, 2CD). They show the Classical era coming to terms (sometimes to blows) with baroque counterpoint. Reicha takes some of the most unlikely fugue subjects, from folk songs to the opening of Mozart's "Haffner" Symphony, and makes them do his bidding. It's all explained in the notes, and the opening of each fugue is printed as well. Beethoven was skeptical, but they were reprinted before Reicha died. Most of the subjects are Reicha's; the treatment suggests the chromaticism of Chopin and Brahms, and sometimes virtual atonality momentarily rears its head. Heady stuff for 1805, played tastefully but with warmth on a hundred-year-old Steinway. Get it before it disappears!

Reicha's vocal works are not very well represented. Only the *Requiem* is presently available in an adequate but somewhat bland reading under **Lubomir Mátl** (Supraphon 332). *The New Psalm* was also conducted rather phlegmatically by Mátl (Panton 810758, NA), and a rousing performance of the dramatic *Te Deum* conducted by **Smetáček** needs reissuing (Panton 800242, NA).   MOORE

Carl Reinecke (1824–1910)

Reinecke's name is all but forgotten now except to flutists and harpists, for whom he wrote important works, yet he was a major figure of his time, an influential conductor and a famous teacher. As director of the Leipzig Conservatory, he turned that institution into a musical powerhouse, numbering Grieg and Albéniz among his students. As a composer, he looked backward rather than forward, seeing himself as a stalwart guardian of Classical tradition. He wrote prolifically throughout his life, however, and continued to grow as a composer. His later works show an eloquent, somewhat Brahmsian nobility.

Reinecke wrote three symphonies, with only 1 in print at the time of writing. It's a youthful work that displays his abundant lyricism and strong orchestration, but it's not among the finest symphonies of its time. Having said that, many listeners will certainly enjoy its synthesis of Mendelssohn and Schumann. **Alfred Walter** and the Rhenish Philharmonic give this music a strong endorsement with their adroit performance (♦Marco Polo 223117).

Reinecke was rightfully famous for his piano music and had a considerable reputation as an interpreter of Mozart, and the cadenzas he wrote for Mozart's concertos were widely used. His own piano concertos owe more to Mendelssohn and Schumann, but they're worthy efforts nonetheless. I especially enjoy 3 and 4, although 1 was the most widely performed in Reinecke's time; musicians and critics of that era regarded it as one of the most important concertos, and it's not hard to see why. Its melodies are beautiful and its thematic development binds it into a gloriously unified whole. No. 2 was somewhat unsuccessful, apparently owing to a general lack of brilliance, but even here there are many exquisite moments. Listeners can judge their merits for themselves with **Klaus Hellwig**'s admirable survey; he plays stylishly, with Alun Francis and the Nordwestdeutsche Philharmonie supporting beautifully (♦CPO 999239, 2CD).

I find Reinecke's chamber music most satisfying, and many of these works should be better known. For an introduction to this music, there is no better starting point than the collection of trios recorded by the **Dallas Chamber Players** (♦Klavier 11050). These lovely works for unusual combinations (piano-oboe-horn, clarinet-viola-piano, and clarinet-horn-piano) are performed with luminous elegance and recorded in a warm acoustic. In these works of his full maturity, Reinecke makes the most of the colors of these disparate instruments, and his melodic gift was apparently inexhaustible. You hear this in other works as well; for instance, the G minor Serenade Op. 242 is a true gem. It can be heard in a lovely disc with three serenades by Robert Volkmann, exquisitely performed by the German Chamber Academy under **Johannes Goritzki** (♦CPO 999159).

Reinecke's three cello sonatas deserve to be better known, too, particularly the magisterial Sonata 3, written at age 74 and dedicated to Brahms. **Claudius Hermann** plays them all with grace, expressivity, and a sumptuous tone, sensitively accompanied by Saiko Sasaki (♦CPO 999342). The earlier sonatas aren't as substantial as 3 but are still fine pieces with many sublime moments. All of them would be welcome recital works, but 3 really deserves a central place in the repertoire.

Some of Reinecke's two-piano works can be heard in a disc along with works by Raff and Rheinberger. These duos are not very substantial, but they're highly enjoyable and full of grace and charm. The **Hitzlberger/Schütz** team plays them with considerable poise and elegance (CPO 999106).

The Flute Sonata ("Undine") is the best known and most often recorded of all his works, and it's well served by several fine recordings. **Galway**'s is excellent, with superb backup by Argerich, and midpriced to boot (♦RCA 61615, with sonatas by Franck and Prokofiev). **Robert Aitken** places it in a different context, with works of Schubert, Bozza, and Marais (♦BIS 183). The sonata also exists in a less-performed clarinet version, but only one performance is available, by **Hans-Rudolf Stalder,** with other Reinecke chamber works that feature the clarinet (Jecklin 602).   McINTIRE

Ottorino Respighi (1879–1936)

Respighi's catalog of works includes no fewer than eight operas, nearly 50 songs, over half a dozen concertos, and even a pair of string quartets. No matter. Respighi will always be remembered for his trilogy of Roman tone poems—*Fountains of Rome, Pines of Rome,* and *Roman Festivals*—whose splashy theatrics display his considerable orchestral gifts and coloristic sense to unforgettable advantage. But it wasn't all

sound and fury, even among the orchestral essays. For every *Roman Festivals,* there's also the muted poetry of a *Brazilian Impressions,* not to mention the songful intimacy of suites like *Gli Ucelli* (The Birds) and *Ancient Airs and Dances,* ingratiatingly arranged from the music of earlier masters. Happily, the record companies have been generous with each, even though this does pose some duplication dilemmas.

ORCHESTRAL MUSIC

Fountains of Rome, Pines of Rome, and ***Roman Festivals.*** For years the solution to the Respighi problem was simple: **Toscanini,** whose recordings of *Pines, Fountains,* and *Festivals* dominated the lists through the mono-LP era. They still command an honored place on CD, even if what once seemed the highest of "high fidelity" now sounds a trifle hard and overly brilliant (♦RCA 60262). Otherwise, here is Respighi's inspiration white-hot from the kiln, with an Italianate verve whose force seems undiminished half a century later. The same might be said of **Sabata**'s *Fountains,* now reissued with his Debussy recordings (Testament 1108). (Too bad they didn't include his *Festivals.*)

It was clearly Toscanini's Respighi **Reiner** had in mind when he remade *Pines* and *Fountains* in stereo, with astonishing success, so much so that they have been reissued with two couplings, first with the Mussorgsky-Ravel *Pictures at an Exhibition* (♦RCA 5407, NA), then with Debussy's *La Mer* (♦RCA 68079). Neither quite equals the splendor of the original LP, but the current remasterings come close to matching the imposing grandeur of the performances, still unsurpassed for power and excitement. They're just not always the last word in poetry.

For that, you could do worse than **Muti,** as Italianate in his way as Toscanini, if without Reiner's heft, sonically or interpretively (♦EMI 47316). Likewise **Daniele Gatti,** who, like Muti, offers all three Roman tone poems in performances of remarkable flexibility and lyricism, even if his Santa Cecilia Orchestra is no match for Muti's Philadelphians (♦Conifer 51292). Nor should you overlook **Bátiz,** whose boldly colorful, vividly articulated readings combine first-rate sound with an old-fashioned interpretive panache (a particularly exciting *Pines*), all at a budget price (♦Naxos 550539).

On a slightly lower rung are **Dutoit**'s readings, luminous and powerful despite some minor quirks of tempo (London); the atmospheric if more restrained **Tortelier,** who happily doesn't overdo the noise factor in *Festivals* (Chandos); the lushly evocative **Ormandy,** at his best in *Festivals* (and less bloated on inexpensive Sony than on RCA); and a CD combining **Sargent**'s somewhat undercharacterized *Pines* and *Fountains* with **Goossens**'s still-potent *Festivals,* which, though not without blemish in the brass, is otherwise spectacular in performance and sound (Everest).

It's no more spectacular than **Mata,** however, whose *Pines* and *Festivals* are especially vibrant and colorful (listen to the way the organ in the latter comes through), as is his appended *Brazilian Impressions* (♦Dorian 90182). **López-Cobos** likewise churns things up impressively in *Festivals,* even if he's a bit less memorable in the evocative middle sections (Telarc). Here, too, the coupling is *Brazilian Impressions,* along with *Church Windows* (see below). His *Pines* and *Fountains,* in a separate CD, also sometimes shortchange the music's poetic content (Telarc). Again, though, the recorded sound is something to hear, as are his antiphonal nightingales in *Pines.*

Fifteen years earlier Telarc also scored sonically with **Louis Lane,** whose *Pines* and *Fountains* are still lease-breakers. Nor are the performances that far down the list, to these ears surpassing the coarse and overemphatic **Dorati** (Mercury), the brilliant but heartless **Sinopoli** (DG), and the over-polished **Karajan** (DG). Certainly the last's EMI *Pines* had more life, if less sonic immediacy. **Maazel**'s latest Respighi recordings (Sony) don't efface memories of his earlier *Pines* (DG, NA) and *Festivals* (♦Decca 466993). All the above, however, are more desirable than the uninspired **Rizzi**, who lumbers his way through these pieces in remarkably unexciting fashion (Teldec). Not so **Bernstein**'s *Pines* and *Festivals*, only here the excitement comes at the expense of warmth, something also true of the hard-edged, metallic recorded sound (Sony).

Among individual performances, **Kempe**'s *Pines* exudes an almost Germanic strength and, like its coupling, **Freccia**'s idiomatic *Fountains* and *Festivals*, is stunningly recorded (♦Chesky 18). **Stokowski**'s *Pines* is even more richly and colorfully projected, if you don't mind Shostakovich's Symphony 1 and Khachaturian's Symphony 2 as discmates (♦EMI 66864). Ditto **Silvestri**'s *Pines* (BBC), coupled with Tchaikovsky's *Manfred*, a little brassy and blatant (e.g., the noisy children at play) but undeniably thrilling (e.g., the concluding march).

Church Windows and *Brazilian Impressions*. Mixing and matching is also something of a challenge with the other major orchestral works in the Respighi catalog. Though *Church Windows* has never achieved the popularity of the Roman trilogy, it bids fair to turn it into a tetralogy. Among current recordings, **Ormandy**'s dynamic reading still holds its own, and at a budget price, though his appended *Birds* is perhaps a bit too well-upholstered (Sony). Nor is fire missing from **Geoffrey Simon** (♦Chandos 8317) or **López-Cobos** (♦Telarc 80356), both spectacularly recorded, even if the organ registers more resoundingly on Telarc. Each also appends a fine *Brazilian Impressions*, if without quite matching **Mata**'s eerily sinuous atmosphere and natural feeling for the rhythms (e.g., the concluding "Song and Dance") (♦Dorian 90182). Moreover, López-Cobos, like Mata but unlike Simon, offers a third piece, his previously mentioned *Festivals*. **Dorati** offers four, though his otherwise estimable *Impressions* (Mercury) seems to lack a center channel (ditto his *Birds*, in the same CD as *Pines* and *Fountains*).

Trittico Botticelliano. Things are even more competitive when it comes to these subtly joyous evocations of three Botticelli paintings— "Spring," "The Adoration of the Magi," and "The Birth of Venus." Two of the best, from **Simon** (♦Cala 1007) and **Orpheus Chamber Orchestra** (♦DG 437533), are no longer available, but there are still **Wolff** (♦Teldec 91729) and **Vasary** (♦Chandos 8913), the first exhilaratingly purposeful and the second luminously vital. Nor will you go wrong with **Marriner**, intimate and alive if just a trifle square (EMI), or **López-Cobos**, also a mite rigid but generally open-hearted and strongly articulated (Telarc). The same tends to be true of their couplings. For Wolff, that takes the form of *The Birds* and Suites 1 and 3 from *Ancient Airs and Dances* (or, for the same money, a 2CD "Ultima" set that includes Rizzi's uninvigorating Roman trilogy). If you can find it, however, the Orpheus CD offered the same pieces, even more characterfully detailed.

By contrast, Vasary's *Birds* and *Trittico* come with full-orchestra versions of the less-often-heard *Adagio con variazioni*, with cellist Raphael Wallfisch, and the lyric poem *Il Tramonto*, with mezzo Linda Finnie. López-Cobos's coupling is all three suites of *Ancient Airs*. But a real bargain set includes not only Marriner's *Birds*, *Trittico*, and complete *Ancient Airs* but also **Gardelli**'s idiomatically colorful *Pines*, *Fountains*, and *Belfagor Overture* (♦EMI 69358, 2CD); if you're not especially keen on the sometimes cacophonous *Festivals*, this could well be the way to go.

Ancient Airs and Dances and *Gli ucelli*. If these are your focus, no one has surpassed **Christopher Lyndon Gee**, whose performances are beautifully shaped and sprung and splendidly effulgent in sound

(♦Omega 1007). Next to this, **Dorati**'s *Ancient Airs* seem a bit close-miked; still, it's hard to resist their manly flavor and generally vigorous interpretive stance (♦Mercury 434304). **Hickox** is at once forthright and sensitive (Chandos 9415, with arrangements of two violin pieces composed by Respighi in 1901). Also in the upper echelon is **Saccani**, a bit distantly recorded but affectionately accented and detailed, and doubly attractive at the price (Naxos 553546).

Metamorphoseon. If you already have **López-Cobos**'s *Pines* and *Fountains*, you don't need another *Metamorphoseon* (Telarc). If not, **Simon**'s is even more richly impassioned, and he has the wit to couple this somber masterwork with the luridly sensual suite from the ballet *Belkis, Queen of Sheba* (♦Chandos 8405).

Sinfonia Drammatica. This hour-long work from 1914 is heavily infused with Mahler and Strauss, at the same time anticipating what was to come in the Roman trilogy (particularly *Fountains*). Neither **Downes** (Chandos 9213) nor **Nazareth** (Naxos) manages to conceal the sprawl of the 18-minute finale. They do, however, bring out the music's Mahlerian overtones, in Nazareth's case with a refreshingly Middle Eastern quality (e.g., the expansive Andante). Since his disc is about one-third the price of Downes's, the choice should be obvious. So too is **Adriano**'s collection of such lesser-known orchestral essays as the Suite in E Major, the Glazunov-inspired *Burlesca*, and *Preludio, Corale e Fuga*, principally because it's the only game in town (♦Marco Polo 223348). Still, for the most part these are enjoyable pieces, not hurt by the lushness of the performances.

Ballets. *La Boutique Fantasque* is undoubtedly the best known of the Respighi ballets, a delightful arrangement of Rossini pieces from the latter's *Sins of My Old Age*. Among the major companies, Decca/London has long had a near lock on the complete ballet, beginning with the mono **Ansermet** LP—still the most fanciful--and continuing through **Bonynge**'s 1981 CD, alive with the spirit of the dance. Neither is available at present, but happily **Dutoit** manages to combine their best qualities in a beautifully recorded, lovingly shaped performance, coupled with an okay *Brazilian Impressions* (♦Decca 455983). **López-Cobos** may be less bouncy and fanciful but serves things up with plenty of zest, taking particular delight in the masterly orchestrations (♦Telarc 80396). **Solti**, by contrast, seems a little short on magic and whimsy, not to mention heart (London).

Among abridged *Boutiques*, **Fiedler** could likewise use a bit more warmth but takes a backseat to no one in the zest department (RCA). **Ormandy** is warmer but also heavier in an unabashed big-orchestra rendition (Sony). **Janigro** is almost as cut and dried in places as Solti, something that extends to his *Rossiniana* in the same CD (Vanguard). A better option for this less-compelling *Boutique* follow-up might be **Patrick Peire**, whose disc in addition to being more curvaceous and atmospheric includes its own *Boutique* suite, tossing in Britten's two Rossini concoctions, *Matinées Musicales* and *Soirées Musicales*, for good measure (René Gailly 87062).

Closer to *Boutique* in spirit is *Le Astuzie di Columbina*, one of three lesser-known Respighi ballets **Adriano** has unearthed, with some composer-authorized cuts (♦Marco Polo 223346). *La Pentola Magica* (The Magic Pot) is sort of a Russian potpourri, and just about everyone will recognize the *Gavotte* from *Sèvres de la vieille France* in this charming disc.

Arrangements and transcriptions. Russia was not far from Respighi's heart when he orchestrated five of Rachmaninoff's *Etudes-Tableaux*.

(He had, after all, spent several years in St. Petersburg studying with Rimsky-Korsakov.) **López-Cobos** offers the whole set as filler to his *Boutique Fantasque* in performances a bit less soulful than some but admirably recorded (Telarc). Nor is soulful the word to describe **Gerard Schwarz**'s recording of Respighi's Bach transcriptions (♦Delos 3098). Here, however, the tastefulness helps more than it hurts.

CONCERTOS

Respighi's concerted works don't generally find him at his best, though those for violin often exude a remarkable beauty. Among current recordings of *Concerto Gregoriano,* that beauty emerges more richly, if more deliberately, with **Mordkovitch** (♦Chandos 9232) than with the lyrically subdued **Takako Nishizaki** (Marco Polo). Moreover, Mordkovitch's CD, like the latter's, offers the lovely *Poema Autunnale* and goes farther in adding Downes's colorful *Ballad of the Gnomes* (though in fact Simon, on Cala, made more of its *Salome*-like overtones). If the *Poema* is your chief concern, no other violinist sinks into it quite as romantically as **Ricci** (♦Reference 15). However, the more straightforward **Igor Gruppman** is also worth hearing in a disc that includes not only *Il Tramonto* (here for baritone and string quartet) but also the only extant *Suite for Organ and Orchestra* I know (Koch 7215).

The most successful of the piano concertos is probably the 1928 *Toccata,* to which **Scherbakov** brings an appropriately Lisztian spark (♦Naxos 553207). What's more, his budget-priced CD also tops the list for the early *Fantasia Slava* and A minor Piano Concerto, as opposed to the more consciously majestic **Tozer** (Chandos). As for the more protracted *Concerto in Modo Misolidio,* Tozer must likewise yield to **Sonya Hanke**'s greater sense of shape and forward motion, as well as her more obvious affection for Respighi's beloved modes (♦Marco Polo 220176). On top of this, hers seems to be the only recording of *Three Preludes on Gregorian Themes* for piano solo, the original form of what was to become the first three movements of *Church Windows.*

GOODFELLOW

OPERAS

I keep hoping that one of Respighi's operas will be effective and interesting, but I continue to be amazed that an Italian composer who wrote such gaudy, successful works for orchestra should have had so little affinity for opera.

Belfagor. Respighi's only comic opera, based on a contemporary Florentine comedy, was staged at La Scala in 1923. It achieved only a modest success at its premiere and immediately disappeared from the repertory. Its musical interest is entirely in the orchestra; the vocal lines are uninteresting, consisting of concise conversational fragments. The result is a uniform mellow blandness with no clear profile or direction. Opera is about voice—what it does and how it does it. Success depends on how interestingly the voice is used, and there is little of interest here. Even if the music were more than serviceable, the only recording leaves much to be desired (Hungaroton 12850, 2CD). **Gardelli** tries gamely to animate the score but despite comfortable playing by his orchestra doesn't manage to bring life to this moribund piece.

La Fiamma. This opera is based on Hans Wiers Jenssen's play *The Witch.* The story is a curious amalgam of witchcraft and the Byzantine world of 7th-century Ravenna. Respighi labored arduously over the opera, making alterations even during the rehearsals for the premiere, and it's probably his strongest. Its clever combination of romantic passion, spirituality, and the menace of witchcraft made for an initial popular success, but after a brief tour around the world it faded into obliv-

ion. As usual, **Gardelli** conducts with authority, sympathetic to the needs of the singers, yet keeping the show steadily on course with no dragging (♦Hungaroton 1259, 3CD). The singers are a strong group, imparting a good degree of dignity to the proceedings.

Lucrezia. This is the last of Respighi's ten operas; his wife Elsa, also a composer, completed the final 29 pages of orchestration after his death. After its 1937 La Scala premiere, *Lucrezia* made the rounds of the Italian opera houses and was broadcast, but even the opera's champions (Maria Caniglia, Fedora Barbieri) couldn't make it an international success or even keep it afloat in Italy. Respighi's music is a continuous stream of melodic fragments allowing for little vocal display, rather like out-takes from Puccini operas; there's much more musical interest in the doings of the orchestra. In the only recording, the **Bratislava Radio Orchestra** turns out a worthy performance, but with a genuinely unpleasant group of singers (Marco Polo 223717).

Maria Egiziaca. Respighi's brief opera based on the *Lives of the Holy Fathers* by Cavalca was originally intended for concert performance; its premiere took place at Carnegie Hall in 1932. A 1980 performance at Assisi by the **Accademia di S. Cecilia** forces has little to recommend it, with ugly singing and playing all round (Bongiovanni). A **Gardelli**-led performance has better sound but except for the orchestra lacks the Italianate romantic spirit the music so generously exudes (Hungaroton 31118).

Semirama. Respighi's first opera bears the solid influence of Strauss. Not only did the music of *Salome*—with its highly charged, voluptuous sounds, and colorful orchestration—influence *Semirama,* but the libretto in a round-about fashion was an influence as well. Strauss's libretto, a German translation of an English translation of a French text by Oscar Wilde, found an imitator in Italian poet Alessandro Cerè. The text is wordy, overly picturesque, full of archaic and curious expressions. The orchestra is the star here, with broad, soaring melodies—exotic, oriental, and all at the expense of the singers. The plot is similar to Rossini's and many others.

I really like this opera; the only recording not so much (Hungaroton 31197, 2CD). **Gardelli** leads a sweeping performance that storms along full of color and passion; a good start, yes—but then the singers must sing. Marton has a big voice, hard-edged, difficult to control, and afflicted with waves of wobble. When she isn't pushing her voice she's fine, but up high and loud, look out! Linda Bartolini belts out everything at a constant forte. It's not a pretty sound; it's irritating, it's boring, it's *very* provincial.

Sleeping Beauty. This was written for Vittorio Podrecca's famous troupe of puppets. A decade later Respighi remade the opera, now called *La Bella Dormente Nel Bosco,* and reorchestrated it for a small ensemble. It's quite graceful, intimate, with much charming appeal. The familiar story, though, isn't quite so familiar here. Respighi updates the finale to 1940 with characters from the past stepping into the present. The only recording is fine, aside from a strained sounding Prince from Guillermo Dominguez; **Adriano** is noted as a Respighi authority and imposes that authority here to keep the show light and lively (♦Marco Polo 223742).

PARSONS

VOCAL MUSIC

Respighi wrote a considerable amount of vocal music besides his voluminous operatic output, although it wasn't really until the advent of CDs that it began to receive regular attention in the recording studios; now almost all of it is available.

The best-known of these works is *Il tramonto*, setting an Italian translation of Shelley's *The Sunset;* its intense, almost cloying, atmosphere recalls Schoenberg's *Verklärte Nacht.* The string-orchestra version can be heard with the Swiss mezzo **Brigitte Balleys** and the Lausanne Chamber Orchestra under López-Cobos (Claves 50-9807, with Giuseppe Martucci's *La Canzone dei ricordi*). Balleys's voice is just slightly hard-edged, though she responds sensitively to the text.

In the smaller-scale scoring with string quartet, the Brodsky Quartet and **von Otter** are first-rate; the Brodskys play with both passion and technical security, and von Otter is in her usual glorious voice (Vanguard 99216, with *Quartetto dorico* and Quartet in D). Their recorded sound is much better than that given the Tokyo String Quartet and **Scotto,** who produces some ugly singing in both *Il tramonto* and the other works on this disc (Vox 7201, with the cycle *Deità silvane* [Gods of the Woodland] and five songs for voice and piano). So, too, does the squally tenor of **Axel Everaert**—to be avoided (Pavane 7375, again with *Deità silvana,* four of the *Cinque canti all'antica* and 13 other songs).

The only recording of a baritone in *Il tramonto* comes from **Christopher Trakas,** tentatively sung and tentatively accompanied by Quartetto di Venezia; the balance of the disc, with the San Diego Chamber Orchestra under Donald Barra, is the lyrical *Poema autunnale* for violin and orchestra and the early Suite for Organ and Orchestra, along with Menotti's *Cantilena e scherzo* for harp and orchestra (Koch 7215).

The orchestral version of *Deità silvane* can be found with *Aretusa,* a cantata for soprano and orchestra, and the "lyric poem" *La sensitiva* (both, like *Il tramonto,* settings of Shelley) in a fine CD led by Richard Hickox; **Linda Finnie**'s glowing account of *La sensitiva* is particularly moving (Chandos 9453). Finnie also contributes *Il tramonto* to another disc, here with the Bournemouth Sinfonietta conducted by Vásáry (Chandos 8913, with *Adagio con variazioni* and *Trittico botticelliano*).

The Swiss conductor Adriano has set about exploring this repertoire systematically. *Aretusa, Il tramonto, La sensitiva,* and Adriano's own orchestration of *Quattro liriche* to texts of d'Annunzio can be found with mezzo **Faridah Subrata** and the Czecho-Slovak Radio Symphony (Marco Polo 223347). Subrata has a bright, clear tone. The soloists in Adriano's recording of the 45-minute "lyric poem" *La primavera,* recorded by the Slovak Radio Symphony with *Quattro liriche su poesie popolari armene,* again arranged by Adriano, are far less impressive (Marco Polo 223595).

Respighi's complete songs for voice and piano have been issued in reliable interpretations by the sweet-toned tenor **Leonardo de Lisi** and pianist Reinild Mees. Vol. 1 contains *Cinque canti all'antica, Sei liriche* (2nd series), *Deità silvane,* and nine individual songs (Channel 9396). They're joined in Vol. 2 by soprano **Andrea Catzel** for *Sei liriche* (1st series), *Sei melodie, Quattro rispetti toscani, Sue canzoni dialetti,* and five early songs (Channel 11998).

Last, we have the earliest substantial piece Respighi composed, the hour-long "biblical cantata" *Christus,* with soloists including baritone Roland Hermann and conducted by **Marco Balderi** (Claves 50-9203). *Christus* is neither individual nor memorable, though it does demonstrate considerable technical assurance for a 19-year-old student.

ANDERSON

Silvestre Revueltas *(1899–1940)*

Known as the "Bartók of Mexico," Revueltas wrote his finest works during the last decade of his short life. In 1931 he burst onto the international musical scene with an original musical style characterized by irresistible energy, vigorous, syncopated, often asymmetric rhythms,

rapidly changing meters, frequent pedal notes and ostinatos, and bold instrumental effects. As Revueltas said, "My rhythms are loud, dynamic, tactile, and visual." His tonal music also shows bitonal and polytonal tendencies and mixes consonance and dissonance. Rooted deeply in the soil and people of Mexico, his sharply etched, often angular melodies are based on the melodic and rhythmic inflections of Mexican folk music, but the melodies are almost always his own.

ORCHESTRAL MUSIC

Revueltas wrote music for seven films, including the 1939 *La Noche de los Mayas.* In 1960, a four-movement suite was drawn from this film by the Mexican conductor José Ives Limantour. **Luis Herrera de la Fuente** conducts this exciting piece on an all-Revueltas release (♦Catalyst 62672). On the same disc, *Homenaje a Federico Garcia Lorca* and *Sensemayá* are led by Mata, and David Atherton leads the remaining works: *Ocho por Radio, Toccata, Alcancías,* and *Planos.* All except *Sensemayá* (discussed below) are alternately soulful and boisterous, rhythmically syncopated works made up of fast and slower sections.

Eduardo Alvarez offers *La Noche* coupled with impressionistic music by José Pablo Moncayo and heavy-footed works by Manuel Ponce (Crescendo 1679). A performance of *La Noche* by **Herrera de la Fuente** is coupled with the Garcia Lorca *Homenaje, Sensemayá,* and *Janitzio* (Spartacus 21005). The same conductor gives us another *La Noche,* this time with two brightly colored nationalist works by Moncayo and Blas Galindo (Spartacus 21007). There's also a fine performance of *La Noche* by **Bátiz,** with Ponce's lovely Violin Concerto (Szeryng as soloist) and Moncayo's *Huapango* (EMI 49785). The recordings of *La Noche* all have some instrumental balance problems, but for best performance, fullest strings, and sheer visceral excitement, I prefer Catalyst.

Sensemayá is Revueltas's most-performed work. He wrote it for chamber orchestra in 1937 but expanded and rescored it in 1938 for 27 winds, strings, and 14 percussion. It's based on a poem by Cuban poet Nicolás Guillén describing the ritualistic killing of a tropical snake. The original version is in "The Unknown Revueltas," with **Enrique Arturo Diemecke** (Dorian 90244). As interesting as this version is, it lacks the barbarism and visceral impact of the expanded revision, often called a Mexican *Sacre du Printemps.* This compelling release also contains short chamber works from the '20s, including the attractive Five Songs for soprano, baritone, and chamber orchestra, and the 1931 *Cuauhnahuac* for strings, Revueltas's first successful work.

Herrera de la Fuente leads *Sensemayá, Ocho por Radio,* and other attractive Mexican compositions (IMP 63). *Sensemayá* and the fine suite of introspective and dramatic music from the film *Redes* are offered by **Mata,** with works by Julian Orbón and Ginastera as discmates (Dorian 90178). *Sensemayá* is also led by **Bátiz,** coupled with *Ocho por Radio, Janitzio,* and seven other worthwhile Mexican works (ASV 394). **Salonen**'s *Sensemayá* is somewhat leisurely but well played; this sonically splendid release contains seven other Revueltas works as well (Sony 60676).

Fernando Lozano conducts *Sensemayá, Cinco Canciones para Niños* for soprano and orchestra on texts by Lorca, *Janitzio, Redes,* and two works by Moncayo (Spartacus 21021). **Tilson Thomas** leads *Sensemayá* with works by five other Latin American composers plus Copland's *Danzón Cubano* (Argo 416737). The fastest, most exuberant reading of *Sensemayá* is by **Stokowski,** recorded in 1947 in surprisingly good sound in a "Centennial Anthology" commemorating Revueltas's birth (RCA 63548, with the material on Catalyst 62672 plus seven other works). This release is rounded out with *Cinco Canciones para Niños y Dos Canciones profanas* with **Margarita Pruneda** as soloist.

All these versions of *Sensemayá* offer rhythmically detailed readings and are coupled with a wide variety of interesting Latin American works. The Mexican conductors have this music in their blood, but Tilson Thomas and Salonen also do a very fine job, with spacious sound to boot. Mata's somewhat tentative reading is the least interesting.

Bátiz presents *Caminos, Ventanas,* and the evocative suite *Musica para charlar* from a film on Baja California, coupled with Chávez's masterly Symphonies 1 and 4 (ASV 653 and 942). **Diemecke** offers the unfinished and uninteresting four-movement "Dance of Life and Death" ballet suite *La Coronela,* completed and orchestrated by other hands (Spartacus 21027, with a vibrant piece by Arturo Márquez and Moncayo's somewhat long-winded Symphony).

CHAMBER MUSIC

From 1930 to 1932, Revueltas wrote four string quartets. The first three are rather conventional melodically and rhythmically but show a few hints of his later style. No. 4 is the pinnacle of the quartets and is characteristic of his mature music. All four are given idiomatic performances by the **Latin American String Quartet** (NALB 62).

DE JONG

Roger Reynolds (b. 1934)

Reynolds is an American avant-gardist whose musical activities have encompassed a wide range of interests and idioms. An experimentalist by nature, he fits into and extends the lineage of Cowell, Cage, and Varèse. He's probably best known for his extensive efforts in electro-acoustic music, and most of his available recordings reflect this. At the same time, he has worked diligently to extend the possibilities of instrumental music, writing many works for performer and tape. One thing that gives his music an engaging aspect is his enthusiasm for collaboration; most of it involves contributions from other artists. Sometimes he uses musicians as sound sources for his electronic music, or sometimes the collaborators determine the parameters of the material, as in the case of his work with Japanese experimental theater director Tadashi Suzuki. Several of his works are concertos, although they are not so described in their titles. He has long been interested in mixed-media events, and has recently begun exploring the possibilities opened up by DVD.

Little of Reynolds's large-ensemble music is recorded, but the recording of *Whispers out of Time* for string orchestra makes us wish to hear more (New World 80401). Reynolds was awarded the Pulitzer Prize for this piece, and it's one of the more challenging works so honored. In six movements, it draws upon quotations from Mahler and Beethoven, evoking an intense pathos throughout its 26 minutes. Although Reynolds employs a wide range of complex compositional techniques, they never intrude on the expressive aspect.

It's coupled with *Transfigured Wind II* for flute soloist, computer-generated tape, and ensemble, a good example of Reynolds's collaborative style; the tape part is created from four recorded flute solos played by **Harvey Sollberger.** Reynolds, through digital processing, creates a stunning backdrop for the instrumentalist generated entirely from the sounds of Sollberger's flute. This disc conveys the essence of Reynolds's music and presents two of his most satisfying pieces. Both works are performed by the San Diego Symphony Ensemble, conducted by Sollberger.

Personae for violin, tape, and ensemble is another notable concerto, coupled with two other fine works that show the range of Reynolds's style very nicely (Neuma 450-78). Soloist **János Négyesy** shows that challenging music need not sound labored, and the SONOR Ensemble under Rand Steiger provides exceptional support. *The Vanity of Words*

is a tape piece built on baritone Philip Larson's reading and singing of a brief text by Milan Kundera. Reynolds unfurls this material into a collage reminiscent of Samuel Beckett. *Variation* is a large-scale solo piano work and one of Reynolds's best pieces, superbly played by Aleck Karis. Not a set of variations, the work is "a set of sonic fragments continuously interacting with one another."

The Dream of the Infinite Rooms is a concerto for cello, orchestra, and four-channel tape (GM 2039). Here the tape part is realized from material played by the soloist, **Regina Mushabac.** Edwin London leads the Cleveland Chamber Symphony, and the disc is filled out with works by Libby Larsen, Salvatore Martirano, and Bernard Rands.

"The Paris Pieces" is a collection of works that resulted from a residency at IRCAM, Pierre Boulez's immense musical research center in Paris (Neuma 450-91, 2CD). *Odyssey* is a disc-long "opera in the mind," which features the Ensemble Intercontemporain under **Peter Eötvös,** soloists Marie Kobayashi and Philip Larson, and an eight-channel tape of computer-processed sound. The second disc has three more pieces that emerged from the IRCAM relationship plus a much earlier work, *Fantasy for Pianist,* here played by Scott Dunn. I heard this work in recital once and thought it rather weak, but Dunn makes a strong case for it, and in his hands its complex architecture is clear.

Another IRCAM commission was *Transfigured Wind IV* for flute soloist and tape (Neuma 450-74). The soloist is **Sollberger** again, accompanied by a tape made of transformations of his playing. The work has much in common with *Transfigured Wind II* but is much leaner in texture. It's coupled with other excellent electronic works by Babbitt, Varèse, and Xenakis.

The Ivanov Suite and *Versions/Stages* are two "suites" of electro-acoustic music that expand our portrait of this composer (New World 80431). *Ivanov* was composed as incidental music for a Japanese production of Chekhov's play, and *Versions/Stages* is a rigorous study of the separability of form and content through the exploration of individual timbres. The resulting five-part work is a good deal more musical than this description probably implies.

COCONINO . . . A Shattered Landscape is a remarkable work for string quartet and is given a superb reading by the **Arditti Quartet** (Gramavision 79440, NA). The title is indicative of this fragmented work with its ever-changing textures and contours. This disc is notable and worth seeking, not only for this piece but for the couplings: Nancarrow's Quartet 3, Seeger's *Quartet 1931,* and a strange and unsettling performance of Beethoven's *Grosse Fuge.*

For the die-hard Reynolds fans, there's *From behind the Unreasoning Mask* for trombone, percussion, and tape (New World 80237). This is one of his more astringent works. Trombonist **Miles Anderson** delivers some extraordinary sounds from the bell of his horn, and though it's quite dramatic, I find I haven't listened to it as much as other pieces by this composer. Another interesting-sounding project (but unheard by me) is Reynolds's foray into digital multimedia on a DVD with three works: *Watershed IV, Eclipse,* and an excerpt of *The Red Act Arias* (Mode 70). This interactive disc features video, surround sound, and interviews with Reynolds and the performers. Though he's of an earlier generation of American composers, Reynolds obviously has no intention of being left behind in the development of new technology.

McINTIRE

Emil Nikolaus von Rezniček (1860–1945)

Perhaps the greatest irony surrounding the Austrian composer Rezniček is that his best-known piece, the sparkling overture to his comic opera *Donna Diana*—set in Barcelona— should be remembered primarily as theme music for the radio program *Sergeant Preston of the Yukon.* Yet in his day Reznicek was revered for far more serious fare, including his opera *Ritter Blaubart,* a violin concerto, and four symphonies. We may be thankful for the few works now available on disc, but as adepts of the tape underground know only too well, there's so much more out there if only some enterprising record company would bring it to light.

The early Symphony in D clearly reflects the influence of Reznicek's teacher Reinecke. He always seems ready to burst into song; it's a thoroughly carefree and captivating exercise. Symphony in F Minor is a far more imposing work, very much in the Austro-German tradition and admittedly somewhat diffuse structurally, yet opulent and richly textured, with an appealing font of melody. Restless and passionate, it offers a heroic opening sally, a rather Mahlerian "Funeral March on the Death of a Comedian," an upbeat Scherzo, and finally a set of variations on an original theme. **Gordon Wright** gives authoritative readings of both works, lacking only that last rush of high spirits in the finale of the D major (♦Schwann Musica Mundi 11091).

Serenade in G for string orchestra deserves to be heard occasionally alongside the more familiar examples of Tchaikovsky, Dvořák, and Suk; it offers a variety of images in the style of Goldmark's *Rustic Wedding Symphony,* culminating in a delightful "Peasant March." It's nicely turned by **Jiři Stárek,** coupled with Violin Concerto in E Minor with **Michael Davis** and Wright (♦Schwann Musica Mundi 311128). While Wright describes the score as "fiendishly difficult," you'd never know it from Davis's seemingly effortless traversal, and his assurance and purity of tone make the discovery all the more rewarding.   HALLER

Josef Rheinberger *(1839–1901)*

Rheinberger, highly regarded during his lifetime as one of the premier European composers and as a teacher who drew students from across the globe, was consigned within a few years of his death to the pages of music history, and his works have all but disappeared from view. This is a misfortune, for he wrote some of the most memorable Romantic music. Nevertheless, a modest Rheinberger renaissance has begun, due in large part to the work of Harald Wanger of the Rheinberger Archiv in Liechtenstein and to the emergence of a new critical edition of his complete works.

ORCHESTRAL MUSIC

Symphony 1 ("Wallenstein"). The first symphony is an expansive four-movement work for large orchestra, with some programmatic aspects. The performance by the Philharmonic Orchestra of Frankfurt (Oder) under **Athinäos** is excellent in all respects (♦Signum 50-00, with the buoyant Overture to the opera *The Seven Ravens*). The young orchestra plays with eloquence and distinction, and the recorded sound is well centered and satisfying. Extensive program notes by Wanger add an extra dimension of value.

Symphony 2 ("Florentiner"). This is again a four-movement work, this time infused with impressions of Rheinberger's trip to Florence in 1874. This work, however, is surer, more gripping, and more innovative in its thematic treatment than its predecessor, and the orchestration is magisterial—an overlooked masterpiece. It's given a fine, spirited, cohesive performance by **Francis** and the NW German Philharmonie, an orchestra with a distinctive Central European sound (♦Carus 83.112). The detailed program notes, with many photos, make this a luxury edition.

A third disc furnishes a cross section of Rheinberger's orchestral works, from early to late, as well as several choral selections (♦Signum 60-00). Of special interest is the *Academic Overture in the Form of a Fugue with Six Voices,* dedicated to the faculty of the University of Munich, which awarded him an honorary doctorate in 1899. The early Overture to *Taming of the Shrew* is a genial, dexterously written work, modeled along the lines of Mozart's *Zauberflöte* Overture. On the basis of these performances, the Philharmonic Orchestra of Frankfurt (Oder) must be rated as a world-class ensemble. The strings are homogeneous and meticulously in tune, the brasses round, dark, and focused, the woodwinds faultless, and the general precision of the highest caliber.

CONCERTOS

Piano Concerto in A-flat. This concerto is unusual for its choice of key, for its virtuosic fashioning of the solo part, and for its superlative artistic qualities. In dimensions, it's comparable to the Schumann, Grieg, or Saint-Saëns 2nd, but wears better than the last two, thanks to its ever-fresh, fascinating themes and consummate scoring. For a long time only one recording existed, by **Adrian Ruiz,** now reissued with well-written program notes by David Dubal (♦Genesis 106). It presents an imaginative, thoughtful performance. Some years later, a superbly assured performance by **Ponti** followed (♦Vox 5065, in "The Romantic Piano Concerto" Vol. 2, 2CD). In 1998 **Jürg Hanselmann** recorded this work in a performance more elegant than either of its predecessors and as thrilling as Ponti's (♦Prezioso 800.034). The Symphonic Orchestra of Liechtenstein is excellent; the sound is superior to the others; and there are notes by Wanger. So we have three very satisfying versions, but Hanselmann's seems to me the most distinguished.

Organ concertos. Rheinberger's "two magnificent organ concertos stand unmatched as monuments of 19th-century literature," wrote E. Power Biggs. Indeed, **Biggs**'s recording, not yet reissued on CD, has not been surpassed. Of the several recordings currently listed, none is without detriment. The Rehfeldt (Bayer) and Juffinger (Capriccio) versions differ sharply. The **Rehfeldt** isn't a particularly distinguished recording, and the organ sound is buried. **Juffinger**'s approach is neo-Baroque in most respects, emphasizing clarity and directness. The acoustics are dry, and the organ, while in good balance with the orchestra, is quite monochromatic, making its presence known via upper work. The instrument isn't distinguished, but at least we can hear it! In between these two, and probably the top choice of the three, is a recording by the Danish organist **Ulrik Spang-Hanssen,** in which spirited, ardent playing and excellent balance of organ and orchestra prevail (♦Classico 252).

CHAMBER MUSIC

Among the 197 opus numbers in Rheinberger's catalog, his genius is most strikingly revealed in his chamber music. The high points of this repertoire are the sublime late Sextet for piano and winds, the priceless Nonet, the Piano Quintet, and the Piano Quartet, widely popular during the composer's lifetime. Also noteworthy are the virtuosic Horn Sonata, with its haunting slow movement, and the expressive, melodious Cello Sonata. Fifteen of these pieces are available in a superb set, a collection of peerless performances, most of them with pianist **Horst Göbel** as the inspiring catalyst (♦Thorofon 2161/6, 6CD). Sound quality is absolutely ideal, and especially pleasing is the perfect balance between piano and other instruments, always a ticklish problem. Some of these discs, though not all, are available singly.

You will also find excellent performances of the four piano trios by **Trio Parnassus** (♦MD&G 3419/20, 2CD), of the Nonet by **Ensemble Wien-Berlin** (♦Sony 58971), of the Sextet by the chamber soloists of the

Staatsphilharmonie Rheinland-Pfalz (♦Bayer 100233), and of the two violin sonatas by **J. Besig** and C. Brembeck, piano (Christophorus 74616). For the last, the Thorofon release is to be preferred because of its superior intonation and balance.

ORGAN MUSIC

Of 24 organ sonatas planned by Rheinberger, one in each key, he was able to complete 20. These are concert pieces rather than liturgical or sacred works, for which Beethoven's 32 sonatas served as distant models. Supplementing the sonatas are 94 smaller character pieces, most of which are also for concert performance. To these can be added 16 more works with one or more obbligato instruments, and the two large concertos—altogether an imposing and invaluable contribution to the concert literature for the instrument.

Nearly all the sonatas have been recorded several times, but two recordings stand out: **Thomas Murray**'s 5 (♦Afka 507), the most visceral reading of a Rheinberger sonata I've heard, and **James Callahan**'s brilliant 7 (♦Centaur 2081). Although **Timothy Farrell** viewed the composer's tempo indications merely as general guidelines (Rheinberger was very explicit in his markings), his performance of the majestic 20, Rheinberger's last completed composition, is exceptional in its musicality. This is in Volume 1 of a 7CD series of the complete organ sonatas, recorded on British organs by four different organists who make nearly every performance a fine one, even if the organs don't always suit the music ideally (Prezioso). **Bruce Stevens**'s beautiful performances, painstakingly prepared and very well recorded on 19th-century American organs, shouldn't be overlooked (♦Raven). Finally, **Wolfgang Stockmeier** has made distinguished recordings of four books of the smaller pieces in three splendid CDs (♦CPO 999040, 999041, 999089).

The novel and arresting Suite for Cello, Violin, and Organ Op. 149 is presented by **Juffinger** in a good, agile performance, along with Six Pieces for Violin and Organ Op. 150 (Capriccio). Unfortunately, the solo strings are much too prominent in the Suite, so that his excellent playing is thrown into the background, where the organ passagework is often inaudible. The same criticism applies to **Ulrik Spang-Hanssen**'s recording of this work. Another Suite for Violin and Organ, Op. 166, is performed by the same duo as Op. 150, **Sebestyen** and **Juffinger**, and here the balance is much better (Capriccio, with the Concertos).

PIANO MUSIC

At the very beginning of his career, Rheinberger aspired to become a concert pianist. Although 35 opus numbers are for solo piano, and von Bülow praised these works and performed them throughout Europe, very few recordings have been made. Heading the list of these piano essays stand four large sonatas that carry forward the line of Schubert-Schumann-Brahms and surely deserve to be programmed much more often than they are.

Along with Sonata 2, **Horst Göbel** offers the charming *Improvisation on Themes from Mozart's Zauberflöte*, a work very much in the manner of Liszt's operatic paraphrases but more provocative than most of them (♦Thorofon 2157). Göbel plays it superbly, with intelligence, wit, and delectable tone. A particularly fine LP recording of 4 ("Romantic") was made by **Adrian Ruiz;** perhaps we can hope for its remastering (Genesis). A valuable CD presents Rheinberger's arrangement of Bach's *Goldberg Variations* for two pianos, with **Adelheid Lechler** and **Ulrich Eisenlohr** (♦RBM 6.3087).

Jürg Hanselmann has recorded all four of the sonatas in 2CDs that contain several other captivating piano pieces as well. His performances are stylish, sympathetic, full of color and nuance, and technically ac-

complished, and the sound is faultless. Sonatas 1 and 2 come with the *Präludium und Fuge zum Konzertvortrag* (dedicated to Anton Rubinstein), *Etude and Fugato,* and *Three Small Concertpieces* (♦Prezioso 800.040); 3 and 4 are grouped with *Toccatina in G Minor* and *Toccata in C Minor* (♦Prezioso 800,009). The pianist has collaborated with his wife, Sandra Hanselmann-Kästli, in a beautiful disc of four-hand pieces, including the exceptional Duo for two pianos Op. 15 (♦Prezioso 800.010).

CHORAL MUSIC

Rheinberger's writing for chorus, like his orchestral works, was expert, and his choral catalog is wide-ranging, from masses and motets to secular part songs. The beautiful and touching Christmas cantata, *The Star of Bethlehem,* deserves first mention. The libretto was by his wife and seeks to portray the Nativity events in a Tyrolean mood. The great Mass in E-flat Op. 109 for double choirs a cappella, the so-called "Cantus Missae," has been called the most beautiful a cappella mass of the 19th century. Two other exquisite Romantic masses, the large Op. 109 in C, with full orchestra, and Op. 151 in G, the "Missa St. Crucis," are still unavailable on CD.

A 1968 performance of *The Star of Bethlehem* led by **Heger,** with the Graunke Symphony Orchestra and soloists Streich and Fischer-Dieskau, can rightly be designated one of the great recordings since WWII (♦Carus 83.111). Soloists, conductor, chorus, and orchestra all seem to have been inspired during the recording sessions; an unmistakable sense of dedication to the work emanates from their performance. Streich's artistry is particularly captivating. The program notes are by Harald Wanger, one of the key figures in making this recording a reality.

Two American choirs, both turning their attention to "Cantus Missae," achieve a choral tone of astonishing sensuousness—a floating purity of timbre combined with a wide range of dynamics and sensitive nuances that holds the listener enthralled. **Gloria Dei Cantores** has recorded five works (three with organ) in the gently luminous acoustical environs of Mechanics Hall in Worcester, Massachusetts. We have here superbly prepared and executed performances, full of atmosphere, spirituality, and many memorable moments, both thrilling and intimate (♦GD 018). An equally entrancing choral sound, though quite different due to the smaller ensemble, is to be heard from **St. Clement**'s **Choir,** Philadelphia (♦Dorian 80137). The all-professional choir of 19 voices offers six sacred works by Rheinberger, all a cappella, including "Cantus Missae," in which their singing is a model of precision, flexibility, discipline, and intonation.

An all-Rheinberger disc by one of the world's oldest and greatest men's and boys' choirs, the **Regensburger Domspatzen,** conducted by one of this century's great choral directors, Georg Ratzinger, includes a wide variety of secular and sacred works (♦Ars Musici 1063). Most are a cappella, but several of the Latin motets have organ accompaniment. Everything about this CD is estimable, as might be expected. Of course, their sound is entirely different from the choirs already discussed.

An even wider range of Rheinberger's choral art is presented by another distinguished European choral conductor, Frieder Bernius (Carus 68.113). However, the **Kammerchor Stuttgart** is neither as well trained and disciplined as the Americans, nor is their performance as evocative. These comments also apply to the performances by **Collegium Vocale Limburg,** a men's choir that sings the Masses in B-flat Op. 172 and F Op. 190 (both with organ), along with choral works by Mendelssohn and Cornelius (Carus 83.125). Still, these are attractive CDs, with excellent, detailed notes, and the performances, while they may not be of the Americans' quality, are good to very good.

SONGS

Like Schubert and Brahms, Rheinberger turned often to that most Romantic of genres, the lied, to which he devoted twelve of his opus numbers. A well-chosen cross section can be heard in an excellent disc, where two female and two male soloists share the assignments (◆Signum 88-00). One of the ladies (the documentation doesn't say who is singing, or when) isn't always pleasant to hear, but the other three vocalists are very good. **Horst Göbel,** at the piano, plays with scrupulous taste and impeccable artistry, and the sound is bright and realistic.

MULBURY

Wallingford Riegger (1885–1961)

Riegger belonged to the generation that included Ives, Cowell, Ruggles, and Varèse, and his music was born of a mindset similar to theirs. He was sometimes facetiously referred to as "the common man's Schoenberg"—I suspect because his approach to serialism had a rhythmic brio that spoke of a common touch foreign to the Viennese master. Even at his thorniest moments, Riegger's music remains appealing and approachable because of its exhilarating propulsive qualities. His approach to serialism is uniquely American-sounding and more thematic than the Viennese methods, making its formal aspects easier to hear. He's widely acknowledged to be one of the most influential American composers of the 20th century, yet his music is performed little and recorded less. Many important pieces, like *Study in Sonority* for strings and his landmark orchestral work, *Dichotomy,* are not to be found.

Only two surveys of Riegger's music are currently available. "Music for Piano and Winds" is a magnificently played collection in which Gilbert Kalish and the New York Woodwind Quintet offer a fine recital of various works (Bridge 9068). Starting with the Concerto for Piano and Woodwind Quintet, this group makes the strongest argument possible for Riegger's music; the work is a masterpiece, a sparkling 12-minute essay in Riegger's eclectic fusion of styles and techniques. Vivid colors, strong melodic writing, and spiky, jazz-inflected rhythms give it immense appeal and downplay its overall dissonance. The disc is nicely paced with lots of variety, alternating between various combinations of woodwinds and pieces for solo piano.

"Music of Wallingford Riegger" is similarly varied, with more emphasis on pieces for larger forces, and it shows off the range of Riegger's music very well (CRI 572). *Romanza* and *Dance Rhythms* display his more ingratiating qualities, whereas *Music for Brass Choir* and *Nonet for Brass* offer some of his more uncompromising moments. The disadvantage of this set is its uneven recording quality; its contents were compiled from a variety of sources and recorded at different times, and while it fills an important need, I'm left wishing for better sound. Symphony 3, for example, is presented in a serviceable performance led by Hanson with the Eastman-Rochester Symphony Orchestra, but the mono sound leaves much to be desired. The same is true (even more so) of *Romanza,* and here the orchestral playing is rather scruffy as well. *Concerto for Piano and Woodwind Quintet* is included and is very well played, but the Bridge recording outpaces it in every respect. Still, the quality of the music shines through in every measure of each piece, and whatever its drawbacks, it's still an important collection of this remarkable composer's work.

McINTIRE

Wolfgang Rihm (b. 1952)

Rihm's music is ferociously Teutonic; it seems to have sprung wholly from that culture with little or no outside influence. He's greatly influenced by Mahler and other 19th-century Austro-Germanic composers, though his own style is much more dissonant and expressionistic. He began composing at an early age, quickly absorbed the methods of Schoenberg and Webern into his vocabulary, and expanded his technique with later studies with Stockhausen and others. Although generally regarded as an avant-garde composer, he has resisted the isolation that accompanies that path, trying to reach a wider, nonspecialist audience as well. His music is somewhat formidable, but he always deploys his technique toward some expressive purpose; indeed, beneath the sometimes forbidding surface lies a heartfelt romanticism.

Rihm's reputation rests largely on his orchestral writing, but little of this repertoire is available on recordings. **Gunther Neuhold** leads the Badische Staatskapelle in a collection well worth seeking out (Bayer 800886). It includes several pieces of modest dimension and shows Rihm's range and style of writing well, including *Dunkles Spiel* for small orchestra, *O Notte* for baritone and orchestra, Viola Concerto, *Schwebende Begegnung* and *Schwarzer und Roter Tanz,* both for orchestra. **Claudio Abbado** leads *Départ,* an intense, harrowing work, in his "Wien Modern" collection (DG 429260). Though brief, this piece is a memorable setting of a text by Rimbaud for two choruses (one speaking, one singing) and large ensemble. **Mutter** has recorded a stunning performance of *Gesungene Zeit* (Time Chant) for violin and orchestra, one of Rihm's more immediately accessible works, with Levine leading the Chicago Symphony (DG 37093). This piece is lean, lyrical, and adagio: a single thread of music spun out with sparse support from the orchestra. It's coupled with Berg's Concerto and is an excellent choice for that work also.

For chamber music there is a wider choice of repertoire. *Music for Three Strings* is an hour-plus exploration (deconstruction is perhaps a better word) of Beethoven's late quartets (CPO 999050). Rihm quotes motifs from these works, creating a fleeting, chaotic unity that is frequently ruptured by sudden outbursts, ostinatos, and fragmentation. Members of **Ensemble 13** give the work a blue-chip reading (CPO 999134). This disc includes two other works: *Kein Firmament* and *Sine Nomine,* among Rihm's more radical and astringent pieces. *Sine Nomine* for brass quintet is unremittingly aggressive, with jagged contours and extremes of register. *Kein Firmament* is more pointillistic—a shifting kaleidoscope of colors punctuated by (sometimes lengthy) silences.

In *Fremde Szenen I–III* (Strange Scenes) for piano trio, Rihm's point of departure is the music of Robert Schumann. This haunting, unsettling work is aptly described by its title and is beautifully rendered by the **Beethoven Trio Ravensburg** (CPO 999119). Quartet 4 is a striking work, full of contrasts, from its energetic, almost Bartókian opening to its slow, melancholy final movement. The **Alban Berg Quartet** gave a stunning live performance that's well worth seeking out (EMI 54660). This might be an ideal entry point into Rihm's chamber music.

Rihm has considerable renown in music theater, although much of that repertoire remains unrecorded. *Die Eroberung von Mexico* (The Conquest of Mexico) is a stunning example. Based on an outline by Antonin Artaud and other sources, this massive work depicts the collision of two cultures, the Spanish of Cortez and the Aztec of Montezuma. Although it's too dramatically static to be described as an opera (the story is conveyed more through the music than the words), the themes and emotive content are certainly as large as anything in that genre. **Ingo Metzmacher** directs the Hamburg Staatsoper chorus, orchestra, and soloists in a vibrant, intense performance (CPO 999185).

McINTIRE

Terry Riley (b. 1935)

Modal-pulse music was an early form of minimalism, and Riley's *In C* (1964) is one of the better pieces in that genre. Composed of 53 snippets of music in C major/modal, any number of performers from a few to full orchestra move at individually or conductor-determined pace from one to the next. The only limit to this indeterminacy is that one must always move forward, but each snippet can be repeated ad libitum. Consequently, *In C* lasts from a few minutes to, theoretically, infinity. Two recordings illustrate the temporal and instrumentational variance: in one (Argo 380) it takes only 21 minutes, played by six musicians; in the other 30, players plus conductor make it last 76 minutes (New Albion 71). I've heard it live a couple of times, and if memory serves, 30 to 40 minutes is about right, and a mixed chamber ensemble is best for holding interest via timbral counterpoint.

Both recordings are acceptable for recorded sound, but for all other reasons except pace and length of recorded time I prefer the Argo disc. First of all, it includes Reich's *Six Pianos,* another example of pulsed minimalism performed very well by **Music Circus** on acoustic and electric pianos, harpsichords, and a vibraphone. *In C* benefits from this instrumentation, a relatively homogeneous timbre but with enough variation to arrest the ear when a new snippet is embraced. However, the music sounds rushed at 21 minutes, as though Music Circus had another gig to play. Maybe they did, because there's plenty of recording time remaining, as the two pieces together require only 43 minutes of disc space. In the New Albion recording the additional timbres don't support the additional half-hour of music; there simply isn't enough there to hold your interest for 76 minutes.

Riley has embraced a variety of music from the vernacular to the exotic. *June Buddhas* brings a lot of it together as a backdrop for Jack Kerouac's poetry, albeit somewhat obviously and pretentiously. The Brooklyn Philharmonic conducted by **Dennis Russell Davies** offers *June Buddhas* and *Etruscan Concerto,* with Keith Jarrett as piano soloist for the latter, and Lou Harrison's *7 Pastorales* (MusicMasters 67089).

A slightly different style of minimalism is offered in *A Rainbow in Curved Air*—very Philip Glass–like, consonant and improvisatory over repetitive arpeggios played by the composer on electronic keyboards (Sony 07315). The disc includes *Poppy Nogood and the Phantom Band* for soprano sax and electric organ, both instruments also played by **Riley.** Despite the title, *Poppy Nogood* reflects Riley's study of Indian music, as consonant drones support free-form jazz licks. He sometimes improvises concerts that last several hours, and I that presume something like these pieces results. An unattributed poem constitutes the entire liner note except for performance information.   ZIEROLF

Nikolai Rimsky-Korsakov (1844–1908)

Youngest of the Russian composers collectively termed "The Five"—along with Balakirev, Cui, Borodin, and Mussorgsky—Rimsky-Korsakov was a driving force behind nationalism in Russian music, not just in opera (like Glinka before him) but in a series of sumptuous works that carried his name around the world. Into his music he incorporated seductive Eastern melodies (as in *Scheherazade* and *Le Coq d'Or*), venturing as far west as Iberia for his *Capriccio Espagnol,* while glorifying the traditions of the Orthodox Church in his *Russian Easter Overture,* the colorful and fanciful tales of Russian folklore in *Skazka, The Snow Maiden,* and *May Night.* It has become popular to disparage Rimsky-Korsakov as a sort of musical alchemist, all surface glitter and no substance; yet with a greater appreciation of his influence on future generations, we may see that the inspired mix of imagination and

orchestrational skill that characterizes his best work is its own reward. Through the wonder of *Scheherazade* the child in us all stands revealed.

SYMPHONIES

There are three symphonies, or four if you count *Sinfonietta on Russian Themes.* The best part of 1, completed while he was still a 17-year-old naval cadet with no formal musical training, is the opening movement—fresh and bracing—though the rest betrays the young man's lack of sophistication, as he himself was later quick to admit. When you hear a wonderful performance like **Boris Khaikin**'s, you forget how immature it is (♦Multisonic 310237). How many other teenagers could write music like this?

And so different from 3, completed in 1873 shortly after becoming professor of composition and orchestration at the St. Petersburg Conservatory. Indeed, he later recalled ruefully that Borodin—who liked it—nevertheless said that Rimsky "appeared to him as a professor who had put on spectacles and composed *Eine grosse Symphonie in C* as befitted his rank." You might think so, too, if all you knew was a turgid performance like **Svetlanov**'s (RCA) or **Anichanov**'s (Naxos); but if you can find it in your import bin, head straight for **Rozhdestvensky,** who's far more invigorating than any of the domestic releases (♦Revelation 10083).

We might call *Antar* Symphony 2, but Rimsky went to great pains to describe it as a suite rather than a symphony; whatever you call it, it's simply gorgeous, a series of Arabian Nights–styled images culminating in an embrace of mature passion far more erotic than that of the innocent young lovers of *Scheherazade.* Of the great LPs, **Scherchen**'s has been reissued, even including a few measures somehow left out of the LP (PRT 6021), but **Paray**'s remains in limbo (Mercury). Switching to stereo does little to help **Maazel,** who is sadly prosaic, with an unbelievably sluggish tempo in the third movement march (Telarc). You'd do better (and cheaper) with **Abravanel** (Vanguard)—though Maazel has far better sound—or check out the "two-fer" that combines **Zinman**'s *Antar* with other pieces, including *Coq d'Or* and *Tsar Saltan* (Philips 442605, 2CD).

There are several complete surveys of the Rimsky symphonies. You might think it a simple matter to buy **Neeme Järvi**'s set and be done with it (DG), but only *Antar* can be recommended; his hyper tempos in 1 and 3 effectively rule out the set. **Svetlanov** recorded all three symphonies twice, first for Melodiya and later for RCA, plus a third try at *Antar* (Hyperion). The RCAs are uniformly flaccid, occasionally pulling ahead—as for example in 3:I, which has an earthy vigor not evident from the early Melodiya—but thoroughly dispensable if you have either the original Melodiyas or the BMG "twofer" (40065, combined with an even worse *Scheherazade*). You may still want Svetlanov's RCA version of 3 for the marvelous *Maid of Pskov* and *Tsar's Bride* overtures. The Hyperion *Antar* has the benefit of a far better orchestra (the Philharmonia), but even though he picks up the pace elsewhere, the lovers' embrace still seems strangely dispassionate.

Butt's coupling of 1 and 2 is preferable to his bully-boy approach in 3 by a wide margin, but he's still sadly dispirited in 1:I and never really seems involved with either the music or the story behind it in *Antar* (ASV). I suppose **Kitaienko** will do if you want 1 and 2 on one disc (Chandos 9178); at least he's properly sensuous in *Antar,* though Khaikin remains supreme in 1. In 3 Kitaienko is better than Butt (admittedly that's not saying much) but he seems slack in the glittering Scherzo (Chandos), and both conducting and engineering are far better for Rozhdestvensky.

Unfortunately, the cheapest set is also the worst, with **Anichanov** presiding over an ensemble easily as ragged as anything ever heard from Svetlanov and apparently recorded in an Aeroflot hangar to boot (Naxos). In *Antar*, the second movement is so hectic that the players fall all over themselves, while Anichanov's use of the earlier edition avails little as the all-important gong is barely audible. The disc with 3 is at least worth considering for the rarely encountered *Sinfonietta on Russian Themes*, notable for its use of a melody familiar from Stravinsky's *Firebird* (550812). **Ari Rasilainen** is better, though saddled with a lackluster Borodin Symphony 1 (Finlandia 14910). **Svetlanov** seems rather sober-sided in this music (Melodiya), while **Maxim Shostakovich**'s LP hasn't come out on CD (Melodiya).

OTHER ORCHESTRAL MUSIC

Scheherazade. If ever there were a score tailor-made for **Stokowski**, it's *Scheherazade,* and not surprisingly he recorded it several times. If there were a stereo recording with Stokowski and the Philadelphia Orchestra in their prime, it would sweep the board. We must be grateful for the exemplary reissue of the highly expressive 1934 performance (Cala 521), though the more straightforward 1927 Philly has its staunch adherents (Biddulph 010). With the Royal Philharmonic, Stokowski is more freewheeling and enjoys superb playing, including concertmaster Erich Gruenberg's solo turn as the seductive Sultana (RCA 62604). There's also a low-cost version, a bit harsher sounding and without filler (Victrola 7743); the newer version has *Russian Easter* (see below). But for sensuous string sound and bold splashes of color, nothing can beat the performance with the London Symphony, a standout in London's low-price Jubilee series (♦41753), though it must be admitted that he saunters through the festival at Baghdad at rather moderate tempos.

Certainly no one can complain about lack of excitement in **Reiner**'s standout Chicago recording, the hair-raising final movement incredibly recorded in a single take and even surpassing Stokowski in virtuosity. Some may find it subject to capricious mood swings—seductive one minute, coquettish the next—yet both the superb playing and glorious sound, still lustrous after some 40 years, remain unsurpassed. There was an earlier Gold Seal pressing (RCA 60875), but the "Living Stereo" release is the one to have (♦RCA 68168).

If you prefer a more elegant, even sophisticated *Scheherazade,* **Beecham** remains unsurpassed, and the Royal Philharmonic of course played wonderfully for him, with Steven Staryk beguiling in the central role (♦EMI 47717). While something of the sensuous nature of the music is lost, we must remember that Scheherazade is no wanton harlot but a beautiful woman desperately trying to save her life by keeping the Sultan interested in what she has to say, and Beecham is a master storyteller himself, with the winds even taking on the quality of the human voice. **Bernstein** knew how to tell a good story too, and his 1959 New York recording still sounds marvelous today, crisply imaged if without quite the spotlighting of Stokowski's and rivaling even the old wizard himself in a highly emotional and exciting reading (Sony 47605, or the "Bernstein Century" reissue, 60737).

There's a grand sweep and wealth of color with **Mackerras**—clearly among the front ranks (♦Telarc 80208). So too is **Jansons,** a rapturous and magical account culminating in an exhilarating and festive finale (♦EMI 55227). Like Stokowski before him, Jansons clearly relishes his role as *griot* and finds just the right "once upon a time" imagery in Sinbad's timeless adventures. The Concertgebouw is in top form for **Chailly**—a lush, highly satisfying rendition in luxurious sound (London 443703)—as indeed they were for **Kondrashin,** a gorgeous recording of an inspired and compelling performance (Philips 400021). **Monteux**'s warm embrace works wonders (London 417028).

Temirkanov and the New York Philharmonic merge the best traditions of Bernstein and Stokowski with lush, warm, string textures and thrilling brass sound, all building to an almost manic account of the festival at Baghdad and culminating in a shattering crash as Sinbad's ship careens into the massive rock (♦RCA 61173). The New Yorkers play as if possessed, and the RCA engineers have surpassed themselves. Those on a budget need not hesitate on finding **Enrique Bátiz;** save for a rather dispassionate account of the young lovers, it offers good value at the price (Naxos 550726).

As with Stokowski, **Ansermet** recorded *Scheherazade* more than once; his later account with the Suisse Romande, once highly praised for its sound, now seems sadly outdated both for performance and sonics and is of greater interest for the various suites (see below; London 443464); his earlier recording with the Paris Conservatoire, should you happen upon it, seems even more ancient. Far more compelling is **von Matačič,** whose potent recording with the Philharmonia has been brought out as part of a set also containing Kletzki's splendid *Tsar Saltan* Suite (EMI 68098, 2CD). **Fedoseyev** is seductive and boasts opulent sound, though at a premium price (Canyon).

Muti seems too cool and detached, and the violinist sounds as if he were seated backstage (EMI). So too does the soloist in **Ashkenazy**'s rather aloof and uninvolved run-through, with a bland and faceless performance by the Philharmonia (London). They play splendidly for **Emmanuel Krivine,** but his reserved reading may not be to all tastes (Denon), any more than **Karajan**'s rather Teutonic view of the music (DG). **Chung**'s routine and impersonal reading is beautifully played but lacking in character (DG), while sluggish tempos and over-reverberant acoustics rule out **Järvi** (Chandos).

The engineers have provided massive sound for **Litton,** especially in the heady finale, but he seems less involved in the quieter passages, and David Nolan's violin is slighted in the process (Virgin; the same performance is in Seraphim 69030, with Leinsdorf's *Russian Easter).* They should have used **Leinsdorf's** *Scheherazade* instead; it still sounds fine (if not as seductive as some), though the main reason to buy the disc is William Steinberg's *Coq d'Or* Suite (EMI 65424).

Mauceri is not as overtly sensual as Stokowski (also with the London Symphony), but flows seamlessly in an absorbing reading distinguished by Michael Davis's beautiful playing of the solo (MCA 25187). **Boughton** is bland and uneventful with low-level sound to match (Nimbus), while **Mehta** (CBS) and **Masur** (Teldec) are prosaic and eminently forgettable (CBS). So is **Barenboim** (Erato). **Dorati** was a top contender in the days of Mercury's "Living Presence" series but is sonically outclassed today, the Minneapolis performance little more than routine. **Ozawa** has given us two equally dull readings, one on EMI and a more recent attempt for Philips. **Frémaux** suffers from thin string sound and a too-distant solo violin; it all sounds pretty homogenized and predictable (Collins).

You may find **Svetlanov** in a 2CD set (Chant du Monde), separately (Melodiya), or reissued with the symphonies; either way it's dead weight, an uneventful account enshrouded in murky sound. His remake with the London Symphony is splashy and anything but subtle; at nearly 50 minutes some may find he overdoes the languor (EMI, with his ponderous Glazunov *Seasons*). **Goossens**'s recording, a marvel of the LP era, still sounds wonderful, if hardly the most seductive account around (Everest 9047). However, it seems positively X-rated next to **Mario Rossi**'s recording—indeed at 7:45 (compared to 11:52 for Stokowski and the London Symphony), the embrace of the Young Prince and the Young Princess sounds more like a picnic in the country (Vanguard).

Suites. Järvi's collection remains essential (♦Chandos 8327/29). There are great recordings by **Ansermet** of the *Tsar Saltan* and *Christmas Eve* Suites plus *May Night* Overture and *Sadko,* unfortunately coupled with his *Scheherazade* (London). Järvi replaces *Sadko* with *Mlada, Coq d'Or,* and *Legend of the Invisible City of Kitezh.* This is a 3CD set totaling 147 minutes, and Chandos should have remastered them onto 2 discs long ago. But Järvi knows how this music should go, and Chandos delivers great sound (though Ansermet is more atmospheric). Another conductor who's done all the suites is **Edward Serov** (Kontrapunkt; *Tsar Saltan, Snow Maiden,* and *Kitezh* on 32117; *Coq d'Or, Maid of Pskov,* and *Pan Voyevoda* on 32247; and *Mlada, Christmas Eve,* and the brief *Sadko* episode on 32261). Vol. 1 is worth having despite cavernous sonics, hampered only by Serov's curious tendency to slow down or speed up at segue points, and this affectation is unfortunately even more marked in Vol. 2, marred especially by the frenetic wedding procession in *Coq d'Or.*

Fortunately, he does a lot better with the harder-to-find *Pan Voyevoda* and *Maid of Pskov* (also known as *Ivan the Terrible*), handily holding his own against **Svetlanov** (Melodiya) and **Ermler** (Multisonic). Actually, there are two recorded suites from *Maid of Pskov* employing different material; Serov uses the same sequence as Svetlanov, while Ermler uses the same version offered by **Michail Jurowski** (Melodiya LP). Even more curious, on comparison the Ermler and Jurowski sound like exactly the same performance. Either is superior to **Golovchin** (Naxos) or—even worse—**Bystrik Režucha** (Marco Polo) in *Pan Voyevoda.* In Vol. 3 Serov is up against stiff competition for both *Mlada* and *Christmas Eve;* it's difficult to choose between Serov and Jurowski (Capriccio) in the latter. Both offer highly atmospheric and richly colored readings, though the Capriccio engineers have let Jurowski down by setting the bells too far back in the closing pages.

Ansermet does beautifully with this music too, but he makes a massive cut near the Introduction, unfortunately losing some glittering harp music in the process (London). You get even less music in the so-called "Second Suite" recorded by **Othmar Màga;** it begins with the harp music omitted by Ansermet and then just as abruptly stops short at the end of the Polonaise (Vox). This Polonaise—one of the most exhilarating pieces Rimsky ever wrote—is treated in such sodden fashion by **Tjeknavorian** that his disc can be ruled out altogether, though his *Tsar Saltan* is pretty good (ASV).

With *Mlada* we have a rather more involved situation, since this strange opera-ballet actually spawned two disparate children, the more familiar Suite—ending with the wonderful "Cortege of the Nobles"—and the curious *Night on Mount Triglav,* wherein the demon Tchernobog holds court; his entrance and the wild dance that follows can't help but call to mind the *Firebird* of Rimsky's impressionable pupil Stravinsky. Yet **Serov** omits this part entirely (Kontrapunkt), while **Režucha** (Marco Polo) fails to put across Tchernobog's manic string writing and snarling brass with anywhere near the intensity of **Golovchin** (♦Naxos 553789). Since Golovchin's *Christmas Eve* is no slouch either, the Naxos may be warmly recommended. For the standard *Mlada* Suite, there's little to choose between **Järvi, Johanos** (Naxos), **Zhuraitis** (Multisonic), or **Jurowski;** indeed, Serov does well with the suite too, it's just that the additional *Mount Triglav* music seems rather pointless without Tchernobog's dance.

Probably none of the Rimsky suites has been recorded more often than *Le Coq d'Or.* Even in less than opulent sound, **Dorati** is as good as it gets, not least for his use of the London Symphony rather than the Minneapolis (♦Mercury 434308). Two others that complement each other rather well are **Lazarev** (Erato) and **Johanos** (Naxos), the former dark and foreboding, broadly paced yet with an infectious swagger to the final cortege, the latter ever alert with a wider range of colors and in the final pages considerably more propulsive. Better recorded than Dorati, if without the brilliance of the Mercury sound, is **Zinman,** who paints both this suite and *Tsar Saltan* in bold primary colors (Philips). **Steinberg's** splendid *Coq d'Or* has been reissued, but few would put the accompanying Leinsdorf *Scheherazade* in the top rank (♦EMI 65424).

In Sony's "Essential Classics" series (♦62647), you'll find the fine **Ormandy** in rather mixed Russian company, notable for his colorful account of the Balakirev/Casella *Islamey.* In "The Magic Kingdom," **Pletnev** fusses needlessly with tempos; the accompanying pieces by Liadov and Tcherepnin are better (DG). **Tjeknavorian's** *Coq d'Or* is little better than his *Christmas Eve*—a sore disappointment from this generally dynamic conductor—while **Maazel** (reissued with Respighi's *Pines and Feste*) belies the "Legend" label with a dreary though sonically potent run-through (Decca). Both **Fiedler** and (should it be reissued) **Leinsdorf** may be set aside with regret due to a big cut near the end (RCA)

The suite from *Tsar Saltan* is one of Rimsky-Korsakov's best, composed when the grand master of the art of orchestration was at the peak of his powers, and every page is saturated with a richness of color and texture that beggars description; indeed, in the second section, depicting the Tsarina and the young Prince set adrift in a barrel, craftsmanship rises to artistry.

No one does it better than **Ansermet,** whose superb recording has been reissued (♦Classic Compact Discs 6012, or in inferior sound, London 443464). Both **Zinman** and **Järvi** do well with this music too, and they even throw in another excerpt from the opera curiously left out of the suite, *Flight of the Bumblebee,* except that Zinman only gives you the usual minute's worth while Järvi plays the longer version. Both *Tsar Saltan* and the accompanying *Snow Maiden* betray their Teutonic sources with **Jurowski** and the Berlin Radio Symphony; the opening scene of the hero setting off for the battlefield suggests Bismarck more than the Tsar, while the dancing birds in *Snow Maiden* seem to inhabit the Black Forest rather than any Russian counterpart; fortunately, his *Christmas Eve* is a lot better (Capriccio).

You'll find a beautiful *Tsar Saltan* in EMI's "Profile" of **Paul Kletzki** (67726, 2CD, also included with von Matačić's fine *Scheherazade* in another 2CD set, 68098), and a splendid *Coq d'Or* and *Snow Maiden* in their equally desirable "Profile" of **Efrem Kurtz** (67729, 2CD). **Ashkenazy** does *Tsar Saltan* well enough, but it's not worth buying his *Scheherazade* to get it (London), and the same may be said of **Barenboim,** who offers the same coupling (Erato)—as does **Johanos,** who's better than Ashkenazy and Barenboim in both pieces and a lot cheaper too (Naxos).

Capriccio Espagnol and ***Russian Easter Overture.*** Space doesn't permit a detailed rundown on these pieces, which usually turn up as the inevitable makeweight for *Scheherazade* anyway. If you like the *Scheherazade,* you'll probably like the other piece too; certainly that's true of *Capriccio* with **Bernstein, Jansons,** and **Mackerras,** or *Russian Easter* with **Temirkanov.** Some conductors have recorded both pieces, including **Svetlanov;** however, he's ponderous in *Capriccio,* while the raw sound of the Soviet brasses effectively rules out *Russian Easter.* **Dorati** is much better—and much better recorded—in both pieces, which come with his splendid *Coq d'Or* Suite (Mercury 434308). You can get **Järvi**'s potent coupling either separately combined with his *1812* (DG 429984) or in the box with his Rimsky symphonies (DG 423604). **Ormandy** always did this sort of thing very well; he offers both pieces (Sony 46537, with *Scheherazade*, or Odyssey 42248). **Argenta**'s classic reading has been reissued (♦Decca 466378 or ♦Classic 6006)

There were two great mono *Russian Easters:* **Paray** remains unavailable (Mercury), but **Scherchen** has resurfaced together with his splendid *Antar* (PRT 6021). **Fiedler**'s reading was a standout of the early stereo era and remains impressive in its "Living Stereo" incarnation (♦RCA 68132). Another favorite, **Leinsdorf**, is in "Portraits in Sound" (EMI 65205) and also shares Seraphim 69030 with Andrew Litton's *Scheherazade* and Felix Slatkin's exhilarating *Capriccio Espagnol.* **Stokowski** recorded *Russian Easter* many times, with the most recent and in many ways most straightforward account (1968, with the Chicago Symphony) serving as filler for his *Scheherazade* (RCA). His 1953 recording with "His" Symphony Orchestra (still awaiting CD reissue) had a bass, Nicola Moscona, intoning the cantor's part rather than the trombone, a curious effect (RCA). **Charles Gerhardt** takes him one step further and uses a full bass choir (Menuet).

You can find the sonorous **Ansermet** in the London "Double Decker" along with the suites or (even better) on Classic 6012 together with *Tsar Saltan* and *May Night* Overture. **Jurowski** is of even greater interest for his splendid *Overture on Russian Themes* and his alert *Mlada* Suite (Capriccio 10776). For both *Capriccio Espagnol* and the Tchaikovsky *Capriccio Italien*, **Kondrashin** reigns supreme (♦RCA 63302). Bracing and rhythmically secure, he yields to no one in the Rimsky piece, taking the opening "Alborada" at a healthy clip and sounding fresh and invigorating all the way through. (Would that RCA finally brings out the Martinon as well!) **Stokowski** touched up *Capriccio* a bit; it comes with his London Symphony *Scheherazade* (London 417753).

Skazka. No one could tell a story better than Rimsky-Korsakov, and in this musical fairy tale based on Pushkin's story of magical cats and enchanted kingdoms, he enthralls the listener in the same wondrous way as *Scheherazade.* Unfortunately **Anshel Brusilow**'s recording never made it to domestic CD—it used to be in the British catalog as EMI 63093—while **Butt** seems content to simply whip up the tempo every few minutes (ASV). Since the best of the lot, **Svetlanov,** may be hard to find, you may have to settle for **Màga** (Vox), who is at least a better deal than Butt.

Overture on Russian Themes. This is the highlight of **Jurowski**'s disc with *Mlada;* it includes two themes you'll immediately recognize from *Boris Godunov* and *1812* (Capriccio 10776). Jurowski fields it in far more chipper fashion than either **Svetlanov** (Melodiya) or **Màga** (Vox) and adds the tuneful *Fantasia on Serbian Themes*, while **Lazarev**'s disc of *Coq d'Or* includes alert readings of the *Tsar's Bride* and *May Night* overtures (Erato 94808). **Golovchin**'s sluggish Overture adds nothing to his disc of *Pan Voyevoda* (Naxos), while ASV's plan of using it to fill out **Butt**'s CD of Symphony 3 and *Skazka* (though not by very much) likewise avails little. A better reason to buy the Naxos—indeed, the *only* reason—is the rarely heard overture to the "prequel" to *The Maid of Pskov, Boyarinya Vera Sheloga*, which includes some of the same material; in fact the Overture that opens the *Maid of Pskov* suite on **Ermler**'s CD (Multisonic) seems identical to the piece heard on Naxos. Actually, you'd do better to seek out **Svetlanov**'s CD of Kalinnikov's Symphony 1 (♦Melodiya 00171), which has perfectly good versions of both *Pskov* and *Boyarinya* as makeweight.

CONCERTO

Rimsky-Korsakov's brief Piano Concerto is tuneful enough but doesn't leave much of a lasting impression. **Richter**'s performance has been around for years, most recently surfacing on RCA 29468. **Geoffrey Tozer** imbues it with the proper spirit, but Kitaienko's accompaniment leaves something to be desired (Chandos). If you can tolerate Gilbert Levine's sluggish tempos in Tchaikovsky's "Polish" Symphony, with it you get as fine a performance of the Rimsky Concerto as ever set to disc, played by **Jeffrey Campbell** (Telarc 80454). **Malcolm Binns** has the measure of this savory morsel too, and his recording has the advantage of far better company in the two rarely performed Balakirev concertos (♦Hyperion 66640).

You can also get the Rimsky coupled with Balakirev's Concerto 1 (plus one by Medtner) played by **Igor Zhukov** (MK 417087), but why settle for just one Balakirev Concerto? Or you can spend the bare minimum for acceptable versions of the *Kitezh* and *Mlada* Suites, *Overture on Russian Themes, May Night,* and *Skazka,* as well as the Concerto with **Michael Ponti** and the *Concert Fantasy* for violin with **Aaron Rosand** (Vox Box 5082). HALLER

OPERAS

All of Rimsky-Korsakov's operas except *Mozart and Salieri* are based on Russian history and folklore. They're often quite long, with many scene-painting diversions from the main plot, but always tuneful, with brilliant, colorful orchestrations. His operatic oeuvre can be divided into three categories: the "Peasant" group (often based on Gogol's stories of peasant life), the "Heroic" group (with larger-than-life characters drawn from Russian history), and the "Fantastic" group (based on Russian folktales and fairy stories). They're rarely staged outside Russia. Except for three minor works, all 15 of his operas have been recorded, albeit not all in their various revisions, and sometimes not particularly well. I will limit my discussion to those most often recorded and best known outside Russia.

The Golden Cockerel. Rimsky's last opera, this is the only one to achieve any sort of international status. He clothed this comic satire and politically symbolic, fantastic tale in brilliant, opulent, exotic music. It also presents a vocal problem: the stratospheric high notes and tessitura of the tenor Astrologer are fearfully daunting.

A 1985 recording favors the voices a bit, but the Sofia National Opera orchestra led by **Dimiter Manolov** makes a fine impression (Capriccio 10760; Fidelio 8809; 2CD). Nikolai Stoilov is a personable King Dodon with a big growling voice and much attention to the text. Lubomir Dyakovski gets most of the Astrologer's notes; just don't expect beautiful singing. Elena Stoyanova's Queen cuts through with a diamond-hard voice, and Yavora Stoilova makes the Cockerel into a Wagnerian heroine where a coloratura soprano is expected.

A 1988 performance was the first at the Bolshoi in more than 60 years; Russian authorities found the opera politically disturbing, even delaying its 1908 premiere until after Rimsky's death (♦Arts and Electronics 10391, 2CD). Arthur Eizen is a sincere Dodon, more lovable than comic. Oleg Biktimirov manages the Astrologer's music quite well, with Elena Brileva a harsh Queen, no frilly coloratura here but an angry, malevolent character. Irena Udalova is a proper Cockerel. A bonus is the rich contralto of Nina Gaponova's Amelfa. **Svetlanov** elicits a grand performance from his forces.

The Legend of the Invisible City of Kitezh and the Maiden Fevronia. Rimsky's next-to-last opera can be considered a summation of his musical life. Here are quotes from his own works, folk tunes and hymn tunes, original and composed by Rimsky. Influences from Mussorgsky and Borodin are found along with those of Wagner. The opera is long, noble, static, and through-composed, with little opportunity for vocal display. More than ever, the orchestra plays an important role in interpreting inward thoughts and motivations, as richly colored as always.

Other than Ivan Petrov's sonorous Yuri, the 1956 performance led by **Vassili Nebolsin** is short on beautiful singing but strong on drama and authenticity (Arlecchino 51/53, 3CD). **Svetlanov** leads an evocative 1983 Bolshoi performance (Chant du Monde 278557, 3CD). The Fevronia of Galina Kalinina is youthful and innocent; Alexander Vedernikov is the dignified Prince Yuri. Vladislav Piavko's Kuterma is strongly sung, but a bit shy on the hysterical drama. In 1994 performances at the Kirov Opera, superb recorded sound catches the orchestral opulence evoked by **Gergiev.** Gorchakova sings beautifully, but is more matron than maiden (♦Philips 462225, 3CD). It would be difficult to improve on Vladimir Galuzin, music and drama poetically combined. Nicolai Ohotnikov and Larissa Diadkova are opulent in voice.

A 1995 performance at the Bregenz Festspielhaus uses an Eastern European cast, with choruses from Sofia and Moscow and the Vienna Symphony conducted by **Fedoseyev** (Koch Schwann 1144, 2CD). It's a festival-quality performance, relatively strong in all departments, but without the sense of ensemble, depth of characterization, and vocal opulence of the Kirov recording.

May Night. One of the "Peasant" operas, this is mainly based on several Ukrainian village stories by Gogol with a healthy dollop of the fantastic by way of a legend about a water nymph. There is lots of local color, a winning love story, and plenty of musical splendor.

A historically important 1948 recording from the Bolshoi conducted by **Nebolsin** enlisted the major talents of Sergei Lemeshev and Veronika Borisenko, but its dated sound relegates it to second or third choice (LYS 342, 2CD). An excellent 1970 version from Moscow Radio led by **Fedoseyev** has lots of dramatic energy and theatrical insight (♦Relief 991044, 2CD). Konstantin Lisovsky is a graceful Levko, at ease and dramatically involved. Ludmila Sapyeghna is a bright-voiced Hanna, with Olga Pastushenko an appealing Pannochka (the water nymph). The Village Mayor of bass Alexei Krivchenya is vocally elderly but dramatically insightful.

A 1994 performance from the Bolshoi led by **Chistiakov** is an all-round good show, with Vitali Taraschenko a winning Levko, a charming Hanna from Natalia Erassova, a brilliant Pannochka from Marina Lapina, but a rather stolid Mayor from Viacheslav Popchapsky (Harmonia Mundi 288103, 2CD; 388054, 4CD, with *Christmas Eve*). Excellent sound and a smoothly beautiful performance from the Kölner Rundfunk led by **Lazarev** are sadly undercut by a relentlessly loud and insensitive Vladimir Bogachev (Capriccio 10792, 2CD). Tatyana Erastova and Elena Brilova are reliable heroines and Viktor Matorin is a generously vocalized Mayor.

Mozart and Salieri. Perhaps due to its brevity, *Mozart and Salieri* is the most frequently recorded of Rimsky's operas. It's a duodrama, almost a vocal duel, based on Pushkin's tale of the rivalry between Mozart and Salieri, but it's a real letdown musically.

The 1951 recording led by **Samuel Samosud** with tenor Ivan Kozlovsky (Mozart) and bass Mark Reizen (Salieri) is still the best (♦LYS 517). Two extraordinary voices well versed in drama contend effectively, with sympathetic support from the orchestra—in monaural sound, of course. A performance in German by Schreier and Theo Adam led by

Janowski is well sung and beautifully played, but it has no filler to augment its brief 38 minutes (Berlin 2089). Another German version with Martyn Hill and Kurt Widmer under **Bamert** is very well sung. It includes a real curiosity: an effective performance of Mozart *Requiem* fragments as written, unedited and with no additions by Süssmayr. I Musici de Montreal play well for **Turovsky,** but his recording is a real dud (Chandos 9149; MHS 513907L). Vladimir Bogachov has little variety or understanding of the Mozart role, and Nikita Storojev is a lightweight Salieri, though he projects the text well. Songs by Rimsky and Glinka fill out the CD.

Sadko. This is the most popular of Rimsky's operas in Russia. Although episodic in story, the continual flow of tuneful music effectively binds the work together. Its fantastic tale is highlighted by Sadko's adventures in the underwater kingdom of the Sea King.

An extraordinary 1952 Bolshoi recording conducted by **Golovanov** has not been issued on CD. Georgy Nelepp (Sadko) and Vera Davidova (Liubava), with Ivan Kozlovsky, Pavel Lisitsian, and Mark Reizen as the three guests, were definitive. However, the 1993 recording from the Kirov authoritatively led by **Gergiev** is as good as it gets today (♦Philips 442138, 3CD, also available on video). It's strongly cast throughout, with many carefully delineated minor characters. Vladimir Galusin is a poetic Sadko, tireless throughout the lengthy role. Valentina Tsidipova sings a charming Sea Princess, but the best of the lot is Larissa Diakova's Minstrel. The three Kirov Guests aren't up to the standards set by their Bolshoi predecessors, but they handle their brief roles effectively.

Snow Maiden. One of Rimsky's "Fantastic" operas, Snow Maiden is full of beautiful melodies, distinctive orchestration, and colorful situations and characters. The trouble is that those characters are not at all developed—they are mere cardboard cutouts—and the story is scarcely enough to stand by itself. It's more of a pageant or festival play than an opera and is quite long.

In a 1984 Bulgarian Radio performance, except for the irritating tenor sound of Avram Andreev (Tsar Berendei), the performance is good if not outstanding (Capriccio 10749; Fidelio 8806; 3CD). Everyone seems to understand what they are singing about, but with a touch of routine. The orchestra plays well for **Stoyan Angelov,** but often with a lack of excitement. A much better choice is a performance with Moscow Radio forces led by **Fedoseyev** (♦MHS 535899Z, 3CD; Chant du Monde 278.1027/09, 3CD). Valentina Sokolik is a radiantly innocent Snow Maiden; Arkhipova doubles as Fairy Spring and as the shepherd Lel. Alexander Vedernikov is an impressive Grandfather Frost, and Anton Grigoryev is a pliant Tsar Berendeja.

The Tsar's Bride. This is one of Rimsky's "Heroic" operas. Its plot is convoluted, complex, wordy, and static, with little dramatic intensity, but it offers a wealth of melodies decked out in colorful orchestration.

The 1943 Bolshoi recording has some felicities, but the sound dooms it to the historical dustbin (LYS 055/66, 2CD). The 1973 Bolshoi recording (Vishnevskaya, Nesterenko, Arkhipova, Borisova, **Mansurov** conducting) was excellent but has not been issued on CD. The 1992 Bolshoi remake under **Chistiakov** is a strong show with better sound, but the singers don't equal their 1973 predecessors (♦Chant du Monde 288056, 2CD). Again the forces of the Kirov Opera led by **Gergiev** are characterful and colorful (♦Philips 462618, 2CD). Borodina serves up equal portions of delicacy and defiance, and Hvorostovsky sings not only beautifully but also with much character insight as the villainous Tsar; Marina Shaguch brings grand intensity to Marfa. It's a splendid performance all round.

SONGS

Rimsky composed a large number of songs in all vocal categories, quite pleasant affairs, but they haven't been taken up by Western singers. The few available recordings (with one exception) are by Russians.

The complete songs were recorded by singers from the Kirov Opera, one for each voice category, using four pianists. It's a viable edition, presenting authentic if not quite great singing (Chant du Monde 288038/40, 3CD). The complete romances (34 of them) are heard in similarly effective performances, again with singers from the Kirov doing the honors, with Yuri Serov at the piano (Russian Disc 10051).

Christoff sings several selections in an overview of Russian song that contains material by other Russian composers; his voice is big and burly with an emphasis on drama (EMI 67496, 5CD). **Vladimir Bogachev**'s loud voice of unbending iron does little with his program, and I Musici de Montreal are overshadowed by the tenor (Chandos). A much better singer and interpreter is baritone **Hvorostovsky** in his album titled "My Restless Soul," which includes Rimsky among other Russian songwriters (Philips 42538). **Vassily Savenko**'s smooth, pleasing voice recommends his recital, highlighted by the cycle *By the Sea* (Meridian 84399).

PARSONS

George Rochberg (b. 1918)

Two crises altered the direction of Rochberg's career: The first was military service during WWII, and the second was the death of his teenage son from brain cancer. Rochberg's wartime experiences (and later, Schoenberg's influence) drove him from neoclassicism to serialism. The second crisis, in 1964, found Rochberg "washing his hands" of serialism and incorporating other musical styles in a collage technique that he called *ars combinatoria*. For example, in *Music for the Magic Theater* (1965), Rochberg quotes snippets of Mahler and Mozart and cross-pollinates them with Stockhausen and Webern (New World 80462, with *Octet* and *A Grand Fantasia*). As the '60s progressed, Rochberg freed himself to shift between tonal, atonal, and chromatic writing as the material and his expressive needs demanded.

A notable example of this freedom is his Violin Concerto (1974), recorded definitively by **Stern** and Previn (♦Sony 64505). Despite jagged opening gestures and virtuosic solo writing, this is an elegiac work of breadth. It's approachable, even when Rochberg turns to a more "difficult" dialect. The economical Oboe Concerto (1984) is more understated; this is modern music that really communicates without condescending. **Joseph Robinson**'s recording with Mehta is first-class (♦New World 80335).

There are two excellent retrospectives. The first includes the Bartókian, preserial String Quartet 1 played by the **Concord String Quartet;** the aggressive, serial—but accessible—Symphony 2 (1955–56), led by Werner Torkanowsky; and *Contra Mortem et Tempus* (1965) for flute, clarinet, violin, and piano, an important transitional work that begins to withdraw from serialism (♦CRI 768). Written shortly after his son's death, it's an alternately angry and reflective meditation on mortality, played by the **Aeolian Quartet.** The second contains two serial works: the Schoenberg-influenced String Quartet 2 (1959-61), played by the **Philadelphia String Quartet** with soprano Janice Harsanyi, and *Duo Concertante* (1955; rev. 1959), which Rochberg called a "composed improvisation," played by Mark Sokol, violin, and Norman Fischer, cello (♦CRI 769). Again, although both works challenge the listener, Rochberg's sincerity and never-failing desire to communicate make their serialism highly approachable.

The other works on this CD are *Ricordanza* (1972) for cello and piano

(Fischer, with Rochberg at the piano), and *Slow Fires of Autumn* (1978–79) for flute (Carol Wincenc) and harp (Nancy Allen). If the latter work conjures up Japanese shakuhachi and koto music, it's probably no accident; it's based on a traditional Japanese lullaby. Although the recordings on these discs were made over a period of many years, the sound quality isn't problematical, and the performances are authoritative. These would be good to try after the Violin Concerto.

String quartets have been nodal points in Rochberg's output. Most were written for or recorded by the **Concord String Quartet** (No. 2 in Vox 5145, 2CD—superior to the CRI recording; 3–6 in ♦New World 80551, 2CD). This is marvelous music, veering between jagged atonality and heartbreaking neo-Romanticism; Beethoven and Berg rub shoulders, and neither is the poorer for it. No. 6 contains moving variations on Pachelbel's *Canon*. Sadly, 7 isn't on CD at this time, nor is the sublime Piano Quintet. Perhaps Nonesuch will reissue their Concord recordings of these.

Of Rochberg's piano trios, the latest (1990) is the strongest. It was inspired, at least in part, by the collapse of the Eastern bloc. Rochberg wrote it for the **Beaux Arts Trio;** their recording (Philips 438866) is gone, but the **Kapell Trio** has ably recorded all three (♦Gasparo 289). Trio for Clarinet, Horn, and Piano is expertly written (ca. 1947), but lacks individuality (cassette only; Crystal 731, performed by **Combs,** Williams, and Covert). Other chamber music includes the Trio for Violin, Cello, and Piano (1964), written at the very end of his purely serial period. More a series of soliloquies and duets than a three-way conversation, it shows Rochberg pushing the expressive borders of serialism (**Kees Cooper,** Fred Sherry, and Mary Louise Boehme; Albany 153). The Viola Sonata (1979) is emotionally open and generous (**Lawrence Wheeler** and Ruth Tomfohrde; ♦Albany 141).

Rochberg's 51 *Caprice Variations* for violin (1970) are modeled on Paganini's you-know-what, and they also nod to Schubert, Webern, and others. Like their model, they are technical studies for the player, but they also gratify the attentive listener. **Zvi Zeitlin** plays all 51 with excellent imagination and technique (Gasparo 1010). **Michelle Makarski** plays a manageable and composer-approved selection of 11 in her recital; slower tempos enhance expressivity (♦ECM 1587).

The piano music contains delightful surprises. **Sally Pinkas**'s set goes from the Brahmsian *Variations on an Original Theme* (1941) to *Four Short Sonatas* (1984), the latter inspired by Scarlatti (♦Gasparo 340/2, 2CD). In between are the teasing *Partita-Variations* (1976) and *Nach Bach* (1966), as well as the unusual *Carnival Music* (1971), with its allusions to ragtime, and the challenging 12-tone *Sonata-Fantasia* (1956). **Martha Thomas**'s selection is a more economical alternative (ACA 20044), but her playing isn't as persuasive as Pinkas's.

Rochberg's recorded song cycles include the violently expressionistic *Tableaux: Sound Pictures from "The Silver Talons of Piero Kostrov"* (1968) for soprano and ensemble (**de Gaetani;** Vox 5145, 2CD) and *Songs in Praise of Krishna,* adapted from sensuous Bengali poetry, and astonishingly performed by soprano **Neva Pilgrim** with the composer at the piano (CRI 817).

TUTTLE

Joaquin Rodrigo (1901–1999)

Rodrigo is, next to Villa-Lobos, the greatest "legitimate" composer of guitar music of the 20th century. In previous centuries guitar music was almost always written by the instrument's players, many of them the greatest performers of their age (Corbetta and Sanz in the 17th century; Sor, Giuliani, Mertz, and Tárrega in the 19th). Though trained in music academies, these players rarely composed for other instruments except for chamber music utilizing the guitar.

In the 20th century, through the instigation and encouragement (and sometimes commissioning) of top players (particularly Segovia and Bream), a very large quantity of music, including some of the best and most lasting pieces, was written by composers who didn't play the guitar but treated writing for it on an equal footing with writing for the piano or violin or any other solo instrument. Although the player-composer tradition didn't completely die out (and in fact at the end of the century was reviving considerably), much of the modern repertoire is by "legitimate" composers of varying degrees of historical and musical stature, ranging from Castelnuovo-Tedesco (who composed for Heifetz as well as Segovia) to Hans Werner Henze (writing for Bream and David Tanenbaum).

Rodrigo, who was blind from the age of three, did not play. This was due as much to his training as an all-round composer for all instruments as to his handicap; like most composers, his instrument was the piano. After training at the Valencia Conservatory, he went to Paris, studying with Dukas and becoming associated with many of the major composers there in the '30s, including Falla and Ravel, two of his biggest influences. He returned to Spain permanently after its civil war in 1939, which was also the year he wrote the piece whose popularity brought him worldwide acclaim, *Concierto de Aranjuez*, a concerto for guitar and full orchestra composed in Paris but redolent of his native country. The remainder of his life was split between his activities in academia (including historical research) and composition (including tours as a lecturer and pianist).

The catalog of Rodrigo's works lists more than 160 compositions, covering the expected range of piano music and songs, chamber music, concertos, and orchestral pieces, plus works for guitar. The success of *Aranjuez* led him to specialize in the concerto form (11 such works), and to some extent the magical qualities of that piece and its success with audiences created a daunting standard for him to match with subsequent works. While guitar music constitutes most of his oeuvre, piano and chamber music are also represented.

GUITAR CONCERTOS

In addition to its exceptional popularity, *Concierto de Aranjuez* is acknowledged as a truly virtuosic work, playable by many but better left to only the best. Therefore, almost all aspirants to that category have recorded it. One reason for its popularity is its hauntingly lyrical slow movement, which has prompted a number of wonderful jazz versions, notably those of Miles Davis and Gil Evans, Jim Hall, and Chick Corea. Incidentally, the piece was written for and premiered by Regino Sainz de la Maza, not Segovia, who held a considerable grudge against it and never played it.

A rapprochement between Segovia and the composer was reached in the mid-'50s, when Rodrigo wrote his second most frequently recorded and played guitar "concerto": *Fantasia para un Gentilhombre*, "inspired by the music of Gaspar Sanz." This four-movement piece uses the folk-like baroque dances (and a fugal ricercare) of the 17th-century guitarist-composer in a neoclassical way similar to Stravinsky's Pergolesi-based *Pulcinella*. Though not a concerto in the strict sense (it has an extra movement and emphasizes "dialogue" between soloist and orchestra rather than "argument"), it feels like one to both player and audience, and is almost invariably paired on recordings with its famous predecessor.

Unlike with concertos for other instruments, even the world's top guitarists often revise the solo part of concertos by nonplaying composers, so (for some) one factor in evaluating the many recordings of Rodrigo's concertos is the player's fidelity to the score. Other factors are the player's characteristic tone and interpretive style, the quality of the orchestral collaboration, and the other repertoire on the recording. With players like Julian Bream and John Williams, you can also choose between the several different recordings they've each made of *Aranjuez* over the last 40 years.

Keeping those factors in mind, I recommend the following as the best recordings of *Aranjuez* and *Fantasia*. For true Spanish style and dazzling technique: **Pepe Romero** with Marriner and the Academy of St. Martin in the Fields (Philips 38016), or **Angel Romero** with Previn and the London Symphony (EMI 47693). For superior musicianship and impeccable technique: **John Williams** with Frémaux and the Philharmonia (♦CBS 45648). For fidelity to the score and technical ease: **Manuel Barrueco** with Placido Domingo (!) leading the Philharmonia (EMI 56175), or **David Russell** with Kunzel and the Naples (Florida) Philharmonic (♦Telarc 80459). Russell's disc also features the rarely encountered *Concierto para una Fiesta,* and Barrueco's includes the beautiful neo-Renaissance solo piece *Zarabanda lejana* and five songs for voice and guitar sung by Domingo.

For Rodrigo's multiple guitar concertos, the four **Romeros** with Marriner and the Academy (Philips 24) are your best bet for *Concierto andaluz,* and the incredible **Assad** brothers with John Neschling and the St. Gallen Symphony are preferable for *Concierto madrigal* for two guitars.

OTHER GUITAR MUSIC

Rodrigo wrote more than two dozen pieces for solo guitar, but only a handful have been played frequently. They tend to be very demanding technically, but as the overall skill of most classical guitarists has risen in recent decades, so too has more of his music become accessible and recorded.

Segovia made an excellent recording in the '50s (NA) of the much-played *Fandango,* which next-generation players like **Williams** also recorded (♦Columbia 44794). However, Segovia and his disciples never played the other two *Piezas Españolas* (a haunting passacaglia and a perpetuum mobile *zapateado*), which the *Fandango* precedes (they're even harder). All three pieces are tossed off with understated taste and the occasional burst of rapid-fire virtuosity by **Barrueco** (♦EMI 66577, with works by Ponce and Falla). That recording also offers a highly poetic version of *Invocation et Danse;* for a more extroverted performance, try **Kazuhito Yamashita** in "Music of Spain"(♦RCA 5913). In "Iberia: Rodrigo, Granados, Albéniz, Llobet," Williams also plays that piece excellently (it's typical of his recent forays into post-Segovia repertoire) and offers a somewhat perfunctory take on *En Los Trigales,* a charming (and easier) piece (Sony 48480).

Vol. 28 of RCA's "Julian Bream Edition" (61611) is all-Rodrigo: the two concertos, the three *Piezas Españolas,* and *Invocation et danse.* If you really enjoy **Bream**'s highly personalized style (exaggerated but never dull), then you'll perhaps forgive his slower-than-acceptable tempos in the more technically challenging pieces. More successful all-Rodrigo recordings include **Angel Romero** (RCA 68767) and **Luigi Orlandini** (Koch 311832). One of the standard works of the modern guitar duo repertoire is Rodrigo's *Tonadilla,* which gets a state-of-the-art account by the **Assad** brothers (GHA 126034).

OTHER MUSIC

Rodrigo's piano music, songs, violin music, and concertos for other instruments are available in a few releases. His complete piano music is performed by **Gregory Allen** and **Anton Nel** (Bridge 9027, 2CD), and selected pieces are played by **Maria Garzón** (ASV 990). "Music for Violin" by **León Ara** contains works ranging from 1923 to 1984 (CPO 999186). In addition to the songs sung by **Domingo** with Barrueco (above), Rodrigo's *Madrigales amatorias* (four love songs for soprano and chamber orchestra) have been recorded by **Ruth Golden** with Donald Barra and the San Diego Chamber Orchestra, an album that also features his *Viejos aires de danza* and a chamber-orchestra version of the lovely *Zarabanda lejana* (♦Koch 7160).

Rodrigo's nonguitar concertos include one for violin, *Concierto de estío,* played by **Michaël Guttman** (ASV 855); one for cello, *Concierto in modo galante,* played by **S. Hess** (Koch 315362); and one for flute, *Concierto pastorale,* played by **Galway** (♦RCA 68428). Galway's recording also includes a flute version of *Fantasia para un Gentilhombre* he arranged with the composer's approval. Unfortunately, a harp version of *Aranjuez* by **Nicanor Zabaleta** is NA.   DINGER

Ned Rorem *(b. 1923)*

Rorem has a way with music and words that is always poetic. Probably America's finest art song composer, he is also a compelling fin de siècle diarist, and his writings and settings say as much about his Francophile personality as his music. His love and natural feel for verse and its musical possibilities have revealed the richness and diversity of America's literary heritage. Equally successful are his many instrumental and orchestral pieces, which he justly regards as songs without words. Although his style has developed over the years, he has never forsaken tonality. Mood and impression matter more to him than structure and form; every Rorem work is ripe with imagery and often bittersweet fragrance.

The haunting Symphony 3, which Rorem regarded as his farewell love letter to France after eight years there, is a good place to start. **Abravanel** gives a fair reading in a set that includes other American orchestral works; it's good value, though the performances show their age (Vox, 2CD, budget-priced). Much stronger playing by the Atlanta Symphony led by **Shaw** and Louis Lane can be found in String Symphony, coupled with the superb tone poem *Eagles* and the evocative and dreamy suite *Sunday Morning* (New World 353). The Symphony has two slow movements, of which "Nocturne" is an impassioned threnody, with a climax equal to any string writing for intensity. It compares well with the last movement of Rorem's Pulitzer Prize winner, the aptly titled and atmospheric *Air Music,* another suite where full orchestra only plays in the outer movements. The Louisville Orchestra gives a reasonable account, with the rather metallic and virtuosic Piano Concerto 3 thunderously played by **Jerome Lowenthal**—a work he has almost made his own (Albany 047).

Three discs of instrumental concertos are well worth the effort. Rorem has proved his facility in writing for the keyboard in Piano Concerto for Left Hand, played by **Graffman** with Previn conducting (New World 80445, with *11 Studies for 11 Players*). The usual "suite" format is found; Rorem clearly feels better able to achieve contrasts of mood and timbre by using differing groups. The Violin Concerto was one of **Bernstein**'s last recordings, with concertos by Glass and Bernstein all played with crystalline purity by **Kremer** (DG 445185). The mystical English Horn Concerto captures the remote, nocturnal tone of the instrument, nobly aided by soloist **Thomas Stacy** (New World 80489, with concertos by Persichetti and Sydney Hodkinson).

Two '80s quintets, *Bright Music* and *Winter Pages,* are unrivaled for scope, musical interest, and quality of playing (by **Ida Kafavian** and friends)—*Winter Pages* for its sad portrayal of the uncertainty of a world asleep and cold, not knowing when rebirth will come, and *Bright Music* for its gaiety and abandon (New World 80416). Also recommended are two suites for violin and piano, *Day Music* and *Night Music,* played by **Jaime** and Ruth **Laredo** (Phoenix 123). From the archives, **Katchen** playing the early Piano Sonata 2 is an absolute gem (in his Philips "Great Pianists" set). Rorem has also made a significant contribution to organ music with two autobiographical suites: the reflective *A Quaker Reader* recalling his own religious upbringing and the more extroverted *Views from the Oldest House.* They are played by the veteran **Catherine Crozier** in stunning form on the Marcussen organ at Wichita State University (Delos 3076).

Rorem's only major opera, *Miss Julie* (1965; text by Elmslie, after Strindberg) compares well as music theater with Barber's *Vanessa* and the best of Menotti. A bleak tale, it's awash with memorable arias and dramatic gestures. The **Manhattan School of Music** live recording is clean, committed and very professional; the lush orchestration, rich vocal writing, and dramatic unity are well captured (Newport 85605, 2CD). Rorem's range is remarkable; he slips easily from Parisian cafe-waltz to brooding angst. Of less substance but still of passing interest are the shorter chamber operas with piano accompaniment: *A Childhood Miracle* and *Three Sisters Who Are Not Sisters* (Newport 85594).

The best of Rorem's many song cycles is also the most recent and the largest: *Evidence of Things Not Seen* for four solo voices and piano, a grand tour of the many poets (mainly American) whom Rorem has set over the past half century, the order following the cycle of life, with a poignant but unsentimental reflection on death at the end (New World 80575, 2CD; a good value though one CD is only 26 minutes long). Also not to be missed is *Poems of Love and the Rain,* which sets each poem twice (Phoenix 108). Rorem (himself a fine pianist) has worked with many singers, and his collaboration with **Phyllis Curtin** in *Gloria* and *Ariel,* two cycles from the early '70s, has been reissued (Phoenix 138, with *King Midas*). They show the more angular idiom he favored at the time, as does the very striking *Missa Brevis,* the only item of his substantial catalog of church music presently available (Vox VB3, a budget-priced 3CD set that includes an earlier song cycle, *Letters from Paris*).

War Scenes finds Rorem in rare angry mood; it's sung by baritone **Donald Gramm** (Phoenix 116, with *Dialogues* for two voices and piano). (These Phoenix discs have been remastered from old Desto LPs, which occasionally left much to be desired, so sound quality can vary.) Last but not least is a combination of three cycles, *Women's Voices, Nantucket Songs* (memorable images of the area where the composer lives), and *Some Trees* (CRI 657).   JOHNSON

Hilding Rosenberg *(1892–1985)*

This composer, pianist, organist, conductor, and teacher was known as "the first great Swedish modernist" and "the grand old man of Swedish music." Rosenberg's early works show national-romantic traces, but in the '20s he modernized his style in an effort to free Swedish music from that tradition. Bach, Hindemith, Nielsen, Schoenberg, and Stravinsky were formative influences in the development of his own cosmopolitan voice. In the middle '50s, Rosenberg adopted his own brand of 12-tone technique, based on melodic and polyphonic principles, without losing his sense of identity. His basically tonal music is classical in its restraint and formal layout and is characterized by arching cantilenas, polyphonic lines, long pedal points, moderate dissonance, vigorous rhythms, and masterly instrumentation. His melodies are sometimes austere, but he's also capable of warm lyricism.

Orchestral music. Rosenberg wrote eight symphonies between 1917 and 1980; 2 through 6 are now on CD. Symphony 2, aptly named "Sinfonia grave," is led by **Blomstedt,** coupled with the vigorous, pithy overture to the opera *Marionettes* and the genial Concerto 3 for orchestra ("Louisville Concerto"), written in 1954 for the Louisville Orchestra (Swedish Society Discofil 1026). **Ehrling** conducts the London Symphony in the overture, **Westerberg** the Swedish Radio Symphony in the concerto.

The epic 3, a work of great expressive power, and the lyrical, intimate 6 (*Sinfonia semplice*), simpler in expression, are given excellent performances by **Blomstedt** and **Westerberg** conducting the Stockholm Symphony (Phono Suecia 100). The 1966 sound is good but has a slight edge. The monumental 80-minute 4 ("The Revelation of St. John"), for baritone, chorus, and orchestra, was recorded with Hagegård, choruses, and the Gothenborg Symphony under **Ehrling** (Caprice 21429). Alternating biblical apocalyptic and sacred visions of St. John with war poetry by Hjalmar Gullberg, this oratorio-like symphony is one of Rosenberg's greatest works. Excerpts of 4 plus six other works, with various soloists in mostly live performances, are in "Rosenberg plays Rosenberg" (Caprice 21510, 3CD). Showing its age, this set was recorded in mono in the '30s and '40s, with **Rosenberg** conducting various orchestras.

The short *Prelude to the Last Judgment* is performed by **Petter Sundkvist** and the Swedish Radio Symphony, coupled with the exciting hour-long ballet *Orpheus in Town,* with **Tommy Anderson** conducting the Royal Stockholm Philharmonic (Phono Suecia 702). It's a memorable disc, beautifully performed and recorded. The lovely *Dagdrivaren* for baritone and orchestra was recorded with Rolf Leanderson as soloist and the Norrköping Symphony conducted by **Göran Nilson** (BIS 55). It's coupled with Allan Pettersson's bleak *Vox Humana* for soloists, chorus, and strings, led by **Westerberg.**

Concertos. The symphonic, predominantly lyrical Violin Concerto 2 has been described as "sunshine all the way" and is offered by **Leon Spierer** and the Stockholm Philharmonic under Arvid Jansons in an excellent performance and fine sound (Caprice 21367, with Lille Bror Söderlundh's more astringent concerto performed by Leo Berlin and the Swedish Radio Symphony under Westerberg's direction). **Mats Widlund** is the excellent soloist in Rosenberg's two very attractive piano concertos, well performed and recorded with Sundkvist conducting the Swedish Radio Symphony (CPO 999573).

A beautifully recorded and performed disc contains the engaging Concertos 1 and 4 for string orchestra coupled with the polytonal, polyphonic *Suite on Swedish Folk Tunes* (CPO 999573) The Deutsche Kammerakademie Neuss under **Goritzki** is at its best in these exhilarating works.

String Quartets. Rosenberg wrote twelve numbered string quartets and several other works in that genre. No. 1 dates from 1920 and 8 through 12 were written in a burst of feverish creativity in 1957. They have been recorded in five Caprice CDs by such leading Swedish groups as the **Fresk, Gotland, Kyndel,** and **Lysell Quartets** in authoritative and eloquent performances and fine sound. No. 1 was recorded in 1956 (slight tape hiss), the remaining works in the '70s and '90s. Nos. 4 and 7 are coupled with the six-movement *Moments Musicaux* (1972). This is a stimulating series marked by individuality, expressiveness, and technical mastery.

Piano music. *Mats Widlund* performs Rosenberg's Suite and Sonatas 2 and 4, dating from the '20s, and *Tema con variazioni* and Sonatina, writ-

ten in the '40s. He provides persuasive and eloquent playing throughout these very fine works (Daphne 1003). Another very good disc offers authoritative performances by **Oyvind Sørum;** here we find Sonatas 1, 2, and 4, coupled with *Tema con variazioni* and *Plastiska scener* (M.A.P 05).   DE JONG

Gioacchino Rossini (1792–1868)

Rossini was the most successful Italian opera composer of his time. He composed nearly 40 operas, comic and serious, not including several major revisions and a number of pasticcios of his music arranged by other composers. His operas were in demand not just in Italy and Paris but throughout the operatic world, including the Americas. Rossini was one of the great exponents of the bel canto style, with its emphasis on a memorable melodic line capable of much embellishment and intended to be sung with a maximum of beauty, brilliance, and virtuosity. Emotion and serious drama are somewhat lacking in his early operas, and it's often difficult to distinguish between the music he wrote for serious and comic situations. Several of his comic operas (*Barbiere, Cenerentola, Italiana*) remained in the standard repertoire, but his serious operas were mostly neglected (except for their delightful overtures) until the early '50s, when they were resurrected as part of the bel canto revival sparked by Callas.

CHORAL MUSIC

Rossini couldn't escape his operatic heritage; thus the style of his sacred music is scarcely distinguishable from that of his operas, comic or serious, with only the Latin text indicating its use for religious services.

Petite Messe Solennelle. This mass was originally composed for voices accompanied by piano and harmonium. Rossini later orchestrated the piece, claiming that if he didn't do it, someone else would. Yet it's the intimate original version that is recorded most frequently.

The Stuttgart Chamber Ensemble led by **Johannes Moesus** is splendid; they sing with exquisite intonation and nuance (♦Tacet 14, 2CD). The soloists blend beautifully, and the magnificent recorded sound captures every detail. **Cleobury** leads a wrong-headed performance with the unauthentic boy treble voices of the King's College Choir, but with satisfactory soloists — Popp, Fassbaender, Gedda, and Dmitri Kavrakos (EMI 688658, 2CD, with *Stabat Mater*). **Romano Gandolfi** favors ponderous tempos, but they're bearable for the sake of the vocalists: Freni, Pavarotti, Valentini-Terrani, and Raimondi are the big-name, big-voiced soloists, turning the piece completely into an *opera seria* (♦Decca 455023, with *Stabat Mater*).

Simon Halsey and the City of Birmingham Symphony and Chorus view the *Messe* very much as an Italian opera, and their performance is a delightful example of the style. It's the soloists that fail (Conifer 184). A very modest approach to a modest piece is by the Cologne Chorus led by **Elke Mascha Blankenburg.** The chorus is excellent but the soloists are merely serviceable (Koch 1419).

The orchestral version lacks the subtleties and inventiveness of Rossini's original, but **Marriner** does a lot with it (Philips 446097). The Academy of St. Martin in the Fields plays with much nuance, and his soloists sing beautifully. **Chailly** leads an even better performance, adding considerable drama and tension, with excellent soloists (♦Decca 444134).

Stabat Mater. This is a kind of miniopera, with a sacred text set to operatic music. The conductor must choose among performing it as a slow and reverential piece, an outright dramatic opera, or a compromise between the two.

The best-known excerpt from the *Stabat Mater* is the very operatic tenor aria "Cujus animam," with its high tessitura and climatic high D, so interest naturally centers on the tenor soloist. Pavarotti has recorded the work several times, all of which find him in fine form. A 1967 performance led by **Giulini** is in monaural sound, but is just about as good as you could wish for (♦Fonit Cetra 2041). Zylis-Gara, Verrett, and Plishka are Pavarotti's excellent colleagues. He's also heard in a moving performance led by **Kertész** (Decca 417766 and 455023, 2CD, with *Messe*). Here Lorengar, Minton, and Sotin are his very fine colleagues.

Schippers is almost as good, and in superior sound (Vox 9017 and Vox Box 5141, 2CD, with five Rossini overtures). It's paced more like an opera, with fleet tempos and only a modicum of reverence. The well-matched soloists, Sung-Sook Lee, Florence Quivar, Kenneth Riegel, and Plishka, are all in fine form. **Scimone** leads a happy compromise between the reverential and the operatic (Erato 75493). His soloists, Gasdia, Margarita Zimmermann, and José Garcia, are pleasant nonentities, and only tenor Chris Merritt is truly effective.

Hickox and the London Symphony Chorus and City of London Sinfonietta have the real goods: lots of silken sounds and authentic Italian drive and style (♦Chandos 8780). Arthur Davies sails through the high-lying tessitura with ease, his sweet-toned tenor a pleasure, but the rest of the cast sings with too much English seriousness. **Bychkov** takes the solemn, stately, and reverential approach for a most impressive performance (Philips 426312). The Bavarian Radio Chorus is outstanding, wending its way with stylistic ease between delicacy and full-throttle outbursts. Araiza copes well with his music, but is workmanlike rather than impressive. Bartoli is rich-voiced and expressive, but Vaness and Furlanetto don't have the agility needed for Rossini's music.

Myung-Whun Chung's approach is big and dramatic, a German rather than an Italian view; for what it is, it works, but it's just not authentic Rossini (DG 449178). The Vienna Philharmonic and Vienna State Opera Chorus are powerful and play Rossini like Beethoven (they performed more correctly for Kertész). The soloists are mixed. Bartoli is again just about perfect, and Giménez negotiates the tenor difficulties with ease. Orgonasova sings beautifully, but with little comfort in the style, and Roberto Scandiuzzi is dull. **Muti** offers a dramatic reading (EMI 68658, 2CD, with *Messe*). Malfitano (uncertain), Baltsa (stuffy), Gambill (a disaster), and Howell (the best of the basses) are the soloists.

OPERAS

Armida. This is perhaps the most difficult to perform of all Rossini operas. Not only does the title role present stupefying vocal difficulties, but the opera also contains six difficult tenor roles. Although a bit shy of drama, it contains a wealth of beautiful melody.

Armida remained almost unproduced for a century until a 1952 revival for **Callas** at the Maggio Musicale Fiorentino (Melodram 2.0012 and 26024; 2CD). Although she learned the title role in only five days, she's in absolute control, easily encompassing every difficulty from bravura display to plaintive tenderness. Her tenor colleagues don't approach such artistry, having neither her flexibility nor her insight. Francesco Albanese omits much of his higher-lying music; Mario Filippeschi is equally inflexible, but at least he can trumpet out his high notes. Alessandro Ziliani barely makes it through his music, though a young Gianni Raimondi shows signs of promise. Grand old maestro Serafin brings experience and authority to the music. The opera suffers some cuts (some lost in radio transmission), and the sound is dim, but this is a major sample of Callas's legacy.

After Callas, *Armida* didn't surface again until 1990 (Koch 350211, 2CD). **Gasdia** does well by the dazzling title role with the requisite vocal agility, but she's small-scaled in voice and in musical and dramatic conception. Merritt isn't quite comfortable in the upper reaches of his role, but in "normal" tenor range he sings quite beautifully. Matteuzzi's blazing tenor excitingly skyrockets into the stratosphere, and Bruce Ford is almost as good. The usually reliable Furlanetto does little with his two roles. I Solisti Veneti under **Scimone**'s energetic leadership are almost a separate show in themselves, playing with great beauty of tone and musicality.

In a 1993 performance, **Fleming** is a stunning Armida (♦Sony 58968, 2CD). She easily encompasses the role's two-and-a-half octave range, sailing through the fioratura gracefully and with great agility, modulating her voice for the intimate scenes, yet with plenty of power and authority for the dramatics. The six tenors are good young singers who are willing to embellish their music properly even in the stratospheric range. The best is Donald Kaasch (Goffredo); the others are adequate. Daniele Gatti is the dutiful conductor.

Il Barbiere di Siviglia. Now the most popular comic opera in the repertoire, this was a resounding failure at its 1816 Rome premiere. The audiences considered Rossini's version of the Beaumarchais play not only inferior to Paisiello's 1782 opera but an insult to the older composer as well. Happily, Sterbini's witty, character-filled libretto and Rossini's wealth of engaging melodies have won the day. Although the composer wrote the leading role for a mezzo, in the past it was most often performed by coloratura sopranos, and that's what we hear in earlier recordings. Modern scholarship has resulted in renewed interest in the mezzo version, and that's what we get in most recent recordings.

Callas sang only five performances of Rosina (at La Scala), yet for many she's indelibly associated with the role. Her 1956 performance, however, finds her in poor voice, heavy-handed in the comedy, tough, and unendearing (Melodram 26020, 2CD). Luigi Alva, early in his career, isn't flexible enough in Almaviva's coloratura, but is in sweet voice. Gobbi does more with the text than any other Figaro, his Venetian accent and dark baritone combining for a remarkably well-sung and well-interpreted Barber. Melchiorre Luise (Bartolo) and Rossi-Lemeni (Basilio) are comic delights, but Giulini has coordination difficulties, and the recorded sound is dim.

In 1957 Callas recorded the opera in the studio, a much better performance (♦EMI 56310, 2CD). She's in superb voice, with a high level of textual interpretation matching Gobbi (again the superlative Figaro) in comic expressiveness. Alva is back for a more agile Almaviva, with Fritz Ollendorf and Nicola Zaccaria, better-voiced than their predecessors and interpretively an equally comic pair. Galliera lightens up the La Scala forces and even restores the cuts generally made in the finale.

The 1962 Glyndebourne production was the first based on modern scholarship (♦EMI 64162, 2CD). Conductor Gui restored Rossini's original orchestration, keys, and notes, and found a happy compromise between soubrette and mezzo for Rosina in **de los Angeles,** whose beautiful voice was delightfully engaged in a charmingly delicate performance. Alva is the elegant Almaviva, with Bruscantini an almost perfect Figaro, brilliantly sung with a thorough naturalism in the recitatives. Equally natural and entertaining are the Bartolo of Ian Wallace and the Basilio of Carlo Cava. Gui molds the show into a sparkling, witty, and graceful treasure.

An almost complete performance from the Metropolitan is an all-round winner (♦RCA 68552, 3CD). Leinsdorf hardly seems like a logical choice to conduct an ebullient comedy, but he pulls it off with sparkling aplomb. **Roberta Peters** sings the traditional soprano rewrite of Rosina's music with all the art and artifice of a true diva, a vocal match for Valletti's light and elegant Almaviva. Merrill is a jolly Barber with plenty of voice to spare. Corena is a broad, sunny Bartolo, and Tozzi's Basilio is magnificently sung, bubbling with malicious glee.

Levine leads a subtly inflected, complete performance with a strong international cast (EMI 66040, 2CD). The recorded sound tends too often to be hollow and cavernous, but it's worth putting up with it just to hear the performance. **Sills** (soprano rewrite again) is a spectacular Rosina, full of character and vocal histrionics. Gedda's golden lyric voice is outstanding, but a bit shy of character. Milnes equals Merrill's vocal performance and adds even more characterization. Capecchi's Bartolo is nasty and strangulated; Raimondi's Basilio is plain and restrained, almost too serious.

Problems abound with Chailly's unsympathetic recording (CBS 37862, 3CD). The bel canto proficiencies of **Horne** (Rosina) and Ramey (Basilio) are in evidence, spectacularly sung but hardly funny. The humorless Figaro of Leo Nucci fits right in, and the Almaviva of Paolo Barbacini is a vocal disaster. Dara is the bland Bartolo. **Bartoli** is a prima donna delight in Patanè's traditionally comic recording, sparkling, witty, almost over-interpreted, but beautifully sung (Decca 425520, 2CD). William Mattinuzzi is a spectacular Almaviva, but again Nucci is a humorless Figaro. Enrico Fissore pulls out the buffo arsenal for a delightful Bartolo, scheming with Paata Burchuladze's ponderous Basilio.

Domingo as Figaro? What a waste! He has no problems getting the notes right, but the timbre is all wrong, and his lack of stage experience in the role makes for awkward, uninteresting patter and recitatives. Lopardo alternates in crooning, belting, and often using a character-tenor splatter as Almaviva. Lucio Gallo and Raimondi are the lightweight, humorless buffo pair. **Battle** manages the high-flung parts of the soprano rewrite, but the low notes go for nothing as she whispers them. Characterization? Soubrette-diva only. Claudio Abbado charges through the opera in record time. The sound is over-engineered and gimmicky too (DG 435763, 2CD).

Although López-Cobos charges energetically through the uncut score, it's a dreary affair (Teldec 74885, 2CD). Giménez is a vocally wan Almaviva, an unpleasant contrast to Hagegård's blustering Figaro. Ramey is a gray, uninteresting Basilio, with only Corbelli (Bartolo) and **Larmore,** both in fine voice, comfortable with Rossini's comic idiom. The Failoni Chamber Orchestra of Budapest are sprightly for Will Humburg in a performance that is complete, inexpensive, but has little to recommend it (Naxos 660027/29, 3CD). **Sonia Ganassi's** heavyweight, unsure, Carmen-sings-Rosina voice is in trouble, though Ramon Vargas is an attractive Almaviva. Roberto Servile (Figaro) and Angelo Romero (Bartolo) are vocal lightweights adept at over-clowning, with Franco De Grandis a crude Basilio.

Gelmetti's recording is another bland affair, and he indulges his singers too frequently (EMI 54863, 2CD). **Susanne Mentzer** is in pleasant (mezzo) voice, but without agility or characterization. Hadley has some vocal difficulties, and Practico ignores vocal niceties in favor of comic effect. Hampson sings stoutly, with agility, confidence, and humor. Once again Ramey is the agile, but too serious Basilio. Gabrielle Bellini's recording is in English, a light and lively performance with the text remarkably clear, particularly in the recitatives (Chandos 7023, 2CD). **Della Jones,** a mezzo Rosina, sings all the notes but creates a prim and proper young lady, hardly the cunning vixen Rossini had in mind. Bruce Ford is a slack Almaviva; Alan Opie is a lively, well-sung Figaro;

but buffos Andrew Shore and Peter Rose have shallow bass voices, lacking the rotundity of proper Italian sound.

La Cenerentola. Rossini's version of the age-old story of Cinderella is a delight, carefully balancing sincerity, pathos, romantic love, and knee-slapping comedy.

A superb midpriced monaural version comes from the 1953 Glyndebourne Festival (♦EMI 64183, 2CD). **Marina De Gabarain** is an unfamiliar name, but she's an exquisite Angelina, darkly rich in tone with striking coloratura agility. Juan Oncina is a fresh-voiced Ramiro. Bruscantini (Dandini) and Ian Wallace (Magnifico) actually sing the required notes while creating delightful buffo characterizations. Gui paces the music with plenty of snap and fizz.

An all-Italian 1963 version would be more satisfactory if de Fabritiis had led a livelier performance (Decca 433030, 2CD). **Simionato,** Benelli, Bruscantini, and Montarsolo have a grand time with the comedy, with some true, high-powered singing. An excellent inexpensive version from the 1971 Maggio Musicale with **Berganza,** Alva, Capecchi, and Montarsolo led by Abbado is available (Opera d'Oro 1212, 2CD). The same cast, but from Edinburgh with the London Symphony, may be heard in a studio recording (DG 459448, 2CD). Berganza is a naturally charming Angelina, singing smoothly with easy grace and without artifice. Alva is the excellent Ramiro, but Capecchi is a woolly, poorly sung Dandini. Montarsolo is a grotesque but funny Magnifico. Abbado enforces a fine sense of ensemble, using the critical edition by Alberto Zedda; the score is a bit more complete and has better sound on DG.

Marriner leads a lively performance (Philips 420468, 2CD). **Baltsa** is more comfortable with the role's pathos, less so with the coloratura, a rather dour heroine. Araiza's second Ramiro is still in fine shape, darkly beautiful. Simone Alaimo slinks through Dandini's coloratura, but is most amusing. Raimondi has no trouble with the coloratura, but is not amusing. Chailly's version has plenty of speed and lightness, but fails to capture the underlying sadness of the opera (Decca 436902, 2CD). **Bartoli** gives a bravura performance, astonishing in its agility, but with only external characterization and no depth of feeling. Matteuzzi (Ramiro) nips around the coloratura with ease, but his voice isn't pleasant, also lacking expressiveness and elegance. Corbelli too is short on vocal beauty, but he does create a bumbling, amusing Dandini. Dara does little with Magnifico's music or comedy.

Larmore provides a most extraordinary performance of Angelina (♦Teldec 99455, 2CD). A true mezzo-soprano, she has plenty of plush vocal darkness, smooth and pure, absolutely beautiful, with amazing agility. Giménez is a youthful-sounding Ramiro. Gino Quilico is hardly an expert Rossinian or bel canto specialist; his voice isn't agile, though he does project plenty of character. Corbelli this time is a vivid, old-fashioned Magnifico. The Covent Garden forces put on a lively show under Carlo Rizzi's baton.

Guillaume Tell. Although Rossini composed *Tell* in French for Paris, the opera is firmly set in the Italian bel canto tradition, with touches of early Verdi. It's a lengthy opera of great drama and depth, with much fine music other than the famous, ubiquitous overture. Rarely performed, the opera is generally produced and recorded in Italian translation.

Many listeners learned their *Tell* from a 1952 recording sung in Italian from RAI Turin (Cetra); unfortunately, it hasn't been issued on CD. Taddei was definitive as Tell, strongly sung, nobly characterized. **Mario Rossi** led a vigorous performance, confident and bold. Rosanna Carteri etched a delicate Matilde, and Plinio Clabasi was a powerful Mechthal, but Corena's buffo mannerisms muddled the tyrant Gessler, and Mario Filippeschi's Arnold was a disaster.

A 1965 performance in Italian from Naples is a rough and ready affair, but its low price makes it a good introduction to the opera (Opera d'Oro 1165, 3CD). Giangiacomo Guelfi is a burly Tell, and although Gianni Raimondi is taxed by Arnold's difficult music, he manages it with decorum. Gencer is a tough-sounding Matilde. **Fernando Previtali** is the energetic but wayward maestro.

In French—and the first absolutely complete recording—the 1972 performance led by **Gardelli** was worth the wait (♦EMI 69951, 4CD). He leads the Royal Philharmonic in a classically restrained performance, no Italian melodrama, elegant and stately French drama instead. Bacquier is a sympathetic Tell, a more intimate portrait than Taddei's, with exquisite tone and diction. Gedda can actually meet the demands of Arnold's music, with lovely tone and sensitivity as well; only in the stratospheric top notes does he spare himself, lightly touching them instead of belting them out. Caballé is an aristocratic, silken Matilde, with Gwynne Howell an imposing Mechthal.

Also complete, but in Italian, **Chailly** leads an inconsistent performance, wildly varying between Italian Rossini correctness and early-period Verdi, heavy on the melodrama; but it's undeniably exciting and has with much to recommend it (♦Decca 417154, 4CD). The big selling point is Pavarotti's Arnold; he's in superb voice, but a bit sloppy musically, failing to make some delicate musical points. Milnes sings a grand and eloquent Tell, black-toned and majestic. Freni brings surprising strength of character to Matilde, plus creamy tone and delicacy. Ghiaurov's Gualtiero is regal and potent.

Muti's recording was made at a 1988 performance at La Scala (Philips 422391, 4CD). He's knowledgeable but beset by recording problems; there's little presence or depth, with an overall muffled sound. It's in Italian, with Giorgio Zancanaro a sturdy Tell of unpleasant voice. Merritt sails spectacularly through Arnold's music, with Studer a strong Matilde of lovely tone.

L'Italiana in Algeri. Rossini's biographer, Stendhal, said of *L'Italiana,* "It makes one forget all the sadness of the world," a well-deserved compliment. A truly funny plot combined with Rossini's array of sparkling arias, duets, and especially vocal ensembles, add up to a package of total delight.

Berganza is hard to beat; she's a finely etched Isabella, silken-toned, yet sly and wily (♦Decca 417828, 2CD). Alva is an attractive Lindoro, with Rolando Panerai and Fernando Corena definitive as Taddeo and Mustaphà. All have particular insight into the Italian text and Rossini's music. Varviso leads the Maggio Musicale Fiorentino ensemble in a sparkling performance.

The listener is the winner in what seems like two performances for the price of one (♦Opera Italiana 12, 2CD). First comes a complete performance with **Horne** (RAI Torino, 1968), then most of Isabella's music by **Berganza** (RAI Milano). Both Isabellas are quite remarkable. No one can compare with Horne in quality or quantity of voice. By contrast, Berganza is a beautifully soft-grained mezzo, not as incisive as Horne, her voice tastefully employed. Horne is more the extrovert. Berganza conquers Mustaphà by feminine wiles, sexily discreet and winning; Horne conquers by sheer bravura. Pietro Bottazzo is a brilliant Lindoro, ready for anything Rossini can throw at him. Walter Monachesi (Taddeo) is dry of voice but amusing. Carlo Rizzi is a driving but sympathetic conductor. The excerpts are from a more subtle performance led by Sanzogno.

In 1980 Horne recorded the opera in the studio (Erato 45404, 2CD). Again it's a spectacular affair, perhaps without all the fizzy delight of an on-stage performance, but a delight all the same. Her colleagues are even better here. Palacio sings beautifully as Lindoro, with ease and grace, and Domenico Trimarchi creates a comic masterpiece as Taddeo. Ramey is vocally awesome, but without much of a comic sense of character. A bonus is Battle in the secondary role of Elvira. I Solisti Veneti play splendidly for Scimone.

Abbado's recording has a fine sense of ensemble (DG 427331, 2CD). **Baltsa** is a coldly calculating Isabella, lightening her usual dark mezzo to move gracefully through the coloratura intricacies. Lopardo is the least experienced in his role, but he uses his dark tenor to good effect, even if he's not quite at home with all the textual subtleties. Ruggero Raimondi (Mustaphà) has no problems with the notes, but is simply not funny. The Wiener Philharmoniker plays beautifully for Abbado, but the overall impression is one of detached seriousness.

López-Cobos leads a truly complete performance, fast and furious, but again not really funny (♦Teldec 17130, 2CD). **Larmore** is the spectacular successor to Horne in the bel canto operas. Her Isabella couldn't be more rewarding, sumptuously sung, with agility, grace, style, and personality. Giménez's attractive, small and light tenor voice has no difficulties. Corbelli's Taddeo is full of character but needs a bit of tolerance for his singing. John Del Carlo is a rather likable Mustaphà, hearty, robust, and agile.

Mosè in Egitto. Rossini's *azione tragico-sacra* has a complex history. First performed in Italian in Naples in 1818, the opera was a success except for its short final act; one year later Rossini presented the Neapolitan audience with an entirely new third act. In 1827 he revised the entire opera for the Paris Opéra, now in French as *Moïse et Pharaon,* and this recomposition soon supplanted the 1819 version in popularity. Finally, *Moïse* was retranslated into Italian and as such has maintained a performance history.

The 1956 monaural recording of the 1827 version from Naples has a regal but woofy-voiced Mosè from **Rossi-Lemeni** and an impressive performance from Taddei as Faraone, but Mario Filippeschi and Caterina Mancini are barely adequate (Philips 442100, 2CD). Serafin deserved a stronger cast. An imposing 1971 performance of the 1827 version, in Italian, comes from the Rome Opera (♦Giuseppe Di Stefano 21036, 2CD). The great **Christoff** gives us a Mosè who is majestically human and humanly majestic, hurling vocal thunderbolts. His act is impossible to duplicate or even to follow, but the cast gives it a good try. Gabriella Tucci sings with sincere simplicity, Tagliavini with passion. Lino Puglisi and Clabassi sing very well with their "merely human" bass voices. Bianca Maria Casoni is all consternation and concern, and Bartoletti rises to the occasion. What a performance!

A 1980 recording from Budapest has idiomatic conducting from Gardelli and a pleasant Mosè from **Jozsef Gregor,** but nothing else to recommend it (Hungaroton 12290, 3CD). In a recording of the 1819 version, **Raimondi** beautifully sings a sensitive Mosè but lacks the authority needed for the character (Philips 420109, 2CD). The young June Anderson sings prettily but is devoid of character; Nimsgern produces lots of character, but his vocal technique is foreign to the musical style. The star here is Palacio (Osiride), an agile singer also capable of characterization. Scimone leads the Philharmonia in a beautifully realized performance but fails to catch the grandeur and majesty of the opera.

For his second try at Mosè (a highly cut 1988 performance), this time in the 1827 version in Italian, Raimondi is much better, singing beautifully and with a reasonable projection of authority (Orfeo, 2CD). **Vaness** is a splendid Anaide, with Doris Soffel a regal Sinaide and Araiza a winning Amenofi. Bodo Brinkman is an unidiomatic Faraone, but the other bass roles are quite good at capturing the majesty of the score.

Semiramide. This is the last of Rossini's serious Italian operas, and it calls for singers of extraordinary vocal skills. The mezzo-soprano (Arsace) lead is a trousers role.

In Bonynge's knowledgeable recording, the cuts are plentiful, but he has the impressive team of **Sutherland** and Horne; the pair are most impressive, the ultimate bel canto artists (Decca 425481, 2CD). John Serge (Idreno) and Joseph Rouleau (Assur) are not. An inexpensive alternative is a 1968 performance in which Sutherland and Bonynge are in fine form, with Monica Sinclair a strong Arsace, but Ottavio Garaventa (Idreno) and Mario Petri (Assur) are sorely tried by their music (Opera d'Oro 1136, 3CD).

A 1980 performance at Aix-en-Provence was a coloratura spectacular (♦Legato 509, 2CD) This is **Caballé** in excelsis! Her Semiramide is one of her best performances; she sings with incredible accuracy, floating those famous ethereal pianissimos, then breaking out in dramatic, fiery utterance as required. Horne is again an astonishing Arsace, even more exciting in this staged performance. Araiza is the big-voiced Idreno. Ramey finds no difficulty in the bass-coloratura extravaganza Rossini composed for Assur—not just a magnificent voice, but one agile enough for every ornament, every phrase, every twist and turn. López-Cobos, so frequently a rapid-fire Rossinian, here holds the pace in check but keeps the adrenaline flowing.

At the 1992 Rossini Festival, Rossini scholar and conductor **Alberto Zedda** presented his version of *Semiramide* (Fonit Cetra). It's absolutely complete, running for almost four hours at his languid tempos, but that's all there is to recommend it. The singers are barely adequate, and the chorus is laughable. Ion Marin uses the Zedda edition, but at zippy tempos shaves almost half an hour off Zedda's performance (DG 437797, 3CD). Everything is too fast, with ensembles bordering on confusion, a condition not helped by the muddled acoustics; voices are distantly miked, lacking any real presence. **Studer** is an uncomfortable heroine, her voice too often unsupported and weak. Larmore is the best singer here, a silken sound, but too womanly for the military hero. Ramey again sails easily through Assur's coloratura, but as is so often the case, remains totally uninvolved in the drama.

Tancredi. Rossini was only 21 when he composed *Tancredi* (1813). This was his first attempt at serious opera, and perhaps due to his youth (both musically and personally), he transformed Voltaire's *Tancrède* from a powerful tragedy into a standard melodrama with a happy ending. For a production in Ferrara later the same year he restored the original tragic ending, composing new music for it.

A performance from Venice uses the tragic ending (♦Sony 39073, 2CD). As usual, **Horne** (Tancredi) is a one-woman coloratura spectacular; no difficulties faze her. Cuberli is a magnificent Amenaide, matching Horne note for note. Palacio is an agile, virile Argirio, but by 1988 Zaccaria could no longer sing Obrazzano's coloratura. Ralf Weikert leads his forces in a melodramatic performance, a bit shy on the bel canto line.

Zedda restores the original happy ending; often a placid conductor, he's just that here, with the period instrument Collegium Instrumentale Brugense often unpleasantly scrawny and scrappy (Naxos 66037, 2CD). **Podles** is in spectacular voice, steady and even through the role's immense range, with fleet coloratura and dramatic energy. Sumi Jo is a bright, chirpy Amenaide, and although Stanford Olsen has no difficul-

ties with the intricacies of Argirio's music, his role is shorn of the high-flying notes of the cadenzas.

A 1995 recording offers both the happy and tragic endings plus an extensive second entrance aria for Tancredi; you can choose which you want to hear (RCA 68349, 2CD). **Vesseline Kasarova** has a fine technique and flexibility along with a dark, warm sound, a fine contrast to Mei's bright soprano (Amenaide). Vargas is an attractive Argirio. **Roberto Abbado** leads Bavarian Radio forces in a sensible performance, with the clear purpose of tightening up Rossini's long recitatives, balancing them with the more compact arias.

Il Turco in Italia. This *dramma buffa* is often mistaken for a rewrite of *L'Italiana,* depicting a similar clash of cultures, but it's a much more intimate work and less of a farce. Its Pirandellian Poet in search of a plot is an unusual framing device. Musically, there are surprisingly few opportunities for vocal display; the opera moves along in a series of extended recitatives, brief, unspectacular arias, and ensembles.

Callas easily captures the subtleties of Fiorilla's character and smoothly interprets the musical ones (♦EMI 56313, 2CD). Gedda is a honey-toned Narciso, delicate yet virile. Rossi-Lemeni's Selim is dry and woolly, but very much a comic character. The big surprise is veteran Mariano Stabile as The Poet, a comic delight. Gavazzeni leads the La Scala ensemble in a distinguished performance.

For just plain beautiful singing, you can't go wrong with **Caballé,** Palacio, Ramey, and Nucci as musically sensitive interpreters (Sony 37859, 2CD). The opera isn't very funny, so their lack of comic interpretation can be forgiven in light of the gorgeous sounds they make. Chailly goes along with the vocal pleasantries, duplicating them with the orchestra (National Philharmonic).

Perhaps it's damning with faint praise, but "pleasant" is the term for Marriner's version with **Sumi Jo,** Giménez, Enrico Fissore, Simone Alaimo, and Alessandro Corbelli (Poeta) the attractive singers (Philips 434128, 2CD). The opera is bland enough without the well-sung but dull performances here. Chailly is again on the podium, this time at La Scala, for an effervescent performance (♦Decca 458924, 2CD). **Bartoli** is a total delight, singing as smooth as silk, agile of voice and characterization, a comic masterpiece. Michele Pertusi is a hearty, grand Selim, relishing the text. Corbelli interprets Geronio as a more sympathetic character than you would expect, avoiding many buffo mannerisms. Vargas is a passionate Narciso, with Robert De Candia a cooly calculating Poet.

ORCHESTRAL MUSIC

Overtures. Recordings of Rossini's opera overtures are so numerous that it's impossible to discuss their various merits and deficiencies in any detail. I offer only a selection of the better collections. For a complete set of all of them, you can't go wrong with **Marriner**'s "The Complete Rossini Overtures" (Philips 434016, 3CD). **Alun Francis** offers an unusual collection in "Early Overtures and Sinfonias," including *Cambiale di matrimonio, Inganno felice, Occasione fa il ladro, Pietra del paragone, Signor Bruschino, Sinfonia di Bologna, Sinfonia di Odense, Sinfonia al Conventello,* and *Grand'Overture obbligato a contrabasso* (CPO 999063).

Claudio Abbado/Chamber Orchestra of Europe (DG 431653)
  Sprightly performances.

Beecham/London Philharmonic (Dutton 7001)
  The smiling face of Rossini himself.

Bernstein/New York Philharmonic (Sony 47606)
  Big, bold, brassy, and sassy.

Chailly/National Philharmonic (Decca 443850, 2CD)
The "new" Italian approach to Rossini.

Dorati/Minneapolis Symphony (Mercury 434345)
Sturdy performances.

Goodman/Hanover Band (RCA 68139)
Period instruments; strong, but without the excitement of Norrington.

Halász/Zagreb Festival Orchestra (Naxos 550236)
A bit on the raw side, but a budget delight.

Levi/Atlanta Symphony (Telarc 80334)
Superior recorded sound and solid performances.

Marriner/Academy of St. Martin in the Fields (Philips 434016)
A joyous selection.

Norrington/London Classical Players (EMI 54091)
A stunning new sound using period instruments.

Orpheus Chamber Orchestra (DG 415363)
Restrained, unsmiling performances sans conductor.

Patanè/Bamberg Symphony (Eurodisc 69011)
An Italian conductor brings out the Italian best in a German orchestra.

Reiner/Chicago Symphony (RCA 60387)
Hungarian fire combined with Italian brio.

Schippers/Cincinnati Symphony (Vox 5141, 2CD)
Dashing, romantic versions of the overtures.

Toscanini/NBC Symphony (RCA 60289); New York Philharmonic 1929–36 (RCA 60318); New York Philharmonic (Pearl 9373)
The real thing, a native's insight into Rossini and Italian bel canto style.

Suites. In 1936 Benjamin Britten arranged for orchestra a sprightly five-movement suite, *Soirées Musicales,* from a variety of Rossini's music. Such was its success that in 1941 he arranged another five-movement suite, *Matinées Musicales.* Tuneful, clever, and charming as the two are, there have been surprisingly few recordings. Both are heard in classically poised 1956 performances by **Boult** and the London Philharmonic (♦EMI 63777). Broadly romantic interpretations are offered by **Alexander Gibson** leading the English Chamber Orchestra (EMI 67492). **Britten** conducts the Covent Garden Orchestra in a sparkling performance of *Soirées,* paired with a more restrained performance of *Matinées* by Bonynge and the National Philharmonic (Decca 425659). Bonynge also conducts the National Philharmonic in both suites: elegant, but not lively enough (Decca). **Patrick Peire** leads the New Flemish Symphony in a rather acidic, French view (René Gailly 87062).

Péchés de Vieillesse (SINS OF OLD AGE) AND SONGS
Although Rossini lived 39 years after composing his last opera (1829, *Guillaume Tell*), he wrote very little more other than some short choral compositions. But he did produce an eclectic anthology of about 180 brief compositions for various instruments, voice, and piano that he called his "Sins of Old Age."

A representative selection is exquisitely, ideally performed by **Augér,** Larmore, Aler, and Steven Kimbrough, with fine piano accompaniment by Dalton Baldwin (♦Arabesque 6623). Another selection with good but unenthusiastic performances is by **June Anderson** and others (Nimbus 5132).

It has been said that performances of Rossini's music can be dated B.H. and A.H., "Before Horne" and "After Horne." Completely identified with Rossini's music, **Horne** is a Rossinian without equal. She's heard in 22 selections, fabulously sung, decorated, and presented with her delightful sense of humor (♦RCA 60811). **Bartoli** is the personable soloist in a selection beautifully realized by her distinctive voice (Decca 430518). **Rockwell Blake** performs a selection of songs from throughout Rossini's career, including some from *Péchés* (EMI 55614). His vocal range and technique are astonishing, his colorations of infinite variety, but the peculiar sound of his voice needs some indulgence.

A notable group of piano selections from *Péchés,* "Album de Chaumière" and "Album de Château," are played by **Dino Ciani** in monaural sound but solid performances (Cetra 2021; Hunt 901; 3CD). **Bruno Mezzena** gives a subdued performance of the "Quelques riens pour album" section of *Péchés* (Dynamic 42, 2CD).   PARSONS

Nino Rota *(1911–1979)*
The trouble with being a chameleon is that you may end up not knowing what color you really are, and to an extent that was the fate of Nino Rota. His prodigious start as a composer was made with tuneful works, full of sinuous melodies, but as he matured and worked more and more in the cinema, his concert music developed a family resemblance to the work of such composers as Malipiero, Pizzetti, and Casella—a liking for linear melodic progressions and a certain coolness of harmonic texture. And whereas his music for films was perforce written fluently, at great speed, Rota's concert works often evolved over a number of years. The music therefore displays a high level of craftsmanship, and, thankfully, this is reflected in the performances on CD: Musicians appear to have embarked on a Rota project because they really wanted to. (His film music is discussed in the article on that subject in Part II.)

Orchestral music. Rota produced three symphonies; a fourth is really a concoction from film music. The first two are four-movement works each lasting half an hour, fresh in melodic inspiration and luminously scored. Symphony 1 had quite a success before the war; 2 ("Tarantina: Anni di pellegrinaggio") was completed in wartime and not heard until the mid-'70s, when Rota revised it without tainting its freshness. **Ole Kristian Ruud** and the Norrköping Symphony give beautiful performances, well recorded (BIS 970).

Rota pupil **Muti** and the Orchestra Filarmonica della Scala have produced several Rota discs, only two of which concern us here. One, of music from the '60s, frames the fine *Concerto per Archi*—superbly played by the Scala strings—with two works with cinematic connections, the ballet suite *La Strada* (based on Fellini's film) and the full versions of the dances for *The Leopard,* as opposed to the rough drafts used in the actual movie (Sony 66279). The other Muti disc couples the two Piano Concertos, that in C dating from 1959–60 and written for Michelangeli, that in E ("Piccolo mondo antico") being Rota's last work, from 1978. They are attractive and splendidly played by the young **Giorgia Tomassi** (EMI 56869). The quality of Muti's accompaniments gives this disc the edge over an equally well recorded rival by **Massimo Palumbo** and Virtuosi Italiani under Marco Boni (Chandos 9681).

Another piano concerto of sorts, *Concerto Soirée* is a delightful piece of light music, while the *Fantasia sopra 12-Note del Don Giovanni* is a typically resourceful comment on Milhaud's discovery of a 12-note figure in the finale of Mozart's opera; both are well played by **Danielle Laval** with the Orchestra Città di Ferrara under Giuseppe Grazioli; the disc includes two early works for chamber orchestra, the Dances of 1932 and the

Sonata of 1937 (Auvidis 1034). As for the 1968 Trombone Concerto, written for the great Bruno Ferrari and displaying Rota's complete understanding of the instrument, your choice between **Christian Lindberg** with the Tapiola Sinfonietta under Vänskä (BIS 568) and **Branimir Slokar** with the Berlin Symphony under Lior Shambadal (Claves 509606) will probably depend on the couplings (works by Rimsky-Korsakoff, Henri Tomasi, and Folke Rabe in the first; Bloch, Launy Grøndahl, and Alexander Harut'unyan in the second); Lindberg is the greater virtuoso.

Chamber and instrumental music. Rota's chamber music has attracted a number of interpreters, and inevitably there is duplication among the various anthologies. None of the music outstays its welcome, and its brevity is matched by idiomatic writing for the various instruments. Sonata for Flute and Harp is a lovely early piece, the original version of Sonata for Chamber Orchestra. It's featured in the well-filled disc by **Ex Novo Ensemble,** which also offers the other most popular chamber work, Trio for Flute, Violin, and Piano, as well as Quintet for Flute, Oboe, Viola, Cello, and Harp (ASV 1072).

All three of these works are also offered by flutist **Mario Carbotta** and colleagues (Dynamic 172), but his two couplings are less substantial, whereas the Ex Novo players include Trio for Clarinet, Cello, and Piano, String Quartet, and the short *Piccola Offerta Musicale* for wind quintet, and are more pleasantly recorded. An even better performance of the String Quartet comes from **Nuovo Quartetto Italiano,** if you fancy the Respighi and Malipiero couplings (Claves 9617).

Trio for Flute, Violin, and Piano crops up again, very well played, in a marvelous grab bag from **Kremer** and the Kremerata Musica. Other substantial works on this disc are the enjoyable *Nonet,* which took Rota from 1959 to 1977 to finish and is his longest essay in chamber music, Intermezzo for Viola and Piano, *Il Presepio* for soprano and string quartet, and *Sarabanda e Toccata* for harp. Kremer himself plays only in the trio, but all the performances (with Gérard Caussé and the Hagen Quartet among the artists) and the sound are of a high standard (BIS 870). Two early and two mature works come from **Ensemble Nino Rota** directed by Palumbo: Violin Sonata, Viola Sonata 2 (inexplicably described as No. 1), and the two Trios already mentioned (Chandos 9832). The trios are as well performed as in the rival discs, and Suela Mullaj doubles effectively on violin and viola.

So does **Luigi Alberto Bianchi,** who, with Marco Vincenzi as his excellent piano partner, provides the Violin Sonata and both Viola Sonatas, getting even further inside the music than Mullaj and playing the version of Viola Sonata 1's finale that Rota altered specially for him when he gave the belated premiere; he adds the virtuosic *Improvviso* for violin and piano and Intermezzo for Viola and Piano (Dynamic 211). So if the lyrical string sonatas are your priority, Bianchi is the man.

An excellent recital of Rota's piano music from **Danielle Laval** is dominated by the first-rate *Variations and Fugue on the Name B-A-C-H,* lasting only 19 minutes but full of content and incident. The other pieces, including two Waltzes, seven *Difficult Pieces for Children,* the early *Ippolito Gioco,* and 15 Preludes, are slighter, but the performances make them worth hearing (Auvidis 1021).

Operas. Rota's best-known opera is *Il cappella di paglia di Firenze,* based on the French vaudeville *The Italian Straw Hat,* in which with some success he sought to revive the Ottocento opera buffa style. The orchestra carries much of the argument, the vocal line proceeding in a mixture of recitative and arioso. The famous RCA recording seems never to have been transferred to CD, but there is an adequate substitute, albeit in rather dim sound, from a performance in Brussels in 1976. The cast includes Olivero, no less, as the Baroness, with Edoardo Giménez and Devia as Fadinard and Elena, the young couple whose wedding is jeopardized when Fadinard's horse eats a woman's straw hat. The Chorus and Orchestra of the Theatre Royal de la Monnaie are well directed by **Elio Boncompagni** (Gala 100.547). Only a sketchy synopsis is provided, but a bonus track features Olivero in a 1979 performance of Poulenc's *La voix humaine.*

The other of Rota's ten operas available is the one most commentators rate as his best, *La visita meravigliosa,* based on H.G. Wells's story *The Wonderful Visit,* about an angel coming down to an English village. The recording, made at a 1993 performance in Rovigo, is in decent broadcast sound. **Giuseppe Grazioli** handles his large cast sympathetically; Danilo Rigosa is authoritative as the vicar; Maurizio Frusoni is excellent as the angel; and considerable justice is done to a really worthwhile opera (La Bottega Discantica 02/03). The libretto is in Italian only, but a detailed English synopsis is given.   POTTER

Christopher Rouse (b. 1949)

Rouse, who teaches composition at the Eastman School of Music, has been considered an important American composer for quite a few years, and very recently, thanks to recordings, he has become widely known and popular. He has produced a steady stream of large-scale, enthusiastically received works: two symphonies; concertos for trombone, violin, cello, and flute; and several shorter orchestral pieces. His Trombone Concerto won the 1993 Pulitzer Prize, and Yo-Yo Ma's recording of his Cello Concerto won three Grammys in 1998.

Most of Rouse's major works are haunted by death: the loss of relatives, friends, and musical heroes. *Phaethon* is dedicated to the memory of the Challenger astronauts; the senseless kidnapping and murder of a two-year-old boy in England haunts the Adagio of his Flute Concerto. Keats might have described his music as "gloom-pleased," but these works are also built to last. His orchestration, even at its most imposing, is perfectly judged, and Rouse has a precise sense of proportion and timing. And while his large-scale works abound in flamboyant dramatic gestures, their sense of tragedy is genuine.

The Trombone Concerto, dedicated to the memory of Leonard Bernstein, ends with an apparently calm acceptance of death; in the Cello Concerto, the noble melodic lines of the soloist are dogged until the very end by the death rattle of percussion instruments. They have the last word, but it's a fight to the finish. Rouse wrestles with his reaction to Stephen Albert's violent death in a car accident in his Symphony 2, a masterly work whose finale grows ever more raucous and defiant, annihilating itself. His music is anything but easy listening, but is well worth the effort. His remarkable recent works come from a well-stocked brain and a battered but resilient heart, and the best of them are as affecting as any contemporary music.

Rouse's Trombone Concerto, *Gorgon,* and *Iscariot* are available with trombonist **Joseph Alessi** (RCA 68410); the concerto is also available in a quite different performance by **Christian Lindberg** (BIS 788). His Symphony 2, Flute Concerto, and *Phaethon* are recorded by **Eschenbach** and flutist Carol Wincenc (Telarc 80452), and his Cello Concerto comes from **Ma,** the recording that got all those Grammys—and deserved them (Sony 66299, with works by Danielpour and Kirchner).
                                                                RAYMOND

Albert Roussel (1869–1937)

Before he was a composer, Roussel was a sailor. He was nearly 30 before he traded ships and sails for counterpoint and orchestration at the

Schola Cantorum of Paris, but he was a quick and thorough study and soon became a teacher at the Schola. (His most famous pupils were two other late bloomers, Satie and Martinů.)

Roussel was a notable composer from the beginning, but his style changed dramatically during his career. The main influence on his early music is Debussyian impressionism, with occasional applications of Indian and Indochinese color, remembered from his naval duty in France's Far Eastern colonies. He later adopted the spiky rhythms and clean, vibrant orchestral color of Stravinskian neoclassicism, adding a particularly French elegance of his own. It was in this style, and relatively late in life, that he produced his most familiar works: the ballet *Bacchus et Ariane* and Symphonies 3 and 4. These grand works suggest that if Lt. Albert Roussel was anything like Composer Albert Roussel, he ran a tight ship. In France, he's admired as a master; elsewhere he's perhaps more admired by musicians than loved by audiences, but he deserves to be better known.

ORCHESTRAL MUSIC

Bacchus et Ariane (1930) may be Roussel's masterpiece. This rhythmically propulsive, sumptuously orchestrated music is one of the great ballet scores of the 20th century, not far below Stravinsky's *Pétrouchka* and *Rite of Spring*. The complete ballet has been recorded decently by **Prêtre** (EMI, NA) and spectacularly by **Tortelier** (♦Chandos 9494). Tortelier, who seldom puts a foot wrong in French music, also offers a complete performance of Roussel's ballet *Le Festin de l'araignée* (The Spider's Feast). If Stravinsky is the prime influence on the muscular *Bacchus et Ariane*, this delicate, transparently scored music (illustrating a rather gory scenario about the activities of mayflies, mantises, and fruit worms) shows the audible influence of Debussy.

The second suite from *Bacchus et Ariane* is Roussel's most popular orchestral work, but there are few good recordings. My current recommendations are **Neeme Järvi** (♦Chandos 7007), the best performance in his Roussel collection, and **Markevitch** (♦DG 449748, with music by Milhaud and Honegger). **Ormandy**'s 1960 recording is highly polished, but the interpretation is forced, almost vulgar (Sony). The recordings by **Dutoit** (Erato) and **Baudo** (Supraphon) are NA, as is **Munch**'s Boston Symphony version (RCA), although his reading with the French National Radio Orchestra is available (Disques Montaigne, generously coupled with Symphonies 3 and 4). Munch's performances are hectic and scrappily recorded, but they have palpable energy.

Roussel wrote four symphonies. Symphony 1, *Le Poème de la forêt* (Poem of the Forest, 1904–06), is in a lush but disciplined impressionistic style. Symphony 2 (1920) is harsher and more "advanced" harmonically; Roussel himself considered it "a rather hermetic work," but also a milestone in his development as a composer of *musique pure*. Both are better than their infrequent performances and recordings would suggest, but the exhilarating 3, written for Koussevitzky and the Boston Symphony in 1930, should be a repertory staple; as Poulenc said after its Parisian premiere, "It is marvelous to combine so much springtime and so much maturity." Symphony 4 (1934) is just as remarkable: definitely *musique pure*, as flawlessly concise and good-humored as late Haydn.

All of Roussel's symphonies have been recorded by **Dutoit** (Erato), and more recently in a fine set by **Janowski** (♦RCA 62511). **Bernstein** recorded 3 twice (New York Philharmonic, Sony 62352; French National Orchestra, DG 445512); the New York performance is preferable, more brash but less "interpreted" than the French one (which, however, is coupled with Franck's D Minor Symphony in a highly "interpreted" but gripping performance). This rigorously neoclassical symphony is an

offbeat vehicle for **Boulez**, but his 1976 recording is one of the best, judiciously if often slowly paced, and outstandingly played by the New York Philharmonic (♦Sony 64107).

Järvi's Detroit Symphony sounds, if anything, even better (♦Chandos 7007), but his interpretation, exciting at first, seems rushed compared with Boulez's; ditto the **Munch** performances (Disques Montaigne). However, Järvi's midpriced collection includes good versions of 4 and *Bacchus et Ariane Suite* 2, as well as *Sinfonietta* for strings; with reservations, it's a good single-disc introduction to Roussel (Boulez's coupling is some fine performances of Ravel songs).

In the delicious 4, **Järvi** has little competition except for Janowski's complete set and a good but outdated '50s mono recording by **Karajan** (EMI). **Cluytens**'s excellent performances from the early '60s of 3 and 4, suites from *Bacchus et Ariane* and *Spider's Feast,* and *Sinfonietta* were once available in an EMI 2LP set that's worth seeking out.

Roussel himself conducted selections from *Spider's Feast* for a 1929 recording, along with his piano accompaniment in several songs with mezzo Claire Croiza (♦EMI 54840). *Evocations* is a lavishly orchestrated memoir (with choral finale) of his honeymoon trip to India; the 1986 **Plasson** recording is NA in the United States (EMI), but a performance by **Košler** was praised by critics (Supraphon 111823). And Suite in F, very similar in mood and style to Symphony 4, is available in a peppy recording by **Paray,** coupled with some even peppier Chabrier favorites (♦Mercury 434303). A third, nearly unknown Roussel ballet, *Aeneas,* was recorded by **Dutoit** along with *Bacchus* and other works (Erato).

Roussel's concerted works are few. The brief, bizarre Piano Concerto is included in a survey of unusual French piano concertos (Lalo, Pierné, Boieldieu, etc.), but **Maria Littauer**'s playing is slapdash, and the recording murky (Vox). Cello Concertino (one of his last works, from 1936) is a little jewel in his most distilled neoclassical style; unfortunately, no recordings are available.

CHAMBER AND PIANO MUSIC

Like many other 20th-century French composers, Roussel wrote a lot of chamber music for many combinations of instruments. His impeccable craftsmanship ensures that even the shorter pieces are substantial. All of it, in excellent performances by Dutch musicians, is available in three discs (♦Olympia 458/60). The best known of his chamber works is probably *Serenade for Flute, Harp, and String Trio* Op. 30; a classic **Melos Ensemble** performance from the '60s is available as part of a toothsome French chamber music program (♦London 452891). Also enjoyable in these discs are the violin sonatas, String Quartet, Divertissement for winds and piano (a *Les Six*–ish work, written in 1906), the witty little portrait for guitar *Segovia,* and the suite *Joueurs de flute* (Flute Players).

Recordings of Roussel's piano music are rare. **Eric Parkin**'s survey includes a formidable performance of the most important piano work, Suite in F-sharp Minor (1910), as well as a lot of other music early and late, much of it with Roussel's trademark acidulous harmonies and dense textures (♦Chandos 8887).

VOCAL MUSIC

Roussel's songs have seldom been recorded. A disc with Roussel and **Croiza** contains the most familiar ones except for *Jazz dans la nuit* (EMI). The imposing *Psalm 80* was recorded by **Martinon** but is NA. Nor is Roussel's lavishly scored "opera-ballet" *Padmavati* available, another souvenir of his visits to India and the culmination of his earlier, Debussy-influenced music. *Padmavati* is hardly a singer's opera, but it makes interesting listening, and is recorded by the starry trio of Horne, Gedda, and van Dam, **Plasson** conducting (EMI).   RAYMOND

Miklós Rózsa (1907–1995)

Throughout a long career, Rózsa resolutely avoided all the isms embraced by many of his colleagues (though not necessarily by their audiences). He remained steadfast to his own highly distinctive, tonal, conservative idiom, unashamedly melodic yet strictly contrapuntal and formal. His success as a film composer helped to keep the other side of his "Double Life" (the title of his autobiography) before the public, and since his death many new listeners have discovered his unique sound, which blends Hungarian fire, German classicism, and French sensuality with a dash of Hollywood spectacle. (His film music is discussed in the article on that subject in Part II)

The logical place to start is with the first five volumes of the unfinished "Complete Orchestral Music" series (Koch). Recorded in 1992–97 and conducted by **Sedares,** these performances are always competent and sometimes more. Rózsa made his orchestral debut with two of the works in Vol. I: *Theme, Variations, and Finale* (championed by Walter, Munch, and others) and *Three Hungarian Sketches* (Koch 79191). Sedares's performances are adequate but pale in comparison to earlier recordings by **Rózsa** himself (Decca, mono; RCA, stereo). The latter is a prime candidate for reissue; it includes two later works, *Notturno Ungherese* and *Concert Overture* (also on Sedares's disc).

The most important of the Koch series is Vol. II, containing the first recording of Rózsa's youthful Symphony Op. 6 (♦Koch 7244). When he failed to find a conductor willing to program the long, four-movement work, Rózsa shelved it, only to be persuaded over 60 years later by musicologist Christopher Palmer to dust it off and allow this recording (minus the lost scherzo movement) to be made. It's a fascinating piece, from its mysterious opening to its final vigorous Hungarian dance. **Sedares** brings out the best from his New Zealand Symphony players in the passionately lyrical central Andante; the composer himself called it "a first performance of exemplary fire and passion." Vol. II also includes *The Vintner's Daughter,* a work with impressionistic leanings better heard in a much older and stunningly remastered performance conducted by **Erich Kloss** (Citadel 88139).

Concerto for Strings is one of Rózsa's finest works, composed during WWII and dedicated to his wife. The first two movements reflect the angst of the period, with twisted, angular lines and profound depth of feeling; the concluding Allegro giusto is more playful and affirmative. Koch has recorded it twice, but the best available performance is led by **Peter Csaba** (♦Ondine 919), although nothing may ever beat **Rózsa**'s own version (Westminster LP).

At the core of Rózsa's concertante works are five concertos, one each for violin, piano, cello, and viola plus a *Sinfonia Concertante* for violin and cello. The Violin Concerto was composed for **Heifetz,** who premiered it in 1958 and recorded it shortly thereafter. That disc stood alone and unchallenged for 40 years (♦RCA 61752). **Igor Gruppman**'s superb performance is somewhat compromised by opaque sound and routine accompaniment (Koch Vol. IV, 7379). Far better, and indeed the one Rózsa disc to buy if you're only going to own one, is **Robert McDuffie**'s brilliant account (♦Telarc 80518). Passionate and fiery, lyrical and dazzling, McDuffie meets the work's considerable technical demands as completely as Heifetz; he's partnered by Levi who, with the help of Telarc's engineers, clarifies Rózsa's sometimes complex polyphony more successfully than either Sedares or Hendl (for Heifetz).

The piano concerto was recorded by its dedicatee, **Leonard Pennario,** and that rare disc is well worth seeking out for its combination of poetic feeling and visceral excitement (♦Pantheon 07124). **Evelyn Chen**'s performance is also very good—exciting, professional, and fleetingly profound, in an overly-resonant acoustic (Koch Vol. V, 7402). Those who choose **Danielle Laval**'s superb performance will be treated to some of Rózsa's film music (Auvidis Valois 4841).

The Cello Concerto is a dark and almost forbidding work, closer to Bartók than anything else Rózsa wrote. **Harrell**'s is the recording of choice almost by default, but it's excellent (♦Telarc 80518, with McDuffie's Violin Concerto). **Starker,** the work's dedicatee, brings special authority to his interpretation (Pantheon, with Pennario's piano concerto).

The Viola Concerto was a late work and found the composer in a valedictory, brooding, and somewhat diffuse mood. Unfortunately, its dedicatee, **Zuckerman,** hasn't recorded the piece (tapes of his premiere performance under Previn are highly prized), but **Paul Silverthorne** communicates all the music's warmth and ardor (Koch Vol. III, 73041). This disc features the only recording of *Sinfonia Concertante,* although **Heifetz** and Piatigorsky recorded a revised version of the middle movement rescored for chamber orchestra (*Tema con variazioni,* also on RCA 61752), as have **McDuffie** and Harrell as filler in their essential Telarc disc.

Rózsa's classically formed contrapuntal skills bring great interest and depth to his chamber music. His two string quartets make a strong impression in performances by the **Pro Arte Quartet** (♦Laurel 842), and **Isabella Lippi** is fiery and brilliant in a release of works for violin and piano (♦Koch 7256). A disc of late works for solo instruments is also worth seeking out (Pantheon 10761), as is a composer-supervised release of the early String Trio, Piano Quintet, and violin/piano Duo featuring **Pennario** (Cambria 1034).

Pennario was the dedicatee of Rózsa's powerful Piano Sonata, but his impassioned and muscular performance is not yet on CD (Angel). **Sara Davis Buechner**'s traversal of the complete solo piano music includes a rhythmically vigorous, dazzlingly virtuosic performance of the sonata's last movement, but elsewhere rubato is occasionally over-applied, and tempo and dynamic choices are not always apt (Koch 7435).

Rózsa's vocal music includes some very fine songs (not yet recorded) and three major a cappella choral works still unrepresented on CD.

DEWALD

Edmund Rubbra (1901–1986)

Rubbra is called the "English Bruckner" because of his long melodic lines, though his music is more polyphonic and not as massive. Most of his ideas grow from "germs" and expand linearly: He repeats them, plays them as canons, or spins them along, changing texture, speed, or sonority, and they often extend for a long time without a cadence. Much is modal or in minor keys. He writes clearly for strings, sonorously for brass, and subtly and colorfully for woodwinds. His tone is beautiful and haunting, sometimes bleak, often introspective or serene, occasionally angry, but always deeply felt and moving.

SYMPHONIES

The first two are large-scaled, brash, energetic, and colorful. The more traditional and controlled 3 begins Rubbra's practice of generating symphonic material from short melodic phrases. Symphony 4 is deeper and more romantic, with an opening described as one of the finest in English symphonies; 5 is lighthearted, bright, and chamber-like; 6 has colorful, contrapuntal outer movements, a balletic scherzo, and a glowing slow movement; and 7 is the most romantic, somber, and long-lined; and 8 is iridescent, particularly the finale; its complex first movement has an air of improvisation. Symphony 9 ("Sinfonia Sacra") is mostly slow in tempo, eloquent and beautiful. It resembles a Bach passion with narrator, soloists, and chorus, and was Rubbra's favorite; each section ends with a Latin hymn followed by a Lutheran chorale as a sign of the unification of Western Christianity. Symphonies 10 and 11 are tightly constructed in one movement; the latter represents the stylistic culmination of Rubbra's symphonies.

Hickox recorded a fine set (♦Chandos: 9538, 1, with *A Tribute; Sinfonietta;* 9581, 2 and +6; 9634, 3 and 7; 9401, 4, 10, and 11; 9714, 5 and 8, with *Ode to the Queen;* 9441, 9, with *Morning Watch*). You can purchase them with confidence, but there are minor drawbacks. Generally, Hickox takes a heavy, broad, and full-textured view, which is fine but can seem puffy at times; he doesn't always delineate the important lines and sometimes glosses over subtleties. Chandos's sound accentuates this, and the fine BBC Wales Symphony isn't quite as polished as the London orchestras.

There are fine recordings of individual symphonies:

2. **Handley** is outstanding (♦Lyrita 96 LP, with *Festival Overture*), making the work sound more clear, controlled and cogent than **Hickox,** who is a bit overblown and up-front.

3. **Del Mar** (♦Lyrita 202, with 4; *A Tribute; OvertureResurgam*) finds more texture and sinew than **Hickox.** He's also more searching and brings out more character; his thinner consistency underscores the work's linear nature and reveals more inner light. He's helped immensely by the New Philharmonia and great sound.

4. **Handley** is best, with cogency and solid articulation and bass, though his II is hurried (♦BBC 91932, with Piano Concerto; *Soliloquy for Cello and Orchestra*). **Del Mar** is expressive and thoughtful in I, but II is forced; III is dark and thrusting but lacks flow and structure (♦Lyrita 202, with 3). **Hickox** is too literal and plods noticeably in I, wanders a bit, then turns too bright in IV; II is delectable.

5. I prefer **Hans-Hubert Schönzeler**'s clear, linear style, with good playing from the Melbourne Symphony (♦Chandos 6576, with Bliss's *Checkmate;* Tippett's *Little Music*). His simplicity pays off in the Scherzo, which **Hickox** blunts. **Barbirolli**'s magisterial 1950 mono is powerful and should be heard, but the work benefits from stereo (HMV).

6. **Hickox**'s weighty and lyrical seeking works better than **Del Mar**'s molded style, particularly in the slow movement (Lyrita 127 LP, with 8). **Boult** is good but has hard sound and a weak coupling (Intaglio, with 8 led by Groves).

7. **Boult** matches **Hickox** in quality and style. He may be slightly better, with more introspection, flow, and attention to line and texture (♦Lyrita LP 119, with *Soliloquy for Cello and Orchestra* led by Handley).

8. **Hickox** smooths over points of light and doesn't catch the upbeat, incandescent spirit as well as the angular, brightly lit **Del Mar** (♦Lyrita LP, with 6). **Groves** is poor, with harsh sound (Intaglio).

9. **Hickox** is terrific, with fine soft playing. Della Jones is eloquent, with Stephen Roberts a lyrical baritone (♦Chandos 9441, with *Morning Watch*). *Morning Watch* builds orchestral sonorities before the chorus enters in traditional British choral fashion, singing words of joy.

10. Comparison between **Hickox** and **Schönzeler** (♦Chandos 6599, with *A Tribute; Improvisations on Virginal Pieces by Giles Farnaby*) parallels 5 but here favors Hickox, who has more control and a better orchestra than Schönzeler's Bournemouth Sinfonietta.

11. **Hickox**'s broad, ripe style produces one of his best Rubbra recordings.

A Tribute. This is a touching honor to Vaughan Williams. **Hickox** (♦Chandos, with 1) is full-sounding, **Del Mar** (Lyrita LP, with 3) is slower and leaner, and **Schönzeler** is a tad behind both (Chandos 6599, with 10).

CONCERTOS

Rubbra's concertos are symphonic in style, with the solo instrument almost part of the orchestra. The Piano Concerto's bright score makes it sound complex and rhythmic. **Malcolm Binns,** with Handley, is terrific (♦BBC Classics 91932, with Symphony 4). **Denis Matthews** with Sargent is more massive but not as deft and colorful (EMI LP).

The Viola Concerto is darker, slower, and richer, with I reminiscent of Symphony 5 and a theme-and-variations finale. The Violin Concerto is brighter and more extroverted, with a starry, symphonic I and an introspective slow movement. Handley is excellent in both with violinist **Tasmin Little** and violist **Rivka Golani** (♦Conifer 51225). Little plays brilliantly, superceding small-toned **Carl Pini** (Unicorn). Golani is almost as good, but with a small, occasionally whiney sound.

Improvisation for Violin begins with an introspective cadenza over tympani, then turns complex and rhapsodic. The effect is "modern" before a serene close. **Sidney Harth** is excellent (♦RCA 25096 LP, with Britten's Piano Concerto). *Soliloquy for Cello and Orchestra* is slow and ruminative, with the cello singing plaintively. **Rafael Sommer** and Handley are decent, though Sommer's high register gets slightly unreliable in intonation (♦BBC 91932, with Symphony 4). Handley is warmer and gets better playing from **Rohan de Saram** (♦Lyrita LP 119, with Symphony 7).

CHAMBER MUSIC

Cello Sonata. This is a mature work, full of life; it stresses the vocal nature of the cello, combining counterpoint, drama, and serenity in a work that sings and flows naturally. An excellent performance by **Raphael Wallfisch** is accompanied by John York (♦Marco Polo 223718, with Moeran and Ireland Cello Sonatas).

Quartets 1–4. These display consistency, retaining the symphonies' linear generation of ideas but containing more chordal passages. The **Sterling Quartet** has a silvery tone and a good feel for this music (♦Conifer 51260, 2CD). The **Amici Quartet** (Golden Guinea LP) is romantic, introspective, and deliberate in 2 but misses Sterling's flow.

Violin Sonatas 1–3. These feature Rubbra's modal harmony and canonic writing in its purest, most hypnotic form; the second is his first masterpiece. **Krysia Osostowicz**'s style and tone are perfect; she's ably accompanied by Michael Dussek (♦Dutton 7101, with *Four Pieces* and *Variations on a Phrigian Theme*).

CHORAL MUSIC AND SONGS

Four Medieval Latin Lyrics for baritone and *Five Spenser Sonnets* for tenor (both with string orchestra); *Amoretti (Second Series)* for tenor and string quartet. These vocal works range from medieval chant to haunting melody (with *Amoretti* set against a bleak string quartet). **Hans-Herbert Schönzeler**'s leadership is okay, but is a warmer approach would help. Martyn Hill's tenor is fine; David Wilson-Johnson's baritone is adequate; and the Endellion Quartet is beautifully austere (♦Virgin, with Sinfonietta for Large String Orchestra). Sinfonietta resembles a more pure and simple Vaughan-Williams "Tallis Fantasy."

Missa Cantuariensis and *Missa in Honorem Sancti Dominici.* These are beautiful, unaccompanied choral works remindful of Vaughan-Williams, if less grounded and vital and more ethereal. They are slow in tempo, and atypically chordal (as opposed to linear) in texture. **Hickox** leads stunning performances with great intonation (♦RCA 5119, LP).

Jade Mountain; Discourse for Solo Cello; Discourse for Cello and Harp; Transformations for Solo Harp (1972) and other works. Rubbra's troubadour-like songs are meditative, flowing, somewhat moody, and quietly expressive. Some touch on Chinese music, others Medieval. The harp works are like ragas—large-scaled, full, and complex. The cello works are equally accomplished. **Tracey Chadwell** and colleagues are excellent (♦ASV 1036 with Berkeley' Nocturne and Howells's Prelude). HECHT

Anton Rubinstein *(1829–1894)*

Founder and long-time director of the St. Petersburg Conservatory, Anton Rubinstein molded the careers of a generation of Russian composers, yet he remained of the old German school, having little interest in "nationalism" as represented by Glinka and The Five. His music is so effortlessly melodic that it seems unfair to point out that it's not very "Russian," though this may explain why many continue to think of him as one of the outstanding pianists of his time rather than as a great Russian composer. Modern audiences are likely to know only two of his pieces, Melody in F and the gloomy *Kamennoi-Ostrow.* For those wishing to learn how wonderfully he wrote for the piano, Concerto 4 is the place to start, while the "Ocean" Symphony (2) is worth knowing, too.

SYMPHONIES

Symphony 2 ("Ocean") was long a favorite with audiences in England and the United States as well as turn-of-the-century Russia. As originally conceived, it had four movements, each with its own "program"; however, 12 years after the premiere Rubinstein added two more, an Adagio and Scherzo (quite upsetting Tchaikovsky, who felt it was fine the way it was), and then 17 years later he added another ("Storm Scene"), in the process evoking images of the fabled "Seven Seas," though he vigorously denied this.

The first recording, with **Richard Kapp,** was ostensibly based on the second (six-movement) version but omitted the Adagio and thus was neither fish nor fowl (Candide), while **Fuat Mansurov** went back to the original four-movement edition (Vista Vera), as did **Golovchin** (Russian Disc). Fortunately Marco Polo has made it possible to program whichever you choose by cramming all seven movements into one well-filled CD (♦220449). Moreover, the performance by **Gunzenhauser** and the Slovak Philharmonic is far superior to either Kapp's Westphalian ensemble or Mansurov's muffled sound. Those preferring the original version would be better off with Golovchin, despite his rather broad view of the opening seascape.

Discussion of the remaining symphonies needn't detain us long; in most cases there's only one recording. Rubinstein wrote his Symphony 1 at the age of 21, and it's understandable that he might refrain from pulling it out of his drawer until long after the great popularity of the "Ocean" Symphony stimulated interest in his other works. Melodic and unassuming, it frequently betrays his love of Mendelssohn, and we may assume **Stankovsky** with his Košiče ensemble does all he can for it (♦Marco Polo 223277).

No doubt you'll hear Mendelssohn in 3 as well, though much of the wind writing seems to have made an impression on Rubinstein's most promising student, a young man named Peter Ilich Tchaikovsky, and

the heroic, even defiant final movement certainly compels attention. Once again there's **Stankovsky,** and you might think that would be the end of it. But he seems content with merely going through the motions compared to **Barry Kolman** and his plucky Slovak players, whose committed reading really makes the music soar (♦Centaur 2185).

Unfortunately, Kolman is rather slack in 5, a hearty mix of "Russian" dance rhythms surrounding a solo turn for the horn in the Andante that clearly points the way for Tchaikovsky's 5. For this you'll want the fine Romanian orchestra directed by **Horia Andreescu** (♦Marco Polo 223320). The more expansive Russian bear hug of **Valentin Zverev** is also very satisfying (Melodiya LP). In between is the massive exercise that is Symphony 4 ("Dramatic"), which lasts for over an hour and at first seems to be based on Beethoven (chiefly the *Eroica*), until the triumphant close of the first movement suggests that the actual model was Liszt. Once again Russian Disc challenges Marco Polo, but there's no contest; not only does the music surge with passion under **Stankovsky** (♦Marco Polo 223319), but the Košiče players are far more proficient. Even worse, the challenger, **Golovchin,** cuts nearly five minutes out of the final movement.

Rubinstein was in his '60s when he wrote his final symphony, 6, yet if there's nothing here we haven't heard before, it's a beautifully constructed and richly lyrical score that nicely sums up the most attractive qualities of his Romantic style. Some may have the LP with **Heribert Beissel** (Turnabout); he's less forceful in the more dramatic passages than **Gilbert Varga** (Marco Polo), yet brings out the yearning quality of the slow movement much better, so the two performances complement each other rather well.

OTHER ORCHESTRAL MUSIC

Though never a nationalist as such, Rubinstein couldn't resist turning to Russian sources on occasion, most notably in the tone poem *Ivan IV* (or *Ivan the Terrible).* An almost unrelentingly grim portrait, it gives full scope to the unspeakable cruelty of the despot, yet also shows us the troubled conscience of the man, interweaving passages of power and triumph with great despair. **Stankovsky** (with Symphony 1) is serviceable enough, but more of the dark Russian coloring comes through with **Golovchin** (♦Russian Disc 11397).

In his overture *Dmitry Donskoy,* Rubinstein honors Grand Prince Dmitri, whose 1380 victory over the Mongol hordes near the Don River—hence the title Donskoy—afforded Moscow a short-lived freedom. An early attempt, it seems hastily thrown together but boasts some wonderful melodies (Marco Polo, with Andreescu's Symphony 5). Also included is the tone poem *Faust,* which began as a symphony after Goethe; perhaps Rubinstein thought better of such a grand plan after hearing Liszt's version, so all that remains is this single movement, limning the inner longing and regret of the aged scholar—not yet under Mephistopheles's spell—and in fact often resembling Liszt though the two men had little good to say about one another. Both pieces are played well enough by the Romanians.

In *Don Quixote* Rubinstein, acting on the advice of Turgenev, took the woeful knight quite seriously, dwelling on the pathos of the unfortunate Don's misadventures while passing over the light-hearted aspects of the novel (including Sancho Panza, who doesn't figure in Rubinstein's game plan). The result is once again not unlike late Liszt, laying bare Quixote's tortured soul and shot through with trenchant phrases and intermittent flashes of color. **Halász** is vigorous without becoming frenetic (Marco Polo), unlike **Khaikin**'s monaural Melodiya LP. **Golovchin** is far more expansive (Russian Disc, with *Ivan IV*). If you buy **Stankovsky**'s Symphony 5, you'll also get the rarely heard *Eroica Fantasia,* despite its title far closer to Liszt than Beethoven, which parades past a wide variety of themes without ever really doing anything with them (Marco Polo). Stankovsky probably does as much as he can for this discursive repast, but no one is likely to place it on his or her short list of essential Rubinstein.

Save for *The Demon,* still occasionally staged today, little of Rubinstein's operatic output is likely to be familiar. The ballet music from *The Demon, Feramors,* and *Nero* is conveniently grouped by **Halász,** but his sluggish tempos frequently prove frustrating (Marco Polo). Many will want the disc for *The Demon,* which contains one melody most people will surely recognize, often serving nobly on screen when an Oriental setting is called for; but you'd be better off seeking out the Turnabout LP containing **Beissel's** Symphony 6. Both **Oue** (Reference) and **Fedotov** (IMP) omit the "Lesginka" (though Fedotov at least breaks a sweat, unlike Oue and Halász). **Golovchin** does much better with the *Feramors* ballet in his disc of the "Ocean" Symphony, and if you search assiduously through import LP bins you may find **Gennady Provatorov's** far superior account of *Nero* as filler with Piano Concerto 4 played by Victor Bunin—though you may have trouble finding a copy with decent surfaces. But if you want all three on one disc, Marco Polo is the only game in town.

CONCERTOS

1. This is no mere tentative attempt but displays at once the leonine quality characteristic of the composer. Since the splendid LP with **Michael Fardink** hasn't been brought out on CD (♦Orion 79347), the coupling of 1 and 2 with **Joseph Banowetz** would seem to be the likely choice, though it's little more than a stopgap (Marco Polo). Banowetz apparently feels that the way to convey poetry is to slow way down; he's more piquant than Fardink in the finale, but his hard, percussive tone and clangy instrument quite spoil the effect.

2. Only one year separates 1 from 2, yet already in 2 we find a greater assurance and sweep that compel our attention, a richness of coloring and texture rare from one so young. Unfortunately, **Banowetz** takes the final movement designation (*Moderato*) too literally, and the music just lies there; **Paley** is better in this regard (Russian Disc, with 4).

3. In 3, with its gently swaying first movement, **Marshev** (with 4) is once again rhapsodic to a fault, and his swaggering account of the final movement is far more satisfying than **Banowetz** (also with 4), where exhilaration is unfortunately achieved at the expense of poetry (and the clangy piano doesn't help). **Valerie Traficante's** assertive style quite overwhelms the music, coming down too hard on the first note of each measure and in the final movement too slow by half (Vox).

4. Among Rubinstein's piano concertos, 4 remains supreme, a soaring, richly colored canvas that fairly bursts at the seams with thrilling cascades of sound and spacious, heartfelt melody. To these ears the final movement can stand beside anything by Tchaikovsky or Rachmaninoff—both of whom clearly drew upon Rubinstein as model—and it's easy to see why this splendid score has been recorded more often than all the others put together. Until recently it might have been impossible to single out one recording, but that changed dramatically when **Lewenthal's** outing was restored to the catalog. Supported ably by Eleazar de Carvalho, Lewenthal's performance stands as the very definition of the Grand Manner, making it an absolute must-have for anyone who loves this music (♦Elan 82284).

Raekallio seems to be trying his hand at the Grand Manner, too, but it comes off as mere affectation, barreling through the final movement

so fast that the notes simply tumble over one another, while the orchestra is little more than a vague blur somewhere in the background (Ondine). **Ponti** is far surer of foot and certainly a master of bravura piano writing, but he tends to come down too hard; it's still a worthy supplement, as are all of the Vox "Romantic Piano Concerto" series. **Marshev** revels in the deepest recesses of the bass register and paints this highly romantic fare in broad strokes that work well enough in the opening movement but greatly impede momentum in the finale (Danacord), while **Banowetz** is too brusque in the finale and also hampered by clangy, metallic piano sound (Marco Polo). As for **Paley,** if this isn't the slowest version on disc it must come pretty close, little more than an exercise in tedium (Russian Disc). Those preferring a more expansive reading should seek out the grand master **Cherkassky** (Decca 448063, still unavailable save as an import).

5. With 5, lasting about three quarters of an hour, you can't help but come away with the feeling that flushed with the success of 4, Rubinstein expanded the contours of his model by maybe a third without once approaching the melodic and harmonic originality that suffuses every bar of that masterpiece. Only in the final Allegro, with its galumphing, almost ribald theme, do we glimpse the true genius of the man, particularly in the recording with **Adrian Ruiz** (♦Genesis 103). **Banowetz's** tendency to simply plow through it may seem all to the good (Marco Polo), but Ruiz brings out the angular quality of the piano writing and also has a far more resonant instrument to work with.

The remainder of Rubinstein's output for piano and orchestra is decidedly of lesser importance, often requiring great virtuosity but without the soaring melodies that make the concertos so memorable. In the case of the Fantasy in C and *Concertstück,* **Banowetz's** slow tempos don't help matters any (Marco Polo). If you can find the rather limited edition of the *Concertstück* with **Blumental,** she pulls ahead of him to good effect (Ars Classicum). The *Caprice Russe* sounds more like Chopin until midway through, when Rubinstein introduces a more Russian-sounding dance to close things out. Once again **Banowetz** (with Concerto 5) simply doesn't get the point; his sodden trudge suggests that these Russian dancers are too full of sausage and vodka to do much more than waddle around in formation. Unfortunately, **Traficante** is no better, and once again comes down way too hard, just as in Concerto 3.

It's not generally known that Rubinstein, the consummate pianist, also composed a concerto for violin and two for cello; unfortunately, they only serve to demonstrate how wonderfully he wrote for the keyboard. The Violin Concerto contains none of the soulful "Slavic" quality of Tchaikovsky's (written some 20 years later), though the elaborate finale with its ingenious juxtaposition of richly varied material is satisfying in its rather Germanic fashion. **Takako Nishizaki** is competent enough but lacks the fire and resplendent tone this music surely calls for (Marco Polo). Nor does cellist **Werner Thomas's** tepid playing do much to redeem the two concertos he offers; though his rich caramel tone may compensate somewhat for his lack of animation, you're left thinking that both final movements in particular are arid and empty exercises (Koch Schwann).   HALLER

CHAMBER MUSIC

Rubinstein's chamber music is full of luscious Romantic melody, and we might wonder why it has made relatively little progress on record. The reason is not far to seek: His structures are loose enough to make almost all his chamber works go on for five minutes or so too long. This problem of length, apart from putting off performers and listeners, made his works awkward to fit on LPs. The greater playing time of CDs has brought a comparative flood of issues, but few of them can be recommended with enthusiasm.

The Viola Sonata is best known, one of the few late romantic works for this lovely instrument. It has done well in recent years; the best versions are by **Svetlana Stepchenko** with Zoya Abolitz (Russian Disc 10 035) and **Thomas Riebl** with Cordelia Höfer (Pan Classics 510111). Both feature top-flight virtuosity, characterful piano playing, and excellent recording quality. Viola aficionados will want to seek out a warmly played version by **Karel Doležal** and Kyoko Hashimoto (Arta 0062-2). Another Czech violist, **Jan Talich Sr.,** gives a rather classical, restrained account with Stanislav Bogunia; it appears unannounced as an adjunct to their Brahms sonatas (Calliope 9696). The distinguished Russian player **Fedor Druzhinin** is in one of his drier moods in his performance with Larisa Panteleyeva, and the recording is gray to boot (Russian Disc 11 061). Japanese violist **Imai** gives a typically sympathetic account with Pöntinen of *Nocturne* Op. 11:2, originally for cello, in "The Russian Viola" (BIS 358).

The only historic recording to appear on CD should be snapped up if it comes your way; it features two great Russian artists, **Galina Barinova** and Alexander Goldenweiser, in the beautiful G major Violin Sonata Op. 13, and the other performances––by different composers and artists––are equally compelling (Multisonic 31 0236). The only other easily available version of this sonata was recorded by **Igor Politkovsky;** he exudes warm tone but lacks Barinova's fragile charm, and his pianist, less charismatic than Goldenweiser, is placed too far back (Talents of Russia 16279).

The two Cello Sonatas are pleasantly played by **Gert von Bülow** and José Ribera (Etcetera 1120), but they need high-powered Russian virtuosity to make the music come to life. Exactly that comes from Rostropovich pupil **Alla Vasilieva;** she's adequately recorded but curiously partnered by two different pianists (Russian Disc 10038). An equally splendid performance of Sonata 1, in a lighter style, is included in the treasurable recital "Forgotten Romance" by **Isserlis** and Hough (RCA Victor 68290). The right kind of heavyweight treatment is brought to Piano Trios 1 and 3 by the **Romantic Trio;** the snag here is that the recording is too close and blatant, verging on distortion (Russian Disc 10 041).

The **Royal String Quartet of Copenhagen** plays less than royally in the G major Quartet Op. 17:1, which betrays Beethoven's influence. The Danish players are more sure of themselves in the Mendelssohnian companion piece in C minor Op. 17:2; the recordings are quite good (Etcetera 1131). On the other hand, some fine Russian musicians including pianist **Alexei Nasedkin** are appallingly recorded in the Quintet for piano and winds Op. 55, so that disc is a nonstarter (Russian Disc 11 061, with the Druzhinin version of the Viola Sonata). Fortunately, the enjoyable if rather garrulous quintet is better served by a recording featuring **Sawallisch** and members of the Munich Residenz Quintet (Calig 50898, with Rimsky-Korsakoff's quintet).

When it comes to the G minor Quintet Op. 99, for the usual combination of piano and strings, you have to ask yourself if you can afford to set aside 50 minutes of your life every time you want to listen to it. It's quite well laid out, with a good deal of melodic interest, and it receives a superb performance from the **Pihtipudas Quintet,** a Finnish-based ensemble that boasts two pianists, husband and wife. She plays with romantic élan in the Rubinstein; he's equally up to the challenge of the coupled Shostakovich quintet; and the recordings are crystal clear (EDA 010).　　　　　　　　　　　　　　　　　　　　POTTER

PIANO MUSIC

Even seasoned concertgoers aren't likely to know much of Rubinstein's solo piano music save for the *Melody in F* from his Op. 3 and *Kamennoi-Ostrow,* Op. 3:22, which has taken on the identity of the entire suite and was frequently played in arrangements by Victor Herbert, Morton Gould, and others. This suite, its various movements describing the inhabitants of the Stone Island, a Russian imperial palace on an island in the Neva River, has been set down with flowing grace by **Joseph Banowetz** (Marco Polo 223846/47), fully supporting the favorable impression of Banowetz's earlier discs of *Album de Peterhof* (223176) and *Soirées Musicales* (223177).

Leslie Howard has recorded Rubinstein's four piano sonatas, handily surmounting their many technical challenges and bringing out the opulent, piquant, even endearing moods of this music to excellent effect (Hyperion 66017, 1 and 3; 66105, 2 and 4). He also offers a wide survey including Op. 3 in a set played with confidence and flair and the rich sound this music needs (Hyperion 22023, 2CD). Etudes Op. 23 (not included in Howard's set) are coupled with Tchaikovsky's Sonata in G by **Morton Estrin,** who unfortunately doesn't have the effortless technique required for both works (Newport 85591).

Alexander Bakhchiev plays well enough in a recital drawing upon various collections, though he lacks the élan and distinctive sound of others before him like Rubinstein, Bolet, or Cherkassky (Russian Disc 11 337). **Tal** and **Groethuysen** offer six *Characteristic Pieces* Op. 50, Dvořak's *From the Bohemian Forest,* and Rachmaninoff's six Pieces Op. 11 in a highly satisfying four-hands recital (Sony 47199).

　　　　　　　　　　　　　　　　　　　　HALLER

Poul Ruders (b. 1949)

"I'm really an orchestra guy," Ruders once said to me, and this statement is easily supported by his output for that medium. His strongest statements to date are all orchestral, and many of his chamber and solo works sound as if they're straining to become something larger. His music is by turns violent and grotesque or Apollonian and elegant, possessed of a wintry Nordicism and capable of moments of transcendental repose. It's all written with an extraordinary transparency of texture, a remarkable ear for color, and an unerring sense of drama and pacing. Ruders isn't dogmatic about technique—tonality or its absence are found with equal frequency in his music—and he uses whatever means seem appropriate to his purpose. When I confessed to him that I found his Symphony 1 extremely powerful but difficult to listen to because of its harrowing emotional impact, he replied, "Well, that's what it's all about, you know."

The orchestral works are dominated by two symphonies, a number of remarkable concertos (two for violin, plus others for cello, clarinet, percussion, and piano), and several tone poems, among which the monumental *Solar Trilogy* stands out. For an immediate one-disc introduction, **Segerstam**'s collection can't be beat (♦Chandos 9179). It includes first-rate performances of Symphony 1, a whirling typhoon of musical extremes that would astound Richard Strauss; the ghoulish tone-poem *Thus Saw Saint John; Gong,* a throbbing, pulsating wonder (the first part of *Solar Trilogy*); and *Tundra,* a brief, beautiful homage to Sibelius. *Solar Trilogy* is a major statement; it presents some challenges for the listener, but with great rewards (♦Da Capo 224054). The single-movement Symphony 2, though written for much more modest orchestral forces than 1, still packs quite a wallop (Da Capo 224125, with the Piano Concerto). The Piano Concerto offers a more restrained side of Ruders (though with plenty of virtuoso display for soloist Rolf Hind), with its overt classicism and emphasis on contrapuntal clarity.

Concertos have been a major interest for Ruders, and those for violin, clarinet and cello offer the full range of his voice (◆Unicorn 9114). Violin Concerto 1 contains overt references to Vivaldi and is marked by that composer's luminous textures. Clarinet Concerto is a virtuoso tour de force that fully exploits the instrument's sardonic qualities. Cello Concerto ("Polydrama") is relentlessly melodic and concludes with a deeply elegiac melancholy. Violin Concerto 2 is much darker in mood than 1 and larger in scale; it's coupled with *Dramaphonia,* a chamber concerto for piano—a bleak, frozen soundscape of icy beauty (◆Da Capo 9308). *Concerto in Pieces* is a concerto for orchestra, celebrating the 50th anniversary of Britten's *Young Person's Guide to the Orchestra.* Ruders's work is a set of ten variations based on a theme of Purcell, and focuses on unusual blends more than on individual instrumental colors. It's glowingly led by **Andrew Davis** and is available in two ways: accompanied by an illustrated book about orchestral music (◆Dorling Kindersley) or coupled with a stunning concerto by Melinda Wagner (◆Bridge 9098).

Two discs of works composed in the '80s offer interesting selections. In one, there are *Four Dances in One Movement* and strong performances of *Dramaphonia* and *Corpus Cum Figuris* (◆BIS 720). The Aarhus Sinfonietta, led by **Søren Kinch Hansen,** plays brilliantly, and the recording is superb. **Eötvös**'s *Corpus Cum Figuris* receives a fine performance (Point 5084), but the sound on BIS is much better, and **Knussen**'s *Thus Saw Saint John* is fine but surpassed by Segerstam's. However, this disc has one dazzling work unduplicated elsewhere—*Manhattan Abstraction,* a tone poem evoking the New York skyline in winter.

The first of two important discs contains an excellent recording of Violin Concerto 1 by **Rolfe Schulte** (surpassing the Unicorn disc in sonic detail); the soundtrack to *The Christmas Gospel,* a short film that's not holiday music of any sort but does have a wonderful darkness-to-light quality; *Etude and Ricercare,* a thorny work for solo guitar played with apparent ease by David Starobin; and a setting of Poe's *The Bells* flawlessly sung by Lucy Shelton (◆Bridge 9057). The second contains three chamber works for mixed ensembles: *Psalmodies* for guitar and nine instruments (played by **Starobin** with Speculum Musicae), *Vox In Rama,* and *Nightshade,* both performed by the chamber group Capricorn (◆Bridge 9037). All three receive committed performances.

"Committed" hardly begins to describe percussion virtuoso **Gert Sørensen**'s recording of solo and ensemble percussion works. Titled "A Drummer's Tale Episode Two," the performances are simply amazing (◆Da Capo 224085). **Sørensen** plays all the percussion parts, and the recording has a vivid in-your-face acoustic that serves the music well.

MCINTIRE

Carl Ruggles *(1876–1971)*
Granitic is the word that comes to mind when listening to the music of this American original, who wrote his atonal pieces on outsize sheets of paper because his eyesight was poor. Somehow the notes seem larger than life even when you listen to them.

The complete works fit easily on two LPs and were recorded by **Tilson Thomas** with the Buffalo Symphony and a supporting cast including pianist John Kirkpatrick, Gregg Smith and his Singers, Gerard Schwarz leading a brass group, and Speculum Musicae. This album covered the ground; it was performed with the conductor's special blend of clarity and passion, and the recordings were outstanding (Columbia LP 34591, NA).

The old recordings of *Men and Mountains* and *Organum* led by **Strickland** (CRI 715) are pinched and lack punch compared to Tilson Thomas. **Dohnányi**'s *Men and Mountains* and *Sun-Treader* in Cleveland are good but not overwhelming (London 443776), unlike Tilson Thomas's (his other, equally impressive *Sun-Treader* with Boston was on DG LP 2530048). The small brass work *Angels* has been recorded effectively by **Arthur Weisberg** with Ensemble 21 (Summit 122), but **Schwarz** was just as good in two different scorings.

The piano suite *Evocations* has fared well. **Roger Shields** did it attractively in his massive collection of "American Music 1900–1945" (Vox 3027, 3CD); **Michael Boriskin** is grander and recorded in richer sound (New World 80402). **Donald Berman** plays it well along with a fine Ives program (CRI 811). But no one holds the work together like **John Kirkpatrick,** and Tilson Thomas also included the orchestral version and several pieces not available before or since: *Toys, Vox clamans in deserto, Exaltation, Portals,* and another version of *Men and Mountains* (Sony, NA). Sony, it's your move!   MOORE

John Rutter *(b. 1945)*
This British composer has been involved with church music since the beginning of his musical life, first as a boy soprano, then as organist, conductor, and composer. He has a superb melodic gift and writes in an appealing, tonal, melodic idiom clothed in individual harmonies. Much of his recorded music is choral, a cappella or with ensembles; it's invariably very attractive, even ravishing. Unless otherwise noted, his recordings are by the Cambridge Singers and the City of London Sinfonia led by the composer, in excellent sonics.

One of Rutter's best-known works is the seven-movement, 37-minute *Requiem.* It's given a warm, sympathetic performance, with the lovely *I will lift up mine eyes* (Collegium 103). Soprano **Caroline Ashton** is ravishing in "Piu Jesu," soprano Donna Deam in "Lux Aeterna." The same performance of the *Requiem* is coupled with the 37-minute *Magnificat,* with **Margaret Forbes** the soprano soloist in the latter (Collegium 504), and this performance of the *Magnificat* can also be found coupled with other choral pieces, including his first large-scale work, *The Falcons,* and *Two Festival Anthems* (Collegium 114). The St. Paul Cathedral Choristers join Rutter's forces in *The Falcons.*

A fine *Requiem* is offered by sopranos Rosa Manion and Libby Crabtree and the Bournemouth Sinfonietta conducted by **Stephen Layton** (Hyperion 66947). Eleven of Rutter's memorable anthems complete this release. **Timothy Seely** conducts the Turtle Creek Chorale and Dallas Women's Chorus in a *Requiem* without orchestra but with organ and eight instrumentalists (Reference 57). Nancy Keith is the soprano soloist in the *Requiem* but sings with too much vibrato. It's a different approach, but I prefer the Rutter's performance with orchestra.

The 17-minute, three-movement *Gloria* is suffused with brass splendor, with the **Philip Jones Brass Ensemble** joining Rutter's forces (Collegium 100). It's coupled with ten memorable anthems, including *The Lord is My Shepherd,* Movement 6 of the *Requiem* (with Quentin Poole's haunting oboe solo), and the gently swinging *For the Beauty of the Earth.* Organist **John Scott** joins Rutter in the seven-minute *Te Deum* and twelve short sacred pieces (Collegium 112).

"Fancies" offers the appealing *Fancies* for choir and chamber orchestra, the lovely *Five Childhood Lyrics* for a cappella choir, and the beguiling *When Icicles Hang* for choir and orchestra (Collegium 117). Rounding out this fine release is *Suite Antique* for flute, harpsichord, and strings, a musical homage to baroque styles and forms, with **Duke Dobing,** flute, and Wayne Marshall, harpsichord.

Narrator Richard Baker joins The King's Singers and City of London Sinfonia, conducted by **Hickox,** in two stories by British author Kenneth Grahame, *The Reluctant Dragon* and *The Wind in the Willows* (Collegium 115). Rounding out this delightful release is Rutter's own story, *Brother Heinrich's Christmas,* which he conducts himself. His lovely Suite for strings, based on British folk songs, is included in "English String Miniatures," with music by seven other British composers. **David Lloyd-Jones** conducts the Royal Ballet Sinfonia in this very attractive collection (Naxos 554186).   DE JONG

Kaija Saariaho *(b. 1952)*

The rise to international prominence of several young Finnish composers during the '80s—including Saariaho and Magnus Lindberg—signaled a revitalization of modernism when it seemed increasingly out of fashion. From this original orientation, Saariaho has developed a strikingly original voice that transcends any particular ideological base. Her music is frequently inspired by visions, dreams, and personal journeys and thus expresses a strong poetic sensibility. This characteristic underlies her compelling juxtapositions and transformations of disparate sounds derived from traditional instruments, electronics, and the natural environment. Moreover, her use of computers facilitates the exploration of continuums between the natural sounds of an instrument and those produced by unconventional playing techniques. This focus on timbre and sensuous textures led her to explore new relationships between harmony and timbre.

An important re-release of the first LP ever made of Saariaho's music provides a fine introduction to her early work from 1981 to 1985 and to some of her continuing genre preferences. The disc includes *Verblendungen* for orchestra and tape, the composer's international breakthrough. Here she creates imaginative sonic vistas—alternately grand and subtle—where the electronic sounds seem to emerge naturally from the orchestral textures. There are two excellent performances: **Salonen**'s with the Finnish Radio Symphony is somewhat more visceral (♦BIS 307), while **Saraste**'s with the Avanti Chamber Orchestra allows more orchestral detail to be heard after the tape's explosive outburst at the midway point (Finlandia 23407, 2CD).

Also in Salonen's CD is one of Saariaho's finest works, the purely electronic *Jardin Secret I,* which uses computer-generated processes. Starting with a deliberately restricted range of color, the composer eventually expands the timbral palette to produce an intoxicating variety of sounds. The disc is completed with the vocal work *Sah den Vögeln* (1981) and two evocative flute pieces, *Laconisme de l'aile* and *NoaNoa.* Performances and sound are excellent.

A set available in Europe nicely complements the BIS recording by rounding out a portrait of Saariaho's development during the '80s. *Lichtbogen,* for chamber orchestra and live electronics, is one of his most accessible and frequently performed works. One performance is beautifully crafted by **Saraste** and Avanti and another by **John Whitfield** conducting the Endymion Ensemble (♦Finlandia 23407, 2CD). The latter proceeds at a much more leisurely pace, clocking in at almost five minutes longer than Saraste's more incisive reading. Representing a synthesis of her previous preoccupations, *Io* is written for a large chamber orchestra and prerecorded tape (like *Verblendungen*) while also presenting live electronic transformations of the instrumental sound (like *Lichtbogen*). Winner of two major international awards, *Stilleben,* a radiophonic work, is another big leap in the composer's output. Though highly controlled, it presents a stream of consciousness of prerecorded instrumental and vocal music, musique

concrète segments of natural environmental sounds, and electronic transformations of these materials. It's a milestone in contemporary music, not just in Saariaho's output. The set also includes the second of her *Jardin Secret* series, for harpsichord and tape, and *Petals* for cello and tape.

During 1989 and 1990, Saariaho produced two major orchestral scores designed to form a complementary pair: *Du cristal* and *Á la fumée* (From Crystal . . . to Smoke). They represent different responses to the same source material and reflect their visual stimuli. *Du cristal* is dense, compact, and symmetrical, achieving a balance between various textures and gestures: continuous surfaces of slowly shifting orchestral timbres, dramatic gestures of regular pulses, and melodic and scalar material. *A la fumée,* a double concerto for alto flute, cello, orchestra, and electronics, is more dynamic and amorphous in its unpredictable course; the frequently intricate, virtuosic dialogue of the two soloists is contrasted with orchestral material that varies between dramatic outbursts and more delicate textures. Petri Alanko (flute) and Anssi Karttunen (cello) are the brilliant soloists and **Salonen** leads the LA Philharmonic in well-balanced performances that maintain dramatic momentum while clarifying the internal orchestral details of these important scores (♦Ondine 804).

This disc concludes with *Nymphea* (*Jardin Secret III*), an important addition to the string quartet repertoire commissioned by the **Kronos Quartet.** It's a resumé of the encyclopedic range of string techniques that were characteristic of Saariaho's writing during the '80s. More important, these techniques have been subsumed into a work of real substance and inventiveness, a worthy descendant of Lutoslawski's Quartet, though in a voice entirely Saariaho's own. Unfortunately, the Kronos performance sounds a bit stiff and unfocused, in contrast to their live interpretations; the **Arditti Quartet** is more effective (♦Auvidis Montaigne 782033). Nevertheless, the Ondine CD is an essential purchase for its landmark offering of some of Saariaho's best music.

The 74-minute ballet *Maa* from 1991 is perhaps the composer's most ambitious work prior to her new opera *L'amour du loin.* Divided into seven movements incorporating various groupings of seven instruments and electronics, the work has no plot but is based on the abstract evocation of various thematic archetypes, like journeys and crossing water. The first three movements have their attractive moments, but Saariaho's imagination and sense of pacing seem more fully engaged in the last four. However, there's no doubt about the commitment of the performers, conducted by **Tapio Tuomela** (♦Ondine 791).

Another release offers an important window into Saariaho's recent output for solo instruments or voice in combination with electronics. *Lonh* is a 1996 setting of a medieval Provençal text. The shapely vocal line is complemented with electronics incorporating subtle, percussion-like sounds, sustained pedal points, and prerecorded voices. **Upshaw** is in top form, presenting a subtly shaded, lyrical performance sensitive to nuances of phrasing and the changing moods of the text (♦Ondine 906). The most ambitious of the remaining works is *Près* (1992), which exploits the technical resources of the cello and **Karttunen**'s virtuosity. The disc is completed with *NoaNoa,* sensitively performed by Camilla Hoitenga, and *Six Japanese Gardens* for percussion and electronics, interpreted by Florent Jodelet.   LONG

Harald Saeverud *(1897–1992)*

During the last decades of his long life, Saeverud was known as the "Grand Old Man of Norwegian Music." His basically tonal compositions embrace national-romantic, neoclassical, neoromantic, and near-expressionist styles, with roots in the Norwegian folk melos. His music is characterized by variation and ostinato techniques, polyphonic lines meeting in consonance or dissonance, and a masterly handling of orchestral colors with emphasis on transparent scoring. He never quoted Norwegian folk tunes but created his own, inspired by the same sources, "the Norwegian landscape and temperament." Sentimentality was never Saeverud's way, but humanity and humor—often sardonic—are always present in his music. Performances and sound range from good to excellent in all the recordings recommended below.

ORCHESTRAL MUSIC

Saeverud wrote nine symphonies, No. 1 in 1920, No. 9 in 1966. No. 1 was divided into two "Symphonic Fantasies" and the second was later published separately as *Ouverture Appassionata*. Neither 1 or 2 is currently available. No. 3 was finished in 1926 and revised in the '80s by bassoonist/composer Robert Rønnes. The result is a powerful, dramatic 44-minute work, the longest of the symphonies, centering on a heartfelt Andante; it has been recorded by **Ole Kristian Ruud** (coupled with the masterly Violin Concerto), performed with deep understanding by the composer's grandson **Trond Saeverud** (BIS 872). The Violin Concerto is again played by the younger Saeverud, coupled with the lovely *Romance* for violin and orchestra, this time with **Karsten Andersen** (Simax 1087). This disc is rounded out by the deeply felt *Elegy* for solo violin and 20 *Small Duets* for two violins, with **Karsten Dalsgaard Madsen** playing the other violin.

Symphonies 4–8 and the very worthwhile *Canto Ostinato, Galdreslåtten,* and *Rondo Amoroso* are led by **Kitaienko** in Vol. 1 of a set of Saeverud's orchestral music (Simax 3124, 2CD). The classically proportioned 4 is transparently scored and enlivened by fugal passages. Nos. 5, 6, and 7 are Saeverud's war symphonies, symbols of Norwegian patriotism. No. 5, "Quasi una fantasia," includes a gentle Andante section and 26 variations on the main theme. The short (12–14 minute) *Sinfonia Dolorosa,* based on several chorale-like themes, is powerful, deeply felt, emotionally moving, and memorable. No. 7, anticipating the end of the war and subtitled *Salme* (Psalm), is based on two chorales, a hymn, a yuletide tune, and a stave-church theme, all of Saeverud's own invention. In its simple themes, this deeply moving work is his most accessible symphony. No. 8 ("Minnesota") was written in 1958 for the 100th anniversary of that state. This accessible work evokes dreamy and pastoral atmospheres and ends with a victory celebration.

Nos. 6 and 7 are led by **Karsten Andersen,** with the fine 1938 Oboe Concerto performed by Erik Niord Larsen (Aurora 4953). No. 6 is also performed by **Alexander Dmitriev,** with *Galdreslåtten* and *Kjempeviseslåtten* (Ballad of Revolt) and the two highly successful, melodic but somewhat austere *Peer Gynt* suites (BIS 762). These suites were written in 1947 to replace Grieg's music, which was considered too romantic for Ibsen's non-romantic play by its producers. The suites were also recorded by **Miltiades Caridis,** coupled with the engaging Piano Concerto with Jan Henrik Kayser as soloist (Aurora 4954).

A passionate performance by **Dmitriev** of 7 is coupled with the lyrical and melodic Bassoon Concerto with Robert Rønnes as soloist (BIS 822). This disc is rounded out with the attractive *Lucretia Suite,* incidental music written in 1935 for André Obey's play *The Rape of Lucretia* (BIS 962). **Per Dreier** is right at home in the majestic 9, expressing the atmosphere of Western Norway in now dramatic, now serene, then whimsical and triumphant music (Norwegian Composers 4913). Also on this release are the short, memorable orchestral pieces *Rondo Amoroso, Galdreslåtten,* and *Kjempeviseslåtten.*

In Vol. 2 of the "Orchestral Music" set with **Karsten Andersen** (Simax 3125, 2CD) contained one disc with the two *Peer Gynt* suites, *Kjempeviseslåtten,* and other short, worthwhile works. The other disc offers several short pieces, the *Romanza* for violin and orchestra with Trond Saeverud again as soloist, the neoclassical *Divertimento for Flute and Strings* with flautist Gro Sandvik, and Piano Concerto performed by Einar Røttingen.

PIANO MUSIC

Compared with his orchestral music, string quartets, and concertos, Saeverud's piano music is more traditional, poetic, lyrical, and melodic. In the composer's words, his piano music expresses "all the feelings and moods of the human soul"; it ranges from quiet contemplation to exuberance and from warmth and tenderness to sardonic humor. Stylistically, it ranges from national romanticism to freer tonality via neoromanticism and neoclassicism.

The complete piano music was recorded in commanding performances by **Einar Henning Smedbye** (Victoria 19084/86, 3CD). In "Saeverud Amoroso," **Jan Henrik Kayser** performs 23 pieces he selected with Saeverud's approval (Simax 1070). This is an imaginatively varied recital of delightful, predominantly diatonic music, constituting nearly half the 50 pieces Saeverud wrote for the piano. 18 selections from *Easy Pieces for Piano* and *Dances from Siljustøl,* performed by five Norwegian pianists, are coupled with the austere, serious-minded String Quartet 3 (1979) performed by the **Norse Quartet** (VNP 97).

DE JONG

Camille Saint-Saëns *(1835–1921)*

"As naturally as a tree produces apples, so do I fulfill the functions of my nature," said Saint-Saëns. Fulfillment meant performing, writing, editing, and, above all, composing music: more than 300 works by the time of his death in 1921. When Saint-Saëns was born, Beethoven had been dead less than a decade; by the time he died, Stravinsky's *Sacre du Printemps* had created a furor eight years before (the 78-year-old composer was there, hissing), Berg had written *Wozzeck, Les Six* were getting their act together in Paris, and Gershwin's *Rhapsody in Blue* was just three years in the future. Saint-Saëns would have approved of none of them. He began as a revolutionary, a champion of Schumann, Liszt, and Wagner, and ended as a reactionary, railing against Stravinsky, Ravel, and Debussy. This is a common enough progression, but it seldom endears you to posterity.

Saint-Saëns's fate was to be born a prodigy worthy of Mozart and to die with a reputation as the heaviest of lightweights. "He is tormented by no passions, and nothing disturbs the lucidity of his mind," wrote the French novelist Romain Rolland. "He brings into the midst of our present restlessness something of the sweetness and clarity of past periods, something that seems like fragments of a vanished world." No, Saint-Saëns surely is not Beethoven or Mahler; his symphonies and concertos don't probe deeply. But they're full of wit, color, melody, and imagination, and his best music is so deftly executed that we no longer realize how original it often is. It's the music of a 19th-century man of the world—a vanished world—and its sweetness, lucidity, and urbanity make it worth keeping in the 21st.

ORCHESTRAL MUSIC

Saint-Saëns wrote five symphonies. The first two are student works without numbers, but with many delightful moments. They were closely followed by the official 1st (written at age 18) and 2nd (age 24, almost as effervescent as Bizet's Symphony in C), and many years later by the 3rd.

The two earliest works are truly prodigious: neatly if conventionally structured, airily orchestrated and with surprisingly powerful finales. **Martinon** recorded all of the symphonies in the '70s, and the set, if sometimes over-reverberant, is a solid buy and will make you wonder where these works have been all your life (♦EMI 62643; MHS 525324; 2CD).

The official 1 and 2 are available in decent if not outstanding performances led by **Prêtre** in an on-again, off-again collection whose only really distinguished moments are Martinon's versions of the colorful tone poems *La Jeunesse d'Hercule* and *Le Rouet d'Omphale* (Erato 24236, 2CD). A better performance of 2 is led by **Butt** (ASV 599, with the charmingly exotic *Suite Algérienne*), and perhaps the best of all is by Kantorow (♦BIS 790, with two Saint-Saëns rarities, the early "Urbs Roma" Symphony and *Africa* fantasy for piano and orchestra).

Then there's 3, a massive work that led Gounod to call Saint-Saëns "the French Beethoven." Well, not quite, but this work's flamboyant scoring and tidy construction give it a deserved place in the orchestral repertoire (that is, if the orchestra's hall has an organ). It also has a honorable recorded history as a "stereo spectacular," and the best of its early-stereo recordings still sound spectacular, for example **Munch**'s performance in RCA's "Living Stereo" series (♦RCA 61500, generously coupled with Debussy's *La Mer* and Ibert's *Escales*). The taut, charmless **Toscanini** from the '40s is definitely not in stereo, spectacular or otherwise (RCA).

Among more modern recordings, **Dutoit** (with organist Peter Hurford) offers wonderful sound and a performance that makes the piece sound even more substantial than it is (♦London 307020). **Bernstein** with Leonard Raver is less sumptuous than Dutoit but exciting (♦Sony 47608). Two fine performances have stayed pretty consistently in the LP and CD catalogs: **Barenboim**'s 1976 recording with the Chicago Symphony (DG 415847), and **Levine**'s early-digital Berlin Philharmonic performance, which still sounds sharp and vivid (DG 415847).

Saint-Saëns was the first French composer to write orchestral tone poems, inspired by the example of Liszt. *Danse macabre, Phaëton, Jeunesse d'Hercules*, and *Le Rouet d'Omphale* (*Omphale's Spinning Wheel*) aren't heard much in concerts anymore, but they still make entertaining listening. If you'd like to have all four on a single disc, **Dutoit**'s is a bargain (London 425021). Many of the more unusual and charming orchestral works are investigated by **Geoffrey Simon** (Cala 1031/32 or 1015/16, 2CD). The array includes the large-scale *Requiem* and Symphony 3, but also a version of *Danse macabre* for solo baritone and orchestra, *Africa, Marche militaire Française*, the Overture to *La Princesse Jaune*, and other rarities.

CONCERTOS

The name Saint-Saëns on a concert program usually signifies the "Organ" Symphony or else one of three delectable concertos: Cello Concerto 1, Piano Concerto 2, or Violin Concerto 3. He was a technically accomplished, reportedly rather cool pianist (he performed a cycle of all Mozart's concertos, unheard of in 19th-century France or probably anywhere else at that time), and his five piano concertos enshrine his style beautifully.

Cello. 1 is often performed and recorded, 2 hardly at all, presumably because of its insane difficulty and comparative lack of memorability compared with its predecessor. Among the great cellists who have recorded 1 are **Rose** (♦Sony 48276), **Starker** (♦Mercury 32010, with Schumann and Lalo concertos), **Rostropovich** (EMI 49306, with the Dvořák concerto), and **Ma** (Sony 35848, also with Lalo). Ma's performance is also

included in a very desirable budget-priced collection (Sony 66935) of three excellent digital recordings of popular Saint-Saëns concertos, with Violin Concerto 3 (Cho-Liang Lin and Tilson Thomas) and Piano Concerto 2 (Cecile Licad and Previn).

Piano. No. 1 was the first important piece of its kind written by a French composer; an early work by a 23-year-old with whiffs of Beethovenian ambition, it has a memorable galumphing finale. No. 2 is markedly eclectic, beginning very seriously with a piano cadenza recalling a Bach organ fantasia that melts into a first movement of Schumannesque lyricism. The dapper scherzo is Saint-Saëns in boulevardier mode, the finale a tarantella whose relentlessness makes up for its lack of inspiration. No. 3 is the longest, with a sultry slow movement and a lively, tuneful finale. No. 4, a clever example of thematic transformation, is probably the best of the bunch. Many years separate these concertos from 5, but Saint-Saëns hadn't lost his touch; this is a dazzling, entertaining virtuoso work, given added piquancy by the use of Egyptian tunes.

Considering how rarely Saint-Saëns's piano concertos are heard in concerts these days, there are a surprising number of complete sets available. The best is **Rogé**'s, with Dutoit conducting several different orchestras: excellent sound and effervescent performances (♦London 443865). **Ciccolini**'s aging set with Baudo has its moments, but their thoughtful, rather placid approach has its problems: The opening of 2 and the finale of 4 just sit there (EMI). **Collard**'s set is good, but full-priced; the discs are available separately, though, in case you don't want all five, and they include a couple of other piano-and-orchestra works, like *Africa* and the delectable *Wedding Cake* (EMI 49757, 47816, 49051).

Entremont's brashly recorded '70s set isn't very elegant, but not bad at its budget price (Odyssey 45624). **Tacchino** and de Froment are stronger contenders: They give good performances, if rather thin recordings, and the couplings include not only Saint-Saëns's other piano-and-orchestra works but also interesting music for violin and for horn with orchestra (Vox 3028).

In 1964, the youthful Entremont recorded 2 and 4 with Ormandy. The pianist has a couple of finger flubs, but the performances benefit from Ormandy's zest and the plush sounds of the Philadelphia Orchestra. The coupling of Cello Concerto 1 (with Leonard Rose) makes this a very attractive proposition if you only want one concerto recording (♦Sony 48276). If you only want these two concertos, **Biret** offers them at budget price (Naxos 550334). **Rubinstein** recorded 2 three times: The two RCA stereo recordings — the first with Wallenstein (61496), the second with Ormandy (61863) — are both excellent.

One would expect the great showman **Earl Wild** to do spectacularly by 2 (Chesky 50), but it's a bit of a surprise to find **Gilels,** the great interpreter of Beethoven and Brahms, just as persuasive (Testament 1029). In 1935, **Cortot** made a marvelous recording of 4, coupled with his equally fine account of Ravel's Left-Hand Concerto (Pearl 9491). The great **Casadesus** is a bit messy in places, but still magisterial (Sony 47608, with a very good Symphony 3). **Johannesen**'s performance of 4, in a set of all kinds of French rarities performed by this excellent pianist, is skimpy in the orchestral department but worth seeking out (Vox 3032).

Violin. Two of the three violin concertos (1 and 3) and *Introduction and Rondo Capriccioso* were written for the great Sarasate; only 3 remains in the repertory. It's grand, tuneful, and virtuosic; every note is in its proper place, and instead of a slow movement that plumbs the emotional depths, Saint-Saëns offers a lovely barcarolle. Critics may sniff, but audiences and violinists don't, and the work is frequently recorded. There's a beautiful performance by **Perlman**, a mid-priced disc that includes Lalo's *Symphonie Espagnole* and Berlioz's *Rêverie et Caprice* (♦DG 29977). **Dong-Suk Kang** isn't as polished as Perlman, but he often has an appealingly ripe romantic quality, and couples the concerto with several engaging shorter Saint-Saëns works for violin and orchestra (♦Naxos 550752).

Shaham's sweet-toned fiddling in one of his first concerto recordings is on as high a level as you can get these days (DG 29786, with Paganini's Concerto 1), and another young violinist, **Chee-Yun,** is sweet-toned and very stylish without seeming artificial (Denon 18017, with a fine Lalo *Symphonie Espagnole*). If you don't mind mono sound, you can hear a special performance from a special violinist in a collection devoted to **Francescatti**'s recordings from the early '50s, including Chausson's *Poème,* Prokofiev's Concerto 2, and the Mendelssohn, Tchaikovsky, and Bruch concertos (♦Sony 62339). They're all very satisfactory, in no small part because of the conductor, Mitropoulos.

Nos. 1 and 2 aren't on the same level, but are pleasing: 1 is a suave little number less than 15 minutes long; 2 is grander in scale but genial and tuneful. **Kantorow** couples 1 with other short violin pieces (Bis 860); **Ricci** plays all three concertos in a collection of violin and cello works (Vox 5084); and **Philippe Graffin** plays all three in a single disc, elegant and highly polished, very French (Hyperion 67074). As for *Introduction and Rondo Capriccioso* and the slightly less famous *Havanaise,* there are very few violinists who haven't recorded them. **Chung**'s performances are included in Dutoit's collection of symphonic poems (♦London 425021); **Perlman**'s in a standard French violin collection that includes Chausson's *Poème* and Ravel's *Tzigane* (♦EMI 47725); **Ricci**'s in a similar collection (London 452309); and **Heifetz**'s in still another (RCA 7709).

CHAMBER MUSIC

Saint-Saëns wrote a lot of chamber music, and he would be mortified to discover that the most famous example—indeed his most famous work—is *Carnival of the Animals,* written as a good-natured (and still amusing) joke. Many years later Ogden Nash furnished a poem for each movement, and the work is often performed and recorded with them, but it's entertaining enough on its own.

An excellent version of the original chamber version features **Argerich** and Freire at the pianos and some famous names in the supporting cast (♦Philips 416841). There are more famous soloists—**Entremont**, Ma, Tortelier—in a bargain-priced disc that also includes a classic 1962 recording of Symphony 3 by Ormandy with E. Power Biggs, along with a few lollipops (Sony 47655). *Carnival* is performed by **Musique Oblique** (Harmonia Mundi 901472).

Big-band versions are led by **Fiedler** (RCA 68131, with Hugh Downs reading Nash), **Bernstein** (Sony 47596, with his own narration), and most sensitively by **Previn** (Philips 442608, with a lovely performance of Ravel's *Mother Goose;* also in Philips 442608, a less generally recommendable "Best of Saint-Saëns" collection). In a class by itself is the famously campy recording of *Carnival* and Prokofiev's *Peter and the Wolf* by **Beatrice Lillie** (London 36105); the great comedienne is so overpowering, you may forget who the musicians are (the London Symphony, led by **Skitch Henderson**).

If he might be irritated by the popularity of *Carnival,* Saint-Saëns would probably be gratified by the relative frequency of recordings of his other chamber music. Much of it came late in his career (he wrote his sonatas for oboe, bassoon, and clarinet in his last year), and if seldom

probing, it's unfailingly euphonious and elegant. The most popular is probably the first of his two violin sonatas, both of which are worth hearing, and both have been recorded by **Kantorow** (Denon 79552) and **Olivier Charlier** (Erato 45017). The early Piano Trio 1 was written in 1863, when chamber music of any kind was rare from a French composer. If not on the level of similar works by Fauré and Ravel, it's assured and elegant. There are solid performances by **Golub/Kaplan/Carr** (Arabesque 6643, with Fauré and Debussy) and the **Rembrandt Trio** (Dorian 90187, with Ravel and Chaminade). If you'd like to try both trios (2 is much later, from 1892, but little had changed), the **Joachim Trio** offers a good inexpensive way to do it (Naxos 550935).

Even more characteristic of Saint-Saëns's genius are his works for winds and piano, which include sonatas for oboe, clarinet, and bassoon and an entertaining *Caprice on Danish and Russian Airs;* these and other woodwind works are played by **Collegium Musicum Soloists** (♦Kontrapunkte 32062, 2CD) and by a group of distinguished British musicians (♦Cala 1017). Both are 2CD sets, but the Cala is offered at the price of a single disc and also includes several delectable Debussy chamber works. (I wonder what Saint-Saëns would have thought of that.)

All the other recordings of these works are in potpourri albums; among the most attractive are **Janet Hilton**'s of the Clarinet Sonata, in a medium-priced collection of other French clarinet works (Chandos 6589), and **John Mack**'s of the Oboe Sonata, with worthwhile pieces by Hindemith, Poulenc, and Schumann (Crystal 324). One of the jolliest chamber pieces ever is the tuneful Septet for Piano, Trumpet, and Strings, available with pianists **Ian Hobson** (Arabesque 6570) and **Previn** (RCA 68181). A serious, almost elegiac side of Saint-Saëns is heard in his two finely fashioned string quartets—very late works (2 was written in 1918), and proof that he retained his lucidity of mind to the end. They're sensitively played by the **Medici Quartet** (Koch Schwann 364842) and **Miami Quartet** (♦Conifer 59291, a beautiful recording job). The Medici have no coupling; the Miami appropriately add another late-in-life French quartet, by Fauré.

PIANO MUSIC

Saint-Saëns's most popular piano music is contained in the concertos and in *Carnival of the Animals.* The solo piano works are difficult to play but anything but difficult to listen to, combining the 19th-century flash and glitter of Liszt with a more objective style. **Piers Lane** recorded all of the etudes, strongly recommended for fans of Saint-Saëns and of the piano (♦Hyperion 67037). **Cortot**'s old recording of the most famous of them, *Etude en forme de valse,* is available in several collections (Adès 203932; Nimbus 8814). A more representative selection, including *Bagatelles,* miscellaneous dances, and the solo version of *Rapsodie d'Auvergne,* is played with suavity and affection by **Anton Nel** (♦MusicMasters 67083). Saint-Saëns also wrote some excellent two-piano music, of which *Variations on a Theme of Beethoven* is the most substantial example. Two identical programs are offered by **Christian Ivaldi** and **Noël Lee** (Arion 68011), and by **Patricia Thomas** and **Erik Berchot** (Chamade 5631).

RAYMOND

ORGAN MUSIC

The organ works of Saint-Saëns come either very early or very late in his career. **Margaret Phillips** has recorded most of them on two discs, playing the Father Willis organs at Exeter Cathedral and St. Michael's, Great Torrington, Devon (York). The playing is far from bad, but somewhat lackluster and pedestrian, so the music sounds less interesting than it really is. The two Victorian English instruments have beautifully refined sound, but seem better suited to accompany the Anglican service than to play French solo repertory. Also disappointing is **James Higdon,** who plays the Cavaillé-Coll organ at St. François de Sales, Lyon (Arkay). Here the instrument is right but the playing is dull and deliberate, with no apparent understanding of how the music ought to move.

Far better are discs by **Georges Bessonet** (♦Accord 243062) and **Hans Fagius** (♦BIS 556). Bessonet plays the Cavaillé-Coll organ at Orléans Cathedral. Some of the quieter stops may sound unclear to ears accustomed to more modern instruments and the action noise may distract the uninitiated, but Bessonet's playing is stylish and elegant, persuading the listener that he really does understand what Saint-Saëns was driving at as Phillips and Higdon do not. Fagius plays a 1976 Marcussen organ at St. Jacob's Church, Stockholm. It's not the Cavaillé-Coll sound that Saint-Saëns would have had in mind, but it has a convincing romantic warmth plus great clarity and is well suited to this repertory. Fagius plays with impressive sweep and energy, favoring brisk tempos but not making them sound rushed. Between them, they cover all the important works except for the *Breton Rhapsodies*. For those I recommend **Marie-Claire Alain,** where they are part of a program of Christmas organ music (♦Erato 10703).

Vincent Genvrin is embarked on a series of recordings of the complete organ works and motets. Judging from the first three volumes (Hortus 011, 014, 015), they will be indispensable for the serious student, bringing together many rarities along with the more familiar works. In many ways, Genvrin's playing is admirable, but much of it is so understated and introspective that many are apt to find it unengaging, perhaps even sluggish and aimless in places. Several historic instruments are used, and in quieter registrations the action noise can be almost as loud as the music. The music is very uneven in quality, so the set may not appeal to the general listener.   GATENS

OPERAS

Samson et Dalila. Saint-Saëns wrote more than a dozen operas, but as far as the opera-going public is concerned, he might have left only one. *Samson* started its existence as an oratorio and still has static patches, but its familiar story, uncomplicated characters, good tunes, and splashy finale have kept it alive. The first complete recording, led by **Fourestier** in 1946, is the most authentically French, and it remains one of the best (♦EMI 65263). Hélène Bouvier has a light, evenly produced contralto and lucid, forthright diction. She comes across as a sophisticated, alluring woman rather than a sultry vamp, but she's believable as the sort of glamorous creature whose aloofness is in itself tantalizing. Her victim is the Corsican tenor José Luccioni, and though his voice is sometimes on the dry side, he has plenty of ringing strength for the big outbursts. His elegant deportment is not, perhaps, what one might expect from the biblical Samson, but the composer turned the character into a noble, urbane hero. The mono sound overloads in loud passages, but the voices are reproduced with reasonable fidelity.

The next recording would preserve some of the French style: **Prêtre** in 1963, who also leads the orchestra of the Paris Opéra (♦EMI 47895). His Dalila, Gorr, is a much tougher cookie than Bouvier. Her voice is ostensibly larger and fuller, but it also has a hard, cutting edge. She's sometimes blandishing, sometimes merely insistent. Samson is Vickers, who in his own inimitable way manages to sound both calculated and blazingly committed. He tends to croon his softer lines, but no one is more thrilling in declamation. I wish for a smoother line and purer French, but none of his successors would do much better.

Patanè, recorded in Munich, has a stolid Samson and High Priest, though both James King and Weikl sing capably (RCA; Eurodisc). What makes the performance special is Ludwig's Dalila; she sings more beautifully than any of her rivals in the complete sets. Her warm, sensuous voice fondles the music, gently easing it into shape, and if her manner has a slight touch of the maternal about it, she's still pretty sexy most of the time.

Barenboim's Dalila, Obraztsova, offers quite a contrast (DG). This is harsh, ugly vocalism, and nothing of the character survives apart from her determination. She ruins the performance, and not even Domingo's Samson affords sufficient redemption. Fortunately, he would record it a second time; more about that presently.

Let's deal next with the two *Samsons* of **Colin Davis.** You wouldn't expect him to have an affinity for the opera, and you'd be right. It's puzzling that he recorded it twice. Very often, the best opera conductors are the ones you notice least, but you can't help being aware of Davis, mostly because he sets such slow tempos for much of the music. In his 1989 performance (Philips), Baltsa is an alert, efficient Dalila with temperament but no tonal voluptuousness. Carreras brings some feeling to Samson, and he sings all-out, as if he has nothing to lose, which is probably true. The listener is more likely to be distressed by the obvious strain under which he labors than moved by the flashes of ardor.

Davis's 1998 recording is more interesting (Erato). Borodina has some of the vocal velvet Baltsa lacks, and her voice flows freely, but it's a bottom-heavy instrument, and the low notes have an unseemly earthiness. She's thrilling in a crude way, and her big voice never turns strident, but we wish for more finesse—a virtue also lacking in José Cura's Samson, though not for want of trying. Cura attempts to sing softly and suavely from time to time, but when he does, his tone is constricted and throaty. He can belt out loud, high notes, and there's no denying he has a certain animal vitality. It's a poorly-trained voice nonetheless, ill at ease when the music demands a smooth line at medium-volume levels. Davis has always been an expert choral conductor, and one of this performance's redeeming features is the deft and even personable singing of the chorus, which really sounds involved in the drama.

If I wanted to sit down and listen to a recording of *Samson* for my own enjoyment, I'd choose either the old Fourestier or the 1991 **Chung** (♦EMI 54470). Domingo is in remarkably good voice, liquid and ringing. He's comfortable at all volume levels, and he can flesh out the mezzo forte lines where Luccioni and Vickers sound rather wan. Waltraud Meier has neither a conventionally beautiful voice nor an idiomatic command of French. The top is strong, but Dalila's lines expand in both directions, and Meier's lowest notes are fairly weak. Nonetheless, she's a cunning and resourceful vocal actress who persuades you that she is, in fact, singing beautifully. She has an unerring instinct for bringing the right inflections and vocal weight to each phrase and knows how to sound amorously seductive. The performance is greatly enhanced by the chorus and orchestra of the Bastille Opera, by a French High Priest (Alain Fondary) and Abimelech (Jean-Philippe Courtis), and by a nice cameo from Ramey as the Old Hebrew. Chung is dynamic but unintrusive, and the sound, recorded at an oddly low level, presents no problems that can't be solved with a healthy volume boost.   LUCANO

Antonio Salieri *(1750–1825)*

Most people know of Salieri only from the movie *Amadeus,* where he's accused of murdering Mozart out of jealousy. That seems doubtful, but a sober audition of his output suggests that his jealousy wasn't entirely unfounded. Much of the same lyrical impulse and dramatic sense that suffuse Mozart's music may be heard from Salieri as well, yet even a superficial comparison demonstrates the great gap that separates the facile but workmanlike Salieri from Mozart's consummate inspiration. Had Salieri paused to reflect that any other composer would pale beside the divine genius that was Mozart, we might have had no movie, but all who treasure music would benefit.

Michael Dittrich's generous collection of overtures is essential (♦Marco Polo 223381; Naxos 554838). Highlights include the witty wind scoring in *La Secchia Rapita,* the intense storm scene from *Cesare in Farmacusa,* and the unexpected brass dissonances in *Les Danaïdes.* Silvano Frontalini duplicates four of these in rather bland fashion and adds four more (Venice Classics 11018). The assortment of overtures, scherzos, and divertimentos offered by Quartetto Amati is dispensable (Tactus). Of greater interest are two symphonies, a concerto for flute and oboe, and *Piccola Serenata* for winds, played elegantly by the Lukas Consort with a sure sense of Salieri's theatrical gestures (Campion 1330). The Symphony in D (*Il Giorno Onomastico*) and Flute/Oboe Concerto are imaginatively combined with Mozart's Symphonies 24 and 33 nicely led by Modest Cichirdan, though the comparison doesn't favor Salieri (Gallo 601). An even better performance of the Concerto is led by Kenneth Sillito (Philips 416359, with concertos by Cimarosa and Stamitz). It's also available from the Budapest Strings, combined with the Triple Concerto for oboe, violin, and cello and Symphony in D (*La Veneziana*); sound and performances are first-rate (♦Capriccio 10530). You may still find the Flute/Oboe Concerto, Piano Concerto in B-flat, and Sinfonia in B-flat (*La Tempesta di Mare,* credited by some to Antonio's older brother Francesco), led in straightforward fashion by Scimone (Erato 45245; MHS 512347).

Two recordings demonstrate Salieri's skill in writing for wind ensemble, at that time a potent medium. Ensemble Italiano di Fiati offer three trios for two oboes and bassoon and three serenades performed with freshness, verve, and spontaneity (Tactus 751902). A much skimpier disc offers the three trios; the playing by Il Gruppo di Roma and the sound seem stifled by comparison (Arts 47319). Both discs include the brief but moving *Music for the Temple of the Night,* written for a Freemason colleague.

Salieri's two piano concertos have been coupled on disc several times. Scimone again steps forward, this time with Ciccolini (Fonit Cetra 10); they're also available from Andreas Staier (♦Teldec 94569, with Joseph Anton Steffan's Concerto in B-flat), and Pietro Spada conducting from the keyboard (ASV 955, with *Variations on "La Follia"* and the overtures to *Semiramide* and *Les Horaces*). Ciccolini sparkles and Scimone offers able support, but the notes are in Italian. Spada, who specializes in this literature, gives a good account of himself, but the Philharmonia seems strangely slipshod and sluggish. Best of the lot is Staier, who employs a period fortepiano, and the plangent sound coupled with the expansive tempos and airy grace of the Cologne players put him well ahead of the competition.

Several of Salieri's operas have surfaced on disc. *Les Danaïdes* is a stolid setting of a stolid text by Metastasio. Danaus hates his brother Aegyptus so much that he marries off his 50 daughters to Aegyptus's 50 sons and then orders the girls to kill their husbands on their wedding night. When Hypermnestra refuses to go along with the plan, he tries to sacrifice her to the gods, but he and the other 49 daughters end up in Hell, damned for all eternity. Gelmetti conducts as if he actually believed in this foolishness and bass Dimitri Kavrakos is properly sonorous as Danaus, but the squally singing of Margaret Marshall as Hypermnestra lets everyone down (EMI).

Falstaff, a rollicking entertainment loosely based on Shakespeare's *Merry Wives of Windsor,* won't edge Verdi aside but remains a joy, with Romano Franceschetto's rich baritone supported crisply by Alberto Veronesi and the Orchestra Guido Cantelli of Milan (♦Chandos 9613); there's also a very fine recording with Gregor as Falstaff and Tamás Pál directing with a refreshing lightness of touch (Hungaroton 12791). Either is preferable to the mono set with Gino Bechi past his prime, though Bruno Rigacci at least provides energetic leadership (Melodram 474).

Harnoncourt with the Concertgebouw ingeniously couples Mozart's *Schauspieldirektor* with the likewise brief Salieri effort *Prima la Musica, Poi le Parole* (First the Music, Then the Words), since both works were commissioned by Emperor Joseph II for an evening's entertainment (Teldec 43336). Harnoncourt omits several incomplete numbers, in which the singers start up but then begin bickering among themselves; it's presented complete by Domenico Sanfilippo, but at the cost of a dreary performance padded out by an equally dreary intermezzo by Alessandro Scarlatti; at 65 minutes it could have been offered by itself for the curious (Bongiovanni). Far more compelling is *Axur, Re d'Ormus,* led by Clemencic (Nuova Era).

Much of Salieri's output for the church is also available. Alberto Turco combines *Te Deum, Jesus in Limbo* and *The Last Judgment,* and the vocal writing demonstrates Salieri's ability to write music well tailored for the human voice as well as his keen understanding of liturgical texts (Bongiovanni). Unfortunately the lackluster singing and slipshod ensemble make this desirable only as a stopgap. In another disc Turco also gives a second-rate account of the *Passion* (Bongiovanni). Far better are the *Magnificat, Dixit Dominus, Kaisermesse,* and Organ Concerto directed by Uwe Christian Harrer, though the vast resonance of the St. Florian's acoustic apparently posed some difficulty for the engineers (Koch Schwann 1288).   HALLER

Aulis Sallinen (b. 1935)

Sallinen effectively combines an eclectic temperament with a strikingly original and vivid imagination to produce colorful and fascinating music. His works in all genres derive from many influences beyond his native Finland, but the strong personality of his style has great drawing power for its masterful orchestration, bittersweet tonality, and quirky, rhetorical irony. His many operas provide the most forceful evidence of his musical character, but he has made his mark with an ever more striking series of symphonies (now seven) and with his chamber music.

The best and most generously filled disc of Sallinen's orchestral music has DePreist playing Symphonies 4 and 5 with the Malmö Symphony (BIS 607). The deeply enigmatic and pivotal 4 (1979) is loaded with sardonic vitriol; its grotesquely bitter opening reflects Sallinen's pessimism and the angry "Dies Irae" his frustration at the stalemate of the Cold War. The prelude *Shadows,* now something of a cult piece that he extracted from his opera *The King Goes Forth to France,* is lighter but scarcely shorter on sarcasm. By the time he wrote 5 ("Washington Mosaics"), some acceptance and resignation had begun to cool the anger, but all is fragmented and the mosaic is razor-edged glass.

It's only with 6, composed following a visit to New Zealand, that a more placid sheen reflects the tranquillity of an Antipodean landscape. This is his biggest symphony, but despite its glowing picture of nature it somehow seems bland compared to his more vituperative outbursts. The Malmö Symphony is back, with Kamu impressively in charge. The startling Second Symphony for Percussion and Orchestra draws close to the sometimes static polytonality of Russian avant-gardists like Kancheli and Avet Terteryan (BIS 511, with *Sunrise Serenade*).

A chamber music disc contains the superb *Kammermusik I* and *II* played by the Stockholm Chamber Ensemble led by Kamu, with performances by six other groups of artists (BIS 64). The string writing is unusual and original, thematic material emerging gradually from the opening soundscape. The early Quartet for Flute, Violin, Cello, and Harpsichord is the most substantial piece, let down by dim sound. The atmospheric *Four Dream Songs* for soprano use material from the opera *Ratsumies* (The Horseman). The disc is worthwhile for this and the *Kammermusik*.

A compilation of some earlier recordings, including Symphonies 1 and 3, is even more interesting (BIS 41). The brief and elegiac 1 is edgy and unpredictable, sometimes claustrophobically intense, with an uneasy tritonic undercurrent in its neoclassical foraging. No. 3 (1974) is overwhelmed by dense harmonies and a heavily brooding atmosphere interrupted by the fateful footfalls of wind and brass clarion calls, never forsaking its rhetorical grandeur. **Kamu** is Sallinen's most persuasive advocate, and the Finnish Radio Symphony is on his wavelength throughout. String Quartet 3 played by **Voces Intimae Quartet,** also on this disc, is a folk-like funeral march.

By contrast, the Flute Concerto is in a much lighter vein, and the mature Sallinen has exorcized many of the ghosts that haunted his earlier pieces. **Kamu** is again at the controls (Naxos 554185, with concertos by Takemitsu and Penderecki). He also leads the Helsinki Philharmonic and baritone **Hynninen** in a major cycle, *Songs of Life and Death,* in which the composer, in a warm post-romantic afterglow, reflects on poems of Lassi Numi to create a sort of Finnish requiem, more allusive than strictly liturgical (Ondine 844). Like so many contemporaries, Sallinen has discovered rich new pastures watered by the wellsprings of tonality.

The same disc contains *Iron Age* suite for baritone, children's choir, and orchestra; the story is taken from the Finnish epic *Kalevala* and is based on a TV series for which Sallinen wrote the music. A dramatic cutting edge returns with a vengeance amid stunning orchestral color and sweeping gestures. Sallinen exults in the pagan atmosphere of this legendary tale with eerily remote vocalises, misty instrumental whisperings, and warlike dances. This is a splendidly recorded and immaculately performed disc of some of his best work.

His opera *Kullervo* also draws on Finnish legend, but the later operas don't quite scale the heights of the early *Ratsumies,* now NA. But *Kullervo,* conducted by **Ulf Soderblom,** is available (Ondine 3-780) and so is *Palatsi* (The Palace), led by **Kamu** (Koch 6465). *Kullervo* is the better one to investigate first. We can hope the earlier operas will find their way back to the catalog soon. JOHNSON

Pablo de Sarasate *(1844–1908)*

Sarasate was the greatest Spanish violinist. He possessed a tone of remarkable purity and a technique that made the most difficult passages sound like child's play. He's remembered as a composer of primarily nationalist music, but it took a while for this inclination to develop. Most of his early compositions are concert fantasies based on tunes from popular operas, and in fact, we might say that Lalo invented his style in 1874 with *Symphonie espagnole,* a remarkable combination of Hungarian Gypsy violin styles and Spanish rhythms and melodies that was written for the Spaniard. After that, Sarasate began writing such works as the *Spanish Dances, Zigeunerweisen,* and the *Carmen Fantasy.*

The complete works for violin have been recorded by **Angel Jesus Garcia** (RTVE 65042, 6CD). The first three discs are devoted to works for violin with orchestra, the last three to violin and piano, as well as *Navarra,* for two violins and orchestra. This set is very well recorded and the orchestra plays beautifully, but Garcia isn't up to the technical demands of these pieces and his playing is often embarrassingly bad.

Carmen Fantasy. Sarasate wrote no concertos, and his non-Spanish opera fantasies are rarely played. Therefore, the only works of any length that need concern us are *Carmen Fantasy* and *Zigeunerweisen.* The former is the longest of his works that is commonly played today. Aside from Bizet's winning tunes, the Fantasy benefits from Sarasate's wonderful adaptation of the material to the idiom of the virtuoso violin. Fine versions in modern sound have been made by **Josefowicz** (Philips), **Mutter** (♦DG 437544), **Perlman** (♦EMI 63533), and **Rosand** (Vox, with orchestral accompaniment). Mutter scores with her imaginative phrasing, but pride of place must go to Perlman for one of his most joyous recordings. **Shaham** (DG 427659) and **Sarah Chang** (EMI) recorded the Fantasy in their debut discs, and Shaham's earlier version is to be preferred to his later concert recording with the Berlin Philharmonic on both technical and sonic grounds.

Zigeunerweisen. Immediately becoming a staple of the repertoire, it has received many exceptional recordings. Although coming out just before the beginning of hi-fi, **Heifetz**'s last recording sounds good enough for all but the pickiest audiophile (RCA 17532). It certainly set a standard for tone, panache, and aplomb. Good recordings in more modern sound are available by **Josefowicz** (Philips), **Mutter** (♦DG 437544), **Perlman** (♦EMI 63533), **Rabin** (EMI), **Rosand** (Vox), **Shaham** (DG, with orchestral accompaniment), and **Lara St. John** (♦Gypsy 5185, with piano accompaniment). All these accounts are fine, but I'm drawn to Perlman for his rich tone and flaming technique, Mutter for her meticulous, imaginative phrasing (though some may find her fussy), and St. John for her powerful temperament and impulsive manner.

Few discs are devoted entirely to Sarasate's music. This is understandable, given the short, encore nature of most of his output. Such discs have been made by **Eduardo Hernández Asiain** and **Ricci** (EMI), **Rachel Barton** (Dorian), **Mark Kaplan** (Arabesque), **Perlman** (♦EMI 63533), and **Rosand** (♦Vox 8160). The Asiain/Ricci disc isn't a top choice, since Asiain, who plays most of the most famous works, shows some wear on his technique (though he's fully attuned to Sarasate's idiom), and the nimble Ricci only some of the least-known. Perlman's disc is mostly but not wholly devoted to Sarasate, and is essential for its fine *Zigeunerweisen,* irresistible *Carmen Fantasy,* and a choice selection of short pieces including a *Zapateado* ready to eat you alive. His remake of *Carmen Fantasy* is also superior (DG). Rosand's disc is an excellent choice for readings of *Zigeunerweisen,* a *Carmen Fantasy* nearly as joyous as Perlman's, and performances of the shorter works that are second to none. Of Barton and Kaplan, Barton has better sound, but Kaplan has more rhythmic snap and doesn't have Barton's rather slow, wide vibrato; however, he lacks her hypnotic powers, which she wields to great effect in *Playera.*

Those who don't wish to sit through an hour or more of Sarasate are directed to the various encore collections by their favorite violinists. His music is ubiquitous and nearly always turns up on such discs.

Among historical recordings, there is a superb *Zigeunerweisen* by **Heifetz** (RCA 61735; EMI 64251; Biddulph 026). An equally fine performance of that work, along with *Romanza Andaluza* and *Jota Navarra,* was made by the superb technician **Příhoda,** though in a more Central European style (111 50200; Magic Talent 48037). **Huberman,** a great virtuoso with a tremendous personality who was active in the first half of the 20th century and is underappreciated today, recorded *Carmen Fantasy* with piano (♦Classical Collector 2003). This performance is legendary for its impulsiveness and daredevil virtuosity, and is accompanied by wildly individual readings of Lalo's *Symphonie espagnole* and Tchaikovsky's Violin Concerto.

Finally, we must consider the 1904 recordings of **Sarasate** himself (◆Opal 9851). They reveal an effortless technique and a pure, pale tone that's hollow on the G string. He tosses off six of his compositions, including an abbreviated version of *Zigeunerweisen,* with little emotional involvement. These recordings provide a window into a lost world where a style resembling calm legerdemain, rather than the grunt-and-snort gymnastic manner common today, could command an audience's rapt attention.   MAGIL

Erik Satie *(1868–1925)*

Satie is an oddity in a nation replete with odd composers. His personality and ideas endeared him to his contemporaries, even though his music seemed obscure to the point of perversity. His work could be seen as a precursor of John Cage's compositional abnegation; for example, to accompany an art exhibit, Satie once wrote music he exhorted patrons not to listen to. His little piece *Vexations* could be considered an early minimalist score—a minute and a half of music to be repeated 840 times. Yet alongside this philosophy of negation is music of much charm and wit.

Most of Satie's music consists of short pieces for piano, and it's through that medium we can most easily follow his development. His music changes over the years, beginning with a period of lyrical simplicity from 1886 to 1890 (*Ogives, Sarabandes, Gymnopédies,* and *Gnossiennes*). Then he met Joseph Péladan, the guru of the Rosicrucians, who inspired him to write several longer pieces of a hieratic, ceremonial nature (1890 to 1892). These are more harmonically assertive though less rhythmically varied than his earlier works and tend to sound dull if played softly or hectoring if played loudly. Variety is not their aim, though they can be fascinating in the hands of a sensitive performer (*Le Fils des Étoiles, Sonneries de la Rose Croix, Danses Gothiques, Quatre Préludes,* and *Prélude de la Porte Héroïque du Ciel*). Following hard on this series are further meditative religious compositions (*Messe des Pauvres* and various chorales), written cheek-by-jowl with some cabaret songs. Then there is a period of several years when he brought forth little music other than the beautiful *Three Pieces in the Shape of a Pear,* written in 1903 in answer to Debussy's complaint that Satie's music lacked form. During much of this time, he was studying at the Schola Cantorum because he felt his compositional technique was lacking. Apparently he took Debussy seriously.

In 1912, he began producing a long series of piano pieces with accompanying text, both music and words written in a witty, lively style. One of the later examples contains an adjuration from the composer not to read the text aloud during the performance, continuing: "Ignorance of my instructions will bring my righteous indignation against the audacious culprit. No exceptions will be allowed." This injunction has been interpreted by most performers as applying to everything Satie wrote. Actually, I doubt that it should even be applied to the piece in question, the composer's righteous indignation notwithstanding. His philosophical relationship to Cage should teach us not to take him so seriously that we destroy half his appeal because he tells us to deprive ourselves of some aspect of his creativity. It's high time someone recorded these works with a really good actor reading the texts. To do them all would take a little over an hour.

The major collection of Satie's piano music is by **Ciccolini.** Originally on six LPs plus another containing most of the songs and violin pieces and the complete *Le Piège de Meduse,* he re-recorded all these and more

on five CDs. At present, only EMI 49702 and 67282 (2CD) are listed, containing a little over half this material. Ciccolini is a sophisticated, lively player, recorded in somewhat dry sound, but it is reliably interesting. The sound on the new discs, however, is shallow and metallic, leaving room for other interpretations. Also, he ends disc 1 of his set with 20 minutes of the most irritating of the Rosicrucian pieces, played in a steely, stultifying tone.

Pöntinen has made two discs in a resonant ambience (BIS 317, 877). Curiously, they share a couple of pieces. His readings are moody and beautiful. A larger collection is by **France Clidat** (◆Forlane 16591/3, 3CD), a pianist whose triumphs in Liszt prompted her to see if Satie would lend himself to bravura treatment. Her approach is perhaps a bit too dramatic at times, but she eventually won me over. Her juxtaposition of contrasting pieces works well over the long haul and she plays a lot of the music, including many of the pieces discovered behind Satie's piano after his death, on well-filled CDs. The opposite approach is taken by **Reinbert de Leeuw** in several discs concentrating on the early works and playing them as dully as possible, a sort of new-age way of eliciting the boredom Satie claimed to be expressing in one of his chorales. Philips 46672 seems to be the only one left, thank St. Cecilia! One of his discs contained 35 performances of *Vexations* which, if played 24 times, will give you the full dosage of 840 performances. That was in LP days, when you had to turn over the record, too.

Klára Körmendi has made four discs, of which only one is presently listed, though Naxos sent me three (Naxos 550305, 696, and 699). Hers are pleasant performances, though the faster music lacks the verve and cabaret insouciance given to it by Ciccolini or Clidat. Highlights from this series are available (Naxos 556688, with an orchestral performance of *Gymnopedies* conducted by **Jerome Kaltenbach** from 554279). **Rogé** also made four discs, but only one is still listed (London 10220). He has a feeling for the more delicate pieces, but the livelier and funnier ones seem to elude him. **Frank Glazer** plays a nicely varied collection including most of the published works (Vox 5011, 2CD). Vol.s 3–5 of the piano music are played by **Olaf Höjer,** which I haven't heard (Swedish Society Discofil 1073/5).

The pieces for piano four-hands may be found by **Körmendi** (Naxos 550699), in **Ciccolini**'s set (EMI 767282), by the **Campion-Vachon Duo** in a singularly lifeless performance (Analekta 3040), and by **Rogé** and **Collard** in a disc that also contains the pieces for violin and piano, *Things seen to right and left (without glasses),* played stylishly by Chantal Juillet (London 455401). The four-hand pieces are also played by **Glazer** and **Richard Deas** in a curious album containing the songs and much orchestral music (Vox 5107). The violin suite is played by **Millard Taylor** so self-effacingly that the violin is almost inaudible. But the album is valuable in several ways: It contains all four of the song cycles plus some cabaret songs, sung by **Elaine Bonazzi** in lively fashion, and it gives us the orchestral ballet *Parade* and the *Entr'acte cinématographique* from *Relâche,* both played in an atmospheric fashion though in dated sound.

The Vox set has still more surprises for us. Friedrich Cerha, who conducts all the orchestral works except *Parade,* has orchestrated the piano suite *Dessicated Embryos* and performs it with its spoken commentary, including preliminary essays on the three creatures described and the running commentary on events depicted in the music. Finally, there is a complete performance of Satie's major work, the cantata *Socrate,* performed beautifully by **Friedrich Cerha** with a good cast. *Socrate* is Satie's longest and most serious composition and is seldom heard. This is the only complete performance presently available and is sung and played to touching effect. Unfortunately, and amazingly, this album comes without texts.

This brings up another disc entitled *Musical Tales,* featuring Poulenc's setting of *Babar, the Little Elephant* and including Satie's *Childish Small Talk, Picturesque Child's Play,* and his major suite, *Games and Diversions,* all played and narrated in English by **Catherine Kautsky** (Vox 7545). This is exactly the kind of performance these pieces need, carefully translated and spoken in an interesting way that complements her lively musical performances without distracting the listener from them. Kautsky has a gift. If only she will follow up this disc with the rest of Satie's pieces with text! There is a performance by **Evelyn Lear** and James Tocco of *Games and Diversions,* also with *Babar* (VAIA 1150),that others like but I haven't heard; I'm happy with Kautsky.

Relâche was Satie's last and largest ballet, in two parts separated by a satirical film featuring cameo appearances by Cocteau and Satie himself. The two parts are played in lively style by **Abravanel,** with *Parade, Mercure,* and other orchestral works (Vanguard 4030). Those three major ballet scores plus the film score from *Relâche* may be found with more modern sound and more idiomatic performances by **Jerome Kaltenbach** and the Nancy Symphonic and Lyric Orchestra (Naxos 554279).

One other vocal (well, partially vocal) piece needs to be mentioned, *Mass for the Poor (Messe des Pauvres),* written in 1894. This is basically an organ mass in the tradition of the early French masses in which the organ played interludes based on liturgical chants in between Gregorian chants. In Satie's work, a choir or soloist sings occasionally during the organ preludes. As in many Satie productions, odd things tend to happen, though they will pass you by if you're not reading the score. The only recording is by **Desarbre** with the vocal Ensemble Paris-Renaissance. This disc also includes a number of other pieces usually heard on piano, here played on organ (Mandala 4896, NA). If you find the thought of Satie in his religious mode daunting, try David Diamond's orchestration of the Mass conducted by **Schwarz** (Koch Schwann 373582). MOORE

Alessandro Scarlatti *(1660–1725)*

Scarlatti has been called the "Father of Neapolitan Opera," establishing the conventions of opera seria by introducing the aria da capo, accompanied recitative, and three-part overture. Recent research has shown that Scarlatti didn't invent these concepts, but was just better at writing them and so popularized the style. His musical output was enormous, with compositions numbering in the hundreds in all the then-current genres. His music is still being discovered by the general public, which is more familiar with the harpsichord sonatas of his son Domenico.

INSTRUMENTAL AND KEYBOARD MUSIC

Scarlatti composed an uncounted amount of instrumental music in all forms. The **Baroque Ensemble of Nice** offers six concerti grossi and two flute sonatas (Pierre Verany 96105). "Sinfonie di concerto grosso & concerti per flauto dolce" features seven selections played by **Ensemble Musica Antiqua** (Pierre Verany 95013). "I Concerti per flauto ed archi" offers the period instrument ensemble **Modo Antiquo** in a collection of nine concertos (Tactus 661902). A superb collection of sinfonies and concertos is beautifully performed by **I Musici** (♦Philips 434160), who also offer an excellent collection with flute, oboe, and trumpet soloists (♦Philips 400017).

Splendid harpsichord performances of a dozen pieces by **Alessandrini** are heard in "Toccate per cembalo" (♦Arcana A3).

CANTATAS AND ORATORIOS

Scarlatti composed more than 600 cantatas, mostly unknown and unperformed today. Only one has had any kind of currency, *Su le sponde del Tebro,* with its challenging trumpet obbligato. His oratorios are numerous as well, some 100 plus.

Adriana Maliponte is a gracious soloist in "Tebro" plus three other cantatas, with the Società Cameristica di Lugano (Nuova Era 1061). **Donath** and Baker are the splendid soloists in "Tebro" and a Christmas cantata; Maurice André's trumpet soars majestically over the English Chamber Orchestra led by Leppard (♦EMI 65735). Another excellent collection has **Lynne Dawson** as soloist in two other cantatas, accompanied by the Purcell Quartet (♦Hyperion 66254).

Cantata per la Notte di Natale and *Abramo* are lively affairs with Concerto Italiano led by **Alessandrini;** unhappily the vocalists are barely adequate (Opus 111). The **Alessandro Scarlatti Ensemble** barely make it through *Abramo* (Nuova Era). It's better served by **La Stagione;** the soloists here are much stronger, and a splendid *Cinque Profeti* rounds out the disc (Harmonia Mundi 77291). Four cantatas with recorder obbligato are nicely performed by **Silvia Piccollo** and Roberto Balconi with Collegium Pro Musica (Nuova Era 7162). *La Colpa, il pentimento, la grazia* is a regal oratorio composed for Holy Week of 1708 in Rome. It bears no resemblance to the passion oratorios of Bach, having a plotless, rather cryptic text by Cardinal Ottoboni. The work is generally well served by **La Stagione** in a tightly controlled performance, a bit shy on emotion, but extremely well sung and played (Capriccio 10411, 2CD).

McGegan offers two volumes of cantatas with the period instruments of the Arcadian Academy; Vol. 1 has four solo cantatas with soprano Christine Brandes (Conifer 51293),and Vol. 2 contains six solo cantatas with the spectacular countertenor David Daniels (♦Conifer 51319). Countertenor **Gérard Lesné** and soprano Sandrine Piau offer six more cantatas with Seminario Musicale (Virgin 45126). Lesné can also be heard in a collection of motets (Virgin Classics 45103).

Il Giardino d'amore was one of the first Scarlatti cantatas to be recorded (1964). The Munich Chamber Orchestra accompanies Catherine Gayer and **Fassbaender** in a joyous performance (Archiv 431122). *La Giuditta* is Scarlatti's setting of the tale of the Biblical Judith. **McGegan,** five fine soloists, and Capella Savaria give an excellent introduction to the piece; emotion flows freely as McGegan interprets the work not as a static oratorio but as a dramatic opera (♦Hungaroton 12910). Zádori, Minter, and Gregor are the purposeful soloists, and Capella Savaria's period instruments glitter brilliantly. A 1995 performance by the **Alessandro Stradella Consort** is best forgotten (Bongiovanni).

The oratorio *Humanità e Lucifero* is a celebration of the birth of the Virgin Mary. **Biondi** leads Europa Galante in a zesty, spirited performance (♦Opus 111 30-129). The soloists are crisp and clear. Two trio sonatas by Corelli are interpolated into the work. The oratorio *Ishmael* sets the story of Ishmael and Hagar in the wilderness. A fine performance by the Brewer Chamber Orchestra led by **Rudolph Palmer** has Baird and Erie Mills among the soloists (♦Newport 85558, 2CD). *Il Primo omicidio* is an oratorio setting of Cain and Abel's story. **Jacobs** leads the Akademie für Alte Musik Berlin in a stirring, well thought out performance with excellent soloists (Harmonia Mundi 901649, 2CD). *S. Filippo Neri,* another oratorio, is available only in a dated but sympathetic performance from Angelicum di Milano under **Franco Caracciolo** (Ars Nova 168; Sarx 2001).

Messa di Santa Cecilia and two motets are impressively rendered by the Choir of St. John's College, Cambridge, under **Guest** (♦Decca 430631). **Norrington** leads the Schütz Choir in the motets. The *Messa* is not as felicitously performed by Voci Angeli and Collegium Antiquum led by **Mary Jane Newman** (Newport).

OPERAS

Scarlatti composed more than 115 operas (only one a comedy, it's said); they're rarely performed today and rarely recorded. His tragic opera *Griselda* is heard in a vocally impressive if not quite stylistically correct 1969 performance from Hanover (Arkadia 015, 3CD; Memories 4154, 2CD). **Freni,** Eugenia Ratti, Haefliger, and Pierre Mollet are the excellent singers.   PARSONS

Domenico Scarlatti *(1685–1757)*

1685 was a remarkable year in music history; it witnessed not only the birth of Domenico Scarlatti but Bach and Handel as well. However, Scarlatti has yet to achieve the kind of popularity his more famous contemporaries enjoy. His music, in particular over 555 keyboard sonatas, remains something of a connoisseur's item. For all their brightness and clarity, their fluidness and accessibility, his sonatas are mostly refined, rarified gestures. In the three or four minutes they manage to say more about the art of playing the keyboard than compositions ten times as long by Bach or Handel. This type of music attracts the serious record collector, not the casual listener, which is probably why there has never been a "Greatest Hits of Scarlatti" album.

In the first part of the 20th century, his stock was considerably lower than it is now. Prior to the appearance of Ralph Kirkpatrick's pioneering study in 1955, his music was regarded as filler to be inserted at the beginning of recitals, useful for filling time while the audience coughed and shuffled about. The sonatas, available only in the corrupt Longo editions, were regarded as little more than practice material, which explains why so many pianists had a high regard for them even if they didn't play them in public. Kirkpatrick changed all that; he ordered them chronologically, grouped them in pairs related by key and style, and suggested an interpretive approach commensurate with the style of composition. The emergence of the harpsichord as a serious performance medium helped matters too. Once performers and audiences heard what was possible with period instruments, the record labels responded with increasing numbers of recordings.

We still know very little about Scarlatti's life. At age 50, for no other apparent reason than the lure of a secure position, he left a promising career in Italy to take the job of harpsichord teacher to Princess Maria Barbara of Braganza, daughter of the King of Spain, later to become Queen of Spain. He lived in almost complete isolation, his only artistic contact and confidant being the castrato Farinelli, who saw to it that bound copies of the sonatas were sent to Italy after the composer's death. To this day, none of the autograph manuscripts have been found; the sonatas are known only from copies made by other hands.

The story of Scarlatti on record must start with a relatively recent development: the complete recording of all 555 sonatas by one artist, the remarkable American harpsichordist **Scott Ross.** From June 1984 to September 1985, Ross was captured on digital tape by Radio France, the result being 34 Erato CDs (45309, budget-priced). By this time Ross had been diagnosed with AIDS, and he died in 1989. His achievement can't be overestimated; certainly his fatal disease had little effect on his powers of communication. Here is playing that's unbounded by the usual constraints of the keyboard: joyous, spontaneous, introspective, stately, magisterial, yet always responsive and appropriate to the music. The fast sonatas go really fast, without a hint of technical limitations; the slow ones are almost too emotional for the relatively sterile medium of the

harpsichord. The range of instruments used is impressive and the recorded sound uniformly excellent, despite the several different venues.

I feel fortunate to have witnessed this major event in the history of recordings; let's hope the set will continue to be available for later generations to sample. But understandably, 34 CDs will be out of the question for many collectors. Erato has come to the rescue by issuing a 3CD compilation, and for many this will be the best way to get started (45422).

Beyond the one complete set, Scarlatti on CD mostly appears in single-disc recitals by the leading harpsichordists of our time. One who has distinguished himself in this music over his long career is **Kipnis.** His recital (Chesky 75) is marked by groupings in Kirkpatrick pairs and full repeats with free ornamentation (most harpsichordists don't bother with either). Chesky's demonstration-quality sound is another attractive feature. **Edward Parmentier** offers his usual thoughtful, insightful playing on two fine Italian-style instruments by American builder David Sutherland (Wildboar 8501). **Pinnock**'s recital, recorded early in his career, presents a wide range of early and late sonatas played on original instruments from the Victoria and Albert Museum in London (CRD 3368). French superstar **Rousset** has recently released a disc performed on an original Portuguese harpsichord much like the ones Scarlatti probably played (Oiseau-Lyre 458165). As usual for this exciting artist, the playing is full of fire and intensity.

Veteran Canadian artist **Colin Tilney** has made two CDs. The first features an original Italian instrument that, with its dry, gesticulating sound, is ideally suited to the music (Dorian 90103). As is usually the case with Dorian, the engineering is very warm and natural. The second is entitled "Scarlatti High and Low" and explores 16 late sonatas that go either too high or too low for the average harpsichord (Music & Arts 907). The instrument, an Italian copy by John Phillips, has all the necessary notes, but more important, a gusty, forceful sound that will surprise those listeners who expect the harpsichord to sound laid-back and pretty. Tilney's playing is both effervescent and authoritative, some of the best on disc.

Many listeners prefer to hear Scarlatti performed on the piano. From a historical perspective, there are certainly arguments to support this approach, as he is known to have played early Cristofori pianofortes during his time in Italy. But it should be noted that no modern pianist has yet dared take the final step and record Scarlatti on a truly historical instrument. For now, it's all modern Steinways and Bösendorfers—not bad, but not ideal, in my opinion. **Horowitz** made headlines in the '60s and '70s with his self-effacing performances for Columbia; most of the original recordings have been reissued in two CDs (Sony 53460, 53466). Another Scarlatti specialist on the piano was **Michelangeli,** though I find him a bit too slow and self-indulgent (Philips 456901, with music of Debussy, Ravel and Baldassare Galuppi). Among the younger generation, **Schiff** has the right instincts (Hungaroton 11806), as does **David Schrader** (Cedille 42).

During his Italian period, Scarlatti wrote much sacred vocal music, no doubt at the urging of his heavy-handed father Alessandro, who was a severe critic and actually tore up many of Domenico's scores in dissatisfaction. Producers have been reluctant to record this repertoire, for no apparent reason other than it doesn't sell as well as the keyboard stuff. But *Salve Regina* is a moving, beautifully written solo cantata for alto and strings, easily the equal of anything Papa wrote, and James Bowman and the **King**'s **Consort** have given it a superb reading (Hyperion 66875, with cantatas by Alessandro Scarlatti and Hasse). *Stabat Mater,* for ten voices with organ, is probably his best-known vocal work, and **Ensemble**

William Byrd under Graham O'Reilly gives it an ethereal, moving performance (Pierre Verany 799111). The disc includes four other sacred works, captured in Verany's usual shimmering, transparent sound.

BRODERSEN

Giacinto Scelsi (1905–1988)

Scelsi's life is something of a mystery. Before the '50s, he had composed in various styles and traveled from his native Italy to Africa and the Far East, where he absorbed Eastern philosophy and found that composing in the 12-tone system brought on a nervous breakdown. His therapy was to play one note on the piano until the sound disappeared, over and over again. His concept of tone as having three dimensions, not just pitch and duration but something spherical, came gradually to infuse his music with a character all its own, including great subtlety of tone production and the use of bent tones, quarter-tones, and other sounds as decorations and color effects, in a subtle use of sound for its own sake.

Scelsi's earlier works, from 1953–1958, are less austere and mostly for single instruments. Pieces for solo piano and solo flute are recorded by **Kristi Becker,** piano, and **Carin Levine,** flute (CPO 999340), while music for clarinet is played by **David Smeyers** (CPO 999266). These are interesting collections, both well played, and they contain a few late works as well; one of the flute pieces is an improvisation accompanied by the composer on the piano. A more controversial look at this controversial music is by **Marcus Weiss,** saxophone, who, with the Contrechamps Ensemble under Jürg Wyttenbach, plays several of the woodwind works transcribed for saxophone, turning them into quite different, more earthy sounding music (Hat Hut 117). That disc also includes an unusual work (even for Scelsi) for bass singer (Johannes Schmidt) and bass instruments, gravelly and weird. Hat Hut provides no texts and little relevant information. Another early solo work, *Four Pieces for Trumpet,* is in "Nobody Knows de Trouble I See," played sensitively by **Reinhold Friedrich** (Capriccio 10482).

In the '80s the then four string quartets appeared in two LPs played by the **Arditti Quartet** (Fore 80, 13-14). No. 1 is a half-hour, tensely expressionistic score that makes an abrupt change of pace at the end, presumably symbolizing the crisis Scelsi came to feel Western music had reached. The LPs included duos for two violins and violin and cello. The re-release omitted the duos but added a fifth quartet, a string trio, and *Khoom,* a work for soprano, horn, and percussion (Salabert 8904/05, 2CD). The trio and several otherwise unrecorded pieces for strings are played by **Robert Zimansky** and colleagues (Accord 20062). The Arditti collection is in more austere sound, fitting the style perhaps better than the smoother, less concentrated Accord sound, but both discs are important.

"Trilogia," a 40-minute series of early pieces for solo cello, was played by **Frances-Marie Uitti** in close collaboration with the composer, according to her notes Etcetera 1136). This collection is harder listening, requiring the cellist to produce a particularly grainy muting effect on the lower strings (in imitation of an Eastern tradition). Uitti plays the entire piece in a rather unclear way, the demands being almost impossible to achieve with real clarity. The fault may be partly in the somewhat vague recorded sound of the Fone LP, which the re-release did little to improve. A transcription by Uitti of *Kotha,* a guitar piece, is more convincing.

Works for larger aggregations begin to appear in 1959, but Scelsi's choice of notes becomes more austere. *Four Pieces for Orchestra* consists of changes rung on one note per piece, while *Anahit, Kya* (for clarinet and ensemble), and *Pranam* (for voice, ensemble, and tape) are almost equally limited, if very colorful in sound. The last two may be heard led

by **Hans Zender** in a program of music otherwise by the conductor (CPO 999485), while *Anahit* is in **Zukofsky**'s disc (CP^2 108) and *Kya* is also in Smeyer's clarinet program. *Four Pieces* and *Anahit* are conducted by **Jürg Wyttenbach,** along with *Uaxuctum* for chorus and orchestra (Accord 20061). Another disc contains *Aion, Pfhat,* and *Konx-Om-Pax,* played by the same forces (Accord 20040). The chorus is rather distantly recorded. A more recent CD continues the documentation of Scelsi's choral works, sung by the New London Chamber Choir under **James Wood** (Accord 20681).

In nomine lucis is a considerable piece for organ, played by **Christoph Maria Moosmann** (New Albion 74). Two late pieces for solo bass viol may be found in two discs: *Le réveil profond* played by **Michael Cameron** (Athena 223) and *C'est bien la nuit* by **Bjorn Ianke** (Simax 1136).

MOORE

R. Murray Schafer (b. 1933)

Schafer is Canada's most original and important composer. I've listened to his music and been challenged by his ideas for years. He avoids easy solutions to musical matters and is utterly unafraid of jarring an audience's sensibilities. Even as a young man, his thinking was independent and unconventional; it's this decidedly individual streak that led to his expulsion from the University of Toronto. He then set out on a path of self-education that included composition studies with Mátyás Seiber and formative encounters with Ezra Pound, whose musical writings he later edited. Supremely literate and a gifted visual artist, Schafer is one of the most remarkable thinkers of our time. In addition to his impressive musical accomplishments, he has written important books on the acoustic environment (*The Tuning of the World*), education (*The Thinking Ear*) and music theater (*Patria and the Theatre of Confluence*). His music defies easy description and draws on a wide variety of techniques; it's extremely idealistic in conception and often explicitly specific as to venue: For example, *The Princess of the Stars,* is to be staged on a lake with the musicians concealed by trees.

While some of Schafer's orchestral works are satirical, intended to shake up an audience's sensibilities, *Dream Rainbow, Dream Thunder* is an evocative, highly impressionistic piece, marvelously played by Toronto's Esprit Orchestra under **Alex Pauk** (CBC 5101). It's coupled with fine performances of four other recent works by Canadian composers and makes a strong case for Canada's current musical scene.

Schafer is uneasy with the concerto medium, feeling it allows for too much opportunity for vanity and self-indulgence on the part of soloists and composers. That hasn't prevented him from composing several marvelous examples of the form. Listeners can hear three of these (for flute, harp, and violin) in one excellent disc (CBC 5114). The Flute Concerto features **Robert Aitken,** who is called upon to employ all manner of extended techniques, but in Schafer's hands they seem to unfold from the music in the most natural way; you're hardly aware of them. The Harp Concerto features Toronto's **Judy Loman,** for whom Schafer has written several fine works. The violin concerto, *The Darkly Splendid Earth: The Lonely Traveler,* is a plangent rhapsody in which soloist and orchestra travel mostly independent paths. **Jacques Israelievitch** plays it with uncommon eloquence. In all these pieces, the orchestral writing is unusually brilliant and rich. (For example, try to think of another flute concerto that features a substantial tuba cadenza in the final movement!)

The female voice is a favorite vehicle for Schafer, and "The Garden of the Heart," a collection of orchestral songs, shows just how brilliantly he composes for it (CBC 5173). His interest in Eastern thought is underlined by his settings of Tagore in *Gitanjali* (scintillatingly sung by soprano **Donna Brown**) and the title work, based on a tale from *The Thousand and One Nights*. The final work on the disc, *Adieu, Robert Schumann* is a poignant, wrenching monodrama with its text adapted from Clara Schumann's diary. Mezzo **Judith Forst** gives this work a memorable reading, and it echoes in your mind long after you have heard it.

Schafer's five string quartets are among his finest musical creations and deserve to be better known. These works concede nothing to the avant-garde quartets of Ligeti, Penderecki, or Lutoslawski, but they are much more than experiments. His writing for this medium can be as astringent as theirs, but also more unashamedly melodic. Underlying the microtonal technique and unusual string effects, though, is a finely calibrated dramatic sense and a lyricism that make these works particularly satisfying. They show a great range of expression, each being quite different from the others. They have been collected in a set splendidly performed by the **Orford Quartet** (Centrediscs 39 4090, 2CD, NA).

"Chimera" presents harpist **Judy Loman** teamed up with the Orford String Quartet in a pair of striking works, plus pieces by two other Canadian composers (Centrediscs 414292, 2CD, NA). *Theseus* is an atmospheric piece for harp and string quartet, while *The Crown of Ariadne* is for solo harpist, who simultaneously plays percussion. The Schafer works are wonderful and the performances are superb, but I was dismayed at paying full price for two CDs whose total music was less than 80 minutes in length (caveat emptor).

Patria is a multifaceted cycle of music theater works that Schafer has been working on since the '60s. They're highly ritualistic, often calling for audience participation and seeking a confluence of artistic media in a manner similar to Wagner's. They vary greatly in their instrumentation. Some of them are to be performed outdoors, others are quite long. *Ra*, for example, takes 11 hours to perform, while *And the Wolf Shall Inherit the Moon* requires a week in a forest. So while it's not quite the same as actually being at Lake Muskoga at dawn, a disc entitled "Patria" presents excerpts of this fascinating project (Opening Day 9307). This collection features the **Schafer Ensemble,** a small group of singers and players that has had a lengthy relationship with the composer, who supervised these recordings. McINTIRE

Xaver Scharwenka (1850–1924)

Grove's says that Scharwenka's music is characterized by "energy, harmonic interest, strong rhythm, many beautiful melodies, and much Polish national character," and all this and more is to be found there. This is Romantic music, with an effusive, heart-on-sleeve quality and thrilling bravura writing that touches the soul and sets the adrenaline flowing. Though he spent most of his life in Berlin, he never forgot his heritage, and there are Polish dance rhythms all through his concertos and salon pieces, notably the *Polish Dance* from his Op. 3 that made him famous almost overnight. Anyone who loves Chopin's concertos should investigate Scharwenka's as well, while recitalists would benefit from including his flavorful solo pieces in their programs.

We're fortunate to have all four of the piano concertos readily available in first-rate performances. For 1 there is the reissued RCA recording with **Wild** and Leinsdorf (◆Élan 82266, with the Paderewski Concerto) and the opening sally in **Seta Tanyel**'s ongoing survey of Scharwenka's music (◆Collins 1263, with Chopin's Concerto 1). The sheer power and thrust of Wild's barn-burning account are hard to resist, yet Tanyel's elegant and committed reading, which benefits from her luscious tone and thorough command of the fiendishly difficult piano writing, is also highly satisfying.

No. 2 is as notable for its richly melodic writing and echoes of the Chopin E Minor Concerto as for its highly entertaining finale: a sly, insouciant rondo built around an almost Yiddish-sounding tune—you keep expecting it to turn into "Fiddler on the Roof"! **Tanyel** (◆Collins 1485) is the one to get, far more captivating than **Ponti** in Vol. 3 of the "Romantic Piano Concerto" series, who is earnest but brusque and humorless (Vox). Tanyel couples 2 with 3, the stentorian horn call at the start miraculously transformed into the effervescent final rondo. Here she reigns supreme, and likewise **Hough** has the field all to himself in 4, its imperious opening statement recycled in the finale, a remarkably Lisztian tarantella (◆Hyperion 66790, with von Sauer's Concerto). Hough fields the formidable passagework with aplomb.

All of Tanyel's performances of Scharwenka's chamber music demonstrate her remarkable affinity for this composer. ◆Collins 1419 contains the Piano Quartet and Piano Trio 2, while ◆1448 holds Piano Trio 1, Cello Sonata, and Sonata and Serenade for violin, in each case joined by other top-rank artists. She has also recorded four volumes of solo piano music, every one of them a must-have for anyone interested in the genre. You'll find the familiar *Polish Dance* in Vol. 1 (◆1325); the others are 1352, 1365, and 1474. This is an absorbing cross-section of Scharwenka's most appealing works for the piano, and all four discs are beautifully recorded into the bargain. HALLER

Peter Schickele (b. 1935)

It's difficult to think of a musician who has worked harder to popularize classical music than Schickele. Perhaps his most effective calling card has been his determinedly anti-establishment stance. As a Juilliard student, he would round up musicians for a public concert around exam time, when everyone needed a break, and perform amusing music, his own and others. This is when his famous first *Quodlibet* got started; or perhaps it was at Aspen, where he spent many summers. There was a performance of *Peter and the Wolf* in which the wolf ate Peter early in the proceedings, bringing them to an abrupt halt, and on another occasion Bottesini's Duo for violin and double bass was passed off as a work by PDQ Bach, convincing many, since the performers hammed it up to suit themselves. Funniest, however, were the works written by Schickele and attributed to various imaginary composers. Gradually PDQ Bach became his only pseudonym.

As a composer, Schickele studied with Harris and Milhaud, then at Juilliard with Persichetti and Bergsma. After he graduated, he taught at Juilliard for a while, and always attributed his departure to the management's objections to his habit of demonstrating retrograde motion by using a passage from *Liebestraum* as interpreted by Spike Jones. His penchant for teaching and his omnivorous love for all kinds of music has led to the radio show he hosts for PBS, *Schickele Mix*, which ranges over the world of sound much like PDQ himself, fascinating and amusing listeners while opening their ears.

A number of works from the late '50s and early '60s exist only on private tapes but would make a fine CD, among them: an *Invention* for orchestra that shows his Harris influences and how they ended; *Serenade* for various parts of the orchestra; a cycle of songs for baritone and bassoon (Schickele's instruments, though he refers to himself as a basso blotto); *Celebration with Bells* (a piece written for youth orchestra); a fine string trio; and many other chamber and piano pieces (another of his instruments). *Cool, Clear Walter* is a lovely piece written for Trampler to play on viola d'amore with a chamber group. These early works are in a sometimes dissonant style based on American harmonies leavened with jazz and sometimes rock influences and the styles of his teachers, but they have great personality of their own and are lively and positive. By the time his works began to be recorded commercially, a lot of the brashness had worn off. Schickele's recent music recalls even earlier influences stemming from his childhood in North Dakota; the wide open spaces seem to call strongly in the recent chamber works. Depth has seldom been a conscious concern, but his recent works attain it without seeming effort.

The earliest disc still listed is of a song cycle for horn and orchestra, *Pentangle,* played by **Kenneth Albrecht** with Mester and the Louisville Orchestra (Albany 24). *Fantastic Garden* ("Three Views from the Open Window") is a crossover piece mixing several styles (Louisville LP 691). The orchestral suite *Thurber's Dogs,* based on the humorist's drawings, is a lovely piece on an odd subject, played by **Timothy Russell** and the Pro Musica Chamber Orchestra (d'Note 1010).

Quartet for violin, cello, clarinet, and piano is a relaxed country-sounding piece played by **Eriko Sato** and friends, along with *Bestiary,* a theater piece for early music ensemble performed by Calliope (Vanguard 4066). Another recording of the Quartet was in a program by the **Viklarbo Chamber Ensemble** (Raptoria 1005). Vanguard releases not yet on CD are Elegies for clarinet and piano, *Summer Trio* for flute, cello, and piano, songs from Beaumont and Fletcher's *The Knight of the Burning Pestle* (LP 71269), and a disc called "Good-Time Ticket" primarily containing orchestral arrangements of popular material (LP 6517).

Serenade for Three (violin, clarinet, and piano), has been recorded by the **Verdehr Trio** (Crystal 745), and *Dances for Three* (two clarinets and bassoon) by **Trio Indiana** (Crystal 734). An all-Schickele disc is offered by the **Chestnut Brass Company** with the composer playing his Piano Concerto 2 (*Olé*) along with *Brass Calendar, Varaiations on a Joke* (a put-on of Mozart's *Musical Joke*), *A Little Mosey Music,* and *Hornsmoke,* a theater piece originally written for the Canadian Brass (Newport 85638).

It took Schickele a long time to get around to string quartets, but it has been worth the wait. His first, *American Dreams,* has always moved me since the **Audubon**'s recording appeared (RCA 7719). Like many of the works above, it moves from Western scenes and folk idioms into jazz and is almost minimal at times, but is unfailingly touching. Quartet 2 continues the trend, though it's even more serious. The **Lark Quartet** has recorded it, with a Quintet and Sextet, all appealing pieces (Arabesque 6719). He has now written a symphony; I can't wait for someone to record it!

Schickele's talents also run to film scores (*Silent Running,* MCA LP 9188), crossover compositions like those he wrote for *The Open Window* (Vanguard LP), and arrangements (*Noel* and *Baptism* for Joan Baez, Vanguard LPs).

See also: PDQ Bach.   MOORE

Franz Schmidt *(1874–1939)*

In his adoptive Austria, Schmidt is accepted as one of the great 20th-century masters; further afield, his reputation is being established more slowly. Yet he certainly belongs among the great composers; his late-Romantic music marries the expressive potential of post-Wagnerian chromatic harmony with a mastery of classical form, making his musical language both emotionally rich and formally satisfying. But for most of his life Schmidt was distracted from composition, first because he was earning his living as a cellist in the orchestra that even now doubles as the Vienna Philharmonic and the opera of the State Opera. Then, as his reputation as a pedagogue grew, teaching made demands on his

time. As a result his compositions are few in number, but everything he wrote bears the hallmark of his individual genius.

ORCHESTRAL MUSIC

The backbone of Schmitt's output is a series of four symphonies that ought to be part of the standard repertoire but are only now beginning to command the attention they deserve.

1. Written in 1899 when Schmidt was still an orchestral cellist, it is full of glorious tunes that tumble over one another in generous profusion; it's currently available in two recordings: one from **Neeme Järvi** and the Detroit Symphony (Chandos 9357, separately in a coupling with Richard Strauss's *Four Symphonic Interludes from Intermezzo,* or 9568, 3CD, in a box of all four), the other from **Halász** and the Budapest Symphony (Marco Polo 223119). Järvi chivvies the tempo rather too much where he should let it breathe; Halász obtains much less distinguished playing from his musicians but gets the pace right. His coupling is the exquisite "Introduction, Intermezzo, and Carnival Music" from the opera *Notre Dame,* these brief excerpts being the only music of Schmidt's to have gained a toehold in the repertoire.

2. Containing some of the richest orchestral writing in the entire symphonic canon, here **Järvi**'s tempo is spot on; indeed, this is one of the finest classical recordings made in the last 20 years. No. 1 was a young man's music, full of good-natured sentiment and striving; 2 is the product of his full maturity and exudes an easy strength and sun-dappled warmth. **Mitropoulos**'s live recording, made with the Vienna Philharmonic in 1958, can't compete with Järvi's for sound quality or technical assurance, but it does give us Schmidt's music played in the style he would have expected, portamenti and all, and some of the musicians here may even have played alongside the composer in his orchestral days (Music & Arts 991). Mitropoulos offers a coupling, Schoenberg's *Verklärte Nacht,* whereas Järvi does not.

3. The understated, emotionally oblique but effortlessly lyrical 3 is the Cinderella of Schmidt's canon; the British composer and writer Harold Truscott, an expert on his music, said that with it "one almost has the impression of eavesdropping on a private conversation." **Järvi** and his Detroiters get the tempo right this time too, but fail to penetrate to the elusive soul of the work. Yet until Supraphon brings back **Pešek**'s first-rate reading from the mid-'80s, it's the only version available (either in the Chandos set or in a separate CD, 9000, with Hindemith's *Concerto for Orchestra*).

4. With this one we reach Schmidt's orchestral masterpiece. It was written in 1932–33, inspired by the death of his only daughter in childbirth, and he poured all his anguish into this profoundly moving work, based entirely on the 23-measure trumpet melody that opens the symphony. **Järvi** is again champing at the bit (Chandos 9505, with Strauss's *Symphonic Fragment* from *Josephs-Legende*), but the clear choice is **Welser-Möst**'s recording with the London Philharmonic (EMI 55518). He has the natural measure of the music, allowing Schmidt's heartache to unfold in its own time, guiding the tensions toward the crushing climaxes of despair. The coupling here is *Variations on a Hussar Song,* which traces the formal outline of a four-movement symphony under the disguise of the title.

Martin Sieghart's recording with the Bruckner Orchestra of Linz is a very close runner-up. The orchestral playing is marginally less distinguished, but the climaxes have a hair-raising bite, and he gets the measured pulse right (Chesky 143). The couplings are interesting as well: three early, prophetic orchestral movements and a march by Bruckner.

Chaconne. A transcription of an organ work, it gives ample proof of his astonishing command of variation technique. The Wiener Jeunesse Orchester under **Herbert Böck** plays with the passion of youth, though the recording could do with more clarity at the climaxes (Pan 510081). It's coupled with the Piano Concerto, written, like all his mature piano compositions, for the left hand on commission from the one-armed Paul Wittgenstein; the soloist is **Karl-Andreas Kolly.** There is no rival account of either work in the catalog.

CHAMBER MUSIC

Schmidt was a consummate chamber musician, both as cellist and pianist, so it's hardly surprising that his chamber music is so perfectly crafted; the surprise is that he wrote so little. There are only two string quartets and three quintets, one a standard piano quintet, the other two blending clarinet and piano quartet—and again, the piano part is for left hand alone. The only available coupling of the quartets comes from the **Franz Schubert Quartett Wien;** they're guilty of some questionable intonation, but there's no competition (Nimbus 5467).

The quintets with clarinet are rather better served. **Aladár Jánoshka** is joined by four Slovakian compatriots in the hour-long Quintet in A: They know exactly how to keep the music moving without snapping at its heels (Marco Polo 223414). Pianist **Rainer Keuschnig** and a team of fellow Austrians couple the B-flat Quintet for clarinet and piano quartet with Piano Quintet in G—intelligent playing, spoiled by rather hard-edged recorded sound (Orfeo 287921). But happy is the composer whose music gets a performance like that of the Piano Quintet from **Fleisher** and friends; it's sparkling and passionate and utterly convincing—one of the great chamber-music recordings (Sony 48253, with Korngold's *Suite* for two violins, cello and piano, another unbeatable reading).

Organ music

Alongside the four symphonies, the other series of compositions that ran through Schmidt's life was music for his first love, the organ, accounting for roughly half his output. Even more than in the symphonies, here he gave himself room for calm, expansive thought; the longest single piece, a Prelude and Fugue in E-flat, takes a full half hour. But these are no inflated Romantic monsters; Schmidt sought clarity above everything else. Only one organist has had the wit to record the complete organ works, the young Austrian **Andreas Juffinger,** in a series of four Capriccio CDs, now deleted, as is the Capriccio 2CD set of the opera *Notre Dame;* it's worth keeping your eye on the second-hand shelves. In 1985, in the St. Augustin Church in Perchtoldsdorf, the lower-Austrian village where Schmidt lived, an organ was built to try to capture the sound he visualized for his music; **Helmut Binder** performs the E-flat Prelude and Fugue, Toccata and Fugue in A-flat, and Toccata in C on that instrument (Motette 11191).

VOCAL MUSIC

The work that occupied Schmidt in his last years was the oratorio *Das Buch mit sieben Siegeln* (*The Book with Seven Seals*), a setting of parts of the *Revelations* of St. John the Divine. It's an overwhelming piece in which Schmidt deployed all the musical resources at his command, an amalgam of the lyrical and monumental that recurs throughout his music, a vast canvas supported by the twin pillars of extensive organ interludes and massive choral fugues. It has been recorded surprisingly often; there are four versions in the current catalog, with a fifth only recently deleted. **Mitropoulos**'s account from the 1959 Salzburg Festival has all the disadvantages of a live recording and aging (Sony 68442), but it's stylistically fascinating—those portamenti again! For several years the best modern studio version was **Lothar Zagrosek**'s (Orfeo 143862),

but in 1998 it was trumped by **Welser-Möst,** a performance glowing with commitment and passion, with the Danish tenor Stig Andersen heroic in the central role of St. John (EMI 56660). It's a deeply moving experience. ANDERSON

Florent Schmitt *(1870–1958)*

Schmitt occupied a prominent position in the French musical community early in the 20th century. He was never an impressionist like Debussy and Ravel, nor was he a member of Cocteau's circle like *Les Six.* While renowned for lush, sensuous melodies (witness his best-known work, *La Tragédie de Salomé),* the modernisms and exotic idioms of Messiaen were foreign to his nature. Perhaps the closest cognate might be Roussel, yet there is a spikiness, a rhythmic *éclat* to his finest work that eclipses that composer. Certainly there's a compelling hothouse passion to works like *Salomé, Antoine et Cléopâtre,* and *Salammbô,* yet balanced against these is a more classical though no less fervent strain in Symphony 2 and *Symphonie Concertante,* compelling homage to the indomitable spirit and formidable invention of the Gallic muse.

ORCHESTRAL MUSIC

Schmitt turned for *La Tragédie de Salomé* not to Oscar Wilde but rather to the poem by Robert d'Humière, in which the Biblical tales of Salomé and Sodom and Gomorrah are effectively juxtaposed; thus Salomé is slain not by Herod's soldiers but instead by a cataclysmic eruption of Mount Nebo. The result seems remarkably close to Stravinsky, who praised the score profusely. **Patrick Davin** offers the complete ballet in its original setting for small orchestra (Marco Polo 223448); however, for maximum effect the far more lavish suite compiled by Schmitt two years later remains unsurpassed, and so does the recording by **Paray,** spectacularly recorded and passionately executed (♦Mercury 434336). Paray omits the seductive soprano solo heard midway through, substituting the oboe instead. Two other excellent recordings are by **Janowski** (Erato 45029) and **Martinon** (EMI 749748), both paired with *Psaume XLVII;* Martinon also includes Debussy's ballet *Khamma,* but his recording may be difficult to find. The sumptuous LP led by **de Almeida** (RCA 3151) is unfortunately still unavailable on CD.

Schmitt set Flaubert's novel *Salammbô* first for silent film and then rescored it as three suites. In this extravagant pagan fresco, his penchant for unashamed hedonism is given full reign by **Jacques Mercier,** with performance and sound as resplendent as the music itself (Adès 203592). *Antoine et Cléopâtre,* inspired by Shakespeare's play, offers images ranging from Pompey's camp to the Battle of Actium and finally Cleopatra's tomb, all fitted out with the requisite voluptuous orgies and passionate love scenes. **Segerstam** pulls out all the stops (Cybelia 842).

Pierre Stoll conducts *Oriane et le Prince d'Amour, In Memoriam, Ronde Burlesque,* and *Légende* for viola; the sound is close and detailed (Cybelia 816). *Oriane* is a lush display in the manner of Rimsky-Korsakov, *In Memoriam* is a heartfelt eulogy for Schmitt's mentor Fauré, *Ronde Burlesque* was intended as an elaborate jest à la Satie, and *Légende* is an unhurried and heroic tale. On another disc we hear even more rarified fare led by **James Lockhart:** *Andante Religioso, Suite sans Esprit de Suite,* and *Soirs Fonctionnaire 1912* (Cybelia 869). These pieces display a more intimate and endearing side of the composer. Most interesting is *Soirs,* a satirical look at the foibles of bureaucracy.

Schmitt's more classical side surfaces in Symphony 2, *Danse d'Abisag, Habeyssée,* and *Rêves* (Marco Polo 223689). The symphony is an attempt to bring the caustic rhythms of *Salomé* and *Salammbô* into line with classical traditions, rollicking outer sections framing a flowing repose. Abisag was the maiden summoned to apply heat to the aged King David, and her dance is suitably sultry though (alas!) unresolved, as the Bible tells us "the king knew her not." *Habeyssée* is a suite for violin, while *Rêves* faithfully reproduces Léon-Paul Fargue's epigram "Watch our days and our dreams pass by . . ." All are beautifully rendered by **Segerstam,** including the same performance of *Rêves* as on Cybelia. **David Robertson** offers *Rêves, Soirs,* and *Symphonie Concertante* for piano and orchestra, joined by Huseyin Sermet (Auvidis 4687). *Soirs* is an attractive suite also meant as a tribute to Fauré. *Symphonie Concertante* may be the most modern sounding of the lot, yet it's not without poetry and is well crafted; it's skillfully played by Sermet, and sound and performance are first-rate.

The tone poem *Le Palais Hanté* (*The Haunted Palace*), based on Poe, finds Schmitt at his most engagingly decadent, and **Prêtre** leads it in similar vein (EMI 47931). Together with André Caplet's *Conte Fantastique* (based on *The Masque of the Red Death*), it fittingly complements Debussy's fragmentary opera *La Chute de la Maison Usher* (*The Fall of the House of Usher*).

CHORAL MUSIC

Psaume XLVII is a glorious fresco effectively juxtaposing awe-inspiring and seductive aspects of the Old Testament. Following the grandiose exaltation of the opening "Gloire au Seigneur!" and the exhortation "Clap your hands together, o ye peoples!", we have a "Danse sacrée" and a voluptuous setting of the *Song of Songs* before all come together in a grand celebration of the Lord God. This is heady music, wonderfully carried off by **Martinon** (♦EMI 749748, with *Salomé*), who imbues the music with tremendous thrust—far more than **Janowski** on his similarly coupled disc (Erato 45029)—while soprano Andréa Guiot makes the most of Schmitt's meltingly beautiful setting whereas Sharon Sweet on Erato sounds too hard and too close. HALLER

Alfred Schnittke (1934–1998)

Schnittke's early works are primarily 12-tone, though his feeling for drama leavens his work with lively sound effects, glissandi, microtonal elements, and other surprises. In 1968, polystylistic elements began to be of major importance and remained so until about 1986, when his music became more abstract but in Schnittke's personal sense, no longer 12-tone. Film music is a significant portion of his work; he wrote no less than 60 scores, and it seems to have been this medium that originally suggested the polystylistic element in his compositions. It's sad that Schnittke died so young, as he seemed to be approaching a greater balance of forces at the end of his life.

SYMPHONIES

1 (1969–1974). A marvelously chaotic-sounding work lasting well over an hour, and polystylistic to a fault, it thrusts together everything from baroque music to jazz, managing to leave few kinds of music unbattered in the process. It must have totally alienated the Russian bureaucracy. Does it do more than *épater le bourgeoisie?* Time will tell.

Rozhdestvensky was its dedicatee and made two recordings, both with Russian orchestras (Melodiya 10-00062, 1987; Chandos 9417, 1996). The Melodiya is raw and brash, harshly exciting, and closely miked. The Chandos is, thank goodness, not much more polite, though the emphases in the scoring are markedly different and the trio of the second movement scherzo (a long improvised cadenza for solo violin and piano), is totally different. The Melodiya release has no entry points

between movements, while Chandos gives us four and takes three minutes longer. A choice between these readings is hard to make. I like the unbuttoned quality of the Melodiya; it has more of the flavor of an important social criticism. The Chandos sound isn't much clearer, though it has more ambience. The question is, do you prefer your Schnittke raw and bleeding or half cooked?

This is the kind of composition that clearly benefits from different interpretations and performers. **Segerstam** gives us an even odder recording (BIS 577). It takes eight minutes longer than Rozhdestvensky's Chandos effort and includes an extensive jazz improvisation. It's the most violently recorded version, though the orchestral balances are still a problem, sometimes too loud, sometimes inaudible, as in the quotation from Haydn's "Farewell" Symphony at the end, which seems to have been prerecorded.

2 ("St. Florian," 1980). It could hardly be a greater contrast to its predecessor. It's a choral work containing most of the text of the mass ordinary, complete with references to the Gregorian melodies associated with that text. The immediate subject, however, is the orchestra, which is large. There are two performances conducted by **Rozhdestvensky** (Melodiya 10-00063 and BBC 91962, which also contains a curious *Pas de Quatre* for orchestra, each dance written by a different composer, one being Schnittke). Both recordings are a little squashed dynamically compared with **Polianski**'s, in which the churchy acoustic surroundings make for a more impressive event altogether (Chandos 9519). **Segerstam** gives a similarly committed performance, in sound of similar resonance and great dynamic range (BIS 667).

3 (1981). This is a self-proclaimed attempt to come to terms with the symphony as a form, something Schnittke's previous symphonies rather sidestep. However, it begins with a study in crescendo in the semi-minimal style Schnittke employs in *Passacaglia* and *Minnesang*, thus continuing to beg the question. A pseudo-neoclassical Allegro follows, though its activity hardly seems determined by sonata principles. The rest of the symphony consists of a Scherzo that builds up another endless crescendo, eventually resolving to a single note that falls over into a huge Adagio finale. This symphony has many beautiful and highly effective passages, some of which recall late Mahler, while one pervasive brass phrase is clearly Bruckner-inspired. This piece could easily become habit-forming.

Rozhdestvensky gives a reading of breadth and passion, recorded with rather exaggerated balances favoring the percussion, particularly the keyboards (Melodiya 10-00064). **Eri Klas** conducts the Stockholm Philharmonic in a neater, less grandiose performance, recorded with more natural orchestral balances and a wider dynamic range (BIS 477). His superior engineering makes this work easier to appreciate, despite Rozhdestvensky's expressive, Stokowskian string section.

4 (1983). A curious work enlisting the aid of a tenor and a countertenor who sing wordless vocalises and a piano soloist who never quite takes on concerto duties its premise seeks to unify the Jewish, Catholic, and Protestant faiths by blending their music. In the course of this over-45-minute piece, we traverse all the emotional schisms and battles you can imagine, in the end reaching a satisfying and beautiful climax combining the musical styles of all three faiths under a single God. **Polianski** couples the work with *Three Sacred Hymns,* short sketches for the Concerto for Chorus (Chandos 9463), while **Kamu** gives us the *Requiem* (BIS 497). I'm inclined to go for Kamu, who pulls this huge work together in a particularly dramatic performance.

Concerto Grosso 4/Symphony 5 (1988). A hybrid that sets out to be a concerto grosso becomes a symphony as early as the second movement and never looks back. A very dramatic, exciting, and basically tragic score, it's conducted by **Neeme Järvi** (BIS 427).

6 (1992) reflects Schnittke's late style, in which mass effects give way to an intensely linear style of almost painful clarity and simplicity of texture. It's shorter than the others.

7 (1993). Even shorter, it almost belongs among the Concerti Grossi, with its solos for various instruments, notably the bass tuba. Both are played by **Tadaaki Otaka** and the BBC National Orchestra Wales (BIS 747).The Russian State Symphony under **Poliansky** seems rather put to the test in their version of 7, with sometimes rather shaky tone, though their soloists are good (Chandos 9852).

8 (1994). More expansive, it is 39 minutes long and, like the Mahler 10th, carries us into a disembodied world where the things of this earth stand out with exaggerated clarity but at a distance. If there was ever music that carries us to the edge of infinity and beyond, this is it. **Rozhdestvensky** plays it with great sensitivity (Chandos 9359).

OTHER ORCHESTRAL MUSIC

Apart from the symphonies and concertos, much of Schnittke's orchestral music consists of film scores. There was an interesting collection led by **Emin Khachaturian** (Olympia 606, NA) and another played by the **Moscow Chamber Ensemble** (Triton 17112, NA, with a suite from *Little Tragedies* and other little-known concertante works). Then there is *The Inspector's Tale* (1980), an incidental piece arranged by Rozhdestvensky from a series of satirical projects on works by Gogol. This is a fascinating and funny score recalling similar moods in Shostakovich's early incidental music. It makes up the major portion of a **Rozhdestvensky** disc (Melodiya 32113, NA). **Lev Markiz** gives it a fine reading plus some narration, along with *Labyrinths*, a ballet score from 1971 (BIS 557). *Passacaglia* and *Ritual* are both studies in wave motion and contain massive crescendos, quite terrifying at times, thanks to **Segerstam**'s interpretation and the realistic sound (BIS 437).

K(ein) Sommernachtstraum (1985) is a study in dislocation and horror in which a nice little Schubertian tune gets caught up in some mad adventures with a large bullying orchestra. This work is also played by **Segerstam** (BIS 437); **Polianski** gives it a somewhat less overwhelming performance (Chandos 9722). *Canon* (1985) was based on an occasional work by Berg written in 1930; Schnittke scored it for strings, adding an extra violin line for Mark Lubotsky. It seems to be a straight transcription, but I must confess that without more research I can't say for sure why the version played by **Lubotsky** (Sony 53357) takes less than four minutes while **Kremer** (EMI 55627) takes more than 10. Lubotsky does play it faster, but I can only guess that Kremer must play the entire work twice. It's hard to tell with a 12-tone canon.

CONCERTOS

Dialogue for Cello and Chamber Group (1965). It combines 12-tone, microtonal, and aleatoric techniques in a 13-minute fight between the soloist and a group of winds and percussion, suggesting the hostile relationship between winds and soloist in Violin Concerto 2. It's played by the **Moscow Contemporary Music Group** (Triton 17002) and a trombone version is played by **Christian Lindberg** (BIS 568).

Violin Concerto 2 (1966). A 12-tone work, it is a highly dramatic piece tracing the events leading to the Crucifixion. Its program only came to light since the end of the Soviet era, adding considerable interest to an already unusual piece. It's in **Lubotsky**'s disc (BIS 487), but **Kremer** is equally impressive (Teldec 94540, NA).

Concerto Grosso 1 (1977). One of Schnittke's polystylistic works, and based primarily on his film scores, it has a wildly emotional effect and features two violin soloists. There are two available recordings, in spite of *Schwann Opus,* which has missed Markiz conducting violinists **Christian Bergqvist** and **Patrick Svedrup**, though they list the rest of the disc (BIS 377). The **Turovskys** are even more unbuttoned (Chandos 9590, with music by Pärt and Górecki).

Violin Concerto 3 (1978). Contrasting tonal and atonal music and a large group of winds against a string quartet (the latter only appears in the last movement), this is a moving and unusual piece as performed by **Kremer** (Teldec 94540, NA). **Lubotsky** gives a dark-hued performance (Ondine 893), and it may also be heard played by **Krysa** in a fine reading (BIS 517, with Violin Concerto 4).

Piano Concerto (1979). Sometimes called Piano Concerto 3, it pits the piano against strings in a work of great contrasts of style all subsumed into one movement. **Igor Khudolei** performs it effectively (Chandos 9564), and **Pöntinen** gives a somewhat larger-scaled reading (BIS 377), while **Gothoni** is particularly dark and romantic (Ondine 893). An also-ran is an older recording by **Hana Dvořaková** and Rozhdestvensky, who play the hell out of it in rather uptight orchestral surroundings (Panton 1309). **Constantine Orbelian** and the Moscow Chamber Orchestra are unusually well recorded in an intense performance in a short program with Shostakovich's Chamber Symphony Op. 110a (Delos 3259).

Concerto Grosso 2 (1982). It is larger and funnier than No. 1. Over half an hour long, it's for violin and cello accompanied by a relatively large orchestra including keyboards and percussion. It picks up Bach and "Silent Night" and treats them with considerable virtuosity and venom. The dedicatees, **Kagan** and **Gutman,** give it a marvelous performance under Rozhdestvensky that should be reissued posthaste (Melodiya 10-00068, NA). **Krysa** and **Thedéen** play it almost as well (BIS 567).

Violin Concerto 4 (1984). Both excruciating and touching, it combines the most nostalgic beauty with its most ghastly negations. It's an important piece, like it or not. **Kremer** mixes it with other works chosen to make a point (Teldec 98440). As he says in the liner notes, "We all need Alfred Schnittke and his works. And we need them more with each passing day." **Krysa**'s performance is less harrowing but more beautiful (BIS 517).

Viola Concerto (1985). Giving us a large landscape, less bitter than some, but lonely and full of sadness, the material recalls tonality and its obverse. It's at this point that Schnittke began to turn away from stylistic quotes and to incorporate their emotional impact into his own style. This can result in a lack of contrast, but it doesn't here. **Bashmet,** the dedicatee, plays a gorgeous performance that should be reissued (Melodiya 10-00068, NA). He takes 35 minutes, while **Kashkashian** takes 29 (ECM 1471), and **Isabelle van Keulen** falls in the middle at 33 (Koch 1523). The major discrepancies are in the long, slow, final movement. It seems to me that Kashkashian's high-pressured performance is least convincing; the work is full of intonational discrepancies intended by the composer but needing to sound more emotionally convincing. She gives the uneasy feeling that she really can't play in tune, while both Bashmet and van Keulen make a more clear-cut emotional statement.

Imai is beautifully controlled and expressive, though the orchestral balances are a little overwhelming (BIS 447).

Cello Concerto 1 (1986). This is a wildly dramatic work lasting 40 minutes in which a huge orchestra frequently drowns the soloist in incipient death and destruction. It's a highly emotional and virtuoso piece that **Thedéen** plays with great dramatic flair, despite the attempts of Segerstam and the BIS engineers to stifle him (BIS 507). The sound is very rich and the music desperately emotional. If you want to hear more of the cello part, **Maria Kliegel** is a little closer to the mike (Naxos 554465). You may find you miss BIS's orchestral clout, however. **Gutman,** the dedicatee, gave an outstanding performance with Rozhdestvensky, though the sound is less impressive (Melodiya 00067, NA, with Concerto Grosso 1). She also recorded an equally outstanding performance with Masur (EMI 54443, NA). **Alexander Ivashkin** really sounds as though he's having a heart attack in his recording with Poliansky, with badly tuned high notes and more effort than beauty of tone. This may have been partially deliberate emotionalism, but it's not good listening, particularly since the orchestral balance favors the cello so he didn't have to strain to be heard (Chandos).

Cello Concerto 2 (1990). It redresses the balance problems between soloist and orchestra that make Concerto 1 so difficult. On the other hand, the cello part in 2 is extremely demanding. It's a unified-sounding work despite its length, with less interruption from other periods of music than usual for Schnittke. The earliest recording is by **Thedéen,** a spacious reading taking 45 minutes (BIS 567). **Rostropovich,** the dedicatee, takes 39 (Sony 48241), while **Ivashkin** takes 42 (Chandos 9722). The balances on Thedéen's recording favor the orchestra, while Rostropovich's favors the soloist. Ivashkin's is somewhere in between, perhaps the most satisfactory of both worlds, though Rostropovich, the most overtly virtuosic and intense, has much to recommend it.

Concerto Grosso 6 (1993). Featuring piano and violin, it is more sparely scored than most of Schnittke's previous works. It's also shorter, less than 15 minutes long, and relatively restrained in its emotional pressure. It may be found with **Rozhdestvensky** conducting (Chandos 9359, with Symphony 8). Another fine performance is by **Boughton,** an unexpected but highly effective proponent of this score (Nimbus 5582).

CHAMBER MUSIC

String Quartets. Schnittke's four quartets have been done to a turn by the **Kronos Quartet** (Nonesuch 79500). The **Tale Quartet** recorded the first three in good but relatively traditional performances (BIS 467), while the Kronos shows the bones and the flesh of these works clearly. The only recording that rivals their insights is the **Berg Quartet**'s recording of 4 (EMI 54660, NA).

Serenade for clarinet, violin, double bass, percussion, and piano (1968). This is early Schnittke: partially aleatoric, chaotic in the way Symphony 1 is, and stylistically diverse. It reminds me of Maxwell Davies's nasty pieces for The Fires of London, though the bells and music are clearly from the Eastern bloc. **Capricorn** pulls it off with gusto (Hyperion 66885).

Piano Quintet (1972/1976). A memorial, originally for Schnittke's mother, later for others, it's an extended work in five movements, extending no hope whatever. There are polystylistic elements, but they're used for a serious contrast between memory and consciousness of death. It's a remarkable 26-minute work and has become one of Schnit-

tke's most frequently recorded pieces. In 1979 the composer arranged the work for orchestra, retitling it *In Memoriam.*

Pöntinen and the Tale Quartet are at their serious best here in a rich ambience that comforts while it mourns (BIS 547). **Lubotsky** and Irina Schnittke give us a wilder, more intense reading (Sony 53357). The **Doelen Ensemble** provide a cooler version (Erasmus 170, with other powerful contemporary Russian works), while **Graffman** and the Moscow Quartet show a dramatic flair for this music that's sabotaged by substandard sound (Finer Arts 9804). **Capricorn** plays a beautifully organized reading in excellent sound in an all-Schnittke program (Hyperion 66885).

Schnittke's orchestration is conducted by **Rostropovich** in a clear recording emphasizing the details of the scoring (Sony 48241). **Polianski**'s performance has a more resonant and churchy sound (Chandos 9466). Turning the work from piano and solo strings to a full orchestra with church bells and organ makes it a much more public affair. Perhaps Chandos's sound gives a more consistent effect; on Sony, I find the increasing orchestra in the latter movements a bit off-putting emotionally, if only because the piece starts out as a lament for an individual and Schnittke keeps upping the ante until the organ blasts in. Similar reservations mar my appreciation of **Markiz** (BIS 447). On Chandos we're in church from the beginning and the later violence is therefore better prepared.

String Trio (1985). A curious two-movement piece, it exists also as a piano trio, arranged in 1992, and in a version for string orchestra arranged by Bashmet. Both movements use the same material, notably a kind of sad minuet passage that seems related to the canon by Berg that Schnittke had just scored for string orchestra, though the BIS program notes suggest it may be related to "Happy Birthday." It was commissioned by the Berg Society, so both interpretations may be correct.

Both movements are relatively slow, which leads to some odd discrepancies in timings. **Marinkovic**/Silverthorne/Hugh come out at 15:00 and 10:47 (ASV 868), the **Tale Quartet** at 12:32 and 13:16 (BIS 547), and **Kremer**/Bashmet/Rostropovich at 14:12 and 11:02 (EMI 55627, NA). The Tale push I along a bit, making II appear more retrospective in contrast. **Capricorn** reverses the Tale proportions and plays with compassion in a warm recording (Hyperion 66885). All these are played with conviction but Capricorn has a particularly sensitive balance between passion and ensemble laying.

Lubotsky/Rostropovich/Schnittke play the Piano Trio version, in which the two movements come out almost identical in length (Sony 53271). Since they are the dedicatees, who are we to question them? The string orchestra version is in a disc called "Dolorosa" conducted with particular care by **Dennis Russell Davies** (ECM 1620, with Shostakovich's Chamber Symphony from Quartet 8 and Vasks's *Music Dolorosa*). **Markiz** leads an equally fine reading (BIS 537, with Concerto Grosso 3 and the chamber version of Violin Sonata 1), so let the disc-mates be your guide.

Violin Sonata 1 (1963). It began Schnittke's career with a four-movement piece in which the opening of the slow movement suggests the harmonies of the Passacaglia from Shostakovich's Piano Trio 2. The work is 12-tone in its organization, but the row is a chain of thirds, making it not particularly dissonant. The composer's sense of tragedy and sarcasm is well in evidence, particularly in the masterly orchestration he made of the work in 1968 with lots of harpsichord dryness and strings *col legno.*

There is a somewhat harshly recorded version of all the violin music, with Sonata 3 played with flair by **Mateja Marinkovic** and Linn Hendry

(ASV 868, 877), and an even more intense and better-recorded but not totally in-tune disc by **Valery Gradow** and Inna Heifetz containing Sonatas 1 and 2, *Suite in the Old Style,* and *A Paganini* (Sonora 22579). The same program plus *Gratulationsrondo* and *Stille Nacht* are played by **Wallin** and Pöntinen in fine sound and style (BIS 527). **Christian Bergqvist** also plays Sonata 1 with Pöntinen, and his broad, lyrical reading makes this varied program outstanding (BIS 364, with the Shostakovich Sonata; unfortunately, only the "Dithyramb" from Stravinsky's *Duo Concertant* is included). The orchestrated version is played by **Lubotsky,** the dedicatee (Sony 53271), and by **Bergqvist** in a more resonant but less intense performance (BIS 537). Another fine version is by **Daniel Hope** in a well-filled disc including works by Weill and Takemitsu as well as Schnittke's Concerto Grosso 6 (Nimbus 5582).

Suite in the Old Style. For violin and piano, it was originally from two 1965 film scores, *Adventures of a Dentist* and *Sport, Sport, Sport.* It's imitation baroque almost throughout and could pass for the real thing unless you looked closely. The last movement is the only one that contains a giveaway, though there are other subtly out-of-style moments that contribute to a creepy effect. **Ilya Kaler**'s disc is particularly concise and well played (Arts & Electronics 10572, NA), while **Gradow** is more intense (Sonora 22579). **Marinkovic** is broader and more lyrical than either (ASV 877). **Dmitri Berlinsky** plays it neatly in an attractive light Russian program (Helicon 1015). A version approximating the original scoring but using viola d'amore and harpsichord, vibraphone, marimba, and bells sounds rather more like the composer than the usual violin and piano version, though the viola d'amorist doesn't sound at ease in places (Consonance 810009).

Violin Sonata 2 ("Quasi una Sonata"). This is from 1968, transcribed for chamber orchestra in 1987. It opens with a G minor thwack in the piano that punctuates the 20-minute work at odd moments, rather like the similar thwack opening Stravinsky's *Symphony of Psalms.* The style is basically G minor fighting a 12-tone battle. **Gradow**'s performance is intense and exciting (Sonora 22579), while **Wallin** is more resonant (BIS 527) and **Marinkovic** more leisurely (ASV 877). The orchestral version has many felicities and a few additions; **Lubotsky** is outstanding (Sony 53271).

Gratulationsrondo (1974). It is a seemingly innocuous piece for violin and piano sounding like Schubert with occasional displacements into the 20th century. About 8 minutes in length, it has been recorded by **Kremer** (Teldec 94540), in a more smoothly polished performance by **Lubotsky** (Sony 53271), and at a more leisurely pace by **Wallin** (BIS 527).

Moz-art (1977). Another insouciant little number, it was originally for two violinists, one of whom should be a good whistler. A longer and more complex version with chamber orchestra called *Moz-art a la Haydn* was recorded by **Kremer** with Heinrich Schiff and the Chamber Orchestra of Europe, along with Concerto Grosso 1 and *Quasi una Sonata;* it should be reissued (DG 429413). A lively reading comes from **Wladimir Astrachanzew** and **Marina Skuratovkaja** in a program of Eastern European violin music of the 20th century, including a major sonata by Arno Babadjanian (Cavalli 233).

Cello Sonata 1 (1978). This is the most often recorded of Schnittke's compositions. It's not polystylistic or particularly exaggerated in any direction, sounding closer to late Shostakovich than anything else, and perhaps its relatively mainstream character has attracted cellists. **Thedéen** included it in "The Russian Cello" in a feeling performance, beautifully recorded (BIS 336), and **Jiři Bárta** turns in an even more virtuosic reading (Supraphon 2131). **Ivashkin** gives an uncompromising and dramatic performance (Chandos 9705), and **Xavier Phillips** provides excitingly virtuosic, if musically somewhat stiff readings of the triumvirate of Russian cello sonatas, by Prokofiev, Shostakovich, and Schnittke (Harmonia Mundi 911628).

A Paganini (1982). It is a solo violin piece that begins in a mood of homage and ends with a pile of Paganini fragments separated by dissonant chords. **Marinkovic** (ASV 877) is less frenetic than **Krysa** (BIS 697) and benefits thereby, while **Gradow** (Sonora 22579) makes the most intense effect, if that is desirable.

Epilogue from Peer Gynt (1986). Transcribed for cello, piano, and tape in 1993, **Rostropovich** performs it in a bonus disc of new recordings in his 13CD set "The Russian Years" (EMI). It's a huge 25-minute span in which the cello plays a long and varied cantilena over a piano and a continuous D major triad with variations sung by a distant taped choir. Rostropovich's performance shows some strain in the more emotional, high-register passages and the tape in his recording has a bit of hiss. **Ivashkin** has the same problems of pitch (Chandos 9705), and I miss the straining intensity of Rostropovich as Gynt recalls his life in the ballet score from which this is the epilogue.

Madrigal in memoriam Oleg Kagan (1990). Commemorating the death of that fine violinist, it is another of the series of solo memorials based on the name of the recipient. It's for violin or cello, and both versions may be found, played by **Krysa** and **Thedéen** (BIS 697). The violin version is also played by **Marinkovic** (ASV 877). Despite its violinistic origin, Thedéen makes the best case for this lyrical piece; his high register climax is most convincing.

Cello Sonata 2 (1994). This is an austere and abstract five-movement work written for **Rostropovich** and played by him in "The Russian Years" (EMI). He's a little more volatile than **Ivashkin,** who concentrates on manner rather than matter (Chandos 9705), while Rostropovich sounds totally committed.

Violin Sonata 3 (1994). It is an intense, linear piece, almost disembodied, like the late symphonies. **Lubotsky** gives a marvelous performance (Ondine 893).

PIANO MUSIC

Schnittke's works for piano have been recorded by **Boris Berman** (Chandos 9704, 8962). Sonata 1 (1987) is nearly half an hour long, tragic and angry, ending with the player falling on the keyboard. **Vasily Lobanov** played the Moscow premiere, and his recording is highly charged, a bit harsh in the highest register, but that repeated note at the beginning is the only really painful moment (Consonance 810009). It's coupled with a really odd rescoring of *Suite in Olden Style* and Shostakovich's Piano Concerto 1 with Mikhail Petukov. Berman is more resonantly recorded, though a little less intense.

Sonata 2 is dramatic in character, perhaps better served by **Irina Schnittke,** whose somewhat more hard-edged tone and more volatile reading (Sony 53271) hold the listener's attention better than Berman. Berman's disc, however, is warmer in sound.

CHORAL MUSIC

Requiem (1972–1975). For choir, four soprano soloists, a mezzo, a tenor, 2 trumpets, electric guitar, electric bass, keyboards, and percussion, it originated when Schnittke's mother died in 1972 but didn't get organized until the composer wrote music for a production of Schiller's *Don Carlos* in 1975. The music is a curious cross between incidental music and a requiem mass. **Polianski** gives a resonant and beautiful performance (Chandos 9564), but **Tonu Kaljuste** pulls this somewhat rambling structure together even more effectively (Caprice 21515), only to be further upstaged by **Kamu**'s even tighter version (BIS 497).

Concerto for Chorus (1984–1985). An a cappella work with words by the 10th-century Armenian poet Gregory of Narek, it is devotional in nature. Although its harmonic language is much more dissonant, the mood is that of the Russian orthodox choral tradition we know from Rachmaninoff's *Vespers*. **Parkman** is excellent (Chandos 9126, with *Minnesang*). Chandos competes with itself, also offering **Polianski**'s view of this work, a little more resonant in ambiance but not as clear in detail as Parkman's, and it has no discmate, making a very short, 44-minute disc (Chandos 9332).

Penitential Psalms (1988). It shares the general liturgical world of Concerto for Chorus, though there's more variety of expression and word painting in Schnittke's settings of these ancient and moving poems. The last number is a wordless vocalise. **Parkman** conducts a beautifully balanced performance (Chandos 9480, with the also wordless *Voices of Nature*). **Kaljuste** takes a little longer and gets even farther inside this strangely archaic but totally untraditional music (ECM 1583).

OPERAS

Life With an Idiot (1991). This is a setting of a short story by Viktor Erefyev, like the composer an anti-Soviet figure who was never able to get published until Gorbachev came along. It tells of a couple who are being punished (presumably by the government) by having to take in an idiot to live with them. The husband hopes to find something in the nature of the traditional "holy fool," but what he ends up with is a man who can say nothing but "Ekh!" and yet manages to bring both the man and his wife down to his level. The opera ends, as we know from the beginning, with the man in the asylum and the wife dead. This is a grisly commentary on the way Soviet equality and repression worked and is handled in a suitably nightmarish way by Schnittke. The singers are required to perform superhuman—or is it subhuman—feats, spending half their time in the falsetto register and an appreciable amount of time vocalising on the syllable "Ekh!"

Rostropovich conducts the Netherlands Opera in the only recording (Sony 52495, 2CD). Not for the faint of heart.

Historia von D. Johann Fausten (1983/1992). This is a central work in the composer's output. It sets a version of the tale written by Johann Spies and published in 1587; the text is in German, bringing Schnittke back to his ancestral roots. The music is austere, with much reference to the *klangfarben* style of melodic disjuncture. There are a narrator and a chorus that plays various roles including Lucifer. Its rather abstract setting breaks down musically at Faust's death, which is accompanied by a raunchy tango. In the context of Schnittke's total output, this seemingly undramatic work (the last act has been around since 1983 as a *Faust Cantata*) is important and full of singular resonances. Faust's three "Laments" turn up in Schnittke's Symphony 6, and, despite the work's deliberately static, archaic quality, it's singularly moving.

The only recording is by the Hamburg State Philharmonic conducted by **Albrecht** (RCA 68413, 2CD). There is evidence that the opera isn't complete, that there is more material that may be recorded at some point, but nothing of this sort is even hinted at in the notes to this production. Be that as it may, it's a convincing performance, considerably more dramatic and well characterized than the third act performed by **DePreist** as *Faust Cantata* (BIS 437).

SONGS

Three Madrigals (1980). A setting of poems by Francisco Tanzer, and sung in three languages, it is quietly cautionary love poetry scored for soprano, violin, viola, double bass, harpsichord, and vibraphone. *Sarah Leonard* performs them with Capricorn and sings it all with musical understanding (Hyperion 66885). The different styles in which Schnittke hears the different languages are fascinating.   MOORE

Othmar Schoeck (1886–1957)

Schoeck studied music in Zurich, then with Reger in Leipzig, and thereafter returned to work as a conductor, accompanist, and composer in his native Switzerland. He's known primarily for his more than 400 songs, though he also wrote eight operas and some instrumental music. Although he began in the Romantic tradition of Schubert, Schumann and Wolf, his works of the '20s show a fondness for experiment and betray the influence of Stravinsky, Hindemith, and others.

His instrumental music doesn't match his vocal music in quality, although his early, Brahmsian Violin Concerto has enjoyed several recordings. The finest is by **Ulf Hoelscher** and the English Chamber Orchestra conducted by Howard Griffiths, with orchestral Serenade Op. 1 and Suite for Strings, op. 59 (♦Novalis 150070). There's also an archival recording with the work's dedicatee Stefi Geyer, with a remarkable live recording of **Dennis Brain** playing Schoeck's Horn Concerto under **Paul Sacher** (Jecklin 715). Schoeck's most popular orchestral work is the tone poem *A Summer's Night* for strings; here again, the recording by Griffiths and the ECO is the finest, coupled with the two short but intense instrumental song cycles *Gaselen* and *Wandersprüche*, with Nathan Berg and Jörg Hering, respectively(♦Novalis 150106).

Schoeck's complete violin sonatas receive as good a reading as they are likely to get from **Paul Barritt** accompanied by **Catherine Edwards** (♦Guild Music 7142). The complete piano music has been recorded by **Jean Louis Steuerman** (MGB 6146), the complete string quartets by the **Minguet Quartet** (MD+G 6030665).

Schoeck's expressionistic operatic masterpiece *Penthesilea* (after Heinrich von Kleist) has enjoyed several recent productions and two CD recordings. **Albrecht** conducts the ORF Choir and Symphony and has a magnificent cast including Dernesch and Adam (♦Orfeo 364942). **Mario Venzago**'s recording can't match Albrecht's soloists or his dramatic intensity, but he allows more of the score's detail to be heard (Pan 510118).

Venzago and the excellent Swiss Philharmonic Workshop Orchestra achieve a rare luminosity in Schoeck's earlier opera *Venus*, with Popp, James O'Neal, and Skovhus in the main roles (♦MGB 6112). Excerpts from the 1943 world premiere of Schoeck's final opera, *Das Schloss Dürande*, are led by **Heger** with the orchestra and choir of the Berlin State Opera and an all-star cast including Anders, Cebotari, Willi Domgraf-Fassbaender, Fuchs, and Greindl (♦Jecklin 692).

A complete edition of Schoeck's songs with piano accompaniment is available on 12 CDs (♦Jecklin 671-82). This set offers an impressive international spectrum of singers and accompanists, including Banse, Nathan Berg, Bostridge, Dawson, Julius Drake, and Cornelia Kallisch, but also equally fine Swiss artists like Christoph Keller (piano) and Niklaus Tüller (baritone). For those seeking a smaller-scale introduction to Schoeck's art, the best is the anthology made by **Fischer-**

Dieskau and Margrit Weber shortly after the composer's death (♦DG 463513). F-D was never in better voice, and never had a better accompanist. Also on this CD are Schoeck's Hesse songs, recorded with Karl Engel in 1977.

Fischer-Dieskau's other recordings are also highly recommended, such as the song books *Unter Sternen, Das stille Leuchten,* and *Das holde Bescheiden,* all with Hartmut Höll at the piano (Claves 50-8606, 50-8910m, and 50-9308/09, respectively). But one of the best is his early recording of the orchestral song cycle *Lebendig begraben,* with Fritz Rieger conducting the Berlin Radio Symphony Orchestra (♦Claves 50-8610). The subject matter may be morbid—it's the monologue of a man buried alive—but its subtlety of text-setting and instrumentation, combined with its mastery of large-scale form, make it one of Schoeck's most extraordinary works. Fischer-Dieskau sings the baritone version made for him by the composer; the original, more claustrophobic bass version was recorded by **Günter von Kannen** in fine voice, accompanied by the Zurich Opera Orchestra conducted by Ralf Weikert (Atlantic 96 205). Schoeck himself was one of the finest song accompanists of his day, as proven by "Othmar Schoeck plays Othmar Schoeck," in which he accompanies **Haefliger** and others (♦Jecklin 714). WALTON

Arnold Schoenberg *(1874–1951)*

Schoenberg is still known by many people (inaccurately) as a composer of harsh, atonal, music. His reputation as a difficult composer comes from the mystique surrounding the 12-tone technique he developed, but while some of his music does need to be listened to carefully, once it becomes familiar the harshness disappears.

After he wrote his first great works in late Romantic style, Schoenberg became concerned about where music—including his own—was going. He realized that the combination of Brahms's rhythmic complexity and Wagner's expansion of chromatic harmony from an expressive device into an environment for a whole piece was leading to the end of the traditional harmonic-rhythmic structure of Western music, and that there was no obvious way for music to move forward from that crisis. His solution was to create a new method of organizing music: A work would be based upon a selection of twelve notes (a tone row) that would be used in a set order. This technique would be a tool for composers and not something for average audiences to know or worry about, any more than churchgoers in Renaissance Flanders cared about canons and inversions built into the music at the services, or listeners to Beethoven symphonies realized what he was doing with sonata form.

Unfortunately, it didn't quite work that way. Although the 12-tone method produced such masterpieces as the unfinished opera *Moses und Aron* and the Wind Quintet, general writing about music was more literate earlier in the century than now (though no less vituperative) and Schoenberg's many enemies made sure the image of "Schoen-bug" (with connotations of noisy, unpleasant music created according to a mad professor's system) was widely disseminated in the intellectual and popular press. The result was that people were so busy debating the compositional method that they barely paid attention to the music. In the fuss, a number of very accessible tonal and nontonal works got lost, including Chamber Symphony 2, Suite for String Orchestra, and *A Survivor from Warsaw.*

Although Schoenberg's music can be easy to understand and appreciate, it's seldom easy to perform. Like many other composers in the early 20th century, he expected a lot from his musicians and the general level of playing (and conducting) has only recently caught up to his demands. This means that most older Schoenberg recordings are compromises, the best that could be done with limited technique, rehearsal time, and understanding.

ORCHESTRAL MUSIC

Chamber symphonies. No. 1 is a remarkable combination of symphony and Lisztian tone-poem, full of energy and spooky-erotic atmosphere; it has become a standard repertory item. Good versions are by **Holliger** (Teldec 46019, with Berg's Chamber Concerto); **de Leeuw** (Koch-Schwann 31100, with various chamber piece arrangements); **Eötvös,** an especially wild reading (RCA); and an **Orpheus** disc with *Verklärte Nacht* (DG 429233).

No. 2, with its Mahlerish slow movement, is available in excellent versions from **Holliger** (Teldec 77314, with *Verklärte Nacht*), **Orpheus** (DG, see above), and as filler to **Boulez**'s fine performance of *Moses und Aron* (Sony). Boulez is fine in all of Schoenberg's orchestral works, especially the earlier BBC recordings that have been reissued by Sony, and **Karajan,** not an obvious conductor for this music, recorded (at his own expense) a magnificent three-disc set of Schoenberg, Berg, and Webern pieces (once DG 423249, now MHS 534926).

Five Orchestral Pieces. These compress a world of atmosphere into a few moments of stunning orchestral color. **Boulez** (Sony 48463) and **Dohnányi** (London 436240, with a fine Mahler 6) are both outstanding. The playing from the Cleveland Orchestra is amazing in its range of colors and precision.

Pelleas und Melisande. **Karajan** leads the recommendations for this lush Straussian tone-poem, and his recording is conveniently coupled with *Verklärte Nacht* (DG 457721). There's strong competition: **Barbirolli** is equally dramatic, more romantic, but less well played (EMI), and **Mehta** has the best recording of all, and a good, more generalized account of the piece (♦Sony 45870). Two Chicago versions are also worth noting: **Boulez,** clear and compelling (Erato), and **Barenboim,** hyper-romantic but a little studied (Teldec).

Suite for String Orchestra. A shapely and winning work, it is seldom performed. There's no outstanding version available, but a good stopgap with the **German Chamber Philharmonic** makes the loss a little easier to bear (Virgin 59018).

Verklärte Nacht (Transfigured Night). This was based on what was considered a lurid poem by Richard Dehmel. The conservative musical authorities were shocked by this piece and it wasn't until 1903, four years after it was written, that it got performed—and was violently rejected by the public. It has since become a beloved and popular composition, in both its original sextet and the string orchestra versions. **Karajan** is very good in the orchestral version, though the sound is a little dry; he captures the warmth and sweep of the piece as nobody else has (DG has reissued this with *Pelleas, see* above, and the set it came from is on MHS). The chamber orchestra version has a number of worthy readings. The **Orpheus** disc is admirable and comes with good performances of both chamber symphonies (DG 429233).

For the string sextet version, the **Juilliard Quartet** with Trampler and Ma puts aside its usual astringent tone and tense music making and gives a lovely reading in a lustrous recording (♦Sony 47690). The **Arditti** version is also worthy, but comes as part of an expensive 2CD set (Montaigne). There's a recording by the **Smithsonian Chamber Players** that attempts to recreate the style of playing Schoenberg would have expected when he wrote the piece (Harmonia Mundi). It's an interesting exercise, though less vital than the playing really in that style by Mengelberg and Bruno Walter included in the disc.

CONCERTOS

Piano. **Brendel** gives a uniquely joyful reading, worth getting despite the routine performances of the chamber symphonies that come with it (Philips 446683). **Ax** is good as well (Sony 53289), as is Brendel's older reading (DG). **Pollini** is less compelling (DG). There are recordings by **Gould** in circulation (CBC and various semi-private labels). Of these, the New York recording with Mitropoulos is probably the best, but the sound quality may be an obstacle (Memories). There was a fine recording by **Peter Serkin** with Boulez, but it seems to have disappeared (Erato).

Violin. A worthy but underplayed work. **Zvi Zeitlin** offers the best modern version (DG 431740, with Brendel's Piano Concerto), although the deleted **Amoyal**/Boulez combination (with Peter Serkin's reading of the Piano Concerto) was a fine alternative (Erato).

CHAMBER MUSIC

Phantasy for violin and piano. This lyrical, capricious, but brainy piece has had inadequate interpreters on commercial recordings, aside from the fine performance embedded in the **Arditti Quartet**'s Schoenberg series (Montaigne 782025) and a technically shaky but musically earnest reading from **Menuhin** and **Gould** (Sony).

Quartets. The most famous is 2, with its haunting soprano solo, but they're all worth hearing and become richer and more communicative with repeated listening. With those of Bartók and Shostakovich, these are the greatest quartets of this century. Of the complete sets, **LaSalle** has wiry playing and sour tone (DG). Spend the extra money for the **Arditti** (Montaigne 782024). Excellent individual performances come from the **New Leipzig Quartet** (MD+G 3462) and the **Pražák Quartet** (Praga 250112/1).

The **Arditti Quartet** has recorded a valuable series of performances of everything, published or not, that Schoenberg wrote for string chamber groups (Montaigne 789011). A multi-disc set of chamber music was recorded in the early '70s by the **London Sinfonietta** under David Atherton (Decca LP). Most of these performances haven't been matched, including a riveting Wind Quintet and a wonderfully intense Chamber Symphony 1, but they never made it either to this country or to CD reissue, except for some odds and ends.

Trio for violin, viola, and cello. A powerful, introverted piece, this has had few recordings and fewer adequate ones. Avoid the **LaSalle** recording for the reasons given above. The **Schoenberg Ensemble** are decent (Philips, with Violin Phantasy and *Verklärte Nacht*). The **Juilliard Quartet** on an old disc with Schoenberg's recording of *Pierrot Lunaire* are intense but abrasive (Sony). Their opposites are the **Vienna String Trio**, who are warm and lyrical but a little out of touch with the underlying intensity of the music (Calig). The great recording of this piece has yet to be made, but the **Arditti** is pretty close (Montaigne 782025).

Wind Quintet. As long as Beethoven's 9th and, when you get to know it, as riveting, this work isn't in great shape on current discs. The **London Sinfonietta** recording mentioned above was available here briefly but seems to be NA now (London 433083). A few recordings have come and gone since, but none that made much of an impression.

PIANO MUSIC

These mostly cryptic pieces are superbly recorded by **Pollini**, with excellent playing and at mid-price (DG 423249), **Paul Jacobs** with more passion (Nonesuch 71309), and less coherently but with lots of technique and personality by **Claude Helffer** (Harmonia Mundi).

CHORAL MUSIC

Gurrelieder. This large and lush post-Straussian cantata tells the legend of a Danish king and the tragic outcome of his love for a young woman. **Chailly** can be recommended, mostly for his strong cast (a disappointing soprano aside) and fine recorded sound (London 430321). This remains the safest general recommendation. **Inbal** is a more imaginative and ultimately more powerful conductor, but his singers are less individual (Denon 9066). **Boulez** is sturdy, but lacking a sense of romantic wonder (Sony). **Claudio Abbado** has the Vienna Philharmonic, but some all-too-human singers, with a fallible tenor, a squally soprano, and a female speaker (good idea) who overacts painfully (bad idea) (MHS).

Stokowski made a recording of the piece in 1932; the sound is obviously less than ideal, but the sweep of the performance comes through (various labels). **Kubelik** has his moments, but has older recorded sound (DG). **Ozawa** (Philips) and **Sinopoli** (Teldec) are eminently missable, one bland and the other eccentric. **Kegel** (Berlin) is lyrical and leisurely, with a wobbly tenor, and **Mehta** (Sony) is nothing special.

A Survivor from Warsaw. This lean and powerful melodrama has had a number of worthy performances. In fact, like Beethoven's 5th, it seems immune to performance quality. The performances by **Reich** with Boulez (Sony 44571, 2CD, with various choral works) and by **Hornik** with Abbado (DG 431774) are both worthy. There was an old **Leinsdorf** recording of limited musical value that achieved stunning power by having a mediocre performance of Beethoven's 9th on the same disc, with its opening measures following the end of the Schoenberg piece after a few moments of silence (RCA).

VOCAL MUSIC

Ode to Napoleon. A nasty piece, using Byron's poetry to call Hitler names; Schoenberg was good at scorn, but it didn't come off well in this music. The best recording is by **Thomas Allen** with the Nash Ensemble (Virgin 91478). It comes with Webern's arrangement of Chamber Symphony 1 for small ensemble and a goodish string sextet version of *Verklärte Nacht*. **Wilson-Johnson** and Boulez are good as well (Sony 48463).

Pierrot Lunaire. This piece, with its odd bridge between speech and song and remarkable use of five instruments, caused as much of a stir in the musical world as Stravinsky's *Rite of Spring,* written at around the same time. There are lots of recordings with many different approaches to the sung-versus-spoken issue, but very few good ones. **Minton**/Boulez is the best sung and the most appealing (Sony 48466). It comes with Jessye Norman's "Song of the Wood Dove" (more like the condor in this rendition) and a good *Erwartung*. Others worth hearing are **Bryn-Julson** (better in her New York performance on GM than in Germany for RCA), **Sukowa** (Koch-Schwann), **de Gaetani** (Nonesuch), and **Jane Manning** with the young Simon Rattle (Chandos). Also don't overlook the strange but compelling version by **Erika Stiedry-Wagner** under Schoenberg's direction (Sony 45695).

Erwartung (Expectation). This expressionistic soliloquy for soprano and orchestra is given a lush reading by **Norman** and Levine (Philips 423231), an interesting contrast to the leaner, more high-strung **Silja** and Dohnányi (London 417348, with Berg's *Wozzeck*). Both are fine.

OPERA

Moses und Aron. The first **Boulez** (Sony 48456) is better than the second (DG). **Solti** is exciting, amazingly well played and recorded, but less satisfying over time (London 414264). CHAKWIN

Franz Schreker (1878–1934)

Schreker represented a modernist blend of post-Straussian romanticism and impressionism. Possibly the most frequently performed opera composer of his generation, his operas used huge ensembles with lush sensuality, shimmering strings, harps, and celeste. His popularity peaked before WWI but waned with the rejection of romanticism after 1922. He responded with a sparer style, but the Nazis discouraged performances of his works and cost the part-Jewish composer his directorship of the Berlin Hochschule für Musik. He died a broken man, and his music disappeared for decades. Some contemporaries considered Schreker either too modern or an uninspired tonesmith whose opulence led him to excess and lurid plots. Today, I hear these weaknesses as virtues and find him representative of 20th-century German music at its most luminous.

Chamber Symphony for 23 Solo Instruments. A lyrical, sparkling rhapsody, it is full of singing lines; colorful, shifting, and shimmering harmonies; and bubbling woodwinds. **Gielen** brings out its modern nature, with the exposed parts cleanly taken; more warmth and molding would have made it special (Koch Schwann 311078, with *Prelude to a Drama;* also *Night Interlude* from *Der ferne Klang* and *Valse Lente* led by Rickenbacher). **Welser-Möst's** romance and darkness supply warmth Gielen lacks but he's not as sparkling (♦EMI 56813, with Schubert's "Death and the Maiden" Quartet as orchestrated by Mahler).

Prelude to a Drama "Die Gezeichneten." This is a suite from the opera, combining the prelude with later material (not to be confused with *Prelude to a Great Drama*). **Sinaisky** and the BBC Philharmonic are slow, warm, and glistening here and in the couplings, to make up the lushest, most sensual Schreker disc I know (♦Chandos 9797, with *Valse lente, Ekkehard;* Symphonic Interlude from *Der Schatzgraber; Night Music* from *Der ferne Klang; Fantastic Overture*). **Gielen** is faster, leaner, more dramatic, incisive, and modern, if not quite as seductive or sensual (♦Koch Schwann 311078, with *Chamber Symphony, Night Interlude,* and *Valse Lente* conducted by Rickenbacher). **Conlon** and the Cologne Philharmonic are less coherent and lack the sumptuous tone this music needs (EMI 56784 with *Intermezzo, Prelude to a Great Drama*).

Der Geburtstag der Infanta. A dance pantomime for orchestra (on the Oscar Wilde fairy tale), it was Schreker's first major work. Its elegant dances make for a lovely combination of color, grace, drama, and opulence. **Jürgen Bruns** leads the original chamber orchestra version with fast tempos and light, lively, and transparent textures (♦EDA 13, with Toch's *Dance Suite*). **Albrecht** leads a glorious reading of the large orchestral suite (minus one scene and the original ending); his slower tempos work beautifully (♦Koch 6591, with *Der Weib der Intaphernes*). **Zagrosek's** Suite is rushed and less gripping and beautiful (London 44182, with Hindemith's *Der Dämon* and Erwin Schulhoff's *Mondsuchtige*).

Prelude to a Great Drama. This was for *Memnon,* a planned opera on an Egyptian subject. It's a fervent piece of lavish romanticism, with exoticisms and color. **Uwe Mund** is full-blooded and dramatic, emphasizing the Orientalisms, woodwinds, and percussion; close recording adds to the lively effect. His *Romantic Suite* is just as attractive (♦Marco Polo 220469, with *Intermezzo, Romantic Suite*). **Peter Ruzicka** is slower, smaller-scaled, and more etched (♦Koch 36454, with *Irrelohe Preludes; Four Little Pieces for Full Orchestra;* and *From Eternal Life*). He's less ample in the strings, less Oriental, and his textures aren't as meaty. The effect is intimate and more academically Germanic. The couplings are the only recordings of fascinating music. **Conlon** is livelier than Ru-

zicka, less colorful and red-blooded than Mund, but not as good as either, though better than in his *Prelude to a Drama* (EMI 56784, with *Prelude to a Drama; Intermezzo;* and *Romantic Suite*).

Der Weib der Intaphernes. It is a melodrama for narrator and orchestra on a Herodotus tale of perversion and treachery. It's in Schreker's late terse style and dominated by story and narrator. **Albrecht** is dramatic, involving, and exciting, with a female narrator, as Schreker specified (the wife is the speaker). The Deutsches Symphonie-Berlin plays with panache and color (♦Koch 6591, with *Der Geburtstag der Infanta*). **Gülke** is more romantic but less dramatic and colorful with the Cologne Radio Orchestra. His male narrator is less appropriate and a bit over the top (♦Capriccio 850, with Symphony 1; Psalm 116). The lack of a translation is a drawback to both. The Symphony and the Brucknerian Psalm are fine early works, the former resembling an early Dvořák Symphony; the latter, for 3-part woman's chorus and orchestra, is part exalted prelude, part exciting fugue.

OPERAS

Der ferne Klang. Schreker's first operatic success is lyrical, beyond Strauss with its French touches, but short of Berg, with youthful ardor and a seamy, romantic plot of love found too late. **Albrecht** is supple and atmospheric, with a nice open sound from the Berlin Radio Symphony (♦Capriccio 60024, 2CD). Soprano Gabriele Schnaut acts well and has a nice dark voice but can be shrill. Tenor Thomas Moser, another good actor, can be hollow, and he too strains. The supporting cast is excellent; the recording is well blended, large in scale, and atmospheric. **Halász** is blunt, square, and he hurries phrases (Marco Polo 223270, 2CD). Neither Elena Grigorescu nor Thomas Harper acts as well as Albrecht's leads, but they're better vocally; the supporting cast is less good. The sound is closer and more detailed, but not as atmospheric or involving. Capriccio supplies a German-only libretto, Marco Polo none. I prefer Capriccio's assets of better sound, drama, conducting, sense of occasion, and involvement to Marco Polo's superior (but not flawless) vocalism and greater intimacy.

Die Gezeichneten Schreker's most opulent opera is set in Italy, the orchestration is full and colorful, and the melodies are exotic and heady, with a touch of Puccini. **Zagrosek** conducts with a sense of color and pace, producing a dramatic, sensuous opera, with sound to match (♦London 444442, 3CD). He's best with the big orchestra parts, helped by an expansive Deutsches Symphonie-Berlin, and the soloists are solid. **De Waart's** Dutch Radio recording is smaller scaled, darker, and more intimate, with a velvet beauty all its own (♦Marco Polo 223328, 3CD). The covered sound adds to the effect. Marilyn Schmiege and William Cochran sound older than their London competition, with Cochran disturbingly woofy. Marco Polo cuts 20 minutes from the last act. London is the choice, but both are worthwhile.

Irrelohe. This one adds trenchant harmony to Schreker's romanticism. The flamboyant plot, with curses, revenge, rape, idealistic love, along with scenes of a castle towering over the village, nobles raping their village-girl brides, and the castle burning at the end, presages silent horror films. The image of fire is dominant. This is a huge, colorful, dramatic opera; much is symphonic, with beautiful preludes and interludes. **Peter Gülke** conducts a fine performance with a good if not great cast, though it could use more shaping, as well as more control from the Vienna Symphony brass (♦Sony 66850, 2CD).

Der Schatzgräber. In Schreker's most popular and balanced opera, he coordinates the opulent with the classical by putting music at the service of drama. The libretto is more wordy than usual, and the moody score is filled with subtle musical references to themes, characters, and events. It's less experimental and daring than *Die ferne Klang,* less lush and more pungent than *Die Gezeichneten,* and less dramatic and powerful than *Irrelohe.* There are many fine lyrical moments. **Albrecht**'s reading is very good (◆Capriccio 60010, 2CD). Schnaut is impressively big but shrill; Protschka is excellent.

SONGS

Many of Schreker's student works resemble Schubert lieder, but signs of the mature composer are present (◆Channel, Vol. 1, 12098). Soprano **Ofelia Sala,** mezzo Anne Buter, baritone Jochen Kupfer, and pianist Reinild Mees are splendid, though Sala wails in some louder passages. Nice.

Five Songs are dark, almost impressionistic, touching upon Debussy's *Pelléas and Mélisande* and beyond toward atonality, with slow tempos and a good deal of low voice. **Ortrun Wenkel**'s rich alto is perfect for this treatment of separation, loneliness, and death (◆Schwann LP, with *The Wind* and *Night Interlude*). *The Wind,* for small chamber ensemble (conducted by Rickenbacher), is a delicate set of skittery breezes, tinted with colorful modern harmonies.   HECHT

Franz Schubert *(1797–1828)*

Because Schubert died so young, displaying so little manly heroism in either his music or his pudgy frame, he was long seen as a Boy Innocent. Gradually over the years, however, his music has revealed more and more substance behind his amazing facility. Where earlier musicians were content to savor his breathtaking shifts of harmony and the sweetness of his lovely melodies, now we see more passion and turmoil in his music. This change probably says more about our penchant for seeing the world psychologically than it does about Schubert. Whatever the reason, we're taking Schubert more seriously than in the past. Perhaps the Viennese had it right in their axiom that music like Schubert's should be experienced with one eye wet, the other dry. In Schubert's works opposing forces—major vs. minor, lyrical vs. painful—merge with the subtlety and complexity of life itself.

SYMPHONIES

The standard number of Schubert symphonies is eight, numbered 1–6 and 8–9. The "Great" C Major was originally No. 7 in Breitkopf's *Critical Edition* (edited by Brahms in 1885), but it was written later than No. 8, the "Unfinished," and has become known as No. 9. The situation is further muddied by several sketches of individual movements that turned up after Schubert's death. To simplify a complicated situation, we now have two additional works: a Symphony in E, which has been reconstructed and sometimes labeled as No. 7, and another fragment in D, thought to be from mid-1828 and reconstructed by Brian Newbould as No. 10. The so-called "Gmunden-Gastein" symphony is either an orchestration of the Grand Duo for piano, four hands, or it may be the symphony we call the Ninth. And finally, a recent edition has renumbered the symphonies, making No. 8 into No. 7 and moving No. 9 up to eighth position. These new numbers are reflected on some recent issues, so use care when shopping. Here we will use the traditional numbering: 8 is the "Unfinished," and 9 is the C Major.

Most listeners know only 8 and 9, and understandably so. These are the mature compositions that show Schubert at the height of his powers. The earlier works, however, are not inconsequential. From 1, written in 1813 when the composer was 16, to 6, written only about five years later, we can find examples of Schubert's wonderful lyrical gift and his sure command of harmony. He certainly knew Beethoven's music at this time, but his models seem to be the earlier Viennese generation of Haydn and Mozart. He finds a more original voice in the final symphonies, and indeed they are finer works. In truth, though, we can hardly call 8 and 9 late works, for they were written by a young man. Consider that Schubert completed his last symphony at the age of 29; when Beethoven was that age, he was beginning work on his first symphony. Who can imagine what music this astonishing man might have produced, given a normal life span?

Complete sets. The field here is limited because so many sets (defined as 1–6, 8–9) are not presently available. Conductors like Karajan, Marriner, Muti, Sawallisch, Barenboim, Groves, Munchinger, Mehta, Kertész, Colin Davis, and Vaughan have recorded complete editions that are missing from the catalog; occasional mention will be made of some deleted issues in the expectation that they will reappear. Years ago, Schubert was played exclusively by full-sized orchestras that usually stressed the lyricism and romantic warmth of the music. In time, influenced no doubt by the period instrument movement and the greater attention given to the earlier, more classical symphonies, performances became quicker, steadier of tempo, taut, and less sentimental. Schubert, instead of being a vessel of all that is good and beautiful, now reflects more angst and psychological depth. Fortunately the catalog is rich enough to support any taste (and allows us to sample differing viewpoints).

The roster of traditional performances is represented solely by **Böhm**'s set with the Berlin Philharmonic (◆DG 419318). His Schubert is unfailingly warm and lovely, well-scaled in the early symphonies and capped by very fine readings of the "Unfinished" and 9. Some may find his conducting too serious in the earlier works, but no one can deny the affectionate elegance of Böhm and his orchestra. You sense the loving hand of a conductor who sees Schubert as wise and mature rather than young and impetuous. These works were recorded in the late '60s and early '70s, but still sound wonderful.

The list of large-scale versions is weakened by the absence of **Karajan** and **Barenboim,** two conductors who were able to combine lightness and delicacy with rich, romantic warmth. Karajan's recordings in particular have long been favorites with many listeners. Rather than scaling down the early works, he used the full complement of Berlin Philharmonic strings and gave performances that were big and grand, a clear step away from the Haydn symphonies they somewhat resemble. These recordings have been sold in complete sets and, until recently, were available separately from EMI (some individual issues are still in the catalog); should the set reappear, it would certainly be recommended.

Another deleted set to seek out came from **Colin Davis** (RCA). If you prefer a less imposing sound for the early symphonies, Davis will seem more stylish than Böhm or Karajan. He uses a modern orchestra to good effect (as he did in the late Haydn symphonies) and brings a flexibility and spirit to early Schubert that seem natural and unaffected, though he's occasionally inclined to push the music too hard. His 8 is controlled and serene, not giving way to extremes of drama, but bittersweet in mood. His 9, though, is saddled with more repeats than the music really needs, lasting about 62 minutes. Should his set return, it would be recommended, but buyers should supplement it with another 9.

We have two fine sets that seek a kind of middle ground, eschewing both the full-sized, big-name orchestras and the more modern view.

The best of these is by **Claudio Abbado** conducting the Chamber Orchestra of Europe (♦DG 23651). Here the extremes of the large symphony orchestra and the reconstructed sounds of period instruments are met halfway: modern instruments playing crisply but with slight adjustments of tempo and agreeable romantic detail. As with Davis, the first six symphonies fare better than the last two, though occasionally (e.g., 4:I) the playing tends to be dull. The later symphonies are certainly very good, but many will want a sharper interpretive profile. Abbado has the further advantage of up-to-date scholarship, reached by a thorough study of the manuscripts, with results that range from small details to the omission of measures long thought to be authentic.

Another fine set, crisply modern but not obsessive or driven, is **Viotti**'s with the Saarbrücken Orchestra (♦Claves 9700). He adopts generally light, fast tempos, but the music isn't pushed and Schubert's lyrical graciousness isn't lost. These offerings from a little-known conductor and orchestra are beautifully recorded, and some are available separately. The other end of the spectrum is covered by **Harnoncourt**, who conducts the Concertgebouw (Teldec 91184). This is, of course, not a small band, but he treats it like a period instrument group. The brass playing is incisive, not heroic or soothing, and string vibrato is spare. The effect is chilling and serious, far different from Böhm, who is serious in a kindly, grandfatherly way; some have described Harnoncourt's Schubert as grim. This may be a useful antidote for those who want to purge the sugar from Schubert. The results are thoughtful and revealing, though most will prefer more geniality than is found here.

At present we have no sets using period instruments. The first such, completed in 1990, was led by **Goodman** and may well reappear (Nimbus). To his credit, he didn't equate period instruments with excessive speed and mannered playing. With Goodman, you often forget that the instruments are period but the performances are often bland and — unusual for such versions — not very clearly recorded.

1. Written in 1813 when Schubert was 16, it is a remarkably assured effort considering his tender age. The music has wonderful variety: a ceremonial slow introduction, a slow movement reminiscent of Mozart, an energetic minuet/scherzo (called simply Allegro), and a fleet finale. It's probably a little longer than it needs to be, but there are no false steps, no moments that betray the composer's youth and inexperience. If you want a big approach, one that makes no apologies for the age of the composer, it would be wise to wait for a **Karajan** reissue. This (with 2) is among the finest of all his Schubert. He treats the music seriously and makes it sound important.

For those wanting a lighter-weight version, the top choice is also unavailable: **Beecham**'s legendary recording of 1 and 2 (Columbia LP). He was able to inject spirit and rhythmic life into Schubert without racing, and his detailing was elegant. With Beecham the music was touching without becoming heavy or too serious. Until this returns, the pickings are slim. **Abbado**'s version is very nice, but not now available separately (♦DG 423652, with 2). **Viotti**'s stylish performance is just as good (♦Claves 9319, also with 2, but not available separately). Abbado, Viotti, and Beecham all suggest a youthful composer better than Karajan, but all four are deeply satisfying.

Blomstedt is similar to Karajan, but a bit stodgy and less interesting (Berlin 9263, with 2). **Rilling**'s version of Nos. 1 and 2 is less polished than the best (Hänssler 98312). Versions by **Freisitzer** (CRD 30001, with 4), **Menuhin** (EMI 73359, with 2-6), and **Muti** (EMI 69834, with 8) are acceptable but don't rise above the routine. **Vasary**'s performance is exciting, but misses the depth of the music and was recorded in concert

with a not very quiet audience (Carlton 6601132, with 2). Those on a tight budget should consider **Halasz**'s version with the Failoni Orchestra; the performance is brisk, lightweight, and stylish in the modern manner, but without the grandeur of Karajan and his Berlin orchestra (♦Naxos 553093). Particularly considering its low price, this may be the best stopgap while awaiting the return of Beecham and Karajan.

2. Like 1, 2 is a full-blown affair — big and exciting with no sign of youthful insecurity. If anything, this symphony is even more self-consciously grand than 1, which it followed by about a year. Here Schubert also experiments with tonal relationships, most notably in his subdominant recapitulation in I. Many of the 2s are coupled with 1s, so the above recommendations apply. **Karajan, Beecham, Abbado, Munch,** and **Viotti** are all fine, but either unavailable or wrapped into complete sets. A reasonable alternative if you don't want to wait is to go with **Halasz,** which would save some money for the later symphonies.

3. This followed 2 by only a few months and was written with incredible speed; the entire piece required little more than a week of working time. Schubert was then a teenager working in his father's school (1815), but his every moment, even in class, seems to have been spent composing. No. 3 may be shorter and less imposing than its predecessors, but it's no less charming or attractive. It would be unreasonable to expect intellectual depth from a work written in only a few days, but Schubert's hand is so sure that he betrays no haste or insecurity.

Great Schubert performances are a delicate balance of contradictory qualities. They should be vigorous and rhythmic, but with no loss of grace; they need to be exciting without being hyperactive; they benefit from careful detailing, as long as it doesn't become episodic; and finally they need romantic warmth, but also enough backbone to head off sentimentality. When all these attributes are addressed and balanced, the music is a sheer delight. Few conductors have met these various needs better than **Beecham,** whose 3 is among the finest of all Schubert recordings (♦EMI 69750, with 5 and 6). Other conductors may whip up more excitement in the finale, but Beecham's charm and careful phrasing are infectious and wonderful. Furthermore, the competition isn't too strong.

No. 3 is one of the less satisfying of **Karajan**'s set because the weight of the Berlin Philharmonic and the conductor's vision work in opposition to this slighter piece. **Abbado** is a better choice here; he balances the lyrical and spirited sections very well, though his finale sounds too fast, perhaps a bit out of control (♦DG 423653). **Halasz** and his Failoni Orchestra are in good shape for this piece and can be recommended for budget shoppers (♦Naxos 553094, with 6). For similar reasons **Viotti**'s light, transparent approach suits the piece well (♦Claves 9619, with overtures).

We have recordings of 3 from conductors like **Järvi** (BIS), **Blomstedt** (Berlin), **Suitner** (Denon), **Schiff** (Chandos), and **Wand** (RCA) that offer perfectly acceptable, somewhat Germanic approaches, but lack the imagination of the very finest versions. One distinctive recording is **Carlos Kleiber**'s, where the playing is exceptionally fine but the music is pressed and driven, particularly in the slow movement (DG 449745, with 8). From here it's only a short step to the anguish and unrest of Harnoncourt, mentioned above among the complete sets.

4 ("Tragic"). It was Schubert himself who designated this symphony "Tragic." To modern ears the word seems a little too strong, but compared to 1–3, 4 is more serious and darker in color. Schubert contributed to the somber mood by placing the outer movements in C minor, the key of Beethoven's 5th, and in the lovely Andante he included a dramatic contrasting section. This work followed 3 by less than a year.

Those wanting to see 4 as a mature 19th-century piece should look for a large-orchestra version. Again **Karajan**'s recording comes to mind. He presents the big, tragic side magnificently, and the Berlin Philharmonic plays as well as anyone. The only possible shortcoming is the slow, ceremonial minuet. **Ormandy** is a little less dramatic, but nonetheless big and lush; he brings out less of the tragic side, but the music is unfailingly grand and beautiful (♦Columbia 60267, with 5). Some conductors like **Suitner** (Denon), **Blomstedt** (Berlin), and **Järvi** (BIS 453) bring a heavy richness to Schubert but don't complement it with enough lightness and grace. With them, the music doesn't sound spontaneous enough.

The versions from **Abbado** (♦DG 23653, with 3) and **Viotti** (♦Claves 9619, with 3 and overtures) are fine for those wanting modern instruments on a smaller scale. (In I, by the way, Abbado cuts eight measures now thought to be inauthentic.) **Harnoncourt**'s dramatic approach is well suited for this piece, and it's one of the best in his complete set (Teldec 91184). Detractors will stress, however, that the rare lyrical moments (like the beginning of the slow movement) need loving care to counterbalance the prevailing stormy moods. If it became available separately, this version would be recommended. **Norrington**'s period instrument version is also interesting. It's well played, but also very fast, giving the impression of impatience; I wonder if he really likes this music. In any case, it's presently deleted.

5. It is a break from the first four, as if Schubert were now realizing what kind of composer he would be. Nos. 1–4 are all grand, impressive works, fairly long and fully orchestrated, with slow introductions, trumpets, timpani, and full winds. Now the orchestra is smaller and the emotional level is restrained. It sounds a great deal like Mozart, whose Symphony 40 was known by Schubert as early as 1809. This symphony, the best known of the first six, is quintessential Schubert, a beacon of spring-like lyricism for a dark, cynical world.

No. 5 has long been popular, so the list of recommendations includes some historical recordings. **Toscanini**'s 1947 recording with the NBC orchestra is still of interest (♦RCA 60291, with 9). His tempos are fast, too fast really, but the music is nicely detailed and, in the slow movement, surprisingly supple; the finale, though, is brusque. This is a fine version if you want Schubert with a minimum of sentimentality, and Toscanini is always a conductor to be reckoned with. **Reiner**'s 1960 recording is somewhat in the same mold. His first movement is even faster than Toscanini's but doesn't sound at all rushed. The biggest difference is in his broad, serious slow movement, along with far better sound (♦RCA 61973, with Brahms's 3). Both of these recordings are of the classical, bracing variety.

The more romantic versions may be safer recommendations. First among these is **Beecham**, beautifully shaped with lovely wind playing (♦EMI 69750, with 3 and 6). Every phrase is elegantly detailed, but the effect is simple and spontaneous. Beecham better than anyone else could make this a carefree work of a youthful composer without ever trivializing the music. **Böhm**'s version with the Vienna Philharmonic is in a richer romantic vein (♦DG 47433, with Beethoven's 6). Here everything sounds wonderfully relaxed, simple in concept and warmly beautiful; note that this is a later recording than the one in his complete set (1979). **Vegh**'s wonderful set of 5, 6, 8, and 9 with the Salzburg Mozarteum Camerata Academia is just as attractive (♦Capriccio 490654). He stresses a warm, loving approach, but with no loss of strength when needed.

Two additional performances from the past are worth looking for. **Casals** in his second version (Marlboro, 1970) is wonderfully affectionate, and the music is strikingly poignant and melancholy, but it's currently NA. **Karajan**'s patrician version is a little more restrained and conventional. A good substitute for an old-fashioned romantic approach can be found in **Walter**'s sympathetic recording (Sony 60267), but on the whole Casals's phrasing and detailing are more special. **Bernstein** has a nice finale in his New York recording, but I is lumpy and bass-heavy, and the slow movement lacks refinement (Sony). **Barenboim** turns in another congenial, loving performance, but the ensemble is sometimes ragged and the finale lacks energy (Sony).

The catalog includes many recent recordings with crisper tempos and more classical lines. As in the earlier symphonies, **Viotti** is impressive because his fairly quick tempos aren't forced or pushed; the music sounds warm and it breathes. **Lubbock**'s recording is also unrushed, with lovely soft playing by the Orchestra of St. John's, Smith Square, and nice balances (♦IMP 819, with Haydn's 49). The coupling is unusual, and Lubbock isn't a household name, but the music-making is first-rate. **Abbado** isn't special here, the opening movement too fast and lacking poise. **Halasz**'s version is less impressive than the best—the sound is boxy—but it makes a satisfactory budget version (Naxos 55045).

Those interested in period instruments should look to **Mackerras** with the Orchestra of the Age of Enlightenment (currently NA, but scheduled for release as ♦Virgin 61305). This performance is crisp without being abrupt and the slow movement is nicely shaped without being sentimental. He couples 5 with Newbould's completion of the "Unfinished." This is an excellent second or third version for those wanting a counterbalance to more traditional readings. **Goodman**, in his complete set, is surprisingly tender and relaxed; if anything, it needs more spirit.

6. Following 5 by a little more than a year, it was finished when the composer had just turned 21. It certainly has more in common with the earlier symphonies than with 8 and 9, but it's no carbon copy. The outer movements have big, climactic codas that hint at Beethoven and the lightweight tunes reflect the Viennese rage for Rossini, whose operas were regularly and enthusiastically heard at this time. It may lack the depth of its companions, but Schubert's hand is very sure in this cheerful, underrated work.

This piece is a natural fit for conductors with a light, deft touch. The music should be buoyant with well-sprung rhythms, and care must be exerted to avoid overplaying. In this context **Beecham**'s recording is a clear choice (♦EMI 69750, with 3 and 5). The music has a wonderful lightness, but never at the expense of careful shading and phrasing. Other performances are almost in the same class. **Schmidt-Isserstedt**'s is another well-regarded 6 (♦Mercury 434354, with Skrowaczewski's 9). **Viotti** gets the right degree of liveliness without putting pressure on the music. Tempos are crisp and the Saarbrücken Orchestra plays with delicacy and grace. The budget-priced **Halasz** is also fine, blending energy and gracefulness to good effect (♦Naxos 553 094, with 3). Neither Viotti nor Halasz is as distinctive as Beecham, but their performances are more than satisfactory.

Abbado's version is less attractive; it's too tepid and needs more spirit. **Norrington** brings out the liveliness and surface excitement of the piece with period instruments, but it goes by too quickly and lacks a sense of affection (EMI).

8. Symphonies 1–6 show a slow, steady evolution in Schubert's thinking, but nothing to prepare us for the leap taken by the "Unfinished." We don't know why the composer left only two movements with no more than sketches of the third. The work has been completed competently by Brian Newbould, building upon Schubert's sketches for III and appropriating a movement from *Rosamunde* for the finale. Many find it arrogant to try to do something Schubert could easily have done if he had wanted to, since he lived for several years after its completion. Besides, the symphony, ending with the slow movement, seems very Schubertian. There's no need for a finale, which in this period would have to be either heroic (and Beethovenian) or lightweight (in the manner of Haydn). Neither of these possibilities fits Schubert's character well, so perhaps its existing form expresses the composer's individuality best of all.

No. 8 has certainly been Schubert's most popular symphony. Its rare combination of beauty and drama (as well as its brevity) have made it a popular classic, a shoo-in for lists of the World's Greatest Symphonies. Don't be misled, though, into thinking the "Unfinished" is all sweetness and syrup. Beneath the surface lies a level of pain and melancholy that go far beyond the lyrical veneer.

Thanks to its long-lived popularity, 8 has been performed by almost every conductor of note, and many older versions are still available. The romantic side of older recordings is covered by conductors like Furtwängler, Koussevitzky, and Mengelberg. With **Furtwängler,** the sound is massive and the tempos are very broad—Schubert in Bruckner's clothing (TAHA 1008). **Koussevitzky** is surprisingly bland (PHS 9037). **Mengelberg** shows his mastery by changing tempo in almost every bar and yet tying the piece into a cogent whole; this is a wonderful example of music-making in a forgotten style (♦Pearl 9154). The scrubbed, more classical style is represented by **Toscanini,** who brings his customary fiery directness to the score, giving us Schubert of dramatic intensity and clarity (RCA 60290). Much the same approach was brought by **Cantelli,** who was widely regarded as a successor to Toscanini before his untimely death (Enterprise 4158).

Beecham, who, it seems, got Schubert right without apparent effort, occupies something of a middle ground. His "Unfinished," dating from 1937, will discourage those who want modern sound, but the performance is certainly worth having (♦Dutton 7014). And finally, **Walter** brought wonderful warmth and affection to Schubert without becoming sloppy or indulgent. He was generally a better conductor before his Columbia Symphony days, so the NY Philharmonic version is preferred (♦Sony 64487, with Beethoven).

Several more modern recordings—often with widely differing approaches—can be recommended. The dark, brooding quality of I is presented with ravishing beauty by **Sinopoli** and the Philharmonia (NA); the music isn't particularly dramatic or exciting, it's just ineffably sad. His II has the effect of calm reassurance. Some listeners may want more pure lyricism and less psychological drama than he provides, though his performance is undeniably well thought out and executed. Another conductor who mines the seriousness of the work is **Carlos Kleiber** with the Vienna Philharmonic (♦DG 449475, with 3). The playing is exceptionally good; he presents Schubert as incisive drama. Both Sinopoli and Kleiber give us a mature, grown-up Schubert, but their undisputably fine performances don't sound spontaneous.

For many collectors the best Schubert is that which flows unimpeded by calculation. These listeners will prefer **Bernstein**'s more overtly emotional version with the NY Philharmonic; here the pitched, intense battle is external, not internal like Sinopoli's, and it's clear how much the conductor cares for this music (♦Sony 47610, with 9). With him, the dramatic qualities come to the fore and the lyricism is unashamedly rich,

yet the music doesn't sound contrived. (He also recorded 8 late in life with the Concertgebouw, also a fine recording, now NA.)

The standard romantic tradition (if we may posit such a thing) is well represented by conductors like Wand and Vegh. **Wand** made his recording with the Berlin Philharmonic in his mid-'80s (♦RCA 68314, with 9). The music is rich, full and dramatic, but never pushed or overdone. It lacks the special qualities that call attention to the interpretation, but for many this is a plus. Also in his mid-'80s, **Vegh** bought central European richness to his Schubert (♦Capriccio 49065, with 5, 6, and 9). Here the nervous intensity of Kleiber or Bernstein is replaced by lyrical warmth and an outpouring of lovely sound. **Karajan** seems too enamored with surface beauty; most will want a tougher approach (EMI).

Some conductors capture the spontaneity of Schubert so well that the music seems to play itself, needing no external guidance. **Krips** conducts an "Unfinished" with the Vienna Philharmonic where everything flows with a minimum of effort. On the surface, at least, he doesn't seem to be doing anything to the music at all (♦London 452892, with 9). In his recording, as in Wand's, the interpretive side is hidden, and the music is played with little sense that outside ideas are being imposed on it. On a slightly smaller scale, **Viotti**'s recording achieves the same elusive ideal (♦Claves 9220).

Special mention should be made of **Mackerras**'s performance, which uses Newbould's completion of the symphony (♦Virgin 61305, with 5). In spite of my misgivings about this enterprise, the performance itself is very satisfying: period instruments, nice balances between strings and winds, with brisk but not violent tempos. Mackerras's other recording, with the Scottish Chamber Orchestra, is also good (with period brass), but the coupling isn't ideal (Telarc 80502, with 9). Another period instrument performance, by **Weil** and the Classical Band, is expertly played, but the music is hyped up with fast speeds that lop off the deeper emotions (Sony).

A few of our better known conductors have made respectable recordings of 8, but the magic of the piece somewhat eludes them. **Reiner** (RCA), **Maazel** (Sony), and **Szell** (Sony) can be bypassed, even though the playing is very good on all three. With **Giulini** the music has wonderful nobility and singing qualities, but there's little sense of struggle or tension (Sony). **Gardiner** is also expendable; his orchestra and sonics are no more than adequate (Erato). **Abbado**'s 8 is a worthy member of his set, but next to the competition it doesn't offer anything special (DG).

9. While it would be unfair to dismiss the first six symphonies as derivative works, we must acknowledge that superficially they are similar, and all were written in quick succession. With 8 and 9, though, it's clear that Schubert was devoting much more attention to symphonic writing and achieving compositions of great originality and depth. These two works, both written when he was but in his 20s, are so vastly advanced over the early efforts that we can only shake our heads wondering what he might have done had death not claimed him. No. 9 has the traditional four-movement format, but every movement is long, especially when conductors take many of the repeats. In its powerful drama, motivic techniques, and structure it's reminiscent of Beethoven, but Schubert is more expansive and melodious in his thematic material. No. 9 is a crowning glory, not only for Schubert, but for 19th-century symphonies as a whole.

As with 8, we have a wide range of historical performances that enrich the catalog. In particular, Toscanini and Furtwängler, whom many consider the most significant conductors of the first half of the 20th century, both left excellent, compelling readings. **Toscanini**'s association with this symphony went back to 1896, when he programmed it in his first orchestral concert. The three surviving recordings, all from fairly late in his career—1941, 1947, and 1953—have the tensile strength and directness that characterized all his work. This is Schubert through a Beethoven lens: dramatic, assertive, and unsentimental. Even if you prefer a more romantic Schubert, these recordings are worth knowing. The 1941 version with the Philadelphia Orchestra is the most subtle and supple of the three, but the recording shows its age (♦RCA 60313). The 1953 with the NBC Orchestra seems a little more pressed, but the sound is fairly good for the period (♦RCA 60290).

Furtwängler's view of 9 is even more special; it's indispensable as a Schubert recording and also stands as one of the finest of all his interpretations. He took great freedom with tempos, characterizing each section individually, but amazingly, everything sounds cogent and logical. The exciting sections are white-hot, and the lyric parts linger, never wanting to end. Among the many versions, the long-available 1951 performance with the Berlin Philharmonic is the one to have (♦DG 447439). The sound is remarkably good and the performance is unforgettable. The 1942 version with the Berlin Philharmonic is even more intense (DG 427781). **Mengelberg** is another who deserves mention, a subjective musician who took rhythmic liberties no one would approach today. His 9 is fascinating, but seems self-indulgent next to Furtwängler, and the sound is weaker (Biddulph 39).

The early stereo era included many fine versions. **Szell** is in the Toscanini camp: bracing, no-nonsense Schubert with splendid orchestral playing, particularly in the finale. He felt close to the piece—it's one of two he asked to see shortly before he died—and saw it in tough, Beethovenian terms. Some find his version to be near the core of mature Schubert, while others find his aggressive style antithetical to the composer's spirit (Sony 48268). **Krips** was a conductor who could see the buoyancy and smile in this work. Unlike Furtwängler's philosophical posturing and Toscanini's determination to take no prisoners, he lets the music unfold without pushing it one way or the other and makes you think this is the only way for the piece to go; the music is genial and Viennese, never overblown or rhetorical (♦London 452892). **Walter** strikes a mediating position between Toscanini and Furtwängler: fairly direct and straightforward, but romantically sensitive. In his 1959 version he makes 9 an important, serious piece, but seems reluctant to let the music smile (Sony 64478). **Skrowaczewski**'s version dates from the same period; it's well recorded but too tense and pressured (Mercury).

In his several recordings **Karajan** showed a strong command of the piece: a tautness reminiscent of Toscanini combined with sweep, grandeur, and ravishing orchestral sound. Next to its competitors, though, it lacks strong personality, and to some it sounds too calculated, but it's a strong reading in the modern, somewhat objective style (♦EMI 66105). **Bernstein**'s performances are anything but cool, one with the NY Philharmonic (♦Sony 47610), the other with the Concertgebouw (♦DG 427646). Both are fairly fast, direct, and full of energy without losing a sense of spontaneity or buoyancy; Bernstein, unlike most others, acknowledges the youthfulness of the composer. Both are very good, but the DG has the better orchestra and a less frenetic finale.

Solti was a conductor whose music seldom sounds relaxed, so he has not generally been associated with Schubert. His 9 with the Vienna Philharmonic makes his case as well as possible—a strong, kinetic performance, complete with Solti accents and played by an orchestra that could do this piece in their sleep (Decca 480311). In a different recording with **Muti**, it's possible they did just that; the music flows without

being shaped and, to make things worse, he takes all the repeats (EMI). Among more modern versions a few are strong and competitive. One with the older style well in hand is **Vegh,** whose version is romantically rich and loving. At the same time, though, Vegh knows how and when to be light and graceful and doesn't push; his performances are an excellent way to hear older-style Schubert in modern sound (♦Capriccio 49065).

Wand is in a similar vein—warm, rich, and free of quirky mannerisms (♦RCA 68314). For listeners wanting to get directly to Schubert, this is a good choice, because he brings a minimum of ego to the piece, keeping a low interpretive profile. **Blomstedt** is similar but less desirable: low profile combined with gritty sound and brass-heavy balances (Berlin). **Gardiner**'s version is straightforward and bracing, with a Haydnesque spirit; the whole performance sounds a little impatient (DG). **Mackerras** seems less nervous with the Scottish Chamber Orchestra, but his period brass (with otherwise modern instruments) don't sound very inviting (Telarc).

As in the earlier symphonies, we can see a movement afoot to perform 9 with more modest forces. **Abbado**'s version is such a recording (though it doesn't sound undernourished), and stands as a fine example of a good, objective performance (♦DG 23656). For those not wanting the piece burdened with heavy romanticism or Beethovenian overtones, he's a good choice. **Viotti** is also fine, and for the same reasons (♦Claves 9220). His reading is refreshing and lovely, virtuosic in the finale, but with a couple of odd textual variants. **Halasz** presents 9 as a taut, classical piece, which is fine, though the first movement has tempo problems and the loud sections lack sufficient impact (Naxos).

Period instruments aren't well represented at present. Mackerras's older version with the Orchestra of the Age of Enlightenment is deleted, as are Norrington's with the London Classical Players and Goodman's with the Hanover Band. So we're left with **Weil**'s Classical Band, which plays expertly with fine attention to detail and musical gesture (Sony). At the same time, though, their kinetic style and swift tempos pretty much assure that Schubert's very beautiful harmonic language won't register. Everything seems sacrificed to surface excitement, and the totality of Schubert's vision is untapped.

In addition to the standard eight we have two additional symphonies plus nine fragments in D major. The first of these originated in 1821, a symphony in E that Schubert left incomplete. The composition date, just one year before the "Unfinished," has allowed it to be put in the No. 7 slot, which became vacant when the old No. 7 became No. 9. The work, completed by later scholars, has never caught on with major conductors. The "Gmunden-Gastein" symphony, supposedly from 1825, may be the same work as 9, or it may be an orchestrated version of the *Grand Duo* for piano four-hands. It was performed by Toscanini and is available in a fine recording in **Abbado**'s set (♦DG 23651).

The nine fragments were discovered among Schubert's papers after his death and now seem to be parts of three symphonies: two movements from 1818 (D 615), four from 1821 (D 708A), and three from 1828 (D 936A). Of these, the 1828 fragments, sometimes played with an added scherzo to make a full symphony, are the most significant, particularly the extraordinary, sparse slow movement. Only one recording is now in the catalog, and it's very good: **Mackerras** with the Scottish Chamber Orchestra (♦Hyperion 67000).

OTHER ORCHESTRAL MUSIC

Schubert wrote relatively little for orchestra alone. Most of what we have are overtures to his many Singspiels along with incidental music from

Rosamunde. Since these are all short pieces, they regularly appear as fillers with the symphonies. In **Viotti**'s fine set, for example, he includes four overtures with 3 (♦Claves 9619). For those wanting overtures without duplicating symphonies, the best choice is **Huss** with the Vienna Haydn Sinfonietta, who present nine Singspiel overtures (♦Koch Schwann 1121). Huss's brisk, direct style matches the music very well, though the orchestra is on the light side. A disc that combines a large number of rarities is violinist/conductor **Carlo Chiarappa**'s recording of the Violin Concerto (*Concertstück*), German Dances, minuets and trios, and *Polonaise and Rondo* for violin and orchestra (Arts 47210).

CHAMBER MUSIC

Schubert's chamber music was written with different purposes in mind. The early string quartets and violin sonatas were private pieces, penned for the family, and other chamber works are consciously light in weight. The public pieces, those that Schubert intended for the outside world and wanted to make a mark with, are few in number but equal in quality to the greatest works in the chamber literature.

The string quartets traditionally number 15, but only the last three are important (plus the one-movement *Quartettsatz*). On the same level are the two piano trios, the Octet, and two quintets—one for strings, the other for piano and strings (the "Trout"). A beginning collection should concentrate on these eight works; the lesser pieces, almost invariably tuneful and well constructed, will often appear as fillers with the major pieces.

Sonatas

It's surprising that Schubert, who was so productive in so many genres, wrote so little for piano and solo instrument. His finest work of this kind was written for an instrument that is now a historical curiosity: the arpeggione. Invented in 1824, this was essentially a cello with six strings tuned like a guitar. Schubert wrote a sonata for the instrument for Vincenz Schuster, who appears to have been its only professional player. Now that the arpeggione is defunct, instrumentalists of every stripe—cello, viola, bass, flute, guitar, clarinet, even trombone—have stepped in to rescue the music; the catalog has some three dozen versions. Other than the Arpeggione Sonata we have slim pickings: a sonata, a fantasy, a rondo, and three sonatinas for violin and piano, and *Introduction and Variations on Tröckne Blumen* for flute and piano.

Arpeggione. The most obvious modern instruments to replace the arpeggione are the cello and viola. In range the piece lies more naturally for viola, but a few notes go too low and require upward transposition. For cellists the work lies very high, which makes the work more of a virtuoso vehicle than Schubert probably intended, but today's finest players seem to toss it off without a worry.

Several cellists have given us great *Arpeggiones*. An excellent choice is **Miklós Perényi,** who with Schiff makes the work sound natural and easy (♦Teldec 13151). The tunefulness and charm of Schubert come through beautifully, and the coupling (piano trios) is terrific too. **Ma** is equally persuasive, and with Ax makes the piece sound smooth and effortless, though it's coupled with a so-so "Trout" Quintet (♦Sony 61964). Another warm, effortless version comes from **Maisky** with Daria Hovora; the coupling—Schubert songs played on cello—is less effective (♦DG 449817). (Too bad Maisky's colorful, sensitive version with Argerich is absent from the catalog.) A nicely-shaped, romantic view is presented in **Lluis Claret**'s version with Alain Planès (♦Harmonia Mundi 1901383).

Pieter Wispelwey and Paolo Giacometti explore the light, delicate side of Schubert more than his overtly romantic side and couple their

Arpeggione arrangement with cello versions of the three violin sonatinas (♦Claves 9696). Another recommended version is played on the five-string violoncello piccolo by **Hidemi Suzuki,** accompanied on fortepiano by Yoshiko Kojima (♦Harmonia Mundi 77396, with Beethoven's Cello Sonata 3). Of all the above, Perényi deserves the highest recommendation on the basis of its wonderful coupling, but if you already have the piano trios, any of the others could be chosen.

Historical versions give a welcome perspective on Schubert performance. **Feuermann**'s rich version from the '30s reveals mannerisms from an earlier day, and his playing may be less perfect than we routinely expect, but he identifies deeply with Schubert and conveys that affection as well or better than modern players (♦Enterprise 99328, with Brahms and Dvorak; EMI 64250, with Beethoven). Equally valuable is **Fournier**'s somewhat more classical account (♦Pearl 9198; ♦Enterprise 99344). Either of these would make an ideal second or third version. Those on a budget should look to **Maria Kliegel** and Kristin Merscher; their playing is sensitive and well-balanced, and the sound is fine (♦Naxos 550654).

Even though the viola is a smaller instrument than the cello, it sounds darker and a bit nasal in the range of the *Arpeggione*. As a result, all viola versions sound more mellow and intimate than the cello versions. One of the finest is from **Yuri Bashmet** with Mikhail Muntian; his expressive range is very wide, and he makes the viola a true solo instrument (♦RCA 60112, with Schumann, Bruch, and Enescu). Former Tchaikovsky Competition winner **Raphaël Oleg** and Gérard Wyss present a leisurely *Arpeggione* that is, in a good sense, unassertive; Schubert is often loveliest when performers take it easy and let the music play itself (♦Denon 75636, with more Schubert). By comparison with these, **Imai** and Vignoles sound retiring and mellow (Chandos), while **Yizhak Schotten** with Katherine Collier (Crystal) seems thin next to Bashmet. **Felix Schwartz** and Wolfgang Küesaellohnl play Schubert with depth and dark colors, depriving us of charm and lyric beauty (Discover).

A few versions for winds should also be mentioned. Flutist **Toke Lund Christiansen** with Elisabeth Westenholz makes an excellent case for a wind version, coupled with a fine Flute and Guitar Quartet and an orchestrated arrangement of *Tröckne Blumen Variations* (♦Kontrapunkt 32024). Another good flute version comes from **William Bennett** and Clifford Benson (♦Camerata 14, with arrangements of famous Schubert songs). A good *Arpeggione* comes from flutist **Emmanuel Pahud** and Eric Le Sage, with still another arrangement, this time of a violin sonatina (♦Valois 4717). These three are all recommended to flute fanciers and those interested in hearing old music in new clothing.

Gervase de Peyer's clarinet version with Gwenneth Pryor is equally compelling; in this performance the unwary could easily think they had discovered a new Schubert clarinet sonata (♦Chandos 8506, with Schumann and Weber). Perhaps the oddest transcription is **John Williams**'s for guitar, accompanied by Giulini and the Australian Chamber Orchestra. The transfer works very well, though the guitar can't sustain lines, which compromises the slow movement in particular (♦Sony 63385).

Violin. Schubert's two instruments, studied in grade school, were violin and piano. He wrote extensively for solo piano and violin in ensemble, but, oddly, little for them together. We have three early sonatas, renamed "Sonatinas" after the composer's death by the publisher Diabelli. Other than these, he wrote a single sonata in 1817 and two late pieces: the *Rondo brillant* of 1826 and *Fantasy* of 1827. All are rather lightweight, excepting perhaps the *Fantasy,* while the *Rondo* is a vehicle for virtuosos.

For those wishing to get the complete violin music in one package, **Stern** and Barenboim command immediate attention (♦Sony 64528, 2CD). This comes from fairly late in Stern's career (1988), when his playing lacked some of the finesse of earlier years, but the joyful spirit of Schubert is there in abundance, and the intonation is very good. Less appealing are **Jaime Laredo** and Stephanie Brown, who suffer from aggressiveness and a lack of delicacy (Dorian). For the budget minded, the set from **György Pauk** and Peter Frankl is a good means to get lots of Schubert for little outlay (♦Vox 3042, 3CD). And for period instruments, **William Steck** and Robert Hill can be recommended for their warm playing—and more vibrato than you would expect (♦MD+G 6200688, 2 CD). The versions by **Kremer** are worth looking for; he plays with a wonderful sound and brings great nuance and detail to the music (♦DG 437092, 431654).

The 1817 Sonata played by **Schneider** and Peter Serkin makes a nice filler to one of the best "Trout" Quintets (♦Vanguard 8005), while fanciers of historical performance will find much to ponder in **Kreisler**'s romantic but somewhat willful 1928 account with Rachmaninoff (on several labels with different couplings).

For the Sonatinas alone, **Angèle Dubeau**'s recording with Kuerti is beautifully musical, though the sound isn't ideally balanced (♦Fleur de Lys 23042). A very fine period instrument recording comes from **Fabio Biondi** and Olga Tverskaya; Tverskaya plays an 1820 Graf fortepiano, and Biondi includes interesting ornamentation in some of the repeats (♦Opus 30126, with Duo Sonata). A good budget release by **Dong-Suk Kang** and Pascal Devoyon includes the Sonatinas and *Fantasy* (♦Naxos 550420).

Introduction and Variations on Tröckne Blumen (from *Die schöne Müllerin*). Particularly effective recordings of this flute piece have been made by **William Bennett** and Clifford Benson (♦Camerata 204) and **Yossi Arnheim** and Daniel Gortler (♦Meridian 84320), and special mention should be made of **Christiansen**'s effective arrangement of the piece for octet (♦Kontrapunkt 32024). Here, though, every recording has different couplings, which will strongly influence your choice.

Trios

Piano. Schubert left two splendid piano trios, both late works. In Schubert's lifetime the first was performed only at a private concert, while the second was part of his only public concert, given in 1828 just months before his death. In addition to these we have two independent movements: the E-flat *Notturno*, a wonderful slow movement probably written in 1827, and a less important single movement in B-flat, written when he was only 15.

Most groups who have done one of the two big trios have also done the other, though they're usually on two CDs (and may be available separately). When spread over two CDs the two shorter works are often included as couplings. Among inclusive sets, first mention should go to Yuuko Shiokawa, Perényi, and **Schiff,** who include both trios, *Notturno*, and a wonderful performance of the *Arpeggione* Sonata (♦Teldec 13151, 2CD). Schiff tends to dominate, but their warm and passionate playing brings importance and grandeur to the music. In addition, they open the standard cut in the finale of Trio 2, extending it to about 20 minutes. The long admired versions of Stern, Rose, and **Istomin** still sound wonderful to those who like Schubert played with affection and a warm glow (♦Sony 64516, 2CD).

If you prefer more crispness and youthful ardor, a better choice would be the **Fontenay Trio;** they have the rare ability to play quickly and passionately without overplaying or making the music sound pushed (♦Teldec 94558, 2CD). For Schubert on a big scale appropriate for a large hall, Zukerman, Harrell, and **Ashkenazy** are a logical choice, and both trios are on one CD (♦London 455685). An excellent middle-of-the-road version comes from Mark Kaplan, Colin Carr, and **David Golub** (♦Arabesque 6580, 2CD, with both short trios). They see Schubert's profound side without losing sight of the lyrical moments, particularly in slow movements. For period instruments, **La Gaia Scienza** can be confidently recommended (♦Winter & Winter 6 and 17 separately, or 18 together). Their performances, as you would expect, are light in tone, but their vivid, immediate playing is very compelling.

Several other recordings of the two trios are available, but they're not at the same level of distinction. The **Beaux Arts Trio** plays with great affection, but their Schubert is heavy, lacking vitality and a sense of abandon (Philips). (Their earlier versions with violinist Daniel Guilet are better.) **Beethoven Trio Vienna** plays too aggressively; they're harsh and brusque (Camerata). **Trio Concertante** plays very beautifully and can be recommended to those who want laid-back, intimate performances; most listeners, though, will want more energy (Vox 5033, 2CD). The versions by Vera Beths, Bylsma, and **Immerseel** are on one CD, but the performances are prosaic and under-characterized (Sony). Other groups, like the **Odeon Trio** (Capriccio), **Atlantis Ensemble** on period instruments (Wild Boar) or Werner Hink, Fritz Doležal, and **Jasminka Stancul** (Camerata) are satisfactory but lack the distinctive profile of the recommended versions.

The Trios from the Prades Festival (1951–2) should be mentioned. These versions, rich and generally slow, are full of revelatory moments and sound very spontaneous. Both trios have Schneider and Casals, but the pianists are different: **Istomin** for 1 (♦Sony 58989), **Horszowski** for 2 (♦Sony 64516).

Among modern versions of Trio 1 by itself, the **Suk Trio** does well in the lyrical sections, but the dramatic ones are weak (Boston Skyline). Many historic recordings reveal performance practices from earlier generations. Those headed by **Gieseking** (Dante 134) and **Hess** (APR 7012) would both be interesting supplements to a collection, but the most revealing is **Cortot**'s recording from the '20s with Thibaud and Casals (♦on four different labels with various couplings). Their mannerisms and approach to Schubert conflict with the way we generally want to hear it played today, but they communicate vividly and remind us of the breadth of possibilities in great music. The old 1941 recording by **Rubinstein,** Heifetz, and Feuermann is worth looking for; it captured these artists at the height of their powers and deserves a permanent place in the catalog (♦RCA 60926).

No. 2 by itself is best represented by **Rudolf Serkin** and members of the Busch Quartet. This performance, part of the Quartet's "Schubert Edition," dates from the '30s and is an indispensable historical document; anyone interested in Schubert performance from the early 20th century should hear these CDs (♦Philips 9141). Among modern versions, the **Bekova Sisters** play beautifully, but their Schubert is too rich and over-indulgent (Chandos).

Strings. Both Schubert string trios are early (1816, 1817) and are among his minor works. Perhaps the best way to pick up the first is as a coupling to the **Raphael Ensemble**'s fine String Quintet (♦Hyperion 66724). Both string trios are available in fine performances by **L'Archibudelli** (♦Sony 53982, with Quartet 10). In this instance, though, the wisest course would be to examine the very different couplings and let them be your guide.

Quartets

Strings. Schubert wrote his first string quartet in 1810 or 1811, around the time he turned 14. This was followed by many quartets, some merely fragments, others completely lost. In any event, the numbered quartets reached 11 by 1816. By and large, they were intended for the family group, in which Franz played the viola, his brothers Ignaz and Ferdinand played violin, and his father the cello. All are slight works, tuneful and entertaining—food for a family dinner rather than a fancy reception. After the first 11, quartets became rarer, but also far deeper and more sophisticated. The first of these is only a single movement from 1820 (generally referred to by its German title, *Quartettsatz*), followed by three quartets of the first rank: 13 (sometimes called "Rosamunde," 1824), 14 ("Death and the Maiden," also 1824), and 15 (1826).

Complete sets. Because of the immaturity of the early works, few groups have recorded all 15, not to mention the many fragments. For those wanting virtually everything, the **Leipzig Quartet** offers all the quartets plus the String Quintet and numerous fragments (♦MD+G 0601-0609, 9 single CDs). Their playing, typical of many European groups, is natural and unforced. They don't play to the gallery or attempt to overwhelm the listener with virtuosity, and they're very well recorded. The couplings are arranged so that when possible a substantial work is paired with juvenilia. Consequently, if you want mainly the mature pieces, or if you have the late works and are looking for the early ones, you'll end up with extra expense or duplications in your collection.

These pieces are also available in two albums from the **Auryn Quartet** (♦CPO 999409/410, each 3CD). Here the early works fare better than the mature ones, which lack the depth and distinctiveness of the best versions. Nonetheless they're much cheaper than the New Leipzig and can be confidently recommended. Both are preferable to the old **Melos Quartet** set (DG, 6CD) and the ongoing **Verdi Quartet** series, where the freshness in the early works is not matched by corresponding depth in the mature pieces (Hänssler).

For most listeners, the best approach is to buy a complete set of 12–15. Here the version of choice is the **Quartetto Italiano** (♦Philips 446163, mid-priced). They bring richness and complete technical assurance to Schubert but also find details and depth that few can match. Their tempos tend to be slow, but their intense commitment makes many rival groups sound superficial. Other versions are less competitive. Opinion is divided on the assertive version by the **Emerson Quartet** (♦DG 459191, 3CD, with String Quintet). Their technique and polish are exceptional, but they approach Schubert with New World directness rather than European warmth; those who want Schubert with muscle and lots of projection will appreciate them. The **Melos Quartet** is a fine group, sympathetic and affectionate toward the composer, but their interpretations lack the distinctiveness of the Italians (Harmonia Mundi). Less desirable is the **Brandis Quartet,** whose playing is comparatively aggressive and unsubtle (Nimbus).

13 ("Rosamunde"). The last three quartets provide an abundance of recordings, many of them first-rate. In 13, nicknamed "Rosamunde" because it reuses music from the romantic play of that name, we have a fine version from the **Lindsay Quartet;** they play with great intensity and poetry, but never lose a sense of beauty and purity (♦ASV 593, with 8). The **Cleveland Quartet** is on the same level; their Schubert is played with wide dynamics and seriousness, but it's coupled with a lifeless "Trout" (♦Telarc 80225). For those who prefer an emotional, slow, romantic approach, the **Kodály Quartet** would be an excellent choice (♦Naxos 550591).

Anyone partial to period instruments will be more than satisfied with the **Mosaïques Quartet;** they adopt slow tempos that bring out the spirit of pathos in the music (♦Astrée 8580). The **Guarneri Quartet** are less desirable; they play beautifully (and somewhat more quickly than in their earlier version), but with too little inner tension (Arabesque). The **Prazak Quartet** seems to underestimate Schubert's ability to make his points without aid; their strong rhythms and fierce attacks diminish the music (Praga).

14 ("Death and the Maiden"). No. 14, nicknamed because of the theme and variations based on the song "Der Tod und das Mädchen," has long been Schubert's most popular quartet. For a dramatic approach, the **Lindsay Quartet** is a logical choice; they emphasize contrasts and angular rhythms to bring a Beethovenian seriousness to the piece (♦ASV 560). The **Alban Berg Quartet** is somewhat more flexible and sensitive; their beauty of tone and technical finish leave nothing to be desired (♦EMI 56470/1, 2CD, with 10, 12, and 15). For many, the top version will be the **Tokyo Quartet,** either their first recording (♦RCA 7990), or (with changed personnel) their second (♦Vox 7207); they're a little cooler than the most dynamic versions, but their poise and sweet sound make for wonderful Schubert. Another group that shouldn't be overlooked is the **Busch Quartet,** recorded in the '30s. Their Schubert is smoother and less emphatic than we usually hear today, but their inwardness brings with it a profundity that hasn't been surpassed. Given the age of the recording, the sound isn't too bad (♦Pearl 9141, 2CD, with other Schubert; or ♦Arkadia 78502, with 15).

Several other recordings are certainly fine, if not at the above level. The **Juilliard Quartet** takes an intense, dramatic view, but in the end the music sounds restless and overplayed (Sony). The **Talich Quartet** is another in the serious vein, but their first movement needs more lyricism; it's too insistent (Calliope). The **Kodály Quartet** is fine for those who want an expansive, unforced performance with warm sound (Naxos 550590 or 504006, 4CD). The **Lydian Quartet** plays the work beautifully, but their shifts in tempo are too obvious, and III and IV are on the slow side (Centaur). The **Petersen Quartet** would be a good choice for those wanting a more poised, classical account, with admirable soft playing (Capriccio 10744). The **Amadeus Quartet** offers a performance of great strength, but it's compromised by excessive violin vibrato (DG). Others, like the **Alcan Quartet** (Fleur de Lys) and the **Aria Quartet** (Novalis), turn in adequate performances without any special qualities to set them apart.

Also of interest is Mahler's transcription of this quartet for string orchestra. Of the recordings now available, **Welser-Möst** brings out the Mahlerian angst the best (♦EMI 56813) and is preferable to **Turovsky** (Chandos) and **Mischa Rachlevsky** (Claves). The deleted version of **Hermut Haenchen** has exceptionally virtuosic playing and is worth looking for (♦Berlin 1064).

15. For Schubert's final quartet, several versions can be recommended. We mustn't forget the **Quartetto Italiano,** whose set, mentioned above, is available in a "two-fer"; their performance yields to none in depth and insight (♦Philips 446163, 2CD). The **Alban Berg Quartet** is also very fine; they may be slightly less perceptive than the Italians but compensate by playing with extraordinary tonal finish and sensitivity (♦EMI 56471, with *Quartettsatz*). By comparison, the **Lindsay Quartet** is more dramatic and strongly projected, but their decisions always seem justified by the music (♦ASV 661). Less desirable is the **Brahms Quartet;** they stress the angular side of the music, sounding impatient and overprojected (Berlin). The **Juilliard Quartet** are intense and gritty in this piece, lacking grace and warmth (Sony). And, as mentioned for 14, the **Busch Quartet** has left us Schubert playing so fine it should never be absent from the catalog (♦Pearl 9141, 2CD, or ♦Arkadia 78502).

Other string quartets. The earliest quartets are available in the complete sets (see above). No. 8 is coupled in the recordings by the **Lindsay Quartet** (♦ASV 593) and the historic **Busch Quartet** (♦Pearl 9141, 2CD, or ♦Enterprise 99364). No. 10 is a coupling for the **Kodály Quartet** (Naxos 550591) and the **Mosaïques Quartet** (♦ Astrée 8580). For a fine *Quartettsatz,* look to the **Alban Berg Quartet** (♦EMI 56471, with 14), the **Tokyo Quartet** (♦Vox 7207, also with 14), or the **Quartetto Italiano** (♦Philips 46163, in their set of the last four quartets).

Flute, viola, cello, and guitar. This is a pleasant but minor work, dating from 1814, usually appearing as a coupling with other works for guitar or flute. Guitar fanciers will want the version by the **Accademia Farnese,** coupled with choral songs accompanied by guitarist Claudio Piastra; the playing is warm, romantic, and soothing (♦Mondo Musica 96023). Flute lovers should look to the versions by **Marc Grauwels** (♦Syrinx 93105, with *Tröckne Blumen Variations*) or **Toke Lund Christiansen** (♦Kontrapunkt 32024).

Quintets

Piano and strings ("Trout"). The "Trout" is the earliest of Schubert's chamber masterpieces. Written in 1819, when the composer was but 22, it captures the carefree, lyrical spirit that dominated his life during a rare happy period. The work is unusual in its instrumentation and movement layout. Schubert's ensemble—piano, violin, viola, cello, and bass—has no precedent in Haydn, Mozart, or Beethoven (though a Hummel quintet does use these forces). And in laying out the work Schubert augmented the normal four-movement sequence with a set of variations on his song "Die Forelle" (the "Trout"), placing it between the third movement scherzo and the finale.

We have never had a shortage of fine performances of the "Trout," though some of the finest are presently deleted. Some performers bring a light, dancey touch to the piece, while others are warmly loving or more intense and dramatic. Near the top of anyone's list are the versions by **Curzon,** a pianist whose luminous tone and natural fluency seem perfect for Schubert. His performance with members of the Vienna Octet has been long prized and the sound shows its age only slightly (♦London 448602). His version with the Amadeus Quartet is in a different vein, recorded in concert and coupled with Brahms's Piano Quintet. These performances, dating from the early '70s, aren't note perfect, but their spontaneity and excitement more than compensate (♦BBC 4009). Another distinguished version comes from **Peter Serkin** and musicians from Marlboro; recorded in 1964 when Serkin was only 18, this "Trout" is romantic and loving with a sense of uninhibited freedom (♦Vanguard 8005).

An older version (available at budget price) is from **Horszowski** and the Budapest Quartet. The main attraction here is Horszowski, whose sweet, affectionate playing will please anyone who doesn't want an energized approach (♦Sony 46343, with a restless "Death and the Maiden" overplayed by the Juilliard Quartet). Those partial to period instruments (and even those resistant to them) should consider **Steven Lubin** with the Academy of Ancient Music Chamber Ensemble; he plays an 1824 Graf fortepiano, and the balances and musicality are top-notch (♦London 455724, 2CD). One last recommended version is also one of the least expensive: **Jandó** and the Kodály Quartet, who combine warmth and energy very effectively, and their sound is very good (♦Naxos 550658).

Several excellent versions belong in the first group, but are deleted and move to the "watch-for" list. Among older recordings, the confident performance of **Rudolf Serkin** with Marlboro friends is both assertive and affectionate; as with almost all the Marlboro recordings, the playing is committed, and the music sounds alive (♦Sony 46252 or 37234). Another fine Schubert pianist is **Brendel,** whose "Trout" is thoughtful and beautifully detailed; his second recording with violinist Thomas Zehetmair (♦Philips 446001) is preferable to his earlier version with the Cleveland Quartet. Another to look for, particularly if you like Schubert with freshness and enthusiasm, comes from **Ax** with Ma; it's coupled with an excellent *Arpeggione* Sonata played by Ma (♦Sony 61974).

Several other recordings are adequate but don't rise to the level of those above. **John O'Conor** and the Cleveland Quartet play the piece lightly and rather quickly, but poetry is in short supply (Telarc). **Ax** and the Guarneri Quartet play warmly and romantically but with too little profile (RCA). **Zacharias** and the Leipzig Quartet are fairly straightforward, relaxed, and expressive without exaggeration (MD+G), while **Andreas Haefliger** and the Takács Quartet show more animation and spirit (London 460034). **Frank Glazer** and the Fine Arts Quartet exhibit a serious demeanor in a dry acoustic (Boston Skyline), while **Kocsis** and the Takács Quartet are insistent and persuasive but not very beguiling (Hungaroton).

Not a first choice, but very rewarding is the 1935 version from **Schnabel** and the Pro Arte Quartet (available on several labels with different couplings). Schnabel's playing is much less perfect than we expect today and the sound is marginal, but the musical insights revealed here never grow old.

Strings. The Quintet for strings, written in the composer's last year (1828), has long been considered one of the finest chamber works, not just by Schubert, but by any composer you care to name. Its fame, though, did not come immediately. Schubert probably never heard the work, and the first public performance did not take place until 1850, three years before its first publication. In this work Schubert added a second cello to the standard string quartet, not a second viola, as Mozart did in his quintets.

Perhaps the finest recording is by Schiff and the **Alban Berg Quartet;** every detail seems perfectly judged (for example, note how violin and viola trade triplets in the development) and the piece has wonderful continuity, with no overplaying (♦EMI 66942). Some will miss the first movement repeat, but for others its absence is a plus. In the same league are Douglas Cummings and the **Lindsay Quartet,** who achieve an inner intensity seldom heard in this piece; the intermingling of Schubertian joy and pain could hardly be better felt, while the slow movement is very intimate and stretched almost to the breaking point (♦ASV 537).

Several other recordings are only a slight notch below these. Ma and the **Cleveland Quartet** caress the piece with great affection, but never wallow in sentimentality (♦Sony 39134); their performance is more direct, less intimate than, say, the Lindsay. The performance by Rostropovich and the **Emerson Quartet** is brilliantly played, with lots of intensity, but they sometimes miss the quiet, inner core of Schubert (♦DG 431972). In any case, it's better than Rostropovich's earlier effort with the **Melos Quartet,** where he dominated the proceedings (DG). The all-star version of **Stern,** Ma, and others is strong and dynamic, with emphasis on dramatic, Beethovenian qualities rather than inner spirituality; their intensity brings out the terror in the music, and the finale has a feverish, manic quality (♦Sony 53983).

Another exceptionally beautiful account comes from the **Raphael Ensemble;** like the Lindsay, their performance is well detailed, and the slow movement seems to presage Schubert's death just two weeks after he completed the piece (♦Hyperion 66724). More neutral emotionally but still very fine are the versions by Perényi and the **Bartok Quartet** (♦Hungaroton 4035) and by Martin Lovett and the **Verdi Quartet** (♦Hänssler 98.726); both are lyrical with a strong inner energy that never gets close to bombast or overplaying.

Several other versions are fine and would be recommended except for the stiff competition. The version by Mischa Milman and the **Borodin Quartet** is beautiful and expressive; it captures the richness of Schubert but relatively little of the pain (Teldec). A few recordings—Wispelwey and the **Orpheus Quartet** (Channel), the **Locrian Ensemble** (Quicksilva), Miloš Sádlo and the **Smetana Quartet** (Testament), and Michael Sanderling with the **Petersen Quartet** (Capriccio)—are all lyrical and elegant but lack intensity and fire; in comparison with the best versions they seem to run on auto-pilot. Sanderling's performance with the **New Leipzig Quartet** is similar; lovely, warm, and musical, but less involved than the best versions (MD+G).

The recording by László Szilvásy and the **Tátrai Quartet** is interesting mainly for the wealth of minor chamber pieces included in the set (Capriccio 49068, part of their Schubert Edition, 2CD). Wolfgang Boettcher and the **Melos Quartet** are intense and dramatic, but suffer from tempos that are too slow and sound that is too bright (Harmonia Mundi). The recording by Harnoy and the **Orford Quartet** suffers from bad balances (Carlton). The version by the **Juilliard Quartet** and Bernard Greenhouse is certainly well played, but it sounds over-analyzed and too calculated: A very slow first movement followed by an introspective slow movement and aggressive, pushed final movements drive the spirit of spontaneity and naturalness from the piece (Sony 42383).

Two special versions should be mentioned. The 1951 Prades Festival version with **Stern,** Casals, and others is marred by poor sound and some imperfect intonation, but the playing has great personality (♦Sony 58992). And finally, for those so inclined, there is a fine version of the Quintet arranged for chamber orchestra, played by the Atlas Camerata conducted by **Dalia Atlas** (ITM 950005).

Octet

Schubert's Octet for strings and winds was commissioned by Count Ferdinand von Troyer, a fine clarinetist who played in the work's premiere in 1824. Schubert wrote the piece quickly, modeling it on Beethoven's well-known Septet; the Octet, however, was expanded to about an hour, roughly double the length of Beethoven's work. Schubert scored his piece for clarinet, horn, bassoon, and string quintet, with most of the thematic material falling to clarinet, horn and first violin. As with so many of Schubert's long pieces, the Octet can be a difficult challenge for performers. The melodies are very lovely and invite the players to indulge in local detail, but then the piece may sound too episodic and "loved to death." On the other hand, too tight a rein or too dynamic an approach will smother its lyric beauty and leave the listener impressed but unmoved. The middle ground, alert and direct while sensitive and yielding, can be hard to achieve. Unlike some composers, Schubert isn't made better simply by making loud sections louder or fast movements faster.

Few groups have achieved the desired balance better than the **St. Martin in the Fields Chamber Ensemble** (♦Chandos 8585). This reading, a little more romantic and even better recorded than their 1977 version (Philips), is sprightly without a sign of virtuosity and tender without becoming sentimental. It's hard to imagine a performance being more right than this one. Several other performances, though, are

almost as strong. **L'Archibudelli** captures the lively spirit of Schubert without losing any sense of grace (♦Sony 66264). For those who like a warm, dramatic approach, the **Cleveland Octet** is very fine; they dig deeply into the music and find its serious side (♦Sony 62655). The tough, mature side of Schubert is revealed by **Kagan** and others (♦Live 101); this, like the **Fine Arts** version (♦Boston Skyline 143), is rich, full-bodied, and intense, with few smiles and little sense of vulnerability.

The **Acht Ensemble**'s performance is brightly lit and youthful, with more emphasis on lyricism than drama (Thorofon 2326). For the budget-minded, the **Melos Ensemble** combines a fine Octet with Beethoven's Septet and Mendelssohn's wonderful Octet (♦EMI 69755, 2CD, mid-priced). Some performances, like the **Cherubini Quartet**'s (EMI 54269) or the **Nash Ensemble**'s (Virgin 61409) are attractive but basically too relaxed and unenergetic. For those partial to period instruments, the **Hausmusik** performance is outstanding in every way (♦EMI 54118).   ALTHOUSE

PIANO MUSIC

Schubert wrote a great deal of piano music, including 21 wonderful sonatas, many exquisite miniatures, and several delightful collections of marches, waltzes, and other dances. He also left a number of works for piano four hands, several of which are remarkable masterpieces.

Sonatas

Schubert composed 21 piano sonatas, but this number is not as firm as Beethoven's 32 or Mozart's 18, since about half of them were left incomplete. But all these works contain a rich vein of harmonic and melodic treasure that demands our utmost attention, and the last three in particular are profound expressions of the composer's deepest feelings. They were unfathomably neglected until several decades into the 20th century, when pioneers like Artur Schnabel brought them before audiences more used to thundering virtuosic display pieces than works of a subtler variety.

Complete and partial sets. "Complete" is an uncertain term when dealing with recorded editions of the sonatas. *New Grove* lists 23, and while Martin Tirimo's survey offers all of these—including fragments—Schiff gives us 19 (Decca), and Kempff, in his "complete" edition, provides us with only 18 (DG). On the other hand, **Michel Dalberto** sought to set down almost every note the composer wrote for the keyboard (Denon). The important thing is that all these sets contain the most important sonatas, especially the final trilogy—19, 20, and 21—set down in the last year of Schubert's unconscionably short life.

Currently **Kempff's** is the best of the sets (DG 423496, 7CD). The simplicity and nobility of his playing are really something special, and his intimate readings penetrate to the heart of each sonata. While he is sometimes cavalier about repeats, he does include the long and controversial repeat in 21, one of the finest performances of this work in the catalog.

Schiff is a probing Schubertian and offers chaste and elegiac readings of great beauty that are infused with unique insights (Decca 448390, 7CD). Here, too, the important repeat in 21 is observed. **Tirimo** is also an effective interpreter, and it's obvious while listening to these stimulating performances that much thought and preparation have gone into them. The one snag here is the sound, which is over-reverberant and tends to blur detail (EMI 2278/85, 8CD, also offered singly).

The set by the brilliant young German pianist **Michael Endres** is a splendid alternative to Kempff (Capriccio, various numbers). When I first listened to these performances, I was impressed by some of the finest Schubert playing I had heard in a long time, and hearing them recently again has reconfirmed that impression. Endres plays with assurance and spontaneity, an unerring sense of pace, phrase, and form, and an unmannered eloquence. He is generous with repeats, and the excellent sound is a bonus, as is the 70+ minute playing time of each disc, which allows the contents to be offered on six CDs rather than the usual seven.

Joining Kempff and Endres among the interpreters of choice is **Walter Klien,** a great Mozartean who is equally persuasive in Schubert. Taped between 1971 and 1973, his superb cycle brings his own distinctive insights to this magical repertoire, revealing his intimate knowledge of these works in readings that are at once perceptive and stimulating and have a Viennese songfulnesss and warmth. Generous playing time allows this cycle too to be limited to six discs (Vox, 5173/5, 2CD each).

Anton Kuerti's individualistic readings of what are called Schubert's "major works" include the 11 sonatas deemed the best by the Austrian-born Canadian pianist (Analekta, 7CD). It's interesting to note which sonatas are considered most important by this profound musical thinker. He adds the "Wanderer" Fantasy, the two sets of *Impromptus,* the six *Moments musicaux,* and the Andante from Sonata 15, the so-called "Relique." Not everyone will agree with his view of the music, but I find the set stimulating and very much worth hearing.

Uchida is a sensitive and thought-provoking pianist, and it's no surprise that she's an especially persuasive Schubertian. Thus far she has recorded nine sonatas in especially probing accounts, and no one who opts for them is likely to be disappointed (Philips, various numbers). A similarly high plane of performance is offered by **Imogen Cooper** in a set entitled "Schubert: The Last Six Years" (Ottavo, various numbers). These beautifully recorded discs contain playing of the utmost sensitivity and a profound understanding of what the composer is trying to convey. This is selfless pianism, solely dedicated to the works at hand, and finer realizations would be hard to find.

Richard Goode, whose complete Beethoven sonata cycle is among the best modern versions, has recorded four discs of Schubert sonatas. Here is honest, unaffected music-making that never draws attention to itself and presents the music directly, with a complete lack of artifice, and this pays off on repeated hearings (Nonesuch, various numbers). Two of the discs are rather short, but their musical values more than compensate. The Danish pianist **John Damgaard** has been described by another critic as a miniaturist and lyricist who, in a recently released set, eschews big effects in favor of communicative playing of beauty, purity, and inner strength (Classico 245, 5CD).

Individual performances. There are many exceptional versions of these works, although they were slow to enter the repertoire. **Schnabel's** influence in bringing them to a wide audience cannot be overestimated. Before the great pianist regularly placed them on his recital programs they were all but unknown. In the 1930s Schnabel committed a fair amount of Schubert's piano music to disc, but EMI has been remiss in reissuing this important legacy in its entirety. They leased the material to Arabesque in the mid 1980s for a brief appearance on CD. At last EMI has released a set in its "Reference" series that includes 17, 19, and 20, recorded between 1937 and 1939 (64259).

These sonatas have not received more potent and insightful performances on record. Schnabel had a unique feel for this repertoire, realizing to a greater degree than many of his contemporaries that Schubert was much more than the naive and charming bumpkin from whom

melody poured forth like water from a mountain stream. No. 21 is especially gripping, but that's not to minimize the profundity and power that infuse the other two, and with the variegated moods of the six *Moments musicaux,* the disc is not to be missed. Excellent transfers of 20 and 21 (Pearl 9271, 2CD) and 17 (Pearl 9272, 2CD) are filled out with the four-hand works the pianist recorded with his son Karl Ulrich, *Moments musicaux,* and the "Trout" Quintet with members of the Pro Arte Quartet.

After Schnabel, many of the greatest pianists championed the cause of the sonatas. **Brendel** is a loyal advocate of Schubert's piano works and has recorded many of them, sometimes more than once. Of the analog series of the late sonatas he taped in the 1970s, there remains a set holding the final three that is a fine example of this great pianist's art and his devotion to these masterpieces (Philips 438703, 2CD, with *Klavierstücke).* These recordings are also coupled with digital versions of Nos. 4 and 13 in an anthology that includes his 1970s tapings of the "Wanderer" Fantasy and a considerable number of shorter pieces (Philips 446923, 5CD). Brendel is adamant in his refusal to observe the repeat in 21:I, mistakenly, I think.

Brendel returned to Schubert in the late 1980s and taped a digital cycle encompassing 14–21 filled out with the "Wanderer" Fantasy and shorter works (Philips 426218, 7CD, also issued singly). I like the elemental strength offered here. Admirers of this pianist's Schubert can also find his fresh 1965 accounts of 15 and 19 in marvelous transfers (Vanguard 119, with the delightful German Dances D 783), and his in-concert recordings from the late 1990s of 9, 18, 20, and 21, which have even greater warmth, depth and flexibility (Philips 456573, 2CD).

Curzon infused greatness into whatever he chose to play, be it a Mozart concerto or a Liszt barnburner. As a recording artist he left too little of his work to posterity, but we do have three magnificent Schubert sonata recordings. His version of 17 remains one of the finest, filled with a lyrical warmth and rhythmic insouciance that combine to create a special listening experience; it remains one of my favorite Schubert recordings (Decca 443570). His account of 21 is also quite remarkable (Decca 448578). His deep feeling for this music is always evident, displaying a unique nobility, and his acute attention to detail enhances the music without loss of structure. Another reading of 21 comes from the 1974 Salzburg Festival (Orfeo 401951). Here the pianist offers an even more intense account, and I'm glad to have them both.

An addendum to **Kempff's** magnificent cycle comes in the form of a 1953 taping of No. 16 in the "Great Pianists of the 20th Century" series that reveals the pianist at his considerable best in a powerful and subtle reading (Philips 456865, 2CD). Unlike his later DG recording, he observes the exposition repeat in I. **Gilels** left little Schubert in his discography, but two sonatas remain. A riveting performance of 17 combines drama with felicitous charm (RCA 61614, with an equally imposing Liszt Sonata). A blazing and commanding reading of 14 comes from the 1977 Salzburg Festival (Orfeo 332930, also with Liszt).

Ashkenazy is another pianist with a special feeling for Schubert. His recording of 21 is excellent (Decca 417327, with "Wanderer"), and his later 1995 account is beautifully crafted (Decca 456148, with *Impromptus* D 899). A splendid recital that stands the test of time includes 13 and 14; Schubert playing doesn't get much better than this (Decca 445799, with shorter pieces). **Perahia's** Schubert is also in this special category. He has recorded only 20 thus far and it's a superb example of his artistry (Sony 44569, with Schumann's Sonata 2), but I'm told that 21 is on the way.

It's unfortunate that **Lili Kraus** left us so little Schubert, as she was so attuned to his unique sound world, but she did record 13, 16, and 21 in the late 1970s (Vanguard 8200, 3CD, available singly, with "Wanderer" and both sets of *Impromptus*). She was in her early 70s, but her technique held up pretty well, although it wasn't as fluid as earlier in her long and distinguished career. What comes through are her loving understanding of this composer and the penetrating depth this perceptive pianist was able to bring to this music. That **Kovacevich** is a profound Schubertian is amply demonstrated in two releases that include 20 and 21; better performances—at once severe and sensitive—would be hard to find (EMI 55219 and 55359).

Bruce Hungerford was a profound Schubertian who left us too soon. Fortunately he taped a remarkable reading of No. 20 that remains one of the best in the catalog (Vanguard 76, 4CD, with Brahms, Chopin, etc.). **Myra Hess** was another pianist who was allergic to recording. Examples of her Schubert include a superb account of 13 recorded in the days of 78s (APR 7012, 2CD)—an LP transfer of this magical reading was my first exposure to this music—and a rare in-concert performance of 21 in 1949 (APR 5520).

Annie Fischer left two versions of 21. Her classic EMI recording has left the catalog, but an even more imposing version is available (Hungaroton 31494, with Liszt's Sonata). **Horowitz** might seem to be the last pianist you would expect to be attracted to the mysteries of 21, but he left two versions of this sonata. The first, taped in Carnegie Hall during his 25th anniversary recital in 1953, has never appealed to me; I find it too tense and literal (RCA 60451). He returned to the work in 1986 in a more expansive and searching account, including the first-movement repeat, omitted earlier (DG 435025, with Schumann's *Kinderszenen*).

Arrau brings his usual integrity to 13, 19, 20 and 21 in a beautifully recorded set (Philips 432307, with shorter pieces). Those who favor this pianist's probing pianism, as I do, will find a treasure trove here; others may find the results ponderous and boring. Regrettably, those words accurately describe his last Schubert sonata recording, made in his late eighties; his reading of 18 is so ponderous it seems to last an eternity (Philips 432987). It's refreshing to turn to **Clara Haskil's** lyrical reading of 21, recorded in 1951 and beautifully refurbished in the "Great Pianists of the 20th Century" series (Philips 456829, 2CD).

The artistry of the distinguished Italian pianist **Sergio Fiorentino** is enjoying a revival on discs. His expressive and fluent reading of 21 is well worth hearing (APR 5553, with Chopin's Sonata 3). **Pollini** has turned to the last three sonatas with predictable results. The readings are, of course, pianistically flawless, but there's more than mere surface perfection on display. This pianist can be cold and uninvolving, but here he has something important to say and doesn't slight either the drama or lyricism in these works (DG 427326/7).

Maria Yudina provides one of the most remarkable versions of 21 to come my way (Dante 123, with Brahms's *Handel Variations*). This is as dark and terrifying a reading as you can imagine; it's as though she were probing the composer's very soul as he contemplates his final days. Despite an occasional hint of overload, the 1947 Soviet recording is quite good. No. 21 is also wonderfully served by **Stephen Hough,** who makes a strong case for the first movement repeat in his illuminating annotation, in one of the finest versions in the catalog (Hyperion 67027, with the unfinished 11 and 14).

Ian Hobson has turned his attention to the last three sonatas with commanding results, offering stylish and idiomatic readings. Here is another pianist who gives you the music unfettered and without interpretive tricks, which is one of the many reasons these well-recorded readings are so satisfying (Zephyr 11800, 2CD, with *Klavierstücke*). All repeats are observed.

Peter Rösel deserves to be better known. I've never been disappointed by any of his recordings, and I'm happy to report that the reissue of his late 1980s tapings of 6, 9, 14, and 21 (with repeat) are eminently satisfying. This is superb Schubert and a bargain at budget price (Capriccio 5076, 2CD, with "Wanderer"). No. 19 is given a blazing reading by the lamented **Yuri Egorov,** who really knew how to set a piano on fire (Channel 9213, with *Moments musicaux*).

Richter stands unique in his perception of Schubert's piano music. He views the late sonatas as the tragic expressions of a man loving life with tender lyricism and fearing death with anger and agony. This is especially the case for the slow movements of the sonatas, which he stretches out painfully while somehow maintaining their rapt and gripping intensity. He plays 19 with verve and 21 with a probing expansiveness that can tax listeners unwilling to accompany him on an extraordinary journey (he spends nearly 47 minutes on 21, compared to Annie Fischer's 33).

Richter's huge discography has many twists and turns; here is a partial list of discs that demand to be heard and experienced. Nos. 9, 12, and 13 (BBC Legends 4010); 9, with the Liszt Sonata and Mozart's Sonata K 283 (Music & Arts 600); 9, 11, and *Moments musicaux* 1, 3, and 6 (Olympia 286); 19 (the finest recording I know of this work) and 21 (Olympia 335); 13 and 14 and *Impromptus* D 899 (Olympic 288). In another superb reading of 19 there is some distortion at the beginning, but it clears up quickly (Doremi 7766, with Chopin, Mendelssohn, and Debussy); a haunting reading of 21 with *Impromptu* D. 899:3 (Praga 254); radiant and dramatic readings of 16 and 17 (RCA 29463). Finally, from the so-called "Authorized Edition" (Richter denied any involvement in the project), a treasure trove offers 9, 15 (a four-movement version played to the point where Schubert left off), and 18 (Philips 438483, 2CD).

Rubinstein is a natural for Schubert, yet strangely this most elegant and insightful of pianists recorded little of the solo music, preferring to play the piano trios. However, he did plan to record the last three sonatas, and eventually a 1969 taping of 21 was approved for release. Unfortunately, it's cool, uninvolved, and uninvolving, one of his few failures in the recording studio. However, harnessed with a superb recording of Beethoven's Sonata 3, its purchase is almost mandatory for his admirers (RCA 63055). A later 1965 performance was on an entirely different level, demonstrating his true feeling for this music (RCA 63054, with "Wanderer"). This all-Schubert recital is one of Rubinstein's finest records and is strongly recommended. The remastering of both discs is superb. Incidentally, it's said that recordings of 19 and 20 exist in RCA's vaults; perhaps their reevaluation for possible release is in order.

Lupu serves his art selflessly and always has something interesting to say. That's the case for his readings of 13 and 21, which he explores in direct, classically pure performances. **Jandó** offers sweet, appealing accounts of 6 and 11, and given their good sound and budget price, this is a remarkable buy (Naxos 550846). Those wondering why a renowned Schubertian like **Rudolf Serkin** is missing from this discussion should know that neither of his two recordings of 21 has been transferred to CD, and that his structured and probing reading of 20 is available only overseas (Sony 63042, with *Impromptus* D 935).

While I think the modern piano is really the ideal instrument to transmit Schubert's full expressive range, two exceptions to this rule should be mentioned. The outstanding fortepianist **Olga Tsverskaya** has recorded two discs of remarkable quality. She is a profound interpreter of this music and her accounts of 20 (Opus 111 30139, with *Moments musicaux*) and 6, 13, and *Impromptus* D 899:3+4 are strongly recommended (Opus 111 310193). **Andreas Staier** offers a vivid realization of 16 (Teldec 11084, with *Klavierstücke*), and 19, 20 and 21 are equally good (Teldec 13143).

Other piano works
In addition to his 21 or so sonatas, Schubert left a significant body of shorter pieces of superior quality.

"Wanderer" Fantasy. The distinguished pianist/scholar Paul Badura-Skoda considers this piece, based on a theme from Schubert's song "Der Wanderer," a work of revolutionary consequence. What other composer of the period could put together a virtually monothematic four-movement piece, utilizing the full (although rather limited) resources of the early 19th-century fortepiano in an almost orchestral manner? The work was composed in 1822 (the year of Beethoven's last sonata) and is truly larger than life. It's also harmonically inventive and filled with that special mixture of passion, drama, and lyricism that is the hallmark of this composer's unique genius.

There are few instances when a recording can be called "definitive," but the term can be applied without hesitation to **Richter's** 1963 recording (EMI 66947, in the "Great Recordings" series in a superb remastering, strangely coupled with Dvořák's Piano Concerto). His interpretation encompasses every aspect of this complicated work, in an act of re-creation bringing everything on the printed page—and more—to the listener. It is for such performances that the recording process was made. Here is a great pianist at the height of his powers, revealing every secret of the music.

After this performance, all others are also-rans, but several deserve mention. First is the classic recording by **Edwin Fischer,** whose musical insights and selfless artistry ennobled everything he played. His superb rendering is best heard in a disc with the complete *Impromptus* (APR 5515). Another imposing account came from **Bruce Hungerford,** taken from a 1961 Berlin recital (IPAM 1203, with other short pieces). Also excellent are versions by **Perahia,** spacious and noble (Sony 42124, with Schumann's Fantasy), **Pollini** (DG 447451, also with the Schumann Fantasy), **Lili Kraus's** combination of a strong sense of structure with a fluent lyricism (Vanguard 8099, with Sonata 21); **Rubinstein** (RCA 63054, with Sonata 21); and **Curzon, Rösel, Kempff, Kuerti,** and **Arrau** in the sets mentioned above.

You should approach with caution the rather relentless **Demidenko** (Hyperion 670091/92, 2CD) and the disappointing **Schiff,** who is too soft-centered for this work (ECM 464320). However, **Leslie Howard's** beautifully realized version of Liszt's solo arrangement of the work is of special interest, entirely different from the garish transcription for piano and orchestra (Hyperion 67203, with other transcriptions). Periodists are directed to **Badura-Skoda's** fine reading (Astrée 7763, with *Moments musicaux*).

Impromptus. Schubert's *Impromptus,* published in two sets of four, D 899 and 935, were composed rather late in his short life. Each of them is a beguiling tone poem that is individual in its means of expression. These masterpieces have long been popular, and sometimes their great depth has been underappreciated. Although they have been recorded by many, there are a few versions (including the performances in the sets recommended above) that reach the highest levels of great art.

Perhaps the finest set ever recorded is by **Edwin Fischer,** whose accounts are truly revelatory, even though he plays the spurious G Major transcription of D 899:3 (APR 5515, with "Wanderer"). **Schnabel's** 1950 set is also of the highest quality; few matched his insight, and these are magnificent readings (EMI 61021). But there's a fly in the ointment here

too: He offers a truncated version of D 899:4, cutting some material to meet the time limit of a single 78 rpm side.

There are some extraordinary contemporary versions as well. Among them are **Zimerman's** thoughtful and original accounts (DG 423612); **Lili Kraus's** authoritative and dark-colored interpretations (Vanguard 4068); **Perahia,** elegant and eloquent (Sony 37291); **Lupu** (Decca 460975), **Uchida,** who conveys the bittersweet melancholy of these enchanting pieces with subtlety and skill (Philips 456245); **Brendel** (Philips 422237), and **Kempff** (DG 453762).

Pires offers readings of poetic intimacy, well proportioned and full of nuances, with an unsettling and entirely idiomatic turbulence (DG 447550, 2CD, with *Klavierstücke*). Periodists should find satisfaction in **Badura-Skoda's** perceptive accounts (Astrée 7764). Finally, don't overlook **Curzon,** whose readings our Editor regards as the finest ever recorded, unique in their affectionate innocence and aching beauty (in the "Great Pianists" series, Philips 456757, 2CD, with "Wanderer," etc.).

Moments musicaux. These pieces embody a wide range of moods and colors. Within a deceptively simple facade there is plenty going on; from the easygoing charm of No. 3 to the *Sturm und Drang* of 5, Schubert distills a great deal of material in a very limited time. Again it is **Edwin Fischer** who reveals the profundity hidden in these tiny jewels, while offering playing of the utmost simplicity (Testament 1145, with *Impromptus*). Also of the highest order are the versions by **Lupu** (Philips 456895, 2CD), **Gilels** (RCA 74321, 2CD), **Schnabel** (EMI 64259 and Pearl 9272, both 2CD), and **Egorov** (Channel 9213).

Marches, dances, etc. There are about 350 of these delightful pieces—marches, *ländler* and other dances, short movements perhaps intended for sonatas that were never completed, and so on. The most important of them—like the *Allegretto* D 915—are included in the various sets recommended above.

LINKOWSKI

Music for piano four-hands
Schubert wrote more music for piano four-hands than anyone else: over 70 pieces (some of them large in scale), including two sonatas, four fantasies, and lots of dances, marches, and other short works. Several of them are among the greatest ever composed in this genre. They have been well represented on disc, individually and in more or less complete sets, presumably because of the low cost of putting two pianists into a recording studio and the great appeal of the music.

Among the sets, **Yaara Tal** and **Andreas Groethuysen** should probably be your first choice; they play with remarkable virtuosity, unity, brilliance, and imagination (Sony). **Begoña Uriarte** and **Karl-Hermann Mrongovius** are a close second, completely in sympathy with each other and with the music, stressing emotional content more than surface brilliance (Calig). A third recommendation is the **Duo Crommelynck,** a husband-and wife team that sadly died in a double suicide a few years ago, who played with strength, intensity, and expressive depth, though they sometimes over-pedaled a bit and were a little heavy-handed (Claves).

Bracha Eden and **Alexander Tamir** have been playing together for a long time; their technique is occasionally faulty and their textures muddy, but their sympathy with each other and with the music makes their performances enjoyable (CRD). **Christoph Eschenbach** and **Justus Frantz** are highly polished and skillful; their interpretations are well thought out and persuasive (EMI 69770, 2CD). **Dana Muller** and **Gary Steigerwalt** somehow make this wonderful music charmless and can be ignored (Centaur), while **Gloria Saarinen** and **Arnold Draper** are too precious to be taken seriously (Doremi, 2CD).

Two of these works in particular deserve individual attention:

Fantasy D 940 is one of the great works in the genre, a sublime mixture of lyricism and drama, pathos and tragedy. Apart from performances in the sets recommended above, the recording by the **Duo Schnabel** (Karl Ulrich Schnabel and Joan Rowland) is powerful and disturbing, with considerable subtlety and a good sense of structure (Sheffield Lab 10054, with shorter pieces).

Sonata D 812 ("Grand Duo") is another of the high points of music for piano four-hands. Named "Grand Duo" by its publisher, Diabelli, it's long, constantly changing in mood, and full of harmonic modulations. The **Duo Schnabel** plays it well enough but rather squarely and without much charm (TownHall). **Richter** and **Britten** offer a rough-and-ready recording, underrehearsed but spontaneous and urgent, and **Barenboim** and **Lupu** give the work eloquence and lyricism (Teldec 17146, with shorter pieces).   MORIN

CHORAL MUSIC

The hallmark of all Schubert's work is simplicity—but coupled with a profound melodic and harmonic underpinning that is ravishing in its exemplary, methodical means of expression. Interpreters must not see this music with the eyes of a simpleton, but they must approach it with the ears of a child and reject the temptation to overindulge the senses with supposed profundities and distortions that bend it to the breaking point. At the same time, and this is especially true in his choral music, they must be bold when presenting music that so obviously cries out for unencumbered expressiveness. Neither a skeletal shakedown nor a Berlioz-like explosion will suit Schubert, and those interpreters that find the middle road are the most successful.

Sacred music

Great arguments have been made about Schubert's religious devotion. Much of this is based on the fact that in none of his masses does he include the words "and in One, Holy, Catholic, and Apostolic Church." Yet we know that these masses (or at least most of them) were intended for actual liturgical performance. No Roman Catholic prelate or priest in his right mind would have approved such an omission without fear of sanction, so it can only be assumed that Schubert was writing according to an established practice or local custom of his time. You can find examples of Schubert both praising the virtues of faith in the traditional sense and decrying the folly and superstition of religion as practiced in his (and every) day. But the truth of the matter must ultimately remain in the pages of this extraordinary music. From the juvenile Mass in G to the innovative, amazing Mass in A-flat, Schubert's devotion emerges fresh and unencumbered from every page. Astonishingly, there are very few recordings of this heavenly music.

Complete Sets. One of the highlights of **Sawallisch**'s long and sometimes distinguished career has to be his near complete traversal of Schubert's choral music (♦EMI 64778, 4CD). The readings of the six masses plus the *German Mass* and five smaller works that make up Vol. 3 of his set feature the stirring playing and singing of the Bavarian Radio Symphony and Chorus. The choir is large, the playing forceful and vigorous, and the line leading to bloating and over-zealous romantic excessiveness is never crossed. The soloists (though Schubert greatly restricts their role) are without peer: Popp, Donath, Fassbaender, Dallapozza, Schreier, Araiza, Protschka, and Fischer-Dieskau. I urge you to acquire this set if you want to hear Schubert the way he was meant to sound.

Yet you can't discount some of the very close also-rans. If you're looking for an economical way to add these wonderful masses to your col-

lection without sacrificing quality (often difficult to do with complete cycles), you will do no better than the set with the Berlin Bach Collegium conducted by **Martin Berhmann** (♦Vox 3040, 3CD). These 1978 recordings leave very little to be desired—modern instruments, big choirs, competent soloists, and a great price. The sound is restricted in some places, but the interpretations are near the Shaw and Sawallisch level. While I definitely prefer the latter recordings, I'd be happy for having heard only Berhmann's. As a bonus, the 1962 recording of *German Mass* by Hans Gillesberger and the Vienna Chamber Choir and Symphony rounds out the release.

In the period instrument world, only one set has been produced, and it's a good one. **Bruno Weil** and his Orchestra of the Age of Enlightenment with the Vienna Boys Choir give us Schubert with a new lease on life. This is much closer to the way the composer would have heard these pieces, having himself been a member of that choir. But more than that, Weil paints these works in a joyous, fresh, featherweight manner, succinctly pointed in their honest, pure vocal coloration. The period instruments sound palatable for once, and the set must be considered a worthy full-price investment (♦Sony 62778, 4CD, with *German Mass* as a bonus).

Sawallisch again must be mentioned for his great efforts in behalf of much of Schubert's ignored or forgotten liturgical music. Many of the shorter, gloriously radiant works are presented by the same forces that gave us the masses in a cornucopia of Schubertian devotion and elegance (♦EMI 64783, 3CD). You can obtain some of these works as fillers in other issues, but this is the only offering of its kind (and the only one needed, as long as **Erwin Ortner**'s 7CD set is unavailable), so it's self-recommending.

1 in F. Aside from the usual caveats (no more than adequate solo singing and some rather piercing sound in the trebles), **Weil** does an excellent job in this 1814 opus by the 17-year-old composer. If you like this sound, then there's really no other reasonable choice. The popular, yet still juvenile 2 is the appropriate coupling (♦Sony 68247). **Andreas Weiser** manages some fine, solid choral work with the Prague Virtuosi and Chamber Chorus, but that and the equally fine price can't offset some of the wretched solo singing found here. This is only for those on a highly restricted budget and approaching desperation (Koch, with a *Magnificat* and *Salve Regina*). The same problem occurs in **George Barati**'s recording with forces in Vienna, plus the soloists are horribly overmiked (Tuxedo, with 4).

2 in G. Led by the sweet singing of Barbara Bonney, **Abbado** gives a lovely performance of this delightful, soulfully searching mass. All the freshness of virgin faith is found here, in one of Schubert's most songful works (♦DG 435486). **Kegel** and Leipzig Radio forces turn in a very nice, modestly priced version with affection and taste, though the timing is short with only the *Stabat Mater* coupled with it (Berlin). **Romano Gandolfi** and the Prague Virtuosi make a good go at this youngster's mass, with some excellent choral work, but the coupled Symphony 5 is better served by other recordings, and so, ultimately, is the mass (Koch). But on the same label, Masses 2, 3, and 4 are offered by the **Prague Virtuosi** in excellent readings at budget price, though the sound is somewhat constricted. You can hardly go wrong here, a terrific introduction (♦Koch 920228).

The set of Masses 2, 4, and 6 plus *German Mass* and *Tantum Ergo in C* by conductors **Martin Haselböck** and **Marcus Creed** can hardly be beat at mid-price (♦Capriccio 490807, 2CD). Creed especially is one of the finest exponents of this music, and this set, part of Capriccio's uneven "Schubert Edition," can't be recommended too highly, though Haselböck's 4 is rather undernourished in a soupy rendition that lacks sufficient definition. Nevertheless, the Creed coupling is worth the outlay. The full period strings give the lie to the idea that authentic instruments sound impoverished in a reading by **Patrick Peire** and his Bruges orchestra. Proportions are well shaped, and the light and airy soloists scent this youthful music with a most agreeable fragrance. Also included is 3, along with the short but intense *Stabat Mater* (which uses only the first four lines of the poem) and *Salve Regina*. This is a nice way to acquire these works (♦Rene Gailly 87140).

Reinhard Kammler gives a folksy, unrefined, and rather provincial account of 2 and *German Mass*, a small, yet very attractive work that has had few US recordings, but the singing is not what we have come to expect these days (Calig). **Shaw**'s classic recording of 2 sets the standard (♦Telarc 80212). The singing is superbly rounded and vitally presented (led by the radiance of Dawn Upshaw's soprano), the orchestra is full of vibrancy and soul, while the recorded sound is nowhere bettered.

3 in B-flat. **Jack Martin Händler** and his Prague Virtuosi present us with a more than competent, positively buoyant recording. The choir is on the small side and the lower voices are a tad weak, but the sound is excellent, and for such a low price you can't really beat this introduction to some early, celestial Schubert. The fine reading of Symphony 6 only adds to the attraction (♦Koch 920218). **Weil**, on period instruments, inspires the Vienna Boys Choir in heightened, backlit readings of 3 and 4 that are caressed almost to a fault, yet maintain a fleetness of foot preferable to more profound recordings. Schubert comes through with an unquestioned sheen and consummate validity (♦Sony 68248). **Gillesberger**, with a set of soloists different from the ones that so disabled his recording of 1 and 4, is much more on track in 3, with a fine chorus that seems fully alive to the spirit of this work; the *German Mass* is a fine coupling (Tuxedo). But this same program is available from the Vienna St. Augustin Choir under **Friedrich Wolf**, along with two pieces by Mozart, *Ave verum corpus* and *Vesperae solennes de confessore,* in even better sound, more vibrant and revealing. The full price shouldn't scare you away (♦Preiser 93325).

4 in C. The Prague Virtuosi and Chamber Chorus under **Ulrich Backofen** turn in a rousing reading of this most splashy of Schubert's masses. The choral and solo work is excellent, with ample reverberation given to the choir in this budget disc. The coupled Symphony 3 is up against almost insurmountable competition, but the low price allows some room for choice here (♦Koch 920235). A generous coupling of Masses 4–6 by **Sawallisch** and forces is now available in an issue that tantalizes with *Tantum ergo* and *Offertorium* as well. This "two-fer" is just the ticket for those interested especially in 4, for this recording has never really been topped for sheer energy and robust singing. Grab it while you can (♦EMI 73365, 2CD). Also at mid-price is a release with just 4 and 5 (♦EMI 69222).

5 in A-flat. With this work we enter into the truly sublime realm of later Schubert. This mass is quite the maverick, even more ambitious than his last in terms of textual manipulation and modulations (Schubert himself called it "Missa Solemnis"). There are many fine recordings, none better than **Sawallisch** (see above). **Heinz Hennig** and the Hanover Boys Choir use period instruments that in no way detract from the beauties of this performance; it's not outgoing in a concert manner, but introverted and serene (♦Ars Musici 1211). **Rilling** gives a smooth, buttery reading of Schubert's daring and original work. Mood is of primary concern here, and the Oregon Bach Festival forces are on top of

every twist and turn of this devotional, yet somewhat religiously defiant piece. The timing is on the short side, so all things being equal, look elsewhere (Hänssler).

Harnoncourt displays a traditional, inflated concert version that wants for nothing in terms of shapeliness, tone, or Schubertian suavity. His choral forces (the Arnold Schoenberg Choir) are unsurpassed (♦Teldec 98422). **Gardiner** has given us a reading that is quite typical of him—clean, well-delineated lines, harmonic clarity (almost sparseness), driven tempos, and a sterility that is either virtue or vice depending on your point of view. This effort lacks any degree of Viennese charm, and the additions of *Psalm 92, Stabat Mater,* and *Hymn to the Holy Spirit* don't make up for a disappointing reading. It's another of those media-hyped recordings to be avoided (Philips). **Schreier** leads a beautiful performance that wants for nothing—choral excellence, fine solo singing, meltingly lyrical orchestral playing. The Tapiola Sinfonietta and the choir are to be congratulated for such a golden offering, fondly coupled with *Salve Regina* and *Stabat Mater* (♦Ondine 917). And of course, **Weil** weighs in here with the best of the period instrument/boys choir offerings, though if pressed I'd be in quite a bind to let go of Sawallisch or Schreier (♦Sony 53984).

6 in E-flat. Schubert's final mass is one of the many miracles of his last year. The form is more standard than the preceding 5, and the chorus assumes most of the spotlight, with the soloists relegated to a more subservient role. The writing is superb, full of sensual flow and dramatic word painting that slowly tilt the form away from the strictness of the Church and toward a bona fide romantic expression. While not perhaps as innovative as 5, it remains his choral masterpiece.

No recording surpasses **Shaw**'s magnificent offering, one of his finest efforts. Unusually for this conductor, hex gives full reign to the implicit romantic surges of chromatic and dynamic fluctuations that send chills down the spine. The choral work is unsurpassed, and this has to be first choice for this superb work (♦Telarc 80212). **Sawallisch** turned in a pre-Shaw standard setter with excellent soloists and wide, spacious sound. The Bavarian Radio Symphony has never sounded better, and if you get this in his complete set—even in the face of Shaw—you can hardly do better. As it is, the bargain set of Masses 4–6 will serve you well (♦EMI 73365, 2CD).

Weil and his period practitioners take a far bouncier view of this work. While Sawallisch and Shaw approach it with an overabundance of *gravitas profundis,* Weil sees this last Schubertian breath as one of lightness and joy. The music is certainly flexible enough to countenance a variety of approaches, and Weil makes a firm case here. My only point of concern (true throughout his set) is the boys' choir—rock solid musically, but tending toward a degree of shrillness that only boy choirs can achieve (♦Sony 66255).

Giulini brings a touch of spirituality and insight to everything he does, but in this instance he proves too overbearing for Schubert's finely constructed choral harmonies. Some parts, like the *Credo,* do have a wonderfully majestic feeling, but for the most part it's bogged down in a lethargic, pseudo-piety that misses the pious points (Sony). **Harnoncourt**'s concert performance with the Chamber Orchestra of Europe and the magnificent Arnold Schoenberg Choir brings much pleasure and a few drawbacks. One of these is the lack of palpable presence, probably due to the distant microphone placement. The soloists (led by Orgonasova), with little to do, are excellent. This isn't the familiar Harnoncourt—he's reserved and devotional in his approach, though he loves to spike the punch by ensuring that all of Schubert's dynamics and accents are emphatically observed (♦Teldec 13163). **Abbado** insists that Schubert's last mass is a precursor to the later Austrians like Bruckner. This is a big, bold performance that isn't without attractions and merit, but probably falls into the specialist category (DG).

Secular music

Few recordings exist of the many and varied songs and choruses that Schubert wrote for all sorts of occasions. The first to be mentioned has to be the exceptional, path-breaking readings by **Sawallisch** that complete his survey of Schubert's choral works. A wonderful collection of part songs and every other category that might get lost in a more specific categorization is to be found here. Couple this with a miraculous hoard of soloists—Behrens, Fassbaender, Schreier, and Fischer-Dieskau—and you have a recipe that satisfies time and time again (♦EMI 66139, 4CD). **Dietrich Knothe** and his Berlin soloists and Radio ensemble offer mostly a selection of male chorus works, using boys at times, along with one track using an orchestra. The price is right for this 1986 recording, but the soloists are a little underdone (Capriccio).

The large set of many and varied part songs by **Die Singphoniker**, who are slowly working their way through this music, may be too much of a good thing—if merely good is your word for this music (CPO, 5CD). But the problem lies in their inconsistency of approach; it's best to hunt and peck among the single issues here. If you would just like a sampling of these miniature marvels, be sure to pick up **Shaw**'s "Songs for Male Chorus." These lovelies are divided into three sections, "Evensong," "Of Narrow Nows and Vast Hereafters," and "Of Spring, Love, Youth and Nature's Gifts." They are, in a word, stunning, and aren't likely to be surpassed any time soon (♦Telarc 80340). RITTER

OPERAS

Schubert started well over a dozen operas but finished only half of them. None were published and only one, *Die Zwillingsbrüder,* was staged during his lifetime. Performances of even his best and grandest operas, *Alfonso und Estrella* and *Fierabras,* have been almost as rare in the 175 years since the composer's death, and only the advent of CDs has enabled us to hear these works. The reasons for this neglect probably include his poor choice of subjects and librettists and the great popularity of Italian opera (to the exclusion of anything written in German) in Vienna during his most productive years. Yet the music in these works is always very beautiful, though the serious operas often lack musical characterization of the principals and dramatic tension.

Alfonso und Estrella. The only available recording of this, Schubert's best and best-known opera, dates from 1978 and, fortunately, it's an outstanding performance with a first-rate cast (♦Berlin 2156, 3CD). The principal roles are all taken by noted interpreters of Schubert lieder (Prey, Fischer-Dieskau, Mathis, Schreier, and Adam) and they make a good case for the work, with **Suitner** conducting. The story, set in medieval Spain, deals with the love that develops between the title characters who must overcome their fathers' enmity and the intrigues of courtiers. They do, nobody dies, and all ends happily.

Fierabras. This opera's background is the war between the Moors and the Franks at the end of the 8th century. There are two pairs of lovers, but each pair consists of a Frank and a Moor. Before true love can triumph (which it does), battles are fought, prisoners are taken, escapes are attempted and thwarted; finally, the wisdom and generosity of the kings (Charlemagne and his Moorish counterpart) set everything right. There's no tragedy, little drama, but much magnificent music. There's also a lot of spoken dialogue and two melodramas. The recommended

recording was made in Vienna in 1988 during a staged performance (♦DG 427341, 2CD). Ably conducted by **Claudio Abbado,** it has a generally fine cast (Mattila, Studer, Hampson, and Protschka). It omits the spoken dialogue. The only other listing is a severely abridged version recorded in 1959 (Myto 89001). Its cast includes Wunderlich, but that's the only point in its favor.

Der Graf von Gleichen. This is Schubert's last opera, which he didn't live to complete. The final scene and the orchestration were supplied by Gunther Elsholz, who used music from the composer's Mass in E-flat for the finale. This version was given its premiere in 1994 by the **Cincinnati College Conservatory of Music** (♦Centaur 2281, 2 CD). It's based on the true story of a Count who, already married, took as his second wife the daughter of a Turkish sultan. It too is worth exploring for its glorious music.

Der vierjährige Posten and *Die Zwillingsbrüder.* These are two of Schubert's more than half-dozen Singspiels, a form of musical entertainment popular in Vienna in the early 19th century. They're based on French farces and are often played together, since each takes less than an hour to perform. Spoken dialogue connects the musical numbers in both. Excellent recordings were made in Munich in the '70s with outstanding casts that included Fischer-Dieskau, Gedda, Donath, and Schreier (♦CPO 999563 and 999556). The conductors are **Heinz Wallberg** and **Sawallisch**. Also available are performances from Cosenza in 1977 (Bongiovanni) Their casts are inferior to those from Munich and the performances, conducted by **Peter Maag,** lack the charm and style that can make these slight works appealing. MOSES

SONGS

Schubert wrote more than 600 songs, and anyone who wants to hear all of them should collect the Hyperion Schubert Edition, which runs to 37 volumes. I don't offer such extravagant advice frivolously. The great songs are scattered far and wide among the various discs and the dedicated performers aren't invariably of the highest caliber, but the achievement is nonetheless monumental. Pianist Graham Johnson, the guiding force behind the project, is accompanist, annotator, and program planner. His notes on the songs deserve to be published separately by themselves; no one has written about them so probingly, exhaustively, and comprehensively. Most of the discs are intelligently organized around a specific theme, and each is instructive and absorbing.

A good starting point might be one of the "Schubertiads," like Volumes 24 (all Goethe) or 26 (many great songs including the rare and gorgeous "Nachthelle" for tenor and chorus). These deploy several singers and exhibit the strengths and weaknesses of the whole series; but having bought one disc, the Schubert devotee will find it difficult to stop. The problem for the average collector may be one of surfeit: the Hyperion Edition offers too rich a bounty, and it won't gratify anyone who wants to hear the most familiar songs conveniently grouped together.

Naxos has just launched its own Schubert series, and so far it seems to be (in more ways than one) the poor man's alternative. The discs cost less than half the price and are packaged with texts and translations, but the annotations are skimpy. The first entry is *Winterreise,* impressively sung by baritone Roman Trekel, who has a certain natural eloquence and a telling way of turning a phrase. His successor in *Schwanengesang,* Michael Volle, is less satisfactory: dry, droning, and legato-deficient. Vols. 3 and 4 bring us—and this is no more than faint praise—two dutiful, straightforward baritones who sing poems by Goethe and Mayrhofer honestly but without sparkle or imagination. By Vol. 3, I sorely miss not only Johnson's notes but also his pianism.

Vol. 5 finally brings some variety in the form of a tenor voice: Christian Elsner addresses *Die schöne Müllerin* capably and sensitively. His voice, more spinto than lyric, is a mature-sounding instrument, ringing on top but thewy and inflexible. The performance is solid but far from the best. It's too early to judge the Naxos project, which hasn't put its best foot forward in the face of formidable competition by starting with the three great cycles. Since the Hyperion singers aren't uniformly first-rate either, the Naxos discs, at best, may offer viable alternatives. At worst, they will at least be valuable resources for students who want to learn the songs but who don't want to be influenced by strong, distinctive personalities.

Light-years away, artistically, is the huge collection recorded by **Fischer-Dieskau** and Gerald Moore between 1969 and 1972—400-odd songs in 18 discs (DG 437215, 437225). In one way, Fischer-Dieskau's feat, accomplished in a remarkably short time, is the more impressive (and Moore's contribution can't be praised highly enough). For more than 25 years, the original LPs served as an invaluable reference tool and more. The performances were not only rewarding and enjoyable but also set high standards for future interpreters to study and emulate, and they will continue to do so on CDs. The problem, again, is overabundance. Not everyone will want so many Schubert songs, especially when sung by the same voice.

A less daunting and more varied prospect may be "Schubert Lieder on Record," two 3CD sets of historical performances by 64 singers, recorded 1898–1952 (♦EMI 566150, 566154). These make for addictive listening, and many collectors will be impelled to seek out other recordings by some of the artists, among them Hüsch, Kipnis, Lehmann, Schiøtz, and Schumann, whose work is fairly well documented on CDs.

Elisabeth Schumann is a particular favorite in Schubert's songs, and all her recordings have been reissued (EMI 63060, 2CD). (26 of them are also in Video Archives 1170, which may be easier to find.) Her light, silvery voice, unaffected warmth, and pure diction afford abiding pleasure, though modern ears might be distressed by her penchant for portamento and a certain matriarchal aloofness. The real problem is the antiquated sound, which drains some of the color out of the tone, lending it a monotony that belies the ear-witness reports of those who heard her in person. The microphones were kinder to the more robust **Lotte Lehmann,** whose soprano had a deeper placement and whose urgent, conversational directness remains irresistible. An assortment of songs, together with her *Schöne Müllerin* and *Winterreise,* is available (Lys 231, 4CD), but grab whatever you can find.

Many collectors will insist on modern sound, however, and many are likely to be more comfortable with singers closer to their own time. In general, lieder recordings don't have a long life expectancy, so it behooves us to recommend discs that have a reasonably good chance of being procurable. A good place to start is with two more Elisabeths, Schwarzkopf, and Grümmer, but first, a cautionary note. Many lieder CDs, especially reissues, fail to supply texts, so the collector will need some assistance. Philip L. Miller's *The Ring of Words* (Norton) offers texts and translations for a large number of German songs (and poems in other languages). Also in paperback is *The Fischer-Dieskau Book of Lieder* (Proscenium), which translates 750 songs. Richard Wigmore's *Schubert: The Complete Song Texts* is out of print but worth a search. One very helpful Internet site is <www.recmusic.org/lieder>, which provides texts for well over 1,000 songs in various languages, though not all are translated into English.

Schwarzkopf's 1952 recital deserves its classic status (♦EMI 64026). The soprano is at her sunniest and least mannered in the 12 songs, the

voice a joy in itself. Listen, in particular, to how her tone glows at the end of each stanza of "An Sylvia." Schwarzkopf made many lieder recordings; few of them are as satisfying as this one. **Grümmer** was treated less well by EMI, who permitted this most eloquent of German sopranos only a single lieder disc (♦Testament 1086). She sings only seven Schubert songs (along with five by Brahms), and each one is treasurable. Her voice is enchanting, her diction impeccable. The loveliest of Schubert's cradle songs is here (the one that begins "Wie sich der Äuglein"), and Grümmer, for all her simplicity, is artlessly spellbinding. A 2CD box offers nine songs, among them a different account of "Wiegenlied" (♦Gala 100.554). There are, unfortunately, no recommendable all-Schubert CDs by the cherishable **Seefried** (but don't miss her "Auf dem Wasser zu singen" in a 2CD DG set or the handful of Goethe songs on Orfeo 297921) or the sparkling **Della Casa** (her early-'50s London recital is out of print, but her Schubert can be sampled in EMI 66571).

The natural successor to these singers was **Janowitz,** who started where Fischer-Dieskau left off. In 1978, DG issued a 5LP set of songs for female voice. The album was labeled "Volume 1"; frustratingly, the project was never completed. 30 of the 52 songs have been reissued, and Janowitz is enticingly intimate, thrillingly grand (a wonderfully operatic "Gretchen"), always delightful to hear (♦DG 437943, 2CD). She returned to the studio in 1989, her voice intact and her artistry riper (Nuova Era 6860). "Der Winterabend" in particular has an inviting coziness.

The Dutch soprano **Ameling** arrived in the '60s like a breath of fresh air, a disarmingly straightforward alternative to the aging and increasingly idiosyncratic Schwarzkopf. Her best Schubert recordings are the early EMIs, one with Jörg Demus and another with Irwin Gage, but they have never been reissued. What is available is her first lieder recording (with Demus on fortepiano), nine Schubert and 19 Schumann songs captivatingly sung. Another good sample of her work is something of a "greatest hits" collection (Philips 420870). Very much like Ameling in the purity of her approach is the American soprano **Augér,** who made two desirable Schubert records. With Walter Olbertz in 1976 (Berlin 6203), she recorded graceful accounts of the songs for Gretchen, Mignon, and Suleika. She revisited Suleika's songs (and "Gretchen am Spinnrade") in 1990, with Lambert Orkis on fortepiano (♦Virgin 61457, 2CD, with Thomas Allen's *Winterreise*—a great bargain), and added a wealth of new material. Her singing had grown more assured without losing any of its youthful spontaneity.

More focused but no less winsome is **Bonney,** whose recital is notable for its combination of sweetness and self-possession (♦Teldec 90873). The Mignon songs are particularly affecting. Collectors on a tight budget might want to try **Lynda Russell,** who offers capable, long-breathed performances of the standard Schubert chestnuts (Naxos 553113). **Lott** brings more polish to a similar program, though she too falls short of the top class (IMP 2016). Tempting on the surface, especially given the dearth of contemporary German sopranos, is a disc from the promising but perverse **Christine Schäfer** (Orfeo). Her assets include crystalline diction and a basically pretty voice, but she squanders her talents by refusing to sing honestly and forthrightly, preferring, instead, to sound flat and anorexic. (She's more pleasing in Hyperion's Vol. 26, recommended above.) Also promising but still unproven is **Christiane Oelze,** who has a fresh, girlish voice and might develop into an Ameling-Augér type of recitalist. The five Schubert songs in her disc of Goethe lieder show her heading in the right direction (Berlin 1030).

Two rather different sopranos, statelier and larger of voice, are compelling in their dissimilar ways. **Margaret Price** has devoted much of her career to lieder, and her recording of 21 Schubert songs shows her still in good form (♦Forlane 16698). She's especially effective when she plumbs the darker side of the too-familiar "Im Frühling" or exploits the contrast between her dusky low register and shining top. More extroverted, linguistically peculiar, and often egregiously hammy, **Norman** is nonetheless overwhelming when she pours out her voice in her 1984 collection of 12 songs (♦Philips 412623). Her manic "Gretchen" is no less hair-raising than her "Erlkönig."

Among modern mezzos, two vie for pride of place. **Baker** matches the inwardness of the best German performers. She's always involved, personal, and enlightening. Her singing doesn't have the earthy warmth of Lehmann's but rather a softer, fire-lit glow; she is a consistently comforting and endearing performer. Her best Schubert is the collection with Moore and Geoffrey Parsons (♦EMI 69389, 2CD), but she's better in 1971 with Moore than in 1981 with Parsons. There's much unusual material here, along with the over-familiar, and she even makes the inescapable "Ave Maria" sound new.

A more assertive interpreter is **Fassbaender,** who reaches out and grabs the listener like no one since Lehmann. A master of rubato, she can toy with the words yet never distend the shape of the musical line. Her first (1974) Schubert recording has been reissued as part of an inexpensive "Double" (♦EMI 72004, 2CD, with Souzay's *Winterreise* and a few bonuses from Ameling). Particularly memorable is the sensuous yet decorous affirmation of her "Nähe des Geliebten."

Blander but still satisfying (and a more refined vocalist) is **Ludwig,** who made two adventurous DG albums in the mid-'70s (now NA). 15 earlier recordings are included in EMI's "Introuvables" collection (64074, 4CD), and Ludwig's readings are fervent and instinctive rather than cerebrally subtle. An efficient but often faceless singer, **von Otter** exceeds her usual standard in a 1997 recital, her customary coolness supplanted by genuine passion (DG 453481). Every Schubert lover should know the lilting serenade with chorus, "Zögernd leise," and since EMI inexplicably omitted Fassbaender's account from the disc recommended above, von Otter's recording makes amends.

Less prodigiously endowed was **de Gaetani,** but her recording of nine Schubert songs is indispensable (♦Nonesuch 79263). Her over-the-speed-limit "Musensohn" remains an oddity, but the disc is worth the asking price for her ethereal, rapturous "Blondel zu Marien," where she surpasses not only the two singers who essayed it in the Hyperion Edition but also Fischer-Dieskau himself. **Lipovsek** assembles the songs of Mignon, Ellen, Suleika, and Gretchen into one neat package and sings them efficiently, in dark, consoling, slightly dry tones (Orfeo 159871).

Because so many of Schubert's songs were written in high keys, it's surprising that few tenors have made all-Schubert discs. A conspicuous exception was the great Bach Evangelist of the '30s and '40s, **Karl Erb;** 21 songs are gathered in an invaluable set (♦Preiser 89208, 2CD, with much other material). His voice is thin and penetrating rather than juicy and warm, but his diction is extraordinary, and his interpretations are enlivened by many individual touches. Among the most notable of his successors is the indefatigable **Schreier,** whose mid-'70s recordings are currently NA and whose contribution to the Hyperion Edition comprises rather esoteric material. **Prégardien** (another Hyperion tenor) is similarly lean and dry in timbre though inclined to sound truculent. He has recorded a disc apiece of Goethe and Schiller settings, serviceable rather than moving, and utterly mirthless (Harmonia Mundi). **Blochwitz** has a more attractive timbre, and his collection of fairly familiar pieces is very appealing (♦Philips 438932). The yearning, plain-

tive songs suit his handsome, heady voice especially well; particularly noteworthy is the horn-accompanied "Auf dem Strom."

Wunderlich has been criticized for lack of insight and imagination, but the beauty of his singing is so seductive you'll hang on every word, and that, after all, is what brings a song to life. Nine songs fill out his *Dichterliebe* recording (♦DG 429933), and the open-hearted warmth of "Der Einsame" and "An die Musik" (to name only two examples) is altogether entrancing. **Bostridge,** despite an entirely different sort of voice, has some of Wunderlich's magic. His tone is slender and delicate but still has ample body. His very personal readings can be too resolutely inflected (this is the sort of thing critics value as "insight"), but he never forgets to sing honestly and alluringly, with a bel canto feeling for the melodic line. His buoyant account of the tricky "Im Haine" is marvelous (♦EMI 56347).

Baritones have dominated the lieder discography, and **Fischer-Dieskau** has dominated the baritones. There is no better starting point for a Schubert collection than a pair of recordings he made with Moore in 1965 (♦EMI 63566, 2CD). Too often regarded as an interpreter first and a singer second, Fischer-Dieskau here demonstrates a vocal mastery built on solid technique. The voice is both beautiful and individual, astonishing in its malleability; the singer's rhetorical facility relies as much on timbral color as on verbal nuance. Many of the songs are familiar, many not; all are worth hearing. The four Rückert songs that open the program should be an epiphany for anyone who has never heard Fischer-Dieskau (though such nescience is scarcely conceivable), and that's only the beginning. No other baritone has won comparable plaudits, and even when he fails to satisfy (he grew more finicky and predictable with age), he always elicits strong reactions.

Fischer-Dieskau is the most recorded of all singers, and familiarity may have bred, if not contempt, indifference among many listeners. He is, nonetheless, a tough act to follow, and quite a few of his successors, unable to escape his influence, sound like pale replicas of the real thing. He's also a difficult act to precede. The most mellifluous of his predecessors, **Hüsch** and **Schlusnus** (both well represented on Preiser CDs), sing handsomely but seem to lack subtlety. For better or worse, Fischer-Dieskau revised our expectations of lieder singers permanently.

The baritones who have stepped out of his shadow are those who didn't try to imitate him. **Prey,** the guiding spirit behind many modern Schubertiads, was a more guileless, more approachable singer, in his own way as edifying as Fischer-Dieskau. His Schubert recordings were made for various labels and have been difficult to find. Philips has issued a four-volume "Hermann Prey Lied Edition" in Europe; Vol. 2 contains six discs of Schubert songs (442692). A late (1982) recital is also available, but you'll probably have to search for that too (Intercord 830.837). Contemporaneous with both Prey and Fischer-Dieskau was the French baritone **Souzay,** who had a style of his own and adds some bracing Gallic urbanity to his lieder performances. Highly recommended are his suave 1961 and 1967 recordings with Baldwin (♦Philips 422418). For all his sophistication, he could still deliver a thrilling "Erlkönig."

Among modern baritones, the Austrian **Holzmair** has recorded (in addition to the three cycles) three discs: Mayrhofer settings (Tudor 764), Goethe (791), and poems by Schubert's friends (762). All are inviting, and all reveal a bright, almost tenorish voice slightly limited in volume but pleasing in texture. His words have clarity and flavor. **Goerne** doesn't have the same verbal crispness; his primary asset is his gorgeous voice, a mellow, velvety instrument enthralling in itself and suitable to a wide range of songs. His recital with Andreas Haefliger, exemplary in its vocal smoothness and virile sensitivity, has earned him much deserved praise (♦London 452917). The more modestly equipped **Opalach** is a smiling, companionable Schubert interpreter, and his inexpensive recording of 13 songs yields substantial enjoyment (Vox 9003).

Bass-baritone **Hans Hotter** had an imperfect voice, woolly, wobbly, and inclined to spread; but its timbre was utterly individual, and not even Fischer-Dieskau surpassed his mesmerizing eloquence. When he wraps his tongue around the words, he compels us to hear them, holding our attention with the merest flickers of nuance. His fortes could be thunderous, yet no one has ever matched the magical beauty of his soft singing. For a good introduction to his wizardry, try the ten songs in ♦Preiser 93145, noting in particular the contrast between "Du bist die Ruh" and "Prometheus." The only other deep-voiced lieder singer as charismatic as Hotter was the riveting **Kipnis,** but his Schubert recordings are scarce. Not nearly in the same class, and rather stertorous of timbre, is the modern bass **Kurt Moll.** His recital is an assemblage of songs particularly suited to dark, weighty tones, and he brings laudable imagination and impressive weight to them (Orfeo 021821).

Schwanengesang. A miscellany rather than a true cycle, it was Schubert's last published collection. It originally comprised 14 songs, but the trend lately has been to fill it out with additional items from the poets Seidl and Rellstab. The extra material may be a strong selling point for some shoppers, but the singer's vocal qualifications are far more important. The lilting, rapturous Rellstab settings are easy enough to manage, but the austere Heine songs demand reserves of power and volume few lieder specialists possess.

The best of the undernourished, "sensitive" interpreters win our sympathy but can be quickly dismissed, even such luminaries as **Bär, Schreier, Haefliger** (better in the early DG with Werba than the late-in-the-day Claves), and **Skovhus. Hagegård** is likable but shallow, his voice on the gritty side (RCA). With crafty inflections and fierce concentration, **Holzmair,** partnered by the scintillating **Imogen Cooper,** just brings it off, and many listeners will appreciate the seven additional songs (Philips 442460). His care and imagination compensate for a certain vocal frailty. **Van Dam** takes an unorthodox approach: charmless and somber in Rellstab, oddly nonchalant in Heine, as though he feels mild regret rather than pain. It's a stimulating interpretation but not a good introduction. Worthy recordings by **Prey** and **Krause** have long vanished.

Terfel meets the vocal requirements, but his 1991 recording is immature and overwrought (Marquis). **Ainsley** and **Rolfe Johnson,** the two tenors who share the cycle in the final volume of the Hyperion edition, do not together make even one Haefliger or Schreier. Ainsley is sporadically winning in the lighter, Rellstab half, but Rolfe Johnson is crushed by the demands of the Heine songs.

Hotter was the man for the job, and his recording with Moore has been restored to the catalog after too long an absence (♦EMI 65196, with 10 additional songs). He could sing the tenderest of serenades, then turn to the eruptions of "Der Atlas" or "Der Doppelgänger" without breaking a sweat. **Kipnis** had the same capability, and though he didn't record the complete cycle, excerpts can (and should) be heard (Music & Arts 661). The best of **Fischer-Dieskau**'s recordings is probably the central one (1962) with Moore (♦EMI 66146). He doesn't match the muscular bulk of Hotter or Kipnis, and he does have to push just a little in the Heine songs. His words are searing and forcefully projected nonetheless, and in the lighter Rellstab settings he works miracles. The variety of color (vocal, not verbal) in "Kriegers Ahnung" is astounding, and his smiling "Taubenpost" doesn't even seem an anticlimax.

Women have generally avoided *Schwanengesang;* the audacious exception is **Fassbaender** (♦DG 429766). She's extroverted but never overblown, time and again finding such felicitous shadings for a phrase that we sit up and take notice. Her reading of the Seidl "Wiegenlied" (not part of the original *Schwanengesang*) is refreshingly original; she sees the song as an evocative whole rather than as a sequence of strophes. Her "Abschied" is striking in a different way, poignantly regretful rather than merely jaunty. In the Heine songs, her tone can be abrasive and she comes perilously close to screaming, but this is the sort of singing that would bring an audience to its feet cheering.

Die schöne Müllerin. The first true narrative cycle, this sequence of songs that tells a tale of unrequited love. Its protagonist is a young, inexperienced man whose lamentations require heartfelt singing rather than cerebral exegesis. **Fischer-Dieskau** took the cycle out of his repertory in the '70s because he felt he was already too old for it, but few baritones have been so principled. Both his mono (EMI 63559, 3CD, with *Winterreise* and *Schwanengesang*) and stereo (EMI 66907) recordings with Moore are absorbing even if rather too disingenuous. DG kept a 1968 account with Demus in its vaults for 32 years before finally publishing it; it's comparable in excellence to the EMI readings but no more revelatory. **Souzay** is too debonair (Philips, NA), **Hagegård** too facile (RCA), **Bär** too self-consciously earnest, and **Hynninen** far too ferocious (Ondine). **Hüsch** sings with tonal fullness and warmth but falls too readily into petulance (Pearl). These are all worthy, respectable performances, though less than ideal.

The best baritone interpreters are the fairly recent ones. **Sanford Sylvan**'s mellow voice and uninsistent manner are most engaging (♦Nonesuch 79293). More authoritative because more at home with the language and style of the songs is **Holzmair,** who recorded the cycle early in his career (1983; ♦Preiser 93337). His voice is almost as much tenor as baritone, and he sings with bright-eyed ardor and personal involvement. His second (1997) recording is more polished and richer in detail (Philips). He's still eager and vulnerable, and though he stops short of sounding calculated, his art is not the sort that conceals art. Much of the endearing spontaneity of his first account is missing, tempered by a more philosophical detachment.

Among the more unusual recordings are one from a soprano, one from a countertenor, and one in English. **Lotte Lehmann,** as always, is searching and communicative, yet doesn't quite persuade us she is the young miller. **Kowalski** controls his falsetto whimpering better than you might expect, but he sings almost without expression, wailing and flouncing for a monotonous 60 minutes (Capriccio). The eccentric **Shura Gehrman** offers the only English-language version currently available; it has novelty but no staying power, and this bass is a crude vocalist (Nimbus 5023).

Müllerin really belongs to the tenors, who can sing it in the original keys and have voices that convey youth and innocence. Even the flawed vocalists have something to offer. **Schreier** sounds wizened rather than young, and in his latest recording he's upstaged by András Schiff, a great pianist but a distracting accompanist (London 430414). An earlier recording paired him with Konrad Ragossnig on guitar (♦Berlin 1123). The guitar transcriptions are brilliant in themselves, and the intimate nature of the instrument allows Schreier to sound more relaxed and genial. Those two adjectives are precisely wrong for **Prégardien,** whose anger and bitterness quickly become tiresome (Harmonia Mundi). Far more appealing is **Blochwitz,** whose words are shapelier than Schreier's and whose voice is handsomer than either Schreier's or Prégardien's

(♦DG 427339). His is an unassuming, touching rendition, a little wan at times but more often poignant and sympathetic. The thoughtful, intelligent **Araiza** is on the tight, nasal side, and sings less beautifully than Blochwitz (DG). The versatile **Gedda** is more commendable, vocally and emotionally generous, fluent in delivery, perhaps a little too worldly. His recording has been reissued in an inexpensive 5CD box that also includes a *Winterreise* from Prey and an assortment of lieder sung with stunning, unfettered operatic splendor by Leontyne Price (EMI 72594). Leinsdorf's classic account of the Mass in E-flat is also included, along with a disc of part songs. It's an irresistible bargain, though it may have to be ordered from a European dealer.

The sexagenarian **Anton Dermota** (in 1977) is altogether astonishing (Preiser 93274). The timbre, despite some mushiness, has an aptly innate mournfulness, the words are shapely, and the top notes ring out with a fullness that puts many younger tenors to shame. **Haefliger** in 1982 was far past his prime (Claves). His 1967 account with Werba is vastly more enjoyable, and a great bargain besides (♦Sony 48287). His voice isn't always produced with exemplary freedom, but for the most part it's steady and appealing. The revered **Patzak** displays much verbal flair in a 1943 recording but has no voice to speak of; avoid this one (Preiser). **Schiøtz,** on the other hand, gave us in 1945 one of the most admired recordings, clean, expressive, and unexaggerated (Danacord). His pale, unresonant voice is deployed resourcefully, but listeners who have no sentimental attachment to the tenor might question whether the recording really deserves its legendary status.

Wunderlich is at or consistently near the top of the *Müllerin* lists, and we appreciate him more and more as we realize how irreplaceable he has been. His 1957 recording had a winning naivete; despite some unripe vocalism, he seemed the very embodiment of the young miller (Eurodisc; RCA). From ringing forte to dulcet mezza voce, his 1966 recording is the most beautifully sung of all (♦DG 447452). Diction and legato are superb; the songs and the character spring to life. Wunderlich has been denounced as inexpressive by critics who are either infuriated by his vocal bounty or impervious to candor and simplicity; don't accept any of this. He makes singing seem as natural as speech, and the sensuous warmth of his voice is intoxicating in itself.

His strongest competitor is perhaps **Bostridge,** who sounds frail next to Wunderlich but addresses the songs in much the same way, with unfeigned naturalness and complete identification, singing the melodies with feeling and affection and not just interpreting the texts (♦Hyperion 33025). He has, moreover, a better accompanist in Johnson than Wunderlich had in the prosaic Hubert Giesen. His performance adds a nice lagniappe: Fischer-Dieskau recites the prologue and epilogue to the cycle, and thus makes a contribution of his own to the Hyperion Edition.

Winterreise. The protagonist of *Winterreise* also ruminates on unrequited love, but his observations are deeper and darker, far more disturbing. He's a more mysterious figure than his *Müllerin* counterpart and can be drawn in many different ways. The number of recordings is mind-boggling: almost 150, including well-circulated piracies. The listener can choose a sepulchral bass like **Moll** (Orfeo) or **Talvela** (BIS), a womanly soprano like **Margaret Price** (Forlane) or **Lehmann** (Lys), the blazing eldentenor of **Vickers** (EMI; VAIA), the unclassifiable **Gehrman** singing in English (Nimbus). Several mezzo-sopranos have essayed the cycle, among them the uncomplicated, rich-toned **Ludwig** (DG). Ten different recordings from **Fischer-Dieskau** have been available in the past two decades; and Hans Zender has contrived a bizarrely orchestrated adaptation, recorded by the game and accommodating **Blochwitz** (RCA).

Like *Müllerin, Winterreise* is written in tenor keys, but no tenor has been widely extolled. One of the more interesting is **Pears,** with Britten at the piano (♦Decca 466382). The strangeness of his voice puts you off at first, but the peculiar sounds and unique manner quickly grow hypnotic. Easier on the ears is **Dermota,** a little sluggish but heartfelt and penetrating (Preiser 93287). The great Bach Evangelist **Equiluz** knows how to tell a story, and his *Winterreise* with Margit Fussi on fortepiano has glowing words and a gentle persuasiveness (Christophorus 74544). Similar but with an even slenderer voice is **Zeger Vandersteene,** whose cool tones vividly conjure up bleak, wintry images (René Gailly 87038). The most engaging of the tenors in the historical category is **Tauber,** who recorded only half the songs with his usual blend of warmth and frankness (Pearl 9370).

Almost half the *Winterreise* recordings have been made by baritones. We have admired the fresh, thoughtful, easy-going **Holzmair** (Philips), the surprisingly unemphatic **Hampson** (EMI), the diligent but vocally limited **Bär** (EMI), the hale, Fischer-Dieskau-like **Andreas Schmidt** (DG), even the all-but-unknown **Nic Møller** (René Gailly), a baritone from Curaçao who has a nice touch of honey in his tone. **Thomas Allen** sings sleekly and proficiently (Virgin 61457, coupled with a mixed program from Augér, recommended above). More incisive and personable than any of these is **Prey,** at his best with Sawallisch (Philips). **Souzay** is, as always, searching and cultivated (Philips). The round tones of **Goerne** are a pleasure to hear, but he hasn't quite mastered the songs (Hyperion). He and Johnson mark the harmonic and verbal contrasts too self-consciously, almost as if the greatness of the music intimidates them and they want to be sure they get it right.

In a very crowded field, three performers stand out, and one of them is **Fassbaender,** who steps boldly into the young wanderer's shoes and assumes his identity with an unabashed, peremptory assurance (♦EMI 49846). Her dark voice flows freely, she handles the vocal ornaments gracefully, and she can fill her tone with warmth or drain the life out of it as the drama requires. The clarity of her diction is extraordinary, and she has an unerring instinct for giving each word its proper impetus and weight in the context of the ongoing musical line. Her accompanist, Reimann, is with her every step of the way. Her gender (which one quickly forgets) makes her an unorthodox protagonist, but so is **Hotter,** as absorbing as Fassbaender though even less believable as a young man. The best of his four recordings is the 1955 with Moore where his big, rugged voice envelops the words with unforced strength and eloquence (♦EMI 67000). The listener is drawn in immediately, then transfixed by the unfolding story. For all its deceptive plainness—Hotter is never as overtly excitable as Fassbaender or Fischer-Dieskau—this *Winterreise* is the most emotionally draining of all.

Of **Fischer-Dieskau**'s recordings, the most nearly perfect is his 1966 account with Demus (♦DG 447421), though the 1962 EMI with Moore is almost as good. The baritone strikes just the right balance between interpretive wisdom and vocal allure. Every note is firmly in place, every word lucidly uttered and firmly bound to the musical line. The awe-inspiring range of colors and dynamics is founded not (as is often presumed) on cerebral effort alone but on a secure and resourceful technique. The singer convinces us at every moment that this is exactly the way the music should sound. Fischer-Dieskau also manages to sound natural and spontaneous. When you listen to him or Hotter or Fassbaender, analysis ceases and captious questions remain unformulated. The only option is to surrender (in T. S. Eliot's words) to "music heard so deeply that it is not heard at all, but you are the music while the music lasts."

LUCANO

Gunther Schuller (b. 1925)

Schuller is among the most prominent living American musicians, given his exemplary contributions as jazz educator, ragtime proponent, conservatory administrator, author, conductor, arranger, and composer. His performing edition of Joplin's *Treemonisha,* for which Joplin was awarded a Pulitzer Prize posthumously, provided the public with the first major American opera, and he remains an ardent spokesman for American music of a variety of styles.

Schuller's best-known orchestral work is probably his seven *Studies on Themes of Paul Klee.* The term *third stream* is credited to Schuller and his music of around 1960, and the *Study* entitled "Little Blue Devil," with its walking bass and jazz-inflected harmonies, is one of the best syntheses of jazz and concert music for orchestra. The Minneapolis Symphony conducted by **Dorati** plays it plus Bloch's *Sinfonia Breve,* Copland's *Rodeo,* and Gershwin's *An American in Paris.* The Copland and Gershwin pieces are better served in other recordings, but *Seven Studies* comes off relatively well (Mercury 434329). An LP by Leinsdorf and the Boston Symphony is worth a search for the excellent performances of *Seven Studies* and Stravinsky's *Agon* (RCA 2879). **Schuller** is an underrated conductor, but sometimes composers aren't the best leaders of their own works. This is true of his *Seven Studies* with the North German Radio Philharmonic; they play this work stiffly, and are only somewhat better in Schuller's other three pieces on the disc: *Arc Ascending* (no reference to Vaughan Williams that I can detect), *Meditation,* and *Vertige d'Eros* (GM 2059). These aren't his best works, but *Seven Studies* deserves a better recording than any of these versions offer.

Schuller's career began as a horn player in the Cincinnati Symphony and Metropolitan Orchestra while still a teenager, and he has maintained relationships with countless professional musicians, but his concertos aren't his best music. A fair sample of three of them is available from Jeanne Kirstein, piano soloist with **Max Rudolf** and the Cincinnati Symphony, and Richard Todd, horn, and Kenneth Pasmanick, bassoon, with Schuller conducting the Saarbrucken Symphony Orchestra (GM 2044). The Piano Concerto was recorded in 1963 and comes off best in performance and recording—remastered, of course—but the others, recorded in the '90s, are at least acceptable.

Composers who lived through the last half of the century were exposed to many styles and combinations of them. Schuller never embraced one over another, usually finding something in each to use in his own way—a little serialism here, some mild aleatory essays there, vernacular references mixed with concert music foundations—and his music often suffers from it. For me, a single recording of three recent pieces shows him at his best: Organ Concerto, with James Diaz and the North German Radio Orchestra of Hanover, with **Schuller** conducting; *Of Reminiscences and Reflections* (Pulitzer Prize 1994) and *The Past Is the Present,* by the Calgary Philharmonic conducted by **Mario Bernardi** (New World 80492). The titled pieces are musical responses to the death of the composer's wife and a return to composition after a hiatus of a year or so; they convey deep emotion.

The **Chamber Music Society of Lincoln Center** presents quite a different side of the composer, with two chamber works commissioned for them and performed superbly (Arabesque 6620). The Octet is redolent of Schubert's, and *Impromptus and Cadenzas* is a substantial challenge easily met by the performers. This is another instance of Schuller's understanding of individual musicians, and the recording is high quality as well.

Still smaller chamber music is exhibited in a curious pairing of Schuller's *Duologue* for violin and piano and John Knowles Paine's sonata (GM 2021). The intent was probably to showcase American music composed about a century apart, but Paine's work is weak compared to Ives's at about the same time, and although, like Ives, Schuller includes vernacular references (in this case a fiddle tune), it also doesn't compare in musical quality to Ives's imaginative precursor to *third stream.* The performances by **Rafael Druian** and Benjamin Pasternak aren't particularly engaging, nor is the sound quality on this 43-minute disc up to standard. A much better performance of *Duologue* is by **Gregory Fulkerson** accompanied by Charles Abramovic (Bridge 9093).

The remainder of this disc offers Schuller's Sextet played very well by the **Miro Quartet,** Abramovic, and bassoonist Michael Fine, and *Fantasy* for solo guitar, played by Starobin. The Sextet refers to ragtime, one of Schuller's favorite vernacular idioms, and *Fantasy* exhibits his intent to write solo music of one sort or another for most instruments. Starobin negotiates the pyrotechnics as well as the lyrical passages, which—despite Schuller's misgivings about writing for guitar—come off as idiomatic. however far extended. Schuller gives interesting interviews, and Starobin's conversation with him is included. This is a well performed and recorded disc.

Another *Fantasy* by Schuller for unaccompanied cello (not to be confused with the *Fantasia,* also for solo cello) is played by **Colin Carr** (GM 2031, with estimable performance of sonatas by Crumb and Kodály and Britten's Suite 3). Schuller's piece comes off as less interesting than the others, but cellists will want the disc for the repertoire offered. The sound is excellent, better than that on the disc by **Steven Honigberg** (Albany 82, with music by Foss, Diamond, and Bernstein). Able piano accompaniment for the latter three pieces is provided by Kathryn Blake. Honigberg's performance is different from but equal to Carr's; however, the GM disc contains better music.

American music is also the only repertoire on a disc with the **Emerson Quartet** offering an accomplished performance of Schuller's String Quartet 2 and widely varying pieces by Cowell, Arthur Shepherd, Harris, and Imbrie (New World 80453). One of the most rigorously serial of his compositions, the quartet provides a challenge to listeners and performers. This kind of music, dissonant and complex, couldn't be more out of favor these days, and in fact Schuller, like Boulez, had reservations about the efficacy of extensively serial music. The recording quality is mixed, but an excellent mini-essay by Schuller describes his astute view of this quartet in the context of the composer's task in the posttonal world. His Quartet 3, also played by the Emersons, is coupled with Harbison's Quartet 2 and Richard Wernick's 4 (DG 437537). Harbison's is by far the most engaging of the three. I prefer Schuller's 2 to his 3, but the latter disc exhibits a more seasoned Emerson (with some different personnel) and equally interesting American music.

Dissonance on a larger scale is presented in Schuller's *Spectra,* Carter's Variations, Babbitt's *Correspondences,* and Cage's *Atlas Eclipticalis* on a disc that may well be the definitive record of American progressive and avant-garde orchestral music at midcentury (DG 431698). The Chicago Symphony under **Levine** is the perfect match for these dissonant, highly constructed pieces that are the epitome of modernism. It isn't easy music, so you should expect to listen many times to appreciate its rich complexity. I doubt that these works will be recorded often or better, so this CD is recommended highly even for those not partial to such music. Schuller's piece is the least substantial, but it too is offered in a definitive rendition by these superb musicians and conductor.

The **Berlin Philharmonic Wind Quintet** performs Schuller's early

Suite for Woodwind Quintet beautifully, and interesting music by other composers from the Americas makes this disc a sure recommendation (BIS 952). Also highly recommended is the **Reykjavik Wind Quintet** performing Schuller's and other chamber music from the Americas (Chandos 9174). Schuller's Brass Quintet 2 is available from the **American Brass Quintet** in their usual splendid form (Summit 187), and his Symphony for Brass and Percussion is equally well performed by the estimable **Summit Brass** (Summit 127). Both discs contain other excellent music, either originally for brass ensembles or excellent transcriptions from other media.

Schuller is a surprisingly prolific composer given his many other activities, and some of his works deserve better recorded performances. His stature and accomplishments suggest that we will have them.

ZIEROLF

William Schuman (1910–1992)

Schuman was one of America's most respected composers and perhaps the finest symphonist the United States has yet produced. He contributed greatly to U.S. cultural life, not only as a composer but as president of Juilliard and Lincoln Center. His scores are highly dissonant at times, but always tonal. His rich, American harmonic language is easily recognized, and he wrote with a visceral, energetic rhythm that is breathtaking. He was a master contrapuntalist and a first-rate orchestrator, and his command of form was unsurpassed. His buoyant and large-boned style is most easily discerned in his symphonies, which comprise the core of his large oeuvre. On records his orchestral music is best documented, though he composed in all genres, and his chamber and piano works deserve to be better known.

"Eight symphonies, numbered 3 through 10" was how Schuman described his symphonic output (he withdrew the first two). It's unfortunate there is not yet a complete survey in good modern recordings, and at this writing, the 9th is not available at all. 3 is the best starting point for those who wish to explore his music. It shows off Schuman's style to a T, and is for me one of the most thrilling symphonies written in this century. Its two movements use contrapuntal forms (passacaglia, fugue, chorale, and toccata) rather than conventional symphonic models. **Bernstein** recorded it twice with the New York Philharmonic, in 1960 and 1985. Both are satisfying, and the work seems tailor-made for his Dionysian conducting. I prefer the earlier recording, which has grainier sound but is better balanced sonically and interpretively (♦Sony 63163). The later one strikes me as overblown, but it would be a good choice for those who prefer digital sound (DG 419780, with Roy Harris's 3). The Sony also has the advantage of being coupled with 5 ("Symphony for Strings") and 8, making this disc an essential volume of the composer's work.

Symphony 4 is only available in a reissue of an old Louisville Orchestra recording, **Jorge Mester** conducting (Albany 27). The performance is acceptable, but a fresh recording would be most desirable. Symphony 6 is perhaps Schuman's best symphony; it's less immediately accessible than 3 and much more grim in its mien, but more refined in orchestration and formal design. **Ormandy** conducts the Philadelphia Orchestra in a fine reading (♦Albany 256, part of their "American Archive" series, with Piston and Harris symphonies). The recording is mono, but has been beautifully remastered and is surprisingly detailed. On a companion disc, Ormandy conducts another of Schuman's finer orchestral statements, *Credendum* (Albany 257).

Two strong performances of 7 are available. **Maazel**'s is more sumptuous and better balanced, and Pittsburgh's string section is much fuller

and sounds warmer (♦New World 80348). **Abravanel** leads the Utah Symphony, which delivers a spirited performance but with less refinement than Maazel's version (Vox 5092, 2CD). The latter set has the attraction of a budget price and is coupled with five other American symphonic works.

Other orchestral works are well presented by **Schwarz** and the Seattle Symphony in an excellent collection (Delos 3115). This disc contains Schuman's superb orchestration of Ives's *Variations on "America,"* *New England Triptych,* Symphony 5, and *Judith.* The recording of 5 is good and has excellent sound but lacks the nervous intensity of Bernstein's version. *Judith* is a striking work for dance written for Martha Graham; it receives a committed reading but has strong competition from **David Effron**'s performance with the Eastman Philharmonia (♦CRI 791). I like the Eastman version a little better; it has more punch than Seattle's. This all-Schuman disc is rounded out with another work written for Martha Graham, *Night Journey* (here played by the Endymion Ensemble), and a setting of Shakespeare titled *In Sweet Music,* beautifully sung by Rosalind Rees. Both discs are strongly recommended.

Other notable orchestral performances include **Otto-Werner Mueller**'s reading of *In Praise of Shahn,* an homage to the American artist Ben Shahn. This disc features the Juilliard Orchestra and is filled out with works by Sessions and Copland (New World 80368). **Bernstein** also recorded this piece, coupled with Schuman's *To Thee Old Cause* and Barber's *Adagio for Strings* (Sony 63088). *Three Colloquies for Horn and Orchestra* is a concerto in all but name and is wondrously played by **Philip Myers** (New World 80326). Schuman's Concerto for Piano and Small Orchestra is available on "**Rosalyn Tureck:** Premiere Peformance" (VAIA 1124, with works by Dallapiccola and Diamond).

Slatkin, an ardent advocate of Schuman's music, has released two important discs. Schuman's *Violin Concerto* gets first-rate treatment from soloist **Robert McDuffie,** with able support from Slatkin and the St. Louis Symphony (♦EMI 49464). This work is a close parallel to Symphony 3, with a muscular vitality that is beautifully offset by an elegant lyricism. It's one of my favorite Schuman works, here paired with Bernstein's *Serenade.* Slatkin's other disc contains the only recording of Symphony 10 currently available, plus an excellent version of *New England Triptych* and the sprightly *American Festival Overture.*

New England Triptych has proved to be one of Schuman's most popular scores, and strong performances abound. **Howard Hanson**'s classic recording with the Eastman-Rochester Symphony still holds its own; the sound is more vivid than many digital recordings (♦Mercury 432755). **Andrew Litton** with the Dallas Symphony is also fine, and a good choice for those who seek DDD recordings (Dorian 90224). I prefer the Hanson, but both are worthy releases. Each is filled out with other mid-century Americana.

Little of Schuman's chamber music is currently available, but a recording of his Quartet 3 makes one long for a complete survey of all five quartets. It can be heard on an "American String Quartets 1900–1950" compilation ably performed by the **Kohon Quartet** (Vox 5090, 2CD).

Schuman also wrote strikingly and prolifically for chorus, and a good selection of those works has been gathered in a fine set by the **Gregg Smith Singers** (♦Vox 3037, 3CD). Some of these are quite unusual, such as the *Mail Order Madrigals,* a setting of entries from the 1897 Sears Roebuck catalog, or *Esses: Short Suite for Singers on Words Beginning with S.* At budget price, this collection is irresistible. **Cleobury** has recorded *Carols of Death,* a powerful setting of Walt Whitman (EMI 66787, with choral works by other American composers). Smith and his group also recorded a short opera, *The Mighty Casey* (Premier 1009). Schuman was an avid baseball fan and this piece shows him at his most quintessentially American.   McINTIRE

Robert Schumann (1810–1856)

SYMPHONIES AND OVERTURES

Schumann is an acknowledged master as far as his solo piano works are concerned; the suites comprised of smaller components are recognized and established masterpieces. It's the larger solo piano works—Sonatas 1 and 3, for example—that fuel the controversy over his mastery of larger structures, and his four symphonies have, from the start, garnered critical disapprobation. Early on, the composer himself had serious doubts about his ability as a symphonist, and his skills as an orchestrator also stirred critical reaction. It has been common for conductors, from Mahler on, to touch up the scoring in search of greater clarity. In fact, little or nothing need be done to these works; all that's required is a scrupulous ear for balance, since the composer painted his scores in the unique instrumental hues he desired.

Schumann was a complex individual and a musical revolutionary, searching for new means of expression. In his symphonies, while mainly adhering to the classical sonata-allegro form, he imparts a unique sense of fantasy, of sometimes disturbing emotional expression, of literary allusion. After careful analysis, we come to realize that his symphonies are as important to their time's furtherance of the evolution of musical exploration as Beethoven's were to his.

Schumann's first symphony, the so-called "Zwickau" (1832–33, named after his home town), was left incomplete. The first two movements were finished; the final two never emerged from a series of sketches. His official first symphony, the "Spring" (nicknamed by the composer after a poem by Adolph Boettger), was completed in 1841. His next symphonic work was the imaginative *Overture, Scherzo, and Finale*, and yet another symphony was to emerge from that year, the one now numbered 4 but actually the second of the cycle. Perhaps the most radical of the batch, it's certainly the most thematically compact; its four movements are tightly interwoven and played without pause. This first version is said to have included a guitar part, now lost (it's included by Georg Schmöhe in his recording for Koch Schwann). Mixed critical response moved its creator to revise the work ten years later (hence its later numbering). The later version is a bit less radical, with exposition repeats added to its outer movements, but it's still one of the most individual of the four—surely the most dramatic, and, in the right hands, the most emotionally harrowing.

Schumann was in emotional turmoil during the composition of his C major Symphony (1845–46), published as number 2 (the aforementioned 4 was not yet offered for publication). Yet despite its quirky scherzo and dark-hued Adagio espressivo, its outer movements are decidedly optimistic, and the work ends in triumph. His final symphony, the so-called "Rhenish" (published as his third), was written in the expansive and heroic key of E-flat major. In five, rather than the usual four, movements, it's a symphonic masterpiece in the grand manner.

Complete sets. Collectors who wish to delve into these richly rewarding works are faced with an abundance of superb offerings, several at mid- or budget price. A number of complete cycles vie for attention.

Bernstein recorded them twice. The first cycle came in the early '60s with the New York Philharmonic and was among the first (if not *the* first) complete stereo sets (Sony 47611, 1 and 2; 47612, 3, 4, and *Manfred*). These are intense, muscular readings, at times tender, reflecting his unique energy and drive at this stage of his career. The *Manfred* overture is simply electrifying. The second set was recorded during concert performances in 1984 and 1985 with Bernstein's beloved Vienna Philharmonic (DG 453049, in a "two-fer"; also separately: 415274, 1 and 4; 419190, 2 and Cello Concerto; 415358, 3 and Piano Concerto). The playing is more refined, as is the sound; the performances remain powerful, if not as overtly driven as before.

Karajan's 1971 cycle has been widely praised ever since it appeared (DG 429672, 2CD). That he loved these works is evident in these glorious readings, opulent and refined, and magnificently played by the Berlin Philharmonic. There's nothing slick or cold about them. Unfortunately, Karajan's superb reading of *Overture, Scherzo, and Finale*, included in the original LP issue, has been omitted (though there's plenty of room for it; it can be had, at budget price, coupled with his 1 in DG 431161), and the transfers lack the full-bodied warmth of the LPs. To hear the beauty of the original sound you have to turn to the reissue of the "Spring" symphony (DG 447408, with his 1964 Brahms 4). Superior renditions are also offered by another great German orchestra, the Staatskapelle Dresden, led by **Sinopoli,** in excellent digital sound (DG 439923).

One of the finest sets also features the Staatskapelle under **Sawallisch.** Few conductors have so successfully negotiated this repertoire (EMI 64815, 2CD, with *Overture, Scherzo, and Finale*). The classic recordings by **Szell** and the Cleveland Orchestra show the human side of that often unbearably controlling martinet (Sony 62349, 2CD). These are stunning performances, masterfully realized by one of this country's great orchestras. Special praise is due to Sony for its superb remastering, allowing us to hear the resplendent beauty of these performances for the first time. *Manfred* is a welcome bonus. **Paray** and the Detroit Symphony offer another classic set (Mercury 462955, 2CD). These are blazing, committed readings that stand among the finest. This beautifully refurbished album includes an equally intense *Manfred*. (Symphony 4 is in mono, though this is hardly a drawback given Mercury's vivid sound.) Refreshingly direct and wonderfully urgent, **Masur**'s cycle is one of the best things he's given us (♦Teldec 46445, 1 and 4; ♦46446, 2 and 3). We're blessed with two complete cycles from the great (though often underrated) **Kubelik.** His first was recorded in the mid-'60s (DG 437395, with *Manfred* and *Genoveva*), and he repeated the cycle in the late '70s with the Bavarian Radio Orchestra (Sony 48269, 1 and 2; 48270, 3, 4, and *Manfred;* budget-priced). The warmth and sensitivity he brings to this music make either set recommendable.

Two others deserve honorable mention. **Haitink** and the Concertgebouw offer invigorating readings, and the playing of this magical orchestra is always a joy to encounter (Philips 442079, 2CD). His *Manfred* and *Genoveva* are equally fresh and vital. **Muti** and the New Philharmonia give us especially vivid readings of 1 through 3, though he falls short of the mark in 4, which I find rather underpowered. The rarely heard overtures *Hermann and Dorothea*, a kind of fantasy on *La Marseillaise* inspired by a poem of Goethe, and *Die Braut von Messina*, after a tragedy by Schiller, make this set most valuable (EMI 67319, 2CD, budget-priced). **Marriner** shapes the music beautifully, though some tempos are on the fast side, and the Stuttgart Orchestra sounds perfect for this music (10063, 1 plus *Overture, Scherzo, and Finale* and *Manfred;* 10094, 2 plus the stillborn "Zwickau"; 10093, 3 and 4). A reissue of **Barenboim**'s bracing Chicago survey would be most welcome (DG, LP).

That **Klemperer** was a great advocate of these works is not in doubt. However, he recorded half the set too late in his career, with often disappointing results (EMI 63613). The one indisputably great performance here is 4, which was also the first to be recorded (in 1960). Fortunately, it has been reissued, coupled improbably (or maybe not!) with Tchaikovsky's "Pathétique," both with the Philharmonia (EMI 67336). The redoubtable Philharmonia had become the New Philharmonia by 1965, when the "Spring" symphony was recorded. This is my second favorite in Klemperer's cycle; I like its earthy quality and measured tempos, and the rhythms are nicely sprung. Symphony 2, recorded in 1968, shows the conductor at less than his best, with some shaky ensemble and plodding tempos, though there is still enough to sustain interest. The "Rhenish," taped in 1969, remains the weakest of the cycle. It's virtually a caricature of a creaking, earthbound Klemperer performance. There are some fine moments, but it can be recommended only to diehard fans of the conductor. The dreary *Faust* overture comes from the same sessions and is truly awful, like a dinosaur mired in quicksand.

Schwarz with his fine Seattle forces has recorded the symphonies, *Overture, Scherzo, and Finale, Manfred,* Piano Concerto (with Bella Davidovitch), *Konzertstück* for Four Horns, and a rarity, two *Symphonic Etudes* arranged by Tchaikovsky (Delos 3146, 4CD). Save for a rather staid finale in the "Spring," these are generally exhilarating performances. **Konwitschny** brings out the lieder character of much of Schumann's writing but sorely downplays his more mercurial nature (Berlin). **Levine**'s stop-and-go treatment would win few converts (DG); he has also done again for RCA. **Florian Merz** is of greater interest for the overtures offered as fillers than for the symphonies; all attempts at suavity or nuance by the strings are drowned out by tympani and brass (EBS).

Solti's larger-than-life set has been brought out as a "two-fer" (Decca, with *Julius Caesar* Overture). **Jordan** is earnest enough, but offers nothing special (Erato). **Hans Vonk** offers direct, rugged readings that serve the music well (EMI). **Dohnányi** with the Cleveland Orchestra at his disposal can seem unyielding at times, but the orchestra fairly glows, even more than with Szell (London). Only its low price distinguishes **Wit**'s prosaic 2 and 4; a pity, as his 1 and 3 are much better (Naxos).

For those attracted to "period" performance there are two outstanding recommendations: **Goodman**'s imposing, imaginative readings with the Hanover Band of the four symphonies (he offers the original 1841 version of 4) and *Overture, Scherzo, and Finale* (RCA 61931, 2CD), and **Gardiner**'s complete cycle with the Orchestre Revolutionaire et Romantique, which offers Symphonies 1 through 3, both versions of 4, the early "Zwickau," *Overture, Scherzo, and Finale,* and the *Konzertstück* (DG Archiv 457591, 3CD). Both offer compelling readings and excellent sonics. The *Konzertstück* gets such an electrifying reading from Gardiner's forces that it's almost worth getting the set for that alone.

Incidentally, the symphonies have also been recorded in Mahler's arrangements, but they could use a more persuasive proponent than **Aldo Ceccato,** whose sluggish tempos and haphazard balances make you wonder why Mahler bothered (BIS).

1 ("Spring"). **Munch** and the Boston Symphony offer an exhilarating "Spring," coupled with a brilliant version of 4 with the BSO led by Munch's successor, **Leinsdorf,** in a budget CD (RCA 60488). **Klemperer**'s imposing reading is also available singly, strangely coupled with Franck's D minor Symphony (EMI 66824). **Chailly** is unimaginative in both 1 and 4 (London), while **Zinman** in the same coupling stresses clarity at the expense of warmth and richness of texture (Telarc).

2. I have heard no finer reading than **Reiner**'s, recorded in concert in 1957. It is as all-encompassing a reading as you can imagine. The excel-

lent mono sound allows this extraordinary performance to shine forth in all its resplendent glory (available from the Chicago Symphony by calling 1-312-294-3000). A more controversial reading comes from **Christian Thielemann** (DG 453482). His is a truly romantic view of this work, a performance of extremes. He stretches the Adagio espressivo to its limits, though it never falls apart. The *Konzertstück* and *Manfred* are also given commanding readings. The great **Celibidache** offers his own special brand of refinement in this work. He always—at least as heard on records—managed to make the Munich Philharmonic sound like a great orchestra, in a league with the likes of Berlin and Dresden—which, of course, it wasn't (EMI 56849, with Brahms's *Haydn Variations*).

Welser-Möst drains the score of passion and drive and comes across as slack and lifeless (EMI). **Marriner**'s 2 and 4 with St. Martin Academy forces (Hänssler) can't match his Stuttgart survey (Capriccio). **Harnoncourt** is fresh and stimulating, but his "Spring" is turgid and earthbound (Teldec). **Zinman** is worse in 2 and 3 than in 1 and 4, workmanlike and unimaginative (Telarc). **Dirk Joeres**'s unexceptional reading is of far greater interest for the orchestrated Schumann offered with it, including selections from *Carnaval* and *Album für die Jugend* (BIS).

3 ("Rhenish"). Several versions of the "Rhenish" are also in the "special" category. Among modern readings few are more imaginative than **Giulini** with the Los Angeles Philharmonic (DG 45502). The sweep and grandeur of this performance are amazing; coupled with an exceptional Beethoven 5, this is a mandatory acquisition at mid price. **Thielemann**'s basically lyrical interpretation isn't quite in this league, though his versions of *Overture, Scherzo, and Finale* and *Genoveva* are among the finest (DG 459680). **Leibowitz,** as usual sorely underrated, gives us a "Rhenish" of great vitality and panache (♦Chesky 96, with *Manfred, Tannhäuser,* and *Mephisto Waltz*). **Wand** embarks in promising fashion but takes the final romp far too seriously (RCA).

Celibidache provides an extraordinary reading (EMI 56525, with a fine 4). Its beauty is breathtaking, but this perceptive performance is about more than beautiful sound: It's about musical truth and faithfulness to the vision of the composer. **Norrington** and his period players are on their best behavior here and in 4, radiant and fleet of foot (EMI or Virgin). **Schønwandt**'s disc suffers from a prosaic final movement, and his major offering, *Des Sängers Fluch,* is little more than a stopgap (Chandos).

Two historical versions are also of great importance. **Toscanini**'s 1949 version with the NBC Symphony has been given a sonic facelift in its most recent incarnation; this great performance has never sounded better and is a must-have for any lover of this work (RCA "two-fer," 59481). So too is Bruno Walter's superb 1941 reading with the New York Philharmonic. Sony's remastering in its "Bruno Walter Edition" (64488) is first-rate, and this rare example of the beloved conductor's special way with this composer is a reminder of what was lost when we were deprived of a complete stereo cycle, planned at the time of his death in 1962.

4. For the original version, it doesn't get any better than **Derek Solomons** with his Authentic Orchestra, not least for the horns' wild whoops of joy on ushering in the finale, and his "Spring" is no slouch either (♦Collins 50022). **Harnoncourt** makes much of the benefits of the earlier version, but his recording is so thickly textured and diffuse that it hardly matters; the same goes for the appended "Rhenish," which is hopelessly earthbound (Teldec).

Furtwängler's performance of the revised version is of such rare stature that it should never be out of circulation. A conductor most uncomfortable in the recording studio, in 1963 he set down a performance of this masterwork that remains the standard by which all others are judged. This reading unfolds with a natural inevitability and organic unity, its lyrico-dramatic power unforced; it is re-creative art at its most exalted. Surprisingly, he ignores Schumann's *attacca* markings between I and II and between II and III, allowing a several-second pause at those points (it's the same in the original LP), a minor blot on a supreme achievement. Anyway this recording belongs in every serious collection (DG 9457722, 2CD, with his massive 2).

Apparently 4 isn't congenial to **Wand,** as his rather businesslike approach robs the music of its magic (RCA). **Harnoncourt** did this one too, but it seems rather brusque (Teldec, with Schubert's 4).

LINKOWSKI

CONCERTOS

Schumann finished only three concertos, one each for cello, piano, and violin (there are also two smaller-scaled works for piano and orchestra and an unfinished draft of a first movement of a piano concerto). There is also an "honorary" concerto in the form of the Fantasy for violin and orchestra, actually an arrangement.

Cello. The Cello Concerto is a great and disturbed work. Where the piano concerto is lyrical, this piece (in the same A minor) is haunted, disturbed, seemingly never at the resting place it so movingly yearns for. There are fewer performances of this work than of the piano concerto, but some are outstanding.

Ma had the good fortune to have Colin Davis as his partner and offers a sensitive and articulate reading (Sony 42663, with other Schumann cello works, or 44562, 2CD, with other major cello concertos). **André Navarra** with Ančerl has a grittier approach, but one with deep humanity (Supraphon 11940). **Du Pré** with Barenboim is emotionally powerful, but a little out of scale (EMI 64626, midpriced). Listening to her performance, it's hard to remember that this is a piece of art with a particular shape and structure; use your own judgment on whether this will appeal or not. **Leonard Rose** was a fine cellist, not as individual an interpreter as the others listed here. He recorded this piece with Bernstein, who was so busy making points that the meaning of the work got lost (Sony 47609, midpriced).

Rostropovich's recording was with Karajan, coupled with their stunning version of Strauss's *Don Quixote* (EMI 66965). Their personalities are pretty evenly balanced, and the result is a subtle, insinuating evocation of despair and madness. **Daniel Shafran** was a cellist's cellist with amazing command of the instrument. His recording with Kondrashin is beautifully played but aristocratically removed from Schumann's deep despair (Vanguard 1026). **Starker** is another of the great masters of the instrument in our time, but his recording with Skrowaczewski is a classical version of a romantic masterpiece (Mercury 432010). It's not as aloof as Shafran's, but still a cool reading of a hot work.

My recommendation is either Rostropovich/Karajan or Ma/Davis. There are also two historical recordings worth mentioning. **Casals** recorded a technically stormy but fervent reading with Ormandy in 1953 (Sony 58993). **Fournier** with Furtwängler is an intriguing combination of cool and hot musical personalities (excerpted in Tahra 1008, 4CD).

Piano. The Piano Concerto in A minor is the quintessential Romantic concerto. Along with the two by Brahms, Tchaikovsky 1, and the Grieg, it's at the heart of the popular piano concerto repertoire, and its heartwarming familiar tunes and plangent melancholy are heard over and over in concert halls around the world. Soloists and conductors often get hopelessly out of synch in the tricky finale, as audiences listen with blissful unawareness. With literally scores of recordings of this concerto in print, it would be foolish to say that any one is "the best." Here are some recommendations and a warning or two.

Among stereo-era performances, a handful wear well. **Rubinstein** with Leinsdorf remains fresh despite some prosaic accompaniment (RCA 68454). **Kovacevich** made a memorable recording with Colin Davis; it's NA at the moment but reappears frequently as a low-priced reissue, so keep an eye out for it (Philips). Davis's partnership with **Perahia** some 20 years later is a little thicker around the middle, but its vision and wit are just as nimble, and Perahia avoids the precious interpretive persona he sometimes falls into (Sony 44899, with the Grieg concerto). Perahia also avoids this trap in his Berlin remake with Abbado (Sony 64577, with other Schumann works for piano and orchestra). **Cliburn** and Reiner (RCA 60420, with MacDowell, or 62691, with Prokofiev) offer straightforward ardor, but the most ardent of all is **Argerich,** whose recording with Harnoncourt has two creative and energetic musicians encountering Schumann (Teldec 90696). The result is sometimes startling, but always vivid and true to the composer's questing spirit.

Lortie offers a restrained and elegant reading (Chandos 9061, with Chopin 2). A typically cool **Pollini** performance with Abbado is available at mid price (DG 445522), while **Brendel** under Sanderling is typically spiky and quirky (Philips 462321). **Serkin** with Ormandy comes with his fiery recording of the Piano Quintet with the intonationally suspect Budapest (Sony 37256) or with Schumann's *Introduction and Allegro Appassionato* and the Grieg concerto (Sony 46543); both are discount reissues, but neither is very compelling. Serkin takes a dry approach to this juicy composer. **Zimerman** is sensitive and articulate, but it's hard to avoid the impression that he feels a little inhibited by his (very senior) partner, Karajan (DG 439015). **Richter** is powerful but a little stern. If you like his style, it's compelling, but if you don't, you'll wish for a little more flexibility (DG 47440). **Geza Anda**'s recording was the opposite of Richter's (DG, NA). Every flower was sniffed and appreciated, every vista admired. It had many admirers and will doubtless be reissued soon.

A younger and less imposing Karajan conducted **Lipatti**'s recording in the late '40s. It was a flowing, classical reading, a little too streamlined for some traditionalists but one that remains fresh despite its elderly sound. The EMI reissue is out of print, but it seems to be available on Enterprise Piano Library 273. A more relaxed Lipatti version with Ansermet was once available on Decca but has vanished. Another classic performance, the 1927 recording by the great **Cortot** with Landon Ronald, has been reissued (Biddulph 003). It's technically sloppy, but to paraphrase Busoni, "Who else could play such wrong notes?" For sheer style and charisma, it's hard to beat. **Gieseking**'s wartime recording with Furtwängler is another reissue; the sound is bad, but the performance has charisma (Piano Library 202). His postwar recording with Karajan had better sound but less "fizz" (EMI 66597). Many **Michelangeli** issues exist, all with brilliant playing and various interpretive oddities. None of them left me feeling that I was listening to the music rather than the performer posing in front of the music.

Perahia/Davis (with the Schumann discmates), Rubinstein, or Cliburn are good choices, in that order. Lipatti is a shining supplement to your main version.

Violin. The violin concerto isn't as fervent as the piano concerto or as grim as the cello concerto. It's in D minor and is grittier than either of its companions—one of those odd Schumann pieces with alternating moments of great darkness and blinding light. Why it hasn't joined the Beethoven, Brahms, Bruch, and Tchaikovsky in the ranks of the most popular 19th century violin concertos is a mystery, but perhaps its quirky personality and demands on listener concentration offer a clue.

In any event, this intense piece has a champion in the most intense violinist of our time. **Kremer** has recorded the work twice, first with Muti in a sturdy and insightful reading, accompanied by a fabulous performance of the Brahms Concerto with Karajan, a powerful Sibelius with Muti, and sonatas with Gavrilov (EMI 69334, 2CD, midpriced). That would seem to end matters, except for his remake with Harnoncourt. This offers Argerich's piano concerto as a discmate and a much more pointed and intense performance of the violin concerto (Teldec 90696, 2CD). There's nothing wrong with the EMI recording, and it's a great bargain, but the Teldec is a lot more alive and responsive to the odd twists and turns of this music.

Serious competitors are the historical recording by the shining-toned **Kulenkampff** (Dutton 5018) and the modern **Jean-Jacques Kantorow** (Denon 1666). Neither offers Kremer's musical insight or his technical address, so the choice is fundamentally between his two versions. The Teldec offers the more fully realized performance, but the EMI set offers so much value that it should be your first choice.

The lesser concerted pieces have few recordings. *Introduction and Allegro Appassionato in G* has a decent recording by **Serkin** and Ormandy (Sony 46543) and an outstanding one by **Perahia** and Abbado (Sony 64577), both backed by the piano concerto. Go for Perahia. Similarly, *Introduction and Allegro in D minor* has a fine recording from **Perahia** on the same Sony disc and a formidable **Richter** reading with his piano concerto (DG 447440).

Fantasia for Violin and Orchestra (actually an arrangement) got a sophisticated reading from **Mutter** and the New York Philharmonic under Masur (DG 475075), and there's also a **Kagan** version (Live Classics 173). The piece is of minimal importance, but Mutter's comes with a lovely recording of the Brahms Concerto. Kagan offers Prokofiev, Ravel, and Saint-Saëns in variable sound.   CHAKWIN

CHAMBER MUSIC

Rarely has a major composer accepted the challenge of chamber music so abruptly, and with such purpose, as Schumann did in 1842. His decision resulted in part from a desire to be taken more seriously as a composer. He felt sidelined when accompanying his wife, Clara, on tour; she was acclaimed as a pianist, while he was regarded as her husband, not as the composer of some of the pieces she played. Chamber music seemed to him the best way forward and, having studied the Haydn, Mozart, and Beethoven quartets, he quickly produced three of his own. Thereafter, his chamber music always featured his own instrument (and his wife's), the piano.

The finest general introduction is **Argerich**'s, with a collection of friends at a live concert in Holland, where they performed most of Schumann's smaller pieces plus the great Piano Quartet and Quintet (♦EMI 55484). The major omissions are Violin Sonatas 1 and 3, the string quartets, and the piano trios, but this is still a vibrant collection, superbly played though apparently thrown together after a single day of rehearsal.

Adagio and Allegro Op. 70 for horn (or violin or cello) and piano. This simple, linked pair of movements has been a great favorite for many instrumentalists, allowing them to display first a delicate restraint and later a more unbuttoned mood. More than with Schumann's other chamber duos, the character of the music changes significantly with different instruments, the horn (for which it was primarily written) having a more heroic bearing than the violin or cello, while the unsanctioned oboe arrangements provide a more poignant view of the piece. There are a good many rather ordinary recordings, but here by instrument are the pick of the litter.

Horn: **Marie-Luise Neunecker** gives a marvelous, enthusiastic live account partnered by Alexander Rabinovich (EMI, as above), but while **Volker Grewel** is more prosaic in the Adagio, his triumphant *Allegro* is irresistible (♦Ars Musici 1164). There is also a recommendable performance by **L. William Kuyper** (Elysium).

Cello: **Truls Mørk** gives a very poetic, expansive performance (Simax 1063), much in contrast to **Heinrich Schiff**'s significantly fleeter, virtuosic account (Philips 422414). **Maria Kliegel** plays the work very fluently; while not everyone's first choice—many will prefer **Ma** (Sony 42663)—Kliegel is excellent value with her mainly Schumann program at budget price (Naxos 550654).

Oboe: **József Kiss** delivers a splendidly swift account, showing how well the music fits the instrument (Naxos). He's less strong on imagery than **Heinz Holliger,** accompanied by Brendel, who is nearly ideal (Philips 426386).

Andante and Variations Op. 46 for horn, 2 cellos, and 2 pianos. Two recordings exist of this minor piece, both part of larger surveys of Schumann's chamber output: the live account led by pianists **Argerich** and Rabinovich (EMI, as above), and one led by **Sandra Shapiro** and Thomas Hecht (Elysium).

Fantasiestücke Op. 73 for clarinet (or violin or cello) and piano. Originally composed for clarinet, Schumann sanctioned performances on the violin and cello, though there are plenty of very successful transcriptions for oboe and—less so—bassoon, saxophone, even oboe d'amore and tuba. It is perhaps the composer's finest set of chamber miniatures, containing some of his loveliest instrumental melodies.

Clarinet: Of some 20 available recordings, several stand out. **Franklin Cohen** accompanied by Ashkenazy has the benefit of top-notch sound but isn't as involving as some accounts (Decca, with Brahms's sonatas). The versions by **Stanley Drucker** (Elysium), the **Melos Ensemble** (EMI), **Emma Johnson** (ASV 732), and **Eduard Brunner** (ECM 21508) all have much to commend them, but for sheer magic, few can equal **Walter Ifrim**'s loving interpretation (♦Ars Musici 1164). Silkiest in tone (and at comparatively swift tempos) is **de Peyer,** accompanied to perfection by Gwenneth Pryor (♦Chandos 8506).

Cello: Of around 15 recordings for cello, two of the finest have Argerich as accompanist: both **Gutman** (live, EMI 55484) and **Maisky** (Philips 412230). They show great technique and are alive to every nuance, though some may find Maisky a little too fleet. **Schiff** is fine, the playing alternately strong and poetic, though the sound isn't as immediate as it might be (Philips). Next to Gutman and Maisky, the mercurially gifted **Mørk** seems coarse-toned and ordinary (Simax). **Ma** is safer here, though some may prefer a more intimate approach (Sony 42663). Some of **Kliegel**'s tempos are exaggerated, but hers is a very fluent account, the cello tone full and firm; it's the leading budget choice (♦Naxos 550654). **Hai-Ye Ni** is similarly rich-toned and fluent in a varied program (Naxos). The brilliant **Wispelwey** has recorded the work to some acclaim with the Cello Concerto and Hindemith's Op. 8 Pieces, a typically imaginative and unorthodox program (Channel Classics). Interesting historical performances are also available from **Fournier** (EMI

69708), **du Pré** (EMI PRCDC 6), **Piatigorsky** (Biddulph 117), and **Starker** (RCA).

Others: There is just one widely available violin version, by **Rolf Schulte** (Centaur). The best of the alternatives is that for oboe, of which two very fine performances exist: by **Holliger,** partnered by Brendel, immaculately played (Philips 426 386), and **Kiss** in an excellent budget-priced release (Naxos 550599).

Märchenbilder Op. 113 for viola (or clarinet or violin) and piano. Not surprisingly, this suite of "Fairy Tales" has been seized on by violists, whose repertory of mid-19th century works is very sparse. Other instrumentalists have tried to appropriate the work, usually misguidedly, as in one disc of transcriptions for tuba! Violist **Imai** has recorded the work twice, once in a fine live performance with Argerich (EMI 55484), and previously in the studio with Roger Vignoles (♦Chandos 8550). The live account, with a finale that has real eloquence, suffers from comparatively recessed sound and—fine as Argerich is—Vignoles is peerless as accompanist. Strong competition comes from **Paul Coletti,** beautifully balanced (Hyperion 66946), edging out both **Bashmet** (on the viola, not violin as Schwann lists it; RCA) and **Kashkashian** (ECM). These accounts lead the field.

Märchenerzählungen Op. 132 for clarinet, viola, and piano. One of Schumann's last works (completed only four months before his final breakdown), these "Fairy Tale Pictures" make a stronger, more imaginative set than the more celebrated *Märchenbilder.* There have been some very fine versions of this unusually scored trio, none better than by **Janet Hilton** with Imai and Vignoles (♦Chandos 8776). This set scores over its close rival by **Sabine Meyer,** Tabea Zimmermann, and Hartmut Höll with an extra degree of sensitivity and a more generous coupling (EMI 49736). Only a little less impressive are **Michael Collins,** Isserlis, and Hough, in a transcription replacing viola with cello (RCA), and **Brunner,** Kashkashian, and Robert Levin (ECM, with pieces by Kurtág). Two other performances worth investigating are by the **Melos Ensemble** in a very varied program (EMI 72643) and **Stanley Drucker,** Dorian Rence, and Sandra Shapiro in an all-Schumann disc (Elysium 709).

Phantasiestücke Op. 88 for piano trio. The final chamber product from Schumann's *annus mirabilis* of 1842 shows the fires burning a little lower, and these four character pieces needed thorough revision before publication in 1850 (hence the late opus number). The **York Trio** gives a fluent and committed account, but its speeds are generally rushed, and there are intonational problems (Meridian). The **Florestan Trio** takes a little more time, making a stronger case for the work; it also benefits from the best recorded sound (Hyperion 67175). The **Borodin Trio** is very leisurely, fully four minutes longer than the York, but is the most poetic (Chandos). Best of all is the **Beaux Arts Trio;** the sound (from 1975) is slightly flat but the playing is top-notch (♦Philips 432165, like the Florestan and Borodin with the three piano trios). Next to them, neither the **Abegg Trio** (Intercord) nor **Trio Italiano** (Arts; with Trio 3) makes much of an impression.

Piano Quartet Op. 47. Written shortly after the more extroverted Quintet in 1842, the Quartet is a work whose subtleties need to be teased out rather more. It's actually Schumann's second, the first being a C minor work dating from 1828–30; its recording by **Previn,** Yong Uck Kim, Heiichiro Ohyama, and Gary Hoffman is NA (RCA).

Contrary to Schwann, the relaxed and intimate account by the **Schubert Ensemble** is of the later work, not the C minor (Hyperion). The **Beaux Arts Trio** with Samuel Rhodes will be many people's first choice,

a technically immaculate performance in a slightly close recording (Philips 420791). **Pressler** (pianist of the Beaux Arts) with members of the Emerson Quartet, is more sensitive (♦DG 445848). Another leading contender is the live account from **Rabinovich,** Dora Schwarzberg, Imai, and Maisky, a wonderfully spontaneous reading (EMI 55484).

These are all coupled with the Quintet, so it may be no accident that the most communicative and sensitive account comes rather with Brahms's G minor Piano Quartet, from the **Ames Piano Quartet.** Their performance has a verve and vitality that sacrifices nothing of the work's elusive subtlety; the sound is warm and clear (♦Dorian 90194). Brahms's Quintet is the pairing for **Gould** and members of the Juilliard Quartet, a consistently fascinating performance even if not first choice (Sony 52684). These are preferable to both recordings featuring **Ax,** with Stern, Laredo, and Ma, which never quite adds up to the sum of its parts (Sony), or with the Cleveland Quartet (RCA). The **Mozart Piano Quartet** provides an assured performance, less overtly romantic than others but expressively a little dull; their coupling is a rarity, Felix Draeseke's Horn and Piano Quintet (MD+G). The **Florestan Trio,** with violist Thomas Riebl, gives a slightly clinical, straitlaced interpretation, beautifully recorded (Hyperion 67175).

Piano Quintet Op. 44. One of Schumann's greatest works—his finest for chamber forces—this is gloriously life-affirming music despite (perhaps because of) the grave, funereal atmosphere of the slow movement. One of the mid-19th century's finest chamber pieces, it was the first of any consequence written for the combination of piano and string quartet, earlier quintets—for example, by Hummel (1802) or Schubert (the "Trout," 1819)—being scored mostly for piano, string trio, and double-bass.

It can be heard in the context of those very predecessors in the recording by the **Schubert Ensemble** (Hyperion, 2CD). It's nicely played, and good value at medium price, but there are more inspirational accounts on disc, not least the live one by **Argerich,** Schwarzberg, Lucy Hall, Imai, and Maisky, a performance full of life and playfulness (EMI 55484). The piano is a touch hard-toned at times, unlike that used by **Pressler** with the Emerson Quartet, a very strong performance in spacious, top-notch sound (♦DG 445848). This is even more impressive than Pressler's regular group, the **Beaux Arts Trio,** in 1975 with Rhodes and Dolf Bettelheim. Technically brilliant, it's comparatively constricted in sound, and there is a disadvantageous detached quality to the playing (Philips, in two different releases). These recordings all include the Piano Quartet.

The example of Schumann's Piano Quintet was emulated by many later composers, from Brahms to Bartók, Dvořák to Dohnányi, their works all appearing as couplings for Schumann's. Of those with Brahms, **Peter Frankl**'s with the Lindsay Quartet is solid and nicely balanced, unusual in their fast treatment of the slow movement, which is noticeably shorter than the Allegro brillante I; in most accounts the first two movements are either virtually identical in duration or else the second is a little longer (ASV). **Jandó** and the Kodály Quartet are even fleeter than Frankl and the Lindsays, with the slow movement a full minute shorter than the first; this is mainly due to their lackluster pace for the opening Allegro, not at all brillante. Their account does pick up in the later movements, however (Naxos). Both of these are preferable to **Paul Komen** and the Rubio Quartet (Globe). The best of all is from 1944, by **Rudolf Serkin** and the Budapest Quartet (Pearl 9275).

A more unusual coupling is provided by **Suzanne Bradbury** and the Silvestri Quartet in Bartók's 1904 Quintet; in a well-articulated but rather literal account of the Schumann, the relatively more measured tempos make the music drag compared to others (ASV Quicksilva).

Several recordings couple the Quintet with other Schumann scores, particularly the string quartets. The best of these is by **Paul Gulda** and the Hagen Quartet, a performance of such extremes that there is almost two minutes' difference in duration between the first two movements. It's a thrilling and exuberant rendition, though several critics found it too wayward (DG 447111, with Quartet 1). **Tacchino** and the Athenaeum Enesco Quartet neither take as many risks nor achieve such heights (Pierre Verany).

A notable live performance is by **Richter** and the **Borodin Quartet**, rather steely and over-accented, with the piano placed too far forward for true chamber music (Teldec, with Schubert's "Death and the Maiden" Quartet). Far more faithful—perhaps the finest live account currently available—is by **Entremont** with the Alban Berg Quartet, lively, poetic, and beautifully balanced, if a touch recessed (♦EMI 55593, with Dvořák's Op. 81).

Other fine historical performances include **Gabrilowitsch** and the Flonzaley Quartet (1927; Biddulph), **Sanromá** with the Primrose Quartet (1940; Biddulph 052/3), and **Victor Aller** with the Hollywood Quartet (1955; Testament mono). Several more unusual versions exist, such as **Richard Burnett** on the fortepiano with the Fitzwilliam Quartet, a fascinating variation in texture (Amon Ra 54), and **Wild**'s arrangement using string orchestra (including double basses), which he performs with the American String Orchestra directed by **Isaiah Jackson** (Ivory 71003). Most bizarre, perhaps, is that for piano and wind instruments arranged by Christian Hommel, oboist of **Ensemble Aventure** (Ars Musici 1164).

Romances Op. 94 for oboe (or clarinet or violin) and piano. Of the 30 or so currently available recordings, little more than a third use the oboe for which Schumann originally scored these charming miniatures. *Romance* 2 has probably Schumann's best-loved instrumental melody, and has been much recorded on its own, not least by **Menuhin** and **Kreisler** (both reissued separately on Biddulph), **David Oistrakh** (Melodiya), and **Accardo** (Fone). Several interpreters use the composer's specified alternatives of violin and (especially) clarinet, but some use arrangements for other instruments, such as flute, bassoon, trombone, tuba, viola, or cello.

Oboe: **József Kiss** offers a beautifully phrased and sensitive account, very clearly recorded, coupled with arrangements for oboe of other Schumann works (such as Violin Sonata 1), almost irresistible at budget price (♦Naxos 550599). **Holliger**'s command always impresses, as does his expressiveness (♦Philips 426386), and he scores over **Christian Hommel**, whose surprisingly dry performance isn't as evocative (Ars Musici). The accounts by **Joseph Robinson** (Elysium) and **Björn Carl Nielsen** (Kontrapunkt) form part of enjoyable selections of Schumann's smaller chamber works, while that by **Burkhard Glaetzner** is coupled with the first two violin sonatas (Berlin). **John Anderson** places his winning account among a host of trifles by French and Italian composers (ASV), while **John Mack** couples it with Britten, Emile Paladilhe, and Saint-Saëns (Crystal). Pick of the historical issues is **Leon Goossens**'s wonderful 1939 performance accompanied by the late, great Gerald Moore (Pearl 9281).

Clarinet: The only recording that makes you forget that this music really does suit the oboe better is **de Peyer**'s lovely account (♦Chandos 8506).

Violin: Two versions for violin stand out, by **Cho-Liang Lin** (♦Sony 39133) and **Rolf Schulte** (Centaur).

Sonatas for violin and piano. Schumann's three violin sonatas were written in a comparatively short time in 1851–53. No. 3 originated in the

collaborative "FAE" Sonata for Joachim, Schumann replacing the movements written by Albert Dietrich and Brahms with his own. Effectively his final completed composition, 3 received a handful of early performances, then had to wait until 1956 to be published. Performances and recordings have been rare until comparatively recently, and some players still seem reluctant to include it in their repertory, as for example **Kremer** and Argerich in their exciting recording of 1 and 2 from the mid-'80s (♦DG 419235).

There are now five complete cycles on the market. That by **Mark Kaplan** and Kuerti is notable for their dexterity and the sensitivity of their slow movements, though some may find the violin tone a little too lean (Arabesque 6662). **Robert Zimansky** and Christoph Keller are less persuasive (Accord); so too are **Maria Egelhof** and Mathias Weber, the latter the better recorded (Thorofon). The fine set by **Andrew Hardy** and Uriel Tsachor deserves special mention for including Clara's *Romances Op. 22* (Olympia 356). Most recently, **Isabelle Faust** and Silke Avenhaus have set down passionate and virtuosic accounts, as strong in structure as texture (♦CPO 999597).

1: One of the most celebrated recordings of 1 is surely **Adolf Busch**'s from 1937, accompanied by Serkin, and much reissued (by some five companies at the time of writing; Biddulph 165 leads the way). **Max Rostal** made a very fine interpretation in the '50s with Colin Horsley (Symposium 1076), to be preferred to **Lucy Russell** and Richard Burnett (Amon Ra). There is also an impressive but uncredited arrangement for oboe and piano, played with zest by **József Kiss** and Jandó (Naxos 550599).

2: This is a more relaxed and far more expansive piece. **Yehudi** and Hephzibah **Menuhin** made a very early recording (1934), lovingly restored (Biddulph 067), but the live account by **Schwarzberg** and Argerich is more strongly lyrical (EMI 55484).

String Quartets. Schumann's three completed string quartets all date from his initial assault on chamber music in 1842, reflected in their grouping as Op. 41. Although successful enough on their own terms (and immeasurably valuable for the composer as a learning experience), he would never again pen a chamber work without his own instrument, the piano, being present. Just how valuable were the lessons learned can be heard in his next chamber work, the great Piano Quintet.

Complete cycles: These are fewer in number than these intimate and delightful works deserve. That by the **Hagen Quartet** is brilliantly played, and full of life, though some may find the music too driven (DG 447111 and 449214). The cycle by the **Melos Quartet** is now NA (DG), but the **Alberni Quartet**'s is still available, though the '80s sound has been surpassed by more modern competition (CRD). Most recently, the excellent **Eroica Quartet** has tackled all three, showing themselves to be fully inside the idiom, unlike their rivals giving glowing accounts on a single disc (♦Harmonia Mundi 907270). The **Takács Quartet** cycle isn't as convincing (Hungaroton, 2CD), and neither the **Manfred Quartet** (Pierre Verany) nor the **St. Lawrence Quartet** (EMI) has made a particularly strong critical impression.

1: This is a remarkable first effort. The polyphonic opening was born out of Schumann's studies of Bach with his wife, but has a Shostakovich-like quality (that is rapidly dispelled), while the Adagio's main theme has a distinctly Mahlerian tinge. The **Gabrieli Quartet** gives a typically well-shaped performance, not without blemish (♦Meridian 84380). Theirs is a more measured response to the music than the **Lark Quartet**'s, whose account is just a little too edge-of-the-seat for this music (Arabesque). Faster still were the **Flonzaley Quartet** in 1927, and there is another interesting historical issue from the **Capet Quartet** from about the same time, with largely French couplings (Biddulph). The **Petersen Quartet**'s is a fine reading, but incongruously coupled with quartets by composers from Mozart to Schulhoff (Caprice). Less persuasive are the **Koeckert Quartet** (Calliope, with 3) and the **Athenaeum Enesco Quartet** (Pierre Verany, with the Quintet).

3: There is currently no separate account of 2, but 3—the most assured of the three—has been issued almost as often as 1, and frequently coupled with it. The **Gabrieli Quartet** (♦Meridian, as above) is again preferable to the **Lark Quartet,** whose breathless approach doesn't always suit the music (Arabesque), and to the **Koeckert Quartet** (Calliope). A recording by the aptly named **Robert Schumann Quartet** forms part of a wide-ranging set of the composer's works, including Symphony 3, the Piano Concerto, and piano pieces (Intercord). The Finnish **Voces Intimae Quartet** gives a stylish account coupled with Sibelius's eponymous quartet, though the overly resonant acoustic at Castle Wik in Sweden will not be to everyone's taste (BIS 10).

Stücke im Volkston Op. 102 for cello (or clarinet or violin) and piano. One of Schumann's slightest sets, these five pieces have nonetheless enjoyed the advocacy of many eminent cellists, like **Casals** (Sony 58993) and **Rostropovich** (accompanied by Britten; Decca 452895). **Ma** with Ax (Sony 42663), **Maisky** (Philips 412230), and **Schiff** (Philips) all turn in first-rate accounts, yet the ones that seem to make the best case for the music are by **Kliegel** (Naxos 550654) and particularly **Mørk** (♦Simax 1063). These outclass the accounts by **Bylsma** (Sony) and **Isserlis** (RCA).

Of other arrangements, **Kiss** gives a highly enjoyable account of the full set on the oboe (Naxos, as above), whereas **Holliger** plays only the middle three (Philips). However, bassoonist **Wolfgang Rüdiger** persuades us that the Studies were written for his instrument, a hugely entertaining and playful account (Ars Musici 1164).

Trios. The three Piano Trios are quite varied in character. The first two both date from 1847, the spur possibly being Clara's production of a trio of her own the previous year. In 1, Schumann finally produced a work for trio on the scale—if not quite the quality—of the Quintet, but 2 is a composition of exquisite intimacy and joy. The slow movement's quotation of one of the *Liederkreis* songs underlines the domestic source of inspiration: It was written ten years after his engagement to Clara. By 1851, Schumann was showing signs of mental strain, and this may account for 3's being less convincing than its predecessors. That notwithstanding, it has many fine qualities and only the finale really fails to gel.

Cycles are more widespread than Schwann would have us believe, listing only the **Trio Italiano** (Arts). For many, the leader of the pack will be the **Beaux Arts Trio,** whom the music seems to fit like a glove (♦Philips 432165). Near perfection in 1, they do yield to the younger **Florestan Trio** in 2, in whose hands it rather than its predecessor strikes one as Schumann's finest chamber work after the Quintet (♦Hyperion 67063, 67175). The Beaux Arts has the narrowest of edges in 3, although the Florestan benefits from better recorded sound. Another notable set comes from the **Borodin Trio,** their interpretations of all three trios informed by a richly romantic palette, beautifully captured in the recording, and the most poetically expressive playing (Chandos 8832/3). However, their tempos are at best rather leisurely, which doesn't always serve Schumann's music well: for example, the finale of 1 really doesn't match the marking *Mit Feuer* ("With fire").

These sets all include the earlier *Phantasiestücke* Op. 88. One cycle that does not comes from **Trio Jean Paul,** who pair them with pieces by

Rihm (who provides an essay on Schumann in the booklet, rendered almost unreadable in the English translation). Their interpretations may strike you as mannered, even eccentric, until you realize that they have incorporated elements from their study of the autograph scores. If not first choices, these are still beautifully played and fascinating readings (Ars Musici 1241-2).

There are several historic issues worthy of note, none more so than that by the **Thibaud-Casals-Cortot Trio** set down in 1928 for HMV and currently available from a variety of labels (EMI, Biddulph, Concert Artists, Magic Talent). Another eminent issue is by **Szeryng-Fournier-Rubinstein** (RCA). Bizarrely, the **Grieg Trio** chose not to couple their recordings of 1 and 2 with 3, replacing it with Mendelssohn's Trios Opp. 49 and 66 (Virgin). RICKARDS

PIANO MUSIC

Schumann is the quintessential Romantic composer of the early 19th century, and his piano music embodies the quintessence of his romanticism. Compounded of passion and tenderness, exuberant fantasy and melodic invention, autobiographical and literary allusions, it often conveys a pervading and disquieting sense of a divided self struggling for coherence, even for sanity. Many of his compositions present great technical difficulties, but their interpretive problems are even greater. Most pianists, including some very good ones, offer performances that are respectful—even beautiful—but miss the wildness that often lies beneath the surface. Surprisingly, this is generally true of the German and Austrian schools, and it's among the French and Russians that we find the deepest understanding of Schumann's music and the most satisfactory performances.

Schumann was most at home in short forms, and the brief pieces that make up his piano suites are miniature dramas that require clear differentiation without losing sight of the fact that their contrasts of ardor and sentiment were (as Arrau said) "parts of the same personality." They also require an intensity of expression that's hard to come by. The longer works, especially Sonata 1 and *Fantasia,* are difficult to hold together and make continuously interesting to listeners, and again their passions can't be tamed without losing the essence of their theatrical effectiveness and compelling emotionality.

Many pianists have recorded a considerable part of this repertoire; some are outstanding, others—including some notable names—are less so. I will deal with the most important of these artists first, followed by a survey of recommended recordings of individual works, in alphabetical order.

Cortot's recordings from the '20s to the '40s are extraordinary in their imagination and lyricism, though they portray more of Schumann's courage and vitality than his anguish. In spite of his often sloppy technique, this great artist's phrasing and coloring are miraculous in everything he touched, creating an atmosphere that is at once tender and robust, exquisitely refined and heroically exuberant. Fortunately, many of his recordings have been transferred to CDs in excellent sound. Good collections are in Music & Arts 858 (2CD), Biddulph LHW 003-005 (3CD), and Pearl 9931/32 (2CD).

Arrau took an entirely different approach to Schumann's music: his performances resulted more from thoughtful deliberation than Cortot's inspirations of the moment. He went to its core, not finding much joy in it but bringing out its contrasts of light and darkness in compassionate interpretations that reveal more at each hearing, playing with a rich, burnished tone that uncovered inner voices and textures with great subtlety. He's at his best in the more extended forms like *Fantasia;* his *Car-*

naval is a bit dull, but *Kinderszenen* and *Waldscenen* are notable for the intelligence and sensitivity with which the episodes are illuminated. His early recordings are preferable to those he made in the '60s and '70s, when he became tediously pedantic. There used to be a set that included most of his Schumann recordings (Philips 412308, 7CD), but these days not much remains in the catalog. One disc includes *Carnaval, Kinderszenen,* and *Waldscenen* (♦Philips 420871), and another offers *Fantasia* recorded in 1959 (Aura 157, with Beethoven and Chopin). Sonata 1 appears on HPC 099. A 1959 *Carnaval* is in an Arrau collection called "The Early Years" (♦Marston 52023) and on Pearl 9928 and 0070. With luck, more will be coming from these sources, but for the present, much seems to be missing.

Horowitz could be guilty of unconscionable distortions of what he played, but this was never the case with his Schumann. Something in the troubled psyche of the composer meshed with that of the also troubled pianist to produce very personal performances of genuine insight, great eloquence, and astonishing brilliance. His first recording of *Kreisleriana* in the '60s remains unmatched in its sweep, fervor, and lyricism (♦Sony 53468); his *Fantasia* has depth and sonority, and he explores its treacherous byways easily and effectively. You'll find many of his best performances in ♦Sony 42408 (*Arabeske, Blümenstück,* Sonata 3) and ♦Philips 456838 (*Arabeske, Fantasiestücke* Op. 12, *Kreisleriana,* Sonata 3, *Toccata*).

Richter was another whose encounters with Schumann produced wonderful responses of fire and understanding. He recorded many of the pieces over and over again, and you can follow in them his transition from the blazing virtuosity of his early days (e.g., a 1958 *Toccata* that's almost as pyrotechnical as Barere's but far more musical) to the deeper penetration of his later years. Like every pianist, he imposes his own interpretation on what he plays, but somehow he seems to disappear into it, letting it speak for itself with the utmost naturalness and conveying an incontrovertible sense of "rightness." Nowhere is this more apparent than in the delicacy and whimsy of his *Papillons* or his incomparable 1956 reading of *Waldscenen* (♦Philips 956452), and nobody has ever given more luminous and moving performances of *Humoreske* (♦Monitor 71022) or *Fantasia* Op. 17. His early performances can be found in ♦Parnassus 96-0001, worth hearing in spite of their poor sound; good recordings of *Fantasia, Papillons,* and *Faschingsschwank aus Wien* are in ♦EMI 64625, and a later *Toccata, Blumenstück,* and *Nachtstücke* are in ♦London 436456.

Many critics and listeners are fond of **Kempff**'s Schumann; I am not, or at least not always. He was certainly a wonderfully skilled pianist, ever facile and always graceful, but he displayed little understanding of the divided and often tortured soul the composer presents to us. His gifts are best heard in light and whimsical pieces like *Papillons* and *Kinderszenen,* not in the larger and more complex works (except perhaps for *Kreisleriana,* where he's very good if somewhat too Schubertian). If you're interested, most of his recordings can be found in DG 435405, 4CD. **Schiff** suffers from similar disabilities (Teldec). On the other hand, you might think the elegant and aristocratic style of **Rubinstein** wouldn't be appropriate for this music, but you'd be wrong. Always poetic and rhythmically alive, his *Carnaval* and *Symphonic Etudes* are among his best recordings and stand beside the best by anyone else. The former is in ♦RCA 63051, along with *Fantasiestücke* Op. 12; the latter seems to be available only in RCA 63039, Vol. 39 of the "Rubinstein Collection"; ♦RCA 63052 contains *Kreisleriana* and *Fantasia* Op. 17.

Album für die Jügend. These 43 pieces were written to be played by children and aren't often recorded; **Alexis Weissenberg** does a nice job with them (EMI 63049).

Arabeske. This piece has long been an over-sentimentalized salon favorite. **Horowitz** (Sony 47409), **Rubinstein** (RCA 63039), and **Kempff** (DG 435045) show how it should be played, and they're joined by a beautiful old recording by **Guiomar Novaes** (Turnabout LP) and a beautiful new one by **Kissin** (Sony 52567). This was one of **Gilels**'s favorites, and his several recordings are glowing masterpieces (Philips 4565799; Music & Arts 747; Melodiya/BMG 40116).

Blümenstück. In this charming piece, **Horowitz** (Sony 42409) is nearly equaled by **Lortie,** a Canadian pianist with skill and intelligence (Chandos 9289).

Bunte Blätter. **Richter** (Olympia 338 or 5013) is again joined by **Lortie** (Chandos 9289) in these light essays in pianistic charm, and there is an outstanding performance of the first eight by the remarkable **Clara Haskil** in "The Clara Haskil Legacy" (Tahra 291).

Carnaval. Here we have recordings by many, many pianists. **Rachmaninoff**'s performance of this mercurial, improbably fanciful suite is about as definitive as we'll ever get, bringing its characters into vivid focus with unrivaled skill (in "Complete Recordings," RCA 61265, 10CD). But **Cortot** and **Rubinstein** are right there with him, and there are others to consider as well: **Novaes** again (Turnabout LP), a deeply insightful reading by **Solomon** (Testament 1084), a fresh look at the music from the great colorist **Sofronitsky** (Arlecchino 155; Denon 80074), and a bold and convincing account from **Magaloff** (FNAC 462331). **Annie Fischer** was a very great pianist whose work has come into clearer focus in recent years, and her *Carnaval* is a garden of spontaneity (EMI 69217, 2CD).

Davidsbündlertänze. Schumann's dualism is most explicit in this piece, personified in the contrasted characters of Florestan the man of action and Eusebius the dreamer. There's wildness beneath its melodious surface, and any pianist who doesn't hear it shouldn't play this music. **Cortot** doesn't quite get it, but delivers a performance so rapturous that everything else can be forgiven (Biddulph LHW 003). **Arrau** comes closer to the mark, but his recording seems to be unavailable. **Berezovsky** is excellent in this music, though for some reason he ends it on an inappropriately subdued note (Teldec 77476); **Perahia** is acceptable, though ultimately too restrained (Sony 32299); and **Kuerti** plays it with a good touch and lovely phrasing, evoking both its manic and extroverted side and its gentle and lyrical aspect (Analekta 23126).

***Fantasia* Op. 17.** This shows us Schumann in extremis, almost incoherent in his passionate self-absorption but still producing music of wondrous beauty. Dedicated to Liszt, it contains many things—a love letter to Clara, a tribute to Beethoven, expressions of inner joy and grief—and it's very hard to bring them all under the same roof. Here **Richter** reigns supreme, in structurally solid performances that negotiate every twist and turn of the piece with absolute authority and preternatural expressivity. His 1961 recording is probably the best (EMI 64625), but others are almost as good (Philips 456952 or 438477; Praga 254033). **Arrau** also delivers a marvelous performance (Aura 157), but **Horowitz**'s rather neurotic reading is less successful (Sony), and **Kempff** doesn't seem to understand the piece at all (DG).

A number of others are worth your attention, especially **Fiorentino**'s dreamy but coherent and communicative interpretation (Appian 7036) and **Backhaus**'s strength and richness of tone (Pearl 0046). **Curzon** is subtle and seductive (Decca 466498); **Egorov** plays it with blazing conviction and a fine sense of line and structure (Globe 6015); **Moiseiwitsch** offers wonderful color and rhythmic subtlety (Testament 1023);

Perahia is calm and convincing if not very exciting (Sony 42124); **Annie Fischer** is inspired, as always (EMI 69217, 2CD). **De Larrocha**'s Schumann is generally more satisfying than most of her essays beyond the Spanish territory over which she's the undisputed monarch, and her 1975 recording is magisterial (Decca 6756, LP; the later one on RCA isn't as good). I haven't heard **Alfredo Perl**'s version (Arte Nova 27804), but one critic described it as "musically enriching and pianistically aristocratic."

Fantasiestücke Op. 12. As David Dubal says, these eight contrasting pieces, planned as a unit, are "the epitome of German Romanticism." **Richter** knows how to evoke their capricious dream world in a performance of six of them (Philips 456942 or 438477; Melodiya 294644), and so does **Arrau** (Philips 432308). **Argerich** offers one of her most mellow recordings (EMI 63576). The relatively unknown **Sylvie Carbonel** captures their manic energy in an invigorating and persuasive reading (Pavane 7259), and **Ax** plays them with his customary sensitivity and thoughtfulness (RCA).

Faschingsschwank aus Wien. **Richter**'s version of this splendid romp is inimitable (EMI 64625), and **Ivan Davis**'s fascinating performance is a favorite of many critics (Audiofon 72004). By and large, **Michelangeli**'s unique style isn't well suited to Schumann, but his depiction of these carnival pranks is brilliantly conceived and executed (Testament 2088; DG 423231). **Perahia** is entirely competent but a shade too tame to be wholly satisfactory (Sony 46437).

Humoreske. Among the quirkier pieces, this has a host of improvisatory ideas elbowing each other aside from beginning to end. Once again **Richter** (Monitor 72022) and **Arrau** (Philips 432308) are authoritative. **Horowitz** is a shade too facile for my taste, though others think he's great in this piece (RCA 6680), and still others like **Kempff** (DG 435045), though I think he too lacks the necessary bite. Otherwise, you can turn to **Goode**'s enriching performance (Nonesuch 79014), **Lupu**'s glowing rendition (London 440496), or the warmth of **de Larrocha** (RCA 68657).

Kinderszenen. These evocative scenes from childhood are the purest expression of Schumann's lyrical gifts, and many pianists evoke their sweet simplicity with great effectiveness. **Kempff** is at his best here (DG 435045); **Cortot** is fine (Biddulph LHW 005), and so is **Horowitz**, though he's a bit abrupt in some of the episodes (Sony 42409). **Moiseiwitsch**'s luminous tone is particularly moving (Decca 710048, LP), as is **Curzon**'s natural gravity and tenderness (Decca 466498). **Annie Fischer**'s glowing *Kinderszenen* is a wonderful example of her inspired performances (EMI 68733 or 69217, 2CD); **Moravec** captures their wide-eyed innocence in beautiful colors (Nonesuch 79063).

Kreisleriana. This has been recorded more often than any other of Schumann's piano works, and you only have to listen to it once to understand why. Dedicated to Chopin, the title refers to the unpredictable Kapellmeister Kreisler, a fantastic character created by E.T.A. Hoffmann. It covers a dizzying range of moods, emotions, melodies, and textures, presenting a challenging test of the performer's technical and interpretive skills. The names that come up first are **Cortot,** whose naturalness and simplicity are altogether winning (Biddulph LHW 005; Philips 456751); **Horowitz,** whose 1969 performance is one of the great piano recordings of our time (Sony 53468); and **Sofronitsky** (Arlecchino 1; Denon 80816). **Arrau** seems surprisingly uninvolved here (Philips 432308), and so does **Rubinstein** (RCA), but **Kempff** is at his best (DG 435045; Philips 456862).

There are others worth hearing, including **Argerich**'s exhilarating though overly aggressive reading (DG 410653); **Egorov**'s blazing conviction (EMI 69537); **Annie Fischer**'s grand sweep (EMI 68733, 2CD); **Perahia** in the best of his Schumann performances (Sony 62786); and **Ashkenazy,** whose Schumann usually strikes me as superficial but here delivers a fresh and vital performance (Decca 425940). **Kuerti** is a much underrated pianist, and his *Kreisleriana* is one of the finest (CBC 2012).

Nachtstücke. These "night pieces" are played beautifully by **Kempff** (DG 435405) and with great facility but less insight by **Schiff** (Teldec 14566). The performances by **Arrau** (Philips 432308), **Gilels** (Mobile Fidelity 871), and **Richter** (Philips 42877 or 454169) are where you should turn for the most natural and effective expression of their colorful scene painting.

Noveletten. These eight charming pieces were described by Schumann as "longish connected tales of adventure." Among our great Schumann interpreters, only **Arrau** recorded them, and he's a little heavy-handed (Philips 432308). There once was a beautiful performance by **Beveridge Webster,** long unavailable (Dover LP); watch for it in case it reappears.

Papillons. In this first of Schumann's character suites, **Cortot** (Biddulph LHW 003) makes the butterflies dance like no one else. **Kempff** is a bit too literal, **Richter** and **Sofronitsky** a little too dramatic, but **Perahia** seems (for once) to be inspired by them (Sony 34539).

Romances Op. 28. You can depend on **Kempff** (DG 435404) to do justice to these poetic miniatures. I haven't mentioned **Gieseking**'s Schumann until now because his delicately shaded performances aren't generally among the most interesting, but in 1 and 2 his mastery of color and nuance are illuminating (Music & Arts 1013).

Sonata 1. This sonata is almost unmanageable; Schumann said it was composed by Florestan and Eusebius. It's a sprawling, incoherent outpouring of emotion barely under control; it was dedicated to Clara, and apparently she thought it was quite wonderful. **Perahia** is warm and intelligent (Sony 62786) whereas **Pollini** demonstrates his uncanny technique without much warmth (Philips 456937). Of **Gilels**'s three recordings, his 1957 account is the most balanced and persuasive (Monitor 72048). **Elissa Virsaladze** gives an effective performance; she's almost brutal in her power and passion, but she makes it all fit together reasonably well (Live Classics 352). **Sofronitsky** is an even better representative of the Russian school, playing with a more controlled intensity and much beauty (Melodiya 25177).

Sonata 2. This is much more concise and more often recorded. **Arrau** is warm and introspective (Philips 432308); **Horowitz** is both tender and passionate; and **Richter** captures its moods with utter naturalness and conviction (EMI 64429). **Kempff** is too whimsical (DG 435045), though his performance is certainly enjoyable. **Fiorentino**'s reading is deeply committed and very colorful (APR 5560). Everyone else seems tame compared to **Argerich,** though as usual she loses its lyricism in her fierceness (Philips 456703); **Benedetto Lupo** (VAIA 1158) is more convincing than **Perahia** (Sony 44569).

Symphonic Etudes. These flashy display pieces are among the most difficult of Schumann's piano works. **Richter**'s accounts seem somewhat undeveloped, better in 1971 (Olympia 339) than 1956 (Praga 254033). **Arrau** offers less pizzazz but more musicality (Philips 432308), and this is among the best of **Rubinstein**'s Schumann renditions (RCA 63039). **Magaloff** is assured and convincing (FNAC 642331); **Perahia** is also persuasive, if less adroit (Sony 34539); and **Pollini** is typically flawless and structurally sound (DG 445522).

Toccata. **Barere** could play anything faster than anyone else, and he out-does himself in his famous recording of this virtuoso showpiece, but he makes it more of a stunt in double-note technique than a piece of music (APR 7001, the best of the transfers; Pearl 0012). **Richter** finds much more in it in any of his recordings; the most exciting is from 1958 (Parnassus 96-001), and the most musical came a year later (DG 435751 or 427198). **Horowitz** is brilliant, as you would expect (Sony 42409); so are **Gilels** (Piano Library 235), **Grigori Ginzburg** (Arlecchino 05), and **Josef Lhevinne** (Philips 456889).

Variations on A-B-E-G-G. This is Schumann's Opus 1, a set of four variations on the name of Countess von Abegg plus an extended finale; it's an astonishing first effort. **Arrau** (Philips 432308), **Eschenbach** (Philips 456763), **Ginzburg** (Melodiya), **Haskil** (Philips 456829), **Kissin** (RCA), and **Richter** (DG) give the most satisfying performances.

Variations on a Theme of Clara Wieck. This is the third movement of Sonata 3. By itself, it's given outstanding performances by **Horowitz** and **Sofronitsky** (Arlecchino 1)

Waldscenen. These forest scenes are at once naive and sophisticated, and like the *Fantasia* with which it's coupled, **Richter**'s 1956 interpretation is incomparable (Philips 456952). **Arrau** captures both their tenderness and their wildness (Philips 42087), **Haefliger** their whimsical and poetic components (Sony 48036). MORIN

ORGAN MUSIC

Schumann's "organ" works consist of three sets of pieces. *Six Canonic Studies* Op. 56 and *Four Sketches* Op. 58 are actually for the pedal piano, the sort of instrument organists used for practice in the days before electric blowers. *Six Fugues on the Name B-A-C-H* Op. 60 was written for the organ, but the title page allows the pedal piano as an option. All the pieces date from 1845, when Schumann's mental and emotional states were declining seriously. At that time both he and Clara resumed serious study of formal counterpoint, leading in his case to these essays in canonic and fugal writing. The Op. 58 *Sketches* are more in the character of Schumann's shorter piano pieces.

In performing these works at the organ, *Canonic Studies* is customarily treated as gentle, intimate works, while *Sketches* and *Fugues* are more extroverted and played with bolder registrations. Of the three sets, *Sketches* is perhaps the least convincing at the organ, since so much of the writing seems to presuppose the sonority and percussive attack of the piano.

Olivier Latry has recorded the three sets on the 1855 Cavaillé-Coll organ in the Church of Notre Dame at St. Omer (RCA Victor/BMG France 74321479452). The performances are nicely shaped with sensitive inflections of tempo and generally effective registrations. Quiet-to-medium volume registrations are quite delicious, but the louder combinations tend to be strident; all warmth and richness disappear. It's hard to tell whether the fault lies with the instrument or with the recording.

As for other recordings of this music, the landscape is pretty bleak. **Lefebvre** recorded them at an instrument by Nicolas-Antoine Lété built in 1845, the same year the music was composed (FY). Alas, the instrument sounds dreadful, alternately squeaky and weedy with reeds that no one could possibly take seriously and so much action noise that quiet passages are badly obscured. Lefebvre's playing is animated, but there isn't much nuance.

Innig plays a dark-toned Klais organ in his recording (MD+G). After

Lefebvre, I was impressed with his tempo inflections in the continuous 16th notes of the first of the Op. 56 *Studies*. Overall, however, Innig (true to his surname) is apt to be overly ponderous and introspective, losing the forest of coherence for the trees of detail. **Georges Delvallée** didn't impress me when I first encountered the belated CD issue of his 1983 recording (REM 311135). It begins to sound good after Lefebvre and Innig, but I stop short of recommending it. The recording quality is far from satisfactory. In particular, the larger registrations have an almost metallic quality and boxed-in sound. There are several clumsy edits, and the playing isn't good enough to override these shortcomings.

GATENS

CHORAL MUSIC

Schumann's choral work is neglected, and while it doesn't measure up to his most noteworthy compositions, to ignore it is to fail to understand him fully. At the very least, it's full of many memorable tunes, with solid writing and a Romantic pungency that rings true as no other composer's does. There isn't a lot to choose from, but we're fortunate that most works have had at least one excellent recording.

Manfred. Byron's poem of the tortured story of Manfred, beset by guilt because of his incestuous love for his sister Astarte, came from a man who was guilty of a real incestuous affair with his half-sister. Manfred travels the earth seeking purification or death, and ends up rejecting the forgiveness of the Church in a desperate, Romantic notion of self-annihilation. As sick as this story is—turning morality on its head for the sake of a sinful individual quest—it nonetheless attracted the attention of many Romantic composers. Schumann seems to have put almost everything he could say about the story into his Overture, one of the great Romantic works, and the remaining 65 minutes really add little to it.

Schønwandt offers an excellent version, emended for performance, and the Berlin Symphony and Radio Chorus are first-rate (♦Kontrapunkte 32181). **Mario Venzago** leads a version that's too dialog-heavy; it sounds like a German poetry recital (Musiques Suisse). **Beecham**'s is the best, in excellent mono sound; he loved the music and spent years trying to put together a viable score. It's in English, and that makes it more tolerable for local audiences. The Overture is searing, one of the best on disc, and if the spoken British mannerisms get on your nerves after a while, just try one of the others (♦Beecham Collection 4)!

Das Paradis und die Peri (Paradise and the Peri). Romanticism run amuck is at the center of Schumann's first major choral composition. He felt that the highest achievements in music were in the union of music and text in a choral setting, so this was a great step for the 33-year-old composer. Thomas Moore's epic poem *Lalla Rookh* chronicled the adventures of the heroine trying to gain entrance to Paradise, which she has been denied due to her descent from a union of a fallen angel and a human; she finally succeeds by offering the tears of a criminal who was moved by the sight of a child praying. The work was a resounding success, and many believed it to be a turning point in the composer's fortunes, but it has fallen from favor, partly because of the story's sentimentality and partly because it lacks the big bang so necessary in a post-Wagnerian, Mahlerian age.

Sinopoli's version reigns supreme, with the wonderful Dresden Staatskapelle and the just-as-wonderful Florence Quivar. By all means race to the store and grab it before it disappears from American shores (♦DG 445875, 2CD). **Wolf-Dieter Hauschild**'s effort is only moderately successful, mainly due to the waywardness of the soloists. The soprano sings fairly well, but without any commitment to the emotional state of the Peri; one simply cannot take on this role without at least pretending to be sympathetic, no matter how strange the story sounds to modern ears. The men also have problems, with the tenors and basses insecure in some of the lower parts. The sound is terrific, as are the chorus and Leipzig Radio Orchestra, but there are too many solo inadequacies to let this one pass (Berlin).

Even with the fabulous Bonney, **Gardiner** has problems because of his white-toned, rather monochromatic sound. The perfectly pitched, strait-laced Monteverdi Choir sings with absolute accuracy, but his periodist tendencies obscure much of the vital color in Schumann's score. If this were the only version, I could live happily with it, but Sinopoli tops him. Yet Gardiner has his strengths, with some exciting full-orchestra passages that are quite emotional in their broad, floating sweep (♦Archiv 457660, 2CD).

Jordan was one of the first to appear on the scene in modern guise, and his Orchestra de la Suisse Romande sports a silvery, soft, supple sound that fits the conductor's concept very well (♦Erato 45456). Edith Wiens has received a lot of criticism for her uninvolved singing, but this isn't really the case. Above all, she places emphasis on beauty of sound to underscore the underlying purity of the Peri and the essential unfairness of her predicament. The chorus is excellent: full-bodied and flexible.

Scenes from Goethe's Faust.
Schumann probably felt obliged to pay some attention to his great countryman but was only moderately successful. The overture was completed last, serving as a summary of the themes, typical for the time. Part 2 of Goethe's play is the subject of most of the drama, and the "Cathedral" scene in particular is a wondrous episode in Schumann's output, full of rapt expression and riveting high drama. Even moderately good Schumann is the equal of most other composer's best efforts, and this one is well worth hearing.

Good sound and excellent choral work are typical of a **Herreweghe** performance, and he's certainly the master of the score in a reading that walks a tightrope of technical finesse, but the soloists are a letdown, with some very wobbly singing, rather bland and lacking in dramatic concept (Harmonia Mundi). **Boulez's** recording with Fischer-Dieskau is fine in all respects, with the conductor entering fully into the dramatic elements of the score. This isn't exactly what we have come to expect from him, so in many ways it's a unique document of a path too little taken. If you can find it, don't hesitate (♦Memories 4489).

In 1973 Fischer-Dieskau sang in a memorable reading led by **Britten** that had one of the best casts ever (Harwood, Shirley-Quirk, Pears, Vyvyan, Palmer). He was no stranger to the dramatic and choral necessities of this work, and the performance is a marvel of controlled mania. To my knowledge it has always been an import, but if you check around you may come across it. Do so; it will more than repay your efforts (♦Decca 452673). But for those who are looking for the best currently available version, the wait is short. **Abbado** and his Berliners give a riveting, superbly sung concert performance that's nearly the equal of Britten's. The cast is almost ideal, again almost a list of all-stars (Terfel, Mattila, Rootering, Bonney, Blochwitz, Graham). This may be the finest effort of Abbado's Berlin sojourn, and we're fortunate that it occurred for a piece that desperately needed a great, great recording (♦Sony 66308).

Der Rose Pilgerfahrt
(The Pilgrimage of the Rose). The idea of a supernatural character taking human form to fulfill some sort of quest or destiny was a recurrent theme in the Romantic era. In Schumann's work, a series of extraordinarily insipid lieder loosely held together, you have to

doubt that a composer of such genius could find any sort of creative inspiration from such trite material. But Schumann often surprises us, especially in his noble failures like this. As in all his works, there are moments of great glory and beauty; in this case, the beauty is better served by the composer's later orchestral version.

Creed gives us the original, and adds insult to injury by accompanying it with a period piano, as ill-conceived an idea as I can think of. Oelze leads a cast of very raw but excellent talent, and they make the best of Schumann's first thoughts, but unless you crave the original, I'd stick with the later version (Harmonia Mundi). **Frühbeck de Burgos,** with soloists that include Donath and Sotin, remains the best choice; his great sound, conducting, and singing win the day (♦EMI 69446). This recording is bound to show up again, so keep alert for it. **Gustave Kuhn** and his Danish Radio performers can't muster comparably excellent forces, but his version may be easier to obtain. It's not bad, with very good singing and very nice sound. Do grab it if you're interested in this Rose who becomes human to experience the wonders of motherhood (♦Chandos 9350).

Other choral music. Rarely heard in our time, *The Minstrel's Curse,* a 40-minute cantata, is available in a superb recording with **Schønwandt** and the Danish National Radio Orchestra. The sound is stunning, and the near-perfect performance will make true believers out of many; a very good "Rhenish" Symphony adds to a well-filled disc (♦Chandos 9760). **Peter Neumann** and the Cologne Chamber Choir offer an illuminating rendition of Mass in C minor, a little-known work that gets a remarkable performance. This isn't the sort of piece Schumann was known for, and that only adds to its interest; three pieces by Brahms round out an attractive program (♦MD+G 3320598). *Nachtlied* for chorus and orchestra is given an excellent performance by **Gardiner** in the album with his questionable *Peri;* proceed with caution and a lot of money (♦Archiv 457660, 2CD).

Isaac Karabtchevsky offers the only recording of the rarely played *Requiem* Op. 148, unfortunately coupled with Liszt's *Via Crucis;* this is an expensive disc, and I'd avoid it because of the Liszt (Mondo Musica). **Miklós Forrai** and the Hungarian State Orchestra take us on a *Requiem* field day, with Op. 148 and the more famous *Requiem for Mignon,* a superb work that deserves every drop of attention it can get (♦Hungaroton 11809). Schumann treated the Requiem form with a real sense of comfort and consolation, not unlike Brahms, bittersweet and nostalgic. And while you're looking, maybe you'll spot the early '90s **Sawallisch** with the Bavarian Radio Symphony—a nice recording, too soon retired (Eurodisc).

Requiem for Mignon is one of Schumann's noblest creations. Using four boys and two invisible choirs, they gradually emerge from sadness and mourning to the hope of new life and the continuation of the human spirit. Some of the music is very poignant, and it's well worth hearing. **Gardiner** couples it with his *Peri* and *Nachtlied* in a moving performance (♦Archiv 457660, 2CD). But it's **Abbado** who really steals the show with a warm, loving, particularly touching version that heals the soul and comforts the afflicted (♦DG 435486). The accompanying *Tantum Ergo, Psalm 23,* and Schubert's Mass in G are hardly less wonderful, and the young Chamber Orchestra of Europe gives them their considerable all.

Horst Neumann and the Leipzig Radio Chorus and Orchestra take us on a delightful tour of some of Schumann's songs and *Romance and Ballades* for chorus. This 1978 recording is an hour of delicious writing that spans an emotional range almost as variable as the composer's own mental state. The performances are quite vanilla, but in this case vanilla is a favorite flavor, with several pieces never recorded before. Bravo to these folks with the courage to record neglected Schumann (♦Berlin 9191)! The double chorus songs are featured in a fine disc with Draeseke's Mass in A minor. Though Schumann wasn't the skilled choral writer that Brahms was (who could compete with him?), these works are skillfully written in homophonic style. The Netherlands Chamber Choir under **Gronostay** gives superb realizations of these rarely heard pieces (♦Globe 5147).   RITTER

OPERA

Genoveva. Schumann made many attempts to write an operatic masterpiece; he considered and discarded subjects ranging from the *Odyssey* to the writings of E.T.A. Hoffmann. He finally settled on the medieval legend of St. Genevieve of Brabant, who was considered a model of marital fidelity. He asked for librettos from two poets, found neither satisfactory, and decided to write his own, based on one of the drafts. But the result was undramatic; the persons in the play weren't well characterized. This has prevented the work from being successful; staged performances have been rare (though Liszt produced it in Weimar), but there have been several recordings. No wonder, since much of the music is from the composer's top drawer; it's melodious, romantic, and quite beautiful.

The best of the three available sets was conducted by **Masur** in 1977 (♦Berlin 2056). It has the strongest cast (**Mathis, Schreier, Fischer-Dieskau**), the best orchestra (Leipzig Gewandhaus) and chorus, and Masur delivers the most cogent and lively performance. A recent release by **Harnoncourt** is inferior in all these respects (Teldec). A concert recording by **Albrecht,** while better than Harnoncourt's, is also not as good as the Berlin release; its cast is not satisfactory (Orfeo).

MOSES

SONGS

"Schumann's songs" essentially means "Schumann's song cycles," even if there are many favorites that are independent of any larger collection. The cycles, *Frauenliebe und -leben* excepted, have no underlying narrative or readily characterizable protagonist. Their unity is a matter of style and atmosphere, more like the *Italienisches Liederbuch* of Wolf than the two great cycles of Schubert or Brahms's *Schöne Magelone.* The number of recordings is staggering. Every lieder singer who ever drew breath, from the tyros to the grand masters, has recorded one or more of them; a manageable discussion must be selective, limited only to the most interesting (or appalling) interpreters. Curiously, the alphabetical list of the cycles corresponds fairly closely to their relative popularity: *Dichterliebe; Eichendorff-Liederkreis; Frauenliebe und -leben; Heine-Liederkreis;* and the less coherent *Kerner-Lieder.* The mixed bag known as *Myrthen,* the miniature cycles, the wonderful and neglected songs from the Spanish, and an assortment of favorites and rarities will be discussed separately.

Since many recordings omit texts, see the suggestions at the start of my article on Schubert's songs. *The Ring of Words* and *The Fischer-Dieskau Book of Lieder* are most helpful, and in this case Eric Sams's *Songs of Robert Schumann* should be added; it's out of print but findable.

Dichterliebe. The poet (Heine) speaks from an unmistakably male point of view, but that hasn't dissuaded some of the more irrepressible ladies, among them **Lehmann** (Vocal Archives), **Fassbaender** (EMI), and **Stutzmann** (RCA). Of these, Lehmann is the most endearing, despite some wayward intonation. She's direct and communicative, almost disconcertingly confessional, but even she fails to make a persuasive case for a female voice, and neither does the more masculine Fassbaender or the careful Stutzmann.

Dichterliebe has been claimed primarily by baritones, and the first great recording was **Panzéra**'s in 1934 (♦Biddulph 5; Pearl 9919). The singing is light and springy, the words forward and shapely, but the Gallic sophistication of both Panzéra and his distinguished accompanist, Cortot, keeps the romantic sentiments of the music at a slight distance. A less dexterous Cortot would be the pianist for **Souzay**'s third recording of *Dichterliebe* (1956; Cetra); Bonneau accompanied him in the first two (Decca), Baldwin in the last (Philips). His voice was at its freshest in the early '50s with Bonneau, and he's more inward than Panzéra though less solid vocally. Another French pair, **Bernac** and Casadesus, are not at all reticent in their interpretations; some listeners may find Bernac insightful and stimulating, others repellent and bizarre (CBS).

Indeed, just thinking about Bernac makes me all the more eager to recall the 1936 *Dichterliebe* of **Hüsch:** uneccentric, direct, and warmhearted, if rather monochromatic and uninflected (Preiser). *Uninflected* could never be the word for **Fischer-Dieskau,** whose first, mono recording (DG) was quickly superseded by one of the best of the stereo versions in 1965, Demus accompanying (♦DG 463505). It's a performance that misses nothing, securely and handsomely sung with an arresting variety of tonal colors and verbal nuances. His 1979 account with Eschenbach finds his voice slightly worn but his interpretive assets intact (♦DG 415190). Two other Fischer-Dieskau recordings, with Horowitz in 1976 and Brendel in 1985, are interesting but unnecessary.

Those who want to hear a less assertive German baritone might turn to **Prey,** who tackled the cycle in 1965 with Engel (EMI) and then twice again with Hokanson (Philips; Denon). The central performance, from the '70s, is the best balanced, the manner candid, the voice at its mellowest. **Bär** is similarly genial, his singing not as secure as Prey's, his accents pushier (EMI). **Holzmair** is altogether winning (♦Philips 446086). His voice is just a little fragile, but he bravely takes the high interpolations and lacks nothing in sensitivity and imagination. He's the most youthful-sounding of the baritones, urgent and disarmingly personal. **Goerne** has a really deluxe voice at his command, and he's working with an uncommonly powerful accompanist in Ashkenazy (London). He's a pleasure to hear, but a mite too slick, willing to sacrifice pure vowel sounds for the sake of timbral beauty.

Wächter took an entirely different approach, one that will remind collectors of his high-strung Don Giovanni and *Figaro* Count (London). This is the most splenetic of *Dichterliebe*s — the ravings, perhaps, of a man who loved not wisely but too well. Gone is Heine's special brand of irony, which waits until the end of a poem to twist the knife. Wächter, seething from the outset, has no place to go. It's a provocative, brilliantly sung reading (the top notes would do credit to a Heldentenor), but an exhausting one. **Van Dam,** in the second of his two recordings, is also on the angry side, and sings with ample gravity and a dizzying variety of nuances (1989; Forlane). **Hynninen** is another brooder, though a more restrained one, with a potent top A (Ondine).

It's a relief to turn to the even-tempered **Thomas Allen,** ardent and flowing, his voice deployed with a bel canto smoothness that's almost distracting — and an astonishing attribute for a British baritone (Virgin). He really curls his tongue lovingly around the notes, and the words too, though it takes a while to notice. **Hampson,** in his first recording, makes the most elementary of mistakes: he over-italicizes the words and forgets to sing (1993; EMI). Surprisingly, he ducks the high options, even though he has an easy, tenory top. His second (1994) traversal is better and also instructive (♦EMI 55598). Hampson, a scholar as well as a singer, goes back to Schumann's original version of *Dichterliebe* and allows us to hear four songs later ejected from the cycle and also some variant readings of the ones that remain. Most listeners will continue to prefer the revision, but it's interesting to hear what Schumann first had in mind, not least in the piano accompaniments, marvelously rendered by Sawallisch.

Hagegård and **Quasthoff** are perfectly respectable but not all that distinctive (both RCA). **Hotter,** on the other hand, is in a class of his own (◆Preiser 93145). His *Dichterliebe* is at once the weightiest and gentlest of all. The voice is deeper and grander than his competitors', and he seldom has to raise it for effect. He hugs the words tenderly, needing only a flick of the tongue to convey a world of meaning; his intimate, consoling warmth goes straight to the heart.

The tenors, on the whole, don't match the tonal beauty of the best baritones. The much-revered **Schiøtz** is white and reedy, and he takes the low options, but his verbal clarity and understated eloquence are hypnotic (1946; Danacord; Pearl). **Schreier** made at least four recordings, and he's perhaps at his best in his 1988 account with Eschenbach, having toned down much of the punchiness and sputtering that marred his earlier readings (Teldec). His tone is still spindly, and he sounds peevish when he expresses strong emotion. He's not without sensitivity, merely without an attractive voice. **Pears** probably deserves to be put in the same category, but even as he seems to totter on every note, he patiently casts a spell that draws you in (◆London 443933). He's idiosyncratic but mesmerizing, the poet's sentiments deeply felt and vividly projected. His low notes are unusually solid for a tenor.

Jerusalem does a fairly good job keeping his big voice under control (Erato). His diction is better than Schreier's or Pears's and his timbre more virile and handsome, but he's a little too cautious. **Blochwitz** is fresh and likable, his voice on the pale side but the words clean and lucid, even more so than Jerusalem's (EMI). He's a candid, vulnerable interpreter who takes no chances. With experience, he may become a little less buttoned up. **Dermota,** caught past his prime in 1975, is thin and whiny much of the time, though his top A is still potent (Preiser).

Haefliger's 1963 *Dichterliebe* (the DG account with Werba, not the depressing later one from Japan on Camerata) has long been out of print, but it's always been a favorite of mine. It's unusually pensive and inward, and the tempos are slow, but there's no lack of intensity, and the stalwart voice easily encompasses the notes from top to bottom, at every dynamic level. **Bostridge**'s willowy timbre is less formidable, but like Pears, he's something of a sorcerer, cannily gauging his inflections and dynamic gradations to make his voice sound larger and more colorful than it is (◆EMI 56575). For all the apparent calculation, he's a singer first, an interpreter second, and he's a winning performer because he doesn't neglect the musical line in favor of the words. He does justice to Schumann's melodies, keeping the tone sweet and liquid, but it's a near thing.

Not so with **Wunderlich,** who, aside from one or two weak low notes, offers the most gorgeously sung *Dichterliebe* on records (1965; ◆DG 429933). If you need to be bludgeoned with "insightful" nuances, look elsewhere. Wunderlich makes singing seem as natural as speaking. He's unaffected and spontaneous, never straining for effect, yet his emotional involvement in the songs is always evident. The very seductiveness of his voice must have won as many converts to *Dichterliebe* over the years as the more overt gestures of Fischer-Dieskau. The "live" 1965 and 1966 performances on Acanta, Myto, and Orfeo are no less appealing and perhaps marginally smoother.

It's impossible to name the "best" *Dichterliebe*. I'd take to my desert island—at the very least—Fischer-Dieskau, Hotter, Pears, and Wunderlich, but I'd keep several others on hand for friends who happened to

drop by. On the other hand, it's easy to name the worst recording: **Esswood** (Hungaroton). He screeches and flounces his way through the songs in a precarious falsetto that sounds ridiculous in such robust, Romantic music. **Kowalski,** another countertenor, ranks a notch higher only because he sings German more idiomatically (Capriccio).

Eichendorff-Liederkreis. The songs of the Eichendorff cycle are Schumann's most atmospheric, filled with evocations of nature that enhance the emotional states of the reciter. They're less gender-specific than *Dichterliebe,* so it's not surprising to find many female recordings. What one wants above all is a voice beautiful enough to do justice to the picturesque images of the poems (moonlight, snow, rippling brooks, rustling trees), and no soprano has brought a more beautiful voice to the music than the young **Jurinac,** in the aptly named Voce della Luna reissue (◆2005). The words are a little too vague, perhaps, and the meter too rigid—she needs more conversational rubato—but the singing ravishes the ear. Ravishing also, with a stiffer spine, is **Margaret Price,** splendidly clean in line, clear in diction, and wide in dynamic range (◆Helios 55011). **Baker** is a little more personable and outgoing, though blander in timbre (EMI).

The never-bland **Fassbaender** is slightly raw in tone but always absorbing (Teldec). **Evelyn Lear,** sincere and approachable, has the right sort of glow in the middle but glares on top (Chandos). **Schwarzkopf**'s recordings (this and *Frauenliebe*) are not among her best and needn't delay us; the younger Schwarzkopf might have been wonderful. **Crespin** isn't always comfortable, finding it difficult to rein in her big voice, but her forthright declamation and exquisite soft singing are transfixing (EMI). One out-of-print performance divides the songs between a mezzo and a baritone: **Ludwig** and **Berry,** near their vocal peak, offer long-breathed, crisply enunciated, appealingly artless readings (DG). Some of Ludwig's contributions are in DG's 2CD 70th birthday tribute; the whole recording should be reissued.

There aren't many tenor recordings. **Schreier** is serviceable but skeletal (Teldec; Eurodisc); **Pears** and Perahia don't quite replicate the necromancy of Pears and Britten (CBS); **Jerusalem** is more substantial but also clumsier (Erato). All three are worth hearing, but not beautiful enough; Schumann's melodies deserve better. **Blochwitz** comes closer to the mark, dreamy, plaintive, pleasing in timbre and firm of line (◆EMI 54042). Among the baritones are **Prey** (EMI; Philips; Denon), the forthright **Quasthoff** (RCA), the urbane **Souzay** (Philips), and the palpitatingly earnest **Bär.** Each is persuasive in his own way, and Prey's longevity remains a marvel. (Souzay was less fortunate.) I favor Bär, whose penchant for time-stopping reverie is particularly apt here. His voice doesn't really have a solid core, so the forte outbursts tax him, but he entices us gracefully into Schumann's world (◆EMI 47397).

The promising **Goerne** is a disappointment (London). He has the vocal velvet, but his interpretation misfires, apparently a casualty of the trendy modern belief that the painfully slow and the inaudibly soft betoken profundity. He's nonetheless a model of restraint next to **Terfel,** who shouts and whispers and generally refuses to let the music speak for itself (DG). If you want someone to speak—or roar—for it, be assured that this irrepressible emoter is in ringing voice.

Fischer-Dieskau is better. His first stereo recording with Moore is nearly perfect and deserves reissue (EMI; 1965). Some of the vocal resonance and roundness was gone by 1977, when he recorded the cycle with Eschenbach, but his interpretive powers didn't diminish in the least (◆DG 415190). He has in his tonal palette all the colors needed for Schumann's word paintings, and he understands exactly how to mold the melodic lines. The understanding was still there in 1985 when he recorded *Liederkreis* again with Brendel, but he was 60 years old and too much of the sap had gone from his voice (Philips).

Frauenliebe und -leben. This is the most personal and potentially cloying of the cycles. Its apparent anti-feminist sentiments haven't repelled interpreters, who see the poems not as statements of submission but affirmations of love, and the number of good recordings is legion.

We'll take a geographical approach this time, starting in North America and taking note of the luminescent, extrovert **Leontyne Price** (RCA), the intent and lucid **Evelyn Lear** (Chandos), and the enthralling, softly glowing **Augér,** who seems to be dreamily recalling events from the past rather than experiencing them in the present (♦Berlin 002186). **Norman** is more complex, more assiduously searching, but she's on the heavy side vocally and very harsh in diction (Philips). **Stich-Randall**'s account is extraordinarily poised and accurate, the turns effortless, the long phrases taken in single breaths, the deportment dry-eyed but sympathetic; it should be reissued (Westminster). More overtly dramatic is **de Gaetani,** her voice steady and plaintive, the emotions intensely felt (♦Bridge 9025).

The Canadian mezzo **Catherine Robbin** is softer but no less affecting (♦CBC 1050). Her singing is supple and unforced, and her youth and innocence make the tragedy all the more poignant. A special place must be reserved for **Marian Anderson,** who recorded *Frauenliebe* in 1950 (♦RCA 63575, with 13 Schubert songs, a hair-raising *Erlkönig* among them). Her voice is lighter than you might expect, even a bit fluttery, but the contralto depth still underpins the tone. She was a well-schooled lieder singer who never lost her natural candor, and she's touching, dignified, and utterly unaffected, completely immersed in her bittersweet narratives.

Many recordings have come from the British Isles, and we pause first to renew acquaintance with one of the most vocally generous and emotionally openhearted accounts, **Ferrier**'s in 1950 (♦London 433471). Her rich, feminine contralto is a joy to hear. **Watts,** another contralto, keeps a stiffer upper lip but sings tidily and warmly in well-turned phrases (Oiseau-Lyre). **Lott** makes a pleasing but not indelible impression (IMP), and the usually reliable **Margaret Price** in both of her recordings is too regally aloof and serious (Classics for Pleasure and Forlane). **Baker** also made two recordings. The second (EMI; 1976) has the better sound and pianist (Barenboim); the first (1966) is vocally fresher and freer (♦Saga 3361). As an interpreter, she's dead-on. The pride in her voice as she declares "Ich will ihm dienen, ihm leben" leaves no doubt that she's describing love, not servility.

Moving onto the continent, we'll circle the German-speaking countries for a while, stopping in Spain to savor the fluency of **Berganza** (Claves); the Netherlands to enjoy the sparkling, plain-spoken **Ameling** (Philips); and Norway to listen in awe to the magnificent **Flagstad,** riveting for all the crushing weight of her voice (RCA). More suitable in scale, perhaps, is the Swedish mezzo **von Otter,** a cool, meticulous performer with a quickly forgettable voice (DG). She holds your attention but has no staying power. **Popp**'s pungent timbre lingers in the memory, but not many details of her slightly finicky performance (Eurodisc). **Jurinac** is meltingly lovely, but her *Frauenliebe* has the same liabilities as her *Liederkreis* (Voce della Luna). It's too rigid and superficial. The hard-working **Stutzmann,** French despite her German surname, is prosaic, though her dark contralto is gratifying to hear (RCA).

The native German speakers offer a great variety of approaches. I'm not won over by the sometimes sloppy **Lehmann** (CBS)—I keep wishing she would back off a little—or the fragile, breathy, wilting **Schumann,** who was having a bad day (EMI). **Ludwig** is on the heavy, mundane side, despite her careful words and sumptuous vocalism (EMI). **Fassbaender** is far more interesting (♦DG 415519). She cuts right through the treacle, like Baker before her, and she's both thoughtful and passionate, though more private than Lehmann. She's also very proficient, the tricky turns and wide intervals taken in stride, and her fondness for portamento lends the songs a most becoming shape. Special notice is due **Jovita Dermota,** known in Germany more as an actress than a singer (Preiser). She's among the most inward of interpreters, yet she has a remarkably ability to project her inwardness vividly and naturally. Her mother, Hilda, accompanies her; the performance does credit to the famous family name. **Della Casa**'s timbre is as lovely as Jurinac's, and she articulates the words more incisively. The voice has more color in it and more dynamic play, and the cool, glittering diction enhances her ability to express exaltation or suffering. Her 1963 Electrola recording should be reissued by EMI; meanwhile her old LP is worth hunting down (♦Turnabout 34125).

Seefried is the most lovable and personable of *Frauenliebe* interpreters, and she left three recordings. The 1965 stereo account with Klien has never been on CD, but it's the weakest (Pearl). The 1957 with Werba is my favorite of all *Frauenliebe*s (♦DG 437348). She's among the most natural and conversational of singers, but also has an attractive, sophisticated air. No one projects the rapture of the first two songs better than she (though she stumbles on the turns), the humor of "Helft mir, ihr Schwestern" (impossible to miss the smile in the voice), the desolation of "Nun hast du mir." Her voice in 1957 still had plenty of bloom and radiance. A 1960 Salzburg concert performance is preserved, and she's almost as good here, darker and less malleable of tone but perhaps even more animated in front of an audience (Orfeo). Since the DG has gone out of print, it may have to do.

We have, finally, a performance by the irreplaceable **Elisabeth Grümmer** (♦Orfeo 506001). She begins tentatively, but by the third song, she's worked herself into an ardor that would befit Sieglinde's "Du bist der Lenz." She's the most sincere and humane of interpreters, euphorically wrapped up in the drama until the bitter denouement. The words are pellucid, the voice tender and radiantly lovely. The recording was made by Berlin radio in 1966; it was worth waiting more than 30 years for its release.

Heine-Liederkreis (Op. 24). This is generally regarded as inferior to the Eichendorff cycle, but I can't imagine why. These songs, with their surprising turns of melody, are among Schumann's most rapturous and improvisatory. Their compositional style is tailor-made for **Fischer-Dieskau,** who often reminds me of a cinematographer suddenly zooming in on a telling detail. His 1965 recording with Demus may have been the best ever (♦DG 463506). I could also live quite happily with **Holzmair,** who projects much the same sense of spontaneous discovery (♦Philips 446086).

Bär is also fine, though I miss a firm, freely produced voice, especially in "Schöne Wiege" (EMI). **Skovhus** is on the flinty side, vigorous but with little apparent love for the German words (Sony). **Hampson** is healthier and more sensitive, and sings with plenty of youthful ardor, though he should curb his tendency to distort vowels, presumably for the sake of heightened expression (EMI). It sounds both unnatural and pretentious. **Allen** is polished and uneccentric (Virgin), but **Goerne** in 1997 is the plushest of all, jaw-droppingly beautiful at "Berg und Burge," as romantically impetuous and sensuously lovely as anyone could desire in the great "Schöne Wiegen" (♦London 458265).

Bär chooses the *Kerner-Lieder* as his coupling, but the other baritones mentioned so far opt, appropriately, for *Dichterliebe*. So does tenor **Bostridge,** but his *Liederkreis* isn't on the same level, probably because his vocal flimsiness doesn't allow him to do justice to the more rhapsodic effusions (EMI). For all his attention to detail, he sounds both fussy and undernourished. The seasoned **Schreier** is more satisfactory, but once again, the drabness of his voice militates against him (Teldec). **Fassbaender**'s predilection for appropriating male songs may strain her audiences' indulgence, but she out-sings both Schreier and Bostridge (◆DG 415519). There's nothing delicate or calculating about her readings; she just dives right into the melodies, as attuned to Schumann's lyricism as Fischer-Dieskau and Holzmair.

Kerner-Lieder. Seldom encountered as a group 40 years ago, the *Kerner-Lieder* have become more popular as the voracious appetites of our young singers have grown. The poems themselves appear innocuously placid on the surface, but Schumann focuses on their dark, bitter undercurrents. The pioneers, **Prey** (EMI) and **Fischer-Dieskau** (Orfeo), are still honorable, but the newer interpreters also have much to offer. **Van Dam** is sardonic and violently explosive, but the songs can take it, especially since his voice is up to the demands he makes on it (◆Forlane 16595). **Hampson** is more subdued, but he's alert to every dramatic twist, and his voice is at its most silken (◆Teldec 44935). **Margaret Price** is comparatively introspective, but there's no doubt that the songs engage her deeply, and her glistening timbre is entrancing.

Myrthen. A loose collection of 26 songs, this was Robert's wedding present to Clara. The songs are seldom performed together, but many of them are among Schumann's most beloved, and often find their way onto recital programs: "Widmung," "Der Nussbaum," "Du bist wie eine Blume." Three readily available integral sets are all good. The relatively unknown **Nellie van der Sijde** and **Maarten Koningsberger** are young, unaffected, and tonally pleasing (◆Globe 5025). **Bär** and **Juliane Banse** are more cultivated and less to my liking (EMI). **Dawson** and **Partridge** might seem an unpropitious pairing, and, indeed, I've avoided mentioning any of Partridge's Schumann recordings until now. In fact, they turn out to be quite appealing, especially Dawson, whose pure, silvery voice is deftly and expressively used. Partridge has a heady, mushy timbre without much tenor ping, but it falls easily enough on the ear, and he's animated and sensitive (◆Chandos 9307).

Spanische Liebeslieder; Quartets; Duets. The *Spanish Love Songs* are the best of the works Schumann wrote for vocal quartet, and they're so delightful that I can't understand why we don't hear them more often. The texts are by Geibel (many were also set by Wolf in his *Spanisches Liederbuch*). The songs are brief, and the solo parts are grateful. **Shirai, Lipovšek, Protschka,** and **Hölle** are fine, in a recording that includes the only slightly less inspired *Spanisches Liederspiel* (Capriccio). **Bonney, von Otter, Streit,** and **Bär** sing with more zest as well as more finesse in a 1994 disc (◆EMI 55430, with Brahms's *Liebeslieder Waltzes*). More desirable are two older recordings that both merit reissue. **Marshall, Sarfaty, Simoneau,** and **Warfield** are incomparably vivacious in a Columbia LP. In particular, no one has matched Simoneau's wry humor in his two songs. **Moser, Schwarz, Gedda,** and **Berry** were rather more serious but still personable, in an invaluable set that included the *Liederspiel* and the two big Rückert quartets, *Liebesfrühling* and *Minnespiel* (EMI, 2CD).

Schumann's duets don't rank with the best of his solo lieder, but two good recordings invite exploratory visits: **de Gaetani** and **Leslie Guinn** (Nonesuch) and **Fischer-Dieskau, Schreier,** and **Varady** (DG). **Streich**

and **Forrester** are also charming in a brief collection (Etcetera), and if you want to hear what Siegmund and Sieglinde might sound like if they burst into Schumannesque song, seek out **Lehmann** and **Melchior** (RCA).

Miscellaneous songs. Overdue for reissue is EMI's splendid "Schumann and Brahms Lieder on Record," once available as an 8LP set. The anthology included recordings made between 1901 and 1952 by a tantalizing array of great singers, from Lilli Lehmann to de los Angeles. Even the oddities—Chaliapin singing "Die beiden Grenadiere" in Russian, Giuseppe Borgatti's "Du bist wie eine Blume" in Italian, Alice Raveau's "In der Fremde" in French—are priceless, and many of the German-language performances are among the century's greatest.

Just as impressive in their own way are the Schumann recordings **Fischer-Dieskau** made in the '60s with Demus (DG), and some of them have been reissued with the *Heine-Liederkreis* (◆DG 463506). I'm happy with the partial restoration, but I still hope for the return, in toto, of the three discs titled "Lieder aus dem Spanischen und aus Myrthen," "Liebesbotschaft: Songs from the Year 1840," and "Songs on Heine Poems." The baritone did it all over again and more in the '70s with Eschenbach, and DG issued the recordings in a couple of deluxe boxes. Now, only the already recommended *Dichterliebe* and *Eichendorff-Liederkreis* survive. I can't think of a better foundation for a Schumann library than these EMI and DG sets; they should be restored.

Schreier is almost as ambitious as Fischer-Dieskau. His Schumann recordings from the early 70s with Norman Shetler are on four discs (Berlin); another 3CD set with Eschenbach was released in the late '80s (Teldec). In the more recent performances, his voice may be drier, but the singing is more refined, less punchy, even veering once or twice toward the beautiful. The earlier collection differs in particulars (the entire set of Kerner songs is here, for example) and has one great advantage over the later: The discs are available separately. Vols. 2 and 3 bypass the cycles and are particularly valuable. **Prey**'s recordings from the '70s have been reissued and are available in the "Hermann Prey Lied Edition," but you can't buy just the Schumann (Philips). The later Denons are more convenient, and his voice, even though it's lost a little resonance and smoothness, is still in good shape.

Many of the song-cycle recordings discussed earlier include additional material. The grotesque, unsettling *Andersen-Lieder* are vividly rendered by **Hampson** (Teldec) and **von Otter** (DG) in recordings already mentioned. **Seefried** (Orfeo) and **Robbin** (CBC) address the austere *Gedichte der Königin Maria Stuart* with sympathy and conviction. So does **Margaret Price** in the second of two Schumann recitals from the mid-'90s (◆Forlane 16761). Both discs are compendia of songs early (the miraculous year 1840) and late, the many unfamiliar items leavened by popular chestnuts. The strange songs from Goethe's "Wilhelm Meister," for Mignon and Philine, are in Vol. 2, and **Augér** tackles them in her *Frauenliebe* disc as well (Berlin). **Fassbaender** (DG) and **Bostridge** (EMI) append some Heine songs to their recordings of the *Liederkreis.*

An excellent mixed recital from **Bär** has "Belsatzar," "Die beiden Grenadiere," the miniature "Arme Peter" threesome, *Andersen-Lieder,* some Geibel settings, and a grab bag of other songs (◆EMI 56199). **Terfel**'s *Eichendorff-Liederkreis* album is generously filled out with 23 additional songs. The extroversion that makes something smashing out of "Die beiden Grenadiere" is less appropriate for the gentler romantic numbers (DG). One of **Ameling**'s earliest (1967) recordings offers 19 short songs, mostly of the "cute," folksy sort, sung with ingenuous charm (♦Harmonia Mundi 77085). A difficult-to-find curiosity is the 1957 collaboration between **Seefried** and the actor Oskar Werner, where she sang some of the Heine songs and he recited other Heine poems. The soprano was at her limpid best, and the original DG recording has been reissued (♦Amadeo 429454). The second half of the disc is given over to Wolf and Mörike, who get the same treatment.

Two complete editions of Schumann's songs are in the works. The less interesting is **Stutzmann**'s (RCA). Her industry is admirable and her dark contralto is rare enough in itself, but she doesn't have the imagination or timbral beauty to generate any real enthusiasm. The Hyperion project is wisely using more than one singer. Vol. 1 includes many of the less approachable songs from Schumann's later years, and **Schäfer** performs them with wonderfully lucid diction but a slightly frosty air; she doesn't improve on either Augér or Margaret Price in the same material. **Keenlyside** includes the *Kerner-Lieder* in Vol. 2 and suffers from the same problem. His stolid reading isn't competitive with the best we've already had.

The centerpiece of Vol. 3 is *Frauenliebe und -leben,* sung conscientiously and sincerely by **Banse** but without any real individuality or tonal radiance. Perhaps she's dominated by the Svengali-like Graham Johnson, who seems to regard vivacity as unseemly in this cycle. Banse also tackles the Mary Stuart songs, and while her voice is always pleasing, she's not illuminating in any way. More interesting are the seldom-heard "Lieder of Elisabeth Kulmann" with their spoken introductions. Hyperion is most useful when offering us music not found elsewhere. Johnson's notes, as usual, are characteristically stimulating, and even if his Schumann series doesn't bring us the joyous discoveries of the Schubert, it will probably prove enticing all the same.   LUCANO

Heinrich Schütz *(1585–1672)*

Probably the most important European composer of the generation following Monteverdi, Schütz was the most significant figure in the transition in German music from late Renaissance to early Baroque. A pupil of Gabrieli, he brought from his studies in Italy a zeal for the new "concerted" style of voices with instruments, balanced by a respect for the older idiom of the Franco-Flemish and Italian polyphonic masters.

Historical circumstances brought out qualities of both musical and human character that reverberate powerfully down to our own time. It was Schütz's tragedy that his career coincided in part with the terrible Thirty Years War that saw Germany ravaged by the conflict between opposing forces at least nominally identified as Protestant and Roman Catholic. As a Protestant himself, and as a composer serving a Lutheran court, Schütz was obliged to adjust his stylistic development to the exigencies of wartime. But he also chose to bridge the confessional gap by writing a great deal of his preponderantly sacred music as serviceable for both Protestant and Catholic purposes, hoping for reconciliation through shared Christian expression. As a result, his music covers a spectrum of scope and styles, invariably put to the highest artistic purposes.

A deeply devout Christian, Schütz wrote music of consistent earnestness and sobriety; it doesn't reflect a sense of humor, though he could often demonstrate a strong flair for the dramatic. But his music is always charged with warm humanity and an exaltation of religious spirit in its most earnest and affirmative sense. There have been three systematic modern editions of the composer's works, and a byproduct of the middle one was a 1960 catalog embodying the *Schütz-Werke-Verzeichnis* ("SWV") system of numbering, used below.

SECULAR MUSIC

Like Monteverdi (and unlike his master, Gabrieli), Schütz was a composer for voices, writing almost no instrumental music as such, apart from the incorporation of instrumental parts in his vocal pieces. Unlike Monteverdi, Schütz wrote very little secular music, devoting almost all of his long career to sacred composition. It must be recognized, however, that our picture of his artistic character is seriously skewed by the loss of parts of his output, notably his theatrical works, including at least one opera, *Dafne.* Nevertheless, it does seem that, after the death of his beloved wife in 1625, Schütz not only never remarried but apparently decided to concentrate on sacred music as well.

The most important surviving exception to his sacred commitment had already served as a kind of postgraduate dissertation, at least in secular writing, marking the completion of his studies with Gabrieli. This was his collection of 19 Italian madrigals (all for five voices, save the last, for eight), which he published in 1611 in Venice while still studying there. It showed his full mastery of the classic and "Mannerist" styles of this Italian idiom, as represented by Luca Marenzio, Monteverdi, and even Gesualdo. This was not only his *Opus primus* (SWV 1–19) but was clearly designated as *Libro primo* of madrigals, presuming his intention to follow with more music in this vein — a presumption never fulfilled.

Given its length, early LP ventures into this relatively neglected side of the composer's output weren't always complete and were sometimes choral and rarely satisfactory. One of the better examples is a recording by eight Leipzig singers (Capella Lipsiensis) under **Dietrich Knothe** (1971: Berlin 2102). Knothe gave the full 19 pieces, without instruments, in reliable if only occasionally striking performances. Recognition of the need for chamber groups with one singer per part came in **Jacobs**'s 1984 recording with his Concerto Vocale, which contained the 18 five-voice madrigals but omitted the final eight-voice, double-choir *Dialogo* (♦Harmonia Mundi 1901162). That omission was remedied by **Rooley**'s Consort of Musicke (1985: ♦Deutsche Harmonia Mundi 77118). Jacobs offers an outstanding vocal blend and a sensitive balance of tempos and inflections, and there are some occasional doublings on the theorbo, but the lack of the final madrigal is a grave deficiency. Rooley's group performs without instruments in a lean and relatively light style; their ensemble singing is a bit more edgy and brittle but marked by undeniable insight and pungency.

Those two recordings seem to be out of print just now, and probably difficult to find, leaving two newer ones as the chief competitors, to each other as well as to Knothe. These are the 1998 recordings of all 19 madrigals by the **Orlando di Lasso Ensemble** (Thorophon 2387) and Cantus Cologne led by **Junghänel** (♦Harmonia Mundi). Both involve instrumental doublings. Junghänel himself plays lute reductions delicately behind his Cologne singers in every piece; by contrast, the Lasso Ensemble adds lute only in some pieces, but throws in harp and harpsichord for the eight-voice finale. Junghänel has nine singers, and they give him richly beautiful and superbly blended madrigal singing. The eight singers of the Lasso Ensemble display a bit less sheen and polish, but they recognize better how much of the Mannerist style Schütz absorbed in Italy: as a result, they dig into the verbal and emotional content more fully, with gripping results. Thus the choice is clearly between probing intensity (Lasso) and vocal suavity and sonority (Junghänel); Knothe remains a respectable but lesser option.

If Schütz never again composed secular music systematically, nor ever collected secular pieces for a coherent publication, we are not to conclude that he never produced *any* secular composition after the 1611 Madrigals. Indeed, we know he composed at least one opera, *Dafne,* staged in 1627 but now lost. There were often smaller efforts, however. In a useful program assembled by **Manfred Cordes** with his Weser-Renaissance Bremen group, the five singers and 12 instrumentalists offer a program of 15 selections setting mostly German texts, some occasional pieces (with topical references), some mythological or casual in subject matter, some (from *Song of Solomon*) quasi-sacred in tone (♦CPO 999518). The writing is generally quite serious and even complex (with some double-choir writing at times), not much different from what we would recognize as the composer's sacred style, but the material is rare and appealing, and it's delivered with spirit and fine period-instrument color.

This is perhaps the place for an elegiac reference to a unique Schütz anthology—the only one to survey all aspects and categories of the composer's output—Vol. III of a series of 3LP Vox Boxes marking the 300th anniversary of his death. This release contained selections not only from most of his published sacred collections but also of the only delvings into his metrical Psalms; not only examples of the Italian madrigals but also some of his "German madrigals" (sacred or otherwise) not included in his publications. Solo and choral singers were directed by **Gregg Smith** in lively performances. So very valuable for its still-rare inclusions, it would be lovely to have this set revived on CD.

SACRED MUSIC

The vast bulk of Schütz's music is sacred in character and format. Some of it takes the form of narrative or quasi-dramatic exposition (Christmas and Easter pieces, Passions, etc.) in the category we would call oratorio: these will be dealt with in the final section. Schütz collected large numbers of his sacred works, for both large and small combinations of performers, into systematic publications, some in Latin, some in German. There have been repeated recordings of all these publications as integral entities, and they can be addressed easily; so can cullings from individual publications. Programs that draw upon more than one of these publications will be treated in their turn under collections, while individual compositions will be treated as a separate category, and programs that draw upon both the composer's published collections and the diverse pieces will be dealt appropriately. For convenience, the following abbreviations will be used: PD: *Psalmen Davids*; CS: *Cantiones sacrae*; SS: *Sinfoniae sacrae*; ME: *Musikalische Exequien*; GCM: *Geistliche Chor-Musik*; KGK: *Kleine Geistliche Konzerte*; DM: *Deutsches Magnificat* SWV 494.

Published collections

Psalmen Davids (1619: SWV 22–47). If the Italian madrigals of 1611 represent what Schütz learned of secular vocal music in Italy, it was his first-hand experience with the expansive and colorful polychoral sacred music of his teacher Gabrieli that found expression in his second published collection, his first issued back home in Germany, and his first of sacred music. This is the "Psalms of David," published in 1619, his Op. 2. It contains 26 Psalm texts, all in German, some set as motets (voices and continuo) or as "concertos" (voices with instruments), but all involving two or more choirs, all allowing for a flexible involvement of instruments, and all reflecting in one way or another the splendor and power of Venetian polychoral writing.

There have been four recordings of the complete publication (all 2CD), plus a number of single-CD samplings. The key to evaluating these recordings is the recognition that Schütz allows us to use (or not use) instruments (in stipulated parts, or doubling, or replacing singers), so it's possible to present the same music in widely differing ways.

The earliest complete recording was a revelation of the color and variety of sound that could be achieved with an expansive exercise of options. This came in 1971/72 from the Regensburg Cathedral Choir and instrumental groups led by **Schneidt.** The boys' choral voices are pungent but not raucous, the instrumental contributions piquant, and the overall spirit lively and extroverted (♦MHS 524775). Essentially the same approach was taken by ten soloists, the Stuttgart Chamber Choir, and Roland Wilson's Musica Fiata Köln, directed by **Bernius** (1991: ♦Sony 48042), and by **Michel Laplénie,** leading the Sagittarius Vocal Ensemble and instrumental groups in concert performances (1996: Accord 205582). Both use forces, including instrumentation, roughly parallel to Schneidt's, though Laplénie's scoring is more limited in range. But both Bernius and Laplénie use solo-voice ensembles more frequently in place of full choirs, which lightens textures a good deal and produces a leaner effect. Bernius's performances are, on the whole, somewhat more polished than Laplénie's, and he provides outstanding satisfaction.

Even leaner and still more polished are the nine singers of Cantus Cologne and the 27 period-instrument players of Concerto Paladino led by **Junghänel** (1997: ♦Harmonia Mundi 901652/53). Junghänel is much freer in his substitution of solo for ensemble voices and of instruments for singers, often producing more minimal vocal textures and exploring more instrumental color, resulting in some renditions totally different in character from the others, generally on a smaller scale. The performances are elegant and refined, offering a more subtle approach to these wonderful works, perhaps better appreciated by the listener familiar with this music than by a newcomer.

Those who want more concise or less complete treatment of this collection can turn to several samplings. A selection of 13 items is offered by the mixed-voice Choir of Trinity College, Cambridge, led by **Richard Marlow** (♦Conifer 190). The singers retain a degree of British restraint, but their work is strong and stylish, joined by organists and the excellent period-wind ensemble, His Majesties Sagbutts and Cornets. The instrumental palette isn't very varied, and I miss any interaction of solo with ensemble voices; still, this is a very enjoyable program and a good introduction to the collection.

Two programs by the Windsbach Boys' Choir under **Karl-Friedrich Beringer** are built around selections from *PD*. The first disc contains six, plus the popular double-choir *DM*; the second contains four, plus settings of two other Psalm texts as well as an Easter motet and a memorial ode. Beringer occasionally uses solo voices from his choir, but there are only four continuo players, with no other instrumental participation. The performances are intelligent, and the recorded sound stands up well, but no texts or translations are provided (1983: ♦Bellaphon 020, 031).

Less satisfactory are several releases that carry these Psalms to extremes. **Jeremy Summerly** leads members of the Oxford Camerata in six, plus settings of two other Psalm texts, *DM,* and a memorial motet for Johann Hermann Schein framed by two of the latter's keyboard pieces (Naxos 553044). The use of only one singer per part, with organ continuo, shows that such minimalism is possible but not necessarily satisfying in this music, despite competent singing. At the other end of the spectrum are a pair of discs offering cullings from a batch of 1965 recordings by the Dresden Kreuzchor under **Mauersberger** (Berlin). The first contains 11 items from *PD,* while the second adds three more, plus three later motets and *DM;* all are delivered in squarish, insensitive, and lumpish performances, roughly sung by the choir, with some limited instrumental support—not at all recommended.

Cantiones Sacrae (1625: SWV 53–93). This collection of 40 Latin motets under the title "Sacred Songs" was published as Schütz's Op. 4. Issued as the Thirty Years War was under way, his recourse to Latin texts might suggest the Lutheran composer's first gesture toward reconciliation with Catholic sentiments, though the texts are all extra-liturgical. But—composed for four voices, and with an organ continuo added only at the publisher's request—these motets also represent the third and final testimonial to his learning experience in Italy, for they represent Schütz's response to what was becoming known in Italy as the *stile antico,* the extension of the old polyphonic idiom of the Renaissance. Not just exercises in archaizing but products of his rethinking of that past idiom in a highly charged synthesis all his own, these are as much "spiritual madrigals" in Latin as they are liturgical motets.

This set is comparatively neglected among the composer's major sacred collections and has had only one partial and three complete recordings. The first was one of the ambitious sets made in the '60s by **Mauersberger** with his Dresden Kreuzchor (Telefunken, 3LP; not yet reissued by Berlin, though it could be at any time). As with his other recordings, this one is burdened by the harsh quality of the boy's voices and by the rather heavy and monotonous approach Mauersberger takes to Schütz's choral writing. Its only value today is for reference purposes. The young **Rilling** made an attempt with his Gächinger Kantorei in the late '70s, but apparently it got no further than two initial LPs (Bärenreiter). Rilling eschewed the organ continuo and offered performances smoother and more interestingly inflected than Mauersberger's.

The second complete recording was made (in the '80s?) by the London Bach Society led by **Paul Steinitz** (♦Meridian 84337/38, 2CD). Filling out space are the complex polychoral Latin *Magnificat* (SWV 468), one item from *PD,* and a setting (of dubious attribution) of a passage from *Song of Solomon* (SWV A4). An esteemed early-music specialist and a longtime champion of Schütz's music, Steinitz leads intelligent and well-shaped performances, retaining the continuo in *CS* and using period instruments (violins, sackbuts, continuo players) in *DM.* The singing is highly capable, though I wish the relatively small choir had been recorded a little more closely. But this is certainly an honorable production, not to be overlooked.

The third complete recording came from **Cordes** (1996: ♦CPO 999405, 2CD). His approach shows the very wide latitude that the composer's music allows; rather than performed as choral works, they're done by one singer per part (including Mona Spägele, Popken, Covey-Crump, John Potter, and Kooy) and with the instrumental part (added by organ and chitarrone) only in four items where it becomes an independent basso continuo instead of just a basso seguente that doubles the lowest part. The singing is superb, and the intimate, closely focused scale presents this music in a very special light, though those who prefer the more conservative choral approach should stick with Steinitz.

If you prefer a choral approach, there are at least two samplings by small, mixed-voice groups, both recorded in 1991. Over half the publication (22 pieces) was recorded by the Currende Vocal Ensemble under **Erik Van Nevel** (♦Accent 9174). The small chorus (numbers unspecified) retains the continuo part (on a discreetly placed organ) but sings with warmth and expressiveness. The 22-voice Chorus of Emmanuel Music is led by **Craig Smith** in the first of a series of surveys of Schütz's motets, presenting 12 of these pieces plus four German works: an extended setting of Psalm 116 (SWV 51) and three items from the later *GCM* (Koch 7085). The continuo is dispensed with, and the singing is smooth and well-drilled but just a bit cool in spirit.

Symphoniae sacrae (1629: 257-276). Schütz's next publication, his Op. 5, repeated the title of *PD* but is totally separate from his 1619 collection; this one, commonly known as the "Becker Psalter," is a systematic repertoire of metrical melodies for all the Psalms in German. It was published in 1627 and then republished in a third edition in 1661, heavily revised, and considered then the composer's Op. 14 (SWV 96–256). Only rare attention has been paid to this collection, the most notable example being the Gregg Smith anthology for Vox cited above.

His next publication was far more significant, his Op. 6, carried out in Venice in 1629 while he was on his second journey to Italy, where he used the opportunity to learn what he could from Monteverdi. For this new collection, he chose the title "Sacred Symphonies," emulating its use by his beloved master, Gabrieli. In it, Schütz again addressed Latin texts with various liturgical and Scriptural origins, but this time writing along the lines of the new Italian concertato style for solo voices with various instruments. The set includes some wonderful pieces, many of them charged with emotional or dramatic feeling, and many of them have long been popular on disc.

There have been two complete recordings. The first was made in Dresden with five adult male soloists (including Schreier) plus several boy trebles and some 30 period-instrument players of the Capella Fidicinia Leipzig, led by **Hans Grüss** (1984: ♦Capriccio 10044/45 as singles; ♦Berlin Classics 9250, 2CD). The other involved six singers (including Covey-Crump, Potter, and van der Kamp), with 16 instrumentalists of the **Concerto Palatino** (1991: ♦Accent 9178; MHS 524215; both 2CD). Grüss's performances are freer and more adventurous in their instrumentation, but while the soloists are generally quite good, the boy trebles are an element of weakness. The Concerto Palatino performances are more refined and generally more reliable; they offer some of the best evidence of how well matched the sounds of cornets and human voices can be.

Musikalische Exequien (1636: SWV 279–281). The march onward in composing short sacred works was somewhat interrupted by Schütz's Op. 7, his remarkable "Musical Exequies." This compilation was composed in 1635 at the request of a local prince, Heinrich Reuss Posthumus, and was used at the latter's burial the following year, when it was also published. It's an extraordinarily innovative assemblage, consisting of three sections of unequal length. The first, assembling Scriptural verses, is a "Concerto in the Form of a Burial Mass" for solo and choral voices with continuo, in complex and carefully explained divisions and subdivisions. The second is a motet for double choir on a Psalm text. The third section, for two unequal choirs, pits the Latin Mass's "Ite missa est" dismissal hymn against the consolatory "Selig sind die Toten" ("Blessed are the dead"). The sum total is one of the greatest, most beautiful, most moving examples of funerary music ever composed. A really good performance makes me want to cry.

There have been at least 18 recordings over the years, making this the composer's second most popular major work on disc. A good number go back through the LP years. One of the very earliest, made in 1953 under **Richter,** now sounds ponderous and overblown, in dated monophonic sound (DG Archiv). Two survivors of the Schütz boomlet in the '60s are back with us to show their age. **Mauersberger**'s recording with the Dresden Kreuzchor is sloppy and heavy-handed; its reissue seems unjustified beyond documenting a performance style no longer acceptable—and feeding fans of Schreier, a young member of the solo team (Berlin 2037, with *Seven Last Words*). Much more durable musically is a version recorded by the high priest of Schütz at the time, **Wilhelm**

Ehmann; somewhat dated in its semiromantic weightiness, it's still an honest and eloquent projection (♦Cantate 57602, with *St. John Passion*).

Two products of the last LP days have returned on CD. **Linde**'s 1979 version has been revived, if ephemerally, and is well worth searching out (♦EMI 749225). Combining *ME* with the fine setting of Psalm 136 from *PD,* Linde used members of the Chiaroscuro vocal ensemble with the Basel Boys Choir and period-instrument players of the Schola Cantorum Basiliensis in a beautifully flowing performance of reverent introspection. This was followed by **Herreweghe**'s aesthetically similar but somewhat more weighty version (1987: ♦Harmonia Mundi 901261). Herreweghe used some of the composer's shorter works as fillers: six astutely chosen examples (several with texts related to those of the grand funeral work), two from *SS* and four from *GCM,* adding up to a beautiful collection.

Gardiner's approach was very different: Characteristically brisk and impassioned, he used a large choir of 30 mixed voices with razor-sharp clarity, with soloists drawn from it, plus splendid instrumental groups (1987: ♦DG Archiv 423405). Four added motets and concertos of various vintage are unrelated but fine musical additions, in a release that charted a new direction for the major work. That direction was extended by **Howard Arman** (1992/93: ♦Berlin 1062; Parnassus 78434). With a much smaller group of only 16 mixed voices, Arman more than matches Gardiner's clarity, with an almost ideal balance of textual, textural, and emotional values. Moreover (at least in the Berlin release), instead of filling up the extra space with odds and ends, Arman and his producers created a thematic assemblage that expands the composer's funerary theme in contemporaneous terms. Interspersed with *ME* sections are three short motets by Praetorius, followed by two short consolatory pieces by Schütz himself and one each by Schein and Johannes Christoph Demantius. The idea is fascinating, and the results are richly rewarding. This is a truly superlative release. The Parnassus disc gives *ME* straight, followed by other sacred pieces.

Three more recent releases (all 1998) offer mixed results. **Christophers** makes another quasi-thematic use of fillers; as prefaces he offers not only the great two-choir *DM* and a German "Lord's Prayer" but also three settings of the *Symeon Canticle* ("Herr, nun lässest du deinen diener") other than the one the composer made for *ME* (Collins 1503). The performances, however, are another of Christophers's near misses: ultrapolished choral work by his singers (here 24 mixed voices), with good period-instrumental participation, but he and his engineer consistently place the choir at such a distance that clarity is sacrificed to blend, disastrous to the spatial definition of Schütz's all-important subdivisional groupings.

Jeffrey Thomas's recording is more satisfying, with his American Bach Soloists (♦Koch 7432, with six short concerted sacred pieces). He has a very good lineup (including Brandes, Nelson, Malafronte, Van Evera, Daniel Taylor, and Thomas himself), and his choir of ten mixed voices is beautifully responsive, refined, and stylish. The tone is something of a return to the Linde/Herreweghe style of gentle reverence, not quite as fully realized, but handsomely carried out nevertheless.

Perhaps the sleeper of this threesome, however, is a recording by **Françoise Lasserre** (♦Pierre Verany 799011). This offers a stirring, deeply felt performance of *ME,* preceded by an outstanding supplemental program: three pieces from *GCM,* one each from *SS I* and *III,* one from *KGK II* (a heartbreaking lament on the premature death of the composer's beloved wife), plus instrumental pieces by Scheidt and Gabrieli. Lasserre's Akademia ensemble fields a mixed-voice group of 14 singers, used both as chorus and soloists, plus the cornets (2) and sack-

buts (4) of the La Fenice ensemble together with six continuo players; the ensemble is sometimes a bit scrawny, but the solo singing is excellent, while the general spirit and stylistic commitment are captivating in a release that gives much pleasure and is admirably annotated to boot.

The most recent entry seems promising on paper: *ME* followed by two other Schütz settings of the *Canticum Simeonis* text and three other pieces, all conducted by **Hennig** with his Knabenchor Hannover (Ars Musici 1267). But here Hennig isn't up to his own best standards; the choir sounds overblown, and the direction is diffident and slack, with quite disappointing effects. Of two relatively marginal performances, one by the Chapelle Vocale of Lausanne University under **Christophe Aubert** is at least sung with more clarity and eloquence than Hennig offers and is well recorded (Gallo). The other, by Bulgarian forces under **Vassil Kazandjiev** (Forlane), is stylistically at sea. But with so many really good recordings of this wonderful work, clear-cut choices are difficult and complicated: perhaps Linde, Herreweghe, and Thomas for devotional approaches, with Gardiner, Arman, and Lasserre for expressive excitement, the latter two especially for the accompanying material.

Kleine geistliche Konzerte I and II (1636, 1639: SWV 282–307). As the 1630s progressed, the debilitating impact of the Thirty Years War on German life took its toll on Schütz's Dresden court, where he was eventually reduced to only a few musicians. With necessity as the mother of invention, Schütz turned this situation into an opportunity for creating musical expression on an economical scale by writing German sacred music for one to five solo voices with continuo only, in his own handling of Monteverdian monodic and concertato styles. In publishing the results of this expedient, Schütz apologized for such alleged trivia, but he surely realized that there was a genuine need for music of this kind: simple and direct but musically compelling. Using the title of "Small Sacred Concertos," he issued them in two collections: Part I (SWV 282–305, German texts only) in 1636, his Op. 8; and Part II (306–337, both Latin and German texts) in 1639, his Op. 9.

There have been two complete recordings of these two sets. The first was a major achievement by **Ehmann,** who directed performances with a team of soloists (including Lisken, Adele Stolte, Rotzsch, and Stämpfli) and instrumentalists, with his Westphälische Kantorei brought in for the few larger-scale pieces (♦Cantate 57603/06, 4 separate CDs). Though you can find better-sung individual performances, his standards were consistently high, and the musical and spiritual values are delivered earnestly. Ehmann's pacing is sometimes stolid, but these performances stand up quite well.

The second cycle was undertaken between 1987 and 1990 by **Gerhard Schmidt-Gaden** with members of the Tölzer Knabenchor and instrumentalists (Capriccio 10293, Part I: 10388 and 10418, Part II). The performances are adequate but not vocally distinguished, and the extensive use of boy trebles may be hard on some ears. No recourse is made to a full choir, while the instrumentation is kept at a Spartan minimum. All this probably recreates honestly the sort of performing sounds the composer would have heard; still, if you must have these cycles en bloc, Ehmann may be preferable for modern musical enjoyment.

A third complete cycle seems to have been contemplated by **Eric Milnes** with his New York Baroque, but it appears to have gone no further than Vol. I, which contains 16 items chosen at random from both parts (PGM 109). There are only five singers (including Brandes and Lane) with organ and cello continuo. The singing is consistently beautiful and expressive; I hope this project still has a future. Recorded programs drawing exclusively upon *KGK* have been rare. Usually, selections from this cycle are mixed with other Schütz material, whether scattered as fillers with larger works or in releases considered below.

Symphonia sacrae II and III (1647, 1650: SWV 341–367; 398–419). Schütz's preoccupation with creating a sacred literature of modest scale (whether for church use or, as some suggest, for courtly concerts) continued through the next decade with two more published collections, his Opp. 10 and 12. For these he revived the title of "Sacred Symphonies," though it covered settings of texts not in Latin but entirely in German. Part II stepped up the scale of *SSI*, adding to the one to three solo voices and continuo the enrichment of two melody instruments (two violins "or the like"). Part III went still further, allowing for the inclusion of vocal (or instrumental) choirs ad libitim, sometimes achieving quite sumptuous textures.

Both of these publications have had complete recordings on CD, Part II in no less than three versions. The earliest dates to 1985–86, again led by **Hans Grüss.** The collection is spread rather carelessly over three CDs, in scrambled order, though tossing in as a bonus two concertato madrigals by Monteverdi juxtaposed with the German sacred piece Schütz adapted from them (Capriccio 10110/112; boxed as 10996). Ten singers are employed (Kowalski and Schreier the only familiar names among them), augmented in a few cases by trebles from the Dresden Kreuzchor, while a nice diversity of period-instrument players of the Capella Fidicinia is also involved. The performances are rarely brilliant or outstanding but, again, thoroughly dependable and eminently listenable.

A second recording had no stipulated director but was credited to the **Purcell Quartet** (1993–94: ♦Chandos 0566/67). Here that group consists of six players who variously play violins, violas, recorders, and cornetti in pairs, plus organ and violone. Vocal assignments are traded by seven singers (Kirkby, Suzie Le Blanc, Bowman, Charles Daniels, Rogers, Wistreich, and Varcoe). Predictably, the singing is of top quality, if just a little cool in spirit, and these are splendidly musical performances, conveniently fitting onto only two discs (and in the published order).

If both vocal and instrumental colors are somewhat spare in the Chandos set, they are more lavishly applied and imaginatively varied by the Musica Fiata led by **Roland Wilson** (♦Sony 68261, 2CD). Here we have not only the full Part II collection (again in scrambled order) but also a bonus: "Vater Abraham, erbarme dich mein" (SWV 477), a dialogue between the Rich Man who spurned the pauper Lazarus and Abraham. Under the label of La Cappella Ducale, there are seven singers (including Spägele, van der Meel, and van der Kamp), all with light and agile voices, who sing with spirit, color, and excellent ensemble. For value and vivacity, this gets the highest recommendation of the three.

Roland Wilson and his Musica Fiata are back again in the only complete recording of the larger Part III, but this time the conductor is **Bernius,** who brings to bear his 30-voice Stuttgart Chamber Choir (1988: Deutsche Harmonia Mundi 77910, 2CD). There are wonderful things in this collection, such as the brief but telling vignette of Paul's vision on the road to Damascus, "Saul, Saul, was verfolgst du mich?" (SWV 415), and they're all given sturdy and stylish if not terribly individualized performances (in exact publication order). The seven soloists (among them Frimmer, van der Sluis, Chance, Elwes, Prégardien, and David Thomas) are augmented (in one piece only, and there appropriately) by a boy treble. Perhaps difficult to find, but indispensable for the serious Schütz collector.

As with *KGK,* there are currently no releases that sample the latter two parts of *SS* exclusively, but a number of programs draw upon both.

The granddaddy is an early Westminster mono LP with four works from each series. With instrumental support led by **Daniel Pinkham,** the small but uniquely plangent and artistic voice of Cuénod achieved something special that was probably the first introduction to the wonderful world of Schütz for those of us whose collecting goes back that far. Those 1950 performances are with us again—a nostalgic trip but still impressive in artistry (Lys 201). **Jacobs**'s splendid program with Concerto Vocale is more up to date (1982: ♦Harmonia Mundi 901097). It offers eight items from both parts of *KGK* and four from *SS II.* Sebastian Hennig, an unusually successful boy treble in adult company, joins instrumentalists including Christie (organ), Coin (cello), and Junghänel (lute), for a very attractive and highly recommended release.

Geistliche Chor-Music (1648: SWV 369–397). As he passed into his '60s, Schütz seems to have wanted to consolidate his output into representative collections, issued in rapid succession. Thus, between the appearance of Parts II and III of *SS* (1647, 1650), he produced in 1648—the year the Treaty of Westphalia ended the Thirty Years War—a collection of 29 motets called "Sacred Choral Music," with the title repeated in Latin and German. The texts are all German. There are 12 each for five and six voices and five for seven; a basso continuo is provided perfunctorily but is expendable for all but five items calling for instruments. For the most part, the collection represented the composer's look back to the idiom of the a cappella motet, but in works of great concentration and textural economy.

There have been no less than six complete recordings (all 2CD unless otherwise stated). In **Mauersberger**'s, instruments are used in five items as appropriate, but the rest are done a cappella by the boys and men of the Dresden Kreuzchor (Berlin 2109). As elsewhere, his performances are dedicated and sturdy, but in quantity they become rather unvaried and heavy, making him a mediocre advocate for this collection. **Ehmann** with his Westphälische Kantorei freely added extensive doublings and instrumentation, and wisely included a motet by Andrea Gabrieli ("Angelus ad pastores ait") that Schütz here adapted as one of his German motets (♦Cantate 57611/12). The spirit is expansive but heavy, but there's a lot of earnest commitment in these performances that gives them enduring value.

Hennig's recording of the early '80s represents a return to choral purity (Deutsche Harmonia Mundi 77171). The trebles of the Hanover Boy's Choir have their woolly moments, but generally these are reliable and effective performances. This set may be hard to find now, but it's of special value because Hennig chose to include the composer's variant versions for seven of the items.

The four most recent complete recordings are quite contrasted. **Cordes,** with his Weser-Renaissance Bremen ensemble, turns his back on a cappella choral performance and will put off anyone who expects or insists upon that (♦CPO 999546). He marshals seven singers (the familiar Spägele, Popken, and van der Kamp again among them) and 13 period-instrument players. The motets are performed with great variety, never with more than one singer per part, but only occasionally with voices alone, more often with instrumental doublings or even replacements of singers, sometimes to great extremes. The performances are alert and handsome, and they certainly add new perspectives on the composer's writing. Cordes adds two bonus selections: the fine five-voice Psalm 116 (SWV 51), done with voices only, and a late German Litany (SWV 458) with organ. Not the only way you want to know this music, but essential for the serious Schütz student.

More of a compromise spirit is offered by **Schmidt-Gaden** with his Tölzer Knabenchor (Capriccio 10 858/59). The 29 motets are presented in strict publication order with no alternatives or additions. Some variety is attempted in scoring, but only one motet is given by a cappella choir; several are done by choir with continuo, but soloists with instruments (with or without choral ripieno) are the most frequently used. Listeners who don't enjoy the edgy tone of boys' voices, not only in choir but as soloists, will find many of these performances a bit trying, especially in quantity. But this approach offers a fair and musically able response to the options the composer allowed.

Two other full recordings represent a return to a conservative choral approach. **Suzuki** does most of the motets with a refined mixed-voice choir of ten, though he does a few with one singer per part (using eight soloists), and soloists are also used in the pieces with instruments (♦BIS 831/32, 2CD). He retains the continuo and uses minimal strings for the added instrumental roles. The singing is very beautiful, but distant miking and a reverberant setting only heighten the overall effect of cool and aloof impersonality. Suzuki is particularly generous with his extra space, however, adding *Seven Last Words* as filler. For those who want a more strictly choral approach, the excellent 21-voice Emmanuel Music choir is led by **Craig Smith** in elegant, restrained, but highly polished performances—again, though, with a somewhat cool character stressed by rather distant miking (♦Koch 7174, with the six-voice motets; 7189 for the five-voice items plus those with instruments). Save for those with instrumentation, the continuo is dispensed with, so these motets can be heard as purely choral music.

To these comprehensive traversals I must add a very fine CD from **Herreweghe** (1994: ♦Harmonia Mundi 901534). He presents ten motets from *GCM* interspersed with six selections from both parts of *KGK*, sung by three soloists (Mellon, Mark, Kooy). The motets are sung with elegant but pointed clarity by a choir of 18 mixed voices; an elementary continuo is maintained throughout. Herreweghe demonstrates that a well-focused choral approach can yield very expressive and moving results.

Schwanengesang (1671: SWV 482–494). After Part III of *SS* was published (1650), the aging Schütz saw only two more publications into print. One was a set of *Zwölf geistliche Gesänge* (Twelve Sacred Songs) Op. 12 (1657) for solo voices and continuo; no complete recording has been made. The other was the final (third) edition of the "Becker Psalter," published in 1661 as his Op. 14. In ill health but creative to the last, Schütz planned a kind of musical testament, to which he gave the personally charged title of "Swan Song." This was to be a vast setting (in German) of the longest of the Psalms, 119, cast in the form of 11 sequential motets (SWV 482–492) for subdivisible double choirs and continuo, to which he chose to append two more double-choir works, a setting (also in German) of Psalm 100 (SWV 493) and *DM*.

Rather than making a commitment to either the older polyphonic/choral or the newer soloistic/concertato styles, the music seems to complete Schütz's lifelong dedication to reconciling and synthesizing those two directions, within the polychoral techniques he loved and learned in Venice. Apparently intending to publish this collection as his *Opus ultimum,* he carefully prepared the score and parts, though having a title page and index set in print. This effort was completed in 1671, but Schütz died the following year; his request to a colleague for instrumentation for the music was unfulfilled, and apparently it was never performed. Nothing more was done about publication, probably because of shifts in taste that were bypassing his

style. (Indeed, some authorities have seen this final compilation as the old man's protest against exactly those stylistic shifts.) The music was left to survive precariously in manuscript, to be reconstructed by Wolfram Steude and only published in 1985.

The first performance was (appropriately) in Dresden in 1981, and two years later the first recording was made there, by vocal and instrumental forces under **Knothe** (♦Capriccio 10049 and 100050; Berlin 1071, 2CD). Knothe used Steude's not yet published reconstruction of the text and instrumentation, which aimed at variety of colors and textures. He used 16 singers (boys and men), half of them as soloists, the rest joining as ripieno, and 20 players on period instruments (winds, strings, and continuo). The continuo is retained throughout, and instruments are used extensively to double or even replace vocal parts. It's done with good taste and fine sonority, while the performances are clear, well-drilled, and vigorous.

With his edition now published, Steude assisted in preparing a broadcast and recording performance involving four boy soloists, the six members of Paul Hillier's Hilliard Ensemble, two period-instrument groups, and the Hanover Boy's Choir, all led by **Hennig** (EMI 749214, 2CD). The instrumentation this time was by Alfred Koerppen, but generally followed Knothe's colorful policies. The vocal element is strengthened by the Hanover choir, but the boys' singing and the ensemble work are sometimes ragged, while Hennig's tempos are generally broader than Knothe's, and his pacing is weightier. Still, this is an impressive feast of sound.

Hillier may have been either dissatisfied with or inspired by his involvement in Hennig's recording, for in 1991 he made one of his own, conducting the Tapiola Chamber Choir (♦Finlandia 522082). He diverged drastically from the two previous recordings. With a mixed-voice chorus of 28 (divided equally into two choirs), supported only by a continuo of organ and archlute, he eschews all solo subdivisions (save for the opening intonations) and avoids any supplemental instrumentation to create a totally choral rendition of great suavity and power.

As if this wasn't sufficiently drastic, a fourth recording has carried it even further, a performance in Sydney under **Roland Peelman.** It's not complete, since it omits *DM*, and it's certainly not (as the booklet cover proclaims) the "world premiere recording" (1996: Celestial Harmonies 13139). What it is, in fact, is an ultimate minimalist reduction of the music; the ensemble, called the Song Company, consists of eight singers divided into two quartets, with only an organ for the simple continuo. The singing is deft, skillful, and undeniably artistic. Thanks to relentlessly speedy and inflexible tempos (plus omitting *DM*), the performance was fitted into a single CD, but such pacing, together with the unvaried colors and thin textures, understates this music's scope, reducing it to madrigalian proportions. For all Schütz's triumph over constraints in his more economical sacred writing, it seems unlikely that he would have wanted performing forces as small as these for his "swan song."

With the Hillier/Hennig recording now of limited availability, and even allowing for Peelman's curiosity value, the choice is clearly between Knothe and Hillier, which is also a choice between a grandly colored vocal/instrumental version and a purely choral one—each making the music sound very different from the other.

Miscellaneous sacred pieces

Schütz never intended people to listen to the published collections as entities, all at one sitting. Of course, recordings of integral collections can be sampled at leisure, but some listeners may prefer programs that offer gleanings rather than completeness. One recent example is a program on a seasonal theme ("A Christmas Collection") by soloists, choir, and instrumentalists of the Academy of Ancient Music under **Paul Goodwin** (♦Harmonia Mundi 907202): one item from *PD*, five from *KGK II*, and four from *GCM*, plus the five-choir Latin *Magnificat* (SWV 468), interspersed with contemporaneous instrumental pieces. The range of choices also allows a range of textures, from soloistic miniatures to grandiose choral frescoes, and the performances are full of vitality and strong stylistic flair; this is an outstanding and highly enjoyable program, ideal for newcomers to Schütz.

A more random selection was recorded by the seven male singers of Pro Cantione Antiqua, with two period-instrument groups led by **Edgar Fleet:** one item from *CS*, four from *SS*, three from *KGK II*, and three from *GCM* (♦ASV 6105; MHS 416504). Here the texture is kept light, soloistic, and minimalistic even in the "choral" pieces (with instruments sometimes replacing singers in some voice parts).

Hans Rudolf Zöbeley has been a recurrent champion of such mélanges; his program leads off with the great *DM*, then offers four items each from *PD* (three of them with instruments) and *GCM* sung a cappella (♦FSM 92207). A good-sized choir is used, and the approach is somewhat sedate and conservative, but these are generally very able and enjoyable performances (though no texts or translations are provided). Zöbeley is also represented in a culling of recordings with his Munich group and by **Bernhard Klebel** with Vienna forces in a program totaling seven items from *PD*, two from *SS III*, plus one of disputed attribution (SWV A11). Zöbeley's performances stand up better than Klebel's, but the program is certainly solid. Again, there is good introductory value in these releases (♦Christophorus 74570 or 0048).

Since we never know what may return from the past, I should note a program that **Robert Craft** put together with eight singers (one of them the young Marilyn Horne) and eleven modern-instrument players, presenting eight selections of smaller scale drawn from *CS* (2), *SS I* (4) and III (1), and *GCM* (1): the performances are meticulously detailed if somewhat dry and hard (Columbia LP).

Beyond the considerable quantity of material Schütz published in his printed collections, he also left us quite a number of other vocal compositions—upwards of 50 or so—that survive either in contemporaneous publications by others or in manuscript. Recordings have dipped into this repertoire occasionally, if all too rarely, but always with rich rewards. Pride of place surely belongs to a striking program of "Psalms, Motets, and Concertos," with 12 singers of the Cantus Cologne (led by lutenist Junghänel), 21 players of Roland Wilson's Musica Fiata, and the Hanover Boys' Choir, all led by **Hennig** (♦Deutsche Harmonia Mundi 77175, 2CD). They offer 16 variously polychoral items (11 in German, five in Latin); most use Psalm or other Scriptural texts, while two set Latin liturgical words, and two more are occasional pieces for public ceremonies with words at least partly devised by the composer himself. Though Hennig is leader in the larger-scaled pieces, these performances are really a collaboration among the three ensemble leaders. They are splendidly stylish and vividly recorded. This is an outstanding Schütz recording, and no collector devoted to his music should be without it.

A smaller gleaning from this repertoire can be heard from the Dresden Kreuzchor led by **Mauersberger** and Capella Fidicinia players led by Grüss, presenting six items in Venetian polychoral style, including the Latin *Magnificat* SWV 468 and the mighty Psalm 24 SWV 476 (1970: Berlin). Good intentions are somewhat compromised by the large choir (with not always tightly controlled boy-treble voices) and a rather ponderous approach; this release is useful for the rare repertoire but doesn't offer ideal realizations.

One group steadfastly devoted to this literature has been the conductorless **Musicalische Compagney** (which includes David Cordier, Ragin, Padmore, and van der Kamp among its singers and Cordes among its instrumentalists). They have produced two very worthwhile releases. One offers a program of "Lamenti and Concerti," subtitled "Love and Grief in the Music of H. S.": eight sacred or occasional pieces, three from *SS I*, the rest from the miscellaneous repertoire (1986: ♦MD+G 310 0230). The other is an interesting demonstration of Gabrieli's influence on Schütz (1985: ♦Ambitus 97843). Intermingled with one instrumental piece and three important choral works by the Italian (including the famous *In ecclesiis*) are eight pieces by Schütz: one each from the two parts of *KGK*, two from *SS III*, and four from the miscellaneous repertoire. This ensemble uses soloists and solo ensembles to stress clarity of texture sometimes lost in fuller "choral" approaches, and the instrumental work is stylish and colorful; equal justice is done to each composer, and this program will also appeal to the Gabrieli collector.

A final anthology offers still further perspective on "Heinrich Schütz and Venice" (to quote its title); here the anchor is the recurrent setting of the *Magnificat*, presented in Latin by Gabrieli and Schütz (SWV 468) and in German by Praetorius (♦Capriccio 10049). There's another Gabrieli piece (a double-choir madrigal done instrumentally) and Monteverdi's great seven-voice *Gloria*, while three other items complete the total of four by Schütz. The performances, led by **Howard Arman,** involve 23 period instrumentalists with only 12 singers; thus the vocal texture is again lean, but the ensemble is nevertheless strong, and all these performances are of the highest quality. (Note, though, that only original texts are given, the last of which is wrong.) Schütz collectors will find this an excellent way to place the composer's music in its contemporaneous context. Six of these shorter works are also available in Parnassus 78434, with *ME*.

Finally, some of Argo's old LP collections have been revived in a splendid bargain-rate set put together around **Norrington**'s recordings of the Christmas and Resurrection oratorios (♦Decca 452188, 2CD). It includes seven double-choir motets from a 1970 program with his Heinrich Schütz Choir: three items from *PD* and three of the supplemental pieces, including *DM* and Schütz's adaptation of a Psalm setting by Gabrieli, all done with flair and period instruments. Added from another 1970 program are five motets from *CS*, rounding out an outstanding passage. But Decca should consider reissuing another, more diverse anthology conducted by **Leppard** called "Voices and Brass," including instrumental and choral pieces by Scheidt and Schein; though containing only three of the supplemental works—notably the magnificent Psalm 24 (SWV 476)—the performances by the Purcell Chorus of Voices and Philip Jones Brass Ensemble are stunning, and will please those who prefer modern-instrument wind sounds.

Oratorios

Composed at intervals throughout Schütz's life, at least three more-or-less narrative works survive—one related to Christmas, the other two to the Passion and Easter themes—cast in the concertato style of voices with instruments. But from his last years also come Schütz's three extraordinary treatments of the Passion accounts in an austere, pseudo-archaic style for voices only. For stylistic reasons, it seems best to consider them chronologically.

Die Auferstehung unsres Herren Jesu Christi (1623: SWV 50). This is the earliest of Schütz's oratorios, and the only one he published in his lifetime (Op. 3). Its full title is *Historia der fröhlichen und siegreichen Aufferstehung unsers einigen Erlösers und Seligmachers Jesu Christi*

(Story of the Joyous and Victorious Resurrection of Our Only Redeemer and Savior Jesus Christ), and its music is not entirely Schütz's own—a practice he followed intermittently but without any deceit throughout his career. Some of his lost theatrical works may have drawn upon the music of others, and we know that several of his short sacred pieces were reworkings of music by Gabrieli and Monteverdi.

In this case, the original composer was Antonio Scandello, a distant predecessor of Schütz at the Dresden Court Chapel. Scandello's work, composed in the 1570s, was in the old style of a completely polyphonic setting of the Latin text compiled from the Gospels. It was still in use in Schütz's time, and in 1623 he undertook a "modernization," recasting it drastically if not completely. The text was put into Latin, and he framed it with a six-part opening chorus and a nine-part closing chorus, while setting a brief six-part *turba* (crowd chorus) midstream. For the narrative, he nominally respected the older polyphonic texture but revised Scandello's part-writing for the characters who speak (*colloqueten*). Such part-writing isn't problematic where three characters (the three Marys) or pairs (Two Men at the Sepulcher, Two Angels, Cleopas and his Friend) can be sung by soloists in the appropriate number of parts, but individual parts (Jesus, Mary Magdalene, a Young Man) are also set as *bicinia* (two-part pieces) for a pair of singers.

A continuo part is provided throughout, set in quasi plainsong for tenor, with an indication of accompaniment by a quartet of viols, but Schütz makes clear that the viols may be replaced with other instruments who may elaborate their parts, while in the *bicinia* he allows one of the two parts to be taken by an instrument or even eliminated entirely. With these changes and allowable options, Schütz single-handedly created the German Baroque oratorio.

Though not the most immediately appealing of the oratorios, it has by no means been neglected. A 1969 venture has happily been restored: one of **Norrington**'s valuable recordings in his younger days as a tenor and choral conductor, then calling his group the Heinrich Schütz Choir, with Christmas Oratorio and motets in a rich bargain-rate set (♦Decca 452188, 2CD). His distinguished vocal team included Pears as Evangelist with Tear, Langridge, Partridge, and Shirley-Quirk among the others. He retained Schütz's official scoring, multiple-singer characters and all, while using vocal doublings by cornets and sackbuts for a highly colored rendition. Also from LP days but now back with us is **Flämig**'s recording with the Dresden Kreuzchor and the Capella Fidicinia, Schreier as Evangelist, and soloists including the juvenile Olaf Bär as one of two boy trebles from the choir (1971: ♦Berlin 9205). Flämig respects the stipulated scoring on all counts (with no added instrumental doublings) in a stylish and attractive performance.

Not until the '90s did we have recordings that give Flämig competition. Two of them continue the practice of preserving Schütz's multivoice *colloqueten*. **Jacobs** offers a polished rendition, somewhat spoiled by quirky recording balances and editing, but with Martin Hummel as a fine Evangelist, ensembles of one or two singers per choral part, and renewed wind doublings (Harmonia Mundi 901311). A bracing version of a German *Magnificat* (SWV 344, from *SS II*) completes the disc. A version led by **Philippe Pierlot** is somewhat smoother (♦Ricercar 206412); Padmore is an outstanding Evangelist, and Schütz's instrumentation is followed without augmentation.

Bernius's version is a stimulating contrast, with his tidy Stuttgart Chamber Choir, Roland Wilson's Musica Fiata Köln, and a fine team of soloists: Prégardien, one of the great Evangelists for many composers, and van der Sluis, Christopher Robson, Cordier, and Kooy among the others (Sony 45943). Bernius not only uses cornet and sackbut

doublings, but is bolder in his acceptance of the composer's license to reduce the three *colloqueten* roles to a single singer for each, which brings the piece closer to the subsequent Baroque oratorio texture we're used to. Finally, thanks to comparatively brisk tempos (with no loss of intensity), he's able to pair this Easter oratorio with the complete *Weihnachts-Historie,* thus challenging Norrington's Decca set for both best-buy status and for the chance to appreciate how the composer honed and refined the German oratorio from his earlier to his later work.

Die Geburt unsers Herren Jesu Christi (Weihnachts-Historie) (1660/64: SWV 435). Schütz's later and far more mature oratorio is officially titled *Historia der freuden- und gnadenreichen Geburt Gottes und Marien Sohnes Jesu Christi, unsers einigen Mitlers, Erlösers, und Seeligmachers* (Story of the Joy- and Grace-Laden Birth of the Son of God and of Mary, Jesus Christ, our Only Mediator, Redeemer, and Savior). In construction, it considerably refines the techniques first explored in *Die Auferstehung*. Again, open and closing choral sections frame the narrative based on the Gospel accounts in German. The narrative proper is again carried by a tenor Evangelist, but this time in the more "modern" *stile recitativo* with continuo. The successive episodes involving various characters in the story (one or more Angels, Shepherds, the Wise Men, High Priests, Herod) are represented in a series of concertato episodes, or *intermedia,* for solo or ensemble voices with diversely appropriate instrumentation.

The work was apparently first performed in Dresden in 1660, and the composer soon became so concerned about its proper performance that instead of publishing the work outright, he tried to control its availability through a combination of restrictions that almost brought about its disappearance. In 1664 he issued a skeletal publication containing only the Evangelist's part and the words of the *intermedia* without their music, reserving that to manuscript copies available only by special application. Those manuscripts disappeared in time, and the work survived only in pathetic fragments until a series of other (though also partial) survivals were discovered in the 20th century, which allowed a reliable reassembly of nearly the entire score save for the opening chorus, whose still-fragmentary state requires editorial reconstruction (so performances will sometimes differ). For all the perils of the work's survival, it has reemerged to become the composer's most popular and most frequently recorded major composition, with at least 20 versions to date.

The first modern performing edition was published by scholar-conductor Arthur Mendel in 1949; he made the first recording in 1950, through which old-time collectors first got to know and adore this delicious work (REB LP). There followed a number of LPs, mostly ephemeral, but no less than five recordings of that vintage have survived. The oldest was made in Stuttgart around 1960 by **Grischkat** (Vox 5095, 2CD, with Bach, Buxtehude, Haydn, and Gregorian Chant Christmas pieces). Not much younger is a 1963 recording by the Windsbach Boys' Choir and instruments under **Hans Thamm,** with excellent solo work by Jelden (Evangelist), Mathis (Angel), and Claus Ocker (Herod). This quite successful performance is, however, in somewhat dated sound, in a kind of sampler of EMI Schütz recordings. The other selections (two Psalms and *DM*) are excellent, and the programmatic idea is fine, but the sound isn't always well reprocessed, and in this bargain-rate issue there is no trace of texts or translations (EMI 565736).

Norrington is more deft in a fine recording made early in his career (1970) with his Heinrich Schütz Choir and ensembles of modern instruments (♦Decca 430632, reissued in 452188, 3CD, a splendid bargain-rate set with Resurrection Oratorio and motets; MHS 531434). Partridge is an unaffected Evangelist and Palmer a heavenly Angel, while Bowman, Langridge, and Hill are in *intermedia* ensembles. The disc is filled out with material from another Argo Schütz release, with Norrington conducting lively (and instrumentally doubled) performances of six double-choir pieces (three from *PD,* two from the uncollected pieces, and *DM*). **Zöbeley** is somewhat more subdued; he gives reliable—if not notably brilliant—performances with his Munich Motet Choir, soloists (Yakar among them), and old/new instruments (1981: Orfeo 002811, with *Magnificat* SWV 468).

Musicology more stringent is the watchword for the conductorless **Musicalische Compagney** (1984: MD+G 3229). Nine singers and 13 period instrumentalists, they make their performance very much a small-scaled ensemble affair, somewhat dry and formal. They use a performing edition of their own, whose most striking feature is the omission of the opening chorus, while the Angel is sung by a countertenor. These forces are also used in two framing pieces, the short *German Magnificat* (SWV 344) and the more substantial *Seven Words.* This is more a backup for the specialized collector than a front-rank choice.

Parrott's 1985 recording is no less scholarly but altogether superior musically (♦EMI 47633, with four Christmas motets by Praetorius). His forces are just about ideal: Nigel Rogers is a caring narrator, Kirkby a truly ethereal Angel, and David Thomas a Herod to reckon with. His 16 ensemble singers are an honor roll of London's early-music specialists, delivering beautifully pointed singing, with lovely instrumental work from 19 equally distinguished period-instrument players. The pacing is vigorous yet judicious. This is a strongly preferred version.

It has close competition, however, in **Robert King**'s recording (1989: ♦Hyperion 66398). His direction is just a tad more crisp, and with Holton and George he has splendid soloists, while the others who make up his character singers and minimalist "chorus" include more carry-overs from previous recordings. His choice of fillers points up yet again Schütz's links with Gabrieli: four of his Christmas motets (three of them polychoral), freshly rethought in performances by solo voices with instruments.

The '90s brought no less than seven recordings, all thoroughly rooted in scholarly exploration and period-instrument coloring, each with its own textual and interpretational perspectives. Leading his Schütz Akademie, **Arman** challenges the Musicalische Compagney in the minimalist department (♦Capriccio 10508). In Jochens and Spägele he has an excellent Evangelist and Angel; they join with nine others to form the vocal complement, along with 23 players. They make a strong showing, with Arman using his own reconstruction of the opening chorus. His release is given distinctive interest by his choice of the partner work, the first and only recording of a Christmas piece by Johann Schelle, which demonstrates the development of the cantata and oratorio idiom in the generations between Schütz and Bach.

But if it's minimalism you want, you can go to the bargain bins for **Summerly** with his Oxford Camerata (Naxos 553514): Agnew is a distinguished Evangelist and Anna Crookes a pretty Angel, though Michael McCarthy is a rather diffident Herod. Aside from Agnew, the singers total ten, with an unspecified number of players. They're quite good in Summerly's intelligent and stylistically aware interpretation of the main work, but they're stretched rather thin in the fillers, three motets from *CS* and Psalm 100 (SWV 36).

For a pullback from minimalism to, let's say, reductionism, we have two options. **Michel Laplénie** leads his Sagittarius Vocal Ensemble of 13 singers and the La Fenice Instrumental Ensemble of 11 players (1992: Adès 202362). ("Sagittarius" was the Latin form of "Schütz.") The only

standout is Samuel Husser as Evangelist; for the rest, everything is reliable and attractive, if unexceptional. The added material includes four well-chosen Christmas pieces by Schütz (two of the unpublished motets, a charming Annunciation scene from *KGK II,* and the Latin *Magnificat* SWV 468), affording genuine value but not pulling this release much higher than the "merely excellent" category.

Jacobs's 1990 recording is quite another matter (♦Harmonia Mundi). True, his forces are on the small side—an ensemble of 12 singers (Kiehr, Scholl, and Türk among them) and 15 players—but he uses them to rich effect. His reconstruction of the opening chorus is imaginative, and his instrumentation is full of clever added touches. He has a warm and dramatically involved Evangelist in Martin Hummel, and Ulrich Messthaler creates a Herod of supple evil. The pacing is brisk and propulsive but never really rushed. Here, too, are enjoyable short pieces with Christmas associations: four items from *KGK II* (including the Annunciation scene) and a double-choir concerto from the supplemental works. This is one of the outstanding recordings of the *Weihnachts-Historie.*

It's closely followed in quality by a 1999 recording under **Kuijken** (♦Deutsche Harmonia Mundi 77511). Stephen Genz is a forthright Evangelist, and from an ensemble of 10 singers come the other two soloists, including van der Kamp as Herod. They and the period group of ten players deliver a not very subtle but colorful performance of particular value for the fillers—five shorter sacred pieces including both the German and Latin *Magnificats,* done in rousing fashion.

A somewhat larger-scaled recording was led by **Bernius** (1990: ♦Sony 45943). He has the substantial-sounding Stuttgart Chamber Choir and a group of solo and ensemble singers (among them such recurrent artists as Frimmer, Cordier, Robson, Müller, Kooy), plus Roland Wilson's Musica Fiata Köln players. The pacing is again brisk but smooth, with Prégardien an experienced and reliable Evangelist. There is, however, a degree of blandness to this performance that puts it just a notch below its generous partner on the disc, the full *Auferstehung*—a combination that pushes the release as a whole into the recommendable category.

Finally, the most recent recording is also the most distinctive: another of **McCreesh**'s enterprising liturgical reconstructions (♦DG Archiv 289046). Made in 1998/99 at Roskilde Cathedral in Denmark, it recreates a "Christmas Vespers, as it might have been celebrated at the Court of Dresden c.1664." The centerpiece, of course, is Schütz's *Weihnachts-Historie,* in which McCreesh leads his Gabrieli Consort (19 singers) plus the Cathedral boy's choir and his Gabrieli Players (32) in a warm, flowing performance held together nicely by the genial Evangelist of Charles Daniels, on a scale nicely between too small and too big. There are additional Schütz pieces: an item from *PD,* a sacred concerto from the unpublished repertoire, and the Latin *Magnificat* SWV 468. All this is set in the context of a liturgical service, with organ pieces, celebrant contributions, congregational hymns, and—as appealing as it is authentic—interpolation by the boys of three German hymns among the verses of the *Magnificat.* We are thus able to appreciate the functional dimensions of Schütz's wonderful work in a way no other recording allows. Nor is the performance at all below the highest standards, its tidy scale captured with splendid clarity within the spacious setting of the Cathedral's atmospheric acoustics. No Schütz collector should miss this release.

With so many fine recordings, there can be no "best," but the strongest contenders are surely Arman, Jacobs, King, and Parrott, with Norrington for those who prefer "modern-instrument" sound, and McCreesh as something absolutely special.

Die sieben Worte (ca.1645?: SWV 478). We know nothing about the circumstances or occasion that prompted Schütz to create his setting of *Die sieben Worte unsers lieben Erlösers und Seligmachers Jesu Christi so Er am Stamm des heiligen Kreuzes gesprochen* (The Seven Words of our Dear Redeemer and Savior Jesus Christ, as He Spoke on the Rood of the Holy Cross). Its date has generally been placed between 1640 and 1650, with 1645 the most likely guess. Latin conflations of the Savior's Words from the Cross as culled from the four Gospel accounts—and bearing the symbolically potent number of seven—had long been a feature of medieval hymnography, and it was a German extension of that focus, the hymn "Da Jesus an dem Kreuze stund," from which Schütz took the words (though not the tune) to create the framing choruses of his work.

Of all Schütz's "oratorios," this least fits the definition, since it's only barely a dramatic work and at least as much a symbolic and ritualistic evocation. Within the framing five-part choruses there is an internal frame of a five-part instrumental symphonia, itself played twice, immediately before and after the setting of the seven episodes, laid out in neat proportions. Briefly setting each scene is the Evangelist (over continuo), sung not by one singer throughout but in rotation by three different singers (soprano, alto, tenor) or, at the end, by vocal quartet; the words of Jesus are sung by another tenor, but with two-part instrumental accompaniment, while in the center, the two Thieves are sung by alto and bass with continuo. Stylistically, then, the work blends the tradition of the so-called "motet-Passion" (Gospel words set in parts) with monodistic solo writing in the Italian tradition. The synthesis is perfect, in music that is solemn and devout but very moving, and it set a precedent for settings of *The Seven Last Words* for generations to come.

Because the work is so concise (well under 20 minutes as a rule), it has always been partnered with other music, almost invariably by Schütz himself, and so might sometimes be overlooked as filler. At least three recordings of LP vintage have made the CD transition. The earliest is a 1966 version under **Mauersberger;** the singers include Rotzsch and Adam, with a young Schreier as Jesus and two boy trebles as the Thieves (Berlin). Unfortunately, the conductor's rather weighty treatment is too ponderous to be fully acceptable now. No more passable is a 1975 recording by an early Schütz champion, **Paul Steinitz,** with four Schütz sacred pieces performed by the Monteverdi Choir under the young Gardiner (Cantate). Steinitz's instincts were correct, but he allowed solo and choral singing styles more appropriate to music of the 19th century than the 17th; as it stands, it's of more interest now for Gardiner's contributions. The conductorless **Musicalische Compagney,** recorded around 1984, breathes musicological purity but is brisk and superficial, suggesting little of the work's spiritual earnestness (MD+G).

Three recordings place the work not as partner to another, larger Schütz composition but as the centerpiece in programs of shorter sacred pieces, effective as introductory samplings of his art. An outstanding recording comes from the five singers of Ensemble Clément Janequin, with five period-brass players of Toulouse and three continuo players (1987: ◆Harmonia Mundi 901255). No conductor is mentioned, but countertenor **Visse** is usually considered the leader of the vocal group, while lutenist Junghänel is likely to be giving cues in any performance he's in. Their performance is on the minimalist side (soloists make up the "chorus"), but it does lean and elegant justice to the work's textures and spirit, though I miss the dimension of ensemble strings. The rest of their admirable program offers minimalist performances of the Latin *Magnificat* SWV 468, its German counterpart (SWV 344) from *SS II,* a pair of Latin pieces from *SS I,* an item each from *PD* and *KGK* II, and two

of the unpublished supplement sacred pieces—a very attractive package in all.

Françoise Lasserre scores in a strongly competitive version with her Akademia ensemble (◆Pierre Verany 700013). Imbedded in the midst of a richly diverse program of a dozen shorter examples from a wide range of the composer's sacred collections is a glowing, genuine realization of his *Seven Words.* Soloists, vocal ensemble, and period instrumentalists are both expert and eloquent in an outstanding release.

Even more frankly an introductory survey, "H. S.: A Musical Portrait" was made in California under **Nicole Paiement,** an introduction hardly aided by inadequate or incorrect identifications and the total lack of texts or translations (Helicon 1037). The surrounding material is well chosen: one motet each from *CS* and *GCM,* and *DM.* Some period instruments are used here and there; among the soloists is the male "sopranista," Randall Wong, and their singing and that of the 23-voice choir is generally healthy if not rigorously stylish.

Two recordings take notably reverent approaches to this quietly sincere work. **Suzuki** added it as filler to his recording of the complete *GCM* (BIS). The substantial chamber choir sings beautifully (if a little too distantly), and all the other elements are in place, but it still emerges as a rather cool and unengaged performance. The period-instrument Ricercar Consort under **Pierlot** is leaner, with five singers, as partner to his outstanding *Auferstehung* (◆Ricercar 206412). Here again we have a "chorus" of solo voices, but the singing is strong and stylish, with Agnew as a fine Jesus and Mellon also in the group.

Your choice will inevitably be affected by the accompanying material, but for its own sake, the outstanding releases are certainly Pierlot and Visse/Junghänel; because of the companion music, the former is perhaps best for advanced Schütz collectors, the latter for novices.

Matthäus-Passion (1666: SWV 478). Entering his eighties, Schütz was still fired by creative imagination and exploratory zeal, clearly demonstrated by his final efforts in the realm of oratorio. Apparently for the first time, he chose to enter the complex and shifting field of Passion settings. One line of that development goes all the way back to singing the Gospel texts in Medieval plainchant; by the 12th century, this was done by solo and unison voices representing the narrator and the characters. Out of that eventually came the so-called "dramatic Passion" of Baroque style, with solo voices in *stile recitativo* for the Evangelist and individual characters and choral *turbae* (crowd outbursts), with instrumental participation, and increasingly with latter-day contemplative texts interpolated—an idiom being developed during Schütz's later years and culminating in Bach's great Passions. Parallel to that line, for a while in the late- and post-Renaissance period, some composers embraced the "motet-Passion" idiom, in which all of the text (individuals and all) was set polyphonically.

Rejecting newer trends, Schütz chose an archaizing and stripped-down approach all his own: Instruments and extraneous texts were banished; the narrative was set entirely in a modal pseudo-plainchant of the composer's very expressive devising; the *turbae* passages, as well as stark but moving opening and closing choruses, were set in a simplified polyphonic style of the old motet tradition. The results of this austere and ultra-simplified approach are works of hypnotic power and intense devotional beauty.

The three works—there is a St. Mark version once spuriously attributed to Schütz—were never published and survive only in manuscript. All three have the parallel titles of *Historia des Leidens und Sterbens unsers Herrn und Heylandes Jesu Christi nach dem Evangelisten*

S. atheum/Lucam/Johannem (Story of the Suffering and Death of Our Lord and Savior Jesus Christ according to the Evangelist, etc.) Their dating is slightly blurred. We know they were performed on successive Sundays in April 1666, but there is evidence that the *Johannes-Passion* was performed the year before, and it's sometimes speculated that the *Lukas-Passion* may have been written still earlier. But there's no question that they are of a piece, and constitute a landmark in the composer's final phase of stylistic development.

Recordings have treated them variously—ironically, more fully in LP years than in the CD era. There was once an integral recording of all three, made in Cologne around 1970 by **Johannes Hömberg** and released by Vox in Vol. II (3LP) of its Schütz 300th Anniversary Edition series. These quite serviceable performances have never been reissued on CD as a set, though at least the St. John has appeared in Germany on an obscure local label.

The Passion story in St. Matthew's *Gospel* is particularly rich in episodes and personalities, making its setting the most varied and dramatic of the Gospel texts. Of Schütz's three settings, the *Matthäus-Passion* has received the most attention, in up to ten recordings. The first stereo recording was an expansive but thoughtful version led by **Klaus Fischer-Dieskau** featuring his brother Dietrich as a very special Evangelist; it's a wonder this hasn't been revived (DG Archiv). A stellar 1971 recording by the young **Norrington** and his Heinrich Schütz Choir, with Pears as a distinctive Evangelist plus Shirley-Quirk as Jesus and Palmer, Langridge, Luxon, and David Thomas among the other high-quality singers, was revived for a while but may be hard to find; a reissue is in order (♦Decca 436221).

A recording by the young **Rilling** with Altmeyer as Evangelist, a well-balanced and soundly paced performance, likewise seems to have sunk out of sight (1972: Cantate). But **Flämig**'s 1973 recording has been resurrected; the Dresden Kreuzchor is again heavy but well managed and boldly assertive, while Schreier is another distinctive Evangelist, in a rendition that effectively represents the 20th-century German tradition of Schütz performance (♦Berlin 9010). **Hillier**'s 1983 recording is a particularly cruel loss; he used members of his Hilliard Ensemble, slightly expanded, in a performance characteristically not only minimalist in scale but freshly rethought in interpretation, with rather stately and pointed pacing in choral passages (♦EMI). Paul Elliott is his light-voiced, agile Evangelist, and Hillier himself sings a mellow Jesus; ten other singers (including Dawson, Fisher, Covey-Crump, and George) serve both as a pool for the various character solos and as the chorus. If not the only or the ideal way to present this music, it's an absorbing performance that no Schütz collector should be denied.

Against so rich an LP background, the contributions of CD vintage have been thin. A recording by the Württemberg Chamber Choir under **Dieter Kurz** is graced by the responsible Evangelist of Blochwitz and is a quite respectable performance at a bargain-bin price, though lacking the all-important text (♦Pilz 160123; Point 2650172). That leaves the only serious recent recording, made in 1989 by **Somary** (♦Newport 60103). His Evangelist, Grayston Hirst, is dependable and sturdy, and Ostendorf is a more than usually dark-voiced and bluff Jesus; lesser parts are ably taken. But, as with the two British recordings, there is a slight lack of the idiomatic delivery that native German speakers offer; witness the successes of Flämig and, going all the way back, Grischkat. The particular strength of Somary's version is its highly polished choral work, even more beautifully blended than Norrington's ringing equivalent, fuller than Hillier's white and stately ensemble singing, though less

aggressive than Flämig's all-male forces. Somary's recording, by the way, is the only recording of this work with added filler: David's lament for Absalom (from *SS I*), powerfully sung by Ostendorf as a curtain-raiser.

With Norrington's somewhat modern-style performance of uncertain availability, and Somary's apparently out of print, the choice for now is inevitably (and reasonably) Flämig, with Kurz as a marginal budget option.

Lukas-Passion. (1666: SWV 479). This is sometimes said to be the first of Schütz's Passion settings in order of composition, thought by some to have begun in the 1650s. St. Luke's Passion account is long and vivid, though without some of the richer details given by St. Matthew, making for slightly less musical variety, though not lacking its own power. It has had a rather limited recording history, entirely of LP dating.

Among LP recordings, the most vital and convincing was by **Jürgens** with his Monteverdi Choir (using a baritone Evangelist and van Egmond as Jesus), a release further notable for pairing the work generously with *Seven Words* (Telefunken). I wish that had been revived on CD, instead of the only survivor, a 1965 recording under **Mauersberger** (Berlin 9207). He has the benefit of Schreier's firmly sung Evangelist, but Adam makes a wobbly and unsteady Jesus; Rotzsch is among the backup cast, with a boy treble taking the one female part. The Dresden Kreuzchor is again the rough ensemble, and Mauersberger's pacing exhibits his usual heavy and foursquare ponderosity. With the absence of any new recordings, this rather unsatisfactory entry has to stand as our only access to the work for now.

Johannes-Passion (1666: SWV 480). St. John's Passion narrative is the most concise of the three set by Schütz, and out of it he made a propulsive and powerful statement. Here the recording picture is quite creditable, if with the important aid of LP carryovers. Once again, the LP pioneer was the hard-working **Grischkat** (Renaissance), with a version of honesty and eloquence. He was eclipsed by the more prestigious stereo version by **Ehmann** (♦Cantate 57602, generously partnered with his parallel recording of *ME*). Ehmann's leadership was ne plus ultra Schütz for its day (1961) but its sweet and heavy qualities seem a bit dated now, and the sound likewise. Still, the cast and chorus are able, and this remains a thoroughly listenable version.

The Ehmann tradition updated is offered in **Flämig**'s 1972 recording (♦Berlin 9009). The Dresden Kreuzchor is in typical fine fettle, providing a boy-treble Handmaid, while Schreier is again the rock-solid Evangelist. The performance is reliable and still valid in its approach. Berlin has filled out the disc with Flämig's 1974–75 recordings of selections from *PD;* there are four of them here, given nicely detailed if somewhat sober renditions, his vocal forces joined by members of Hans Grüss's Capella Fidicinia period-instrument ensemble.

Rupert G. Frieberger's recording was made around 1989 by six singers comprising the Collegium Musicum Pragense (Christophorus). They take all the parts and as an ensemble fulfill all the "choral" duties, for a degree of singing-round-the-cantor's-stand minimalism that goes even beyond Parrott's *Matthäus-Passion*. They're competent but uninspired vocalists, and the pacing of the work is lethargic. As filler, there are eight motets from *CS*, given scrawny performances (one singer per part) with the director at the organ. Especially with no divisional tracks in the *Passion* and with no translation of the text, this isn't much of a contribution. Old Ehmann and less-old Flämig are the best choices for now.

BARKER

Joseph Schwantner (b. 1943)

Schwantner, born in Chicago and now teaching at the Eastman School of Music, is a creator of large orchestral canvases rich with imagery of time and space and the awesome beauty of natural phenomena. While his music isn't usually overtly experimental, his major works of the '80s abound with sudden, pulsating gestures, decaying enharmonics, and microtonal glissandi against a background of fluid or static tonality. The feeling of timelessness and otherworldliness in some works is enhanced by his use of unusual musical instruments, such as a glass harmonica in his Pulitzer Prize–winning *Aftertones of Infinity*. He has made a vital contribution to the American orchestral revival of the last 20 years with a series of wonderfully crafted works creating a unique sound world.

Schwantner's music of the '60s and early '70s followed the then-established American serial avant-garde. Some of his early chamber works, such as *Consortium I* and *IV,* can be heard in a **Boston Musica Viva** disc (Delos 1011, with pieces by Ives, Mario Davidovsky, and Berio), but he was already preparing the ground for his highly acclaimed *Aftertones of Infinity* (1979), a 20-minute tone poem of striking originality. **Slatkin**'s recording with the Juilliard Orchestra is very highly recommended (New World 381, with Druckman's *Chiaroscuro* and Albert's *Into Eclipse).*

One of his most startling pieces is the 1995 Concerto for Percussion and Orchestra, played with quite extraordinary panache by **Evelyn Glennie** and Slatkin with the National Symphony (RCA 68692); the disc includes *Velocities,* a sort of *moto perpetuo* for marimba, and the rather portentous *New Morning for the World* (1982), where a narrator intones parts of speeches by Martin Luther King against a suitable background of orchestral pyrotechnics. The latter is also conducted by **DePreist** with Flagello's *Passion of Martin Luther King* (Koch 7293); both discs are superb, but Slatkin's has a more brilliant sheen.

The ethereal *From Afar,* a fantasy for guitar and orchestra (1987) ravishingly played by **Sharon Isbin,** is one of Schwantner's mystical works (Virgin 55083, with guitar concertos by Foss and Corigliano). Another is *A Play of Shadows* for flute and orchestra (1990), a delicate 15-minute concerto played by **Ransom Wilson** with the exquisitely fragile *Black Anemones* for flute and piano (New World 80403, with works by Robert Beaser and Paul Schoenfield). The tone picture *And the Mountains Rising Nowhere* (1977) for wind orchestra served as a template for *Aftertones* but has its own eerie remoteness and is worth hearing (Klavier 11079, with contemporary works by five others).   JOHNSON

Alexander Scriabin (1872–1915)

Had Scriabin lived longer, he probably would have gained wide recognition as one of the great musical innovators of the 20th century—which he most certainly is—but his music fell out of favor, and only in recent decades has he begun to get his due as a composer. He favored solo piano music and orchestral works; his oeuvre contains virtually no chamber music, certainly none from his maturity. He was a gifted pianist (second only to Rachmaninoff at Moscow Conservatory) and is best recognized for his contributions to the solo literature. His single concerto for the instrument is notable for its restraint and lyricism. He strove for much more, however, and even now his gifts as an orchestrator are under-rated.

He began his compositional career modeling his work primarily on Chopin. As time went on, his harmonic language evolved to such an extent that this model no longer worked for him, and it's no coincidence that he stopped writing mazurkas around the time he began blurring and ultimately abandoning tonal harmony. His music is patently and profoundly sensuous, often explicitly sexual. He was attracted to various philosophical pursuits, especially Nietzsche, and eventually fell under the influence of theosophism. In his last years he had become obsessed with a vast project entitled *Mysterium,* which exists only in extensive sketches and poetic descriptions. (Always an egoist, in this phase he began to see himself as a messianic figure, and *Mysterium* was intended to usher in a new age of enlightenment for mankind.) At the same time, his piano statements from that time show him becoming ever more terse and aphoristic, as in the Op. 74 Preludes. We can only speculate on his ultimate reputation as a composer, but it's clear he was headed on a singularly individual path.

SYMPHONIES

Scriabin's symphonic writing began with a highly expansive conception of the medium, proceeding from the examples of Liszt and Wagner. He wrote three numbered symphonies plus two further works, *Le Poème de l'extase* and *Prométhée, le poème du feu,* sometimes referred to as his fourth and fifth symphonies, though they are single-movement works.

Symphony 1 is in six movements and is formally the weakest, though even here there's much pleasurable writing. Ambitious in scope, it calls for a chorus and two soloists in the last movement, singing a text by the composer in praise of art. Symphony 2 is laid out more traditionally (in four movements with a clear sonata design) and is wholly instrumental. The tunes are memorable, and the work is a good example of the late-romantic symphonic tradition. Symphony 3 ("The Divine Poem") is in three movements and the heady voluptuousness that Scriabin is famous for is found in greater abundance. The outlines of symphonic form are blurred, but still audible. *Poème de l'extase* is a shimmering evocation of sexual delirium that has found a permanent place in the concert repertoire. *Prométhée* is in many ways Scriabin's finest orchestral work, featuring a concerto-like piano solo and wordless chorus.

Complete sets. **Muti** (recorded in Philadelphia) is my first choice (♦EMI 54251, 3CD, NA). The orchestra plays marvelously under his direction, and Muti does superb justice to the innumerable transitions in the music. His particular attention to the molding of phrase endings is one of the most satisfying aspects of this cycle, and his *Poème de l'extase* is one of the best ever. **Segerstam** is close behind in his cycle recorded with the Stockholm Philharmonic, a very underrated set (♦BIS 475, 534, 535). He's completely in tune with the sensuousness of the music and brings out the various shifts of color and mood beautifully. **Ashkenazy** has recorded a set now offered as a "two-fer," full of fine music making, though it lacks *Prométhée*. The Deutsche Symphony Berlin plays very well, and the recording is warm and detailed, though not as atmospheric as the others mentioned so far (Decca 460299, 2CD). The price is right, though Symphony 1 is split between the two discs. **Inbal**'s cycle was highly regarded in its time, and I took great pleasure from it when it was just about the only cycle available on LP. It's back as a "two-fer" (again, without *Prométhée*), but the competition has stiffened considerably in the intervening years. I recommend Ashkenazy over this one.

Golovschin has recorded the symphonies with the Moscow Symphony, but it falls short of those already mentioned (Naxos 553580/82, 550818). The playing is fine, and Golovschin has a good overall grasp of the works, but much of the result feels rather workmanlike. Naxos's rather neutral recording perspective doesn't help; it seems to sacrifice both detail and atmosphere. For Scriabin completists, the set does contain some enticing bon mots: the early *Symphonic Poem,* written around the time of the Piano Concerto, coupled with Symphony 2, and some orchestrations of the Op. 32 *Poèmes,* coupled with 1.

Though they're presently NA, **Svetlanov**'s recordings of the orchestral works have acquired almost mythical status, and they're well worth looking for (Russian Disc 11056-58). Richter is the soloist in a legendary reading of *Prométhée,* and all the performances are celebrated for their blazing intensity.

Poème de l'extase. This is probably Scriabin's most popular orchestral work. I confess to having had a minor obsession with the piece at one time, listening to every version I could get my hands on. While it's sometimes referred to as Scriabin's fourth symphony, its relation to symphonic architecture is tenuous; it's in a single movement, though it does convey a hazy outline of sonata form. More obvious is the intensive motivic development that gathers momentum in a series of climaxes of ever-increasing intensity. The erotic implications of the piece are palpable, and the release in C major at the final burst is truly orgasmic. It's also notable for the demanding trumpet obbligato that runs throughout, one of the most difficult in the orchestral literature.

Järvi's reading with the Chicago Symphony is among the finest, and you can choose between two different couplings (♦Chandos 8849 with a sizzling *Pictures at an Exhibition* or 2405, 2CD, an all-Scriabin set with Symphonies 2 and 3 and *Rêverie*). The great Adolph Herseth's playing of the trumpet solo on this recording is one of the summits of brass performance.

Boulez (whose name doesn't usually leap to mind when we think of noted Scriabin interpreters) has turned in a superb all-Scriabin disc, also with Chicago, and Herseth plays the solo here as well (♦DG 459647). Boulez offers a restrained *Poème,* downplaying its overt eroticism, but the orchestral textures are among the most transparent I've ever heard, and the result has a sensuality of a different kind. I think he misses the point of the work, or chooses to ignore it, but the French connection in Scriabin's music is readily apparent. Also on this disc are a wondrous *Prométhée* and the Piano Concerto; Anatol Ugorski is the soloist in both, and it's my top recommendation among recent recordings.

Mysterium. This is the massive project that obsessed Scriabin in the last years of his life. It was to be a week-long ritual of music and drama that would transform the consciousness of mankind, intended to take place in a specially-built temple in India and to utilize every physical sense in its realization. All that exists are 53 pages of sketches and a 1,000-line poem that Scriabin wrote for it, although he's known to have played large sections for friends. The sketches lay untouched on his desk until 1970, when Alexander Nemtin decided to have a look at them and then spent the next 26 years working on realizing the work that came to be known as *Preparation to the Final Mystery,* really a prequel to the actual *Mysterium.* Nemtin completed the first section ("Universe") in 1972, and it was recorded by **Kondrashin** (♦Russian Compact Disc 16301). This section of the work runs 40 minutes all by itself.

Nemtin then completed two more sections, ("Mankind" and "Transfiguration"), bringing the total time to nearly three hours. This has been recorded by **Ashkenazy** with Deutsche Symphony Berlin and is a major event in classical recordings (♦London 466329, 3CD). I'm not sure how many listeners are able to handle three hours of unrelenting voluptuousness, but for those who can it's quite an experience. The question of how much of this work is Scriabin and how much is Nemtin I will leave to other critics and scholars. In fact Nemtin has absorbed Scriabin's late compositional style to an uncanny degree, and has cleverly borrowed material from his late piano works to expand on the sketches. The result is much more than a pastiche, though it's probably quite different from whatever Scriabin himself might have done, had he lived longer.

The two *Mysterium* recordings have a great deal to offer, and any serious Scriabin fan would probably want them both. The piano soloist in both recordings is **Aleksey Lubimov,** a major interpreter of Scriabin's piano music. Obviously, the Ashkenazy recording offers the complete work, and the Berlin group plays very well indeed. He does well, too, in giving some shape to the sprawling score. The Moscow State Orchestra musicians with Kondrashin play somewhat more colorfully, and Lubimov's piano is more forward on that disc. The remastering is excellent too, with much better sound than in my old LP version. The London recording is more diffuse and atmospheric. That set also offers *Nuances,* a ballet work Nemtin created by orchestrating some of Scriabin's late piano works.

PIANO MUSIC

Sonatas. The ten piano sonatas are the core of Scriabin's entire corpus, and along with the preludes they best illustrate his evolution as a composer. They comprised the first important contributions to the genre by any Russian composer and set the precedent (if not the stylistic models) for the later sonata cycles by Medtner and Prokofiev. Sonatas 1 and 3 are the most traditional—the genuine four-movement article. Sonata 2 is called a "Sonata-fantasy," a title that may hint at the struggles Scriabin had with its structure. These earlier sonatas all owe much to Chopin, though the influence of Liszt appears to grow with each succeeding work. Sonata 4 is the shortest, in two movements, although it's closely related to the one-movement 5, and both are in the key of F-sharp major.

From 6 onward, Scriabin's harmonic language had evolved to the degree that keys are barely hinted at, if they exist at all. These last sonatas are all in a single movement. Sonatas 6 through 10 were written in an incredible blaze of compositional activity from 1911 to 1914, and they show his music becoming ever more complex and abstracted. At this point his rhythms and keyboard writing become so elaborate as to often require three and sometimes four staves. Sonata 7 was his favorite sonata, and he suggested that it was a model for *Mysterium,* while 8 is somewhat subdued and enigmatic; 9 is the famed "Black Mass" sonata, so-called because of its diabolical mood; and 10 is built on an ever-expanding proliferation of trills and tremolos.

Among the complete sets, my top choice is **Hamelin** (♦Hyperion 67131/2, 2CD). His accounts (which include the early *Sonate-Fantaisie*) are by far the most polished and fully realized. His clarity of execution and attention to detail allow him to execute ferociously complex passages more cleanly than I've ever heard them done before; he seems to play literally *everything* in the score. Some have found the set lacking in the intensity that many feel is characteristic of Russian music, but I don't find it so. Nor is Hamelin excessively fussy or mannered; rather, I think he shows us how palpably French Scriabin's music was in many ways.

Ashkenazy has established himself as a major Scriabin interpreter as pianist and conductor. His set is attractive, especially for the price (Philips "Double-Decker" 452981). His grasp of the sonatas is on a par with Hamelin's and is perhaps more "Russian-sounding" for listeners who favor that style. The recordings are from the early '70s, but they sound fine in their remasterings. For those who seek DDD recordings, **Boris Berman** has prepared an excellent set, beautifully recorded, though at full price (♦ Music & Arts 4865, 2CD). His interpretations are comparable to Ashkenazy's, perhaps in part because they both studied with Lev Oborin at Moscow Conservatory.

Another "two-fer" worth considering came from **John Ogdon** (EMI 72652, 2CD). This set came out in the early '70s and was a revelation at the time. Many of the individual performances have since been surpassed by others, but there's much to savor, and Ogdon was in fine form for these sessions; it's one of the glories of his career. Besides the ten sonatas, he plays a hefty selection of shorter works, including *Vers la flamme* and the Op. 74 Preludes; the discs are filled to the brim. Ogdon emphasizes the fleeting gestures and darting play of these works, taking some risks that frequently pay off. It's arranged in chronological order to provide a sense of Scriabin's progress as a composer, and for those on a budget, it's one of the best values around.

Bernd Glemser has begun a sonata cycle that shows considerable promise; Vol. 10 offers Sonatas 2, 5, 6, 7, and 9, plus the *Fantasy in B Minor* (Naxos 553158). I wouldn't recommend it as a first choice, but there's some fine playing to be heard, and it's one of the best discs among all the Scriabin recordings Naxos has done. **Ruth Laredo**'s set was a favorite with listeners for years, but it has been eclipsed by recent recordings (Nonesuch 73035). Her playing has many fine points, though ultimately she lacks the command or the technique of those previously mentioned. When her recordings were originally issued by Connoisseur Society, they were valuable for filling a distinct need in the discography. They were also beautifully recorded, but Nonesuch's remastering hasn't done justice to the warmth of the original LPs.

Etudes. Of the current accounts of the complete Etudes, **Chitose Okashiro**'s is by far the finest available (♦ProPiano 224510). Here is a pianist with an extraordinary technique, a fine musical mind, and more than ample power when needed. Though it's still early in her career, her Scriabin recordings are a major accomplishment. She leaves no detail of the score unattended, highlighting inner voices and shading dynamics beautifully. I find her sense of rubato and pacing to be just right—never overdone, but never pulling back from the big moments either. The recording is exemplary as well, providing an immediate and detailed perspective. **Alexander Paley** also offers a survey of the Etudes that provides some pleasant listening but ultimately falls short (Naxos 553070). His readings never exceed the bounds of good taste, but they don't risk much either. He doesn't probe these works as deeply as Okashiro, and his technique isn't on a par with hers.

The Op. 8 Etude cycle makes up nearly half the etudes Scriabin wrote. **Kuerti** performs this set along with Sonata 6 and Glazunov's Sonata 1, and while his fire-breathing approach may be exciting to some, it's decidedly short on poetry, and the music is rarely allowed to breath (Fleur de Lys 3044). To cite only one example, he whizzes through the No. 9 G-sharp minor Etude in 3:28, whereas both Okashiro and Paley take more than 5 minutes in their accounts. The result is an overdriven, breathless interpretation that utterly ignores any moments of repose. It should also be noted that many of the keys for these etudes are incorrectly listed in the liner notes.

Mazurkas. Scriabin's 23 mazurkas don't display the revolutionary and innovative aspects of his work. Rather, they show how thoroughly he had absorbed the compositional models established by Chopin and his deep grounding in the Romantic piano tradition. Dismissed by some as derivative, they're more than that (and for those listeners who savor Chopin but find late Scriabin too weird, they're just the ticket.) They are brief works, based on a Polish dance in 3/4 with the accent placed on the second beat, and in Scriabin's hands this folk form becomes a vehicle for highly improvisational flights of fancy.

Beatrice Long's complete survey is one of the best available (♦Naxos 553600). Doubly recommended at budget price, she plays with a clean, unfussy musicianship that works beautifully. Her phrasing is elegant

and her interpretations eloquent without ever exceeding the composer's wishes; it's a very satisfying disc. **Marta Deyanova**'s highly regarded recording is also worth looking for, though the reverberance is a problem (♦Nimbus 5446, NA).

Preludes. Scriabin's Preludes proceed from Chopin's example, but they continually developed throughout his career. Though he eventually stopped composing mazurkas, he wrote preludes right up until his death. They show a continuous progression away from tonality, becoming ever more abstract. For a complete survey, I recommend **Paul Komen** (♦Globe 5088, 5098). His playing is intense, sometimes a tad too intense, but most of the time he's faithful to the score and fiercely engaged with every bar of this music. Some of them (such as Op. 11:5) are over-driven, and his rubato can be swooningly excessive, but most of the time his approach works.

I greatly prefer Komen to **Evgeny Zarafiants,** whose set seems flat and underpowered by comparison (Naxos 553997, 554145). He has a nice legato and decent technique but takes a rather square approach to rhythm and uses negligible rubato. He's frequently under tempo, especially in the faster pieces. At budget price his account has some attractions, especially as an alternative view, but not as a first choice.

For a middle path between these two interpretations, **Pletnev** is quite satisfying, though ultimately I prefer Komen. He plays the entire Op. 11 set, plus a handful of mid-career preludes and other short works, plus Sonatas 4 and 10, giving a nuanced reading of these pieces without taking any inordinate license (Virgin 45247). **Marta Deyanova** has recorded a fine account of Op. 11 as well, coupled with Shostakovich's Op. 34 Preludes, which were modeled on Scriabin's cycle and follow the same arrangement of key relations (♦Nimbus 5026). One caveat: This recording is recorded in the highly reverberant acoustic that characterizes many Nimbus recordings. When I first heard it, I had a momentary sensation of being lowered into a cistern, but became accustomed to it after a few moments.

Recitals and collections. In all the Scriabin discs I've listened to throughout this project, **Aleksey Lubimov**'s is one of the most impressive (Russian Compact Disc 16301). His reading of the Op. 74 Preludes is as close to ideal as I think possible; it's perhaps the most remarkable six minutes of Scriabin I've ever heard, and I found myself playing it again and again. On this disc he's also the soloist in the opening movement of *Mysterium* (a piano concerto in all but name) and in a white-hot performance of Prokofiev's Concerto 1. This is essential listening for fans of the Russian piano school.

Horowitz is frequently mentioned as one of the great Scriabin interpreters, and he certainly has a considerable number of partisans, but my own reaction is less than enthusiastic. He was undoubtedly instrumental in making Scriabin's music more popular in the West, but I find few of his recordings as essential as their reputations would imply. His Sonata 3 was highly regarded in its day, and for me it's one of his better Scriabin performances, but I find it loose and disjointed compared to others. His Sonata 5 is downright weird, with jarring, oddly placed accents and voicings that make little sense. Many of his interpretive decisions seem calculated more for dramatic effect than for any inherent musical reason—what Virgil Thomson used to call the "O wow" technique.

Horowitz was at his best in music that suited his own personality, and sometimes Scriabin did, but sometimes he didn't. "Horowitz Plays Scriabin" compiles recordings made over 30 years, including the aforementioned sonatas plus some preludes and etudes (RCA 6215). Sony has collected many of the recordings he made for CBS in "The Complete Masterworks Collection" Vol. IX (Sony 53472, with works by Medtner and Rachmaninoff). Also, Horowitz fans will want to seek out "Alexander Scriabin," which features his accounts of Sonatas 9 and 10, some etudes, and *Vers la flamme* (CBS 42411, NA).

Achatz and **Pöntinen** are combined in one well-filled Scriabin recital that has some highly satisfying moments (BIS 119). Achatz performs a wide variety of shorter pieces plus a heroic reading of Sonata 5, while Pöntinen plays Sonatas 7, 9, and 10. The playing is of a very high caliber, though I wouldn't say that any of the performances are first choices. The recording quality is completely up to BIS's usual standard of excellence, though Achatz is AAD, while Pöntinen's pieces are DDD.

John Bell Young is an American pianist who has established himself as a Scriabinist of international repute. His recital disc features striking readings of Sonatas 5 and 7, plus a number of shorter works (Americus 1013). His reading of 7 is memorable; he plays it significantly more slowly than most, and it works; he obtains a ritual atmosphere entirely in keeping with the sonata's "White Mass" appellation. Sonata 5 is paced beautifully, and Young makes more of its contrasts than do many pianists; the slow passages are particularly ruminative. Throughout this disc you hear a musician who has reflected deeply on this music and has strong and original ideas about how it should be performed. Young's disc also contains some non-Scriabin works, including his own lovely transcription of Mahler's Adagietto from Symphony 5, played with a melting pathos.

Some pianists have chosen to concentrate on the mystical and highly innovative portion of Scriabin's career, from about 1911 to 1914. Australian virtuoso **Roger Woodward** presents "Late Piano Works," a collection that includes the late preludes, Sonatas 6 and 10, and *Vers la flamme,* a five-minute elaboration of a single chord (Etcetera 1126). **Donna Amato** offers a nearly identical collection that includes most of the above, but has Sonatas 8 through 10 (Altarus 9020). Amato is an enthusiastic exponent of this repertoire, and she conveys the atmosphere well, but Woodward outstrips her in most respects. Where Amato's *Vers la flamme* suggests a glowing candelabra, Woodward evokes the incandescence of a plasma furnace. Woodward's playing is cleaner in general, and he makes more sense in the larger gestures too. **Mikhaïl Rudy** also takes this approach in the late solo piano works from Op. 65 to Op. 74 (♦Calliope 9692, NA) and Sonatas 6 and 7 (♦Calliope 9687, NA, with Mussorgsky's *Pictures*). His recordings won numerous awards in their day and still hold their own with just about any around.

Okashiro is a major new talent and one of the best Scriabin interpreters around. Her recording of Léon Conus's two-piano version of *Poème de l'extase* is absolutely stunning. She made some adaptations to Conus's score to expand its range of power and nuance and plays both parts herself by overdubbing; the result is an extraordinary work of transcription (♦Pro Piano 224519). She takes the work slower than most orchestral versions, but the performance is mesmerizing nonetheless; the long lines are beautifully spun out, and her pacing of the material is wonderfully judged—there's never a slack moment. The disc is completed with other mature Scriabin, mostly shorter works like the Op. 74 Preludes and an excellent *Vers la flamme.* Highly recommended.

Richter is one of the century's finest Scriabin interpreters. That said, you need to be somewhat cautious about which discs to choose. His playing could be quite uneven, and in his last years he chose to make only live recordings, often in rather backwater locations. Many of the pianos he played weren't in top condition and often were alarmingly out of tune. Still, Richter performing on an out-of-tune piano somewhere in

Bulgaria could offer rewards that rendered those issues superfluous. One of his best Scriabin recitals was recorded in Warsaw in 1972 (♦Music & Arts 878). This disc shows him in excellent form, playing Sonatas 2, 5, and 9 plus Preludes from Op. 11, 37, and 74, some etudes, and other short works. A 1992 recital recording couples four Chopin Polonaises with Scriabin's B minor *Fantaisie, Poème Nocturne, Deux Danses,* and *Vers la flamme* (♦Live Classics 441). This *Vers la flamme* is one of the slowest on record, but his shaping of its growth is truly organic, and the sense of arrival in the final bars is magical. Another notable disc to look for is his solo turn in *Prométhée* with Svetlanov (Russian Disc 11058, NA, with Symphony 3).

Many of the best interpreters of Scriabin were musicians of his own time, some of whom knew him personally. The most notable was **Sofronitsky,** one of the great Russian pianists and a superb Scriabin interpreter. His readings of the sonatas are magnificent and should be studied by anyone seeking insight into this material. Reissues come and go, but the collection of Sonatas 3 through 5 and 8 through 10 is well worth hunting for (Chant du Monde 278764, 2CD, NA). The remastering is a bit harsh, but the playing is of the highest caliber. His artistry can also be heard in 1948 recordings of Op. 8 Etudes (selections), plus the B minor *Fantaisie* and the Op. 32 Poèmes (♦Piano Library 282). This disc also offers a selection of Chopin's mazurkas and waltzes, and the remastering is quite good.

Neuhaus is another pianist whose contribution to our understanding of Scriabin's music is immense. He was a pupil of Godowsky and possessed an unusually delicate touch. He was also a great pedagogue (Richter, Gilels, and Lubimov were just a few of his more notable pupils), and his own recorded legacy is quite substantial. Much of it is NA, but a superb sampling of his Scriabin is available. It offers a selection of Preludes, the B minor *Fantaisie,* and a limpid and poetic reading of the Piano Concerto (♦Russian Compact Disc 16247). The recordings are all from the late '40s and early '50s, but the sound is quite good. The 1946 reading of the Piano Concerto is surprisingly warm and detailed.

"Scriabin and the Scriabinians" is another collection worth seeking out; it features Scriabin himself, plus examples by Sofronitsky, Neuhaus, and others. The recording quality is variable (Scriabin is extremely murky), but it's an important document nonetheless (Chant du Monde 288032, NA).   McINTIRE

Peter Sculthorpe (b. 1929)

Sculthorpe was the first Australian composer to establish a music that was consciously Australian in its material and affect. He seeks to convey his sense of the country's history, its landscape, and the harsh, incessantly blazing sun. He's that country's most renowned composer, but his slim discography in the United States and Europe doesn't reflect his true importance. His music is highly original and disarmingly direct—what he calls "music of straightforward line and structure"—tending toward leanness and transparency and often rather short in duration. He often uses aboriginal material in his writing and tends to favor stringed instruments, piano, and percussion. His melodies are spare and simple, with an emphasis on repetition and variation of timbre rather than tonal development. He frequently rearranges his works for various forces; many of his works exist in more than one realization.

While he hasn't composed any symphonies, he has written a considerable body of orchestral music. "Chamber Music from Australia" presents four selections of Sculthorpe's works for string orchestra, and I think many listeners will be attracted to their lyrical melancholy and lean, lovely melodies; both are found here in abundance (♦Southern

Cross 1016, NA). *Lament for Strings* and *Irkanda IV* both convey a distinct sense of isolation. *Port Essington* and *Sonata for Strings* (an arrangement of String Quartet 10) are more varied in tempo, mood, and texture, but also consistently pensive.

Sculthorpe admits that his Piano Concerto is "more European" than most of his works, but it's still a far cry from what most listeners would expect from this genre (♦Tall Poppies 113, with concertos by David Lumsdaine and Carl Vine). It's more expansive than many of his pieces but not especially extravagant in gesture; essentially ruminative for most of its 25 minutes, it has some powerful moments nonetheless. I find its conclusion one of the most finely judged and satisfying endings I've ever heard. **Ian Munro** handles the solo part beautifully, with Diego Masson conducting the Australia Youth Orchestra.

Sculthorpe has used the medium of the string quartet often throughout his career. The first four are lost or exist only in fragments. I find the mature quartets to be the most substantial and satisfying, though the others are certainly enjoyable. No. 8 is probably the best known, having been recorded several times, especially in the **Kronos Quartet**'s best-selling disc (♦Nonesuch 79111). For those who want to hear more of the quartets, the excellent **Goldner Quartet** has undertaken a more comprehensive survey, and the results are well worth seeking. "String Quartets" Vol. 1 offers a quartet version of *Irkanda IV, Small Town* (a charming, melodic, and somewhat atypical vignette), and 6 through 9 (♦Tall Poppies 089). Vol. 2 offers material both earlier and later: 10 and 11, plus some juvenilia and quartet arrangements of other works (♦Tall Poppies 090).

Sculthorpe has written a considerable amount for piano, and "Piano Music" shows this facet of his music, much of it played by the composer himself (♦Move 3031, NA). This included all his piano works as of 1990; they are mostly very short, primarily brief mood pieces or children's music.   McINTIRE

Roger Sessions *(1896–1985)*

A distinguished teacher (based at Princeton), Sessions is best known for his orchestral works, including nine symphonies, many in a dense but compelling contrapuntal style that during the '50s naturally gravitated toward the 12-tone method. Although his music baffled audiences at the time, it's increasingly being heard on disc.

SYMPHONIES AND OTHER ORCHESTRAL MUSIC

All nine symphonies have been recorded, though the last four are NA. Symphony 1 is written in an exuberant tonal language with a nod or two to Stravinsky and Hindemith; on a disc that contains 1 through 3, **Akeo Watanabe** catches its youthful vigor nicely (♦New World 573). Sessions's decisive step toward atonality, 2 has never been performed more compellingly than in **Mitropoulos**'s 1949 account, despite indifferent sound. Symphony 3 was the first unequivocally to embrace dodecaphony, and does so in shimmering orchestration that's quite beguiling in **Igor Buketoff**'s pioneering recording (CRI).

Symphony 4 opens with that rare beast, a cheerful 12-tone movement. The most immediately appealing of his serial symphonies, it's available with 5, whose three movements play continuously and in which orchestral fantasy and structural cohesion are in perfect balance. The accounts by **Christian Badea** could scarcely be bettered, making this the finest Sessions disc available (♦ New World 345). Unfortunately, **Dennis Russell Davies**'s meticulous accounts of 6, 7, and 9 are now NA (Argo 44519); **Frederick Prausnitz**'s 8 has never been released on CD (Argo, NA).

The *Black Maskers* suite originated in incidental music to Andreyev's play. Betraying the influence of Sessions's teacher, Ernest Bloch, it has remained one of his most often-heard scores. **Hanson** set down a fine account (Mercury 34310), but **Zukofsky** has a better understanding of the music's darker side (♦New World 368).

Concerto for Orchestra was Sessions's last major orchestral score, composed for the Boston Symphony's centenary in 1981. **Ozawa** directs somewhat clinically and without much understanding, but the music's quality shines through (Hyperion 0). *Rhapsody* is richly scored, dynamic and varied in mood; it receives a near-perfect performance from **Christian Badea** (♦New World 345).

CONCERTOS

The Piano Concerto is one of Sessions's earliest pure 12-tone works and, like Symphony 3, is a kaleidoscope of mood and color. **Taub** rises to its virtuosic challenges in a finely wrought interpretation (New World 80443). The Violin Concerto is a relatively early piece from the '30s that is ferociously difficult to play. Its language is tonal, but less happily than in Symphony 1. **Zukofsky**'s account is most persuasive (CRI 676).

CHAMBER MUSIC

Quartet 1 dates from 1936, just after the Violin Concerto. It has been recorded very acutely by the **Group for Contemporary Music,** along with *Canons in memoriam Stravinsky*, six Pieces for solo cello, and String Quintet, one of Sessions's most important chamber scores (Koch 7616). The transitional and atonal Quartet 2 has been recorded by the **Juilliard Quartet** alongside works by Babbitt and Wolpe (CRI 587).

PIANO MUSIC

Sessions's three piano sonatas give a good cross section of his career, from the often playful, neoclassical language of 1 to the tonal ambiguity of 2 and the classical 12-tone manner of 3. **Robert Helps,** who knew the composer well, is highly polished (CRI 800). In 1984 **Helps**—not Randall Hodgkinson, as listed in *Schwann*—took a slightly more measured view of 3, coupled with **Hodgkinson**'s brilliant account of 2 (♦New World 80546). **Christopher O'Riley**'s performance of 1 is also effective (Albany).

From My Diary is a seminal set of piano miniatures from the late '30s, the turning point in Sessions's movement away from tonality. **Helps** has the measure of this very diverse set (CRI 800), and so does **Roger Shields** in his 3CD survey of American piano music (Vox 3027).

VOCAL MUSIC

When lilacs last in the dooryard bloom'd, Sessions' elegiac Whitman cantata, presents a prospect very different from Hindemith's more famous piece. **Ozawa** directs with care and secures an eloquent and surprisingly moving performance (♦New World 296).   RICKARDS

Rodion Shchedrin *(b. 1932)*

The composer who comes to my mind in describing Shchedrin is Morton Gould. Both are virtuoso composers, able to translate moods and emotions into sound in a direct way that lets an orchestra play at its best. Both are less successful when they try to express deep emotions. Shchedrin tends to resort to bombast and sarcasm when confronted with unpleasant emotions, occasionally resulting in bad taste (i.e., his *Stalin Cocktail*). His early works make use of a Russian folk style called *chashtushki*, a form of limerick, used to great effect in his Concerto for Orchestra 1, *Naughty Limericks*, and the ballet *The Humpbacked Horse*, based on a fairy tale. During the '60s and '70s he experimented with modernistic techniques and large collections of pieces (Symphony 2 consists of 24 preludes for orchestra). More recently, he has become more retrospective and more calmly concentrated on concertos.

SYMPHONIES

Symphony 1 is a half-hour work in three movements, a serious, exciting piece typical of Soviet symphonies of the post-Stalin era but more cleanly and effectively expressed than most. There was a recording by **Nikolai Anosov** and the Moscow Philharmonic (MK LP 9185/6a, NA).

Symphony 2 (25 Preludes for Orchestra) is dissonant, experimental in technique, and impressive in its vehemence. Fifty-two minutes long, it's on the order of Shostakovich's 4; not easy listening, but it repays study. **Rozhdestvensky** made a fine recording with the USSR Radio Orchestra, played with almost desperate intensity (Melodiya 90). More recently, **Sinaisky** recorded it with the BBC Philharmonic, taking three minutes longer and without the Russian sound but impressively recorded (Chandos 9552).

BALLETS

Shchedrin's wife is the dancer Maya Plisetskaya, and he has written a number of ballet scores; the most important are discussed here.

Anna Karenina (1972). This is based on Tchaikovsky but treats his music much more freely than Shchedrin's *Carmen* did Bizet. The mood of this hour-and-a-half ballet is surreal and disturbing. The Tchaikovsky quotes contribute to the weird atmosphere, totally unlike the fairy-tale clarity of Stravinsky's *Baiser de la Fée*. It's beautifully performed by **Yuri Simonov** and the Bolshoi Orchestra (Russian Disc 10030, 2CD), though the recorded quality is not as good as on my excellent LP set (EMI 4126). A 25-minute suite is conducted by **Svetlanov**, along with Rozhdestvensky's performance of *Carmen* (Melodiya 36908).

Carmen Ballet (1968). By far Shchedrin's most often-recorded work, perhaps somewhat to the composer's annoyance, this is basically a rescoring of Bizet's music for string orchestra and 47 percussion instruments. There are many original touches; I particularly like the accompaniment to the "Toreador Song" without its melody but with the obbligato from Act IV hovering in loneliness over it, and the slow music is intense throughout, particularly as played by the Russians. The work was written with the traditionally strong, vibrant Russian string sound in mind, and the original recording by **Rozhdestvensky** and the Bolshoi is still a winner (♦Melodiya 36908).

Schwarz didn't match them in Los Angeles (EMI); the Helsingborg Symphony with the Kroumata Percussion Ensemble under **Harold Farberman** beat them in recorded sound, but not in performance (BIS 382). The Young Russia Symphony under **Mark Gorenstein** didn't even come close (Pope). The Ukrainian State Symphony with **Kuchar** did a highly creditable job, coupled with more Shchedrin (Naxos 553038), and **DePreist** with the Monte Carlo Philharmonic made an outstanding recording, lacking only the last ounce of wit and immediacy (Delos 3208). The **Ethos Percussion Ensemble** does a fine job, but the Philadelphia Virtuosi are too small a band to match them (Connoisseur Society 4213). **Fiedler** and the Boston Pops are good, though a bit staid (RCA 63308).

The Humpbacked Horse (1955). This is a fairy tale somewhat reminiscent of the folk entertainment provided by Prokofiev in *The Stone Flower,* but geared more toward children, judging by the 1961 film made by the Bolshoi starring Plisetskaya (Corinth 1204). The presentation and photography seem geared for children, with a narrator and numerous close-ups and visual tricks, and the recorded sound is miserable mono, but it isn't every day you can see this company, and the dancing

is fun. A 45-minute suite was recorded by **Zuriatis** (Angel LP 40106). The complete ballet is recorded by **Georgi Zhemchuzin,** with the attractive *Chamber Suite* for massed violins and folk instruments (Olympia 219, 2CD).

The Seagull (1980). A full-length ballet on Chekhov's play, this represented a further stage in Shchedrin's development. As in *Anna Karenina,* the action is mostly within the minds of the characters; outside activity is suggested by a percussion group recalling the sounds of early Shostakovich, though the mood is much milder and less circusy. Curiously, the composer divides the score into 24 preludes, as in Symphony 2. Like *Anna,* this is a harrowing piece to listen to, particularly in the sound on Russian Disc 10050, emphasizing the high frequencies. The basic sound is there, it just needs to be adjusted at your console. Otherwise, it's a fine 1982 recording by **Alexander Lazarev** and the Bolshoi Theater Orchestra.

OTHER ORCHESTRAL MUSIC

Concerto for Orchestra 1 ("Naughty Limericks"). Shchedrin's early apotheosis of the *chashtushka* is one of his most original works. This under-10-minute romp is a takeoff on everything from Chabrier's *España* to a number of Russian popular tunes we won't recognize, set as a kind of racing piece that probably influenced John Adams when he came to writing his zany minimalist Fanfares. There was a marvelous recording by **Kondrashin** that may turn up again in the next round of Russian imports (Angel 40011). Till then, **Kuchar** does a fine job with the Ukrainian State Symphony (Naxos 553038).

Concerto for Orchestra 2 ("Chimes"). This and "Naughty Limericks" are both conducted by **Svetlanov,** along with *Solemn Overture* and a suite from the opera *Not Love Alone,* in excellent readings (Melodiya 91).

Concerto for Orchestra 3 ("Old Russian Circus Music"). This concerto is longer than the others but is still a single-movement work, relatively light, performed by **Sinaisky** (Chandos 9552, with Symphony 2). Another Chandos release gives us an amusing *Humoresque* and *In Imitation of Albeniz,* little miniatures also heard as violin pieces elsewhere (9288). This disc also contains *Carmen* and *Stalin Cocktail* (as in Molotov cocktail), a curious send-up of the dictator.

CONCERTOS

Piano. Concerto 1 is Shchedrin's graduation piece of 1954, his earliest recorded work. It's a catchy and amusing piece blending popular and classical elements in a somewhat early-Prokofiev manner. Concerto 2 (1966) ranges farther afield into dissonance and jazz elements, while 3 (1972) is made up of dissonant variations on a dissonant theme that's heard only at the end. **Shchedrin** played all three at a 1974 performance; he's a fine pianist, and these readings are authoritative (Melodiya 36907). The same performances, substituting **Nikolai Petrov** for 2, are in Russian Disc 11129. The Melodiya disc sounds less harsh and brittle, though the originals are rather dry to begin with, albeit clean and with very little audience disturbance.

Cello. Sotto voce (1994) is a 40-minute concerto for cello, autobiographical in nature. It was written for **Rostropovich,** who recorded it with Ozawa and the London Symphony (Teldec 94570). It makes a strong impression.

Violin. Concerto cantabile (1998) is a 28-minute work in Shchedrin's more lyrical recent style, though with an exciting scherzo in the middle. **Vengerov,** with Rostropovich and the London Symphony, makes an excellent case for it (EMI 56966).

PIANO MUSIC

The piano music consists of mainly two cycles, 24 Preludes and Fugues (1963–70) and a *Polyphonic Book* of 25 preludes, most of them with didactic titles (1973). **Shchedrin** recorded both sets in his inimitably energetic style (Melodiya 36906, 2CD). This pretty much replaces **McLachlan**'s identical program (Olympia 438, 2CD), which was warmer but less intense, mixing the two books together for variety, a messy idea (the composer unifies them). **Alexander Malkus** recorded the *Polyphonic Book* (Arts & Electronics 10210) in a lyrical way that took some of the curse off this mostly abstract and dissonant music, though the composer is still the authority. **Anna Ouspenskaya** isn't as characterful as the others, and individual entry points on the disc are omitted, making it frustrating for the listener who wants to hear a particular piece (Altarus 9006). Shchedrin made an earlier recording of his Piano Sonata and a number of small works and transcriptions, as well as Piano Concerto 1 (Melodiya 259).

VOCAL MUSIC

The Sealed Angel (1988). This is an hour-long, mostly a cappella choral work in the general style of Russian pre-Soviet liturgical music, though there are many stylistic updatings that would shock traditionalists. The words are based on a story by Nikolai Leskov, so the text is not traditional, and the only instrumental accompaniment is a very occasional flute. **Vladimir Minin** conducts the Russian Choir; the effect is strong, but no texts are included (Melodiya 36905). **Lorna Cooke de Varon,** with singers from the New England Conservatory and the Longy Chamber Singers, goes to the other extreme, including readings from the story between sections of music (Sonora 22582). As you might expect, a work so clearly from the Russian tradition sounds odd transported to America, and there are technical mishaps and offstage noises that tend to relegate this disc to the realm of an interesting but unsuccessful experiment.

Dead Souls (1977). This is an opera full of avant-garde effects and populist songs, mixed in a way that may make more sense to Russians than it does to us. At any rate, it's an exciting and colorful work on the order of Shostakovich's *The Nose;* though less subtle, it's equally colorful and zany as performed by the Bolshoi Theater under **Temirkanov** (Melodiya 29347, 2CD). MOORE

Dmitri Shostakovich *(1906–1975)*

In a totally bogus yet undeniably thought-provoking scene from Tony Palmer's film on Shostakovich's life, *Testimony,* the dying composer (played brilliantly by Ben Kingsley) hallucinates on his deathbed that his nemesis Stalin walks into the room and says something to the effect of, "I made you into a great composer." Well, it's possible that the dictator unknowingly did just that. Would Shostakovich have turned out the anguished masterpieces of his maturity had there been no Stalinist terror campaigns, no secret police, no persecution of his friends and colleagues, no denunciations of his work by *Pravda* and the Composers' Union? No one would conscionably condone the idiocies that produced such suffering, yet they provoked from Shostakovich a response that serves as a soundtrack for the dark side of the 20th century.

At the same time, there are many other facets of Shostakovich. He had a riotously funny light side that produced some of the most uproarious examples of musical humor ever heard—before it turned dark with sarcasm. In his youth, he could embrace the wacky avant-garde as fervently as any child of the 20s, leaving us to wonder how he would have developed if political constraints had not been imposed on him. He was

a classicist who revered Bach and Mahler and kept the symphonic and string quartet genres very much alive to the three-quarter-century mark. He did what he had to in order to survive—hence his large output of film scores of variable quality—but his public in Russia (if not necessarily in the gullible West) knew where he stood.

Veteran Russian conductors like Mravinsky, Kondrashin, Rozhdestvensky and Svetlanov seemed to know all along that Shostakovich was no Soviet stooge; their recordings, most of them made before *Testimony* came out, seethe and bite. Even with the advantage of hindsight, many Western conductors simply don't get it as they smooth away the edges and slow down the tempos in the vain pursuit of "profundity"; a few got it right away—Bernstein, Ormandy—and others like Haitink gradually warmed to the idiom. Unfortunately, Shostakovich recordings tend to go out of print quickly, so the older Russians—with the major exception of Mravinsky—aren't as well represented as they once were.

Finally, if you want to get a bead on the real Shostakovich, read *Testimony,* the bitter, corrosively funny—and, I think, genuine—set of memoirs smuggled out of Russia and edited by the unfairly maligned Solomon Volkov. The musical establishment bore down hard on Volkov over the authenticity of these memoirs—to this day, he can't get a position at a major American university—but *Testimony*'s text rings true. It reads the way Shostakovich's music sounds, with all the galloping rhythms and sarcasm and compassion and veneration for Russian tradition. If you listen as you read, you can't miss the point.

SYMPHONIES

Complete sets. It's startling to realize that nearly a half-century of Shostakovich's life's work—often composed at the risk of his life—now fits into a space smaller than a greeting card box. For such a diverse, sprawling series of 15 compositions, buying a single box may be convenient, even cost-effective, but they each have mixed strengths and flaws.

Though **Rostropovich**'s cycle came about because he promised Shostakovich he'd do it, it can't be considered a composer-sanctioned set; the conductor is much too idiosyncratic and unpredictable for that. He follows the emotional Russian school of Shostakovich conducting, highlighting the sarcasm, pain, and humor. In some he ranks with the best. Symphony 1 has impudent dash and fire; 4 is extraordinary; and he makes a coherent, compelling case for the misbegotten 12. His 5 is also superb, the daringly slow tempo in IV and all, and so are the racy last two movements of 6. His 14, the same 1973 Moscow performance that has been knocking around on a number of labels, has an unmatched combination of wild raw fury and tears; no wonder he figured he couldn't top it.

But Rostropovich can seem strangely uninvolved (7 and 8), or mar a fascinating performance with a strange decision (the terribly slow massacre tempo in 11), or treat 2 as if it were a casual satire when it ought to be played flat out. Somewhere in the middle are a broad but dramatically effective 10, a sufficiently rousing 13, and a surprisingly subdued 15. Recorded mostly from 1988 to 1995 in Washington and London, some of the best performances are only available in the box, and given Rostropovich's personal ties with the composer, plus the midpriced tag and mostly excellent sound, it's worth having (♦Teldec 17046, 12CD).

Rozhdestvensky's electric, provocative cycle from the '80s is at last available in the West in one big box (♦BMG/Melodiya 72915, 14CD). Like Rostropovich, he comes from the generation of Russian conductors after the pioneers. He not only is committed to emotional extremes (if not universally fast tempos), but he goes further out on a limb into grotesquery and truly black humor as well. These recordings have been attacked for the harsh, close-miked Soviet engineering and the less-than-perfect execution by the U.S.S.R. Ministry of Culture Symphony, but I see these alleged defects as assets. The Soviet players may huff and puff, but they're grappling audibly and fervently with this music, and the sonic spotlighting—which may or may not be Rozhdestvensky's doing—brings out all kinds of strange details that heighten the conductor's sardonic viewpoint.

Symphony 1 is full of grotesque pinpointing and energy, as is the march in 7; the latter's coda brings out snarling brass dissonances that leave no doubt of Shostakovich's sarcastic intent. Symphony 5 opens mysteriously and continues with lean textures at standard speeds, punctuated by raucous brass; in 9, Rozhdestvensky hosts a fun house of mocking winds and razzing brasses. Rarely have the crunches in 8 sounded so mean and cataclysmic, with a dynamic range as wide as a battlefield. Symphony 3 has a majestic brutality and imaginative malevolence; 10 is strong and coherent despite the two-faced extremes of jauntiness and malice; 15 is full of either mischief and mockery or stark, blaring fear. The slow tempos and pinpointed details render 2 ineffective, and 14 is surprisingly restrained, especially the singers, but there aren't many misfires. You also receive a bunch of fascinating, little-known manuscripts that Rozhdestvensky unearthed and reconstructed, many of which explore Shostakovich's wacky experiments in the '20s and '30s before the crackdown, plus several song cycles and other fragments. These performances may be the last of their kind, a Russian team with its own wild, no-holds-barred Shostakovich sound.

Haitink's cycle straddles the analog and digital ages and a large gap of perception. The early analog entries (4, 10, 15) are uninteresting because the mild-mannered conductor simply lays out the architecture straight-forwardly without digging any further (although 10 has passages of fierceness). But starting in 1979 with a deeply felt, exciting 7, Haitink began to penetrate Shostakovich's emotional world. From this point onward, he has a lot to say, and Decca's engineering in London and in the Concertgebouw is spectacular, to date the best sound these symphonies have received. Symphonies 2, 3, and 12 are actually strengthened by the conductor's cool head and organizing skills, but he can loosen his tie and produce exciting playing in 2's central weirdness and even find dignity and grace in 12's awful finale. In 8 he builds toward well thought-out yet passionate climaxes without quite going over the top, and just captures the antic spirit of 9, though the coda lacks sufficient ignition.

There are relapses into indifference—the soft-grained attacks in 1, an unexciting 5. There's also a problem in 14; while Haitink's conducting is superb, with much drive and insight, Fischer-Dieskau and Varady sing the poems in the composer-sanctioned original languages, which feels wrong to me. In general, though, the further Haitink goes into the cycle, the better he gets. He feels the pain of 6's largo but keeps it moving, gets the flippancy right in II, and though a little cautious, is vigorous enough in III. Symphony 11 is the best in the set—loaded with orchestral weight; uninhibited fury; driving, thrusting rhythms, and a full sense of horror—and he led a massively fervent, technicolor 13. Though the whole cycle is available in a minibox (London 444430, 11 CD), it's better to pick among the reasonably priced Decca Ovation single discs that have been widely imported here.

The all-purpose, price-busting Naxos catalog has two considerably chunkier boxes of Shostakovich symphonies led by **Ladislav Slovák,** who was a protégé of Mravinsky and knew the composer (Naxos 505017, 5CD, and 506003, 6CD, also available in single discs). Alas, the quality of the performances varies wildly, as does the sound. Most of the time, Slovák applies a poised, almost classical sense of proportion, most effectively in 1, 3 and 7. His tempos are usually on the slow, cautious side; he can't see the humor in 9, his Czecho-Slovak Radio Symphony sometimes plays coarsely (6, 8, 12), and most often, he simply lacks intensity, which in many cases is the whole ball game in Shostakovich.

Yet in the last three symphonies, Slovák reaches down deeply and finds that missing depth; indeed, his 14 is one of the best at any price. In 13 and 14, he has a magnificent bass (Peter Mikuláš) richly versed in malevolence and satire, and 14 pairs Mikuláš with an electrifyingly expressive soprano, Magdaléna Hajóssyová. He concentrates on 15's lyrical bent while still managing to conjure up a thoughtful trance in the finale. As with Haitink's, a later recording date often means a deeper, more satisfying rendition.

1. The 19-year-old Shostakovich first shook the world with this brash symphony, which has its awkward moments but displays most of the composer's personality from beginning to end. **Bernstein** really catches its zesty, smart-alecky tone in his 1971 recording, although he leans on III a bit heavily and the New York Philharmonic doesn't always execute neatly (♦Sony 47614). When he got hold of the Chicago Symphony in 1988, the heavyset quality of III in New York sprawled over the whole piece, but they play fantastically well for him, and the sound is glorious (♦DG 427632, 2CD).

Ormandy is the great sleeper among Shostakovich conductors; just listen to his marvelous 1, full of telling details, not as youthful-sounding as Bernstein/New York but with plenty of dash, understanding, and outstanding Philadelphia playing (♦Sony 62642). In a fair-sounding early-stereo session with the Symphony of the Air, **Stokowski** stamps his personality all over the piece; the first two movements are surprisingly slow; the last two are dominated by brooding sonorities more suited for later Shostakovich (EMI). **Lawrence Leighton Smith** recorded a straightforward, not too eventful rendition, with the bite of Moscow brass crisply captured by the engineers (Sheffield Lab). **Temirkanov** and a subpar St. Petersburg Philharmonic are very fast and militant, laying bare its unpredictable twists (RCA), and **Neeme Järvi** simply lacks intensity (Chandos). I've always had a fondness for **Martinon,** which has poise and mischief (♦Classic 2322).

2 ("To October"). Revived only in the '60s, this is an astonishingly advanced work for a 21-year-old, with an opening of fantastic spacey clusters, a wildly exuberant eruption in the center, and a choral finale with a spoken ode to Lenin at the close. In those pre-Stalin years, Shostakovich was probably absolutely sincere, leaving today's conductors with a dilemma; do you take the agitprop stuff at face value or undercut it? **Morton Gould,** who made the world premiere recording that BMG ought to reissue pronto, had the best solution: let 'er rip (♦RCA 3044, NA). His opening is marvelously spooky and nebulous; the central section goes deliriously wild; and the Royal Philharmonic Chorus conveys not political ecstasy but the fervor of discovery of a marvelous piece of music. No one has done as well since.

3 ("The First of May"). This is similar to 2 in period (the '20s), structure (instrumental turmoil with a choral resolution), and theme (glorification of the Revolution). But the resemblance ends there, for 3 is 50 percent longer, less abrasive in language, more prophetic of future works, and far more discursive (and weaker) than 2. Again, **Gould** struck the right balance of transparent textures, drive, edge, and the thrill of discovery (♦RCA 3044, NA).

4. This didn't come to light until the '60s—a frightened Shostakovich withdrew it in rehearsal after the Soviet denunciations of *Lady Macbeth*—and it didn't catch on until recently. But now that it has, we can perhaps thank the Mahler revival, for this work is stamped with Mahler's expansive embrace of a huge sound world, even quoting a few of his themes. It stands alone in Shostakovich's symphonic output, an hour-long laboratory of wild ideas in a buckling structure.

Ormandy gave the American premiere, and he got it right away with a stark, powerful, splendidly played performance in good 1963 sound that spares no pain or barbed humor (♦Sony 62409, 2CD). **Rozhdestvensky** takes its experiments even further in an explosively biting performance (♦Melodiya 63462, 2CD). He lays into its dissonances and *fugato* madness more boldly than anyone, he turns II into an ironic grotesquery; and his coda—one of Shostakovich's greatest threnodies—is ink-black in tone, totally desolate. Either of these will pound home what this work is about.

Treated to spectacular sound, **Rattle**'s disc starts out grandly, working up to a ferocious climax; for two movements, it sounds like a classic rendition, but then he loses his focus in III, all emotion spent by the time we get to the mighty perforation (♦EMI 55476). **Previn**'s opening may be heavyset, but it feels right and leads to a well thought-out conception, with plenty of dry wit, inexorable climaxes, and superbly hefty playing by the Chicago Symphony (♦EMI 72658, 2CD). **Järvi**'s honest, sober reading comes in highly praised resonant sound, but I find the sonics a bit diffuse in detail in the wild stretches, and his orchestra isn't world class (Chandos).

5. No Shostakovich work was put through such a fundamental change of intent by the publication of *Testimony* as this, his most popular symphony. For decades, the Finale was interpreted as a triumphant apotheosis, but the composer said it was like being beaten with a stick and being forced to repeat "Our business is rejoicing." His disciple **Rostropovich** says it's like being "stretched on the rack," and his first recording leaves no doubt as to the way an excruciatingly slow tempo in the coda can turn those dissonances into agonizing torture (DG 445577). **Kondrashin** achieves the same effect at the end, and the rest of his performance is fast and lacerating (Melodiya 19845). So does **Rozhdestvensky,** who opens mysteriously and continues with lean textures at standard speeds, punctuated by raucous brass (Melodiya 49611, 2CD).

Which is not to say that the old way is no longer effective, for **Bernstein**'s tempo-fluctuating, thrusting, justly famous 1959 performance—which received the composer's approval—still grabs the emotions from the first and doesn't let go right through to the uninhibitedly energetic final bars (♦Sony 47615). He remade it in Tokyo 20 years later, again with the New York Philharmonic, broader and not quite as ecstatic this time, but there's enough left to rank it among the more powerful versions (♦CBS 44903). One of my favorites is the electrifying **Skrowaczewski** performance, loaded with high-strung tension, with a grip like a vise (♦Mercury 434323). **Previn**'s London Symphony recording is full of the fire of his early conducting days, beginning slowly, intensely building steam to a starkly powerful climax (♦RCA 68456). The scherzo has satirical bite, the largo is thoughtful, the coda triumphant. Alas, the edge he had in 1966 was gone by the time he remade it in Chicago a dozen years later (EMI 72658, 2CD).

The legacy of **Mravinsky** becomes important at this point, for he gave the premiere of 5 (as well as 6, 8, 9, 10, and 12). A live taping from near the end of his life (1984) reveals many highly charged passages, a

perfectly gauged II, some roughneck brass and strings (his absolute control over the Leningrad Philharmonic had frayed a bit), and a tortured understanding of the coda (♦Erato 45752). **Stokowski** was another early advocate of this symphony, and he heard it in heroic technicolor terms with a fast, triumphant close. There are a lot of Stokowski 5s floating around; the easiest to find is his mostly literal 1958 recording, where he places his main imprint on a lush-sounding Largo (Everest 9030). **Ormandy** is as reliable as the sunrise, a little slow and perhaps not as electric as in other symphonies, but beautifully played, especially the Largo (Sony 53261).

Levi goes the direct route in a satisfying way, with some bite in I, soulful playing in III, and terrific sound (♦Telarc 80215). The same can be said for one of **Järvi**'s best Shostakovich recordings, with warmth and sweep and a slow, beaten-down coda (♦Chandos 8650). **Jansons**'s lightweight 1987 Oslo rendition zips through the symphony in about 41 minutes (EMI 49181, NA); his Vienna remake a decade later is much broader, with more orchestral weight and thrust in the rhythms (EMI 56442). **Maazel** has the advantage of the Cleveland Orchestra and deep, rich sound, but the performance is uneven: a ponderous I, a sharp II, a not very gripping III, and a hot-and-cold Finale (Telarc). **Inbal** has the right idea, pacing himself well, but there's little fire in the Frankfurters' playing (Denon). **Temirkanov** is surprisingly routine for an heir of Mravinsky, trundling along at mostly brisk speeds; the coda is slow, but there's little emotion driving it (RCA).

6. Here we have one of Shostakovich's more schizophrenic works: a long, mournful opening followed by a flippant dance and a bawdy, galloping circus of a Finale. Such a piece invites conductors who like extremes, and no one had it both ways quite like **Bernstein,** whose recording is in turn anguished, hushed, light as a feather, brash, and tremendously uplifting (♦Sony 47614). With a thin-sounding orchestra, **Järvi** somehow manages to make I seem lush, then cranks up the speed almost beyond his players' abilities; he's good but not as exhilarating as the best (Chandos). The flatly recorded **Mravinsky** opens grimly and thoughtfully, then turns light and snarling, but the coda is a mess (Melodiya). The Leningrad Philharmonic's playing is a lot better on an earlier Mravinsky from 1955, as is, astonishingly, the sound (Chant du Monde 7254017).

In a special category was **Kondrashin,** whose rage at the Soviet system seemed to boil over in this piece. The very fast tempo in I has a fury that speaks of anger rather than melancholy, and the performance gets even more ferocious and vehement as it goes on (♦Melodiya 19847). **Temirkanov** also zips through the Largo, though without Kondrashin's anger, and II and III have great lithe energy (♦RCA 68844). Though the surprisingly well-engineered 1945 **Reiner** recording is being recirculated as some kind of historical treasure, it's not, for he displays little feeling for Shostakovich's rhythms and closes with a terrible unauthorized ritard (Sony). A better historical choice would be **Stokowski**'s imaginative, luminously played world premiere waxing, if you don't mind a slow III (Dutton 8017).

7 ("Leningrad"). Now that the early fame and subsequent denigration of this wartime piece have faded into history, we can hear it as another of Shostakovich's "tombstones"—albeit lengthier and more unwieldy than the others. It demands a master of structure and elasticity, and once again **Bernstein** fits the bill. His 1962 New York session first demonstrated his grip on this piece, with irresistible momentum in the notorious march (though one variation is missing), highlighting its lyricism and poignancy as well as its agitation (♦Sony 47616). His more emotional 1988 Chicago recording takes an agonizingly slow 85 minutes to reach its mark, yet with his incisive rhythms and carefully judged feeling for the work's ebb and flow, you always want to know what's around the next bend (♦DG 427632, 2CD). The sound is stunning, but some will balk at the prospect of buying two full-priced CDs.

Masur comes loaded for bear, driving this exciting live performance home with brutal force, a good feel for rhythm, and pacing that feels just right (♦Teldec 21467). The New York Philharmonic seems to play with the coarse power of a Russian orchestra; this is a top choice despite the coughing and stage noises. **Järvi** opens each movement subtly or perfunctorily but builds to satisfyingly intense climaxes; the Scots play beautifully; and the sonics are a pleasure (♦Chandos 8623). Though Shostakovich hated it, **Toscanini**'s pioneering 1942 broadcast has a brutality, urgency, and lyric feeling that almost override the old, boxy sonics (RCA 60293).

Jansons offers an ironically controlled, cultivated reading that doesn't cut deeply enough (EMI). **Temirkanov** hails from the same city—now St. Petersburg—and while the march is pretty good (though hampered by claustrophobic sound) and the brisk sections everywhere else have drive, the lyrical stretches are inert emotionally (RCA). Are the city's musicians in denial? They understood in **Mravinsky**'s heyday, playing with cultivation and biting urgency in a sweepingly unified performance; the march has a unique percolating groove, and 24-bit remastering reveals unexpected warmth and depth in the 50s-vintage mono tape (♦Omega 1030).

8. This bitter canvas of war and oppression was difficult to find in the LP era, but curiously, now that the piece has caught on as a digital spectacular, there are fewer great performances per capita. No recent recording has matched the impact of **Mravinsky**'s seething, furiously driven live recordings; they have a sarcastic bite that no one this side of Kondrashin and Rozhdestvensky catch. The best-sounding is a March 1982 taping that was transferred about three eighths of a tone too sharp (♦Philips 422442, NA).

Previn, in his less abrasive, suavely brooding way, also gives you a full dose of the work's intensity in his first London Symphony recording, with smooth transitions and a nightmarish climax in V (♦EMI 65521). **Gergiev**'s Kirov Orchestra has the rough-cut Russian sound, but there's curiously little emotion driving it; indeed III and IV sound downright listless (Philips). **Litton** also excels in the Largo, capturing its sullen stillness, but earlier there are some blandness and misjudgments of expression balanced by passages of urgency (Delos). **Levi**'s recording is well played, astutely gauged, and warmly recorded; it just doesn't grab me by the collar (Telarc). **Solti** is fiercely overbearing; he had never recorded Shostakovich before and often wields a bludgeon (London).

9. Humor in music wasn't particularly appreciated by Stalin's gang, who expected a grand, solemn 9th and got this dangerously cheeky, nose-tweaking wisp of a symphony. Nor is it much appreciated today, judging by the shortage of recordings that bother to emphasize Shostakovich's jibes and jokes. **Bernstein** knew what to do, at least in New York (♦Sony 47615). Listen to the way he underlines the musical gags, the way the brasses jeer and interrupt, the way the coda takes off in a frivolously impudent way. **Temirkanov** whizzes through it lightly with a twinkle in his eye (♦RCA 68548). **Järvi** is a serious citizen who doesn't quite crack a smile, though he gets a huge brass sound and superb engineering (Chandos). **Levi** gets beautiful, soft-grained playing from his Atlantans, but he observes the music soberly, and nothing cuts loose (Telarc). Fans of a roughhouse Russian approach may want to hunt down **Kondrashin**'s dashing recording (♦Melodiya 19846).

10. This was the piece that finally convinced many Western listeners that Shostakovich was truly a force to be reckoned with. *Testimony* gave it even more credibility with the revelation that it was about the Stalin years, and that the furiously sinister second movement constituted a portrait of Stalin himself. Ironically, most of the recordings that cut most deeply were made before *Testimony* came out, so the connotations must have been subliminally obvious. The first (1954) Western recording by **Mitropoulos** and the New York Philharmonic is a searing experience that burns through the mellow mono sonics (♦CBS 45698); man, do they tear into that Stalin scherzo!

This was the only Shostakovich symphony that **Karajan** conducted, yet this magician saw through to its emotional core while preserving his own conception of sound. His first recording has a tight, sleek Berlin string sheen in I that bursts open in unbridled fury in the Scherzo; the whole disc has a brooding power and energy that have eluded most of its successors (♦DG 429716). His remake is more luxuriously played, not quite as harrowing and furious, but still very impressive (♦DG 439036). **Ormandy** also commanded a polished instrument that could get to the heart of this piece. His Scherzo is crisp and vigorous, IV isn't as agitated as Karajan's, but in general, everything goes right in Philadelphia (♦Sony 62409, 2CD). A 1976 **Mravinsky** tape has a deeply felt I and terrific Russian-flavored rhythmic energy in III, but the full fury of II barely emerges through the thin, compressed sound, and IV is not well played (Melodiya).

Previn is urgent and passionate in I and understands the ironic humor of IV as few do, but the Scherzo has little real violence; it almost sounds formal. The London Symphony sounds great, but the early digital sound is a bit harsh (♦EMI 73368, 2CD). **Rattle**'s tediously slow tempos don't have redeeming intensity, and even though II is fast, it lacks drive, content only to make a big noise (EMI). **Levi** is even slower, with a tame Scherzo, and the great engineering can't compensate (Telarc). **DePreist** offers fine playing and sound but not much out of the ordinary interpretively (Delos); ditto **Jansons** (EMI). **Litton** at least keeps the London Philharmonic moving with some drive (Virgin), but he too can't penetrate into this piece as deeply as its pioneers.

11 ("The Year 1905"). Here's a minority viewpoint: This is one of the *great* Shostakovich symphonies. Though it purports to chronicle the aborted 1905 Russian Revolution, with its tremendous emotional sweep and atmosphere, we can easily imagine this music as a soundtrack to the 1956 Hungarian uprising (the implied model). **Stokowski** got the message right away with his electrifying, intensely moving outing with the Houston Symphony (♦EMI 65206). No one conveys the lush, magically still sound of the Palace Square episodes, the shocking violence of the massacre, or the overall unity of the hour-plus score quite like Stokowski—and while the 1958 sound isn't as clear as the more recent digital wonders, it still has tremendous warmth and impact (Capitol). A 1967 Czech Radio broadcast from **Mravinsky** in Leningrad hurtles along with nervous tension at the outset and enormous drive everywhere else; the strings really dig into the massacre. The sound is mediocre, but his ferocity comes through forcefully (♦Chant du Monde 7254018).

Järvi is too hasty to capture any atmosphere; nothing is savored, and the massacre and coda are a mess (DG). **Inbal** also lacks atmosphere from the get-go, but he does a better job with the massacre (Denon). **DePreist** conjures the atmosphere well enough at slow speed; the horror is vividly conveyed; and he gets excellent sound; but he doesn't tie the huge canvas together as tightly as the best (♦Delos 3080).

12 ("The Year 1917"). Unlike its brethren, this symphony stubbornly refuses to be rehabilitated, for it's simply an uninspired piece of work, perhaps deliberately so ("the material put up resistance," the composer confessed). Indeed, the blunderbuss finale—with its mirth-inducing title, "Dawn Of Humanity"—is the low point of his symphonies. **Järvi** understandably doesn't have much to say about it; the blitzkrieg tempos in I are fun, but the rest has no conviction whatsoever (DG 431688). **Mravinsky**'s I also takes off like a rocket, yet his jubilant finale does have conviction; he was, after all, an obedient Soviet citizen who wouldn't take on the politically dangerous 13. Either that, or this is a case of a great musician making lemonade out of a lemon (♦Chant du Monde 7254017)

13 ("Babi Yar"). Once again, Shostakovich was in hot water with the authorities after writing this granitic choral symphony to the protest poetry of Yevgeny Yevtushenko. The irony is that the score contains the simplest, most emotionally direct musical language of all his symphonies, so even the dullest commissar (or conductor?) couldn't miss the message. Consequently, there is a bumper crop of fine recordings, right from the first highly charged live taping made only two days after its controversial Moscow premiere (♦Russian Disc 11191). You can feel the intense nervous heat of **Kondrashin**'s gutsy leadership—II especially has bite and snap, only V seems too breathless—and bass Vitaly Gromadsky articulates the texts with crisp anger.

Masur gives it an urgency and sting that aren't surprising, coming from an old East German freedom fighter (♦Teldec 90848). The New York Philharmonic plays bitingly well, Leiferkus has a reedy bass, and Masur has Yevtushenko himself reciting his poem and a sequel, "The Loss." Also conceiving it in grand terms, **Previn** has his best moments down the stretch, coaxing real terror from "Fears" and ridicule from "A Career," overcoming bass Dimiter Petkov's indistinct pitch (♦EMI 73368, 2CD). Hunt for **Ormandy**'s powerful, blunt, splendidly played and sung Western recorded premiere, last seen in a box with 14 and 15 (♦RCA 1284, 3LP, NA).

14. Even by today's loose definition that a symphony is whatever a composer says it is, 14 doesn't fit. It's a relentlessly grim, eleven-part song cycle on the subject of death, for two voices, 19 strings, and percussion, using 12-tone techniques within a tonal center. It's also unequivocally great music whose realism doesn't get in the way of its creative vitality. **Bernstein** and the New York Philharmonic bravely explore its extremes, starting and ending in the depths, capturing the bleakness, tearing into "Loreley" with vigor and malice, supporting two excellent vocal soloists, Teresa Kubiak and Isser Bushkin (♦Sony 47617). **Inbal** also does well, with some intensity, good Russian voices, and fine sound (♦Denon 78821). The once-esteemed Ormandy LP now pales against its successors with its bland American soloists (RCA), and **Lazarev** is sluggish to the point of torpor (Virgin).

15. From its lightly ironic "toy shop" opening through its somber brooding to the death-rattle coda, this is a wistfully autobiographical piece, a quizzical yet deeply absorbing end to a monumental cycle. Everyone seems to have a different take on it. My favorite has been strangely locked in the vaults since the '70s: the witty, spiky premiere recording led by **Maxim Shostakovich** in his father's presence (♦Melodiya 40213, NA).

This symphony caught the erratic **Järvi** on a good day: He leads vigorously with somber, sonorous climaxes and his treatment of the percussion at the end is among the most accurate (♦DG 427616). **Ormandy**'s beautifully played recording suggests a gentle refraction of

childhood, with some emotional depth (♦RCA 63587). Serious, boisterous, rawboned at the start, **Mravinsky** works his way toward a surprisingly gloom-free, crystalline finale, like a resurrection (Melodiya 25192). And though this was one of **Solti**'s last recordings, there's no foreboding at all in his high-powered, life-affirming conducting with robust Chicago bass underpinning (♦Decca 458919).

OTHER ORCHESTRAL MUSIC

Chamber Symphony for Strings Op. 110a. This is really Quartet 8 blown up for string orchestra by Rudolf Barshai, which had the effect of placing the original version solidly in the basic repertoire. **Barshai** himself recorded a warm, thrusting performance, coupling it with his transcription of Quartet 10 (♦DG 429229, NA). **Spivakov** looks imaginatively inward, with a driving edge and bitter lilt in the center and bleakness in the outer movements (♦RCA 7947), and **Turovsky** offers an even more intense experience along the same lines (♦Chandos 8357). **Dennis Russell Davies** is superficial, lacking warmth and tension, going slack when he should move (ECM).

Festive Overture. For sheer open joy, there's little in music to compare with this vivacious piece. **Temirkanov**'s Russians race through it with plenty of joie de vivre (♦RCA 68844); **Kostelanetz**'s edited version is even more rambunctious (♦Sony 62642). **Litton** keeps the lid on tight (Virgin) and **DePreist** actually drags (Delos); both performances are oddly coupled with their emotional flip side, Symphony 10. **Järvi** produces only controlled jubilation (Chandos); **Leighton Smith** takes a while to get pumped up but eventually it moves (♦Sheffield Lab 27). **John Williams**'s fitfully rousing performance is part of a grab bag of miniatures saluting the 1996 Olympics (Sony).

Ballet music. It's amazing that the dance music of Shostakovich still isn't well known, for here is some of the funniest, most melodic, most openly charming music ever composed. Lev Atoumian compiled bits and pieces into four ballet suites; **Järvi** has recorded all of them, plus *The Bolt* as No. 5 (Chandos 7000, 2CD).

The wickedly parodistic music for *The Golden Age* is best known in a four-movement suite. **Martinon** is wonderfully droll (♦Classic 2322), and **Haitink,** for all his sensible nature, still catches the fun (♦London 421131, NA). **Järvi** is often much too fast—the Polka is ridiculous—and the jokes fall flat (DG). Naturally **Stokowski** has his own ideas about balance, timbre (is that an accordion in "Dance"?), and reverse tempo relationships, but it all comes together with lots of flair and humor (♦RCA 70931, 2CD). If time and budget allow, do try the complete ballet as essayed by **Rozhdestvensky** in Stockholm, because it contains some impishly jazzy dances and other inspired or funny episodes that the all-too-brief suite bypasses (♦Chandos 9251/2, 2CD).

The Bolt juxtaposes flippancy with more serious, hectoring ideas, only not as vividly as *Golden Age*. **Järvi** gives you eight numbers (♦Chandos 8650), while **Chailly** performs six (London) and **Mark Gorenstein** only five (Pope)—and Järvi also has the best grip on the slapstick bits. As for the so-called *Jazz Suites*, 1 is an open homage to Kurt Weill, while 2 reverts more to the delicious, lighter-than-air language of the ballets. **Chailly** does both of them nicely, though 1 could be looser (♦London 433702); **Rozhdestvensky** offers a more tart 1 (♦Melodiya 156, NA). But the best (and cheapest) way to discover Shostakovich's light side is to invest in **Kostelanetz**'s irresistible compilation of bits from Suites 1 and 2, *Moskva Cheryomushki*, and *Golden Age*; he knew exactly how to play them (♦Sony 62642). **Mark Elder**'s elegant 1 rounds out a disc of rarities headlined by the screwball *Hypothetically Murdered* suite (♦Cala 1020).

Film music. Thanks in part to film music's current high profile, more and more of Shostakovich's huge output—roughly 36 scores from 1928 to 1971—are emerging from mothballs. His light or satirical personas generate the best music; so far, alas, there is nothing on the epic level of his colleague Prokofiev's great film scores. Also, scores that have received multiple recordings often come in differing editions, which makes things tricky for consumers who just want one version.

The Gadfly is the score that pops up most often by far; it has moments of light fun, lyrical meditations, and grandiose rhetoric that grow on you. **Vakhtang Jordania** sumptuously recorded a 45-minute suite compiled by Atoumian (Koch 7274). **Kuchar** gives a brisker, more flavorful rendition of this suite that, coupled with *Five Days and Five Nights* (with its echoes of Beethoven's 9th and Shostakovich's 11th), makes a fine bargain (◆Naxos 553299). **Chailly** offers a 31-minute suite that purports to retain Shostakovich's original cues and orchestrations, but his heavier-set performance has less life (London). On his light music CD, **Kostelanetz** distills *The Gadfly* down to five numbers, hitting many of the best ones and making them sparkle (◆Sony 62642).

About nine minutes from the score for *Hamlet*, with its high-strung reminders of Symphony 13, turns up on Jordania's disc, while Chailly delivers 17 minutes in his "Film Album," along with scraps from seven other films in luxuriously resonant Concertgebouw sound (London 460792). The latter also contains a prophetic funeral march from the 1938 film *The Great Citizen* that turned up in Symphony 11's slow movement nearly 20 years later. A 12-minute suite from *Alone* by **Rozhdestvensky** has mock military writing and some mild slapstick (BMG/Melodiya 72915, 14CD). Chailly's album has a 20-minute version that reveals a striking snow storm sequence complete with a theremin for wind effects, and **Walter Mnatsakanov** gives you a whopping 71 minutes with choir (Russian Disc 10007). If you see it, grab Rozhdestvensky's LP of Shostakovich's first film score, *The New Babylon*, a zany, Offenbach-laced bit of tomfoolery from the '20s (◆Columbia/Melodiya 34502, NA).

CONCERTOS

Cello

1. The first cello concerto is on a par with Violin Concerto 1 as a memorable, brooding, sardonic, post-Stalin document; its four-note motto is a quizzical variation on Shostakovich's DSCH musical signature. **Rostropovich** already had the work firmly in his grasp in the 1959 premiere recording, fully characterizing the solo line in all its humor, highwire angst and frenzy, with Ormandy and the Philadelphia laying down a plush yet still emphatic backdrop and the composer supervising everyone (◆Sony 63327). Rostropovich's 1987 performance (but not Ozawa's backing) is also larger than life (Erato 75485, NA).

A still spry Ormandy also accompanies **Ma**'s 1982 rendition (it was Ormandy's last recording); Ma is more legato, more high-strung, coarser in tone (he sounds warmer and better balanced in the LP), approaching Slava's depth but not there yet (CBS). **Heinrich Schiff** gets off to a crisp start with sharply pointed rhythms, yet takes a more lyrical approach overall, finally catching some of the angst in the cadenza, while Maxim Shostakovich offers sturdy backing (◆Philips 412 526).

Maria Kliegel goes her own way with much on-edge tension, idiosyncratic phrasing in the opening movement, and real bleakness in the slow movement, and Wit leans meaningfully and emotionally into each phrase. With excellent sound, this is a formidable rival for Rostropovich I, and by far the cheapest (◆Naxos 550813). **Carlos Prieto,** despite an edgy tone, produces some broad intensity, but the threadbare Mexican

orchestra lets him down (IMP). The performance in the Rozhdestvensky box is more notable for the conductor's light, chamber orchestralike commentary (despite the strident horn) in I and sardonic outlook elsewhere than for **Mikhail Khomitser**'s decent, not particularly charismatic playing (BMG/Melodiya 72915, 14CD).

2. Like Violin Concerto 2, this is an unflashy artifact of the mid-'60s, at once bleak and strange. The quirky third movement really grows on you with its weird fanfare for horns and skeletonic percussion that anticipates the coda of Symphony 15. **Rostropovich** is brooding, songful, with his dark-walnut tone always maintaining tension; Ozawa and the then-magnificent Boston Symphony are also thoroughly caught up in the mood (◆DG 2530 653, NA). **Schiff** is more subdued and mischievous, and Maxim Shostakovich really appreciates his dad's off-the-wall wit (◆Philips 412526). **Kliegel**'s tone and outlook are broad and plush, and Wit's backing penetrates the most deeply into the piece's strangeness (◆Naxos 550813).

Piano

1. This is a bright, irreverent piece that pokes fun at all piano concertos, with a solo trumpet adding its own brand of sass and a lyrical interlude to focus on more serious matters. The 1962 combination of the young, unspoiled **Previn** on piano and Bernstein at the rambunctious peak of his New York tenure is just about ideal; this performance has all the fizz, swing and impudence those two erudite wits can provide (◆Sony 47618). The 16-year-old Kissin is a ball of fire in the outer movements; although his wit isn't as sharp as Previn's, he gives each note a distinct character and offers an emotional second movement (◆RCA 7947).

Shostakovich himself provides formidable, more straightforward competition; with Cluyten's scampering though thinly recorded support, the composer still had enough technique left in 1957 to show how he might have sounded in the silent movie theatres of his youth (◆EMI 54606, NA). Brautigam and Chailly bring a street-smart edge and raucous energy into the Concertgebouw (◆London 433702). A newsworthy CD unites three generations of **Shostakoviches**—the father's concerto, his son Maxim conducting in Montreal, and his grandson Dmitri Jr. racing along with lots of technique and elegance—but there's not much wit or unique insight (Chandos). **Bronfman** with Salonen brings his customary powerhouse technique, shafts of vehemence, and little humor or emotion; the outstanding contribution comes from the Los Angeles Philharmonic's then-principal trumpeter Thomas Stevens (Sony 60677). **Carol Rosenberger,** Schwarz, and the Los Angeles Chamber Orchestra offer a poetic second movement and receive breathtaking sound, but much of the zaniness eludes them (Delos). **Andsnes** is as polished and thoughtful a pianist as there is—but again, where are the laughs? (EMI).

2. An older, wiser, presumably disillusioned composer nevertheless managed to come up with an even zanier concerto for Maxim, then a teenager. Some call it vulgar, but don't mind them; it's a nonstop delight. **Shostakovich** knocked it out with panache shortly after its 1957 premiere (◆EMI 54606, NA), and **Dmitri Jr.** and Maxim have followed suit (Chandos). Conducting from the keyboard, **Bernstein** is a little slower, perhaps more dogged, but still conveys a lot of fun (◆Sony 47618). **Bronfman** and Salonen are seemingly disinterested in most of the hijinks (Sony 60677); oddly enough, Bronfman's more pointed performance of the first movement with **Levine**/Chicago on the *Fantasia/2000* soundtrack shows what's missing (Walt Disney 60023).

Violin

1. Written in secret during the campaign against "formalism" and not revealed until after Stalin's death, 1 has an undercurrent of high tragic emotion that isn't realized as often as one would hope. **David Oistrakh** set the example in the work's first (1956) recording, with tiny variations of tempo, phrasing, and dynamics producing a wealth of expression from every phrase, with darkly shaded, driving accompaniment from Mitropoulos and the New York Philharmonic (♦Sony 63327). Later that year in Leningrad, Oistrakh recorded it again for the Soviet market, sounding bleaker, more anguished, and more on edge, and Mravinsky drives as hard as Mitropoulos, with an extra dash of savagery (♦RCA 72914, 2CD). Oistrakh's playing has even more expressive tragedy and a darker tone in his 1972 stereo remake with Maxim Shostakovich in London (with the composer listening), though Maxim lacks Mitropoulos's demonic streak (♦Angel 36964, NA).

More recently, **Vengerov** and Rostropovich feel the pain nearly as deeply as Oistrakh; Vengerov's finale is terrifyingly brilliant (♦Teldec 92256). **Mordkovitch** approaches Vengerov's vehemence in the finale and intensity elsewhere, and her reading with Järvi is most notable for its gorgeously plush sound (♦Chandos 8820). **Salerno-Sonnenberg**'s thick, mauve-colored tone pours heavily over the slow movements, and she sounds suitably unhinged in the fast ones, while Maxim Shostakovich keeps her on course (♦EMI 54314). **Perlman** hasn't a clue, offering schmaltzy little portamentos and a jaunty spirit without a hint of tragedy as Mehta plods alongside (EMI). **Sitkovetsky** does nothing to inflect the music, using very little vibrato, and Andrew Davis officiates sedately; only the Presto coda has any edge (Virgin). I haven't heard **Repin**'s disc with Nagano (Erato), but his live performances (slower than the CD) reveal an intense, songful conception that stops short of real angst. **Ilya Kaler** gives the slow movements a movingly bleak quality, though the scherzos are mild-mannered (Naxos).

2. This concerto looks more bleakly inward than 1, with fewer concessions to virtuoso flash and greater demands on the listener. Again, **Oistrakh** gave the premiere and set the standard with an emotionally gripping, sharply focused recording (♦RCA 72914, 2CD). **Vengerov** meets Oistrakh's challenge and raises the bar with a performance of emotional extremes, played with a lean intensity that cuts to the bone. If this CD doesn't propel this concerto into the repertoire, nothing will (♦Teldec 13150). Though his tone has a nice cutting edge, **Kremer** sounds like a cool modernist next to Vengerov, and he and Ozawa have trouble sustaining the piece's line (DG). **Mordkovitch** and Järvi don't let luxurious sonics get in the way of intensity (♦Chandos 8820); **Kaler** and Wit take a surprisingly absorbing lyrical approach (Naxos 550814); and **Sitkovetsky**'s unrelievedly bland playing simply will not do (Virgin 61633, 2CD).

CHAMBER MUSIC

String quartets

In the final days of the 20th century, it dawned on performers that Shostakovich's 15 quartets might well be the most imposing and enduring chamber music monument of that period. For all of the diversity of the works—their span ranges from 11 to 38 minutes in length, one to seven movements—it's a remarkably unified cycle, with a continuous story to tell despite switchbacks in mood and construction.

Shostakovich launches his ship with a short, classical, not entirely carefree 1, expands to near-symphonic proportions in 2, and really hits his stride in 3, 4, and 5, whose quintessentially Russian rhythms and outgoing, propulsive passages balance their introspection and confound those who claim that the whole cycle represents only the private

Shostakovich. No. 6 serves as a relaxed breather, and 7 is brief and intense. No. 8 is the one we hear most often by far, a harrowing, tightly wound autobiography constructed in a perfectly shaped arc, full of self-quotations and memorable tunes; it was said to be meant as a suicide note, but the process of writing brought Shostakovich out of his depression—for a while.

It gets wilder from there, with nerve-prodding dissonant stretches in 9 and 10. The experimental 11 is probably the cycle's transition point as the composer makes his permanent turn inward, adopting 12-tone procedures sparingly in 12. The downcast spirit increases in 13, only to lift somewhat toward wistfulness in 14. No. 15 is the end—a daring six movements of Adagios, bleak, funereal, and profoundly depressing if you're in a susceptible mood. The composer talked of writing 24 quartets—one in each key—and he did sketch a 16th, but it's hard to see how he could have followed 15.

Complete sets. Given this fascinating evolution, it's not surprising that the quartets often appear in boxed sets. That's how many of us in the West first experienced them in the '60s, through a pair of budget-priced LP boxes from the **Borodin Quartet;** at the time, they were an astounding revelation of mostly newly minted masterworks. For the most part, these come off as fresh, high-strung, often abrasive, sometimes brutally honest readings—the burning edge of the violins often lacerates the ear—putting these works out there as challenging Russian contemporary music. Even today, to my knowledge, no set catches the rhythms of the early quartets with as much of a rustic, tripping motion as the early Borodins. Alas, only 1 through 11 of this cycle were issued in the United States (Melodiya/Seraphim 6034/35, 6LP, NA). The rest hadn't been composed yet, and in 1974 British EMI expanded the collection to 1 through 13 (Melodiya/HMV 879, 6LP, NA), with 14 and 15 remaining unissued in both countries. The sound was wiry and shaggy on Seraphim, and only a little smoother on HMV.

The Borodins recorded the cycle again from 1979 to 1984, and it's available in an economically priced box (♦Melodiya/BMG 40711, 6CD). Since Borodin I, the quartet had acquired two new violinists; as a result, the old abrasiveness is largely gone, and the ensemble sounds more technically assured, warmer, and more refined in tone—more of a single-minded unit, yet without losing an iota of their former intensity and drive. Their tempos are usually slower, but their dynamic range has increased dramatically. Not only that, they play far more expressively; the brooding passages are bleaker than before, and they can still bite your ears off in the passages of madness in 7, 9, and 10. No other complete cycle digs in as deeply or as consistently into the contradictory emotions of the cycle as Borodin II; given the low price, the couplings (Piano Quintet with Richter, two pieces for octet), and decent sound, this has to be a first choice in this repertoire.

The **Emerson Quartet**'s set was considered a breakthrough when it was released, since it was the first time that a major, world-class, non-Russian group had recorded all of them (♦DG 463284, 5CD). For the most part, it lives up to much of the hype, often battling the Borodins toe-to-toe with a different, more aggressive approach, all recorded live at the Aspen Festival over a five-year period. The Emerson's tempos are consistently faster than Borodin II, and some of the flawless technical feats they pull off at those speeds (the scherzo of 7, for example) are astonishing. They also like to lean into the phrases in the early quartets, squeezing more juice out of the Jewish tunes in 4, and they leave nothing but scorched earth in their wake when they work themselves into their most furious moods.

Yet the Emersons can also be inconsistent, sometimes within the same piece (11 alternates between listlessness and brutal fury), and in a handful of quartets, 12 in particular, their concentration seems to flag. The finest examples of their cycle are 3, 9, and 10; the tough, hostile episodes of the latter two are especially cutting, and they offer a uniquely lonely yet warmly played view of 15. The sound is excellent, and DG squeezed the cycle onto five discs, but the price is more than twice that of Borodin II. You can, however, get a cheap taste of the cycle by purchasing a CD single of 8; the playing isn't immaculate, but the performance is driving, passionate, and at the end, emotionally spent (♦DG 459670).

The British **Fitzwilliam Quartet** was the first Western group to record the cycle; the recording emerged gradually through the '70s and is now available in a minibox (London 455776, 6CD). Though they were coached by the composer toward the end of his life, their recordings don't sound anything like their Russian counterparts; they are a smoother, more polished, warmer lot, with sonorities that sometimes sound symphonic. They can come out of the chute pretty forcefully at times and generate some intensity; their 12 is the best in that regard since Borodin I. But most of the time, their rhythmic impulses are subdued, the playing very much on-the-string; in the later quartets, they tend to be more consoling than forbidding—the bleak chill of the Russians is almost entirely absent. This may be appealing for listeners who don't cotton to heaps of acerbic gloom and doom but want to hear these works, especially in opulent sound.

The **Brodsky Quartet**'s versions can be safely bypassed; they seem to give their wardrobe designer almost as much credit as Shostakovich (Teldec, 6CD). Despite their stance as chamber music rebels, this young group doesn't really grapple with the music, resulting in bland runthroughs with little anger, intensity, drive, compassion, or much of anything else. Their anonymous string tone contributes to the blandness, and they aren't as technically accomplished as their rivals. They do improve somewhat in the late quartets, where a bleak, expressionless tone becomes an asset (especially in 15), and they muster some grit in parts of 11, but at full price, this is not competitive.

The performances I've heard from the **Beethoven Quartet**, Shostakovich's frequent dedicatees in this repertoire, have considerable drama, lots of drive, a Romantic temperament, the requisite bleakness, and not always reliable intonation. As historical documents, they're highly instructive. There is an almost-complete cycle from 1956 to 1975 broadcasts, with only 5 missing (Consonance 3005/09, 5CD), and individual performances on Melodiya have been leaking out to the West since the '60s. From what I've sampled of the **Eder Quartet**'s cycle, it's an accomplished, plush-sounding, cultured foursome with a Central European approach, bringing lush warmth to some chilly music, and much lyricism without irony or savagery; the third movement of 3 sounds almost Viennese! (Naxos 550972/77, 6CD). Although the price is tempting and the discs are available individually, since Borodin II is priced as low as Eder, why not spring for the best?

Formed in 1967, the **Shostakovich Quartet** recorded all 15 between 1978 and 1985 (Olympia 531/5, 5CD). Their cycle has been acclaimed for the accomplished soloists in the group, yet they don't dig in very intensely as an entity (7, for example, is zipped off very lightly, tersely, with feathery textures). The Soviet analog engineering isn't bad, though it's a bit dry and not as listenable as the contemporaneous Borodin II. Like the Brodskys, the **Manhattan Quartet** sometimes seems to struggle with the more furious writing, but at least it tries to play with spirit, fire, purpose, and slyness when needed. It's just not up to the level of the best cycles, especially at upper mid-price (ESS.A.Y 1021, 6CD).

One really promising cycle that fell victim to corporate axe-wielding was by the **St. Petersburg Quartet** (founded in 1985), a group that has a deeply felt grip on this music. They recorded 1, 2, and 4 on one disc (♦Sony 64584, NA) and 3, 5, and 7 on another (♦Sony 66592, NA) in performances that were full of crackling drive, roughhouse vigor, and thrilling climaxes, with lots of expression and authentic feeling for each contour. Their 4 is the best I've heard—three movements of all-out passionate arcs of construction—and they find more depth in 1 than any of the Borodin recordings. Alas, this cycle was halted when Sony scrapped its St. Petersburg Classics label, but now the group has started a new cycle, rerecording 2 through 4, 6, and 8 to a chorus of mostly favorable reviews (Hyperion 67153/4, 2CD).

Individual recordings. In addition to their two complete cycles, the Borodins have recorded selections from the cycle over the decades (counting the cycles, there are at least six Borodin recordings of 8 alone). A smoothly recorded 1962 8, made after an appearance at the Aldeburgh Festival, is noticeably faster than those in their cycles but not as intense; the notorious knocks on the door aren't as brutal as they would become (Decca 425 541). Persistent LP collectors may find a different 1962 Borodin 8, recorded in Moscow and paired with 4, that catches them in an even faster, wilder, more devilish mood in glassy Living Presence sound (Mercury 90309, NA). By 1990, the Borodins had traded some of their intensity for more inward expression and even more closelyknit and polished playing; a bargain "two-fer" combines 2, 3, 7, 8, and 12 (Virgin 61630, 2CD). They also rerecorded 1 and 15 in 1995, and their playing is more mature, warmer, with more variety of lyrical expression than before, but not without moments of the old passion (♦Teldec 98417).

In 8, the iconoclastic **Kronos Quartet** zeroes in on the piece's bleakness; the fast raps on the door are positively totalitarian (they've evidently been reading *Testimony*). Fine-tuned liberties with the score and all, this is one of the most communicative versions around (♦Nonesuch 79242). The veteran, second-generation **Fine Arts Quartet** plays extremely well in its single-disc sampler of the cycle, but the performances are inconsistent; 3 is free-thinking in tempo and dynamics yet surprisingly lacking in drama; 7 lacks all-out involvement though the tempos are fast enough; but 11 is just fine (Adés 14.161).

Yuri Bashmet and the Moscow Soloists play Alexander Tchaikovsky's transcription of 13 for viola and strings at an extremely slow tempo; the expanded forces make it easier to sustain tension for the listener, the dissonances become even more ear-bending (♦Sony 60550). **Kremer** and his ad hoc all-stars have penetrated the last three quartets even more deeply than the established groups. Taped at the Lockenhaus Festival, his 13 is the slowest of all but cries out in anguish and the tremolos shudder; he and his friends see 14 in more downcast, despairing terms than their rivals (♦ECM 21347, 2CD). In 15, Kremer gets the right bleak yet emotional tone, and Yo-Yo Ma's cello solos are charged with overwhelming drama and sensitivity (♦CBS 44924).

Other chamber music

Adagio and Allegretto. The Adagio is an elegy from *Lady Macbeth,* and the Allegretto is the familiar, funny Polka from *The Golden Age,* in nifty quartet transcriptions that predate the quartet cycle. **Kremer** and friends are surging and emotional in the Adagio, build to a scratchy apex, and offer slurping humor and galumphing dance steps in the Allegretto (ECM 21347, 2CD). As an appendage to their quartet cycle, the **Emersons** are gentler, much more refined in the Adagio, and they resist the urge to ham it up in the Allegretto (DG 446384, 5CD). The

Fitzwilliam has the loveliest playing of all in the Adagio, and they find the right level of fun in the Allegretto (London 411940, NA).

Piano Quintet. With its symmetrical five-movement structure—a typical scherzo in the center, a magnificently arching Adagio fugue and somber matching Intermezzo surrounding it, and serious proclamations and musings as bookends—the Quintet seems to have something for everyone, and it made an impact on the world long before the quartets. **Richter** and the Borodins, recorded live in Moscow, would seem to be self-recommending, and indeed, the Borodins are in appropriately bleak-toned form, doing the most methodically effective job of working through the fugue and Intermezzo, giving the Scherzo a rough edge (♦Melodiya 40711, 6CD). But **Ashkenazy** and the Fitzwilliams in their own way are just as moving, if not more so: the pianist establishes his extreme dynamic range within the first two minutes; the quartet launches the fugue in a lovely, hushed manner; and the Scherzo has a rollicking quality (♦London 411940, NA).

For all of the Hollywood String Quartet's deservedly vaunted latter-day reputation, its fast-paced, more romantically phrased 1952 version doesn't sound as emotionally in touch with the music as the others, and the sound is thinly transferred, while **Victor Aller**'s piano dominates (Testament 1077). **Bronfman**'s tough-sounding piano tone and the Juilliard's occasional throbbing and drive aside, their performance tends to look on the bright side; everything goes well, but you aren't moved (Sony 60677). **Shostakovich** himself can be heard with the Beethoven Quartet in a performance of savage intensity; it's also in touch with the quintet's folk-like elements (Vanguard 8077).

The **Borodin Trio**—a spinoff of the Borodin Quartet that was founded in the West by the Quartet's defecting first violinist—takes on an additional violinist and violist for a smooth, sumptuously recorded performance, which sometimes crawls even more slowly than Borodin/Richter yet has less compensating tension (Chandos 8342).

Piano Trios. There are two. A wartime piece written just after Symphony 8, this can be a grinding emotional experience, particularly in the finale, where its Jewish-sounding theme—familiar to those who know Quartet 8—is hammered into a brutal march (no wonder it was banned for a while in Russia after the war). The **Borodin Trio**'s founder Rostislav Dubinsky writes movingly of this work's extra-musical meaning in the notes to their recording, which lays into the music in a broadly paced, luscious-toned way, pulling and tugging at the fortissimo phrases, quite oxcart-like in its bludgeoning agony (♦Chandos 8342).

Curiously, this painful work was used by EMI as a vehicle for marketing two glamor-girl trios in 1998 with similarly fetching cover photos and the same companion piece (Dvořák's "Dumky" Trio); even the catalog numbers are consecutive. The **Ahn Trio** didn't identify with it at all; their performance, however immaculately played, doesn't have any weight, rhythm, or emotion. It could be Haydn for all they seem to care (EMI). But the **Eroica Trio** makes something out of it, attacking with emphasis, though I'm not sure that they get Shostakovich's droll humor (♦EMI 56673). The ghostly, delicate **Oslo Trio** recording is the opposite of the Eroica's—they understand the jokes but not the hostility—but they include one of the earliest Western recordings of the 17-year-old Shostakovich's rambling, romantic Trio 1 (Simax 1014). The competent **Stockholm Arts Trio** gives the same coupling at a much lower price (Naxos 553297).

For historians, the trio of **Shostakovich**, Oistrakh, and Milos Sadlo, circa 1947 in Prague, is invaluable for its furious tempos and thrust; the Scherzo and Finale seem to leap off the pages (♦Eclectra 2046).

Sonata for Cello and Piano. Shostakovich was riding high in 1934 when his only cello sonata was written, and much of the piece radiates confidence, but the brooding passages perhaps subconsciously predict trouble ahead in his life. **Rostropovich** gives it a technically flawless, high-powered, emotional performance with his friend, the sometimes reticent but always instructive composer at the keyboard (the mono Soviet engineering may be to blame here) (♦Revelation 70005). The composer also recorded the sonata with the lyrical-minded **Daniel Shafran** in 1946; here Shostakovich is far more assertive, and the sound is surprisingly good, virtually high-fidelity (♦Eclectra 2046).

Russian émigré **Yuli Turovsky** is, if anything, even more emotionally gripping in I, gruff and boisterous in II, and a bit too exaggerated and broad in IV, with pianist Luba Edlina a fierce, equally balanced partner (♦ Chandos 8340). **Carlos Prieto** has considerable energy, a solid and intelligent conception, and Doris Stevenson as a formidable, assertive pianist, but the buzzing, unpleasant recorded tone of his cello works against them (IMP). The beautifully played **Ma** and Ax rendition (Sony 44664) and **Isserlis** with Mustonen (RCA 68437) are highly regarded.

Sonata for Viola and Piano. Shostakovich's last work, almost literally composed on his deathbed, isn't a requiem per se, yet it does convey resignation, with a few half-hearted outbreaks of turbulence and an extended reverie on fragments of Beethoven's "Moonlight" Sonata as the closing Adagio. As a reflection of the composer's last thoughts, it's compelling for that reason alone, though the inspiration seems to be flickering. **Kashkashian**'s tone is wonderfully ripe, underpinned delicately and forcefully by Robert Levin; for them, the piece is about beauty, not tragedy, and supported by equally gorgeous engineering, they make the composer's last moments quite bearable (♦ECM 1425). On the other hand, the prickly opening, forbidding scherzo, and intensively severe finale—all at the slowest of tempos—mean that the team of **Raphael Hillyer** and Reinbert de Leeuw offers no compromise and little consolation; the tremolos in I are icy death itself (Koch Schwann 3-1161).

The world premiere recording by dedicatee **Fedor Druzhinin** (of the Beethoven Quartet) and Mikhail Muntyan grapples with the darkness and drifts along in sullen, colorless contemplation, recorded at a distance so that it sounds almost otherworldly (Melodiya/Columbia 35109, NA). The performance by **Tabea Zimmermann** and Hartmut Höll is good; the scherzo has a lot of spirit and drive, and the "Moonlight" finale has plenty of contrast in dynamics and mood (♦EMI 54394, NA). **Bashmet**'s acclaimed, searing interpretations come in two versions, a 1985 recording with Richter (Olympia 625) and a slower, better-recorded 1991 performance with Muntyan (RCA 61273).

Sonata for Violin and Piano. Written for David Oistrakh's 60th birthday, here we have two mostly spare, bleak, large outer movements surrounding a demonic scherzo, not one of Shostakovich's more interesting utterances as a whole. Since it is a sonata for violin *and* piano, you'd expect the keyboardist to be more than a mere accompanist; both are given showoff cadenzas in the finale. We do hear this balance when **Oistrakh** joins Richter, live in Moscow when the work was barely back from the printers, an intense, inward, concentrated performance that nevertheless erupts in the Scherzo and conjures a chilling death rattle at the end (♦Melodiya/BMG 34182 or 40710, 5CD). There is also an Oistrakh recording with Shostakovich, taped by an amateur in Oistrakh's apartment before the work even saw print; it was probably the first performance ever. Again, the balance is equal, with faster tempos, seat-of-the-pants fire, and understandably imperfect playing (Eclectra 2046).

The husband/wife team of **Dubinsky** and Edlina is also a full partnership, with Dubinsky's edgy violin tone and Edlina's often menacing piano bearing down equally hard in a full-blooded performance that's far from consolatory (Chandos 8343). Meanwhile, the intimate, impulsive, fragile, deliberately desicated **Kremer** dominates the very young Gavrilov in an interesting performance where the Scherzo turns into a relentlessly percussive machine but parts of the score barely hang together (Melodiya/Columbia 35109, NA). **Mordkovitch** likewise dominates her emotionally neutral pianist Clifford Benson in a beautifully recorded but not very involving disc; she can be as rough-hewn as you'd like, yet not much really takes hold (Chandos).   GINELL

PIANO MUSIC

In contrast to his stirring public symphonies and introspective chamber music, Shostakovich composed relatively little piano music. This information is not only odd but paradoxical when you consider that the piano was his instrument. In 1927 he won a prize at the inaugural Chopin Piano Competition in Warsaw and later in life played piano in several of his chamber music recordings, such as the Piano Quintet (Vanguard 8077).

While Bach inspired Shostakovich's 1951 24 Preludes and Fugues Op. 87, the earlier Preludes Op. 34 (1932-3) owe much to Chopin. They are among his first forays into "private" music: intimate, moody, furiously inventive, and aphoristic, some only a page in length. The brief Sonata 1 (1926) is filled with both daring innovation and reflections of Scriabin, Liszt, and Berg. The more worldly Sonata 2 (1943), composed a month before his Symphony 8, has a curious but effective structure. Its edgy Allegretto has nearly symphonic intensity, its Largo is a lament for his colleague Leonid Nikolayev; and its final movement forms an ingenious set of variations on a persistent theme.

Tatiana Nikolayeva gives a highly individualistic reading of the three *Fantastic Dances*, 24 Preludes, and Piano Sonata 2, with pronounced sforzando and rubato (Hyperion 66620). She can be deliberate and slow, as she savors every note. She transforms the sentimental E-flat major prelude, like squeezing tart juices from a ripe kiwi. Her interpretation of Sonata 2 is equally sensitive, nearly a perfect rendition. It's full of dark spaces and trembling anxiety. The engineering could be better; the piano sometimes sounds echoey and rumbly.

Johan Schmidt is quick and businesslike in Sonata 2 and 24 Preludes (Cyprus 2622). His low registers can be muddy, and he could use a keener sense of pianissimo, though the sonic effects are room-sized and not overpowering. He misses the point of Sonata 2, however: He's too hurried in the Allegretto and Moderato, not somber enough in the Largo. For her version of 24 Preludes and Sonata 2, **Inger Wikström** had her picture taken with Shostakovich, so he may have liked the contemplative, gentle touch she gave his work (Discofil 1031). However, her atmospheric effects sometimes occur at the expense of drama. She infuses the poignant E-flat major prelude with more sentiment than other performers. For some odd reason, the producers have grouped the pieces at six per track, which can be annoying if you need to find one. Her performance of Sonata 2 is a hurried affair, seven minutes shorter than Nikolayeva's. It turns into too much of a competent exercise with not enough angst.

Vladimir Viardo is confident, rapid, and slick in 24 Preludes and Sonata 2 (Nonesuch 979234). In most of the Adagio and Moderato preludes (such as the F-sharp major), he displays an excellent feel for pianissimo. For Sonata 2, he's prickly—almost impatient—in the magnificent Moderato, with its palpable minor key. Overall, the sound engineering is excellent. **Oleg Volkov**, another Russian, loves to use bold, dramatic gestures and favors thrilling scalar leaps and startling contrasts in sound and tempo (Brioso 119). In the G major prelude, the sud-

den fortissimo bursts like the tutti chord in Haydn's "Surprise" Symphony. His Sonatas 1 and 2 are both impressive affairs, the former with its in-your-ear acoustics and youthful energy, the latter with the relentless progression of its variations. The piano has a clean, steely sound.

Shostakovich wrote his monumental 24 Preludes and Fugues after attending the 200th anniversary commemoration of Bach's death in Leipzig. There are three prominent contenders for this work: Nikolayeva (BMG 98492, 1987; Hyperion 666441/3, 1991), Keith Jarrett (ECM 437189), and Ashkenazy (Decca 289466). Of the three, **Nikolayeva** was Shostakovich's dedicatee in 1951 and performed the work frequently after that; she died while playing it in 1994. Her style is elegant, perceptive, almost aristocratic, but with an unforced intensity. Her performance in both albums doesn't vary much, though she's two minutes faster in the second. However, the Hyperion disc sounds like it was recorded in a medieval cathedral; the piano's tone is echoey and probably was distantly miked. **Jarrett**'s performance is muscular and tense. He plays the allegro pieces like 2 really fast—2:10 as opposed to Nikolayeva's 2:27 (BMG) and Ashkenazy's 2:18. Yet to his credit, he takes Shostakovich's metronome markings seriously, playing 1 at a leisurely 8:10, while Ashkenazy clocks in at 4:59.

Ashkenazy's rendition is wholly idiosyncratic and unpredictable. Sometimes he plays so softly you need to turn the volume up, as in the jaunty 2. (I first thought there was something wrong with the mike.) Elsewhere he plays more rapidly than Jarrett; his 13 ends at 5:49, Jarrett's at 7:03. More significant are the three performers' respective sense of nuance. Nikolayeva plays the raucous 21 with striking subtlety, imbuing its sections with distinctive character and treating the right-hand ostinato as an equal partner. Ashkenazy and Jarrett whip right through it, interpreting it as musical slapstick, with the ostinato relegated to sidekick. Theirs aren't wrong interpretations; Shostakovich said there were no correct interpretations of his music, only credible ones. Ironically, Jarrett's strict but beguiling 1 *sounds* unorthodox because others perform it more quickly.

Richter played some of these pieces and explores regions the others don't even approach. His selections (Supraphon 11-1421, 2, 3, 6, 7, and 18; Philips 438627, 4, 12, 14, 15, 17, 23) produce an insatiable craving for the others.

Shostakovich composed the Concertino for Two Pianos Op. 94 in 1953 as a rollicking, jocular piece he could play with his 15-year-old son Maxim. He certainly created that; at its liveliest moments, its puckish rhythm sounds like a giggling carnival rider. During the adagio segments, he injects a nostalgic folk melody that inexplicably blends in well. **Inger Wikström** convincingly plays both parts herself by overdubbing (Discofil 1031). But why? Were there no other decent pianists in the locale? Were the producers trying to save money? Or was Wikström just showing off? **Seta Tanyel** and Jeremy Brown play the Concertino better as two people (Chandos 8466). Their different styles effectively play off each other, one playing the daffy treble role, the other the straight-man bass. The sound is acceptable in both renditions but sharper on Chandos, with the performers deftly handling the *pp* bars. The disc also contains the charming Suite for Two Pianos, which Shostakovich composed when he was 15.

Perhaps inspired by Prokofiev's *Sarcasms*, a brief collection of fugitive piano pieces written in 1914, Shostakovich wrote *Aphorisms* when he was 21. But while Prokofiev creates his strange harmonies and jagged rhythms within a context of simple forms, Shostakovich builds his unpredictable pieces from the ground up. As if in training for the later 24 Preludes, he proves he's a master of small forms as well as the large-scale symphony. Sometimes he subverts expectation: His Nocturne isn't dreamy, but nightmarish; his parodistic Funeral March isn't the least bit respectful. Yet just when you expect his Lullaby to startle the most drowsy child, he gives us a work of crepuscular beauty. **Volkov**'s waggish theatricality is perfect for these pieces. BATES

OPERAS

The Nose. This is Shostakovich's first completed opera; written in 1927–28 when the composer was in his early twenties, it's based on a famous 1835 novella by Gogol. This rather ridiculous tale deals with a minor bureaucrat who one day finds his nose missing from his face and wanders about St. Petersburg trying to get it back. In this he's hampered by the stupidity and inefficiency of the officials, police and others who are supposedly helping him. The music is written in the composer's early, exuberant style and is clearly influenced by the Stravinsky of the '20s and by Berg. It's witty and parodistic, and includes polkas, waltzes, distorted Russian folk songs, and popular songs of the time. It was premiered in 1930 but was soon withdrawn on "official orders." The only available recording is coupled with Shostakovich's last opera, *The Gamblers* (♦Melodiya 60319, 2CD); it was made under the composer's supervision in St. Petersburg by the artists responsible for its 1974 revival. The huge cast is very good, the orchestra well balanced, and the sound excellent.

The Gamblers. This opera was completed immediately after Symphony 7, in 1942. It's also based on a Gogol story, and the composer apparently intended to set it without cuts, using Gogol's language as much as possible. But he abandoned the project in December 1942 after writing 50 minutes of music to about one third of the text, reportedly feeling that the work would be too unwieldy. The story deals with a card shark who's cheated by his intended victims in a cleverly executed set-up. The musical style of this incomplete work is similar to *The Nose,* clever and pungent. In addition to the above-named Melodiya set, there's an older recording by Moscow's Bolshoi Opera that's not as well done (Saison Russe).

Lady Macbeth of Mtsensk. This is Shostakovich's best-known opera. Based on a story by the 19th-century Russian writer Nikolai Leskov, it deals with the passions that drive Katerina Ismailova, the wife of a provincial merchant, to murder her husband and father-in-law for the love of a serf. Leskov is unsparing in his condemnation of Katerina, but the composer tried to portray her as a victim of her environment. It's his grandest and most realistic opera (with much sex and violence) and includes his most lyrical as well as much parodistic music. It was a huge success at its premiere in 1934 and made the composer into an international celebrity, but Stalin denounced it, and it had to be withdrawn, effectively putting an end to the composer's operatic career. After the dictator's death, Shostakovich revised the work; that version, known as *Katerina Ismailova,* was premiered in 1963 and, though widely performed, hasn't supplanted the original.

There are only two recordings in the current listings. The better one is a studio version made in London in 1979 (♦EMI 44955, 2CD); the principals are Vishnevskaya (in her prime) and **Gedda,** and the excellent conductor is the composer's friend **Rostropovich.** A later recording (1993), made on the stage of Paris's Bastille Opera, (DG 437511, 2CD) is not as well cast. The leading roles are taken by Ewing and Sergei Larin, and the able conductor is **Chung.**

SONGS

Although Shostakovich's songs, like his operas, are only a small part of his total compositional output, they are by no means insignificant. Long neglected, they're becoming better known in the West through several fine recordings released in the last few years. The discs recommended here are all-Shostakovich, but several of these compositions, for example the wonderful *From Jewish Folk Poetry,* can also be found in releases that include orchestral works or songs by other composers. Those performances are, however, no better than what we are recommending.

Two very commendable selections have been issued. One includes *Verses by Michelangelo,* one of the composer's last and most philosophical works, three more romantic Pushkin settings (from 1937), and *Romances on Words by Japanese Poets,* a much earlier work (from 1928). The other contains *From Jewish Folk Poetry,* six poems by Marina Tsvetayeva, and six romances to English texts (Shakespeare, Burns, and Raleigh, translated by Pasternak), all with orchestrations by the composer, sung by an accomplished vocal quartet (♦Capriccio 10777 and 10778). A third commendable disc duplicates the "English" songs and also includes six songs based on Spanish melodies, five hilarious settings of words from the comic magazine *Krokodil,* four songs about love and motherland (poems by Dalmatovsky), and seven to poems by the symbolist poet Alexander Blok (♦René Gailly 92041). The accompaniments here are piano, and in the Blok, also violin and cello; the latter are especially beautiful and haunting. This CD also has the best singers. All the discs include notes and English translations, but only the Gailly includes transliterations of the Russian words. MOSES

Jean Sibelius (1865–1957)

Sibelius's innovative romanticism bridged the gap between the 19th and 20th centuries. Like Beethoven, he struggled with nature and fate, but his musical geography is northerly, mountainous, and touched by cool forests and icy streams. He's often joyous and colorful, but more often dark and brooding. His genius for symphonic structure, harmony, and tone color parallels the pioneering efforts of the French impressionists, but the influence of Finland's turbulent history and legends gives his music a broad, epic power.

SYMPHONIES

Sibelius's seven symphonies fit easily onto three or four CDs, and complete cycles by the same conductor are plentiful. These are usually issued one disc at a time, then sold in boxed sets or two-for-one packages.

Complete sets. Complete cycles, though interesting, are rarely uniform in quality. Conductors always excel in some works but not in others, and I won't mention every mediocre performance that's part of a complete cycle. For those who are compelled (as I sometimes am) to collect every recording in a cycle, I suggest **Colin Davis** (RCA or Philips), **Vänskä** (BIS), **Ashkenazy** (London), **Rattle** (EMI), or **Berglund** (EMI)

Berglund's melodious, consistently fine Helsinki series may be the best complete introduction at reasonable cost; they're being rereleased at super-budget price. His earlier '70s cycle is also recommendable, though the sound isn't quite as warm and tempos are slower (Royal Classics). **Barbirolli**'s excellent, admired, though somewhat emphatic Hallé recordings are again available as a complete set; the sound is good but could be smoother during a handful of fortissimos (♦EMI 67299, 5CD). Avoid **Abravanel,** who is quite dull (Vanguard). **Anthony Collins** has '50s cult status, and his cycle contains excellent musicianship, but I can't give him a blanket recommendation (Beulah). It's better to get great individual performances in modern sound than to indulge in sets or historic performances too soon.

1. This is Sibelius's most youthful and rhapsodic symphony. **Stokowski** gave us a great recording with the National Philharmonic in a 1976 LP (Columbia M-34548). The 94-year-old conductor delivered a wild, intense performance with wonderful detail and phrasing. The final movement is too quick, and there is some imperfect ensemble, but these criticisms should be taken as an aside. Some still prefer the sound of the LP, but the CD is now issued in a "two-fer," accompanied by Francescatti's fine performance of the Violin Concerto (♦Sony 63260).

My favorite, **Maazel**'s 1963 Vienna Philharmonic recording, was the jewel of his earlier cycle; it has excellent sound to match its sweeping power and romantic spirit (♦Belart 325). His complete Vienna cycle is also being rereleased (London/Decca). **Sanderling** has dramatic strength and focused delicacy (♦Berlin 9267). For a slightly more even-tempered approach, **Ashkenazy** is appealing (♦London 455402, 2CD), as is **Ormandy,** who displays his familiar virtues of ideal tempos, an exceptional Philadelphia Orchestra, and keeping out of the composer's way (♦Sony 63060). Both the Sony and DG **Bernstein** readings have much to offer, but I prefer **Gibson** and the Royal Scottish National with its clean lines, massively weighted first movement, and excellent brass (♦Chandos 6555).

Vänskä, in an otherwise superior cycle, seems lost here, as does **Davis,** whose bloated RCA can't equal his earlier, less self-conscious Philips version. **Berglund** is interesting in a recent recording with 24-bit sound (using all vacuum tube recording equipment), a smaller orchestra, and a crystalline temperament—though the best disc in his series contains 4 and 6 (Finlandia). **Jansons** has been praised by some critics (EMI). **Neeme Järvi** is well recorded but delivers an awkward reading with odd balances (BIS). **Segerstam,** with his habitually slow tempos, gets mixed results, and although he provides some powerful individual moments, he's too cumbersome in the last half of a nearly 15-minute IV (Chandos). **Karajan** is always interesting in this repertoire; he too elects somewhat eccentric tempos that make it a risky but not bad choice (EMI, NA).

At budget price, **Petri Sakari** is satisfactory, but the effect is generic, and the sound isn't up to the label's usually high standard (Naxos). **Levi** has good sound, but this can't help him compete with the finest versions (Telarc). Nor can **Rattle,** who has garnered good reviews from English critics but remains a weak alternative (EMI). **Leaper** has an enervated dynamic in I that destroys the sweep and power of the line, and elsewhere is merely competent (Naxos).

Historic performances may not be essential to everyone, though **Robert Kajanus** must be considered (Finlandia, NA). He discussed and shared ideas with the composer, and his authority is legend. Another attraction is **Ormandy**'s 1941 Philadelphia performance (♦Biddulph 062), which can now be compared with his even earlier 1934 Minneapolis version (LYS). **Paul Kletzki**'s dignified but passionate 1955 reading is coupled with a fair 3 (♦Testament 1049). It may seem odd to some older readers that a 1955 recording is "historic," but a new century has arrived, and the recording is mono.

2. This romantic, inventive symphony is the composer's most popular, with a radiant and irresistible climax. Recordings abound. Anyone needing an introduction can opt for one of its greatest performances with **Ormandy** in an inexpensive disc (♦Sony 53509), or at mid-price with **Mackerras** (♦IMP 927). Ormandy has a smooth vitality, perfectly judged tempos, and is coupled with an excellent 7. His later RCA is conservative by comparison. Mackerras is imaginative and lyrical, with powerful climaxes, and offers an atmospheric *Swan of Tuonela* second to none.

Ashkenazy's Philharmonia account, my favorite, offers exquisitely polished emotions and a transcendent climax (♦London 455402). His more recent recording in Boston, though worthwhile, has a prosaic finale.

Barbirolli's Royal Philharmonic reading is iridescent and colorful, full of beauty and drama, and excellently remastered (♦Chesky 3). The classic **Szell** account deserves reissue as one of his finest moments on the podium (♦Philips, NA). I also like **Kletzki**'s swiftly flowing version (♦EMI 767726, 2CD). **Paray** conducts a sinewy, no-nonsense reading that has tremendous force in the climaxes (♦Mercury 434317). The sound is slightly wiry but quite listenable, and this dramatic version deserves to be better known. **Bernstein**'s New York Philharmonic recording is passionate, brisk, and exciting, but with a IV that's overdone in the Bernstein manner (♦Sony 46719, 2CD). His Vienna Philharmonic recording is even more exaggerated, with a II that runs to more than 18 minutes (DG). Nevertheless, it's hard to ignore these recordings as alternative, emotionally committed performances by a conductor who is never bland.

Davis on RCA seems to be admired by critics across the board. The truth is that the results are mixed, in both this and his earlier set. His lush, seductive 2 on RCA is an improvement on his unmemorable Philips; he's also given outstanding sound, but in its broad, heavily weighted lines, there's too much that sounds calculated, too many endlessly hovering phrases. **Vänskä** is just as sonically resplendent, with fervent expression, a subtle sense of anticipation, and (like Davis) a sense of epic proportion (BIS). Yet it too seems to lack the natural flow and spontaneity that are the hallmarks of a great rather than a worthy performance.

Temirkanov whips up a lot of sound and fury but signifies very little (RCA). **Berglund** gives us supreme textural clarity and a reading that falls just short of an all-out recommendation (Finlandia). **Järvi** remains a standard choice for some, but his reading has a fragmented "here's *this,* now here's *that*" quality, so the music never flows (BIS). **Maazel** gives a polished reading and little else (Sony). **Levine** is muscular and expressive, but also eccentric and overwrought (DG). **Mehta** is routine (Teldec), and **Sakari** can't get the Iceland Symphony to emote (Naxos). **Segerstam** is bulbous and slack (Chandos). Of the lesser Sibelian lights, **Mata** offers a good, sympathetic reading (Pro Arte).

Among historic recordings, **Toscanini** is skillful but cold (RCA). **Koussevitsky** is admired, though he fiddles with Sibelius's orchestration (Pearl, NA). **Beecham** is always good, but I don't think essential here (Dutton). More interesting is **Karajan**'s sober, concentrated recording from 1960 (♦EMI 66599). This dramatically controlled reading reveals a number of surprisingly tragic elements before ending on a note of optimism.

3. This three-movement symphony broke with tradition. Structurally creative outer movements and an Andantino of timeless, almost cosmic contemplation brought Sibelius into close relationship with a younger generation of composers. Beware the critic who accepts an Andantino that's less than 10 minutes long. Kajanus, Sibelius's friend, took 11 minutes—though timing doesn't guarantee profundity. **Davis,** however, is the most profound I know (♦RCA 61963). He conveys genuine understanding, and his cycle with the London Symphony has some of the best sound RCA ever produced. I also like his earlier Boston reading; it's highly refined, though some find it too austere (♦Philips 446160).

A warmer reading can be found with **Segerstam;** the sound is nearly as good as RCA's (♦Chandos 9083). **Vänskä** falls into the warm category as well, and his (also great-sounding) recording gives heartfelt expression without sacrificing profundity (♦BIS 862). The fluent lyricism of **Kamu** is unfairly missing from the catalog (♦DG, NA). **Sakari** is acceptable at budget price (Naxos). **Berglund** is better in his desirable '80s cycle (♦EMI 68643, 2CD). His later 3 is analytic—if not pedantic—by comparison (Finlandia).

This symphony is one of the best or worst of a number of cycles. It's surely the worst of **Bernstein**'s New York series (Sony). He doesn't have a clue to what the music is about, which is certainly not typical. **Maazel**, in his good Vienna cycle, has a fast Andantino that causes the bass line to sound like '50s doo wop (London, NA). You may like it, but its mood is sunny rather than timeless and thoughtful, and he does the same thing in his slick, routine Pittsburgh recording (Sony). The otherwise admirable **Kletzki** (Testament) is just as speedy as Maazel. Going way back to 1932, **Kajanus** set the standard, but the sound is dated; it's for aficionados only (♦Koch 7133).

4. This is the composer's darkest and perhaps finest work, written soon after a bout with throat cancer. It also accounts for the highest percentage of good recordings of a Sibelius symphony. Performances tend to fall into a spectrum of more or less bleakness, though the piece is full of great beauty as well. On the bleakest end is **Davis**'s earlier account with the Boston Symphony (♦Philips 446157, 2CD). This has a striking modernist sensibility and illuminates the composer's amazing flexibility. His more recent London Symphony recording isn't as bleak, but it's more powerfully expressive and has the latest sound (♦RCA 68183). Up there with Davis is **Vänskä**, whose emotional fidelity to this work is the equal of any. His performance has profound depth, heart-wrenching nuance and establishes him as an indispensable interpreter. **Rattle**'s recording is sensitive, analytical, yet passionate, and can be had at mid-price (♦EMI 764121). **Bernstein**'s 1966 recording is one of his most affecting, finely judged performances (♦Sony 47622, 2CD).

Another standard was set by **Karajan**, whose dedication to harmonic texture and refinement of expression made the Berlin Philharmonic a natural for this work. Of his DG and stereo EMI recordings, the latter are recommended for their warmer, richer sound; unfortunately, they're currently NA. For 4, we have his historic (mono) EMI, which is far too studied and lacks flow. But his DG remake is a stunning example of how starkly beautiful this symphony can be. It shouldn't be missed, and it's available at midprice with his other fine readings (♦DG 457748, 2CD). The controversial DG sound has clarity, heft, and smoothness but is slightly lean in the midrange where the strings produce their natural warmth. Whether you will mind I can't say, but with the EMI stereos gone, these are essential.

Segerstam's slow tempos create a darkly brooding atmosphere; this is the best of his cycle (♦Chandos 8943). **Maazel** in Vienna is also excellent (London/Decca). For those wishing a less depressing but still melancholy touch, there are two fine recordings: **Ashkenazy,** falling just short of a top recommendation, and a remarkable Chamber Orchestra of Europe recording with **Berglund** (♦Finlandia 14951). Though lacking the orchestral opulence we're used to, Berglund's smaller group reveals an amazing amount of fresh harmonic detail and is coupled with an equally revealing 6. One of the rare misfires is **Blomstedt,** who seems uninvolved (London, NA). Historic recommendations are difficult, for this symphony can't easily come to life without great sound. **Beecham** has the advantage of skilled remastering, and the work is given its full emotional scope (♦EMI 764027). **Stokowski** is coupled with Ormandy's excellent 1 from 1941, but the sound is thin, and the reading lacks coherence (Biddulph).

5. After a bleak 4, Sibelius returned with a romantic but still unconventional 5. The big, syncopated tune in III is a particular favorite, and it's odd that so few conductors bring it off. In the talented minority is **Bernstein,** who achieves an inspiring grandeur unequaled by anyone before or since (♦Sony 47622, 2CD). This New York Philharmonic performance is also on a single disc coupled with Ormandy's excellent 1 (♦Sony 63060); Bernstein's later account with the Vienna is excellent too, and some listeners prefer its somewhat greater refinement (♦DG, NA). **Karajan**'s 1960 stereo reading with the Philharmonia is another fine rendition (♦EMI, NA). Nothing is taken for granted, but the intense focus is achieved with some loss of spontaneity. His EMI recording is preferred, with the DG a good alternative.

Lately I've begun to appreciate **Rattle** in this work, where earlier I kept comparing his more subtle style with the powerful examples of Bernstein or Karajan. Rattle recorded this twice, once with the Philharmonia in 1981 and then in 1987 with the City of Birmingham Symphony (♦EMI, NA). Some English critics make no distinction between the two, but in the earlier recording, the Philharmonia plays more sensitively, and because Rattle's vision of the work is gentler and more atmospheric than most, this competes on its own terms. The Birmingham recording is stronger but more prosaic. I'd like to see EMI put the Philharmonia recording back in the catalog. Conversely, **Davis**'s newer RCA is an improvement over his earlier Philips—but the big tune in III continues to elude him, and the reading is generally colorless. It's not a bad performance, but Davis is least effective in Sibelius's more traditional, romantic symphonies (1, 2, and 5), and superlative in the modern, innovative ones (especially 3, 4, and 7).

Salonen aptly senses a great deal of melancholy in Sibelius, but a somber approach to 5 is controversial. His reading is curious: I'm not outraged by it, but I don't think it works. Also curious is **Vänskä,** who brings us not one but two versions of 5 in the same disc (BIS). The first is one we're used to and the one Sibelius wanted; the second is the original of 1915, before revisions. Both performances are quite good, and the standard version falls just short of a recommendation, but the 1915 truly sounds unfinished and is difficult to enjoy, however interesting it may be academically. **Berglund** in his '80s set does a fine, relaxed 5 (EMI), and would garner a recommendation if it weren't for Bernstein, Karajan, and Rattle/Philharmonia. His later 5 is clear and level-headed, but not up to his best (Finlandia). The same goes for **Ashkenazy;** this is perhaps the weakest of his London cycle. **Gibson** is better (Chandos), but there's no use pretending it's as good as Bernstein or Karajan.

Kajanus may again please the historically curious (Koch), and EMI offers **Karajan**'s 1953 mono account coupled with an oddly rigid 4.

6. Had I the need to hire a conductor or orchestra, I'd use this symphony as an employment test. Musicians must coax exquisite beauty and emotion from a score that is cool, even-tempered, and structurally abstract, yet not lose the qualities that make the music unique. Many fail.

Of those who succeed, I put **Vänskä** at the top (♦BIS 864). He does two things: He shapes the music into a heartfelt symphony (rather than the extended tone poem it often becomes), yet he never loses his grip on the work's cool objectivity—a neat trick. **Rattle,** whom I also recommend, elicits great sensitivity from his City of Birmingham orchestra, and his may be the warmest version (♦EMI 764121). For those who like 6 cool and austere, **Karajan**'s magical reading is available (♦DG 457748, 2CD). His more natural-sounding EMI stereo recording is NA, and his mono Philharmonia recording for the same label isn't nearly as good an interpretation as his DG or EMI in Berlin.

Leaper gives us the best of his cycle, though it's coupled with a weak 1 (♦Naxos 550197). **Davis,** on both RCA and Philips, is good, but not among the best. **Bernstein** is better (Sony), though I wish he'd lived long enough to rerecord this for DG (and the same goes for 3). **Berglund,** in his newer Chamber Orchestra of Europe reading, brings a hint of sunlight to the cool Alpine meadows, and the 24-bit recording is of demonstration quality (♦Finlandia 14951). The textures are wonderful, and it's coupled with an equally fascinating 4 (see above).

Beecham's fervid, sympathetic 1942 NYPO reading is now available in an excellent remastering that surpasses its previous incarnations (♦Dutton Labs 8013), but his 1954 Royal Philharmonic is even more compassionate and refined (BBC 4041).

7. This single-movement work was christened a symphony after its premiere as *Fantastica sinfonia.* Sibelius realized that although it was a single movement, it was of a high and serious nature and should be included in his symphonic canon. But even the original title is puzzling, for it doesn't convey the work's disconsolate yearnings. In a way, it's Sibelius's Tchaikovsky 6.

Performances must have intense concentration in the strings, and a number of the conductors I've been recommending elsewhere can't quite manage this. The exceptions begin with **Davis,** who again shows his understanding of one of Sibelius's less romantic works. With both the Boston (♦Philips 46160, 2CD) and the London Symphonies (♦RCA 68312), the strings play so sensitively at critical moments that all competition is swept aside. It can't be fortuitous that they do, for here is the same conductor with two different orchestras creating the same heart-wrenching effect.

Bernstein nearly matches Davis in emotional intensity (♦DG, NA). **Ormandy** and the Philadelphia are superbly focused, and hard to beat at budget price, coupled with their outstanding performance of 2 (♦Sony 53509). **Sanderling** has a smooth current of emotion and doesn't miss the yearning (♦Berlin 9281) .**Vänskä** doesn't quite have the feel for it, but he's not bad either (BIS). Some critics recommend **Järvi,** but he's unsympathetic to the spirit of the work and perfunctory where it should be heartfelt (BIS). **Maazel** and **Ashkenazy** have received praise, and they're certainly better than Järvi but aren't quite top choices (both London).

Beecham's fervid, sympathetic 1942 New York Philharmonic reading of 7 is now available in an excellent remastering that surpasses its previous incarnations (♦Dutton 8013), but his 1954 Royal Philharmonic is even more compassionate and refined (BBC 4041). **Koussevitzky's** account is brilliant and intense, the keystone of his Sibelius interpretations (Pearl and EMI, NA).

Kullervo. This early work, written before *En Saga,* made the composer's reputation. Although not often thought of as a symphony, it's a five-movement, 80-minute composition of epic proportions. A number of good recordings have appeared in the last few years, of which **Davis** (♦RCA 68312) and **Salonen** (♦Sony 5263) are the best. **Järvi** is dramatic, but feels a bit rushed (BIS).

OTHER ORCHESTRAL MUSIC
Sibelius's shorter orchestral works were written between 1892 and 1926. Many were inspired by the *Kalevala,* a book of Finnish legends published in 1835. If Sibelius had never written a symphony, his high reputation would have been firmly established by his shorter masterpieces.

The Bard. This is the first piece written after the somber Symphony 4, its moody chords accented by delicate harp arpeggios. It's the jewel of

Gibson's fine set of tone poems (♦Chandos 8395, 2CD; also available with *The Legends,* ♦Chandos 6586). He elicits a truly haunted atmosphere that no other recording quite matches, though **Berglund** isn't far behind (EMI), and neither is **Beecham** (♦EMI 764027, mono). **Järvi** is graceful and elegant, in an excellent program of lesser-known works (♦BIS 384).

Belshazzar's Feast. This is incidental music for a little-known play. The suite, though of high merit, has been in and out of the catalog for years. **Järvi** and the Gothenburg Symphony have great sound and play with feeling, though whether they have probed the colorful possibilities to the utmost is difficult to say without more comparisons (♦BIS 359). **Vänskä** delivers the complete theater score, not just the suite, in a fine performance (♦BIS 735).

The Dryad. This came just before Symphony 4 and is associated with that darkly reflective period. Once again, **Gibson** has an affinity for its delicate mood, and inasmuch as this and *The Bard* are relatively rare, not to mention extremely well played by the Royal Scottish National Orchestra, this fine-sounding set becomes essential to the Sibelius collector (♦Chandos 8359, 2CD).

En Saga. Written in 1892, though it's the 1901 revision we're used to hearing, this work has an exotic, fairy-tale quality, though without a programmatic source; Sibelius insisted that it came directly from his own youthful emotions. Two of the best recordings came nearly 40 years apart, and, luckily, both have excellent sound. The first is **Sargent** in an inexpensive set (♦EMI 69134, 2CD). His *En Saga* is not only thrilling, it's loaded with exotic atmosphere and sumptuous orchestral detail as well. The relatively unknown Tampere Philharmonic led by the young Finnish conductor **Tuomas Ollila** isn't far behind, however (♦Ondine 871). Ollila's penchant for sensuous drama combines with state-of-the-art sound to deliver a disc full of Sibelian wonders. If his orchestra isn't quite the Vienna, they play imaginatively and without the complacency that can plague big-name ensembles.

Ormandy gives a rousing account with the familiar Ormandy virtues (♦Sony 48217). **Ashkenazy's** recording has slightly lower voltage but superb atmosphere and focus (♦London 452576, CD). **Salonen** programs his smoothly powerful reading with controversial renditions of *Legends* (♦Sony 48067, see below). **Segerstam** has fine orchestral detail and excellent sound, but his tempos are sluggish (Chandos).

Boult gives us excellent monaural recordings of the tone poems; his *En Saga* has great momentum and a quiet, ghostly quality in the center section (♦Omega 1027/28). **Furtwängler's** tempered power is worth pursuing, in a release with both his 1943 and 1950 performances (♦Music & Arts 799). You can get yet another Furtwängler *En Saga* from 1943 along with his famous Tchaikovsky 6 (DG 78558), though the 1950 recording is best for the tone poem.

Finlandia. Composed in 1899, this is the composer's most famous and patriotic work. It must be performed with passion and drama—and bring a tear to the eye with its beautiful inner melody. Of the dozens of available versions, only a handful capture the true spirit of the work. My hands-down favorite is **Ashkenazy,** who seems even more adept at the tone poems than the symphonies (♦London 452576, 2CD). He insists on the greatness and emotional intensity of these works and communicates that attitude in each and every rendition. **Ollila** has outstanding sound and finds the music's stature as well as its emotion (♦Ondine 871), but **Berglund** is even more worthy with the Helsinki Philharmonic (♦EMI 68646, 2CD). Berglund is sensitive rather than sentimental in the beautiful latter section, and elicits great power from his Finnish orchestra that *must* play this work well.

Sakari excels in Sibelius's shorter works, and he has just the right emotive balance here, with sound that seems more transparent than the early symphony releases in his cycle (◆Naxos 554265). Davis has great sound also, and the music is gorgeously played by the London Symphony (◆RCA 68770). Karajan's reading is good but not in the top rank (EMI). Speaking of sound, the temptation to get Levi's recording should not be indulged (Telarc). Ondine's and RCA's sound are just as good, if not better, and both Ollila and Davis are better interpreters.

Ormandy provides a fine supplementary *Finlandia,* with the patriotic hymn written for the broad finale sung by the Mormon Tabernacle Choir (◆Sony, NA). Hans Rosbaud is consistently convincing in this repertory, and as a true Sibelius advocate often transcends far better-known conductors (◆DG 447-4523, mono).

Karelia Suite. This was distilled from a lengthier work that came on the heels of *Kullervo.* Though only about 15 minutes long, it has a buoyant, captivating, epic sweep. Sargent and the Vienna Philharmonic have the measure of the music's three disparate movements (◆EMI 69134). Ashkenazy gives it a slightly Russian flavor, but there's great skill and subtlety in his rendition (◆London 452576). Barbirolli is undoubtedly great, but available only in his complete symphony set (EMI). Of the newer readings, Davis gives an eccentric and utterly prosaic performance that's best passed by, though his disc has other virtues (RCA, see below). I'd pick Sakari for its wonderfully hushed rhythms and lithe melodies (◆Naxos 554265). Don't miss the complete original score for *Karelia* with Vänskä (BIS 915) or Ollila (◆Ondine 913).

King Christian II. In suite form, this was the piece that introduced Sibelius to the European world of 1898. Collectors may want the complete theater version with Vänskä (◆BIS 918), while those seeking the familiar suite may be satisfied with Jussi Jalas, the composer's son-in-law, in a set of orchestral works (London). Yet Jalas's refined sensibilities are bettered by Berglund and the Bournemouth's melodic sensuality and rhythmic vigor (EMI 69773). Sakari has a strong soloist in "Lied des Narren," and is elsewhere ardent and rhapsodic (◆Chandos 9158).

Kuolema. This word means death, and here it is taken from a play by Sibelius's brother-in-law, Arved Järnefelt. Vänskä gives us the complete score (◆BIS 915, with the complete *Karelia*). The more familiar incidental music for *Kuolema* is also well served by Järvi and Jalas. Berglund gives us the two most familiar pieces, *Scene with Cranes* and *Valse triste.* They are poignant, vivid, and affecting.

Legends from the Kalevala. These are derived from the book of Finnish mythology and follow the adventures of the young hero, Lemminkäinen. Their moody central scene, *The Swan of Tuonela,* is often recorded separately. The complete four *Legends* are a must, however, and I'd start with Gibson at mid-price, both for its poignantly dark rendering of *Swan* and the drama of all three *Lemminkäinen* sections (◆Chandos 6586). For audiophiles, Segerstam and the Helsinki Philharmonic are hard to beat. The sheer power of sound makes this a compelling choice, though be prepared for the conductor's slower-than-usual tempos in all but the exciting *Lemminkäinen's Return* (◆Ondine 852).

The Los Angeles Philharmonic also has great sound, and Salonen delivers readings of intense sophistication (◆Sony 48067). His performances combine to form a deeply flowing river of music that grows more profound with each hearing. Critics are in a quandary about the reversed order of the two central sections, *Swan* being third (which was the composer's original intent). No one should be without these soul-stirring readings, whatever their order. The reversed sections are also picked up by Segerstam and Sakari. The latter's performance is magical, delicate, and blazingly incisive (◆Naxos 554265). Though the sound is excellent, Järvi is routine (BIS). The same can be said about Vänskä, whose reading has surface appeal but lacks depth (BIS). Ormandy is a better choice (RCA, NA). This is considered one of his best recordings, but I like his earlier *Swan* better than this one (◆Sony 48271), and some of the *Lemminkäinen* sections seem slack. Newcomer Mikko Frank is given superior sound; his readings are satisfying, though they are tightly controlled and would benefit from more spontaneity (Ondine).

The Swan of Tuonela is readily available in a number of outstanding individual performances. Apart from the Sony Ormandy, Mackerras's reading has true *gravitas,* coupled with an outstanding Symphony 2 (◆IMP 927). Stokowski may be best of all; he's remarkably expressive and shapes the piece with astonishing originality, yet never loses its melancholy atmosphere (◆Sony 63260, 2CD). Many admire Karajan, but I find him a bit glossy (EMI). Berglund seems exactly right—vivid, sensitive, detailed, and ideally played, this time by the Bournemouth Symphony (◆EMI 69773, 2CD). Sargent is certainly in the top class, and his recording has smooth sound that belies its late '50s vintage (◆EMI 69134, 2CD).

Toscanini and the NBC Symphony offer a lush and expressive *Swan,* but they're too dynamic and don't quite capture the morbid atmosphere (RCA, mono). Boult comes through with what may be the best *Lemminkäinen's Return* (◆Omega 1027). The mono sound seems to emphasize, not compromise, the orchestral texture, and the reading is packed with excitement. Another volatile performance is by Beecham, coupled with a truly classic reading of Symphony 7 (◆Dutton 8013).

Luonnotar. This is a beautiful, melancholy masterpiece, with a difficult role for soprano. It's hard to imagine a better performance than Söderström's with Ashkenazy (◆London 452576, 2CD). Her combination of vivid lyricism and ideal execution, accompanied by the orchestra's velvet-black calm, is unparalleled. Also competitive is Taru Valjakka's account with Berglund (EMI).

Night Ride and Sunrise. This is a journey across a dark, imaginative landscape. Gibson is exciting and straightforward; his set of tone poems can be recommended for its high points and overall consistency (◆Chandos 8395, 2CD). Järvi is equally exciting, but coupled with his impatient Symphony 7 (BIS). Davis is a bit tame (RCA). Segerstam is sleek and musical, with a sedate tempo that generates a subtly mournful atmosphere in the latter half (◆Ondine 9142). Rattle is more sprightly, and he loses none of the beauty (◆EMI, NA). The classic account by Horst Stein also attains the top rank, and his excellent program is shared with Ashkenazy's in a terrific "two-fer" (◆London 452576, 2CD).

The Oceanides. This is an impressionistic tone painting of the sea in all its moods. Segerstam and the Helsinki Philharmonic are powerful in this work, with spectacular climaxes delivered in audiophile sound (◆Ondine 9142). Andrew Davis finds grandeur as well as atmosphere (◆Finlandia 15242). Gibson is downright salty, and although his Royal Scottish National can't quite match Segerstam's dynamic weight, his carefully wrought atmosphere compels a recommendation (◆Chandos 8395). Boult's historic reading perfectly builds the wind and waves from quiescence to climax (◆Omega 1028, mono).

Pelléas and Mélisande. This work comes in two forms: the incidental music Op. 46 and the complete theatrical version. **Ollila,** this time with the Tapiola Sinfonietta, captures the poetry and drama of the suite as few others have, in gorgeous sound (♦Ondine 952). With subtle emotional restraint, **Boughton** and the English String Orchestra play the incidental music beautifully, though some may prefer more warmth (Nimbus 5169). Slightly less restrained but still refined is the ever-dependable **Berglund** with the Bournemouth Symphony (♦EMI 69773). Their "Death of Mélisande" is very sensitive, yet without an overabundance of pathos. **Sakari** is smooth and lyrical (Chandos). For more music, **Vänskä** plays the original theatrical version, along with the original versions of *Karelia Suite* and *King Christian II* (♦BIS 918). For the collector, **Beecham** gives four selections from the incidental music (Dutton Labs 8013), while **Barbirolli** and the Hallé are now reissued in his symphony set (EMI).

Pohjola's Daughter. A major composition inspired by the *Kalevala,* this piece brings out every fiber of the composer's emotive tapestry. From its expressive opening, **Bernstein**'s performance has a passionate, hair-raising temperament that never lets up (♦Sony 48271). Nothing quite matches its almost cinematic virtues, and it appears on a budget release with some of Ormandy's best. **Salonen** has a slower tempo that colors the music from the beginning, and as may be expected, there's nothing ordinary about his detailed, introspective reading, which may be loved or hated alongside his cheerless Symphony 5 (Sony 42366). **Sargent** is good, but this particular selection (with the BBC rather than the Vienna) has slightly lesser sound quality (EMI). **Berglund** (EMI) and **Gibson** (Chandos) are dependably excellent, while in the historic category, **Toscanini** is well played but ordinary (RCA).

Rakastava (*The Lover*). This is a ravishing musical gem, seamlessly reworked for string orchestra from an early choral piece, and relatively unknown on records. This tender, personal music is eloquently communicated by **Boughton** in a CD that brings together a number of lesser-known pieces (♦Nimbus 5169). No less fine is **Gibson** (♦Chandos 6591), who is always sympathetic to Sibelius's shorter masterpieces.

Scènes Historiques. Taken from various stories and settings, these pieces come in two sets of three that usually accompany one another on disc. This is somewhat prosaic Sibelius compared with the better-known works, but definitely worth hearing. **Järvi** does an excellent job (♦BIS 295), as does **Gibson** (♦Chandos 6591). **Jalas** has a light and airy touch and an excellent program in his "two-fer" (London).

Spring Song. This is a lovely eight-minute work, elegiac in tone, is nicely played by **Berglund** in his set that is a marvel of consistently fine interpretations (♦EMI 69773, 2CD). **Gibson** is equally good (♦Chandos 8395, 2CD).

Scaramouche. This is a pastiche of music from a "ballet-pantomime" by Poul Knudsen, greatly varied in mood, and about an hour in its entirety. The excellent-sounding **Järvi** delivers the necessary atmosphere and eerie charm (♦BIS 502). **Jalas**'s "two-fer" set contains a shorter, 21-minute suite, which will be all that's needed for many of us (♦London 448267). It's very well played by the Hungarian State Orchestra, and the disc is a good value.

Swanwhite. This was commissioned by the Swedish Theater for a production of a Strindberg fairy tale. Memorable melodic lines are scant in this atmospheric music, accented by harp and influenced by Tchaikovsky and Rimsky-Korsakov. I like **Berglund**'s affectionate

poignancy, with its hint of melancholy from the Bournemouth Symphony musicians, though it's a shortened (15-minute) program of selections (♦EMI 69773. 2CD). **Jalas** offers the complete 24-minute suite, nicely played but without Berglund's depth (London). **Järvi** has excellent sound, the complete suite, and fine musicianship in the Gothenburg Symphony (♦BIS 359). **Sakari**'s 19-minute program is graceful, charming, atmospheric, and gorgeously played by the Iceland Symphony (♦Chandos 9158). **Vänskä** offers the original theater version, but it's only a couple of minutes longer than the suite and seems more disjointed with its 14 separate sections (BIS).

Tapiola. Sibelius's last major work, this is a stunning impressionist fantasy of the primeval forest inhabited by Tapio, the forest god. First on many reviewers' lists is **Karajan** (♦EMI 64331). I think it's recommendable, but not as good as the more recent **Davis** with the London Symphony (♦RCA 68770). These musicians lead us down the shadowy paths into the misty grottos of Sibelius's nature music with an ecstatic vision that captures every lush detail, and the RCA engineers deliver the glowing definition and power the music requires.

Vänskä is also polished and atmospheric, but a bit slack (BIS 864). **Berglund** is stronger in his symphony set (EMI 68646, 2CD). His faster tempo generates vitality, but he doesn't dig into the atmosphere of the piece as well as he might. **Segerstam** uses a slow tempo again (Ondine 852), but it's no slower than EMI/Karajan. The storm music is spectacular, as is the sound, but lethargy in the first half keeps the performance from the top rank. **Gibson** is straightforward, exciting, and detailed (Chandos). So is **Rosbaud** (DG, mono), and collectors should keep their eyes out for **Koussevitzky;** this was one of his best Sibelius performances.

The Tempest. This work is taken from Shakespeare, and apart from the complete version, there are two suites. In this case, the historic album comes first, for I know of no one who's topped **Beecham** and the Royal Philharmonic in this music (♦EMI, NA). Rhythmically alive, warmly sensuous, delicately enchanting, awesomely powerful, you name it. Beecham doesn't play all the music in the two suites and chooses his own order of selections, but that's just the way it is. The remastered sound, though mono, might have been recorded yesterday. We must assume it will return to the catalog. Don't confuse Beecham's London Philharmonic recording of just four sections of the music (Dutton Labs 8013) with this one, although it's a must for Symphony 7 (see above).

Both suites from *The Tempest* are played with great authority—and in audiophile sound—by **Segerstam** (♦Ondine 914). He not only whips up awesome climaxes, but is tenderly poetic in "Berceuse" and elsewhere. By programming *The Tempest* along with *The Oceanides,* this disc becomes a sea-music spectacular, and Segerstam stands right alongside Beecham in interpretation. This is a must. For value, **Jalas** is tempting; he conducts with tenderness and charm, and is only just shy of the very best in the storm section (♦London 448267, 2CD). **Järvi** and the skilled Gothenburg Symphony have sound nearly as good as Segerstam's; they play with power and commitment and provide an interesting, out-of-the-way program. Both **Vänskä** (♦BIS 581) and **Saraste** (♦Ondine 813) give us the complete score. The latter, with the Finnish Radio Symphony, may have a slight edge in one or two climaxes, but overall there is much poetry in both and little to choose between them.

Valse triste. This is music almost everyone knows; it was originally part of *Kuolema.* It comes close to being "conductor proof." Of special interest, though, is **Davis** (♦RCA 68770). By taking it slower than usual (just over 6 minutes), he makes it melancholy and eerily beguiling. **Ormandy**'s is a more conventionally fine performance, with several other superior readings and at budget price (♦Sony 48217).

The Wood-Nymph. This legend appears in four of Sibelius's works, three of which share the same thematic material. **Vänskä** and the Lahti Symphony ardently deliver the premier recording of the 21-minute tone-poem version (♦BIS 815). This magical, magisterial reading is a must, and an unusual bonus (along with the complete *Swanwhite*) is the little-known short piece, *The Lonely Ski Trail.*   HALDEMAN

VIOLIN CONCERTO

Heifetz and Beecham were first to record this concerto, in 1935 (♦EMI 64030 et al.), and minor technical imperfections plus dated sound haven't scared collectors away for 65 years. Equal parts fire and ice, Heifetz was born to play this work. His tempos are the fastest I know, apart from his own even fleeter stereo version (1959) with Hendl (RCA 63470). Here the performers occasionally seem on the verge of spinning out of control. Nevertheless, this is a galvanizing reading, even if it does seem rushed. Heifetz's tone was more secure in 1935.

There are other notable prestereo recordings. **Anna Ignatius** (1943), while not a great technician, plays passionately yet without a shred of ego; the conductor is Sibelius's brother-in-law (Finlandia 810). Another vintage performance, recorded in 1945, comes from **Neveu** with Susskind (♦Dutton 5016). Neveu played with such concentration that she literally drew blood. Hers is a tough-as-nails interpretation, and the music has seldom been recorded with such intensity and technical command. A slower tempo in the finale increases her precision, with results that are more exciting, not less.

In 1951, Beecham joined **Stern** and another memorable recording resulted (in Sony 45956, 3CD). Stern, unfazed by technical challenges, is wondrous, and his noble and plaintive tone galvanizes the listener. The dim recording may give some pause, however. Stern's 1969 remake with Ormandy is emotionally generous and is much better recorded (♦Sony 66829). **Oistrakh**'s Sibelius has influenced generations of violinists, Russian and otherwise. He is at his straight-ahead and romantic best with Ormandy, and this version is recommended to those who want opulence but little neurosis (Sony 47659). A 1954 version with Ehrling also has good playing but is short-circuited by bad sound (Testament 1032).

Francescatti, whose classical violinism is right for Mozart, is too plain for Sibelius (Sony). **Sarah Chang** is like Francescatti with more temperament; her version with Jansons is poised and uncomplicated, and her tone is attractive (EMI 56418). **Chung** is similar but stronger (Decca 425080). She's emotionally responsive—coolly exciting, but always respectful of the score—and Previn complements her perfectly. The grand and assured **Perlman** is better still (EMI 47167). His unselfconscious virtuosity makes the music shine with brilliant Nordic lights, and again Previn is a fine partner. An earlier Perlman account with Leinsdorf finds him reveling in his technique (RCA 63591), but the EMI version goes deeper in every way. **Midori** plays with cool intensity, as if she were a Nordic priestess (Sony 58967). She and Mehta favor slow tempos, but there's no danger of boredom, given her concentration and beautiful tone.

Compared to the dramatic Salonen, **Cho-Liang Lin** lacks something in individuality, though his beautiful pure tone partly compensates (CBS). A pairing of **Joshua Bell** with Salonen works better; here Salonen adopts a different approach entirely (Sony 65949). The first movement is daringly slow; eerie shadows glide in the moonlight. Bell's tone is an-

gelically pure, and he's not frightened by the music's demands. Slow but exciting describes **Vengerov**'s version with Barenboim (Teldec 13161). He plays with personality but not at the expense of the composer, and his range of colors is impressive. **Kennedy** belies his "punk" image with a reading that gently insinuates and is more pretty than assertive (EMI). Rattle pulls out plenty of subtle orchestral detail; he's too excitable in II, though, and contrast is lost.

Now we come to the more unusual recordings. **Tossy Spivakovsky** and **Ivry Gitlis** play the concerto as if it were for gypsy violin and fill their part with swooping, gurgling, and edgy tones. Spivakovsky makes my hair stand on end, and Gitlis plays particularly loose with the score; both are guilty pleasures. The former has the benefit of near-audiophile recording quality and solid support from conductor Hannikainen (♦Everest 9035). Gitlis is partnered by Horenstein (in Vox 5505, 2CD). **Salerno-Sonnenberg,** with Tilson Thomas, also goes to extremes but less successfully (EMI). She attempts to chill—the work is "ice and bleakness" for her—but her interpretation is mannered and uninvolving.

Leonidas Kavakos shares her viewpoint but with more rewarding results (♦BIS 500). He and conductor Vänskä strip away all the surface glitter, leaving the score tough and bracing. There's no ego in this reading, and Kavakos's technique is top-flight. A bonus is the inclusion of the concerto's original version. Although the final version is clearly superior, it's fascinating to hear how radically different (and strange) the work was when Finnish audiences first heard it in 1904. At budget price, **Kremer** with Muti is worthwhile (Seraphim; EMI). His tone is wiry, however, and the heaviness of his interpretive points verges on affectation. The slow movement is very slow indeed, and the finale starts at a brave, fast tempo but soon settles down. Interpretively as well as sonically, this is a bit coarse.

In contrast, **Dong-Suk Kang** is relaxed and content to let the music speak for itself. I is under-seasoned, but II is outstanding, and the macabre elements of the finale are played down in favor of dance—a most interesting reading. The conductor is Leaper (Naxos 553233 or 550329). Another good budget reading, part of a "two-fer," comes from **Christian Ferras** and Karajan (DG 437949, 2CD). Ferras's muscular playing raises the music's emotional stakes, and while it's possible to criticize Karajan for grooming the music excessively, the pairing of soloist and conductor is provocative.

Accardo and Colin Davis have their admirers, but this is an oddball performance: maddeningly slow, willful, and unidiomatic (Philips). **Leila Josefowicz** plays the work well in her debut CD; unfortunately Marriner's soft-grained conducting works against her (Philips). **Vadim Repin** is similarly romantic, and he has better company in Krivine, yet he's not memorable either (Erato). Another Russian, **Spivakov,** works hard to personalize the music, but the results are superficial, not incisive (RCA). **Shaham,** with Sinopoli, aggressively slashes away, squandering his opportunities to express himself sympathetically (DG).

Only a few recordings dispense with a second concerto (usually Tchaikovsky's) in favor of Sibelius's shorter works for violin and orchestra. **Mutter,** although she emphasizes the music's dark side, brings a remarkably human quality to her expressive playing (♦DG 447895). Two Serenades and a *Humoresque* are the coupling, and Previn (yet again) conducts imaginatively. **Joseph Swensen** plays well too, but not with Mutter's distinction (RCA 60444). He has a good conductor in Saraste, though, and a coupling of the six *Humoresques* is an asset. Maazel's early recordings of Sibelius's symphonies are treasurable, but his later recording of the concerto with **Julian Rachlin**—a fine player—suffers from too many interpretive distortions (Sony 53272). They offer only the second of the two Serenades and *En Saga* as couplings.   TUTTLE

CHAMBER MUSIC

Sibelius is almost unique in his near-total abandonment of chamber music after his first great orchestral successes in 1892, ceasing to write music for three or more players—with the exception of two string quartets—and abstaining from duos for fourteen years (1900–14). Much has been made of his substantial chamber juvenilia, including the string trios and piano quartet (Ondine 826), *Loviisa* Piano Trio, and G minor Piano Quintet (♦Finlandia 95858). **Erik T. Tawaststjerna** and the Sibelius Academy Quartet are more polished in the last than **Anthony Goldstone** and the Gabrieli Quartet (Chandos).

Cello and piano. Sibelius' entire output for cello has been idiomatically recorded by **Thedéen** and Folke Gräsbeck (♦BIS 817), marginally preferable to **Mørk** and Thibaudet in *Malinconia* and the cello versions of the Opp. 77 and 78 sets (Virgin) or **Heinrich Schiff** and Leonskaja in *Malinconia* (Philips).

String quartets. Three of the four complete string quartets are student works, the best the fine B-sharp (1890)—not in the least Sibelian-sounding. Only the **Sibelius Academy Quartet** has recorded all four, in beautifully shaped, loving performances (♦Finlandia 95851). Their understanding of Sibelius' earliest manner in the A minor (1889) is superior to **Sophisticated Ladies** (BIS), the **Wilanow Quartet** (Accord), and even the **Jean Sibelius Quartet** (Ondine).

Voces Intimae, Sibelius's one mature quartet (the brief *Andante festivo* aside), has been recorded many times. The **Sibelius Academy Quartet** plays with great refinement (Finlandia, as above). The restoration of the 1933 **Budapest Quartet** recording has earned much critical praise (Biddulph 098). There are nicely phrased performances from the aptly named **Voces Intimae Quartet** (BIS 101, with Schumann's Quartet 3), **Sophisticated Ladies** (BIS, see above), and the **Gabrieli Quartet,** the finest all-round (♦Chandos 8742). The **Wilanow Quartet** is earnest but not competitive (Accord), the **Juilliard Quartet** curiously coupled with Verdi (Sony). Sadly, the **Lindsay Quartet**'s excellent version, coupled with Delius' *Late Swallows* Quartet, is NA.

Violin and piano. Sibelius' complete mature output for this combination has been recorded by **Nils-Erik Sparf** and Bengt Forsberg in exemplary accounts and excellent sound (♦BIS 525, 625), preferable to **Yoshiko Arai** and **Eero Heinonen**'s more selective recordings, which include some juvenilia (Ondine). The "Complete Youth Production" for violin and piano has been recorded by **Jaakko Kuusisto** and Folke Gräsbeck in two discs, the second including the early Suite in E, Sonata in F, and four solo violin pieces (BIS 1023). Their accounts stake a greater claim for the music than did **Pekka Kuusisto** (Jaakko's brother) and Raija Kerppo in the Suite or **Ernst Kovacic** and Juhani Lagerspetz in the Sonata (both Ondine).

PIANO MUSIC

For a composer who declared "the piano cannot sing," Sibelius wrote a great deal for the instrument, mainly collections of miniatures, but including a vigorous early sonata, three sonatinas, and a suite, *Kyllikki*, derived from the *Kalevala*. **Tawaststjerna** recorded a complete cycle (BIS, 6CD), adding a further pair of the composer's arrangements of his orchestral works (BIS 366/7), performances that still hold up remarkably well. However, **Annette Servadei**, in just five CDs, is now clear first choice in the original works, her performances yielding nothing in understanding or technique to any rival (♦Olympia 631-5). The "essential"

piano music, including the sonata and sonatinas plus *Finlandia,* appear in a fine disc played with authority by **Marita Viitasalo** (♦Finlandia 98984). The sonatinas and *Kyllikki* were also recorded individualistically if not idiomatically by **Gould** (Sony). **Gothóni**'s recital includes *Finlandia* and *Kyllikki,* plus the Opp. 34, 75, and 114 sets and excerpts from Op. 24 (Ondine).

CHORAL MUSIC

Sibelius' complete songs for male chorus have been recorded in winning performances by **Matti Hyökki,** including *Finlandia Hymn, Rakastava,* and *Jaeger March* (♦Finlandia 95849). A complete set for mixed chorus came from the Jubilate Choir directed by **Astrid Riska** (Ondine 805), repertoire they later reprised in couplings with *Cantatas for Helsinki University* (BIS 825 and 998). The occasional cantatas of the 1890s, including that for the *Coronation of Nicholas II* (Ondine), are generally uninspired; but later works derived from Finnish history—*Sandels*—or myth—*The Origin of Fire*—are stronger, confirmed by the thrilling performances of the Helsinki University Male Chorus, the Gothenburg Symphony, and **Neeme Järvi** (♦BIS 314, with *Jaeger March, Har du mod?,* the political "hit" *Song of the Athenians,* and a version of *Finlandia* with the choral hymn overlaid). **Eri Klas** conducts the Finnish National Opera Chorus and Orchestra in an equally well sung (and more generous) program of later cantatas including *Oma maa, Väinö's Song, Maan virsi,* plus *Finlandia* for mixed chorus and orchestra (♦Ondine 754).   RICKARDS

SONGS

Sibelius wrote most of his more than 100 songs to Swedish texts; only a few are settings of Finnish or German poems. No doubt that's one reason these attractive compositions were neglected for years; only native Scandinavians seem to be comfortable singing in Swedish. (One of the few exceptions was Marian Anderson, who had a number of Sibelius songs in her repertory). But in recent times, perhaps because of CDs, these romantic songs, mostly written in the composer's early years, have achieved wider popularity, though nothing comparable to that of his symphonies and tone poems.

Sibelius's vocal style is often declamatory, yet many of his songs have beautiful melodies, for instance the popular "Black Roses" and "Maiden coming from a tryst." Many of them are about nature; 30 of these are to poems by his favorite poet, J.L. Runeberg. Sibelius was very adept in creating a musical atmosphere by very simple means that reflect the poem's sentiments and pictures. The songs don't often explore deep feelings (unlike those of his contemporaries Mahler and Wolf), and whatever emotional content they have is easily perceived. The piano is seldom an equal partner, most often relegated to the background, perhaps because Sibelius was a violinist, not a pianist.

Three of today's Scandinavian artists have recorded many of these songs. The best is Swedish mezzo **von Otter,** whose all-Sibelius discs top the current listings (♦BIS 457 and 757). She has a rich, beautiful voice of wide range, excellent diction, and a highly musical and intelligent approach. Her shaping of phrases and coloring of words always seems right, and she never exaggerates. Another fine interpreter is the Finnish baritone **Hynninen,** who has recorded two CDs, both with orchestral accompaniments, only some of which are by Sibelius. In the better of these, he has the disc all to himself (♦Ondine 823); in the other, he shares the work with the Swedish soprano **Marie-Ann Håggender,** who's not his equal in vocal range, flexibility and diction (BIS 270 or MHS 512462).

Hynninen's fellow-Finn, bass-baritone **Tom Krause,** has also recorded a fine selection (♦Finlandia 96871). He's a more dramatically expressive singer than Hynninen or von Otter, sometimes at the expense of tonal beauty. Older recordings by **Söderström** and **Flagstad** have either been deleted or never transferred to CD. If and when they become available, grab them, especially Söderström's.   MOSES

Robert Simpson (1921–1997)

Simpson was an English composer whose music didn't fall into the chameleon-like style changes that afflict many of his contemporaries. His music recalls the general characteristics of several of the composers he about wrote in articles and books, namely Nielsen, Bruckner, and Beethoven.

He wrote 11 symphonies; the first ten are available from **Handley** in well-played performances, recorded with clarity and ambience. This Hyperion series also includes his 14 string quartets, the first nine and 13 played by the **Delmé Quartet** in clear and committed performances, not technically perfect but good nevertheless. The **Coull Quartet** plays 10 through 12 in similarly satisfactory fashion, somewhat more assertively than the Delmé. The **Vanbrugh Quartet** plays 13 and 14 very well. Much of Simpson's other chamber music and the complete piano music and other works for organ and chorus are also recorded in this admirably comprehensive series. I deal separately only with pieces that have been recorded more than once or aren't part of this collection.

Symphony 3 (1962) is in two long movements; the first employs an insistent rhythmic figure that recalls the single-minded ferocity of Beethoven's 5th, the second is in the form of a 15-minute accelerando. This work has been recorded twice, in **Handley**'s series and by **Horenstein** in an equally impressive recording and a somewhat more starkly dramatic reading (Unicorn-Kanchana 2028).

The Piano Concerto of 1967 is the only concertante work presently recorded, by **John Ogdon** (BBC 91762). It's an effective and enjoyable work in one long, sectional movement, a curious piece containing more evidence of humor than Simpson usually shows.

The string quartet is the genre that most involved Simpson, with its association with the purity of the classics. No. 1, written, like his Symphony 1 in 1951, plays off the same two keys, A and E-flat, but in a more intense way. The second of its two movements is a set of variations on a palindromic theme in which the theme moves from E-flat to A and back again. The work ends with a mighty fugue in which the two keys battle it out together, ending with an odd little dance of reconciliation. No. 2 (1953) is a one-movement work in which a continuous metronome speed serves to unify several contrasted sections. The mood is uneasy, a contrast between a winsome little tune and disturbing interruptions. No. 3 (1954) is again in two movements ending in hard-won but convincing triumph.

These first three quartets are subtly related in material and mood and were recorded together by the **Element Quartet** in the mid-'50s (Pearl 0023). The performances are good, rougher in outline and more direct than the smoother renditions by the **Delmé** (Hyperion 66376, 66386, 66419, with 4-6 and String Trio). Technically there's little to choose between these versions, but the superior Hyperion sound may be significant.   MOORE

Christian Sinding (1856–1941)

As long as there are students of the piano, Sinding's music will live on. What aspiring keyboard virtuoso hasn't struggled with that quintessential recital piece, *Rustle of Spring*? This one piece has far overshadowed the remainder of Sinding's prolific output for the keyboard, let alone his works for orchestra. We should hope for better for the man who—together with Grieg and Svendsen—made up the grand triumvirate of the Golden Age of Norwegian music; there's no question that anyone who's fond of Grieg will want to know the others as well.

Sinding wrote four symphonies and may have wanted to write more, but his publishers demanded more small (and profitable) pieces after the great success of *Rustle of Spring*. Symphony 1, while clearly cast in late Romantic mold, contains passages of dark foreboding and innate Nordic grandeur; 2 is broadly rhapsodic, with rich writing for the horns. The Norwegian Cultural Council has reissued 1 under **Øivin Fjeldstad** (NKF 50016, with Piano Concerto); 2, conducted by **Kjell Ingebretsen,** remains unavailable on CD (NKF 30025, with *Rondo Infinito*). You'll want to seek out 1 and 2 with **Ari Rasilainen;** more sweeping than Fjeldstad in 1, he favors more expansive tempos than Ingebretsen in 2, but the muted NKF sonics can't match the soaring Oslo horns (♦Finlandia 27889).

Cyclical in form, the Piano Concerto is closer to Bayreuth than Oslo, with a heroic quality and a taxing part for the soloist. Here the choice is **Eva Knardahl** (♦NKF 50016, with Symphony 1) or **Roland Keller** (Vox 5068, with other concertos). There's no comparison; Keller's ham-fisted approach, with massive cuts in both outer movements, can't compete with Knardahl's far more sympathetic treatment.

Still awaiting CD reissue is **Arve Tellefsen** in Violin Concerto in A, *Suite im alten Stil,* and *Légende* (♦NKF 30020). At the outset strongly reminiscent of the finale of the Bruch G minor, the Concerto (the first of three) continues with a central passacaglia and a buoyant final rondo. *Suite* is modeled after Bach, a nonstop Presto followed by an expressive Adagio and a stately but upbeat courante. It's available with the redoubtable **Heifetz** (RCA 61740, mono) and also with **Ricci** (111 96050). There used to be a **Perlman** recording, but this is no longer listed (EMI 47167, with the Sibelius Concerto). The *Légende,* melodically very like Bruch, is played by **Dong-Suk Kang,** and the music responds well to his sweet, relaxed tone (Naxos 550329, with the Sibelius and music by Halvorsen and Svendsen).

Neither Sinding's Piano Quintet nor its Sibelius counterpart is well known, making the **Pihtipudas Quintet** pairing highly desirable—all the more given that Sibelius was probably inspired by Sinding's effort to write his own, and both are beautifully played and recorded (EDA 007). **András Kiss,** Tamás Koó, and Ilona Prunyi offer Piano Trios 1 and 2 (Marco Polo 223283).

Kjell Baekkelund plays *Rustle of Spring,* with the Sonata in B minor and several smaller pieces, as if he believed in every note, not daunted by the Lisztian scale of the sonata, and he's joined ably by **Robert Levin** in Variations for 2 Pianos (♦NKF 50017). **Knardahl** plays the Sonata (BIS 36), while **Helge Antoni** offers *Rustle of Spring, Caprices,* and *Fatum Variations* (Etcetera 1047), and there used to be a disc by **Adrian Ruiz** with a half dozen short pieces (Genesis). **Jerome Lowenthal** is highly sympathetic in the shorter pieces, but sometimes seems rambling and awkward in the Sonata, suggesting that he isn't in full command of the score (Arabesque 6578); Knardahl's tauter treatment works better, while Baekkelund's cohesive reading shows great affection for the music.

Sinding wrote nearly 300 songs; folk-like in their simplicity, they repay repeated hearings very well. There used to be a pair of LPs by **Edith Thallaug** and Kurt Skram presenting 41 songs (NKF 30012 and 30015), but they had little exposure in the United States. **Flagstad** only offers three of them, but this is gorgeous singing (♦Acanta 431893); these are also among the 28 offered by **Bodil Arnesen,** a bit lighter in tone but ably sung (Naxos 553905).

For all its Wagnerian philosophizing, Sinding's opera *Der heilige Berg* (The Holy Mountain) is richly textured and beautifully orchestrated. The monks cloistered on Mount Athos believe the mountain will collapse should a woman ever tempt one of them to sensual desire; when one young monk falls in love, he leaps off the cliff in his despair, and only after he's revived by his mother's kiss are the others persuaded to grant the lovers sanctuary. Along the way there is much declamation and powerful orchestral support, as you would expect from a staunch Wagnerian like Sinding. It's persuasively put across by a strong cast including Toril Carlsen as the young monk and Kjersti Ekeberg as his beloved, **Heinz Fricke** conducting (CDN 31002, 2CD). HALLER

Bedřich Smetana (1824–84)

As with so many such long established stereotypes, the common distinction posited between the two great Czech composers—Dvořák the humble Bohemian *musikant,* Smetana the fiery nationalist—has at its core more than a kernel of truth, and yet doesn't tell nearly the whole story. Smetana like his compatriot embraced the folk traditions of his native land, incorporating images of the Czech people both in his monumental cycle of symphonic poems *Má Vlast* and in his works for the stage, not only the overtly patriotic *Dalibor* and *Libuše* but also the work generally considered the Czech national opera, *The Bartered Bride,* which is beloved the world over—in whatever language.

ORCHESTRAL MUSIC

Má Vlast. In his great cycle of symphonic poems Smetana sought to draw a parallel between his nation's glorious past and a vision—however naive—of its future glory and freedom. Immediately embraced by the Czech people as a symbol of their intense national pride, it has become the traditional offering every year to open the Prague Spring Festival. Some recordings split the cycle between two discs; however, it can fit quite comfortably on one.

It's difficult to avoid having **Kubelik** represented in your collection; he recorded the score no less than five times. His first recording, made only four years after he left Czechoslovakia to come to the United States, is also one of the best it has ever received, with the fiery playing of the Chicago Symphony handily transcending any sonic shortcomings—not that there are very many, as this classic recording taped with a single perfectly placed mike still sounds glorious today when played at the full room volume it deserves (♦Mercury 434379).

It actually sounds better than the stereo recording Kubelik made seven years later with the Vienna Philharmonic, more mellow than the Mercury yet stirring just the same, and irresistible at its "Weekend Classics" price (London 421167). With the Boston Symphony, Kubelik was even more laid back; the sound is translucent but bass-shy (DG). His last recording, with the Czech Philharmonic from the 1990 Prague Spring Festival, may serve as his valedictory; taped in concert soon after he returned to his native land following more than 40 years of forced exile, this was an emotional experience for everyone, and it shows in this heartfelt and highly charged performance (♦Supraphon 1208). Although the sound quality varies—as if someone were fiddling with the controls—the riveting performance makes it a must-have just the same. The runt of the litter is with the Bavarian Radio Symphony; it lacks intensity, and the orchestra is undisciplined, while this earlier pressing, spread over two CDs with no filler, is an even less attractive proposition (Orfeo).

Other than Kubelik, the conductor most closely associated with this music is **Talich,** whose 1954 recording with the Czech Philharmonic is

generally considered one of the classic performances (♦Supraphon 1896). It was Talich who raised this orchestra to greatness before the Soviets took over, and this fervent, committed performance is as much a product of the players' love for Talich as for the music, making any discussion of the mono sound—here the best it has ever been—quite irrelevant. An even earlier version from 78s—the first complete recording—is at least respectable sonically, and its historical value remains unquestioned (Koch). Talich's successor with the Czech Philharmonic, **Ančerl,** offers a thrilling performance in sound only a few steps up from Talich (stereo notwithstanding); this 1963 recording has had more lives than a cat, most recently in a Supraphon CD.

Among other Czech conductors, **Krombholc** is intensely dramatic—without the impulsive tempo variations frequently indulged in by Kubelik—but the sound betrays the 1973 taping (Multisonic). **Bělohlávek** has recorded the cycle twice; sound and ensemble are variable, though the mastery of the performances shines through (Supraphon). Also with the Czech Philharmonic, **Smetáček** never lets up for a minute, galvanizing his players into giving their best, though the recording lacks richness—a small matter given the thrilling performance (Supraphon 0082).

Some may remember the London LPs with the Leipzig Gewandhaus directed by **Neumann;** these were transformed first into a Teldec set and later Berlin, in both cases spread over two discs thanks to Neumann's expansive tempos. The warmth of the performance is matched by the sound, but some may find it lacking in excitement next to Kubelik. Neumann's later performance with the Czech Philharmonic, taped in concert in Japan, is more detailed and fits comfortably on one disc but boasts no special qualities of its own (Denon). His 1982 Prague concert is quite different—genial, affectionate, and marvelously played (Denon 17017, with Janaček).

Pešek's recording has been reissued, but the performance is hardly idiomatic and the nondescript sound is no help (Virgin, in its Ultraviolet budget line); his remake with the Czech Philharmonic, as you might expect, is far superior on all counts (Lotos). **Sejna**'s 1950 recording is highly musical though sonically outdated (Supraphon). **Košler** shows that even the Czech Philharmonic can have an off day; both conducting and playing seem routine and the sound is lackluster as well (Emergo). Both **Susskind** and **Macal** are Czech-born and thoroughly familiar with the idiom. Susskind's tempos are relaxed (though not nearly as slow as Neumann) and his understated account is nevertheless highly colored, but the recording is dull and constricted; it's probably a more attractive prospect on its own than combined unnecessarily with an equally expendable Holst *Planets* on two discs (Vox). Macal gives a mellifluous if perhaps too homogeneous reading, though beautifully played with smoothly blended sonics to match (Telarc).

There are quite a few recordings of *Má Vlast* that have no particular connection with Prague. **Levine**'s exciting recording was originally offered on two CDs, coupled with excerpts from *Bartered Bride;* its reissue on a single disc is good news, as Levine's performance is everything Macal's is not: highly characterized with sharply focused ensemble detail (♦DG 431652). **Inbal** leads a sweeping, epic reading that combines the pastoral and heroic qualities of the music like few others (Teldec, also coupled with *Bartered Bride* excerpts, 2CD).

Surely the Israeli musicians who recorded this highly patriotic score with **Weller** understand its meaning as much as the Czechs, and this is reflected in their soulful, committed performance (London 443015, a mid-priced "Double Decker" with other works by Smetana and Dvořák). Would that the same could be said for their recording under

Mehta, whose brusque and unidiomatic account never allows the music to breathe (Sony)—or for that matter **Neeme Järvi**, who seems eager to get it over with, with the great Hussite hymn at the end rushed to the point of mere tub-thumping parody (Chandos). **Swarowsky** offers an earnest but workmanlike account (Intercord).

Should you happen upon **Dorati**'s recording, keep going; while it sounds a lot better than his old mono Epic LPs —also with the Concert-gebouw—the lackluster remake suggests that in the intervening years he lost all interest in the music (Philips). **Berglund** has a splendid orchestra to work with—the Dresden Staatskapelle—and his richly textured and expansive reading is offered as a "two-fer" (EMI 68649, with Dvořák and Grieg). **D'Avalos** makes much of the drama of the music, less of the poetry perhaps, and the recording is occasionally opaque (IMP). **Norrington** makes much of the use of original instruments, but the colors never blend into a convincing mix, and the lack of energy in the performance makes the result little more than a curiosity (Virgin). Many will be tempted to pinch pennies and go with the Polish Radio Orchestra under **Wit;** however, this coolly efficient and rather stuffy-sounding account is no more than a stopgap (Naxos).

A couple of old favorites are listed in British sources and will repay the diligent willing to seek them out. **Sawallisch** offers a highly charged and vivid reading (RCA), while **Sargent** is fresh and direct, with warm and atmospheric sound that belies its 1965 recording date (EMI).

Other symphonic poems. Like Saint-Saëns, Smetana was inspired by the example of Liszt to compose three symphonic poems on various subjects, or four if you count *Prague Carnival* (sometimes called an overture). *Richard III*—based on Shakespeare's play—tells of his harrowing dream the night before he is destined to fall in battle, when the spirits of those he has slain appear ominously before him. *Wallenstein's Camp,* taken from Schiller, offers a colorful look at barracks life, ending with a spirited march. *Hakon Jarl* is a tyrant who attempts to reestablish heathen ways in feudal Norway but is defeated by the Christian king Olav Trygvason. *Prague Carnival,* intended as the first of a new cycle of symphonic poems in the years following *Má Vlast,* was Smetana's last completed score, a swirling montage of festive rhythms and bright colors that belies the composer's sad fate, dying only a few years later in a Prague sanitarium.

All four pieces are often recorded together, and there's really little to choose between **Kubelik** (♦DG 437254) and **Neumann** (Supraphon 0198), though the Kubelik is better played. The even older set with **Sejna** (minus *Prague Carnival*) has been reissued in respectable '50s mono sound, and the performances are certainly persuasive (Supraphon). In addition, a compelling account of *Hakon Jarl* is included by **Weller** with *Má Vlast* (see above).

Festive Symphony. Conceived as a sort of peace offering for Emperor Franz Joseph I on the occasion of his marriage to Elisabeth of Bavaria—with the unspoken goal of facilitating home rule for the Czech people—*Festive Symphony* instead became effectively barred from the concert hall because of its pervading use of the Austrian national anthem, a stigma that only became worse when the same melody came to be associated with the Nazis. (The fact that it was actually written by Haydn apparently made no difference.) **Zagrosek** offers the only complete recording, but his sluggish treatment of the final movement precludes a firm recommendation (Marco Polo). Even with a couple of cuts in the last movement, **Sejna**'s fresh and vital recording remains the preferred version (♦Supraphon 1914). **Košler** cuts it a lot more than Sejna, so you can forget that one entirely (Supraphon).

Operatic excerpts. Even people who have never been fortunate enough to see *The Bartered Bride* in the opera house will no doubt recognize the bustling Overture—a "Pops" concert staple—as well as the three dances that make up the standard suite: Polka, Furiant and "Dance of the Comedians." Even children will know "Dance of the Comedians," used in many "Roadrunner" cartoons. Unfortunately **Levine**'s spirited reading is now going begging since DG has reissued his *Má Vlast* on one disc. **Dorati** is a non-starter thanks to the slack Overture and the over-prominent piccolo at the close of the comedians' dance (Mercury). British Decca has not yet brought out **Dohnányi**'s recording in the United States. It's of most interest for the other overtures noted below, as the Cleveland strings seem strangely disheveled in the Overture; however, Dohnányi earns a few brownie points for including a chorus in the Polka and also (like Levine) plays the longer version of the "Dance." So does **Geoffrey Simon**, and he goes Dohnányi one better by prefacing it with the comedians' little march on stage (though Scherchen was more convincing on his old Westminster LP), even throwing in "Dance of the Villagers" as a bonus (Chandos).

As you might expect, **Chalabala** includes both the march *and* the chorus, since his wonderfully bracing suite is taken from his classic recording of the complete opera and is well worth seeking out (♦Urania 5174). In a highly enjoyable but brief CD, **Kempe** takes about as long for the Overture as Dorati, but his alert and pointed account makes all the difference (Classics for Pleasure). **Bernstein**'s exhilarating performance has been reissued, but you'll have to put up with his hopelessly self-indulgent Dvořák 7 to get it (Sony). **Bělohlávek** may be hard to find (Supraphon), while **Inbal** (filler for his *Má Vlast*) is no longer listed (Teldec). **Kertész** (filler with Weller's *Má Vlast*) is hampered by omission of the "Dance of the Comedians," while the Dances but not the Overture may be had with **Szell** in a Sony "Essential Classics" collection in a bizarre combination with Rachmaninoff's *Symphonic Dances* and the Offenbach/Rosenthal *Gaité Parisienne* (both Ormandy).

Once you have *The Bartered Bride,* you'll want to know Smetana's other operas, and there's no better introduction than **Stankovsky**'s collection, which brings together in one disc overtures and other short excerpts from all of the remaining stage works as well as *Oldřich and Bózena,* one of two overtures written for the puppet plays of Matěj Kopecky (♦Marco Polo 223326). The other such piece, *Doctor Faust,* is included in another Stankovsky-led collection, with a variety of other music and a suite arranged from Smetana's sketchbook by Jaroslav Smolka (Marco Polo 223705). In the remainder bin you may still find **Gerhard Pflueger**'s *Wedding Scenes* (♦Urania 5174, the same disc as Chalabala's *Bartered Bride* excerpts)—a different arrangement than the one on Marco Polo and a more spirited reading than Stankovsky's. I might add that Stankovsky's *Shakespeare Festival March* is better played than Neumann's, included with the symphonic poems (above). Should London bring out the Dohnányi *Bartered Bride* suite mentioned earlier, you'll also get fine performances of the overtures to *Libuše, The Two Widows,* and *The Kiss.*

Quartet ("From My Life"), orchestral version. As you might expect from its title, this first of Smetana's two string quartets is largely autobiographical, culminating with his tragic and sudden deafness. Szell arranged the score for orchestra, finding in it many passages that he felt cried out for a more varied tonal palette, and the result—not surprisingly—sounds remarkably like the dances from *The Bartered Bride,* at least until near the end of the final movement, when Szell creates a harrowing effect by using both violin (in its highest register) and piccolo to reproduce the high-pitched whistle heard by the composer at that terrible moment when deafness overtook him. **Szell**'s own 1944 recording has been issued (Sony, with the last three Dvořák symphonies); it certainly has the stamp of authority, yet can't help coming off almost as a curio next to **Geoffrey Simon**'s sumptuous stereo recording (♦Chandos 8412, with *Bartered Bride* excerpts, above). HALLER

CHAMBER MUSIC

Though not voluminous, Smetana's chamber music is of high quality and is historically important because it initiated a Czech tradition of autobiographical chamber works.

Piano Trio in G Minor (1855) was written in response to the death of the composer's daughter. It's a powerful work of considerable originality in three movements, culminating in a finale that combines virtuoso display (especially for the piano, Smetana's own instrument) with interludes of nostalgia. The **Guarneri Trio** includes a great pianist, Ivan Klánský, and its CD, well recorded, has the advantage of including the music for violin and piano: the early *Fantasy on a Bohemian Song* and the two beautiful pieces from 1880 that make up *From My Homeland* (Supraphon 1515). **Cenĕk Pavlik** and Klánský play all of these well, but in the 1880 duos, **Suk** is even better. He made two fine recordings, one with Jan Panenka in 1962 (Supraphon 0270) and one with Josef Hála in 1995 (Discover 920317). Various violinists have recorded one or another of the duos, but you'll surely want to have both.

With the string quartets, it's definitely better to have both. The E minor, "From My Life" (1876), in its finale heralds Smetana's tragic deafness with a terrifying high E on the first violin. This work was also influential in liberating the viola, to which he gave an exposed, demanding part; the instrument has the first theme, a searing fanfare-like motif. The D minor Quartet (1882–83), once thought confused and chaotic, can now be heard to be a work of power and originality. The **Smetana Quartet** campaigned for this music for more than 40 years and recorded both works four times. A relatively recent release combines this great ensemble's 1962 E minor with its 1976 D minor (Supraphon 0070). Anyone wanting the best digital sound can happily invest in the 1992 disc from the **Panocha Quartet,** which is also superbly played (Supraphon 3450).

If you want the traditional coupling of *From My Life* and Dvořák's *American,* the historic mono recordings by the **Hollywood Quartet** are typically compelling, and you also get a stereo version of Kodály's fine Quartet 2 (Testament 1072). The late lamented **Cleveland Quartet** supplied a fully digital *From My Life* along with Borodin's lovely Quartet 2 (Telarc 80178). Both performances are up to this ensemble's high standard. POTTER

PIANO MUSIC

If you love Dvořák's *Slavonic Dances,* you should try Smetana's dances too. He had little patience with rigorous exercises in sonata form, instead turning out an endless supply of little gems in the same dance styles as Dvořák—polkas, furiants, dumkas—in many cases subsequently arranged for orchestra as well. This is tuneful, lilting, endearing music that often conceals in its seeming simplicity ideas both fresh and challenging.

The complete piano works were recorded by **Vera Repková** on 11 Supraphon LPs and have conveniently been nestled on four CPO CDs (close to nine hours of music), splitting each disc into two mono channels (999 010). All these pieces have since been rerecorded in stereo with redoubtable soloists like František Rauch, Pavel Stĕpán, and Jan Novotný (Supraphon), and there have been marvelous recordings of indi-

vidual pieces, notably by Firkušny; but Repková is as good as it gets, and this is an incredible bargain. For **Firkušny,** seek out the set combining his spirited and idiomatic Smetana dances with other Czech fare (Vox 5058 or EMI 66069, with Debussy).

Schiff gives us a splendid recital, with a distinct feel for the music's lyricism and poetry, beautifully recorded into the bargain (Teldec 21261, Polkas Opp. 7, 8, 12, 13). **Kubalek** brings great joy to his recital of polkas and Czech Dances and has been afforded warm and natural sound (Dorian 90122), or you may enjoy Czech Dances with other pieces in an earlier and just as winning recital (Citadel 88112). **Claudius Tanski** does very well in a collection of dances and other short pieces but fails to capture the Czech idiom as well as Repková, Firkušny or other home-grown talents (MD+G 3120483).

Macbeth and the Witches is a startling, even dissonant work that goes far beyond simple village dances, very well played by **Kvapil** together with several pieces in polka style (Unicorn 9152). It's also included by **Jan Novotný** in a set ranging from polkas to bagatelles and impromptus, well worth seeking out for those not wishing to buy the entire CPO survey (Supraphon 3374, 2CD), or for an even briefer survey, his Czech Dances and Characteristic Pieces (Supraphon 3070), while Kvapil offers several bagatelles and impromptus in an earlier disc (Unicorn 9139). **Igor Ardašev** brings together Smetana's *Dreams* (also offered by Kvapil) with Suk's *Spring* and Novak's *My May* in a winning recital (Supraphon 3183). **František Rausch** offers a satisfying recital that also includes *Macbeth and the Witches* (Supraphon 0080). HALLER

OPERAS

Smetana was the most important Czech composer of opera in the last half of the 19th century and can truly be called the father of Czech opera. His eight completed stage works encompass both serious and comic works, but only one of the latter, *The Bartered Bride,* has enjoyed worldwide popularity, though *Dalibor* and *Libuše* are sometimes heard in non-Czech countries as well.

The Bartered Bride. This is one of the most charming operas ever written, and any decent performance will leave the audience in smiles. A good recording will do the same, and there are several in the current listings. The work has been recorded in Czech and German; it's a repertory item in many German theaters. The best Czech versions are conducted by **Chalabala** (♦Supraphon 0040) and **Košler** (♦Supraphon 3511). The former, from 1959, is in early stereo but has been remastered, and the sound of the CDs is good. Košler's digital sound, from the early '80s, is much better, but it has unaccountably been spread over three discs, making it more expensive. Both releases have very good all-Czech casts, fine orchestral playing, and idiomatic conducting.

But the best singers (Lorengar, Wunderlich, and Frick) and the best conductor, **Kempe,** are found in a 1963 German-language recording (♦EMI 64002, 2CD). It also has good sound, but the German translation, while singable, doesn't always fit the music as well as the Czech words.

Dalibor. One of Smetana's serious operas, this is based on a historical 15th-century event: The knight Dalibor, accused of various crimes including the murder of Milada's brother, is condemned to life imprisonment, but Milada has fallen in love with him and decides to rescue him. She disguises herself as a boy (like Leonore in *Fidelio*) and becomes assistant to the jailer, but their plot is discovered, and in the ensuing fighting, Milada and Dalibor are killed. All this is set to some of the composer's most appealing music.

The best of the available recordings is, again, conducted by **Košler,** with a fine cast headed by the Czech soprano Urbanová as Milada (♦Supraphon 0077). This is a 1995 release in good sound. Also available is a 1977 set led by **Krombholc** (one of the better Czech opera conductors), but neither its cast nor its sound is as good as Košler's (Praga). A badly cut German-language version from Vienna is conducted by **Krips,** but it has only the Milada of the great Rysanek to commend it, and that's not enough (Myto or, in much better sound, RCA).

Libuše. This nationalistic work is often performed in the Czech Republic as a festival opera on days of national celebration. Its claim to that honor seems to rest on its final scene, in which Libuše, the Ruler of Bohemia, who has just married, peers into the future of her nation. Famous Czech historical characters appear, and at the end, Libuše proclaims that the Czech Nation will never die. The rest of the plot has to do with family quarrels and Libuše's decision to marry. The music is very melodious and quite appealing.

The only two recordings are both from Prague. The more recent and better set is a concert performance conducted by **Oliver Dohnányi** (♦Supraphon 3200), with the excellent Urbanová in the title role. Benačková, another splendid Czech soprano, sings Libuše in **Košler's** 1983 recording, which commemorated the reopening of Prague's National Theater (Supraphon 111276). It's also a good performance, but it takes three CDs instead of Dohnányi's two.

There is only one recording each of three other Smetana operas: *The Devil's Wall* (Supraphon 2201), *The Kiss* (Supraphon 2180), and *The Two Widows* (Supraphon 112122). These are all enjoyable works, and all these sets can be recommended.   MOSES

Padre Antonio Soler *(1729–1833)*

Soler is often dismissed as a "mere" pupil of Scarlatti, but there's more to the story than that. He ranks as the most important Spanish musician of the 18th century, a composer who blended native Spanish (actually, Catalan) tendencies with nascent Classical and Romantic traits. Like Scarlatti, he's a solitary figure who was attached to the Spanish court during the most creative period in his life. He nevertheless managed to stay in touch with developments in European music, and it shows in the greater diversity of his music.

A brief comparison of the two composers' styles is in order. Whereas Scarlatti wrote only single-movement sonatas, Soler wrote many multimovement works in addition to those in one movement. For most of his life, Scarlatti restricted himself to the keyboard; Soler wrote a lot more, including chamber music, masses, and concertos for two keyboards. Almost all his output shows greater thematic development; indeed, it's this patchwork or mosaic of themes that is often most striking. Soler had a predilection for the Alberti bass, a repeating three-note pattern in the bass; Scarlatti almost never used it. The Spanish flavor that is hinted at occasionally in Scarlatti is overt in Soler, the most famous example being the 12-minute *Fandango,* a work Ravel must have had in mind when he wrote *Boléro.* Given all his variety and exoticism, it's a shame there's so little of his work currently in the catalog.

A complete set of the keyboard sonatas is in the works featuring the Scottish harpsichordist **Gilbert Rowland.** Vol. 5 has appeared, but I can only recommend it with reservations; the playing is fine, but the harpsichord, a rather thin-sounding Taskin copy, is entirely wrong for the music (Naxos 554434). Until Astrée sees fit to reissue **van Asperen's** excellent 4CD set from about 10 years ago, you'll have to make do with just two other single-CD versions. The best is undoubtedly **Scott Ross's** (Er-

ato 45435). Recorded just a year before his untimely death from AIDS in 1989, the playing is full of verve and personality, especially the "Fandango," easily the catchiest on records. Another to consider is the slightly less flamboyant rendition by American harpsichordist **David Schrader,** played on a very idiomatic-sounding Italian copy by Paul Irvin (Cedille 90000 004). The recorded sound is more intimate than on Ross's disc, giving the feeling of a private recital in an anteroom of the Spanish King.

The six concertos for two keyboards have long been a favorite of organists. It's not often that two baroque-style organs (hopefully with a few Spanish reeds to spice things up) can be found in one room, which explains why the music has been recorded so infrequently. **Bernard Brauchli** and **Esteban Elizondo** have shown considerable good taste by varying the instrumentation; not only are two organs used, but two harpsichords and two clavichords as well, and the results are just about ideal (Titanic 152).

Soler's chamber music is worth exploring. His *Quintettes* for two violins, viola, cello and harpsichord are delightful Rococo works, rather superficial but quite charming. They are reminiscent of Boccherini, who was also attached to the Spanish court at the time. Harpsichordist **Jean-Patrice Brosse** and Concerto Rococo have recorded all six (Pierre Verany 792111 and 799041). The sparkling, spirited performances are served up in state-of-the-art sound, as usual for Verany.

BRODERSEN

Fernando Sor *(1778–1839)*

Sor was one of the leading virtuoso player-composers for the guitar in the first few decades of the 19th century. He was referred to in his day by the prominent critic Fétis as the "Beethoven of the guitar," a comment that had as much to do with his composing "properly" for the instrument (using correct four-voice part-writing!) as his abilities as a player. In fact, Sor is much closer in spirit to Mozart; he never sought to rewrite the rules, just to operate under them with maximum taste.

His first musical success came not with the guitar but with an opera, *Telemaco,* written at age 19 and successfully staged in Barcelona. The late 18th-century style of Italian composers fashionable in Spain and his strict musical training account for the conservative, "by-the-rules" aspects of his music. The influence of opera, perhaps, accounts for his gift for melody, uncommon for guitar composers of this period. He achieved success in London as a ballet composer; many of his songs (with piano accompaniment) were published there, and he became the first (and only) guitarist to appear before the Philharmonic Society.

He ultimately settled in Paris, where he remained for the rest of his life. He became the leading guitarist of the city, performing (one concert also featured a youthful pianist named Franz Liszt), teaching (and writing a remarkably thorough *Method*), and composing for his instrument, but he died in some obscurity. His music, though, never died out; his pupil, player-composer Napoleon Coste, revised and revived Sor's *Method,* and in the 20th century Segovia made Sor the cornerstone of his early 19th-century repertoire. Currently, the newest generation of players are investigating his less-familiar pieces, trying to balance them with the handful of his works that have become warhorses.

Sor was particularly adept at variation form but also wrote sonatas, including two large-scale works. His published pieces include a myriad of shorter pieces (often issued as "divertimenti") and a large quantity of excellent etudes still in use today. His most famous (and often-recorded) variations are Op. 9, on a theme ("Das klinget so herrlich") by Mozart from *The Magic Flute.* These also became the most over-played of his pieces in the '60s and '70s, but there's no denying their superior writing, particularly when the somber and chromatic Introduction is included. Although **Segovia** certainly put this piece on the map, I can't recommend either of his versions, in 1927 (in EMI's "Great Recordings of the Century") or 1952 (in "5 Centuries of the Spanish Guitar," MCA 42071, or in "A Centenary Celebration," MCA 11124) due to his frequently bizarre rubato, changes to the score, and the missing Introduction.

Many of those mannerisms are repeated in smoother form by his protégé **Parkening** in "Tribute to Segovia" (EMI 115499). Sor's music needs tastefulness, with excessive virtuosity and a performer's distinctive persona kept in check. Therefore, with **Williams**'s "Virtuoso Variations" unavailable (Columbia LP), my choices for Op. 9 are **Bream** (♦"The Classical Heritage," Vol. 24 in the "Julian Bream Edition," RCA 61607), elegant but marred by a weak ending; **Barrueco**, spirited and tasteful (♦EMI 749368); or, for Williams-like virtuosity with uncharacteristic self-control, **Fisk** (♦"Guitar Fantasies," MusicMasters 60169F). An interesting period-instrument version is available from **Nigel North** on an 1828 Panormo guitar (♦Amon Ra 18).

Barrueco's disc is devoted to music of Sor and, appropriately, Mozart, and includes settings of "Six Airs" from *Magic Flute, Gran Solo* Op. 14 as revised by Dionisio Aguado (another leading guitar virtuoso of the day), a complete Mozart piano sonata (K 283), and the Adagio from K 576; the Mozart transcriptions are superb, and very unusual. Bream's disc also contains two fantasies, Op. 7 (with its usually neglected variations) and Op. 30, plus music by Aguado; his vivid interpretations serve music of this period very well, although his tone color manipulations can wear out their welcome, as does a whole record of Sor and his contemporary. Therefore I highly recommend **Bream**'s mid-'60s recording of Op. 7's brooding Largo and the minuet of the Op. 25 sonata (♦"Baroque Guitar," RCA 60494).

As for Sor's two multimovement sonatas, Op. 22 and Op. 25, two of the best versions are unavailable on CD (look around for the LPs): **Bream**'s mid-'70s version of the more interesting Op. 25 (RCA) and both of them by **Pepe Romero** (Philips). Both sonatas and the rather drab single-movement Op. 15 are played by **Fernando Moretti** (Stradivarius 33475). For the pure Sor (non-Aguado) version of his single-movement *Gran Solo* get Bream (♦"Classic Guitar" Vol. 10, RCA 61593) or **Diego Blanco** (BIS 133). The latter contains, besides the expected Op. 9, several other pieces, including the ethnically interesting *Introduction and Variations on the Scottish Tune "Ye Banks and Braes"* Op. 40.

Although some guitar authorities might say Sor was at his best in short character pieces (like his many etudes), he was quite capable of larger, multisectional pieces (in fact, more so than many of his lesser contemporaries), and many of his works are such offerings, often titled "fantasias" and often incorporating variations. Perhaps the fact that many of these works have not been easily available in print until fairly recently and the surfeit of new repertoire for guitarists (particularly 20th-century and newly discovered earlier composers) has kept guitarists from looking into Sor's musical attic.

However, several recordings of less frequently encountered music stand out: **Nicholas Goluses** plays two Fantasies, Opp. 58 and 59, and a set of Etudes Op. 60 (Naxos 553342); **Adam Holzman** plays *Fantasie* Op. 52, *Morceau de Concert* Op. 54, the interesting *Souvenir d'une soirée à Berlin* Op. 56, and Waltzes Op. 51 (Naxos 553450). An excellent compendium of the familiar and not so familiar comes from **Raymond Burley,** including Opp. 7 and 40, the Mozart "Airs," and *Fantasie Elégiaque* Op. 59 (♦ASV 6223). **Pepe Romero** plays a recently discovered Fantasia

in D minor in an album of Renaissance to 20th-century Spanish music (Philips 106959).

With **Williams**'s treasured recording of Segovia's selection of 25 etudes unavailable (Westminster LP), recordings come down to either a choice few by a major artist or a large helping by a newcomer. For the former, **Segovia** himself plays a batch in each of two volumes in "The Segovia Collection" (MCA Vol. 3, 42069; Vol. 7, 42073). **Parkening** recorded two of the most romantic (17 and 19) in "In the Spanish Style" (EMI 747194); 3 has also been reissued (EMI 115570). The late **Narciso Yepes** offers an interesting collection of 10 etudes, mixing well-known with less familiar, in a reissue of "Guitarra Espanola" Vol. 1 (♦DG 100065). Another type of short piece at which Sor excelled was the minuet; choose either a selection of three by Segovia (MCA 42071) or twelve by **Norbert Kraft** (♦Naxos 553007).

Sor wrote a large number of guitar duos, often for himself and a student, but also for two equal players (including *Les Duex Amis* Op. 41 for himself and Aguado). **Robert Kubica** and **Wilma van Berkel** have recorded the complete duos in two discs; I recommend Vol. 1 for its inclusion of Op. 41 and *L'encouragement* Op. 34, one of Sor's best pieces (Naxos 8553302). Unfortunately, these discs also include quite a bit of rather tedious "valse facile" music. Therefore, for an inspired reading of Op. 34 (and lots of other great duo repertoire by Falla, Granados, Fauré and others) get Bream and Williams's "Together" (♦ RCA 61450).

DINGER

Kaikhosru Shapurji Sorabji (1892–1988)

Sorabji's work is a fascinating byway in this century's music. Although of Spanish and Parsi descent, he lived most of his life in England in relative obscurity. He was known in his lifetime mostly as an oddity: a world-record holder for writing the longest nonrepetitive, nonimprovised piano composition ever, his over 4-hour *Opus Clavicembalisticum*. He was also a perceptive music critic whose championing of Alkan, Szymanowski, and Mahler was far ahead of its time. He was eccentric, reclusive, and had a prickly temperament, although he had lasting friendships with many people.

Sorabji belongs to the tradition of virtuoso piano writing of Liszt, Busoni, Alkan, and Scriabin. He forbade public performances of his music for most of his life, but toward the end he heard some pianists whom he approved and who were permitted to perform and record his works. His writing for the piano is prodigiously difficult: dense, highly contrapuntal, florid in style. The harmonies are voluptuous and colorful and often owe more to the Orient than the West. The music frequently has to be notated on three or more staves and sometimes as many as seven are needed to present the individual lines clearly. Many passages seem impossible to execute.

However excessive, this is clearly music that is meant to be played, not merely perused. The pianists who have taken up the challenge all attest to the satisfaction they get from performing it, and Sorabji's exotic sound world is like no other. A steady diet might prove too much for many of us—this is very rich fare—but it's fascinating nonetheless. Many of Sorabji's works are still in manuscript and unrealized; virtually everything is written for or includes the piano. All recordings so far have been for either solo piano or organ.

Opus Clavicembalisticum is the largest work to be recorded, though there are unrecorded pieces that are even longer. Amazingly, the work been issued complete three times—once from **Madge** in an LP set released in 1982; then in 1988 by the great **Ogdon** shortly before his death (Altarus 9075, 4CD, NA). It's now available in a new set with Madge again, taken from a 1983 Chicago concert (BIS 1062/64, 5CD). This is the only account currently available, and at five discs for the price of three, it's reasonable value as well. I heard the Madge LPs years ago, but didn't have either of his recordings available for direct comparison with Ogdon's. Both pianists have much to offer, and both have been enthusiastically reviewed. Ogdon was ideally suited to play this work; with his formidable technique and penetrating intellect, he was equal to its enormous demands. His set stands as one of the major achievements of a distinguished if uneven career.

Another large-scale work was released in a highly praised recording by the English organ virtuoso, **Kevin Bowyer**. *Organ Symphony* 1 displays Sorabji's complex counterpoint with the benefit of registration, and away from the monochromatic piano timbre we get an inkling of what his orchestral music might sound like (Continuum 1001/2, 2CD, NA).

Even the very curious might balk at the notion of purchasing and listening to a piano work that takes up four discs. Fortunately there are some good single-disc introductions to this intriguing composer. **Donna Amato**'s recording of *Fantasie Espagnole* is an excellent place to start (Altarus 9022). This is an early piece in which you can plainly hear the influence of Ravel, Szymanowski, and Scriabin in its suave Spanish rhythms. The disc is low-priced and contains only this 17-minute piece. Amato has also recorded an excellent full-length disc that has two pieces written in the '40s plus some late works, including *Passeggiata arlecchinesca*, Sorabji's last major composition (Altarus 9025).

The Altarus label has made Sorabji's music a special cause and has released several other low-priced discs with various pianists. These are modestly scaled works (for Sorabji, that is) that run from 20 to 30 minutes. The noted virtuoso **Hamelin** has recorded Sonata 1, and the results are superb (Altarus 9050). Sonata 2, dedicated to Busoni, has been recorded by **Tellef Johnson** (Altarus 9049), and *"Gulistãn" (The Rose Garden)—Nocturne for Piano* is played by **Charles Hopkins** (Altarus 9036). I haven't heard the last two.

Michael Habermann was one of the first pianists whose virtuosity met with Sorabji's approval, and he has recorded four excellent discs, three of which are presently NA but well worth hunting for. Habermann is my favorite interpreter of this music. Although Amato's reading of *St. Bertrand de Comminges: "He was laughing in the tower"* is very good, I think Habermann makes the rangy work into a more coherent whole and is better gesturally too. Habermann's disc is a live recording, and the audience's snuffling is a bit distracting at times (MusicMasters 60118, NA). Habermann also recorded the opening sections of *Opus Clavicembalisticum*, along with some shorter works including a bizarre pastiche on Bizet's "Habañera" from *Carmen* (MusicMasters 60015, NA). "Le Jardin Parfumé" contains that extended study in exoticism, along with *Nocturne (Djâmî)* and others (MusicMasters 60019, NA). Habermann rerecorded the latter piece along with new performances of *Gulistãn* and some others a few years later; that disc (Elan 82264) is better filled, but I like his MusicMasters performances a little more. These are minor quibbles; for a one-disc introduction to Sorabji, I think either Habermann's Elan disc or Donna Amato's is the best available right now.

McINTIRE

John Philip Sousa (1854–1932)

Inveterate dabbler in several musical forms, primarily the stage; frustrated novelist (you can still find his lurid tale *The Fifth String* in used bookstores); bandsman extraordinaire; these and other undeniable talents combine in Sousa, but towering above all of them is his unchallenged reign as The March King—a soubriquet bestowed on him by an anonymous writer for a British brass band journal, which the proud American was only too pleased to accept. By the age of 13 he was playing alongside his father in the U.S. Marine Band, becoming Bandmaster in 1880; 12 years later, he formed his own band and soon gained an international reputation. It was while sailing home from Europe that he began to hear a rhythmic beat playing incessantly within his brain, unfolding the same noble refrain over and over; on reaching shore he immediately wrote it down, calling it *Stars and Stripes Forever*—in Frederick Fennell's words "America's march for Americans"—and that alone would be more than enough to elevate him to the ranks of the immortals.

MARCHES

More than 100 Sousa marches survive, many of them for both band and theater orchestras, either in his own arrangements or others commissioned by his publishers. Duplication is unavoidable, since nearly every collection offers his best-loved efforts, including *Semper Fidelis, Washington Post, The Thunderer*, and of course *Stars and Stripes Forever*. Hopes soared in the heyday of Mercury Records with announced plans to record them all with Fennell and the **Eastman Wind Ensemble;** sadly, these plans came to naught with only 31 marches spread across four LPs (reissued on two CDs). Several years later the **U.S. Marine Band** issued all of Sousa's band music in nine 2LP sets, unfortunately not for sale in stores but only for "public affairs purposes." At about the same time Leonard B. Smith and the **Detroit Concert Band** brought out ten LPs comprising 116 marches (against 129 for the Marines). These are now available on CD, while the Marine Band has reasserted itself on Altissimo (reissued by MHS), though not the same performances as the LPs. It would be folly to try to review the flood of Sousa discs that now engulfs band music bins, but a number of stand-outs should be noted.

There's no point in trying to pass off the Eastman performances as reflecting the "Sousa style," which as heard from the Marine Band and the Detroiters is a highly rhythmic, sturdy yet dignified distillation of the parade ground. But these earnest and well-played accounts by students of the Eastman Rochester School of Music, brilliantly recorded by the Mercury engineers, are quite simply in a class by themselves and lift the spirits like no others. Fennell's later Eastman recordings, dating from the early '60's, offer brighter colors and a wider array (♦Mercury 434300); his earlier sally, including some of the best-known marches, has a bass drum that will rattle your windowpanes, most of all in *King Cotton* (♦Mercury 434334). The later Eastman recording with **Donald Hunsberger** (Kem-Disc 1004) continues a proud legacy, but the Mercuries are very special. (An earlier Mercury issue, 416147, offers 22 marches, but the later discs are the ones to have.)

The first two Altissimo CDs with the Marine Band have been reissued (MHS 515391, 515392), with more to follow, and they come up against stiff competition from **Smith**, who was not only first-chair cornet with the Goldman Band for six years but drew upon the experience of several of Sousa's own men and his biographer, Paul Bierley. Decked out in spanking white uniform as to the manner born, Smith and the marvelous Detroit Concert Band for many years offered as close to the sound of Sousa's own band as anyone was likely to hear, and his authoritative readings have been transferred expertly to a 5CD set (♦Walking Frog 300), unfortunately shedding the extensive LP notes and archive photos in the process. Comparison between the two approaches is not so much a matter of tempo as rhythmic emphasis, with the Marine snare drummer spurring everyone on smartly against Smith's warm and effusive embrace.

The **Wallace Collection** offers a wide range, from familiar marches to waltzes, rags, and even a chariot race (inspired by Lew Wallace's *Ben-Hur*), all played with tremendous zest and swagger (♦Nimbus 5129). Another splendid collection from the **Great American Main Street Band** likewise offers Sousa's marches merely as the nucleus of an impressive array of dance styles (♦EMI 54130), though neither is able to convince me that waltzes were Sousa's strong suit. Highlights of the latter include military trumpet and drum tattoos that found their way into *Semper Fidelis* and *The Thunderer,* plus a replica of the Liberty Bell that adds a wonderful sonority to the march so beloved of *Monty Python* fans. Even better, only two marches are common to both discs, and you can probably guess what one of them is.

Her Majesty's Royal Marines offer no less than 43 marches, including several otherwise unavailable except for Smith's set; but either the leader or the engineers have reduced everything to melody plus bass drum, with the euphoniums seemingly off in another room (Angel 64671/2, 2 CD). The **Coldstream Guards Band** offers a mix of Sousa and European marches, and balances are a lot better than on the Angel CDs, but tempos and lung power are a mite restrained (Denon 73807). That certainly isn't the case with the **Grenadier Guards Band,** who dig right in and revel in the rich (and loud!) mix of winds, brass and drums, though the "Stirring Marches of the USA Services" coupled with it come across as rather gimmicky (London 448957). Even so, it's far more upbeat and colorful than the Grenadier Guards' earlier CD (Teldec 96061), let alone Fennell and Eastman.

Keith Brion had the imaginative idea of coupling modern and archive recordings, including seven marches led by Sousa himself, though the ultimate effect is to make you want to hear more from Brion's splendid ensemble (Delos 3102). In addition, he has brought out three discs with the Razumovsky Symphony, a talented group of Czech players who play this music as beguilingly as Sousa's own theater orchestra. Of course there are marches, but best of all Brion has given us music for the stage, including *The Bride Elect* and *El Capitan* (Naxos 559008) and the highly characterful suites *Dwellers of the Western World* (559013) and *Three Quotations* (559029), rich in turn-of-the-century imagery. Even more trenchant accounts of the two suites are offered by **Richard Kapp,** unfortunately combined with vapid excerpts from Kapp's own Roosevelt-era musical *Teddy and Alice* based on Sousa's songs (ESS.A.Y 1003). Hershy Kay has gone even farther, making over Sousa's beloved march rhythms as a ballet, *Stars and Stripes;* it's enjoyable on its own terms as played by **Fiedler** (RCA 61501) but hardly a substitute for the real thing.

OPERETTAS

Sousa hoped to combine in his operettas both Gilbert *and* Sullivan; unfortunately his lyrics are no match for Gilbert's, and his attempts at a light romantic style all too often fall flat. Even so, *El Capitan* provides a highly enjoyable evening's entertainment, quite apart from the nonsensical plot about the Peruvian rebel leader El Capitan and his efforts to unseat the evil Spanish viceroy Don Medigua (think Zorro with singing), crowned by the familiar march that went on to enjoy a life of its own. **Ian Hobson** leads an enthusiastic and properly hambone group of students from the University of Illinois, and the University band joins in with relish in the spirited martial strains (♦Zephyr 11097). *Désirée,* set in the time of Richelieu, is a skillful assimilation of the European operetta style familiar to Sousa from Offenbach and Johann Strauss, nowhere as memorable as *El Capitan* but enjoyable nonetheless, well sung and fielded with verve by **Jerrold Fisher** leading the Pocono Pops (Amdec 101).   HALLER

Leo Sowerby *(1895–1968)*

When Sowerby died, his friend Howard Hanson wrote, "Leo's technique was impeccable. He had one of the finest "ears"—aural imagination—I have observed . . . It is safe to say that in church music his name stands at the top of the list of all American composers."

Sowerby was a prolific composer, with about 550 scores in every medium except opera. He received many awards, including the first American Prix de Rome. He had a long career at the American Conservatory in Chicago and as organist-choirmaster at St. James's Episcopal Church. His music is complex—a unique mixture of romantic and modernist idioms—beautiful, sometimes haunting, and frequently profound. It usually requires several hearings to establish itself in the mind of the listener, but once there, it finds its way inexorably to the heart.

Sowerby's contrapuntal technique and orchestral flair were outstanding. Shortly after his centenary in 1995, two superb recordings of his orchestral works were issued. The first includes the captivating Symphony 2, *Passacaglia, Interlude and Fugue, Concert Overture,* and *All on a Summer's Day* (Cedille 39); the second offers *Comes Autumn Time, Prairie* (a symphonic poem), *Theme in Yellow,* and *From the Northland: Impressions of the Lake Superior Country* (Cedille 33). These performances by **Paul Freeman** with the Czech National Symphony and Chicago Sinfonietta are of the highest quality and in bright, pure recorded sound. The extensive program notes by Francis Crociata, President of the Leo Sowerby Foundation, are an invaluable bonus.

The great American organist **David Craighead** and the Fairfield Orchestra under the magisterial direction of John Welsh collaborated to record one of Sowerby's masterworks, *Mediaeval Poem* for organ and full orchestra, at St. Bartholomew's Church, New York City, in a stirring, colorful performance of this opulent work. Any recording by Craighead is a collector's item, in this case especially so by the inclusion of his live performance of *Pageant,* a display piece par excellence for the pedal organ. *Classic Concerto* for organ and strings and *Festival Musick* for organ, brass, and kettledrums are also on this disc, both with David Mulbury as soloist (Naxos 559028). The lovely Concerto for Harp and Small Orchestra receives a beautiful performance from **Stephen Hartman** and the Monadnock Festival Orchestra under James Bolle (Gasparo 315, with a number of songs and *Rhapsody for Chamber Orchestra*).

Sowerby's extensive, richly varied list of chamber music (about 50 works) is underrepresented on CD. Three treasurable releases are Trio in C-sharp minor and Trio for Violin, Cello, and Piano, played by the **Musica Gioiosa Trio** (New World 365); Sonatas in B-flat and D and *Two American Pieces,* played by **Robert Murray** and **Gail Quillman** (Premier 1049); and Trio for Flute, Viola, and Piano, played by **Zizi Mueller** with Jesse Levine and Emma Tahmizian (Premier 1029, with pieces by Hanson, Barber, and others).

Catherine Crozier's CD is a classic among organ recordings, offering the monumental Symphony in G, the difficult and beguiling *Fantasy for Flute Stops,* and the moving *Requiescat in Pace* (Delos 3075). Crozier is a greatly respected artist who has long promoted Sowerby's organ music and has a rare feeling for it. Meticulous, fluid, and eloquent playing characterizes **Lorenz Maycher**'s attractive organ program (Raven 310). Eight works are included, among them the early *Comes Autumn Time* and *Carillon* and the midperiod *Whimsical Variations and Arioso.* A third fine CD is by **Robert Parris**—eight pieces, including free-flowing performances of *Pageant of Autumn* and *Carillon* and a brilliant *Jubilee* (Premier 1039). Completing a quartet of organ discs is a program played by **Faythe Freese** on the E.M. Skinner organ in Trinity Episcopal Church in Toledo, including the wonderful four-movement *Suite* and the dissonant, austere *Rhapsody* (Albany 368). For each of these splendid recordings, the chosen instrument is large and apt for Sowerby's color-saturated organ style.

Two admirable piano recordings are the Sonata in D, Suite, and *Passacaglia* played by **Gail Quillman,** a student of Sowerby's (New World 376), and *Florida Suite, From the Northland,* and other smaller pieces played by **Malcolm Halliday** (Albany 226). This CD offers the original piano version of *From the Northland,* whose third section is one of Sowerby's most evocative creations, *Burnt Rock Pool.*

An exquisite CD heads the choral genre: "Love Came Down at Christmas," 18 of his anthems and carols sung by **ConVivium,** an ensemble conducted by Patricia Snyder and John Delorey and accompanied on the organ by Ronald Stalford (a former pupil of Sowerby) and Snyder (Albany 187). All enthusiasts of 20th-century music should own this exceptional disc with its incomparable performances.

The expressive Good Friday cantata, *Forsaken of Man,* is one of the monuments of American church music. A sovereign performance is by the William Ferris Chorale of Chicago, conducted by the late William Ferris (another student and friend of Sowerby's), with Thomas Weisflog playing the ambitious organ part (New World 80394). Another disc by the Ferris Chorale consists of a cross section of Sowerby's later choral works recorded live. The centerpiece of this excellent CD is *The Throne of God* for full orchestra and chorus, composed for Washington Cathedral (Albany 232).

A broad selection of sacred music has been beautifully recorded in historic Mechanics Hall, Worcester, by **Gloria Dei Cantores** (Gloria Dei Cantores 016, 2CD). The disc includes solo songs with organ, anthems, canticles (including the solemn *Magnificat and Nunc Dimittis in E minor,* a masterwork), five organ pieces (one of them the challenging *Canon, Chacony, and Fugue*), and *Festival Musick.* MULBURY

Ludwig (Louis) Spohr *(1784–1859)*

The saga of Spohr is a story of contradictions, beginning with his name; although born in Braunschweig, he's called "Louis" in *Grove's* and in most recordings. In addition, while he often experimented with formats unheard of in the music of Mozart or Beethoven, for all his rich lyricism and good humor there's precious little that marks it as his alone, and it has a "considerable sameness" in Paul David's words. David further describes Spohr's music as "monotonous," but there we part company; there's too much that is immensely likable about it, and I for one enjoy a program of Spohr's symphonies or concertos as much as Haydn's. That brings us to the final contradiction, and by far the most curious: Spohr, who in his day was considered by many to be a far greater composer than Beethoven, is now almost unknown in the concert hall, surviving only in the pages of *Schwann* and in the array of recordings that beckon to us in the store. Record buyers should be encouraged to come hither.

SYMPHONIES

Spohr wrote ten symphonies; the last remains unpublished and wasn't included by Marco Polo in their survey. Arguably the finest of the lot is 3, or at least it's been recorded most often, and the glorious swaying theme of the opening movement, once heard, will surely haunt your memory long afterward. I often return to **Albrecht,** in most respects a beautiful reading, but his funereal pace in the Larghetto rules it out as first choice (Musica Mundi 11620). **Hager** is very good too, but the recording is rather thick-textured (Amati 8904, intriguingly coupled

with a violin arrangement of Schumann's Cello Concerto—most likely by Joachim). Best of all is **Alfred Walter** with his splendid Košice forces; alert, propulsive, and beautifully recorded (♦Marco Polo 223439, with 6).

Rickenbacher gives you 6 and 9 (♦Orfeo 094-841). Both are highly programmatic. Symphony 6, subtitled "Historical," is a curious exercise, each of the four movements concerned with a different period in musical history; I represents Bach and Handel, II Haydn and Mozart, and III Beethoven, while IV, "The Newest of the New," parodies music at least new to Spohr, mostly early Verdi. Unfortunately, Walter seems to be mired in the period of Haydn and in particular *The Seven Last Words of Christ on the Cross,* presenting a series of four slow movements without a shred of vitality even in the final Allegro vivace.

The idea comes off a lot better under Rickenbacher, though even he can't instill in the symphony convincing simulacra of Bach, Haydn, and Beethoven where none exist: It all sounds like Spohr. Rickenbacher's coupling is Spohr's setting of the four seasons (*Die Jahreszeiten*). As one critic has pointed out, it's an old man's view of the passing year, nowhere as robust as Haydn's or Vivaldi's yet enjoyable nonetheless. Rickenbacher brings out the programmatic imagery more effectively, though the Largo (Summer) flows better under Walter (Marco Polo 223454, with 2).

Choo Hoey also performs 2. Tempos are about the same, but Hoey's Singapore winds overshadow the rather wan strings, making for a brighter, sprightlier repast (♦Marco Polo 220360, with Lachner's Symphony 1); Walter at broader tempos brings out the "noble melancholy" of the music, though both do very well with the bustling finale. Walter is the only game in town for 4, again programmatic in intent; if 6 tells how various composers approached the art of music, 4 tells of the origins and uses of music itself, *Die Weihe der Töne* (The Consecration of Sound). Walter nearly loves the music to death but fields the contrasting moods of the two final movements in exemplary fashion (♦Marco Polo 223122).

In the remaining symphonies, Walter stands alone (♦Marco Polo 223363, 1 and 5; 223432, 7 and 8). Symphony 7 bears the unwieldy title *Irdisches und Göttliches im Menschenleben* (The Earthly and Divine in Human Life) and is unique in setting an 11-piece chamber ensemble against full orchestra, with the smaller group representing the spiritual side of human nature, the orchestra the secular. No such program attends its successor, perhaps in deference to the more traditional tastes of the English audiences for whom it was written; the music sings throughout, at times suggesting Raff, at others (including the finale) its counterpart in Schubert's 6th. Symphony 1 was obviously the product of happier times; by contrast, 5 gives us "Sturm und Drang" with a vengeance, perhaps reflecting the abrupt fall in fortune for Spohr who in only a few years lost first his brother and then his wife. Here Walter puts aside the *Gemütlichkeit* of the other symphonies with a driven and committed reading, making both discs essential.

Spohr's *Faust* was written 10 years before *Der Freischütz,* and those who hold that it was Spohr rather than Weber who pioneered the ideals of romanticism in opera will nod knowingly at the wide array of supernatural elements summoned on stage; it's easy to see how the burgeoning romantic spirit might have come about in Spohr's operas. All this compels interest in the overtures, fortunately brought together in a splendid collection by **Christian Fröhlich** (♦CPO 999093). Both *Faust* and *Jessonda* are treated in rather perfunctory fashion by **Walter** (Marco Polo, with Symphony 4), *Jessonda* rather more stylishly by **Albrecht** (Schwann, with Symphony 3).

CONCERTOS

As a violin virtuoso, Spohr was the equal of Paganini in technique but surpassed him in warmth and richness of tone. His large hands allowed him to negotiate the most difficult double-stops and stretches, and he cultivated a refinement of expression and singing tone—insisting that the violin should mimic the human voice at all times—that made him wildly popular throughout Europe.

He wrote 18 concertos for his own use; of these, all but two unpublished efforts have been gathered by **Ulf Hoelscher** and the Berlin Radio Symphony under Christian Fröhlich (♦CPO 999657, 6CD, priced as 3; also available separately). These performances are excellent; it's difficult to listen all the way through without coming away impressed with the great rhythmic lift, singing tone, and joyful shaping of phrases that come so easily to Hoelscher, seconded by the energetic and stylish orchestral support, with warm and resonant sonics. Perhaps it's unfair to set Hoelscher against the peerless **Heifetz** in 8, the popular *"In Form einer Gesangszene"* (RCA 7870), but for a complete survey we're not likely to see the equal of the CPO set anytime soon. There's a wealth of highly attractive melody, gracefully spun turns of phrase, and grateful give and take between soloist and orchestra, and you'll surely want to add the entire set to your collection.

Other recordings of the violin concertos are few. A coupling of 7 and 12 with **Takako Nishizaki** and 2 and 9 with **Christiane Edinger** is available (Marco Polo 220406 and 223510). In 7 Nishizaki's burnished tone contrasts effectively with Hoelscher's lighter coloring; she brings more importance to I, but her moribund account of the final Rondo is worlds away from Hoelscher's joyous romp, and a similar comparison (though not as extreme) applies to 12. Likewise Edinger displays marvelous purity of tone but seems sorely deenergized in 2:I compared with Hoelscher, who also invests the final Alla Polacca with far more insouciance; meltingly lyrical in 9:I, she takes the good-humored double-stopping of the final Allegretto too seriously set against Hoelscher's high spirits. Both Marco Polo discs are more resonant than the CPOs, though not enough to prove distracting. **Hyman Bress**'s LP of 8 and 9 is now NA (Oiseau-Lyre 278), as is **Suzanne Lautenbacher**'s LP of 8 with *Potpourri on Themes from "Jessonda"* (Candide).

You may want a disc combining Concertante in A for 2 Violins (one of two written by Spohr) with two works for violin and cello, Concertante in C and *"Jessonda" Potpourri,* all in excellent performances by Antje Weithaas and Mila Georgieva (violin) and Michael Sanderling (cello) with **Hermann Breuer** conducting (♦Es-Dur 2029). The sparkling final rondo of Concerto for String Quartet and Orchestra should have ensured its popularity long ago; there are two available recordings, by **Albrecht** and four accomplished string players (♦Koch Schwann 311088, with two sets of variations for violin and string trio) and by the Lark Quartet with the San Francisco Ballet Orchestra under **Jean-Louis LeRoux** (Arabesque 6723, with works by Handel, Schoenberg, and Elgar). The Koch is mellower in tone and a bit more urgent, the Arabesque deeper and richer sounding, though either will afford much pleasure.

There have probably been more recordings of Spohr's four clarinet concertos than all those for violin combined. They were written for the virtuoso Johann Simon Hermstedt, who modified the instrument to permit more challenging passage work and was effectively challenged by Spohr with four pieces far more advanced and demanding than anything written up to that time, yet richly melodic and heartfelt. They've been brought together three times, by **Karl Leister** (♦Orfeo 088101, 088201), **Eduard Brunner** (♦Tudor 7009, 7043), and **Ernst Otten-**samer (♦Naxos 550688/89), and one critic has perceptively likened the selection to "choosing among Oistrakh, Milstein, and Heifetz."

Those who choose the Naxos for low cost won't be disappointed; Ottensamer, principal clarinetist with the Vienna Philharmonic, has a robust and full-bodied tone and breath control worthy of Pavarotti, and Spohr's daunting passage work poses no problems for him. Leister, who holds a similar post with the Berlin Philharmonic, is cooler of temperament, but also fields the technical hurdles with aplomb—though the ensemble isn't quite up to the competition—and Brunner, principal with the Bavarian Radio Orchestra, plays extremely well, with seamless, confident delivery and tempos often a bit quicker than those of his colleagues.

Part of this impression may be traceable to the fact that both Leister and Ottensamer employ the darker, more mellow Oehler clarinet while Brunner prefers the brighter, sweeter Boehm instrument. Two others who play the Boehm model are **Thea King,** who recorded 4 (Meridian 84022, with the Mozart Concerto), and **John Denman,** who offers a rather more reserved coupling of 3 and 4 (IMP). Three LPs are not yet on silver disc: 1 with **Gervase de Peyer** (Oiseau-Lyre 60035, with Weber's Concerto 1), 2 with **John Denman** (Oryx 1828, with Stamitz's Concerto 3) and both 1 and 2 with **Anthony Pay** (Argo 920).

CHAMBER MUSIC

To Spohr, even Beethoven's middle quartets remained incomprehensible, let alone the later ones; thus we shouldn't expect any great musical revelation from Marco Polo's projected cycle with the **New Budapest Quartet.** Moods range from rapt lyricism to hearty vigor and otherworldly imagery, sometimes with the usual give and take and at other times with the first violin as *primus inter pares.* So far we have Vols. 1 though 9 (various numbers), with some seven or eight discs presumably still to come. Some may demur at the restrained playing, hoping for a more virtuoso display; nevertheless, the fact that the project has thus far only proceeded to nine volumes perhaps confirms the extreme difficulty of these scores, and we're not likely to have the luxury of comparing a wide array of performances, so any perceived flaws in the New Budapest presentation must be deemed irrelevant. Occasional entries by other sources have also surfaced, including 5 and 7 with the **Amati Quartet** (Jecklin-Disco 593) and 7 and 22 with the **Sonare Quartet** (MD+G 1144, LP), the former resonant and lyrical, the latter more close-to and spirited.

Where Spohr definitely one-upped (or rather four-upped) Beethoven was in his Double Quartets, not octets but alternately combining and pitting against each other two separate foursomes in ingenious fashion. You'll find all four in stimulating accounts by the redoubtable **St. Martin Academy Chamber Players** and need look no further (♦Hyperion, 22014; also available separately, 66141 and 42). However, the first of these has surfaced fairly often on its own, most notably from **Heifetz** and friends (RCA 7870). We must also note **Kammermusiker Zürich** (Jecklin-Disco 547, with Raff's Octet), as well as worthier versions by the **Melos Ensemble** (EMI 65995, with Berwald's Septet and Weber's Clarinet Quintet) and an LP by the **Kreuzberger** and **Eder Quartets** that thus far seems to have evaded silver disc (MHS 7028).

Marco Polo also offers all seven of Spohr's String Quintets, pleasing if perhaps somewhat formulaic: 1 and 2 by the **Danubius Quartet** (223597); 3 and 4 with the **New Haydn Quartet** (223599); 5 and 6 with the **Haydn Quartet** (223598); 7 plus the Sextet in C and *Potpourri on Themes of Mozart* by violinist **Atilla Falvay** with the New Haydn Quartet (223600). These works, like the quartets, aren't easy to play, and if the all-out playing on these discs precludes subtlety, perhaps that's all to the good. The "Grande Quintette" in G is coupled with Sextet in C and Double Quartet in D Minor by **Archibudelli** and the Smithsonian Chamber Players (Sony 53370), joyous period-instrument readings that even outshine the Heifetz-led account of the Double Quartet (RCA), while the Sextet and *Potpourri* are offered along with Quintet 4 by the **St. Martin** forces (Chandos 9424).

Even today some critics rank Spohr's Septet above Beethoven's, an irrepressible display that builds to a boisterous finale. The version by musicians from the Chicago area collectively called **Midsummer's Music** is beautifully played and recorded, and the coupling (works of Sigfrid Karg-Elert and the Swedish composer Elfride Andrée) is certainly off the beaten path (Centaur 2448). The rather liberally chromaticized Nonet is available from the **Czech Nonet** (Supraphon 1270, with Berwald's Septet), and from the **Linos Ensemble** in exceptionally warm and alert readings (Capriccio 10473, with Beethoven's Septet).

The Octet, with its final movement ingeniously working up Handel's familiar *Harmonious Blacksmith,* may be heard combined with the Nonet in irrepressible, even bumptious performances by the **Berlin Octet** and friends (Berlin 9012) and in stylish, buoyant readings by the **Gaudier Ensemble** (Hyperion 66699). Or if you can find them, there's an excellent pair of CDs by the **Nash Ensemble** offering the Septet and C minor Quintet for Piano and Winds (CRD 3399) and the Octet and Nonet (CRD 3354); these recordings date back a way and lack the richness of more recent versions, but the adroit and spirited playing allays all hesitation. (I yearn for a silver disc of the **Vienna Octet**'s warm and affectionate London pairing.)

The Quintet may also be found with **Sawallisch** at the keyboard, coupled with a Danzi quintet for similar forces—actually the better piece (Claves 8101). It's available with Sextet in C in an elegant and beautiful recording by **Ensemble Villa Musica** (MD+G 3448), who also offer Piano Quintet in D and Septet (MD+G 0534). You may also obtain the C minor Quintet combined with the Octet in stylish and fluid performances, as we would expect from clarinetist Dieter Klöcker and his colleagues who make up the **Consortium Classicum** (Orfeo 410961). These worthies also offer Nonet in a pairing (Orfeo 155871) with more offbeat fare (even for Spohr), the Janissary-styled Nonet for Winds and Turkish Band, a delightful piece and probably more immediately smile-provoking than the **Ensemble Wien-Berlin**'s coupling of Martinů's Nonet (DG 427640). There was also a very nice LP with **Leslie Jones** and the winds of the Little Orchestra of London, unfortunately NA (Oryx 1830, with Hummel's Octet-Partita for winds).

Spohr's five piano trios are richly romantic and joyful, with comfortable interplay of piano and strings—miniature piano concertos, if you will. Two integral sets are available, by the **New Munich Piano Trio** (Orfeo 352952) and **Ravensburg Beethoven Trio** (CPO 999246. The New Munich's brisk tempos occasionally seem to nudge the music along, but they get all five trios on 2 CDs; the Ravensburg needs 3, but it's worth it for these loving, lyrical readings, though it would have been nice to have the Piano Quintet too to fill out the 31-minute third disc. You can get warmly sympathetic readings of 3 and 4 played with real feeling by the **Borodin Trio** (Chandos) or more prosaic accounts by the **Hartley Trio,** which together cost not that much more than the Chandos (Naxos 553206, 1 plus the Piano Quintet; 553205, 2 and 4; 553164, 3 and 5). For those who prefer the plangent sound of period instruments, you can supplement the other recordings with 1 and 2 played by the **Beethoven Broadwood Trio,** though their intonation is a problem (Kingdom 2004).

Peter Csaba and **Vilmos Szabadi** are excellent Hungarian violinists, and in their disc of duets for two violins (*Duos Concertant*) they put singing tone ahead of virtuoso display, though the steady diet of legato is better taken in small doses (Hungaroton 31866). Or you can buy the affectionate and polished readings of Op 67:1–3 by **Heinz Schunk** and **Ulrike Petersen** (CPO 999343). **David** and **Igor Oistrakh**'s performance of Op 67:2 is legendary (Doremi 7714; Chant du Monde 278906).

Though a violinist himself, Spohr lavished great affection on music for the harp, gifts for his beloved wife (and harpist) Dorette. Flutist Peter-Lukas Graf and harpist **Ursula Holliger** play Spohr's Sonata in E-flat, a mixed bag but nicely done (Claves 50-708). Two like pieces, the Sonata Concertante in G and the Sonata in C Minor, are offered by Martin Ulrich Senn and **Chantal Mathieu** (Jecklin-Disco 548, with Johann Andreas Amon's Sonata in E-flat), while the C minor sonata is included in a collection with Marc Grauwels and **Catherine Michel** (Marco Polo 220441). **András Adorján** and **Marielle Nordmann** offer the C minor and E-flat sonatas with the *Fantasy on Themes of Franz Danzi and Abbé Vogler* (Orfeo 129881).

You can also obtain two sonatas for violin and harp with **Philipp Naegele** and **Giselle Herbert,** played with an appealing directness and handily negotiating the more difficult trills and embellishments (Bayer 100264). **Helga** and **Klaus Storck** (harp and cello) and violinist **Kurt Guntner** offer the Sonata in C minor for Violin and Harp, Sonata in D for Harp and Cello, and Trio in F minor for Harp, Violin, and Cello, for those who can never get enough Spohr harp music (Calig 50887). Such partisans will also want the disc by **Ursula Holliger** and **Thomas Füri** containing two sonatas in E-flat for harp and violin, Fantasy in C Minor, and Variations in F on the air "Je suis encore dans mon printemps" (Jecklin-Disco 573). Concertante 1 in G for violin, harp, and orchestra is more substantial fare, offered with Mozart's Flute/Harp Concerto by Hansheinz Schneeberger and Holliger with **Graf** conducting (he's also the flutist in the Mozart) (Claves 50-208).

CHORAL MUSIC

Of the three large-scale oratorios left to us, only *Der Fall Babylons* (The Fall of Babylon) remains unrecorded, though I have a BBC radio dub from 1984 conducted by **Meredith Davies** that suggests it would be welcome on disc as well. *Die letzten Dinge* (The Last Judgment), in many respects not unlike Brahms's *German Requiem,* is a fascinating setting of the *Book of Revelations,* ultimately more elegiac than apocalyptic for all the dramatic power of the Judgment Scene. **Gustav Kuhn**'s recording (Philips 416627) is somewhat cramped sonically but far more compelling than the performance by **Siegfried Heinrich** (Jubilate LP), a dreary account lasting nearly a quarter of an hour longer.

Des Heilands letzte Stunden (The Last Hours of the Savior, or Calvary) was also a great success with English audiences; though intended as a Passion Oratorio for Easter services, the text is not entirely biblical but explores human feelings and emotions as well and was perhaps a source of inspiration for Mendelssohn, who was working on *St. Paul* at the time. The performance by the Wiesbaden chorus, orchestra, and soloists under **Klaus-Uwe Ludwig** is competent, but the notes are entirely in German save for the libretto, which offers both German and English but not side by side (Motette 50201, 2CD).

Devotees of a cappella music will want the Mass in C for five soloists, not so much a polyphonic exercise as a maelstrom of chromatic harmonies. It's offered along with three psalms, beautifully sung by the Berlin Radio Chorus and soloists led by Michael Gläser and **Dietrich Knothe** (CPO 999149). **Jaroslav Brych** leads the Prague Philharmonic

Choir in the same coupling and throws in three psalms by Mendelssohn, but many of his tempos seem uncomfortably rushed (Praga 250117).

OPERAS

Unlike Gounod and Berlioz, Spohr turned for his setting of *Faust* not to Goethe but a retelling of the familiar legend by Josef Carl Bernard, in which Faust has already made his pact with the Devil before the curtain rises; however, there's a wild *Walpurgisnacht* as well as not one but two fallen maidens, thus providing gainful employment for two sopranos instead of one. In a Bielefeld production with **Geoffrey Moull** conducting, the singing ranges from impressive to less so, but it may be recommended *faute de mieux* (CPO 999247, 2CD).

Once popular with German audiences, *Jessonda* is best known today for its sparkling overture, close cousin to Weber's *Preciosa*. The rajah's widow Jessonda is compelled by custom to commit *suttee* (ritual death by fire) upon her husband's death but is rescued by Tristan d'Acunha, leader of the invading Portuguese forces. Unfortunately the grand tableaux and visual effects are lost on disc, but the presence of Varady and Fischer-Dieskau in the major roles at least offers sumptuous aural splendor, despite **Albrecht**'s rather stodgy conducting (Orfeo 240912, 2CD).

Zemire et Azor, a reworking of the text employed by Grétry, suggests a colorful coming together of the familiar "Beauty and the Beast" story with the *Arabian Nights,* skillfully put across by principals of the Nordhausen Theater led by **Anton Kolar** (Deutsche Schallplatten 1064).

SONGS

Soprano **Marjorie Patterson** offers three complete cycles of six songs each (Opp. 25, 41, and 72, plus 5 from Op 37); her rather colorless readings fail to impress, and she's all too often overpowered by Daniel Sarge's piano (Marco Polo 223869). You may gravitate naturally to **Varady** and **Fischer-Dieskau** on a rather brief but beautifully appointed recital (Orfeo 103841). Songs by Spohr and Norbert Burgmüller are sung beautifully by **Mitsuko Shirai** (MD+G 3244).   HALLER

Carl Stamitz (1745–1801)

Mozart was rude about the Stamitz brothers, Carl and his brother Anton, five years younger; but in truth they were thoroughly congenial men. Their father Johann was Czech and a mainstay of the Mannheim court orchestra and the school of composers that grew up around it. Born into this musical background, both brothers became not just proficient composers but expert violinists and violists as well; indeed Carl must be accounted one of the earliest traveling viola virtuosi, and he wrote idiomatically for the instrument—as did Anton, who is mentioned here because the few recordings of his music are coupled with works by his brother or father.

Carl Stamitz's music is consistently agreeable, but you wouldn't insult any of it by listening to it while eating a meal or working at the computer. It makes no demands and is soon forgotten, although at the time it seems gracious and the embodiment of the Classical style. Take the four symphonies, which are beautifully performed by the London Mozart Players under **Bamert** in the "Contemporaries of Mozart" series (Chandos 9358). All are in three movements; the opening movements bustle cheerfully, the slow ones have a pleasant lilt, and the finales are delightful. The fourth work on the disc, actually the earliest, is full of hunting rhythms and offers splendid opportunities for the horns. The CD, highly recommended as long as you're not looking for Mozartian profundity, is well recorded.

The wind concertos are fun. There's only one recording of the jolly Bassoon Concerto, and it will satisfy anyone who doesn't remember the inimitable version by Archie Camden. **Yoshijuko Nakanishi** is the soloist, and Cleobury conducts the London Mozart Players; couplings are Weber and Hummel bassoon concertos (ASV 6159). For the Clarinet Concertos the choice is mainly between the high-gloss combination of **Sabine Meyer** with the Academy of St. Martin under Iona Brown and the slightly earthier **Kálmán Berkes,** who directs the Nicolaus Esterházy Sinfonia himself. Both offer two volumes. Meyer's first disc has Concertos 3, 10, and 11, with the concerto by father Johann thrown in (EMI 54842); her second has 1 and 7, along with concertos for basset horn and for clarinet and bassoon (EMI 55511). Berkes's first CD has just Concerto 1, with the concertos for two clarinets and clarinet and bassoon (Naxos 553584); his second has 7, 8, 10, and 11 (Naxos 554339). Meyer is better artistically and more clearly recorded, but Berkes has a huge price advantage.

Eduard Brunner is also competitive in 1, 7, 8, and 11, with the Munich Chamber Orchestra under Hans Stadlmair (Tudor 739). A useful disc has Concerto 11 played by the late **Bohuslav Zahradník** and the E major Horn Concerto played by **Zdeněk Tylšar,** with the concerto for two flutes by Anton; František Vajnar conducts the Prague Chamber Orchestra (Supraphon 11 1424). For the G major Flute Concerto it would be hard to beat **Irena Grafenauer**, whose disc with the Academy of St. Martin under Marriner is still available in Europe (Philips 426318). But if a period flute is preferred, **Bart Kuijken** is just as good in his own way, with excellent support from Tafelmusik led by Lamon (Sony 48045).

The idiomatic D major Sinfonia Concertante for violin and viola was recorded on LP by **Stern** and **Zukerman** and an even more sympathetic Czech team, **Suk** and **Josef Kočousek;** neither is now available. In an excellent 1994 recording, Suk took to the viola with **Oldřich Vlček** on violin and Rudolf Krečmer conducting the Virtuosi di Praga. As the price and the couplings by Dittersdorf and Haydn are attractive, this disc is a winner (Discover 920274). You can safely disregard another Czech version in which **Lubomír Malý** plays both violin and viola (Panton 81 1045). The work in C for two violins is available in a rather humdrum disc of various sinfonie concertante by the London Festival Orchestra and soloists under **Ross Pople,** along with the D major (ASV 6140).

Sinfonia Concertante in A for violin, viola, and cello has been recorded only once, by **Collegium Aureum** and its fine soloists. Although it inevitably becomes something of a procession, with three soloists needing to have their say, it's enjoyable, and a bargain CD reissue may still be found in Europe (Deutsche Harmonia Mundi 77457). That disc also includes a sterling account of the popular D major Viola Concerto played by the late Ulrich Koch.

For this work there are several fine alternatives, though **Zukerman**'s superb version has never appeared on CD. The young Italian player **Marcello Defant** directs the Zandonai Ensemble himself, offering concertos by Franz Anton Hoffmeister and Dittersdorf as well (Symposion 0106). The strong Czech soloist **Jan Pěruška** has an equally interesting program, adding concertos by Johann and Anton; he's nicely supported by the Prague Chamber Philharmonic under Běhlolávek (Panton 81 1422). **Wolfram Christ** is another front-rank contender available in Europe, with the Cologne Chamber Orchestra under Müller-Brühl (Schwann 11060). Versions by **Ernst Wallfisch** (Vox 0011) and a very young **Tabea Zimmermann** (Hyperion 55035) will interest viola fans.

The three hitherto unknown cello concertos are well played by **Christian Benda,** directing the Prague Chamber Orchestra himself (Naxos 550865). The recently discovered No. 4, in which the cello writing shows even more of Boccherini's influence, is superbly played on a period instrument by **Werner Matzke,** backed by Concerto Köln, in "Mannheim: The Golden Age" (Teldec 28366).

No great claims can be made for Carl Stamitz's chamber music. The *Harmoniemusik,* for instance, falls a long way behind that of Mozart or Krommer. A selection is played better than it deserves by **Consortium Classicum** (CPO 999081). Similarly, the Oboe Quartet in D hardly merits the artistry lavished on it by **Paul Goodwin** and Terzetto; this exquisite period-instrument recital is more notable for its Mozart, Krommer, and Louis Massoneau performances (Harmonia Mundi 907220). The pleasant Viola Sonata is weakly played by **Anna Barbara Duetschler,** although Ursula Duetschler almost saves the day with her handling of a fortepiano (Claves 50-9502); **Robert Verebes** sounds a little past his best, even if both he and Mireille Lagacé play with spirit, she on another early piano (SNE 569). If you can find the Czech disc by **Malý** with František Kuda on a modern piano, it's one of the better efforts by this often dull player; he offers Hummel and Vanhal as well as the Stamitz in well-shaped interpretations (VARS 0013).   POTTER

Charles Villiers Stanford *(1852–1924)*

Born in Dublin and trained in Germany, Stanford was very much an English composer, the leading example of his time before Elgar. He paved the way for Elgar, both with his breakthroughs in English song, choral, and especially cathedral music and with his willingness to conduct Elgar's music. Stanford may still be England's leading church composer, and he also wrote some fine chamber music. His more uneven symphonies had less effect, but they include some unjustly neglected works. Stanford's music is strongly reminiscent of Schumann, Brahms, and Mendelssohn with an English accent, and, in some works, a heavy dose of Irish folk song. It's well crafted, with few unnecessary or theatrical gestures, and much is very beautiful. In addition to composing, Stanford was an organist and conductor, and he taught at the university level for many years. Many English composers, including Vaughan Williams, Holst, Ireland, and Howells, studied with him at the Royal College of Music and at Cambridge. They may be his greatest legacy.

ORCHESTRAL MUSIC

The symphonies and Irish Rhapsodies have all been recorded by **Handley** leading the Ulster Orchestra. The symphonies alone are available in ♦Chandos 9279 (4CD) and the rhapsodies in ♦Chandos 7002 (2CD). They can also be obtained one symphony to a disc with a Rhapsody as coupling (listed below). These are excellent performances with a pleasant, delicate touch, good spring to the rhythms, and fluid motion. The sound is excellent if a bit rounded in the upper frequencies in some recordings. The Rhapsodies find Stanford at his most charming and eloquent; the hinges sometimes show in the symphonies, but they contain many fine moments and are well worth exploring.

1. This pleasant, spirited work was mainly the product of a composer learning his craft, but it has its moments (♦Chandos 9049, with Rhapsody 2, "Lament for the Son of Ossian"). The mature Rhapsody is a dark-toned account of Ossian's story with wistful, glowing Irish tunes.

2 ("Elegiac"). This symphony is more concise and assured (Chandos ♦8991, with Clarinet Concerto). Underlying the work is a seriousness reflecting its nickname, from Tennyson's *In Memoriam.*

3 ("Irish"). This is Stanford's most famous symphony. It has marvelous moments with Irish tunes, particulary the Scherzo, the spirited finale, and a deep slow movement whose theme echoes that of Brahms's 3rd. Anyone who likes Vaughan Williams and Holst folk song suites will love

both this movement and the excellent Rhapsody 5. **Del Mar** is weighty and a bit clunky, though the finale is darkly appealing (EMI 65129, with Elgar's *Scenes from the Bavarian Highlands*). **Handley** catches the dance and folk qualities better and with more finesse; the Rhapsody is a must (♦Chandos 8548).

4. This is an assured, mostly upbeat work (♦Chandos 8884, with Rhapsody 6 for violin). The Rhapsody has a lovely, slow Irish introduction, with a more academic Allegro. It's beautifully played by **Lydia Mordkovitch.**

5. Based on Milton's *L'Allegro ed il Penseroso,* this is Stanford's most mellow, Brahmsian symphony, particularly the lyrical Andante and complex finale, with a striking organ passage (♦Chandos 8581, with Rhapsody 4, "The Fisherman of Loch Neagh and What He Saw"). The Rhapsody, perhaps the finest of the group, is typical of Stanford's Irish vein, with some lively, varied tunes.

6 ("In Memoriam to G.F. Watts"). This is the weakest of the mature symphonies, with a not very interesting Schumannesque I and a too-long finale (♦Chandos 8627, with Rhapsody 1). Each movement is dedicated to one of the British painter's works; the touching slow movement is best. The Rhapsody combines two tunes, including "Londonderry Air." It's better than the symphony, though not the strongest of the rhapsodies.

7. This is the most sparingly orchestrated symphony (♦8861, with Rhapsody 3 for cello; Concert Piece for organ and orchestra). The Rhapsody is a lyrical, full-toned treatment of Irish tunes. Cellist **Rafael Wallfisch** is outstanding. The Concert Piece is reminiscent of Strauss, but in simpler harmonic language with noble organ music, heady brass, and contemplative string writing.

CONCERTOS

Clarinet. This concerto was written for Richard Mühlfeld, who didn't care for it and refused to play it. Its dark coloring, particularly the warm Andante, fits the clarinet well. **Emma Johnson** is the most lyrical, singing, and warm of three readings, particularly in her romantic treatment of the slow movement; Charles Groves and the Royal Philharmonic are excellent (♦ASV 787, with *Three Intermezzi;* Finzi's Clarinet Concerto; *Bagatelles*). **Janet Hilton** is more straightforward, animated, aggressive, and brighter (♦Chandos 8991, with Symphony 2). She's not as moving or subtle, particularly in II, where she's much faster and less romantic. If you don't want Symphony 2, Johnson is the choice. **Thea King** is more aggressive and angular than Johnson or Hilton, a tendency exaggerated by conducting that lurches a bit (Hyperion, with Finzi's Clarinet Concerto).

Piano. No.1 is intimate, close to Schumann, Mendelssohn, and Saint-Saëns, with the pianist often working like a chamber player filling in orchestral textures. It's a delicate and sophisticated work, with an expressive slow movement and a good-humored finale. **Piers Lane**'s performance and the recorded sound are fine (♦Hyperion 66820, with Parry's Concerto 1). No. 2 isn't a great work, but it's more assured and entertaining than 1. It has a stirring, Brahmsian flow with touches of Rachmaninoff, particularly in the rolling opening theme before stern horns announce the main motive. **Binns** brings out its dark, weighty romanticism and accents the parallel with Rachmaninoff (♦Lyrita 219, with Rhapsody 4 and other works). **Fingerhut** is more extroverted and flowing, if not as poetic (♦Chandos 8736, with *Concert Variations upon an English Theme*). Her reading has a lighter, brighter touch and a faster tempo than Binns's. The exciting *Concert Variations* takes a strong theme ("Down among the Dead Men") and spins variations that just roll along.

Violin. Recordings of Stanford's reputedly two fine violin concertos are lacking.

CHAMBER MUSIC

Organ Sonatas. Stanford was the leading British composer for organ. His style is most notably Mendelssohn with traces of Bach counterpoint, culminating in the romanticism (but not the chromaticism) of his era. Of his organ sonatas, all but 1 are based on hymns or folk tunes that he combined with classical elements to produce solidly structured works that are immediately appealing. Much of the writing is pianistic, with arpeggios, hemiola, staccatos, etc. **Joseph Payne** is an excellent advocate (♦Marco Polo 223754). Fine sound.

Piano Trio 2. This represents Stanford at the peak of his powers. Listeners will think they've found another Brahms trio, with the sturdy rhythms and characteristic Brahmsian lurch in the Presto. The **Pirasti Trio** effortlessly delivers power and flow (♦ASV 925, with piano trios by Bax and Holst).

VOCAL MUSIC

Magnificat. **Marlow** and the Trinity College Choir, Cambridge, offer magnificent choral tone and intonation (♦Conifer 51155, with other choral works including Parry's *Songs of Farewell*). Written for double choir, the *Magnificat* is beautifully crafted, the most complex of Stanford's choral pieces and one of the few with quicker tempos.

Orchestral songs. Stanford orchestrated a number of songs originally written for piano. They are more eloquent, involving, and moving (if less heroic) than the "sea" songs reviewed below. "Chieftain" is almost Elgarian. Baritone **Christopher Maltman** brings the words to life more than Luxon in the "sea" songs, but is less good vocally, straining in the high register and in loud passages (♦Hyperion 67065). This will bother some more than it does me: I enjoyed this disc. It offers good sound and fine direction from Martyn Brabbins with the BBC Scottish Symphony.

Requiem and *Veiled Prophet.* *Requiem* is sweet-toned, intimate, yet dramatic. It's Mendelssohnian in style, with hints of Verdi's *Requiem* and the *Messiah*. There are many serene, sublime moments. *Veiled Prophet* is Stanford's first opera. You hear his symphonies in the overture; the remaining items are in operetta style. **Leaper** leads very fine performances, though the "Offertorium" and the faster music could use more energy (♦Marco Polo 223580, 2CD). The sound is boxy but clear enough.

Songs of the Sea and *Songs of the Fleet.* These are both stirring, dealing with England's glory at sea, with the latter (and later) work more serious, deeper, and more sophisticated. They are direct, without the exoticism of Elgar's *Sea Pictures,* and range from the martial and rousing (particulary "Drake's Drum" from *Sea*) to the touching and sad. Baritone Luxon sings firmly and with sympathy, though **Del Mar**'s straightforward conducting could use more imagination. The Bournemouth Symphony sounds a bit hard, a combination of the playing and the sound. Worth exploring but not Stanford's or EMI's best work (♦EMI LP 4401).

Stabat Mater and *Bible Songs.* Stanford called his *Stabat Mater* a "symphonic cantata," and the work does begin with a long, symphonic introduction. The choral sections are mainstream and more dramatic than *Requiem:* Any lover of Mendelssohn or Brahms will feel at home. It's energetic in the Victorian church manner, and the final choral section is heavenly. **Hickox** leads a fine performance, though Ingrid Attrot is squally at times. On the same disc are *Bible Songs,* set mostly to Psalmic texts; they have a churchly English ring. They're let down slightly by some groping by Varcoe in the low register and a few pitch problems. The sound is good, but a bit bloated. Still, it's an interesting disc (♦Chandos 9548).

HECHT

Robert Starer *(b. 1924)*

Starer is a composer of highly evocative, eerily dark-hued music of crystalline clarity. His razor-sharp sensibilities and exceptionally acute ear for unusual sonority inform his work with a sometimes brittle, glassy edge, and his transparency of texture serves as a vehicle for the exploration of color and shade rather than as a window for the transmission of light. His music shows some characteristics of Webern and Berg (he was born and spent his childhood in Vienna), but he developed a personal style derived from many influences. His large output includes works in most genres, including three operas and several ballets, and his recorded catalog includes a body of distinctive and eloquent chamber music.

One of his finest works is the wistful Clarinet Quintet, based on Catskill folk songs and notable for its lovely string writing, offered by **Music in the Mountains Festival Players** (Albany 152). This disc continues with Duo for Violin and Piano and *Episodes* for viola, cello, and piano, which, although sad, is resigned and compliant. The viola seems to be an especially expressive instrument for him. **Melvin Berger** and the English Chamber Orchestra give a memorable performance of Concerto for Viola, Strings, and Percussion (Vox 5158, with concertos by other American composers). The string writing is bittersweet and taut, the solo instrument yearning and brooding, the percussion stark and insistent.

"Remembering Felix" for cello and piano is a series of portraits of an imaginary musical character, narrated by **Robert Lurtsema** (Albany 151). The narrator represents acquaintances reminiscing about their encounters with him, in a sort of light burlesque manner. More serious is the ensuing song cycle on Whitman poems, *To Think of Time* (1984), sung by soprano **Ann Kerl Donaldson** with the Mariani String Quartet. Again the string writing is poignant and rich, and the famous texts include "Darest thou now O soul, walk out with me toward the unknown region . . . ," treated in a rather less optimistic vein than by Vaughan Williams. *Night Thoughts* for vocal quartet and piano is gestural and theatrical.

Two discs of solo piano music contain works spanning Starer's entire career. **Gerald Berthiaume** (Albany 205) includes *Sketches in Color,* a series of short and straightforward reflections designed for younger players, and the jazzy, urbane *Excursions for a Pianist.* This excellent disc also includes *At Home Alone,* another set of short impressions, which are of much more than pedagogical interest. The same can be said of *Three Israeli Sketches.* The spooky, almost Debussyian *Electric Church* is a brief tone painting of a church shrouded in mist during an electrical storm, and the much earlier and more complex *Five Caprices* and Sonata 1 reveal great emotional breadth and expressive power.

Justin Kolb's offering (Albany 228) contains a wealth of substantial pieces, including the lyrical Sonata 3 and the very early but remarkably contemporary and bluesy *Prelude and Toccata. Sketches in Color,* Set II adds three more to the earlier seven, and a set of advanced studies, *The Contemporary Virtuoso,* is a challenging addition to the repertoire. *Twilight Fantasies,* after a poem by Shelley, shows the impressionistic Starer at his best and is highly recommended. A set of three *Preludes for Trum-*

pet and Organ played by **Keith Benjamin** and **Melody Turnquist** is also interesting (Gothic 49067).

Sadly, little of Starer's music for larger forces is currently available. The dark and brooding oratorio *Ariel, Visions of Isaiah,* performed by the Camerata Singers and Orchestra under **Abraham Kaplan,** is in rather raw and dated sound (CRI 612), but the neoclassical *Concerto a Tre* on the same disc (with a youthful **Gerard Schwarz** on trumpet) sounds better. Again, Starer's skill in contrasting a wind trio with string orchestra is displayed. The more recent Cello Concerto with **Starker** and the Boston Pro Arte Orchestra is certainly worth investigating (CRI 618, with concertos by Richard Wernick and Richard Wilson), and another release includes the very impressive symphonic poem *Samson Agonistes* with **Vladimir Vlasák** leading the Czech Radio Symphony and the very Jewish-sounding Clarinet Concerto with Orit Orbach and the Haifa Symphony (MusicMasters 2048). Last but not least is an excellent recording of the colorful and approachable *Hudson Valley Suite* played by **David Alan Miller** and the Albany Symphony (Albany 244, with *Evanescence* for brass quintet and Francis Thorne's Symphony 7). This is music in English pastoral style with occasional jazz and dance inflections, very well performed and recorded.   JOHNSON

Wilhelm Stenhammar *(1871–1927)*

Stenhammar was an accomplished composer, pianist, and conductor. He was a late romanticist with roots in the music of Haydn, Beethoven, Liszt, Wagner, and Brahms and a spiritual kinship with Sibelius, but these stylistic elements don't overshadow his individual musical language. Among his orchestral and vocal works are some of the finest treasures in Swedish music.

Four of Stenhammar's most profound orchestral compositions appear in excellent sound and performances by **Neeme Järvi** and the Gothenburg Symphony (DG 445857, 2CD). Nordic touches, expressed in majesty, long melodic lines, and dramatic intensity, are found in the impressive 50-minute Symphony 1, described by Stenhammar himself as "idyllic Bruckner." The splendid Symphony 2, written 12 years later (1915), is based on Swedish folk idioms and ancient church modes. Straussian opulence and passionate lyricism mark the *Excelsior!* Overture, expressed in a still largely German vernacular. Stenhammar's crowning achievement is his magnificent Serenade. The *Excelsior!* Overture and Symphony 2 are also heard in inspired readings by **Petter Sundkvist** and the Royal Scottish National Orchestra (Naxos 553888). Not quite matching Järvi's orchestra in fullness and warmth of strings and brass, this is still a very worthwhile release.

Although Stenhammar was an excellent pianist, he wrote few solo pieces for that instrument, concentrating instead on large-scale works. The two piano concertos, coupled with the two symphonies and other important music, are in a set with **Järvi** (BIS 714, 4CD). Concerto 2, Serenade, and the love-ballad *Florez and Blanzeflor* are heard with Janos Solyom in a well-balanced performance of the concerto and Ingvar Wixell the fine baritone soloist in the haunting ballad (EMI 65081). Pianist **Greta Erikson**'s lyrical, commanding interpretation of Concerto 2 is coupled with Tor Aulin's Violin Concerto 3, among the finest of all Swedish violin concertos (Musica Sveciae 622).

Stenhammar was primarily interested in strings and voices and applied them to excellent use in several majestic works for vocal forces and orchestra. Two cantatas, *Stockholm Exhibition Cantata* and the patriotic *Ett Folk* (One People) have been recorded (Sterling 1023). Soloists, choir, and orchestra are outstanding in these popular works; the latter is simpler in melodies and harmonies. The cantata *Sången* (The Song) was

Stenhammar's last major work, written in 1920–21. Scored for four vocal soloists, massive choral forces, and orchestra, *The Song* has been recorded with mezzo von Otter among its performers, with **Blomstedt** conducting the Swedish Radio Symphony (Caprice 21358). It's coupled with Stenhammar's beloved *Two Sentimental Romances* for violin and orchestra and *Ithaca* for baritone and orchestra; Arve Tellefsen is the fine violinist, Håkan Hagegård the sensitive baritone, and Stig Westerberg and Kjell Ingebretsen conduct the Swedish Radio Symphony.

The wonderful orchestral Interlude (*Mellenspel*) from *The Song* is often performed as a separate work. **Järvi** offers an excellent performance, coupled with the Wagnerian cantata *Snöfrid,* the symphonic poem *Midwinter,* and the theater suite *Lodolezzi Sings* (BIS 438). *Interlude* is also in a delightful CD of "Swedish Orchestral Favourites," ably interpreted by **Kamu** directing the Helsingborg Symphony (Naxos 553115).

Lucia Negro is the excellent pianist in Sonatas 1 through 4 and the *Fantasy*—all early works (Sonata 1 and *Fantasy* were written when Stenhammar was 9)—in Volume II of the complete piano music (BIS 634; Volumes I and III are on BIS 554 and 764.). Although there is much to like in these compositions, I don't always find them interesting or memorable.

Of Stenhammar's seven lyrical, melodic string quartets, 1 and 2 are in Caprice 21337, 3 in Swedish Society 1032, and 6 in Opus 3 19702. Nos. 1, 2, and 3 are youthful works, while 6, along with 7 considered to be his finest quartets, dates from his mature period. Various ensembles are involved in these performances.

Four of Stenhammar's choral works, coupled with music by Alfvén and Wilhelm Peterson-Berger, may be found in outstanding performances by the **Uppsala University Chamber Choir** led by Stefan Parkman (Musica Sveciae 612).   DE JONG

William Grant Still *(1895–1978)*

Still is a difficult composer to come to terms with. He studied with both W.C. Handy and Varèse and was adept in the commercial field of arranging and writing for Hollywood films. His serious music is as attractive and immediately effective as his film scores, yet there is greater depth in them than appears on first hearing. He wrote many songs and operas, but none of the latter are available at present.

Three of Still's five symphonies have been recorded. Symphony 1 ("Afro-American") is among his early compositions, but he's already amazingly assured in handling orchestral sounds and adept at mingling the idioms of the blues with the unwieldy forces of a full orchestra. For a long time **Krueger**'s 1965 recording with the Royal Philharmonic was the only one (Bridge 9086), but **Paul Freeman** recorded a considerable collection of music by black composers, including this piece, with the London Symphony in 1974, demonstrating that Krueger's tempos were too slow (Columbia LP 32782). Finally, an American orchestra recorded it, though with an Estonian conductor, **Neeme** with the Detroit Symphony (Chandos 9154). Curiously, this issue doesn't mention the poems by Paul Lawrence Dunbar that are quoted in the score as inspiration for the four movements. Freeman is more natural, but Järvi beats Freeman for idiom and also offers better sound. Another recording, by **Jindong Cai** and the Cincinnati Philharmonia, is less incisive and less idiomatic, though it also contains two important pieces for piano and orchestra, *Kaintuck'* and *Dismal Swamp,* otherwise unavailable (Centaur 2331).

Symphony 2 ("Song of a New Race") follows the progress of black Americans with a sense of positive accomplishment, as opposed to the more nostalgic "Afro-American." **Järvi** is the only one to record it, in a warmly played if sometimes matter-of-fact reading (Chandos 9226). There may be five symphonies, but 3 ("Sunday") has also been listed as Still's last. It has been recorded by the North Arkansas Symphony under **Carlton Woods** in a somewhat rough and ready reading in a disc with Arthur Bennett Lipkin's serviceable performance with the Royal Philharmonic of *Festive Overture* (once available from CRI), *Folk Suite 4, Romance* for saxophone and piano, three *Rhythmic Spirituals,* and *I Feel Like My Time Ain't Long* for choir (Cambria 1060). This disc has a good deal of little-known music for the Still enthusiast, though perhaps it shouldn't provide an introduction to his art. *Romance* is also played beautifully by **Lawrence Gwozdz** in an unusual "American Concerto Tribute to Sigurd Rascher" album (Albany 331).

Schwann lists the ballet *Sahdji,* but the recording they cite doesn't contain it, being a piano album. There are two recordings, one by **Hanson** in "Fiesta in Hi-fi" (Mercury 434324). This is an incisive performance in which the Eastman School Chorus plays an important part, singing with beautifully clear diction. **Freeman** also recorded this work in his black composer series in an even more idiomatic reading with the excellent Morgan State College Choir (Columbia LP 33433). Their diction isn't as clear, but the quality of their final yell is worth the price of admission. A reissue of the entire 8LP series is called for.

Miss Sally's Party, a light-hearted ballet, is in a disc containing *And They Lynched Him on a Tree,* a work for orchestra, narrator (William Warfield), mezzo (Hilda Harrison), and a chorus that comments on the lynching, all conducted by **Philip Brunelle** (Collins 1454). This disc also contains two organ pieces, *Reverie* and *Elegy.* Another early ballet score, *Guiablesse,* is full of beauty and energy. It may be found in another of the many mixed-genre discs that mark Still's discography, making them difficult to categorize. This ballet is played by the Berlin Symphony under **Isaiah Jackson** (Koch 7154). They also play *Danzas de Panama* in rather polite fashion, and the 36-minute disc (!) is filled out with two short transcriptions for flute and piano, played by Alexa Still (apparently no relation to the composer) in New Zealand.

There is another disc by Alexa Still containing these same transcriptions plus one of *Pastorela,* originally a piece for violin and orchestra, two movements from *Suite for Violin,* and four song transcriptions (Koch 7192). Two pieces here are played in their original scorings, *Folk Suite 1* for flute, string quartet, and piano, and a four-movement *Prelude* for the same instruments plus double bass. Still plays with some taste, though it must be said that the flute is no substitute for the violin sound as the composer used it, and the ear tires of the transcriptions.

Two early orchestral works, *From the Black Belt* and *Darker America,* are in an album containing a number of relatively light American works conducted by **Siegfried Landau** (Vox 5157, 2CD). These are somewhat heavy readings, but most of the music is unavailable elsewhere, so thanks to Vox for keeping them around.

A curiously underpowered disc comes from the Manhattan Chamber Orchestra under **Richard Auldon Clark** with soprano Margaret Astrup, containing three suites titled *The American Scene,* representing impressions of the Southwest, Far West, and East, mixed with shorter orchestral pieces: *Serenade, Phantom Chapel,* and *Mother and Child* (an arrangement for strings of the slow movement of Violin Suite). There is also a song cycle, *From the Hearts of Women, The Citadel,* and *Golden Days* (Newport 85596). The performances aren't bad, particularly those of Astrup, and the choice of material emphasizes the quiet side of Still, yet the range of volume is so wide that much of the soft music is practically inaudible. Add performances that are a bit wispy, and you have an unsatisfactory disc that should have been lush and emotional.

Folk settings make up a significant part of Still's output. *Folk Suites 2–4* are found in a relaxed program by the **Cambria Winds** (Cambria 1083) that also includes *Incantation and Dance,* the usual transcriptions, and another suite of folk settings, *Miniatures* for flute, oboe, and piano, also available played a bit more stiffly by **Gretel Shanley,** flute, Peter Christ, oboe, and Sharon Davis, piano (Crystal 321).

A historical disc gives us the complete *Violin Suite, Pastorela,* and three transcriptions, played by their dedicatee, **Louis Kaufman,** the Suite played with orchestra. There are also two of the *Danzas de Panama* in their original string quartet versions, *Songs of Separation* and *A Song for the Lonely* sung with character by mezzo Claudine Carlson, and the ballet score *Lenox Avenue,* played by Howard Barlow and the CBS Symphony with the original narration (Cambria 1121). Some of the Kaufman material was once available from Orion, along with a number of other Still recordings that languish in limbo.

Speaking of *Violin Suite,* a good performance with piano is by **Fritz Gearhart** and Paul Tardiff in "American Violin," though the listed timing is 14 minutes longer than the performance (Koch 7268, with Copland's *Duo,* Cowell's *Suite,* and Dello Joio's *Variations and Capriccio).* "Here's One" contains six transcriptions played in an insouciant popular style by violinist **Zina Schiff** with Cameron Grant (4Tay 4005, with sonatas by Cowell and Hoiby and other unusual material).

Another pair of discs is by **Videmus,** a group that fields vocalists as well as strings, piano, harp, and, at one point, steel pans. One gives us the violin/piano version of *Violin Suite, Incantation and Dance* (originally for oboe and piano, here played by flute), *Ennanga,* a three-movement suite for harp and string orchestra, an arrangement by Still for chamber orchestra of *Out of the Silence* (a movement from his piano suite *Seven Traceries),* and *Songs of Separation* and several other fine art songs sung by baritone Robert Honeysucker (New World 80399). A second disc is primarily vocal, including *Caribbean Suite* arranged by Vivian Taylor for three singers, with the East Carolina University Steel Orchestra conducted by **Mark Ford** (Cambria 1112). This is a steel band, in case you wondered, and it's an odd performance of an odd piece, the whole affair somewhat reminiscent of Lou Harrison with his gamelan orchestras. The original work included chorus and orchestra, here replaced by piano and steel drums.

The rest of this disc mixes spirituals and art songs, as well as a saxophone and piano piece called *Breath of a Rose* and the inevitable *Summerland,* which turns up on at least half the Still discs in one transcription or another. This is an unbuttoned program, though there's something ersatz about the project that disturbs while it entertains. Contralto Ruth Hamilton is so ethnic she's a bit of a caricature, while soprano Louise Toppin is pure and polished. Honeysucker has a fine voice, although it's a mite hard to control in high registers.

Still's piano music is played with style by **Denver Oldham,** including *Bells, Seven Traceries,* five *Preludes, Africa,* and some miniatures (Koch 7084). **Natalie Hinderas,** in her remarkable collection of African-American piano music, plays *Three Visions* with vigor and poetry (CRI 629, 2CD). **Richard Crosby** presents a dreamy performance of *Seven Traceries* in a conservative American program (Capstone 8671).

MOORE

Karlheinz Stockhausen (b. 1928)

Stockhausen is a visionary and modernist whose music can be kitschy and his visions bewildering, what with his interest in astrology, arcane theorization, theater, electronics, and ritual. Certainly no composer has gone into greater eclipse with the aesthetic changes of recent decades.

You'll now find very little of his work in the catalog: DG chose to dump their entire Stockhausen list in the mid-'80s, and starting in 1991 the composer has made his vast output available on his own label. The discs are expensive, can only be ordered through the mail, take weeks to arrive, and can only be paid for with a check that includes high bank fees. There are now more than 60 releases available from Stockhausen-Verlag; their coverage here (with works listed in chronological order) is unavoidably incomplete and rather arbitrary; see <http://www.stockhausen.org/cd_catalog.html> for a more complete listing.

If Stockhausen's *Licht* operas are his big canvases, the *Klavierstücke* are pen and ink sketches. **David Tudor** was the virtuoso pianist who inspired Stockhausen to continue the sequence (Nos. 5–8 are dedicated to him). Tudor recorded cliff-edge (and often very fast) performances of 1–8 and 11 in 1958–59 and makes the music sound hot off the press (♦Hat Hut 6142). **Herbert Henck** takes fewer risks in his set of 1–11 (Wergo, 2CD), but his tone and rhythm are more centered than Tudor's, making this an approach for those who might want to study the music more than they want to tangle with its abrupt, rude physicality (which is not to say he's dull). **Bernhard Wambach** also taped 1–11 and doesn't have Tudor's muscularity or Henck's crispness and clarity of texture; he lacks nuance and is rather clumsy (Koch-Schwann). **Aloys Kontarsky** has elegant rhythmic control in 1–11 as well as a bright and ultra-focused sound, but the close miking limits his dynamic and color range (CBS/Sony).

Gesang der Jünglinge (1955–56) is one of Stockhausen's more durable works, in which his imagination transcended the rudimentary technology of the time. A taped boy's voice, singing a text from the third *Book of Daniel,* is manipulated alongside electronically produced sounds that often resemble dripping and rushing water. The disc (♦Stockhausen-Verlag 3) also includes an interesting 1952 *musique concrete* etude produced by the most rudimentary means—basically a piano, tape recorder, and pair of scissors. Two more electronic studies (1953–54) are also on the disc, along with the electronic-tape version of *Kontakte* (1959–60). All in all, this fascinating compilation shows a Promethean imagination starting to take wing.

There are two recordings of the "live" version of *Kontakte* with soloists as opposed to the tape version. One contains a fine-sounding 1960 Cologne tape with Stockhausen's electronics, **David Tudor** again on piano, and **Christoph Caskel** as percussionist (♦Wergo 6009). The imagination and sonic variety of this piece makes a mockery of the dreary tape works produced by more academic composers. The Cologne performance is much more vivid, with a closer balance, than the recording with pianist **Bernhard Wambach** and percussionist **Mircea Ardeleanu** (Koch-Schwann). The Cologne rhythmic interplay is particularly crisp and immediate. Typically, the Wergo offers only *Kontakte* (35 minutes of music), while the transparently engineered Koch-Schwann throws in the percussion score *Zyklus* and *Refrain* for piano and percussion.

Gruppen (1955–57) is the most compelling representation of Stockhausen's "music in space" concept. Thinking the concert hall an archaism, he wrote for three separate and independent orchestras that encircle the audience on three sides. No recording duplicates the effect *Gruppen* can have in concert, but **Abbado** and the Berlin Philharmonic give a spellbinding and beautiful account. I sometimes wonder if the Berliners' consummate tonal blend is really appropriate to Stockhausen's primary colors, and DG offers a rather muted sonic picture (♦DG 447761). But they're certainly more on top of the score than the 1965 German Radio performance led by **Boulez, Maderna,** and **Stock-**

hausen (Stockhausen-Verlag), where some passages send the recording engineers scrambling. The latter disc also includes *Carré* for four orchestras and choruses (1959–60). Here the forces more literally surround the audience in quadraphony, yet the music tends to be less explosive or impressionistic. The 1960 Hamburg performance is rather scrappy, and mixing the quadraphonic tape down to two necessitated some artificial fading and panning between channels.

With the idea of moment-form, Stockhausen negated the continuous musical narratives that have been cultivated for centuries. The concept is manifest in *Momente* (1962–64, 1969), a theatrical work for choruses, vocal soloists, electronic organs, and instrumental ensemble. With its choral shouting, growling (snorting, even), and theatrics, this is the kind of opus that has led some critics to consider Stockhausen a crank. The Hammond organ doesn't do anything to make the music sound any less dated, but approach the score with an open mind and you'll notice the poetry—and sporadic musicality—of its quieter moments. **Stockhausen** leads a vivid West German Radio performance that would have been helped by a more sympathetic acoustic (Stockhausen-Verlag).

Mixtur (1964) calls for five orchestral groups, sine-wave generators, and ring modulators. It's one of the first works (Boulez's *Répons* is a later example) to use real-time electronic transformation of orchestral sounds. The result is a prismatic, poetic, and often gutsy intercession between orchestral and electronic music. The disc (♦Stockhausen-Verlag 8) holds two versions, one with the musical events in score order, the other in reverse. There are some hints of peaking on the tape, but the performances (led again by **Stockhausen**) are crisp and do just what is needed.

Hymnen (1966–67) is Stockhausen's monument to *musique concréte,* and a typically grandiose attempt to bring together the national anthems of various countries. The piece proceeds by geographical region, and the discs (♦Stockhausen-Verlag 10) typically include a version for tape alone and one with instrumental soloists. The music is a sonic feast with its tape manipulations and synthesized sounds; its effects haven't dated at all, and some of the language-lab collisions of languages are amusing.

Stimmung (1968) is a kind of vocal chamber music. So as not to disturb his little children, he composed using only the sounds he was able to create in his head. The piece spins out an a cappella texture on a single Bflat and explores its overtones by constantly manipulating the mouths and throats of the singers, offering a unique combination of intimacy and vocal exoticism. The English vocal group **Singcircle** enjoys every note and buzzy nuance, the engineers offer perfect warmth and accessibility, and the texts are included so you get all the obscene bits (♦Hyperion 66115). (My only quibble is a half-second dropout at 1:06 in track 8.) **Wolfgang Fromme** and **Collegium Vocale Köln** (Stockhausen-Verlag, formerly DG) are labored and also more heavily miked; the Hyperion performance definitely has more grace and panache.

Stockhausen wrote *Mantra* (1970) for two pianos and ring modulators. I think of this work as his answer to Bartók's Sonata for Two Pianos and Percussion, or perhaps Cage's early prepared piano works. **Janka** and **Jürg Wyttenbach** (♦Accord 202252) are more consistently interesting than **Yvar Mikhashoff** and **Rosalind Bevan** (New Albion). The Wyttenbachs' rhythms are sharper and more forceful (they also take seven minutes less to get through the piece), the subsections set into harder relief, and the ring modulation of the pianos is a bit more colorful, more extreme. Likewise, the New Albion sound gives a deeper and richer perspective on the instruments, but things are also a little smoothed over. The **Kontarsky Brothers** have a rhythmic integrity and ensemble crispness all their own, but the recorded sound is very artificially balanced, with little of the unaltered piano sound coming through in the mix (Stockhausen-Verlag, formerly DG).

In *Tierkreis* ("Zodiac"), Stockhausen had the delightful idea of writing for music boxes, and this delectable music displays his skills as—believe it or not—a charming miniaturist (Stockhausen-Verlag). But the second work on this disc, *Musik im Bauch* (1975), is negligible both musically and dramaturgically: gong and bell strokes, footsteps, whips, and finally the tinkling music-boxes heard in *Tierkreis*. Still, the 25-minute *Tierkreis* alone makes this disc worth hearing: where else can you hear music-boxes chiming off atonal melodies in mixed meters?

Stockhausen wrote *Der Jahreslauf* (1977) for the Imperial Gagaku Ensemble in Tokyo. On the Stockhausen-Verlag recording, Western instruments impersonate the Gagaku. It's always fascinating to hear modern-day composers writing for this ancient Japanese court orchestra (Takemitsu did likewise in his *In an Autumn Garden*), but I wish Japanese instruments had been used on the disc. Stockhausen's group also becomes a background for some inscrutable "temptations" and "incitements," which range from a lion roaring to a cook pushing along a cart "with exquisite food." Like the instrumental timbres, the acting and sound effects could have been done with more flair. *Samstag* and *Donnerstag* are two operas—more like masques or arcane allegories than stage narratives—from Stockhausen's mammoth *Licht* cycle. In *Samstag* Scene 1 ("Lucifer's Dream"), **Majella Stockhausen** gives a commanding performance of *Klavierstück* XIII for Lucifer (sung by **Matthias Hölle**), with added vocalizations and miniature rocket ignitions. Also playable as a concert piece, Scene Two ("Kathinka's Chant") is written for solo flute (the virtuoso **Kathinka Pasveer**) and six percussionists. Scene Four ("Lucifer's Farewell") is the most haunting: Male choir, organ, and seven trombones perform in a large church, and the music has some of the same mysterious poetry as Nono's *Promoteo*. Though uneven in inspiration, *Samstag* is at its best hypnotic and never less than engrossing. Compiled over several years by DG and West German Radio, the recording (♦Stockhausen-Verlag 34, formerly DG 423596, 4CD) is fine, though the perspective and acoustic differ between scenes.

Michael's Reise is the second act of *Donnerstag*. Stockhausen made a reduced touring version for solo trumpeter, nine *Mitspieler* ("co-players"), and sound projectionist. An outstanding disc displays the trumpet virtuosity of the composer's son, **Markus Stockhausen** (♦ECM 21406). The sounds are refreshing, even intoxicating: electronic effects including suave washes and piquant bell sounds, counting out loud from the players, flutter-tonguing, and smack-tones (sucking noisily on a woodwind reed). Unexpectedly accessible, this is a work for those who might think they don't like Stockhausen and an ideal place to start looking into his music. ECM has typically created an extremely poetic and listenable sound picture, with real depth and the timbral edges slightly rounded off.

Unsichtbare Chöre is a 48-minute tape piece (Stockhausen-Verlag, formerly DG) that serves to fill out the texture in two scenes of *Donnerstag*. The **Chorus of West German Radio, Cologne** is a lusty group and they've been miked up close. Despite the ear-catching innovations (some rhythmic aspirants, torrents of cheek-clicking), this music is a thin brew, questionable as a stand-alone listening experience.

Some have dismissed the *Helikopter-Quartett* from *Samstag* (1993) as a stunt: The quartet goes up in four helicopters that circle the performance locale, the sounds of the rotors mixed with the strings' ever-present drones and tremolandos before it's all piped into the concert hall. As sheer sound, there's no denying the interest of tremolo strings mixing with the machinery. There are also some campy theatrics as the players count off, Germanically rolling their "r"s and sounding slightly mad. It's fun and exhilarating, if also ephemeral, and the **Arditti Quartet** more than hold their own with the Dutch Army's aircraft (♦Montaigne 782097). Shouldn't the pilots get a credit?   ASHBY

The Strauss Family

We're talking about four gentlemen: Johann Strauss Sr. (1804–49) and his three sons, Johann Jr., aka the Waltz King (1825–47), Josef (1827–99), and Eduard (1835–1916). This dynasty is responsible for some of the most exhilarating and joyous feel-good music ever written. Johann Sr. in his heyday was one of Vienna's top producers of dances who had his own orchestra. His rivals were Joseph Lanner and, in a sense, Johann Jr., for at the end of the elder Strauss's life his son had attracted notice as a conductor and composer, despite his father's opposition to his sons pursuing musical careers. Only the Waltz King composed operettas (on which he based many of his dances), but all four turned out waltzes, marches, polkas, polka-mazurkas, galops, and quadrilles, often based on the music of others (*Carmen* and Verdi Viennese style are lots of fun), and Johann Jr. turned out some ambitious fantasias. Some of these pieces are really sophisticated tone poems. *Tales from the Vienna Woods*, for example, with its lengthy introduction and sweeping waltz melodies, is as ideal a portrait of nature and life in Imperial Austria as is humanly possible.

These men were more than clever tune-smiths, especially the Waltz King and Josef. Typical of this music are its sophisticated harmony and orchestration, incredible rhythmic confidence, plus, in the case of the two greatest Strausses, sometimes startling uses of minor keys. Johann Jr. considered Josef the most talented Strauss, but all four captured their times as expertly as any historian (the sociopolitical background of many of their works makes for wonderful reading)—and of course there are those marvelous melodies!

Counting posthumously published works, Johann Jr. has more than 600 compositions to his credit and Josef nearly 300. The bulk of the Strauss music on CD is devoted to these two, but Johann Sr. and Eduard are respectably represented. Most all-Strauss recordings contain works by two or more of the family, while many other recordings pair them with other Viennese masters of the dance such as Lanner, Lehár, Schubert, Suppé, and Carl Millöcker. Many staples from the waltz and polka repertory can be found in discs also featuring more "serious" music.

If you'd like to check out discs devoted to one Strauss, a good starting point is the 51-volume ♦Marco Polo complete orchestral works of Johann Jr., available separately. Some of the pieces haven't survived in their original orchestrations, but expert Straussians working from the published piano scores or sparse orchestral sketches have come up with orchestrations that sound like the real McCoy. The orchestras come from Austria, Poland, and the Czech and Slovak Republics. The conductors include Alfred Walter, Johannes Wildner, Peter Guth, Jerome Cohen, Christian Pollack, Alfred Eschwe, Michael Dittrich, Oliver Dohnányi, Richard Edlinger, and Franz Bauer-Theussl. A variety of different approaches, from leisurely dances to a grandly symphonic point of view, are in evidence, but each conductor and orchestra contributes sparkling performances with plenty of *luftpausen* and rubato to satisfy discerning Straussians. Among the reasons for my enthusiasm for these recordings, other than the delightful music making, is that listeners can hear a wealth of unjustly neglected works. All these dances, marches, fantasias, and overtures are a great sonic adventure.

Also on ♦Marco Polo is a Josef Strauss project. Thus far the results are as appealing as the label's work on behalf of his big brother Johann. Conductors have included Walter, Dittrich, Pollack, John Georgiadis, and Mikka Eichenholz leading Hungarian and Slovak orchestras in delightful performances. Eighteen volumes have been issued at the time of writing, and the variety and personality of Josef's music is very well served in these recordings. There is also a generously filled disc devoted to Johann Sr. in which Eichenholz leads the Slovak Philharmonic in yet another distinguished look at the dynasty (♦Marco Polo 223617). There's definitely more to the elder Strauss than the ubiquitous *Radetzky March*.

In the '70s, four LP sets were devoted to mostly unfamiliar works by the four Strausses featuring the Vienna Chamber Orchestra under **Paul Angerer**. The performances were delightfully *gemütlich* and are now on CDs, one Strauss per disc, unfortunately with some of the LP selections left out for what I assume were time considerations (♦Concerto 820.745/46, 4CD), Also, be reassured: These collections, and all the others mentioned in this article, don't present selections in order of composition, so listeners get a sort of total immersion in the music.

Many celebrated maestros have tackled the Strausses with varying degrees of success. **Fiedler** and **Ormandy** are highly regarded in this repertory, and I, like many Americans, learned many of these pieces through their LP recordings with the Boston Pops and Philadelphia Orchestras. I can't share the enthusiasm many Straussians have for their performances; to me they're often bland, mechanical, driven, and merely efficient. Of course, there's something to be said for hearing two major ensembles under the men who made them that way (and those gorgeous-sounding Philadelphia strings!). But like them or not, I'm talking about two of the most famous Strauss conductors, so I do recommend exposure to their recordings. For Fiedler and the Pops, RCA 61608 is a representative sample, while the CBS "Johann Strauss' Greatest Hits" release at budget price is a good way to check out Ormandy and the fabulous Philadelphians. An American Straussian I *do* like is **Bernstein** (Sony 47626). The New York Philharmonic sounds like a great virtuoso ensemble playing with grandly symphonic exuberance. Bernstein with a light touch is something to hear.

While on the topic of Strauss interpreters who don't appeal to me, let me mention two other names. First, **Dorati**. He was a noted dance conductor most famous in this regard as arranger of the pastiche Strauss ballet *Graduation Ball*, which has been periodically available in the delicious Boskovsky/Vienna Philharmonic edition (London/Decca). As a kid growing up in Minneapolis during the Dorati years, I heard lots of his Strauss. Then and now, I find it the work of a speed demon, lacking warmth—dancing to his Strauss can't be done! Mercury has issued some of this material; proceed with caution.

Reiner is another example of charmless, driven Strauss. I yield to no one in my admiration for his *Richard* Strauss, but the Viennese Strausses are not his thing. RCA 601771 contains wonderful playing by the Chicago Symphony, and you may find more here than I do. I should point out that many of the waltzes, quadrilles, and polka performances in Strauss recordings contain varying degrees of repeat cuts—a common practice that occurred during the Strausses' lifetimes. Some prolific Strauss maestros, such as Boskovsky and Karajan, don't always use exactly the same cuts for works they've recorded several times. Although I prefer to hear them in their absolute entirety, I wouldn't let repeat omissions rule out a recording unless they destroy a piece's structure.

The Vienna Philharmonic is to the Strauss family what the Czech Philharmonic is to Dvořák and Smetana. This orchestra could probably play a Strauss waltz or polka in its collective sleep, and it's not surprising that many CDs with this ensemble belong in the collection of anyone devoted to the light Viennese repertory. For me, the greatest Straussian on disc is **Clemens Krauss.** Krauss reestablished the celebrated VPO New Year concerts after WWII and initiated the custom of studio recreations (usually abridged) of these concerts. (After Krauss's death in 1954, the New Year recordings continued with different conductors, some of them performances from the actual concerts.) Krauss's recording based on the 1951 concert, filler for his classic *Fledermaus,* shows what makes him so terrific: The music dances, sings, sounds positively exhilarating, has a brilliant rhythmic verve, is treated with affection at all times, has a great symphonic feel, and sounds like the work of no other conductor (♦London/Decca 425590).

The joy in Krauss's Vienna, including lots of *luftpausen* and rubato, and of course his magnificent orchestra playing at its best, make his recordings a delight many times over—therefore shame on London for putting so little of this material on silver disc. To hear more of the 1951–54 New Year material than they have issued, you need to locate the 3CD ARL 93-85 set (Vol.1 of a Krauss series) that also includes HMV and Telefunken material from the 30s and 40s. More Krauss 78 rpm recordings have been issued by Preiser, Biddulph, Enterprise, and Iron Needle.

If Krauss is the No.1 Straussian, then **Willi Boskovsky** is a very, very close No. 2. A distinguished violinist, he was a long-time Vienna Philharmonic conductor and founder of the Boskovsky Ensemble who often led Strauss performances with violin in hand à la Johann Jr. Boskovsky took over the New Year concerts in 1958 and led his last one in 1979 (in toto in ♦London/Decca 443473). With the exception of the 1979 program, Boskovsky's Strauss recordings are studio versions of the concerts plus a few pieces not connected with these events; much of this material has been recycled on Decca here and abroad, often at mid-price. Boskovsky is less symphonically oriented than Krauss and has been imitated often. He's not the rugged individualist Krauss was, but when you hear the love and joy in his performances, with all those scrumptious tempo and rhythmic inflections, you know you're hearing something extra special. And, like Krauss, He shows that the Strausses had a lot of emotion underneath all those notes. He is a Straussian Titan with whom any devotee of this repertory should be familiar.

He also made a number of recordings of light Viennese repertory for EMI with the Vienna Symphony and Vienna Johann Strauss Orchestra; many of them have been issued on CD in various compilations. These orchestras aren't the VPO, but they play very well indeed for Boskovsky, who apparently was skilled at making any good orchestra sound great in this repertory (including such unlikely Strauss ensembles as the Chicago Symphony and Hollywood Bowl Orchestra).

Maazel took over the New Year concerts from 1980–86 and returned to the podium several times in the '90s. The recorded documentation of the 1983 program shows him (as does much of his other recorded repertory) to be cold, driven, and sometimes maddeningly fussy—he doesn't know how to relax (DG). However, his 1994 and 1996 recordings (Sony and RCA, respectively, the latter a 2CD documentation of the entire program taped in concert) find Maazel in more relaxed mood some of the time and even charming on occasion. And of course the VPO sounds great in this repertory no matter who the conductor is. **Mehta**'s New Year programs of 1990 and 1995 reveal a strong affinity for matters Strauss, perhaps due to the years he spent in Vienna as a student. These discs, recorded in concert, don't have the easy *gemütlich* feel of

Boskovsky or the graceful symphonic grandeur of Krauss, but there's charm and rhythmic sweep aplenty (Sony).

The reclusive **Carlos Kleiber** led the 1988 and 1992 concerts (the former was recorded in toto in two ◆CBS CDs with a Sony abridgment as well). A great Straussian in the making, also shown by his leadership of an uneven *Fledermaus,* he loves the music, plays it with warmth, embraces it, and makes it dance. More, please. Carlos's father, **Erich Kleiber,** was also a distinguished Straussian, and ◆Biddulph 002 is a wonderful excursion to the past. I want to like **Muti**'s 1991 (Philips) and 1997 (EMI) concerts better than I do. They have character and excitement but no really relaxed charm. His most recent New Year program, however, reveals that he is currently a more *gemütlich* Straussian (EMI).

DG, as a tribute to the Vienna Philharmonic's 150th anniversary, issued a 2CD tribute (now available only as an import) of the orchestra's legendary way with the Strausses, spanning the years 1929–80. The best-known VPO Straussians are included as well as some unexpected names: Walter, Szell, Furtwängler, Knappertsbusch, Abbado, and Böhm. Furtwängler lacks a truly light touch, and Knappertsbusch's *Emperor Waltz* is one of the performances that refute the notion that he was a stodgy, leaden maestro.

Karajan gets my vote as the third greatest Straussian on disc. He didn't lead a VPO New Year concert until 1987, and Karajan being Karajan, much of the time the music sounds like tone poems of the dance, perhaps as Liszt or Richard Strauss might have composed them; but the grand symphonic approach works for him, and he knows how to smile and tease the listener with *luftpausen* and rubato. The disc, like several of the in-concert CDs, includes participation by the Vienna Boys Choir (do they ever give an unwinning performance?); often, Strauss Jr. and others set lyrics for chorus or solo voice to the Waltz King's tunes. An example of the latter on this disc is Battle's radiant, winningly virtuosic *Voices of Spring.*

Even the weakest of Karajan's performances from the late '40s to that 1987 New Year concert can't be labeled boring, and many of them have been recycled on silver disc umpteen times. On EMI, his orchestras are the Philharmonia and the Berlin Philharmonic, on London/Decca the VPO, and on DG the BPO. My comments about Karajan's 1987 New Year concert apply to these CDs as well. In some of the '70s discs for DG he's sometimes fussy and unwilling to smile, but at his best, he makes the best possible case for the Strausses as lords of the dance. I wouldn't recommend Karajan to folks who like to dance to the Strauss family's tunes, but he knew how to make the music spring to life.

Anton Paulik's set with the Vienna State Opera Orchestra, "The Strauss Dynasty," is worth your attention (Vanguard, 3CD). Actually, the orchestra was created for recording purposes and is a combination of musicians from the VPO (the usual Staatsoper orchestra), the Vienna Symphony, and freelancers. Paulik was music director of the Volksoper from 1939 to 1975—formidable credentials, and a Straussian to be reckoned with. His '50s Vanguard LPs were my first exposure to some of the then rarer Strauss pieces. He has an ingratiating light touch—lots of sparkling rhythms and a sometimes very vigorous take on the music—but he does know how to relax. He may not extract as much as my three favorite Straussians or the best maestros on Marco Polo achieve, but I forget that whenever I listen to his work.

There are some excellent discs from England. Highly recommended are the three "Vienna Premiere" CDs featuring **Jack Rothstein** and his Johann Strauss Orchestra (Chandos; Strauss competitors including Millöcker and the two Phillip Fahrbachs are included); also "Johann Strauss and Family in London" with the London Symphony under **John**

Georgiadis (also Chandos). These two conductors have a real feel for Old Vienna, and so do their responsive orchestras. Their ability to coax schmaltzy (in the best sense of the word), often *echt* Viennese style from their ensembles (no stuffy Englishmen here) will be a pleasant surprise for any listener not wanting any disc lacking a "Made in Vienna" stamp. And for the ultra-curious, both Rothstein and Georgiadis have included one work by Johann Strauss III (1866–1939), the elder of Eduard's two sons. They are more suggestive of the family's successors, like Carl Michael Ziehrer, but tuneful they definitely are. There's more Georgiadis for Straussians to savor, all recommended, on ASV Quicksilva, PWK, and Concert Classics.

Other recommendations, sparkling, affectionate performances all: **Fricsay** (DG), **Kamu** (BIS), **Krips** (Accord), **Knappertsbusch** (Melodram and Preiser), **Guth** (Discovery), plus some surprisingly good budget discs on various labels by Viennese ensembles under **Peter Falk.**

Listeners looking for just a few of the chestnuts, such as *Blue Danube, Emperor Waltz, Radetzky March,* etc., are advised to check the Boskovsky recordings; he has recorded every well-known orchestral piece at least once for London and/or EMI. Karajan's London, EMI, and DG performances include many of these warhorses. Krauss, too, committed many of them to disc. Ormandy and Fiedler, for those readers not dissuaded by the comments in this article, might be good choices. Of course the Johann Jr. and Josef series from Marco Polo contain laudable versions, and all the New Year concert CDs contain them as the traditional encores at these events.

For the super-duper curious Straussian, Johann Jr.'s incomplete ballet *Aschenbrodel* (Cinderella) has been recorded in a 2CD midline London Jubilee edition by **Bonynge,** with Douglas Gamley, an arranger often used by Bonynge and his wife Joan Sutherland, having realized the composer's sketches and other material for a completed version. Gamley seems to have gone his own way in matters of orchestration, but the effects aren't too jarring. Bonynge, so expert in classic ballet, is also an expert Straussian; you really have a sense of dancers on stage here. Also in this set is ballet music from *Pasman,* Johann Jr.'s only "serious" opera (a flop), and the *Blue Danube* ballet pastiche arranged by Roger Désormière —very entertaining offbeat *schlag,* this.

It would be very strange to spend a day in Vienna and not encounter Strauss tunes played by small ensembles in restaurants and coffee shops, city streets, and parks. **Boskovsky** and the Boskovsky Ensemble (a small complement of strings and winds) were very busy during the '50s and '60s recording the Strausses, Mozart, Haydn, Beethoven, Schubert, and Lanner dances (◆Vanguard). This is intimate drawing-room Strauss—I always feel they're making music for me alone. Everything on the CDs that has been culled from this material is irresistible and guaranteed to tempt listeners to get up and dance. Boskovsky's beguiling violin inflections tease the listener, yet it's not just his show. This is really give-and-take chamber playing, and the tempos, rhythms, and balanced precision must make many orchestras feel frustrated. These are classic performances that entertain and yet are far more than surface readings. Be prepared to smile and chuckle a lot.

It's not widely known that 12-tone titans Schoenberg, Berg, and Webern each arranged waltzes by Johann Jr., not in weird atonal editions but in versions that thoroughly respect the master's ideas. They're charming. Three of these waltzes—the arrangements are for string quartet, with bass, harmonium, piano, flute, and clarinet putting in appearances—have been recorded by the **Alban Berg Quartet** and others, with Johann Sr. and Joseph Lanner completing the program (EMI 54881). Spirited and very Viennese.

The Waltz King was a favorite target of virtuoso pianist-composers, including Godowsky, Lhevinne, and Rosenthal. Often the original tunes are mere departure points for pieces of staggering pianistic pyrotechnics. Some of this repertory is presented in performances by Bolet, Rachmaninoff, and Moiseiwitsch (VAIA 1019). It's exciting, visceral stuff, even when primitive sonics are involved.   MARK

Johann Strauss II *(1825–1899)*

We should be grateful that Waltz King Johann Strauss Jr. turned to the operetta stage; he might very well have continued just writing dance music and would have still retained his throne, but when he saw how lucrative the results were for Offenbach, he decided to try his hand in the theater. Possibly this resulted from a suggestion from Offenbach himself, visiting Vienna, but more likely because of his wife's pushiness. Certainly, as Europe's dance master he was the perfect composer to enter operetta, the very basis of which is dance rhythms, and he cleaned up financially not only with his stage rights but with the publishing royalties he received from his own dance arrangements of music from each of his operettas.

In modern recordings and productions, Strauss is represented principally by *Die Fledermaus*—arguably the greatest (and most recorded, with *Die lustige Witwe*) of all Viennese operettas—*Eine Nacht in Venedig, Der Zigeunerbaron,* and the pasticcio *Wiener Blut. Fledermaus* (1874) has noble operetta ancestry, based on a Parisian vaudeville by Offenbach's genial genius-librettists, Meilhac and Halévy. Strauss takes the plot's frippery—suggesting Offenbach's *La Vie Parisienne* (1866)—a step further, however, bathing it in a distinctively Austrian wash. This liquid gold is a solution made up of Viennese musical comedy, folksy wine-garden sentiment, and a classical refinement that echoes composers from Mozart to Schubert.

Die Fledermaus. There are a large number of Fledermice to choose from, ranging from CD reissues of acoustic 78s to radio transcriptions from the Nazi era (when Strauss's part-Jewish ancestry was kept from the public for reasons of cultural propaganda) to modern studio versions. Which of these darling flying rodents you want to call your own may not depend so much on the leading singers—as in an opera, or a Tauber-Lehár operetta—as it does on the ensemble performance, as in a Parisian operetta. The conductor will thus bear a great responsibility for shaping the performance, which is why I prefer the 1960 **Karajan** rendition for its considerable vivacity (Decca/London 421046). It has a theatrical flair and speed without the roughness of a live broadcast, wonderful sound, and a terrific cast.

Gueden's Rosalinde has piquancy and elegance, Kmentt's Eisenstein is admirably flustered but beautifully sung (as a baritone), Köth is a winning Adele, Wächter and Berry are marvelous as the two subsidiary baritones. And Resnik is one of the most distinctive of all Prince Orlofskys—it's resolute, smoky Resnik, similar to no one else. This is one recording that includes well-performed, very theatrical dialogue, all the dance music, and the now-famous gala that has numerous oddities including Birgit Nilsson's "I Could Have Danced All Night." Karajan, however, is the star; from his shaping of the overture to the acid test of the many moods of the great second act finale to the champagne-soaked close, this *Fledermaus* constantly flies.

This was Karajan's second *Fledermaus.* His first was assembled in 1955 with a perhaps even superior cast: Schwarzkopf, Gedda (a tenor Eisenstein), Streich (darling as Adele), and—for his fans—Erich Kunz's Falke, though I find him too genteel here (EMI 69531). But

Rudolf Christ, whom Volksoper visitors may remember from the '50s, sabotages the recording with a misconceived Orlofsky, and Karajan's mono performance doesn't have the theatrical vivacity you find in the 1960 version, even with its dialogue snippets.

Two earlier complete studio recordings have their virtues. One, conducted by **Krauss** in 1950, must have seemed a joyous return to the Vienna of old after the Nazi years (Decca/London 425990). It starred many of the singers who made the famous visit of the Vienna Staatsoper to London in 1947 (but let it not be forgotten that most of this cast was active during 1938–45 in various Third Reich companies). Gueden's first Rosalinde is a joy, but only a dress rehearsal for her 1960 rendition. Lipp's Adele is somewhat less joyous but still pleasant. Patzak's Eisenstein isn't vocally memorable, but he acts well (even without dialogue), and Dermota's Alfred is ideal. Less so Sieglinde Wagner's Orlofsky—the voice is there, but not the vocal characterization. The flatness of several of the numbers is mirrored in the flat mono sound, and Krauss, for all his champions, doesn't turn my head very often. Lipp and Dermota repeat their roles in a 1959 performance led by **Otto Ackermann,** the first in stereo (EMI). This has its adherents, but it lacks fizz. Dermota is still good, but Karl Terkal (Eisenstein) and Gerda Schreyer (Rosalinde) are stodgy much of the time, and Ludwig is an annoying Orlofsky.

From the same year comes one of the oddest of Fledermice—a version of the famous "Fledermaus" (no article) that was a huge hit for the Metropolitan Opera in a Garson Kanin-Howard Dietz English version. What Welitsch (Rosalinde) and Pons (Adele) do to poor Dietz's words is actually what makes this record so perversely enjoyable, especially in such phrases (in the Act III trio) as "You call me an improper noun" and "the legal mind." The rest of the cast lacks the Broadway zip of such performers as Kitty Carlisle, containing instead old-timers like Martha Lipton, John Brownlee, and Charles Kullmann. Magyar **Ormandy** has a good time with the Act II csardas, but the performance lacks Broadway and 39th Street flair.

Proceeding chronologically, a 1963 version has a most interesting line-up of stars (RCA 7029, 2LP): Adele Leigh (a creditable if not too suavely Viennese Rosalinde), Rothenberger (Adele), Risë Stevens (a terrific Orlofsky), Wächter (a good, baritone Eisenstein), and London (a bass-ier than usual but still fascinating Dr. Falke). **Oscar Danon** leads a pert Vienna Staatsoper chorus and orchestra in that ebullient stereo era. From the same period came **Robert Stolz**'s version (Eurodisc), which proceeds with a convincing swing but with a cast that can't match its competitors, led by Lipp's unexceptional Rosalinde and Schock's unsubtle Eisenstein (though some may like his blustery quality in this part). However, it has attractive performances from Cesare Curzi (Alfred) and Renate Holm (Adele).

Holm repeats and improves upon her Adele in an excellent 1971 set with a Volksoper chorus and the Wiener Symphoniker under Strauss specialist **Boskovsky** (EMI). Rothenberger here graduates to Rosalinde, and she's excellent, but the real female star is Fassbaender as Orlofsky. Even Resnik must bow to her superiority in delivering the part as written while maintaining character—a very difficult challenge. Gedda is (properly) more boorish, less lyrical an Eisenstein than he was in the '50s, and another surprise is Fischer-Dieskau as Dr. Falke, who gets to sing an interpolation from *Waldmeister* in the party act. But Boskovsky's tempos are sometimes dull, and the dialogue is similarly untheatrical.

Also from 1971 came a version under **Böhm,** a conductor less well-disposed to operetta, and he's not helped by a cast that seems second-hand, with stars of earlier versions (Wächter, Kunz, Kmentt, and Holm)

sounding less agreeable than they once did, often in different parts (Decca/London). **Carlos Kleiber**'s 1974 rendition may have a fresher cast, the best contribution coming from Popp (Adele), but the baritones (Prey as Eisenstein and Weikl as Frank), smooth though they may be, don't sound idiomatically correct (DG). And there is a famously awful falsetto Orlofsky from the once-popular Ivan Rebroff.

In 1986, Popp devolved into Rosalinde (not too memorably) for a performance conducted by **Domingo** (EMI). It's advisable only for fans of late Popp or middle Domingo, who also (of course) sings Alfred, and nicely, too. The rest of the cast is forgettable except for Baltsa's Orlofsky. There are also too many *Der Zigeunerbaron* interpolations as party pieces. (Why doesn't Domingo record that, too? He'd make a fine Barinkay.) The following year saw what was touted as a more musically significant *Fledermaus* conducted by **Harnoncourt** (Teldec). Yes, all the notes are there (including the ballet sequences), but the Concertgebouw and Netherlands Opera chorus, at least here, don't seem the ideal forces for a Viennese operetta, and the soloists aren't very scintillating. Still more objectionable than the dull if well-meaning musical values is the awful narration that replaces the dialogue.

A 1990 set under **Previn** also fails to bite orchestrally, even with the Vienna Philharmonic (Philips 432157). Some of the soloists are good: once again Fassbaender's Orlofsky, Wolfgang Brendel's fine baritone Eisenstein, and, in particular, Richard Leech's Alfred. Te Kanawa has a welcome verve and vocal sheen as Rosalinde, but Gruberová's Adele is a less happy realization.

There are of course other bats in this cave: recent issues of performances recorded off the radio and in theaters from Germany in the Nazi era (with Anders in the cast), a fun reissue in hoary acoustic sound of the first semi-full set from 1907, and odd performances in German, Russian, Hungarian, French, and other tongues. It's unnecessary to own any but the 1960 Karajan, a model of what a modern *Fledermaus* should be, with or without the gala sequence.

Eine Nacht in Venedig (*A Night in Venice*). I have great fondness for this, as it was my very first theater visit as a child, at Jones Beach in 1951 in Mike Todd's colossal outdoor production. I've seen it countless times in Austria and Germany, indoors and out, and while its plot will never reach the level of *Fledermaus,* it's a convenient peg on which to hang some of Strauss's most sumptuous, often Italianate music. The two long finales are wonderful, especially the first act, and it's usually a visual treat as well, like Gilbert & Sullivan's *Gondoliers* set in a very picturesque 18th century Venice.

The original version (1883) was a notorious fiasco in Berlin, with near riots over the silliness of some of the lyrics. The Zell and Genée libretto lacks intelligence and wit and it has therefore been subjected to several revisions, the most famous and successful being Korngold and Ernst Marischka's in 1923. Variants of this are usually heard in theaters and on recordings today, though newer recordings have gone back to the original manuscript, recently published.

The Korngold version beefed up the part of the Duke of Urbino by giving star tenor Tauber two new numbers, one from the (up-to-now) neglected *Simplicius,* the other from a formerly female solo. One is in praise of Venice, the other champions infidelity, both are superb showpieces, and Tauber singing them even more so. But Gedda is our model modern Duke, both in 1954 and 1968 (EMI). In the former, he has Schwarzkopf as the fisher girl Annina, and in the latter, Streich, and both are excellent. I have a heartfelt preference here for Streich, though Schwarzkopf has more to sing in her album. In both, Gedda is a sexy,

suave womanizer, one of his best operetta parts. However, the 1968 version (EMI 69363) is superior for several reasons: its very theatrical stereo sound and pacing, under musicals-operetta specialist **Franz Allers** and his Munich forces, its superior Caramello in Cesare Curzi (Kunz underperforms in the role), and the excellent chorus work. It also has more delectable Strauss interpolations for Prey and Rothenberger (two from the '20s Berlin pasticcio *Casanova* that also gave birth to the famous Nuns' Chorus). Until we have a thoroughly redone *Venedig,* this remains the recommended version—especially when you hit the middle of Act 2 and the spectacular duet between Pappacoda and Caramello and chorus ("Noch sah Ciboletta ich nicht").

However, BASF, CBS, and RCA on LPs and later a deleted CD (Acanta 43809), offered in 1976 what was supposedly the "first recording of the original version," conducted by **Märzendorfer** with a Budapest orchestra and chorus. Well, not really, but at times reasonably close to it, though there were all sorts of changes in song order, vocal assignments, and so forth. Two vocalists shine out: Jeanette Scovotti as the fisher girl and Wolfgang Brendel, arguably one of the best (and lowest-lying) Caramellos on discs.

Two open-air versions have been recorded, each with their fruity pleasures. The 1951 Bregenz Festival production was the first major semi-complete recording of the work, and it has its values, including excellent singing from Karl Friedrich (the Duke) and Kurt Preger (Caramello); the conductor was **Anton Paulik.** It also eschewed the Korngold revisions. The Jones Beach version from exactly the same time—a more spectacular affair—received a stereo version some time later, using the Ruth and Thomas Martin translation and several soloists from the Mike Todd production (Everest 9036). Wholesale alterations were made and the presentation is something like a 1940s' radio condensation, with linking dialogue including such memorable lines as "Look! Here comes Pappacoda!" delivered in very broad US accents that have precious little Viennese or Venetian lilt. Likeable singers abound, however, including Laurel Hurley and Enzo Stuarti. I have cherished childhood memories of the "Spaghetti" song and the "Ni-nana" ensemble as they were staged in the dim, windy distance over the canal, which are only brought back by this recording, but this is admittedly hardly an ideal *Nacht in Venedig.*

Other excerpted versions of the Korngold edition of various vintages are around: one with Schock (Caramello) and Cesare Curzi (this time as the Duke) is an amiable extraction (Eurodisc 258375). A 1960 RCA set of excerpts has Wunderlich as Caramello and Schock as the Duke, a dream duo for many (LaserLight 16045). And any Tauber operetta compendium with his two *Venedig* numbers will demonstrate how refreshing the 1923 version must have seemed in its day.

Der Zigeunerbaron (*The Gypsy Baron*). This offers a weightier, more thoughtfully constructed score than was the norm for 1880s Viennese operetta, with vocal opportunities and romantic sections that often steer it into opera houses. (Strauss paid more attention to his libretto after he was roundly criticized for having haphazardly set some tedious situations and awful lyrics in the original *Night in Venice.*) This doesn't mean that *Zigeunerbaron* is without stock operetta mannerisms or broad humor, but these are well balanced by thickly set ensembles. Indeed, the melodic and harmonic rapture running through most of Strauss's operettas, and particularly *Zigeunerbaron,* is what makes them so attractive to modern ears. Often, these moments are brief: a tiny bit of Alfred's farewell to Rosalinde in Act 1 of *Fledermaus* that recalls Schubert, Saffi's "O Heimat so wunderbar" in *Ziguenerbaron,* and of course the memorable waltz refrains in the latter, led by Barinkay's "Ja! Das alles auf Ehr."

But this was—and still is—a comic operetta, with lighter portions complementing the more lush moments, and several versions make this perfectly clear by including most of the original score. However, most of these were taken from double-LP sources, and not all the music could possibly have fit on four LP sides, given the usual dialogue incursions. Thus various numbers have had to be cut (as they usually are in modern performances) until we arrive at the most recent recording. This, under **Harnoncourt,** offers all the score, including what is advertised as "+40 minutes of newly-discovered music" (Teldec 94555). It's too much for any actual theater performance, but fascinating nevertheless. Unfortunately, the vocal renditions aren't quite up to previous standards.

For these, you have to turn to older versions. First and foremost is the one under **Otto Ackermann** with Schwarzkopf as Saffi, the gypsy-Turkish princess, and Gedda as Barinkay, the titular would-be gypsy baron (EMI 69526). Kunz is the pig farmer, Zsupán, and is once again a bit underwhelming for so broad and coarse a part, but he sings admirably and is amusing. Köth is delightful as the soubrette Arsena, and the young Prey shows his mettle as the lusty Hungarian army recruiter, Homonay. I have to concur with others and declare this vocally the best of the *Barons,* though there some will find the mono sound too limited.

For a more theatrical rendition from the same period, you may enjoy the 1956 Vienna Volksoper version led by **Paulik,** which has a brassy pit-orchestra sound wedded to an extremely lively presentation (Vanguard 8082). I like Loose's Arsena more than Gerda Schreyer's Saffi, and some may find it odd to have mild Erich Kunz doing the recruiting song here when Wächter was on hand (as Carnero, the bureaucrat). This version includes the delicious "Decency Commission" trio, often cut, and also offers on its cover the glorious poster from the first production at the Theater an der Wien. Loose also does her Arsena in the very first complete *Zigeunerbaron* from 1951, with Patzak as Barinkay and the Vienna Staatsoper chorus and orchestra conducted by **Krauss** (Phonographe). It's a slow-going, boxy performance, and, besides Loose and Patzak, practically the only pleasures come from Rosette Anday as the gypsy crone Czipra and Alfred Poell as the army man.

Of the later stereo editions, there are some things to be admired in the **Franz Allers**-led version with the curious casting of Bumbry as Saffi opposite an older Gedda (EMI 65971). Hers is a smoky performance, and at the time I rather enjoyed its lively quadraphonic sound, though Gedda isn't quite as lyrical as he was 16 years earlier. But the rest of the cast is good, Streich (Arsena), Prey (Homonay), and Wolfgang Anheisser (Carnero) in particular.

Go forward another 15 years or so and you find a version under **Boskovsky** that was even less noteworthy than its predecessors (EMI). Boskovsky did not (to my knowledge) have the operetta-house experience that Allers and Paulik very much had, and this is all too evident in his lackluster performance. The recorded sound, with the Munich radio orchestra and chorus, is fine, but not the excitement or pacing. Of the principals, Fischer-Dieskau has the most oomph and presence as Homonay, which demonstrates the vocal deficiencies of this set. The same criticisms might be leveled at Harnoncourt's album, but this, unlike all the EMIs, was taken from a live recording. However, as Harnoncourt includes all the usually deleted numbers plus a bit more (and copious notes), it's worth acquiring.

Wiener Blut. Before his death, Strauss gave his approval for this pasticcio fabricated out of various waltzes and other music lying around. Un-

successful at first in Vienna, it subsequently became broadly popular and to this day is one of the most played of Strauss stage operettas. Why, I've often asked, as I am not and never will be one of its admirers. It must have something to do with the Congress of Vienna setting, or the pre-sold popularity of such memorable tunes as the title number. The libretto itself is dauntingly dull (though concocted by Leon and Stein, who would later write *The Merry Widow*) and the word-setting to pre-existing music is at times atrocious. What a Vienna Volksoper performance will reveal is a vague connection to the vaudeville characters and situations that were popular on the Viennese stage in Nestroy's day. If these moments are well played, a certain amount of amusement can be obtained, even if this has little to do with the musical content of the work.

A recording, however, will hardly reveal much of this. My advice is to avoid any complete version and settle for the breeziest excerpts you can find. The one with Schock, Gueden, Margit Schramm, and Lipp will do quite well, conducted in appropriately vigorous style by **Stolz** (Eurodisc 258370). Otherwise, you can find two sets from EMI. The first was the **Ackermann**-conducted '50s version, sung by Gedda, Schwarzkopf, Loose, and Köth, which used to be available on an odd three-sided LP set (69529). I never warmed to it, and also didn't care for its replacement, done in the '70s under the often-boring **Boskovsky,** but this does at least offer more of this score in much better sound. And once again it has Gedda, paired this time with Holm and Rothenberger, both in good voice.

Other operettas. No matter what critics may say about Strauss being injudicious with his librettos, he was definitely a man of the theater and (obviously) had his finger on the public's pulse a good deal of the time. Simply listening to the first-act finales of the operettas will bear this out. When recording companies thoughtfully provide every note written for an operetta like *Zigeunerbaron,* they do modern scholarship a great service but not necessarily the theater. Cuts and choices were made by Strauss, his librettists, and his managers; hits were hits, and flops were flops—and the public was often the best judge of all this.

But tastes do change. In the 1880s, especially here in the United States, Strauss operettas like *Das Spitzentuch des Königin* and *Die lustige Krieg* were substantial touring triumphs. Today they're forgotten, while a minor, fairly gloomy work like *Simplicius,* an 1880s failure, has recently been rewarded by a reconstructed production in Zürich and a subsequent live recording, not received in time for these notes (EMI). Also forthcoming is a radio broadcast of *Die lustige Krieg* on the ORF (Austrian Radio) label that I'm certain will reveal a far more lively affair than *Simplicius,* which I saw in Zürich.   TRAUBNER

Richard Strauss (1864–1949)

Strauss was a comfortably public composer, not a practitioner of abstract, purely musical ideas. The best Strauss conductors are those who can give full rein to this programmatic, quirky, and demonstrative nature—the sheer pleasure in the music—without ever making it sound cheap or insincere. Perhaps no music is open to a greater variety of approaches. The interventionist Mengelberg took to the verbose and prose-like qualities of the music, Furtwängler the challenge of his large-scale symphonic edifices, Reiner to his professionalism, and Karajan to the sheer sonic possibilities of the music and its vaulting lines.

ORCHESTRAL MUSIC

Eine Alpensinfonie (Alpine Symphony). "What a sound!" was Dietrich Fischer-Dieskau's excited response to **Karajan's** *Alpine Symphony.* It is indeed a spectacular demonstration of the unique sonic dynamism, at the same time controlled and fiercely uncontrolled, that he created in his later years with the Berlin Philharmonic (♦DG 439017, the much improved "Karajan Gold" remastering). If the 21 tableaux of Strauss's last great tone poem tend to sprawl in lesser hands, Karajan knows exactly where he is and where he's going at every moment. His "Sunrise" has never been matched in grandiosity, his "Storm" never rivaled for its fury: The orchestral sound erupts like a force of nature. It's a performance to make you wonder how this score could ever have been thought a lesser light in the Strauss canon. DG's 1981 early digital sound is dry, occluded, and murky, not up to Karajan's conception; even so, the intensity of the performance comes through, and any sonic caveats don't amount to much in the face of such an irreplaceable reading.

The only version that really challenges Karajan is Mehta's 1975 recording with the LA Philharmonic (♦Decca/London, NA). Mehta is even more impulsive; he moves the score excitingly from one heady moment to another, and the return of the brass fanfare at "Vision" is all the more majestic for the way he has prepared for it—yet the spontaneity is such that it sounds like the music is being made up as it goes along. After this the more reflective pages following the storm are a bit disappointing, but this is perhaps Mehta's best Strauss recording. The orchestra plays very well. The sound is a bit more recessed than expected, but the organ comes through clearly. Mehta's second version, with the Berlin Philharmonic, can't compare (Sony). It has a vigorous, *al fresco* sound that recalls Karajan, though Mehta's tempos are generally slower and his phrasing less far-reaching; by the end it comes up as a reading without much vision. Yet again, the Berlin sound falters on its own beautiful smoothness, without the Karajanian thrust to take the players just to the verge of ugliness.

Solti and the Bavarian Radio Symphony take a similar approach, but are generally faster and don't give the music as much time to breathe (♦Decca/London 414676 or 440618, a twofer Strauss collection). It's a virtuosic, bracing jaunt, while Karajan does more to uncover the darker and more mysterious elements of the score. But Solti isn't breathless or lacking in poetry—there's a nice onrush of melancholy at "Sunset," for example—and this long piece certainly holds together well in his hands. The sound is warm without quite the frequency and dynamic range that digital recording made possible soon after, and the organ is fine. Kempe's lyrical Bavarian manner proves unexpectedly illuminating in Strauss's bit of delicious sensationalism (EMI). The Dresden Staatskapelle are more interested in the humanity of the music than its pyrotechnics: More showmanship would not have gone amiss. However, the harmonic suspension at "Sunset" draws forth more melancholy than in any other performance, and the playing is stunning in its deep-set and tonally blended way. The sound is a bit dated, though the blurred tonal edges make for easy listening. MHS 5959311, 9CD, contains all of Kempe's EMI recordings

Böhm is typically farsighted, the opening not milked for dark impressionism but rather a slow and expectant preparation for "Sunrise," which is gloriously strong and sure (DG). More than anyone, he reveals a beautiful wealth of musical (rather than pictorial) detail. No other conductor makes "Wandering by the Brook" such a luxurious statement, so logical and elementary that it could have come from a Brahms symphony. In his hands, Strauss's rambling structure makes perfect and inevitable sense. Only "Storm" seems undercooked. The Dresden Staatskapelle plays superbly, but it's a pity the engineers supply slightly harsh sound that suggests 1940 rather than the recording date of 1957. This, of all Strauss scores, needs up to date stereo.

Barenboim and the Chicago Symphony, unlike Karajan and Solti, give the impression of not wanting to risk any hint of bombast (Erato). The orchestra often sounds reined in, even in "Storm"; there is some telling dusky lyricism in the Chicago strings in "Elegy," but a lot more that sounds tentative. If the sound had been more direct and engaging, such an approach might have worked. Blomstedt's tempos are also on the slow side, with a similar lack of rhythmic tension, and maybe he purveys too much musicality for Strauss's welter of banal gestures and naturalist sounds (Decca/London). With his acute observation of detail and careful scaling of dynamics, he loses some of the forest for the trees; the raindrops at the start of the storm are more pedantic than expectant, and "Sunset" sounds strictly counted out. The San Francisco Symphony plays remarkably, without quite the timbral niceties of Berlin or Dresden, but the hall is rather small for the huge orchestra—the far-off yodeling horns in "The Ascent" sound dubbed in.

It's a surprise that Järvi also tends to be more interested in local moments than the larger picture and any sense of transcendent grandeur (Chandos). The cathedral sound may be the most vibrant of all, with a wide frequency range and a nice, gut-rattling bass drum. As usual, the Scottish National Orchestra creates an astonishingly full-throated sound, partly a matter of the resonant recording. A more farsighted reading in this straightforward vein is Haitink's with the Concertgebouw (♦Philips 416156). He gives a better account of the large picture than Blomstedt or Järvi, for example making more of the return of the big brass fanfare at the end of "Vision." The recording is more trenchant, too, and the Amsterdam brass and drums are imposing and darker in color. A fine recording, though as a performance it isn't as exciting as this conductor's *Heldenleben*, and it doesn't really displace Karajan.

It's a surprise that as an interpretation Haitink is almost put in the shade by Waart and the Minnesota Orchestra (Virgin). Less immediately imposing than most, Waart is even more patient than Haitink, and with graceful molding of phrases and plenty of detailing presents the lyrical side of the piece. Listen to his "At the Summit" and "Vision" and you'll hear songfulness and nostalgia rather than Karajan's heroism or Solti's precipitous exultation. The Minnesotans are well recorded (though the distant, yodeling horns are almost inaudible), and they play beautifully, with all departments putting on a good show. Previn also boasts obvious musicality in his Vienna Philharmonic recording (Telarc), with less interest in minutiae than Blomstedt. Interpretive calculation can be deadly in this music, and here there's a bluff sound to things that aligns well with the work. But there are also some unfortunate longueurs, for instance "In the Mountain Pasture." Previn's earlier EMI disc with the Philadelphia is recognizably from the same interpreter, neither thrusting and symphonic in the Karajan or Solti vein, nor lyric and humanitarian like Kempe, nor as discursive and self-conscious as Barenboim. But the nasal and disembodied sound is a drawback, no comparison with the Telarc disc, though the latter lamentably has only one track for the entire piece and the former has some impressive drums in the storm.

Maazel with the Bavarian Radio Symphony is quite different (RCA). There's much more of a sense of resources marshaled, which means there's a stepping back from the climaxes that can be a bit frustrating after you hear Karajan. Maazel tends to throw sonic and interpretive weight behind the passages that are not so obvious; he's not such a "big moment" kind of conductor. In the last analysis, his is a refreshing alternative view, especially as he's wont to capitalize on the darker colors in Strauss's palette, particularly the trombones, who make a menacing entrance in "Sunrise." Too bad someone saw fit to insert a cheesy electronic thunder clap toward the end of the storm in lieu of the orchestral thunder-sheet.

Also Sprach Zarathustra. One of the first *Zarathustras* on record came from **Koussevitzky** and the Boston Symphony in 1935 (RCA). The interpretive sweep and intensity of orchestral sound would go unchallenged until Karajan's 1974 Berlin recording. Apart from an eccentrically slow "Sunrise," this is an outstanding performance from the BSO's golden age; Koussevitzky is always personal, to the point of causing some precarious ensemble, and he often reaches heights of Nietzschean ecstasy. The sound is good, though the considerable surface swish and relative lack of presence will cause many listeners to gravitate to more recent engineering.

Strauss himself made a *Zarathustra* recording with the Vienna Philharmonic in 1944 (Preiser). It's easy for us to forget his tremendous skills as conductor, and he gets the utmost from this great orchestra. His reading is streamlined and not indulgent, the kaleidoscopic moods and tricky tempo changes faultlessly brought together into an organic whole. I haven't heard the Preiser CD, but presumably it suffers same the wateriness in sustained wind passages heard in the Vanguard LP but corrects the cut toward the end of the *Grablied;* was one of the acetates missing?

No one did more to establish Strauss performance traditions on records than **Clemens Krauss** and his Vienna Philharmonic, who did a famous survey of the symphonic poems for Decca in the very early '50s. His *Zarathustra,* recorded in 1950, is charming and fairly lightweight, not reaching for Olympian peaks like Solti and Karajan (Testament). Down to the free Viennese vibrato, this is Strauss with a Viennese elegance that is long gone. Krauss and his orchestra sound most at home in the quiet and enigmatic ending, which for once doesn't sound anticlimactic. Sadly, Decca's engineering is so piercingly bright as to be all but unlistenable; turning the treble way down helps, but can't alter the engineer's boxy take on the Musikverein.

Unexpectedly, a more gratifying reading in a similar vein—emphasizing color, melody, and charm over taut rhythms and pile-driving climaxes—came from the admirable Slovak Philharmonic under **Košler** in 1989 (♦Naxos 550182). Apart from a rather lackadaisical "Science" fugue, this performance is beautifully conceived and full of character and musicality. The Slovak strings won't be putting the Berlin or Vienna orchestras out of business, but there's nothing second best to this ensemble's work. It may not be the most unforgettable rendition, but it's one to hear.

Reiner and the Chicago Symphony recorded *Zarathustra* twice; the first, from 1954, is better (♦RCA 61494, with an equally fine *Heldenleben*). Some dryness and the Chicago trumpets cutting through the texture at climaxes are the only hint that this well-balanced stereo tape, made before stereo was even in most engineers' vocabulary, isn't a modern audiophile product. In sound it's far preferable to Krauss. (I'm not sure the "Living Stereo" remastering improves upon the 1986 Red Seal version; the latter had slightly less firm bass and a bit less depth, but also more presence and a smoother high end.) Reiner's interpretation strikes the perfect balance between control and abandon, reminiscent of the composer's own readings. There's plenty of intensity in the Chicago phrasing and bowing where it's called for, and the performance is never bland in the manner of Haitink, Ozawa, or Blomstedt. Reiner's 1962 recording, one of his last in Chicago (RCA), is weak by comparison to the 1954, though the sound is a bit more lucid than before.

Bernstein is to be avoided (CBS/Sony). The organ is quavery, elec-

tronic, and over-prominent (especially in "Of the Great Longing"), and the New York Philharmonic—given a fairly shallow sound picture that doesn't encourage any tonal blend and makes the start of the fugue seem prosaic—has sounded better. His tempos tend toward inorganic extremes. If you desire the unblended and unbridled New York style of playing, better turn to **Sinopoli** (♦DG 423576). He often gets the Philharmonic down to surprisingly quiet dynamic levels, and much of the piece has a wonderfully vague, impressionist feel without going limp. The timpanist really earns his paycheck at the beginning, but the organ sometimes sounds out of tune with the ensemble.

Solti and the Chicago Symphony are fantastic (in the recommendable twofer, ♦Decca/London 440618). The orchestra was at its absolute peak, and Solti's trademark intensity is sympathetic to the detail in this score above all others. Yet he's unexpectedly spacious in this music, which is all to the good, though he's perhaps a bit blank with the question-mark ending. The sound could use more transparency and detail; perhaps a new remastering will come to the rescue. His remake with the Berlin Philharmonic has much of the same electricity and a touch more old-world finesse in the playing (Decca). Unfortunately, the sound is dry and unforgiving, the Philharmonie organ something of a monstrosity.

Haitink and the Concertgebouw are beautiful and cultured, and quite well recorded, but the reading never surprises you in this, Strauss's most unpredictable symphonic poem after *Don Quixote*, and perhaps his most "modern" one (Philips). It's well paced, very well played, and a shapely performance with enviable tonal blend from the orchestra, but in the end it's inappropriately relaxed and more than a bit prosaic. *Zarathustra* brings out the best in **Mehta**, and he went bicoastal with his recordings, one made in Los Angeles and the second in New York. The LA version is one of his best Strauss excursions: well played, sweet in its characterization, and not at all self-conscious, even if the question-mark ending does sound a bit arbitrary and rushed (♦Decca/London 452 910, with some John Williams nonsense). The engineering still holds up well, though there is an audible splice right before the big repeat of the C Major "Sunrise." The New York reading is less spontaneous and less distinctive in detail, without the sweep and eager pressing forward of the LA rendition. The playing overall is second rate after hearing the LA, the sound more ordinary. The CD follows the LP side-break, which doesn't match up with the composer's score designations.

After an explosive "Sunrise," **Tilson Thomas** lacks tension in the first half and continuity in the second (CBS/Sony). The London Symphony strings, which are often overwhelmed by the brass, never really reach the glowing transcendence that's mandatory in this score. The sound is weighty, transparent, and impressive overall. **Dorati** and the Detroit Symphony will appeal to organ fanciers, as the instrument is in fine shape and is encouraged to make itself heard (Decca/London). Otherwise, this concise and compact reading tends to disappoint with its shortage of charm and lyrical expansiveness. The sound is impressive, though. **Ormandy**'s 1980 recording is impressive and surprisingly lively, considering the octogenarian conductor was entering an undependable phase in his recording career (♦EMI 47636). The famed Philadelphia sound is still intact, but the early digital recording can get glassy in the high range. This is less stoic than Ormandy's earlier accounts, indeed often brilliant.

In his well-recorded San Francisco reading, **Blomstedt** is crisp rather than ecstatic (Decca/London). Everything is done with care, and all the score's details make themselves heard. Still, the sum of his attractive parts isn't great, and much of the articulation and rhythm seems too relaxed, the timpani muddy. His earlier Dresden Staatskapelle reading is recognizably the work of the same musician, but the tensions run higher (♦Denon 2259). The sound is also a bit more realistic, though perhaps not as dynamic as Decca/London. A very fine reading comes from **Tennstedt** and the London Philharmonic, though to be hypercritical, the white heat familiar from his Mahler recordings is in only sporadic supply (EMI). The sound is likewise naturalistically recessed, Strauss's percussion balanced to the back.

Böhm has the same sense of scale that marks Karajan's famous recording with the same orchestra, the Berlin Philharmonic: grand but never falsely grandiose, the climaxes never detracting from the smaller details (DG). But Karajan was less stern and better at making the music dance, and Böhm was taped in 1958, with sound that becomes threadbare in places, at least as remastered. There's also some spot-miking, especially of individual winds. **Kempe** tended to make Strauss sound true to his Bavarian roots: songful and fairly easy-going, even rhythmically lax at times. His *Zarathustra* with the Dresden State Orchestra is stylish, sometimes ecstatic, but basically lyrical rather than symphonic, virtuosic, or transcendent, certainly not a Nietzschean performance (EMI). You sense that the emotion comes from within the music instead of being applied to it, and many will enjoy that lack of grandiloquence. The sound is warm but not particularly detailed, which means the strings sound very well in the remastering, and EMI gets a black mark for giving the piece only one track.

Maazel's Vienna Philharmonic recording has tremendous grip, with energy and thrust similar to Karajan's first Berlin version and homogeneous orchestral sound (♦DG 439739). This is volatile and inspired music making, with massed strings that can take on a powerful, glowing fire; they inspire similes of incandescence, luminosity. Only the early digital sound—a touch harsh and opaque—gives pause. Maazel's later performance is exciting, and the Bavarian Radio Symphony surely hasn't sounded better on records (RCA). But while the reading is taut and impressive, it has no particular originality or individuality. The sound is big and a bit glaring, the opening timpani much larger than life.

Though not quite in that same league of orchestral performance or interpretive ecstasy as Maazel in Vienna, **Schwarz** and the Seattle Symphony achieve a considerable accomplishment with this difficult score. It's more engaging than Haitink or Ozawa, and the dynamic yet ungimmicky sound is a pleasure. A pity the "midnight" climax hangs fire, and after that the reading eschews rhapsody for strictness—and Delos gives the piece only one track. **Järvi** brings rather more podium prowess to his recording with the Scottish National Orchestra, and his interpretation is more affectionate, energetic, and detailed than Schwarz's (Chandos). *Zarathustra* finds Järvi at his Straussian best, though the loose and echoey church acoustics tend to cloud some of Strauss's delectable writing for solo and divided strings. That apart, the sound is dynamic and vibrant.

Ozawa has smoothed-over engineering with no genuine highs or lows, especially in comparison with Previn or Schwarz (Philips). Balances also reek of the mixing board. His interpretation verges on the generic, with precious little rhythmic tension or individuality of phrasing. **Prêtre** and the Philharmonia tend to tempo extremes, with speeds alternately pushed and dragging (RCA). This "Sunrise" was obviously designed to impress audiophiles—the timpanist is really in your face—but right after, in "Of the Backworldsmen," the conductor lets the pulse go slack. Considering that he wields a latter-day version of the Philadelphia sound, **Sawallisch** gets a surprisingly weak contribution from the strings; it would be hard to describe them as especially confident or secure, let alone voluptuous (EMI). The orchestra as a whole can

muster plenty of tone in climaxes, but it's not a very welcoming sound. This reading has no particular warmth or individuality—and he is yet another *Zarathustra* conductor who doesn't quite know how to make the more exuberant rhythms dance.

Previn turns in one of his finest Strauss performances, and the Vienna Philharmonic is again unmatched in tone (♦Telarc 80167). He has perfected the art of giving orchestras their natural voice without getting in their way; the results aren't always exciting, but there's certainly considerable tension here. The sound helps, with its natural balance and width of frequency response, though again the lack of internal cuing is lamentable. This is a memorable and effective middle of the road performance, with some glorious playing. Considering the distance—incompatibility, even—between Strauss and **Boulez**'s own esthetic lineage, he conducts with surprising stylistic savvy (DG, with Mahler's *Todtenfeier*). He doesn't quite turn the x-ray eye on Strauss's texture and partwriting that you might expect; the sound is consistently warm and comfortable, and climaxes open up pretty well. After getting off to an exciting, taut start, though, he and the Chicago Symphony go a bit off the boil. He's never particularly interested in making Strauss sing, and other conductors kick up more dust in the transitional passages.

Finally, we come to the *pièce de resistance:* **Karajan**'s 1974 *Zarathustra* from Berlin may well be the finest Strauss orchestral recording ever made, indeed one of history's great performances of any orchestral composition (♦DG 447441). Having tremendous vision and musical initiative, it's the kind of rendition that leaves you gasping for air and grappling for words. Just listen to the stunning glow of the Berliners' divided strings in "Of the Backworldsmen" and the intoxicating, ecstatic crescendo that follows. The weight and intensity of orchestral sound are astonishing, as are its delicacy and mystery, and Karajan's intense grip on the structure of the work means that it flows by as one uninterrupted, organic whole. DG's earlier Galleria remastering was harsh on top, while the "Originals" version restores much of the warmth of the LP, though the high strings still aren't perfectly smooth. This release offers a wellnigh perfect blend of digital and analog virtues. It's a recording that no man, woman, or child can do without.

Karajan's 1961 disc has much the same intensity, though the Vienna Philharmonic sounds a bit more hoarse than the Berlin (Decca/London). Part of this is the rather brash sonics, but then the Viennese intonation is also a hair less predictable, Karajan is wont to punch out details more emphatically than later on, and some moments are a touch more listless than in Berlin. The Vienna rendition is fine, but the 1974 Berlin is preferable at just about every moment. His 1984 Berlin remake is also very good, the strings not as shrill above the stave as in 1974, but the new Philharmonie acoustics are drier than the Jesus-Christus Kirche (DG). Relaxed and unhurried, with a soft-pedaled solo violin, the later performance has less fire in its belly but also an affecting lyricism. The steely, electric Philharmonie organ almost ruins the music in exposed passages early on, but the digital sound is improved in the "Karajan Gold" remastering.

Aus Italien. Strauss's early (and long!) evocation of Italy relies more on luxuriance of orchestration than any melodic or harmonic felicities, so full, up to date sound is required. On these grounds, it's difficult to recommend **Krauss**'s Vienna Philharmonic performance (Testament) or **Kempe**'s 1975 Dresden version (EMI). The former suffers from the disappointingly metallic sound of Decca's Vienna master tapes of this period, with good balancing but sonorities that are very bright, not to mention the mono reproduction, which has a limited range and little sonic bloom. Krauss does offer the best playing *per se*, full of character and tonal depth, and Kempe does bring appropriate simplicity, and often gentleness, to this music.

Järvi does everything right, giving shape to Strauss's melodies and always keeping the music moving even when the composer is at his least inspired (♦Chandos 8744). The Scottish National Orchestra sounds galvanized by this off-the-beaten-path assignment, always caught up in the music, and the engineers supply resonant and transparent sound. For once the Decca engineers produced less than optimum sound for **Ashkenazy** and the Cleveland Orchestra; together, the massed brass and strings can get harsh. Next to Järvi, Ashkenazy also tends to go slack; maybe he doesn't want to oversell this modest but attractive piece, but Järvi's greater incisiveness and abandon carry the day. **Košler** and the Slovak Philharmonic are more convincing than in some of their other Strauss outings, partly a matter of the limited competition (Naxos). Košler is closer to Järvi than Ashkenazy in his wish to keep things moving. The engineering lets you hear more detail than the Chandos, but Järvi's orchestra and sound allow for more tonal weight.

Burleske. For this work for piano and orchestra, the catalog is still dominated by Rudolf Serkin's 1955 recording with Ormandy and the Philadelphians (last reissued in a set of his "Legendary Concerto Recordings, 1950–1956," ♦Sony 47269, 3CD). Things begin with very in-tune Philadelphia timpani, ensemble is razor-sharp, and the rhythmic precision and spring are extraordinary. The sound is mono, but sounds to these ears like undemonstrative, well-balanced stereo. Serkin and Ormandy's stereo recording has a wider aural spread, and some of the same splash and precision (CBS/Sony). A bit of the earlier spunk and panache has gone by the wayside, though; even the newer sound, which is rather over-bright, isn't an improvement on the mono version.

The only modern performance that has the same kind of propulsion is by **Barenboim** with Mehta (CBS/Sony). If anything, Mehta's *tuttis* have more energy than Ormandy's, but next to Serkin/Ormandy, this fairly unvaried rendition leaves behind a slightly battered memory. As a filler for Mehta's outstanding *Sinfonia Domestica*, though, it's certainly worth hearing. **Janis** and Reiner are sweatier in interpretation, more concerto-like in their recording balance, with the conductor typically eschewing charm (RCA). Janis's piano has a starchy, shallow tang to it that's not inappropriate, and he kicks up quite a bit of dust in the fast music of the coda. The reading from **Malcolm Frager** and Kempe (EMI) is in a similar vein: engrossing, but in a way that's often heavy rather than scintillating, and I don't hear any real chemistry between conductor and soloist.

Margrit Weber is fleet, if not as scintillating and rhythmically sharp as some others, but her *Burleske* is worth hearing for Fricsay's accompaniment with the Berlin Radio Symphony; he gives the orchestral parts rare sweep and power, but without heaviness or recklessness, in probably the best conducted account on record (DG, mono). If you want a freewheeling romp of a performance, something muscular and kinetic (if also less flippant than usual), then **Gulda** is your man (♦Decca/London 460296, a Strauss concerto twofer; Philips 456820, in the "Great Pianists of the 20th Century" series). Conductor Anthony Collins doesn't seem to enter into the equation much; this is really Gulda's show, and he takes a muscular, Beethovenian, and very exciting view of the piece. At times it seems as if he's eager to leave the orchestra trailing in the dust, and in the coda you actually fear for his life. The 1954 sound is bright and metallic, but with music-making like this, who cares?

Hobson enjoys the conducting of Strauss authority Norman Del Mar,

who brings out some telling details, but the piano is a bit lost in the balance and the Philharmonia has its spotty moments (Arabesque) The other items on the disc, *Parergon* and *Stimmungsbilder Op. 9*, come together with more confidence. **Ax** and Sawallisch's Philadelphians have plenty of drama and weight to their sound, probably too much; the overall clangor can get rather ugly, and again I miss Serkin/Ormandy's effervescence (EMI). **Argerich** and Abbado demonstrate just what they're missing: Theirs is the most impulsive, mischievous performance on offer, with plenty of shape and thrust in the climaxes and also lots of expressive detail in the quieter music (♦Sony 52565). These two are particularly exciting in the later stretches of the work, with Abbado and the Berliners delivering explosive detonations when the timpani motto returns.

Carol Rosenberger and Schwarz provide more thought and detail than Ax/Sawallisch, and the Seattle sound is better controlled (Delos). These interpreters, though, lack something in personality and in fact are somewhat prosaic. The same goes for **Jeffrey Kahane** and López-Cobos, who are dispiriting (Telarc). There's plenty of rhythmic motion, but little crispness or energy behind their rhythms. **Glenn Gould** and Golschmann dignify *Burleske* without weighing it down; it's the most substantial and musical rendition available, Strauss without the fluff (♦Sony 52687, with an indifferent "Emperor" Concerto). This 1967 reading is a good six minutes longer than most others, mostly a matter of Gould investing the reflective solo passages with the kind of attention you might expend on late Beethoven or Brahms. Nevertheless they often surprise you by revealing the purely musical strengths of this early score, and the performance is never boring, certainly not heartless. Decent mono sound, from a CBC TV broadcast.

Don Juan requires an impulsiveness, the sense that the bar lines at the opening are being rushed off their feet and the cross accents will derail the music. It's this kind of metric freedom—some would say eccentricity—that was a **Mengelberg** specialty, though none of his tempos are particularly fast. With the Concertgebouw in great form, his recording is to the manor born (♦Teldec 28409 and Dutton 5025, both with his outstanding *Heldenleben*). The sound is astonishingly fresh in the Dutton remastering, with a delightful tang to the orchestral bells and high violin writing—more lively than the Teldec reissue, though Dutton's added reverb may dismay some purists. Mengelberg's is a personal take on the music—an antidote to the streamlined slickness of modern renditions—that all Straussians should hear. A different performance tradition—charming and non-interventionist, but full of delightful details of characterization—can be heard in **Krauss**'s 1952 Vienna Philharmonic rendition (Decca/Testament). The sound is ungratefully thin, as usual in Krauss's Strauss series for Decca. Still, the honeyed sound of the Viennese strings is recognizable, and this is as exciting and beautifully phrased an interpretation as you're likely to hear.

"Modern" Strauss interpretation undoubtedly began with Strauss himself, who as a conductor suffered none of Mengelberg's 19th-century mannerisms. Strauss's *Don Juan*, recorded in 1944 with the Vienna Philharmonic, presents a trim and straightforward protagonist (Preiser). The Vienna Philharmonic sounds just as beautiful as it does under Krauss, even if they exhibit slightly less delight in the music. The sound is respectable and well balanced, but a bit watery in sustained wind passages.

As an example of a modern reading that could use some of Mengelberg's rhythmic capriciousness, **Blomstedt**'s rendition with the Dresden Staatskapelle is all about suavity; the transitions are seamless, the vaulting string lines careful never to risk unbalancing the texture, the oboe solo in the love music faultlessly controlled (Denon). This beautiful reading seems square after you hear Mengelberg. Blomstedt has a touch more flair in his 1990 recording with the San Francisco Symphony, and the sound is also more resonant. But there's slightly less timbral character, and discretion is still the watchword (Decca/London). **Böhm** taped *Don Juan* in Dresden in 1957, a performance more idiomatic and fanciful than his *Till Eulenspiegel* (DG). As he so often does, he makes Strauss's structures sound perfectly, beautifully inevitable. The tonal magnificence of the Staatskapelle, astonishing so soon after the war, shines through the mono setup right away. Stereo is less of a requirement here than in the *Alpine Symphony* that serves as coupling, and this is easy to recommend to those who aren't especially interested in showing off their stereos.

Haitink has more verve in his 1974 Concertgebouw rendition, though there isn't much in the reading to recommend it over, say, Karajan, Previn, or Tennstedt (Philips). The rhythm of the massed violins can lack flair, even giving an occasional walking-on-eggs feeling. Philips fails to compensate with much sonic presence, the sound coming up shallow and smooth in the remastering. Haitink's 1983 remake (♦Philips 441442) is much better, a matter of the clearer and more vivid and transparent sound, but also crisper and more decisive articulation.

Toscanini responded to the heroic and virtuoso elements in *Don Juan,* and his 1939 NBC Symphony broadcast is undeniably bold and brazen (Music & Arts). It catches fire at the return of the opening music toward the close, but some will find the dryness of sound unappealing. In all, this disc is more valuable for the Maestro's 1941 *Heldenleben* (see below). More readily recommendable, his 1951 recording is an enjoyable "straight" antipode to Mengelberg (RCA). There's no lack of fantasy or tenderness in the interpretation, and on this occasion Carnegie Hall proved kind to the NBC Symphony strings. Only the central love music could relax more.

It's just that section that is so memorable—so bittersweet, and so deliciously reluctant to give way to the returning heroic music—in **Furtwängler**'s 1942 version (♦Music & Arts 829). As is so often the case, this conductor is beyond compare. He has his own deeply rooted and deeply felt views on the music, and inspires one of the great orchestras—a group that knew his every wish and whim—to a performance of irreplaceable spontaneity. Be warned that the sound is thinner than elsewhere on the disc, and there are some fairly obvious coughs from citizens of Hitler's Reich. His later studio recording (EMI) with the Vienna Philharmonic is comparatively earthbound, the textures and accenting heavier, though the music-making is still more beautiful and individual than just about every other recording except his own in 1942. **Kempe**'s rendition with the Dresden Staatskapelle never quite finds its center; contrasts are underplayed between the opening and the quiet music at the middle of the work (EMI). There's a good zip to the opening, but the love music seems fairly impersonal, and the '70s recording could use better definition.

Stokowski and the New York Philharmonic offer a fine 1959 performance, recorded with a vivid frequency range if also the slightest hint of tape flutter (Everest). But the relative lack of Stokowskian panache and charm would leave some unable to name the conductor in a blind test, and this isn't terribly distinctive in the end. It's a surprise that **Szell** proves far more charismatic (♦Sony 48272, or a bit more vivid on Sony 63123, with his exceptional *Don Quixote*). He encourages the Cleveland violins to an astonishingly confident, even swashbuckling account of their opening paragraphs, the rhythmic figuration chugging away feverishly. But there's plenty of flexibility at the big lyrical moments, and there's plenty of intense emotion behind the climaxes. The sound is a touch bright and dry (with some occasional faint and intermittent tape noise), but this underlines the vividness of Szell's classic performance.

Much the same applies to **Solti** and the Chicago Symphony, though he's not open to all of the music's voluptuousness, and in 1975 the Chicago strings had an audacious brilliance that some may think unidiomatic (♦Decca/London 440618). He certainly gives the tumbling out of the opening music an electrifying brashness. In the love music, he offers some of the most personally molded phrasing on record, and after this, there's a spectacular entrance by the Chicago horns, who prove as dazzling (and loud) as the entire string section. In sum, this is a reading to have you on the edge of your seat, though listeners with velvet ears will probably demur. **Previn** drew a lush and stylish reading from the Vienna Philharmonic in 1980 (EMI). The interpretation isn't dull, but there's a generalized quality to the sound that prevents the music (particularly the brass and percussion) from sparkling as it should. His 1991 account with the same partners is far more exciting, with a beautiful fluidity of phrase and a more specific sound picture (♦Telarc 80262). Here he does equally well in the thrusting rhythms of the opening and the languorous, tender phrasing of the love music.

Karajan's 1973 recording is suave and lush, with an unbelievably beautiful moment where the horn theme enters the second time and is then taken up by the strings (♦DG 447441). Some of the Berlin players complained that he didn't allow them time to articulate, and there's some of that all-cosseting string legato here, though part of the impression comes from the loose church acoustics. The 1984 remake has more variety of articulation, though the close Philharmonie acoustics mean the sounds are tougher, less obviously lovely (♦DG 439016). His 1961 Vienna Philharmonic recording is rougher still, with the typically boxy sound of the Sofiensaal and some slightly less predictable tuning in the Viennese winds (Decca/London). His 1952 Philharmonia rendition is the most electrifying of his four, probably the most intense version ever recorded (EMI). Here he holds the tension astonishingly tight, making the minor-key climax overwhelming and the big horn passage majestic. This is a must-hear for anyone not addicted to stereo, though the EMI tapes are lamentably thin-sounding.

Bernstein is idiomatically impetuous, with some nicely rhapsodic moments (CBS/Sony). But the clipped articulation wears thin after a while, and the orchestra and engineering rather let him down. The New York trumpets tend to bray, and in climaxes the ensemble sound often has constituent instruments poking out here and there. **Mehta**'s 1965 recording was one of his very first in Los Angeles (RCA). He does all the right things in this fresh and enjoyable performance, and there's plenty of fire in the heroic passages. RCA also marked the occasion with fine sound; the two small drawbacks are the shallow acoustics of the spanking-new Los Angeles Pavilion, and the occasional less-than-ironclad intonation of brass and winds. **Maazel** takes to *Don Juan* like a fish to water, and the Bavarian Radio Symphony is with him every step of the way (RCA). Too bad the sound is rather bright and uninviting, and the dark ending a bit arbitrary and inconclusive. **Sawallisch** has the nonpareil Philadelphia strings at his beck and call, but there's a good sparkle to response from all sections (EMI). Still, there isn't quite the rhythmic certainty and pizzazz of Mengelberg, Karajan, or Maazel, and the *Zarathustra* coupling isn't a front-runner. **Tennstedt** gets a full-throated, cushioned sound from the London Philharmonic strings—almost dreamy in the love music, and suitably dark and oppressive at the end (♦EMI 73560, bargain-priced). But the opening music also has an enviable rhythmic sureness, and this is a reading with some real Straussian panache. The engineers hit on the perfect combination of opulence and detail.

Järvi has a rhythmic flair that suits *Don Juan,* and the Scottish National has just the right rhapsodic touch for Strauss (Chandos). This record would be a winner if the sound wasn't so bright at the top and echoey enough to make the climaxes sound cluttered. **Masur** and the New York Philharmonic employ similarly explicit rhythms, though the tempos are generally a hair slower (Teldec). This is one of the finest *Don Juans* to come along in recent years. The mikes are a bit close to minimize audience noise, and this helps give the reading an imposing sonic up-frontness (more appropriate here than in the coupled *Death and Transfiguration*), but it's a pity the setup precludes any true pianissimos in the love music. **Tilson Thomas** and the London Symphony have more charm than expected, though the dryish recording emphasizes the brass and winds at the expense of the strings (Sony, with *Zarathustra*). This conductor's Strauss tends to be more heavy than crisp, and a lack of bloom in the orchestra's sound adds to such impressions.

Dohnányi manages to trim the high-cholesterol Vienna Philharmonic into a low-fat kind of sound, though the engineering seems to have helped out in that respect, increasing their rhythmic amenability but also making the timbres a bit anonymous (Decca/London). The reading does all the right things, but comes up sounding generic. **Ashkenazy** starts off at a nice clip in Prague (♦Ondine 943). As usual with this conductor, the performance offers more professionalism than originality—but if the naturalness of the reading is deceptively easy-sounding, there's also plenty of swagger at Don Juan's second theme on the horn. Only the protagonist's last, fatal encounter could be more cataclysmic. The 24-bit engineering renders Strauss's orchestration more transparent and "true" than any other, though Previn's Telarc sound is almost its equal. Ashkenazy's earlier Cleveland version is very similar in outline, but he has a more concentrated, rapturous take on the love music in Prague (Decca/London, with *Aus Italien*). The Czech Philharmonic also has a more immediately distinctive sound, with its dark woodwinds.

The virtues of Ashkenazy's Ondine disc certainly come out when you compare it with **Košler,** who sports some nice shaping of phrases but takes slowish tempos that lessen Juan's virility (Naxos). The Slovak Philharmonic winds produce a few purplish sounds. Better to turn to **Waart** and the Minnesota Orchestra, who turn in a beautifully played and heartfelt account, if one that doesn't quite match the electricity of their *Till Eulenspiegel* (Virgin). Other readings bring back Juan's luscious horn theme with more obvious majesty, relishing the moment. Though the playing isn't quite equal to Minneapolis, **Mata** and the Dallas Symphony are better at keeping the narrative interesting, leaving you to guess how it will all turn out (♦RCA 60135). This is beautiful conducting, with nothing escaping Mata's attention, and the orchestra commands a greater timbral variety than many more renowned groups.

Abbado's Berlin Philharmonic version sounds unsettled, with some iffy rhythms in the difficult opening paragraphs and a relative shortage of the poise that is his trademark (Sony). Still, there's some very fine playing, and the string swells early on are particularly exciting. He made an earlier recording with the London Symphony that has some similarly unfocused rhythms, and again none too much charm (DG). **Dorati** is more conventional and consistent, with excellent playing by the Detroit Symphony and 1980 digital sound that is still warm and outstanding (Decca/London). Reactions to this will depend on how you take to his ironing out of the surprises in the music—the drum detonations, surprise

horn calls, etc., all get their edges rounded off. **Barenboim** produces one of his more convincing Strauss excursions with the Chicago Symphony (Erato). That said, there's still a heaviness to the playing that I don't hear in his moving *Heldenleben,* and there are some unusual things that might not bear a lot of repetition, like the speeding up of the opening music when it returns for Juan's last exploit, and a daringly long pause before his death.

Don Quixote. Unlike Strauss's other tone poems, *Don Quixote* (for cello and orchestra) is essentially chamber music. He tends to use soloists and divided sections more than in his other orchestral scores, eschewing the thrusting *tuttis* that give *Heldenleben,* say, its heroic sound. (Quixote is, after all, an anti-hero.) In a nutshell, *Don Quixote* needs lightness.

Fournier and Krauss (Decca/Testament) are light but not frivolous, more a charming Max and Moritz comic panel than a prognostication of Hemingway. It doesn't come together into much of a grand statement, but Fournier is, as always, personable without indulgence, and the Viennese Philharmonic string solos are as sweet and delectable as spun candy. The 1953 sound is among the best in Krauss's series, far preferable to his *Zarathustra* and *Heldenleben.* Lightness is missing in the transfers of the 1938 acetates from **Feuermann** and Toscanini because of the painfully dry acoustics (Music & Arts). It's hard to say how much of the recording's musical over-stringency is owed to the sonic deficiencies, which include some surface noise that could have been easily removed. There's little affection, humor, or charm in evidence, and there's nothing here that later accounts don't supply.

There's not as much levity as expected from Beecham in his 1935 New York recording with **Alfred Wallenstein** (RCA). Ensemble and intonation aren't quite what you might hope for, and Beecham's charm is in sporadic supply. The sound is surprisingly lively and well balanced, though a bit dry, but the surfaces have some audible wear in the 1992 "Legendary Strauss Recordings" box. **Janigro** and the Chicago Symphony under Reiner in 1959 are lightness incarnate (♦RCA 68170). These musicians truly play the piece as chamber music; there are no thick or occluded sounds, and everyone seems to be listening closely to everyone else. Reiner isn't lacking in wit, and the discretion of the performance means it all comes together satisfyingly at the end. This glorious orchestra makes sensuous sounds and the sonics are astonishingly clear.

The Columbia engineering was even more spot-on for **Fournier** and Szell, and it's Szell who seems a bit more spontaneous (♦Sony 63123). The Clevelanders sound like they're enjoying themselves, even if the sheep in the second variation bleat with frighteningly precise rhythm and pitch, and Fournier always brought a uniquely aristocratic touch to this music. He's a bit freer than in his later recording with Karajan, who, in contrast to Reiner and Szell, was wont to portray a Technicolor *Quixote.*

Karajan's 1975 recording with **Rostropovich** is awe-inspiring in its energy and grandeur, and the engineering is appropriately beefy (EMI). But he and his soloist overstate the piece, and the conductor's less grandiloquent 1965 account with **Fournier** is more on the mark(♦DG 457725, with Horn Concerto 2). Less muscular, but certainly not lacking in character, the earlier interpretation responds more to the music bar by bar. The twinges of melancholy are wistful rather than tragic, and the remastering is ideal—very warm, yet dynamic. Where the EMI record is in some respects a star turn for Rostropovich, on DG the aristocratic Fournier is perhaps more at a level with the Berlin Philharmonic front desk players—that chamber music ideal again. That said, it's hard to escape the feeling from either recording that Karajan didn't respond to *Don Quixote* and its intimacies quite as he did to Strauss's other great tone poems. His 1987 version with **Antonio Meneses** suffers from tired, sclerotic direction and over-miked engineering (DG). The recording is admirably clear—probably *too* clear—but there's a metallic echo to much of the playing, and the mixing-board perspective means there's never a real sense of interaction among the players. *Till Eulenspiegel* is the filler, and there Karajan is splendidly dynamic—though the sound again has a bit of steeliness to it.

Tortelier and Kempe are arrestingly vital, in a way that may be surprising for this conductor (♦EMI 64350). If there is any performance that manages to encompass both the symphonic and chamber music characteristics of this score, it's this one. Their rhythmic spring is unequaled, yet they never brutalize the music. Tortelier paints such a vivid title character that he makes you feel you know the daft knight personally. New York Philharmonic first cello **Lorne Munroe** is one of the more characterful orchestral principals on record, and Bernstein gives him plenty of interpretive leeway (CBS/Sony). But the reading is odd, with heavy languorousness where you don't anticipate it, unexpected tempo pushes, and enough mikes to catch chairs squeaking and music pages rustling. It takes a Reiner, Szell, or Karajan to bring all *Don Quixote's* loose ends together after its 40 far-flung minutes; Bernstein doesn't even try.

Haitink is predictably equable with Concertgebouw principal **Tibor de Machula** (Philips). The sound is likewise smooth and unsurprising. Conductor and cellist have some musical insights, but the soloist isn't very individual. The feeling arises that everyone too readily falls back on the plush delivery of the orchestra. **Kurt Reher** and Mehta are generous and affectionate, though they also tend to fragment the score (Decca/London). Mehta's later recordings with the New York Philharmonic were a consistent letdown after his incisive and beautifully recorded LA discs like this one, though the LA winds start off with offish intonation.

Ma and Ozawa are given a sound picture that robs the Boston Symphony of clarity and detail (CBS). Partly because of the recessed sonics, partly because of the absence of turn-on-a-dime interpretive detail, the performance is rarely gripping, or even attention-getting. Previn recorded *Quixote* with the Vienna Philharmonic and front-desk cellist **Franz Bartolomey** in a reading of introversion, freedom of phrasing, and spontaneous energy (♦Telarc 80262, with Previn's equally outstanding *Don Juan*). In "Quixote's Vigil During the Summer Night" (Variation 5), which is often sort of passed over in performance, they get very quiet and are heartfelt enough to induce tears; this and the hero's death make up the heart of the interpretation. The engineering gives the orchestra astonishing depth (why can't all Vienna Philharmonic records sound like this?) and the lower brass and timpani tremendous focus. Bartolomey is balanced rather far back, almost in the orchestra, which adds to the fresh and very believable impression.

Slatkin is surprisingly Toscaninian in the *tuttis,* in fact very taut and energetic but not overblown like Rostropovich/Karajan; as a result, his reading tends more toward verismo than farce—there isn't much funny about this Quixote (RCA). The sound is spectacularly clear and weighty, and **Starker** gives the sense of knowing precisely what he wants to do with each passage, illuminating many details that other soloists don't appear to notice. There's a kind of unsettling, manic edge to this performance I haven't heard elsewhere. **Levine,** with the Met Orchestra stunningly at the ready and DG providing trenchant sound, is impressive; if

you're seeking a stirring and consummately played account, look no further (DG). The score isn't overblown like Karajan/Rostropovich, but Levine makes every detail count, and by the end I was left limp. Typically, he makes Quixote's death a dark moment— the later part of the passage sounds like the beginning of *Götterdämmerung*. This performance seems too good to be true, its fantastic professionalism hiding the fact that it doesn't have much to say.

Wallfisch and Järvi are of similar persuasion; they don't have quite as much *chutzpah* as Levine but rather more individuality (Chandos). But the reading doesn't come together particularly well by the last page, and there's more incisiveness than affection. By contrast, Barenboim and Chicago principal **John Sharp** are somewhat loose-limbed and sprawling (Erato). Barenboim is unusually tender with the opening, and neither Sharp nor violist Charles Pickler has the aural personality to help pull the score together. This is disappointing.

Ein Heldenleben. **Beecham**'s mono and stereo versions with the Royal Philharmonic are complementary, the earlier one (Testament) played with a bit more confidence by the orchestra, but the second (♦EMI, NA) more astutely paced and brimming over with sincerity and soul. Of contrasting interest is **Reiner,** a controlled reading with plenty of room for joy and spontaneity (♦RCA 61494, with his equally commendable 1954 *Zarathustra*). The Chicago Symphony plays magnificently, with well-nigh perfect rhythm and ensemble, but also plenty of tonal warmth in both strings and winds. Recorded in 1954, this discreetly miked and almost hiss-free stereo recording sounds like it was made yesterday, except for very slight compromises at the high and low ends in climaxes.

Of similar vintage, **Ormandy**'s 1959 reading in Philadelphia boasts a more obviously unanimous orchestral response than the Beechams and string sections that are almost superhuman in their sheen and tactile richness (CBS/Sony). But it's disappointingly superficial; for one thing, why is the episodic string writing toward the opening of "The Hero's Retreat from the World" so stiff and metronomic? There and elsewhere, his 1980 remake is more thought through and deeply felt (RCA). Still, the later reading is of no tremendous distinction either, partly because of Norman Carol's labored account of the violin solo and the general feeling that no one is enjoying the music much. The sound, too, is a bit unusual, with all the violins piled up well left of center stage.

To his credit, **Kempe** divides the Dresden Staatskapelle violins left and right (in the ♦EMI 68110 twofer or the set 64342). This account will disappoint those looking for swashbuckling orchestral virtuosity and symphonic thrust, but get past the opening and into "The Hero's Companion" and especially "The Hero's Retreat from the World" and you'll hear music-making of rare humanity. With his utterly natural pacing and characterization (his concertmaster is one of the finest soloists heard in this music), Kempe also manages to avoid fragmenting the work, as so often happens. The recording suffers from some roll-off in climaxes.

Those looking for an ideal combination of orchestral virtuosity, Technicolor interpretive vision, and beauty of execution will be very happy with any of the three **Karajan** recordings with the Berlin Philharmonic. Like Kempe, he never cheapens the music or condescends to it. That said, you won't find Kempe's warmth and compassion; instead, the sections of his Berlin orchestra have a bit more individuality, and he makes Strauss's lines surge and sweep as no other conductor did. Karajan's 1959 version combines youthful fire, characterization, and sonic presence with audible space around the orchestra (♦DG 449725). This was Karajan's first DG album in years, and the engineers went out of their way to impress him; it still sounds extremely well and has almost no hiss to speak of. The second version, recorded in 1974, has a touch more of the expected Karajanian panache and grandiloquence, but also less life and rhythmic energy (EMI). The orchestra sounds splendid, but the music's edges are smoothed away.

In Karajan's 1985 recording, Berlin concertmaster Leon Spierer drops a fair number of notes in his portrayal of Frau Strauss's shrewish moments, and generally gives her an unfortunate, hectoring quality (♦DG 439039). The live recording can make the orchestra sound pretty thin, but the sound is still good, and the interpretation is one of the finest efforts from Karajan's last half-decade and distinctly preferable to the 1974 version. Indeed, the 1985 is Karajan's most characteristic, humane, and convincing reading. The old wizard's grip is still very much intact, though the playing doesn't have all the rhythmic poise it did in 1959, and the end has a very moving valedictory sense that you won't hear in his earlier efforts.

Solti recorded *Heldenleben* with the Vienna Philharmonic in 1978 (♦Decca/London 440618). He presents Strauss's self-portrait in wide-angle Panavision, with a thrilling portrayal of the Hero and a manic, homicidal, near-tragic battle scene that sounds like the cauldron finale to Mahler's Sixth. A highlight is his tight coordination between solo and orchestra in the Frau Strauss section, with none of the usual rhythmic approximations allowed. The conductor isn't blind to the intimacies and domestic warmth of this music, even though you may wish he'd relax a bit more in the earlier sections, and in this he's helped by the Vienna Philharmonic, which—recorded with the non-showy warmth Decca gives it here—couldn't make an ugly sound if it tried.

Ashkenazy has the Cleveland Orchestra in extremely fine fettle, and also some of the clearest yet warmest and most listenable orchestral sound on records (Decca/London). But the conductor was fairly new to the podium, and the interpretation has a touch of greenness to it. The grand pauses are strangely inorganic, and there's little or none of the cumulative sweep and urgency that marks great (or even competent) Strauss performances. **Dohnányi** and the Cleveland offer a more coherent reading, perhaps less remarkable moment to moment but with cumulative impact (♦Decca/London 436444, with one of the finest *Tills*). He never makes Ashkenazy's or Ozawa's miscalculations, and the orchestra sounds absolutely wonderful in its refinement and tonal splendor. He goes for detail rather than weight in the battle scene, and his conclusion has a quiet dignity to contrast with Karajan's splendiferous life summation. Strange that neither the box nor the notes name concertmaster Daniel Majeske as the stylish soloist.

Blomstedt balances the orchestra almost to a fault, with the all-important horns unusually discreet. Portamentos are in fairly liberal supply, which is refreshing. But if his reading often has an under the breath quality like Dohnányi's, it also tends to sound fussier. This is very musical, and Blomstedt's restraint means the grandeur of the closing pages isn't pre-empted, but it's also too obviously and consistently controlled for my taste. **Haitink** and the Concertgebouw make self-control less of a fetish; the impulsiveness and energy are something of a surprise for this conductor, and the orchestra has a strength and purpose that haven't always been heard on other occasions (Philips). The 1970 sound is a bit dry and threadbare in the remastering; this could be one of the very best *Heldenlebens* if it were to get a 24-bit facelift.

Ozawa's reading suffers from indifferent engineering (Philips). It takes some doing to make Boston's Symphony Hall disagreeable, but the multi-miking does the trick, and there are even some traces of electric hum (not to mention the conductor's vocalizing). Better sound might have made it easier to respond to Ozawa's generous but slick and ultimately uninvolved reading. **Previn** and the Vienna Philharmonic are treated to very natural and musical engineering (Telarc), though the orchestral picture is less transparent and open than for Oue and the Minnesota (see below). Previn eschews any kind of thrust at the opening and in the battle music, but get beyond those moments of dispiriting limpness and you will hear unique tenderness and warmth in the love music, backed up by glowing Viennese playing. If introversion is desired, though, Blomstedt is a better choice, and Telarc's lack of tracking is a major inconvenience.

A Dresden Staatskapelle reading from **Sinopoli** is almost a perfect inversion of Previn's: The opening and the battle against critics are electrifying, with fantastic rhythmic tension, yet the more inward-looking passages sound a bit blank, and "The Hero's Works of Peace" doesn't bring a tear to the eye as it does with Karajan and Kempe (DG). The sound has its dryish moments but is generally good. **Oue** and the Minnesota Orchestra are better at balancing the music's extremes (♦Reference 83). The disc is marvelous, a must-hear, not only for the audiophile but anyone who wants a recent, strong performance with something to say. Oue paces *Heldenleben* sensitively and beautifully, and his concertmaster gives a heartfelt portrayal of Frau Strauss. The orchestra sounds only one-ninth of a notch below the Vienna Philharmonic. In terms of energy and the will to deliver, the Minnesota is beyond the Vienna, and the sound, with unmatched but unostentatious dynamic range, gives the lustrous strings plenty of room to bloom in climaxes and lends good weight to the drums in the composer's battle with his critics.

Neither of **Maazel**'s two recordings is entirely satisfactory. His 1978 rendition is marked by the Cleveland Orchestra's typically crystalline virtuosity, and the sound is vintage analog, even if more recent versions have more transparency (CBS). Concertmaster Daniel Majeske is even better than Ashkenazy; he's near perfect—fluent, elegant, sardonic. Maazel's reading is very impressive up until the battle scene, where a fragmentation sets in that keeps the performance from concluding properly. Part of this moment-to-moment, detail-oriented quality comes from the conductor's failure to articulate and set apart the bigger cruxes of the score. Maazel's second version shows the Bavarian Radio Symphony to be distinctly inferior to the Cleveland in balance and finesse, especially in the battlefield scene (RCA). The sound has a compensating warmth and richness, but Maazel's interpretation is more mannered and disjointed than before.

In his reading with the New York Philharmonic, **Mehta** tends to go slack—gooey, even catatonic—in the more reflective passages (CBS). The string *tuttis* aren't particularly attractive, and there's little or none of the timbral glow that's a necessity in Strauss. His Berlin Philharmonic remake is rather better, particularly when it comes to the strings (Sony). But in Berlin the more rhetorical moments protest too much compared with the successful "less is more" approaches of Dohnányi, Kempe, or Oue, while paradoxically the tension again tends to go slack. This is a live recording, and the close miking means the overall picture has a manufactured quality; the sound also tends to cramp in climaxes. Mehta's best *Heldenleben* is his first, recorded in Los Angeles (Decca/London). This has some of the indulgence of the New York version but is the most spontaneous and genuine reading among his three, rising to quiet eloquence in the hero's "Works of Peace" and retirement. The sound is still very good (the off in the distance effects particularly well done), even when they expose the LA orchestra to be less alert than it later came to be under Giulini, Previn, and Salonen; it's a good bargain-priced choice (Australian Decca 466669, with *Rosenkavalier Waltzes*).

Barenboim and the Chicago Symphony might seem too relaxed at the start, but he goes on to unfold a strikingly wide-ranging performance; his extraordinary sensitivity to the quieter dynamic markings makes the central battle all the more dramatic, and the autumnal closing pages (which offer a genuine crescendo and rock-solid wind tuning) all the more moving (♦Erato 45621). His generous rubato also helps make sure this is a performance with soul. Yet the discreet sound (with no over-conspicuous width to the stereo spectrum) means this is one of the more musical jobs to come from Orchestra Hall. It isn't the most rhapsodic, tightly drawn, or heroic performance—the Chicago strings are lovely without offering anything like the all-enveloping, old world sound of Karajan, Kempe, or Haitink—but it's a refreshing and loving view from musicians who refuse to weigh the music down.

From Tilson Thomas comes a showy, virtuosic, fragmented, soulless performance, impressive from moment to moment, by turns swooning and apocalyptic (Sony). If all great *Heldenlebens* are more than the sums of their parts, this shapeless account fails utterly, fearless as the London Symphony horns are and despite the beautiful recording job. Would a real hero have to try this hard, I wonder? Järvi is almost as impressive, and a good deal more musical and mindful of Strauss's long line (Chandos). Except maybe for the strings, the Scottish National Orchestra needn't fear the other orchestras in this listing, especially given the resonant, vivid recording. What Järvi lacks are the glimmers of humanity and personality that make you smile when you hear the likes of Beecham, Karajan, Kempe, and Barenboim. This is a beautiful reading of no great humanity, and humanity should be the mainstay of *Heldenleben*.

I prefer Schwarz and the Seattle Symphony, who, though not quite as polished as Järvi's Scots or as impressive as Oue's Minnesotans, do more to make the music their own than Järvi, Ozawa, or Tilson Thomas (Delos). The Seattle horns are very fine, in the soaring *Till Eulenspiegel* quote and elsewhere, and the unpretentious engineering is among the best: Watch out for the apocalyptic drums at the start of the battle scene. Sawallisch and the Philadelphia return to Strauss's original, quiet ending—which, perhaps only in hindsight, now seems inconclusive and disappointing (EMI). More important are the disappointments of Sawallisch's performance, which is marred by some surprisingly lax ensemble, suspect intonation, and a general lack of tension. Just about any other listing here is preferable. Markson and the National Symphony of Ireland turn in a performance of surprising strength, and the conductor works within his resources to create a touchingly introverted, personal reading with some particularly beautiful phrasing (Naxos). The Irish strings, though, want for presence when you compare them with other renditions. The sound is just fine—dynamic but warm and easy on the ear.

Turning to historic performances, Mengelberg and the Concertgebouw have some priority: After all, Strauss dedicated the score to them (♦Dutton 5025). The orchestra returns the favor with affection to spare in their 1941 recording, and Mengelberg typically leaves no stone unturned. He's no slave to the score, but the inimitable Mengelbergian rubatos are all of a piece with the music, and the absolutely glorious orchestral playing has never been surpassed. The only drawbacks are a bit of suspect intonation from the concertmaster and some occasional hollowness in the middle to lower strings induced by Dutton's CEDAR processing. As usual for this time, there are some eccentricities in the balances; the oboes and snare drum, for instance, are almost inaudible. Mengelberg also made a recording in 1928 with the New York Philharmonic, with which he and Toscanini then held joint appointments

(RCA). That performance has many of the virtues of the 1941—Mengelberg was quite consistent in his inconsistencies—and the New York playing has even more thrust and confidence. The sound, though outstanding for the late '20s, is inevitably limited compared to the 1941 discs, with surface noise omnipresent though ignorable. Still, the utter and extreme magnificence of orchestra and interpretation always comes across. What a wonderful ensemble the Philharmonic was in those days!

Strauss himself recorded *Heldenleben* in 1941 with the Bavarian State Orchestra (Lys, Koch, and other transfers). The contrasts with the ultra-romantic Mengelberg couldn't be stronger; Strauss is comparatively modern-sounding in one of the straighter renditions on record, with almost none of the Dutchman's rubato and portamentos. The Bavarians play wonderfully, though the conductor emphasizes efficiency over rhapsodic opulence. Volume levels are inconsistent on the Lys reissue, the sound is rather thin, and there is some low level buzz in quieter moments—Dutton's transfer of Mengelberg is definitely more pleasant listening. Much the same goes for Strauss's 1944 Vienna Philharmonic recording, though the sound is a good deal better and the playing comparable only with Mengelberg's Concertgebouw (Preiser). As usual for Strauss, this is an unusually strict, modern-sounding interpretation. It's certainly worth hearing, beyond its documentary value, and is likely the best installment in Strauss's Vienna Philharmonic series. But Mengelberg's two renditions are so much more interesting.

Monteux's 1947 San Francisco performance is glorious: spontaneous, taut and eager—he protects the final pages from soup and sentimentality—yet always carrying itself with dignity (♦RCA 61889). Concertmaster Naoum Blinder is a major asset, and the orchestral response is thrilling, often downright ecstatic, and it's astonishing that the performance was never released until the 1994 CD reissue. The only caveat, and it's a pretty strong one, is the thin and surfacey sound: This sounds like an engineering job from the early '30s rather than the late '40s, but at least it's consistent and well balanced. Krauss and the Vienna Philharmonic (Decca/Testament) have comparable fire, and their 1952 Musikverein recording has a slightly more forgiving acoustic. This is likely the finest of Krauss's postwar Strauss recordings, though the sound is disappointing—bright and whistley, with some slightly confusing balances. The resonance of the Vienna Philharmonic strings survives, and concertmaster Willi Boskovsky is still unsurpassed for his beautiful sound and abundance of character. Much the same could be said of Krauss's interpretation as a whole, which is typically Viennese in its elegant but vibrant insouciance; given more palatable remastering, this would make another prime recommendation.

Böhm paces *Heldenleben* with unerring skill; there are none of the longueurs, bombastic fragmentation, or inorganic pauses that can often be heard elsewhere. Indeed, he has no peer in the difficult task of presenting this score as a single, indivisible whole (DG). The Dresden Staatskapelle plays beautifully, but the 1957 mono sound is rather echoey and hardens a bit in climaxes. Not a central recommendation, given the sound, but still a reading to hear. A 1941 Toscanini performance of extraordinary intensity has been resurrected (♦Music & Arts 754). The NBC musicians play as though their lives depended on it, though without the under-the-gun impression that mars many of Toscanini's performances; indeed, the playing has a beautiful inner glow that is idiomatic for Strauss. But be warned that you won't listen to this for the sound: There are some audience coughs, M&A hasn't tried to remove the persistent surface pops and scratches, and the acoustics are dry. Still, the sound is immediate and has plenty of presence—and Toscanini's performance rises above any limitations.

Metamorphosen. Strauss's elegy to Munich and Dresden, cities bombed to kingdom come at the end of WWII, was recorded only two years after its composition by **Karajan** and the Vienna Philharmonic (♦EMI 66390). The performance is a *cri du coeur* of its own, cut on hard-to-procure wax in a devastated city where producer Walter Legge had to run his equipment with gasoline-powered generators. Yet EMI's sound, agreeably distant and rounded, is easier listening than Karajan's 1983 remake (♦DG 410892). DG's mikes are so close and plentiful that sometimes each of the 23 solo strings seems to have one of its own. The sound can get so heavy that you wonder if he's doubling the lines, and in climaxes, the dryness becomes unacceptable. But what makes the later record necessary is the exceptional intensity of Karajan's performance; the tension and weight of sound are absolutely extraordinary at the final piling up of the dissonant chord. The middle recording among Karajan's three—recorded in the Jesus-Christus Kirche, Berlin, in 1971—is his least direct and weighty; the articulation is more smoothed over, the delivery more impassive, the music's edges rounded off. The mikes are also a good deal farther back than for his 1983 Philharmonie reading. Though the Berlin sounds are beautiful, this makes the least engaging Karajan choice.

A 1947 concert reading by **Furtwängler** and the Berlin Philharmonic has been preserved in dim sound, with the tone coming apart in louder climaxes (Music & Arts). *Metamorphosen* is in some ways Strauss's most daring and organic structure, and no other performance I've heard makes the piece unfold so naturally and inevitably. The intensity of the reading also surpasses Karajan's at times—the players dispatch the last climax as if their lives depended on it—but there are also some moments where the Berliners sound taxed, understandably enough.

Kempe and the Dresden Staatskapelle strings don't try for Karajan's apocalyptic and Germanic style, but something lighter-toned and more variable—more *Winterreise* than *Götterdämmerung* (♦EMI 64351). **Previn** and the Vienna Philharmonic are more variegated than either Karajan or Kempe, and perhaps more immediately and consistently interesting (♦Philips 420160). Maybe because of the Musikverein acoustics, there's greater differentiation here between solo strings and ensemble. The ensemble sound is light, but with that sweetness and bright (though never harsh) tone that is so typically Viennese: creamy in a highly focused way. This makes for a central recommendation. **Dohnányi** gets a tougher and less honeyed sound from the Vienna Philharmonic (Decca/London). The reading itself also sounds calculated, wanting in lyricism, spontaneity, and more freedom from the bar line. The sound is impressive, something of a waste of effort.

A similarly strait-laced performance comes from **Gielen** and the Cincinnati Symphony (Vox). It's tightly argued and well played, but the lightweight sound of the orchestra conspires with the conductor's over-literal approach to make the experience entirely unmoving and unengaging. **Blomstedt** and the Dresden Staatskapelle operate at a markedly lower level of tension, though the very end is movingly quiet and sustained (Denon). **Rattle** is painfully stiff at Strauss's piling-up of his climactic dissonant chord, and the climactic pause is strangely inorganic (EMI). This performance suffers from too much rhythmic clarity at the expense of bowing through one note to the next. **Järvi**'s excellent performance with the Scottish National Orchestra is an alternative for those who might find Karajan oppressive, Marriner and Previn lightweight, and Kempe not up to date in sound (♦Chandos 8734, with his less recommendable *Death and Transfiguration*). He displays a sure hand in shaping this dark tapestry; certainly he creates far more intense climaxes than the anodyne Dohnányi, and the close is poignantly articu-lated. The recording is powerful and rather bass-heavy but not opaque, and the climaxes expand nicely too.

Barbirolli was originally a cellist, and he and the Philharmonia really took to the dark string colors of *Metamorphosen* (EMI). Like Marriner (another string player), he finds the perfect variety of bow weights, not playing too heavily or too quickly and emphasizing the climax through rhythm and articulation rather than just playing loud. But he was more inclined than Marriner to slow things down for expressive effect, partly because his body of strings was larger. Some will respond to the extra weight and emphases, others will think this is gilding the lily. Barbirolli's reading is nothing if not deeply felt; much of his expressiveness lies in denying some of the music's need to move forward. Similar concepts can be found in **Richard Stamp**'s recording with the Academy of London (Virgin). The articulation is very connected, like Karajan, and Stamp clearly has some passionate and well-thought-through ideas about the music. It's enjoyable, though it tends to fall between the Marriner and Karajan stools: not as detailed or astutely argued as the former, not as sonorous and overwhelming as the latter.

Salonen has clearly worshiped at different musical altars, and his recording with the New Stockholm Chamber Orchestra seems to owe more to the proto-modernism of Schoenberg's *Verklärte Nacht* than to late romanticism (CBS/Sony). Transparency of texture is delightfully wedded to rich sonorities that belie the setup of one player to a part, and he's clearly interested in local detail (the agogic point-making in the opening section will exasperate some listeners). Though it shouldn't be the only version in your collection, the performance is very refreshing for its new ideas and the playing outshines both Marriner and Stamp, particularly in its sheer strength. **Boughton** and the English String Orchestra are praiseworthy, less oppressive than Brown and the Norwegians (see below) but not as full of ideas as Salonen (Nimbus). The ensemble plays and listens more as a chamber group than Brown's, but isn't always ironclad perfect in blend and intonation. What really makes this hard listening, though, is the echo; I usually enjoy Nimbus's back-in-the-hall miking, but here I consistently hear some parts of the orchestra twice.

Thanks in part to a recording that has more edge, presence, and detail, **Marriner** and the Academy of St. Martin in the Fields pull you into the work more quickly and keep you there (♦Decca/London 430002). This might not have quite the inner tension of the Karajan recordings or the bottomless sonority of his larger string groups, but Marriner's climaxes really open up and the warm analog sound tells at every moment. I like very much the shape and continuity of the phrasing—the obvious long-range thinking, the feeling that the players know exactly where they're coming from and where they're going—and the smoothness of the Londoners' bowing. They also lend the music rare grace and dignity; not everything here is funereal, Marriner seems to say.

An Academy of St. Martin alumnus, **Iona Brown,** has committed *Metamorphosen* to disc with the Norwegian Chamber Orchestra (Chandos). As in the coupled Tchaikovsky *Serenade,* the sound and perspective are skewed to the bottom of the ensemble; at times I swear the violins stop playing, or are outnumbered by their colleagues, so opaque and bottom-heavy does the tone get. There's little here of Marriner's far-sighted phrasing, no real *pianissimos* whatsoever (or even *pianos;* does Brown have a Karajan complex?), and Chandos supplies boomy and ill-focused sound. Instead of that depressing experience, turn to **Pople** and the London Festival Orchestra, who have much of Marriner's structural foresight with a bit of extra spontaneity (ASV). What Pople lacks is Marriner's attention to detail and the transparency of texture that allows

Strauss's contrapuntal details to be heard—fine points tend to get swallowed up in the press toward the big climax. The playing *per se* is beautiful, never actually heavy.

The reverse applies to **Jordan** and the Lausanne Chamber Orchestra (Erato). This ensemble isn't top-flight; Jordan sometimes seems to be asking for more than they're quite capable of, and they're left with nowhere to go in trying to expand their sound in the unison passage after the big culmination. And Jordan's reading could use a bit of Pople's urgency in passages that seem to stagnate a bit. The sound tends to get top-heavy in louder climaxes.

Sinfonia Domestica. **Karajan** again proves himself to be the *sine qua non* in Strauss. He rarely has sounded so unbuttoned, so out-and-out gleeful, than he does in the closing pages of his Berlin Philharmonic recording (♦EMI 66107). What's more, the fairly resonant Salle Wagram acoustics in Paris afford more space around the orchestra than its home base, the Berlin Philharmonie. As one Strauss contemporary put it, the baby truly makes more of a ruckus than the fall of Valhalla in *Die Götterdämmerung,* yet the domestic love-making is quiet and intimate, beautifully phrased, and presented with string textures that are luxurious but not saccharine. An irreplaceable recording, though the remastering does bring some harshness at the end.

Sawallisch doesn't push the music nearly as hard as Karajan, and elicits particularly lush playing from the Philadelphians, with generally slower tempos (♦EMI 55185). Some passages—the lullaby, for instance—are almost dreamy in their softness, timbral delicacy, and intimate phrasing. EMI recorded the orchestra live in Tokyo, but the audience is utterly silent until the final applause. The sound *per se* is extremely good. **Szell** pulled an astonishingly precise and detailed realization of Strauss's score from his Clevelanders (CBS/Sony). Especially given the low asking price, many will enjoy this beautifully played performance, well recorded except for some over-miking (the harp) and a few minute executive noises from the orchestra. If the warmth and refinement of the Cleveland strings prove moving in the lullaby, though, Szell neglects the more exuberant and melancholic moments of the score.

One of the earliest accounts was recorded in 1944 by **Strauss** himself with the Vienna Philharmonic (Preiser). It's a very satisfying reading, intimately emotional rather than indulgent—I'm tempted to call it a domestic rather than public rendition. The violins are absolutely without equal in the nocturnal love-making, with some sliding between notes (typical of the period) to add beautifully to the sense of ecstasy. The engineers got more resonance and character from the Musikverein acoustics than Decca did for Krauss, but the sound can get a bit occluded and hard in climaxes.

Krauss and the Vienna Philharmonic taped *Domestica* in 1952 (Decca/Testament). It's an inconsistent rendition, charming and sweet-toned at the beginning and rather stiff yet wayward in the Adagio. As with the other Krauss discs, the remastered sound comes up shrill and metallic. **Reiner** recorded the piece with the Chicago Symphony in 1956, a very detailed reading that renders even Strauss's most complicated passages—his orchestra here is particularly large—with complete clarity (RCA). The phrasing, too, is most shapely, but in the end I'd categorize this next to Szell as a carefully crafted version of the score that neglects its more manic moments, especially in the finale.

Maazel tends to be obvious and rather heavy-handed in Munich, different from Sawallisch (RCA). Each movement threatens to grind to a halt, so slack does the structural tension get at each midpoint. The

sound, too, is peculiarly boxy and lacks the bloom heard in both the Karajan and Sawallisch discs, making the Bavarian Radio Symphony's high strings sound grainy and the timpani and basses very indistinct. His earlier Vienna Philharmonic version is far better, with a fair measure of spontaneity and some truly splendid but not showy playing (DG). He keeps a cooler head with all the domestic surprises than Karajan or Ashkenazy, but thereby presents the purely musical and structural strengths of this score. The only concern is the close but not very detailed balance, which causes some cramping of the sound picture in the exuberant closing sections. A bit more charm wouldn't have been inappropriate either.

That's in more ample supply from **Mehta.** Like Maazel, Mehta doesn't drive the music quite as hard as Karajan, nor does he allow it to luxuriate like Sawallisch. Yet his Berlin Philharmonic reading is very engaging, indeed one of his finest recordings—a superb performance, though the sound isn't ideal, with the harp sometimes over-miked and climaxes rather hard (♦CBS/Sony 42322). The spontaneity infecting practically every bar makes one wonder all the more at the antiseptic music making on many of his other Berlin recordings. His 1970 LA Philharmonic reading is also very fine, with some of the best LA playing on record (not as beautifully sounded as Berlin, but more emphatically articulated) and deeper perspectives than CBS (Decca/London). Orchestra and engineers work together to produce beautifully sustained sonorities in the love-making passages. Decca needs to reissue this.

Previn and the Vienna Philharmonic are in a similar vein (DG). The very last pages go off the boil a bit, and as so often the Musikverein proves a temperamental acoustic for recording; there are some occlusions in the bigger climaxes. **Waart** and the Minnesota Orchestra offer a recording with warm perspectives, but the texture—too homogenized, too Schubertian—wants for detail, and the interpretation lacks individuality and the phrasing a strong sense of direction (Virgin). **Schwarz** and the Seattle Symphony offer more to interest the ear, and the engineering lets you hear more of what's going on (♦Delos 3082). Though not quite as distinctive an interpretation as Karajan, Mehta, or Sawallisch, there's much to enjoy here, and audiophiles will be happy with the sound.

In his allegiances and nonsensationalist "old school" approach, **Kempe** reminds me of Bruno Walter. It's not surprising, then, that he should sound a bit embarrassed by the musical voyeurism of *Sinfonia Domestica.* His recording with the Dresden Staatskapelle is one of the lesser lights in his Strauss cycle, with some coarse playing and stiff phrasing in the amours of the Adagio and an opening and closing that fail to catch the attention (EMI). If a more understated approach is desired, Sawallisch and Previn have more character, charm, and variety.

Ashkenazy has matured immensely as a conductor since his first Strauss records (e.g., his Cleveland *Heldenleben*), and this shows in his *Sinfonia Domestica* with the Czech Philharmonic (♦Ondine 943). This isn't an interpretation to astonish you with revelations or make you swoon sympathetically, but the reading has a spiffy, energetic professionalism that's very attractive. He doesn't control detail to the detriment of the players' spontaneity, and is more willing than most to give finer shades of detail and meaning to the opening phrases. A big benefit is the very transparent 24-bit recording, which combined with the natural miking makes this one of the most realistic-sounding *Domesticas* around, even if the orchestra could have more presence. The Rudolfinum's loose acoustics have been managed very well, and the mikes are back far enough that there's plenty of air around the sound of the ensemble.

Sonatinas for winds. These two works are big, symphony-sized pieces—scored for 16 players, the second actually subtitled "Symphony"—that served as occupational therapy during the latter part of WWII. 1 (subtitled "From an Invalid's Workshop"—Strauss was recovering from influenza) is probably the more cogent and interesting of the two, with a darkness that shows he hadn't completely forgotten the horrors of the world outside. The **Orpheus Chamber Orchestra** are a bit more "on" than in their recording of 2 (DG). Still, they're rather too matter of fact in the *Romanze,* the tempo too quick to allow meaningful phrasing. The **Netherlands Wind Ensemble** is better recorded in 1 than they are in 2, though the acoustic is still a bit dry (♦Philips 438733, an uneven but desirable set of the "complete music for wind ensemble"). But they find a measured tempo—nice and slow—for the *Romanze,* and the performance has plenty of character.

The **London Winds** are just a bit too suave and undetailed to be completely enjoyable (Hyperion). Besides, they're competing with a marvelous reading by the **Vienna Philharmonic Winds** under Previn, a performance with everything: full and rich tone colors with lots of character (thanks in part to the distinctive Viennese double-horns), beautiful phrasing, well-chosen tempos, and ample sound (♦Philips 420160, with a memorable *Metamorphosen*). My second choice is the **Norwegian Winds** under Gerard Oskamp, who are the stateliest and most shapely of all in the *Romanze* (♦Victoria 19045). All that's missing is the last ounce of timbral character that you hear in Vienna.

Strauss's *Sonatina 2* ("Happy Workshop") was written while the old man was waiting for the war to wind down to its grisly end. Its neoclassical cheer makes light of the ingenuity that went into constructing this 38-minute set of four movements. For quality of wind playing and sonic warmth, the **London Winds** are the only real possibility; their fluency falls beautifully on the ear (♦Hyperion 66731/2, a set of the complete wind music). But they could find more variety in the music; in the march-like second movement, for instance, the rhythm could be more pointed. In such matters, the **Netherlands Wind Ensemble** under Waart is more consistently lively and interesting, though their phrasing has its pedantic moments (Philips). The 1970 sound, though, comes up a bit dry and sour. Hyperion, on the other hand, gives a fluent and lovely sheen to the Londoners, who are recorded in a distinct space, and this account really gives you the chance to hear the bass clarinet and contrabassoon at the bottom of the texture.

The **Orpheus Chamber Orchestra** wind players can be unsteady in exposed moments, and it's also surprising that their tuning proves undependable at the dark introduction to the finale (DG). The good news is that these players often give the music more life than the London Winds, and with the brilliant but comfortable sound, you're free to enjoy the music-making. Your choice will depend on whether you like urbane and slightly unvariegated playing in fine sound (Hyperion), lively and straightforward musicianship with no great emphasis on sound (Philips), or a spiffy and decisive performance by a great ensemble not caught absolutely in top form (DG).

It's cruel to come to **Sarah Chang** after Heifetz, but her tone color is too uniform—as if applied with a spray can—while Heifetz shakes myriad colors from his sleeve (EMI). Her accompanist, Sawallisch, doesn't exude the confidence of Smith (let alone Sandor) in the majestic piano opening, where the quick note values should be sharp and mercurial. Because of these and other shortcomings, the performance outstays its welcome. If **Kremer**'s enervated (but not monochromatic) tone is an unlikely vehicle for a youthful piece by an arch-romantic, he turns that unsuitability to his benefit by capitalizing on the music's "modern"

rhythmic whims instead of its 19th-century luxuriance (♦DG 453440). In the outer movements, he and pianist Oleg Maisenberg dispatch the young Strauss's rhythms with the most precise weighting. This is engrossing musicianship.

On the surface, **Kyung-Wha Chung** and Zimerman are more idiomatic (DG). They're freer with rubato, and respond more to the music's harmonic and melodic richness. They offer beautiful playing and impeccable musicianship, yet it must be said they gloss over the rhythmic and narrative quirkiness in the music, as in the strange piano interjections in I. **Sitkovetsky** and Pavel Gililov hear the restlessness as a kind of *Sturm und Drang* storminess that lurks just below the surface, and in that sense, this is a Brahmsian reading (♦Virgin 61766, a twofer). With vibrant and sometimes echoey sound, their performance is certainly distinctive and exciting.

Symphonies. Strauss wrote two *Eroica*-length symphonies in his late teens; the precocious composer already knew his way around the orchestra well, but his schematic structures aren't well argued. And the movements tend to ramble when they don't sound formulaic. They are, in a word, boring. It's the isolated moments, like the dark colors opening Symphony Op. 12, that stay in the memory, rather than any of the rather threadbare musical ideas. **Michael Halász** taped Op. 12 with the Slovak Philharmonic in a distantly recorded performance that makes the music attractive without eloquently arguing its case (Marco Polo). **Järvi** and the Scottish National Orchestra sound more excited and their sound is less recessed (Chandos). The earlier Symphony in D Minor is a more modest work, and maybe more appealing because of that. **Schermerhorn** and the Hong Kong Philharmonic do the music justice, though the orchestra isn't the last word in refinement and solid tuning (Marco Polo). Only die-hard Straussians need apply.

Till Eulenspiegels lustige Streiche. **Strauss**'s 1944 recording with the Vienna Philharmonic is unusually straitlaced, even rather dull up until Till's last exploit and trial (Preiser). The Vienna Philharmonic plays beautifully, though the sound is more closely balanced and echoey than others in the Strauss-Vienna series. **Toscanini**'s 1952 performance is dead serious, even though all the tempos are quick (RCA). Maybe it's the dry sound and close miking; we know the wiry sound the Maestro habitually got from his NBC Symphony, but how the engineers could have made Carnegie Hall sound so jejune is anyone's guess. His 1949 NBC Symphony version is similar, though here there are also some intrusive surface noise and dim sound to contend with (Music & Arts).

As always, the contrasts between Toscanini and **Furtwängler** are mind-boggling. Even in the biggest climaxes, Furtwängler and the Berlin Philharmonic, recorded in 1943, manage to retain a special lightness (♦Music & Arts 829). This is a live recording—always the best setting for this conductor—and his spontaneity more than compensates for the few coughs. The sound is amazingly good, except for a touch of pre-echo and one or two buzzy notes at the biggest climaxes. His later Vienna Philharmonic version, done in studio conditions around 1950, sounds cautious by comparison, though phrases are still beautifully turned and the piece is sensibly paced (EMI). But for the patented Furtwänglerian spontaneity, his ability to make you feel that the music was being conceived at that very moment, the 1943 version is the one to hear.

Reiner's 1956 recording with the Vienna Philharmonic is poker-faced, and the trial scene quite slow and lacking in impetus; naturally, he gets exceptional playing from the orchestra, but the sound hasn't aged very well (Decca, RCA). **Szell** and his Cleveland Orchestra are wonderfully free and vivid (♦Sony 63123, with his marvelous *Don Quixote,* or 36721). This should be heard by those who say that Szell's exactitude inhibited spontaneity; his preparation hasn't kept the players from investing a lot of character in their sound and rhythms, or rather, rehearsal has given the orchestra the freedom to be impulsive. This is rare music-making, thrilling and exhilarating. **Haitink** and the Concertgebouw are a bit more even-tempered, but still very vivid (♦Philips 411442, and in the more uneven Duo 2CD collection, 442281). I can't think of a more exciting Haitink recording; there's real mischief here, and the ensemble sounds nice and crisp in this digital remastering.

Waart is similarly middle of the road, and enjoys superbly agile and confident playing from the Minnesota Orchestra (Virgin). Next to Haitink, though (and most certainly Szell), his reading lacks the last degree of interpretive and timbral distinction. The kind of reading you might anticipate from Szell comes instead from **Böhm** and the Berlin Philharmonic (DG). His Till wears a pedicure; this is fastidious music-making, but the rogue and mischief-maker in the protagonist have disappeared. There could be no greater contrast than **Stokowski,** whose reading with the New York Philharmonic is the most hair-raising on record, bar none (♦Everest 9004). Things get so heated that the strings and winds part company completely in one passage (at 8:05): a major gaffe, but it hardly matters given the thrilling performance. The *Don Juan* coupling is comparatively staid, but this *Till* is worth the cost of the entire disc. Everest's sound is also very good.

Bernstein also has the New York Philharmonic, if in rather more grotesque (and heavily miked) form, in a disc that's not recommendable because of a failed *Zarathustra* (CBS/Sony). He's in his metier with *Till;* he's wonderful with the ever-shifting textures, the manic surprises, the explosions of lyric charm, and Strauss's orchestral groans and grunts. But he also fragments the work more than most conductors, repeatedly losing the narrative thread for the sake of the moment. Very different is **Previn**'s unassertive Vienna recording (EMI). The early digital sound is a bit muted, which may be partly responsible for the impression of even-temperedness; his trial scene is one of the limper ones on record, the music coming to a stop with the grand pauses. The Viennese playing itself is marvelous, of course.

Karajan's accounts are the most magnificent, but also the most affectionate. The 1973 version has a generous church acoustic to help the more luxuriant string passages glow beyond belief (♦DG 447441). The 1987 version was taped in the closer and drier Philharmonie, and he appropriately takes a slightly tougher, more matter of fact approach (DG, with a non-recommendable *Don Quixote*). These Berlin accounts both come highly recommended in their different ways. But Karajan also recorded *Till* in Vienna in 1961, and that is the most irrepressible of all (♦Decca/London 466388). The sound is wide-ranging, if also a bit raspy even in the latest remastering and with some tape noise in the right channel. Going back even further, his 1952 version finds him coaching Walter Legge's Philharmonia Orchestra to displays of turn-on-a-dime virtuosity that even the Berlin and Vienna didn't match (EMI). This is even more impetuous than the Vienna version, though later on Karajan would prevent the march-like sections from dragging as they do here. The mono sound is also disappointing, rather like the shrill tapes Decca was making of Krauss and the Vienna in this period: Did they use the same mikes?

If **Kempe** and the Dresden orchestra usually accentuate the easy-going, Bavarian aspect of Strauss's make-up, their *Till* is more demonstrative (♦EMI 64342). Their recording is the most consistently beautiful—as opposed to circusy or self-conscious—and the engineering is

crisp enough to allow the violins a touch of bravado and the winds and brass a nice range of colors. **Solti**'s two recordings are similarly high-powered, Till's rhythmic shenanigans almost allowed to get out of hand. It's hard not to like his Berlin Philharmonic reading, where the maestro's urgency is tempered a bit by the Berliners' timbral blend (Decca/London, with *Zarathustra*). Still, his earlier Chicago version is the one to go for; if anything, there's a bit more rhythmic flexibility in Chicago, and the generous acoustics and studio conditions make for more gratifying sounds, with less spotlighting (♦Decca/London 440618). And this is one to hear: Few works are better suited to Solti's grand, often unsubtle, style than Strauss's boisterous *Till.*

Too many details are elided by **Slatkin** and the Bavarian Radio Symphony, the grand moments going by like any others (RCA). Despite a deep and clean recording, this is an unworthy coupling for Starker's valuable *Don Quixote.* The very things glossed over by Slatkin are brought out by **Maazel** (♦RCA 68775, with his less satisfactory *Heldenleben*). He's wonderfully adept at the subtle, playful tempo changes needed to make *Till* come alive. The Bavarian orchestra doesn't have the beautiful sound of many other ensembles, but it hardly matters with Maazel's talents as a story teller. The sound is vivid, though again there isn't much bloom in *tuttis.* **Abbado** proves refreshingly thoughtful with the London Symphony (DG). His avoidance of bombast means the performance is a bit slow to gather momentum. However, he reaches real tension by the last prank and the trial scene, and the "once upon a time" music is beautifully phrased at its concluding return. With the London Symphony playing both with the weight of a hammer and the lightness of thistledown, there's much to recommend this record. His later Berlin Philharmonic account is different: The playing style is rather heavier than in London, though he never burdens the music, and the performance is more inclined to extremes and surprises (Sony). With excellent sound, this is smashing stuff, though it doesn't quite match Szell, Kempe, Karajan, or Stokowski.

Blomstedt in San Francisco (Decca/London) is generally more attentive to detail. His usual care for balanced textures and dynamics is appropriate to this piece (though surely the famous horn solo could be more conspicuous and bragging), and this is a far cry from the usual programmatic-picturesque bloodbath. The splendid sound makes Sony's climaxes in Berlin seem a bit coarse. All that said, Blomstedt is disappointing in the horn-led climax before the trial, where he fails to deliver the big structural payoff that Abbado supplies. He had less gutsy and open sound in his Dresden recording (Denon), so that reading comes up with an even less convincing account of the piece as a whole. Compared to both Abbado and Blomstedt, **Tilson Thomas** and the London Symphony are more conventionally heavy and Hollywoodish, more impressive from one moment to the next, but entirely lacking in warmth and affection (CBS/Sony). Still, as a virtuoso account of a virtuoso score, this can be hard to resist. The sound is likewise heavy-set.

There's also more of the juggernaut than the grin to **Barenboim** with the Chicago Symphony (Erato). With some loud and showy playing, this tends more toward empty, ill-willed rambunctiousness than humor. Instead of bringing in some lightness or affection, the slower music tends to meander. **Dorati** (Decca/London) doesn't fall into the trap of over-weighting this music, and the Detroit Symphony—unlike Tilson Thomas's and Barenboim's orchestras—plays it as chamber music. But some of the performance also sounds a bit stiff and duty-laden, as in the scene where Till impersonates a priest. Some of the same phlegmatic tempos and rhythms that spoiled **Košler**'s *Don Juan* also affect his *Till* (Naxos). This is a fairly relaxed reading, with a decent and alert orchestra and a transparent recording job that doesn't try to fatten up the ensemble's thinnish sound. In a smaller field of competition, it would be a good choice. But at budget price, the Szell is far better.

Then there's **Horenstein** and the Bamberg Symphony (♦Vox 5529, a bargain twofer with Mahler, Schoenberg, and more Strauss). The sound is mono, and a modern-day producer would probably blanch at the occasional hints of the conductor taking his orchestra by surprise. You wouldn't mistake this orchestra for the Vienna Philharmonic. But this is very rare music making in that the score is so wisely and beautifully conducted; the tempos are all interrelated into a single whole, and the wide palette of characterization used to instill character without cheapness. Like the *Death and Transfiguration* coupling, this is a performance to acquire and hear if sound isn't of overriding importance.

Tod und Verklärung (Death and Transfiguration). **Furtwängler** wasn't very closely associated with Strauss's music, finding much of the composer's programmatic specifics distasteful. His 1947 recording with the Hamburg State Philharmonic is, as always, a fiery interpretation that convinces totally from first bar to last despite some imperfections (Music & Arts). He also inspires this second-string orchestra to heights of tone and expression. The acoustics are boxy, the sound thins out at climaxes, there is plenty of coughing at the start, and a bit of irritating tape noise here and there. Nevertheless, as a document of this great conductor's Strauss, this is very valuable: Just listen to how nostalgically the protagonist's "memories of youth" steal in.

Still, Furtwängler's 1950 Vienna Philharmonic version is the one to hear—indeed, one of the very greatest Strauss orchestral records ever made (♦EMI 65197). There is no grandstanding whatsoever in this intensely musical and noble performance; the work unfolds as one organic whole, the climaxes somehow cut from the same cloth as the tender moments. The pulse is ever pliable but molded with exquisite taste, the playing is profoundly luminous at every moment, and nothing is forced. This is an unforgettable document, and it's an added blessing that the sound is so good. **Strauss**'s own 1944 Vienna Philharmonic rendition is typically straightforward, never milking the music for expression (Preiser). The orchestra plays wonderfully, but Furtwängler in 1950 certainly had more to say about the music. On this occasion, the sound gets a bit ragged in climaxes.

Karajan's 1983 rendition is one of his great Strauss documents; there is more nobility than carnage, and the gripping reading rises to an all-enveloping transfigurative climax (♦DG 439039, with *Heldenleben*). He was at the peak of his powers, and the Berliners are in top form. Though things get a touch hard at the very top, the sound is also fine—a close but believable image of the orchestra. His 1974 performance is more suave, and the church acoustics give the orchestra a sweeter, more distant sound (DG). They're both great performances; the first is easier listening, but Karajan had had some harrowing brushes with mortality himself by the early '80s, and the second reading is more truthful and engrossing. His 1953 Philharmonia recording is his most intense, the furious death throes sometimes imperiling ensemble, yet he never lets the brass swamp the rest of the orchestra at bigger climaxes (EMI). This is a sterling performance, even when Karajan is a bit heavy-handed. The sound, thin, and unkind to the high strings, is also a drawback.

Horenstein taped *Death and Transfiguration* twice. The first is a '50s mono production with the Bamberg Symphony (♦Vox 5529). This is a most beautiful and thoroughly considered performance—very typical of Horenstein, and one of the finest renditions in the catalog. Every detail makes sense within the larger picture, and he never lets the orchestra sound as though its expressivity lay in playing as loud as it can, as is all too familiar in Strauss. With a well balanced and hiss-free recording (though the strings could have more presence), this is easy to recommend to those for who don't need the most up to date sound. Horenstein's stereo version was one of his final recordings (Chandos). Maybe because of failing health, his grip on the proceedings is weaker and the climaxes flower less readily. This seems to have been a bad stretch for the London Symphony; they sound like a third-rate group, and the engineers homed in on the timpani at the expense of the winds and strings.

Reiner's stereo 1957 recording with the Vienna Philharmonic is one of the best (RCA, NA). He responded particularly well to *Death and Transfiguration,* giving it great tension without allowing any occluded climaxes or bloodbaths, though some may think that his lucidity comes at the expense of flexible phrasing. His 1950 mono rendition with the RCA Victor Orchestra is, of course, impeccably prepared (RCA). The amount of detail is impressive in the opening, but the tempos don't always mesh well further on, and his love of detail means a sense of cathartic release is never really achieved. The pickup orchestra impresses except in tonal blend, and the recording tends to accentuate the first desk players at the expense of the rest of the sections.

The perspectives are actually much better in **Stokowski**'s 1934 recording with the Philadelphians (RCA). This is a romantic, well-paced, string-based conception that never involves an ugly sound. Some of the sliding between pitches sounds anachronistic to modern ears, but the climaxes are splendidly sonorous, their majesty shining through the 78 rpms, which are fairly quiet if a little dim-sounding. In the introduction, **Monteux** coaxed impressively dark, old world sounds from the San Francisco Symphony strings in 1960. However, but the double-reed woodwinds were painfully thin, and the playing wasn't quite up to the better performances (RCA). The rich sound tends toward glare and blattiness in the climaxes.

Kempe impresses right off with his fine grading of dynamics and dovetailing of phrases (EMI). The climaxes are impeccably balanced (no insolent brass work here), yet typically for this conductor this Technicolor music never becomes a bloodbath. A truly noble performance; only the sound, very listenable but lacking in crispness and detail, gives pause. **Sinopoli** is more of a storyteller; a furious drum stroke announces the death throes, and the climaxes are grand. But there's nothing bombastic here; he has the patience of a great narrator, and doesn't rush the apexes (♦DG 423576). The quiet ending, particularly, has a special radiance. Sinopoli had a certain camaraderie with the New York Philharmonic, and they often sound luminous here.

Tennstedt is wonderful at the recitative-like music, the transitions that lie between death and transfiguration (EMI). This means the last, brass-led arrival of the idealism theme is a real event. Here and elsewhere, he can make Karajan sound almost noncommital. But the London Philharmonic, great as it sounds here, doesn't have quite the resplendent, organ-like tone of the Berlin (or even New York), and so the expertly prepared climaxes don't have quite the effect they might. While **Abbado** is great at sorting through the stylistic and esthetic duplicities of Mahler, he can seem less at home with the more straightforwardly "bourgeois" Strauss. His recording with the London Symphony is beautifully done, with no lack of sincerity, and is very knowingly paced, the spaciousness of the opening creating vivid expectations for what follows (DG). Yet there isn't quite the sense of humanity that marks the great renditions, and the interpretation is rather lightweight in emotion and empathy.

That said, it's very enjoyable and certainly to be preferred to many others, particularly **Dorati** and the Detroit Symphony, who move through the piece in fits and starts with no real long-range thinking (Decca/London). The best thing about this is the full-blooded sound, which gives a lot of presence to the lower brass. **Mata** and the Dallas Symphony, on the other hand, have a structural acumen similar to Abbado's with more obvious emotional outlay (♦RCA 60135). The orchestra's tone lacks Straussian glamor, and the chromatic rising figures in the lower strings (the incipient death pangs) are strangely feeble. Yet Mata's interpretation is strong enough to outweigh any such caveats—it's a real performance, full of detail. This was one of RCA's earliest digital recordings, and a good deal of care clearly went into it.

Szell takes a sectionalized approach not very different from Dorati's, and the transfiguration itself is unusually strict in time—maybe the conductor was saying we meet our redemption through a metronome? Apart from an over-prominent harp, the recording is warm and well proportioned (CBS/Sony). **Gielen** has the Cincinnati Symphony sounding better than it has during the more recent López-Cobos tenure (Vox, 2CD). The strings, in particular, play with great confidence, and this makes for a majestic final transfiguration. His orchestra sounds fine, with excellent blend and internal balances. There may not be the obvious emotional commitment of Karajan or Sinopoli, but anyone who takes a liking to the unusual bargain-priced program (Berg, Strauss, and Lutoslawski) will be happy with this.

Maazel has a special relationship with *Tod und Verklärung,* and his '60s version with the Philharmonia was a highlight of the Phase Four catalog, though the miking sounds contrived nowadays (Decca/London). Likewise, his remake with the Bavarian Radio Symphony is one of the best performances in his RCA cycle: a fine reading, if not the most individual or communicative. **Dohnányi** and the Vienna Philharmonic enjoy very fine sound, and this would be truly enjoyable solely for the gleaming orchestral sounds; as usual, he gets an unusually clean-limned sonority from the ensemble (Decca/London). It doesn't add up to very much as an interpretation, though; I don't feel that much emotional distance has been traveled between the first bars and last.

For this kind of non-interventionist performance, I prefer **Blomstedt** in San Francisco (♦Decca/London 448815, with his rather less convincing *Zarathustra*). The pained wind and string lines of the introduction are beautifully shaped, quite free. In the death throes and elsewhere, he's exceptionally intense, yet he never condescends to the music; his credentials as a Brucknerian mean the climaxes are convincingly articulated without preempting one another. As icing on the cake, the engineers give even more presence and weight to Blomstedt's orchestra than they did Dohnányi's. Blomstedt's earlier version is less committed—or more introverted, maybe—and wears its musicality less obviously, though the tone of the Dresden Staatskapelle is a bit sweeter and more cultured than the San Franciscans (Denon). The sound, too, tends to be more shallow and a bit drier.

Haitink also presents a valid middle of the road view (♦Philips 442283). The Concertgebouw oboe solos near the opening have exceptional breath control and support, and the death struggle becomes surprisingly passionate. The 1983 digital sound is fine, but ultimately it can't quite compare with Blomstedt's Decca or Previn's Telarc engineering. **Masur** and the New York Philharmonic have been recorded live, so prepare yourself for distant shuffles and stifled coughs (Teldec). Masur clearly enjoys and identifies with this early Strauss piece, and his orchestra sounds better than on many another Strauss outing. Yet the close miking gives the group a hulking, rather claustrophobic atmosphere; the wind solos and brass are a bit too forward to be believable.

Košler is very good but not distinctive (Naxos). The Slovak Philharmonic plays well but isn't one of the best orchestras in Naxos's stable; the brass, for one, tend to bray and the group's beautiful and coherent sound in pianissimos doesn't carry over into the climaxes. **Previn** and the Vienna Philharmonic have realistic and sonorous sound, the violins sweet above the stave in true Viennese style, the brass believably balanced with everyone else, and the timpani having just the right presence (Telarc). The interpretation, though, fails to make much of an impression. His 1980 reading with the Vienna had more poise and also more generalized, softer-edged sound (EMI). The reading even seems tired in a way that's not out of keeping with the music. With **Järvi**, the Scottish National wind solos are often ungrateful in tone and the interpretation doesn't have much vision and offers a rather sprawling conception of the score (Chandos). The sound is predictably good, though the orchestral tone tends to spread in climaxes and there could be more depth to the picture.

CONCERTOS

Horn. Strauss's two horn concertos were written at the beginning and end of his career, in 1883 and 1942. **Dennis Brain**'s verve and confidence still astonish almost half a century after he recorded them in 1957 (♦EMI 47834, with Hindemith's concerto). It's tempting to think that his cleanness and clarity have never been matched; others might exhibit more showmanship and panache and be more evocatively romantic in the slow movements, but certainly no one is more precise in the rhythms, articulations, and dynamic changes of the opening call of 2. The Philharmonia under Sawallisch are equally sharp and attentive, and the mono sound is excellent even if modern recordings inevitably give the soloist more presence. **Peter Damm** and Kempe (EMI) are relaxed. They make unfailingly beautiful sounds, but there isn't any audible interaction between conductor and soloist—the kind of quicksilver exchange of ideas that really makes these scores come alive. At times it almost sounds as if Damm had been dubbed in after the orchestral sessions. Nevertheless, many have enjoyed these performances, and the soloist's relatively fruity vibrato does give the music a certain luxuriance.

Tuckwell made classic recordings with Kertész and the London Symphony (♦Decca/London 460296, a twofer with Gulda in *Burleske,* Belkin in the Violin Concerto, Gordon Hunt in the Oboe Concerto, and a concerto by Strauss's father, Franz, described by Von Bülow as "the Joachim of the horn"). The soloist's manner is smooth and assured, and some have found him unresponsive to the more romantic, penetrating moments of 2. However, Kertész is so light on his feet that he inspires character left and right. Decca helps with plenty of presence for the orchestra. Tuckwell is a bit more forward in the mix in his 1991 remake with Ashkenazy and the Royal Philharmonic, which helps give the solo parts more character, though some of that is counteracted by the slightly slow tempos (Decca/London). While Ashkenazy supplies an agile if sometimes rather inert accompaniment, it's unquestionably the Hungarian who gives the delightful finale of 2 glitter and verve, the rhythms bristling with childlike energy.

For a round, full tone and affectionate, old-world character, **Hermann Baumann** proves very attractive (♦Philips 412237, with Weber's *Concertino* Op. 45). He has a bit more vibrato than British horn icons like Tuckwell and Brain, and is helped immensely by Masur's all-knowing, personality-laden accompaniments. The engineers give the Leipzig Gewandhaus a becoming warmth, the solo woodwinds distinctive in tone in the slow movements. These are probably the most amiable, immediately likeable performances on disc, though not the choice if chrome-plated virtuosity is what you're after. **Marie-Luis Neunecker,** an extraordinary young virtuoso with faultless technique, is heir to Dennis Brain's mantle (EMI, with Britten's *Serenade*). If anything, she has more spirit and variety of character, encompassing a greater contrast of smooth legato, cheeky clarion passages, and brassy near-growls. Ingo Metzmacher provides an alert backdrop, but I miss Masur's Dvořákian warmth and charm, not to mention Kertész's vim and vinegar.

Berlin Philharmonic first horns **Gerd Seifert** and **Norbert Hauptmann** offer the concertos as couplings for Mehta's *Alpine Symphony* (1 with Seifert) and *Heldenleben* (2 with Hauptmann). Hauptmann and Mehta are professional in 2, but also rather faceless (Sony). The close acoustics of the Berliner Philharmonie makes the *tuttis* sound busy. Seifert's 1 is a different matter: Soloist and conductor are more spontaneous, pressing ahead eagerly in the finale, and the horn has a less fat and "comfortable" tone. Hauptmann had already recorded 2 with the Berlin Philharmonic under Karajan, who burdens the orchestral part with too much interpretive and textural detail (DG, with *Don Quixote*). Cleveland Orchestra principal **Myron Bloom** recorded 1 with Szell, a performance remarkable for the close-knit integration of horn and ensemble and for Bloom's wonderful variety of sound—wide but not self-conscious, more characteristic of a solo player than an orchestral section member (♦Sony 63123, with the wonderful Szell/Fournier *Don Quixote*).

Oboe. Just about every record of the Oboe Concerto has something to offer, and reactions are likely to hinge on more subjective aspects, like the soloist's tone and phrasing. First, the fairly big and romantic conceptions, with players who are orchestra principals rather than soloists and thus party to conceptions that are basically symphonic.

Richard Woodhams, with Sawallisch and the Philadelphians, tends to make creamy sounds, with little of the "American" double-reed buzz that is an important aspect of Ray Still's tone, for example (EMI, with *Heldenleben*). Woodhams sometimes sounds as though he were playing a clarinet. As recorded, the Philadelphia Orchestra has a particularly healthy bass to their sound, and this clarity works nicely to give impetus to Sawallisch's genial and fairly relaxed take on the music.

From the opening string quavers, Karajan instills more rhythmic tension (♦DG 423888, with his 1971 *Metamorphosen* and Janowitz in *Four Last Songs*). He also seems to exert more control over Strauss's textures and dynamic changes. As part of this, his orchestra never gives any impression of heaviness, which is good considering the mellowness and rounded edges of DG's engineering. Karajan's soloist is Berlin principal **Lothar Koch,** smooth of delivery like Woodhams but with a little more buzz. This recording shows Karajan's consummate qualities as accompanist, following and leading at the same time, never even getting close to swamping the player, and never giving any feeling of marking time or treading water. **Manfred Clement** is the oboist with **Kempe** and the Dresden Staatskapelle (EMI). The soloist is assisted in the mix, which doesn't help the impression that there's not much communication going on between conductor and player. That said, if there's a work where the laid-back Kempe style is appropriate, it's this concerto. If only Clement were able to add some personality to the proceedings.

Holliger is one of the few touring solo oboists, and he infuses the solo line with more personality than heard elsewhere, accompanied by the Philharmonia under Waart (Philips, with the *Sonatinas* and other wind music). He also sounds much more the bright, soprano instrument than Woodhams and Koch. Holliger is unsurpassed in breath control and

breadth of phrasing. His tone is thin and nasal to these ears, however, and that often makes it hard to believe the lyricism of the music—and this concerto exceeds just about any other Strauss work, vocal or instrumental, in that respect. Holliger's second recording, with the Cincinnati Symphony, is brisk and workmanlike, with little or nothing to be heard of the autumnal Strauss (Vox). To make matters worse, he's recorded so closely that his key clicks are audible, and his tone is even more astringent than before.

Neil Black with Barenboim and the English Chamber Orchestra fails to make much of an impression (CBS/Sony). He doesn't have as much rhythmic alacrity as some others, and the conductor alternates between brusque *tuttis* and inertia. The sound is echoey and indistinct. **Ray Still,** veteran first chair of the Chicago Symphony, has just a touch of sharpness to his sound, in contrast with some of the European players (♦Virgin 61766). Richard Stamp imposes himself more than most conductors in this work; he makes the rhythmic insistences in Strauss's first movement almost obsessive at the climax. Some might want more obvious relaxation in this late score, though he certainly brings out the felicities of Strauss's minimalist orchestral scoring. **Gordon Hunt,** with Ashkenazy and the Berlin Radio Symphony, offers a fine account, the soloist exhibiting plenty of interpretive initiative as well as a sweet tone, and the conductor (and recording engineers) helping to clarify the strands of interaction between solo and orchestra. Next to Stamp and Still, the orchestra can sometimes sound deferential. Decca's sound is warm.

Violin. Strauss wrote this concerto at the age of 18, and it's far from his best work. Still, music that can sound like second-string Bruch truly comes alive in the hands of **Ulf Hoelscher,** abetted by Kempe and the Staatskapelle Dresden (♦EMI 64346). Hoelscher is helped by a very slight forward balance, and firm yet resonant backup from the Dresdeners. He isn't afraid to strain his tone in louder and high-lying passages. Next to this, **Belkin** and Ashkenazy can sound a little ponderous and bland, the violinist's tone smaller, but they're certainly enjoyable, particularly given the transparent and well-proportioned sound (Decca/London). **Sarah Chang** and Sawallisch lack crispness, and this in combination with their more temperate speeds can make the music sound labored. Chang does have a bit more personality than Belkin, though not quite the variety of color. The conductor tries for a Mozartian sound, rather than the tougher Beethovenian statement of Kempe. **Xue-Wei** and the London Philharmonic under Jane Glover are a bit slower still in I, and the soloist's tone is the thinnest of the four violinists considered here (♦ASV 780). But he compensates with lots of color and timbral liveliness, and this makes the solo line "speak" and helps give each movement more shape. Glover could have brought out more musical detail in the orchestra.

BALLET MUSIC

Le Bourgeois Gentilhomme. **Mata** and the Canadian National Arts Centre Orchestra are admirable in this suite adapted from Lully's music for the Molière play, but give the impression of holding the music at arm's length (RCA). The accenting tends to be heavy, almost clumsy at times; the sound is dry and reverberant. **Jordan** is more intimate and good humored (Erato, with his less recommendable *Metamorphosen*). There's some elegant and dynamic playing from his Paris pickup band, though not quite the ear-tickling variety Kempe and Krauss get from each number. **Reiner** doesn't have a parodistic bone in his body; the Chicago solos aren't blatant, but neither are they retiring (RCA). The clarity that served so well in the chamber-like textures of *Don Quixote* works against the on-the-sleeve charms of this score, and the recording comes up grainy on CD. **Maazel** is stiff rather than elegant or whimsical with members of the Vienna Philharmonic, and their sound is clattery (Decca/London).

The **Orpheus Chamber Orchestra** has a similar brilliance, but is more flexible in phrasing (♦DG 435871, with the Op. 86 *Divertimento*). They prove electrifying in the overture—though not in Maazel's heartless way—and the contrasting central section has plenty of warmth. This is delectable music-making, with everything clear yet without glossiness. Sometimes you wish the players would relax more, as **Kempe**'s Dresdeners often do (♦EMI 64346). Kempe shows an affectionate warmth for this score that eludes just about everyone else. You could wish for more transparency in the engineering, but the performance has an artlessness to inspire smiles. The playing is always elegant, without the up-front virtuosity of Orpheus or the anemic sonorities of Reiner.

Yet **Krauss** manages to outdo Kempe, thanks to the delightfully winsome sounds of the Vienna Philharmonic, especially the solo strings (♦Testament 1184, with his less consistent *Sinfonia Domestica*). Like the rest of Krauss's Decca's series, the mono sound is glassy and fairly shrill, but this is less of a problem for these chamber textures than in the larger scores. *Gentilhomme* premiered in Vienna, and there's more of that city in this music than in most other Strauss scores, so Krauss's sweet, pliant, *echt-Wienerisch* performance is a reference recording, and a most enjoyable one. **Marriner** is in his element, and his winning account with the Academy of St. Martin in the Fields really offers the best of all worlds (♦Philips 446696, with a generous helping of Strauss's orchestrations of Couperin). There is much of the Orpheus's bravado and rhythmic precision, but also Kempe's and Krauss's affection. With a group of virtuosos who play regularly together, there's more natural and easy balancing than with Jordan or Schwarz. Marriner always finds the right tempos and sense of scale, instilling uncommon transparency and grace in the Lully adaptations, and the recording is the most natural sounding of all.

Barenboim and the English Chamber Orchestra tend to be listless whenever they aren't mannered and brutal, and the harsh recording doesn't help matters (CBS/Sony). Then there's **Schwarz**, who offers seven additional numbers beyond the usual suite—about an extra half hour of music (♦Pro Arte 448). The original overture is shorter, and when Strauss converted his stage music into a concert suite, most of the pieces he jettisoned had vocal parts. It's good to have *all* the incidental music on disc—there's some charming and memorable music that fell between the cracks when Strauss and Hofmannsthal's original stage conception disintegrated, including a rare chance to hear the composer as exoticist (in "The Turkish Ceremony," the choral number). And if Schwarz's New York Chamber Symphony and chorus aren't entirely a match for Marriner's group or Orpheus, they have plenty of verve. The recording itself could be warmer.

Josephslegende is the most ambitious of Strauss's ballets, written for Diaghilev in 1914 to a scenario by Hofmannsthal, and it's music to investigate if you want to go beyond the tone poems. It's usually heard as a 24-minute "symphonic fragment," and was recorded thus by **Schwarz** and the Seattle Symphony, in an outstanding performance with slightly boomy acoustics as the only quibble (♦Delos 3082, with his equally fine *Sinfonia Domestica*). He's at his absolute best in Strauss's more kaleidoscopic vein, music without the heavy Nietzschean baggage; he makes the piece glitter. **Kempe** also taped the fragment with the Dresden Staatskapelle in a reading that sometimes finds the orchestra in less than optimal form (EMI). The sound, too, tends to cloud over in climaxes.

So Schwarz is the recommendation for the shortened score, but all Straussians will want to hear the complete ballet. The orchestra is one of Strauss's largest, just about every bar is a delightfully orchestrated morsel of the composer in his prime, and the usual "symphonic fragment" leaves out some of the most erotic and highly charged numbers. **Sinopoli** recorded the complete ballet, all 64 minutes of it, with the Staatskapelle Dresden (♦DG 463493). He can sometimes make the music heavy and menacing, aligning it with the "Dance of the Seven Veils" or the maniacal apotheosis that ends *Elektra* (DG). But there's no shortage of lightness, the Dresden orchestra again proves itself second to none, and the sound is outstanding.

Schlagobers, "a merry Vienna ballet in two acts," also uses a large orchestra. The post-*Nutcracker* scenario set in a Viennese confectioner's shop didn't succeed with the Austro-German public in the lean and hungry mid-'20s, and it also failed to draw any distinctive music from Strauss—he often switches into a generic kind of Johann Strauss balletic mode. There's always much to enjoy of his inimitable genius for orchestration, even if it becomes the main course rather than the condiment. **Hiroshi Wakasugi** manages to get a very good semblance of Vienna sound from his fairly light-toned Tokyo Metropolitan Symphony (Denon). Still, he doesn't exactly alchemize the work, as Gerard Schwarz might if he were to pick it up.

Verklungene Feste was a compilation of orchestrated music by Couperin that Strauss wrote for Krauss in 1941. He added six new arrangements to his 1923 *Dance Suite after Couperin;* two additional orchestrations were added a bit later for *Divertimento*. While various conductors and ensembles have recorded those two scores, **Wakasugi** has reconstructed the 1943 ballet. His disc with the Tokyo Metropolitan Symphony sounds heavy and dutiful, out of sorts with the French baroque idiom. Denon's sound is also more edgy than in their *Schlagobers* production. It's better to compile your own *Verklungene Feste* with **Kempe** in the Dance Suite (EMI) and the **Orpheus Chamber Orchestra** in the *Divertimento* (♦DG 435871, with their *Bourgeois Gentilhomme*). Both those performances are more stylistically aware, with some transparency, and Kempe's harpsichord is actually audible from time to time in the Dance Suite.

MUSIC FROM THE OPERAS

Der Rosenkavalier. The various suites and anonymously compiled medleys of R*osenkavalier* music are legion as couplings, and it's hard to keep up with the available versions. For the first waltz suite, it's difficult to beat **Reiner,** particularly on account of some heroic Chicago horn playing (RCA). He's more stylish than **Mehta** and the Berlin Philharmonic, who are laid-back in a comfortable, cocooned-in-eiderdown (or narcoticized?) kind of way (Sony). **Maazel** recorded a much more suave and stylish Vienna Philharmonic rendition of the first waltz suite in 1967, notable for its transparency and utter lack of bombast (Decca/London). **Košler** did the first waltz set with the Slovak Philharmonic, a measured and careful reading that nevertheless has some orchestral mistakes in it (Naxos). **Schwarz** recorded both sets of waltzes with the Seattle Symphony, accounts that are more flexible than Reiner's but also—on record, at least—a bit veiled in tone and sometimes a touch sleepy musically (Delos). For idiomatic elegance in the first waltz set, **Kempe** and his Dresdeners are irreplaceable (♦EMI 64346). The strength in mellowness of the Dresden violas and cellos makes a world of difference, and there's warmth and affection lavished on every bar.

Contrary to legend, not all of *Rosenkavalier* is in three-four time.

More satisfying than the waltz suites is one of the more comprehensive third-party compilations, which run to about 24 minutes of pure and delicious Hapsburg decadence. It's impossible to resist **Järvi**'s high spirits or the Scottish National Orchestra's ecstatic, gleaming tones (♦Chandos 8758). The sound, too, is less reverberant than in the coupled *Capriccio* selections. The Bavarian Radio Symphony has a more streamlined and controlled sound in **Maazel**'s similar compilation (RCA, with *Zarathustra*). Typically for him, there are many felicities of phrasing, blend, and balance; there's no lack of high spirits, and he also knows when and where to be delicate with the music. RCA's sound, though, tends to be ungratefully thin next to Chandos's.

López-Cobos and the Cincinnati Symphony take a more nostalgic, autumnal perspective (Telarc). In tone and rhythm the orchestra isn't the equal of Järvi's or Maazel's, not to mention the Vienna Philharmonic, and we're audibly farther away from a true Vienna style. But Telarc's deep, transparent, and colorful sound makes the best possible case for the performance. Three discs of orchestral suites and medleys come from **Previn** and the Vienna Philharmonic (♦DG 437790), **Mehta** and the Berlin Philharmonic (Sony), and **Tate** and the Rotterdam Philharmonic (EMI). **Previn** is at the Mecca of Viennese style, the Musikverein, and he doesn't exactly languish; typically, the Vienna Philharmonic somehow proves more relaxed, colorful, and stylish than any other ensemble on earth. The microphones are too close, but this helps convey the ecstasy of the music-making. For the extended suite, I'd choose Previn for sheer style, Järvi for the well-proportioned sound.

Other operas. Strauss's mastery of the orchestra made it inevitable that suites would be drawn from a number of the operas. **Mehta** and the Berlin Philharmonic are consistently stylish and enjoyable in arrangements from *Rosenkavalier, Die Liebe der Danae, Intermezzo,* and *Die Frau ohne Schatten* but, as often with this partnership, there's a comfy gloss to the performances that prevents them from going much below the surface of the music (Sony). **Previn,** on the other hand, never sounds automatic in a more varied program with the Vienna Philharmonic of the "Dance of the Seven Veils" and music from *Rosenkavalier, Intermezzo* and *Capriccio.* Especially in the 24-minute "Four Symphonic Interludes" from *Intermezzo,* the Viennese are both glamorous and achingly beautiful (♦DG 437790). The orchestra has that unmistakable Viennese glimmer, though the sound is again a bit shallow, the orchestra closely observed. **Tate** is perfectly at home in the nervous "Reisefieber" that begins the *Intermezzo* music and opens his disc (EMI). He's wonderfully incisive with Strauss's rhythms, but the slower and more lyric numbers are lethargic and shapeless, the phrasing nonexistent.

Other orchestral extracts can be found as filler in various discs. The dark, trombone-heavy coloring of much of *Die Frau ohne Schatten* comes across imposingly in Krauss's compilation from that opera— and here **Oue** and the Minnesota Orchestra are not to be missed, partly on account of the wonderful sound and clarity of the percussion (♦Reference 83, with their outstanding *Heldenleben*). By comparison, **Schwarz** and the Seattle Symphony are pretty lightweight in an opera where weight of tone and utterance are important (♦Delos 3109). Yet he brings out a vein of lyrical beauty, notable right away with the lovely phrasing of the major-mode string melody after the opening chords— and surely the Seattle violins and horns have never sounded better. In the four interludes from *Intermezzo,* Previn's main competition comes from **Järvi** and the Detroit Symphony (Chandos, with Schmidt's Symphony 1). He tends to be more forceful and emphatic, introducing a kind

of energy that's not always idiomatic. **Schwarz** is, as usual, more lyric and transparent—in this case, even a bit dull (Delos).

Cello sonata. Strauss wrote this sonata at the age of 19, and it's unfairly neglected: Considering the wealth of musical ideas and expert writing, it's gratifying for both cello and piano. The only two widely available recordings are by **Rostropovich** and **Ma,** and my choice hinges on what the pianist does with the keyboard part, which is much more than accessory. Ma and Ax make a true partnership (♦CBS 44980, with Britten's sonata) while Rostropovich's Vasso Devetzi sounds more the accompanist (EMI, with a pair of Beethoven's fairly insipid variations). Both are admirable, but Ma and Ax strike me as more inside the piece, with an especially intimate account of the slow movement. Rostropovich is fairly chilly and pushes the music rather hard.

Violin sonata. Strauss's swaggering sonata, a product of his 23rd year, was a **Heifetz** favorite, and he left three recordings. In several respects the second (with longtime accompanist Brooks Smith, taped in 1954) is the best, with a bit more poise than the others (♦RCA 61763, with chamber works by Brahms and Dohnányi). The sound also finds the best compromise between smoothness and dynamism, while the 78s of the 1934 performance with pianist Arpad Sandor aren't always kind to Heifetz's unique, silky tone (♦RCA 61733). Where the 1934 version is better, though, is in Sandor's spontaneity; Smith was so firmly under the great violinist's thumb that their collaborations were more strictly planned solo vehicles than spur-of-the-moment interactions. Heifetz was also audibly more of a romantic in 1934 than 20 years later, his tone and vibrato slightly richer. The 1972 version is from Heifetz's final recital, and the "live" situation means the sound is boxy if still acceptable. (RCA also includes *everything,* including tuning between movements and the occasional imprecision.) Even at age 72, the Heifetz magic was still intact, though the vibrato sounds less inhibited in the other two recordings.

It's cruel to come to **Sarah Chang** after Heifetz, but her tone color is too uniform—as if applied with a spray can—while Heifetz shakes myriad colors from his sleeve (EMI). Her accompanist, Sawallisch, doesn't exude the confidence of Smith (let alone Sandor) in the majestic piano opening, where the quick note values should be sharp and mercurial. Because of these and other shortcomings, the performance outstays its welcome. If **Kremer**'s enervated (but not monochromatic) tone is an unlikely vehicle for a youthful piece by an arch-romantic, he turns that unsuitability to his benefit by capitalizing on the music's "modern" rhythmic whims instead of its 19th-century luxuriance (♦DG 453440). In the outer movements, he and pianist Oleg Maisenberg dispatch the young Strauss's rhythms with the most precise weighting. This is engrossing musicianship.

On the surface, **Kyung-Wha Chung** and Zimerman are more idiomatic (DG). They're freer with rubato, and respond more to the music's harmonic and melodic richness. They offer beautiful playing and impeccable musicianship, yet it must be said they gloss over the rhythmic and narrative quirkiness in the music, as in the strange piano interjections in I. **Sitkovetsky** and Pavel Gililov hear the restlessness as a kind of *Sturm und Drang* storminess that lurks just below the surface, and in that sense, this is a Brahmsian reading (♦Virgin 61766, a twofer). With vibrant and sometimes echoey sound, their performance is certainly distinctive and exciting.

PIANO MUSIC

Again these are works by a teenage composer. The impossible choice rests between **Stefan Vladar** (Koch) and **Glenn Gould** (CBS/Sony), the former beautifully turned but conventionally Schumannesque, the latter brilliant and often exasperating. Gould loved Strauss's music, and he clearly felt deeply about the Op. 5 Sonata and Five Pieces Op. 3, the items on his disc. He felt so strongly about the Largo from Op. 3 that he dragged it out to a funereal 10 minutes while Vladar takes six. And so it goes: Gould never really went as far with these stylistic deviations as he did with his Mozart, yet the more distantly recorded Vladar is certainly easier to listen to. What might really direct inquiring minds to the Gould disc, besides the great pianism, is his dramatic and Beethovenian account of the outer movements of the sonata. Vladar includes *Stimmungsbilder,* which as Schumannesque character pieces (complete with titles) might have appealed less to Gould. **Hobson** also taped *Stimmungsbilder,* and his renditions are more intimate than Vladar's; indeed, he renders these subtle miniatures perfectly (♦Arabesque 6567, with his less dependable *Burleske* and *Parergon*).   ASHBY

OPERAS

The Strauss operas were almost all written in this century, and because they resisted falling into 78-rpm-sized chunks, the best recordings came after the LP was developed. Shortly after, in fact: Most of my first choices were recorded before 1970. This isn't old-fogeyism on my part. The supply of soaring Straussian sopranos, at home with the language and style of the operas, has dwindled sharply in the past two decades. The older performers were simply more personable and accomplished, and the technology of the '50s and '60s captured their voices with substantial presence and fidelity. Of course, Strauss's orchestra is important too, and while I feel that the sound fabricated by RCA's engineers for Fritz Reiner's '50s recordings, or by Decca's John Culshaw in the '60s, is as stunning and detailed as anyone could want, other listeners may insist on state-of-the-art digitalization. If that's the case, the most recent recommendable recordings should be satisfying.

Salome. Strauss (tongue in cheek?) wanted Salome to be a "16-year-old princess with the voice of Isolde." He couldn't quite write it that way and regarded the Isolde part of the description as more practicable. A slimmer voice with ample thrust and focus will also do, and the opera's recordings allow us to hear various types of sopranos surmounting the role's obstacles.

Nilsson with Solti is the most assured of all (♦London 414414, 2CD). Solti's performance is loud, powerful, bloodcurdling; something is always happening, though I don't mean to imply that it's vulgar or unsubtle. The Vienna Philharmonic plays wonderfully, and the listener never feels the orchestra or conductor are losing control. Nilsson's Salome is the most accurately, securely sung on records. Her voice flows forth wherever and whenever she wants it, at every dynamic level, and easily rides over the orchestra. She is, perhaps, a cool singer, the words clear and insinuating but understated. She never sounds uninvolved, however, and the eruptions of tone in the Final Scene are overwhelming. Her Jochanaan is the virile and handsome-sounding Wächter and her Herod is the egregiously hammy Stolze.

For my second choice, I'd go for something completely different: Leinsdorf's account with **Caballé** (♦RCA 6644, 2CD). She's the most lyrical and sensuous of Salomes; no one sings more beautifully. She has an uncanny knack for accenting the musical line in exactly the right places, and she can soar brightly above the orchestra. Milnes is an eager young Jochanaan, Richard Lewis a restrained Herod, and Resnik a venomous, impatient Herodias. Leinsdorf is stolid but correct.

Karajan finds more color and detail in the score, and the Vienna Philharmonic plays with proprietary confidence (♦EMI 67080, 2CD).

Behrens is also a lyrical Salome, and she's a good vocal actress who relishes the words. Her upper range is more impressive than her middle, however. Van Dam's noble bearing and bass-baritone timbre are made to order for the implacable Prophet. **Studer** offers a more evenly sung Princess with Sinopoli, and her voice has a hot, sultry quality well suited to the character (♦DG 431810, 2CD). Rysanek, a riveting Salome on stage (see below), is a chilling Herodias, and Terfel is a perfervid Jochanaan. The music loses momentum at odd moments, but that's typical of Sinopoli and doesn't do too much damage here.

Christel Goltz was an acclaimed Salome in the '50s, and she recorded the role three times. Most effective is the 1954 performance led by Clemens Krauss (London), with Patzak a spooky, obsessive Herod and Dermota setting a standard for Narraboth. Goltz's voice actually has a touch of girlishness in it, and she flings it out with vigor. She's competent and interesting, more persuasive than the calculating **Norman,** the squally **Marton** (a really ugly performance), and the over-parted **Catherine Malfitano,** none of whom should have recorded the role. I remember **Gwyneth Jones** as an effective Salome in the theater, but her singing with Böhm is too often inaccurate (DG).

The youngest-sounding Salomes are Anja Silja and Inga Nielsen. **Nielsen** recorded the role in the studio under Schønwandt in 1999 (Chandos). She sounds sweet and ingenuous, and her singing at soft and medium levels is lovely. When more volume is required, she can't produce it, and the high, expansive climaxes find her sounding and pretty desperate. The recording has a solid Jochanaan in Robert Hale and an unusually dignified Herod in Reiner Goldberg. Herodias is played by **Silja,** who was an imprudent Salome in her salad days. Myto has preserved a performance staged in 1965, when the soprano was in her '20s. She must have been something to see, and her acting skills are vividly discernible, but she's no more able to slice through the orchestra than Nielsen. Her Narraboth is **Wunderlich,** as striking as Dermota but with more honey in his voice. Wächter is a lyric Jochanaan with strong top notes.

Next to these two miscast lyric sopranos, **Rysanek** comes on like a blast furnace. She's a knowing, masterful princess; you don't believe for a moment that she's a young girl. She's capable of delicate pianissimos and flexible, subtle shadings, and her blazing upper range is matchlessly huge and thrilling. She may not be unswervingly accurate, but no one else hurls out lightning bolts of sound in quite the same way. At the Vienna Opera in 1972, her conductor was Böhm; once again, Wächter sang Jochaanan. The stereo sound is fairly good but not ideally clean (♦RCA 69430).

Two recordings of the Final Scene belong in every collection. **Borkh** was a softer, more feminine Salome than Nilsson, and she's heard to best advantage with Reiner, even though the conductor and his Chicago Symphony pretty much upstage her (♦RCA 60874). The orchestra explodes with volcanic force at the climax, but the clarity and control remain astonishing. **Welitsch,** the most sensational Salome of her time, also recorded the Final Scene with Reiner (Sony), and again with von Matačič (EMI). Both recordings convey her unique suitability for the role. The timbre is bright and womanly, with enough thrust and focus to cleave through the orchestral clamor but still not wound the ears. Like Nilsson, Welitsch sounds preternaturally unruffled as she pours out her voice with complete abandon and no hint of strain.

An appreciative nod, finally, to the most unusual *Salome* recording. Shortly after completing the opera, Strauss, in collaboration with Romain Rolland, decided to write a French version. He wanted the text to adhere as closely as possible to Oscar Wilde's original and altered the vocal lines in the score to fit the French words. The differences are slight but often jarring. The one available recording is led by **Nagano** (Virgin). Van Dam is a natural for the French Jochanaan, even if the words have less bite than they do in German. (It's easier to sink your teeth into "Du bist verflucht" than "Tu es maudite.") The title role is sung with steely determination by Karen Huffstodt, who is efficient rather than sensuous.

Elektra. Once again, there's no getting around Solti (♦London 417345, 2CD). He and **Nilsson** leave you exhausted, and that's exactly what should happen. Nilsson's power and security are awesome; no one in recent years has matched her. She has a formidable opponent in Resnik's regal, malicious Klytämnestra, though it's better acted than sung. Chrysothemis is the fragile Marie Collier, vulnerable beyond the demands of the drama. She reaches the notes easily enough, but the voice has no real power and nothing is left in reserve. Tom Krause is a sturdy Orestes, and Solti's orgasm-a-minute conducting isn't inappropriate in this opera. When he comes to a Big Moment, he lets you know it, not by putting on the brakes but by asking the orchestra to play more intensely. The Vienna Philharmonic never sounds discomfited, and the 1966 sound is still a marvel.

Böhm and the Dresden Staatskapelle are more subdued (♦DG 445329, 2CD). **Borkh** is a warmer, more womanly Elektra than Nilsson. She doesn't have the same vocal strength, but she turns to dramatic ends the desperation that understandably creeps into her voice from time to time. Jean Madeira's Klytämnestra is deeper and richer than Resnik's but less pointed, Fischer-Dieskau is an unusually lyrical Orestes, and Marianne Schech is a competent Chrysothemis. What I admire most about this performance is the clarity of the words; what I should deplore is the omission of part of the second Elektra-Chrysothemis scene (a standard cut), but I don't.

Ozawa's recording has excellent sound and one of the most gripping of all mother-daughter confrontations (Philips). Both **Behrens** and Ludwig are riveting vocal actresses, but both (it must be ungallantly added) were a bit over the hill. Ludwig is still in fairly good shape, but Behrens's voice lacks the solid core of Nilsson's. Her top notes shine forth like laser beams, but she comes too close to speech in many of the low-lying passages. You stay with her nonetheless, even though she's drained and wobbling well before the end of the opera. She's more interesting than the heaving Marton with Sawallisch (EMI), the uneven **Deborah Polaski** with Barenboim (Teldec), and the fairly steady but almost unintelligible **Alessandra Marc** with Sinopoli.

Sawallisch's performance is uncut, and I must admire **Marton,** at least, for learning the unfamiliar passages. She varies her dynamics only from loud to louder, however, and rides roughshod over the most lyrical passages. It's a shame, because Sawallisch has a richly sung Klytämnestra in Lipovšek, softer and less vitriolic than the norm, and he also has in Studer the best Chrysothemis on commercial discs. Her voice is shining, well-focused, and reliably produced, and if her ardor seems at odds with a certain lack of comprehension, that suits the character. Voigt, with Sinopoli, sings about as well as Studer but sounds anonymous.

Rysanek was an incomparable Chrysothemis, and she can be heard to best advantage in an inexpensive recording of a 1953 Cologne broadcast led by the capable Richard Kraus (Gala 100512, 2CD). The monaural sound is remarkably good though certainly limited. Rysanek's intensity was absolutely transfixing, and so were the sounds she could pour out in her upper range. On top, she produced even more volume than Nilsson, and while a mono recording from the '50s won't accurately con-

vey the true size of the unleashed Rysanek voice, you'll certainly get the idea. Her Elektra is Varnay, always a vivid, perspicacious actress (with a rather cutting voice); Hotter is the imposing and mysterious Orestes.

Like Varnay before her, Rysanek sang Klytämnestra late in her career, but she also undertook the role of Elektra once (with Varnay playing her mother!), for a video performance led by Böhm (♦London 071500; excerpts on Orfeo 504991). It's a must for *Elektra* collectors. Rysanek's vocal splendor rivals that of her old partner Nilsson, and she's more blazingly intense. The stereo sound is excellent, and the uniqueness of the performance makes it urgently recommendable even in its video format.

Reiner and **Borkh** (RCA), with the always-perceptive Schöffler as Orestes, again demand attention in two excerpts: the Recognition and Final Scenes. Reiner can be best appreciated, I think, in comparison with Sinopoli, who draws louder sounds out of his orchestra (the Vienna Philharmonic) but not more precise playing. At the moment when Elektra recognizes her brother, Sinopoli is all sound and fury, and you know what that signifies. Reiner's orchestral sonorities are almost as immense, and far more expressive.

Der Rosenkavalier. Erich Kleiber's recording set an extraordinarily high standard (♦London 425950, 3CD). No one has yet bettered Jurinac's Octavian or Ludwig Weber's Ochs. Jurinac's boyish eagerness almost convinces you she's really a young man, yet her singing is never less than luminously beautiful. She creates an endearing, specific character, and she's such a miraculous vocal actress she actually persuades you Mariandel is a boy impersonating a girl. Weber's deep, rolling bass and colorful declamation make him a vivid Ochs, a boor who still has the trappings of an aristocrat. Gueden's irrepressible Sophie has spirit and a rather sharp tongue. She sings flawlessly, but ingenuousness isn't quite there.

Kleiber conducts with a real feeling for the music's lilt and flow. Like his son Carlos (who doesn't make enough opera recordings), he has an uncanny ability to get the orchestra (here the Vienna Philharmonic) to sing. The smaller roles are in practiced hands, but there are two problems: the monaural sound and Maria Reining's Marschallin. Reining was a classy singer who often performed with Strauss himself, but she was past her prime in 1954. Her pale voice is just a little too threadbare—I admire what she tries to do with it, but it won't respond with any tonal fullness. It's true Octavian and Ochs do most of the singing, but the Marschallin is still at the opera's heart, and no performance can be satisfying with a poor one.

Schwarzkopf with **Karajan** was a much healthier, more resourceful Marschallin (♦EMI 49354, 3CD). She has presence and personality, and she pays meticulous attention to textual nuance. Some listeners will find her too artificial, but she certainly creates a well-defined character, and has the sense to ease up on the inflections when the line has to soar. Ludwig sumptuously fleshes out Octavian's music but sounds far more feminine than Jurinac. Stich-Randall's Sophie has a rarefied purity, but I wish she didn't bleach all the color out of her tone. Otto Edelmann is a routine Ochs, far less plush than Weber. Wächter is a vibrant Faninal, and Gedda sings the tenor aria gracefully. Many of the *Rosenkavalier* recordings acknowledge tradition by casting veteran singers in cameo roles, and here we have Welitsch as Sophie's duenna. Karajan conducts elegantly and supports his singers grandly, really bolstering them at their big moments. The stereo sound has been nicely refurbished for CD. Avoid the mono issue released to indulge Schwarzkopf, who fancied it flattered her voice.

Karajan's second recording (1982; DG) has a great Ochs in Moll, but the ladies aren't on the same level. At this point in his career, the conductor was apparently more comfortable working with his protégés than with great singers. DG passed over a studio *Rosenkavalier* in favor of a 1969 Salzburg performance. Ludwig was the Marschallin, a role she also recorded under **Bernstein** (Sony). Her bottom notes are solid and she can reach the top ones, but I prefer the timbre of a true soprano. **Böhm**'s 1969 Octavian is another mezzo, Troyanos, and that really throws the listener off balance. In both recordings, Ludwig sounds rather matronly and unglamorous, and the supporting casts, aside from Bernstein's Sophie (Popp), need not detain us.

Solti's *Rosenkavalier* sounded spectacular in its day and still does (♦London 417493, 3CD). Crespin's Marschallin is more aloof than Schwarzkopf's and to me more appealing. She shapes the words lucidly, has no eccentric mannerisms, and conveys a more aristocratic (but never an unfeeling) aura. Her vocalism has a few bumpy spots but the big voice is always pleasing. Donath's Sophie may be the best on records. She's fresh, girlish, and enthusiastic; her top notes come easily and never seem detached from the rest of the voice. You readily understand why she would turn a young man's head. Minton's Octavian is strongly sung but not memorably individual, and Manfred Jungwirth's Ochs is something of a phenomenon in that he has very little voice to work with but knows how to make us hang on every word. The Italian tenor is Pavarotti, more toilsome than Gedda or Dermota (who turns up on Solti's recording as a clarion Landlord). After his harrowing accounts of *Salome* and *Elektra,* Solti shows he knows how to relax, and he underlines the big moments by having the orchestra dig in and play with more feeling (not just more loudly or slowly).

The best-sounding recording is **Haitink**'s (♦EMI 54259, 3CD). The conductor is on the phlegmatic side, but the Dresden Staatskapelle is as quintessential a Strauss orchestra as the Vienna Philharmonic. Te Kanawa sings with lovely, creamy tone but doesn't etch the words sharply enough in the memory. Rydl's Ochs is the strongest cast member, even if he lacks the timbral rotundity of Moll and Weber. Hendricks's pretty Sophie is sometimes just a little flat on top, and von Otter's Octavian is well sung but leaves no impression whatsoever.

EMI's legendary 1933 abridgement, led by **Robert Heger,** is the Parthenon of *Rosenkavaliers,* a remnant that still suggests the splendid whole. Lotte Lehmann, Elisabeth Schumann, Maria Olczewska, and Richard Mayr sing with an assurance and authority that few of their successors have duplicated. My favorite Marschallin on the complete recordings is Crespin, but another interpreter very much like her (or the other way around) is Lisa della Casa. No other soprano, aside from Rysanek, served Strauss's cause so devotedly, yet she left us too few studio recordings. A 1960 Salzburg performance, led by **Karajan,** has finally been released officially (♦DG 453200; also Arkadia and Gala). Joining her are familiar *Rosenkavalier* stalwarts: Jurinac, Gueden, Edelmann. A better-recorded sample of her Marschallin is in Berlin 0090012. Even though we get only highlights, I recommend them warmly for the sake of her disarmingly pure voice, her perfect ladylike poise, and the unemphatic clarity of her words.

Since I'm recommending excerpts, let me cast my net a little wider in another direction to include a sensational performance of the Act 1 tenor aria. A 1965 Munich broadcast not only preserves the touching Marschallin of the underrated American soprano Claire Watson but also a star turn from **Wunderlich** in the aria that had (on sundry recordings) each of the Three Tenors sweating (Orfeo 425963). Queen Elizabeth II attended the performance, and it was reported that when Wunderlich

started to sing, she sat up and took notice, and raised the royal binoculars. You will, metaphorically, do exactly the same.

Ariadne auf Naxos. Strauss returned again and again to mythological subjects after *Der Rosenkavalier. Ariadne* leans in that direction, but the world of *Rosenkavalier* still trails after it. The final version (the one generally played) is the most peculiarly constructed of the Strauss operas. The Prologue is set in the house of the richest man in Vienna, and only one of its main characters (Zerbinetta) also makes the trip to the island of Naxos for the opera proper, which takes place, in effect, just down the hall. The singers in the conversational Prologue must seem like real human beings; the leads in the opera act in a more contrived fashion, unshaken even by the antics of the *commedia dell'arte* troupe around them. At least four accomplished singers are required to put the opera across, and two of them (the Composer and Zerbinetta) must be fine actors as well.

Karajan's recording (already reissued three times on CD) is the one I'd take to my desert isle, mono sound and all (♦EMI 67007, 2CD). The conductor knows exactly how to balance the score's buoyancy and grandeur, and the Philharmonia plays superbly. Schwarzkopf, that great mistress of operatic artifice, is a stunning Ariadne, her lines carefully shaped, and though her top notes could be more expansive, they're still bright and shining. Seefried's Composer is one of my favorite operatic creations. She immerses herself in the role completely, delivers the words with miraculous spontaneity, and sings with an enchanting freshness. Streich's captivating Zerbinetta tosses off the coloratura effortlessly, and there are some unforgettable vignettes from the supporting players. Prey is a warm, solicitous Harlekin, and Cuenod sings the Dancing Master's brief solo with an unforgettable dandyish flamboyance. Rudolf Schock's strangulated Bacchus is competent but of a lower order of achievement.

The Ariadne of Rysanek, on the other hand, glories in the highest passages, where her voice takes off like a rocket (London). Her conductor is **Leinsdorf,** who rushes through the comedians' music as if he wants to sweep the intruders off the stage, and her Bacchus is Jan Peerce, who can reach his top notes easily but never sounds like a *junger Gott.* Roberta Peters has the agility for Zerbinetta, but her upper and middle registers are poorly matched. Jurinac's Composer, however, is almost on the Seefried level. It's as beautifully sung, but the words aren't as crisp. A second London recording, led by **Solti** in 1977, came too late in the day for Leontyne Price, who should have been a wonderful Ariadne.

Kempe's *Ariadne* is the best of the stereo recordings (♦EMI 64159, 2CD). Janowitz is more sumptuous than Schwarzkopf. Her voice has more strength on top, although its tight focus sometimes constricts the vowels so that the words aren't as clear as they ought to be. It's still a gorgeous piece of singing. His Bacchus, James King, doesn't make his music sound either facile or graceful, but at least his voice has some youthful ring. Zylis-Gara and Silvia Geszty sing efficiently, and sometimes beautifully, as the Composer and Zerbinetta, and once again Prey is an exemplary Harlekin. The conductor, leading the Dresden State orchestra, was a great Straussian, as attentive to detail as Karajan.

The soprano who sings her lines most lucidly is della Casa, the Ariadne of a 1954 Salzburg performance led by **Böhm** (DG 445332; Gala 100513). Once again, DG passed up his unremarkable studio recording in favor of a far more interesting account. Seefried is still a peerless Composer, Schock (alas) still a thuggish Bacchus. Gueden's Zerbinetta is precise, sexy, and keenly focused.

Levine has the sprightly Zerbinetta of Battle, the Music Master of veteran Prey, and the playing of the Vienna Philharmonic to commend it, but not much else (DG). His Ariadne, Tomowa-Sintow, has a strong top but a jumbled, tremulous middle. More engaging is **Masur** (Philips). Norman's acting captures to perfection the self-centered, self-pitying Ariadne, but her voice, despite its voluptuousness in the middle, doesn't soar freely on top; she delivers less than she promises. Gruberová is a fluent Zerbinetta, and Varady's Composer has gleaming top notes, though her diction is peculiar. Paul Frey is a capable Bacchus, Bär a velvety Harlekin, and Fischer-Dieskau an eloquent but hard-pressed and often wobbly Music Master. We could have used a hybrid of the two.

In a class by itself is **Nagano**'s recording of something approximating the original version of *Ariadne,* without the Prologue (Virgin). Margaret Price (like Leontyne) waited too long to record Ariadne, but her customary poise remains intact. Zerbinetta has a larger role than she does in the revision, and Sumi Jo is sufficiently agile but charmless. Gösta Winbergh is probably the best Bacchus of all. His lyrical singing makes the strenuous music flow as smoothly as possible.

Die Frau ohne Schatten.

Die Frau ohne Schatten. Strauss and Hoffmannsthal regarded *Der Rosenkavalier* as an opera in a Mozartian vein, their own *Figaro,* as it were. *Die Frau ohne Schatten* (which they wryly called "Frosch" for short) was to be their *Zauberflöte.* It exists in a similar fairy-tale world, but its ponderous, convoluted libretto is absurd. The story is too long, weighed down by too much Straussian din and babble, but the music at its best is glorious, and it deserves its place in the repertory. That it became a repertory piece at all is probably due in large part to the advocacy of its tireless champions in the '50s and '60s — Böhm, Rysanek, Ludwig, King, and Walter Berry. I don't believe they ever performed the opera complete, and it wasn't until 1987 that we were able to hear all the music, when Sawallisch recorded it — but more of him anon.

Pride of place must go to **Böhm,** whose slightly abridged 1955 recording with the Vienna Philharmonic was a revelation (♦London 425981, 3CD). Rysanek pretty much owned the role of the Empress for a good quarter-century, and her febrile intensity and soaring high notes remain incomparable. Schöffler is a humane, eloquent Barak, Hopf a hard-working but not insensitive Emperor. Christel Goltz and Elisabeth Höngen are on the squally side as the Dyer's Wife and the Nurse, but they hurl out the words with such conviction they make us listen.

A 1977 Böhm performance was stereophonically recorded live in Vienna (♦DG 445325, 3CD), and it brought Rysanek together with Berry (a warm, dignified Barak — one of his best roles) and King (noble but not entirely comfortable). It was about a decade too late for all of them, and Böhm truncated the score even more than he did in 1955, but the singers are still pretty exciting. Nilsson, rather than Ludwig, is the Färberin, a role she undertook late in her career. Both she and Rysanek are striking (if less than precise), and it's good to hear them together again in hearty competition. (One of them — I wouldn't bet on it but I think it's Nilsson — holds on to the final high C just a fraction of a second longer than the other.) Ludwig should have recorded the Färberin in the studio. The fullest memento we have of her is another live and very incomplete performance led by **Karajan,** where she's joined by Rysanek, Berry, and Jess Thomas (DG). She's assertive and down-to-earth, but she knows how to make her music as shapely as possible, especially in the upper reaches.

Sawallisch has Studer as the Empress, a worthy successor to Rysanek (EMI). She doesn't manifest the same sort of identification with the role and she can't match the sunbursts of tone at the top, but she sings strongly and urgently. Hanna Schwarz is the first satisfactory Nurse on records; she manages the tricky musical line accurately and expres-

sively. Kollo's Emperor has a certain lofty air, but he wobbles, and Mr. and Mrs. Barak are entrusted to competent, unimaginative singers. Sawallisch, a better opera conductor than he's usually given credit for, understands the music as well as Böhm, and by opening up all the usual cuts, he makes slightly more sense out of the story.

Solti, with the Vienna Philharmonic is also complete and has a better cast and spectacular sound (♦London 436243, 3CD). Domingo is a suave, lyrical Emperor, uncomprehending (as usual when he sings German) but not inappropriately so. Varady's Empress is passionate and resplendent on top. Van Dam is a tender, loving Barak, but his voice doesn't always sound solidly supported. Neither does Behrens's, but her top is bright and penetrating and she's a compelling actress.

Sinopoli's recording is badly cut and wouldn't be worth bothering about if he didn't perversely find the best Emperor of all, Ben Heppner (Teldec).

Arabella.

Arabella. We're back in *Rosenkavalier* territory, even if the characters are a few rungs down the class ladder. *Arabella* is ostensibly more of a piece than *Ariadne,* but there's still a dichotomy here. The main characters are likable and interesting, but when they're not interacting with each other the music becomes rather empty and banal. *Arabella* may, in fact, have Strauss's most irritating, unnecessary character, the Fiakermilli — no matter how well she sings those yards of ridiculous coloratura, we just wish she'd go away.

The title part is a wonderful role, and della Casa made it one of her specialties. Aloof but alluring, with a warm heart and a cool head, Arabella suited her temperament perfectly. **Solti** is just about perfect (♦London 43037, 2CD). London's rough-hewn baritone and charismatic manner are ideal for Mandryka, Dermota's yearning, naive Matteo has never been bettered, and Gueden's Zdenka is firmly, brightly sung, with full-bodied high notes. Della Casa is ravishing, and she brings such sincerity and personal involvement to the role that the character springs unforgettably to life. The Vienna Philharmonic plays wonderfully, and the sound holds up well. The producer of this recording, John Culshaw, disowned it after it was released, claiming the recording sessions were so difficult (the two sopranos didn't get along) he never wanted to hear the results again. He shouldn't have denied himself the pleasure; it was a great achievement.

Della Casa sang Arabella again with **Keilberth** (♦DG 437700, 3CD). She was slightly less secure vocally but even more sparkling; singing in front of an audience always seemed to make her more communicative. Her Zdenka is Rothenberger, more feminine than Gueden, with a softer, lovelier timbre. Fischer-Dieskau is rather too knowing a Mandryka, entirely without London's apt earthiness. When his wife, Varady, recorded *Arabella* in 1981 with **Sawallisch,** his voice was pretty much gone, and he tended to substitute over-emphatic orating for honest singing (Orfeo). Varady had the range for the part, but she can't begin to enunciate the German language with anything like della Casa's clarity and flavor. Donath's Zdenka is delightful, almost on a par with her Sophie.

Arabella became one of Te Kanawa's signature roles, and she recorded it with **Jeffrey Tate** (London). Like Della Casa, her lovely voice, glamorous appearance, and natural reserve are most appropriate, but she doesn't quite go far enough in creating a detailed, personal character. The rest of Tate's cast is no more than serviceable.

My favorite Arabella after della Casa is Janowitz, who made only a video recording of the role, with **Solti** and the Vienna Philharmonic (♦London 440071). In her own way, she's as vocally stunning as della Casa, and she's partnered by the handsomely vocalized Mandryka of

Weikl and the tender Zdenka of Sona Ghazarian. She doesn't look quite right for the part, so I recommend this as an audio-only experience.

Capriccio. The conversational style that Strauss and Hoffmannsthal developed for *Rosenkavalier,* the *Ariadne* Prologue, and *Arabella* here finds its apotheosis. *Capriccio* is indeed a conversation piece, so through-composed it's almost impossible to winnow out excerptable material. **Sawallisch** is unbeatable (♦EMI 67591, 2CD). Schwarzkopf has never sung more beautifully; her words are unusually clear and her voice glitters like sunbeams playing on a stream. The young Gedda is a zealous, sweet-tongued Flamand, and Olivier, his adversary, is Fischer-Dieskau, eloquent and in sappy voice. Hotter is a vivid La Roche, and Wächter, Ludwig, and Moffo excel in smaller roles. The mono sound does little damage to the intimate music. The Philharmonia must have learned the score for the occasion but you'd never know it.

Böhm's 1971 stereo set (♦DG 445347, 2CD) is also praiseworthy. Janowitz sings almost as beautifully as Schwarzkopf but without the inflectional variety, Prey is as fine an Olivier as Fischer-Dieskau, and Ridderbusch is perhaps less insightful but more mellifluous than Hotter. Schreier's dry, petulant Flamand is no match for Gedda's, intelligent though his singing is. Fischer-Dieskau takes the small part of the Count, and Troyanos and Augér stand comparison with Ludwig and Moffo.

Ulf Schirmer enjoys the services of the Vienna Philharmonic, Uwe Heilmann's youthful Flamand, and Bär's meticulous Olivier (London). Te Kanawa's Countess is gorgeously sung and conscientiously acted. She's less subtle than Schwarzkopf or Janowitz, but I applaud her devotion to so recondite a role.

Other operas. Late in his life, Strauss modestly described himself as a "first-class second-rate composer." Listeners who explore the other eight of his 15 operas might unkindly wonder whether he was being self-deprecating enough. There are beautiful moments in his three reversions to mythology, *Der Ägyptische Helene, Die Liebe der Danae,* and *Daphne,* but the first two still lack fully satisfactory stereo accounts (though you'll find, and should seek, **Rysanek** in unauthorized mono recordings). If you must have modern sound, **Gwyneth Jones** is a spirited Helen in a 1979 recording led by Dorati (Decca), but she was in better voice in a "live" 1970 Vienna performance when her conductor was **Krips** and her tenor partner Jess Thomas (RCA, unfortunately without a libretto).

Daphne has been luckier. **Böhm** conducted it at the opening of the 1964 Vienna Festival (♦DG 445322, 2CD), and in his cast were Gueden, Wunderlich, and King. The excellence of their singing holds our unflagging interest; Gueden, in particular, soars to radiant heights in the Transformation Scene, where Strauss's old magic is in evidence. **Haitink**'s studio recording (EMI) has Popp in the title role, and she has just a little more bloom and float on top than Gueden. Schreier and Reiner Goldberg sing less handsomely than Wunderlich and King, but Moll is a deluxe Peneios.

Popp is the heroine (anti-heroine, actually) of the only recording of the quasi-autobiographical *Intermezzo* (EMI). **Sawallisch** is the conductor and Fischer-Dieskau the composer's alter ego, but despite their commitment to the score, this is a conversation opera smothered by its own talkiness.

Die schweigsame Frau is Strauss's transmutation of the *Don Pasquale* story, though far heavier on its feet. **Janowski**'s recording is certainly adequate (EMI), but **Böhm** at Salzburg in 1959 led an extraordinary assemblage: Gueden, Wunderlich, Prey, and Hotter, performers so appealing they make the best possible case for the opera (♦DG 445335, 2CD).

There are two stereo recordings of *Friedenstag.* **Robert Bass** at Carnegie Hall in 1989, with Alessandra Marc and Roger Roloff, is impressively grand (Koch). **Sawallisch** in Munich the previous year is even better, distinguished by fine contributions from Sabine Hass, Weikl, and Moll (EMI). The currently available recordings of *Guntram* (CBS), *Feuersnot* (Acanta), and *Friedenstag* (Koch) are less persuasive, but the Strauss devotee will be glad to have them until something better comes along.

SONGS

Solo songs. Strauss was the most eclectic of the great song composers, setting whatever texts struck his fancy and not too concerned about their literary merit. He never wrote a unified cycle like *Dichterliebe,* never thoroughly explored a great poet as Wolf did with Goethe and Mörike. The songs that can be grouped topically—the Ophelia and Brentano lieder, or the witty *Krämerspiegel*—are not among his best efforts, which were published a few at a time.

Once again, the collector owes a great debt to **Fischer-Dieskau** and Gerald Moore, who more than anyone else have made the rough places plain. Their set (♦EMI 63995, 6CD, recorded 1967–70) includes all the songs suitable for baritone voice, and even some that aren't (two of the Brentano lieder, written for high soprano). This is an absolutely indispensable collection, and not just for its bounty. The songs are arranged in order of publication, and the first two discs contain the most familiar items and could stand nicely on their own. The last four discs allow us to explore Strauss's development as a lieder composer, and it's absorbing to study his experiments with various poets and musical trends: a whiff of Berg here, Bartok or Mahler there, always filtered through his own characteristic style.

It was the older Strauss who turned finally to Goethe, Heine, and Rückert, and even Hans Bethge, famous as the wordsmith of Mahler's *Das Lied von der Erde.* **Fischer-Dieskau**'s readings are unfailingly thoughtful and authoritative, and quite beautifully sung. He easily meets all vocal demands, from the low notes of "Im Spätboot" to the ringing high B-flat of "Drei Masken sah ich" (both on disc 5). Moore colors the accompaniments perfectly, always listening to the voice and the sense of the words. It's almost impossible to resist citing the virtues of a multitude of songs: Sweetness, warmth, humor, verbal shapeliness, vocal strength are all here in abundance.

There's even some novelty in hearing the familiar songs sung by a baritone. Strauss was very much a ladies' man, and few male singers have left us extensive recordings. The most valuable are those that offer a voice and an approach that contrasts with Fischer-Dieskau's, but there aren't many options. **Souzay** brings sophistication and a confiding manner to 17 items (♦Philips 442744, 2CD, with Wolf's *Italian Songbook*), and **Hotter** has also left us a good handful, recorded rather too late (1967) in his career (♦Preiser 93367).

Strauss himself accompanies Maria Reining, Lea Piltti, Hilde Konetzni, Dermota, and Alfred Poell in a series of wartime recordings (Preiser 93621/2, 2CD). The composer apparently regards himself as subsidiary to the singers and remains in the background, and he also allows them considerable rhythmic latitude. All the vocalists are interesting, Dermota most of all. His sincere manner, ringing top notes, and eloquent diction have scarcely been matched by later tenors—certainly not by the pasty, inelegant **Schreier** (Orfeo and Berlin) or the stentorian **Winbergh** (Nightingale). The much-superior **Gedda** and **Wunderlich** have recorded Strauss songs only in mixed, hard-to-find recital discs.

The recordings to set beside Fischer-Dieskau's are those from the great sopranos and mezzos. **Elisabeth Schumann** is a perennial favorite, and gave us 12 prime recordings, some with orchestra (♦Pearl 9379). Just as lovely, in better sound, and wondrously graceful in diction is **della Casa,** whose recording of 17 songs is the best available short introduction to Strauss (♦Eurodisc 69313, originally RCA). Her refined demeanor doesn't preclude subtlety—just listen to the gentle nuances of "Allerseelen"—and her singing is well-nigh flawless. Seven additional items, including "Schlechtes Wetter" and an ethereal "Morgen," fill out her disc of excerpts from *Ariadne* (♦Testament 1036). Among the most accomplished of her successors are **Margaret Price** and **Popp,** who share an inexpensive reissue (♦EMI 572569). They have something of the same poise, the same exquisitely pure tone. (You'll get more music, and pay more money, if you can locate the two individual discs conflated on EMI Red Line.)

Not quite in the same league but a most agreeable singer nonetheless is **Marie McLaughlin** (Hyperion 66659). She has a seemingly instinctive feel for the melodic contours of the songs, and she's a winning interpreter for the most part. The drawback is her propensity to take the bloom off her upper notes by stinting on vibrato. Her program of 26 songs is varied and unhackneyed. **Alexander** revitalizes more familiar fare, singing with fresh tone and a sense of discovery (Etcetera 1028). **Bonney** brings a perky, girlish voice, keen diction, and a delicate manner to 10 songs (DG 429406, coupled with 10 by Wolf).

In the larger-than-life class are **Nilsson** (BIS) and **Norman** (Philips). Nilsson is thrilling in "Cäcilie" and "Zueignung," and there's something endearing about her strapping "Wiegenlied" and "Ständchen." Norman is also striking in a program of 20 songs. She's stagy, and her words can sound peculiar, but she's ear-catching all the same. More comfortable with the idiom is **Fassbaender** (♦DG 419238). She performs 11 songs (coupled with nine by Liszt) with her usual blend of dark tone, sharply chiseled diction, and sense of the long line.

Fassbaender is the last of the singers on my short list, which perforce must include many half-Strauss recordings. There isn't much general agreement about the others, which are, in any case, few in number. Many admirable recordings from the past have probably vanished for good: Gueden, Moser, Baker, Prey. Some critics have praised, with varying degrees of enthusiasm, recitals by **Gruberová** (two well-filled Teldec discs that, oddly, fail to fill the gaps left by Fischer-Dieskau (EMI), **Varady** (Orfeo), **Mathis** (Denon), and **Evelyn Lear** (VAI), but there's no real consensus.

Songs with orchestra. Strauss wrote 14 orchestral songs and orchestrated 22 of those originally conceived for piano. **Lott** has recorded most of them in two CDs: serviceable performances, sometimes quite lovely but lacking magic (Chandos 9054, 9159). **Schwarzkopf** is a more individual interpreter, and she brings deep personal involvement to 12 songs (♦EMI 66908). She knows how to project their wistfulness and how to sculpt the melodies, even if her voice (in 1965–68) isn't always responsive. Her technique doesn't always allow her to place the tone on pure vowels, and some of the sounds she emits are very strange.

She's still more vivid than Lott, or **Te Kanawa,** who filled out her first recording of *Four Last Songs* with six gorgeously sung, blandly articulated additions (Sony). **Norman** and **Fleming** also append some orchestral songs to their *Four Last Songs.* Fleming is like Te Kanawa: beautiful tone, no special insight (RCA 68539). Norman is thrilling in her clarion "Cäcilie," and the warmth of her voice is all-enveloping in "Wiegenlied" and "Ruhe meine Seele" (♦Philips 411052).

Perhaps even more admirable, and certainly purer of diction, is **Janowitz,** who returned to the studio in 1988 after a long absence to

record nine songs (♦Virgin 90794). Her voice was in fine shape, aglow with a raptness perfectly suited to the quiet songs on her program. "Befreit" is particularly stunning and builds to a spine-tingling climax. Similarly rapt and sadly deleted is **Baker** (EMI). A version for the library is a set that includes all the orchestral songs, shared by seven singers (Nightingale, 3CD). The best of them are **Gruberová** and—in two songs only—Moll; the other participants are devoted, hard-working, and rather pedestrian.

In the gone-but-not-forgotten department is an invaluable disc from **Jerusalem** (Philips). Tenors rarely venture into this repertory, and Jerusalem acquits himself honorably. His voice (in his pre-Tristan days) was an attractive lyric instrument, his instincts aptly poetic. **Wunderlich** sings five songs in another disc (Philips)—and that pretty much exhausts the commendable males.

Four Last Songs. More than 50 recordings have been issued, but we can whittle that number down quite a bit. The songs were written in 1948 and first performed by **Flagstad** and Furtwängler in 1950 at the Albert Hall. We have, miraculously, a recording of the event, but it's a mixed blessing (Simax 3 and others). The sound is awful, and Flagstad ducks the top B in "Frühling" and sounds unsettled in "September." Through the sonic murk, you can nonetheless discern why Strauss had her voice in mind for "Beim Schlafengehen" and "Im Abendrot," where she patiently unleashes vast floods of burnished, billowing tone. She sang three of the songs (omitting "Frühling") at a 1952 concert in Berlin, which has also been preserved (Hunt 576). Flagstad muffs a few words and sounds jittery in "September," but the sound is far better. The listener still needs to exercise some reconstructive imagination, but the two documents together give us a fair idea of how the great soprano sounded.

After Flagstad, most of the recordings have been made by Marschallins and Sophies rather than Isoldes. The first studio recordings date from the same year, 1953, and it's to their credit that they have been available almost continuously ever since: **della Casa** (♦London 425959) and **Schwarzkopf** (♦EMI 61001). Both performances are on the brisk side and both are exquisitely lovely. Della Casa is the cooler, crisper vocalist; Schwarzkopf's delivery is smoother, her voice slightly richer in texture. These recordings have probably introduced thousands of listeners to these songs, and they remain cherishable. Schwarzkopf revisited them again in 1966. Her voice was no longer pristine; she transposed "Frühling" down a half-step, but her understanding had deepened and she took her time (♦EMI 66908). The second performance is dreamier and more languorous than the first and even more enthralling.

Two other early, non-studio recordings have recently come to light. **Jurinac**'s voice was at its freshest in 1951, when she sang the songs with Fritz Busch (EMI 63199). She pretty much skates across their surfaces, however, with a metric rigidity that precludes expressive urgency. A later (1960) performance finds her digging deeper, but the sound is poor and her voice has lost some of its bloom (Voce della Luna 2005). **Edita Grümmer,** on the other hand, is easily in the della Casa-Schwarzkopf class. She was born to sing these songs, and we're lucky that a 1970 performance was preserved, albeit in somewhat constricted mono (♦Melodram 16523, or a better buy, Gala 100.554). Her voice has strength, tenderness, and a serene, consoling warmth. I wish she had recorded the songs earlier in her career, when she was a little more secure, and in high-quality sound.

Janowitz has much of Grümmer's serenity, but she's more aloof, almost angelically disembodied. Her recording is one of the most beautiful, polished accounts of all (◆DG 447422). She sings with an instrumental ease and purity, her voice a luminous strand in the orchestral fabric, even if we wish for sharper words and greater compassion. **Rothenberger** was one of nature's Sophies, and her voice is a little too shallow and fluttery for the music (EMI). Among the other Sophie-like interpreters are **Popp** (twice, but better on EMI than Sony) and **Hendricks** (EMI); like Rothenberger, they don't bring enough tonal fullness to the vocal lines. **Augér** has the same type of voice but manages it more resourcefully (◆Telarc 80180). Her singing has more color and variety, and an appealing luster. She's also more probing, and she seems to feel the sentiments of the poetry very deeply.

The first American soprano to record the songs in the studio was **Stich-Randall;** her recording is long gone but deserves reissue (Westminster). She's even cooler than Janowitz, but her breath control is phenomenal. Very few sopranos try to sing the phrase "tausendfach zu leben" from "Beim Schlafengehen" exactly as Strauss wrote it; Stich-Randall does, and it's wonderful to hear the long phrase in one almost unbroken span. **Leontyne Price** should have been stunning, but she and Leinsdorf rush through them without a trace of affection (RCA). Concert performances by the dependable, astute **Evelyn Lear** have been preserved, but she didn't quite have the flow and soaring top for the songs (VAIA), and by **Steber,** who certainly did but was caught too late in the day (1970).

Norman comes close to duplicating the breadth and amplitude of Flagstad, and her recording is the most magisterial of all modern accounts (◆Philips 411052). Once her voice settles down (after "Frühling"), she plumbs the depths of the music with an almost contralto richness, and when she opens the floodgates at "Und die Seele unbewacht" in "Beim Schlafengehen," the power and beauty of her singing make your knees buckle. Extraordinary!

Caballé, so striking as Salome, is inexplicably clumsy (Erato). **Freni,** performing on stage, is far more careful and surprisingly at home in the music, though she starts running out of breath before the end of the third song (Legato). **Teresa Zylis-Gara** is another surprise, her voice sleek and shining, her bearing lofty, her words not quite idiomatic (Rodolphe). **Te Kanawa** recorded the songs twice. The first time (Sony) she sounds pretty and emotionally blank, but the second account, with Solti, has more insight and variety (◆London 430511). The voice pours out as easily as before, but she has found richer vocal colors. She fills out the disc with 13 songs, accompanied by Solti at the piano. It's a diverse group, and she has the vocal mettle for the folksy numbers as well as the ruminative and the operatically expansive; it should be on the list of piano-accompanied recommendations above.

Voigt has the right basic feeling for Strauss, and she has become a fine Ariadne, but she sounds bland and clumsy in *Four Last Songs,* her voice short of luster and purity (Sony). **Karita Mattila** limns a smoother, firmer line, but her potential would probably have been better realized in the studio. Singing in concert, she's too cautious, and her odd phrasing ruins "Beim Schlafengehen." Claudio Abbado, her conductor, is in his own world, more concerned with highlighting instrumental details that strike his fancy than in helping the soprano (DG). More promising is **Eaglen,** whose voice has the flow, amplitude, and incandescence to do justice to the songs (Sony). Her recording is, at least, a pleasure to hear, but her words are bland, almost zombie-like. The ear quickly starts aching for some verbal relish or individuality.

The two best recent recordings have come from Americans. **Studer** has a bright, vibrant soprano with a sensuous tingle (◆DG 439865). Like Janowitz, she evinces a slight reserve, as though ecstasy isn't something to be shared, but her commitment is manifest, and she curls her tongue around the melodies with care and warmth. Her round, lovely voice and the marvelous playing of the Dresden Staatskapelle under Sinopoli are captured with a fidelity we wish Flagstad, della Casa, and Grümmer had enjoyed. **Fleming** has, perhaps, an extra dollop of ardor and humanity but sings less well than Studer (RCA). Her basically gorgeous voice isn't emitted with complete freedom; it takes on a touch of astringency when pushed.

The best-sounding performances are these two, along with Te Kanawa, Norman, and Augér. Janowitz is certainly satisfactory, however, and so is Schwarzkopf with Szell. The singing of della Casa, Schwarzkopf, and Grümmer on the older, mono recordings transcends sonic limitations and is no less treasurable.   LUCANO

Igor Stravinsky (1882–1971)

He was a chameleon, or perhaps a magpie, spending nearly all of his career latching onto this and that for sustenance, from Gesualdo to Webern. But except for the very earliest works and some of the last atonal pieces, it is Stravinsky's signature sound—the pungent harmonies, the ingenious orchestrations, the shafts of wit, and above all, those driving rhythms and ever-shifting meters—that we notice first. Indeed, Stravinsky tapped into something that classical composers had been politely sidestepping for centuries: rhythm. As a result, we have to listen to him in a different way, responding to the feeling that he stirs in our limbs as well as our hearts and minds. It is no wonder that younger people raised on pop music take so wholeheartedly to Stravinsky; a good, cracking performance of *Rite of Spring* is as exciting as any rock concert. And it's also small wonder that a lot of performers avoid his music or don't get much out of it; they aren't trained to relate to the intricacies and energy of rhythm. Unless you're a magician like Karajan, smoothing out Stravinsky usually waters him down.

Stravinsky always set great store in the value of his own recordings, and despite contemporary carping about his being a mediocre conductor, don't believe it. Whatever his technique, whatever the fluctuating quality of his ensembles, whatever the controversial role that his right-hand man Robert Craft played in preparing the ensembles for the sessions, most of the recordings issued under Stravinsky's name have a life-affirming vitality and rhythmic urgency that lights up a room. The legend has sprouted among collectors that Stravinsky's mono recordings on 78s and LPs were always better than the later stereo editions, but now that the monos are increasingly appearing on CD, the nasty secret is that quite often, the stereos match or trump the monos in performance and sound. The proof is in the listening.

(By the way, beware of what current *Schwann* catalogs—once paragons of accuracy but now riddled with careless errors—say about the contents and availability of Stravinsky recordings. To cite but two weird faux pas, they insist upon referring to a world-renowned Swiss conductor as "Pierre" (instead of Ernest) Ansermet, and list a *Scherzo Fantastique* under Dorati on Mercury where no such performance exists.)

COMPLETE EDITIONS

The "Igor Stravinsky Edition" is a reissue of the CBS 31LP set issued for his centenary, consisting mostly of the stereo recordings he and Robert Craft made from 1957 to 1969 (◆Sony 46290, 22CD). Certain things in the CD edition have changed; the set is better-organized now, some deletions were made, and the set was slightly expanded to include ballet suites and a few 78 rpm and mono recordings. But Sony has repeated CBS's marketing mistake by not releasing the discs separately in the United States (except for *The Rake's Progress*). However, I have spotted imported pieces of the set in large record shops, so they probably can be ordered. As a reference, I have listed the catalog numbers of the individual volumes as I go, and in any case, several mostly well-known works remain available on single discs, the residue of CBS's half-hearted Stravinsky reissue program.

A second complete Stravinsky project, entitled "The Composer," took shape in the '90s under Craft's direction, who, after complaining for years about the inaccuracies and alleged defects in the Sony set, is trying to set the record straight (MusicMasters). The series got off to a disheartening start, but within a few volumes, there has been a remarkable improvement. He likes lightning-fast tempos, and as the series has evolved his performances have shown more wit, more flexible rhythms, and particularly after he shifted his base from New York's Orchestra of St. Luke's to London ensembles, a newly-found lyricism. Craft is our most authoritative living link to Stravinsky's performing style; he deserves to be heard out. The series reached eleven volumes in 1998, most of which contain hodgepodges of works from all periods, and some have fascinating chips from the workbench that had not been recorded before.

ORCHESTRAL MUSIC (INCLUDING CONCERTOS, IN CHRONOLOGICAL ORDER)

Symphony 1. There's hardly a hint of the composer of *Firebird*, let alone the cosmopolitan musician to come, in this conventional yet fascinating romantic Russian symphony, save for the opening strains of a Russian folk song that was later used in *Pétrouchka*. **Stravinsky** himself doesn't slight his Tchaikovsky heritage but neither does he linger in his direct, vigorous recording (♦Sony 46294, 2CD). **Dorati** takes a more spacious, softer-focused view of the piece (London), while **Pletnev** turns on the wide-screen, heart-on-sleeve (though unmannered) treatment as if he had discovered a long-lost Rachmaninoff symphony (DG). **Ashkenazy** and the St. Petersburg Philharmonic offer the best combination of classical clarity and Russian passion; they sound the most convinced of the piece's worth (♦Decca 448812).

Scherzo Fantastique. With this 12-minute score, composed in 1907–1908 while still under the tutelage of Rimsky-Korsakov, Stravinsky begins to display some foliage of his own, with lots of delicate instrumental lines, exotic colors derived from Rimsky, a strong whiff of French impressionism, and some premonitions of the motor energy that would animate much of his output. **Stravinsky**'s own recording is deliciously light and lovely, well played by the Columbia Symphony (♦CBS 42432), and **Boulez** also captures the composer's transparency with the NY Philharmonic (NYPO), but with more attention to detail and expressive phrasing (♦Sony 45843). Both are clear choices, with **Ashkenazy**'s swift, luminous performance (London 458142) and **Chailly**'s slower, less airborne, but gorgeously detailed recording in the Concertgebouw (Decca 448812) coming in right behind. **Schwarz**'s broader, fussier, though lusciously recorded Seattle Symphony performance (Delos) and **Dorati**'s rhythmically slack Detroit reading (London) are at a somewhat lower level.

Fireworks. A brief yet vivid impression of a pyrotechnical display with a center section that brazenly alludes to Dukas's *Sorcerer's Apprentice*, *Fireworks* is a succinct preview of immediate coming attractions— namely *Firebird*. The recording of choice, **Stravinsky** and the Columbia Symphony, is brightly lit, mobile, and light on its feet (♦CBS 42432), and

his more tart live performance with the Moscow Philharmonic is also worth hearing (♦Melodiya 33220). **Dorati**'s taping is also very agile, if trebly in sound (♦Mercury 432012). **Ashkenazy** is tasty and fast, deliciously recorded, and a delight (♦Decca 448812).

Craft is somewhat more subdued in character (MusicMasters), as is **Boulez**'s stunningly recorded Chicago Symphony performance (♦DG 437850). **Inbal**'s glistening recording is quite good, a bit heavier in texture yet well-paced (Teldec 18964, 2CD). **Schwarz** opens at a fast tempo but swoons to the languorous perfumes of the Dukas episode soon thereafter (Delos). Ruled out are **Ozawa**'s hard-charging, thinly-recorded reading (RCA), **Chailly**'s spectacularly recorded but routine performance (London), **Iwaki**'s earthbound session in Melbourne (Virgin), and **Maazel**'s soft-focused rendering in Vienna (RCA).

The Firebird. The ballet that rocketed Stravinsky to world fame at the age of 28 is also, in its various forms, the gateway for many (if not most) listeners into his sound world. Yet ironically, the piece that launched Stravinsky was the final flowering of his dazzlingly colored, gorgeously melodic, Rimsky-influenced manner.

Only in recent years has the complete ballet taken a solid hold in the repertoire; it may be performed more often now than the popular 1919 suite. **Stravinsky**'s Columbia Symphony recording has a lot of rhythmic springiness perhaps more appropriately applied to what came after *Firebird*, but is irresistible nonetheless and still clearly in the top ranks of available versions (♦CBS 42432). **Craft** also approaches *Firebird* with a decidedly rhythmic approach, but he's not quite as resilient as the composer (MusicMasters). However, his recording is valuable for hitherto unrecorded restorations from the original score, most of them very minor but some that add to its theatricality down the stretch.

With **Ansermet**, we're dealing with a pioneering Stravinsky interpreter who nevertheless would not be bound to the rhythmically tough Stravinsky performing style. His last *Firebird* is leisurely (sometimes overly so), luminous in texture yet understated in ambience, and almost totally at odds with the ideas of the composer (London). His earlier stereo recording with the Suisse Romande, though not as well played, is still available in a bargain double-decker (London). **Dorati** has the London Symphony (LSO) streaking through the score in record time in his first recording, one that despite a thin treble edge still sounds detailed and thrilling (♦Mercury 432012); his stunningly recorded digital Detroit disc isn't nearly as urgent (London).

Boulez's second *Firebird*, with the Chicago Symphony, came as a pleasant surprise after earlier disappointing Stravinsky ballet remakes (♦DG 437850); this one blazes with finely detailed color and power, outdoing his lustrous yet lighter NYPO recording (CBS). Of the younger conductors, **Tilson Thomas**'s *Firebird* is great; the colors are lit superbly and lightly, the rhythms beautifully sprung, and the tempos always comfortable, combining the rhythmic resilience of the composer with the polish and thrust of the San Francisco Symphony at its peak. It's available only as part of a boxed set, but RCA gives you a big price break (♦RCA 68898, 3CD).

Salonen is light on his feet and has some good ideas but doesn't really electrify the Philharmonia; he does it much better live nowadays with the LA Philharmonic (CBS). **Rattle** takes a more lyrical approach that brings out the impressionistic Stravinsky but tends to drag some of the swifter dances (EMI). **Gergiev**'s tempos are among the broadest on discs but he uses them to phrase in idiosyncratic ways; his textures are surprisingly light and balletic, and the Kirov brasses display their distinctive Slavic bite (Philips). Some ideas don't come off, but at least

Gergiev takes risks, and he throws a killer Scriabin *Prometheus* into the deal.

Stravinsky would fashion three different suites from *Firebird,* in 1910, 1919, and again in 1945, reducing the size of the orchestra somewhat in the latter two. The 1919 version is the one most often played and recorded, but both the 1910 and 1945 suites contain additional numbers (the 1910 deletes some, too).

Always devoted to the 1919 suite, **Stokowski**'s first recording came in 1924 in two Victrola acoustic 78s. It's a fascinating curio of another age, with old-fashioned string portamentos re-orchestrated for the acoustic horn, yet fresh and fast with a sense of adventure around every bend. (Remember, this was contemporary music at the time.) He recorded another one with basically the same interpretation in 1927 (Dell'Arte LP) and yet another in 1935 (Dutton), all with his miraculous Philadelphia Orchestra. Nor did he stop there, recording five more (!) with different orchestras until 1967, his interpretation changing radically, broadening and luxuriating deeply. Listen to the ravishing phrasing and tone that he drew from the Berlin Philharmonic in 1957 in reverberant early Capitol stereo; obviously he could mesmerize any band (♦EMI 65207). Though coupled peculiarly with Orff's *Carmina Burana* on CD, it's still an excellent choice, more so than the less idiosyncratic 1967 LSO version (London).

With **Bernstein,** who grew fussier in Stravinsky as he aged, a sound rule of the thumb is always to go for the NYPO over the Israel Philharmonic. The New York performance, a few gushing rubatos aside, is full of life and energy (♦Sony 47605 or 60694); the ponderous Israeli remake, though it reveals some intriguing dissonant inner voices, is to be avoided (DG). **Szell** and his disciplined Clevelanders put a brilliant finish on the 1919 suite; their furiously scintillating "Infernal Dance" is a marvel (♦Sony 47664). **Ozawa**'s early recording is marked by lovely playing and a straightahead conception that stays out of the Boston Symphony's way (RCA). Octogenarian **Monteux**'s elegant performance carries the patina of history, but the orchestra isn't first-class (London). Though **Giulini**'s third recording of the 1919 suite beautifully captures the mystery of the Introduction and Berceuse, the rest is much too sleepy (Sony); search out his first luminous Philharmonia disc instead (♦Seraphim 60022, LP).

The latest reissue of **Claudio Abbado**'s smooth, mellow 1919 Suite is part of a bargain-priced release containing all his Stravinsky recordings with the LSO (DG 453085, 2CD), a safe way to acquire a good deal of the composer's best-known ballet music on the cheap. **Skrowaczewski** is one of the most effective advocates of the composer's performing style; the opening is unusually rhythmic, and despite a few broad tempos, textures are clear and unsentimental (Vox 3016, 3CD).

The enterprising **Boulez** is one of the few who chose the 1910 Suite, which lacks resolution by omitting the Berceuse and Finale but nearly compensates with more extensive lesser-known material and the original orchestrations, carefully etched by the BBC Symphony (♦Sony 45843). Ashkenazy also goes for 1910, applying more lightweight flair and fantasy, with heartfelt playing from St. Petersburg (♦Decca 448812). Even more inventive was **Leinsdorf** who, for a direct-to-disc session with the LA Philharmonic, added the Berceuse and Finale to the 1910 suite (Sheffield). The LAPO plays well under these tough conditions, but the sound is bone dry.

Stravinsky preferred his 1945 suite; his first version with the NYPO is often dark-hued in timbre and well-recorded for its time (Pearl). The 1967 remake in Hollywood with the Columbia Symphony, his last recording, is remarkable; even at 84, Stravinsky could convey much vi-

tality (♦Sony 46293). **Pletnev** and the Russian National Orchestra, almost indistinguishable in timbre from your average Western ensemble, opt for 1945 in a conventionally paced, highly polished reading (DG).

Song of the Nightingale. This vivid orchestral poem condensing the music of Acts II and III from the opera *Le Rossignol* ought to be as popular as the big three ballets but hasn't really caught on; perhaps its lengthy, quiet coda disturbs the egos of conductors who like to close with a bang.

Early stereo days produced many of the finest *Nightingales* on records. **Reiner,** in a rare Stravinsky outing, provided lots of finely detailed glitter and precisely etched clarity in a famous 1956 Living Stereo issue (♦RCA 68168). **Dorati** can be very swift, maybe a bit brusque in spots, but crisp and invigorating in a strikingly transparent acoustic (Mercury). *Nightingale*'s sensuality and color were perfectly suited for **Ansermet,** who led the premiere in 1919 (♦London 15011). This would be my first choice if it were in print, but it shouldn't be too hard to find it second-hand on LP.

Dutoit sumptuously continues the coloristic Ansermet tradition, and there is some bite, too, in his excellent performance (♦London 417619). *Nightingale* also brings out the best in **Boulez** with the NYPO (♦CBS 42396) and the Orchestre National de France (♦Erato 45382); both discs illuminate the colors with a high-powered laser, but Erato has better sound. **Chailly** is given truly spectacular sound, but as usual he can't phrase or tie anything together properly—great engineering, stilted interpretation (London). **Craft** is hasty and clinical, with hard, close sound to match (Sony). **Maazel** isn't one for spreading glittering color across the soundscape, yet he does allow a thoughtful mood to emerge and the Vienna Philharmonic produces some seductive portamentos (RCA 57127).

Pétrouchka. Now Stravinsky really becomes uniquely his own man and a deeply Russian one at that, moving beyond Rimsky into folk song, some abrasive polytonal clashes and above all, irresistible, driving, motorized rhythms. *Pétrouchka* is immediately winning, and unlike the complete *Firebird,* consistently inspired from stem to stern. Yes, there is a *Pétrouchka Suite* that runs about 18 minutes; **Stravinsky**'s bustling but sonically old recording with the NYPO (Pearl), a Columbia Symphony remake (Sony), and a frisky live recording in Moscow (Melodiya) cover that ground, and **Koussevitzky**'s brilliantly-played and paced 1928 recording is another historic treat (BSO 171002). But since the complete ballet is only a little more than a half hour in length anyway, it's best to get the whole thing.

A more pertinent decision would be the choice between the opulently scored original 1911 version and the leaner, meaner 1947 revision that Stravinsky wrote to earn royalties lost to him after he left Russia. The 1911 *Pétrouchka,* with its ever-fascinating extra details and additional instruments, has been winning more advocates since the composer's death, but in some ways the 1947 version is more invigorating.

1911 Edition. **Boulez,** the master of color, has always favored the original version. His New York recording savors the detail with glittering clarity, combined with the streetwise brashness that the NYPO could still summon in 1971 (♦Sony 64109). His remake in Cleveland has more refined playing and much better sound, but there is a noticeable drop-off in vitality (DG). While **Ansermet**'s lithe, clearly-etched stereo recording with L'Orchestre de la Suisse Romande has long been prized by sound buffs (London 443467, 2CD), his most electric rendition was the London Philharmonic set issued just after WWII on five English

Decca 78s. These records set the postwar world on its ear, ushering in the age of high fidelity, and they still vividly convey the resonance around Ansermet's splashy, broadly paced, balletic performance. This recording received its first reissue in 1998 (Avid 600), albeit in so-called "3-D Sound" and CEDAR processing. Dating even earlier, to 1937, **Stokowski** and the Philadelphians hurl themselves into the score in a driving, wildly colorful, sometimes oddly balanced sonic whirl, a thrilling performance not too restricted by the sound (Dutton).

Monteux, who led the premiere, luxuriates broadly at 83 in the 1911 edition with the Boston Symphony, an absorbing, lustrously detailed rendition that leaves out the drum rolls between tableaux (♦RCA 61898). There is an earlier, closely recorded Monteux with the Paris Conservatoire with much the same interpretation; that's Julius Katchen on prominently spot-lit piano (London). The opulent **Dutoit** was hailed as the digital 1911 standard of the '80s, and it still makes a gorgeous impression (♦London 417619). Despite excellent sound, **Schwarz**'s performance has very little lift or fire; the broader tempos aren't compensated by strong rhythm and attacks are often tame (Delos). The Vienna Philharmonic plays splendidly for **Maazel** but the results are smoothed over, uninvolved, a mismatch of orchestra and idiom (RCA). **Inbal** is so slow and dragging in Tableaux I–III that he sounds like he's sleepwalking, and the "Coachmen's Dance" in IV is sabotaged by a crude thumping beat (Teldec). Another "two-fer" yields more routine—a pale, unshaded run-through by **Iwaki** (Virgin).

1947 Edition. Again, **Stravinsky**'s stereo recording of the 1947 version—not 1911, as the liner inexcusably insists—sets a crackling, vigorous pace for all who follow (♦CBS 42433). Everything is alive, rhythmic, and buoyant in the composer's hands, despite a few outbreaks of scrappy playing from the Hollywood edition of the Columbia Symphony, and the sound is much improved on CD over the LP. Coupled with a powerful *Rite*, there's no better starting point for a Stravinsky collection. **Dorati** runs with the composer's example and turns in an even more deliciously driving, rough-and-ready, pointed performance (♦Mercury 434331); the same team's mono LP has a slightly keener edge. **Skrowaczewski** took the renamed Minnesota Orchestra on a less driven, equally unsentimental return trip, now liberated from the old crummy LP surfaces (Vox 3016, 3CD).

Craft's performance is a delightful surprise—mellower, more flexible, and less uptight than some of his other recordings but with plenty of rhythmic spring and detail, a fine case for his spirited manifesto for the 1947 edition in the booklet (♦MusicMasters 67184). Caught near the end of his term (1969) as NYPO music director, **Bernstein** is impulsive and excitable, prone to some willful tempo fluctuations but generating tremendous vitality, wit, and a great feeling for rhythm (♦Sony 47629). The remake with the Israel Philharmonic is one of his better Stravinsky performances with that group (DG), weightier but with an even more galvanic rhythmic punch, but New York gets the edge.

Pétrouchka is the best of **Abbado**'s Stravinsky performances; it has energy, drive, and bite along with the inevitable polish; pay no attention to the liner, this is 1947, not 1911 (♦DG 453085, 2CD). **Salonen** again has sound instincts—his "Danse Russe" has a particularly nice swing to it—but he remains a cool customer; the Philharmonia plays well for him but without much heat or momentum (Sony). After opening with a full head of steam, **Rattle**'s performance becomes unpredictable, with passages of impressionistic refinement, massive sheets of sound and jolts of energy—an imaginative conception treated to exceptionally wide-range recording (EMI).

Mehta is out of the running; Tableaux II and III are slow and fussy, the rhythm is weak in IV, a Eurocentric approach without elegance, wrapped in indistinct, early digital sound (CBS). And **Nagano** goes nowhere; all the life and dance feeling are sucked away with leisurely tempos, little rhythmic definition, and an obsession with refinement, refinement, refinement (Erato).

The Rite of Spring. How times have changed. Whereas Boulez used to recall the days when rehearsing *Rite* was like "driving on ice," nowadays not only is the piece easily navigated in lots of places (indeed, one of my recommended choices is by a semi-pro ensemble), it has become the most recorded Stravinsky work, period. Yet when the piece is played all-out, it still can be—and ought to be—a cathartic, shocking rabble-rouser, just as it was in 1913 at its wild Paris premiere.

Stravinsky set a thrilling example with the New York edition of the Columbia Symphony in 1960, with mostly swift pacing, steady unrelenting drive, lots of revealed detail (including some wrong notes), and a raw vitality that will lift you from your chair (♦CBS 42433). His 1940 version with the NYPO is pushed harder in sections, with more variations of tempo in Part II (Pearl). Too bad the period technology couldn't capture the full impact of this performance; it's like a black-and-white photo viewed at a distance. The orchestra handles it superbly until the tumultuous final minute of "Danse sacrale" where things turn really clumsy.

Craft's highly anticipated recording, made 30 years after rehearsing Stravinsky's stereo edition, is even faster (MusicMasters). Yet the music nearly suffocates from a lack of oxygen in the phrasing and shortage of spring in the rhythms, although Part II is more acceptable than Part I. **Monteux** was the imperturbable maestro in the pit during the 1913 *Rite* riot, so what he has to say is certainly worth hearing. He recorded it four times; the third, a 1951 mono with the Boston Symphony, has a savage grandeur where tempos may be a bit slow at times but the cumulative effect of the crescendos is amazing (♦RCA 61898). The sound is pale and opaque on this transfer; the "Monteux Edition" issue is reportedly better.

Though **Ansermet**'s Swiss orchestra is sometimes not up to the job, he combines a light touch with an implacable determination that keeps the momentum going (London 443467, 2CD). The *Rites* by **Markevitch,** Diaghilev's last protégé, have acquired cult status for reasons that are hard to confirm. His 1951 mono recording is well-paced, not radically different from many others except for some spot-lit hidden details in Part II that add to an impression of mysterious *nachtmusik.* His 1959 stereo *Rite* is a less interesting and faster run-through much of the way, although the whirling close of Part I has an intensity the mono performance lacks. Both have been reissued back-to-back in a single CD for the cultists (Testament 1076).

In many ways, **Bernstein** was the ideal conductor for *Rite*, at home with all the score's complexities, gifted with a matchless feeling for rhythm, thoroughly in control of an orchestra, and capable of a level of excitement that could blow the roof off a concert hall. His 1958 NYPO recording from the early charged-up days of his tenure got all of this together in one mighty wallop with plenty of room for expression and a barbaric momentum that is positively frightening (♦Sony 47629). He never could match his first *Rite*—not in his close-but-not-quite electrifying enough quadraphonic attempt with the LSO (Sony) nor his final, more deliberately paced, sonically rawboned recording in Israel (DG).

A handful of eccentric rubatos aside, **Salonen** clearly buys into the composer's approach—fleet, driving, and violent—but he applies an appealingly lighter, more linear touch and delivers a slam-bang coda, a cool young Finn reveling in the score's complexities and his remarkable control of the Philharmonia (♦Sony 45796). For all the expected ferocity of **Solti**'s conducting and the fabled brawny power of the Chicago brass, their recording also strikes me above all as superbly controlled, with tempos exactly on target and nothing left to impulse (♦London 417704). **Tilson Thomas** sees *Rite* as the ultimate apotheosis of the dance; his live performances have been irresistibly rhythmic, rock'em sock'em affairs. Alas, his rhythmically restrained, resonant-sounding Boston recording, made when he was in his 20s, doesn't really capture what he can do with the piece (DG). His 1996 San Francisco performance, recorded live, comes a lot closer (♦RCA 68898, 3CD); the rhythms are more alive, the playing is superb, "Dance sacrale" snarls—yet even so, I can imagine an even hotter *Rite* from MTT.

Muti's hell-for-leather 1979 *Rite* was one of the best of its time and it remains a stunner—a tough, hard-driving workout in powerful analog sound that captures the Philadelphia Orchestra while it still had its own character (♦EMI 64516). The most vehement, take-no-prisoners *Rite* that I've ever heard belongs to **Dorati,** a performance so furiously fast, searing, and brutal that you can almost see flames coming through the speakers (♦Mercury 434331). The piece can take such an uncompromisingly violent approach jolly well, too, though it isn't for everyone.

Moving on to less inflammatory approaches, **Dutoit** sounds wonderfully polished and elegant, and he keeps a taut enough hand on the rhythms and attacks to maintain some degree of virulence (♦London 414202). The sound is Decca/London digital at its finest; this is a good first choice if ultra-violent *Rites* drive you mad. **Boulez**'s first *Rite* with the Cleveland Orchestra is a rigorously objective piece of work, with every detail precisely examined and projected but curiously lacking in drive or real intensity—an analysis as opposed to a performance (Sony). He went at it again in Cleveland in the '90s; the sound is considerably better, even the level of playing is better, and though the interpretation is even more maddeningly sane, at least this recording has some sensual allure (DG).

Maazel also has the benefit of the Cleveland Orchestra, with clear, spectacular early digital sound that remains in the demonstration class, and a middle-of-the-road yet satisfyingly brassy interpretation marred only by some ridiculously drawn out trombone glissandos in Part I (Telarc). In a mid-priced "Basic 100" package, **Ozawa** secures lustrous playing and sufficient force from the Boston Symphony in fine analog sound; it lacks liner notes, though (RCA). The resilient, not-too-vehement **Skrowaczewski** *Rite* is a good bargain in a set loaded with top-drawer Stravinsky and Prokofiev (Vox 3016, 3CD). **Mehta**'s 1978 recording has a certain heavyweight charisma and bludgeoning power, but some of the pacing is so sodden that this can be recommended only as a budget-priced supplement (Sony). Though **Abbado** doesn't really tap into the *Rite's* full power, he allows some vehemence to creep into his highly refined performance (DG).

Rattle and his well-recorded City of Birmingham Symphony open tamely and often take a deceptively mild approach before surprising you with ear-opening hidden detail and huge gusts of energy and power (EMI). It's exciting in spots but not consistent enough to weigh in with the top choices. In an enterprising mid-priced coupling with *Perséphone,* **Nagano** doesn't see the forest for the trees, bringing forward some fascinating, glistening inner details at the expense of forward momentum—like Rattle, different but spotty (Virgin). **Inbal** opens slowly and indifferently but starting with "Ritual of the Two Rival Tribes" he begins to feel the piece's heat, and Part II goes fairly well,

with the details caught superbly in the Maltings acoustic (Teldec 18964, 2CD).

A most valuable disc is by **Benjamin Zander** and the Boston Philharmonic, paced according to the pianola roll that the composer supervised, with distinctly different tempos than Stravinsky's own metronome markings, especially the pell-mell "Danse sacrale" (♦IMP 25). The character of the work changes amazingly, and Zander enforces the concept with gusto. The orchestra is a mixture of pros and amateurs, but you'd never guess it from their assured playing—recorded live at that! **Levi** also takes a furious closing tempo in an otherwise solid, straight-shooting, brilliantly recorded reading with hardly any other distinguishing tics or marks (Telarc).

Now a word or two about **Karajan,** whose first recording Stravinsky absolutely tore apart point by point in a famous article. Yes, Karajan can be inappropriately plush, but this performance has mesmerizing power; listen to the awesomely ethereal way he drifts through the opening of Part II. No more eloquent dissenting opinion can be imagined (♦DG 429162).

Finally, reeling back into the past, we behold one of the great gambles of the 78 rpm era—**Stokowski** unleashing the *Rite* upon a world that still considered it to be weird, far-out stuff. The recording was made with the Philadelphia Orchestra over several sessions in 1929–30 (Pearl 9488), a lush, glamorous-sounding thing (despite the faded sonics) where the sections of Part I seem to blend seamlessly and the opening of Part II has a breathtaking sweep the likes of which we wouldn't hear again until Karajan. Don't bother with Stokowski's horribly cut and reordered *Rite* on the *Fantasia* soundtrack unless you're curious about primitive stereo effects circa 1939 (Buena Vista).

Suites for Small Orchestra. These transcriptions of eight piano-four-hands pieces are wonderful little examples of slapstick **Stravinsky,** an attitude conveyed nowhere with more wicked fun than by the composer with the Columbia Symphony (Sony 46296), and even more emphatically in Lugano circa 1955 (♦Aura 164). **Craft** also catches much of the humor (at racier tempos), a performance that rivals the composer's (♦MusicMasters 67110). **Boulez** has a go with a more deadpan expression, hampered by airless sound (Sony), while **Chailly** pushes harder and receives the best sound by far (London). The **Orpheus Chamber Orchestra** is also a hard-charging band, and some of the humor slips between their fingers (DG). **Rattle** has a sardonic laugh with this music's mischievous qualities, but the second-rate Northern Sinfonia and dry engineering weaken this recording (EMI).

Four Studies for Orchestra. More mordant, humorous transcriptions for orchestra; the first three were originally written for string quartet and the last was an etude for pianola. **Stravinsky**'s recording catches the fun perfectly (♦Sony 46296), with **Craft** and the Philharmonia huffing and puffing a bit harder but with good results (MusicMasters). With broader tempos and more inflated, gorgeous textures, **Boulez** and the Chicago Symphony do well with this piece (♦DG 437850); there is also an earlier, less-relaxed Boulez version with Ensemble InterContemporain (Erato). **Rattle** displays an especially ample sense of humor in his recording (♦EMI 49178). **Dutoit** gives it a more rounded, luxurious texture (London), while **Dorati** is a bit too hard-edged (Mercury).

Pulcinella. Besides being the work that kicked off Stravinsky's long neoclassical period, *Pulcinella* is great fun, an unabashed love letter to what the composer thought was the music of Pergolesi (actually, it was spurious), with dashes of 20th century spice. The best way to enter this piece is through the irresistible 22-minute suite that includes most of the best numbers, but extended acquaintance with the whole ballet (which sports a soprano, tenor, and bass) will yield new delights every time you hear it.

Here is a clear case where the **Stravinsky** stereo beats the mono, for the composer's 1965 recording (♦Sony 46292, 3CD) has more life and animation than his 1953 taping (Sony 63325, 2CD), despite the presence of the mighty Cleveland Orchestra in the latter. The West Coast Columbia Symphony is more rhythmically alert, and though quite often the 1965 tempos seem faster, it's because the articulation is crisper. Also 1965 has a far more pleasing vocal cast than 1953. Yet 1953 does have its virtues—the Clevelanders sail through passages that the Columbians scrape away at—and it's easier to acquire now on Masterworks Heritage.

Compulsive educator **Christopher Hogwood** was the first to execute what should have been an obvious idea, coupling *Pulcinella* with a few of the original pieces (why not more?) that inspired Stravinsky (♦London 425614). What we do hear is illuminating, demonstrating that Stravinsky didn't alter the material as much as you would think; his manipulations were often diabolically subtle. In the ballet itself, Hogwood has the St. Paul Chamber Orchestra running alertly at brisk tempos; the rhythms are a bit stiff but the vocal soloists are OK.

Hickox's account is a most attractive dark horse in this derby—vigorous in tempo and lively in rhythm, light and fragrant in texture, and cushioned in velvet sonics (♦Virgin 61107). No texts, but this is still one of the best *Pulcinellas* around. **Abbado** is also very good, highly invigorating and floating despite the heavier LSO textures, with a fine vocal trio on board (♦DG 453085, 2CD). **Marriner** made a lovely digital *Pulcinella* that disappeared much too soon (♦Angel 37899).

Following the composer's example, **Salonen** has a lot of energy, wit, and textural clarity—a fine realization that just misses the extra sparkle of Stravinsky's versions (Sony). **Rattle** was in his very early 20s when he recorded *Pulcinella,* yet already he knew how to project the droll qualities of the music (EMI). Alas, he couldn't prevent some of the tempos from sagging a bit nor completely control the sometimes scrappy playing of the Northern Sinfonia, and the sound is unpleasantly dry. **Boulez**'s interest in Stravinsky stops almost cold with *Pulcinella;* he rarely plays anything dating after 1920, owing perhaps to his hostility to neoclassicism in his youth (as recently as 1984, he referred to it as a "cancer"). His complete *Pulcinella,* with its draggy phrasing and distinct lack of lift in the rhythms, may reflect this lack of interest more than he would like us to think (Erato).

The best recording of the suite, alas, is still not available on CD: **Ansermet**'s wonderfully witty, elegant, early stereo account (♦London 15011). He conducted the premiere in 1920 and evidently loved it ever since. The best-of-the-rest award goes to the **Orpheus Chamber Orchestra** which, minus a conductor and not missing one in the least, turns in a polished, poised, beautifully paced gem of a performance (♦DG 445541). **Marriner**'s mostly sparkling edition of the suite almost makes up for the complete version's unavailability (♦London 443577).

Stravinsky's stereo recording, while nicely paced, is not as essential as his complete ballet; the magnifying-glass engineering is unflattering to his Hollywood pickup group (Sony 46293). **Bernstein**'s New York rendering opens a bit heavily with thick 19th century textures, but things soon pick up as the conductor's rhythmic resiliency starts to kick in (Sony). His Israel recording is heavier still, but follows the same basic blueprint, however raucously played (DG). **Craft** is so highly pointed in rhythm and so swift in tempo that the piece begins to lose some of its high spirits; everything is rush-rush-rush (MusicMasters). As in his

complete version, **Boulez** is much too poker-faced and leisurely in the Suite; only the Tarantella and Finale come off with some fizz (Sony). **Levi** and his Atlantans display few of their competitors' eccentricities but offer few strengths of their own, a safe, nicely played reading with a fast closing kick (Telarc).

Symphonies of Wind Instruments. This mordant, compact, slightly forbidding, misnamed piece is rarely heard in the concert hall, but it marks an important transition between the repeated cells of *Rite of Spring* and Stravinsky's emerging neoclassical style. **Craft**'s recording claims to be the first of the accurate original version, and at the conductor's fast tempos, it does sound more coherent and less icy (♦MusicMasters 67103). **Salonen** is alert and buoyant, an attractive, airy performance that's anything but austere (♦Sony 45797). **Dutoit** gets exceptionally lovely results from the Montreal Symphony winds and brasses—and the best sound (♦London 414202).

Since no stereo composer version exists, Sony reached back to **Stravinsky**'s 1951 mono recording with the Northwest German Radio Orchestra for the "Stravinsky Edition" (♦Sony 46297, 2CD; the LP set used Craft's first stereo version), a stark, highly pointed, well-played performance. **Fennell**'s recording is unusual in that it uses a real working wind band; this gleaming, sharply etched performance should get be reissued (Mercury). **Boulez** doesn't have as much spring in his step, but he savors the transparencies of texture with the NYPO (Sony). Its discmates in the "Boulez Edition," two big works by Messiaen, aren't as bizarre a coupling as you might think. His newer Berlin recording is even softer in focus and not as interesting (DG 457616).

Concerto for Piano and Wind Instruments. Allowing Stravinsky to make a quick buck (or franc) as a touring pianist, it reflects his percussive piano technique, his austere and spiky neoclassical persona as a composer, and his infatuation with syncopated jazz. The pianist who balances the jazz and Bach most convincingly is **Béroff** in a rollicking recording with a frisky Ozawa and the so-so Orchestre de Paris (♦EMI 67276, 2CD). **Stravinsky** brings his usual quota of energy and well-sprung rhythms to the Columbia Symphony, but the bland soloist, **Entremont,** is fatally miscast (Sony). **Seymour Lipkin** is all brittleness and baroque clarity; Bernstein and the NYPO offer vigorous support, but the sound is clattery and dry (Sony). **Crossley** is altogether more self-effacing and rounded while allowing the work's percussiveness to shine through, and Salonen's accompaniment is light and playful (♦Sony 45797). Salonen/Crossley easily beats the others in sound.

Apollo. This ballet for string orchestra may be the most poised and beautiful of Stravinsky's neoclassical scores, filled with many melodic passages that haunt the memory and just enough harmonic unease to keep our ears planted in the 20th century. While sporting the lean edge of most of his recordings, the tenderness in **Stravinsky**'s rendering (♦Sony 46292, 3CD) betrays his lifelong affection for this score (as does the rehearsal excerpt in the "Stravinsky Edition"). **Ansermet** scores again with a subdued and lovely performance in nice early stereo that, alas, remains a casualty of the deleting axe (♦London 15028).

Perhaps surprisingly for a conductor with a hard-driving reputation, **Mravinsky** took on *Apollo* in a 1965 live performance with the superb Leningrad Philharmonic strings and hit the bull's-eye (♦Melodiya 25197). This is a gorgeous performance, full of elastic phrasing, unstylistic yet effective portamentos, and some nervous energy when needed, the work of a first-class maestro, and it's decently reproduced. **Rattle** leans toward a lyrical appreciation of the music, but his version tends to drift along without much sensual appeal or countervailing toughness

(EMI). **Salonen** indulges in some odd slowdowns and pauses; otherwise, his way is mobile and fluid, aiming for transparency, a not-incompatible mixture of classical sound and romantic tempo practices (Sony). His Stockholm Chamber Orchestra strings, however, aren't the best.

The strings of the Orchestra of St. John's Smith Square produce a dark, rich timbre that validates **John Lubbock**'s leisurely viewpoint (♦ASV 618). Normally an also-ran with this composer, this is one of **Chailly**'s better Stravinsky performances; he's more flexible, more expressive than usual, and permits the marvelous Concertgebouw strings to sing out (♦London 458142). The English String Orchestra receives perhaps the most opulently resonant sound of all, and **Boughton**'s mostly straightforward interpretation can't help but luxuriate at slower tempi in this cushioned setting (Nimbus). While **Marriner** gets bogged down in some passages, his forces are athletic and lovely in others, which is more like the Academy way (London). **Dorati** also takes the slow road, but with heavier, lackluster results (London). **Koussevitzky**'s heartfelt 1928 performance of the "Pas de deux" only, recorded just seven months after the ballet's premiere, makes you want to hear more (BSO 171002).

Le Baiser de la fée and *Divertimento.* Not for the first or last time, Stravinsky shocked the world in 1928 by proclaiming his love for Tchaikovsky's music in this transformation of some of his piano pieces, songs, and a few symphonic quotes into a ballet in the neoclassical idiom. A sweeping, attractive, tuneful score spiced with Stravinsky's harmonic pungency, at last *Le Baiser* is achieving some measure of popularity, a far cry from a recent time when there were exactly zero versions in print.

Stravinsky made two recordings, a 1955 mono with the Cleveland Orchestra (♦Sony 63325, 2CD) and a more spaciously recorded Columbia Symphony session a decade later (♦Sony 46292, 3CD). I like both; the Cleveland is sharper in articulation while the Columbia is lighter and more graceful, and the playing of the Hollywood musicians is not all that inferior (both have their woolly moments in the horns). **Muti** and the La Scala Orchestra have dash and fire as well as delicacy when needed but also some unyielding stiffness in manner, particularly in the crucial "Village Fête" section (Sony). **Järvi** maintains a mostly brisk pace with the competent Scottish National Orchestra, wrapped in nicely resonant sound and coupled appropriately with *Bluebird Pas de Deux,* Stravinsky's arrangement of excerpts from *Sleeping Beauty* (Chandos).

Divertimento distills the best of *Le Baiser* into four movements adding up to roughly half the complete ballet. **Reiner** and the Chicago Symphony are the long-running undisputed champs in this suite; their blend of crispness, delicacy, strong rhythmic feeling, and orchestral virtuosity is tough to beat, and the sound is amazingly up to date for a 1958 recording, tape hiss notwithstanding (♦RCA 61957). **Chailly** makes a good run at the Reiner standard and gets plenty of help from the engineers; if only he didn't charge a bit too hard in spots (London). As if to prove that a Franco-Russian team is well suited for 1928 vintage Stravinsky, **Bychkov** and the Orchestre de Paris are also very good, with a graceful medium-weight approach and excellent sound (Philips).

Capriccio for Piano and Orchestra. This is a more immediately winning piece than the Piano Concerto, embedded with a carefree, scampering quality that brings the composer's sense of humor into play. As a pianist, **Stravinsky** can be heard, albeit dimly, in a 1930 recording with Ansermet and the Walther Straram Concerts Orchestra in Paris's dead-sounding Théâtre des Champs Elysées (EMI). A percussive, brusque pi-

anist, though capable of some color, Stravinsky is in greater command of his brand-new score than many of the players in this wretchedly recorded orchestra.

Béroff is head-and-shoulders above the pack with his pointed, witty articulation at racy tempos and Ozawa's irreverent conducting; this is lots of fun (♦EMI 67276, 2CD). Craft's first recording with the Columbia Symphony is saddled with the characterless playing of **Entremont** and too-close miking (Sony), whereas his second with the Orchestra of St. Luke's features the more playful **Mark Wait** (MusicMasters). Indeed, the second performance as a whole has far more color and shade than the first. **Crossley** and Salonen trip lightly and fragrantly through the score, generating some drive in the finale, balancing Crossley's piano against the orchestra as equal partners (♦Sony 45797). **Ogdon** and Marriner are more opaque, less pointed in the first two movements, but pull off a nice finale (London).

Violin Concerto. No high-flown, romantic virtuoso piece is this tangy, spiky, Spartan, concertante-style concerto; indeed, it's almost an anti-violin concerto as far as some show-off fiddlers are concerned. On the other hand, other violinists find it a cleansing experience right from the fabulously acidic spread-out chord that launches each movement.

Although **Stern**'s recording with Stravinsky (now available separately in the "Isaac Stern: A Life in Music" edition) has been attacked for inaccuracies, I think his cutting-edge tone and incisive rhythmic sense were a good match for the composer's pointed conducting of the Columbia Symphony (♦Sony 64505). The sound is closely-miked stereo (the date of the recording is 1960, not 1951 as the booklet says). A '30s recording led by Stravinsky with the violinist who gave the premiere, **Samuel Dushkin,** has been revived after decades in limbo, but is for scholars and masochists only; tempos are more deliberate, Dushkin's playing is very scrappy, and the Lamoureux Orchestra is just adequate (Biddulph).

Mutter is one of the best we currently have for 20th century violin music; sporting a somewhat thinner tone, she has much of Stern's incisiveness and more expressive phrasings (♦DG 423696). Her alert collaborators are Paul Sacher, now the keeper of the Stravinsky archives, and the Philharmonia, and this valuable disc includes two Lutoslawski concerti conducted by the composer. **Perlman** with Ozawa is direct, witty, and technically dazzling (♦DG 447445); his live remake with Barenboim and the Chicago Symphony is silkier in tone but has more pointed orchestral support (♦Teldec 98255).

Cho-Liang Lin is somewhat scrappier, as is Salonen's LA Philharmonic (Sony). Everyone has the right idea, light, springy, and grotesque, but other recordings have more flair. An improved Salonen/LA team got another, more intimate crack at the concerto with a silkier-toned **Mullova** in 1997 (Philips), yet it sounds claustrophobic next to the more spaciously-recorded Lin performance. **Chung**'s lyrical rendering with Previn has been praised to the skies—which beats me, for I find it too soft-focused, rhythmically flaccid, and veiled in sound (London). Presumably Craft is as accurate as a measurement in an MIT lab, but the corrected tempos result in slack pacing; soloist **Krzysztov Smietana** lacks personality and is recessed too far into the orchestra (MusicMasters).

Vengerov and Rostropovich are highly stimulating and controversial. Vengerov gives the outer movements a cutting Slavic rasp and sharp-edged panache, and flaunts an extravagantly Romantic temperament in III, while the conductor and the massive LSO enliven their often broad tempos with sly phrasing that actually has a lot of character. As an unorthodox, deeply felt alternative, this beautifully recorded release is worth a try (◆EMI 56966).

Jeu de Cartes Another attractive, witty, brilliantly pointed, neoclassical ballet score is slowly becoming better known, with mischievous swipes from *Barber of Seville, La Valse,* and other totems among its delights. Again **Stravinsky** leads the way with his lively, scampering, rhythmically alert stereo recording with the Cleveland Orchestra (◆Sony 46292, 3CD). His pioneering 1938 Telefunken account with the Berlin Philharmonic, with reproduction startlingly good for its time, is actually faster than the remake, but it comes off as heavier-set and less humorous (Biddulph).

Salonen's high-powered account is also good (◆CBS 44917), a little mannered in spots, but fully aware of the ballet's sharp wit and better executed than Stravinsky/Cleveland. **Karajan** recorded *Jeu de Cartes* in glassy-sounding mono in 1952; despite the heavyweight texture, it's a powerhouse performance that, in its regal way, doesn't short-change the ballet's satirical shafts (EMI). The super-refined **Abbado** account has a lot of vitality but also some ponderous episodes and a general shortage of humor (DG). The same goes for **Järvi**'s disc, though the gorgeous sound and mid-price make it very tempting (◆Chandos 7120).

Dumbarton Oaks Concerto. Although Stravinsky probably didn't mean this as a satire of Brandenburg Concerto 3, with its deliberately repetitive blocks of baroque-like motives, the arch flavor of the Allegretto middle movement, and scampering outcropping in the Finale, it succeeds deliciously in that role. **Stravinsky** is at his most ingratiating in his Columbia Chamber Orchestra recording, delectably pointing out every witty detail (◆Sony 46296). The sound is almost analytical, as if every instrument were individually miked, but this concerto grosso can take it. There are earlier composer recordings, too—a 1947 rendition (Pearl 0065) and a scrappy, spirited 1954 Lugano broadcast (Aura 164). **Craft** also gets it right, with highly pointed accents and faster tempos (◆MusicMasters 67113). **Hogwood** has the right deadpan stance, fine soloists, and excellent sound, though he falls just short of underlining the humor as effectively as the composer (London).

From Ukraine, **Virko Baley** and the Kiev Camerata play *Dumbarton* with plenty of vigor and wit as part of a very mixed program; this long-shot is thoroughly competitive (◆Cambria 1403). The **Orpheus Chamber Orchestra** takes it noticeably slower, but their version has the most impressive ensemble and concertante work of the lot, and their more elegant performance retains most of the piece's barbed spirit (◆DG 445541). Not so with **Boulez,** who, in a rare Stravinsky venture beyond 1920, is sober, deliberate, and rather humorless (DG). As for **Günter Wand,** who turns in a ponderous, lead-weighted performance in a grab-bag program, it's surprising that this Teutonic veteran would take it on at all (RCA).

Symphony in C. The composition of this piece came at a very difficult time for Stravinsky (1938-40), when tuberculosis claimed the lives of his wife, daughter, and nearly his own, and he made the move from Europe to America. Despite his protestations that the music didn't mean anything other than a means to keep his mind busy, you can hear desperation breaking through the orderly neoclassical surface in I, and the *angst* is rarely far from sight in the remaining three movements.

Stravinsky's own stereo performance with the CBC Symphony captures that despair in abrupt, jagged rhythms; the playing is mostly quite good, save for the fourth movement (◆CBS 42434). His 1952 mono Cleveland disc takes a similar tack, has somewhat better playing, but doesn't quite convey the force of the stereo performance (◆Sony 63325,

2CD). It's not that he doesn't try, for the new Masterworks Heritage reissue comes with a brief rehearsal excerpt where he repeatedly asks for more staccato. **Craft**'s rendering is even tougher, faster, more driving, and all the more effective as a result; the piece can take his ruggedness and then some (◆MusicMasters 67086).

With **Tilson Thomas,** in one of his best Stravinsky recordings, the basic pushing energy is there, strewn with gusts of violence, and he also receives a more polished orchestral surface, courtesy of the LSO (◆Sony 53275). **Bernstein** confronts the symphony's underlying angst directly; his view is darker and broader, while preserving a yen for strong rhythm that keeps the music from assuming a beaten-down quality (DG). The Israel Philharmonic's playing is raw at the climaxes and the sound is dry but listenable; if only he had taped it earlier in his career in New York. **Colin Davis** and the LSO are deliberate and classical at first, kicking it up to a cracking tempo in the finale; avoid his later, heavier-set digital rendition with the Bavarian Radio Symphony (both Philips). **Karajan** delivers his usual stuff—a supremely buffed surface, broad pacing (again, except for the finale), and the Berlin Philharmonic's strong playing, but in this work, he won't sweep you away (DG).

Tango. When the sentimentality of Astor Piazzolla gets too cloying, Stravinsky's sardonic take on the tango is the perfect antidote. **Dorati** catches the sly spirit perfectly (◆Mercury 432012); **Craft** is more elegant but still quite winning (MusicMasters 67195). The **Orpheus Chamber Orchestra** takes Dorati's brisk tempo, with a whiff of cabaret added (◆DG 453458). **Stravinsky**'s Columbia Jazz Ensemble sounds way too slow to me—too sinister (Sony). In the solo piano version, **Béroff** is nicely brisk and acerbic (◆EMI 67276, 2CD), **Gloria Cheng** is relaxed and waywardly expressive (Telarc 80549), while **Aleck Karis** drags too much (Bridge).

Danses Concertantes. The abrupt, jocular eruptions and general optimism of these concert dances can be read as an expression of relief, for this was Stravinsky's first work written entirely in America. The composer's first recording (◆Pearl 0065), made in the late '40s, is a hearty, robust affair with adequate playing by the RCA Victor Chamber Orchestra, and an even heartier Stravinsky-led 1954 broadcast with Lugano's Orchestra della Svizzera Italiana has surfaced (◆Aura 164). **Craft**'s recording was once deliberately, and wrongly, credited to Stravinsky; it's leaner in texture and more ascetic in atmosphere (Sony). The **Orpheus Chamber Orchestra** plays with brio and precision, just lacking that extra crackling edge (DG). **Hickox** resembles Craft in texture but applies an appealing balletic grace—and thus, with an outstanding *Pulcinella* as a coupling, captures the prize (◆Virgin 61107).

Four Norwegian Moods. As star-struck as any tourist, but not at any price, Stravinsky tried several times to write for an uncomprehending Hollywood, and these pleasing neoclassical takeoffs on the idiom of Grieg were a salvage job from the rejected score to the film *The Commandos Strike at Dawn.* **Stravinsky**'s stereo recording with the CBC Symphony bounces along delightfully (◆Sony 46296), while **Craft** is much quicker, more military in bearing in "Intrada" and has better playing from the Orchestra of St. Luke's (◆MusicMasters 67110). A roughhouse Russian alternative is by the young **Järvi** and the Moscow Radio Symphony (Melodiya/HMV).

Circus Polka. Perhaps Stravinsky's strangest commission, *Circus Polka* was written for a baby elephant, bumping along with good cheer and taking Schubert's *Marche Militaire* along for the ride. **Stravinsky**'s own stereo recording will give you the right galumphing idea (◆Sony 46296);

his mono rendition with the NYPO is introduced by Jack Benny! (Pearl). **Craft** is jauntier and stiffer, almost a goose-step (MusicMasters), and **Tilson Thomas** brings an almost Ivesian exuberance and lightness to the dance (♦RCA 68865). **Karajan** and his Berliners are wonderfully droll (♦DG 2530 267)—you'd be surprised how well they get it—while **Järvi**'s recording is a raucous hoot (Melodiya/HMV). I also like **Inbal**'s truly elephantine stomp through the piece (Teldec 46327).

Ode. Breaking a bit from the good-times atmosphere of his early American pieces, the three-movement *Ode* forms an elegiac sandwich around a lively central hunting scene, another fragment of an abandoned film score (*Jane Eyre*). While **Stravinsky** (Sony) is totally unsentimental and invigorating with the Cleveland Orchestra (although the horns aren't as good as they should be), I prefer his surprisingly emotional 1962 live recording with an inspired USSR Symphony in decent, close-up stereo (♦Melodiya 33220). **Craft** coaxes a lean, quick, pointed performance from the Orchestra of St. Luke's in Vol. 5 of "The Composer" series (MusicMasters). **Tilson Thomas** is generally more lyrical in approach, receiving plush support from the LSO (RCA).

Scherzo à la Russe. Written for the Paul Whiteman band, this reminiscence of the mood of *Pétrouchka* from a neoclassical viewpoint exists in two versions, one for orchestra and the other for an augmented jazz big band, and contains yet more strains from an attempted film score. Though the jazz version has saxophones, the difference in ambience is surprisingly slight. The enterprising **Rattle** gives you both versions; he takes the orchestral version at a slightly slower pace while romping through the jazz band edition (♦EMI 49178). If only it weren't coupled with an uneven *Firebird,* it would be an easy first choice. **Inbal** also did both in galumphing, lavishly-recorded performances (the jazz version tugs more emphatically), once inconveniently available on separate discs (Teldec 44938 and 46327).

Stravinsky's late '40s recording with the RCA Victor Symphony is brisk, bouncy, and delightfully raucous (♦Pearl 0065); his remake with the Columbia Symphony is microscopically slower but has more robust vitality (♦CBS 42432). Both use the orchestral versions, whereas **Craft** opts for the jazz band but rushes the tempos so much that the Orchestra of St. Luke's can't breathe (MusicMasters). On the orchestral side, **Dorati** and the LSO have the pounding rhythm and bright, brassy timbre of a parade-ground performance (Mercury). **Tilson Thomas** leans a bit heavily into the accents; otherwise he pulls it off with as much élan as Rattle (♦RCA 68865). **Pletnev** is unbearably draggy and lifeless, no fun at all (DG). The relentlessly bouncy, fast **Orpheus Chamber Orchestra** claims they play the orchestral version, but I hear saxophones (DG).

Scènes de ballet. Written for Billy Rose, who called it a "great success" but thought it could be a "sensational success" if the orchestrations were redone (Stravinsky's reply was, "Satisfied with great success"), these are graceful, mostly light-hearted dance gestures of no great distinction, yet engagingly easy to live with. Both **Stravinsky** studio performances are excellent. On the mono edition the performance has warmth and vigor, the NYPO is in superb form, and the sound is old but listenable (♦Pearl 9292, 2CD). As is the general pattern, his stereo remake is leaner in texture, with more spring in the rhythms; the CBC Symphony isn't as brilliant as New York but certainly up to the task, and the spotlighted sound reveals a lot more detail (♦Sony 46292, 3CD). A third Stravinsky performance comes to us via a 1952 Paris concert, but its vigor is compromised by sour orchestral playing (Disques Montaigne).

Craft is lighter still in texture, even quicker than Stravinsky (MusicMasters). **Tilson Thomas** takes a more expressive, lush, leisurely trip,

astutely upholding the Russian balletic tradition from Tchaikovsky through *Le Baiser de la fée* to this piece (RCA).

Ebony Concerto. Though roundly criticized by purists on both sides of the classical/jazz fence when it came out, the *Ebony Concerto* is a wonderfully acerbic Third Stream piece with its own idiosyncratic way of swinging that's difficult but not impossible to replicate. **Stravinsky** actually led the Woody Herman First Herd in the premiere recording on 78s. The reading is rather clunky; the great jazz soloists, perhaps intimidated by the great composer, sound stiff (Pearl). He does much better in his remake with **Benny Goodman;** this one swings just enough in the work's peculiar rumba-like manner, and the Columbia Jazz Ensemble creates a more convincing big-band sound than did the real working Herman group (♦Sony 46297, 2CD). Long after a second, often downright inept attempt in 1959 (Everest), Herman's band—now the Thundering Herd—tried *Ebony* for a third time in 1987 with **Richard Stoltzman** conducting instead of the ailing leader; it's an able but colorless reading with almost no rhythmic bite (RCA).

The Chicago Symphony's brilliant clarinetist **John Bruce Yeh** leads the field in a swaggering, idiomatically right performance with Donald DeRoche and the De Paul University Wind Ensemble; the sound is staggeringly clear and rich (♦Reference 55). Onetime jazzman **Rattle** has the most genuine feeling for the subtler aspects of swing, particularly in the slow movement (♦EMI 47991). **Boulez** does surprisingly well in a workout of his preferred Stravinsky time period: a fast, pointed, precisely etched outing that even has some swing (♦DG 447405). **Tilson Thomas** and the young New World Symphony are oddly smoothed out, even overrefined—an anomaly in a CD of otherwise brash performances of jazz-tinged classics (RCA). But then, so is **Craft,** suggesting a questionable trend toward the taming of the *Ebony* (MusicMasters)

Symphony in Three Movements. Stravinsky's most popular—and best—symphony is a wartime piece of craggy power and rhythmic punch; a great performance should make you unable to sit still. Both of the composer's studio recordings do that. **Stravinsky**'s (and the piece's) first recording with the NYPO, magnificently played with much driving fire in surprisingly full 1946 sound, is a touchstone; when played straight from the shoulder, the work generates its own force (♦Pearl 9292, 2CD). The stereo remake is leaner, jazzier, full of life-affirming rhythm; the Columbia Symphony plays with enormous vitality—but how did they let that awful wrong trumpet note in the last chord slip by? Never mind, it's still a superb recording (♦CBS 42434)

Craft tries to follow the composer's example at faster tempos, lacking only the composer's rhythmic resiliency—and that's half the game conceded right there (MusicMasters). **Tilson Thomas** has no such handicap; his performance has plenty of pizzazz and swings along with a more polished surface (♦Sony 53275)—though oddly, the second half often drags (his live performances have always been on the dot). **Rattle** is a touch more relaxed at first, with a nicely sly II and rugged III, and receives the best sound of the pack (EMI). **Salonen** skates lightly over the rhythms of the I and glides through II, producing light, almost delicate textures from the Philharmonia (Sony). His is virtually a balletic performance, a novel idea in this field.

Colin Davis's exciting, still-competitive LSO recording (♦Philips 442583, 2CD) has more rugged drive and life than his overrefined remake in Munich (also Philips), though the Bavarian Radio Symphony is a better ensemble. **Maazel** gets things cracking at a lively tempo in I with just enough rhythmic snap; the Bavarian refinement doesn't get in Stravinsky's jagged way, though the finale could use a bit more of an edge (RCA). **Bernstein** starts up slowly but enforces sharp rhythms with craggy details protruding and develops a pounding vitality in the end—a valid conception as punched out by the Israel Philharmonic, but not among the best (DG). **Boulez**'s I is just adequate, with no particular rhythmic animation—not his strong suit in any case; II is draggy and headed nowhere and III has a bit more life (DG 457616). While it's good to see him reassessing areas of Stravinsky that he once disdained, he still doesn't sound convinced.

Concerto in D for String Orchestra. This is another lovable neoclassical masterpiece, where passages of perpetual motion run through the landscape and cool beauty is deflated by a pungent joke now and then. **Stravinsky** plays it straight and lean, with clipped phrasing (except in the Arioso) and transparent textures (♦Sony 46296); he was more expressive in a 1954 live performance in Lugano, captured in very good mono (♦Aura 164). **Craft** leads an excellent, beautifully recorded turn—alive, pointed in rhythm, and catching the droll humor, one of his best recordings in his series (♦MusicMasters 67177).

Salonen also gives it a mostly clear-cut treatment—his tempo fluctuations aren't meant to convey emotion—and he's definitely aware of the fun (♦Sony 46667). The **Orpheus Chamber Orchestra** is very invigorating as their tempos shoot along; their unguided strings sound like they're having a ball (♦DG 453458). And then there's **Karajan,** who does it his defiantly Germanic way—plush, sleek, and slow but with powerful playing from the Berlin Philharmonic (♦DG 423252 or 447435). Indeed, the second subject of I has a unique languorous beauty I wouldn't want to do without.

Orpheus. The composer's most enigmatic ballet, it is mostly contemplative and inward, dominated by spare, sometimes angular, solitary instrumental lines and silences that look forward to his serial adventures, becoming more difficult to penetrate as it unfolds. **Stravinsky**'s stereo recording makes a poised, refined case for its elusive qualities; the Chicago Symphony—especially the many soloists—responds magnificently (♦Sony 46292, 3CD). Another Stravinsky-led *Orpheus* comes from Russia, a rough, slightly trimmed live reading with the USSR Symphony that gradually becomes bogged down, aimless, and undisciplined (Melodiya). **Järvi** starts out a bit fast but that sets up a polished, fluid, mostly lush rendition with gorgeous sound from the Concertgebouw (♦Chandos 7120).

Obviously the **Orpheus Chamber Orchestra** just had to have a crack at this, yet after a lovely introduction, there's neither tension and life, nor compensating darkness (DG). **Lubbock**'s very well-played performance has a lot of dark, suave atmosphere, an analog dark horse that has worn well over two decades (♦ASV 618). Ultimately it's **Salonen** and the Philharmonia who have made the most cohesive recording of this score, flying through the pages with lightness, clarity, and drive (♦Sony 53274).

Agon. It was the last of Stravinsky's amazing half-century-long string of ballets, and though parts of it use the composer's still-controversial serial procedures, it has a lightness and blithe spirit that are winning more converts. We need good recordings of *Agon,* and the two most recent ones are the best yet. **Craft**'s is tightly played and very fast, three minutes quicker than the composer, but he gets the Orchestra of St. Luke's to dance in an airborne recording (♦MusicMasters 67113). The assured **Tilson Thomas** performance has playful panache and bounce as well as mystery; it goes straight to the top (♦RCA 68865).

Stravinsky's disc, recorded the day after the world premiere, gives

you the idea, but it sounds like a very brave first draft; the ad hoc "Los Angeles Festival Symphony Orchestra" doesn't quite have the piece in its grasp (Sony). As part of a tribute album to Balanchine, **Robert Irving** offers a sturdy, plain-wrap version that again gives you the idea and little more (Nonesuch). **Iwaki** and his Melbourne ensemble are cautious and remote, though they make a game stab at a difficult score (Virgin). Give **Mravinsky** and the Leningrad plenty of credit for playing the partly serial *Agon* in the Soviet Union, and this live, raw-boned, pungent, even sinister performance isn't like any Western recording (Melodiya). The mono sound, however, is hard and abrasive.

Movements for Piano and Orchestra. These are tough, super-concentrated, quiet, Webernesque jewels from deep within the composer's serial period, laced with a few rhythmic irregularities and orchestrational signatures to remind us that indeed Stravinsky is the composer. **Rosen** and Stravinsky give us a sharply outlined, brightly recorded look at this elusive quarry (Sony), while **Crossley** and Salonen are more polished and not quite as arch (Sony). **Béroff** and Ozawa are a touch faster in the first and fourth movements, with a little more bite (♦EMI 67276, 2CD), and Craft, with pianist **Christopher Oldfather,** delivers the slowest but also the most characterful rendition of all (♦MusicMasters 67195).

Instrumental Miniatures A delicate, witty 1962 arrangement of Stravinsky's eight *Easy Pieces* for piano written a half-century before, it is totally at odds (except maybe in texture) with the rigorous serial direction he was then pursuing. **Stravinsky** and members of the CBC Symphony are light on their feet, pointed in rhythm, and very much aware of the Russian quality in the music (♦Sony 46296). **Craft** is quicker, sometimes too hard-pressed, but good overall (MusicMasters). The **Orpheus Chamber Orchestra** scores with more expressive extremes in a recording now, alas, cut off from its old companions, *Pulcinella Suite* and *Dumbarton Oaks* (DG). **Boulez** offers dry precision and not much personality (DG).

Variations "Aldous Huxley in memoriam" for Orchestra. Less than six minutes in length, Stravinsky's last orchestral piece is his most concentrated and most difficult to perform or comprehend. The secret to unlocking it is to pretend it's Webern, listening repeatedly until each note shines like a refracting gem. **Craft** made two recordings, the first a hasty, not quite coalesced effort with the Columbia Symphony (Sony); the second with the London Philharmonic, slower yet still brightly lit, acerbic in tone, and indelibly stamped with the Stravinsky sound despite the Webern esthetic (♦MusicMasters 67177). **Oliver Knussen**'s is even sharper and more fully characterized (♦DG 447068).

CHAMBER MUSIC

Pastorale. The quiet *Pastorale* received **Stravinsky**-directed recordings in an arrangement for violin and wind quartet—a fairly tense one from 1933 (EMI) and a lovely, relaxed rendition from 1965 (♦Sony 46297, 2CD). **Boulez** gives you the unusual original version for wordless soprano (Bryn-Julson) and four winds (♦DG 413751).

L'Histoire du Soldat (*A Soldier's Tale*). Nothing like this deliciously satirical, jazzy, acidic, addictive theater piece had ever existed before, a play based on the Faust legend separated by a parade of marches, a tango, a waltz, an off-kilter ragtime dance, and mordant little interludes pumped out by a compact, unorthodox seven-piece group that needs not a player more. The complete piece used to be a rarity but now receives increasing numbers of scurrilously updated stagings—and for those impatient with all the talking, there exists a marvelous suite that gives you just about every important idea in the score, plus chamber versions in various editions for smaller groups.

The best recording I know of the whole work, alas, was available only briefly in the late '80s (♦Pangaea 6233). It sports an all-star cast of expert British actors—rock star Sting as a superb, salt-of-the-earth Soldier, Ian McKellen as the narrator, and in a bizarre but inspired bit of casting, Vanessa Redgrave as the Devil—and **Nagano**'s marvelously pointed, rhythmically swinging conducting of seven crack members of the London Sinfonietta. In a highly unusual appearance with a chamber ensemble, the 85-year-old **Stokowski** is delightful; he produces highly-delineated rhythms that convey plenty of kick and sly humor. The cast, led by narrator Madeleine Milhaud (Darius's wife), performs the dialogue in French (♦Vanguard 8004; an English version is also available in ♦Vanguard 92). In the absence of Nagano, Stokowski's is the *Histoire* of choice.

One-time horror flick actor Christopher Lee takes all three parts quite authoritatively in another complete recording, but the pacing of the dialogue is too slack, as is the articulation of **Lionel Friend** and the Scottish Chamber Orchestra (Nimbus). In **Boulez**'s version, his conducting is also often slack, and the dialogue is in French (Erato). Contrary to myth, there is actually little to choose between **Stravinsky**'s mono recording of the suite in New York (♦Sony 63325, 2CD) and his stereo remake in Hollywood (♦Sony 46291, 3CD); both of them are terrific, rhythmically uplifting recordings. The West Coast cats are as accomplished as their Eastern rivals, the sound is warm and full in the mono, brighter in the stereo. Only a much slower tempo in the mono "Soldier at The Brook" episode and greater swing in the stereo "Ragtime" distinguishes them.

Bernstein's sole recording of the suite comes from the Tanglewood summer of 1947 in an indifferent-sounding transfer (♦RCA 68101). Though a bit broader than most and with some of the pieces in inverted order, his control of a Boston Symphony septet is full of thoughtfully nuanced phrasing and strong rhythm; his "Ragtime" really swings. **Craft**'s recording comes with a restored original percussion part; better still, it's a fine, tough, brisk, driving rendition, well recorded and well played by members of the Orchestra of St. Luke's (♦MusicMasters 67152). **Maazel** not only leads a polished and often very swift-paced performance, he also plays the violin part himself expertly and diabolically (♦RCA 68470). **Schwarz** and the LA Chamber Orchestra have the right idea but lack the extra snap of the others (Delos). **Järvi** too is vital, yet just a bit too genteel—or is the lush sound coloring our perceptions (Chandos)? The most common small-group version consists of about half the suite, for clarinet, violin, and piano; **Richard** and **Lucy Stoltzman** and Richard Goode turned out a cracking good performance (RCA).

Ragtime for Chamber Ensemble.
Stravinsky learned everything he knew about ragtime and jazz from printed sheet music—which is definitely not the jazz way to go about it—and this bouncy little concoction with its jangling cimbalom is his purest expression of homage while remaining completely Stravinskyan in attitude. His 1934 recording with a French pickup group (EMI 54607, 2CD) has fairly stiff rhythms but also tons of period charm—the trombonist is delightfully loose—but a Lugano radio group swings it more (♦Aura 164), and the Columbia Chamber Ensemble in his spacious stereo remake sounds more like a big band (♦Sony 46297, 2CD). **Salonen** stays very close to the composer's earlier tempo but remains fairly cool and composed (Sony). The **Orpheus Chamber Orchestra** matches the composer's tempo, with sharply angular rhythms (♦DG 453458). **Craft** perks up the tempo and gives it more rhythmic pizzazz (♦MusicMasters 67110).

Pieces for String Quartet.
As the listener will quickly discover, these three scratchy-sounding pieces are the first three of the four *Etudes for Orchestra* in their original acerbic garb. The **InterContemporain Quartet**'s dry, spiky performance provides an instructive comparison with Boulez's orchestral recording in the same set (Erato 98955, 3CD). An easier purchase would be the **Alban Berg Quartet**'s more humorous recording on a disc that gathers together nearly all of the Stravinsky string quartet literature—all 14 minutes of it—along with quartets by Roman Hauberstock-Ramatt and Gottfried von Einem (♦EMI 54347). The **Goldner Quartet** also gives you all the Stravinsky works for string quartet (plus some Szymanowski), a lower price, and an alert, nearly competitive performance (Naxos 554315).

A quartet of **Orpheus Chamber Orchestra** strings offer a sly, arch take as part of an excellent collection of Stravinsky miniatures (♦DG 453458). The **Brodsky Quartet** (Silva) serve up a performance of extremes—either very fast, ultra-spiky, and percussive, or scratched out at a funeral pace—in a grab-bag album of maximum hipness called "Lament" (one of their disc-fellows is rock singer Elvis Costello). The **Lafayette Quartet**'s collective tone becomes somewhat unstable in III after catching some of the abrasive humor of II (Dorian).

Concertino for 12 Instruments.
Originally written for string quartet in 1920, the composer rearranged this arch piece for six winds, four brass, violin, and cello in 1952, where it fits at the tail end of his neoclassical period. **Stravinsky** and the Columbia Chamber Ensemble give it a really acerbic edge, miked to within an inch of their instruments (♦Sony 46297, 2CD), and **Boulez** lays into it with a cool X-ray beam (Erato). **Craft** delineates the prickly wit and sharp angles marvelously well (♦MusicMasters 67103). So does **Tilson Thomas** at a somewhat slower tempo, placing it half-accurately on his "Stravinsky in America" album (RCA). The **Orpheus Chamber Orchestra** is miraculously cohesive, their brasses bite, and their tempos race through the tricky syncopations without a care (♦DG 453458). In the original string quartet edition, a Boulez LP of chamber music finds an **InterContemporain Quartet** offering a good, rhythmic account (DG), the close-miked **Goldner Quartet** scrapes away with sufficient gusto (Naxos 554315), but the **Alban Berg Quartet** is more aggressive and more in tune with the piece's ripping energy (♦EMI 54347).

Octet.
While some have called this work a watershed in Stravinsky's development, I believe that *Symphonies of Wind Instruments* is a more important transitional work, leaving this pointed, humorous, neoclassical bagatelle to bedevil the tongues and fingers of wind players. **Stravinsky**'s first recording from 1932 has much spirit and bounce, but also a wind group of unreliable intonation and extremely dry sound that gives the second movement a cartoonish feeling (EMI). In the '50s, a much more polished New York crew and solid mono engineering are on hand to bring his buoyant conducting to life (♦Sony 63325, 2CD). In stereo, Stravinsky's Hollywood octet is just about as good, the concept rhythmically a bit feistier (♦Sony 46297, 2CD). Take your pick between the latter two, but the mono will be easier to obtain. There's also a lively 1955 composer recording from Lugano (♦Aura 164).

The *Octet* figures significantly in **Craft**'s career, being the first work he ever conducted in public, and he brings to it a fine robustness and humor at racetrack tempos, which the winds of the Orchestra of St. Luke's handle with disarming ease (♦MusicMasters 67103). Another snapshot of **Bernstein** at Tanglewood in 1947 finds him with eight members of the Boston Symphony a tad slower than the competition but full of expression and rhythmic bite; the sound is adequate mono with a bit of rumble early on (RCA). The nimble **Orpheus Chamber Orchestra** winds and brasses are as chipper and polished as anyone's, and they appreciate the *Octet's* occasional jazzy swerves more than most (♦DG 453458). **Chailly** receives a sharp, clear recording for his agile, though sometimes stiffly phrased performance with the London Sinfonietta (London), while **Salonen,** using the same band, gets a wittier, more flexible, more rhythmically alive performance out of them (♦Sony 45965).

Septet. Opening in the composer's neoclassical vein, the *Septet* eventually moves over the line into using tone rows, but the concluding contrapuntal "Gigue" where it happens has such a marvelous screwball theme that you won't care about the tonality unless you're looking for an argument. In I, **Stravinsky** (♦Sony 46297, 2CD) has somewhat more rhythmic excitement than **Craft** (♦MusicMasters 67158), but Craft is more propulsive in the "Gigue" and receives better playing and warmer sound overall. There is a mellower composer-led performance in mono as well (Columbia).

Transcriptions. The flagship release in a valuable series called "Composers in Person" includes several transcriptions from the '30s with Stravinsky as pianist and his sidekick **Samuel Dushkin** on violin, plus their exciting recording of *Duo Concertant* (♦EMI 54607, 2CD). Dushkin was the kind of highly percussive, tonally dry player the composer preferred, a prophetic style-setter for the avant-garde later in the 20th century, but technically he leaves a lot to be desired by today's standards.

Most of the music Stravinsky fashioned for violin and piano with the assistance of Dushkin can be found in a now-deleted boxed set by the refined young team of **Isabelle van Keulen** and Mustonen (Philips 420953, 2CD). Both are exponents of the generic romantic/objective international style, but they can generate enough rhythm when necessary. Mustonen provides his own stylish staccato arrangement of *Tango,* and alone, van Keulen plays the violin version of the stark *Elégie*. And while we're at it, let's gang up on EMI to bring back **Perlman**'s marvelous recordings of *Divertimento, Suite Italienne,* and *Duo Concertant* with pianist Bruno Canino (♦Angel 32014).

PIANO MUSIC

"Complete." **Martin Jones** has by far the most comprehensive survey of Stravinsky's surprisingly small solo piano output (♦Nimbus 5519/20, 2CD). He seems most at home with music that can take a conventional Romantic virtuoso treatment, from the earlier student pieces right through *Firebird,* whereas he offers a tame *Pétrouchka* and some rather square-cut readings of the rag pieces and neoclassical works. But there are a lot of compensating rarities in this set--the very early Scherzo, the ultra-chromatic, Scriabin-like Etudes Op. 7, transcriptions of major works like *Song of The Nightingale,* the last half of *Firebird Suite,* and *Symphonies of Wind Instruments*. (The latter fits surprisingly well on the piano, with pungent harmonies and stabbing dissonances.)

Three Movements from Pétrouchka. Written for Arthur Rubinstein—who, alas, didn't record it commercially—this is the only Stravinsky solo piano work, and a transcription at that, which has secured a prominent place in the piano repertoire. In Rubinstein's absence, the first choice, hands down, is **Pollini** with an astounding performance (♦DG 447431). Perfectly gauged in tempi, Stravinsky's rhythms humming along, lots of coloristic shading, and a refined, non-clattering Steinway tone, this disc has been praised every which way—and for once, you can believe it. **Béroff,** as part of his complete Stravinsky piano survey, is a strong contender (♦EMI 67276, 2CD), jaunty in a Parisian way; **Bronfman** is good too (Sony). The **Labèques** whack away at the two-piano

arrangement with lusty abandon, willing to exploit the percussive properties of the pianos to the hilt (Philips).

On the next level is **Aleck Karis,** who sports a formidable technique and favors more expression, but not very much drive (Bridge). **Ilana Vered** was very good on LP, getting some throbbing, steel-fingered momentum going in Part III (London). In a 1973 Czech Radio tape, **Gilels** has rock-solid rhythm going for him in "Danse Russe" and clearly-etched textures elsewhere that, alas, reveal a lot of wrong notes (Philips). **Cherkassky**'s performance is hopelessly pulled about in tempo to the point of flaccidity, especially in "Danse Russe" a case study of eccentricity gone haywire (Nimbus).

Pianola Works. **Rex Lawson,** who claims to be the world's only professional concert pianolist, presumably makes as good a case as can be made for Stravinsky's piano roll editions of the complete *Pétrouchka* and *Rite* (MusicMasters). Although the performances still sound unnervingly mechanical—especially the trills—*Rite* is fascinating for its unorthodox composer-stipulated tempos; "Danse sacrale" now sounds like a blueprint for the finale of Prokofiev's Piano Sonata 7! The short *Etude For Pianola,* of course, receives a totally idiomatic rendering of the music as intended. Another Lawson *Rite* performance can be found in Benjamin Zander's disc of the orchestral *Rite* (IMP 25).

Piano Rag Music. No, this isn't real ragtime, just a rambunctious little exercise in convoluted rhythm with a whiff of American rags now and then. **Stravinsky** in 1934 is jagged, unpolished, and full of life (♦EMI 54607, 2CD, or Sony 46297, 2CD). **Béroff** applies a more brittle touch, sharply delineating the sudden changes in rhythm (♦EMI 67276, 2CD). **Karis** is smoother and propulsive, keeping the rag influence under wraps (Bridge), while **Mark Wait** generates more drive and has a more pronounced rhythmic feeling (MusicMasters).

Serenade. Though this 1925 foursome of stylistically varied, not terribly inspired pieces was famously written to order for a projected set of two ten-inch 78 rpm records, **Stravinsky** didn't get around to recording it until 1934 (♦EMI 54607, 2CD, or Sony 46297, 2CD). Not a virtuoso pianist, the composer nevertheless gives you the basic idea with considerable lilt and energy. As for the virtuosos, **Karis** is more relaxed and rounded and not as interesting (Bridge); **Béroff**'s I and IV are so languorous and out of shape that they wouldn't fit on a ten-inch 78, while III races like Prokofiev unchained (EMI).

Concerto for Two Pianos. Here you don't have to imagine the composer pounding out his latest ballet or choral piece on his out-of-tune upright composing piano, for this exciting, percussively polyphonic duo-piano piece goes straight from the keyboard onto the page and back. **Stravinsky** and his son **Soulima** reveal the most telling nuances and turns of phrase while also generating much vitality in a worn-sounding recording from 1938 (♦EMI 54607, 2CD, or Sony 46297, 2CD). **Mark Wait** and **Tom Schultz** generate similar drive at faster tempos in a recording buried within Vol. V of Craft's Stravinsky series (MusicMasters). The **Labèques** are even more brittle, incisive, and feverish in tempo—they seem happiest when the volume and speed go up—and Philips's microphones easily contain their most clangorous passages. **Benjamin Frith** and **Peter Hill** are the most relaxed of the lot, almost too refined (Naxos).

Piano Sonatas. The early half-hour Piano Sonata in F-sharp Minor from 1903–4, lost until 1973, would make a great name-the-composer parlor game. Like the E-flat symphony, it sounds like long-lost Rachmaninoff in the first movement, with touches of Tchaikovsky the rest of the way. Both **Crossley,** who gave the recorded premiere (Philips), and **Béroff** (♦EMI 67276, 2CD) approach the piece with un-selfconscious 19th-century bravura.

The official Piano Sonata dates from 1924 and is in a more recognizable neoclassical Stravinsky idiom, with motor-like propulsion, tricky rhythms, and mordant wit. **Béroff** treats it to a brilliant, pointed performance (♦EMI 67276, 2CD), while **Karis** offers a much mellower alternative (Bridge). The Sonata for Two Pianos receives a dry, faceless performance by **Gold** and **Fizdale** in the "Stravinsky Edition" (Sony). **Frith** and **Hill**'s controlled yet more musical account is a much better bargain, and you also get an invigorating, rhythmic account of Stravinsky's four-hands arrangement of *Rite of Spring* (♦Naxos 553386).

CHORAL MUSIC

Zvezdoliki (*King of the Stars*). Nestled between *Pétrouchka* and *Rite of Spring* on the time line, *Zvezdoliki* is just as starkly original and unique—a five-minute cantata with an eerie, placid surface and mind-bending harmonies that seem to anticipate Ligeti by half a century. **Stravinsky**'s recording has a spiky, scary, primeval power, though the singers aren't precisely in tune (Sony). **Craft** takes you inside the piece to watch the gears turn at the expense of some atmosphere (MusicMasters). It's **Tilson Thomas** who takes the piece's measure, conjuring up a much slower, mysterious slice of science fiction, with luminous Symphony Hall sound for the Boston Symphony and New England Conservatory Chorus (♦DG 435073).

Les Noces. Once again, **Stravinsky** invented a genre of his own with this pounding, clattering, vibrant theater piece for four pianos, percussion section, vocal soloists, and chorus, a Dionysian celebration of a Russian peasant wedding. He unleashed his daring score in a 1934 performance with an English-translated text, enforcing his will vigorously on the ad hoc piano/percussion ensemble, the BBC Chorus, and vocal soloists, who pronounce everything with crisp British diction (EMI). Alas, the recessed sound in the transfer greatly dilutes this brave recording's impact. For the stereo version, he assembled a piano quartet of blue-chip composers—Barber, Copland, Foss, and Sessions—yet they, the Columbia Percussion Ensemble, the American Concert Choir, and soloists don't generate as much juice as the occasion would seem to require (Sony).

Craft has had a long, complex recorded involvement with *Les Noces.* His first LP in the '60s used the published edition in Russian, setting sometimes deliberate tempos (Columbia). Then around 1974, he made two more fascinating recordings in a single LP (Columbia M33201)—one using a dynamic but rejected complete version for winds, brass, string octet, percussion, and cimbalom; the other a radical attempt for pianola, two cimbaloms, harmonium, and percussion that breaks off after the first two parts. For recording No. 4—or 3½?—Craft went back to the published edition and generated a driving, hurtling performance with the Gregg Smith Singers and members of the Orchestra of St. Luke's (♦MusicMasters 67086).

While Stravinsky's celebrity coup didn't quite pay off, **Bernstein** proved the idea can work (♦DG 423251). Though deliberate in tempo, he delivers a tremendous wallop of rhythmic force, thoroughly turbocharging the excellent English Bach Festival percussionists, noted pianists Argerich, Zimerman, Katsaris, and Francesch, and chorus—a barbaric, ecstatic, life-affirming, *echt*-Russian performance in excellent analog sound. An early **Boulez** recording (in French) uses forces from the Théatre National de L'Opéra (including a young, strong José van Dam) in a noisy but emotionally neutral performance, more mid-

century avant-garde than Russian in sound; and flatly recorded (Adès). **Ansermet** also does it in French, softer in focus as was his style, yet some of the piece's rowdy spirit comes through in astonishingly good 1961 sound (London 443476, 2CD). **James Wood**'s singers are recessed and the energy level is low; however, the performance comes with a fascinating preface of five genuine, enthusiastically performed Russian bridal folk songs (Hyperion 66410).

Oedipus Rex. Though Stravinsky set out to write a "waxworks opera"—a static opera-oratorio on a Greek legend further distanced by its use of a Latin text—what resulted was not a pretentious bore but a theater piece of tremendous dramatic power and irony with strong roots in, of all people, Verdi. **Stravinsky**'s dramatic 1951 recording was justly famous for Pears's heroic but vulnerable Oedipus, librettist Cocteau's deliciously haughty narration—recorded in Paris some eight months later—and Martha Mödl's Wagnerian Jocasta (♦Odyssey 33789). This ought to be a priority reclamation project for Sony, along with **Bernstein**'s fervent Boston recording (Columbia). The composer's remake in Washington on the day of President Kennedy's inauguration isn't as good (Sony). The Chester Watson Chorus and Washington Opera Society Orchestra are strident, nearly defeating Stravinsky's pinpointing of his mocking wind writing; George Shirley is a sturdy Oedipus but no Pears; John Westbrook's English narration is a plus, though. Until the 1951 recording reappears, a 1952 Stravinsky-led live performance from Paris, with Cocteau and a decent cast, delivers enough force to serve as a stand-in (♦Disques Montaigne 8760, 2CD).

Salonen realizes the score's power and irony, bringing out the latter in his spotlighted pointing of the wind obbligatos while maintaining mobile, lucid textures (♦Sony 48057). His narrator (in French) is the radical stage director Patrice Chereau, Vinson Cole is an adequate Oedipus, Sotin a subtle Tiresias, and von Otter a touchingly human Jocasta. **Colin Davis** also scores in a 1983 performance of direct, incisive force that ranks with Salonen's among the best digital editions (♦Orfeo 071831). Thomas Moser is persuasive as Oedipus, the narration is in French, and Davis has the current gold-standard Jocasta, Jessye Norman.

Norman also appears in **Ozawa**'s lugubrious recording (Philips). **Craft,** who can be impressively craggy in this work live, skips hastily over the surface, missing the dramatic weight and impact, and the Orchestra of St. Luke's and the New York Choral Artists aren't at their best (MusicMasters). An older, shakier, but still eloquent Pears returns and nearly redeems the **Solti,** which is more refined and not as hard-driven as you might guess—and thus, not too effective, in Stravinsky English-oratorio-style. (London).

Symphony of Psalms. Perhaps more than any of his other works, this choral symphony—whose austerity can't quite contain Stravinsky's deeply religious feelings—refutes those who accuse the composer of being a cold, congenital curmudgeon. In the hands of an inspired conductor, the piece can move you right down to your toes—and with tempos slower than usual, every bar of **Bernstein**'s recording throbs with controlled passion, capped by an extraordinary coda that places him ahead of the pack (♦Sony 47628). Bernstein links the piece to the liturgical masterworks of Mozart and Verdi and perhaps his own music too, using strong rhythm in the right spots, drawing precision and fervor from the LSO and Bach Festival Chorus. And despite their differing esthetics, it's worth quoting Stravinsky's own reaction on hearing Bernstein's *Symphony of Psalms* live: "Wow!"

Stravinsky's first recording dates from 1931, only two months after the premiere, and despite the worn, faded sound, you can feel the dark, fervent power of the performance he drew from the Walther Straram Concerts Orchestra and Alexis Vlassov Choir (♦EMI 54607, 2CD). His stereo performance some 32 years later with the CBC Symphony and Festival Singers of Toronto reveals a changed man, more fastidious and emotionally close to the vest, enforcing clipped phrasing and lighter textures (CBS). It simply doesn't have the intensity he produced when the piece was hot off the press. **Craft** does even worse in an early installment in his cycle before it began to jell (MusicMasters). He whisks through the piece as if he couldn't wait to get it over with; the Orchestra of St. Luke's plays well; the New York Choral Artists are ordinary.

Tilson Thomas scores well with the LSO and smooth-as-silk LSO Chorus in a very competitive recording, not nearly as emotional nor as deep a performance as Bernstein's, yet strewn with bursts of brassy exuberance (♦Sony 53275). You'll get fine choral singing out of **Robert Shaw** and his Atlanta crew, with tempos close to those of Stravinsky's stereo disc, lovely sound, and an uneventful performance (Telarc). **Maazel**'s recording has some bite and considerable momentum at first, but the more devotional passages later on don't have the intense concentration of the best performances; moreover, the Bavarian Radio Chorus sounds recessed and not too involved (RCA).

Chailly is stiff-jointed as usual, though his coda is rather nice and the choir excellent (London), and **Gary Bertini** produces a lot of hasty forward momentum and little sense of shape (Orfeo). **Karajan**'s curious outing is streaked with passionate, almost wild choral singing and strange lapses of concentration, a performance a few takes short of realization (DG). **Boulez** came to this work late in life, and his cool, matter-of-fact Berlin Philharmonic/Radio Chorus recording doesn't indicate any special affinity for it (DG 457616).

Perséphone. A lyrical cantata that can last nearly an hour, *Perséphone* has yet to win a wide audience due to its specialized performance requirements (orchestra, a high tenor, an expert youngish female French speaker, and regular and boys' choirs), many stretches of weak musical material, and a set of rather slow-marked tempos that make it seem even weaker.

Stravinsky's first recording is often slower than his own metronome markings in Part I (albeit a bit faster in Parts II and III) in a very placid, dark-colored performance (Columbia). The Mitropoulos-era NYPO doesn't play well, Vera Zorina is a fine speaker, tenor Richard Robinson is ordinary, the Westminster Choir also sings the boys' parts, and the mediocre sound was old before its time. In his second recording, Stravinsky got a lighter, crisper, more delectable choral/orchestral sound from the Columbia Symphony and Gregg Smith Singers; there is a real boy's choir (which makes a big difference), a better tenor (Michele Molese), the return of Zorina, and more spacious sound. Though the tempos are even broader, especially in Part III, the sharper articulation makes the piece less tedious, though still not convincing (Sony).

It fell to **Craft** in 1992 to throw out the metronome markings and radically kick up the tempos (his recording runs only 42 minutes compared with the Stravinsky remake's 56). Yet the piece works much better at his speeds; it's a lot less lugubrious, more coherent, and more in the arch Stravinsky style. Craft's speaker, actress Irène Jacob, is almost ideal, Aler is bright and assured, and the Orchestra of St. Luke's, the Smith Singers, and Newark Boys Chorus are excellent (♦MusicMasters 67103).

Nagano performs it in a polished, suavely French manner; in Part I, you can hardly believe it's Stravinsky, with tempos about halfway between those of the composer and Craft, and good showings from

speaker Anne Fournet and Rolfe-Johnson (Virgin). A stronger challenge to Craft comes from **Tilson Thomas,** who, like Nagano, finds a middle ground in pacing (48 minutes), but also captures the Stravinsky tang the piece needs (♦RCA 68898, 3 CD). Stephanie Cosserat is the sexiest Perséphone of the lot, and tenor Stuart Neill is first-class.

Babel. This stirring, compact Biblical cantata is part of a collective work called *Genesis Suite,* with each section written by an eminent California composer (including Schoenberg and Milhaud) circa 1944. **Stravinsky**'s recording is a bit tangled in the *fugato* but quite beautiful elsewhere, with narrator John Colicos doing the dignified honors (♦Sony 46301, 2CD). The smooth backing of **Bertini** and the Stuttgart Radio Symphony Orchestra and Chorus almost redeems Fischer-Dieskau's heavily accented English narration (Orfeo).

Mass. Stravinsky's "pocket mass" has a simplicity and terseness that look ahead to both the serial works and to the passage in *Rake's Progress* just after Tom has been rendered insane. **Stravinsky**'s recording is touchingly devotional, terse, and hushed, with plain-voiced soloists and the Gregg Smith Singers and good playing from members of the Columbia Symphony (Sony 46301, 2CD). **Craft** is more polished, reticent, and inward, and lacking passion in the "Sanctus" (MusicMasters). **Bernstein** adopts considerably broader tempos and more incisive attacks from the voices, producing a more forceful, larger-scaled performance than the others (♦DG 423251).

Cantata. The 1952 *Cantata* is a sleeper in Stravinsky's output, a touchingly beautiful piece that might almost be termed neoRenaissance, whose contrapuntal manipulations in the "Ricercar II" section helped open the door to his final period. **Craft**'s performance has a forthright clear-eyed innocence that's exactly right, with guileless vocal solos from Mary Ann Hart and Thomas Bogdan, and the Orchestra of St. Luke's and Gregg Smith Singers are caught in gorgeously etched sound (♦MusicMasters 67158). **Stravinsky**'s less-nuanced recording with the Columbia Chamber Ensemble and the Smith Singers (Sony 46301, 2CD) is given a piquant flavor by Adrienne Albert's plain, non-operatic mezzo; this recording and Craft's suggest that the composer probably preferred such a voice in this part (Sony). **Salonen** gives the music a slight edge, anticipating big changes ahead for the composer (♦Sony 46667). Kenny and Aler put more of a performer's finish on their singing; the London Sinfonietta and Chorus are lovely.

Canticum Sacrum. A solemn tribute to St. Mark's church in Venice, *Canticum Sacrum* is austere but not unapproachable; the brassy I and V form a diatonic sandwich around three inner movements composed in the 12-tone system. It receives a powerful, solidly recorded performance from **Craft** (♦MusicMasters 67152). **Stravinsky**'s is slower in tempo but brighter in timbre, though I can't hear some of the blazing brass writing very well at the beginning and end, and the LA Festival Chorus cuts almost abrasively through the early stereo sound (Sony).

The Flood. Having the misfortune of being unveiled on prime-time television, it quickly alienated a mass audience perhaps expecting a sequel to *Firebird.* That figured, given that Stravinsky wrapped his Biblical tale in spare, often harsh, serial regalia, but only recently have its dramatic virtues emerged on recordings. The 1962 premiere recording, originally credited to both Stravinsky and Craft but reverting to **Craft** in the 1981 LP edition, is a dry, desiccated affair, where the spoken voices often don't bother to follow the score's rhythmic values or stay in sync with the Columbia Symphony (Sony). (Paul Tripp's silly Caller is downright embarrassing.) After hearing this, I'm amazed by the amount of vitality that **Knussen,** the London Sinfonietta, and New London Chamber Choir pull from this score, pointing out links going back to *Symphony in Three Movements* and *Rite* (♦DG 447068). And there's a world of difference between Craft's first recording and his warmer, more polished, and expressive remake; it now sounds like a viable concert work instead of a stagey radio play with music (MusicMasters).

Requiem Canticles. Although a few chips and sketches would follow, this oddly moving requiem-in-miniature is the leave-taking, Stravinsky's final major work. But *Canticles* isn't nearly as forbidding as your typical Stravinsky serial work—as he admitted himself—for you can hear several poignant echoes of the past (*Oedipus* in "Tuba Mirum" *Symphonies of Winds* in the Interlude, and *Noces* in the gleaming Postlude). The first recording with **Craft** makes a stark impression, especially the "Libera me" with its vivid babel of voices behind the vocal quartet (Sony 46302). His remake with the Orchestra of St. Luke's and New York Choral Artists is brisker and altogether more refined and approachable (MusicMasters). But **Knussen** again comes out on top in late Stravinsky; while matching Craft's speeds, he's sharper and more brutal in "Dies Irae" and more delicate in the Interlude, finding a wider spectrum of emotion (♦DG 447068). He also has superior singers in the New London Chamber Choir and the expert London Sinfonietta.

Late choral works. Several rare Stravinsky-led choral works from all periods can be found (♦Sony 46301, 2CD). *Threni*—the biggest piece he wrote after *Rake's Progress,* a stern, forbidding, half-hour of serial writing at extremely slow tempos—has yet to receive another recording. Also standing alone is *A Sermon, A Narrative and A Prayer,* which Craft claims is a scandalously inaccurate recording, yet still makes a dramatic impact (presumably Craft will offer his own views in the near future). A high point of the collection is a late-period choral piece that will appeal across the board, the beguiling *Chorale Variations on J.S. Bach's Vom Himmel hoch.*

OPERAS

Le Rossignol (*The Nightingale*). Begun before *Firebird* and set aside until after *Rite of Spring* was finished, *Le Rossignol* is the culmination of Stravinsky's Rimsky period and also an anomaly for its strong Oriental flavor. This is **Boulez**'s kind of Stravinsky, particularly in the impressionistic Act 1 where he savors the colors with exquisite clarity (♦Erato 45627). Throughout, he sees it as an extension of Debussy and performs it as he would *La Mer,* with delicate, vividly glittering timbres—and as the complexion of the music changes in Act 2, Boulez's command of color becomes even more impressive. **Bryn-Julson,** one of Boulez's favorite singers, is in lovely, radiant voice as the Nightingale, Neil Howlett is a richly textured Emperor, Ian Caley is a plaintive, sweet Fisherman, and the BBC Symphony plays even more expertly for Boulez in 1990 than they did in the '60s.

Though **Craft** isn't quite as transparent or alluring, he's still able to relax and luxuriate in this score even at faster tempos, receiving gorgeous playing from the Philharmonia (♦MusicMasters 67184). Robert Tear's Fisherman is a bit shaky but exceptionally moving, Olga Tr'fonova gives the Nightingale a slight Slavic edge, Paul Whelan is an adequate Emperor. **Stravinsky** doesn't do anything to illuminate the colors of the score—at times, you'd swear he was leading one of his serial pieces— and the forces of the Washington Opera Society sound barely professional (Sony). Overall, the composer can't compete with Boulez or Craft, sonically or otherwise. Likewise **Conlon** doesn't savor anything; his conducting isn't clinical, it's just emotionally uninvolved, and the forces of the Paris National Opera are indifferently balanced and recorded

(EMI). But he does field an idiomatic Russian-sounding cast, with Vsevolod Grivnov as a forthright, Slavic Fisherman, and Dessay an acceptable Nightingale, ditto Albert Schagidullin's Emperor.

Renard. A spiky quarter-hour burlesque set in a barnyard, *Renard* is another wartime theater piece that falls between the genre cracks; on records (as opposed to stage performances), it plays like a mini-opera. Since Stravinsky insisted that *Renard* be performed in the language of its audience, the naturalized composer and his hand-picked American disciple both present performances in English. **Stravinsky**'s lively, highly rhythmic performance with the Columbia Chamber Ensemble and four good soloists is the most fun (♦Sony 46291, 3CD). **Craft**'s recording is off to the races, a driving but lucid performance with crystal-clear diction by the cast and highly pointed playing by the Orchestra of St. Luke's, with properly prominent attention paid to the cimbalom (♦MusicMasters 67110). For a more subdued and rounded English version, seek out **Ansermet** on LP (London).

In the Russian version, which I prefer in terms of sheer sound, **Salonen** displays energy and wit but not much bounce and drive; his excellent singers and the London Sinfonietta are thinly recorded (Sony). Conversely, **Chailly**'s turn in front of the same group receives bright, tangy sound, enhancing a spirited, reasonably pointed performance with adequate rhythm and characterful work from his British singers (London). **Conlon**'s recording has little bounce or life; it sounds like a runthrough (EMI). **Ansermet**'s first, somewhat more animated recording in good early stereo, uses a French text (London).

Mavra. Less than half an hour in length, *Mavra* is a frivolous one-act opera buffa whose main strength is its bouncy, heartfelt music that looks backward at Mother Russia, as scored for a wind-dominated chamber group. The principal recording available is **Stravinsky**'s marvelously nostalgic outing with a capable Russian cast (♦Sony 46298, 2CD), but a trip to used LP shops may yield **Ansermet**'s softened, understated English version (London) or **Rozhdestvensky**'s rough-hewn, vodka-and-borscht-laced performance (Melodiya/HMV).

The Rake's Progress. Now that all the saber-rattling between the serial and neoclassical crowds has died out, Stravinsky's only evening-length opera has at last been recognized as a 20th century masterwork. *The Rake* is blessed with one of the most literate librettos (by W.H. Auden and Chester Kallman) ever written for an opera and a score brimming with ideas whose sharply angular rhythms slam against the graceful verses. In spite of Stravinsky's increasing determination to avoid emotion, there's plenty of it here, along with a rumbling energy and sense of fun that recall Verdi's *Falstaff.*

After a long period when the composer's two recordings had the field to themselves, there is now plenty of competition; three appeared in the mid-'90s alone. Still, **Stravinsky**'s sets have all kinds of little inflections that have eluded most of the others, along with an unquenchable vitality and dramatic power. His pioneering 1953 mono set was a Metropolitan Opera production prepared by the exacting Reiner (♦Columbia 125, 3LP). Mack Harrell is the best Nick Shadow on records, a commanding voice capable of different colors and flexible expression, and Thebom offers the only fully characterized Baba the Turk in all her coquettish, frivolous, temperamental ways. Both steal the show from Gueden's Anne and Eugene Conley's Tom. You won't need a libretto for this performance, which, alas, has been out of print for decades.

The 1964 Stravinsky stereo set has different virtues: more rhythmically alive conducting and theatrical atmosphere; Alexander Young's remarkable evolving Tom, a likeable cipher in Act I who acquires stature in Act II and transforms into a sweetly insane denizen of Bedlam in Act III; the way John Reardon's often jolly Nick colors his words with sinister intent; and better sound, greatly improved on CD (♦Sony 46299, 2CD). Raskin is a rather formal Anne; the Royal Philharmonic isn't letter-perfect; and the Royal Opera Chorus makes open, well-enunciated sounds, though not as good as the Met's—but all in all, this still sets the standard.

Of the sets that have emerged recently, **Craft**'s displays the most highly developed sense of phrasing, the most pointed rhythms and appreciation of the score's wit, and the fastest speeds (♦MusicMasters 67131, 2CD). He can be a little abrupt, but that's within the style; Act III in particular bristles with sharp edges and the Epilogue is full of zip, the best since Stravinsky's stereo set. The casting isn't world-class, but they do their jobs efficiently. The Gregg Smith Singers are as agile as ever with Craft's rhythmic angles, the Orchestra of St. Luke's offers a lean chamber orchestra sound.

The Rake can comfortably handle disciplinarian **Gardiner**'s own brand of abruptness (♦DG 459648, 2 CD). With tempos consistently faster than the composer's, he and the LSO are a little stiff in rhythm but not damagingly so, and his Monteverdi Choir is the best since Stravinsky's. The two box-office stars happen to turn in the best performances; Terfel rises to full evil stature as Nick Shadow and the against-type casting of von Otter as Baba was a brilliant stroke, for she fills out the portrait with striking word-pointing and she's got a temper, too. Bostridge's piping ninny of a Tom is pushed around by everyone, Deborah York sings a lovely, liquid Anne, and the sound is superb.

Nagano has a good feeling for the jagged phrasing and bursts of energy, almost as good as Craft and the composer (Erato). But he loses concentration after the Act III auction; the graveyard scene is routine, and the Epilogue is not crisp. Upshaw, in beautiful voice, is probably our best Anne, perhaps too much the diva in the Act I aria but displaying heart-rending emotion from Act II onwards. Hadley projects a winningly naive bravado in Tom, but Ramey's Nick is a letdown, shakier and heavier-set than in his earlier Decca recording. Though the Opéra Lyon Orchestra is the best of the '90s pack, the chorus sounds lusterless and the voices are recessed.

Ozawa is the main problem with his Saito Kinen Festival recording; he's too low-key, not pointed enough, not getting everything he can out of the notes, though his touching Bedlam scene is his best moment (Philips). McNair produces her lovely, sexy, trademark gliding effect as Anne, which makes you wonder why Tom would wish to stray, yet it also signifies yearning. Plishka is a hollow-voiced, one-dimensional Nick; Rolfe-Johnson is an acceptable Tom; and Jane Henschel is a formidable, suitably frivolous, not necessarily repulsive Baba. This set's strongest point is in the minor role of Trulove, for it has that noble Savoyard, Donald Adams, making a rare recorded appearance in a non-Gilbert & Sullivan role (sadly, his last ever), his proper British diction and unique bass as sturdy as ever.

Chailly may have the most consistent cast of all, but his stiff, square conducting of the London Sinfonietta and the muddy choral work rule it out, despite excellent sound (Decca). Ramey is in more flexible, clearer voice here, really digging into Nick as charmer and monster. Langridge is a vibrant Tom in Act I and the character grows; Cathryn Pope is a crystal-blue, pure Anne, and Sarah Walker is an imperious English Baba.

VOCAL MUSIC

In Memoriam: Dylan Thomas. In a brief, stark threnody for the late poet, two dirges for string quartet and four trombones surround an atonal setting of Thomas's poem "O do not go gentle into that good night," one of the earliest examples of Stravinsky embracing the sound world of Webern. Jon Humphries sings the verse in an alternately sweet and fervent tenor voice in **Craft**'s authoritative recording (♦MusicMasters 67158). **Stravinsky**'s stereo version isn't as beautifully blended as Craft's but has a more magnetic tenor in **Alexander Young** (Sony). **Boulez** has the most interesting tenor of all in Robert Tear but also the coolest instrumental backing (DG). For collectors, Richard Robinson is the plaintive tenor in **Stravinsky**'s mono recording (Columbia).

Abraham and Isaac. Dedicated to the people of Israel, this was a startling project for an 80-year-old composer, a Biblical ballad marked with a knotty sustained urgency and sporting one of the most difficult parts ever written for a baritone. In his premiere recording, **Craft** claims that Richard Frisch had to be overdubbed with the Columbia Symphony to get the synchronization right—and indeed, baritone and ensemble sound musically and emotionally disconnected in this harsh reading, closely miked within an inch of their lives (Sony). Craft's second attempt is a much more coherent and musical performance, with the hollow-sounding but compassionate Varcoe blending organically with the Orchestra of St. Luke's (♦MusicMasters 67158). The gruff-sounding David Wilson Johnson and **Knussen** are tougher and on-edge with a fine grasp of the score's rhythms, giving the piece real dramatic momentum (♦DG 447068). The score sounds crabbed and epigrammatic in the hands of **Bertini**, with Fischer-Dieskau in uneven voice (Orfeo).

Songs. From his early conducting days, **Boulez** offers a collection of four wartime mini-song cycles in French-language performances that are as dry as the sonics (Adés). His 1982 collection with Tear, Bryn-Julson, Shirley-Quirk, Ann Murray, and Ensemble InterContemporain is far more valuable (♦DG 413751)—better sung and played, ranging in repertoire from *Pastorale* through the wartime songs to some of the 12-tone miniatures, as well as Stravinsky's arrangements (his last published project) of two of Hugo Wolf's Spanish lieder.

The "Stravinsky Edition" gives you the widest range of material (♦Sony 46298, 2CD)—35 selections, from the 1906 romantic song cycle *The Faun and the Shepherdess* all the way to his last song, 1967's "The Owl and the Pussycat." The quality of singing is variable—with the terrific Berberian, expressive Lear, and poised Gramm faring best—but **Stravinsky**'s inflections almost always strike sparks with the Columbia and CBC Symphonies, and **Craft**'s contributions are also noteworthy. For collectors, the primary attraction of a mono disc of composer-led song cycles in English is hearing a very young **Horne** as a high soprano; the performances here are lively but dry (Columbia).

So far, the Craft project has yielded only a scattering of songs. **Katherine Ciesinski**'s somewhat harsh mezzo and Craft's crisply articulated leadership of the Orchestra of St. Luke's can be heard in *Pribaoutki* and *Berceuses du chat* (MusicMasters 67152) and the three *Songs from William Shakespeare* (MusicMasters 67158). A refined a cappella version of *Russian Peasant Choruses* is in MusicMasters 67086 and the exotic "Sektanskaya" for soprano, flute, and cimbalom turns up for the first time anywhere in MusicMasters 67195.   GINELL

Morton Subotnick (b. 1933)

Hear ye, all those who claim that electronic music is cold and faceless. Morton Subotnick's music has personality. Aggressive, motoristic rhythms and a brooding introspective bent drive his recorded output, which divides itself roughly into three genres. First, there are the pure electronic pieces, then the ghost works in which a silent score of taped instructions triggers electronics that modify the sounds of acoustic instruments, and finally the post-1984 unions of acoustic instruments and MIDI electronics. Though Subotnick's evolution was amply documented through the '80s, a large portion of it is currently unavailable, including most of the ghost pieces and a lot of the electronic music, and several recent works like *Hungers* and *Intimate Immensities* have yet to be recorded.

ELECTRONIC MUSIC

The spectacular *Silver Apples of The Moon* was Subotnick's breakthrough, and it still provides a thrilling experience more than three decades after it hit the record shops in 1967. *The Wild Bull* digs somewhat deeper into the psyche, the dances are more complex, the general tone more ominous. Both works have been transferred satisfactorily onto one CD (♦Wergo 2035), but the original Nonesuch LPs still pack a big sonic punch and are easy to find second-hand. *Touch* is exactly what the title implies, a toccata for the Space Age, with even more highly developed structure and drama; it comes with the acoustic-electric monodrama *Jacob's Room* (♦Wergo 2014).

Gradually, Subotnick's electronic pieces would become more austere in tonal palette, sparer in texture, and less approachable. Each part of *Sidewinder* begins with a rattling that suggests its title, as subdued drones become the driving engines (Columbia, NA). *4 Butterflies* is most notable for unveiling the butterfly metaphor—a three-part structure corresponding to the caterpillar-chrysalis-butterfly cycle—that would dominate his work into the '80s (Columbia, NA). *Until Spring* has more energy and tension than the previous two works but unfolds in fits and starts before belatedly belting home the ostinatos near the close (Odyssey, NA). *A Sky of Cloudless Sulphur,* the best choice from the '70s, says similar things far more succinctly and organically (Nonesuch 78001, NA).

Return—commemorating the return of Halley's Comet in 1986—came as a big surprise to electronic music buffs, for it was a return to tonality as well, with flashy allusions to Scarlatti, Mozart, Liszt, and ragtime as it sweeps through the comet's history. Though not at all typical of Subotnick's all-electronic work, it's the easiest to approach (New Albion 012).

ACOUSTIC/ELECTRONIC MUSIC

An early (1968) fusion of orchestra with electronics, *Laminations* reflects the circus world of *Silver Apples* as Subotnick overlays flamboyant pitchless electronics on the dissonant layers of Lukas Foss and the Buffalo Philharmonic, often in funky rhythmic patterns (Turnabout 34428, NA). However, the main thrust of Subotnick's acoustic/electronic fusions would commence in the '70s with his ghost pieces. *Parallel Lines* for orchestra and ghost score isn't nearly as showy as *Laminations;* the language is sterner, the electronics alter the acoustic instruments in subtle ways, as Tilson Thomas leads the nonplussed Buffalo Philharmonic (CRI, NA).

Liquid Strata, expertly played by the work's dedicatee, **Ralph Grierson** (Town Hall 24), is a moody, challenging canvas of extremes (with a couple of Chopin pastiches) where a piano is fuzzed and warped by the ghost score. *Passages of The Beast* exhaustively explores electronically bent timbres from a solo clarinet (Owl 30, NA), while *The Wild Beasts* does the same for trombone and piano (Nonesuch 78012, NA), and the truly wild *After the Butterfly* crystallizes the format for trumpet and chamber group (Nonesuch 78001, NA).

Subotnick's magnum opus, *The Double Life of Amphibians*—a 70-minute multimedia tour de force unveiled at the 1984 Los Angeles

Olympic Arts Festival—wasn't recorded in toto, but you can assemble a nearly complete facsimile of the work on LP by sequencing *Ascent Into Air* (♦Nonesuch 78020, NA), *The Last Dream of The Beast* (Nonesuch 78029, NA), and *A Fluttering of Wings* (Nonesuch 78020, NA). These pieces, especially the stunning *Ascent,* introduced something new and exciting for Subotnick, a growling, expressive Hebraic quality to go along with the aggression (composer William Kraft once told him, "You're always writing *Schelomo*"). Another version of *A Fluttering Of Wings* has since appeared in the giant, invaluable **Southwest Chamber Music** box, not quite as feverish in tempo and stunningly recorded (♦Cambria 8800, 12CD).

The Key to Songs (New Albion 012) marked a turning point in 1985, a jazzy, thoroughly tonal series of toccatas and lyrical meditations for chamber group and computer-generated sound. His favorite metaphor turns up again in *And the Butterflies Begin to Sing* (New World 80514), with his newfound lyricism and glistening digital electronics still in charge, along with unison passages that sound like Indian ragas. Thus far, the only '90s works we have on disc are *All My Hummingbirds Have Alibis* (New World 80514), which indulges in Subotnick's occasional weakness for pretentious spoken texts, and *Echoes From The Silent Call of Girona* for string quartet and CD-ROM, a yearning, deeply-moving tone poem inspired by a long-extinct Jewish community in Spanish Catalonia, with a searing union of strings and phase-shifted electronics at the close (♦Cambria 8800, 12CD).   GINELL

Josef Suk *(1874–1935)*

Suk and Novák were the inheritors of Dvořák's mantle during the early 20th century. Both studied with him, and Suk married his daughter, who died a year after Dvořák, causing a marked alteration in Suk's outlook. From a talented and inspired user of folk-inspired materials, he abruptly became a dark, almost Mahlerian composer of large canvases.

ORCHESTRAL MUSIC

Taking the music in chronological order, the earliest works are two overtures. First came *Dramatic Overture,* a fine effort recorded by **Altrichter** (Supraphon 111825). Then came *A Winter's Tale* (after Shakespeare), evocative and stirring, presently available in a polished reading by **Mogrelia** (Naxos 553703). Symphony 1 is a broadly conceived work in the Dvořák tradition, a little blocky in structure but with beautiful melodies and powerful climaxes. There have been a couple of recordings, notably one by **Neumann** and the Czech Philharmonic, a mite heavy but well played (Supraphon 1964, NA).

One of Suk's most popular scores is *Serenade for Strings.* Modeled on Dvořák's example, they are frequently programmed together. **Bělohlávek** does this in his version in a light but leisurely reading (Supraphon 3157). **Suk** is livelier with his own chamber orchestra. He has recorded this combination twice, once in 1985 (Supraphon 104136) and again in 1996 (Vox 7540). Both have been castigated for close miking of a very small string group, but to me, this works well, particularly in the Dvořák. Suk needs a larger ensemble, and the feeling of teetering on the edge of sonic disaster lends a not entirely desirable frisson to the experience, yet he does have a crack group here.

A more lush reading may be had from **Krček,** an unqualified success, recorded in natural and spacious sound (♦Naxos 550419). A similar relaxed impression with a feeling of personality second to none is **Talich**'s recording, in rich mono sound (♦Supraphon 1899, with his indispensable Dvořák "New World" symphony). **Vlček** substitutes Suk's *St. Wenceslas Meditation* and Janáček's *Suite* for Dvořák in relaxed readings

(Discover 920234). More tension is provided by the **Orpheus Ensemble** (DG 447109 with two little-known works by Kodály).

There are two major scores of incidental music to plays by Julius Zeyer, *Raduz and Mahulena* and *Under the Apple Tree*. The former became one of Suk's best-known works under the title *Fairy Tale*. For this score, Suk invented love themes, introduced by solo violins, that he reused in later years. The classic recording is by **Talich,** made in 1949, now coupled with his indispensable *Ripening* (♦Supraphon 111904). There have been two readings by **Pešek,** one with the Czech Philharmonic (Supraphon 103389) and one in 1997 with the Liverpool Philharmonic (Virgin 45245). **Bĕlohlávek** also did it twice, first in 1991 with the Prague Symphony and Suk playing the violin solos (Supraphon, NA), then again two years later (Chandos 9063). All the Czech recordings are good; so is Liverpool if an authentic Czech sound doesn't concern you.

Under the Apple Tree has never been as well known. There were two Czech recordings of the work, neither presently available. **Pešek** recorded an Overture, "Bacchanale" "Epilogue" and two songs sung by Eva Dĕpoltová with the Czech Philharmonic (Supraphon/Denon 1372, with a fine *Serenade*, NA). **Otakar Trhlik** with Bohuslava Jelinkova and the Ostrava Janáček Philharmonic omitted one song and the "Epilogue" but added two substantial choral numbers (Supraphon, NA). A complete version would go well with the late *Epilogue* Op. 37, written for similar vocal forces and using sung text from this play.

The next orchestral piece enlists a solo violinist. Suk's only concertante work is a *Fantasy*, a long, rambling, but exciting movement in folk style. **Suk** himself has made two recordings, the first and feistiest with Ančerl, in a disc that also contains Dvořák's *Concerto* and *Romance* (♦Supraphon 111928). A later and more resonantly recorded reading was with Neumann, but his relaxation doesn't suit this piece (Supraphon 701, NA). **Pamela Frank** plays it with Mackerras, also with the two Dvořák pieces (London 460316). All of the above are with the Czech Philharmonic. **Gabriela Demeterová** plays it with the Prague Symphony, omitting the Dvořák *Romance* and lacking something in personality (Supraphon 3385).

Fantastic Scherzo followed, one of a curious lot of orchestral scherzos of the period, perhaps beginning with Dvořák's *Scherzo Capriccioso*. It's an exciting piece, available in two versions by the Czech Philharmonic under **Bĕlohlávek** (Chandos 8897) and **Mackerras** (Decca 466443) or the Prague Symphony under **Vladimir Valek** (Praga 250018). Mackerras is probably the most exciting and best recorded.

Then there's *Praga*, a patriotic tone poem based on a recognizable variant of the Hussite hymn used by Smetana in *Tabor and Blanik*. Impressive and powerful, it ends with a massive passage including the organ. From here on, the widened dynamic range of Suk's orchestral music becomes apparent. **Altrichter**'s otherwise effective performance with the Prague Symphony (Supraphon 111825) is a bit less rich in sound than **Pešek** with the Czech Philharmonic, with less presence for the organ (Supraphon 103389).

Soon after, Dvořak died and Suk began a symphony in honor of his memory, only to have his own wife, Otylka (Dvořák's daughter), die while he was working on the fourth movement. Canceling its plan as a paean to Dvořak's memory, he wrote the two final movements as a tribute to Otylka, titling the symphony *Asrael*, "the Angel of Death. It's a long and passionate work, the first of four tremendous orchestral outpourings of grief and attempts to come to terms with life and death. The classic performance is by **Talich,** coupled with his equally important reading of Dvořák's *Stabat Mater* (♦Supraphon 111902, 2CD). Though

recorded in 1952, it's a remarkably good-sounding recording of a powerful reading.

Another recording on a high interpretive level is by **Kubelik,** recorded in 1981 (Panton 1101, NA). **Neumann** gives a less visionary performance with the Czech Philharmonic, but it's marvelously played and recorded (Supraphon 110278, or 111962, 2CD). **Bĕlohlávek** is more fiery, with the same orchestra (Chandos 9640, 2CD). **Válek** is a fine interpreter, but the Prague Radio Symphony in a live performance isn't the Czech Philharmonic's equal, nor is the recording consistent (Praga 250018). **Svetlanov** gives a surprisingly effective performance, recorded in good if not outstanding sound (Russian Disc 11011).

A Summer's Tale is Suk's next study of his own psyche under stress. On the same scale as the hour-long *Asrael,* it's a panorama of scenes and feelings of equal intensity, if less unity. There is a fine performance by **Sejna** in serviceable mono (Supraphon 111923). Richer stereo sound is provided by **Pešek** in two recordings, with the Czech Philharmonic (Supraphon 111984) and with the Liverpool Philharmonic (Virgin 45057), the Czechs more detailed, the Liverpudlians more richly blended. Perhaps most impressive of all is **Mackerras,** an intense and impressively recorded performance (♦ Decca 466443).

Ripening is a single-movement rhapsody culminating in a mighty fugue representing the liberating character of work. There is also a wordless women's chorus near the end. The 1918 premiere was conducted by **Talich,** and he included it in one of his last sessions with the Czech Philharmonic in 1956, in mono sound but an incandescent performance (♦Supraphon 111904). **Neumann**'s well-recorded but somehow matter-of-fact performance with the same ensemble is available (Supraphon 103640, or 111962, 2CD). There was a 1962 **Ančerl** version in a coruscating live performance in sound no better than Talich's (Multisonic 310150, NA; this reading may well be on Supraphon 111996, 2CD). **Pešek** did a fine reading in Liverpool (Virgin 59318, coupled with an impressive *Praga*, NA).

Three short patriotic works are usually coupled together. *Legend of the Dead Victors, St. Wenceslas Meditation* for string orchestra or quartet, and a march called *Towards a New Life* are incidental to Suk's psyche, yet they represent his reaction to the upheavals of WWI. *Meditation* appears with the string quartets (Supraphon 111531), but all three works are together on two discs at present, a historically important issue by **Kubelik** in mono (Supraphon 111911) and a modern recording by **Altrichter** (Supraphon 111825). I recall more flavor in an old LP with **Alois Klima,** but times change (Supraphon 50476, NA).

Finally, *Epilogue* makes a fitting end to Suk's musical life. Like *Ripening,* it's a 40-minute symphonic poem, this time enlisting soprano, baritone, and bass soloists as well as chorus. The words are from the Bible and from the play *Under the Apple Tree,* set by Suk many years before. In this one, he comes to terms with death itself. There are two recordings at present, **Neumann** in one of his most involved performances (Supraphon 110116, or 111962, 2CD), and **Pešek** in one of his best, impressively recorded (Virgin 45245).

CHAMBER MUSIC

Most of Suk's chamber music came early in his career. The Piano Quartet, Trio, String Quartet, and Quintet are full of enthusiasm, idiomatic writing, and memorable melodies. His initial nationalistic style has tended to be overshadowed by his later grandeur, but these pieces are most attractive. All of them have been recorded in outstanding performances in three Supraphon discs, the Piano Trio, Quartet, and Quintet in 111532, the pieces for violin and piano plus many other short works in 111533, and the two String Quartets in 111531. All these discs are outstanding, made more valuable by the participation of the composer's grandson, one of the outstanding violinists of our generation. The **Suk Quartet** plays the quartets, and the pianists are Pavel Stepan, Jan Panenka, and Josef Hala. That disc contains an alternate finale to Quartet 1, *St. Wenceslas Meditation,* and other pieces.

There is a recording of Piano Trio and *Elegy* by the **Joachim Trio** (Naxos 8553415, with Smetana and Novák). This group plays with passion and polish, though they're not as natural and idiomatic as the Czechs. Information is lacking about another recording by the **Kubelik Trio** (GZ Opera 144).

PIANO MUSIC

The piano is where Suk developed his private thoughts, sometimes in the form of extended suites, particularly in his later years. **Pavel Stepan** made recordings of all of it in the '70s, according to Supraphon, but only one 2LP album was released (Supraphon 2471, NA) and only one CD is presently available (♦Supraphon 31). That's a pity, because he's still the best. It contains some works not on the LPs but omits more. **Niel Immelman** has two discs out but they show less insight (Meridian 84269 and 84317), likewise with **Fingerhut** (Chandos 9026, 2CD). A good recording by the excellent **Kvapil** would have supplemented Stepan's program neatly, but it seems to have disappeared (Unicorn 9159, NA).

Vocal music

A collection of ten songs for female chorus and piano four-hands has been recorded twice, once in a disc called "Classical Czech Choruses by Foerster and Dvořák" performed by various groups (Supraphon 3114), once by the Prague Chamber Choir under **Josef Pancik** in a disc containing choruses by Smetana and Petr Eben and arrangements of Dvořák's *Moravian Duets* sung by a choir (Chandos 9257). The Supraphon also contains the only recording of three Songs for Mixed Choir Op. 19 and is chock full of rare material. No texts are provided, however. The ten Songs are more richly recorded on Chandos and that disc contains the texts, a significant inclusion.   MOORE

Arthur Sullivan (1842–1900)

Sullivan with Gilbert remains a highly marketable commodity on both sides of the pond, yet save for that hoary staple of concert bands *The Lost Chord,* Sullivan without Gilbert is encountered far less often; a pity, as the same fresh and spontaneous music-making that informs the operettas readily surfaces in his concert works as well. Indeed, for England in the time of Queen Victoria, Sullivan's reputation was made long before his collaboration with Gilbert, his studies in Leipzig leading directly to *Irish Symphony* and *Overture di Ballo.* Though disdained by some critics for having the effrontery to write for the popular stage, with renewed interest in Sullivan's music has come much deserved appreciation for his undeniable melodic gifts even without Gilbert's trenchant satire. He was a devoted admirer of Mendelssohn, and perhaps we may consider these works as his "songs without words."

The same font of glorious melody that suffuses Mendelssohn's *Scotch Symphony* flows through Sullivan's *Irish Symphony,* though the composer hesitated to call it that until Stanford wrote one too. He needn't have worried; for all his claims of "real Irish flavor" the score seems closer to Mendelssohn's fairy realm than the Emerald Isle. Honors are evenly divided between **Groves** and his splendid Liverpool ensemble (EMI, with *Patience* on 64406 or separately on ♦64726) and **Owain Arwel Hughes** (CPO 999171). Groves's more restless tempos impart an almost Gothic character to the opening movement (but he omits the re-

peat) while Hughes pulls ahead of him in the finale. Probably Groves will wear better with repeated hearings.

With Groves you also get Cello Concerto and the brilliant *Overture di Ballo,* in effect a skillfully scored sequence of polonaise, waltz, and galop rhythms, also nicely played, though **Boult** is even more bumptious in his "Concert Favorites" collection (Chesky). Hughes offers the suite from *Victoria and Merrie England,* the *Imperial March,* and the overture *In Memoriam,* making both discs well worth owning. **Fiedler**'s recording of *Overture di Ballo* remains tantalizingly out of reach (Polydor).

The ballet *Victoria and Merrie England,* written for the Diamond Jubilee of Queen Victoria, presents eight scenes of British history from the time of the Druids to the Victorian Era, along the way making use of familiar tunes and closing out in grand style with imposing statements of "Rule Britannia" and "God Save the Queen." The complete ballet, some 78 minutes long, comes off in fine fettle from **Andrew Penny** (Marco Polo 223677); certainly it's a far more substantial entertainment than the brief suite offered by Hughes as well as **Royston Nash** (London, with *Utopia Limited*).

On another disc **Penny** favors us with more ballet music, *L'Ile enchantée*—originally commissioned by Covent Garden to fill out a production of Bellini's *La Sonnambula*—and *Thespis,* a tuneful pastiche concocted by Sullivan for his first endeavor with Gilbert, clearly modeled on Offenbach if without quite the same vein of bawdy good humor (Marco Polo 223460). These too may be safely recommended. Penny continues his survey with the incidental music for *King Arthur* (set to a different text from Elgar's far more compelling score), *Macbeth,* and *The Merry Wives of Windsor* (Marco Polo 223635). The music for *Macbeth,* richly depicting both the Witches and Banquo's Ghost, greatly expands on the Overture available from **David Lloyd-Jones** (Hyperion), **Marriner** (Philips) and **Nash** (London, with *Utopia Limited*), and Penny can readily hold his own.

Only in his remaining Marco Polo outing does Penny come up against serious competition, offering music from *The Merchant of Venice* and *Henry VIII* in addition to the overtures *In Memoriam* and *The Sapphire Necklace* (Marco Polo 223461). The first of these is expertly set forth by **Vivian Dunn** (Klavier 11033), but Penny offers even more music, including the "Barcarole" (with tenor Emmanuel Lawler as the gondolier).

The heartfelt and deeply moving overture *In Memoriam,* dedicated to Sullivan's father, builds to a glorious peroration with the organ standing proud against the stentorian brass. **Penny** does well enough, **Dunn** even better, but best of all is **Hughes,** who really brings out the organ at the end (CPO). Dunn offers a suite from Sullivan's setting of *The Tempest,* his first great success, unfortunately omitting the vocal portions included by **Karl Adler** in his Unicorn LP but well worth having nonetheless (Klavier). *Marmion Overture,* inspired by Scott's romance, is also included by **Nash** with *Utopia Limited,* and I regret London's failure to bring out all of Nash's fillers on one disc. That includes *Imperial March,* though Nash's rather superficial run-through pales beside the overpowering grandeur of Hughes's *nobilmente* treatment.

The ballet *Pineapple Poll* is a delightful entertainment compiled by **Mackerras** from the G&S repertoire and based on the same story line as *HMS Pinafore* (Arabesque 8016). Devoted Savoyards will have a grand time trying to spot tunes familiar (or not) from the various operettas; Mackerras writes with evident glee, "I have come across only two people who were able to 'place' the source of every tune in the ballet!" The recording has a real theater feel to it and still sounds very good, though for warmth and atmosphere his later Philharmonia recording, fitted out with *Overture di Ballo,* is hard to beat (London

436810). Mackerras also recorded a suite from the ballet with the London Philharmonic, notable for the coupling with his boisterous Verdi pastiche *The Lady and the Fool* (Classics for Pleasure 4618). Another suite (in an older recording) may be had from John Hollingsworth along with a suite of "Savoy Dances" compiled and conducted by **Stanford Robinson** (EMI 63961).

Though it may seem disingenuous to refer to Sullivan's many curtain-raisers for the Savoy Theatre as "Gilbert and Sullivan Overtures," it's difficult to think of them any other way, even though Sullivan often merely selected the themes and had an assistant write the overture, not wishing to expend great effort when he knew the audience would only talk over the music anyway. The classic set by **Sargent** first surfaced on CD as Classics for Pleasure 67111, but the more recent "two-fer" (♦Seraphim 69137) is far more valuable for its inclusion of the dances from Edward German's *Henry VIII* and *Nell Gwynn*. Sargent finds much infectious good humor in these little gems.

Alexander Faris leads sprightly performances too and even includes *Overture di Ballo* (omitted by Sargent), but the unforgivable absence of *The Mikado* makes it difficult to recommend the disc (Nimbus). **Marriner** offers *Overture di Ballo* as well as *Macbeth* in addition to the standard complement, an insouciant *Mikado* and *Pinafore* set beside a rather breathless *Pirates* and *Iolanthe* (Philips). There are two collections of interest featuring a wide variety of conductors (IMP 9014): a hasty *Pinafore* from James Walker and a limp *Overture di Ballo* from Anthony Collins alongside more gratifying performances of the usual pieces led by **Sargent** and Isidore Godfrey. And one derived from the D'Oyly Carte recordings is notable for its inclusion of two versions of *Ruddigore*, the original plus the more familiar arrangement by Geoffrey Toye (TER 8316).

At the price it would be difficult to top the redoubtable **Penny** offering all the G&S overtures, even *Cox and Box* which Gilbert had nothing to do with (♦Naxos 554165). If Penny fails to summon quite the grace and charm of Sargent, he certainly keeps his players on their toes, and his wonderful first chair oboe Alaster Bentley makes all the others sound nasal by comparison. Penny and Sargent top the charts, though **Alan Ward**'s splendid RCA LP (with its wonderful gong strokes in *Ruddigore*) and **Groves**'s disc would be welcome on CD too (EMI).

Sullivan's highly appealing Cello Concerto was written for the Italian cellist Alfredo Piatti, who performed it a couple of times before the score inexplicably faded from the repertoire, then disappeared altogether when the parts were lost in a fire. Mackerras, who had conducted the concerto for the BBC, reconstructed the score from memory and recorded it with **Lloyd Webber** (EMI, first issued with Herbert's Concerto 2 in 47622 and with *Irish Symphony* in 64726). Tuneful and ingratiating in the manner of Mendelssohn, Sullivan's score complements either partner more gratefully than Friedrich Gulda's rather jazzy concerto combined with it, though suavely played by **Martin Ostertag** and **Klaus Arp** (Amati).   HALLER

Franz von Suppé *(1819–1895)*

The full name is too good to overlook: Francesco Ezechiele Ermenegildo Cavaliere Suppé-Demelli. Born of mixed Belgian and Italian heritage, Suppé began his career in the prescribed fashion with a studiously orthodox Roman Catholic mass but was soon attracted to the stage, and taking to heart the models of Offenbach (then highly popular in Vienna) tried his hand, beginning with *Das Mädchen vom Lande* in 1847 and turning out one success after another. It's his tuneful and rollicking overtures that hold the floor today, with *Poet and Peasant, Light Cavalry,*

Pique Dame, and *Morning, Noon and Night in Vienna* being central to nearly every recorded collection.

There are several versions of his overtures to choose from, most of them including the above listed foursome, hereafter designated "the basic 4" to save space; all of those listed below include other overtures, mostly but not always by Suppé. The basic 4 are the only ones offered by **Solti;** a sonic blockbuster on LP, he now seems slapdash, even hectic (London 421170 or 460982). The more recent effort by **Dutoit** seems bland by comparison, he's content to sidle uneventfully from one tune to the next (London 414408). **Mehta** is even worse, adding cymbal crashes where they're not called for (even a gong in *Pique Dame*) and showing no trace of sentiment in the wonderful cello solos (CBS).

Marriner has gone to the well twice. His first effort is amiable enough and he obtains crisp ensemble from the London Symphony (Philips 420892 or 411450); in his second try, with his St. Martin players, he picks up the pace nicely in some pieces (EMI 54056). All but the completist will surely derive the greatest pleasure from the wonderful recording by **Paray,** a glorious bouquet that still sounds fresh and bracing (♦Mercury 434309). The splendid collection by **Barbirolli** substitutes a roaring good *Jolly Robbers* for Paray's very special *Boccaccio* (♦EMI 64196). Unfortunately EMI has tacked on muffled, dispirited accounts of *Boccaccio* and *Fatinitza* from Boult's old mono Westminster LP, but you don't have to play them. **Suitner** is nearly as good; his robust, hearty approach pays rich dividends (Berlin 2153).

For those on a budget, **Janos Sandor** is nothing spectacular, but a good (and cheap) cross-section (LaserLight 15611). There's a welcome swagger to **Karajan,** though the sound isn't as suave as some (DG). Few conductors have issued more than one disc of Suppé overtures; one exception is **Gustav Kuhn,** who recorded two collections. His tempos are expansive even unto indulgence, but the sonorous environs and the superlative playing by Beecham's Royal Philharmonic help make amends. Vol. 1, offering the basic 4 plus *Galatea* and *Jolly Robbers* is expendable (Eurodisc 69037); of far greater interest (and also much harder to find) is Vol. 2 containing seven even rarer examples (Eurodisc 69226).

Even more ambitious is Marco Polo's project to record all of Suppé's overtures, with five volumes at hand thus far, all but one led by **Alfred Walter** and in all cases filled out with marches and other short pieces. If there's a sameness to the general format, there's more than enough sheer joy and soaring melody to recommend looking into this series. However, Walter is not the most pixilated of conductors, and he lacks the sort of broad humor this music needs. Christian Pollack picks up the pace in the waltzes but doesn't work up much of a sweat elsewhere. Pollack has also recorded an assortment of marches, waltzes, and polkas with even more dispiriting results; they all sound the same, and the players seem bored out of their skulls (Marco Polo). Avoid this one unless you have to have every note Suppé ever wrote.

Requiem has been recorded surprisingly often. Its melodious character confounded many who considered its Italianate style too much like operetta, though it's closer to accepted form than Verdi and far more restrained than Berlioz. **Edmund de Stoutz** sets such broad tempos that he needs two CDs, but he has the most mellifluous soloists of the lot, and the rich orchestral backdrop and strong chorus are in his favor (Novalis 150112). The music flows more smoothly under **Roland Bader** and the orchestra is nicely detailed, though the male soloists are occasionally swamped by the women; his approach is unimaginative, but it serves the music well and can be recommended for a more reverent treatment (Koch Schwann 1248). **Wolfgang Badun,** with smaller forces, sometimes exercises reckless abandon and can seem superficial, but offers a beguiling freshness (BNL 112774). Those mainly concerned with the vocal line may prefer de Stoutz despite his dreary tempos, but you'll probably be quite happy with Bader. However, the sheer joy of this most undogmatic *Requiem* comes across most winningly with Badun.

HALLER

Johan Severin Svendsen (1840–1911)

Svendsen was perhaps the greatest Norwegian composer after Grieg, but such a comparison seems beside the point, as the two were not competitors but lifelong friends. Their styles complement each other rather well—Grieg the exquisite miniaturist, the poet of the piano and the human voice, Svendsen the great symphonist and conductor. Not as intense a nationalist as Grieg, Svendsen remained firmly planted in the Romantic mainstream, faithful to the legacy of Mendelssohn and Schumann; yet so skillfully did he fashion his melodies that many took them to be authentic folk songs, in effect, as one writer put it, "fusing the legacy of the Viennese classics with the Norwegian folk tradition." Both of Svendsen's symphonies deserve your attention, along with a healthy sampling of his shorter works.

SYMPHONIES

1 and *2*. Grieg was so impressed on hearing Svendsen's far grander score that he suppressed his own Symphony in C Minor. Indeed, Svendsen's Symphony 1 is a stronger piece, more stimulating and rhythmically assured (though the Grieg contains some of his freshest and most winning music), and yet it frequently seems prophetic of Grieg's later works. In Svendsen's Symphony 2 you can hear echoes of Grieg's Norwegian Dances in the Scherzo, while the giddy final romp closes things out in marvelous fashion.

These works are almost never played in concert in the United States but have now been paired on disc five times. The pioneering LPs by the Norwegian Cultural Council have come out on CD, with 1 (plus the Violin Concerto) conducted by **Miltiades Caridis** (NKF 50010) and 2 (with various short pieces) by **Oivin Fjeldstad** (NKF 50011). However, they have been handily superseded both musically and sonically. With the second wave of recordings came **Neeme Järvi** (BIS) and **Jansons** (EMI), both very well played and recorded, with Järvi's Gothenburg strings perhaps pulling ahead of Jansons's Oslo players. Yet even these expert readings were supplanted by **Terje Mikkelsen** and the Latvian National Symphony (♦La Vergne 260741) and **Ari Rasilainen** and the Norwegian Radio Orchestra (♦Finlandia 19055), as well as by the Bournemouth Symphony led by **Bjarte Engeset** (Naxos).

1. Both Rasilainen and Mikkelsen offer an energetic account of I where Järvi leans on it too much and Jansons seems even more breathless; they both take a relaxed view of the Andante, though it flows a bit better with Mikkelsen, and both are crisp and alert in the Scherzo where Jansons is too fast and Järvi too slow. In the finale both conductors are refreshingly buoyant, where the others merely press on. Engeset offers good value, spirited and pointed in both outer movements and deeply felt in the Andante (Naxos). You may also find an LP of No. 1 with **Odd Grüner-Hegge,** robust and richer sounding and boasting a very fine reading of *Zorahayda* as filler (Philips 838051).

2. Much the same comparison obtains in No. 2, with **Järvi** pulling ahead of **Jansons**—not least for his impassioned approach to I—but again it comes down to **Mikkelsen** and **Rasilainen,** both so splendid it would be easier to buy both than try to choose between them. **Engeset** is very good too, but his tendency to punch up the closeout occasionally proves distracting, as does the more reverberant sound. Certainly Engeset will

be easiest to find and at the Naxos price makes an excellent introduction to Svendsen's music. Another recording of 2 by **Grant Llewellyn** is also very good, but you really need both of Svendsen's symphonies—though the shorter pieces included by Llewellyn (see below) are highly attractive (Chatsworth).

OTHER ORCHESTRAL MUSIC

The four *Norwegian Rhapsodies* are about as close to authentic folk songs as anything Svendsen ever wrote; this is comfortable, joyful music filled with lively tunes and inventively scored, and you'll be happy to have them in your collection. **Karsten Andersen** leads spirited performances coupled with *Zorahayda* and *Norwegian Artists' Carnival* (NKF), but the ultimate choice lies between **Ole Kristian Ruud** (Simax 1085) and **Mikkelsen** (♦La Vergne 260748). Ruud is a bit more relaxed, particularly in 4, but worth having for Johan Halvorsen's two *Norwegian Rhapsodies;* Mikkelsen is vibrant and colorful and offers the only available version of the Prelude to Bjørnson's drama *Sigurd Slembe*, an absorbing work perhaps closer to symphonic poem than overture, with a story very much like *Peer Gynt.* There's also a very good reading of Rhapsody 4 included with Symphony 2 under **Llewellyn** (Chatsworth).

While little of Svendsen's output may be described as programmatic, both *Romeo and Juliet* and *Zorahayda* surely qualify. Bright colors and buoyant rhythms inform *Norwegian Artists' Carnival, Carnival in Paris,* and *Festival Polonaise.* Svendsen's most often-heard piece, *Romance* for violin, has probably never been played poorly on disc, and thus will only be noted in passing here. In *Romeo and Juliet* there is little of the white-hot passion of Tchaikovsky's masterpiece; the pensive opening measures suggest instead a eulogy for the star-crossed lovers with everything after that meant as a flashback. *Zorahayda* is a Moorish princess who hesitates when asked to follow her lover, a Christian knight, to his homeland and remains trapped in the Alhambra by evil spirits; she tells her story to another forsaken maiden, Jacinta, who releases her from her curse by baptizing her in the fountain and is herself transfigured by joy in return. We hear Zorahayda in the violin, Jacinta in the oboe.

Norwegian Artists' Carnival symbolically celebrates the marriage of the cold North with the warm-blooded South, while *Carnival in Paris* draws upon the composer's fond memories of his stay in France as a young man—though given the rollicking saltarello rhythms he could just as easily have called it "Carnival in Rome." *Festival Polonaise* was written for a grand ball held in Christiania (now Oslo) where the King and Queen of the joint Swedish-Norwegian monarchy led the festivities.

All these pieces are offered both by **Ruud** (♦Virgin 45128) and **Mikkelsen** (La Vergne 260745), with **Llewellyn** including the two carnival pieces with Symphony 2, and there are the NKF reissues (50009, *Zorahayda* and *Norwegian Artists' Carnival;* 50011, *Carnival in Paris* and *Festival Polonaise* with Symphony 2). It would be good to praise the La Vergne collection as highly as the symphonies, but unfortunately it sounds damped and colorless—was a different mike set-up used? In *Romeo and Juliet* both Mikkelsen and Ruud bring out its roiling passions with admirable intensity, while **Andersen** is more lyrical.

Grouping together works based on Shakespeare's play (IMP), **Dalia Atlas** is more expansive in *Romeo and Juliet,* with passions more full blown and better sound than the La Vergne. In *Zorahayda,* Ruud's solo players (violin and oboe) aren't as mellifluous as Mikkelsen's, while both Andersen and **Grüner-Hegge** (Philips LP, with Symphony 1) suffer from a queasy-sounding violin. Ruud seems slack in *Norwegian Artists' Carnival,* and conversely he's much more alert than Mikkelsen in *Carnival in Paris,* while Llewellyn's crisp, brassy account of both pieces makes a nice complement. **Fjeldstad** recorded *Carnival in Paris* twice, once as part of the NKF survey plus a more slapdash Mercury LP. Unfortunately both Fjeldstad and Mikkelsen curtail the reprise of *Festival Polonaise;* it expands far more winningly with Ruud and Andersen.

CONCERTOS

The Violin Concerto lasts just over half an hour; the Cello Concerto is close to 20 minutes and styled as a single movement cyclical in form. They were paired on an LP by NKF; on CD I could only locate the Violin Concerto. **Arve Tellefsen** gives an effective if not tonally alluring performance aided by Andersen (NKF 50010, with Symphony 1). **Hege Waldeland** does well with the Cello Concerto (30 002, LP), but the larger than life solo recording pretty much relegates Anderson and the Bergen Symphony to the background; the Violin Concerto is better.

CHAMBER MUSIC

It's surprising that ensembles which commonly include Mendelssohn's Octet in their programs don't make the same effort on behalf of Svendsen's Octet, which draws on the same rich font of flowing melody and sparkling rhythms as its far more frequently played counterpart. Fortunately, there are several excellent recordings. The pioneering LPs from the Norwegian Cultural Council are available, with both the Octet and Quintet; the **Hindar Quartet** is joined by violinist Arve Tellefsen and friends (NKF 50012). (Their A Minor Quartet appears to be NA.) The **St. Martin** players led by Sillito are more elegant, lacking the gritty peasant quality of the Hindar but superbly recorded (Chandos 9258, with Nielsen's Quintet). The **Risor Festival Strings** couples the Octet with several very nice pieces for string ensemble, more dryly recorded than the Chandos (Simax 1097). The augmented **Kontra Quartet** offers the Octet and A Minor Quartet (Svenden's first, actually; a second quartet was abandoned when no publisher could be found) in inspired performances, beautifully recorded. The **South German String Octet** has had the good sense to couple Svendsen's Octet with Gade's, and for those interested in the form, that may be the most practical choice (Stieglitz 10294).   HALLER

Jan Pieterszoon Sweelinck (1562–1621)

Sweelinck was influential in his day as an organist, teacher, and composer. His father, he himself, and then his son Dirk successively held the position of organist at the Oude Kerk in Amsterdam, a musical dynasty that lasted nearly 100 years. Though Sweelinck traveled little, his abilities as a musician were widely known and organ students flocked from all over Europe to study with him. His vocal works form the largest part of his extensive oeuvre, with a substantial number of keyboard works as well. (It's owing to copies made by his students that we know any of the latter, since all manuscripts have been lost.)

Sweelinck is the last of the great composers from the Netherlands, closing a rich chapter in music history. His music shows him to be a craftsman of the highest order, well acquainted with the English keyboard style of the day. It isn't as colorful as that of some of his contemporaries—he rarely wrote with any of the effects used to great advantage by Frescobaldi, for instance—but it's entirely without pretense or artifice, at times almost monastically austere. His discography is minuscule but is growing.

My first encounter with Sweelinck was via the artistry of **Glenn Gould**'s reading of the Organ Fantasy in D in his remarkable 1959 Salzburg recital (♦Music & Arts 667, NA, or his CBC broadcast of the same piece, Sony 52589). His performance (on piano) was spellbinding and sent me on a search for other works by this composer. Listeners who

wish to hear Sweelinck's keyboard music can do no better than with **Anneke Uittenbosch**'s disc (♦Globe 5030). Her generous recital offers 13 of his compositions played on harpsichord, virginal, and organ. I like the variety of colors she uses in this recital and her unmannered performances; she plays eloquently and with restraint, allowing the music to speak for itself.

Though Sweelinck's musical life was largely dedicated to the organ, his compositions for voices vastly outnumber his extant keyboard music. *Cantiones Sacrae* is a collection of 37 five-voice Latin motets published in 1619. The texts are largely biblical in origin, with many from the *Psalms*. (Sweelinck also set the entire psalter in French.) Two fine recordings are available, each with strong attractions, depending on the listener's tastes. Timothy Brown and the **Choir of Clare College,** Cambridge, present the work in a complete set, energetically performed (♦Etcetera 2025, 2CD). Strong competition is found in Richard Marlow's survey with the **Trinity College Chapel Choir** (♦Hyperion 67013/14). Both use women in the upper voices, with Marlow favoring a more solemn and refined approach while Brown takes a brighter slant, sacrificing ensemble to a slight degree but obtaining a more pungent result, which suits the music just fine.   McINTIRE

Karol Szymanowski (1882–1937)

Born into an aristocratic Ukrainian family, Szymanowski led an artistically stimulating turn-of-the-19th-century youth. He was well traveled, spending time in Vienna and finding it depressing and provincial; Paris and London (and his encounters with *Pelléas et Mélisande, The Firebird,* and *Pétrouchka*) were more congenial. He also set out for more exotic climes: Italy, Sicily, North Africa, and the Middle East. His early music had some predictable influences: Chopin, Schumann, and Scriabin in his piano music, Wagner and Richard Strauss in early orchestral works. In the '20s he became more and more interested in Polish folk music, particularly that of the Tatra Mountains. Somewhat like his contemporary Bartók, Szymanowski injected the elements of this music into a pared-down, more modern sound, in such works as the ballet *Harnasie,* mazurkas for piano, Quartet 2, and the work many critics consider his masterpiece, *Stabat Mater*. He also had a brief, ambitious, but frustrated academic career as director of the Warsaw Conservatory, where his progressive ideas on music education were opposed by the conservative members of the faculty.

ORCHESTRAL MUSIC

If you like Richard Strauss's tone poems and Stravinsky's ballets, Szymanowski did too, and you'll probably like his orchestral music, which is almost always plangently melodic, intensely emotional, and opulently orchestrated. His appeal to the ear can obscure his adventurousness; he was open to all the musical trends of his time, filtering them through his own sensibility.

His most familiar orchestral works are probably his two violin concertos. These have been lucky pieces, beautifully served on almost every recording. The classic account is by **Wanda Wilkomirska** with Rowicki; she beautifully captures the ecstatic quality of 1 and the gutsy folk inflections of 2 (Polskie Nagrania 64). There's also a generous coupling, the Op. 9 Violin Sonata.

If you want a more modern recording (and the more sumptuous and wide-ranging the sound, the more it brings out Szymanowski's sensuous, detailed orchestration), you can't do better than **Mordkovitch** with Sinaisky (Chandos 9496) or **Zehetmair** with Rattle, who dig into the juicy and virtuosic solo writing and resplendent orchestration (EMI

55607). **Chantal Juillet** is pointed and elegant, with a small but beautifully focused tone occasionally swamped by the orchestra, but these are satisfying performances, pushed into the winner's circle by Dutoit's sympathetic conducting and the excellent sound (London 436837). (The Stravinsky Concerto coupling isn't bad either.) The Juillet/Dutoit recording of Concerto 2 is also included in a London "two-fer" of music by Szymanowski and Lutoslawski (London 448258). Any of these performances will have you wondering why these terrific pieces aren't repertoire staples.

These single discs are all full-priced but worth the money; however, the low-priced coupling by **Konstanty Kulka** (in 1) and **Roman Lasocki** (in 2) isn't much of a bargain; the violinists' tone and command and the quality of the recording aren't in the same class as the others (Naxos 553685). Kulka's performances of both concertos with conductor Jerzy Semkow are better (EMI 65418), but any of the above-mentioned are preferable.

Szymanowski's four symphonies pretty much cover his career and the course of his musical development. Nos. 1 and 2 are big, romantic, rather overbearing pieces indebted to Strauss. No. 3 ("The Song of the Night") shows the composer in full ecstatic-Oriental mode; it includes a chorus and solo tenor. No. 4, an extremely beautiful work full of folkish melodies, is a sophisticated cross between a symphony and a piano concerto. If you want to get to know all four, **Karol Stryja**'s recordings with the Polish State Philharmonic are an economical way to do it (Naxos 553683/4, 2CD). The conducting is persuasive and idiomatic, but the orchestra sometimes leaves something to be desired, a problem with music that so obviously revels in orchestral sound. At present, this is the only available recording of 1, but there are some luxury-class choices for the others. **Dorati**'s Detroit Symphony readings of 2 and 3 are still among the most impressive early digital recordings, rich and detailed (London 448258, 2CD, with Violin Concerto 2 and some fine pieces by Lutoslawski). **Sinaisky** holds the sprawling 2 together better than anyone else, and his 4 (with pianist Howard Shelley) is even finer (Chandos 9478).

Rattle's 3, coupled with the magnificent *Stabat Mater*, has won awards and been praised to the skies everywhere, and it deserves the accolades; it may be *the* Szymanowski recording to have (EMI 55121). **Rubinstein** recorded 4 with Wallenstein, but it doesn't seem to be currently available (RCA, mono). The coupling of 4 with Violin Concerto 1—two of Szymanowski's most appealing pieces—may sound like a tempting introduction to his music, but apart from **Mescal Wilson**'s 4, there's little to enjoy in the scrawny orchestral playing of the Janáček Philharmonic under Dennis Burkh or the over-parted violin soloist, Robert Zimansky (Centaur 2153).

The rest of Szymanowski's orchestral music includes *Concert Overture,* in the composer's early, lavish style (**Sinaisky**'s recording with the BBC Philharmonic is an attractive filler for his outstanding Violin Concertos with Mordkovitch, Chandos 9496); the strange commedia dell'arte ballet *Mandragora,* a sort of Szymanowskian version of Stravinsky's *Pulcinella;* and another ballet that's one of the composer's best works, *Harnasie,* full of pungent folk themes and brilliant orchestration. The ballets are coupled in recordings by **Stryja** (Naxos 553686) and **Satanowski** (Koch Schwann 311064). *Harnasie* is abridged in Stryja's recording, and Satanowski's gutsy performances have the edge too.

CHAMBER MUSIC

There's only one recording of Szymanowski's string quartets listed in the catalog, but it's a beauty: The **Carmina Quartet** combines a rich-textured sound with a refined, rather aristocratic approach to the music, which is a short recipe for good performances of this music (Denon 79462). Quartet 1 (1917), densely scored and ecstatic, is similar in style to Violin Concerto 1; 2 (1927) is in the harder-edged, folk-inspired style he adopted after WWI. If you have a taste for the Debussy and Ravel quartets, or even the early ones of Schoenberg and Bartók, you'll thoroughly enjoy Szymanowski's (as well as the coupling, Webern's early *Langsamer Satz*).

Violin Sonata in D Minor, a very early work, is more popular than the quartets. Some excellent violinists have taken to its late-Romantic style. **David Oistrakh** and Vladimir Yampolsky are pre-eminent and probably ideal (Testament 1113, with sonatas by Khachaturian and Prokofiev). **Mordkovitch**'s full-blooded style suits this sonata to a T, as well as the other violin pieces on her disc, *Myths* and *Notturno e Tarantella* (Chandos 8747, with Marina Gusak-Grin). Available as an import but worth seeking out is a satisfying violin collection—*Notturno e Tarantella, Myths,* a *Romance,* and three *Paganini Variations*—by **Ulf Hoelscher** and Béroff (EMI 55169).

PIANO MUSIC

Szymanowski wrote a considerable amount of piano music: 3 sonatas, 22 mazurkas, numerous etudes, and larger works like *Métopes* and *Masques* (containing *Don Juan's Serenade,* sometimes played on its own). All of it can be heartily recommended to anyone who enjoys Ravel's *Gaspard de la Nuit,* Debussy's Preludes, or Scriabin's sonatas. They often have a "hothouse" atmosphere, but it's usually counterpointed by boiling energy and biting harmonies.

There are two series of Szymanowski's piano music, by **Martin Roscoe** (Naxos 553016 and 553300) and **Martin Jones** (Nimbus 1750, 4CD, or Nimbus 5405, 5406, 5435, and 5436 individually), both excellent, sympathetically and virtuosically performed, and brightly recorded. Roscoe's discs are potpourris; Jones presents the music chronologically, allowing insights into Szymanowski's development as a composer. If I had to choose only one disc by either pianist, it might be Jones's Nimbus 5435, which includes *Métopes* and *Masques* as well as a selection of the enjoyable mazurkas, late works whose bitonal textures and irregular rhythms sound as authentically Polish as say, Bartók sounds Hungarian. (Rubinstein recorded several of them for RCA, NA.)

Among other highly-praised piano discs, **Fialkowska**'s recording presents the sometimes riotously complicated textures with exemplary clarity (Opening Day 9305: Op. 4 Etudes, Op. 10 Variations, *Métopes,* and *Masques).* **Dennis Lee** offers shorter measure but equally outstanding playing (Hyperion 66409: Op. 4 Etudes, *Masques,* and *Métopes).* Complementing either of them we have **Danielle Vernède**'s disc of the Opp. 4 and 23 Etudes, Op. 10 Variations, and Op. 62 Mazurkas (Channel 9110).

VOCAL MUSIC

Stabat Mater (1926) is one of the towering modern choral works, on the same exalted level as Stravinsky's *Symphony of Psalms.* It combines the rich, complex textures of Szymanowski's earlier music with the toughness and compactness of his later style, adding a genuinely ecstatic religious feeling. It's in Polish, which means it has seldom been performed in the West, but it's becoming more and more popular. **Rattle**'s recording is a stunner, with strong soloists and a rich, full choral sound (EMI 55121, with Symphony 3 and another brief but extremely beautiful choral work, *Litany to the Virgin Mary).* If you prefer the coupling of Poulenc's *Stabat Mater,* **Shaw**'s performance with the Atlanta Symphony is highly recommendable; as is often the case with his recordings, the soloists are less strong than the competition, but the choral singing is impeccable (Telarc 80362). For idiomatically Polish if not ideally polished performances, check out **Maksymiuk**'s 1974 recording (Koch Schwann 1265, with Symphony 3 with a soprano soloist instead of tenor) or **Stryja**, who has a good orchestra and chorus and uneven soloists, including a wobbly soprano (Naxos 553687). It does have fascinating and rare Szymanowski couplings, decently performed: the cantatas *Demeter* and *Penthesilea* and the late choral work *Veni Creator*.

Szymanowski's orchestral songs are extremely attractive and, as titles like *Songs of the Fairy-Tale Princess* and *Songs of the Infatuated Muezzin* suggest, they contain some of his most uninhibitedly exotic music. Four Polish singers offer some strong, idiomatic singing in the above-mentioned songs plus *Love Songs of Hafiz, Three Fragments by Jan Kasprowicz*, and one of Szymanowski's most famous works, "Roxana's Song" from his opera *King Roger* (Naxos 553688). This is one of the best in the long line of **Stryja**'s Szymanowski recordings.

OPERA

Which bring us to Szymanowski's surviving opera, his largest work, and one of his most important: *King Roger*, which occupied him from 1918 to 1924. A comparison of Dionysian and Apollonian religious attitudes (to put it over-simply), *King Roger* was the result of Szymanowski's travels in the Mediterranean and Middle East and his study of early Christianity. While it's hardly a repertoire piece, the music certainly deserves to be heard more often. Its music has the same qualities as *Stabat Mater*, voluptuous and severe, hard and glowing like a Byzantine icon. This is one of those operas that doesn't quite work on stage, and not just because of the Polish libretto. It's perhaps best experienced as a kind of sacred oratorio; the choral writing is plentiful and gorgeous.

There is a **Satanowski**-led performance (Koch Schwann 314014), but **Stryja**'s performance is the one to get; the solo and choral singing is uniformly excellent, the recording clear and full, and the price hard to beat (Naxos 660062/63). Instead of an English libretto, there's a very full and useful synopsis; don't let that keep you from hearing this beautiful music.   RAYMOND

Toru Takemitsu *(1930–1996)*

ORCHESTRAL MUSIC

Takemitsu's orchestral music displays to the fullest his subtle cultural and timbral collisions, his cross-pollination of Viennese modernism with a beautiful Franco-Japanese brand of impressionism. For him the orchestra was not an instrument of power and dynamic extremes, but a pool of timbres—a string of sonic possibilities.

A Flock Descends into the Pentagonal Garden. This is Takemitsu's most-recorded orchestral score, and his most beautiful and cogently thought out. **Ozawa**'s premiere recording is still the best; he places the work squarely in late-romantic performing traditions, making the symmetrical structure clear and delivering all the rich detail without false delicacy. Now deleted from the American catalog, this very fine performance, coupled with *Quatrain* for orchestra and a quartet of soloists and four earlier and negligible modernist pieces is still worth seeking out (♦DG 423253).

Two other performances of *A Flock Descends* are more readily available: **Hiroyuki Iwaki** is a bit more impetuous and indulgent than Ozawa (♦ABC 77000), and **Tadaaki Otaka** is beautifully delivered if rather drawn out and episodic (BIS 760). I also prefer Iwaki's program to Otaka's; he and the Melbourne orchestra give us *Dreamtime* and a fine *Vers, l'arc-en-ciel, Palma* with solo guitar and oboe d'amore. ABC's

mikes are less close than Sony's in their otherwise worthy performance with John Williams and **Salonen** (Sony 46720). *Nostalghia* for violin and orchestra is the real discovery in Iwaki's disc: It flaunts burnished—and nostalgic?—lyricism and a gloriously rich, Bergian harmonic palette. Otaka fills out his disc with two pieces that are less decisive in style. Among these, *Orion and Pleiades* finds a sure stylist in cellist Paul Watkins, and proves a showcase for Otaka and his orchestra's lush, ear-tingling pianissimos. As usual, BIS's sonics are very transparent and truthful.

From me flows what you call Time. A commission for the Boston Symphony's appearance at the Carnegie Hall centennial, it is another great orchestral work, and Takemitsu's longest. **Carl St. Clair**'s recording surveys the 36 intoxicating minutes with affection, grace, and mystery (♦Sony 63044). The Pacific Symphony puts it across with deftness, delicacy, and a lovely tone, and the percussion ensemble Nexus helps us relish Takemitsu's quietly orgasmic plethora of colors, among them the bent tones of traditional Japanese flute music, luminous string pedals, steel drums, cowbells, bells, water gongs, and crotales. Sony's sound is magnificent, giving the orchestra considerable depth. The discmates are *Twill by Twilight* for large but subtly deployed orchestra and *Requiem* for strings, which Stravinsky declared a masterpiece in 1959. A Francophile, Takemitsu often leaves his forms tantalizingly open in ways I recognize from Stravinsky as well as Debussy and Ravel.

Riverrun. An extraordinary piece for orchestra and piano solo, it trails off into tolling, bell-like fifths in the piano, the gentle tones charging the encroaching silence with the most powerful tension. *Tree Line,* for chamber orchestra, has a similarly unforgettable, blissful ending: a single oboe in the wings, trailing off to a simple melody shot through with quietly erotic pitch-bends. **Knussen** includes both pieces in his beautifully-prepared program with pianist Paul Crossley (♦Virgin 91180).

Takemitsu has also found faithful advocates in pianist Peter Serkin (as soloist and member of the quartet TASHI) and clarinetist **Richard Stoltzman**. He wrote the gorgeous one-movement concerto *Fantasma/Cantos* for Stoltzman, who plays it as he has played many Takemitsu compositions—impeccably yet personably, as though he had written it himself (♦RCA 62536). Filling out this disc are several chamber pieces originally issued in the late '70s: *Quatrain II* is simply the *Quatrain* heard in Ozawa's DG disc minus the orchestra. *Waterways,* also in Knussen's CD, is a score for eight players that is all bell-sounds and sighs; be sure to listen for the plangent chords on plucked strings, hardly recognizable as a pair of retuned harps. *Waves* is more ritualistic and forbidding, a sort of homage to Noh theater and Japanese folk music.

Traditional Japanese instruments have also figured into some of Takemitsu's orchestral tapestries, and hearing the way he writes for them leaves you more aware of the non-Western melodic slides and intonations heard in much of his concert music. **Ozawa** and the admirable Saito Kinen Orchestra, joined by biwa and shakuhachi players, make the best case for *November Steps* and *Eclipse* (Philips 432176), and **Imai** joins the orchestra for the gentle viola concerto *A String Around Autumn*. If exoticism is your thing, you would be better advised to look into Takemitsu's piece for gagaku, the traditional orchestra of the Japanese royal court: *In an Autumn Garden* is an ear-opening experience and may still be available (♦Varèse 47213).

Takemitsu's music can occasionally be cinematically facile; his lyricism, ease of communication, and skill with texture sometimes causes him to undershoot the structural challenges of his material. These tendencies have free reign in his many film scores, for Kurosawa and Masaki Kobayashi among others. **Rudolf Werthen** (Telarc 80469) conducts I Fiamminghi in some 18 minutes of Takemitsu's film music, and continues his string-oriented and rather soft-centered release with the full-string arrangement of the quartet *A Way A Lone* and the more considerable *Nostalghia* for violin and strings (also in Iwaki's ABC disc). **Hiroshi Wakasugi** conducts several of Takemitsu's weaker and more cinematic concert works: *Gemeaux, Dream/Window,* and *Spirit Garden* (Denon 78944). **Ryusuke Numajiri** leads the same group in *Autumn* and again *Twill by Twilight* (Denon 80462); he also includes *A Way A Lone II* and, the finest piece on the disc, *I Hear the Water Dreaming* for flute and orchestra.

PIANO MUSIC

Several pianists have given us Takemitsu's more-or-less complete piano output, which fits well on a single CD. Containing works written between 1952 and 1992, these discs let us hear him integrating the influences of Debussy, Ravel, Berg, Messiaen, and Boulez into his own idiom. The more recent scores are the most introverted and sensual: *Rain Tree Sketch* sounds a bit like some of the sweeter of Messiaen's *Vingt Regards,* while *Les yeux clos* and *For Away* recall Ravel's *Oiseaux tristes.* **Noriko Ogawa** (BIS 805) and **Kumi Ogano** (Philips 432730) have encompassed these varied works well, but it's **Peter Serkin** who is most idiomatic and sensitive in the composer's delicately sifted gradations of tone, difficult and painstakingly notated multi-pedal effects, and characteristic rubato (♦RCA 68595). This is a very beautiful disc; every note seems to speak. Serkin also includes *Rain Tree Sketch II,* written in 1992 as an epitaph for Messiaen.

Almost as recommendable in his less quixotic way is Australian virtuoso **Roger Woodward,** who leaves out this final keyboard essay but superimposes two earlier Cagean exercises in indeterminacy and graphic notation that haven't been recorded elsewhere: *Corona* and *Crossing* (Etcetera 1103). Their inclusion makes Takemitsu's journey toward a serene, personal brand of impressionism all the more attractive.   ASHBY

Thomas Tallis (c. 1505–1585)

Tallis was a much-admired composer of primarily vocal works for English church services. He skillfully navigated through the shoals of religious turmoil, shifting among both political allegiances and the changing musical styles of his time with apparent ease. Though a lifelong Catholic, he wrote copiously for both Catholic and Protestant liturgies. His music is always assured and competent but not egoistic. He wrote in a somewhat conservative style of imitative counterpoint based on plainchant; this style was generally rather restrained, especially compared to that of his younger colleague and pupil, William Byrd. He was something of a monastic craftsman, and his music always places liturgical needs above any desire for technical display or innovation. Yet occasionally he wrote music that soared beyond all expectation, as in *Spem in alium,* and he is regarded as one of the finest composers of his time.

Tallis is probably best known for his 40-voice motet, *Spem in alium,* and no wonder. This astounding work for eight five-voice choirs is absolutely without precedent, and nothing else in his output suggests anything like it. It's a feat of technical mastery that stands as one of the finest examples of counterpoint ever written, but this fact is rendered superfluous by the work's emotional power and beauty. It's extremely difficult to perform, as you might guess, and requires absolute security of pitch from all the singers.

In spite of this, several excellent recordings are available. The estimable **Tallis Scholars** recording is a good first choice; this group is renowned for its impeccable control and perfect blend, and that's in full evidence here (Gimell 54906). But there's plenty of competition. **The Sixteen** are equally satisfying, and their interpretations and tempos are very similar (Chandos 0513). Both use women's voices in the soprano and alto parts, and in fact they share a number of the same singers. For some, the deciding factor may be the other works on the discs: The Sixteen's is somewhat fuller and includes Tallis's wonderful setting of *Lamentations of Jeremiah.*

For a more radical view of *Spem in alium,* but one I enjoy immensely, check out **Pro Cantione Antiqua** (Carlton 6600952). Two features distinguish it. First, their tempos are much slower; it's a full four minutes longer than the other two. Second, they use countertenors rather than women altos, and there's much more individual vocal color, as opposed to the creamy blend favored by the others. This helps set off the individual parts, and in spite of the slower tempos, they never let the lines go slack. The result might not be to everyone's taste, but I find it extremely compelling. This disc is filled out with a selection of mostly Latin works, including a stunning reading of *Lamentations of Jeremiah.* They use a single male voice in each part and place each line in sharp relief, eschewing the more lush sound obtained by The Sixteen or Tallis Scholars.

A less successful interpretation of this work was attempted by the **Kronos Quartet,** who made an overdubbed transcription of *Spem,* but the result was unexciting (Nonesuch 79242). With all the parts played on stringed instruments and the text removed, the piece loses all drama and is overly homogenized in sound; it sounds as if it's being played on a harmonium. An earlier recording (the first I ever heard) that I still think is exceptionally good is the classic version by **Kings College Choir,** Cambridge, in a "two-fer" with many other choral favorites (London 452949, 2CD). Their reading is more old-fashioned and less scholarly than the others, but wonderful nonetheless. This choir made a later recording under Cleobury that was well reviewed, but I find it comparatively dull (Argo).

The **Tallis Scholars** have recorded many other Tallis works, including a disc with *Lamentations of Jeremiah* and several motets (Gimell 54925). This group deserves its reputation for excellence and consistency, and this recording is highly recommended. With their complete English Anthems (Gimell 54907) and the *Spem in alium* already mentioned, they offer an excellent cross-section of Tallis's lengthy career. Another notable version of *Lamentations* is by the **Hilliard Ensemble.** As with their other recordings, this all-male group performs with a single voice in each part. They have a more blended sound than Pro Cantione Antiqua and some listeners may prefer them.

Completists will be pleased to learn that **La Chapelle du Roi** has begun a "Complete Works of Thomas Tallis" project, with three volumes completed so far (Signum 1, 2, and 3). Vol. 1 contains all Latin texts; 2 presents Mass for Four Voices, some English anthems and other works; 3 is all Latin material. *Spem in alium* has not yet been recorded by this group.

The **Choir of St. John's College,** Cambridge, offers a fine selection of works composed for Latin services, interspersed with some of Tallis's organ pieces performed by Robert Wooley (Chandos 0588). Using all male voices, they give us a fine example of the classic English choral sound. The works themselves are beautiful; many are based on plainchant, and the texts are set with a humble simplicity. More of Tallis's motets plus his Mass for Four Voices can be heard sung by the **Oxford Camerata** (Naxos 550576). Though not quite as refined in sound as either The Sixteen or Tallis Scholars, this group is excellent and the price is right. It's a worthwhile disc that will give great pleasure.

McINTIRE

Sergei Taneyev (1856–1915)

A student of Nikolai Rubinstein and Tchaikovsky at the Moscow Conservatory, Taneyev in turn served as mentor to such disparate talents as Rachmaninoff, Medtner, and Scriabin. While his strong grounding in classical counterpoint and mathematics and his avoidance of the lush orchestral textures of Tchaikovsky and Rachmaninoff have often led to his categorization as "the Russian Brahms," this rather superficial designation only addresses the architecture of his music and fails to explain the virility, the flow of Romantic melody, and the triumphant nobility of his greatest achievements.

SYMPHONIES

There have been maybe half a dozen recordings of Taneyev's Symphony 4 (long erroneously labeled 1), beginning with the pioneering mono LP by **Alexander Gauk,** which save for the completist may be set aside with respect. With stereo came the LP led by **Yuri Ahronovitch** (Arabesque), an admirably straightforward account by this sometimes eccentric conductor that paled beside the more robust and pointed approach of **Rozhdestvensky,** who worked wonders, his great affection everywhere in evidence (♦Chant du Monde 278931). **Arnold Katz** (Russian Disc) comes off as routine next to Rozhdestvensky, who constantly finds new things to show us. **Svetlanov** gives a fiery account (Melodiya), but the USSR Symphony plays better for Rozhdestvensky. **Gunzenhauser** with a fine Polish orchestra combines 2 and 4 (Marco Polo 223196); he does very well with both, perhaps the most recommendable pairing if you can't find the Rozhdestvensky.

However, there are also two very fine recordings that combine 4 with other material. **Neeme Järvi** has the Philharmonia at his disposal, and despite the rather resonant sound stage he compels attention, his brawny approach to the outer movements building with the power of a juggernaut (♦Chandos 8953). **Peter Tiboris** moves forward implacably as well, though the Moscow brasses can't match the heft of the Philharmonia and his rather hasty tempo smudges things a bit in the Scherzo (Bridge 9034). Thus the buyer may find himself torn between the imposing *Oresteia* Overture on Chandos and the even more rarified Bridge makeweight, Taneyev's sumptuous arrangement of sketches left by Tchaikovsky for an opera based on *Romeo and Juliet.* Those fortunate enough to find **Rozhdestvensky's** Rimsky-Korsakov Symphony 3 will also obtain an intense account of the *Oresteia* Overture (Revelation 10083). **Järvi's** recording of the *Romeo and Juliet* duet can be had as makeweight for his Rachmaninoff *Bells* (Chandos 8476).

Symphony 2 was never completed; Taneyev left only the outer movements in full score and a piano four-hands sketch of the Andante, with no indication of a scherzo. In 1973, Vladimir Blok orchestrated the Andante and also altered the first movement following Tchaikovsky's suggestions. The resulting three-movement symphony has been recorded twice, first by **Fedoseyev** (Russian Disc) and then **Gunzenhauser** (Marco Polo), in both cases combined with 4. This fascinating experiment is passionately Russian in its cumulative effect, bracing and richly scored for the brass. Fedoseyev is more impetuous; Gunzenhauser seems tepid by comparison.

Occasionally reminiscent of Brahms or Bruch, the curiously structured Concert Suite for violin and orchestra is an imposing score in five movements; the fourth is almost a suite in itself, an extended theme and variations leading to an exhilarating Tarantella. **Oistrakh** was long a proponent of this score, and his 1956 recording is available (EMI 65419). Your best bet is the bright, clear-eyed account by **Yuval Waldman** (Newport 85517), since the duskier, more soulful **Andrei Korsakov** may be hard to find (Melodiya 00147), and the even earlier Melodiya LP with **Eduard Grach** hasn't made it to silver disc. It's also played very beautifully by cellist **Werner Thomas-Mifune** (Koch Schwann 1135)—though the finale hardly seems like the indicated Presto—but the source of the arrangement isn't identified (was it the composer's own?).

CHORAL MUSIC

The cantata *Saint John of Damascus* was Taneyev's first published work, filled with religious fervor and some thrilling sounds from the choir. There used to be an exciting and highly colored Melodiya LP by **Fedoseyev** that hasn't made it to CD. **Andrey Chistiakov's** recording might turn up in the stores listed under its companion piece, Tchaikovsky's cantata *Moscow* (♦Saison Russe 288069). It must yield to **Poliansky** in sound but not passion (Chandos 9608, with the Tchaikovsky 4th). *At the Reading of a Psalm* is a more extended work (lasting over an hour) calling for four soloists, chorus, and orchestra; here too is vivid and dramatic singing and impassioned and soulful writing for the orchestra. Unfortunately the only available recording, with **Svetlanov,** is taken from a 1977 concert and is anything but subtle, either in performance or sound; still, this is such an earnest and fascinating score that it's worth the effort to meet it halfway (Russian Disc 10044).

HALLER

Alexandre Tansman (1897–1986)

Tansman belonged to a group of composers from Eastern Europe who spent time in Paris during its bohemian flowering in the '20s and whose outlook was shaped, leavened, and marinated by the cosmopolitan influences encountered there. Born in Poland, he soon espoused the modernism of Scriabin, Honegger, and Milhaud, and later Stravinsky. An exceptionally facile and technically accomplished craftsman and pianist, Tansman left a vast legacy of works in all forms, and developed his own highly distinctive and diverse style. Renewed interest in his work has led to a spate of recent recordings that reveal a musical master of sophisticated tastes and kaleidoscopic personality.

Two facets of that persona are emphatically revealed in a recording of his ballet *Bric-a-Brac*, an airy divertissement described as an "answer to Pétrouchka," very well played by the Bamberg Symphony led by **Israel Yinon** (Koch 6558, with the urbane Symphony 4). Even more interesting is a release by the Virtuosi di Praga (again under Yinon) of four works for chamber orchestra, including the two Sinfoniettas (the first a sort of pastoral Stravinsky), the *Sinfonia Piccola* (a substantial and keenly felt piece that belies its title), and the mercurial, modally inflected *Divertimento* (Koch 6593). Equally worthwhile is a superb first recording of the Violin Concerto, another lost post-romantic masterpiece. **Beata Halska** and the Polish Radio Symphony Orchestra under Bernard Le Monnier also present the folk-oriented five *Pieces* for violin and small orchestra, the nostalgic Polish Rhapsody, and four Polish Dances, all first recordings (Olympia 685).

Almeida and the Moscow Symphony Orchestra offer three late works in Tansman's complex post-Stravinskian style: Concerto for Orchestra, the sometimes demonic six Etudes, and *Capriccio* (1955), which is something of a misnomer for this serious, thoughtful work (Marco Polo 223757). Sadly, Symphony 5 (*Stele*), in memory of Stravinsky, and four

Movements for Orchestra are NA (Marco Polo 223379): I hope Naxos will reissue it. Suite for two pianos and orchestra played by **Joshua Pierce** and **Dorothy Jonas** with David Amos conducting the Slovak State Philharmonic is another release not to be missed for its scope and variety (Centaur 2269, with works by Nicolai Lopatnikoff and Gian Francesco Malipiero).

There is a good range of chamber and keyboard music to be considered. Especially notable are the complete Mazurkas for piano played by **Mark Andersen;** these are fascinating miniatures (Talent 39). Equally recommended is a release including Sonatine for bassoon and piano, Suite for bassoon and piano, *Sonatine Transatlantique,* Blues Preludes, and Suite for clarinet, oboe, and bassoon (Arion 55401). *Berceuse et Danse* for guitar is just part of a large output for the instrument, little of which is yet recorded; it can be heard played by Segovia (AURC 115, with pieces by several other composers).

Tansman's rapidly growing reputation as a 20th century master is reflected in his lengthening representation on disc. His remarkable consistency of quality and sustained interest over such a wide range of works will undoubtedly secure that reputation. JOHNSON

Giuseppe Tartini *(1692–1770)*

This fine violinist and composer contributed much to violin technique. With his countrymen Locatelli and Nardini, he helped prepare the way for the virtuosity of Paganini in the next century. He also contributed to the diabolical image of the violinist, likewise taken on by Paganini, through his sonata "The Devil's Trill." He wrote 135 other sonatas and a like number of concertos, many of great technical difficulty. He was famous for his purity of tone and accurate intonation (he discovered the difference tone, a third tone heard when two are played together). His music has an energy of expression comparable to Vivaldi, though his imagination is less far-ranging and full of variety than that master's.

"Devil's Trill." Tartini is remembered today principally for the "Devil's Trill" or "Devil's Sonata," purportedly composed after a dream he had of the devil, who inspired him to play music far better than he could normally conceive.

Among the artists who use the original edition, **Manze** plays the sonata unaccompanied as Tartini claimed to have done (Harmonia Mundi). His expression is ghostly at first, but a degree of monotony eventually sets in, as his ornaments are sparse and unimaginative. **Rachel Barton** employs a harpsichord and cello continuo and supplies her own ornaments (♦Cedille 41). Her articulation is authentically Baroque, her vibrato chaste, and her ornamentation ample and imaginative. The performance has a light, delightful air.

The following violinists use the popular arrangement by Fritz Kreisler, which smoothes out some dissonant harmonies and adds a cadenza to the last movement. **David Chan** plays in a straightforward manner (Ambassador). He has chosen not to adopt the more articulated manner of bowing advocated by period performance practitioners like Manze, so his bowing is mostly very legato. His performance is bland and inexpressive. **Shaham** is very similar to Chan (DG). While he articulates more, he's also inexpressive and mechanical, and only Jonathan Feldman's sensitive pianism is interesting. **Rosand** is much more emotionally involved, in an unabashedly romantic manner with a full-bodied tone, a wide, continuous vibrato, and portamento (Biddulph LAW 006).

Milstein is also romantic in manner, more expressive than Shaham but less than Rosand (EMI). **Gerhard Taschner** (Tahra) and **Menuhin**

(Biddulph) are passionate and romantic but not thoughtful. **Príhoda** is very much in the grand style of the old school. His playing has strong character and is spontaneous and exhibitionistic, with a wide range of articulation and expression (111 50200). **Mutter** plays with almost operatic melodrama in a tasteless arrangement for violin and orchestra by Riccardo Zandonai (DG).

Concertos. The technical agility required to play Tartini effectively limits the success of a surprising number of recordings. **Menuhin** tends to sound tentative, despite an interesting reading of D12 and 36 (EMI LP 38039). **André Gertler,** whose 1962 recordings of four concertos have been re-released, also tends to be a little loose in intonation, though his performances, like Menuhin's, have a sweetness and musical energy that some of our more recent early music types have chosen to avoid (Hungaroton 31529). **Accardo** offered five in performances that show similar character and technical limitations (Philips LP 6500784 and 9502089). Perhaps the idea of a healthy vibrato just doesn't fit Tartini's style very well.

The next generation of recordings is represented by Scimone and I Solisti Veneti, who accompanied several performers in this repertoire during the '80s. **Uto Ughi** recorded three (Erato 88096) with this lively string group, while **Piero Tosi** did five more (Erato 12988). Both violinists take their technical duties with a lighter touch and less aggressive vibrato than those mentioned above, with more satisfying results. **Felix Ayo** plays only one of the two different slow movements of D96 in his recording, which also includes concertos in D minor (D45) and E (D53), both listed without their D numbers, and a Symphony in A (Dynamic 92). He's another smoothie, not yet an early musicker but easy-going and beautiful in tone. Vol. 2 of his series contains D15, 56, and 125 (Dynamic 131) and Vol. 3 offers D12, 67, and 78 and shows a falling off, mostly due to an inferior orchestra (Dynamic 163).

The period instrument movement took its time getting to Tartini, perhaps because of the ambiguity of his style, so clearly heart-on-sleeve romantic that it seems a pity to deprive him of that period's expressive style. The first to try it was **Carlo Chiarappa,** who played four concertos with enthusiasm, if with a somewhat wiry tone at times (Denon 78969). The very small l'Arte dell'Arco group recorded the twelve Op. 1 concertos with three soloists in somewhat rough and ready readings (Dynamic 160, 3CD). However, this album of early works is not duplicated elsewhere. **Giovanni Guglielmo** appears to be the most polished of the three players; he offers the Op. 2 concertos (Dynamic 190, 2CD). Other volumes of this series have appeared; they seem to be working their way in chronological order (Dynamic 196, 220, 239). I only wish the playing were more polished.

Gordan Nikolitch's two volumes of concertos include five in one of them (Olympia 475) and three in the other (Olympia 176). This lively and accurate violinist gives effective performances with a modern sound.

Chamber music. Besides the "Devil's Trill," Tartini wrote as many sonatas as he did concertos. Due to ambiguities in Italian performance practices of the time, it's not easy to determine whether many of these works are supposed to include a keyboard continuo or not, the richness of Tartini's double-stops inviting many performers to do them in a bare-bones way with only a melodic bass line. **Elizabeth Wallfisch** with her Locatelli Trio has chosen to include the keyboard in her two releases (Hyperion 66430 and 66485), while **Manze** takes Tartini at his word when he remarked that the bass line itself was an afterthought, and plays his disc with no bass whatsoever, including the Devil himself (Harmonia Mundi 907213). **Giovanni Guglielmo** gives us a collection with harpsichord alone, perhaps the least effective solution, though well played (MusicaImmagine 101).

The Art of Bowing is more specialized, a primarily didactic set of 50 variations on a Corelli gavotte for unaccompanied violin. **Gilles Colliard** is the only one to play it all, though Eduard Melkus and others have been given us excerpts over the years. Colliard does a good job, though it would take a god to keep us on the edge of our seats for 55 minutes (Doron 3007). **Andrea Cappelletti** takes on a somewhat similar task in a series of *Piccole Sonate* for solo violin (Koch 1126). He plays well, but Tartini isn't as imaginative as Schmelzer or Biber. Try Manze's collection first; he's the best of the bunch.   MOORE/MAGIL

John Tavener (b. 1944)

The English have enjoyed great sacred choral music for centuries, and the 20th is no exception. The great cathedrals have provided optimum settings for the distinctive British sound produced by unparalleled choirs and conductors as well as solo and accompanying instrumentalists. Tavener has formed close relationships with several of these marvelous performers and their distinct locations for a couple of decades now.

Tavener's music is amply available on CD; all performances and recording quality are at least acceptable. This is fortunate, because his compositions are very much in vogue these days, with audiences for both classical and New Age music finding much to like—and others finding equally much to dislike. English ensembles are the most avid practitioners, and their audience is likewise overwhelmingly English, with those of other nationalities more likely of the sort that buys Gregorian chant and Wyndham Hill discs primarily for background music or chilling out. The mostly consonant musical surface is a warm sonic bath, and the unabashed spirituality nurtures those so inclined. Detractors are equally adamant that for all Tavener's commitment to religiosity in text and sonic reference, this is merely soporific pretension at profundity, or at least it comes across that way despite Tavener's sincere, confident religious faith and concomitant musical expression of it.

Labels for his music include "spiritual (or holy) minimalism," "New Age choral chic," "Neoancient," and "Mystic Minimalist." Not all of these monikers are intended as complimentary, but all are apt; all are subsets of the New Consonance that was the prevalent style of composition in the last quarter of the 20th century. Perhaps more than others Tavener is inextricably bound to digital recording for the clean sound this harmonically triadic, rhythmically static, and aurally spacious music requires. Therefore, the digital recording is in a sense a part of the composition itself. The tradeoff is a lack of the warmth analog recording would provide, but the resonance of most of the spaces and attentive engineering result in a sound that modern listeners of whatever esthetic persuasion are now accustomed to.

A fine example of this sound and Tavener's esthetic premise and compositional style is "Thunder Entered Her, God is With Us," in which the **Winchester Cathedral Choir** presents the title pieces and four other sacred works (Virgin 45035). The similarity between pieces is alleviated somewhat by accompaniments ranging from handbells to organ to strings, and superb solos against mixed and women's choirs. "Ikons: Choral Music of John Tavener" is a disc of nearly comparable quality that includes the two works identified above (United 88023). The **BBC Singers** are marginally less successful than the Westminster musicians, and the digital sound is more apparent than on the Virgin CD. For those who relish Tavener's religious choral music, both are recommended.

Initiates would be better off with either of these discs before proceeding to Tavener's most extensive single work, *Akathist of Thanksgiving* (Sony 64446). The text of this 78-minute strophic, ritualistic music was written in a Siberian gulag by the Russian Orthodox priest Gregory Petrov and deals with Christ's life and resurrection. The recorded sound is good, and the performance by the **Westminster Abbey Choir** captures the spirit of the music well, marred only by the basses, who seem overextended in the extremely low range. My ear wants the Russian bass sound for the intonations that begin each of the ten strophes. On the other hand, countertenors James Bowman and Timothy Wilson are superb.

Tavener isn't alone as composer of consonant sacred music, linked often with Pärt and Górecki as "New Monasticists." Two excellent recordings by exemplary British choirs offer a sample of the three. The former features the Oxford **Pro Musica Singers** in nine short works by Tavener, two by Pärt, and three by Górecki (Proud Sound 136). All are performed with attention to stylistic differences within their generally similar approach to composition. The recording by the **King's College Choir,** Cambridge, offers some of the same music (Pärt's *Magnificat* and Górecki's better-known *Totus tuus*). The estimable Cleobury's take on the music is less somber than Smedley's, and the differences between Tavener's direct expression versus Pärt's more elaborate and Górecki's more Latin Catholic are more clearly delineated (EMI 55096).

The **Tallis Scholars** are one of the best of several choral groups specializing in Medieval and Renaissance music, usually sacred, and late 20th-century composers of retro or similarly styled compositions. No call here for vibrato or equal temperament, but precise intonation and blend are an absolute necessity. The group exemplifies the epitome of this style in an all-Tavener CD (Gimell 54905). The featured work, *Ikon of Light,* was composed for them. The original Greek Orthodox text by the Medieval mystic St. Simon the New Theologian is compelling in its metaphysical simplicity, and Tavener's setting is more formally synoptic than many of his other works. The easily followed arch form and canons are richly consonant, and repetition of text at the beginning of strophes provides a comfortable progress through the ritualism. The performers project clearly, and the ambiance of Merton College Chapel at Oxford provides the ideal forum for *Ikon* as well as *Funeral Ikos* (inexplicably and to lesser effect sung in English), and *Carol: the Lamb.*

For those made skeptical, even annoyed, by the sameness of Tavener's work, *Ikon of Light* is a good (re)introduction to his sacred choral music. The schema and poignant dissonances add a sense of continuity generally lacking in his shorter pieces. An alternative recording of *Ikon* by **The Sixteen** isn't comparable in quality to the Tallis offering (Collins 1405). The performance is less engaging and marred by intonation problems and imprecise attacks. However, it does contain 12 minutes more of Tavener's music, settings of two of Blake's texts (*The Lamb* and *The Tiger),* as well as four other short pieces.

Fall and Resurrection is an hour-long oratorio that will interest those who want the mood Tavener conjures up to last for a while. The title gives the story away, and this "crushing bore of a work," according to one reviewer, takes on myriad effects, including eerie sounds from a shofar and some massive dissonance aided by electronics. Four soloists join the **BBC Singers** directed by Hickox in a fine performance (Chandos 9800). Paradoxically, perhaps perversely, I suggest this disc to those who don't know Tavener's music. If they are engaged, they should then proceed to the discs containing several shorter pieces of more recent vintage, perhaps the '80s compositions that are largely all of one stylistic piece.

Tavener joined the Orthodox Church in 1977, but he remained interested in the Anglican service and music in addition to the newly acquired Byzantine realm. We have some of each performed by the **St. George Chapel Choir** of Windsor (Hyperion 66464). The several '80s pieces include *Ode to St. George of Crete* as well as *Nunc Dimittis* and, again, settings of Blake's mystical *The Lamb* and *The Tiger*. Excellent quality of performance and recording throughout.

I wonder whether Tavener can sustain this compositional style successfully without running dry. There's no shortage of comparable texts, and the audience for consonance-cum-spirituality is, if anything, growing daily. However, two reviewers of more recent music question whether he has perhaps mined out that lode. I refer to reviews of the disc that contains *Annunciation* (1992), *Song for Athene* (1993), and *Innocence* (1995), performed by a few soloists, the **Westminster Abbey Choir** and English Chamber Orchestra, all conducted by Martin Neary (Sony 66613). The music is perfectly suited to the performers and recording space; in fact, Tavener worked closely with these musicians in this space while composing. The performances are all one could wish for, and even reviewers less than enthusiastic about the compositions praise the recording. On the other hand, a third reviewer recommends this disc above all other Tavener CDs for these works as well as the often-recorded Blake songs. I'm neither as negative as the first pair nor as enthusiastic as the third. Choral sound, a cappella, or accompanied, seems to be the best medium for Tavener's work, and his favorite. However, there are other media through which he expresses his spirituality. His fans will enjoy *Eis Thanaton* and *Theophany,* two extended works, 67 minutes total, for solo voice and orchestra. **Hickox** conducts the City of London Sinfonietta with Patricia Rozario and Stephen Richardson as soloists in *Eis Thanaton,* and the Bournemouth Symphony, Margaret Feaviour, and Jeremy Birchall (on occasion his voice is electronically altered) as soloists in *Theophany* (Chandos 9440). The performances are sincere, but the music is at best self-indulgent, at worst soporific. A few exotic instruments add to the orchestral timbre.

For purely instrumental music, *The Protecting Veil* is popular enough to receive numerous live performances and a half-dozen recordings. My preference is about equal for three: Justin Brown conducting the Royal Philharmonic Orchestra with **Wallfisch** as cello soloist (Tring 48); Rozhdestvensky and the London Symphony with **Isserlis** (Virgin 59092; see also his top-of-the-charts hit recording in 91474); and Zinman with the Baltimore Symphony and **Ma** (Sony 62821). The musical personalities of these fine artists differentiate their otherwise equally gratifying performances. The 45-minute work was composed for Isserlis, so it may be that his relatively restrained rendition is closest to Tavener's intention. It's an austere reading, more akin to the choral music than are the others. Wallfisch's rendition is more dramatic, calling attention to the music itself more than to the spiritual program implied by the title. Ma's rendition is more presentational, as you might expect, as though adding yet another work to his instrument's repertoire is at least part of the reason to perform the piece.

Another purely instrumental work is *The Repentant Thief* for clarinet and orchestra, which refers to one of the other victims crucified with Christ (Collins 2005). This 20-minute work features the clarinet in a high-register, vaguely Middle Eastern folk idiom as well as Tavener's typical drones in the chalumeau register.   ZIEROLF

John Taverner (c. 1490–1545)

We know a lot less about Taverner than we thought we did. We still know that he was born in the early or mid-1490s and came to the attention of

Bishop Longland, who recommended him for the choirmaster post at Cardinal Wolsey's newly established Cardinal College in Oxford. Taverner would have found there the sixteen singers common to an established college choir of the time (thus the name for Harry Christophers's estimable early music ensemble, The Sixteen), and "twelve clerkes skilled in polyphony," one of whom was an organist.

Then comes the muddy bit. A marginal note made four decades after the composer's death in John Foxe's 1583 edition of *Actes and Monuments* begins the confusion; Foxe writes that Taverner "repented him very much that he had made Songes to Popish Ditties in the time of his blindness." There was Lutheran sentiment afoot at the college, and while some were arrested for heresy, Taverner was apparently pardoned, since he had hid the heretical texts "under the bordes of his schoole, yet the Cardinal for his music excused him, saying, that he was but a Musitian, and so he escaped."

After Wolsey fell out of favor, Taverner left in 1530 when Henry VIII reformed the college to create Christ Church. Then, back to speculation: It's thought that he returned to Lincolnshire, giving up composition to become "a cruel and fanatical agent in the suppression of monastic establishments" (as Philip Brett wrote). The truth is at once more subtle and more poignant. It's likely that he remained a Catholic, perhaps adjusting his public statements to survive the fractious times. He returned to the parish of Boston in Lincolnshire, where at the time of his death, he had been elected one of the 12 aldermen of the church, and was given the signal honor of being buried beneath the "stump" (bell tower) of the parish Church of St. Botolph, the second person so honored.

It's probable that while the main body of his work was composed while at Oxford in the high and florid style we associate with the festal masses, there were some later works that show a more clear and placid expression. His surviving correspondence with Cromwell reveals a cleric concerned with the welfare of the monks at Boston; even "Popish Ditties" may just refer to the movement away from Marian antiphons— certainly the subsequent history of English music in the 16th century can't be written without those composers who were allowed to remain Catholic.

All this misses the point, according to that most eloquent proponent, Tallis Scholars director Peter Phillips: "'The first great English composer' has been used as a banner to describe Purcell, yet it was Taverner who was the first English composer of sufficient breadth and scope to establish an identifiable school of composition in his native land." The argument is wonderfully persuasive. Nearly every composer in England from Taverner's death to Purcell himself wrote a variation of the "In Nomine" theme from the "Benedictus" of the *Missa Gloria tibi trinitas,* and he was the first Englishman to write a mass on a popular song ("Western Wind"). Phillips notes his direct influence on Byrd, and rhapsodizes on Taverner's ear for sound: "His sense of vocal spacing, like the most perfectly realized perspective in Renaissance painting, unfailingly enthralls the listener."

There's almost nothing I can't commend in discs dedicated to this master, but in the confusion of releases and re-releases featuring the **Tallis Scholars,** my first recommendation must be their 1995 disc commemorating the 450th anniversary of Taverner's death (♦Gimell 995). It features their recording of *Missa Gloria tibi Trinitas* and *Western Wind Mass,* with the passionate defense of Taverner's genius in Phillips's notes. (Don't be confused by the nearly-eponymous modern composer John Tavener; Phillips, a personal friend, also recorded the latter's first compositions, and a recent *Schwann* listed "The Protecting Veil" and "Village Wedding" as being by Taverner, which they clearly are not.)

The Sixteen have given us *Western Wind* and a body of motets, including some written in the later style we associate with the composer's return to Lincolnshire (◆Hyperion 66507). Worth seeking out is their earlier essay of *Gloria tibi trinitas* with yet another motet, *Audivi vocem* (Hyperion 66134). Taverner's home choir of **Christ Church, Oxford,** gives us a lovely reading of *Mater Christi* and the work composed as a prayer dedicated to Wolsey as the College's founder, *O Wilhelme pastor bone* (◆Nimbus 5218). The oddities of the recording world have given us the 1962 performance of *Western Wind* by **King's College, Cambridge,** but without three motets and *Kyrie Le Roy* that filled out that LP (London "Double Decker" 452170). It would be lovely if they had given us the much rarer *Missa Corona spinea* with the **Oxford Schola Cantorum** from 1973 (Saga LP 5369, NA), or *Western Wind* with the **Choir of New College, Oxford,** from 1979 (Bach Guild 78, NA).

However, an indispensable item from 1989 does float back and forth in availability: the **Taverner Choir** with two works each by John Browne of the *Eton Choirbook,* Scotland's Robert Carver, and Taverner (◆EMI 749661). The spacious *O splendor gloriae* is paired with the mysterious *Quemamodum,* a masterpiece from those late years at Boston that makes us long for the works of this long misunderstood composer we have lost.   DAVIS

Piotr Tchaikovsky *(1840–1893)*

Tchaikovsky's immense popularity belies the fact that his instrumental works are ad hoc in a number of ways. Prized now for his Slavic soulfulness (and described by an admiring Stravinsky as "the most Russian of us all"), he was thought too Westernized by his composer confreres. Certainly he tried to unite the stringent construction of the symphony with the most subjective and theatrical content (hosted in instrumental music up until that time only by the symphonic poem), and came up with a conflation that works inspite of itself—that moves the listener *because* of its fragile paradoxes. If Tchaikovsky's large-scale structures tend to sound improbable, he was no miniaturist either. Great Tchaikovsky performers manage to boil the music down to its barest essentials; they tend neither to the sentiment nor the forms, but convey the emotions with such sincerity (as opposed to obviousness) that the structures take care of themselves. And they never forget to make the music sing, even when the composer tips into depression and savagery.

SYMPHONIES

Complete sets. What a marvelous Tchaikovsky orchestra **Masur**'s Leipzig Gewandhaus is! The slight tinge of Eastern vibrato to the brass and winds helps separate the playing from so much modern, Western anonymity (Teldec). His winds have great color and character, the strings are just as cosseting and just as muscular as Karajan's in Berlin, and Teldec's sound is full, crisp, transparent—absolutely first-rate. Masur's 4 isn't quite up to the rest of the cycle, and the conductor's disinclination to linger leads him to neglect some of 3's beauties; highlights are 5 and 6. If Masur's quick tempos aren't to your taste, you may prefer **Haitink** and the Concertgebouw's more considered choices (Philips). Their crushed-velvet sound and generous acoustics are palpably idiomatic, yet the partnership is really distinctive only in 2 and *Manfred,* where the conductor confers the necessary emotional weight and bowing energy to the strings.

Maazel's Vienna Philharmonic cycle is host to some exquisite playing as well as some surprisingly scrappy sounds (Decca/London); it's sometimes hard to reconcile this with the uniformly ethereal playing heard on his later Vienna recording of Suite 3 or his Sibelius cycle. In interpretation, at this fairly early stage he tended to sound perfunctory and hasty in Tchaikovsky; the exception is his taut and extremely fine 3. London's remastering of the Vienna Sofiensaal tapes tends to be bright and harsh in climaxes. **Slatkin** and the St. Louis Symphony are uniformly unengaged, except perhaps in 4 (RCA). The best thing here is the rich, solid, and ungimmicky sound. If **Abbado** had been given similar treatment from the recording engineers, his cycle would be recommendable, but the Orchestra Hall acoustics conspire with the brass-laden edge of the Chicago orchestra to make for difficult listening in 1 and 6. Best are his 2, 5, the inner movements of 3, and the two rare tone poems, *The Voyevoda* and *The Storm.*

Jansons and the Oslo Symphony made an international reputation with their Tchaikovsky cycle in the early '80s (Chandos). There's no question that the orchestral playing is remarkable, at least for rhythmic clarity and intonation, but executive preparedness tends to leave the music behind, and Masur is to be preferred if limpidity, musicality, and refinement are desired. **Markevitch** and the London Symphony gave us one of the first cycles, and it still has fans praising it for its rhythmic energy (Philips). I find many of these performances aggravatingly mechanical, the exception being 1. **Wit** and the Polish National Radio Symphony have the benefit of super-budget price and turn in some of the best performances available regardless of price (Naxos). But since the discs are all available separately, it's best to pick and choose; the highlights are a 2 and 5 full of character and energy, and also well enough played and recorded to rank with any others. Wit is least convincing in 4 and 6.

Orchestral sonority is the primary drawback to **Svetlanov** and the USSR Symphony (Melodiya/RCA). The strings are vibrant, maybe even more so than Karajan's, but the winds and brass are coarse and unpredictable with their ungainly '60s Russian vibrato. At louder moments the whole orchestral sound spreads and becomes ugly, thanks to an acoustic that sounds like a high school gymnasium. The best installments here are 2 and *Manfred.* For the noncommital **Pletnev**, the Russian National Orchestra is a truly great group in fine rhythmic fettle, with strings to dispatch Tchaikovsky's nervous vamping and tremolos with refreshing crispness. The orchestra is also carefully balanced, actually too much so. Here it doesn't help that DG supplies ill-focused timpani and a lower range that's generally indistinct. This might, in fact, be the first Tchaikovsky cycle to have no marks of distinction, good or bad.

Those listening to **Karajan**'s cycle will react differently to the close miking and dry sound of the Philharmonie in Berlin and the slightly metallic echoes produced there (DG). This is an inconsistent cycle, with 4–6 taped before the onset of Karajan's health problems, and the early symphonies recorded several years afterward in an even drier and closer acoustic setup. But Karajan had vision even when he was inconsistent, and there's always something to learn from what he does. A 20-bit remastered double holds his remarkable mid-'70s versions of the last three symphonies, more generally recommendable than his first three (◆DG 453088). A new 7CD bargain box substitutes his '60s recordings of the last three for those from the mid-'70s, which is an advantage with 4 and a drawback when it comes to 5 (DG).

The best all-round recommendation is **Rostropovich** and the London Philharmonic, who never skimp on the atmosphere and emotional import of each movement (◆EMI 65714, including *Manfred*). A large asset is the ear-warming Kingsway Hall acoustic, as captured in some of EMI's most sympathetic analog engineering. Recorded for the most part in the same hall, **Muti** is less consistent, though on occasion more brilliant. Some disingenuousness creeps into his interpretations, but he isn't an interpreter to be stereotyped (EMI). He's at his best in 1 and 5, and is one of few conductors to note a real difference of tone and style between 1 and 2. Kingsway Hall sound is again a big benefit in this cycle.

1 ("Winter Dreams"). If I had to choose one over all others, it would be **Rostropovich** (♦EMI). His stunning, well-nigh perfect reading is brisk but poetic and emotionally strong, a real curtain-raiser to his cycle. The tempos are expertly chosen, the rhythms are dynamic and passionate, and the London Philharmonic plays beautifully. This is irreplaceable, but running him close are **Haitink** and the Concertgebouw (Philips). If anything, Haitink is more energetic in the opening *Allegro tranquillo*, and the deep sound of the Concertgebouw is perfect for Tchaikovsky's soulful but frosty woodwind parts. Unfortunately, the slow movement and scherzo tend to sag, lacking the shape and sense of direction they have under Rostropovich.

Markevitch and the London Symphony turn in the finest performance in their cycle; he holds your attention from beginning to end, with an overall flexibility that's sorely missed in the other symphonies (Philips, a twofer with 2 and 3). But he's easily supplanted by **Leaper** in a single budget-priced disc (♦Naxos 550517). Here Leaper replaces Wit in the Naxos Tchaikovsky cycle and offers a fine performance, one of the best available at any price. I only had reservations about the ending: An orchestra with more tone could have better supported the deliciously pompous closing pages of the finale, which don't reach quite the climax here as they do elsewhere. The engineering is crisp, transparent, resonant—in a word, marvelous. The kind of tone that isn't quite supplied by Leaper's Polish orchestra is provided in spades by **Muti**'s Philharmonia (♦EMI). This is another outstanding reading where everything comes together; his version is more knowing and beautifully played than Leaper's and also more cunning, less obviously showy, than Rostropovich's.

The kind of embattled rhythmic tension and strictly held tempos you'd expect from Muti came instead from **Dorati** and the London Symphony (Mercury). In the outer movements, at least, this is very exciting—even fairly manic—music-making. But the performance is also generally labored. Mercury's vivid sound has a typically wide range, though the busyness of high-frequency detail tends to sound dated now. **Slatkin** has his St. Louis Symphony playing with the deep, multicolored tone of a centuries-old central European ensemble, but rhythmic tension is consistently lax and the interpretation often tired-sounding (RCA). I could say similar things about **Ormandy** and the Philadelphia, who give a nicely cool interpretation of I but seem unarticulated and heavy in the other movements (RCA). The rather over-resonant engineering conspires with Ormandy's ultra-thick orchestral textures to create an echoey and mushy sound.

Tilson Thomas and the Boston Symphony hear more tautness in Tchaikovsky's neurasthenic sequences and ostinato patterns (♦DG 463615). The music-making is always crisp and clear, avoiding any impression of soupy, soft-centered romanticism. Slavic melancholy is there, but in Tilson Thomas's hands it lies just below the music's surface. Conveying more ambience than usual, DG gives a most beautiful (and recognizable) account of the Symphony Hall acoustics. **Bernstein**'s 1 with the NY Philharmonic is a marked improvement over his 2 and 3, where the speeds and decisions sound cursory and only half thought through (see below). He seems to relate well to the Mendelssohnian lightness of the scoring, and the orchestra does well; however, there are still some patches of bad intonation in both winds and strings, especially the basses (Sony). All told, Bernstein has

sounded more intimate and sensitive elsewhere, and Rostropovich and Karajan reveal more of the music.

Karajan and the Berlin Philharmonic are consistently weighty in their approach, but not in the least fleshy or ponderous (♦DG). As always, this partnership takes Tchaikovsky the reluctant symphonist and, by reducing the music to its essentials, reveals all its strength, simplicity, cohesiveness, and tension. In the finale, some listeners will dislike DG's dry and slightly claustrophobic balance, but it helps support just the kind of musical and sonic immediacy Karajan strove to achieve. **Maazel** and the Vienna Philharmonic are stylistically questionable in early Tchaikovsky; the string sound is opaque rather than transparent, and the horn solo in the slow movement so grand and brazen as to make the *Andante cantabile* sound like Wagner (Decca/London). The sound is bright and edgy. **Schwarz** and the Seattle Symphony are easy to rule out because of their I, where the performance careens clumsily between two ill-chosen tempos (Delos). It's hard to move beyond this flaw, but the sound is excellent, the playing is fine, and the disc is worth getting for Schwarz's much more recommendable 2 (see below).

Svetlanov comes up with one of the better readings of 1 in his cycle with the USSR Symphony (Melodiya/RCA). It's similar to Dorati in its basic outlines and even in its sonic processing. If you aren't overly bothered by the slightly garish acoustics and Russian-school woodwind vibratos, this makes a good recommendation. **Jansons** and the Oslo Symphony are proficient rather than memorable, though the conductor's equanimity and Oslo's chilly timbres are perhaps better suited to this music than to some of the other symphonies (Chandos). There is a hefty, workaday sound to much of I in **Abbado**'s performance with the Chicago Symphony (Sony). The structural tension is also lax: Abbado seems most interested in the famous horn dissonances before the recap. In general the phrasing doesn't have much direction, and the jubilation of the finale is held at arm's length despite the coarse power of the brass.

2 ("Little Russian"). Conductors tend to essay 2 with all the fiery *Sturm und Drang* they cultivate in the late symphonies. The reason is that the piece's tension-filled I, which can set the tone for many performances, is in fact a late composition: Tchaikovsky went back in 1878 and heavily revised this movement, making it more obviously symphonic, linear, and rhetorical in the manner of his Symphony 4 (which he was then working on). **Beecham** premiered 2 on vinyl and, being more in sympathy with early Tchaikovsky than late, made it a bracing rather than an oppressive statement (Columbia/CBS). His Royal Philharmonic plays with sensitivity as well as surprising power when needed. The performance was put on tape (not wax) in the mid-'50s, and the sound is extremely good and steady mono; this is a very fine, from-the-heart reading that needs to be reissued without delay.

In 1957 came **Giulini**'s early stereo recording with the Philharmonia (EMI). The sound still holds up, though there is some glare in climaxes. The orchestra plays with ease and real virtuoso gloss, and the conductor helps make sure that just about every bar of this grandstanding music stays musical. Giulini is a joy to hear, but his tempos don't sound as natural or mesh as well as Previn's; he also makes two cuts in the finale that were apparently standard practice at the time. But Giulini is much to be preferred to **Solti**'s version with the Paris Conservatoire (Decca, with some brilliant and beautiful later recordings of Glinka, Mussorgsky, and Borodin). The Paris orchestra is patently deficient in the outer movements, the early stereo recording takes on a lot of glare in climaxes, and Solti is inflexible in a way that makes the music more graceless than exciting.

Previn and the London Symphony are better than most at making 2 a human experience rather than a scalding, intimidating symphonic *tour de force* (RCA, not yet on CD). Next to Beecham, Previn's is the most natural, flowing 2 to be had. The only possible controversy is that he, like Giulini, makes two cuts in the finale; interestingly, one of them excises the ultra-dramatic pre-tam-tam material that almost brings Muti to an aneurysm (see below). **Schwarz** and the Seattle Symphony do well musically and are well recorded (♦Delos 3087). Their climaxes aren't as full in tone as Previn's or many others, but Schwarz marshals their resources wisely and gives phrases a real sense of direction. This may not be a great performance, but it's fresh and rewarding. The sound is top-notch—warm, resonant, and wide-ranging.

Haitink and the Concertgebouw are another and rather better played choice in the moderate category (♦Philips 442061). He doesn't overstate the music, yet he gives it plenty of character and good cheer; this is the best performance in his cycle. Even so, **Wit** and his Polish National Radio Symphony have more character and drama, and the orchestral playing is surprisingly close to the Concertgebouw's in color and richness (♦Naxos 550518). This is yet another outstanding installment in Wit's cycle, extremely well recorded. **Jansons** lacks personality, for all the clarity of orchestral execution and the superb engineering (Chandos). His tempos sound as though they were calibrated to give the Oslo Philharmonic just enough time to execute the rhythms with no hint of strain or imprecision.

Ormandy and the Philadelphia (RCA, not yet on CD) turned in one of the more exciting performances in the autumn of their partnership (taped in 1979, the year before he stepped down as music director). The tempos tend to be slow, but the playing has plenty of energy and force, and the finale comes to a real climax. What's more, RCA had singular success here in capturing the "Philadelphia Sound" in all its richness. Along with his 5, this is the best installment in his cycle. The contrast couldn't be stronger with **Bernstein,** whose tempos are all fast and strictly held (CBS/Sony). The Philharmonic plays rhythmically and in tune, but the conductor sets speed records in just about every movement and rarely if ever relaxes the pulse. The sound is fine, but this is a musical travesty.

Maazel's Vienna Philharmonic rendition proves almost as fast and cursory (Decca/London). He pays more attention to the score and its details than Bernstein, but this still amounts to a fairly empty (though bravura) experience. For a fast and furious 2, I'd rather turn to **Muti** and the Philharmonia, who are electric but not stiff in the Bernstein manner (EMI). All of Muti's movements are white hot except perhaps II, and even that sometimes threatens to go over the edge. Over the top, certainly, but all in good fun. **Rostropovich** is really at home in 2 with its very symphonic first-movement development and its heavily rhetorical, Glinka-style finale (♦EMI). At the opening of this last movement, he announces the impending theme with red-velvet pomp and ermine circumstance and lays out the following variations with irresistible verve. **Markevitch** and the London Symphony are heavy and lumpish—unmusical, even; sequential and repeated passages, of which there are many, are for the most part turned out with no variance of dynamics or color (Philips). I can't remember a Tchaikovsky recording where the conductor engaged in so little expressive shaping; no wonder he was Stravinsky's first choice to conduct the premiere of *The Rake's Progress*! **Dorati** and the London Symphony are likewise heavy going, though at least he has some bar-to-bar reactions to the music (Mercury). There's nothing terribly wrong with the performance except its steadfast refusal to relax or smile. **Svetlanov** and the USSR Symphony turn in one

of the best installments in their cycle; the tempos all sound natural and the playing has a confidence and centeredness that aren't always in evidence in their other recordings (♦Melodiya/RCA 34163, a twofer with his good 1 and less recommendable 3). The Soviet winds still steadfastly refuse to blend, though.

Masur and the Leipzig Gewandhaus are properly muscular in I and the variations finale, where the strings are a strong and imposing presence (♦Teldec 44943). The orchestra never sounds less than beautiful; with its pronounced vibrato, the opening horn melody reminds us that Leipzig was once in the Eastern Bloc. Teldec did a wonderful job with its refined yet resonant recording, but RCA gave them a good run for their money when they taped **Slatkin** and the St. Louis Symphony (RCA). This is, if anything, an even warmer and more believable sound. Slatkin is at his best and most energetic in I, though it doesn't have quite the spontaneous variety of Masur's; unfortunately, he tends to be rather square in the other movements.

Abbado has recorded 2 twice. His '60s London Symphony version is almost as tense as Muti's and one of the more exciting on disc (DG). He's especially delightful in the *Andante marziale,* which has very chipper woodwinds and perfect tempo modification—subtle, yet expressive within the basic tempo. This is coupled with his fantastic Vienna 4, and that reading points up the fact that his 2, for all its energy, lacks something in soul. His excellent 1984 Chicago Symphony recording is a good deal more personal, and the sound is weighty and impressive (♦CBS/Sony 39359). Chicago's take-no-prisoners brass still cause some climaxes to cloud over, but that rather suits this symphony, which is in Tchaikovsky's grandest, most "public" style.

Typically, **Karajan** holds quite strictly to his tempos (DG). Unlike Bernstein, though, he chooses them very wisely. What's more, and here we get into matters of Karajan's particular genius, their strictness never becomes oppressive. I very much enjoy this recording for bringing out the sheer, no-nonsense strength in this music—for not condescending to it. But at the same time, some will find a lack of crispness: He takes half a bar to get the whole orchestra to sound the opening chord. Some listeners will want more variety, more obviously beautiful sounds, and more natural miking. Such a version comes from **Maazel,** who makes many of the same tempo choices in his second reading, with the Pittsburgh Symphony (Telarc). This is fairly light in weight, more cool-headed than his earlier Vienna version—beautifully played and recorded, one to live with. Yet I wish some of the headlong impetus of his Vienna reading had carried over.

Geoffrey Simon and the London Symphony play Tchaikovsky's original version, where the first-movement development and much of the recap are different from the later, printed one (Chandos). (The composer went back and rewrote much of I later in his symphonic career, and also tinkered with instrumentation in the other movements, did some small-scale trimming, and made a very large cut in the finale. He had trouble deciding which version to publish, but finally went with the revision.) It would be hard not to conclude that the revisions are an improvement, but it's always interesting to hear a great composer's first thoughts, and this is one of Simon's finest performances. The sound is very good.

3 ("Polish"). **Rostropovich** makes heavy going of the outer movements, but the balletic *Alla tedesca* and *Andante elegiaco* are nicely turned, with some exquisite quiet playing (EMI). A fine reading, though not the best in his cycle. **Dorati** falls between two stools in this work, neither procuring a momentous and symphonic reading nor a diaphanous, balletic performance (Mercury). It's a kind of makeshift that comes up short on charm and grace, and in the mid-'60s the London Symphony wasn't the virtuoso band it later became. Mercury's sound is big and beefy. **Abbado** and the Chicago Symphony, by contrast, manage to encompass both the balletic and symphonic aspects of the music (Sony). This is the freshest reading in their cycle; the music-making is very beautiful in the heartbreaking *Andante elegiaco* and similar qualities benefit the scherzo. However, but the orchestra's tone hardens in I and V, where the brass conspire with the Orchestra Hall acoustics to coarsen all *tuttis* above *mf*. Abbado is also sticky, almost careless, in his interpretation of the slur marks at the opening of I.

Litton, on the other hand, hits upon a nice combination of the balletic and the symphonic (Virgin). He may not be the wisest and most farseeing when it comes to choosing and personalizing tempos, and the Bournemouth Symphony strings aren't equal to Chicago's, but they're very clean rhythmically, and we get the impression the conductor has put them on a fairly tight dynamic leash until the end. Virgin's discreet balancing is definitely an asset, and every climax is clean and transparent. **Gilbert Levine** and the Royal Philharmonic are caught in a drier acoustic setting, and the playing has a little more character (♦Telarc 80454). This is a more plain-speaking rendition, less transparent and refined than Litton, appropriate perhaps to such a modest piece with so many folksy elements. Telarc's sound is absolutely ideal: warm and full but crisp and detailed, with climaxes that open up impressively without being splashy. The coupling is a delightful surprise, but appropriate: Rimsky-Korsakov's rarely encountered Piano Concerto, with soloist Jeffrey Campbell.

Masur tries the opposite tack, taking consistently speedy tempos and making I and V outwardly exciting (♦Teldec 46322). But if the tempos look fast on paper, they certainly work well in performance. It's an extremely pleasant reading, with typically beautiful, sensitive, and limpid playing from the Leipzigers and sound that's rich in overtones and ambience. Much the same could be said of **Haitink,** though his tempos tend to be more moderate, and I find the Concertgebouw Orchestra's winds less distinctive than those in Leipzig and the timpani more muddy (Philips). In the moderate performance category, Masur is less bland and wins out for his more obvious temperament.

Maazel tends to be just as straightforward, almost stiff and hard-hitting at times, but his 3 has more energy than anyone else's (♦London/Decca). It's also marked by a refreshing joy and spontaneity: This sounds like an off-the-cuff concert performance recorded in a single take. Decca's bright sound, though tameable with the controls, doesn't help alleviate these impressions. No matter; it's extremely enjoyable, especially in the slow movement, where those gold-spun Vienna strings and butter-and-cream winds come gorgeously into their own. A similar approach comes from **Muti** and the Philharmonia, who enjoy a smoother, sweeter, and more consistently natural production (EMI). But Muti's excitement can verge on brutality; he pushes too hard, and doesn't let up at all in I and V. 3 has been more affectionately shaped by other hands, though the playing itself is stunning here.

Karajan and his Berliners do an amazing job of sidestepping the possible pitfalls, and Tchaikovsky's five non-symphonic movements hang together wonderfully. On the other hand, the dry and rather harsh Philharmonie acoustics mercilessly underline some off-color horn intonation and less-than-tight ensemble rhythms in the outer movements (DG). **Ormandy** and the Philadelphia got excellent 1980 sound from the RCA engineers; the ultra-rich strings create a lush curtain for the slow movements, but the reading as a whole sounds tired, with consistently slow speeds and little if any tension or cumulative impact. As usual,

Markevitch is insensitive to Tchaikovsky's quieter dynamics, and his interpretation tends to be vacant and lumbering; still, his reading does have its fans (Philips). 3 almost sounds like it could have been written for **Beecham,** but he's unusually businesslike in his 1947 recording (EMI/Beecham Trust). The 78s have been well transferred, but the acoustics prove rather harsh and surfaces sound a bit worn in I and V.

Recorded in 1967, **Svetlanov** conducts a performance of extremes, with 3 as a kind of sketch for *Francesca da Rimini* (Melodiya/RCA). He lurches suddenly into the *Allegro* tempo at the first real *tutti* of I, and there you quickly get a picture of the USSR Symphony's frayed sound, which is worlds away from the bourgeois lushness of Haitink's and Ormandy's orchestras. The finale provides a particularly unfortunate combination of approximate intonation, slow tempo, and a matter-of-factness that makes the music seem even slower than it is. This might appeal to those who want a purebred Russian performance. **Pletnev** and his Russian National Orchestra are, by comparison, just as sleek and glossy as any other supersonic touring ensemble (DG). **Jansons** and his Oslo Philharmonic essay unremarkable minutiae (Chandos). The ensemble has been well prepared and coached, but Maazel and others sound more engaged with the music. Though their pitch is impeccable and their dynamic control even more so, the Norwegians have a chilly sound that tends to get clattery in climaxes, especially in the loose church ambience.

By far the most disappointing 3 came from **Bernstein** in 1971 (CBS/Sony). The Philharmonic is scrappy, its intonation and ensemble unpredictable. Bernstein gives the work an empty, contractual-obligation read-through in a tinny, ugly acoustic. It's depressing to think that unwary people will try to acquaint themselves with this beautiful piece through the much-reputed Bernstein while paying no attention to **Wit**'s thoughts (♦Naxos 550518). He and his stylish Polish National Radio Symphony don't quite take the up-tempo Maazel approach, but in the fast movements take enough time to smell the roses, while the climaxes are pressed along with exhilaration. Not everything is perfect: Rhythms could be a shade crisper, and Wit can typically engage in last-minute rubato at the ends of movements. The sound is the most transparent and faithful on offer, a beautiful job. Regardless of price, Wit's outstanding performance could well be a first choice for anyone wanting 3 on a single disc.

4. Previn and the Pittsburgh Symphony are light and airy, rendering 4 almost as ballet music (Philips). The approach presents wonderful possibilities, especially given the bludgeoning this music is usually subjected to. But considering the light-and-easy approach, Previn should have offered more compensating variety and character of phrasing and articulation. The orchestra's astonishingly light tone is made even lighter by the recording, which rounds off all corners and shirks response in both bass and high treble. Any suspicions that **Beecham** might be a similarly *laissez-faire* presence, not sympathetic to the emotional weight of Tchaikovsky's late symphonic works, prove unfounded. His recording is superbly tense and dramatic in the outer movements, with the Royal Philharmonic playing better than they have on just about any other recording, before or since (♦EMI 63380). (The curmudgeon in me would nevertheless like a weightier orchestral presence.) Beecham was a master of phrasing and color, and this makes his II and III utterly delectable. EMI's mono sound is just fine, if a bit constricted in climaxes; you don't miss stereo at all.

Previn's teacher, **Monteux,** gets a lovely response from the Boston Symphony, with no hint of hysteria, interpretive stridency, or orchestral boredom (RCA). It's a golden-age reading of integrity that many remember with affection, and his splitting of first and second violins left and right provides some nice antiphonal effects in the scherzo and elsewhere. Yet his II strikes me as superficial, and he doesn't quite seem to get under the skin of the grandiloquent finale. The sound in the "Monteux Edition" mastering could have been produced yesterday, except for a hint of peaking in the loudest brass.

Another Monteux pupil, **Zinman,** has different problems in his recording with the Baltimore Symphony: His interpretation is generally disjointed and lacking in any subtlety (Telarc). The engineering is superb, though, more immediately impressive than Maazel's recording (see below). **Kubelik** conducts the Vienna Philharmonic in a 1960 performance that's a pleasure to hear but has no distinction at all (EMI). And, as with some other recordings by this great orchestra from the '60s (Maazel's set of the symphonies, for one), the playing is surprisingly substandard.

Dorati is typically bright, alert, and dramatic in an exterior way (Mercury). In sound if not in tempo, this is one of the more intense readings. Sometimes I found myself wishing for more grace in the inner movements and more deeply rooted orchestral sound, built from the bottom up à la Karajan. Much depends on your reaction to Mercury's sound, which is very substantial and covers a wide frequency range but tends to sound frayed at the top and hollow at the bottom. **Solti** and the Chicago Symphony take to 4 like oil to oil, you might say. Their 1987 performance is superb, with the streamlined sound giving the trademark Chicago brass more of a regal, striving aspect than the tooth-and-nail quality sometimes heard (♦London/Decca 414192). This might not be a deep, multilayered, long-considered view—and as such is very different from Barenboim's Furtwänglerian vision with the same orchestra—but there's no arguing with Solti's unblinking conception and the strength and confidence of the playing.

Barenboim with the same orchestra brings appropriately firmer rhythms and greater drive to 4 than to 5 and 6, yet he also lets a telling, Furtwänglerian flexibility and expectancy into the argument (Teldec). To add to the central European ethos, he's actually able to tone the Chicago brass down into a blend with the rest of the orchestra, which neither Solti nor Abbado were able (or wanted) to do. This carefully balanced, highly musical reading would be all the more recommendable if the sound had more bloom and if the players sounded just a bit more interested in what they were doing.

Maazel's 1981 Cleveland recording is the most convincing of his three late symphonies (CBS/Sony). There's much to enjoy here, though he could have more panache and rhapsodic flair in the finale; a bit more showmanship there would have made this a definite keeper. His 1979 Cleveland recording is a bit less cogently argued, with more reticent brass and some tempos that seem a touch more arbitrary (Telarc). The unobtrusive digital engineering sounds entirely natural, but also weighty enough and with good presence for the low brass in the finale. Maazel's 1964 recording is more impulsive and excitable than the later two (London/Decca). Yet the Vienna Philharmonic's phrasing is short-winded, and the playing is rather scrappy—not helped by the brash sonics, with a fair amount of audible mixing-board work.

Markevitch's 4 is far less inhumane and stiff than his 5 and 6 and is very satisfying (in the Philips twofer, 438335 saddled, lamentably, with his much less recommendable later symphonies). He neglects the quieter dynamics, but the scherzo is one of the more lively ones on record, the finale has a nice variation of tempos, and he gets a fairly rich, Slavic sound from the London Symphony. **Masur** takes his usual approach of dynamic sensitivity, well-coordinated tempos, and attention to the long line, though the formula isn't perhaps as conspicuously successful here as in his 5 and 6 (Teldec/Erato). Still, the Gewandhaus woodwinds are full of wonderful color, in a class by themselves. This recording is best appreciated for the silken beauty of the Leipzigers' playing and the equally ravishing recording job, which catches the hall's ambience and all the orchestral overtones like no other.

Bernstein's 1974 recording is spoiled by some of the most slovenly playing ever heard from the Philharmonic, with squalling high trumpets in the outer movements and his unwillingness to maintain a strict rhythm for any length of time (CBS/Sony). In the 20-bit remastering, the strings sound fierce above the stave and there's barely any bass response. His second New York version is even more directionless (DG). In the introduction to I, he pulls the tempo around so much that you wonder if the *Moderato con anima* will ever arrive; his slow movement is one-third slower than anyone else's, and after an unremarkable scherzo, his tired-sounding finale plays host to all variety of special nudges and *tenutos*. DG's sound is disappointing.

Karajan's five recordings are typically consistent. His EMI Berlin recording has long been out of the catalog. The most striving, cinematic conception is the 1976 Berlin Philharmonic rendition (DG). "Cinematic" is the right word: It's overwhelming, beautiful, and vehement by turns, with the blanket-like orchestral sound stretching deep and luxurious. I have enjoyed the recording for many years, particularly for the sound and Karajan's astute pacing and unfailing sense of timing. But there are also hints of grandiloquence and overstatement; almost too good to be true, it's too aurally and musically grandiose to be a comfortable experience. DG got a large amount of ambience from the Philharmonie in this Technicolor production, showing in this case that it's not the hall but the engineering that counts.

Karajan's outstanding 1966 version is more credible, often gentler and less single-minded. It helps that DG apparently used fewer mikes (♦DG 445195, and in his complete 7CD set). The articulation has the gluey quality that afflicts many of his '60s recordings, and the Berlin trumpets of this time are also a trial. But the reading burns with a steady, inner intensity that offsets any reservations, and the finale has spontaneity and tremendous panache. Karajan's 1954 mono recording with the Philharmonia is more obviously emotional, almost blowzy (EMI). Again, it's amazing how similar the sound, conception, and articulation are to the '70s Berlin recordings. The Philharmonia's playing is stunning and the mono sound is lively and believable, even if the orchestra tends to lack weight in the finale. Yet somehow Karajan's 1966 and 1976 interpretations prove more memorable. By comparison, his 1984 Vienna Philharmonic recording is lumbering and overworked, with some of the interpretive details now sounding sadly automatic (DG). It's heavy going, particularly with the up-front microphones, but it must be said that even at this late stage Karajan's grasp of the music's color, structure, and style is outstanding.

Szell and the London Symphony are pretty uneventful, and this orchestra has neither the tonal weight nor the transparency of Szell's home band in Cleveland (Decca/Penguin). It's a fairly anonymous sound, and there isn't much clarity of rhythm to compensate. **Stokowski** essentially rewrites the piece in his American Symphony performance (Vanguard). Hardly a bar goes by without a change of scoring, a reversal of Tchaikovsky's dynamic markings, an echo effect, or an unindicated tempo change. Unfortunately, these touch ups do nothing to enhance or illuminate the music; they only get in the way. A pity, because the music comes very alive in his hands, his orchestra plays fantastically, and the sound is rich, warm, and well detailed. I suppose this is worth a spin if you fancy a Stokowski arrangement—and this does qualify as a arrangement. He must have toured with his own parts, since he performed the same edition with the Japan Philharmonic in Tokyo in 1965 (Music & Arts, with 5 and 6). While the American Symphony is in full command, the hard-working Japanese make many gaffes and short-winded moments.

Mengelberg also indulged in some tinkering, though more in the realm of rubato and dynamics than instrumentation. His temporal eccentricities are much more revealing than Stokowski's. His 1929 Columbia reading isn't quite as fierce as his unforgettable 1928 5 for the same company, but it does have an intensity of its own (Music & Arts, with 5 and 6). Considering the importance of woodwind and brass interjections in this score, it's too bad the set-up is imbalanced by placing the winds far away while the strings are close. **Ormandy** may not plumb the highest highs and lowest lows (♦CBS/Sony 46334). His tempos are unfailingly moderate, and some will regret his resolute avoidance of excitable pressing ahead in I, but all those sighing interjections create a visceral response, thanks to the almost overwhelming gravity and intense confidence of the Philadelphia strings. Though the finale never goes beyond a stately basic (rather march-like) tempo, he somehow winds up instilling more structural tension and exhilaration than just about anyone else. Sony's "Essential Classics" mastering is just fine.

Muti enjoys much the same kind of Philadelphia sound, but his concentration and structural tension tend to sag in the outer movements, though his tempos are in fact quicker than Ormandy's, his touch more brash (EMI). His 1979 recording with the Philharmonia is better, with a more immediate and personal response to the music (EMI). With its showmanship and intensity, this is probably the Tchaikovsky score most suited to Muti. Yet there are some odd agogic touches in II, and hints of impatience elsewhere that seem to cut against the grain of the music.

Abbado's Vienna Philharmonic recording is electrifying, the orchestra unfailingly beautiful as well as intensely powerful (♦DG 429527; also in his double with 5 and 6, ♦437401). Indeed, this is the most thrilling musical playing to be heard anywhere in recordings of 4. As usual, he has chosen his tempos perfectly. My only concern is DG's bargain-price remastering, which has reduced the weight and body heard in the original LP; hope for a 20-bit remastering. Abbado's Chicago version isn't quite as tightly drawn, and the brass-led climaxes in Orchestra Hall sound pinched at the top compared to Vienna (Sony). Still, this is an admirable reading in its own right.

Haitink has the intrinsically Tchaikovskian sound of the Concertgebouw, and his reading isn't boring (Philips). However, I find myself wanting more variety of articulation and tonal weight. **Slatkin** in St. Louis has more direction and drama, and in that respect is more of a success than his 5 and 6 (♦RCA 60432). Another attraction of this release is the couplings: Tchaikovsky's two rarest tone poems, *Fatum* and *The Voyevoda*, in their best-played performances. **Wit** reminds me of Masur: elegant but powerful, extremely well but unostentatiously played, and recorded with refinement and transparency when so many engineers aim for a kind of aural bludgeoning (Naxos, with 2). Many will want this disc for its outstanding sound and low price.

Rostropovich is superbly dramatic from the first horn fanfare (♦EMI). He makes the piece a real spectacle of emotions without flying in the face of the score or pulling tempos around, and he also—here is the wonder of the reading—manages to sustain the tension with no hint of flagging. The London Philharmonic responds to his direction in the

grand manner and with a full-throated yet sensitive response, though maybe not as cogent in sound as Abbado's Vienna Philharmonic.

There are interesting and profound contrasts to be drawn between Rostropovich and **Mravinsky,** who with his Leningrad Philharmonic gives a reading that is less Slavic but just as obviously "Russian" (♦DG 419746, with 5 and 6). The orchestra plays as though their lives depended on it, which, considering Soviet artistic policies, was probably the case. Easy listening it's not: The intensity of the reading is often blinding, given the acidic upper woodwinds and trumpets, not to mention the cadaverous lower brass and the conductor's do-or-die rhythmic severity. Yet Mravinsky is also very free with the pulse when need be, and his contrasts of gentleness and relentless strength make it a *sui generis* reading, one to remember. Considering this is a studio recording made in England in 1960, it's hard to understand how DG allowed the climaxes to get so coarse. **Pletnev**'s Russian National brass are positively genteel, miles away from Mravinsky's Soviet-regime sound (DG). The orchestra is almost too carefully balanced, and you won't hear much of the bass drum at all.

5. Among Tchaikovsky's symphonies, this is probably the one that least plays itself: The piece needs constant shaping and direction, and the tempo relationships are difficult to articulate, especially in the finale. If you want someone who rethinks and re-creates this subjective and difficult score as his very own, **Furtwängler** is the only answer (♦Music & Arts 712). Unfortunately, the recording is pretty dim 1952 mono, from a radio broadcast preserved with occasional static, surface noise, and even some faint and occasional crosstalk from another radio frequency. Get beyond those sonic faults (and the sound of the Turin Radio Orchestra itself is certainly steady and listenable), and you will hear an extraordinary performance the likes of which are not to be found anywhere else.

Similar adjectives apply to **Mengelberg**'s remarkable 1928 Columbia rendition, one of the most white-hot accounts (♦Music & Arts 809, with his less recommendable 4 and 6). Mengelberg is a kind of obverse to Furtwängler's introspection. His I and IV blaze away with fire, the orchestra's rich and imposing tone shining through a limited sound that's still dependable, steady, and good for the time. His rubato is less inorganic and mannered than elsewhere, and the period string portamentos add much to the reading.

A commanding and substantial 5 from **Fricsay** and the Berlin Philharmonic, weightily recorded in 1949 with a few edits and no surface noise at all, has been reissued (Urania). The orchestral playing is superlative—indeed, I've never heard the Berliners in finer form—and the rhythms of the outer movements have tremendous tension without sacrificing tone. If the remastering were better, this would be a strong recommendation. A modernistically straightforward performance, it's already worlds away from the likes of Furtwängler and Mengelberg.

Szell put down a superb 5 that achieves almost as inspiring results of a very different kind (♦CBS 37767, and in a clumsily arranged twofer, ♦CBS/Sony 63281). The Cleveland Orchestra plays with the kind of transparency, attention to detail, and eagerness to listen to their confreres that are more usually heard in chamber music. The orchestral texture is seamless and refined, but also emphatic when it needs to be. It's interesting and unexpected from Szell to hear the strings occasionally using more vibrato than you hear elsewhere. The fundamental difference from Furtwängler is that Szell isn't improvisatory: The symphony is presented as a whole, always knowing where it will wind up and sounding as if written in a single master stroke. Yet this is the relatively rare Szell performance where no trace of calculation remains in the music-making.

Stokowski is surprisingly energetic, even extreme, considering that he and his American Symphony were taped in 1967 when he was 85 (Music & Arts, with 4 and 6). His extremity lies in the fast tempos, pressing the outer movements along fairly hard, and he shapes the music like no one else. Stokowski fans will have to hear this, and it's a beautiful rendition of its kind, though the audience does some coughing, there's hiss and a slight flutter to the tape speed, and also the odd touch-up from the conductor.

A surprisingly strong rendition comes from **Monteux** and the Boston Symphony, who produce one of the more incisive and bustling first movements on record (RCA). There's a lot to like in this always fresh and never overweight interpretation. To be hypercritical, though, I found myself wanting both more weight and occasional relaxation in the outer movements, a lighter touch in the inner ones, and more dependable pitch from the woodwinds. As remastered in the mid-priced "Monteux Edition," the recording sounds as if it had been made yesterday.

I prefer Monteux to **Slatkin** and the St. Louis Symphony, who present a performance that's soft at the center, with the music's edges rounded off (RCA). Given the orchestra's fluid woodwinds and old-world, blended string sound, it can be a lovely experience in a languid, easy-going kind of way. Slatkin coordinates tempos well in the finale, but even there not much seems to happen. **Klemperer** and the Philharmonia come up with a taut, up to tempo, and well-characterized 5 (EMI). Kingsway Hall provides its usual natural sound, and the music-making has real shape and character. All that prevents complete enthusiasm are some moments of surprising insecurity in the winds and Klemperer's touch of stodginess in the finale and stiffness in approaching the new tempo for the second theme of I. Worth hearing, nonetheless.

Prêtre recorded 5 with the same orchestra at around the same time (EMI). The playing is cleaner than under Klemperer, though the interpretation doesn't have quite the same tension. This is as good as, and possibly better than, many more famous versions, but Prêtre holds too strictly to his tempos, indulges in little personal shaping of phrases, and his phrasing tends to be pedantic (particularly in the slow movement), with notes seemingly counted out rather than played through to the next.

Any 5 with arbitrary-sounding tempos is dead in the water before it begins, and it often seems that **Markevitch** barely bothered to look at the score (Philips). Having heard it many times, I still can't help but tune out this performance entirely as soon as I hear him sail into the gorgeous second theme of I with no change in tempo and then proceed to dispatch it so quickly the notes barely have time to sound. The London Symphony plays well, but the conductor's interpretation (or lack thereof) makes this a total loss. **Dorati** and the London Symphony are full of character, though as a whole their reading is more efficient than grand (Mercury). His plainness and slightly workaday phrasing prove detrimental in a work so full of sequences and repetition, and the London strings, recorded in Mercury's usual bony manner, are unattractively coarse in every *forte*—the finale's coda in particular.

Maazel and the Cleveland Orchestra begin the symphony sounding more at home than in the *Pathétique,* a score that more readily "plays itself" (CBS/Sony). The Cleveland wind lines intermesh with cool elegance, and in the introduction to II the strings achieve beautifully unanimous pianissimos. Commitment flags as the work goes on, though, and Maazel is unconvincing with the difficult, changing tempos of the finale. I prefer his 1964 Vienna Philharmonic version, a more direct and straightforward reading (London/Decca). The Vienna orchestra has more presence, the brass especially, though the treble needs taming. All told, though, this isn't a distinctive or memorable performance.

We get a distinguished realization from **Inbal** and the Frankfurt Radio Symphony (♦Denon 76364). It's suitably tough and farsighted in the outer movements, graceful in the inner ones. His orchestra plays with real character, and his thrilling performance—very much in the Karajan manner in its ability to bring this sprawling work together—is highly recommended. **Jansons** with the Oslo Philharmonic is basically similar in outline and recorded with a bit more body (Chandos). But this business-as-usual reading differs from Inbal in giving no sense of the music feeling its way into interpretation. It's unremarkable, leaving nothing to linger in the memory. Despite the superb engineering, I prefer Inbal for his more heightened emotion and more interesting ideas.

Haitink and the Concertgebouw also offer a telling contrast to Jansons; unforced but never dull, the performance is more subtly individual and the playing better (Philips). Every one of his tempos and inflections is perfectly chosen, as are Jansons's, but the orchestral coloration is more assured and kaleidoscopic and the rubato more varied. The cool, rich, deep Concertgebouw tone colors suit the music perfectly. This is one of the best installments in Haitink's cycle, and Philips's engineering sounds more natural than in their *Pathétique.* The only thing preventing an all-out recommendation is a finale that goes a bit off the boil. Though **Masur** and the Leipzig Gewandhaus have much the same elegant, central European tone colors, the conductor does more shaping (♦Erato 18966, a twofer with 4 and 6, or with no notes whatsoever in the identically arranged ♦Teldec 95981). The Leipzig strings seem less restrained in dynamics and bow weight, the winds more beautifully colored by the Gewandhaus acoustics. This is a fine, very genuine performance. It also helps that Teldec's recording opens up so impressively in climaxes.

Abbado also has much to interest the listener's ear and mind. His superb early reading with the London Symphony is still one of the finest in the catalog (♦DG 437401, with his excellent 4 and cooler 6 from Vienna). Full of the kind of spontaneity that came in shorter and shorter supply in his later recordings, this performance has electricity as well as subtlety. The sound has plenty of bloom, and my only complaint is that the bass has a slightly hollow ring. Twenty years on, the edges of the score are more rounded off in his Chicago Symphony rendition, the momentary touches of dynamic inspiration smoothed over (CBS/Sony). Still, this is the best performance in Abbado's Chicago cycle, and while the sound isn't very attractive, it unites strong orchestral playing with a farsighted and trenchant understanding of the score. His 1993 remake with the Berlin Philharmonic completes his interpretive aging process: The little dynamic surges in the second theme of I are pretty much gone, expression in the slow movement standardized, and the finale's structural mine field negotiated without incident (Sony). The Berlin Philharmonie provides a claustrophobic acoustic, and ugliness often comes along with dynamism.

Muti in Philadelphia procures an impersonal, hulking performance; much of the score is loud and unyielding in an impersonal rather than exciting way (EMI). Better to turn to his 1978 Philharmonia version, which is one of the best at effortlessly bringing together the music's rhapsodic, introverted, and martial aspects (♦EMI). The playing and direction are surprisingly sensitive and graceful, the wind solos beautifully turned, the conductor atypically elastic and flowing in tempo and never stooping to agit-prop gestures. This is also the rare performance that doesn't go slack in the finale. As for the perfectly proportioned sound, what to say except that EMI was working again on its glorious old stomping grounds, Kingsway Hall? The timpani are again over-miked, but this is a top-ranked 5.

Sian Edwards and the London Philharmonic hold to consistent tempos, creating shades of difference within them à la Karajan (EMI). (Indeed, Edwards and Karajan are so similar that I wonder if she might have grown up with the Austrian maestro's 1975 recording.) This is *echt* symphonic and well played, but in the last reckoning doesn't have the personality, originality, and profile of Karajan, Muti, or Masur and fails to add anything those interpretations don't already provide. **Previn** turns in a very disappointing performance (Telarc). His 5 starts promisingly with nicely molded phrasing, but the Royal Philharmonic gets distressingly coarse (both in playing and as recorded) at louder dynamics, and the playing is often surprisingly shaky for an internationally known ensemble. **Kazuhiro Koizumi** recorded 5 with the same orchestra several years later, and the fact that the results are similar reflects badly on both the orchestra and the acoustics (Royal Philharmonic/Pickwick).

Turn to **Wit,** one of the finest accounts at any price, and marvel at the far truer response of the Polish National Radio Symphony (♦Naxos 550716). He shows how a performance can scrupulously follow the score and still be remarkably powerful. What's more, the sound is more transparent and dynamic than most others in this listing. An extraordinary achievement in all respects. Wit is more incisively "Slavic" sounding than **Svetlanov** and the USSR Symphony (Melodiya/RCA). There's certainly tension here, but it doesn't amount to excitement when there isn't any real contrasting relaxation. The orchestral sound has a certain garishness that couldn't really be called particularly Russian, let alone "authentic" in this music. I'd much rather listen to **Bernstein,** whose final recording has plenty of emotional weight but also lightness when it's required (DG). There's more rhythmic focus than usual with this conductor, and the engineers got more transparency than usual in Avery Fisher Hall. I prefer this recording to his 1960 New York performance, which is too single-minded in approach to be convincing (CBS/Sony). He makes the music oppressively unrelenting in tempo and characterization, though the remastered recording still sounds excellent.

Ormandy's outer movements present a very different kind of dilemma (CBS). Though not as mechanical as Markevitch, much of it is so plain-vanilla straight as to be objectionable. He inspired far more tension, variety, and flexibility in the orchestra in his bewitching 1973 remake (♦RCA 61853). The engineers also got a richer perspective on the Philadelphians, and added more bloom into the bargain; this is one of the better-sounding 5s on record. And surely the orchestra never played better! By itself, the gleam to the strings would qualify the ensemble as one of the world's greatest; when the cellos take up the horn line shortly into the slow movement, and take it higher than before, the ascent is truly a kind of benediction. This is a dazzling recording.

For Ormandy's 1981 recording, Delos wisely moved out of the Academy of Music (where they did the *Pathétique*) and into the more spacious acoustics of the old Met (♦Delos 3015). The disc is beautifully and truthfully recorded with lots of presence, perhaps the best the Philadelphians have ever sounded on record (some of RCA's tonal sweetness has been swapped for extra transparency). As a performance, this lies somewhere between Ormandy's two earlier renditions: more musical and flexible than the CBS but not quite as rhapsodic and volatile as the RCA. The 1981 III and finale have a bit less shape and direction than before. Very enjoyable, nonetheless.

Karajan recorded this symphony five times. His 1975 performance is magnificent, one of his very finest achievements (♦DG 453088, with his

1976 4 and 6). He relates tempos unerringly and apportions energy gradually, perfectly, in the outer movements; the "seams" that Tchaikovsky lamented finding in his own arguments utterly disappear here. Offsetting and enlivening Karajan's sustained articulation is the orchestra's cogent and often tough sound. They are also all-enveloping; the only other group to provide such astonishing groundswells of string tone in the slow movement are Ormandy's Philadelphians in 1973. His subtle inflections of pulse could serve as a lesson in Tchaikovsky interpretation. DG provides more believable and transparent sonics here than they did in the 1976 4 and 6.

By comparison, Karajan's 1965 performance is in the suaver, slightly sleepy, and smoothed-over style that generally marked his interpretations in the mid-'60s (DG). The articulation is more connected, even gluey, and in conjunction with a more distant and light-in-the-bass perspective on the orchestra, this makes the music more soporific than rugged. His earliest recording was with the Philharmonia, taped in mono in London in 1953–54 (EMI). It's very similar to his 1975 version in its toughness and strength and lack of late-Romantic perfumery. If anything, the performance is even more combustible than the 1975, and the phrasing in the slow movement even freer (a freedom that becomes slow and mannered in III). All's the pity, then, that this wasn't captured in stereo.

Karajan recorded his last 5 with the Vienna Philharmonic in 1984, and neither the performance nor the sound is up to the 1975 version (DG). Tempos are uniformly slower (his health was deteriorating at this time), and the only point of interest is hearing the aging maestro add some dynamic shading and details of phrasing not heard earlier (the slower tempos make this possible, of course). The sound is imposing and very acceptable in the remastering, and it catches well the darkness of the Viennese woodwinds in their low register.

Barenboim and the Chicago Symphony sound more at home in 5 than they do in 6 (see below), the interpretation more thoroughly considered (Teldec). This is well worth hearing, particularly as the coupled *1812* is very good, but Barenboim's interpretation is still rather anonymous. This conductor has professed to owing much to Furtwängler, but comparisons with the master show him to be less creative and personal, to say the least. I prefer **Solti**'s 1987 Chicago recording, which is more intense, even blistering (London/Decca). While a similar approach didn't quite work in Solti's *Pathétique* (see below), in 5 the Chicagoans' playing is stronger and more consistent. Some will find this just too much, but the locomotive-edged CSO tone does make for heady music-making that's not to be forgotten. Beware the *Swan Lake* suite coupling, though, where the solos are badly pitched and the brass work can be mindlessly brutal.

Celibidache's account with the Munich Philharmonic has creativity and individuality in spades (♦EMI 56522). This is a highly unusual reading, best heard by those who already know the work. It's more compelling than his *Pathétique,* the very slow tempos in this instance not sustained with quite the same maniacal single-mindedness and not precluding structural tension. The orchestra also sounds more convinced and a bit more alert than they do in 6. The concert tapes from 1991 sound very well, though there are big swells of audience noise between movements. **Pletnev** and the Russian National Orchestra are at their best in 5, where they traverse some real emotional distance in I and the brass actually stand out when they need to in the finale (DG). But other accounts offer more immediate expression and musicality— **Rostropovich** and the London Philharmonic, for example, who are nevertheless on the stodgy side. Always moving and enjoyable, they still turn in one of the more uneven performances in their cycle.

Gergiev recorded 5 with the Vienna Philharmonic, and the booklet is full of encomia over their partnership (Philips). The playing is fine, but Gergiev isn't as skilled at choosing and varying tempos as he needs to be in this difficult work. He also loses some credibility by inserting unmarked and ineffective speedings up. In short, this is a fairly shapeless reading. Recorded live at the Salzburg Festival, the orchestra has a slightly shallow sound. **Mravinsky** isn't known for a particularly steady hand in tempos, yet his I unfolds with an inevitability that eludes Gergiev (◆DG 419746, with 4 and 6). The musical argument is intense in the outer movements, the Leningrad Philharmonic tone more glaring than sumptuous or depressive, yet he knows when to relax. The sound is fairly well balanced, but there is coarseness and overload in climaxes. Isn't it high time DG remastered these famous recordings?

6 ("Pathétique"). The earliest recordings that still enjoy currency and discussion are by Koussevitzky, Furtwängler, and Mengelberg and then, to move on several years, Karajan and Toscanini. **Mengelberg**'s 1937 performance can sound archaic today, refreshing or annoying depending on your perspective (Music & Arts, with 4 and 5, *Serenade*, and *Romeo*). The Concertgebouw violins are close enough to the mikes to drown out much of what's going on in the winds and the sound is rather dim overall. This reading is notable for the string portamentos, which are sometimes positively Hollywoodish, and also for the rubatos. His tempos rarely stay the same for more than two bars, and at his extreme his changes in pulse can be amazingly inorganic (and non-vocal sounding). The recitative sections of the finale invite such freedoms, and here (especially with the intense Amsterdam string sound) you begin to think he really was in touch with idiomatic performance practices that we have impoverished ourselves by losing.

Some of the same period portamentos are heard in **Koussevitzky**'s 1930 recording (RCA). Next to Mengelberg, it's a straightforward, meat-and-potatoes interpretation with few if any surprises and not a lot of emotion. The Boston orchestra plays very well in this not very memorable rendition, but the 78s used for the transfer sound rather worn. **Toscanini**'s live 1941 Carnegie Hall performance is surprisingly sensitive, and beautifully phrased (◆Music & Arts 956, with *Manfred* and Horowitz's Piano Concerto 1). The NBC Symphony, caught away from their home turf in the infamously dry Studio 8H, sounds like a major orchestra, without the oppressed, under-the-gun quality that makes many of Toscanini's recordings empty as musical experiences. His studio recording with the same orchestra is far drier in sound and has less of the feeling of spontaneity that makes the Music & Arts version so compelling (RCA).

Furtwängler and the Berlin Philharmonic recorded the *Pathétique* in 1938 (◆Music & Arts, a collection of the conductor's "early recordings"). His renowned, small-scale fluidity of tempo—here perfect, and perfectly ingenuous—moves him to a fairly wide variety of speeds that all sound natural and inevitable. As so often with Furtwängler, it's cause for wonder how anyone could be so loose and yet so straightforward with the music's pulse; nothing is forced, and no hint of mannerism taints the blissful sense of temporal freedom. With its infinitely malleable sound, the Berlin is of course inseparable from this conception; there are many moments where the sonority is simultaneously intense and incredibly light in weight, and I know of no performance that wrings so much musicality from III and IV. Furtwängler is preferable even to Toscanini's 1941 Carnegie Hall performance, and this is the historical version to recommend to people who are more interested in musical than acoustic perfection (though the Berliners provide a compensating aural perfection of their own).

Solti and the Chicago Symphony were caught in 1976, at the height of their abilities (Decca/London). The reading is short on the variety, charm, transparency, and grace in the music, between and among the bloodbaths. Also, Solti shortchanges the composer's quieter dynamics, though the sound picture doesn't help with its minimal depth. **Reiner** got a much more shapely and musical performance from the same ensemble back in 1958, and he also maintained better instrumental balances (RCA). There is good metric flexibility to the recitative opening of the finale; this movement is intensely eloquent and moving, not at all upstaged by what preceded it, and it surely represents Reiner and his orchestra at their best.

Recording in Chicago almost 30 years later, **Abbado** attempted a Reiner-like refinement and control, though with longer bow strokes and freer phrasing (CBS/Sony). His reading also has more intensity than Reiner's, but its merits are compromised by some occasionally hoarse playing by the orchestra and a recording that gets harsh in climaxes. His Vienna Philharmonic recording is far preferable, indeed one of the more beautifully paced, well-played, and lucid performances (DG). But emotions are held at arm's length and the performance as a whole will strike some as too cool. This is a reading to hear but not a central recommendation.

Munch's Boston reading is more interesting than Koussevitzky's with the same orchestra some 30 years earlier, and the playing not as slapdash and undisciplined as Munch allowed on other occasions (RCA). It's shapely in phrasing, well paced, and quite exciting. However, but his development in I is surprisingly prosaic, and the recording suffers from a lot of glare in the louder climaxes. **Markevitch** has some fine moments, including a second-movement trio with a nice strong pull to the hairpin dynamics (Philips). As usual, though, his phrasing tends to be stiff, and it's hard to tell if the absence of any truly quiet sounds is the conductor's doing or the fault of the engineers (probably both).

By contrast, **Giulini**'s two readings, especially the first, overflow with humanity and sincerity. His 1960 performance with the Philharmonia is an unforgettable classic (◆EMI 67789, or in the ◆EMI/Seraphim double, 68537). Giulini's phrasing could serve as a model: Take any other performance and you'll find it wanting compared to the impeccable cantilena and direction he instills in each movement. He perfectly captures each of this score's many moods, whether it's the dignified processional at the end of I, the jingoistic swagger of the March, or the disconsolate leave-taking of the finale. Though a bit bright, EMI's sound is fine in this super-bargain mastering. Giulini returned to the piece during his short but miraculous tenure in Los Angeles. That 1981 recording is a bit less dramatic and also slightly less intimate than the 1960, but some of the greatness remains (DG). He utterly transformed the tone of this ensemble, darkening it to the rich, aging colors of a Rembrandt, so all's the more pity that the engineers hadn't yet accustomed themselves to the locale and wound up giving the players a slightly hard and dry sound.

There are similarities of approach between Giulini and **Sanderling,** who made an early (1979) digital recording with the Berlin Symphony (Denon). Everything Sanderling does is worth hearing, and this performance has its moments of quiet eloquence—especially in the lyrical passages, which breathe very naturally and with a disingenuousness even Giulini didn't achieve. He never hurries the music, glamorizes it, or turns it into podium virtuoso fodder. But the performance will inevitably strike some as too non-glamorous, the climax of the March not pressed home strongly enough, the despair of the finale not sufficiently urgent or hard-edged. The recording tends to glare at climaxes, and the bass is unusually indistinct: You can't even make out the timpani strokes in the trio of II.

Barenboim made his vastly inferior recording in Chicago (Teldec, with Beethoven's "Pathétique" Sonata). The microphones are too close, probably to cut down on audience noise, and the tension is lax. The music often fails to move under his portentous tempos. By contrast, **Masur** and the Leipzig Gewandhaus supply a wonderfully fluid, humane reading (♦Erato 18966, a twofer with his equally desirable 4 and 5, or on the identically arranged ♦Teldec 95981). This benefits immensely from the East German wind timbres, which have both character and elegance. You could say the same thing of the Leipzig strings and brass, which are unsurpassed. With just the right intensity in the outer movements and a beautiful recording, transparent and deep with a real sense of the Leipzig hall, this is one of my favorite *Pathétiques*.

Slatkin in St. Louis is heavier in sound and labored and obvious in interpretation, never letting the music find its own way (RCA). The playing is expert, of course. RCA's engineers weren't quite as successful as on previous outings at taming the resonance of Powell Hall. **Ashkenazy**'s reading was one of his first recordings as a conductor, and it's marked by signs of inexperience. A lack of farsighted shaping and tempo fluctuations make much of the work drag even though the tempos themselves seem fine at any given moment (Decca). Whatever its flaws, the reading has plenty of empathy, and the engineers did a great job with the Philharmonia: The sound is full without being fruity, as orchestral recordings sometimes were on this label.

Gergiev makes a genuinely grand statement, turning in a performance with his Kirov Orchestra that brims over with character, though in the final analysis it doesn't quite come together (Philips). This was taped in Finland rather than in the Mravinsky Theater, so the sound is good, though still a bit dry. A similar approach comes from **Rostropovich,** who has much of the same heavy emphases as Gergiev but with more consistently well-judged tempos (♦EMI). He traverses Tchaikovsky's highest highs and deepest depths, making the March a great, triumphant procession to victory and the finale a desperate and end-all farewell to all possibility of happiness. The sound of the orchestra is among the weightiest on records, and Rostropovich pulls a particularly all-enveloping sound from the London Philharmonic strings.

Mravinsky's two recordings with the Leningrad Philharmonic, the first in mono, will always be controversial for some fast tempos (DG, with 4 and 5). Both versions blaze with intense conviction, though their intensity is worlds away from the lush theatricality of, say, Stokowski, and it's possible to feel that Mravinsky's style didn't align with 6 quite as it did with 4 and 5. If you find the heart of this work in the lyricism heard in the second theme of I (and Tchaikovsky does return to it more as a refrain than a typical first subject), you'll likely find Mravinsky prosaic: His cantilena had an under-the-gun quality. The Leningrad orchestra still had a heavily non-Western sound in the second recording (1960), the strings lean and not playing with very long bow strokes, the woodwinds keen and penetrating, the brass playing with Slavic vibrato. DG's sound is a bit glassy to match the playing style.

Svetlanov is more sensitive to Tchaikovsky's lyricism without softening the drama (Melodiya/RCA). Still, the reading has its mechanical moments, the March especially; this conductor is really more suited to the high-Romantic rhetoric of *Manfred*. The remastering is a success, though I wish the Melodiya original were sweeter, the acoustics a bit less hard and dry. **Ormandy** is a model of clarity and dignity, with few fences rushed or hankies soaked (CBS/Sony). The Philadelphia Orchestra made beautiful and utterly unanimous sounds in 1959, and the contrapuntal lines and interchanges in the first-movement development are crystal clear. Poise is replaced by fatigue and uneventfulness in Or-

mandy's third and final recording (Delos). While the CBS/Sony was taped in the forgiving acoustic of the Bloodwood Hotel in Philadelphia, Delos recorded in the notoriously dry, bandshell acoustic of the orchestra's own Academy of Music, so even the smallest discrepancy in wind intonation becomes glaringly obvious.

When **Muti** took the reins from Ormandy, there was much hand-wringing over his streamlining and sharpening of the famously unstreamlined "Philadelphia sound." But his 1989 recording is stunning, primarily for the orchestra's new flexibility and transparency of tone, achieved at no cost to the gargantuan string sound and timbral beauties (♦EMI 54061). This reading is less phlegmatic than Ormandy's, and it has just about everything: muscle as well as lush nostalgia and elegiac tenderness, and the Memorial Park acoustics are perfectly judged. Muti isn't one to draw special dignity from the music (à la Giulini, Ozawa, or Reiner), nor one to infuse the score with much originality or personal emotion (as per Bernstein or Mitropoulos), so this may not be a reading for the ages or a version to change the way you hear the piece. But it's extremely enjoyable, and at Seraphim's price makes a good super-budget recommendation (especially as it includes Muti's outstanding Scriabin *Poem of Ecstasy* as filler). I prefer the Philadelphia rendition to his earlier (1979) Philharmonia recording, which has a more fallible sense of structure, emotion, and proportion (EMI). The Philharmonia's playing is more obviously exciting than the Philadelphia's, and the sound is better focused, but the conductor does some occasionally implausible point-making and lingering.

Maazel in Vienna is efficient without being particularly memorable (Decca/London). He creates more obviously powerful sonorities with the Cleveland Orchestra, and the early digital sound comes up better than expected on CD (CBS/Sony). The Clevelanders' playing is, of course, stellar, but the reading tends to sound calculated and dry-eyed. The same kind of patrician reading, though more generous in pathos and nostalgia, comes from **Dohnányi** (Telarc). It's a fine performance of its kind, preferable to Maazel. This performance primarily impresses for the outstanding, fine-grained playing of the Clevelanders. The 1987 sound is vivid and well balanced, though recent recordings have more transparency.

Though not the same kind of technician, **Pletnev** is a conductor in the Maazel tradition of quality orchestral playing and non-invasive conductorial professionalism. His first recording with the Russian National Orchestra (Virgin) is rather less perfunctory in tempo than Maazel/Cleveland. He isn't as sensitive to lower dynamics as Dohnányi, Masur, or Ozawa, and has a naughty tendency to have timpani rolls follow along with any crescendos in the strings even when none are marked (Jansons does something similar; maybe it's a Russian tradition?). The sound could be more dynamic. Pletnev's remake is rather different: That reading, again with the Russian National Orchestra, is more individual than the earlier symphonies in his cycle, but here I'm more aware of an interpreter consciously and not always convincingly molding the music to his whims (DG). In this, he's at odds with Richard Taruskin's revisionist liner notes which improbably claim that there is nothing of a "man in torment" in the *Pathétique;* those throbbing low Bs in the basses mark the end of a garden party, I suppose.

Turn to **Ozawa** (♦Erato 45261) and you'll hear each movement take on a more convincing shape. It's a moving rendition that confers dignity on music that can all too easily become, as Neville Cardus once put it, a series of "charnelhouse descents." Similar restraint comes from **Monteux** and the Boston Symphony (RCA), though his march movement is lax and inconsequential, and in the finale he unexpectedly and perversely pulls the tempos around, speeding up at climaxes and slowing as he moves out of them. **Haitink** doesn't have Masur's or Ozawa's nobility and luminosity in the closing paragraphs of the first-movement exposition, nor does he have their subtle flexibility of pulse (Philips). He's more emotionally engaged than Maazel or Dohnányi, but Ozawa is just as dramatic and the Boston sounds rather superior to the Concertgebouw. Still, this *Pathétique* does make a satisfying capstone to his complete cycle. The Philips disc has more presence than Ozawa's, but is also a bit raw in the loudest climaxes.

Another mainstream reading comes from **Jansons** and the Oslo Philharmonic (Chandos). The Oslo band is very serviceable without having anything like the tonal weight or distinction of the great European and American orchestras. This reading's success in some quarters would seem to stem from the fact that the conductor does nothing untoward (or very interesting) interpretively and from the beautifully resonant and truthful sound. Admittedly, his phrasing is more idiomatic than **Dutoit**'s, who also enjoys beautiful and spacious sound (Decca/London). But the Montreal Symphony's lack of idiomatic tonal weight (especially in the outer movements) is exacerbated by the conductor's inability to instill much tension or variety of tone color, and his phrasing can be rather stiff.

Wit is also disappointing, and for similar reasons, though the Polish National Radio Symphony plays with more color than the Montreal and the excellent sound is vibrant and transparent (Naxos). Interpretive commitment is sporadic, and Wit's is not a particularly well-sustained, symphonic argument. Barenboim once quipped that **Celibidache** made the interesting mistake of conducting everything the way Furtwängler conducted slow movements. Celibidache's *Pathétique* with the Munich Philharmonic tends to prove his point, since I and III are impossibly slow (EMI). Tempo *per se* is a non-issue when evaluating a performance, but Celibidache makes nonsense of the slowness by doggedly holding onto the same speeds, not personalizing the pulse and articulating individualities within it. The Munich playing is so-so, with not very true woodwind tuning in II to make a lie of the legend that this conductor took fantastic care over tuning his orchestras. In all, this is a reading to make you question the whole Celibidache mythology; despite all its surface individuality, the performance is surprisingly ordinary.

Mitropoulos reversed the Celibidache situation, taking most of I fast enough that the tortures of the development section grow organically out of it rather than being spit out as a kind of nightmarish illusion (CBS). Even when it might sound rushed, this is every inch a genuine performance, the kind that makes you sit up immediately. If this 1958 rendition never really seems to find a *tempo giusto*, that's undoubtedly appropriate to the restless side of the music. The Philharmonic plays gloriously, with a non-oppressive discipline that makes you wonder how the critics could have accused him of being lax with the group. The stereo sound is fine, though it needs a treble cut and isn't as rich as some RCA masters of this vintage.

If you want a slow and autumnal approach like Celibidache's, a far more eventful and non-doctrinaire performance comes from a nonagenarian **Stokowski**, quite drily recorded with the London Symphony in 1973 (Music & Arts). There are many of the conductor's typical touchings up and also a few grotesquely heavy-handed effects, including some Mengelbergian tempo changes. The pre-Dolby broadcast sound is hissy, with a too-heavy bass. Still, unlike Celibidache, the old magician succeeds in coming up with a bona fide interpretation of the work. Like Celibidache, **Bernstein** and the NY Philharmonic slow the work down trying to plumb its depths but end up sounding prosaic (DG). Once you

get past the inorganically slow Adagio he chooses for the finale (which occupies him for more than 17 minutes, when 10 is the common timing), the reading is surprisingly ordinary.

Karajan clearly had a special relationship with the *Pathétique* and made all of seven recordings for commercial release. Over the 50 years documented by these performances, his interpretation remained startlingly consistent; even the timings for each movement barely changed. He was less interested in momentary, local detail than the larger picture, and you get the feeling that the first three movements as Karajan interprets them feed cumulatively into the finale. But his finale itself is on the quick and non-indulgent side, its variety supplied by an enviable flexibility of pulse that (though very different from that heard in Amsterdam) was surpassed only by Mengelberg.

Karajan made cantish statements about trying to join the apparently irreconcilable approaches of Toscanini and Furtwängler, and his Tchaikovsky does combine crispness of rhythm and ensemble with an innate flexibility of pulse. The first of the seven was his 1939 Berlin Philharmonic version, reissued only recently (DG). DG made some lovely-sounding recordings during the war, and this is one, with an unexpectedly wide dynamic range. The 78 rpm surfaces are unusually quiet, and the sides have been joined extremely well. Not surprisingly, the 31-year-old Karajan had a slightly freer approach to tempo than he would later, but the reading is just as continuous, sonically all-enveloping, and powerfully shaped.

In 1948 Karajan recorded the *Pathétique* with the Vienna Philharmonic (♦EMI 66392). It's a stoic but exquisite performance, particularly notable for the beautiful sweetness of the playing, which easily surpasses his 1985 Vienna version (DG, see below). Here II and IV are Karajan's slowest, with a bittersweet poignancy that certainly had something to do with the miserable postwar conditions in Vienna. EMI's 1948 sound is more open than the earlier DG, and in its way more realistic than the 1958 stereo version, though there are some noticeable side joins in the 1997 "Karajan Edition" remastering. But the surfaces are almost silent.

The most spontaneous and compassionate among Karajan's versions is the 1958 stereo recording with the Philharmonia (♦EMI). He had worked Walter Legge's recording orchestra into a virtuoso touring ensemble, one of Europe's finest, and his success there in the early '50s surely served as a blueprint for his later endeavors in Berlin. If anything, the Philharmonia climaxes are more moving than the Berlin by virtue of the conductor's less obvious control. CD audiophiles might not warm to the hints of shrillness in climaxes, the fact that loud passages don't open up as they do in more modern recordings, but the balances and stereo spread still sound very natural. In the 2CD "Karajan Edition" set, EMI apparently couldn't find a stereo master for the first three minutes and inserted a stereo-reprocessed bit of the mono tape.

Karajan's 1963 Berlin Philharmonic recording is a bit less volatile than the later two Berlin versions, but the Jesus-Christe Kirche in Berlin provided looser, more believable acoustics for this disc; to judge from the lack of audible edits, the movements must have been done in long or even complete takes (DG). The least satisfactory of Karajan's seven *Pathétiques* is the 1971 Berlin recording (EMI), followed by the final Vienna recording (DG; see below). The 1971 Berlin is heated, indeed fantastically intense in the first-movement development and finale. EMI also did their usual fine job with the Philharmonie acoustics, but the sound on this mid-priced disc is impossibly glaring and distorted in climaxes (can this really be on the master tape?). Distortion or no, the performance has its grandiloquent, unfeeling moments—not least the

March, which has an almost careless edge that isn't characteristic of Karajan.

When we get to his final Berlin recording, made in 1976, the effect is like a painter who draws a master canvas from a landscape he has visited and revisited over the decades (available singly on Penguin 460609, but preferable in 20-bit remastering in the twofer, ◆DG 453088). The expressive rubato is intensely personal but perfectly judged. Though rather dry and inconsistent, the sound is the most all-enveloping of all seven recordings. And what a sound Karajan could produce! The passage toward the end of the first-movement development sounds as if all the molten lava of Hell had risen up to surround you and singe the flesh off your mortal bones. Karajan's 1985 performance with the Vienna Philharmonic (DG) is attractive but can't compare, partly a matter of not sustaining the structural tension as well, though the sound on the "Karajan Gold" mastering reeks less of the mixing board than the 1976 Berlin disc.

"7". Between 5 and 6, Tchaikovsky did extensive work on a symphony that he gave up on and later salvaged for Piano Concerto 3. In the '50s, Semyon Bogatyryev tried to reconstruct the original symphony, and his edition has been recorded by Ormandy and Järvi in an interesting and pleasurable marginalium rather than a vital addition to the Tchaikovsky canon. **Ormandy** is to be preferred (CBS/Sony). **Järvi's** London Philharmonic is cleaner with the rhythms, but the Chandos recording has a hard edge, and Ormandy's slightly homely sincerity is more attractive than Järvi's hard sell.

Manfred. Muti's *Manfred* with the Philharmonia could well be the most electrifying orchestral recording ever made and is the highlight of his Tchaikovsky cycle—indeed, one of the highlights of the entire record catalog (◆EMI 47412). The engineering gives a dramatic, wide spread to the orchestra, and the timpani are wonderfully present and incisive. The tam-tam strokes in the first and last movements are heart-stopping, and the big melody's return has tremendous drama. Maybe Muti could do with more charm in III, but who's going to complain? This is animalistic music-making that's brimming over with nervous, even sexual energy.

The reading clearly has its roots in **Toscanini,** who put great store in *Manfred* at the expense of some other Tchaikovsky scores—apparently so much that he saw fit to make significant changes to the piece, most notoriously by cutting over 100 bars of the finale. (He also makes some scoring changes, like throwing some cymbal crashes into the end of I for the sake of effect. All this makes a mockery of the music and of Toscanini's mythical *com'e scritto* adherence to the scores.) His 1949 NBC Symphony performance is of course taut and exciting (RCA). It's also surprisingly musical, though the outer movements take on a time-beating, tub-thumping bombast. The strings are also more deficient in body than in any other recorded performance, partly because of the notoriously dry Studio 8H acoustics. His 1940 broadcast with the same ensemble is in all respects an improvement (◆Music & Arts 956). The cuts are still there, but the group has a sweeter and fuller sound, and Toscanini reacts more willingly to the expressive cues in the score. The sound is very listenable, though compared to the RCA there is some roll-off in climaxes and muting of high frequencies.

Svetlanov is a bit more humane than Muti and Toscanini and just about as exciting (◆Melodiya/RCA). This is the best installment in his cycle, particularly effective in instilling a sense of anxious flux in II and III. While you can question the appropriateness of the naked and slightly ragged USSR Symphony tone in other Tchaikovsky scores, here they're perfectly suited to the music's raw nerve endings. I also hear greater un-

animity and weight in their string sound than elsewhere. RCA's remastering is good, the top tamed a little but the bass a bit lacking.

Masur is much freer and more rhapsodic with the yearning "Astarte" theme than Muti, but when the big theme comes in at the end of I, he's not as broad and squelches the tam-tam, and thereby builds up less tension (Teldec). The whole performance has beautiful playing, and the recording is impeccable. Nevertheless, I come out feeling that this symphony is too turgid and melodramatic for his taste and that his sympathies lie with other Tchaikovsky scores. **Silvestri** and the Bournemouth Symphony taped *Manfred* before an almost silent audience (BBC). The orchestra starts off rather unsure of itself, and with some offish woodwind intonation. Things improve, but the ensemble never quite calls up the firm, weighty bass sonorities or molten strings of Muti's or Svetlanov's ensembles. The value of Silvestri's reading lies in its lyrical detail: The "Astarte" theme in the outer movements is treated freely, lovingly.

Recording some 30 years later with the same orchestra, **Litton** is just as personal and free in his phrasing, the orchestra has improved markedly, and the sound is much better. I especially like his detail in the big *tutti* passages of the outer movements, which are not just set into motion, juggernaut-like, as with some other conductors. This is a fine reading that has something to say about the music, though in the last analysis the ensemble doesn't have quite the tonal weight of Muti's Philharmonia or Tilson Thomas's Los Angeles, and this causes some disappointment in the outer movements. But Litton is preferable to **Jansons** and the Oslo, who don't have the necessary tonal resources for this music (Chandos); I can't think of another work where Tchaikovsky requires his orchestra to sustain such chordal, organ-like sounds. In such textures, all the rhythmic clarity and transparency of the Oslo orchestra don't amount to very much. **Kazuhiro Koizumi** and the Royal Philharmonic (RPO/Pickwick) are more solid and engaging than in their numbered symphonies for the same label. I would be happy to hear this fine performance in the concert hall, but on records it's not as distinctive as others, though at least the organ at the end is a massive and imposing hulk of an instrument.

Like many of **Ormandy's** Philadelphia performances from the late '70s, his *Manfred* is stodgy and rounds off the music's edges; he takes 59 minutes, about six more than most, and it seems even longer because the music has lost its ability to surprise (RCA). Compared to Muti, **Tilson Thomas** and the London Symphony are more musical, more centered, generating more warmth than light (◆CBS/Sony 36673). This is concentrated but not showy music-making, deeply sympathetic with the treacherous emotional undertow of the piece. CBS's sound, with its rather hollow bass and some edge and lack of clarity and bloom on top, needs remastering as well as a higher transfer level. Still, it's naturally balanced. **Chailly** and the Concertgebouw have a similarly dusky and idiomatic sound, and this is splendidly caught by the engineers (Decca/London). But this reading is unremarkable, hosting little if any of Muti's explosive rhythmic tension or Tilson Thomas's powerful moodiness.

Haitink gives a much more distinctive reading with the same orchestra (◆Philips 442061). It has more energy and fiber than Chailly, and his sense for detail is also very telling. This music also seems perfectly suited to the fine-grained playing of the Russian National Orchestra under **Pletnev** (◆DG 439891). This could well be the best-played *Manfred* in the catalog, with plenty of subtlety to the phrasing and an overwhelming beauty and strength to the strings (this is easily the best orchestra Russia has ever produced). It's the most skillfully shaped performance on offer, with every bar of the outer movements full of direction and significance. With their Mendelssohnian lightness, these artists' inner movements are often light as a feather. For its part, DG offers the perfect combination of dynamism, transparency, weight, and warmth: an outstanding job. I would rank this at the top of the pile, right next to Muti.

Lenard and the CSR Symphony of Bratislava are out of their league here; the brass are especially lacking in presence, and there are no interpretive insights as compensation (Naxos). The same goes for **Abravanel** and the Utah Symphony: Their performance is well conducted, but the orchestra isn't up to today's standards, especially the winds (Vox). *Manfred* could have been custom-written for that Byronesque musical dramatist, **Rostropovich** (♦EMI). Muti and Pletnev are better at keeping the music on the move, but Rostropovich is a master at sustaining and coloring the kinds of organ-like sonorities that are heard almost everywhere in this great work. Like Litton, he inserts hairpin dynamic changes in the big drum rolls concluding I: naughty, but certainly exciting. EMI's Kingsway Hall sound gives an especially good account of the lower brass.

BALLET MUSIC

Complete scores

The Nutcracker. **Lanchbery** is so complete as to include his own scoring of the 40-second "English Dance" that Tchaikovsky wrote for the Act 2 divertissement but didn't orchestrate (♦EMI 49399; ♦MHS 522054; and 61 minutes of highlights on a bargain-priced disc, ♦EMI 73574). As in his other Tchaikovsky ballet sets for EMI, Lanchbery's experience in the ballet pit (as principal conductor of the Royal Ballet, Sadler's Wells, and American Ballet Theater) means he knows which tempos work and which don't. Even though his tempos aren't extreme, the score has great shape at every turn and the music comes intensely and immediately alive: This is a very engaging performance, without a dull moment. The engineering is discreet studio multi-miking at its best, serving up a rich and brilliant orchestral panoply. My only complaint is that the Ambrosian Singers in the "Waltz of the Snowflakes" aren't childlike at all, but sound like a bunch of muscular (and loud) aunties. Still, this is a *Nutcracker* to submerge yourself in — a reading that's unsurpassed for piquancy and style.

The same Ambrosian muscle-building aunties are back for **Previn**'s London Symphony version, though here they have a bit less vibrato (♦EMI 4706; also in his highly recommended box of all three ballets, ♦EMI 73624). Don't judge this *Nutcracker* by the first half of Act 1, which tends to be smooth and sedate, the tempo choices unchallenging, the battle with the mice not very vivid. But as the battle wanes, you realize Previn has been keeping things in reserve, working to give the act a larger shape. The London Symphony playing is more enjoyable than for Bonynge (they're much more willing to play quietly), and the group presents many tender moments. In Previn's 1986 Royal Philharmonic version, he summons up less energy and radiance than he did earlier. The differences are small, but differences there are, and the Royal Philharmonic is a bit less confident than the LSO.

Bonynge and the National Philharmonic are prone to pretty heavy accents and some forced tone in climaxes (Decca/London, taped in 1974). Things can sound forced and inelegant, and his *stringendos* tend to aim for excitement at the expense of ensemble. His orchestra is agile, eager, and full of character, but not exactly sumptuous. That this is such good listening despite these reservations has much to do with the Kingsway Hall acoustics and the depth of Decca's sound, and with the fact that Bonynge seems incapable of phoniness — it may be heavy, but it's also a reading of happiness and naivety.

Gentle but always fresh and immediate, **Ozawa**'s *Nutcracker* is one of the finest recordings he has made, with none of the sense of auto-pilot and rhythmic inelegance that sometimes mar his *Swan Lake* (♦DG 435621). Instead, it has an enviable spontaneity and rhythmic flow, with all the tempos expertly coordinated and climaxes perfectly underlined. The Boston Symphony has rarely sounded this transparent on CD, or so light on its feet. The coupling is the standard *Sleeping Beauty* suite, in a performance that's not quite as refreshing as his *Nutcracker*. **Jansons** is less adept at sustaining the flow that characterizes the best performances (EMI). Though rhythms are always clear and clean, tensions are surprisingly lax and the grandeur and affection quotients rarely get very high; too often, he sounds like he's doing a lovely and extremely musical job of treading water. The London Philharmonic does play with more character than the Oslo Orchestra in his symphony cycle. Balances aren't always as sensitively handled as in other renditions, but the crisp and refined sound is hard to dislike.

If you want a crisp performance in a cool, elegant, and somewhat distant ambience, then skip Jansons for **Ermler** and the Royal Opera House Covent Garden Orchestra (♦Conifer 16074). Ermler is excellent at preparing for and supporting exciting, expansive climaxes. The orchestra's potentially fearsome brass, the large and echoey acoustics, and the audiophile-level, 20-bit recording (probably the most transparent engineering given any *Nutcracker*) all help open up the orchestra's sound at those moments. Ermler thus gives the ballet a far more distinct overall shape than Jansons and makes it more exciting overall.

Tilson Thomas and the London Symphony contrast with Jansons and Ermler (CBS/Sony). A big issue in ballet music recordings is the conductor's ability to inflect and personalize the music within extended uniformities of meter and rhythm, and this often comes with experience in the ballet pit. Listen to Monteux or Lanchbery take on one of the waltzes, and you'll hear infinite small-scale variety within the meter. Tilson Thomas isn't interested in such subtleties, and as a result his *Nutcracker* — though very impressive from one moment to the next, and many will love it — doesn't add up to more than the sum of its exhilarating parts. The sound is dynamic and gutsy but not coarse — less chaste and pristine than most other sets listed here, and that might appeal in itself.

The Bolshoi is of course the epicenter of Russian ballet traditions, which makes it all the more surprising that **Rozhdestvensky**'s version with the Bolshoi Orchestra tends to sound so turgid and nonterpsichorean (Melodiya). These bright, garish timbres and fairly heavy-handed tempos and phrasing almost give a socialist-realist impression. The Soviet-period miking is typically idiosyncratic: There's a strong echo, and individual players often seem to change position between one number and another. The playing is colorful but not flawless, with some especially watery brass work. **Mackerras** and the London Symphony enjoy splendid sound: a marvelously solid bass and impeccable balancing, but a natural concert-hall perspective that's less open and less obviously spectacular than Ermler (Telarc). The orchestra plays extremely well and passionately when required. Still, this leaves the ears with a slightly dour aftertaste, and I hear a lack of character when comparing it with others. It's a fine performance of its dry-eyed kind, but to these ears it's an interpretive and emotional compromise.

In his Concertgebouw version, **Dorati** has a lighter and charming touch when need be, but also gets the Amsterdam players to dig in deeper at the right moments; I can't remember a recording where this orchestra sounded so caught up in the music (♦Philips 442564). The deep Concertgebouw sound is a pleasure, as always in Tchaikovsky. Dorati's earlier recording with the London Symphony is even faster than Gergiev (see below), so Mercury really missed a trick by failing to reissue it on a single, 78-minute CD (Mercury). (It comes on two mid-priced discs, coupled with his not-front-rank *Serenade*). The performance is rhythmic and quick, only occasionally to the point of sounding offhand. The London Symphony plays very well and stylishly, if without quite the old-world distinction of the Concertgebouw. Mercury's 35mm-film recording is one of their best, with a smooth upper register and no hiss whatsoever; this sounds as though it could be a digital recording made last Tuesday.

Schermerhorn and the National Philharmonic are similarly bright and buoyant (CBS, awaiting reissue). If anything, there's a touch more spontaneity to this picturesque performance, but the playing isn't as cushioned and sumptuous as the Concertgebouw's and Schermerhorn is less consistent than Dorati when it comes to rhythmic energy. **Andrew Davis** and the Toronto Symphony are less of a success in both recording and performance. The balancing is rather odd and the acoustics dry, and the workaday interpretation doesn't invoke much splendor, excitement, or eloquence. In **Ansermet**'s *Nutcracker* with the Suisse Romande, he isn't very interested in subtleties of phrase or dead-on accuracy of pitch; he's interested in rhythm (Decca/London). He doesn't work toward luxurious sound, but brings out Tchaikovsky's tangy, proto-Stravinskian tone qualities. It would be easy to dismiss this out of hand because of the iffy intonation and the sometimes insensitive approach, but he does give the work a real overall shape, noticing details unearthed by no one else. There is definitely character here—earnest, if not romantic—that comes up missing in many other performances.

Temirkanov is weighty, unsubtle, and undetailed (RCA). The performance doesn't lack character; indeed, the conductor pulls from the Royal Philharmonic a strong and garish brass sound that often makes it sound like a Soviet band. Most damaging is his inflexible phrasing, and again the orchestra turns in a disappointing performance with some approximate intonation, lack of rhythmic finesse, and opacity. **Rodzinski** has a relaxed, old-world charm, but it's hard to get past the rather bizarre and sometimes shoddy production. The London Philharmonic is multi-miked with a vengeance in a dry acoustic setting, and the sound picture was obviously assembled at the mixing board (MCA). A very professional but ultimately routine outing comes from **Bychkov** and the Berlin Philharmonic (Philips). There's no lack of variety, or of the loudness and rhythmic force that constitute "excitement" in common terms, but there could be more affection for the music.

Far better to turn to **Gergiev** and his Kirov Orchestra, who give us the only performance with all 24 numbers complete on one disc, at over 81 minutes (◆Philips 462114). The sound is warm and intimate in just the right way, without much ambience but with vivid yet natural perspectives—the performance is direct and energetic. Some listeners will find the tempos too uniformly borderline-quick, and some of the numbers segue pretty quickly into each other (to fit it all on the disc, no doubt). As far as symphonic, string-based sheen goes, the Kirov isn't in the same league as Pletnev's Russian National Orchestra, but it's a theater ensemble with its own insights. This is one of the best things the Kirov has done on records, and one of Philips's best engineering jobs.

A big contrast comes from **Slatkin** and the St. Louis Symphony, who offer an eminently comfortable ride but in the last analysis are dull and uninspired (RCA). Compare it with just about any other performance and you'll encounter phrasing with more direction. Part of the reason these discs sound so tepid is the sound, a fairly colorless 1984 digital recording that can't begin to compare with RCA's recent productions.

Single discs of *Nutcracker* excerpts, often at mid price or lower, are offered by **Tilson Thomas** and **Mackerras** (from their sets mentioned above), and also **Ormandy** and **Zinman.** The format has become dubious, since these performances usually substitute trumpets for the chorus at the end of Act 1, and for about the same price you can get Dorati's delightful Concertgebouw set or Gergiev's gripping edition. Ormandy offers few insights in his earlier "highlights" disc (CBS/Sony); the Philadelphians' articulation is uniformly heavy and smoothed over, tempos are on the slow side, while the engineering is quite shrill and glassy on top. Ormandy's 1973 highlights disc is far preferable: It has more variety of articulation, and the sound is more firm, smooth, natural, and consistent in frequency response (RCA). If it were still available, this would be a good recommendation—though you still have to do without the children's chorus and there are finer renditions of the entire score.

Zinman conducts a fleet and elegant performance in the Dorati-Schermerhorn fashion (Nonesuch). He must owe much of its stylishness to the New York City Ballet Orchestra, which sounds like a pit-sized group—leagues away from the gargantuan Philadelphia sonority, yet it doesn't lack punch or strength. None of Zinman's tempos go to concert-hall extremes, and this is what *Nutcracker* sounds like if you sit near the pit (with your eyes closed) when an outstanding ballet orchestra is playing on a very good evening. The sound is excellent, but some of the cue titles in the booklet are unrecognizably rendered. Among the many recordings of the composer's own suite distillation (aside from collations from complete recordings described above), special mention must be made of **Beecham**'s (◆EMI 63380, with his very fine Symphony 4). He's not always as light and frothy as you might expect, but grabs hold of the music and comes up with an ungimmicky reading that has both depth and beauty. EMI's mono engineering sounds for all the world like stereo.

Karajan and the Berlin Philharmonic have a superbly thrusting March (these sound more like Prussian foot soldiers than children), and everywhere a centered, luxuriant, solid sound that's a joy (DG, recorded in 1982). But the rest of the numbers are unnuanced and severely lacking in charm; he sparkled more in his earlier DG recording (see ballet suites below). **Solti** and the Chicago Symphony are straightforward to a fault (Decca/London). Offsetting some of that lack of character and charm are the personality of individual woodwinds. There are amazing contrasts with **Reiner** and the same orchestra: Reiner presents 38 minutes of excerpts, and the Chicagoans' extremely clear rhythmic detailing and transparent tone add much to the more delicate moments of the score (RCA, with Gilels's least successful take on Concerto 1). The grander, more symphonic moments are less convincing and the score's more confessional emotions go unspoken. The early stereo sound comes up extremely well.

Marriner and the St. Martin Academy (Philips) are cushy and comfortable; things are fairly easy-going even in "Trepak," where many conductors have achieved a liftoff worthy of *1812*. But Marriner and his players are really at home in something more intimate like "Arabian Dance," which has subtle shape and telling details of articulation.

Sleeping Beauty. **Previn** and the London Symphony again reign supreme (◆EMI 54814 and in Previn's ballet set, ◆73624). His sense of scale is impeccable, and he hears and conducts the music in a single sweep, without giving the impression (as others so often do) of being more at home in either the dramatic-symphonic effusions or the characteristic "at the ball" numbers. The London Symphony doesn't have the perfect, ultra-smooth, anonymous sheen of some more recent recordings (this was taped in 1974), but I would count that as an asset. Specifically, it may not always be as suave and nimble as, say, Pletnev, but I prize the character of the playing and the sense of human music-making and expression in just about every bar. The remastering is very acceptable, though there's some glare at the top and the climaxes don't open up very well and can even sound coarse. Previn omits the 2 1/2 minute Sarabande from Act 3, probably for reasons of disc space.

Those wanting the most up-to-date sound will turn to **Pletnev** and his very fine Russian National Orchestra (♦DG 457635). This recording offers plenty to delight the ear, particularly with the stunningly crisp and transparent engineering. The climaxes are impressive both in orchestral tone and their consistent warmth and focus. There's plenty of lift to the rhythms in climaxes, and the division of first and second violins left and right enhances the character of the reading. The orchestra has the tonal refinement and blend, both within and between sections, to put it in the international *crème de la crème,* and the performance is very enjoyable for the fact that Pletnev—though fairly dramatic—entirely avoids any hint of the rhythmic heaviness perpetrated by others. If I have any reservations about this set, it concerns a certain non-balletic quality to his direction: I hear less stiffness, and also more charm and better-considered tempos, from Previn and Dorati. I imagine his perception of the music would gain in nuance if he were to conduct it in the pit.

But then **Gergiev** presumably has done just that, and he has some similar tempo miscalculations; he's at home in the grand numbers, but there and elsewhere can fall victim to heaviness (Philips). Philips has acclimated to the smallish acoustics of the historic Maryinsky Theater, the Kirov's home turf; the full ensemble sound doesn't come apart in climaxes, as it sometimes has in previous recordings, and the St. Petersburg strings never get strident. Still, when it comes to clarity and vividness this doesn't match DG's production for Pletnev. Like Gergiev, **Bonynge** and the National Philharmonic opt for weight rather than sprightliness (Decca/London). His plain-vanilla rendition can be refreshing, and the sound is a good deal better than Previn's; however, this isn't as memorable as others, either in tonal affluence or interpretive detail.

If you prefer warmth of sound to Pletnev's crystalline transparency, then you'll find **Dorati** and the Concertgebouw the best on offer; the hall's acoustics embrace this often brassy music like a warm blanket (Philips). Dorati doesn't find as much drama in the score as some others, and doesn't organically coordinate the numbers to flow into and through one another as Previn does. Still, this is an undoubted pleasure, and there's certainly evidence here of the grace and naturalness that almost always characterized Dorati's approach to the Tchaikovsky ballets. This would be my choice if you want a budget-priced *Beauty* without the other two ballets, but be advised that fitting the music onto two discs has necessitated dropping the six-minute Entr'acte from Act 2.

The Czecho-Slovak Philharmonic is serviceable for **Mogrelia,** but not much more than that (Naxos). Their stylish performance lacks nothing in efficiency and punch, but the sound has a frosty tinge, and there's little or no lingering or luxuriating allowed (or desired) here. For this kind of performance—emphasizing theatrical vigor over subtleties of phrase or timbre—I prefer Bonynge. **Rozhdestvensky** leads the BBC Symphony in a strident and brittle performance that rarely relaxes (BBC). The studio where this was recorded is too small for Tchaikovsky's grander, more symphonic gestures, and the orchestra—brightly recorded—offers precious little of the succulence and weight we hear elsewhere.

Slatkin and the St. Louis Symphony turn in one of their finest Tchaikovsky recordings, and the sound is at the same time elegant and gutsy—more substantial than DG's for Pletnev (RCA). Slatkin isn't the most subtle, astute, or affectionate of Tchaikovskians, but he gives the music an appropriate rhythmic tension. Like Rozhdestvensky and Lanchbery, **Ermler** comes with a long pedigree of experience in ballet theater, including more than 25 years at the Bolshoi. His recording with the Royal Opera House Orchestra is fine; his pit experience is evident in the near-perfect choices of tempo for each number (Conifer). In this respect, he is to be preferred to Pletnev, who misjudges a fair number of tempos and might be thought Ermler's main competitor in the dynamic, well-prepared, and transparently recorded category. Ermler avoids Pletnev's occasional hints of stiffness, and also the occasional longueurs of that performance, but then Pletnev wins out when it comes to character and quality of orchestral playing. The orchestra is all you could ask for and sounds a good deal larger than many other pit orchestras (partly a matter of the church acoustics, which give the group real resonance and presence), but Pletnev's Russian National is one of the world's great orchestras, with something to delight the ear in every bar, and interpretively Pletnev makes Ermler sound just a little generic. As in the rest of his series, Ermler's sonics are outstanding, even more flattering to the ensemble than Pletnev's.

Ormandy taped an extended series of excerpts that goes well beyond the usual suite (♦Sony 46340). This is his most consistent and recommendable Tchaikovsky ballet recording: His tempos had not yet slowed and ossified as they did later in the RCA readings. There's more sparkle to the articulation, and his phrasing is only rarely breathless. **Litton** adds some extra numbers to flesh out the usual suite to 28 minutes (Delos, with *1812* and *Voyevoda*). It's stunningly recorded, more for its concert-hall naturalness than for any ostentation, but the performance, though very enjoyable, rarely reaches the level of inspiration or pulse-quickening splendor of others. The Dallas Symphony's string sound, for instance, is splendid but doesn't breathe the way the sections did in Berlin, Philadelphia, and London. **Fistoulari**'s 1962 set with the London Symphony was more stylish and gripping, with strong and no-nonsense music-making that becomes inelegant only on rare occasions. Philips has happily reissued 50 minutes of this as filler for Dorati's superb Concertgebouw *Nutcracker* (♦Philips 442 562).

Swan Lake. **Slatkin** gets characteristically smooth playing from his St. Louis orchestra, and the quieter, more lyrical moments are beautifully done, but he doesn't have the rhythmic subtleties within the unchanging dance meters achieved by the better conductors (and those with some experience in the ballet pit). In a word, this tends to be dull (RCA). Turn to **Previn** and you'll immediately hear more variety in tonal weight and bow pressure and the subtle rhythmic inflections that are so hard to describe and yet so necessary in this music (in his set of the three ballets, ♦EMI 73624, which restores the Act 3 *Pas de deux* that EMI dropped for the earlier 2CD release; the *Pas Berrichon* remains missing; also separately as EMI 49531). He doesn't choose his tempos with quite the skill of Monteux or Lanchbery, but the music-making is always passionate and engaging, with not a slack moment. He never forces his hand, yet his acute sense for shape and line makes everything comes alive. The remastered sound is a touch on the bright side, but Kingsway Hall again proves itself one of the world's great acoustic spaces.

Tilson Thomas and the London Symphony are more inclined to push the music and less sensitive to its subtleties; he's out to underline points in the score at the expense of its gracefulness and lyric flow

(Sony). Yet the interpretation is somehow more anonymous than Previn's, perhaps because the later London Symphony proves so confident. The good news here is the beautiful 1990 sound—firmer and smoother than Previn's, but with much of the same depth. Still, those wanting drama are better directed to Bonynge and Svetlanov, who are more varied and interesting (see below). For modern sound **Dutoit** wins the laurels by virtue of greater bloom and openness (London/Decca). Still, he has something of the concert conductor's tendency to take the uniform dance meters blandly at face value and over-inflate the louder numbers—he pushes sequential and climactic passages without divining the finer shades of drama uncovered by Previn, Lanchbery, and sometimes Dorati, and takes some jackrabbit tempos that wouldn't work in the theater. Decca/London's tracking is inadequate.

A similar verdict applies to **Ermler** and the Covent Garden orchestra: splendid sound, with crispness alongside alluring depth and suavity, in an extremely listenable performance that nevertheless lacks something in character (Conifer). **Lanchbery** isn't far behind Dutoit and Ermler in sound, and he also gets some of the most sumptuous Tchaikovsky orchestral playing on disc from the Philharmonia (♦EMI 49173). One of the great things about his account is that every tempo is perfectly chosen, doubtless because he has many years of pit experience with this music under his belt. Yet he sometimes doctors up the dynamics (apparently this is consistent with theater traditions), and non-balletomane purists may resist the occasional extra hairpins and crescendos. But it's hard not to be swept up in Lanchbery's vivid sense of theater.

Sawallisch and the Philadelphia Orchestra make some gorgeous sounds, and the engineers have finally found just the right mix of depth and brightness in taping the Philadelphian glories, but his rigid rhythmic insistence in the ballroom waltz of Act 3 almost drove me round the bend (EMI). There's plenty of balletic point-making, but lyricism is in short supply and the climactic moments are heavy rather than dramatic. **Dorati** has some typically astute detailing and you can often hear the enviable naturalness that was typical of his Tchaikovsky, but the sound is boomy mono, so the orchestra seems raw, bottom-heavy, and lacking in transparency (Mercury). To judge from this performance, in the late '50s the Minneapolis orchestra wasn't quite up to the international standard it has achieved more recently.

Ozawa, like Dutoit and Tilson Thomas, is rather anonymous for all the beautiful playing and symphonic impressiveness (DG). Quite a few of his transitional numbers are regrettably inert, and he omits the beautiful *Pas de deux* from Act 3. There is much more excitement to **Bonynge**'s 1975 rendition (London/Decca). He's another man of the theater, but the miking tends to give the National Philharmonic a heavy, even Wagnerian sound, and Svetlanov's version is the one to recommend to those wanting lots of drama. Like Rozhdestvensky and Dutoit, Bonynge is so complete as to include the Act 3 *Danse Russe* and *Pas de deux* that were dropped for the 1895 Drigo-Petipa-Ivanov revival of the ballet and published only in the late '50s.

Recorded in 1988, **Svetlanov** and the USSR Symphony have the best of all worlds: the keen, sometimes piercing woodwinds and high brass that keep the music from falling into sentimentality, lean and powerful strings, energy and drama to keep the music always moving along, and also a degree of lyricism and "give" in the phrasing that's perhaps surprising for this conductor (♦Melodiya 00403, 3CD, with his orchestrated *Seasons*). He's no subtle colorist; there are more primary colors than pastels here, but the playing is consistently more reliable than it was in

his '60s symphony cycle. There's plenty of evidence of **Rozhdestvensky**'s astute musicality in his recording with the Moscow Radio Symphony, and comparisons with Svetlanov's phrasing and balancing of textures are usually to Rozhdestvensky's credit (Melodiya). But Svetlanov offers greater panache and grandeur, and the Moscow orchestra isn't a pleasure to hear at much of anything above *mf.*

Swan Lake was initially a limited success and was dropped from the Kirov repertory in 1883. Two years after Tchaikovsky's death, composer and conductor Riccardo Drigo and choreographers Marius Petipa and Lev Ivanov mounted the ballet to great popular success and set the work on its path to high popularity. Unfortunately (but entirely in line with theater practices of the time), they heavily altered the score, reducing the four acts to three, transposing some numbers, abridging or eliminating others, and inserting orchestrations of three piano pieces from Op. 72. Some older recordings followed that corrupt edition, and **Fedotov** and the Maryinsky Theater Orchestra (another name for the Kirov ensemble?) for some reason returned to it in 1994 (JVC). The cover inscription "complete" thus takes on ironic connotations. Their performance is rather lightweight and colorless, like Ozawa but with some finer dynamic detailing. As if in corroboration, JVC's sound is fairly pale and weak in bass response.

Ansermet uses a version of the Drigo edition, which means almost one-fourth of the score is missing (London/Decca). Those who don't particularly mind the omissions (and none of the famous numbers heard in the standard suite are dropped) will find the Suisse Romande orchestra more on top of things than in Ansermet's *Nutcracker,* but the winds still have moments of obvious insecurity. What isn't in doubt is this conductor's astute understanding of Tchaikovsky's phrasing and drama. Though not the last word in refinement, the 40-year-old sound is still pretty spectacular.

Fiedler offers a disc of excerpts with the Boston Pops, and it's a non-starter; his interpretation is short on transparency and subtlety and strong on obvious, tub-thumping theatrical effects and foursquare rhythms (RCA). For a single disc, **Monteux** is far better; it's a lesson in Tchaikovsky ballet style, with nothing forced but not a slack or dull measure to be heard, and all the rhythms pointed without a hint of rigidity (out of print, but with five excerpts now on a bargain disc, ♦Philips 422265).

Suites and excerpts

Taking in a Tchaikovsky ballet through one of the suites is as frustrating (and sacrilegious) as getting to know a Tolstoy novel through Cliff's Notes. But I have to make some mention of the suites here, especially as a great Tchaikovskian like Efrem Kurtz never got around to doing the complete scores. It's become standard to couple the three ballet suites on one disc, and the following listings hold the same selection of numbers from all three unless indicated otherwise.

You simply haven't heard Tchaikovsky's ballets until you've heard **Kurtz** (♦EMI 62861 or 67791). He's often surprisingly quiet and his touch is light but never dull. Subverting some of the energy that most conductors expend on getting the music to be as loud and outwardly impressive as possible, Kurtz is free to do all sorts of miracles of phrasing, shaping, characterization, and variation in tonal weight. The Philharmonia was playing wonderfully in 1958–59, and the clear, expertly balanced, and hiss-free sound is better than most recordings nowadays. Except for *Nutcracker,* his suites are rather different from most: He doesn't include the fiery opening number from *Sleeping Beauty* or the Act 1 waltz from *Swan Lake,* but does have the Bluebird *pas de deux* and

Menuhin soloing gorgeously in the two concertante numbers from Act 2 of *Swan Lake*. This is not to be missed. Apparently Kurtz's excerpts come from single-LP compilations of each ballet; if so, EMI should lose no time in making every bit of these great performances available again.

By contrast, **Rostropovich** presents the ballet suites at their most symphonic (DG). That's great, except that much of the freshness that characterized his London symphony cycle has vanished, and about all that's left is heaviness. He does get a tough musicality out of Karajan's orchestra that few others managed to educe, but compare him with Kurtz and you'll be surprised at how shapeless his phrasing is.

Karajan has four separate accounts of the suites to his name, and his Berlin Philharmonic accounts are stunningly luminous (♦DG 419175, recorded in 1966 and 1971). There is some of the over-smooth non-articulation that he advocated at this time, and those late-'60s, bawling Berlin trumpets can be a trial, but the depth and living vibrancy of the Berlin string tone are absolutely miraculous. Though not satisfying through and through, this is a must-have for its flashes of all-enveloping, astonishing music-making, the likes of which we will never hear again.

Karajan taped the conventional *Swan Lake* and *Sleeping Beauty* suites with the Vienna Philharmonic only a year earlier, and for his "Legends" CD, his 1961 Vienna *Nutcracker* has been added (Decca). This is one of Karajan's more disappointing discs. The articulation is a good deal less gluey here, but the readings don't have the intoxicating sonic extravagance and intense level of concentration heard in the Berlin recording. He also recorded the standard *Sleeping Beauty* and *Swan Lake* suites with the Philharmonia in stereo and all three with the same orchestra in mono (EMI). The 1952 mono tapings are nothing special, but the later stereo versions are magnificent, probably Karajan's best all-round versions—the phrasing less glutinous than on DG, but the performances also a hair less splendiferous (NA). With the Philharmonia in fantastic form, this is a wonderful recording that EMI must return to the catalog.

Muti is often surprisingly intimate in his Philadelphia coupling of the *Swan Lake* and *Sleeping Beauty* suites, and the 1983 sound has held up well, but his performances aren't distinctive enough to offset the fact that only two suites are included (EMI). **Mackerras** also pairs *Swan Lake* excerpts with numbers from *Sleeping Beauty,* but his selection runs over 65 minutes and his readings with the Royal Philharmonic are exceptional (♦Telarc 80151). With the sometimes problematic RPO sounding radiant here, the music-making is more deeply felt than in his complete *Nutcracker,* and this is one of the better discs of ballet excerpts in the catalog—and one of this conductor's finest projects. Telarc goes along with some of its very best engineering, deep-set but subtly transparent rather than bombastic, with a luscious (but not overdone) helping of hall ambience.

Levine gets a remarkably intense response from the Vienna Philharmonic in Tchaikovsky's more symphonic moments, and reaches new heights of spontaneity, fervor, and eloquence in the *Swan Lake* finale (DG). But his quieter numbers don't hold quite as much interest, and he sounds totally out of his element—more efficient than inspired—in the shorter numbers of *Nutcracker*. DG's engineering is only a mixed success; as so often happens, the Musikverein becomes bright and clattery in louder passages. Though his orchestra might not be in quite the same league, **Mehta** and the Israel Philharmonic are to be preferred for their more humane contact with the music (Decca/London). This is one of Mehta's best discs, with the Israelis playing particularly well and the Decca engineers getting more sympathetic results with them than anyone else.

Bernstein's three suites were recorded in different years and locales and vary in credibility and sound. *Nutcracker* is best, with tempos that are less offhanded than usual and the NY Philharmonic and the engineers making a fairly rare commitment to tonal beauty and depth of sound. *Swan Lake* is burdened by some off-color wind tuning and the dry, acoustic disaster that was Philharmonic Hall before its remodeling (CBS/Sony).

Ormandy's 1972–73 coupling of excerpts is inconsistent: The "Panorama" from *Sleeping Beauty* is diaphanous and lovely, but the big *Swan Lake* waltz is elephantine and stiff (RCA). His earlier versions are more variegated and stylish in sound and tempo, but along with that comes glassy sound, some spot-miking, and some startling cuts of repeated material in individual numbers (CBS/Sony).

SUITES

Tchaikovsky's four suites have had a variable fate on records, jet-set maestros dropping in on them occasionally only to inflate them with symphonic rhetoric. **Järvi,** beautifully and transparently recorded as his complete set is, tends to follow in this unfortunate tradition of playing the music for heavy effect rather than sensitivity, wistfulness, delicacy, or wit. He's at his best in 1, which is recommendable in its separate issue (♦Chandos 9587), especially as it's coupled there with the fairly rare overture to *The Storm* and the even rarer early tone poem *Fatum*. His tempos tend to be fairly quick, which is all to the good, and the marvelous depth of the recording adds a lot. But dropping in on the other three less symphonic scores, I find him unsubtle, even a bit stiff.

Dorati's set with the Philharmonia has long been a standby, though I find him only intermittently successful in Tchaikovsky's agglomeration of symphonic and balletic characteristics (Philips). His phrasing can be very nice in 3, and the strings can sound wonderful (as well as taxed in figuration), but the conductor's tempos and dynamics often strike me as stiff and effortful. All you have to do is compare him with **Marriner,** who is my first choice if you want the same performers doing all four scores. He finds the elusive *tempo giusto* in all the suites, and with the help of his very fine Stuttgart orchestra, he also gets the quietest and most naturally bowed and effortlessly phrased playing I've heard in these works. His success is consistent in each of the four, whether it's the balletic piquancies of 2 (♦Capriccio 227) or the more symphonic emotional scale of 3 (♦Capriccio 200).

A complementary view comes from **Stefan Sanderling** and the National Symphony of Ireland, who have recorded the suites on a pair of cheap discs (Naxos). Sanderling can make Marriner's response sound a little generalized, but I prefer the greater weight and body of the former's Stuttgart Radio Orchestra to Sanderling's admirable Irish band. In general, he's a good deal more obvious than Marriner, and some of his tempos are rather ponderous.

Svetlanov and the USSR Symphony taped the suites in the early '80s, and these performances are generally better (and better recorded) than their '60s symphony set (1 and 2, ♦Melodiya 117099; 3 and 4, ♦117100). The sound is warmer, for one thing, though just as echoey, and climaxes can still get a bit blatty. Svetlanov's luscious strings are the highlight of these discs, though the winds want for nothing in character. His performances are all vivid and recommendable, though I sometimes find them overstated: These are suites, not symphonies, and he often loads up the outer movements with all the weight and emotion deserved by, say, the *Pathétique*.

Bělohlávek and the Prague Symphony recorded the suites in the early '90s and turned in the toughest, most symphonic renditions available (Supraphon). Tempos are quick and the interpretations are straightforward—maybe too much so. Among performances of this kind, Marriner's have more character, more interpretive detail, even more symphonic weight when required (the Prague Symphony isn't to be confused with the great Czech Philharmonic). **Tilson Thomas**'s virtuoso and punchy renditions of 2 and 4 with the Philharmonia are the most enjoyable in his series (♦CBS/Sony 46503). He taped 3 with the LA Philharmonic in a sympathetic reading that's hampered by less than stellar playing and some acoustic dryness (CBS, not yet on CD). He can be heavy, and his tendency to over-interpret fractures the theme and variations into an unrelated set of segments, each of them characterized as heavily as a separate symphonic movement.

3 is the most substantial of the suites (I have sometimes thought of it as a kind of symphony in the way its movements offset and complement one another cumulatively), and is a favorite with many by virtue of its wistful melancholy and large theme-and-variations finale. It's also the work recorded most often by conductors who drop in to do just one. **Boult** and the London Philharmonic did this in 1974 and produced a pleasing if fairly stiff and literal performance (EMI). By contrast, **Maazel** and the Vienna Philharmonic taped an intoxicatingly elegant performance in the mid-'70s that represents the pinnacle of their Tchaikovsky collaborations (Decca/London, not yet on CD). The Viennese playing is beautiful and refined, and the sound likewise. All that disappoints is the conductor's rather vacant, literal reading of the long theme-and-variations movement. Decca needs to reissue this.

Kondrashin and the Moscow Philharmonic take the same kind of personal view of 3 as Tilson Thomas, but are more able to pull the four movements together (Icone). What prevents me from recommending this distinctive performance is the mastering, which makes the orchestra sound distant, small-scale, and a bit shrill. Just about every **Rozhdestvensky** performance has its revelations, though his orchestras and recording engineers don't always keep their part of the bargain. His 3 with the USSR Ministry of Culture Orchestra is a case in point: This is beautifully and wisely paced and well recorded, but the orchestra's sound tends to come apart in climaxes (Erato).

James Judd and the English Chamber Orchestra reverse that situation and offer a performance of 4 ("Mozartiana") that's charmless and joyless, but marked by orchestral playing that's always graceful (Novalis, with *Serenade*). The theme-and-variations finale seems dispatched out of a sense of duty. **Koizumi** and the Winnipeg Symphony come up with an even less remarkable 4 (CBC). They rush through most movements: The exception is the *Preghiera,* which is sincere and unusually slow. CBC's sound isn't gratifying.

OTHER ORCHESTRAL MUSIC

1812 Overture. **Dorati**'s stereo recording for Mercury is famous, mostly for the special effects: "authentic" cannons manned by historical munitions experts, a relay of the carillon from Harkness Tower at Yale University, etc. Most impressive is the carillon, which really does fill the air with tolling bells like no other recording. But the Minneapolis Symphony is recorded in a dry, boxy setting (they sound like they're playing in a bunker, which might not be an inappropriate impression), the sound of the orchestra itself doesn't give any pleasure, and the reading is neither very exciting nor affectionately phrased. Dorati's last recording, made in 1978 in Detroit, is less gimmicky and better recorded, except that the acoustics are cavernous, causing some aural confusion at the end (Decca/London). But his interpretation isn't very convincing or

charismatic, the cannons coming in toward the close with utter predictability.

Like the first Dorati, **Kunzel**'s rendition with the Cincinnati Symphony is another gimmick disc: The cannons get star billing and reproduce well enough, but the reading is depressingly slow and tedious, with no sense of shape or line (Telarc). For a recent and good all-the-bells-and-whistles performance (chorus, carillon, real cannons), try **Litton** and the Dallas Symphony (Delos). He gets real mileage from his chorus, having them sing any and all snippets of hymn, folk song, and anthem material. It's too bad the performance never quite got this listener to the edge of his chair, and that it hangs fire conspicuously at the end. But Litton really adds luster to this release by including the very rare *Moscow,* a cantata Tchaikovsky wrote in 1883 for the coronation of Tsar Alexander III. It's a beautiful if not terribly deep work, with a stunning mezzo aria that the composer re-used for *Queen of Spades.* Litton's honesty is the perfect approach, and with fine sound this is very enjoyable.

You could do far worse than choose **Maazel** and the Vienna Philharmonic, who offer the very finest in orchestral playing (CBS/Sony). The Vienna State Opera Chorus intones the hymn at the opening in pretty sober fashion. Maazel is coolheaded at the climax in descending unison strings, but the playing is luminous and elegant and he paces the piece very well. His remake with the chorus-less Bavarian Radio Orchestra is more mannered and less exciting: The tempo gear shifts don't always ring true, the lyrical string tune seems fairly pedantic in its phrasing, and the last big brass statement of the hymn hardly gets above *mf* (RCA).

Haitink and the Concertgebouw are surprisingly trenchant, and the brass are absolutely ideal, adding extra force and color whenever they enter, but not making the paint peel off the walls either (♦Philips). He chooses each tempo astutely and puts it to work without any nonsense or obvious point-making. At the final climax, he bolsters the Amsterdam brass with a military band, and brings in the best and most resonant carillon after Dorati's. Philips's miking is natural and discreet, refusing to shove tambourine or cannons in our face and allowing the music to create its own spectacle.

Of fairly recent *1812*s, **Barenboim**'s is among the best: Orchestra and conductor actually sound like they're enjoying themselves, and the lyrical tune is done affectionately, though there's not much to make the pulse race (Teldec, with a slightly less desirable Symphony 5). There's a touch more excitement to his earlier recording, again with the Chicago Symphony (♦DG 445523). The orchestra plays a bit more cleanly and energetically, and the engineering is likewise smoother, with more presence for the strings. I prefer Barenboim's DG issue to **Solti**'s Chicago performance (Decca/London). But if you want sheer weight of orchestral tone, brass dominating, look no further: The end spills forth more sound than just about any other. Still, the brass don't mesh with the rest of the orchestra nearly as well as they do under Barenboim; this is another disc to make you lament Decca's decision to go back to recording in Orchestra Hall.

Slatkin and the St. Louis Symphony are extremely well recorded, with the depth and richness RCA typically gets in Powell Hall (RCA). They also dub in an academic carillon (from an Indiana Girls Academy!), but the orchestra and interpretation don't get much cumulative tension going. **Muti** and the Philadelphians sustain the tension from first bar to last (♦EMI 47022). It's hard to think of a more consistently exciting recording, or one that calls up such a visceral response. The huge Philadelphia string sound is a definite asset. It's also a nice touch that the cannon fire is splayed across the stereo spectrum. The sound is a bit raw at the very top, and the acoustics a bit dry, but this is impressive in all respects. **Ormandy**'s own reading with the Philadelphia has its impressive moments, especially the massive opening intonation (in English) by the Mormon Tabernacle Choir (CBS/Sony). Following them up with organ is overkill, though, and would seem to put us in a church service. The huge Philadelphian string sound also pays dividends in the many string-led assaults and sequences, but the climaxes tend to be heavy, without the rhythmic lift that Muti and others produce, and the sound is disappointing: The climaxes break up, the cannons sound like someone dubbed in a bad cassette recording of ammunition, and the engineer hastily fades out the panoply of bells at the very end.

In their powerful but temperate account, **Reiner** and the Chicago Symphony (RCA) make a massive 80-bar cut in the middle of the piece and don't deign to give us cannons (or even an imitation thereof). That will limit the performance's popularity, but he certainly gets a stunningly poised and substantial sound from his orchestra. **Abbado** combines some of the same musicality and feel for the shape of the work with a more freewheeling approach. I love the way he and the Berlin Philharmonic press ahead, almost stumbling, from the opening string choir into the main argument of the piece. The orchestra sounds stunning, with the strings especially lithe, silky, and powerful. Unfortunately, the climax holds a few disappointments that prevent an unconditional recommendation: The cannon shots don't sound cannon-like at all (certainly it would have been easy to over-dub something more realistic), and things start to sound tentative at the final windup. Still, this is preferable to Abbado's Chicago reading, which has nothing of the eager spontaneity of the Berlin version (CBS/Sony).

Temirkanov recorded *1812* with the Leningrad Philharmonic (in "Tchaikovsky Gala in Leningrad"), and though the orchestra can sound glorious at times, the performance disappoints with its hasty and rather empty pressing-ahead quality. His cannons sound like someone axing a tree next to a microphone, and the music ends amid fireworks and rhythmic applause. It seems a good time was had by all, except maybe the home listener. A far better reading in this block party style came from **Fiedler** and his Boston Pops—a top recommendation that DG must reissue. Fiedler and his engineers did absolutely everything right, dispatching the lyrical material with grace and playing the more rambunctious passages with flair and real affection. What's more, this is one of few renditions where cannons, bells, and orchestra somehow sound as though they're coming together in one believable acoustic setting.

Bernstein in New York turns in a pretty exciting performance, though the sound is disappointing: There isn't much range for the orchestra to expand in climaxes, and in lieu of cannons someone seems to be hitting a piece of plywood very, very hard with a big stick (CBS/Sony). One complaint can be laid at the conductor's doorstep: There should be more quiet playing. Bernstein's Israel Philharmonic reading is far better in all respects, with a much smarter and more sensitive approach to phrasing and dynamics and bristling climaxes (♦DG 415379). The DG engineers have also done a great job with an uncooperative hall, though they do let the bass get a bit hollow when things go loud. **DePreist** and the Oregon Symphony catch the ear right away with a regally phrased introduction that rises to a climax of real grandeur (Delos). This is a musical and rather mellow reading; he paces the piece extremely well, so the climax is eagerly awaited and makes an impact when it does arrive. The orchestra is very alert but can't quite summon the needed tonal heft at the cascading unison string transition. **Sian Edwards** and the Royal Liverpool Philharmonic are fresher in approach and more lively than many others, but her reading isn't memorable (EMI). For instance, she's completely upstaged by **Leaper**'s thrilling performance with the Royal

Philharmonic (♦Naxos 550500). He phrases the opening hymn flexibly and knowingly, and it's clear by the first climax that the brass are more than a match for their assignment. His last grand climax is as noisy and joyful as any other, but also ungimmicky.

Karajan recorded *1812* twice. His first version, with the Philharmonia, has panache and sonic depth to spare (EMI). But giving pause are the oboist's painfully thin tone and the conductor's rather labored and sleepy renditions of the lyrical string melody and unduly protracted final hymn in the brass. The cannon shots show the limitations of period technology, sounding like they're amplified out of a small loudspeaker. But Karajan's Berlin version gets the strongest of recommendations: The sequential figures crackle with electricity, the orchestra makes a very imposing sound, and things hold up through to the end, where there's also a fairly good carillon (♦DG 463614, with *Schehérazade* and *Capriccio Italien*). There are three drawbacks, small ones given the general splendor of what's on offer: For the opening hymn he uses Serge Jaroff's Russian choir, a group Karajan much admired for their intensity of sound, but the intonation of their tenors and women goes insanely awry under pressure (you're almost grateful he doesn't bring them back toward the end); similarly, the Berlin trumpets are thin and whinnying at the final hymn peroration; last, the gain on the orchestra obviously gets turned down during the cannon shots and then turned up again when they're over.

As always, **Stokowski** is *sui generis*. He has the Royal Philharmonic and keeps his massive choir mum until the big climax for the sake of effect (Decca/London). There are also the inevitable scoring retouches and some mannered aspects to the phrasing early on. But all this hardly matters when the piece is dispatched with such cinematic flair and has so much cumulative impact. This was a multi-miked Phase Four issue, and I haven't yet heard how well the production has transferred to CD.

Capriccio Italien. No one matches, let alone surpasses, **Kondrashin** and his pickup orchestra for color, vividness, shapeliness of phrasing, and thrilling energy (♦RCA 63302). The performance is smiling even before the trumpets and orchestral bells come in for the big Neapolitan tune, and the end is extraordinarily taut and energetic even though the last statement of the Neapolitan melody is rhetorically slow: He puts quotation marks around it. Forty years on, RCA's sound is still warm and all-enveloping. Similar flair comes from **Mravinsky** and his Leningrad Philharmonic, recorded in 1949 (Melodiya/RCA). This isn't a version for sound buffs, obviously, but the mono production (though it tends toward glare in climaxes) comes more readily alive than EMI's recordings of the same period. More important, this rendition has more personality and life in each bar than many other performances have in their entirety. It's one of the very best.

You might expect **Mitropoulos** to take Tchaikovsky's tempos and run off with them, but his NY Philharmonic performance sails on a consistently even keel except for the last statement of the Neapolitan tune with tambourine, where he slows down (CBS/Sony). This isn't to say the performance doesn't have character: The ability to infuse life and color into a score without playing havoc with tempos is a secret that only great conductors have had, and Mitropoulos makes this very memorable. The CBS "Portrait" mastering has a hissy high end, and seems to convey cistern-like acoustics.

As a similar surprise, **Bernstein** and the Israel Philharmonic never weigh this music down (DG). Still, it does sometimes cry out for a lighter and more obviously charming touch, and the slightly boxy acoustics somehow prove a bigger limitation here than they did in the coupled

1812. While **Kunzel** and the Cincinnati Symphony were disappointing in *1812,* their *Capriccio* is a good deal more lively, if still fairly modest in vision and resources, with a sudden lurch ahead in tempo for the end in lieu of long-range interpretation (Telarc). **Litton**'s Symphony 3 gets added luster from its discmate *Capriccio;* he's right at home in sunny, public showpieces like this. Maybe he goes too far with some of the rhythmic detailing, but his Bournemouth group plays very well, and *Capriccio*s don't come much better than this.

Haitink and the Concertgebouw enjoy beautifully resonant acoustics, and this pays off in Tchaikovsky's spatial effects (Philips). They bring plenty of energy and color to the assignment, but the piece never really lifts off. **Dorati** in London is matter of fact, and beefy engineering works against any sense of lyricism, caprice, or lightness (Mercury). His Detroit version is far better in sound: The strings are lithe, the rhythmic backdrops to the opening melodies more appropriately distant (♦London 443003, a twofer of Tchaikovsky's single-movement orchestral works). It's a fine performance, relatively direct and refusing to take the piece too seriously, but at the same time showing a loving touch.

Sterner stuff comes from **Karajan** and the Berlin Philharmonic (DG). They also have some circusy tempos, with a very broad and portentous take on the opening string melody, a narcotically slow start to the big Neapolitan tune, and a final coda that presses ahead. But the orchestral sonorities are very imposing and the performance never fails to leave an impression. It's interesting that **Beecham** takes a similar approach in his late '40s recording, starting the work off slowly and speeding up gradually until the last bars (CBS, not yet on CD). We could definitely use a reissue of this, even though it doesn't sport the sharp rhythmic snap of some later performances.

Svetlanov and the USSR Symphony give a counterexample, starting off quickly with the Neapolitan tune and not getting much faster overall (Melodiya/RCA); the Beecham/Karajan approach gives the work a more definite shape. Your view of Svetlanov will also depend in part on how you take to the Eastern-bloc vibrato in the brass, not to mention his acidic trumpets. This orchestra is an assemblage of garish and unblended poster-paint colors, which may or may not oversell the vulgarity of Tchaikovsky's music. Next to Svetlanov, **Jansons** and the Oslo are a paragon of good manners and well-heeled coloration, and that may be their undoing (Chandos). He meshes the tempos with typical skill, giving the piece shape without extremes or letting anything get bogged down. It's very enjoyable, but it has less cumulative effect than Kondrashin.

There are instructive contrasts with **Maazel** in Munich, who goads his orchestra to a very impressive and imposing display but at the same time lends the score some character (♦RCA 68471, with his less recommendable *1812*). The Bavarian Radio Orchestra plays better than I've ever heard it, and he keeps the piece moving with no longueurs. The sound is gutsy and impressive. No cheap shots either from **Ormandy,** who manages to make everything sound natural (♦CBS/Sony 47657). He doesn't vary tempo much over the course of the piece, but the Philadelphians' sound lets him open up broad, impressive vistas at just about every turn. This isn't a virtuoso orchestral version like the Kondrashin, but something that emerges all of a piece, like a symphonic movement created to fit into a larger whole. The sound is very fine in the remastering, without even a trace of tape hiss.

Barenboim and the Chicago Symphony are suitably rhapsodic and stylish, and the sound is conspicuously successful—one of DG's best early digital efforts (DG). The woodwinds have a keen tone, the brass are properly balanced against a rather dark body of strings, and the overall sound comes wonderfully alive when the orchestral bells come in. Still, the audiophile choice must be **Leaper** and the Royal Philharmonic (♦Naxos 550500, with his equally fine *1812*). Here the climaxes open up wonderfully and with real transparency, and his interpretation is among the more exciting on discs. Both as recording and performance, this has a flair to beat most others.

Francesca da Rimini. All *Francesca*s (and probably all Tchaikovsky orchestral recordings) rest in the shadow of **Stokowski** and the pseudonymous NY Philharmonic (♦Everest 9037, with his equally splendid *Hamlet* overture; avoid the earlier Dell'Arte transfer). The devastating drama of Dante's depiction of Hell, the gentle but terrible nostalgia of recalling happiness amid eternal suffering—Stokowski encompasses all this with tremendous sweep and lyricism. Everest's sound is remarkable in the 20-bit remastering, though some hiss remains.

Hell must be a rather small and boxy place, to judge from the acoustics Mercury gave **Dorati** and the Minneapolis Symphony. The woodwinds are miked so close you can almost hear each player breathing and pressing down keys. His orchestra, too, places more emphasis on rhythmic energy than on tone. Still, this is probably the Tchaikovsky score where timbral luxury is not the highest criterion, and Dorati turns in one of his more wide-ranging performances: sensitive in the love music and savage when the composer is imitating the winds of Hell. Yet there's no question that his 1973 National Symphony version is better (Decca/London), mostly because the sound is more distant and flattering. The Washington performance is likeable, musical, and well paced, but doesn't inspire gooseflesh as Stokowski and Markevitch (in Paris) do.

Markevitch was really suited to *Francesca,* and he left us two recordings. The 1967 Philharmonia reading starts out with rare intensity (Philips 446148, with Symphonies 1–3, or in the more recommendable set of complete tone poems, ♦442586). The playing doesn't have the bold edge of Svetlanov's USSR Symphony (see below), but that makes it all the more listenable. Nor does it have much in the way of tonal allure, but then this conductor was much more interested in rhythmically induced drama. Markevitch's early '60s version had some less consistent playing from the Lamoureux Orchestra, and a few unusual balances, but the drama was even more remarkable, indeed just as stunning as Stokowski's (DG). Whereas the latter was in a Hollywood vein, Markevitch's was sparer, more raw and expressionistic, like a Schoenberg opera or a Buechner drama. DG must reissue this.

Ormandy's version is typically unhurried, but the Philadelphia Orchestra offers the kind of palatial sonority that can only pull you helplessly into Tchaikovsky's hellish and divine tone poem (RCA). A drawback is the unnatural recording job, which sounds like it relied on multiple close-placed mikes with balancing done at the mixing board. Taking no cue from the score, **Bernstein** seems to wallow in a drunken stupor in his second New York recording (DG). His earlier New York version is tauter, the rhythms far better focused, the orchestra more brightly lit (CBS/Sony). This is one of the more fetchingly brash and hellish versions, though other accounts have more dependable playing, and Bernstein tends to dawdle in the early chromatic passages. **Slatkin** brings unusual sensitivity to the entrance of the idyllic love music in the strings, but is generally pedantic and over-literal (RCA). You suspect that he's continually holding back for a final climax that never arrives.

Similarly conspicuous holding-back for the payoff comes from **Sian Edwards** and the Royal Liverpool Philharmonic (EMI, with *Romeo, Marche Slave,* and *1812*). The Liverpool strings lack body and force in the chromatic scales (Tchaikovsky's winds of Hell), and this distinctive if soft-centered performance can't rank with the likes of Stokowski and Svetlanov. **Muti** and the Philadelphia are surprisingly noncommital, and all the orchestral tone can't rescue the performance from its lack of shape and direction (EMI). **Haitink** is certainly distinctive, particularly with that deep Concertgebouw sound, so perfect for this score both in its loud and soft moments (Philips). The strings are plush and the woodwind solos distinguished. Haitink is superb at forging the piece into one uninterrupted narrative, but his central section is rather lacking in direction and quiet ardor.

Rostropovich and the London Philharmonic give us wide-screen drama in Technicolor, with an unusually weighty and sustained opening and winds of Hell that swirl and bite ferociously (EMI, in his symphony set). My only hesitation is that the recording hasn't been remastered well: The sound is bright and edgy. **Svetlanov** is very different, splendidly intense (♦Melodiya/RCA 37880, with his less recommendable Symphony 6). Given the conductor's energy and the thin, unblended USSR Symphony timbres, these climaxes can peel the paint from your walls. Even so, subtleties do mark the more delicate moments, and the thrilling and very powerful string sections balance the brass and winds. No holds barred here.

Romeo and Juliet. It's surprisingly difficult to find a through-and-through satisfying *Romeo*. **Toscanini**'s 1947 recording is still the tautest on records, and the maestro isn't as austere in the love music as you might expect (♦RCA 78800, with his slightly less satisfying *Pathétique*). The performance benefits from the tonal weight of the NBC Symphony, which comes across even in the dry and limited studio sound. The young **Muti** was sometimes declared Toscanini's successor, but his *Romeo* with the Philharmonia, though generally emotional and idiomatic, tends to wilt when it isn't pushing home dramatic cruxes (EMI). As in the rest of his Tchaikovsky cycle, the mikes home in on the bass drum and timpani—for the sake of impact, I suppose.

The word "Toscaninian" would never apply to **Abbado** and his brilliant musicality. His first and most spontaneous *Romeo,* with the Boston Symphony, rises to the heights of passion: The love theme overwhelms at its last appearance in the soaring violins, and the death-stroke in the timpani is heart-stopping (♦DG 427220). But the magic of the reading is that it impresses just as strongly with its moments of subtle introversion. The sounds are a tad worn and could use a fresh remastering. Abbado's Berlin Philharmonic version is also among the most dramatic and ecstatic on records, with his patented perfection of phrasing, but the sound gets hard in climaxes and the end is unduly rushed (DG). His Chicago recording has a drier ambience, and the love music tends to go slack (CBS/Sony).

The most tightly drawn feud music (with fantastic clashing of swords) comes from a septuagenarian **Bernstein** (♦DG 429234, with his fine Symphony 5). This is an original reading, strong, always interesting, and well proportioned. He searches out the deepest veins of Mahlerian melancholy at the end of the introduction, the faster music has tight rhythmic focus, and if the love music is quite slow, it also has emotional strength. **Slatkin** is unremarkable, the culminations hardly making the listener's pulse race, though his St. Louis band is always rich and nuanced (RCA). Though their sound isn't as impressive, **Haitink** and the Concertgebouw have a good deal more energy (Philips). Still, the reading stops short of being memorable or recreating Shakespeare's more tragic depths.

Beecham's 1946–47 recording is variable; the recording was made in two sessions some months apart, and the Royal Philharmonic takes on an enviably rich and dark sound in one of them and a harsher sound in the other (Beecham Trust). A pity, since the opening is remarkable in its concentration and phrasing. **Ormandy**'s performance is one of the very best, a top recommendation (♦RCA 61853, with his equally outstanding Symphony 5). Most impressive is his ability to sustain the music in all its darker intensity. In that, he is to be contrasted with **Dorati** and the National Symphony, who are disappointingly episodic, sometimes impatient, and prosaic (Decca/London). Similar comments apply to **Sian Edwards** (EMI). She does get more affectionate and subtle detail from the Royal Liverpool Philharmonic than Dorati gets from his group, and the engineering is excellent, but her drum-filled climaxes tend to get noisy. **Giulini** also presents a fairly episodic account, with a larger variety of tempo than is often heard (♦EMI 67789, with his spellbinding *Pathétique*). But the reading has plenty of intensity and vision and is very distinctive and memorable.

Karajan's 1967 Berlin recording is similarly sustained, the orchestra sounding as if its sonority had been painstakingly built and anchored from the bottom up (♦DG 423223). His 1981 version is more forceful and passionate, a very impressive document of the Indian summer in his recording career (DG). The "Karajan Gold" remastering helps put a bit more space around the big orchestral sound, and the balancing is fine, but in climaxes the drums take on an unfortunate steely quality and also produce a strange overload effect in transients. Karajan recorded *Romeo* in 1946 with the Vienna Philharmonic, a patient but fairly intense reading, the conductor making more immediate human contact with the music than in his other versions. EMI's rather shrill sound, however, makes this something for the Karajanophile, or the person wanting to hear the remarkable 1948 *Pathétique* it's coupled with.

Munch combines nobility, toughness, and drama in this overplayed work, making it sound fresh without the ragged ensemble he sometimes condoned (RCA). The Boston Symphony strings have a dark gravity that is beautifully appropriate. My only reservation about the remastering is the rather raucous climaxes, with the sound losing some focus. In 1964, **Maazel** took the Vienna Philharmonic into the studio (actually, the trusty if rather aggressive-sounding Sofiensaal). This is still one of the best versions for brilliant playing and tautness and power of argument, categories where it's challenged only by Toscanini, though some will find him too cool and non-interpretive in the love music. **Rostropovich** invokes similar dramatic tension but also indulges in considerable (but never overdone) rubato and engages the work's passion like no one else; when the apexes arrive, you know it (♦EMI, in his symphony cycle). He pulls a rich, living-and-breathing, almost overwhelming sound from the London Philharmonic, and Kingsway Hall ensures that there's a beautiful bloom on *pianissimos* and climaxes alike.

Svetlanov elicits considerable heat and excitement from his USSR Symphony, and not inconsiderable tenderness, but the climactic feuds between warring families are spoiled by the boxy acoustics and the orchestra's tin trumpets (Melodiya/RCA). **Leaper** and the Royal Philharmonic enjoy clear and well-proportioned engineering, though again it's not the warmest sound imaginable (Naxos). The reading is fine, but in the final analysis, it isn't the most distinctive performance around. **Barenboim** and the Chicago Symphony get a fine recording job, one of the best from the remodeled Orchestra Hall, but his interpretation tends to be shapeless and pinnacles are afflicted by over-emphatic brass (Teldec).

In his digital (second) version with the same orchestra, **Solti** is surprisingly attentive to detail and nuance (Decca/London). Balances are also good within the ensemble, and though the sound is a bit dry, this will appeal to those wanting a reading that's strong, bordering on coarse. Its only real drawback is its neglect of the long line, the kind of care for narrative that comes from **Colin Davis** and the Boston Symphony (Philips). Still, Davis in his turn tends to pass over the work's surface and ulterior tensions, and the reading doesn't have much cumulative impact. **Dutoit** is also attentive to the shape of the work and its moody darkness of sound, but climaxes fall short of being inspiring. (Decca/London). The best thing here is the sound, full and warm but with plenty of detail. **Geoffrey Simon** offers the original 1869 version, which is almost a different work altogether than the familiar 1880 revision (Chandos). There's no question this version is weak and very episodic, but in Simon's fine rendition with the London Symphony it leaves you with a fresh perspective on Tchaikovsky's most famous (maybe over-famous?) tone poem.

Serenade for String Orchestra and *Souvenir de Florence.* There should be some kind of law requiring those who direct the *Serenade* to be string players. **Yuri Bashmet** is one of the great virtuosos, and he and his Moscow Soloists prove revelatory in this frequently played score (♦RCA 60368). You come to feel that just about everyone before him has misunderstood the music. Taking great care over texture, balance, chording, articulation, and dynamic variety, Bashmet makes the piece sound utterly new. The playing is miraculous, at times light as thistledown and at others heavy as an entire symphonic string section. Some might find the music-making too fastidious or even mannered, but I would say the forest is seen just as well as the trees. I only wish Bashmet had given us *Souvenir de Florence* instead of his Grieg couplings.

Vladimir Spivakovsky takes a similar approach with the Moscow Virtuosi (probably the same players as Bashmet uses), though he's more conventional (RCA, with his orchestration of Tchaikovsky's *Album for the Young*). He's also less interested in the myriad possibilities made possible by a smaller band of strings; clarity of texture is really its only advantage over the full-section sounds of Karajan and Munch. **Scott Yoo** and the Metamorphosen Chamber Orchestra bring fresher and more joyful music-making to the score (Archetype). These Boston-area youngsters don't have quite the seamless blend of the Moscow groups, nor do they snap their way through Tchaikovsky's rhythms as virtuosically as the Orpheus or react as immediately and personally to details as Bashmet's group. They more than compensate by bringing to their task the kind of relish and vigor that prove so rare in professional ensembles. Yet at times I found myself wishing Yoo would push his players harder, or indulge himself and his group a little more.

Carl Pini has had a long and distinguished career as first violin in London orchestras, and he has coached the Australian Chamber Orchestra to the perfect combination of classical lightness and symphonic weight (♦Omega 1010). The recording engineers have helped what sounds like a pretty large ensemble with a sympathetic balance that's colored by ambience and never dry, but never clumsy either; all it needs is some added bass. Their *Souvenir* was taped in a different acoustic, and here the sound is a little thinner; likewise, this admirable performance lacks some of the distinctly Slavic "soul" (with its throbs, sobs, and slides) that's so audible in, say, the Borodin Quartet recordings of the sextet version.

Entremont and the Vienna Chamber Orchestra are attractive, agile, fairly lightweight in sound, and not inexpressive in both *Serenade* and *Souvenir* (Naxos). They're definitely enjoyable, especially given the crisp and transparent sound, but their performances aren't very distinctive; efficiency is the primary impression left by the Waltz, and Pini (for one)

finds more detail throughout *Souvenir.* Yet I prefer Entremont to **Orbelian** and the Moscow Chamber Orchestra, who usually make the right moves and generate pleasant sonorities but offer an interpretation that doesn't jell into a memorable whole (Delos, with *The Seasons*). For one thing, he tends to dull the first movement by rounding off its corners and softening its higher ascents.

The **Orpheus Chamber Orchestra** recording isn't inconsiderable, and has some original interpretive contributions (DG). The absence of a conductor liberates them to explore the strange, almost atonal passage toward the close of the *Elegie* and the recitative-like opening of the finale, where they beautifully rethink the articulations. But I find them less interesting in the big, *tutti* passages: They start I sounding pedantic and unsustained, with an accent on each note of the opening melody. Their delivery soon loosens up, and the rationale was probably to give some room to move toward a softer address in the following pages, but this is at best a mixed success. **Lev Markiz** and the Nieuw Sinfonietta Amsterdam are consistently slow, cool, and dispassionate (Globe), but the string playing by this very young group is always a joy, full of ingenuous detail but never heavy or pretentious. If only the conductor sounded a bit more emotionally caught up in the music.

Marriner and his Academy of St. Martin in the Fields have recorded the Serenade at least twice, and their 1982 version contrasts with the Orpheus in that it's easy listening, with consistently light textures and smoothed-over edges—no feathers ruffled, not many questions asked (Philips). His crisp and slightly abrupt way with the cross-rhythms of the Waltz is surely the right way, but in most other places, this is just too cozy and easy to make much of an impression. Still, the Academy's textures are perfect for this work, and those who like their Tchaikovsky done in an old-fashioned way will find a lot to enjoy here.

Iona Brown and the Norwegian Chamber Orchestra are more variable: wonderfully free—and often blissfully quiet—in the *Elegie,* but extremely heavy and opaque in the first and last movements (Simax). I don't think I've ever heard the opening material, and its return in the finale, put across with less charm; rather than chamber music, this is a symphonic wannabe that sounds like it's yearning angrily for a full string section. **James Judd** and the English Chamber Orchestra enjoy a more wide-ranging recording—lower lows, and also higher highs with more overtones audible (Novalis, with Suite 4). Partly because of this greater variety of sound, they exude more character and variety than Marriner or Brown, but they convey less joy and affection for the music than Marriner. Their conception ultimately comes across as stern and unsympathetic.

Turning to large-scale orchestral renditions, **Mravinsky** recorded *Serenade* with the Leningrad Philharmonic in 1949: a beautiful performance, the string playing sustained just as well as Karajan's (see below), and the phrasing rather more free (Melodiya, with *Francesca* and *Capriccio*). In fact, his subtle tempo inflections in the *Elegie* and at the start of the finale could serve as lessons in how to pace and shape this music. His Waltz has elegance galore, and he effortlessly and lovingly supports the lyrical line here and elsewhere, while the finale has a relaxed kind of symphonic strength. If this had been recorded in modern studio sound, it would be a version to top all others. But the sound is very acceptable (even if it tends to overload a bit in the loudest passages), and it's strongly recommended to anyone not allergic to mono.

Bernstein and the NY Philharmonic strings make some lovely sounds (CBS/Sony). This is as "expressive" as you'd expect, and many have enjoyed it. Yet to these ears the ossified expressiveness becomes relentless after a few minutes, and I soon find myself yearning for a lighter touch, or some crispness rather than sheer sonic ballast. Things aren't helped by CBS's close miking, which makes the ensemble sound grainy and spot-lit, even sledgehammer-ish in climaxes. Much of Bernstein's shaping and rubato sounds elephantine, stiff, and awkward, more a caricature of musical expression than the real thing.

For this kind of grand symphonic experience I'd rather turn to **Karajan** and the Berlin strings, who are much more supple in interpretation and enjoy a less shrill recording with more body to it (♦DG 400038, with his equally lovely version of Dvořak's String Serenade). Not having heard the disc for a few years, I expected the early digital recording to make for hard listening but was pleasantly surprised. The string sound is huge, undoubtedly more appropriate to a Wagner music drama than a work that Tchaikovsky initially conceived as a string quintet, but note the care with which Karajan (and his engineers, probably) cultivates a wide dynamic range; from the start, he gives the sound somewhere to go. His 1966 recording is even fresher in approach, and the sound (recorded in the Jesus-Christus Kirche in Berlin-Dahlem) allows more air around the instruments (DG, not yet on CD). Perhaps there's also a touch more evidence of Karajan's '60s tendency toward over-legato phrasing here, but be sure to grab this as soon as DG reissues it.

Stokowski and the London Symphony are magical (in the Philips twofer, ♦438386). What the performance may lack in lightness and elegance it more than makes up in shapeliness; there isn't a single inert bar. No doubt encouraged to further opulence by the free bowing this conductor espoused in held notes and chords, the London Symphony produces a succulent, wall-to-wall string sound. **Ormandy** and the Philadelphia present a dilemma (CBS/Sony, with Symphony 5). They're alert and responsive in rhythm, with articulation that's less sticky than either Karajan or Bernstein, and outer movements (and *Elegie*) that aren't as self-consciously slow. Ormandy's Waltz also has more grace and crispness than either of the others, even if Karajan wields his forces with more sensitivity, but his string sound is so consistently thick that the effect is like an artist applying so much paint to a canvas that the image becomes difficult to see. Even worse are his large and pointless cuts in I and the finale; with this abridged finale heard at Ormandy's quick tempo, the work comes to a distinctly premature end.

I much prefer **Munch** and the Boston Symphony, who don't butcher the score and also pick a tempo for I that, even if it seems brusque at first, prevents the kind of marmoreal impression given by other conductors (♦RCA 61424). His *Elegie*, with its impeccably blended sound and light touch, is absolutely perfect; moderation enables him to make much more of the quiet ending and transitional opening to the finale. RCA's admirably remastered 1957 recording has plenty of body, bite, and detail. The rest of Munch's program—Barber and Elgar—is just as rewarding. **Solti** and the Israel Philharmonic—a recording from the late '50s—are more sensitive than you might expect (Decca/London). Indeed, this is more sympathetic music-making, more pliable in its phrasing, than Bernstein's. Only the Waltz is pressed rather hard—it sounds like Hussars dancing—and the early Decca engineering does nothing to soften the Solti-steeled tone of the Israeli strings.

Dorati is often over-emphatic, but this is more joyful music-making than I've heard from him on other occasions, and the London Symphony strings play very well (Mercury). A version to hear, maybe, but not one of the best or more distinctive readings. **Poliansky** and the Russian Philharmonic recorded *Serenade* in cistern-like cathedral acoustics, with close miking probably intended to cut down on reverberation (Opus 111). This makes for some beautifully washy if slightly confusing sounds, but has also prevented a real pianissimo and neces-

sitated slow tempos that don't combine happily with his rather glutinous phrasing. And as an interpretation, this strikes out in no new directions.

Be sure to hear **Dejong Victorin Yu** and the Philharmonia strings in *Serenade* and *Souvenir de Florence* (IMP). These may not be the most stylish or sensitive renditions, but they certainly sound well and the disc is cheap. The main drawing point is Yu's smart redistribution of *Souvenir's* parts for a performance with full string orchestra. He makes the excellent point in his liner notes that doubled strings have in the past just played from the sextet parts (the basses playing the second cello line, which is often higher than cello 1) with unbalanced and muddy results. His careful and faithful "orchestration" clarifies the texture wonderfully, especially as he sometimes reverts to soloists. And such a large body of strings really brings out the symphonic style of the music.

At least one disc offers *Souvenir de Florence* without *Serenade* as coupling. **Iona Brown** and her Norwegian Chamber Orchestra are characteristically professional and spot-on in ensemble and intonation and smooth in phrasing, but even though this is excellent string playing, I find it pretty blank as a musical statement (Chandos). There are no real pianissimos, and that imparts a kind of unrelenting sameness to the straight-faced and dry-eyed proceedings.

Among sextet (one-player-to-a-part) renditions, special mention has to be made of the augmented **Borodin Quartet** (♦Melodiya/EMI 49775, with their quartet cycle), and also the gloriously-toned **Schubert Quartet,** almost sounding like a chamber orchestra, though their rhythmic near-mannerisms and tendency toward stately tempos are less appropriate than in the quartets (Nimbus). Nevertheless, the viola at the start of the slow movement is to die for.

Other tone poems and orchestral music. Tchaikovsky's early *Tempest* is one of his finest tone poems, engrossing right off with its quiet and evocative bass drum roll before it moves on to "storm" music that's worthy of *Francesca da Rimini,* delicate, chimerical music for Ariel, and then finally one of his most impassioned string melodies. It's strange that the piece isn't heard more often.

Pletnev and his fine Russian National Orchestra catch the music's delicate balance between impressionism and romanticism, and the sound—both deep and transparent—is outstanding (♦DG 439891, with their excellent *Manfred*). **Abbado** in Chicago has slightly less cooperative acoustics but is just about as poetic and powerful, with real passion in the ecstatic love theme (♦CBS/Sony 39359, with Symphony 2). The engineering is better than in most of the CBS/Sony Chicago cycle.

Another outstanding rendition comes from **DePreist** and the Oregon Symphony, who also supply one of the most thoughtful and memorable versions of *Hamlet* (♦Delos 3081). As far as single discs of Tchaikovsky's tone poems go, the Delos is not to be missed, and the sound is great; though there's a touch of hiss, the engineers easily pass the bass drum test that opens *The Tempest*. **Stokowski** essays *Hamlet* with intense, blistering drama and aching lyricism, fully worthy of the coupled and unmatched *Francesca* (♦Everest 9037). **Bernstein's** Israeli *Hamlet* is also one to hear, though the claustrophobic acoustics hollow out the bass sonorities and limit the climaxes (DG).

Marche slave is especially well served by **Karajan** (DG, NA), who is the perfect guide in this dark-hued, sonorous, processional music. **Ormandy** is also idiomatic (CBS/Sony), while **Bernstein** works himself up into more of a Slavic froth (CBS/Sony). **Maazel** and the Vienna Philharmonic (♦CBS/Sony 37252) are consistently fast, but this helps them convey the stern, martial quality of the music (♦CBS/Sony 37252). The orchestra plays with just the right tension and fervor, and the early digital recording still sounds fine.

The rarer tone poems are well served by **Abbado** and the Chicago Symphony, who recorded some of them as fillers for their variable symphony cycle (Sony). For instance, his account of the Sibelius-like "symphonic ballad" *Voyevoda,* one of Tchaikovsky's last pieces, is among the tauter and more exciting performances; released as filler for his Symphony 5, it should be made available separately with his account of *The Tempest.* The early tone poem *Fatum* can be painfully banal in the wrong hands, but it's certainly not as played by **Slatkin** and the St. Louis Symphony, who do well with the fetching lyrical melody and redeem the noisier opening section (♦RCA 60432, with their Symphony 4 and a *Voyevoda* that's almost as fine as Abbado's).

And don't forget **Toscanini**'s accounts of *Voyevoda* and *Tempest,* rather dimly recorded. His 1944 Studio 8H broadcast of the latter is too indistinct in sound and routine in interpretation to be very useful, but his 1941 Carnegie Hall version of the former has much of the fiery banality that makes his *Pathétique,* Piano Concerto 1, and *Manfred* so remarkable (Music & Arts, 2CD). **Litton**'s *Voyevoda* gets the most faithful recording of the lot, and these days the Dallas Symphony is a virtuoso group in fine fettle. But Litton isn't as good as Abbado at sustaining the work's dramatic tensions, and his bar-by-bar response to the music is rather generalized.

The two available doubles of Tchaikovsky's complete tone poems are valuable mostly as mop-ups, since most of the individual performances can't compare with those described above. It's difficult to choose between the **Dorati** edition (♦Decca/London 443003) and the set with **Inbal, Markevitch,** and **Haitink** (Philips), but in the final analysis I'd choose the former. The Philips twofer is more inconsistent, offering Markevitch's exciting *Francesca* but also his labored *Hamlet* (a score where Dorati is very much to be preferred). The Frankfurt radio studio recording is a bit glaring and clinical for Inbal's *Fatum, The Storm, Tempest,* and *Voyevoda,* while Markevitch's sound is warmer and more appealing. I also think Inbal tends to oversell a modest early piece like *Fatum,* while Dorati takes it a touch more lightly. Inbal's rhythmic focus is better than Dorati's in *Voyevoda,* but Decca's sound contains the climaxes much better.

Though it doesn't include all these works, a good cheap set holds renditions of *Tempest,* the overture to *The Storm,* and *Fatum* that are a lot better than Dorati's or Inbal's (♦Vox 5079, 2CD). **Othmar Maga** and the Bochum Symphony Orchestra pace and shape these rare pieces well, neither trying to wring another *Pathétique* out of them nor breezing through them. What's more, Vox gives the orchestra very fine depth and a wide frequency range, though details can get a bit muddy. In addition to Abravanel's none-too-desirable rendition of *Manfred,* the set includes 46 minutes of music from the operas *The Voyevoda, The Oprichnik,* and *Mazeppa.* Here the Bamberg Symphony has a far thinner tone and the acoustics are echoey, but Janos Furst inspires some shapely phrasing and fine rhythmic pointing. At the price, though, the box is worth getting if only for Maga's eloquence in 50 minutes of rare Tchaikovsky.

Colin Davis made a useful disc in 1977 of ballet music and orchestral portions of some of Tchaikovsky's operas, ranging from the familiar Polonaise and Waltz from *Eugene Onegin* to music from the far more obscure *Oprichnik, The Maid of Orleans, The Sorceress,* and *Les Caprices d'Oxana.* Though always a pleasure, some of this is very thin brew and not up to anything in Tchaikovsky's three great ballets. The Covent Garden orchestra plays well and the sound is fine, but this fairly short disc

(though bargain-priced) is really for the Tchaikovsky completist. It would have been much enhanced if Davis had thrown in the splendid orchestral numbers from *Mazeppa,* which are unfairly neglected on record.

"Battle of Poltava" and "Cossack's Dance" from *Mazeppa* do appear in **Geoffrey Simon**'s collection of little-known overtures and incidental music (♦Chandos 8310, 2CD). In addition to those gems, this set is most desirable for the incidental music to *Hamlet,* a late product (1891) that takes up all of the second disc. By comparison, the early *Overture on the Danish National Anthem* is an empty piece, though the writing and orchestration are recognizably (and attractively) Tchaikovskian. Simon and the London Symphony are consistently superb in all these late Romantic byways. **Zuraitis**'s performance of the *Hamlet* music has more tension, but also more blatant and high-strung sounds from the USSR TV & Radio Symphony to counter the music's lyricism (Mobile Fidelity). Simon is generally preferable, though the Soviets do give the *Elegy*'s melancholy a certain intensity.

Tchaikovsky's 1873 incidental numbers for Ostrovsky's *The Snow Maiden* are shorter and less individual (more folk-based and "incidental") than the *Hamlet* music. In most cases, you'd be hard-pressed to name the composer if you didn't know the music already. But Tchaikovsky completists will want to hear this, if only for the occasional glimmer of that unmistakable lyricism (as in the recurring cantilena). The choice is easy: **Golovchin** and his Moscow forces (Naxos) are able but pretty blank, the chorus is under-rehearsed, and the Russian sound engineers are up to their old spotlighting tricks, putting microphones right in front of the full-throated tenor and mezzo (who with her operatic delivery hardly sounds like a shepherd boy). Chandos's engineering is less claustrophobic for **Järvi,** and his two singers have a lighter delivery. Both discs have texts and translations, but the Chandos is distinctly preferable.

CONCERTOS

Piano

1. Let's take the historic recordings first. **Rubinstein** recorded No. 1 three times. In his 1932 rendition, one of his first concerto recordings, he was partnered with Barbirolli and the London Symphony (RCA). Barbirolli acquits himself with typical poetry, and the pianist is open to every lyrical and virtuoso opportunity. The recording comes up extremely well in its 20-bit "Rubinstein Edition" remastering, but the performance never quite finds its center. Rubinstein's 1946 recording with Mitropoulos and the Minneapolis Symphony finds its feet much more quickly and is very satisfying (RCA). This conductor's tensile rhythm and dynamics seem particularly suited to the music, and Rubinstein follows along almost too eagerly; it would have been absolutely tremendous if only the pianist were more sensitive to the composer's quieter dynamics and interacted more sympathetically with the orchestral solos, if the finale's rhythms didn't have such a forced, even gawky feel. The 20-bit remastered sound is outstanding, except for some swishy surfaces and a metallic tinge to the piano. That said, I prefer that 1946 version to Rubinstein's 1963 tape with Leinsdorf and the Boston Symphony, where the passions run a good deal cooler (RCA). The fire you hear in his tone in 1946 had dissipated by 1960, and Leinsdorf's contribution sounds like so much rote, unnuanced recitation when heard after Mitropoulos.

The contrasts between Rubinstein and Horowitz are immense. **Horowitz** and Toscanini can be heard in three recordings made between 1941 and 1943, all with some very small cuts. Common opinion has it that the third and last of these is the finest, while I would nominate the first, more heated live version as one of the very greatest Tchaikovsky Firsts. This collaboration, quite well recorded in Carnegie Hall, has been preserved with minimal surface noise and a slightly damped-down treble (◆Music & Arts 956, with the *Pathétique* and *Manfred*). The broadcast catches the duo at all the expected white heat and clocks in two minutes faster than the third rendition (1943). Toscanini was supposedly so demanding and dictatorial in the 1941 rehearsals that he left his son-in-law limp with exhaustion, and this is indeed an astounding (if not always very musical) performance, especially in the finale's high-speed dove-tailings and cutting interchanges of piano and orchestra.

Two months later, pianist and conductor officially preserved their collaboration in a performance that was also recorded in Carnegie Hall, though this time without an audience (in RCA's "Toscanini Collection," Vol. 43). The sound is brighter and tinnier than in the Music & Arts 1941 issue; RCA's mikes are pulled back to the point of making the pianist sound off-mike. In all three movements, this performance also sounds a bit less spontaneous, though the *Andantino* is a hair slower than on Music & Arts.

The Toscanini/Horowitz collaboration had mellowed by the famous 1943 rendition, a spectacle engineered to sell war bonds, though in cadenzas the pianist's brittle octaves still swirl like smoke in the third circle of Dante's Hell (RCA, either with Horowitz's *Pictures at an Exhibition* or his Beethoven "Emperor" with Reiner, ◆RCA 7992). This is a more superficial yet heavier interpretation than Argerich's, the *Andantino* less a songful vehicle than a tense intermezzo between a pair of titanic outer movements, but in its own way it's even more dangerous and subversive. Part of that is due to the dry sound and a bit of surface crackle. Horowitz also joined forces with Bruno Walter in No. 1 several years later, and enjoyment of that reissue is immediately limited by the brittle, primitive recording (Music & Arts). The famous double-octave passages in I all but break up into distortion, surfaces can be poor, and there are also some bad side-joins. Still, Walter does give the tuttis of I real nobility, and you can hear the pianist experimenting (with pedaling, for instance) and generally opening up under Walter, who evidently deferred far more to his soloist than Toscanini did.

Cherkassky teamed with the Berlin Philharmonic and Leopold Ludwig in 1956 (DG, with his more consistently rewarding Concerto 2). The reading must have seemed wildly unconventional at that time, and it surprises even today. Ludwig and the orchestra are fairly staid and businesslike while the soloist works his mischief: The pianist's agogic touches, Gouldish x-ray dissection of accompaniment figures, and hairpin dynamic changes sound spur-of-the-moment and would almost seem to indicate boredom with the music. This is worth hearing, but recommendable only as the coupling for Cherkassky's fantastic Concerto 2.

Cliburn made his famous recording shortly after his historic first prize at the 1958 Tchaikovsky Competition, at the height of the Cold War (coupled variously by RCA, including a more assured Rachmaninoff Concerto 2 with Reiner). The pianist's career has since had its ups and downs, and the world is now a very different place, but this reading still holds interest. In conception it's more knowing and lyrical than electrifying, though Cliburn and Kondrashin are more adept than most at doing justice to the score's manic variety of emotions. The pianist's technique isn't transcendental, his tone anything but plush, and the pickup orchestra (not helped by a rather dry Carnegie Hall recording) is one of the weakest Tchaikovsky ensembles anywhere on record (though Kondrashin did wonders with them given the hurried circumstances). But

all this only underlines the all-too-rare human element of the rendition; it's not stellar but it's never dull, a performance from next door, as it were.

Cliburn's generation spawned an incredible crop of American pianists, most of whom succumbed to various disorders or simply failed to live up to their early promise. One such was **John Browning,** who took the piece into the studio in 1966 (RCA, with Friedman's Violin Concerto). The reading is quite adventurous, with good attention to quieter dynamics and rubatos and other fair liberties taken with the cadenza passages. The finale is also taken daringly fast. Ozawa and the London Symphony are wonderfully alive and dynamic as accompanists. Though this is an interesting rendition, Pletnev and Pogorelich (see below) have more character.

One of the rising American virtuosos of the late '50s and '60s, **Gary Graffman,** was felled by carpal tunnel syndrome. His No. 1 with Szell and the Cleveland reminds us of our loss (◆CBS/Sony 46460). It's a fleet, clean, and brilliant performance—powerful but, typically for Szell, always unquestionably controlled—that might disappoint some wanting a grand statement. But the finale does end with a healthy surge of adrenalin. The virtuosic Horowitz pupil **Byron Janis** was eventually sidelined by arthritis, but his recording with Menges and the London Symphony remains a document of his impressive virtuosity in the '60s (Mercury). The reading tends to be heavy, with lightness and sensitivity to the score's quieter dynamics in short supply, and neither pianist nor conductor ever seems to relax into Tchaikovsky's lyricism. The best part of this is Mercury's bold, full-frequency recording.

For fire-breathing virtuosity, the choice has to be **Argerich,** who has made at least two recordings that are mandatory listening. Her 1981 reading in Munich matches her with the great, irreplaceable Kondrashin in a perfect partnership (◆Philips 446673, with a less single-minded Rachmaninoff 3, where Chailly is the collaborator). Together, they are master story tellers who leave us hanging white-knuckled on the smallest detail of their narration. Every moment is an event, even if that means Argerich starts her cadenzas at twice the speed of all mortal pianists, though any accusation of virtuosity for its own sake would be beside the point. There's more fire and brimstone in her tone in the 1981 performance than in her other two, and also greater tenderness in the *Andantino semplice,* though the finale is a mite disappointing after the first two movements. The recording is quite natural and the audience silent except for their final applause.

Argerich's 1970 recording with Dutoit operates on a more even keel and is uniformly slower, though there's some added enticement in that the studio setup lets us hear more details of the pianist's sorcery (◆DG 415062). The orchestral contribution is among the best on record, though Dutoit is no Kondrashin and doesn't consistently pull the listener to the edge of his chair. Argerich's 1994 version, with Abbado and the Berlin Philharmonic, is somewhere between the two earlier readings, more spontaneous and daring than the 1970 and not quite as volcanic as the 1981 (DG). Abbado's responsiveness is a gain over Dutoit (what you can hear of it, since the piano is very forward). There's a bit more orneriness and point-making from the pianist this time, and some may not like her mannerisms; her rhythms are more often spasmodic than grand and flowing. For a coupling, she joins Nicolas Economous in his two-piano arrangement of *Nutcracker Suite.*

A reading in the Argerich vein came from **Cziffra** and the ORF Orchestra under Dervaux (EMI). Dating from 1958, this is, if anything, more quixotic, seething, and unpredictable than the Argentinean tigress's. But unlike Argerich, Cziffra lacks limpidness in the simpler passages. Another reading in the grand manner is **Wild**'s with Fistoulari and the Royal Philharmonic (♦Chesky). There isn't a hint of slickness to this, and Wild can convince you the piece was written for him. If anything, he and Fistoulari are at fault for not relaxing the tension until the reprise in the slow movement, where we finally feel an excuse to inhale. Wild doesn't have Argerich's ability to charm at the same time she bewitches you, but this is powerful music-making. His coupling is a drawback: Dohnányi's faded *Variations on a Nursery Song,* with an unsatisfactory orchestral backdrop.

Richter has at least two Tchaikovsky performances available, which are typically virtuosic without quite redefining the rules as Argerich and Horowitz do, and they could thereby be considered less imposing; I might even call his track record with this work disappointing. His tempos are less free (or less indulgent?) than Argerich's, but his tone is more exposed and even more restlessly kinetic. Richter made his earlier record with Ančerl and the Czech Philharmonic before the Soviet government let him concertize in the West (Supraphon). It's a solid and often exciting account, with an orchestra that matches the pianist's naked tone, but overall it isn't very memorable. The coupling, Prokofiev's Concerto 1, is in even more rudimentary sound. Richter's 1961 studio recording with the Vienna Symphony bears traces of disagreement between him and Karajan; the pianist later said the conductor did "unforgivable things" in the rehearsals, and some of the unusual touches have a blank obviousness that gives the impression the soloist is cooperating only under duress (DG). The pianism remains stunning, and the sound comes up amazingly transparent and dynamic in the remastering (though the piano can get a bit metallic).

Karajan went on to make a more imposing recording with **Lazar Berman,** who (or so one imagines) fell more readily in line with the conductor's conception; everything comes together here, the pianist's Rachmaninoffian weight of sound perfectly matched with Karajan's intensely rousing and sonorous account of the orchestral part (♦DG 429166, with Ferras's Violin Concerto; see below). Structural pinions are sunk deep in the musical bedrock, yet each musician also offers very beautiful detailing of the quieter, more lyrical effusions. There is nothing cheap or circusy to this Germanic, very symphonic conception, and I'd rank this recording among the top three or four ever made. (It's also probably the finest example of Karajan's accompaniments on records.) Typically, Karajan makes sure all the music has plenty of time and room to breathe—some find him self-consciously slow—and there's more transparency and ambience than usual with his Philharmonie productions.

Concerto 1 was ideally suited to **Gilels**'s temperament, and three of his recordings are widely available. The first is his performance with Reiner and the Chicago Symphony, which is rather disappointing (RCA): The piano tone is wooden, tensions are sporadically held, some mono re-edits of cadenza passages were obviously pasted in, and there isn't the same kind of soloist/conductor chemistry as in his 1972 recording. That performance with Maazel and the Philharmonia has more tension and more charm, and comes as a "two-fer" with Gilels's accounts of Nos. 2 and 3 in the abridged Siloti editions (♦EMI 68638). His No. 1 with Maazel has tremendous panache and rhythmic tension with no cheap effects, and the listener can only be helplessly swept up by their music-making. Conductor and pianist, equally known for their severe but often volatile perfectionism, are perfectly matched. EMI's recording has a hard edge, quite easily tamed with the treble control, but it gives a good account of Tchaikovsky's wind writing and Gilels's high-strung but weighty sound.

That performance is consistent with Gilels's taut 1980 concert recording with Mehta in New York (CBS/Sony, with Oistrakh's Violin Concerto). Mehta is rather freer than Maazel, less acute in his rhythm and characterization, and overall the rendition isn't quite as pinpoint-sharp from moment to moment as the EMI. And then there are the applause and occasional coughs to deal with, especially in the slow movement—the mikes are well back, which gives a natural account of the players and hall but lets in quite a bit of audience noise.

Though the engineering is resonant and imposing for **Gutierrez** and Zinman's Baltimore Symphony, their performance is a disappointment (Telarc). This is a commonplace interpretation, without a single splash of originality. Both the pianistic and orchestral contributions lack tension, and the orchestra is second-string. Another Telarc release has the more imposing and consistent Atlanta Symphony, with **Watts** offering a more detailed account of the solo part, though he's further back in the mix. Still, despite an exciting finale, the performance somehow amounts to less than the sum of its parts—partly a matter of the pianist's insufficient dynamic variation. **Jon Kimura Parker** is more sensitive and compliant and enjoys a more sympathetic accompaniment from Previn and the Royal Philharmonic (Telarc). As a whole, though, this dependable performance boasts no particular distinction or memorable moments.

Werner Haas is handicapped by an efficient but tonally (and intonationally) meager contribution by the Monte Carlo Opera Orchestra under Inbal (Philips). He tends toward a kind of unvariegated heaviness. **Andrej Hotéev** has been berated for slow tempos and a less-than-penetrating keyboard attack (Koch-Schwann). It's surely wrong to impute to inadequate technique his taking the double-octave passages and cadential explosions fairly slowly, for he sounds quite secure at the speeds chosen. But hopes really dim at the first-movement cadenza, where the piano takes up the furious double octaves from the orchestra, since at this point his lack of incisive keyboard attack really shows. Fedoseyev's orchestra is distinctly tepid before this tradeoff, and when the pianist comes in you realize it's because he'd have trouble matching the players at a fuller volume. The insecure cello solo in the slow movement is just one disappointment among many.

By contrast, **Ousset** has sonority and fluid technique to challenge anyone, and Masur gets a full-throated, attentive, near-ideal response from a luminous London Philharmonic, beautifully recorded (♦EMI 54157, with Schumann's concerto). Some listeners might want more fire and brimstone, but this partnership has points of telling sensitivity, and also a particularly good grasp of Tchaikovsky's phraseology—the linear aspect of the music that goes beyond the bar lines. Ousset also observes some revealing details of the score, especially points of articulation, that just about everyone else glosses over. This is fresh and unrushed musicality that somehow allows more of the grand statement than most renditions.

A contrasting approach comes from **Gavrilov,** who is in the Richter/Neuhaus lineage and thus, rather than offering Horowitzian arrays of splintered color, sports an about-to-go-off-the-rails kind of intensity. He first recorded No. 1 immediately after his Tchaikovsky Competition victory in 1978 (Melodiya/CBS, an intensely exciting reading yet to appear on CD). His second, similarly exciting performance with Muti had much of the same intensity (EMI 64329). Especially after his fiery earlier accounts, his third recording, with Ashkenazy and the Berlin Philharmonic, is a disappointment: It's painfully perfunctory until the beginning of the finale, where some of the old Gavrilov fire burns through for a few moments, and even the recording sounds filtered of its highs and lows (EMI, with Dumay's Violin Concerto).

A similarly superficial account comes from Greek prodigy **Dimitris Sgouros,** who made his recording while in his teens (EMI). Sgouros's tone is shallow; surely this work needs a grown person's musculature? And at the manic double octaves in I, he essays what has to be some of the most mechanical pianism on record. Like Gavrilov, **Ashkenazy** was a Tchaikovsky Competition medal winner, and it's rumored that he didn't return to this work because the Soviet regime forced it down his throat for the contest. He recorded it in 1963 with Maazel and the London Symphony, and it's a very fine reading (Decca/London). There's a freshness to his early performances that dissipated by the late '70s, and this is a reading in the mainstream tradition that still represents a spontaneous voyage of discovery. The orchestral contribution is taut and exciting, and only the pianist's rounded sound and relative lack of tonal weight might disappoint some listeners.

Ogdon was co-winner with Ashkenazy in 1962, and his recording with Barbirolli is marked by amazing keyboard facility and brilliance but also a certain anonymity and joylessness (EMI, reissued by Dutton). The conductor does ensure that the orchestral part is always shapely and alive. **Ohlsson** has Marriner and the St. Martin Academy (Hänssler), and that means there is a chamber-music kind of intimacy between soloist and orchestra (and orchestral soloists). This automatically makes this reading preferable to half the others listed here, where it can sound like pianist and conductor hadn't even met until they arrived at the studio. The engineering is outstandingly full and warm. But neither Marriner nor Ohlsson is a particularly individual artist, nor are they noted partisans of late Romanticism. Each of their movements are confident and well shaped, but each also tends to be insubstantial when it comes to formal argument; the finale, for one, sounds less like a capstone in symphonic style than it does a light-hearted caprice.

Far better to turn to a super-bargain alternative: **Glemser** has the wonderful Wit and his fine Polish Radio Orchestra, and dispatches the solo part with plenty of fire, weight, and also piquancy and lightness where required (♦Naxos 550819). The reading isn't the most original, and the *Andantino* is perhaps a shade wanting in intimacy. All told, however, this is one of the better recordings, regardless of price, and the sound is just fine. **Joseph Banowetz** and conductor Ondrej Lenárd are admirable but don't have the temperament of Glemser and Wit, and Banowetz's sound isn't as full as Glemser's (Naxos). **Ponti** has more character, but Kapp's Prague Symphony can't match Wit's Polish Radio group for Glemser, and pianist and conductor aren't as sensitive to the lyrical moments as they are to the more virtuoso passages (Vox). This is an exciting but unnuanced reading, not helped by a busy and big-boned sound picture.

Dichter offers a better interpretation of this kind; he has the Boston Symphony in its prime and a rather blank if often exciting partner in Leinsdorf (RCA, with Perlman's first and better recording of the Violin Concerto). Dichter's account is thrilling, with just as much temperament as Ponti and greater lyrical sensitivity; if the conductor were a bit more responsive and if RCA hadn't included static in the right channel (consistently audible in the mid-priced reissue, especially in the slow movement), this would be recommended. The young **Alexei Sultanov** made his recording shortly after winning the Van Cliburn Competition (Teldec). It's a technically assured performance, but dull musically. There's no originality or personality in evidence, no vision of the work we are asked to share, and the longer line takes a back seat to bar-to-bar detail.

Barry Douglas and Slatkin are prosaic; the pianist offers very few interpretive details or nuances compared with his later recordings of Nos. 2 and 3, and conductor and orchestra debilitate the outer movements with sludgy rhythms and soft attacks (RCA). The recording is not well focused, and is generally uninviting. **Feltsman** is cool, civilized, and unremarkable, which is surprising considering Rostropovich is the conductor (Sony, with 3). The National Symphony sounds very well in Sony's expert engineering. **Postnikova** and Rozhdestvensky are powerful enough in characterization and shape the concerto with a sure hand, but the tempos tend to be slow and the structural tension is fairly lax throughout (Decca/London). The sound is rich and bold, and if Postnikova is uniformly heavy-handed, Rozhdestvensky is, as always, an insightful and convincing Tchaikovsky conductor.

If an off-the-beaten-path view is wanted, **Pogorelich** is the one to hear (♦DG 415122). This is an intensely original reading of a fairly ambiguously notated warhorse that's been heard so often we can only wonder if musicians have been listening to each other for 125 years more than they have listened to and scrutinized the score. While some will be startled by Pogorelich's reading, I find it intensely convincing. Immensely to its credit, it's not a show-off performance; he could undoubtedly play the double octaves and cadential passages twice as fast as just about anyone else, but more often than not he takes a measured approach to such moments. Most notably, he takes unprecedentedly slow tempos in the cadenzas. Many have thrown up their hands at this, but look at the score and you'll see that the composer consistently marks these passages "ad libitum," "molto espressivo," "a tempo rubato," and so on. More important, Pogorelich's divergence from tradition at such moments illuminates passages that are often raced through so fast the listener can hardly hear them. In that respect, he de-virtuosizes this music. In the finale, which is entirely up to tempo, he pays scrupulous attention to the interweaving of piano and orchestra, and the result truly sounds as if everyone involved is actually listening to everyone else. Abbado and the London Symphony enter entirely into the conception.

An unusual, de-virtuosized performance of a different kind came from **Arrau** and Colin Davis (Philips). First, there is Arrau's tone, which will disappoint some: dark and bottomless, a far cry from the brittle and exciting sound produced by so many other pianists. Articulation is uniformly smooth, with nothing punched (or, heaven forbid, pounded) out. Like Pogorelich, he's willing when necessary to retreat into the orchestral sonority. The tempos are never rushed (an aging Arrau misses the occasional note here and there) and pianist and conductor spend much of their time illuminating details of phrasing and harmony. In much of the slower and chromatic music, the first-movement cadenza, or parts of the slow movement, Arrau is fascinating and confers a new dignity on the music. Still, this isn't one of his better recordings.

Kissin's reading provides a footnote to Pogorelich's fascinating recording (DG). Rumor has it that Karajan was originally scheduled to be Pogorelich's accompanist but bolted as soon as he heard of the pianist's ideas for the piece. Some four years later, he taped the concerto with the young Kissin, and was presumably responsible for a depressingly enervated and poorly controlled rendition that serves the reputation of neither pianist nor conductor. For listeners who fancy a score-based attempt at authenticity and stripping away bad traditions, **Lowenthal** startles right off by rolling the big piano chords, which is indeed how the composer marked them (Arabesque). This forces the orchestra to go lightly in this grand passage, which is probably one reason why the chords have come to be de-rolled. But such urtextual revelations are few and far between, and Lowenthal and Commissiona are neither thrilling nor distinctive in any of the three movements. They sound a good deal more at home in the coupling: the rather trivial Concert Fantasy Op. 56, which is far, far rarer on records.

To end this listing, I will mention an outstanding performance that manages to electrify in the conventional fast-loud-virtuoso sense as well as impress the listener that the players have thought the score through in their own terms: **Pletnev** renders Tchaikovsky's octaves with spine-tingling thunder, just as Fedoseyev does with the orchestra (♦Virgin 61465, a "two-fer" with Pletnev's less desirable 2 and 3). No detail escapes his attention. His finale has a unique, slightly mad capriciousness, on occasion coming close to barroom banality, and thereby harkening back to Nikolai Rubinstein's complaints when the composer first showed him the music.

2. The major issue with 2 is the cuts made by Tchaikovsky for a performance he conducted in 1888 and the far more extensive excisions proposed by pianist Alexander Siloti and commonly restored in performances and recordings only in the past 20 years. The composer's own 24-bar cut in the first movement (not long after the second big cadenza) shortens a sequential and thematically repetitious passage, and is if anything an improvement. In II, Tchaikovsky condoned only two fairly small cuts toward the end, while the Siloti edition adds in two other, more substantial deletions that aim to lessen the double-concerto character of the movement by pruning back the violin and cello solos. Under Siloti, the movement becomes a lot shorter and the piano also becomes the first soloist to enter, by playing a version of Tchaikovsky's starting violin solo.

If you refuse to accept these cuts—and we live in a time when all original texts have become sacrosanct—you'll miss out on what are well and away the two most memorable recordings. In **Gilels**'s rendition with Maazel, they take all the cuts (♦EMI 68638, with 2 and 3 in slightly harsh remasterings). But this partnership brings irreplaceable, blazing intensity to this neglected work, and the tension—which they maintain from first bar to last—is enough to make this structurally flawed piece fly by as if conceived and played in a single breath. Specifically, they miraculously prevent the impression created by lesser performances that the piece is constantly arriving and re-arriving at B sections and codas.

Cherkassky and the Berlin Philharmonic under Richard Kraus also give 2 the Siloti treatment (♦DG 457751, with 1). Even in the pretty distant 1951 mono sound, the Berlin orchestra's tonal splendors in its Furtwängler period come through loud and clear. Indeed, from a purely orchestral standpoint this could well be the most splendid recorded version of 2, though the first violin seems to be having an off day in intonation in the slow movement. Though more quixotic and unpredictable than Gilels in his detailing, Cherkassky has an unmistakable grip on this music. Indeed, it's probably the soloist's impishness that gives the reading so much energy and character, especially in the white-hot finale.

Another fine account of Siloti's heavily pruned edition is **Gary Graffman**'s with Ormandy (♦CBS/Sony 46460). This is less impulsive music-making than Gilels/Maazel; Graffman and Ormandy know just where and when to pull back so the heavily rhetorical I doesn't become empty and overbearing. This is multi-miked—though done well enough—so don't expect a natural concert-hall account. But what makes this in some ways more distinctive than Glemser/Wit is Ormandy's perfect pacing and impeccable tailoring of the orchestral part to his soloist. Also listen to the beautiful shape he lends to the doleful opening phrase of the slow movement.

None of these partnerships overstate the piece, the failing of **Dono-**

hoe's account with Barshai, which uses the complete text (EMI). They make the mistake of pushing I along too fast (Tchaikovsky's marking is "*Allegro brillante*," but brilliance doesn't necessarily involve speed), which instead of helping it cohere only makes it more episodic. The Bournemouth Symphony sounds second-rate, and EMI's sound gives a dry, bright, and slightly ragged edge to tuttis. The violin and cello solos in the slow movement are taken by bona fide soloists (Kennedy and Steven Isserlis), but they become star turns that make everything stop. A better account of this kind of bluff, fairly hard-hitting approach comes from **Magaloff** and Colin Davis, who also play the score complete (Philips). Magaloff is fleet and has a big sonority, but avoids banging. Likewise, Davis and the London Symphony are emphatic without battering any of the tuttis, and their pacing is very nice.

Werner Haas and Inbal play the complete text and are certainly enjoyable, but the Monte Carlo orchestra's contribution is only a bit more distinguished than in their No. 1 (Philips). At least the musicians don't take the piece as seriously as Donohoe/Barshai, and Barshai could take some lessons from Inbal on scaling back the orchestral backdrop when necessary. The recording is smooth and refined, the soloist up in front. But it's hard to understand why Philips reissued this when the Arrau is better and Magaloff more interesting. Like Donohoe, **Ponti** and Kapp rush and fragment I, and they also open up all the cuts. If anything, they're more wooden and poorly recorded than Donohoe/Barshai, the Prague Symphony sounding rattier than the Bournemouth.

Postnikova and Rozhdestvensky take the opposite tack, essaying the opening tempo of I so slowly that any symphonic pretensions are immediately thrown out the window for an incidental conception that could be called balletic if it weren't so heavy (Decca/London). The impression of fragmentation is underlined by their attention to detail, which is quite remarkable, though always tasteful; although the overall structure is lax in their hands, every detail finds its place. With sound that's sonorous almost to the point of heaviness, this is very enjoyable if you don't resist their deliberate and regal interpretation; they also play the complete score. The players couldn't be better attuned to each other; it's worth hearing.

An instructive comparison comes from **Andrei Hotéev,** whose tempos are also slow but without Postnikova/Rozhdestvensky's sharp rhythms or compensating interest in fine points (Koch-Schwann). Even more than in No. 1, Fedoseyev's pickup orchestra sounds distinctly second-rate. The notes claim this is an authentic rendition, but this isn't the first such account, and who will care about such matters when the disc isn't likely to be taken down from the shelf? **Lowenthal** also opens up all the cuts, but his account suffers from slightly muffled sound, the pianist doesn't have a lot of personality, and the London Symphony sounds a bit under par under Comissiona (Arabesque). As with most recordings, though, the slow movement is quite beautifully done.

Pletnev (Virgin) doesn't luxuriate as much as Lowenthal in the first-movement lyrical music. He gives the whole piece a rather nervous energy without tapping into the wonderful grandeur that Gilels and Maazel bring out of I. Also, he and Fedoseyev tend to make light of the big moments, the structural junctures of the first two movements. Quite a bit of Pletnev's grunting can be heard. Though invigorating and engaging, this comes as a disappointment after his electrifying No. 1. He plays the complete text, except for observing the composer's 16-bar cut at the end of the slow movement. I prefer **Glemser,** though he and Wit lack the sweep of Gilels/Maazel and some of the tension and attention to detail of Pletnev/Fedoseyev and Postnikova/Rozhdestvensky (♦Naxos 550820). Much of my preference can also be attributed to the sound, which is warmer and has more presence than the Virgin. Here, too, the solos are extremely well done by orchestral players. This is a good first choice if Gilels's Siloti-fication offends and Postnikova is found to be too eccentric.

If something slightly more relaxed and easier on the ear is desired, try **Douglas** and Slatkin (♦RCA 61633). They play the complete text, and Slatkin and the Philharmonia's suave way with the orchestral part is hard to beat. This may not be immortal music-making in the Gilels/Maazel vein, but these musicians do well by not trying to squeeze a Grand Statement out of this music. Pianist and conductor also find details in the witty finale that elude most others, and the full and vibrant sound is a delight.

3. If No. 2 is neglected, 3 has had an even more checkered history. It originated in a symphony that Tchaikovsky began after his Fifth, but he soon became dissatisfied with it and put it aside; after the *Pathétique* was completed, he turned the abandoned music into an "Allegro de concert" and by the time he died had (whether because of continuing doubts or another reason) orchestrated only the first movement. Usually the only music heard in performances of "Piano Concerto No. 3" is that movement, but the other two are also available in score as orchestrated by Tchaikovsky's faithful pupil Taneyev. The only recordings to include all three movements (essentially Bogatyryev's "Symphony No.7" minus its scherzo) are from Ponti, Glemser, Haas, and Hotéev.

Fortunately, **Ponti**'s three-movement No. 3 is far and away the finest installment in his concerto set, and the cheap box is worth getting for this superb performance alone, though the rendition could be criticized for neglecting warmth and refinement for brilliance (♦Vox 5024). With its strange, music-being-pieced-together opening, 3 often starts off limp and doesn't improve much along the way. With Ponti and Froment, the tension is palpable and it holds.

Haas and Inbal are a bit more polished, easier on the ear, and less exciting than Ponti, and Haas's lively, plain-vanilla presentation is well suited to this rather shallow work (Philips). **Graffman** and Ormandy do less with No. 3 than they do with 2, and this performance sounds pretty weak when compared with Ponti, Gilels, and Douglas. **Postnikova** and Rozhdestvensky are by turns celebratory, tense, and tender in the one-movement version, but this impressive performance is paired with their No. 1, and not many listeners will warm to that (Decca/London). For a three-movement No. 3 on a single disc, **Glemser** is the choice; he brings his usual full-toned virtuosity and poise to the music, though there are also some suave sonorities and smoothed-over phrasing and rhythms that I'd gladly trade for Ponti's electricity (♦Naxos 550819, with his fine 1, at super-bargain price). The deep and transparent sound helps this music sound the best it ever has on disc, and for this and other reasons, the slow movement is more immediately attractive here than on Vox.

Hotéev is even more consistently slow and autumnal than in his Nos. 1 and 2, and again he does without the compensating detail of Postnikova/Rozhdestvensky (Koch-Schwann). His lukewarm, methodical trudge through the finale is particularly objectionable, though he almost rescues the performance with some passionate phrasing in I and II. By contrast, **Pletnev** and Fedoseyev are brusque and impatient in their one-movement rendition, and evince neither charm nor particular interest in the piece (Virgin). (It's a pity that Pletnev's electrifying 1 is only available now in a double with his 2 and 3; the record industry is going two-for-one crazy.)

Except for Gilels (with 1 and 2 on ♦EMI 68639, filled out with Richter's enigmatic Prokofiev 5 and Bartók 2), none of the one-movement 3s on a single disc surpass Ponti and Glemser in the three-movement version. **Gilels** and Maazel start off especially slowly, but their impeccable rhythmic control keeps the work in motion; they prove gripping in every bar, as always, the pianist's and conductor's characterizations equally acute. **Lowenthal** and Comissiona pair their one-movement 3 with 2, and the reservations expressed above about that also apply to their 3: Operating at a far lower level of tension than Gilels/Maazel, it's an unremarkable performance (Arabesque). You could say the same of **Feltsman,** though he sounds more caught up in this score than in the coupled 1; Rostropovich does give the orchestral part power and shape, and the engineering is fine (Sony). This is eminently respectable, but not equal to the others.

Gavrilov and Ashkenazy in Berlin sound more interested in the music, which they were probably playing for the first time (EMI). Both the pianism and orchestral playing are striking assets; it's more dazzling than the 1 from these artists. Too bad their one-movement No. 3 is saddled on disc with Sgouros's depressingly uneventful No. 1 as coupling for their No. 2 (♦RCA 61633). **Douglas** and Slatkin include 3 as coupling for their 2 (♦RCA 61633). It's very enjoyable, more so than this team's No. 1. **Douglas**'s workaday but artless pianism is suited to this pleasant but non-profound piece, and Slatkin shapes and details the accompaniment as few others have, bringing the music to a considerable climax. The rich, warm sound is a pleasure through and through. **Tozer** and Järvi pair their one-movement No. 3 with the Tchaikovsky/Bogatyryev "Symphony 7," giving the listener a chance to hear the music in its two different guises (Chandos). The concerto has plenty of drama, typically for Järvi, but turn to the Gilels/Maazel and you'll hear stronger rhythmic focus and more stringent orchestral control. It doesn't help that the London Philharmonic takes on a harsh glare in fortissimos, an unexpected flaw in a Chandos production.

Violin

Mention the Tchaikovsky Violin Concerto and half of the world's population will immediately think of **Heifetz**—something of an irony, since his renowned teacher, Leopold Auer, will go down in history as the violinist who rejected the piece when the composer offered it to him in 1878. Heifetz's 1937 Victor recording, with Barbirolli and the London Philharmonic, catches the virtuoso in his absolute prime, though it's interesting to note that he sounds as if he had to work harder with the first-movement passagework than adolescent virtuosos of today like Sarah Chang and Leila Josefowicz. But Heifetz's style is nonpareil here, perfectly suited to the music. The old canard that he was the first modern violinist holds true: With its rhythmic clarity, very moderate vibrato, and lack of shenanigans, the performance could have taken place yesterday. Especially in the *Canzonetta,* Heifetz's Slavic heritage comes to the fore with his subtle vibrato and perfectly placed slides. Barbirolli's orchestra can be surprisingly sloppy at times, but like the soloist they're perfectly attuned to the music's style. Avoid the EMI "Great Recordings of the Century" disc and search out the less shrill mastering in a set that also holds other classic Heifetz concerto recordings from the '30s; though obviously not hi-fi, the mono sound is perfectly listenable, with almost pristine surfaces (♦Pearl 9157, 2CD).

By the time Heifetz re-recorded the piece in 1957 with Reiner and the Chicago Symphony, much of the earlier spontaneity and excitement within confidence had evaporated (RCA). The tape is in stereo, and Reiner's orchestra is more on top of things than Barbirolli's, but the thrill is gone; it only reinforces the 1937 as one of the classic readings. A final note: In both earlier and later recordings, Heifetz used the Auer edition with the occasional small cut and jazzed-up solo passage (e.g., before the big tutti in I).

Mention the Tchaikovsky concerto to the other, non-Heifetzian half of music-loving humanity and they will rhapsodize over **David Oistrakh.** It's a tribute to his musicianship, and that of Ormandy and his Philadelphians, that there's so little to say about their extremely fine recording (♦Sony 46339, with Gilels's Piano Concerto 1 with Mehta). Nothing is obvious, and yet not a bar is dull. Rehearing the interaction of solo line and orchestral solos toward the middle of the *Canzonetta,* I'm struck anew at the incredible variety that infuses Oistrakh's work, and how Ormandy manages to stick to him like glue through all the subtle rubato and dynamic inflections. But then there's also the soul of the music-making in the quieter episodes of the finale. And so on. This is truly a performance to live with, and it's at bargain price.

That said, Oistrakh's 1954 rendition with Konwitschny and the Staatskapelle Dresden finds the violinist more outgoing and spontaneous, and given more presence by the microphones (♦DG 447427, 2CD, with Brahms and Bach concertos). It's hard to remember Oistrakh ever being more exciting on records. I find this version even more captivating than the Ormandy, especially as the Dresden sound (which is mono but could just as well be stereo, for all I can tell) is less hissy and more vibrant. The couplings might make the DG set more clumsy as an acquisition, but the more of Oistrakh's artistry you have around the house, the better.

Menuhin was not usually associated with the Tchaikovsky, but it was one of the first concertos he learned as a child. His 1959 EMI recording with Boult has drifted out of the catalog, but as a memorial DG has reissued a fine-sounding 1949 recording with Fricsay and the Berlin Radio Symphony. Menuhin was one of the first Jewish musicians to concertize in postwar Germany, and many Germans (Anne-Sophie Mutter among them) revere him for this reason, just as some Jews never forgave him. Perhaps his humanitarian mission is one reason for the dignity and communicativeness of this great performance. The first and last movements are cut, the finale severely, and the violinist's intonation is fallible and his tone often wiry, but none of this matters, especially given Fricsay's unrushed poetry and authority in shaping the orchestral contribution. Not a first choice, then, but a performance to hear. DG fills out the disc with three of Menuhin and Kempff's 1970 Beethoven sonata recordings. The same performance also comes on a Urania disc, more suitably coupled with Fricsay's Symphony 5, but there the mastering is inferior, with volume changes, more distortion, and some artificial reverb.

For a similarly aristocratic approach in modern sound, **Joshua Bell** is highly recommended (♦London/Decca 421716). He lacks nothing in passion or technical address, and yet the concerto doesn't become the usual Hollywoodish vehicle; there's no mooning in the *Canzonetta* and little schmaltz in the finale. The sound is beautifully transparent, as is appropriate to the honesty of the music-making, with a nice ambient wash. In Ashkenazy's hands, the Cleveland Orchestra is lucidity incarnate. **Shaham** aspires to a similar non-Heifetzian authority, but he's closer to the microphone, Sinopoli isn't much of an inspiration, and some of Shaham's detailing sounds a bit insecure after you hear Bell (DG).

Mullova is a bit more demonstrative than Bell, yet her interpretation somehow emerges as having less personality (Philips). She's a soloist of true stature, more than equal to every musical and technical hurdle in the music. What sets this record apart, in addition to the very fine sound, is Ozawa, who supplies a consummate example of the accompanist's art. He's right there when he needs to be and out of the way when

that's necessary. He also sounds more caught up in things, with plenty of rhythmic tension, than he sometimes has in the past. If only there were a dash more character to the proceedings, especially in the finale, where Mullova doesn't compare with Kremer (see below).

The only other violinist to offer the same kind of purity and authority is **Midori,** who teamed up with Abbado (Sony, with a fine Shostakovich Concerto 1). She justifies her superstar status here. This reading displays her supremely confident bowing, but the reading almost sounds valedictory with its spacious tempos, frequent slowdowns, and many spontaneous, fleeting *subito pianos.* The performance tends to droop on occasion, and I suspect she'd do it with more integrity in the studio; Bell has more poise and grace, and his London/Decca sound is more inviting than Sony's in-concert job, where applause is included.

Leila Josefowicz is another young and most impressive artist, more assertive and risk-taking than Bell, Midori, or Shaham (Philips). But each moment in her performance somehow becomes the same as any other; the end of the first-movement cadenza and re-entry of the orchestra, for example, shouldn't sound so much like a glib afterthought. And Marriner presents few ideas of his own to challenge the soloist. Menuhin declared an adolescent **Sarah Chang** the perfect violinist, and her concerto is indeed a more soulful and memorable interpretation than Josefowicz's or Shaham's (EMI). Colin Davis no doubt helped her give the score direction and shape. This impressive performance only misses out a bit in lightness and chamber-music translucency, especially in the orchestral contribution and in any real chemistry between soloist and conductor. The finale would have been more fun and invigorating if there had been some sparks struck between the violinist and the man on the podium.

Milstein and Abbado give some idea of what's missing: They're impressive for their teamwork, the seamless dovetailing of their sound and ideas (DG). The Vienna Philharmonic also has a touching and tender thoughtfulness after the cadenza in I. But the actual emotional outlay from both parties is strangely minimal, especially in I. On all counts, even sound (though there's some faint static in the left channel), I prefer Milstein's 1958 version with Steinberg and the Pittsburgh Symphony; soloist and conductor are more consistently engaged, though Milstein's innate aristocracy is naturally in force and the violin and orchestra are more faithfully and warmly rendered (♦EMI/Seraphim 69035, with his even finer Brahms concerto under Fistoulari, or ♦EMI/Seraphim 67101, with Steinberg's Brahms Symphony 1). I don't prefer Milstein/Steinberg to Bell, Kremer, or Oistrakh/Ormandy, but it ranks very high among the super-budget versions.

Abbado returned to this concerto with **Vengerov** as soloist, and performance and engineering are much richer than in either the Milstein or Midori renditions (♦Teldec 90881). Vengerov is one of the most demonstrative, stylish, and engaging soloists the work has had in recent decades. He stops just short of indulgence; in that respect, it helps that the production is rich but not fruity in sound, and the soloist-orchestral balance is tasteful.

Perlman has recorded the concerto three times. In his reading with Ormandy, he's a bit "straighter" than Vengerov within the same kind of romantic approach, with less terracing of dynamics and less obvious affection in phrasing (EMI). Many will like this ultra-smooth approach, with no corners cut or taken at high speed, but I find his playing rather wooden. Like Perlman, Ormandy and the Philadelphians are not as immediately attentive to bar-to-bar details as Abbado and the Berliners. Perlman's 1990 Leningrad recording with Mehta and the Israel Philharmonic is a little more personal and directly involved with the music, but their approach is so smooth and comfy as to be inconsequential (EMI). Perlman's fabled cleanness isn't always up to its reputation here, with little slides and approximations. I far prefer Kremer's more wiry energy, or—if you want something in Perlman's general style—Stern is more caught up in the music in his version with Rostropovich. The best of Perlman's three recordings is his first, where the soloist isn't favored so much in the balance and Leinsdorf and the Boston Symphony are less heavy and portentous (if not particularly imaginative) than either Ormandy or Mehta (RCA).

Stern made four recordings, in 1949 with Alexander Hilsberg and the Philadelphia Orchestra, in 1958 with Ormandy and the Phillies, in 1973 with Bernstein and the NY Philharmonic, and in 1978 with Rostropovich and the National Symphony. The Ormandy has more than the standard small cuts in orchestral passages, and in terms of intonation, Stern has sounded more secure elsewhere. Still, this is a noble reading, he and Ormandy effect what is surely the perfect soloist-accompanist relationship, and the sound is very nice if a bit echoey (Sony). The Hilsberg rendition doesn't benefit from the same seamless partnership, and the violinist is even less secure (in Sony's "Early Concerto Recordings" box). He does make a more soulful sound in the slow movement, though, with more vibrato. In the performance with Bernstein, the conductor tends to hold up I with some slow and bloated tuttis. The critic Hanslick took famous exception to the vulgarity of Tchaikovsky's finale, and here Stern and Bernstein (with their lunging at notes) are perhaps more at home. Their *Canzonetta* is more appealing, though it too is heavy and overwrought and sounds like Wagner.

My favorite Stern rendition is the last, with Rostropovich; it's the most original of his readings, fairly slow and everywhere suffused with wistful melancholy, even in the finale (♦Sony 64127). Rostropovich and his fine orchestra pull the score together into a gripping whole despite the slow speeds. This is emphatically not one to hear if you're after fireworks and effortless virtuosity, and Stern's technical grip in the finale is only iffy by early 21st-century standards, but his soulful sound ennobles just about every passage, and for that reason and others the slow movement is particularly moving.

Kremer has the most exciting and muscular accompaniment imaginable from Maazel and the Berlin Philharmonic, and the soloist is also a remarkably dynamic presence, immediately identifiable as a musical personality (♦DG 400027). This is a non-romantic, unconventional reading in the best sense; the exuberant edge to Kremer's tone lends the perfect spark, and his bow strokes can also be light as air when necessary. The spunky finale is a particular thrill, a real joy. DG taped these players in the problematic Philharmonie in 1980, but even 20 years later the sound is still outstanding. In 1987 Maazel returned to the work with soloist **Frank Peter Zimmermann** and again the Berlin Philharmonic (EMI). It's very enjoyable, and indeed finer than many other readings, but the performance still falls short of real distinction. It's tempting to impute the greater electricity of Kremer's reading to a near-clash of personalities, whereas in the Zimmermann disc things seem more comfortable between soloist and conductor.

A reading in the Kremer vein comes from **Erik Friedman** and Ozawa, who are just as exciting and exuberant even if they don't get below the skin of the music quite as much as Kremer or have the same wistfulness in the slow movement (RCA, with John Browning's piano concerto). Some of Friedman's passagework can also sound mechanical, but at budget price this is certainly worth hearing. It would be hard to imagine a bigger contrast to Kremer than **Grumiaux,** who leaves you with memories of the music's subtleties (Philips). Though the recording doesn't

have much dynamic range, he sometimes seems to play more quietly than anyone else on record. Still, the Philharmonia is a fairly heavy and cumbersome presence under Jan Krenz, and the transitional passages tend to be aimless. Grumiaux sounds too much a classicist—stylistically unassertive in a way that runs against the music—in all movements except the *Canzonetta,* which is lovely.

There's much more of interest in **Szeryng**'s account with Munch and the Boston Symphony, and also a more audible cooperation between soloist and conductor (RCA). The music-making is nice and decisive, but the recording gives the violinist a nasal and emaciated sound. At the same time, the narrow dynamic range tends to inhibit any real pianissimos. This would be a rendition of some stature if a future remastering were to solve these sonic problems, especially as Munch's impulsiveness-without-heaviness is perfect for this music. Szeryng has a better tonal profile, but also a touch more anonymity, in his less symbiotic relationship with Haitink and the Concertgebouw (Philips). It's a rare Szeryng performance that doesn't give real pleasure, and this rendition has an affectingly chaste eloquence. To sweeten the pot, this "twofer" ("The Best of Tchaikovsky") also contains Stokowski's uniquely stylish *Serenade* and his rather less memorable *Capriccio Italien.*

Mutter made her recording with Karajan and the Vienna Philharmonic only several years before her mentor's death, and the orchestral side of the performance has its longueurs, with tired-sounding tuttis dragging against the basic tempo (DG). The soloist has an almost exaggerated vibrancy in the outer movements, as if by way of compensation, and the mikes are close to her. Without any filler, the disc is extremely short. Still, Mutter and Karajan should be heard for the most hauntingly nostalgic *Canzonetta* on records, with a whispered inwardness that often sounds otherworldly.

Karajan recorded the concerto once before, though French-born, **Christian Ferras** gave one of the more Slavic-sounding performances, to the point of sounding affected or even grotesque on occasion, as at the start of the finale (DG). Karajan's accompaniment is one of the most exciting ever recorded—dynamic, yet superbly shaped and controlled. This recording is worth hearing, but leaves one pondering the possibilities if Karajan had gone into the studio with Mutter when he still had this much energy. (The cheap DG disc with Ferras is worth getting for the coupling alone, Karajan's majestic and passionate rendition of Piano Concerto 1 with Lazar Berman; see above.)

Kennedy and Okku Kamu work very hard, but the music tends to sound empty when it is host to so little interpretive charm or virtuosity (EMI). The interpretation falls between two stools, but the sound is excellent, and the coupled Sibelius concerto with Simon Rattle and the Birmingham orchestra is much more memorable. **Dumay** is both more technically assured and more personable; next to Kennedy, he even sounds rhapsodic (EMI). But he also lacks charm, and he doesn't have the bright and centered tone or ear-catching variety of bow weight of Kremer. Tchakarov and the London Symphony are a shade directionless in the purely orchestral passages, except in the *Canzonetta.* **Chung** has some of Perlman's sweetness and suavity in her second recording with Dutoit, but also more personality (♦Decca/London 410011). Her intonation isn't as straight down the middle as Bell's or Vengerov's, but this recording has beautifully resonant sound and genuine interaction between soloist, conductor, and orchestra; this is a fine choice. (The coupled Mendelssohn concerto is just as good, but Decca earns a gripe for running the Tchaikovsky's II and III together into only one track.)

Zukerman recorded the piece as a young man with Dorati and the London Symphony; the performance is refreshingly vibrant, if also uneven (CBS Odyssey, with Freire's Piano Concerto 1). Zukerman is everywhere admirable, his playing beautiful in every bar, but the sound has hints of distortion and the conductor's commitment flags; the sequential wind-up leading into the first-movement cadenza is heavy and unnuanced. I wonder if conductor and soloist had much time to work together. **Takako Nishizaki** gives a strong, eager, and honest reading, with Kenneth Jean and a vibrant if slightly glassily recorded Slovak Philharmonic (Naxos). She doesn't offer the variety of some others, which isn't a bad thing when you compare her with Midori's more self-conscious music-making. This is an honorable go at the score, but for a few bucks more you can have Oistrakh's peerless account with Ormandy.

Mariko Honda is a vibrant soloist and has more variety in her tone, but is saddled with Keith Clark's rather literal account of the orchestral part; something auspicious might have come of pairing her with Nishizaki's Kenneth Jean (Naxos). Of the super-budget versions, in addition to Milstein's EMI/Seraphim disc, the obvious choice is **Aaron Rosand,** who is assured, personal, engaged, and always interesting (♦Vox 8207). There's nothing trendy or circusy to this interpretation, just poetry, rousing musicality, and many years of this outstanding player's experience with the score. Froment conducts the Radio Luxembourg Orchestra, which the engineers give a bit of a ragged edge in the loudest passages, but the balances are good, and this is easy to recommend; just sample the effortless, flowing poetry of the finale. Rosand's coupling, the Mendelssohn concerto, is just as fine—indeed, the engineering is a bit better there.

Variations on a Rococo Theme

Rose and Ormandy hit the stylistic bull's-eye with their *Rococo Variations* for cello and orchestra (♦CBS/Sony 46453). They're charming, vibrant, spirited, and elegant, Classical and Romantic at the same time. Rose plays with a long bow and phrases with wonderful confidence (though, to be over-critical, his tone does thin out when he gets high up). Ormandy and the Philadelphia are equal partners, leading the argument when they need to and accompanying when that's their role. The sound is a bit glassy, but that's easy to correct with a treble reduction.

Maisky and the Orpheus Chamber Orchestra have clearly worked up their recording as a listening-to-each-other chamber music effort (DG). But the orchestral passages without solo leadership tend to be pedantic and shapeless, and when playing alongside Maisky they're too deferential, too wallpaperish. The disc also includes arrangements of *Andante Cantabile* and Lensky's aria from *Eugene Onegin;* only Maisky, who has the vibrancy and personality of a great singer, could bring these off so wonderfully. Then the Orpheus are back to their pedantic selves for a non-thrilling, Maisky-less *Souvenir de Florence* in the string orchestra version. Maisky has also recorded *Rococo Variations* with Sinopoli and the Philharmonia (DG). This lacks the crispness heard in his account with Orpheus, though there's definitely more personality with a conductor in tow. The coupling is the Elgar Concerto, an interpretation that is both powerful and willful.

Though **Isserlis** doesn't quite have Maisky's personality, I prefer his recording with the Chamber Orchestra of Europe under Gardiner (Virgin). Gardiner commits the orchestra to a much more obvious presence, though he isn't one for much tenderness and delicacy or for memorable phrasing. Also on this Russian recital disc are Tchaikovsky's *Nocturne, Andante Cantabile,* and *Pezzo capriccioso,* as well as some Glazunov, Rimsky-Korsakov, and others. **Ofra Harnoy** has the authority of Mackerras leading the London Philharmonic (RCA, with a delectable set of

Tchaikovsky arrangements for cello and orchestra). But I'm tempted to attribute any stylishness to the conductor; the cellist's phrasing tends to be pedantic, and the close mikes make her tone sound wooden.

A justly famous account came from **Rostropovich** and Karajan (♦DG 447413, with the Dvořák Concerto). You only have to see the photos from these sessions to recognize the affection and respect the cellist and conductor had for each other, and this is audible in the music-making. They come together entirely in interpretation and support each other infallibly. The cellist's tone is ever-reaching but dusky in color and never the least bit shrill, his intonation is perfect, and the phrasing just as subtly flexible as Karajan's. They don't overstate the music or overdramatize it—these are recognizably Rococo variations, lush but in an elegant way. Rostropovich's 1985 remake with Ozawa and the Boston Symphony (Erato) is a good deal cooler, even bland, the exchanges between soloist and orchestra less charged with tension. It sounds like he is leading Ozawa and the orchestra more often than the other way around. His earlier rendition is graced by Rozhdestvensky's firmer sense of direction, but the Soviet recording—hardly lush—makes it very much a second choice to the performance with Karajan (Melodiya).

Ma and Maazel are both alive to every fleeting whim and moment in the music (Sony). Each phrase is beautifully shaped and the hyperactivity (and hyper-expressiveness) brings this score close to the garish world of the Violin Concerto's finale (where, in Hanslick's infamous words, the violin was "beaten back and blue"). This is an entertaining and invigorating conception, though Ma isn't as memorable as I had expected in the slow, more poetic variations. **Maria Kliegel** and Gerhard Markson with the National Symphony of Ireland breeze through the theme, and also do no dilly-dallying in the rest of the score (Naxos). Kliegel has real personality as a soloist, but her tone is rather nasal, and to my ears her vibrato often has her playing flat. Markson's orchestra is good but not up to others. Naxos should have given the work more than one track.

A Norwegian account comes from **Truls Mørk** and the Oslo Philharmonic, with Jansons conducting (Virgin). Mørk is superior at sustaining a long, high melodic line. This is a very clean, bright-hued, and beautifully proportioned performance that classicizes the music without giving it the compensating rhythmic drive that should also mark such a reading. Virgin has done a very fine job recording the orchestra, making them less echoey than Chandos does in their symphony series.

All of the accounts discussed thus far give us the *Rococo Variations* as they were ordered (and even cut) by the first soloist, cellist Wilhelm Fitzenhagen. **Raphael Wallfisch** was the first to record the composer's own original (1876) version, with Geoffrey Simon leading the English Chamber Orchestra (♦Chandos 8347). Scholars can debate the merits of the two versions, but it's great to enjoy Variation 8 (which Fitzenhagen cut altogether) and also to hear the piece end with the variations that Tchaikovsky planned as the finale. (Fitzenhagen moved the third and fourth to the end, transplanted the cadenza, made various smaller changes, and also added gratuitous repeat signs to the theme itself.) Wallfisch's performance is modest, with little of the suave phrasing, vibrancy of tone, and bowing fireworks heard from some of the superstar soloists, but it's eloquent in its own small-scaled and intimate way. The sound is warm, and the fairly short disc also contains some of Tchaikovsky's own transcriptions for cello and orchestra, as well as *Pezzo Capriccioso* Op.62.

Andrew Lloyd Webber and Maxim Shostakovich also revert to the composer's original 1876 version rather than the published score (Philips). They are rather prosaic and don't sound like they're having much fun, and the cellist isn't as much a joy to listen to as Rostropovich or Maisky. Perhaps cellist and conductor were influenced by the dark (but very rewarding) Miaskovsky concerto and Shostakovich ballet excerpt also on the disc. But Lloyd Webber is grander and more confident in style than Wallfisch, and this sounds as though you'd dropped in on a concert performance. The sound is pretty spectacular, easily the best this score has yet enjoyed.

CHAMBER MUSIC

Piano Trio in A minor. Written in memory of pianist and conductor Nikolai Rubinstein, it has a piano part as powerful as those in his concertos, and so the work has often been destroyed by a keyboard virtuoso doing a star turn and drowning out his or her partners, and also by recording engineers not taking care to balance the piano against the violin and cello. The dramatic and psychological crux of this intensely moving but problematic work is its twofold return to the tonic key in I and the return to the same music in the finale — points of stifled despair, mourning, and the measured tread of a funeral cortege. A worthwhile performance makes these moments haunt the memory and weigh heavy on the spirit.

To contrast with both these scenarios, the second **Beaux Arts Trio** reading (with cellist Peter Wiley replacing Bernard Greenhouse) is one of genteel introspection and impeccable balance (Philips). Pianist Menahem Pressler is anything but domineering; indeed, I sometimes found myself wanting a larger sonority from him. Except for an unsteady first page, the performance also has the unerring sense of pace you expect from this group. But at their return to A minor on the final two pages of I (marked *dolce espressivo*), the regularity of Tchaikovsky's accent marks is taken as an excuse for prosaic and rhythmically square phrasing. They have been multi-miked for detail, and this tends to make the sound dry, colorless, and unappealing. All around, this group's earlier recording (with Greenhouse) had a more sensitive feel for the music's lyrical ebb and flow (Philips).

In much of I, taken fairly quickly, the **Suk Trio** brings out the tension of Tchaikovsky's chugging figuration, but the performance doesn't have many subtleties to offset the tension (Denon). In the theme and variations, this almost becomes palm-court music-making, entertaining and glossy in execution but not really going beneath the surface of the music. Violinist **Andres Cardenes**, cellist **Jeffrey Solow**, and pianist **Mona Golabek** make up a less than inspired partnership (Delos). The violinist has a bright and attractive but easily submerged tone; the admirable pianist has perhaps more intelligence than sensitivity; and the cellist irritates with his inability to play less than mezzo piano, his bald interpretation of rests, and his covered tone. The **Chung Trio** has very little to say about the piece (EMI). These three siblings show more interest in sound, efficiency, and sleekness than affection for or particular interest in the music. Each instrument's tone is on the cold side, not helped by fairly harsh acoustics. The pianist is too emphatic for my taste; alongside his obvious skill in I is a third variation where the arpeggios are a bit lumpy.

Perlman, Ashkenazy, and **Harrell** are solid and beautiful and pleasant enough on the surface, but with perfunctory passages that make you question how long they've lived with this piece (EMI). They don't personalize or shape the music, and not much characterization goes on in the theme and variations. Perlman is best, whose vibrant and soulful sound adds a great deal to the performance. **Vovka Ashkenazy** is joined by violinist **Richard Stamper** and cellist **Christine Jackson** in a disappointing performance; it's rough going, but in a way that seems more mannered than passionate. There's no intimacy whatsoever, and the sound tends to be shrill and chilly (Naxos).

At bargain price, a far better option — indeed, one of the best performances available — comes from the **Eastman Trio** (♦Vox 3021, with chamber scores by other Russian composers). Straightforward but at the same time commanding and audibly caught up in the music, they hit on the perfect solution of shaping the big first movement through dynamics and phrasing rather than distortions of rhythm — the pulse is kept quite steady. Everyone makes a lovely sound; the 1979 sonics need taming in the treble and could have more dynamic range, but balances are excellent.

Except for the Eastman Trio, none of the above discs supplant the **Vienna Haydn Trio,** who offer a performance of wistful rather than oppressive melancholy (♦Teldec 43209). This is one of the best balanced performances, with the pianist never drowning out his partners. Indeed, in this often tense music I almost wished for a bit more feeling of competition among the players. Rather more invigorating, and far more Slavic, was the astonishing reading with **Pletnev, Oliveira,** and **Rosen** that CBS issued on vinyl in 1980. (These were three Tchaikovsky Competition winners, which probably served as the rationale for bringing them together.) This is a great performance that needs to be reissued, though the ill-balanced and bony sound will need some help when that happens. A reading in a similar vein — a commanding piano virtuoso joined with soulful string players — comes from **Bronfman, Lin,** and **Hoffman** (Sony). This is a less deep performance, though one that's always fascinatingly in flux, rarely at rest. When I return to this disc, it will be to hear Bronfman take full command of the taxing piano part without banging or drowning out his partners — he's especially thrilling with the powerful return of the funereal music at the end.

These three players also have an elegance that tends to elude **Licad, Salerno-Sonnenberg,** and **Meneses,** who are more intent on point-making and bar-to-bar intensity (EMI). Their local detailing (and not always perfect tempo choices) tends to keep the theme and variations in particular from cohering. I wish they'd trust the music more. There's even more point-making from **Argerich, Kremer,** and **Maisky** in their Tokyo recording (DG, with wild applause following and a "Tango pathétique" encore!). The playing is brilliant and I found it endlessly fascinating, especially since the sonics are a bit thin and bright; however, I'm not sure it's an experience I'm eager to repeat.

A once-in-a-lifetime performance that everyone should hear comes from the **Borodin Trio,** who are the most soulful on offer (♦Chandos 8348). Violinist Dubinsky and cellist Turovsky come up with that particularly from-the-heart manner of phrasing and moving from note to note that is so ineffably Russian. These idiomatic qualities more than offset some agogic mannerisms and the pianist's less-than-ideal address; she isn't the rock-solid lynchpin, undeclared virtuoso that Gilels, for instance, was so perfectly. All told, though, this is a kind of personal music-making that's becoming all too rare these days — their wispy "Andante flexibile" variation is a gem. In their second recording, the performance is more labored and less spontaneous (Chandos).

A famous recording came from the "million-dollar trio" of **Rubinstein, Heifetz,** and **Piatigorsky** (RCA). I find their 1950 reading businesslike and brusque, despite the wonderful sounds heard at any given moment, and the bloom-less Hollywood studio doesn't give their considerable sonority any room to expand. The recording with **Gilels, Kogan,** and **Rostropovich** (a "two-million-dollar trio"?) would be my candidate for an unforgettable historical performance — indeed, the one Trio recording I'd grab if the floods were to come. They don't hear the work as needing any kind of special pleading; they only play the score very naturally, with tremendous musicality and an impeccable sense of the music's shape, color, and charm. This Melodiya tape from the early 50s, with quite murky and all-round low-fi sound, appeared most recently on an Arlecchino CD that I haven't heard. Maybe Melodiya or the Russian Revelation label will give us a reissue.

String quartets. For Tchaikovsky's three quartets, all entries are judged by the three **Borodin Quartet** cycles (early '70s and again 1978–79 for Melodiya, and 1993 for Teldec). For style, the first (with violinists Dubinsky and Alexandrov) has never been surpassed (♦Chandos 9871). Now 20-bit remastered and with their nonpareil *Souvenir de Florence* thrown in (where they're joined by Rostropovich and violist Genrikh Talalyan), it stands as a central recommendation for interpretation and musicianship. But the sound comes up thin, and there's some low-frequency tape noise, a narrow dynamic range, and a hint here and there that the tapes have seen better days.

Those wanting better sound can go for the 1978–79 Melodiya cycle (with violinists Mikhail Kopelman and Andrei Abramenkov), though that tends to sound a bit plummy in the reissue (♦EMI 49775). It has the same natural flow, beautiful pacing, and gorgeous playing as the first cycle, though I do miss Dubinsky's little heart-wrenching, vocal-style slide about three minutes into the *Andante cantabile* in the early '70s version of Quartet 1. But the sound is a bit airless, and the lovely B-flat movement wasn't included. In the third set, the sound is very fine, with good balance and nice acoustics, but the players have lost some of their original naturalness, composure, and finesse, nor is there quite the same blend and homogeneity heard earlier; some of the louder dynamics sound forced (Teldec). Anyone coming to the Teldec without hearing the earlier Melodiya/EMI won't be disappointed, but why settle for second-best?

The young **St. Petersburg Quartet** dispatches the quartets with spirit but not much subtlety (Sony). Things tend to be fairly heavy, though they do have all the glorious trademarks of a Russian group; everyone has a vibrant and succulent tone, and the solos display those little aching, Slavic slides now and then. As an addendum, they include the magnificent early movement in B-sharp as well as four rare juvenile movements that are among the 24-year-old Tchaikovsky's first compositions. They're all short but full of the melodic grace and ineffable sadness of his greatest music. With a romantic and personal, almost Stokowskian approach, the **Schubert Quartet** has the Tchaikovskian melos down better than anyone else (♦Nimbus 5380; MHS 525222). They make everything their own, and in beauty and dark intensity of tone they take a back seat to no one; there's an idiomatic Slavic warmth and blend to their sound, with the cello a strong underpinning to the ensemble. At times I even prefer them to the Borodin because they're more individual and bring out more detail, which particularly suits 2: Here their I is an absolute joy, though the lamenting *Andante* is more pensive and low-key than the Borodins, at least at the start.

The **New Haydn Quartet** is less distinctive, simpler and more refined in style, though for the most part idiomatic (if not always imposing) in sound (Naxos). Their sequential and transitional sections can get just a little mechanical, but the dynamic terracing and sensitive bowing often make their slow movements delectable, moments of true introspection and peace. They're more successful with the classicism of No. 1 than in the grand, elegiac rhetoric of 2.

On to individual quartets. Sensitive but never sentimental in No. 1, the **Hollywood Quartet** offers music-making of rare simplicity, candor, and integrity (♦Testament 1061). They produce a rich and beautifully blended sonority, but the vibrato is fairly minimal in the outer movements and this isn't an especially dark or Slavic sound. The recording dates form the early '50s and the acoustic is fairly small, but then this is a pretty intimate, chamber-size rather than symphonic conception. It's recommended to listeners not necessarily committed to "Russian" sobs or hifi stereo. In their 1976 recording of No. 1, the **Gabrieli Quartet** are almost as soulful as the Borodin and almost as rich and generous in sound. Actually, they have the best of all worlds: a dash of ensemble clarity, slightly clearer rhythm, and a springier scherzo added to the Borodin-style blend and beautiful tone. Unfortunately, they come up sounding thin in the remastering.

The **Emerson Quartet** have less blend, freedom of vibrato, and less of an inner glow to their ensemble sound (DG). The leader's rhythm is more conspicuously accurate than his intonation, and when any of the players try a "Russian" sob or slide, it sounds rehearsed. It's less idiomatic, and the four movements don't unfold as naturally as with the Hollywood, Borodin and Gabrieli; you get the feeling that the style just isn't in their bones. They're best in the scherzo. The **Lafayette Quartet** is more within the style, with their warm sound, their blend, feeling for phrase shape, and generous vibrato (♦Dorian 90163). Even their ever-so-slight laziness of rhythm tends to make this sound like East European music-making. They aren't quite as stylish as the Gabrieli, but their dynamic sensitivity and the fine sound make this very attractive. Certainly they're second to none in the famous *Andante cantabile,* and the Shostakovich couplings (including Quartet 8) are just as idiomatic.

The **Koeckert Quartet** is more finicky in both rhythm and sound, and you can almost hear them counting at the Schubertian opening of I (Calig). They're especially wooden in the high-register, Russian melody in the finale. Similar comments apply to the coupled No. 3. The **Carmina Quartet** is delightfully alive in sound in it, but some matters of balance, phrasing, and emphasis suggest inexperience (Ex Libris).

Discs devoted entirely to Tchaikovsky's works for violin and piano come along no more than once in a blue moon. All the more fitting, then, that the only one now in the catalog is so superb: A pupil of Oistrakh, the Latvian **Oleg Kagan** had that unmistakable deep and sentimental sound that puts the listener in direct contact with the darkest recesses of the Slavic soul (♦Ondine 733). The wistful melancholy he brings to *Sérénade mélancolique* is unforgettable, as are the subtle rubato of *Meditation,* the pungent characterization of the outer sections of *Valse-Scherzo,* or the lightness he brings to *Humoresque.* The composer's own arrangement of the *Andante funèbre* from Quartet 3 is a bit of a letdown; even in the hands of the able Vasily Lobanov, the rather staid piano part is no replacement for the mournful vibrancy of three strings. But what a sound Kagan had, given free rein here by impeccable engineering. It's a great memorial to a great violinist, tragically taken from us at the age of 44.

PIANO MUSIC

Tchaikovsky often turned to writing for piano as an easy way to make money, but he was hardly capable of churning out potboilers, even under financial duress. As evidence, consider his two greatest piano sets: *The Seasons* was written on a tight schedule for a music magazine, and the often sublime Pieces Op. 72 was produced for quick money after Nadezhda von Meck's termination of her allowance to the composer. The less appealing pieces in his piano oeuvre are early and show him sorting through influences that somehow proved less oppressive in his orchestral and chamber music. Lisztian pyrotechnics pop up (*Valse-Caprice* from Op. 2), but the more common model is Schumann, a composer Tchaikovsky loved dearly and who supplied the prototypes for the noisy and sequence-ridden Sonata in G Major. Even as late as Op. 72, though, one of the pieces almost amounts to a paraphrase of Liszt's famous *Liebestraum.*

Two pianists have recorded the complete piano works. **Postnikova** is a good guide through these pieces, both the obscure and the more familiar (Erato, 7CDs available separately). Her *Seasons* is fine (though not preferable to some others discussed below), and in her slightly more sensitive account of Op. 72 she succeeds in making each of these pieces her own. In this she outdistances **Ponti,** who in his comprehensive survey cleaves through much of this music at high speed and with equal stiffness (Vox). Sometimes Postnikova tries to invest too much variety and pyrotechnics in this wistful and sometimes even inconsequential (though almost invariably lovely) music; surely *Souvenir de Hapsal* and the Sonata would benefit from a lighter, simpler, and more straightforward touch? Erato's sound is also a bit cramped and clattery at louder moments. The not-entire-completist will want to acquire one of the more sensitive accounts of *The Seasons* mentioned below and then supplement it with Postnikova's complete Op. 72 (♦Erato 45996) and Opp. 40 and 51 (♦Erato 45995), in that order.

The twelve character pieces of *The Seasons* (perhaps better called "The Months") represent Tchaikovsky's best-known keyboard opus, and different hands have even orchestrated them (see below). Whereas many pianists take to either the lyrical aspect or the showier side of these pieces, **Ashkenazy** usually manages to encompass both. He's consistently slow in the more reflective numbers, which, however, can become a bit uniform and shapeless, and yet in the March "Song of the Lark" he's rare in conveying some of the brittleness of bird calls rather than a generic melos (Decca). His tone takes on a harder edge than **Lydia Artymiw**'s, who takes the prize for pianistic sensitivity, beauty of sound, and variety; she moves between quiet and loud fluently, without sounding self-conscious (♦Chandos 8349). Her fluid, Chopinesque account of these miniatures is abetted by the most beautiful sound on disc, always lucid but also full and rounded; it's colored by ambience without verging on the clattery, as Ashkenazy's does. My only misgiving is that you can hear the pedal mechanism.

Something like Artymiw's sensitive approach, though on a smaller scale and with more controlled acoustics, comes from **Antonin Kubalek** (♦Dorian 90102). His dynamic and expressive range is fairly narrow, but his powers of natural evocation and concentration carry their own powerful charms. His sound is just as good as Artymiw's, if more closely miked. This is the most intimate performance available, and often the most direct. An extraordinarily ordinary reading, on the other hand, comes from **Bronfman** (Sony). There's no doubt about his technique, which is indeed flawless, or his astute observance of the score's markings, but his lyrical pieces don't sound song-like, and in the heavier works (the February "Carnival") he doesn't capture the fleetness and energy of Artimiw or Pletnev or the lightness of Kubalek. **Luba Edlina**'s edition is nothing very special either; she tends toward plainness, neither floating the lyrical numbers effortlessly nor impressing with keyboard fluency in the more virtuosic months (Chandos).

Katin gives *The Seasons* a Mozartian elegance, but neglects to do much tonal and dynamic shading within that classical approach (Olympia). As a result, he lends an enviable and moving aura of perfection to the brooding and aloof "June" Barcarolle, but seems to skim over the surface of the music elsewhere. **Pletnev** has recorded *The Seasons* twice, in 1986 and in 1994. The second version is typically keen and astutely characterized, discreetly pedaled, and never overstated (Virgin, a "two-fer" with his Symphony 6). But his earlier version, where the 1980 recording sounds like it dates from 40 years earlier, finds him with a fresher response to the music, even if the sound has some hiss (♦Chant du Monde 278952/53, with the Op. 72 pieces). His slower speeds (as in "June") have also become a bit more impatient the second time around.

Among mixed Tchaikovsky piano recitals, **Richter**'s 1983 compendium truly stands out (♦Olympia 334). He captures the innate simplicity of Tchaikovsky's piano muse, but also catches the abrupt humor of the G major *Humoresque* like few others. Initial impressions of plainness are immediately banished by his varied touch and wide range of temperament. His very generous program includes four of the *Seasons,* which he characterizes unerringly and without preciousness. **Ilona Prunyi** is a very able guide through an attractively wide-ranging recital of 16 piano works (not including anything from *The Seasons*), but she tends to be loud and over-emphatic, even in the more nocturne-like pieces (Naxos).

Barry Douglas offers a disc with the big G major Sonata, a notoriously intractable piece, and five pieces from *The Seasons* (RCA). In the sonata (Tchaikovsky's piano writing at its most bombastic), I find him preferable to Postnikova, though still not ideal. Part of the success of his reading comes from his fleeter tempos in I and the scherzo. He's also helped by RCA's more sympathetic, more controllable acoustics, but then Postnikova also takes some blame for failing to adjust her Bechstein's large sound to her somewhat cramped recording space. Even given that, it's Douglas who is more tempted to bang in the finale. **Richter**'s 1956 concert reading of the Sonata is out of the running because of barely listenable sound, but the music-making also needs a greater sense of nuance for this remarkably unnuanced work (Melodiya). **Katin** goes in the other direction, correcting the sonata's symphonic pretensions and playing it as though it were Haydn (Olympia, with *The Seasons*). This makes it far easier listening, but seems a falsification of the composer's intentions. For all their flaws, Douglas and Postnikova are the choices.

Several orchestrations of *The Seasons* are available. **Svetlanov** and the USSR Symphony taped the Alexander Gauk orchestration in 1975, and this is now coupled with their more recent *Swan Lake* (♦Melodiya 405). Though not perfect (the phrasing can go beyond expressiveness to being gluey, and some of the clarinet's intonation is awful), this is a more communicative and memorable performance than **Orbelian**'s with his Moscow Chamber Orchestra (Delos). The Delos engineering is preferable in the quieter numbers, but the sound gets crowded at louder moments. Another recording, by **Leonid Grin** and the Tampere Orchestra, is to be avoided: The playing is often very bad, the group hardly sounding up to international standards (Ondine).

There are transcriptions of *Album for the Young* for strings and for string quartet. **Spivakov**'s version for chamber orchestra is tastefully done, but not played with much affection except for the numbers where some charming percussion is brought in (RCA, with *Serenade*). It sometimes sounds as though they're sight-reading, though not with the spontaneity that it could bring. The augmented **Borodin Trio** recorded a more intimate version for quartet (Chandos), and coupled this with Luba Edlina playing the piano original (Erato). These quartet versions are often more affected than Spivakov's, and one of the violins has suspect intonation. Likewise, Edlina's performance of the piano version is less elegant and assured than Postnikova's.   ASHBY

CHORAL MUSIC

Vespers. The little-known *Vespers* is a series of 17 liturgical pieces based on the service of all-night vigil performed in the Russian Orthodox church on the eves of Sundays and feast days. It's Tchaikovsky's most important and best-written choral work, far superior to the feeble *Liturgy* of earlier years, where he, like Rachmaninoff, strayed from the use of canonical Russian melodies and tried inventing his own.

Neglect continues to plague this work; only one recording has been generally available, with the Leningrad Glinka Choir conducted by **Chernushenko,** and it has had to fill the gap for some time. The choir is generally expert, though and unrelenting in its unchanging choral color. The 1979 sound is serviceable, but now can be safely retired in favor of the recording by the Russian Chamber Chorus of New York directed by **Nikolai Kachanov** (♦Koch 7420). Finally a recording fully worth the measure of this work, Kachanov and company sing splendidly, the 29-voice choir completely attuned to the nuance and style of this music, with sound that's second to none. This is one of the best Russian sacred music releases in quite a while, and I hope others take up the challenge to pull Tchaikovsky's vintage opus out of obscurity.

Liturgy of St. John Chrysostom. Tchaikovsky's earliest complete liturgical opus has seen a number of recordings over the years, few of them complete. This isn't surprising, as it's substandard for his work and as an example of Russian liturgical music. Nevertheless, a few of its selections have attained some status with dedicated listeners and church choir singers, like "Cherubic Hymn," "Holy God." and "Our Father." These and a few others can be found scattered about in various choral compilations, whether Russian or not, and most people will—and should—be satisfied with that.

For diehards who need the complete work, or at least a large selection from it, the choices are not good. The Bulgarian National Choir led by **Georgi Robev** offers a nearly complete liturgical reconstruction that should satisfy most listeners (♦Capriccio 10518). Even though this recording is an improvement over Robev's ealier outing (EMI) in the same location (the notorious St. Alexander Nevsky Cathedral in Sofia), problems with the aural tsunami that overwhelms all but the most talented record producers still plague the disc. The choir is finely balanced, though recessed, and sings with vigor and resolution. Not the greatest, but far from the worst. **Nikolai Korniev** and the St. Petersburg Chamber Choir attempt a dramatic, pathos-laden reading that all but destroys the liturgical dimension of the work. Add the foggy sound that negates the bass spectrum entirely, and you end up with a mix that fails to present the piece properly.   RITTER

OPERAS

Tchaikovsky's best and most popular operas are *Eugene Onegin* and *The Queen of Spades.* Both have been recorded several times, in Russia as well as in the West. While there's often an aura of greater authenticity in the Russian recordings, some of the Slavic voices sound strident to our ears, and there isn't a Russian recording in which at least one soloist (usually a soprano or mezzo) doesn't have a wobble. Unless that's a minor role, those recordings are not recommended.

Eugene Onegin. Three recordings can be recommended. In one, **Bychkov** leads an excellent cast headed by Hvorostovsky, who sings the title role more beautifully than any of his recorded competitors, and Nuccia Focile, who captures Tatiana's girlishness and innocence in a well-sung portrait (♦Philips 438235). An older mono set from the '60s, led by **Khaikin,** features the young and fresh-voiced Vishnevskaya's irresistible Tatiana, Eugene Belov as a smooth, elegant Onegin, and Sergei Lemeshev an appealing Lensky (♦Legato 163). In Vishnevskaya's 1970 recording conducted by **Rostropovich,** her voice already sounds edgy and sometimes shrill, and her husband's slow tempos don't help the drama (Chant du Monde).

A recording by the Sofia Opera led by **Tchakarov** is generally well sung, especially by Gedda and Mazurok, but Tomowa-Sintow's Tatiana doesn't capture the girlish innocence of that fascinating character (Sony 45339). Similarly, in **Solti**'s recording, Kubiak's portrayal of Tatiana doesn't measure up to the competition (Decca, NA). An English version led by **Mackerras** can be recommended to Russian-averse listeners who want to get to know the work better (♦EMI 55004). Hampson sings the title role in honeyed tones though a bit stiffly at times and Te Kanawa's beautiful voice makes for a lovely Tatiana, though she really sounds too mature for the part in Act 1. Unfortunately, **Levine**'s gorgeous recording, with Freni and Thomas Allen, has been deleted; if it reappears, grab it (♦DG 428959).

Iolanta Tchaikovsky's last opera, it's in one act and based on a Danish play about a blind princess in medieval times who is made cruelly made aware of her condition when she tries to find a lover. In one recommended recording, **Gergiev** conducts the Kirov Opera (♦Philips 442 796); in the other, an international group of young singers (no well-known names) led by **Hans Rotman** was recorded in 1993 (♦CPO 999456). That cast sounds fresher, younger, and more enthusiastic than the Kirov singers, but the set lacks a libretto, a serious handicap to listeners who don't understand Russian. However, **Rostropovich**'s 1984 recording with Gedda and Vishnevskaya is also recommended; it includes the libretto (♦Erato 45793).

Mazeppa. This is based on a Pushkin poem about Peter the Great's governor of the Ukraine, who betrayed his monarch for the cause of Ukrainian separatism. But in Tchaikovsky's opera, the emphasis is on Mazeppa's love for Maria, the daughter of his friend Kochubey. When the latter objects to the marriage and denounces Mazeppa to the Tsar, Mazeppa has him tortured and beheaded, and Maria goes mad. Tchaikovsky's score is one of his most lyrical; the love scenes are especially well crafted. There are only two recommendable recordings, both with the same principal singers: **Neeme Järvi** conducts the Gothenburg Symphony in one (♦DG 439906) and **Gergiev** the Kirov in the other (♦Philips 438141). Gergiev is the better conductor, but the DG set has better sound; either recording will give much pleasure.

The Queen of Spades. Considered Tchaikovsky's operatic masterpiece, dramatically as well as musically, it's also based on a Pushkin story. Hermann, a poor young officer, has overheard that the Countess has a secret for invariably winning at cards. He tries to wrest it from her by pretending to love the Countess's ward Lisa, but only succeeds in destroying Lisa, the Countess, and himself.

The best recordings are those by **Ozawa** (♦RCA 60992) and **Tchakarov** (♦Sony 45720). Both have superb sound, but the RCA set has a somewhat better cast and therefore is the better all-around choice. Freni (RCA's Lisa) has a warmer and more beautiful voice than Stefka Estafieva (Sony) and Vladimir Atlantov is a more dramatic Hermann than Sony's Wieslaw Ochman. Also, the Sofia Orchestra doesn't play with as wide and rich a range of tonal colors as the Boston Symphony. But in the supporting cast, Yuri Mazurok (Sony) sings Yaletsky's aria with more authority than Hvorostovsky, and Stefania Toczyska sings Polina's music more firmly than Katherine Ciesinski (RCA). Also, Penka Dilova's Countess (Sony) sounds more convincing than Maureen Forrester's rather hysterical interpretation. Of more recent vintage is **Gergiev**'s Kirov Opera performance (Philips 438141). It's admirable in many, ways but neither the cast nor the sound are quite as good as RCA's and Sony's.

SONGS

Tchaikovsky wrote more than 100 songs, most of them for the female voice, so it's not surprising that the best recorded recitals are by female artists. One of them is **Zara Dolukhanova** (♦Russian Disc 11342, with selections by Medtner, Rachmaninoff, and Scriabin); her rich, colorful voice and compelling interpretations have also been recorded in other discs that are NA. **Borodina,** a mezzo who is one of today's best Russian opera singers, has also recorded a disc of Tchaikovsky's songs; her creamy, rock-solid voice and dramatic expressiveness make it an outstanding selection (♦Philips 442013). Finally, I recommend a disc by the Rumanian soprano **Varady** (♦Orfeo 053851). She also has a smooth, beautiful voice and is an imaginative interpreter. By contrast, **Hvorostovsky** sings nine of the songs quite well but he doesn't plumb their emotional content deeply (Philips), and neither does **Leiferkus** (Conifer). MOSES

Georg Philipp Telemann (1681–1767)

The early years of the 19th century witnessed the energetic rediscovery of the music of the German Baroque, a movement spearheaded by several avant-garde musicians, among them Mendelssohn, Schumann, and Brahms. Bach and Handel were studied by music historians and recognized for their considerable achievements, but their contemporary Telemann was not so lucky. He came to be branded as an overproductive, largely superficial composer, and this verdict has stuck despite the efforts of many over the years to change it. Telemann's catalog is enormous, including more than 1,000 church cantatas, 40 operas, 44 Passions, hundreds of orchestral suites, and countless smaller-scale chamber works—in sheer volume probably the greatest single legacy by any composer of art music.

But as late as 1954, the consensus had not changed; the fifth edition of *Grove's Dictionary of Music* accuses Telemann of "originating nothing" and "lacking an earnest ideal" in his compositions—this despite the high regard in which he was held by his contemporaries. Bach was a close friend, and we may judge the esteem he had for Telemann by his many borrowings from his music and by the fact that Telemann stood as godfather for Bach's second eldest son, Carl Philipp Emanuel. In fact, Bach was rejected in favor of Telemann for the post of Music Director of Hamburg's five principal churches, a real plum of a position that everybody and his brother wanted, and he was accepted for the job in Leipzig (the final stage of his career) only after Telemann had told the Leipzig town elders "no thanks" and was off to Hamburg! Amazingly, none of this seems to have affected their friendship.

The issue of Telemann's relative merit as a composer need not be decided here and now--or perhaps ever. The recent growth of the period-instrument movement has allowed us to re-examine his compositional skill; arguably, his music sounds far better when played on the instruments appropriate to his time, and particularly when played with the correct feeling and stylistic awareness. Record collectors have responded to the recent wave of period-instrument recordings by making him one of the best-selling baroque composers on CD. The issue of his superficiality has subsided somewhat; even the latest edition of *Grove's* is far kinder to him than before. What remains is an imposing body of work, much of which (opera, cantata, and oratorio) begs for a first recording. Although many of his compositions are small-scale works written to entertain, it's difficult to find a truly bad piece. There are many gems out there, and record collectors are likely to find a winner almost anywhere they look.

Telemann wrote in all the forms and genres common to the Baroque,

but none is perhaps as familiar as the sonata, either in solo or trio format. In these compositional forms, one or two solo instruments are pitted against a basso continuo, usually a harpsichord and a bass instrument like a cello or bass viol. Music theorists have likened this ensemble to a typical jazz trio or quartet, with the basso continuo functioning as the rhythm section. A further similarity with jazz is the fact that the solo instruments were usually required to vary their part with free ornamentation.

Nearly every available melodic instrument of the time found its way into a sonata by Telemann, but the one that seems to have interested him most is the transverse flute. There is no finer collection of his flute music than "Concerto da Camera," by the phenomenal Dutch musician **Wilbert Hazelzet** (Glossa 920803). Every disc from this extraordinary artist is a treasure, and this one is no exception. Hazelzet's teacher **Barthold Kuijken,** also a noted performer, has recorded the 12 *Sonate metodiche,* along with 12 more sonatas, in a set marked by solid musicianship and excellent engineering (Accent 94104, 2CD). Although the recorder was often interchangeable with the transverse flute in the baroque era, recorder players can nonetheless thank Telemann for much first-rate music written specifically for their instrument. For this, check out the excellent disc by **Dan Laurin** (BIS 855).

Telemann also had a special fondness for the oboe (which he played quite well, in addition to nearly a dozen other instruments); his music forms the backbone of the oboist's Baroque repertoire. Two distinguished oboists have recently released collections of this music, and both can be highly recommended: **Paul Goodwin** (Harmonia Mundi 907152) and **Marcel Ponseele** (Accent 95110). In addition to the solo sonatas, the latter also offers a trio sonata for two oboes as well as an unusual quartet for two oboes, trumpet, and basso continuo.

As with many other German Baroque composers, Telemann wrote extensively for the viola da gamba, which during the first half of the 18th century vied for popularity with the up-and-coming violoncello. French gambist **Christophe Coin** has released an excellent cross-section of Telemann's gamba music; the disc includes three quartets and two sonatas, and is the ideal introduction to this aristocratic instrument (Astrée 8632). Ultra-realistic sound, too.

Telemann's unaccompanied solo music was usually written either for flute or violin. The twelve Fantasias for violin constitute an important precursor to Bach's sonatas and partitas, and **Manze** has given them his usual bang-up treatment (Harmonia Mundi 907137). The twelve Fantasias for flute are equally important to flutists; **Bart Kuijken**'s version is highly recommended (Accent 57803). Akin to the solo music are the 24 duets for two flutes. American transverse flute players **Tom Moore** and **Kimberly Reighley** have put together an excellent recording of the last six (Lyrichord 8019). Another excellent CD presents the first set of six, here labeled "Six Sonatas Op. 2," ably played by **Stephen Schultz** and **Mindy Rosenfeld** (Naxos 554132).

Telemann's best chamber music can be found in several important collections published by the composer himself. By acting as his own publisher, he ensured that his music would be preserved for posterity in readable, easily obtained editions—and he made a lot of money in the process too. His typical approach was to solicit subscriptions to a new series of publications from connoisseurs and prominent personages; as each installment was completed and engraved, copies were dispersed throughout Europe and beyond. The most famous of these collections is *Essercizii Musici* (*Musical Exercises*), his last chamber series published before he took up the job in Hamburg. Look no further than the superb set featuring **Camerata Köln** with star soloists Karl Kaiser, baroque flute, and Hans-Peter Westermann, baroque oboe, for the definitive recording (Deutsche Harmonia Mundi 77361, 4CD). If 4CDs are too much, then the outstanding distillation of *Essercizii Musici* by the **Aulos Ensemble** is for you (MHS 522080W, 2CD).

Many would argue that Telemann's *Tafelmusik* (Music for the Table) is an even finer collection. The work is divided into three large suites, each with a distinct tonal center, beginning with a stately Overture followed by a variety of smaller-scaled pieces (trios, quartets, etc.). It's debatable whether this is chamber or orchestral music, although the chamber approach (one player to a part) is more or less the norm nowadays. I have the utmost admiration for the recording by Musica Antiqua Köln under **Reinhard Goebel** (Archiv 427619, 3CD). For some, his approach to Telemann may be too hard-hitting, and certainly there are other recordings that treat the music with greater *Gemütlichkeit* and relaxation. Ultimately, I relish the vitality Goebel and his players bring to the music; everyone else sounds dull by comparison. An excellent version of the third Suite can be found by the Belgian ensemble Il Fondamento under **Paul Dombrecht** (Accent 78643). Too bad they never recorded the whole thing.

Telemann's *Paris Quadri* (Paris Quartets) of 1730, 1738, and 1752 were also released on subscription, this time with the goal of capturing a wider audience among the French, and also to forestall any pirated editions of his music there. He had a special affinity for French music, and these works for transverse flute, violin, viola, cello, and harpsichord (the cello and harpsichord count as the fifth instrument) were written in the most up-to-date, *galant* style. **Hazelzet** has again lent his inimitable touch to the 1752 set (Globe 5146). The **Boston Museum Trio**'s recording of the 1730 set is also excellent, with flutist Christopher Krueger (Centaur 2260). Those seeking a more or less complete compilation should investigate the **Kuijkens** and Leonhardt playing the 1730 and 1738 quartets in the late '70s (Sony 63115, 3CD). This is more than just a historical document; the playing is fresh and alive and the sound is surprisingly good.

For listeners new to Telemann who are daunted by the prospect of listening to a complete collection, there are several samplers of his chamber music that should fill the bill. A recent issue by the Dutch period-instrument group **Ensemble Senario** presents trios, quartets, and chamber concertos delightfully played on a wide variety of instruments, including recorder, violin, oboe, viol, and harpsichord (Globe 5154). The British group **Bandinage** has released a similar collection (Meridian 84347); this one includes such unusual items as a bassoon sonata and several of Telemann's seldom-performed harpsichord pieces. Another British group, **Collegium Musicum 90,** headed by violinist Simon Standage, is represented by an excellent collection of sonatas, cantatas, and selections from *Serious and Lighthearted Odes* (Chandos Chaconne 525). Finally, a disc recorded in 1981 at the Oberlin Baroque Performance Institute includes a veritable who's who of this country's leading period instrument performers, and the program, featuring four sonatas and a cantata for soprano and bass, is both interesting and varied (Gasparo 1008).

Telemann's concertos for solo instrument(s) and orchestra constitute a relatively small portion of his output, but they have received a lot of attention. One of the oldest and most venerable is the reissue of the Vienna Concentus Musicus under **Harnoncourt** playing double concertos, including the rollicking *Concerto à 6* for recorder, bassoon, and strings, with a young Frans Brüggen as recorder soloist (Teldec 43773). By today's standards, the orchestral playing, particularly the violin vibrato, is a trifle outdated, but overall the disc is still quite enjoyable. From the early '80s comes **Hogwood**'s recording of double and triple concertos (Oiseau-Lyre 411949). The CD begins with the stirring Concerto for three trumpets and strings and concludes with the charming Concerto for flute, oboe d'amore, viola d'amore, and strings.

A recent entry from La Stravaganza Köln under violinist **Manze** includes several concertos *per molti strumenti* in the style of Vivaldi and concludes with a Concerto for transverse flute, chalumeau (forerunner of the clarinet), oboe, 2 double basses (!), and strings (Denon 78933). The spectacular recorded sound is a further recommendation. Telemann wrote a significant number of trumpet concertos, in many respects the most important body of Baroque trumpet music. An excellent sampler features the young Italian trumpeter **Gabriele Cassone** performing two concertos and three excerpts from *Tafelmusik* (Arts 47320). While the latter can be heard to better advantage elsewhere, the two concertos are brilliantly performed on the valveless, seven-foot long natural trumpet, the same instrument used in Telemann's day.

Another **Reinhard Goebel** disc explores six of Telemann's wind concertos: a flute concerto, one for two chalumeaux, two trumpet concertos, and the famous concerto in E minor for flute and recorder (Archiv 419633). As in their *Tafelmusik* set, the music-making is energetic and exciting but occasionally over-driven. Lest you think Goebel has neglected the strings, check out a release that presents a varied assortment of seven solo and ensemble concertos, played with Musica Antiqua's usual precision and verve (Archiv 463074).

Some of Telemann's best music can be found in his 134 extant orchestral suites, more than 90 per cent of which remain unrecorded. In the late '70s, **Harnoncourt** rendered a valuable service by unearthing and recording four of them (Teldec 42986 and 42589). These CDs bear witness to the magic that his pioneering ensemble was capable of working in the right music. In 1984 Goebel and gang made one of their finest discs: a recording of *Water Music* (subtitled "The High and Low Tides of Hamburg") along with three concertos. The recorded sound is still remarkably satisfying, the full-bodied playing even more so. The **Freiburger Barockorchester,** another topnotch German period-instrument band, has made an excellent disc of Telemann *ouvertures* (suites) that includes the captivating *Ouverture in G* "Bourlesque de Quixotte" (Deutsche Harmonia Mundi 77321). Finally, the **Akademie für Alte Musik Berlin** presents the "La Chasse," "Alster," and "Tragicomique" suites (Harmonia Mundi 901654). The last is quite a shocker; with all its sarcasm and dissonance, it could well be a work by Hindemith or Bartók.

In comparison to Bach and Handel, Telemann was only a fair keyboardist. He never made the keyboard a priority as his two great contemporaries did, so his harpsichord and organ music is minuscule compared to the rest of his oeuvre. Needless to say, it's virtually untouched by the record companies, which is why the 1998 release of 20 Fantasias by British harpsichordist **John Butt** was such a surprise (Harmonia Mundi 907176). Here is music heavily influenced by the French tradition, highly listenable, and superbly performed on two magnificent original instruments from the Russell Collection in Edinburgh.

Telemann's sacred and secular vocal music is the most neglected of all; like some vast uncharted continent, it lies waiting to be rediscovered. The few items that have trickled out in recent years are both tantalizing and frustrating. Chief among these is the first complete recording of a Telemann opera, *Orpheus*, by **Jacobs** conducting the Akademie für Alte Musik Berlin (Harmonia Mundi 901618/19, 2CD). Historical arcanum this is not; Telemann wrote 40 operas and was regarded as the finest German opera composer after Hasse. *Orpheus* is a good example of his theatrical prowess; written in the pastiche style popular at the Goose-Market in Hamburg, it vibrantly mixes arias and ensemble pieces in three different languages and as many different musical styles. This is one of the most convincing recorded performances of opera I've ever heard--all concerned cover themselves with glory. We'll be lucky if future Telemann operas get half as enterprising a treatment, but for the moment, that's all there is.

The stats on Telemann's cantata output are quite mind-boggling: seven complete cycles of cantatas (at an average of 30 per cycle) composed at Eisenach, over 800 at Frankfurt, and so many during his 46 years at Hamburg that scholars still haven't sorted them all out. Perhaps it's just as well that only a few have been recorded. A complete edition on CD is unthinkable--no record label or group of performers could muster the time and capital outlay necessary, nor, I dare say, would very many collectors be interested. If it takes ten years to do Bach's measly 200 church cantatas, just think how long it would take to do Telemann!

Two recent CDs of Christmas cantatas recorded by the Kammerchor Michaelstein and the Telemann-Kammerorchester Michaelstein under **Ludger Rémy** are a good way to start your cantata pilgrimage (CPO 999419 and 999515). The music is unfailingly delightful, more outgoing, and in fact better suited to the season than many of Bach's Christmas cantatas. The semi-professional choir, period-instrument orchestra, and soloists have found just the right combination of lightness, clarity, and fervent expression; be sure to check out the joyous pealing of the trumpets in several of the chorale movements ("Von Himmel hoch," "In dulci jubilo").

Another excellent collection presents excerpts from the *Harmonischer Gottes-Dienst* (*Harmonious Worship-Service*), a subscription series of cantatas published by Telemann during his Hamburg tenure (Capriccio 10795/97, 3CD, available singly). These are simple works scored for solo voice with small instrumental ensemble, and are divided into three short movements--aria, recitative, and aria. The 21 cantatas recorded here are evenly apportioned between Christmas, Easter, and Pentecost, and post-Trinity. Once again, a small group of German early music specialists (the best-known name is likely to be soprano Monika Frimmer) have scored big-time with performances of great beauty and simplicity. In addition to the vocal part, each aria includes an obbligato instrument (violin, flute, oboe, and cello), making for a small-scale but captivating listening experience.

To appreciate Telemann's large-scale oratorios, you must be careful not to compare them with similar works by Bach. Above all, Telemann excelled in writing simple, tuneful melodies that go straight to the heart, and there's very little of the harmonic and contrapuntal complexity and symbolism found in Bach's music. Instrumental accompaniments are bound to be disappointing when compared with Bach, too, although Telemann does throw in the occasional obbligato flute or oboe. The *Matthäus-Passion* (*St. Matthew Passion*) of 1746, the last treatment of this text by Telemann, is a good case in point. Overall, this is a much lighter, more tuneful piece than Bach's, but no less effective in its directness of expression. **Hermann Max,** the Rheinische Kantorei, and Das Kleine Konzert have made a magnificent recording (Capriccio 10 854). The solo singing is distinguished, the chorus motivated, the instrumental work accomplished, with the whole captured in a pleasantly resonant acoustic.

In addition to the Christmas cantatas, **Rémy** and his forces have worked their wonders on two of Telemann's large-scale oratorios. *Die Auferstehung* (*The Resurrection*), which contains, as you might expect, much jubilant trumpet-and-drum music, but also moments of great awe and wonder, as befits the subject of the resurrected Christ (CPO 999634). *Der Tod Jesu* (*The Death of Jesus*) is a much more spare, introspective work that benefits from Rémy's dramatic leadership (CPO 999720). Perhaps the most famous of Telemann's oratorios is *Der Tag des Gerichts* (*The Day of Judgment*), a rousing but not especially terrifying work recorded by **Harnoncourt** and Concentus Musicus in 1966 (Teldec 77621, 2CD). Fortunately, this pioneering recording sounds as fresh and imaginative as the day it was released. BRODERSEN

Ambroise Thomas (1811–1896)

This French composer was for many years known chiefly for *Mignon,* first performed in 1866. It's based on Goethe's *Wilhelm Meister's Lehrjahre* and was an instant hit, racking up 500 performances in its first dozen years and 1,200 by the end of the century. Its popularity endured into the '30s; it was the first opera commercially broadcast from the Met (1933). But it's rarely performed these days, perhaps because of casting difficulties but more likely because, in spite of its appealing and expressive melodies, its libretto relies on coincidence rather than characterization and its happy ending seems contrived to please the Paris audiences of the day.

Mignon. Its title role has appealed to many great mezzos. The most recent full-length recording has a fine cast headed by Horne, Von Stade, and Vanzo, led by **de Almeida** (♦Sony 34590, 3CD). There's also a 1949 staged performance of dubious provenance from Mexico City (Legato, 2 CD).

Hamlet (1868). Based loosely on Shakespeare's play, is the best of Thomas's more than a dozen operas. But Shakespeare's ending is altered in a very significant way: After Hamlet kills Claudius, he reigns as the new King of Denmark! The work has been revived in recent years thanks to Milnes and Hampson, both of whom have performed and recorded the title role. The work also includes a famous Mad Scene that has appealed to sopranos from Christine Nilsson to Sutherland. The best available recording has Hampson, June Anderson, and Ramey heading the cast, with **de Almeida** again the conductor (♦EMI 54820). A fairly competitive set conducted by **Bonynge** has Milnes and Sutherland in the leading roles (London 433857, NA). Unfortunately, it caught both singers late in their career, and their work here, as well as Bonynge's, is inferior to the EMI set. MOSES

Randall Thompson (1899–1984)

Thompson's music is tuneful and melodically simple, with a homespun, folk-like quality (though he never actually quoted any folk or popular tunes) that earned him the label of the Norman Rockwell of American music. It's colorful, moving, and often deep, without ever being harsh or acerbic. Thompson studied with Bloch and Malipiero and was affected by Respighi and Duke Ellington, though the strongest influence on his work may have been the more conservative John Knowles Paine. His popularity peaked in the '30s, but by the '50s he was declared "superfluous" in foolish and unfortunately influential pronouncements by composers like Boulez and Sessions. He is perhaps America's most famous choral composer; his vocal music often uses Renaissance polyphonic devices, and even his instrumental works have a vocal quality. He taught for years at Harvard, where he worked to leave his exacting standards upon American music education.

SYMPHONIES

1. It was partly based on a vocal work, and some of the vocal manner remains. It's more abstract, neoclassical, impressionist, and transparent than the other two symphonies and not as folk-like. Its rhythms are subtle and important. **Sedares** sees it as a modern work, bringing out its transparency in an energetic, tightly structured performance (♦Koch 7181, with Gould's *Fall River Legend;* also 7413, with Symphonies 2 and 3 conducted by Andrew Schenk). He is probably more idiomatic than the slightly slower and more romantic **Abravanel** (♦Angel 37315, with *Testament of Freedom).*

2. A great American symphony, it is big, romantic, and full of variety, powerfully combining elements of folk tunes, jazz, spirituals, impressionism, and hymns. **Bernstein** and the NY Philharmonic capture its warmth and good spirits in a generous reading that set the standard (♦Sony 60594, with Diamond's Symphony 4 and Harris's Symphony 3). **Järvi** provides a leaner and more urgent alternative with a startling dark quality of mystery, menace, and even anger (Chandos 9429, with works by Chadwick). **Schenk** and the New Zealand Symphony are straightforward but underpowered (Koch 7074, with 3, or 7413, with 1+3); they miss the music's richness and are no match for Bernstein, Järvi, and their orchestras. My recommendation is based on the couplings.

3. It isn't as inventive or advanced as 2, but more rapt and moving. The sad and lyrical I and hymnlike III are entrancing, and the defiant, brassy II and cheerful finale are almost as good. **Schenk** (♦Koch 7074 with 2 or 7413 with 1+2) is better here than in the more difficult 2, getting a slightly fuller sound and greater concentration in the slow movements.

CHAMBER MUSIC

Quartets 1 and *2.* These are in Thompson's pleasant, conservative style with bold rhythms, American-sounding melodies, and fast, fiddle-like tunes and jigs. The serious 1 was called "neo-Razumovsky" by the composer, referring to its Beethoven model; 2 is sunnier. Neither is pretentious, but these are major American quartets. The **New Jefferson Chamber Players** offer clean performances with bold recorded sound (♦Citadel 88119, with Hanson's String Quartet; Bay Cities 1036, with two piano works).

Suite for Oboe, Clarinet, and Viola. This is a fluent, folk-based piece, lyrical and hymnlike, with contrasting dance tunes. It's very enjoyable in a fine performance by **Peter Christ**, David Atkins, and Alan de Veritch (♦Crystal 321, with oboe-based works by others).

CHORAL MUSIC

Frostiana; Feast of Praise; Alleluia; other choral works. Frostiana is a setting of Robert Frost poems and is in the same spirit as the more famous *Testament of Freedom*, though quieter, more reflective, and more hymn- and folk-like (heard here in the original version with piano). *Feast of Praise* is stirring, with its brass and harp accompaniment, and more modern with its modulations, quartal harmony, and mixed meters. These and more appear in an entertaining collection, nicely varied in mood, in which Voces Novae et Antiquae led by **Robert Ross** have a full, balanced sound. They aren't highly polished and there are a few strained moments, but in a way this adds to the directness and appeal of the music, and they sing with affection and understanding in fine recorded sound (♦ARKAY 6110).

Nativity According to St. Luke. Thompson's music drama for Christmas is singable by amateur soloists and chorus, though professional instrumentalists are best used for the chamber orchestra. It's in a neo-baroque format of recitatives, arias, chorus, etc. According to the program notes for **Frances Burmeister**'s recording, "The individual scenes were designed to recreate the mood and ambiance of cinque-

cento Italian nativity scenes, another legacy of Thompson's Roman years." The music is lyrical, tonal, simple, and pious in the most attractive way—a sort of reined-in American counterpart to Vaughan Williams's *Hodie*). It should be a Christmas standard (♦Koch 7210, with *Pueri Hebraeorum; Feast of Praise;* and *Morning Stars*). The couplings, two stirring works for chorus and brass and *Morning Stars* for chorus and organ, are first-rate Thompson.

Peaceable Kingdom; Odes to Horace; Alleluia; other choral works. This collection by the American Repertory Singers conducted by **Leo Nestor** covers mostly different repertoire from the Ross disc and is sung a cappella. It features solid singing and intonation, but the sound is so distant that the words aren't clear, and the sopranos and tenors dominate, tilting it toward the treble. This is relaxing, almost serene music and quite enjoyable, though the performances are blander than Ross's (♦ARSIS 103).

Testament of Freedom. For male chorus and orchestra, it is a stirring setting of writings by Thomas Jefferson and is irresistible, rousing Americana. **Richard Auldon Clark** leads the New York Choral Society and Manhattan Chamber Orchestra in an intimate, small-scaled performance that has a lot of life and feeling. Here *Frostiana* is performed with chorus and orchestra and is very effective. The disc is a must for fans of Thompson and American choral music (♦Koch 7206). **Timothy Seelig** leads the Turtle Creek Chorale and Dallas Wind Symphony in a fine *Testament,* more dark and solemn than stirring, but still moving (♦Reference 49, with works for chorus and wind ensemble by Hanson, Bernstein, and Copland). **Abravanel**'s large-scale version starts slowly and is a bit languid, but he comes on strong until, by the end, he is more powerful and stirring than Seelig, though Clark still leads the way (♦Angel 37315, LP, with Symphony 1). HECHT

Virgil Thomson *(1896–1989)*

Thomson was a prolific composer, writing in most musical forms, and a mordant critic. Influenced by Satie, he embraced simplicity, yet he achieved real expressivity, if not opulent color. His music is sprightly and entertaining, filled with folk and hymn tunes, spiked with dissonance, quartal harmony, and bold, sometimes stark but never dull or severe orchestration. His pieces evoke early-American folk dances, Main Street, fire barns, etc., particularly of the South and Midwest. The works he wrote in Paris were as American as any of his others because he wanted Parisians to know what music sounded like in his native Kansas City.

ORCHESTRAL MUSIC

Symphonies. All three are symphonic Americana. No. 1 ("On a Hymn Tune") is heavily colored by its basic pentatonic hymn and strongly reflects rural American religion; 2 is outgoing, lyrical, jolly, and sometimes militaristic. No. 3 began as a Schubertian quartet, then became a symphony; it's classical and often dance-like, and the orchestration makes it sound piquant and modern. **Sedares**'s recordings of all three with the New Zealand Symphony are large in scale with full, deep sound; price and performances are irresistible (♦Naxos 559022, with *Pilgrims and Pioneers*). **James Bolle** and his recorded sound are more buttoned down and less spirited (Albany; Citadel). I prefer Sedares's more striking presentation and sound; he brings these works up a notch. All Bolle's couplings are worthwhile: The *Lord Byron* excerpts appear to be from his Albany recording of the complete opera. Hanson's colorful, more punchy 1 with the Eastman Rochester Symphony is well worth seeking out; the couplings are from classic LP recordings: *Feast of Love,*

McPhee's *Tabuh-Tabuhan,* and Sessions's *Black Maskers* (♦Mercury 434301).

Louisiana Story. This is a Depression-era film score that deals with the reaction of the Acadians of northern Louisiana to industrialization and the arrival of an oil drilling crew. The score, particularly the beautiful "Pastoral," is influenced by French music and Cajun folk melodies; in some ways, it's the most evocative of Thomson's film scores. **Siegfried Landau** does a decent job with the Westphalian Symphony (♦Excelsior 5256, with Barber's Symphony 2, *Music for a Scene from Shelley,* and *Essay 1,* all with Sedares). I prefer **Ronald Korp**'s better-played if too-laid back British rendition that includes more music from the film (♦Hyperion 66576, with *Plow that Broke the Plains,* and *Acadian Dances, Fugues and Cantilenas*).

Parson Weems and the Cherry Tree. It is a ballet set to the classic tale of George Washington chopping down his father's cherry tree. This chamber orchestra piece is full of charm as Thomson runs a number of old folk tunes through his compositional mill. The result isn't biting, often sounding Baroque with its bright woodwind colors, light dance music, and gently militaristic brass, and it's expertly done by **Donald Teeters** and the Boston Cecelia (♦Newport 85621, with Menotti's *The Unicorn, The Gordon, and the Manticore*).

The Plow that Broke the Plains and ***The Rive.*** Written for Depression-era documentaries made by the US Department of Agriculture, the folk tunes, blues, and hymns, blended with Thomson's arch, sardonic style, make the films come alive. The most complete recording (containing about eight extra minutes of music for both suites) followed performances with the films by **Richard Kapp** and Philharmonia Virtuosi (♦ESS.A.Y 1005). Suites are played by **Stokowski** and the Symphony of the Air (♦Vanguard 8013, with Stravinsky's *Histoire du Soldat Suite*) and **Marriner** and the LA Chamber Orchestra (♦Angel 64307, with *Autumn*). Stokowski is forward and powerful; Marriner is more lyrical and warmer. Both are slower, more expressive, better played, and better recorded than Kapp's lightweight reading, though the latter will do if you want the nearly complete scores. **Korp** with the New London Orchestra is more laid back and polished; it lacks some of the bite of the others, but is extremely well played. The couplings are spirited works that Thomson fans will want (♦Hyperion 66576, with *Acadian Dances, Fugues and Cantilenas*).

CHAMBER MUSIC

Portraits. Thomson wrote 147 short musical descriptions of friends and colleagues for small ensembles. Their style is generally linear and quirky, varying in character from dry, simple pieces to more substantial works. They are said to capture their subjects well. The most interesting collection was put together by pianist **Anthony Tommasini,** containing thirteen selected *Portraits* for solo piano; *Five Ladies* for violin and piano, and *A Portrait of Two* for oboe, bassoon, and piano, along with some major works like the Violin Sonata. (♦Northeastern 240). "Portraits," with **Jacquelyn Helin,** includes only piano portraits and the piano version of *Parson Weems.* It's well played, but there is a sameness about the pieces if you listen to them all at once (♦New World 80429).

OPERAS

Four Saints in Three Acts. More of a plotless stage piece than an opera, it's a work of religious faith with a text of repetitious words by Gertrude Stein, often selected for sound rather than meaning. All this is spun over and contrasted with lyrical music full of hymns, folk songs, psalms, marches, and ballads, like a rapid-fire Singspiel. There are few arias; the most memorable part is a big chorus near the end. The effect is meant to be hypnotic. It's certainly clever, colorful, and full of high spirits and humor, but some may find it irritating, especially on records. Still, this is an important American work, and the performance with soloists and chorus led by **Joel Thome** and the Orchestra of Our Time is fine (♦Nonesuch 7905, 2 CD). I haven't heard the abridgement conducted by **Thomson** himself in 1947 in a while, but remember it as an interesting, quite personal performance (♦RCA 68163).

Lord Byron. This is a clever memoir about Byron as seen by other poets. The music is hymn-like, with flowing, conversational melody. There are no soaring moments, but it's tuneful and listenable, with singing strings and resonant brass. This is the most mature and romantic of Thomson's operas, and **James Bolle** leads a fine performance. The soloists have young, pleasant, and expressive voices, the smallish orchestra plays well, and the clear sound is perfect for the literary libretto (♦Koch 71242Y6, 2CD).

The Mother of Us All. Thomson's second opera and collaboration with Gertrude Stein deals with Susan B. Anthony's life as told and seen by historical characters (including Thomson and Stein), many of whom didn't know each other or live at the same time. The style is conversational and vocal (the orchestra is mostly supportive), with several arias and three orchestral pieces. The music is at times folksy, hymn-like, humorous, sardonic, and often catchy, and a mood of nostalgia prevails. It's interesting with fine moments, but might be more powerful in the theater. **Leppard** leads the Santa Fe Opera Chorus in a lively performance with Mignon Dunn excellent as Anthony (♦New World 288, 2CD).

SONGS

Thomson was adroit with language, taking pains to match music carefully to text. (This was true in his operas as well.) A fine collection of songs, including *Preciosilla, La Belle en Dormant, Stabat Mater, Five Songs from William Blake,* and more (25 in all), demonstrates this admirably. They're very well sung and enunciated in a variety of styles, many sharp and humorous, by soprano **Dora Ohrenstein,** tenor Glenn Siebert, and baritone William Sharp, with pianist Phillip Bush and the Cassatt Quartet (♦Albany 272).   HECHT

Michael Tippett *(1905–1998)*

Tippett felt a strong attachment to America, and perhaps we have to look to Ives to find the same quirkiness, romanticism, mysticism, daring, and naivete. By way of introduction, two multi-disc collections are available at reduced prices: Nimbus has a 4CD set of some chamber works, choral works with Darlington and the choir of Christ Church Cathedral, and orchestral scores conducted by the composer, and EMI has pulled together a miscellany of '60s recordings (*Fantasia Concertante on a Theme of Corelli,* Quartet 1, Piano Concerto and Sonatas 1 and 2 with John Ogdon, and Concerto for Double String Orchestra). The EMI box has second-drawer sound and chancy performances (the *Corelli Fantasia* teeters on the brink of ensemble breakdown under the composer's baton). The Nimbus renditions and sound are more dependable, though the composer doesn't bring much snap to the rhythms and the orchestra can lack focus.

Orchestral music. Tippett's four symphonies offer an exhilarating journey, from the Hindemithian classicism of 1 to the cutting rhythmic energy of 2, the commingling of Beethoven's 9th and the blues in 3, and the darkly conceptual single-movement 4. **Colin Davis**'s readings of 1–3 have a fantastic freshness, almost as if conductor and orchestra were having a joyful time of sight-reading. These were joined in a complete set with Solti's Chicago 4 (♦DG 425646, 3CD; NA but certainly worth looking for). In 1:I, Davis produces a bony, sprinting athleticism that **Hickox** can't achieve with the more generalized, more rounded tone of the Bournemouth Symphony (♦Chandos 9333). But Hickox's 1 is now the only game in town, and also comes recommended because the sound is more transparent in the slow movement. Hickox is a good deal slower than Davis in 2:I, but Chandos's sound does account beautifully for the solo trumpet and strings in the Adagio (♦Chandos 9299, with Shelley in the Piano Concerto). In 3, Hickox brings clarity to the insane melange of Beethoven quotes while Davis more appropriately plows into the music and lets the pieces fall where they may. The truly exceptional reading in Hickox's series is his exciting 4 (♦Chandos 9233, with an outstanding *Corelli Fantasia*), preferable to **Solti**'s because of the greater depth of sound and flexibility of phrase.

Davis went on to give both Concerto for Orchestra and Triple Concerto (♦Philips 420781), two of Tippett's greatest scores, a coherent shape and constant sense of direction that the more ordinary-sounding **Hickox** can't match (Chandos). Hickox does more to emphasize Tippett's antiphonal brass effects in the first movement of the Triple Concerto, but Davis's detail and more ecstatic touch in the South Asian exoticism of the slow movement make his disc irreplaceable. If I had to choose a single Tippett disc above all others, it would be this one. But **Tippett**'s own recording of the Triple Concerto is the highlight of his Nimbus series, outstanding for the expressive latitude he gives his soloists and for their own passionate advocacy.

Four discs of orchestral Tippett center around the pairing of the Concerto for Double String Orchestra and *Corelli Fantasia,* to which **Marriner** and his Academy of St. Martin in the Fields added *Little Music for Strings* (Argo). The playing has a lightness that's missing in most full-orchestra performances, but the remastering of the 1971 recording is a bit musty and edgy. In 1995 the same artists brought a fresher approach to a recital that leaves out the *Corelli Fantasia* but adds the deliciously erratic Sonata for Four Horns and the delightful *Divertimento on "Sellinger's Round,"* whose finale is sure to turn any breathing music-lover into a hopeless Tippettophile. This is one of the finest records Marriner and his group ever made (♦EMI 55452).

Andrew Davis adds "Ritual Dances" from *The Midsummer Marriage* (this last with choral contribution) to the standard pairing. These are excellent performances, though the BBC strings have an edge and more dynamic sensitivity wouldn't have gone amiss (♦Teldec 94542). Davis is touchingly expressive in the Adagio cantabile from the Double String Concerto. **Tippett** himself did the standard pair and threw in the embarrassing and entertaining *Songs for Dov* for tenor and orchestra (Virgin). Here his tempos were even slower than in the Nimbus releases and the articulation gluey with what sounds like a large group.

Tippett's last orchestral piece, *The Rose Lake,* is a half-hour tone poem, unusually meditative for him, with some extraordinarily evocative orchestration. **Colin Davis** conducts the London Symphony, and the coupling is Tippett's own 1971 performance of his great but rather forbidding oratorio *The Vision of St. Augustine* (♦Conifer 51304).

Chamber music. Tippett's five string quartets (1934–91) span an even wider chronology than the symphonies—indeed, almost his entire compositional career. Choice isn't easy between the **Lindsay Quartet** (ASV) and **Britten Quartet** (Collins). The Britten certainly offers finer quartet playing. This makes a particular difference in Tippett's slow movements, where the Brittens outshine the Lindsays in ensemble, intonation, and tonal blend. But the Lindsays are more flexible and personable in Tippett's fast movements, and springier in some of the opening movements. The Collins discs give the quartet more presence, which I prefer, but many will find this set less attractive because 5 was omitted.

Piano music. **Paul Crossley** commissioned and premiered Piano Sonata 3 and worked with the composer during the composition of 4, and his cycle of all four sonatas (1937–1984) is easy to recommend (♦CRD 34301, spread not very generously over 2 discs). **Nicholas Unwin** also taped all four works, but on separate releases, with 1–3 on one disc (Chandos) and 4 on another (Metier, with works of contemporaries). Crossley is as consistently alive to the composer's quirky cross-accents and rhythmic drive as he is to the naive lyricism. He's more apt to rely on the sustaining pedal than Unwin, and he isn't quite as impressive in technique, but there's more variety and spontaneity to his approach. **Perahia** also recorded 1, a beautifully lyrical performance that's only available in a 4CD Perahia 25-year retrospective (Sony).

Choral music. Tippett's best known and most often recorded work is his oratorio *A Child of Our Time* (1939–41), initially conceived as a pacifist's outcry against war. The finest recording overall, the one most sensitive to the work's dark lyricism and also most able to bring the startling variety of music together into a coherent and moving whole, is **Previn**'s with the Royal Philharmonic and an unbeatable lineup of soloists including Armstrong and Langridge (♦MCA 6202). The orchestral tone is particularly beautiful, with ensemble balances carefully tended to, even if the sound is a bit recessed (and the disc insufficiently cued). **Tippett**'s recording is generally faster and sharper in characterization, that impression backed up by multi-miking and greater sonic transparency (Collins). Despite Tippett's bigger, more operatic voices, Previn and his singers give the impression of getting deeper beneath the music's skin.

John Pritchard's more British-sounding 1959 performance has a special intensity, with the chorus clear and up-front, if also some occasional stiffness (♦Decca 461123). The sound is a touch frayed and the soloists don't have the poise, sensitivity, and individuality of Previn's. **Colin Davis** has Norman and Baker, but Richard Cassilly's strident tenor doesn't fall easily on the ear (Philips). Davis tends to fragment the structure of the piece, and the unflattering acoustics and off-mike soloists make for fairly disappointing sound.

Inspired by Jacob Bronowski's cultural-anthropological TV epic *The Ascent of Man*, Tippett's *The Mask of Time* (1980–82) is a non-denominational meditation for voices and large orchestra on mankind, time, the universe, and the transcendental. There are glimmers of brilliance in this no-holds-barred work, and all aficionados will want to hear it. But it's a mannered and pretentious creation—not least for Tippett's text, which is among his most freewheeling and opaque. **Andrew Davis**'s 1986 live recording is fine, though the sound is rather one-dimensional (EMI).

Songs. Tippett's songs have rarely been recorded, but **Martyn Hill**'s disc includes the two fine tenor cycles he wrote for Pears and Britten: *Boyhood's End* and *The Heart's Assurance* (Hyperion). Hill's delivery is very reminiscent of Pears, even to the fact that his voice isn't aging very well. *Byzantium,* Tippett's half-hour work for soprano and large orchestra, is in a tough and vigorous style reminiscent of the Triple Concerto. Tippett favorite **Faye Robinson** recorded the work with Solti and the Chicago Symphony, and it appeared as a coupling for Solti's CD reissue of Symphony 4 (London). Though it's an imperfect performance, given a fairly one-dimensional sound-picture, I hope it will soon reappear.

ASHBY

OPERAS

In his operas, composer-librettist Tippett constructed his own mythology. Often the situation can be emotionally gripping, full of intent and import, but all too often the story degenerates into a logic-defying haze. Self-knowledge and reconciliation are recurrent themes.

The Midsummer Marriage. This one uncomfortably blends Hindu and Celtic elements. The text is thick with heavy-handed spirituality imbedded in a literary and literal (stage) fog. The singers at the premiere said they had only the haziest idea what the opera was all about. I haven't been able to find the recording of the world premiere performance in 1955, but—with Sutherland, Monica Sinclair, and Otokar Kraus led by **Pritchard**—it looks promising (Gala 100.54, 2CD). A recording based on the 1970 revival contains some cuts sanctioned by the composer (♦Lyrita 2217, 2 CD). Joan Carlyle isn't the coloratura technician that Sutherland was, but she sounds quite lovely and copes well with the technical difficulties, and the rest of the cast is attractive. The choral forces of Covent Garden are impressive, with seeming mastery of the score's intricacies, and **Colin Davis** leads the orchestra with equal parts spirit and control.

King Priam (1962). Perhaps because it invents no new mythology but contents itself to reinterpret Homer's story, *King Priam* is easier to understand and more emotionally effective. Even here, though, the death of Priam is of a perfunctory suddenness, almost a footnote to a story about choice and its consequences. A series of orchestral outbursts relieves the spare quality of the dialogue; rarely do the singers have a chance at full-blown vocal outcry. In the only recording (1980), Norman Bailey, nasally focused but regal in presence, dominates the proceedings (♦Chandos 9406, 2CD). Thomas Allen is too bland but sings nicely. Langridge sounds unpleasant as character and singer, and Robert Tear shouts Achilles. The ladies all sound vocally healthy and soothing to the ear. **David Atherton** sorts out the orchestral strands with clarity and care.

The Knot Garden (1970). It recycles Shakespeare's *Tempest,* but casts it in a more realistic light summed up in the defiant line "Simply the thing I am shall make me live" (Parolles in *All's Well That Ends Well*). This is the least complex, least artificially contrived of Tippett's operas and has the most sympathetic characters. It also has received the best all-round recording of any of his operas (Philips 446350, 2CD). This is the complete original cast and they're immersed in their roles, singing with easy familiarity and much beauty. Barstow remarkably creates a sympathetic character out of the freedom fighter Denise, a role that could all too easily degenerate into a harridan. Tear sings well, but his tough tenor voice is inappropriate for the delicate musician Dov. **Davis** paces the work with careful delineation of parts smoothly connected through their transitional passages.

The Ice Break (1977). This invents a new politically correct mythology. This is Tippett's shortest opera, its three brief acts passing at an accelerated pace with all transitions removed, achieving a cinematic effect. The title has both actual and symbolic meanings, recalling the exhilarating sound of ice breaking in the great rivers of the north—the arrival of spring—and also drawing our attention to the main premise of the opera: "whether or not we can be reborn from the stereotypes we live in." Tippett calls this "the central problem of our time"; it's expressed

through the struggles of opposing generations (young and old) and racial groups (black and white). The opera is about the need for conciliation.

Tippett visited the United States for the first time in 1965 and translated this experience into his opera, employing a lot of American slang. This—especially the four-letter words—can be distracting, and much strikes the listener as silly and outdated. Tippett characterizes his protagonists by using the very stereotypes he protests against. The music is anything but hummable, with seemingly random dislocations of rhythm and emphasis. What is truly effective is the motif of the ice break—a brass and percussion chord of manipulated minor and major thirds, which begins the opera and recurs at climatic moments.

The only recording derives from concert performances at the Proms in 1990 (♦Virgin 91448). Most impressive is David Wilson-Johnson, a mellow-voiced Lev, strongly sung. Carolann Page handles her vocal gymnastics with precision and ease. Cynthia Clarey's Hannah is sung with warm beauty, and Thomas Randle's tenor is at ease with the silly banalities required of him, Heather Harper has some difficulty early on keeping the awkward musical line from squawking, but the longer she sings the better she gets—a humane, caring Nadia. Sanford Sylvan's Yuri is a little too petulant for my taste, but it does derive legitimately from the text. Much is required of the chorus, and they rise to the challenge. **David Atherton** keeps things firmly under control.

PARSONS

Rudolf Tobias (1873–1918)

Tobias is often referred to as "the father of Estonian music," and rightly so; as the first composer to tackle one musical form after another, he pretty well kick-started Estonian art music. He obtained a thorough grounding in the rudiments from his father, a church organist, and began composing at the age of nine—for organ, of course—and studied organ with Louis Homilius and composition with Rimsky-Korsakov at the St. Petersburg Conservatory.

His dramatic overture *Julius Caesar,* written in 1896 while still a student, was the first orchestral piece composed by an Estonian. The language, dark and driven, muscular and meaty, owes more to Schumann than to his Russian teachers, yet for a first essay it's strikingly assured, as **Neeme Järvi**'s taut recording makes clear; it's in the second of two discs of Estonian orchestral music he recorded in the late '80s (♦Chandos 8656).

After his graduation Tobias remained in St. Petersburg as organist and choirmaster of an Estonian church, and it's there that he wrote both his surviving string quartets (a third was left a torso at his death). Quartet 1 (the first Estonian string quartet) has its stylistic feet in Schubert, though the craftsmanship is Tobias's own—a blend of derivative language and independent technique that makes it a close cousin to the early Sibelius quartets. No. 2 opens with an imperious gesture announcing more ambitious aims and, indeed, a Beethovenian sense of scale and momentum runs through the entire piece—the homage made explicit at the opening of the finale with a quote from one of the Rasumovsky quartets. The performances by the **Tallinn String Quartet** are both passionate and articulate and are unlikely to be bettered (♦BIS 704).

Tobias moved back to Estonia in 1904, to the provincial city of Tartu. Around 1905 he began to write his massive German-language oratorio *Des Jona Sendung* (*The Mission of Jonah*), a huge outburst of overwhelming power and majesty. For all its scale, it remained a matter of local pride until the 1995 release of **Järvi**'s electrifying performance (♦BIS

731/2, 2CD). The influences on Tobias are clear, Bach's passions, Mendelssohn's "Lobgesang" Symphony, and Brahms's *German Requiem* chief among them. But the work, based on the Old Testament *Book of Jonah*, has a kind of exultant solidity that is a Tobias hallmark: "Heilig, heilig," for example, the 19th of its 32 movements, is both prodigiously mighty and refreshingly direct—it packs a physical punch that raises the hairs on the back of your neck. At other moments *Jona* can be extraordinarily beautiful, unfolding melodies of exquisite loveliness. This is, quite simply, great music.

Aware that he was working on a scale unlikely to find a local outlet and keen to discover what was happening in modern music, Tobias headed west, settling in Leipzig in 1908; it was here that he completed *Des Jona Sendung*, and here that it had its disastrously under-prepared premiere the next year, conducted by the composer. He learned from his mistakes, re-wrote parts of the work and conducted the "Introitus" and "Sanctus" at the opening of the Estonia Concert Hall in Tallinn in 1913. At last he had his triumph and, emboldened, returned to Germany, where he now had a teaching post at the Königliche Hochschule für Musik in Berlin, having stepped in for the indisposed Engelbert Humperdinck.

As choirmaster and organist, Tobias wrote music for practical religious purposes throughout his career. None of it has yet been taken up by a Western recording company, though the Estonian label Forte—available only intermittently even in Estonia, though still worth keeping an eye open for on the import shelves—has released three CDs: one of motets and sacred songs where the chamber choir Eesti Projekt is conducted by **Anne-Liis Treimann** (♦0013/2); another of his organ music with **Ines Maidre** (♦0028/2); and the piano music, most of it on a fairly small scale, played by **Vardo Rumessen** (♦0029/2), the pianist-musicologist whose selfless labors in reconstituting Tobias' scores have made possible his rediscovery. A marginal master, perhaps, but a figure of world standing nonetheless.   ANDERSON

Ernst Toch (1887–1964)

Austrian by birth and highly successful in Europe, Toch came to the United States in 1935, where he became, in his own words, "the most forgotten composer of the 20th century." His early music was influenced by Brahms, but he soon developed his own style, characterized by long-lined, chromatic melodies, often large interval-leaps, linear counterpoint, tonal flexibility, frequently changing meters, and an acute sensitivity to colors and textures. Toch wrote: "I believe in the conciseness and concentration of musical expression, in well-balanced form, in utter economy of artistic means, in the functional life of independent voices more than in the compilation of harmonies." His closest cognate is Hindemith, but Toch's music is warmer and more optimistic.

Toch wrote seven symphonies during the last 15 years of his life. In the masterly 3, his orchestra contains a Hammond or pipe organ, a glass harmonica, glass chimes, and a "hisser," a tank of compressed carbon dioxide gas controlled by a valve. Scurrying fugatos, lively dances, marching themes, and quiet, contemplative passages mark the melodic riches of this genial work. It won the 1956 Pulitzer Prize and was written for **William Steinberg** and the Pittsburgh Symphony and recorded by them in 1956 (EMI 5658682, with Hindemith's *Mathis der Maler*, performed by the same forces, and Frank Martin's *Petite Symphonie Concertante* with Stokowski conducting his own orchestra). The sound, in remastered stereo, is clear but sometimes sharp-edged, especially in the high strings and trumpets, and there are a few microphone pops in the loud passages near the end; a new recording is urgently needed.

The powerful 5, 6, and 7 were recorded in excellent sound and solid, secure performances by **Alun Francis** (CPO 999389). No. 5 is also known as the symphonic poem *Jephtha*, written for the Louisville Orchestra and recorded by them in 1966, led by **Robert Whitney** (Albany 21). Nos. 6 and 7 are characterized by frequently thinning textures; orchestral tuttis are rare. Prominence given to individual instruments brings these two works within the realm of "concertos for orchestra."

The 6 movements of *Dance Suite* are serious dances, often dark-hued, now capricious, then wistful and melancholy. Some are typical Viennese dances, but not of the bon-vivant type. They are well performed by **Jürgen Bruns** leading the Kammersymphonie Berlin, though they sometimes sound under-miked (EDA 013, with Schreker's *Birthday of the Infanta* suite). *Spiel* is a 9-minute suite that is considered a standard in the wind band repertoire (CRS 9051, with wind music by five other composers). Toch's felicitous Cello Concerto and masterly Piano Concerto have lingered too long on LP (Contemporary Records 8014)—more than 30 years—and are badly in need of new interpretations and recordings.

The delightful Divertimentos, for violin and cello and for violin and viola, are performed with verve by the **Mendelssohn Quartet,** but the sound is sometimes on the thin side (Laurel 850, with the impressive Quartets Opp. 26 and 70). The Op. 26 quartet marks the turning point toward Toch's more adventurous works of the '20s. Its melodic and harmonic vocabulary is still similar to the earlier ones, but the music is more dissonant, subdued, and introverted. Toch's early Brahmsian Sonata for Violin and Piano (1912) is given a fine performance by **Eudice Shapiro** and **Ralph Berkowitz** (Crystal 302, with violin and piano music by Stravinsky).   DE JONG

Giuseppe Torelli (1658–1709)

In his time, Torelli was best known as a virtuoso violin and viola player and had a major role in the development of both the concerto grosso and the solo concerto. He spent most of his career at the basilica of San Petronio in Bologna, his home town, with an interlude as a touring musician.

Recordings haven't been kind to him in recent years. All the discs currently available are trumpet recitals, ignoring the fact that most of his output was for strings; "The Art of the Trumpet" offers an acceptable introduction to his work (♦Naxos 550531, 550567). **Ivor Bolton** and the St. James Baroque Players have been praised (♦Teldec 91192), but not the series from San Petronio led by **Sergio Vartolo,** poorly played and recorded and rather dull (Bongiovanni). Several other discs offer Torelli works as part of trumpet recitals; I haven't heard them all, but most will be at least acceptable. Your choice of couplings will be a deciding factor in most cases.

Anyone who wants to get serious about Torelli's music has two choices: Wait for record companies to delve more deeply into his large output (don't hold your breath) or turn detective and search out LP-era recordings. Of these, by far the best is a 2LP set offering all twelve of the Op. 8 concertos played by violinist **Louis Kaufman** and a fine French ensemble (Oiseau-Lyre 166/67). Smaller in scope but equal in artistry are discs with five Op. 8 concertos played by I Musici (Epic 3217), and one with **Newell Jenkins** leading a superb group of Milanese players in a selection of Torelli works (Washington 9405). The Washington is stereo, the other two good mid-fifties hi-fi mono.   McCLAIN

Francesco Paolo Tosti (1846–1916)

Tosti was the classiest of the composers we think of as purveyors of Neapolitan songs. Although he came from the opposite side of Italy, he was a son of Naples by adoption, having studied there with Mercadante, and the most famous interpreter of his songs was that inimitable Neapolitan tenor Enrico Caruso. Tosti was singing master to both Italian and British royalty, and Edward VII knighted him in 1908. He responded to his English fame by writing such Victorian ballads as "Parted" and "Goodbye," with the immortal line "Kiss me straight on the brow and part." But his true genius lay in the simple Italian song, and he often set quite good words by such poets as d'Annunzio.

The Istituto Nazionale Tostiano, based in the composer's native town of Ortona sul Mare on the Abruzzi coast, is sponsoring a complete edition of the songs. Four volumes feature the veteran baritone **Renato Bruson.** If the disc of 1878–1882 songs to Italian texts with Robert Kettelson as pianist is typical, the edition will be of a high standard but the CDs will give short measure. This one ends with three of the most famous songs, "Patti chiari!," "Ideale," and "Povera mamma!," all from 1882, and Bruson is in good voice (Nuova Era 7272).

The most beguiling modern singers to have tackled Tosti are **Pavarotti,** who includes four songs in one of his popular recitals with orchestra (Decca 425037), and **Bergonzi,** who devotes a whole disc to 17 of them, again with orchestra (Orfeo 073831). The young bass **Michele Pertusi** sings three and six respectively in fine style in two of his recital discs with the Parma Opera Ensemble (Stradivarius 33472/73). We could do with a reissue of **Luigi Alva's** lovely LP.

Most of the great singers of the past have recorded Tosti's songs and here is a quick checklist of unmissable performances: "A vucchela": Caruso (a wonderful mezza voce), Ponselle, Schipa; "L'alba separa dalla luce l'ombra": Caruso, Björling (clearly imitating Caruso); "Aprile": Tetrazzini, Gigli; "Ideale": Caruso; "Luna d'estate": Caruso, Ponselle; "Marechiare": Schipa, Gigli; "La mia canzone": Caruso; "Non m'amate più": Smirnov (in Russian); "Pour un baiser": Caruso; "La serenata": Nezhdanova (in Russian), Battistini, Ponselle; "L'ultima canzone": Pinza (his loveliest record), Pertile (a truly anguished performance); "Voi dormite, signora!" De Luca; "Vorrei morire": Schmidt, Pattiera.

POTTER

Charles Tournemire (1870–1939)

Tournemire, *titulaire* organist at Ste. Clotilde for more than 40 years, is best known for incidental organ pieces, especially those transcribed by Maurice Duruflé. But beyond these works, Tournemire wrote not only the mammoth *L'orgue mystique*—a series of 51 five-movement collections that accompany the liturgical year—but also eight symphonies and some chamber pieces. While the organ music is improvisatory in nature and based on chant, the symphonies tend to be somewhat uneven, with lovely moments offset by episodes of meandering.

Symphony 1 (subtitled "Romantic") makes for pleasant listening, with attractive solos for violin and double reeds. No. 3 (subtitled "Moscow" after Tournemire's visit there) may be his best in terms of logical form and memorable melodies. The third movement—"The Bells of Moscow"—with its deftly handled orchestration, deserves repeated hearings. Two conductors have made a specialty of Tournemire's symphonies: **de Almeida** with the Moscow Symphony (Marco Polo) and **Pierre Bartholomée** with the Liège Philharmonic (Adda). Almeida is best for 1, 2, 4, 5, and 8; Bartholomée offers the only recording of 6 and is preferable in 3 and 7, though de Almeida is adequate.

As for his organ music, only one recording of the complete 51 offices of *L'orgue mystique* exists, from performances in 1989–90 in the Basilica of St. Mary (Minnesota). **Katherine Handford,** the series organizer, invited 50 prominent organists to join her (interested readers can write

to Digital-on-Location, 4340 Penfield Ave S., Afton, MN 55001). Most discs contain portions of various Offices. You can get a taste of the Minnesota marathon from ♦Sonus 105, with Offices 3, 26, 31, and 48; the discs by Delvallée and Cogen both contain extracts that are worth examining. **Harald Feller** performs music from the Pentecost cycle on a splendid Klais instrument in Ingolstadt (Calig 50939); **Jacques Boucher** incorporates choral sound with his interpretations (♦Real Music 31131); **Pierre Moreau** performs six selections at Notre-Dame paired with a disc of Vierne favorites, in excellent sound and interpretation (♦Charlin 106/7, 2CD).

The seven *Chorals-Poèmes* are based on the Last Words, and several excellent performances are available. Certainly one of the best is **Georges Delvallée** at St. Quentin and St. Sernin, though the instrument at St. Sernin doesn't please everyone (♦Arion 68158). Langlais's successor at Ste. Clotilde was **Pierre Cogen,** who delivers a first-rate performance from there (Cybelia 883).

Tournemire's best known organ music, however, consists of five improvisations he recorded in the early '30s that were transcribed from wax audio cylinders by Duruflé: settings of the *Te Deum, Victimae paschali laudes, Ave Maris Stella, Petite Rhapsody,* and *Cantilene.* The first can be heard to good advantage from **Suter** (JAV 105), and there are three fine interpretations of the *Ave maris* from **Colin Walsh** (Priory 648), **Mary Beth Bennett** (World Library 2914), and **Donald Foster** (Towerhill 71988). Look in the LP bins for more complete recordings: **James Kibbie** (Spectrum 173) performs all five; **Marie-Madeleine Duruflé** does only four, but hers are the most rewarding interpretations (MHS 1016).

METZ

Joan Tower (b. 1938)

Tower writes music that is both dynamic and approachable. Her orchestral pieces are striking in their directness of expression: She uses a contemporary language in a strongly personal way and builds drive, energy, and excitement by rapid and repeated figurations and ostinatos. Her first orchestral work, *Sequoia* (1981), was an instant success, and when Leonard Slatkin, then Music Director of the St. Louis Symphony, came across it he immediately invited Tower to become the orchestra's composer-in-residence. So began a fruitful collaboration that led to the commissioning of a number of pieces played by **Slatkin** and his orchestra (Electra/Nonesuch 79245).

Both *Sequoia* and *Silver Ladders* (1986) suggest the idea of rising upward; ascending scales (often at differing tempos) depict the great tree and the ladders. The concept of growth from a single point both outward and upward gives shape and body to Tower's fertile imagination and resource. If the '80s and '90s saw a rebirth of interest and confidence in American orchestral music after the lean, experimental years of the '60s and '70s, Joan Tower is a central figure in that revival.

Her continuing success in this vein is further illustrated by a release of more orchestral pieces led by **Alsop,** including a number of snappy and effective curtain-raisers for brass called *Fanfares for the Uncommon Woman* (Koch Schwann 37469). This disc features the 1990 Concerto for Orchestra, a tornado of a piece that illustrates how Tower's art has developed. More quiescent and poetic but no less assured is the 1995 *Duets,* which, although a chamber orchestra commission, still manages to encompass a very broad range. Her highly charged Piano Concerto ("Homage to Beethoven") is played by **Paul Barnes** (Koch Schwann 31333, with concertos by David Ott and Victoria Bond).

Two discs of chamber music are worth mentioning: "Black Topaz" includes the ethereal **Snow Dreams** for flute and guitar with **Carol Win-**

cenc and **Sharon Isbin,** and the two-piano version of the ballet *Stepping Stones* with **Double Edge** (New World 80470). *Black Topaz* for piano and instruments is full of exciting and exotic imagery. A number of clarinet pieces played by **Robert Spring** make up another disc (Summit 124). *Fantasy . . . those harbor lights* is a shimmering, remote nocturne, and the clarinet and piano version of the 1990 Clarinet Concerto achieves both spontaneity and controlled tension; long, mysterious piano trills and nervous augmented fourth figurations often darken the mood. The earlier *Breakfast Rhythms I and II* for ensemble are marginally experimental but still expressive.   JOHNSON

Eduard Tubin (1905–1982)

Until the early '80s, when Neeme Järvi began his pioneering series of recordings for BIS, Tubin was a composer of purely local importance, a source of pride in his native Estonia and an object of rather detached respect in his adoptive Sweden where, with 25,000 other Estonians, he had fled in the fall of 1944. Now he is increasingly recognized as one of the major 20th-century composers from the Nordic-Baltic area.

The backbone of Tubin's output is formed by his ten magnificent symphonies (he was working on an eleventh at the time of his death). Although the dark, Sibelian atmosphere and sense of grim, inexhaustible strength of 1 were to prove characteristic of the subsequent works, he later learned how to generate energy more compactly; 1 shares a disc with the less successful *Balalaika Concerto,* where some marvelous orchestral writing alternates with a workaday solo part, and the tightly argued, Bartókian *Music for Strings* (BIS 351). **Järvi** conducts the Swedish Radio Symphony, and the unconvincing balalaika soloist is Emanuil Sheynkman. The same conductor and orchestra tackle 2, bearing a title, "The Legendary," that Tubin intended as an indication of mood rather than a reference to any specific tale (BIS 304). Nos. 2 and 5 form Vol. 1 of a new Tubin cycle underway with the Estonian National Symphony under **Arvo Volmer;** these readings are just a shade underpowered (Alba 41). Nos. 3 and 6 turn up the temperature (Alba 147).

The grim, bitter determination expressed in 3, recorded again by **Järvi** (BIS 342), is explained by its dates: When Tubin began it, in 1940, Estonia was occupied by the Soviets; by the time he finished it two years later, his country had been overrun by Hitler's troops, and the defiant tone sounds a call to resistance. No. 4, though, offers a striking contrast; subtitled "Sinfonia lirica," its tone and orchestration, the woodwind writing in particular, are uncannily close to George Butterworth's sound world. **Järvi** here conducts the Bergen Symphony (BIS 227).

No. 5 is perhaps the most successful of them all and deserves a place in the international concert repertoire—audiences who enjoy Shostakovich and Vaughan Williams would take to it immediately. It shares a disc with the suite he drew in 1961 from the ballet *Kratt,* draping symphonic muscle around Estonian folk tunes (BIS 306). **Järvi** again conducts the Swedish Radio Symphony. No. 6 reveals how much more adept Tubin was becoming at focusing his material (BIS 304, with 2). March rhythms pervade almost everything he wrote, and the tramp of war sounds through all three movements here, with one as fierce and angry as anything in Shostakovich in the central *Molto allegro.*

Most of Tubin's symphonies are in three movements (4 and 8 are four, 9 in two, and 10 forms a single span, though in four clear sections). So, too, is the *Sinfonietta on Estonian Motifs,* inspired by the folk-music research of Bartók and Kodály; given the somber tone of much of Tubin's music around this time, it's a remarkably good-natured work, though his customary reserves of power can be sensed behind the even temper. A less rigorous composer would have included

it in his canon of numbered symphonies. Nor is it clear why Tubin gave the label "Concertino" to what is clearly a piano concerto, the first work he composed in his Swedish exile. After the black fury of 6, 7 begins as if it inhabits a more relaxed world, but the tension soon builds, given added bite by the (relatively) lighter scoring; the finale is another of Tubin's driving marches. **Järvi** again conducts; this time the orchestra is the Gothenburg Symphony, and the soloist in the *Concertino* is **Pöntinen** (BIS 401).

No. 7 introduced a note of harmonic obliquity into Tubin's language; it's consolidated in 8 (BIS 337, with 3). The style is still grand, heroic, proud, but the thematic material is more abrupt—the old certainties, even of justified anger, have gone. There was no "ninth-symphony problem" for Tubin: He disarmingly called his 9 "Sinfonia semplice", though it continues the rarification of his harmony. The structure is unusual for Tubin: I develops a sonata allegro out of a slow introduction and II enfolds a fugal scherzo within an *Adagio.* It's coupled with 4, where they are complemented by the bouncy orchestral *Toccata;* **Järvi** conducts, of course, this time with the Gothenburg Symphony (BIS 227).

Tubin's last completed symphony, 10, continues the stylistic evolution of the previous three: It's as if 6 represented all he could say in the more romantic Sibelian-Shostakovichian vein of the earlier works and he began to plough a sparser furrow—though ten obviously bears the Tubin hallmarks of long-legged basses, brass-powered counterpoint, and those ever-present march rhythms, and there are passages as bleak as anything in late Holst. That characteristic is emphasized by being heard alongside *Requiem for Fallen Soldiers,* set aside for 19 years and finally completed only in 1979. The scoring—contralto soloist, male-voice chorus, trumpet, side-drum, timpani, and organ—has military overtones and the music is dignified and anti-sentimental. **Järvi** conducts the Gothenburg Symphony in 10 and the Lund Student Choral Society in *Requiem* (BIS 297).

When Tubin died, he had completed the first movement of 11, though not its orchestration; that task was undertaken by fellow Estonian Kaljo Raid in 1987. It was recorded by the Estonian State Symphony under **Arvo Volmer** and shares a disc with Tubin's brief, elliptical *Elegy* for strings (written for two violins and two cellos and arranged by Raid) and Raid's own Symphony 2 (Koch 7291).

Tubin's concertante works are generally less successful than the symphonies. The Waltonian *Prélude solennel* prefaces **Lubotsky**'s performance of the slight and forgettable *Suite on Estonian Dance Tunes* (1974) and the rather more substantial Violin Concerto 1; he's accompanied by **Järvi** and the Gothenburg Symphony—but, compared with the best of his music, this is second-rank Tubin (BIS 286). As a man who was to write a balalaika concerto, he must have regarded a commission for a double-bass concerto with equanimity; it sits between Symphonies 5 and 8 and shares some of their martial strength, though it loses focus in the more relaxed passages. The soloist is **Håkan Ehrén,** who rubs shoulders with **Gustavo Garcia** in the Violin Concerto and *Ballade* for violin and orchestra, neither of them particularly convincing (BIS 337). **Järvi** throws in *Valse Triste* (and yes, it does indeed recall Sibelius) and the jolly *Estonian Dance Suite.*

Almost all the running on Tubin's behalf has been by BIS, through the efforts of two Estonian musicians in particular: Neeme Järvi, of course, and the pianist-musicologist **Vardo Rumessen,** who performs the complete piano music (BIS 414/416, 3CD) and joins **Arvo Leibur** (violin) and **Petra Vahle** (viola) in an anthology of the complete music for violin, viola, and piano (BIS 541/542, 2CD). A *Suite of Estonian Dance Tunes* and some smaller pieces aside, it consists principally of two sonatas for violin and piano, another for solo violin, and two for viola and piano, one of which is a transcription of the Alto Saxophone Sonata. The original saxophone version, played by Pekka Savijoki and Pöntinen, can be found in a Tubin miscellany with an earlier recording of Violin Sonata 2 and the *Ballade in the form of a Chaconne on a Theme of Mart Saar;* the unexpected closing tracks offer two choral works, *The Retreating Soldiers' Song* and *Ave Maria* (BIS 269). **Järvi** conducts the male voices of the Lund Student Choral Society.

Tubin wrote two operas, *Barbara von Tisenhusen* and *The Parson of Reigi.* Both are concerned with thwarted love: The aristocratic Barbara runs away with the scribe, a commoner below her station, and is killed by her unforgiving brothers for bringing shame on the family name; Catharina, the lovely young wife of the Parson, falls in love with a newcomer to the village of Reigi and is put to death along with the man who brought her brief happiness. The earlier work is a technical tour de force; in Tubin's tonal equivalent of the Schoenbergian note-row, the entire opera is based on a single theme, presented in its basic form, in version, retrograde, retrograde inversion, etc. The approach does produce the atmosphere of implacable fate required by the plot, but at the cost of musical variety; in purely dramatic terms *The Parson of Reigi* is more effective. Both works have been recorded by the Estonian Opera Company in 2CD sets, *Barbara* conducted by **Peeter Lilje** (Ondine 776) and *The Parson* under **Paul Mägi,** accompanied by *Requiem for Fallen Soldiers* conducted by **Eri Klas** (Ondine 783).

Even more than in his many orchestral and instrumental works based on Estonian folk tunes, it's in Tubin's choral music that his roots are outlined most clearly. Before his wartime flight to Sweden he was active as a choral conductor, so his writing for chorus is extraordinarily resourceful, capable of generating a startling degree of power in only a few bars. The excellent Estonian National Male Choir R.A.M., conducted by **Ants Soots,** copes easily with the considerable difficulties of the complete songs for male-voice chorus (Forte 0056/2). Stocks of Forte CDs come and go even in Estonia; keep your eye on the import shelves.

ANDERSON

Joaquín Turina *(1882–1949)*

The generation following Albéniz and Granados in Spain is traditionally thought to consist mainly of Falla and Turina. Two more unlike composers can hardly be imagined, Falla acerbic and gutsy, Turina unfailingly beautiful and romantic. It's perhaps possible to dismiss Turina as a purveyor of picture postcard Spain, but if so, he writes the most collectible musical postcards. The majority of his 104 opus numbers consist of music for his instrument, the piano: A projected complete edition is expected to fill no less than 16 CDs.

ORCHESTRAL MUSIC

Turina recordings tend to come and go, perhaps reflecting the evanescent quality of his music. His only symphony, *Sinfonia Sevillana,* is in an all-Turina program led by **Miguel Gómez-Martínez** with the Hamburg Symphony (MD+G 3290744). This lyrical but somewhat underpowered performance replaced an earlier version by **de Almeida** and the Bamberg Symphony that had energy but somewhat short-changed the more delicate moments in this colorful score (RCA 60895, with *Danzas fantásticas* and *La procesión del Rocio*). Alert readers will note that in both cases we have a Spanish conductor attempting to nationalize a German orchestra. The latest contender is **Leaper** with the Canary Islands Philharmonic, an Englishman meeting a Spanish orchestra on their own island (ASV 1066). This performance is dreamy and atmospheric, and it

complements the MD+G issue, including two works omitted there— *Evangelio* and *El Castillo de Almodóvar*—not otherwise available, both substantial, lovely compositions.

Danzas fantásticas and *La procesión del Rocio* are also available from **Enrique Fernández Arbós** and the Madrid Symphony in an interesting program called "Spanish Orchestral Favorites" (VAI 1046), while the well-known *La oración del torero* is perhaps best heard in **Gerard Claret**'s performance with the National Chamber Orchestra of Andorra (Nimbus 5570, with the lovely Serenade for Strings and other string orchestra works by modern Spanish composers). The recording is somewhat harsh in loud passages, but played well. The Serenade is also played in virtuoso fashion by I Musici di Montreal under **Turovsky** in "Latin Impressions," a disc containing works by composers from the New World as well as the old (Chandos 9804).

A less polished reading is in an all-Turina disc entitled "Andalusian Concertos," containing several pieces not otherwise recorded, in which **Isidro Barrio** plays piano and conducts the Chamber Orchestra of the Empordá (Figueres) (Koch 1258). *Symphonic Rhapsody* for piano and strings and *Oración* are here, as is an excerpt from the opera *La Anonciación* and string orchestrations of three piano works. The performances are idiomatic but rather labored technically. The *Rhapsody* is also heard in **Eileen Joyce**'s disc in a celebrated performance transferred from 1936 78s (Dutton 5505); **Joaquin Soriano**'s reading is recorded in your face (ASV 775, with *Oracion*). **Juan de Udaeta**'s disc with Ricardo Requejo would be a most idiomatic choice for both of these pieces and the *Serenade* if it were available (Claves 9215, NA).

Apparently help is at hand. The Centro de Documentation Musical de Andalucia has issued an album containing performance tapes and historical recordings (Almaviva 128, 2CD). The set includes a 1954 performance of *La Procesion del Rocio* played by the National Orchestra of Spain under **Ataulfo Argenta** in respectable mono sound, *La Oracion del Torero* with the Barcelona Symphony under Eduardo Toldra, and the *Rapsodica Sinfonica* with Lympany and the Philharmonia under Susskind. The sound is variable, but the album has a feeling of historical value, a frisson of authenticity. It also includes several arrangements from the 1920s, interesting for their period charm and some interesting castanet improvisations.

CHAMBER MUSIC

There is a string quartet, only one movement of which was recorded by **Guitars a quattro** in a disc with something approximating the original scoring of *Oracion* for lutes (Intim 51). Then there is a piano quartet, nicely played by the **Amabile** (Summit 199) and **Philarte Piano Quartets** (Gaspaaro 2003). The discmates will determine your choice: Brahms and Bridge quartets for Amabile, Bernhard Heiden and Mozart for Philarte.

There are two piano trios. No. 1 has been recorded by the **Mompou Trio** (RTVE 65011; Schwann incorrectly believes it's also on RTVE 65013). Don't get them mixed up with the trio by Jose Luis Turina (RTVE 65014). These discs are all part of a series of Spanish trios performed by this excellent group. Both trios used to be available, together with the little-known *Circulo,* also for trio, played by the **Munich Trio** in particularly good readings (Calig 50902, NA), and they are offered by the **Philadelphia Trio** (Centaur 2259, with Martinů's *Bergerettes*). The two violin sonatas plus the earlier *Sonata Española* come from **Scholl** and Lourdes Ramirez (Amati 9702) and by **Felix Ayo** and Bruno Canino (♦Dynamic 208), the latter winning in both personality and recorded sound.

PIANO MUSIC

The complete piano compositions are being recorded by **Antonio Soria**. At least eight discs of a projected 16 have been released, eliciting modified rapture (Moraleda, various numbers). He's good, but a little lacking in temperament. Our taste for Spanish piano music has been whetted by the marvelous **Alicia de Larrocha;** after her, nobody seems quite good enough, though her Turina is presently NA. Other collections include those by **Mirian Conti,** fluent and lively (Koch 7322); **Albert Guinovart,** both vigorous and subtle (Harmonia Mundi 987009); **Lourdes Ramirez,** a little clumsy and a short program (Amati 9404); and **Ricardo Requejo,** who includes Turina's first and last compositions for piano, along with the favorites, *Danzas Fantasticas* and the sonata *Sanlucar de Barrameda* (Claves 9904). Between Conti, Guinovart, and Requejo, you can get a good taste of Turina while sampling Soria's more esoteric wares at your pleasure.

GUITAR MUSIC

There is a little less than half an hour's worth of original guitar music by Turina, effective and exciting as played by **Barrueco** (◆EMI 66574, with the soloist's arrangement of Albéniz's *Suite Española*). **Rafael Andia** plays this music much more moodily, taking three minutes longer for his program (Harmonia Mundi 905246, with his own transcriptions of the Tango from Op. 8 and Five Gypsy Dances Op. 55). Shorter programs may be found, but these are the most extensive and useful collections.

SONGS

Turina's songs are dominated by *Canto a Sevilla,* a cycle usually heard in its orchestral arrangement. In its complete form, with instrumental introduction, interlude, and epilogue, it lasts well over half an hour. This version is sung by **Alfredo Kraus** with piano in somewhat shallow sound and with no discmate, making a 38-minute recording (RTVE 65017). The orchestral version may be heard sung by **Yannula Pappas** (Mercury 84134), though the absence of texts is a turn-off. **Manuel Cid** is less distinctive but well sung and offers a longer program with Requejo on piano, a better buy (◆Claves 9602). An odd disc is by **Yannula Pappas** with orchestra, an interesting program unfortunately omitting the orchestral sections and with no printed texts.

The same problem besets the elaborate album of historical recordings put out by the Cultural Society of Andalucia (Almaviva 128, 2CD). This includes two versions of the *Canto,* one recorded in concert by **Victoria de los Angeles** with Dorati, one with **Lola Rodriguez Aragon** in which the composer plays piano with colorful expression. Neither version includes the interludes. There are other single songs with Aragon and Turina, and one with **Supervia.** But no texts.   MOORE

Johann Baptist Vanhal (*1739–1813*)

Few composers have risen as far as Vanhal, who was born in Bohemia into a family of bonded peasants. He studied the organ and violin but was a good enough cellist to play quartets with Haydn, Dittersdorf, and Mozart. In 1760, when he was a 21-year-old choirmaster, Countess Schaffgotsch took him to Vienna, where he studied with Dittersdorf and was so successful as a teacher that he was able to buy his freedom. From 1769 to 1771, thanks to another noble sponsor, he traveled in Italy. Up to this time Vanhal was clearly driven by a creative demon as strong as that which impelled Haydn and Mozart, but following a mental crisis—he apparently heard voices telling him to compose only religious music—his creativity declined and his last years were spent teaching and writing relatively small pieces.

Vanhal composed at least 76 symphonies, and those that have been

recorded are of splendid quality, often providing interesting solo opportunities. The best disc to start with is by **Concerto Köln;** it contains five works, including one of the G minor symphonies that were such a feature of the Viennese classical era (Teldec 13141). A disc in the "Contemporaries of Mozart" series by **Bamert** contains three fine works but duplicates the G minor (Chandos 9607). So too does the disc by **Michael Helmrath,** which has three of the same works as the Teldec collection (Orfeo 320941), while **Thomas Kalb**'s has only two symphonies out of four to itself (Koch Schwann 367152). **Saraste** offers a nice F minor symphony that no one else has recorded, but their trump card is the marvelous Concerto for Two Bassoons, with soloists Annika Wallin and Arne Nilsson (BIS 288). **Bruno Meier** offers excellent E-flat Flute Concerto alongside works by Friedrich Witt and Josef Mysliveček (Koch Schwann 311104).

The violin concertos have tended to come from Czech and Slovak players over the years, and so it is at present, with the terrific young Czech fiddler **Ivan Zenatý** playing a Concerto in D with the Prague Virtuosi under Oldřich Vlček in a bargain disc (Discover 920265, with Mysliveček and Dvořák), and **Andrea Sestaková** coupling a C major Concerto with one by Benda, sturdily accompanied by the Slovak Chamber Orchestra under Warchal (Opus 2334). A delightful all-Vanhal disc contains the Double-Bass Concerto in E-flat and the Viola Concertos in C and F (the latter a recent discovery); the brilliant soloists are the Romanian bassist **Ovidiu Badila** and the French violist **Pierre-Henri Xuereb,** with the Prussian CO well conducted by Hans Rotman (Talent 291055). The familiar Viola Concerto in C gets a gemütlich performance from the late **Ernst Wallfisch,** with the Württemberg Chamber Orchestra under Jörg Faerber in a memorial disc devoted to the soloist (Bayer 200028).

Of at least 72 string quartets by Vanhal, only three are available at present, but the works are all mature and the disc is a good one. It was the first recording by the well-known **Stamitz Quartet** of Prague after its change of leader in 1995, but the playing is assured (Panton 1431). The six *Quartette concertante* Op. 7 for oboe and string trio are beautifully written, though not in the same class as Mozart's work for the same forces, and the performances by senior British players, including oboist **Sarah Francis** and violinist Frances Mason, are fine (Helios 55033). The little Divertimento in G for violin, viola, and double-bass is a jolly surprise; it comes in an entertaining disc spotlighting the bass playing of **Barbara Sanderling** with pieces by Michael Haydn, Rossini, and Couperin (Berlin 0093552).

No doubt Vanhal could list playing the viola among his accomplishments; he certainly wrote well for the instrument. Versions of the well-known Sonata in E-flat by **Anna Barbara Duetschler** (Claves 9502) and **Robert Verebes** (SNE 569) can safely be overlooked—both are outclassed by their keyboard partners—but **Karel Spelina** of the Czech Philharmonic is a different matter. Superbly partnered by the veteran Josef Hála on harpsichord or piano, he plays the four slightly earlier Op. 5 sonatas as well as the E-flat (Supraphon 3285). Six highly enjoyable flute sonatas are superbly played by **Bent** and Sverre **Larsen** in a disc that's well recorded but poorly presented—we aren't even told if the artists are related. Like the viola sonatas, these works each feature a strong first movement, a lyrical central movement and a finale in popular style (Classico 237).

The best possible introduction to Vanhal's religious music is *Missa solemnis in E-flat,* magnificently performed by four young soloists, the Prague Chamber Choir, and the Virtuosi di Praga under **Neumann** at his relaxed best. The mass has stirring choral passages and the soloists all have impressive moments. They generally sing one at a time; there's just one duet and one concerted section. This mass is only a notch below those of Haydn and Mozart in quality and is beautifully recorded (Orfeo 353951). POTTER

Edgar Varèse (1885–1965)

"The contemporary composer refuses to die," Varèse once wrote, and while he left only a dozen completed works, their beauty and originality ensure that he is very much alive. Initially trained as an engineer, he studied music in Paris and Berlin, becoming well known as a composer and conductor. He came to the United States in 1915 and had a lively, controversial career as a promoter and composer of new music that sounded much too new for most tender ears. He returned to Paris from 1928 to 1933, and then went back to New York, living for many years in obscurity in Greenwich Village. In the '50s, Varèse's engagement in the burgeoning field of electronic music brought more public recognition. He died a grand old man of modern music and has been revered ever since, his influence spreading even into pop music; his most famous admirer was undoubtedly Frank Zappa, who probably introduced more people to Varèse than anyone else.

Varèse's musical output is, as Ezra Pound once wrote of good poetry, "News that *stays* news." It's eternally invigorating and an essential part of any 20th-century collection. The cornerstones are two huge orchestral works, *Arcana* and *Amériques*. Varèse's preface to the latter offers a good description of the appeal of this music, which he considered "symbolic of discoveries—new worlds on earth, in the sky, or in the minds of men."

The other works are, for lack of a better term, chamber works, although their precisely sculptured brawniness (Varèse preferred to call music "organized sound") doesn't easily fit the cliché of chamber music as genteel conversation. *Hyperprism*, *Octandre*, and *Intégrales* are strictly instrumental, for winds, brass, and percussion. *Ionisation* is the prototypical percussion ensemble piece, much copied and still provocative. *Offrandes*, *Ecuatorial*, and *Nocturnal* (Varèse's last, unfinished work) call for voices. *Density 21.5* is a brief, shapely, cool piece for solo flute. *Déserts* alternates electronic and instrumental passages (which can be performed alone); *Poème électronique* is strictly, proudly electronic, a wonderfully original approach to a brand new way of writing and presenting music.

You have to be a true believer to play Varèse's music, and most of the available recordings are excellent. The complete, or nearly complete, works are available, outstandingly played and performed, from Boulez, Nagano, and Chailly. (Neither Boulez nor Nagano offers *Poème électronique*, which of course doesn't require an interpreter.) It's hard to choose among them, and frankly I like having them all.

When the **Boulez** recordings originally appeared in the '70s and '80s, they represented a high new standard for Varèse performance, and they still don't disappoint. The gutsy performances still sound excellent, particularly the NY Philharmonic's virtuosic run-throughs of *Arcana*, *Amériques*, and *Ionisation* (Sony 45844, with *Intégrales* and *Density 21.5*). Boulez's Ensemble Intercontemporain versions of *Déserts*, *Ecuatorial*, and *Hyperprism* are available (Sony 68334, with Elliott Carter's *Symphony of Three Orchestras*). These discs omit *Offrandes* and *Nocturnal*.

Nagano's readings are as compelling as Boulez's but in a different way; they're more overtly emotional, finding unexpected lights and shades in Varèse's music. The performances of the chamber and vocal works are especially haunting. *Ecuatorial*, *Density 21.5*, *Intégrales*,

Déserts, *Nocturnal*, and *Ionisation* are on a well-filled disc (Erato 14332). His *Arcana*, *Amériques*, *Offrandes*, *Hyperprism*, and *Octandre*, aren't currently listed (Erato 92137). If Nagano's performances are eventually collected in one of Erato's "two-fers," it will be a great bargain.

Chailly's truly complete Varèse collection offers the best of both worlds (♦London 460208). It includes a few unusual items unavailable from Boulez and Nagano, notably the original version of *Amériques* (which has even more percussion than the revised edition), and it offers the original tapes of *Poème électronique* (also to be heard in Neuma 45074 with electro-acoustic music by Babbitt, Xenakis, and Roger Reynolds). Chailly also offers two versions of the song "Un grand sommeil noir," the sole surviving sample of Varèse's early music; all the rest was either lost, or destroyed by the hypercritical composer. The Concertgebouw plays *Arcana* and *Amériques* with predictable smoothness and beautiful sound. The informative booklet, with notes by Varèse's pupil and assistant Chou Wen-Chung, is also a plus.

Like snowflakes, no two Varèse discs are quite alike. A live recording of *Intégrales* and *Octandre* in bright, hard-edged performances is outstanding (Col Legno 31872, imaginatively coupled with Feldman's ethereal *Rothko Chapel*). **Arthur Weisberg** collects topnotch performances of *Ecuatorial*, *Offrandes*, *Intégrales*, and *Octandre*, performed by the cream of '70s New York City freelancers, including the peerless mezzo de Gaetani (Nonesuch 71269). **Mehta**'s performances of *Arcana*, *Ionisation*, and *Intégrales* are brash and exciting (not the whole story in this music, but not inappropriate either) and given a highly colored, brightly defined recording (London 448580). The collection led by **Abravanel** is less flashy but also satisfying: *Amériques*, *Ecuatorial*, and *Nocturnal* make their discmate, Honegger's *Pacific 231*, sound positively genteel (Vanguard 40). The **Hague Percussion Group** and ASKO Ensemble collect *Intégrales*, *Ionisation*, *Déserts*, and *Poème électronique* in spiffy Dutch performances from 1984 (Attacca 9263).

If you'd like a quick, inexpensive education in three important 20th-century composers, check out Vox 5142. Besides works by Ligeti and Penderecki, **Friedrich Cerha** (an important 20th-century composer himself; he completed Berg's *Lulu*) leads authoritative performances of *Ionisation*, *Density 21.5*, *Hyperprism*, *Intégrales*, *Octandre*, and *Offrandes*, in brilliantly clear 1969 sound.

Two Varèse recordings are in a class by themselves. **Martinon**'s lucid, precise *Arcana* is paired with ballet suites by Hindemith and Bartók, all in outstanding 1967 recordings (♦RCA 63315). **Dohnányi**'s *Amériques* may tame some of the wildness of Varèse's "new worlds," but compensates with beautifully detailed sound, rich but not plush; ditto the coupled performance of Ives's Symphony 4 (♦London 443172). RAYMOND

Pēteris Vasks (b. 1946)

This Latvian composer studied the contrabass and played in orchestras from 1963–74; although he later studied composition at the Music Academy in Riga, he's largely self-taught as a composer. From a welter of influences, including Pärt, Shostakovich, and the modern Polish School (especially Lutosławski), he forged a diatonic to chromatic musical language characterized by simple hymn-like and folk-like melodic lines, a basic lyricism spiced with moderate dissonance, shimmering luminosity, cellular themes that grow organically, billowing, densely polyphonic lines, and aleatory techniques. In his deeply felt, intensely emotional music, Vasks expresses profound religious and passionate feelings about nature, the environment, the human species, life, death, and the tragic suffering of the Latvian people under the Soviet heel. His music contains sadness but also life-affirming optimism and idealism. Many of his works evoke the songs of birds, to Vasks "voices of life and freedom." "In my music I speak Latvian," he says, but his prize-winning works are immediate, personal, and universal.

Vasks has a predilection for writing for strings. His three most famous, most often performed works in that medium are the stunning, life-giving *Cantabile*, the tragic, soulful *Musica Dolorosa,* and the masterly, deeply expressive Symphony 1 ("Voices"). An all-Vasks CD offers *Cantabile* and *Musica Dolorosa,* lamenting the death of his sister, rounded out with the dramatic *Message* for strings, two pianos, and percussion, and the "Voices" Symphony (Wergo 6220). The music is well recorded and beautifully played by the Latvian National SO under **Pauls Megi** and the Latvian Philharmonic Chamber Orchestra led by **Tovijs Lifčics.** Vasks is especially partial to this disc.

Another well-recorded and performed all-Vasks release, much admired by the composer, is conducted by **Kriss Rusmanis** with the Riga Philharmonic, playing *Cantabile, Musica Dolorosa,* the "Message" Symphony, and the lyrical English Horn Concerto with Normunds Schnee as soloist (Conifer 51236). Also on this CD is *Lauda* for orchestra, a heartfelt tribute to the Latvian people. **Rudolf Werthen** conducts I Fiamminghi in stunning performances of *Cantabile, Musica Dolorosa,* the "Voices" Symphony, and *Lauda* (Telarc 80457). As much as Vasks admires this release, he told me that he considers *Cantabile* played too fast (6:23 versus the usual eight to nine minutes). Werthen's urgent, white-hot approach lends a more dramatic aspect to the music.

Juha Kangas and the Ostrobothnian Chamber Orchestra play *Cantabile* with finesse and intensity, coupled with some astringent but predominantly tonal works for string orchestra by five Estonian and Lithuanian composers (Finlandia 97893). Kangas and his ensemble also recorded the "Voices Symphony," coupled with attractive music for strings by two Lithuanian composers, in fine performances and sound (Finlandia 97892).

Latvian-born violinist/conductor **Kremer** leads the Deutsche Kammerphilharmonie in a sensitive reading of *Musica Dolorosa,* with tonal and more modern works by five other Estonian and Latvian composers (Teldec 14654). They include Pärt's popular *Fratres,* here in the version for violin, strings, and percussion, and *Nevertheless,* a delightful concerto for violin, piano, and strings by the Latvian composer Georgs Pelecis, with Vadim Sacharov as piano soloist; a very worthwhile release. *Musica Dolorosa* was also recorded by **Dennis Russell Davies** conducting the Stuttgart Chamber Orchestra, coupled with Rudolf Barshai's string orchestra version of Shostakovich's String Quartet 8 and Schnittke's 1985 String Trio in the string orchestra version by violist Yuri Bashmet (ECM 21620). This stunning release was voted one of the best CDs of 1997 by *BBC Music Magazine.*

Vasks's powerful Cello Concerto with David Geringas as soloist and the "Voices" Symphony are well performed, in fine sound, by **Jonas Aleksa** and the Riga Philharmonic (Conifer 51271). **Kremer** and his Kremerata Baltica offer the "Voices" Symphony and the masterly Concerto for Violin and String Orchestra, called "Distant Light," referring to the distant memories of childhood expressed by the solo violin (Teldec 22660). The powerful performances elicited high praise from Vasks.

Vasks's gripping, evocative String Quartets 1–3 are given rich, detailed performances by the **Miami String Quartet** (Conifer 51334). In "Baltic Elegy," the **Duke Quartet** offers Quartet 2, coupled with Pärt's quartet version of *Fratres* and a fine quartet by Estonian composer Sven-Erki Tüür, performed with finesse and insight (Collins 14752). Vasks is also very pleased with the recording of Quartet 2 by the **Riga String**

Quartet (Caprice 21635, with Quartet 3). The composer also expressed his admiration for the performance of his *Musica Adventus,* the string orchestra version of Quartet 3, performed by **Juha Kangus** and the Ostrobothnian Chamber Orchestra, This stunning CD is rounded out with evocative string works by one Lithuanian and two Estonian composers, includng the recently deceased Lepo Sumera.

An all-Vasks release offers *Landschaft mit Vögeln* (*Landscape with Birds*) for solo flute; *Landscapes of a Burnt-out Earth,* an intense, emotional piece for piano; the eight-movement *Episodi e Canto perpetuo,* a homage to Messiaen for violin, cello, and piano; the nostalgic *Musik für einen verstorbenen Freund* (*Music for a Deceased Friend*) for wind quintet; and *Gramata cellam* (*The Book*), a tour de force for solo cello, well performed in good sound by flutist Dita Krenberga, pianist Inara Zandmane, cellist Kristine Blaumane, and the **Riga Quintet** (Conifer 51272). *Episodi e Canto perpetuo, Landschaft mit Vögeln,* and *Musik für einen verstorbenen Freund* are also well performed by members of the **North German Radio Symphony** (Koch 6496). They're coupled with *Eine kleine Nachtmusik* for piano, starting quietly, building up to thundering chords and then subsiding, the delicate *Weisze Landschaft* (*White Landscape*), also for piano, and *Eine kleine Sommermusik* (*A Little Summer Music*) for violin and piano, alternating dance-like and contemplative movements.

Vasks's majestic *Te Deum* is in "Baltic Organ Music," with works by five Estonian, Latvian, and Lithuanian composers, in fine performances and sound by Swedish organist **Hans-Ola Ericsson** (BIS 561). Available as imports are two Latvian Radio releases (Māte Saule, unnumbered, and LRCD 031). On the first we find four of Vasks's memorable choral pieces performed by the Latvian Radio Choir conducted by **Kaspars Putninš** and Sigvards Klava, with seven pieces by the Latvian composer Pēteris Plakidis. On the second are Vasks's masterly, prayerful *Dona Nobis Pacem* for choir and organ and shorter choral works by eleven other Latvian composers—a very worthwhile release. *Dona Nobis Pacem* is also in "Baltic Canticles" in a fine performance by the Latvian Versija Chamber Choir, **Juris Voivods** conducting, with works by six other composers (Jade 8126).

Another import has the Latvian **Sacrum Chamber Choir** performing five short choral pieces by Vasks and music by nine other Latvian composers, with various conductors and assisting performers—a very attractive release (Sacrum 009).   DE JONG

Ralph Vaughan Williams (*1872–1958*)

Vaughan Williams's music is a cornerstone of 20th century romanticism. In his conductor's notes to RVW's symphonies (EMI), Roger Norrington says: "I want to hear a marvelously individual composer who just happened to be English: a composer who chose his tonalities as freely as Debussy and Ravel, his unique rhythms as deftly as Stravinsky and Bartok. I want to celebrate a master . . . whose soul was ablaze with glory, pity, and anger. I want to do honour to a man whose sense of social duty made him seek to write music for everybody. The Sea, the City, and Land, War, Peace and War again; heroism, suffering, anxiety, longing, transfiguration."

SYMPHONIES

Most RVW symphonies have been recorded as part of complete cycles. I've heard nearly all of them and they're of generally high quality. Boult's EMI cycle still offers the most consistently satisfying interpretations in modern sound, though many prefer his earlier Decca/London recordings for their briskness. Boult worked intimately with the composer for many decades and had a special flair for the English idiom. But starting with Previn in the late '60s, Boult's hegemony slowly succumbed to the wide selection we have today.

For someone who wants the most effective rendition of each work, no cycle by one conductor will suffice. To those wishing a convenient introduction to the composer via the shorter orchestral works, I recommend "A Portrait of Vaughan Williams" (♦Nimbus 1754, 4CD). Conductors **Boughton** and **Darlington** have a good feel for the music, and nothing in this set is less than excellent—though top choices still have to be purchased separately. My preferences lean toward those recordings that capture the composer's unique sense of beauty and timelessness, and hence toward those conductors who create a harmonic blend and a melodic sensibility that isn't too literal or analytical.

1 ("Sea Symphony"). RVW made a stunning symphonic debut by combining huge orchestral and choral forces, choosing a timeless subject and importing the bold American poetry of Walt Whitman. For years, **Boult**'s mono recording from the early '50s set the standard; it's still a potent reading (Belart 144). His stereo remake with the London Philharmonic is even better—epic in scope, with an exquisite sense of mystery in "The Explorers," due in no small part to soprano Sheila Armstrong (♦EMI 64016).

Previn's cycle began before Boult's stereo remakes were completed (RCA). The soloists seem a bit too operatic and stilted for Whitman's text. **Handley** is better, for he and the Royal Liverpool capture not only the mood but the epic range of the score. Because of criticism that the soloists were too distant, the recording was remastered after its initial release, though it's now unavailable except as part of a complete set. It should also be noted that Handley's series as a whole has wide-ranging sound that falls into the demonstration class (♦EMI, NA).

Thomson emphasizes clarity of harmonic texture with a tendency toward literal interpretation (Chandos). Although the musicianship is fine, the atmosphere of the quieter sections is compromised. **Slatkin** has great sound, excellent choral and orchestral intensity, but goes oddly numb in the latter half of the mystical final movement (RCA). Reviews of **Andrew Davis**'s recording haven't been especially favorable, citing an overall lack of inspiration (Teldec, NA). Along with Boult's EMI, my favorite is **Haitink.** Although he's not quite as mystical as Boult, his version with the London Philharmonic has truly inspiring soloists and stunning orchestral playing from beginning to end (♦EMI 49911).

2 ("London Symphony"). This is an urban portrait by turns dramatic, atmospheric, jaunty, and somber. You might think its programmatic nature might make it relatively conductor-proof, but that's not the case. The dynamic and emotional contrasts are challenging, and few orchestras succeed in delivering it all. **Boult,** in the final recording of his later cycle with the London Philharmonic, gives us an expressive, flowing, superbly idiomatic reading (♦EMI 64017). His earlier mono recording is tighter, more intense, and not as broadly conceived (Belart 008). Right alongside Boult is **Barbirolli,** whose energetic, wonderfully expressive recording is badly in need of reissue, as is his earlier Vanguard recording (♦EMI, NA).

Previn's recording with the London Symphony is unmatched—breathtaking in its power, beauty, and balance, not to mention the darkly evocative Epilogue of the closing minutes (♦RCA 60581). His second recording is unique (♦Telarc 80138). He tempers the brighter aspects of the music, presenting a heavy, cataclysmic view that would seem to have England sinking into the sea—the fall of an empire—

and it's an awesome audiophile recording with the Royal Philharmonic .

Slatkin is the opposite of Previn: exciting and affirmative. It's appealing, but its uncompromising forward momentum costs something in grandeur and atmosphere (RCA). **Thomson** pushes the pendulum in the other direction—with dignity and grandeur but little momentum (Chandos). **Handley** is uncharacteristically cool (e.g., in the Andante of IV), though he has plenty of English charm (EMI, NA). **Andrew Davis** is also cool, and lacks charm altogether, though some may like the brooding atmosphere he gets in certain sections (Teldec, NA). **Kees Bakels** elicits excellent, concentrated playing from the Bournemouth Symphony, takes nothing for granted, and may be self-recommending at a low price—but I'd like more refinement of atmosphere in the critical Epilogue (Naxos).

Owain Arwel Hughes offers a broad, slightly uneven performance with real dramatic weight coupled with hushed sensitivity. Though I like it a great deal, it's the slowest on records and hence a bit controversial (ASV). **Haitink** has splendid sound and fine orchestral balance, but seems to lack a true understanding of the English idiom, which in this symphony, at least, is crucial (EMI). Besides Boult's mono recordings, historic performances include **Henry J. Wood**'s 1936 version. It's mainly for collectors, and has an older clipped style of conducting, but it generates plenty of excitement and is superbly remastered (♦Dutton 8004).

3 ("Pastoral Symphony"). It breathes the air of the English countryside, although the composer was inspired by sunset recollections in wartime France. The score allows the use of a wordless soprano or tenor solo in the last movement, though it's almost always a soprano. Two are especially evocative. **Previn** and the London Symphony have a blended harmony that is both vivid and atmospheric, with Harper ideally suited for the haunting beauty of the closing measures (♦RCA 60583). **Norrington** may seem an unlikely candidate because of his early-instrument recordings, but he and the London Philharmonic achieve a ravishing blend of orchestral sound with a natural, flowing grace. Rosa Mannion's wordless solo is iridescent (♦Decca 458357).

Both **Thomson** (Chandos) and **Slatkin** (RCA) share excellent engineering and fine musicianship but fail to find the soul of the work, with Thomson too literal and Slatkin dull. More to my liking is **Handley,** whose Royal Liverpool Orchestra delivers a fluent, expressive account in excellent sound that is coupled with one of the best 4s (♦EMI, NA). **Andrew Davis** has superior sound as well, and though not quite in the top rank, it's an expressive reading with especially clear orchestral textures (Teldec, NA). **Boult**'s stereo remake has excellent remastered sound and a polished lyricism that seems just right (♦EMI 64018). His earlier mono recording is equally good, interpretively similar to the stereo version (Belart 118).

Haitink takes the composer at his word regarding the wartime source of the music and gives us a somber, subtle, and effective reading(♦EMI 56564). Amanda Roocroft's solo seems to emerge out of a twilight landscape, and the London Philharmonic maintains a refined tension. **Bakels** and the Bournemouth arrive on the budget rack with a traditional reading whose orchestral balances and passionate mood hold their own with the best (♦Naxos 550733).

4. This tumultuous symphony has become associated with the eve of WWII, though the composer referred to it in purely musical terms. Given the violent BBC Symphony performance under **Vaughan Williams** himself in 1937, it's hard to imagine that the musicians weren't thinking of deteriorating conditions in Europe (♦Dutton 8011).

The piece doesn't work very well when it's subtly toned down, as it is by **Norrington** (Decca) and **Haitink** (EMI), though they may please those who want something less aggressive. **Thomson** is broad and massive, but the music never comes to life (Chandos).

I prefer performances with the drama and fire of the composer's own rendition, starting with **Handley**'s intense, heavily weighted opening movement and his mesmerizing contrasts (♦EMI, NA). **Bernstein** excels with a broader approach, creating a swirling vortex rather than whiplash violence, but displaying his penchant for rhythmic emphasis. It's also one of the best-sounding of the "Royal Edition" (♦Sony 47638).

Boult is no less effective with the London Philharmonic. His stereo recording still sounds good and is coupled with an outstanding 6 (♦EMI 764019), but his earlier mono recording is unequaled. It has a broad, frighteningly dramatic I; in fact, this whole reading is the most concentrated and tense of all, and an absolute must for aficionados, though the sound is bright and not up to standard (Belart 117). **Previn** and the London Symphony's tempos are heavy with anticipation and cataclysm, and the playing is first-rate (♦RCA 60583). **Sargent**'s in-concert recording is exciting, though not as telling in quieter passages (IMP). **Berglund** is again available overseas; it's been occasionally admired, but it's one of the very few I haven't heard (EMI). The 1956 **Mitropoulos** is of far more than historical interest—a strong, visceral reading with the NY Philharmonic (♦Sony, NA, with Stokowski's lesser 6).

5. Virtually another pastoral symphony, this piece surprised audiences during WW II with its tranquillity. The yearning third-movement "Romanza" is surely the soul of the work, and a recording has to get this right. **Barbirolli**'s early '60s performance not only does that, but sweeps the listener into the idyllic landscape from the first measure to the last. It's one of those rare recordings whose emotional concentration and careful shaping of phrases result in greatness, and the Philharmonia has never sounded better (♦EMI, NA). His 1946 recording is nearly as good, but in mono sound (Dutton). **Boult**, as usual, is dedicated, magical, and only slightly less moving in III than he might be (EMI).

Previn has recorded this symphony three times. He takes I at a fairly slow tempo in both his first and last recordings, building an impassioned warmth that culminates not only in heartfelt "Romanzas" but stunningly dramatic final movements as well. His London Symphony recording is one of the jewels of his earlier cycle (♦RCA 60586), while his last, with the Curtis Institute orchestra, is smooth, refined, and passionate (♦EMI, NA). His middle recording isn't up to the other two; it has excellent sound, but lacks the final ounce of emotional commitment (Telarc).

Five other recordings avoid succumbing to flatness. **Handley**'s enchanting Royal Liverpool recording is second to none, and it's coupled with a superb *Flos Campi* (♦EMI, NA). **Rozhdestvensky** conducts the BBC Symphony in concert with both strength and tenderness (♦IMP 9125). Equally good is **Norrington**, whose blended yet detailed recording comes with his superb 3 (♦Decca 458357). **Thomson** delivers a flowing, attractive, and stately account in his London Symphony cycle (♦Chandos 8554), while **Bakels** offers a less poignant "Romanza" than ideal (Naxos). **Boult**'s earlier mono reading is worth pursuing for collectors (Belart), and there are some rewarding moments in **Slatkin** (RCA), **Haitink** (EMI), **Hickox** (Chandos), and others, though I don't consider them first choices.

6. Written between 1944 and 1947, this work was also associated with WWII, its bleak finale thought to describe a nuclear wasteland. Instead, the composer suggested themes involving the storms of life ending in eternity, though he always preferred his work to be taken as pure music. Whatever the case, the movement is bleak and eerie. Few conductors have trouble conveying the overall score, but many fail to get this finale right. I used to think a slow tempo was of primary importance, but **Andrew Davis** and the BBC Symphony are so concentrated and delicately balanced that even at a fast 9:36, their recording has the right atmosphere. I consider this a must-have, and it's coupled with an outstanding *Tallis Fantasia* and a tasteful *Lark Ascending* (♦Teldec 73127).

In the finale, **Previn** is bereft of all feeling or atmosphere (RCA). **Stokowski** is on the speedy side, and although his is a generally sympathetic reading, IV just doesn't work at 8:38 (Sony, NA). The standard is **Boult,** whose final 6 with the London Philharmonic is nearly definitive—and at 11:20, IV certainly has that nuclear wasteland feeling (♦EMI 764019). Neither can you go wrong with any of his several earlier recordings (Belart, IMP, EMI). The 1990 release of his 1949 performance has the original version of the Scherzo as a bonus track (EMI, NA). Conversely, the 1949 is available using the original Scherzo, but offers no revised Scherzo at all (Pearl). **Bakels** reveals a modern, angular side of the finale, and the Bournemouth plays excellently in all four movements. This CD presents an outstanding example of a talented conductor who has something new and valuable to say (♦Naxos 550733).

Of the rest, **Norrington** lacks energy (Decca), **Haitink** is routine in IV (EMI), and neither **Thomson** (Chandos) nor **Slatkin** (RCA) offers anything noteworthy. More interesting is **Handley,** whose Royal Liverpool musicians punctuate the power and drama with terrific force, while the finale swirls with what seems to be darkly forested, rather than stark, imagery (♦EMI, NA).

7. ("Sinfonia Antartica"). This five-movement powerhouse was culled from RVW's film score for *Scott of the Antarctic*. The otherworldly orchestration reminds us that the South Pole is second only to outer space on a list of inhospitable places, its history one of triumph and tragedy. **Bakels** and the Bournemouth emphasize the dark side of the ill-fated Scott Expedition as well as the horror of the Antarctic wastes. He downplays the heroism through careful balances (and a powerfully cryptic organ) and emphasizes the cruel and deathly aspects of the struggle without compromising its eerie beauty. This superb recording also uses the advantages of CD programming to make the spoken prefaces to each movement optional (♦Naxos 550737).

Thomson and the London Symphony have been underrated. They deliver a big, broad, haunting performance that is tensely controlled and starkly noble (♦Chandos 8769). **Haitink**'s widely praised version is atmospheric and dramatic, but has a fake-sounding wind machine that detracts from the closing minutes (EMI). **Andrew Davis** has the same problem; the sound is so clear that you can't think of anything but the barrel of the machine rubbing against its fabric. Otherwise, he gives us a black, somber reading that has huge climaxes but borders on the ponderous. **Handley**'s is a traditional reading, carefully shaped, and with good sound, but too even-tempered (EMI, NA). **Slatkin** can be similarly described, and though competent, has little to recommend it (RCA).

Boult, as might be expected, is ablaze with the traditional English heroism that is the ostensible nature of the piece; neither does he miss the tragic drama. Both his mono and stereo recordings are powerful and essential. The former has John Gielgud as speaker; it's slightly more energetic and literal (♦Belart 116). The latter omits the spoken prefaces and is more carefully shaped (♦EMI 64020). **Barbirolli** conducted the premiere, and his energetic 1953 recording was made shortly afterwards. Though the mono sound lacks dynamic range and Margaret

Ritchie's wordless solo is closely miked, this can be recommended as an interpretive touchstone (EMI). His Helsinki 7 combines willful inflection with strong emotion and is similar to his Hallé/EMI recording (Intaglio, NA).

Previn may be better than either Boult or Barbirolli. He has a traditionalist's temperament, not as extroverted as Boult in the climaxes nor as briskly self-assured as Barbirolli, but the London Symphony perfectly captures the eerie mood of the work as well as its nobility, while Ralph Richardson's masculine voice sweeps the field in the spoken introductions and Harper delivers a spooky, evocative solo (♦RCA 60590).

Special mention must go to Leppard and the Indianapolis Symphony. In combination with the brief prefaces using snippets of poetry from Shelley, Donne, and Coleridge, Leppard includes big chunks of Scott's own diaries (he says Vaughan Williams suggested this to him), not only at the beginning of movements but between thematic sections. While this breaks up the music considerably, the narration is cleverly chosen and adds a unique dimension. This recording is only an alternate, but the music is well served and the presentation is fascinating (♦Koss 2214).

8. It separates itself from the rest in a jaunty splash of unusual orchestration. Apart from the wide variety of percussion instruments, the two inner movements are scored, respectively, for winds only, then strings only. The outer movements are a complex rush of bold, almost fragmented themes and linkages. It's difficult to know how it should go, but several conductors offer a satisfying picture. Bakels is always searching for the right details, and his tightly controlled version with the Bournemouth is both tense and passionate, with a tender violin solo in the "Cavatina" (♦Naxos 550737, with his insightful 7 at bargain price). If I had to choose only one, it would be Stokowski's 1964 Promenade Concert recording. By emphasizing orchestral color as no one but he can do, the whole piece comes alive with clarity and rhythm. The dramatic structure is coherent and lyrical, and the BBC Symphony is given excellent sound (♦IMP 91312).

I like Boult's 1952 London Philharmonic recording better than the later one with the same orchestra (EMI). The earlier one is atmospheric, imaginative, and energetic—and interestingly, it was recorded in stereo (♦Belart 116). Previn is smooth, dynamic, spacious, and refined (♦RCA 60590), while Thomson chooses somewhat controversial tempos and has a "bricks-and-mortar" approach that lacks coherence (Chandos). Slatkin isn't very searching in the opening measures, or early on in the beautiful "Cavatina" but he has fine soloists, excellent sound, and his reading is generally warm and expressive (RCA). But Handley sounds just as good, if not better, and he presents a joyful, coherent symphony tinted with buoyant delicacy (♦EMI, NA). Barbirolli, the dedicatee, conducted the premiere; his 1956 recording has both advocates and detractors. It was originally available on Mercury, so collectors will want to watch for it.

9. RVW's later innovative period continued with this distinctive and powerful work, written in his mid-80s. It set a new direction, with the composer in peak form. No one does it better than Handley, and in demonstration sound to boot. The opening is big and powerful, tense and controlled, with an epic quality. The interweaving saxophones in III are magically rendered and the *Andante tranquillo* has refined brass and string playing. The final measures are awesome under his dynamic stewardship. We must hope that his cycle will again become available as single discs (♦EMI, NA).

Of earlier recordings, Boult and the London Philharmonic once

again demonstrate their understanding with a powerful, thoughtful interpretation that clearly connects this last symphony to all that has come before (♦EMI 64021). His interpretively similar first recording with the same orchestra has an edge of freshness, and the 20-bit remastering is excellent (♦Everest 9001). Bakels uses quick tempos and ends up with a tense, engaging, but somewhat breezy rendition (Naxos). Slatkin has been praised for his direction of the latter two symphonies. His 9 is serviceable, in excellent sound, but isn't especially noteworthy (RCA). Thomson falls into the same category (Chandos). For a smoother, somewhat enigmatic yet highly effective performance, I'd go for Previn, though it's unfortunately coupled with his misfire of 6 (RCA).

OTHER ORCHESTRAL MUSIC

Lovers of RVW's orchestral music are luckier than most, for it's difficult to find a truly unsatisfactory performance.

Fantasia on a Theme of Thomas Tallis. This is a 20th-century masterpiece. Anyone who believes that great music ended with Brahms can be made to seem foolish by this profoundly passionate composition for string orchestra. At this count, nearly 30 recordings are available. I sometimes divide *Tallis Fantasias* into those that use an "a tempo" approach with those that mine the score for maximum expression. The effect of the former is to project a breathless urgency that carries right through the climax; the latter projects a deeply expressive ecstasy. The mysticism of the quieter passages is usually effective regardless of metric nuances, though it's especially dependent on the soloists. Concerning urgency vs. ecstasy, I have usually leaned toward the latter, though I'm learning to appreciate the former.

Two recordings may be said to exemplify these approaches. Best of the "espressivo" school is Morton Gould, who conducts his own orchestra in a timeless, profoundly satisfying reading that has not to my knowledge ever been released on CD (it was last seen in a Camden "Quintessence" LP, but was originally on RCA in 1964). That such a recording can be neglected by record executives doesn't inspire confidence, for there is a soul-stirring, mystical quality here that has not been duplicated (♦RCA LP 2719, NA). Akin to Gould, and also unavailable, is Dalia Atlas conducting the Israel Philharmonic in what must be considered a top choice, though the strongly accented musicianship isn't seamless (♦Stradivari, NA). Also taking after Gould is Slatkin, who has genuine regard for the mystical side of this piece; the St. Louis Symphony is marvelously recorded (♦Telarc 80059).

Handley exemplifies the urgent approach; he builds his argument slowly at first, then neglects every opportunity for expressive emphasis (EMI). Although he's not a good defender of the "a tempo" school, there are at least two who are. At just over 14 minutes, Andrew Davis and the BBC offer one of the fastest performances on records, but it's a superbly refined rendition—darkly expressive in calmer passages, fluently passionate in forceful ones, and vividly compelling in the dynamic climax. The rich, deep sound ideally complements the silky atmosphere, and to cap it off, the recording is coupled with a good *Lark Ascending* and a top-notch 6 (♦Teldec 73127). Another in this category shows its breathless urgency mainly in the climax: Karajan's fine-sounding mono recording from the early '50s with the Philharmonia. Its interpretive excellence is apparent in every measure, and it must be considered a classic (♦EMI 66601).

But some of the best recordings fall into a middle ground: neither indulgent nor impatient, but flexible, lyrical, and expressive. Again we find Boult the standard bearer. His wonderful London Philharmonic provides a baseline of sympathetic refinement and superior musicianship (♦EMI 64017). Where Boult is enchanting and refined, **Stokowski** is ardent and lyrical. He recorded his famous rendition with the Royal Philharmonic in 1975 in a radiant, fine-sounding performance that's among his best work (♦EMI 66760). **Ormandy** is flowing and mystical, with silky remastered sound, superb instrumental soloists, and the bonus of a top-choice *Lark Ascending* at budget price (♦Sony 62645). **Bernstein** is carefully wrought, deeply felt, and beautifully played by his New York soloists. It may be a bit less than spontaneous, but highly recommendable with its Symphony 4 coupling (♦Sony 47638).

Of newer recordings, **Thomson** is one of the most interesting (♦Chandos 9775). His approach has strength and nobility; and after a slightly tempered opening, the reading builds to a potent dynamic climax. **Boughton** is delicate and a bit tentative, but poignant and compassionate (Nimbus). **Marriner** is warm and graceful, but not as effective as we might wish at full price (Philips). **Christopher Warren-Green** is broad and forceful; he rushes the climax, but not without overall sensitivity (Virgin). **Previn** is nicely recorded and his recording with the Curtis Institute orchestra is one of the best ever (Telarc). These musicians play so beautifully, so passionately, you might think they were giving the premiere; unfortunately, as is so often the case with this label, it's deleted (♦EMI, NA).

Five Variants of "Dives and Lazarus". It is taken from one of the composer's favorite folk tunes and scored for string orchestra and harp. Perhaps because of the basic melody, this is one of the few pieces I've found to be relatively conductor-proof. **Hickox** and the London Symphony have the best sound and deliver a flowing, folk-like legato that has great expressiveness (♦Chandos 9593). Not even the redoubtable **Willcocks** quite achieves this level of rhapsody in his recommendable rendition (♦EMI, NA). **Thomson**, as in his *Tallis Fantasia*, brings purposeful nobility to the piece (Chandos). But you can't go far wrong choosing this work primarily as a companion to another (recommended) selection. This also applies to the popular *Fantasia on Greensleeves,* with slight tempo variations being the primary difference among the better conductors.

In the Fen Country. Another piece in the pastoral mood, it's one of RVW's first to use English folk melodies. **Boult** is straightforward and not very atmospheric, but sympathetic nonetheless (EMI). **Haitink** makes a better case for the work, with a touch of melancholy and plenty of atmosphere, revealing details of counterpoint (♦EMI 56762, with his routine 6 and a nicely sung *On Wenlock Edge*). **Wordsworth**'s overall program is better; his *Fen* is by turns sensitive and passionate (♦Argo 40116).

Job: A Masque for Dancing. Yet another masterpiece written for a ballet that follows the story of Job in the Bible, it sounds like one of the composer's greatest symphonies. **Boult** recorded it five times that I know of and all five are worth hearing. The 1946 performance is sharply articulated, frank and powerful, well paced, and very much like his later readings (♦Dutton Labs 8016, in "English Gramophone Premieres"). The sound is good but obviously can't match modern engineering. Still, the otherworldly atmosphere in V is well captured and the violin solo in VII is lovely and affecting. As in a number of Boult's performances, an older monophonic version stands out. Here it's his early '50s recording—a nearly ideal interpretation (Decca). All my enthusiastic remarks apply to this almost diabolically expressive reading, from the powerfully inflected orchestral climaxes to the sweetly sarcastic saxophone solo in "Job's Comforters"; it's available in relatively dated sound (♦Belart 122).

Boult's next recording can't match this, though it has its moments, and the sound is a bit rough in the highs during fortissimo passages (Everest). If you're looking for more modern sound from this conductor, better to go to 1971, the best-known of his stereo versions (EMI). It's broader than the early ones, slightly bloated in places, but noble and dramatic. A lesser-known, hard-to-come-by Boult recording beats all but the early Decca: the Vaughan Williams centenary performance of 1972 from Royal Festival Hall, strikingly passionate and detailed. The musicians played their hearts out on this special occasion, and while the recording's dynamic range could be better, the sound is excellent overall. I hope this will be reissued so that more listeners can discover it (Intaglio, NA).

For sheer sound quality, **Handley** is unbeatable; almost all of his mid-priced EMI recordings are in the demonstration class, and *Job* is no exception. After a lugubrious start, his reading becomes a powerful, atmospheric, and ironic traversal that exactly suits the composer's intentions (♦EMI, NA). **Lloyd-Jones** attempts to fill the gap among newer versions, and many feel this is one of the best. It's certainly forceful and dynamic, but also a bit straight-laced; neither is it ideal in atmospheric passages (Naxos). **Andrew Davis** has received a lot of attention and is worth hearing for those who appreciate his approach in the symphonies (Teldec, NA); reviews of **Bostock**'s 1999 recording have been only fair (Classico).

The Lark Ascending. A "Romance for Violin and Orchestra," it is perhaps the most poetic, and one of the most English, of RVW's compositions. The soloist conveys not only an airy lightness of being, but a timeless pastoral beauty that seems to grow more and more out of reach. Twenty recordings are currently listed, and most are satisfying. First among my favorites is **Hugh Bean,** who brings an indescribable rightness to this piece, with ideal phrasing and a graceful, yearning intonation that lifts you into the clear English sky (♦EMI, NA). **Raphael Druian** has exquisite control, excellent remastered sound, and an expressive fluency second to none (♦Sony 62645). **Barry Griffiths** is oddly self-effacing, but subtle and effective (Telarc). **Christopher Warren-Green** has garnered accolades; he takes a virtuosic, rather than an idyllic approach, but I'm not completely convinced (Virgin).

Unfortunately gone is **Zina Schiff.** In a rather closely miked presentation, she's individual and expressive, but also warm and unpretentious (Stradivari, NA). **David Nolan** is smooth and flowing but a bit straight-laced (EMI). **Kennedy** is broadly expressive at 17 minutes, the slowest on records, and appealing as an alternate (EMI). **Tasmin Little** is tasteful and refined (Teldec). **Iona Brown** might be considered were it not for some low-frequency hash on the CD (London). I like **Michael Bochman,** who sees the piece as sweet and lyrical (♦Nimbus 5208). **Hagai Shaham** has purity of tone, is gorgeously expressive, and offers a lovingly optimistic conclusion; the New Queen's Hall Orchestra under Wordsworth provides an especially sympathetic accompaniment (♦Argo 40116). **Anne Akiko Meyers** also achieves a beautiful tone with her 1718 Stradivarius (RCA). **Michael Davis** is sweetly flowing, but lacks the final touch of emotional yearning that I seek (Chandos). **Bradley Creswick** is better in this regard, and very pleasing, though he loses purity of tone in the final two notes (EMI). **Mordkovitch** is especially interesting in a version for violin and piano. She's dazzlingly expressive, a little too much so, but Julian Milford's piano provides an attractive, calm, pristine quality to this version (♦Carlton 00132).

Partita for Double String Orchestra. This one ought to be purchased by anyone who likes the *Tallis Fantasia.* Like the better-known work, it's a richly textured piece full of wonderful—though far more angular—

sonorities. I find **Handley** particularly persuasive in his emotional urgency (♦EMI 2179), while both **Boult** (EMI, NA) and **Thomson** (Chandos) aren't far behind.

The Wasps. This piece from 1909 is melodic and lighthearted music written for a comedy by Aristophanes. It's been a popular filler in both "Overture" and longer "Incidental Music" form (subtitled *Aristophanic Suite*). For the latter, **Handley** goes all out in a brisk, lively rendition that clearly has the musicians enjoying themselves (♦EMI 9508). **Boult** is again excellent, in both his Everest and EMI recordings.

CONCERTOS

Though they are technically difficult, RVW's concertos aren't strictly geared to show off the virtuosity of the soloist; rather the solo instrument is used as a powerfully expressive orchestral tool. The Piano Concerto is a case in point, for in the outer two movements it's easy to imagine the piano part transposed along orchestral lines like those in the symphonies. Yet the beautiful "Romanza" shows the composer making excellent use of the instrument's character and timbre.

Shelley has recorded this concerto twice, once with Handley (Lyrita, NA), and once during Thomson's London Symphony cycle. The latter is excellent in its ability to convey, without too much stridency, both the percussive aspects of the score and the calm inner Lento (♦Chandos 8941). **Piers Lane** is no less accomplished under Handley, also with a lovely central movement (♦EMI, NA). Both recordings have excellent sound. For the composer's two-piano version, written at Boult's behest, the one I'm familiar with was recorded by **Boult** with Vronsky and Babin; it sets an excellent standard (♦EMI 67220).

The Oboe Concerto is the most popular of the concertos. **Maurice Bourgue** gives a lively and lyrical account under Boughton in excellent sound, but it's only available in a 4CD set (♦Nimbus 1754). **Jonathan Small**'s with Handley is less likable for its too-even temperament (EMI), which leaves **David Theodore**'s traversal under Thomson open for recommendation (Chandos). Still better is **Robin Cantor,** whose satiny tone is very attractive (♦IMP 660021).

The Tuba Concerto is a marvelous testament to the flexibility of the instrument and an excellent work musically. **Patrick Harrild** with Thomson is a fine exponent (Chandos), but I can't recommend the Symphony 6 coupling so I'd opt for the full-bodied and delightful **John Fletcher** (♦RCA 60586, with Previn's Symphony 5).

RVW's violin concerto is called "Concerto Accademico"; it's formal and propulsive and has none of the pastoral mood of *The Lark Ascending.* **Kenneth Sillito** is poignant and expressive under Thomson, but it's coupled with Thomson's less-than-desirable Symphony 4 (Chandos). A better choice is **James Buswell;** his rich, sharply articulated reading comes along with Previn's outstanding Symphony 2 (♦RCA 60581).

CHAMBER MUSIC

Perhaps because of its limited scope, RVW's chamber music is considered secondary to his orchestral works, but there is wonderful music to be found, as fine as any of the rest. First on my list is the *Phantasy Quintet,* with its beautiful "Alla sarabanda." It's exquisitely played by the **Music Group of London** (♦EMI 65100) and barely less so by the **Mendici** (♦Nimbus 5191). On the same discs, these two groups also play the mystical String Quartet 2, with my preference here going to the Mendici. The Nimbus recording includes String Quartet 1, while the EMI has the lovely Violin Sonata in A Minor and six *Studies in English Folk Song* for cello and piano. The Sonata, *Studies,* and two Pieces for violin and piano are gorgeously captured by **Mordkovitch** along with her *Lark Ascending* (♦Carlton 00132).

CHORAL MUSIC

Dona Nobis Pacem (*Grant Us Peace*). This was written during the rearmament of Europe in the '30s. Symphonic in length, its text comes from imaginatively mixed sources, including Walt Whitman, the Latin Mass, the Old Testament, and John Bright's House of Commons speech during the Crimean War. Its beauty is not only resplendent but powerful and insistent. **Hickox** and the London Symphony and Chorus bring these qualities to the fore. The performance is exemplified by Kenny's enthralling voice, which carries an appropriate urgency, and Terfel's powerful and resonant baritone. The fine orchestra and chorus are recorded with wide dynamic range in an excellent acoustic (♦EMI 54788).

Yet I have to say that no one has surpassed the London Philharmonic and Choir under **Boult,** which makes me wonder how this conductor so consistently brings such a transcendent quality to this composer's music. Part of the answer can be found in the harmonic blend. Maybe choir master John Aldis was mostly responsible here, but there's something gorgeously ethereal in this recording, something that lifts the listener into another realm. Sheila Armstrong and John Carol Case are not only perfectly suited to convey the work's emotions, but they do so with peerless lyricism. I hope this recording will find its way back into the catalog soon (♦EMI, NA).

Best and his Corydon Singers and Orchestra aren't far behind; they have both clarity and understanding, but I can't recommend them in the same company as either Hickox or Boult (Hyperion). **Henry Wood**'s early broadcast recording with the BBC Chorus and Orchestra is of historical interest (Pearl, NA).

Flos Campi. It is a suite containing six movements without pause. Expressly about sensuous desire, it's a haunting tone poem in the impressionist mold of Ravel or Debussy and features a wordless choir. Two recordings are so exceptional that they must be considered above the competition. The first is **Willcocks** conducting the King's College Choir and Jacques Orchestra, with Cecil Aronowitz providing the important viola solo (♦EMI 67221); the second is **Handley** directing the Royal Liverpool Philharmonic and Choir with Christopher Balmer the soloist (♦EMI 9512). The King's College Choir under Willcocks sings with an incomparable, timeless passion; Aronowitz's viola is rapturous, warm, and eerily heartfelt. Handley's choir is slightly more mellow, emphasizing atmosphere, while Balmer plays with a tender beauty that could melt lead.

Of the rest, **Darlington,** the English String Orchestra with the Christ Church Cathedral Choir and Roger Best's refined viola playing, make a vivid alternative (Nimbus). So does **Hickox** with the Northern Sinfonia. No separate chorus is credited on the jacket or in the notes, but they achieve a blend that is both strong and atmospheric, while Philip Dukes plays with graceful poignancy (Chandos). **Del Mar** and Frederick Riddle do a serviceable job (Chandos), and violist Imai provides the compelling heart and soul of **Matthew Best**'s straightforward but compassionate account (Hyperion).

Mass in G minor . In one of the most beautiful liturgical pieces in all music, **Willcocks** conducts an irreplaceable performance with the King's College Choir. The ethereal beauty and ravishing mysticism of this recording transcend every other attempt (♦EMI 65595). Of the remaining performances, **Darlington** and the Christ Church Cathedral Choir are in top form, and an excellent alternative (♦Nimbus 5083).

Sancta Civitas (*The Holy City*). It was the composer's favorite of his choral works—an oratorio whose theme is spiritual and material renewal. Using the boys of the King's College Choir, the Bach Choir, and the London Symphony, **Willcocks** achieves a blend of forces ideally suited to the uncompromisingly sincere and spiritually transcendent music (♦EMI 67221). **Hickox** falls just short of achieving an equally ethereal balance with the Choristers of St. Paul's, but makes up for it in strength and inspiration. If it weren't for Willcocks, he would be the top choice (♦EMI 54788). **Rozhdestvensky** is also very satisfying, with strong soloists and a fine orchestra and choir (IMP).

Serenade to Music. This one was arranged in two versions for voices and also one for orchestral. The piece was originally written for 16 soloists—famous singers associated with conductor Henry Wood—with a text from the last act of *The Merchant of Venice.* Although a number of fine performances are available in the instrumental arrangement, I'd first consider the vocal version with **Boult,** the London Philharmonic, and soloists chosen to replace the originals of 1938. It's a sweetly serene, affectionate, incomparable performance (♦EMI 64022). Alternatively, and amazingly, you can hear the original 16 artists in **Wood'**s own 1938 reading; it's highly listenable and a must for collectors (♦Dutton Labs 8004). A fine but expensive newer recording is by **Matthew Best** with the English Chamber Orchestra (Hyperion). **Bernstein'**s group of soloists really doesn't sound that good as an ensemble, with the men often dominating. Yet it has its moments, and the excellent soloists are good when taking turns in the spotlight (Sony).

HALDEMAN

FILM MUSIC

RVW thought he might like to try writing for motion pictures at the age of 69, and later described his work on *The 49th Parallel* (called *The Invaders* in the United States) as "one of the best composition classes I ever had." Many have been introduced to his film music through the heartfelt prelude to that film, then continued on with *Scott of the Antarctic,* which he transformed into *Sinfonia Antartica* some years later. His writing for films, as you might expect, ranges from bucolic to intensely patriotic, and **Andrew Penny'**s wonderful disc of *Story of a Flemish Farm, The England of Elizabeth,* and *Coastal Command,* filled out with the Prelude to *49th Parallel,* makes a marvelous introduction (♦Marco Polo 223665). **Kenneth Alwyn'**s *Coastal Command* is very fine, if somewhat less evocative (Silva America 1011) ,while **Previn'**s *England of Elizabeth* is also essential (RCA 60586, with Symphony 5 and Tuba Concerto). **Bernard Herrmann'**s sodden tempo in the *49th Parallel* prelude shouldn't dissuade those who love British film music from buying his otherwise splendid Phase 4 CD (448954).

HALLER

SONGS

RVW was a prolific and venturesome song composer, eager to break away from the traditional voice-and-piano forms. He had a gift for melody and a deep appreciation of folk music, and the traditional and the innovative often dwell side by side in his songs. There have been many recordings over the years, and most of them have disappeared. We will pay homage to some that are gone, hoping for their reissue, but enough remain to afford a broad picture of his achievement.

On Wenlock Edge. The six Housman settings for tenor, piano, and string quartet might strike some listeners as too sophisticated for the down-to-earth verses. The poet himself was distressed to learn that the "football" stanzas of "Is My Team Ploughing?" were deemed too trite to set to music, and the thrilling, expansive climax of "Bredon Hill," is, perhaps, grander than the words would suggest. *On Wenlock Edge* nonethe-

less remains one of RVW's most popular vocal works, and few British tenors have been able to resist it.

The first recording was made in 1917 by **Gervase Elwes,** the composer's favorite interpreter, and is still available (Opal). Elwes was a communicative if somewhat amateurish singer, but his performance is of historical interest. I would sooner see reissues of the stronger-voiced **George Maran** (Decca) and the always compelling and lucid **Alexander Young** (Westminster). Pears's '40s recording, characteristically pungent and individual, is buried in a 2CD album (Pearl). **Partridge'**s sensitive, keenly enunciated stereo account is a worthy replacement (♦EMI 65589). **Martyn Hill** is almost as polished, though even paler in timbre (Hyperion), while the scratchy-toned **Adrian Thompson'**s reading is less enticing than its discmates (two Gurney cycles sung by Varcoe; Hyperion).

Rolfe Johnson brings his sweet, mellow voice and smooth style to a performance that's as satisfying as any other, included in one of the most essential issues of RVW songs (♦Collins 14882). **Tear** has recorded the effective version for full orchestra (made by the composer in the '20s), and it's worth hearing (♦EMI 64731). The sensitive, imaginative **Bostridge** will please collectors who admire his intimate manner, but his slender voice is taxed by much of the vocal writing and sounds rather pallid (EMI). Like Tear, he chooses the orchestral arrangement; he might have been more impressive pitted against a string quartet.

Songs of Travel. This is the most approachable of the song cycles. Set to verses by Robert Louis Stevenson, it's filled with tunes that instantly lodge in the mind. Many of the songs have been recorded individually, by such venerable singers as **Elwes** and **Peter Dawson. Richard Standen,** best known as the bass soloist in Scherchen's *Messiah* recordings, left us a spirited account, but it vanished years ago (Westminster). Still among the most likable interpreters is **Shirley-Quirk,** whose combination of robustness, tonal beauty, and observant nuance is well-nigh perfect (♦Saga). **Brian Rayner Cook** is fluent and sincere though he has even less voice (Unicorn). **Thomas Allen** offers the most handsome, urbane singing of all, but he's not quite as personable as Shirley-Quirk (♦EMI 64731).

There's no ignoring **Terfel,** whose popular appeal may have sold the songs to more collectors than any singer since Shirley-Quirk (♦DG 445946). Stevenson's lusty verses suit his brawny style, and his splendid voice and crisp declamation are undeniably apropos here. The young Canadian baritone **Gerald Finley** is less assertive than Terfel, but mellow and unaffected (♦CBC 1115). Among the tenors, **Tear** is sturdy and knowing, if perhaps somewhat burly of voice. Better is **Rolfe Johnson,** whose voice has enough good, clean ring to make the climax of "Youth and Love" really pulse-quickening (♦IMP 1065).

Other Cycles. The most recorded is *The House of Life,* settings of six sonnets by Dante Rossetti, of which the exquisite "Silent Noon" is the best known. It often appears in anthologies of English song, too many to enumerate—but don't overlook **Ferrier, Roy Henderson,** and **Bostridge. Rolfe Johnson'**s recording of the entire cycle is regrettably missing (Polydor), but in its absence, **Allen** will do quite nicely (♦Virgin 91105). **Luxon** (Chandos) and **Cooke** (Unicorn) are also acceptable. The ten *Blake Songs* for tenor and oboe have been recorded by **Partridge** (♦EMI 65589) and **Tear** (Argo). Partridge's disc includes *Four Hymns* with viola and the Chaucer setting *Merciless Beauty.*

Ainsley's indispensable collection bypasses *Four Hymns* but gathers together the great cycles that are accompanied by something other than solo piano: *On Wenlock Edge, Along the Field, Merciless Beauty,* and

Blake Songs (♦Hyperion 67168). His firm, glinting tenor and immaculate diction are just right for the music, and his voice blends well with the various instruments. American soprano **Lois Winter** once recorded *Along the Field* (for voice and violin) as part of an album that included the Blake and Chaucer songs (Desto LP). **Ruth Golden,** another American, sings it in a wide-ranging recital of songs hard to find elsewhere (♦Koch 7168). She's more operatic than intimate, and she seldom sings softly, but her enterprise earns our gratitude and serviceably fills some gaps in the catalog.

More difficult to track down is the second Housman cycle, *Along the Field,* for soprano and violin. **Winter** once recorded it as part of an album that included the Blake and Chaucer songs (Desto LP).

Miscellaneous Songs. *Linden Lea, The Water Mill,* and *The New Ghost* are often anthologized and easy enough to find. I'll spare a word only for the haunting, appropriately icy reading of *The New Ghost* offered by **Jennifer Vyvyan** in her English song recital because this wonderful but neglected soprano is more in need of an advocate than Ferrier, Baker, or Bostridge (Belart). My recommendations are otherwise for discs devoted exclusively (or at least extensively) to Vaughan Williams songs.

One of the most desirable is by **Rolfe Johnson** and **Keenlyside,** who divide a glorious selection of songs, some with instrumental accompaniment (♦Collins 14882, Vol. 2 in the English Song series). Also indispensable is **Partridge**'s Warlock-Vaughan Williams album, originally part of a generous English song collection issued by Oxford University Press and now on Etcetera (♦1078). The nine piano-accompanied songs here are a sampling of the composer's best. **Luxon** proffers interesting material (Chandos), and so does **Peter Savidge** in settings of Whitman and Tennyson, along with four Barnes settings, four Shove settings, and the poignant four *Last Songs* (Trax). The five *Mystical Songs* and five *Tudor Portraits* are neatly conjoined by **Henry Herford** and **Sarah Walker** (♦Helios 55004). **Allen** is a mellifluous interpreter of *Mystical Songs* (Hyperion, with *Serenade to Music* and *Fantasia on Christmas Carols*), but **Keenlyside** is no less satisfactory on that indispensable Collins disc. **Shirley-Quirk** is perhaps most eloquent of all in *Mystical Songs* (EMI), and Willcocks's recording of *Tudor Portraits*, with **Elizabeth Bainbridge** and **John Carol Case,** appends an electrifying account of *Benedicite*, sung by **Harper** (EMI)—but we're moving too far from the song repertory proper.

The nine piano-accompanied songs that filled out the fourth side of **Partridge**'s English song recital from Oxford University Press, once on Peters International LPs, are eminently worthy of reissue. Partridge was also one of the soloists in a defunct collection of folk song arrangements (mostly for chorus), titled "The Spring Time of the Year" (EMI). Its loss is not quite so grievous given the availability of "Over Hill, Over Dale," another folk song collection, with **Bostridge** and **George** among the soloists (♦Hyperion 66777).   LUCANO

Giuseppe Verdi (1813–1901)

In 1962, the gentleman critic Max de Schauensee published a slim volume entitled *The Collector's Verdi and Puccini,* which discussed the operas, surveyed the LP recordings available at the time, and made sensible recommendations. With (for example) only seven *Traviata*s, four *Ballo*s, two of *Don Carlos*, and one *Macbeth,* he had an easy time of it. Many of the early operas hadn't been recorded at all. Now we're deluged with Verdi, and the number of recordings dictates a certain ruthlessness in evaluating them. Hard-core opera fanatics, passionately devoted to singers they idolize, may be unfazed by poor sound , but it's unfair to expect the average listener to have the divinatory skills needed to appreciate many pirate recordings, or most professional recordings made before 1950. The 1928 *Aïda* conducted by Sabajno, the 1930 *Rigoletto* with Stracciari in the title role, even the 1940 *Otello* with Rethberg, Martinelli, and Tibbett, may indeed enshrine individual performances of unsurpassed merit, but collectors accustomed to modern sound will hesitate to genuflect before them.

It might have been safe, at one time, to advise consumers to stick to the major labels if they wanted good sound, but now that the majors have jumped on the pirate bandwagon, the number of unauthorized recordings has proliferated and many of them masquerade as legitimate. As more and more copyrights expire, Sony, RCA, and DG have invaded what used to be the underground market, but EMI is the worst offender, dressing up Maria Callas's *Macbeth* and *Traviata* to look exactly like studio recordings. Anyone but a Callas cultist is bound to be sorely disappointed by the all-but-unlistenable sound of the *Macbeth* and will feel cheated at having paid even half price. Recordings of live performances account for more than 90 per cent of the listings in the latest catalogs; most of these should be left to dedicated specialists. Proceed with caution.

I'm not turning my back entirely on older recordings, and certainly not the splendid monaural ones from the '50s. The golden age of Verdi singing predates even that decade, however. It's fortunate that we have an abundance of arias and ensembles recorded by Rethberg, Ponselle, Caruso, Gigli, Ruffo, Battistini, Pinza, et al.—the list can be extended into the dozens. Labels like Romophone, Pearl, Preiser, Marston, Nimbus, Minerva, Symposium, Enterprise, and more have preserved the voices of the great Verdi singers. The best way to learn the Verdi operas is through good-sounding modern recordings, like the ones recommended below, but by all means investigate the singers of the past.

OPERAS

Early operas

The 16 operas that precede *Rigoletto* are generally classified as early works, even though several of them have become almost as popular as the later masterpieces. The unsung hero of early Verdi is conductor **Lamberto Gardelli,** whose '70s Philips recordings of *Un Giorno di Regno, I Lombardi, I Due Foscari, Il Corsaro, La Battaglia di Legnano,* and *Stiffelio* pretty much have the field to themselves. With singers like Caballé, Norman, Carreras, Domingo, Cossotto, and Raimondi in the casts, the collector needn't feel deprived. Gardelli has also recorded *Nabucco* (♦London 417407), the negligible *Oberto* (Orfeo), and the much-maligned *Alzira* (Orfeo). His *Nabucco,* with the fiery Souliotis (who was soon to flame out meteorically) and Gobbi, has some competition (led by **Sinopoli** and **Muti**) but is still the best choice. Bergonzi and Ghena Dimitrova head the *Oberto* cast, and the performance is superior to the more recent effort led by **Marriner** (Philips). *Alzira* is performed by Cotrubas, Araiza, and Bruson, a cast not likely to be bettered in an opera not likely to be recorded often.

Bonynge's *I Masnadieri* (London), with Sutherland and Ramey, is a viable alternative to Gardelli's, with Caballé and Bergonzi. Despite the contributions of Bergonzi, Milnes, and Raimondi, **Gardelli**'s *Attila* is ruined by the bizarre Deutekom. In this case, the better choice may be **Muti** (♦EMI 49952), with Studer splendid in the soprano role and Ramey singing a part he performed many times on stage. Gardelli missed *Giovanna d'Arco,* but **Levine**'s EMI recording has a glamorous cast (Caballé, Domingo, and Milnes). Neither Gardelli nor anyone else has recorded *Jérusalem,* the French version of *I Lombardi,* in the studio.

His *Ernani,* originally on Hungaroton and later appropriated by Philips, is poorly cast.

The three most popular of the early Verdi operas deserve to be treated individually.

Ernani. **Muti**'s is the best-conducted recording (EMI). He whips up plenty of excitement and brings out lots of instrumental details, but he can also seem overbearing and frenzied. Freni toils with her aria, and Ghiaurov's voice has lost much of its plush, but Domingo is a diligent Ernani and Bruson, despite his colorless timbre, is the most impressive of recorded Carlos. The problems: Muti, for whom the *Urtext* is the final word, omits the bass's cabaletta, a later addition; Freni can't soar in the ensembles; and the recording is, unnecessarily, on three rather than two CDs.

Sutherland, in the **Bonynge** recording (♦London 421412), doesn't have Freni's feeling for the Italian words, but once past the aria, her voice shines out brightly and powerfully. Pavarotti's ardent Ernani gives much pleasure, but the other two principals are just passable. The performance has a winning vitality and directness nonetheless.

Probably the best choice is **Leinsdorf** (♦RCA 6503). Leontyne Price can't manage the aria either (for that we have to go back to Ponselle, de los Angeles, or the young Sutherland), but she's wonderful everywhere else. She always knows how to run with the ball, so to speak, energetically and thrillingly, her upper notes steadier and more beautiful than Freni's or Sutherland's. Bergonzi's dignified Ernani is the one that sticks in the mind, and the baritone and bass have solid voices, if little personality.

For the most exciting *Ernani* of all, try to find a recording of the 1956 Met broadcast with Milanov, Del Monaco, Warren, and Siepi, **Mitropoulos** conducting (available in Europe).

Macbeth. **Leinsdorf**'s recording still satisfies (♦RCA 4516). Warren is a stagy villain, but no one sings Macbeth more refulgently. Despite some ungainly moments, Rysanek is a sizzling, unforgettable Lady. Macduff's aria flows smoothly off Bergonzi's golden tongue. **Schippers**'s recording (♦London 433039) has the finest of Macbeths in Taddei, an underrated singer. He is a resourceful actor, and his baritone is round and warm. Nilsson, as his wife, lacks the agility for the drinking song, but her icy resolve and vocal steel are entirely apt.

Muti (♦EMI 67128) has a striking Lady Macbeth in Cossotto, who knows how to sing on the words, biting into them until her fangs drip venom. She has to stretch her mezzo a bit, but her singing is admirably firm and full. Milnes, like Warren, is on the hammy side but has glorious top notes. Carreras is a good Macduff. The much-praised **Claudio Abbado** (DG) is on the bland side, with neither Verrett nor Cappuccilli demonstrating the individuality of their competitors. The complete **Callas** piracy on EMI (and elsewhere) should be passed over in favor of her studio recordings of the arias.

Luisa Miller. The first major-label recording, led by **Cleva**, is still the most enjoyable (♦RCA 6646). Moffo is agile and vulnerable, lacking only upper-range power. Bergonzi's Rodolfo and MacNeil's Miller are mellifluously sung, and the two basses, though less memorable, are smooth and sonorous. Ricciarelli's swoony heroine, under **Maazel,** is not unappealing, and she has laudable colleagues (Domingo and Bruson), but Maazel is too meddlesome a conductor (DG). **Levine** is more considerate and also has Domingo, but the rest of his cast is unpersuasive (Sony). **Maag**'s *Luisa* is thoughtful and penetrating, and many collectors will be pleased by Pavarotti's trenchant Rodolfo and Milnes's robust Miller (♦London 417420). Caballé is more diva-ish, less personal than Moffo,

but she sounds stunning and fills out the expansive passages more satisfactorily.

Middle period

Rigoletto. Now it really gets tough. Since Caruso walked into the Milan studios of the Gramophone and Typewriter Company in 1902 and started it all, *Rigoletto* has been one of the best-represented Verdi operas on record. New singers must risk comparison not only with their contemporaries but with a century's worth of great voices. It's impossible to dispel the ghosts of the past, but the best modern recordings of *Rigoletto* are very good indeed and worthy of our gratitude—after all, one can't live by excerpts alone, no matter how spectacular the singers.

For dramatic vitality, **Serafin** with Callas, Gobbi, and di Stefano still leads the field (♦EMI 66667). None of the stars is vocally impeccable, but all are caught up in the drama and draw us inexorably into it. This isn't golden-age vocalism, but it certainly is *Rigoletto.* The performance makes the standard cuts, the most regrettable of which is not the Duke's bumptious cabaletta but the missing half of the "Veglia, o donna" duet. (It's inexplicable that anyone could regard this as dispensable.)

Complete, and the most vocally opulent of all recordings, is **Bonynge,** with Sutherland, Pavarotti, and Milnes (♦London 414269). La Stupenda takes all the traditional high interpolations and adds another (a mighty top D at the end of the Act 3 trio) of her own. Pavarotti and Milnes are at their healthiest. The end of Act 2 typifies the performance: an attempt at sensitivity in "Tutte le feste" and "Piangi, fanciulla" (superficial next to Callas and Gobbi), then a sensational gallop through "Si vendetta." Sutherland rockets to a brilliant high E-flat, but Milnes's own tremendous A-flat upstages even her. Touchdown, extra point, the crowd roars—and the characters get rather lost in the exhilarating spectacle.

One place to find them again is in **Kubelik**'s offbeat but stimulating recording (♦DG 437704). He's not a conductor we readily associate with Italian opera, but he keeps the La Scala orchestra alert in a piece they could play in their sleep, setting sensible tempos and powerfully underlining the drama. His almost all-Italian cast guarantees an idiomatic performance. Scotto is an involved, often affecting Gilda, though very acidulous in the upper register. Bergonzi is more attuned to the patrician aspects of the Duke than the rakish, but he sings ingratiatingly. Cossotto is a full-tongued, noticeable Maddalena. The odd man out is Fischer-Dieskau as Rigoletto, and yes, his voice is wrong for the part, but his acting is so shrewd, so alive, you soon stop fretting. He really makes you remember the character.

Fischer-Dieskau is a far more interesting Rigoletto than many baritones who might seem more natural in the role: Bastianini, Merrill, Warren, and MacNeil (though the sumptuousness of the last two is something to be savored, on RCA and London respectively). Björling was Merrill's first Duke, Alfredo Kraus, his second (both EMI). Kraus, elegant but charmless, recorded his role on two other occasions: with Scotto and Bastianini (Ricordi) and with Sills and Milnes (EMI). Pavarotti would also return to the part again: with Anderson and Nucci (London) and with Studer and Vladimir Chernov (DG). Fans of these (and other *Rigoletto* singers) have plenty to choose from, but the three great recordings remain the ones praised above.

Il Trovatore. Caruso's oft-quoted dictum was right on the mark: *Trovatore* simply needs the four best singers in the world. The characters materialize in unlikely places at the librettist's whim, but when they stand and deliver, the dramatic inconsistencies of the story vanish. Milanov, Barbieri, Björling, and Warren in the 1952 **Cellini** recording come fairly close to filling Caruso's prescription (♦RCA 6643). Milanov has a few wild, strident moments, but her dark, creamy voice has a majesty few of her successors have matched. Björling's Manrico, incomparably clean in line, at once plaintive and ringing, hasn't been surpassed, and no modern baritone has brought more sheer voice to di Luna than Warren. Barbieri is a solid, authoritative Azucena. The performance is slightly cut.

Callas's Leonora, on the first **Karajan** recording (1956), is more human than Milanov's, and she addresses her music with more feeling and finesse (♦EMI 56333). Panerai and di Stefano, a bit light, shape the words keenly. Barbieri is again Azucena. Karajan has a firmer hand than Perlea, but the discipline he imposes on the La Scala orchestra pays off dramatically. A second (1962) La Scala performance led by **Serafin** has much of the same authentic Italian flair, but Stella is an uninteresting Leonora and Cossotto had yet to grow into the great Azucena she would soon be (DG). Bergonzi and Bastianini sing handsomely and rather too politely.

The best all-around stereo set is **Mehta**'s, though not everyone may be sold on his conducting, with its punchy, arbitrary accents (♦RCA 39504). Leontyne Price's Leonora is the most breathtakingly beautiful on records. In 1959, under **Basile** (RCA), she sang ravishingly; ten years later, her voice was even firmer, her musical insights more fully developed. Listening to the soaring phrases of the arias is a physical sensation so exquisite that you hunger for more. This is profoundly sensuous singing; you feel it with your entire body. Cossotto's words are great blocks of sound, smoothly joined together from bottom to top and delivered with irresistible vigor. She was the last of the great Italian mezzos, and after her most Azucenas seem insubstantial. Domingo and Milnes are in lusty form, vocally resplendent though without any special insight. When Price recorded Leonora for the third time, with **Karajan** in 1977, much of the magic was gone (EMI).

Another good stereo choice is **Giulini** in 1983, just before his self-imposed mummification became permanent (♦DG 23858). His fastidiousness and commitment enhance the drama, which is further bolstered by the savagely sleek di Luna of Giorgio Zancanaro and the dependable Manrico of Domingo. His leading ladies are unorthodox interpreters. The brainy Fassbaender has the darkness but not the weight for Azucena, yet her intensity and concentration carry her through. Plowright's big voice doesn't encompass Price's glorious top notes, but she's an uncommonly thoughtful Leonora, a crafty actress who takes the character seriously and brings her to life as vividly as anyone since Callas.

Domingo sang Manrico again for **Levine** in 1991, without offering anything new (Sony). Zajick's Azucena is vibrant and voluminous, though less polished than Cossotto's. Morris's timbre is wrong for di Luna, and Millo's Leonora is a pastiche of Italian-soprano mannerisms. She's learned too much from Tebaldi, and it's more satisfying to have the real thing. Tebaldi's Leonora, with **Erede**, has the grandeur of Milanov's with some added warmth, but she's uncomfortable on top and the rest of the cast, Simionato excepted, is unsatisfactory (London).

Simionato recorded Azucena again in 1964 under **Schippers**, when her resources had diminished. Merrill is a bland but sonorous di Luna; Tucci, an anonymous Leonora. What's special about this recording is Corelli's Manrico, the most viscerally thrilling of them all. He's sloppy, and the words are often hewn out laboriously, but when he lets loose, he silences criticism.

La Traviata. No Verdi opera depends so fully on a single performer. A poor Alfredo or Germont may be distressing; a poor Violetta destroys the entire show. Personal tastes differ widely; the best Violetta is the one who touches the individual listener most deeply. I offer suggestions more tentatively than usual in this case. There is no one recording that can be proclaimed superior to the rest.

Violetta was one of Callas's signature roles. She recorded it early in her career for Cetra, and in so doing was prohibited from recording it again for EMI. The company has unapologetically issued two live performances instead, the so-called "Lisbon *Traviata*" and the more engaging 1955 La Scala production conducted by **Giulini** (♦EMI 66459). With Giulini, Callas falters only at the start of "Dite alla giovine," where she veers sharp. Everywhere else, she's riveting, unmistakably herself but somehow Violetta in the flesh as well. No other soprano finds such haunting, memorable colors for the music. The singing may not be conventionally beautiful, and the sound is distressingly substandard, but it's impossible to be unmoved by the performance. Di Stefano and Bastianini, unlike Callas, sound more like robust opera singers than dramatic characters. The tenor, at least, has his trademark fervor and forward diction, but the baritone is maddeningly blank, never modulating his rich tone toward any dramatic end.

Another great recording from the '50s was led by **Monteux** (♦RCA). Never on CD, it deserves to be. Carteri and Valletti are a most believable pair of protagonists, both utterly immersed in their portrayals. She sings Italian with extraordinary clarity and eloquence; he heeds Verdi's dynamic markings more scrupulously than most tenors, to great expressive effect. Germont is Warren, whose big, barreling voice champions propriety with crushing weight. He's a visitor from another world, and in that sense, he's not unlike Fischer-Dieskau on **Maazel**'s recording (♦London 443036). Dieskau, of course, barely has half Warren's voice, but he's no less sure of himself. Lorengar and Aragall are, like Carteri and Valletti, personal and specific, the tenor involved and articulate, the soprano (if you can get past the pronounced Spanish vibrato) febrile and vulnerable—and absolutely ravishing on top. No one lofts her voice up to the As of "Dite alla giovane" more beautifully.

Another lovable Spanish Violetta is de los Angeles, **Serafin** conducting (EMI). The natural plaintiveness of the timbre is most apt for the tormented heroine, but she also rips through the coloratura of "Sempre libera" with blinding speed. Her colleagues are capable, no more. Moffo, under **Previtali**, also has irksome partners (Merrill's bland Germont and Tucker's pushy Alfredo), but she herself sings honestly and warmly. Her voice may be on the colorless side, but her performance wants little in emotional involvement and communication. She's one of the few Violettas equally at home (and persuasive) in "Sempre libera" and "Addio del passato" (♦RCA 68885).

All these recordings make the traditional cuts, though Maazel allows his tenor and baritone one verse of their cabalettas. A complete *Traviata* should include both verses, along with the second verses of Violetta's two arias and the repeat in "Parigi, o cara." A good uncut version for the library is by the utilitarian **Prêtre**, who has Caballé, Bergonzi, and Milnes putting in a good day's work in the recording studio (RCA). The uncut **Ceccato** is notable for Sills's thoughtfully drawn heroine (EMI). Gedda is a lithe Alfredo; Panerai's Germont is short on plush, lucid in elocution. **Muti** is also complete, but he seems to think the opera is his show rather than Violetta's, and his loud, self-aggrandizing approach is infuriating (EMI). Scotto, his Violetta, is reflective and probing. All the traditional *accenti* are in place, but the vinegar in the voice is unalluring.

Freni sings far more beautifully with **Gardelli**, and if you like her, you'll want this unheralded but very touching performance (Acanta). Her colleagues are the avuncular Bruscantini (who was more at home in buffo roles) and the slightly oafish but impassioned Bonisolli. **Carlos Kleiber** has garnered much praise, but he has also been criticized for his rigidity (DG). He does drive the music hard, but the real problem is his cast. Domingo and Milnes are efficient, as always, Cotrubas is very poignant, exploiting her voice's innate melancholy to fine effect, but it's difficult to remember anything specific about her performance once it's finished.

Levine, strong but flexible, is not at all inferior to Kleiber, and Studer's Violetta is almost as touching as Cotrubas's (DG). She too leaves no indelible mark, but the performance is involving enough while it lasts. Pavarotti is an expert Alfredo, and Pons, with less voice to work with than Merrill, Milnes, or Bastianini, sings with a far greater command of nuance.

Gheorghiu sings Violetta prettily but vaguely under **Solti** (London). The same might be said of Te Kanawa with **Mehta,** a performance that taxes credulity by casting as Germont a baritone (Hvorostovsky) who sounds younger than Alfredo (Kraus) and Violetta (Philips). Tiziana Fabbricini, with **Muti,** is the opposite of Gheorghiu and Te Kanawa: anything but vague but decidedly unlovely, for all her commitment (Sony).

I Vespri Siciliani. Two good recordings here. **Levine** is the more easygoing, with a heroine (Arroyo) luxuriant in tone but laid-back in demeanor (♦RCA 63492). Domingo and Milnes are at their considerable best, and they sweep the listener away in the surging melodies of the three tenor-baritone duets. The important bass role is entrusted to Raimondi, proficient but not quite plush enough. **Muti** is more dynamic, though his climaxes are unnecessarily explosive (♦EMI 54043). Studer is more keenly focused than Arroyo, more intensely involved, and Zancanaro matches Milnes's extroverted frankness. Merritt and Furlanetto are acceptable but less magnetic than their counterparts under Levine. Still waiting to be recorded is *Les Vêpres Siciliennes,* the original French version of the opera.

Simon Boccanegra. Again, two good recordings do justice to Verdi's gloomiest opera, and two others deserve honorable mention. **Santini,** in slightly congested mono, gets a searching performance of the title role from Gobbi and an exquisite Amelia from de los Angeles (♦EMI 63513). Giuseppe Campora is an impassioned, dignified Gabriele, though his tenor isn't a first-class instrument. Christoff's Fiesco is unidiomatic, overacted, and utterly gripping.

Abbado has much better sound, a classier Gabriele (Carreras) and Fiesco (Ghiaurov), and Freni is enthralling if slightly undersized as Amelia (♦DG 449752). Cappuccilli is more suave than Gobbi but less interesting. He was also the Boccanegra of the first stereo recording, under **Gavazzeni,** an honorable effort distinguished primarily by Domingo's Gabriele (RCA). Raimondi's Fiesco is on the mild side; Ricciarelli's Amelia, delicate and rather self-contained. Te Kanawa's Amelia is the one redeeming feature of **Solti**'s recording (London).

Un Ballo in Maschera. Serafin's 1943 recording has the potent Gigli and Caniglia; **Toscanini**'s in 1954 stars himself. **Votto** comes closer to the opera's heart, and once again we must marvel at the extraordinary dramatic talents of Callas and Gobbi (♦EMI 56320). Di Stefano's amiability is perfect for the benign, warmhearted Riccardo, Barbieri has the chesty strength Ulrica requires, but Eugenia Ratti is a brittle Oscar. Less theatrically alive but more beautifully sung is **Leinsdorf**'s *Ballo,* with Leontyne Price resplendent as Amelia, Bergonzi a flowing Riccardo (more noble than di Stefano), and Merrill a resonant Renato (♦RCA 6645). Grist is a charming Oscar; Verrett a welterweight Ulrica. The two performances complement each other; together, they leave little to be desired.

Ballo has been lucky on records, however, and there are other accounts too good to be neglected. Bergonzi recorded Riccardo (one of his best roles) for **Solti,** replacing the originally scheduled Björling (London). His Amelia is Nilsson, surprisingly animated and heroically secure. MacNeil's Renato is rounder and richer than Merrill's, and Simionato is an electrifying Ulrica. She's matched by the even more secure Cossotto, under **Muti** (EMI). This was one of his earliest (1975) Verdi recordings, and he supports his singers strongly rather than dominating them. Arroyo, Domingo, and Cappuccilli, none of them natural firebrands, benefit greatly from his propulsiveness. Grist, a second time, is a tidy, sparkling Oscar.

Domingo recorded his role again in 1989 under **Karajan,** who leads a weighty, stimulating performance, lacking momentum but full of grandeur—it's more operatic than dramatic (DG). Karajan's Amelia is the unidiomatic Barstow, strangely interesting but not really in the same league as Callas and Price.

Riccardo was a felicitous role for Pavarotti, who, like Domingo, recorded it twice. The first (1970) is led by **Bartoletti** and pairs Pavarotti with an over-the-hill Tebaldi (London). It's a pity his best years didn't intersect with hers. It was also too late in the day for Resnik's Ulrica. **Solti** conducts the second, which unfortunately finds the tenor less free of voice than he was 12 years earlier (1982; London). There's some unorthodox casting here too, not just Ludwig's Ulrica but also Margaret Price as Amelia. Because Amelia is the one Verdi heroine who never has a single carefree moment, Price's reserved, queenly bearing is not entirely inappropriate. The timbre isn't quite right, but all the notes are there, often radiantly beautiful. Ludwig's professional acumen carries her through Ulrica; Battle is a cute Oscar; and Bruson is a boring but acceptable Renato.

La Forza del Destino. Verdi's most sprawling, uncohesive opera, its long scenes of splashy local color are jarringly juxtaposed with the intimate tragedy of the main characters. The still-rousing but sonically inferior 1941 Cetra (now Arkadia) recording led by **Gino Marinuzzi** and the 1954 EMI with Callas are cut, but most of the others are complete. Callas's conductor is the trustworthy **Serafin,** but the two of them can't offset the inadequate contributions of their colleagues.

A better starting point is **Molinari-Pradelli** (♦London 421598). The conductor, an indulgent collaborator rather than a motivating force, is redeemed by his superb cast. Tebaldi, aside from some slightly flat top notes, is luscious, and the stentorian del Monaco manages a modicum of sensitivity. Simionato and Corena are authoritative in the comic roles, and the mellow, compassionate Siepi remains the best Guardiano in the complete sets. Bastianini's vibrant voice is well suited to Carlo, one of Verdi's most one-dimensional roles; the baritone sounds implacable and unimaginative, that is, just right.

A second London recording (originally RCA) dates from 1958 and is conducted by **Previtali.** It's compromised by the tribulations of the cast but rescued by their grand-opera flamboyance. Milanov, past her prime, is often raw and unsteady, but the legato is intact, and so is the dark richness of the timbre. She's every inch the prima donna. When di Stefano takes the trouble to modulate his tone, he's absolutely spellbinding, the most vivid, personable Alvaro on records though far from the most tidily sung. Warren alternates slightly tremulous vocalism with matchlessly beautiful, powerful outpourings of tone. (He was singing Carlo when he collapsed and died on the Met stage two years later.) Both Tozzi and Elias are light for their roles.

Leontyne Price recorded Leonora twice, and the more satisfactory of her performances came in 1976 under **Levine** (◆RCA 39502). Its only weakness is the Guardiano of Bonaldo Giaiotti, who pumps out one desiccated tone after another. Cossotto's crisp words and ripe, chesty tones make Preziosilla an unusually positive character (even if a few top notes land a hair below pitch). As Melitone, Bacquier tempers his nastiness with some dignity; he's less verbally adroit than Corena. Milnes is a dynamic Carlo with ample upper-range thrust, and Domingo's earnest manner is well suited to the anguished Alvaro. The two of them are thrilling in the duets. Price's glorious upper range and inherently serious demeanor are ideal for her role. She was, perhaps, in even better voice in 1964 with **Schippers,** but the differences are small (RCA). Levine swings back and forth between lethargy and excitability.

Domingo recorded Alvaro again with **Muti** in 1986, when he had another fine baritone partner in Zancanaro. The conductor races through the score, however; the Guardiano is unsteady; and Freni's Leonora, though often captivating, is not quite big enough. Arroyo, with **Gardelli,** has the requisite amplitude, but for all the voluptuousness of her singing, she comes across as rather gloomy and sluggish (EMI). The best thing in Gardelli's recording is Bergonzi's Alvaro, short on upper-range ring but wonderfully steady and responsive. The lofty eloquence of his phrasing makes a lasting impression. Cappuccilli is a passable Carlo; Raimondi has the manner but not the depth of tone for Guardiano. **Sinopoli's** eccentric recording has an unorthodox and provocative Leonora in Plowright but little else to commend it (DG).

A curiosity is **Gergiev's** recording of the original (St. Petersburg) version (Philips). It's performed well enough to make a strong case for itself, but the revision is a better opera and collectors should get to know it first.

Late operas

Don Carlos. There are, roughly speaking, three versions of *Don Carlos* to contend with: the original French grand opera and the four- and five-act Italian translations. The four-act abridgement helped popularize the opera but omits too much music, so only the impatient should seek a recording. (**Karajan** on EMI, with Freni and Carreras, will do.)

Solti offered the first complete recording of the five-act Italian *Don Carlo* (◆London 421598). The best of his performers are the unfailingly capable Bergonzi in the title role and Ghiaurov in magnificent voice for King Philip. Tebaldi's Elisabetta has stature and authority, though the singer was past her prime. Bumbry's Eboli is skillfully vocalized but blandly acted. "What is this Fischer-Dieskau doing?" asked Tebaldi, when she encountered her very untraditional Rodrigo. He's singing with punctilious care (not a trill goes unmarked) and real attention to the drama, and even if the voice isn't quite right, the character makes an indelible impression. Also unidiomatic is Talvela's Grand Inquisitor, and though he's less vivid than Fischer-Dieskau, we're grateful for the resonant solidity of his voice. Solti, as usual, supports his singers strongly but also indulges his fondness for loud, crunching orchestral climaxes.

Giulini offers a more polished reading, but it has far less life (EMI). Caballé, Verrett, Domingo, Milnes, and Raimondi sing well but prosaically; only the coarse Grand Inquisitor of Giovanni Foiani seems really involved in his role. **Muti** reverts to the four-act version; his cast, despite the presence of Pavarotti, need not detain us (EMI). Stronger competition comes from two '90s recordings. **Levine** leads a cast of Met regulars in a performance that would probably have been absorbing in the theater but doesn't stand up to repeated hearings (Sony). Millo's Elisabetta is counterfeit Tebaldi, Ramey is a mild Inquisitor, and Furlanetto, who sings Philip, is no *basso cantante.* Michael Sylvester, Vladimir

Chernov, and Zajick are adequate, though the recording doesn't quite convey the power and projection the mezzo has on stage.

Haitink, though slightly more subdued than Levine, has a more effective cast (◆Philips 454463). Borodina is a smooth, seductive Eboli; Richard Margison a cleanly sung, affectingly plaintive Carlo. Galina Gorchakova's big voice is sometimes ungainly, but she sings with admirable tonal fullness. Hvorostovsky's bel canto Rodrigo is gorgeously vocalized. Roberto Scandiuzzi doesn't have the sort of bass that rolls out majestically, but he deploys it most expressively. He makes his aria a profoundly doleful private meditation, not a public address, and he's heart-rending.

The French *Don Carlos* differs not only in language but also in musical detail, most noticeably at the appearance, after the death of Posa, of the theme Verdi would use as the "Lacrymosa" of his *Requiem.* **Claudio Abbado's** recording has a mostly Italian cast, comfortable with the style but not the language: Ricciarelli, Valentini-Terrani, Domingo, Nucci, and Raimondi (DG).

Pappano's account is more incisive, weakened only by the Eboli of Meier, a fine actress but an inflexible singer (◆EMI 56152). Mattila's Elisabetta is one of her finest recordings, the voice flowing easily, like molten metal into a mold. Hampson has the fervor and sophistication for Posa, and Alagna and van Dam, though lightweight, offer authentic French diction as Carlo and King Philip. It's generally assumed that *Don Carlos* in French is vastly preferable to *Don Carlo* in Italian, but that's a debatable opinion. Pappano's recording makes the best case so far for the French version, so listen and decide for yourself.

Aïda. The old-fashioned, full-throated singing on **Perlea's** 1955 *Aïda* remains irresistible (◆RCA 6652). Milanov, Barbieri, Björling, and Warren make most of their successors sound tentative. No one since has sung Radames with more gleaming, beautiful tone than Björling, or Amonasro with a plumper, richer voice than Warren. Milanov has some unruly moments, but she phrases much of the music exquisitely and makes a very regal princess indeed. Barbieri is less distinctive, not superior to Simionato and Cossotto on later recordings but imposing enough all the same. The mono sound is a drawback in the triumphal scene, but the solo voices are captured with a fidelity that modern technology has scarcely improved on.

Muti's stereo recording has blander performers, but their singing is almost as beautiful (◆EMI 56246). Cossotto is an imperious Amneris with a solid chest register. Both words and notes are perfectly articulated, and the voice can really move. Caballé is a singer first, an actress second, but she's not without temperament and she surpasses the finesse of even Milanov and Leontyne Price in many long-breathed phrases. Domingo and Cappuccilli approach the drama more rhetorically than personally, but they're in good form, and Ghiaurov is a suitably August Ramfis. **Maazel's** recording has a surprisingly accomplished Aïda in Maria Chiara but will probably appeal most to diehard fans of Pavarotti, an over-parted Radames (London).

Karajan's first *Aïda* (1959) brings together the splendid Vienna Philharmonic, the meaty baritone of MacNeil, and three seasoned Italian stars (◆Decca 460978). Tebaldi has some awkward moments on top, but when the music lies well for her ("Ritorna vincitor"), she fleshes it out with full-bodied tone and an instinctive feel for dramatic verity. Simionato is a formidable Amneris, at her best in the last act with Bergonzi's liquid Radames. The tenor isn't quite heroic enough, but his lines are always shapely. Karajan is a potent presence and renders the music with unusual care. The sound, typical of Decca recordings around 1960, keeps the voices at a slight distance. Karajan's second recording, made 20 years later, attempted to turn *Aïda* into a chamber opera (EMI). The singers—Freni, Carreras, and Baltsa—are undersized, but the conductor tries not to overwhelm them. The missing grandeur is offset by many felicitous details.

Mehta's recording, with Nilsson and Corelli, couldn't be more different (EMI). It's unsubtle but rousing, especially when the two protagonists are hurling out their voices on an epic scale. **Abbado** also has a good ear for detail (DG). His *Aïda* is bigger than Karajan's second, yet lacks nothing in transparency. Domingo is the only first-class vocalist here; for various reasons, Ricciarelli, Obraztsova, and Nucci are unqualified for their roles. Domingo recorded yet a fourth *Aïda* in 1990, **Levine** conducting (Sony). The performance is similar to the *Don Carlo* on the same label: absorbing enough at first hearing, then forgettable. Zajick sounds uneven and slightly unsteady, and Morris's voice isn't juicy enough in the middle register for Verdi. You won't mistake Domingo for Björling or Corelli, perhaps not even for Radames. He's the world's busiest tenor, once again delivering a sound, competent account of one of his typical roles. Millo's Aïda is a compendium of affectations gleaned from sopranos going back to Muzio, or perhaps even Pozzoni-Anastasi (Cairo, 1871). It's difficult to discern a single quality uniquely hers, and her timbre is plain and serviceable rather than beautiful.

The last great soprano to make Aïda her own was Leontyne Price, and she brings to the role an intensity and fervent identification that elude Milanov, Caballé, and Tebaldi (but not Callas, dismissed parenthetically here because her 1955 EMI recording finds her and her colleagues below their best). Her voice is close to its most pristine in 1961, with **Solti,** and she's surrounded by interesting singers (♦London 417416). Neither Gorr nor Vickers sounds traditionally Italian, but they deploy their big voices with passion and dramatic verve. Merrill's stolid Amonasro is handsomely vocalized, and Solti's gusto keeps events moving, though he knows how to hold back for the lyrical episodes. The sound favors the orchestra and chorus over the soloists. **Leinsdorf** is an efficient but stiff conductor (RCA). Price had polished her Aïda in the decade since her first recording, but her voice isn't quite as free and fresh. Bumbry, who also sang Amneris for Mehta, is a high mezzo without the vocal depth for the role, and Domingo's first Radames is the least perceptive of his four.

Otello. **Toscanini**'s *Otello,* recorded in 1947, still sounds absolutely right (♦RCA 60302). He combines proper tempos with wonderfully precise orchestral playing, startling clarity (despite the mono recording), perfect rhythms, and an unsurpassed depth of understanding. His outstanding cast member is Giuseppe Valdengo as Iago, so crisply enunciated, so musically and dramatically alert, that not even Gobbi betters him. It doesn't matter whether this was alchemy on Toscanini's part or an extraordinary effort by the baritone, but Valdengo gives the performance of a lifetime. The passive Desdemona suits the passive Nelli better than the other roles she recorded with Toscanini. We want a more colorful voice, but she's still very touching. Vinay has the heft and passion for Otello, but his strangulated, baritonal voice won't please everyone. (Later in his career, he would sing Iago.)

Toscanini misses nothing of importance, but his singers do, and for partial remediation, we can turn to **Karajan**'s first (1961) account, where Tebaldi, in one of her most congenial roles, demonstrates what Nelli lacks: a passionate identification with the character and an opulent voice with an imposing chest register (♦London 411618). Del Monaco trumpets "Esultate" the way you hope to hear it but seldom do, then goes on to sing most of the rest of the music in the same stentorian way.

Although he's not without sensitivity and he does try to modulate his tone, his blaring becomes wearisome. Aldo Protti's Iago is no better than routine; at least he puts some Italian flavor into his words. Karajan's second *Otello* has the sweet Desdemona of Freni and Vickers's Moor but is disqualified by some inexplicable cuts (1973; EMI).

Vickers is better appreciated in an earlier (1960) recording led by **Serafin** (♦RCA 63180). The timbre is peculiar next to del Monaco's burnished instrument, and the middle range can be oddly hollow, but the top notes have ring and power, and the words are inflected so pregnantly you hang on his every utterance. This is a more complex, tortured, sympathetic character than del Monaco's or even Vinay's, the work of a great tragedian who might have bestrode the legitimate stage. Rysanek has some ungainly moments and you wouldn't suppose her temperament is suited to the wilting Desdemona, but the tonal bulk doesn't preclude vulnerability, and the character, much like Chrysothemis in *Elektra,* is sympathetically drawn. Gobbi's maleficent, insinuating Iago isn't dwarfed by his powerhouse colleagues. Serafin's tempos, like Karajan's, veer toward the stately, but he sustains them without flaccidity.

Barbirolli in 1968 is much slower, and he also has an Otello with an idiosyncratic, non-Mediterranean timbre (♦EMI 65296). McCracken at his best is as hypnotic as Vickers, but he's more histrionic and less polished. What's never in doubt is his complete immersion in the role. The young Gwyneth Jones is a lovely Desdemona. She floats some graceful pianissimos and takes care to articulate notes many sopranos slur. Fischer-Dieskau is an adroit Iago, but the villainy is built into the music and the baritone is savvy enough not to exaggerate what Verdi has already made plain. We often wish for more sheer voice. Barbirolli's performance is deeply absorbing, despite its deliberateness; it's an *Otello* that confronts the tragedy uncompromisingly and really wrings the heart.

Domingo, the foremost Otello of recent days, has recorded the opera three times. **Levine** is highly regarded, but it doesn't move me (1978; RCA). The omnivorous conductor has a good grasp of the score; he has clearly learned much from Toscanini. Domingo sings well but impersonally, and Milnes is a hearty, precise Iago, but Scotto's inability to utter pleasing sounds undermines the performance. **Maazel** was Domingo's second *Otello* conductor; the droopy Ricciarelli was his Desdemona (EMI). The recording places the voices so far away from the microphones that it can't be considered seriously. The third time around, in 1993 with **Chung,** Domingo is master of his role (♦DG 439805). His voice has grown richer (if not bigger) with time and his bearing is more confident, even more noble. He lacks the *squillo* of del Monaco or Martinelli, but his voice still fills out the musical lines generously. Studer's Desdemona gets off to a tentative start, but the juices start to flow in Act 3 and she has many powerful, affecting moments. Leiferkus's Iago can be deemed either striking or downright weird. The gritty timbre is not appealing, but it lends the character a definite profile. Chung, like his Desdemona, doesn't catch fire until Act 3, and he's proficient enough, though more febrile than subtle.

Those adjectives might describe **Solti** as well. He recorded the opera twice, in 1977 and 1991, but neither of his tenors—Carlos Cossutta the first time, the imprudent Pavarotti the second—is much of an Otello (London).

Falstaff. **Toscanini** once again achieves the striking clarity of his *Otello* recording (♦RCA 72372). The busy ensembles of *Falstaff* are rendered with astonishing transparency, the mono sound notwithstanding. Every tempo seems right, every musical impulse just. Valdengo doesn't quite pull off another miracle here; the dry, snarling timbre that served

Iago so well is less apt for Falstaff. The outstanding cast members are Cloë Elmo, a fruity, old-fashioned Italian contralto; Stich-Randall, a dainty Nannetta; and Merriman, one of the few Megs you really notice. Frank Guerrera is a likable, underpowered Ford; Nelli a pallid Alice. If the conductor had rounded up the young Tebaldi and di Stefano for Alice and Fenton, and somehow persuaded Warren and Merrill to sing Falstaff and Ford, this would have been the Verdi recording of the century.

Few of us regard **Karajan** as another Toscanini, but his 1956 recording has a far better cast (♦EMI 67162). Gobbi has a more colorful voice than Valdengo, and he's a more gifted actor. Panerai's Ford, though a bit on the gravelly side, is a model of meaningful elocution. Barbieri brings more voice and panache to Quickly than Elmo did. The young lovers are endearingly portrayed by Moffo and Alva, so sparkling and elegant they really do seem to inhabit a different world. Schwarzkopf doesn't sound particularly Italian, but her sophistication and radiant top notes are ample compensation. The conductor in his early days was less mannered than he would become, more inclined to let the music flow naturally.

His second (1980) recording finds him more finicky, but he brings back Panerai's Ford (for the third time on records) and casts, in the title role, the 64-year-old Taddei (Philips). This underappreciated baritone made his Met debut as Falstaff in 1985, when he was almost 70, and scored a triumph. He still had plenty of voice left, and his command of an almost defunct style was peerless. The 1980 recording is not as well cast as the earlier EMI, and Taddei himself was in far better voice when he recorded Falstaff for Cetra in 1949, but there's still plenty to enjoy.

Like Karajan, **Solti** made two recordings. The second is dispensable; the first is a great one and probably has the best cast of all (♦London 417168). Geraint Evans has a fatter, richer voice than Gobbi or Valdengo and he's a cunning actor. Among his colleagues are the plush Merrill, the ravishing young Freni, the delectable Simionato, and the excellent but underrated Ligabue, who made something of a specialty of Alice Ford. A *Falstaff* conductor must be energetic, flexible, and attentive, qualities that certainly characterize Solti's work.

The *Falstaff*s of **Colin Davis** (RCA), **Giulini** (DG), **Muti** (Sony), and **Will Humburg** (Naxos) are sporadically enjoyable, but they seem mirthless next to the fourth great recording of the opera, by **Bernstein** (♦Sony 42535). The two young lovers (Sciutti and Juan Oncina) sound a bit long in the tooth, but Ligabue and Panerai expertly repeat their usual roles, and Resnik is a spirited, funny Quickly. Fischer-Dieskau acts so well he makes you forget he has the wrong sort of voice for Falstaff, and Bernstein, at his best, leads a rollicking, theatrical account that sweeps you along from start to finish.

CHORAL MUSIC

Requiem Mass. The *Requiem*, in its own way, has as much dramatic force as any of the operas, but it is less easy to bring off on records. The thundering choruses demand the best possible sound, and the cruelly exposed soloists can't take refuge behind their characterizations. No recording gets everything quite right, and I find myself hanging on to several of them for the sake of one or more soloists: Björling and Leontyne Price with **Reiner** (London); Caballé and Cossotto with **Barbirolli** (EMI); Bergonzi with **Leinsdorf** (RCA); Pavarotti with **Solti** (London); and even Wunderlich with the unrenowned **Hans Müller-Kray** (Myto).

It would be impractical to suggest that all collectors do the same, and it's also unfortunate that some of the most stirring performances have the worst sound: the 1939 **Serafin** with Gigli and Pinza (EMI), the 1940 **Toscanini** with Milanov and Björling (Music & Arts), and the 1951 **Toscanini** with di Stefano and Siepi (RCA). **Reiner**'s 1960 recording was

one of the first to enjoy full-bodied stereo sound, but the conductor is too cautious and uneven. He has his moments, however, and so does the forthright and uneccentric **Ormandy** (Sony). The old Columbia sound is full and natural, with window-rattling bass; the soloists are decent (especially Forrester, a true contralto), and the price is low.

The first—and almost the last—great stereo *Requiem* was **Giulini**'s (♦EMI 556250). It's an intense, powerful reading; every tempo seems perfectly chosen, and the soloists (Schwarzkopf, Ludwig, Gedda, and Ghiaurov) are musically impeccable. You might not want to hear Schwarzkopf and Gedda step into *Il Trovatore*, but listen to how well she shapes her upper lines (no worries here about the soft high B-flat) or how sensitively he observes the trills in "Hostias." The drawback is the sound. It's been cleaned up a bit on CD, but there's still distortion at the loud climaxes. No such problems beset **Shaw**, probably the best-engineered *Requiem* of all (♦Telarc 80152). Shaw is a more restrained conductor than Giulini—he lacks Italian passion—but his chorus is splendid, and his soloists (Susan Dunn, Diane Curry, Hadley, and Plishka) are, like their EMI counterparts, unprepossessing but conscientious.

Shaw and Giulini complement each other rather well but still leave the listener hankering for a great solo quartet. Sutherland, Horne, Pavarotti, and Talvela don't quite jell for **Solti** in 1967 (London); neither does the foursome led by Leontyne Price and Janet Baker under the same conductor in 1976 (RCA). Solti's supercharged approach is compelling nonetheless, and both his recordings are engrossing. Caballé, Cossotto, Vickers, and Raimondi were undermined by **Barbirolli**'s lethargy in 1969 (EMI). **Muti**'s performance is tremendously impressive and exciting—his chorus stays with him on what often seems like a wild roller-coaster ride—but his soloists, however good they look on paper (Studer, Zajic, Pavarotti, and Ramey), are slightly too tentative (EMI). **Giulini** is a great disappointment, torpid and lifeless (DG).

Far more satisfying are the older recordings led by **Leinsdorf** (RCA), **Mehta** (CBS), and even **Karajan** (DG). Better overall than any of these is **Abbado,** smoothly played and sung by the Vienna Philharmonic and the Vienna State Opera Chorus (♦DG 435884). The quartet is compromised by the sorely taxed Carreras, but Studer, Lipovšek, and Raimondi are very good, and the sound approaches the Telarc level. Abbado can be a bland conductor, but he seems galvanized here, effortlessly blending musical precision and beauty with blazing fervor.

Gardiner uses original instruments, a choice that might put off as many listeners as it attracts, but it turns out to be hardly noticeable (♦Philips 442142). More important is the torrential energy of the performance (like Solti without the brashness, or like Toscanini himself) together with its rapt devotional air. The dynamic range is (perhaps too) huge—'Tuba mirum' will knock you out of your seat, while the beginning of "Hostias" is barely audible—and the soloists (Orgonasova, von Otter, Luca Canonici, and Alastair Miles) are well matched but even more modest than Giulini's first group, and less individual. This is, nonetheless, a mesmerizing account, one that really stays with you for a long time.

Four Sacred Pieces. Abbado's *Requiem,* like Giulini's and Gardiner's, is supplemented by the austerely lovely choral works known collectively as the *Four Sacred Pieces.* (Shaw chose some opera choruses as his filler.) They are also appended to the Reiner *Requiem,* but the conductor is Mehta, and to two of the Toscanini packages on RCA. No need to look for a separate recording; they will automatically find their way onto your shelf beside the *Requiem.* LUCANO

OVERTURES AND BALLET MUSIC

Collections of Verdi overtures provide a satisfying font of melody from the operas as well as a filling repast heard on their own. Basic to most collections are *La Forza del Destino*, *I Vespri Siciliani*, and *Nabucco*; often *Luisa Miller* and the preludes to *Aïda* and *La Traviata* are included as well. If you're lucky, you'll get a sampling of his grander efforts such as *Oberto*, *Aroldo*, *Giovanna d'Arco*, and *La Battaglia di Legnano;* yet even a CD can only hold so much, and you may wish to seek out one of the complete sets. With the ballet music the choices are even more limited, as few conductors have recorded all of it, and in many cases it's left out of the opera recordings.

One quick solution is the set by **Edward Downes,** which combines the overtures and ballets (♦Chandos 9787, 4CD; also issued separately: 9510, 9594, 9696, 9788). Even without *Aïda,* de **Almeida**'s splendid set of the ballet music is a bargain, and if you have that you don't need to look any further (♦Philips 422846).

Karajan's set of the complete overtures is a classic, but he overloads the climaxes with cymbal crashes and lets pass some surprisingly slapdash playing from the Berliners (DG 439972). His readings, while superficially exciting, are likely to wear a lot less well than **Pier Giorgio Morandi**'s ripely robust and warmly contoured accounts (♦Naxos 553018 and 553089). **Muti** offers a stirring *Battaglia di Legnano* and his *Luisa Miller, Oberto,* and *Stiffelio* are highly charged, but that isn't enough to make him a first choice given his hectic tempos in *Vespri* and *Nabucco,* and he puts up with some sloppy wind playing in *Alzira* too (Sony 68468 and 62373). Downes is just as variable as the others; he too does very well with *Oberto, Alzira,* and *Battaglia,* but his *Giovanna d'Arco* lacks swagger and he really spins out of control in *Nabucco.*

Among the less complete collections, **Dorati** is one of the few who gets *Nabucco* just right, and his *Forza* and *Vespri* are top-rank too; what a pity that the appended Rossini overtures are entirely expendable (Mercury 434345). Likewise **Serafin** is unbeatable in *Giovanna d'Arco* — so why did EMI leave it off when they transferred his splendid Angel LP to CD (62609)? **Claudio Abbado** with the Berlin Symphony (DG 457627) is far less satisfying than his version with the London Symphony (♦RCA 31378); not only is the smooth Berlin ensemble no match for the more characterful playing and visceral excitement of the London players, but RCA gives you the *Aïda* overture written for Milan, later suppressed by Verdi in favor of the familiar prelude (Downes gives you both versions). **Chailly** offers *Aroldo* and *Oberto,* while his fine accounts of *Forza* and *Vespri* make up for the usual too-fast *Nabucco* (London 425052). **Markevitch** fields incisive accounts of the usual suspects plus *Giovanna d'Arco, Luisa Miller,* and the *Macbeth* ballet music in a budget entry (♦Philips 426078).

The often willful **Sinopoli** channels his efforts into highly characterful and compelling accounts of the standard overtures plus several of the preludes (Philips 411469). An inexpensive collection is more notable for several preludes led passionately by Gardelli than for the rather stolid full-scale overtures with **Karolos Trikolidis** (Hungaroton). **Jacek Kaspszyk**'s extreme tempos rule him out (Collins 1072), while **Choo Hoey**'s collection of Verdi's rarer overtures (should it ever come out on CD) may be passed up, as both performances and sound are second-rate (Marco Polo LP).

Downes offers strong competition to de Almeida in the ballet music, though his tempos in *Vespri* are occasionally a bit distracting. **Levine** and the Met Orchestra would seem to be a match made in heaven, but his experience conducting the operas proves to be irrelevant for the ballet music; in *Vespri* he wavers between too fast and too slow, though the

awesome lung power of the Met low brass makes amends (Sony 52489). I wish EMI would reissue **Mackerras**'s LP of *Vespri* and *Il Trovatore;* he only did about half of each, but he included all the best parts and makes Levine sound like a *routinier* (Angel). **Roberto Abbado** does well with *Vespri* but elsewhere tends to nudge phrases a bit too much, to the point that ensemble suffers and the notes tumble over one another (RCA). **Chailly** offered excellent accounts of *Vespri, Don Carlos, Macbeth* and *Otello* (London 425108); unfortunately this has been replaced by the overtures with the ballet music from *Macbeth, Otello,* and the *Aïda* "Ballabile" tacked on (Decca 448238, mentioned above). Likewise missing are **Muti** (Angel) and **Maazel** (London). As I said, there's a lot to choose from, and you can never really have too much Verdi; still, the overtures with Morandi plus the ballet music with de Almeida pretty much say it all.

CHAMBER MUSIC

Traveling to Naples in 1872 for productions of *Aïda* and *Don Carlo,* Verdi wrote his only string quartet while waiting for his star soprano to recover from her illness, which may explain its rather introspective nature. When filled out with a larger complement of strings as with **Scimone** or **Steinberg** it can seem quite lush; unfortunately these are unavailable on CD. It's played by the **Juilliard Quartet** in their usual forceful and extrovert manner (Sony 48193, with the Sibelius Quartet), and the **Britten Quartet** gives a highly sympathetic reading in warm and full sound (Collins 1267, with Cherubini's Quartet 1 and Turina's *The Bullfighter's Prayer*). The ensemble spirit of the **Delmé Quartet** is engaging, with plenty of vigor where needed (Hyperion 66317, with the Strauss Quartet).

Accardo and colleagues are warm and exhibit great affection for the music (Dynamic 47, with Borodin's Quartet 2). There is great integrity to the **Vermeer Quartet**'s playing, though the recording could be more spacious (Teldec 43105, with Dvořák's Quartet 10), and they give off more energy than the **Nuovo Quartetto** (Denon 1029, with Boccherini's Quartet in E-flat and Quartettino in G). While the Verdi piece makes a rather strange discmate for Berg's *Lyric Suite,* the **Vogler Quartet**'s supercharged account stands out (RCA 60855), especially when compared with the **Joachim Quartet**'s rather restrained approach (Thorofon 2037, with the Strauss Quartet).   HALLER

Tomás Luis de Victoria *(c. 1548–1611)*

Victoria lived and died in Spain but spent 20 years in Rome. Unlike his older contemporaries Palestrina and Lassus, he composed only sacred music. Of his two acknowledged masterpieces, *Officium Hebdomadae Sanctae* (Office for Holy Week) was published at the end of his Roman period (1585) and Officium Defunctorum (a Requiem Mass with several shorter pieces) was his last published work (1605). The Holy Week music covers the period from Palm Sunday to Easter, but the most familiar parts are the lamentations and responsories for Tenebrae (the solemn night office of the last three days of the week).

Officium Hebdomadae Sanctae. David Hill's Westminster Cathedral Choir has recorded the 18 responsories for Tenebrae, one of their finest achievements; the sound of this choir of men and boys is especially suited to the composer (♦Hyperion 66304). There are other good recordings of the responsories by Bruno Turner's Pro Cantione Antiqua (Harmonia Mundi 77056), Peter Phillips's Tallis Scholars (Gimell 454922), and Harry Christophers's The Sixteen (Virgin 561221). Earlier, the Westminster Cathedral Choir recorded a memorable set under George Malcolm (Decca 433914, 2CD).

For the nine lamentations, I prefer Musica Ficta for their native grasp of the style (♦Cantus 9604). The Sixteen also sing them beautifully (Collins 15182). The Ensemble Vocal Jean-Paul Gipon has recorded an almost complete set of the Holy Week music, including the *St. John Passion* and eight shorter pieces but omitting the *St. Matthew Passion* (Champeaux 0001, 3CD). While it can be recommended for its completeness, the singing isn't equal to the best of the recorded excerpts. Almost as complete was the collection of lamentations, responsories and several shorter pieces from Ireneu Segarra's choir of Montserrat, a treasurable set that was long on atmosphere and short on refinement (Harmonia Mundi/EMI 169572, 3LP, NA). A vocal quartet was too light in sound for the most complete set of all, with both Passions somewhat abridged (Columbia [Spain] 991/5, 5LP, NA, with *Officium Defunctorum*).

Officium Defunctorum. Hill's Westminster Cathedral Choir recorded a fine version of this work, another example of their ideal Victoria style (♦Hyperion 66250). McCreesh's Gabrieli Consort (Archiv 447095), the Tallis Scholars (Gimell 454912), and Segarra's Montserrat choir (Harmonia Mundi/BMG 77423) are also excellent in this masterpiece.

Missa O magnum mysterium. One of two other masses that have been recorded more extensively than the rest, this is based on the composer's Christmas motet. Hill couples it with **Missa Ascendens Christus in altum,** based on a motet for the Ascension, for one of the choicest discs on this list (♦Hyperion 66190).

Missa O quam gloriosum. This equally popular mass is also based on a motet, this one for All Saints. Hill pairs it with *Missa Ave maris stella,* which has a Marian cantus firmus, for another exceptional entry (♦Hyperion 66114). The two popular masses appear in Jeremy Summerly's Oxford Camerata disc, a satisfactory coupling from a consistently worthy group (Naxos 550575).

Missa Vidi speciosam. Based on a Marian motet, Hill couples this mass with several motets and hymns, including the composer's most popular single work, the simple four-voice *Ave Maria* (♦Hyperion 66129).

Missa Trahe me post te. Hill's successor at Westminster Cathedral, James O'Donnell, couples this mass, based on a Marian motet, with four Marian antiphons and a *Magnificat* (♦Hyperion 66738).

Missa Dum complerenter. O'Donnell's choir fills out their recording of this mass, based on a Pentecost motet, with more motets and hymns (♦Hyperion 66886). Stephen Darlington's version (below) is also sung very well (Nimbus).

Missa Simile est regnum caelorum. Darlington's Christ Church Cathedral Choir couples this Mass with the one just above (♦Nimbus 5434). This choir matches the Westminster singing very closely.

Missa Laetatus sum. This mass for 12 voices (triple choir) is one of the large-scale works published late in the composer's life. Christophers has recorded it with several motets in a superb performance (♦Collins 15212). Peter Conte's choir of St. Clement's in Philadelphia couples it with *Missa Ascendens Christus in altum* (Dorian).

Missa Salve. This mass for eight voices (double choir) is filled out with four Marian antiphons, a *Magnificat,* and the eight-voice *Ave Maria* on Christophers's other disc (♦Collins 15012).

Missa Gaudeamus and **Missa pro Victoria.** Andrew Carwood's Cardinal's Musick couples these two Masses with eight short antiphons (♦ASV 198).

Missa Surge propera. Peter Schmidt's Mixolydian ensemble pairs this with a mass by Juan Gutierrez de Padilla (Carlton).

Three more masses were once available on LP, but we had best look for new recordings of **Missa pro defunctis** for four voices (RCA Victor), *Missa quarti toni* (Erato), and *Missa Alma redemptoris*(Vox) rather than reissues. In addition to the motets mentioned above (and the mass recordings are invariably coupled with their related motets), Savall's Capella Reial de Catalunya has grouped ten Marian motets and a *Magnificat* in "Cantica Beatae Virginis," in a superbly atmospheric recording (♦Astrée 8767). WEBER

Louis Vierne *(1870–1937)*

In spite of being born almost blind and undergoing operations that were never completely successful, Vierne's musical talent was apparent early in life. While the organ was his primary instrument, he was exceptionally gifted on the piano and violin. Elected unanimously to be organist *titulaire* at Notre-Dame in 1900, he maintained that position until his death at the console in 1937. His six organ symphonies are his best-known efforts, though he composed a symphony, a work for piano and orchestra, masses, works for organ and brass, songs, and some splendid chamber music.

SYMPHONIES

There are three excellent complete symphony collections available, with some of the best performances, and you can't go wrong with any of these: **Pierre Cochereau** at Notre-Dame (♦FY 028/29 and 064), **Ben van Oosten** (♦MD+G 3211/14, 4CD), and **Günther Kaunzinger** (Koch 315000, 3CD). Kaunzinger invariably chooses the fastest tempos, which tends to dilute the seriousness; Cochereau can be unpredictable, whizzing through some movements and luxuriating in others; van Oosten tends toward conservative tempos. Of special interest with van Oosten is that he performs on three Cavaillé-Coll organs—two symphonies each at St. Francis-de-Sales, Lyon; St. Ouen, Rouen; and St. Sernin, Toulouse. There are many very respectable performances of individual symphonies.

1. Both **Colin Walsh** at St. Albans (♦Priory 236) and **Michael Murray** at St. Ouen (♦Telarc 80329) compensate for church resonance with somewhat slower tempos. The Pedal at St. Ouen, however, has the edge for awesome sound. **Marie-Clair Alain** at St. Etienne (Caen) does 1–4 on an instrument with enough edge to give it a more visceral quality (Erato 45485). **Boucher** and others do 1, 2, and 4 acceptably from Montreal (REM 11047-1/2, 2CD). For all these interpretations, the instrument, acoustics, and style are outstanding.

2. **Walsh** at Lincoln (♦Priory 446) and **Harald Rise** at the 3-60 stop organ in Lulea Cathedral in Sweden (♦Victoria 19062) are excellent. Lincoln's sound is heavier and not as clear as that from Sweden. My favorite is early **Cochereau,** issued in the '50s; the tempos are mercifully conservative and appropriate (Solstice 177/78, 2CD, with Dupré's Passion Symphony).

3. **Bruno Mathieu** at St. Sebastien (Nancy) (♦Naxos 553524) and **Alain** (♦Erato 45485) are excellent. Both instruments have muscle and a hard edge, and the engineering reproduces the resonance and clarity.

4. **Alain** has a strong interpretation with superb engineering (♦Erato 45485), but **Bjorn Boysen** playing the new Ackermann organ with Cavaillé-Coll influences, in St. Catherine's, Stockholm, is surprisingly convincing (♦Simax 1050).

5. Rise is remarkably appealing from Lulea Church, Sweden, in this seldom heard symphony (♦Victoria 19062). **Van Oosten** at St. Sernin (MD+G 316072) and **Cochereau** (FY 029/30) also contribute outstanding interpretations

6. David Craighead is splendid, musically and stylistically (♦Delos 3096). Another top choice is **Mathieu** (♦Naxos 553524). The snarl and power of the Dalstein-Haerpfer installation are clearly appropriate for this acidic work.

OTHER ORGAN MUSIC

For the 24 *Pièces en style libre* (1913), **Jacques Amade** is best overall (♦Chamade 5651/2, 2CD). **Kaunzinger** provides clean, intelligent readings (Koch 315009, 2CD; **George Baker** does 13 of them, coupled with Widor's Symphony 9 (FY 128)). Although she plays only three or four from each suite of the *Pièces de Fantasie* (1926–27), get **Susan Landale** (♦Adda 581246). **Kaunzinger** is excellent for the complete suites (♦Novalis 150132); **Wolfgang Rübsam** is adequate (Bayer 100014/15). In *Triptyque*, **Cochereau** at Notre-Dame is outstanding, with close miking and suitable tempos (♦FY 064), and **Walsh** is a good second choice (Priory 319). The best newer recording of *Marche Triomphale* (1921) is by **David di Fiore,** with Kershaw and the Auburn Symphony, even though the brass dominates (♦ARC 1019). A fine old performance has **Bernard Gavoty** at Les Invalides (Paris)—good balance with the added benefit of improvisations by Dupré (Erato 3082, LP).

SACRED MUSIC

Messe Solennelle. Op. 16 (1903–5) was written for choir and two organs. The runaway favorite among recordings is from **Notre-Dame,** where the choir is the clearest (♦FY 064). The **Sacre-Coeur** forces are good, but the overwhelming echo reduces choral articulation considerably (Motette 40081). The **Chartres** performance is disappointing; in spite of being the only recording that includes five brass and three timpani with the two organs and choir, at quarter note=58 it's positively funereal (Valois 4627). **David Briggs** does a decent job from Gloucester Cathedral with just the one primary organ (Priory 597).

CHAMBER AND PIANO MUSIC

A little known treasure trove, these pieces were written between 1894 and 1928. The best recording of his piano works is by **Georges Delvallée** (♦Arion 68270). For the complete chamber works, get "La musique de chamber," which includes the important sonatas for violin and for cello, the string quartet, and the piano quintet, in intensely-felt performances (♦Timpani 2019). METZ

Henri Vieuxtemps *(1820–1881)*

This Belgian violinist was one of the archetypal 19th-century virtuoso soloists. He helped create the image of the virtuoso as hero, nobly battling the difficulties in the score at hand. In contrast to the circus showmanship of Paganini and his works, Vieuxtemps had an air of dignity in his playing and compositions. He was an uneven composer and much of his music has not aged well, but his first five concertos are fine works.

Aside from 4 and 5, Vieuxtemps's violin concertos are sparsely represented on disc. **Mischa Keylin** is recording the complete set, and he's a very fine violinist; he has plenty of technique and a virtuoso's panache, and both discs released so far are excellent investments. No. 2 shows the influence of Paganini in its Italianate lyricism and refusal to take itself too seriously, but 3 opens with a more forceful movement before returning to Paganinian influences in its waltz-like rondo finale (Naxos

554114). No. 1 is a sprawling work with a first movement nearly as long as all of 4, but there are no longueurs. No. 4 is Vieuxtemps's most popular concerto; it's full of imagination, and Berlioz called it a "magnificent symphony for orchestra with principal violin" (Naxos 554506).

No. 5 is perhaps Vieuxtemps's most difficult concerto, written as a competition piece for the Paris Conservatoire. It's formally his most peculiar work, since he kept adding to it over the years; it's in three movements, but these are to be played without pause, so it feels as if it's in one. In the past few decades, 5 has overtaken 4 as the favorite among recording artists. The cause of this is easy to spot: In 1961, **Heifetz** made a stunning recording (♦RCA 6214, 61745). This wasn't his first go at the work; he had recorded it in 1947 with the same conductor, Sargent (EMI 65191). The two recordings are very similar, but the later one has a real sense of occasion and is blessed with excellent sound—Heifetz's tone burns like a laser. It's also a remarkable achievement for a man of 61. It has more recently been recorded by **Chang** (EMI), **Chung** (London LP, NA), **Alexander Markov** (Erato), and **Zukerman** (Sony), but they all come across as mere imitators at best.

Perlman recorded 4 and 5 in 1977 with the Orchestre de Paris under Barenboim in one of the best recordings he has made (EMI 47165 or 566058). He has his own ideas about how things should go, and he uses slightly slower tempos than Heifetz to enhance the drama and dignity of the music. He and Barenboim realize the expressive potential of the concertos better than anyone else before or since. Nos. 6 and 7 have been recorded by **Gérard Poulet** (Valois 4797). They lack the inspiration of the earlier concertos, and Poulet isn't exactly a dashing virtuoso, though he's technically up to the task.

Příhoda recorded 4 in 1925; his central-European warmth and flashy technique are a rare combination these days (♦Biddulph 135). **Heifetz** recorded 4 with Barbirolli in 1935 (♦Pearl 9167; Monopoly 2043). This is a high-voltage reading, and Heifetz's tone really soars. **Huberman** made a sensitive recording of *Ballade and Polonaise* in 1922 that oozes personality (♦Biddulph 077/78; Pearl 9332). Vieuxtemps's Cello Concerto 1 has an especially treasurable slow movement; 2 is perhaps more virtuosic, in the style of the violin concertos. Both have been beautifully recorded by **Heinrich Schiff** and Marriner (EMI 47761).

Vieuxtemps's salon compositions haven't aged well. Steeped in 19th-century sentimentality, they haven't found a place in the modern repertoire and are rarely recorded. The best of them is the witty *Greeting to America,* variations on "The Star-Spangled Banner" and "Yankee Doodle" that were the composer's present to the young republic on his first tour here in 1844. They have been ably recorded by **Poulet** with orchestral accompaniment (Valois 4797). **Michael Guttman** has recorded *Grand Sonata* with selections from longer salon works (ASV 1050). The Sonata demonstrates Vieuxtemps's elementary grasp of this form and idiom, and Guttman lacks the tone, charisma, and virtuosity to hold the listener's attention through such an empty program. **Philippe Koch** fares somewhat better with his disc, containing six *Salon Pieces* and *Voices of the Heart* (Cypres 3613). These are light as a feather as far as substance goes, but they may be enjoyed if you are in the proper mood.

Vieuxtemps owned a fine Maggini viola, for which he composed works for his own performance. They aren't bad, so we may conclude that he enjoyed playing the instrument. **Pierre Lénert** has recorded the complete works for viola with Jeff Cohen (Syrius 141340). He's a sensitive musician who phrases naturally and doesn't let the longer movements outstay their welcome. **Pierre-Henri Xuereb** recorded the Unfinished Sonata, but he isn't the musician Lénert is (Classic). MAGIL

Heitor Villa-Lobos (1887–1959)

Villa-Lobos was a Brazilian phenomenon: self-taught, unabashedly idealistic, unrepentently flaunting his wide range of European and native influences, pouring out music in the same natural, uncontrollably easy way that a fertile orchard bears fruit. He wasn't crazy about rules, inventing his own musical forms and letting pieces sprawl every which way, but at the same time, he strove for respectability by managing to write symphonies, concertos, and quartets that number well into the teens. His corpus supposedly numbered over 1,000 works, many of which have yet to be catalogued, let alone recorded.

Today, Villa-Lobos would be considered a prophet of eclecticism and world music, but we don't know the whole story. There are still giant gaps in his discography, some of which are gradually being filled by enterprising labels like Marco Polo and Dorian, but others await deep pockets that are becoming increasingly loath to invest in big projects—not to mention internationally famous interpreters who could give some of these pieces a shot at invading the repertory. What is known is that however wildly uneven and often undisciplined his output, there is a lot of cherishable, tuneful, exciting, even emotionally powerful music beyond the famous *Bachiana brasileira* No. 5.

BACHIANAS BRASILEIRAS

Villa-Lobos created his own unique genre here, a nine-work series written between 1930 and 1945 that operates on the same premise as Satchel Paige's legendary all-purpose pitch, the be-ball—"be anything I want it to be." In other words, Villa-Lobos pays tribute to his idol Bach by hijacking some of his musical and dance forms, contrapuntal techniques, and melodic patterns, and fusing them freely to his own tunes, structures, and original treatments of Brazilian folk influences, sometimes abandoning Bach altogether. He didn't want to know about categories like orchestral, chamber, and the like; a *Bachiana brasileira* can be a solo piano piece, a showcase for a huge orchestra, or almost anything in between. So if he didn't care, why should we? Hence the *Bachianas Brasileiras* as its own category.

Complete sets. Pathé Marconi recorded Villa-Lobos as a conductor extensively from 1954 to 1958, and almost all the results can be found in an indispensable boxed set, "Villa-Lobos par lui-même" (♦EMI 67229, 6CD). Included is the first recording of the complete *Bachianas brasileiras,* which appeared only in fragments in the United States during the LP era. Despite the occasionally ragged playing of the Orchestre National de la Radiodiffusion Française and the pallid mono sound, you get a clear sense of Villa-Lobos's unquenchable vigor and desire to air all the loose ends and complicated textures of his music, trusting the listener to sort things out. For instance, 7 may be a little messy in execution but has irresistible forward drive, coming to an impressive conclusion in the Fugue. The "Dansa" in 4 isn't as well played as the digital contestants, but it sounds wilder and more exotic in the composer's hands—and conversely, he stretches the Preludio and Aria out lovingly and luxuriously; it almost sounds like Stokowski. Though not listed in *Schwann,* this box is available everywhere—I've even seen it at Best Buy—at ridiculously inexpensive prices ($33 to $45 for a six-CD set!), a super-bargain by any measure.

There is a stereo set, albeit hard to find, of the complete series with **Isaac Karabtchewsky** and the Brazil Symphony, which plays capably if not impeccably most of the time (Iris 143, 3CD). The set does have its unique pleasures, particularly the uninhibited use of native percussion instruments—just listen to how these Brazilians can swing "The Little Train of the Caipira"—but many of the performances lack the com-

poser's drive, and the sound and balances can be somewhat murky. Besides, there's more than twice as much music for less money in the EMI box.

1. To start off the cycle on an eccentric note, Villa-Lobos writes for a cello and orchestra, but within seconds, we realize this is no mere oddity. The Introduction is a big, exuberant essay with zesty massed syncopations; the *Prélude* contains one of his great soaring melodic passages, and the concluding Fugue takes a merry theme and runs it through the Bachian processes. **Villa-Lobos**'s own recording has fire and fervor; the sound is a bit thin yet adequate to project the composer's intentions (EMI 66964). **Bátiz** and the Royal Philharmonic take slower tempos and use a softer focus that makes the work seem mournful, and the syncopations in the Fugue don't have much snap. Moreover, the digital sound isn't much better than the composer's disc (EMI 47433). Falling somewhere between these two are **Aldo Parisot** and the Yale Cellos, who display nearly as much zest as the composer, more weight in the lower-clef parts, perhaps too much freedom in the *Prélude,* and a good stab at the syncopations. Parisot was a friend of Villa-Lobos for nearly 20 years, and he's on the right track (Delos 3041). The leaderless 12 cellists of the **Berlin Philharmonic** are unparalleled in their ability to sail through the Fugue effortlessly at a hair-raising clip; more Bach than Brazil, they make the whole thing sound like the work of a European neoclassicist (EMI 56981).

2. With full orchestra this time (with saxophone and trombone leads), the Bachian element is still present in traces of melody and in the layout of the movements—Preludio, Aria, Dansa, and Toccata—but the key to the work is in the descriptive subtitles. These are really tone poems about various aspects of Brazilian life, the most famous being the Toccata finale ("The Little Train of the Caipira"), which clatters along on a tune of pure genius, perhaps the composer's best. In **Villa-Lobos**'s ingratiatingly saucy recording, listen to how he treats the Toccata in a complex, unsentimental manner, with all kinds of jungle and train sounds making a delightful cacophony (EMI 66964).

Though **López-Cobos** and the Cincinnatians are lush, smoothed over, and a bit inflexible in rubato, this approach works wonders with the Toccata; the big tune soars in its full glory. Ultimately there's more to this music, yet the results are undeniably beautiful and mobile (Telarc 80393). **Paul Capolongo** gets expressive, delicate, deeply-layered playing from the Orchestre de Paris in excellent analog sound. Only the Toccata's massive symphonic treatment disappoints; it sounds like an overweight diesel train (EMI 47357). **Morton Gould** vividly characterizes the quirks of the Toccata in his "Jungle Drums" album (RCA 68173); likewise, **Goossens** and the London Symphony just play the Toccata—slowly (Everest 9007). Schwann's listing of a Bernstein recording is wrong; there ain't none.

Villa-Lobos also arranged three of the four movements for cello and piano, where his marvelous melodies stand out in more direct relief. **Tania Lisboa** and pianist Miriam Braga perform all three movements (Meridian 84357); **Rebecca Rust** and David Apter are more driving and less wayward in the Toccata (Marco Polo 223527).

3. The third in this strange series of works is a 27-minute piano concerto of sorts where, despite the prescribed integration of the keyboard into the texture, the piano has frequent passages to itself. Bach makes only fleeting paraphrased appearances in the solo part and the tread-like procession of the Aria, while the Toccata has a relentless Indian flavor, aptly subtitled "Picapao" (a woodpecker-like bird). The only major-label alternative to **Villa-Lobos**'s rough-hewn recording in the boxed set is **Cristina Ortiz**, who flashes more of a virtuoso technique while Ashkenazy leads a smoother, more understated Philharmonia (EMI 72670, 2CD).

4. This one maintains the four-movement structure and several musical aspects of 2 and 3, but the composer gives the options of performing the work on solo piano or with full orchestra. The "Preludio" is a perfect amalgam of Bach and Brazil, mournful and courtly in the Central European Baroque manner while also an unabashedly lush Brazilian cousin of the Bach-Stokowski style (small wonder that the two hit it off immediately). **López-Cobos** conscientiously takes the repeat in "Preludio"; though he's a trifle bland at times, he serves up the requisite lush sound and receives excellent engineering (Telarc 80393). **Tilson Thomas** omits the "Preludio" repeat, which doesn't allow the mood to develop; elsewhere he impulsively produces gusts of passion amid oceans of stasis, an intermittently involved performance (RCA 68538).

5. Here Villa-Lobos breaks the mold and only writes two short movements for soprano and eight cellos (originally the lead instrument was a violin). The world knows this work only from its first movement, the "Aria," whose ineffably haunting tune for wordless soprano has made this his most popular piece; only "The Little Train of the Caipira" can rival its fame.

The first recording, in 1945, originally just an experiment to try out the newly written soprano part, is a classic (Sony 62355): **Bidù Sayão**'s defining moment on records is passionate, direct, and spine-chilling, with the composer conducting and Leonard Rose on solo cello. Interestingly, Sayão is the only singer in this survey who sails through the "Aria's" final treacherous octave interval seamlessly; all the others need a pause. Only the "Aria" was recorded; the "Dansa" wasn't written until later that year. A more emotional Villa-Lobos recorded it again in 1957, this time with the cooler soprano of **de los Angeles** recessed in the mix, but now we hear the beautiful, agitated "Dansa." This performance, too, is a treasure (◆EMI 66964).

Expanding to 12 cellos and 2 basses, Stokowski makes absolutely ravishing, creamy work of the "Aria," with **Moffo** in sexy form in the vocalise, and he captures the red-blooded vitality of "Dansa" (RCA 70931, 2CD). With Bernstein, you get a Romantic temperament mostly held in tasteful check, less-than-ravishing NY Philharmonic cellos, the penetrating soprano of **Davrath**, a winning rhythmic vitality in "Dansa," and superb Latin American disc companions (Sony 60571). Tilson Thomas is on the fast side in the Aria, not really at home with this music, though he approaches Bernstein's vigor in "Dansa." **Fleming** makes gorgeous, world-class sounds, but she's not very believable emotionally (RCA 68538).

Parisot's Yale Cellos follow **Augér**'s meltingly executed main line with real passion and elasticity in the "Aria," and "Dansa" has plenty of vigor and unusual tempo ideas; this is a strong contender (Delos 3041). **Mady Mesplé**'s tiny soprano, Capolongo's swift tempo in the "Aria," and the slightly wayward "Dansa" produce a less emotional effect than the top recordings (EMI 47357), while Bátiz's hasty, faceless performance is partially redeemed by the lovely singing of **Hendricks** (EMI 47433). **Te Kanawa** glides in a swoon from note to note in the "Aria" and sounds lost at sea in the rapid passages of "Dansa"; furthermore, Lynn Harrell's cello ensemble lacks definition (London 411730). The 12 red-blooded Berlin cellos are absolutely stunning in "Dansa" yet surprisingly indistinct in the "Aria," while **Banse** maintains a cool distance in the vocalise and brandishes a diva's thick tone quality in the verses (EMI 56981).

The **Eroica Trio** works from a transcription of the "Aria" only, with the violin taking the vocal line, and they rise to a slightly overwrought climax (Angel 57033). Barenboim's Brazil disc contains an arrangement of the "Aria" for piano, three winds and bass which comes off as mellow and uninvolving (Teldec 21482). In a transcription of the "Aria" for cello and piano, the instruments split the melodic line between themselves; the **Rust/Apter** recording (Marco Polo 223527) is more animated than **Lisboa/Braga** (Meridian 84357).

The universal appeal of the "Aria" inspired several moonlighters from other fields to give it a go. As Abravanel indulges in lots of rubato, folk singer **Joan Baez** does indeed hit all of the notes, though her fluttery vibrato gives the performance a distractingly lightweight quality (Vanguard 79160). From the jazz world, **Branford Marsalis** offers a smooth, bloodless rendition on soprano saxophone with Litton and the English Chamber Orchestra, a pointless exercise (CBS 42122). **Camerata Brasil** combines the soprano sax of Paulo Sergio Santos with an arrangement for a native Brazilian ensemble of plucked string instruments; this has considerably more life (EMI 56939). But Lalo Schifrin has the temerity to offer an imaginative bossa nova arrangement for trumpeter **Markus Stockhausen** and big band that actually works (Aleph 002). Check it out.

6. The shortest, most eccentric work in the cycle, Villa-Lobos scales his forces all the way down to a flute and a bassoon, who intertwine contrapuntally through a Bachian Aria and a fluttery Fantasia that follows entirely unpredictable flight patterns. Flutist **Fernand Dufrene** and bassoonist **René Plessier** work their way delicately through the piece in the Villa-Lobos box, **Michel Debost** and **André Sennedat** let their imaginations run more freely in the Aria (EMI 47357), while **Emmanuel Pahud** and **Friedrich Edelmann** are faster, more forceful, and better recorded (Marco Polo 223527).

7. Back to a full orchestra and four movements, this is the lengthiest in the series by a few hairs and also the most exciting, a chug-chugging journey over the Brazilian land mass with motor-driven ostinatos and a momentum that reminds me, believe it or not, of Sibelius. Then Villa-Lobos throws us a curve in the final Fugue, a broad, grandiose allusion to Bach's organ pieces. No. 7 fires up **Tilson Thomas**'s engine and analytical tools; this is one of the more successful performances in his spotty collection, and his youthful New World Symphony is leagues better than the composer's French band (RCA 68538). **Bátiz** does well here too, with a slightly softer focus and differing balances; it's the best thing in his disc (EMI 47433). Overall, MTT pulls it off best.

8. With a four-movement, full-orchestra layout similar to 7, substituting an Aria for the Gigue as a second movement, 8 is generally a less turbulently driven, more elusive work. Yet as was his wont, **Villa-Lobos** pulls a fast one and introduces some agitation into the center of the Aria, and the Toccata is filled with weird sonorities and home-grown percussion. In contrast to the composer's recording, **López-Cobos** would rather luxuriate in the main lines as he finds them, yet he can muster enough vigor when needed, and he has a superior ensemble and Telarc's powerful surround sound on his side (Telarc 80393).

9. Only ten minutes long in a single *Prélude* and Fugue movement, 9 serves as an eloquent, often reflective epilogue to the series, with its own set of demands. Villa-Lobos intended the piece to be performed by a voice orchestra, but realizing that he may have gone too far beyond the capabilities of his performers, he also made a version for string orchestra. Even with the limitations of indifferent sound, **Villa-Lobos**'s recording is rich and dark in hue, with the strings digging deeply—if not with the utmost technical finish—into the Fugue (EMI 66964). **Capolongo** also uses a string orchestra, getting a plusher, more full-bodied texture; though his recording time is shorter, he seems slower than the composer, probably because he doesn't feel the rhythms as incisively (EMI 47357).

The lean-textured **Turovsky** outraces everyone and tries to give the rhythms of the Fugue some oomph, fighting a cloud of reverberation in a disc that also includes the rare, early, nostalgic Suite For Strings (Chandos 9434). **Tilson Thomas** pulls the dynamic levels of the *Prélude* like taffy, skips lightly through the Fugue without much involvement, and contrary to the promises of the liner notes, does not use a chorus with his strings (RCA 68538).

ORCHESTRAL MUSIC

Symphonies. Here we stumble into one of the largest black holes in the Villa-Lobos discography. He wrote 12 symphonies but only a handful have made it onto discs, perhaps due to the extravagant forces needed to perform them.

The rambling, hectoring, super-Romantic, hour-long 2 exists in an old, muffled recording by **Villa-Lobos** and the Maracana Symphony (Aries 901, NA). No. 4 ("A Vittoria"), part of a trilogy marking the end of WWI, is half as long, highly bombastic like many politically inspired pieces (even quoting "La Marseillaise"), and you don't begin to hear any interesting ideas until near the end of the Andante III. **Villa-Lobos** lays out all this hot air with a lot of energy and confidence; the competing street band in the Finale is very saucy (EMI 67229, 6CD). But even he can't convince us of this bloated piece's worth—and neither digital sound nor **Enrique Diemecke**'s more refined leadership makes it any better (Dorian 90228).

Symphony 6, however, is quite dramatic and inventive. The idea of basing the melodic material on the contours of Brazil's mountains as plotted on graph paper predates Cage's chance theories, and somehow the results sound remarkably Brazilian, with a beautifully idealized jungle garden of a slow movement topping the bill. **Roberto Duarte** and his sometimes overstretched Slovakians make a fine case for the piece, coupled with the spectacular symphonic poem/ballet *Ruda* (Marco Polo 223720). The fascinating, restless 10 ("Amerindia") is an exotic "Symphony of a Thousand" for the founding of São Paulo, with large orchestra, three choruses, three vocal soloists, and a wild trilingual text (Portuguese, Latin, and Tupi Indian dialect), punctuated by erotic, windswept, wordless choral swoops. It receives a spectacular recording from **Gisèle Ben-Dor** and the Santa Barbara Symphony (♦\Koch 7488).

Another California-based conductor, **Carl St. Clair,** has recorded the diffuse 1 ("The Unexpected"), which tosses off fleeting, unrelated, often Romantic ideas in search of a common thread. Its discmate, 11, is exactly the same length (26 minutes), with exactly the same classical four-movement layout. But oh, what a difference 40 years made, for this piece warps the classical mold into a bundle of restless energy, thickly-textured polytonal lushness, crazy motion, and a marvelously-orchestrated finale. This is a work Villa-Lobos fans should definitely get to know (♦CPO 999568).

Amazonas. It is a truly radical slice of early Villa-Lobos, a short ballet that plays fast and loose with tonality under the vague influence of Debussy, with all kinds of slithering, blasting, lightly streaking orchestral effects. "After *Amazonas* I lost all modesty and shyness for writing daring things," wrote the liberated composer. **Diemecke**'s performance from Venezuela slithers and bumps sensuously and boisterously about in stunning recorded sound (Dorian 90228). **Duarte,** working in

Bratislava, shines a broader-paced, more analytical X-ray upon these weird textures in a disc that includes such occasionally riveting orchestral rarities as *Genesis, Erosao,* and *Dawn in a Tropical Forest* (Marco Polo 223357).

Discovery of Brazil. Always thinking of performance possibilities, Villa-Lobos fashioned four suites out of the reams of music that he wrote for the film of this name. It's a cinematically effective, surprisingly consistent score, lasting 72 to 79 minutes, slipping uninhibitedly from music with Iberian and Moorish flavors toward wild, idealistic fusions of Brazilian Indian and Latin vocal traditions. The first three suites are short and orchestral in format, while the half-hour fourth contains all the Dionysian choral carryings-on as the Europeans settle into the New World. **Duarte** and his Slovakians (Marco Polo 223551) give **Villa-Lobos** and his French forces (EMI 67229, 6CD) a really hard run in the first three suites, with Duarte's clear advantages in sound and execution nearly trumping the composer's vitality. However, in the fourth suite the composer creates more excitement even with antiquated sonics, making Duarte and his Slavic-sounding chorus seem plodding.

Forest of the Amazon. One of the composer's last works, this is an expanded, unified concert version of a score he wrote for the failed film *Green Mansions* (they threw almost all of it out in favor of a Bronislaw Kaper score!). It's an exciting, imaginative, emotional, wide-screen, yet still an exotic summary of everything he had tried to evoke about Brazil in the past. The recording **Villa-Lobos** made with the Symphony of the Air only six months before his death is the best way to hear this music (EMI 65880). Though the score is trimmed to 47 minutes, the performance teems with vitality and color, a startling example of his undiminished vigor as well as a final reunion with Sayão, who came out of retirement to record it. In 1994, Villa-Lobos disciple **Alfred Heller** put together a virtually complete 73-minute version with the Moscow Radio Symphony and Renée Fleming; the restored sections and passages generally aren't too striking and the performance is slicker, more Hollywoodish in feeling (Consonance 81-0012).

Mómoprecoce. Its subtitle, "Fantasy for Piano and Orchestra," is as a good label as any for this free-flowing, strung-together, near-concerto of eight pieces originally written as a piano suite called *Brazilian Children's Carnival.* **Magda Tagliaferro** and the composer maintain a light, whimsical touch and toward the end, good pounding rhythm in their 1954 recording; the original LP has more body than the CD transfer in the boxed set (EMI 67229, 6CD). **Ortiz** and Ashkenazy are a sleeker, more polished, rhythmically tame pair—not as much fun, but a decent alternative (EMI 72670, 2CD).

Rudepoema. While this turbulent, sometimes dissonant piece has already found a place in a corner of the piano repertoire, the rarer orchestral version doesn't have quite the same slashing visceral impact, except at the pile-driving close. **Duarte** does well here, coupling it with three ingratiatingly tropical early works, *Dança frenética, Danças caracteristicas africanas* (No. 3 is surprisingly jazzy), and *Dança dos mosquitos* (Marco Polo 223552).

Uirapurú. Written in the same year as *Amazonas* (1917), *Uirapurú* also flirts with atonality and abounds with exotic effects, yet assumes a more coherent, even cinematic shape, with greater emphasis on melody. *Uirapurú* was one of **Mata**'s last recordings, and he takes the Simón Bolívar Orchestra for a stirring ride (Dorian 90211). But **Eleazar de Carvalho** and the Paraiba Sinfonica give the opening a richer, broader, more brooding feeling, treat the agitated sections with more savagery, and seem more deeply in touch with the mysterious ethos of the Amazon (Delos 1017). As fine as Dorian's sound is, Delos's is even more spaciously spectacular.

CONCERTOS

Cello Concerto 2. Given that Villa-Lobos was an excellent cellist and loved the instrument above all others, it shouldn't come as a surprise that this is one of his more ingratiating concertos, scored lightly, with several affectionate passages and references to the *Bachianas Brasileiras* cycle in the slow movement. **Andrés Diaz** plays with silky ardor for Diemecke and a top-notch engineering team (Dorian 90228). Also worth hearing is the pungently played world premiere LP by Gustav Meier and the dedicatee, **Aldo Parisot,** who assisted Villa-Lobos in the work's creation (Westminster 8278, NA).

Guitar Concerto. See below.

Piano Concertos. After WWII, his international career back on track, Villa-Lobos cranked out a dozen concertos on commission, including five for the piano. Alas, they're mostly makework, safe and settled for this composer, with lots of melody but very few striking ideas, each with its own extensive, labored cadenza. For a complete cycle, the only choice at this writing is **Ortiz** with Miguel Gómez-Martinez and the Royal Philharmonic in a series of cool, highly-polished, not very exciting readings (Decca 452617, 2CD). In 5, which is a cut above the rest—particularly when Villa-Lobos reaches back to the *Bachianas Brasileiras* idiom for a poised tune in the slow movement—Ortiz faces formidable, more emotionally involved competition from **Felicja Blumental** and the composer (EMI 67229, 6CD).

THEATER MUSIC

Magdalena. This protean, ultra-prolific composer actually wrote a Broadway musical. Originally, it was supposed to be another Robert Wright/George Forrest cut-and-paste adaptation of existing music by a famous composer (*Song Of Norway, Kismet*). But rather than have them use his old music, Villa-Lobos energetically wrote a whole new score, and it's a mostly marvelous, joyous, atmospheric, operetta-like piece where the composer's melodic gift adapts very comfortably to a snazzier Broadway idiom. The reason few know about *Magdalena* is that a strike by the Musicians Union in 1948 prevented a cast album from being made.

A suite commissioned and recorded by **Kostelanetz** surfaced in 1974 but it's a syrupy confection that doesn't do Villa-Lobos justice (Columbia 32821, NA). In any case, the show closed quickly and lay dormant until the 1987 Villa-Lobos centenary, when a recording was finally made, with a combination of Broadway babies like **Judy Kaye** and opera stars like Faith Esham and Jerry Hadley (CBS 44945). Although the disc doesn't reveal any obvious hit tunes that might have leaped from the never-recorded cast album, the performance strongly suggests the ripe flavor of what might have been.

CHAMBER MUSIC

Chóros. As strange and individualistic as the *Bachianas Brasileiras* seem, the earlier *Chóros* are even more radical in conception and sound. Here is where Villa-Lobos really got involved with the folk, Indian and urban popular music of Brazil, immersing himself in their idioms to the point where European influences occasionally disappear altogether. Moreover, their formats are totally unpredictable, from a single solo instrument to several odd combinations of instruments and voices of every size, from a folk-like song for a single guitar lasting only a few minutes to an extravaganza carrying on for over an hour. Hence, a *Chóro* is whatever Villa-Lobos says it is.

No one has yet attempted an integral edition of all 16; I imagine that the logistics of rounding up so many diverse performing groups stops that idea in its tracks. In the **Villa-Lobos** box (EMI 67229, 6CD), you can hear tangy composer-conducted or supervised performances of the tiny 2 for flute and clarinet; 5 played by pianist Aline Van Barentzen; a rowdy rendition of the at first languid, then wildly primal 10 for large orchestra and chanting chorus; the lavishly textured 11 for piano and orchestra that sprawls for 63 minutes (a lot of it holds up surprisingly well, though it's still too long); and two unnumbered *Chóros Bis* for violin and cello, one jaunty, the other acerbic.

With the more refined yet no less enthusiastic New World Symphony and BBC Singers, plus better sound, **Tilson Thomas** catches the wildness and rhythmic charge of 10 spectacularly well (RCA 68538). **De Carvalho** receives even more brilliant sound in his superb performance of 8, a sensational, exuberantly rhythmic tone poem for two pianos and large orchestra that careens toward the limits of tonality (Delos 1017). **Kenneth Schermerhorn**'s 8 from Hong Kong is somewhat clumsy and congested, though coupled with the rarer, more restrained 9 for orchestra (Marco Polo 220322). The **Quintet of the Americas** and Sine Nomine Singers issued a sampling of 1–4 and 7 that will give a good impression of how diverse and how similar these small early works are (Newport 85518, NA).

Pequena Suite. This one is a souvenir of 1913, a romantic time when Villa-Lobos and a newly acquired pianist/girlfriend were stranded on Barbados after gambling all their money away and were forced to eke out an existence playing in bars. But if you're looking for emotional turbulence, you won't find it in this mostly gentle, lyrical score, although you will hear a precursor of *Bachianas Brasileiras* in the Fugato. **Rust**'s warmer, darker tone and greater animation with Apter on piano (Marco Polo 223527) makes for a more appealing performance than the **Lisboa**/Braga team (Meridian 84357).

Piano Trios. The piano trios are early works on the Villa-Lobos time line, and while 1 sounds like derivative Brahms-with-a-French-accent student music—pleasant and no more—3 plays with impressionism, the pentatonic and whole-tone scales a bit and even suggests the Brazilian jungle. 3:II is especially beautiful, even haunting. **Antonio Spiller** (violin), Monique Duphil (piano), and Jay Humeston (cello) have the only recording of 1–3 (Marco Polo 223182 and 223164), while the **Ahn Trio** makes an even more expressive, sweeping, perhaps at times over-the-top statement with 1 (Chesky 124).

String Quartets. The ever industrious Villa-Lobos wrote 17 string quartets—one more than Beethoven, two more than Shostakovich—and he was sketching an 18th the year before his death. In his quartets, the erratic Brazilian rule-breaker was never more consistent; all but the suite-like 1 are cast in the traditional four movements, almost all are 16 to 24 minutes long, and their inspiration level is remarkably even, with unquenchable vitality from first to last. No. 1 is a Dumky-Trio-like series of mood swings between lively, folk-like dances and conventional Romantic lyricism, while 2 through 4 are very much influenced by Debussy. No. 5 is full of popular tunes and distinct Brazilian rhythms, while 6 consolidates all of that in a unique manner. With 7, we hear a new seriousness of intent, more expansive in language, veering into near dissonance in 8 and neoclassical drive in 9, emerging into a conciliatory maturity from 10 onward with the Brazilian influences now tucked away within the classical string framework.

Here is one of the most extensive, likeable chamber music collections of the 20th century, just begging for a major quartet to take them on and punch them into the repertory. So far, only Hungary's plush-sounding, Romantic-grounded **Danubius Quartet** has recorded the whole cycle, treating it to handsome digital sound and chopping it into surveys that are most useful when selecting an early, middle and late quartet per disc (Marco Polo.223389/94, 6CD, available separately). For those new to the cycle, I would first try the disc that has the immediately winning 5, the invigorating 9, and 12 (Marco Polo 223392) and if they grab you, explore the others at random.

The **Cuarteto Latinoamericano,** which has a somewhat tougher, leaner approach, is currently finishing up a cycle for Dorian, after first issuing tantalizing tastes of 5 (Elan 2234) and 17 (Elan 2218) coupled with more incendiary quartets by other Latin American composers. Available from Dorian as of this writing are 1, 6, 17 (90205), 3, 8, 13 (90220), 7, 15 (90246), 5, 10, 13 (93211), and 2, 12, 16 (93179).

Other chamber works. *Jet Whistle* for flute and cello is a charming three-movement piece from 1950 lasting approximately ten minutes, beautifully played by flutist **Doriot Anthony Dwyer** and cellist Judith Glyde (Koch 7001) and with more of an edge by **Pahud** and Apter (Marco Polo 223527). The moody pastorale *Distribuçao de Flores* exists in a version for girls' choir, yet sounds especially good in its oboe/guitar incarnation, with guitarist **Simon Wynberg** and oboist John Anderson presiding (Chandos 6581).   GINELL

PIANO MUSIC

Villa-Lobos wrote hundreds of colorful pieces for solo piano. Most are miniatures and are often organized in collections based on Brazilian folk themes that reflect his interest in children's music. Currently it isn't possible to acquire all of the solo piano works, but **Débora Halász** seems to be engaged in a complete cycle, with two volumes available thus far (BIS). It's a pity she uses a harsh instrument and has been given congested sound, because she has a suitably fiery temperament; perhaps she will be recorded more naturally in future releases. The recorded sound is also a hindrance for two other artists working on series. **Alma Petchersky** is more introspective than Halász, but the details of her equally colorful playing are slightly suppressed by the cloudiness of the recording (ASV). **Sonia Rubinsky** faces a different problem in her first disc: She's recorded so closely that any attempt at subtlety is nullified (Naxos).

Some listeners may not be concerned by sound quality, but **Christina Ortiz** recorded many of Villa-Lobos's best and best-known works more than 20 years ago in a clear, realistic acoustic (♦EMI 72670, in the budget-minded "double fforte" series). No pianist has surpassed Ortiz in this repertoire; her performances abound in variety of tone, articulation, and mood. **José Feghali** comes close in three short works included in a collection of primarily Latin American dance music (♦Koss 1018). Ortiz is arguably better than the composer's contemporary advocate, **Magda Tagliaferro,** many of whose authoritative recordings were once available (♦EMI 69476). If you're looking for supplements to Ortiz and Tagliaferro, try the understated but satisfying **Marcelo Bratke** (♦Olympia 455). Also, **Rubinstein**'s *A Próle do Bébé* should be in every library (♦RCA 61445).

Tagliaferro and Ortiz both recorded *Mómoprecoce*, a zesty fantasy for piano and orchestra, and **Marco Antonio de Almeida** has a fine if less immediate account (♦Arte Nova 54465). For concertante works off the beaten track, look for Ortiz's version of the piano concertos (available in Europe on EMI) and **Gothoni** in the massive and unusual *Chóros 11* (♦Ondine 916).   LOVELACE

GUITAR MUSIC

Villa-Lobos wrote for the guitar in a revolutionary way, letting its open strings (mostly fourths apart) suggest harmony, texture, and even melody to a degree unheard of before him; yet this music seldom seems to fall victim to mere gimmickry. He frequently finds a chord voicing and moves it up and down the fingerboard (sometimes with open strings embedded as a drone element) in parallel harmony, akin to similar procedures used by Bartók and the Impressionist composers in their instrumental music. For the musically conservative guitar repertoire of the early 20th century this was a major breakthrough, bringing dissonances and unusual harmonies to the instrument in a way that is undeniably and innately guitaristic. The simplicity of his method is often allied with simple ABA forms, clear-cut yet distinctive melodies, jazzily tonal harmonies, with a very appealing result.

Concerto. Villa-Lobos was one of the few major composers to write for the guitar prior to recent years, yet despite his big name value to the repertoire, his Concerto for guitar and small orchestra hasn't been recorded frequently. Although Segovia premiered it (and requested the majestic cadenza that transformed the piece from a "fantasia" to a "concerto") he never recorded it. The two most important post-Segovia players offer excellent performances with top level orchestral collaboration; which one to choose is a matter of personal preference for the players, and also depends on the couplings. **Bream**'s version with the London Symphony and Previn is part of an all-Villa-Lobos disc (♦RCA 61604); **Williams** offers it as part of the "Great Guitar Concertos" package with Barenboim and the English Chamber Orchestra (♦Columbia 44791, 2CD, with concertos by Vivaldi, Rodrigo, Ponce, and Giuliani). Should you ever find it, **Angel Romero** gives an excellent reading paired with the rarely encountered Guitar Concerto of Hollywood's Lalo Schifrin, with López-Cobos and the London Philharmonic (EMI/Angel 38126).

Etudes. Though the Etudes were composed with a clear scheme of related keys (like Bach's *Well-Tempered Clavier* and Chopin's Preludes), they're not always presented or recorded in their given order; often some are left out or a new sequence is created. **Barrueco** did both in his awesome 1978 debut recording (Vox 3007, 3CD). For selected Etudes, try **Parkening**'s 1 and 11 in "In the Spanish Style" (♦EMI/Angel 447194) and 3, 4, 11, and 12 from **Norbert Kraft** in an otherwise mostly Spanish disc (♦Chandos 8857).

The most satisfying recording of the complete set, in their original order and with a thorough explanation of it, is by **Eliot Fisk** in an album of South American guitar music (♦EMI LP 14-6757). You can also get the complete etudes, preludes (in a new order), and Guitar Concerto all in one disc, played in his inimitable way by **Bream** (♦RCA 61604, Vol. 21 of the "Bream Edition"). His interpretations are always vivid; however, his serendipity can become a bit much, even with such colorful music. A piece perfectly suited to his sense of humor and melodrama, however, is *Choros 1,* which can be found in a highlights disc from the "Bream Edition," the reissued "Popular Classics for Spanish Guitar," and a recent "Ultimate Guitar Collection" with two preludes as well (♦RCA 61848, 61591, or 68814, and 33705, 2CD).

Preludes. These are Villa-Lobos's most popular guitar pieces, each one a gem. Though they're not hard to play—any decent player can manage them—they sound especially wonderful in the hands of a virtuoso. Unfortunately, guitarists tend to memorize the fingerings quickly and often ignore the composer's quite precise instructions as to dynamics, tempo, etc.; furthermore, the published editions have more than their fair share of errors, discrepancies, and inconsistent notation. **Segovia** often included an etude or prelude in his concerts, and you can find his treatment of the first Prelude (exaggerated) and Etude (dazzling) as part of the "Centenary Celebration" (MCA/Decca 11124). Early in his career his protégé **Parkening** gave beautifully atmospheric readings of the first three in "In the Spanish Style" (♦EMI/Angel 447194).

For the complete Preludes, I recommend either **Williams**'s earthy, early 70s recording (♦Sony 62425, with superb performances of Scarlatti, Paganini, and Giuliani), or for a more precise approach and discreet interpretation, **Barrueco** in an all-Latin American disc including *Choros 1* (♦EMI 66576).

Suite Populaire Bresilienne. It was neglected for quite a while by guitarists because it's comparatively lightweight and less guitaristically adventurous than the preludes or etudes. It consists of various European dances (mazurka, waltz, schottische, etc.) Brazilianized into the "choro," hence the joint titles (e.g., "Valsa-choro"). **Bream**'s colorful version serves the music's parodistic qualities well (♦RCA 61591, while **Barrueco** offers an understated civility that suggests a deeper level to these pieces than is often found (♦Vox 3007, 3CD).   DINGER

Giovanni Battista Viotti *(1755–1824)*

By all accounts, Viotti was not only a great violinist but a very pleasant person. His compositions certainly project a sunny disposition, and it's sad to think that he died in some disillusionment with music. As a composer he was influenced by Mozart but also by such Italian compatriots as Boccherini, and many of his works hark back to a slightly earlier age, being in only three movements. On the other hand, much of his music can take a bel canto Romantic approach and many violinists enjoy playing it.

CONCERTOS

If Viotti still has a place in today's concert life, it's due to his 27 violin concertos, especially 22 in A minor, a beautiful work with a well-defined classical form and memorable themes. Kreisler never made his planned commercial recording, but among those who did set it down were Oistrakh, Menuhin, and **Grumiaux;** the latter's performance, in fine stereo sound, is much missed. One classic analog recording that's still around is by **Lola Bobesco** with the Rheinland-Pfalz Philharmonic under Redel (Talent 291013). She plays Ysaÿe's cadenzas and adds 23, which has an exquisite central Andante. **Rainer Kussmaul,** a top German violinist, plays 22 with elan, well supported by Johannes Goritzki and the Deutsche Kammerakademie Neuss; his coupling is 19, another favorite (CPO 999324). The chief attraction of **Elizabeth Wallfisch**'s ear-piercing performance of 22 on a baroque fiddle is hearing Ferdinand David's embellished edition (Hyperion 66840).

Perlman includes a breezy account of 22 in a program of student concertos (EMI 56750), and **Mark Kaplan** enjoys himself in Nos. 4, 22, and 24, with his colleague David Golub (best known as a pianist) conducting (Arabesque 6691). But perhaps the most beautiful digital 22 is by **Uto Ughi,** who directs the Santa Cecilia Chamber Orchestra himself; perhaps he slows down too much for the lovely second subject of I but he plays with glowing tone and adds Mozart's slightly questionable K271a (P&P Classica 010). A cheap but excellent version of 23 comes from **Mauro Ranieri** and the Accademia dei Filarmonici (Naxos 553861); he makes much of the Andante, and his colleagues Roberto Baraldi and Alberto Martini team up convincingly in the two enjoyable Sinfonie concertante for two violins. **Adelina Oprean** plays 13 with fire but adds a meager coupling, a frothy concerto by Viotti's contemporary Federigo Fiorillo (Hyperion 66210).

The ongoing series of the concertos by **Franco Mezzena,** who directs the Symphonia Perusina himself, can be given a blanket recommendation. The soloist is superb, if without the touch of individuality that makes for greatness, the little orchestra plays well for him, and the recordings are uniformly good. A good starter is the disc containing 27, which Adolf Busch used to play but hasn't been recorded before (Dynamic 206). It has a beautiful slow introduction to I and an unusually elaborate finale; the couplings are 4 and 20. Two enjoyable compilations of Viotti arrangements can be left to the fanatics (Bongiovanni 5077 and 5567), as can **Harnoy**'s unstylish performance of a dubious cello concerto (RCA 61228).

CHAMBER MUSIC

Some of Viotti's most enjoyable music can be found in his duets and serenades for two violins. Busch loved playing them and often programmed the big G major Serenade. **L'Arte dell'Arco** plays it reasonably well, along with two other serenades and two trios, which add a cello (Dynamic 101). Another disc of duets and serenades is a disappointment, however, as the playing of **Duo Deschka** is scratchy and ill tuned (Dynamic 2008). A beautiful G major duet, Op. 2:3, was recorded in the mono era by Busch's pupil **Menuhin** with de Vito, and this performance—available only in a French box devoted to Menuhin—is worth looking out for (EMI 573819). At present the best Viotti duetting can be heard in a mixed recital by two leading Czech players, **Pavel Hůla** and Bohumil Kotmel (Supraphon 1868)

A major surprise has been the series of Viotti's 12 sonatas for violin and piano (Dynamic 2002/4). The artistry of the veteran Spanish virtuoso **Felix Ayo,** whose fingers are still in great shape, transforms what could be rather bland sonatas into little gems; he's ably partnered by Corrado de Bernart, the recordings are superb and the three discs are available separately.

Viotti's string quartets have lost out to those of Boccherini, Giuseppe Cambini, and even Donizetti. The Busch Quartet used to play the C major from Op. 3, but not until 1992 was a recording made of this charming, melodious set. It's a winner: The Belgian-based **L'Arte del Suono** foursome led by Lola Bobesco plays with bewitching grace and glorious tone, getting all six works on one disc (Talent 291046). The three quartets published in 1817 and dedicated to his brother André are Viotti's best, in which he graduates to the four-movement form; the first violin still dominates, but there is interest for the other parts; the opening movement of Quartet 2 features cadenzas for both the violins and the cello. **Quartetto Aira** plays the set adequately, but we miss Bobesco's charisma (Dynamic 138).   POTTER

Antonio Vivaldi *(1678–1741)*

Venice's most famous composer was recognized only in the 20th century, when the identification of his music as the source of some of Bach's arrangements stimulated curiosity and turned Vivaldi himself into a limitless growth industry. He was regarded as an eccentric in his time for the daring and descriptive effects in his music that have endeared him to us. His life was one of aspirations never quite fully or directly fulfilled. A musician by family background, a priest by vocation, and a splendid violinist, his most important employment was as music teacher to the girls at a monastic foundling home (the Ospedale della Pietà), allowing him to explore both instrumental and vocal composition, secular and sacred, for his ladies, who became famous for their contribution to Venice's musical life. But he aspired for years to break into success as a composer of opera for the commercial theater. Feeling that his chances for recognition and rewards were insufficient in Venice, he spent his later years wandering in search of new patronage, as a result of which he died far from home, in Vienna, where (in anticipation of Mozart just 50 years later) he was buried in a pauper's grave.

Latter-day attention has unbalanced our perception by focusing on his instrumental works, especially his concertos, notwithstanding the waggish observation (variously credited) that Vivaldi composed the same concerto 500 times. The commercial fixation on two not wholly representative works ("Four Seasons" and *Gloria*) has risked reducing him to a caricature, but recordings have gradually helped provide some balance by exploring a wider scope. While it's true that he was no great choral composer, he did understand solo voices, and he wrote well for them in both secular and sacred forms. As recordings continue to probe and update his music, they can only confirm our recognition of Vivaldi as one of the greatest composers of the late Baroque.

CONCERTOS

The number of recordings of Vivaldi's concertos is very large and growing daily. It's almost as if his bright, orderly music has been sought as a panacea against the chaotic shadows of the late 20th century. In addition, period-instrument performances have produced even more recordings than might otherwise have been made and have added to the confusion about what to buy. The most important things you can do are (a) learn whether you enjoy modern or period instrument sound and (b) decide which ensembles and conductors satisfy you the most. My own bias tends toward modern-instrument ensembles that are heavily influenced by period performance practices; modern renditions of Vivaldi's music have profited greatly from recent scholarship. But you will probably also find, as I have, that any good ensemble, whether modern or period instrument, will speak to the heart, and you'll find yourself discarding the artificial categories that I have, nonetheless, set up here for ease of reference.

Collections

There are substantial Vivaldi collections, some from producers and others from conductors who have recorded a substantial part of Vivaldi's work for various labels.

Modern instruments. Philips has released all of Vivaldi's numbered opuses in two large boxes labeled "Vivaldi Edition." Vol. 1 (♦456185, 10CD) contains Opp. 1–6, which includes the well known and loved "L'Estro Armonico"; Vol. 2 (♦456186. 9CD) has Opp. 7–12, with the popular "Four Seasons" as the first four concertos of Op. 8 (Vol. 3 offers the Sacred Music; see below). In most cases, well-known soloists are used, and these recordings, though ranging over time from 1959 to 1977, are excellent and can be recommended, unless otherwise noted in the separate sections below. This set, though attractively packaged and very convenient, is quite expensive. For the budget-minded, Philips has also released some of these performances as mid-price duos; these will be noted below where available.

Even if your pocketbook is too slim to accommodate mid-price discs, you're not out of luck, thanks to Naxos, who have embarked on a project to record all of Vivaldi's concertos. Many are now available, with more planned in the near future. These will be discussed in their proper order below; they are turning out to be excellent, in some cases equal or even superior to Philips, and any Naxos collection is a very good risk. They can best be described as modern instrument recordings heavily influenced by period performance practices—the best of both worlds.

Period instruments. You can always rely on **Hogwood** and the Academy of Ancient Instruments for energetic yet delicate, nuanced work. Many of his recordings were issued on LP and have been transferred to CD, and because they have appeared on various labels, it's best to watch for his name. Another good choice is any of the various pieces recorded by **Pinnock** and the English Concert (Archiv). Some of them have been picked up by other labels, such as MHS, so again, watch for the conductor. Some reviewers find Pinnock less expressive than Hogwood, but I've always enjoyed the dash and vigor he brings to Vivaldi. Tactus, an Italian label, has undertaken a series of Vivaldi's 12 numbered opuses; some of them are good, but they're generally below par in both sound and performance. Exceptions will be noted below.

Most listeners like to begin with Vivaldi's violin concertos, especially the familiar "Four Seasons" and "L'Estro Armonico," so they're discussed first, in order of opus number. Concertos for other instruments follow in alphabetical order according to instrument, with miscellaneous concerto collections and chamber music after that. In general, for each instrument I discuss either complete collections or programs devoted solely to that instrument; concertos scattered throughout collections for various instruments will be found in the "Miscellaneous" section.

Violin concertos

Opus 3 ("L'Estro Armonico")

Vivaldi's Op. 3 is probably the second most popular of the sets of violin concertos. All 12 are justly famous and made more so by Bach, who adapted some of them for organ.

Modern instruments. There's no lack of choices for complete performances of Op. 3 using both modern and period instruments, but the modern-instrument versions are generally older. A good standard continues to be the Philips set, with I Musici and **Roberto Michelucci,** available both in the multi-disc "Vivaldi Edition" and as a separate "Duo" (♦44616). It's bright, brisk, and reliable, with good sound. I also highly recommend a great London "Double-decker," recorded in 1972 by **Marriner** and the Academy of St. Martin in the Fields (♦London 443472). This version is rich and mellow but not overly romantic. Both harpsichord and organ provide the continuo, with Hogwood as harpsichordist. It's a particularly good value, with four lesser-known Vivaldi concertos added as filler for over 144 minutes of music.

Mario Rossi directs the Chamber Orchestra of the Vienna State Opera in somewhat over-romanticized performances, recently released with digital remastering and consequently fantastic sound (♦Vanguard 66). Even with some slow tempos in spots, fast movements are generally brisk, and this is sunny Vivaldi, done with love. Listeners who enjoy the leaner period-instrument approach will probably find it dated, as well as **Renato Fasano**'s approach with the Virtuosi di Roma (EMI 69376); nonetheless, you will enjoy the rich sound of these older recordings.

Jozef Kopelman and Capella Istropolitana offer a 1988 recording of 1, 2, 4, 7, 8, 10, and 11; it isn't especially good or bad, with some bright spots, but it seems to lack energy at times (Naxos). **I Filarmonici**'s recording is best avoided; it's beset with hollow sound, imprecise intonation, and tumbling, over-hurried tempos (Tactus). The St. Petersburg soloists with **Michail Gantvarg** did a fiery, sometimes delightfully impetuous reading, but it's a bit spotty, with idiosyncratic tempos (Arte Nova).

Period instruments Leading the way are **Hogwood** and the Academy of Ancient Music (♦London 458078). This mid-priced set is almost unbeatable for value and beauty; soloists include Huggett, one of the stellar names in the early music firmament, and all is done with energy, sparkle, and good cheer. Harpsichord and organ are alternately used for continuo, contributing warmth, and variety. **Pinnock** leads the English

Concert and Standage in a vigorous rendition, unique for using one instrument per part. You might expect a thin sound, but not to worry; this is a worthy competitor (♦Archiv 23094).

For something different, try the explosive reading by **Biondi** and Europa Galante (Virgin 45315). This is a high quality, unconventional approach. The playing is a delight, but differences startle at every turn; for example, the concertos aren't played in normal order, and tempos are stretched and manipulated freely. The sound is pristine, and even if this isn't a first choice, it's fun. A more conventional approach may be found with **Estevan Velardi** and the Allessandro Stradella Consort in their 1997 recording; it's vigorous and straightforward, only slightly less desirable than Hogwood because of a few idiosyncratic moments (Bongiovanni 5597).

Opus 5 ("La Stravaganza")

Modern instruments. Philips offers a full and exciting rendition of these 12 concertos with a vigorous organ continuo, and **Felix Ayo**'s playing is lovely in this 1963 recording. If you've become used to a leaner Vivaldi but still enjoy modern instruments, two more excellent choices await. **Carmel Kaine** and Alan Loveday, with Marriner and the Academy, give a rich but not unduly romantic version on a mid-priced "Double-decker" (♦London 444821). For a recording even more obviously influenced by period performance practice, try **Andrew Watkinson** with the City of London Sinfonia under Nicholas Kraemer (♦Naxos 553323/24). The sound is beautiful, and these are lively, exciting, and expressive readings.

Period instruments. The best without a doubt is by **Huggett** with Hogwood and the Academy of Ancient Music (♦Oiseau-Lyre 417502, NA); her performance makes you wonder why these concertos aren't recorded more often.

Opus 6

These six concertos are seldom recorded, but the ever-reliable Philips edition awaits with **Pina Carmirelli** as soloist in a 1977 reading. Carmirelli's playing is soft and velvety; it may seem a bit too syrupy for Vivaldi, but it's still really lovely. **I Solisti Italiani** (♦Denon 18024) and I Filarmonici with soloist and director **Alberto Martini** (Tactus 672229), both conductorless ensembles, have recorded these concertos; the former is an admirable performance with crispness and energy, obviously influenced by period practice; the latter has occasional problems with ragged playing, and hollow sound that blurs the notes. **Mintz** has done a wonderful job with these concertos in Vol. 9 of his 10CD set (see below in "Miscellaneous").

Only one period-instrument version exists, but with stellar forces: **Manze** performs with Christopher Hogwood and the Academy of Ancient Music in a recent release (♦Decca 455653).

Opus 7

For whatever reason—questions regarding authenticity?, run-of-the-mill composition?—these 12 concertos have rarely been recorded as a group. Michael Talbot believes three of them to be spurious and also thinks Vivaldi didn't approve their publication. Whatever the cause, there are only two choices here: first, the Philips edition, where **Accardo** gives the violin concertos very good treatment indeed; likewise for Heinz Holliger and the two oboe concertos in this opus. Second, **I Solisti Italiani,** with the help of oboist Hansjörg Schellenberger, has done a beautiful job, with lively, sensitive playing (♦Denon 75498). (It should be noted that Bach apparently found some of them to be musically interesting: He arranged 8 for harpsichord and 11 for organ.)

Opus 8 ("Il cimento dell'armonia e dell'inventione," including "The Four Seasons")

These 12 concertos begin with the four most famous, "The Four Seasons." When they were written, with their highly descriptive tone painting of the seasons of the year, they were exceedingly daring and inventive. Today even the most jaded listener can enjoy a good recording with a score in front of him to serve as a reminder of just how many vivid effects Vivaldi packs in.

Modern instruments. These recordings can be divided into two categories: traditional and those influenced by period performance practices. A good representative of traditional is I Musici and soloist **Ayo** in the Philips set. This has a "big orchestra" sound and is full and sweet, with lingering tempos, especially in the slow movements. Emphasis is placed on making beautiful music rather than bringing out the effects Vivaldi tried to create. This version, along with the other eight concertos, is in the 9CD set as well as in a "Duo" budget issue (438344). Another comparatively early version that wins rave reviews from modern instrument fans is **Fasano** with the Virtuosi di Roma (EMI 68625, 2CD)**.**

Bernstein produced a surprisingly scaled down, fresh and vigorous "Seasons" in the early '60s with violinist John Corigliano; it has survived the transition to CD well, with only minor sound problems thanks to expert engineering (Sony 63161). Most people find **Karajan**'s versions heavy, dated, and lacking in freshness; it's more Karajan than Vivaldi (DG 439422; MHS 515322). Also avoid **Stern**'s rendition, a relatively insensitive reading, though some other numbers in this set are good (Sony 66472, 2CD). A better choice—and budget-priced to boot—features violinist Konstanty Kulka with **Münchinger,** the Stuttgart Chamber Orchestra, and harpsichordist Igor Kipnis (London 417712). This recording from the '70s is brisk, vigorous, and expressive, with crisp attacks throughout; it's rich without undue romanticism, and the sound is excellent.

My first choice here is a re-release of a 1969 recording by Alan Loveday with **Marriner** conducting the St. Martin Academy (♦Decca 466232). The performance was revolutionary for its time, with swift tempos, lean, lovely execution, and vivid tone-painting, with no sacrifice of musicality. In addition, this recording has the incomparably jaunty Bassoon Concerto in A Minor (RV 498) with bassoonist Martin Gatt, as well as a 2-oboe concerto (RV 535) and a recorder concerto (RV 443) played with piccolo.

A similar approach may be found with I Solisti di Zagreb and soloist Jan Tomasow, directed by **Janigro** in 1957 (♦Vanguard 2536 or VBD-15). It's a lively, cheerful performance; while the remastered sound is a little harsh, it makes this version only a little less desirable than Kulka/Münchinger.

Perlman's rendition is slightly more romantic and wistful; the violinist plays and directs the London Philharmonic (♦EMI 64333). Programmatic aspects aren't emphasized in this 1976 recording, but neither are they downplayed as much as in the Philips version. **José-Luis Garcia**'s rendition with the English Chamber Orchestra is adequate, though occasionally lumbering; there's little here to attract the buyer compared to the others (ASV 6148).

Accardo's traditional reading with I Solisti delle Settimane Internazionali di Napoli is of special interest to collectors (♦Philips 422065). Accardo plays with passion and fire; the effects—for example, the summer thunder—are fine. But an added attraction is his choice of instruments: For each concerto, he uses a different Stradivarius violin, most of them from his private collection; the booklet has detailed pictures of one of the most famous. This release is both interesting and of very high quality musically. **Muti**'s recording falls in the crack between tradition and period styles (◆EMI 55183). He directs I Solisti dell'Orchestra Filarmonica della Scala with soloist Giulio Franzetti in a very good program that includes two other programmatic concertos: "La tempesta di mare" (RV 570) and "La notte," the G minor flute concerto from Op. 10. The orchestral sound is full and immediate with tight, fiery solo playing, but sometimes the orchestra is a little blurry, perhaps because there's a little too much reverb. Nonetheless, this is a high quality rendition that emphasizes musicality.

Occasionally, recordings actually deserve all the publicity they get, except they always deserve better than hokey hype. This is true of **Shaham**'s 1994 "Seasons," probably the best example of the happy marriage that can occur between period instrument practice and modern instrument usage (◆DG 439933). Here we have bright sound with snappy tempos, meticulous attention to programmatic aspects without eccentricity. Shaham's playing is pure and clear, musical and expressive; the soft organ continuo adds warmth. The Orpheus Chamber Orchestra gives a very clean performance, with crisp, brilliant sound. This is an exciting and fresh rendition without the eccentricities that can mar those simply trying to be different.

A surprise, also from 1994, was a performance probably as under-advertised as Shaham's was over-publicized: **Ivan Zenaty** and the Virtuosi di Praga give a more than solid rendition, and you can hardly beat the budget price (◆Discover 920219). The orchestra is jaunty, fleet-footed, and effortless where better-known ensembles seem labored, and Zenaty's playing is excellent, as is the sound. Another version with wonderful sound and character is by **Zehetmair** with Camerata Bern (◆Berlin 1164). Many reviewers like **Mutter**'s 1999 release with the Trondheim Soloists (DG 463259). Certainly it has its moments: The summer storm is brilliant, for example. But it often strikes me as too lingering and clingy, and some of the slow movements are drawn out to agonizing lengths. Nor does Mutter have command of these concertos as Shaham does.

Takako Nishizaki trails in this category; her playing is brisk and pleasing but not as expressive as it might be (Naxos 550056). This is one of Naxos's earlier recordings, and the company has come a long way sonically in the past twelve years. Here it seems harsh, especially on high notes, and the balance is none too good, with the harpsichord fading into oblivion at times. Avoid **Kennedy**'s eccentric version; it's unimaginative and given over to cheap effects (EMI 56253). Also avoid unconventional performances of these concertos, like **Galway**'s substitution of flute for violin or "Seasons" played on recorders or mandolins. Vivaldi wrote these concertos for violin; unless a musician of Bach's caliber transcribes them, they sound strange if performed.

Period instruments. These versions can also be divided into two schools: the "standard" and what I have dubbed the "speeding bullet" school. This moniker sprang to mind because of the evocative—some would say provocative—picture on the cover of Il Giardino Armonico's 1993 rendition of "Seasons"; a bullet ripping through a violin represents quite well the attempts by some ensembles to emphasize, perhaps to the point of over-emphasis, the pictorial aspects of these works.

First, the "standard" versions; there are many very good ones. Three spring readily to mind as models: **Hogwood** and the Academy of Ancient Music with various soloists, including Huggett (◆Oiseau-Lyre 417515); **Standage** with Pinnock and the English Concert (◆Archiv 400045); and **Huggett** again with the Raglan Baroque Players and Nicholas Kraemer (◆Virgin 61172). All of them are performed with en-

ergy and finesse, with Pinnock having a bit more intimate sound than the others, and Huggett leaning heavily to the expressive side with her creative stretching of tempos. Her version may be a little less exuberant than the other two, but she plays with elegance and a beautiful crispness. Hogwood's version contains the entire Op. 8, which is a great bonus, considering that the other eight concertos in this set are vastly underrated and underperformed, but Kraemer's set is also a good value that includes concertos 5, 6, 10, and 11.

A very solid performance—musical but expressive, sprightly, and cheerful—comes from violinist and director **Christopher Warren-Green** with the London Chamber Orchestra (◆Virgin 61466, 2CD). This 1989 recording has excellent sound with good balances, and the set includes a good survey of Vivaldi's wide-ranging compositional skill with two concertos from "L'Estro Armonico" and one each for oboe, cello, bassoon, and two trumpets. **Biondi** gives a fiery, entertaining reading with Europa Galante, with a bonus of two extra concertos (◆Opus 111 912). Another excellent version, but a poor value at full price for just "Seasons," is by the Drottningholm Baroque Ensemble with violinist **Nils-Erik Sparf** (BIS 275). The 1984 recording is the equal of any in terms of musicality, expression, and sound. Andrew Parrott and the Taverner Players have released two fine versions: **John Holloway** is soloist in 1984 (Denon 7283), and **Chiara Banchini** and others take turns as soloists in a release that's a much better value than the Denon, as it includes three other concertos (◆Virgin 45117).

As for the "speeding bullet" school, it's only fair to say that these recordings have been controversial, with some reviewers finding them horridly unmusical and others finding them fun and intriguing. I think they're fun and that they add to our understanding of these concertos, but I don't advise having them for your only recording. Vivaldi's music is wonderfully versatile, and it can bear a variety of interpretations, but some will wear better than others.

Harnoncourt's version with soloist **Alice Harnoncourt** was one of the first to provoke controversy, with some reviewers labeling the team "stunning" and others finding much of the performance to be distastefully eccentric (Teldec 97983). The 1968 recording with conductor Giovanni Antonini and violinist **Enrico Onofri** proved a good forerunner to the Giardino Armonico version (Teldec 97671). Listeners will probably find it harder to adjust to the stretching of tempos here than to the vociferous strings; at the least, the recording is quite vivid, designed to present in the boldest possible musical colors the pictures Vivaldi painted. For an interesting variation on this theme, try **Gottfried von der Goltz**'s 1997 recording, where he functions as both violinist and conductor of the Freiburg Baroque Orchestra (◆Harmonia Mundi 77384). The continuo is provided by Andrew Lawrence-King and the Harp Consort, which makes for some great effects, especially for the storms and buzzing bugs.

For a toned down version, go to **Jeanne Lamon** with Tafelmusik; this recording is wonderfully pictorial without sacrificing musicality, and the sound is great (◆Sony 48251). **Rainier Schmidt** and the Deutsche Kammervirtuosen have released an expressive chamber version, with one instrument to a part and lute continuo (◆Melisma 7118). Though its emphasis is on pictorial aspects, the effects aren't excessive and the sound is full and immediate. "Seasons" is the only work on the disc, but there's a beautiful booklet with facsimiles of portions of the score and the original sonnets, plus gorgeous full-color replicas of famous paintings of each of the seasons. The text is in German, but that's not an insurmountable difficulty.

Now to the unjustly neglected concertos 5–12 of this remarkable opus: Modern-instrument performances are scarce. **Ayo** is absolutely beautiful in the Philips edition, and the whole Op. 8 is available as a "Duo" (♦438344). I quite like **Béla Bánfalvi**'s 1988 recording of Nos. 5–8 and 10–12 with the Budapest Strings (♦Naxos 550189). No. 9 is inexplicably left out, possibly because it can be found in its oboe incarnation in another Naxos CD (see oboe section below). They play a very tuneful set with aggressive tempos, fast and crisp; the sound is immediate with one minor defect, a lack of clarity. If you don't know these concertos, this is a good and inexpensive way to acquire them.

My favorite version of Nos. 5–12 is a 1978 period-instrument recording with **Pinnock** conducting the English Concert; the performance is stirring, energetic, and expressive (♦CRD 3325; Vanguard; MHS 11085Z, 2CD; NA). If you find it in one of its three incarnations, you should grab it. Hogwood's version is also excellent (see above). **Carlo Chiarappa** as violinist and conductor with the Accademia Bizantina offers the entire opus in a serviceable but not very exciting recording (Denon 75352, 75447).

Opus 9 ("La Cetra")
The little attention these 12 works has received is at least of high quality: **Ayo**'s 1964 recording for the Philips edition is marvelous, as is **Iona Brown**'s, in a somewhat leaner version with the St. Martin Academy (♦London 448110). **I Solisti Italiani** offers a crisp rendition (Denon 79475/76).

Huggett's 1986 period instrument version is delightfully warm and lively (♦Virgin 61246). A cooler and more reserved rendition came from **Standage** with Hogwood (Oiseau-Lyre 421366, NA).

Opus 11
For modern instruments, **Accardo** gave a clean, vigorous 1974 performance in the Philips set. A 1997 recording from I Filarmonici and **Alberto Martini** is better than others in his series, played with plenty of energy (Tactus 672237). A crisp 1993 period-instrument version comes from **Stanley Ritchie** (violin) and Frank de Bruine (oboe) with Hogwood and the Academy of Ancient Music (♦Oiseau Lyre 436172), my top choice here.

Opus 12
Accardo plays a beautiful and exciting version of these six concertos that highlights the latent pathos you often hear in Vivaldi's music (in the Philips set). **I Solisti Italiani** does well in a release with excellent sound (♦Denon 78974), and **I Filarmonici**'s rendition is also lively and interesting (Tactus 672238).

Pavlo Beznosiuk's 1997 period-instrument version, with Hogwood and the Academy of Ancient Music, is top-notch (♦Oiseau-Lyre 443556). Beznosiuk has a gentle sound, and the performance overall is full of pep and verve—completely delightful, and my first choice for this opus.

Other violin and string concertos
Vivaldi wrote many violin concertos that were not assigned to an opus; these tend to be performed less frequently than the more popular opus numbers, but a few attempts have been made to collect them in various ways.

Modern instruments. The most comprehensive collection so far is a 10-volume set with **Mintz** as both soloist and conductor of the Israel Chamber Orchestra. These are solid performances; there's no lack of energy and crispness. The first set in this series (♦MusicMaster 67085, 2CD) uses FI numbers rather than the standard RV, which is frustrating; this is a minor problem, though, nor does it apply to the rest of the volumes. The set contains a mixture of well- and lesser-known pieces; even some from Op. 3 are included. Vols. 3, 4, and 5 are boxed together (♦MHS 533192); 3 is a collection of "string symphonies," which are sinfonias or ripieno concertos written without a solo instrument. Vols. 4 and 5 are solo violin concertos; a few of the "Dresden" concertos are here.

Vols. 6 and 7 were released together as the "Anna Maria concertos," so designated for one of Vivaldi's star pupils at La Pietá, who was renowned for her ability on many instruments (♦MHS 523435H). Vols. 3–7 consist entirely of concertos outside the numbered opuses, so you won't find duplicates even if you have the whole Philips edition. Vols. 8, 9, and 10 (♦MHS 533639H) make up the last set; 8 consists of more miscellaneous violin concertos, while 9 is mostly Op. 6 (arguably the best recording of this seldom-heard group), and 10 has the first five concertos of Op. 11. All these less familiar concertos need to be performed with conviction, as they easily become wallpaper otherwise, and they are well served here.

A large number of Vivaldi's concertos were dedicated to the composer's student and friend, the distinguished German violinist Johann Georg Pisendel. These survive in manuscript form and are all played by **Accademia I Filarmonici** with Alberto Martini as director and as violinist in the first of four volumes (Naxos 553792, 553793, 553860, 554310). They're probably not Vivaldi's most distinguished works, and these certainly aren't Naxos's most distinguished recordings. I Filarmonici is not my favorite ensemble either; their attacks are often neither crisp nor true, and fast passages frequently sound blurry and consequently sloppy. This may be partly a result of faulty engineering, as the recordings are plagued with a slight hollowness. Soloist Cristiano Rossi does a lot to redeem Vol. 4 with his fiery, expressive playing, and I also enjoyed Roberto Baraldi's full, confident tone in Vol. 2. But you'll probably want these for the rarely heard music they contain rather than for repeated listening.

The **Budapest Strings** play with emotion, passion, and great beauty in three volumes of concertos and symphonies (♦Nuova Era 6937, 7047, 7113, all NA). These are all without solo instrument and are denoted, approximately, by RV numbers 109–169. Béla Bánfalvi, who has recorded for Naxos, is concertmaster in these early '90s recordings, which have warm, immediate sound and are very much worth having. About half the concertos and sinfonias can be found here, including the well-known "Alla Rustica."

Besides the more or less systematic string collections, there are a large number of single CD collections; these aren't to be sniffed at, as they often have some of the juiciest Vivaldi you can find. A good example is a 1997 recording of concertos for strings, played by an all-female ensemble called **La Pietá** with their director, Angèle Dubeau (♦Analekta 3128). This is a beautifully varied program with five ripieno concertos for strings (including "Alla Rustica"), concertos 1 and 11 from Op. 3, the "L'Amoroso" violin concerto, and the "La Follia" variations. La Pietá's playing is stunningly crisp and precise; they play with much energy, yet with feeling and delicacy.

This release is well worth its full price, but if you'd like to have a budget sampling, try **Accardo** as violinist and conductor with I Solisti delle Settimane Musicali Internazionali di Napoli (♦EMI 69847). None of the violin concertos (RV 243, 270, 277, 286) are very familiar; one is a Christmas concerto. This program also includes two cello concertos, played by Harrell with the English Chamber Orchestra, Zukerman conducting. Accardo is an old hand at Vivaldi, which he plays very warmly; I prefer the violin concertos here to the cello concertos, which seem a little cold (see the cello section for better ideas). Don't miss **Zukerman** as both violinist and conductor of several lesser known concertos (RV 187, 195, 197, 204, 209, 242, 364) with the English Chamber Orchestra (♦RCA 68433). His playing is warm, rich, and alive, his virtuosity breathtaking; this recording wears well.

Period instruments. Here there are many choices. For some of the string symphonies, you can turn to **Simon Standage** conducting Collegium Musicum 90 (♦Chandos 0647). Standage is a veteran of period-instrument Vivaldi, so he knows what he's doing. A second volume is planned in the near future. An outstanding program was recorded under the direction of Rinaldo Alessandrini, whose Vivaldi is reliably snappy (♦Tactus 67200101). Violinists **Fabio Biondi** and Adrian Chamorro, with Concerto Italiano, contribute to this sparkling 1988 recording.

A great program was done in 1993 with several of the same people and serves as a good supplement (♦Opus 111 3086). Here Biondi plays the violin and directs, with Alessandrini at the harpsichord. This attractive program includes an unusual double concerto (RV 541) for violin and organ, as well as the Concerto for Two Cellos in G Minor (though I must say the Naxos set has the best recording of this concerto I've heard). Another outstanding release from Biondi offers a program exploring Vivaldi's theatrical dimension in several of his most programmatic concertos. Another recording of the G minor Two-Cello Concerto is here in a fascinating, expressive reading that, however, is less compelling than the Naxos version (♦Virgin 45424).

A thoroughly admirable program comes from violinist **Manze,** who plays and directs the Academy of Ancient Music in "Concert for the Prince of Poland," a reconstruction of a gala event put on for Frederick Christian, Prince of Poland, who was visiting La Pietá (♦Harmonia Mundi 907230). The four concertos Vivaldi wrote for the occasion still exist in the manuscript presented to the prince as a souvenir of the evening, as do notations in the Prince's diary about how much he enjoyed the music. The disc has been rounded out with a stirring performance of "La Tempesta di Mare" and "Il Piacere," both programmatic pieces from Op. 8.

Bernard Labadie and Les Violons du Roy have produced another great program that includes "Alla Rustica," Op. 3 concertos 3, 8, 9, and 11, and three ripieno concertos, RV 114, 120, and 157 (♦Dorian 90255). The sound is topnotch for these vigorous, aggressive, and tuneful performances. Jeanne Lamon and Tafelmusik have produced two discs crammed with miscellaneous concertos, mostly for strings (Sony 48044, 62719). Both discs include cellist **Anner Bylsma.** Those who like a gentle sound that is nonetheless very period-instrument will enjoy these outstanding programs. **McGegan** and Capella Savaria give a much more brusque treatment to various concertos and sinfonias; the playing is lively and energetic, so some may like this program (Hungaroton 12547). I find it too harsh, Vivaldi with nearly all the underlying pathos squeezed out.

Bassoon concertos

Strangely enough, only one complete set of these 37 charming concertos exists, and the two sets I mention here both use modern instruments. **Daniel Smith** has recorded all of them, the first half with Ledger and the English Chamber Orchestra, the rest with the Zagreb Soloists (♦ASV 971/75; also MHS, NA). The concertos have been rearranged to fit on five discs instead of six; since they're full-priced, that's considerate of them! Smith's tone is dark and velvety. His attack isn't always precise—some concertos are downright sloppy—but his performances are well worth having. I prefer **Klaus Thunemann**'s performances with I Musici, but only 19 have been recorded and these are now NA, at least in the United States (♦Philips 416355, 432124, and 446066). Thunemann has a leaner and brighter tone than Smith, and he's more brisk and whimsical. I've spent many hours listening to them, and I think they're some of Vivaldi's finest works.

The good news in terms of complete sets is that Naxos plans to release these concertos at the rate of two CDs per year, beginning in 2001, name of soloist unknown.

Cello concertos

There are two comprehensive sets for modern instruments. My favorite is from **Raphael Wallfisch** with the Nicholas Kraemer and the City of London Sinfonia (♦Naxos 550907/10, 4CD). This set grows in beauty with each listening. Wallfisch's playing is aggressive and a bit lean but has great energy and expression, and each line is carefully shaped. The set includes the scrumptious Concerto in G Minor for Two Cellos (RV 531) and a concerto for cello and bassoon (RV 409). Kraemer plays harpsichord or organ for continuo, with another cello or lute sometimes added. For a completely different approach, **Harnoy**'s set, recorded with Paul Robinson and the Toronto Chamber Orchestra, is rich and sensuous—I think a little too much so for Vivaldi—but beautiful all the same (♦RCA 7774, 60155, 61578, 68228).

To sample these concertos, try **Heinrich Schiff** with Iona Brown and the St. Martin Academy (♦Philips 411126). This 1983 recording includes five concertos, all aggressively but smoothly rendered, with warm, immediate sound. You might be attracted by **Pieter Wispelwey**'s name in the catalogue, but unless you like Vivaldi in bits and pieces, avoid this release (Channel 10097). Wispelwey is a good cellist, but his program consists mostly of his favorite movements from various concertos combined in various odd ways and with various instrumentations to suit himself. For further sampling, this time with period instruments, try **Christopher Coin**'s whimsical reading of RV 406, 402, and 414 with Hogwood and the Academy of Ancient Music—if you can find it (MHS 514181X). Coin also recorded the two-cello concerto with Il Giardino Armonico; this recording is fine if you like the orchestra's explosive approach (Teldec 94552).

Flute concertos

Vivaldi's Op. 10 is devoted to flute concertos; all six are among his best-known and best-loved works—the first flute concertos by an Italian ever to appear.

Modern instruments. The top choice here is **Béla Drahos** with the Nicolaus Esterházy Sinfonia (♦Naxos 553101). The energy Vivaldi's music needs sometimes degenerates into nothing but rip-roaring tempos, but Drahos's set is wonderfully musical, played with feeling as well as energy and cheer. The tempos are occasionally a little more languid than you might be used to, but the musicianship is so good that it doesn't really matter. The sound is full and gentle.

Severino Gazzelloni's version with I Musici in the Philips set is also solid. If the nine CDs don't interest you, Philips has issued Op. 10, along with nine of the other flute concertos scattered through the catalog, as a "Duo" (♦454256). **Jennifer Stinton** with Christophers and the Concertgebouw Chamber Orchestra is another good choice (Collins Classics 1324; MHS 514231X, NA). Stinton plays a delicate, soaring flute line—a bit less aggressive than I like, but still a good reading. **Patrick Gallois** has gotten good reviews for his rendition with the Orpheus Chamber Orchestra (DG 437839). He's certainly virtuosic and the orchestral playing is tight and crisp, but I find the performances whimsical to the point of idiosyncracy, with too much stretching of tempos. Those who enjoy **Galway**'s flamboyant style will go for his version with the New Irish Chamber Orchestra, but he's first of all a virtuoso and second a musician, which shows in this recording, where the slow movements are played with little feeling (RCA 61351). The sound is a little too bright, bordering on harshness.

Where does one discuss the flute concertos performed on a recorder? In the case of **Petri**, all instruments except the recorder in her two versions are modern. The first is a 1980 Philips recording with the St. Martin Academy and Iona Brown, re-released by MHS (514163Z). I don't know whether this is still in print, but in some ways it doesn't matter, as her second recording with Spivakov and the Moscow Virtuosi is better (♦RCA 68543). Petri's playing is marvelous, lively and crisp, her pure tone and facile execution a delight. There's just a tad too much reverb, but it doesn't seriously harm the overall high quality.

Period instruments. Options are fewer here, but they're good. Hogwood with **Stephen Preston** would be my first choice (♦London 458078), with Pinnock and **Liza Beznosiuk** a close second (Archiv 423702). Another recording with lesser known forces proves to be very good: **Frederic de Roos** playing recorder with La Pastorella (Ricercar 206392). Though this is a fine performance, the length (49 minutes) is something of a cheat, especially for a full-priced disc and considering the amount of material available for possible fillers.

Vivaldi wrote many other widely scattered flute concertos, but Naxos has thoughtfully gathered many of them into two convenient releases. Vol. 1, with **Drahos,** consists of chamber works for a few instruments and continuo (*Schwann* lists them under "Chamber Concertos"). They're infrequently heard, so it's nice to have them assembled and excellently performed (♦553365). In Vol. 2, "Famous Flute Concerti," Jiri Válek and Jiri Novotny are ably accompanied by the Capella Istropolitana and conductor Oliver Dohnányi (♦Naxos 550385) This performance returns to flute and full orchestra and includes three concertos (RV 443-45) for "flautino," played by Jiri Stivin; I assume from the notes this is a sopranino recorder rather than a piccolo.

Guitar, lute, and mandolin concertos

Though quite a number of Vivaldi's "guitar concertos" have been recorded, it's misleading to speak of them as such, since he only composed music for lute or mandolin. They have often been adapted for guitar, and this works very well, resulting in first-rate music-making. But don't pass up the original versions. There are only a handful of these concertos, but being deservedly popular, they turn up in many recordings.

Modern instruments. My favorite program of mandolin concertos is, I fear, no longer in print (♦MHS 11057L; originally Erato). Soloists **Ugo Orlandi** and Dorina Frati team up with Scimone and I Solisti Veneti to play all four. Even though the timing is short at 43 minutes, this is certainly worth picking up if you can find it, and we can always hope that Erato or MHS will take the hint and reissue this wonderful recording. A fine program of lute and mandolin concertos has been re-released, in traditional performances from 1972 by **Narciso Yepes** and other soloists with conductor Paul Kuentz and a chamber orchestra (♦DG 429528). The sound shows its age, but it's very good.

Most of the in-print concertos have been transcribed for guitar, and the choices are good. **Parkening** gives three of them stylish treatment (♦EMI 555052, with Warlock's *Capriol Suite* and a Praetorius suite). **Pepe Romero,** with Iona Brown and the St. Martin Academy, play a similar program with miscellaneous Vivaldi violin concertos as fillers

(Philips 412624), and **Angel Romero** gives an uproarious performance—for those who want something more lively—also with the ASM (RCA 68291). **Fisk** and **Williams,** with their performances scattered in various places, are also worth hearing. Fisk offers an all-Vivaldi disc with both lute and mandolin concertos transcribed for guitar—pleasant and energetic, if a bit heavy on pluck (♦MusicMasters 67097). These pieces are like potatoes; you have to work hard to ruin them.

Period instruments. The best complete collection is by **Paul O'Dette** and the Parley of Instruments, directed by Roy Goodman and Peter Holman (♦Hyperion 66160). This is a delightful and beautiful program that softens what otherwise might be a pluck-heavy ensemble with an organ continuo instead of a harpsichord. Il Giardino Armonico, directed by **Giovanni Antonini,** has recorded an identical program with the addition of one concerto for two mandolins (RV 558); this ensemble, with its excellent soloists, serves up a much more rambunctious program (Teldec 91182). It's fun to listen to, but I think O'Dette will wear better over the long term. Two labels have released excellent collections—all four pieces—of Vivaldi's lute music; I slightly prefer **Rolf Lislevand** (♦Astrée 128587) to **Jakob Lindberg** (♦BIS 290), but this, except for a difference in sound, is a matter of taste. Lislevand's 1996 version has better sound—for Lindberg the continuo is insistent, almost overbearing—and the tempos are a little quicker, with expressive playing. Lindberg has Huggett as one of the violinists, though, and her rich tone is always a pleasure.

Oboe concertos

The oboe concertos, like those for bassoon, are charming, and they turn up in many collections with diverse instruments, but the small number of oboe collections is surprising. Naxos leads the way here with two volumes, the most thorough on the market (♦550859/60). **Stefan Schilli** (joined by Diethelm Jonas for the two-oboe concertos) and the Failoni Chamber Orchestra directed by Pier Giorgio Morandi, gives a smooth and lively rendition of most of them. Unless you're adamantly against anything other than period instruments, this sets a fine standard and is all you'll need. **Alex Klein**'s expert rendition of eight oboe concertos is, regrettably, out of print, but pick it up if you see it; most of the performances are even more jaunty than Schilli's sprightly versions (♦MHS 513905X). A release from **Jiří Krejčí** lags behind these two, with slightly muddy sound and only five concertos (Supraphon 73189).

There are two choices for period instruments, with an overlap of only two concertos, RV 457 and 535 for two oboes. **Stephen Hammer** and Frank de Bruine offer a surprisingly reserved performance with Hogwood and the Academy of Ancient Music (London 433674). **Marie Wolf** with Capella Savaria isn't much more aggressive, but the sound is more immediate, warmer, and smoother than the London (Harmonia Mundi 1903018). Both offer very good interpretations, but I think the Naxos set is a better choice.

Recorder concertos

Modern instruments. The limited number of recorder concertos is not to be confused with the Op. 10 flute concertos performed on recorder. Vivaldi wrote Op. 10 for the developing flute, but his works specifically for recorder are discussed here. Available recordings are almost all by period-instrument groups, the exception being **Petri**'s program of RV 108 and 441–445 with Scimone and I Solisti Veneti (♦RCA 7885). Petri's virtuosity makes this an excellent choice if you dislike period instruments. Another program, a favorite of mine for many years, hasn't made it to CD (I hope someone at Vanguard is reading this): The Bach Guild's

1976 recording with **Julius Baker** and I Solisti di Zagreb, Janigro conducting, is as compelling now as it was then, with Baker playing a piccolo as flautino.

Period instruments. Don't miss **Dan Laurin**'s performance with the Bach Collegium (♦BIS 865). For both content and length (68 minutes), this is the best program of recorder concertos you can find, and Laurin's playing is outstanding—a treat you owe yourself if you've never heard it. Here he performs most of the recorder concertos along with a couple for flute, using a sopranino recorder for the "flautino" specified by Vivaldi: RV 92, 108, 428, 435, 443–45. **Piers Adams**'s playing is virtuosic and expressive in a shorter program with Robert King on continuo (♦Cala 88015). Three concertos here are from Op. 10 for flute, with RV 440, 441, and 443 for recorder.

A collection for recorder only includes RV 108, 441–445 by **Peter Holtslag** and the Parley of Instruments with director Peter Holman (Hyperion 55016). Holtslag has a strong tone and negotiates the fast passages beautifully. I slightly prefer both Laurin and Adams, but this is nonetheless a very good survey of the recorder literature. Another release that lags behind any of these for quality and length contains five concertos for various recorders and transverse flute, performed by **Michael Schneider**, Konrad Hunteler, and the Capella Coloniensis with director Gabriele Ferro (RCA). At only 48 minutes and with an occasionally lackadaisical approach, it's a poor value.

Miscellaneous concertos for diverse instruments

Vivaldi wrote more violin concertos than any other kind, but in addition to sets for one instrument—like bassoon, oboe, or cello—he wrote many for various combinations of solo instruments, like flute and bassoon, violin and organ, or viola, two horns, two oboes, and bassoon. The reason for these intriguing combinations lies in the diversity of talent at La Pietá; he wrote for the instrumentalists he had, resulting in an astonishing diversity.

Modern instruments. The *sine qua non* for the concertos for diverse instruments is a 1964 recording by I Solisti di Zagreb, with **Antonio Janigro** conducting and soloists Julius Baker and Rudolf Klepac (♦Vanguard 2006; originally Bach Guild LP 70665). This release—with concertos for two mandolins; flute, bassoon, and strings; strings and harpsichord; bassoon; and violin, two string choirs, and two harpsichords—is as bright and beautiful as the day it was recorded. I hope it will always be available to introduce new generations to Vivaldi. More recent recordings include "Concertos for the Court of the Elector of Saxony," a polished and elegant program in fine sound from Virtuosi Saxoniae and **Ludwig Guttler** (♦Berlin 1082).

Another interesting selection comes from I Solisti Veneti with **Scimone** conducting (♦Teldec 97404). Oddly, this is subtitled "Trumpet Concertos." Vivaldi wrote only one concerto for two trumpets (RV 537), which is included here; the rest are for other instruments, including the Bassoon Concerto in E Minor RV 484. This last is one of his most poignant pieces, though this rendition is a little rushed and doesn't quite convey the mood; Pinnock's is much better (see below). Everything else here is excellent.

A well-recorded assortment entitled "Famous Concerti" has bright sound, with good presence and warmth, and some of these are extraordinarily fresh. The Op. 12:1 Violin Concerto is magical, as is Lute Concerto RV 93 arranged for guitar (♦Naxos 550384). The only real lemon is the alleged trumpet concerto, which wasn't written for that instrument by Vivaldi but is a transcription by Jean Thilde; it's irritating. The G minor Concerto for Two Cellos is very warm but a little slow; Wallfisch's

version (Naxos) is better. A note of caution: The works are not tracked correctly. The list indicates 18 tracks; in reality there are only six.

A polished program with warm sound comes from the Scottish Chamber Orchestra with director **Jaime Laredo;** however, there are only five concertos, so you pay quite a lot for 42 minutes of music (MCA 25960; Carlton Classics 92252). A better value comes from the City of London Sinfonia with **Nicholas Kraemer** and various soloists; sound and performance are both excellent (♦Naxos 553204). In another, earlier recording of wind and brass concertos by these forces, everything is played with a refined energy, but the release has several drawbacks: The sound is a bit harsh, with a few balance problems, and the two transcribed trumpet concertos are annoying (Naxos 550386). The E minor Bassoon Concerto is a little flippant, but František Herman is warm and wonderful. Quite a different program of Telemann and Vivaldi concertos for recorder, bassoon, and strings comes from the **Drottningholm Baroque Ensemble** and soloists Clas Pehrsson and Michael McCraw (MHS 515408F, from a 1985 BIS release). Tempos are deliberate, but the woolly bassoon is a delight, and the whole recording is warm, with great presence.

Period instruments. Two of the best releases, recorded in 1986 and 1987, come from **Pinnock** and the English Concert (♦Archiv 415674, 419615). The first, entitled "Alla Rustica," has a lovely version of the concerto of that name; the second, entitled "L'Amoroso," has the best available rendition of the E minor Bassoon Concerto (RV 484). Their Vivaldi brims with energy but also with feeling, and the sound is full and immediate. A very good value with stellar forces may be found in (as described on the box) "a richly varied programme of fourteen Vivaldi concertos," performed by various ensembles: the New London Consort directed by Pickett, the Bach Ensemble with Rifkin, and the Academy of Ancient Music with Hogwood (♦Oiseau Lyre 455703, 2CD). This has one of the best versions of the G minor Concerto for Two Cellos, with soloists Anner Bylsma and Anthony Pleeth. One gripe: I can't imagine why Hogwood drags out the two-trumpet concerto for nearly nine minutes, when everyone else takes a little over seven. It's way too slow!

A reliable collection, though not as exciting as the Oiseau-Lyre, may be had from the **Aulos Ensemble** (MHS 522474X, 2CD). This set has many of the concertos for flute and other instruments that aren't part of Op. 10. The ensemble is small, so the recording has an intimate ambience. For those who enjoy **Il Giardino Armonico**'s rambunctious style, they have released four volumes of various concertos (Teldec 73267, 73268, 73269, 74727). These may not wear as well as more elegant versions, but they do make you listen to familiar works with new ears.

Three other period-instrument recordings are similar in that they all have several of Vivaldi's concertos for horns—a risky proposition for lovers of authentic instruments. The best of these is "Concerti con molti istromenti," with the King's Consort and **Robert King;** this has full, warm sound and is played with gusto (♦Hyperion 67073). Second best is a 1997 recording from **McGegan** and Philharmonia Baroque (Reference 77). Here the sound is good, though the performances don't have quite the pizzazz of the King's Consort. Modo Antiquo, directed by **Federico Maria Sardelli,** comes in last, with hollow sound and overbalanced percussion on some numbers; the horns are well played, but they sound far away, as does nearly everything except the timpani (Tactus 672206).

Several labels have released programs of various wind concertos. One of the best is again with **Pinnock** and the English Concert (♦Archiv 445839). Paul Goodwin has done an outstanding program of Albinoni and Vivaldi wind concertos with **King** and the King's Consort (♦Hyperion 66383; MHS 513388H). Goodwin's oboe playing is elegant.

Don't overlook Vivaldi's double concertos; he wrote many of these, and there are a few good programs of some choice ones. For modern instruments, try **Marriner** and the St. Martin Academy, with violinist Iona Brown and other soloists (♦Philips 412892). But beware: There is no indication that the first work is not the Concerto for Two Trumpets but rather one for two oboes arranged for two trumpets. Nonetheless, this is a worthy release. For a lovely period-instrument sampling having little overlap with the Philips, try the Wiener Akademie with director **Martin Haselböck** (♦Novalis 150074). This 1990 recording has refinement and polish, and includes the unusual F major Concerto for Violin and Organ.

CHAMBER MUSIC

Sonatas. Those who approach Vivaldi's sonatas looking for music that sounds like his concertos will be disappointed. Many of them tend toward the French style, though Vivaldi could never quite suppress his fiery Italian musical approach; still, they seem much more grave and introspective—especially the cello sonatas—than his flamboyant concertos or joyful sacred music. Opp. 1, 2, and 5 are all sonatas.

Op. 1 consists of 12 sonatas for two violins and continuo; they bear obvious marks of homage to Corelli and end with the "La Follia" variations so many composers used. Most recordings are for period instruments, but a modern instrument version may be found in the Philips edition; these used to be available separately (Philips 426926), but no longer. They are played with cello and harpsichord continuo and are very attractive.

The best period-instrument recording is from the **Sonnerie Ensemble** (♦CPO 999511, 2CD). These 1999 performances have wonderful vitality and verve, topped off by pristine sound. They're also a great value, as the disc includes not only sonatas 1–12 but also five others (RV 43, 60, 70, 72, and 83), and the "La Follia" variations are subtracked. A good 1998 version comes from **Ensemble Mensa Sonora** with director Jean Maillet (Pierre Verany 798021, 2CD). As in the CPO version, they add a theorbo to the continuo, which makes for full sound. The performance, while fine, isn't quite as attractive as Sonnerie's. Soloists **Roberto Baraldi** and Alberto Martini have also released Op.1; the playing is good, but the sound is very close up and dead (Tactus 672220, 672221). Harpsichordist **Iakovas Pappas** has recorded an interesting version of them for solo harpsichord, quite justifiable historically (♦Arkadia 1202). It works quite well; I like them about as well as the original versions.

The selection for Op. 2 is limited, with only two complete recordings currently available. The Philips version is smooth and lively, and very lovely. If you find the separate set now NA, it would be a good buy (♦Philips 426929 2CD). A period-instrument version, recorded in 1992, is by **Fabrizio Cipriani** and adds a theorbo to the continuo (♦Cantus 9608). Cipriani's tone is full and melodious; he plays with little vibrato, though, which I think is needed for these sonatas. Nonetheless, this is an excellent recording that period-instrument fans will like.

The Op. 5 sonatas as a whole have been recorded even less; the only available version is in the Philips edition. As with almost all of Philips's Vivaldi, the performances are solid.

A few words should be said regarding the alleged Op. 13 sonatas for flute or oboe and continuo entitled "Il pastor fido." These six sonatas were published under Vivaldi's name and for many years were regarded as authentic. Peter Ryom—he of the RV numbers—raised serious questions about their authenticity in 1974; other scholars agreed with him, but nothing was really proved until Philippe Lescat, in 1989, discovered a document proving beyond a doubt that though they contain melodies borrowed from Vivaldi, they were really composed by one Nicholas Chedeville. He deliberately published them in Paris under Vivaldi's name, hoping to attract attention and promote his own instrument, the musette. The ploy didn't work, but Vivaldi's name stuck to these sonatas for over 200 years. Vivaldi did write some oboe sonatas, however, and some have been recorded. One program of interest is **Paul Goodwin**'s; two of the works are from "Il pastor fido," but the notes designate them as faux Vivaldi (♦Harmonia Mundi 907104).

Other violin sonatas of interest include the "Manchester Sonatas," not discovered until 1973 in a library in England where they had been brought by a series of strange events. These 12 sonatas were recorded twice in 1992: **Biondi** gives a gentle performance (♦Arcana 942004) and **Manze** gives a slightly brighter one (♦Harmonia Mundi 907089). Both are excellent, but the notes for Arcana are more thorough and interesting. Biondi, Alessandrini, and Naddeo have also done a good recording of the "Dresden Sonatas" (♦Opus 111 30154). As with the "Dresden" violin concertos, these are yet another indication of Vivaldi's connection with German violinist Johann Georg Pisendel.

Miscellaneous violin sonatas RV 60, 68, 70, 71, 74, and 77 receive excellent treatment from violinists **Giovanni** and **Federico Guglielmo**; this is a very spirited and tuneful performance, produced in 1992 (♦Musicaimmagine 10012). It claims to be a world premiere recording, but at least three of the sonatas were recorded in 1990 by the **Purcell Quartet** (♦Chandos 0502, 0511). They play two volumes of various sonatas, including some from Opp. 1 and 5—a nice program with excellent sound.

Chamber music. Not much of Vivaldi's oeuvre can properly be called chamber music, but he did write about 20 works for a small number of instruments. One program of flute concertos consists of just such pieces (Naxos 553365). Another very similar release, entitled "La Pastorella" after the first concerto, came from **Marion Verbruggen** and colleagues (♦Harmonia Mundi 907046). The use of a recorder instead of a flute works very well here; these performances are delightful. Another release by **Nuovo Quintetto di Venezia** duplicates some of the works from Verbruggen and others (Tactus 672205). The instruments used here include oboe, flute, violin, bassoon, and harpsichord; the bassoon is prominent, making these numbers warm and lively. Sound and performance are both very good.

CHORAL MUSIC

Only about 50 of Vivaldi's choral works have survived, but like the rest of his compositions, they are very popular; many recordings have been made, with more coming out all the time. If you want to make short work of the bewildering array, two excellent sets are either on the market or in the making. Modern instrument fans can't go wrong with Philips's 1998 release, a 10CD set compiling all the sacred works they released separately in the late '70s and early '80s (♦462234). **Vittorio Negri** with the English Chamber Orchestra and the Concertgebouw Chamber Orchestra commands a star cast, including such eminent soloists as (along with many others) Lott, Murray, Ameling, Hamari, Kowalski, and Rolfe Johnson. Each of the individual works discussed here is in the Philips set, unless otherwise noted; likewise, each is recommended unless stated to the contrary.

Period instrument enthusiasts, on the other hand, will enjoy collecting **Robert King**'s set of the sacred music with the King's Consort and various singers as each volume emerges. Vols. 1–5 have been released, and everything so far has been top-notch for performance and sound (♦Hyperion 66769, 66779, 66789, 67281, 66799). Indeed, the sound is so beguiling that even listeners dedicated to modern instruments might enjoy these performances. Hyperion plans to record all of Vivaldi's sacred music, whereas the Philips set, while a thorough overview, is not complete. (In what follows, numbers from the RV catalog follow the titles to help identify the work being discussed.)

Perhaps these two recommendations are too much for the budget, but you'd still like to sample Vivaldi's most popular works. If so, a "Double-decker" by **Guest** with the St. John's College Choir and Wren Orchestra, **Ledger** and the King's College Choir, Cambridge, and St. Martin Academy, and **Cleobury** leading the English Chamber Orchestra has the two *Glorias* (588 and 589), *Dixit Dominus* 594, *Magnificat* 610, and *Beatus Vir* 597 (♦London 443455). These two choirs are all male, so this is a good choice only if you like boy sopranos. The outstanding adult soloists include Watts, Partridge, and Shirley-Quirk. **Corboz** conducts the Lausanne Vocal and Instrumental Ensembles in a magnificent 1975 rendition of *Gloria* 589, *Beatus Vir,* and *Magnificat* 610 (♦Erato 17919). This is a re-release of an LP set that contains some other fine recordings, if you still listen to LPs.

Two recordings that are difficult to categorize contain excellent period-instrument recordings of various works. **Malgoire** has put together a remarkable *Vêpres pour La Nativité de la Vierge,* a reconstruction of a Vespers service as Vivaldi might have composed it around 1715 (♦Astrée 8520, 2CD). Seven compositions are included: *Dixit Dominus* 595, *Laudate Pueri* 600, *Nisi Dominus* 608, *Magnificat* 610, *Confitebor Tibi* 596, and two short choral psalms, *Laudate Dominum* and *In Exitu Israel.* The children's choir La Maitrise Boréale has good support in La Grande Ecurie and Le Chambre du Roy so the sound is full, and the soloists—Dawson, Bowman, Elwes, and Varcoe—are stellar.

A similar, less ambitious project has come from **Jeffrey Skidmore** conducting the Ex Cathedra Chamber Choir and Baroque Orchestra, also with good soloists (♦ASV 137). This bright, vigorous reconstruction, entitled "Vivaldi Vespers," includes the *Stabat Mater, Magnificat* 610, and *Beatus Vir* 597.

Beatus Vir 597. **Negri** (Philips) and **Corboz** (Erato) take first place for modern-instrument versions of this beatific work with its haunting repetitions of the ethereal opening theme. A good budget choice comes from the reliable team of **Jeremy Summerly** and **Nicholas Ward,** directors of the Oxford Schola Cantorum and the Northern Chamber Orchestra, respectively; it's excellent, with immediate choir sound and crisp orchestra (♦Naxos 550767, with *Gloria* 589). It also has English translations, which Negri does not.

For period-instrument performance, the blue ribbon goes to **Robert King** and his King's Consort; they have done the lesser-known *Beatus Vir* 598 as well (♦Hyperion 66789). The version in "Vivaldi Vespers," directed by **Jeffrey Skidmore,** is also commendable for its vigor, brilliance, and exceptional smoothness (ASV 137).

Dixit Dominus 594 and 595. 594 is the grander of the two, but both have been recorded several times. The best version for modern instruments again comes from **Negri,** who includes both. **Malgoire**'s version of 594 with Watts and Partridge is a good budget choice (Sony 48282). This 1977 *Dixit Dominus* has better sound than the other pieces on the disc (*Stabat Maters* by Vivaldi and Scarlatti), and the interpretation is fresh and vigorous. I like **Corboz**'s performance of 594, but the sound is a little muddy and the choir seems far away (Erato).

Dixit 595 has superior representation of period instruments with King and Consort (♦Hyperion 66789). Another excellent 595 comes from the reconstructed Vespers (mentioned above) with **Malgoire** and

others. Those who enjoy boy singers should try 594 with **James Litton,** the American Boychoir, the Albemarle Consort of Voices, and the 18th Century Ensemble (MusicMasters 67084). It's done well, and the sound is very bright.

Gloria 589. Collectors may groan when they hear about another *Gloria* 589 as much as they do with *Four Seasons,* but this highly accessible, radiant piece remains Vivaldi's most popular and frequently recorded sacred work. My two top choices for modern instruments are in the **Negri** and **Corboz** sets. But if you like big, operatic sound and large forces, try **Muti**'s 1977 version with the New Philharmonia and soloists Berganza and Lucia Valentini Terrani (♦EMI 67002). This is a splendid recording with brisk tempos, beautifully-shaped lines, good enunciation, and great sound.

A 1966 recording from **David Willcocks** and the King's College Choir is another very reliable choice (♦Decca 458623). This beautifully remastered release includes soloists Elizabeth Vaughan and Janet Baker, and the program is an excellent value, presenting Haydn's *Nelson Mass* and Handel's "Zadok the Priest" in addition to the *Gloria.* The singing is both joyful and reverent; I wouldn't mind having this as my only version.

Marriner presents a cool and correct *Gloria* that needs a bit more warmth, despite the wonderful owl-like organ continuo; the soloists are Hendricks and Murray (EMI, with Bach's *Magnificat*). Other reviewers have liked **Shaw**'s version, and Upshaw is truly a delight (Telarc 80194). But the orchestra outbalances the choir on occasion, enunciation isn't as clear as it might be, and there's a tad too much reverb. A good budget choice again comes from **Summerly** and **Ward**—a little slow, but very well done (Naxos 550767, with *Beatus Vir 597).* Stay away from a 1996 Bulgarian recording led by **Stoyan Kralev** that's ponderous and sloppy (Gega 199).

Period instrument choices probably increase as I write. **Hickox,** with the Collegium Musicum 90 and soloists Kirkby, Tessa Bonner, and Chance, has done a superb job, making it my first choice for either modern or period instruments (♦Chandos 0518). It has beautifully-shaped lines and great sound, the all-adult chorus sings with feeling, and the organ continuo adds warmth. Countertenor Chance is outstanding, better than an alto, and the orchestral sound is clean and lovely. The introduction to the *Gloria,* "Ostro picta, armata spina" 642, is included, flawlessly rendered by Kirkby.

Two releases are close seconds to Hickox, both with adult choirs: **Christophers** and The Sixteen deliver a spirited yet delicate and nuanced performance (♦Collins 13202) or, for freshness and energy, try **Pinnock** and the English Concert Choir (♦Archiv 423386). **Ludwig Güttler** with his Virtuosi Saxoniae has a good recording; soprano Andrea Ihle is very capable, with a light, facile voice (Berlin 110003). This version's atmosphere is more operatic than sacred; nonetheless, it's a good choice. **Radu** gets off to a lame start that fulfills all the stereotypes you may have of period instrument performances, and the sound is hollow (Newport).

There are two choices for period instruments with all-male choirs. **Preston** directs the Academy of Ancient Music and the Christ Church Cathedral Choir, Oxford, with soloists Kirkby, Nelson, and Watkinson (Oiseau-Lyre 455727). The same choir recorded the two *Glorias* with **Darlington** conducting—a grave performance (Nimbus 5278). And, for something entirely different, listen to the Taverner Choir and Players with **Parrott** conducting an all-female choir (♦Virgin 59326). It's sweet and ethereal, especially interesting considering that for many years Vivaldi composed for such a choir.

Gloria 588. Much less popular, this version for modern instruments and adult choir in **Negri**'s set is solid, as is **Cleobury**'s for all-male choir (London). The period-instrument recording by **Francesco Fanna** and I Madrigalisti Della Polifonica Ambrosiana is ragged around the edges, with an amateurish-sounding choir (Agora 001). **Darlington** is better (Nimbus, with 589).

Magnificat. Vivaldi's setting of the *Magnificat* is available in several versions—610, 610a and b, and 611. He wrote it around 1715, probably for the Pietá. In the 1720s, he rewrote the tenor and bass parts for male voices and added a pair of oboes. The final version, 611, was for a performance at the Pietá in 1739; it retains six of 610's nine movements but adds five new arias.

For big choir, modern instrument sound, the top choices are **Corboz** (610, Erato 17919) and **Muti** (611, EMI 67002). **Negri**'s set has both 610 and 611 in more restrained but very good performances (Philips), and **Güttler** is precise and delicate (Berlin 110003). **Ledger/Cleobury**'s 610 is the weakest; it's the only one not recorded with adult soloists, and Peter Castle's treble is too thin (London).

Between two outstanding period-instrument versions, the leader is 610a performed by **King** and others (♦Hyperion 66769). The sound is warm and beautiful, the choir, with specially-picked boy singers, is exceptionally rich. Those preferring an all-adult mixed choir can turn to **Lamon**'s 1987 recording of 610 with Tafelmusik (♦Hyperion 66247). Though brought from LP to CD, it has excellent sound, big and immediate. The all-female choir directed by **Parrott** offers an admirable 610b (Virgin 59326). **Radu**'s performance is pedestrian (Newport).

Stabat Mater 621. The best modern-instrument *Stabat Mater* is in Negri's set (Philips). The performance, with organ continuo, is dark, quiet, and measured, and the driving rhythm of "Eia, Mater" is stark, with very little orchestral support. **Kowalski**'s voice is rich and satisfying. **Stutzmann** has recorded a close second with Spivakov and the Moscow Virtuosi, though I prefer Philips's organ to Spivakov's harpsichord continuo (♦RCA 60240). Malgoire's 1977 recording with **Watkinson** is easy on the budget, but the sound isn't the best and the soloist seems far away (Sony).

Period-instrument collectors fare much better here: Most recordings have been with countertenors, which is probably more authentic, since it's thought to be an early work. **Andreas Scholl** delivers a near flawless performance with Chiara Banchini and Ensemble 415; this is the best all around (♦Harmonia Mundi 901571). But **Robin Blaze** with King and Consort is no slouch either; here "Eia, Mater" is extremely rough—almost ugly, as it should be—to symbolize the words piercing Mary's heart (♦Hyperion 66799). **Charles Brett** has also recorded this work; his voice is a treat, but the sound is overbearing, and too much reverb makes it slightly muddy (Pierre Verany).

I generally prefer male singers in the *Stabat Mater,* but two women are worth mentioning: **Catherine Robbins,** with Bernard Labadie conducting Les Violons du Roy (Dorian 90196), and **Sara Mingardo,** with Alessandrini and the Concerto Italiano (Opus 111 30261). The former is good but unremarkable; the latter is outstanding for its atmosphere of devotion and for Mingardo's luscious contralto. Unfortunately, both the organ continuo and the orchestra badly override her voice in many places, marring an otherwise fine performance. This recording is called "Sacred Music, Vol. 1," so I'd look for other work from these truly superior musicians.

Other sacred works. There is room to mention only a few other works. Vivaldi did three settings of *Salve Regina,* and they're beautiful in Ne-

gri's set. An excellent period instrument version of 616 and 618 is offered by countertenor Gerard Lesne, **Biondi** conducting Il Seminario Musicale, in a spare, quiet rendition befitting the material (♦Virgin 59232).

Vivaldi's motets reward exploration; indeed, the third movement of *Nulla in mundo pax sincera* captured the hearts of many people in the movie *Shine.* This, along with five others, is included in **King**'s series (♦Harmonia Mundi 66779). Various motets are often used as filler with the larger works, but two more releases deserve mention: Canadian soprano **Karina Gauvin** has done an outstanding job with *Sum in medio tempestatum, O qui coeli terraeque,* and *Laudate pueri Dominum* 600, accompanied by Les Chambristes de Ville-Marie with director Jean-Francois Gauthier (♦Analekta 3099). **Suzie LeBlanc** repeats *O coeli terraeque* in her recording with Stubbs and the Teatro Lirico, but the rest of the program is different: *Laudate pueri* 601, *Salve Regina* 617, and *Vos aurea per montes* (♦ATMA 2225). All the foregoing are with period instruments; the representation of modern instruments is hit or miss. Several motets are included in **Negri**'s set, but a particular favorite of mine, *In turbato mare,* is missing. **Susan Gritton** gives a virtuoso performance of this for King (Hyperion 66799).   CRAWFORD

CANTATAS

The demand for short secular vocal pieces was so great in Vivaldi's time that he could have composed them as much for wide salon consumption as for use by his Ospedale girls; those that survive were all intended either for soprano or contralto voice, though many could well have been sung by a castrato. They are formulaic, lightweight pieces, generally dealing with one or another aspect of amorous longing; many contain music of considerable charm, and they often make strong virtuosic demands. Peter Ryom's catalogue ("RV") lists 39: 22 for soprano and 8 for contralto with continuo, 5 for soprano and 4 for contralto with obbligato or ensemble instruments and continuo. They have only been pecked at by recordings—scantily in LP days, but with more momentum on CDs.

At least three projects have been launched proclaiming the goal of a "complete recording" of all or a subdivision of them. The only one more or less realized is a series that aims to present all 22 of the soprano-with-continuo cantatas (Mondo Musica 90011, 90021, both 2CD). Actually, it gives 20 of those listed by Ryom (RV 649-657, 659-669) and one (with flute obbligato) not so listed, for a total of only 21. The singer is Gasdia, a distinguished artist who is here not at her best, somewhat mannered and tentative, ultimately tedious in such quantity. She's given strong support by **Claudio Ferrarini**'s Barocco Veneziano, a pool of continuo players (who sometimes, though, make free with instrumentation); but the reading of some of the cantata texts by a female reciter is distracting and needless, while the absence of printed texts and translations is a serious drawback. (Note also that the last cantata on the third disc, *Sorge vermiglia in ciel* RV 667, is misidentified as *All'or che lo sguardo,* which appears in the second disc correctly as RV 650.)

A more comprehensive and systematic approach has been launched by **Federico Maria Sardelli** and his Modo Antiquo ensemble (Tactus). The cantatas for soprano and continuo have been undertaken to date in the first three of an eventual four discs, six to each (672207/8/9), sung in turn by Rossana Bertini, Elena Cechi Fedi, and Niki Kennedy. The continuo work is solid and intelligently spicy, but the singers are variable—Kennedy is the best of them, while the others aren't always up to the technical demands of the style. Texts are given without translations. No further along is another series with a different road map, again with six cantatas per disc (Agora 101, 147, 189). The first two feature the accomplished and solid-voiced soprano **Invernizzi,** who includes two of the cantatas with obbligato instruments. In the third, **Caterina Calvi,** who has a firm contralto sound that she uses to good lyric or expressive effect, sings six of the eight alto/continuo cantatas. The instrumentalists of the Conserto Vago group provide imaginative and (in their continuo role) nicely varied support. The recording acoustics are overly cavernous, though, and, while the notes are good, once more texts appear without translations.

A fourth series has moved from promise to puzzlement. A proclaimed "Vol. I" of Vivaldi's *Cantate da camera* was issued with the mercurial **Robert Gini** leading instrumentalists in five continuo cantatas, three sung by the slightly woolly and wobbly soprano Alessandra Ruffini and two by the ever-reliable Calvi (Nuova Era 6859). No more seem to have appeared, though Gini led a chamber orchestra in later recordings of the two most popular cantatas for alto with obbligati and *Stabat Mater,* all with Calvi (Nuova Era 6877).

Three recordings have drawn upon the cantatas to showcase countertenors. With a small chamber group, the high-flying sopranista **Randal Wang** has recorded three of the soprano/continuo cantatas and two for soprano with obbligato instruments (Helicon 1032). Wang manages a genuine soprano range, with perhaps a hint of what castrato sound might have sounded like, but not without some strain in the florid passages. **Ragin** (with harpsichord and cello support) recorded five of the alto/continuo cantatas and one for soprano and continuo (Etcetera 1069). Technical confidence is his strong suit, and his capacity to negotiate the wide leaps in vocal lines is almost as striking as his agility, most notably in RV 667 (also done by Wang), which is normally sung by soprano, not alto.

Finally, **Marco Lazzara** has recorded all four of the cantatas for alto with ensemble, whose parts are taken by a small chamber orchestra led by Antonio Plotino (RV 683-86). His is the most contralto-like voice in this roundup, and his singing is quite agreeable. Retrospectively, however, we should not forget a fine program recorded in 1977 in which **Jacobs,** supported by an ensemble under Alan Curtis, presented three of the alto/ensemble cantatas plus one of the alto/continuo items, stylishly sung and played; an LP gem worth searching out (DG Archiv).

Vivaldi's chamber cantatas are often found mixed in with other works. An outstanding collation in a bargain-rate set combines sacred works (*Gloria, Nisi Dominus,* and a motet) with the *La Follia* Trio Sonata (Op. 1:12) and four outstanding cantata performances (♦Oiseau-Lyre 455727, 2CD). **Kirkby** sings one of the soprano/continuo cantatas with her usual agility and pointed diction, and **Bott,** supported by a chamber ensemble led by Philip Pickett, delivers three of the soprano/obbligato cantatas with richer voice and particularly intense expressiveness. The nimble Kirkby can also be heard singing a soprano/obbligato cantata and a motet in a mixed program led by Lamon (♦Hyperion 66247, with a *Magnificat* and three string-ensemble concertos).

SERENATAS

The cantata category leads easily into its expansion as the serenata, usually an extended, quasi-oratorio format for 2 to 4 characters (with chamber orchestra) on pastoral or allegorical themes, meant to be performed as a concert work. These formulaic scores are usually pleasant but rarely memorable, as they were intended for ephemeral presentation. Vivaldi is known to have composed at least eight, of which five are lost; the surviving three have all been recorded.

Two are occasional pieces, for celebrations in honor of King Louis XV of France. *Gloria e Imeneo* RV 687 has received two recordings. One is a

serviceable but rather insensitive performance by mezzo and contralto, with **Carlos Gubert** conducting a period-instrument orchestra in 1994 (Dynamic 125). The other, of the same vintage, was recorded by **Jean Estournet** with two countertenors (♦Ligia 202016). Though his singers aren't particularly pleasing, Estournet's performance is far better in shape and nuance, and he adds two orchestral concertos to fill out the remaining space; his is the better choice if you can find it. The other occasional piece, *La Senna festeggiante* RV 693 was recorded in 1978 by **Scimone,** using the period instrument Cappella Coloniensis, with a superlative team of singers: Cuberli, Helga Müller, and Nimsgern (♦Fonit Cetra 25, 2CD).

The remaining work is a stylized fantasy of pastoral romance: an untitled *serenata a 3* beginning "Mio cor, povero cor" (RV 690); it has had three recordings. The first was an abridged version, done around 1960 by Italian forces under **Edwin Loehrer** (Vox LP). This was followed by a much superior full version, recorded in 1982 by **Scimone** with his modern-instrument Solisti Veneti and a much more stylish cast (♦Erato 97417, 2CD). A still more stylish, better-sung, and more strenuously authentic performance (embellishments, period instruments, and all), was led by **Clemencic** in 1988 (♦Harmonia Mundi 1901066, 2CD).

OPERAS

Vivaldi hungered after operatic success and labored extensively at the form. He claimed to have composed 95 operas, and computing the true number is difficult because he revised or recycled some of his scores, reviving them under other titles, while participating in collaborative works or compiling pastiches (with other composers' music involved). Ryom reckons some 46 operas, of which 5 were not completely by Vivaldi; of the remainder, 25 have been lost in full, and 2 more survive incomplete. To date, 12 operas have been recorded, in three cases twice over, though few of them have survived long in circulation.

Catone in Utica RV 705. We have a lone recording of what survives—Act 1 (itself a pastiche) is almost completely lost—in a recording ably led by **Scimone** but with a very uneven cast (of whom the forceful Palacio and the uneven Gasdia are best known), in one of Vivaldi's weaker works (Erato 88142, 2CD).

Dorilla in Tempe RV 709. It survives only in a revived version as a partial pastiche, reconstructed by **Gilbert Bezzina** (♦Pierre Verany 794092, 2CD). He leads a period instrument ensemble with Elwes (in a role written for contralto) leading a generally fine cast including Kiehr, Philippe Cantor, and countertenor Jean Nirouet as a castrato stand-in.

Farnace RV 711. One of Vivaldi's stronger operas, he revived it several times and its score went through some transformations. It's one of the operas that has been recorded more than once, in all cases using divergent editions. A 1970 production led by **Newell Jenkins** circulated unofficially for a while, dealing freely with the problems of vocal casting, its team including Elaine Bonazzi and Fortunato. Two commercial releases have since appeared, one documenting a 1982 staged performance in Genoa led by **de Bernart** (Hunt 110, 2CD), the other a 1991 (studio?) recording led by **Massimiliano Carraro** (Nuova Era 7213/14). Vivaldi's original casting was for four female singers and three castrati; both of these versions replace the castrati with more females, making for a somewhat top-heavy vocal palette for modern listeners. Dessi and Kate Gamberucci are the best of the seven singers for de Bernart, who leads with spirit; unfortunately, the microphone balances are very poor. Carraro isn't much better, though Susan Long Solustri, Marina Bolgan, and Tiziana Carraro deliver some smooth singing. The orchestra is rather too strong against the more distant singers, but the balances are not as bad as de Bernart's. In truth, neither set is more than a stopgap. The accompanying booklet in each gives only the Italian libretto, with no translation, though Nuova Era does give an English synopsis.

La fida ninfa RV 714. There are fewer problems with this tedious story of love-tangles in a pirate's lair (with some anticipations of Mozart's *Abduction from the Seraglio*). Its only recording has been out of print for a long time. Made in 1964 in Milan with local singers under **Raffaello Monterosso,** it transfers the two castrato parts to females in a mediocre and rather dated interpretation (Vox).

Griselda RV 718. From fairly late in Vivaldi's output, it sets a libretto by Apostolo Zeno with revisions provided by the young Goldoni, and is regarded as one of his better operas. Another taped performance, this time of a 1992 concert presentation in Montpellier, is directed by **Francesco Fanna** (♦Arkadia 122/23, 3CD). The three castrato roles are given to women and, some rough moments aside, the singing is very good, while the overall interpretation, if on the expansive side, is intelligent. A libretto and synopsis are provided but without translation.

L'Incoronazione di Dario RV 719. Conductor-editor **Gilbert Bezzina**'s 1986 recording misuses the talents of a fine cast to turn the casting into confusion compounded (Harmonia Mundi 1901235/37, 3CD). Vivaldi's intended lineup—with a male character given to a "trousers" female singer and a castrato male character singing in a female range—is jumbled enough, but Bezzina turns it into a parodistic mess; one soprano takes the "trousers" part and another takes the castrato role, but three of the four female characters are taken by countertenors, in travesty reversal. No matter that Lesne, Ledroit, and Visse are quite theatrical in their impersonations, or that Poulenard and Mellon sing with style, or that the admirable tenor Elwes and baritone Michel Verschaeve bring needed weight to their lone male/male roles; the period instrument playing is skimpy, Bezzina's leadership is scrappy, and the whole thing is a musical as well as a dramatic travesty. Harmonia Mundi did help with its then-current practice of giving the libretto in an illegible original-print reproduction, with only synopses instead of translations.

Montezuma RV 723 presents textual problems of a very different kind, for this opera doesn't actually exist; Vivaldi's score has been lost altogether. But the libretto survives, so **Malgoire** turned the 18th-century practice of the pasticcio on its head by taking arias out of a dozen surviving Vivaldi scores, fitting them to this text, providing unidentified recitative settings, and thereby making an authentic-fake new Vivaldi opera (Astrée 8501, 2CD). It has no more integrity, in fact, than a simple concert of Vivaldi arias, and the performance standards are not high at that: Baritone Rivenq stands out as Cortez, but Visse as Montezuma and Poulenard as his daughter are below their best and the rest of the cast is indifferent, while the period instrument playing is sometimes rough. Strictly a curiosity.

L'Olimpiade RV 725. Telling of love and intrigues at the original Olympic Games, it uses an admired libretto by the prestigious Metastasio and contains much fine music. It was the first Vivaldi opera to be revived in modern times (1939), in Virgilio Mortari's rather modernized edition. That was used in the first complete recording, made in Budapest in 1988 under **Ferenc Szekeres** and originally on three LPs; only a single CD of highlights has appeared (Hungaroton 073). The Mortari version updates the vocal scoring, setting the castrato roles down for a male singer who heavily dominates the cast. The Budapest lineup includes some of the finest Hungarian singers of the day, who generally de-

liver an excellently sung performance; but there is little vocal embellishment and Szekeres displays good musical sensitivity but limited stylistic insight in his conducting, a bit on the heavy side by subsequent performing standards.

Quite in contrast is the 1990 concert recording by **Clemencic,** which trims away Mortari's fat, uses a soprano and countertenors in the castrato roles, with a period-instrument ensemble (Nuova Era 6932/33, 2CD). Generally, the voices are good, though of the two countertenors, Lesne is below his own best standards while Aris Christofellis (a singer who makes the most countertenor-friendly listener recoil in despair) is unbearable; the orchestral work is a bit choppy. This will do for now, but there certainly could be better. Italian libretto without translation.

Orlando (furioso) RV 728. Vivaldi's contribution to adaptations of Ariosto's great poem, it has received the most stellar attention of any of the composer's operas, in a 1977 recording led by **Scimone** (♦Erato 45147, 3CD). Horne's powerful performance in the title role (one of her greatest on discs) and the sweet voice of de los Angeles in her last opera recording stand out, but there is also very fine singing from Valentini-Terrani, Lajos Kosma, Bruscantini, and Zaccaria. Scimone's leadership is polished and steady, but he has come in for much criticism for his high-handed performing edition, which shifts a castrato part down to a baritone and, above all, cruelly abridges the score by omitting many of its arias (while inserting one from another Vivaldi opera). As a realization in Vivaldi's terms, then, the recording falls far short, but as a piece of full-blooded singing in Baroque opera, it remains something of a classic.

Ottone in villa RV 729. This was Vivaldi's first opera (1713), sporting historical Roman characters of the age of Nero who opera-lovers may already have encountered in treatments by Monteverdi and Handel. Vivaldi's newness to the idiom is evident in the score's unevenness, but it does include some lovely music. How much its viability depends upon a quality performance is demonstrated by its two recordings, under **Flavio Colusso** (Bongiovanni 10016/18, 3CD) and **Hickox** (♦Chandos 0614, 2CD). Both use period-instrument ensembles but differ in their casts. Patrizia Pace and Anna Maria Ferrante for Colusso are quite good as the soprano romantic objects, but the handling of the two important male characters is unfortunate. The title role of Ottone was written for a female contralto, a voice certainly easy to find, and it's pointless to force countertenor Nirouet into the role, even if he's reasonably competent. But the part of Caio, written for a very virtuosic soprano castrato, is foolishly assigned to "sopranista" Christofellis whose ugly squawkings and squallings, here as elsewhere, blight everything he participates in.

Fortunately, the Hickox cast is a joy, in both comparative and absolute terms. Of the two male characters, Ottone is back as a contralto, smoothly portrayed by Monica Groop, while soprano Argenta is dazzling as Caio; Gritton is a particularly sprightly Cleonilla. Also, as against Colusso's stolid direction, Hickox runs things briskly, allowing economical compression to bring down the number of discs. Considering not only this opera but the full picture of Vivaldi's operas, Hickox/Chandos offers the best recording made so far.

Il Teuzzone RV 736. With *Il Teuzzone* led by **Sandro Volta,** we are back to seat-of-the-pants Baroque opera recording (Tactus 672280, 3CD). The addition of a Chinese setting's pseudo-oriental touches to the usual Baroque tangle of love and intrigue hardly makes for a very sane piece of lyric drama, but Vivaldi's growth as an opera composer is evident in the solid and characteristic score. The quirky vocal scoring is only partly replicated by Volta's cast. The title character, the heroic Teuzzone, was written for a female soprano, while his beloved was meant for a contralto, making for an odd balance in their interchanges. The contralto range works for a scheming stepmother, and one of her co-conspirators was and is a bass; but the other was written for a soprano castrato, and his replacement, countertenor Angelo Manzotti, is decent but tends to bellow to compensate for a pallid volume. Finally, a minor role for castrato is abandoned here to a bass. For the most part, the cast is competent if never outstanding, though Fernanda Piccini has some genuinely dramatic moments as the Empress. The period-instrument group is small and their playing thin and strident, if enthusiastic, in vivid sound. Italian libretto but no translation.

Tito Manlio RV 738. Produced at the same time as *Teuzzone* (1719), it is both longer and less consistent as a score. Based on a Roman legend of stern duty, the opera is very long. Its only recording, made in the late '70s, hasn't been revived on CD (Philips, 5LP). The performance, conducted by **Vittorio Negri,** is dutiful, never less than competent, but with a fairly prestigious cast in variable estate. The two castrato roles are given to women, Norma Lerer and the really splendid Margaret Marshall. Finnilä and Hamari are strong presences, while two basses—Giancarlo Luccardi in the title role, Domenico Trimarchi as a servant— are outstanding.

Those who wish only to sample Vivaldi's operatic writing have a few recourses. A mid-'70s recording by **Scimone** with his Solisti Veneti offered a valuable survey of 11 of Vivaldi's opera overtures, 5 of them to operas as yet unrecorded (Erato and MHS). That is long gone, but more recently **Hogwood** has directed an orchestral program that includes overtures to eight operas, duplicating several of Scimone's choices (♦Harmonia Mundi 77501).

In the vocal department, we have **Bartoli**'s program of opera arias, with Giovanni Antonini leading his period-instrument Giardino Armonico (Decca 466569). Two independent items aside, her program contains 11 arias from 9 operas (3 of them still not recorded in full) plus 2 isolated aria pieces. While the singer's new-found enthusiasm for Vivaldi's vocal music is genuine, her performances are hard-driven and unstylish, at times even overbearing; and Antonioni's ensemble seems drawn by her vehemence into harsh excesses of its own. The disc is really of interest more to Bartoli fans than to Vivaldi-lovers.

There are more pretensions to authenticity but no better musical values in a program of opera arias featuring "sopranista" **Angelo Manzotti,** with the Baroque Orchestra of Bologna under Paolo Faldi (Tactus 672214). There are ten arias from as many operas (two unrecorded), plus multi-movement overtures to two of these; the material is of honest interest and even considerable appeal, but you're distracted from enjoying the music by constant fear that the singer's scrawny voice and precarious intonation won't make it from one phrase to the next.

Fortunately, a more balanced program provides access to both realms of Vivaldi's operatic writing. **Kirkby,** backed by Roy Goodman's period-instrument Brandenburg Consort, has recorded a program of eight arias and one duet from six operas (one not yet recorded), interspersed with overtures to three operas, one otherwise unrecorded save for Scimone's counterpart (♦Hyperion 66745). While Kirkby conveys little dramatic variety, her vocal agility is on a level few other singers have offered in this literature, and she and Goodman thoroughly understand the music's style and spirit.

ORATORIOS

Vivaldi is securely known to have composed three sacred dramas between 1714 and 1722 with a possible earlier one in 1713. The first, on

Moses in Egypt (in Latin), and the last, on the Adoration of the Magi (in Italian), are lost, but the middle one, ***Juditha triumphans devicta Holofernes barbarie*** RV 644, survived and has received no less than six recordings. Composed in 1716, with the subtitle *Sacrum militare oratorium,* it retold a familiar story (from the Apocryphal *Book of Judith*) of the Hebrew heroine's seduction and murder of an invading army's general. But the para-Biblical characters and situation were clearly intended as an allegory of current events of the day, Venice's last great struggle with the Ottoman Turks, turned into a prophecy of a great Venetian victory that, in actuality, did not come. Vivaldi used the occasion to compose the work for the women of the Pietà: All five characters are for female singers, though male choristers must have been imported. If it might formally be classified as a sacred work, it's nevertheless of a piece with his operatic writing.

The first recording, a brave but rather crude affair made in the '50s by **Angelo Ephrikian,** established a dubious principle of rationalizing the roles of the three male characters by shifting them down an octave to male voices to appeal to latter-day expectations of vocal verisimilitude (Period, 3LP, mono). This practice was followed by **Ferenc Szekeres**'s 1968 recording (Hungaroton 4022/23, 2CD). Using an edition by Alberto Zedda, Szekeres conducts with smooth but stately and bloodless pacing; Margit László stands out as the servant Abra, but Zsuzsa Barlay is a deadpan and hollow-voiced Judith, while the three men are good singers but undistinguished here and recording balances are not well handled. Of interest nowadays only if you want an old-fashioned approach at a low price.

Zedda recorded his edition himself, also in 1968 (RCA, 2LP). He at least respected Vivaldi's all-female vocal assignments, but his cast, ensembles, and recorded sound were on the rough side and would be quite unacceptable now. A distinct move to greater authenticity was made by **Negri,** who prepared a new edition, restoring music previously omitted and honoring Vivaldi's instrumentation more strictly (as well as adding some variant numbers in an appendix). This he recorded in a splendid production still memorable for high-quality singing from a cast that included Finnilä in the title role, supported by Ameling, Hamari, and Burmeister (Philips, 3LP).

McGegan prepared his own edition for the first period-instrument treatment in 1990, differing in a few details from Negri (Hungaroton 31063/64, 2CD). Banditelli's Judith is full-voiced but somewhat bland, and Zádori brings some personality to the role of Abra, but the other three singers lack individuality. McGegan's leadership is understated and less robust than Negri's, but has its advantages in catching subtleties here and there. But his contribution is put in the shade by **Robert King**'s stunning recording (♦Hyperion 67281/82, 2CD, Vol. 4 of his series of Vivaldi's sacred music). He too has prepared his own edition, and he's the first to provide an overture for the work, in the form of abridgments of the first two movements of one of Vivaldi's "diverse-instruments" concertos (RV 555). The all-female cast is uniformly outstanding, with Susan Bickley a vivid Holofernes and Murray bringing Judith to life for the first time as a woman of sensual power. King also wrings maximum color and charm out of the period-instrument playing, especially in the obbligatos. This is a truly great Vivaldi recording!

BARKER

Robert Volkmann (1815–1883)

The German-born Volkmann adopted Hungary as his homeland and became fast friends with Liszt, and at the same time somehow remained on good terms with both German musical camps, Schumann and

Brahms on the one hand and Wagner and Bruckner on the other. In a sense, this gift for diplomacy extends to his music as well; you might struggle in vain to find a unique central quality before settling back and accepting the music on its own amiable terms. His symphonies, steeped in Viennese classicism, may be seen as bridging the gap between Beethoven and Brahms, though the endless flow of melody and strong rhythmic sense that characterize his best efforts are very much his own. Certainly anyone who loves Brahms and Schumann will find Volkmann well worth investigating.

For all the Mitteleuropean traditions of Volkmann's heritage, the similarity between the opening statement of his Symphony 1 (1862) and Borodin's Symphony 2, written some 15 years later, is far too striking to overlook, and it's instructive to note that Volkmann's symphony was extremely popular with Moscow audiences when it was played there in 1864. Beethoven might be the model for Symphony 2, not least for the final Allegro vivace, which, while veering dangerously close to Beethoven's 8th, dispels all thought of imitation with an infectious and vivacious cheerfulness. Both symphonies serve as the focal point of an indispensable set led by **Albert** labeled "Complete Orchestral Works" (it isn't, really), with performances and sound quite beyond reproach (♦CPO 999151, 2CD).

Of the four Volkmann overtures mentioned in the CPO booklet, two are included in the set. The Overture in C shares with the final movement of Symphony 1 a tendency toward rhythmic rather than full-blown thematic material. More impressive is the concert overture *Richard III;* dark and desolate, it mirrors the events of the play faithfully, beginning with a highly evocative introduction before plunging full tilt into an intense depiction of the Battle of Bosworth (no doubt modeled after Beethoven's *Wellington's Victory*) while further characterizing the combatants by subtle use of the familiar tune "Garry Owen." Albert throws himself into this music with abandon, far more exciting than **Ondrej Lenard** (Naxos, part of his "Battle Music" collection), if without quite the manic intensity of **Rozhdestvensky** (Melodiya LP).

Volkmann's three Serenades for string orchestra date from near the end of his creative life and are imaginatively thought out and highly appealing. None of them is more than 15 minutes long, so even hearing all three in succession is a stimulating experience. In No. 3, Volkmann adopts a concertante style with a featured role for solo cello, an engaging effect. The performances led by **Goritzki** (CPO 999159, with Reinecke's Serenade) far surpass the thin-sounding ensemble under **Janos Petro** (Hungaroton 31622, with Schubert dances), as well as **Karl Ludwig Nicol,** which is nicely played but a dry recording (Christophorus 73973, with Bruch's *Serenade on Swedish Melodies*). Serenade 2 makes a not very satisfying filler for **Suitner**'s recording of Tchaikovsky's *Serenade for Strings* (Berlin 9194)—all three would have easily fit—and there's a nice reading of No. 1 conducted by **Jiři Stárek** in the collection called "A Serenade for You from Germany" (Koch Schwann 311067).

Volkmann's Cello Concerto is expansive and songful, a fairly compact exercise not unlike the Schumann Concerto. In the box with the symphonies, **Johannes Wohlmacher** tends to press onward more than **Jörg Baumann,** a more expressive reading accompanied by Miltiades Caridis (Koch Schwann 1205, with d'Albert's Cello Concerto). The *Konzertstück* for piano offers a rather eclectic mix, the reflective opening pages suggesting Liszt while both Brahms and Schumann surface as the piece progresses. It's nicely played by **Jerome Rose** aided by Pierre Cao in Vol. 7 of the "Romantic Piano Concerto" series (Vox 5098).

HALLER

Richard Wagner (1813–1883)

Wagner was one of the greatest composers of opera and the most influential musician of the last half of the 19th century. *Tristan und Isolde* is the fountainhead of modern music in its development of chromaticism and its use of dissonance to an unheard of degree. In addition, he tried to revolutionize staging and lighting so that the presentation was an integrated work of art, and greatly increased the importance of the orchestra. In his works, it's no mere accompanist to the singer; to the contrary, the orchestral score often carries the argument.

Some of the preludes to his operas and orchestral interludes have found a place in the concert hall, like *Siegfried's Rhine Journey,* the Funeral March from *Götterdämmerung,* and the Good Friday Spell music from *Parsifal.* His scores include musical phrases (leitmotifs) that are specifically associated with characters in the opera, their feelings, and dramatic situations; these are often played by the orchestra rather than sung. His last operas are difficult to cast, especially *The Ring of the Nibelung* and *Tristan und Isolde,* so we're fortunate to have several fine recordings of these works; most stage presentations today suffer from a scarcity of tenors and sopranos who can sing the leading roles.

Wagner wrote 13 operas, three of which were youthful works in which he had not yet developed his own operatic vision. The other ten, however, irrevocably transformed not only the art of opera but the world of music. Wagner called his mature works "music dramas," by which he meant that in them, text and music are tightly integrated and that both, along with scenery, costumes, and attention to dramatic expression on the part of the singers, are essential elements of what he termed the *Gesamtkunstwerk,* the complete and total work of art. To show how this could be done, he established his own festival at Bayreuth and, after more than 120 years, that's still the pre-eminent Wagner theater. Many of its presentations have been released on CD. The "Bayreuth sound," particularly the balance between singers and orchestra as well as the orchestral balances, are considered ideal for his operas, though not all Bayreuth recordings reflect that.

He demanded much more from his singers than most composers of his time, both in vocal strength and stamina, as well as dramatic expression; this accounts for the scarcity of great Wagner singers. In the period between the two World Wars, however, there were a remarkable number of such artists, and although few complete recordings of his operas exist from that time, even the excerpts and shortened versions that we have demonstrate vocal standards that have rarely been equaled in the last 50 years. Therefore I've included many of these older recordings in my recommendations, though listeners should keep in mind that their mono sound is almost always below today's standards, sometimes considerably so. The operas are listed below in the order of their composition, followed by a discussion of orchestral excerpts.

OPERAS

Die Feen (1833–34). The only available commercial recording of the composer's first opera is a 1983 Munich performance by the Bavarian Opera, part of a Wagner Festival to mark the 100th anniversary of his death (Orfeo). **Sawallisch** conducted a cast that included Alexander, Moll, Roland Herrmann, and June Anderson.

Das Liebesverbot (1835). Based on Shakespeare's *Measure for Measure,* this comedy was also recorded at the 1983 Munich Festival (♦Orfeo 345953). **Sawallisch** is, again, the fine conductor, and the excellent cast includes Prey, Robert Schunk, Sabine Haas, and Pamela Coburn. An older version was taken from a 1962 Austrian Radio broadcast (Melodram). **Heger** conducted and the cast included Hilde Zadek, Dermota,

Equiluz, and Ludwig Walter. Except for Dermota, this cast is quite inferior to Orfeo's. Other pirate recordings may exist.

Rienzi (1838–40). This tragedy, set in 14th-century Rome, is based on a novel by Bulwer-Lytton and is heavily influenced by Meyerbeer's grand operatic style. It's very long, and all recordings have cuts, sometimes drastic. The shortest is a 1960 concert version conducted by **Krips;** the cast includes Svanholm, Ludwig, and Paul Schöffler (Melodram). This performance was once available with only a German libretto, and includes less than half of Wagner's score (Laudis). Some of the singing is quite good, but the mono sound is poor.

A better choice is the 1983 Munich staged performance. Although it lacks a libretto, it has 196 minutes of music and better sound (♦Orfeo 346953). The generally fine cast includes Kollo, Studer, and John Janssen. **Sawallisch** shortened many scenes but unlike Krips, didn't omit any—though he did cut the ballet music, as did Krips. This is the best *Rienzi* now available. A 1976 Dresden version, also with Kollo and conducted by **Heinrich Hollreiser,** seems to have disappeared from the listings.

Der fliegende Holländer (*The Flying Dutchman,* 1843). The first of the ten Wagner operas still in the repertory of the world's opera houses, it is one of the most listener-friendly of his works. It has conventional arias, duets, and choruses, as well as dramatic, exciting music that should stir the listener as much as the artists on stage. Like all of Wagner, it benefits from modern sound, a topnotch orchestra, and a theater-minded conductor who's not afraid to whip up a storm. But it's essential that the leading roles, the Dutchman and Senta, are filled by artists who not only sing well but who can project and convince us of their larger-than-life characters.

In the stereo age, Rysanek and London have been the best Senta and Dutchman. Their 1960 recording is still preferred by most critics (including me), though **Dorati**'s conducting is rather pedestrian (♦London 41731). This pair can also be heard, in more exciting surroundings, in a 1959 Bayreuth performance that's better conducted (by **Sawallisch**) but has poorer mono sound (♦Melodram 26101; no libretto). Varnay and Hermann Uhde are the runners-up and their 1955 Bayreuth outing led by **Knappertsbusch** is a fine second choice (♦Music & Arts/Arkadia 421; mono, but acceptable sound). Another is a 1983 studio recording by **Karajan;** it's the best-led *Dutchman* and has excellent sound (♦EMI 64650). Van Dam offers a beautifully nuanced rendition of the title role and Dunja Vejzovic is a strong Senta, though she lacks Rysanek's thrilling top notes and dramatic sensibility. The supporting cast is as good as London's.

By comparison, the other stereo recordings are deficient in one way or another. **Levine**'s Met recording (Sony) is too slow and has a dull, bland Dutchman (Morris). **Klemperer**'s Dutchman (Theo Adam) is vocally and dramatically unattractive though Silja is a committed and intermittently appealing Senta (EMI). **Dohnányi**'s cast lacks passion and dramatic instincts, vitiating strong contributions by conductor and orchestra and excellent sound (London). **Konwitschny** (Berlin) and **Böhm** (DG) have generally inferior casts.

Since most *Dutchman* recordings are on two CDs, it makes little sense to buy a disc of excerpts, but there's one exception: parts of a 1937 Covent Garden performance led by **Reiner,** with the incomparable Flagstad in her heyday as Senta. No other recorded Senta matches her in vocal splendor (♦SRO 8081).

Tannhäuser (Dresden version 1845, Paris version 1861). These versions differ primarily in the Venusberg Scene of Act 1, which Wagner revised thoroughly for the Paris production. At that time, he had already composed *Tristan und Isolde* and this is reflected in the music that he rewrote; it's now more sensuous and erotic, thus putting it stylistically somewhat at odds with the rest of the opera. Other changes include the elimination of Walther's song in the Act 2 contest and other minor alterations. I prefer the Paris version, and it's the one most often performed.

This opera requires a real Heldentenor, and that's a rare species (it probably always was). Of all the tenors I've heard over the last 50 years, only Melchior filled out the part more than adequately and you can only hear him in a noncommercial Met recording from a 1941 broadcast in mono but fairly decent sound, with a stellar cast including Flagstad, Thorborg, and Janssen, conducted by **Leinsdorf.** This was available from the Met, but only on LP, for a sizable contribution.

Of the stereo recordings in good sound, **Solti**'s is the best (♦London 414581). This well-engineered 1970 set is the Paris version and offers the best Venus (Ludwig), a fine Elisabeth (Dernesh), and a good supporting cast. Kollo is caught here in his youth, before he got the wobbles and serious intonation problems. He's an acceptable Tannhäuser and better than Hopf and Windgassen. A Dresden version by **Franz Konwitschny** (♦EMI 632214) has the best Elisabeth (Grümmer), a notable Wolfram (Fischer-Dieskau), but a poor Tannhäuser (Hopf). Wunderlich (Walther) is an added attraction.

A more recent Paris version, in excellent sound, is very well conducted by **Sinopoli** (♦DG 427625). Domingo sings the title role lyrically and beautifully but strains in the more dramatic passages. The supporting cast is average to good, Studer's Elisabeth being the most contentious. I don't like her cold, steely voice in this role, but others do. If the complete Met recording is too much money for you, buy a disc that includes Melchior singing the Rome Narrative and Flagstad in Elisabeth's two arias (Preiser 9049).

Lohengrin (1846–48). This romantic story of a knight in shining armor rescuing a princess in distress has long been Wagner's most popular opera. It's easier to cast than *Tannhäuser* primarily because it doesn't require a Heldentenor for the title role. Heldentenors have sung it, of course, often to considerable acclaim, but lyrico-spinto tenors like Domingo, Sandor Konya, and Torsten Ralf have often done better with it (Björling was ready to try it at the time of his death). Indeed, it's often more difficult to find a good Ortrud; that role needs a big-voiced mezzo with a solid top up to a high B.

There's a general consensus that the best recorded *Lohengrin* is the 1964 version conducted by **Kempe** with the excellent cast of Jess Thomas, Grümmer, Ludwig, and Fischer-Dieskau (♦EMI 49017). Its sound is still quite good, the orchestra (Vienna Philharmonic) superb, and Kempe as good a conductor as you'll find. No one in the competing recordings is better than Grümmer and Ludwig, and while you may prefer Konya or Domingo to Thomas, or the more dramatic Uhde to Fischer-Dieskau, the sets where they appear have other problems. As a second choice, I suggest **Solti** (♦London 425530). Its strength is the beautifully lyrical singing of Domingo in the title role (though his German isn't perfect) and of Fischer-Dieskau, its stunning sound, the fine playing of the Vienna Philharmonic, and Solti's cogent and exciting leadership. Its weakness is the poor singing of Eva Randova (Ortrud). Norman (Elsa), though in great voice, isn't right for the part; her characterization lacks vulnerability and ingenuousness.

Konya's Lohengrin can best be heard on a recording from the 1959 Bayreuth Festival led by **Cluytens** (♦Myto 89002). Varnay and Uhde are a powerful pair of villains (with Nilsson and Windgassen as the lovers) in a 1954 Bayreuth set conducted by **Keilberth** (♦Melodram 36104). The sound of these sets is, of course, not as good as that of the commercial recordings. The best of today's Lohengrins is Heppner, but his 1995 recording, led by **Colin Davis,** is flawed by the poor performances of Marton and Sharon Sweet (RCA 62646).

Tristan und Isolde (1857–59). This opera has rarely been recorded or performed in recent years, and that's entirely due to the absence of satisfactory, not to mention great singers, for the title roles. The Met hasn't put it on for nearly 20 years, and the performances I remember from the late '70s were, to put it mildly, forgettable. The same may be said for any recording made in the last 25 years or so; there just hasn't been an Isolde or a Tristan to do justice to this great music since Nilsson and Vickers.

Fortunately, there are at least two earlier recordings to turn to. A critical consensus exists in favor of the 1966 Bayreuth performance, in stereo, conducted by **Böhm,** with Nilsson, the pre-eminent Isolde of the 1955–75 era, and Windgassen as a more than acceptable Tristan (♦DG 419889). It has a fine supporting cast and benefits from having been recorded on stage. The sound is quite good, and Böhm leads a theatrically compelling performance. A 1953 mono set documents a studio version by **Furtwängler,** with Flagstad and Ludwig Suthaus as the lovers (♦EMI 47231). There are better recordings of Flagstad's magnificent Isolde, her greatest role, but they suffer from poor sound, and Suthaus isn't much better than Windgassen as Tristan; Furtwängler's smooth and flowing pacing is a definite plus. Vickers was surely the best Tristan since Melchior and he can be heard in **Karajan**'s recording, but his Isolde, Dernesh, an admirable singer, isn't compelling, especially in her top register (EMI).

Vickers is better paired, with Nilsson, in a recording from the 1973 Orange Festival, also conducted by **Böhm,** but that's NA and may be hard to find (Rodolphe). If your ears can adjust to its poor sound, the 1936 Covent Garden performance led by **Reiner,** with Flagstad and Melchior at their best, should appeal to you (♦VAIA 1004). They set the standard for this work, and it's sad that none of their successors, except for Nilsson, have come close to meeting it.

Die Meistersinger von Nürnberg (1845–67). Except for the early *Das Liebesverbot,* this is Wagner's only comedy. It has retained its popularity over the years (second only to *Lohengrin*) in spite of its nationalistic rhetoric and its sometime association with the Nazi regime. Excellent recordings are easier to find than for most Wagner operas; except for the crucial part of Hans Sachs, it's relatively easy to cast. A tenor who can sing Lohengrin well will most likely be a persuasive Walther von Stolzing (as Konya and Torsten Ralf proved) and a soprano who is appealing as Elsa will also do well as Eva Pogner (as Grümmer has shown us). As for Sachs, the standard was set by Schorr, whose recording (led by **Böhm**) of much of Sachs's music is now available, a must for everyone who loves this opera (Preiser 9944). The best of the post-WWII interpreters of the old cobbler was Schöffler, whom you can hear from 1944 Vienna also led by Böhm, the fine Eva of Seefried but a poor Stolzing (Preiser 90234).

For complete recordings in modern sound, the best all-around choice is a 1967 Bavarian Opera release by **Kubelik** (Myto and Calig ♦5097); the latter has better sound. Thomas Stewart is a pleasing, warm-hearted Sachs, Janowitz an exquisite Eva, and Sandor Konya one of the best Stolzings on records. Other fine releases include a set from Dresden by **Karajan** in superb sound and with a generally fine cast, though I don't care for Adam's thin-voiced Sachs (♦EMI 49083). Karajan's conducting is more stately than either Kubelik's or **Kempe**'s, whose 1955 recording,

in decent mono sound, offers the best podium leadership (♦EMI 64154). Its main vocal distinctions are Grümmer's warm and passionate Eva, Benno Kusche's well-sung (and not overacted) Beckmesser, and Gerhard Unger's stylish David. Ferdinand Frantz offers a well-routined, solidly sung Sachs that's a bit lacking in warmth and humanity.

Solti's cast (London) doesn't measure up to any of the three recordings mentioned, specifically the Eva (Mattila) and Sachs (van Dam). The latter, whose work I usually admire, may have waited too long to record this role; his voice seems to have lost much of its color. Another Solti recording, also with the Bavarian Opera, features Heppner, today's premier Stolzing, but Studer's matronly Eva and Weikl's patchy and only intermittently appealing Sachs are not to my taste (EMI).

Parsifal (1877–79). Like *Tristan* and *Tannhäuser, Parsifal* is difficult to cast nowadays. The best recordings date back more than 35 years and the end of the drought is barely in sight. Domingo, a recent Met interpreter, was quite taxed by the title role, and Heppner, as far as I know, hasn't tried it yet, so we must do with Messrs. Windgassen, Thomas, Kollo, and Jerusalem, none of whom is vocally thrilling.

For that, look to Vickers, the best Parsifal of the recent past. Unfortunately, he never recorded the part commercially, but you can hear him in a 1964 *Parsifal* from Bayreuth that's apparently based on a radio broadcast (Melodram 10004). It's led by **Knappertsbusch,** the best conductor of this opera in the post-WWII period, and the supporting cast is quite good, though the sound is inferior to the other two Knappertsbusch *Parsifals* that have long been available. Of these, the 1962 recording has the better sound (♦Philips 416390), the 1951 issue is slower but has the better cast (Teldec).

For up-to-date sound, **Barenboim** (♦Teldec 74448) and **Solti** (♦London 417143) can be recommended; the former has somewhat better sound, the latter a better cast. Of all the principal singers, the best Kundry is Ludwig (Solti), the best Gurnemanz is Ludwig Weber (Knappertsbusch 1951), and the best Amfortas is London (better in 1951 than in 1962) who sings the part in both the Bayreuth sets. The rest of Solti's cast (Frick and Papp) are somewhat better than Barenboim's Matthias Hölle and Jerusalem, and Solti is a more forceful and majestic conductor than Barenboim. What this opera must have sounded like in the '30s can be gleaned in excerpts sung by Flagstad and Melchior (RCA 7915).

DER RING DES NIBELUNGEN

While we are literally being deluged with *Ring* recordings, none of them made within the last few years can be recommended. The reason is that—as with *Tristan* and *Tannhäuser*—adequate singers for the main roles are few and far between and, in the case of Siegfried and Brünnhilde, practically nonexistent. Specifically, this is the case for the cycles conducted by **Barenboim, Dohnányi,** and **Levine.** Their sound is, of course, very good to excellent, and so is the orchestral playing. None of these conductors is less than very competent, but nowhere is there a conductor active today of such extraordinary talent that his readings would persuade me to overlook his cast's vocal deficiencies. So for the best *Ring* cycles, we must go back to the **Solti** and **Böhm** recordings, which were made in the '50s and '60s. And it's best to consider each of the four operas individually, since no cycle is consistently superior in every one of the operas.

Das Rheingold. Here the best selection is **Solti,** who was the first to record this opera in modern sound in 1958 (♦London 414102). That sound is still very good by today's standards and Solti's cast has never been equaled, let alone surpassed. For example, London's dark voice and expressive declamation are more appropriate for Wotan than the relative blandness of James Morris for Levine; ♦DG 427607) who, to be sure, sings the part very beautifully but not dramatically enough. Nor does Adam (for Böhm), who doesn't even have Morris's vocal allure. The role of Fricka has never been sung with more sumptuous tones than in Flagstad's work for Solti, and Svanholm's delivery of Loge's lines is as compelling as his competition's, though he sometimes shouts his words at the expense of the vocal line. Gustav Neidlinger (who also sings the role for Böhm) was then the world's best Alberich, and the supporting roles are all well portrayed. Still, **Böhm** (♦Philips 412475) is an appropriate second choice for those who prefer a more laid-back approach—but I think this opera benefits from Solti's more exciting way with the score. **Levine**'s cast also includes Ludwig's wonderful Fricka and Jerusalem's splendid Loge.

Die Walküre. This is the most popular of the four operas and often performed apart from the cycle, but none of the complete recordings are ideally cast in the leading roles. The best Sieglindes are Rysanek (**Böhm**; ♦Philips 412478), Crespin (**Solti**; ♦London 414105), and Janowitz (**Karajan**; ♦DG 415145); the best Siegmund is Vickers (**Karajan**) though James King (**Böhm** and **Solti**) is quite acceptable. But for the role of Brünnhilde, only Nilsson (**Solti** and **Böhm**) will do; Dernesh (**Karajan**) and Behrens (**Levine**; DG) can't match her in vocal opulence and thrills. The best Wotan interpreter is Hotter (**Solti**), though his somewhat woolly voice was beginning to fray around the edges when he recorded the role. Adam (**Böhm**) is vocally more secure and often affecting in the long stretches of Act 2. Morris (**Levine**) and Stewart (**Karajan**) offer the smoothest singing and the most beautiful voices; Stewart is the more cogent interpreter.

No one should be without the 1934 recording of Act 1 with Lehmann, Melchior, and List conducted by **Walter** (♦EMI 61020). Though far from up-to-date sonically, this is still the gold standard for both singing and conducting. It's one of the greatest opera recordings ever made.

Siegfried. This opera rests almost entirely on the shoulders of the singer entrusted with the title role. Windgassen, who sings it for both **Solti** (♦London 414110) and **Böhm** (♦Philips 412483), has been its most persuasive interpreter since the '50s, but that's only a mild compliment. Jerusalem (**Haitink**; EMI) has a more lyrical approach but his voice lacks the heroic ring for the climaxes. Jess Thomas (**Karajan**; DG) and Reiner Goldberg (**Levine**; RCA) are inadequate. Nilsson is, again, the indispensable Brünnhilde for both Böhm and Solti and Hotter (Solti) is a much better Wanderer than Adam (Böhm). As Mime, Böhm's Erwin Wohlfart sings with more character than Solti's Gerhard Stolze. Again, Solti's conducting is more dynamic than Böhm's, notably in the first and second acts (where it's needed). Böhm, however, shapes the final duet in a warmer, more romantic manner. A close call, but I prefer Solti.

Melchior was the best Siegfried ever recorded. Much of the music for the title role can be found on Danacord 319-21 and EMI 69789. Although surrounded by dim orchestral sound, he sings the role with a heroic ring, yet still offers a warm, appealing tone; no one else has come close.

Götterdämmerung. Again, **Solti** (♦London 414115) offers the best cast. In addition to Nilsson, Windgassen, and Neidlinger, whom he shares with **Böhm** (♦Philips 412498). Solti's Hagen, Gottlob Frick, sings with more menace in his voice than Böhm's Josef Greindl. Most of the supporting roles are also better cast in the Solti recording. Both conductors give us cogent and dramatic readings of the score; Solti has the better orchestra, Böhm the better chorus.

Historic excerpts from this opera that are highly recommended include the Immolation Scene with Flagstad and Furtwängler (EMI

63030), **Frida Leider**'s Brünnhilde (Pearl 9331), and excerpts from Act 1 with **Traubel**, Melchior, and Toscanini (RCA 60304).

WESENDONCK SONGS

These five songs were composed in 1857–58 when Wagner was given refuge in Zurich by Otto and Mathilde Wesendonck, a wealthy couple who loved his music. Mathilde, who wrote the banal and pedestrian texts, also served as one of the composer's muses. Two of the songs, "Im Treibhaus" ("In the Hothouse") and "Träume" ("Dreams") were labeled by Wagner as studies for *Tristan und Isolde*, the opera on which he was working at the time. A third song, "Schmerzen" ("Pain") starts with the same dissonant orchestral chord as Act 2, and "Der Engel" ("The Angel") also has a Tristanesque flavor.

The songs were written for female voice and piano; they were later orchestrated by Felix Mottl under Wagner's supervision. But the composer himself scored "Träume" for small orchestra, and that version was once performed under Mathilde's window as a birthday greeting. In 1976, Hans Werner Henze produced his own orchestration using smaller and more wind-dominated forces; this was later recorded by **Jard van Nes** (Chandos 9354). I wasn't happy with the thin-sounding result that seems deliberately to de-emphasize the *Tristan* connection.

While other mezzos and contraltos, and even a tenor or two, have recorded this work, it has fared best when sung by an Isolde-type voice, a real Wagnerian soprano. In particular, **Flagstad** made it her own. She recorded the songs several times in the studio, and several of her concert performances have also been released. Recommended are her studio recording with orchestra (part of a Memories 2CD set, ♦4456/7) and one with pianist Gerald Moore (♦EMI 63030). The latter, from 1948, shows the soprano in characteristically sumptuous voice; even her somewhat glacial expression contributes to the grand effect, as it does in her recording of Isolde. Other fine recordings are by **Eileen Farrell** (♦Sony 47644), who sings with even less passion than Flagstad, and **Norman** (♦Philips 412653), whose undeniable vocal prowess is handicapped by indifferent and sometimes unnatural diction. MOSES

ORCHESTRAL MUSIC

Early, Wagner came to the realization that for the propagation of his music, it was necessary that he cull orchestral passages from the complete operas for presentation at concerts. The Overtures and Preludes were easy, but the so-called "bleeding chunks" that he and his musician friends excised—minus the normal vocal line—have remained controversial to this day. Yet the amazing thing about Wagner is the independence of the singing line from the orchestra. Some people, hearing the complete operas for the first time, are startled at how different the music sounds with voices (some even preferring the singers' silence).

Many conductors now reject the so-called "concert endings" that were grafted onto selections taken from an opera mid-stream, and many have created large symphonic suites based on their own sense of Wagnerian style and decorum. No matter the guise, this music is some of the greatest the world has heard, and even radical deviations from the original don't seem able to quell its beauties or stifle its influence. Many people who don't spend a lot of time with the complete operas and music dramas will spend hours with the selections—and there's a large variety to choose from.

Klemperer was involved with Wagner's music throughout his career, and the results are mixed, though leaning toward the positive. "The Klemperer Legacy" gives us two jam-packed CDs with every note he ever recorded in the studio (♦EMI 66806). *Rienzi* can be stop and go, with congested sound at the climaxes, while *Dutchman*, as might be anticipated in the light of his superb opera recording, is completely in sync with the composer, with the transitions between sections, so crucial in this piece, deftly handled. His climax in *Lohengrin* lacks fire and passion, though he clearly catches the warmth and religious pageantry of the descent of the Grail. *Meistersinger* is given a fine, standard reading without any excesses. But it's in the *Ring* excerpts where he really shines, with impressive sound and swollen, boldly proclaimed winds and brass. These discs are available separately; the second is the one to have.

Right from the beginning of **Barenboim**'s first set of overtures and preludes, you notice a sound problem (Teldec). Recorded as if at a great distance and at a fairly low level, the strings are often drowned out and much important detail is lost. You can't have effective Wagner without soaring strings, and this is much more of a brass-dominated reading, always a mistake in this music. His *Tristan* is very fast, substituting speed for the intense holding-back that's so important here. *Dutchman* and *Tannhäuser* are both taken at rapid clips—the former can take it, the latter can't. *Meistersinger,* because of the string problem, sounds weak and pallid. *Lohengrin,* perfectly paced in the Act 1 Prelude, falters yet again because the strings cannot (or aren't allowed to) carry the day. This recording demonstrates what a difference recorded sound can make.

Barenboim's second set, recorded after Orchestra Hall in Chicago underwent a much needed revamping, is better in every way (♦Teldec 24224). Though there remains an audible haze in this recording, the orchestra's sonic presence is much more palpable and lively. The strings remain the primary weakness, though the winds are strong, as has always been the case in Chicago. *Rienzi* sounds great, with the brass really bellowing as only the Chicago brass can. *Meistersinger* Act 3 is as good as any, with the "Prize Song" played by hornist Dale Clevenger. *Siegfried Idyll* is given a familial, tender reading that surely would have brought tears to Cosima's eyes that Christmas morning in 1870. The Act 3 Prelude from *Tannhäuser* is given a rousing performance, while *Parsifal* is somber and suggestive, but the *Good Friday Music* isn't as affecting as with someone like **Levine**—though his disc is rather lackluster (Philips).

Barenboim also recorded *Ring* scenes for Erato; he gives the standard tour with Deborah Polaski and the Chicago Symphony in a very well-recorded disc, much better than the first Teldec outing (♦Erato 45786). In almost the same program with the addition of *Siegfried Idyll,* Teldec increases its impressive store of great Wagner recordings with the Dresden Staatskapelle under **Donald Runnicles.** A more impressive album is hard to find, with rich sound and perfectly judged conducting, not surprising considering his experience heading the San Francisco Opera. Ravishing orchestra sound is complemented by a superb sense of color in every bar (♦Teldec 17109).

Chailly's Concertgebouw recording has thrilling brass and superb strings, but it lacks clarity (Decca). *Meistersinger* is taken at a fast pace that sounds even faster, with little contrast among sections or delineation of the complex contrapuntal strata. *Ride of the Valkyries* is fine, a nice conception that still remains miles away from the blazing, vibrant excitement generated by Stokowski. *Rhine Journey* has a lot of short, clipped orchestral articulations, as does every piece in this disc, and it feels completely out of place. This is a very anti-Romantic reading of these works, and nothing suffers more than the *Funeral March,* though the brass have their day. *Tannhäuser* is rushed and short-changed, with even the usually unassailable "Venusberg Music" lacking exoticism and flavor. *Lohengrin* comes across well, a puff piece that rounds out a really disappointing recording. Look to Haitink as a Concertgebouw corrective.

Boulez gives us a mixed bag that may be worth pursuing at mid price (Sony). *Meistersinger* is a surprising, almost Romantic recording that falters only toward the end where the conductor slows down inappropriately to prepare for the big three-chord concert ending. This can be avoided by using the opera ending instead. *Tannhäuser* lets us down with less than angelic trombones, lacking force and impact. *Faust Overture* is a marvel, exciting, lithe, and played with a visceral mania that suits the music perfectly. *Tristan* is standard, with no special impact, though Boulez does make a point of rushing through the "Liebestod." But *Siegfried Idyll* is another story altogether, a burnished, soft, heart-warming account that would melt lead. I would buy this for it and *Faust Overture* alone—maybe.

Jansons is another who seems determined to cover Wagner in a glow of anti-Romanticism (Seraphim). His orchestra (Oslo Philharmonic) is for the most part very good, though the brass can be a bit raw, with the strings not as strong as they should be. *Meistersinger* is a good reading, taut, clean, and contrapuntal. *Tristan* is shorn of passion, too calculated for cheap effect. *Tannhäuser* (non-Venusberg edition) is also very good, noble and inspiring with no histrionics. *Funeral March* is too matter of fact, with not enough build-up to the climax, though the brass are wonderful. *Ride of the Valkyries* is straightforward and routine, while *Lohengrin* Act 3 cruises along at a high speed blur. The real prize here is *Rienzi,* a fine, fatty reading that enlivens and glows.

Thielemann shows no fear of the romantic in this music; he pulls back where necessary, shapes phrases, caresses notes, and contours as the master would have wanted. *Meistersinger* is wonderful, broad, spacious, and texturally rich. *Lohengrin* is glowing and auburn, the Philadelphia strings sounding like Ormandy of old. The Act 1 Prelude and *Good Friday Music* from *Parsifal* almost comprise a symphonic suite when played alongside one another, and this lush account is the equal of any. *Tristan* is given an especially rapturous rendering, tender and caressing with ecstatic climaxes. An excellent offering (♦DG 453485).

Though the playing of **Boult**'s three orchestras (New Philharmonia, London Philharmonic, London Symphony) isn't the most refined—a rugged individualism is especially prevalent in the brass—his underestimated Wagner must be ranked with the best. You wouldn't expect such full-bodied, powerful playing from this old English gentleman, but he delivers the goods with a blended precision and bite that compares well with any of the noted masters of this music (♦EMI 62539, 2CD). You only have to hear the noble aggressiveness of *Tannhäuser,* the strenuous, arching melodies of *Meistersinger,* or the tender, devotional passages of *Parsifal* to understand that Boult's knowledge of this composer is thorough and far-reaching. All the standards are here, including the usual suite from the *Ring,* a must-have collection at bargain price that's something of a sleeper among Wagnerians. It awaits your delighted discovery and their enlightenment.

Aside from an intriguing 45-minute rehearsal segment and one of the most sensitive and utterly gorgeous readings of *Siegfried Idyll* on record, **Walter** treats us to some of the most illuminating Wagner ever. He didn't leave a large Wagnerian legacy, and he never recorded any of the operas or conducted at Bayreuth. Nevertheless, we know from his own words how important Wagner was to him, and it shows in every one of these wondrous recordings. Just listen to the glowing, translucent bass of *Meistersinger,* or the pious, heartfelt radiance of *Parsifal; Dutchman, Tannhäuser,* and *Lohengrin* are all among the best. I wish there had been much, much more (♦Sony 64456).

You really want to like **Schwarz**'s recordings (♦Delos 3053 and 3120,

3CD). Seattle has been the site of a noted *Ring* festival for many years, and the orchestra is well attuned to the Wagnerian manner. Yet Schwarz is not always so. In the first of his set, *Tannhäuser* and *Meistersinger* selections are wonderful, smoothly played in fabulous sound. But in the *Rheingold* selections, the horns falter miserably at the climax of "Entry of the Gods into Valhalla," and the tempo transitions in "Twilight of the Gods" are wayward and unthinking, to say the least. The second disc is much better, with an excellent *Dutchman,* and wonderful, sensual accounts of the Preludes to Acts 1 and 3 plus *Good Friday Music* from *Parsifal.* I haven't heard it played better. *Lohengrin* is okay, but the Act I Prelude needs a string section of great nuance and flexibility, and the Seattle strings just don't cut it; one of the great weaknesses of the set is its lack of potent, powerful strings.

Disc 3 is sonically the best, with a ravishing *Forest Murmurs,* an equally luscious "Elsa's Dream" from *Lohengrin* (sung radiantly by Alessandra Marc), and a vigorous *Faust Overture* that rehabilitates the strings with some truly fine playing. Round it off with Schwarz's own *Tristan* suite, again with Marc, all in sumptuous sound, and you have a fine release by any standard. These three are available as a complete set, but I'd stick with 2 and 3.

Tennstedt's compilation is a major disappointment (EMI, 2CD). Willful and disoriented, his Wagner is beset by all sorts of balance problems, with the strings totally dissolved at critical points and winds completely out of focus. The Berlin Philharmonic doesn't seem to respond to him as they did for Karajan and others. He's not willing to let the music unfold at a natural pace as dictated by the score, and instead we hear choppy phrases, badly tapered cutoffs, and some generally sloppy workmanship. Disc 1 of this collection focuses on the *Ring* music and is the less impressive of the two, with *Magic Fire Music* the best thing here—and that's not saying much. *Rhine Journey* and *Funeral March* are ineffective, lacking the intense psychological drama Wagner imparted to these pieces. Disc 2 is better, a collection of Overtures from *Tannhäuser, Rienzi, Lohengrin,* and *Meistersinger.* Only *Rienzi* is worth repeated hearings, a very fine performance, while *Meistersinger* is plagued with a triangle that sounds like a dull, off-tone dinner bell.

In a rare example of intelligent programming, **Sawallisch** offers an album of less played Wagner esoterica. A delightfully tensile, committed reading of the Overture to the early comic opera *Das Liebesverbot* opens this recording; you have to wonder why it's not played and recorded more often. The one-movement Symphony in E follows, a thoroughly enjoyable marvel that heightens your sense of being deprived of something important all these years. *Faust Overture* and *Rienzi* are both here, in two of the finest performances I have heard of these wonderful warhorses. And it's a unique privilege to be exposed to Hans Werner Henze's chamber arrangement of *Wesendonck Lieder,* performed by a 30-member ensemble. This is a revelation, fervently and delicately portraying Wagner's songs in an intimate, sweetly secure manner. The Mottl arrangement is still wonderful, but there's something special in Henze's version I wouldn't want to be without (♦EMI 56165).

López-Cobos's recording is fine for the most part (♦Telarc 80379). The strings are warm and blanketing, the brass, while not overly sharp and pointed, are very chaste and rounded, and the woodwinds play with style and commitment. All the performances are mainstream, played by an orchestra (Cincinnati) that has a long tradition with the German Romantic repertory. Tempos are generally relaxed, without forcing the music at all, and while there are more exciting renditions of several of these works, good, solid craftsmanship isn't to be slighted. If you desire steady readings of the standard Overtures (*Meistersinger, Rienzi, Faust,*

Dutchman, Tristan, Tannhäuser) in excellent, slightly recessed sound, don't hesitate .

Bernstein, had he spent more time with the composer, could have been a phenomenal Wagnerian. As it is, we have to be satisfied with his complete *Tristan* (Philips) and a smattering of "bleeding chunks." And bleed they often do, as his often raucous and rough-edged NY Philharmonic seems to care little for the finer things in musical life, like tone quality and intonation. The trumpets especially have a hard time negotiating pitch in *Dutchman* and *Rienzi,* while the strings aren't the best in *Lohengrin,* Act 1. But *Meistersinger* fares well, as do *Tannhäuser* (Paris version) and the most searing *Tristan* on disc, relentlessly erotic in its excruciatingly slow, methodical tempo. We're treated to the final scene of *Twilight of the Gods* with soprano Eileen Farrell, who also gives a superb performance of the *Wesendonck Lieder* (though perhaps not as beautiful as Norman with **Colin Davis,** also including *Tristan;* ♦Philips 12655). But scrappy or not, Bernstein keeps the heat turned way up in every reading here, and these two discs demand recommendation (♦Sony 47643, 47644).

The Concertgebouw under **Haitink** gives us what may be the single best recorded and played Wagner program ever assembled. *Meistersinger* is nonpareil—only Szell comes close to its clarity and gorgeous orchestral sheen. You can hear every strand of counterpoint in Wagner's magnificent comic opera. The *Parsifal* Prelude isn't as saccharinely devotional as others have made it, and the lusciously vibrant string sound and perfectly back-dropped winds and brass make for stunning listening. The strings also shine in *Lohengrin* Act 1, expertly judged in all respects. *Tristan* is solid and middle of the road—there are better readings, but none with more aplomb. *Siegfried Idyll* is relaxed, joyous, and tempered, an icon of Wagner's domestic tranquility (♦Philips 420886).

Stokowski was a phenomenal Wagnerian, and he spent a lot of energy on Wagner over his long career. His 1966 recording of *Ride of the Valkyries, Dawn and Rhine Journey, Siegfried's Death, Funeral March, Entrance of the Gods into Valhalla,* and *Forest Murmurs* has attained legendary status. The London Symphony was very uneven at that time, but he had them playing like the greatest orchestra in the world. The "Phase IV" recording, now transferred to CD, is superior in every respect. This is an absolute classic, a must for even the sparsest of Wagnerian collections (♦Decca 443901).

Hardly less impressive is RCA's 2CD series (part of the Stokowski "Stereo Collection"). Only four selections are duplicated with his London album (*Entrance of the Gods, Ride of the Valkyries, Rhine Journey, Funeral March*). Stokowski treats us to a sizzling *Rienzi,* Act 3 Prelude to *Tristan,* and a passionate Paris *Tannhäuser* in 1, while 2 feasts us with three selections from *Meistersinger* (but not the Overture), the Prelude and "Liebestod" from *Tristan,* and *Rhine Journey, Funeral March,* and *Immolation Scene* from *Twilight of the Gods.* These are stunningly recorded, fervently emotional, highly engaging readings that shouldn't be passed over by anyone who takes Wagner seriously (♦RCA 62597, 62598).

Szell was another excellent Wagnerian. He never did anything to beef up the music. His was the quintessential anti-Romantic approach, not dissimilar to Toscanini, yet both of these conductors were able to present Wagner in a most sympathetic manner. Szell recorded all the symphonic chestnuts, and most are now available on two CDs (♦Sony 48175, 62403). Ormandy and the Philadelphia are substituted in *Tannhäuser*—a real shame, for the power of Szell's reading has to be heard to be believed—and the Act 3 Prelude to *Lohengrin,* a fine version. But *Lohen-*

grin Act 1, *Dutchman, Rienzi,* and *Faust Overture* are all superb. The other CD has the standard *Ring* excerpts (including an overwhelming *Funeral March*), the *Meistersinger* Prelude (the only real competition to Haitink), and a very good *Tristan.* At budget price, failing to purchase these two discs would be inexcusable; they offer some of the finest Wagner on record.

Levine leads two CDs of integrated, forward-moving performances that are for the most part played marvelously by the Metropolitan Opera Orchestra. The sound is rather cloudy in the *Lohengrin* Prelude, and the same spatial ambiguity appears at the climax of *Ride of the Valkyries.* One of his best readings is the evocative, almost impressionistic *Forest Murmurs,* aptly capturing the magic and mystical allure of the hero in the forest. But elsewhere Levine stretches the music in climaxes, leading paradoxically to a colder emotional feeling. The playing is beyond comment, it's so fine, but the bloodless readings lead to an emotional detachment that serves Wagner poorly. Some of the slow accounts transform the music into parody instead of the boisterous current of symphonic statement the composer desired. For great playing, you can't get any better, but that's only half the story (DG).

You can't fault **Dorati** in any way for the rather vibrant, sun-lit sound the people at Mercury afforded him. I like very much his recordings of *Parsifal Good Friday Music, Meistersinger* Act 1 Prelude, *Lohengrin* Acts 1 and 3 Preludes, *Tristan* Prelude and "Liebestod," and the Paris *Tannhäuser.* The London Symphony was on fairly good behavior, though they don't come near the later Stokowski effort. But if you're a Dorati fan, you'll be pleased. **Maazel** decided to create his own vast symphonic suite from the *Ring,* and he has toured with it around the world. The sound is rather close and constricted, but the Berlin Philharmonic sounds great. The breakdown among the four music dramas is 12 minutes for *Rheingold,* 15 for *Walküre,* six for *Siegfried,* and a whopping 37 for *Twilight of the Gods.* If you want to hear the best parts of the *Ring* without sitting down to 17 hours or so, this is your best bet (♦Telarc 80154).

Solti, whether in Chicago or Vienna, offered athletic, sometimes clipped readings that won't be to all tastes. His *Meistersinger* has long been one of the finest around, yet he's impatient and impertinent in works like *Tristan.* His *Ring* was something of a specialty, and those wanting sharply delineated, crisp readings of this music can't go wrong with either of his two discs (Decca, one with Chicago and Vienna, the other a 2CD set with Vienna alone). But some of us want more from this composer than Solti offers.

Reiner set down his 1959 recording in early stereo, but its latest incarnation retains the somewhat boomy sound that could often plague the early Chicago recordings. His *Meistersinger* is broad and vast, while the highlights from *Twilight of the Gods* are very affecting, but the pounding pulsation coming from this disc may be too much for many (RCA). **Paray,** on the other hand, is quite ascetic in this music, austere, unyielding, and iconoclastic. Just listen to his *Dutchman*—not willing to pause, linger, or caress in the least. His *Rienzi* is the same—hurried, as if he must go out of his way to rehabilitate Wagner's Romanticism (Mercury).

For many, **Furtwängler**'s Wagner remains the ultimate example of fluid, long-lined conducting, the kind that supports a singer with ease and flexibility and molds a perfect architectonic structure over music that by nature seems impervious to structure. He could indeed do this, and his Wagner is something special. But most of the recordings are in fairly insubstantial mono, and only his EMI set (now deleted) is really worth the effort. Do look into it when it becomes available again, but by

no means should this conductor be a primary choice in Wagner's orchestral works (the operas are another story).

Toscanini is another conductor whose Wagner must be considered with sound taken into consideration. Wagner was a passion for this Italian maestro, and he was an excellent Wagnerian, giving undiluted, passionate, but very clean-cut performances. The best recording you can get (partly because of its 1954 stereo sound and also for its historical value) is the "final concert" in Carnegie Hall, where the conductor lost his way in the *Tannhäuser* Overture. He recovered, and the rest of the program (*Lohengrin* Act 1, *Forest Murmurs, Dawn and Rhine Journey, Meistersinger*) is superb. Pursue its acquisition with a vengeance (♦Music and Arts 3008). His two RCA recordings have surprisingly good mono sound, though the typical compression and closet feeling of these releases are present. Nonetheless, if you can abide mono and like this conductor, don't hesitate.

D'Avalos tries hard on three discs with mixed results. The first is the best—*Die Feen, Das Liebesverbot, Rienzi, Dutchman,* and *Tannhäuser* all played fairly well in somewhat swallowing acoustics, but the program is attractive and enjoyable (♦ASV 996). The second, with *Meistersinger, Tristan, Parsifal* Prelude Act 1 and *Good Friday Music,* and *Siegfried Idyll* is more problematic; *Tristan* is plodding and lethargic and absent are Bernstein's unerring sense of line and arch (not to mention passion). The third is to be avoided, a collection of *Ring* music with a *Funeral March* that just dies away, so stretched and musically disconnected is the phrasing. Just as Bernstein is plagued by strange balances in some of his Vienna recordings, so **Böhm** has similar difficulties. But his flawless sense of urgency, of which strata to highlight and which to leave alone, plus the incredible playing of the Vienna Philharmonic, make it an immensely satisfying reading. *Dutchman,* the two Preludes from *Lohengrin, Parsifal* Act 1, *Rienzi,* and *Tannhäuser* are splendid, broad, and exceptionally spacious (♦DG 453989).

The news is good and bad for **Karajan,** perhaps the premier Wagner conductor of the 20th century. A disc with the Paris *Tannhauser,* Act 3 *Meistersinger,* and *Tristan* is rather short shrift for the price, and there are problems with the sound (EMI). A steely brilliance surrounds the orchestra, and a claustrophobic sense of suffocating sound won't release its grip on the listener. Avoid it. *Siegfried Idyll, Tannhäuser,* and a searing *Tristan* are available with the Vienna Philharmonic in Salzburg in 1987 (♦DG 23613). This was a widely distributed performance, with many viewing the documentary that accompanied it on worldwide television. The performances are magnificent, with Norman singing at the height of her considerable powers. But Karajan's best efforts all stem from the mid '70s, previously released in discs coupling Bruckner and Strauss, now criminally withdrawn. These are the conductor's best recordings, and we can only hope EMI comes to its senses and re-releases them. The sound is much better than on the original Angel CDs, which left the impression of a sonic diffusion that was not what was recorded. Their refurbishing was wonderful, allowing the flowers to bloom.

Ormandy wasn't recognized for the fabulous Wagnerian he was, and he definitely had the orchestra for it. The gargantuan, singularly possessive sound is overwhelming in both of his recordings. One provides stunning performances of *Valkyries, Magic Fire Music, Forest Murmurs, Entrance of the Gods into Valhalla, Dawn and Siegfried's Rhine Journey, Funeral Music, Immolation Scene* from *Twilight of the Gods,* and strangely, only the "Liebestod" from *Tristan* (♦RCA 61850). These recordings were unsatisfactory in their LP guise, with constricted and narrow sound. An earlier recording has the same *Valkyries, Tannhäuser*

Overture and *Fest March,* both halves of *Tristan* (with a sweep that has to be heard), Act 3 *Lohengrin,* and *Meistersinger* (♦Sony 38914). There are more where these came from, but this is all Sony offers for the moment (the same applies to RCA). But do sample Ormandy's Wagner; his way is quite unique. The Sony disc is budget-priced, so little harm can come from a purchase.

Finally, **Mehta** weighs in with a spectacular recording of the standard *Ring* excerpts. The NY Philharmonic was undergoing a transition in the early Mehta years, and his new hires had their effect—this is Wagner playing so pointed, rich, and powerful that it can stand comparison with any in the world. The sound is marvelous, clear as a bell, with all sonic fog dispelled. And at mid-price—well, you figure it out (♦Sony 44657).

DG's album of Wagneriana by assorted conductors and orchestras is very much a mixed blessing. I detest the practice of excising segments from the complete opera recordings; thus, in several of the *Ring* offerings, the normal, expected ending of one of these works dovetails into the next section of the opera, then is faded out by the engineer, a wholly unacceptable practice. In *Tristan,* Böhm's 1966 Bayreuth recording is used for the Prelude, and the Vienna Philharmonic studio recording for the "Liebestod," making for a rather disconcerting juxtaposition. Highlights include a breathless *Dutchman* and sturdy *Meistersinger* with Böhm, an evocative *Rhine Journey* with Karajan, and a gorgeous Act 1 Prelude to *Parsifal* with Jochum. But these and everything else on this disc are equaled or excelled by others.   RITTER

William Walton (1902–1983)

Walton's musical talent was his ticket out of his dingy northern industrial home town. At the age of 12 he became a chorister in Christ Church Cathedral, where he encountered not only church music but, thanks to a far-seeing tutor, the works of Stravinsky, Debussy, and Prokofiev. Soon after, he began to compose on his own, partly in an attempt "to make myself interesting somehow" after his voice changed. Essentially self-taught, his early efforts were remarkably mature; his anthem "Drop, Drop, Slow Tears" and the Piano Quartet offer plenty of clues to the mature composer.

In his early 20s, Walton took up with the highly (and self-consciously) artistic Sitwell family; the well-connected trio of Edith, Osbert, and Sacheverell gave him entrée into London society and the leisure to pursue composition at his own pace (usually slow). Edith also gave Walton the bizarre and original poems he set for speaker and chamber ensemble as *Façade,* whose first performance in 1924 was a succès de scandale and put Walton on the cultural map in England. This jazzy, clever music wasn't nearly as avant-garde as many said, so it wasn't surprising that his next big work, a viola concerto, was primarily lyrical and quite traditional in style. *Belshazzar's Feast* (1931) turned the dowdy, earnest Victorian oratorio into a De Millean Biblical spectacular, and Symphony 1, whose prolonged composition created an amazing atmosphere of anticipation, was hailed by British critics as the equal of Beethoven and, more accurately, Sibelius. This is music so masterly in workmanship and individual in sonority that the adjective "Waltonian" immediately conjures up its essential qualities: wit, dashing and brilliant orchestral color, sure craftsmanship, lyricism, and emotional appeal.

Walton had the good fortune, or perhaps the misfortune, to hit it big in his 20s and early 30s, producing a string of outstanding works that remained his best known. His wartime music included the Violin Concerto, commissioned by Heifetz, and acclaimed scores for Laurence Olivier's films of *Henry V* and *Hamlet.* His later works were often greeted with some disappointment as skillful rehashes of familiar elements, and his conservative musical style definitely went against the fashions of the times. But times change, and have proved such late works as the Cello Concerto (1956), Symphony 2 (1960), and *Variations on a Theme of Hindemith* (1963) to be as satisfying as the earlier ones: conservative, perhaps, but beautifully written, and every bar could be taken for no other composer.

Walton may have played down his talent (he once told an interviewer that he became a composer "because I was too damned stupid to do anything else"), but he never played it false. His biographer Michael Kennedy compared him to Flaubert in his single-minded concentration on his art, which led him to constantly revise successful works. So brilliant, individual, and enjoyable a composer deserves a high place in 20th-century music.

SYMPHONIES

1. Like most of Walton's music, No. 1 didn't come easily. In fact, only three movements were completed in time for the work's first performance in 1934. Finished or not, it was hailed as a profound and brilliantly constructed work, and even more so when it was performed with its finale in 1935. This is truly one of the best 20th-century symphonies, a grand, powerful work in the tradition of Sibelius (very much in the British air in the '30s) or contemporary works by Shostakovich and Prokofiev.

Recordings soon followed. **Harty's** 1935 performance still conveys a sense of excited discovery and is still worth hearing (Dutton 8003, with Frederick Riddle's Viola Concerto). **Walton** himself recorded it with the Philharmonia in the '50s (NA), and there have been many good stereo recordings (EMI has produced no fewer than seven over the years). The classic is probably the 1967 London Symphony recording by a young **Previn,** which established him as an outstanding Walton interpreter and is still rightly considered one of the best of his many recordings (RCA 7830). Previn also made a digital version, a worthy performance of lower voltage but sumptuously recorded (Telarc, with splendid renditions of the *Orb and Sceptre* and *Crown Imperial* marches).

The best of the current crop are a predictably brilliant and intense **Rattle** (EMI 56592, with a whopping coupling in an urgent performance of *Belshazzar's Feast*) and a slightly less taut but highly expressive **Paul Daniel** (Naxos 553180). Daniel has produced a Walton series for this label including both symphonies and concertos, and they're all worth getting. A nice surprise in the super-budget category comes from **Leaper** conducting the Canary Islands Philharmonic in a solid, energetic performance (Arte Nova 39124).

2 (1962). Coolly received, its first recording was made not by a British conductor but by **Szell** and the Cleveland Orchestra (Sony 62753, with *Variations on a Theme of Hindemith,* NA in the US). Walton found both performances "flawless in every aspect," and they remain remarkable demonstrations of virtuoso conducting and playing. Szell's lack of sentimentality keeps No. 2 from sounding too lush, and his sense of musical architecture makes both works sound like worthy successors to No. 1. They remain the best recordings of both and are worth a search.

The runners-up, however, are very good. **Previn** is more romantic than Szell (EMI, a "two-fer" including a worthy 1 with Haitink, an excellent Violin Concerto from Haendel, and a beautiful Cello Concerto from Tortelier). **Daniel** makes the English Northern Philharmonia sound almost as alert and brilliant as the Cleveland (Naxos 553402, with a very fine Viola Concerto). **Bryden Thomson** is less satisfying (Chandos); his slowish speeds and the sumptuous recording make the work sound a little too luscious and enervated (ditto the coupling, a suite from *Troilus and Cressida*).

OTHER ORCHESTRAL MUSIC

Besides the symphonies, Walton's largest exercises in pure orchestral music are *Variations on a Theme of Hindemith* (1963) and *Improvisations on a Theme of Benjamin Britten* (1970). Both are tributes to esteemed colleagues, and both are concise, ingenious works on their own, full of musical subtleties that surface with repeated listening. The Hindemith work has the unshowy solidity we associate with that composer, and in his Britten tribute, Walton nicely captured the spare, luminous orchestral sound of a composer quite different from himself.

As noted above, the best *Hindemith Variations* remains **Szell**'s (Sony), but since it's not readily available in the US, **Daniel**'s performance is a more than acceptable substitute (Naxos). To date the only recordings of the *Britten Improvisations* have been **Previn**'s, now coupled with *Belshazzar's Feast* and two lively Walton overtures in a very recommendable CD (EMI 64723), and **Thomson**'s, with the entertaining *Partita for Orchestra* and Wallfisch's excellent account of the Cello Concerto (Chandos 8959).

In addition to these largish sets of variations, Walton wrote many short and extremely pleasing orchestral works; chips from the workbench, perhaps, but chips of the highest quality wood and workmanship. Like Berlioz, he produced a number of short, dazzling orchestral overtures. At 23, his lively *Portsmouth Point* was performed to great acclaim and hasn't left the repertoire since. Several years later came the even livelier, more sophisticated, and charming *Scapino*, commissioned by the Chicago Symphony. **Previn**'s peppy recording of both overtures is coupled with his exciting first recording of *Belshazzar's Feast* (EMI 64723). In the '50s, Walton wrote a *Johannesburg Festival Overture* incorporating native African tunes and percussion. For many years **Walton**'s own recording was the only one; **Daniel**'s is a brightly recorded successor to it, serving as a colorful prelude to his outstanding disc of the Viola Concerto and Symphony 2 (Naxos 553402).

Thomson offers a disc of most of the short pieces, alert and richly recorded. Besides the overtures mentioned above, there is the sparkling *Capriccio Burlesco*, written in 1967 for the New York Philharmonic (an undiscovered gem among Walton's later works), and the first recording of his very last work, a gnomic, shadowy *Prologo e Fantasia* written for Rostropovich and the National Symphony (Chandos 8968).

Other short orchestral works include the very popular coronation marches *Crown Imperial* and *Orb and Sceptre*, the first written for George VI, the second for Elizabeth II. Their tuneful, richly orchestrated pageantry makes them worthy successors to Elgar's famous *Pomp and Circumstance* marches. Outstanding among the many recordings are **Walton**'s own, in mono; **Previn**'s lavishly played and recorded versions, coupled to an underpowered account of Symphony 1 (Telarc); and **Willcocks**'s, with other pleasing examples of Walton at his most "English," including the lively cantata *In Honour of the City of London* (Chandos 8898). Both pieces predictably show up regularly at Proms Concerts, and you can hear them played in that context in "Rule Brittania!," with English items by Elgar, Parry, and others—essential for Anglophiles (Naxos 8553981).

One of Walton's most treasurable pieces is *The Wise Virgins*, arrangements of pieces from Bach cantatas for a Frederick Ashton ballet. Using a fairly large modern orchestra, they're often compared to Stokowski's Bach arrangements, but Walton's are much less technicolored, in fact a model of restraint in comparison. The highlight of the suite is the delicate, inspired arrangement of "Sheep may safely graze" (sometimes played separately). There are two current recordings: **Thomson**'s is coupled with a Walton obscurity, the ballet *The Quest* (Chandos 8871), while **Robert Irving**'s is paired with his vintage recordings of an equally tasty 18th/20th century confection, the Scarlatti/Tommasini *Good Humored Ladies,* and Glazunov's tuneful ballet *The Seasons* (EMI 65911).

FILM MUSIC

Walton wrote music for movies throughout his entire career, for financial as well as artistic satisfaction. In the process he joined forces with the great actor and director Laurence Olivier and completed brassy, sumptuous scores for three Shakespearian films that are not only effective as background scores but contain some of his most colorful and characteristic music: *Henry V, Hamlet,* and *Richard III*. **Walton** conducted a celebrated recording of selections from all three in the '60s (EMI LP 30139 or 5246), but they have more recently had a lively life as "Shakespeare Scenarios" devised by Christopher Palmer, combining orchestra with actors declaiming selections from the plays, and in the case of *Henry V*, with a chorus, used sparingly. They're played by Marriner and the Academy of St. Martin in the Fields.

Henry V is the most famous of the three and usually considered a high-water mark of movie music—Shakespeare in sound. As with most film scores, playing it nearly whole (as in the "Scenario") diminishes it somewhat. There are plenty of tedious background bits, but there are also many beautiful passages, as profoundly English as Prokofiev's *Alexander Nevsky* is profoundly Russian. In the recording of the whole thing led by **Marriner,** Christopher Plummer declaims magnificently, the Academy of St. Martin in the Fields plays splendidly, and the chorus sings its heart out (♦Chandos 8892).

The suite from *Henry V* contains most of the goodies from the score (including two short, quiet, but very moving pieces for strings), and **Previn**'s satisfying performance with the Royal Philharmonic is an appropriate filler for *Belshazzar's Feast* (♦Intaglio 6701862). There is an equally pleasing and similar-sounding suite from *Richard III*, recorded by **Herrmann**—a nice tribute from one master of movie music to another, and quite spectacularly recorded (London 455156, with two more worthy film scores, Rósza's *Julius Caesar* and Shostakovich's *Hamlet*).

Famous as *Henry V* is, Walton's gloomy score for Olivier's *Hamlet* is perhaps his best, crowned by a magnificent Funeral March. Palmer devised another "Scenario" for this music, and the combination of declamation and music works even better, with more substantial music and fewer longueurs. **Marriner** also recorded *Hamlet,* this time with the late John Gielgud, again an impeccable performance musically and verbally (♦Chandos 8842). There's a respectable budget alternative conducted by **Andrew Penny,** with a much younger Hamlet in Michael Sheen (Naxos 8553344).

Both these *Hamlet* recordings are coupled with a fourth Shakespeare-Olivier-Walton score: *As You Like It,* a delightful example of what this composer could do in the English-pastoral vein. There's also an outstanding mid-priced sampler of Marriner's four recordings (♦Chandos 7041). He has recorded plenty of Walton's other film music, including a swaggering performance of Walton's best-known non-Shakespearian movie item, *Spitfire Prelude and Fugue* (Chandos 8870). This was also recorded by **Walton** (EMI LP 30139 or 5246) and **Paul Daniel** (Naxos 8553869, with *Sinfonia Concertante* and *Variations on a Theme by Hindemith*).

CONCERTOS

All three concertos for strings are substantial works, similar in structure: a rather slow, lyrical opening movement with agitated interruptions; a brief, brilliant scherzo; and a long movement in moderate tempo that acts as an emotional and musical summing-up. The composer took great pains with all of them, and was rewarded with popularity—less quickly than in the case of the Violin and Cello Concertos, but now all three are among the most-performed 20th-century works in this genre.

Cello. The Cello Concerto, written for Piatigorsky in 1956, is perhaps the subtlest and darkest-hued of Walton's concertos. Its opening, a lulling melody for the cello against tick-tocks in the orchestra set off by vibraphone chords, is the most haunting of the three. After a slow start, it caught on with cellists as well as conductors, since, like its predecessors, it offers plenty of interest for the orchestra. And like its predecessors, it has plenty of good recordings, starting with **Piatigorsky**'s own, with Munch conducting the Boston Symphony (RCA 61498). With its abundance of slow tempos and melancholy mood, it can seem soft-centered, but this original performance is rather tough, with fairly fast tempos. RCA's sound was fiercely up front on LP but has been tamed considerably for the CD, generously coupled with an even more propulsive Piatigorsky-Munch Dvořák Concerto.

Most other recordings emphasize what one critic happily called its "lotus-eating" qualities; the best of them, like **Ma** with Previn (Sony 39541), **Wallfisch** with Thomson (Chandos 8959), or **Tim Hugh** with Daniel (Naxos 554325), balance lassitude with energy. (This isn't necessarily true of their conductors; Previn and Thomson underline the music's lushness, but are much less pointed than Daniel.) The combination of **Julian Lloyd Webber** and Marriner works like a charm here, the conductor's precision matching the soloist's romantic passion (Philips 454442). Fans of the Walton may not like Britten's longer, drier Symphony for Cello and Orchestra (Walton didn't), but the soloist and conductor also do this difficult piece most persuasively, and the recording presents these very different works with wonderful clarity.

Piano. Before the three string concertos, Walton wrote his *Sinfonia Concertante* for piano in the '20s—twice. The first version, for piano and jazz band, he destroyed, at least according to his friend, the composer Constant Lambert. The second version survived, and while it's hardly performed as often as the others, it has been recorded several times and is enjoyably Waltonian in its tunes, rhythms, and high spirits. The recording in Paul Daniel's series, with **Peter Donohoe** a muscular soloist, is an excellent bargain, considering that the other big work on the CD is the beautiful *Variations on a Theme of Hindemith* (Naxos 553869). **Eric Parkin**'s performance is part of an entertaining collection of Walton's jazz- and popular-influenced music, including the orchestral suites from *Façade* and the delightful south-of-the-border miniature *Siesta* (Chandos 9148).

Viola. Listeners to *Façade* or *Portsmouth Point* who considered Walton brilliant but shallow had to reconsider after hearing his 1929 Viola Concerto (first played by no less than Paul Hindemith). A work of definite brilliance but profound feeling expressed in a very individual voice, it was almost immediately accepted as perhaps the greatest concerto ever written for the viola and is still accepted as such eight decades later, when the competition is stiffer. If there seem to be a surprising number of recordings, it's because all violists play it; it's to their repertoire what the Beethoven and Brahms concertos are to violinists.

There are two versions of this work: In 1964 Walton decided to lighten and brighten the orchestration, reducing the brass and adding a harp.

Most recordings are of the newer version, but the darker, more restrained original is effective and appropriate. The great violist **Primrose** recorded the original twice: in 1946 for EMI with Walton conducting (Dutton, with the first recording of Symphony 1), and in the '50s with Sargent (Columbia).

Among recordings of the second version, **Nigel Kennedy** (before he dropped his first name) plays the Viola and Violin Concertos with virtuosity, affection, and style, abetted by Previn (EMI 49628). **Menuhin** recorded it in 1968 with Walton conducting, but to much less assured effect (EMI). The estimable **Imai,** with conductor Jan Latham-König, plays the lyricism of this piece for all it's worth, and while the slower sections are quite a bit slower than Walton's indications, the sumptuous result is hard to resist (Chandos 9106). Closer to the Waltonian norm, and playing with a smallish, finely focused tone that brings the music's melancholy home, **Lars Anders Tomter** is accompanied by Daniel (Naxos 553402). At its bargain price, and coupled with Daniel's first-class performance of Symphony 2, this is worth getting even if you decide on one of the others.

Violin. The 1939 Violin Concerto sounds like the Viola Concerto with its defenses down; written for Heifetz, it's more lyrical, more virtuosic, even more sumptuous, and even more swankily orchestrated. Not as exalted as the Viola Concerto is in its repertoire, it's still one of the most enjoyable 20th-century concertos if the soloist can summon up enough style and lustrous tone, while maintaining a degree of gravity that is definitely beneath the music's sophisticated high gloss.

As with the Viola Concerto, the composer rewrote the piece considerably after its first performances. **Heifetz** recorded the Walton Concerto twice. The only recording of the original is his 1941 performance, predictably brilliant but surprisingly warm, with Goossens and the Cincinnati Symphony (Biddulph 016); he set down the second version in the '50s with Walton conducting (RCA). Heifetz may be authoritative, but there are quite a few excellent modern recordings. Besides **Kennedy**'s, there are, in approximate chronological order: **Chung** with Previn (London/Decca 460014, with the Beethoven Concerto; the young violinist's elegant performance, also her looks, had Walton's enthusiastic approval); **Haendel** with Berglund (EMI 64202, with an equally rich performance of Britten's Violin Concerto); **Mordkovitch** with Latham-König (Chandos 9073, with the Violin Sonata arranged, not altogether convincingly, for orchestra); **Bell** and Zinman (London 452851, cannily coupled with its songful American cousin, Barber's Concerto); **Tasmin Little** with Litton (London 444114); and **Dong-Suk Kang** with Daniel (Naxos 554325, with the Cello Concerto).

You could reach into the CD bin blindfolded and pick a good one: these violinists all match elegant showmanship with juicy tone, the conductors have Walton's style down pat, and the recordings are rich and full. I think the couplings should determine your choice, or perhaps the price; Chung's is mid-priced and Kang's is budget-priced.

CHAMBER MUSIC

Walton wrote very little chamber music, only three works in fact. The early Piano Quartet is impressive stuff for a 16-year-old and quite listenable. The not-quite-assimilated influences include Ravel and Vaughan Williams. With his string of orchestral and choral successes, Walton didn't really take up chamber music until after WWII, producing two beautiful works: a string quartet and a violin sonata for Menuhin. This is unusually refined music even for Walton, and has an underlying melancholy that gives it a unique place in his output.

The Piano and String Quartets are coupled in red-blooded performances by the **Maggini Quartet** and pianist Donohoe (Naxos), or you can hear the former with the Violin Sonata from **Kenneth Sillito** and friends (Chandos 8999). The **Hollywood Quartet**'s magnificent mono recording (the work's first) is available, in the congenial company of quartets by Hindemith and Prokofiev (Testament 1052). The **Coull Quartet** couples it with the equally elegiac Elgar Quartet (Hyperion 66718), and the **Endellion Quartet** offered a finely etched performance, with an excellent coupling in Frank Bridge's visionary Quartet 3 (Virgin 59026). The Violin Sonata benefits from **Lorraine McAslan**'s juicy tone and openly emotional playing (ASV 6191, with an equally convincing Elgar Sonata).

CHORAL MUSIC

Belshazzar's Feast bowled the audience over at its premiere in 1931, and it's hardly less exciting now. There's plenty of flash in this piece, but profoundly emotional passages too, in the lamentation of the enslaved Hebrews. It's easy and more immediately impressive for a conductor to emphasize the former over the latter, but an ideal performance balances both. **Walton** recorded it twice, in mono and stereo (and sat in on more than one session with other conductors, notably Previn and Solti), and to many he remains the ideal interpreter of this work (EMI LP 32036 or 5246, unfortunately NA).

Litton's gutsy and splendid recording boasts perhaps the best soloist of all, Bryn Terfel (London 448134, with *Henry V Suite*). Both of **Previn**'s recordings are still available: His 1972 London Symphony performance with Shirley-Quirk works up quite a lather; his Royal Philharmonic version with Luxon is just as good and has a more detailed and lucid recording (Carlton 6701862, with *Henry V Suite*). **Willcocks**'s tempos are the closest to Walton's, making this performance as musically satisfying as any (Chandos 8760). However, the "warm bath" acoustic of most Chandos recordings isn't ideal for all of Walton's music, particularly this piece. The couplings, though, are ideal: Walton's snazzy settings of *Te Deum* (first sung at Queen Elizabeth II's coronation) and *Gloria*. **Hickox** offers a fine performance with an equally interesting coupling, the cantata *In Honour of the City of London* (Classics for Pleasure 2225).

Ormandy's excellent rendition with the Philadelphia Orchestra and Temple University Choir is a surprise, none too subtle, maybe, but full of drama and energy, with the orchestra digging in (Sony 63039). The coupling (Mahler's *Kindertotenlieder*, sung by Tourel) is bizarre but a first-class performance, and it's hard to resist at its budget price.

Befitting a former chorister, Walton also wrote a significant amount of a cappella music throughout his career. **Darlington** leading the Christ Church Cathedral Choir (of which Walton was an alumnus) offers sensitive performances of most of it in an appropriate church acoustic, from Walton's first acknowledged composition, *Drop, Drop Slow Tears*, to some late church music, including some delectable little songs and carols (Nimbus 5364).

OPERA

Walton toiled mightily over almost all his music, but never more than on his grand opera *Troilus and Cressida*, which took seven years from idea to stage. Initial reviews ranged from ecstatic to cautiously approving, and the composer's reputation ensured an initial run of performances, but the work never really caught on. He revised the words and music thoroughly after librettist Charles Hassall's death, and completely rewrote the original soprano part of Cressida so mezzo-soprano Janet Baker could sing it at Covent Garden in 1976. Audiences liked the opera well enough, but the reviews were even more lukewarm, and it remains Walton's biggest disappointment.

Troilus and Cressida contains some genuinely beautiful music in a red-blooded Puccinesque fashion, but dramatically it never takes off, and perhaps it's best experienced in a recording. An Opera North revival offers the final version, incorporating Walton's structural revisions but reinstating the lead for soprano, by all accounts more effective (Chandos 9370). With the sympathetic **Hickox** in charge and a uniformly strong cast, this is probably as good as it's apt to get.

Walton never recorded the complete opera, but he did conduct excerpts with Richard Lewis and **Schwarzkopf**; she was his original choice to play Cressida, but her English is iffy and she's often overparted by the richly scored music (Angel LP, NA). **Baker** and the rest of the 1976 revival cast recorded it (EMI, NA), and a suite of some of the more sumptuous moments was recorded by **Thomson** (Chandos, with the contemporaneous Symphony 2). All in all, not a bad track record for one of 20th-century opera's near-misses.

Walton's one-act *The Bear*, an adaptation of a Chekhov farce written for the Aldeburgh Festival, was a happier experience. It's silly and entertaining, and the fast-paced, sparkling music includes some nifty parodies of Britten and Stravinsky among others. This is one of the brightest spots in the Chandos Walton series, done to a turn by Della Jones, Alan Opie, and Shirley-Quirk, with **Hickox** bringing out every detail in the music (Chandos 9245).

SONGS

This is as good a place as any to put Walton's most famous piece, *Façade*. Scandalous it may have been in the '20s, but it now seems simply very clever and entertaining, in both Edith Sitwell's rhythmic, allusive poems and the sophisticated musical response they drew from the 20-year-old Walton.

For many aficionados, the original 1929 recording with Walton conducting and Constant Lambert and **Sitwell** as the reciters has never been surpassed, and it certainly has the air of authenticity (Symposium 1203, with other British music of the '20s). (Sitwell re-recorded it in the '50s with Peter Pears, NA.) An outstanding modern version presents **Lynn Redgrave** as an excellent speaker, rhythmically precise and full of character but never overdoing it; the same can be said for the members of the Chamber Music Society of Lincoln Center who accompany her (Arabesque 6699). Walton added to, subtracted from, and rearranged *Façade* throughout his life, and every item is included in a disc by **Pamela Hunter** and the Melologos Ensemble (Discover 920125). This is valuable for more than completeness; it's an excellent, clearly recorded performance and worth investigating at its budget price.

Solo songs are rare in Walton's output. There are a couple of early efforts and arrangements for soprano and piano of three numbers from *Façade*. His other works for solo voice are cycles, delectable both musically and verbally: *Anon in Love* for voice and guitar, written for Peter Pears and Julian Bream (also orchestrated by the composer) and *A Song for the Lord Mayor's Table*, originally performed in 1964 by Schwarzkopf and Gerald Moore. Happily, **Pears** and Bream recorded *Anon in Love*, re-released in an engaging mid-priced collection of 20th-century music for voice and guitar (RCA 61601). Walton's orchestration of this piece is sung by **Martyn Hill**, along with *A Song for the Lord Mayor's Table*, the *Façade* songs with soprano Jill Gomez, and some other interesting vocal odds and ends (Chandos 8824).　　　　　　　　　　　RAYMOND

John Ward (*c. 1571–c. 1638*)

Ward deserves better than to be the somewhat shadowy figure he is to most of us. During his relatively long life—for those times—the greater talent of Orlando Gibbons came and went, but the best of Ward's music stands up to comparison with that of Gibbons. Had the then Prince of Wales not died inopportunely in 1612, Ward's patron Sir Henry Fanshawe would have had preferment and so would the composer, on his coat-tails.

It was that genius of early music, **Alfred Deller,** who first alerted the world to Ward's qualities, with recordings of three madrigals. You can still obtain that recital and the performances by the Deller Consort have a magic only they could distill (Vanguard 8103, with music by Byrd and Gibbons). Five madrigals recorded in 1998 by the **Trinity Consort** don't have quite the same impact (Beulah 2, with music by Byrd, Alfonso Ferrabosco, etc.).

The 1984 disc of madrigals and viol fantasies by the **Consort of Musicke** under Rooley promises more than it delivers, although with Kirkby on the top line and the firm Richard Wistreich on the bottom the singing has much to recommend it (Musica Oscura 070981). The problem is the resonant acoustic of Forde Abbey. The program is also badly arranged, with seven madrigals followed by seven instrumental pieces—and viol playing has moved on apace in the past 16 years. The companion disc of psalms and anthems, recorded four years later, is infinitely more satisfying. This time the acoustic is better handled and the performances have a missionary zeal that carries all before it. The soloists, led by Kirkby, are excellent; so is the chorus, and the viols are palpably more engaged than in 1984. The music, with its constant use of imitation, could mostly be by Gibbons, so anyone who has run out of Gibbons pieces to enjoy should hasten to investigate this superb disc (Musica Oscura 070982).   POTTER

Peter Warlock (1894–1930)

Warlock, born Philip Heseltine, is widely regarded as the greatest English song composer since Purcell and Arne. His scope was broad, and his inspiration was kindled by the elegiac, the amorous, the supernatural, the dipsomaniac, or whatever else struck his fancy: Shakespeare and the minor Elizabethans, poets of his own time (notably Yeats and Belloc), or a multitude of folk songs. He also wrote choral music and was an accomplished and enthusiastic carolist. Once heard, the best of his melodies are eternally haunting. They spring out of the natural rhythms and inflections of the poet's words, but like Wolf's, they're also singable and memorable. His folksy, boisterous side may be a problem for Americans, who are likely to quail at the prospect of yet another "Hey diddle," "Hoyda," or "Rantum Tantum," but many of the serious songs are deeply affecting and delightfully original.

Warlock's masterpiece is *The Curlew,* settings of four Yeats poems for tenor, string quartet, flute, and English horn. Yeats didn't like Warlock's music any more than Goethe liked Schubert's, but posterity has taken the composers' sides. Warlock captures the spirit of the poems perfectly, and his instrumental accompaniments are aptly bleak and atmospheric. Perhaps the best of all recordings of *The Curlew* was **Alexander Young**'s in the early '50s, now long out of print (Argo). His eloquent diction, telling nuances, and strong, well-focused voice are impossible to forget. Young included 12 additional songs with piano, and if you need to be reassured that the English language can actually sound beautiful in itself, listen to him sing "Sweet and Twenty." It may seem cruel to praise an unavailable recording, but take my accolades as an urgent plea for its reissue.

There is, fortunately, no shortage of other fine *Curlew*s. **Partridge** is earnest and sensitive, though his monochrome, featherweight voice is pallid (EMI). A collection of 12 piano-accompanied songs on a different label serves Warlock better; here Partridge is sensitive and engaging,

and his selections are choice (♦Etcetera 1078). **James Griffett** (Pearl) is another lightweight, but he brings to *The Curlew* some of the crispness and ring Partridge lacks, as well as a becoming youthfulness. **Martyn Hill** (Arte Nova) is also wan—even the one or two spoken lines veer toward the inaudible—but his very fragility is touching, and his recording is the least expensive of all. It's recommendable, but not for the sake of *The Curlew* (see below).

Ainsley comes closest to filling Young's shoes (♦Hyperion 66938). His is a handsome and substantial voice, well defined and smoothly produced, and his readings of the poems are as eloquent as Partridge's or Thompson's. His disc includes not only the two best-known orchestral compositions but also a bonanza of 15 songs in arrangements for tenor and string quartet. Ainsley has another Warlock disc to his credit: A slightly earlier recital has piano-accompanied songs only, 34 in all, mostly in a serious vein (♦Hyperion 66736). Here are some of Warlock's greatest songs, and Ainsley's two records make the demise of Young's seem less catastrophic.

Adrian Thompson is thin and reedy but not without bite and clarity. What makes his recording worthwhile is the assortment of songs that fills out the disc (♦Collins 15002). He shares them with **Christopher Maltman,** a baritone of lucid diction and keen imagination. Maltman's tone is basically appealing, but he's unable to keep the wobbles away. Since Thompson is also shaky, the recital profits from the contrast between the two voices; when we tire of one, the other brings surcease. **Luxon,** a light baritone, and **Norman Bailey,** a renowned Wotan, offer the best of the recordings that omit *The Curlew*. Luxon sings 32 songs, clearly and straightforwardly, in a relaxed if slightly bland manner (Chandos). More imposing and personable is Bailey (♦Belart 461608). He's magisterial in a Hotter-like way, and he imparts to many of the songs (26 in all) a gravity that eludes the lighter tenors, but he also has plenty of swagger for the folksy numbers.

By and large, female singers haven't been drawn to Warlock. That leaves **Ruth Golden** in a class of her own (Koch). She's not an ideal interpreter—her voice grows too fulsomely operatic when the tessitura rises—but her words are clear (in mid range), her tone sweet, her delivery sincere and often touching in detail. Many Warlock songs can be found, two or three at a time, on various anthology discs. The avid collector might want to seek out English song recitals from Ferrier (Decca), Baker (Saga), Elizabeth Ritchie (IMP), Roy Henderson (Dutton), Pears (Belart), Rolfe Johnson (IMP), Graham Trew (Hyperion), and Bostridge (EMI). The composer's antic side was best served by "A Peter Warlock Merry-Go-Down," once on Unicorn and worthy of reissue.

Recordings of Warlock's choral music are in short supply. One of the best, from the **Elizabethan Singers,** was issued in 1972 on Pearl but has not survived. The "Warlock Centenary Album" includes, besides Partridge's account of *The Curlew* and a few miscellaneous songs, a brief sampling of choruses and carols along with the two orchestral pieces (♦EMI 65101). "The Frostbound Wood," a disc of Christmas music from the **Allegri Singers,** is highly desirable(♦Somm 11).

Warlock's two famous orchestral works are *Capriol Suite* (based on Elizabethan tunes) and *Serenade for String Orchestra* (dedicated to Delius). *Capriol* was scored for string orchestra or two pianos, but several performers have concocted arrangements of their own: the **Los Angeles Guitar Quartet** (Delos), **Equale Brass Ensemble** (Nimbus), and—rather elaborately—guitarist **Christopher Parkening.** The version for strings is included in the *Curlew* recordings by Ainsley (Hyperion) and Hill (Arte Nova). The Arte Nova disc also offers the only available recordings of six *English Tunes* and six *Italian Dance Tunes,* played by **Ross Pople** (♦37868). There's no dearth of other recordings of both *Capriol* and *Serenade*. **Marriner** leads deluxe performances (as good as any) in a set that also contains instrumental music by Butterworth and a generous selection of Vaughan Williams, Delius, and Elgar (♦Decca 452707, 2CD). LUCANO

Carl Maria von Weber *(1786–1826)*

If Weber did not single-handedly create the Romantic Era with his operas *Der Freischütz* and *Oberon*, he nevertheless brought to the stage an admirable blend of drama and lyricism, in many cases mingled with elements of the supernatural, and this is reflected in his overtures, which remain as popular in the concert hall as in the theater. His two symphonies seamlessly blend high spirits with flowing melody much in the manner of Schubert; if the fluency and grace of the works for piano (particularly the *Konzertstück*) almost go without saying—given that Weber was a pianist himself—the quality of the clarinet concertos is all the more remarkable as he never studied that instrument. Even setting aside the operas, Weber's two symphonies, the concertos, and a healthy sampling of his overtures should be in every collection.

SYMPHONIES

Weber wrote both of his symphonies at the age of 20 while in service to Duke von Württemberg-Öls of Karlsruhe, and not surprisingly they contain much graceful writing for the Duke's beloved oboe. But horn players can't complain of short measure; the horn chorale heard midway through the slow movement of No. 1 looks ahead to the "Wolf's Glen" scene of *Der Freischütz* and the final movement opens with glorious horn roulades.

There used to be a very fine LP with **Victor Desarzens** that approached the pellucid scoring of the Duke's house orchestra (Westminster 17034); fortunately, much of this intimate music-making comes across in two splendid recordings for period instruments, by **Roy Goodman** (♦Nimbus 5180) and **Roger Norrington** (♦EMI 55348). Of these, the remarkable Hanover Band horn section nearly makes up for the strident sound of the violins and the reverberant locale, in performances that give much pleasure. However, Norrington's strings, if hardly plush, come off better than Goodman's—especially the solo viola in the Adagio of No. 2—and his broadly assertive approach to both scores reaps rich dividends. Both conductors earn high marks for bringing out the puckish humor of the final Presto of 2, that last fillip by the bassoons in each case bringing a smile to the face where too many conductors simply hurtle past with scarcely a moment to take breath.

Most culpable in this regard is **Marriner** (Vanguard), while **Flor** is also too fast and unfortunately omits the repeat in 1:IV (RCA). Elsewhere Flor invests both scores with a gratifying vigor, but his *Freischütz* Overture—as good as it is—isn't much of a filler though it's more than you get from Marriner. The fillers are the best part about **John Georgiadis**'s performance, which includes a number of selections from *Turandot*, *Silvana*, and *Die drei Pintos* (Naxos). Perhaps conscious of Weber's debt to Beethoven (these two symphonies would fall somewhere between Beethoven's 5 and 6), Georgiadis is more sturdy, less buoyant than some, but it's his incredibly slow tempo in the Menuetto of No. 2 that drags everything down. **Sawallisch** is more *gemüutlich* than ebullient and omits the repeat in 2:I (Orfeo).

One recording has everything: **Hans-Hubert Schönzeler** brings out all the alert rhythms, the great good humor of this music, and he gets that little Presto in No. 2 just right (♦Guild 7138). Moreover, the early symphonies contrast nicely with the music from *Turandot*, which Hin-

demith transformed with such obvious affection and zest in his *Symphonic Metamorphoses.*

OVERTURES

And that leads to Weber's Overtures, the exotic *chinoiserie* of *Turandot* and sparkling Janissary music of *Abu Hassan* set beside the compelling drama of *Der Freischütz*, the wide-eyed fairyland of *Oberon*, the mysticism of *Euryanthe*, the Spanish coloring of *Preciosa*. There are 10 in all, though some were used over again; *Das Waldmädchen* became *Silvana*, while *Rübezahl* was recycled as *Der Beherrscher der Geister* (*Ruler of the Spirits*). Rounding out most collections is *Jubel* (*Jubilee*), concluding with the rousing strains of "Heil dir im Siegerkranz" (you'll recognize it as "God Save the Queen" or "My Country 'Tis of Thee"); if you're lucky, you'll also get *Peter Schmoll*, a pert oboe tune leading into a buoyant Allegro.

The only one to offer all 10 is **Neeme Järvi**, which he unfortunately achieves mainly by going way too fast in *Oberon* and (even worse) the otherwise unavailable *Silvana; Euryanthe* and *Peter Schmoll* fare better, but *Beherrscher der Geister* is strangely sluggish and there's too much striving for effect in *Der Freischütz*, while the crisp wind writing of *Abu Hassan* and *Preciosa* is all but swallowed up by cavernous sound (Chandos). You may find many of the same performances—including *Turandot*—in an earlier disc coupled with Hindemith's *Symphonic Metamorphoses*, but only *Euryanthe* and *Turandot* are worth the duplication (Chandos). If only **Skrowaczewski** had included *Silvana* and *Turandot*, his CD would sweep the board; it's more expansive perhaps in the lyrical passages but bubbling over in *Preciosa* and *Peter Schmoll* and closing out in sturdy fashion with *Jubel,* the Hallé players no doubt humming the British anthem all the while (♦IMP 1105).

The most notable thing about **Lawrence Foster**'s survey is not the splendid playing—we may take that as a given with the Birmingham orchestra—but the curious omission of the best known pieces, *Der Freischütz*, *Oberon*, and *Euryanthe*, here replaced by not one but two arrangements of *Invitation to the Dance*, the familiar Berlioz and the more elaborate Weingartner, whose splashes of percussion and contrapuntal display make it sound like a different piece entirely (Claves). **Goodman** is not as successful as he was with the symphonies, the pleasurable wind scoring quite overwhelmed by the strident strings (Nimbus). Those who don't mind a few slips and slides would be better off seeking out **Scherchen** in typical wing-and-a-prayer mode, though only six of the ten are included (Adès).

Two other classic sets from LPs are available: **Karajan**, filled out with the Berlioz arrangement of *Invitation to the Dance* (DG), and best of all, **Sawallisch;** no filler, but he gives you seven overtures in readings that still sound crisp and fresh (♦EMI 69572). **Suitner**'s half dozen (omitting *Der Freischütz*) have been augmented by Janowski in *Euryanthe*, but this isn't enough to recommend it over more substantial collections (Berlin).

CONCERTOS

Piano concertos. Both of Weber's piano concertos date from about the same time as the *Emperor*, yet though Weber was clearly inspired by Beethoven's score—which he purchased shortly before embarking on Concerto 2—these are far more unassuming, buoyant exercises, for all the swagger of the title "Grand Concerto" given to each of them. **Frager**'s winged traversals were included in the RCA LP set of the symphonies under Schönzeler, and I hope they will resurface soon; but they're played so beautifully by **Rösel** with superb support from Blomstedt that further comparisons seem superfluous (♦EMI 49177, remastered as Berlin

1058). Even where Weber seems somewhat less than inspired, as in the Hummel-like figurations of the final Rondo of 2, Rösel is clearly having so much fun it hardly matters, while the Dresden wind players dance with joy. Moreover, his bardic temperament is perfectly suited for the rather episodic *Konzertstück,* the forlorn maiden pining away until her lover returns triumphantly from the Crusades with banners flying, a glorious march in Weber's most winning manner.

Not surprising given his mastery of the Beethoven concertos, **Oppitz** does beautifully with all three pieces, imbuing this music with a healthy vigor, yet warmly poetic where called for and alternately rhapsodic and impetuous in the *Konzertstück;* only the appended *Polonaise Brillante* disappoints, sounding a bit four-square and stiff (♦RCA 68219). Colin Davis offers exemplary support from first to last. **Frith** does very well with both *Konzertstück* and *Polonaise,* but in the concertos he lavishes so much effort on the sheer beauty of the writing that the music doesn't really go anywhere (Naxos). Far better as a budget choice are the light and airy readings by **Dana Protopopescu** (Discover 920222). **Roland Keller** and **Siegfried Kohler** have resurfaced in Volume 7 of the "Romantic Piano Concerto" series (Vox). **Elizabeth Rich** offers an inspired coupling—Clara Schumann's concerto—but her ravishing tone avails little against Dennis Burkh's limp orchestral support (Centaur).

Demidenko is rhapsodic in the opening pages of the *Konzertstück,* then ruins everything by barreling through the final Presto, and unfortunately this is true of the concertos as well, which become hectic and slapdash (Hyperion). **Melvyn Tan** plays an instrument modeled on a fortepiano of Weber's time; it sounds more like a cimbalom, quite distracting the listener from his graceful reading (EMI, coupled with the symphonies under Norrington). Even worse is **Christopher Kite** playing an out-of-tune 1840 Viennese grand as filler for Chopin's Concerto 1, for which he uses an equally excruciating Broadwood once played—surely better—by Chopin himself (Nimbus). (Incidentally, it's a good idea to check the Liszt bin too, since he reworked both the *Polonaise Brillante*—that's his version mentioned above—and the *Konzertstück.* For example, the Polonaise may be found in **Leslie Howard**'s Vol. 1 of the Liszt concert works on Hyperion, while the *Konzertstück* is included in Vol. 2.)

Wind concertos. Those interested in Weber's output for winds need look no further than the impressive set with clarinetist **Dieter Klöcker** in the Clarinet Concertos and Concertino, the Bassoon Concerto and the delightful *Andante and Hungarian Rondo,* the Horn Concertino plus another for oboe and winds, Divertimento for Clarinet, Romances for bassoon and flute, and *Adagio and Rondo* for two clarinets, two French horns and two bassoons (♦Novalis 150104, 3CD). As if that weren't enough, Klöcker even offers a second version of Clarinet Concerto 1 incorporating changes made by both Weber and the work's dedicatee, Heinrich Baermann, with cadenzas supplied by Busoni. You can find more sumptuous sound elsewhere, but you won't find a more dedicated or comprehensive survey, and the three discs are also available separately.

If your primary concern is the clarinet concertos, there are several fine recordings coupling them with the Concertino, to the point that it seems pointless to try to pit one against another; among the top rank you'll find **David Shifrin** (Delos 3220), **Charles Neidich** (DG 435875), and **Emma Johnson** (ASV 747), a convenient way of obtaining all three pieces plus the *Grand Duo Concertante,* originally spread over several discs. Also worth your interest are **Paul Meyer,** robust and sure-footed (Denon); **Janet Hilton,** stylish if not the last word in sheer virtuosity (Chandos); and for good value, **Ernst Ottensamer** (Naxos).

Some may find Neidich on the brisk side, in which case the more mellow version with Neville supporting his son **Andrew Marriner** should be just the ticket (Philips). You may be fortunate enough to find **Benny Goodman** and Jean Martinon, appropriately coupled with Goodman's equally stylish Nielsen Concerto conducted by Morton Gould (RCA). **Antony Pay** is light and charming in a "period instrument" survey (Virgin). I should also note the performances of No. 1 by **Stoltzman** (RCA) and **Meyer** (EMI), supplemented by No. 2 with either **Thea King** (Hyperion) or **de Peyer** (Decca), if you prefer to mix and match.

Weber's output for bassoon is sparse outside the Novalis set, but **Klaus Thunemann** sets things aright with marvelous accounts of both the substantial Concerto and the *Andante and Hungarian Rondo,* the latter originally written for viola (and occasionally recorded in that form) but sounding much more delightful on the bassoon (Philips). **Valeri Popov** offers a typically Slavic, larger than life account of the Andante and Rondo (Chandos); but you'd be better off buying the classic version with **Bernard Garfield** and the Philadelphia under Ormandy in peak form, coupled with concertos by Mozart and Strauss (Sony).

The wide range of solo effects and tongue-in-cheek humor that characterize the Concertino for Horn require the utmost virtuosity, and that it obtains from **Hermann Baumann** (Philips, with the two Strauss concertos). **Anthony Halstead**'s nimble account adds to the pleasures of Goodman's disc of the symphonies (Nimbus). You may also find an excellent performance by **Zdeněk Tylšar,** combining the Weber with other fare including Schumann's wonderful *Concertstück for 4 Horns* (Supraphon).

It should also be noted for those with access to budget imports that a number of fondly remembered Turnabout LPs have been reissued in England on the Carlton Turnabout label; these include Piano Concertos 1 and 2, the Clarinet Concertos and Concertino, and a variety of other works, all very attractively played.

CHAMBER MUSIC

Weber's quintet for clarinet and strings is more of a mini-concerto than a chamber work, not a subtle or profound piece but highly entertaining. **Jon Manasse** and the Manhattan Quartet make it all seem easy (which it's not, not by a long shot) and the sound is very good (XLNT 18004, with *Grand Duo Concertant, Introduction, Theme and Variations*—attributed to Weber, though authorship is in doubt—and *Seven Variations on a Theme from "Preziosa"*). You can find the same program with **Ensemble Walter Boeykens,** solid performances if without quite the panache and no-holds-barred approach of Manasse (Harmonia Mundi 901481). **Kálmán Berkes,** Jandó, and the Auer Quartet offer one of the most satisfying accounts of these four pieces at any price (♦Naxos 553122). **David Shifrin** and colleagues are also recommended (Delos 3194). **Luc Fuchs** and colleagues omit *Introduction, Theme and Variations,* and the metallic clarinet sound and sluggish tempos are no incentive to settle for less (Gallo). You can get the same three pieces with **Janet Hilton** and the Lindsay Quartet, a model of ensemble if not as mellifluous as some (Chandos 8366).

Eduard Brunner with the Hagen Quartet pairs the clarinet quintets of Weber and Mozart, a short program but beautifully played (♦DG 419600). Another fine pairing is led by **Emma Johnson,** with splendid sound (♦ASV 1079). **Charles Neidich** and the Mendelssohn Quartet also pair Weber and Mozart in a beautiful recording (MusicMasters 60178), and the choice isn't an easy one, though Neidich adds variety by using a basset clarinet in the Mozart. In his later recording of the Weber with L'Archibudelli, he makes a splendid case for period instruments;

you'll never believe this is an old-style clarinet when it's played this beautifully (Sony 57968, with music by Hummel and Reicha). Another easily recommendable pairing of Weber and Mozart finds **Steven Karoff** with the Allegri Quartet (Collins 10872). Brunner offers *Grand Duo Concertant* and *Preziosa* Variations along with a far rarer work, Weber's Trio in G minor for flute, cello, and piano (Orfeo 187891), or you can get the Trio coupled even more effectively with Weber's Flute Sonatas Op. 10, played by **Aurèle Nicolet** and colleagues (Novalis 150065).

The Quintet and *Grand Duo Concertant* are joined with Mendelssohn's two Concert Pieces for clarinet, basset horn, and piano by **Kari Kriikku** and the New Helsinki Quartet; here too the discmates may be the selling point, though the performances throughout are first rate (Ondine 820). That also applies to **Paul Meyer** and the Carmina Quartet, who pair the Weber with Robert Fuchs's rarely heard Clarinet Quintet (clearly modeled after Brahms), which complements the Weber rather well (Denon 78801). **Stoltzman** and the Tokyo Quartet (♦RCA 68033) and **Eddie Daniels** and the Composers Quartet (Reference 40) both pair the Weber and Brahms Quintets, and again the choice is difficult; both artists display spectacular technique and enviable musicianship—all the more remarkable for Daniels, better known in some circles as a jazz musician—but Stoltzman adds just that much more shading and nuance, putting him ahead even though he throws in a few roulades in the finale (Weber didn't think of this). **Béla Kovács** with the Kodály Quartet offers an exceptional pairing in rich and lustrous sound (♦Hungaroton 31463).

Two recordings of the Piano Quartet merit mention, in both cases combined with works for winds. **Jean-Louis Haguenauer** and flutist Jean-Christophe Falala lead a session of joyous music-making, joining the Quartet with the Flute Trio and *Norwegian Variations* (Tympani 1007). **Philippe Corré** joins clarinetist **Jean-Louis Sajot** in the Piano and Clarinet Quartets and *Introduction, Theme and Variations* in pointed and nicely shaded readings of some delightful music (Pierre Verany 792021).

Weber's violin sonatas are brief but highly characterful; there are six, the shortest not quite five minutes in length. **Emmanuele Baldini** and his father Lorenzo play them with style and spirit (Agora 36, with *Norwegian Variations* and Mendelssohn's Sonata in F). There's also a fine version by **William Steck** and Lambert Orkis of the sonatas and *Norwegian Variations,* though without the Mendelssohn sonata (Gasparo 263). Flutist **Roberto Fabbriciani** with Massimiliano Damerini is less inviting; he plays only the sonatas (total disc length 47 minutes) and has problems with pitch (Arts 47566). The Flute Sonata in A-flat is a more substantial and dramatic work, though the flute often seems to be accompanist to the piano. It's played beautifully by **Emmanuel Pahud** and Eric Le Sage, with six Sonatinas originally written for piano but well suited for the flute (Valois 4751).

PIANO MUSIC

Weber's piano sonatas have always hovered on the fringe of the repertoire, nowhere resembling Beethoven's far more formidable essays, yet thoroughly rewarding on their own terms. **Ohlsson** offers all four plus *Invitation to the Dance, Rondo Brillante,* and *Momento Capriccioso* in stylish and elegant readings that beautifully present the florid figurations and near-operatic gestures of this immensely melodic music, and the plangent sound of his Bösendorfer is faithfully captured by the engineers (♦Arabesque 6584, 2CD)—though he doesn't entirely efface memories of **Leon Fleisher**'s LP of No. 4 (Epic). **Milne** substitutes *Po-*

lacca Brillante for *Momento Capriccioso;* he's a good deal freer than Ohlsson in the sonatas and his Steinway is far richer in tone (♦CRD 3485/86). **Brendel**'s account of No. 2 is scholarly and erudite, more a lecture in musicology than a performance (Philips 426439, with Brahms Ballades).

Lucia Marrucci and **Maurizio Galli** offer the complete works for piano 4-hands in a very well-filled CD—charming music, played ideally in a light, graceful, and rhythmically acute manner without the least affectation or condescension (Rodolphe 32521). For a few bucks more you can get Weber's entire output for piano on three discs ably performed by **Alexander Paley;** he is everywhere sympathetic to the needs of the music, but is let down by the engineers, with little or no bass resonance and jarring climaxes (Naxos 550988/90). **Eva Schieferstein** offers several nicely turned dances and other short pieces (Koch 6731). For historical collections, there are the classic **Richter** account of Sonata 3 (Ermitage 113), **Arrau** in 1 (RCA), and **Cortot** in 2 (Biddulph 002 or Music & Arts 662).

CHORAL MUSIC

Just as Weber's two symphonies combine classical tradition with the burgeoning Romantic style, so the two masses written in 1818–19 for his patron, the King of Saxony, may be seen as bridging the gap between the grand examples of Haydn and Mozart and the choral works of Mendelssohn and Schumann; there is reverence here, but there's joy as well. The first was written at about the same time as *Der Freischütz* and shares some melodic material—hence the name *Freischütz-Messe*—yet it's entirely devotional, as befits its commission for the feast of the King's patronage. The shorter *Jubel-Messe,* written for the golden wedding of the King, is properly joyous, with glorious writing for the horns in the "Sanctus."

The *Jubel-Messe* is led by **Roland Bader** and the *Freischütz-Messe* by **Ernst Ehret** in recordings that show their age, the former with sound that wavers throughout while the latter sounds shallow and the chorus recessed (Koch Schwann). They are likewise coupled by **Gerhard Wilhelm** and **Horst Stein** (EMI 47679); both works are far better recorded and sung, with both groups of soloists more mellifluous than their Koch counterparts. The Offertorium (*Gloria et Honore*) and *In Die Solemnitatis Vestrae* have been brought out in a different disc coupled with Schubert's *Stabat Mater* (Koch Schwann 313055).   HALLER

OPERAS

Weber has the ironic distinction of being a composer whose seminal importance in operatic history is universally affirmed but whose operas are seldom performed. Stereo recordings of *Abu Hassan* (CPO), *Silvana,* and *Peter Schmoll* (both Marco Polo) are available, and we once had an RCA account of Mahler's reworking of *Die drei Pintos.* The majestic *Euryanthe* has been recorded only once (originally EMI, later Berlin), and imperfectly at that. Everyone agrees *Der Freischütz* is a great opera, but the chances of seeing a staged performance in this country are slim. Recordings have come along at regular intervals, however, often enough to remind us how delightful the music is. Weber's last opera, *Oberon,* has enjoyed something of a revival lately, and the collector can now face the agreeable prospect of acquiring more than one recording.

Der Freischütz. It has four main singing roles: Agathe, Annchen, Max, and Caspar. No conductor on records has managed to put a first-rate singer in each part, but **Keilberth** probably comes closer than anyone else (♦EMI 69210, 2CD). His Max is the burly and sometimes oafish Rudolf Schock, a tenor whose popularity in Germany seems almost inexplicable to outsiders. His voice is strong rather than beautiful, but Schock has sound musical instincts and is an excellent vocal actor who knows how to put the words across. Karl Christian Kohn, the Caspar, also acts well and has the requisite agility. His voice is bone dry, but he's an energetic, believable villain. Prey makes the small role of Ottokar both noble and noticeable, and Frick is as effective as possible in the anticlimactic aria of the Hermit.

The ladies are the glory of this performance. Annchen is pretty much a sure-fire role, but Lisa Otto's vivacity and verbal elan are exceptional even so. Grümmer's Agathe is, quite simply, perfect. The voice, utterly individual in timbre, has a consoling, feminine softness, but it's also strong and well-defined (barring, perhaps, the high B, which doesn't quite pop out as resplendently as it should). She sustains the lines of her two arias with ethereal poise, and she has a unique way of uttering the words so they seem to glow from within. When she sings German, no one could possibly regard it as a harsh language. Keilberth's conducting is solid and correct if not really propulsive, and the Berlin Philharmonic plays marvelously. The CD sound is an improvement over the previous issues, and much of the dialog has been retained.

Jochum remains the best of the *Freischütz* conductors (♦DG 439717, 2CD). He brings exactly the right weight to the music without ever becoming ponderous, and he makes the most of both the drama and the composer's colorful orchestration. Richard Holm's Max doesn't substantially improve on Schock's. His voice is lighter and deployed with slightly more finesse, but he sounds taxed at times and his diction often veers toward the slurpy. Kurt Böhme's thunderous bass rumbles so ominously through Caspar's lines that he never has to reinforce his maliciousness by overacting. His voice is surprisingly flexible; it seems unimportant that it's not in any way beautiful. The Hermit is poor, but Wächter is a fine Ottokar. Streich's Annchen is slightly less personable than Otto's but more prettily sung. Seefried was past her best days when she recorded Agathe. The top notes don't come easily and she needs to stop too often for breath, but when she's in her comfortable middle register, she sings with the disarming directness of old, the words round and clear, the manner warm-hearted and engaging.

Von Matačić's recording brought us a second Max from Schock and what should have been a classic Caspar from Frick (Eurodisc). His black bass, never all that smooth around the edges, has gained some roughness and lost some solidity, but it still moves spryly and the words are thrust forth with point and panache. The American soprano Claire Watson knows how to sing Agathe's music, and she can govern the long lines of the two arias; but the timbre is a little too flat and pallid, especially in contrast with Grümmer or Seefried. Von Matačić is a fairly exciting conductor, and the Wolf's Glen scene, filled with gimmicky stereo effects, is really gripping.

Robert Heger's *Freischütz* has, I think, been underrated by most commentators (EMI). Gedda, as Max, etches a cleaner, firmer line than Schock or Holm. He's lyrical, articulate, and just a bit namby-pamby, which suits the character very well. Berry is a baritone rather than a bass, but he has Caspar's low notes, and his suavity adds a second dimension to someone who is, after all, human. Erika Köth is another charming, practiced Annchen, and Crass is a noble, sonorous Hermit. Agathe is Nilsson, not a natural choice for the role. She keeps her voice reined in, for the most part; it's remarkable how she fines down its Wagnerian amplitude in the two arias, which she shapes with care and understanding. Her coloratura is cautious, however, and she brings too much Turandot-like aloofness to her impersonation. Heger is a genial conductor, perhaps too broad and heavy in the opera's first scenes. The waltz that precedes Max's aria is pachydermatous, but the score's theatrical moments are rendered with conviction.

Carlos Kleiber is at the opposite pole (DG). This was his first opera recording and his least likable. He drives the music too vehemently, blasting away all traces of rollicking, peasant-like unsophistication. A separate cast of actors recites the dialogue with brusque, military precision. Kleiber relaxes only when the two ladies are singing, as if he wishes to emphasize that they live in a more refined world. His Max and Caspar have unattractive voices and spit the words out too emphatically. Crass repeats his exemplary Hermit. Mathis is an unusually full-bodied Annchen, one you can almost imagine stepping into Agathe's shoes — but not in this performance, where **Janowitz** sings the role better than anyone since Grümmer. Her voice doesn't have the same roundness and warmth, but it's stronger on top. The arias are sung with perfect control and composure, "Und ob die Wolke" so angelically ravishing it holds you spellbound. Janowitz and Mathis together are reason enough to acquire the recording, and anyone who likes Kleiber's rip-snorting Beethoven conducting might also be thrilled by his Weber — but my own preference is for more graciousness.

After Janowitz, the pure, radiant, German lyric soprano went right onto the endangered species list. Agathe may be a passive character, but *Der Freischütz* revolves around her nonetheless, and no performance can satisfy unless her arias — the most beautiful in the German Romantic repertory — are given their due. Their neglect leaves a hole at the opera's center. I pass quickly, therefore, over **Janowski** (EMI), who hotfoots it through the opera even more callously than Kleiber and whose Agathe is a disaster (though I'm sorry to ignore his Max, Peter Seiffert, and Annchen, Ruth Ziesak). The estimable **Colin Davis** is more sensitive, but his scrupulous ministrations can't compensate for poor casting (Philips).

Kubelik is at least sporadically enjoyable (London). Donath is a fetching Annchen, and Kollo's crisply enunciated Max sounds, appropriately, like a hero gone to seed. Peter Meven is an effective enough Caspar even though his baritonal voice is rather monochromatic and his consonants too soft. Behrens is too intelligent a singer and too fine an actress to fail as Agathe. Her voice is precariously supported and has no bottom at all. She strives stalwartly to keep the arias smooth and steady, but the effort is noticeable. Kubelik is sometimes slack, more often forthright and unobtrusive. Despite its shortcomings, this is the last acceptable *Freischütz* recording. Kubelik had faith in the opera, and unlike the conductors after him, he felt no need to tweak the score, apologize for it, or try to fix what wasn't broken in the first place. London's sound is notably excellent.

The best recordings of *Der Freischütz* have come out of Munich (Jochum, Heger, Kubelik) and Berlin (Keilberth, von Matačić). **Harnoncourt** should have been on that list, but his *Freischütz* is the most maddening of all (Teldec). His first act is wonderful: lively, incisive, unexaggerated. Salminen is the suavest of the Wagnerian-bass Caspars; Endrik Wottrich's youthful, ringing voice has just the right touch of neuroticism for Max; and Holzmair is the best Kilian I've ever heard. In Act 2, unfortunately, Harnoncourt is in the grip of one of his Ideas. He believes time should stop when Agathe sings (which is exactly what happens naturally when Grümmer or Janowitz arrives at the arias), and to drive home the point, he goes into slow motion.

Orgonasova has phenomenal breath control and knows how to float her lines, but her voice hasn't much shimmer and the words aren't always clear. Still, she might have been the best Agathe after Janowitz, but the music and the character disappear behind the technical exertion. Christine Schäfer's Annchen has some bite to go along with the vocal prettiness, but she doesn't bother to execute the trills of her first aria.

Moll, who might have been a great Caspar, sings the Hermit for the third time (after Kubelik and Davis). Harnoncourt's *Freischütz* may come to seem less nerve-racking in time, so I recommend it grudgingly as the most interesting recording in 15 years. Buy it, if only to read (in the accompanying booklet) the conductor's provocative thoughts on the opera before going back to Keilberth or Jochum.

Oberon. The best recordings of *Der Freischütz* were made before 1970, but *Oberon* wasn't recorded at all until 1971. **Kubelik** was the pioneering conductor, and he's at home in both the magical elfin music and the prophetic Wagnerian adumbrations (DG 435406, 2CD). The score doesn't actually demand Wagnerian voices, but dramatic sopranos from Flagstad to Farrell have found Rezia's "Ozean, du Ungeheuer" irresistible. Nilsson sings it thrillingly, in tones that seem to well up from great oceanic depths, but she also knows how to mute the power of her voice for Rezia's Prayer. I presume that sopranos of Weber's time would have been unfazed by the role's mild floridity, but Nilsson picks her way rather cautiously through the coloratura of the Act 1 finale.

Domingo made his first foray into German opera as Huon, and he brings flowing, Italianate tone and surprising agility to his first aria. His words are often unintelligible, but his singing is very beautiful indeed. The opera's title role is a small one, and Donald Grobe, a light *Spieltenor*, handles it capably. Capable as well is Julia Hamari as Fatima, and Prey's Scherasmin is still unmatched—he really brings the part to life. *Oberon* has a great deal of spoken dialog, and in this performance, a spurious character ("Droll") is added to deliver most of it. He's an irritating, effusive fellow, one who makes me glad CD players have remote controls with skip buttons.

James Conlon also has a cast of Wagnerians (♦EMI 54739, 2CD). Oberon himself is lent some muscle by Heldentenor Gary Lakes. Voight has a warmer, more feminine voice than Nilsson, but she's comfortable in the role's high tessitura, easily pours out floods of tone, and leaps smoothly across the wide intervals. Like Nilsson, her coloratura in Act 1 is gingerly. Heppner is a remarkable Huon, his passage-work clean and precise, his voice ringing and shiny, his words much clearer than Domingo's. The smaller parts are well managed, and Conlon addresses the music with respect and conviction. He includes an extra aria for Huon in an appendix. The dialogue is replaced by narration, an acceptable (but not ideal) solution. The libretto of *Oberon* was written in English—the opera had its first performance in London—and the dialogue is laughable in the original language ("The scourge of the desert o'er my heart hath pass'd, and the tree that's blighted fears no second blast"). A German narration may not be what Weber intended, but it spares the singers much potential embarrassment.

Janowski, who also made recordings of *Euryanthe* and *Der Freischütz,* leads the third *Oberon* (RCA 68505, 2CD). Peter Seiffert, the Huon, is another tenor who has drifted toward Wagnerian roles; but I first encountered Inga Nielsen as Mozart's Constanze, and that takes us in an entirely different direction. Nielsen has gone on to sing Salome and Chrysothemis, but she is still the most agile of the Rezias, and she alone makes the coloratura sound natural and congruous. She musters the strength for "Ozean," but her top notes are somewhat constricted; her high As and Bs don't blaze forth like Nilsson's or Voight's. Seiffert's tone also narrows in his high register, but he demonstrates that Huon's music lies within lyric tenor limits. He brings to his arias a touch of elegance that eludes his rivals. Vesselina Kasarova is the most vivid and flexible of Fatimas, and Deon van der Walt, though he tends to squeal, is an acceptable Oberon. Skovhus's Scherasmin, fine though it is, doesn't make

me forget Prey's. Janowski's conducting is less frenetic than it was for his *Freischütz,* and he makes the music by turns enchanting and noble. The dialogue is severely abridged and spoken by the singers themselves, the best option of all.

It's difficult to recommend any of these three recordings above the others. In their diverse ways, they're all enjoyable. Kubelik has the most thrilling vocalism, but the more mundane Janowski is better proportioned—Weber rather than Wagner. Conlon is poised somewhere in between, and pressed to make a single choice, I'd opt for him.

LUCANO

SONGS

Weber wrote more than 100 songs, but they're hardly ever heard in recital. In these pieces he stands somewhere between Beethoven and Schubert, less concerned with form than the former but without the font of memorable melody of the latter. There have been LPs by Schreier, Martyn Hill, and others, all long gone. We can be thankful to **Fischer-Dieskau** for making this music available again, and the wonder is that these songs, which he recorded around his 66th birthday, find him in fine form, not fresh and youthful to be sure but wrapping his very soul around their naive melodies with great artistry, particularly in the more humorous pieces (♦Claves 9118). As expected, Höll provides expert support. Soprano **Karin Ott** offers selections from *Preziosa, Peter Schmoll,* and *Silvana* along with several concert arias to Italian texts. While her upper register has a rather pronounced edge, she clearly understands the idiom, and she's given strong support by the Italian Swiss Radio Orchestra led by Marc Andreae (Ex Libris 6060). HALLER

Anton Webern (1883–1945)

Few composers took such a long path to arrive at their mature styles. Beginning as a Symbolist, Webern progressed swiftly into extreme expressionism, adopting a late atonal/early twelve-tone style with tortuous melodic lines, and finally developing a highly classical style that treated the tone row very differently from his teacher Schoenberg. In Webern's hands, the row became a crystalline substance, and its permutations were presented as the major object of interest. He also developed *Klangfarbenmelodie* (tone color melody), in which notes of a melodic line are passed from instrument to instrument, changing the tone color on nearly every note.

For complete recordings, **Boulez**'s first set contains only those works to which Webern assigned opus numbers, plus his orchestrations of Fugue 2 from Bach's *Musical Offering* and Schubert's *German Dances* (Sony 45845, 3CD). Boulez's second set contains all the works with and without opus numbers, save for some student compositions for piano (DG 457637, 6CD).

ORCHESTRAL MUSIC

Passacaglia Op. 1. In a letter of 1912, Webern confessed to Alban Berg that most of his compositions from the *Passacaglia* on "relate to the death of my mother." It's his graduation piece upon completing his studies with Schoenberg and is very significant, because it's the first work that embodies the grief and associated feelings he had about his mother's death in 1907, the year before.

Claudio Abbado has the narrowest dynamic range and lacks drama and momentum (DG). **Kegel** is usually too loud and fails to clarify the music's structure, though he does have a strong ending (Berlin). **Roelof van Driesten**'s beginning is too loud and lacks mystery; he makes the structure clear, but it's obvious that the Netherlands Ballet Orchestra is challenged by the demands of the score (Koch). **Sinopoli** draws gorgeous sounds from the Dresden Staatskapelle, but he lacks drama and momentum (Teldec).

Boulez and the London Symphony are good, with a spooky atmosphere appropriate to the inspiration of the piece (Sony). He and the Berlin Philharmonic have a far wider dynamic range and are more dramatic, with huge climaxes (DG). Dohnányi also has a very wide dynamic range (London 444593). His reading is dramatic, with a greater variety of mood and colors; it's also more clearly episodic. Karajan is in a class by himself (♦DG 457760). He has almost all Dohnányi's virtues (except for the wide dynamic range afforded by the digital recording) and adds some of his own. His reading isn't just dramatic, it's simply thrilling, and there is no orchestra today to rival the Berlin Philharmonic of the early '70s for character, virtuosity, and depth of string tone.

Pieces Op. 6. These six pieces relate directly to the death of Webern's mother, and the movements are programmatic. No. 1 depicts the expectation of a catastrophe, 2 the certainty that it will happen, 3 is "the most tender contrast," representing flowers around a bier, 4 is a funeral march, 5 remembrance, and 6 resignation.

There are two versions of this work, the original for very large orchestra from 1909 and one for a normal-sized orchestra from 1928. In the original version, Dohnányi is excellent in No. 1 (London 444593) and Abbado nearly so (DG 431774). In 2, Abbado is truly terrifying, while Dohnányi comes close. In 3, Dohnányi is very melodic and flowing, Abbado nearly as fine. In 4, Dohnányi does a good job, followed by Boulez and the London Symphony (Sony). In 5, Levine is good (DG, NA), while Dohnányi is the next best. In 6, Dohnányi is best, followed by Abbado.

For the 1928 version, Sinopoli does a good job in No. 1 (Teldec 22902). Sinopoli and Kegel (Berlin 9020) tie for 2, and van Driesten (Koch 1069) is best in 3. In 4, Sinopoli conveys wonderful atmosphere and dread, while Kegel expresses sheer terror. Kegel is the most grieving in 5, while Sinopoli is very good at handling Webern's *Klangfarbenmelodie*. In 6, van Driesten is excellent. Unfortunately, there is no clear first choice for either version. Dohnányi is perhaps the all-around best for the original, while Sinopoli and Kegel are best in the revision. In general, those who play the original do better in the first three pieces, while those who play the revision excel in the last three.

Pieces Op. 10. Sinopoli comes out on top in these five pieces (Teldec 22902), as he's marginally more fluent than Boulez (DG) and Dohnányi (London). The old analog recordings by Boulez (Sony) and Doráti (Mercury) are recorded at too high a level and with too narrow a dynamic range to do justice to the music.

Symphony Op. 21 (1927) is Webern's first twelve-tone work for orchestra. It's also the first work in his fully mature, classical style. Sinopoli is the best interpreter, as his performance has real emotion (Teldec). Dohnányi (London) is a close second. Kegel (Berlin) and both versions by Boulez (Sony and DG) lack emotion.

Variations Op. 30. This is Webern's last orchestral work. It's surprisingly eventful for such a severely classical composition, and Sinopoli does a superb job conveying its emotions (♦Teldec). Van Driesten does the next best job of clarifying the work's structure (Koch 1069), while Abbado (DG), Dohnányi (London), and both Boulez versions (Sony and DG) are mediocre.

Im Sommerwind (1904). Webern's earliest composition for orchestra, it was inspired by a poem from the novel *Revelations of the Juniper Tree* by the German social philosopher Bruno Wille. It's gorgeous music, recalling Strauss, Mahler, and early Schoenberg. Sinopoli's reading is flowing and powerful, and his orchestra revels in Webern's beautiful textures (Teldec 22902). Dohnányi isn't bad, though a bit too slow (London). Boulez is dead on arrival (DG), and van Driesten's group lacks the tonal resources to do justice to such a score (Koch).

Pieces for String Quartet Op. 5 (orchestral version, 1909/29). These are Webern's arrangements of his five pieces for string quartet. Kegel's Leipzig Radio Symphony plays cleanly and expressively (Berlin 9020), Boulez and the London Symphony are rough and ready but expressive (Sony), while he and the Berlin Philharmonic are clean but dull (DG).

CHAMBER MUSIC

Pieces for String Quartet Op. 5. Here the pain Webern experienced upon the death of his mother two years earlier is expressed without restraint for the first time. The five pieces are drenched in expression marks, and the Artis Quartet isn't quite up to the task of playing them; actually they're not bad, but other more virtuosic ensembles outclass them (Sony). The Emerson Quartet is much better (DG). The Juilliard Quartet recorded this music at least twice, once on LP in the early '60s (RCA 2531, NA) and again in 1970 as part of Boulez's "Complete Works" (Sony 45845, 3CD). Both performances are superb; the earlier one is more virtuosic and dramatic, the later one more atmospheric and colorful. The Arditti Quartet plays this music like no one else (♦Disques Montaigne 789008). They sound wildly spontaneous, as if they're improvising.

Pieces for Violin and Piano Op. 7. Stern doesn't quite achieve the *innigkeit* needed in the slow movements of these four pieces (Sony), Kremer is much better at communicating their quiet moods, and no one else conveys their grotesquerie with as much relish (♦DG 447312, 457637, 6CD). On LP, Ida Kavafian of Tashi recorded them with Peter Serkin (♦RCA 4730, NA). She tends to take slower tempos than either Stern or Kremer and makes the slow movements downright hypnotic. There's an unmatched delicacy in this duo's playing.

Bagatelles for String Quartet Op. 9. The Artis Quartet can't quite make these six pieces flow; they're not as subtle or as comfortable with this idiom as other groups (Sony). The Emerson Quartet is much better, but again they don't quite inhabit the music (DG). The Juilliard Quartet is excellent in both their early (RCA LP 2531, NA) and later (Sony 45845, 3CD) recordings, with more atmosphere in the later one but sharper ensemble in the earlier. The Arditti Quartet is wonderful (♦Disques Montaigne 789008). They play Webern's *Klangfarbenmelodie* like old friends who finish each other's sentences in a truly great performance.

Little Pieces for Cello and Piano Op. 11. Piatigorsky conveys much tenderness and *innigkeit* in a performance of great delicacy (Sony 45845 3CD). Clemens Hagen has a fine understanding of the three pieces and plays with a much greater dynamic range (♦DG 447112, 457637, 6CD). On LP, Fred Sherry, with Tashi mate Peter Serkin, performed miracles of tone color; time seems suspended in this performance (♦RCA 4730, NA).

String Trio Op. 20. This is a pointillist, twelve-tone work of the most daunting sort for interpreters and listeners, and neither the Arditti Quartet (Disques Montaigne) nor the Emerson Quartet (DG) seems able to unite its expressionist and classical aspects. The Juilliard Quartet plays this music as to the manner born (♦Sony 45845, 3CD). They're more colorful, the music flows in their hands, and there's greater variety among the sections of the two movements. There's more of a sense of drama, and they even knit the short notes together so you can hear melodies. A remarkable achievement, given the difficulty of the task.

Quartet for Violin, Clarinet, Tenor Saxophone, and Piano Op. 22. **Ensemble Intercontemporain** isn't quite playful enough and not good enough at smoothing out Webern's *Klangfarbenmelodie* (DG). Members of the **Cleveland Orchestra** are much better (Sony 45845, 3CD), but pride of place must go to **Tashi**, who are able to relax and have fun with this music (♦RCA LP 4730, NA).

Concerto Op. 24. **Sinopoli** does the most seamless job of knitting together the *Klangfarbenmelodie* (Teldec 22902), but **Rattle** is much more expressive, with a wider range of moods, and really brings out the coarse humor of the finale (♦Chandos 6534). The ensemble led by **Boris Brott**, which includes Glenn Gould (Sony), and both ensembles led by **Boulez** (Sony and DG) just aren't expressive enough.

String Quartet Op. 28. The **Artis Quartet** isn't up to the music's intellectual demands (Sony). The **Emerson Quartet** (DG) is better, but not at the level of the **Juilliard** (♦Sony 45845, 3CD) and **Arditti Quartets** (♦Disques Montaigne 789008). The Juilliard is very good in I and II, but the Arditti is better at clarifying their structure, and they make the music flow better. In III they play with more dramatic contrast, while the Juilliard is better at distinguishing the various sections.

Slow Movement for String Quartet (1905). The **Emerson Quartet** plays beautifully but can't get the music to flow (DG). This is no problem for the **Artis Quartet,** which creates several magic moments (Sony). Their first violinist distinguishes himself with some lovely playing. The **Arditti Quartet** plays more slowly but brings out more of the music's drama; it's a lovely performance (Disques Montaigne). The **Carmina Quartet** is excellent in this music (Denon 79462). Taking a full minute longer than the Arditti (and more than two minutes longer than the Artis), they play with more color and *innigkeit* than the other groups and are about as dramatic as the Arditti.

String Quartet "1905." The **Arditti Quartet** seems more comfortable with Webern's atonal and twelve-tone works, and there is a lack of feeling and formal clarity here (Disques Montaigne). The **Emerson Quartet** is similarly unsuited to this music (DG). The **Artis Quartet** is much better, with a beautiful and very vocal ensemble sound (Sony). The **Hagen Quartet** really shines here; their beginning is excitingly dramatic, and they contrast the sections very clearly, with great changes of tempo (♦DG 437836).

Rondo for String Quartet (1906). The **Emerson Quartet** is intense but tedious, quite missing the point (DG). The **Artis Quartet** is better, producing striking tonal effects and communicating the humor nicely (Sony). The **Arditti Quartet** is right on target (♦Disques Montaigne 789008). They play this piece as a twisted little waltz, alternately lyrical, dramatic, and impish, and are tonally opulent.

Pieces for String Quartet (1913). Nos. 1 and 3 were later appropriated as 1 and 6 of the *Bagatelles.* No. 2 adds a female voice singing a remarkably terse, haiku-like text by Webern about his feelings at his mother's funeral. In the **Emerson Quartet**'s recording, mezzo-soprano Mary Ann McCormick has a pleasing, dark timbre that suits the words and music, but her singing is a bit wooden (DG). Dorothy Dorow with the **Schoenberg Quartet** (Koch 314005) milks every last ounce of feeling out of the words, but the Schoenberg scratches and scrapes in 1 and 3 and can't compare with the virtuoso Emerson.

PIANO MUSIC

Variations for Piano Op. 27. All the performances I will discuss have considerable merit. **Gould**'s account is the driest and spikiest (Sony

52661). His exceptionally sensitive touch clarifies Webern's voice leading like no one else; perhaps the work's similarity to Bach's keyboard music attracted him. **Charles Rosen** is smoother and quieter, and III ends more movingly (Sony 45845, 3CD). **Peter Hill** is the slowest of all in III, the main movement; he's more expressive in I than Rosen and II ends well, but III is a bit mediocre (Naxos 553870). **Peter Serkin** has recorded the Variations twice. His first, on a Tashi LP, had an intense concentration and *innigkeit* to it, with an ending to III that will make you hold your breath (♦RCA 4730, NA). His second recording doesn't quite achieve this level of concentration, but he finds more humor in II (Koch 7450).

Pollini has a tone of crystalline clarity—perfect for this music—and he shines in II, where it sounds as if each of his fingers has its own brain, so carefully does he distinguish each note's dynamic level (DG 447431). He misses much of the work's feeling, though he isn't as dry as Gould (or as arch). **Zimerman** takes a more romantic approach to I, and this is enhanced by the more resonant acoustic (DG 457637, 6CD). He misses the humor in II, though, and doesn't clearly differentiate the sections of III.

CHORAL MUSIC

Entflieht auf leichten Kähnen Op. 2. This very brief setting of a poem by Stefan George already shows Webern's preference for canon. The **Netherlands Chamber Choir** has recorded it under Reinbert de Leeuw with wonderfully clear diction and a lovely ending (Koch 314005). They include the 1908 original and the 1914 revision. It has been recorded twice by Boulez, first with the **John Aldis Choir** (Sony) and later with the **BBC Singers** (DG 457637). The latter are much more successful at conveying the grief at the end of the piece.

Songs for Mixed Choir Op. 19. A setting of two poems by Goethe, this is Webern's first choral work using the twelve-tone technique. **Boulez** recorded it twice using the same forces as in Op. 2. The **BBC Singers** are smoother and more blended, making it harder to make out the words (DG), while the **John Aldis Choir** is more staccato and clearer, and they bring out the songs' good cheer (Sony 45845).

Das Augenlicht for Mixed Choir and Orchestra, Op. 26. This is Webern's first choral setting of a text by his friend Hildegard Jone. Boulez's first recording with the **John Aldis Choir** is mechanical and inexpressive (Sony); his second with the **BBC Singers** is far superior, as there is more tone painting and the singers really express the text (DG 457637).

Cantata 1 Op. 29. It consists of settings of three poems by Jone. Boulez's second recording with the **BBC Singers** and soprano Christiane Oelze (DG 457637) is preferable to his earlier recording with slightly less refined singers (Sony).

Cantata 2 Op. 31. Here, Webern sets six poems by Jone. Again, **Boulez** has recorded it twice, and again the singing is superior the second time, as is the conducting (DG 457635).

SONGS

A selection of songs spanning most of Webern's career has been released (Orfeo 411951). Unfortunately, the delivery by the several female singers is wooden and none of them distinguishes herself.

Soprano **Heather Harper** recorded Webern's early songs with opus numbers for Boulez's first complete set (Sony 45845, 3CD). She has a beautiful voice and effectively conveys the angst of the earliest songs, but she's lost by the time she reaches Op. 14, the last song. Soprano **Halina Lukomska** took over for Opp. 15 to 25. These songs are more demanding, with frequent leaps from low to high register and back, and Lukomska nails each note, but the meaning of the texts completely escapes her and her voice is not beautiful.

In Boulez's second more complete set, soprano **Françoise Pollet** sings most of the early songs up to Op. 14, while soprano **Christiane Oelze** sings all the rest (DG). Pollet has a much heftier voice, appropriate to the darker moods of the early Symbolist and expressionist songs, while Oelze has a fresh, girlish voice that can handle Webern's leaps like an Olympic gymnast. Unfortunately, both Pollet and Oelze utterly fail to express the feeling of the texts.

Roswitha Trexler has recorded the early songs through Op. 13 (♦Berlin 9049). Coached by Webern confidant Rudolf Kolisch, she sings with a delightful Viennese swing. She gets into the texts and, best of all, sounds like she's having fun. **Dorothy Dorow**'s approach is similar to Trexler's, without quite so much Viennese swing; she has obviously devoted a great deal of thought to how each text should be expressed and her effort has really paid off (Etcetera ♦1051 and ♦2008; ♦Koch 314005).

MAGIL

Kurt Weill (1900–1950)

Weill's career had two distinct phases, European and American. Before 1935, when he relocated from Germany to the US to escape the Nazi regime, he had been one of the most successful opera composers of the '20s and '30s. He wrote in a directly accessible yet modern style, and he knew how to write tunes that were eminently memorable and singable. His librettos, many written by the leftist Bertolt Brecht, dealt with common folk, even with the dregs of society, rather than with kings and generals, and often advocated social or economic reforms. Once in America, Weill quickly changed his style to one appropriate for Broadway musicals, and he became one of that genre's best practitioners. In addition to his stage works, Weill wrote many songs and a fair amount of instrumental music, including two symphonies. Much of this music has only recently been recorded.

SYMPHONIES

While his stage works are surely his most important musical legacy, Weill did write two symphonies. The first, from 1921, was scorned by his teacher Busoni, who urged him to destroy it. It's a gloomy single movement in a style that's partly late Romantic, partly expressionist. It's not a very likable piece and wasn't performed in the composer's lifetime. But there exist at least four recordings, paired with his Symphony 2. The latter, from 1934, evokes the Weill of the '20s without the vocal parts. It's in three contrasting movements, with clearly characterized motifs, fanfares, and sardonic marches à la Mahler. It was premiered by Bruno Walter and the Concertgebouw in 1934. Walter championed the work and conducted it repeatedly, even with the NY Philharmonic. Two of the available recordings can be recommended, one by **Gary Bertini** (EMI 65869) and the other by **de Waart** (Philips 6500642). De Waart does better with No. 1, Bertini with 2.

OPERAS

Down in the Valley. It was first written as a "radio opera" in 1945, and later considerably expanded and revised for performance by schools and other nonprofessional groups. The music for the simple story is based on the folk song of the title; it includes four other American folk songs. The work is singable even by untrained voices and yet it haunts your memory. While it's simple and folksy, Weill treated his material seriously, using the compositional techniques he had successfully employed throughout his career. This is an excellent work for introducing

youngsters to opera. There's only one CD version in the current catalog, led by **Willi Gundlach** (Capriccio 60020).

Der Jasager. Weill's other "student opera," it is also contained in the Capriccio set. It dates from 1930; its libretto was written by Brecht, who based it on a Japanese Noh play. Weill considered it his most important European work.

Threepenny Opera. This is, by common consent, Weill's (and Brecht's) masterpiece; from its premiere in 1928, it has been their most popular stage work. Based on John Gay's 1728 *Beggar's Opera,* Brecht shifted the action to Victorian England and produced a brilliant social satire, and Weill responded with a wonderfully melodious score that fits it perfectly and has more hit tunes than many Verdi operas. At the same time, it's one of the cleverest parodies of opera ever written. It has often been imitated but never equaled.

The best of the available recordings is the first (1958), which included all the musical numbers but not the spoken dialog (CBS 42637, mono). The splendid cast includes Weill's wife **Lotte Lenya** and Trude Hesterberg, both of whom took part in the premiere. Lenya supervised this production, thus lending it an air of authenticity. This performance is in German. English versions, like the one by **Marc Blitzstein** (produced, unforgettably, in New York in the '50s), once issued by MGM, seem to have vanished. If it ever reappears, grab it! A disc that transfers many of the original 78s made in Germany right after the premiere has been issued (♦Teldec 72025). It includes 14 of the most popular numbers from this work, two from *Mahagonny* (sung by Lenya), and several Berlin cabaret songs from the '20s, two of them sung by the young Marlene Dietrich. It's also highly recommended.

Rise and Fall of the City of Mahagonny. Weill's most operatic work, it employs all the means of that genre, including an overture, bel canto arias, choruses, and large ensembles. Still, it's hardly a traditional opera. Its subject is the excesses of capitalism, such as the high cost of living relative to wages, the uneven distribution of wealth, and a judicial system favoring the wealthy. All this leads to the decline of a city built by entrepreneurs. While the opera was well received at the Met in the '80s, revivals have been sparsely attended. Its characters seem to be stereotypes rather than human beings, and its tunes, except for "Alabama Song," aren't as catchy as those of *Threepenny Opera.* Some of the action, such as political slogans carried on placards by members of the cast, seems anti-operatic.

There are two fine recordings. A stereo version from the late '80s has excellent sound and an able cast headed by **Anja Silja** and Anny Schlemm (Capriccio 10160). An earlier mono recording from the '50s has **Lenya** (the original Jenny) and Gisela Litz (CBS 37874). Lenya's performance adds authenticity and frisson to that set but Capriccio's much better sound gives it an edge.

The Tsar Has His Photograph Taken. This 46 minute opera buffa was first performed in 1928. It was a sensational success; 35 German opera houses produced it within a year. It's a satirical comedy; its story includes a conspiracy to commit murder, false identities, and a love interest. There are no set pieces, yet the music is recognizably Weill's: tonal, jazzy, not complicated, but clever. The only available recording, from 1984, is by the Cologne Radio, with a fine cast and good sound (Capriccio 60007).

SONGS

There are more than a dozen recordings of Weill songs in the current listings. Most also include excerpts from his stage works; the most popular ones, like "Pirate Jenny," "Surabaya-Johnny," and "Lost in the Stars," are included in many of them. Highly recommended are discs by **Lenya** (CBS 42658, entitled "American and Berlin Theater Songs"), **Stratas** (Nonesuch 79019 and 79131), and **Angelia Réaux** (Koch 7087). Of these, Stratas has the best voice and is the most affecting, and Lenya is, sometimes, the best interpreter in spite of her raspy voice. Réaux is somewhere in between.

Discs by **Lemper** (London 425204) and **Gisela May** (Capriccio 10180) have their admirers but they are diseuses rather than singers. For those interested in the Broadway Weill, "Kurt Weill on Broadway" is recommended (EMI 55563). The singers include **Hampson**, Hadley, and Elizabeth Futral. Somewhat off the beaten path is "Unrecorded Songs," a collection of mostly American songs including the Walt Whitman cycle, sung by **Steven Kimbrough** (Arabesque 6579).

MOSES

Jaromír Weinberger *(1896–1967)*

Weinberger was a classic "one-work" composer. His *Schwanda der Dudelsackpfeifer* (*Schwanda the Bagpiper*), completed in 1927 when he was 31, is the most famous Czech opera after *Bartered Bride*, but other than its "Polka and Fugue" we hear nothing else by this composer, though he wrote more operas and other works. Many of the latter appeared after he fled Hitler, first for England and then the US, where he wrote several pieces that celebrated his adopted country. Perhaps never resigned to his fate, Weinberger committed suicide in Florida.

Schwanda is a sophisticated and complex folk opera. It's not strictly based on folk material but rather is written around traditional Germanic operatic structures and colored with folk songs and dances (similar to Smetana's approach, as opposed to Janáček's). The folk element is always present in the subject matter, tuneful arias, and lively Czech dance music, but the opera is very orchestral in the German late-Romantic manner in accompaniment and major set pieces. The influences of Smetana, and to a lesser extent Janáček, are obvious. We also hear the Germans—Strauss, Schreker, and Korngold—in the prominent orchestra and in harmony and melody that are more complex, exotic, and chromatic than usual in folk operas. There's also some Reger in the extensive counterpoint.

The plot concerns the piper Schwanda, who wins the heart of the Ice Queen, but she finds out he's married and orders him put to death. He's saved by his music and the intervention of the magician Babinsky—until he tells his wife, Dorotka, "let the devil take me" if I kissed her (the Queen). The Devil does, but eventually the couple is reunited after Babinsky wins him back in a poker game.

The only recording is a German-language version led by **Heinz Wallberg**, with Popp, Jerusalem, Prey, and the Munich Radio Orchestra, sadly not yet on CD (♦CBS LP, NA). It's large-scale and lively, with sound to match. Prey is outstanding, and Jerusalem is ardent if not always beautiful; Popp is charming if sometimes strained in the high notes. None of these quibbles detracts from a recording that should appeal to anyone fond of late Romantic German and Czech opera, and even those who avoid folk operas should like it—if they can find it!

HECHT

Leó Weiner *(1885–1969)*

With roots in Beethoven, Mendelssohn, and Bizet, the music of this Hungarian composer remained true to a Romantic expressiveness marked by lyricism, clarity, classical balance, and expert instrumentation. His music is tonal, melodic, accessible, and memorable. Most recorded works are from his nationalist period of the '20s and '30s, spiced with Hungarian folk idioms. Living up to his motto, "The two principles of art are beauty and comprehensibility," he has secured a firm place in 20th-century Hungarian music.

The 5-movement *Csongor és Tünde* (1937) is a delectable ballet suite still influenced by the Viennese Classical composers. Weiner incorporated authentic Hungarian folk music for the first time in the charming 4-movement *Hungarian Folkdance Suite for Orchestra* (1931); in III, listeners will recognize the "swineherd dance" used by Bartók in his *Hungarian Sketches*. **László Kovács** does full justice to these fine works in excellent sound (Hungaroton 31740). The Suite is also performed by **Neeme Järvi** in excellent performances and spacious sound (Chandos 9029, with Bartók's *Miraculous Mandarin* ballet).

Also from Weiner's nationalist period is the lovely Divertimento for strings (1931, subtitled "Old Hungarian Dances"); like Kodály's *Galánta Dances*, it's more an arrangement of existing folk melodies than an original composition. It has been recorded in a delightful disc by **György Győriványi-Ráth** (Hungaroton 31467, with Bartók's Divertimento and eight familiar pieces by Fritz Kreisler). Divertimento 1 was also recorded in 1945 by **Reiner** (Sony 62343, in digitally remastered mono, with works by Bartók and others). In surprisingly good but somewhat grainy sound, Reiner's interpretation is the most fiery on record, and the one I prefer, with startling dynamic contrasts and rhythmic flexibility. But why include a trumpet and flute in IV, in this work scored for strings? Long deleted from the catalogs, this may still be available in specialty stores.

Weiner's early (1906) Serenade for Small Orchestra is in the capable hands of **Solti** in "Georg Solti: The Last Recordings" (London 458929, with Bartók's *Cantata Profana* and Kodály's *Psalmus Hungaricus*). In "Mephisto Magic," Solti conducts Weiner's 1927 ballet suite *Prinz Csongor und die Kobolde* (London 43444, with works by Bartók, Kodály, and Liszt). Fine performances and sound.

An all-Weiner release offers the lyrical, elegant, 23-minute, two-movement Concertino for Piano and Orchestra (1923); it's transparently scored, with Hungarian folk music touches, and is a grateful vehicle for pianist Isabelle Oehmichen. Also imbued with folk idioms are the Romance for Cello, Harp, and Orchestra (1949), with soloists Katalin Sin and Melinda Felletár, and Divertimentos 1 and 2 for strings. Richard Weninger and the Hungarian Chamber Orchestra of Szeged do the fine honors (Marcal 981101).

The complete works for violin and piano are performed by **Vilmos Szabadi** and **Márta Gulyás**; well-played, memorable music in good sound (Hungaroton 31663). Weiner's string quartets show his intimate side and are well worth exploring. 1 is in his early style, while 2 and 3 partake of Hungarian folk idioms (2 won the Coolidge Prize in 1922). All three are performed by the **Auer Quartet** (Hungaroton 31687).

DE JONG

Silvius Leopold Weiss *(1686–1750)*

Weiss was the foremost lutenist of the first half of the 18th century. He was famous throughout Europe in his lifetime and remembered after his death as the greatest player-composer of his instrument (which completely disappeared as a "living" instrument during the latter half of the century). He also shares almost the exact birth and death years of Bach, whom he encountered in his career (one such meeting was an improvisation competition) and whose lute music—though its true intended instrument remains in dispute—may have been written for Weiss; its excessive difficulty suggests the need for a great virtuoso. At his best, some of Weiss's compositions achieve a level of excellence and profundity comparable to Bach's.

Typical of Baroque musicians, Weiss came from a family of players; his father and brother were also lutenists. He held court appointments in Dusseldorf, then Italy (where the musical style had a significant impact on his compositions), and finally Dresden, where by 1744 he was the highest-paid instrumentalist in town, a notable measure of his stature. Weiss is the origin of the joke that if a lutenist had been playing for 20 years, 10 of them had been spent tuning; by his time the lute had acquired an inordinate number of strings, which considerably lengthened the tuning process—a factor in its demise.

Weiss composed over 70 suites for lute (he called them either "sonatas" or "partitas"), the largest body of music for the instrument of any composer, and a few single-movement pieces including fugues, chaconnes, tombeaux, and several fantasias. Particularly in these pieces he's sometimes startlingly chromatic (like Bach), while in most of the dance movements of his suites his melodic and harmonic style is similar to Handel's. The preludes to his suites were often unmeasured (like Couperin's), and many of his concluding gigues have a rhythmic/melodic character again comparable to Bach. Sometimes his music flows on with little melodic or harmonic distinction, and his use of sequence (the same melodic idea repeated many times but starting on different notes) occasionally rivals Vivaldi in monotonous effect; however, note again the comparison to a great composer. His music is best represented in lute performances, though it's encountered quite often, both live and in recordings, in classical guitar programs.

Perhaps the most technically brilliant current lutenist is **Lutz Kirchhof**, whose double CD of lute works contains five suites, several characteristic preludes and single pieces (an elegiac plainte and a vigorous capriccio), and a terrific *Praeludium, Courante, Fuga and Presto* in D minor, not a suite but apparently intended to be played as a unit (♦Sony 48391). Weiss's most emotionally riveting piece, *Tombeau por M. Comte de Logy,* isn't in that collection, however. **Hopkinson Smith** recorded it on a surviving instrument from 1755 (♦Astrée 8718, with two sonatas and a fantasia). Or try **Nigel North**'s "Baroque Lute," with a suite and more by Weiss as well as some of Bach's lute music (Linn 5006), or **Jakob Lindberg**'s "Baroque Music for Lute & Guitar," also including a sonata in F, pieces by David Kellner and Bach (a prelude and fugue), and Baroque guitar music by Ludovico Roncalli and Robert de Visée (BIS 327).

Tombeau was recorded on guitar with great intensity by **Bream** in the '60s, and is now available in two "Baroque Guitar" reissues, along with Weiss's two other most popular pieces transcribed for guitar: a fantasia—which Bream unfortunately rushes through—and a passacaglia (♦RCA 60494 and 61592, "Bream Edition" Vol. 9). Better paced, and featuring expertly rendered state-of-the-art ornamentation, are guitarist **John Williams**'s versions of the latter two pieces, with another less frequently encountered (but nearly as wonderful) tombeau for "M. Cajetan," among the selections in "The Baroque Album" (♦Sony 44518). Williams used to play half-Weiss/half-Barrios programs in the '70s (Pio Augustín Barrios was called the "Chopin" of the guitar), but until fairly recently hadn't recorded any Weiss. **Eliot Fisk** avoids the expected pieces and plays a Weiss *Menuet, Fantasie and Fugue* with jaw-dropping speed and scope of phrasing in "Guitar Fantasies," which runs the gamut from Renaissance (Alessandro Piccinini and Alonso Mudarra) to Baroque, Classical (Sor and Mozart), Romantic (Barrios), and modern (Henze), all delivered with Fisk's typical and occasionally overwhelming intensity (♦MusicMasters 60169F). DINGER

Charles-Marie Widor (1844–1937)

Born in Lyon into a family of Hungarian extraction with considerable musical talent, Widor was recommended for the post as organist at St. Sulpice when 25 by none other than Cavaillé-Coll. Besides performing, Widor composed works for every musical genre and became a respected music critic. A professor of organ and, later, composition at the Paris Conservatoire, he maintained his St. Sulpice post until 1933, retiring after 64 years. On his death in 1937, a former student replaced him: Marcel Dupré. In spite of his fame during most of his life, his compositional style fell out of favor, and he's known today almost solely by his organ works. Only those will be considered here.

There are 10 organ symphonies, and Widor reworked and revised them over and over, deleting here, adding there. Many of them have individual movements that have become popular over time—for instance, in No. 1 it's the "Marche Pontificale," heard frequently at weddings and ceremonies demanding something big and pompous, and the flowing *Andante sostenuto* and Finale of 9 are often heard.

Several organists have recorded all or most of them. **Charles Krigbaum** at Woolsey Hall presides over the imposing Skinner organ, providing well-paced but not especially exciting performances, with somewhat remote miking (Afka). For those interested in historically correctness, **Patrice Caire** plays on a 3-91 Callinet-Merklin in St. Bonaventure (Lyon), the very make of organ Widor used while composing the first four symphonies (Real Music). However, the pungency of the reeds results in a hard-edged sound without much smoothness. The two preferable versions are by **Ben van Oosten** (♦MD+G) and **Günther Kaunzinger** (♦Novalis). The former chose a number of different Cavaillé-Coll instruments; they don't overwhelm, yet they have all the potency required. Kaunzinger recorded all the symphonies on the massive organ in the Waldsassen Basilica. His tempos are kept in check and the clarity is quite good. In terms of sound quality, van Oosten's is golden, Kaunzinger's silver.

There are also good recordings of individual symphonies. **Marie-Claire Alain** recorded three of the five movements of No. 3 in 1977 at St. Germain on the bright, 3-62 Haerpfer-Erman (Erato). The recording has considerable hiss, but the performance is typical Alain—clean, well articulated, closely miked. In No. 4, **Suzanne Chaisemartin** at Ste. Trinité has the right tempos—though the miking could be better, the sound is potent and well balanced (♦Motette 11131)—and **Odile Pierre** has one of the best recordings from St. Sernin, with good engineering, speed, registration, and an aggressive approach seldom encountered (♦RCA 37394).

There are three very rewarding interpretations of No. 4 apart from van Oosten's—all French—and little differentiates one from another except reverberation time, tempo, and degree of articulation. **Kåre Nordstoga** at St. Etienne (Caen) gets a wonderful sound from the 3-70 Cavaillé-Coll, with conservative tempos (♦Simax 1073). **Jane Parker-Smith** commands the massive installation at St. Eustache; the Pedal is occasionally too heavy, and the engineering not quite as clear as that for Nordstoga (♦ASV 958). **Latry,** co-titulaire at Notre-Dame since 1985, adopts fairly fast tempos (like Parker-Smith), and the organ has that familiar hard-edged quality (♦BNL 112617). However, his interpretation is accurate and compelling. For history fans who wonder how **Widor** played his famous *Toccata,* you can hear this, along with other vintage selections, in a recording made at St. Sulpice when Widor was 88 (EMI 55037).

There are three excellent performances of No. 6, each with resonant acoustics, competitive tempos, and appropriate registration: **Nord-**

stoga (♦Simax 1073), van Oosten again (♦MD+G 3160403), and **Latry** (♦BNL 112617). Nordstoga's venue (St. Etienne) provides the cleanest recording, while Latry at Notre-Dame works with a clearly recorded but still somewhat hard-edged sound. Any one of these discs will satisfy. No. 7 is the least familiar to audiences; fortunately, three exceptional interpretations can be found. **Daniel Roth** at St. Sernin has the most deliberate (but not slow) pace, which allows more detail to emerge (♦Motette 11241); **Kaunzinger** provides an accurate reading, though sometimes the Pedal is a bit hooty (♦Novalis 150098). Without doubt the most exhilarating performance is from **Parker-Smith** (♦ASV 958). At the helm of the massive van den Heuvel installation at Guillou's church (St. Eustache), she combines appropriate tempos and proper registration with a flair and verve all too rarely encountered. Her recording might make this work more popular.

No. 8 presents some of the most challenging pages of music for organ you will find, and two splendid interpretations reveal its seldom heard beauty: **Kaunzinger** and **Pierre** (♦RCA 37394), who provides a surprisingly deliberate, clear performance without his usual rush. **Alain** puts some life into the opening movements of No. 9 ("Gothique"), but the Pedal dominates in the toccata, and the constant though not ruinous background hiss may bother listeners (♦Erato 98534). **George Baker** at St. Ouen has a murky start, but the Andante is lovely; distant miking emphasizes the top and bottom, the Pedal often dominates, and the overall sound is syrupy (♦Solstice 128). One of the best recordings is a **Dupré** LP at St. Sulpice (Westminster 18871). Balance is good, the buildups are gradual, and proper mike placement lets the polyphonic detail come through. For history buffs, **Widor** plays excerpts at St. Sulpice from 1932 (EMI 55037). And finally, for Symphony 10, **van Oosten** (♦MD+G 3160406) and **Pierre** (♦RCA 37394) provide the best interpretations.

Three versions of the Mass in F-sharp Minor for Two Choirs and Two Organs Op. 36 (1890)—all by German ensembles—are available. This is a very approachable work, with smooth melodic writing throughout. The **Hannover Boys Choir** led by Heinz Hennig are just fair, with less than ample acoustics (Ars Musica). A more rewarding performance comes from the **Altenberg and Gürzenich Choirs**, Cologne, led by Volker Hempfling (Motette). Miking favors the voices, though they overdo some of the pronunciation. There are some lovely moments here, but this disc is just edged out by the **Munich Madrigal Choir** with Franz Brandl (♦FSM 97735). They possess a more homogeneous sound, and the organ isn't timid. The sopranos are luminous in the "Benedictus."

Widor fans may wish to sample two of his organ symphonies. No. 8 in G minor, a transcription of three movements from the earlier Nos. 2 and 6, is recorded by **Franz Hauk** with the Ingolsadt Philharmonic (Guild 7182) and by **Ulrich Meldau** with the Zurich Orchestra (Motette 40441). No. 3 is notable for its final movement, nicely captured by **Ian Tracey** and the BBC Philharmonic in Liverpool Cathedral (Chandos 9785).   METZ

Henryk Wieniawski *(1835–1880)*

Wieniawski referred to himself as "the last of my breed." His breed was that of the trail-blazing super-virtuoso violinist who was able to play in a bold, new manner. Think of Paganini and Liszt and you'll get the picture. He was also the first of a new breed, thanks to his extensive teaching in Russia and Belgium, where Ysaÿe was one of his pupils. To play Wieniawski properly, a violinist must have what he had: a lush, abundant tone; a sensuous, pulsating vibrato; a daredevil technique that in-

cludes a brilliant staccato; plenty of swagger; and the ability to play the most banal melody as if it were a divine revelation.

As a composer, Wieniawski was called "the Chopin of the violin." His compositions hardly approach the brilliance or novelty of his countryman's, but in a sense this comparison is accurate, as, in his modest way, Wieniawski did for the romantic violin idiom what Chopin did for the piano. They both did it by the appropriation of Polish folk music and by the heightened sensitivity they brought to the tonal resources of their respective instruments. There is none of Wieniawski's combination of sensuousness and drama in the music of his great predecessor, Paganini, who modeled his idiom on the coloratura aria.

Concerto 1, a juvenile work, is more long-winded than the more popular 2, but it's also more grandiose and exhibitionistic, with a lovely II that is a showcase for the soloist's tone. **Shaham** wins the prize for technique, with flawlessly tuned octaves and a staccato that even surpasses Heifetz in speed, evenness, and ease (♦DG 431815). In fact, he's so technically perfect that some of the drama is lost from the piece, as he gives no clue to the gruesome difficulty of the passages that he's playing, and thus the listener has none of that cliff-hanging suspense over whether the soloist is going to be able to pull it off—the real psychological basis for the virtuoso repertoire. **Rabin** is nearly as immaculate as Shaham but more involved in the music, in an electrifying performance (♦EMI 64123, 6CD).

Perlman plays with the greatest emotional involvement, and he nearly succeeds in making the listener forget the concerto's excessive length (♦EMI 64617, in "The Art of Perlman," 4CD). In II, he works wonders of tone production that have never been equaled. **Marat Bisengaliev** (Naxos) and **Vadim Brodsky** (Arts) are nearly as fine in this concerto, with Brodsky having the edge for style and technique and Bisengaliev for tone.

Wieniawski is best known for Concerto 2, a mature work with irresistible tunes in all three movements and plenty of opportunities to show off. **Bell** possesses the technique to pull off this finger twister, but lacks Slavic soul (London). **Bisengaliev** has all the Slavic soul the work needs, but lacks the last ounce of technical wizardry needed to really make your jaw drop (Naxos). The classic recordings of this work are by **Perlman** (his first one, ♦EMI), **Shaham**, and **Stern**. All are thrilling, with great affinity for Wieniawski's style. As he does in 1, Shaham performs technical miracles (♦DG 431815). Stern is strong on drama and intensity (♦Sony 66830). These two are surpassed in tone and panache by Perlman, whose tone is plushly carpeted from wall to wall. Of the three, Perlman musters by far the most enthusiasm. His digital remake is nearly as good (♦DG, NA), but there has been a general cooling off in his emotional involvement since the '70s.

Wieniawski is just as famous for his shorter works as his concertos. The two polonaises, *Légende*, and *Scherzo-Tarantelle* are irresistible. The problem for serious Wieniawski collectors is that these works rarely show up more than two to a disc, usually interspersed among other encore-type material by other composers. Discs consisting entirely of short pieces by Wieniawski are rare, and I know of only five: by **Stefan Stalanowski** (Pavane), **Joanna Mdroszkiewicz** (MD+G 6030863), **Bisengaliev** (♦Naxos 550744), **Levon Ambartsumian** (♦ACA 20053), and **Corey Cerovsek** (♦Delos 3231). All are technically adequate, though Bisengaliev and Ambartsumian have the edge in tone and style. There is a feeling of caution in Stalanowski's playing that by all accounts was absent from Wieniawski's. Mdroszkiewicz has a real flair for this music and is always willing to take risks, but there are a few moments on her disc when she reveals that her technique is less than perfect.

Cerovsek stands out in this crowd. He has a tremendous technique, and he plays Wieniawski's own magnificent Guarnerius violin, a late work of the master with an irresistibly dark, rich, velvety tone superbly captured by the Delos engineers. Cerovsek also has a strong affinity for Wieniawski, and his disc has the best *Fantasy brillante on Themes from Gounod's Faust* I've ever heard.

There is a disc of violin duets by **Ilya Gringolts** and **Alexander Bulov** that includes Wieniawski's *Etude-Caprices* Op. 18 (♦BIS 1016). These were conceived as didactic works, but they're so well written that they are a joy to hear. The short but scintillating 6 has been in the solo repertoire since it was published. **Ricci** has recorded *L'Ecole Moderne,* another didactic work (Dynamic 28). His execution isn't quite immaculate, but then, these studies are fiendishly difficult.

For the shorter pieces, you would do well to look for recordings by your favorite virtuoso violinists. The key word here is virtuoso, meaning someone with a daredevil technique and a strong temperament. Fodor, Heifetz, Milstein, Perlman, Shumsky, Zukerman, and Vengerov, for example, have all recorded superb Wieniawski. **Shaham**'s concerto disc is filled with a very fine reading of *Légende,* the work that according to legend, the composer wrote in one night to convince Isabella Hampton's father of the strength of his love for her, causing him to relent in his opposition to their marriage. **Vadim Brodsky** offers delightful readings of two mazurkas, *Scherzo-Tarantelle* and *Fantasie brillante on Themes from Gounod's Faust* (♦Arts 47313). The use of the orchestral arrangements here is a definite improvement over the piano arrangements that are usually recorded.

As for historical recordings, **Heifetz** recorded Concerto 2 at least twice, in the '30s with Barbirolli (♦EMI 64251) and in 1954 with Izler Solomon (♦RCA, NA). Both are mono, but in the later recording he's still in top form and his tone cuts like a razor. A warmer, more old-fashioned central European take on the concerto can be heard from **Příhoda** (♦Biddulph 135). On Sony's wonderful disc of the complete recordings of **Ysaÿe,** you can hear the "Obertass" and "Kujawiak" mazurkas performed with gusto by Wieniawski's prize pupil (♦Sony 62337). Wieniawski's countryman, **Huberman,** recorded the "Romance" from Concerto 2, the "Dudziardz" mazurka, and *Capriccio Valse* in the early '20s. These readings are distinguished by Huberman's powerful personality and intensity of feeling (Biddulph 077/78). MAGIL

Alec Wilder (1907–1980)

This American composer combined elements of the classical, jazz, and popular idioms. His compositions number in the hundreds, ranging from orchestral to band to chamber music, film scores to opera, musical theater, and popular song. He's at least as well known in the latter category as for any of his concert music. Nevertheless, those compositions reveal a remarkable originality and a broad range of musical expression, often in miniature terms. He generally avoided the larger orchestral canvas in favor of smaller, more intimate ensembles where his unique melodic gift and his skill at counterpoint would be displayed more effectively.

Wilder first attracted attention with a series of octets scored for woodwinds and a rhythm section consisting of bass, drums, and harpsichord. Light, airy, whimsical and eminently pleasing, they were considered too classical by the jazz world and too jazzy by the classical music establishment, but they occupy a unique position in 20th century American music, a harbinger of what Gunther Schuller has called the "Third Stream."

Wilder's next breakthrough came from none other than Frank Sinatra, the young vocalist who had just achieved his initial stardom. During the many hours between performances, he entertained himself by playing classical recordings, among them a group of off-the-air tapes of "Airs" for solo instrument and strings that Wilder had recently written. They captivated the young singer, and learning that they hadn't been recorded (and realizing there would probably be little interest in them by the powers that be), Sinatra decided to record and conduct these and other Wilder pieces himself. In this landmark recording (Sony A4271), my favorite track is entitled "Slow Dance," an engaging piece for woodwinds, strings, and percussion. In a contrapuntal pairing of two themes, a jazz-inflected up-tempo woodwind chorus and a slow and wistfully romantic string melodic line, the effect is enchanted, at once exhilarating and haunting. Reissues of several of the original recordings of the octets are added to this CD as a bonus.

Following the advice and encouragement of two friends, the virtuosos John Barrows (horn) and Harvey Phillips (tuba), Wilder composed a large body of works for solo instruments, many of them written for these two musicians. (More often than not, Wilder's compositions were written with a particular instrumentalist or individual in mind.) An excellent sampling can be found in the complete works for horn and piano played by **Thomas Bacon** (Summit 170) and the complete works for solo flute by **Laurel Zucker** (Cantilena 66014). In Sonata 1 for Horn and Piano, Bacon displays an amazing agility, particularly in the Gershwinesque II and the rollicking III, where his skill at jazz-like phrasing is most clearly in evidence. Zucker has the same ability and is comfortable with Wilder's style of combining a standard classical form with a jazz-influenced rhythmic underpinning and melodic language. This is especially noteworthy in the delicate Small Suite for Flute and Piano, written for the actress and would-be-flutist, Judy Holliday.

In later years, Wilder wrote pieces for favored jazz musicians in a more classical setting than usually found. Among these, I would cite the exemplary Suite 1 for Tenor Saxophone and Strings (aka "Three Ballads for Stan"), as recorded live at Tanglewood by **Stan Getz** with Fiedler and the Boston Pops (RCA/Bluebird 6284).

Among many fine examples of Wilder's skill at setting music to lyrics, often his own, I recommend *Songs for Patricia,* setting a text by Norman Rosten, as recorded by soprano **Margaret Astrip** and the Manhattan Chamber Orchestra under Richard Auldon Clark (Newport 8854). With a woodwind accompaniment in a style not unlike Barber's, Wilder creates a warm and tender background and melodic thread for this lovely poem, tracing a young girl's journey to adulthood. The singing is first rate. A second example, on a smaller scale, is the art song "Did You Ever Cross Over to Sneden's?," written for the legendary cabaret singer, Mabel Mercer. You should consider the exceptional rendering of this song by **Roberta Alexander** (Etcetera 1190). This crossover CD also contains a number of the popular songs for which the composer is justly well known. PRATHER

Dag Wirén (1905–1986)

This Swedish composer is best known for his lyrical, engaging *Serenade for Strings.* Throughout his life, Wirén's guiding star was the Nordic tradition represented by Nielsen and Sibelius. During the '40s, his neoclassical music became more serious, trenchant, and austere, based on a metamorphosis technique in which a theme is subtly and continuously transformed. His individual lyrical, tonal language is lucid, elegant, life-asserting, and meticulously crafted. Even the darkening chromaticism of his later years doesn't conceal the fresh immediacy of this fine composer's music.

Thomas Dausgaard leads the Norwegian Symphony in the romantic, pastoral Symphony 2 and the dramatic, more austere but still accessible 3, coupled with two light-hearted concert overtures (CPO 999677). Dausgaard really has the feel of this music, in excellent sound. The lyrical, expressive 4 is monothematic, each theme derived from the opening clarinet tune. A 1956 recording is well performed by **Westerberg, Ehrling,** and **Lennart Hedwall** conducting the Stockholm Philharmonic, Swedish Radio Symphony, and Örebro Chamber Orchestra, with *Serenade for Strings, Sinfonietta,* and *Music for String Orchestra,* the last three recorded in the '60s and '70s (Swedish Society Discophil 1035). It also appears in a splendid, well-recorded release with **Dausgaard** at the helm of the Norrköping Symphony, coupled with the masterly, more laconic 5 and the often humorous *Oscarbalen* suite (CPO 999563).

The often-recorded *Serenade for Strings,* suffused with spirited, healthy humor, is well performed by **Göran Nilsson** and the Örebro Chamber Orchestra, rounded out with other first-rate Swedish string music (Bluebell 019). **Petri Sakari** conducts the Swedish Chamber Orchestra, cellist Mats Rondin, and pianist Mats Widlund in an excellent release that contains *Serenade,* Cello Concerto, Piano Concerto, and *Divertimento* (Caprice 21513). **Somary** is outstanding in the *Serenade* (Vanguard 45, with string music by Britten and Grieg), and another fine performance is by **Richard Studt** and the Bournemouth Sinfonietta (Naxos 553106, with well-known string music by Grieg, Nielsen, and Svendsen).

For his Violin Concerto, Wirén turned to Sibelius for inspiration. It's well performed by **Nils-Erik Sparf** with Comissiona conducting the Stockholm Philharmonic (Caprice 21326). Also in this fine disc are Jan-Olav Wedin leading the Stockholm Sinfonietta in *Tryptich* and the austere, but still accessible, Quartet 5 played by the **Saulesco Quartet,** and the Wind Quintet played by the Stockholm Wind Quintet. **Jan Bengtson** is the capable flutist and Stefan Karpe conducts the Dala Sinfonietta in absorbing, spirited performances of the *Romantic Suite,* derived from stage music for *The Merchant of Venice,* the sprightly Flute Concertino (1972), Wirén's last work, and the engaging 1957 ballet suite *Plats på scenen* (*Take Your Places on the Stage*) (Nosag 041).

Wirén's witty 1945 piano suite *Ironiska småstycken* (*Ironical Miniatures*) is well played by Stefan Bojsten, who joins violinist Dan Almgren and cellist Torleif Thedéen as the **Stockholm Arts Trio** in sonatas for violin and piano, cello and piano, and piano trios, in a fine all-Wirén disc (BIS 582). Foreshadowing the bon vivant atmosphere of *Serenade for Strings* is the engaging Quartet 2, performed by Swedish musicians, coupled with the more soul-searching, austere, sparsely scored Quartet 5 by the **Ferro Quartet** (Caprice 21413). This disc also contains the gentle Little Serenade for solo guitar, with guitarist **Per Skaveng** as soloist, and the sprightly Quartet for Flute, Oboe, Clarinet, and Cello, played by Swedish musicians.

Göran Söllscher's Little Serenade is also a fine performance (Caprice 21514). Sharing this all-Swedish disc are solo guitar works by Hilding Hällness and Daniel Börtz and lyrical guitar concertos by Erland von Koch and Ulrik Neumann performed by Söllscher, with Jan Risberg conducting the Sonanza Chamber Orchestra. Quartets 3 and 4 are much like 2 in atmosphere, but more chromatic. Fine performances of both by the **Fresk Quartet** are rounded out by the Gotland Quartet playing string quartets by Bo Linde and Daniel Börtz (Phono Suecia 16).

Examples of Wirén's tuneful vocal music may be found in the three *Sea Poems* for a cappella choir and two songs for soprano and piano, sensitively performed by the Jubilate Choir conducted by **Astrid Riska,** soprano Christina Hogman, and pianist Stefan Bojsten, who also plays

a delightful *Sonatina* and other engaging solo piano pieces. Cellist **Torleif Thedéen** joins Bojsten in the *Miniature Suite.* Life-enhancing joy marks the music in these excellent performances (BIS 797).

DE JONG

Hugo Wolf *(1860–1903)*

Lieder represent by far the major part of Wolf's musical works. Not only did he compose more than 250 songs, he changed the vocabulary and structure of the lied by making it more sensitive to poetic values and meanings and by the intensity with which he expressed those values. His musical style, while clearly based on his predecessors (Brahms, Schumann, and Schubert), is more compact and terse. His melodies aren't as long-limbed; often, indeed, the piano carries whatever melody there is, and the vocal line is declamatory. The singer, therefore, must take great pains to make the words expressive and clear; these songs make no sense otherwise. A generalized, uninflected delivery of a Wolf lied is unsatisfactory, no matter how beautiful the singer's voice, the listener can't understand the song's depth and meaning.

In the '30s, the Hugo Wolf Society sponsored a series of albums, available by subscription, for which they engaged many of the best lieder singers then before the public. These recordings were widely admired; unfortunately the series had to be discontinued at the outbreak of war in 1939. But in 1998, all these recordings, plus some never released, were transferred to CDs. This set, which includes 150 tracks of 147 songs (there are three duplications), is highly recommended for its scope and the high quality of the performances by the principals: Elena Gerhardt, Hüsch, Kipnis, Rethberg, Erb, and Janssen (♦EMI 66640, 5CD).

The superb accompanists are Coenraad V. Boos, Michael Raucheisen, and Gerald Moore. The release includes most of *Italienisches Liederbuch* (41 of 46), much of *Spanisches Liederbuch* (22 of 44), and 35 of the 55 *Mörike Lieder*. Also, here are 24 of the 51 Goethe songs and 9 of the 20 to Eichendorff texts, and many others. The songs are parceled out; thus eight singers participate in *Spanisches Liederbuch,* similarly for the other Mörike songs and *Italienisches Liederbuch*. The singers are all well-captured, but much of the time the tone of the piano isn't as brilliant as in more recent recordings.

The post-WWII generation has also produced excellent Wolf interpreters. Their vocal and interpretive style differ in some instances from the previous generation, but their work is just as compelling, sometimes even more so. The best, and most consistent in the records they have left us, are Schwarzkopf, Fischer-Dieskau, and, to a somewhat lesser extent, Seefried. In general, their discs have pleased us, though age and venue sometimes make a difference both in sound quality and in their singing.

In particular, **Schwarzkopf** emerged as almost a Wolf specialist; she seems to have programmed more of his songs than anyone else. Her Salzburg recital discs from the '50s show her at her best, particularly one from 1953, accompanied by Furtwängler (♦Fonit Cetra 21), and those from 1957 and 1958, both accompanied by Moore (♦EMI 65749 and 64905). Schwarzkopf was a master of tonal coloring; every word gets its due, sometimes too much so, to the point of fussiness. This is more apparent in her studio recordings; in the Salzburg recitals, these mannerisms don't intrude much. Her singing then was always beautiful and secure, and often tonally ravishing.

Fischer-Dieskau's way with Wolf lieder is just as compelling, and that's true even when, as in his later recordings, his voice had lost some of its tonal appeal. A disc of early Wolf songs to texts by Heine and Eichendorff is notable for this singer's canny sense of drama and superlative diction (♦Claves 8706). Another recommended recital disc is one of *Möricke Lieder* (♦Music & Arts 870, accompanied by Sviatoslav Richter), but a 1990 release of orchestrated songs found the 65-year-old in poor voice (Orfeo).

Italienisches Liederbuch. **Fischer-Dieskau** and **Schwarzkopf** teamed up with Moore for one of the best Wolf recordings, made in 1969 when both singers, but especially the baritone, were still in fine vocal shape (♦EMI 63732). Both had by then deepened and sharpened their ideas through many years of performing these songs. An older Salzburg performance, from 1958, where F-D was partnered by the irresistibly natural-sounding **Seefried,** is also recommended, though Seefried's charm and vocal allure aren't captured as well as they should be (♦Orfeo 220901). This disc, incidentally, includes many of Wolf's most accessible songs.

There are several other recordings of interest but somewhat below this level of excellence. In some cases, only one of the two singers is outstanding, the other merely competent. The best of them is by **Bonney** and **Hagegård;** both are excellent in the "cute" songs but don't plumb the depths of the heavier ones, and the soprano sometimes sounds a bit whiny (Teldec). **Upshaw** and **Bär**'s work lacks the tonal variety and expression of the best renditions, though both singers have attractive voices (EMI).

An older version by **Ameling** and **Krause** includes some of the Goethe and Keller lieder (Globe, 2CD, NA). It will please those listeners who respond to the Dutch soprano's charm and tonal beauty, but it too lacks dramatic expression in the heavier songs. **Lott** does well with her share of the songs in the recording she made with **Schreier,** but the tenor's thin, whitish tone is this set's liability (Hyperion). Similarly, **Ziesak,** a fresh-voiced young soprano, is winsome; her partner, **Andreas Schmidt,** is not, especially when he sings louder than piano (RCA). Finally, there was a recording from the '50s, with **Berger** and **Prey,** that gathered unanimous praise but is unavailable at present (Vox).

Spanisches Liederbuch. Not been recorded as often, its 44 songs, which include ten "Spiritual Songs," are more serious and not as tuneful. Here the piano's lines are sometimes the more "vocal." A fine 1968 recording with **Schwarzkopf, Fischer-Dieskau,** and Moore has vanished from the listings but we can hope it will return (DG). So has an excellent effort by **Seefried** and **Wächter;** they sang some of the spiritual songs as duets (DG). A more recent set by **von Otter** and **Bär** was not favorably received (EMI). **Ameling** also recorded this work, but the same comments apply to this as to her other Wolf discs (Hyperion, with seven Möricke songs).

Other Wolf discs of more than casual interest include those by **Augér** (♦Hyperion 66590), **Ziesak** (♦Sony 53278), and **Thomas Allen** (♦Virgin 59221). Also, many recital discs by lieder singers like **Lehmann, Anders, Mathis,** and **Margaret Price,** include some Wolf songs. These are usually chosen to display the singer's art, not the composer's. However, Lehmann in particular was an outstanding Wolf interpreter. Unfortunately, she offers only six by Wolf in one of her recital discs (Claremont 785057) and three in another (RCA 7809) amid much Schubert, Schumann, and Brahms—but lieder lovers can't go wrong with these releases.

Der Corregidor. This is Wolf's only completed opera, based on Alarcón's novel *The Three-Cornered Hat* (also used by De Falla). It hasn't been successful in the theater because it lacks drama; it's almost a sequence of (very fine) songs. The only modern recording fortunately has

a very good cast (♦Schwann 11641, 2CD). The principal roles are taken by Doris Soffel, Fischer-Dieskau, and Werner Hollweg, and **Albrecht** is the exemplary conductor.

Italian Serenade. Wolf's most celebrated and often-performed non-vocal work, it is a short piece that the composer scored for string quartet as well as chamber orchestra. It's in one movement and is a very lyrical, light-textured composition that seems to have unlimited energy. It must be performed without a break or even a change in tempo.

There are fine recordings of both versions, but because it takes little of the space on a CD, most listeners will want to consider the couplings. Thus, the **Orpheus Chamber Orchestra** has recorded, on one disc, "seven romances by seven composers" as well as the Wolf work (♦DG 431680). A more substantial program by **William Steinberg** includes Beethoven's Symphony 7 and Mendelssohn's "Italian," but you wouldn't want to invest in this unless you liked Steinberg's performances of the symphonies (EMI 65611). The work also turns up in a collection by **Bychkov** that includes Barber's Adagio, Tchaikovsky's *Serenade,* and Elgar's *Introduction and Allegro* (Philips 434108). A more attractive program by the **Budapest Strings** includes the Elgar and Suk Serenades and Chausson's *Poème* (♦Capriccio 10527).

Commendable quartet versions include the **Hagen Quartet,** where it's coupled with the two Janáček quartets (♦DG 427669) and an older recording by the **Hollywood String Quartet** that includes Schubert's 14 and Dohnányi's Quartet 3 (Testament 1081).   MOSES

Ermanno Wolf-Ferrari (1876–1948)

Like Peter Pan, Wolf-Ferrari refused to grow up; even in his 60s, with the premiere of *La Dama Boba,* he could recapture the youthful sparkle and innocence of his best-known scores, *Il Segreto di Susanna* and *I Quattri Rusteghi* written 30 years earlier; quoth he, "A real child I was, I am, I always will be." Those who know only the sparkling overture to *The Secret of Susanna* owe it to themselves to look further, for is there not still a bit of the child in us all?

Two splendid collections gather together the best of Wolf-Ferrari's orchestral excerpts, by **Marriner** (♦EMI 54585) and **Serebrier** (♦ASV 861). Both include a number of overtures and dances, including the familiar *Danza Napolitano* often played at "Pops" concerts as "Dance of the Camorristi"; to these Marriner adds a couple of intermezzos for good measure. Those who remember **Nello Santi**'s excellent London LP will find a similar rough-hewn heartiness from Serebrier; Marriner is more polished and usually faster—though there's no point in splitting hairs; both are wonderful. **Heinz Rögner** offers some of the same pieces combined with the *Serenade for Strings,* an early work that shows Wolf-Ferrari's love of Mozart while suggesting Rossini's string sonatas (Berlin 9177). His Teutonic reading is handily surpassed by **Alun Francis**'s ebullient account (CPO 999271), while **Roberto Padoin** is betrayed by execrable sound (Rainbow).

Sinfonia Brevis calls for a large orchestra, yet in its pellucid scoring almost seems like chamber music. Here **Francis** seems curiously nonchalant, though the essence of the music still comes across (CPO). The gentle and rhapsodic *Sinfonia da Camera* for piano and small orchestra is available in two fine versions, from **Horst Göbel** in Berlin (Thorofon 2078, with the Sextet by Wolf-Ferrari's mentor Rheinberger) and **MiNesemblet** in Norway (Marco Polo 223868, with Bloch's *4 Episodes*).

Surely the heartfelt passion that informs the Violin Concerto by the nearly 70-year-old Wolf-Ferrari owes much to his affection for the raven-haired 20-something violinist Guila Bustabo, who gave the premiere. It's beautifully played by **Ulf Hoelscher** (♦CPO 999271, with *Serenade*). The Cello Concerto is more broadly expressive and closes with a sparkling saltarello. Here Francis is less successful; either he or cellist **Gustav Rivinius** is too cautious in the finale (CPO 999278, with *Sinfonia Brevis*). The *Idillio Concertino* for oboe and *Concertino* for English horn are imaginatively played by **Omar Zoboli** (Koch Schwann 311113).

The two trios for violin, cello, and piano, Piano Quintet in D sharp, and String Quintet in C are gathered together in excellent performances by the **Munich Piano Trio** and Leopolder Quartet with Sawallisch on piano (MD+G 3310, 2CD). The trios are warm, attractive music in the manner of Schubert or Brahms; the Piano Quintet is closer to Dohnányi, while the Quintet, written during WWII, understandably has a dour, unsettled quality. This set is far more satisfying than the **Raphael Trio**'s two trios (ASV 935); it's better recorded, but the violin is often out of tune. The **Trio di Venezia**'s account is even worse (Nuova Era). The two trios for violin, viola, and cello are admirably presented by the **German String Trio** (CPO 999624). The third of Wolf-Ferrari's three violin sonatas isn't as spontaneous as the first two, but the totality is rewarding as heard from **Cristiano Rossi** and Marco Vincenzi (Dynamic 68).

The Secret of Susanna remains Wolf-Ferrari's most popular opera. (Susanna's secret, incidentally, is that she enjoys an occasional cigarette—hot stuff in those days!) There used to be LP sets with **Scotto** (CBS 40134) and **Maria Chiara** (London 1169); neither appears to be on CD, but a set led by ? contains *Susanna,* Suppés *Beautiful Galatea,* and Massenet's *Portrait of Manon,* unfortunately not available separately (Mondo Musica 10605, 3CD). His third opera, *Sly,* vaguely based on *The Taming of the Shrew,* replaces Shakespearean comedy with verismo tragedy; but even with Carreras as the drunkard Christopher Sly, distant voices and dreadful sound make **Frühbeck de Burgos**'s recording no more than a stopgap (Legato).

I Quattro Rusteghi (*The School for Fathers*) finds four equally boorish men given lessons in sociability by their wives and daughters; the singers led by **Daniele Callegari** seem competent, but who knows what they're singing? There is no English libretto (Arkadia). Far more entertaining is *Il Campiello,* a rollicking comedy of bickering neighbors, with expert singers expertly led by **Niksa Bareza** (Fonit Cetra 2014, 2CD). **Gerhard Markson** conducts the sparkling *Das Himmelskleid* (*The Garment of Heaven*), based on Perrault's fairy tale *The Donkey Skin,* competently sung and recorded (Marco Polo 223261, 3CD).

The oratorio *La Vita Nuova,* based on Dante, is a passionate setting of unrequited love, sublimely sung by soprano Celina Lindsley, less so by baritone George Fortune, with **Roland Bader** conducting; chorus, orchestra, and sonics are all excellent (♦Koch Schwann 1267). Wolf-Ferrari's double heritage (German and Italian) surfaces in his songs, particularly *Edelweis* (in German) and *Italian Songbook,* expressively sung by soprano **Maria de Francesca-Cavazza** (Koch Schwann 314004), while mezzo **Yvi Jänicke** offers the *Songbook* and eight *Rispetti* played by pianist Bruno Canino (CPO 999270).   HALLER

Stefan Wolpe (1902–1972)

Often referred to as a kind of modernist "outsider," Wolpe is difficult to categorize; he had connections with the Darmstadt modernists as he did with jazz and working-class-conscious Marxists like Eisler, yet his music is undoctrinaire and often tinged with humor. Pitch repetitions and local tonal gestures let wit and light into his textures, at least in the more streamlined works of the '60s. Wolpe's impishness might make you think of cabaret. Impeccable craftsmanship meets individuality, and brief lyrical effusions are integrated with disruptive gestures.

Each of the five available Wolpe discs presents a balanced and varied program, though one of them puzzlingly includes Webern's two-piano arrangement of Schoenberg's *Five Pieces for Orchestra* (Koch 7315). Still, that well-recorded disc is important for its patient and very musical performance of the late String Quartet (1969), a Wolpe *opus ultimum.* (See below for two competing renditions of this score.) Apart from a brief solo violin work, the rest of this disc is taken up with the half-hour *Man from Midian* for two pianos. This is a fairly early (1942) but startlingly skilled ballet score in short tableaux, with a harmonic language resembling Hindemith or even Messiaen. This performance fairly convinces, even if the slightly relentless players don't keep the listener from missing the lost orchestrations.

A rendition of the 1969 String Quartet has a shallower recording, and the less sensitive (and quicker) players are also wont to strain for accents (CPO). The 1955 Quartet for Oboe, Cello, Piano, and Percussion is another considerable and beautiful opus, but the 1963 Cantata that fills out this disc might strike some as idiosyncratic and awkward with its weird assortment of German and English texts, occasional speech, and sometimes punishing soprano line.

The 1969 String Quartet was also recorded by the **Juilliard Quartet** (♦CRI 587), some 20 years after first violin Robert Mann commissioned the work and helped encourage it along to completion through the composer's illness. Though not as ingratiating as the Koch performance mentioned above, with a recording that's brighter and more echoey, the Juilliard version is invested with the expected astonishing degree of detail. Hearing them after the Koch rendition—with its perhaps unidiomatic melodic warmth—not to mention the more generic "modernity" of the CPO performance, the Juilliard's intense musicality seems just right for this engrossing, important, and very enjoyable score. Also on the disc are very authoritative performances of Sessions's Quartet 2 and Babbitt's Quartet 4, this last marred by some shoddy mastering.

The best version of the mercurial 1955 Quartet can be heard on a release where **Harvey Sollberger** directs a sensitive performance that responds to the music bar-by-bar (♦Koch 7112). And Koch's more distant mikes—fewer in number, too—give more color to the piano and percussion. This issue continues with the refined Trio for Flute, Cello, and Piano (1964) and the uncompromising Violin Sonata (1949), truly a grand concert-stage statement that would rank as one of the great duo sonatas of the mid-century if it didn't go on so. Here **Jorja Fleezanis** finds an ideal partner in virtuoso pianist **Garrick Ohlsson;** the difficult keyboard part requires no less.

One of Wolpe's longest and most difficult mature works is his Symphony (1956), premiered complete only in 1965. In a complex and dense work such as this, with its manic and slippery rhythms and its restless dovetailings of tone-color, Wolpe shows his true Schoenbergian pedigree; the finale, especially, tends to sound like Schoenberg's orchestral Variations with the intermittent lyricism removed. It is not one of Wolpe's most characteristic works, probably because the composer felt the historical weight of the genre, but there is still a typical streak of humor, especially in the opening bassoon material. A live recording from 1975 finds **Arthur Weisberg** leading a New York performance that is extremely competent but not much more than that—the opening, for one, finds the group in tentative ensemble (CRI). As so often with CRI sonics, the balance is fairly good but the stereo spread is so narrow and the sonic image so noncommittal that the disc might as well be mono. The coupling is a fine performance, better recorded than the Wolpe, of Sessions's Violin Concerto by **Paul Zukofsky.**

Another disc (♦Bridge 9043) presents a wide cross-section of Wolpe's styles, including the droll *Suite im Hexachord* (1936) for oboe and clarinet, the Quintet with Voice (1957), and *Piece in Three Parts* (1961). The Quintet is again Schoenbergian, in disruptiveness of gesture if not in pitch vocabulary. (Wolpe's brief period of study with Webern likely purged his style of Schoenberg's brand of "wrong-note" classicism.) By the *Piece in Three Parts,* though—or even the beautiful finale of the Quintet—Wolpe was very much striking out in his own direction. The performances, by **Speculum Musicae** and the **Chamber Music Society of Lincoln Center,** are outstanding, neither bullying the music à la Parnassus (see below) nor romanticizing it unduly. Bridge gives us *Piece in Three Parts* in an excellent 1992 live recording, with **Oliver Knussen** conducting the 17 players and **Peter Serkin** on piano. This is another major score. Indeed, the whole disc is a must for Wolpians; the only duplication with other issues is *Suite im Hexachord,* and if this performance doesn't find quite the wit (and occasional sultry pitch slides) of the Col Legno version (see below), it compensates with a final Adagio of particular depth.

An outstanding disc encompasses six works written between 1929 and 1969 and gives perhaps the widest and best Wolpe survey, ranging from jazz influences to Schoenbergian aphorism (♦Col Legno 31809). The longest pieces included are *Suite im Hexachord* and the Quartet for trumpet, saxophone, percussion, and piano (1954). The German performances are extraordinarily vivid and spot-on without sounding at all stiff or unvaried, and the same goes for the ambient and dynamic sound. All told, this is one of the easiest Wolpe discs to recommend. Yet another disc, with the virtuosic group **Parnassus,** provides a similar selection (Koch), but here the performances tend toward a kind of superficial brilliance; compare it with the outstanding CPO performance described above and there's no questioning the greater musicality and variety of response in the latter. The Koch is also marred by heavy-handed and overmiked performances of two song sets.

Geoffrey Douglas Madge offers a hefty slice of Wolpe's piano music (CPO 999055). Again, such a cross-section of his output (ranging here from one of his earliest pieces, a song without words dated 1920, to *Form IV* from 1969) telescopes diverse experimentation in popular dances, Viennese-style 12-tone studies, and the more personal and pared-down works of later years. Madge is a fine technician, but he favors a close microphone balance and tends to get bombastic whenever Wolpe increases his demands and dynamic markings. You will want Madge's disc for the 24-minute *Battle Piece* in which the composer registered his horror of war. But if a 20-minute sampling of Wolpe's keyboard music will satisfy, turn to **Peter Serkin**'s tauter and more piquant and majestic accounts of *Form IV, Passacaglia,* and the early *Pastorale* (♦New World 344). Serkin's disc-mates are slightly overpedaled renditions of Stravinsky's Serenade in A and Sonata, and some short works by the pianist's friend Peter Lieberson.   ASHBY

Charles Wuorinen (b. 1938)

Wuorinen has been at the forefront of American new music for four decades. Perhaps more than anyone else, he has demonstrated through his very large output the variety and potential still to be realized in combining serial and tonal formats and disciplines. His imagination and facility enhance the scope and breadth of his musical expression, and his capacity to articulate and expand ideas with fluency results in powerful large-scale images of the textural, motivic, and timbral possibilities he

explores. He was the youngest composer ever to win the Pulitzer Prize. Wuorinen is an accomplished pianist and conductor and the founder of the Group for Contemporary Music, a chamber ensemble that has recorded many of his works since the early '60s.

The Group can be heard to very good effect in the brilliant Violin Sonata, played by **Benjamin Hudson** and Garrick Ohlsson (New World 385). It's an example of artistic integrity achieved through absolute clarity of vision, unity of purpose and consistency of means, and the disc is a good place to start an exploration of Wuorinen's work. String Quartet 3 demands even closer attention, structural unity being achieved through the firm anchor of a tonal G to and from which all peregrinations radiate. The *Fast Fantasy* for cello and piano (with **Fred Sherry** and Wuorinen himself) displays ideas that have an uncanny knack for capturing interest and then compounding it with more ideas, declinations, slants, and revisits. Another excellent disc from the Group includes the Piano Quintet, an expansive, intricate, and kaleidoscopic essay in which Wuorinen assimilates the language of mainstream 19thand 20th-century music into a complex, ornamented style (Koch 7410). Conceived as a ballet, *The Mission of Virgil* for piano duet serves as a commentary on episodes from Dante's *Inferno,* the mood being more ironic and grotesque than apocalyptic. The Percussion Quartet is a stunningly virtuosic exploration of the sonorities of a wide range of tuned and untuned instruments.

String Quartet 2 seeks the reconciliation of opposites, unity from dichotomy (Koch 7615, with quartets by Jonathan Harvey and Wayne Petersen). A disc of trios features the Horn Trio, much less concerned with opposites and more with fluency and classical grace (Koch 7617). A trio for tuba, bass trombone, and double bass makes serious fun of the instruments' obvious gaucheries. The Trombone Trio achieves contrast and interest by combining marimba, vibraphone, and piano. The often explosive Piano, Violin, and Cello Trio gives the players ample scope for pyrotechnics, and the substantial *Double Solo* for Horn, Violin, and Piano is another example of Wuorinen's inventive and coherent fluency.

Alan Feinberg has explored the keyboard music (Koch 7308, with a piece by Morton Feldman). In some ways Wuorinen's debt to one of America's early disciples of Schoenberg, Stefan Wolpe, is shown in the extended range of expression, highly gestural, virtuosic brush strokes, and the sense of molding order out of primeval disorder that are the hallmarks of the often vertiginous Piano Sonata 3. The more static *Bagatelle* couldn't be in greater opposition to the edgy, elusive, and enigmatic *Capriccio,* which comes from a crucial period in Wuorinen's development. Amid this array of turbulence sits Feldman's Satiesque *Palais de Mari.*

An especially fine disc of music for voice and larger chamber ensemble presented by the **Chamber Music Society of Lincoln Center** includes *A Winter's Tale,* with Bryn-Julson. This disc also contains erudite and illuminating sleeve notes by the composer Peter Paul Nash, who astutely observes that Wuorinen's music is pure artifact rather than political. *New York Notes* for seven players reverts to the fluid mechanics of opposites and the fragmentary coalescence of order and chaos, overlain with computer-generated sounds. Earlier Wuorinen can be heard on a disc that includes the Varèse-like essay *The Winds* for large chamber ensemble, played by **Parnassus** (New World 80517). Also worth exploring is "Music of Two Decades" (Music & Arts 4801, 4802 and 4932, 3CD, available separately). The first disc is a useful introduction to the orchestral music, including the 1971 Concerto for Amplified Violin and Orchestra in a recording of fair quality by **Paul Zukofsky** and the

University of Iowa Symphony. The Group for Contemporary Music and Speculum Musicae also make a number of appearances.

As for large-scale orchestral works, two discs stand out. One includes the masterful *Two-Part Symphony*, a brilliant study in variation form, with the American Composers Orchestra under **Dennis Russell Davies** (CRI 744). The Piano Concerto is perhaps less distinctive, but the Tuba Concerto is a work of early maturity: multi-layered polyphony finding its way into the vocabulary, gradually unfolding as the piece gains momentum, played by the **Group for Contemporary Music.** From the '80s comes the sonorous and mystical (not an adjective usually applicable to Wuorinen) *Mass for the Restoration of St. Luke's,* for instruments, voices, and organ (Koch 7336). Perhaps the ultimate accolade goes to the final work on this disc, *Genesis,* in which Wuorinen captures both the physical violence of Creation and the loving gentleness of God. One of the finest and most profound American choral works of recent years, it is well served by the Minnesota Orchestra and Chorale led by **Edo de Waart.**   JOHNSON

Iannis Xenakis *(b. 1922)*

Xenakis's music is remarkable for its daring, originality, and utter lack of compromise. While his works receive several hundred performances each year around the world, he's an important force in contemporary music in the US even though only a dozen or so take place here. His training was initially in engineering, mathematics, and architecture, and his music is composed exclusively by various mathematical procedures. This suggests that the results might be dry and academic, but the reality is the opposite. His music possesses tremendous vitality, a primal aspect that is provocative and thrilling; it conveys remarkable power, rhythmic vitality, and force of emotion, devoid of sentimentality, but with real heart. He's also capable of composing with great subtlety and refinement, a delicate elegance. Once you've become acclimated to the sound world he creates, his music satisfies—and deeply.

In spite of the formidable challenges posed by Xenakis's music, recorded performances abound, especially solo and chamber music. Some works like *Eonta* or the solo piano pieces have been recorded many times. Orchestral works are recorded much less often, and little of his large-scale orchestral music is currently available. A landmark recording of his two earliest orchestral works, *Metastasis* and *Pithoprakta,* is no longer in print (Chant du Monde 278368). **Juan Pablo Izquierdo** with the Carnegie Mellon Philharmonic has begun to address this lack, offering several compositions including *Metastasis* and *Jonchaies,* a stunning piece that's quite accessible, even melodic, and deserves to be much better known (♦Col Legno 20504, and in a wonderful but costly anthology, Col Legno 31830, 5CD). Mode's excellent series also includes a fine rendering of *Dümmerschein,* a dense, swirling kaleidoscope of sound that could be mistaken for electronic music (♦Mode 58, with two other ensemble pieces plus a fine reading of Varèse's *Amériques).*

In chamber and solo music matters are better, often with several choices of many works. Two labels are offering collections that provide an excellent introduction to Xenakis's music. Disques Montaigne's Vol. 1 contains chamber music for strings and piano written between 1955 and 1990 (782005, 2CD). The **Arditti String Quartet** plays with its customary verve and precision, both as an ensemble and individually in several solo pieces, while pianist Claude Helffer draws out the lyrical aspect of the music without sacrificing any of its ferocity or rhythmic punch. In the Mode series, the quartets aren't yet represented, but the piano works are (Mode 80). **Aki Takahashi** negotiates their technical

demands with great ease. Overall, her approach is drier and spikier than Helffer's but equally satisfying. Both pianists have had a long association with this music, and both play with unswerving commitment. Another exponent of Xenakis's piano music, **Yuji Takahashi,** made an important earlier recording of *Evryali* and *Herma;* it's excellent but a very short disc (Denon 1052, NA).

The Mode series includes many other fine performances. Vol. 1 (Mode 53) has excellent performances led by **Charles Bornstein,** including a superb version of *Eonta* for brass and piano and *Rebonds* for solo percussion. **Charles Pelz** leads an exuberant reading of *Palimpsest* in Vol. 4 (Mode 80), the best recorded of the three versions I've heard. In general, these performances are equal or superior to any others. One exception is **Irvine Arditti**'s second recording of *Dikthas* (Disques Montaigne), which has much greater intensity than **Jane Peters** on Mode. Other recommended collections of ensemble music include **ASKO Ensemble**'s live recording (Attacca 9054); it has much to savor but isn't as sonically detailed in the pieces duplicated on Mode. A fine collection under the direction of **Guy Protheroe** is well performed but short on playing time (Wergo 6178).

The sweeping percussion cycle *Pléiades* gets a strong performance by the **Kroumata Percussion Ensemble** (BIS 482), sonically superior to the earlier recording by **Le Percussions de Strasbourg.** The BIS disc is completed by **Gert Mortenson**'s amazing reading of *Psappha,* for solo percussionist. Die-hard fans of Xenakis's percussion music will be pleased to get the **Demoé Percussion Ensemble**'s disc, which presents three important works (Stradivarius 40001). The performances are adequate, but Mortenson's *Psappha* is much better, and the versions of *Okho* and *Persephassa* are outstripped by the recordings in ♦Mode 56 and 58.

Xenakis has also written extensively for voice. His choral works are somewhat gentler in aspect than his instrumental music, and a wonderful collection entitled "Pupils of Messiaen" with three of his finest pieces is highly worthwhile (♦Chandos 9663, with choral works by Messiaen and Stockhausen). Another collection is offered by **James Wood** and Critical Band; I haven't heard it, but it's highly regarded and more extensive (Hyperion 66980). Xenakis has long been interested in Greek tragedy, and the stark intensity of that dramatic form is well-matched to his music. His setting of *Oresteia* is emotionally harrowing and very challenging, but compelling (Salabert/Actuels 8906, NA).

Xenakis was an early pioneer in electronic music, and unlike many of his contemporaries, he has kept pace with changes in technology and continues to compose in this medium. I find his earlier analog electronic works more satisfying; they've held up better than many others of their time. They are available in a superbly mastered collection (♦Electronic Music Foundation 003). Later computer-generated pieces are just as rigorous but less dramatic, and have less sonic warmth. Two examples, *Gendy3* and *Tauriphanie,* are included in a notable all-Xenakis collection (Neuma 450-86, with two ensemble works).   McINTIRE

Eugène Ysaÿe *(1858–1931)*

This great Belgian violinist bridged the gap between the 19th century with its cult of personality and the 20th with its cult of tone. Trained by two of the great virtuosos, Vieuxtemps and Wieniawski, he inspired the first generation of tonalists in Western Europe. No other performer resembles him in his mercurial, bigger-than-life temperament. You can hear him in a 1913 recording of his mazurka, *Lointaine passé,* and *Rêve d'enfant,* a lullaby-like work he wrote for his youngest son. His performance of the mazurka is suave, his *Rêve* full of a dreamy tenderness you won't hear in any other recording. Sony's engineers outdid themselves in transferring these acoustic recordings from their original masters (◆Sony 62337, N/A).

Ysaÿe is best known for his unique set of six sonatas for solo violin, Op. 27. After hearing a performance of one of Bach's solo violin sonatas by his young colleague, Joseph Szigeti, Ysaÿe conceived the idea of writing a set of works each of which would evoke the performing style and personality of its dedicatee; their composition was an act of love by a big-hearted man for those he inspired. They are dedicated, in order, to Szigeti, Thibaud, Enescu, Kreisler, Mathieu Crickboom, and Manuel Quiroga, and range in length from one movement (3 and 6) to four (1 and 2). They are fascinating, evocative, highly original works that are also superb virtuoso display pieces. It's good to see them beginning to receive the attention they deserve, judging by the number of recordings that have become available in the past ten years or so. Perhaps they will inspire modern performers to explore the rest of Ysaÿe's oeuvre.

Several complete recordings exist. **Charles Castleman** suffers from inflexible bowing and vibrato and frequently crude execution; he shines in 3 and 6, but he can't hold the longer ones together (Music & Arts). **Philippe Graffin** is up to the music's technical demands but lacks the emotional range these works require (Hyperion). **Evgenia-Maria Popova** plays them with ferocious energy; they would benefit from some contrasting calm, but she's quite exciting, if a bit rough-edged (Leman). **Frank Peter Zimmerman** made a good, if not electrifying, recording that included fine performances of *Poème élégiaque* and *Rêve d'enfant* (EMI, N/A).

Tomoko Kato (Denon 18011) and **Leonidas Kavakos** (BIS 1046) have made the most technically immaculate readings, with the best recorded sound to boot. **Shumsky** recorded them in 1982 in majestic readings, and he draws a rich, sweet tone from his Stradivarius that erupts like lava in the more explosive passages (Nimbus 7715). **Kremer** is more mercurial than Shumsky, even nervous, with more tonal flexibility and often faster tempos, and brings out the works' quirkiness better (Mobile Fidelity 1000921). **Vincenzo Bolognese** is remarkably similar to Kremer in approach and temperament (Arts 47175).

Takayoshi Wanami (◆Somm 012) studied Sonata 1 with its dedicatee, Szigeti. These lessons paid off, as Wanami has developed so much insight into these works that even the most seemingly gratuitous virtuoso display passages have purpose. While he's fully up to its technical demands, Wanami is the least virtuosic of the violinists considered here; but he's not afraid to dazzle, and his readings are the most satisfying. He even resembles Szigeti in his slow, wobbly vibrato, which is a great advantage in 1.

There are some fine performances of individual sonatas. **Vengerov** gives a fine reading of 3 in his debut disc (Biddulph 001). **Josefowicz** rips into 3 and 4 with obvious relish in an excellent release (Philips 446700). **Gringolits** has recorded 3 and 6; this remarkable boy has technique to burn and his own ideas about whatever he plays (◆BIS 1051). These performances are very stylish, and his insight into this music rivals Wanami's. Excellent sound too, with lots of hall ambience. On **Fodor**'s debut LP, 3 burns right through the speakers in a delirious performance (RCA 0735). **Rabin** recorded 3 and 4 in 1955 in beautifully shaped, high-octane performances (EMI 67020).

Among Ysaÿe's shorter works, *Caprice d'après l'Etude en forme de valse de Saint-Saëns* is a whimsical arrangement for violin and orchestra of Saint-Saëns's famous etude that deserves greater popularity. It's that rare thing, a virtuoso showpiece with more humor than bravura. **Bell** recorded the only CD incarnation known to me in his *Poème* disc

(London 433519). *Extase* Op. 21 is a rapturous Symbolist work recorded by **David Oistrakh** and pianist Vladimir Yampolsky in the late '50s and is available in the super-budget "Violin Classics" set (EMI 69114). *Amitié* (*Friendship*) Op. 26 is scored for two solo violins and orchestra; it's a lovely piece that also deserves to be better known. There is a fine performance by **David** and **Igor Oistrakh** (Revelation 10039).

Ysaÿe wrote his Sonata for Solo Cello Op. 28 for the cellist in his string quartet, Maurice Dambois. Its four brief movements exploit that instrument's tonal and technical possibilities just as effectively as the violin sonatas do. **Gordon Epperson** has recorded the piece, but he fails utterly to make any sense of the music and merely draws a succession of rude noises from his instrument (Centaur). **Erling Blöndal Bengtsson** could hardly provide a greater contrast. A real virtuoso and an intelligent musician, he deftly characterizes each movement and draws a refined, beautifully controlled tone from his finely recorded Nicolas Lupot cello (Danacord 372). MAGIL

Isang Yun (1917–1995)

The more of Yun's music I hear, the more confounded I am that he isn't better known. The body of work he left behind is enormous, and enormously satisfying. He wrote an important cycle of five symphonies, several concertos and a wealth of chamber music. His life was marked by political turmoil and great personal suffering, and this comes through in many of his works. From an expressive standpoint, his music resembles Shostakovich, though Yun's techniques are different and he's more dissonant. His music is an intriguing synthesis of East and West; he combines elements of Korean court music with serialism and other contemporary western compositional techniques. The result is a powerful music that's quite unlike anyone else's.

Yun's five symphonies are central to his output. They can also be regarded as a five-section "hypersymphony," although they stand alone just fine. I recommend the cycle by **Takao Ukigaya** with the Pomeranian Philharmonic (CPO 999125, 999147/48). This has the advantage of being all recorded in a consistent acoustic, and the orchestra plays quite well. Alternative performances are offered in a remarkable set by a variety of performers that gives a fine overview of Yun's oeuvre, but the symphonies were recorded in different venues with different orchestras and the results are inconsistent (Camerata 231/40 10CD, NA). Some of the recordings are live, and the performance of 1 under **Byung-Hwa Kim** is especially weak. The performances of 2, with **Georg Schmöthe** conducting, and 4 under **Hiroyuki Iwaki,** are better.

This set is balanced out with many superb chamber and concerto performances, some not otherwise available, such as the excellent Violin Concerto with **Akiko Tatsumi** as soloist and Macal conducting the Bavarian Radio Orchestra. Yun's more nationalistic (and optimistic) side can be heard in the sweeping *My Land, My People!* for soloists, orchestra, and chorus (CPO 999047). This work is offset by the darker *Exemplum in Memoriam Kwangju*. These two works are also in the Camerata set, in the same performances.

Yun wrote a number of notable concertos; the Cello Concerto is an outstanding example. **Siegfried Palm** plays this harrowing work with appropriate intensity; it recalls Yun's political imprisonment and torture in the late '60s (Camerata 22). The fiercely difficult Clarinet Concerto is also worth your attention, and **Eduard Brunner** plays it with uncompromising brilliance (Camerata 46).

In Yun's chamber music, there is a wealth of excellent works to sample. Start with the two Clarinet Quintets, exquisitely played by **Eduard Brunner** and the Amati String Quartet (CPO 999428). Amati also offers a wonderful reading of Quartet 6 on this disc. More music for string quartet is offered in "Chamber Music" with Quartets 3 and 4, *Tapis* for string quintet, and *Concertino* for accordion and string quartet (CPO 999075). In "Chamber Music II" **L'Art pour L'Art** presents a more instrumentally varied assortment, with solos, duos and trios of flute, violin, harp, cello, and guitar (CPO 999118). "Music for Wind" has three works for wind quintet, plus *Sori* for solo flute and *Rondell* for oboe, clarinet, and bassoon, all played by members of the **Albert Schweitzer Quintet** (♦CPO 999184). Everything here is impressive for its originality, eloquence, and elegance of writing, and all of these pieces display Yun's uncommon understanding of instrumental color.   McINTIRE

Frank Zappa *(1940–1993)*

In his lifetime Zappa took up plenty of limelight as a guitar idol, politically incorrect rocker, and fighter against US government initiatives like the Parents' Music Resource Center and its successful campaign in the mid-'80s to put warning labels on parentally offensive recordings. But much of Zappa's music is worth our attention and respect; he claimed his first music was written for classical ensembles, and that he had formed his bands only because he had no other way of hearing it.

The man was a workaholic, and it's impossible to generalize about the 60-some albums he released between 1966 and 1993. But Zappa's initiative as a composer for acoustic ensembles took many by surprise when EMI released "The Perfect Stranger: Boulez Conducts Zappa" in 1984. It might have seemed a collision of worlds when Boulez, doyen of the European avant-garde, taped three scores with his Ensemble InterContemporain only two years after Zappa—in collaboration with his daughter Moon Unit—had topped the pop charts with "Valley Girl." But Zappa heard no such divisions, and it must be said that a top-40 Zappa song like "Teenage Prostitute" owes as much to Rossini and Schoenberg as an orchestral score like *Sinister Footwear* owes to Johnny "Guitar" Watson.

Two of Zappa's first musical encounters, and figures he venerated all his life, were Varèse and Stravinsky, and they rank among the strongest influences on his music of the '60s and '70s, whether it be pigeonholed as rock or classical. Add to the developing mix his interest in progressive big-band jazz, musique concrète, and doo-wop, his aspirations as a filmmaker, his hateful amusement with lounge-lizard vocalizations, and his later love of the sampling Synclavier. A few of the early albums are worth mentioning as parallels to what some of the "classical" avant-garde was doing at about the same time. *Lumpy Gravy* offers some of the most entertaining musique concrète ever produced, though the album does revert too much to spoken extemporizations from friends and band members (♦Rykodisc 10504). Entertainment is enhanced, though, by some astute satires of commercial pop music from the '60s. (Zappa made a substantial remix of the album decades later, almost amounting to a revision; that's found in tandem with a re-release of "We're Only in it for the Money": fascinating for Zappaphiles, but the original single album remains preferable.)

Zappa's sixth album, *Uncle Meat,* is an astonishing melange of Stravinskyan and rhythmically uncentered banality, parodies of cheap pop, and musique concrète (♦Rykodisc 10506/07). It's unlike anything heard before or since. It was originally designed as a film, but the audio discs were the only thing released. Alongside a film-like narrative, the album represents a set of double variations and is therefore one of his more stringently classical products. And, like most of Zappa's albums, it's impeccably recorded and produced. (When he realized he was dying of cancer, he went back and carefully remixed and remastered most of his albums; these can be identified by the "FZ" imprimatur on the back of the Rykodisc jewel boxes.)

Another video project, one that was released as a film, was the grand and outrageous *200 Motels*. (Zappa takes as his subject the boredom of a rocker's touring life on the road, pace Nicolas Slonimsky and his contention in *Baker's* that the movie is about "itinerant sex activities.") The soundtrack, made with the combined forces of Zappa's band and the Royal Philharmonic, presents some of his most fascinatingly astringent serious music ("Dental Hygiene Dilemma") alongside white-trash country music send-ups ("Lonesome Cowboy Burt") and utter inscrutables (though often with less inscrutable titles) like "Shove It Right In" (Rykodisc 10513/14, 2CD). *200 Motels* is a central document for Zappologists, but this album—especially as the recorded sound is atypically dim and messy—is best recommended to converts.

Burnt Weeny Sandwich and *Weasels Ripped My Flesh* are equally brilliant stylistic centrifuges, though the more frequent infusion of straight-out rock might limit their appeal to card-carrying classical listeners. Both these recordings date from 1970 and both carry typical *épater-les-bourgeois* titles. With its echoes and rethinkings of the jangly, harpsichord-dominated *Uncle Meat* style, *Burnt Weeny* probably has broader appeal. But anyone who misses *Weasels* will miss out on the weird if self-indulgent "Prelude to the Afternoon of a Sexually Aroused Gas Mask" and the "Eric Dolphy Memorial Barbecue," not to mention standbys like "My Guitar Wants to Kill Your Mama." Zappa suffered severe injuries after falling from a stage not long after he made these two albums, and his slow convalescence pushed him in new directions—specifically, jazz-fusion and dada-rock styles that needn't concern us here.

There are four albums of bona fide orchestral music. His orchestration is neither warm and fuzzy nor coloristic, and his textures—involving multi-doubled but improvisatory melodies over bass lines—and his structures—based not upon development of material so much as jazz-pop models of "heads" and solos, and also on cartoon-style streams of consciousness—will disappoint or confuse those who come to the music with strong art music expectations, not to mention hopes for good tunes.

Zappa's greatest "classical" hit, a delightful piece that's been performed often, is "Duprée's Paradise." This originated as a piece for his own rock bands, but he revised the work for Boulez, and the avant-garde maître's recording happily captures the music's syncopated exuberance and Coplandesque, al fresco textures (♦Rykodisc 10542). Also on this necessary, if rather short, disc is a 13-minute Boulez commission that gives a clearer picture of Zappa's serious modernist aspirations (The Perfect Stranger"), the wonderfully mysterious "Naval Aviation in Art?," and four examples of his work with his home-studio Synclavier (anthropomorphized on the disc package as "The Barking Pumpkin Digital Gratification Consort"). He was led to the Synclavier through his frustration with orchestras and other acoustic performing ensembles and, with a few exceptions ("Outside Now Again"), these electronic pieces contain some of his more daring experiments. *Jazz from Hell* consists almost entirely of such pieces, though here the evocation of drum sets and pop-style chords might strike you as self-indulgent (Rykodisc).

In a biographical denouement worthy of fiction, the Ensemble Modern and arranger Ali Askin hooked up with the dying composer in 1992 to do some spectacular virtuoso concerts of Zappa's more difficult music, recorded and excerpts preserved for posterity under the title *The Yellow Shark* (♦Rykodisc 40560). The way these young German players latch onto Askin's arrangements of his dizzying and complex Synclavier pieces "The Girl in the Magnesium Dress" and "G-Spot Tornado" has to be heard to be believed. Zappa's political posturing continued into his last illness (as in the narrative piece "Food Gathering in Post-Industrial America, 1992"), and you also have to contend with an audience that enjoys itself hugely between works, but there's no escaping the exhilarating and undoctrinaire creativity of the music or the impression that this is exactly how it was meant to be played. Hear the disc, and you'll also have the rare experience of hearing some atonal and difficult music meeting up with loving, expert performances and rapturous, knowing applause.

Zappa recorded some of his longer and more ambitious orchestral and ballet scores with Nagano and the London Symphony (Rykodisc 10540/41, 2CD; avoid the old single-disc issue with only half the pieces). None of the music overlaps with the Boulez or Ensemble Modern discs, so the album is a must-hear for interested parties, particularly as it offers some large scores like the 28-minute "Mo 'n Herb's Vacation," premiered as a ballet one year after these sessions by Nagano and his own Berkeley Symphony. But the composer—a perfectionist for all seasons—was unhappy with the LSO and with the sessions, and in truth some playing is ambivalent. He did his own earlier taping of three of these scores and two additional ones with a smaller, more versatile, and more electric and studio-miked group ("Orchestral Favorites," ♦Zappa 45); that album is a lot of fun, not as slow and labored as the LSO album, and at times more characterful than the *Yellow Shark* renditions. (The "Orchestral Favorites" are also available interspersed in the three-disc *Läther* album, per Zappa's original intentions; ♦Rykodisc 10574/76.)

Zappa's final album, released after his death, is the dark and Orwellian *Civilization Phaze III* (Rykodisc). Here he went back to some of the earlier taped *Lumpy Gravy* material and melded it with his latest Synclavier work, some Ensemble Modern playing, and samples he made with those players. Some of the music here ranks among his finest in a classical-modernist vein (e.g., *Gross Man*), but the overall result—like so much of his work—is willful and best heard cinematically. And the weird but uninteresting *Lumpy Gravy* life-inside-a-piano narrative can't hold up in a 2CD album as well as it did in the earlier release.

A posthumously released compilation entitled *Strictly Genteel: A "Classical" Introduction to Frank Zappa* puts together bits and pieces of the classically inclined musician, taken from the various orchestral and electric albums described above (Rykodisc 10578). This would make a good introduction, including as it does favorite larger orchestral scores like "Dupree's Paradise" and "Pedro's Dowry" alongside some of the fascinating rock-classical intercessions from the *Uncle Meat* period of the late '60s. Still, it should be said that Zappa took great care over the song-to-song macrostructure of each of his albums, and hearing pieces out of context like this means missing out on a vital aspect of his creative thinking.

Four albums released after Zappa's death show how enthusiastically other groups and arrangers have taken to his music. *Zappa's Universe* (Verve 513575) is a flop, though it's hilarious to hear a new version of the narrative song "Jazz Discharge Party Hats." This live album brings together guitar virtuoso Steve Vai with a rock group, the Persuasions, and Joel Thome conducting the Orchestra of Our Time. There's rarely anything heard of the orchestra at all, the end-of-song fadeouts are annoying, and many of the vocals fall flat without Zappa's own wry and inimitable touch. The 12-member Omnibus Wind has made a disc of their own arrangements (Opus 3). There's some good solo work, but the ensemble sound is variable and one doubts this group could have gotten past the front doorstep of the militantly hard-to-please composer.

A stricter, more uptown sound comes from Jean-Michel Bossini and

Le Concert Impromptu, a French wind quintet (♦ED 13071). The disc holds only 47 minutes of music, and the close balance gives a larger-than-life image to the ensemble, but the performances (including old favorites like "The Black Page," "Uncle Meat," and "The Idiot Bastard Son," alongside "Outside Now Again," originally heard in Synclavier on the "Perfect Stranger" disc) are spot-on. Maybe too spot-on, since the "chaos" interlude in "Strictly Genteel" sounds over-rehearsed and humorless. But "Peaches en Regalia" sounds magnificently spiffy here, and Zappa would no doubt have loved the sheer professionalism of this group.   ASHBY

Jan Dismas Zelenka *(1679–1745)*

It's tempting to account for a certain austerity in Zelenka's music by referring to his disappointments in employment. He worked for the court of Dresden, starting as a double bass player in 1710, then filling in as conductor for five years, only to be passed over in favor of Hasse, whose music was much more forward-looking. After 1735, Zelenka worked and composed for the Dresden court church. His studies with Fux in Vienna and Lotti in Venice gave him a contrapuntal fluency perhaps equal to Bach's, leavened with an Italianate feeling for sound, drama, and lyricism. His personal life appears to have been solitary; he never married. There's a sense of humor in some of his music, particularly the trio sonatas and some of his orchestral works, but there's also a concentration on technical demands and a single-mindedness that leads him to write longer and harder single movements than most of his contemporaries. To present his music well, you must give him the same attention one would Bach.

Orchestral music. These consist primarily of five Capriccios, multi-movement works for oboes, horns, bassoon, and strings in a variety of moods and styles, sharing characteristics of the suite and sometimes the concerto. They contain stratospheric parts for horns, and the mixture of styles makes them challenging. There are several other works: a Sinfonia (more a Sinfonia Concertante, in five movements), a concerto for four soloists and strings, an *Ouverture,* and a three-movement piece called *Hipocondrie.* All of these pieces were recorded by Camerata Berne conducted by **Alexander van Wijnkoop,** played with technical polish and warmth, if a mite staid at times (Archiv 423703, 3CD).

The complete orchestral works were also recorded by the Suk Chamber Orchestra conducted by **František Vajnar** (Panton 1234/5, 2CD). These were beautifully played but much less lively than Camerata Bern. A more incisive early-music collection was played by Virtuosi Saxoniae under **Ludwig Güttler** (Berlin 1102, 1150). The most recent attempt at a complete edition is a soggy one by Das Neu-Eroffnete Orchestre under **Jurgen Sonnentheil** (CPO 999458/9). It's hard to get all these works onto two discs unless you take lively tempos, so these sets all omit something.

The four non-capriccios were recorded by **Combattimento Consort Amsterdam** in neatly turned performances (Astoria 90015). The Freiburg Baroque Orchestra under **Gottfried von der Goltz** was the first to give them an early-instrument treatment; they recorded all but the *Ouverture* in a program that included several rare works by Johann Pisendel (Deutsche Harmonia Mundi 77339). An early-music treatment was also recorded by Collegium 1704 under **Xavier Julien Leferriere,** including Trio Sonata 3 (Supraphon 9). This lively performance omits three movements from the Sinfonia, which appears in an otherwise Bach program played by Fiori Musicali under **Penelope Rapson,** spirited if not technically perfect (Metronome 1019). And finally, all four non-capriccios have been recorded on period instruments by Il Fondamento under **Paul Dombrecht** (Vanguard 99724).

Chamber music. The only chamber music pieces we know of are six trio sonatas. They are demanding and quirky pieces that require both subtlety and stamina for effective performance. The earliest complete edition was led by **Heinz Holliger** (Archiv 423937, 2CD, NA). It was estimable but used an edition that mixed up the separate bassoon part with the basso continuo line and had other problems. **Burkhard Glaetzner** recorded a better edition but didn't use a violin for Sonata 3 (Berlin 1070, 2CD). Neither is as sensitive or easy on the ears as **Dombrecht,** here as oboist, who not only sorts out the bass lines as the composer intended but uses early instruments played with great variety of tone color and a sense of humor absent from the other versions (Accent 8848, 2CD).

Ensemble Zefiro offered even more variety of sound and virtuosity, including theorbo and double bass in the continuo (♦Astrée 511, 563). Soloists of the **Chamber Orchestra** of Europe turned in a modern-instrument version, excellent though not as subtle as the early-instrument versions and a little muddy in the double bass (Claves 50-9511-12). Then **Holliger** re-recorded them, even better than before, though still with a vibrato that won't please everyone (ECM 462542, 2CD). His is the best of the modern oboe recordings.

Choral music. Zelenka's religious music shows a surprising variety of styles, always returning to his contrapuntal roots. The most striking contrasts are among the three *Requiem*s that have been recorded. The first, in D minor, was probably written in 1721, one of his earlier religious works. It's austere, scored sparingly for strings, flutes, oboes, and that odd predecessor of the clarinet, the chalumeau, It contains no less than seven fugues, each expressive and full of variety. Ensemble Baroque 1994 and the Czech Chamber Choir under **Roman Valek** play it with a tender simplicity, their early-music style contributing to the effect (Supraphon 52).

In 1733 Zelenka wrote a *Requiem* in D, complete with trumpets and drums and Italianate arias, giving the uneasy impression that it's for someone the congregation was glad to be rid of. This work also includes the chalumeau, though in **Lubomir Matl**'s performance it's replaced by a number of instrumental expedients, and two sections are omitted (Supraphon 1596/7, 2CD, NA). The *Requiem* in C minor is possibly one of Zelenka's last works, full of odd, sometimes naive, sometimes very moving touches. The "Tuba Mirum" without brass is an oddity in itself. **Jorg Ewald Dahler** conducts an effective performance with the Berne Chamber Choir and Orchestra (Claves 508501, NA).

There are a number of settings of the Mass Ordinary. *Mass for the Circumcision* (1728) is scored for a large orchestra and makes a festive sound, though the 1989 recording by **Konrad Wagner** sounds a little boxy, and the disc is only 40 minutes long (Christophorus 87). At the end of his life Zelenka began a series of six "last" masses but only completed three. *Missa dei Patris* is a large-scaled 70-minute mass performed in modern style by **Guttler** and Virtuosi Saxoniae (Capriccio 10285).

Missa Dei Filii is a Lutheran-style mass consisting of only the "Kyrie" and "Gloria," recorded by the early music group Tafelmusik under **Bernius** (Deutsche Harmonia Mundi 77922). This disc also includes a setting of *Litaniae Lauretanae,* a more Italianate work of considerable charm. Another short mass in D, sometimes called *Gratias agimus tibi,* is performed by **Bělohlávek** with the Czech Philharmonic in a full-blooded but not very sensitive performance (Supraphon 110816). This disc also includes five *Responsoria pro Hebdomada Sancta* and the Marian antiphon *Sub tuum praesidium* No. 3.

A complete performance of the responsories is offered by Capella Montana under **Ludwig Gossner,** who play all 27 of them (MD+G 6050954, 2CD). These are simply scored but musically varied works for chorus, strings, and trombones, but make rather an unvaried sonic diet. They were meant to be sandwiched between the lessons during Holy Week, which would also include performances of *Lamentations of Jeremiah,* where they would serve as an effective contrast to the Italianate warmth of solo voices, strings, and woodwinds. The latter are to be found in an English recording with singers Chance, Ainsley, and George and the **Chandos Baroque Players** in a beautiful performance, recorded atmospherically. A more recent version is from Amsterdam, with Ulla Groenewold, Hein Meens, von Egmond, and the Academy of the Begijnhof under **Roderick Shaw** (Globe 5050). The Dutch version is more emotional, the English smoother.

Two of Zelenka's *Litanies* have been recorded. *Litaniae omnium sanctorum* received a rather clunky performance from **Lubomir Matl** and his forces (Supraphon 3315, with *Magnificat* in D, Psalm 129, *De Profundis,* and the little *Salve Regina* based on Frescobaldi). *Litaniae Lauretanaeis* is on Bernius's disc (above) and is in a collection of little-known religious pieces, conducted by **Thomas Reube** with an early music group called Metamorphosis Baroque Orchestra (Thorofon 2181).

One of Zelenka's best-known religious works is his setting of Psalm 51, the *Miserere,* written on the death of his father. This 14-minute setting is touching and beautiful, with a lovely soprano aria as centerpiece. The performance by **Roman Valek** with the *Requiem* in D minor is good (Supraphon 52), but the one included on an entire disc of Zelenka's psalm settings conducted by **Pavel Baxa** is more polished, and the other psalms aren't available elsewhere (Supraphon 112175). Best of all is the performance by **Hermann Max** in a disc also containing *Misereres* by Hasse, Johann Heinichen, and Gottfried Homilius, all Dresden composers (Capriccio 10557). Zádori sings the aria in a touching and sweet-voiced manner, while the instrumentalists are clearer than under Valek and less jaunty than under Baxa.

Another interesting disc is a collection of *Magnificats* by Bach, Kuhnau, and Zelenka's in C and D. The Bach Collegium of Japan is conducted by **Maasaki Suzuki** in nicely shaped performances (BIS 1011).

MOORE

Alexander von Zemlinsky *(1871–1942)*

Zemlinsky took German music beyond Mahler and Strauss, up to but not crossing the bounds of tonality. He wrote his early works when budding composers had to subordinate their creative impulses to the norms of the time—in Zemlinsky's case, Brahms (especially) and Wagner. It was not until later that we hear the rich, dark, and complex sound that synthesized Mahler and Strauss, suggesting where Mahler might have gone had he lived longer or Strauss had not pulled back from *Elektra.* Zemlinsky wrote large-scaled orchestral works and operas, the latter often dominated by the orchestra. Even his chamber music was ripe and emotive. Many pieces were autobiographical, particularly those involving his agony over losing his erstwhile lover Alma Schindler to Mahler (whom he always respected). Zemlinsky's neglect is undeserved. He appeals to anyone who likes Mahler, Strauss, and even Berg.

SYMPHONIES

Lyric Symphony. For soprano, baritone, and orchestra and with texts by Tagore, this is Zemlinsky's answer to Mahler's *Das Lied von der Erde.* It's richly scored, evocative, and dramatic. One of the composer's most popular works, my minority opinion is that it's the equal of the Mahler masterpiece.

Sinopoli's is the most powerful version, with Voigt and Terfel; their Wagnerian voices fit the conductor's concept (♦DG). Terfel is the best of the baritones, but good as Voigt is, I prefer a leaner-toned soprano. Sinopoli and the close recording bring out many often hidden instrumental lines, revealing a more complex, vibrant, and eerie score than most. The Vienna Philharmonic's expression, color, and robustness are heard nowhere else. **Chailly,** with Alessandra Mark and Hagegård, is large-scaled and beautifully sung, with moderate, relaxed tempos (♦London 443569, with *Symphonische Gesänge*). The music flows naturally, and the Concertgebouw colors the music masterfully, if not as strikingly as the VPO. Mark's covered soprano is outstanding; Hagegård is the beautifully focused lieder singer, straining only occasionally; the sound is dark but clear.

Flor is romantic in a different way (♦RCA 68111, with six lieder). His tempos are slow in most of the songs, but his touch is light and ethereal. The light voices and focus of Orgonasova and Skovhus fit his conception, and the soundstage is large and distant. **Michael Gielen** is dramatic and bold, but sharper-edged than Sinopoli (♦Arte Nova 27758, with Berg's *Three Pieces from "Lyric Suite"* and *Five Orchestral Songs*). Tempos are fast but not rushed, attacks are strong, and textures are lean and brightly lit. Vlatka Orsanic is small but lyrical; James Johnson is similar to Hagegård but brighter. The recording is open and dry.

Bernhard Klee (♦Koch Schwann) and **Gabriele Ferro** (♦Fonit Cetra 70) are similar. Both are small-scaled and straightforward, and both use the BBC Symphony. Klee is clean and forward looking, with good tension and anticipation. For Klee, Söderström uses head tone to create an eerie, dreamlike effect and is my favorite soprano for this work. Dale Duesing's slightly unfocused voice seems overwhelmed in I; he does better later. Ferro's version is more rounded and not quite as modern. Dorothy Dorow's smaller, darker soprano punctuates the line and makes VI sound Bergian; Nimsgern has a brighter, larger tone than Duesing. Both recordings have clear, open sound.

Armin Jordan sounds French with a decent Suisse Romande orchestra (♦Aria 592011, with *Maeterlinck Lieder*). The performance is brightly lit, even impressionistic, with a sheen on the strings, prominent winds, and fast, forward-leaning tempos. Andreas Schmidt is outstanding in the high tessitura; Edith Wiens is best in the quieter music. **Maazel** is too urgent, and neither Fischer-Dieskau nor Varady sounds rich or expansive enough (DG). **Vladimir Valek** conducts well, but his singers let him down (Praga, with Quartet 3).

1 and *2.* No. 1 was a student work influenced by Brahms, Bruckner, and Schubert. Originally we had only three movements (including a moving Adagio), but a delightful Dvořakian fourth has been discovered and appears in the Conlon and Beaumont recordings. No. 2 is more independent but still influenced by Dvořak and Bruckner. Both are worth knowing.

Conlon pairs the symphonies (♦EMI 56473). His approach is weighty and full, though not always flowing, with a glow that accentuates their Germanic qualities. No. 2 is especially involving. The sound isn't first-rate, but it's full and detailed. **Ludovít Rajter** leads the Czecho-Slovak Radio Symphony in a resplendent, glowing 1 that's lighter and more lyrical than Conlon's (Marco Polo 223166, with *Das gläserne Herz Suite*, the most complete version of the ballet music). **Anthony Beaumont** and the Czecho-Slovak Radio Symphony give a middle of the road performance almost as good as Rajter and more flowing than Conlon (♦Capriccio 10740, with *Waldgesprach* and other pieces). **Edgar Siepenbusch** isn't particularly accomplished or involving and has poor sound (Marco Polo).

OTHER ORCHESTRAL MUSIC

Cymbeline Suite; Tanzpoem. The Suite is incidental music to Shakespeare's play. Much of it is pretty, and there's some dramatic battle music with trumpet fanfares. *Tanzpoem* is a ballet full of warmth and cheer. Both lack the dark, rich color and post-Straussian chromaticism that make Zemlinsky so compelling. **Conlon**'s performances are excellent (♦EMI 56474). Note that the best work on this disc, *Frühlingsbegräbnis,* can also be obtained in Conlon's more interesting collection of choral works (EMI 56783).

Die Seejungfrau. A beautifully lush treatment of Hans Christian Andersen's *Mermaid,* it is filled with visions of the sea and the sweet songs of the mermaid. This may be Zemlinsky's richest and most popular work. **Dausgaard**'s tempos are beautifully gauged, sonorities are rich and lyrical, and his Danish Radio Symphony shines (Chandos 9601, with *Sinfonietta* and *Sarema Overture*). **Zoltán Peskó** isn't bad, but some tempos are too slow, balances aren't always there, and it lacks magic and flow (Wergo). **Chailly** (London) is more superficial and less rich than Dausgaard. **Conlon** is lean and dry; he seems uneasy with the work's opulence, his effects and cohesion aren't consistent, nor is his orchestra as good as Dausgaard's. Dausgaard has the best sound; Chailly's is thinner.

Sinfonietta. This one is late, astringent, and angular. **Conlon** (♦EMI 55515, with *Die Seejungfrau*) and **Klee** (♦Koch Schwann LP, with *Maeterlinck Songs*) capture the pungent, modern tone of the piece. **Dausgaard** is rounder, more romantic, and slightly out of character (♦Chandos 9601, with *Sarema Overture* and *Seejungfrau*).

CHAMBER MUSIC

String Quartets. There are two complete sets of all four from the **Artis Quartet** (♦Nimbus 5563, 1+2; ♦5604, 3+4, with Johanna Müller-Hermann's Quartet) and the **LaSalle Quartet** (♦DG LP, with Hans Apostal's Quartet). The LaSalle is more romantic, with bigger attacks and a darker sound. The Artis is more modern, rhythmically crisper, less weighty, but bold and virtuosic. They indulge and romanticize less than the LaSalle, but aren't dull because their uncanny sense of pace, proportion, and tonal balance allows the music to breathe naturally, creating a sense of rightness in all four works. The LaSalle, while not always so unerring in flow, produces its own riches, though 4 is weaker than the others.

1. This early work is Brahmsian in style, but more varied metrically and less complicated in structure and texture, with a bit of Beethoven and Dvořak in the finale. The **LaSalle Quartet** brings out its Brahmsian qualities with its broad, lyrical phrasing and attacks in an excellent version. The **Artis**'s lighter, less warm performance, with its more tightly sprung rhythms, makes the work sound more modern. The **Prašák Quartet** is still lighter (♦Praga, with Quartet 4 and two Movements for String Quartet). Their textures aren't as warm, their sound is more seamless, and their phrasing and pacing are more indulgent, slowing here and there to explore a nuance and vary the dynamics. You could find this performance penetrating or halting. Praga's acoustic is brighter as well.

2. Zemlinsky's most ambitious, massive, and longest quartet, it stretches tonality and romanticism to their limits. Its one movement is difficult to hold together, given its changes in tempo, dynamics, and mood. It's partly an angst-ridden emotional reworking of the scandalous affair involving Schoenberg's wife (who was Zemlinsky's sister) that resulted in tension between the two composers; it's rife with symbolism of their relationship.

Comparison between the **Artis** and **LaSalle** versions reflects what was said above. The **Schoenberg Quartet** are closer to the Artis if more linear, with a brighter, more streamlined tone and more tensile strength (◆Koch 310118, with 3). At the same time, their textures are less full, weighty and bold, their pacing not as irresistible, and the sound needs more clarity in the bass. It's a good performance with a terrific coupling, but the Artis and LaSalle are better.

3. This one pulls back from the romanticism of 2. Post-war Europe wasn't open to emotional outpouring, and Zemlinsky was determined to be sparer with his resources. The result was a four-movement quartet written within classical structures in a way that gently mocks the atonalists. The **Artis Quartet** excels in its usual way, but the Schoenberg and LaSalle prove that this seemingly dry and acerbic piece can take to more warmth than Artis's bravura suggests. **LaSalle** is darker, sweeter, and more romantic, with heavier rhythms. The **Schoenberg**, my favorite, displays the same linearity and bright sound of their 2. There they seemed too controlled, but here these qualities provide strength, warmth, and real passion (◆Koch 310118, with 2). The **Kocian Quartet** is similar but more subdued and quieter. They add a degree of eeriness and mystery that is interesting if not overwhelming, but the coupling is a weak *Lyric Symphony* (Praga).

4. Zemlinsky interrupted work on *Der König Kandaules* to write this 1935 memorial to Berg. It's in the form of a six-movement suite, with themes from previous works, some Wagner, and a Beethovenian double fugue. The **Artis Quartet** is straightforward, full of energy, and well-paced. (The coupling, Müller-Hermann's 1908 Quartet, is in a style similar to Zemlinsky's but more soft-toned and wistful). The **Prašák's** reading is similar to their 1 but less indulgent, and their lean qualities work better here (◆Praga 250107, with 1 and Movements for String Quartet). They make the work seem airier, leaner, more mysterious, and less urgently electric. The **Lark Quartet** is lyrical, sweeter, much slower in the slow movements, and more relaxed; they may seem bland at first, but their concentration is winning (◆Arabesque 6671, with Schoenberg's Quartet 1). The **LaSalle** is weakest here; harsh in tone, severe in interpretation, and too forward in the recorded sound. It's certainly not bad enough to disqualify a fine set, but the others are better.

Trio for Clarinet, Cello, and Piano. This early Brahmsian trio is one of Zemlinsky's finest works. The **Amici Trio** is warmly lyrical, flowing, yet strong and surging (Summit 151, with Beethoven's Clarinet Trio and Chan Ka Nin's *Among Friends*). Their tempos are slightly slow, their manner broad. The clarinetist plays with a warm sound, full of low harmonics, the pianist provides dark Brahmsian pianism, and the cellist matches both. The sound is excellent and immediate. **Eduard Brunner**, Dagid Geringas, and Gerhard Oppitz are bright-toned, angular, and a bit restless (Tudor 717, with an arrangement of Schoenberg's Chamber Symphony 1). They aren't as Brahmsian, so the playing isn't as flowing or warm; it's enjoyable, but the Amici are more compelling and heartfelt. The **Boeykens Trio** is pedantic and heavy, especially in I, where there is no flow or sense of movement (Harmonia Mundi, with Bruch's Pieces for Clarinet, Viola, and Piano). The piece doesn't quite come together, and the cellist is either too heavy, too close, or both. The piano is a bit tinny at loud volumes.

Among readings that substitute violin for clarinet (this instrumentation works very well), the **Beaux Arts Trio** gives the best performance of all—rich, dark, Brahmsian, played with the understanding of real pros (◆Philips 434072, with Korngold's Piano Trio). The **Clementi Trio** has a lean, compelling tone and style. Not as warm as the Amici or as utterly natural as the Beaux Arts, they go for intensity and make the work sound more modern; the results are interesting (Largo 56666, with Schoenberg's *Verklärte Nacht* arranged for piano trio).

Pieces for String Quartet; Pieces for String Quintet. The two quartets are late, dark, richly scored, and full of post-Straussian harmonies and a major quote from "Yankee Doodle." The early quintet is Brahmsian; the later is a Prestissimo with touches of Korngold. The **Corda Quartet** plays with a full, ripe sound that lends weight, impact, and nobility (Stradivarius 33438, with Schoenberg's Quartet 1 and String Trio). The **Prašák Quartet**'s tempos are similar, but their sound is a bit more raw and less blended (◆Praga 250107, with Quartets 1 and 4). These pieces offer only 15 minutes of music, so the couplings may be the most important issue.

CHORAL MUSIC

Conlon provided a compelling collection of Zemlinsky's choral works, and his weighty and resonant readings, with good work by Voigt et al., the Düsseldorf Musikverein Chorus, and the Cologne Orchestra, are easy to recommend (◆EMI 567830). The only drawback is diffuse, distant sound that you get used to. *Frühlingsbegräbnis*, for large orchestra and chorus, is rich in color and variety, Psalm 13 depicts the horrors Zemlinsky escaped in Europe, Psalm 83 is in the Brahmsian choral tradition, and the five other works in the disc are glowing and stirring.

Antony Beaumont's *Frühlingsbegräbnis* is lighter, slightly faster, and less resonant (◆Capriccio 10740, with Symphony 1). The early *Waldgespräch* for soprano and strings reflects Wagner, but Zemlinsky's operatic voice is present in the lyrical but pessimistic *Maiblumen blühten überall*. Good performances, though this *Waldgespräch* isn't as impressive as Conlon's. Mathis and Roland Hermann have lighter voices than Conlon's soloists; the sound is just as distant and diffuse as EMI's, if a little brighter. **Chailly** recorded Psalms 23 (◆London, with *Die Seejungfrau*) and 83 (◆London 460213, with Janáček's *Glagolitic Mass* and Korngold's *Passover Psalm*). Both are fine, but neither coupling ranks among the best performances of these works. Chailly gets better playing and sound than Conlon, but the latter's slower, more lyrical, and dramatic conducting is more enjoyable.

OPERAS

Es War Einmal (*Once upon a Time*). Slightly reminiscent of Wagner and *Hansel und Gretel*, Zemlinsky's second opera is charming and full of atmosphere and color, with plenty of beautiful and humorous moments and evocative orchestral passages. The vocal lines are light and pleasant. Mahler helped with the opera and composed the final 50 bars of Act 1. **Hans Graf** leads a delightful performance with the Danish Radio Symphony (◆Capriccio 60019, 2CD). Kurt Westi and Eva Johansson have attractive light voices, and I like the deep bass of Aage Haugland's King. Good sound.

Eine Florentinische Tragödie. It crosses the florid Richard Strauss with Mahler, with much polyphony, structure, and complex harmony. The plot—man rediscovers charms of wife after killing her boyfriend—is from Oscar Wilde. **Albrecht**'s leadership is supple, flowing, subtly expressive, and Straussian (◆Koch-Schwann 314012). Doris Soffel sings with her accustomed light soprano, tenor Kenneth Riegel is balanced and lyrical, Guillermo Sarabia is heavy on top but powerful and ominous. **Chailly**'s recording is lusher, heavier, and well paced, if not as understanding (♦London 455112, with Alma Mahler's *Six Songs*). Iris Vermillion is a bit heavier but just as fine as Soffel; Heinz Kruse is brighter and lighter than Riegel; Albert Dohmen is dark and menacing, and his less heavy tone is more songful than Sarabia's. (Kruse's and Dohmen's roles are reversed in the London notes.)

Conlon is exciting, flashy, and sometimes driven, but he lacks Albrecht's understanding and finesse and Chailly's sumptuousness. His singers are bested slightly by both, as is his orchestra, while EMI's close sound lacks depth. **Friedrich Pleyer** provides fine conducting and singing, but his Venetian orchestra isn't up to the score and also too distantly recorded (Fonit Cetra).

Der König Kandaules. After arriving in America, Zemlinsky showed the short-score of his last opera (based on an André Gide play from Herodotus) to Met conductor Artur Bodansky, who rejected it because of its risqué libretto about adultery in ancient Lydia. Zemlinsky died leaving the orchestration unfinished until Antony Beaumont completed it in the '90s.

This dark, moody opera about marital betrayal and murder is rooted in the orchestra, a kind of vocal symphony more approachable and less thorny than *Florentinische Tragödie*. **Albrecht** leads a dramatic, evocative, and involving performance with an excellent Hamburg Philharmonic, in fine sound and with good solo singing but for some early strain from James O'Neal and stress in the loud music from Nina Warre (♦Capriccio 071, 2CD).

Der Kreiderkreis (*The Chalk Garden*). Zemlinsky's seventh and last completed opera is based on a play (from a Chinese fairy tale) that again involves adultery, this time in ancient China, and ends in a Solomonic decision about the paternity of a child. The influences of Weill's *Mahagonny* and Krenek's *Jonny spielt auf* (Zemlinsky conducted both) are strong in this work, for example, in the moody tenor sax opening, the sparer orchestration, and the decadent jazzy atmosphere. The music isn't as rich as most Zemlinsky; some of the vocal writing is declamatory, but there is some darkly cinematic writing in the orchestra, including a sprinkling of Orientalisms. The problem is the plethora of spoken dialogue with and without orchestra. A good performance is led by **Stefan Soltesz** with soloists and the Berlin Radio Symphony (♦Capriccio 60016, 2CD), but it's not the place to start with Zemlinsky operas.

Sarema. This opera deals with a Circassian peasant woman who falls in love with an enemy Russian commander, betraying her Circassian boyfriend; she's ostracized and then redeemed but kills herself in disgrace. It's exciting, with plenty of Slavicisms, a bit of Wagner, and the appeal of *Cavalleria Rusticana*. **István Dénes**'s recording is stirring and dramatic (Koch 6467, 2CD). Most of his singers are fine but for Karin Clarke's upper register problems and Juri Zinovenko's strained Prophet.

Der Traumgörge (*Gorge the Dreamer*). Zemlinsky's third opera was a nonentity until lost parts were discovered in the '70s. It's colorful and lyrical, far less thorny than *Florentine Tragedy* but more advanced than *Es War Einmal*. It has touches of Humperdinck but is more adventurous. The richly textured orchestra is thematically more important than the voices.

Görge is so obsessed with fairy tales that when his fiancee abandons him, he runs off to find a "fairy princess." She turns out to be Gertraud, a beggar thought by her neighbors to be a witch; when he returns home with her, he founds a family and school. This is another "Alma" work, in which Alma is the princess of Gorge's (aka Zemlinsky's) dreams. There

are some opulent and magical scenes, as well as beautiful and exotic arias and ensembles. Protschka is sweetly lyrical, but Janis Martin is less good, though adequate. **Albrecht** is in his element. Fine sound and an excellent introduction to Zemlinsky's operas (♦Capriccio 242, 2CD).

Der Zwerg. Mahler's death in 1911 drove Zemlinsky to come to grips to what had happened between him, Alma Schindler, and the dead composer. Zemlinsky turned to Oscar Wilde's *Birthday of the Infanta,* whose theme of goodness and innocence hidden behind ugliness and unappreciated by the shallow to the point of tragedy made it the ultimate "Alma" work. (Zemlinsky was short and gnome-like in appearance, described by Alma before her infatuation with him as "chinless and short, with bulging eyes.") *Der Zwerg* contains some of Zemlinsky's most beautiful and touching music, both for voice and orchestra.

Albrecht's recording of a 1980 Hamburg production employs an adaptation of the original libretto that brings the story closer to Wilde's original, including Wilde's original title (♦Schwann 1626, LP). This version is crueler, changes some of the characterizations and imagery, and moves away from the words that inspired Zemlinsky's music. It also cuts 13 minutes of music. **Conlon** recorded the original (and preferred) version, with updates by the composer, and restored the cuts and Zemlinsky's title (♦EMI 66247, 2CD). Fortunately, his performance is superior to Albrecht's. Riegel's lyrical dwarf for Albrecht is better sung than David Kuebler's occasionally strident performance, but Conlon's other leads are excellent, and his orchestra and sound are more lush and attractive.

SONGS

"Posthumous Songs." Spanning Zemlinsky's whole career, they are often intimate and conservative in style, and admirers of Wolf won't find them too adventurous. They appear in a consistently fine collection sung by **Ziesak**, Vermillion, Blochwitz, and Schmidt, with Cord Garben (♦Sony 57960). The songs in light baritone **Steven Kimbrough**'s beautifully sung collection, also accompanied by Garben, sound more like Zemlinsky and are more interesting (♦Acanta LP).

Songs to Poems by Maurice Maeterlinck. These are elusive and erotic, with a dream-like quality and French overtones that reflect the text. **Cornelia Kallisch**'s dark, flexible soprano works well in a sensuous and perfumed interpretation, with Armin Jordan and the Suisse Romande. **Von Otter**'s light, slightly dry voice expresses the poetry clearly (♦DG 439928, with Mahler songs). She and Gardiner produce a lean sound that brings out modern elements of the score, and DG's thin sonics fit their interpretation. **Glenys Linos**'s creamy alto goes well with Bernhard Klee's clean conducting of the Berlin Radio Symphony (♦Koch 311053, with *Lyric Symphony*). Klee isn't as modern as Gardiner, but he's less romantic than the near-Wagnerian approach of John Carewe with mezzo **Birgitta Svenden** (Forlane 16642, with Elgar's *Sea Pictures* and Mahler's *Kindertotenlieder*). Svenden's darker, more opulent, and heavier approach has its attractions but seems out of place here.

Symphonische Gesänge. A product of Zemlinsky's exposure to '20s American jazz and to *Afrika singt,* this is an anthology of works by black poets of the Harlem Renaissance that furnished the texts of these songs. They are a synthesis of American poetry dealing with oppression and Zemlinsky's dark, dramatic, late German romantic style. **Franz Grundheber**'s lyric baritone is sometimes absorbed by the busy orchestra (he's set somewhat far back) but he sings with subtlety and expression. Albrecht gets dramatic and colorful playing from a responsive Hamburg State Orchestra (♦Capriccio 448, with excerpts from *Triumph der Zeit* and *König Kandaules*).

More of a bass-baritone, **Willard White** has greater power, depth, and earthiness than Grundheber and is more closely recorded, but he's not as lyrical or expressive and he wobbles in the high tessitura. Chailly's conducting is blockier and not as supple or expressive as Albrecht's, and the Concertgebouw sounds blander and less dramatic (♦London 443569, with *Lyric Symphony*). **Ortrun Wenkel** sings a version for alto with a clear tone, accuracy, power, and expression. Neumann's conducting is similar to Albrecht's, if lighter overall and not as demonstrative in the big moments. Wenkel's higher voice makes the work sound more modern and icy (♦Wergo 286209, with *Die Seejungfrau*).

A wonderful collection of Zemlinsky's orchestral songs with **Conlon** and the Cologne Philharmonic playing with a nice glowing texture is a near must (♦EMI 557024). Violetta Urmana could use a bit more expression, but she sings the Maeterlinck songs warmly. Half the disc contains very important recording premieres of *Waldgesprach, Maiblumen blühten überall* (sung by Soile Isokoski), and two Songs for Baritone (orchestrated by Antony Beaumont and sung by Schmidt). The first two are lush, beautiful works from Zemlinsky's Wagnerian period (note the touches of *Siegfried Idyll* in *Maiblumen*).   HECHT

Ellen Taaffe Zwilich (b. 1939)

Zwilich's earliest music fairly defines the '70s "uptown" New York style, natural enough given her graduate study with Carter and Sessions at Juilliard, and since the mid-'80s her music fits squarely into the prevailing New Consonance. All her work is cast in traditional forms and genres, mostly instrumental, and she never requires unusual sonic tricks from the performers. Widely performed and for the last couple of decades fully commissioned, a fair sample of Zwilich's music has been recorded well by first-rate performers and ensembles.

An accomplished violinist before she gave up performing in favor of composition in the mid-'70s, Zwilich writes precisely and appropriately for the symphony and concerto. In 1983 she was the first woman to win a Pulitzer Prize for composition. The award was for her Symphony 1, and although I don't find this work equal to her subsequent symphonies, it exists in a good recording with **John Nelson** conducting the Indianapolis Symphony (New World 336). This disc also contains *Celebration* and *Prologue* and *Variations for String Orchestra,* actually more interesting pieces.

For an introduction to Zwilich's music, NY Philharmonic musicians offer two full orchestra pieces and two chamber works (New World 372). Of the former, *Concerto Grosso 1985* is true to its traditional form: multimovement with varying tempos and characters. Conducted by **Mehta,** the five movements form an arch (I and V are maestoso; II and IV are presto; III is largo). Composers throughout history have borrowed from their predecessors and sometimes have been criticized for it. Zwilich mostly favors fellow 20th-century composers, as is evident in the unmistakably Coplandesque gestures in the first movement of the *Concerto Grosso,* despite its inclusion of a bit of Handel's Violin Sonata in D. Shostakovich's influence is evident elsewhere in this work as well as in the second full-orchestra piece on the NYPO disc, the one-movement *Symbolon* (1988).

Zwilich has been criticized for these references, especially for the Shostakovichisms in this and other works (for example, the Bassoon Concerto) and for emulating obvious characteristics of Stravinsky's music (for example, in the Trumpet Concerto). I find this absolutely unwarranted, no more valid than similar criticism was for Stravinsky, because she makes her own engaging music, and who cares whom it references! I contend she simply has good ears and makes use of them.

Besides, this sort of criticism goes away over time. The chamber works in this disc are the Concerto for Trumpet and Five Players , an idiomatic piece played superbly by principal trumpeter Philip Smith, and the Double Quartet for strings. Like so many of her time, Zwilich doesn't mind consonance and uses it well with this rich string sonority.

Based on number of works completed, the concerto in its various forms is Zwilich's favorite genre. She has composed solo concertos for flute, oboe, trumpet, trombone, bass trombone, and piano; also a duopiano concerto; a double concerto for violin and cello; and a concerto grosso. More are on the way. They vary somewhat in style and widely in accompaniment, and all were written expressly for first-desk players in major orchestras. Some of these performers have recorded them with their own or other ensembles, and I find nothing wrong with any of the performances except a quibble here and there based on my own taste. All exhibit some expected virtuosity, but none is merely a showpiece.

The Flute Concerto refers to topical music of its day—lush movie-music sounds, "Music from the Hearts of Space" passages, and a viscerally thrilling conclusion. **Doriot Anthony Dwyer** (who commissioned the piece) is soloist with the London Symphony, Sedares conducting, for an all-round satisfactory performance of this easy-to-digest music (Koch 7142). Piston's Flute Concerto and Bernstein's *Halil* complete this short (49-minute) disc. The sound is better than usual from Koch.

In addition to his exceptional work as principal oboist with the Cleveland Orchestra, **John Mack** is revered as a teacher and has recorded much of the important solo repertoire from all periods. For Zwilich's Oboe Concerto (1990), he's just right (Koch 7278). Appropriately expressive for the instrument, this two-part single-movement concerto isn't much of a challenge, but the Louisville Orchestra (led by Sedares) sounds a bit under-rehearsed, and I would have preferred a recording with Mack's own orchestra. The other works on this disc are Symphony 3 and *Concerto Grosso;* the latter is better performed and recorded by Mehta (see above).

Zwilich's Bassoon Concerto (1993) was composed for **Nancy Goeres** and the Pittsburgh Symphony, and these musicians, conducted by Maazel, recorded it (New World 80503). The bassoon lacks an extensive concerto repertoire, so I expect this piece will receive considerable attention from advanced students and orchestra principals. It's conceived idiomatically for the instrument and presents the usual varied challenges of its genre. The excellent recording includes Lees's Horn Concerto and Leonardo Balada's *Music for Oboe and Orchestra: Lament from the Cradle of the Earth.*

Trombone concertos are likely all from the 20th century, and **Christian Lindberg** provides four of them in "American Trombone Concertos," a disc with DePreist conducting the Malmö Symphony (BIS 628). The performance wants for nothing, but the music isn't Zwilich's best work, though Lindberg makes the most of it. Other works in this disc are Creston's Fantasy for Trombone and Orchestra, George Walker's Concerto for Trombone and Orchestra, and Schuller's *Eine Kleine Pausanenmusik.* Zwilich has also composed a concerto for bass trombone.

The Louisville Orchestra and its conductor, Lawrence Leighton Smith, commissioned Zwilich's Concerto for Violin, Cello, and Orchestra; they accompany **Jaime Laredo** and **Sharon Robinson** in the recording (Louisville Orchestra First Edition 9). These fine soloists also appear in a recording of the Trio (see below), with a good deal more to work with in the chamber piece. Other works in this disc are David Dzubay's *Snake Alley,* Adolphus Hailstork's *An American Port of Call,* and Schuller's *Four Soundscapes.*

Zwilich has composed chamber music all along, and three of her earliest works in that genre are available on a single disc. The Violin Sonata (1974) shows her not fully formed as a composer, but the three movements offer **Joseph Zwilich**'s excellent musicianship, suitably accompanied by James Gemmell (CRI 621). The String Quartet from the same year is likewise not yet Zwilich in full bloom, but the **New York String Quartet** plays it well. Joseph Zwilich was the composer's husband; he died after recording the sonata, and the Chamber Symphony (1979) is surely something of an elegy despite its generic title. Composed for six players with mixed instrumentation, this is to my mind Zwilich's first truly mature work. The performance by Boston Musica Viva, led by **Richard Pittman** (the work doesn't seem to require a conductor), is sensitive. Three short pieces by Eleanor Cory fill out the 72 minutes in the CD.

The **Kalichstein-Laredo-Robinson Trio** is one of the world's premier ensembles, and they exhibit their considerable prowess in Zwilich's Trio (Arabesque 6676). A three-movement work of marvelous contrasts, this piece might become a staple for piano trios in concert and the recording studio. If so, performers must reckon with this exemplary recording that also includes trios by Kirchner, Pärt, and Stanley Silver-man. The listener will note the disparate styles of the four composers, and other than instrumentation the only connection between them is that they were written for these musicians. I recommend the disc for Zwilich's piece; none of the others are of nearly the same quality. The sound quality is equal to the superb performances.

Sound quality of the opposite sort is only one of the drawbacks of a recording of *Passages,* a song cycle for **Pierrot Players** instrumentation plus percussion (ACA 20027). Zwilich writes well for the voice, but so far hasn't composed much for it. Other pieces in the disc are Schoenberg's *Pierrot lunaire* (I suspect it was included as a well-known work to attract attention to the disc as a whole) and Lewis Nielsen's forgettable *Black Magic* for flute and piano. Nielsen conducts the **University of Georgia Contemporary Music Ensemble** and wrote the liner notes—you get the picture. Soprano Leslie Boucher's diction and uneven but generally poor sound quality make the texts of the six poems by A. R. Ammons all the more necessary, but they're not provided. *Passages* should be recorded by better performers, and given Zwilich's rising star probably will be, but in the meantime you might look for **Janice Felty**'s LP (Northeastern 218). ZIEROLF

PART II: GENRES

Christmas Music

The hundreds of Christmas albums are an embarrassment of riches at best and a cornucopia of kitsch at worst. I have divided the recordings into eras and genres and have listed only some of the best of each, all of fairly recent vintage with some re-releases. All are recommended. Only a brief description of contents is given.

For major liturgical and concert works, see: Bach's *Christmas Oratorio* and cantatas; Britten's *A Ceremony of Carols;* Handel's *Messiah;* Rutter's *Gloria;* and Vivaldi's *Gloria.*

CHANT

"Christmas Hymns": Greek Byzantine Choir (Jade 91006)
　　Greek Orthodox chant by the experts.
"Christus Natus Est": Abbey of Ligugé (Studio SM 1612)
　　24 Gregorian chants in straightforward performances.
"Christus Natus Est Nobis": Schola Gregoriana Plagensis (Christophorus 77179)
　　Premonstratensian Chant for Christmas Eve.
"In the Golden Age of Icons": Rybin Chorus of Moscow, Sofia Radio Chorus, Bulgarian Chorus (Capriccio 10758)
　　Traditional, folk, plus music by Dmitri Bortnyansky, Dobri Hristov, Rachmaninoff, and Gretchaninoff based on Russian Orthodox chant.
"Le Temps de Noël": Choirs from the Abbeys of Ligugé, Timadeuc, En Calcat, and the Pères du Saint-Esprit de Chevilly and Bec-Hellouin (Studio SM 1910, 2CD)
　　Chant sampling the full liturgy from Advent through Christmas.

MEDIEVAL

"Aquitanian Monasteries": Sequentia (Harmonia Mundi 77383)
　　Polyphonic music from the monastery of St. Martial in Limoges.
"Carols and Motets for the Nativity": Deller Consort (Vanguard 5066)
　　Music from medieval and Tudor England.
"Carols and Motets of Medieval Europe": Deller Consort (Vanguard 70680)
　　A variety of medieval music from Europe.
"Creator of the Stars": Pomerium (DG 449819)
　　Music from plainchant to polyphony.
"In Natali Domini": Niederaltaicher Scholaren (Sony 66317)
　　Medieval Christmas songs.
"Legends of St. Nicholas": Anonymous 4 (Harmonia Mundi 907232)
　　Chant and polyphony for the patron saint of Christmas.
"Noël, Noël!": Boston Camerata (Erato 75569)
　　French Christmas music, 1200–1600.
"Nova Stella": Altramar Medieval Music Ensemble (Dorian 80142)
　　A medieval Italian Christmas.
"Now Make We Merthe": Purcell Consort of Voices, London Brass (Boston Skyline 121)
　　Medieval English lyrics, rounds, and carols.
"On Yoolis Night": Anonymous 4 (Harmonia Mundi 907099)
　　Medieval carols and motets. Surely this is the sound of Heaven.
"A Star in the East": Anonymous 4 (Harmonia Mundi 907139)
　　Medieval Hungarian chants and polyphony for Christmas.

RENAISSANCE

"Beyond Chant: Mysteries of the Renaissance": Voices of Ascension (Delos 3165)
　　Palestrina, Victoria, Sweelinck, Josquin, Gibbons, Schütz, Byrd, etc.

"A Christmas Legend": Niederaltaicher Scholaren (Sony 66242)
　　22 vocal and instrumental variations on *Resonet in laudibus.*
"In Natali Domini": La Colombina (Accent 96114)
　　Vocal quartet singing music from 16th Century Spain and the Americas.
"Old Christmas Return'd": The York Waits (Saydisc 398)
　　The town band with a glorious gaggle of unusual musical instruments.
"Oyez! La Nouvelle": Rossmarin (ATMA 9718)
　　Mainly French music for two male voices, lute, viol.
"Psallite! A Renaissance Christmas": Chanticleer (Chanticleer 8806)
　　Brilliant realizations by the vocal ensemble.
"There is No Rose": Virelai (Virgin 45286)
　　Unusual vocal and instrumental music.
"Villancicos and Ensaladas": La Capella Reial de Catalunya (Astrée 8723)
　　Music from the 16th-century court of the Duke of Calabria at Valencia.

BAROQUE

"A Baroque Christmas": Collegium Aureum (RCA 61882)
　　Italian Baroque Christmas concertos.
"Baroque Christmas": Netherlands Brass Quintet (Helicon 1012)
　　Brass music from Holland from the 16th through the 18th Century.
"Baroque Christmas in Leipzig": Leipzig University Choir and other forces (Thorofon 2275)
　　Choral and instrumental music by Fasch, Johann Christoph Pezel, Johann Hermann Schein, Johann Schelle.
"Cantiones Natalitiae": Camerata Trajectina (Globe 6033)
　　Music from the time of Rubens, in Dutch and Latin.
"Christmas Adagio": Karajan/Berlin Philharmonic (DG 449924)
　　Italian Baroque Christmas concertos, plus Handel and Respighi.
"A Christmas Concert": Karajan/Berlin Philharmonic (DG 419413)
　　More Italian Baroque Christmas concertos.
"Christmas Concerti": Capella Istropolitana (Naxos 550567)
　　And more Italian Baroque Christmas concertos.
"Christmas Concertos": I Solisti Italiani (Denon 78912)
　　Still more Italian Baroque Christmas concertos.
"Christmas Concertos": I Musici (Philips 412739)
　　Italian Baroque Christmas concertos—but I Musici did it first and they did it best.
"Mexican Baroque": Chanticleer (Teldec 96353)
　　Music of Manuel de Zumaya and Ignacio Jerusalem from Mexico City Cathedral.
"Puer Natus in Bethlehem": Capella Savaria (Capriccio 10558)
　　Music of Pal Esterházy, Buxtehude, Telemann, Michel Corrette, Georg Böhm.
"Sanctus": Ex Cathedral Choir (ASV 166)
　　Music of Bach, Gabrieli, Gibbons, Handel, Monteverdi, etc.
"Weihnachtskonzerte mit dem Collegium Aureum" (Harmonia Mundi 770048)
　　Christmas concertos by Corelli, Francesco Manfredini, Johann Christoph Petz, and Tartini.

CLASSICAL

"An American Christmas": Boston Camerata (Erato 92874)
　　Carols, hymns, and spirituals, 1770–1870.

"Christmas in Early America": Columbus Consort (Channel 5693)
   Instrumental, mostly for viols.
"While Shepherds Watched": Psalmody, Parley of Instruments (Hyperion 66924)
   Music from English parish churches and chapels, 1740–1830.

MODERN

"December Stillness": Dale Warland Singers (American Choral 121)
   Twelve selections, mostly 1987–93. Some of it is not for the faint of heart, but nothing is outrageous.
De Vocht: "Flemish Christmas Carols": Camerata Ostendia (René Gailly 87004)
   Mystical, gentle, and reminiscent of a more quiet time, heavily romantic with just a discreet touch of modernism.
"Essentially Christmas": East London Chorus, Locke Brass Consort (Koch 7202)
   Music by English composers, including Bliss, Grainger, Rutter, Walton, and others.
"Nativitas: American Christmas Carols": Kansas City Choral (Nimbus 5413)
   Music by American composers, including Carter, Cowell, Dello Joio, Rorem, Sowerby, and others.
"O Magnum Misterium": Polyphony (Hyperion 66925)
   20th-century carols by Howells, Warlock, etc.
"A Peter Warlock Christmas": Allegri Singers (Somm 011)
   24 Christmas carols, all composed by Peter Warlock.
"A Rose in Winter": Dale Warland Singers (D'Note 1022)
   Music by a variety of 20th century composers including Messiaen, Poulenc, and Taverner
"Sing We Christmas": Chanticleer (Teldec 94563)
   Heavy on the modern (Ives, Stephen Sametz, Joseph Jennings), but a lot of more traditional material as well.
"Welcome Christmas": American Repertory Singers (Arsis 108)
   Music by a wide range of more-or-less contemporary composers
"What Cheer!": Gloriae Dei Cantores (Gloriae Dei 012)
   Music by Walton, Warlock, and others, plus some early Colonial and traditional carols. Five traditional carols arranged for handbells are dynamically explosive.

TRADITIONAL

"Angels on High: A Robert Shaw Christmas" (Telarc 80461)
   A Robert Shaw Christmas—the best.
"The Bach Choir Family Carols": The Bach Choir (Chandos 8973)
   Lots of carols.
"Black Christmas" (ESS.A.Y 1011)
   Emotionally communicative spirituals in the African-American tradition.
"Carols Around the World": Quink (Telarc 80202)
   Five Dutch voices in 26 carols in a variety of styles and languages.
"Carols From Trinity": Trinity College Choir, Cambridge (Conifer 51754)
   56 items, traditional and modern.
"Celebration": Welsh Guard Trumpeters, BBC Welsh Chorus (Nimbus 5310)
   26 fanfares, carols, and readings in a judicious mixture.
"Christmas Carols From Tewkesbury Abbey": Tewkesbury Abbey Choir (Naxos 553077)
   16 pieces, nothing fancy, but very familiar and comfortable.

"Christmas Day in the Morning": Rutter/Cambridge Singers (Collegium 121)
   A traditional English celebration.
"A Christmas Gloria": Mormon Tabernacle Choir, Canadian Brass (Bonneville 196)
   Big, noisy, festive, fluffy, and friendly; includes Rutter's *Gloria*.
"Christmas Hymns and Carols" Vols. 1 & 2: Robert Shaw Chorale & Orchestra (MHS 524314, 2CD)
   From the master choral conductor himself.
"Christmas Treasures": Marian Anderson and others, Robert Shaw Chorale, Norman Luboff Choir, Boston Pops, Chicago Symphony (RCA 61867)
   A big, generous, mixed bag of reissues.
"Christmas with the Boys Choir of Harlem" (Unencumbered 2301)
   Traditional and modern.
"Christmas with the Cambridge Singers" (Collegium 111)
   John Rutter conducts brilliant choral singing.
"Christmas with the Canadian Brass and the Great Organ of St. Patrick's Cathedral (RCA 4132)
   Spectacular!
"Christmas with the Vienna Boys Choir" (RCA 7930)
   Traditional German music.
"Favorite Carols at Christmas": York Minster Choir (Chandos 6588)
   23 of the best-known carols, nothing unusual here.
"Joy to the World": Tanglewood Festival Chorus, John Williams/Boston Pops (Sony 48232)
   Very commercial, spiritual, and secular.
"Noël": Canadian Brass, Robert Stoltzman and others, King's Singers (RCA 62683)
   Something for everyone.
"Season's Greetings: A Musical Christmas Card from the Thomas Choir" (Philips 446344)
   J.S. Bach's own Thomas Choir, Leipzig, in German.
"The Vienna Boys Choir" (Sony 48590)
   With the London Symphony Orchestra.
"Welcome Yule": Bristol Bach Choir (Saydisc 375)
   Extraordinary, expressive, exquisite.

There are also many estimable recordings on Decca by the King's College Choir, Clare College Choir, and St. John's College Choir.

OPERATIC

"Along the Road to Bethlehem": Heppner, Toronto Children's Chorus (CBC 5151)
   An unusual variety highlighted by Frederick Thury's *Last Straw,* a heartfelt cantata for children.
"Barbara Hendricks" (EMI 55536)
   Soprano Hendricks sings 33 favorites.
"The Best of Christmas in Vienna": Domingo (Sony 62696)
   Big voice, big sounds.
"A Carnegie Hall Christmas Concert": Battle, Marsalis, and others (Sony 48235)
   Impressive singing and trumpet playing, but the arrangements are jazz-heavy.
"Christmas Favorites from the World's Favorite Tenors": Carreras, Domingo, Pavarotti (Sony 53725)
   The Three Tenors celebrate Christmas.
"Christmas with Marilyn Horne and the Mormon Tabernacle Choir" (Sony 63305)

Great singing all around.

"Christmas with Pavarotti" (LaserLight 21373)
A surprisingly unhackneyed program, some in Italian.

"Christmas with Plácido Domingo" (Sony 37245)
With the Vienna Symphony.

"Christmas with Ramon Vargas" (Claves 9612)
A variety, old and new, tastefully sung by tenor Vargas.

"Christmas with Renata Scotto at St. Patrick's Cathedral" (VAI 4136)
A lovely selection of favorites.

"Christmas with Thomas Hampson" (Teldec 73135)
A traditional program.

"In the Spirit": Jessye Norman (Philips 454640)
The grande dame of opera in a collection of standards.

"The Magic of Christmas": Price, Sutherland, Te Kanawa, Von Stade, Pavarotti, St. John's College Choir, King's College Choir (Decca 443401)
A repackaging of material, but an impressive variety of serious music.

"Mario Lanza at Christmas" (RCA 63178)
All favorite carols, no sleazy pop music.

"Our Christmas Songs for You": Te Kanawa, Alagna, Hampson (EMI 56176)
Hollywood Christmas sleaze by big-name opera stars.

"Plácido Domingo and the Vienna Boys Choir" (RCA 3835)
Big voice and little voices.

"Renata Tebaldi Christmas Festival" (Decca 455214)
Twelve favorites, some in English, some in Italian, some in German.

"The Ultimate Christmas Album": Pavarotti, Te Kanawa, Price, Sutherland, King's College Choir (Decca 448614)
A repackaging from a variety of Decca CDs.

INSTRUMENTAL

"Beautiful Christmas Melodies": Ayako Shinozaki, harp (Sony 62677)
Restrained, gentle playing of traditional carols.

"A Cello Christmas": 24 Cellos of the London Cello Sound, Clare College Choir (Cala 55003)
An unusual mixture of old and new.

"A Christmas Experiment": Canadian Brass, Bach Children's Chorus (RCA 68880)
20 arrangements by Christopher Dedrick.

"A Christmas Festival with Arthur Fiedler and the Boston Pops" (RCA 6428)
Mainly a secular Christmas.

"Christmas Music Box" (Vanguard 6020)
24 carols performed alternately by the Canterbury Choristers (unaccompanied) and 150-year-old music boxes.

"Empire Brass Christmas" (Telarc 80416)
Christmas music arranged for the New Age.

"Hark!": Guildhall String Ensemble, Boys' Choir of Harlem (RCA 61272)
Laid-back, jazz-oriented, ear-catching, sprightly arrangements.

"Hear Them Ring! The Bells of Christmas": Gloriae Dei Ringers (Gloriae Dei 019)
Lots of music, all for handbell choir.

"James Galway's Christmas Carol": BBC Singers, Royal Philharmonic (RCA 5888)
The flute dominates the music.

"Noël! Noël! Noël! Christmas with Michala Petri": Westminster Abbey Choir (RCA 60060)
The fabulous Petri at full tilt in brilliant recorder-dominated arrangements.

"Rejoice! A String Quartet Christmas" Vols. 1 & 2: Ad hoc quartet (John Marks 12 & 18, 2CD)
Traditional carols played simply and sincerely.

"Weihnachtliche Harfenmusik": New York Harp Ensemble (Orfeo 122841)
Lots of harps in Italian Baroque music.

ORGAN

"Celestial Christmas Organ": Franz Lehrndorfer (Celestial Harmonies 1309)
Music by Bach, Georg Böhm, Sigfrid Karg-Elert, etc. from Munich Cathedral.

"Christmas Organ": Kevin Bowyer (Nimbus 7711)
A wide variety from *The Oxford Book of Christmas Organ Music.*

"Christmas Organ Music": Paul Wisskirchen (Prezioso 80011)
An unusual conglomeration from Altenberg Cathedral.

"Noëls pour Orgue": Marie-Claire Alain (Erato 45455)
17th- and 18th-century Noëls by Claude-Bénigne Balbastre, Jean François Dandrieu, Louis-Claude Daquin, Legegue.

"Noëls Romantiques et Modernes": René Oberson (Gallo 700)
French music old and new.

"Serenade for a Christmas Night": Philip Brunelle (Virgin 79108)
An unhackneyed program of music from Bach to Paul Manz.

PIANO

"Christmas at the Movies": Michael Chertock (Telarc 80485)
Selections from popular and unusual movies associated with Christmas.

"Christmas Piano": Eteri Andjaparidze (Naxos)
Rare Christmas music by Sergei Liapunov, Reger, Tchaikovsky, etc.

"O Christmas Tree": Christopher Boscole (Centaur 2137)
Strange arrangements.

UNUSUAL

"Christmas Revels": Christmas Revels (instrumentalists, singers, and actors at Harvard's Sanders Theater (Revels, 5CD; available boxed and singly)
These boisterous, sometimes amateurish performances vary widely in quality, but the repertoire is heavy on the unusual.

Vol. 1 (1078): "Traditional & Ritual Carols, Dances, and Processionals in Celebration of the Winter Solstice"
A Yuletide banquet of unusual lessons and carols.

Vol. 2 (1082): "Wassail! Wassail!: An Early American Christmas"
Instrumentals, vocals, and spoken poetry.

Vol. 3 (1087): "Christmas Day in the Morning: Carols, Processionals, Ritual and Dance"
Mostly Old English.

Vol. 4 (1091): "Sing We Now of Christmas: Six European Centuries"
A folk and classical mixture.

Vol. 5 (1093): "A Child's Christmas Revels"
Music from around the world performed by children.   PARSONS

Eastern Chant

Most people are not familiar with Eastern chant's most common guise, the Byzantine, still the only "canonical" chant in use in the Greek Orthodox Church. Those who come across it often don't return because of its perceived difficulties with quarter tones, strange modes, and a rather sharp, acerbic nasal quality that too often passes for the genuine thing (but in fact is not). There are also many variants of this chant, such as those found among the so-called "Oriental Orthodox" churches of Syria,

Egypt, India, and elsewhere, and even in Milan and Venice there were echoes of a long-gone Byzantine Empire, when these churches were either independent of Rome or directly under an Eastern Patriarchate.

More familiar, both in practice and in temperament, is the chant of the Russian Orthodox Church, a body of work that, though early influenced by Byzantine models, quickly followed its own path, including a devastating encounter with all things Western around the time of Peter the Great and afterwards that threatened to rob it of its uniqueness. But this century has seen a resurgence of the influence of the ancient Russian chants, and we can hope for the future.

There are literally hundreds of albums now available on the market. Russian chant predominates by a large factor, not surprising since the fall of the former Soviet Union, and there has been a tidal wave of recordings coming out of there ever since, most of them pure junk. I will list a small but superb collection of albums that should be more than enough for anyone wanting an introduction to this music. (Note that some chant music by composers like Rachmaninoff and Tchaikovsky are listed in their own articles.) For a further perusal of current offerings, I suggest logging on to the web site <www.musicarussica.com> to keep track of these albums, including some excellent releases off the beaten path. The reviews you find there tend to be overly generous, so caution is advised, but the site is an important resource.

Byzantine Chant. One of the best ways to appreciate the spiritual power of Byzantine chant is to hear it sung in English, and there are some very fine albums that have successfully imported the intricacies of this body of work into our language. Vassillis Hadjinicolaou and the **Byzantine Chorus of the Sign of the Theotokos Orthodox Church** of Montreal show us just how warm, comforting, and splendidly tuneful this music can be. Two albums, "Byzantine Music in the New World" and "Orthodox Saints," are beautifully done, though the playing time is less than generous (STOC 100, 200; they can be found at the above web site). The **Boston Byzantine Choir**'s "First Fruits" is a compendium of hymns from different services, sung with sensitivity and attention. This 10-member mixed choir serves notice that you don't have to be of any particular ethnic origin to enter fully into the spirit of this chant, and the tone quality and sound are both excellent, though this is by no means a professional ensemble (BBC 1, also available at the web site).

"Byzantine Orthodox Vespers and Matins" by the **Bucharest Madrigal Choir** under Marin Constantin is a gentle, quietly loving account of traditional chant from a Romanian choir perspective (Koch 312472). **Sister Marie Keyrouz,** of Lebanese descent, has been gaining a well-deserved reputation for mastery of many styles of chant, first and foremost the Byzantine. Her "Byzantine Chant—Passion and Resurrection" is one of the finest examples of the genre, superbly sung with exquisite taste and a real flair for the idiom (Harmonia Mundi 901315). The **Greek Byzantine Choir** directed by Lycourgos Angelopoulos has long been considered one of the best exponents of traditional chant in Greece. They have many CDs available, some of uneven quality, but none better than *The Divine Liturgy of St. John Chrysostom,* recorded in wonderfully vibrant, clear sound (Opus 111 3078).

Russian Chant. Viewed by many as the most beautiful choral music in the world, Russian chant has undergone singular changes over its 1000 years of existence. From the stark, haunting monody of Znamenny chant to the elaborate, chorally rich compositions of Pavel Chesnokoff, there are a wide variety of styles to choose from. The **Patriarchal Choir of Moscow,** directed by the indomitable Anatoly Grindenko, has been leading the way in recent years, mining the riches to be discovered in this ancient body of work. "Early Russian Plain Chant—17th Century Liturgy" attempts to reconstruct some of this music in marvelous fashion (Opus 111 3079). If you're only familiar with later Russian choral work, you owe it to yourself to hear some of this remarkable music. With the same forces, you can enjoy *Vigil for the Feast of the Protecting Veil of the Mother of God,* recorded in the Monastery of the Caves, Kiev, a recording powerful in its impact and devotional in its spiritual message (Opus 111 30223). Just as good is *Divine Liturgy for the Feast of Sts. Peter and Paul,* another tremendous example of Grindenko's art (Opus 111 30161). Truly, almost any Eastern Chant recording you buy from this company is guaranteed to please, and they lead the way with glorious sound and excellent recording techniques.

A splendid liturgical ceremony was captured by the engineers at the Cathedral of the Transfiguration in St. Petersburg, the wonderful choir directed by **Alexander Prodan** (DG 445653). This is a "don't miss" for those who like "live" liturgical experiences, and the choir is wonderful. One of the most Western-style chants is surely the lovely Kievan tradition, influenced by Italian and Polish models but still maintaining a distinctly Russian flavor. Westerners find it particularly satisfying, and it has become the style of choice for most Orthodox parishes in the New World and elsewhere, including Russia. The **Moscow Liturgic Choir,** under the knowing guidance of Father Amvrosy, show the attractiveness of this music in a "Celebration of the Nativity," a delightful change of pace from the usual Christmas fare (Erato 45961). If you're just making your acquaintance with this music, you'll do no better than the solidly done, excellent introductory album called "Russian Chant for Vespers." Offering a mixture of chants by a variety of composers, the **Novospassky Monastery Choir** (all male) gives far more expensive albums a run for their money (Naxos 553123).

But Russian choirs aren't recording all, or even the best, albums. Elizabeth Patterson and **Gloriae Dei Cantores** give a splendid, exceptionally well-sung recital of works by Tchaikovsky, Rachmaninoff, Georgy Sviridov, and others that offers quality of tone and precision of ensemble second to none (GDCD 100). This may be the best all-around Russian chant recording on the market. The **Washington Cathedral Choral Society** under J. Reilly Lewis offers a miscellany of the more popular liturgical chants in a splendid recording called "Millennium," made at the beautiful American cathedral in fine, open sound (Centaur 2038).

From England, the irreproachable **Holst Singers** directed by Stephen Layton have crafted a similar program that even includes compositions by Pärt and Górecki. With magnificent singing and a real sense of style, "Ikon" mixes Russian fervency with the cool clarity of the English choral tradition (Hyperion 66928). For a survey that includes some fascinating examples of the Polish influence in certain parts of Russia as well as a glance at the Orthodox Church works of Stravinsky, try "Russian Orthodox Music" by the **Tallis Scholars,** an unusual and fascinating look at a body of work largely unheard. This group brings its usual impeccable intonation and technique to bear in a style that, while seemingly incongruous at first, works amazingly well (Gimell 2).

Other Traditions. The *Great Canon of St. Andrew of Crete* is a magnificent poetic ode that is chanted during the first and fourth weeks of Great Lent in Orthodox Churches, deeply penitential in nature but full of hope and joy at the Resurrection. "Have Mercy on Me, O God" is a rendition primarily in Carpatho-Russian Chant, a unique body of work found only in the Carpathian mountains and among the people who emigrated from there. It's subtly beautiful, extremely accessible, and a very desirable byway in the history of Eastern Chant. The **Schola Cantorum of St.**

Peter's in the Loop, Chicago, under J. Michael Thompson, has devised an English program that features the *Canon* in this peculiar, devotionally sweet chant (Liturgical Press; see the web site).

The **Choir of the Theological Seminary and St. Mark Cathedral** of Cairo give us one of the few examples of Coptic Chant, in great sound; the splendid recording selects hymns from the various Holy Week celebrations (Christophorus 77200). The first national Christian church, the Armenian, celebrates one of its most famous native sons, Vardapet Komitas more than anyone else envisioned a national Armenian religious music, dedicating his life to the cause until the Armenian genocide of the early 20th century precipitated a mental breakdown. His *Divine Liturgy* is a wonderful tribute to his efforts, and a testimonial to the endurance of the Armenian people. The **Choir of St. Gayane** performs it splendidly in a must-have album for Chant devotees (New Albion 33).   RITTER

Electronic Music

The electronica trend in the pop music world—where once-obsolete analog synthesizers like the Moog have been brought out of mothballs by the young for use in dance and trance music—is having a welcome side-effect, for it has triggered a rediscovery of classical electronic music. But sadly, the major record labels are no longer interested in documenting serious electronic compositions the way they once did.

Back in the '60s, many labels (Columbia and Nonesuch in particular) had new music series, sometimes at budget prices, where you could sample the latest experiments for two or three bucks. Nonesuch would commission new works just for the phonograph; DG kept its Stockhausen connection going into the '80s. These days, their electronic catalogs have almost completely vanished, and the demand for early, seminal, never-reissued pieces has pushed the prices of the original LPs into double or even triple figures. So it's harder now to document the evolution of this still-young art form, but not impossible; those old LPs can still turn up at reasonable prices and CD reissues are coming more frequently from a swarm of smaller, if sometimes poorly distributed boutique labels.

Once you get past the recognized technological landmarks and better-known personalities, electronic music becomes maddeningly diverse and diffuse, especially in the post-'80s digital synthesizer era. With so many directions in play and so little of the music in widespread distribution (perhaps the Internet and MP3 will improve things in the near future), it's impossible to sort out definitively what is significant and what's ephemeral. All I can do in this space is skim the surface, using my own taste as a guide, knowing that we're going to leave out many worthwhile things. Also, the line between so-called classical music and popular music is nowhere so blurred or even obliterated as it is in electronic music, so I hope you don't mind if this personalized survey occasionally crosses over the line to talk about something compelling on the other side of the divide. More detailed consideration of many of the composers discussed below will be found in Part I.

A useful tutorial for electronic music beginners is Wendy Carlos's illuminating 1987 lecture/demonstration "Secrets of Synthesis," which includes excerpts from her own recordings (♦CBS 42333). If you can find them (libraries are the best source), also try either "The Nonesuch Guide to Electronic Music" by Bernie Krause and the late Paul Beaver (♦Nonesuch 73018, 2LP, NA) or Krause's updated (1981) "The New Nonesuch Guide to Electronic Music" (♦Nonesuch 78007, NA). True, much has happened since they were released—the universal adoption of MIDI (Musical Instrument Digital Interface), the rise of computers, sampling, etc.—but the raw sounds (especially the cool early Moog timbres in the older "Nonesuch Guide"), techniques, entertaining pieces,

and accompanying literature will give you an idea of where electronic music has been.

Musique Concrète. Just after the end of WWII, Frenchmen Pierre Schaeffer and Pierre Henry championed the idea of *musique concrète,* now brought under the "electronic music" umbrella but at the time a completely separate, thoroughly French genre. Here, natural or found sounds were systematically dissected, filtered, modulated, reversed, rearranged and otherwise altered electronically without resorting to electronic sources. Nowadays, Schaeffer's and Henry's pieces can sound quaint, distant, quirky—due partly to the primitive recording quality—though they must have seemed like shocking apocalyptic soundscapes to 1948 ears. Yet the plunge from madcap jazziness to surreal, nightmarish noises in *Music Without a Title* is still pretty chilling. There was even a 1953 *musique concrète* "opera" by Henry called *Orpheus,* from which a sample cantata, *The Veil of Orpheus,* reveals a gripping, dramatic quality in its best passages. This work has been reissued along with Henry's classic 1963 *Variations on a Door and a Sigh* (Harmonia Mundi 905200).

Until recently, this music was accessible mainly to those lucky collectors who owned the long-out-of-print, '50s-vintage LP anthology "Panorama of Musique Concrète" (London 903090, NA). Yet a boxed set has emerged containing Schaeffer's complete output, which may be a bit much for the explorer, but at least this music is out there again (♦Electronic Music Foundation 114, 3CD).

It took a great composer, **Edgar Varèse,** to put together *musique concrète's* first masterwork, *Déserts* (he preferred the term "organized sound"). *Déserts* is actually a hybrid piece in which four sections for acoustical ensemble are juxtaposed with three grinding, jolting stretches of manipulated natural sound, a vision of a hostile industrial wasteland. Here, the voyager has to watch out; while the pioneering Robert Craft (♦Columbia 31078, 2LP, NA) and recent Chailly (♦London 460208, 2CD) and Nagano (Erato 14332) recordings contain Varèse's original tape, Boulez's version (Sony 68334) leaves it out, and the piece suffers greatly (Boulez claimed the tape is unusable, but that has been disproved).

Varèse's second and last "organized sound" outing, *Poème Electronique,* is equally compelling, a combination of electronic and altered acoustic sounds meant to be played over 400 loudspeakers, but two will do just fine. This has surfaced many times; both the Craft set and the more readily available Chailly Varèse box mentioned above include it, and it has also been reissued in a "classics-of-electronic-music" collection with works by Babbitt, Xenakis and Reynolds (Neuma 450-74).

Unlike *Déserts,* where the electronic and instrumental sections are separated, the tape part plays nearly continuously throughout Roberto Gerhard's Symphony 3 ("Collages," 1960), a harrowing, powerful work—possibly his masterpiece in any genre—that manages to fuse symphonic and electronic elements with amazingly cohesive results. The BBC Symphony has recorded it twice, first in a stunning LP performance under Frederik Prausnitz (♦Angel 36558, NA) and then as part of Bamert's recent Gerhard symphony cycle (Chandos 9556).

Iannis Xenakis produced some powerful *musique concrète* in the '50s and early '60s, using sounds like burning charcoal (*Concret P-H II*), jet planes and trains (*Diamophoses II*), ionospheric signals (*Orient-Occident III*), and Oriental jewelry (*Bohor I*), to produce cohesive, often seething compositions (♦Nonesuch 71246, NA). The moody *Bohor I* builds to one of the most alarming, deafening crescendos ever composed (though the record pales next to live performances). This remarkable music is at long last available again, and beautifully remastered (Electronic Music Foundation 003). Xenakis has kept pace with changing technology and continues to compose electronic music, now using his own UPIC system, developed in the '70s.

Though the development of synthesizers placed *musique concrète* behind the avant-garde curve in the '60s, it continued to exert a large influence. **Steve Reich**'s frightening phase pieces *It's Gonna Rain* and *Come Out* both fall into the *musique concrète* camp (♦Nonesuch 79169). **Frank Zappa**, a Varèse disciple, introduced *musique concrète* techniques in Part II of *The Return of The Son of Monster Magnet,* which is exuberant satirical fun (in "Freak Out!," Rykodisc 10501). He continued this in his next few releases as well: "Absolutely Free" (Rykodisc 10502), "We're Only In It for the Money" (Rykodisc 10503) and "Lumpy Gravy" (Rykodisc 10504) all feature well-realized *musique concrète* pieces interspersed with Zappa's caustic, satirical pop stylings. **Hans Werner Henze**'s entertainingly eclectic *Der langwierige Weg in die Wohnung der Natascha Ungeheuer* has a *musique concrète* tape running effectively through parts of the score, including some overt quotes from Mahler near the end (♦DG 449873)

The most emotionally wrenching piece of *musique concrète* I've ever heard is **The Beatles**'s *Revolution 9* in "The White Album," a brilliant collage of orchestras, voices, sound effects, backwards tapes, and that infamous disembodied voice repeating "number nine" over and over (♦Capitol 46443, 2CD). It's an unsettling kaleidoscope of the heightened emotions of 1968, a direct stylistic descendant of *Orpheus,* that no contemporary music fan should miss (though I can't say the same for John Lennon's disappointingly lame concurrent venture, *Two Virgins*) (Rykodisc 10411).

Karlheinz Stockhausen. On the other side of the Franco-German border, the born-again serial movement started exploring electronic composition at Cologne Radio's electronic studio. At first, the exacting Germans, dominated by Stockhausen, preferred to use only electronic tone generators, but within a few years they began to use natural sources as well. "Cologne-WDR: Early Electronic Music" is a very interesting album that documents pieces composed between 1951 and 1958, essentially the heyday of this studio (BVHAAST 9010). It features several notable composers, including two striking compositions by Ligeti, though it contains none of Stockhausen's own work.

One of Stockhausen's best electronic pieces from the '50s, *Gesang der Jünglinge,* was also the first to capture the world's imagination, a *tour de force* of electronic sounds and boys' voices that whisks inventively from speaker to speaker in the two-channel version of the original five-track tape. Coupled with the spectacular all-electronic *Kontakte* (♦Stockhausen 3), the LP edition was a required purchase among the hip in the '60s and remained available for over two decades (equivalent to a lifetime in this idiom). Another great Stockhausen electronic work is *Hymnen,* which uses several national anthems as a launching pad for a tightly organized electronic/concrète collage that keeps you riveted despite its nearly two-hour length, for there is a surprise around nearly every bend (♦Stockhausen 10, 4CD).

Opus 1970 tries to do the same thing with taped and live performances of Beethoven's music, but the results are less cogent; the great man is sometimes trivialized (DG 139461, NA). *Spiral*—which exists in two different versions—and *Pole* are more succinct, absorbing collages of panned deep-space electronics, short-wave radio transmissions, and miscellany like a lounge saxophonist playing Lerner and Loewe (♦Stockhausen 15). *Mikrophonie II,* with its disembodied voices distorted by ring-modulated electronics, is a denser and more fascinating score than the roaring, scraping organized noise of *Mikrophonie I;* both, however,

are worth hearing (♦Stockhausen 9). 1967's *Prozession* takes off from *Mikrophonie,* with stunning outbreaks of ring-modulated electronics and some self-conscious fits and starts elsewhere (once available in Varèse 81008 and in a more coherent 1971 performance in DG 2530 582). A later, predominantly electronic piece, *Sirius,* mixes live electronic drones and decorations with two singers, trumpet and bass clarinet, but between the striking electronic bookends at the opening and close, the pace bogs down (Stockhausen 26, 2CD). Stockhausen's huge discography, mostly on DG, has disappeared almost entirely from the shops, but the composer is gradually making all his recordings available on his own mail order label. The prices are extremely high ($44.75 for *Mikrophonien!*), so you might find better deals even in the inflated used LP market. Check out his web site (<www.stockhausen.org>) for information.

Luciano Berio. From the Milan electronic studio he co-founded with Bruno Maderna, Berio's *Thema (Omaggio A Joyce)* is a ghostly, sometimes madly swirling, always theatrical electronic piece with Cathy Berberian's voice intoning the beginning of the 11th chapter of *Ulysses. Visage*—Berberian's nonsense syllables, sexy laughter, crying, howling, etc., set against electronic murmurs and violence—breaks through the silliness with chilling electronic rushes toward the end (BVHAAST 9109, with two works by Maderna).

John Cage. As in many other areas, Cage was an electronic music pioneer, using two sine-tone records on variable-speed turntables as sources as early as 1939 in *Imaginary Landscape No. 1* (Hat Art 6179). The pure tape version of *Fontana Mix* is a busy, humorous electronic/*musique concrète* collage (♦Turnabout 34046, NA). Another recording uses *Fontana*—one of Cage's indeterminate compositions—as a base for a Max Neuhaus realization employing feedback from percussion instruments resting on loudspeakers; it's not terribly stimulating except as background (Columbia 7139, NA). Yet another version has Berberian superimposing the equally mirthful *Aria* upon it; it's all the same to Cage (Mainstream 5005, NA). Later Cage can be endearing and/or infuriating; his expansive, gentle, burbling collaboration with David Tudor and Takehisa Kosugi, *Five Stone Wind* (1988), is the former, and the various abrasive scrapings of phono cartridges in *Cartridge Music* (1960) is most emphatically the latter (Mode 24).

The Columbia-Princeton Center. In the U.S., electronic music started to sprout under the aegis of the universities, first at Columbia in 1951 where **Vladimir Ussachevsky** and composer/flutist **Otto Luening** began experimenting with the music department's new tape recorder. Separately and together, they came up with a synthesis of *musique concrète* and Stockhausen, using acoustic and electronic sources at will.

A fascinating, absolutely essential disc, "Pioneers of Electronic Music," collects several of their earliest pieces; Ussachevsky's *Sonic Contours* and Luening's ethereal *Low Speed, Invention in Twelve Tones,* and *Fantasy in Space* follow each other in the same order Stokowski presented them at a 1952 concert (♦CRI 611). For all their otherworldly spookiness, this music is quite beautiful, capturing something that today's infinitely more advanced digital equipment misses. As the disc goes on to include Ussachevsky's terrific *Piece for Tape Recorder* and some later computer-generated works, we hear that his basic abstract esthetic never really changed. His appropriately disembodied music for Orson Welles's film of Sartre's play *No Exit* and the sprawling, occasionally pretentious score for *Line of Apogee* are also examples of this early abstract style —period pieces, actually (New World 80389).

For over a decade after 1959, the Columbia-Princeton Electronic Music Center's RCA synthesizer—a large, unwieldy instrument programmed by punching holes in paper—dominated electronic music composition, attracting several noted composers who were staunchly devoted to serial music. **Milton Babbitt** was widely regarded as a virtuoso of the RCA synthesizer; his *Ensembles for Synthesizer* is a rapidly changing, high-speed streak of events, strictly serial and complicated as hell but a *tour de force* that holds your attention (♦Columbia 7051, NA). Scarcely less complex is Babbitt's *Reflections,* parallel monologues for acoustic piano and electronics that are part of pianist Aleck Karis's stimulating disc of piano/tape pieces (♦CRI 707).

Another collection offering this piece contains a good selection of Babbitt's other music for tape and performer, including the fascinating *Philomel* for soprano and tape, *Phonemona,* and *Post-Partitions,* with **Robert Miller** on piano (New World 80466). Babbitt's early, more severe *Composition for Synthesizer* is less interesting (Columbia 6566, NA). **Jacob Druckman**'s antic dialog between a trombone and burbling Columbia-Princeton electronics, *Animus I,* can be hunted down (Turnabout 34177, NA). *Animus III* for clarinet and tape is even more animated and inventive, including some comic vocal banter and some intergalactic drifting and gliding (♦Nonesuch 71253, NA). **Ilhan Mimaroglu** produces ingenious manipulations of sounds from a rubber band (Prelude No. 11, *Bowery Bum*) and a somber march from oscillators, piano and Turkish voice in Prelude No. 12 (Finnadar 91305).

Charles Wuorinen's *Time's Encomium* won the 1970 Pulitzer Prize, the first for an electronic score, yet this highly abstract, serial-grounded 31-minute piece doesn't really get interesting until some complex, kaleidoscopic, Babbitt-like madness takes over midway through (♦Music & Arts 932). **Mario Davidovsky**'s brief, ruminative, ultimately dramatic *Synchronisms No. 6* for piano and tape won the Pulitzer the following year—it can be found on Karis's disc (♦CRI 707)—while *Synchronisms No. 5* is a spare, wry discussion between appropriately matched sparring partners, a percussion group and electronics (♦CRI 611).

William Hellermann's absorbing *Passages 13—The Fire* juxtaposes gentle RCA synth effects against an irreverent processed text by Robert Duncan and an often jazz-slanted trumpet played by a young Gerard Schwarz (Nonesuch 71275, NA). And as late as 1980, **Mel Powell** was still composing music like his tumbling, delicate, abstract *Three Synthesizer Settings* in a Columbia-Princeton-related style, though realized on Moog and Buchla equipment (Nonesuch 78006, NA).

The Columbia-Princeton studio's influence continued to be felt well into the mid-'70s; since then it has been eclipsed by other electronic music centers. "Columbia-Princeton Electronic Music Center 1961–1973" is a vibrant, wide-ranging compilation of tape music from some of its finest exponents that documents the period from 1961–73 quite well, with selections by Mimaroglu, Bülent Arel (who assisted with much of the tape work for Varèse's *Déserts*), Charles Dodge, Ingram Marshall, Daria Semegen, and Alice Shields (New World 80521). While some of these names may be unfamiliar, these composers were and are highly influential in academic circles.

Morton Subotnick was the leading advocate of Donald Buchla's synthesizer, one of the two portable, flexible, modular, voltage-control instruments (the other was the Moog) that took electronic music out of academia into the public arena. Using the Buchla's touchplates instead of a keyboard, Subotnick created spectacular, aggressive, tightly organized, abstract compositions that had wide appeal among the young. The whirling *Silver Apples of the Moon* still gives you a buzz today—it was a best seller for Nonesuch in its time—and it has been combined in a single CD with its moodier, more ominous immediate successor, *The*

Wild Bull (♦Wergo 2035). Although Subotnick later turned to electronic "ghost" scores for live instruments and tape, occasionally he returned to the all-electronic medium, as in the energetic toccata *A Sky of Cloudless Sulphur* (♦Nonesuch 78001, NA) or the exuberant celebration of Halley's Comet, *Return* (♦New Albion 012).

Wendy Carlos looms as a giant, the instigator of nothing less than a revolution. Once she began working with Robert Moog on developing his synthesizer, her volatile imagination was turned loose, and her first Moog album, *Switched-On Bach,* set music on its ear in 1968 (♦CBS 07194). It's impossible to underestimate the importance of this recording; it showed the world that electronic music need not be pitchless blips, bleeps, and blats, and that the synthesizer can be used to make attractive music. Glenn Gould called it "the record of the decade," but it could easily be called the record of the half-century, for it opened the door for the domination of the synthesizer in everyday music, for good and ill. What's more, *SO-B* is still a lot of fun, for Carlos's realizations are witty, intelligent, and full of invention, taking Bach's polyphonic possibilities to their limit while being faithful to the scores. (Carlos's own CD transfer is richer, more reverberant but not as pointillistic as the original LP).

Naturally, there were several sequels—as well as crassly inferior imitations like *The Moog Strikes Bach, Everything You Always Wanted to Hear on The Moog,* etc., that aren't worth bothering with—but Carlos's *The Well-Tempered Synthesizer* is actually a better-balanced, more densely harmonized, more musically and technically sophisticated record, one that imaginatively translates Handel, Monteverdi and especially Scarlatti to the electronic medium (♦Columbia 7286, NA). 1973's *Switched-On Bach II* is smoother, more assured, less irreverently far-out than its famous predecessor (Columbia 32659). Having already done Brandenburgs 3, 4, 5, and part of 2, Carlos completed the series in 1979 with *Switched-On Brandenburgs* (♦CBS 35895, 2CD)—though not without some revisions; the sober second movement improvisation of 3 is less cheeky than the one in *SO-B*. All the above albums were deleted and then gathered into a box (East Side Digital 81422, 4CD), but the original Columbia and CBS LPs and CDs are still commonly found—and yes, the ones labeled "Walter Carlos" are the real McCoys (that was Wendy's name before her sex-change operation in the early '70s).

In 1992, Carlos revisited her old stomping grounds with *Switched-On Bach 2000,* remaking her hit album—plus the Toccata and Fugue in D minor—with digital synthesizers, a Mac computer, and a few exotic tunings (Telarc 80323). But the results are sedate, overly legato, and lacking the old audacious spark; I prefer her Bach when she was young and foolish.

Perhaps more important for electronic music's evolution have been Carlos's original electronic compositions, some of which are among the most brilliant in the medium's history. A student of Ussachevsky and Luening, her early pre-Moog pieces like *Variations for Flute and Electronic Sound, Dialogues for Piano and Two Loudspeakers* (Turnabout 34004, NA), and *Episodes for Piano and Electronic Sound* (Columbia 32088, NA) were strictly in the Columbia-Princeton academic mode, although you can hear a playfulness that sets them apart.

But *Timesteps,* the flagship of Carlos's score for the 1971 film *A Clockwork Orange,* was a sign that the medium had given birth to a major composer (♦East Side Digital 81362). A stunning, nearly 14-minute-long canvas of dread, transcendental escape, martial airs, and inexorable angst, it unfolds like a movement of a Mahler symphony, flamboyant yet tightly unified, moving between emotional extremes. Along with some very clever transcriptions of Beethoven, Rossini, and Purcell,

East Side Digital's softly remixed *Clockwork* CD also includes three shorter Carlos pieces: *Orange Minuet,* a pleasant classical pastiche, the portentous *Biblical Daydreams* (both released for the first time), and a powerful electronic march to the scaffold, *Country Lane.*

Right on top of *Clockwork* came another Carlos masterpiece: *Sonic Seasonings*—a sprawling, haunting depiction of the four seasons through gentle electronic nocturnes, brooding abstract soundscapes, and unaltered natural sounds (♦East Side Digital 81372, 2CD), It has been called a forerunner of "New Age" music, but the depths and ambiguous emotions that Carlos taps into are not to be compared with those of that flaccid, feel-good idiom.

Though her technical expertise has more than kept pace with the march of technology, the artistic road has been spotty for Carlos since 1972. *Pompous Circumstances* (1975) is a clever quodlibet of assorted classical quotes and gags that sometimes border on the silly, an electronic Peter Schickele circus act (Columbia 32088, NA). The 1982 soundtrack for *Tron* is mostly a series of uninspired cues for electronics mixed with the London Philharmonic (CBS 37782, NA). 1984's *Digital Moonscapes* does away with the orchestra altogether as Carlos uses a library of some 500 complex timbres to create two suites of thoroughly tonal, Romantic-orchestra-inspired, electronic tone poems; *Cosmological Impressions* is more inventive than *Moonscapes,* but neither repays repeated listening (East Side Digital 81552).

Far more intriguing is 1986's *Beauty in The Beast* where Carlos's imagination was fired up again once she started de-tuning her Synergy synthesizers to exotic scales (♦Audion 200, NA, to be reissued on East Side Digital). The music is eerie, radical, impressionistic, flavored with Balinese, Arabic, and other Third World spices, likely to be uncomfortable for anyone cursed with so-called perfect pitch, yet hauntingly beautiful. Another winner, *Land of The Midnight Sun,* a gorgeous, flowing, layered 40-minute electronic improvisation, dates from the same year but wasn't released until 1998 as a companion to *Sonic Seasonings* (♦East Side Digital 81372, 2CD).

To date, the only original Carlos music from the '90s on disc is *Tales of Heaven and Hell,* an extravagant attempt to scare the bejeepers out of us, using male voices, *musique concrète* techniques, advanced synth technology, centered around *Clockwork Black,* an elaborate satanic fantasia on her *Clockwork Orange* score (East Side Digital 81352). The cover says, "Use caution when listening alone or in the dark"; I found it more creepy than frightening.

Other Switched-On Classics. Of Carlos's successors, longtime Disney employee **Don Dorsey** is probably the most popular; his albums "Bachbusters" (Telarc 80123) and "Beethoven Or Bust" (Telarc 80153) were bestsellers in the '80s. Though Dorsey had the advantage of using polyphonic synthesizers, steering mostly clear of the repertoire Carlos covered, "Bachbusters" doesn't stretch the boundaries of the art much beyond Carlos's transcriptions on the Moog, nor is it as timbrally imaginative (sometimes he even falls back on a tacky rhythm machine). "Beethoven" is marred by lapses of taste—the infernal electronic percussion section returns, a sickening auto crash ends a bagatelle—and some pieces sound like little more than electrified harpsichord renditions, yet others do display a resourceful selection of sharp timbres. The fitfully interesting "Busted" finds Dorsey second-guessing his record company with a collection of out-takes from the Bach and Beethoven albums, some hyped-up Mozart from an unfinished album, pop-flavored Dorsey compositions, and a slick classical quodlibet from a Disney project (Telarc 80473).

Best-known as a jazz keyboardist and arranger, **Bob James** made two albums of tasteful electronic arrangements of Baroque music. "Rameau" uses mostly analog synthesizers, abounds in attractive, unusual timbres and attacks that approach Carlos's achievements (♦CBS 39540). "The Scarlatti Dialogues" employs digital instruments, and to my ears, sounds slicker, less fresh (CBS 44519, NA). In a similar vein, **Frank Zappa,** believe it or not, made some innocuous Synclavier transcriptions of the innocuous, Scarlatti-like music of his 18th-century namesake, Francesco Zappa (Rykodisc 10546).

Isao Tomita broke completely with the Carlos example, hijacking classical pieces as launching pads for outer space sound voyages with his own signature, departing from the score at will. Using Debussy piano pieces as his initial vehicles in "Snowflakes Are Dancing" was a brilliant stroke, for Debussy's hazy impressionism and wit adapted beautifully and often movingly to Tomita's shimmering, vibrating, pitch-drifting, phase-shifting electronic technique (♦RCA 63587); *The Engulfed Cathedral* is a classic (♦RCA 60579). The whimsy and brooding grandeur of *Pictures at An Exhibition* also translates very well into Tomita's idiom, a few cutesy spots aside (♦RCA 60576). His version of Holst's *The Planets* (RCA 60518) was controversial—the Holst estate even tried to force it off the market—and though the timbres aren't as radical as *Snowflakes* or *Pictures,* it often does amount to a recomposition, placing the vast suite in the context of a space trip (there's a nasty asteroid belt between Jupiter and Saturn).

After his breakthrough albums, Tomita seemed content to repeat most of his tricks too often, but there are times in later albums where he hits it just right—a thoroughly idiomatic Ives's *The Unanswered Question* (from "Cosmos," RCA 2616), a gorgeous rendition of Vaughan Williams's *The Lark Ascending* (from "Live at Linz," RCA 5461, NA). There are also three anthologies: "Greatest Hits" (RCA 5660), "A Voyage Through His Greatest Hits," Volume 2 (RCA 4019, NA), and "Space Walk" (RCA 5037, NA), the latter of which has the most interesting selection.

IRCAM. When **Pierre Boulez** opened his Parisian dream music laboratory, IRCAM, in 1977, it seemed to signal the second great French contribution to electronic music. So far, the most visible and tangible results have come from its founder; once Boulez started merging real-time computer-generated sound with live acoustic instruments, he found a new, wildly colorful, more listener-friendly voice.

His first big electro-acoustic piece, *Répons,* is a sprawling, mesmerizing masterwork that just washes over you; the introduction of glistening electronics all over the listening space about six minutes into the piece is a great dramatic coup (♦DG 457605). With its electronically altered triple-flute lead voices, . . . *explosante fixe* . . . is a fluid, lighter-textured, no less colorful work (♦DG 445833). *Anthèmes 2* electronically multiplies, harmonizes, and places a solo violin in a gorgeous electro-acoustic space; you can actually detect a delectable French sense of atmosphere in this work (♦DG 463476). How ironic that "chilly" electronics have actually made a more warmly expressive composer out of Boulez; let that be a riposte to its critics.

When Boulez founded IRCAM, he placed **Jean-Claude Risset** in charge of computer music. Risset is a composer whose technological savvy is matched by his musicianship and his work is of the highest importance in this idiom. He has a knack for creating seemingly "impossible" acoustic phenomena through digital synthesis and has developed many important techniques without which much of his and other composers' work would not exist. His music can be heard in two fine compilations that document his work from Bell Labs in the late '60s to his later projects at IRCAM and elsewhere (Wergo 2013 and INA GRM 1003). Both contain his masterwork *Sud* (*South*), a breathtaking three-movement exploration of *musique concrète* realized from sounds collected in various southern places.

Another significant IRCAM composer is **Jonathan Harvey,** who subjected *musique concrète* techniques to computer processing in the sustained voices and bell-like sonorities of *Mortuos Plango, Vivos Voco*—a direct descendant of *Gesang der Jünglinge* (Erato 71544, NA). More of Harvey's IRCAM work can be sampled in "Music of Jonathan Harvey" (Bridge 9031), with *Ritual Melodies,* a delicate and evocative tapestry of shimmering exotic sounds that transmute from one to another. *Bakti* for chamber ensemble and quadraphonic tape is an extended meditative essay that again shows his indebtedness to Stockhausen (NMC 1 or Disques Montaigne 782086). His music has a humane warmth that makes it especially appealing. An invaluable 1983 introduction to IRCAM was available on LP for several years, demonstrating computer techniques and offering samples from works by Harvey, Subotnick, Machover, York Höller, and an enlightening extract from an early version of *Répons* (♦IRCAM 0001, NA).

Many other centers for computer music have emerged whose contributions often rival IRCAM's. In the U.S. there is CCRMA (pronounced "karma") at Stanford and the studio at MIT, to mention but two. The composers associated with these places are too numerous to mention, but some anthologies have been released that will help the curious explore this interesting world. "Cultures Electroniques" was a multi-volume series released in the late '80s that offered prize-winning compositions from all over the world and is well worth searching for (Chant du Monde). "Music With Computers" is an ongoing series that includes important surveys of composers like John Chowning and Jean-Claude Risset, as well as multi-composer volumes under the heading "Computer Music Currents" (Wergo).

Ingram Marshall found his voice with haunting, drifting, relaxed soundscapes that transcend the musical wallpaper laid down by less-inspired musicians. A ghostly, somber piece for live brass ensemble and a tape of foghorns and oceanic sound effects, *Fog Tropes* is a direct descendant of parts of *Sonic Seasonings* as well as Ives's *The Unanswered Question.* Fellow composer John Adams leads both recordings(♦New Albion 002 and ♦Nonesuch 79249); the tape of sound effects is mixed more up front in the New Albion disc, the Nonesuch performance (in a disc called "American Elegies") offers a more detailed sonic panorama. Also on New Albion is *Gradual Requiem,* a graceful succession of looped episodes whose eerie vocal sequences remind one of Ligeti.

Alcatraz is a quietly atmospheric collaboration with photographer Jim Bengston shaped roughly in an arch, with an inner core of desolate electronic music surrounded by concentric rings of slamming cell doors, growling voices in solitary, somber minimalist piano/electronics, and peaceful, fog-shrouded ambient electronics (♦New Albion 040). No doubt about it, the piece powerfully evokes its landscape. Another Marshall/Bengston collaboration, *Three Penitential Visions,* manipulates tape loops of acoustic sounds into a haunting fresco, while its companion, *Hidden Voices,* which uses a digital sampler and soprano voices from Eastern Europe, is an untypically disturbing piece (Nonesuch 79227). A compilation of Marshall's text/sound compositions from the '70s is available; these earlier pieces are quite different from but just as evocative as those described above (New World 80577). Through the course of the disc, you hear a progressive evolution toward his present style, rounding out our portrait of this composer.

Charles Dodge's computer music has been making a quietly significant contribution for many years; "Any Resemblance is Purely Coincidental" is a fine survey from all periods of his lengthy career (New Albion 043). His music is remarkable for its high level of craftsmanship, understatement, and a gentle wit rarely experienced elsewhere. The title piece is a digital transformation of a Caruso recording of "Vesti la giubba" with piano accompaniment (here played by Alan Feinberg); it's simultaneously comic and sadly poignant, restrained but exuberantly dramatic. Other works on the disc offer a similar richness, from the early, oddly remote *Speech Songs* to the recent *Viola Elegy* for viola and tape (written to commemorate the death of Morton Feldman), eloquently performed by Dodge's son, Baird.

Electronic Miscellany. An absorbing, wide-ranging sampling of several generations' work circa 1989 can be found in "Imaginary Landscapes," ranging from **Alvin Lucier**'s clattering brain-wave amplifications and **David Tudor**'s Cage-ian collage to digital synthesizers and microcomputers (♦Nonesuch 79235). And to top it off, **Christian Maclay** reverts to Cage's primeval idea of spinning turntables (hence the title) in *Black Stucco.*

Women in Electronic Music—1977 is a misnomer; not everything here qualifies as electronic music, particularly the CD's primary selling point, a pair of gabby early pieces by now-famous performance artist **Laurie Anderson** (♦CRI 728). Yet there are some things here that will grab your attention—an "updated" performance of Johanna M. Beyer's *Music of the Spheres* for oscillators (from 1938!) and **Pauline Oliveros**'s inventive manipulation of oscillators and an opera disc, *Bye Bye Butterfly.* A cohort of Subotnick in the '60s, Oliveros's gripping interstellar fantasy *I of IV* is also worth hunting down (♦Odyssey 32160160, NA).

Alwin Nikolais spanned almost every era of electronic music from *musique concrète* of the '50s through owning Moog's first synthesizer in the '60s to his highly rhythmic, sometimes pop/funk-flavored compositions for the EMULator in the '70s and '80s. A single-disc survey of short electronic dances bypasses all of his early stuff and includes only two Moog pieces, but it's entertaining (♦CRI 651).

Joel Gressel, meanwhile, unrepentantly continues to ply the old roads of twelve-tone rows in his computer music. Even modern digital technology merely places a gleaming face upon these tough, atonal abstractions from the mid-'70s and mid-'90s, though you can hear a softening of his stance in the '90s in "Cold Fusion III" (CRI 797).

Barton and **Priscilla McLean** created some smashing electronic pieces on analog equipment in the '70s—clearly structured, full of drama, with arrestingly complex timbres—and they were particularly effective in long forms. Several of their best, including Barton's *Song of The Nahuatl* and Priscilla's *Dance of Dawn,* have been gathered together, along with Barton's dazzling 1982 etude *Etunytude* on a digital Fairlight synthesizer (♦CRI 764). Barton's eerie, inventive, disturbing *A Little Night Music* and *Demons of The Night* can be heard in Vol. 7 of the CDCM Computer Music Series, which at 30 volumes and counting is easily the most extensive—though hard to find—collection of electronic music in the catalog (Centaur 2047). Elsewhere, the series features a cross-section of a few well-known composers like Subotnick, Oliveros (whose surprisingly genial gamelan-fest *Lion's Tale* is also in Vol. 7), Joan LaBarbara, and a host of unheralded figures.

A major figure in West Coast electronic music, **Carl Stone** likes to manipulate found and electronic sounds into well-organized, recycling, mesmerizing, very listenable patterns, often naming his pieces after Chinese restaurants. The best-known example of his music is *Hop Ken,* which, almost as a response to Teammate, exuberantly turns *Pictures at An Exhibition* inside out. This is combined with *Wall Me Do*, a syncopated toccata, its cunningly constructed successor *Sonali,* and the ethereal *Shing Kee* (♦EAM 201).

Normally associated with rock music, **Brian Eno** has also been a pioneer in ambient electronics; his *Discreet Music* is a gorgeously hypnotic, peaceful, half-hour meditation designed to be heard just above the threshold of audibility (♦Antilles). I also recommend the second, mostly electronic half of his collaborative album with David Bowie, "*Low*"; the last section, *Subterraneans,* is a surprisingly emotional musical catharsis (♦Rykodisc 10142). "Music for Airports" was another influential Eno ambient recording (Editions EG 1516), and it was recently presented by the Bang-On-a-Can All-Stars in a lush production with the musicians playing acoustic and electronic instruments in real time (Point).

Frank Zappa recorded some accomplished, often rhythmically complex electronic music on the Synclavier as the "Barking Pumpkin Digital Gratification Consort" (♦Rykodisc 10542); the most interesting are the tumbling *The Girl in The Magnesium Dress* and the appropriately ominous *Jonestown.* "Jazz From Hell," a 1986 release consisting mostly of Synclavier compositions, is also intriguing (Rykodisc 10549). Most noteworthy, though, is Zappa's posthumously-issued masterpiece "Civilization Phaze III," a haunting, dark, and weirdly coherent exploration of a group of characters who live inside a large piano (UMRK 01, 2CD). **George Harrison**'s *No Time Or Space* from "Electronic Sound" is a flamboyant, dramatic, structurally tight Moog tone poem, although unbilled collaborator Bernie Krause deserves much of the credit for its success (♦Zapple/EMI 55239).

Paul Dresher's *Dark Blue Circumstance* (New Albion 053) and *Liquid and Stellar Music* (Lovely Music 2011) are attractive, revolving pieces for looped solo electric guitar. **George Todd** has a recording of abstract compositions realized on the Synclavier, shifting easily between tonal, vocal and pitchless sounds; there are a few grand moments, but the music mostly drifts indulgently (Electronic Music Foundation 001). **Tod Machover**'s *Bounce* for piano, electronic keyboard and "hyperinstrument electronics" is a highly percussive piece that turns into a Nancarrow-like high-speed multi-keyboard extravaganza (Bridge 9040).

Douglas Leedy's huge, two-hour-long *Entropical Paradise* uses pure Moog and Buchla electronics to create "sonic environments"; the sounds are fascinating, but the premise pretty much rules out concentrated listening (Seraphim 6060, 3LP, NA). Finally, dipping again into the minimalist camp, **John Adams** has produced some attractive electronic music in "Hoodoo Zephyr" (♦Nonesuch 79311), and **Terry Riley**'s *A Rainbow In Curved Air* is a gorgeously floating, loopy series of loops produced on electronic organs (♦CBS 7315, with *Poppy Nogood's Phantom Band*). GINELL, WITH THE ASSISTANCE OF McINTIRE

Film Music

Music and film have been entwined since the dawn of the cinema, with some great names participating: Walton, Vaughan Williams, Copland, Prokofiev, Shostakovich (discussed in the articles on those composers). Others, no less distinguished, made composing for the screen their primary careers; it's the latter group we treat here.

Richard Addinsell (1904–77) is best known for *Warsaw Concerto;* Pennario's is the best (EMI 63661). The ghostly suite from *A Christmas Carol* is memorable (Telarc 88801); compilations from Kenneth Alwyn are on Marco Polo and ASV.

John Barry (b. 1933). The magnificent *Lion in Winter* is Barry's one great score (Sony 5127). *Deadfall* is interesting for its guitar concerto (Retrograde 80124).

Elmer Bernstein (b. 1922). *The Magnificent Seven* defines his outdoorsy Americana style. The soundtrack is a manly romp, in burly mono sound (Rykodisc 10741). Sedares (Koch 7222) and Bernstein (RCA 63240) have sumptuous acoustics but aren't as lively. *Return of the Seven* is the same score, briefer and with a smaller ensemble (Rykodisc). *True Grit* (Colosseum 47236 or Varèse 47236, NA) has magical moments, but avoid the jazzed-up Capitol. *The Comancheros* is archetypical Western music (Silver Age FSM 2/6).

To Kill a Mockingbird is Bernstein's masterpiece—a sensitive work not far removed from chamber music. The composer's latest reading is unsurpassed (Varèse 5754); the soundtrack is an appalling mono transfer (Mainstream, NA). *The Field* (Varèse 5292), *Summer and Smoke* (RCA 73592), and *The Age of Innocence* (Epic 57451) are in the same mold. *The Ten Commandments* is bold and emotional (MCA 42320). Others worth mentioning are *Zulu Dawn* (Silva 22) and *The Great Escape,* with its well-known march (Rykodisc 10711)—Bernstein's remake has better sound (RCA 63241). A composer-led anthology is lethargic (Denon); John Wayne suites are more effective (Colosseum 47264 or Varèse 47264, NA).

Bruce Broughton (b. 1945). While his magnificent *Young Sherlock Holmes* awaits reissue, I recommend the exhilarating *Silverado* (Intrada 7035) as well as *Honey, I Blew Up the Kid* (Intrada 7030), *The Boy Who Could Fly* (Varèse 47279, NA), and *Lost in Space* (Intrada 7086).

Patrick Doyle (b. 1953). *Henry V* (EMI 49919) and *Dead Again* (Varèse 5339) are remarkably creative. *Much Ado About Nothing* shows a gift for sophisticated comedy (Epic 54009).

Danny Elfman (b. 1953). His shadowy *Batman* music is well represented (Varèse 5766), but with *Edward Scissorhands* Elfman paints an enchanting sketch of childlike wizardry (MCA 10133). *Sommersby* (Elektra 61491), *Black Beauty* (Giant 24568, NA), and *Dolores Claiborne* (Varèse 5602) reveal new depths.

Hugo Friedhofer (1901–81). Stromberg's collection is the best introduction to this respected composer (Marco Polo 223857). *The Best Years of Our Lives* is considered the pinnacle of his work (Preamble 1779, NA).

Jerry Goldsmith (b. 1929) studied with Jakob Gimpel, Castelnuovo-Tedesco, and Rózsa, then burnished his skills in radio and television. The use of the Lydian mode gives a longing, heavenly feel to *The Blue Max.* The sound in the reissue (CBS 57890) is a tad inferior to the original (Varèse 47238, NA), but one of the two belongs in every collection. *Patton,* with its reverberating fanfares and militant passacaglia, has been newly recorded by Goldsmith (Varèse 5796), but the soundtrack is definitive (Silver Age FSM 2/2).

Star Trek: The Motion Picture is a panoply of luminous melodies and inventive development (Columbia 66134). Goldsmith returned to the series for *Star Trek V* (Epic 45267), *First Contact* (GNP Crescendo), and *Insurrection* (GNP Crescendo 8059). Some consider *Planet of the Apes,* with its advanced atonality, Goldsmith's best; Varèse 5848 is longer than previous issues, with music from a sequel.

Poltergeist is, by turns, childlike, charming, and ferocious (Rhino 72725). The choral chants of *The Omen* (Varèse 5281) set a standard for satanic music, followed in two sequels (Silva, NA, and Varèse 47242, NA). *Logan's Run* makes resourceful use of orchestral colors (Chapter III

136, with *Coma*). Nostalgia and a horror parody highlight *Matinee* (Varèse 5408); *Explorers* combines wonder and wit (Varèse 5261). Also recommended are *The Mummy* (Decca 466458) and *Alien,* conducted by Cliff Eidelman (Varèse 5753).

Rio Conchos is overshadowed by its disc-mate, the exquisite prologue to *The Agony and the Ecstasy* (Intrada 6007). *Stagecoach* is sophisticated and disarming (Silver Age 1), and *The Wind and the Lion* is a coruscating mélange of Arabian Nights rhythms and soaring themes (Intrada 7005). *Lilies of the Field* (Pendulum 009), *A Patch of Blue* (Intrada 7076), *Rudy* (Varèse 5446), and *QB VII* (Intrada 7061) are more introspective. Goldsmith conducts extracts from his sci-fi scores in Varèse 5871. A well-chosen anthology from Nic Raine is fervent, in splendid sound (Silva 1091, 2CD).

Ron Goodwin's (b. 1925) splashy *Battle of Britain* shares a disc with Walton's discarded score (Rykodisc 10747). The capricious Miss Marple music is in an import with *Force 10 from Navarone* (Label X 706). *Valhalla* is an ambitious score for an animated film (Label X 709); Chandos 8811 is a good sampler of his work.

Bernard Herrmann (1911–75) was working at CBS when Orson Welles brought him to Hollywood for *Citizen Kane.* Joel McNeely is a superior Herrmann conductor and captures the essence of the score (Varèse 065806); Tony Bremner is uninspired (Laserlight or PRCD). Gerhardt's authoritative suite misses the lighter moments (RCA 0707), but these can be had in Herrmann's concert work, *Welles Raises Kane* (Unicorn 2065). That disc includes a suite from *The Devil and Daniel Webster* plus *Obsession* (see below). Sedares leads a less energetic *Devil,* but he has the latest sound (Koch 7224).

After *Kane* came *The Magnificent Ambersons;* with these films Herrmann was creating his own darkly nostalgic American idiom. Bremner is more successful here (Preamble 1783, NA); Label X 2008 pairs condensed versions of Bremner's *Kane* and *Ambersons. The Ghost and Mrs. Muir* is intensely romantic but not sentimental, with striking passages for woodwinds (Varèse 5850). Bernstein's recording is no less gorgeous, and the sound is exceptional (Varèse 47254, NA). In *Jane Eyre,* Adriano creates a dark, brooding atmosphere; still, some find it overlong (Marco Polo 223535). A selection from the soundtrack (Fox) retains its strength despite faded sound; Herrmann's brief suite is lovingly played (London 448948).

The Seventh Voyage of Sinbad is imaginative: a snake dance written for winds and percussion, a skeleton attack scored for percussion and brass. The soundtrack is a profusion of color and melody (Varèse 47256, NA), while John Debney's survey is longer and sonically up to date (Varèse 5961). The composer's Phase-4 excerpts are sabotaged by lethargic tempos. Except for a few scenes, there are no strings in *Journey to the Center of the Earth,* but there are multiple harps, a pipe organ, and four electronic organs. The original tracks make an immense effect (Varèse 5849); the composer's Phase-4 suite is impressive (London 443899). Theremins, electronic organs, electric violins, dual pianos, and brass dominate *The Day the Earth Stood Still;* Varèse 11010 is mostly mono but eerily effective. Herrmann's suite has phlegmatic tempos and doesn't use a true theremin, and one track is off-speed (London). *Jason and the Argonauts* is mammoth and multicolored; Broughton's recreation (Intrada 7083) is stunning.

Scored for strings and percussion, *Fahrenheit 451* offers passion, menace, and incomparable beauty. The Phase-4 extracts are valuable (London 443899), but Joel McNeely's longer suite uncovers new layers of inspiration, in radiant sound (Varèse 5551). Salonen is in the same league (Sony 62700). For the mysterious, unsettling *Psycho,* Herrmann used only strings. Unicorn 2021, credited to Herrmann, was in fact conducted by Laurie Johnson, whose stiff tempos were dictated by the composer. McNeely delivers the full score, brilliantly played and recorded (Varèse 5765). "Narrative for Orchestra" is Herrmann's adroit distillation (London 443895). Salonen offers a different set of excerpts, as does Bateman (Silva)—both are spirited, but Salonen has the better orchestra. Elfman's reworking of the music for the recent remake is close in spirit to the soundtrack readings (Virgin 47657). Elmer Bernstein (Milan) and Broughton (Intersound) are not in the running.

Herrmann's collaboration with Hitchcock continued with *North by Northwest,* a wild frolic with a recurring fandango rhythm. Laurie Johnson is enthusiastic if not always urtext (Unicorn 2040); an earlier issue has more distant sound and incorrect sequencing (Varèse, NA). Rhino 72101 offers the original tracks in vivid stereo. *Vertigo* is music of almost hypnotic impact; apart from the film, its minimalism can be harder to take. McNeely's reading is near-perfection (Varèse 5600); the original tracks can't compare (on Varèse—the Mercury has inferior audio and less music). Among short suites, Herrmann's sounds unromantic in sterile Phase-4 acoustics; Salonen is refined; Bateman (Silva) and Broughton are unremarkable.

Herrmann's *Torn Curtain* music—with its sixteen French horns, twelve flutes, and nine trombones—was rejected by Hitchcock and ended their alliance. McNeely is spectacular (Varèse 5817), rendering Bateman's suite superfluous (Silva). *Obsession* uses a huge orchestra, plus chorus and pipe organ. The Phase-4 soundtrack delivers the goods and then some (Unicorn 2065).

The Night Digger is in the *Psycho* mold: strings plus a sinister harmonica; *Battle of Neretva* offers towering blocks of sound. These two are combined in Label X 2003. *Mysterious Island* is a *tour de force,* highlighted by an outrageous fugue (Cloud Nine 7017, NA). Herrmann's final score, *Taxi Driver,* is an atypical, bluesy mood piece—its defenders argue it's suited to the film's wasted urban nightlife (Arista 19005). Also noteworthy are *The Trouble with Harry* and *Marnie* (McNeely, Varèse 5971 and 066594), *Garden of Evil* (Stromberg, Marco Polo 223841), *Anna and the King* (Varèse 302 066 091), TV scores for *The Twilight Zone* (McNeely, Varèse 066 087), and *Cape Fear* (MCA 10463, adaptation by Bernstein).

Among compilations, Herrmann's Phase-4 series has some perverse tempos but is a good introduction. It includes suites from *The Trouble with Harry* (443895), *The Snows of Kilimanjaro* (443948), and the witty, neoclassical *Three Worlds of Gulliver* (443899). The Mobile Fidelity reissues sound no better, have shorter running times, and cost three times as much. Gerhardt's collection is a standout, the best such on record (RCA 0707). Besides *Kane,* it includes a suite from *Beneath the 12-Mile Reef,* with its huge orchestra and nine harps, and the ultimate reading of the *Hangover Square* Piano Concerto.

Salonen's anthology reflects the increasing penetration of serious film music into the concert hall (Sony 62700). The *North by Northwest* prelude is frantic, but overall he brings considerable finesse to the program. Bernstein's is marred by wrong notes and missing instruments but is redeemed by the stirring *Storm Clouds Cantata,* composed for *The Man Who Knew Too Much* by Arthur Benjamin, reorchestrated and expanded by Herrmann (Milan 35643). Bateman has too many brief snippets, sloppily played (Silva).

James Horner (b. 1953). Horner's eclectic output is uneven. *Glory* (Virgin 91329) is an inspiring rhapsody for chorus and orchestra that some rate his masterpiece (others hear echoes of Prokofiev). His best work includes *Star Trek III* (GNP Crescendo 8023), *Krull* (STSE 01/02, 2CD), *The Rocketeer* (Hollywood 61117), *Brainstorm* (Varèse 47215), and *Willow* (Virgin 86066).

Erich Wolfgang Korngold (1897–1957). A child prodigy, Korngold adopted a grand, romantic style, making his scores more like tone poems. *Adventures of Robin Hood,* led by Varujian Kojian, is all but complete (Varèse 47202); shorter suites have been recorded by Gerhardt (RCA 0912), John Scott (Denon), Malcolm Nabarro (ASV), and Korngold himself (Facet, NA). While Gerhardt takes top interpretive honors, Kojian is close and offers the most music.

In *The Sea Hawk* Kojian is again unlikely to be outdone (Varèse 47304). Gerhardt's two suites are brilliant (RCA 7890 and 0912, combined in 60863, NA). Stanley Black's are exaggerated (London and Bainbridge); Bateman is routine (Silva). For *King's Row,* Gerhardt led a full-length recording (Varèse 47203)—no one, other than the composer himself, had his feel for Korngold. I also endorse *Elizabeth and Essex* (Carl Davis, Varèse 5976), *Anthony Adverse* (John Scott, Varèse 5285), *Juarez* and *The Sea Wolf* (Sedares, Koch 7302), and Stromberg's recordings of *The Prince and the Pauper* (RCA 62660), *Another Dawn* (Marco Polo 223871), and *Devotion* (Marco Polo 22503).

Among compilations, Gerhardt's are compulsory. The LP release of *The Sea Hawk* launched the "Classic Film Scores" series and helped bring about a critical reappraisal of film music (now on RCA 7890). A second volume includes the *Deception* Cello Concerto, still the best on record (RCA 1085). More than a decade before Gerhardt, Lionel Newman recorded an album of excerpts; the orchestra is small and the sound dry (Stanyan or DCC). Two discs from Korngold's original sessions sound shrill and noisy, but the tangy performances are worth having (Rhino 77243).

Joel McNeely (b. 1959). *Iron Will* is a rousing, outdoorsy enterprise (Varèse 5467, NA); *Gold Diggers* (Varèse 5633) and *Samantha* (Intrada 7040) are entrancing.

Jerome Moross (1913–83). Nothing typifies his Americana style more than *The Big Country*—few will fail to recognize its broad, pentatonic theme. The soundtrack is authoritative, in strong mono sound (Screen Archives 1R), but Tony Bremner's impassioned stereo version is better listening (Silva 030). Also meritorious are *The War Lord* (Varèse 5536), *The Proud Rebel* (Screen Archives 2), and Bateman's collection with *The Valley of Gwangi* and the fetching *Adventures of Huck Finn* (Silva 1049).

Alfred Newman (1900–70). Though he was classically trained, Newman came to Hollywood from Broadway. The "Newman string sound" was legendary, and its heart-touching sonorities permeate *The Song of Bernadette.* Gerhardt includes a suite in his compilation (RCA 0184), but the full score is not to be missed (Varèse 6025). The *Captain from Castile* march is one of those pieces everyone knows but can't name. The soundtrack is mono, but crisply performed (Facet 8103).

The harmonic progressions in the opening bars of *The Robe* may be Newman's most inspiring creation. The original tracks in stereo sound great (Fox 11011), displacing the old mono recording (Varèse). Gerhardt's suite is a little stiff but still captivating. *The Greatest Story Ever Told* is music of transcendent beauty; a 3CD set for the first time presents the score before it was tampered with (Rykodisc 10734). *The Egyptian,* a once-in-a-lifetime collaboration with Herrmann, is unique and legendary; Stromberg's brilliant reading (Marco Polo 225078) sweeps aside the mono Varèse.

The orchestral portions of *How the West Was Won* are rich in Americana without resorting to Western cliches; an Indian attack is accompanied not by tomtoms but instead a sharp scherzo (Rhino 77458, 2CD). The earlier Sony (NA) omits much. Kunzel's short suite is poky (Telarc); Raine's is 22 minutes, but soggy (Silva). Other memorable works include *How Green Was My Valley* (Fox 11008), *All About Eve* and *Leave Her to Heaven* (Golden Age FSM 2/7), and *Prince of Foxes* (Golden Age 2/5). Richard Kaufman's collection highlights *Wuthering Heights* and *Prisoner of Zenda* (Koch 7376). Even better is Stromberg's with *Hunchback of Notre Dame* and *Beau Geste* (Marco Polo 223750).

Alex North (1910–91) studied piano at the Curtis Institute, then struggled as a telegraph operator while attending Juilliard. Elia Kazan brought him to Hollywood where North composed *A Streetcar Named Desire.* This amazing synthesis of jazz, classical, and haunting melody is well captured by Goldsmith (Varèse 5500). The soundtrack is no less essential (Capitol 95597); Eric Stern's abbreviated Nonesuch suite is maladroit. *The Sound and the Fury* is another of North's exceptional jazz-influenced scores (Varèse 5297).

Spartacus is dramatic, full of counterpoint (a North trademark), with one of the most compassionate love themes ever (MCA 10256). The sound is clear but shrill, with distorted highs in spots. The Nonesuch suite has balance problems (excerpts from *The Bad Seed* fare no better). *The Agony and the Ecstasy* is bitterly majestic (Cloud Nine 5001); Goldsmith's longer rendition (Varèse 5901) is less pointed but has resonant sound—the same applies to his remake of *Viva Zapata!* (Varèse 5900). In *Dragonslayer,* chromaticism, discontinuous rhythms, and dissonant harmonies are punctuated with ravishing, bittersweet melodies—North at his unorthodox best (Southern Cross 3, NA). Goldsmith's recordings of *Who's Afraid of Virginia Woolf?* (Varèse 5800) and the rejected score to *2001* (Varèse 5400) are also interesting.

Basil Poledouris (b. 1945) has done his share of explosive action films: *Conan the Barbarian* (Varèse 5390) and *Starship Troopers* (Varèse 5877) are representative. More varied are *The Hunt for Red October* (MCA 6428), *Jungle Book* (Milan 35711), and *Lonesome Dove* (Sonic Images 8816).

Rachel Portman (b. 1960). Hers is the charming ambience of *Emma* (Miramax 62069) and *War of the Buttons* (Varèse 5554, NA). *Only You* is gorgeous, but extraneous songs clutter this release (Columbia 66182).

André Previn's (b. 1929) best work is not yet on CD, but *Elmer Gantry* (Rykodisc 10732) captures a fervently American idiom, and *Irma La Douce* (Rykodisc 10729) is likeable gaiety.

David Raksin (b. 1912). *Laura* is regarded as a classic for its famous theme. The soundtrack (Fox) doesn't sound as good as his suite (RCA 1490); the latter is coupled with *Forever Amber,* whose original tracks are captivating (Varèse 5857).

Leonard Rosenman (b. 1924). A student of Sessions and Schoenberg, Rosenman (and North) moved motion picture music into the 20th century. His score for *East of Eden* is a brooding, complex slice of Americana. John Adams conducts an excellent reading, with the more desolate *Rebel Without a Cause* (Nonesuch 79402). *Fantastic Voyage* (Silver Age FSM 1/3) and *Lord of the Rings* (Intrada 8003) are typical of his modernist sci-fi scores.

Laurence Rosenthal (b. 1926). *Clash of the Titans* (Pendulum 014) evokes Richard Strauss, and *Meteor* (Windemere 42348) shines with bright colors and melodies. *The Island of Dr. Moreau* (Windemere 42347) and *Becket* (Windemere 42349) are also interesting.

Nino Rota's (1911–79) gaudy scores for Fellini are best known, but there is more merit in *Romeo and Juliet* (Silva 200; avoid the dialogue-laden Capitol). *The Taming of the Shrew* can be had in DRG 32928; *The Abdication* (Legend 14) and *The Leopard* (Cam 010) are available as imports (Muti's suite from the latter is on Sony). *War and Peace* (Varèse 5225) is in need of a stereo remake; truncated suites (like Gelmetti on EMI) are insufficient.

Miklós Rózsa (1907–95). An established composer of serious music, Rózsa brought the same integrity to his film work, leading one studio bigwig to scold him for supplying "Carnegie Hall music." With *The Jungle Book* and *Thief of Bagdad* Rózsa became known as a specialist in romantic exotica. A suite (with narrator) from the former became the first commercially recorded film score—the 78 rpm audio is primitive (Flapper). Klauspeter Seibel has modern sound, but no narrator (Varèse 47258, NA). Rózsa's suite from *Thief* is colorful (Varèse 48258, NA, or Colosseum 8044); Bateman does well by four movements (Silva 1081), but a comprehensive recording is needed.

Using a theremin in *Spellbound* made the composer the leading musical spokesman for neurosis. Two archival recordings appear on Flapper in dreadful sound. Ray Heindorf's is lightweight (Stanyan). In his compilation, Gerhardt gives us one chilling sequence (RCA 0911). But *Spellbound* is best known for the piano concerto arranged from the film's themes— Pennario and Rózsa are unrivaled (EMI 63735); Santiago Rodriguez (Elan) has more modern sound but is disqualified—there's no theremin! Earl Wild rewrites it extensively—his tighter edition makes sense (Ivory 70801). Elmer Bernstein recorded an expanded two-piano version with the *New England Concerto,* but the readings lack finesse (Varèse, NA).

Quo Vadis was one of Rózsa's proudest moments. A concert suite is in strong mono but minus one movement (Angel 59932). His Phase-4 of the original score is a collector's item (London 820200, NA). Alwyn's haphazard suite has brilliant sound (Silva). *Julius Caesar* is dark and powerful—Bruce Broughton's conducting is matchless (Intrada 7056). There are eloquent recordings of the overture (Gerhardt, RCA 2792) and a suite (Herrmann, London 455156). *Ben-Hur* is a complex work of beauty and turmoil. Older releases (Sony, NA) are not faithful to the score and sound fuzzy; Rózsa's Phase-4 has wonderful sound (London 820190). However, the virtuoso playing and vibrant sound of the original tracks are unmatched (Rhino 72197, 2CD).

The finale to *El Cid,* with organ, chorus, and orchestra, is striking. Sedares (Koch 7340) adds much not heard in the soundtrack rerecording (Sony 47704, NA), but the conducting is a little slack, and the organ wheezes electronically. *King of Kings* is carelessly edited (Sony 52424, NA). Alwyn (Silva) and Rózsa (Angel 59932) offer a few selections. The stereo *Sodom and Gomorrah* reappeared on CD in mono (Cambria, NA). Broughton gives a sensational reading of *Ivanhoe* (Intrada 7055); *The Power* (Prometheus 122) is a complex sci-fi score spotlighting the cimbalom, while the ghostly, nostalgic *Providence* (Cam 085) is unforgettable. *Lust for Life* and *Background to Violence* (Varèse 5405, NA) and *The Private Files of J. Edgar Hoover* (Citadel 117118) are worth looking for.

Rhino's double-disc set of MGM scores (75723) is essential; Alwyn's collection is variable, but the sound is sumptuous (Silva). Critics liked Sedares's program, but his *Double Indemnity* and *Lost Weekend* lack the grit of the originals (Koch 7375). Gerhardt is more telling, and includes a scary suite from *The Red House* (RCA 0911). An elaborate fantasy from *Young Bess* (the full score is on Prometheus 133) is a highlight of brass-and-organ arrangements (Citadel 77111). Rózsa recorded bits and pieces for Capitol over the years; many of these are in Angel 59932.

Richard Müller-Lampertz's Varèse compendium is so unidiomatic that the *El Cid* love theme emerges in a crisp staccato! It's a must-miss.

Hans J. Salter (1896–1995) and **Frank Skinner** (1898–1968) defined the sound of the Universal horror and mystery films. Salter's masterpiece is *Ghost of Frankenstein;* Andrew Penny's devitalized distortion is painful (Marco Polo), but the chills come through in fine form in Stromberg's new recording (Marco Polo 225124). *House of Frankenstein* is another triumph (Marco Polo 223748), and *The Wolf Man* (Marco Polo 223747), written with Skinner, is even better. It's coupled with the latter's best work, *Son of Frankenstein,* solidly directed by Stromberg. A suite from Salter's horror tracks is in Citadel 77115.

Max Steiner (1888–1971) wrote simple, emotional melodies, but he had another side, as evidenced by *King Kong.* Oscar Levant said the film "should be advertised as a concert of Steiner's music with accompanying pictures." Fred Steiner's rendition (Laserlight 21354) has its moments, but Stromberg offers the entire score and recreates its power and mystery as never before (Marco Polo 223763). *Son of Kong* is worth having, but its discmate, the severe *Most Dangerous Game,* steals the show in Stromberg's sensational reading (Marco Polo). The mystical *She* is another of the composer's best (Marco Polo 104).

More typical of Steiner is *Gone with the Wind,* one of his most-loved works. Nearly every note is in Rhino 72269, 2CD, in 1939 sound. Fred Steiner (RCA mono), Walter Stott (Pickwick), and Muir Mathieson (Stanyan or Laserlight) recorded orchestral suites, but Gerhardt's expanded version is tops in all departments (RCA 0452). *The Flame and the Arrow* is exciting (BYU 102 mono); Alwyn leads a good suite in modern sound (Scannan 1502). An inadequate Slovak orchestra stumbles through *Charge of the Light Brigade* and *Sierra Madre* (Centaur), but Stromberg's *Sierra Madre* (Marco Polo) and *They Died with Their Boots On* are stimulating (Marco Polo 225079).

A short suite from the magnificent *Informer* is in coarse mono (Capitol), but Gerhardt offers a sample, along with *The Fountainhead* (RCA 0136). Alwyn incorporates a selection from *Helen of Troy* (Silva); Stromberg provides a macabre suite from *The Beast with Five Fingers* (Marco Polo).

Dimitri Tiomkin (1894–1979) studied with Glazunov and had visions of a career as a pianist until he was sidetracked into cinema. His music is restless and sometimes overorchestrated, but he could write a simple, lovely tune, as in *The Alamo.* The soundtrack has some great moments (Varèse 5228, NA); the CBS reissue is cluttered with dialogue. Lawrence Foster's lengthy selection is pointlessly reorchestrated (RCA 62658)—if there is one composer whose music doesn't need *more* added to it, it's Tiomkin! Foster includes the moving *55 Days at Peking,* but the soundtrack is more authentic (Varèse 5233, NA).

The enormous forces used for *Fall of the Roman Empire* render it a wealth of self-indulgent sonorities (Pendulum 029); the additional music on Cloud Nine (NA) is mostly mono. *The Old Man and the Sea* is picturesque (Pendulum 028); some consider *It's a Wonderful Life* Tiomkin's best (Telarc 88801). Gerhardt's collection includes the exotic *Lost Horizon* (RCA 1669); the complete original tracks are in BYU 103. David Willcocks conducts *Rhapsody of Steel* (a 22-minute tone poem composed for U.S. Steel), with a suite from *Guns of Navarone*—the student orchestra has its hands full (Unicorn 9047). Laurie Johnson leads a selection from the cowboy films (Unicorn).

Franz Waxman (1906–67) wrote both classical and film music in Germany and added a conducting career when he came to America. Many consider *The Bride of Frankenstein,* with its shifting harmonies and odd dissonances, Waxman's best work, but Alwyn's survey needed a more proficient ensemble (Silva 135). Adriano renders *Rebecca* lugubrious (Marco Polo); John Scott (Delos) and Paul Bateman (Silva) conduct abridged versions of Waxman's suite. *Peyton Place* is, by turns, inventive, wistful, ironic, and ravishing; the import from Spain has been worth the wait (RCA 73612), and Frederic Talgorn's gorgeous remake is no less intoxicating (Varèse 066 070).

The Spirit of St. Louis depicts the beauty, the peril, and the majesty of flight. The mono soundtrack is definitive (Varèse 5212); a concert version is well conducted by Lawrence Foster, and adds narration from Lindbergh's autobiography (Capriccio 10711). *Taras Bulba* is a vivid, rousing romp—Rykodisc 10736 is essential. Richard Hayman's suite is torpid (Naxos). Elmer Bernstein's longer selections are poorly played (RCA); Bateman cuts these to 12 minutes, but is otherwise superior (Silva 1081). Bernstein couples the botched *Taras* with three more successful suites, including the lyrical *Adventures of a Young Man* (RCA 62657). Stromberg's recreation of *Objective Burma!* is a knockout; *Mr. Skeffington* (Marco Polo 225037) and *The Nun's Story* (Stanyan 114, NA) are also worthwhile.

Among compilations, Gerhardt (RCA 0708) includes suites from *Sunset Boulevard* and the joyous *Prince Valiant* (the soundtrack in Golden Age FSM 2/3 is a delight). Hayman isn't as invigorating (Naxos 990034) but has the *Medal of Honor Suite* (culled from war movies). Four discs conducted by Richard Mills (Varèse 5242, 5257, 5480, 5713) contain much of value, particularly *Demetrius and the Gladiators* (5242).

John Williams (b. 1932). For many, Williams is *Star Wars* and its sequels, works evocative of Korngold swashbucklers. The soundtracks have seen a variety of issues, but the current double-disc sets (RCA 68746, 68747, 68743) are the standard. Each is unabridged, properly sequenced, with refurbished sound. *The Phantom Menace* continues the series's tradition (Sony 61816).

Gerhardt does a spectacular job with the *Star Wars* concert suite (RCA 2698); Mehta's is stiff (London), and Kunzel's luxurious (Telarc). Gerhardt's full discs of *The Empire Strikes Back* (Varèse 47204) and *Return of the Jedi* (RCA 60767) sometimes surpass the originals. Williams's own suites from *Empire* and *Jedi* are mundane (Philips). The composer recorded highlights from all three films, but they sound listless (Sony); Kojian's "trilogy" is much more fervid (Varèse 47201).

Long before *Star Wars,* Williams wrote a stirring backdrop for *The Cowboys.* The Overture is an expert synopsis (Philips 420178); the complete score is in Varèse 5540. *Dracula,* with its whooping French horns, is far more satisfying than the film (Varèse 5250); *The Fury* was ridiculous, but the elegiac strings are indelible (Varèse 5264). *E.T.* offers sequences of heavenly beauty and soaring melodies. Rerecordings of the LPs are in MCA 37264 (NA); an expanded version presents the superior performances heard in the film (MCA 11494). Kunzel's excerpts are exhilarating (Telarc 80094).

In *Close Encounters of the Third Kind,* atonality alternates with inspiring spirituality. The suite covers most of the ground nicely: Williams (Philips) and Mehta (London) recorded it, but Gerhardt's is the finest (RCA 2698). Arista 19004 offers the complete soundtrack. Some of the beautiful nostalgia is cut from *Superman* in Warner 3257 (NA); the Japanese import is longer (Warner 3859), but the Rhino 2CD set is full-length perfection (75874). John Debney has the best sound, though the London Symphony sounds a little uncertain (Varèse 5981, 2CD).

Beautiful Irish melodies and an exciting land race appear in the superb *Far and Away* (MCA 10628). *Jaws,* with its Stravinskian shark and bracing sea music, is celebrated (MCA 1660; Decca 467045 is an expanded version using the actual film tracks), but *Jaws 2* is even better (Varèse 5328, NA). The "Indiana Jones" scores are rousing and expertly crafted (DCC 090, Polydor 821592, Warner 25883). Also recommended: *Home Alone* (CBS 48595), *Empire of the Sun* (Warner 25668), *Midway* (Dick Wentworth, Varèse 5940), *Jurassic Park* (MCA 10859), and *Amazing Stories* (Varèse 5941).

The Reivers is rife with rural warmth and wit (CBS 66130). A concert suite, narrated by Burgess Meredith, highlights an anthology; the accompanying *Born on the Fourth of July* is powerful (Sony 64147). A collection includes fanfares, marches, and NBC News themes (Philips 420178); Kunzel's is one of his best performances (Telarc 80094). A Hayman assemblage is limp (Naxos); the Orlando Pops lacks Hayman's intensity (Excelsior).

Victor Young (1900–58) was a traditionalist in the mold of Max Steiner. *The Quiet Man* suite is light as a flea's wing, but pleasant (Varèse mono). Alwyn's complete recording is amiable, but the orchestra isn't the best (Scannan). A miscellany typifies this composer's simple gifts (Koch 7365); Stromberg offers some of his best scores in *The Uninvited* and *Gulliver's Travels* (Marco Polo 225063).

This survey would not be complete without mention of such singular achievements as the inventive *Time Machine* by **Russell Garcia** (GNP Crescendo 8008); *Watership Down,* a bewitching delicacy from **Angela Morley** (Pendulum 022); **David Newman**'s stirring *The Phantom* (Milan 35756); the enduring *Victory at Sea* by **Richard Rodgers** (RCA 60963, 60964); **John Lanchbery**'s clever orchestrations of Cole Porter for *Evil Under the Sun* (DRG 12615); and the beguiling *Return to Oz* by **David Shire** (Bay Cities 3001, NA).

COLLECTIONS

Gerhardt's program devoted to Errol Flynn offers Steiner's colorful suite from *Adventures of Don Juan* (RCA 0912). (Bateman's shorter version in Silva 1081 omits many percussion parts.) Tiomkin's ingenious *The Thing* is part of RCA 2792. Varèse 5207 offers a refulgent overture to Korngold's *Constant Nymph,* with Gerhardt's own edition of Walton's *Henry V* suite (the best around).

A set from *The Twilight Zone* showcases Herrmann, Goldsmith, Waxman, and Rosenman (Silva 2000, 4CD). "Warriors of the Silver Screen" has the first stereo recording from **Mario Nascimbene**'s *The Vikings* (Silva 1081). "Disasters" (Silva 1092) includes Williams's *Towering Inferno* and Shire's *Hindenburg,* but a much longer selection from *Inferno* can be had in Varèse 5807. Silva's albums of Hitchcock scores (1030, 1045) and sci-fi music (1083) cover many seldom-met works.

John Mauceri's Philips discs include Tiomkin's mind-boggling treatment of Johann Strauss (438635) and the only uncut recording of Newman's *Street Scene* (432109). The best of Kunzel's Telarc spectaculars are "Star Tracks II" (80146) and the well-programmed "Fantastic Journey" (80231).

Hayman's Naxos series has its moments but usually sounds tired. Several Varèse anthologies are well played but favor overfamiliar snippets. Two Marco Polo collections from Richard Kaufman sound indifferent. Stanley Black's are mostly overstated and pointlessly embellished (London and Bainbridge).

CBS 66691 is an extraordinary Hollywood Bowl concert, with Rózsa, Newman, Raksin, Herrmann, Tiomkin, and North conducting their own music. Fred Steiner conducts Herrmann (*The Kentuckian*), Newman (*Down to the Sea in Ships*), and Waxman (*Sunrise at Campobello*) in an important issue (Preamble 1777, NA). And Stromberg makes some second-level film noir suites sound better than they are (RCA 68145).

Piano concertos are a popular undertaking. A collection from Santiago Rodriguez is mostly rewarding (Elan 82268); Naxos 554323 mixes in esoterica like **Jack Beaver**'s *Portrait of Isla.* Koch 7225 contains David Buechner's reading of Waxman's *Paradine Case;* Pennario's Hollywood Bowl compendium is first rate (EMI 63735). And Earl Wild plays a dazzling program (Ivory 70801).   KOLDYS

Gilbert and Sullivan

The operettas of Gilbert and Sullivan (hereafter referred to as "G&S"), all of which are now well over a century old, have provided a source of "innocent merriment" to countless English-speaking audiences. But things have changed greatly in the last two decades, not only in performance styles and statistics, but also in the recording domain, with the demise of the original D'Oyly Carte Opera Company (hereafter referred to as "DCO") in the early '80s. The absence of "standard," copyright-protected DCO performances has opened the floodgates to a host of new productions and recordings that have reexamined the G&S *oeuvre.*

This is all well and good and, for artistic experimentation, certainly as it should be, because it forces us to reevaluate these classical works much as we do Shakespeare. But the artistic backbone that was the old DCO has ceased to exist, and it's as if suddenly Britain were without its Royal Shakespeare Company in London and Stratford-on-Avon. Unthinkable? Well, the DCO—a private and lucrative producing concern in its heyday—was allowed to collapse not merely because of devastating reports from the British Arts Council of the company's slipshod standards (mainly, and ironically, due to a lack of prior government funding), but also because of the general perception in the UK that the G&S operettas were too lowly or too bourgeois to be treated as national treasures.

Of course, the general international decline in operetta production in the last quarter-century and the celebration of rock-and-roll are partly to blame for the decreased interest in G&S. These Victorian relics have less and less appeal to young people who consider the Beatles or the Rolling Stones the last word in nostalgia. Contrarily, current scholars and musicologists have brought G&S into a renaissance of reappreciation, and much of their work has gone into recent recordings. But in my youth, schools, community groups, and camps all did G&S, spreading interest at impressionable ages. This is not the case now, and G&S, although today treated with the respect and artistic admiration it deserves, has become a much more marginal, specialist form of musical theater, something like Baroque opera (although that seems far more popular internationally than G&S today).

Luckily, in the CD era we have access not only to the latest digital reexaminations of the Savoy canon but also to reissues of older recordings, from an era when the DCO set the gold standard. Many of us who remember the company in its heyday (and slightly thereafter), or at least grew up treasuring their records from the '20s and '30s, will be inclined to prefer the old performance styles, which indeed date back to Gilbert and Sullivan themselves as filtered through successive DCO performers or directors. We also tend to champion certain star performers, such as Martyn Green or Henry Lytton.

It's hardly fair to compare legendary stars to those available today, but I can state with confidence that in many cases those I actually saw in the past had far more charisma and vocal distinction than the current

crop of G&S singers. Martyn Green, as just one example, was a much more exciting performer than Richard Suart, who for some unfathomable reason is the actor called upon most frequently today to perform the patter-comedian parts. Still, if you listen to recordings from the DCO's golden era objectively, you can imagine the problems younger listeners encounter: the boxy 78 rpm sound, the plummy singing style that no longer exists in operatic singing and has gone out of fashion in operetta singing as well, the fruity West End diction that has also become passé, the ridiculous tempos that were often a result of the duration of a 78 rpm side, the often lackluster orchestras and choruses. Furthermore, many of the nonstar DCO performers weren't really very good, or at least come off rather badly in their recordings.

Little of this will matter to the nonobjective, older listener (like me) who tends to revel in the past, either by experience or association. Having spent night after night at age 13 listening illicitly after bedtime (with huge headphones) to a reel-to-reel tape of the 1927 *Gondoliers* is one of my cherished memories, and one reason no other recording of this work will ever please me as much.

The fact that I listened to this recording two generations after it was made proves that even in the late 50s many people found earlier versions more exciting, for whatever reasons. Similarly, digital-era listeners may still relish certain older recordings for their considerable style, personality, and presence, qualities some find lacking in today's state of the art (and state of the scholarship) G&S CDs.

In the early '60s, at the time the first stereo recordings appeared, I remember the endless discussion about the "tradition" of performing G&S in the correct or "received" DCO style. The reason it was an important issue at that time is because the Gilbert copyright was to expire at the end of 1962, permitting other companies to perform and record G&S, and any kind of monkeying around with them could take place. In the UK, protection for Sullivan had already ceased in 1950, but the main result of that was the much-admired ballet *Pineapple Poll,* arranged by Charles Mackerras, an Australian champion of Sullivan's music of long standing.

The result of G&S's going into the public domain was initially good: The DCO weathered fine competition from then-admired productions from the Sadler's Wells Opera and various TV and record companies, like the BBC and HMV/Angel recordings. Many relished the thoughtful creativity of the Sadler's Wells shows (recorded for HMV) and the operatic grandeur of some of Malcolm Sargent's recordings. But this evidence that G&S could be effectively produced without the DCO tradition eventually rang the death knell for the company, which by the '60s was already suffering from a combination of problems: increased touring and union costs; lack of adequate funding, whether government or private; genteel, Victorian-age publicity that had nothing to do with modern methods; and an unwillingness to move to more adventurous and modern theatrical practices. The company was tired and demoralized by the '70s, and it sounded that way in its recordings. Although the 1975 Centenary was an exciting event, with every operetta performed in order at the Savoy Theatre, one had an eerie sense that this was a dying company. I remember playing hooky one night during that wonderful fortnight and being far more excited by the English National Opera's *Patience,* then playing at the London Coliseum.

But G&S now seems to be in the ascendant in terms of recordings. Not only has the new DCO recently been recording the works all over again (on the Ter/Jay label), but other companies have joined the fray. Stage-based and studio releases on Philips and Teldec were released in the mid-'90s, with participation from such companies as the New

Sadler's Wells and English and Welsh National Operas and with such renowned conductors as Mackerras, returning to one of his loves. Furthermore, new, conscientious scholarship has cleaned up incorrect orchestra parts for some of these recordings and expanded the standard operetta scores to include numbers that were cut or changed. And there have even been exciting new projects like the Papp *Pirates of Penzance,* the film *Topsy-Turvy,* and such bizarre items as recordings of *Pirates* and *Mikado* in Catalan!

In going through the operettas in chronological order, it's useful to point out the older recordings that have reappeared on several labels in the UK and US, some of which may no longer be available. The majority of DCO recordings made from the late '40s until the '70s are under license to Decca/London, which presumably will release the series of the 40s and 50s starring Green as these copyrights expire. Pearl, which has many valuable older G&S recordings in its catalogue, will also be issuing some of these in 2001. Ter/Jay now does the new DCOs. HMV/EMI/Angel still reissues Sargent's Glyndebourne series, but its pre-1936 exclusive DCO recordings (from the golden age) are now cropping up — also thanks to lapsed copyrights — on various labels, from Romophone to Symposium. It's best to check the G&S sections of the larger stores.

Trial by Jury (1875) is the perfect G&S work to record *in toto* because of its operatic form; there is no possibility of rancorous arguments whether or not to include Gilbert's dialogue, because there isn't any. That said, the "dramatic cantata" (as it was originally billed) has prospered well over the years in recordings, with excellent DCO and non-DCO renditions to choose from. Of course, by its very operatic nature and the operatic parody that abounds, it's a work that can stand Sargent's often heavy-handed treatment quite well; the surprising thing is that his 1961 version for HMV has the most theatrical atmosphere of any of the *Trials.* The sense of being at a real performance is very present, with lots of stage reactions and tittering, all done in lively fashion. The cast is excellent.

But the best cast of all is in the DCO's first *Trial,* recorded in 1927, with the peerless, sparkling Leo Sheffield as the Judge and the powerhouse romantics Derek Oldham and Winifred Lawson as the legal sparrers (Pearl 9961). It doesn't get much better than this. The 1964 DCO production on Decca/London had the advantage of good stereo, a far better cast than in the dull, now-forgotten 1949 mono version, and (in its LP release) excerpts from the then-unheard *Utopia Limited,* making it then a collector's must. If John Reed's Judge has a tad too much of the raspychortly, it's balanced by Kenneth Sandford's austere portrayal of the Counsel (a role he didn't do on stage). In all, there's an excellent choice that will be dictated to some extent by the couplings. If it's ebullience and gusto you go for — and you should — I'd choose between the 1927 on Pearl because it's with the greatest of all G&S recordings, the same year's *Gondoliers,* or the bubbly 1961 Sargent.

The Sorcerer was the second full-length G&S work. (*Thespis,* whose music has disappeared, was produced in 1871.) It's a pastoral, English country-house affair that finds G&S still tweaking formats and recipes that they'll get right by *H.M.S. Pinafore,* their next work. As such, it continues to fascinate, but it doesn't have the amazingly lively brilliance we find in *Pinafore* or its successors, which is why it rarely gets produced or recorded.

The '50s DCO mono version I grew up with was easily superseded by a good 1966 stereo rendition, with a sharp John Wellington Wells from Reed (a role he did very, very well in a DCO revival a few years later, with a cockney accent, amid memorable scenery by Osbert Lancaster). The

1966 also beats the only other recorded *Sorcerer,* the 1933 abridged version with Darrell Fancourt's smooth Sir Marmaduke and Leslie Rands's very dry country parson. Stick with the 1966 on Decca/London.

H.M.S. Pinafore (1878) has no shortage of versions available; in the 78 rpm era, there was even one in Yiddish, now reissued on CD. What makes the work so popular is the sea spray of its setting and the salty tang of its shipboard denizens, contrasted with the mature visitor from London and his "admiring" female relatives. Gilbert's book continues to work like a charm; there's no fat in it, and the operetta still startles much as it must have done originally. The jokes remain amusing, and many lines are instantly memorable, especially to those who may not have heard them before. The social satire still works in its trim way, rather like having a long Shaw comedy slimmed down. Sullivan must have been so braced by the libretto that he produced one of his happiest efforts. The operatic and patriotic burlesques shine, but he goes beyond them with a number like the Italianate scena in Act II, "The Hours Creep On Apace," that nowadays still stops the show, not only because of its intensity but because of Gilbert's fascinating portraits of the contrasts of rich and poor society.

The DCO put its official stamp on no less than five *Pinafores;* the best was the penultimate, done in 1961 for Decca/London just before the copyrights expired. It was the first to be recorded with its dialogue — possibly a gimmick at the time to increase interest and sales in yet another *Pinafore,* but one that paid off for an operetta with such a tight libretto. Fortunately, the cast was very good: Reed was a fine, reedy Sir Joseph Porter, Jeffrey Skitch a martini-dry martinet of a Cap'n Corcoran, and Donald Adams a definitively dastardly Dick Deadeye, while Thomas Round was an ardent Ralph and Gillian Knight an appealing Little Buttercup. Isidore Godfrey was a frolicsome G&S conductor, and the whole performance bears the shipshape succulence of a company on its toes. That is hardly the case in the final DCO version of 1971, where everything is beclouded by the extraneous sounds of seagulls and lapping waves in an effort to justify the "realism" of the Phase-4 process.

The historically minded will be attracted to the DCOers of 1930, among them the great Lytton as Sir Joseph, Bertha Lewis as Buttercup, Fancourt as Deadeye, and Charles Goulding as Ralph. Lytton and Fancourt are the star attractions, but this *Pinafore* is by no means as engaging as some of the other records from this era. Certainly, Sargent's conducting in 1930 was more spirited than in his 1958 version for HMV, and the later rendition tends to go overboard (as it were) in its pompously operatic singing. Shall we give Sargent and his singers the benefit of the doubt — that they were doing this entire *Pinafore* as an operatic parody? I wonder . . .

The two most modern recordings are also shot through with opera singers, but are more successful in creating an operetta atmosphere. Mackerras and his Welsh forces manage to put the whole shebang on one disc (bravo!) and still offer excellent orchestral and choral work (Telarc). The soloists — especially Adams and Thomas Allen — are of interest too. The New Sadler's Wells rendition contains cleaned-up orchestra parts and scholarly variants (Ter/Jay). But both lack the naval discipline of a DCO ensemble at its crispest; for that, you need only go to the 1960 London/Decca.

The Pirates of Penzance. Some have called *Pirates* a dry-land *Pinafore,* but this is misleading and unfair to the special merits of an operetta that in this era has surpassed its predecessor in popularity. For one thing, the operatic buffoonery is stronger in *Pirates,* and the vocal demands generally weightier, especially for the romantic leads, Frederic and Mabel.

Sullivan offers seething Verdian drama in the ludicrous confrontation between Frederic and his nurse, Ruth, early in the first act, when he accuses her of lying about her attractiveness. There is the spectacular ensemble in Act II where Mabel and her sisters send a reluctant police force off to grisly glory, and there are other hilariously inappropriate moments, like the choral ode to poetry at the end of Act I, which define the topsy-turvy nature of Gilbert and Sullivan's combined wit. To these morsels, add such superb moments as the thrilling "Paradox" trio, the Major General's famous entrance song, and the faux music-hall couplets of the Police Sergeant, and you have one wonderful work — plus a tight, very amusing book to boot. (Offenbach and Meilhac & Halévy would have loved it, once they got past the borrowing from their own *Brigands*, which Gilbert had previously translated for the London stage.)

There are potential longueurs, however, like the churchy, very English duet "Ah, Leave Me Not to Pine," the Major General's silly second-act ditty, or Ruth's three-verse expository number in which a misheard word accounts for their being pirates in the first place, but they can be judiciously performed. Savoyards will still dote on these — they have a tendency to be utterly forgiving when it comes to anything by G&S — but others may be wearied. In *Pinafore*, after all, nothing is allowed to linger long enough to bore the listener. Yet the whimsy of *Pirates* is so successful and its score so wondrous that it weathers any squalls and can even survive (or, according to some, be enlivened by) the synthesized jolt the music received in the famous Joseph Papp Central Park version of 1980. William Elliot's tinkly "modernization" will probably date faster than Sullivan's original scoring, so listeners are advised to steer to the latter.

I remember the DCO doing a magisterially right *Pirates* in the early '60s, with a definitive performance from Adams as the Pirate King underscoring the elegant seriousness and "sense of duty" that must come through for the work to succeed in its mockery. Some of this appears in the first stereo DCO recording, the 1958 *Pirates* under Godfrey, which also has a dry Major General in Peter Pratt, a sonorous Policeman (Sandford) and a first-rate Frederic (Round) and Mabel (Jean Hindmarsh). It was certainly a better all-around recording than two earlier DCO ones, in 1929 and 1950. And yet there are delights in these as well, among them Oldham's Frederic and Australian baritone Peter Dawson's Pirate King in 1929 and Green's cocktail-dry Major-General in 1950. (The truly antique 1920 DCO, on Sounds on Disc, gives us an even younger Oldham and Dawson, but the ladies don't come off quite as gracefully in acoustic reproduction.)

The 1968 DCO had a dialogue advantage with Godfrey and Adams again, Reed a merry Major-General, Philip Potter a really jejune Frederic, and Valerie Masterson a lovely, limpid Mabel. In fact, as a reference to the departed DCO style, in excellent sound, this is an ideal recording. It meets its almost-match in the 1961 EMI. The operatic weightiness that characterizes Sargent's EMI recordings would seem to be ideal for the main satirical thrust of *Pirates,* and his 1961 version perfectly realizes this. The sound from that era remains splendid, and the soloists, particularly the lovers Richard Lewis and Elsie Morison and the strong Ruth of Monica Sinclair, make this one of the very best of the Glyndebournes. **Mackerras's** reading from 1993, nearly complete on one disc, has a very late Adams reprising his Pirate King and a latter-day Gillian Knight as Ruth, with an uninteresting Richard Suart as the Major-General. Despite some nice singing elsewhere, the recording doesn't cohesively grip the melodramatics of the work (Telarc).

Patience (1881) and *Iolanthe* (1882), even more than *Pirates,* require an utter suspension of disbelief for them to work their full Gilbertian effect.

Both weave their spell, *Iolanthe* perhaps more memorably because of its fairy nature. But musically they're quite different: *Iolanthe* is Germanic-English romantic (echoes of Wagner-Mendelssohn) with 18th-century neoclassic embellishment, while *Patience's* score perfectly mirrors — for satirical purposes — the earnest, lugubrious church and parlor music so popular in mid-Victorian Britain. (Sullivan was a famous purveyor of this in his nonstage works.) Thus *Patience* can tax the listener's patience (pardon!), whereas *Iolanthe* is usually more rewarding on disc.

Having the dialogue included in the recording makes *Patience* more savory as satire; without it, many recordings have seemed flat. The 1962 DCO rendition is a classic, with all the fun and frolic you usually encountered in their stage performances at this time. Reed and Sandford are marvelous as the rival poseur esthetic poets, Adams is once again peerless in his bass-baritone range as the blustery Colonel of the Heavy Dragoons, Philip Potter is an effective silly-ass Duke, and Mary Sansom is a charming butterball of a dairymaid. Only Gillian Knight, as the formidable Lady Jane, is less than massive in her vocal effect, especially in the dialogue — she was then just too young. The whole thing coalesces with avidity on disc, something you can't really say about the earlier 1930 set with George Baker's Bunthorne or the 1952 one with Martyn Green's. However, each has certain likable elements. From the 1930 version we get Bertha Lewis's Jane, Oldham's Duke, Rands's fruity Grosvenor; in the 1952, Green himself, with his purred, creamy Bunthorne, and Ella Halman's heavy Jane.

The 1958 Sargent *Patience* would have benefited from dialogue, because musically it got a lot very right vocally (especially in the smaller parts and chorus). The mock gravitas achieved here (listen to Sinclair as Jane) isn't too amusing without the sprightly dialogue to balance it, and George Baker was really too old then for Bunthorne, a role he also sings more spiritedly in the 1930 recording. Unfortunately, I haven't heard the new DCO *Patience,* never released in the US.

Iolanthe also had a full-dialogue version in the early '60s for Decca/London, which I relished at the time. On hearing it again, I find it somewhat more labored in the dialogue sections than the contemporary *Patience,* but musically sound and sonically sparkling. Godfrey conducts — with happy results — a cast led by Reed's twinkly Lord Chancellor. Alan Styler (Strephon) is perhaps a trifle pallid at times, but I was very used to him at the time; Mary Sansom is pleasant (Phyllis), and those in the other parts and the chorus sing well. If this recording doesn't quite enter the realm of fairyland, it comes off better than the 1959 Sargent version (EMI), which is on the whole more operatically sung and lacks the fullness of a DCO conception because its dialogue is missing. Still, George Baker is an adorable Lord Chancellor, Elsie Morison and John Cameron are a sweet pair of lovers, and Sargent dwells positively on the Englishness of the music.

But Sargent's real *Iolanthe* accomplishment came in 1929–30, in a brilliant DCO realization (Arabesque). Bertha Lewis is the finest Fairy Queen of all, swooping down on her notes sublimely. Lawson (Phyllis) and Oldham (Tolloller) demonstrate once again how the '20s productions could be both plummy and playful, and Rands is the embodiment of English elegance as Strephon. George Baker isn't as effective a Chancellor as his older self was 30 years later. If the flat sound of the late '20s bothers you, seek solace in the 1991 new DCO version, which has far superior sonics but not nearly as distinctive a group of singers (Ter/Jay). The best of these are Jill Pert (the Queen) and John Rath (Private Willis). This version also omits the dialogue, which may bring you back finally to the 1960 DCO after all. When and if Decca/London releases its 1950

DCO, you can savor Green's highly susceptible and superbly succinct Chancellor.

Princess Ida (1884), appearing in between the ethereal *Iolanthe* and the majestic *Mikado,* is prime-cut G&S. If Gilbert made a mistake in offering his dialogue in blank verse and in three acts, Sullivan made few errors with his magical score, delineating the proto-medieval setting with more jolliness, spice and suavity than in *The Yeomen of the Guard* a few seasons later. G&S reach what some consider their zenith in Act II, with such moments as Princess Ida's entrance aria, the biting "hoity-toity" duet, the delightful entrance of the drag trio, the incredible contrasted ensembles "The World is But a Broken Toy" and "The Woman of the Wisest Wit," and the stirring finale coda. The Handelian burlesque in the third act is another triumph for the collaborators, recalling in its satire the freshness of *Trial by Jury.*

Ida is ideal for records, if more difficult to bring off on stage. Fortunately, the 1965 DCO version brought Sargent over from EMI, plus the Royal Philharmonic, and the results were sterling. Elizabeth Harwood is a commanding princess, Reed a terrifically raspy King Gama, Sandford a sonorous King Hildebrand, Philip Potter a charming Hilarion, Valerie Masterson a melodious Melissa, and Christene Palmer a rather good Lady Blanche. I thought the LP sound was truly spectacular, and I'm sure Sargent had something to do with that; his pacing is alternately grand and lively, as required. His 1932 version isn't as sumptuous, although it does offer Lytton in old age as a marvelously scabrous Gama, but not, sadly, paired with Bertha Lewis (Arabesque LPs). As the Decca/London 1965 recording also gives you the 45-minute Mackerras-Sullivan ballet *Pineapple Poll,* it's irresistible.

The only *Ida* competition is an Ohio Light Opera production, which gives the full dialogue—not a good idea for this particular operetta, and not spoken in the Queen's English throughout (how could it be, in Wooster, Ohio?). But Julie Wright is a winning Ida (Newport).

The Mikado remains, worldwide, the most popular G&S operetta. The reasons for this are physical as much as musical or lyrical. Gilbert made the happy decision to set his grotesque story in a mythical Japan conjured up from Victorian-esthetic decorations and tell it with a lot of opportunities for slapstick. These matter little when it comes to listening to a recording, and the listener has no sense of the visual splendor or silliness that will appear in any decent performance. The question of how well sung is this or that *Mikado* is almost peripheral to your enjoyment, and you should opt instead for as much "harmless merriment" as possible in a recording.

Bubbling joy and burlesque melodrama can be found abundantly in the historic 1926 version, the first to be recorded electrically by the DCO. The cast is the summit of golden-age greatness, headed by the marvelous team of Lytton and Lewis as the befuddled little ex-tailor and the overbearing daughter-in-law-elect. Sheffield adds an amusing twinkle to his aristocratic Pooh-Bah, and Oldham remains the most ardent of all DCO tenors, his Welsh diction only making his Japanese prince even more exotically regal. Fancourt set the standard with his fearsome Mikado, and at this time the company was chockablock with dazzling soubrettes. By the time you get through the first-act finale and its "For He's Going to Marry Yum-Yum," you'll realize this is truly a vintage performance.

You can't quite say that about any subsequent *Mikado* recording now available. The 1936 DCO comes closest, with Green's smoother, much younger Ko-Ko and a pretty good male contingent, but the females are a lesser lot, save for Marjorie Eyre's Pitti-Sing. In 1957, the Sargent-

Glyndebourne series (named after the pick-up orchestra and chorus) began on HMV/Angel/EMI as a rival to the DCOs available on Decca/London. This *Mikado* is among the most staid ever put on vinyl, with a very heavy Ko-Ko from the unsuitable Geraint Evans and only John Cameron's tasteful Nanki-Poo to salvage it. The same year saw a new DCO with another less-than-twinkling Ko-Ko in Pratt (though it's not a bad performance) buttressed by good stereo sound, Godfrey's lively pacing, an exemplary Mikado from Adams in his prime, and a youthful Nanki-Poo from Round. I also liked Ann Drummond-Grant's Katisha very much in those days—probably because she was my first stage Katisha.

Many like the Sadler's Wells version (EMI Classics for Pleasure) from the '60s, with comedian Clive Revill as Ko-Ko, but it's not a performance I've found as gratifying as the more spirited *Iolanthe* excerpts from the same era. The new overture by arranger Hamilton Clarke is unnecessary, even granting the patchwork quality of the original. However, the appeal of getting both the complete *Mikado* and the *Iolanthe* bits in one cheap CD reissue is considerable, even if you don't get the spectacular color photo that graced the original LP cover.

The 1973 DCO version has a mediocre cast that all too well demonstrates the company's decline. Reed on stage was a winningly wistful Ko-Ko, but his chortles and gasps can become wearying on disc. John Ayldon's Mikado seems like a watercolor copy of the Fancourt-Adams rendition, and Lyndsie Holland's Katisha is ghastly, but Masterson is a sweet Yum-Yum.

In 1986, the English National Opera staged and recorded a notorious and very popular *Mikado* set in a '20s English hotel, directed by Jonathan Miller. To this critic, such de-Japanning was fatal; my ears couldn't really concentrate when my eyes were so cruelly robbed of the spectacle I expected. On disc, this is a less urgent problem, and there is some fun to be had from Bonaventura Bottone's limpid Nanki-Poo, Eric Idle's nasal upstart of a Ko-Ko (with new verses for the "Little List" song), and—especially—Felicity Palmer's plummy, showy Katisha (Ter/Jay).

More recent *Mikado*s are best recommended for their conductors rather than their casts. Mackerras's well-judged and nearly complete version, using forces from the Welsh National Opera, is like the English National version conveniently on one CD and has the dearly missed Adams's last portrayal of the title role (Philips). It also has the uninteresting Suart as Ko-Ko; is this inheritor of the mantle once worn so memorably by Grossmith, Workman, Lytton, Green, and even Reed the best Britain can offer at this *fin de siècle*?

The 1990 new DCO version has a scholarly score cleansed by David Russell Hulme and conducted competently by John Pryce-Jones, but it has nothing particularly distinctive about it (Ter/Jay).

Granting that *The Mikado* is something to see as much as to hear, I recommend the DVD of the lovely 1939 film with Green, Granville, and a winning Kenny Baker. Of course, vast chunks of the score are gone, and they're sorely missed. If you want a glance at the DCO at its confident finest, you merely have to dip back into the '20s for the great *Mikado* with Lytton and Lewis to get some indication of what G&S at its perkiest must have been like.

Ruddigore, like *Princess Ida,* has considerable lodes of pure gold and certain longueurs. While many like the ghostly second act, I think the first, with its mixture of salt, silliness, and mock melodrama, is among the finest things the partners ever did. Although it has never been as popular as the works surrounding it, to me *Ruddigore* represents G&S at the peak of their joint perfection, nearly every bit as winning as *Gondo-*

liers and with equally gorgeous moments. Mad Margaret's entrance in Act I and her poignant garden aria move me more than almost all of *Yeomen*, and I've always had a soft spot for the often-cut duet between Richard and Robin in the same act, "The Battle's Roar is Over," which has a whiff of the story's Napoleonic setting.

Unlike the *Mikados*, most of the recorded *Ruddigores* are shipshape, tight little crafts. The New Sadler's Wells '90s version has the most music, including a great deal that was (wisely) excised by Sullivan after the first night in 1887; trust the composer to know better than scholar David Russell Hulme. Geoffrey Toye also made some changes and cuts for the 1921 DCO revival (its first), and in some cases these were wise—his revised overture is excellent (Ter/MCA). This *ur*-version is admirably done, with a winning pairing of Marilyn Hill Smith (Rose) and the robust baritone of Gordon Sandison (Robin). Linda Ormiston is a characterful Margaret and Harold Innocent surely the strangest of Despards on disc. If Simon Phipps's conducting can't be described as intensely dramatic, he was probably preoccupied with presenting the public with the new or varied music. Certainly the original finale ultimo is preferable to the revised version.

But in *Ruddigore* you want melodrama—guyed, to be sure, but melodrama nonetheless. You get this in the two performances of the standard '20s version from the early '60s. Sargent's Glyndebourne recording is a fluid, lively affair, with a fine cast including Brannigan as Despard and Sinclair as Dame Hannah (EMI). It moves briskly and humorously and attempts some terror in the ghost scenes. The Godfrey-led DCO 1962 essay is even better, in superbly crisp stereo and with a truly excellent cast (London/Decca). Adams and Sandford are sublimely, fruitily pungent as the wicked baronets (one deceased). Reed is a properly dry Robin (true, the young Green was smoother in 1950), and Round is first-rate as the ardent foster brother. The ensemble numbers are attacked with glee, like the Act I double chorus, and the moving moments are memorable, among them Jean Allister's singing of Margaret's aria. If the dialogue had been included, it might have been even better, but no matter. The sound quality is (with the contemporary *Princess Ida*) among the best of the DCO recordings, and having it with the irresistible *Cox and Box* (even in slightly abridged form) makes this a must-own album for the sensitive Savoyard.

There are some fine points in Sargent's 1931 DCO recording, tops being the Mad Margaret/Sir Despard pairing of Nellie Briercliffe and Sydney Granville, but listeners are steered to the '60s for a better *Ruddigore*.

The Yeomen of the Guard is well represented on disc, as befits what is perhaps the most opéra-comique-ish work in the Savoy canon. In some ways, it's even better to listen to *Yeomen* than to see it, because the ersatz Tudor dialogue strains one's patience and the score reverts to Sullivan's fondness for the quaint olde-English rather than the ebullient (a fault abundantly corrected in his next work, the super-lively *Gondoliers*). I'm going through a phase in which *Yeomen* has become the scapegoat G&S operetta, disliked because of overexposure. It may be very touching at times, but it leaves me yawning. A thoroughly revolutionary stage production might jolt me out of my boredom; in the meantime I can review the many disc versions.

Of the older versions on CD, one of the least satisfactory is the 1929 DCO conducted by Sargent (Pro Arte). Despite a great cast, this performance fails to register, possibly because the 78 rpm sides failed to allow the music to really breathe. Even with Oldham, Lawson, Sheffield, Dawson, and company (wow!), I remain unmoved. The chorus isn't very good, nor is the orchestra. Perhaps it's the transfers? The second Sargent

DCO from 1964 is obviously a vast improvement in sound and space, if without as stellar a cast (London/Decca). Reed, Elizabeth Harwood, and Philip Potter were all better in their *Princess Ida* around the same time; Sandford, however, is a memorable Shadbolt, if a rather elegant one. Sargent also had his own Glyndebourne-EMI version in 1958, with the standout stars easily being Richard Lewis as Fairfax and Brannigan as Shadbolt.

No less than three new versions appeared in the '90s, among them a new DCO in 1993 under John Owen Edwards (Ter/Jay). In the same year, Marriner led an ad hoc group of soloists plus the forces of St. Martin in the Fields (Philips), and in 1995 Mackerras conducted the Welsh National Opera version of the previous year (Telarc). All have their points (including their Jack Points). The DCO does have supplemental songs (Savoyard scholars take note); the original version of "Is Life a Boon?" is most interesting. Marriner has abridged dialogue and a notable cast, including Terfel as Shadbolt, Anne Collins as Dame Carruthers, and Thomas Allen as a heavy Point, somewhat akin to but better than Geraint Evans in the 1958 Sargent. The Philips is also the cheapest new version, being available as a "two-fer"—a big incentive. Mackerras manages to find room to include *Trial by Jury* in his album. It also has the late, late Adams reprising his dear Sergeant Meryll from the old DOC days and an okay Point from Suart.

It's difficult to choose which *Yeomen* to own, but I wouldn't lose my head over it—as it were. The Philips is certainly the most intriguing of the newer versions, while the 1964 DCO has its stately, traditional merits. It will be interesting to hear the 1950 Martyn Green version when it gets reissued, as it's the one I grew up on and loved—especially near the beginning of the Act I finale, when you had to turn over the LP.

The Gondoliers is to many the perfect G&S work, and, indeed, in England its popularity has remained consistently high. I'm convinced that part of this has to do with its sunny Italian ("Baritarian") setting, so warm and inviting after the misty Cornwall of *Ruddigore* and dank, dour Tudor London of *Yeomen*. The pretty 18th-century costumes also help set a Canaletto-ish if not Mozartian mood, which Sullivan happily exploits in several delightful ensembles. Gilbert's book is a deft reworking of old themes (baby-switching, social inappropriateness, etc.) but written with great aplomb, and because the lower-class gondoliers and their brides are the center of the show, the dialogue moves very briskly and is very funny. Other memorable characters abound, especially the Spaniards visiting Venice: the parvenu Plaza Toro ducal party and the grave Grand Inquisitor. The overlying republican satire, which works very well if you're a British aristocrat or at least a member of the upper middle classes, has ensured this work's general unpopularity in the US, where equal rights are held sacred, even more so in 1999 than in 1889.

Once again, a '20s DCO version of the show wins the recording sweepstakes hands down. Lytton's rough Duke and Lewis's hooty Duchess are without peer. The gondolier contadine quartet of Oldham, George Baker, Lawson and Aileen Davies is ingratiating and invigorating, and Sheffield is a grand Grand Inquisitor, though extraordinarily light on his feet. The chorus and orchestra are remarkably lively under Harry Norris in this literally and figuratively electric recording. I'm not sure the CD transfers on Pearl or Arabesque bring out all the underlying bass you hear from real 78s on a period gramophone, but no matter—this is the DCO at its lofty summit even in a scratchy transfer.

There are three other versions from more recent decades. First, we can dismiss the unsatisfactory 1958 Sargent-Glyndebourne (EMI). The tempos are at times agonizingly slow, and many have voiced disapproval with Geraint Evans's Duke. To be fair, he sings the part better than Lytton, but that's not quite good enough. The other soloists also have a touch of the blahs, and I wish Sargent had done his *Gondoliers* a decade or so later. The 1961 DCO version under Godfrey has all the dialogue, very, very smartly delivered, and an irrepressible liveliness and gaiety that almost make it a match for the 1927. All the singers are good, and Reed and Gillian Knight make a fine ducal pair, though without the attack of Lytton and Lewis. Round and Alan Styler are very stylish gondoliers, and Mary Sansom and Joyce Wright are their delightful brides. Sandford's Don Alhambra is probably the definitive portrayal, and hearing his dialogue alone brings the palmy (late) DCO company that I loved back to me with nostalgic force.

Thirty years on, in 1991, the new DCO came up with a scenically notorious production (I recall corrugated floors and a running rat) but a not-bad recording (Ter/Jay). John Pryce-Jones leads the crispest sounding orchestra on disc, and he has a few fine singers, most particularly John Rath as the Inquisitor. But this is hardly a dream *Gondoliers,* despite some effective moments; stick with either of the DCOs.

Utopia Limited and ***The Grand Duke.*** No amount of Savoyard arm-twisting will convince me that the original audiences at the Savoy Theatre were wrong: these two works are simply not as effective as their predecessors in any way, and their short runs proved this, despite (in both cases) super-elaborate productions that would cost a mega-million pounds today. Those audiences had seen the original versions of the other great works and were making direct comparisons. Gilbert's long-windedness (page after page of unwieldy dialogue between numbers) and his often numbingly pointless and repetitious lyrics were calculated to bring out the very worst of Sullivan. It's amazing that the composer managed to come up with as much enchanting music as he did in both works, and these are the attractions of the two final operettas on disc.

Both of the complete DCO stereo versions from the '70s briefly on CD were the best—indeed the only—versions available (though, as mentioned, I found the excerpts of *Utopia* done in the previous decade and appended to the 1964 *Trial* LP more scintillating). A complete *Utopia* from Ohio Light Opera is forthcoming, with the unwise inclusion of all the dialogue (Newport). There are agreeable morsels in each score. In *Utopia,* the duet entrance of the English-schooled Utopian princesses, a waltz from the first-act finale, the fabulous minstrel ensemble in Act II; in *Grand Duke* such delights as the sausage-roll anthem, the "cheap" duet of the Duke and the Baroness that takes off from the Duke-Duchess duet in *Gondoliers,* the neoclassical choral opening of Act II, the entrance of the "Prince of Monte Car-lo" and the Frenchified roulette number. A more advantageous presentation would be a single CD of highlights from both operettas.

There are all manner of G&S highlights, overture assemblages, and other whatnots available, as well as Sullivan items sans Gilbert; the latter are discussed in the article in Part I. I'll mention only one to look for and one to avoid. Pearl had the valuable "Art of the Savoyard," with vintage performances in a single CD of no less than 29 tracks. If it's a program of G&S excerpts you want, the soundtrack of *Topsy-Turvy* isn't really advisable (Sony). *The Mikado* and other excerpts may look grand in this fascinating film, but don't sound it at home. TRAUBNER

Gregorian Chant

Sung worship in the Latin rite of Christendom began when Greek was replaced in Christian worship in the West. A cycle of chants for feast days of the year was completed by the early 8th century in Rome. Introduced into the Frankish kingdom under Pepin and Charlemagne, the Roman chant underwent some modifications and its tones were systematized in eight modes. (These modes survived in western European music until they were replaced in the Baroque era by the major and minor keys.) By about 900 the chants of the mass are found in surviving manuscripts, and a century later the chants of the office (the daily hours of prayer in monasteries and cathedrals). In this Frankish redaction, it's known as Gregorian chant. All itemized discs are recommended except as noted.

Dominique Vellard's Ensemble Gilles Binchois has given us an excellent introduction to the modes in "Les Tons de la Musique," singing an introit and one other mass chant in each of the eight modes (Harmonic 8827). For an overview of the way the mass and the office use all the different forms of chant, some recordings of complete services are useful. Jean Claire's Monks of Solesmes sing the mass of Maundy Thursday (Paraclete 831). Karlheinrich Hodes's Choralschola of Düsseldorf sings the three Christmas masses in three single discs (Motette 50321 1/3). The same group sings complete masses of St. Martin, St. Stephen, Easter, Pentecost and Assumption (Motette 50311, 50331, 50341, 50351 and 50361). Their equally fine Mass for the Dead (with *Dies irae*) still awaits CD reissue (Motette 50370, LP).

For the office, the Monks of Solesmes recorded the important Tenebrae service (matins for the last three days before Easter) on three single discs (Paraclete 833, 834, 836). The same group sang Sunday Vespers and Compline, the most familiar of all the offices, using a new Latin translation of the psalms (Paraclete 826). These monks under their previous director Joseph Gajard sang the same offices in traditional form (Accord 222012). For a complete office of a major feast day, the Nuns of Mariendonk Abbey recorded the feast of the Assumption on four single discs, but the last two still await CD reissue (Motette 50381; 50391; 50410 and 50420, LP).

The Proper parts of the mass assigned for each day of the year, which existed in large part before 750, are considered to be the truly authentic chant repertory. The Choralschola of Düsseldorf has grouped examples of each form in single discs. Their collections of Offertory, Introit and Alleluia (Motette 50471, 50441, 50431) are invaluable, as is Gradual (Motette 50490, LP). The Ordinary parts of the mass, medieval chants of a later era, are also gathered in the same group's discs as Kyrie, Gloria and Sanctus/Agnus Dei (Motette 50451, 50501, 50461).

Two fine single discs from the Monks of Solesmes offer mass Propers from the early repertory of saints' feasts (Paraclete 827, 828). Other discs on these two labels are also well sung. The monks of Solesmes made many older recordings for Decca, many of them sets of mass Propers. Only a few are available on CD, but Palm Sunday (Accord 201472) and two discs of the Sundays after Easter (Accord 201492 and 201502) are worthy of special note. The path-breaking 1930 recordings made at Solesmes are available again in either complete or partial fashion (Pearl 9152, 2CD; Paraclete 835). A collection of chants recorded by other choirs at about the same time is useful mainly to show the different interpretations that existed before the Solesmes approach prevailed (Parnassus 96015/6, 2CD).

Even without such a systematic approach, the most satisfying chant discs keep within bounds. Alberto Turco's Nova Schola Gregoriana has an excellent collection of mass Propers, several of each type (Naxos 550711). The same group offers the service of Good Friday (Naxos 550952). Turco's women's ensemble In Dulci Jubilo sings a series of Propers that follow the course of the year (Naxos 550712). Alessio Randon's women's ensemble Aurora Surgit sings the Mass for the Dead with *Dies irae* (Naxos 553192) and a collection of Easter chants including the complete *Exsultet* for the vigil (Naxos 553697). Earlier, Nova Schola Gregoriana recorded an interesting group of graduals, or mass Propers (Arion 68068), and an Easter mass (Arion 68094).

The Monks of Ligugé recorded many programs. The singing is uniformly excellent, but noteworthy is "Rorate Caeli" for the mass Propers of the four Sundays of Advent (Studio 121696). Gloriae Dei Cantores recorded three unified programs offering all the masses of Easter week, the four masses of Christmas, and the Mass for the Dead including *Dies irae* (Gloriae Dei 015, 005, 021). Johannes Berchmans Göschl's Monks of St. Ottilien have recorded five discs that are well organized and nicely sung (Calig 50858, 50883, 50884, 50919, 50922). They are devoted mostly to mass Propers, but the first and third include a Vespers as well. Somewhat less successful are seven thematic discs from Hubert Dopf's Hofburgkapelle (Philips 416808, 432089, 446658, 446665, 446087, 446088, 446703).

The Nuns of Argentan Abbey made a fine group of recordings, but only "The Mysteries of the Rosary" is on CD (Jade 29490). A later recording is "Rex Pacificus" with mass and office chants of Epiphany and Christ the King (Jade 33327). Godehard Joppich's Essen Schola developed an interesting theme of penance with profound effect in "Deus Deus meus" (Novalis 150009). Joppich also directs Die Singphoniker in two programs (CPO 999111, 2CD; 999267). Choeur Grégorien de Paris has recorded chant for several labels, but one of their best is "Job" (Jade 29060). The same group, with tenor Hervé Lamy, developed an intriguing program about Christ the King (Jade 91010).

In general, the foregoing discs were sung from modern printed editions, based on a selection of early manuscripts. Chants composed in the later middle ages include mass Ordinaries, hymns, sequences, tropes and rhymed offices. The last three categories are not generally found in modern printed chant editions, but they have appeared on records much more commonly since about 1980. Ensemble Gilles Binchois devoted a disc to sequences and tropes from the famous monastery of St. Gall (Harmonia Mundi 905239). Rhymed offices, those composed when new feasts were added to the calendar, generally used texts in verse and a regular use of the chant modes in numerical order. Recorded examples vary greatly in quality, but one of the best is "St. Elizabeth of Hungary" from Schola Hungarica (Hungaroton 31605). The same group offers "Historia Sancti Emmerammi" (Calig 50983).

Schola Hungarica is one of many ensembles that sing chants as they are found in single manuscripts rather than the modern editions. Schola's choice usually falls on Hungarian or other central European sources, which are variant versions of the familiar chants. Schola has recorded more chants than any other group except the monks of Solesmes. As a group their discs (on Hungaroton, and a few on Quintana/Harmonia Mundi) are uniformly fine, though tempos are consistently fast and the ensemble of men, women and children (well distributed among the various chant selections for best effect) is unlike the more homogeneous sound of most choirs.

In addition to Gregorian chant, several other repertories of chant also exist: Old Roman, Milanese, Beneventan and Mozarabic. Schola Hungarica can be recommended for the first three of these (Hungaroton 12741 and 31574; 12889; 31168). In a more controversial fashion, marked by slow tempos and an argument for Greek influence (not widely adopted), Marcel Pérès's Ensemble Organum has recorded selections from all four repertories (Harmonia Mundi 901218, 901382 and 901604; 901295; 901476; 901519). Other Milanese (or Ambrosian) chants can be heard from In Dulci Jubilo (Naxos 553502), Luigi Benedetti's group (Sipario 29), Jan Boogaarts's student group (Van-

guard 99011), and Duomo di Milano (Archiv 435032, 4CD). Other Mozarabic chants have come from the Monks of Silos (Archiv 445399; also 435032, 4CD), Schola Antiqua (Jade 39410), and Leo Massó's choir (MEC 1009), all preferable to Organum. WEBER

Jewish Music

Jewish musical traditions are thousands of years old and were probably influenced initially by the music of the Egyptians and Assyrians. The musical traditions of Babylonia, the oldest Jewish settlement in Israel, developed separately from those of Yemen in South Arabia, a community virtually secluded for 1300 years from all other Jewish settlements. Spain developed a Jewish community that thrived until the 15th century, when the Jews were exiled, and those who left Spain because they wouldn't convert to Christianity developed communities in areas of Syria, Turkey, North Africa, and Italy. These people, called the "Sephardim," retained their identity as Spanish Jews.

During the 5th century, German-Jewish musical traditions developed in settlements in southwestern Germany, and the musical traditions of these German Jews, called the "Ashkenazim," influenced those who later formed communities in Eastern Europe. As civilizations and cities developed, there was a great deal of cultural diffusion between the musical traditions of the Jewish communities and those of the countries that surrounded them, but a distinctive Jewish musical culture developed within each community.

MUSICAL TRADITIONS

Sephardic Music. Many of the songs of the Sephardim have to do with the rituals of daily life and were passed orally through the generations, mainly by women. The music is rich with modal melodies, history, and drama. **Voice of the Turtle,** a group of four musicians interested in medieval music, started a recording project called "Paths of Exile" in 1992 to commemorate the exile of the Jews from Spain. Each recording in this monumental collection concentrates on a different tradition of Sephardic music—Turkey, Morocco, Bulgaria and Yugoslavia, Rhodes and Salonika, and Jerusalem (Titanic, various numbers).

Chassidic music. We owe the development of the Chassidim to Baal Shem Tov (1700–1760), a music lover who revitalized eastern European Judaism with music. He introduced the *Nigun* (plural: *Nigunim*), a song without words created on the premise of King David's statement that "words alone cannot relate the greatness of God." Chassidic *Nigunim* fall into three categories: the *rikud* (a dance), the *tish nigun* (a table song), and the *dveykut* (a slow, introspective melody). The Chassidim borrowed melodies from all cultures, even absorbing melodies by Schubert and Verdi, who, it seems, might have learned something from the Sephardim.

Chassidic melodies made their way into liturgical music and can be heard often in music for the synagogue, as opposed to the large body of daily-life music sung by the Sephardim. The most important 19th-century eastern European composer of liturgical music was Louis Lewandowski (1821–1894). Most famous for his setting of the *Kol Nidre* and the *Kiddush* prayers, Lewandowski combined Chassidic traditions with Germanic schooling. His music can be heard in synagogues everywhere and has been recorded in "Jewish Masterworks of the Synagogue Liturgy" (Harmonia Mundi 77388) and "Thank God it's Friday: The Music of Shabbat" (Vox 7546). Another fine disc that includes some of Lewandowski's works is "Masters of Jewish Music," a recording of violin and piano music by Leila Rasonyi and Erika Mayer (♦Hungaroton 31758).

Cantorial music. The role of the *Chazzan,* or Cantor, has always been important in Jewish religious services. By the 18th century, with the development of Chassidic music, the *Chazzan* was considered a true artist in the Jewish communities of eastern Europe. His role was to satisfy the desire for music that would express Jewish sentiment and give tonal expression to the Jews' sorrows. He had to have a good voice and a thorough musical understanding of all aspects of liturgical music, folk music, and folklore. Many of the great *Chazzanim* were important composers, and there are claims that they were more capable of inspiring people by singing than the rabbis were with their preaching. Such is the power of music.

The great cantors were known throughout all of Eastern Europe, and their traditions were (and still are) passed through the generations. Thanks to recent interest in Jewish music, recordings by important cantors of the past like **Mordechai Hershman** (Israel Music 5026), **Leibale Waldmann** (Israel Music 5028), **Mosche Koussevitzky** (Israel Music 5002), and **Yossele Rosenblatt** (Israel Music 5001), once virtually impossible to find, are now available. Excellent samplers include "The Golden Age of Cantors" (Tara 10D) and "Great Voices of the Synagogue" (Tara 602). These recordings are available from Tara Publications on the Internet (www.jewishmusic.com).

Klezmer music and Yiddish songs. The term "klezmer" comes from the Hebrew word *kle-zemer,* which means "musical instruments." *Klezmorim* were music makers. During the Middle Ages every city had its *Klezmorim,* and some gained fame as court musicians to kings, dukes, caliphs, and even popes. By the 19th century a typical European Klezmer band was made up of five musicians: two violinists, a clarinetist, a cellist, and a hackbrett or hammer dulcimer player. These bands played for weddings and festivities throughout the cities and Jewish communities of Eastern Europe, sometimes engaging Gypsy musicians when an additional player was needed. The Jewish and Gypsy musicians learned much from each other, and it is through a few Gypsy musicians who survived the Holocaust that musicians have been able to preserve the traditions of this particular kind of Klezmer music.

"Maramaros: The Lost Jewish Music of Transylvania" is an enlightening recording of reconstructed Hungarian Klezmer music, played by **Muzsikas** (Hannibal 1373). Another recording that sprang from Transylvanian traditions is by **Shony Alex Braun,** a Rumanian violinist who, after surviving both the Auschwitz and Dachau concentration camps, came to the US and studied with Joseph Gingold. His "Shalom" (Shony 5009, available by calling the company at 323-939-7485) is a heartfelt collection of traditional Jewish melodies and his own compositions. "Khevrisa" is an excellent recording of European Klezmer music (with great liner notes), by violinist **Steven Greenman** and Klezmer dulcimer (tsimbl) player Walter Zev Feldman (Smithsonian Folkways 40486).

The modern Klezmer revival that started in the '70s is really a revival of Yiddish-American musical traditions. Of course, these traditions had their roots in Eastern Europe and in the music of the Jewish people who emigrated to America around the turn of the 20th century. Yiddish, like Ladino to the Sephardim, was spoken and sung (with many regional variations) throughout the countries of Eastern Europe, and it became the language of Jewish music in America, where Klezmer and music from the Yiddish theater thrived from the '10s through the '50s. In 1959 **Leon Lishner** and Lazar Weiner made an excellent recording of Yiddish-American music called "Out of the Ghetto: Songs of the Jews in America" that was rereleased in 1997 (Vanguard 6012).

For a number of political and social reasons, the popularity of Yiddish song and Klezmer music declined, and for about 20 years both were nearly forgotten. In the '70s musicians began to copy the playing of great players like clarinetists Naftule Brandwein (1889–1963) and Dave Tarras (1897–1989) that they heard on 78 rpm recordings from the '20s. Eventually, thanks to the dedication of ensembles like the Klezmer Conservatory Band, The Maxwell Street Klezmer Band, The Andy Statman Klezmer Orchestra, The Klezmatics, and Brave Old World, Klezmer music has once again become a vibrant part of Jewish musical culture.

A valuable introduction to the history of Klezmer music and its modern development is a "Musical Expeditions" book called *Klezmer Music: A Marriage of Heaven & Earth* that includes excellent essays, pictures, and a disc with music from the Klezmatics, Ray Musiker, The Flying Bulgar Klezmer Band, Di Naye Kapelye, and other musicians (Ellipsis Arts 4090). Clarinetist **Glora Feldman's** recordings are finally being rereleased on CD. "Klezmer Celebration" is an excellent collection of traditional Klezmer music (Pläne 88809), and "Soul Meditation Harmony of Song" is a recording of "classical" Jewish music by **Ora Bath Chaim** and Bloch (Koch 36501).

In 1995, when violinist **Itzhak Perlman** began playing Klezmer music, wonderful things began to happen. Perlman's "In the Fiddler's House" (Angel 55555) is an excellent collection of the most prominent and innovative Klezmer ensembles in the world. This recording and its companion PBS television program ignited a widespread interest in Klezmer music that reached beyond the Jewish communities. Another excellent collection called "Esquisses Hébraïques" includes music by American and Eastern European composers for clarinet and strings played by clarinetist **Dieter Klöcker** and the Vlach Quartet of Prague (CPO 999630). The focus of the music is more "classical" than Klezmer, but the recording offers a wide range of Klezmer-influenced 20th century music. FINE

Latin Sounds and Rhythms

Flamenco. Created by either the Gypsies or the Andalusians (some of Spain's non-Christian outcasts) during the 16th century, flamenco has both an important vocal (singing) tradition and an instrumental tradition. The **Gipsy Kings** made several fine flamenco recordings, including "Tierra Gitana" (Nonesuch 79399) and "Cantos de Amor" (Nonesuch 79510). "The Story of Flamenco" is a useful compilation (Hemisphere 855680). Excellent guitar recordings include **Paco Peña** playing music by Ramón Montoya and Nino Ricardo (Nimbus 5093) and **Lorenzo Dominguez's** "Alma Gitano" (Sevilla/Window 11602).

Fado. The Portuguese term "fado" means "fate." This music expresses a kind of dignified despair in its words and a kind of bittersweet optimism in its melodies. The guitar used by fado musicians has six sets of double strings (like an extended mandolin) and is called the *viola.* "The Story of Fado" (Hemisphere 855647) includes some of the greatest fado singers from the '50s through the '80s. A wonderful contemporary singer, **Mísia,** sings with the accompaniment of conventional instruments in "Garras dos Sentidos" (Detour 22731).

Tango. The best-known Argentinean music is the tango. It was born in the brothels of the ports along the Rio de la Plata and flourished primarily in Buenos Aires. As a dance, the tango evolved from the *milonga,* a relative of the Spanish *habañera.* Through the white slave trade, the tango made its way to Europe via the sin-ridden city of Marseilles, and eventually became dance music for the upper social classes. After World War I, the tango became popular with the elite in Argentina as well. European composers wrote their tangos far differently than did the Argentineans. A classic example of a European tango is "Jealousy," by the Danish violinist and band leader **Jacob Gade** (Marco Polo 224090).

The most celebrated Argentinean tango singer was Carlos Gardel (1890–1935), who toured Latin America and Spain, singing, making films, and writing wonderful music. When he died in a plane crash, tens of thousands of Argentineans watched his funeral procession and his tomb became a place of pilgrimage. Gardel was succeeded by **Roberto Goyeneche** (1926–94), the male Argentinean equivalent to Edith Piaf. Two of his many recordings are "Tangos Del Sur" (Milan 35812) and "Evita's Tango" (Milan 35794). The latter is a collection of recordings from the '40s—a golden age of tango singing in Argentina. Another wonderful compilation is "The Story of Tango" (Hemisphere 855646). It includes the **Sexteto Major** playing Villoldo's "El Choclo" and Piazzolla's "Adios Nonino," the bandoneon virtuoso Anibal Troilo, and Gardel singing "El Dia Que Me Quieras" and "Mi Buenos Aires Querido."

Samba. Brazilian music is a mixture of music of the native Brazilians, the Portuguese explorers who settled in Bahia in the 16th century, and their African slaves. By the 19th century, a strong African element had entered Brazilian popular music, due to the large African population. *Samba* is derived from the African word "semba," the act of thrusting forward and contacting navels before the beginning of the dance. "Semba" also appears in the Bunda language, meaning prayer, supplication, or adoration. "Sounds of Bahia" is a compilation of Afro-Brazilian music played by **Djalma Oliveria**, Jo Santana, and Chocolate da Bahia (Sound Wave 98003).

Bossa Nova. A Brazilian style created in the '50s by guitarist and singer João Gilberto and composer **Antonio Carlos Jobim,** bossa nova is a "high-class," instrument-dominated offshoot of samba. Recordings by Jobim include a reissue of the 1963 "Antonio Carlos Jobim the Composer of Desafinado" (Verve 521431), "An Antonio Carlos Jobim Songbook" (Concord 45212), "The Art of Antonio Carlos Jobim" (Verve 36253), and "Eliane Elias Plays Jobim" (Blue Note 793089). **Gilberto** recordings include "The Legendary João Gilberto" (World Pacific 93891) and "João" (Polydor 848507).

Choro. Brazilian choro music is the result of European polkas and waltzes crossed with African rhythms played on Mediterranean instruments. It first appeared in printed form in the '20s and was made popular by Villa-Lobos (who played guitar in a choro band). Two excellent choro recordings are "Os Ingenuos Play Choros from Brazil" (Nimbus 5338) and "Rio Nights," a recording that features the greatest composers and players of this music (Milan 35648).

Afro-Peruvian Music. During the 16th century, the Spanish slave traders brought many small groups of Africans from different tribes to Peru to discourage rebel movements. Lacking strong tribal traditions, the Afro-Peruvians became absorbed in the culture of their new country. Their music is still developing as a blend of Spanish, Andean, and African traditions with very unusual instrumentation. In addition to the guitar, it employs a resonant wooden box upon which the player sits and plays with his hands, a burro's jawbone with vibrating loosened teeth, and a cajita—a wooden box with a lid that's opened and shut rhythmically. An excellent recording of Afro-Peruvian music is "The Soul of Black Peru" (Luaka Bob/Warner 945878).

Cuban Music. When the Spanish slave traders came to Cuba, they brought slaves from the Congo; and in the 1800s, when Yoruba's Oyo empire (in the area that is now Nigeria) collapsed, Yoruba people were sold into slavery and sent to Cuba. Music was (and is) central to the Yoruba religion, and the music of Cuba is rich with Yoruba influence. The African influence continued for centuries in Cuban culture, religion, and popular music, and the music kept changing and adding rhythmic sophistication. **Rolo Martinez's** "Para Bailar Mi Son" is one of the finest recordings of Cuban popular music (Ahi Nama 1020), and "Cubanissimo!" (Hannibal 1429) is also a good (although more commercial-sounding) recording.

Cha Cha Cha. At the end of the 18th century, French and Haitian immigrants brought the quadrille to Cuba. Cuban musicians added rhythms and Cuban instruments and created the *Creole quadrille,* which in turn became the *danzón.* Enrique Jorrin created the cha cha cha in 1951. A wonderful collection of this music by various artists is "La Cha Cha Cha de Cuba" (Milan 35740).

Charanga. Like the cha cha cha, the charanga grew out of the *Creole quadrille.* The instrumentation of the Orquesta Tipica Cubana includes a five-keyed flute, a piano, two violins, a bass, a pair of pailas (drums), and a güiro (a scraped, ribbed instrument). "La Charanga de Cuba" (Milan 35742) has a great collection of charangas, and the **Orquesta Aragón's** "Cha Cha Charanga" (Candela 4384752) not only has wonderful music but also gives explicit dance directions.

Rumba. The rumba, an erotic Cuban dance consisting of small, quick steps, developed in the 19th century and became popular in North America and Europe in the '30s. A fine example of the new Cuban rumba music, called "son," can be heard in **Los Guanches'** "The Corpse Went Dancing Rumba" (Corason 128).

Afro-Cuban Music. When Cuban music reached Africa in the '40s and '50s, it became popular over the whole continent and is now one of the most popular forms of Latin music in the world. An interesting compilation recording that features Afro-Cuban music by African musicians is "Afro Latin" (Putumayo 139).

Mexican Music. Cortés brought musicians with him when he conquered Mexico in the 16th century. After they were too old to be soldiers, they began teaching music to the natives, thus creating a rich European-influenced musical culture. The Spaniards brought African slaves with them to Mexico, which added an African element to the developing folk styles. There are eight different styles of *son* in Mexico, and Discos Corason (distributed by Rounder) has made their first recording of a series illustrating these traditional styles. "La Iguana: Sones Jarochos" (Corason 127) has Jarocho music from Vera Cruz in a highly rhythmic style. "La Bamba" is one of the traditional *sons jarochos* popular all over Mexico.

Salsa. Salsa (literally, "sauce") is made of many different ingredients. It often is a mixture of many Cuban styles, with heavy helpings of influences from other Latin and North American, African, and European countries. "Salsa, Merengue, Mambo" (Hemisphere 831791 2) is a collection of just about everything, a very tasty salsa indeed.

Guitar Collections. **Paulo Bellinati** (b. 1950) is a spectacular Brazilian guitarist-composer. His "Lira Brasileira" (GSP 1016) is a series of pieces reflecting the dance styles of different regions of Brazil. Bellinati's "Choros and Waltzes of Brazil" (GSP 1005) includes music by other important Brazilian composers: Antonio Carlos Jobim, Laurindo Almeida, Dilermando Ries, and Baden Powell. The Cuban guitarist **Manuel Barrueco** made a fine recording in "Manuel Barrueco Plays Brouwer, Villa-Lobos and Orbon" (EMI 49710), and **Marcello Kayath's** "Latin Guitar" (MCA 25963) features music from all over Latin America. FINE

Medieval Music

No record catalog can list early music comprehensively. This article generally follows the structure of Richard Hoppin's textbook *Medieval Music* (Norton 1978) to provide an overall perspective on music before about 1420 by listing recordings in the principal categories.

Gregorian chant is discussed in a separate article, but some early medieval vocal music falls outside that category. The *Song of the Sibyl*, traditionally sung at Christmas, is best heard in a series of versions recorded by Montserrat Figueras. The first disc of the three, offering Latin, Provençal, and Catalan versions, is the most interesting (♦Astrée 8705). Submerged in the Deller Consort's collection of Gregorian chants are four early laments for kings and princes from the 9th to the 11th centuries (♦Harmonia Mundi 190235/37). From the 12th century comes the Gothic Voices collection of "Music for the Lion-Hearted King" (♦Hyperion 66336) and Ensemble Venance Fortunat's "Rituel" for the early Capetian kings of France (♦Empreinte Digitale 13068).

Liturgical plays developed in the 12th century from the simple dramatizations that had been added to liturgical celebrations on the major feast days. The most famous is the *Play of Daniel*, the first to be revived (and recorded) in modern times by New York Pro Musica. Andrew Lawrence-King has recorded the play for the first time according to the insights of Margot Fassler, who connects it to a reform of the Feast of Fools at Beauvais (♦Deutsche Harmonia Mundi 77395). Janka Szendrei's Schola Hungarica presents the play with the least embellishment of the manuscript version (♦Hungaroton 12457). Similarly unadorned is the recording by David Wulstan's Clerkes of Oxenford (Calliope 9848). Conversely, Mark Brown's Pro Cantione Antiqua version is greatly embellished (Decca 433731).

Four *Plays of St. Nicholas* are the first of ten plays in the *Fleury Playbook*. A fine recording of all four came from Frederick Renz's New York Ensemble for Early Music (MHS 824437, 2LP, NA). Schola Hungarica recorded three of them with careful attention to their probable place in the celebration of the saint's feast day (♦Hungaroton 12887/88, 2CD). Another *Fleury* play is *Visitation to the Sepulchre*, recorded by Thomas Binkley (♦Deutsche Harmonia Mundi 99925/26, 2LP, NA, with the Easter Mass in Notre Dame polyphony). For the Easter Play of Origny-Ste-Benoîte, Dominique Vellard's Ensemble Gilles Binchois gives a superb rendition (♦Virgin 545398, with a troped Easter mass). Another Easter play from St. George in Prague comes from David Eben's Schola Gregoriana of Prague (♦Supraphon 111562). Marcel Pérès's Ensemble Organum recorded The Pilgrims at Emmaus in a version written at the Norman court of Sicily and preserved in Madrid (♦Harmonia Mundi 901347).

With reference to the *Play of Daniel*, we may take note of its predecessor, the liturgical parody known as the *Feast of Fools*. This is the sort of thing the Clemencic Consort did superbly, but the indispensable texts have not been carried over from the original LP (♦Harmonia Mundi 1901036). Philip Pickett's New London Consort recorded a similar program without the magic (Oiseau-Lyre 433194), as did the Berry Hayward Consort (BNL 112746).

Early polyphony can be found in fragmentary form beginning in manuscripts of the 9th to 11th centuries. Ensemble Gilles Binchois recorded "Eleventh-Century French Polyphony," the most representative collection of these pieces (♦Virgin 545135). Mary Berry's Schola Gregoriana recorded a selection from the earlier (10th century) Winchester Troper in "An Anglo-Saxon Christmas" (♦Herald 151). Earlier, the same group recorded a similar disc, "An Anglo-Saxon Easter" (♦Archiv 413546, LP,

NA). The Orlando Consort sang 25 selections from the *Worcester Fragments* (♦Amon Ra 59).

In the mid-12th century we find more systematic collections of polyphony for two voices in the *Codex Calixtinus*, a manuscript compiled for Santiago de Compostela, and four manuscripts preserved for a long time at St. Martial de Limoges, all five of French origin. Both Sequentia (♦Deutsche Harmonia Mundi 77199) and Ensemble Venance Fortunat (♦Empreinte Digitale 13023) have recorded a complete set of the polyphonic pieces from Compostela, while the Spanish ensemble Coro Ultreia sang the complete chant and polyphony of this manuscript (♦Punteiro 301, 4CD). Marcel Pérès's Ensemble Organum recorded some of the St. Martial repertory (♦Harmonia Mundi 1901134), as did Sequentia in "Shining Light" (♦Deutsche Harmonia Mundi 77370) and "Aquitania" (♦Deutsche Harmonia Mundi 77383).

Notre Dame polyphony developed when the new cathedral in Paris, still under construction, began to be used for services about 1180. The two musicians usually identified as its composers are Leoninus and Perotinus (the forms Léonin and Pérotin are a 19th-century French conceit). Few pieces can be attributed to either, since the four surviving Notre Dame manuscripts date from the mid-13th century and the first citation of the two names is even later. Several of the principal works, including two quadrupla (graduals of the mass in four-voice organum), *Viderunt* and *Sederunt* (c. 1198), are attributed to Perotinus.

The Hilliard Ensemble groups nine Notre Dame polyphonic works, including six attributed to Perotinus by the later writer known as Anonymous IV, framing the program at beginning and end with the two great quadrupla (♦ECM 21385). Fine earlier recordings of the two quadrupla came from David Munrow (Archiv 453185, 2CD) and Alfred Deller (Vanguard 8107 and Deutsche Harmonia Mundi 77416, both with Machaut's Mass). The Red Byrd ensemble sings nine organa for two voices, giving them the conventional attribution of Leoninus (♦Hyperion 66944). Two excellent but rather broad collections come from Ensemble Gilles Binchois (♦Harmonic 8611) and the Orlando Consort (♦Archiv 453487).

Carmina Burana is a German manuscript of secular songs of the 13th century that owes its fame to Carl Orff's setting of its texts for a concert work of the same name. Thomas Binkley's Studio der frühen Musik first recorded selections from this source (Teldec 95521, 2CD). Konrad Ruhland's Capella Antiqua München offers 13 songs (Christophorus 16). The Clemencic Consort recorded a substantially complete version that captures the irreverent and profane hilarity uncommonly well (♦Harmonia Mundi 190336-38, 3CD). Philip Pickett's New London Consort has made another complete version (Oiseau-Lyre 443143, 4CD), while Joel Cohen's Boston Camerata offers 21 songs (Erato 14987).

Troubadours were singers of secular songs who flourished in southern France from 1100 to 1290. Hendrik van der Werf lists 42 composers in his modern edition. Three recordings are devoted entirely to a single composer. Martin Best sings 12 songs by Bernart de Ventadorn (♦Hyperion 66211), the Kecskés Ensemble sings 14 by Gaucelm Faidit (♦Hungaroton 12584), and Martin Best's ensemble sings 8 by Guiraut Riquier (♦Nimbus 5261). Other troubadours often found on records are Peire Vidal, Raimbaut de Vaqueras, and Comtessa Beatriz de Dia. Others recorded less often include Arnaut Daniel, Bertran de Born, Folquet de Marseilla, Guiraut de Borneil, Jaufre Rudel, Marcabru, Peire Cardenal, Peirol, Raimon de Miraval, and Raimbaut d'Aurenga. Collections of these songs come from Sequentia (♦Deutsche Harmonia Mundi 77227), Alla Francesca (♦Opus 111 30170), Paul Hillier (♦ECM 21368), the

Clemencic Consort (♦Harmonia Mundi 2901524-27, 4CD, with Alfonso el Sabio), Thomas Binkley's Studio der frühen Musik (♦Teldec 97938, 2CD) and Russell Oberlin (♦Lyrichord 8001).

Trouvères were singers of secular songs who flourished in northern France from 1140 to 1300. Thibaud (1201–53), count of Champagne and king of Navarre, is by far the most famous, with some 60 songs surviving. Ensemble Athanor recorded nine of his songs in excellent fashion (♦Gallo 30374, LP, NA). Adam de la Halle, who also composed polyphony, is well known. Thomas Binkley's Schola Cantorum Basiliensis performed his *Jeu de Robin et Marion* in the context of additional music of the period (♦Focus 913), as did Guy Robert's Ensemble Perceval (♦Arion 68162). Adam also figures extensively in the collection of trouvère songs by Sequentia (♦Deutsche Harmonia Mundi 77155, 2CD). Other collections come from Christopher Page's Gothic Voices (♦Hyperion 66773), Ensemble Venance Fortunat (♦Empreinte Digitale 13045), Paul Hillier (♦Harmonia Mundi 907184), the Studio der frühen Musik (♦Teldec 97938, 2CD), Russell Oberlin (♦Lyrichord 8001), and the Augsburg Ensemble (Christophorus 77117).

Minnesingers were singers of secular songs who flourished in Germany from 1200 to 1445. Walther von der Wogelweide (1160–1230), the first, was best known for *Unter den Linden* and the *Palestinälied*, both heard in the Studio der frühen Musik collection (♦Teldec 97938, 2CD). Neidhart von Reuental (c. 1180–c. 1240) was very popular in his own time, judging by the number of manuscripts that preserve his work and that of his imitators. The Augsburg Ensemble recorded 14 of his songs (♦Christophorus 77108). Frauenlob (Heinrich of Meissen) enjoys a full disc sung by Sequentia (♦Deutsche Harmonia Mundi 77309). The Monk of Salzburg wrote polyphonic as well as the usual monophonic songs. The Augsburg Ensemble offers 16 (♦Christophorus 77176), while the Paul Hofheimer Consort Salzburg sings 17 (♦Arte Nova 37316).

The one-eyed Oswald von Wolkenstein (1377–1445) was the last of these, his songs (some of them polyphonic) collected in two large manuscripts (Codices A and B). Consequently, more discs have been devoted entirely to his songs than to those of any other medieval writer. Sequentia recorded a superb collection (♦Deutsche Harmonia Mundi 77302). Pickett's New London Ensemble offers 16 of his songs (♦Decca 444173), while the Augsburg Ensemble sings 24 of them stylishly (♦Christophorus 74540). Thomas Binkley's Studio der frühen Musik (♦EMI 763069), Wilfred Jochims (Aulos 53516, LP, NA), and Othmar Costa's chamber choir (Telefunken 641139, LP, NA) have also devoted entire discs to this composer.

Laudario di Cortona is a 13th century manuscript of popular devotional songs, mostly in Italian. La Reverdie captures their spirit well (♦Arcana 34 and 304, 2CD), while Ensemble Organum is less successful (Harmonia Mundi 901582). *Llibre Vermell* is a 14th century manuscript at Montserrat containing 10 songs of popular devotion. Savall's Hesperion XX has not been surpassed in these songs (♦Virgin 561174), but Pickett's New London Consort is an alternative (Oiseau-Lyre 433186).

Les Miracles de Notre Dame of Gautier de Coincy (c. 1177–1236) was a collection of devotional songs that may have influenced Alfonso el Sabio, recorded by Alla Francesca (♦Opus 111 30146). Also lovely were earlier versions by Ensemble Guillaume de Machaut (Arion 38347, LP, NA) and Ensemble Alegria (Pierre Verany 794113). At Vigo on the northwestern coast of Spain, Martin Codax wrote a cycle of seven songs of remarkable simplicity on lost love; the music was found in a book binding in 1914. Though secular, not devotional, they are considered here because the language of their poetry is that of Alfonso's cantigas.

Hartley Newnham sings them most affectingly in an Australian disc (♦Move 3044). Catherine Bott's version in the New London Consort's collection of Spanish medieval music may be more accessible (♦Oiseau-Lyre 433148, 2CD).

The *Montpellier Codex* and *Bamberg Codex* are the two largest collections of 13th century motets. These pieces, not to be confused with sacred music, were the work of composers who had learned their trade by singing in the cathedrals. They took the familiar melodies and built up polyphonic structures using French (less often Latin) texts sung simultaneously over the original chant tenor. Anonymous 4 sings 29 motets from the *Montpellier Codex*, in some cases usefully grouping different motets based on the same tenor (♦Harmonia Mundi 907109). A disc drawn from the *Bamberg Codex* comes from Luigi Taglioni's Camerata Nova (♦Stradivarius 33476). Other motets from both of these codices are scattered among medieval collections.

Codex Las Huelgas contains Spanish compositions along with much French material. Collections of these pieces come from Sequentia (♦Deutsche Harmonia Mundi 77238), Discantus (♦Opus 111, 3068), Paul van Nevel's Huelgas Ensemble (♦Sony 53341), and Luis Lozano Virumbrales' Voces Huelgas (♦Sony 60844 and 60846).

The *Roman de Fauvel* was an early example of the Ars Nova, with monophonic songs and motets inserted into a satirical attack on the royal and papal courts around 1316. Three discs have offered partly different selections from the poetry and music. Thomas Binkley's Studio der frühen Musik was adept at making the first recorded version attractive (Electrola 30103, LP, NA; also a 6CD set). The Clemencic Consort captures the spirit of this satire remarkably well, just as it did in *Feast of Fools* and *Carmina Burana*. The booklike issue cited, however, is the only one of several CD issues that reproduces the indispensable notes and texts from the original LP (♦Harmonia Mundi 590994). Joel Cohen has also recorded selections from this source (Erato 96392).

Philippe de Vitry (1291–1361), a contemporary of Machaut during the Ars Nova, is known for at least four motets composed around 1320, but about ten more have been attributed to him. Five are found in the *Roman de Fauvel*, the rest in *Codex Ivrea*. The Orlando Consort collected 19 motets composed at about this time (♦Amon Ra 49). On a slightly more varied disc, Sequentia collects 13 motets and five chansons attributed to Vitry, adding two organ intabulations, or arrangements (♦Deutsche Harmonia Mundi 77095). Since 12 motets are common to both discs, you may settle for one or buy both for the additional selections on each. Jehan de Lescurel was an earlier innovator. His songs in several forms are heard from Ensemble Gilles Binchois (♦Virgin 545066).

The *Messe de Tournai* is the most important of several anonymous polyphonic masses for three voices that were assembled from separately composed pieces in the decades before Machaut's four-voice polyphonic mass was composed. Ensemble Organum recorded it from the original manuscript, with chant propers from the same manuscript, superseding all the preceding half-dozen recordings (♦Harmonia Mundi 1901353). Emmanuel Bonnardot's Obsidienne ensemble recorded the *Barcelona Mass* with chant propers included (♦Opus 111 30130, with *El Cant de la Sibilla*).

Italian secular song developed in the Trecento (the 1300s). The earliest manuscript source is the *Rossi Codex* (before 1350) and the most splendid is the *Squarcialupi Codex*. The first generation of composers included Jacopo da Bologna and Giovanni da Cascia. Of the second generation, Francesco Landini (c. 1325–1397), a blind organist, was the leading Italian composer of the entire Trecento. Studio der frühen Musik (♦Electrola 30113, LP, NA) and Andres Mustonen's Hortus Musicus (Chant du Monde/Melodiya 78666, LP, NA) recorded programs of his music. His contemporaries included Bartolino da Padova. Matteo da Perugia (died c. 1418) worked in Milan and Padua after 1402, composing in the Ars Subtilior style and was the most important Italian composer of that period. The Huelgas Ensemble offers a superb collection of nine of his sacred pieces (♦Sony 62928). The Medieval Ensemble of London sings or plays a dozen of his secular songs (♦Oiseau-Lyre 577, LP, NA). A few manuscripts have survived that transcribe songs for instrumental use. Ensemble Organum offers 10 of these from *Codex Faenza* along with the original songs (♦Harmonia Mundi 901354). A remarkable collection of Italian songs comes from Esther Lamandier in "Decameron," including a lovely anonymous *Per tropo fede* (♦Astrée 7706).

Johannes Ciconia (c. 1370–1412), the first Flemish composer to go to Italy, was the leading figure of the Ars Subtilior, a period of complex notation that flourished in the decades between Machaut and Dufay. His biography had formerly been merged with that of his father, who was born about 1335 and traveled to Avignon. The son lived in Rome after 1390, then in Padua. The Huelgas Ensemble recorded substantially the complete works, a remarkable project for a composer of this era (Pavane 7345/47, 3CD). While the ensemble is more than competent, some of these performances have been bettered. The Orlando Consort includes nine works in a program that focuses on northern Italy around 1400 (♦Archiv 459620). Pedro Memelsdorff's Mala Punica groups all 10 of Ciconia's motets (♦Erato 21661). Alla Francesca collects 19 sacred and secular pieces in different forms, but 12 of them are only performed instrumentally (♦Opus 111 30101). The Little Consort (Channel 290) and Ensemble P.A.N. (New Albion 48) duplicate some of these pieces.

Other collections that group Ciconia and his lesser contemporaries include single discs from the Orlando Consort (♦Metronome 1008), Mala Punica (♦Arcana 21, 22, 23) and Crawford Young's Ferrara Ensemble (♦Arcana 32, 40). The last group also has a program focused on the Visconti court in Pavia (♦Harmonia Mundi 905241), while the New London Consort offers "Ars Subtilior" (♦Linn 039). Ensemble Organum recorded a collection from the *Codex Chantilly* (♦Harmonia Mundi 901252) and Ensemble P.A.N. gave us "Ars Magis Subtiliter" (♦New Albion 021).

The *Old Hall Manuscript*, compiled around 1410–20, is the principal surviving source of medieval polyphony from England. John Dunstable and Leonel Power are well represented, but many pieces are anonymous or attributed to little-known composers. The Hilliard Ensemble offers a superb collection of 21 pieces (♦Virgin 561393).

Power (d 1445) was an older contemporary of Dunstable. Far more works are attributed to him in the *Old Hall Manuscript* than to any other, but only his sacred music survives. The Hilliard Ensemble recorded a fine collection of his music, including the complete cycle *Missa Alma Redemptoris Mater* (♦Virgin 561345). The most important piece not included there is the motet *Beata progenies*, which the same group included in their survey of the *Old Hall Manuscript* (see above).

Dunstable (d 1453) was the most important English composer of his time. Like Power's, his mass movements were written singly or in pairs, though each composed a complete cycle in his later years. The Orlando Consort collects a dozen works, including the complete cycle *Missa Rex seculorum* (♦Metronome 1009). The Hilliard Ensemble offered nine motets, only two duplicating the Orlando program (♦Virgin 561342).

Wilfried Jochens et al. sang four motets, including the important *Sancta Maria non est* (Christophorus 41).

See also: Gregorian chant, Hildegard of Bingen, Alfonso el Sabio, Machaut.   WEBER

Music for Children

There are many fine recordings now available for children and parents, especially those unfamiliar with the world of classical music who need to have some idea where to begin helping their children explore that world. Based on experience, I believe that children need to hear good music and will like it when they hear it. Actually, there is relatively little music written specifically for children. Some that we connect with childhood isn't really for children; for example, Schumann said of his *Scenes from Childhood* that the pieces were composed by an adult for adults. Of course, this doesn't mean the music is unsuitable for children's listening; no piece of great music can be considered off limits to children. Parents and teachers can present a wide variety, from early music to 20th-century compositions, and they will probably be amazed at what captures the child's imagination.

MUSIC FOR EARLY DAYS

Logically, the first music specifically addressed to a child will be a lullaby. Of all the lullaby discs I examined, "Lullabies" is my top choice (ESS.A.Y 1054). This CD is rich with traditional songs familiar to me from my childhood, including my favorite, that magical combination of Tennyson and Barnaby, "Sweet and Low." **Julianne Baird** sings most of the solo numbers, but 12-year-old Madeline Kapp sings some of the songs, and she joins Baird in a few numbers, her young voice adding charm, freshness, and simplicity. The mingling of voice, piano (Richard Kapp), and violin or viola (Mela Tannenbaum) is sweet without sentimentality. In a few places, I thought the piano a bit overmiked, but it's a minor nit to pick with an otherwise unusual and delightful performance.

Another charming album, "Dreamscape: Lullabies From Around the World," comes from the Aureole Ensemble and **Heidi Grant Murphy** (Koch 7433). This gentle album is unusually interesting, including traditional lullabies from many countries in excellent performance and sound. Among lullaby discs, I must put pianist **Carol Rosenberger**'s excellent entries very near the top. Her first album, "Perchance to Dream" was rarely put back on the shelf after its purchase (Delos 3079), and "Such Stuff as Dreams: A Lullaby Album for Children and Adults" is a worthy sequel (Delos 3230, 2CD). Rosenberger and the producers at Delos have managed to make albums appealing to children without making them seem condescending to adults. Each booklet has copious notes, with one section for adults, giving good background on the making of the CDs as well as some information about each composer and each piece, and one for children that includes the proper pronunciation for each composer's name. The composers on both releases include all the familiar names from Bach to Bartók.

A similar release, "Listen, Learn, and Grow Lullabies," provides a mix of soft piano and orchestral music, many specifically lullabies, from a list that includes such unusual composers as Warlock, Suk, and Parry, along with more familiar ones like Brahms, Mozart, and Mendelssohn (Naxos 554790). A companion disc is aimed at newborns through preschool children and designed for their waking hours, with lively selections from Mozart, Bach, Rossini, and Vivaldi (Naxos 554569). Both are beautifully done and may be used with confidence. Every selection is taken from another Naxos recording, and the numbers are given for each so that parents and children can easily explore where their inclinations lead them.

"Baby Sleep" is another excellent disc for children and adults — short pieces of quiet music for various instruments, including piano, guitar, and harp, as well as a few orchestral works (Erato 18311). All performances are of high quality, with familiar artists and conductors, for example Katsaris, Gardiner, and Hampson. There are no notes, only a list of each piece with performer. Don't be put off by the sappy cover on **Julian Lloyd Webber**'s "Lullaby: Sweet Dreams for Children of All Ages" — a picture of the father cellist cuddling his infant son (Philips 111925). The music is lovely. All arrangements are for cello and piano, with Webber playing the cello, various pianists accompanying. A few selections are certainly in the category of light classical, but there are many interesting pieces here. In terms of sound and variance in volume level, this is one of the better lullaby discs on the market; sudden changes in volume aren't conducive to lulling anyone to sleep, and this one maintains a desirable level of uniformity through the entire program.

"Baby Needs Mozart" is, I suppose, a response to the recent research showing that Mozart's music increases your IQ, even if only temporarily, and makes rats run through mazes better (Delos). Whatever the motivation behind its production, it's not a bad purchase as a Mozart sampler, as it contains excerpts from many of his works. All the performances are very good, with well-known artists. I'm much less sympathetic to "The Mozart Effect: Music for Children Vol. 1" (The Children's Group). Don't bother with this disc. The music on it is OK, but it's only a Mozart sampler marketed under the guise of a musical pill to increase your child's IQ. And if I were one of the performers, I would be angry, as no individual artists' names are given except for the piano solo.

"Classical Princess: Music for Dress-Up" is for little girls, perhaps ages 4-10 (Delos 3215). This is all music chosen by a little girl, her favorites for playing "dress-up" with her friends, and most of it is music for dancing. Some is exactly what you would expect: several waltzes from Tchaikovsky, for example. I'm surprised there is no Strauss, but it includes some more serious pieces: part of Grieg's *Holberg Suite* and two movements from Dvořák's *Serenade for Strings*. There are also a couple of lighter classical works, edging toward pop, but nothing that would prevent me from buying it for any child on my gift list. All selections may be found in other Delos releases; the number for the CD with the fuller rendition is given after the title. A clever marketing ploy, but also a good technique for drawing both children and parents into the larger works. Little girls will also enjoy the packaging; it comes with a few stickers inside — what kid doesn't love stickers? — and the little princess pictured on the front is admiring herself in a mirror consisting of the silver surface of the CD shining through a mirror-shaped hole in the paper.

A successful series for young children is "The Classical Child," which includes "The Classical Child is Born," "The Classical Child Dreams," "The Classical Child at Play," "The Classical Child's Christmas," and "The Classical Child at the Ballet," with a sixth release on the way, "The Classical Child at the Opera" (Metromusic). These are the brainchild of **Ernest Mavrides;** to quote an advertising flier from the company, "It occurred to him to try using sparkly and unusual percussive sounds to play the parts of traditional orchestral instruments." Mavrides himself says, "I haven't tried to replace the traditional presentation of classical music, but rather see it as a playful interpretation." His characterization is accurate; he hasn't mutilated the music. Rather, familiar classical themes are played on a synthesizer, but without a lot of weird noises. I don't like these recordings much, but I'm not a big fan of such tricks as Beethoven's 9th on panpipes or the *St. Matthew Passion* performed by

accordions either. I wouldn't hesitate to recommend them to parents who don't have much familiarity with classical music, since I think it would be much better for children to become familiar with the classics in this way than not at all. But parents who are classical music lovers will become tired of these renditions, since the sameness of the synthesizer sounds tends to make them monotonous. These recordings have received considerable acclaim, however, and there's nothing harmful here, especially if they're combined with plenty of more traditional versions of the pieces. A wide range of composers is introduced, with a good deal of emphasis on baroque and classical periods, and the Christmas and ballet albums are the best.

"Classical Zoo" is a nice idea that doesn't quite come off (Telarc). Most children can't fail to be interested in music about animals. The program starts with Rossini's *Thieving Magpie* overture and continues with Respighi's *The Birds,* Sibelius's *Swan of Tuonela,* and Saint-Saëns's *Carnival of the Animals.* All the performances are with the Atlanta Symphony with **Levi** conducting, except for the Respighi, where Louis Lane conducts. The renditions are uniformly good, but this version of *Carnival* really kills the disc. The problem is the new poetry by Bruce Adolphe, whose attempts at versifying this splendid music put me off. His poetry ranges from mildly witty to heavy-handed to distinctly unfunny, compared to Ogden Nash's inimitable, sly, and understated humor. In defense of this release, it's narrated by Itzhak Perlman, and he does an excellent job; he's funny, with his use of different accents and inflections. And parts of the musical performances are very lively, with lots of dash and energy. The most desirable *Carnival* with new poetry comes from Johnny Morris with the Slovak Radio Symphony Orchestra, **Lenárd** conducting (Naxos 554463). It's very well done, and the program is rounded out with Ravel's *Mother Goose* and Dukas's *Sorcerer's Apprentice.*

For an excellent, traditional performance of *Carnival of Animals,* along with many other good selections for children, try "Classics for Children" with **Fiedler** and the Boston Pops (RCA 68131). This is 76 minutes' worth of the best children's music on the market; the sound is good, and the notes by Fiedler's daughter are entertaining and affectionate. Best of all, the Ogden Nash verses are used, narrated with aplomb by Hugh Downs. Also included here is Britten's *The Young Person's Guide to the Orchestra* (with narration), music by Grieg and Gounod, a fairy tale medley from the 1952 movie *Hans Christian Andersen* by Frank Lesser, and several kid's songs arranged by Richard Hayman. The sound is excellent, rich and sonorous. I can't think of a better all round children's disc, and it's mid-priced.

MUSIC WITH STORIES

With Prokofiev's *Peter and the Wolf,* we encounter a different way of introducing children to good music: with a story. The strictly musical merits of the many recordings of this piece are discussed in Part I; here we're concerned with their suitability for children. It's a perennial favorite of children, and each time I listen to it, I can see why. It's also a great way to introduce children to themes in music and their significance. One good and economical choice is **Ormandy**'s 1957 recording with the Philadelphia Orchestra, Cyril Ritchard narrating (Sony). Also on this release are very good concert versions (no narration) of *Carnival of the Animals* and Britten's *Young Person's Guide.*

Another good choice is **Claudio Abbado** conducting the Chamber Orchestra of Europe, Sting narrating (don't laugh; his favorite music for listening is classical, and he does rock only for a living.) The rest of the CD is excellent for introducing children to some of Prokofiev's more accessible works; the program opens with his March in B-flat and is nicely rounded off with *Overture on Hebrew Themes* and the Classical Symphony (DG 429396).

I don't like the narration in "Sneaky Pete and the Wolf" (Telarc). The music is fine (the same recording as in Telarc's "Classical Zoo"), but the narration is written by **Peter Schickele,** and it's very lame. His story for the traditional music is slightly humorous but nothing more, and the ending is simply asinine. I wouldn't even characterize this CD as one for children, though it may have been intended that way.

A topnotch *Peter* is narrated by **Dame Edna Everage** with the Melbourne Symphony Orchestra, John Lanchbery conducting (Naxos 554170). The sound is wonderful, the performance expressive and exciting. Two other chestnuts are included on this program: Poulenc's *Babar,* narrated by Barry Humphries, and Britten's *Young Person's Guide,* also narrated by Everage. This *Babar* is the best on the market with its combination of Humphries's genteel narration and Jean Françaix's luminous orchestration of Poulenc's masterpiece. Considering the quality of performance, the composition of the program, and the price, this is a contender for the best children's disc available.

This is only one of three good recent releases of *Babar.* The other two are done with the traditional piano. **Catherine Kautzky** performs Poulenc's original version as both pianist and narrator (Vox 7545); **Evelyn Lear** as narrator chooses a later version to which Poulenc added a cello obligato, and she adds a bit to the usual text (VAI 1150). Both Kautsky and Lear also perform Satie's delightful *Sports et divertissements,* and Kautsky gives us the piratical *Shiver Me Timbers* by contemporary composer Jon Deak. For children, the clear first choice is Naxos, but collectors might be interested in having all three, given the substantial differences in the versions of *Babar.* All are very well done and provide enjoyable listening.

"Maestro Orpheus and the World Clock" (MOP 101) is a good way to sneak in some classical music for children who love stories. A little boy named Fred wonders why his grandfather, whose house he is visiting, is so interested in old clocks. After Fred is in bed one night, he discovers to his horror that time has stopped, and he gets up to see what he can do about it. He encounters Maestro Orpheus, who takes him through the corridors of time to wind up the World Clock. Along the way, Fred is introduced to many composers, from Bach to Janáček. Fred, who starts off feeling a little impudent, learns some important lessons about life and death and what his grandfather really means to him. This musical tale is good for either home or classroom use, since a teacher's guide is available with many ideas for musical activities and discussion questions.

A good group of discs combining a great deal of music with stories is the "Classical Kids" series; it includes "Mr. Bach Comes to Call" (84235), "Beethoven Lives Upstairs" (84236), "Mozart's Magic Fantasy" (84237), "Vivaldi's Ring of Mystery" (84238), "Hallelujah Handel!" (84263), and "Tchaikovsky Discovers America" (84226). Each disc introduces children to the music of one composer, and each is packed with as many selections as possible, with some excellent performances. In "Mr. Bach Comes to Call," the composer, along with some choir boys and an orchestra, magically drops in on a girl who is supposed to be practicing the piano, shows her how his pieces are supposed to be played, and tells her a little about his life. "Beethoven Lives Upstairs" is put together as an exchange of letters between a boy named Christoph and his uncle. Christoph's father has died, and the mother lets out the room upstairs to lodgers. Mr. Beethoven moves in, and Christoph writes many letters to his uncle about the composer's odd habits, which convince the child that he's mad. The others are similar in tone.

The amount and variety of music on the discs are impressive, and the music isn't a mere sidelight, an excuse for the stories; rather, it dominates. There's only one drawback to these delightfully creative programs, and that is an annoying modernism that creeps in at times. Especially in the Bach and Vivaldi stories, the children are sometimes a bit fresh at best and disobedient at worst. Of the six, the Beethoven and Handel are my favorites; the music on both is exceptional, and the stories are well done, especially the accounts of Mr. B's many eccentricities. There are few notes with these discs, mostly a list of tracks and credits for the performers. Their value would be much enhanced if there were more copious notes with a short biography of each composer, especially since most of the stories are entirely fictional.

Delos has released some of the most charming and artistic children's story discs on the market, consisting of Russian fairy tales combined with Russian music. These CDs may be purchased separately or in a gift pack with all three: "Prince Ivan and the Frog Princess: Music of Prokofiev" (6003); "The Snow Queen: Music of Tchaikovsky" (6004); and "The Firebird: Music of Igor Stravinsky" (6005). To accompany the first, pianist **Carol Rosenberger** has used Prokofiev's *Music for Children* to illustrate the story. The two fit together so well that you would think the pieces were composed especially for this fairy tale; also included are three of the *Visions Fugitives.* The narrator is Natalia Makarova, best known as the famous Russian ballerina who defected from the Soviet Union in 1970. She is a gifted narrator, speaking with expression and enthusiasm in her rich Russian accent and dramatizing the stories in a way children (and adults) will enjoy, and since each booklet includes a good printed version of the story, children can follow along, Especially funny is her rendition of Baba-Yaga, as she chortles in a satisfyingly wicked, witchy way.

Rosenberger also provides the music for "The Snow Queen," for this tale, she has used music from Tchaikovsky's *Album for the Young.* Accompanying "The Firebird" is, of course, the music of Stravinsky's ballet, performed by the Seattle Symphony, Gerard Schwarz conducting. After both "Prince Ivan and the Frog Princess" and "The Snow Queen," there is a reprise of all the music previously incorporated with the fairy tales, played through without interruption. This helps acquaint children with the music for its own sake. "The Firebird" is narrated entirely with the music, the performance taking up the entire disc.

Another Delos release of a classic children's tale with music, *Peter Pan,* can't be recommended too highly (6007, 2CD). This is the product of a talented team: Jane McCulloch, who skillfully adapted and abridged the text; **Derek Jacobi,** who narrates it with love and charm; and Donald Fraser, who composed the music for accompaniment. Anyone who buys this set should also take a hard look at "An Awfully Big Adventure: The Best of Peter Pan (1904–1996)" (Delos 3201). Here is the complete music, as well as arrangements of Peter Pan music from other productions, like Mary Martin's and Disney's. While the story CDs have no notes (they don't really need any), the music release has copious notes, with a synopsis of the portion of the story that goes with each musical selection.

There are a couple of somewhat unusual recordings not made specifically for children that are excellent for young listeners. The first is "Down on the Farm," with **Kunzel** and the Cincinnati Pops (Telarc 80362). This is a thoroughly delightful pastiche of music associated with country living. It begins with farm animal sounds—a pig snuffling at his trough, the crow of a rooster, and finally a turkey gobble—from which the orchestra bursts into a spirited arrangement of "Turkey in the Straw." Other traditional arrangements for orchestra include "Shenandoah" and "Old Folks at Home," and then there is John Denver's "Thank God I'm a Country Boy," sung by Tom Wopat. A highlight is a stylish performance of "Old MacDonald Had a Farm" by a Cincinnati children's chorus. There's a medley of music from TV farm shows and a medley of old American songs—like "The Farmer in the Dell," "She'll be Comin' Round the Mountain," and "On Top of Old Smoky"—done as a sing-along. The words are printed in the booklet so children can sing along, too.

The other disc I wish to recommend is "John Amis—Amiscellany: Music Making with Old Friends" (Nimbus 5342, NA). Amis is probably more familiar to the British than to Americans for his BBC radio programs, "Music Now" and "My Music." This CD is exactly what the title says, music making with old friends. It isn't high art—the singing leaves a lot to be desired—but it's down-to-earth, a charming aural portrait of old friends having fun together. I recommend it for children especially for Poulenc's delightful *Babar the Elephant*, with Amis narrating, Leslie Howard at the piano. Following Babar is Alan Ridout's *Ferdinand the Bull*, done with a Spanish accent by Amis and accompanied by Levon Chilingirian on the violin. Then come several songs that Amis has sung or whistled on his show over the years, accompanied by various of his friends, some of them familiar to a knowledgeable classical music audience, like Jeffrey Tate and Donald Swann. The last song on the program will interest those familiar with Tolkien's great work, *The Lord of the Rings*: "Bilbo's Last Song," sung by Amis and Swann together. Children may miss the poignancy here, but this is another disc for both children and adults.

GROWING OLDER

As children mature, learn to read for themselves, and become more independent in choosing their listening, the combination of music with stories will gradually be left behind. At this point, the whole wide world of classical music and of books is open to them, but here are a few suggestions to bridge the gap.

Recordings of Tchaikovsky's three great ballets—*The Nutcracker, Swan Lake,* and *Sleeping Beauty*—are discussed in Part I, but I should call your attention to the following releases: *The Nutcracker,* with **Jansons** and the London Philharmonic (EMI 293514), and from RCA, *Swan Lake* (62557), *Sleeping Beauty* (61682), and *The Nutcracker* (61704), with **Slatkin** and the St. Louis Symphony. All are attractively packaged in colorful boxes, and each contains a booklet telling the story of the ballet and providing a listening guide for children, with cues to help them distinguish the various instruments of the orchestra and match the music to the story. Parents can buy these recordings without fear; they're all excellent renditions with good sound—the very best in classical music for children.

Some of the best recordings for introducing children and young people to the great masters are in the Vox Music Masters series, available on either CD or cassette at a budget price. Composers included in this series are Bach (8500), Mozart (8501), Chopin (8502), Mendelssohn (8503), Schubert (8504), Schumann and Grieg (8505), Handel (8506), Beethoven (8507), Haydn (8508), Wagner (8509), Vivaldi and Corelli (8510), Dvořák (8511), Tchaikovsky (8512), Brahms (8513), Johann Strauss Jr, (8514), Foster and Sousa (8515), Berlioz (8516) and Verdi (8517). Each program has a simple, straightforward narration with a story of the composer's life, suitable for children ages 8 to 12, accompanied with many samples of his music.

The number and range of musical samples is quite comprehensive; for example, the Handel disc has excerpts not only from his best-known works, such as *Water Music* and *Messiah,* but also from those not as well known to the general public, such as *Israel in Egypt, Julius Caesar,* and some of the organ concertos and concerti grossi. After the story and music samples comes a complete work: for Handel, *Water Music;* for Schubert, Symphony 5; for Brahms, nine Hungarian dances, etc. The sound is good enough, considering the age of the original tapes, and the level of both education and enjoyment is high, the performances excellent.

Don't miss the relatively new line of Naxos Audiobooks. I will give them only brief mention here, since the use of music on these CDs is limited, but they are excellent, and their number is growing at typical Naxos speed, which is to say *fast!* The "Junior Classics" include such works as *Alice's Adventures in Wonderland* and *Through the Looking Glass, Pinocchio, Tales of King Arthur,* Kipling's *Jungle Book* and *Rikki-Tikki-Tavi, Treasure Island, Huckleberry Finn* and *Tom Sawyer,* and there are many titles for those of high school age to adult, including Greek classics (*The Iliad* and *The Odyssey*), Dante's *Inferno* and *Purgatorio, Hamlet,* Greek love poetry, and several other poetry discs. Though not a lot of music is included, the liner notes lists what is used. *Alice in Wonderland,* for example, includes portions of Delius's *Brigg Fair, In a Summer Garden,* and *Scherzo;* Parry's *Lady Radnor's Suite;* Roger Quilter's *Where the Rainbow Ends;* and Bruckner's *Lancer's Quadrille.* The story is read most beautifully and expressively by actress Fiona Shaw.

My final recommendation, suitable for ages 12 to adult, is conductor **Gerard Schwarz**'s series, "Musically Speaking." As far as I know, these CDs are available only by subscription to the series. Each mailing contains a 2CD set about a given composer, and all the major composers are covered. Schwarz narrates one CD with information about the life of the composer and about the music, explaining how the music fits together and introducing such concepts as introduction, theme, exposition, development, and recapitulation; the other contains the pieces under discussion. Each set also comes with two booklets, one with information about the composer and his music, the other with a detailed guide, with timings on each track, to point out where themes occur and how the music develops.   CRAWFORD

Overtures

In LP days, collections of overtures may well have introduced more people to good music than anything else. Usually parceled out three to an LP side, they provided bite-size helpings of rich melody and swirling color that may have stimulated many beginners to seek out the entire opera to hear the tunes in context. You may indulge in a rich repast or save them for dessert after more filling fare; but whatever your pleasure, there's every good reason why overtures continue to be immensely popular. The key to bringing off this kind of music is an absolute lack of affectation or condescension, and all the great conductors knew it. Because bright sound and witty repartee between winds and strings are essential, I must regretfully set aside the pre-stereo classics like the **Toscanini** and **Beecham** reissues, which partisans will surely seek out anyway. In stereo you'll treasure Beecham's memorable *Cambiale di Matrimonio* (Rossini) and *Fair Melusina* (Mendelssohn); surely the Royal Philharmonic horns are alone worth the price of admission (♦EMI 63407).

No one did French overtures with more élan than **Paray** and the Detroit Symphony in their Mercury recordings. One combines French fare, including an unsurpassed Massenet *Phèdre* (♦432014), while another bubbles over with Gallic joie de vivre—*Si j'étais Roi, Dame Blanche, Orpheus, Belle Hélène,* and *Tales of Hoffmann*—plus a rip-roaring *William Tell* (♦434332). And don't forget his *Masaniello, Bronze Horse* and *Fra*

Diavolo (♦434309, with Suppé) or his *Mignon* and *Raymond* (♦434321, with *Carmen* and *l'Arlésienne*). As a displaced Detroiter I'm probably not all that objective, but you won't be either once you've heard these bracing renditions.

Bernstein benefitted from more billowy, airier sound than Paray and also embraced a more wide-ranging repertoire; one of his best efforts offers thrilling accounts of *William Tell, Poet and Peasant, Zampa, Mignon,* and *Raymond* (♦CBS 37240). On a "Royal Edition" disc, *Mignon* returns in the company of *Merry Wives of Windsor, Bartered Bride, Marriage of Figaro, Donna Diana, Die Fledermaus,* and rather indulgent readings of *Der Freischütz, Oberon* and *Euryanthe* (CBS 47601). *Beautiful Galatea* and *Orpheus* are included with his peerless Bizet Symphony (♦Sony 47532), *Poet and Peasant* and *Light Cavalry* with his Rossini overtures (♦Sony 47606).

RCA continues to hold back its **Fiedler** material, making his earlier disc essential (♦5479); of course you get the standards, but even more valuable are his wonderful *Martha* and still unsurpassed *Fatinitza* (Suppé). "Boston Pops Tea Party" is notable for Michael Balfe's exuberant *Bohemian Girl* (RCA 68793), while *Il Guarany* (Carlos Gomes), part of his "Jalousie" program, is currently available only on a private label (Collector's Choice 2747). The other great Pops orchestra, the Cincinnati, may be heard in familiar fare (*Zampa, Fra Diavolo, Poet and Peasant, Light Cavalry, Orpheus, Donna Diana, William Tell*) in vigorous readings by **Kunzel** (Telarc 80116). **Stokowski** recorded this material far too infrequently, but one highly desirable disc contains his vivid *Leonore 3, William Tell, Rosamunde, Don Giovanni* and *Roman Carnival* (EMI 64140). We can't forget **Barbirolli,** who like Beecham transcended the familiar boundaries of British music to embrace the operatic stage in *William Tell, Semiramide, Forza, Oberon, Hansel and Gretel, Merry Wives,* and *Don Pasquale* (EMI 64138).

Klemperer's overtures have the same virtues as his Beethoven and Brahms symphonies—rock solid playing and warm, rich sound from the Philharmonia—but also the same slow tempos, which work well enough in *Hansel and Gretel* and the more deeply felt emotions of *Oberon, Der Freischütz* and *Euryanthe,* less successfully in *Manfred* and *Genoveva* where more passion is clearly called for; actually they work best of all in Gluck's elegant *Iphigenie en Aulide,* but *that* one they left out (EMI 63917). **Karajan,** like Stokowski, was strangely silent in this repertoire, but one reissue offers plush accounts of *Hansel and Gretel, Der Freischütz, Hebrides, Gypsy Baron* and *Anacréon* (Cherubini) together with several operatic intermezzos (EMI 64629).

Norrington's "Early Romantic Overtures" followed hard upon his controversial *Symphonie Fantastique,* and as expected it's Berlioz's *Francs-Juges* that benefits the most from his "period instruments" treatment, where the massive low brass take center stage, and likewise the horns in *Genoveva;* most interesting is *Flying Dutchman,* where Norrington uses the original 1841 draft instead of the more familiar 1860 ending. *Oberon, Hebrides,* and *Rosamunde* complete an absorbing program (EMI 49889).

If **Leibowitz** fails to bring out the insouciance of familiar French fare as infectiously as Paray, he comes pretty close, and his *Reader's Digest*-derived recordings offer more bloom than the Mercuries; *Crown Diamonds* is included along with *Prince Igor* and *Marriage of Figaro* in one (Chesky 61), *Orpheus* in another (Chesky 57), both filled out with other highly desirable material from that "Festival of Light Classical Music" box I know you all have hidden away somewhere. Other *Reader's Digest* material with **Gerhardt** is available from Chesky in two volumes of "Light Classics," including *Le Roi d'Ys* and *Der Freischütz* in Vol. 1 (102),

Khovantschina, Orpheus, Colas Breugnon and Dvořák's *Othello* in Vol. 2 (108).

Redel is afforded sumptuous sound for his "Grandes Ouvertures Françaises," including some wonderfully brazen horns in Méhul's *La Chasse de jeune Henri,* but the Méhul, Cherubini's *Medée,* and André Grétry's *Le Magnifique* suffer from sodden tempos, and he doesn't even come close in the sparkling items by Ferdinand Hérold (*Zampa*), Auber (*Masaniello*), Adam (*Poupée de Nuremburg, Si j'étais Roi*) and François-Adrien Boieldieu (*Calife de Baghdad*) (Pierre Verany). **Tortelier** offers several French standards (*Zampa, Si j'étais Roi, Bronze Horse, Mignon, La Belle Hélène*), but his tempos are frequently wayward while Aimé Maillart's *Dragons de Villars* is impossibly bloated (Chandos). **Scherchen**'s blowzy but delightful French overtures (*Masaniello, Mignon, Si j'étais Roi, Dragons de Villars, Dame Blanche, Roi d'Ys*) have been reissued (ReDiscover 015). **Jean-Pierre Wallez**'s collection of French operetta overtures is harder to find but worth the effort; it includes *Le Fille de Madame Angor* (Charles Lecocq), *Les Cloches de Corneville* (Robert Planquette), *Véronique* (Messager), *Les Saltimbanques* (Louis Ganne), *La Mascotte* (Edmond Audran), and lots more (Forlane 003).

Collections of British overtures are far fewer; one of the best is **David Lloyd-Jones**'s "Victorian Concert Overtures," balancing Elgar's *Froissart* and Sullivan's *Macbeth* against less familiar but equally stalwart fare, all beautifully rendered (♦Hyperion 66515). Another disc gathers together pieces on a Scottish theme under the knowing hand of **Alexander Gibson,** including the obvious—*Hebrides, Tam O'Shanter*—and the not so obvious—Hamish MacCunn's *Land of the Mountain and the Flood,* Berlioz's *Waverley,* and Verdi's *Macbeth* ballet music (Chandos 8379).

We travel from Scotland to 18th-century Sweden for an absorbing collection of music written under the beneficent *noblesse* of King Gustav III; this music is all top-drawer and beautifully set forth by **Claude Génetay** (Musica Sveciae 407). You'll also want "Overtures for the Royal Theater," which offers more romantic Swedish fare, including Berwald, Kraus, and Ludwig Norman plus even rarer examples (Sterling 1009). While the sound varies, the performances by Stig Westerberg and Mats Liljefors are excellent. But the Danes outshine them all with a wonderful disc led superbly by **Johan Hye-Knudsen:** marvelous accounts of Kuhlau's *William Shakespeare,* Jean-Baptiste Du Puy's *Youth and Folly,* J.P.E. Hartmann's *Little Kirsten,* Peter Heise's *King and Marshal,* and Christian Horneman's *Aladdin,* all played with immense gusto by the Royal Danish Orchestra (♦Sterling 1018).

Among the highlights of EMI's "Artist Profile" of **Silvestri** (68229) are several Russian favorites: *Prince Igor, Russlan and Ludmilla,* and *May Night,* plus an electrifying Elgar *In the South.* I could wish for a modicum of Silvestri's white-hot inspiration from other Russian collections; **Chistiakov** does well with *Prince Igor* and *A Life for the Tsar,* and the seldom heard "Temple of Apollo at Delphi" from Taneyev's *Oresteia* is welcome, but the rest of his bits-and-pieces grab-bag suffers from the excesses of the Bolshoi ensemble (Chant du Monde 288053). Even more frustrating, given its unhackneyed program, is **Pletnev**'s collection; his tendency to push too hard spoils Glazunov's *Ouverture Solennelle* and Tchaikovsky's Overture in F, while Shostakovich's *Festive Overture* is little better and *Russlan* nothing but a blur (DG 439982). Only Rimsky's *Tsar's Bride,* Prokofiev's *Semyon Kotko* and Kabalevsky's *Colas Breugnon* salvage the project. Farther off the beaten track, but no less welcome, is **Andrei Korsakov**'s program of Alexander Alyabiev, Evstigney Fomin, and Dmitri Bortnyansky—the latter probably better known for his choral music—

which may give you some idea where Russian opera was headed before Glinka made it a whole new ball game (A&E 10370).

You expect superb Italian fare from a grand old man of the theater like **Serafin,** and you get it from a program of mostly Verdi but also Bellini, Rossini and Donizetti (EMI 62609). Of the two London "Operatic Highlights for Orchestra" LPs still fondly remembered by many, **Gavazzeni** at least has surfaced on CD, highlighted by *Norma, Linda di Chamounix,* and Mascagni's *Le Maschere* (Decca 448548). **Piero Gamba**'s recording, with its glorious *Cleopatra* (Luigi Mancinelli), is still missing. More unexpected treasures are offered by **Ezio Rojatti,** who offers Cimarosa's *L'Italiano in Londra, I due sopposti Conti,* and *Li due Baroni di Roccazzura,* and Paisiello's *Il Barbiere di* Siviglia, *Le zingare in fiera,* and *Nina,* plus two Rossini favorites, tuneful music played with great spirit (♦Nuova Era 6726).

Solti's blistering Suppé foursome is included among a wide array ranging from *Les Francs-Juges, Hansel and Gretel,* and *Egmont* to Wagner and his Russian favorites, *Russlan, Prince Igor* and *Khovantschina,* most of them already available elsewhere but conveniently grouped together at a budget price (Decca 460982). If this is too much Solti for your taste, you can find the "Weekend Classics" issue with the four Suppé items plus a handful of others including Boskovsky's *Die Fledermaus* (Decca 421170, 2CD). Vol. 5 in Decca's "Wiener Tanzgala" series is far more attractive (♦436785), with **Boskovsky** offering some of the best Johann Strauss around (*Prinz Methusalem, Cagliostro in Wien, Indigo und die vierzig Raüber, Carneval in Rom, Das Spitzentuch der Königin,* and *Waldmeister*) plus *Donna Diana, Beautiful Galatea, Merry Wives* and Richard Heuberger's *Der Opernball*—a wonderful disc!

Even British aficionados must send to Australia for the richest treasure of all: **Bonynge**'s marvelous London recordings, with one set (♦466434, 2CD) of 18th-century overtures (Haydn, Kraus, Florian Gassmann, Boieldieu, Ferdinand Paër, Grétry, Antonio Sacchini, Salieri, and Handel—lots of Handel) and another 19th-century (♦466431, 2CD), including the best Donizetti *Roberto Devereux* you'll ever hear, plus *Torvaldo e Dorliska* (Rossini), *La Fille du Tambour-Major* (Offenbach), *Giovanni d'Arco* (Verdi), Led Dragons de Villars (Maillart), and much, much more, all worth their weight in gold.

Another import, from **Marriner,** offers prosaic accounts of *Merry Wives, Hansel and Gretel, Fledermaus, Euryanthe, Poet and Peasant,* and *Donna Diana,* and his slapdash treatment of the rarer *Zar und Zimmermann, Hans Heiling* (Heinrich Marschner) and *Die Opernball* (Richard Heuberger) makes no amends (Philips). You can do a lot better for a lot less with **Alfred Walter,** who offers *Hans Heiling,* Lortzing's *Der Waffenschmied* and *Der Wildschütz,* Humperdinck's *Koenigskinder,* and more familiar Weber fare, a true bargain (Naxos 550146). You might also haunt the import bins for **Florian Merz**'s rather eclectic grouping, labeled "Vol. 1" though so far I haven't seen a Vol. 2 (Koch Schwann 6505); certainly if there's more planned like the initial program of *Hans Heiling, Die beiden Schützen* (Lortzing), *Martha* (Flotow), and *Taming of the Shrew* (Hermann Goetz), I'll be keeping an eagle eye out.

You won't find a better *Bartered Bride* anywhere than **Ančerl**'s with the Czech Philharmonic; indeed, the other pieces, including *Leonore 3, Magic Flute* and *1812,* almost seem like icing on the cake, fitting tribute to this great musician (Supraphon 3397). Unfortunately **Neumann** with the same orchestra is no bargain, offering no serious competition to Bernstein or Fiedler in *Poet and Peasant, Light Cavalry, Orpheus* and others (Supraphon). They may be heard to far better effect under **Vladimir Válek** in a (mostly) Viennese program: *Poet and Peasant, Light Cavalry, Beautiful Galatea, Fledermaus, Gypsy Baron, A Night in Venice, Orpheus,* and *Belle Hélène* (Canyon 389).

One mono recording offers several pieces you're unlikely to find anywhere else, unless (like me) you used to tape David Berger's "Music from Germany" off the radio on a regular basis; this disc includes Lortzing's *Die beiden Schützen, Hans Sachs, Der Grossadmiral, Andreas Hofer,* and *Regina,* Marschner's *Der Vampyr,* E.T.A Hoffmann's *Undine,* and Peter Cornelius's *Barber of Bagdad,* with a laundry list of stalwart German conductors (Memories 4556). Only *Der Vampyr* is in stereo, and *Undine* is badly cut, but as a gap-filler it's worth having, and anyway *Hans Sachs* and *Regina* are mono on the Marco Polo CD too. **Hans Vonk** also offers *Barber of Bagdad* with other hard-to-find items, including *Zar und Zimmerman,* Flotow's *Alessandro Stradella* and *Martha,* alongside the more familiar *Merry Wives, Fra Diavolo, Si jétais Roi,* and *Donna Diana,* comfortable readings warmly recorded (Ars Vivendi 036).

A rather mixed but very attractive bag includes *Nachklänge von Ossian* (Gade), *The Naiads* (William Sterndale Bennett), plus *Hebrides* and Schumann's *Overture, Scherzo and Finale,* very well done by **Dirk Joeres** (IMP 00152). There's also a valuable collection bringing together overtures by Beethoven (a very fine *Leonore 1* from Colin Davis), Weber (*Oberon* and *Euryanthe* with Inbal, *Preziosa* with Markevitch), and some rare Schubert (in B-flat and E minor, affectionately rendered by Leppard), plus *Die Meistersinger* and *Hebrides* (Davis), all priced to go (Philips 426978). **Leppard** may be heard separately in a splendid collection of 18th-century overtures (Philips 446569; reissued as "Curtain Up!," ♦454426). Included in "Kaleidoscope" are nicely turned readings of *Jolly Robbers, Merry Wives, Abu Hassan, Mignon* and *Orpheus* with **Mackerras,** along with other equally delightful lollipops (Mercury 434352).

Finally, to conclude on a hopeful note, I need to mention some other LP collections that would be welcome on CD, beginning with the disc that started it all for me: **Pierre-Michel Le Conte** in French overtures (Audio Fidelity); **Raymond Agoult**'s "Overtures—In Spades!" (RCA); **Albert Wolff**'s "Overtures in Hi-Fi" (a very fine *Domino Noir, Merry Wives* and *Si j'etais Roi;* London); **Münchinger** with the Vienna Philharmonic (London); **Claudio Scimone** in Italian overtures, especially Spontini's *La Vestale,* Mancinelli's *Cleopatra* and Ponchielli's *I Promessi Sposi* (Erato); an even more rarified assortment from **Kurt Herbert Adler** including Nicolai's *Der Tempelritter,* Goldmark's *Merlin,* Goetz's *Francesca da Rimini* and Schreker's *Die Gezeichneten* (London). The list goes on: "**Fiedler**'s Favorite Overtures" (Polydor); **Kostelanetz**'s "Festive Overtures" (Columbia); "Sparkling Overtures" by **Vilem Tausky** (EMI). (MVCW-18043). Happy hunting!   HALLER

Renaissance Music

"Renaissance," a name taken from art history, refers to the revival of learning after the rebuilding of Rome began around 1420. It also identifies the music that stretches from the mature polyphonic works of Dufay to the *oeuvre* of Palestrina. Gustave Reese treated it as a unit in *Music in the Renaissance* (Norton, 1954). This style is sharply different from the *seconda prattica* that arose in Italy around 1600 and flowered in the works of Monteverdi. Still, it's only one way to define an era. It would be instructive to compare how *The New Oxford History of Music* (Vol. 3, 1960; revised edition in preparation) covers the period 1300–1540 and then to see how Reinhard Strohm devotes *The Rise of European Music* (Cambridge, 1993) to the period 1380–1500. Although this article is long even while omitting a dozen composers who have their own place in the book, there isn't enough room to mention everyone, let alone every worthwhile recording. But it's a start.

Several generations of French and Flemish singer-composers, beginning with Johannes Ciconia (see Medieval Music), dominated European music both at home and in Italy. Guillaume Dufay (q.v.) was the leading figure of the early decades of the Renaissance. Reginald Liebert, a younger contemporary of Dufay at Cambrai, is interesting for a plenary Mass (one that consists of both Ordinary and Proper), *Missa de beata Virgine* (ca. 1430). Schola Discantus sings it capably (Lyrichord 8025).

Gilles Binchois (1400–60), who served at the Burgundian court, is Dufay's most important contemporary. The Clemencic Consort recorded a selection of his sacred and secular music, including a mass cycle assembled from separate movements (Harmonia Mundi 10069, LP, NA). Two newer discs of Binchois's music by Ensemble Gilles Binchois (Harmonic 8719, with Dufay) and Gothic Voices (Hyperion 66783, with contemporaries) each include half a dozen pieces.

Later in the 15th century **Johannes Ockeghem** (q.v.) was the dominant figure. Among his contemporaries, Antoine Busnois (ca. 1430–92) composed songs and some sacred music at the Burgundian court. Pomerium sings a sampling that includes *Missa O crux lignum triumphale* and his lament for Ockeghem, *In hydraulis* (Dorian 90184). Alexander Agricola (1446–1506), well regarded in his own time in France and Italy, is poorly represented. A fine disc from the Huelgas Ensemble collects songs, motets and single movements from five different mass cycles (Sony 60760). Ensemble Unicorn offers a collection of songs (Naxos 553840), and the Ferrara Ensemble recorded another collection (Deutsche Harmonia Mundi 77038).

Jacobus Barbireau (1455–91) spent his life in Antwerp. The Clerks's Group sings his *Missa Virgo parens Christi* (ASV 188). Guillaume Faugues served at Bourges in 1462, where he was respected in his own time. The Obsidienne ensemble recorded *Missa La basse danse* (Opus 111 30222, with Ockeghem motets). Johannes Regis (d. 1496) served at Cambrai. In an important contribution to the repertory, Schola Discantus recorded both his masses, *Missa Ecce ancilla Domini* and *Missa Dum sacrum mysterium* (Lyrichord 8044). Johannes Tinctoris (ca. 1430–ca. 1511) is remembered best as a writer on musical theory. The Clerks's Group repaired the long neglect of his music by recording *Missa L'homme armé* and *Missa sine nomine* (Cyprès 3608). Roger Blanchard once recorded the latter work for Discophiles Français/Nonesuch.

At the end of the 15th century **Josquin des Prez** (q.v.) was preeminent and Jacob Obrecht (q.v.) was also outstanding. An important contemporary of these two is Pierre de La Rue (ca. 1460–1518), whose *Requiem* was much recorded in the LP era. Ensemble Clément Janequin coupled it with *Missa L'homme armé* (Harmonia Mundi 901296). Ars Nova also recorded both the *Requiem* (Kontrapunkt 32001) and *Missa L'homme armé* (Kontrapunkt 32008). *Missa cum jucunditate* has had two fine recordings, by the superb Hilliard Ensemble (Virgin 561392, with seven motets) and by Henry's Eight (Etcetera 1214, with various works). Gothic Voices has recorded *Missa de feria* and *Missa Sancta Dei genitrix* (Hyperion 67010, with four motets). Schola Discantus offered *Missa de Sancta Anna* and a set of three Lamentations for Tenebrae (Lyrichord 8021). Charles Ravier's *Missa Dolores gloriose* on a Philips LP needs replacement.

Heinrich Isaac (ca. 1450–1517) worked at the Hapsburg court after serving Lorenzo de' Medici, at whose death he wrote *Quis dabit capiti meo aquam*, recorded by Fabio Lombardo (Christophorus 77132, with music of Florence). Capella Pratensis recorded *Missa paschale* with impeccable style (Ricercar 206692). Another dependable group, the Tallis Scholars, recorded *Missa de Apostolis* (Gimell 545923, with motets). The

Munich Cathedral Ensemble offered *Missa Virgo prudentissima* (Christophorus 77218), and Capella Lipsiensis gave us *Missa Carminum* (Berlin 3102, with Pierre de la Rue's *Requiem*). Gerd Ziemann's *Missa Ein fröhlich Wesen* on a Schwann LP needs replacement.

Ludwig Senfl (ca. 1486–ca. 1543) was Swiss, but he fits here as a pupil of Isaac, whom he succeeded at the court of Maximilian. Ensemble Officium recorded a selection of his Latin sacred music including *Missa super Nisi Dominus* (Christophorus 77226). Weser-Renaissance recorded mostly German songs (CPO 999648). The Clemencic Consort presented a more varied selection of his works (Accord 149163).

Antoine Brumel (ca. 1460–ca. 1520) concluded a peripatetic life at the court of Ferrara. His *Missa Et ecce terrae motus* for 12 voices is unusually elaborate for its time. The Huelgas Ensemble (Sony 46348) and the Tallis Scholars (Gimell 454926) have both done justice to the music. The Daltrocanto ensemble sings his *Missa A l'ombre d'ung buissonet* (Opus 111 30162, with a *Requiem* by Engarandus), while Chanticleer sings his *Missa Berzerette Savoyenne* (Chanticleer 8805). Matthaeus Pipelare (ca. 1455–ca. 1515) served in Antwerp and nearby cities. The Huelgas Ensemble recorded sacred and secular works including *Missa L'homme armé* (Sony 68258). Loyset Compère (ca. 1450–1518) was Flemish, but he's known for a brief stint in Milan. The Orlando Consort sings one of his three Milanese motet-masses along with some motets and songs (Metronome 1002).

The first half of the 16th century was the generation between Josquin and Orlando Lassus (q.v.). Secular music grew in importance. French chansons, many based on poems of Ronsard, and Italian madrigals, frequently based on poems of Petrarch, were new forms that inspired composers. Ensemble Clément Janequin has several collections of chansons, including "Songs on Poems of Ronsard" (Harmonia Mundi 901491), "Une fête chez Rabelais" (Harmonia Mundi 901453), and "Fricassée Parisienne" (Harmonia Mundi 1901174). Similarly, the Scholars of London sing "French Chansons" (Naxos 550880).

Clément Janequin (ca. 1485–1558), the leading French song composer of this period, is best served by his namesake Ensemble Clément Janequin (Harmonia Mundi 1901099 and 1901271). Other collections come from A Sei Voci (Astrée 8571) and Charles Ravier's ensemble (Astrée 7785). Ensemble Clément Janequin also sings his *Messe "La Bataille"* and *Messe "L'Aveuglé Dieu"* (Harmonia Mundi 901536, with a motet). The same group sings three lamentations for Tenebrae and six motets of Claudin de Sermisy (ca. 1490–1562) (Harmonia Mundi 1901131). Pierre Certon wrote chansons and a *Messe "Sus le pont d'Avignon."* The Boston Camerata offers a selection (Harmonia Mundi 1901034).

Claude Le Jeune (1527–1600) composed sacred music, including Huguenot psalms, as well as vocal and instrumental pieces of a secular nature. Ensemble Clément Janequin offers a selection of chansons and viol fantaisies (Harmonia Mundi 901182), while Ensemble Vocal Sagittarius recorded seven of his psalms (Accord 206752). His Latin sacred music is also well represented. I prefer *Missa Ad placitum* sung by the Choir of New College Oxford (Hyperion 66387) to the capable work of Ensemble Clément Janequin (Harmonia Mundi 901607). Nine motets are found on a disc from Ensemble Jacques Moderne (Adda Musica Nova 7), but the group includes a *Magnificat* and motet heard on both discs just noted and another motet heard on the latter disc. Another composer of Huguenot psalms was Paschal de l'Escotart (ca. 1540–91). Ensemble Clément Janequin recorded a set of Huguenot poems titled "Octonaires de la Vanité de la Monde" (Harmonia Mundi 1901110).

Elzéar Genet (d. 1548), known as Carpentras from his birthplace, served at the papal chapel. A Sei Voci recorded his nine Lamentations for Tenebrae (Erato 45021). Jacob Arcadelt (ca. 1505–68) also served at the papal chapel, but he was an important composer of madrigals; the Consort of Musicke recorded a selection (Deutsche Harmonia Mundi 77162). Henry's Eight included his *Missa Noe noe*, based on Jean Mouton's motet, in a mixed program of Christmas music of the time (Etcetera 1213). Jacob Clemens non Papa (ca. 1510–ca. 1556) remained in the Netherlands while his compatriots went south. The Tallis Scholars recorded *Missa Pastores quidnam vidistis*, based on his own motet (Gimell 454913). Nicolas Gombert (c1495-c1560) directed the chapel of Charles V. Henry's Eight recorded two significant collections of his music, *Missa Tempore paschale* (Hyperion 66943, with motets) and a group of eight more motets (Hyperion 66828). Odhecaton recorded *Missa "Sur tous regrets"* for the coronation of Charles V (Bongiovanni 5083).

Adrian Willaert (ca. 1490–1562) was the last of the Flemish composers in Venice, since his successors at St. Mark's (after Rore, who stayed only a year) were native Italians. A recording of his complete works was announced, but issues (five so far) are proceeding slowly. Antonio Eros Negri led *Vespers of the Blessed Virgin* (Stradivarius 33326) and Marco Longhini directed *Christmas Vespers* (Stradivarius 33373). Negri also recorded the *Villanesche* (Stradivarius 33311). Negri and others recorded 21 *Ricercari* by Willaert and his circle (Stradivarius 33355), while Il Desiderio ensemble recorded his intablatures (instrumental arrangements) of Philippe Verdelot's madrigals (Stradivarius 33325) and Romanesque presented a collection of his songs (Ricercar 151145). The Oxford Camerata sang *Missa Christus resurgens*, based on Jean Richafort's motet (Naxos 553211, with two motets). Giaches de Wert (1535–96) served at the Mantua court. The Consort of Musicke recorded his Madrigals Book 7 (Virgin 790763), while Cantus Cölln sang a broader selection of five-voice madrigals (Harmonia Mundi 901621). The Currende ensemble collected a group of motets and *Missa Dominicalis* (Accent 9291).

Pierre de Manchicourt (ca. 1510–64) was the first director of Philip II's chapel. The Huelgas Ensemble recorded motets, chansons and *Missa Veni Sancte Spiritus* (Sony 62694). Cipriano de Rore (1516–65), Flemish despite the name, served in Venice, Ferrara and Parma. The Hilliard Ensemble recorded his masterpiece, *Le Vergine* (Harmonia Mundi 1901107), while the Huelgas Ensemble presented his St. John Passion (Deutsche Harmonia Mundi 77429). The Tallis Scholars recorded *Missa Praeter rerum seriem*, based on Josquin's motet (Gimell 454929, with motets), and Weser-Renaissance offer a set of sacred and secular motets (CPO. 999506). Guillaume Boni (ca. 1530–ca. 94) lived in the south of France. Ensemble Jacques Moderne recorded 18 of his Book 1 motets (Adda Musica Nova 8). Philippe Rogier (ca. 1561–96) was the last Flemish director of Philip II's chapel. The Magnificat ensemble recorded his *Missa Ego sum qui sum* and six motets (Linn 109)

Philippe de Monte (1521–1603) served at the imperial court in Vienna and Prague. The Hilliard Ensemble recorded a selection of secular and sacred works including *Missa La dolce vista* (EMI 763428). His assistant, Jacobus Regnart (ca. 1540–99), served the court at Prague and then Innsbruck. Weser-Renaissance recorded his motets for the Virgin Mary (CPO 999507).

ITALIAN COMPOSERS

Giovanni di Palestrina (q.v.) was Lassus's great Italian contemporary. In secular Italian music, this was the era of the *frottola*, which flourished at the court of Mantua, where its two most prolific composers resided. The *frottole* of Bartolomeo Trombancino (ca. 1470–ca. 1535) can be heard

from the Consort of Musicke (Oiseau-Lyre 593, LP, NA). In addition, Ensemble Les Nations offers a collection of his sacred music (Tactus 472001). Marchetto Cara (ca. 1465–ca. 1525) stayed at Mantua longer. Consort Veneto recorded a collection of his *frottole* (Bongiovanni 5086). The first Italian composer who achieved international fame was Costanzo Festa (ca. 1490–1545), who worked at the papal chapel. The Huelgas Ensemble offers a varied collection of sacred and secular music, including *Quis dabit oculis nostris* for the death of Anne of Brittany, a motet later arranged by Senfl for the emperor Maximilian's death (Sony 53116).

Francesco Corteccia (1502–71) can be heard in austerely appropriate responsories for the first two days of Tenebrae from the Cantori di Lorenzo (Dynamic 187). Marc'Antonio Ingegneri (1547–92), Monteverdi's teacher and the director at Cremona cathedral, composed a complete office of Tenebrae. The nine lamentations, 27 responsories, canticle *Benedictus* and psalm *Miserere* (along with the *Improperia* for the Good Friday service) are sung in proper fashion though not quite in liturgical sequence (Adda 581129/30, 2CD), far superior to a partial collection on an Audivis disc. Emilio de' Cavalieri (ca. 1550–1602) composed a Tenebrae service of which the Madrigalisti di Padova recorded nine lamentations and nine responsories (Tactus 550501). At this time the huge basilica of San Petronio in Bologna attained its peak under Andrea Rota (ca. 1553–97). The San Petronio Cappella performs his *Missa Resurrectionis* with contemporary works (Tactus 551801).

Girolamo Cavazzoni (ca. 1510–ca. 1577), following the lead of his father, composed organ elaborations of chant masses, hymns, and *Magnificats*. The organ would play and the choir would sing alternate verses. Organist Sergio Vartolo recorded his Book 2 with the Nova Schola Gregoriana (Tactus 510390, 2CD). Claudio Merulo (1533–1604) composed similar works. Frédéric Muñoz recorded a *Missa Apostolorum* and a *Magnificat* with Dante Andreo's chant group (Naxos 553420/1, 2CD). Andrea Gabrieli (1533–1585) was organist at St. Mark's in Venice. His Majestys Consort recorded motets, instrumental music and *Missa Pater peccavi* (Hyperion 67167), a mass that had once appeared on a mono LP. Giovanni Gabrieli, Andrea's nephew, succeeded him (q.v.). In addition to Don Carlo Gesualdo (q.v.) and the other madrigal composers already mentioned, Luca Marenzio (ca. 1533–99) was a leading figure. Concerto Italiano recorded his Book 1 (Opus 111 30117), while Concerto Vocale gave us a broader selection (Harmonia Mundi 1901065).

ENGLISH COMPOSERS

The Eton Choir Book is the main source of late 15th-century sacred music in England (as the *Old Hall Manuscript* is earlier). Harry Christophers's The Sixteen has the most extensive recording of this music (Collins 13142, 13162, 13422, 13952, 14622, 5 single CDs). The group also made two earlier discs, each accounting for one piece not found in the newer set (Meridian 77039 and 77062, LP, NA). Richard Davy's *St. Matthew Passion* (along with works by Walter Lambe and John Nesbet) comes from the Eton College Chapel Choir (Chatsworth 1004). The music of Walter Frye (d. 1475), one of the most significant composers represented in the manuscript, is sung superbly by the Hilliard Ensemble in a disc that includes his *Missa Flos regalis* (ECM 1476). William Cornysh (d. 1502), no longer to be confused with another (probably his son), is included in the Cardinall's Musick collection (ASV 164). Music by both father and son (d. 1523) occupies a Tallis Scholars collection (Gimell 454914).

The leading composer of the early Tudor era is **John Taverner** (q.v.). His older contemporary Robert Fayrfax (1464–1521) is less obscure since Cardinall's Musick recorded his complete works. A mass is featured on each disc, filled out with motets: *Missa O quam glorifica* (ASV 142), *Missa Tecum principium* (ASV 145), *Missa Albanus* (ASV 160), *Missa O bone Jhesu* (ASV 184) and *Missa Regali ex progenie* (ASV 185). Nicholas Ludford (ca. 1485–1557) enjoys a similar complete set from Cardinall's Musick. Again a mass is found on each disc, filled out with motets: *Missa Videte miraculum* (ASV 131), *Missa Benedicta et venerabilis* (ASV 132), *Missa Christi virgo dilectissima* (ASV 133), and *Missa Lapidaverunt Stephanum* (ASV 140). Two forgotten composers of this period share a set of discs. The Christ Church Cathedral Choir Oxford recorded Thomas Ashwell's *Missa Jesu Christe* and Hugh Aston's *Missa Videte manus meas* (Metronome1030, 2CD). Robert Carver is a Scottish composer of the same period (ca. 1485–ca. 1568). Cappella Nova recorded his complete works, principally masses: *Missa Dum sacrum mysterium* (ASV 124), a *Mass for Six Voices* and *Missa L'homme armé* (ASV 126), and *Missa Fera pessima* with *Missa Pater Creator omnium* (ASV 127).

The leading figure after Taverner was **Thomas Tallis** (q.v.), and Christopher Tye (ca. 1505–ca. 1572) was his exact contemporary. The Oxford Camerata recorded his *Missa Euge bone* (Naxos 550937, with two anthems and two pieces by John Mundy). Other versions of this mass by the Winchester Cathedral Choir (Hyperion 66424) and Cambridge University Chamber Choir (Guild 7121) are less satisfactory. The Choir of New College, Oxford, recorded his "Western Wind" mass (CRD 3405, with four other pieces), but this last mass can best be heard in a Tallis Scholars disc containing Taverner's and Sheppard's masses based on the same tune (Gimell 454927). The Ely Cathedral Choir recorded all three of Tye's masses, useful primarily for including the first recording of the "Peterhouse" Mass (ASV 190, 2CD). Hespèrion XX recorded Tye's complete consort music (Astrée 8708).

From the same period, **John Sheppard** (ca. 1516–ca. 1560) has been recorded extensively. The Sixteen devoted four discs to 11 anthems (Hyperion 66259), *Cantate* Mass (Hyperion 66418, with five anthems), 10 more anthems (Hyperion 66570), and "Western Wind" Mass (Hyperion 66603, with anthems). But for the great responsory *Media vita*, the Tallis Scholars recording is a must (Gimell 454916, with seven other pieces). The Christ Church Cathedral Choir, Oxford, duplicates eleven pieces (Nimbus 5480).

A lesser-known contemporary was **Robert Johnson** (ca. 1500–ca. 1560). Cappella Nova recorded nine of his anthems (ASV 154). Another contemporary, John Merbecke, (ca. 1505–ca. 1585) is best remembered for setting the Book of Common Prayer to music, but Cardinall's Musick recorded his earlier Latin church music (ASV 148). William Mundy (ca. 1530–ca. 1591) is best represented by The Sixteen's collection of his more familiar works (Hyperion 66319). Robert White (ca. 1538–74) wrote two sets of *Lamentations*, the setting for five voices being more familiar. The Tallis Scholars recorded it with six other pieces (Gimell 454930). The last Catholic composer of the Tudor era was William Byrd (q.v.).

SPANISH COMPOSERS

Johannes Cornago (fl. 1455–75), who worked in Aragon and its Neapolitan outpost, wrote *Missa de la mapa mundi*. Paul Hillier led an ensemble in its first recording (Harmonia Mundi 907083). A Spanish school of composition arose with the unification of Castile and Aragon, Juan Anchieta (ca. 1462–1523) being an early example. Dario Tabbia's chorus from Turin sings his *Missa quarti toni* (Bongiovanni 5015, LP, NA, with works of his contemporaries). Francisco de Peñalosa (1470–

1528) was a contemporary. Pro Cantione Antiqua recorded his complete motets (Hyperion 66574), while the Westminster Cathedral Choir presented his *Missa Ave Maria peregrina* and *Missa Nunca fué pena mayor* (Hyperion 66629). Juan del Encina (1486–1529) composed romances and vilancicos, superbly interpreted by Hespèrion XX (Astrée 8707). Mateo Flecha the elder (1481–1553) is best known for *ensaladas*, a sort of burlesque unique to Spain in this period. The Huelgas Ensemble offers three of these works (Sony 46699), while Ensemble Clément Janequin includes two others in a mixed collection of the period (Harmonia Mundi 901627).

Cristobal de Morales (ca. 1500–53) was the leading Spanish composer of his generation, whose work in several cathedrals was interrupted by a decade in Rome. The Westminster Cathedral Choir sings *Missa Quaeramus cum pastoribus* (on Jean Mouton's motet) with notable sympathy for the idiom (Hyperion 66635). The Gabrieli Consort recorded two superb discs, the *Requiem* (Archiv 457597) and *Missa "Mille regretz"* (Archiv 449143). Capella Reial de Catalunya offers an equally fine version of the *Requiem* (Astrée 8765). Juan Vasquez (1500–60) enjoys a disc devoted to his Office of the Dead (RNE 640036). Bartolomeo de Escobedo (1515–63) honored his king in the dedication of *Missa Philippus Rex Hispaniae*. I prefer the a cappella Westminster Cathedral Choir (Hyperion 67046) to a generally fine A Sei Voci version with instruments (Astrée 8640).

Francisco Guerrero (ca. 1527–99) achieved new recognition as his quatercentenary arrived. The Westminster Cathedral Choir recorded *Missa Sancta et immaculata* unaccompanied (Hyperion 66910, with motets) and *Missa de la Batalla escoutez* (on Janequin's famous song) with instruments (Hyperion 67075, with motets). The Choir of the Church of the Advent in Boston recorded this latter mass unaccompanied along with *Missa Simile est regnum caelorum* (Arsis 113). His *Requiem* has been recorded with and without accompaniment. On that basis, I prefer Chapelle du Roi (Signum 17, with *Vespers of All Saints*) to the Orchestra of the Renaissance (Glossa 921402). Capilla Peñaflorida recorded *Missa Puer natus est* (Almaviva 126), Capella Reial de Catalunya recorded 16 *Sacrae Cantiones* (Astrée 8766), while Musica Ficta gave us 10 motets (Cantus 9619).

Alonso Lobo (1555–1617) was Guerrero's pupil. The Tallis Scholars sing all seven motets and *Missa Maria Magdalene* (Gimell 454931). For a collection mostly of Guerrero and Lobo, hear the Westminster Cathedral Choir (Hyperion 66168). The greatest figure of this period was Tomás Luis de Victoria (q.v.).

Instrumental music, especially for vihuela (a lute), flourished as well. Hopkinson Smith plays this instrument in music of Luys de Narvaez (Astrée 8706) and Luys Milan (Astrée 7748), while Savall's ensemble plays music of Diego Ortiz (Astrée 8717). The Milan disc is complemented by his vocal music with Montserrat Figueras accompanied by Smith (Astrée 7777), while the same duo offers music of Alonso Mudarra (Astrée 8533).

Portuguese music blossomed during a 60-year union with Spain. Duarte Lôbo (ca. 1565–1646) wrote *Requiems* for six and eight voices. The Tallis Scholars sing the six-voice work (Gimell 454928, with *Missa Vox clamantis*). The William Byrd Choir sings the earlier eight-voice work (Hyperion 66218, with a mass by Felipe de Magalhães). The Schola Cantorum of Oxford also sings the latter setting (Naxos 550682, with Cardoso's *Requiem*), as does The Sixteen (Collins 14072, with Cardoso's *Missa Regina caeli* and motets).

Manuel Cardoso (1566–1650), in addition to the two couplings cited, can be heard in Herreweghe's recording of *Missa Miserere mihi*

Domine (Harmonia Mundi 901543, with *Magnificat*). The Tallis Scholars also sang his *Requiem* superbly (Gimell 454921, with motets). There are collections of music by these composers and their contemporaries, including those by the Westminster Cathedral Choir (Hyperion 66512), Pro Cantione Antiqua (Hyperion 66715), A Capella Portuguesa (Hyperion 66725), Ars Nova (Naxos 553310) and the Studium Chorale (Globe 5108).   WEBER

Zarzuela

The zarzuela is a popular operetta form indigenous to Spain. It occupies a place in nationalistic music similar to the German Singspiel, the English ballad-opera, and the French comédie while retaining its own individual characteristics. The name is derived from one of King Philip IV's hunting lodges known as "La Zarzuela," situated in a remote area thick with *zarzas* or brambles. It was there the musical form originated with Pedro Calderon de la Barca's "El Laurel de Apollo," with music by Juan de Hidalgo (1657). Although zarzuelas were composed sporadically over a long period of time, it's the second half of the 19th century that's called "The Golden Age of the Zarzuela."

The zarzuela is an exotic mixture of genres: some musical numbers reminiscent of Donizetti and Rossini, some sophisticated dialogue mixed with flashes of flamenco, popular songs, rowdy stories, and low-life comedy. The standard pit orchestra is tricked out with castanets, guitars, lots of hand-clapping, and vocal cries. Some zarzuelas are lengthy works, operatic in scope—the *genéro grande*. Most are brief, one-act farces, the *genéro chico* and *sainete,* telling titillating tales set in the unsavory parts of Madrid.

Some of the more popular composers of "The Golden Age" were Pascual Arrieta, Francisco Asenjo Barbieri, Tomás Bretón, Ruperto Chapí, Manuel Fernando Caballero, Federico Chueca, and Joaquin Valverde. The first half of the 20th century produced immensely popular works by Pablo Sorozabal, Federico Moreno Torroba, José Maria Usandizaga, and Amadeo Vives.

Many of the great Spanish singers—Supervia, de los Angeles, Berganza, Caballé, Carreras, Domingo, Kraus, and Lorengar—have recorded songs from the zarzuelas; some, notably Domingo and Kraus, have recorded complete works as well.

EMI-Hispavox has issued a bargain-priced "La Zarzuela" series with almost thirty works now available. These are classic recordings from the late '40's through the '50s and '60s. Sorozabal and Torroba conduct some of their own works as well as zarzuelas by other composers. The singers are generally excellent with lots of hot-blooded temperament and plenty of passion. Recommended recordings include Barbieri: *El Barbarillo de Lavapiès* (4731); Chapí: *La Revoltosa* (67328); Chueca: *Agua, azucarillos y aguardiente* (67331); Emilio Serrano: *La Dolorosa* (67334); Usandizaga: *Las Golondrinas* (67453); and Vives: *Bohemios* (67322)

BMG is in the process of re-issuing materials from the Alhambra, Columbia, and RCA catalogs from 1950 to the early '70's. Argenta and Frühbeck de Burgos lead some first-rate singers. The original sound was on the dim side and hasn't been improved by the CD transfers. Recommended from BMG are Chapí: *La Bruja* (Alhambra 75125, 2CD); Chueca: *El Chaleco blanco* (Alhambra 74389); Chueca: *La Gran via* (Ariola España 71587); Reveriano Soutullo: *La del Soto del Parral* (Alhambra 71582); and Vives: *Maruxa* (Ariola España 71584, 2CD)

Auvidis Valois is issuing an ongoing series of new recordings of zarzuela classics using some of Spain's best contemporary singers. Domingo is the guiding light here and often a principal performer as well. Some of their better recordings are: Arrieta: *Marina* (4845, 2CD); Tomas Bretón: *La Verbena de la Paloma* (4715; Granados: *Goyescas* (4791); Torroba: *Luisa Fernanda* (4759); and Vives: *Doña Fracisquita* (4710). A compilation of zarzuela songs, "Viva la Zarzuela!," with Bayo, Domingo, Kraus, and Pons, makes an excellent introduction to the genre (4765).

A most interesting addition to the zarzuela discography is a recording of a vibrant 1999 performance at Ohio Light Opera of Breton's *La Verbena de la Paloma* (Albany 405). It's sung in an English translation by Richard Traubner, has plenty of gusto and excitement, and is a good introduction to the genre.   PARSONS

PART III: INSTRUMENTS AND ARTISTS

Brass Instruments

HORN

Period instruments. Descended from such conical objects as conch shells and rams' horns, the horn was for centuries a signalling device used by hunters and postmen. Its first use in a musical setting was in Venetian operas of the 1630s, where it played—surprise!—hunting calls. During the 1680s some fine hornists from Paris were imported to Bohemia, giving rise to the name "French horn" and to a school of outstanding Bohemian players. During the mid-18th Century, Anton Hämpel discovered that by manipulating his hand in the bell of the horn he could make the tone mellow, produce chromatic pitches, and adjust intonation. Once this "hand-horn" technique was perfected, great composers began to write great music for the instrument.

The rowdy sound of the hunting horn is captured in excellent recordings of hunting-horn ensembles led by **Hermann Baumann** (Philips 426301) and **Michael Höltzel** (MD+G 324-0143), while the refined yet variable tone produced by hand-horn technique is heard in recordings by such artists as **Anthony Halstead** (Nimbus 5190) and **Kirsten Thelander** (Crystal 677). A beautiful disc by **Jeffrey Snedeker** (Snedeker 0) demonstrates how some mid-19th century hornists may have used the newly invented valve, combining hand-horn with valve techniques.

Solo horn collections. Few musicians have ever been more highly regarded than **Dennis Brain,** whose life was cut short in an automobile accident in 1957. No collection of great horn recordings should be without his accounts of the Mozart concertos (EMI 56231) or Britten's Serenade for Tenor, Horn, and Strings (with tenor Peter Pears, Pearl 9177). Brain's compact tone was much like those of Poland's prolific recording artist **Zbigniew Zuk** (Zuk 100955 and 310355 are the best of his seven discs) and Australia's **Hector MacDonald** (Tall Poppies 42).

Most of today's premier hornists have a big, dark tone. Perhaps the best is **David Jolley,** whose series of superb recordings includes a collection of French recital pieces (Arabesque 6678) and the jazz-infused horn works of Alec Wilder (Arabesque 6665). **James Sommerville,** principal hornist of the Boston Symphony, made a ravishing recording of the Mozart concertos, one that shows the very interesting results of recent scholarship (CBC 5172). A thrilling all-Strauss disc, recorded in concert by Bavarian Radio Symphony hornist **Johannes Ritzkowsky,** has some of the most incisive piano accompaniment I've heard, by Sawallisch (Arts 47261).

Superb artistry by pianist Friedrich Wilhelm Schnurr also helps to elevate the very personal accounts of works by Schumann, Strauss, Ferdinand Ries, and Rheinberger by **Michael Höltzel** (MD+G 324-0908). The beautiful horn works of Hindemith and Bernhard Heiden are given compelling readings by **Janine Gaboury-Sly** (Mark 1924), while superb horn-soprano recordings have been made by **Gregory Hustis** (Crystal 675) and **Adam Friedrich** (Hungaroton 31585).

Of the many excellent contributions by earlier generations of hornists, I am most fond of a spectacular Weber *Concertino* by **Hermann Baumann** (Phillips 412237), a fiery Beethoven Sonata by **Albert Linder** (BIS 47), and a set of classical concertos by **Tuckwell** (EMI 69395, 2CD).

Horn ensembles. A number of terrific recordings by horn quartets and large horn ensembles have appeared in recent years. The reading of Schumann's *Konzertstück* by the **Berlin Philharmonic Horn Quartet** is

electrifying (Koch-Schwann 311021). Also dazzling is the **American Horn Quartet** (EBS 6008). Hindemith's Horn Quartet fares well in interpretations by the **NFB Horn Quartet** (Crystal 241), **Summit Brass Horns** (Summit 115), and **American Horn Quartet** (EBS 6038). I love the dark, space-filling sound of the large horn ensemble, so I treasure beautiful discs by the **Salzburg Mozarteum Horns** (Koch Schwann 310090 and Koch 1535) and the **German Horn Ensemble** (Koch 1594).

TROMBONE

Period instruments. With a design that dates back at least to the 14th Century sackbut, the trombone is one of the oldest of all instruments. Ideal for accompanying singers and often teamed with the cornetto in ensembles, sackbuts came in sizes ranging from soprano to bass. Not many solo sackbut discs have been made in this era of period-instrument recording. Only one, by **Christian Lindberg** and mezzo-soprano Monica Groop, is truly satisfying (BIS 548). Otherwise, to hear good sackbut playing, listen to groups like **Concerto Palatino** or the **QuintEssential Sackbut and Cornet Ensemble** (see Brass Ensembles).

Solo trombone collections. The trombone world of the past 15 years has been dominated by **Christian Lindberg,** a Swedish virtuoso who may be the greatest trombone soloist who ever lived. His output of recordings is staggering—more than 25 at last count—and nearly all could be recommended here. I'll hold it to four concerto collections (BIS 478, 568, 628, 658), a disc of unaccompanied pieces (BIS 858, which includes exemplary work on alto trombone), and the best of all, "Trombone Odyssey" (BIS 538). This incredible disc includes Jan Sandstrom's *Motorbike Concerto,* one of the most astonishing concertos ever written for *any* instrument. High recommendations also go to three superb discs by **Joseph Alessi,** principal trombonist of the NY Philharmonic. Two are recital collections (Summit 130 and Cala 508), while the third is a stunning account of Rouse's Pulitzer Prize-winning concerto with Alsop and the Colorado Symphony (RCA 68410). Lindberg's reading of that work is also excellent (BIS 788).

Before Lindberg and Alessi, German trombonist **Armin Rosin** and Los Angeles Philharmonic principal **Ralph Sauer** led the field. Sauer's three impeccable LPs are summarized in one fine disc (Crystal 380). Avant-garde techniques and the ability to make sense out of complexity are the strengths of Israeli trombonist **Benny Sluchin** (Adda 581087). Concerto collections by **Warwick Tyrell** (ABC 77000) and **Alain Trudel** (Naxos 553831) and recital collections by **Stanley Clark** (EBS 6023) and Trudel (Amplitude 2015) are outstanding. The best recordings of the Hindemith Sonata, a cornerstone of the trombone literature, are by **Ben Haemhouts** (René Gailly 92024) and **John Kitzman** (Crystal 386). The alto trombone, given prominent roles in Mozart's *Requiem* and symphonies by Beethoven, Schumann, and Mendelssohn, has been the object of renewed interest in recent years. Fine recordings have been made by Lindberg and Trudel (Naxos 553831).

No brass instrument is in greater need of recordings than the bass trombone, and the one by **Blair Bollinger** (d'Note 1033) stands head and shoulders above the rest. Before his came along, the best were LPs with relatively poor acoustics—collections of standard recital literature by **Donald Knaub** and **Jeffrey Reynolds.** A disc of complex, often improvisatory works by **David Taylor** has good sound but is a stretch for most listeners. Some of the best recorded examples of bass trombone playing are by ensemble members **John Rojak** (American Brass Quintet), **Hermann Bäumer** (Triton Trombone Quartet), and **Hans Ströcker** (Vienna Trombone Quartet).

Trombone ensembles. The best trombone-ensemble recordings, showing gorgeous tone and remarkable virtuosity, are by the **Triton Trombone Quartet** (BIS 644, 694, 884) and **Vienna Trombone Quartet** (Camerata 445 and 573). Both groups have a sort of graduated sound that is clear at the top and dark at the bottom, like that of **High Anxiety Bones** (Albany 346). Two fine quartets—**Datura** (Ars Musici 1094 and 1154) and **Rotterdam** (Erasmus 176)—offer more extreme examples of that sound, with very bright high voices. A different concept has four dark, nearly identical tone qualities, as in recordings by the **Summit Trombone Quartet** ("Four of a Kind" is the perfect title for its collection, Summit 123) and **Westphalian Trombone Quartet** (MD&G 324-0094). **Datura** (Ars Musici 1094 and Ars Musici 1154) and **Rotterdam** (Erasmus 176). Few large trombone ensembles have made recordings since the **Eastman Trombone Choir** decades ago. "The London Trombone Sound" is a terrific one, though, with works by Gabrieli, Barber, Brahms, and Eric Clapton, plus a lively arrangement of "76 Trombones"—played by 76 trombonists (Cala 108).

TRUMPET

Period instruments. The earliest trumpets were simple, straight brass tubes with mouthpieces and flared bells. These instruments played the pitches of the overtone series, with large intervals between low notes and small ones between high notes. Eventually, people discovered that melodies were best played on high overtones, that a long tube made more high overtones available, and that coiling the tube made it much easier to hold. Such instruments are now called natural trumpets. Some trumpeters became adept at relatively low-pitched fanfares, while others became the high-note artists for whom Torelli, Corelli, Vivaldi, and Bach wrote exciting sonatas and concertos.

In recent years, several recordings of natural trumpet have been made, the best of them by **Crispian Steele-Perkins** with the period-instrument Tafelmusik (Sony 57365). A well-balanced and in-tune natural-trumpet ensemble like the **Friedemann Immer Trumpet Consort** makes a very impressive sound (Deutsche Harmonia Mundi 77027). Another remarkable recording is by the **Edward Tarr Trumpet Ensemble,** which plays stirring fanfares on 24 beautiful silver trumpets from the King of Portugal's royal trumpet corps (MD+G 3348).

A slightly more advanced instrument is the so-called Baroque trumpet, a natural trumpet with a couple of tone holes added for better intonation. Its leading exponent is the remarkable young Swedish virtuoso **Niklas Eklund,** whose collection of concertos (Naxos 553531) and trumpet-soprano works (Naxos 553735) are gorgeous. Another ancestor of the trumpet is the cornetto (also known as cornett or zink), a leather-covered wooden tube with tone holes—a recorder with a cup mouthpiece. Quite popular in the Renaissance, it produced a sweet tone and was capable of amazing virtuosity. While some fine solo discs have been made by **Doron David Sherwin** and **Jeremy West,** the best cornettist on record is **Bruce Dickey,** leader of the cornetto-sackbut ensemble Concerto Palatino (Accent 8861).

Late in the 19th century, keys were applied to the length of the trumpet, thus enabling its players to produce complete chromatic scales. Although its tone was awful (each pitch had a different tone, and few were resonant), the instrument inspired Haydn, Hummel, and Johann Neruda to compose their wonderful concertos. A few modern recordings have been made on keyed trumpet in recent years, all showing how

bad the instrument sounded. Most interesting is the Haydn Concerto by **Friedemann Immer** (Oiseau Lyre 417610).

Solo trumpet collections. Once the valve was invented in 1813, and once the system of three valves was perfected, a trumpeter could play a chromatic scale with good tone from low to high register. The first successful 19th-century brass instrument was the mellow-voiced cornet, and its leading virtuoso was Jean-Baptiste Arban. The more brilliant-sounding trumpet gained ground early in the 20th century, given a significant boost by the dazzling recordings of Cuban virtuoso **Rafael Méndez.**

The best trumpeters play with flair yet beguile with warm, beautiful tone and deeply expressive phrases. "No Limit," a recent album by the young **Sergei Nakariakov,** includes the most astonishing trumpet playing I have ever heard (Teldec 80651). His performance of Saint-Saëns's *Introduction and Rondo Capriccioso,* a violin showpiece, will leave you agape at his virtuosity, taste, and charm. Also on the disc are a number of cello pieces, beautifully played—at their original pitch—on the mellow-voiced flugelhorn. A previous effort includes wonderful accounts of Mendelssohn's Violin Concerto, Franz Anton Hoffmeister's Viola Concerto, and Haydn's Cello Concerto (Teldec 24276). Only 23 years old when he made this recording, Nakariakov now seems to be in a class of his own.

Gerard Schwarz—now better known as a conductor—made a series of trumpet recordings that show timbral variety, brilliant technique, singing style, and audacious music-making. His Haydn Trumpet Concerto is one of the best of all solo brass recordings (Delos 3001), and his "Cornet Favorites" (with trombonist Ron Barron and pianist William Bolcom) makes corny, old-fashioned pieces sound like great music (Elektra/Nonesuch 79157). Also outstanding are recitals by NY Philharmonic principal **Philip Smith** (Cala 516) and LA Philharmonic principal **Thomas Stevens** (Crystal 761).

Of the many recordings of solo trumpet with organ accompaniment, perhaps the best is by **Bernhard Kratzer** (Fermate 20008). Only **Maurice André,** for decades the world's best-known trumpeter and most prolific recording artist, could make a 4CD set of baroque and classical concertos (EMI 64100). Unusually elegant and even more stylish recordings of that literature have also been made by **John Wallace** (Nimbus 7016), **Reinhold Friedrich** (Capriccio 10-529), **Stephen Burns** (Dorian 80132), **Günther Beetz** (Amati 9104), and **Rolf Smedvig** (Telarc 80227). The modern repertory is presented in spectacular fashion by **Jouko Harjanne** (Finlandia 96868), **Eric Aubier** (ADDA 590027) and **Geoffrey Payne** (ABC 426990).

Trumpet ensembles. Professional-caliber trumpet ensembles are rare and tend to be short-lived. Best-known and still making recordings is the **New York Trumpet Ensemble,** led by Gerard Schwarz in the early 1980s (Delos 3002). The **Paris Trumpet Ensemble** made a recording that showed obvious care and taste (Arion 68195). **Anthony Plog** and Nick Norton put a fine trumpet group together for a Baroque program (Summit 108), while Chicago Symphony principal **Adolph Herseth** was the most famous of the virtuosos heard in "Contrasts for Trumpets" (Doyen 009).

TUBA

For centuries, the lowest voice in the brass family was the bass sackbut, although the more mellow-sounding serpent (a wooden, s-shaped relative of the cornetto) was also in extensive use. Around the turn of the 19th century, not long after key mechanisms revolutionized the trumpet, they were applied to low-pitched instruments, and so the ophicleide, a relatively robust instrument with lousy intonation, was born. A few decades later, after the valve was invented, the tuba was created. It was the first satisfactory bass-voiced brass instrument. Berlioz rescored the ophicleide parts of his *Symphonie Fantastique* for tuba, and Wagner used it in his music dramas.

Still, although the tuba was considered a member of the orchestra by the end of the 19th century, its first concerto was written in 1954 (Vaughan Williams), its first sonata in 1955 (Hindemith). Since then, outstanding performers have made recordings and prodded composers to write for them. William Bell (NY Philharmonic and Indiana University), Harvey Phillips (New York Brass Quintet and Indiana University), John Fletcher (London Symphony and Philip Jones Brass Ensemble), and Roger Bobo (LA Philharmonic) were the most prominent of the pioneers who elevated the instrument's status.

Despite their efforts, the list of solo tuba recordings is not extensive. The reading of Vaughan Williams's Tuba Concerto by **John Fletcher** and the London Symphony is a gem (RCA 60586). **Roger Bobo** has been making spectacular recordings since the 1960s (the best are Crystal 125 and Crystal 690). The Chicago Symphony's **Eugene Pokorny** has the best Hindemith Tuba Sonata on record (Summit 115). A wonderful recording by Norwegian virtuoso **Oystein Baadsvik** (Simax 1101) and an entirely unaccompanied disc by Hungarian tubist **Jozsef Bazsinka** (Hungaroton 31642) have raised tuba-playing standards to their highest levels yet.

EUPHONIUM

Even more rarely recorded than the tuba is the solo euphonium recording. A small cousin of the tuba with an important solo voice in the British-style brass band, the euphonium is a more robust version of the baritone horn and is also known, in orchestral works, as tenor tuba. Most of its chief proponents have roots in the tradition of American armed-forces bands. Like the tuba, the euphonium has a small solo repertory, much of it composed since the mid-'60s and not very good. Aside from a few fine recital pieces, the literature consists of turn-of-the-century virtuoso cornet solos and transcribed music for cello, bassoon, flute, etc.

The traditional sound of the euphonium soloist, which dates back to the days of Simone Mantia and Sousa's Band, is dominated by a very prominent vibrato—a sound that seems odd given the instrument's thick tone. The best recording in that tradition is a collection of old-fashioned pieces by the most famous euphonium soloist in the world today, **Brian Bowman** (Klavier 11060). He has that traditional euphonium vibrato, but it's balanced by a remarkably clean and impressive technique, from-the-heart expressiveness, and a sense of calm assurance. My favorite euphonium recording is by **Mark Fisher** (Albany 162), whose technique, taste, and style make a Bach flute sonata sound wonderful on euphonium. [Editor's note: a recording by the author of this article, **Barry Kilpatrick,** containing compositions written for him by Alec Wilder, John Davison, Walter Hartley, and Hilmar Luckhardt, has been highly praised by critics (Mark 2535).]

Most euphonium-tuba ensembles exist in college music schools, so most recordings are uneven in quality. The best are by **Symphonia** (Mark 1982) and **Gerhard Meinl**'s Tuba Sextet (Angel 54729).

BRASS ENSEMBLES
Period instruments.
Period instruments. Ensembles of cornettos and sackbuts have come a long way since the 1960s, when they were interesting but wobbly and out of tune. Now such groups are as technically accomplished as the best chamber ensembles, and their beautiful sonorities make me wonder why on earth the instruments became obsolete. The cornetto-sackbut ensemble **Concerto Palatino** raised the standard in the early 1990s (Accent 8861). A lovely disc by the **QuintEssential Sackbut and Cornett Ensemble** combines period brasses with strings (Meridian 84367). Perhaps the best period-brass recording to date is "Music for San Rocco 1608," where Paul McCreesh's **Gabrieli Consort** and **Players** blend voices with old instruments to make a stunning case for the genius of Giovanni Gabrieli (Archiv 449180).

Other excellent period brass-with-voices recordings are by **Les Saqueboutiers de Toulouse** (ADDA 581245) and **His Majesties Sackbutts & Cornetts** (Meridian 84096). Music of the American Civil War is the focus of fine recordings by **Americus Brass Band** (Summit 126), **Classical Brass** (MusicMasters 67075), and the **Dodworth Saxhorn Band,** whose collection focuses on the remarkable works of 19th-century New York City-band leader Claudio Grafulla (New World 80556). It's impressive to hear nearly perfect intonation from these supposedly primitive instruments.

Brass quintets. The quintet (two trumpets, horn, trombone, and tuba) became the standard brass chamber medium during the '60s, and many excellent recordings have been made since then. Professional quintets tend to specialize either in transcriptions and pop music or in new works and serious literature. The best of the former are **Canadian Brass** and **Empire Brass.** Canadian, the most famous brass ensemble ever, has made excellent recordings of imaginative arrangements for decades, and recently reaffirmed its stature with a beautiful account of Bach's *Goldberg Variations*. Personnel changes have slowed Empire's recording pace, but its recent foray into the new-age genre is a first among brass groups.

American Brass Quintet is in a class of its own; it's one of the few groups that use bass trombone instead of tuba and is now over 40 years old. Its adherence to serious concert music is encapsulated in "American Brass Quintessence" (Summit 263), but its best recording ever is of new music (Summit 187), and a collection of stirring solo music by Eric Ewazen shows the artistry of its individual members (BMG 63610).

Stockholm Chamber Brass has a great sound and makes a powerful statement with whatever kind of music it plays. Its collections of new music (BIS 544, 699) and of the music of Victor Ewald (BIS 613) are among the best quintet recordings ever made. Another outstanding quintet, **Meridian Arts Ensemble,** is the Kronos Quartet of the brass world. Its recordings mix non-Western influences, new concert works, and arrangements of the music of Frank Zappa. Like Stockholm and American, Meridian has the remarkable ability to make complete sense out of highly complex music (Channel 9496 and 2191)

Three other outstanding recordings are by lesser-known groups. **Center City Brass Quintet,** founded when its members were students at Philadelphia's Curtis Institute, reconstituted itself recently and gave seemingly effortless accounts of some of the medium's most challenging literature (Collins 14892). A collection by the **Wisconsin Brass Quintet** includes a superb reading of John Stevens's *The Seasons*. Finally, exciting new works by Margaret Brouwer and others are presented by the **New Mexico Brass Quintet** (Crystal 563).

Brass choir. The best brass choirs (usually with four trumpets, four horns, four trombones, tuba, and percussion) make truly impressive sounds yet can play delicately too. Those at the professional level tend to assemble only occasionally, so their recordings are often uneven in quality. The most famous of these is a celebration of the music of Giovanni Gabrieli by the combined brass sections of the Cleveland, Philadelphia, and Chicago symphonies (Sony 62353). That was a truly influential recording, but those who want to hear Gabrieli's great music played with greater taste, refinement, and nuance on modern instruments should listen to **Summit Brass** (Summit 101) and the trumpets and trombones of **London Symphony Brass** (Naxos 553873).

The best American brass ensembles on record are **Summit Brass** (Pro Arte 278 and 318, and best of all, Summit 171) and **Burning River Brass** (Dorian 90277). Excellent recordings by a number of elite English groups bear mention, including those by the **Wallace Collection** (Collins 12292, 12272), **London Brass** (Teldec 46442), **London Symphony Brass** (Collins 12882), **London Gabrieli Brass** (Hyperion 66275, 66517), and **London Brass Virtuosi** (Hyperion 66870). Fine efforts are also contributed by the German groups **Frankfurt Radio Symphony Brass** (Capriccio 361) and **Brass Partout** (BIS 1054).

KILPATRICK

Choirs

The legacy of choral music is as wide and rich as the people whose musical aspirations it represents. Something innately profound, a deep, intrinsic spiritual vibrancy resonates loudly when the human voice, gathered *en masse* as if it were some gigantic, all-compassing conduit of God himself, manifests itself in the masterworks of the vocal idiom. There are few emotive efforts that can match a well-trained choir exhibiting all the subtleties the vastly versatile human voice can muster. Every country has its own sense of vocal artistry and accomplishment, many unique, some difficult to penetrate, yet all born of a need to sing, and sing from the heart.

Most major symphony orchestras have a chorus that records only with them, some of them (like the Chicago Symphony Chorus) of great distinction. Other distinguished groups are independent but sing primarily in opera and oratorio performances, like the Monteverdi Choir. They make important contributions to the recordings in which they participate, but won't be discussed further here. I can't give you a guided tour of all the world's vocal music, but I can point out some of the best choral albums to appear in the last few years (all of them recommended), while concentrating primarily on the two countries that have emerged as perhaps the two most brilliantly adept at choral art—England and the United States.

But we must first turn to Russia. Her history of peasant vocalizations and village songs is second to none in profuseness and quality. Nowhere is this captured better than by Anatoly Grindenko and the **Moscow Male Voice Choir** in "Songs of Old Russia." This superb disc flirts with mastery in every bar, a tuneful, wonderful excursion into the heart of Mother Russia (Opus 111 30164). A marvelously sung release by **La Capella Dumka,** the National Choir of Ukraine, treats us to sacred and secular music from that region in an explosively gorgeous soundstage that simply must be sampled (K617 86).

The **Danish National Radio Choir** under Stefan Parkman offers "Nordic Light," a regionally flavored recital that will pique your interest in the choral art of that part of the world (Chandos 9464). There is perhaps no more frequently recorded ensemble than the trusty **Mormon Tabernacle Choir,** yet compared to many of today's color-laden ensembles, they can appear a bit staid and bland. You can sample them best in one of their patriotic, heart-on-sleeve performances like "God Bless America" (Columbia 6721).

The English are second to none in their choral tradition, believed by many to be the finest in the world. Their sounds are cool and clear, highly delineated, white-toned, and often marked by the inclusion of boys, a tradition that has been challenged somewhat successfully in recent years but one I hope will never disappear. The **Tallis Scholars** directed by Peter Philips have made many worldwide tours, spreading the gospel of carefully prepared, flawlessly executed programs that give many their first palatable taste of early choral music. Among the most delicious of their recordings is "Western Wind Masses," a recital of Tavener, Christopher Tye, and John Sheppard in a well-filled CD that is an exemplary example of their art (Gimell 27).

One of the most brilliant and perspicacious of recent discs is "Mexican Polyphony" by James O'Donnell and his **Westminster Cathedral Choir,** a surprisingly complex and beautiful disc of composers we never knew about but who were just as proficient as their European counterparts (Hyperion 66330). Two English composers, Holst and Vaughan Williams, are given affable readings of various shorter choral works in a program by the **Finzi Singers** under Paul Spicer. The unity and harmonic beauty of this group are something to hear (Chandos 9425).

When you speak of the **King's Singers,** you speak of an ensemble that has a recorded history of excellence second to none. With a range extending from the early classics to the most modern pop songs (always made to sound like classics in their sterling arrangements), this group is tough to beat for sheer musicality. But stick with one of their non-instrumental recordings, unaccompanied voices being the preferred way to sample their work. "Watching the White Wheat: Folksongs of the British Isles" is a demonstration disc of native gems given by the native boys—it's superb! (EMI 47506). "All at once well met: English Madrigals" is as good as you'll ever hear for these much-performed, time-honored jewels (EMI 49265). And for a little spice, be sure to pick up "The Beatles Connection," 19 songs by the Fab Four sung in a more fab fashion than they ever imagined (EMI 49556).

Christophers and **The Sixteen** are another bunch of trend-setters; you could pick a recording blindfolded and come up a winner. But nothing they've done in their illustrious career ranks as highly as the five disc series of "Music from the Eton Choirbook." This unbelievably varied, stunningly conceived project contains some of the most spiritual, wondrous music to ever reach the eardrums. I must list them, in volume order: "The Rose and the Ostrich Feather" (Collins 13142), "The Crown of Thorns" (Collins 13162), "The Pillars of Eternity" (Collins 13422), "The Flower of All Virginity" (Collins 13952), and "The Voices of Angels" (Collins 14622).

For big-band English processional anthems at their very best, try to track down "Jerusalem," a compendium of works by Parry, Stanford, and Elgar that will rock your house with the volume turned up. The **Winchester Cathedral Choir** directed by David Hill do the honors in this sumptuously recorded disc (Argo 430836). Rutter and his for-recording-purposes-only **Cambridge Singers** have entertained us with many discs spanning a great volume of music in all styles, including Rutter's own considerably popular idiom. If you feel confused, you can always just dive in; chances are you won't be disappointed. But for an only slightly more informed option, try either "Faire is the Heaven," a collection of English church music from the Latin Rite to the Reformation, landing squarely on the Anglican Revival of the 20th century (Collegium 107), or a wonderful sampler that takes up the best of the best: "A Portrait of the Cambridge Singers" (Collegium 500).

I would be remiss if I didn't mention at least one album by the always reliable **King's College Choir.** Out of hundreds of discs over the years, a collection of music by the "God Squad" (Pärt, Tavener, Górecki) called "Ikos" stands out as one of the best of the best, a true tribute to their traditional and traditionally superb art (EMI 55096). "Be Still My Soul: The

Ultimate Hymns Collection" is just that—all your favorites sung in the classic English manner by a variety of classic English choirs. The beauty of these pieces is timeless, and you will find no better collection (Decca 452212).

America, as the child of Britain and inheritor of the finest choral tradition in the world, has more choruses—amateur and professional—than any other country, and we take to singing the time-honored classics of the motherland as well as our own uniquely styled compositions, the equal of any. Despite the name **His Majestie's Clerkes,** this Chicago-based ensemble is able to sing Vaughan Williams's *Mass in G,* Stanford's three Motets, and Parry's soulful *Songs of Farewell* as well as any counterpart from across the Atlantic, though to be fair, the group has a close connection to English luminaries like Willcocks and Preston (Cedille 36). The album is appropriately called "Hear My Prayer." In recent years the well blended, tonally keen **Kansas City Chorale** under Charles Bruffy has been making a few but well-received discs of Americana that are stunningly presented. "Fern Hill" is a classic example of modern yet traditionally grounded compositions by composers like Corigliano, Jean Belmont, Barber, and James Mulholland. The singing is full of Midwestern clarity and vigor (Nimbus 5449).

The greatest contribution America has made to the repertory, and the most unique, is its early psalmody and folk hymns. Luminaries like William Billings, M. Keys, and Amos Bull adorn "Make a Joyful Noise—Mainstream and Backwaters of American Psalmody" by the **Oregon State University Choir** directed by Ron Jeffers. You wouldn't think Oregon would be in the forefront in interpreting this music, but their chorus is fully involved (New World 80255). For a touch of the genuinely authentic, with rugged vocal choruses and spirited music making, it's hard to top "Rivers of Delight, American Folk Hymns from the Sacred Harp Tradition." Sacred harp or shaped-note singing had its beginnings in congregational New England, but over time migrated to the South, still a bastion of its preservation. The **Word of Mouth Chorus** is delightful, and you'll want to hear this again and again (Nonesuch 71360).

No one did as much for American music as Gregg Smith and his **Gregg Smith Singers,** and their "America Sings: The Founding Years," despite the rather sun-glare bright sound, is not to be missed. Covering music from the *Ainsworth* and *Bay Psalters,* the sacred and secular music of the Revolutionary period, 18th-century American tune books, and—best of all—music of the American Moravians, this disc is a one-of-a-kind insight into the kind of scholarship and commitment only Smith could bring to the table. Don't miss this, and at about 10 dollars for two CDs, who would want to? (Vox 5080, 2CD).

Joel Cohen and his **Boston Camerata** have been doing yeoman work for many years trying to bring the riches of a forgotten past to a slowly awakening American public. His "American Vocalist" is based on a book of the same name surviving in the American Northeast, and the selections of hymns and tunes couldn't be better (Erato 45818). Entering the rarefied world of American spirituals—is there anything like it anywhere else?—Cohen again solidifies his reputation with "Trav'ling Home: American Spirituals 1770–1870." His recreations are heartfelt and breezily honest (Erato 12711).

Not to be outdone, and dressed in a more modern guise—though hardly any less beautiful—is Shaw's "Amazing Grace," a collection of 20 hymns and spirituals guaranteed to lift your spirits (Teldec 80325). The **Robert Shaw Festival Singers,** a handpicked group that personified the conductor's choral excellence, sings these pieces like Palestrina. Choosing among Shaw discs is like fishing for catfish in a fully stocked pond, whether sea shanties or Irish songs, but two of his later discs stand out

as must-haves. "Evocation of the Spirit," a collection of works by Gorecki, Pärt, Barber, Martin, and Schoenberg, gives some of the finest performances these works have ever had, in spectacular sound (Telarc 80406). "Appear and Inspire" shows the versatility of Shaw's ensemble in Britten, Debussy, Ravel, Poulenc, Henk Badings, and Argento. Again, the readings are as good as can be imagined (Telarc 80408).

The **National Gallery Vocal Arts Ensemble** demonstrates how versatile an American group can be with "Four Centuries of Vocal Music." Ranging from the 1550s to spirituals, this 5-voice ensemble gives us a very well executed, vocally nimble recital that is a demonstration sampler of some wonderful music (Koch 7038). The **Harvard University Choir** engages us emotionally and artistically in a wonderful disc of New England choral chestnuts ranging from the "Old Hundredth" psalm to "Arise, Shine!" by Rorem. This recording is superb in all respects, sensitively sung while eliciting a wave of emotion (Northeastern 247). One of the best choral recordings of the last 10 years emerged from **Musica Sacra** in a fabulous recording from St. John the Divine in New York City. The resonant, radiant music of Strauss, Schoenberg, Bruckner, Scarlatti, and Gabrieli, just to name some of its contents, has never sounded more glorious, and the singing is beyond compare (RCA 60970).

"Radiant Light: Songs for the Millennium" offers, among others, "Song for Athene" by Tavener (which achieved instant worldwide fame as the exit processional at Princess Diana's funeral), the sublime "Ave Maria" by Franz Biebl, and Thompson's "Alleluia," in bold, emotive fashion by the **Trinity Choir** in Boston. Brian Jones is the wizard behind the mastery, and the sonics are some of the widest and deepest on disc; you'll be calling it one of the best things you've ever heard (Dorian 93191). **Chanticleer** has been offering sparkling, integrated recitals for 20 years, and to choose one over the others almost seems like an insult. But "Colors of Love," with contemporary music by Steven Stucky, Tavener, Zhou Long, Chen Yi, Steven Sametz, and Augusta Read Thomas is a milestone in recorded art. To present admittedly modern but not inaccessible works in such an attractive format and so sympathetically rendered is a true victory for modern choral music. This is some of their finest work (Teldec 24570).

The **Ambrosian Singers** are a group that has been around for years and made some stunning recordings (though few spotlighting only themselves). One of the best ways to hear them in action is to listen to the album of spirituals they made with the wonderful Jessye Norman (Philips 416462), or for a stroll down memory lane, listen to their marvelous *Messiah* with Mackerras (EMI 62748). Finer singing is hard to come by. **La Chapelle Royal** under the indomitable Herreweghe has created a number of superb albums, yet few featuring themselves. For a great sampling of their art, try the album of music by Josquin, truly a fine example of quality singing (Harmonia Mundi 901243). It wouldn't be out of line to expect Stephen Darlington and **Christ Church Cathedral Choir** to perform well in musical staples performed for the Oxford chapel over a number of years; this is magnificent testimony to the sublimity of their art, and a darned good listen (Nimbus 5440).

Jacobs and **Concerto Vocale** have been making great music together for a number of years, as their many albums testify. For an off-the-wall yet beautiful choice, listen to Buxtehude's *Membra Jesu Nostri,* an extraordinary work that showcases this choir to the fullest (Harmonia Mundi 901333). The airy, haunting sound of the **Corydon Singers** under Best is one of the most distinguishable sounds on record today. Almost any choice is a good one, but for me their Bruckner Mass in F minor will always be something special (Hyperion 66599). The **Deller Consort** has been involved in an uncountable number of recording projects over the years, with a style all their own, though somewhat dated if we listen attentively to the older recordings. But this is a group that simply must be sampled, and one of the ways to do so is to get their set of Gregorian Chant. It isn't authentic by any means, but it's never been done more splendidly (Harmonia Mundi 190235, 2CD).

Lovers of the sound of San Marco Cathedral will cherish a chronological survey of music from the time of Gabrieli by Elizabeth Patterson and **Gloriae Dei Cantores;** you won't find a sweeter sounding choir (Paraclete 015). The **Hilliard Ensemble** is another American group that has achieved a worldwide reputation. An unusual, completely modern "Hilliard Songbook" contains song cycles and choral pieces by composers as diverse as James MacMillan and Morton Feldman; it's a must for aficionados of the modern choral scene (ECM 453259).

For a Dutch look at English choral music, you can hardly do better than the album by the **Netherlands Chamber Choir** under John Alldis. Their fresh, clean, stark, but still colorful sound suits classics by Vaughan Williams, Howells, Holst, Britten, and David Bedford to a T (Globe 5179). "Early One Morning," a delightful album of folk music from the 13th century to the present, is gloriously rendered by the **New College Choir** of Oxford under Edward Higgenbottom. Though those seeking more pristine versions of these works may wish to look elsewhere, others who appreciate fine choral arranging as an art unto itself will be entranced by these lovelies (Erato 19065). Jeremy Summerly and the **Oxford Camerata** have received mixed reviews, and there is some truth in the accusations of thin ensemble, less than stellar singing, and stylistic inconsistencies. But I said *some* truth—for while this group may fail to compete in the big leagues, the amount of repertory they cover for the price is unbeatable, especially if you're just sampling some obscure music. That's why "Renaissance Masterpieces" is such an attractive disc; you get Josquin, Ockheghem, Morales, Lassus, Palestrina, et al., at a very low price. If you don't like it, no harm, no foul. The singing is excellent (Naxos 550843).

The Holy Week music and *Requiem* by Lassus have never had more radiant performances than those given by **Pro Cantione Antiqua.** To add frosting to the cake, it's offered as a spectacular two-fer in peerless sound (Hyperion 22012, 2CD). The **St. John's College Choir** folks from Cambridge have been making a big splash for many years, and if you want to see what the fuss is all about, go out and buy "Set Me as a Seal Upon Thine Heart." This miscellany of 20th-century choral masterpieces is a wonderful introduction to artistry that needs no introduction (Lindenberg 55).

The medieval chant meisters **Sequentia** have made a killing in our artificially meditative world, but their pseudo-serious "Ancient Music for a Modern Age" has much to recommend it, including unity and purposefulness of ensemble (RCA 61868). You may want to investigate their many other recordings if this one appeals. Andrew Parrott's **Taverner Consort** has made many excellent recordings, but none so exquisitely beautiful as "Latin Church Music by Tallis." This was originally in two volumes, so we should be glad that Vol. 1 is available. Grab it while it lasts, it's that good, and if you come upon Vol. 2, know you are truly blessed (EMI 49555). The richly varied collection of choral pieces called "Glorious Trinity" from the **Trinity College Choir** under Richard Marlow is only one of many discs by this ensemble worth your hard-earned dollars (Conifer 15355).

It's difficult to know where to begin when speaking of the **Vienna Boys Choir,** perhaps the most prolifically recorded choir of all time. So let's start with the obvious: No collection of choral music is complete without this group singing Strauss, and a disc called "Strauss Celebra-

tion" will fill the need quite nicely (Koch 340392). "Panis Angelicus" is a wonderful collection of many different religious styles by composers of differing times and places. Finally, discs by the U.S. women who have fashioned themselves into a cohesive, white-toned wonder called **Anonymous 4** have been selling like hotcakes. Leaving aside the question of how authentic an ensemble like this is, you can't deny the musicality and commitment of these talented singers. Their first album, "An English Ladymass," is still one of their best (Harmonia Mundi 907080).

RITTER

Guitar and Lute

GUITAR

The modern classical guitar (the kind used by recording players) has hardly changed in physical dimensions from the design of a late 19th century Spanish maker, Antonio Torres: the familiar figure-eight body shape, simple decorative design and 6 individual strings. This was, however, a considerably different instrument from the one used for nearly 300 years prior to that time.

The 16th-century guitar had only four strings, each a pair tuned in octaves (the pair called a "course"), and a much smaller and more elongated body, with simple design details. The early 17th century found the addition of a new bass course, giving the instrument more range; the instruments were also extremely ornate in design, with elaborate inlays everywhere, consistent with their new standing as favorites of the nobility (Louis XIV employed two of the more famous composer/players of his day). The 18th century, when the instrument almost died out in popularity, was also a period of experimentation, with makers (including Stradivarius) trying six courses, single strings, and combinations of the two.

Single strings won out in the 19th century, though body size remained small until Torres, and a "nonornate" design (like that of other stringed instruments) prevailed. Greater numbers of strings were tried by players like Coste and Mertz but didn't catch on; if fact the increasingly difficult music and limited volume of the instruments again drove the guitar's standing down until the advent of players like Segovia (in Europe and America) and Barrios (in South America). Modern guitar makers (now all over the world, not just in Spain) continue to experiment with design and materials to increase the instrument's range, playability and volume. And there remain some players still intrigued by the possibilities of greater numbers of strings: the late Narciso Yepes pioneered the 10-string, and currently two of the most impressive players, Stephan Schmidt and Paul Galbraith, play 10- and 8-string guitars, respectively (Galbraith holding his like a cello, with an endpin, too!).

Individual artists

Let's begin with the three most important modern guitarists, go on to their better-known successors, and conclude with a brief alphabetical list of others worth your attention.

Andrés Segovia (1893–1987). His early HMV recordings from 1927–39 reveal startlingly fleet fingers coupled with an expressiveness that, despite occasional banal lapses, is very endearing; his artistry is so sincere we're inclined to forgive his indulgences and "wrong" Baroque performance practices. I prefer Vol. 1 of these reissues (EMI 61048), which includes 18th and 19th century pieces by Bach, Weiss (actually a Ponce counterfeit), Mendelssohn, Sor, and others. Segovia's romanticism, plus a more mature playing style and sound (modern recording on nylon—not gut—strings) work to great effect for many pieces included in "The Romantic Guitar," Vol. 9 of "The Segovia Collection" (MCA 110281); and for many of his most frequently performed concert pieces, such as *Leyenda* and *Sevilla* by Albéniz, Granados's *Tonadilla*, and several etudes by Sor, look for Vol. 3, "My Favorite Works" (MCA 42069).

Julian Bream. Beginning in the mid-'50s, Bream began to redefine the sensibility of the classical guitar. Suddenly there was a player with a technique equal to (or better than) Segovia and a distinctive voice; he could invest the standard Segovia repertoire with new life, and his predilection for a more modern repertoire truly brought the guitar to a par with other instruments. Bream's almost continual use of tone-color nuances in his phrasing lends an orchestral quality to his playing, and his musical perceptions are always very clear; at his best he's a great musical communicator, at his worst he threatens to parody himself.

Several CDs from RCA's "Julian Bream Edition" stand out. "Popular Classics for the Spanish Guitar" (61591) has a mixture of lively and accessible works by Villa-Lobos, Falla, Giuliani, and others, recorded in the earlier '60s. His intense expressiveness and dark sound are very satisfying in "Baroque Guitar" (61592) with music by Frescobaldi, Bach, Scarlatti and others. And for sheer involvement and authority, few players can top him when dealing with "Twentieth-Century Guitar"; Vol. 1 (61595) contains great recordings from 1959 to 1973 of pieces by Roussel, Berkeley, Martin, Henze and Walton. His landmark recording of Britten's *Nocturnal* (probably the greatest piece of music ever written for guitar) is, oddly, found in Vol. 18, "Music for Voice and Guitar" by Britten, Walton and Mátyás Seiber. Excellent examples of his playing from the last 20 years can be found in Vol. 27, "Guitarra: The Guitar in Spain" (61610), with music from 1540 to 1930, featuring his recent taste for period instruments for the earlier music. Bream is also a great lutenist (although not always historically accurate in his technique), so look for Vol. 3, "Dances of Dowland" (61586).

John Williams (b. 1942). Following on the heels of Bream's accomplishments by a few years was this gifted British Segovia pupil (not to be confused with the American conductor and film music composer with the same name). Williams took Bream's technical precision to an even higher level, attaining a pianistic sweep to his playing (both he and Bream had to enter the Royal College of Music as pianists, since guitar wasn't a major). Though his expressive style is less distinctive than Bream's, he is perhaps more musically direct, his interpretations offering an elegance and fire less affected by guitaristic tricks. His non-self-indulgent style and superb technique were particularly influential on the newest generation of players.

Williams's interpretations in "Spanish Guitar Favorites" smooth out Segovia's rough edges and add a new level of excitement with their technical aplomb (CBS 44794). Several of my favorite recordings from the late '60s and early '70s are reissued in "Guitar Recital," an "Essential Classics" disc including an awesome first-time-on-guitar rendering of Paganini's *Caprice 24*, five Scarlatti sonatas, and Villa-Lobos's popular Preludes (Sony 62425). His great first recording of Bach's *Chaconne* isn't on CD (look for "Virtuoso Variations," a Columbia LP), but in the '80s he rerecorded it in "The Baroque Album," with more mature pacing and a surprise in the arrangement at the end, and the Scarlatti sonatas plus an assortment of pieces by others, (Sony 44518).

An excellent example of his recent concert repertoire and sound (he switched in the '80s from a Spanish-made instrument to an Australian one) is found in "The Seville Concert," its highlights including a variety of fascinating works ranging from Bach to Nikita Koshkin (Sony 53359, also available as a video). Williams also offers the best compilation of guitar concertos (Sony 44791). I will always enjoy his versions of Bach's

Lute Suites (Sony 42204), although he has been eclipsed in style by newer players.

Manuel Barrueco. In the late '70s three players emerged as the best of the next generation; they all record now for major labels, each with their own distinctive sound and approach: Barrueco, Fisk, and Isbin. Barrueco is noted for his crisp rhythms, elegant phrasing, and razor-sharp technique; his exciting playing often seems to be on the edge of exploding. His first few LPs have been reissued as "300 Years of Guitar Masterpieces," offering stunning playing of the standard repertoire; in the Spanish music his playing is notably free of guitar gimmicks, reminding me more of de Larrocha than Segovia (Vox-Turnabout 3007). His albums for EMI are thematic, often centered around a pair of composers. My favorites: Mozart and Sor (749368), Albéniz and Turina (754382), and Leo Brouwer, Villa-Lobos and Julian Orbón (566576). His recent "Cantos y Danzas" (556578) is devoted to accessible South American pieces plus excellent performances with flutist Emmanuel Pahud (Piazzolla's *Histoire du Tango*) and soprano Barbara Hendricks (the "Aria" from Villa-Lobos's *Bachianas Brasilieras 5*).

Eliot Fisk. If Barrueco is Apollonian, then Fisk is Dionysian. His extravagant technique often seems to defy physics, and his interpretive style is nearly as extroverted as Bream's, with a personal quality reminiscent of his mentor, Segovia. While his live performances are truly jaw-dropping, his recordings for MusicMasters add a layer of structural interest in their often symmetrically structured programs. A Fisk concert has to have some newly transcribed Scarlatti and Paganini, and "Für Eliot" couples them with selections by Ponce and Frank Martin (his wonderful *Quatre Pièces Brèves* with alterations from the unpublished manuscript) and the title piece by Relly Raffman (1008). "Guitar Fantasies" (60169F) runs the historical gamut from Renaissance to modern, mixing familiar with new, and "Bell'Italia" (67079) ranges almost as widely. All of these are very absorbing discs, for the mind as well as the adrenal glands—and Fisk is responsible for one of the most amazing transcription and playing feats ever: all 24 of Paganini's *Caprices* in their original keys! (67092)

Sharon Isbin falls somewhere between Fisk and Barrueco in style. Her technique is cutting-edge without the bombast; her musicianship is tasteful but leans toward the romantic—except for Bach, where she has created new versions of the four Lute Suites with pianist/scholar Rosalyn Tureck, employing state-of-the-art ornamentation (Virgin 790717). "Road to the Sun: Latin Romances for Guitar" (Virgin 59591) features Spanish and South American pieces. Isbin's commitment to modern music (she has premiered several concertos) is demonstrated with good variety in "Nightshade Rounds" (Virgin 45024). If you can find it, I still treasure the playing (and program) in Vol. 2 of her two debut LPs for Sound Environment (1013): Britten's *Nocturnal,* Brouwer's *Eternal Spiral,* and Bach's Lute Suite 1. Her recent Teldec albums of South American pieces and folk-inspired music have a somewhat "crossover" style that she does well, though I prefer her more serious classical discs.

Norbert Kraft, from Canada, plays with disarming ease and tonal beauty and offers refreshingly musical interpretations (and new transcriptions, for those interested) of very familiar repertoire (Albeniz, Agustin Barrios, Federico Morena Torroba, Turina,, Villa-Lobos, etc.) in "Guitar Favorites," a great meet-the-classical guitar sampling (Naxos 55399).

Christopher Parkening. In the early '70s the American Parkening made a debut that for a few years catapulted him to the ranks of Bream and Williams. His career soon sputtered, and in its revival it has become clear his main talent was in duplicating many of Segovia's tonal and interpretive trademarks with, as it were, an airbrush covering his imperfections. However, his first album, "In the Spanish Style" is a totally enticing sample of his talent: short, Segovia-repertoire Spanish and South American encore pieces lovingly and beautifully played (Angel 747194).

David Russell. Lately the pendulum has shifted away from the pyrotechnics of Fisk and Yamashita to a more subtle virtuosity, where even difficult music sounds effortless. A wonderful player of this persuasion is this Scottish guitarist, who combines the tone of Parkening and technical clarity of Barrueco with a warmth and innate musicality of his own. I particularly recommend his Teldec discs: all Barrios (80373), all Torroba (80451) and Celtic music (80492).

Stephan Schmidt. Look for his superb all-Scarlatti (Astrée) and all-Bach (Naive) discs, the latter utilizing a 10-string instrument with an extended lower range making it possible for him to play the Lute Suites in their original keys.

Göran Söllscher (violinist Gil Shaham's duo partner) tosses off an album of sophisticated and artful Beatles arrangements (his own and those of Takemitsu and others) in "Here, There and Everywhere" (DG 447104), my favorite crossover classical guitar disc.

Kazuhito Yamashita. You should also have at least one example of the larger-than-life playing of Yamashita, whose claim to fame, beyond his phenomenal technique and huge expressive range, will always be his transcriptions of complete orchestral works (and big ones at that). His RCA LPs haven't been issued on CD; they include an amazingly convincing version of *Pictures at an Exhibition* (4203), Dvořák's "New World" Symphony and Stravinsky's *Firebird* (7929), and he even manages Rimsky-Korsakov's *Scheherazade* in duet with his sister Naoko (6777). His Bach recordings are also controversial (Crown Classics), some movements startlingly profound and others marred by a virtuosity almost out of control—but amazingly so. For great playing of tough guitar music I recommend his inspired version of Castelnuovo-Tedesco's seldom tackled *Caprichos de Goya* (Crown Classics 8006).

Among the other big names of the classical guitar concert world, a collection would be well filled out with some recordings by the late **Narciso Yepes** (look for two discs of "Guitarra Espanola" DG), either **Pepe** (Phillips) or **Angel Romero** (EMI/Angel), and perhaps **Alirio Diaz.** Unfortunately, many of these players are inconsistent in their quality. Yepes can be downright unmusical in his pedantic interpretations of some pieces (Alonso Mudarra's Fantasia 10 or Albeniz's *Torre Bermeja*) yet stunning—musically and technically—in other pieces (Sor's Etude Op. 29:14, or Falla's *Cancion del fuego fatuo*). Similarly, while the Romero brothers' technique never fails to deliver, their interpretations and choice of repertoire often do. However, while Diaz never fulfilled the promise of his "Masterpieces of the Spanish Guitar" (Vanguard OVC 5004), it's a treasure of superb Segovia-style playing and repertoire.

Period instruments. Several performers have made recordings on period instruments or replicas thereof. With the guitar this can vary from the lutelike vihuela of Spain's Renaissance to the 5-course (five double strings) Baroque guitar to the smaller and more intimate-sounding 19th century guitar (with the modern guitar's six single strings). **Bream** brings the virtuoso touch to replica instruments of the Renaissance and Baroque in "La Guitarra" (RCA 61610). **Nigel North** is less dazzling but more thorough in his exploration in "Guitar Collection," using instruments from the 17th to 19th centuries, including some favorites by Mudarra, Sor and Giuliani plus two keyboard-guitar duets (Amon Ra 18).

Duos and ensembles

Duos. Although the first important guitar duo was **Ida Presti** and **Alexandre La Goya,** their recordings don't hold up well. Much more satisfying, though their precision wasn't absolutely flawless, was the partnership of **Bream** and **Williams** in LPs from the early '70s and 1978; the reissues are very listenable, my favorite being "Together Again" with music by Granados, Albéniz, and others and three famous piano pieces by Debussy (RCA 61452). The best current duo is the brothers **Sergio** and **Odair Assad.** Their precision and technique are breathtaking, with musicality to match in a disc of Baroque keyboard music (Elektra/Nonesuch 979292).

Ensembles. Several multiguitar ensembles (trios and quartets) currently exist, but the most important and impressive so far is the **Los Angeles Guitar Quartet.** They're very successful at arranging and playing piano and orchestral music (look for "Evening in Granada," which includes Falla's complete *El Amor Brujo* and Rimsky-Korsakov's *Capriccio Espagnol* plus the title piece by Debussy). But they're most distinctive with their unique repertoire of new compositions (often by their own Andrew York) and jazz, folk or world music arrangements; try "Labyrinth," with the title piece by Ian Krouse based on a Led Zeppelin song and works by Copland and Count Basie (Delos 3163). You'll also encounter some very impressive ensemble work from the **Amsterdam Guitar Trio,** including excellent versions of Vivaldi's "Four Seasons" and some of the Brandenburg Concertos (RCA).

Guitar with other instruments. The most common and effective instrument to pair with the guitar is the flute, and there are many fine duo recordings available. **Galway** chose Yamashita (several decades his junior) to partner him in an "Italian Serenade" disc that rates highly (RCA). For a more representative program I recommend "Two American Virtuosi" by **Carol Wincenc** and Fisk (who subsequently switched partners to Paula Robison), a fine album with Giuliani's often-played Sonata Op. 85 and short pieces by Ravel, Poulenc, Milhaud and Bartók (MHS 4969). For violin and guitar duos, try a recent all-Paganini disc by **Shaham** and Söllscher (DG) or **Perlman** and Williams playing Paganini and Giuliani (an LP from the '70s reissued by Sony).

LUTE

Like the harpsichord, the lute has returned as a concertizing instrument; unlike the harpsichord, it hasn't attracted new compositions. There are a small number of excellent players, and the plucked or fretted string record collection could also include an assortment of lute recordings. The Renaissance lute is somewhat different from the Baroque: the earlier instrument had about as many strings as the guitar and was tuned similarly; the later one had many more strings (some of which are only plucked, not fretted) and a completely different tuning. The greater difficulty of the Baroque lute's features accounted for its demise.

The best music for the Renaissance lute are the fantasias of Francesco da Milano (mid-16th century) and the compositions (dances and fantasias) of Dowland (early 1600s.). In 16th century Spain, lute-style music was composed for a guitar-shaped instrument called the "vihuela"; it, too, enjoys a minor comeback today.

Today's leading Renaissance lutenist (also branching out to Baroque guitar) is **Paul O'Dette,** and any of his Dowland recordings (of the complete works) are heartily recommended (Harmonia Mundi). He also offers an excellent disc of Vivaldi concertos (including the often-played

"Guitar" Concerto) and trios for lute, with The Parley of Instruments led by Roy Goodman (Hyperion). For Italian repertoire, look for his "Dolcissima Et Amorosa" (Harmonia Mundi). **Lutz Kirchhof** offers a fine assortment of Renaissance lute music taken from Robert Dowland's "Varietie of Lute Lessons" (RCA/Seon 71967). His specialty, though, is the Baroque lute and he has double CDs of music by the two main composers for that instrument, Bach and Weiss (Sony/Vivarte).

Among the other best recording lutenists to look for (some albums specializing in one composer, but more typically presenting an assortment within a style or period) are **Hopkinson Smith** (Astree), **Nigel North** (Linn), **Konrad Junghänel** (Deutsche harmonia Mundi) and **Ronn McFarlane** (Dorian).   DINGER

Harp

The harp has been an important instrument since ancient times. Harp-like instruments have been found in the burial chambers of Ur in Mesopotamia, and large harps have been found in Greece, China, and Egypt. By the 14th century it was extremely popular in Ireland, but it declined in popularity after Queen Elizabeth, who considered harps instruments of rebellion, issued a proclamation to "Hang harpers wherever found and destroy their instruments." In the middle of the 17th century Cromwell furthered the instrument's demise by burning 500 harps in Dublin.

Luckily lute makers in continental Europe considered the harp worth saving. Until the middle of the 17th century all harps were diatonic (they could only play in one key), but then Austrian harps began to appear with tuning hooks along their necks. In 1720 Jacob of Donauworth created a pedal mechanism to operate the hooks, so the hands of the harpist were free. The pedals shortened the length of the strings half a step, allowing some chromatic flexibility, producing an instrument referred to as the single action pedal harp. In 1810 the harp achieved complete chromatic flexibility when Sebastian Erard developed the double action pedal harp with seven pedals (one for each set of strings for a given diatonic pitch) that have three positions: flat, natural, and sharp. There have been improvements in construction and changes in style, but this system of pedals has remained pretty much the same.

Around the turn of the century there were two dominant styles of harp playing in America, those of Carlos Salzedo (1885–1961) and Marcel Grandjany (1891–1975). Both studied in Paris with the same teacher, Alphonse Hasselmans, and both came to the US to teach. Harpists used to play in either the Salzedo or the Grandjany style, but now they strive for the best qualities of both, with musicianship as their main goal. Unfortunately there are no recordings by Salzedo on CD, but **Grandjany** can be heard playing Debussy, Ravel, and Handel with the Budapest String Quartet (Bridge 9077). He also recorded some of the same music with the Hollywood String Quartet (Seraphim 60142, LP), but it hasn't yet been released on CD.

Because Salzedo and Grandjany both taught in the US, some of the finest harpists now making recordings are American. **Nancy Allen,** principal of the NY Philharmonic, studied at Juilliard with Grandjany, began her career by winning the Israel Harp Competition in 1973, and has made many excellent recordings. They include Ginastera's Harp Concerto (ASV 654; MHS 513274T) and a solo disc called "A Celebration for Harp" that includes music by French Baroque composers, Bach, and Prokofiev. Allen also recorded Louis-François Dauprat's Sonata and a transcription of Satie's *Gnossiennes* with horn player David Jolley (Arabesque 6678).

Nancy Allen's sister **Barbara Allen,** who plays a good deal of con-

temporary music, recorded Druckman's *Divertimento* (New York Philomusica 30005) and music by Griffes with the Perspectives Ensemble (Newport 85634). She also recorded chamber music by Ravel, Fauré, and Ibert with the Auréole Trio (Koch 7102) and music by Harald Genzmer, Nielsen, and Gubaidulina (Koch 7055).

Yolanda Kondanasis, the first harpist to win the Ima Hogg National Artists Competition and the Darius Milhaud prize, now teaches at Cleveland Institute of Music and Oberlin. Her recordings include Vivaldi's "Four Seasons" in transcription (Telarc 80523) and "Pictures of a Floating World," a collection of miniatures (Telarc 80488). "Scintillation" offers solo music of Debussy, Gershwin, Grandjany, and Carlos Salzedo, as well as a wonderful reading of Ravel's *Introduction and Allegro* with an excellent chamber ensemble (Telarc 80361).

Judy Loman, who studied with Salzedo, has been principal of the Toronto Symphony since 1960. Her excellent recordings include "20th Century Masterworks for Harp" (Marquis 165), "Britten Canticles" (Marquis 185), "The Genius of Salzedo" (Marquis 117), and "Meditations" with cellist Daniel Domb (Pro Arte 3414). Another important Canadian harpist, **Erica Goodman,** made many recordings of standard and unusual repertoire. Her disc of trios by Debussy, Ravel, and Fauré with Trio Lyra is one of the best I know (Opening Day 9309). Her two discs of horn and harp music with Sören Hermanssohn are remarkable (BIS 648 and 793), as are her chamber recording, "Erica Goodman and Friends" (Musica Viva 1054), her solo "The Virtuoso Harp" (BIS 319), and her recording with flutist Robert Aitken (BIS 143).

A number of important harpists aren't part of the Salzedo or Grandjany "schools." One of the finest French harpists, **Lily Laskine** (1893–1988), studied only with Hasselmans (she was the first beginning student he ever accepted and never worked with anyone else) and won first prize at the Paris Conservatory in 1906. She had an important career as an orchestral musician, inspired scores of composers to write for the instrument, and some of her recordings have been reissued. She plays the Handel concerto in "The Best Ever Harp Classics" (Toccata 70342), and has a solo recording that includes music by her teacher, Marcel Tournier, Schumann, Grandjany, and Ibert called "The Magic of the Harp" (Erato 92131).

The British harpist **Osian Ellis,** principal of the London Symphony from 1961 to 1994, inspired Britten to write for the instrument. His 1972 *Ceremony of Carols* remains my favorite recording of the piece; last reissued in 1987 (EMI 47709), it's in serious need of reissue again. His recording of Britten's Folk Songs with Shirley-Quirk and Suite is still available (Mercury 84119), and his beautiful Handel Concerto for harp and lute appears in "Masterworks for the Harp" (Boston Skyline 119). This disc also contains performances by **Marisa Robles,** whose playing I don't like very much except for her Handel Concerto in F, a transcription of the F major recorder sonata. Ellis plays and sings medieval music in "Now We Make Merthe" with the Purcell Concert of Voices (Boston Skyline 121).

The Spanish harpist **Nicanor Zabeleta** (1907–93), who made his American debut in 1934 and had a huge international solo career, continues to have his recordings reissued. Two compilations of his work are available: "La harpe du siècle," with concertos (DG 39693), and a disc with solo music as well as concertos (Ermitage 134).

"Music from the Middle Ages to the Twentieth Century" is a good introduction to the harp repertory (Vox 33019, 3CD). It contains much music in excellent performances by **Marie-Claire Jamet** and **Susanna Mildonian;** Jamet also plays Debussy's Dances in "The Best Ever Harp Classics" (Toccata 703492). "In Flanders' Field," a recording of 20th century Belgian music by **Sophie Hallynck** (Phaedra 92012), and French harpist **Fabrice Pierre's** Debussy Dances (Calliope 9837) are both excellent recordings by lesser-known artists.

Some of the finest harp recordings are in dire need of reissue. **Heidi Lehwalder's** 1983 recording of music by Salzedo remains one of the finest I know (Nonesuch 79049, LP). There was also an excellent recording of Chopin transcriptions by **Deborah Hoffman**, principal harpist of the Metropolitan Opera Orchestra, with flutist Elizabeth Mann (Arabesque LP).   FINE

Harpsichord

Like the phoenix rising from the ashes, the story of the harpsichord in the 20th century is one of rebirth from total oblivion. At the turn of the century, the harpsichord was not taught at any conservatory in Europe or the U.S. No established school of performance existed, nor were there any professional harpsichordists to speak of. If a concert pianist wished to try his hand at it, he likely would have found no reliable instruments to play. The few surviving original instruments in museums were either totally unplayable or so badly restored that it was impossible to gain a true impression of their original sound. Early opinions of the harpsichord as a "feeble, jangling box of wire" were usually based on such encounters between pianists and museum instruments.

A few visionaries, like Arnold Dolmetsch in England, had a vague idea of the instrument's possibilities. Around the turn of the century, Dolmetsch actually built several "reproductions" and played them in recital, but it wasn't until the '20s that a handful of piano makers, chiefly Pleyel in France and Neupert in Germany, started the production-line manufacture of harpsichords. However, these massively built, iron-framed monsters bore little resemblance to the originals. The Polish-born pianist Wanda Landowska began concertizing and recording on a Pleyel and became a star in her own right. In the process, she spread the word about the instrument and its music, single-handedly educating a whole generation of listeners in its vast literature and potential.

Gradually, other keyboardists took up the harpsichord (many were Landowska pupils), and many began investigating historical performance practice. It soon became clear that a pianist's technique, which relies on power generated through the shoulders and arms, is completely wrong for this instrument. A few contemporary composers, like Poulenc and Falla, recognized this and were mildly successful at writing idiomatic music that exploited its gentler voice. This "mini-Renaissance," as it turns out, was based on a complete misunderstanding. The large, double- and triple-manual factory machines actually had a minuscule, bass-shy sound in comparison to well-restored originals or faithful historical reproductions. The Pleyel was especially disadvantaged in volume when pitted against a symphony orchestra or played in a large recital hall. Audiences grew tired of trying to hear it, and the novelty wore off.

Even today, most people know the sound of the harpsichord only from the theme song of the "Addams Family" TV show, which features Lurch playing an electronic fabrication that is as close to the real thing as an accordion is to a pipe organ. The historical harpsichord, by such celebrated 17th and 18th century makers as Ruckers, Baffo, Taskin and Kirckman, is a surprisingly robust-sounding instrument, usually with a booming bass register capable of carrying over a fairly large chamber orchestra. Historical harpsichords have a warm, singing, sustaining tone that aids the performer greatly in executing musical ideas.

Many European museum instrument collections underwent extensive reorganization and restoration after WWII. This was also the time

of a harpsichord "rebirth" almost as strong as the first. Starting in the early '50s, a young American scholar and instrument builder named Frank Hubbard visited the great collections and made a systematic study of the remaining instruments. His contribution to the corpus of harpsichord knowledge is unique; his book, *Three Centuries of Harpsichord Building* (Harvard University Press, 1965), which contains the distillation of his ground-breaking research, is both fascinating and essential reading for anyone interested in the subject. Other recommended introductory books include *A Plain and Easy Introduction to the Harpsichord* by Ruth Nurmi (Scarecrow Press, 1986); *A Guide to the Harpsichord* by Ann Bond (Amadeus Press, 1997); and *Early Keyboard Instruments in European Museums* by Edward L. Kottick and George Lucktenberg (Indiana University Press, 1997).

In 1949, Hubbard set up a workshop in Cambridge, MA, and with his partner William Dowd began producing historical reproductions of harpsichords, clavichords and fortepianos that quickly found their way into studios and conservatories across the county. Many apprentices went through the Hubbard and Dowd workshops, with the result that a genuine "school" of harpsichord building sprang up in the Boston area. Activity picked up in Europe as well, and all contributed to a better understanding of the historical instrument.

Performers took advantage of the improved sound and playing characteristics now available, producing increasing numbers of recordings with markedly greater insight and stylistic awareness. The Telefunken/Das Alte Werk recordings of Gustav Leonhardt from the '60s, using a mix of old instruments and several highly successful reproductions, were particularly effective in garnering a larger audience. Likewise, the recordings of Concentus Musicus Wien, which featured a prominent continuo harpsichord, gave the first clear picture of its dominant role in the Baroque orchestra.

A true cross-fertilization was at work: as more builders hung out their shingles, more keyboardists were drawn to the harpsichord. Teaching the harpsichord became a priority, and professorships were endowed at major universities and conservatories. More early keyboard graduates meant more harpsichord owners, and so on. Indeed, the growth of the entire period instrument movement coincides to a large extent with the burgeoning of interest in the harpsichord, and in many ways was spurred on by it.

Today, there are hundreds of harpsichord builders across the world, and it's no longer difficult or unusual to find one of distinction in your own area. Medium-size, custom instruments suitable for recital and ensemble work are as affordable and commonplace as a good upright piano. For those who have the necessary skills, do-it-yourself kits can represent an even greater cost saving while approximating the musical qualities of a custom instrument. Harpsichords in kit form are one of the most dramatic cultural indicators of the late 20th century; no other instrument, not even the guitar, has been made available to the general public in this way.

Professional harpsichordists abound as well, many holding university positions and pursuing the life of a recitalist or recording artist. The wealth of music (and instruments) currently available on CD is staggering, even more so when one considers that exactly 100 years ago, the harpsichord was essentially nonexistent in Western concert halls. What follows, then, is a highly personal selection of the best performers currently available on CD. This list doesn't strive for all-inclusiveness, nor is it even representative of, say, the top 20 players in the world. Many important figures in the historical harpsichord movement, such as Thurston Dart and Sylvia Marlowe, are totally absent from the catalog.

Some, such as Alan Curtis and Christopher Hogwood, have seen their earlier recordings withdrawn. The few historical items are included for their general interest, but don't necessarily constitute a ringing endorsement.

John Butt (b. 1960) is one of England's leading young keyboardists. An organist as well as harpsichordist, he studied in the UK, and from 1989–99 was Professor and University Organist at the University of California, Berkeley. He's also a noted Bach scholar and has done much valuable work in the service of neglected German literature for the harpsichord. CDs devoted to the music of Johann Kuhnau (Harmonia Mundi 907097) and Telemann (Harmonia Mundi 907176) are two recent examples.

David Cates (b. 1958) is an example of the outstanding talent to be found in America's newest generation of harpsichordists. A student of Parmentier, he now makes his home in Berkeley, which is in many ways the New Mecca for America's period instrument movement. Cates's recent Bach recital reveals an unusually insightful interpreter at work (Wildboar 9902). The CD concludes with what I consider the most successful rendition of the difficult *Chromatic Fantasy and Fugue* ever recorded.

William Christie (b. 1944) was born in New York and moved to France in 1972, where he founded Les Arts Florissantes, the first period-instrument ensemble to specialize in French Baroque opera. His early discs are treasured by many as benchmarks in the recorded history of the harpsichord; unfortunately, most have been withdrawn from the catalog. One that remains is his recording (with Christophe Rousset) of the two-harpsichord versions of Couperin's *L'Apothéose de Lully* and *L'Apothéose de Corelli* (Harmonia Mundi 2901269, in Rousset's complete Couperin set).

Thurston Dart (1921–71) was one of the seminal figures in the history of performance practice. His book *The Interpretation of Music* (London, 1954) created widespread interest in a field that had previously been the exclusive property of academics. As a harpsichordist, he made many solo recordings, performed as continuo player in such famous groups as the Philomusica of London and Boyd Neel Orchestra, and taught many famous students. Although none of his long-playing records seems to have been reissued digitally, they may still be found in shops specializing in LPs. His recordings of the "Complete Music for Harpsichord and Clavichord of Purcell" (Sp. Arts 207/8) and the music of William Bull (Oiseau-Lyre S-255) and Louis Clérambault (Oiseau-Lyre 50183) are still sought after.

Richard Egarr (b. 1963), another of England's exceptional young talents, is perhaps best known for his work with the chamber ensemble Romanesca, which includes violinist Andrew Manze and lutenist Nigel North. Egarr has made many fine CDs; his "Restoration Harpsichord Music" (works of Purcell and others) explores neglected but worthwhile territory (Globe GLO 5145), while "Four Harpsichord Suites for the Sun King" is one of the most successful recordings of the works of Louis Couperin (Globe 5148).

Albert Fuller (b. 1930) is generally regarded as America's premier pedagogue of the harpsichord. A student of Kirkpartrick, Fuller has taught at the Julliard School of Music since 1964 and is a founding member of Aston Magna and the Helicon Ensemble. You should try his recording of selected pieces by Rameau (Reference 27) or Bach (Reference 51), both distinguished by excellent-sounding instruments and superb engineering.

Elaine Funaro (b. 1952) studied at Oberlin and in Amsterdam with Leonhardt and Koopman and is regarded as one of the leading performers of new music for harpsichord. Her "Into the Millennium" explored several award-winning harpsichord compositions from around the world (Gasparo 331). "Overture to Orpheus" features music written for the important women harpsichordists of the 20th century, such as Landowska, Sylvia Marlowe, Antoinette Vischer, and . . . Ms Funaro (CRC 2517).

Kenneth Gilbert (b. 1931) is a Canadian who studied organ with Duruflé and harpsichord with Leonhardt. Since the early '70s Gilbert has held forth as the leading harpsichord teacher on French soil, with many illustrious pupils to his credit. He's also an important researcher in the field of harpsichord music, having published complete editions of Couperin, Rameau, Scarlatti, Jean-Henri d'Anglebert, Charles Dieupart, and others. His aristocratic style can be heard to good advantage in his recording of Bach's English Suites (Harmonia Mundi 91074/5) and *Goldberg Variations* (Harmonia Mundi 2951240).

Igor Kipnis (b. 1930) is the son of the famous Russian basso Alexander Kipnis. Since the late '50s, the younger Kipnis has specialized in early music and toured as a harpsichord and fortepiano recitalist. Thanks to his activities as researcher and music critic, his flashy, virtuosic style of playing is balanced by a thorough understanding of the history behind the music, as in "A Treasury of Harpsichord Favorites" (Music & Arts 243).

Ralph Kirkpatrick (1911–84), the first internationally acclaimed American performer on the harpsichord, clavichord and early piano, was also a scholar and researcher who wrote the definitive study of Domenico Scarlatti (1953) and, together with Kenneth Gilbert, published a complete facsimile edition of Scarlatti's sonatas (1971). Kirkpatrick had many illustrious students, recorded extensively, and was widely respected for his meticulous keyboard technique. Unfortunately, he was often conservative in his choice of instrument; his recordings are therefore often less than ideal. Sample the reissue of the historic 1952 Haydn Society recordings of music of Bach, Rameau, Couperin, etc., to hear some of his best work (Music & Arts 4976, 4CD).

Wanda Landowska (1897–1959) is remembered today as the person who, thanks to the force of her personality and the magnetism of her music-making, single-handedly dragged the harpsichord into the 20th century. Although she devoted much effort to the study of historical performance practice, her recordings reveal an artist who was more concerned with flamboyance and showmanship than historical niceties. She was a real "star," which explains why many modern composers were drawn to her playing (Falla, Poulenc, Martin). Her instrument, an enormous three-manual Pleyel, is a disappointment compared to almost present-day harpsichords. Even the post-WW II recordings, made in the US with the benefit of the latest in electrical techniques, are a chore to hear. You can judge for yourself in Pearl 9489 (music of Bach) or Pearl 9490 (suites of Handel).

Gustav Leonhardt (b. 1928) can be credited with starting the ball rolling in earnest for the historical harpsichord. His early LPs on the Telefunken/Das Alte Werk label introduced many (myself included) to the sound of well-restored museum originals. More important, Leonhardt has influenced the early music movement as few others, his greatest accomplishments coming as an orchestral conductor rather than a performer (his complete recording of the Bach cantatas with Harnoncourt made recording history in the '70s). As a keyboardist, Leonhardt has his detractors; his "micro-management" style of phrasing is considered expressive by some, fussy by others. The earlier recordings are mostly unavailable on CD, leaving only a few recent discs as samples of his highly personalized style. Try Sony 53114 (works of Georg Böhm) or Sony 62732 (works of Matthias Weckmann and Froberger) to hear two of this taciturn Dutchman's infrequent recent harpsichord outings.

Trevor Pinnock (b. 1946) has, like Christie, abandoned the harpsichord in favor of a conducting career. He's most familiar to American record collectors as the founder and conductor of the English Concert, but several of his earlier, highly successful CDs are still in the catalog, including "The Harmonious Blacksmith" (Archiv 413591), a collection of favorite Baroque pieces, and "Chaconne" (Archiv 410656), a selection of pieces by Handel.

Edward Parmentier (b. 1947) studied with Fuller and Leonhardt and is professor of harpsichord at the University of Michigan. He has made many distinguished recordings, featuring a wide range of music. His recent CD of Bach toccatas has met with unanimous critical acclaim (Wildboar 9402), while the fascinating disc entitled "Splendor of the Harpsichord" presents music of Bach, Frohberger, Couperin, Marais, and others performed on six different historical styles of harpsichord (Wildboar 9606).

Rafael Puyana (b. 1931) is perhaps Landowska's best-known pupil. Born in Colombia, he settled in New York in the late '50s and made several highly regarded records for Mercury. Puyana inherited both Landowska's flair and (unfortunately) her predilection for the Pleyel harpsichord. "Puyana plays Bach" (Mercury 434-395), recorded in the early '60s, is much better engineered than any of Landowska's recitals, making the Pleyel almost tolerable. In his later years, Puyana moved to Paris, where he began collecting antique keyboards. Unfortunately, he hasn't made any recordings on them.

Scott Ross (1951–89) holds the distinction of being the first and for many years the only winner of the International Harpsichord Competition at Bruges, Belgium (1971). He's also the only artist (so far) to record all of Domenico Scarlatti's keyboard sonatas, a massive undertaking encompassing 34 CDs that was completed just before his tragic death from AIDS. Ross possessed remarkable powers of communication, nowhere better evidenced than in a live 1979 recital in Paris of music by Antoine Forqueray, Jacques Duphly, and Bach (INA 262021). This is perhaps the most exciting harpsichord recital ever committed to disc, wrong notes and all.

Christophe Rousset (b. 1961) is unquestionably France's outstanding young virtuoso on the harpsichord. A pupil of Gilbert, Rousset holds the distinction of being only the second artist, after Ross, to have won first prize at the Bruges Competition (1983). He's also a noted conductor; he and his ensemble Les Talens Lyriques have won many international awards. His complete recordings of Couperin and Rameau have been widely praised, while his *Goldberg Variations* shows him to be an uncommonly insightful Bach interpreter (Oiseau-Lyre 444 866). Sample Rousset's CD of the music of Pancrace Royer to hear some of the most invigorating keyboard work of recent years (Oiseau-Lyre 436127).

Byron Schenkman (b. 1966) is another up-and-comer on the American scene. He has performed extensively as a recitalist and chamber musician throughout North America, and in addition to his keyboard work is artistic director of the Seattle Baroque Orchestra. His "The Bauyn Manuscript: 17th-Century French Harpsichord Music" was widely ac-

claimed (Wildboar 9603), while his disc of suites and variations by d'Anglebert filled an important gap in the catalog (Centaur CRC 2435).

Andreas Staier (b. 1955) is the finest harpsichordist of his generation to come out of Germany. In the '80s, he was active as a continuo player with several leading orchestras, including Musica Antiqua Köln and the Freiburg Baroque Orchestra, and since 1987 he has been a lecturer at the famed Scuola Cantorum Basiliensis. In recent years, he has turned his attention increasingly toward the fortepiano, so his harpsichord recordings have become rather infrequent. The last to appear, it seems, is his 1994 set of Bach's *Clavierübung I & II*, including the six Partitas and *Italian Concerto* (Deutsche Harmonia Mundi 77306, 2CD). Staier is a formidable keyboardist whose playing commands attention.

Colin Tilney (b. 1933), British-born and educated, has lived in Canada since 1979, where he is professor of harpsichord at the Royal Conservatory of Music in Toronto. He's one of the founding fathers of the British early music movement, having performed with virtually all the important period instrument groups as well as teaching many of the world's great players. He's an active recording artist; some of his many celebrated discs include the seven Bach toccatas (Dorian 90115) and *Well-Tempered Clavier I* and *II* (Hyperion 66351/4, 4CD).   BRODERSEN

Organ

COLLECTIONS

Organ collections can come and go very quickly in the catalogs, and each is essentially one of a kind, so it's difficult to make meaningful comparisons in the face of so many variables. It's worth noting that most of them can almost be described as "vanity" recordings, and many of the companies issuing organ and sacred choral recordings bring out nothing else. Of course, the companies won't produce a recording for just anyone able to pay for it, but in most cases it's necessary for the artists to secure their own financial backing for the projects. Some of these recordings are of the highest quality, others are not, and opinions differ as to which are which. The sheer number of recordings can be bewildering, and no one can listen to all of them.

One factor that distinguishes organ recordings from other instrumental collections is that their chief purpose may be to exhibit a particular instrument. This is because pipe organs differ greatly in size, tonal design, acoustical setting, and other factors, making each instrument to some extent unique. Furthermore, the instrument has a longer history than most others, so there has been a great deal of evolution in the organ builder's art from period to period and from one national style to another within the same period. Music ideally suited for one style of organ may become no better than a caricature when played on an instrument of very different style. Further complicating the issue is the fact that sometimes a given organ will be extremely effective in playing music originally intended for a quite different style of instrument. I was astounded, for instance, by a recording of Hans Fagius playing music by Saint-Saëns on a large 1976 organ by the Danish builder Marcussen at a church in Stockholm (BIS 556).

A recording that seeks to exhibit a particular instrument's qualities to best advantage will most often consist of a program carefully chosen to suit those qualities. When this is the primary purpose of the recording, the instrument itself will be identified prominently on the CD booklet cover, usually with a photograph of its case. Two good examples come to mind: one is of a fairly recent instrument, the other a great organ from the 19th century.

The first is a showcase for the two-manual Charles B. Fisk organ, completed in 1991 for the First Presbyterian Church of Evansville, IN (Mulberry St. 1001). It's a versatile instrument but not a large one, so **Douglas Reed** plays a program of baroque, romantic, and contemporary pieces that don't exceed the instrument's capabilities (Opus 98). The second is "Music for a Grand Organ" played by **David Drury** on the five-manual William Hill organ completed in 1890 for the Town Hall of Sydney, Australia (ABC 770019). Since this is a large, late Victorian concert organ, the program is very different. Drury includes orchestral transcriptions by W.T. Best and E.H. Lemare (both of whom played the instrument on their recital tours), some turn-of-the-century fluff, original works by Franck, Eugène Gigout, Dupré, and Stanford, an improvisation by Drury himself, and a toccata by contemporary Australian composer Graeme Koehne. Again, a well-played and nicely varied program of works exceptionally well suited to the instrument.

In addition to the instrument itself, the factors that determine an organ collection's personality and composition are the same as any other vocal or instrumental collection: the repertory and the performer(s). While most organ collections are played by a single artist on one instrument, some notable sets involve multiple performers and multiple instruments. Each year, the **Organ Historical Society** (OHS) holds a convention in a different American city or region with recitals on instruments in the area, and selections from these recitals are issued on sets of two to four CDs in a continuing series under the title "Historic Organs of. . . ." As you might expect, the performances and instruments vary greatly in quality. Many of the instruments are small Victorian organs designed primarily to accompany congregational singing rather than to play the solo organ repertory. Others are large church and concert hall organs. In any case, these sets offer welcome documentation of historically significant instruments. OHS (P.O. Box 26811, Richmond, VA 23261; <www.ohscatalog.org>) also provides a valuable service to seekers after organ recordings through a substantial catalog that includes theater organ discs as well as classical offerings, sheet music, and books, often at reduced price to members. Many of them are hard-to-find items.

"Historic Organs of Europe" is a most remarkable collection, a reissue of recordings originally issued on LPs from the mid 1960s to the early 1970s (Harmonia Mundi 290060, 6CD). It includes ten instruments from Majorca, Spain, France, Italy, and Germany played by four different organists. One of its great virtues is that a substantial amount of solid repertory is played on each instrument, including all twelve toccatas from Georg Muffat's *Apparatus Musico-Organisticus,* nearly all of the organ works of Nikolaus Bruhns, six of the twelve *Noëls* of Louis-Claude Daquin, the complete Convent Mass of François Couperin, as well as generous helpings of Frescobaldi, Pachelbel, and others. In this way the listener can really get a sense of the organ's character, and the performances are competent if not always exciting.

In 1992 there were many releases of Spanish music to coincide with the 500th anniversary of the conquest of Granada and Columbus's first voyage. Among them was "The Historic Spanish Organ," a set of organ music from the 16th to the 18th century including performances on 20 organs by ten artists (Valois 4645-54, 10CD). Most of the instruments were built in the 18th century and restored in the 1980s. The discs were issued separately, so you aren't obliged to buy all ten. Like the more wide-ranging Harmonia Mundi set, the Valois gives each instrument a generous exposure in music well suited to it. The performances vary in quality, but the standard is generally high. I was especially impressed with the young Uruguayan organist Cristina Garcia Banegas in a program of works by Juan Cabanilles (Vol. 3), and with veteran Montserrat Torrent in Catalan music of the 18th century (Vol. 8).

A whole subcategory of organ releases consists of reissues of recordings by great organists of the past. Some of these are single artist and single composer compilations as, for example, a pair of Bach discs recorded by **Albert Schweitzer** in the mid-1930s (Magic Talent 48039, 48045). While I don't wish to take much space here on pre-high-fidelity recordings, I must mention an extraordinary disc of music by Widor, Vierne, Dupré, and Messiaen in performances by the composers themselves (EMI 55037). The first three date from between 1926 and 1932; Messiaen's *Le Banquet céleste* and *L'Ascension* were recorded in 1956 and also appear in "Messiaen par lui-même" (EMI 67400, 4CD).

INDIVIDUAL ARTISTS

Opus currently lists nearly 200 artists under the rubric of "Organ Collections," and that's in addition to multi-artist collections. Space doesn't permit a consideration of them all. What follows is one listener's personal and inevitably quirky survey of a large and complicated field.

Marie-Claire Alain (b. 1926) is something of an aristocrat among organists, an artist of consummate technique and artistry whose recordings cover a wide spectrum, from Bach and the French Baroque masters through the great Romantics to the 20th century. She's perhaps most attuned temperamentally to the Baroque repertory. Barry Millington writes in *New Grove* of her "scrupulous attention to the details of articulation and ornamentation" as well as her preference for mechanical-action organs of appropriate character. She may not always gratify the thrill-seeking listener, and more serious listeners may disagree with some details of her interpretations, but you can count on her for well-considered, subtly nuanced, impeccably tasteful performances with no hint of cheap ostentation.

"Famous Music for Organ" includes several works of Bach and individual pieces by others (Erato 45976), "Great Toccatas" (Erato 94812) and "Organ Encores" (Erato 92888) are two of her other collections. I'm especially fond of her collections of Christmas music, like a 1978 release that includes ten *Noëls* by Louis-Claude Daquin and three by Claude-Bénigne Balbastre (Erato 88161). A more recent (1990) issue offers an anthology of baroque *Noëls* (Erato 45455), and a still more recent (1995) disc branches out from the French Baroque to include the *Breton Rhapsodies* of Saint-Saëns, a selection of Christmas music by Bach, and four excerpts from Messiaen's *La Nativité du Seigneur* (Erato 10703).

E. Power Biggs (1906–77) was a giant among American organists around the middle of the 20th century. Generations of listeners made their first serious acquaintance with the organ and its literature through his recitals, broadcasts, and many recordings. Some of his interpretations and registrations may seem wayward by today's standards, but he was a pioneer who had to forge his own performance style in early music at a time when authoritative models and scholarly guidance were sparse. To his credit, he could make the classic organ repertory accessible without dumbing it down or making it sound cheap. It's astonishing that there are no available collections by Biggs. Some single-composer recordings have been reissued: three Bach discs (CBS 30539; CBS 42644; Sony 46551), the Handel concertos on "Handel's organ" at Great Packington (Odyssey 45825, 3CD), and the Saint-Saëns Organ Symphony with Ormandy and the Philadelphia Orchestra (Odyssey 38920 and Sony 47655).

David Britton (1942-92) brought an adventuresome flair to recorded collections of organ works. His "Gargoyles & Chimeras: Exotic Works for Organ" contains Bach and others, including the Vierne *Fantasy Piece* that gives the disc its title (Delos 3077). It's a fascinating program of picturesque and extravagant pieces brilliantly played on the 1987 Rosales organ at Trinity Episcopal Church, Portland, OR, and it was for a time the company's most popular organ recording. Britton followed it in 1991 with a disc I particularly admire: "Organo Deco: Sophisticated American Organ Music c1915–1950," played on the 1938 Kimball organ at St. John's Cathedral, Denver (Delos 3111). It uncannily presents a musical counterpart to the art deco school of architecture and design and is an imaginative and thoroughly coherent program played superbly on what may be the ideal instrument for such pieces.

Pierre Cochereau (1924–84), appointed in 1955 as organist of Notre-Dame in Paris, was one of the most celebrated recitalists of his generation and a noted exponent of the art of improvisation, on a par with his teacher Marcel Dupré. A miscellaneous program played on the Notre-Dame organ is available but doesn't exhibit the artist to best advantage (Fnac 642301). A disc of great historical interest documents Cochereau's last recital at St. Thomas Church, New York, in 1970 (August Classics 9001). This recording wasn't made under studio conditions and some extraneous audience noise and subway trains are audible, but it's worth bearing with the disc's technical shortcomings for the thrill of listening to a recital by one of the great organists of the 20th century.

David Craighead (b. 1924) is one of the most highly respected of American organists. After study at the Curtis Institute, he began a brilliant career as a recitalist in 1944 at the age of 20. A rather lightweight program of Americana is played on the great concert organ at Mechanics Hall, Worcester, MA (Gothic 49021). The depth and seriousness of his artistry are perhaps heard to better advantage in his recording of Reger's Sonata 2 and Vierne's Symphony 6 on the 1987 Rosales organ at Trinity Episcopal Church, Portland, OR, a rare instance of romantic repertory convincingly played on a modern instrument (Delos 3096). In addition to his solo recitals, Craighead often performed organ duets with his wife, Marian Reiff Craighead (1919-1996). Their combined artistry can be heard in a varied selection of works played on the Austin organ of Asbury Methodist Church, Rochester, NY (Pro Organo 7046). The disc was issued in her memory.

Catharine Crozier (b. 1914) is another highly respected American organist. Although her repertory is large and wide-ranging, she's especially celebrated for her interpretations of 20th-century organ literature. I'm not convinced that she's heard to best advantage in a recital disc from Alice Tully Hall in New York, largely because of an acoustic unfriendly to the instrument (Gothic 49041). The fourth side of the original 1979 LP release contained selections from Ned Rorem's *A Quaker Reader,* superseded by Crozier's much finer 1989 recording of that work in its entirety plus the same composer's *Views from the Oldest House* on the Marcussen organ at Wichita State University (Delos 3076). Among her other outstanding recordings are pieces by German Romantics played at Grace Cathedral, San Francisco (Delos 3090), and an all-Sowerby disc including the complete Symphony in G played at the Groton School Chapel (Delos 3075).

Jeanne Demessieux (1921–68), organist of St. Esprit, Paris, at the age of 12 and in 1962 appointed to La Madeleine, was a brilliant performer, but her artistry went beyond mere technical brilliance. In her short career, she created a sensation not only in France but also in England and the United States, where she toured extensively. Felix Aprahamian, writing in *New Grove,* observes that toward the end of her career she revealed

greater involvement with the music she played, suggesting that she had barely reached "the zenith of her powers as an interpreter." This is already apparent in her 1959 recordings of the 12 Franck masterworks (Festivo 155, 2CD). I prefer her Franck (especially her hair-raising Chorale 3) to most others I have heard. Festivo has also reissued her performances in a wide variety of repertory, including some of her own compositions (131, 132, 141).

Marcel Dupré (1886–1971), who succeeded his teacher Widor as organist of St. Sulpice, Paris, in 1935, was the most celebrated French organist-composer-improviser of his generation. His recordings aren't as readily available as they used to be, but a disc was released in 1992 of music by Widor and Franck, recorded in 1957 at St. Thomas Church, NY (Mercury 434311). Although Dupré continued to play (and teach) the French Romantics at a time when they were out of fashion, this disc reveals that his artistic temperament was quite unromantic. The performances are hard-edged and straightforward, almost prosaic, yet authoritative. There is a recording of Dupré improvisations at Cologne Cathedral (Motette 60011), and OHS advertises their importation of a disc of improvisations from 1953 and 1957 produced by L'Association des amis de l'art de Marcel Dupré.

Hans Fagius (b. 1951) has recorded extensively for the Swedish BIS label, mostly on Scandinavian instruments. Some critics have faulted his performances as lacking in stylistic insight, but I have hardly ever felt that way about them. I enjoyed his Saint-Saëns program more than most other recordings of this music (BIS 556), and I've long been fond of his organ duet disc with David Sanger (BIS 273). His collections include a miscellaneous program at Härnösand Cathedral (BIS 156), a French program on the same instrument (BIS 7), and Swedish Romantics at Katarina Church, Stockholm (BIS 191).

Virgil Fox (1912–80) was easily the most flamboyant (and highest paid) organist of his generation, and even after his death, he still has something of a cult following. In terms of sheer manual and pedal technique and his ability to manipulate the registers of a large instrument, he was unrivaled. His esthetic legacy, however, is more controversial. He was more than a mere popularizer, but for him there was no conflict, almost no difference, between serious music-making and showbiz. He had a haughty contempt for neoclassical organ building and Baroque performance practice. Other organists had to take his enormous talents seriously, but few followed his artistic example.

Many of his recordings have been reissued, most of them made on the huge Aeolian-Skinner organ of the Riverside Church in New York, where he was organist from 1946 to 1965. "The Art of Virgil Fox" comes from LP recordings for Capitol (EMI 65426, 65913, 66386), as does "A Virgil Fox Christmas" (EMI 66088). They contain mostly transcriptions and arrangements. "Virgil Fox Encores" stays closer to the legitimate organ repertory (RCA 61251). Perhaps more interesting than any of these is "Soli Deo Gloria," documenting Fox's last recital at Riverside in 1979, complete with his spoken commentary (Bainbridge 8005, 2CD). Also noteworthy is a disc recorded on the John Wanamaker department store organ in Philadelphia (Bainbridge 2501).

Jean Guillou (b. 1930) can in many ways be regarded as the French Virgil Fox. He forcibly injects his personality into everything he plays, and if you like that, well and good, but if you're mainly interested in the music he plays, then his personality gets in the way. There's no denying that he is enormously talented and imaginative, but the program notes that try to make him the artistic equal of the great composers can be simply laughable. I love his hair-raising recording of Bach's *Goldberg Variations* (Dorian 90110), but I can barely sit through his centennial recording of the 12 masterworks of Franck at the spectacular organ of St. Eustache, Paris, where he has been organist since 1963. His interpretations and registrations seem to me unendurably grotesque. Among his collections is the 1989 inaugural recording of the new organ at St. Eustache (Dorian 90134) and a rather disjointed disc of encores played on an exquisite small organ he designed for a church in the French Alps (Dorian 90112).

Naji Hakim (b. 1955) succeeded Messiaen as organist of La Trinité, Paris, in 1993. Born in Beirut, he is by education (Paris Conservatoire and Jean Langlais) and temperament a secure part of the French organ world, with a reputation as performer and composer that is growing steadily. A recording of his debut in Boston's Mission Church includes works by Bach, Franck, Langlais and himself (AFKA 323). A more recent (1998) "Debut" recording was made at La Trinité (EMI 72272). His Franck and Vierne on that disc are too reserved and rigid to be really convincing. His playing is essentially unromantic, better suited to Langlais and Messiaen. His original works are characterized by pungent harmonies and vivid rhythms, showing the influence of Langlais.

Christopher Herrick (b. 1942) was a chorister and later assistant organist at St. Paul's Cathedral in London, and afterward served for ten years at Westminster Abbey. He has been recording the organ works of Bach for Hyperion in a somewhat academic performance style, though he's not as severe as some others. At the opposite end of the pole, however, his series of "Organ Fireworks" collections consists mostly of lighter virtuoso pieces of the 19th and 20th centuries, with eight discs so far (Hyperion, various numbers). I find such programs tiresome, like a seven-course meal consisting entirely of desserts; I haven't heard all the discs, but what I have heard doesn't greatly impress me. The playing is capable enough, but it's rhythmically unsteady, awkwardly unflowing, and doesn't quite achieve the pizzazz necessary to justify the choice of that repertory. Other critics have reacted more favorably, even enthusiastically. It just goes to show that after all the reviews are in, listeners have to judge for themselves.

Frederick Hohman (b. 1955) is not only a highly talented organist, but the head of Pro Organo Records, with an impressive catalogue of solo organ and choral discs by a wide variety of artists, including quite a few by himself. His specialty is the Anglo-American symphonic school of virtuoso organ composition and transcription, but only an overactive sense of history can justify dredging up the appallingly bad compositions of Edwin Henry Lemare and his contemporaries on two of Hohman's discs, "Lemare Affair" (Pro Organo 7007) and "Lemare Affair II" (Pro Organo 7018).

Other Hohman discs are showcases for specific instruments. "Opus 190" is a program of mostly turn-of-the-century fluff played on the 1912 E.M. Skinner organ at the Grand Avenue Methodist Temple in Kansas City, MO (Pro Organo 7042), claimed to be oldest surviving original four-manual Skinner. "The English Connection" is a mostly English Baroque program, plus Mendelssohn's Sonata 3 and some works of Bach, played on the 1969 N.P. Mander organ at the Winston Churchill Memorial and Library in Fulton, MO (Pro Organo 7029). "Forever Methuen" is a surprisingly mainstream program, played on the Walcker/Aeolian-Skinner organ at the Methuen Memorial Music Hall in Methuen, MA (Pro Organo 7066).

Michael Murray (b. 1943) is one of the last generation of organists to study with Dupré and the author of a fine biography of his teacher. He has recorded extensively for Telarc, including a good deal of Bach and a centennial recording of the Franck masterworks (Telarc 80234, 2CD). His collections include works by Franck, Vierne, Bach, and others at the Cathedral of St. John the Divine, NY (Telarc 80169); Bach, Widor, Dupré, and Franck at Davies Symphony Hall, San Francisco (Telarc 80097); a program of French encores (Telarc 80104); and a mixed program at Salisbury Cathedral (Telarc 80255). (Warning: *Schwann* erroneously lists several of Thomas Murray's recordings under Michael Murray's name.) "Bach Organ Blaster" is a sampler (Telarc 80316). Murray is always professional and solid, but he tends to play it safe, avoiding extremes of tempo and unorthodox registrations—reliable, but not always exciting.

Thomas Murray (b. 1943) is University Organist and Professor at Yale, where he commands the magnificent E.M. Skinner organ at Woolsey Hall. Though his specialty is the Romantic repertory, including the Anglo-American literature, his performances don't suggest egotistical flamboyance in the manner of, say, Jean Guillou. Some listeners may find him less than exciting for that reason, but I value his blend of a scholar's historical understanding with solid performing technique. His landmark recording of the Mendelssohn sonatas on two mid-19th-century organs in Boston has been reissued (Raven 390).

One of his finest collections is a showcase for the 1863 E. & G.G. Hook organ at Boston's Church of the Immaculate Conception (AFKA 507). There is an all-Edwin Lemare program (yawn) on the 1912 Kotzschmar Memorial organ at Portland, ME (AFKA 515) and a French program including Widor's Symphony 6 on the 1987 Schoenstein organ at SS Peter and Paul Church, San Francisco (AFKA 512). Murray's more lightweight program on the 1929 Aeolian organ at Longwood Gardens is one of the finest recordings ever made on that instrument, but at least 90 per cent of what has been recorded at Longwood is utter rubbish (DTR 8305). Murray's recording of Henri Mulet's *Byzantine Sketches* on the 1990 Austin organ at the National Shrine of Our Lady of Czestochowa in Doylestown, PA, is also noteworthy (Arkay 6111).

Anthony Newman (b. 1941), who made waves in the 1970s as a kind of hippie-Zen-Bach guru, continues to produce recordings that bear his own unmistakable stamp. He has recorded a great deal of Bach, mostly too fast, much of it too loud, and quite a bit of it not very cleanly played. There are also collections of Romantic organ masterworks played on the brash neoclassical Rieger at Holy Trinity Church in New York (Newport 60050, 60150). Here as in Bach, Newman's fast tempos are too fast, so that all subtlety and nuance go out the window. There must be listeners (and producers) who actually like this kind of playing.

Frederick Swann (b. 1931) succeeded Virgil Fox as organist at the Riverside Church in New York and was there for 25 years before going to Robert Schuller's Crystal Cathedral in California in 1983. He is a consummate artist enjoying the highest regard of his colleagues, but unlike Fox, he seems to appeal most to other organists. This must be due, at least in part, to his tendency to overload his repertory with pieces churned out or arranged by organ composers mainly for their own and their colleagues' use.

For example, a collection recorded at St. Andrew's Cathedral, Honolulu, consists of works by Jean-Joseph Mouret, Alexandre Guilmant, Alexander Russell, Norman Cocker, Sowerby, John Stanley (not one of his legitimate voluntaries but an arrangement), Vierne, Parry, and an arrangement of a devotional song by Queen Liliuokalani (Gothic 49092). In such company, even the pieces by Sowerby and Vierne seem somehow diminished. In "The Mystic Organ," recorded at the National

Shrine of the Immaculate Conception in Washington, DC, the theme is spiritual ecstasy, a sense of numinous contemplation brought off in large part because of the spacious acoustics of the room and the superb engineering of the recording (Gothic 49053). The program itself is less impressive.

Peter Sykes (b. 1958) is a remarkable artist who has demonstrated that he can play many different kinds of repertory and different styles of organs very well. My first acquaintance was with his "From the Heartland," and based on that he might be pegged as an academic scholar-organist, though a very good one, who's most at home on no-nonsense neoclassic instruments (Titanic 181). Then he turns around and records his own transcription of Holst's *The Planets* on the mighty E.M. Skinner at Girard College, PA (Raven 380). What's more, he makes it sound glorious and proves that he can play most of today's transcription jockeys under the table! More recent is a staggering Reger disc on the restored 1931 Steinmeyer organ at the Cathedral of the Blessed Sacrament in Altoona, PA (Raven 430). Note also his collection, "A Nantucket Organ Tour" (Raven 320). Keep your eyes (and ears) on this man.

And here, almost arbitrarily, I draw the line, fully aware that there are literally dozens of other organists worthy of mention, some of them—for example, Simon Preston, Gillian Weir, John Scott, Gerre Hancock, Lionel Rogg—artists of the first magnitude. In many cases, their recorded output has not centered on collections, and they should be receiving due attention under individual composer entries in this volume. In many other cases, I simply had to make difficult choices for purely practical reasons and sometimes based on the inevitable limitations of my own listening experience. I don't expect anyone to agree with all my decisions, but if I have sparked some curiosity or induced anyone to go exploring in this fascinating field, my time and effort won't have been wasted. GATENS

Percussion Instruments

Although percussion instruments are probably the oldest of all in music, they didn't attain anything beyond a supporting role in Western classical music until comparatively recently. For long, the only percussion member in the standard orchestra was the timpani (kettledrums), descended from the nakers brought to Europe by the retreating Crusaders in the 1200s. During the 18th century unpitched instruments, such as the side drum, bass drum and cymbals (often thought of as Turkish), began to appear in concert and operatic works, as in Marais's opera *Alcyone* (1706; Astrée 8525 for selections) and Beethoven's Symphony 9 (1823, which also—along with Berlioz's *Symphonie Fantastique*—revolutionized timpani writing), but only toward the end of the 19th century did they begin to appear regularly. One view of the growth of the percussion within the orchestra has been presented by the great ensemble **Nexus**, narrated by Bill Moyers (Nexus 10306).

The 20th century saw an explosion of membership of the "kitchen department" (to quote Vaughan Williams's quip about the percussion, which he used to great effect in *Sinfonia Antartica* and with glee in his Symphony 8). Several of Stravinsky's ballets were crucial in this respect, like *The Rite of Spring, The Soldier's Tale* and *Les Noces,* this last for an ensemble of four pianos and a large battery of percussion. Other composers quickly caught on to the elemental sound and dramatic qualities of expanded percussion roles, as for example Nielsen in his last three symphonies and Antheil in his notorious *Ballet mécanique* (RCA 68066). Bartók, who scandalized musical opinion with his earthy, percussive approach to the piano, was scrupulous when writing for the reg-

ular percussion instruments in the orchestra, notating precisely what type of stick to use, or where to strike a drum or cymbal, as in his Piano Concerto 1 and *Music for Strings, Percussion and Celesta.*

Few went as far as Varèse, who in the 1920s wrote hugely complex parts for percussion in orchestral scores such as *Amériques, Hyperprism* and *Intégrales,* culminating in 1931 with *Ionisation,* for a 13-strong unaccompanied percussion ensemble (♦Decca 460208, 2CD). Another such innovator was Havergal Brian in his *Gothic Symphony,* with its demonic xylophone solo, six timpanists (playing 24 drums) and enormous array of other instruments including two bass drums, African long drum, bird-scare, chains and thunder machine (♦Marco Polo 223280).

Even before WWII, solo and ensemble works were being composed with increasing regularity, particularly in the United States. This was partly a consequence of growing interest in the percussion orchestras of Asia, notably the gamelans of Java and Bali, which influenced the music of Colin McPhee, as in his vivid orchestral suite *Tabuh-Tabuhan* (Mercury 34310), John Cage, and Lou Harrison, the last two of whom even created their own instruments from bits of cars and household items. Emancipated percussion sections spread to composers around the globe, like Britten in his ballet *The Prince of the Pagodas* (Virgin 59578), Crumb, and Henze, in a variety of pieces.

By the 1960s, the percussion section had become enlarged to include the xylophone, vibraphone and marimba, glockenspiel, bells, celesta, large gong (or tam-tam), cymbals of all sizes, all manner of drums, triangle, tambourine, whip, wood blocks, and other exotica derived from as far afield as Latin America (not least due to the impact of the music of Villa-Lobos, Chavez and Revueltas) and China. Often instruments have been specially created for certain works, for example Maxwell Davies's *St. Thomas Wake* (Collins 1308) and Ligeti's *Aventures* and *Nouvelles Aventures* (Sony 62311).

SOLO COLLECTIONS

Sadly, there are no extant solo recordings on CD of **James Blades,** who did much to champion the cause of percussion instruments around the world. Another British percussionist, **Tristan Fry** (best known through his association with guitarist John Williams), is only represented by solos in larger works by Britten and Maxwell Davies; his pioneering recordings of Daniel Jones's *Kettledrum Sonata* (written not for the modern pedal instrument but its screw-tightened predecessor) and Stockhausen's *Zyklus* are now NA. A similar situation pertains with the Japanese **Stomu Yamash'ta,** present only in two ensemble works by Henze.

However, the deaf Scottish percussionist **Evelyn Glennie,** who has dominated solo percussion playing in the past decade, has made many recordings. These range from "Rhythm Song," arrangements with orchestra (by Christopher Palmer) of popular classics by Chopin, Joplin, Rimsky-Korsakov and others (RCA 60242), to "Light in Darkness," a typically diverse collection featuring music from as far afield as Keiko Abe in Japan and Ross Edwards in Australia (RCA 60557). Her "Drumming" is something of a curate's egg: there are several classic scores here, like Roberto Sierra's *Bongo-O,* Askell Massón's *Prím,* and Frederic Rzewski's *To the Earth,* cheek by jowl with lesser-known pieces and a string of improvisations by Glennie herself (BMG 68195). One such rarity is *Pezzo da Concerto No. 1* by percussionist-composer **Nebojša Jovan Zivkovic,** who has recorded a whole disc of his dynamic and vibrant compositions, "The Castle of the Mad King" (BIS 1098). Zivkovic's mercurial talent as creator and executant is evident in both miniatures and larger-scale conceptions, like the title work, *Trio per uno*, or *Ultimatum II*.

More recently, Glennie has ventured along a completely improvisatory path with her "Shadow behind the Iron Sun," a brave but ultimately unsatisfying attempt that for all its textural variety seems to plough the same furrows over and again (RCA). Pieces by Abe are included by **Christian Roderburg** alongside other marimba solos by Masanori Fujita, Gordon Stout (also recorded by Glennie, RCA), Toshiya Sukegawa and Michael Ranta (Koch 311692). Devotees of improvisation may find "Live at Vatnajökull" of interest, recorded in Iceland by the Swedish organ-and-percussion duo **Matthias Wager** and **Anders Astrand** (Opus 3).

Rainer Kuisma is currently under-represented in the recorded catalogue, with a collection of solo pieces by Sibelius (an arrangement), Oscar Lemba, and Leonid Bashmakov, plus the Milhaud concertos (BIS 149), as well as Crumb's ensemble work *Makrokosmos III* (BIS 261). **Dave Samuels** presents an enterprising program of mostly Australian works for vibraphone or marimba by Ross Edwards, Peter Sculthorpe, Nigel Westlake and Samuels himself, plus Cage's *First Construction* (Tall Poppies 30; several other works by Edwards involving percussion in chamber and vocal compositions are available on the same label). Of more marginal interest are **Kai Stensgaard**'s "Marimba Classic" (Danacord) and **Brian Slawson**'s "Bach on Wood" (Sony), transcription collections both.

Several of Elliott Carter's eight *Timpani Pieces* are available, 1, 6 and 8 by **Jonathan Faralli** as part of a stunnningly recorded program including Stockhausen's *Zyklus,* Henze's *Prison Song* and Smith Brindle's *Orion M42* (♦Arts 75582). **Peter Sadlo** includes 1 and 8 in a very varied disc of solo items, including pieces for marimba, snare drum, and clashed cymbals, concluding with Xenakis's riveting *Rebonds* (♦Koch 36569). Sadlo has also set down 4 and 5 in a joint venture with Nexus (Koch 315572), and has recorded Smith Brindle's *Orion M42* with short items by Abe, Siegfried Fink, Toshimitsu Tanaka, and others (Koch 310141).

Xenakis has been one of the seminal forces in post-WW II avant-garde music, and has composed many works either involving percussion (such as the drama *Oresteia* with **Silvio Gualda** the percussion soloist; Salabert), or for percussion alone. Aside from *Rebonds*, the best known is *Psappha*, which **Gert Mortensen** has recorded spectacularly (with Nørgård's *I Ching* and Pelle Gudmundsen-Holmgreen's concerto *Triptykon* (BIS 256).

Jonny Axelsson's solo program "Percussione con Forza" will appeal mainly to avant-garde specialists, comprising six works in advanced styles by young Swedish composers, all but one written in the 1990s (Phono Suecia 126). Highlights are Kerstin Jeppson's *Prometheus* and Karin Rehnqvist's remarkable *Strömar* ("Streams"), the latter for Axelsson's own invention, the bass cimbalom.

DUO COLLECTIONS

Bartók's Sonata for Two Pianos and Percussion is a staple of the percussion duo repertoire, yet on disc pride of place is usually given to the pianists. This may be commendable in the case of the historic 1940 recording by Bartók and his wife Ditta Pásztory-Bartók, with **Henry J. Baker** and **Edward J. Rubsam** (Hungaroton 12326/31, 6CD), but the marketing reasoning is less apparent for the version by the Labeque sisters, with **Silvio Gualda** and **Jean-Pierre Drouet** (EMI). Discs where the percussionists are seen to be equal tend to be the more persuasive accounts, as for example that by Argerich and Freire with **Sadlo** and

Edgar Guggeis, coupled with arrangements for the same combination by Sadlo of Ravel pieces including *Mother Goose* (♦DG 439867), or by the **Safri Duo**—with pride of billing—and the Slovak Piano Duo, coupled with Marta Ptaszynska's arrangement of Lutoslawski's *Paganini Variations* and Kim Helweg's Bernstein tribute, *America Fantasy* (Chandos 9398).

The Safri Duo has made several electrifying discs, the best of them containing four works by modern Danish composers (including Nørgård) and Minoru Miki's *Marimba Spiritual II* (♦Chandos 9330). Their "Goldrush," named from Jacob ter Veldhuis's brilliant piece, juxtaposed transcriptions of Bach, Chopin, Mendelssohn and Ravel with original scores by Nørgård, Soren Barfoed and Rolf Wallin (Chandos 9482). I should also mention their electric playing of Reich's *Nagoya Marimbas* and a duo version of *Music for pieces of wood* (Chandos 9645, with Wayne Siegel's *42nd Street Rondo*). *Nagoya Marimbas* is played by **Sam Walton** and **Colin Currie** in "Striking a Balance," alongside original works by Toshi Ichiyanagi, Chick Corea, and Ney Rosauro, and arrangements of Bach and Ravel (EMI 72267).

ENSEMBLE COLLECTIONS

The Hungarian group **Amadinda** was one of the first to record regularly. Their CD transfers can be tricky to find and are of LP length, but the sound is generally excellent and the musicianship exemplary, as in their collection of Varèse's *Ionisation,* Chavez's *Toccata* and three Cage scores including *Third Construction* (Hungaroton 12991). Their recordings of Reich's music are important for their non-Californian approach (Hungaroton 31358; Amiata 0393). Chavez's *Toccata* is featured in the **Düsseldorf Percussion Ensemble**'s only available CD, coupled with Michael Denhoff's *Bacchantic Dance Scenes* and three works by Iannis Vlachopoulos (Koch 312342).

Ensemble Bash is a four-man British group whose concert appearances have attracted much critical attention; their sole album to date is a characteristically challenging collection of new scores by largely unknown composers (though including Howard Skempton), but also a group composition—*Dash Me Something*—and an arrangement of a Senegalese circumcision ritual (Sony 69246).

The six-man Swedish ensemble **Kroumata** is among the most dynamic groups currently recording; their series of discs is consistently stunning for sheer technical prowess as well as clarity. Three discs will give some idea of their great range: one with Sven-David Sandström's invigorating *Drums* and flutist Manuela Wiesler in Jolivet's *Suite en Concert* and Lou Harrison's First Concerto (♦BIS 272); a second with legendary marimba player Keiko Abe—amazingly, her only currently available recording (♦BIS 462); and a third that includes Cage's *Third Construction* and Sandström's *Kroumata Pieces* (♦BIS 932).

To describe the status of **Nexus** as legendary would be a distinct understatement, yet their available recorded legacy is rather sparse. Their discs range from Bryars's quartet *One Last Bar, Then Joe Can Sing* (Point Music 454126) to their invigorating recitals of works by George Hamilton Green (Nexus 10273, 10284) to compositions and improvisations by Nexus members themselves (Koch 315572; Nexus 10262, 10295). A "Best of Nexus" compilation is also available (Nexus).

The **New Music Consort**'s "Pulse," named from Henry Cowell's pioneering work, features Cage's *Second* and *Third Constructions* (perhaps not quite as exciting as Amadinda or Kroumata) plus his collaboration with Lou Harrison, *Double Music,* as well as Lukas Foss's Percussion Quartet (♦New World 80405). The **Continuum Percussion Quartet** also features a splendid Cage *Third Construction,* along with Irwin Bazelon's

Fourscore, Rouse's *Ku-Ka-Ilimoku* and Harrison's Concerto for Violin & Percussion Orchestra (New World 80382). Yet another coupling of the *Second* and *Third Constructions* comes from the fine four-man **Mainz Percussion Ensemble** in an all-Cage program (Col Legno). In complete contrast, the **Pekarsky Percussion Ensemble** has made a splendid disc of works by the Russian Vyacheslav Artiomov (♦Olympia 514), as well as two of his percussion-and-orchestra pieces (Olympia 515).

Les Percussions de Strasbourg has been a dominant force in experimental percussion ensemble writing in Europe since the 1970s. Their recorded repertoire includes works by Edison Denisov (Pierre Verany) and Miloslav Kabeláč (Praga), Messiaen's *Et exspecto resurrectionem mortuorum* (♦Sony 68332), Stravinsky's *Les Noces* (Pierre Verany) and Xenakis's *Pleïades* (Harmonia Mundi). Another modernist-minded ensemble is **Percussive Rotterdam**, who have recorded works by James Wood (Mode 51) and, directed by Wood, Scelsi's *TKRDG*, with male voices (Accord).

The Mexican **Tambuco** ensemble has made several recordings, especially of chamber pieces involving percussion. An excellent example of their range and virtuosity can be found in *Rítmicas*, named after two pieces by Amadeo Roldán, in collaboration with Camerata de las Américas (Dorian 90245). The same combination has also recorded chamber and percussion works by Chavez (Dorian 90215).

Steve Reich achieved a hypnotic and euphonious use of percussion instruments on a large scale in works like *Drumming, Music for Mallet Instruments, Voices and Organ*, and *Six Marimbas*, all of which have been recorded by several groups, most authentically perhaps by his own ad hoc group, **Steve Reich and Musicians** (Nonesuch 79451, 10CD; though see **Amadinda**, above). That Nonesuch collection also included **The Hague Percussion Group;** music from Senegal and Mozambique form the cores of their "Skin Hits" and "The Wooden Branch," mixed in with works by Cage, Ron Ford, Xenakis and others in performances and contexts as exciting as they are unusual (Globe). The group also recorded Birtwistle's modern classic percussion sextet *For O, For O, The Hobby Horse Is Forgot* in an all-Birtwistle disc (Etcetera 1130).

Wendy Mae Chambers' *Twelve²* is a hugely ambitious work in eleven movements for twelve players, directed with finesse by **Howard van Hyning.** If it doesn't quite sustain its 45-minute-plus length, it's undeniably fascinating (New World). Equally ear-opening, for entirely different reasons, is a brief program by the **All Star Percussion Ensemble** of arrangements by Harold Farbermann of music from Bizet's *Carmen*, Beethoven (Symphony 9's Scherzo), Pachelbel's famous Canon, and Berlioz's *March to the Scaffold;* over-familiar music in a bizarre context that sheds light on the originals (Vox 8195). Bizet is a recurrent choice for arrangers, as for the **Horsholm Percussion and Marimba Ensemble** who include a *Carmen* suite—arranged by Klaus-Dieter Zimmer—and reworkings of Joplin (*The Entertainer*), Chick Corea, and others (Danacord), and **Repercussion** in their program of classical favorites by composers like Rachmaninoff, Mussorgsky, Vivaldi, Chopin, and Debussy (Analekta). The **O-Zone Percussion Group** cast their net wider with arrangements of music from Bizet's *L'Arlésienne* (for a change), Bach and Debussy to *Greensleeves* and Billy Joel (Klavier).

On the very edge of the classical and crossover divide is a disc of works for Balinese gamelan orchestra, played mainly by the Californian **Sekar Jaya,** ranging from real kebyar music in arrangement to Wayne Vitale's remarkably faithful *Khayalan Tiga*, played by Seka Gong Abdi Budaya from Bali (♦New World 80430). There's also a varied program by **Gamelan Pacifica** (¿What Next?). Over the divide, perhaps, is the album by **Drums A'Plenty,** featuring treatments of *It's a Long, Long Way to Tip-* *perary* with tracks entitled *The Sledgehammer Strikes Back* and *Bedtime for Drums* (Bandleader).

CONCERTOS

Percussion concertos have been a growth area in 20th-century music, although their presence on disc is not yet as widespread as percussion-only issues. However, there are some curiosities from earlier centuries, like Jean Baptiste Prin's suite *L'Echo et Psyché*, written in the first half of the 18th century, Johan Wilhelm Hertel's Concerto for 8 Timpani, Winds and Strings from the late 1700s, and the roughly contemporaneous (but anonymous) *Adagio and Allegro* for timpani and bass strings, all played by **Nicholas Bardach** and coupled with **Werner Thärichen** performing his own 1954 Timpani Concerto (Koch 311052).

Perhaps the most played recent work is *Veni, veni, Emanuel* by the Scottish Catholic composer, James Macmillan, premiered and later recorded by **Glennie** (♦RCA 61916). **Colin Currie**—finalist in the BBC's "Young Musician of the Year" with a brilliant premiere of Errolyn Wallen's Percussion Concerto (scandalously still unrecorded)—has also made a splendid account of it (Naxos 554167). Glennie has recorded the classic Milhaud concerto, as well as others by Richard Rodney Bennett, Akira Miyoshi and Ney Rosauro (♦RCA 61277). A fine rival version of Milhaud's concerto—with its companion for marimba and vibraphone—was set down in the 1970s by **Rainer Kuisma** (BIS 149).

Nørgård's incandescent *Bach to the Future*, based on three Bach preludes, has been recorded by the **Safri Duo** along with Jacob ter Veldhuis' elemental *Goldrush Concerto* (♦Chandos 9645). **Gert Mortensen** has also recorded Sallinen's masterly and attractive *Symphonic Dialogue* for percussionist and orchestra, now counted as his Symphony 2 (BIS 511). Another symphony with a substantial percussion part is *Metasinfonia,* the Polish composer Andrzej Panufnik's 7th, who also wrote a Concertino for Timpani, Percussion and Strings. **Kurt-Hans Goedicke,** formerly principal timpanist of the London Symphony, recorded both works under the composer's direction, though *Metasinfonia* is currently only available on cassette (Unicorn-Kanchana); the Concertino—with **Michael Frye** playing the additional percussion part—is still available in a peerless performance (♦Unicorn-Kanchana 2020). **Richard Benjafield** (a member of Ensemble Bash) and **Graham Cole** provide spirited competition (Conifer 217). Perhaps the most bizarrely titled concerto is James Wood's Paul Klee-inspired *Two men meet, each presuming the other to be from a distant planet,* which includes parts for Wood's invention the xyl, a huge microtonal evolution of the xylophone (NMC 044).

In ensemble percussion-and-orchestra works, **Nexus** has set down Takemitsu's epic *From me flows what you call time* in a highly evocative performance (Sony 63044; a live account from the 1993 BBC Proms has been released in a cover disc of the *BBC Music Magazine*, Vol. 2 No. 11), as well as Canadian Harry Freedman's *Touchings* (CBC 5154). **The Hague Percussion Group** has also been active in this field, with recordings of works by their countrymen, Cornelius de Bondt (*Donemus*) and Louis Andriessen's *De Tijd* (♦Nonesuch 79291), Messiaen's *Des Canyons aux étoiles* (Auvidis), and Reich's *Tehilim* (Nonesuch).   RICKARDS

Piano

The last two centuries have produced three identifiable schools of piano playing and technique: the French school; the musical descendants of Chopin and Liszt, sometimes called the German school; and the Russian school. Few of the great pianists fit these categories easily, but it's helpful to describe these schools, as they have influenced nearly all the artists listed here.

The French school is characterized by an elegant, refined, logical, and precise style. The fingers are generally held close to the keys, and the resulting economy of motion facilitates the clean, light runs idealized as "jeu perlé." Fidelity to the score is essential. The great examples of this school are Cortot and Casadesus.

The German school is more forceful, profound, massive, and serious. This is also true of the German pianos built by Bechstein, Steinway, and Bösendorfer, which are much heavier and produce a more powerful tone than the French Erards and Pleyels. The best examples of this style are Rosenthal, Backhaus, and Kempff.

The Russian school is sensuous and intuitive, even mystical. It's more concerned with cultivating deep emotional expressiveness than with developing mechanical technique. The school emphasizes using the whole body and playing from the shoulders rather than the fingers as in the French style. The Russian school is a later development, begun by Anton Rubinstein in the 19th century, and it takes much from the German and French traditions. The products of the Russian school include Rachmaninoff, Sofronitsky, Richter, and Gilels.

The library of recorded piano music gives us a nearly complete picture of the range of performing styles from the mid-18th century, when the instrument was perfected, to the present. Today you can obtain an overview of the entire field with just one purchase. The Philips series entitled "Great Pianists of the 20th Century" is a 200-CD set that claims to be the largest project in the history of recordings. It includes contributions from 74 artists and about 25 record companies. Taken as a whole, it's a mixed bag. The selection of artists is reasonable, but some pianists just don't belong here and others are unaccountably missing. In the first category are Previn, Barenboim, Eschenbach, Kissin, Uchida, and Watts. In the second are von Sauer, Rosenthal, Barere, Bauer, Gabrilowitsch, Petri, Annie Fischer, Goode, Sokolov, and Hamelin, all of whom are described below.

Regrettably, too many of the selections in "Great Pianists" are commonly available and too few are rare. The experienced collector will find it frustrating to buy a two-disc set for the sake of a few minutes of music that can't be found elsewhere. The newcomer will find better choices in other releases. The best examples of the latter are Edwin Fischer's complete *Well-Tempered Clavier* (EMI); Gieseking's complete Debussy piano music and Mozart piano sonatas (both EMI); Brendel's complete Beethoven sonatas (Philips); Gavrilov's complete Bach *French Suites* (DG); Haebler's complete Mozart sonatas (Philips); Katchen's Brahms (Decca); Moravec's Beethoven (VAI); and the complete legacy of Lipatti (EMI). If you don't see your favorites here, you can find all our references to them in the Index of Artists.

The rarities and essentials in the series include Kovacevich's Beethoven sonatas; Rosalyn Bach; the Backhaus and Bolet live recitals; Ogdon's Alkan; all of Godowsky, Yudina, Sofronitsky, and Ginsburg; and the Cziffra Chopin etudes.

Martha Argerich (b. 1941) took the musical world by storm in 1960 at the Chopin Competition in Warsaw. In the same year, she made her first recording, including works by Chopin, Brahms, Ravel, Prokofiev, and Liszt—a very ambitious and successful program (DG 447430). A few years later, in 1965, she recorded Chopin's Sonata 3, Polonaise Op. 53, and other short works (EMI 56805). Both this and the DG debut disc make excellent introductions to this performer.

Argerich's other early recordings, including the Liszt Sonata (also on DG 447430), a Ravel Concerto (DG 447438), Bach's Partita 2, and Prokofiev's Concerto 3 (Philips 456700), are highly prized for their en-

ergy and enthusiasm. Her live Rachmaninoff Concerto 3 with Chailly from 1982 is legendary for its wild abandon but isn't for everyone (Philips 466673). She's subject to the same criticism as Horowitz, that her playing is often about herself and not about the composer. Still, her performances are exceptional for their persuasiveness and risk-taking.

Argerich hasn't made any solo recordings since the mid-1980s. She now plays primarily concertos and chamber music, with good results, though her loyal admirers aren't happy that her solo appearances are rare. One of the best sets of Beethoven's violin sonatas is by Argerich and Kremer (DG 453743). Another high point is a disc featuring the Tchaikovsky and Shostakovich piano trios with Kremer and Maisky (DG 459326).

Claudio Arrau (1903–91) resists classification. Gifted with superb technique and a temperament that included romantic and analytical aspects, his playing was always insightful and entertaining. However, it can also be glib and self-indulgent. His early recordings are the best, including Chopin etudes (EMI 61016) and Sonata 3 and Schumann's *Carnaval* (EMI 64025). Also fascinating are Balakirev's *Islamey* and Busoni's *Carmen Fantasy,* a CD from the 1930s that includes Liszt's *Spanish Rhapsody* (Dante 001).

In the 1960s and 70s Arrau recorded most of the mainstream piano repertoire for Philips, with mixed results. Best are his Liszt, Beethoven, and Debussy; the Brahms and Chopin solo works are less successful. A Beethoven set includes all the sonatas, concertos, and variations, recorded between 1962 and 1985; this is one of the great traversals of the sonatas, and a real bargain (Philips 462358, 14CD). Beware of the "Final Sessions" on Philips. These four releases from 1993, with music of Bach, Debussy, and Schubert, are an unfortunate postscript to a great career.

Vladimir Ashkenazy (b. 1937). Before he turned to conducting, Ashkenazy recorded much of the standard repertoire. The high point is his early Chopin etudes; this is perhaps the most successful set of this music on record, integrating flawless technique with understanding and emotional depth (BMG/Melodiya 33215). His later complete Chopin piano music is consistently good but rarely reaches the same heights of inspiration (Decca 421185). He has also recorded sets of Beethoven sonatas (Decca 425590) and Mozart piano concertos; these are solid but not exceptional (Decca 425557).

Although Ashkenazy now rarely records solo piano music, two recent items are worth hearing. Brahms's Sonata 3 is serious and unsentimental (Decca 430771, with *Handel Variations*). By contrast, he makes Shostakovich's Preludes and Fugues Op. 87 sound almost Romantic, smoothing out the difficult parts. He's the first to have taken this approach to this music, and it's very successful (Decca 466066, 2CD).

Wilhelm Backhaus (1884–1969), one of the first modern artists of the keyboard (see Cortot for his antithesis), played with a clean, spare, and objective style. In spite of this analytical approach, his performances are full of feeling. One of the first pianists to record, he had a long career on the concert stage and in the studio and left us a great legacy. Generally associated with Beethoven and Brahms, he was also the first to record the Chopin etudes, in 1927; this is still regarded as one of the best recordings (Pearl 9902 and others). Backhaus plays them smoothly and softly, overcoming their technical challenges without apparent effort. A live recording from 1953 includes seven of the Op. 25 etudes and shows the changes that occurred in his playing style over the years (Aura 119). His technical command is the same, but he's more relaxed and confident and more willing to let the music speak for itself.

His 1939 recording of Brahms's Waltzes Op. 39 runs just over 13 minutes; it's difficult to imagine anyone actually dancing to this version, but it's exhilarating nevertheless (EMI 66425). His studio recordings of the complete Beethoven sonatas, made in the 1960s, display awesome technique for a man in his 70s (Decca 433882), as do the two Brahms concertos from about the same time (Decca 433895). His live Beethoven recordings are in some ways even better, freer and more vivid (Orfeo 300921).

Simon Barere (1896–1951) owned the fastest set of fingers ever to play at Carnegie Hall. His Schumann *Toccata* runs to less than five minutes—one of the shortest on records—yet never sounds rushed. His early HMV recordings from the mid-1930s have been reissued (Appian 7001, 2CD), as have his Carnegie Hall recordings (Appian 700809, 2CD). The first set includes works by Liszt, Chopin, and Schumann, as well as pieces by Balakirev, Scriabin, and Glazunov. Liszt's *La leggierezza,* which opens the program, is the epitome of lightness, and Balakirev's *Islamey* is a brilliant showpiece; both are astounding for speed and accuracy. Few pianists could match Barere's precise runs of notes or rapid-fire staccato. The Carnegie Hall discs feature concertos by Liszt and Rachmaninoff and the Liszt Sonata. The sound quality of these private acetate recordings is poor, but they are rare and essential documents of one of the great keyboard artists.

Harold Bauer (1873–1951). Overshadowed by Rachmaninoff in his time, Bauer made relatively few recordings. We're fortunate that a sweeping and powerful rendition of Brahms's Sonata 3, one of his specialties, gives us a chance to hear this master at his best (Biddulph 009). Also on this disc are short pieces by Brahms, Grieg, Debussy, Schubert, Chopin, Couperin, Scarlatti, Handel, and Bach. The baroque works show Bauer's sensitive handling of contrapuntal lines, which merge with his subtle use of crescendos. Another disc opens with an exceptionally gentle and lyrical set of Schumann's *Fantasiestücke* and includes short works by Liszt and Grieg (Biddulph 011). The Grieg pieces in particular are distinguished by a light touch and a warm, romantic spirit.

Jorge Bolet (1914–90). One of the greatest piano recitals of all time took place in Carnegie Hall on February 25, 1974, when Bolet played the Bach/Busoni *Chaconne* and Chopin preludes, plus encores; the entire recital is now available (Philips 46724). This is a rare example of the convergence of energy, brilliant inspiration, and flawless technique, all expertly captured on disc. Bolet's best-known recordings covered much of Liszt's piano music in consistently beautiful, refined, and smooth-toned performances (Decca). Liszt's *Transcendental Etudes* are shown from another angle in a 1970 Barcelona recording; here Bolet takes more risks, and the results are exciting and persuasive (Ensayo 9711). A solid and persuasive Reger *Variations and Fugue on a Theme by Telemann* plus Brahms's *Handel Variations* are available (London 417791). Bolet was always able to produce lovely sounds, and his pianissimo was second to none.

Alfred Brendel (b. 1931) is a thoughtful and analytical musician. He has recorded three complete sets of the Beethoven sonatas, which are his specialty. The first of these, though not as well recorded as the others, is the liveliest and most interesting (Vox 5028, 5042, 5056, 5060). The earlier of the two Philips sets is consistently rewarding (412575); the later one has better sound (446909). Brendel is able to convey the individual character of each piece. His recordings of Beethoven's short pieces and variations are also valuable, since they include many early works (without opus numbers) that no other first-rate pianist has ever put on disc

(Vox 3017). For anyone with a strong interest in Beethoven, Brendel is essential.

There's a lot more to Brendel than Beethoven, however. His Haydn sonatas are exemplary; he understands this music thoroughly and presents it effectively (Philips 456727). Schubert is another composer with whom he has a strong affinity; he has surveyed the piano sonatas twice, and the second set is one of the best recordings of these works and one of Brendel's best (Philips 438703). His *Pictures at an Exhibition* is a curiosity and recommended mainly to those who already know this piece well (Philips 420156). Brendel's forays into 20th-century works, including Schoenberg's Concerto, are very successful and worth hearing (DG 432740).

Ferruccio Busoni (1866–1924) is better known today as a composer and transcriber, and most of his recordings are on piano rolls, not on discs. This isn't the ideal way to hear a performer, as the reproducing piano is not an accurate medium. However, the excellent sound of a set that contains works by Liszt, Chopin, and Busoni's own arrangement of the Bach *Chaconne* has its compensations, and the playing is convincing (Nimbus 8810).

Robert Casadesus (1899–1972) was scrupulous in his fidelity to the score and the composer's intent. His recordings of Ravel's complete piano music are precise and meticulous; his close association with the composer helped greatly in this regard (Sony 63316). He also excels in the music of Ravel's contemporary and compatriot, Debussy. The set of preludes he recorded in 1953/54 is one of the most idiomatic and persuasive readings of these pieces (CBS 45688).

Mozart's Concertos 21 and 26, in collaboration with Szell, are elegant and refined (Sony 67178). The four works by Rameau that open the volume devoted to Casadesus in the Philips "Great Pianists" series are fine examples of delicate filigree presented with confidence and strength. The set continues with Bach's *French Suite* 6 and six Scarlatti sonatas, all wonderful interpretations of Baroque music on a modern instrument (Philips 456739).

Alfred Cortot (1877–1962) represents the end of an era. He was the last exponent of a personal, subjective style that gave intuition and interpretation the same weight as precise technique. This approach was replaced by the modern objective way of playing, which places logic and precision at the forefront. Cortot was an artist and a law unto himself, and to enjoy his playing you must come to terms with his idiosyncrasies. Modern ears may find him cavalier, willful, approximate, and even sloppy, but beneath that surface lie great depth and insight.

Cortot's recordings are highly variable. Spirited and passionate, they're also technically imperfect, and some from his late career show a decline in his technique. A Chopin set is a good survey but a mixed bag; it's probably the best general introduction, as it concentrates on a composer with whom Cortot was strongly identified, but it doesn't always show him at his best (EMI 67359). An earlier set of etudes from 1933 and 1934 is superior in many ways, especially in note accuracy (Philips 46751). The great Schumann sets, *Papillons, Kinderszenen, Kreisleriana, Carnaval,* and the *Symphonic Etudes,* were all recorded when he was in his prime (Biddulph 003/5).

Clifford Curzon (1907–82). A master of analysis, Curzon was especially effective at interpreting the more difficult large works, for example, Brahms's Sonata 3 (Decca 448578) and the Liszt Sonata (Decca 452306). He combined an understanding of their large-scale structure with attention to detail, bringing these pieces to life. His style never calls attention to itself; instead, it draws the listener deeper into the music, revealing much beauty and truth. Two Schubert sonatas, D 850 and D 960, are especially well served by this approach (Decca 443570; 452399). Mozart's Concertos 26 and 27 and Schubert's *Impromptus* and *Wanderer Fantasy* are all played with insight and charm (Philips 456757).

György Cziffra (1921–94). Phenomenal technique and a complete lack of inhibition combined to make Cziffra controversial. Some listeners are put off by his extroverted manner and aggressive showmanship, but no one presents a more persuasive reading of the great works of Liszt. For those who enjoy this approach, the good news is the "Introuvables" set that contains about two hours of Liszt plus many other showpieces (EMI 67366, 6 CDs). His *Hungarian Rhapsodies* and complete *Années de pèlerinage* are available (EMI 64882), and so is one of the most over-driven sets of the *Transcendental Etudes* ever recorded (EMI 69111). The Chopin etudes get a similarly extreme presentation (Philips 456760). These performances must be heard to be believed.

Annie Fischer (1914–94) was an inspired and intuitive artist whose performances were very much of the moment, in pursuit of an elusive ideal of total spontaneity. In 1977 and 1978, near the end of her career, she recorded the complete Beethoven sonatas (Hungaroton 31626/34, 9 separate CDs). Generally uncomfortable with recordings and self-critical, she wasn't satisfied with these sessions and would not approve their release. In the late 1990s these exceptional performances were at last made available, and they are among the finest Beethoven cycles.

Two other recordings show her unique approach: the final Schubert Sonata, D 960, is restlessly searching, in contrast to the spacious sound world presented by many other artists; the Liszt Sonata is probing and driven, always near the edge of what she and the instrument can handle (Hungaroton 31494). Schumann's *Kinderszenen* and *Kreisleriana* are less intense and more lyrical; they are part of an "Introuvables" set that includes seven Beethoven sonatas recorded between 1958 and 1961 (EMI 69217).

Edwin Fischer (1886–1960) was an unusually headstrong performer, throwing himself into every piece he played with great determination. The results are always impressive and persuasive, but they may not be to everyone's taste. His complete *Well-Tempered Clavier* is one of the landmarks of Bach discography (Pearl 0017; EMI). Recorded between 1933 and 1936, it's forward-looking in that Fischer is faithful to Bach's terraced dynamics and doesn't use the resources of the modern instrument artificially to embellish the score. This may be one of the earliest historically informed performances on record.

His early recordings of Beethoven's Sonatas 8 ("Pathétique"), 23 ("Appassionata"), and 31, from 1935-38, exhibit a great sense of drama, but Fischer has an occasional tendency to rush (Appian 5502, with Handel's Suite in D minor and *Chaconne* in G). Seven Beethoven sonatas recorded between 1948 and 1954 demonstrate that his energy level and penetrating intellect remained strong through the end of his career (Music & Arts 880). In spite of occasional technical problems (both in the recordings and the performances), these broadcast tapes are a valuable part of Fischer's legacy. His Schubert *Impromptus* are simultaneously intense, lyrical, and romantic in their abandon (Testament 1145).

Leon Fleisher (b. 1928) recorded two of the finest sets of concertos available, with Szell conducting, by Brahms (Sony 63225) and Beethoven (Sony 48397). These bold, athletic performances are exhilarating and exceptionally accurate, both technically and in interpreta-

tion. His Grieg and Schumann concertos, also with Szell, have been reissued only as a CBS "Masterworks Portrait" import (44849). In 1964 Fleisher's career was cut short by arthritis, which limited the use of his right hand, and for many years his repertoire was limited to such works as Ravel's Concerto for the Left Hand and Prokofiev's Concerto 4 (Sony 47188).

Ignaz Friedman (1882–1948) was a Chopin expert from Poland, born in the same town as Hofmann (Podgorze, near Cracow). Friedman brings an authentic feel to the mazurkas, and he also excels in Mendelssohn's *Songs without Words* (Philips 456784, with more Chopin and Beethoven's "Moonlight" Sonata; the Chopin and Mendelssohn are also on Biddulph 044). Friedman's complete recordings have been released (Pearl IF 2000).

Ossip Gabrilowitsch (1878–1936). One of the most famous and popular artists of his time, and like Bauer overshadowed by Rachmaninoff, Gabrilowitsch left a very small recorded legacy, all of it valuable. The Arensky *Waltz*, a duet with Bauer, is legendary. An odd collection of short pieces by various composers, plus two versions of the Schumann Quintet Op. 44, with the Flonzaley Quartet — all of them gems — are collected on CD (Dante 51/52). This set includes a number of orchestral pieces with Gabrilowitsch as conductor and provides his complete recordings, lasting a little over two hours — enough to prove his greatness.

Walter Gieseking (1895–1956) was a natural and intuitive pianist. According to legend, he never practiced except in his own mind. He apparently would study the score, imagine playing it, and then perform it flawlessly. His complete Debussy piano works are the best ever recorded (EMI 65855, 4CD). When listening to him play the music of the Impressionists, it's easy to forget that the piano is a percussion instrument; his legato is perfect, and his handling of the musical line is inspired. Gieseking's interpretation of some of Grieg's *Lyric Pieces* is ideal; his sensitive phrasing and delicate tonal palette capture the varied moods of these charming miniatures perfectly (EMI 66775, with selections from Mendelssohn's *Songs without Words*).

Gieseking could also play Beethoven and the great Romantic concertos with aplomb. All his live recordings are enthusiastically recommended, especially a magnificent "Emperor" Concerto from 1944 in excellent sound, and the best-ever Schumann Concerto from 1942, with Furtwängler conducting (Music & Arts 815). Four Beethoven sonatas, including the "Waldstein" and "Appassionata," are available (VAI 1088); an all-Schumann disc includes *Symphonic Etudes* and Grand Sonata 1 (Music & Arts 1013); another has Brahms's Sonata 3 (Arbiter 103); and still another features music of Bach, Beethoven, and Schumann from broadcast recitals of 1949 to 1951 (Music & Arts 743).

Emil Gilels (1916–85). Somewhat overshadowed by his countryman Richter, at least in the West, Gilels is nevertheless in the same class. Neither pianist recorded all the Beethoven sonatas; Richter avoided a number of them, and Gilels didn't live to finish his studio cycle, but he recorded nearly all of them, and the results are consistently excellent (collected as DG 453221, with some also available separately). An overview of Gilels's repertoire is presented in a 1959 London recital captured by the BBC; it begins with graceful Scarlatti sonatas and Bach variations and continues with Schumann, Tchaikovsky, and Prokofiev (BBC Legends 4015).

One of the greatest Tchaikovsky recordings is a set of the three concertos Gilels made with Maazel (EMI 68637). He imbues the familiar

Concerto 1 with lyrical fire and serious passion without slipping into soft, self-indulgent romantic excess. His earlier recording of this concerto with Reiner is similar in tone (RCA 68530). Another important recording is the two Brahms concertos with Jochum (DG 447446). A selection of Grieg's *Lyric Pieces* is among the finest recorded versions and one of the high points of Gilels's discography (DG 419749). For those inclined to explore this pianist further, there is a boxed set that includes both concertos and solo works, many recorded live, and all richly rewarding (Melodiya 40116, 5CD).

Grigory Ginsburg (1904–61). Little known outside Russia, Ginsburg's brilliant recordings of Liszt's opera paraphrases are among the finest examples of the bravura style of the Russian piano school, and a number of them have been collected (Melodiya 33210; Philips 456802). The Philips set includes six of Liszt's *Hungarian Rhapsodies,* Tchaikovsky's Grande Sonata, Medtner's *Sonata reminiscenza,* and Prokofiev's Sonata 3. A disc with Rachmaninoff's two Suites for piano four-hands is a nice complement; Ginsburg is joined by his teacher, Alexander Goldenweiser, another great Russian master (Talents of Russia 16260).

Leopold Godowsky (1870–1938) was possibly the finest and most subtle technician ever to play the instrument. Known as the pianists's pianist, he was at his best when performing at home for his friends, and many great keyboard artists of his day came to hear him. However, his recordings are somewhat dry and literal, thoughtful rather than exciting. Godowsky was very conscious of the limitations of the recording process of his day, and he did his best to compensate for them, but his recorded performances remain earthbound. For the listener who prefers delicacy to display, his playing can be a delight. The high points can be found in a CD that includes several Chopin nocturnes, the B minor Sonata, and Grieg's *Ballade* (Philips 456805). Perhaps the greatest examples of his work are his own transcriptions of two Schubert songs, "Morgengrüss" and "Gute Nacht."

Richard Goode (b. 1943). A student of Serkin and similarly reticent in style, Goode gets out of the way of the music and lets the voice of the composer come through. He has produced a fine complete set of Beethoven sonatas (Nonesuch); the best single discs are Op. 10, Op. 31, and the late sonatas (Nonesuch 79211/13). His clean, unmannered approach to Schubert also recalls Serkin (Nonesuch 79271 for the earlier sonatas, D 845 and 850; 79064 for D 958). His Bach *Partitas* are careful and detailed, with subtle effects; these performances are understated but rewarding for the patient listener (Nonesuch 79483).

Glenn Gould (1932–82). A perfectionist, Gould left a large legacy of highly polished performances. He retired from the concert stage early to concentrate his efforts on the recording studio. His most famous recordings are of Bach's *Goldberg Variations;* the first and last are available, and both are fascinating examples of his analytical approach (Columbia/Sony 38479 and 37779, respectively). Inner voices are emphasized, lines are clarified, and yet this is a hyper-intellectual presentation, particularly in the later version. A reissue of Gould's first twelve Bach LPs gives a more complete picture of his unusual insight into this music (Sony 64226).

Gould's real strength was not in the music of the Baroque or Classical periods—although he played a great deal of it—but in the 20th-century repertoire, especially the atonal Berg; there are broadcast recordings of music by Berg, Schoenberg, and Webern (CBC 2008). His Beethoven is a favorite of some listeners and certainly worth hearing, in particular the "Hammerklavier" (Sony 45821). Other Beethoven

sonatas seem strangely distorted or are played much too fast. It's said that Gould recorded the Mozart sonatas just to show how little he thought of this composer.

Marc-André Hamelin (b. 1961). At the end of the 20th century there has been a trend toward super-virtuoso technique and refuge in the "standard" repertoire. Hamelin's technique is second to none, and his bold championship of obscure and modern composers shows that he's more concerned with artistic worth than with commercial success. In addition, he's a great entertainer. This is an unbeatable combination.

Hamelin's traversals of the complete sonatas of Scriabin and Medtner are twin pillars of his discography (Hyperion 67131 and 67221), his Alkan Sonata is dazzling and a lot of fun to hear (Hyperion 66794), and his performance of Alkan's Concerto for Solo Piano is a major achievement (Music & Arts 724). His recordings of Rzewski's *The People United Will Never Be Defeated* (Hyperion 67077) and works by Georgy Catoire are to be applauded for his determination to bring these obscure composers the attention they deserve (Hyperion 67090).

Josef Hofmann (1876–1957). Famous as a child prodigy in Poland, Hofmann spent most of his career in America. He made many recordings, from 1903—the earliest days of acoustic 78s—through the 1950s. They display a refined and precise technique with shimmering surfaces but limited depth. Because the medium allowed only six or seven minutes per side, Hofmann was forced to choose short, showy pieces, but this doesn't diminish the performer's artistry or the listener's pleasure. He was very much aware of the limits of recording technology and his audience's tastes and tailored his presentation for best effect under the circumstances.

His collected recordings are available (VAIA 1002, 1020, 1036, and 1047, Vols. 1 through 4; Marston 52004 and 52014, Vols. 5 and 6, with two additional volumes planned). The Brunswick recordings of 1922 and 1923 are the best introduction to his art; they have reasonably good sound and capture the artist in his prime (VAIA 1047). The earliest items are flashier but very noisy; the rest are later live recordings that don't show him at his best (VAIA 1036).

Vladimir Horowitz (1903–89). A great showman and probably the most famous concert pianist of his day, Horowitz was prone to excess and self-indulgence. Even his earliest recordings (from the 1930s) show these traits, but this is exactly what endeared him to his audiences. The best single Horowitz disc is his Metropolitan Opera recital that contains six Scarlatti sonatas, a Chopin ballade, and music of Liszt and Rachmaninoff (RCA 61416).

His early recordings show him at his most confident and technically secure (EMI 63538). This set includes four sonatas by Scarlatti and one by Haydn, four Chopin etudes, the Liszt Sonata, and Rachmaninoff's Concerto 3, among other works. Horowitz was at his best in Schumann's music, especially the short pieces like *Arabesque, Kreisleriana* (both in CBS/Sony 42409), and *Kinderszenen* (RCA 61414). Scriabin's Sonatas 3 and 5 are available (RCA 6215), and there is a fine selection of works by Schumann (RCA 6680). Tchaikovsky's Concerto 1 is the ideal vehicle for him, and there are two versions with Toscanini; both are electrifying and have attained legendary status (RCA 60449 and 7992). The earlier studio recording (RCA 60449) is faster and comes across as rushed and glib; the later live recording is steadier and more serious but still brilliant and exciting.

Mieczyslaw Horszowski (1892–1993). In the late 1980s, as Horszowski was approaching the age of 100, his longevity as a performer brought him much attention from the media. Unfortunately this came long after his technique had faded. The recordings of the late Beethoven sonatas from about 1950 (Vox 5500) and *Diabelli Variations* are both excellent (Vox 5511); the 1990s recordings of Bach and Schumann aren't as good (Nonesuch). Mozart is the composer with whom he had the strongest affinity, and his complete cycle of the sonatas has been issued, recorded live between 1958 and 1969 (Arbiter 101 and 104). These recordings present him at his best; Horszowski dramatizes the sonatas successfully, an unusual approach that is difficult to achieve. Many performers find Mozart"s music facile but shallow; Horszowski presents these works with the full understanding that Mozart was the master of operatic form. Similar examples of his delightful singing tone and phrasing are found in the Mozart Concertos recorded in the 1960s with Waldman (Pearl 9138 and 9153).

William Kapell (1922–53). Many critics considered Kapell the most promising American pianist of the postwar generation; unfortunately, his brilliant career was cut short when he died in a plane crash at the age of 31. His style was direct, clear, and energetic, his technique impeccable, and his repertoire eclectic and adventurous. A valuable survey contains his legendary Chopin mazurkas and sonatas and Rachmaninoff and Khachaturian concertos (RCA 68442, 9CD). It also has many lesser-known items, including Shostakovich preludes, Scarlatti sonatas, and Copland's Sonata. Chopin's Sonata 2 is profound, moody, and complex; the mazurkas are brought to life with subtle accents.

Broadcast recordings of Rachmaninoff's Concerto 3 and Khachaturian's Concerto are available (VAIA 1027), and another disc features part of Beethoven's Concerto 3 and Shostakovich's Concerto 1 (Arbiter 108); the latter includes *Pictures at an Exhibition,* which also appears in the RCA set and in a 1953 Australian recital (VAIA 1048). Of the three, the version on Arbiter (from 1951) is the most colorful and varied, the RCA (from 1953) is steadier and sustains a dreamlike mood, and the VAIA is wild, daring, and free. All three are live recordings, but RCA has by far the clearest sound. It's fascinating to hear three such different interpretations of this piece, all recognizably by the same person.

Julius Katchen (1926–69). Katchen's 1949 recording of Brahms's Sonata 3 was credited as the first piano LP. From then on he was identified with this composer, and later recorded a fine set of Brahms's piano music, an important part of any serious collection of piano recordings (Decca 430053, 6CD). Katchen brings vitality and a perfect sense of timing to these works, and he's especially successful in the larger pieces, like the *Handel* and *Paganini Variations.* The early version of the Brahms Sonata, Franck's *Prelude, Chorale and Fugue,* Chopin's *Ballade* 3 and Fantasy, as well as Ned Rorem's rarely heard Sonata 2, are available (Philips 456856). Katchen's earlier recording of Rachmaninoff's Concerto 2 from 1951 remains one of the brightest readings of this piece (Dutton 2504).

Wilhelm Kempff (1895–1991). With Kempff, the young firebrand— listen to the Beethoven sonatas of the 1920s! (Dante 109)—gradually gave way to a thoughtful, dry, and professorial pianist. His early recordings are full of slips and faults but brimming with enthusiasm and discovery; the late recordings of the same works sound sensible, measured, and correct. Between these two phases, Kempff recorded a complete set of Beethoven sonatas in the 1950s that stylistically falls between the two periods (DG). In excellent monophonic sound, it's preferable to the 1964 stereo version (DG 429306 or 453724).

Kempff was among the first to record the complete sonatas of Schubert, long before these works became popular (DG 423496). His ten-

dency to under-romanticize them, although controversial, is quite effective. His Schumann is less successful (DG 435045), but his Brahms short pieces are beautiful and idiomatic (DG 437249 and DG 437374). Various Bach works and transcriptions are appealing; his Bach is always solid, weighty, and profound (DG 439672).

Stephen Kovacevich (formerly Bishop-Kovacevich, b. 1940). Kovacevich's 1970s Beethoven recordings have an unerring sense of drama (Philips 456877, 456880). Earnest and driven, they can seem a bit too fast at times, but few other pianists are as clearly in touch with the revolutionary spirit of the composer. He has recorded two of the late Schubert sonatas, and these interpretations exhibit the same strong sense of musical architecture that is so effective in his Beethoven (D 960 in EMI 55359, D 959 in 55219).

Josef Lhevinne (1874–1944). All of Lhevinne's recordings have recently been reissued (Philips 456889; Dante 008). His performance of the Schulz-Evler arrangement of the *Blue Danube Waltz* is one of the most famous piano recordings of all time. It combines brilliant technique and high spirits to give us a glimpse into the lost world of *fin-de-siècle* Vienna. But Lhevinne is closer in spirit to the modern style of playing, in which fidelity to the score is considered primary.

Dinu Lipatti (1917–1950). Everything Lipatti played was full of poetry and grace. Sadly, there are few recordings of his performances, but all show outstanding sensitivity and assurance. One disc opens with Chopin's Sonata 3 and includes music by Liszt, Enescu, and the best Ravel *Alborada del Gracioso* ever recorded (EMI 63038). Most of this material, along with the Schumann and Grieg concertos, a Bach Partita (also on EMI 66988), and Chopin's *Barcarolle,* can be found in his "Great Pianists" set (Philips 456892). Don't miss his Chopin waltzes, presented with authority and variety (EMI 66904).

Radu Lupu (b. 1945). Dark and brooding, Lupu's Schubert (Sonata D 960, Decca 440295; D 959, Decca 425033; *Impromptus,* Decca 460975) and Brahms (Sonata 3, Decca 448129) are unusually profound. He has recorded all five Beethoven concertos with Mehta (Decca 448000)—a solid achievement—and two of them (3 and 5) live in Bucharest (Electrecord; Seven Seas 145).

Arturo Benedetti Michelangeli (1920–95). Hailed as the greatest technician of his time, Michelangeli often displayed a detached and dispassionate approach. He could be impulsive and willful and sometimes edited the music to suit his interpretation, but he also conveyed deep concentration and communion with the spirit of the composer. His Debussy preludes are the most successful example of his style (DG 427391). His highly personal approach is evident in his Brahms *Paganini Variations* (EMI 64490; Music & Arts 817). A live BBC broadcast from 1959 includes Chopin's Sonata 2, Clementi's Sonata Op. 12:1, and a dark and moody performance of Ravel's *Gaspard de la Nuit* (Music & Arts 955). Beethoven's Sonata 32 and Scarlatti and Galuppi sonatas are a typically idiosyncratic program (Decca 417772). A recording of Beethoven's Concerto 5 with Celibidache is restless and passionate (Music & Arts 4296), much better than the lifeless version with Giulini (DG).

Benno Moiseiwitsch (1890–1963) excelled in the quiet and lyrical passages of Romantic works. An expert colorist, he brought a personal approach to the music and played with beauty and variety of tone, though he could also seem scattered and inconsistent. His talents are most evident in Schumann, for example in the *Fantasie* Op. 17 and *Fantasiestücke* (Testament 1023). Moiseiwitsch lets these pieces glow from within. His Chopin is represented by a disc containing *Barcarolle,* two ballades, two scherzos, and two nocturnes; the *Barcarolle* starts with a sweet, caressing motion and builds to an effective climax (Philips 456907). This set also features works by Kabalevsky, Medtner, and Prokofiev, and ends with a wonderful rendition of Rachmaninoff's Concerto 2. Two different recordings of Brahms's *Handel Variations* have appeared (Testament 1023, from 1953, and Pearl 9135, from 1930). The former has much better sound; the latter includes Mendelssohn's Concerto One and short pieces by Schumann, Liszt, Debussy, and Ravel.

Ivan Moravec (b. 1930). In the 1960s Moravec made a series of Beethoven and Chopin discs for Connoisseur Society; these highly idiomatic and sensitive performances, in exceptionally fine sound, have been reissued. His Beethoven Concerto 4 is the sweetest and most lyrical version of this piece on disc (VAIA 1021). Four popular Beethoven Sonatas—the "Appassionata," "Pathétique," "Moonlight," and "Les Adieux"—are in another (VAIA 1069); Chopin preludes, Scherzo One, and *Barcarolle* in a third (VAIA 1039); and the ballades and mazurkas in a fourth (VAI 1092). They are all fine examples of Moravec's smooth and unaffected style; he has a unique ability to find the essence of this complex music. His complete Chopin nocturnes are very refined, though slow in some places (Nonesuch 79233). The artist seems lost in his own world, thoroughly involved and self-satisfied. His Debussy, including *Images* and *Estampes,* provides successful examples of his measured approach (Vox 5103).

John Ogdon (1937–89). For courage bordering on recklessness, few pianists can match Ogdon, and none with this much daring can match his technique. Who else would or could sit down to play Sorabji's massive, five-hour *Opus Clavicembalisticum* in what is essentially a single take? Without the score in hand it's impossible to gauge the accuracy of his playing, but there's no mistaking his energy and dedication in this bizarre work (Altarus Records 9075, 4 CD). Other Ogdon recordings not to be missed are Scriabin Sonatas (EMI 72652), Beethoven's "Hammerklavier" (RCA 3123, which might make it to CD one day), and Alkan's Concerto for Piano Solo (Philips 456913). Busoni is another composer for whom Ogdon had a special affinity; *Toccata* and *Fantasia Contrappuntistica* are given bold, dramatic readings (Altarus 9063). There is more poetry in Rachmaninoff's Suites for two pianos, with Brenda Lucas, which show Ogdon's lyrical side (ASV 636).

Murray Perahia (b. 1947). Early in his career, Perahia made outstanding recordings of Schumann's *Fantasiestücke* (CBS/Sony 32299), Chopin's Sonatas 2 and 3 (CBS 32780) and Schubert's Impromptus (CBS/Sony 37291). His complete Mozart concertos are highly regarded for their clear and careful interpretations (Sony 46441, 12 CD, also available separately). Perahia's Schubert *Fantasy* for piano four hands, D 940, with Lupu, is the best version of that music extant (CBS/Sony 39511), and his 1996 recording of four keyboard Handel Suites and seven Scarlatti sonatas is elegant and graceful (Sony 62785).

Egon Petri (1881–1962). Bold and energetic but also highly polished and refined, Petri was full of contradictions. His technique was exceptionally precise but never drew attention to itself. The 1929 Electrola platters of Chopin and Liszt etudes and transcriptions that open the first of two sets are exuberant almost to the point of recklessness (Appian 7023). The Liszt recordings from the 1930s in the same set display an exceptional command but convey a darker mood and tone. Late recordings include the last three Beethoven sonatas, Bach transcriptions, Chopin preludes, Schumann's *Fantasiestücke,* and Busoni's *Fantasia*

Contrappuntistica; the last is especially valuable, as Petri and Busoni were close colleagues (Music & Arts 772, 4CD).

Maurizio Pollini (b. 1942). One of the few pianists to study with Michelangeli, Pollini exhibits a precise technique and emotional restraint reminiscent of his master. His early Chopin performances were widely praised and won the 1960 Warsaw Chopin Competition; excerpts are available (LaserLight 15961; Polskie Nagrania). These are cool, assertive, confident, and somewhat aggressive readings. Pollini has recorded more Chopin in the studio (the Etudes in DG 413794, Preludes in 413796, and sonatas in 415346). The earlier sets, in particular the Etudes and Preludes, are the best for their clarity and direct approach; the later recordings are heavily edited and less persuasive.

Pollini's late Beethoven sonatas are very good (DG 429569, 429570), and his late Schubert sonatas are deft and restrained and show great insight (DG 427327, 427326). Finally, Pollini is very much at home in the 20th century. He has programmed music for piano and tape by Nono in recitals, and his recordings of Stravinsky's Three Movements from *Pétrouchka,* Prokofiev's Sonata 7, Boulez's Sonata 2, and Webern's Variations for Piano are the best available (DG 447431).

Sergei Rachmaninoff (1873–1943). A huge figure, both literally and figuratively, Rachmaninoff towered over his contemporaries. With deep roots in both the Russian and German Romantic traditions, he was an unsurpassed interpreter of the piano repertoire. His recorded legacy isn't large but all of it is valuable. The most important and enjoyable pieces are his own four concertos, recorded in the 1930s by RCA and recently reissued in superior transfers (Naxos 110601/02). His chamber music recordings include a marvelous Grieg Sonata Three for violin and piano with Kreisler (RCA 61826). His Chopin Sonata Two is idiosyncratic and persuasive (RCA 62533).

Sviatoslav Richter (1915–97). Regarded by many as the greatest pianist of the 20th century, Richter had an unsurpassed range of repertoire and depth of interpretation. His recording career spans nearly 50 years, from the early 1950s in Moscow to the 1990s in Europe and Japan. An "In Memoriam" set presents an excellent overview of his work, including a selection of Preludes and Fugues from Bach's *Well-Tempered Clavier,* two Chopin ballades, Debussy's *Estampes,* and seven Rachmaninoff preludes (DG 457667). His early Schumann recordings (from the late 1950s), including *Toccata, Fantasiestücke,* and *Waldszenen,* have not been surpassed (DG 435751). Schumann's *Symphonic Etudes* from Prague (1956) are stunning (Praga 254033). This disc is part of a larger set that includes Beethoven concertos, Mozart sonatas, Chopin ballades, and much more (Praga). A London recital from 1961 includes the best Debussy preludes ever recorded (BBC Legends 4021). A 1972 Scriabin recital from Warsaw, featuring Sonatas 2, 5, and 9, and a selection of preludes, is hypnotic (Music & Arts 878).

The Russian recordings from the 1950s and 1960s are consistently exciting and energetic, which largely makes up for their variable sound quality (BMG/Melodiya 29460, 10 CD, available separately). This set contains music by composers from Bach to Prokofiev, both solos and concertos, and includes a fine studio version of *Pictures at an Exhibition.* The more famous live *Pictures* is plagued by noise from the audience—a flu epidemic was raging in Sofia at the time—but the quality of the playing keeps the listener enthralled (Philips 454946). Also in this set are Prokofiev's three "War Sonatas" (6, 7, and 8); Richter is closely identified with these works, having premiered or given the first public performance of each, and these recordings can truly be called definitive.

On his first visit to the United States in 1960, Richter performed Brahms's Concerto 2 with Leinsdorf, a recording that has deservedly achieved legendary status (RCA 6518). His interpretation of the last Schubert Sonata, D 960, is famous—and controversial—for its very slow tempos (Music & Arts 642, a live 1964 recording from Aldeburgh; or Olympia 335, a 1972 studio recording from Salzburg). Even near the end of his career, he continued to add new works to his repertoire. His late recordings of Bach's sonatas and English and French Suites will please anyone who is not a strict early-instrument purist with their beautifully sculpted sound and considered architecture (Stradivarius 33323, 33333/35).

Richter was an exceptional accompanist, working with violinist David Oistrakh, among others. A fine example of this partnership is found in Brahms and Prokofiev sonatas from Salzburg in 1972 (Orfeo 489981). The set of Beethoven cello sonatas with Rostropovich is another example of this side of Richter's art (Philips 412256).

Moriz Rosenthal (1862–1946). A student of philosophy and a performer with tremendous stage presence, Rosenthal left few recordings. All of them, however, are great examples of a tradition now lost. He was one of Liszt's last pupils and thus provides an invaluable link to the generation that invented the piano virtuoso. Rosenthal's best recordings have been collected, including a Chopin piano concerto, *Berceuse,* two etudes, and three mazurkas (Pearl 9339). Another collection contains his complete American recordings: works by Chopin, Strauss, and Handel. Both sets include Rosenthal's first recording (1928), his own arrangement of Strauss's *Blue Danube Waltz* (Biddulph 039). He takes great liberties with the original, at times rendering it almost unrecognizable; however, these creative tangents are both extremely entertaining and very subjective. The Biddulph disc, apart from a staid and solemn "Harmonious Blacksmith" (Handel), features works by Chopin: various mazurkas, preludes, etudes, and Sonata 3, recorded in 1939. All of them have a subtle suggestion of improvisation and a special brand of poetry derived directly from the composer.

Artur Rubinstein (1887–1982). Possibly the best-loved pianist of his day, Rubinstein's enthusiasm for music was contagious. His interpretations are often light and always pleasing, but there are "cannons among the flowers," and he displays a wide range of feeling. His Chopin recordings are his most famous, made both early and late in his career. The early recordings are bright and full of vitality (EMI 64933, 6 CD); the later ones are more polished but no less energetic (RCA 60822, 10 CD). Don't overlook his Schubert and Brahms sonatas (RCA 6257 and 61862, respectively). Short pieces by Grieg in a disc that includes the Concerto are energetic and more earnest than usual for these light works (RCA 61883).

Rubinstein was also an outstanding chamber musician, partnering with Szeryng, Heifetz, Piatigorsky, the Guarneri Quartet, and others in the music of Brahms, Schubert, and Dvořák. Some of the best examples are the two Brahms piano quartets (RCA 5677), the Schubert and Schumann trios (RCA 6262), and Dvořák's Piano Quintet (RCA 6263). He has recently been the subject of an 82-disc retrospective set (RCA 63000, also available separately). There is no other pianist for whom so grand a tribute would even be possible, for none recorded so extensively, and there are few for whom it would be as well deserved.

Emil von Sauer (1862–1942). Although a few early pianists left recordings (for example, the piano rolls of Reinecke and Saint-Saëns), Sauer's constitute the strongest link to the performing style of the middle and late 19th century. A student of both Nikolai Rubinstein and Liszt, Sauer

made about four hours of recordings between 1923 and his death in 1942, and his technique remained strong in later life. Fortunately, all of his solo commercial recordings are available (Marston 53002, 3CD), and in addition there is a live recording of works by Schumann, Chopin, and Schubert from 1940 (Arbiter 114).

These recordings are the inevitable starting point in any serious study of the development of piano playing in the last 100 years. The most characteristic example of Sauer's performances is Schumann's *Carnaval.* This piece offers a microcosm of his style. Its most striking feature to modern ears is the great delicacy of his playing; he caresses the keyboard, producing a sound as smooth as silk and as sweet as honey. Even the unavoidable surface noise of 80-year-old acetates doesn't mar the clarity of his subtle tone colors. There is no thunder or display, only pure seduction.

Artur Schnabel (1882–1951). Schnabel's approach to music was intellectual, intense, and often severe; listening to him requires commitment and effort. He avoided anything resembling light entertainment, which restricted his repertoire. He also tended to disregard his own technical limitations in pursuit of a musical ideal, sometimes leaving it up to the listener to figure out what he had in mind.

The best transfers of Schnabel's pioneering (1930s) Beethoven cycle for HMV are by Pearl (9083, 9099, 9123, 9139, 9142, 9378). These include not only the 32 sonatas but also *Diabelli Variations* and *Bagatelles.* An excellent alternative for those not wishing to invest in the Pearl sets, which total 11 discs, is the Philips "Great Pianists" set that includes Beethoven's Concerto Four, Sonatas 21, 30, and 31, and *Diabelli Variations* (Philips 456961). His Schubert sonatas (D 850, D 958, D 959, and D 960) are fine as well (various labels, including Pearl 9271/72 and EMI).

Rudolf Serkin (1903–91). Not a natural performer or technician, Serkin maintained an arm's-length relationship with his music, taking refuge in a cool detachment that may not be to everyone's liking, but the results are nevertheless refined, thoughtful, and precise. His *Diabelli Variations* are a classic recording and an excellent starting point, though some may find his treatment perfunctory (CBS Masterworks 44837). His Beethoven sonatas are fine but also remote (Sony 64490). However, Schubert's last sonatas (D 959 and D 960) are among the best recordings of these serious works; his methodical style is very effective in conveying the overall structure of these large pieces (Sony 60033). In Brahms's *Handel Variations,* Serkin produces a clear and rational sound that is not without sweetness; his playing is exceptionally lucid and analytical, almost the antithesis of Horowitz (Aura 124). The Brahms concertos with Szell are similarly deliberate in style (Sony 48166 and 53262).

Vladimir Sofronitsky (1901–61) is another colossal Russian talent poorly served by recordings. Sadly, he made very few studio discs, and recordings of his live recitals are often noisy and rough. A good survey of his repertoire is in a set that includes Mozart, Schubert, Schumann, Chopin, Rachmaninoff, Scriabin, and Prokofiev (Melodiya 25177, 2CD). Sofronitsky excelled at all of these, especially Scriabin. Extroverted, technically dazzling, and yet sensitive, in many ways he seemed larger than life. One volume in the Philips "Great Pianists" series concentrates on Chopin and Scriabin and shares one piece with the Melodiya release (Philips 456970). This isn't nearly enough, but, alas, no other recordings are available.

Grigory Sokolov (b. 1950). Almost unknown outside Europe, Sokolov's recordings are hard to find. Most of the early Soviet releases are currently unavailable, with the notable exception of Tchaikovsky Concerto

One and Saint-Saëns 2, with Järvi (Melodiya 40721). Sokolov has a superlative technique and unsurpassed concentration, and his recent solo recitals are worth seeking out. Music by Scriabin, Rachmaninoff, and Prokofiev is a good starting point (Opus 111 40-9104), followed by the Chopin preludes (Opus 111 30-9006).

Solomon (1902–88). Solomon Cutner was supremely elegant, aristocratic, and very English. He eschewed display and his performances are understated to great effect. His concerns are architectural, not superficial, and his recordings require a certain concentration from the listener. His Chopin is sensitive and finely wrought, surprisingly successful for an artist whose style seemed the antithesis of Romanticism (Testament 1030). His late Beethoven sonatas are among the very best versions of these difficult and profound works (EMI 64708), and his Beethoven concertos are eloquent and direct (EMI 65503). The mainstream Romantics are represented by Schumann's *Carnaval* in a brisk and exciting rendition, and a very good Brahms Sonata Three (Testament 1084).

Maria Yudina (1899–1970). Wild, daring, fiery, and highly idiosyncratic, Yudina was fearless. She even dared to refuse a direct request by Stalin to perform. Unfortunately, few high-quality recordings of her art exist. One set includes Bach's *Goldberg Variations* and Beethoven's *Diabelli* and *Eroica* Variations. These episodic pieces show Yudina at her best; she's able to exploit their kaleidoscopic potential to the full (Philips 456994). A "Great Russian Pianists" set includes Stravinsky's Sonata and Schubert Impromptus Op. 90 (Harmonia Mundi 1905170). A disc in the "Russian Piano School" series presents her in works by Stravinsky, Bartók, Hindemith, Berg, and Krenek; she delights in playing these difficult 20th-century pieces and probably enjoyed the challenge they presented to her audience as well (Melodiya 25176).   GEFFEN

Singers

This article lists those great singers of the past 100 years or so who have left us significant recordings of their art. Singers still in early or mid-career have not been included because voices often decline rapidly, for any number of reasons, and we're frequently disappointed by an artist's inability to fulfill his or her initial promise. However, an exception is made for well-established artists like Domingo and Pavarotti; their work merits inclusion even if they never sing another note. If you don't see your favorites here, you can find all our references to them in the Index of Artists.

Complete opera sets are discussed by composer in Part I, so they are omitted here. In the case of very popular singers (Caruso, Björling, Tauber, et al.), performances are often recycled on different labels with different discmates so that duplication of arias and songs is unavoidable; buyers should examine each disc to minimize this. Sound is not a primary factor in determining my recommendations, except for those cases where it's so poor that it affects one's enjoyment or distorts the voice. Many CD transfers of old recordings have pops, crackles, and hiss. Some labels filter these out; others (like Pearl) don't. My preference is usually for the unfiltered product, since filtering often distorts the artist's voice. For the same reason, Nimbus's controversial Ambisonic method of transferring acoustical recordings is not recommended. Where a Nimbus and a Pearl or Romophone disc of the same material exist, the latter are most often recommended. Since I don't expect everyone to agree with all my selections of artists or their recordings, I have also indicated the preferences of other critics whose opinions I respect.

SOPRANOS

Victoria de los Angeles (b. 1923). This Spanish soprano achieved worldwide fame as the lyrical heroine of Puccini's *La Bohème, Manon,* and especially *Madama Butterfly*. She also sang the lighter Wagner roles (Eva, Elisabeth, and Elsa) with success, as well as Desdemona, Mélisande, and Marguerite. She made up in vocal charm what she lacked in amplitude. Her voice was sweet and pure and she was a communicative artist on stage and in recitals, notably in Spanish songs and zarzuelas (EMI 69078) and Catalan songs (Collins 1318). Her recorded repertory includes discs of Baroque and religious arias (Testament 1088), opera arias (Seraphim 60262 and EMI 63495), and live recitals (VAIA 1025). "The Fabulous Victoria de Los Angeles" is devoted mainly to songs and is recommended as an overview of this fine singer's art (EMI, 4CD).

Arleen Augér (1939–96) was a pure-voiced, stylish coloratura soprano who specialized in Baroque music as well as the light Mozart roles. Her career was centered in European opera houses. She was noted for her charm as well as for her astute phrasing and fine diction. She made nearly 150 recordings; among the best are "The Art of Arleen Augér" (Koch 7248), "Love Songs" (Delos 3029), Baroque arias (Delos 3026), and Mozart arias (London 440414).

Erna Berger (1900–90) was one of the best coloratura sopranos of her day, noted for her singing of Mozart's Queen of the Night and Konstanze. Her career was centered in Dresden and Berlin but she made guest appearances in London and New York. She was also a well-liked recitalist, especially in her native Germany. At her best, her coloratura had an uncommon force and dramatic thrust, and this has been captured in her opera aria discs (Preiser 89092 and 89035). A set of postwar recitals displays her talents in that genre, notably clarity of diction and a direct and unmannered approach (Koch, 3CD).

Montserrat Caballé (b. 1933). This Spanish soprano is noted for the seamless beauty of her voice and her ability to sing long legato phrases, as well as for her ability to float high pianissimos. While retired from opera (which she sang in all the world's great houses), she is still giving recitals. She made many complete opera recordings. Among her aria and recital discs, the following cover most of her repertory and are recommended: Bellini and Donizetti arias (RCA 61458); Bellini and Verdi arias (EMI 69500, 65575); lieder (Schubert, Strauss) and arias (RCA 23675, 60865); Rossini, Donizetti, and Verdi rarities (RCA 60941, 2CD); duets with Shirley Verrett (RCA 60818); and opera arias (Memories 4279).

Maria Callas (1923–77). One of the most famous post-WWII singers, her stage career was relatively short, lasting only from the late 1940s to the early 1960s. By then, growing vocal troubles forced her to curtail and then eliminate her stage appearances, though she concertized for many years after that. At her best, she was one of the great singing actresses of our century, though her vocal production was often flawed by noticeable register breaks, excessive vibrato, and unreliable notes above the staff. However, her stage performances were fascinating because they were so intelligently conceived and compellingly acted.

Callas made many recordings of complete operas. The following list of excerpts and arias includes duplications unavoidable with compact discs; most of the selections show Callas at her best: "The Art of Maria Callas" (EMI 63244); arias from French operas (EMI 49059); arias and scenes from Italian and French operas (EMI 54103, 2CD); "La Divina" I, II, III (EMI 54702, 55016, 55216); "Five Heroines" (arias from *Norma*,

Lucia, Tosca, Traviata, Butterfly) (EMI 64418); mad scenes and other arias (EMI 47283); and off-the-air opera excerpts (Melodram 36513, 3CD, and Legato 162, in uneven sound).

Emma Calvé (1858–1942). This famous French soprano was especially noted for her Carmen. Massenet wrote two roles for her, the heroines in *La Navarraise* and *Sappho*. She left the opera stage in 1908 but concertized until 1927. Her voice was pure throughout its large range (though she used head tones above the staff) and she was known as a dramatic and sometimes impulsive interpreter. She didn't make many recordings, and the few we have vary in quality and don't always show her at her best. A set of her complete Victor recordings 1902–19 (Pearl 9482, 2CD) and two single discs (Music Memories 30365 and Romophone 81024) are more than adequate to demonstrate her talents.

Regine Crespin (b. 1927). This French soprano was noted for her stylish interpretations of French and German roles, including Sieglinde, Strauss's Marschallin, Berlioz's Dido, and both Madame Lidoine and Madame de Croissy in Poulenc's *Dialogues of the Carmelites*. She was also a noted recitalist, at home in the German as well as the French repertory. Her large voice was characterized by warmth and flexibility, her range of tonal colors was very wide, and she was a fine singing actress. Though her vocal timbre wasn't as suited to Italian opera, she was a fine Desdemona, Amelia (in *Ballo*) and Tosca. She retired from opera in 1989. In addition to her complete opera recordings, a disc of French opera arias (London 440416) and excerpts from her complete sets (LaserLight 14263) are interesting.

Lisa della Casa (b. 1919). Her smooth, warm, and lovely voice and exceptionally beautiful appearance, as well as her refined singing and taste, contributed to her success as one of the finest Mozart-Strauss singers of the post-WWII era. She triumphed in the three leading soprano roles in Strauss's *Rosenkavalier* and was the best Arabella and Countess Almaviva of her generation. She was an enchanting Eva (*Meistersinger*) and created several roles in modern operas, among them von Einem's *The Trial*. She retired in 1973. A fine disc of operatic arias has been reissued (Melodram 26526), and so has a lieder recital from late in her career, but still enjoyable (Relief 1825).

Emmy Destinn (1878–1930). One of the greatest opera stars of her generation, this Czech soprano made more than 200 78 rpm records. She was an admired member of the Berlin State Opera from 1898 to 1908, triumphed as Senta in Bayreuth in 1901, and was acclaimed at Covent Garden and the Met, where she made her debut as Aida (with Caruso and Toscanini) in 1908. She created Minnie in Puccini's *Girl of the Golden West* at the Met in 1910; in fact, she was the first great Puccini prima donna. Her dark voice was projected with intense passion but also, sometimes, with some unsteadiness and intonation problems. Some of this is evident in her recordings, which are also sonically variable. All of them have been issued in "The Complete Destinn" (Supraphon 112136, 12CD). A single disc of selected arias is available (Supraphon 111137), and so are Destinn's Victor recordings (Romophone 81002, 2CD). All are recommended.

Emma Eames (1865–1952). This American lyric soprano had a pure, beautiful voice with considerable power. Her vocal technique was considered excellent and she sang a large repertory that included Mozart, Wagner, Gounod, and Verdi. She made her Met and Covent Garden debuts in 1891 and stayed at the New York house until 1909 as one of its leading singers. Available and recommended are her complete Victor

recordings (Romophone 81001, 2CD) and opera excerpts with Pol Plançon (Nimbus 7860).

Geraldine Farrar (1882–1967). This glamorous and popular American artist made her debut in Berlin in 1901, joined the Met five years later, and stayed there as the company's leading lyrico-spinto soprano until 1922. She was as acclaimed for her acting ability as for her clear, powerful tone and fine phrasing. A beautiful woman, she was one of the first opera stars to make films. Farrar created the role of Suor Angelica in 1918 and the Goose Girl in Humperdinck's *Königskinder* in 1910. She made many records for Victor. Her most famous role was Madama Butterfly; ten excerpts from this role are on CD, and most of the other selections are also from Puccini works (Nimbus 7857). Also recommended is a collection of excerpts from *Carmen, La Bohème,* and *Madama Butterfly* (Pearl 9420).

Eileen Farrell (b, 1920) had a large, lustrous voice, warm and well controlled, that seemed ideal for Wagner, but she sang only excerpts in concert; it was claimed at the time that she didn't like to sing this repertory. She appeared in San Francisco and at the Met, but only sporadically for five years at the latter. She found a soul-mate in Leonard Bernstein; their recording of the Immolation Scene from *Die Götterdämmerung* shows Farrell at her best (Sony 47644). Other aspects of her repertory can be found in discs of operatic arias and songs (Testament 1073), Verdi arias (Sony 62357/8, 2CD), and popular songs (DRG 91436).

Kirsten Flagstad (1895–1962). This Norwegian dramatic soprano ranks among the greatest singers of the 20th century; indeed, many critics called hers "the voice of the century." To quote *New Grove:* "No one within living memory surpassed her in sheer beauty and consistency of line and tone." Her voice was pure and powerful, and at her peak, combined the solid register of a contralto with brilliant, reliable high Cs. She was the greatest Isolde and Brünnhilde of her generation, but unfortunately her only complete opera recordings were made after WWII when her voice was in somewhat of a decline (though still superior to all other contemporary Wagnerian sopranos). Her recorded excerpts from Wagner operas from the 1930s and early 40s, many with Melchior as her partner, belong in the library of every opera lover. She wasn't as highly regarded as a recitalist, though in that setting her magnificent vocalism and vivid coloring of the words often more than compensated for a lack of emotional identification. But she was a superb interpreter of Grieg, Sibelius, and other Scandinavian composers.

She made many recordings, all now on CD, though there is duplication among different labels. The complete 1937 Victor recordings show Flagstad in her prime (Romophone 81023, 2CD), and a selection of these is also recommended (Nimbus 7847). Live as well as studio recordings are available (Memories 4456, 2CD), and lieder (Grieg and Strauss) as well (Hunt 576, 2CD). There are two unique discs of duets with Melchior, one of Wagner excerpts (Pearl 9049) and another, recorded in Copenhagen, that also includes Norwegian songs (Danacord 325). Simax has issued a complete discography, including the singer's early recordings before her worldwide fame (Simax 1821).

Amelita Galli-Curci (1882–1963). This Italian coloratura soprano was known for her florid yet natural-sounding singing, the exceptional beauty of her voice, and her ability to go as high as E above the staff. Of her many recordings, the acoustics made before 1925 are generally judged to be the best. Her discs were very popular and many are still in the catalog. Her voice began to deteriorate in the 1930s. Her singing is best sampled in an issue containing the complete acoustic recordings

(Romophone 81003, 2CD). Her later recordings from 1925–28 have also been reissued (Romophone 81202, 2CD), and smaller selections can be found (RCA 61413 or Nimbus 7806).

Frieda Hempel (1885–1955). This German coloratura was best known for her Queen of the Night and Marschallin. Her large repertory also included Euryanthe and Eva and many of the lighter Verdi, Rossini, and Donizetti roles. She was at the Met from 1912 to 1919, when she retired from opera to concertize. Pearl 9032 and Nimbus 7849 contain arias and songs; the former is preferred for sonic reasons.

Lotte Lehmann (1888–1976) was one of the most beloved singers of the period between the wars, adored in Vienna and also a great favorite in London and New York. Her voice was warm, smooth, and quite beautiful, and her operatic portrayals were admired for the refinement and dramatic temperament she brought to them. Few singers have been so closely identified with their principal roles; she long set the standard for the Marschallin, Fidelio, Eva, Sieglinde, and Elisabeth. She was also a wonderful recitalist; her ability to communicate the essence of a song simply and without artifice or mannerism was exceptional. She retired from opera in 1945 and from the concert stage six years later.

Her early recordings from 1914–25 (Preiser 89302, 3CD) and from the 1920s and early 30s (Pearl 9409/10, 2 CD) show her in better voice than some of her later ones, but the latter show a deeper penetration of the texts and music that often compensates for vocal deficiencies. Among them are concert recordings from 1943-50 (Eklipse 20) and her New York farewell recital in 1951 (VAIA 1008). A fine disc of lieder is highly recommended as prime Lehmann (RCA 7809).

Frida Leider (1888–1975) was for 15 years the principal dramatic soprano of the Berlin State Opera, where she appeared in many Mozart, Verdi, and Strauss works as well as Wagner. She gained international fame mainly as Isolde and Brünnhilde; in her Wagner roles, only Flagstad was her equal. Her voice was ample, rich, and warm, and she was a compelling vocal actress. Her complete recordings from 1921–26 have been issued (Preiser 89301 and 89098), and there is also a disc of opera arias from 1927–31 (Preiser 89004). They show this remarkable singer at her best.

Nellie Melba (1861–1931). This Australian soprano was prized for her beautiful tone, her vocal technique, and her musicianship. Her operatic base was Covent Garden, where she sang from 1888 to 1926. In her prime, her voice was said to be beautifully equalized from B-flat below the clef to high F above. Her early acoustic recordings, dating from 1907–16, find her in her best voice (Romophone 81011, 3CD). Single discs have been issued covering the years 1907-26 (Pearl 9353 and Phonographe 5043, which includes her farewell recital). One disc is devoted entirely to French arias and songs (Pearl 9471), and another offers a wider range of opera arias (RCA 61412).

Claudia Muzio (1889–1936) was an important member of the Met from 1916–24, where she created the role of Giorgetta in Puccini's *Trittico;* subsequently she sang for nine seasons in Chicago, at La Scala (under Toscanini), and in Rome. She sang all the important Verdi and Puccini roles as well as verismo operas, and was noted for her sweet voice, nobility of expression, and intense dramatic involvement. Her early recordings don't do justice to her voice and artistry, while in the far better electrical recordings made in the 1930s, her voice had already lost much of its tonal allure. Her early recordings have been reissued (Romophone (81010, 2CD) and so have her Columbia electrics (Romo-

phone 81015, 2CD). A selection of her "Finest Edison Recordings" (1920-25) is in Pearl 9072 (2CD).

Birgit Nilsson (b. 1918). This Swedish soprano was the mainstay of the Wagner repertory at the large international opera houses from the early 1950s to the late 1970s. She had an accurate, powerful voice with a brilliant, reliable top register, even throughout its range. She was unquestionably the finest dramatic soprano of her time. In addition to most of the Wagner roles, her repertory included Strauss's Salome, Elektra, and the Dyer's Wife, Puccini's Turandot (she was the ideal interpreter), and several Verdi roles (Aida, Amelia, and Lady Macbeth). Her Isolde and Brünnhilde were matchless. Fortunately, many of her operatic roles are available in complete recordings. Nilsson also concertized, though opera seemed to be her preference. A recital disc has been issued (Melodram 18027) and one of opera arias, the latter taken from Swedish radio concerts (Bluebell).

Rosa Ponselle (1897–1981). Ponselle's voice was one of the most beautiful of all 20th-century singers. It was rich, even, warm, and technically perfect. She was the leading soprano for the Italian repertory at the Met from 1918 to her retirement in 1937. Her early recordings show this great singer in her prime. These include her Columbia acoustic recordings from 1918–24 (Pearl 9964, 2CD), single discs of arias and songs (RCA 7810 and Pearl 9210), and "The Best of Her Acoustic Recordings" (Grammofono 78576). After her retirement from the stage, she made a series of recordings (1939, 1954), the latter privately at her home, which still show a remarkable voice, though more limited range and darker color. These include mainly songs (Romophone 81022, 3CD).

Leontyne Price (b. 1927). One of the best lyrico-spintos of the last 50 years or so, Price had a lush, warm, and beautiful voice, with a wide range of colors, smoothly produced up to high C. She was one of the Met's leading sopranos from her debut in 1961 to her retirement in 1985, and has concertized since then. She was most admired in the Verdi and Puccini operas and created the role of Cleopatra (in Barber's opera) for the opening of the new Met in 1966. In her prime, she was a very expressive interpreter of her roles, bringing to them considerable theatrical know-how. RCA has included her in their "Prima Donna Collection," which contains the entire contents of five LPs by this artist (RCA 61236, 4CD); a single CD of operatic highlights is also available (RCA 62596).

Elisabeth Rethberg (1894–1976). The German-born Rethberg was one of the Met's stars for 21 consecutive seasons. Her repertory extended from Mozart to the lighter Wagner roles (Elisabeth, Elsa, Eva, and Sieglinde) and the title role of Strauss's *Die Ägyptische Helena,* which she sang at its world premiere in 1928. Hers was a pure, even, and very attractive voice; her legato was much admired. Her complete Brunswick (1924–29) and HMV, Parlophone, and Victor recordings from 1927 to 1934 can be found in two 2CD sets (Romophone 81014, 81212); there are single discs with similar content (Preiser 89051 and Pearl 9199).

Leonie Rysanek (1926–98). This Austrian soprano thrilled opera audiences for more than 40 years with her rich voice, exciting upper register, and dramatically compelling interpretations of many roles in the German and Italian repertories. Among her brilliant achievements were the Empress in Strauss's *Die Frau ohne Schatten,* which she "owned" for many years. She was notable as Strauss's Chrysothemis and Klytämnestra, Verdi's Lady Macbeth, and as Tosca, Senta, and Sieglinde. She was a mainstay of the Met and the Vienna Opera throughout her career. Unfortunately, she made few recordings, but an Italian aria disc (RCA

68920) and one of Strauss opera excerpts (HRE 1005) display her talents rather well.

Elisabeth Schumann (1888–1952). This silver-voiced German soprano was equally successful in opera and song. Her charm, well-focused voice and acting ability won praise in the light Mozart roles (Zerlina, Susanna, Despina), and she made the role of Sophie in Strauss's *Rosenkavalier* her own. She also made many lieder recordings, in which she excelled, and many of them are available (Preiser 89031, Pearl 9379 and 9445). A collection of her early recordings (1915-23) represents some of her best work and includes Mozart and other arias (Romophone 81028).

Elisabeth Schwarzkopf (b. 1915) is one of the best lieder singers of her time as well as one of the finest interpreters of the lyrical Mozart and Strauss operas that she performed. Her beautiful, flexible voice, combined with her consummate musicianship and penetrating intelligence, made her an outstanding recitalist. Her many recordings of the songs of Wolf, Strauss, Schubert, and Mozart are classics, as are several of her opera recordings. In her later years, her renditions were often criticized for excessive artfulness and over-inflection; she relied on such techniques increasingly as her voice became less flexible. But at her best, as in most recordings made in the 1950s and 60s, her interpretations were models of style, beauty of line and tone, and emotional identification with the meaning of the work. She retired from the stage in 1972.

In addition to her complete opera recordings, there are single CDs of arias (EMI 65577, 63657) and encores (EMI 63564). More complete collections can be found in "The Schwarzkopf Edition" (EMI 63790, 5CD) and "The Schwarzkopf Song Book" (EMI 65860, 3CD). There are many recordings of her concert appearances. Although the sound isn't always very good, these discs often show us a more spontaneous, less mannered, and less careful artist than her work in the studio. Some of the better recorded recitals are a 1956 lieder recital in Salzburg (EMI 66084); a 1953 all-Wolf recital also in Salzburg (Fonit Cetra 21); Amsterdam recitals in 1962 and 1967 (Verona 27021); her 1956 Carnegie Hall recital (EMI 61043); a 1960 Strasbourg recital (Chant du Monde 278899); and a 1962 Hanover recital (Movimento Musica 051-015).

Irmgard Seefried (1919–88). This Austrian artist was a great favorite in Vienna and Salzburg in the post-WWII era. She had a lyrical voice of great beauty and purity. She specialized in the Mozart and Strauss operas but was also an excellent recitalist, mainly in German lieder. Her stage interpretations were characterized by charm and verve, and she was always a compelling actress. She also participated in several complete opera recordings. Single CDs that illustrate her accomplished singing in opera and lieder include opera arias (DG 437677), arias and songs (Testament 1026), and Schubert lieder (Adés 13227).

Joan Sutherland (b. 1926) was the outstanding bel canto singer of the post-WWII era until her retirement in 1990. She had a magnificent voice of great power and beauty, enormous range (up to E above the staff) and flexibility, and unusual warmth. She enjoyed great success in the operas of Handel, Rossini, Bellini, and Donizetti, many of which were revived for her after decades of neglect. She wasn't as successful in Verdi, where her poor diction was much criticized. She made many complete opera recordings from which excerpts are liberally sprinkled on the discs listed here. All can be recommended, but the first two are the best in showing this singer's unique abilities: "The Age of Bel Canto" (London 421881); "The Art of the Prima Donna" (London 425493, 2CD); "Home Sweet Home" (London 425048); "Operetta Gala" (London 421880);

"Romantic French Arias" (London 421879); "Command Performance" (London 421882); "Tribute to Jenny Lind" (London 421883); live opera excerpts 1955-64 (Melodram 26515, 2CD); and "Romantic Trios" with horn and piano (London 421552).

Renata Tebaldi (b. 1922). This Italian lyrico-spinto dominated the Verdi and Puccini roles at major opera houses in the 1950s and 60s. Her voice had a rare beauty and warmth, as well as a purity and evenness not matched by her competitors, but she could be a placid interpreter, unlike her rival, Callas. This was more the case at the beginning of her career; later she gave more evidence of dramatic involvement. She was the leading soprano for Verdi and Puccini at the Met for 20 years, and she was equally admired at La Scala. In addition to her many complete opera sets, excerpts and arias are on single CDs. They include early recordings 1949–52 (London 425989), operatic arias (London 440408, 430481, 421312), and concert recordings (GOP 721, 2CD).

Luisa Tetrazzini (1871–1940) was a highly accomplished singer whose technical gifts were outstanding. Her voice was agile, accurate, and produced easily, and is reputed to have had a warm, clarinet-like beauty. She was noted for her coloratura in Bellini and Donizetti as well as in her French roles, like Thomas's Ophelia and Philine, Meyerbeer's Marguerite de Valois, and Delibes's Lakmé. Her operatic career in the United States was relatively short, though she did sing in Boston and Chicago and briefly at the Met, and for Hammerstein's Manhattan Opera, where she scored a notable triumph as Violetta. She made many recordings, but only a few are still available, among them a set that includes her 1904 work for Zonophone (Victor's "cheap" label) and those issued by Victor from 1911–20 (Romophone 81025, 2CD). They are representative of her art and are as good as or better than a competing issue that offers more selections (EMI 63802, 3CD).

Ljuba Welitsch (1913–96). The Bulgarian soprano was one of the most arresting and sometimes provocative singers to emerge after WWII. She had a gleaming, intensely focused voice that, in her prime, easily cut through orchestral storms. Her flamboyant temperament heightened the dramatic expressiveness she achieved by vocal means, yet she could sing lyrically and softly as well. Her most famous role was Strauss's Salome, with which she conquered the world's opera stages, but she was also a fine interpreter of Aida, Amelia, Jenufa, Donna Anna, and Rosalinde. Much of what made her a unique and thrilling artist can be heard in her all too few recordings, especially excerpts from concert and opera performances (Melodram 26511, 2CD; IMC 204004, 2CD). Her studio recordings are quite as valuable and in better sound (Sony 62866, 2CD).

MEZZO-SOPRANOS AND CONTRALTOS

Marian Anderson (1899–1996). This American contralto will always be known for being the first African-American artist to sing at the Met (in 1955), but her accomplishments as an artist go far beyond that. She had a large, rich voice that was strikingly beautiful and was an artist of uncompromising integrity in all matters, artistic and personal. She concertized extensively throughout the world (she wasn't allowed to sing opera until late in her career); her lieder recitals included mostly 19th-century songs, as exemplified in a disc devoted to Bach, Brahms, and Schubert lieder (RCA 7911). She was one of the greatest interpreters of spirituals, and you can find selections in Pearl 9069.

Janet Baker (b. 1933) was for many years the queen of English singers and song. She had a warm, rich, and flexible voice, and her work in both opera and song was invariably expressive and committed. She spent most of her operatic career with English companies but concertized extensively in Europe and North America, retiring from opera in 1982. The breadth of her repertory is indicated by her recordings, all of which are recommended. They range from an "Anthology of English Song" (Saga 3340) to "Arie Amorose," a collection of love songs (Philips 434173). Lieder are represented by a disc of Brahms, Schumann, Duparc, Chausson, and Ravel (EMI 56866, 2CD) and Schubert (EMI 69389, 2CD).

Teresa Berganza (b. 1935). Berganza's warm, even, and agile voice led her to many operatic triumphs, notably in the Rossini operas but also in Baroque works by Cherubini, Cesti, and as Mozart's Sextus. As her voice darkened with age, she sang Carmen and Charlotte, which added to her operatic laurels. She concertized extensively in the 1980s. Representative recordings, all recommended, include a disc of cantatas by Monteverdi, Vivaldi, Haydn, and Rossini (Claves 9026), Spanish songs of Granados, Turina, and others (Claves 8704), and zarzuelas (Koch 321949).

Kathleen Ferrier (1912–53) was one of the most beloved singers of her time and her premature death sent shock waves through musical circles. She had a dark, large but warm, and very beautiful voice that was secure and even throughout its range, and a winsome stage personality. She was still deepening her always expressive interpretations when a fatal illness struck her down. Still, her recorded legacy is significant and documents her artistry quite well. Her only operatic roles were Lucretia, in Britten's opera, and Gluck's Orpheus. Her recitals and concert appearances were usually the highlight of a music season. "The Art of Kathleen Ferrier" includes all her commercial recordings (London 433802, 10CD). Singles from this set are available. Especially recommended are Vols. 7 (Bach and Handel arias), 8 (British folk songs), and 10 (Mahler and Brahms).

Marilyn Horne (b. 1934). One of the greatest bel canto singers of her generation, she was peerless in the operas of Rossini, Bellini, and Handel. She was one of the outstanding vocal technicians of her day, noted for her even, sparkling coloratura, her large vocal range, and her brilliant top and chest tones. She was also a fine vocal actress, with a gift for comedy. In her assumption of standard roles like Carmen, Azucena, and Eboli, she didn't enjoy the same successes as in her bel canto parts. Horne retired from opera in the early 90s but was still giving recitals in 1997. She has also championed American songs with great success. Recommended recordings include a disc of opera arias (London 440515), a spectacular one of Rossini opera scenes (London 421306), a Handel aria release (Erato 45186), and "Rarities from Her Repertory, 1966-76" (SRO 822).

Christa Ludwig (b. 1928) has been one of the most admired mezzos of the 1960–90 era. She has a large, creamy voice, evenly produced, with a range that could, in her prime, go up to high B. Her operatic characterizations range from Dorabella and Cherubino to Dido, Kundry, Ortrud, and the Marschallin. She has participated in several opera premieres, including von Einem's *Der Besuch der alten Dame* and Liebermann's *Die Schule der Frauen,* both on discs. She is an excellent vocal actress and one of the premier lieder singers of our time; her recordings of Mahler, Brahms, and Strauss songs are among the best. They can be heard in "Les Introuvables de Christa Ludwig," which includes many Brahms, Schumann, Mahler, and Strauss songs, as well as Bach, Handel, and some French songs (EMI 64074, 4CD). "Live in Opera (1955–74)" presents scenes from some of her operatic roles (Orfeo 365941), and "Farewell to Salzburg 1993" is a lieder recital (RCA 61547).

Ernestine Schumann-Heink (1861–1936). This singer's fabulous operatic career extended from 1878 to 1932. She sang under Mahler as a

member of the Hamburg Opera in 1892, in Bayreuth from 1896 to 1914, at the Met from 1898 to 1903, and she returned to that house for several seasons thereafter. Her extensive concert tours in the United States contributed much to her fame. She returned briefly to the scene of her operatic debut in Dresden to sing Clytemnestra in the world premiere of *Elektra,* but she was most renowned for her Wagner roles. Some of her recordings survive (Nimbus 7811).

Ebe Stignani (1903–74) was a pre-eminent interpreter of the big Verdi mezzo roles during her operatic career, which began with her La Scala debut in 1926. She was also a famous Adalgisa (which she sang to Callas's Norma), and sang some non-Italian roles like Ortrud, Delilah, and Brangäne. She had a large, rich voice that ranged from F to high C, and her operatic characterizations were usually large-scaled and expressive. Opera arias (Preiser 89014) and opera arias and duets with Rossi-Lemeni (Fonit-Cetra 5013) present her art well.

Conchita Supervia (1895–1936). This Spanish mezzo made her operatic debut at the age of 14 and two years later sang Octavian at the Rome premiere of *Der Rosenkavalier.* While her repertory was large and included Carmen, Cherubino, and Charlotte, she was best known for her Rossini (*La Cenerentola, Il barbiere,* and *L'Italiana in Algeri*). Her voice was warm, rich and very flexible, she had excellent diction, and she was a charming actress. Her early death after childbirth was a great loss. She made many recordings, some of which, her contemporaries tell us, made her voice seem more strident than it actually was. Still, there's much to enjoy in her characterizations as heard in "Supervia in Opera and Song: Odeon recordings 1927–32" (Nimbus 7836, 2CD), "Spanish and Other Songs 1930-32" (Pearl 9165), and "The Unknown Supervia 1929–34" (Pearl 9969). The last contains rare operatic excerpts and songs in Catalan, Spanish, French, and Italian.

Kirstin Thorborg (1896–1970). This Swedish mezzo was best known for her Wagner roles, but her repertory also encompassed Ulrica, Clytemnestra, Delilah, and Herodias. She was a member of the great Wagnerian casts of the 1920s and 30s. After seeing her as Kundry, the renowned critic Ernest Newman called her "the greatest Wagnerian actress of the present day." She sang at the Met from 1936 to 1951 and in the famous *Ring* cycles at Covent Garden from 1936 to 1939. Thorborg had a dark, rich voice with a strong top. She didn't make many recordings, but a disc entitled "Opera Arias and Songs" gives a fair idea of her art (Preiser 89084).

TENORS

Peter Anders (1908–54). When Anders died prematurely, as the result of an auto accident, he was about to become the reigning German tenor, both in opera and as a recitalist. His many recordings, which include several complete operas, attest to his vocal endowment as well as his intelligence and musicianship. He was a lyrical tenor at the outset of his career but was beginning to take on dramatic roles, including some of Wagner's, when he died. His voice had much tonal beauty, a range up to a high B, and it was smoothly and firmly produced. He had excellent diction. A disc of opera arias (Teldec 95512) and one of operetta excerpts (Acanta 43812) are recommended. His recordings of German lieder don't show him at his best (Berlin 2166).

Carlo Bergonzi (b. 1924) started his career as a baritone but achieved outstanding success as a lyrico-spinto tenor, primarily in Verdi and Puccini. He was noted for his stylish, smooth, and tasteful singing and his fine diction. He never forced his voice and always preserved an elegant sense of tone and line. He was a reliable, communicative artist, though not a very imaginative vocal actor. He had a long operatic career, singing at the Met, for example, from 1956 to 1988. Among his recommended recordings are a disc of opera arias 1968–73 (Bongiovanni 1100), one of his early opera recordings from the 1950s (London 440417), and one of operatic duets with Fischer-Dieskau (Orfeo 028821).

Jussi Björling (1911–60). One of the most celebrated and recorded tenors, Björling had one of the most consistently beautiful voices. It was smooth, velvety, and mellow, with an excellent top register. His legato was widely admired and served him well in the French and Italian operas in which he specialized. His voice recorded unusually well and there's hardly a poor selection among the three dozen or so Björling CDs (but avoid RCA 5934 for its poor sound). Opera arias and duets 1936–1949 (EMI 64707), a similar CD that includes some unusual items (Legato 705), a disc of radio recordings in good sound (Verona 27022), operetta arias and songs (Pearl 9042), and a selection of Swedish songs (SWE 1010) should satisfy all but the most ardent Björling fan.

Enrico Caruso (1873–1921) is, by almost universal agreement, the greatest tenor of the 20th century. His many recordings contributed as much to the acceptance of phonograph recordings by the public as they did to his own fame. His recorded legacy has been in print ever since his death, and all of it is on CD. Carus's fame is based as much on his technical abilities (his smooth legato, tasteful portamento, and secure intonation) as it is on the warmth and brilliance of his voice, his clear and dramatic declamation, and his elegant phrasing. Perhaps it was coincidental that his voice recorded very well, or perhaps this was because, as most critics agree, it was the perfect tenor voice.

Of the "complete" Caruso sets, Pearl EVC (12CD) is the best; the comparable Bayer and RCA sets suffer from poorer reproduction and higher noise levels. Single CDs from the Pearl set are also available. Nimbus 7809 and 7803 used the Ambisonic method and the results are somewhat controversial. Pearl 9030 (2CD) is, by contrast, an electrical reproduction of the acoustic originals that most critics find more acceptable. RCA 61640 presents the tenor in a song recital with acceptable sound.

Franco Corelli (b. 1921) was a leading lyrico-spinto tenor from his La Scala debut in 1954 to his virtual retirement from opera in the early 1970s. He had a gorgeous voice, notable for its strong top register, but smooth and evenly produced throughout its range, and very expressive. A handsome stage figure made him a matinee idol. His voice was quite large and warm, and it seemed that he could assume dramatic tenor roles like Otello, but that didn't happen; he retired early from the stage, apparently for personal reasons. He didn't leave us as many recordings as some of his competitors, but his opera arias (EMI 47851), religious and Neapolitan songs (EMI 69530), and recital recordings (Melodram 16503 and 16521) are recommended.

Giuseppe di Stefano (b. 1921). At the beginning of his career, in the late 1940s and early 1950s, di Stefano had a beautiful lyric tenor voice, comparable to the best in an age when such voices weren't as rare as they have become more recently. It was rich, warm, and smooth, and it was produced with a honeyed tone that recalled Gigli. Unfortunately, it deteriorated quite rapidly, perhaps because he tried to sing dramatic roles like Canio and Radames. After the mid-1960s, his operatic appearances became less frequent, for example, at the Met where he had been very popular since his 1948 debut. He made several concert tours with Callas that didn't add to either singer's reputation. A disc of early aria recordings (EMI 63105), one from Chicago and San Francisco (Myto 92467),

and a set of arias and songs entitled "The Glory of Italy" (Cantabile 704, 2CD) present the tenor's best efforts.

Placido Domingo (b. 1941). It's no exaggeration to say that in the last 20 years of the 20th century, this Spanish artist has been the best dramatic tenor in opera. His repertory is exceptionally large, encompassing not only most if not all of the Verdi and Puccini roles but also such rarities as Paolo (in Zandonai's *Francesca de Rimini*), Berlioz's Aeneas, many French roles (Samson, Hoffmann, Don José and Werther), and several Wagner parts (Lohengrin, Siegmund, Parsifal). He has made Otello his own and is generally considered to be one of the best ever in this difficult role.

Domingo's voice is rich and powerful, easily produced, and has a solid low register. Its main limitation is at the top, B-flat and above, which sometimes sounds too effortful. Still, Domingo, who also conducts opera and concerts, is one of the most intelligent and stylish tenors within memory. He's probably the most recorded tenor of our time already, and he's not done yet. Of his opera aria discs, London 440110 and EMI 66532 are recommended, as are CBS 37207 (Donizetti, Puccini, and Massenet), and an RCA issue (61356) entitled "Domingo sings Caruso." He's also well regarded for his way with zarzuelas, as documented in Angel 49148 and Acanta 49390.

Nicolai Gedda (b. 1925). Gedda's versatility in language (he speaks and sings in seven) is one reason for his large operatic repertory, which includes Russian, German, French, and Italian roles, all of which he performs with a fine command of vocal styles. At his best (and most of his work is that), his singing is a model of taste, refinement, and musicianship. His essentially lyric voice is sweet, smooth, and easily produced. He was at the Met for 22 years, where he created the role of Anatol in Barber's *Vanessa*, and he has also participated in the revival of rarely heard works such as Berlioz's *Benvenuto Cellini* and Pfitzner's *Palestrina*. He is also a fine recitalist, especially in Russian and Scandinavian songs. The latter skill is evident in a disc of Russian songs and romances (Melodiya 244) and a Salzburg 1961 recital (EMI 65352). A CD of opera arias is also available (Foné 85FO2-6).

Beniamino Gigli (1890–1957) had one of the sweetest and most beautiful lyric voices of the century. Many critics considered him to be Caruso's heir in lyric and romantic opera, and he was the Met's principal tenor for 12 successive seasons, singing 29 roles (his repertory included more than 50). He was the very model of a natural singer, though stylistically his work was often marred by sentimentality, excessive portamento, sobbing, and a stance that seemed to beg for applause. He was most at home in Puccini and other verismo works (*Andrea Chenier,* for example) and in lyric operas such as Flotow's *Martha,* Donizetti's *L'Elisir d'amore,* Bizet's *Pearl Fishers,* and Gounod's *Faust.* He made many recordings throughout his career and most of them have never lost their appeal. The most complete set has been issued as "Complete Victor Recordings, 1921–1932" (Romophone 82003-5, 5CD). A set of his complete acoustic recordings can also be found (Pearl 9423, 2CD). Recommendable single discs include arias 1921–1930 (RCA 7811), arias and ensembles (Pearl 9367), and arias and songs (Pearl 9033).

Giacomo Lauri-Volpi (1892–1979) was considered one of the finest lyrico-spinto tenors of his day and was especially admired for his beautiful legato. He had a bright voice with metal and ping that enabled him to sing dramatic roles like Manrico, Otello, and Raoul. His recordings demonstrate his unmannered approach and the rather odd mix of chest and head tones, including falsetto, that he employed. Some of his French and Italian opera aria recordings from 1920–1934 have been reissued (Pearl 9010), and so have two CDs of Italian opera (Preiser 89012, 89133).

Giovanni Martinelli (1885–1969) succeeded Caruso at the Met, where he sang for 31 successive seasons (in 38 operas) in the latter's dramatic repertory (Manrico, Don Alvaro, Radames, among others). He was also the leading Otello of his time and even made a stab at Tristan (with Flagstad, in Chicago). He had a powerful and brilliant voice with a bright ring in his upper register, excellent diction, and, at the same time, the ability to sing legato in lyrical passages. Unlike some of his colleagues, he didn't indulge in sobbing, excessively slow tempos, or other mannerisms. He made many recordings, some of which—like the excerpts from *Aida, Trovatore,* and *La Forza,* in which he was joined by Ponselle, Pinza, and De Luca—are still models of singing and interpretation. He's best heard in excerpts from *La Forza* and other arias (Pearl 9350), excerpts from *Aida* and *Il Trovatore* (Pearl 9351), and operatic arias (Pearl 9184).

Lauritz Melchior (1890–1973) started his operatic career as a baritone but became the greatest Heldentenor of the century. During his operatic career, which ended in 1950, he was unmatched in the heavy Wagner roles (Tannhäuser, Siegmund, Siegfried, Parsifal, and Tristan), partly because of his great vocal strength and stamina, but mainly because of the size and brilliance of his heroic voice that, in its prime, easily encompassed high C. He also had a strong low register, and in addition to its enormous size, his voice had a baritonal warmth over much of its range that enhanced its appeal in lyrical passages, as did his clear and forward diction. He could sing softly without crooning, rare for a Wagner tenor. He wasn't a great actor and, in his later years, often sloppy in rhythm (to the despair of some of his conductors), but his popularity never waned. He sang Tristan more than 200 times (his best role) and each of the other parts listed above more than 100 times. In the almost 50 years since his retirement, no one has come close to his achievement.

Melchior sang only a few non-Wagner roles (Otello and Radames, for example); this was mainly the work of opera managers who "saved" him for their Wagner operas where he was indispensable. He recorded extensively, though not, unfortunately, complete operas. The classic recording of Act One of *Die Walküre* remains one of his best efforts (EMI 61020); others include duets with Leider (Preiser 89004 and 89301) and Flagstad (Pearl 9049, Danacord 325). Most of Melchior's recordings are now on CD. A complete anthology of his early records (1913–1932) has been preserved (Danacord 311-321, 11CD). For those not wanting that much Melchior, arias, songs, and duets with Lehmann (RCA 7914), *Otello* excerpts and Wagner arias (Nimbus 7816), and Wagner arias (Preiser 89086) are suitable alternatives.

John McCormack (1884–1945). One of the most famous lyric tenors of the 20th century, McCormack achieved most of his renown as a recitalist; his operatic career was relatively short, as he abandoned the stage in his early 30s. He was noted for the sweetness and smoothness of his voice, his sense of style, and his virtually flawless technique, which included excellent breath control. He recorded extensively, sometimes in collaboration with other famous artists like violinist Fritz Kreisler. Much of his recorded work consists of Irish, English, and American popular songs of the time, including many Victorian tear-jerkers, which he sang with uncommon sincerity and grace. Pearl 9338, EMI 64654, and Romophone 82006 (2CD) are representative of his approach to these songs. His singing of opera arias is equally esteemed (Pearl 9335,

Angel 63306, and Romophone 82007, 2CD); his way with German lieder has been well captured (Symposium 1164).

Luciano Pavarotti (b. 1935). One of the most popular lyric tenors of our time, not least for his frequent television and arena appearances, Pavarotti has become known as a larger-than-life personality that threatens to overshadow his talents and achievements as a serious artist. In the early phases of his long career (the 1960s and 70s), he was the best lyric tenor then before the public who specialized in Italian opera, specifically Donizetti, Bellini, Puccini, and the lighter Verdi roles. In more recent times, he has tried more dramatic parts such as Don Carlo, Radames, and Otello, not always successfully.

His bright, smooth and very appealing voice seems to have been little affected as yet by the ravages of time and physical ailments. His excellent forward diction (in Italian only) makes him a highly communicative singer, and even a pop star. He is a prolific recording artist, but many of his recital discs are quite repetitious and some are flawed by a routine delivery of his rather narrow repertory. Recordings from his early days show more involvement and expression, notably RCA 62541 and Legato 846; both include arias and Italian songs. Other representative opera aria programs include London 440400 and 443220.

Tito Schipa (1888–1965) had a light, lyrical voice, sweet but somewhat lacking in color and volume. But it was flexible, easily produced, quite beautiful, and used with taste and style. His excellent diction and forward placement made it carry even in a large house. This tenor concentrated on the more graceful and lighter Italian and French operas. A three-volume set of his recordings is representative of his art (Pearl 9322, 9364, 9290). There are single discs that will also give much pleasure (Memories 437 and Pearl 9017).

Aksel Schiøtz (1906–75). This Danish tenor's meteoric rise as a Mozart and lieder singer was interrupted by a severe illness that affected his voice in mid-career; he never regained its full use thereafter. At its best, his light tenor was silvery and well focused, and applied with elegance and a highly developed sense of style. He left us recordings of German lieder and Mozart and Handel arias that rank with the best. Danacord has collected his legacy in 10 volumes (451–460) that are sold individually. Vols. 1–3 are the best; they include his Schubert, Schumann, and aria discs. Vol. 10 is all Nielsen; it's a must for fans of that composer. There are other discs that offer Scandinavian songs (Pearl 9140) and Schubert's *Die Schöne Müllerin* (Preiser 90293, also in Danacord 452).

Leo Slezak (1873–1946) was one of the leading tenors at the Vienna State Opera from 1901 (when he was hired by Mahler) to the mid-1920s, and he sang there as late as 1933. He also sang at the Met from 1909–1912 (under Toscanini) and at Covent Garden. He was a true dramatic tenor, at home in most of the Wagner roles and the heavier Verdi parts, but he was also successful in Puccini and French opera and was a noted lieder singer. Most of his recordings have been reissued and all of them are recommended. They consist of French and Verdi arias (Preiser 89020), lieder and Wagner (mainly) arias (Preiser 89203, 2CD), and diverse opera arias (Preiser 89136).

Francesco Tamagno (1850–1905) was known for his heroic trumpet-like voice, with a brilliant and secure top register. He may have been the ideal Otello, a role he created under Verdi's guidance at the world premiere in 1887. He also created several other roles, including Gabriele Adorno in the revised *Simon Boccanegra*. A good sampling of his recordings has been issued, including several *Otello* excerpts and selections from other Verdi and French operas (Pearl 9846). His complete recordings (1903–4) are available (Symposium 1188/7, 2CD; Opal 9846); these sets include several takes of some arias and will be of interest only to the most dedicated vocal fans.

Richard Tauber (1891–1948) was one of the most popular tenors in the interwar period, equally at home in opera (especially Mozart) and operettas and other lighter music. He had a beautiful, warm, and smooth voice and was a stylish singer who appealed to his audience with his charm and diction as much as with his smooth legato. He was also an accomplished lieder and folk song singer, and delivered this repertory straightforwardly and without mannerisms. He is said to have made more than 700 records; they encompass opera, operetta, and lieder, and many are still available. Individual discs offer a fair number of Tauber's opera arias (Pearl 9148), his work in operetta (Angel 69787), and songs as well as some arias (Pearl 9327).

Georges Thill (1897–1984) was the most distinguished French heroic tenor of his time, the leading tenor at the Paris Opera from 1924–1956. In addition to all the major tenor parts in French opera, he sang Wagner (Lohengrin, Walter, Tannhäuser, and Parsifal) and Italian dramatic parts (Calaf, Radames, and Canio). He was noted for his brilliant, clarion tone, fine diction, and elegant phrasing. Not many of Thill's recordings are now available, but 11 arias (all in French) from Italian and French opera as well as eight Fauré and two Gounod songs recorded for Columbia in 1925–1936 are on CD (Pearl 9947). Another disc offers 18 arias from all parts of the singer's repertory (Music Memories 30190).

Jon Vickers (b. 1926). Vickers, now retired, was the only true heroic tenor of his generation. He had a huge but well-controlled voice that, when let out, could thrill listeners in the last row of the top balcony in any opera house in the world. He was a committed vocal actor who sometimes dug so deeply into his roles that the musical line and tone suffered. He made many roles his own by the vividness and passion of his characterization and his dominant stage presence, among them Florestan, Siegmund, Peter Grimes, Otello, Parsifal, and Samson. He was expected to be the great Wagner tenor of his generation and the successor to Melchior, but specializing in Wagner evidently had no appeal for him; he refused to sing Tannhäuser and Siegfried though the Met (and others) begged him to do so. Although his singing could turn to crooning and become quirky, no other tenor with his vocal and dramatic power has been seen on any stage since the days of Melchior.

Vickers didn't make many single discs. Excerpts from five of his complete opera recordings (*Fidelio, Otello, Walküre, Carmen,* and *Medea*) are in Memories 4394 (2CD). There is also a single disc of Italian opera arias, recorded in London in 1961 (VAIA 1016). A recital from 1967 shows a deep understanding of Schumann's *Dichterliebe*, but his analytical dissection of its text may not be to everyone's taste (VAIA 1032).

Fritz Wunderlich (1930–66) had a short career; he was struck down in his prime by an avoidable accident. Had he lived longer, he might have become one of the great lyric tenors of the century. He surely had all the prerequisites: a gorgeous voice, smooth and even, a direct manner of singing free of affectations, and a wonderful sense of style and taste, especially in Mozart operas. He left us a significant number of recordings, all of which can be recommended. They include operetta (Acanta 43567), a set of opera and operetta arias (Angel 62993, 3CD), a single disc devoted to German opera (Acanta 43267), and a large set of arias and songs (DG 435145, 5CD). There's very little duplication among these releases. His last lieder recital, recorded in Salzburg in 1965 and Edinburgh in 1966 (his last concert), shows an increasing artistic maturity that was, alas, to be unfulfilled (Myto 89011).

BARITONES AND BASSES

Pasquale Amato (1878–1942). After a stint with Toscanini at La Scala (1907–8), Amato joined the conductor at the Met where he sang the principal Italian baritone roles, many French roles including Valentin and Escamillo, as well as Kurvenal and Amfortas. He had a fine voice, with a wide range and a brilliant top, and was known as a reliable artist. He suffered a vocal crisis in mid-career, so his early recordings (1909–14) are his best. His Victor and Fonotopia recordings from that period include arias, songs, and duets with Hempel and Matzenauer (Preiser 89064). There is also an aria disc that contains some of the same material (Pearl 9104). Either will do for an introduction to this splendid singer.

Mattia Battistini (1856–1928) was one of the most famous singers of his or any other day. His voice was a vibrant and strong baritone, almost a tenor. He was known for his superb phrasing, perfect diction, command of vocal colors, and especially his flawless technique, including his *mezza di voce*. He was called "the Paganini of Song" and was widely admired in Europe, but didn't sing in the United States. Many of his 100 or so recordings have been transferred to CD, including three discs of arias and songs (Pearl 9936, 9946, 9016) and several single discs (Symposium 1210 and Nimbus 7831); the first two are highly recommended.

Michael Bohnen (1887–1965) was often described as "the German Chaliapin." He had a large, "black" voice with a wide range and could sing baritone as well as bass parts. His repertory was also large, ranging from Ochs and Sarastro to Escamillo, Scarpia, Amonasro, and many Wagner roles. He was reputed to be a very good actor and participated in many silent and sound films. He sang at the Met from 1923 to 1932 and in many German opera houses. Bohnen's acoustic recordings have been rereleased and are well worth listening to, though almost everything is sung in German (Preiser 89215, 2CD).

Feodor Chaliapin (1873–1938) was considered the greatest singing actor of his day, if not of all time. He had a very large, flexible voice and could take on baritone as well as bass parts. Judging from his more than 200 records, his voice wasn't really beautiful, but it was highly expressive and had a wide dynamic range. However, vocal beauty and purity were never this artist's main objectives on stage; they were always subservient to dramatic expression and, sometimes, theatricality. Indeed, his acting often distorted the music, sometimes to the point of travesty. He was, essentially, a law unto himself. Chaliapin also participated in films; his last, *Don Quixote,* still in print, had a score written for him by Ibert. Chaliapin's most famous role was Boris Godunov. He recorded excerpts from the opera several times, also taking on the roles of Pimen and Varlaam.

All of Chaliapin's recordings are now on CD, and all are recommendable. They include several devoted to Russian opera and songs (Pearl 9920, 2CD, and 9921), all opera (Pearl 9182 and Preiser 89030), and all songs (Preiser 89207 and 89087). A set that includes 36 arias and songs is a good overview of his achievement; Nimbus's Ambisonic method in this case has produced as good a sound as Preiser and Pearl (Nimbus 7823, 2CD).

Boris Christoff (1914–93). This Bulgarian bass was often hailed as Chaliapin's successor because of his identification with the latter's most famous roles and also because he too was a very good actor. But he was a more conventional performer; he never distorted the music or went "over the top" dramatically. His voice, a penetrating black bass, was smooth and even, well focused and controlled, and very expressive. Boris was his most celebrated role (he also sang Pimen and Varlaam) and he was very successful as Philip II, in most other Verdi bass roles, and in several Wagner parts (King Marke, Hagen, and Gurnemanz). Recommended recordings are a fine program of Russian arias and five songs (EMI 64252) and an all-Russian song program (EMI 67496).

Giuseppe de Luca (1876–1950). For 20 years (1915–35), this Italian baritone was a leading singer at the Met, where he was featured in all the important Italian opera baritone roles. His vocal technique was so good that he sang well into his 60s (his last concert was in 1947). He was a stylish artist in the bel canto tradition, with a voice that wasn't large and a bit dry, but well focused and quite flexible. As is evident from his recordings, he sang in a direct, unaffected manner. Discs of arias and ensembles, mostly from Italian operas, that were originally recorded by Victor (1907–30), and Fonotopia (1902–30) are recommended (Pearl 9159, 9160 and Nimbus 7815). 14 arias from 1917–24 are in somewhat poorer sound (Preiser 89036). The early recordings find this singer in more brilliant voice.

Dietrich Fischer-Dieskau (b. 1925) has been one of the outstanding singers of our time, in opera and even more so on the recital stage. He is now retired but has left us a huge discography that encompasses the works (often the complete works) of many composers. His solidly produced baritone was warm, vibrant, and secure, his vocal technique impressive. Above all, his powerful intelligence was evident in the depth of his interpretations of everything he undertook, in opera and in lieder. These interpretations were always tasteful and refined but, as his vocal powers declined, they sometimes became over-inflected and a bit precious, as if to compensate for vocal shortcomings, so the recordings from the early part of his career (1950 to 1970 or so) are, in general, his best.

A fine selection from the 1950s has been assembled that includes songs by Classical (Beethoven, Brahms, Schumann, and others) as well as modern composers (EMI 68509, 6CD). A valuable disc contains a 1970 Salzburg recital of lieder to texts by Goethe (Orfeo 389951) and another offers a 1975 Salzburg recital devoted to songs on texts by Eichendorff; it includes some hard-to-find songs by Pfitzner and Bruno Walter (Orfeo 185891).

Gerhard Hüsch (1901–84) was renowned as one of the premier lieder singers of the 1920s and 30s. He was among the first to record the Schubert and Schumann song cycles in the 1930s; these, as well as his opera discs, have stood the test of time. His singing had depth and beauty, but it was always virile, straightforward, and free of mannerisms. He had a warm, lyric voice, not very large but resonant and smooth, and under superb dynamic control. His diction and vocal coloring were exemplary, and his work was always tasteful and refined. His Schubert and Schumann cycles are still in the catalog and are highly recommended. An all-Schubert song program (Preiser 89017) and a disc of opera arias (Preiser 89226) are also recommended.

Marcel Journet (1867–1933). This French bass had a powerful voice with a wide range; he sang baritone roles like Tonio and Scarpia as well as many leading French and Italian bass parts. He was also a renowned interpreter of Wagner's Klingsor, Hans Sachs, Wotan, and Gurnemanz. His vocal delivery was firm, pure, and expressive, and he could scale his voice down and sing softly and with lyrical feeling. He performed almost to the day of his death. A sampling of his early recordings (arias and songs) is available (Preiser 89106); he's in better voice there than in a compilation of arias from late in his career (1925–33) (Preiser 89021). Both discs demonstrate his great artistry. Recently, Marston has announced a four-volume series of Journet's recordings. The initial set (52009, 2CD) presents opera selections by Wagner, Massenet, Gounod, Boito (*Nerone*), and others, mostly sung in French, and some French songs.

Alexander Kipnis (1891–1978). This Ukrainian-born bass had a powerful yet very flexible voice that served him well in opera and recitals. He was best known for his Mozart and Wagner roles (in addition to Boris); as a lieder singer, his Brahms and Wolf recordings are wonderful examples of tasteful, refined, yet virile interpretations. His best recordings date from the 1930s, though they're not as good technically as his later ones. A set of opera arias and lieder captures his voice well (Preiser 89204, 2CD). From his later work, we have Russian opera arias and songs, including excerpts from *Boris Godunov* (RCA 60522), and many of his best lieder interpretations, including songs by Wolf, Schumann, and Schubert (Music & Arts 661, 2CD).

Ezio Pinza (1892–1957) was a true *basso cantante*, perhaps the best of this century. He had a velvety smooth yet manly voice that was flexible, even, and easily produced. He was also a natural singing actor, with a commanding stage presence and a winning personality. All this made him the best Figaro and Don Giovanni of his time. His repertory was quite large; it encompassed tragic roles like Boris, Fiesco, Oroveso, Guardiano, and other High Priests, including Sarastro. He also sang French parts, notably Gounod's Mephisto and the bass parts in *La Juive*, *Le Cid*, and *Mignon*. He was a leading bass at the Met for 22 consecutive seasons, after which he embarked on a successful Broadway career (*South Pacific*). All the Pinza recordings I've heard are excellent. A fine collection is available (Memories 4411, 2CD). Also recommended, all singles, are one where he is accompanied by Bruno Walter and the Met orchestra (Preiser 89132), one containing mostly Italian opera, 1923–7 (EMI 64253), and one of arias from 1927–30 (Preiser 89050).

Pol Plançon (1851–1914) was considered the greatest bass at the turn of the century. His elegant, stylish singing and stunning technique, which included flawless trills and rapid scales, were highly praised. Witnesses differ as to the size of his voice, but all agree on his excellent legato. His complete Victor recordings have been reissued (Romophone 82001, 2CD), as have 24 arias and songs in a single disc (Pearl 9497). No bass is currently active with Plançon's technical abilities.

Hermann Prey (1929–98) was one of the great lieder singers of our time and his operatic portrayals are treasured for some of the same qualities that he showed in song: a pleasing, honeyed baritone and a direct way of communicating a song's essence to the listener. He was a genial artist, particularly in his Mozart roles (Papageno, Guglielmo, and Almaviva), as well as his few excursions into Wagner (Wolfram and Beckmesser). His diction was excellent and his characterizations often persuasively original (his Beckmesser was not a parody). His recordings include all the classical lieder cycles and many discs of songs by Brahms, Schubert, Schumann, Wolf, and others, all commendable—for instance, a selection of 14 songs by these and other composers (Denon 1254) and another that includes mainly German opera arias (Capriccio 10054).

Mark Reizen (1895–1992), like Kipnis, was born in Ukraine, but unlike the latter, never traveled to the United States. He spent most of his career at the Bolshoi Opera in Moscow, where he was the principal bass for many years. He was reputed to be an excellent actor, with a big, beautiful voice that was warm and flexible. Two discs of arias have been reissued, one all Russian, recorded between 1948 and 1955 (Preiser 89059), and another all Italian, recorded at about the same time (Preiser 89080). Both are recommended.

Titta Ruffo (1877–1953) was one of only three vocal "miracles" that conductor Tullio Serafin said he had experienced in his lifetime, the others being Caruso and Ponselle. His baritone was notable for its tenor-like ring in its upper register, its huge size and range, and its warmth and purity. It had a dark color, almost like a bass. Ruffo was a very expressive and dynamic singing actor at a time when most operatic singing was still in the more refined Classical tradition of the 19th century. There is a collection of 70 selections from 1912–29 (Preiser 89303, 3CD) and another presents 47 items from 1906–12 when Ruffo was at his best (Preiser 89220, 2CD). Most of the contents are the usual selections from Italian opera, but some are off the beaten path. For example, the latter set includes eight arias and duets from *Rigoletto* and six from Thomas's *Hamlet*, plus a few Mozart arias. A single disc of some of these selections can be found in Pearl 9088. Ruffo also recorded many Italian songs, which can be sampled in either Minerva 17 or Club 99 63; there are many duplications in these discs.

Heinrich Schlusnus (1888–1952) was the leading Verdi baritone at the Berlin Opera, where he was active from 1917 to 1945. He was also a renowned recitalist, specializing in German lieder, and concertized all over the world. His smooth voice had a noticeably brilliant top, his diction was always excellent, both in German and in Italian, and he could sing legato with the best. Many of his recordings have been reissued; most were made in the 1920s and 30s, his best years. A set of arias and songs (Preiser 89212, 2CD) and one of lieder (Preiser 89205) provide a good survey of his discography. A single disc has about half the arias from the first (Preiser 89006), another has most of the rest (Preiser 89110).

Friedrich Schorr (1888–1953). The Hungarian-born Schorr emerged as the world's leading Wagner bass-baritone in the 1920s, when he sang these roles at the Berlin Opera, Bayreuth, Covent Garden, and the Met. At the Met, he sang for almost 20 seasons and "owned" such roles as Hans Sachs, the Dutchman, and Wotan. His beautiful voice was notable for its smoothness and power. At a time when others succumbed to the notorious "Bayreuth bark," Schorr sang with a fine legato even in Wagner's many declamatory passages, still maintaining superb diction. His Wagner and other interpretations have been captured in his recordings (unfortunately, no complete roles). The best are excerpts from *Meistersinger* and *Flying Dutchman* (Pearl 9944), a variety of opera arias and lieder (Pearl 9398), and early recordings 1921–22 (Preiser 89052).

Cesare Siepi (b. 1923). A member of the Met for 24 years where he sang all the major bass roles except Wagner, Siepi was the successor to Pinza as that company's leading *basso cantante*. Like Pinza, he was especially admired for his Mozart (Don Giovanni, Figaro) and Italian parts like Philip II, Fiesco, Ramfis, and Oroveso. Others were Mephisto in Gounod's *Faust*, Boris, and Gurnemanz. Siepi was a very reliable performer and a good singing actor, with a warm, rich, even, and flexible voice with an attractive velvety sheen. A fine all-opera aria recital shows Siepi's art (Myto 93591); it's better than Cetra 107, a similar disc. Many of Siepi's best performances can be found in London complete opera sets.

Lawrence Tibbett (1896–1960) was one of this country's preeminent opera singers as well as a star of radio and the movies. He had a dark, flexible but powerful voice and was a vivid stage actor. He was a principal baritone at the Met for 27 seasons and was enormously popular. There is a good collection of his opera arias (many from Met broadcasts), some spirituals, and some popular songs (Delos 5500, 2CD). Some of this material can also be found elsewhere (Nimbus 6005 and Legato 706); the Delos release has the better presentation and sound. Yet another disc contains opera arias, including some by Gershwin, Hanson, and Gruenberg; Tibbett sang the premieres of operas by the latter two composers (RCA 7808). All of these demonstrate his art.

Leonard Warren (1911–60) died on the Met stage while singing Carlo in *La Forza del destino;* it was one of that house's most tragic moments. He had made his debut there in 1939 and was for many years its principal Verdi baritone. He had a huge and powerful but warm voice that was well-controlled and very smooth, with an unusually high top, up to C. In his best roles, like Rigoletto, Germont, Renato, and the Count De Luna, he was also a persuasive vocal actor. He appeared on many Met broadcasts and a compilation of 14 arias from them (Legato 707) and a reissue of many of his Victor recordings from 1941–47 (Preiser 89145) are recommended. Some of Warren's best performances are in RCA's complete opera recordings.　　　　　　　　　　　　　　MOSES

Strings

CELLO

Historical collections

In 1977, **Thomas Clear** released a 5LP album called "Augmented History of the Cello (1910–1940)" that brought us recordings of short pieces played by cellists till then known mostly by rumor: Victor Herbert, Hans Kindler, John Barbirolli, Felix Salmond, and many others. This was a valuable set, well recorded and historically and musically important, partly as a gauge of how playing styles have changed over the century. Herbert and others from the early period play almost without vibrato. It appears to have been partly the influence of the Russians that changed that.

A larger collection, ranging farther afield and containing some fine material as well as some dross, is in "The Recorded Cello" (Pearl 9981 and 9984, 3CD each). These albums include recordings made as late as the '60s and include excerpts from longer works, interesting for their rarity, but they don't all invite repeated listening. Pearl believes in giving you the original sound of a disc, warts and all, rather than smoothing out the surface noise along with the high frequencies. I agree with this philosophy; this is why we have filters built into our preamplifiers, so we can control the sound ourselves. 78 rpm discs were pressed on shellac surfaces that made surface noise when played, but if you tame them too much you lose the highs.

Individual artists (discussed in roughly chronological order)

Pablo Casals (1876–1973). A good case in point is "Encores," a reissue of early recordings by Casals (Sony 66573). The sound is so flattened to remove the surface noise that at times you can't hear the notes he's playing. Casals was one of the most satisfying of early cellists, and his rich tone and gutsy performances come across with surprising immediacy. For early recordings, there is "The Complete Acoustic Recordings," recorded with audio warts you may remove to taste (Biddulph 141–43, 3CD). "The Victor Recordings (1926–28)" continues the series (Biddulph 17), and "Bow & Baton" gives us recordings from 1929–30 and introduces Casals as conductor as well (Pearl 9128). There are also a number of trio recordings from this period with violinist Thibaud and pianist Cortot, as well as a Brahms Double Concerto with Cortot conducting. The early concerto recordings of Boccherini-Grutzmacher, Haydn-Gevaert D major (two movements only), Elgar, and Bruch's *Kol Nidre* are available (Biddulph 144). RCA has released its own version of the 1926–28 recordings, but the Biddulph discs are better.

Casals didn't record from 1930 to 1936; then he completed the cycle of Beethoven sonatas with Horszowski that he had begun in 1930 with Otto Schulhoff, Brahms's Sonata in F, the six Bach solo cello suites, and the Dvořák Concerto; much of this material has been reissued (Pearl 9935, 4CD). The Bach Suites and other Bach-Siloti transcriptions are available in particularly good transfers, but watch out for early pressings that replace the Gigue of Suite 1 with the opening of Suite 6 (Naxos 110915/16). The Elgar and Haydn concertos were his last recordings before he stopped performing in 1947 to demonstrate his opposition to the Franco regime. Most of these recordings were included in a huge compendium from Japanese sources, using the infamous Cedar system of removing surface noise (Monopoly, 11CD). Perhaps it wasn't the system itself but the way it was used; whatever the case, it removed the mid-register growl of surface sound along with the guts of the cello sound, leaving us with a sort of attenuated high and low register with little in the middle.

A series from the Prades Festival (1953–59) includes a number of chamber performances, recorded in rather grainy sound (Music & Arts 688/89, 4CD each). By this time Casals was in his late 70s, and his series of Bach and Beethoven sonatas with Rudolf Serkin is slow and stolid compared to his earlier work, though musically moving. The chamber music livens him up a bit; his Schubert, Brahms, Schumann, and Beethoven trios are memorable. The even later Marlboro Festival series features him primarily as conductor. I might mention an aircheck of the immense Donald Francis Tovey concerto, made in the mid–40s (Symposium 1115). No other cellist from the early days has been recorded as much as Casals.

Gregor Piatigorsky (1903–76) was perhaps the greatest cellist after Casals. However, he was not usually at his best in the recording studio, though choice recordings of his early work may be found (Biddulph 117 and Music & Arts 674), while we also have his early Dvořák and Saint-Saëns Concertos and Bruch's *Kol Nidre* (Sony 62876). His fiery performance of Walton's Concerto (written for him) is a classic (RCA 61498). His series of chamber recordings with Heifetz is also important.

Emanuel Feuermann (1902–42) was probably the smoothest technician of all the earlier cellists and recorded a good deal in his short life. Material from 1930–1939 is on three CDs (Pearl 9442, 9443, 9446; the first of these is listed in *Schwann* as by du Pré). Recordings from the '20s are available (Pearl 9077; Magic Talent 48025; Enterprise 99354). Columbia-Japan recorded a number of pieces that were never released here: they may be found in "The Lost Feuermann" (Music & Arts 1075). An outstanding repressing of the Haydn D major and Dvořák concertos, complete with alternate takes, has been inexpensively reissued (Naxos 110908). And let's not forget a number of concertos with the National Orchestral Association under Leon Barzin (Connoisseur Society, 4162/63). Performance tapes of his 1938 Strauss *Don Quixote* with Toscanini surface occasionally.

Maurice Maréchal (1892–1964) is a less well known but very musical earlier cellist, whose legacy may be found (Enterprise 99301, 99316, and 99356). **André Navarra** (1911–19) is a gutsy cellist who once contem-

plated a career as a boxer. His recordings turn up from European sources, and a disc of short pieces is also worth investigation (Lys 348). Recordings by **Gaspár Cassadó** (1897–1966), a pupil of Casals and a fine composer, have been collected in performances with orchestra (Vox 5502, 2CD). **Pierre Fournier** (1906–86) is the best known of this group of European cellists. He made patrician recordings of much of the literature, including all the Beethoven Sonatas with Kempff (DG 453013, 2CD) and an equally interesting set with Schnabel (Enterprise 99357, 2CD). A different issue of the Schnabel Beethoven sonatas along with other works is undermined by misuse of the Cedar reproducing system, thinning out the sound (Monopoly, 3CD).

More recent cellists who have rated major collections are the short-lived but brilliant **Jacqueline du Pré** (EMI 68139, 6CD)

Mstislav Rostropovich's "The Russian Years, 1950–74" contains many items of interest to collectors of contemporary music as well as lovers of this outstanding cellist's playing (EMI 72016, 13CD). He's also presented in an album with the Berlin Philharmonic in recordings made at about the time he left Russia; some fine performances may be found here (DG 437952, 2CD). Rostropovich has recorded nearly everything in the repertoire over the years. His recordings of the Dvořák Concerto with Talich (Supraphon 111901), his Schumann Concerto with Rozhdestvensky (DG LP, NA), and his Beethoven Sonatas with Richter (Philips 442565, 2CD) are prime examples of his protean abilities. I am less enamored of his Bach Suites, though the video of his performances is interesting.

Leonard Rose's album of early recordings may be heard on Pearl 9273 (2CD). This fine cellist's trio recordings with Stern and Istomin are classics. My favorite solo recording is the early *Schelomo* he did with Mitropoulos while he was principal cellist in the New York Philharmonic, more exciting than his later remake with Ormandy (Sony 48278).

János Starker is an outstanding technician who has recorded most of the repertoire over the years. Several miscellaneous discs may be found, including encore pieces (Denon 8117 and 8118), Baroque sonatas (Mercury 434344), and "The Road to Cello Playing", a solo release containing a number of etudes as well as solo pieces by Hindemith, Bernhard Heiden, and Gaspár Cassadó (Parnassus 97008). His Kodály Sonata is outstanding (Delos 1015). Most of his EMI recordings are no longer listed, such as his Prokofiev and Milhaud Concertos and Dohnányi's *Konzertstück*, but no doubt they will return.

Yo-Yo Ma's many discs show a polished technique wedded to a deep emotional involvement. He's particularly fine in music from the 19th and 20th centuries. I can't recommend his Bach or Beethoven as highly as yet, though his recent explorations of early music performance practice suggest that he's about to make a breakthrough in this area. He is the most omnivorous of cellists, crossing over in every direction, playing Cole Porter with violinist Stephane Grappelli (Sony 45574), songs with Bobby McFerrin (48177), and country style with fiddler Mark O'Connor and bassist Edgar Meyer (Appalachia Waltz, 68460). There is a disc of "Japanese Melodies" that Sony should reissue. If you want to study the crossover process in depth, the six videos he made of each of the six Bach Suites in collaboration with some highly unlikely artistic partners are worth seeking out.

Stephen Isserlis is an outstanding British cellist. He usually records single-composer programs and has done some particularly fine ones of

Saint-Saëns, Fauré, Liszt, and Martinů for Hyperion and RCA. "Cello World" deals with material he has arranged, some of it quite unusual (RCA 68928). **Julian Lloyd Webber** is another interesting British artist. Where Isserlis is energetic and intense, Lloyd Webber is pastoral and relaxed, making his recordings of the more traditional virtuoso repertoire sound a bit under-energized, but some of his collections are highly effective: "Cradle Songs" (Philips 442426), "English Idylls" (Philips 442530), and a "Romantic Cello" program (ASV 6014).

Mischa Maisky is a Russian cellist with the outgoing, romantic sound we associate with that country. Besides some fine recordings of the Russian concerto literature, he has made a number of specialty discs, a collection called "Adagio" with orchestra (DG 435781), another with piano called "Cellissimo" (DG 39863), and "Meditation" (DG 431544).

Werner Thomas-Mifune could make the phone book interesting; his three potpourris, one with orchestra (Orfeo 131851), one with piano (Orfeo 443961), and one with more cellos (Calig 50967) are all worth hearing. The title of the last, "Magic Cello," shouldn't be confused with a disc by an older cellist, **Frederic Lodéon,** whose "Magic of the Cello" covers a lot of ground, including excerpts from many longer works (Erato 94689). **Torleif Thedéen** is a fine player who brings distinction to his many recordings. One valuable disc contains three major works by Schnittke, Shostakovich, and Stravinsky (BIS 336).

Miscellaneous collections

Encores have always been an important part of the cello repertoire, but full discs of them are usually too miscellaneous in organization to be easily described or recommended. Besides the mood-oriented programs mentioned above, there are some interesting goodies, particularly a number of discs of music from specific countries. **Coenraad Bloemendal** plays an unusual program of Jewish music (Dorian 90208). A fine French cellist, **Lluis Claret,** pays tribute to Casals and his artistry (Valois 4733). **Andrés Diaz** performs a Russian program with lots of Tchaikovsky (Dorian 90188), while **Leonid Gorokhov** plays more unusual Russian fare (Olympia 641). **Bernard Gregor-Smith** fills in the gaps, including a few good European numbers with his primarily Russian program (ASV 2103).

Bryndis Halla Gylfadóttir plays a curious program of contemporary Nordic composers (Music from Iceland 804). **Mats Lidstrom** offers Swedish cello works (Caprice 21460), and **Louise Patterson** offers a Bohemian program (Querstand 9606). **Erkki Rautio** plays an entire disc of pieces from his native Finland (WEA/Atlantic 95871). Australian cellist **David Pereira** plays a program from his homeland (Tall Poppies 75) and another of interesting continental pieces, some with clarinet (Tall Poppies 10). **Beatrijs Schilders** introduces us to composers from the Belgian Conservatory (René Gailly 87135). **Peter Schuback** plays a mixed program of contemporary works (Phono Suecia 45).

There are a couple of almost identical contemporary programs. Both **David Geringas** (Es Dur 2020) and **Patrick Demenga** (ECM 21520, 2CD) play *Homages,* written for Paul Sacher's birthday celebration by 12 composers. Demenga is more warmly recorded and includes more music; Geringas was dealing with the limits of a single-CD format, I suspect. Try his other disc, "Solo for Tatjana," also a primarily contemporary program (Es Dur 2019). Americana is covered nicely by **Terry King** in two pleasant discs (Music & Arts 603 and 685). The sunny South gets its innings in a program by **Dorothy Lewis** (Gasparo 274), and she may also be heard in an unusual miscellaneous program (ACA 20013). Crossing the border, **Ignacio Mariscal** has an unusual Mexican pro-

gram (Spartacus 21016), and **Carlos Prieto** spreads his net throughout South America (Urtext 14 and 15)

"The Last Song of Summer: Romantic Music for Cello and Organ," played by **Donald Moline** and **Randall Swanson,** is an unusual collection of original pieces (Dorian 80148). Both this disc and "Original Music for Cello and Guitar," played by **Michael Kevin Jones** and **Agustin Marari,** contain fascinating material from the Classical and Romantic periods (EMEC 1 and 21). A similar program with some duplication is by the **Levy** and **Ben Attar** (FCM 9569). The combination of cello and guitar is also exploited in two discs of mostly transcriptions, "Serenade Espagnole" by **Marek Jerie** and **Konrad Ragossnig** (Bayer 100173) and "Romance" with **Gunter Ribke** and **Bernard Hebb,** all Granados and Tchaikovsky (Ambitus 97880). I'm a sucker for the sound, so I tend to be not too critical of these last performances.

Finally comes every cellist's favorite, discs for multiple cellos. We've mentioned **Thomas-Mifune's** contribution of transcriptions. Another disc by the **Kölner Cello Trio** transcribes the entire Dvořák *Terzetto,* among other unexpected items (FSM 97757). The larger **Philharmonische Cellisten Köln** has recorded "Cellicatissimo," another exercise in transcription, beautifully performed (Koch Schwann 1152). **Vier Cellisten,** on the other hand, sticks to originals (Bayer 100069). The **Peter Buck Cello Ensemble** gives us Villa Lobos's *Bachianas Brasilieras 1* and suites by David Funck and Julius Klengel, then falls back on transcriptions (Harmonia Mundi 905240). An unusual program is in "Subliminal Blues & Greens," sort of a jazzy New Age program played by an all-female quartet called **Cello** (d'Note 1011). And finally, among its several discs, the **Conjunto Iberico Cello Octet** offers a disc mostly of transcriptions for soprano and cellos of Spanish and South American material, also including Villa Lobos's *Bachianas 5* with Clara McFadden, an unlikely name for a singer of Spanish material. I've heard better *Bachianas,* but there's meat here otherwise (Channel 9323).

DOUBLE BASS

The bass viol, or double bass, was seldom used as a solo instrument until the Romantic era when Beethoven's preferred bassist, Domenico Dragonetti, wrote some music for it. So did Giovanni Bottesini in the middle of the 19th century. Here we deal primarily with the most important and representative collections for the instrument.

Dragonetti's Concerto, Bottesini's *Allegro* and *Capriccio di Bravura,* Henry Eccles's Sonata, and other works by Giambattista Cimador and Bloch transcribed for bass and strings are played by **Massimo Giorgi** in "Il Contrabasso Italiano", though the name doesn't refer to the composers (Koch Schwann 1424). "Salon Music for a Double Bass" is an equally misleading title for a disc by **Frank Coppieters** containing Adolf Mišek's Sonata 2, Bottesini's *Elegie in D* and *Tarantella,* three works by Koussevitzky, and other pieces; they're well played, and none of them strike me as salon music (René Gailly 86006). Mišek's Sonata 1 may be heard on an ambitious disc with sonatas by Eccles, Hindemith, and Vilmos Montag and a solo sonata by Wilfried Jentzsch, all played by **Ferenc Contos** in fine style (Hungaroton 31758). Both the Mišek sonatas and two sonatinas by Fritz Skorzeny have been recorded by **Roelof Meijer** (Partridge 1134).

Michael Reiber plays five pieces by Bottesini, three by Glière, and a *Legende* by Mišek before he becomes seduced by the lure of the transcription and tears into Paganini's *Moses Fantasy* (on the Prayer from Rossini's opera) and Rachmaninoff's *Vocalise.* **Klaus Stoll,** in "Virtuosity Contrabass," offers a number of unusual early works, relying little on transcriptions and branching out into pieces with harpsichord and other strings (Camerata 2061). **Barbara Sanderling** plays works with strings by Rossini, Haydn, Couperin, and Johann Baptist Vanhal in "Rarities," mostly original, though not all actually feature the bass. "Virtuoso Reality" features **Joel Quarrington** in a program employing a string orchestra for Eccles's Sonata and two contemporary works plus Bottesini's *Grand Duo* for violin and bass, before giving us a duet with viola by G.B. Borghi and a fine *Sonatina Tropicale* by Mannino. He ends by showing the violinists how to play Sarasate's *Zigeunerweisen.*

Gary Karr, in "The Spirit of Koussevitzky", gives us four of his own works and four by Glière before resorting to transcriptions from Rachmaninoff and Scriabin (VQR 2031). Another disc emphasizing originals is "Lady Plays the Bass" by **Mette Hanskoy,** which ends with settings of Danish folk songs (Danacord 378). **Ivan Sztankov** begins his "Virtuoso" disc with no less than 12 transcriptions, then launches into an 11-minute Solo No. 10 by contemporary Hungarian composer Laszló Dubrovay, finally bringing in the Budapest Symphony for Koussevitzky's Concerto (Hungaroton 31518).

Transcriptions are a major source of material for the bass, of course, and a number of discs are more than half full of them. In this category should be put **Jeff Bradetich,** whose "Classics for All to Hear" contains not one original bass piece (Music for All to Hear 9101). **Yoan Goilav** also offers an entirely transcribed program, including Brahms's Cello Sonata in E minor, not as good an idea as you might expect, at least in these hands (Gallo 675). **William Xucla** gives only the first movement of the Brahms in "The Bel Canto Double Bass," but follows it up with Beethoven's 12 *Magic Flute Variations* (another cello piece) before going back to Bottesini. This is a nice disc with other good things on it, made in New York, but it shows no company, number, or distributor.

Another rather mixed bag comes from **Eugene Levinson,** who gives us Beethoven's Horn Sonata, Bruch's *Kol Nidre,* and ends with Rachmaninoff's *Elegaic Trio 1,* in which he plays the cello line; Hindemith's Bass Sonata and a couple of other bass pieces are here too (Cala 507). **Klaus Trumpf** divides his time well: Only 18 minutes of his 55-minute program isn't originally written for bass (Berlin 93962). **Gerd Reinke** has given us several discs: "Scherzando" is mostly transcriptions of the high-flying variety (Colosseum 9509), while "Zeitgenössische Raritäten" is entirely originals, mostly contemporary but all conservative and neoclassical (Rare Classics 105). Reinke is an energetic but not always accurate player. **Jorma Katrama** divides his program about evenly in "Con Bravura" (Finlandia 95864), while **Jean-Marc Rollez** is all transcriptions except for two sets of Bottesini Variations in "Encores! Bis!" (Maguelone 350507). **Ludwig Streicher**'s "Encores" is almost entirely transcriptions as well (Orfeo 225911). This doesn't reflect on the abilities of the players, of course; frequently the transcriptions are harder to play.

There are a few contemporary programs. **Bjorn Ianke** offers a particularly demanding group of works by Stockhausen, Dallapiccola, Henze, and Françaix, among others (Simax 1039). Another solo disc is by **Corrado Canonici,** containing works by Cage, Berio, Scelsi, and others (Capstone 8628).

Duets by cello and bass are represented by the **Rossini Duo.** Where you go from there, however, is anyone's guess. **Odile Bourin** and **Bernard Cazauran** head for the 20th century with *Six Bagatelles* by Harald Genzmer and a *Fantasie* by Mikhail Boukinik, varying the fare with teaching pieces by August Franchomme and Auguste Lindner (Gallo 795). **Duo di Basso** faces in both directions at once with classical duets by Ignaz Pleyel, Benda, and Jean Barrière and modern ones by Gemrot and Lukas (Canyon 331). Then, having done their Rossinian

duty, they offer a further disc of Boccherini, Haydn, Couperin, and Hus-Desforges on the classical side, Lukas, Thomas Christian David, and Rehor on the modern (Canyon 403). The **Berlin Philharmonic Duo** evade the Rossini issue by working with a harpsichord in a mostly baroque setting, with music by Pergolesi, de Fesch, Zumsteeg, François Francoeur, and Boccherini, mostly but not always featuring the cello.

Quartets of bassists seem to have as much fun as cello quartets, judging by the number of recordings they make. They seem to be associated with particular cities or orchestras. A quartet drawn from the Berlin Philharmonic offers a short program of music from the baroque to the contemporary by David Funck, Bernhard Alt, Theodor Findeisen, Helge Jorns, Paul Chihara, Erich Hartmann, and Mozart (how did he get in there?) (Camerata 20-62). Another group from Brussels is even more light-hearted; they record a number of humorous arrangements. Though they also play Alt's suite, even though he was from Berlin (Pavane 7254). In Frankfurt the Brussels Quartet plays music by Van Herenthals, as well as others both classical and modern (MD+G 6030634). And the New Colophonium combines with the Berlin Quartet in "What a Wonderful Contrabass World!", mostly transcriptions for masses of basses (Camerata 60).   MOORE

VIOLA

The viola has had to fight for its status as a solo instrument. Its somber tone, unstandardized size, slowness of response relative to the violin, and the difficulty of playing an instrument of its size that's too big to hold on the shoulder but also too small to hold between the legs like a cello, make it unappealing to many composers and performers. Most violists, no matter how accomplished, have had to content themselves with playing in orchestras or string quartets. I have restricted myself to writing about those who have pursued major careers as soloists.

If you wish to hear all the great violists of the last century, sometimes recorded as members of a chamber ensemble rather than as soloists, you may wish to invest in Pearl's ambitious "Recorded History of the Viola," in four volumes of two CDs each (Pearl 9148-50, 0039). See the section on the violin below for the history of the schools of viola playing; the two are identical except for the groundbreaking 20th-century British violists exemplified by Tertis and Primrose.

Yuri Bashmet (b. 1953). Like most great violists, Bashmet has an unostentatious demeanor. There is no flash in this Russian's playing, but an extraordinary inwardness and intense concentration in his best performances rank him among the greatest artists on the viola instrument, in spite of the rather thin, dry tone he draws from his Testore instrument. His recital disc has superb performances of Schubert's *Arpeggione* Sonata and Schumann's *Märchenbilder* (RCA 60112). With Richter, he has recorded the definitive performance of Shostakovich's Viola Sonata, along with great readings of Hindemith's Viola Sonata Op. 11:4 and Britten's *Lachrymae* (Olympia 625).

Gerard Caussé is a musician of taste, but this Frenchman's tone production and vibrato are a bit insecure. He can be heard in Berlioz's *Harold in Italy* with Gardiner (Philips 46676).

Paul Doktor (1919–89) was the son of the violist of the great Busch Quartet. A superb technician, this Austrian's style was rather somber, but he had a beautiful tone. None of his recordings is currently available.

Lillian Fuchs (1903–95) was a tiny woman who played an enormous Gasparo da Salò from which she drew a magnificent tone. A very spirited player with an impeccable technique, this great American was the opposite of the stereotypical violist struggling with too large an instrument. Sadly, her recordings are no longer available. Her LP of Mozart duos with her brother, violinist Joseph Fuchs, was delightful, alternately vigorous and sensitive (Columbia, NA). She also made wonderful, much-sought-after recordings of Bach's cello suites for Decca in the '50s.

Paul Hindemith (1895–1963). In addition to being a major composer, Hindemith was a major viola soloist. He played the premiere performance of Walton's Viola Concerto after Tertis turned it down because the score was too modernist. Hindemith was trained in the German school of string playing, so his technique was anything but immaculate, but he had a strong character, a full tone, and could play with great emotion. He can be heard in his own works, including his great *Der Schwanendreher* Concerto (Biddulph LAB 087).

Nobuko Imai (b. 1943). An artist of great subtlety and sensitivity, Imai can make you forget the passage of time. She avoids flash and draws a gorgeous sound from her Andrea Guarnerius. Her "A Bird Came Down the Walk" is the finest viola recital disc I know, with many rare but wonderful works perfectly suited to the instrument's character (BIS 829).

Kim Kashkashian (b. 1952) is a remarkable talent, with a unique combination of purity of tone and intonation and an effortless technique. The size of the instrument has no effect on the perfection of her nuances. This American émigré draws a silvery tone from her compact Brothers Amati viola. Listen to her faultless Brahms viola sonatas, and she will dispel the myth that the instrument can't be played immaculately (ECM 1630).

Kennedy (formerly Nigel Kennedy, b. 1956). Like Zukerman, the English Kennedy isn't normally thought of as a violist, but he occasionally performs on that instrument. I include him here because his recording of Walton's Viola Concerto, my choice as the finest concerto written for the instrument, is the best I've heard, surpassing the versions by Primrose (EMI 49628).

William Primrose (1904–82). This Scotsman was the greatest violist of all time. While Tertis revealed the viola's tonal and expressive possibilities, Primrose showed that it was also a vehicle for the virtuoso; listen to his arrangements of Paganini's Caprices 5, 13, and 17 and you'll become a believer (Pearl 9453). He also introduced greater subtlety of nuance into viola playing than Tertis could achieve; just compare their recordings of Bax's Viola Sonata (Tertis: Pearl 9918; Primrose: Pearl 9453 or Biddulph LAB 148). He could be big and bold in manner, making him a superb concerto soloist. His first recording of Walton's Viola Concerto from the mid-'40s is the only one that gets II up to tempo (Pearl 9252), though his second, with Sargent, is more soulful (Columbia LP, NA). Many feel his recording with Koussevitzky of Berlioz's *Harold in Italy* is the finest ever (Dutton 5013).

Primrose's career is split into halves. In the '30s and early '40s he played an Amati viola his father had owned that had a deep, alto tone; in the mid-'40s he obtained an Andrea Guarneri instrument with a more penetrating, mezzo-soprano timbre. His playing became bolder and more emotional after the switch. He's one of the most-recorded violists ever, largely because he was a favorite chamber music partner of Jascha Heifetz.

Lionel Tertis (1876–1975) was the man who sparked interest in the viola at the turn of the century. This Englishman began as an orchestral violinist, but after realizing that he had an uncanny knack for the viola, he switched to that instrument and embarked on what was probably the first major solo career for any violist. Playing a large Domenico Montag-

nana, he drew ravishing sounds from the viola no one had thought possible. He also confidently explored the instrument's higher positions. His recordings of Bach's Chaconne, Brahms's Viola Sonata 1, Delius's Viola Sonata 2, and Bax's Viola Sonata are priceless documents of an artist who took an instrument most had found dull and made it thrilling (Pearl 9918).

Walter Trampler (1915–97) continued the tradition of Tertis. This German played a large Brothers Amati viola and drew a huge, virile tone from it. He favored contemporary repertoire and can be heard in Richard Wernick's Viola Concerto (Composers Recordings 618).

Pinchas Zukerman (b. 1948). The Israeli-born Zukerman is the greatest living tonalist playing the viola. His Guarneri produces a ravishing sound in his hands, and he's just as comfortable on it as he is on his violin. His recording of Brahms's viola sonatas with Paul Neikrug is a lesson in tone production every violist and viola lover should hear (RCA 61276).

VIOLIN

In the 19th century, three distinct national schools came to dominate violin playing: the German, Franco-Belgian, and Russian. The German school, surviving into the third quarter of the last century, was distinguished not for its virtuosity but for the cultivated musicianship and depth of feeling of many of its leading members, and especially for their probity in interpreting music of the Classical era. The Franco-Belgians had a reputation for nobility and urbanity, and the Russians were renowned for their fiery temperament and tonal intensity. (Of course, these are generalizations and there have been many violinists who were exceptions.) The Italian school, which had been very important since at least the early 17th century, went into decline after the deaths of its last important exponents, the great Viotti (1755–1824) and, greatest of all, Paganini (1782–1840). Italy then turned its back on instrumental music and devoted its energies to opera.

These schools distinguished themselves by their approaches to bowing. The German school, which extended its influence into Austria-Hungary and Poland, advocated an extremely low right elbow that, together with a delicate grip of the bow with the fingertips, often made bowing difficult and robbed the tone of power and fullness. The Franco-Belgians began to hold their right elbows higher by the mid-19th century and used a more secure grip, and their tone production and bowing virtuosity were usually superior to the Germans.

The Russian school was profoundly influenced by the Polish virtuoso Wieniawski (1835–80), who taught at St. Petersburg for several years. He appears to have invented a very secure grip that has the bow held very close to the base knuckle of the index finger. He also seems to have been the first to bow from the shoulder, a method of moving the right arm with a more natural swing and of using its weight, rather than pure muscular effort, to press the bow into the string. This results in a far fuller, more powerful tone than the Germans and even the Franco-Belgians. With the example set at the turn of the century by such popular tonalists as Ysaÿe, Kreisler, and Elman, the German school's days were numbered.

Putting the example of the great tonalists before the public every day, the phonograph and radio helped speed the decline of the various national schools. This process was accelerated by the mass emigration of musicians from European countries that adopted totalitarian regimes. Major artists and teachers from all three schools moved to Canada, the United States, and the United Kingdom and trained a new generation of musicians. This had a cross-pollinating effect. Starting as far back as the second quarter of the last century, it has become increasingly difficult to distinguish the schools because an amalgam of Russian and French techniques and styles has been adopted the world over and German musicianship has become the model for interpreting the classics.

For those who would rather have just a taste of many of the artists discussed below than buy numerous CDs, each devoted to just one player, Pearl has assembled a superb collection of performances of short works by the most important violinists who recorded from the early acoustic era to the advent of stereo (♦Pearl BVA1 and 2, both 3CD).

Salvatore Accardo (b. 1941). Italy's leading violinist, Accardo has a full-bodied tone and a patrician style. One of his best recordings is the Sibelius Concerto with Colin Davis conducting; they have a unique approach to the slow movement (Philips 46160).

Fabio Biondi (b. 1961). Italy's premier period performance violinist, Biondi combines a virtuoso technique with surprising tonal allure. His recording with Alessandrini of Bach's six sonatas for violin and harpsichord set the benchmark for this music (Opus 111 30127).

Adolf Busch (1891–1952). Fritz Kreisler said Busch was the true heir to Joachim's mantle as the leading conservator of the classical tradition in Germany. The last great exponent of the German school, Busch was anything but a tonalist, but his keen intellect gave his interpretations a unique lucidity that grips the listener. Because of this, his recordings of Brahms's Sonatas 1 and 2 are unsurpassed (Pearl 0025).

His most important recordings are not as a soloist but those he made with the Busch Quartet of the Classical repertoire and of Brahms, the great neoclassicist. A nervous intensity of a distinctly post-romantic sort marks their best work; the players' concentration in these recordings is almost palpable. Their recordings of Beethoven's late quartets are definitive (Pearl 0053, 3CD), and those of Brahms's chamber music—Clarinet Quintet with Reginald Kell (Pearl 0007; Testament 1001; Arkadia 78559), Horn Trio with Aubrey Brain (Pearl 0007; Testament 1001), and Piano Quintet with Rudolf Serkin (Arkadia 78559; Pearl 9275)—are just as great. The quality of Busch's playing became variable after his heart attack in 1940.

Giuliano Carmignola is one of the stars of the new wave of Italian period performance specialists. His recordings of Vivaldi's "Four Seasons" (Sony 51352) and "Nature" concertos show that he is a musician with immaculate technique and great panache (Erato 80225).

Cory Cerovcek (b. 1972). This young Canadian has a mellifluous tone and tremendous technique and can bring the virtuoso repertoire to life. His Wieniawski recital disc is one of the best recordings of that composer's music (Delos 3231).

Kyung-Wha Chung (b. 1948). Co-winner of the Leventritt Competition with Zukerman in 1967, the Korean Chung made a splash with her excellent recording of the Sibelius Concerto (London 425080). Her greatest achievement on record, though, is her spellbinding account of Walton's Concerto (Decca, NA), which, with its sinuous eroticism, surpasses both recordings by Heifetz, who commissioned the work.

Mischa Elman (1891–1967) was the first great tonalist to come out of Russia. He was a very small man with a huge, rich, vibrant tone the likes of which no one had ever heard before. His early electric recordings give the best idea of his sound. Tchaikovsky's Concerto was among his specialties (Pearl 9388).

Georges Enescu (1881–1955) was a world-class violinist with a beautiful, seductive tone, a conductor, pianist, and Romania's greatest com-

poser. He was a powerfully charismatic artist who could enchant his audiences with subtle nuances delivered at low dynamic levels, whereas most others must play fortissimo to gain their listeners' attention. His recordings are scarce. A disc with some Baroque music and some Kreisler (Biddulph 066) and a set of Bach's sonatas and partitas for solo violin (Idis 328) display the spiritual force of his playing. There is also a superb set of Enescu playing his own compositions, accompanied by Lipatti, Romania's greatest pianist and Enescu's godson (Dante 91, 2CD).

Eugene Fodor (b. 1950), an American, made a big splash in 1974 when he won the silver medal at the Tchaikovsky Competition (no gold was awarded, probably for political reasons). His debut LP shows a virtuoso violinist with great energy and a searing tone playing short, virtuoso works with unsurpassed brilliance (RCA, NA). He hasn't been able to sustain his career at the same level since the '70s, largely due to his apparent inability to grow musically and play longer, serious works with sufficient probity and individuality.

Zino Francescatti (1902–91) was a sort of French Kreisler. He was a virtuoso with a lovely, vibrant tone, an affable manner, and showed little of the demonic in his playing. His early electric recordings have been collected (Lys 325), and his concerto recordings from the '50s are available (Sony 62339, 2CD). He's most effective in the very lovely and very French Saint-Saëns Concerto 3.

Pamela Frank (b. 1968). Daughter of Schnabel student Claude Frank and herself a student of Szymon Goldberg, Frank is an accomplished classicist. This American seems to need a stimulating partner to bring out her best, though, and she has one in Peter Serkin in her superb disc of Brahms sonatas (London 455643). Her recording of Mozart concertos with Zinman is exquisite (Arte Nova 72104, 2CD).

Szymon Goldberg (1909–93). A student of Carl Flesch and concertmaster of the Berlin Philharmonic under Furtwängler, Goldberg was one of the great classicists. Forced into a solo career when the Nazis expelled Jewish musicians from German orchestras, Goldberg formed a legendary duo with Lili Kraus. Their bold approach to the classics, with stark dynamic contrasts and elastic tempos, has rarely been equaled. Their magnificent recordings of Mozart sonatas and, especially, Beethoven's Sonatas 5, 9, and 10 are the cornerstone of any collection of music for the violin (Music & Arts 4665, 3CD).

Ilya Gringolts (b. 1982). This teenager from St. Petersburg is already a fully mature musician. He possesses a perfect technique, a beautifully even tone, and the musical insight of a seasoned adult. His Paganini CD shows a mature lyricism and concentration on musical values over flash that is almost never heard in this music (BIS 999). His "Solo" disc shows the same virtues applied to superior music (BIS 1051). We'll be fortunate indeed if his musical growth continues along these lines and he keeps sharing his insights with us.

Arthur Grumiaux (1921–86). Grumiaux was the last important representative of the Belgian school of violin playing. Not content to dazzle with charisma or technique, he was a thoughtful musician and noted classicist. His recordings of Mozart and Beethoven sonatas with Clara Haskil from the 1957 Besançon Festival show the joy in music making this duo communicated (Music & Arts 4860).

Jascha Heifetz (1899–1987). Not since Paganini has a violinist had such a profound influence on other musicians. Heifetz amazed the music world with his Carnegie Hall debut in 1917 after emigrating from revolutionary Russia; not in living memory had anyone heard such perfect, effortless virtuosity wedded to such vigor. His early American recordings reveal a youth with no apparent technical limitations (RCA 61732, 3CD). Heifetz later greatly refined his tone, making it the envy of every violinist. His recordings were exemplars for aspiring artists who practiced until they could approximate his tonal refinement and spit-polish technique. More than anyone, he helped raise the technical standards of modern violinists and establish a radically new tonal ideal.

Among his finest recordings are his stereo version of the Beethoven Concerto (RCA 68980), a tour de force of tone production, and Bruch's *Scottish Fantasy* with Vieuxtemps's Concerto 5, breathtaking displays of virtuosity with great élan (RCA 61745, 6214, 61779, 5CD). The list of important Heifetz recordings is very long. Fortunately, RCA has assembled all his recordings from 1917 to his farewell recital in 1972 into one magnificent collection (61778, 65CD).

Bronislaw Huberman (1882–1947). This Pole had a brilliant technique and a powerful temperament. Although a spellbinding performer, his playing has fallen out of style because of his idiosyncrasies and lack of modern tonal refinement. No one today dares to play as impulsively. The Tchaikovsky Concerto was one of his specialties, and his thrilling concert recording with Ormandy (Music & Arts 4299) is superior to his earlier studio version with Steinberg. His accounts of Lalo's *Symphonie espagnole* and Sarasate's *Carmen Fantasy* are among the most freewheeling on records (Pearl 9332; Biddulph LAB 077/78, 2CD). He recorded an explosive Beethoven Sonata 9 with Ignaz Friedman (Biddulph LAB 081/82, 2CD), and his Beethoven Concerto with Szell is justly famous (Naxos 110903).

When he was 13, Huberman played Brahms's Concerto for the composer and brought tears to the old man's eyes. His concert recording of the slow movement of Brahms's Sonata 1 is one of the most ardent and lyrical on records (Arbiter 105). Those unfamiliar with the Viennese romantic style (for the Viennese, technical untidiness was almost a virtue) may be put off by the slovenliness of some of his concert recordings, but his tremendous force of character and strength of feeling can overcome these reservations.

Joseph Joachim (1831–1907). In 1903, an old man stood before a recording horn in Berlin and recorded two movements of unaccompanied Bach, two Brahms *Hungarian Dances,* and his own *Romance.* This was a historic occasion, because Joachim, the greatest violinist of the 19th century after Paganini and paragon of the German school, preserved for us the sound of a playing style soon to vanish. Sparing of vibrato, liberal of slow, languid portamento, and tonally weak, his dreamy performances give us a hint of what was considered the pinnacle of taste in mid-19th-century violin playing. His complete recordings have been collected (Pearl 9851).

Leila Josefowicz (b. 1978). The Canadian-born Josefowicz is a fresh young artist with good instincts and plenty of spunk. She shines in her recital disc "End of Time" (Philips 456571), with an outstanding performance of Falla's *Suite populaire espagnole,* and in "Solo" (Philips 446700), a very fine collection of works for unaccompanied violin, including Bartók's solo sonata.

Kennedy (formerly Nigel Kennedy, b. 1956) is an artist always striving to improve; this Englishman's playing has become more imaginative and has acquired greater depth of feeling over the years. Compare his two recordings of the Elgar Concerto: The earlier one is lovely and autumnal, the later one is alternately turbulent and introspective (EMI 63795, 56413). He also dared to improvise his own cadenzas to the Beethoven Concerto in concert (EMI 54574). His foray into pop hasn't produced any memorable music, but it does seem to have freed him from the constraints imposed by the modern conservatory system, which is designed to produce indistinguishable, cookie-cutter artists.

Fritz Kreisler (1875–1962) was part of the tonalist revolution in violin playing at the turn of the century. This Austrian possessed a warm, round tone and was the first to use continuous vibrato, even in fast, difficult passages. He was also the last of the great violinist-composer/arrangers, and his works are staples of the repertoire to this day. Kreisler was an intellectual and a consummate gentleman, and his gentle nature is evident in his playing. His early recordings have been collected (Biddulph LAB 019/20, 2CD; Monopoly 2041, 2CD). He was a fine sonata partner too, and his recordings with Rachmaninoff are classics; together, they recorded the best Grieg Sonata 3 ever (Monopoly 2042, 2CD).

Gidon Kremer (b. 1947). Though he is David Oistrakh's most important student, the Latvian Kremer is anything but a copy of his teacher. He doesn't possess Oistrakh's incomparably rich tone; indeed, he seems to scorn beauty of sound. Not a stately classicist either, Kremer is attracted to the bizarre and exotic. His slashing, explosive accounts of Beethoven's last five violin sonatas with Argerich probably would have pleased Beethoven but shocked Oistrakh (DG 445652, 447054, 447058, 4CD). A thinking person's violinist, Kremer has recorded a superb Beethoven Concerto with Harnoncourt (Teldec 74881). His taste for the exotic and bizarre produced the excellent "Impressions d'enfance," with music by Enescu, Schulhoff, and Bartók (Teldec 13597).

Jan Kubelik (1880–1940). This Czech-born Hungarian was the Paganini of the turn of the century. The prize student of Otakar Sev#ik, the first teacher to take a radically analytical approach to teaching violin technique, it was Kubelik, not Heifetz, who was the first virtuoso to play with machine-like accuracy. He was famous for practicing until his fingertips bled. His best recordings are his earliest acoustics (Biddulph LAB 033/34).

Sigiswald Kuijken (b. 1944) was part of the first wave of period-performance practitioners of the '60s. He made a name for himself as concertmaster of the Leonhardt Consort, and then went on to found his own group, La Petite Bande. Some of his best solo work can be found in his recording of Corelli sonatas (Accent 48433).

Georg Kulenkampff (1898–1948) was the most tonally refined violinist of the old German school. His performances were more lyrical than, say, Adolph Busch's, and lacked his nervous charge. His Beethoven Concerto was a technical benchmark for the recording industry and is beautifully played (Dutton 5018).

Cho-Liang Lin (b. 1960). This Taiwanese virtuoso is a master of nuance and can convey feelings of great tenderness. He has a special affinity for Stravinsky, and his recording of that composer's music for violin and piano is outstanding (CBS 42101).

Sergiu Luca (b. 1943). Romanian-born Luca was trained on the modern violin at Juilliard but has created a reputation as a Baroque specialist under the guidance of musicologist David Boyden. He plays one of the best accounts of Bach's sonatas and partitas on a fine Nicola Amati, one of the most beautiful-sounding Baroque violins ever recorded (Nonesuch, 2CD, NA).

Yehudi Menuhin (1916–99) was one of the giants of the music world in the 20th century. He came to the public's attention with his Carnegie

Hall debut in 1927 at the age of 11. There was great warmth and joy in this American émigré's playing, along with the peculiar "Gypsy" vibrato that he copied from his teacher Enescu. Many feel he made his best recordings while still in his teens and twenties (Testament 1003). He could really dazzle back then, before his technique began to deteriorate and become unreliable, which happened gradually after WWII. Those who are only familiar with his more recent work may be surprised to find that he was originally a real virtuoso, as his recordings of Paganini attest (Biddulph LAB 102). More willing to forgive the enemy after the war than many other Americans, Menuhin made some excellent recordings with his recital partner Adolf Baller, a superb pianist, in Japan in 1951 (Biddulph LAB 162, 2CD), and a classic recording of the Beethoven Concerto with Furtwängler (EMI 66990).

Midori (b. 1971). Unlike other musicians, Japanese-born Midori knows that the way to get others' attention is to whisper, not shout; she's the virtuoso of the pianissimo. Listen to what she does in her recording of the Tchaikovsky Violin Concerto (Sony 68338). Her soft passages will have you holding your breath.

Nathan Milstein (1903–92). An Auer pupil, the Russian-born Milstein had a dazzling technique, but he developed a much higher level of musicianship than most of his classmates. He lacked their distinctive, intense tone but had just as strong a personality. He played encore-type music with extraordinary finesse and concentration (EMI 66871), and also had a great affinity for music of the Baroque (EMI 66873).

Shlomo Mintz (b. 1957). Not a musician with a powerful personality, Mintz's forte has been his ability to collaborate with others and not hog all the attention. His recordings of the two Prokofiev concertos (DG, NA) and the Brahms Concerto (DG, NA), both with Abbado, are exemplary in the way he holds chamber-music-like dialogues with the sections and soloists in the orchestras.

Erica Morini (1906–95). One of the last of the great exponents of the German school, the Viennese-born Morini was a wonderful combination of grace and verve. Her concert recording of Wieniawski's Concerto 2 is exemplary, as is her Sarasate (Doremi 7762).

Viktoria Mullova (b. 1959). Russian émigré Mullova is a virtuoso with a brain but no heart. She's no sensualist, and her tone is just this side of being wiry. She excels in repertoire where intellectual penetration of the score's structure is essential. She made a superb recording of Brahms's sonatas with Piotr Anderszewski and lets her partner take the lead, as he should in this music (Philips 446709).

Anne-Sophie Mutter (b. 1963). This German is an uneven artist. She can be tasteful, as in much of her "Berlin Recital" (DG 445826) or her "Carmen Fantasy" disc of showpieces with Levine (DG 37544), or she can be tasteless, fussy, and frumpy, as she is in her Vivaldi "Four Seasons." Either way, she has a finely spun tone and a flawless technique.

Ginette Neveu (1919–49). Tragically killed in a plane crash at the age of 30, this French artist was one of the greatest woman violinists. She played with a ferociously masculine style when many girls were still being told it was unladylike to play like a man. A great classicist and a fire-breathing virtuoso, her 1946 recording of the Brahms Concerto with Issay Dobrowen is one of the finest (IDIS 320).

David Oistrakh (1908–74) was the equal and antithesis of Heifetz in the mid-20th century. With a superb technique and rich, golden tone, the Russian Oistrakh placed his supreme artistry at the service of the music. While Heifetz was accused, sometimes justly and sometimes not, of using the music as a vehicle for displaying his virtuosity and unique tone, this was never the case with Oistrakh. A fine classicist, he eschewed display and often did his best work in slow movements. An excellent collection of recordings spanning his career is indispensable for his admirers (Melodiya 40710, 5CD). He also made one of the great recordings of the Brahms Concerto with Szell (EMI, NA), and his recording of Prokofiev's magnificent Sonata 1 with Richter is definitive (Orfeo 489981). The list of great Oistrakh recordings is long.

Itzhak Perlman (b. 1945). Israeli-born Perlman's career was almost stillborn. When he made his Carnegie Hall debut, the New York City newspapers were on strike; fortunately, some members of the national press were there to hear this young sensation. Perlman quickly showed that he was ready to take on the world. He made one great recording after another until the '80s, when his style mellowed and he lost his ability to leave listeners breathless. Among his finest early recordings are Lalo's *Symphonie espagnole* and Ravel's *Tzigane,* both bursting with joy (RCA, NA); Prokofiev's Concerto 2 and Sonatas 1 and 2 (RCA 65454); a collection of encores (EMI 49514); Wieniawski's Concertos 1 and 2 (EMI, NA; 1 is in "The Art of Itzhak Perlman," EMI 64617, 4CD); Vieuxtemps's Concertos 4 and 5 (EMI, NA); the Brahms Concerto (EMI 66992); and some delightful arrangements of Scott Joplin rags for violin and piano (EMI 47170).

Váša Příhoda (1900–60) was the greatest virtuoso of the Czech school after Kubelik. His manner wasn't as mechanical as Kubelik's, though their technique was equal; he had a warm, Central-European style with a slow vibrato and languid portamentos. He preferred the virtuoso repertoire, and made acoustic recordings of abbreviated versions of Paganini's Concerto 1, Vieuxtemps's Concerto 4, Wieniawski's Concerto 2, and his own arrangement of Paganini's fiendish *Nel cor piu non mi sento* (Biddulph LAB 135). He can also be heard playing shorter works, including his own fine arrangement of Richard Strauss's *Rosenkavalier* waltzes (111 50200).

Michael Rabin (1936–72) astonished the music world in 1950 when he made his Carnegie Hall debut at age 13 playing the fiercely difficult Vieuxtemps Concerto 5. Already possessing a flawless technique, the young American recorded 11 of Paganini's 24 Caprices that year, and these were followed by recordings of other short virtuoso showpieces that have never been surpassed (Sony 60894). "Mosaics" is a fine collection of mostly shorter works (EMI 67020). He developed mental problems in the early '60s that curtailed his career and died accidentally in 1972.

Vadim Repin (b. 1971). This Russian started as a virtuoso *wunderkind* but has matured into a formidable musician. His "Vadim Repin au Louvre" contains memorable performances of works by Debussy, Prokofiev, Schubert, Ravel, and Grigoras Dinicu (Erato 26411).

Ruggiero Ricci (b. 1918) is a highly variable artist. He favors the virtuoso repertoire, which he plays in a mechanical but very efficient manner. In more serious fare, his vibrato loosens, his tone deepens and becomes more flexible, and he shows that he is capable of greatness. A fine example of his excellent interpretive abilities is his recording of Beethoven's Sonatas 5 and 9 and Debussy's Sonata (111 96010).

Arnold Rosé (1863–1946) was concertmaster of the Vienna Philharmonic from 1881 to 1938 and had enormous power and influence during those 57 years. He presided over the development of what was probably the first modern virtuoso orchestra during Mahler's tenure as music director. He can be heard playing Bach and with his quartet playing Beethoven's Quartets 4, 10, and 14 (Biddulph LAB 056/57, 2CD).

Lara St. John (b. 1971) is that rare musician who combines the wild instincts of the Gypsy with an uncanny ability to clarify the voice leading in Bach's works for solo violin. An electrifying performer, this Canadian's phrasing is always individual, and her pianissimos are just as spellbinding as her fortissimos are thrilling. Her fusion of the feral and the intellectual makes her a uniquely satisfying artist. Her recording of Bach's Partita 2 and Sonata 3 is a classic (Well-Tempered 5180), and her "Gypsy" contains great performances of Sarasate's *Zigeunerweisen,* Waxman's *Carmen Fantasy,* and Ravel's *Tzigane,* along with an astonishing account of Bartók's Rhapsody 2 (Well-Tempered 5185). Both discs have superb 24-bit sound.

Nadja Salerno-Sonnenberg (b. 1961). This Italian-born artist is noted for her emotionalism on stage, but she is most of all a thinking person's violinist. Her interpretations are invariably very carefully thought out and very imaginative. Her Sibelius Concerto is one of the finest ever, and no one has laid bare the peculiar logic of Chausson's *Poème* as clearly as she and Tilson Thomas (EMI 54855). She's also a superb chamber musician; listen to her outstanding performance of Tchaikovsky's *Souvenir de Florence* in "Bella Italia" (EMI 56163). She's one of the most intelligent and tasteful people ever to hold a violin under her chin and, I suspect, considerably underrated.

Albert Sammons (1886–1957) was that *rara avis,* a self-taught virtuoso. Exemplifying all that's British, he played with a very stiff upper lip. He was one of the last of this type, as later generations of English musicians have adopted a more hot-blooded style in emulation of more expressive continental virtuosos. His recording of the Elgar Concerto (Pearl 0050 or 9496) makes a tremendous contrast with Kennedy's second recording of that work.

Pablo de Sarasate (1844–1908). Spain's greatest violinist, Sarasate represented a by-gone era that accepted a glib style and lack of tonal intensity if the performer had a facile technique. He was one of the last important violinist-composers, writing in the style of Spanish folk music. His complete recordings, made in 1904, are available (Pearl 9851).

Toscha Seidel (1899–1962). This great Russian was a classmate of Heifetz in St. Petersburg. He had a similarly intense, penetrating tone, but his style was midway between Heifetz and Elman. He had a brief international career in the '20s and '30s before he settled in Hollywood to play film scores, and can be heard playing the solos in the Hollywood version of *Intermezzo.* He recorded Brahms's Sonatas 1 and 2 and Grieg's Sonata 3 in the late '20s and early '30s (Pearl 0059) and Korngold's lovely *Much Ado About Nothing* Suite and Franck's Sonata in the late '30s and early '40s (Biddulph LAB 138).

Gil Shaham (b. 1971) is a flawless technician. This American-born Israeli's recording of Wieniawski's concertos gives the listener no hint of the devilish difficulty of the music (DG 431815). He can be somewhat blank, but he can also be an engaging musician, as he is in his debut recital disc, which is very stylishly played and has a fine account of Strauss's Sonata (DG 427659).

Oscar Shumsky (1917–2000). One of the great violinists of the 20th century, the American Shumsky spent more of his career working as a concertmaster and freelance musician than pursuing the life of a soloist. He was a remarkable virtuoso and an intelligent musician. Some of his early recordings have been reissued (Biddulph LAB 136, 137), with an excellent I from Beethoven's Concerto and electrifying accounts of two of Wieniawski's *Polonaises.*

Albert Spalding (1888–1953). An American aristocrat, Spalding was one of this country's leading native-born soloists in the early part of the last century. Not a flaming virtuoso, he was a tasteful, self-effacing musician, and these qualities are evident in his recording of Mozart's *Sinfonia Concertante* with Primrose (Pearl 9045).

Isaac Stern (b. 1920). The dean of American violinists, Stern is almost as famous for his teaching and charitable activities as he is for his playing. He began his career as a virtuoso but has continued to grow musically, and some of his finest work has been his recordings of chamber music with younger musicians. His Wieniawski Concerto 2 and Bruch's Concerto 1 are superb (Sony 66830), and his recording of the Brahms piano quartets is wonderfully intense (Sony 45846, 2CD; 64520, 3CD). Sony has collected some of his finest performances in "A Life in Music" (67195, 12CD).

Josef Suk (b. 1929) is a descendant of Czech musical royalty: Dvořak and Joseph Suk the composer. He's a warm, genial artist with a very musical, self-effacing style. He recorded the definitive Dvořak Concerto with Ančerl (Supraphon 111928).

Henryk Szeryng (1918–88) was another intellectual Carl Flesch student and was renowned for his fine unaccompanied Bach (DG 453004). Discovered by Artur Rubinstein, this Pole and his countryman formed a duo that made some excellent sonata recordings for RCA in the late '50s and early '60s. Szeryng's performance of the slow variations movement from Beethoven's Sonata 9 is a miracle of tone production (RCA 61861). After this, Szeryng traded his Stradivarius for the great "Leduc" Guarnerius of 1743 and lost in tonal finesse what he gained in tonal heft.

Joseph Szigeti (1892–1973) was a thinking man's violinist, but unlike his intellectual peers Adolf Busch and Szymon Goldberg, he was also a very distinctive virtuoso. His early recordings reflect his training by Jenö Hubay in the Hungarian virtuoso tradition of the late 19th century, as they consist mostly of musical fluff (Biddulph LAB 043). Around the time he made these early records, he met his true music teacher, the great Italian pianist Busoni. With Busoni's encouragement, Szigeti explored more serious repertoire and developed a taste for the classics and the avant-garde. As he matured, his vibrato widened, becoming a slow, strangely expressive wobble, and he developed an uncannily vocal tone. His was one of the most distinctive personalities in the history of the violin.

Two of his greatest recordings are concert recital discs: His recital with Bartók at the Library of Congress in 1940 is one of the most important musical events captured on records (Vanguard 8008; Hungaroton 12326-31, 6CD), and his legendary Frick Collection recital with Schnabel shows his exemplary *innigkeit* in the slow movements of Beethoven's Sonata 10 and Mozart's Sonata K 481 (Pearl 9026).

Kyoko Takezawa. This Japanese artist is an intelligent, tasteful young violinist who shows signs of developing real insight. Her recording of Debussy's Violin Sonata is the most impish and mercurial I have heard (RCA 61386).

Christian Tetzlaff (b. 1966) is a cool-headed intellectual. A born classicist, his recording of the Mozart concertos is outstanding, and very impressive because Tetzlaff is both soloist and conductor; his conducting ranks with the best (Virgin, NA). He has also released an excellent set of Bach's sonatas and partitas for solo violin (Virgin, NA).

Jacques Thibaud (1880–1953) was the model French violinist of the 20th century, a virtuoso with Gallic suavity and imperturbability. He was a member of the great Thibaud-Cortot-Casals piano trio and recorded one of the greatest accounts of Franck's Sonata with Cortot in 1923 (Biddulph LAB 014; the electric remake from a few years later isn't as inspired). The pair later recorded Debussy's Sonata (Pearl 9348).

Maxim Vengerov (b. 1974) is a violinist who amazed the world with his consummate technique and his victory in the Carl Flesch competition at a tender age, but his musical development hasn't met expectations. This Russian can be heard to best effect in his debut CD, with a delightful performance of Schubert's Fantasy in C, an intense rendition of Ysaÿe's solo Sonata 3, and a stupefyingly virtuosic account of Heinrich Wilhelm Ernst's *Variations on The Last Rose of Summer*.

Eugène Ysaÿe (1858–1931) was a giant in the music world at the turn of the last century. A huge man with a huge temperament and a whimsical style, the great Belgian was the kind of artist that no longer exists in this era of machine age uniformity, where musicians are filtered into concert halls through the sieve of competitions all judged by the same international elite of artists and teachers. He could be explosive, as in his recording of the finale of the Mendelssohn Concerto, or he could be hushed and tender, as in the hypnotic *Rêve d'enfant,* a lullaby-like work he composed for his son. All his recordings have been carefully remastered and put on one disc (Sony 62337, NA).

Efrem Zimbalist (1889–1985) was the thinking man's violinist from the great pedagogue Leopold Auer's stable of Russian virtuosos of the first third of this century. He had a warm, full tone like his fellow students but didn't develop an instantly recognizable personality like Heifetz, Elman, or Seidel. He was content to let the music be the center of attention, and his recordings have stood the test of time for their good taste and lack of idiosyncrasy. He can be heard playing Brahms's Sonata 3 and Ysaÿe's solo Sonata 1 (Pearl 0032).

Pinchas Zukerman (b. 1948). Co-winner of the Leventritt Competition with Kyung-Wha Chung in 1967, the Israeli-born Zukerman is a master of nuance and the greatest living tonalist alongside Perlman. As a young man, he had a wonderfully spontaneous-sounding manner, but as he has matured, his performances have come to sound highly calculated. This difference is subtle but easily discernible: Listen to his gorgeous, dreamy cantabiles in the Tchaikovsky Concerto, recorded in 1969 (Sony 46268). One of his best recent recordings is of Brahms sonatas; due to its classicism, this music doesn't suffer under his severe discipline (RCA 61697).

MAGIL

Woodwinds

BASSOON

The bassoon, like the oboe, is a double-reed instrument. Its direct ancestor is the dulcian, a hairpin-shaped instrument with a long, folded bore and a single key; developed in the first half of the 16th century, it remained in use until the 17th. An early reference to the dulcian as a "fagotto" (the Italian name for the bassoon, which literally means "a bundle of sticks") was made in 1619 by the composer Michael Praetorius. Around 1700, Johann Christoph Denner developed a 3-keyed bassoon, the English instrument maker Thomas Stanesby, Jr. added a 4th key in 1747, and by 1800 the bassoon had seven keys. Theobold Boehm used his metalworking skills to make a bassoon with 30 keys.

Baroque bassoon

In her "Bassoon Collection," **Frances Eustace** plays an array of instruments from three centuries (Amon Ra 35). She plays Mozart's Duo K 292 for bassoon and cello on a four-keyed Grenser instrument from Mozart's time, a Giovanni Bertoli sonata on a dulcian, Schubert's "Trout" song on a contrabassoon from around 1800, and a Romance by Elgar (who was a bassoonist himself) on a Buffet instrument from 1910.

There are excellent readings of Mozart's Bassoon Concerto played on classical instruments by **Danny Bond** (L'Oiseau-Lyre 417622) and **Dennis Godburn** (MusicMasters 67157). Godburn, who plays both baroque and the modern instruments equally well, also recorded some Vivaldi chamber concertos with recorder player Marion Verbruggen (Harmonia Mundi 907046, 907040). He plays modern bassoon with Previn in recordings of Poulenc's Sextet (RCA 68181) and has also recorded Beethoven wind music (Sony 53367), chamber music by Mozart, Rossini, six Zelenka Sonatas for oboe and bassoon (Accent 8848), and six sonatas by François Devienne (Accent 9290).

Michael McCraw, another excellent baroque bassoonist, has recorded music by Vivaldi and Fasch (Harmonia Mundi 77438), Bach's Orchestral Suites (DG Archiv 415 671), and a Telemann concerto (Harmonia Mundi 77201).

Modern bassoon

As the bassoon continued its development into the 20th century, it branched off into two distinct styles of instrument-making and playing (not to mention reed-making): the German and French systems. Both instruments have the same range, but the French bassoon requires varying degrees of air pressure for different notes. Though this could be taken as a disadvantage, it actually enhances the possibilities of nuance and color. The lower register is gentler in the French bassoon than in the German, and the upper register speaks freely. Other major differences between the two systems are in the ways of fingering notes and making reeds. These differences make switching between the two systems very difficult, and therefore bassoonists usually dedicate themselves to one system or the other.

French. There has been a rise in interest in the French (Buffet) system of bassoon playing during the last generation, but there are few recordings of French playing available. None of the LPs by **Maurice Allard,** the former solo bassoonist of the orchestra of the Paris Opéra and a fine exponent of the French system, are available on CD. Some that should be reissued are his Mozart Concerto (DG 18631), Vivaldi concertos (Erato 70837), and the Saint-Saëns Sonata (Calliope 1819).

Fortunately, Allard's student **Gilbert Audin,** his successor at both the Opéra and as professor at the Conservatoire, has made some excellent recent recordings. They include Françaix's Concerto (Cybelia 650), and Haydn's "London" Trios (Sony 48061). **Jean-François Duquesnoy** has recorded Poulenc's Trio (Harmonia Mundi 911556), and Belgian bassoonist **Luc Loubry** has recorded music by several French composers (Discover 920193). **Alexandre Ouzounoff** made a fine recording of Poulenc's Trio (Accord 205192) and a superb recording of Villa-Lobos chamber music (Adda 581074).

American and Canadian. In the early days of American orchestras the woodwind players were almost all French and therefore the bassoonists played French instruments. Gradually American players moved toward the simpler German system, and eventually most of them adopted the Heckel system.

The principal bassoon seat in the Philadelphia Orchestra has been the home of some excellent musicians. **Sol Schoenbach,** the principal in Philadelphia until 1957, was a great bassoonist and teacher. He made only one solo recording: Burrill Phillips's *Concert Piece* is on in LP that showcases the principal players of the orchestra (Columbia 4629). I hope Columbia will reissue it on CD. Columbia did reissue a recording that features Schoenbach's successor **Bernard Garfield** playing the Mozart Concerto and Weber's *Hungarian Rondo* (Columbia 62652). Garfield can also be heard playing Poulenc's Trio (Boston Records 1026) and Hindemith's *Kleine Kammermusik* with the New York Woodwind Quintet (Boston Skyline 139).

David McGill studied with Schoenbach at the Curtis Institute and since 1988 has been principal of the Cleveland Orchestra. He has many excellent recordings, including Saint Saëns's Sonata and Poulenc's Trio, in "Musique Française" (Boston Records 1022), and Mozart's Bassoon Concerto (London 443176). He also made a novelty recording of Peter Schickele's *Dutch Suite* with tuba player Ronald Bishop (Telarc 80307), and one of orchestra excerpts with spoken commentary (Summit 162). Another student of Schoenbach, **Christopher Millard,** principal of the Vancouver Symphony, has also made a set of orchestral excerpts (Summit 220) as well as some other exceptional recordings. "Duos" is a wonderful collection of pieces for bassoon with other instruments—piano, cello, flute, and percussion (Summit 224), and "Mélange" (Summit 128) is a collection of French music with flute and piano. Millard also recorded some Italian concertos with the CBC Orchestra (CBC 5185).

David Carroll, associate principal with the NY Philharmonic, is another fine American musician with a Canadian past. He plays beautifully in a recording of Poulenc's Trio (Cala 0518). **Sherman Walt,** former principal of the Boston Symphony, made many LPs with the Boston Symphony Chamber Players that should be reissued (RCA 6184, 6167, 6189). He can be heard playing Mendelssohn's *Konzertstücke* (Boston Records 1025), recorded in concert in 1983 and 1986 with the great clarinetist Harold Wright and pianist Gilbert Kalish.

European and others (Heckel system). The German **Klaus Thunemann,** former principal of the NDR Hamburg Symphony, made several recordings with the Academy of St. Martin in the Fields. These include fine concerto by Mozart (Philips 422390), Telemann (Philips 454417), and Hummel and Weber (Philips 432081). He has also recorded three volumes of Vivaldi concertos (Philips 432124, 416355, 446066) and chamber music by Heinz Holliger, Carter, and Varèse (Philips 446095).

Croatian-born **Milan Turkovic** plays both modern and baroque bassoon. The former principal with the Vienna Symphony, he plays with Concentus Musicus Wien, Ensemble Wien-Berlin (a woodwind quintet of principal players from Vienna and Berlin orchestras), and the Chamber Music Society of Lincoln Center. Turkovic plays a modern instrument in his Mozart concerto recordings (Orfeo 223911 and Teldec 8.44056); in his recording with Concentus Musicus he plays a 7-keyed instrument (Teldec 77603); for his Vivaldi concertos (DG Archiv 419615) and his quartets from Telemann's *Tafelmusik* Baroque Soloists (Denon 9613) he plays a baroque instrument. Recently Turkovic made a modern bassoon recording of sonatas with pianist Karl Engel that includes fine transcriptions of Schumann's Romances Op. 94, and Brahms's Clarinet Sonata Op. 120:1, as well as Saint-Saëns's Sonata and Ibert's *Carignane* (Denon 32CM).

In addition to his excellent recordings of classical bassoon literature, **Rino Vernizzi,** solo bassoonist of the RAI Turin Symphony, also plays jazz, and has made a fascinating recording with the Rino Vernizzi quartet (Scatola Sonora 008, available from Tirreno Gruppo Editoriale, Via Volta 4 2036, Cernusco S. N. Milano, Italy). His recording of Villa-Lobos wind music is remarkable (Arts 47200), as are his wind transcriptions of Rossini overtures with the Ottetto Italiano (Arts 47162).

Masahito Tanaka's "Bassoon Fantasia" includes transcriptions of pieces by Kreisler and a great *Hora Staccato* (Pavane 7252); "French Music for Bassoon" includes music by Pierné, Dutilleux, and Saint-Saëns (Pavane 7349; "The Magic Bassoon" has music by Hindemith, Jean-Lois Tulou, Weber, and Saint Saëns (Thorofon 2099). Tanaka has also made a recording of Devienne sonatas (Pavane 7416).

Bassoon ensembles. It's rare to find a bassoonist without a sense of humor. When two or more of them get together to make recordings, the result is often hilarious, and in the case of the great musicians making recordings today, often quite beautiful. "United Sounds of Bassoon," by Milan Turkovic and three other bassoonists, includes novelty pieces like Schickele's classic *Last Tango in Bayreuth* and a setting of "In My Merry Oldsmobile," as well as duets by Hindemith, Stravinsky, Mozart, and Bizet and quartets arranged from music by Desprez and Prokofiev (Koch Schwann 3-1374).

The **Bassoon Brothers,** who are "wanted for low-down playing and bass behavior," are the bassoon section of the Oregon Symphony. Their recording includes great transcriptions of Grieg's "Hall of the Mountain King" (from *Peer Gynt*), Rodgers and Hart's "Bewitched," Hoagy Carmichael's "Georgia on my Mind," and Dave Brubeck's *Blue Rondo a la Turk,* as well as Schickele's *Last Tango* and *Blue Set No. 2 for Four Bassoons* (Crystal 873). (You might have guessed that Schickele, known as the discoverer of PDQ Bach, is a bassoonist.)

The **Caliban Quartet** is a Canadian group that takes its name from the monster in Shakespeare's *The Tempest.* Their exquisite recording of tangos and novelty transcriptions, including arrangements of Gershwin's "I Got Rhythm" and Leroy Anderson's *Bugler's Holiday* (renamed *Bassoonist's Holiday*), is called "BassOOnantics!" (CBC 1116).

Contrabassoon. Though it has been in use since the time of Handel and Beethoven wrote parts for it in some of his symphonies, the modern contrabassoon was first developed in 1879 by William Heckel. Almost every orchestra has one, and so does every bassoon quartet. More than a dozen pieces of standard orchestral literature include a part for the instrument (with its 18 feet of tubing), but only recently has it become distinguished as a solo instrument. **Susan Nigro,** who has made a solo career playing the contrabassoon, has recorded "Little Tunes for the Big Bassoon" (Crystal 348), and some commissioned pieces in "The Big Bassoon" (Crystal 346). **Gregg Henegar,** the contrabassoonist of the Boston Symphony, recorded Donald Erb's Contrabassoon Concerto (Leonarda 331) and his *Five Red Hot Duets for 2 Contrabassoons* with the St. Louis Symphony's **Bradford Buckley** (Albany 092).

CLARINET

Forerunners

The chalumeau is the instrument that eventually, due to the work of Jacob Denner (1655–1707), developed into the classical clarinet (Denner invented it in 1690, but the term "clarinet" first appeared in 1716). Telemann's concerto for two chalumeaux has been recorded by **Erik Hoeprich** and Lisa Klewitt with Musica Antiqua Köln, who bring out the finest qualities of this interesting and unusual instrument (DG 419633). Another recording of this work by clarinetists **Colin Lawson** and **Michael Harris** includes a Telemann sonata for two chalumeaux (Chandos 0593).

Telemann's contemporary, Christoph Graupner, used a pair of chalumeaux in his cantata "Es begab sich, dass Jesus in eine Stadt mit Namen Nain ging," recorded by the **Kleine Konzert** (CPO 999592), and **Ensemble Mensa Sonora** made two recordings that feature pairs of chalumeaux: "The Baroque Chalumeau: Unpublished Concertos" (Pierre Verany 795103) and a group of Graupner overtures (Pierre Verany 794114). The **Accademia Daniel** also recorded music by Fasch that features the chalumeau (CPO 999674).

Another precursor and relative was the basset clarinet—a cross between the basset horn and the classical clarinet. Mozart wrote his A major Concerto (K 622) for this instrument, though the piece was published in 1801 (after the composer's death) for the clarinet; **Colin Lawson,** principal of the Hanover Band, made a fine recording on the earlier instrument (Nimbus 5228).

The clarinet of 1800 had a cylindrical bore with a flared bell, a separate mouthpiece from its boxwood body, and five or six brass keys. Because of the need for a soft reed and a multitude of forked fingerings, it was difficult to play. By the mid-1830s many clarinets had up to 13 keys, but the six-keyed instrument remained the standard until Theobald Boehm began working with clarinets in the 1850s.

Modern clarinet

The clarinet is the most fortunate instrument of the woodwind family because of its rich chamber music literature. Mozart, Schubert, Beethoven, Brahms, Schumann, Bruch, Weber, Mendelssohn, and Messiaen wrote some of their finest music for the clarinet, and because of this wealth of material, many performers have developed into superior musicians. There is controversy about the use of vibrato. Both Anton Stadler, for whom Mozart wrote most of his clarinet music, and Richard Muhlfeld, the clarinetist for whom Brahms wrote, used vibrato. However, the traditional clarinet sound, unlike that of the rest of the instruments in the orchestra, is pure, clean, and devoid of vibrato.

The uninhibited use of vibrato by the British clarinetist **Reginald Kell** (b. 1906) once prompted Furtwängler to stop the Covent Garden orchestra and tell Kell that he was the first clarinet player he had heard who played from the heart. Kell was a wonderful musician whose recordings are finally being reissued on CD. His performances of Beethoven's Clarinet Trio and Schumann's *Fantasiestücke* are available (Testament 1022), as is his beautiful 1937 Mozart Quintet with the Busch Quartet (Pearl 0007; EMI 64932). His 1958 recordings of the Mozart and Brahms Quintets with the Fine Arts Quartet have been reissued together (Boston Skyline 135).

Perhaps the antithesis of Kell (but certainly his equal in musicianship) is **Robert Marcellus,** former principal of the Cleveland Orchestra. He played with a pure and open sound that was free of vibrato, and his Mozart Concerto from the '60s with Szell is a beautiful recording (CBS 37810), a convincing argument for the virtues of playing the clarinet without any vibrato, provided the clarinetist is a superior musician with infinite tonal resources. Unfortunately Marcellus had a brief career and made no other solo recordings.

The former principal of the Boston Symphony, **Harold Wright,** combined the heartfelt qualities of Kell's vibrant sound with the pure linear beauty of Marcellus. His sound and extraordinary musical creativity and sensitivity made Wright a true poet of the instrument, an inspiration for a whole generation of clarinetists who followed him. Many of his chamber music recordings with the Boston Symphony Chamber Players have not been reissued, but after Wright's death in 1993, many tapes of his solo and chamber music concerts have turned up on CD. Wright's recording of the Brahms sonatas with pianist Peter Serkin is wonderful; their reading has extraordinary substance, and Wright and Serkin have an inimitable musical rapport.

There are also three recital recordings (Boston 1023/25): "Live Recital 1," a concert from 1992 with pianist Luis Batlle, includes sonatas by Saint-Saëns and Poulenc and music by Martinů, Debussy, and Lutoslawski; "Live Recital 2" contains a 1960 recording of Schubert's *Shepherd on the Rock* with soprano Benita Valente and pianist Rudolf Serkin, as well as music by Weber, Ingolf Dahl, Pierre Sancan, and Debussy; "Live Recital 3" includes some wonderful chamber music: Mendelssohn's *Konzertstücke* 1 and 2, Mozart's "Kegelstatt" Trio K 498, and Weber's Clarinet Quintet.

Wright's student **John Bruce Yeh,** assistant principal of the Chicago Symphony, also studied with Marcellus. Yeh was a prizewinner in the 1982 Munich International Competition and the 1985 Naumburg Clarinet Competition and has made many excellent recordings. His 1997 "Dialogues with My Shadow" includes solo music by contemporary composers, including a fascinating work by Boulez called *Dialogue de l'ombre double* for computer-multi-tracked clarinets (Koch 7088). Yeh also recorded some multiple clarinet music with Larry Combs and Julie DeRoche (Helicon 1028), and made two concerto recordings with the Chicago Chamber Orchestra: the Nielsen (Centaur 2024) and Kent Kennan's transcription of Prokofiev's Flute Sonata (Centaur 2154).

His recording of music by Reger and Blackwood is extremely interesting (Cedille 022). Blackwood wrote his two sonatas, for clarinet and for piccolo clarinet, in 1994 for Yeh, and both use the harmonic and structural vocabulary of the 19th and early 20th century, yet they sound original and fresh. They are bold statements advocating the inventive use of traditional harmony.

Larry Combs, Yeh's colleague in the Chicago Symphony, has been principal there since 1978. His recording of Copland's Sonata (transcribed by the composer from his Violin Sonata) with Deborah Sobol is beautiful (Summit 172). Also on this disc are a sonata by Bernstein, James Cohn's arrangement of Gershwin's Preludes, and Gould's *Benny's Gig for Clarinet and Double Bass,* which Combs plays with Chicago Symphony bass player Bradley Opland.

Another Wright student, **Jonathan Cohler,** has made many excellent recordings of both the standard literature and music by relatively unknown composers. He plays with a good deal of energy and a gentle touch of vibrato. "Cohler on Clarinet" (Ongaku 024-101) and "More Cohler on Clarinet" (Ongaku 024-102) include the Brahms Sonatas, music by Poulenc, Stravinsky, Schumann, and Milhaud, and lesser-known pieces by Heinrich Joseph Bärmann and Simon Sargon. "Moonflowers Baby" includes Hindemith's Sonata, Honegger's *Sonatine,* and a lilting performance of Kupferman's magical *Moonflowers Baby* for solo clarinet (Crystal 733). In "The Clarinet Alone," Cohler plays a legato version of Paganini's *Moto Perpetuo,* as opposed to the double-tongued staccato way it's played by flutists (Ongaku 024-105, with music by Messiaen and others). In order to achieve the illusion of perpetual motion, he either uses circular breathing or has had his stops for breath electronically removed from this four-page-long string of sixteenth notes. It's so well done that I can't tell.

Another exceptional student of Marcellus, **David Schifrin,** is a very active chamber musician. He's Artistic Director of the Chamber Music Society of Lincoln Center and also Music Director of Chamber Music Northwest. He has made many recordings with both ensembles, including Brahms's Quintet (Delos 3104), Messiaen's *Quartet for the End of Time* and Bartók's *Contrasts* (Delos 3043), and music by Weber (Delos 3194).

Jon Manasse, principal of the American Ballet Theater Orchestra and the NY Chamber Symphony, is a wonderful performer with a beautiful sound and an elegant approach. He also has made some fine recordings of Weber's music, including concertos with Lukas Foss leading the Brooklyn Philharmonic (XLNT 18005) and chamber music with pianist Samuel Sanders and the Manhattan String Quartet (XLNT 18004). He has also recorded music by Spohr, Mozart, and Gershwin (XLNT Music 18009).

Richard Stoltzman is a clarinetist with a very different approach to the instrument. Though he spent ten years at Marlboro working with Casals, Serkin, and Marcel Moyse, he seems to have found his real voice in playing jazz-influenced classical music, collaborating with jazz musicians, and commissioning new music. Stoltzman was a founding member of Tashi, an ensemble that based its instrumentation on Messiaen's *Quartet for the End of Time;* they made a wonderful recording of the piece in 1976 that hasn't been re-released (RCA 1667). Stoltzman's discography is diverse. Recently he recorded Latin music in "Danza Latina" (RCA 63281), as well as Beethoven and Mozart trios with Ma and Ax (Sony 57499). Also of special interest is "Amber Waves," a recording he made with pianist Irma Vallecillo of music by American composers (RCA 62685).

Karl Leister, the German counterpart to Harold Wright, is a clarinetist of extraordinary artistry, with a huge and expressive dynamic range, exceptional taste, and a beautiful sound. Luckily he has recorded a good deal of the clarinet literature with excellent partners. His Brahms sonatas and Clarinet Trio (Nimbus 5600) and his Brahms Quintet with the Brandis Quartet (Nimbus 5515) are wonderful. His Mozart Concerto is included in the Academy of St. Martin in the Fields's collection of wind concertos (Philips 445232), and his Poulenc Sonata with pianist James Levine is intimate and expressive (DG 427639). He also plays in a wonderful reading of Poulenc's Sextet in that recording, with Levine and Ensemble Wien-Berlin.

In 1982 Karajan appointed Leister's countrywoman Sabine Meyer as principal of the Berlin Philharmonic. At that time women weren't accepted by the orchestra, and there was a rather ugly controversy that resulted in Meyer leaving after one year. She did, however, begin an extremely successful solo career, and even established her own wind ensemble, the Sabine Meyer Wind Ensemble. She recorded Beethoven's Octet with that group (EMI 56817), and has made dozens more excellent solo and chamber music recordings, including the Mozart and Brahms quintets (EMI 56759), Stamitz concertos (EMI 548422), and "Belcanto," Mozart opera aria transcriptions (EMI 55513). She has even made a partially crossover recording called "Blues for Sabine" that includes music by Poulenc, Françaix, Stravinsky, and Billy Strayhorn (EMI 55253).

No discussion of the clarinet would be complete without mentioning the Argentinean-born Giora Feidman, whom *Jewish Monthly* once called the "undisputed king of Klezmer." At the age of 20, when he was principal of the Israel Philharmonic, Feidman began a project to reintroduce Jewish music to the still new state of Israel. He's a musician of boundless energy and creativity; his inventiveness, uninhibited romanticism, and endless variety of tone colors make him one of the real masters of the instrument. Among his most interesting discs are a recording of Argentinian tangos called "Clarinetango" (Pläne 88796), one called "Gershwin and the Klezmer" (Pläne 88717), and another called "Schubert and Juddishe Lieder" with guitarist Walter Abt (Pläne 88820).

ENGLISH HORN

The English horn is an alto version of the oboe pitched in the key of F. Its music is written five notes higher than it sounds when played (English horn players aren't required to transpose). There are subtle differences in reed-making and tone production, but otherwise the instrument is played and fingered like the oboe. The common saying that "the English horn is neither English nor a horn," may not be true. Some say it got its name because due to its size it's held at an angle, as revealed in its French name "Cor anglais." The instrument developed from the hunting oboe, the "Oboe da caccia," and could have been given its name because the French had already named their advanced hunting horn the "French" horn. Nobody really knows.

Whatever the origins of its name, the English horn is a strong voice in the modern orchestra. There isn't much solo music, but people like Thomas Stacy, the English horn player of the NY Philharmonic, have been very active in promoting the instrument and finding and commissioning new works for it. Stacy has a valuable recording in the "New York Legends" series that includes a piece for English horn and actress (called "Why else do you have an English horn?"), and many other interesting (and relatively unknown) pieces (Cela 0511). He has also recorded *Canto XV* by Samuel Adler (Albany 306), and can be heard in the many NYPO recordings of music with English horn solos.

Pamela Pecha Woods has recorded music by Alexandre Guilmant and Jan Koetsier (Crystal 721), and Carolyn Hove made a recording that includes works by Hindemith, Salonen, Persichetti, and Carter (Crystal 328). Cynthia Steljes, the Canadian oboe and English horn player of Quartetto Gelato, can be heard along with the rest of her versatile ensemble (where everyone doubles on another instrument) in three excellent recordings (Marquis 600/02).

FLUTE

Baroque flute

In the '70s and '80s, flutists who sought a new approach to the literature of the 16th through the 18th centuries began experimenting with copies of instruments that had conical bores, a single key, and were made of wood. These instruments have an entirely different sound from the modern flute, are tuned roughly one half step below standard orchestral pitch, and have a different fingering system. The baroque flute was the instrument of Frederick the Great of Prussia (1712–1786), and was used in Haydn's orchestra as well as all German orchestras into the 19th century.

Frans Brüggen, who plays baroque flute as well as recorder, and Frans Vester (Brüggen's teacher) are largely responsible for the instrument's revival. As they learned to play the instruments, baroque flutists began to make recordings and flute makers started making better instruments. We now have a wealth of well-played, well-recorded Baroque flute music on disc, after the instrument had been virtually silent for more than 100 years.

Brüggen's student Barthold Kuijken (b. 1949) was the first to make a significant contribution to the art of baroque flute playing. Kuijken studied recorder with Brüggen and taught himself to play the baroque flute. Music for Kuijken was a family affair, and with his brothers, violinist Sigiswald and cellist Wieland, he had a substantial influence on the historically-informed performance movement. Some excellent Kuijken family recordings are Mozart flute quartets (Accent 48225), Haydn trios Op. 38 (Accent 47807); French music for flute and continuo (Accent 67909); Italian flute sonatas (Accent 9177); Bach sonatas and trio sonatas (Harmonia Mundi 77026); Handel flute sonatas (Accent 9180); and Telemann's Paris quartets (Sony 63115).

Wilbert Hazelzet is another important (and self-taught) baroque flute player. He learned about 18th-century style from reading treatises and from his colleagues, and in 1978, eight years after devoting his energies exclusively to baroque flute playing, he joined Musica Antiqua Köln. Hazelzet is also first flutist of the Amsterdam Baroque Orchestra and teaches at the Royal Conservatory in The Hague. He made some fine recordings of music by CPE Bach (Philips 416615; Channel 0790; Globe 5110) and recorded chamber music by the Bach sons (Globe 5116); music by Bach's students (Glossa 920802); Danzi quartets and quintets (Musicaphon 56825); Haydn trios (Globe 5061); Locatelli sonatas Op. 2 (Philips 416613); Mozart Concertos K314 and 299 (Erato 91724); and Telemann's Paris quartets (Globe 4146).

Stephen Preston was largely responsible for the ascent of the baroque performance movement in England. He began as a modern flutist and, like the other pioneers, taught himself the baroque instrument. He was a founding member of the Academy of Ancient Music and is featured in many of the Academy's first Baroque recordings, made between 1973 and 1991 (for example, Oiseau-Lyre 443267). A reissue of "Preston's Pocket," a 1983 collection of music by Louis-Claude Daquin, Jacques Hotteterre, and Quantz, is available (Amon Ra 19).

The next generation of baroque flutists studied the instrument—they didn't have to teach themselves. **Konrad Hünteler,** who studied with Hans-Martin Linde and developed into one of the finest baroque flutists in the world, continues to play modern flute. He also plays just about every flute-like instrument between the one-keyed, conical-bored baroque flute of the 18th century and the modern Boehm instrument. Hünteler has been active in researching and recording unknown pieces of particular merit. A few of his many recommended recordings are "Boehm: The Revolution of the Flute" (MD+G 0708); Reicha quartets (MD+G 0630); CPE Bach's complete flute concertos (Erato 75536) and flute quartets (Ex Libris 6021); Haydn trios (Harmonia Mundi 901521); and Schubert's *Introduction and Variations* (EMI 49999).

A colleague and student of Stephen Preston, **Lisa Beznosiuk** is the flutist of the English Concert, the Orchestra of the Age of Enlightenment, the New London Consort, and several other ensembles. Some of her excellent recordings are Bach's *Brandenburg Concertos* (DG 432492); Bach's B minor suite (Oiseau-Lyre 417834); Mozart flute concertos (Oiseau-Lyre 417622); flute music of the 16th and 17th Centuries (Hyperion 66298); and Handel sonatas Op. 1 (Hyperion 66921/3). Beznosiuk's student **Rachel Brown** won first prize at the 1984 American National Flute Association's Young Artist Competition. Three of her excellent recordings are Quantz flute concertos (Hyperion 66927), "Music at the Court of Louis XIV" (Harmonia Mundi 77176), and "French Baroque Flute Music" (Chandos 544).

Modern flute

The modern flute is a cylindrically-bored instrument with a fingering system perfected in the 1870s by Theobald Boehm. Though some modern flute players do play wooden Boehm-system flutes, most use instruments made of silver, gold, or even platinum. Of course, only music written after around 1850 was written specifically for the modern flute. The Boehm flute came into use in France soon after it was introduced in the latter part of the 19th century, and by the beginning of the 20th it became the instrument played in orchestras all over the world.

There are roughly four generations of modern flute players currently available on recordings. I haven't listed recordings of important flutists from the first generation (like Marcel Moyse and William Kincaid) because the sound quality doesn't accurately capture the best qualities of their work. My selection of representative flutists is mostly chronological, and I have tried to present an internationally broad sample.

The American **Julius Baker** (b. 1915) was principal of the New York Philharmonic from 1964 until his retirement in 1983, and was the first to play the instrument with a truly beautiful, full-bodied sound. His playing is the standard by which all flutists are and will continue to be judged. His recordings not only show superb musicianship and extraordinary technical accomplishment, they reflect an entire era of musical life in New York, one of experimentation and exploration in newly written music and the wonderful rediscovery of Baroque music.

Baker made many important recordings for Decca and Oxford in the '50s; the latter are being reissued on CD in the "Oxford Julius Baker Limited Edition" and are available from the Manhattan Flute Center (96 Enoch Crosby Road, Brewster, NY 10509). Other recommended recordings include "Pastorale" (VAIA 1133); "Music from Cranberry Isles" (Centaur 2084); "Julius Baker in Recital" I and II (VAIA 1022, 1033); and "Suites for Flute and Orchestra" (Vox 8194). Excellent reissues from the '60s include "The Virtuoso Flute" I–III (Vanguard 42, 53, 55) and Nielsen's flute concerto with Bernstein and the New York Philharmonic (Sony 47599).

Jean-Pierre Rampal (1922–2000) had a very long and prolific recording career. He recorded much of the 18th and 19th century literature in the multi-volume "Rampal Edition" (Erato 45828/45837). Françaix, Jolivet, Martinon, Poulenc, and Boulez wrote works for him. Though he was an important flutist and teacher, I don't like many of his recordings. His playing is flashy but rather bland and empty.

William Bennett (b. 1936) offers an interesting contrast to Rampal. Bennett is an excellent musician so devoted to perfect intonation that he developed his own flute "scale" and had an instrument made to his specifications. Many of his recordings, like "Concert Live at Nova Hall" (Camerata 25CM-204) and his Schubert recording (Camerata 25CM-014) include interesting transcriptions.

James Galway (b. 1939) served as principal of the BBC and London Symphonies, Royal Philharmonic, and Berlin Philharmonic. Since 1976 he has maintained an impressive solo career and recorded a large variety of music. He's known for his bright, full sound and his intense wide vibrato. Many of his recordings I can do without, but there are some that demonstrate both excellent flute playing and fine musicianship, like "The French Recital" (RCA 68351), Bach sonatas (RCA 62555), and "Galway Plays Bach" Vol. 2 (RCA 68182).

A student of Julius Baker, **Paula Robison** was the first American to win First Prize at the Geneva International Competition. Robison has made interesting and beautiful recordings of flute music and music transcribed for the instrument. Her Vanguard reissue (OVC 8089) remains one of the finest recordings available of virtuoso Romantic flute music, and her newer recordings show exceptional artistic sophistication and imagination. They include "By the Old Pine Tree" (music by Stephen Foster and Sidney Lanier; Arabesque 6679) and music by Joachim Andersen and Grieg (Arabesque 6668).

Robert Stallman studied as a child with Rampal. He plays Baroque music very well and 20th-century music with insight and intelligence. His recordings include "Incantations: 20th Century Works for Solo Flute" (VAIA 1112), "The American Flute" (VAIA 869), and Bach violin sonata transcriptions (VAIA 1138). **Alexa Still,** a native of New Zealand, studied and now lives in the US. She has made some exceptional recordings of American music (Koch 7063 and 7144).

There are some exceptional recordings made by young European flutists. The Slovenian-born **Irena Grafenauer** won first prize at the Belgrade (1974), Geneva (1978), and Munich (1979) competitions, and in 1977 she was appointed principal with the Bavarian Radio Symphony. Since 1987 she has maintained an extensive international solo career while teaching at the Salzburg Mozarteum. Some of her best recordings include Bach's complete works for flute and harpsichord (Philips 434996), Mozart concertos (Philips 422399), and the Mozart flute quartets (Sony 66240). **Emmanuel Pahud** has been principal of the Berlin Philharmonic since 1993, when he was 23 years old. He has an exquisite sound, perfect intonation, and highly developed musical sophistication. His recordings are all spectacular and include music by French composers (EMI 56488), Weber sonatas (Valois 4751), and Mozart concertos (EMI 63652).

Among these soloists and competition winners, there are some excellent chamber musicians. **Philippe Bernold** (b. 1960), who won first prize in the Jean-Pierre Rampal International Flute Competition in 1987, made a fine recording of chamber music by Debussy (Harmonia Mundi 901647) and another of music by Schubert and Weber (Harmonia Mundi 911535). The principal of the Israel Philharmonic, **Yossi Arnheim,** made some excellent solo and chamber music recordings, including "Modern Masters II" (Harmonia Mundi 90611) and chamber music by Martinů (Kontrapunkt 32205). Arnheim is also a member of Sheshbesh (an ensemble of flute, oud, bass, and percussion) that plays traditional Mediterranean and Middle Eastern music arranged by Israeli composers. Some other fine Arnheim recordings include "Sounds of Love and Legend" (Meridian 84320) and "SheshBesh" (Enja 888830).

Susan Hoeppner is another fine chamber musician who has made some fine recordings, including "Histoire du Tango" with guitarist Rachel Gauk (Marquis 177) and another with the Chinook Trio (Marquis 141).

OBOE

Baroque oboe

The baroque oboe is not as different from its modern counterpart as the baroque flute is from the modern instrument (Boehm's cylindrically-bored flute was a drastic departure from its conically-bored predecessor). The oboe was in a constant state of evolution from the mid-1600s until the mid-1800s. Its bore gradually became narrower, which helped the instrument's sound project over larger orchestras, and it acquired metal keys to facilitate passage work. By around 1830 the oboe achieved its modern form.

The wider bore of the baroque oboe gives the instrument a rounder and less penetrating sound than the modern one. It doesn't require as intense air pressure, and the range of articulations possible on separately tongued notes is greater. True legato playing and slurring larger intervals are far more difficult on the baroque oboe. Another important distinction is pitch. Baroque oboes (and their modern copies) are usually pitched at A=415, about one half step lower than the modern A=442. Because of this, their lesser volume, and their darker, warmer timbre, they are always played in conjunction with other period instruments.

There are several excellent recordings by baroque oboe players. **Gonzalo Xavier Ruiz** made a beautiful recording of Handel sonatas (Well Tempered 5174). He plays in tune very well and has a warm, lilting sound. **David Reichenberg** made some fine recordings with the English Concert, including Bach's *Brandenburg Concertos* (DG Archiv 423492), C minor double concerto (BWV 1060) and oboe d'amore concerto in A (DG Archiv 413731), and chamber music by JC Bach (DG Archiv 423385). There is an admirable recording of Mozart's *Divertimenti* for winds by the Ensemble Zefiro that includes **Alfredo Bernardini** and **Paolo Grazzi** (Astrée 8629), and a *Messiah* by the Boston Baroque with

wonderful playing by **Marc Schachman** and **Fredric Cohen** (Telarc 80322).

Modern oboe

American oboists. Since the oboe's solo literature is limited, and since the instrument takes so much physical stamina to play, it's rare for an oboist to have a career as soloist. Luckily many of the world's finest orchestral players have made recordings of the instrument's limited yet excellent solo and chamber music.

Modern American oboe playing has its roots in France. Three students of the French oboist Georges Gillet came to America in the early years of the 20th century: Georges Longy, who joined the Boston Symphony, Alfred Barthel, who joined the Chicago Symphony, and Marcel Tabuteau (1887–1966), who first played in the Metropolitan Opera Orchestra and later joined the Philadelphia Orchestra. These oboists were also extraordinary teachers. Longy founded the Longy School of Music in Boston and Tabuteau was invited to be on the original faculty of the Curtis Institute, where he remained for 40 years and influenced several generations of students.

There is an illuminating recording of **Tabuteau** teaching called "Marcel Tabuteau's Lessons" (Boston 1017). In this recording, made by Wayne Rapier, one of his students and founder of Boston Records, Tabuteau discusses many important technical and musical aspects of oboe playing. There is also a recording of orchestral solos from 1924–1940 with the Philadelphia under Stokowski (Boston 1021). His influence was considerable; most of the last two generations of principals in major American orchestras are either Tabuteau's students or students of his students.

John Mack, a student of Tabuteau and principal of the Cleveland Orchestra, made extraordinary recordings of Britten's *Metamorphoses* and Mozart's Oboe Quartet (Crystal 323) and sonatas by Hindemith and Poulenc (Crystal 324). He made a teaching recording of orchestral excerpts that includes some breathtaking playing and offers interesting insights about oboe playing and musicianship in general (Summit 160). Another splendid Mack recording is Mozart's Oboe Concerto with Dohnányi leading the Cleveland Orchestra (London 443176).

Alfred Genovese, the recently-retired principal of the Boston Symphony, who studied with Tabuteau, made several solo and chamber music recordings. His recording with pianist Peter Serkin includes Poulenc's Sonata and Schumann's *Romances* (Boston 1004). He also plays Mozart's Piano Quintet with clarinetist Harold Wright and others. "Musique Française" is another of his fine chamber music recordings with Serkin (Boston 1022). Here bassoonist David McGill joins them in a voluptuous reading of Poulenc's Trio and Lalliet's *Terzetto*, as well as many shorter treats for oboe, piano, and bassoon.

Robert Bloom (1908-94) studied with Tabuteau at the Curtis Institute and went on to became solo oboist of the Rochester Philharmonic, and in 1938 became a founding member and solo oboist of the NBC Symphony under Toscanini. Boston Records has released the first of a many-volume set called "The Art of Robert Bloom" that includes concert performances from the '60s and '70s (Boston 1031). It contains a wonderful Bach Double Concerto with violinist Joseph Silverstein and Bloom's own *Requiem*, as well as a conversation with Bloom recorded on his 80th birthday in 1988.

Bloom's student **Ray Still** began his 40 years as principal of the Chicago Symphony in 1953, and at the age of 80 is still making recordings. He has made many excellent solo and chamber music recordings, and like his teacher, has a brilliant vocal approach to oboe playing. Still's use of dynamics is extraordinarily expressive; he can achieve the intensity of a loud fortissimo while playing an extremely quiet pianissimo. In 1960 Still recorded Mozart's Oboe Quartet with members of the Fine Arts Quartet (Boston Skyline 142) and later recorded it again, along with oboe quartets by Stamitz, J.C. Bach, and Vanhal, with Perlman, Zukerman, and Harrell (Angel 5237756). Unfortunately the entire recording isn't yet on CD, but the Mozart is in Vol. 2 of "The Perlman Collection" (EMI 317926). In Vol. 1 there is a recording of Still and Perlman playing Bach's Concerto for Violin and Oboe, BWV 1060 (EMI 317827). In 1985 Still recorded the Mozart Concerto with the Chicago Symphony under Abbado (DG 415104), and in 1989 he made a wonderful recording of Strauss's Oboe Concerto, a concerto by Marcello, and some Bach Sinfonias (Virgin 90813).

John de Lancie (another Tabuteau student) was solo oboist with the Pittsburgh Symphony under Reiner in 1940 and became principal of the Philadelphia Orchestra in 1946 after his teacher retired. De Lancie remained with the Philadelphia until 1977, when he left to become director of the Curtis Institute. He can be heard in hundreds of recordings under Ormandy, including concertos by Marcello, Mozart, Strauss, Ibert, and Françaix, but the only one that has been released on CD is Strauss's Oboe Concerto (RCA 7989).

In 1977 **Richard Woodhams** succeeded his teacher De Lancie as principal of the Philadelphia Orchestra. In addition to all his orchestral recordings, he made a lovely recording of Poulenc's Trio with bassoonist Bernard Garfield and pianist Kiyoko Takeuti (Boston 1026). After Woodhams left the St. Louis Symphony, **Peter Bowman** became principal oboist. His only solo recording, of Vivaldi's Oboe Concerto in F, is well worth hearing (Summit 118). Like Woodhams, Bowman has a perfectly balanced sound and a singing quality to his playing. Another De Lancie student, **James Gorton,** co-principal of the Pittsburgh Symphony, is a young musician whose extraordinary playing deserves mention. His 1996 "Pavanes, Pastorales, and Serenades for Oboe and Harp" contains some interesting and beautiful 20th-century music, as well as attractive music from the 16th through the 19th centuries (Boston 1015).

Alan Vogel, who studied with Bloom at Yale, is solo oboist of the LA Chamber Orchestra. He's an extraordinary musician who has made excellent recordings of some neglected pieces of chamber music. His performance of Prokofiev's Opus 39 Quintet with Chamber Music Northwest is marvelous (Delos 3136). He also recorded the Mozart and Beethoven piano and wind quintets (Delos 3024), and made a fine solo recording of Baroque chamber music called "Bach's Circle" (Delos 3214).

Joseph Robinson, who since 1978 has been principal of the New York Philharmonic, studied with both Tabuteau and Mack. He made a recording of Rochberg's Oboe Concerto with Mehta (New World Records 335), and is also featured in chamber music by Madeleine Dring and Poulenc in "New York Legends" (Cala 0518) and playing Barber's *Summer Music* with colleagues from the NYPO (EMI 555400). Robinson plays Schumann's *Three Romances* in a recording of the complete wind and piano works (Elysium 709), and a Haydn Concerto with the NYPO (WQXR 89.5).

Brazilian-born **Alex Klein,** the Chicago Symphony's new principal, has won several major international competitions. He has recorded all the Telemann solo *Fantasies* and several transcriptions of pieces by Bach, including Partita BWV 1013 and several movements from the unaccompanied violin sonatas and partitas (Boston 1029). No discussion of American oboe recordings would be complete without mentioning **Pamela Pecha Woods**'s excellent recording of the Bax and Bliss Quintets for oboe and string quartet and Britten's *Phantasy Quartet* with the Audubon Quartet (Telarc 80205). Woods, assistant principal of the Cleveland Orchestra, also recorded the Strauss and Vaughan Williams concertos with the Moscow Philharmonic (Carlton 00652).

European oboists. **Heinz Holliger** has a strikingly different approach to sound from the Americans discussed above. Though his sound certainly isn't unrefined, it carries a refreshing lack of inhibition. He doesn't strive for the ultimate evenness valued by American oboists; rather, he tries to extend the tonal spectrum of the instrument in all directions. He's a restless musician who is constantly striving for new ways to express himself, an excellent conductor and composer, as well as a champion of both Baroque and avant-garde music.

Holliger's recordings of Bach are well worth hearing. His transcriptions of Bach's organ trio sonatas are extremely colorful (Philips 422348), as are his oboe concertos (Philips 412851). His recording of oboe concertos by Dittersdorf and Ludwig Lebrun is also very exciting, but out of print (DG 427125). There are two available Holliger recordings of Strauss's Oboe Concerto, one with de Waart and the New Philharmonia (Philips 438733), and one with Holliger acting both as soloist and conductor with the Chamber Orchestra of Europe (Philips 466105). His Mozart concerto from the '80s has been reissued (Philips 411134), but unfortunately most of his recordings are no longer available.

Hansjörg Schellenberger studied with Holliger in Darmstadt and joined the Berlin Philharmonic as principal in 1980. He is the oboist of the Ensemble Wien-Berlin (made up of principals from both the Berlin and Vienna Philharmonic) and is one of Europe's finest players. His solo recordings include two beautiful Vivaldi concertos from Op. 7 (Denon 75498), concertos (Campanella Musica 130045), and duos (Denon 6611). He has recorded Italian music (Denon 7908) and French music (Denon 73088), and made an excellent recording of the Mozart Concerto with Levine and the Berlin Philharmonic (DG 429750).

Anthony Camden was solo oboist of the London Symphony from 1972 to 1988 and is now with the London Virtuosi. His recordings include Grace Williams's oboe concerto (Lyrita 323), some Albinoni concertos (Naxos 50739), and some Italian oboe concertos (Naxos 553433); "The Art of the Oboe" includes selections from the latter discs (Naxos 553991).

RECORDER

The recorder flourished in England and Europe from the 15th through the first part of the 18th centuries; its players included Henry VIII and it was a favorite instrument of Louis XIV. Its decline in popularity began with the rise of the transverse flute, the instrument of Frederick the Great of Prussia.

During the Classical period the recorder was almost forgotten, until Arnold Dolmetsch (1858–1940) revived the instrument. In the '20s he began organizing concerts devoted to early music, and soon instrument makers in Germany started making reproductions of recorders that would have been used during different periods of their popularity. In the '50s recorder players started releasing good recordings, and now, nearly 250 years after it virtually disappeared as a serious instrument, there are dozens of excellent makers and its performers are among the finest and most innovative musicians making recordings.

David Munrow (1942–1976) began his musical life as a bassoonist and in 1960 became interested in early flutes. In 1968 he formed the Early Music Consort of London, and during his brief career he made many excellent recordings. "Early Music Festival" (London 452976), "The Medieval Experience" (DG 449082), and "Musiques de la Renaissance Française" (EMI 569555) are among those re-released on CD.

One of the most influential musicians in the recorder revival is **Frans Brüggen** (b. 1934), who studied flute and recorder at the Amsterdam Conservatory and joined the faculty there in 1955, at the age of 21. An excellent teacher, he has been an inspiration to generations of recorder players and other musicians interested in historical performance. Brüggen founded Sour Cream, an ensemble dedicated to new music (as well as very old music) for recorders. As a conductor, he founded the Orchestra of the 18th Century and is a frequent guest conductor for many "modern" symphony orchestras. Many of his recordings have been reissued, and the best are in the "Frans Brüggen Edition" (Teldec 97465/71).

A student of Brüggen, **Walter van Hauwe** founded the Quadro Hotteterre to play 17th and 18th century chamber music. Along with Brüggen, he founded Sour Cream and the Little Consort (an ensemble that plays music of the 15th–17th centuries), and performs often with Japanese marimba virtuoso Keiko Abe. His recordings reflect both a reverence and appreciation for old music and a search for new music for the recorder to ensure that it doesn't die a second death. His recordings include "Blokflutes 3—The Early 17th Century" (Channel 3392); "Ladder of Escape 3," solo recorder music from the 13th through the 20th centuries (Attacca Babel 8847-5); "Japanese Poetic Scenes for Recorder and Marimba," with Keiko Abe (Denon 33446); and Xenakis's *Theraps* (Neuma 450-71).

Van Hauwe's colleague in Sour Cream, the Little Consort, and the Quadro Hotetterre, **Kees Boeke** studied recorder with Brüggen and cello with Anner Bylsma. Boeke has written a good deal of contemporary music for the recorder, including a piece for 40 recorders and electronic tape called "A Little History of Mankind." Like van Hauwe, he considers the recorder to be an avant-garde instrument. Among his recordings are Frescobaldi's *Canzoni* (Nuova Era 7131), Philippe de Monte's sacred and secular works (EMI 63428), and "The Image of Melancolly," with the Amsterdam Loeki Stardust Quartet (Channel 2891). Boeke and van Hauwe have made a number of recordings together, including Telemann's trio sonatas and quartets (Teldec 97455), "A Little Consort Music" (Etcetera 1005), and "The Passion of Reason" (Glossa 921102).

Another Brüggen student, **Marion Verbruggen,** tends to concentrate on fairly standard literature, like Jacob van Eyck's *Der Fluyten Lust Hof* (Harmonia Mundi 907072) and Telemann's *Les Plaisirs* (Harmonia Mundi 907093). She made some other excellent recordings of Vivaldi recorder and chamber concertos (Harmonia Mundi 907046/7) and her own transcriptions of the Bach cello suites (Harmonia Mundi 907071).

Michala Petri began her career as a young virtuoso playing "The Flight of the Bumblebee" and other transcriptions with her mother playing harpsichord and her brother the cello. Her approach is far different from that of Brüggen and his students. While they often use copies of instruments made for the music they perform (17th-century instruments for 17th-century music) and play at the lower baroque pitch, nearly a semitone lower than modern, Petri prefers commercially-made recorders set at the modern A=440. She plays in an elegant yet straightforward manner and seems to have bypassed the historically-informed performance movement altogether. Still, she never plays a note of Baroque music that sounds inappropriate; her virtuosity and musicianship are immaculate, and she's one of the finest instrumentalists to make recordings. Some of her best include "Greensleeves" (Philips 420897); Italian sonatas (Philips 412632); concertos for recorder and strings (Philips 400075); "The Modern Recorder" (RCA 7946); "Souvenir" (RCA 62530); "Moonchild's Dream" (RCA 62543); Vivaldi concertos, Opus 10 (RCA 68543); and "Air" (RCA 62530).

Dan Laurin studied in Denmark with Ulla Wijk, a student of

Brüggen. Like Petri, he plays many transcriptions, and like Brüggen and his students, he plays a good deal of contemporary as well as baroque music. His recordings include "The Japanese Recorder" (BIS 655); "The Swedish Recorder" (BIS 685); contemporary music for recorder and strings (BIS 685); "The French King's Flutists" (BIS 685); Baroque music and transcriptions of everything under the sun in "Your Favorite Classics" (BIS 750); and "Recorder Graffiti" (Intim Musik 1012)

Though it has taken a while for the recorder to catch on in the US (very few American conservatories and colleges teach the instrument to the extent that they do in Europe), there are some fine American recorder players. **Elissa Berardi,** a founding member of Philomel, a Philadelphia-based early music ensemble, has an excellent recording of Telemann concertos (Centaur 2366), and **Judith Linsenberg,** a member of Musica Pacifica, made a fine recording of transcriptions of Bach organ trio sonatas (Virgin 5 451922). FINE

SAXOPHONE

The saxophone is unique among woodwind instruments in that the majority of its history has passed during the age of recording. Belgian instrument maker Antoine Joseph Sax, better known as Adolphe, patented the saxophone in Paris in 1846. His patent covered a choir of fourteen saxes: an orchestral group and a band group, ranging from the sopranino pitched in F to the contrabass in E-flat. In spite of enthusiasm from such composers as Berlioz, Bizet, and Massenet, the saxophone did not become part of the regular orchestral instrumentation.

However, a few composers have required one or more saxophones in orchestral compositions; the best known include Strauss's *Symphonia Domestica,* Ravel's *Boléro,* and Ravel's orchestration of Mussorgsky's *Pictures at an Exhibition.* It found a more stable home in French military and civilian bands. When special classes for military instruments were created at the Paris Conservatoire in 1857, Adolphe Sax was named professor of saxophone and held the post for 13 years.

The French tradition

Marcel Mule was the second saxophone professor appointed to the Paris Conservatoire (in 1942) and established himself as one of the instrument's premier teachers. To many he is the father of the classical saxophone. Beginning in 1925, he gave many solo concerts throughout Europe and became known as an outstanding virtuoso. The body of literature dedicated to him still forms the heart of the classical saxophone repertoire. Mule's approach to tone and vibrato became the standard upon which the "French" school is based. The sound is brilliant without being shrill, and incorporates a relatively fast and nearly constant vibrato. He was considered a master musician and teacher who "legitimized" the saxophone as a serious solo concert instrument.

Mule made many recordings that are, sadly, out of print. However, two excellent collections of many of these early recordings have been reissued, called "Marcel Mule—'Le Patron' of the Saxophone" (Clarinet Classics 0013) and "Marcel Mule—'Le Patron' of the Saxophone—Encore!" (Clarinet Classics 0021). These disks contain a wealth of insight into the classic French saxophone literature and performance style. In them we hear Mule as soloist on alto, as well as leading his quartet on soprano, performing works by Ibert, Rameau, Glazunov, and many others.

Daniel Deffayet, one of Mule's students, succeeded him as Professor of Saxophone from 1968 to 1988. His recordings reveal a very similar approach to vibrato and tone. Like Mule, most of Deffayet's recordings are no longer available. He may be heard, however, with the Berlin Philharmonic conducted by Karajan, in Bizet's *l' Arlésienne* Suites (Musikfest 431160).

Jean-Marie Londeix is also a Mule student who taught at the Bordeaux Conservatory of Music, and his influence upon saxophonists has been immense. Over 130 students have traveled from around the world to study with him, many of them Americans, further disseminating the French tradition. He has 13 LPs and six CDs to his credit and at least 100 of the most important works for saxophone have been written for and dedicated to him. Londeix may be heard performing Debussy's *Rapsodie for Saxophone and Orchestra* in "Debussy: Orchestral Works" Vol. 2 (EMI 72673). Commissioned in 1901 by Elise Hall, the *Rapsodie* is one of the first works by a major composer for the instrument.

Claude Delangle succeeded Deffayet in 1988 as professor of saxophone at the Paris Conservatoire and is considered a master of the French school in classical and contemporary music. While clearly demonstrating roots in the Mule tradition, Delangle has recorded a variety of music from around the world and in many styles. He has made wonderful recordings, called "The Russian Saxophone" (BIS 765) and "The Japanese Saxophone" (BIS 890), featuring works from composers of those nationalities. "The Solitary Saxophone" provides an opportunity to hear his technical control in an unaccompanied setting (BIS 640). This CD includes pieces by Stockhausen and Berio, and Delangle proves that he is equally adept with saxophones other than the alto. His reading of *Episode quatrième* for tenor saxophone solo by Betsy Jolas is particularly interesting.

The American school

The saxophone was introduced to America as a band instrument. In 1892, French saxophonist Edoard A. Lefebre joined Sousa's new professional civilian band. The positive response of audiences and critics to the new instrument led to its use by the burgeoning recording industry in the 1890s. According to Allen Koenisberg's *Edison Cylinder Records, 1889–1912*, Bessie Meeklens recorded twelve Edison cylinders of saxophone solos with piano accompaniment in 1892. Another important soloist who recorded in this period was H. Benne Henton. Henton recorded for Victor and in 1910 made a two-minute cylinder playing his own composition, *Laverne Waltz Caprice.*

Rudy Wiedoeft (1893–1940) was the soloist most responsible for the American "saxophone craze" of the '20's and early '30's. While he performed classical transcriptions, the works he was most popular for included novelty selections such as *Saxema, Saxophobia,* and *Saxophun.* Wiedoeft displayed incredible technique, particularly his lightening fast staccato articulation. He was also one of the first to exploit techniques such as growling, slap-tongue, flutter-tongue, and other humorous effects. Fortunately, a collection of 24 of these early recordings is available in "Rudy Wiedoeft—Kreisler of the Saxophone," where he's featured with Percival Mackey's Band, his own Wiedoeft Saxophone Sextet, and pianist Oscar Levant—a must have for anyone interested in this lost era of saxophone style (Clarinet Classics 0018).

Frederick Hemke (at Northwestern University since 1975) was one of many modern classical saxophonists who owe much to the French tradition after studying in Paris. One of America's foremost teacher/performers, he was the first American to receive the Premier Prix du Saxophone from the Paris Conservatoire in 1956. However, a subtle change in approach has developed in the US, perhaps in response to new repertoire.

Donald Sinta has taught at the University of Michigan since 1974 and is currently the Chair of the Winds Department. He has championed saxophone music by American composers and made a classic recording called "American Music for the Saxophone" featuring sonatas by Bernard

Hieden and Paul Creston (NA). Sinta's playing is an archetypical example of the American adaptation of the "French" classical approach. His sound is slightly darker and his vibrato a bit narrower and more flexible than that heard from Mule. Two recent releases are Walton's *Façade* with the Lincoln Center Chamber Players (Arabesque Recordings 6699) and Crumb's *Quest* with Speculum Musicale (Bridge 9069).

Eugene Rousseau has combined his teaching position at Indiana University with a distinguished career as a performer. Much like Mule, Sinta, and Larry Teal (Sinta's predecessor at the University of Michigan), Rousseau has influenced scores of younger saxophonists through his role as teacher. Two of his recordings are "Saxophone Colors" (Delos 1007) and "Saxophone Vocalise" (Delos 3188). The latter is a wonderful disc featuring Rousseau with the Winds of Indiana conducted by Fennell.

Sigurd Rascher was born in 1907 in Germany, began teaching saxophone at the Royal Danish Conservatory in Copenhagen in 1934, and from about 1940, spent the rest of his life in the US. The normal range of the saxophone is about two and one-half octaves; Rascher did much to remove that limitation by developing a nearly four-octave range through use of the "altissimo" register. From the early '30's through 1977 he distinguished himself as one of the instrument's finest soloists, appearing with principal orchestras throughout the world.

Almost as identifiable as Rascher's unusual range was his sound. His recordings reveal an extremely dark sound that doesn't emphasize the upper harmonics. One reason for this is the type of mouthpiece he used—a large-chamber type, similar to Sax's original design. He may be heard performing Erland von Koch's Saxophone Concerto with the Munich Philharmonic Orchestra conducted by Stig Westerberg (Phono Suecia 55). Just as most of the recordings by Mule, Deffayet, and Londeix are out of print, so too with Rascher. Anyone who wishes to hear the archetypical classical saxophone recordings by these true masters should search libraries and used record dealers for LPs recorded in the '50s, '60s, and '70s. Many of these were on the Golden Crest label and were sponsored by the Selmer Company.

John-Edward Kelly was chosen by Rascher to succeed him in the Rascher Quartet. Kelly is an American who has lived in Germany as a free-lance artist since 1982 and is currently a professor of contemporary chamber music at the Robert Schumann Academy in Düsseldorf. He plays a saxophone built in 1928 "according to the original acoustical specifications of Adolphe Sax." His "Ibert, Martin, Larsson: Works for Saxophone" is an excellent example of a performance by a Rascher disciple with orchestra (BMG/Arte Nova 27786).

Harvey Pittel teaches at the University of Texas at Austin. He recorded "Moving Along" with pianist Jeff Helmer, which includes several important works for the alto saxophone, such as Ingolf Dahl's Concerto and Paule Maurice's *Tableaux de Provence* (Crystal 655).

John Sampen of Bowling Green State University is known for his performances of contemporary literature. He has worked to expand the repertory through commissions and premieres of over 40 new works, including compositions by Bolcom, Cage, Vladimir Ussachevsky, Stockhausen, and Tower. Several of these composers and others are represented in Sampen's 1997 recording, "The Electric Saxophone" (Capstone 8636).

Lynn Klock teaches at the University of Massachusetts and has made several excellent recordings. Two of these, with pianist Nadine Shank, are "Vintage Flora" (Open Loop 007) and "Chant Corse" (Open Loop

003). The first includes several standard works for alto and the second features music for tenor and baritone saxophones.

James Umble is Associate Professor of Music at Youngstown State University's Dana School and won First Prize in Saxophone Performance from the Bordeaux National Conservatory of Music. His "Dejeuner sur l'herbe" is an excellent example of saxophone chamber music (Dana 001). It was recorded with the Cleveland Duo and received Grammy nominations in five categories in 1993, including best chamber music disc.

Dale Underwood came to prominence as saxophone soloist with the US Navy Band; he held that position for 31 years and performed all over the world. He may be heard performing contemporary works such as Robert Muczynski's Sonata and Robert Whitney's *Introduction and Samba,* as well as transcriptions of sonatas by Handel and Henry Eccles, in "Classic Pastiche" (Open Loop 009).

Griffin Campbell, Professor of Saxophone at Louisiana State University, has performed throughout the United States, Britain, and Japan. "Tableaux," with pianist Jan Grimes, includes several standard repertory works as well as the premiere recording of Paul Hayden's Concerto (WorldWinds 1). This is an exciting and difficult work based upon Latin dance rhythms and demanding total command of the altissimo register of the alto saxophone.

Steve Mauk is Professor of Saxophone at Ithaca College School of Music and has recorded several albums with pianist Mary Ann Covert. His "The Saxophone & Me" features mostly transcriptions of music by JS and CPE Bach (Open Loop 029). While baroque adaptations for saxophone are common, transcriptions for the instrument from the Classical period are somewhat rare, but "Classical Bouquet" includes a transcription of Mozart's Concerto in C (Open Loop 008). Contemporary compositions are featured in "Distances Within Me," which includes Alfred Desenclos's exciting *Prelude, Cadence, et Finale* (Open Loop 012). Mauk has dedicated one recording, "Tenor Excursions," to literature for the tenor sax (Open Loop 019).

Tenor specialists
The alto has traditionally been favored over the other members of the saxophone family as a solo instrument in classical music. However, in recent years, a few artists have used the tenor sax as a primary solo instrument and thereby proven its usefulness in the concert realm.

Roger Greenberg, professor of saxophone at the University of Northern Colorado, is a versatile performer on alto and tenor saxophone. However, he has made the tenor something of a specialty, having recorded and toured as tenor saxophonist with the Harvey Pittel Saxophone Quartet. Also, several original compositions for the tenor instrument are dedicated to Greenberg, including William Schmidt's Concerto for Tenor Saxophone and Symphonic Winds. Greenberg has made two of the very few classical recordings that primarily feature the tenor instrument and Schmidt's music in particular. The first, recorded in 1980, is entitled "Art of the Saxophone" Vol. 1 (WIMR 18) and the most recent is "The Art of the Tenor Saxophone" (WIMR 131).

James Houlik has been one of the leading proponents of the tenor saxophone, having performed exclusively on that instrument throughout his career. He currently teaches at Duquesne University, has recorded several albums of tenor saxophone literature, and has commissioned and had dedicated to him more than 60 works for the instrument. "American Saxophone" features Houlik in three major works: Morton Gould's *Diversions,* Robert Ward's Concerto, and Russell Peck's *The Up-* *ward Stream* (Koch 7390). Houlik recorded two wonderful LPs of mostly contemporary literature for tenor saxophone for the Golden Crest label around 1977 and 1978. They have long been out of print, but those interested in this repertory should search libraries and specialty dealers for "James Houlik Plays the Tenor Saxophone" (Golden Crest 7060) and "A Tenor Saxophone Recital" (Golden Crest 7088).

Europe and Asia
Arno Bornkamp is Professor of Saxophone at the Amsterdam Conservatory and a member of the Arrelia Saxophone Quartet and Netherlands Wind Ensemble. He is one of the most technically and musically capable artists playing today. "Saxophone Sonatas" offers perhaps the definitive contemporary recordings of several staples of the repertoire (Globe 6049). Included are Creston's Sonata Op. 19, Alfred Desenclos's *Prelude, Cadence et Final,* and Hindemith's Sonata for Alto Horn and Piano; in particular, the disc displays the skill and musicianship of pianist Ivo Janssen.

Kenneth Tse is a graduate of Hong Kong Academy for the Performing Arts and Indiana University (under Rousseau). He debuted in Japan, "the classical saxophone capital of Asia," in 1977. Tse's first recording, "Saxophone Works," with pianist Kari Miller, includes works by Bernstein and Heiden and the premiere recording of Jind#ich Feld's Sonata for Alto Saxophone and Piano, among others (Crystal 656). Feld's compositions have become something of a specialty for Tse, and his performance reflects this insight. "Sonate" is a collection of sonatas by Saint-Saëns and other less well-known composers (RIAX 2002).

Saxophone quartets
The standard soprano, alto, tenor, and baritone instrumentation of the saxophone quartet was established by Marcel Mule around 1928 with three of his colleagues from the *La musique de la Garde Republicaine* band. The group inspired a significant part of the medium's now large repertoire. Today saxophone quartets are numerous and serve as the primary, classical chamber ensemble for the instrument. Virtually all the soloists mentioned above have performed and recorded with a quartet.

The formation of the **Rascher Saxophone Quartet** is among the accomplishments of Sigurd Rascher. This group is now led by his daughter, soprano saxophonist Carina Rascher, and has long been considered one of—if not the—leading saxophone quartets. They are heard in "The Rascher Saxophone Quartet" (Caprice 21349).

The **Prism Saxophone Quartet** has distinguished itself as among the best. This American group was founded in 1984 and has served as Artists-in-Residence at Settlement Music School in Philadelphia since 1994. One of their excellent recordings is "The Prism Quartet," featuring standard and contemporary repertoire (Koch 7024).

The **Jean-Yves Fourmeau Saxophone Quartet** has made two wonderful recordings. "French Masterpieces" contains several of the original and now standard pieces for the medium, such as Eugène Bozza's *Andante and Scherzo,* Pierné's *Introduction and Variations for Saxophone Quartet "sur une ronde populaire,"* and Jean Rivier's *Grave et Presto* (René Gailly 87134). Arrangements of a variety of pieces running the gamut from Bach to Barber to Brubeck may be heard on "The Art of the Jean Yves Fourmeau Saxophone Quartet" (René Gailly 87088). The performances on this recording are musically expressive, and the technical precision, the intonation in particular, is among the best to be found in modern saxophone quartet recordings.   FAGALY

INDEX

Angerer, Paul, 331, 380, 893
Anghelescu, Cristina, 527
Angus, David, 189
Anichanov, André, 350–51, 486, 759–60
Anievas, Agustin, 728, 731
Anissimov, Alexander, 346–48
Anonymous 4, 441, 1116
Anosov, Nikolai, 12, 709, 856
Anselmi, Susanna, 570
Ansermet, Ernest, 18–19, 72, 151–52, 164, 213, 253, 255, 275, 323, 347, 380, 428–29, 455–56, 517, 534, 560–61, 710, 739, 752, 760–62, 923–25, 927, 934, 936, 964, 966
Antal, István, 50–51, 501
Antalffy, Gabor, 21
Antheil, George, 11
Anthony, Adele, 669, 693
Anthony, Ryan, 308
Antolini, Anthony, 734
Anton Quartet, 352
Antonelli, Claudia, 263
Antonellini, Nino, 597
Antoni, Helge, 875
Antonini, Alfredo, 615
Antonini, Giovanni, 23, 1028
Antonioli, Jean-François, 559, 736
Apap, Gilles, 306
Applebaum, Judy, 164
Apter, David, 1018
Ara, León, 766
Arad, Avner, 474
Aragon, Isabel, 333
Aragon, Lola Rodriguez, 998
Arai, Yoshiko, 874
Araiza, Francisco, 822
Arambarri, Jesus, 309
Arbós, Enrique Fernández, 997
Arcata Quartet, 165
Archer, Malcolm, 290
Ardašev, Igor, 286, 289, 678, 731, 878
Ardašev, Renata, 289
Ardeleanu, Mircea, 891
Arden, David, 137
Arditti, Irvine, 203, 675, 1064
Arditti Quartet, 81, 133, 198, 203, 208, 251, 279, 316, 439, 501, 514, 661, 675, 755, 781, 791, 800–801, 892, 1053–54, 1064
Arena, Maurizio, 127
Arensky, Anton, 11–13
Argenta, Ataulfo, 616, 997
Argenta, Dario, 252
Argenta, Nancy, 43, 45, 138, 723, 762
Argento, Dominick, 13
Argerich, Marta, 82, 103, 112–13, 179, 221–22, 228–30, 431, 520, 530,

576, 586, 631, 645, 712, 730, 733, 740–42, 784, 827–29, 833, 901, 975, 983, 1129
Aria Quartet, 810
Ariel Quartet, 500
Arienski Ensemble, 12–13
Arion Ensemble, 322
Arita, Masahiro, 33
Arkhipova, Irina, 735
Arman, Howard, 609, 843, 846, 848
Armiliato, Marco, 696
Armstrong-Ouellette, Susan, 375
Arne, Thomas, 13–14
Arnell, Johann, 699
Arnesen, Bodil, 875
Arnheim Yossi, 563, 809
Arnold, Malcolm, 14–17
Arnold Wind Quintet, 446
Aronowitz, Cecil, 445, 452
Aronsky, Peter, 736
Arp, Klaus, 941
Arpin, John, 478
Arrau, Claudio, 102, 106, 109, 113, 116, 121–22, 173–74, 178–79, 199, 220–23, 225–31, 520, 523, 644–45, 814–15, 831–34, 977, 1050, 1129
Arriaga, Juan Crisostomo, 17
Arroyo, Martina, 78
Arthur Grumiaux Trio, 12, 512
Artis Quartet, 133, 288, 577, 1053–54, 1069–70
Artymiw, Lydia, 578, 985
Asawa, Brian, 572
Asbury, Stefan, 443
Asch, David van, 65, 404, 406, 614
Ashkenazy, Vladimir, 80, 222, 226–27, 229, 254, 347, 488, 629, 631, 645, 660–61, 709, 712, 727–33, 738, 741, 760–61, 809, 813, 833, 851–52, 865–71, 901, 903, 905, 908, 923, 960, 977, 983, 985, 1129
Ashkenazy, Vovka, 12, 97, 102, 112–14, 117, 122–23, 131, 133, 164–65, 172, 176–77, 179, 197, 983
Ashrafi, Mukhtar, 351
Ashton, Caroline, 780
Asia, Daniel, 17–18
Asiain, Eduardo Hernández, 787
ASKO Ensemble, 1064
Asma, Feike, 579
Asperen, Bob van, 21, 25, 383, 386, 879
Assad, Odair, 765, 1118
Assad, Sergio, 765, 1118
Aston Magna, 641

Astrachanzew, Wladimir, 798
Astrand, Anders, 1127
Astrand, Christina, 676
Astrip, Margaret, 1059
Atamian, Dickran, 486, 712
Athena Ensemble, 256, 463, 670
Athenaeum Enesco Quartet, 831
Atherton, David, 131, 150, 993
Athinäos, Nikos, 292, 615, 756
Atkins, John, 451
Atlanta Chamber Players, 10, 240
Atlantis Ensemble, 809
Atlas, Dalia, 155–56, 812, 942, 1003
Attar, Ben, 1147
Attenelle, Albert, 332
Atterberg, Kurt, 18
Atzmon, Moshe, 699
Auber, Daniel-François, 18–19
Auberson, Jean-Marie, 735
Aubert, Christophe, 843
Aubier, Eric, 1112
Audin, Gilbert, 1154
Audubon Quartet, 288, 308, 489, 793
Auer Quartet, 1056
Augér, Arlene, 43, 206, 388, 438, 658, 772, 819, 839, 922, 1018, 1061, 1136
Augsburg Ensemble, 442
Aulos Ensemble, 988, 1029
Aulos Quintet, 446
Aura Ensemble, 534
Auric, Georges, 19
Aurora Quartet, 578
Aurora Quintet, 714
Auryn Quartet, 186, 810
Austbø, Hakan, 586
Australian Festival of Chamber Music, 564, 702
Avalos, Francesco d', 234, 323, 517, 574–75, 735–36, 877, 1042
Avshalomov, Jacob, 422
Ax, Emanuel, 112, 114, 123, 180, 221–22, 431, 434, 520, 730, 801, 811, 829, 831, 833, 901
Axelsson, Jonny, 1127
Ayo, Felix, 577, 948, 997, 1022, 1024, 1026

B

Baadsvik, Oystein, 1113
Babbitt, Milton, 19–20, 1081
Babin, Stanley, 451
Bach, Carl Philipp Emanuel, 20–21
Bach, Johann Christoph Friedrich, 21
Bach, Johann Sebastian, 21–71, 987, 1081, 1102, 1131
Bach, PDQ, 71, 792
Bach, Wilhelm Friedemann, 71–72

Bach Aria Group, 39
Bachauer, Gina, 174, 221
Bachmann, Maria, 423
Baciu, Ion, 305
Backhaus, Wilhelm, 102, 106, 116, 122, 174, 178, 180, 832, 1129–30
Backofen, Ulrich, 817
Bacon, Thomas, 1059
Baddings, Vera, 251
Badea, Christian, 78, 582, 855
Bader, Roland, 357–58, 477, 594, 686, 941, 1050, 1062
Badila, Ovidiu, 166–67, 998
Badinage, 162
Badun, Wolfgang, 941–42
Badura-Skoda, Paul, 643, 645, 815
Baekkelund, Kjell, 875
Baez, Joan, 1018
Bagratuni, Suren, 245, 713
Bailey, Norman, 1047
Baileys, B., 559
Baillie, Alexander, 186, 299
Bainbridge, Elizabeth, 1007
Baird, Julianne, 43, 50, 322, 389, 391, 696, 1100
Bakels, Kees, 667, 1001–3
Baker, George, 1016, 1058
Baker, Henry J., 1127
Baker, Janet, 45, 142–43, 182, 193, 217, 271, 275, 303–4, 315, 438, 526, 556, 743, 820, 837–38, 921, 1046, 1139–40
Baker, Julius, 324, 636, 638, 668, 1029, 1158
Bakhchiev, Alexander, 779
Balakirev, Mily, 72–73
Balakleets, Olga, 169
Balanescu Quartet, 198
Balboni, Enrico, 423
Balderi, Marco, 210, 754
Baldini, Emmanuele, 1050
Baley, Virko, 929
Balkanyi, Janos, 155–56
Ball, Andrew, 332
Ballerini, Luca, 210
Balleys, Brigitte, 136, 142, 754
Ballo, Pietro, 567
Balogh, Josef, 176
Balsam, Artur, 114, 289
Baltsa, Agnes, 567, 769–70
Bamert, Matthias, 264, 307, 332, 358, 438, 492–93, 498, 558–59, 660, 691–92, 735, 763, 886, 998
Banchini, Chiara, 508, 1025
Bandinage, 988
Banditelli, Gloria, 392
Bánfalvi, Béla, 1026
Banfield, Volker, 355

Bang on a Can, 748
Banks, Anne Victoria, 689
Banks, Kevin, 668
Banowetz, Joseph, 520, 778–79, 977
Banse, Juliane, 136, 451, 839–40, 1018
Bar, Alwin, 731
Bär, Olaf, 126, 821–22, 836–39, 1061
Bar-Illan, David, 616
Baraldi, Roberto, 1030
Barati, George, 67, 816
Barbagallo, James, 321, 532
Barber, Graham, 458
Barber, Samuel, 73–79
Barbican Trio, 503
Barbireau, Jacobus, 1106
Barbirolli, John, 11, 84–85, 91–92, 94, 97, 172, 185, 260, 281–84, 294–96, 298–99, 302, 323, 362, 368–69, 540, 545–46, 550, 618, 664, 776, 800, 867–68, 871–72, 907, 941, 1001–3, 1012–13, 1104
Barbizet, Pierre, 213
Barcelona Trio, 287
Bardach, Nicholas, 1128
Barenboim, Daniel, 58, 89–90, 103, 107, 109, 111–14, 117, 122–23, 125–26, 135, 137, 151–52, 168, 171, 173–74, 181, 196–97, 199, 207, 233, 242, 253–54, 295–98, 310, 314, 516–17, 530, 544, 578, 586, 629–30, 641, 643–45, 647, 656, 760–61, 783, 785, 800, 803, 805, 816, 825, 898, 901, 903, 906, 910, 914, 955, 958, 960, 968, 970–71, 1038, 1040
Barere, Simon, 225, 523, 834, 1130
Bareza, Niksa, 1062
Barinova, Galina, 779
Barlow, Jeremy, 331
Barnard, Trevor, 154–55
Barnes, Paul, 995
Baron, Samuel, 702
Barone, Marcantonio, 247
Baroque Ensemble of Nice, 789
Barra, Donald, 16, 75, 155–56, 711
Barrault, Jean-Louis, 681
Barrett, Nerine, 360
Barrio, Isidro, 997
Barritt, Paul, 458, 466, 799
Barros Classical Concert, 161
Barrueco, Manuel, 344, 703, 765, 880, 998, 1021–22, 1097, 1117
Barry, John, 1084
Barshai, Rudolph, 634, 861
Bárta, Jiří, 798
Bartholdy Quartet, 324
Bartholomée, Pierre, 512, 995

Bartók, Béla, 79–83, 114
Bartók Quartet, 176, 812
Bartoletti, Bruno, 268, 704, 721, 1010
Bartoli, Cecilia, 126, 438, 743, 769, 771–72, 1035
Bartoli, Sandro Ivo, 210
Bartolomey, Franz, 904
Barton, Hanuš, 278
Barton, Rachel, 235, 384, 787, 948
Barton Workshop, 315
Bartos, Michael, 356
Bärtschi, Werner, 449
Barzin, Leon, 710
Bashkirov, Dmitri, 715
Bashmet, Yuri, 139, 195, 306, 352, 448, 484, 796, 808, 829, 864–65, 972, 1148
Basile, Arturo, 595, 1009
Basquin, Peter, 463
Bass, Robert, 125, 920
Bassano, Peter, 328
Bassoon Brothers, 1155
Bate, Jennifer, 278, 524, 586
Bates, Robert, 180
Bátiz, Enrique, 139, 152, 165, 217, 283, 309, 312, 374, 513, 702, 751, 754–55, 760, 1017–18
Battistini, Mattia, 1143
Battle, Kathleen, 49, 78, 215, 392, 769
Baude-Delhommais, Eric, 439
Baudo, Sergio, 124, 252, 455, 464, 774
Bauer, Andrzej, 531
Bauer, Harold, 13, 1130
Bauer, Ivo, 448
Baumann, Christiane, 387
Baumann, Gerhard, 573
Baumann, Hermann, 218, 250, 351, 637, 912, 1049, 1111
Baumann, Jörg, 1036
Bäumer, Hermann, 1112
Baumgartner, Paul, 22–23, 27, 355, 491
Baumont, Oliver, 35
Bax, Arnold, 83–86
Baxa, Pavel, 1068
Baxtresser, Jeanne, 76
Bay, Emanuel, 113
Bayer, Roland, 272
Baynov Piano Ensemble, 248
Bayo, Maria, 391
Bazsinka, Jozsef, 1113
BBC Philharmonic, 443
BBC Singers, 949, 1054
BBC Symphony Chorus, 333
Beach, Amy Marcy Cheney, 86–87
Bean, Hugh, 300–301, 1004
Beardslee, Bethany, 20, 697
The Beatles, 1080

Beaumont, Antony, 1069–70
Beaux Arts Trio, 12, 109, 114, 176, 287, 313, 433, 459, 494, 577, 639, 642, 731, 764, 809, 829, 831, 983, 1070
Beaver, Jack, 1089
Beck, Janice, 276, 579
Becker, Kristi, 791
Becker, Markus, 746
Beckett, Edward, 16
Bedford, Brian, 185, 188–89, 191–92
Beecham, Thomas, 72, 91, 94, 99, 138, 141–42, 151–52, 172, 213, 219, 260–62, 298, 323, 362, 369, 392, 397, 400, 416, 428–31, 435, 503, 517–18, 573, 575, 618–23, 625, 651, 656, 760, 771, 804–6, 834, 868–72, 904, 952, 954, 964, 970–71, 1103
Beekman, Bram, 325
Beethoven, Ludwig van, 87–127, 1102, 1130
Beethoven Broadwood Trio, 885
Beethoven Quartet, 864
Beethoven Trio, 287, 758, 809
Beetz, Günther, 1112
Behrens, Hildegard, 916–17
Behrmann, Martin, 479
Beinum, Eduard van, 79, 172, 196, 378, 429, 554, 575, 744
Beissel, Heribert, 777–78
Bekova Sisters, 12, 325, 563–64, 731, 809
Belardinelli, Danilo, 130
Belkin, Boris, 175, 349, 713, 913
Bell, Joshua, 76, 336–37, 496, 741, 873, 980, 1045, 1058, 1065
Bellavance, Michel, 563
Bellezza, Vincenzo, 720
Bellinati, Paulo, 1097
Bellini, Gabriele, 269
Bellini, Vincenzo, 127–30
Bellows, Beverly, 423
Bellugi, Piero, 398
Bělohlávek, Jiří, 281–83, 285, 290, 442–44, 470–71, 560–61, 565, 677, 876–77, 938–39, 967, 1068
Belyayev, Mitrofan, 349
Ben-Dor, Gisèle, 343, 1019
Benačková, Gabriela, 292, 566
Benda, Christian, 161, 210, 563, 886
Benda, Sebastian, 563
Benedek, Tamas, 693
Bengtson, Jan, 1060
Bengtsson, Erling Blöndal, 449, 747, 1065
Benjafield, Richard, 1128
Benjamin, Keith, 889

Bennett, Mary Beth, 995
Bennett, Richard Rodney, 130–31, 453
Bennett, Robert Russell, 144
Bennett, William, 33, 211, 384, 808–9, 1158
Benoit, Jean-Christophe, 707
Benyamini, Daniel, 445
Benzi, Roberto, 151, 323
Berardi, Elissa, 1161
Berberian, Cathy, 137, 608
Berchot, Erik, 784
Berezovsky, Boris, 73, 226, 520, 730, 732, 742, 832
Berg, Alban, 131–36
Berg, Nathan, 582
Berg Quartet, 797
Berganza, Teresa, 152–53, 368, 438, 769–70, 838, 1140
Bergen Wind Ensemble, 446
Bergen Wind Quintet, 77, 670
Berger, Erna, 1136
Berger, Julius, 156, 160–61, 493, 658, 1061
Berger, Melvin, 888
Berglund, Paavo, 283, 491, 663–65, 867–72, 877, 1002
Bergman, Lisa, 462
Bergmann, Hans, 200
Bergonzi, Carlo, 720, 995, 1140–41
Bergqvist, Christian, 796, 798
Bergsma, William, 136–37
Berhg, Øivind, 377
Berhmann, Martin, 816
Beringer, Karl-Friedrich, 64, 841
Berio, Luciano, 137–38, 1080
Berkel, Wilma van, 880
Berkes, Kálmán, 498, 886, 1049
Berkowitz, Ralph, 994
Berlin, Leo, 148
Berlin Akademie für Alte Musik, 23, 28
Berlin Octet, 148, 885
Berlin Philharmonic, 701, 1017
Berlin Philharmonic Academy, 240
Berlin Philharmonic Duo, 1148
Berlin Philharmonic Ensemble, 161
Berlin Philharmonic Horn Quartet, 1111
Berlin Philharmonic Octet, 112, 177, 446
Berlin Philharmonic Sextet, 494
Berlin Philharmonic Wind Quintet, 250, 446, 823–24
Berlin Philharmonic Winds, 627–28
Berlin Radio Choir, 747
Berliner Streichquintet, 578
Berlinsky, Dmitri, 714, 798

Berlioz, Hector, 138–43
Berman, Boris, 204, 472, 520, 712, 714, 798, 852
Berman, Donald, 468, 780
Berman, Lazar, 730, 976
Bern Quartet, 745
Bernac, Pierre, 213, 259, 707, 836
Bernard, Anthony, 413
Bernard Roberts Piano Trio, 184
Bernardi, Mario, 22, 460, 823
Bernardini, Alfredo, 1159
Bernart, Massimo de, 233, 1033
Bernasconi, Giorgio, 160
Bernius, Frieder, 52, 354, 437, 608, 613, 844, 847–48, 1068
Bernold, Philippe, 1159
Bernstein, Elmer, 1084
Bernstein, Leonard, 58, 62, 74, 79–80, 89–91, 93, 95–98, 100, 125, 129–30, 138, 141, 143–46, 151–52, 157, 165, 171–72, 185, 207, 219, 235–41, 252–55, 275, 281–82, 298, 322–23, 333–34, 356, 362, 369, 374, 401, 413, 421, 428, 430, 435–36, 442–44, 453, 455, 467, 475, 517–18, 534, 537–39, 542, 544–45, 547–49, 551, 553, 574–76, 587, 590, 592, 618–23, 631, 649, 651, 659, 662, 664–65, 683, 705–6, 708–9, 739–40, 752, 760–61, 766, 771, 774, 783–84, 805–7, 824–25, 858–62, 868–70, 872, 877, 893, 899, 902, 910, 918, 924–25, 927, 929, 931–32, 934–35, 952–55, 958, 961, 967, 969–73, 990, 1002, 1004, 1006, 1013, 1041, 1104
Béroff, Michel, 519, 521, 586, 712, 740, 927, 929, 931, 933–34
Berry, Walter, 556, 837, 839
Bertelsen, Lars Thodberg, 674
Berthiaume, Gerald, 888
Bertini, Gary, 935, 937, 1055
Bertoldi, Francesco, 352
Bertrand, Emmanuelle, 245
Berwald, Franz, 146–48
Besch, Eckart, 114
Beschi, Paolo, 31
Besig, J., 757
Bessette, Louise, 469
Bessonet, Georges, 785
Best, Martin, 197
Best, Matthew, 77, 123–24, 140, 145, 240, 314, 458, 582, 734, 1005–6
Beths, Vera, 109, 114, 433
Bettina, Judith, 20
Bevan, Rosalind, 504, 891

Beyer, Franz, 264
Beznosiuk, Lisa, 636, 638, 1028, 1158
Beznosiuk, Pavlo, 634–35, 1026
Bezzina, Gilbert, 1033–34
Bianchi, Luigi Alberto, 459, 688, 747, 773
Biber, Heinrich von, 148–49
Biegel, Jeffrey, 248
Bieler, Ida, 448
Biery, James, 276
Biggs, E. Power, 38, 323, 328, 381–82, 756, 1123
Bilek, Zdenek, 677
Billeter, Bernhard, 449
Billman, Per, 247
Bilson, Malcolm, 630, 640–41
Bima, Jeanne Marie, 689
Binchois Consort, 274
Binder, Helmut, 794
Bindina, Jean-Luis, 390
Binns, Malcolm, 227, 426, 762, 776, 887
Biondi, Fabio, 32, 241, 332, 397, 527, 789, 809, 1024–25, 1027, 1030, 1032, 1150
Biret, Idil, 169, 178–79, 220–22, 225–31, 731–32, 783
Birkeland, Oiven, 370
Birkelund, Poul, 668
Birtwistle, Harrison, 149–50
Bisengaliev, Marat, 183, 301, 576, 1058
Bishop, Henry, 14
Bizet, Georges, 150–53
Björlin, Ulf, 126, 147, 511, 704, 720
Björling, Jussi, 1141
Blacher, Boris, 153
Blacher, Kolja, 26, 445
Black, Neil, 913
Black, Robert, 571
Black, Stanley, 374, 486
Black, William, 262, 730
Black Dyke Mills Band, 569–70
Blackburn, Olivia, 343
Blackwood, Easley, 153–54, 210, 240, 469
Blades, James, 1126
Blake, Rockwell, 772
Blanco, Diego, 880
Blankenburg, Elke Mascha, 767
Blase, Dörte, 391
Blase, Heidrun, 391
Blau, Andreas, 638
Blaze, Robin, 1032
Blees, Thomas, 591
Blerk, Gérard van, 445
Bliss, Arthur, 154–55

Blitzstein, Marc, 1055
Bloch, Ernest, 155–57
Blochwitz, Hans-Peter, 820–22, 837
Block, Michel, 367, 741
Bloemendal, Coenraad, 1147
Blomdahl, Karl-Birger, 158
Blomstedt, Herbert, 88, 126, 147, 181, 442, 444, 539, 621–23, 662–67, 676, 684, 767, 804–5, 807, 869, 889, 898–902, 905, 907, 910, 912
Bløndal-Bengtsson, Erling, 451
Bloom, Myron, 913
Bloom, Robert, 1159
Blow, John, 158–60
Blume, Norbert, 352, 445
Blumental, Felicja, 12, 499, 686, 689, 778, 1020
Blumenthal, Daniel, 13, 211, 234, 248, 258
Blyme, Anker, 331
Boatwright, Jo, 246, 308, 469
Bobesco, Lola, 512, 1022
Bobo, Roger, 1113
Boccherini, Luigi, 160–62
Boccherini Quintet, 161
Bochman, Michael, 1004
Bochmann Quartet, 184
Böck, Herbert, 560, 794
Bocquillon, Patrice, 358–59
Boegner, Michele, 228
Boehm, Mary Louise, 87, 321
Boehm Quintet, 208, 698
Boeke, Kees, 326–27, 1161
Boepple, Paul, 410
Boettcher, Wolfgang, 114
Boeykens, Anne, 498
Boeykens, Walter, 498, 668
Boeykens Trio, 1070
Boffard, Florent, 168
Bogaart, Jacob, 246
Bogachev, Vladimir, 353, 764
Bogár, István, 173
Bogard, Carole, 43, 390
Bohemian Ensemble Los Angeles, 564
Böhm, Karl, 90–91, 93–98, 100, 124, 134–35, 196, 353, 428, 430, 434, 616–17, 619–25, 636, 648, 651, 653–57, 744, 803, 805, 895, 898, 900, 902, 906, 910, 918–20, 1037–39, 1042
Bohnen, Michael, 1143
Boismortier, Joseph Bodin de, 162
Boito, Arrigo, 162–63
Bok, Joszef, 67
Bolcom, William, 163–64, 591
Bolet, Jorge, 222, 229, 520–22, 616, 712, 730, 732, 746, 1130

Bolle, James, 990–91
Bollinger, Blair, 1111
Bolognese, Vincenzo, 1065
Bolstein, Leo, 372
Bolton, Ivor, 399, 607, 994
Bonaventura, Anthony di, 732
Bonazzi, Elaine, 788
Boncompagni, Elio, 773
Bond, Danny, 162, 635, 1154
Bongartz, Heinz, 745
Bonisolli, Franco, 696
Bonney, Barbara, 78, 181, 241, 582, 658, 706, 819, 839, 921, 1061
Bonucci, Rodolfo, 527
Bonynge, Richard, 127, 129–30, 232, 259, 267–68, 272, 354, 362–63, 392–93, 395, 398, 401, 437, 483, 568, 680, 683, 689, 721, 752, 894, 963, 965–66, 989, 1007–8, 1105
Boothby, Richard, 32
Bordas, Ricard, 159
Borgonovas, Pietro, 532
Boriskin, Michael, 179, 250, 424, 583, 696, 780
Borkh, Inge, 721, 916–17
Bornkamp, Arno, 1163
Bornstein, Charles, 1064
Borodin, Alexander, 164–66, 432
Borodin Quartet, 165, 176, 433, 812, 830, 863, 973, 984
Borodin Trio, 12, 114, 184, 287, 352, 459, 642, 741, 829, 831, 865, 885, 983, 985
Borodina, Olga, 987
Borowicz, Zbigniew, 166–67
Boskovsky, Willi, 199, 517, 624–26, 893–95, 897, 1105
Bossert, Christoph, 746
Bosso, Ezio, 166
Bostock, Douglas, 15, 67, 84, 452, 663–65, 677, 1004
Boston Byzantine Choir, 1078
Boston Camerata, 479–80, 1115
Boston Composers String Quartet, 487
Boston Museum Trio, 200, 557, 988
Boston Musica Viva, 851
Boston Symphony Chamber Players, 240, 318, 446
Bostridge, Ian, 192, 319, 820, 822, 837, 839, 1006–7
Bostrom, Erik, 587
Botstein, Leon, 195, 264, 372, 425, 478, 581
Bott, Catherine, 14, 389, 723, 1033
Bottesini, Giovanni, 166–67
Boucher, Jacques, 995, 1015

Boughton, William, 74, 183–86, 236–39, 260, 298, 318, 452, 574, 691–92, 760, 797, 872, 907, 928, 1001, 1004

Boulanger, Francois, 139

Boulanger, Lili, 167

Boulanger, Nadia, 314, 597

Boulez, Pierre, 79–80, 82, 123, 131–33, 135, 137–38, 142, 150, 167–69, 207, 254, 258, 275, 309, 316, 378–79, 501, 514, 537, 542, 544, 546, 548, 550, 556, 586, 674–75, 739–40, 774, 800–801, 835, 852, 891, 900, 923–24, 926–27, 929–32, 934–35, 937, 999, 1040, 1052–54, 1082

Boult, Adrian, 84–85, 92, 95–97, 173, 234, 294–96, 298–99, 302–3, 323, 401, 406, 444, 452–54, 536, 592, 691–92, 772, 776, 870–71, 940, 968, 1001–6, 1040

Bouquet, Michel, 167

Bour, Ernest, 742

Bourbon, Maurice, 597, 611

Bourgue, Maurice, 1005

Bourin, Odile, 1148

Boutry, Roger, 573

Bowers-Broadbent, Christopher, 586–87

Bowles, Paul, 169–70

Bowman, Brian, 1113

Bowman, James, 44, 391–92, 723

Bowman, Peter, 1160

Bowyer, Kevin, 38, 181, 251, 449, 671, 881

Boyce, William, 170

Boyd, Douglas, 637

Boyd Neel Orchestra, 185, 380

Boysen, Bjorn, 1015

Brabants Chamber Choir, 277

Brabbins, Martyn, 187, 495

Brabec, Lubomír, 688

Bradbury, Suzanne, 829

Bradetich, Jeff, 1148

Bradshaw, Susan, 453

Brahms, Johannes, 170–82

Brahms Quartet, 810

Brain, Aubrey, 176

Brain, Dennis, 113, 176, 445, 636, 640, 799, 912, 1111

Brain, Gary, 465

Brainin, Norbert, 634

Braithwaite, Nicholas, 183–84, 261, 452, 743

Braito, Eva, 562

Brake, Kathryn, 493–94

Brandeis String Quartet, 625

Brandes, Christine, 723

Brandis, Thomas, 114, 448

Brandis Quartet, 177, 810

Brass Partout, 1114

Bratislava Radio Orchestra, 753

Bratke, Marcelo, 1021

Bratkef, Marcelo, 240

Brauchli, Bernard, 879

Braumann, Suzanne, 557

Braun, Shony Alex, 1096

Brautigam, Ronald, 445, 644

Bream, Julian, 16, 29, 273, 344, 382, 440, 559, 744, 765, 880, 1021–22, 1057, 1117–18

Brembeck, Christian, 55

Brendel, Alfred, 35, 101, 106, 115–16, 121–23, 434, 520, 523–24, 629–30, 639, 644–45, 661, 801, 811, 813, 815, 827, 1050, 1130

Bress, Hymen, 157, 884

Bressan, Filippo Maria, 212

Bresso, Silvio, 166

Brett, Charles, 159, 1032

Breuer, Hermann, 884

Breuer, Paul, 264

Brewer, Aline, 698

Brewer, Bruce, 526

Brezina, Alexander, 362

Brian, Havergal, 182–83

Bridge, Frank, 183–84

Bridge, John Schneider, 693

Bridge Quartet, 184

Brigandi, Loredana, 615

Briggs, David, 276, 375, 1016

Brindisi Quartet, 132–33, 184, 186

Brion, Keith, 361, 365, 440, 668, 882

Britannia Building Society Band, 570

Britten, Benjamin, 23, 65, 183–93, 256, 302, 366–67, 413, 428, 431, 575, 618–22, 624, 639, 646, 726, 772, 816, 835

Britten-Pears Ensemble, 559

Britten Quartet, 185–86, 992

Britton, David, 1123–24

Brizio, Edoardo, 689

Brodsky, Vadim, 1058–59

Brodsky Quartet, 261, 301, 864, 932

Bronfman, Yefim, 12, 642, 661, 712, 715, 729–30, 862, 865, 933, 983, 985

Brooke, Gwydion, 635

Brooks, Tamara, 698

Brookshire, Bradley, 725

Brosse, Jean-Patrice, 879

Brott, Boris, 1054

Broughton, Bruce, 1084

Brouwenstijn, Gré, 126–27

Brown, Donna, 792

Brown, Emily, 462

Brown, Ian, 177

Brown, Iona, 185, 329, 331, 380–81, 384, 618–20, 624–26, 633, 907, 972–73, 1004, 1026

Brown, Jeremy, 705

Brown, Mark, 404

Brown, Niall, 446–47

Brown, Rachel, 508, 726, 1158

Browning, John, 76–77, 109, 732, 975

Brownridge, Angela, 338–39

Broyhill Chamber Ensemble, 571

Bruce, Edwin, 733

Bruch, Max, 193–95

Bruck, Charles, 354, 565, 716

Bruckner, Anton, 196–97

Bruffy, Charles, 734

Brugalla, Emilio, 367

Brüggen, Frans, 63, 66, 89, 384–85, 428, 430, 575, 736, 1161

Bruk, Lyubov, 733

Brumel, Antoine, 1106

Brund, Bert, 483

Brunelle, Philip, 13, 241, 496, 890

Brunner, Eduard, 239, 250, 444, 501, 745, 828–29, 884, 886, 1049, 1065, 1070

Brunner, Richard, 319

Brunner, Robert, 319

Brunner, Wolfgang, 149

Bruns, Jürgen, 802, 994

Bruns, Peter, 31, 175

Brusca-Solastra Duo, 210–11

Brusilow, Anshel, 73, 165, 217, 762

Bruson, Renato, 266, 995

Bryars, Gavin, 197–98

Brych, Jaroslav, 885–86

Brymer, Jack, 234, 626–28, 635, 642

Bryn-Julson, Phyllis, 168, 193, 209–10, 374, 514, 587, 801, 936

Bucharest Madrigal Choir, 1078

Buchberger Quartet, 446

Buchbinder, Rudolf, 630

Buchman, Noam, 668

Buckel, Ursula, 49

Buckley, Bradford, 1155

Budapest String Quartet, 111, 176, 288, 373, 433, 641, 731, 874

Budapest Strings, 731, 786, 1026, 1061

Budapest Wind Ensemble, 627–28

Budiardjo, Esther, 355, 578

Buechner, David, 289

Buechner, Sara Davis, 775

Buenos Aires Symphony, 701

Buketoff, Igor, 359, 727, 855

Bulov, Alexander, 1059

Bülow, Gert von, 779

Bunin, Stanislav, 226–28

Bunnell, Jane, 145

Burdick, Owen, 402

Burge, David, 246

Burkh, Dennis, 284

Burley, Raymond, 880

Burmeister, Ellen, 698

Burmeister, Frances, 990

Burnett, Richard, 360, 830

Burning River Brass, 1114

Burns, Stephen, 1112

Burton, Gary, 701

Busch, Adolf, 22, 25, 29, 113, 175, 198, 380, 830, 1150

Busch, Fritz, 653

Busch Players, 27

Busch Quartet, 111, 745, 810–11

Buschnakowski, Andreas, 580

Bushkov, Yevgheny, 714

Busoni, Ferruccio, 198–99, 1130

Büsser, Henri, 362

Buswell, James, 702, 1005

Butt, John, 298, 327, 347–48, 356, 489, 518, 686, 735–36, 759, 762, 783, 988, 1121

Butt, Yondani, 346

Butterman, Michael, 441

Butterworth, George, 199

Buttmann, Bernhard, 746

Buttrick, John, 746

Buxtehude, Dietrich, 199–201

Buzzarté, Monique, 203

Bychkov, Semyon, 151, 279, 768, 928, 964, 986, 1061

Bylsma, Anner, 21, 31–32, 112, 114, 161, 433, 445, 750, 831, 1027

Byrd, William, 201–2

Byzantine Chorus of the Sign of the Theotokos Orthodox Church, 1078

C

Caballé, Montserrat, 266, 269–72, 368, 566, 569, 587, 718–21, 771, 916, 922, 1136

Caballero, William, 509

Cabestany, Rose Marie, 489

Caeyers, Jan, 666–67, 749

Cage, John, 202–6, 1080

Cahuzac, Louis, 444, 667

Cai, Jindong, 889

Caillard, Philippe, 479

Caire, Patrice, 1057

Caldwell, Sarah, 267

Caliban Quartet, 1155

California EAR Unit, 315–16
Callahan, James, 757
Callas, Maria, 126, 129, 153, 215, 266, 269, 271, 343, 353, 566, 718–19, 721, 768, 771, 1008, 1136–37
Callegari, Daniele, 1062
Calusio, Ferruccio, 601
Calvé, Emma, 1137
Calvet Quartet, 111
Calvi, Caterina, 1033
Cambreling, Frédérique, 477, 591, 680–81
Cambria Winds, 890
Cambridge Musik, 384
Cambridge Singers, 706, 722, 1114
Camden, Anthony, 383, 1160
Camerata Bern, 185, 378
Camerata Brasil, 1018
Camerata Köln, 384, 726, 987–88
Camerata Quartet, 512
Cameron, John, 199
Cameron, Michael, 791
Camozzo, Adolfo, 271
Campanella, Bruno, 128, 268, 585
Campanella, Michele, 461
Campbell, Griffin, 1163
Campbell, James, 255, 642
Campbell, Jeffrey, 762
Campion-Vachon Duo, 788
Campoli, Alfredo, 301
Canadian Brass, 685, 1113
Cani, Roberto, 81
Canin, Stuart, 558
Canino, Bruno, 210, 431, 443
Canonici, Corrado, 1148
Cantalupi, Diego, 327
Cantamen, 332
Cantelli, Guido, 172, 323, 574–75, 806
Canteloube, Joseph, 206
Cantilena Ensemble, 241
Cantor, Robin, 1005
Cantores, Gloria Dei, 46
Cantus Köln, 340, 686
Capecchi, Renato, 696
Capella Alamire, 480
Capella Istropolitana, 21
Capella Savaria, 696
Capella Sebaldina Nuremberg, 686
Capet Quartet, 111, 831
Capolongo, Paul, 1017, 1019
Cappelletti, Andrea, 949
Capricorn, 797
Capsir, Mercedes, 269
Capua, Katia, 148
Capuana, Franco, 129, 162, 232
Capuano, Tindaro, 166
Caracciolo, Franco, 789

Caramiello, Francesco, 209
Carbonel, Sylvie, 833
Carbotta, Mario, 773
Carchiolo, Salvatore, 426
Cardenes, Andres, 983
The Cardinall's Musick, 201
Cardoso, Manuel, 1108–9
Carella, Giuliano, 130, 584–85
Caridis, Miltiades, 782, 942
Carignani, Paolo, 271
Cariven, Marcel, 684
Carl Nielsen Quartet, 669
Carlos, Wendy, 1081–82
Cármina, Coral, 333
Carmina Quartet, 176, 255, 288, 944, 984, 1054
Carmirelli, Pina, 1024
Carney, Jonathan, 669
Carola, Maria Pia, 731
Carr, Colin, 30, 245, 784, 823
Carraro, Massimiliano, 1033
Carreras, José, 720
Carroll, David, 1155
Carroll, Edward, 378
Carroll, Paul, 508
Carter, Elliott, 207–10
Carter, Jason, 162
Carter, Roy, 186
Carteri, Rosanna, 696, 717
Carthy, Nicholas, 735
Caruso, Enrico, 1141
Carvalho, Eleazar de, 1019–20
Carver, Lucinda, 618–19
Casa, Lisa della, 819, 838, 921, 1137
Casadesus, Jean-Claude, 140, 151, 254, 258, 456, 705
Casadesus, Robert, 213, 313, 323–24, 630, 741, 783, 1130
Casals, Pablo, 22, 30, 97, 112, 114, 174–75, 195, 285, 300, 574, 805, 827, 831, 1145–46
Case, John Carol, 1007
Casella, Afredo, 210–11
Casella, Leopoldo, 735
Caskel, Christoph, 891
Cassado, Gaspar, 30, 1146
Cassard, Philippe, 258
Cassone, Gabriele, 988
Castagnet, Yves, 276
Castellani, Luisa, 138
Castelnuovo-Tedesco, Mario, 211
Castle, Joyce, 583
Castleman, Charles, 1065
Catalani, Alfredo, 211–12
Catalucci, Gabriele, 427

Cates, David, 327, 1121
Cattaneo, Pieralberto, 570
Catzel, Andrea, 754
Caussé, Gérard, 139, 459, 1148
Cavalli, Pier Francesco, 212
Cavallo, Enrico, 576
Cavani Quartet, 308
Cavazzoni, Girolamo, 1107
Cavina, Claudio, 597, 600
Cayzer, Albert, 458
Cazacu, Marin, 305
Cazal, Olivier, 705
Cazauran, Bernard, 1148
Ceccato, Aldo, 348, 826, 1009
Celibidache, Sergio, 54, 91–93, 96–99, 196–97, 252, 429, 659, 826, 958, 961
Celine, Annette, 232
Cellini, Renato, 268, 512, 1008
Center City Brass Quintet, 1113
Centro Musica Antica di Padova Madrigalisti, 341
Cerha, Friedrich, 788–89, 999
Cerminaro, John, 434
Cerovcek, Cory, 1058, 1150
Chabrier, Emmanuel, 212–13
Chadwell, Tracey, 777
Chadwick, George Whitefield, 213–14
Chailly, Riccardo, 124, 172, 344, 445, 475, 495, 517, 536, 545, 552–53, 556, 574, 585, 684, 739, 760, 767, 770, 772, 801, 826, 861–62, 923–24, 926, 928, 933, 935–37, 962, 999, 1014, 1040, 1069–71
Chaim, Ora Bath, 1096
Chaisemartin, Suzanne, 276, 1057
Chalabala, Zdenek, 292, 877–78
Chaliapin, Feodor, 568, 660, 1143
Challan, Annie, 701
Chamber Music Northwest, 441, 713
Chamber Music Society of Lincoln Center, 23, 256, 823, 1063
Chamber Orchestra of Europe, 626, 1068
Chamber Orchestra of Europe Soloists, 461
Chamberlain, Robert, 452–53
Chambon, Jacques, 459
Chaminade, Cécile, 214
Champs-Elysées Wind Ensemble, 627
Chan, David, 948
Chance, Michael, 723
Chancel Choir of the Episcopal Church of the Incarnation, 342
Chandos Baroque Players, 1068
Chang, Hae-won, 459, 461, 701, 1016
Chang, Helen, 431

Chang, Sarah, 577, 687, 787, 873, 909, 913, 915, 980
Chanticleer Ensemble, 201, 480, 1115
Chapelin-Dubar, Anne, 243
Chapelle Royale, 480
Chapman, Lucy, 82
Chapman, Richard, 82
Chapuis, Michel, 38, 200
Charbonnier, Jean-Louis, 558
Charivari Agréable, 243
Charlier, Olivier, 167, 279, 332, 784
Charpentier, Gustave, 214–15
Charpentier, Marc-Antoine, 215–16
Charvet, Jean-Loup, 392
Chase, Roger, 634
Chausson, Ernest, 216–17
Chávez, Carlos, 217
Chee-Yun, 256, 784
Chen, Evelyn, 775
Chen, Pi-Hsien, 169
Chen Liang-Sheng, 415
Cheng, Gloria, 929
Cherkassky, Shura, 231, 325, 521, 578, 730, 778, 933, 975, 978
Cherkassov, Alexei, 12
Cherkassov, Gennadi, 165
Chernushenko, Vladislav, 733–34, 986
Chernykh, Lydia, 572
Cherrier, Sophie, 209
Cherubini, Luigi, 217–20
Cherubini Quartet, 812
Chestnut Brass Company, 793
Chiara, Maria, 1062
Chiara Banchini, 241
Chiarappa, Carlo, 26, 808, 948, 1026
Chiaro, Giovanni de, 479
Chicago Chamber Musicians, 262
Chicago Pro Musica, 208
Chicago Symphony, 301, 323
Chilingirian Quartet, 17, 81, 148, 287–88, 370, 433, 494
Chistiakov, Andrey, 763, 947, 1104
Chiu, Frederic, 198, 228, 578, 714
Chiuri, Anna, 211
Chmura, Gabriel, 429, 575
Choi, Young-Hee, 232
Choir of Clare College, 943
Choir of Hallgrim's Church, 512
Choir of New College, 170, 342, 951
Choir of St. Gayane, 1079
Choir of St. John's College, 946
Choir of the Theological Seminary and St. Mark Cathedral, 1079
Choir of Trinity Church, 451
Choir of Trinity College, 507
Chojnacka, Elizabeth, 358, 515

Chopin, Frédéric, 220–32
Chopin Trio, 222
Chorus of West German Radio, Cologne, 892
Chorzempa, Daniel, 382
Christ, Peter, 990
Christ, Wolfram, 80, 445, 634, 886
Christ Church Cathedral Choir, 187, 201, 569, 722, 951, 1115
Christensen, Toke Lund, 668
Christian, Thomas, 616
Christiansen, Toke Lund, 499, 808–9, 811
Christie, William, 381, 393, 396, 403–4, 406, 598, 600–601, 609, 613, 648, 651, 653, 656, 724–25, 736, 1121
Christoff, Boris, 163, 166, 248, 353, 363, 660–61, 735, 764, 770, 1143–44
Christophers, Harry, 48, 52, 59, 65–66, 69, 77, 387–89, 400, 404, 407, 409, 411, 414, 506, 611–13, 724, 843, 1031
Chuchkov, Victor, 520
Chuchro, Josef, 562
Chun, June, 234
Chung, Hae-won, 25, 81–82, 256, 280–82, 577, 585, 663–67, 710, 741, 760, 784–85, 867, 873, 928, 981, 1012, 1016, 1045
Chung, Kyung-Wha, 30, 132, 140, 152, 194–95, 286, 300, 324, 713, 909, 915, 1150
Chung, Myung-Whun, 768
Chung, Sarah, 356
Chung Trio, 983
Ciccolini, Aldo, 211, 359, 730, 783, 786, 788
Cichirdan, Modest, 786
Ciconia, Johannes, 1100
Cid, Manuel, 998
Ciesinski, Katherine, 210, 292, 937
Ciesinski, Kristine, 167
Cilea, Francesco, 232
Cillario, Carlo Felice, 128, 601
Cimarosa, Domenico, 232–33
Cincinnati College Conservatory of Music, 818
Cincinnati College Conservatory of Music Wind Symphony, 749
Cinco, Atril, 500
Ciompi, Arturo, 491
Cipriani, Fabrizio, 1030
Cirri, Riccardo, 233
Civil, Alan, 176, 637
Claret, Gerard, 997

Claret, Lluis, 489, 808, 1147
Claritas Ensemble, 340
Clark, Andrew, 113, 115, 640
Clark, Keith, 74–76, 237–38, 350–51, 421–22, 467
Clark, Richard Auldon, 10, 244, 394, 400, 440, 463, 890, 990
Clark, Robert Haydon, 22, 28, 151
Clark, Stanley, 1111
Clarke, Raymond, 569
Claudel Quartet, 714
Clear, Thomas, 1145
Clegg, John, 744
Clemencic, René, 601, 786, 1033–34
Clemencic Consort, 149, 274
Clemencic Ensemble, 274
Clement, Manfred, 913
Clement Janequin Ensemble, 480
Clementi, Muzio, 233–34
Clementi Ensemble, 288
Clementi Trio, 1070
Clemmow, Caroline, 452–53
Cleobury, Nicholas, 66, 86, 131, 145, 240, 314, 387, 404, 411, 469, 475, 649–50, 767, 824, 1031–32
Cleobury, Stephen, 458
Cleva, Fausto, 212, 362, 1008
Cleveland, Douglas, 276
Cleveland Orchestra, 1054
Cleveland Quartet, 76, 110, 165, 176, 242, 255, 288, 578, 741, 810–12, 878
Clevenger, Dale, 637
Cliburn, Van, 106–7, 173–74, 179–80, 222, 257, 370, 520, 712, 729–30, 732, 827, 975
Clidat, France, 788
Cliff, Lluis, 489, 808, 1147
Cluytens, André, 89–91, 93, 95–97, 99, 140, 314, 323, 362–64, 460, 679, 706, 739, 742, 774, 1037
Coates, Albert, 53
Coates, Eric, 234
Coburn, Pamela, 509
Cochereau, Pierre, 275–76, 505, 1015–16, 1124
Cogen, Pierre, 995
Cohen, Franklin, 175, 255, 828
Cohen, Fredric, 1159
Cohen, Joel, 596
Cohen, Robert, 286, 300, 433
Cohler, Jonathan, 1156
Coin, Christophe, 433, 987, 1027
Colalillo, Martha, 211
Cold, Ulrik, 674
Coldstream Guards Band, 882
Cole, Graham, 1128
Cole, Jo, 332

Colegium Pro Musica, 311
Coleman, Donna, 469
Coleridge-Taylor, Samuel, 235
Coletti, Paul, 184, 829
Collard, Catherine, 464
Collard, Jean-Philippe, 313, 783, 788
Collard, Jeannine, 505
Collegium Aureum, 28, 46, 59, 378, 380–81, 383, 886
Collegium dell'Arte, 628
Collegium Musicum 90, 508, 988
Collegium Musicum Soloists, 784
Collegium Vocale Köln, 597, 891
Collegium Vocale Limburg, 757
Colliard, Gilles, 949
Collins, Anthony, 260, 867
Collins, Michael, 16, 82, 109, 208, 319, 829
Colom, Josep, 310
Colomer, Edmon, 310, 332
Colonna, Leonardo, 166
Colorado Quartet, 176, 462
Columbia-Princeton Center, 1080–81
Colusso, Flavio, 207, 1034
Combattimento Consort Amsterdam, 1067
Comberti, Michael, 508
Combs, Larry, 764, 1156
Comissiona, Sergio, 323, 699
Command, Michèle, 587
Comparone, Elaine, 698
Complesso Barocco, 206
Composers Quartet, 208
Comte, Franck-Emmanuel, 406
Con Vivium, 883
Concertante Chamber Players, 578
Concerto Amsterdam, 445
Concerto Köln, 263, 495, 998
Concerto Palatino, 328, 842, 1111, 1113
Concerto Vocale, 1115
Concilium Musicum, 438
Concord Quartet, 165, 246, 764
Conde, Mas, 574, 576
Conjunto Iberico Cello Octet, 1147
Conlin, Thomas, 247
Conlon, James, 517–18, 580, 705, 802, 936, 1052, 1069–72
Consort of Musicke, 273, 340, 507, 1047
Consortium Classicum, 148, 615, 626–28, 750, 885, 887
Constable, John, 310
Constant, Marius, 455
Conta, Iosif, 305
Contemporary Chamber Players, 737
Conti, Diego, 166

Conti, Mirian, 361, 698, 998
Contiguglia, John, 164, 366
Contiguglia, Richard, 164, 366
Continuum Ensemble, 244
Continuum Percussion Quartet, 1127–28
Contos, Ferenc, 1147
Convivium Ensemble, 385
Conzelmann, Kurt, 562
Cook, Brian Rayner, 199, 234, 292, 1006
Cooke, Antony, 446, 482
Coombs, Stephen, 12–13, 258, 348–49, 376, 514, 568, 576, 591
Coop, Jane, 226, 229, 231, 434
Cooper, Emil, 364
Cooper, Imogen, 646, 813, 821
Cooper, Kees, 764
Copenhagen Quartet, 330, 499, 669
Copenhagen Schola Cantorum, 480
Copenhagen Trio, 330
Copenhagen Young Strings, 666
Copland, Aaron, 235–41
Coppieters, Frank, 1147
Coppola, Piero, 252, 254–55, 258
Corbato, Emily, 321
Corboz, Michel, 54, 57, 61, 64, 68, 124, 212, 400, 559–60, 581, 596, 601–2, 608, 611–12, 1031–32
Corda Quartet, 1070
Cordes, Manfred, 841–42, 844
Corelli, Arcangelo, 241
Corelli, Franco, 704, 720, 1141
Corigliano, John, 109, 241–42
Cornago, Johannes, 1108
Cornet Ensemble, 1111
Corporon, Eugene, 697
Corré, Philippe, 1050
Cors, Anna, 333
Corteccia, Francesco, 1107
Cortese, Paul, 136, 444–45, 447–49, 698
Cortot, Alfred, 114, 118, 224, 226–27, 257, 324, 577, 741, 783–84, 809, 827, 831–33, 1130
Corydon Singers, 277, 1115
Cossotto, Fiorenza, 566
Costa, Sequeira, 729–30
Cotrubas, Ilpana, 215
Coull Quartet, 184, 301, 577, 714, 875, 1046
Couperin, François, 242–43
Couraud, Marcel, 597
Covert, Mary Ann, 463
Cowell, Henry, 243–44
Cox, Nicholas, 744

Garrison, Jon, 210
Garrus, Bernard Fabre, 609
Garzón, Maria, 278, 766
Gasdia, Cecilia, 719, 768
Gast, Arvid, 746
Gates, Marcia, 500
Gatti, Daniele, 79, 544, 710, 751
Gatti, Enrico, 160–61
Gaudier Ensemble, 112, 288, 322, 885
Gauk, Alexander, 351, 947
Gauk, Rachel, 701
Gauvin, Karina, 1032
Gavazzeni, Gianardrea, 129, 162, 211, 343, 395, 588, 703, 1010
Gavoty, Bernard, 1016
Gavrilov, André, 25, 34, 372, 386, 976, 979
Gawriloff, Saschko, 515
Gay, John, 331
Gazzelloni, Severino, 533, 1027
Gearhart, Fritz, 262, 890
Gecker, Chris, 697
Gedda, Nicolai, 126, 153, 477, 510, 526, 734, 822, 839, 867, 920, 1141
Gedge, Nicholas, 45
Gee, Christopher Lyndon, 465, 752
Gehring, Wolfgang, 276
Gehrman, Shura, 821–22
Gelber, Bruno-Leonardo, 179
Gelland, Cecilia, 700
Gelmetti, Gianluigi, 786
Geminiani, Francesco, 331–32
Genberg Trio, 745
Gencer, Leyla, 219, 266, 270–71, 570
Gendron, Maurice, 30
Genet, Elzéar, 1106–7
Génetay, Claude, 1104
Genovese, Alfred, 1159
Gens, Véronique, 390
Gentile, Norma, 442
Genvrin, Vincent, 785
Genz, Stephan, 126
George, Michael, 1007
Georgescu, Remus, 304–5
Georgiadis, John, 312, 894, 1048
Gérard, Jean-Claude, 33, 447
Gerasimova, Natalia, 353
Gerelli, Ennio, 397, 696
Gergiev, Valery, 164–65, 353, 569, 660, 710, 715–17, 763, 860, 923–24, 959–60, 964–65, 986, 1011
Gergor-Smith, Bernard, 563
Gerhard, Roberto, 332–33
Gerhard Trio, 332
Gerhardt, Charles, 372–73, 419, 465, 762, 1104

Geringas, David, 160, 444–45, 1147
Geringas Baryton Trio, 434
Gerlin, Ruggero, 24
German Chamber Philharmonic, 800
German Horn Ensemble, 1111
German Natural Horn Soloists, 749
German String Trio, 745, 1062
Gershwin, George, 333–39
Gertler, André, 82, 425, 446, 948
Gesualdo, Don Carlo, 339–42
Gesualdo Consort, 341
Gewendhaus Quartet, 264
Gheorghiu, Angela, 718–19
Ghiaurov, Nicolai, 568
Ghielmi, Lorenzo, 327
Ghione, Franco, 513
Ghitalla, Armando, 438
Giardino Armonico, Il, 148
Gibbons, Jack, 339
Gibbons, John, 726
Gibbons, Orlando, 342
Gibson, Alexander, 16, 139, 152, 185, 295, 297–98, 303, 362, 378–79, 426, 453, 664–66, 772, 868–69, 871–72, 1104
Giebel, Agnes, 43, 50, 390
Gielen, Michael, 133, 135, 207, 514, 549, 802, 907, 912, 1069
Gielgud, John, 711
Gieseking, Walter, 104–6, 111, 114, 119–20, 210, 256–57, 324, 371, 578, 631, 640, 643–44, 742, 809, 827, 833, 1131
Gigli, Beniamino, 343, 567, 704, 720, 1141
Gilbert, Kenneth, 34–36, 38, 242, 327, 386, 726, 736, 1121
Gilbert, Laura, 714
Gilbert and Sullivan, 1089–94
Gilberto, João, 1097
Gilels, Emil, 102, 105, 119, 121, 173–74, 177–78, 180, 221, 371–72, 433–34, 481, 631, 644, 715, 729, 742, 783, 815, 833–34, 933, 976, 978–79, 983, 1131–32
Gillesberger, Hans, 817
Giménez, Raúl, 343
Gimse, Havard, 370
Ginastera, Alberto, 343
Gingold, Joseph, 489
Gini, Roberto, 597, 600–601, 610, 1033
Ginsburg, Leo, 589
Ginzburg, Grigori, 834, 1132
Giordano, Umberto, 343–44
Giorgi, Massimo, 166–67, 1147
Giovane Quartetto Italiano, 722

Gipsy Kings, 1096
Gisler-Haase, Barbara, 447
Gitlis, Ivry, 81–82, 194, 576, 688, 873
Giuliani, Luciano, 218
Giuliani, Mauro, 344
Giulini, Carlo Moria, 54, 91, 95, 141, 196, 212, 254, 281–82, 309, 314, 323, 550, 621–22, 638, 647, 653–54, 659, 739, 768, 806, 817, 826, 924, 952, 959, 971, 1009, 1011, 1013
Giunta, Joseph, 335–36
Giuranna, Bruno, 115, 139, 634–35
Glaetzner, Burkhard, 25, 830, 1068
Glass, Philip, 344–46
Glass Ensemble, 345–46
Glavany, Maria, 570
Glazer, Frank, 788, 811
Glazier, Richard, 339
Glazunov, Alexander, 346–49
Glazunov, Elena, 348
Glazunov Quartet, 482
Gleeson, Derek, 716
Glemser, Bernd, 530, 715, 729–30, 853, 977–79
Glenn, Carroll, 576
Glennie, Evelyn, 130, 851, 1126, 1128
Glenton, Robert, 723
Glière, Reinhold, 349–51
Glinka, Mikhail, 351–53
Gloria Dei Cantores, 757, 883, 1078, 1116
Glorian Duo, 262
Glover, Jane, 192, 430, 618–19
Gluck, Christoph Willibald, 353–54
Glushchenko, Fedor, 465, 486
Glyndebourne Touring Opera, 189
Gmür, Hanspeter, 263
Göbel, Horst, 153, 248, 756–58, 1061
Göbel Trio, 355, 494
Godburn, Dennis, 1154
Godowsky, Leopold, 223, 226, 354–55, 1132
Goebel, Reinhard, 23, 28, 32, 149, 601, 686, 988
Goedicke, Kurt-Hans, 1128
Goehr, Walter, 395, 406, 410, 605
Goeres, Nancy, 1072
Goerne, Malthias, 45, 820–22, 836–38
Goerner, Nelson, 731–32
Goetz, Hermann, 355
Goff, Scott, 373
Goilav, Yoan, 1148
Golabek, Mona and Renée, 705, 983
Golani, Rivka, 139, 300, 445, 776
Gold, Arthur, 576, 705

Goldberg, Szymon, 634, 638, 641, 1150
Golden, Ruth, 78, 766, 1007, 1047
Goldenweiser, Alexander, 731
Goldmark, Karl, 355–57
Goldner Quartet, 855, 932
Goldray, Martin, 20, 208
Goldsmith, Jerry, 1084–85
Goldstein, Boris, 351
Goldstone, Anthony, 452–54, 874
Golebiowski, Karol, 525
Golovanov, Nikolai, 347, 482, 763
Golovchin, Igor, 72–73, 348–50, 761–62, 777, 851, 974
Golschmann, Vladimir, 75, 77, 138, 156, 253, 421, 481
Goltz, Christel, 916
Goltz, Gottfried von der, 33, 1025, 1067
Golub, David, 283–84, 437, 729–30, 784, 809
Golub-Kaplan-Carr Trio, 255, 287, 577, 731
Goluses, Nicholas, 880
Gomez, Jill, 368, 570, 743
Gómez-Martínez, Miguel, 272, 997
Gonella, Claudio, 459
Goni, Antigoni, 593
Gönnenwein, Wolfgang, 45, 47, 57, 61, 64, 67, 70, 389, 412, 434, 648
Goodall, Reginald, 191
Goode, Richard, 116, 180, 630, 697, 813, 1132
Goodman, Benny, 239, 361, 635, 667, 930, 1049
Goodman, Erica, 279, 1119
Goodman, Roy, 14, 23, 28, 50, 67, 89, 144, 147, 380, 428, 431, 453, 573–74, 695, 772, 804–5, 826, 1048
Goodwin, Michael, 362, 651
Goodwin, Paul, 27, 63, 529, 846, 887, 987, 1030
Goodwin, Ron, 1085
Goossens, Eugene, 11, 138, 751, 760, 1017
Goossens, Leon, 830
Gorchakova, Galina, 353
Gordon, Judith, 421
Górecka, Anna, 358
Górecki, Henryk-Mikolaj, 357–58
Gorenstein, Mark, 856, 861
Goritzki, Ingo, 447
Goritzki, Johannes, 160, 329, 377, 438–439, 700, 751, 767, 1036
Gorli, Sandro, 533
Gorokhov, Leonid, 713–14, 1147

Gorton, James, 1160
Gossec, François-Joseph, 358–59
Gossner, Ludwig, 1068
Gothic Voices, 441, 532
Gothoni, Ralf, 576, 796, 874, 1021
Gotland Quartet, 767
Gottschalk, Louis Moreau, 359–60
Gould, Glenn, 25, 34–35, 386, 434, 449, 497, 632, 643–45, 705, 801, 829, 901, 915–16, 943, 1054, 1132
Gould, Morton, 102, 104, 107, 115, 119, 121, 173, 178, 180, 237, 239, 360–61, 374, 466, 663, 855, 858, 1003, 1017
Gounod, Charles, 361–65
Goyeneche, Roberto, 701, 1097
Grach, Eduard, 947
Gracis, Ettore, 695
Gradow, Valery, 798
Graf, Erich, 246, 617–18, 620–23, 626, 885
Graf, Hans, 1070
Graf, Peter-Lukas, 384, 447, 498, 745
Grafenauer, Irena, 636, 886, 1158–59
Graffin, Philippe, 784, 1065
Graffman, Gary, 712, 729–30, 766, 797, 975, 978–79
Graham, Susan, 142, 376
Grainger, Percy, 257, 365–67
Gramm, Donald, 766
Granados, Enrique, 367–68
Grandjany, Marcel, 1119
Grante, Carlo, 355
Grauwels, Marc, 447, 811
Gray, Harold, 493, 495
Grazioli, Giuseppe, 773
Grazzi, Paolo, 1159
Great American Main Street Band, 882
The Greate Consort, 507
Grebanier, Michael, 714, 730
Greek Byzantine Choir, 1078
Green, Nancy, 211
Greenberg, Noah, 597
Greenberg, Roger, 1163
Greenhouse, Bernard, 208
Greenman, Steven, 1096
Greer, Ludwig, 176
Greevey, Bernadette, 304
Gregg Smith Singers, 318, 322, 824, 1115
Gregor, Bohumil, 263, 285, 475–77, 561
Gregor, Jozsef, 770
Gregor-Smith, Bernard, 85, 713, 1147
Greif, Haridas, 169
Grenadier Guards Band, 882

Gressel, Joel, 1083
Gressier, Jules, 680
Grevillius, Nils, 18
Grewel, Volker, 828
Grieg, Edvard, 368–72, 942
Grieg Trio, 831
Grierson, Ralph, 938
Griffes, Charles Tomlinson, 372–74
Griffett, James, 438, 1047
Griffin, Susan, 357
Griffiths, Barry, 318–19, 1004
Griffiths, Howard, 217–18
Griller Quartet, 641
Grimaud, Hélène, 106, 336, 729
Grimbert, Jacques, 359
Grin, Leonid, 708, 985
Grindenko, Tatjana, 693
Gringolts, Ilya, 687, 1059, 1065, 1150
Grinke, Frederick, 466
Grischkat, Hans, 57, 68, 408, 612, 847, 850
Gritton, Susan, 1032
Grodd, Uwe, 263
Groethuysen, Andreas, 179, 248, 733, 747, 779, 815
Grofé, Ferde, 374
Grohs, Wolfgang, 647
Grøndahl, Launy, 662, 664, 672
Gronostay, Uwe, 273, 450, 497, 649, 836
Groop, Monica, 51, 372, 492
Groote, Steven de, 493
Groslot, Robert, 13, 258
Grossman, Ferdinand, 68–69
Grossman, Jerry, 489
Group for Contemporary Music, 20, 274, 315, 855, 1064
Groves, Charles, 15, 183–84, 186, 261, 302–3, 454, 618–19, 621, 711, 776, 940–41
Gruber, H. K., 11
Gruberová, Edita, 266, 269–72, 658, 921
Grubert, Ilya, 713
Gruenberg, Erich, 86, 586, 692
Grumiaux, Arthur, 26, 31, 108–9, 113, 139, 633–34, 638, 642, 687–88, 981, 1022, 1150
Grumiaux Trio, 115, 641–42
Grümmer, Edita, 921
Grümmer, Elisabeth, 126, 819, 838
Grundheber, Franz, 1071
Grüner-Hegge, Odd, 942
Grünfarb, Josef, 700
Gruppman, Igor, 17, 139, 753, 775
Gruppman, Vesna, 17
Grüss, Hans, 842, 844

Grychtolowna, Lidia, 101
Guadagno, Anton, 130
Gualda, Silvio, 1127
Guarneri String Quartet, 17, 110, 473, 578, 641, 810
Guarneri Trio, 175, 287, 750, 878
Gubaidulina, Sofia, 374–75
Gubert, Carlos, 1033
Gudmundsdóttir, Thórunn, 512
Gueden, Hilda, 509, 511
Guerrero, Francisco, 1108
Guerrini, Marcello, 210
Guest, George, 435, 610–11, 648, 789, 1031
Guggeis, Edgar, 1127
Guggenheim, Janet, 730–31
Guglielmo, Federico, 1030
Guglielmo, Giovanni, 948–49, 1030
Gui, Vittorio, 127, 220, 653
Guibbory, Shem, 748
Guildhall String Ensemble, 381
Guillou, Jean, 38, 325, 1124–25
Guilmant, Alexandre, 375–76
Guinn, Leslie, 839
Guinness, Alec, 711
Guinovart, Albert, 998
Guitars a quattro, 997
Gulda, Friedrich, 112, 901
Gulda, Paul, 830
Gülke, Peter, 749, 802
Gulli, Franco, 576
Gulyás, Márta, 1056
Gundlach, Willi, 1055
Guntner, Kurt, 885
Gunzenhauser, Stephen, 99, 155, 164, 236–37, 239, 280–82, 284–85, 349–51, 356, 513, 709, 777, 947
Gurovsky, Mark, 732
Gurtne, Heinrich, 38
Gürzenich Choir, 1058
Gustafsson, Jan-Erik, 713
Gustafsson, Ralph, 331
Guth, Peter, 894
Gutierrez, Horacio, 173–74, 712, 729–30, 976
Gutman, Natalia, 375, 796–97, 828
Guttenberg, Enoch zu, 64, 69
Güttler, Ludwig, 64, 432, 445, 620–22, 1029, 1031–32, 1067
Güttler, Wolfgang, 166–67, 447
Guttman, Michael, 157, 286, 445, 766, 1016
Guye, François, 563
Gwozdz, Lawrence, 462, 890
Gyfadóttir, Bryndis Halla, 1147
Györiványi-Ráth, György, 1056

H

Haas, Bernhard, 746
Haas, Rosalinde, 445, 449, 746
Haas, Werner, 177, 627–28, 976, 978–79
Habermann, Michael, 881
Hacker, Alan, 319
Haden, Charlie, 198
Hadley, Jerry, 192–93, 510–11
Haebler, Ingrid, 113, 641, 643, 645
Haefliger, Andreas, 126, 477, 800, 811, 821–22, 834, 837
Haemhouts, Ben, 1111
Haenchen, Harmut, 71, 429–30, 517, 810
Haendel, Ida, 109, 113, 186, 300, 306, 700, 1045
Haffner, Barbara, 208
Haffner Wind Ensemble, 10
Hagegård, Håkan, 46, 372, 821, 837, 1061
Hagen, Clemens, 174, 1053
Hagen Quartet, 81, 177, 433, 473, 530, 830, 1054, 1061
Hager, Leopold, 183, 437, 529, 628, 691, 883
Hägerston Motet Choir, 201
Haggart, Margaret, 460
Håggender, Marie-Ann, 874
Hague Percussion Group, 999, 1128
Haguenauer, Jean-Louis, 1050
Hahn, Hilary, 76, 109, 144
Hahn, Reynaldo, 376
Haider, Friedrich, 269
Haimovitz, Matt, 195, 449
Haitink, Bernard, 79, 89, 125, 151, 191, 194, 196, 254, 295–96, 298, 453, 518–19, 534, 536, 538, 540–41, 544–45, 547, 549, 551, 555, 574, 656–57, 739, 825, 858, 861, 898–99, 902, 905, 910, 912, 918, 920, 951–54, 956–57, 961–62, 968, 970–71, 974, 1001–2, 1004, 1011, 1039, 1041
Hakim, Naji, 505, 586, 1125
Hala, Josef, 288
Halász, Débora, 1021
Halász, Michael, 99, 125–26, 356, 518–19, 589, 695, 772, 777–78, 793, 802, 804–5, 807, 909
Hale, Richard, 711
Halévy, Jacques Fromental, 376
Hallgrimskirkja Motet Choir, 277
Halliday, Malcolm, 883
Hallynck, Sophie, 1120
Halsey, Louis, 261, 302, 612
Halsey, Simon, 767

Halska, Beata, 947

Halstead, Anthony, 23, 113, 495, 637, 1049, 1111

Halvorsen, Johan, 376–77

Hamari, Julia, 44

Hamelin, Gaston, 255

Hamelin, Marc-André, 8, 164, 198, 355, 366, 469, 493, 523, 572, 746, 852, 881, 1132

Hamerik, Asger, 377

Hamilton, Robert, 671

Hamilton, Stephen, 276

Hammann, James, 579

Hammer, Moshe, 688

Hammer, Stephen, 1028

Hampson, Thomas, 78–79, 126, 322, 470, 526, 556–57, 822, 836, 838–39, 1056

Hampton String Quartet, 685

Hamrahlid Choir, 512

Hanani, Yehuda, 685

Hancock, Judith, 505

Handel, George Frideric, 377–418, 1104

Handford, Katherine, 995

Händler, Jack Martin, 817

Handley, Vernon, 15–16, 84–86, 154, 183, 185, 260, 262, 282, 284, 295, 297–98, 302–4, 319, 368–69, 453, 458, 570, 592, 776, 875, 887, 1001–5

Handt, Herbert, 601

Hanini, Yehudi, 30

Hanke, Sonya, 753

Hannisdal, Henrik, 669

Hannover Boys Choir, 1058

Hanselmann, Jürg, 756–57

Hansen, Jørgen Ernst, 671

Hansen, Lisa, 668

Hansen, Søren Kinch, 676, 780

Hanskoy, Mette, 1148

Hanson, George, 273

Hanson, Howard, 75, 136, 155–56, 207, 214, 335, 360–61, 374, 418–21, 467, 532, 615, 701–2, 824, 855, 890

Hantai, Jerôme, 558

Harbison, John, 420–21

Harbison, Rose Mary, 421

Harden, Wolf, 265

Hardenberger, Håkan, 459

Hardgrave, Barbara, 501

Harding, Daniel, 99, 654

Hardy, Andrew, 830

Hardy, Rosemary, 501

Hargis, Ellen, 389–90

Harjanne, Juoko, 425, 445, 1112

Harle, John, 130, 150, 198, 255, 463

Harnoncourt, Alice, 1025

Harnoncourt, Nikolas, 23, 28, 31, 42, 46–48, 50, 55, 62, 65, 69, 89–93, 95–99, 124, 171, 281–82, 285, 378, 380–81, 390, 403, 407–9, 411, 413–15, 417, 428, 430–32, 434–35, 437, 557, 574–75, 601–2, 604, 606, 612, 617, 620–23, 625–26, 628, 646, 649, 651, 653, 655–57, 695, 726, 786, 804–5, 817, 826–27, 836, 896–97, 988–89, 1051–52

Harnoy, Ofra, 157, 286, 684, 982, 1022, 1027

Harper, Heather, 426, 1007, 1054

Harrell, Lynn, 30, 112, 114–15, 286, 300, 307, 441, 445, 741, 775, 983

Harrell, Mark, 44

Harrer, Uwe Christian, 786

Harrer, Wolfgang, 166–67

Harrild, Patrick, 1005

Harris, Johana, 422

Harris, Michael, 505, 1155

Harris, Roy, 421–22

Harrison, Beatrice, 300

Harrison, George, 1084

Harrison, Lou, 422–24

Hart, Mary Ann, 469

Harth, Sidney, 776

Hartley Trio, 885

Hartman, Stephen, 882

Hartmann, Johann Peter Emilius, 424

Hartmann, Karl Amadeus, 424–25

Harty, Hamilton, 283, 298, 425–26, 1043

Harvard University Choir, 1115

Harvey, Jonathan, 1083

Harvey, Keith, 747

Harvey, Richard, 237

Haselböck, Martin, 431, 445, 461, 525, 816, 1030

Hashimoto, Eiji, 160

Haskil, Clara, 105, 113, 120, 222, 434, 443, 632, 642, 644, 814, 832, 834

Hasse, Johann Adolph, 426–27

Hassler Consort, 707

Haugsand, Ketil, 34

Hauk, Franz, 375, 570, 746, 1058

Hauptmann, Norbert, 913

Hauschild, Wolf-Dieter, 410, 467, 834

Hauser, Ursula, 375

Hausmusik, 218, 461, 578, 641, 812

Hauwe, Walter van, 1161

Havlikova, Klara, 562

Hayami, Kazuko, 500

Hayashi Duo, 563

Haydn, (Franz) Joseph, 427–38

Haydn, Michael, 438–39

Haydn Baryton Trio, 434

Haydn Quartet, 165, 884

Haydn Trio, 287

Haydon Clark, Robert, 378

Hayman, Richard, 333

Hazelzet, Wilbert, 21, 987–88, 1157–58

HCD Ensemble of Frankfurt, 169

Heard, John, 498

Heatherington, Alan, 155

Hebb, Bernard, 1147

Hedwall, Lennart, 1060

Hegedüs, Endre, 590

Heger, Robert, 320, 661, 700, 757, 799, 918, 1036, 1051

Hegyi, Julius, 213

Heifetz, Galina, 261

Heifetz, Jascha, 12, 25, 29, 108, 113–15, 157, 174, 194–95, 211, 216, 301, 324, 337, 349, 370, 493, 503, 576, 634, 642, 703, 713, 775, 784, 787, 873, 875, 884, 915, 979, 983, 1016, 1045, 1059, 1150–51

Heiller, Anton, 25

Heinonen, Eero, 874

Heinrich, Siegfried, 602, 885

Heinrich, Suzanne, 558

Heisser, Jean-Francois, 133–34

Helbich, Wolfgang, 52, 67, 388–89

Heled, Simca, 534

Helffer, Claude, 82, 169, 591, 801

Helfgott, David, 730

Helin, Jacquelyn, 991

Heller, Alfred, 1019

Hellermann, William, 1081

Hellfter, Claude, 82, 311

Hellwig, Klaus, 751

Helmerson, Frans, 286, 449

Helmis, Fritz, 638

Helmrath, Michael, 470, 998

Helps, Robert, 855

Heltay, László, 183, 437

Hemke, Frederick, 699, 1162

Hempel, Frieda, 1138

Hempling, Volker, 559

Henck, Herbert, 169, 204, 469, 491, 593, 891

Henderson, Roy, 199, 1006

Henderson, Skitch, 338, 784

Hendl, Walter, 109, 421

Hendricks, Barbara, 79, 259, 658, 922, 1018

Henegar, Gregg, 307, 1155

Hengelbrock, Thomas, 56, 725

Henkel, Christoph, 447, 700

Hennig, Heinz, 47, 290, 410, 525, 613, 817, 843–46

Henning Braaten, Geir, 371

Henriot-Schweizer, Nicole, 464

Henry, Yves, 352

Henry Trio, 503

Henry's Eight, 506

Henze, Hans Werner, 439–40, 1080

Heppner, Ben, 126

Her Majesty's Royal Marines, 882

Herbert, Giselle, 885

Herbert, Kurt, 1105

Herbert, Victor, 440–41

Herbig, Gunther, 294, 425

Herford, Henry, 1007

Herkenhoff, Ulrich, 726

Herman, František, 749

Hermann, Claudius, 751

Hermann, Roland, 556

Herrera de la Fuente, Luis, 217, 754

Herreweghe, Philippe, 41–42, 46, 49, 52–53, 56–57, 59, 62–63, 66, 69–70, 98, 124, 140, 314, 341, 507, 529, 580–81, 611–12, 627–28, 651, 722–23, 835, 843, 845

Herrick, Christopher, 38, 375, 1125

Herrmann, Bernard, 441, 453, 1006, 1044, 1085

Herseth, Adolph, 1112

Hershman, Mordechai, 1096

Herskowitz, Matthew, 349

Hesperion XX, 726

Hess, Myra, 104, 107, 120, 434, 809, 814

Hess, S., 766

Hesse-Bukovska, Barbara, 229, 686

Heward, Leslie, 592

Hewitt, Angela, 34–36

Heyerick, Florian, 387, 439

Heyghen, Peter van, 385

Hickman, David, 697

Hickox, Richard, 9–10, 15, 56, 59, 96, 145, 151, 181, 186–87, 189–92, 194, 236, 238, 260–62, 277, 302–3, 365, 367, 378, 393, 403, 431, 435, 452–54, 457–58, 561–62, 580, 583, 607, 646, 724–25, 752, 768, 776–77, 781, 888, 927, 929, 950, 992, 1002, 1004–6, 1031, 1034, 1046

Higdon, James, 785

Higginbottom, Edward, 458

High Anxiety Bones, 1112

Hildegard of Bingen, 441–42

Hilgers, Walter, 447

Hill, David, 159, 303, 314, 389, 689–90

475, 517, 535, 537, 539–41, 543, 547, 549, 552, 555, 801, 851, 859–61, 876–77, 923, 925–26, 930, 957, 974

Incanto Ensemble, 446

Indermühle, Thomas, 562

Indy, Vincent d', 464

Ingebretsen, Kjell, 875

Ingham, Michael, 470

Inghelbrecht, Désiré Emile, 253–54, 258

Ingólfsdóttir, Rut, 511

Innig, Rudolf, 181, 578–79, 587, 834

Institutioni Harmoniche, 207

InterContemporain Quartet, 932

Invernizzi, Roberta, 390, 1033

Ippolitov-Ivanov, Mikhail, 465

IRCAM, 1082–83

Ireland, John, 465–66

Irving, Robert, 259, 347, 931, 1044

Isaac, Heinrich, 1106

Isbin, Sharon, 242, 703, 851, 996, 1117

Isoir, André, 37–38, 325

ISOS Quartet, 195

Israelievitch, Jacques, 166, 194, 791

Isserlis, Stephen, 76, 184, 186, 248, 299, 312, 370, 563, 577, 713, 741, 779, 831, 865, 950, 982, 1146–47

Istomin, Eugene, 109, 113–14, 175–76, 809

Italian Octet, 626–27

Ivaldi, Christian, 237, 289, 449, 784

Ivanov, Konstantin, 12, 347, 589

Ivanovs, Jānis, 466

Ivashkin, Alexander, 797–98

Ives, Charles, 466–70

Iwaki, Hiroyuki, 923, 925, 931, 945, 1065

Izquierdo, Juan Pablo, 1064

Izquierdo, Luis, 309

J

Jablonski, Peter, 530

Jablonski, Roman, 531

Jackson, Christine, 983

Jackson, Frederic, 401

Jackson, Isaiah, 830, 890

Jacob, Jeffrey, 245–47, 571

Jacobi, Derek, 1102

Jacobs, Paul, 56, 69, 159, 200, 207, 209, 212, 257–58, 391, 395, 598, 603–4, 607, 609, 613, 656, 789, 801, 840, 847–48, 988, 1033

Jacobs, Peter, 184, 214, 692

Jacobs, René, 695

Jacobson, Julian, 332

Jacottet, Christine, 24, 34–35

Jacques, Reginald, 61

Jacquillat, Jean-Pierre, 376

Jakowicz, Krzysztof, 531

Jalas, Jussi, 511, 871–72

James, Bob, 1082

James, Ifor, 218, 431

James St. Bride's Church Choir, 197

Jamet, Marie-Claire, 1119

Janáček, Leos, 470–77

Jancsovics, Antal, 483

Jandó, Jenö, 35, 80, 107, 109, 115, 117, 173–74, 286, 369, 434, 520, 629, 642–43, 646, 811, 814, 829

Janequin, Clément, 1106

Jänicke, Yvi, 1062

Janigro, Antonio, 74, 170, 752, 903, 1024, 1029

Janis, Byron, 519, 521, 661, 712, 728–29, 901, 975

Jánoshka, Aladár, 794

Janowitz, Gundula, 451, 658, 819, 921–22, 1051

Janowski, Marek, 695, 763, 774, 794–95, 920, 1051–52

Jansons, Mariss, 281–82, 709, 728, 760–61, 859–60, 868, 942, 951–54, 957, 961–63, 970, 1040, 1103

Janssen, Werner, 158

Jarman, Derek, 187

Jarrett, Keith, 386, 423, 866

Järvi, Neeme, 72, 74–75, 79, 83, 87, 147, 164–65, 173, 185, 213–14, 218, 236, 244, 280–82, 284–85, 304–5, 317, 329, 346–48, 368–69, 421, 442, 444, 455, 466–67, 471, 482–83, 485–86, 503, 513, 518, 543, 560, 572, 659, 663–66, 673, 692, 708–12, 715–17, 727, 733, 745, 759–62, 774, 793, 796, 804–5, 852, 858–61, 868, 870–72, 874, 877, 889–90, 900–901, 903, 906, 909, 912, 915, 928–32, 942, 947, 962, 967, 974, 986, 993, 996–97, 1048, 1056

Järvi, Paavo, 143–44, 627, 692

Jaya, Sekar, 1128

Jean Sibelius Quartet, 874

Jean-Yves Fourmeau Saxophone Quartet, 1163

Jekowsky, Barry, 423

Jelinek, Hubert, 638

Jelvakov, Vasily, 481

Jenkins, Neil, 510

Jenkins, Newell, 218, 264, 496, 627–28, 994, 1033

Jensen, Thomas, 662–63, 665–66, 672–73

Jensen, Wilma, 504–5

Jerie, Marek, 1147

Jerusalem, Siegfried, 837, 921

Jespersen, Holger-Gilbert, 668

Jílek, František, 317, 470–71, 475–76, 677

Jo, Sumi, 771

Joachim, Joseph, 29, 477–78, 1151

Joachim Quartet, 745, 1014

Joachim Trio, 255, 592, 677–78, 741, 784, 940

Jobim, Antonio Carlos, 1097

Jochum, Eugen, 54, 60, 63, 68, 171–74, 196, 297, 428, 430, 435, 444, 554, 601, 653, 655–56, 684, 745, 1051

Jochum, Veronica, 198

Joeres, Dirk, 151, 329, 331, 826, 1105

Jóhanesson, Einar, 155

Johannes Ensemble, 330

Johannesen, Grant, 275, 312–13, 783

Johanos, Donald, 151–52, 237–39, 307, 350, 465, 761

John Aldis Choir, 1054

John Oliver Chorale, 209

Johnson, A. Robert, 623–24, 627–28

Johnson, Anthony Rolfe, 192–93, 199, 821, 1006–7

Johnson, Charles Anthony, 532

Johnson, Emma, 16, 166, 247, 319, 828, 887, 1049

Johnson, Evan, 149

Johnson, Gilbert, 447

Johnson, Graham, 365

Johnson, James, 39, 481

Johnson, Robert, 1108

Johnson, Sarah, 321

Johnson, Tellef, 881

Johnson, Wayne, 457

Johnsson, Bengt, 504

Jolivet, André, 478

Jolley, David, 637, 1111

Jonas, Dorothy, 245, 562, 564, 576, 948

Jones, Angela, 373

Jones, Brian, 276

Jones, Brynmor Llewelyn, 394

Jones, Della, 259, 304, 367–68, 769

Jones, Gwyneth, 916, 920

Jones, Jonathan Hellyer, 23

Jones, Joyce, 505

Jones, Karen, 16

Jones, Leslie, 885

Jones, Louise, 261

Jones, Martin, 256, 318, 366–67, 578, 733, 933, 944

Jones, Mason, 447

Jones, Michael Kevin, 1147

Jonsson, Anders-Per, 127

Joó, Arpád, 518–19

Joplin, Scott, 478–79

Jorda, Enrique, 309, 703

Jordan, Armin, 213, 258, 275, 826, 835, 908, 913, 1069

Jordania, Vakhtang, 456, 862

Jørgensen, Jesper Grove, 358, 451

Josefowicz, Leila, 81, 577, 787, 873, 980, 1065, 1151

Joselson, Tod, 76, 715

Josquin, Desprez, 479–81, 506, 1106

Josquin Des Prez Chamber Choir, 506

Journet, Marcel, 1144

Joyce, Donald, 345, 746

Joyce, Eileen, 12, 466, 997

Jucker, Rama, 747

Judd, James, 294, 453, 490, 537, 588, 968, 972

Judd, Roger, 746

Juffinger, Andreas, 756–57, 794

Juillet, Chantal, 82, 493, 944

Juilliard Quartet, 20, 38, 81, 110, 133, 176–77, 208, 255, 279, 318, 324, 432, 436, 448, 468, 473, 577–78, 640, 741, 800–801, 810–12, 855, 874, 1014, 1053–54, 1062

Junghänel, Konrad, 42, 52, 200, 206, 614, 840–41, 1119

Junkin, Jerry, 17

Jürgens, Jürgen, 46, 602, 610, 614, 850

Jurinac, Sena, 837–38

Jurowski, Michail, 18, 424, 483, 662, 710, 737, 761–62

Jutland Ensemble, 670

K

Kabalevsky, Dmitri, 481–82

Kachanov, Nikolai, 986

Kafavian, Ida, 766

Kagan, Oleg, 375, 448, 639, 641–42, 796, 812, 828, 984

Kahane, Jeffrey, 901

Kaine, Carmel, 1024

Kajanus, Robert, 868–69

Kakhidze, Djansug, 483–84, 486

Kalb, Thomas, 998

Kaler, Ilya, 286, 450, 687–88, 798, 863

Kalichstein, Joseph, 576–77

Kalichstein-Laredo-Robinson Trio, 1073

Kalinnikov, Vasily, 482–83

Kalish, Gilbert, 207–8, 240, 246, 258, 469

Kalitzke, Johannes, 150

Kaljuste, Tonu, 799

Kallisch, Cornelia, 1071

Kálmán, Imre, 483

Kaltenbach, Jerome, 788–89

Kammerchor Stuttgart, 757

Kammerensemble Neue Musik Berlin, 316

Kammermusiker Zürich, 884

Kammler, Reinhard, 649, 817

Kamu, Okko, 147, 324, 369, 506, 663, 699, 786–87, 795, 799, 869, 889, 894

Kancheli, Giya, 483–84

Kang, Dong-Suk, 109, 256, 300, 312, 370, 669, 784, 809, 873, 875, 1045

Kangas, Juha, 1000

Kanka, Michal, 161

Kannen, Günter von, 800

Kansas City Chorale, 1115

Kantorow, Jean-Jacques, 216, 432, 487, 512, 784, 828

Kapell, William, 104, 173, 180, 225, 228, 486, 661, 729, 1133

Kaplan, Abraham, 889

Kaplan, Gilbert, 538

Kaplan, Mark, 80–82, 784, 787, 830, 1022

Kapp, Richard, 311, 321, 735, 777, 882, 991

Karabtchevsky, Isaac, 467, 835, 1017

Karajan, Herbert von, 22, 54, 58, 60, 72, 88, 90–91, 93, 95, 97–98, 100, 124–25, 132–33, 138, 152, 171–73, 181, 194, 196, 218, 254, 258–59, 282–83, 362, 368–69, 428, 430, 434, 436, 443, 453, 455, 460, 512, 517–19, 542–43, 545, 552, 574–75, 605, 619–26, 638, 647, 650–51, 655–57, 659–60, 664, 683, 685, 708–9, 739, 752, 760, 774, 800, 803–7, 825, 860, 868–69, 871–72, 894–95, 897–98, 900, 902, 904–5, 907–8, 910–11, 917–19, 926, 929–31, 935, 941, 951–55, 958, 961–62, 964, 967, 969–71, 973, 1003, 1009–14, 1024, 1037–39, 1042, 1048, 1053, 1104

Karis, Aleck, 204, 209, 929, 933–34

Kärkkäinen, Jaana, 492

Karoff, Steven, 1050

Karr, Gary, 1148

Karttunen, Anssi, 781

Kasarova, Vesseline, 142, 771

Kashkashian, Kim, 80, 445, 448–49, 483–84, 501, 634, 642, 796, 829, 865, 1149

Kasman, Yakov, 715

Kaspszyk, Jacek, 1014

Kassai, István, 157, 308

Kastelsky, Valery, 180

Katahan, Enid, 214

Katahn, Enid, 671

Katchen, Julius, 106, 123, 125, 173, 176, 178–79, 333, 519, 729–30, 766, 1133

Katin, Peter, 180, 231, 234, 371, 576, 731, 985

Kato, Tomoko, 1065

Katrama, Jorma, 1148

Katsaris, Cyprien, 520, 576

Katz, Arnold, 947

Katz, Florence, 456

Katz, Mindru, 107

Kauffmann, Jacques, 505

Kaufmann, Julie, 127

Kaufmann, Klaus, 359–60

Kaufmann, Louis, 562, 890, 994

Kaunzinger, Günther, 1015–16, 1057–58

Kautsky, Catherine, 789, 1102

Kavafian, Ida, 244, 1053

Kavakos, Leonidas, 687, 873, 1065

Kavina, Lydia, 564

Kawahara, Yasunori, 167

Kawalla, Szymen, 694–95

Kayath, Marcello, 1097

Kaye, Judy, 145–46, 1020

Kayser, Jan Henrik, 782

Kazandjiev, Vassil, 843

Kee, Piet, 201, 449, 686, 746

Keene, Christopher, 263, 532

Keene, Constance, 373, 731–32

Keene, Dennis, 141–42, 277

Keenlyside, Simon, 840, 1007

Kegel, Herbert, 89, 135, 153, 187, 442–44, 536, 684, 694–95, 801, 816, 1052–53

Kehr, Günther, 22, 27, 380, 617

Keilberth, Joseph, 450, 476, 553, 745, 919, 1038, 1050–51

Keiser, Marilyn, 278

Keleinert, Rolf, 573

Kell, Reginald, 114, 1156

Keller, Roland, 875, 1049

Keller Quartet, 81, 501

Kelly, Frances, 638

Kelly, John-Edward, 1162

Kempe, Rudolf, 90, 93, 95, 172, 460, 492, 752, 877–78, 898, 900–902, 904, 907–8, 910–11, 913–14, 918, 1037

Kempf, Freddy, 731–32

Kempff, Wilhelm, 101, 106–7, 112, 114, 116, 121–22, 178–80, 631, 644–45, 812–13, 815, 832–33, 1133

Kenedi, Mary, 82

Kennedy, Nigel, 82, 108, 174, 301, 496, 873, 981, 1004, 1025, 1045, 1149, 1151

Kenny, Yvonne, 389

Kent, Fuat, 246–47

Kentner, Louis, 631

Kerdoncuff, François, 328

Kernis, Aaron Jay, 484–85

Kertesi, Ingrid, 43

Kertész, Istrán, 82, 267, 280–82, 284–85, 489–90, 648, 768, 877

Kertész, Otto Jr., 165, 172

Ketèlbey, Albert W., 485

Keulen, Isabelle van, 279, 577, 796, 933

Keuschnig, Rainer, 794

Keveházi, Jenó, 176

Keylin, Mischa, 1016

Keyrouz, Sister Marie, 1078

Khachaturian, Emin, 711, 796

Khaikin, Boris, 346, 349–50, 759, 777, 986

Kharitonov, Dimitri, 734

Khatchaturian, Aram, 485–87

Khersonsky, Grigory, 155

Khomitser, Mikhail, 862

Khudolei, Igor, 796

Kibbie, James, 995

Kiehr, Marina-Christina, 390, 610

Kilanowicz, Zofia, 357

Kilbey, Reginald, 234

Kilenyi, Edward, 225, 523

Kilpatrick, Barry, 1113

Kim, Byung-Hwa, 1065

Kim, Soovin, 81

Kim-Ma-Ax Trio, 287

Kimbrough, Steven, 495, 1056, 1071

Kinderman, William, 122

King, David, 527

King, Robert, 55, 159, 200, 379, 388, 396–97, 406–9, 412–13, 695, 723, 848, 1029–32, 1035

King, Terry, 422, 1147

King, Thea, 16, 176, 247, 319, 458, 635, 640, 744, 884, 887, 1049

Kings College Choir, 187, 358, 693, 946, 949, 951, 1114

King's Consort, 722–23, 790

King's Singers, 184, 480, 507, 1114

Kinton, Leslie, 13, 289

Kipnis, Alexander, 1144

Kipnis, Igor, 24, 34, 182, 310, 386, 790, 821, 1121

Kirchhof, Lutz, 1057, 1119

Kirchner, Leon, 487

Kirkby, Emma, 14, 43, 200, 389–91, 610, 658, 723, 1033, 1035

Kirkpatrick, John, 469, 780

Kirkpatrick, Ralph, 34–35, 424, 1121

Kirschbaum, Ralph, 30, 76–77, 109, 174, 300

Kiss, András, 494, 875

Kiss, Gyula, 520

Kiss, Josef, 21, 639–40, 828–31

Kissin, Evgeni, 104, 107, 123, 180, 221, 325, 431, 434, 712, 730, 832, 834, 977

Kitaienko, Dimitri, 236, 329–30, 373, 481, 709–10, 728, 733, 759, 782

Kite, Christopher, 1049

Kitzman, John, 245, 1111

Kiviniemi, Kalevi, 492

Kjekshus, Helge, 370

Klami, Uuno, 487–88

Klánský, Ivan, 472, 474, 615

Klas, Eri, 795, 874, 997

Klebel, Bernhard, 846

Klee, Bernhard, 123, 529, 649, 661, 1069

Kleiber, Carlos, 94, 96, 172, 653, 804, 806, 894, 896, 1010, 1051

Kleiber, Erich, 93, 283, 894, 917

Kleigel, Maria, 701

Klein, Alex, 1028, 1160

Klein, Elisabeth, 133, 676

Klein, Emil, 381

Klein, Franz, 746

Klein, Kenneth, 321, 360, 689

Kleine Konzert, 1156

Kleinert, Rolf, 716

Klemperer, Otto, 54, 60, 89–91, 93, 95–98, 100, 124–25, 138, 172, 181, 196, 323, 401, 428–29, 538, 541, 548, 551, 553–54, 574–75, 618–24, 655–56, 825–26, 957, 1037, 1039–40, 1104

Klerk, Albert de, 445

Kless, Yair, 562

Kletzki, Paul, 530, 536, 541, 553, 761, 868–69

Kliegel, Maria, 109, 157, 195, 222, 265, 286, 299, 489, 797, 808, 828, 831, 862, 982

Klien, Walter, 123, 643, 645, 813

Klima, Alois, 939

Klinda, F., 431

Klint, Jørgen, 674

Klobucar, Berislav, 320
Klock, Lynn, 245, 1162–63
Klöcker, Dieter, 431, 498, 1049, 1096
Kloss, Erich, 775
Kluttig, Christian, 414
Kmentt, Waldemar, 511
Knappertsbusch, Hans, 894, 1037–38
Knardahl, Eva, 370–71, 875
Knaub, Donald, 1111
Kniazev, Alexander, 157
Knothe, Dietrich, 408, 818, 840, 845, 885
Knushevitsky, Sviatoslav, 731
Knussen, Oliver, 185, 207, 488, 516, 676, 780, 931, 936–37, 945, 1063
Kobayashi, Rinko, 686
Kober, Dieter, 377, 380, 711
Koch, Helmut, 377–79, 389, 401, 408, 410–12, 416, 450, 601
Koch, Lothar, 637, 639, 913
Koch, Philippe, 512, 1016
Koch, Ulrich, 745
Kocian Quartet, 317, 446, 448, 1070
Kočousek, Josef, 886
Kocsis, Zoltán, 25, 80, 82, 501–2, 520, 523, 645, 730, 732, 811
Kodály, Zoltán, 488–90
Kodály Quartet, 255, 265, 432–33, 464, 489, 741, 810–11
Koechlin, Charles, 490–91
Koeckert Quartet, 831, 984
Koehlen, Benedikt, 11
Kogan, Leonid, 433, 983
Koh, Jennifer, 669
Köhler, Markus, 497, 610
Köhler, Siegfried, 349, 1049
Köhn, Christian, 179, 289
Kohon Quartet, 373, 824
Koito, Kei, 38
Koivula, Hannu, 451
Koizumi, Kazuhiro, 958, 962, 968
Kojian, Varujian, 138, 158, 516
Kojo, Kullervo, 668
Kokars, Imants, 466
Kokkonen, Joonas, 491–92
Kolacny, Steven, 179
Kolacny, Stijn, 179
Kolar, Anton, 886
Kolb, Justin, 888
Kollar, Zsuzsa, 646, 747
Kollontai, Mikhail, 73
Kolly, Karl-Andreas, 348–49, 794
Kolman, Barry, 11, 462, 777
Kölner Cello Trio, 1147
Komen, Paul, 829, 853
Komischke, Uwe, 726
Komsi, Anu, 501

Kondanasis, Yolanda, 685, 1119
Kondo, Fusako, 456
Kondrashin, Kiril, 165, 210, 282, 351, 353, 481–82, 486, 589, 665, 716, 733, 760, 762, 852, 856, 859–61, 968–69
Koningsberger, Maarten, 839
Kontarsky Brothers, 169, 674, 891–92
Kontra, Anton, 330, 676
Kontra Quartet, 330, 370, 489, 504, 669, 943
Konwitschny, Franz, 745, 826, 1037
Koopman, Ton, 23–24, 28, 38, 40, 42, 48–52, 59, 63, 66, 70, 200–201, 379, 382–83, 404–5, 619, 643, 646, 650, 724
Kooy, Peter, 45
Kopelman, Jozef, 1023
Koppel, Herman D., 671
Koppel Quartet, 669
Korcia, Laurent, 216
Korevaar, David, 35
Korf, Anthony, 464
Körmendi, Klára, 502, 788
Korn, Michael, 386
Korngold, Erich Wolfgang, 492–95, 1086
Korniev, Nikolai, 734, 986
Kórodi, András, 356, 517
Korp, Ronald, 991
Korsakov, Andrei, 947, 1104
Korsimaa-Hursti, Anna-Maija, 247
Korupp, Reimund, 745
Koshin, Valentin, 72
Košler, Axel, 151
Košler, Zdeněk, 284, 471, 475, 565, 621–23, 648, 678, 708–9, 774, 876–79, 901, 903, 910, 912, 914
Kostelanetz, André, 374, 861–62, 1020, 1105
Koster, Ab, 431, 637
Koten, Frank van, 532
Köth, Erika, 658
Kotkova, Hanna, 562
Kotmel, Bohumil, 560–61
Koussevitzky, Mosche, 1096
Koussevitzky, Serge, 22, 61, 79, 124, 236, 253, 421, 429, 659, 708, 710, 806, 868, 870, 872, 899, 924, 928, 959
Ková, Pavel, 459
Kovacevich, Stephen, 80, 82, 101, 107, 115, 118, 122, 173–74, 369, 814, 827, 1133
Kovacic, Ernst, 564, 874
Kovács, Béla, 81, 642, 1050
Kovács, János, 308

Kovács, László, 272, 1056
Kowalski, Jochen, 45, 390, 405, 821, 837, 1032
Kožená, Magdaléna, 678
Kraemer, Nicholas, 398, 1029
Kraft, Norbert, 211, 688, 880, 1021, 1117
Kraft, Walter, 39
Kraggerud, Henning, 370
Kralev, Stoyan, 1031
Krapp, Edgar, 38, 385–86
Krasavin, V., 255
Krasko, Julia, 82, 349, 496
Krasner, Louis, 132
Krastev, Anatoly, 563
Kratzer, Bernhard, 1112
Kraus, Alfredo, 153, 998
Kraus, Eberhard, 386
Kraus, Joseph Martin, 495–96
Kraus, Lili, 82, 434, 631, 643, 813–15
Krause, Tom, 821, 874–75, 1061
Krauss, Clemens, 123–24, 429, 893, 895, 897, 899–901, 908, 914
Krauss, Lili, 123
Kravchenko, Sergei, 351
Krebbers, Herman, 108
Krebs, Dietmar, 440
Kreček, Jaroslav, 283, 331–32, 527, 938
Krecher, Andreas, 194–95
Krečmer, Rudolf, 284
Kreger, James, 463, 577
Kreisler, Fritz, 108, 113, 370, 496, 576, 634, 687, 809, 830, 1151
Krejčí, Jiří, 1028
Kremer, Gidon, 81, 107–8, 113, 132, 144, 174, 306, 345, 374–75, 432, 448, 484, 576, 633–34, 642, 693, 701, 766, 773, 796–98, 809, 828, 830, 863–64, 866, 873, 909, 915, 981, 983, 1000, 1053, 1065, 1151
Kremlin Chamber Orchestra, 330
Krenek, Ernst, 496–97
Krenz, Jan, 530–31, 594
Kreplin, Gordon, 593
Krettly Quartet, 313
Kretzschmar, Hermann, 169, 501
Kreutzer Quartet, 332
Kreuzberger Quartet, 473, 884
Krigbaum, Charles, 1057
Kriikku, Kari, 1050
Krimets, Konstantin, 348
Krips, Henry, 683
Krips, Joseph, 88, 616, 620, 651, 654, 806–7, 879, 894, 920, 1037
Krist Brothers, 746
Krivine, Emmanuel, 151–52, 760

Krogh, Grethe, 671
Krombholc, Jaroslav, 317, 476–77, 565, 678, 876, 879
Krommer, Franz, 497–98
Kronjäger, Brigite, 279
Kronos Quartet, 246, 315, 345–46, 358, 423, 484, 701, 748, 781, 797, 855, 864, 946
Kröper, Andreas, 66
Krosnick, Joel, 208, 147, 714
Kroumata Percussion Ensemble, 1064, 1127
Krozinger Musik-Collegium, 33
Krueger, Karl, 87, 213–14, 321, 440, 532, 688, 889
Kruse, John, 667
Kruszewski, Adam, 531
Krysa, Oleg, 81, 157, 374–75, 563, 796, 798
Kubalek, Antonin, 878, 985
Kubelik, Jan, 1151
Kubelik, Rafael, 80, 97, 99, 138–39, 142, 165, 171, 196, 280–82, 284–85, 288–89, 291, 378–79, 398, 412, 425, 435, 444, 450, 471–72, 475, 534, 536, 539, 541, 543, 545, 547, 551, 561, 617, 620–21, 623, 625, 659, 661–62, 665, 700, 801, 825, 876–77, 939, 955, 1008, 1038, 1051–52
Kubelik Trio, 940
Kubica, Robert, 880
Kubin Quartet, 264, 670
Kuchar, Theodor, 11, 482, 574, 708–9, 711–12, 856
Küchl, Rainer, 432
Kudo, Yoshido, 634
Kuentz, Paul, 64, 581
Kuerti, Anton, 111, 118, 123, 248, 640, 813, 815, 832–33, 853
Kuhlau, Friedrich, 498–99
Kuhlau Quartet, 749
Kuhn, Gustav, 156, 835, 885, 941
Kühn, Pavel, 564
Kuijken, Barthold, 20, 384, 726, 736, 848, 886, 987, 1157
Kuijken, Sigiswald, 23, 26, 28, 52, 59, 161, 241, 243, 393, 397, 429–32, 434–435, 437, 557–8, 627, 736, 848, 988, 1151
Kuijken, Wieland, 557–58, 726
Kuisma, Rainer, 1127–28
Kuivanen, Juha, 695
Kulenkampff, Georg, 108, 114, 828, 1151
Kulka, Konstanty, 445, 944
Kun, Hu, 76, 145, 487

Lenti, Tony, 211, 355
Lenya, Lotte, 1055–56
Leonard, Sarah, 198, 799
Leonardy, Bernhard, 278
Leonardy, Robert, 186
Leoncavallo, Ruggero, 512–13
Leonhardt, Gustav, 23, 34–36, 46, 49, 56, 62, 159, 327, 598, 601, 609, 722, 724, 736, 1121–22
Leonhardt Consort, 33
Leoninus (Léonin), 1098
Leonskaja, Elisabeth, 730
Leopold Trio, 114–15
Leppard, Raymond, 23–24, 27, 46–47, 61, 84, 160, 212, 284, 354, 378–81, 383, 392, 394, 401, 414, 429, 573, 596–97, 599, 604–5, 651, 725–26, 846, 991, 1003, 1105
LeRoi, Nancy, 355
LeRoux, Jean-Louis, 884
Les Adieux, 161–62, 250
Les Arts Florissants, 340
Les Percussions de Strasbourg, 1064, 1128
Les Saqueboutiers de Toulouse, 1113
Les Talens Lyriques, 508
Lesné, Gérard, 390, 610, 695, 789
Lessing, Kolja, 450
Lester, Richard, 161–62
Letzbor, Gunar, 28, 149
Leusink, Pieter Jan, 41, 46
Levant, Oscar, 337, 455
Levi, Yoel, 74–75, 99, 236, 238, 284, 443–44, 546, 659, 709–10, 772, 859–60, 868, 871, 927, 1101
Levin, Robert, 24, 103–6, 112–13, 123, 433, 501, 632, 640, 875
Levinas, Michael, 324
Levine, Carin, 791
Levine, David, 746
Levine, Gilbert, 659, 954
Levine, James, 20, 79–80, 92, 124, 128–29, 131, 141, 172, 181, 203, 207, 237, 252, 268, 283, 298, 335, 344, 360, 435–36, 453, 541, 544, 546, 550, 552, 554, 574–75, 617–18, 622–23, 625, 650–51, 654, 656–57, 684, 709, 823, 826, 862, 868, 876–77, 904, 918–19, 967, 986, 1007–12, 1014, 1037–40, 1042, 1053
Levine, Joseph, 11, 683
Levinson, Eugene, 1148
Levinson, Max, 82
Levitz, Jodi, 459
Levitzki, Mischa, 224
Levy, Ernst, 645, 1147

Levy, Mark, 342
Levy, Robert, 245
Lewandowski, Louis, 1095
Lewenthal, Raymond, 8, 521, 778
Lewin, Michael, 373–74
Lewis, Anthony, 399, 415, 612, 726
Lewis, Dorothy, 1147
Lewis, Henry, 588
Lewis, J. Reilly, 59, 140
Lewis, Richard, 405
Leygraf, Hans, 158
Lhevinne, Josef, 224, 834, 1133
Liadov, Anatoly, 513–14
Licad, Cécile, 221, 225–26, 230, 983
Licata, Andrea, 127–28
Licht, Daniel, 44–45
Lichtmann, Theodor, 444
Lidsky, Mikhail, 572
Lidström, Mats, 482, 486, 490, 1147
Lieberman, Carol, 149
Lifčics, Tovijs, 1000
Lifschitz, Constantin, 36, 645, 732
Ligabue, Ilva, 219
Ligeti, András, 517
Ligeti, György, 514–15
Lilje, Peeter, 304, 997
Lill, John, 729–32
Lillie, Beatrice, 784
Lin, Cho-Liang, 194–95, 577, 633–35, 668, 705, 713, 741, 830, 873, 928, 983, 1151
Lin, Gillian, 186, 240
Lincer, William, 139
Lind, Michael, 447, 451
Lindberg, Christian, 155, 245, 273, 447, 773, 796, 1072, 1111
Lindberg, Jakob, 1028, 1057
Lindberg, Magnus, 515–16
Linde, Hans-Martin, 23, 28, 206, 311, 379–80, 385, 843
Linden, Jaap ter, 31
Linder, Albert, 18, 1111
Lindgren, Ingrid, 245
Lindgren, Stefan, 148
Lindsay Quartet, 110, 287–88, 432–33, 810–11, 874, 992
Line, Ildikó, 474
Linnu, Hannu, 738
Linos, Glenys, 1071
Linos Ensemble, 283, 885
Linsenberg, Judith, 1161
Lipatti, Dinu, 225–26, 306, 369, 630–31, 827, 1133
Lipkin, Seymour, 370, 927
Lipovšek, Marjana, 559, 820, 839
Lippi, Isabella, 775
Lisboa, Tania, 1017–18, 1020

Lishner, Leon, 1096
Lisi, Leonardo de, 754
Lisitsa, Valentina, 731
Lisitsian, Pavel, 734
Lislevand, Rolf, 1028
Liss, Dmitri, 350–51
List, Eugene, 359–60, 366, 419, 521, 576
Liszt, Franz, 516–26
Littauer, Maria, 12, 774
Little, Tasmin, 261, 286, 776, 1004, 1045
The Little Consort, 532
Litton, Andrew, 235, 238, 297, 299, 338, 373, 453, 467, 492, 536, 538, 540, 545, 824, 860–61, 954, 962, 965, 968, 970, 974, 1046
Litton, James, 387, 1031
Litwin, Stefan, 145
Lively, David, 73, 179, 520, 729
Llewellyn, Grant, 235, 569, 942
Lloyd, George, 526–27
Lloyd-Jones, David, 84–85, 154, 260, 298, 452, 454, 743, 781, 940, 1004, 1104
Lloyd Webber, Andrew, 982–83
Lloyd Webber, Julian, 184, 186, 198, 261, 300, 370, 441, 590, 730, 744, 941, 1045, 1101, 1147
Lobanov, Vasily, 798
Lobo, Alonso, 1108
Locatelli, Pietro, 527–28
Locke, Matthew, 528
Locke Brass Consort, 154
Lockhart, James, 264, 794
Locrian Ensemble, 812
Lodéon, Frederic, 1147
Loehrer, Edwin, 212, 600–601, 1033
Loewe, Carl, 528
Löffler, Peter Klaus, 446
Logemann, Sally, 707
Lohmann, Ludger, 746
Loman, Judy, 449, 791–92, 1119
Lomardi, Daniele, 11
Lombard, Alain, 363–64, 682
Lombardi, Daniele, 685
Londeix, Jean-Marie, 1162
London Baroque, 14, 507–8, 557, 726
London Brass, 1114
London Brass Virtuosi, 1114
London Fortepiano Trio, 642
London Gabrieli Brass, 1114
London Mozart Players, 287
London Sinfonietta, 801
London Sinfonietta Voices, 514
London Symphony, 261
London Symphony Brass, 1114

London Winds, 515, 909
Long, Beatrice, 853
Long, Marguerite, 312–13, 740
Long, Michael, 457
Long Island Chamber Ensemble, 463
Longhini, Marco, 611
López-Cobos, Jésus, 17, 151–52, 196, 233, 275, 309–10, 323, 356, 429, 552, 624–25, 740, 751–53, 915, 1017–18, 1041
Loré, Carlo, 610
Loré, Jean-Pierre, 573
Loreggian, Roberto, 327
Lorengar, Pilar, 354, 368
Lorenz, Siegfried, 44
Loriod, Yvonne, 169, 586
Lortie, Louis, 118, 222, 226, 519, 521, 740, 742, 827, 832
Lortzing, Albert, 528–29
los Angeles, Victoria de, 142, 153, 206, 311, 368, 438, 566, 658, 718, 768, 998, 1018, 1136
Los Angeles Guitar Quartet, 1047, 1118
Los Guanches, 1097
Lott, Felicity, 376, 509, 658, 707, 838, 921, 1061
Loubry, Luc, 1154
Loughran, James, 183, 294–95, 453, 570
Lowenthal, Jerome, 520–21, 766, 875, 977–79
Lower, Janna, 423
Löwlein, Hans, 662
Lozano, Fernando, 217, 754
Lubbock, John, 361, 628, 805, 928, 931
Lubimov, Aleksey, 852–53
Lubin, Steven, 103, 811
Lubotsky, Mark, 186, 796–98, 996
Luca, Giuseppe de, 1144
Luca, Sergiu, 30, 1151
Lucarelli, Bert, 242
Lucas, Brenda, 733
Lucewicz, Andreas, 747
Lucier, Alvin, 1083
Lücker, Martin, 445
Ludwig, Christa, 182, 460, 556, 820, 822, 837–38, 1140
Ludwig, Klaus-Uwe, 885
Ludwig, Michael, 235
Ludwig Quartet, 133
Luening, Otto, 1080
Lugansky, Nikolai, 731–33
Luisada, Jean-Marc, 367
Luisi, Fabio, 129, 268, 460
Lukas Consort, 786

Lukomska, Halina, 1054
Lukšaité-Mrázková, Giedré, 32
Lully, Jean-Baptiste, 529–30
Lundlin, Bengt-Ake, 148
Luolajan-Mikkola, Markku, 557
Lupo, Benedetto, 833
Lupu, Radu, 121–23, 179–80, 370, 641, 645–46, 814–16, 833, 1133
Lurtsema, Robert, 888
Lutosławski, Witold, 530–31
Luxon, Benjamin, 193, 199, 1006–7, 1047
Lydian Quartet, 468, 810
Lympany, Moira, 576, 743
Lynch, Andre, 525
Lyndon-Gee, Christopher, 154
Lyric Quartet, 265, 343, 349, 419, 494
Lysell Quartet, 148, 767

M

Ma, Yo-Yo, 31–32, 76, 80, 109, 112, 114, 156–57, 174–75, 186, 286, 299–300, 375, 431, 441, 482, 487, 503, 642, 701, 713–14, 730, 773, 783, 808, 827–28, 831, 862, 865, 904, 915, 950, 982, 1045, 1146
Maag, Peter, 89, 354, 574–75, 617–18, 624, 626, 818, 1008
Maazel, Lorin, 88, 100, 125, 138, 249, 254, 282, 309, 323, 333, 338, 374, 440, 453, 519, 535–36, 538–39, 541, 544, 546, 549–50, 569, 655, 710, 720, 727, 739, 742, 752, 759, 761, 806, 824, 859, 868–70, 893, 898, 900, 902, 905, 908, 910, 912, 914–15, 923–26, 930, 932, 935, 951–55, 957, 960, 968, 970–71, 973, 1008–9, 1011–12, 1014, 1042, 1069
Macal, Zdenek, 98, 140, 250, 280–82, 284–85, 290, 350, 425, 659–60, 711, 715, 876
Macalester Trio, 87, 214
MacDonald, George, 239, 278
MacDonald, Hector, 1111
MacDowell, Edward, 531–32
MacGregor, Joanna, 150, 186, 240, 469
Machaut, Guillaume de, 532
Machek, Miloš, 462
Machover, Tod, 1084
Machula, Tibor de, 904
Mack, John, 784, 830, 1072, 1159
Mackay, Ann, 387, 390, 438
Mackerras, Charles, 17, 88, 99, 139, 171, 182, 189, 218, 234, 261–62, 282, 284–85, 292, 295, 297–98,

362, 378–80, 383, 395–96, 400–401, 410, 413, 415, 429, 443, 452–53, 471, 474–77, 489, 561, 565, 575, 617–18, 624–25, 627, 653, 657, 683, 760–61, 805–7, 868, 871, 939–41, 963–64, 967, 986, 1014, 1091, 1105
Mackie, Neil, 193
Mackintosh, Catherine, 26, 32, 724
Maclachlan, Murray, 715
Maclay, Christian, 1083
MacMillan, Ernest, 61
MacNamara, Hilary, 733
Macomber, Curtis, 209
Maderna, Bruno, 532–33, 605, 891
Madge, Geoffrey Douglas, 355, 497, 571, 880–81, 1063
Madojan, Nicolai, 714
Madsen, Karsten Dalsgaard, 782
Maestri, Fabio, 426
Maga, Othmar, 498, 761–62, 974
Magaloff, Nikita, 832–33, 978
Maggini Quartet, 184, 301, 592, 1046
Maggio-Ormezowski, Franco, 305
Mägi, Paul, 997
Magnard, Albéric, 533–34
Magnin, Alexandre, 161
Magnússon, Orn, 511
Mahler, Gustav, 534–57
Maidre, Ines, 994
Maile, Hans, 425, 478, 745
Mainardi, Enrico, 745
Mainz Bach Choir, 747
Mainz Percussion Ensemble, 1128
Maioli, Renaldo, 533
Maisenberg, Oleg, 733
Maisky, Mischa, 30–32, 112, 286, 299, 713, 808, 828, 831, 982–83, 1147
Makarski, Michelle, 764
Maksymiuk, Jerzy, 22, 329, 369, 686, 727, 945
Malcolm, George, 24–25, 378, 380–82, 611
Malcuzynski, Witold, 222
Malfitano, Catherine, 916
Malgoire, Jean-Claude, 152, 378, 380–81, 395, 397–400, 403, 573, 600, 606–7, 613, 1031, 1034
Malicki, Waldemar, 686
Malinova, Olga and Margarity, 698
Maliponte, Adriana, 789
Malko, Nikolai, 513, 708–9, 716
Malkus, Alexander, 857
Malling, Amalie, 370, 499
Malloch, William, 28
Malmö Brass Ensemble, 446
Maltman, Christopher, 888, 1047

Malý, Lubomír, 263, 886–87
Mamikonian, Vardan, 729
Manalov, Dimiter, 481
Manasse, Jon, 1049, 1157
Manchicourt, Pierre de, 1107
Mandeal, Cristian, 304–5
Mandel, Alan, 359, 361, 468–69
Manfred Quartet, 830
Manhattan Quartet, 864
Manhattan School of Music Opera Theater, 188, 766
Mann, Alfred, 388
Mann, Robert, 82, 208
Mannberg, Karl-Ove, 158, 700
Mannheim Quartet, 195, 745
Manning, Jane, 801
Manno, Ralph, 447
Manolov, Dimiter, 762
Manson, Anne, 511
Mansurov, Fuat, 465, 763, 777
Manz, Wolfgang, 733
Manze, Andrew, 26, 28, 149, 379, 381, 383, 948, 987–88, 1024, 1027, 1030
Manzotti, Angelo, 390, 392, 1035
Mar, Norman del, 84, 183–84, 190, 260, 592, 743, 776, 887–88, 1005
Marais, Marin, 557–58
Maran, George, 1006
Marari, Agustin, 1147
Marbá, Ros, 333
Marc, Allesandra, 917
Marcante, Emanuela, 597
Marcellus, Robert, 635, 1156
Marcovici, Andrea, 349
Mardjani, Jahni, 453, 659
Mare, Anthony de, 205, 243, 424, 468
Maréchal, Maurice, 1146
Mareš, Vlastimil, 498, 750
Margraf, Horst-Tanu, 396–97
Mari, Jean-Baptiste, 259
Mariano, Joseph, 373
Marinkovic, Mateja, 572, 747, 797–98
Marinotti, Bruno, 585
Marinov, Ivan, 352
Marinuzzi, Gino, 1010
Mariozzi, Vincenzo, 166
Mariscal, Ignacio, 1147
Mark, Peter, 395
Markevitch, Dimitry, 30
Markevitch, Igor, 19, 138, 140, 147, 167, 218, 352, 362, 436, 455, 592, 659, 664, 682, 774, 925, 951–55, 957, 959, 970, 974, 1014
Markham, Richard, 16–17
Markiz, Lev, 155, 574, 626, 796–97, 972

Markov, Alexander, 687, 1016
Marks, Alan, 360
Markson, Gerhard, 157, 906, 1062
Marlboro Festival Players, 627, 670
Marlboro Music Festival Orchestra, 77
Marlow, Richard, 38–39, 314, 610, 841, 888
Marriner, Andrew, 319, 635, 1049
Marriner, Neville, 27–28, 58, 75, 99, 144, 151, 170, 183, 199, 218, 238–39, 245, 281–83, 297, 314, 362, 369, 378–80, 383, 388, 392, 402, 406, 411, 429–30, 434–36, 453, 455, 467, 505, 575, 580, 616–18, 624–26, 628, 646–47, 650, 654–57, 682–83, 685, 694, 752, 767, 771–72, 825–26, 907, 914, 927–28, 940–41, 964, 967, 972, 991–92, 1004, 1007, 1023–24, 1030–31, 1044, 1048, 1061, 1105
Marrucci, Lucia, 1050
Marsalis, Branford, 1018
Marsalis, Wynton, 311, 432, 438, 447, 459, 478
Marschik, Peter, 402–3
Marsh, Ozan, 520–21
Marshall, Deborah, 490, 839
Marshall, Ingram, 1083
Marshev, Oleg, 504, 714, 732–33, 778
Martin, Barbara Ann, 245–46, 463
Martin, Frank, 558–60
Martin, Jean, 313, 747
Martin, Laurent, 8
Martin, Philip, 360
Martin, Thomas, 166–67
Martinelli, Giovanni, 1142
Martinez, Rolo, 1097
Martini, Alberto, 1024, 1026
Martini, Joachim Carlos, 405, 408, 415
Martinon, Jean, 82, 138, 151–52, 165, 252–54, 275, 443, 456, 463, 503, 665, 708–9, 712, 739–41, 774, 783, 794–95, 858, 861, 999
Martins, João Carlos, 34–36
Martinů, Bohuslav, 560–66
Marton, Eva, 718, 721, 916–17
Marvin, Frederick, 278, 615
Marwood, Anthony, 286
Märzendorfer, Ernst, 896
Mascagni, Pietro, 566–67
Mase, Raymond, 211
Masó, Jordi, 332, 593
Mason, Patrick, 209, 279, 315, 743
Masselos, William, 240, 469
Massenet, Jules, 567–69

Massis, Annick, 365
Masson, Diego, 168
Masters, Rachel, 10, 351
Masur, Kurt, 95, 125, 171–72, 181,
    187, 194, 254, 282, 323, 472, 475,
    516–19, 537, 573–75, 580–81,
    660, 709–10, 712, 760, 825, 836,
    860–61, 903, 912, 919, 951,
    953–55, 957, 960, 962
Mata, Eduardo, 144, 216–17, 237,
    239, 296, 309–10, 343, 368, 421,
    453, 684, 709, 715, 751–52, 754,
    868, 903, 912–13, 1019
Matačič, Lovro von, 73, 409, 513, 612,
    760, 1051
Mathe, Christianne, 246
Mathé, Ulrike-Anima, 496, 747
Mathews, Shirley, 21, 327
Mathias, William, 569–70
Mathieu, Bruno, 276, 505, 1015–16
Mathieu, Chantal, 885
Mathis, Edith, 49, 181, 438, 658, 836,
    921, 1061
Mátl, Lubomir, 750, 1068
Matoušek, Bohuslav, 562
Mattax, Charlotte, 72
Mattes, Willy, 483
Matthews, Denis, 114–15, 121, 743,
    776
Matthews, Ingrid, 30
Matthies, Silke-Thora, 179, 289
Mattila, Karita, 922
Matuz, Gergely, 502
Matuz, István, 701
Matzke, Werner, 887
Mauceri, John, 760
Mauersberger, Erhard, 46, 53, 60,
    841–42, 844, 846, 849–50
Mauk, Steve, 1163
Maurer, Laurel Ann, 500
Mauser, Siegfried, 425, 443–45, 449
Mavrides, Ernest, 1101
Max, Hermann, 56–57, 63, 66, 72, 614,
    989, 1068
Maxian, František, 286, 481, 678
Maxwell, Linn, 13
May, Angelika, 286, 444
May, Gisela, 293, 1056
Maycher, Lorenz, 882
Mayer, Steven, 520–21
Mayes, Samuel, 684
Mayr, (Johannes) Simon, 570
Mazzola, Denia, 267
McAslan, Lorraine, 186, 301, 1046
McCabe, John, 432, 434, 449, 458,
    570, 671
McCallum, Stephanie, 9

McCapra Quartet, 17
McCarthy, John, 611
McCaw, John, 668
McCawley, Leon, 77
McCormack, John, 1142
McCraw, Michael, 1154
McCreesh, Paul, 57, 149, 328, 404–5,
    722–23, 848
McDermott, Anne-Marie, 715
McDuffie, Robert, 76, 144, 194, 262,
    345, 577, 775, 824
McFarlane, Ronn, 273, 1119
McFrederick, Michael, 211
McGegan, Nicholas, 14, 241, 379, 387,
    393–97, 399, 403, 405, 413,
    417–18, 598, 600–601, 736–37,
    789, 1027, 1029, 1035
McGill, David, 1155
McGinnis, Patrice, 424
McGreevy, Geraldine, 155
McInnes, Donald, 139
McIntosh, Kathleen, 34
McKinley, Daniel Jay, 277
McKinley, William Thomas, 570–71
McLachlan, Murray, 482, 590, 857
McLaughlin, Marie, 656, 921
McLean, Barton, 1083
McLean, Priscilla, 1083
McMahon, Richard, 366, 733
McNair, Sylvia, 78, 153, 387, 723, 743
McNeely, Joel, 1085–86
Mdroszkiewicz, Joanna, 1058
Measham, David, 74, 481, 589
Medici Quartet, 301, 473, 784
Medieval Ensemble, 274
Medlam, Charles, 33, 159, 385, 602
Medtner, Nikolai, 571–72
Medveczky, Adam, 283
Megi, Pauls, 1000
Mehlhart, Ulrich, 444
Mehta, Zubin, 75, 98, 236–37, 274,
    296–97, 452, 517–19, 536–37,
    540, 544, 546, 627, 653–54, 664,
    684, 688, 721, 760, 800–801, 868,
    877, 893–94, 898–99, 902, 905,
    908, 914–15, 925–26, 941, 967,
    999, 1009–10, 1012–13, 1043,
    1072
Méhul, Étienne-Nicolas, 572–73
Mei, Eva, 390
Meier, Bruno, 498, 998
Meijer, Roelof, 1147
Meinl, Gerhard, 1113
Meintz, Catherine, 558
Meister, Barbara, 671
Melba, Nellie, 1138
Melbourne Quartet, 592

Melchior, Lauritz, 839, 1039, 1142
Meldau, Ulrich, 277, 1058
Melia, Roland, 590
Melik-Pashayev, Alexander, 352, 717
Meliora Quartets, 578
Melkus, Eduard, 149, 241, 384
Mellon, Agnes, 213, 723
Meloni, Fabrizio, 459
Melos Ensemble, 112, 256, 288, 473,
    670, 741, 774, 812, 828–29, 884
Melos Quartet, 218, 473, 810–12, 830
Melton, James, 322
Mendelssohn, Felix, 573–82
Mendelssohn Duo, 179
Mendelssohn Quartet, 994
Méndez, Rafael, 1112
Mendici, 1005
Mendoza, Francisca, 714
Meneses, Antonio, 904, 983
Mengelberg, Willem, 60, 88, 181, 255,
    323, 540, 806–7, 901, 906, 956,
    959
Mennin, Peter, 582
Menotti, Gian Carlo, 583–84
Mentzer, Susanne, 769
Menuhin, Jeremy, 288
Menuhin, Yehudi, 25–27, 29, 31, 72,
    80–83, 91, 107–9, 113, 139, 194,
    228, 295, 297, 299, 301, 306,
    378–79, 381, 384, 451–52, 503,
    576, 633–34, 664, 668, 687, 801,
    804, 830, 948, 980, 1022, 1045,
    1151–52
Menuhin Festival Piano Quartet, 639
Mera, Yoshikuzu, 44
Mercadante, Saverio, 584–85
Mercier, Jacques, 794
Mergio, Evenzia Mario, 427
Meridian Arts Ensemble, 1113
Mertanen, Janne, 492
Mertens, Klaus, 21, 45, 70
Merz, Florian, 826, 1105
Merzhanov, Victor, 523
Mesplé, Mady, 260, 376, 1018
Messiaen, Olivier, 585–87
Mester, Jorge, 77, 214, 238, 321, 360,
    421–22, 697, 702, 824
Métamorphoses Ensemble, 340
Metheny, Pat, 749
Metzmacher, Ingo, 425, 468, 758
Meunier, Alain, 114
Mewton-Wood, Noel, 113
Meyer, Kirsten, 304
Meyer, Paul, 145, 239, 250, 425,
    1049–50
Meyer, Sabine, 144, 239, 250, 255,
    627–28, 635, 638, 829, 886, 1157

Meyer, Wolfgang, 498, 640, 642
Meyerbeer, Giacomo, 587–88
Meyers, Anne Akiko, 195, 240, 713,
    1004
Mezzena, Bruno, 772
Mezzena, Franco, 1022
Miami Quartet, 784
Miami String Quartet, 313, 1000
Miaskovsky, Nikolai, 588–90
Michael Thompson Quintet, 250, 472,
    750
Michael Thompson Wind Ensemble,
    498
Micheau, Jeanne, 19
Michel, Catherine, 885
Michel, Danielle, 505
Michel Piquemal Vocal Ensemble, 277
Michelakakos, Michel, 490
Michelangeli, Arturo Benedetti, 35,
    104–6, 178–79, 225–28, 231, 369,
    632, 730, 741–42, 790, 827, 833,
    1133
Michelucci, Roberto, 1023
Midori, 80, 195, 286, 301, 324, 687,
    873, 980
Midsummer's Music, 885
Migdal, Marian, 148
Migenes, Julia, 706–7
Mihály, András, 501
Mikhashoff, Yvar, 891
Mikkelsen, Terje, 377, 942
Mikkola, Laura, 738
Milan, Susan, 559
Milanov, Zinka, 566
Mildonian, Susanna, 1119
Milenkovich, Stefan, 29, 687
Milhaud, Darius, 590–92
Milkov, Mikhail, 734
Millard, Christopher, 1155
Miller, David Alan, 360, 420, 422, 582,
    889
Miller, Leta, 423–24
Miller, Mina, 474, 671
Miller, Robert, 246, 1081
Millet, Danièle, 681
Millinger, Andrew, 458
Milne, Hamish, 57, 1050
Milne, Lisa, 465
Milnes, Eric, 66, 843
Milnes, Sherill, 374
Milstein, Nathan, 29, 113–14, 174,
    194, 216, 286, 349, 356, 503, 576,
    713, 948, 980, 1152
Mimaroglu, Ilhan, 1081
Mimura, Kazuko, 288
MiNesemblet, 1061
Ming, Liu Xiao, 248

Nasedkin, Alexei, 348, 779
Nash, Royston, 940
Nash Ensemble, 17, 85, 112, 148, 155, 256, 284, 288, 461, 498, 639–40, 642, 741, 812, 885
Nasveld, Robert, 246–47
Nat, Yves, 117–18
National Gallery Vocal Arts Ensemble, 1115
National Youth Chamber Choir, 744
Navarra, André, 157, 299, 713, 827, 1146
Nazareth, Daniel, 659, 752
Neale, Alasdair, 485
Neary, Martin, 159
Neblett, Carol, 718
Nebolsin, Vassili, 763
Neel, Boyd, 299, 380
Negri, Vittorio, 233, 328, 1030–32, 1035
Negro, Lucia, 889
Négyesy, János, 755
Neidich, Charles, 459, 627, 636, 750, 1049
Neikrug, Marc, 641
Nel, Anton, 765, 784
Nelson, John, 142, 358, 416, 1072
Nelson, Judith, 390–91, 438
Nelsova, Zara, 156
Németh, Gyula, 387, 438–39, 519
Németh, Pal, 311
Neriki, Shigeo, 731
Nes, Jard van, 1039
Nesterov, Valentin, 610
Nestor, Leo, 990
Netherlands Chamber Choir, 489, 747, 1054, 1116
Netherlands Guitar Trio, 369
Netherlands Wind Ensemble, 150, 472, 628, 909
Nettle, David, 16–17
Neuhaus, Heinrich, 715, 854
Neuhold, Gunther, 140, 323, 758
Neumann, Horst, 835–36
Neumann, Peter, 66–67, 415, 597, 835
Neumann, Václav, 280–82, 284–85, 292, 471, 475–76, 538, 544–45, 551, 560, 565, 649–51, 876–77, 938–39, 998, 1105
Neunecker, Marie-Luise, 351, 445, 828, 913
Nevel, Erik van, 200, 507, 842
Neveu, Ginette, 109, 873, 1152
New Amsterdam Singers, 318
New Arts Trio, 12
New Bochmann Quartet, 564
New Budapest Quartet, 464, 572, 884

New Chamber Opera Ensemble, 724
New College Choir, 201, 480, 1116
New England Conservatory, 203
New England Piano Quartette, 463
New Haydn Quartet, 884, 984
New Jefferson Chamber Players, 990
New Jersey Chamber Music Society, 278
New Leipzig Quartet, 801, 812
New London Chamber Choir, 480
New London Children's Choir, 187
New London Quintet, 301
New Mexico Brass Quintet, 1113
New Millenium Ensemble, 315
New Munich Piano Trio, 12, 885
New Music Consort, 423, 1127
New Prague Trio, 678
New World Basset Horn Trio, 628
New World Chamber Ensemble, 373
New World Quartet, 494
New York Chamber Ensemble, 373
New York Concert Singers, 211
New York New Music Ensemble, 209
New York Philomusica, 274
New York Pro Musica, 479
New York String Quartet, 246, 1073
New York Trumpet Ensemble, 1112
New York Vocal Arts Ensemble, 127
New York Woodwind Quintet, 77, 318
Newband, 694
Newman, Alfred, 35–36, 1086
Newman, Anthony, 39, 65, 379, 386, 434, 1125
Newman, David, 1088
Newman, Mary Jane, 790
Nexus Quintet, 198, 1126–28
NFB Horn Quartet, 1111
Ni, Hai-Ye, 828
Nibley, Reid, 359
Nice, Carter, 74
Nicholson, Paul, 13, 383, 386
Nickel, Timothy, 355
Nicol, Karl Ludwig, 1036
Nicolai, Otto, 661–62
Nicolaievsky, Yuri, 131
Nicolesco, Mariana, 270
Nicolet, Aurèle, 358–59, 668, 750, 1050
Nicolet, Christine, 210
Nicolosi, Francesco, 732
Niekrug, George, 157
Nielsen, Carl, 662–74, 830
Nielsen, Inga, 916
Nieuw Ensemble, 332
Nigro, Susan, 1155
Nikolaiev, Leonid, 514

Nikolaieva, Tatiana, 117, 121–22, 715, 866
Nikolais, Alwin, 1083
Nikolitch, Gordan, 948
Nilson, Göran, 767
Nilsson, Bengt, 329
Nilsson, Birgit, 126, 718, 721, 916–17, 921, 1138
Nilsson, Göran, 1060
Nimsgern, Siegmund, 425
Niquet, Hervé, 162, 213, 530, 737
Nishizaki, Takako, 26, 324, 478, 633, 635, 642, 753, 778, 884, 982, 1025
Nitschmann, Martin, 273
Nixon, Marnie, 457
Nobel, Felix de, 611
Noble, Jeremy, 480
Noehren, Robert, 38, 275
Nojima, Mineru, 742
Nolan, David, 1004
Nolte, Irmela, 490
Nomos Quartet, 161, 326
Nono, Luigi, 674–75
Nopre, Gilles, 464
Noras, Arto, 299, 491
Nørby, Einar, 674
Nordmann, Marielle, 885
Nordstoga, Kåre, 180–81, 325, 1057–58
Nørgård, Per, 675–77
Norman, Jessye, 136, 142, 153, 217, 353, 587, 681, 743, 801, 820, 838, 916, 921–22, 1039
Norrington, Roger, 98, 139, 172, 379–80, 574, 646–47, 724, 772, 789, 805, 826, 846–48, 850, 877, 1001–2, 1048, 1104
Norse Quartet, 782
North, Alex, 1086
North, Nigel, 880, 1057, 1118–19
North German Figural Choir, 747
North German Radio Symphony, 1000
Norwegian Winds, 909
Nosek, Václav, 565
Novacek, Steven, 211
Novaes, Guiomar, 106–7, 221, 227–31, 631, 644, 832
Novák, Vítězslav, 677–78
Novák Quartet, 473, 677
Novospassky Monastery Choir, 1078
Novotný, Jan, 278, 511, 878
Nowakowski, Mieczyslaw, 393
Numajiri, Ryusuke, 946
Nuñez, Antonio, 423
Nuns of Rüdisheim-Eibingen, 441
Nuoranne, Timo, 738

Nuovo Quartetto, 1014
Nuovo Quartetto Italiano, 773
Nuovo Quintetto di Venezia, 1030
Nuvolone, Félix, 682

O

O-Zone Percussion Group, 1128
Oberfrank, Géza, 61, 68, 272
Oberlin, Russell, 272, 577
Oberlin Baroque Ensemble, 557
Obermeyer, Janet, 526
Obetz, John, 505
Oborin, Lev, 370, 731
Obraztsova, Elaha, 566
Obrecht, Jacob, 678
Obstfeld, Frieder, 564
Ockeghem, Johannes, 678–79, 1106
O'Conor, John, 317, 811
Odeon Trio, 809
O'Dette, Paul, 273, 1028, 1118
O'Donnell, James, 475, 506, 559
Oelze, Christiane, 658, 819, 1055
Offenbach, Jacques, 679–84
Ogano, Kumi, 946
Ogawa, Noriko, 661, 729–30, 946
Ogdon, John, 8, 10, 173, 198, 348, 520, 576, 671, 733, 852–53, 875, 880–81, 928, 977, 1134
Ogrinchuk, Leonid, 352
Ohlsson, Garrick, 103, 118, 220–22, 225–31, 240, 257, 434, 715, 729, 977, 1050, 1062
Ohrenstein, Dora, 991
Ohrwall, James, 56, 58, 387, 402
Oistrakh, David, 26, 81, 108–9, 174, 195, 216, 349, 370, 445, 482, 486, 577, 633, 710, 713–14, 731, 741, 830, 863, 865, 873, 885, 944, 947, 980, 1065, 1152
Oistrakh, Igor, 300, 324, 590, 885, 1065
Okashiro, Chitose, 853–54
Okatsu, Shuya, 624
Oland, Anne, 671
Oldfather, Christopher, 208, 931
Oldham, Denver, 373–74, 890
Oleg, Raphaël, 808
Olevsky, Julian, 384
Oliveira, Elmar, 76, 320, 463, 478, 512, 983
Oliver, John, 249
Oliveria, Djalma, 1097
Olivero, Madga, 232, 343, 567
Olivero, Patrick, 354
Oliveros, Pauline, 1083
Ollila, Tuomas, 487, 870–72
Olmi, Paolo, 130

Peelman, Roland, 845
Pehrsson, Clas, 385
Peinemann, Edith, 745
Peire, Patrick, 752, 772, 817
Pekarsky Percussion Ensemble, 1128
Pekinel, Güher and Süher, 576
Pellegrini Quartet, 244, 425
Pellicia, Arrigo, 634, 638
Pelucchi, Pierangelo, 570
Pelz, Charles, 1064
Peña, Paco, 1096
Penderecki, Krzysztof, 694–95
Penin, Jean-Paul, 123, 213
Pennario, Leonard, 360, 519, 577, 775
Penny, Andrew, 15–16, 183, 234, 691–92, 940–41, 1006, 1044
Pepicelli, Angelo, 210
Pepicelli, Francesco, 210
Pepusch, Johann Christian, 331
Perahia, Murray, 34, 82, 101, 104, 106–7, 111, 121, 134, 179–80, 221, 225–27, 325, 369, 576, 578, 629, 640, 644–46, 813, 815, 827–28, 832–34, 992, 1134
Percussive Rotterdam, 1128
Pereira, David, 208, 714, 1147
Perényi, Miklós, 502, 808
Pérez, Victor, 332
Pergamenschikov, Boris, 30, 279, 348, 459, 714
Pergolesi, Giovanni Battista, 695–96
Perl, Alfredo, 118, 122, 833
Perl, Hille, 32
Perle, George, 696–97
Perlea, Jonel, 1011
Perlemutter, Vlado, 227–29, 231, 742
Perlman, Itzhak, 26, 29, 76, 81–82, 109, 113–15, 132, 139, 144, 174–75, 194–95, 211, 216, 286–87, 301, 324, 344, 349, 356, 486, 493, 496, 503, 508, 577, 633–34, 638, 641, 687–88, 703, 713–14, 741, 784, 787, 863, 873, 875, 928, 933, 980–81, 983, 1016, 1022, 1024, 1058, 1096, 1118, 1152
Perotinus (Pérotin), 1098
Perrett, Danielle, 279
Perrin, Cecile, 358
Persichetti, Vincent, 697–98
Perspectives Ensemble, 373
Pertusi, Michele, 995
Pěruška, Jan, 886
Pešek, Libor, 185, 280–82, 284, 470, 677, 793, 876, 939
Peskó, Zoltán, 1069
Petchersky, Alma, 1021
Peter, Hans, 438

Peter Buck Cello Ensemble, 1147
Petermandl, Hans, 449
Peters, Jane, 1064
Peters, Roberta, 269, 769
Petersen, Ulrike, 885
Petersen Quartet, 153, 370, 810, 812, 831
Petit, Jean-Louis, 361–62
Petitgirard, Laurent, 275
Petkova, Marietta, 731
Petracchi, Franco, 166
Petrella, Clara, 567
Petri, Egon, 199, 1028, 1134
Petri, Michala, 385, 451, 1161
Petro, Janos, 1036
Petrov, Nikolai, 481, 856
Pettersson, Allan, 698–700
Peyer, Gervase de, 175, 319, 640, 808, 828, 830, 884, 1049
Pfitzner, Hans, 700
Pflueger, Gerhard, 877
Phantasm, 38
Phelps, Cynthia, 306
Philadelphia String Quartet, 764
Philadelphia Trio, 997
Philarte Piano Quartet, 997
Philharmonia Quartet, 745
Philharmonische Cellisten Köln, 1147
Philip Glass Ensemble, 345
Philip Jones Brass Ensemble, 154, 328, 780
Philippe, Les Amis de, 21
Philippe de Vitry, 1099
Phillips, Daniel, 489
Phillips, Edna, 252
Phillips, Margaret, 784
Phillips, Matthew H., 214
Phillips, Peter, 507
Phillips, Xavier, 534, 714, 798
Piano Circus, 748
Piatigorsky, Gregor, 112, 115, 174–75, 286, 829, 983, 1045, 1053, 1146
Piau, Sandrine, 392
Piazzolla, Astor, 700–701
Piccollo, Silvia, 789
Pichaureau, Claude, 358, 573
Pickett, Philip, 23, 28, 57–58, 69, 385, 528, 599, 602–3, 613, 707
Pierce, Joshua, 204, 245, 519–21, 562, 564, 576, 948
Pierlot, Philippe, 431–32, 557, 847, 849
Pierné, Gabriel, 701
Pierre, Fabrice, 1120
Pierre, Odile, 375–76, 1057–58
Pierrot Players, 1073
Piesk, Guenter, 635

Pieterson, George, 176
Piguet, Michel, 379, 638
Pihtipudas Quintet, 779, 875
Pikaizen, Viktor, 304
Pikal, Guido, 327
Pilgrim, Neva, 764
Pini, Anthony, 114, 300
Pini, Carl, 776, 972
Pinkas, Jiří, 292
Pinkas, Sally, 764
Pinkett, Eric, 183
Pinkham, Daniel, 51, 844
Pinnock, Trevor, 23–24, 27–28, 36, 170, 241, 342, 378, 380–81, 386, 392, 403, 406, 408–9, 413–14, 430–31, 435, 437, 617–18, 650, 686, 723, 725, 790, 1023–24, 1029, 1031, 1122
Pinza, Ezio, 1144
Piquemal, Michel, 277, 706
Pirasti Trio, 86, 888
Pires, Maria João, 228, 370, 631, 642–43, 645
Pirzadeh, Maneli, 349
Pischner, Hans, 35
Piston, Walter, 701–2
Pittel, Harvey, 1162
Pittman, Richard, 1073
Pittsburgh Orchestra, 443
Pizarro, Artur, 482, 591, 730
Plagge, Rolf, 439, 733
Planchart, Alejandro, 274
Plançon, Pol, 1144
Plane, Robert, 319
Planès, Alain, 474
Plasson, Michel, 151–52, 164, 213, 216, 275, 277, 361–64, 455, 464, 518–19, 533, 573, 591, 681–82, 684, 774
Plessier, René, 1018
Pletnev, Mikhail, 115, 121, 123, 284, 352, 514, 644, 709, 715, 717, 727, 730, 732, 761, 853, 923–24, 930, 951, 954, 956, 958, 960, 962, 965, 973, 978–79, 983, 985, 1104
Pleyer, Friedrich, 1071
Plog, Andrew, 697
Plog, Anthony, 1112
Pludermacher, Georges, 700
Pobbe, Marcella, 271
Podger, Rachel, 30
Podles, Ewa, 735, 771
Pogorelich, Ivo, 661, 742, 977
Pokorny, Eugene, 447, 1113
Polaski, Deborah, 917
Poledouris, Basil, 1086
Polekh, Valerie, 351

Polianski, Valery, 11, 290–91, 346–47, 349, 659–60, 795–97, 799, 947, 973
Polidori, Massimo, 167
Politkovsky, Igor, 779
Polk, Joanne, 87
Pollack, D., 77
Pollet, Françoise, 706, 1055
Pollini, Maurizio, 106, 118, 123, 134, 169, 173, 177, 222, 257, 715, 801, 814–15, 827, 833–34, 933, 1054, 1134
Polyansky, Valery, 11, 347
Polyphony, 693
Pomarico, Emilio, 218
Pomerium, 274, 480
Pommer, Max, 23, 294, 380–81, 383, 409, 625–26, 737–38
Ponce, Manuel, 702–3
Ponchielli, Amilcare, 703–4
Ponkin, Vladimir, 711
Pons, Lily, 269, 309–10
Ponse, Luctor, 82
Ponseele, Marcel, 987
Ponselle, Rosa, 1138
Ponti, Michael, 73, 147–48, 286, 355, 499, 521, 572, 615–16, 731, 736, 756, 762, 778, 792, 977–79, 985
Pöntinen, Roland, 370, 474, 576, 731, 796–97, 854, 996
Pope, Richard, 470
Pople, Ross, 16, 160, 314, 378, 402, 453, 472, 574, 886, 907, 1048
Popov, Valeri, 1049
Popov, Yuri, 481
Popova, Evgenia-Maria, 1065
Popp, Lucia, 529, 658, 685, 838, 921–22
Poppen, Christian, 425
Poppen, Christoph, 439
Poroshina, Inna, 289–90, 514
Portal, Michel, 642
Portland Quartet, 157
Portman, Rachel, 1086
Porto, Heriberto Calvalcante, 701
Portugheis, Alberto, 343, 486
Postnikova, Viktoria, 472, 474, 977–79, 985
Potter, Stephen, 273
Pougnet, Jean, 261, 592
Poulenard, Isabelle, 389
Poulenc, Francis, 704–7, 1102
Poulet, Gérard, 512, 634, 641, 1016
Powell, Mel, 1081
Powell, Ross, 308
Powers, Marie, 583

Reiber, Michael, 166–67, 1147
Reich, Steve, 747–49, 801, 1080
Reicha, Anton, 749–50
Reicha Trio, 750
Reichenberg, David, 383, 1159
Reichert, Hubert, 356
Reighley, Kimberly, 987
Reinecke, Carl, 750–51
Reiner, Fritz, 79, 90–91, 94–96, 98, 100, 172, 252–53, 283, 309, 431, 456, 481, 541, 555, 620, 622–23, 625, 659, 711, 715, 727, 740, 751, 760, 772, 805–6, 826, 859, 893, 899, 904, 908–9, 911, 913–14, 924, 928, 959, 964, 969, 1013, 1037–38, 1042
Reinhardt, Rolf, 51
Reinke, Gerd, 1148
Reisman, Michael, 345
Reizen, Mark, 1144–45
Rejto, Peter, 563
Rembrandt Trio, 214, 287, 784
Reményi, János, 649
Remeš, Václav, 473
Remoortel, Edouard van, 355
Rémy, Ludger, 21, 989
Renardy, Ossy, 687
Renaud, Madeleine, 681
Renz, Frederick, 614
Renzetti, Donato, 217–18
Renzi, Frances, 696, 698
Repercussion, 1128
Repin, Vadim, 633, 713–14, 863, 873, 1152
Repková, Vera, 878
Requejo, Ricardo, 998
Rescigno, Nicola, 127, 129, 219, 393, 395
Resnik, Regina, 153
Respighi, Ottorino, 751–54
Rethberg, Elisabeth, 1138
Reube, Thomas, 1068
Reuter, Rolf, 140, 408, 700
Rév, Livia, 228, 578
Revolutionary Drawing Room, 161
Revsen, Joel, 505
Revueltas, Silvestre, 754–55
Reykjavik Wind Quintet, 87, 824
Reyne, Hugo, 385
Reynish, Timothy, 130, 365, 444, 454
Reynolds, Jeffrey, 1111
Reynolds, Roger, 755
Rezníček, Emil Nikolaus von, 755–56
Režucha, Bystrik, 761
Rheinberger, Josef, 756–58
Riber, Anders, 671
Ribke, Gunter, 1147

Ricci, Ruggiero, 26, 76, 186, 286, 356, 486, 503, 509, 583, 687, 713, 753, 784, 787, 875, 1152
Ricciarelli, Katin, 271, 718, 721
Ricercar Academy Orchestra, 507
Ricercar Consort, 384, 557
Rich, Elizabeth, 1049
Richards, Deborah, 491
Richman, Stephen, 376
Richter, Karl, 22, 36, 354, 382, 386, 392, 401
Richter, Sviatoslav, 27, 34–35, 40–42, 45–48, 53, 58, 60, 63–64, 68, 80, 82, 104, 109, 111–12, 114, 119, 121–22, 124, 178, 180, 186, 225, 229, 257, 286, 288, 348, 370, 395, 414, 434, 445, 519, 524, 590, 632, 641–42, 644–46, 648, 661, 712, 715, 729, 731, 742, 747, 762, 814–16, 827–28, 830, 832–34, 842, 854, 866, 976, 985, 1050, 1134–35
Rickards, Steven, 272
Rickenbacher, Karl Anton, 123, 125, 425, 443–44, 460, 462, 518, 662, 883
Riddell, Wayne, 47
Riddle, Frederick, 638
Rider, Rhonda, 208
Riebl, Thomas, 779
Rieger, Fritz, 425
Riegger, Wallingford, 758
Rifkin, Joshua, 41, 46–48, 55, 59, 62, 478, 618, 625
Riga String Quartet, 1000
Rigacci, Bruno, 786
Rigai, Amiram, 360
Rigby, Jean, 86, 193
Rigutto, Bruno, 491
Rihm, Wolfgang, 758
Riley, Terry, 759, 1084
Rilling, Helmut, 22, 28, 39–40, 42, 46–51, 53–55, 57–58, 61, 64–65, 68, 70, 125, 290–91, 400, 408, 436–37, 439, 525, 574, 581–82, 804, 817, 842, 850
Rimbu, Romeo, 262
Rimsky-Korsakov, Nikolai, 759–64
Ringborg, Tobias, 148
Ringeissen, Bernard, 8
Rischner, Alfons, 651
Rise, Harald, 1015–16
Riska, Astrid, 874, 1060
Risor Festival Strings, 943
Risset, Jean-Claude, 1082–83
Ristenpart, Karl, 22, 27

Ritchie, Stanley, 1026
Ritzkowsky, Johannes, 1111
Riva, Douglas, 367
Rivinius, Gustav, 1062
Rivoli, Gianfranco, 363
Rizzi, Carlo, 364
Rizzi, Marco, 210
Robbin, Catherine, 838–39, 1032
Robbins, Gerald, 289, 355
Robert Schumann Quartet, 831
Robert Shaw Chorale, 187, 322
Robert Shaw Festival Singers, 1115
Roberts, Bernard, 35, 115, 117, 121–22, 449
Roberts, Timothy, 328
Roberts Wesleyan College Choral, 422
Robertson, David, 795
Robertson, George, 747
Robev, Georgi, 733, 986
Robilliard, Louis, 325
Robin, Mado, 260
Robinson, Christopher, 458, 582
Robinson, Faye, 389, 992–93
Robinson, Joseph, 764, 830, 1160
Robinson, Sharon, 1072
Robinson, Stanford, 941
Robison, Paula, 279, 384, 639, 1158
Robles, Marisa, 638, 1119
Robson, Christopher, 14
Rochberg, George, 764
Rochette, Jacquelin, 276
Rodde, Anne Marie, 259
Rodenhäuser, Ulf, 447
Roderburg, Christian, 1127
Rodgers, Richard, 1088
Rodrigo, Joaquin, 764–66
Rodriguez, Santiago, 211, 221, 520, 732–33
Rodzinski, Artur, 253, 323, 715, 964
Rogé, Pascal, 324, 705, 740, 742, 783, 788
Rogeri Trio, 287
Rogers, Eric, 485
Rogers, Nigel, 598, 614
Rogg, Lionel, 37, 382
Roggeri, Marcela, 240
Rogliano, Marco, 148
Rögner, Heinz, 745, 1061
Rojak, John, 1112
Rojatti, Ezio, 1105
Rolla, János, 28, 218, 378, 380, 624–25, 627
Rollez, Jean-Marc, 1148
Romantic Trio, 352, 779
Rome Opera, 660
Romero, Angel, 765, 1021, 1028, 1118
Romero, Gustavo, 593

Romero, Pepe, 211, 344, 765, 880, 1028, 1118
Rônez, Marianne, 149
Ronstadt, Linda, 345–46
Rooley, Anthony, 159, 272–73, 596, 598–600, 603, 840
Roos, Frédéric de, 385, 1028
Rorem, Ned, 766
Ros, Pere, 557
Ros-Marbá, Antonio, 367
Rosand, Aaron, 12, 29, 108, 113, 478, 762, 787, 948, 982
Rosbaud, Hans, 167–68, 354, 442, 444, 653, 871–72
Roscoe, Martin, 87, 264–65, 944
Rosé, Arnold, 1152–53
Rose, Gregory, 470
Rose, Jerome, 1036
Rose, Leonard, 32, 109, 114, 157, 174, 286, 503, 783, 827, 982, 1146
Rose Consort of Viols, 507, 726
Rösel, Peter, 109, 123, 178, 180, 431, 728–30, 814–15, 1048
Rosen, Charles, 121–22, 209, 931, 983, 1054
Rosen, Jerome, 520
Rosen, Marvin, 457
Rosen, Nathaniel, 30, 463
Rosenbaum, Poul, 373–74
Rosenberg, Hilding, 766–67
Rosenberg, Richard, 359
Rosenberger, Carol, 373, 419, 431, 862, 901, 1100, 1102
Rosenblatt, Yossele, 1096
Rosenfeld, Jayn, 246
Rosenfeld, Mindy, 987
Rosengren, Håkan, 667
Rosenman, Leonard, 1086
Rosenstock, Milton, 360
Rosenthal, Laurence, 228, 254–55, 683, 1086
Rosenthal, Manuel, 252
Rosenthal, Moriz, 221, 223, 521, 1135
Rosin, Armin, 1111
Roslak, Roxolana, 451
Ross, Alexander, 422
Ross, Pamela, 34
Ross, Robert, 990
Ross, Scott, 327, 386, 790, 879, 1122
Rossi, Cristiano, 715, 1062
Rossi, Mario, 232–33, 760–61, 769, 1023
Rossi-Lemeni, Nicola, 770
Rossini, Gioacchino, 767–72
Rossini Duo, 1148
Rossler, Almut, 587
Rost, Andrea, 269

Rost, Jürgen, 559
Rost, Martin, 375
Rostal, Max, 830
Rostropovich, Mstislav, 31, 109, 112, 115, 156, 174–75, 184, 186, 256, 279, 285, 431, 433, 484, 531, 590–91, 660, 708, 713, 717, 731, 734, 783, 797–99, 827, 831, 856–57, 859, 862, 865, 867, 903, 915, 951–53, 956, 958, 960, 963, 967, 971, 982–83, 986, 1146
Rota, Nino, 772–73, 1087
Roth, Daniel, 325, 525, 1058
Rothenberger, Angelica, 509, 922
Rother, Artur, 460
Rothkopf, Andreas, 746–47
Rothstein, Jack, 894
Rotman, Hans, 986
Rotter, Jorge, 573
Rotterdam Quartet, 1112
Rotzsch, Hans-Joachim, 41–42, 46–47, 49, 58, 64
Rouen Choir, 277
Rouits, Dominique, 359
Rouse, Christopher, 773
Rousseau, Eugene, 1162
Roussel, Albert, 773–74
Rousset, Christophe, 24, 34–36, 242–43, 397–98, 651, 695, 736–37, 790, 1122
Rowe, Tony, 182
Rowicki, Witold, 280–82, 530, 594
Rowland, Gilbert, 879
Rowland, Joan, 289
Royal Consort, 342
Royal String Quartet of Copenhagen, 779
Rozhdestvensky, Gennadi, 12, 72, 164–65, 261, 304–5, 346–49, 369, 443, 458, 465, 504, 588–89, 660, 663–67, 708–12, 716, 759, 795–97, 856–59, 861–62, 936, 947, 963, 965–66, 968, 1002, 1006, 1036
Rózsa, Miklós, 775, 1087
Rubbra, Edmund, 775–77
Rubens, Sybilla, 50
Rubinsky, Sonia, 1021
Rubinstein, Anton, 777–79
Rubinstein, Arthur, 102, 105–6, 114, 120–21, 174, 177–80, 221–22, 225–31, 257, 289, 310, 324, 369, 372, 434, 520, 522, 524, 630, 639, 644–45, 705, 729–30, 742, 783, 809, 814–15, 827, 831–33, 944, 974, 983, 1021, 1135
Rubio, Consuelo, 367

Rubsam, Edward J., 1127
Rübsam, Wolfgang, 38, 746–47, 1016
Rudel, Julius, 129, 163, 395, 568–69, 605, 679
Rudenko, Vadim, 733
Ruders, Poul, 779–80
Rudich, Rachel, 423–24
Rüdiger, Wolfgang, 831
Rudin, Alexander, 348, 481, 713
Rudner, Ola, 158
Rudolf, Max, 823
Rudolph, Pierre-Paul, 701
Rudy, Mikhaïl, 472, 728–30, 854
Ruffo, Titta, 1145
Ruggles, Carl, 780
Ruhland, Konrad, 480, 506
Ruhlmann, François, 268, 364
Ruiz, Adrian, 355, 756–57, 778, 875
Ruiz, Gonzalo Xavier, 1159
Rumessen, Vardo, 304, 994, 996
Rummel, Martin, 562
Rundel, Peter, 445
Rundell, Clark, 365
Runnicles, Donald, 354, 460, 1040
Rupp, Franz, 113
Rusha, Stanley de, 462
Rusmanis, Kriss, 1000
Russell, David, 344, 765, 1118
Russell, Linda, 322
Russell, Lucy, 830
Russell, Lynda, 819
Russell, Timothy, 793
Russo, John, 137, 208, 447
Rust, Rebecca, 184, 1017–18, 1020
Rutter, John, 313–14, 780–81
Ruud, Ole Kristian, 376–77, 772, 782, 942
Ruzicka, Peter, 699, 802
Ružičková, Zuzana, 386, 562
Ryabchikov, Victor, 352
Rybar, Peter, 562
Rybrant, Stig, 18
Rysanek, Leonie, 916–17, 920, 1138–39

S

Saariaho, Kaija, 781
Saarinen, Gloria, 815
Sabajno, Carlo, 267
Sabata, Victor de, 751
Sabine Meyer Wind Ensemble, 627
Sabrié, Isabelle, 167
Saccani, Rico, 752
Sacher, Paul, 799
Sacrum Chamber Choir, 1000
Sádlo, Milos, 285
Sadlo, Peter, 591, 1127

Sado, Yuraka, 145
Saeverud, Harald, 781–82
Saeverud, Trond, 782
Saffer, Lisa, 391
Safri Duo, 1127–28
Saint-Saëns, Camille, 782–85
Sajot, Jean-Louis, 750, 1050
Sakari, Petri, 369, 487, 511, 868–69, 871–72, 1060
Sala, Ofelia, 803
Salerno-Sonnenberg, Nadja, 76, 174, 194, 496, 577, 863, 873, 983, 1153
Salieri, Antonio, 785–86
Sallinen, Aulis, 786–87
Salman, Mark, 8
Salo, Per, 676
Salomon String Quartet, 433, 639–41
Salonen, Esa-Pekka, 147, 249, 254, 258, 369, 506, 515–16, 531, 540, 542, 553, 586, 663–66, 672–73, 710, 754, 781, 869–72, 907, 923, 925–36, 945
Salter, Hans J., 1087
Saltire Singers, 272
Saltzman, Harry, 389, 410–11
Salzburg Mozarteum Horns, 1111
Salzedo, Carlos, 1119
Sammons, Albert, 261, 301, 592, 1153
Samoilov, Yevgeny, 589
Samosud, Samuel, 763
Sampen, John, 1162
Samuels, Dave, 1127
Samuels, Gerhard, 422, 467
San, Ludovic de, 213
Sanchez, Esteban, 310
Sanderling, Barbara, 998, 1148
Sanderling, Kurt, 171, 407, 533–34, 868, 870, 959
Sanderling, Stefan, 574, 967
Sanderling, Thomas, 699
Sándor, Frigyes, 437
Sandor, György, 80, 82, 714
Sandor, Janos, 941
Sanfilippo, Domenico, 786
Sanger, David, 326
Sanromá, Jesús-Maria, 449, 830
Santambrogio, Claudio, 533
Santi, Nello, 513, 595, 1061
Santiago, Enrique, 448
Santini, Gabriele, 343–44, 720, 1010
Sanzogno, Nino, 219, 233, 268
Saorgin, Rene, 200
Saperton, David, 227
Saram, Rohan de, 208, 776
Sarasate, Pablo de, 29, 74, 151, 279, 516, 618–20, 622–23, 660,

663–65, 710, 781, 787–88, 872, 998, 1153
Sardelli, Federico Maria, 1029, 1032
Sarfaty, Regina, 839
Sargent, Malcolm, 261, 297–98, 303, 331, 400, 410, 453, 659, 711, 751, 871–72, 877, 941, 1002
Satanowski, Robert, 593–94, 944–45
Satie, Erik, 788–89
Sato, Eriko, 793
Sauer, Emil von, 520, 1135
Sauer, Ralph, 1111
Sauer, Thomas, 197
Saulesco Quartet, 1060
Savall, Jordi, 17, 23, 28, 32, 149, 273, 379–80, 529, 557–58, 597, 613, 646, 725
Savenko, Vassily, 764
Savidge, Peter, 1007
Savijoki, Jukka, 703
Savijoki, Pekka, 447
Savino, Richard, 162
Savinova, Natalie, 445
Savonlinna Opera Festival Chorus, 492
Sawa, Kazuki, 82
Sawallisch, Wolfgang, 90–91, 93–94, 96–98, 281–82, 285, 290, 443–44, 450, 518, 580, 657, 685, 700, 779, 816–18, 825, 835, 877, 885, 900, 902, 906, 908, 919–20, 966, 1036–37, 1041, 1048
Say, Fazil, 335, 644–45
Sayão, Bidù, 1018
Scaglia, Ferrucio, 212
Scandinavian Chamber Players, 670
Scapoli, Gli, 747
Scarlatti, Alessandro, 789–90
Scarlatti, Domenico, 790–91
Scelsi, Giacinto, 791
Schachman, Marc, 1159
Schadeberg, Christine, 138, 210
Schaenen, Lee, 679
Schäfer, Christine, 43, 50, 819, 840
Schafer, R. Murray, 791–92
Schafer Ensemble, 792
Scharwenka, Xaver, 792
Schele, Marta, 193
Schellenberger, Hansjörg, 639, 1160
Schenck, Andrew, 74–75, 77, 236, 360, 443, 990
Schenkman, Byron, 386, 1122
Schepkin, Sergey, 36
Scherbakov, Konstantin, 122, 355, 571–72, 753
Scherchen, Hermann, 41, 48, 54, 58, 60, 63, 89–90, 141–42, 249, 350,

377, 401, 432, 435, 517–19, 548, 648, 683, 711, 744, 759, 762, 1048, 1104

Scherman, Thomas, 412–13

Schermerhorn, Kenneth, 248, 348, 419, 467, 909, 964, 1020

Schernus, Herbert, 359

Scherzer, Manfred, 745

Schickele, Peter, 711, 792–93, 1102

Schidlof, Peter, 634

Schiefen, Guido, 747

Schieferstein, Eva, 1050

Schiff, András, 25, 34–36, 80, 101–2, 109, 286, 299, 434, 474, 576, 578, 629, 639, 642–43, 645–46, 730, 746–47, 790, 804, 809, 812, 815, 828, 831–33

Schiff, Heinrich, 531, 828, 862, 874, 1016, 1027

Schiff, Zina, 211, 890, 1004

Schifrin, David, 1156

Schilders, Beatrijs, 1147

Schill, Ole, 668

Schilli, Stefan, 1028

Schiøtz, Aksel, 673–74, 822, 837, 1142

Schipa, Tito, 1142

Schippers, Thomas, 74–75, 123, 219, 583–84, 768, 772, 1008–9, 1011

Schirmer, Ulf, 134, 664, 672, 920

Schirmer Ensemble, 310

Schleiermacher, Steffen, 204

Schlick, Barbara, 70

Schlusnus, Heinrich, 820, 1145

Schmalfuss, Gernot, 194

Schmid, Benjamin, 687

Schmid, Georg, 444–45

Schmid, Ulrich, 157

Schmidt, Andreas, 822, 1061

Schmidt, Felix, 300

Schmidt, Franz, 793–94

Schmidt, Johan, 866

Schmidt, Nanette, 273

Schmidt, Ole, 329, 503, 662, 665

Schmidt, Rainier, 1025

Schmidt, Stephan, 1118

Schmidt-Gaden, Gerhard, 843, 845

Schmidt-Isserstedt, Hans, 147, 442, 651, 745, 805

Schmiege, Marilyn, 526

Schmitt, Florent, 794–95

Schmitt-Walter, Karl, 528

Schmitz, E. Robert, 257

Schmöthe, Georg, 1065

Schnabel, Artur, 103–6, 112, 115, 117, 121–23, 174, 180, 631, 639, 644–45, 811, 813, 815, 1135

Schnabel, Karl Ulrich, 289

Schnabel Duo, 289

Schnanda, Michael, 426

Schneeberger, Hansheinz, 209, 745

Schneider, Alexander, 114, 161, 283, 621, 623, 638, 809

Schneider, John, 423–24

Schneider, Michael, 385, 398, 437, 1029

Schneider, Urs, 735–36

Schneiderhan, Wolfgang, 106, 108, 113, 633

Schneidt, Hanns-Martin, 53, 55, 69, 71, 611, 841

Schnittke, Alfred, 795–99

Schnittke, Irina, 798

Schock, Rudolf, 510

Schoeck, Othmar, 799–800

Schoenbach, Sol, 1155

Schoenberg, Arnold, 800–801

Schoenberg Ensemble, 801

Schoenberg Quartet, 133, 1054, 1070

Schola Cantorum, 511–12

Schola Cantorum of St. Peter's in the Loop, 1078–79

Schola Hungarica, 274

Scholars Baroque Ensemble, 52, 387, 724–26

Scholl, Andreas, 392, 997, 1032

Schöne, Wolfgang, 425

Schönwandt, Michael, 329–31, 499, 503, 663–65, 667, 826, 834–35

Schönzeler, Hans-Hubert, 154, 776, 1048

Schopper, Michael, 45

Schorr, Friedrich, 1145

Schotten, Yizhak, 808

Schrader, David, 35, 790, 879

Schramm, Margit, 509–10

Schreier, Peter, 27, 41, 50, 55, 57–58, 60–61, 64, 68, 126, 192–93, 292, 406, 438, 582, 658, 817, 820–21, 836–37, 839, 920, 1061

Schreker, Franz, 802–3

Schröder, Jaap, 26, 445

Schroeder, Marianne, 316

Schroeder, Rolph, 29

Schuback, Peter, 1147

Schubert, Franz, 803–23

Schubert Ensemble, 265, 461, 493–94, 829

Schubert Quartet, 264, 973, 984

Schulhof, Otto, 112

Schuller, Gunther, 464, 467, 479, 689, 823–24

Schulte, Rolf, 20, 208–9, 780, 829–30

Schultz, Stephen, 162, 987

Schultz, Tom, 933

Schultze, Richard, 379

Schulz, Wolfgang, 638

Schuman, William, 824–25

Schumann, Elisabeth, 49, 819, 920–21, 1139

Schumann, Robert, 825–40

Schumann-Heink, Ernestine, 1140

Schunk, Heinz, 885

Schuricht, Carl, 196

Schütz, Heinrich, 751, 840–50

Schwalbé, Michel, 577

Schwantner, Joseph, 851

Schwartz, Felix, 808

Schwarz, Gerard, 75, 79, 82, 90, 95–96, 98, 155, 157, 207, 209, 217, 236–39, 245, 249, 262, 309, 360, 368, 372–74, 378, 406, 418–20, 422, 432, 455–57, 484, 488, 571, 574, 582, 623, 701, 710, 739–40, 753, 789, 824, 826, 839, 856, 889, 900, 906, 908, 914–15, 923, 925, 932, 952–53, 1040–41, 1103, 1112

Schwarzkopf, Elisabeth, 43, 49, 126, 509, 556, 658, 819, 830, 837, 921, 1046, 1060–61, 1139

Schweitzer, Albert, 1123

Schweizer, Rolf, 614–15

Schwieger, Hans, 73, 347

Scialdo, Mary Ann, 482

Sciannameo, Franco, 273

Sciascia, Stefano, 167

Scimone, Claudio, 272, 402, 617, 722, 768, 786, 1014, 1029, 1033–35, 1105

Scott, Cyril, 258

Scott, John, 160, 277, 375, 388, 525, 569, 579, 780

Scott, William Fred, 647

Scotto, Renata, 266, 270, 696, 718–21, 754, 1062

Scotts, Donald, 592

Scriabin, Alexander, 851–54

Sculthorpe, Peter, 854–55

Seattle Chorale, 263

Sebestyen, Ernö, 351, 757

Sebestyen, Janos, 386

Sebok, Gyorgy, 256

Sedares, James, 17, 156, 238, 262, 307–8, 360–61, 441, 583, 775, 990

Sedazzari, Felice, 584

Seefried, Irmgard, 126, 658, 819, 838–40, 1061, 1139

Seeley, Gilbert, 77

Seelig, Timothy, 420, 990

Seely, Timothy, 780

Segarra, Ireneu, 613

Segerstam, Leif, 158, 487, 490, 495,

503, 511, 537, 546, 660, 672–73, 675, 698–99, 727, 737–38, 779, 794–96, 851, 868–72

Segovia, Andrés, 211, 310, 344, 702–3, 765, 880, 1021, 1116–17

Seibel, Klauspeter, 262, 575

Seidel, Toscha, 1153

Seifert, Gerd, 637, 640, 913

Seifried, Reinhard, 574

Seivewright, Peter, 671

Sejna, Karel, 281, 284–85, 317, 560, 677, 876–77, 939

Sellick, Phyllis, 729

Semionov, Yuri, 351

Semkow, Jerzy, 166, 476, 593

Sempé, Skip, 200, 243, 601

Sender, Ernst-Erich, 201

Senfl, Ludwig, 1106

Senn, Martha, 311

Sennedat, André, 1018

Senor Ensemble, 316

Seow, Yitkin, 730

Sequardt, Ivan, 562

Sequentia, 442, 1116

Sequoia Quartet, 81

Serafin, Tullio, 128–29, 163, 219, 267, 269, 272, 420, 513, 720, 1008–10, 1012–14, 1105

Serebrier, José, 164, 214, 216, 282, 442, 444, 467, 470–71, 1061

Serebryakov, Pavel, 731

Serenata of London, 745

Sergeyev, Nikolai, 589

Serkin, Peter, 118–19, 288, 576, 586, 632, 639, 646, 747, 801, 811, 946, 1054, 1063

Serkin, Rudolf, 103, 106–7, 109, 111, 113–14, 118–19, 122–23, 125, 173–74, 177, 576, 630–31, 642, 645, 745–46, 809, 811, 814, 827–29, 1135

Sermet, Hüseyin, 449

Serov, Edward, 11–12, 659, 663–67, 673, 761

Servadei, Annette, 874

Serviarian-Kuhn, Dora, 486

Sessions, Roger, 855

Sestaková, Andrea, 998

Sestetto Classico, 461

Sestetto Italiano Luca Marenzio, 597

Sexteto Major, 1097

Sgouros, Dimitris, 977

Sgrizzi, Luciano, 386

Shafran, Daniel, 30, 431, 481–82, 827, 865

Shaham, Gil, 76, 80, 82, 109, 194, 240, 286, 324, 482, 493, 496, 577,

Sørenson, Per Dybro, 251

Soria, Antonio, 998

Soriano, Joaquin, 997

Sorrel, Jeannette, 24, 67, 404, 614, 618

Sorrel Quartet, 186

Sørum, Oyvind, 767

Sosa, Raoul, 494

Sourrisse, Jean, 581–82

Sousa, John Philip, 881–82

Souter, Matthew, 457

South African Chamber Music Society, 351

South German Octet, 330

South German String Octet, 943

Southwest Chamber Music Society, 713, 938

Souzay, Gérard, 44, 126, 217, 259, 315, 365, 743, 820–22, 836–37, 920

Sowerby, Leo, 882–83

Spacagna, Maria, 718

Spada, Pietro, 107, 233, 318, 689, 786

Spain, Anthony, 136

Spalding, Albert, 1153

Spang-Hanssen, Ulrik, 579, 671, 756–57

Spanjaard, Ed, 316

Spányi, Miklós, 21

Sparf, Nils-Erik, 311, 874, 1025, 1060

Spectre de la Rose, 557

Speculum Musicae, 209, 1063

Speidel, Sontraud, 747

Speiser, Elisabeth, 387

Spelina, Karel, 998

Spence, Patricia, 14, 209

Spencer, David, 308

Spering, Christoph, 62, 218, 406, 414, 581

Spicer, Paul, 302, 319, 458

Spiegelman, Joel, 318

Spierer, Leon, 148, 767

Spiller, Antonio, 1020

Spiller Trio, 512

Spillman, Herndon, 277, 698

Spivakov, Vladimir, 26–27, 425, 861, 873, 985

Spivakovsky, Tossy, 873

Spivakovsky, Vladimir, 972

Spohr, Ludwig (Louis), 686, 883

Spring, Robert, 996

Springuel, France, 484

Spruit, Henk, 124

St. Clair, Carl, 945, 1019

St. Clement's Choir, 757

St. George Chapel Choir, 950

St. John, Lara, 30, 82, 787, 1153

St. John, Scott, 688

St. John's College Choir, 187, 277, 506, 1116

St. Lawrence Quartet, 830

St. Petersburg Quartet, 864, 984

St. Thomas Church Choir, 489

St. Thomas Episcopal Choir, 187

Stacy, Thomas, 697, 766, 1157

Stade, Fredericka von, 145, 206, 456, 707

Stader, Maria, 43, 658

Stadler, Sergei, 12

Stadlmaier, Hans, 558

Staier, Andreas, 21, 34–35, 318, 632, 640–41, 786, 814–15, 1122

Stalanowski, Stefan, 1058

Stalder, Hans-Rudolf, 751

Stallman, Robert, 384, 1158

Stamitz, Carl, 886–87

Stamitz Quartet, 287–89, 564, 998

Stamp, Richard, 907

Stamper, Richard, 983

Stancul, Jasminka, 809

Standage, Simon, 26, 170, 381, 390, 392, 508, 633, 1025–27

Standen, Richard, 1006

Stanford, Charles Villiers, 887–88

Stankovsky, Robert, 571, 589, 777–78, 877

Stanzeleit, Susanne, 81–82, 287, 744

Stárek, Jiři, 272, 362, 756, 1036

Starer, Robert, 888–89

Starker, János, 30, 32, 109, 211, 256, 263, 286, 300, 431, 444, 489, 503, 563, 577, 582, 713, 731, 775, 783, 827, 829, 889, 904, 1146

Starobin, David, 209, 247, 344, 780

Stasevich, Abram, 715

State Prokofiev Quartet, 572

Statkiewicz, Edward, 136–37

Staufenbiel, Brian, 169

Stauffer String Quartet, 446

Steber, Eleanor, 79, 127, 922

Steck, William, 809, 1050

Steele, Jeffry Hamilton, 480

Steele-Perkins, Crispian, 432, 1112

Steen, Piet van der, 277

Steen-Nøkleberg, Einar, 370–71

Stefano, Giuseppe de, 1141

Stefanski, Andrzej, 686

Steigerwalt, Gary, 815

Stein, Horst, 220, 744–45, 871, 1050

Steinberg, Pinchas, 128, 139, 212, 568, 682, 735

Steinberg, William, 95–97, 155–56, 171, 297, 453, 622, 624–25, 761, 994, 1014, 1061

Steiner, Christian, 733

Steiner, Max, 1087

Steinhardt, Arnold, 29–30

Steinitz, Paul, 842

Steinmetz, Paul, 57

Steljes, Cynthia, 1157

Stenhammar, Wilhelm, 889

Stensgaard, Kai, 1127

Stenz, Markus, 445

Stepán, Pavel, 481, 940

Stepansky, Alan, 77

Stepchenko, Svetlana, 352, 779

Stéphane Caillat Choir, 277

Stephens, John, 698

Stephens, Patrick, 35

Stephenson, Mark, 15–16

Stephenson, Ronald, 198

Stephenson, William, 198

Stepner, Daniel, 405, 468

Sterling Quartet, 776

Stern, David, 662

Stern, Isaac, 25–26, 76, 80–82, 109, 114, 144, 174–75, 178, 240, 251, 279, 286, 324, 448, 496, 503, 625–26, 633–34, 642, 713, 764, 809, 811–12, 873, 886, 928, 981, 1058, 1153

Stern-Istomin-Rose Trio, 577

Steuerman, Jean Louis, 799

Steve Reich and Musicians, 748, 1128

Stevens, Bruce, 757

Stevens, Denis, 331, 597, 608, 612

Stevens, Risë, 153

Stevens, Thomas, 500, 1112

Stevenson, Ronald, 366

Stevensson, Kjell-Inge, 668

Stevove, Milos, 637

Stewart, John, 192–93

Stewart, Malcolm, 457

Stewart, Paul, 730

Stich-Randall, Teresa, 43, 510, 658, 838, 922

Stiedry, Fritz, 354

Stiedry-Wagner, Erika, 801

Stignani, Ebe, 1140

Still, Alexa, 16, 490, 1158

Still, Ray, 638, 913, 1159–60

Still, William Grant, 889–90

Sting, 711

Stinton, Jennifer, 373, 698, 1027

Stirling, Michael, 445

Stobart, James, 527

Stockhausen, Karlheinz, 674–75, 890–92, 1080

Stockhausen, Majella, 892

Stockhausen, Markus, 892, 1018

Stockholm Arts Trio, 865, 1060

Stockholm Chamber Brass, 446, 1113

Stockmeier, Wolfgang, 757

Stokes, Sheridan, 160–61

Stokowski, Leopold, 79, 92, 96, 98, 100, 138, 151–52, 157, 173, 252–55, 275, 283, 298, 305, 309, 323, 350, 365, 379, 453, 485, 517–18, 538, 548, 575, 583, 586, 627, 659–60, 684, 727, 739, 752, 754, 760, 762, 801, 858–61, 868–69, 871, 902, 910–11, 924–26, 932, 955–57, 961, 969–70, 973, 991, 1002–4, 1041, 1104

Stoll, Klaus, 166, 1147

Stoll, Pierre, 794

Stolper, Mary, 668

Stoltzman, Lucy, 932

Stoltzman, Richard, 114, 144–45, 175–76, 239, 242, 307, 319, 635, 640, 642, 749, 930, 932, 945, 1049–50, 1157

Stolyarov, Grigori, 351

Stolz, Robert, 895

Stone, Carl, 1083–84

Stone, Dorothy, 20

Storck, Helga, 449, 885

Storck, Klaus, 885

Storojev, Nikita, 353

Stott, Kathryn, 184, 313, 732, 742

Stoutz, Edmund de, 941

Strahl, Tomasz, 222

Straka, Peter, 477

Strakova, Daniela, 678

Stratas, Teresa, 1056

Stratton, Kerry, 457

Strauss, Johann, II, 892, 894–97

Strauss, Paul, 512

Strauss, Richard, 897–922

Strauss family, 892–95

Stravinsky, Igor, 922–37, 1102

Stravinsky, Soulima, 933

Streep, Meryl, 705

Strehle, Wilfried, 445–46

Streich, Rita, 658, 839

Streicher, Ludwig, 263, 1148

Streit, Kurt, 839

Strickland, William, 615, 780

Strieby, Lawrence, 447

Stringer Alan, 432

Ströcker, Hans, 1112

Stromberg, William, 374

Strong, David, 449

Strub Quartet, 745

Stryja, Karol, 944–45

Stubbs, Stephen, 70, 598–99

Studer, Cheryl, 78–79, 127, 269, 771, 916, 922

Studt, Richard, 1060
Stupel, Ilya, 503
Stupka, František, 677
Stuttgart Chamber Choir, 747
Stutzmann, Natalie, 44–45, 182, 217, 259, 391, 836, 838, 840, 1032
Stych, Jan, 317
Subotnick, Morton, 937–38, 1081
Subrata, Faridah, 754
Suderberg, Elizabeth, 246
Sudzilovsky, Sergei, 351
Suitner, Otmar, 173, 280–82, 427, 460, 529, 700, 744, 804–5, 818, 941, 1036, 1048
Suk, Josef, 22, 31, 262, 283, 286, 288, 324, 562, 878, 886, 938–40, 1153
Suk Quartet, 677, 940
Suk Trio, 287, 809, 983
Suliotis, Elená, 266, 566
Sullivan, Arthur, 940–41, 1089–94
Sultan, Grete, 205
Sultanov, Alexei, 977
Summerly, Jeremy, 506–7, 841, 848, 1031
Summit Brass, 307, 446, 824, 1111, 1114
Summit Trombone Quartet, 1112
Sund, Robert, 8
Sundkvist, Petter, 495, 737, 767, 889
Supervia, Conchita, 368, 998, 1140
Suppé, Franz von, 941–42
Suske, Karl, 26, 29
Suso, Foday Musa, 346
Susskind, Walter, 236, 360, 453, 709, 876
Sutej, Vjekoslav, 585
Suter, Hermann, 995
Sutherland, Donald, 524
Sutherland, Joan, 128, 260, 266, 269–70, 351, 393, 658, 721, 771, 1139
Sutherland, Robin, 36
Suwanai, Akiko, 194–95
Suzuki, Hidemi, 31, 34, 40, 42–43, 59, 63, 66, 69, 161, 200, 808, 845, 849
Suzuki, Masaaki, 36, 404, 1068
Svarovsky, Leoš, 291
Svedrup, Patrick, 796
Svenden, Birgitta, 304, 1071
Svendsen, Johan Severin, 942–43
Svensson, Petja, 491–92
Svetlanov, Evgeni, 11–12, 72–73, 155, 164–65, 296, 346–48, 351–52, 452, 482–83, 513, 540, 727, 759–63, 852, 856, 939, 947, 951–54, 958, 960, 962, 966–67, 970–71, 985

Swann, Frederick, 375, 1125–26
Swann, Jeffrey, 169, 523, 616
Swanson, Randall, 1147
Swarowsky, Hans, 395, 437, 462, 877
Sweelinck, Jan Pieterszoon, 943
Swensen, Joseph, 391, 873
Swierczewski, Michel, 573, 683
Swoboda, Henry, 561
Sykes, Peter, 453, 1126
Sylvan, Sanford, 78, 241, 315, 821
Symphonia, 1113
Szabadi, Vilmos, 80, 82, 264, 306, 885, 1056
Szábo, Peter, 502
Szathmáry, Zsigmond, 515
Szefcsik, Zsolt, 438–39
Szegedi, Ernö, 265
Szekeres, Ferenc, 1034–35
Szell, George, 88, 90–92, 95–97, 99–100, 172–73, 253, 281–82, 284, 324, 379, 430–31, 444, 471, 489, 542, 546, 575, 621–25, 628, 639, 641, 659, 709, 711, 806–7, 877–78, 908–10, 912, 924, 955–57, 1041, 1043–44
Szeryng, Henryk, 26, 29, 108–9, 113–14, 174, 324, 577, 633–34, 641, 688, 703, 831, 981, 1153
Szidon, Roberto, 522
Szigeti, Joseph, 29, 81–82, 108, 113–14, 198, 256, 448, 576, 641, 713, 1153
Szmytka, Elzbieta, 231, 357
Szokolay, Balázs, 82, 234
Sztankov, Ivan, 1148
Szymanowski, Karol, 943–45

T

Tabuteau, Marcel, 1159
Tacchino, Gabriel, 705, 712, 715, 783, 830
Tachezi, Herbert, 382
Tachner, Gerhard, 114
Tacit, Ilona, 567
Taddei, Giuseppe, 266
Tafelmusik, 383
Taffanel Quintet, 750
Tagliaferro, Magda, 1019, 1021
Tagliavini, Ferrucio, 163, 567
Taimonov, Mark, 733
Takács Quartet, 81, 830
Takahashi, Aki, 316, 1064
Takahashi, Yuji, 204, 586, 1064
Takemitsu, Toru, 945–46
Takezawa, Kyoko, 76, 82, 301, 1153
Tal, Yaara, 179, 248, 733, 747, 779, 815
Tale Quartet, 155, 797

Talich, Jan, 562, 779
Talich, Václav, 281–82, 284–85, 677, 876, 938–39
Talich Quartet, 110, 288, 432–33, 473, 639–41, 810
Tallinn String Quartet, 993
Tallis, Thomas, 946–47, 1108
Tallis Scholars, 201, 341, 479, 946, 949–50, 1078, 1114
Talmi, Yoav, 139, 141, 155, 350
Talvela, Martli, 822
Talvi, Ilkka, 263, 487
Tamagno, Francesco, 1142–43
Tambuco Percussion Ensemble, 1128
Tamir, Alexander, 815
Tan, Margaret Leng, 204, 245
Tan, Melvyn, 103, 106, 1049
Tanaka, Masahito, 1155
Taneyev, Sergei, 947
Taneyev Quartet, 590
Tannenbaum, David, 423, 439–40
Tanski, Claudius, 273, 746, 878
Tansman, Alexandre, 947–48
Tanyel, Seta, 616, 705, 792, 866
Tapestry, 442
Tarasova, Marina, 481–82, 590
Tarr, Edward, 447
Tartini, Giuseppe, 948–49
Taruskin, Richard, 678
Taschner, Gerhard, 948
Tashi, 586, 1054
Tate, Jeffrey, 125, 295, 461, 575, 604, 624, 626, 680, 915, 919
Tatlow, Mark, 496
Tatrai, Vilmos, 625
Tatrai Quartet, 433, 812
Tatsumi, Akiko, 1065
Tatum, Art, 289
Taub, Robert, 20, 116–17, 697, 855
Tauber, Richard, 510–11, 822, 1143
Tausky, Vilem, 10, 683, 1105
Taverner, John, 949–51, 1107
Taverner Choir, 341, 693, 951
Taverner Consort, 480, 532, 722, 1116
Tawaststjerna, Erik T., 874
Taylor, Daniel, 723
Taylor, David, 1111
Taylor, Millard, 788
Tchaikovsky, Piotr, 951–87, 1102, 1104
Tchakarov, Emil, 166, 352, 986
Tchavdarov, Zahari, 747
Tchistiakov, Andrei, 734
Te Kanawa, Kiri, 153, 206, 215, 275, 391, 658, 719, 921–22, 1018
Tear, Robert, 193, 477, 734–35, 1006
Tebaldi, Renata, 718–20, 1139

Tees, Stephen, 452
Teeters, Donald, 583–84, 991
Tegzes, Maria, 293
Telemann, Georg Philipp, 987–89
Tellefsen, Arve, 148, 668, 875, 943
Telmányi, Emil, 29, 668–69
Temianka, Henri, 384
Temirkanov, Yuri, 715–16, 760–61, 857–61, 868, 964, 969
Temple University Wind Symphony, 712
Tenenbaum, Mela, 29, 31–32, 527
Tennesen, Terje, 368
Tennstedt, Klaus, 196, 535–36, 538, 540, 542–47, 549–51, 554, 900, 902, 911, 1041
Terakado, Ryo, 32, 332, 384, 508
Terfel, Bryn, 199, 392, 821, 837, 839, 1006
Terry, Carole, 698
Tertis, Lionel, 1149
Tetourova, J., 678
Tetrazzini, Luisa, 1139
Tetzlaff, Christian, 80–81, 472–73, 633, 1153
Thallaug, Edith, 875
Thamm, Hans, 847
Tharaud, Alexander, 591
Thärichen, Werner, 1128
Tharp, Steven, 532, 580
Theatre of Voices, 480, 693, 749
Thedéen, Torleif, 157, 186, 445, 447, 491, 563, 714, 731, 796–98, 874, 1147
Thelander, Kirsten, 1111
Theodore, David, 1005
Thibaud, Jacques, 114, 216, 313, 324, 1154
Thibaud-Casals-Cortot Trio, 831
Thibaudet, Jean-Yves, 179, 257, 455, 520, 729–32, 741
Thielemann, Christian, 95, 97, 123, 700, 826, 1040
Thiem, Barbara, 273
Thill, Georges, 1143
Thiollier, François, 324, 464, 731, 733, 740
Thiry, Louis, 586
Thomas, Ambroise, 989
Thomas, Bryden, 42, 46–49, 51–52, 64, 68, 84, 185
Thomas, David, 391
Thomas, Jeffrey, 41, 55, 435, 843
Thomas, Kurt, 41, 58
Thomas, Martha, 764
Thomas, Patricia, 784
Thomas, Ronald, 16, 170, 185

Válek, Vladimír, 131, 317, 560, 939, 1069, 1105
Valente, Benita, 259, 333
Valjakka, Taru, 871
Valletti, Cesare, 567
Vallin, Ninon, 215
Valta, Jan, 561
Valtsa, Tapani, 492
van Dam, José, 365, 568, 743, 821, 836, 839
Vanbrugh Quartet, 240, 473, 570, 592, 875
Vanden Eynden, Jean-Claude, 324
Vandersteene, Zeger, 822
Vandeville, Jacques, 491
Vandré, Philipp, 204
Vaness, Carol, 354, 771
Vanessa-Mae, 195
Vanhal, Johann Baptist, 998–99
Vänskä, Osmo, 247, 487, 491, 511, 667, 738, 867–73
Varady, Julia, 566, 839, 886, 921, 987
Varcoe, Stephen, 199, 319, 367, 692
Varèse, Edgar, 999, 1079
Varga, Gilbert, 777
Varga, Laszlo, 500, 713
Varon, Lorna Cooke de, 857
Vartolo, Sergio, 206, 327, 596, 600, 603, 994
Varviso, Silvio, 710
Vásáry, Támás, 265, 520, 561, 729, 752, 804
Vasilieva, Alla, 779
Vasks, Pēteris, 999–1000
Vassiliades, Christopher, 500
Vaucher, Jean-François, 278
Vaughan Williams, Ralph, 61–62, 1000–1007, 1113
Vedehr Trio, 463
Végh, Sandor, 28, 81, 624–25, 628, 805–7
Végh Quartet, 81, 110
Velardi, Estevan, 1024
Veldhoven, Jos van, 61
Vengerov, Maxim, 349, 669, 687, 713, 856, 863, 873, 928, 980, 1065, 1154
Venhoda, Miroslav, 597
Venice Quartet, 161
Ventadorn, Bernart de, 1098
Venzago, Mario, 735, 799, 834
Verbit, Marthanne, 685
Verbruggen, Marion, 385, 1030, 1161
Verchi, Nino, 268
Verdehr, Walter, 583
Verdehr Trio, 793
Verdi, Giuseppe, 1007–14
Verdi Quartet, 810, 812

Verdin, Joris, 375
Verebes, Robert, 562, 747, 887, 998
Vered, Ilana, 933
Verhehr, Trio, 308
Verlet, Blandine, 35–36, 386, 641
Vermeer Quartet, 110, 432, 1014
Vermeulen, Dirk, 378
Vermillion, Iris, 747
Vernède, Danielle, 944
Vernet, Isabelle, 365
Vernet, Olivier, 35, 201, 580
Vernizzi, Rino, 1155
Veronesi, Alberto, 786
Verrett, Shirley, 587
Vertavo Quartet, 670
Vetö, Tamás, 205, 329, 504, 666–67, 672–73, 675–76
Veyron-Lacroix, Robert, 24, 641
Viard, Maurice, 255
Viardo, Vladimir, 732, 866
Vickers, Jon, 822, 1143
Victoria, Tomás Luis de, 1014–15
Vidal, Luis, 310
Videmus, 890
Viderø, Finn, 671
Vienna Boys Choir, 187, 1116
Vienna Chamber Ensemble, 628
Vienna Concerthall Quartet, 432
Vienna Haydn Trio, 983
Vienna Kangforum, 316
Vienna Motet Choir, 507
Vienna Octet, 885
Vienna Philharmonic Quintet, 197
Vienna Philharmonic Winds, 909
Vienna Piano Trio, 433, 577
Vienna Schubert Trio, 642
Vienna Sextet, 746
Vienna String Quartet, 288
Vienna String Quintet, 444
Vienna String Trio, 287, 745, 801
Vienna Tonkünstler Chamber Orchestra, 626
Vienna Trombone Quartet, 1112
Vier Cellisten, 1147
Vieru, Andrei, 661
Vieuxtemps, Henri, 1016
Vignoles, Roger, 195
Viitasalo, Marita, 874
Viklarbo Chamber Ensemble, 793
Villa-Lobos, Heitor, 1017–22
Villa Musica Ensemble, 446–48
Villier, David de, 497
Vinikour, Jory, 36
Viotti, Giovanni Battista, 268, 344, 804–8, 1022
Virágh, András, 524
Virsaladze, Elissa, 833

Vishnevskaya, Galina, 735
Visse, Dominique, 849
Vistula, Camerata, 712
Vivalda, Janette, 510
Vivaldi, Antonio, 1022–35
Vlach Quartet, 287–88, 433, 473
Vlachová, Jana, 473
Vladar, Stefan, 915–16
Vlasák, Vladimir, 889
Vlatkovic, Radovan, 447, 637
Vlaud, Marie, 490
Vlček, Oldřich, 283, 561, 886, 938
Voces Intimae Quartet, 738, 787, 831, 874
Voces Quartet, 17, 306
Vogel, Alan, 21, 1160
Vogel, Jaroslav, 476, 677
Vogler Quartet, 81, 133, 473
Vogt, Lars, 103, 121, 369–70, 445
Voice of the Turtle, 1095
Voices of Ascension, 441
Voigt, Deborah, 922
Voivods, Juris, 1000
Vojtisek, Martin, 678
Volger Quartet, 1014
Volkmann, Robert, 1035–36
Volkov, Oleg, 729–30, 866–67
Vollestad, Per, 372
Volmer, Arvo, 996
Volodos, Arcadi, 730
Volonday, Pierre-Alain, 313
Volta, Sandro, 600, 1034
Vonk, Hans, 19, 92, 628, 826, 1105
Vorster, Len, 310, 452–53
Votapek, Ralph, 705
Votto, Antonino, 703, 1010
VoxAnimae, 442
Vronsky, Petr, 561
Vyvyan, Jennifer, 658, 1007

W

Waart, Edo de, 144, 347–48, 362, 369, 627, 727, 749, 802, 898, 903, 908, 910, 1055
Wachner, Julian J., 69
Wächter, Eberhart, 836, 1061
Wachthorn, Peter, 34
Wager, Matthias, 1127
Wagner, Friederike, 50
Wagner, Konrad, 1068
Wagner, Richard, 1036–43, 1142
Wagner, Roger, 46, 314, 597
Wait, Mark, 928, 933
Wakao, Keisuke, 76
Wakasugi, Hiroshi, 914, 946
Walcha, Helmut, 35, 37–38
Waldeland, Hege, 943

Walden Quartet, 136
Waldhans, Jiri, 565
Waldman, Frederic, 407, 410
Waldman, Yuval, 947
Waldmann, Leibale, 1096
Walevska, Christine, 431, 713
Walker, Frances, 235
Walker, Nicholas, 73
Walker, Sarah, 1007
Wallace, John, 432, 1112
Wallace Collection, 882, 1114
Wallberg, Heinz, 293, 320, 460, 512, 653, 818, 1056
Wallendorf, Klaus, 750
Wallenstein, Alfred, 493, 903
Wallez, Jean-Pierre, 424, 1104
Wallfisch, Elizabeth, 241, 384, 508, 527–28, 948, 1022
Wallfisch, Ernst, 886, 998
Wallfisch, Ralph, 186
Wallfisch, Raphael, 26, 30, 76, 154, 261, 286, 318, 444, 482, 486, 562, 776, 887, 904, 950, 982, 1027, 1045
Wallin, Ulf, 264, 448, 473, 745, 798
Wallstroem, Tord, 166
Walsh, Colin, 278, 505, 995, 1015
Walsh, Diane, 373, 559
Walt, Sherman, 1155
Walter, Alfred, 324, 327, 750–51, 883, 941, 1105
Walter, Bruno, 61, 90–92, 94–98, 124, 138, 171–72, 282, 429–31, 535, 538, 541, 543, 549–50, 554, 617–23, 625–26, 628, 632, 647–48, 805–7, 1039–40
Walter Boeykens Ensemble, 586, 713
Walther, Geraldine, 445, 447
Walton, Bernard, 636
Walton, Sam, 1127
Walton, William, 1043–46
Walz, Wilhelm, 148
Wambach, Bernhard, 169, 891
Wanami, Takayoshi, 1065
Wand, Günter, 92, 171, 804, 806–7, 826–27, 929
Wandel, Waldemar, 498
Wang, Jian, 77
Wang, Randal, 1033
Warchal, Bohdan, 22, 25, 27–28, 185, 378, 380, 438
Ward, Alan, 941
Ward, John, 1046–47
Ward, Nicholas, 58–59, 429–30, 452, 573, 617–18, 1031
Warfield, William, 839
Warlock, Peter, 1047–48
Warner, Wendy, 446–47

Warren, Leonard, 1145
Warren-Green, Christopher, 283, 311, 345–46, 634, 748, 1004, 1025
Washburn, Jon, 52
Washington Cathedral Choral Society, 1078
Watanabe, Akeo, 500, 855
Watanabe, Reiko, 132
Watkins, Richard, 16, 351
Watkins, Sara, 13, 186
Watkinson, Andrew, 452, 1024
Watkinson, Carolyn, 438, 1032
Watson, Janice, 184
Watts, André, 44, 339, 434, 520, 838, 976
Watts, Helen, 389
Watts, Jane, 375
Waxman, Franz, 1087–88
Weaver, James, 403
Webber, Geoffrey, 67
Weber, Carl Maria von, 1048–52
Weber, Helga, 274
Weber, Janice, 374, 523, 685, 733
Weber, Margrit, 562, 901
Webern, Anton, 1052–55
Webster, Beveridge, 209, 833
Wecrzyn, Krysztof, 439
Wehr, David Allen, 179, 261
Weigle, Jörg-Peter, 273, 744
Weil, Bruno, 428, 430, 435, 624–26, 628, 646, 653, 683, 806, 816–17
Weilerstein Duo, 157
Weill, Kurt, 1055–56
Weinberger, Gerhard, 38, 52
Weinberger, Jaromír, 1056
Weiner, Leó, 1056
Weingartner, Felix von, 138, 170
Weir, David Allen, 733
Weir, Gillian, 326, 586
Weisberg, Arthur, 247, 274, 590–91, 780, 999, 1062
Weisenberg, Alexis, 104, 257, 729, 732, 832
Weiser, Andreas, 816
Weiser, Manuela, 423
Weiss, Marcus, 791
Weiss, Sidney, 301
Weiss, Silvius Leopold, 1056–57
Weissenborn, Günther, 397, 414
Welin, Karl-Erik, 515
Welitsch, Ljuba, 916, 1139
Weller, Walter, 88, 347, 708–9, 876–77
Wells, David, 500
Welser-Möst, Franz, 197, 483, 492, 574–75, 647, 684–85, 793–94, 802, 810, 826

Welsh, Moray, 167, 457
Wenkel, Ortrun, 803, 1072
Wenzinger, August, 387, 602
Werff, Ivo van der, 745
Werner, Fritz, 41–42, 64
Werthen, Rudolf, 357, 456–57, 484, 693, 946, 1000
West, Charles, 352
West, Jeremy, 1112
West Jutland Chamber Ensemble, 670
Westbrook, James, 366, 422
Westenholtz, Elisabeth, 331, 671
Westerberg, Stig, 18, 158, 402, 506, 698–700, 767, 1060
Western Quintet, 463
Westi, Kurt, 674
Westminster Cathedral Choir, 187, 277, 480, 505, 722, 949–50, 1114
Westphal, Barbara, 745
Westphalian Trombone Quartet, 1112
Westrup, Jack, 429
Westwood Wind Quintet, 136, 208
Wetton, Davan, 453–54, 692, 735
Wey, Fritz ter, 450
Weyand, Eckhard, 64
Wheeler, Kimball, 509
Wheeler, Lawrence, 764
White, John, 307
White, Robert, 127, 322
White, Willard, 1072
Whiteman, Paul, 337
Whitfield, John, 781
Whitney, Robert, 421–22, 457, 701, 994
Whittlesey, Christine, 501
Wick, Denis, 454
Widlund, Mats, 767
Widor, Charles-Marie, 1057–58
Wiedoeft, Rudy, 1162
Wieniawski, Henryk, 1058–59
Wiesler, Manuela, 214, 463, 478, 714
Wiget, Ueli, 445
Wihan Quartet, 473
Wijnkoop, Alexander van, 1067
Wikström, Inger, 866
Wilanow Quartet, 370, 874
Wild, Earl, 77, 179, 221, 227–29, 240, 265, 335–36, 339, 370, 520–22, 572, 583, 661, 686, 728, 730, 732–33, 783, 792, 830, 976
Wilder, Alec, 1059
Wilhelm, Gerhard, 1050
Wilkinson, Stephen, 86
Wilkomirska, Wanda, 943
Wilks, Nicholas, 190
Willaert, Adrian, 1107
Willcocks, David, 62, 65, 314, 387–88,

407, 413, 435, 437, 454, 613–14, 1004–6, 1031, 1044, 1046
Williams, Gail, 447
Williams, John, 29, 211, 344, 453, 685, 688, 703, 765, 808, 861, 880, 1021–22, 1028, 1057, 1088, 1117–18
Williams, Lorraine, 184
Williams, Roger Bevan, 13
Wilson, John, 234
Wilson, Mescal, 944
Wilson, Ransom, 748–49, 851
Wilson, Roland, 507, 609, 844
Wilson, Todd, 276, 278
Wilson-Johnson, David, 801
Winbergh, Gösta, 920
Wincenc, Carol, 639, 995–96, 1118
Winchester Cathedral Choir, 201, 722, 949, 1114
Windbacher, Samine, 562
Winter, Lois, 1007
Winter, Quade, 441
Wirén, Dag, 1059–60
Wirtz, Tiny, 750
Wisconsin Brass Quintet, 1113
Wispelwey, Peter, 31–32, 175, 245, 299, 446, 449, 747, 808, 828, 1027
Wit, Antoni, 284–85, 530–31, 540, 545–46, 616, 686, 826, 877, 951, 953–54, 956, 958, 961
Witten, David, 703
Wittgenstein, Paul, 740–41
Wobisch, Helmut, 432
Wodiczko, Bohdan, 686
Wodnicki, Adam, 686
Wohlmacher, Johannes, 1036
Wojciechowski, Tadeusz, 369
Wöldike, Mogens, 61, 414–15, 424, 435–36, 672
Wolf, Friedrich, 290, 435, 817
Wolf, Hugo, 1060–61
Wolf, Marie, 1028
Wolf-Ferrari, Ermanno, 233, 1061–62
Wolfe, Paul, 386
Wolff, Albert, 152, 236–38, 283, 347, 485, 752, 1105
Wolfgang, Randall, 637
Wolfsthal, Josef, 108
Wolpe, Stefan, 1062–63
Wood, Henry J., 1001, 1005–6
Wood, James, 475, 791, 934, 1064
Woodhams, Richard, 913, 1160
Woods, Carlton, 890
Woods, Elaine, 127
Woods, Pamela Pecha, 1157, 1160
Woodside, Lyndon, 400

Woodward, Roger, 316, 854, 946
Woolley, Robert, 34, 726
Woolley, Scot, 493
Worcester Cathedral Choir, 672
Word of Mouth Chorus, 1115
Wordsworth, Barry, 85, 154, 570, 618–23, 628, 1004
Woudenberg, Pierre, 746
Woytowicz, Stephania, 357
Wright, Desmond, 466
Wright, Gordon, 756
Wright, Harold, 177, 235, 640, 1156
Wulstan, David, 342
Wummer, John, 384
Wunderlich, Fritz, 126, 438, 511, 820, 822, 837, 916, 918, 920–21, 1143
Wunderlich, Heinz, 746
Wuorinen, Charles, 1063–64, 1081
Wyatt, David, 637
Wynberg, Simon, 688, 1021
Wyner, Susan Davenny, 210
Wyttenbach, Janko, 891
Wyttenbach, Jürg, 209, 791, 891

X

Xenakis, Iannis, 1064, 1079–80
Xiao, Hong-Mei, 80
Xuclá, William, 167, 1148
Xue-Wei, 913
Xuereb, Pierre-Henri, 998, 1016

Y

Yablonskaya, Oxana, 349, 486
Yablonsky, Dimitri, 12, 466, 486
Yakar, Rachel, 376
Yale Quartet, 111
Yamashita, Kazuhito, 211, 344, 765, 1118
Yamash'ta, Stomu, 1126
Yampolsky, Vladimir, 642
Yanagita, Masako, 361
Yannatos, James, 702
Yates, Sophie, 327, 386, 726
Yeh, John Bruce, 168, 361, 668, 930, 1156
Yepes, Narciso, 1028, 1118
Yggdrasil Quartet, 148, 511
Yinon, Israel, 947
Ylonen, Marko, 738
Yoo, Scott, 283, 318, 972
York Trio, 829
Yoshino, Naoko, 210
Young, Alexander, 937, 1006, 1047
Young, Alison, 263
Young, Emma, 714
Young, John Bell, 854
Young, Victor, 1088

Ysaye Quartet, 741
Yu, Dejong Victorin, 973
Yudin, Gavriil, 346
Yudina, Maria, 121–23, 814, 1136
Yun, Isang, 1065–66

Z
Zabaleta, Nicanor, 638, 766, 1119
Zacharias, Christian, 109, 631, 644–45, 811
Zádori, Maria, 50, 387, 389–90
Zagrosek, Lothar, 442, 450, 497, 794, 802, 877
Zahradník, Bohuslav, 886
Zampieri, Mara, 718
Zander, Benjamin, 94, 96, 283, 926
Zander, Hans, 316, 551–52
Zapolski Quartet, 670
Zappa, Frank, 1066–67, 1080, 1082, 1084
Zaradnik, Bohuslav, 640
Zarafiants, Evgeny, 853
Zaretsky, Michael, 71
Zarinš, Valdis, 466
Zaritzkaya, Irina, 229, 231, 482

Zaslav, Bernard, 180
Zayas, Juana, 226–27, 229
Zazofsky, Peter, 571
Zeani, Virginia, 696
Zedda, Alberto, 128, 130, 607, 689, 771, 1035
Zehetmair, Thomas, 132, 425, 472, 943, 1025
Zeitlin, Zvi, 764, 801
Zelenka, Jan Dismas, 1067–68
Zeltser, Mark, 109
Zeltsman, Nancy, 701
Zeman, Dietmar, 635
Zemlinsky, Alexander von, 1068–72
Zěnaty, Ivan, 32, 286, 472, 998, 1025
Zender, Hans, 90, 249, 252, 425, 546, 791
Zeuthen, Morten, 676
Zhemchuzhin, Georgy, 481, 856
Zheng, H., 563
Zhukov, Igor, 73, 571, 716, 762
Zhukov, Mikhail, 715
Zhuraitis, Algis, 347–48, 350–51, 486, 710, 761, 856, 974
Ziegler, Robert, 311

Ziesak, Ruth, 43, 451, 1061, 1071
Zigante, Frédéric, 688
Zimansky, Robert, 745, 791, 830
Zimbalist, Efrem, 1154
Zimdars, Richard, 422
Zimerman, Krystian, 102–3, 179, 221, 225–27, 257, 520, 523–24, 531, 740, 815, 827, 1054
Zimmer, Hans, 294
Zimmerman, Frank Peter, 108–9, 132, 633, 687, 981, 1065
Zimmerman, Richard, 479
Zimmermann, Tabea, 515, 865, 886
Zinman, David, 74–75, 89, 91–92, 94–97, 99, 138–39, 143–44, 237, 239, 259, 295, 297, 336, 357, 362, 465, 467, 485, 490, 759, 761, 826, 955, 964
Ziporyn, Evan, 749
Zitterbart, Gerrit, 431
Zivkovic, Nebojša Jovan, 1126
Zöbeley, Hans Rudolf, 846
Zoboli, Omar, 533, 1062
Zsigmondy, Denes, 81
Zucker, Laurel, 1059

Zuckerman, Eugenia, 87, 775
Zuk, Zbigniew, 445, 1111
Zuker, Lauren, 214
Zukerman, Eugenia, 463
Zukerman, Pinchas, 26, 80–82, 109, 113–15, 132, 174–75, 194, 256, 300, 312, 324, 496, 503, 508, 577, 624, 626, 633–34, 638, 641, 676, 886, 981–82, 1016, 1027, 1149, 1154
Zukofsky, Paul, 20, 203, 208, 345, 468, 511, 748, 791, 855, 1063
Zukovsky, Michele, 565
Zumbro, Nicholas, 367
Zuponcic, Veda, 209
Zürcher, Liliane, 211
Zurich Kammermusiker, 746
Zurich New Music Ensemble, 246–47
Zverev, Valentin, 777
Zwilich, Ellen Taaffe, 1072–73
Zwilich, Joseph, 1073
Zygel, Jean-François, 169
Zylis-Gara, Teresa, 45, 49, 593–94, 922

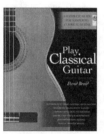

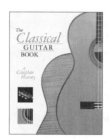